Welcome to this special 5
of your Good Sam RV Tra

This year marks twin milestones for the two biggest names in RV living and travel: the **Good Sam Club and Camping World are both celebrating 50 years** as part of the growing RV lifestyle. Over the past five decades, the Good Sam Club has brought savings, fellowship, convenience and assistance to RVing families across the U.S and Canada. During that same time span, Camping World has grown from a single campground store to a nationwide network of over **115 full service, one-stop SuperCenters**, offering thousands of RV and camping products, new and used RV sales, and professional installation and service.

To celebrate this **Golden Anniversary,** we have a host of special events and special savings coming your way. During the 50th anniversary celebration, **Camping World shoppers visiting any SuperCenter between January 4 and September 11, 2016, will receive a Golden Giveaway scratch-off game card** with any purchase. Just scratch the ticket to see if you are an instant winner of **five 2016 Coleman travel trailers** that will be awarded to lucky winners. You could also win a portion of $5 million in free camping that will be given away during the anniversary celebration. Not an instant winner? You still have a chance to win the Grand Prize of a **2016 Thor Windsport Class A motorhome valued at $140,000.** Simply go online to CampingWorld.com/Golden Giveaway to register. See page 7 for more details. We've also included a special 50th Anniversary Retrospective section in this RV Travel & Savings Guide (starting on page 5).

As always, this ***RV Travel & Savings Guide*** also includes information you need for saving money and getting the most out of your RV travels, including information on over **12,500 public and private parks and campgrounds across North America. Among them are listings for over 2,100 Good Sam Parks offering members a discount on camping fees.** Good Sam's trusted rating system lets you easily choose the best park or campground with the amenities you want. We've also included **coupons worth $1,500 in savings at Camping World locations nationwide, online at CampingWorld.com or when you place an order by phone or mail,** for the exclusive use of Good Sam Club members.

Both Good Sam and Camping World have always had one thing in common: a passion to help RVing families enjoy their active lifestyles to the fullest, with peace of mind that comes from knowing they are not alone out there on the road. And today, **Good Sam members enjoy the broadest range of benefits ever**, including discounts on camping fees at Good Sam Parks; savings every day on merchandise, service and installation at Camping World; discounts on fuel and LP gas; savings on RV insurance, roadside assistance, travel assistance, RV financing, prescriptions and mail forwarding, plus **Smile & Save discounts** with Good Sam partners, among others. Members also have access to the **Standby Sams network** for help from fellow members if needed; **Action Line consumer advocacy** problem resolution; **RV Parking Rights advisory council**; and **Sam Alert RV recall notification**. Members can also share the fun and fellowship at local, state and regional Good Sam events.

Good Sam and Camping World have come a long way over the past 50 years, and the future of both has never looked brighter. **Count on Good Sam and Camping World to continue to grow, evolve and expand**, giving members even more ways to make RV travel more affordable, enjoyable and worry-free through the decades ahead.

Happy Camping!

Marcus Lemonis
Chairman & CEO
Good Sam & Camping World

Table of Contents

WELCOME
GOOD SAM
CLUB MEMBERS
GOOD SAM
RECREATIONAL VEHICLE CLUB
CAMPING WORLD
IT'S GREAT TO HAVE CUSTOMERS LIKE YOU. KEEP ON CAMPING!

Photos from our archives

Find it fast! **We've color-coded our guide to help you reach your destination: red indicates discounts, products, services and information available through Good Sam and Camping World; blue means articles that help you get the most out of your RV lifestyle; green denotes special travel features and itineraries for every RVer.**

Fun, Families and Camping page 62

Snowbird Destinations page 71

2016 Directory Listing Section

Chairman & CEO
Marcus Lemonis

CFO and EVP - Operations
Tom Wolfe

COO, Good Sam
Mark Boggess

SVP - Sales, Marketing & Strategy
Seth Rosenberg

Chief Marketing Officer
Tamara Ward

President, Good Sam Club
Mike Siemens

Vice President & Publisher
Ann Emerson

Director of Sales
Dawn Watanabe
Bob Chamness

Sr. Product & Marketing Manager
Ellen Tyson

Business Managers
Christina Din, Christine Distl

Traffic Supervisor
Tanya Paz

Application Systems Administrator
Kristen Marozzi

Account Coordinators
Kimberly Carter, Robyn Elzie,
Siera Samaniego, Lori Wiseman

Content Editor
John Sullaway

Editorial Design
Gabriel E. Herrera

Pre-Press
Rob Roy

Graphic Design
Doug Paulin

Marketing Coordinator
MaryEllen Foster

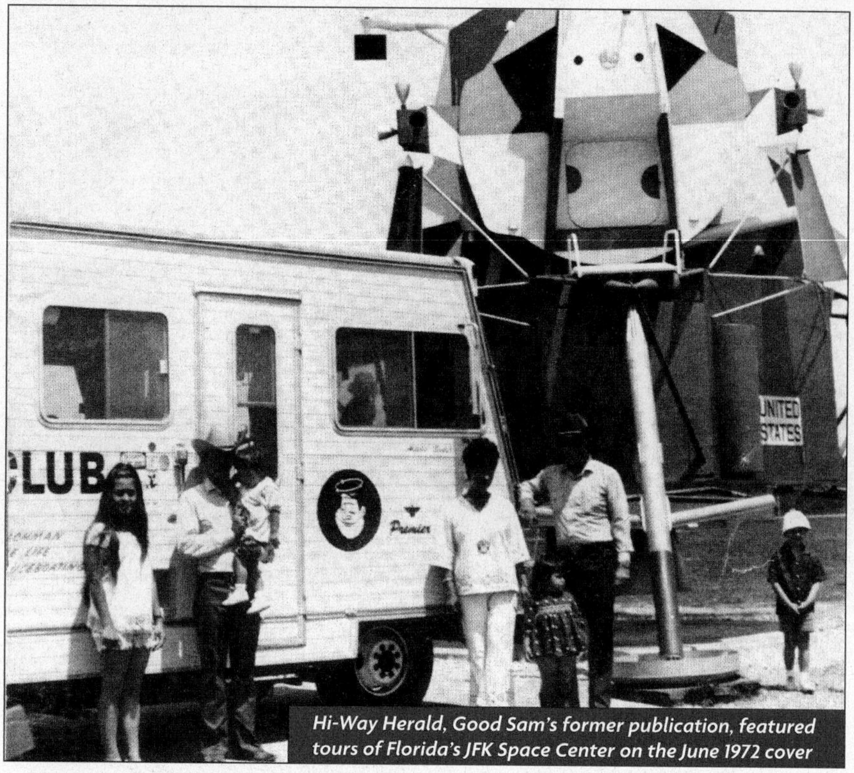

Hi-Way Herald, Good Sam's former publication, featured tours of Florida's JFK Space Center on the June 1972 cover

Sales Consultants

Bob & Vicki Auer
Greg & Maureen Baron
Bob & Becky Bazemore
Randy & Debbie Block
Dan & Annette Bramos
Alan & Teresa Breuer
John & Shirley Bujnovsky
Joe & Rita Comer
Chip & Pat Dennis
Fred & Susan Denischuk
Ed & Susan DeWitt
Mike & Mary Lou Dillon
Duane & Bev Finger
Jim & Julie Golden
Henry & Anne Goldman
Stan & Julie Grabiec
Charles & Alyce Grover
Jeff & Peggy Harmann
Dave & Donna Harmon
Tim & Sheryl Heath
Ron & Margaret Hobkirk
Dan & Flo Kleine
Fain & Lynda Little
Bob & Raissa Maroney
Chip & Karen May
Jim & Chris Mays
Frank & Linda Mintken
Mike & Donna Oliverio
Gary & Leesa Palmer
Mark & Wendy Pitts
Craig & Debbie Rice
Marcia Waggoner
Ken & Kathy Wente
Frank & Suzy Whitmore
Gary & Sherry Wilcox

Contributors

James Adinaro
Stefany Adinaro
Rene Agredano
Jennifer Alexander McCall
Marisol Basil
Tracy Bibler
Margot Bigg
Allison Brunner
Kristopher Bunker
Seana Dawson
Bonnie Denmark
Greg Donahue
Nina Fussing
Doug Gelbert
Cathy George
Estera Hayes
Caroline Lascom
Joy Neighbors
Brittany Nelson
Alan O'Sullivan
Chris Odegard
Jeremy Puglisi
Stephanie Puglisi
Lynn Seldon

Published by Good Sam Enterprises, LLC
2750 Park View Court, Suite 240
Oxnard, CA 93036
(800) 765-7070
GoodSamCamping.com

Printed in the U.S.A. Printed on Recyclable Paper
Book Trade Distribution by National Book Network
(800) 462-6420

ISBN: 978-1-937321-35-2 (bookstore)
ISBN: 978-1-937321-27-7 (other circulation)

Celebrating 50 Years!

CAMPING WORLD | Good Sam

1966-2016

Happy 50th Birthday!
Camping World & Good Sam

The RV lifestyle's two biggest names reach the half-century mark

Get ready to light the candles: Camping World and the Good Sam Club each turn 50 years old in 2016, marking a combined century of providing stellar value, great products and excellent service to RV travelers.

To recognize the twin 50th milestones of the RV industry's biggest retailer and largest membership organization, respectively, we're inviting every RVer to join us in celebrating five decades of RV excellence.

To help us celebrate, head to your nearest Camping World SuperCenter and enter the Golden Giveaway. You could be the lucky winner of a new 2016 Class A motorhome, one of five new travel trailers, or a portion of over $5 million in FREE camping to be awarded. See page 7 for details on how to enter for your chance to win.

But you don't have to scratch a lucky ticket to be a winner with Camping World and Good Sam. They offer fantastic values to everyone every day, from discounts on camping and RV products to fantastic service and benefits.

CAMPING WORLD
IT'S GREAT TO
HAVE CUSTOMERS
LIKE YOU.
KEEP ON CAMPING!

Today, as members of the same corporate family, Camping World sells RV supplies and accessories at over 115 SuperCenters from coast to coast, most of which also offer sales of new and used motorized and towable RVs, while the Good Sam Club provides a suite of exclusive benefits, services and discounts to over 1.6 million members across North America.

Buckle up and enjoy the ride as you learn more about the remarkable journeys of Camping World and Good Sam in the following pages. We're eagerly anticipating our next 50 years, and we'd love for you to join us!

WELCOME
GOOD SAM
CLUB MEMBERS

GOOD SAM
RECREATIONAL VEHICLE CLUB

The Journey Begins

Nineteen-sixty-six was a momentous year. The Beatles embarked on their final world tour, and NASA launched the first spacecraft to orbit the moon. On television screens, "Star Trek" went where no man had gone before.

In the RV world, two equally momentous events occurred: a small RV park store in Kentucky named Camping World sold to campers and RV travelers eager for supplies, and the California-based Good Sam Club began enrolling its first members.

The rollouts of these two RV brands didn't attract as much hype as the Fab Four or outer space missions, but these companies would eventually make their mark on the RV lifestyle after years of hard work, outstanding products and exemplary customer service.

An RV Boom For both companies, it was a fortuitous time to enter the RV industry. Winnebago introduced its first motorhome, just one of many companies entering a growing RV market. The national Interstate Highway system had just turned 10, and miles of new interstates were added seemingly every day. Parents of the Boomer generation were taking their kids out on the road to experience America's beauty and history. Today, many of the kids who enjoyed those trips enjoy the RV lifestyle as adults. A number of them enjoyed the trip more with the help of Camping World and Good Sam, two companies that started in two very different places yet eventually came together to form a partnership that would bring unprecedented value to camping and RVing families.

Camping World With a $5,000 loan from his father, a 23-year-old entrepreneur named David Garvin set up a small camping supply store in Beech Bend Amusement Park & Campground in Bowling Green, Kentucky, which his father also owned. From day one, Garvin built Camping World by focusing closely on customer service. After each purchase, a customer received a letter requesting feedback. Each response was sent to Garvin himself.

Garvin eventually branched out into mail order, and began opening new locations throughout the United States, offering both RV parts, supplies and accessories plus installation and service on all types of RVs. Customer service still ranked number one: David Garvin's motto was "No Unhappy Customers – Not Even One!"

Good Sam It all started with a simple letter. A small RV periodical named *Trail-R-News* received a letter from a reader who suggested the magazine form a club built on the principles outlined in the biblical story of the Good Samaritan. The publisher printed up stickers of the smiling, haloed mascot, and members were encouraged to help each other on the road in the event of a breakdown or other emergency.

When magazine publisher Art Rouse purchased *Trail-R-News*, he received the Good Sam Club as part of the bargain. The legendary industry innovator began adding discounts and benefits to the club, from RV park discounts to chapter membership. As membership gradually grew, the club became a significant force in the RV industry.

As you'll see in the following pages, both companies would eventually join forces to serve every aspect of the RV experience. Camping World and Good Sam continue to chart new territory in the RV world today.

Plus, We Are Giving Away $5 Million In FREE CAMPING!

As Camping World and Good Sam turn 50, it's your chance to take a drive down Memory Lane in a brand new motorhome or travel trailer. Camping World shoppers visiting any of over 115 SuperCenters nationwide between January 4 and September 11, 2016 will receive a Golden Giveaway scratch-off ticket with any purchase.

Just scratch the ticket to see if you are an instant winner of one of five 2016 Coleman travel trailers that will be awarded to lucky winners. You could also win a portion of over $5 million in free camping that will be given away during the anniversary celebration.

Not an instant winner? You still have a chance to win the Grand Prize of a 2016 Thor Windsport Class A motorhome valued at $140,000. Simply go online to CampingWorld.com/GoldenGiveaway to register for a chance to win.

Commemorative reusable shopping bags will also be given away with any purchase of $50 or more while supplies last at various times throughout the year. For special savings, look for events celebrating each decade of the last 50 years at Camping World SuperCenters, including free gifts to the first 50 customers, event-only product specials, free lunch and more!

For more information about the Camping World and Good Sam 50th Birthday Celebration, call or visit your nearest SuperCenter.

NO PURCHASE NECESSARY. VOID WHERE PROHIBITED. For full Official Rules, by which this sweepstakes is governed, go to: *www.CampingWorld.com/GoldenGiveaway.* Must be 18 or older and a legal resident of the U.S. or Canada. Promotion begins 1/04/2016 and ends 9/11/2016 @11:59:59 p.m. EDT.

50 Years of Camping World and Good Sam

Important milestones on the half-century-long journey of the RV industry's two biggest brands.

1966

First Camping World store opens inside Beech Bend Park after founder David Garvin successfully launches business selling RV parts and supplies from the back of a pickup truck in the park's campground. Corporate offices are located in an old farmhouse nearby. A simple black-and-white catalog is printed and mailed to customer addresses collected in the store and at the campground.

1968

Trail-R-News and the Good Sam Club are acquired by publisher Art Rouse. The magazine is renamed *Trailer Life* and is later joined by sister publications *MotorHome* magazine and the *RV Buyers Guide*.

1968

The Ute Salt Shakers from West Valley, Utah, becomes the first Good Sam chapter. Today, chapters are in almost every state and province.

1969

Good Sam launches the first comprehensive RV insurance program. Today, Good Sam provides a wide choice of insurance products.

1974

The first Samboree launches at Devonshire Downs in Northridge, California, and ends at Lion Country Safari. Attendees enjoy an old-fashioned 4th of July picnic, fireworks and Caraventure stretching 10 miles along the freeway.

National Good Samboree Attracts Record Number

1966 1967 1968 1969 1970 1971 1972 1973 1974 1975 1976 1977

1966

Trail-R-News, a small RV lifestyle publication, receives a letter suggesting that the magazine provide bumper stickers encouraging RVers to assist each other on the road. The magazine's publisher conceives the idea of the Good Sam Club.

1967

Hi-Way Herald is launched, providing news for members of the Good Sam Club. Today, club news is available in *Trailer Life* and *MotorHome* magazines.

1969

Mail order catalog becomes full color, featuring more pages and more products for camping and RVing.

1972

Good Sam publishes the Good Sam Club's *1972 Recreational Vehicle Owners Directory*, which lists RV parks and businesses that offer discounts.

Staffers review listings for Good Sam's inaugural 1972 directory.

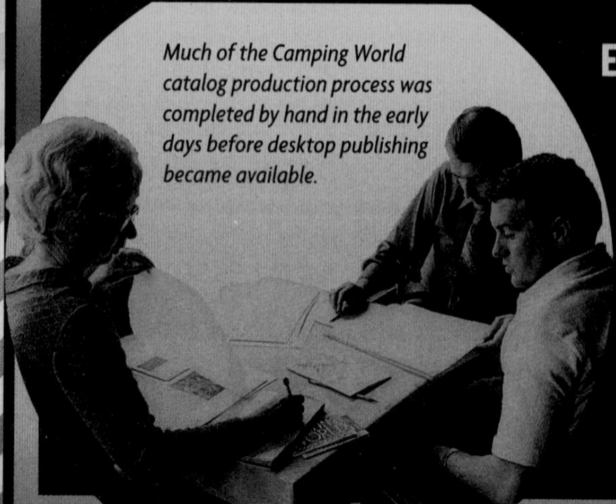

Much of the Camping World catalog production process was completed by hand in the early days before desktop publishing became available.

Early Catalog Production—Ahead of the Curve

Two key decisions made in the first few years of Camping World's existence were pivotal in the success today of the world's largest retailer of RV and camping products and accessories. Those decisions were to collect the names and addresses of Camping World customers at the retail store, and to publish a print catalog of essential RV, camping and towing accessories. Not only was catalog ordering from anywhere in the U.S. convenient for customers, but Camping World became a well-known source of RV parts and supplies within the rapidly expanding RVing community.

DOGS for the DEAF inc.

1980

The Good Sam Club adopts Dogs for the Deaf as its official charity.

1985

The President's Club is launched, offering members savings of at least 10% off every item sold by Camping World, installation discounts, special members-only savings events, product testing and more.

1973-1979

New Camping World store with four service bays and offices opens on Beech Bend Road, a short distance from the park. First store outside Bowling Green opens in Myrtle Beach, South Carolina. First Florida store opens in Kissimmee.

1981

The first Action Line letter is sent to Good Sam. Since then, Good Sam's Action Line program has netted more than $1 million for customers seeking to resolve disputes with RV companies.

1984

A Mobile RV SuperCenter provided products and services at off-site events, utilizing a team of Camping World crewmembers and service technicians.

1985-1989

New warehouse facility and corporate office built on Three Springs Road, adjacent to warehouse.

1978 1979 1980 1981 1982 1983 1984 1985 1986 1987 1988 1989

1980-1989

14 more Camping World stores open in six states including the first one in California.

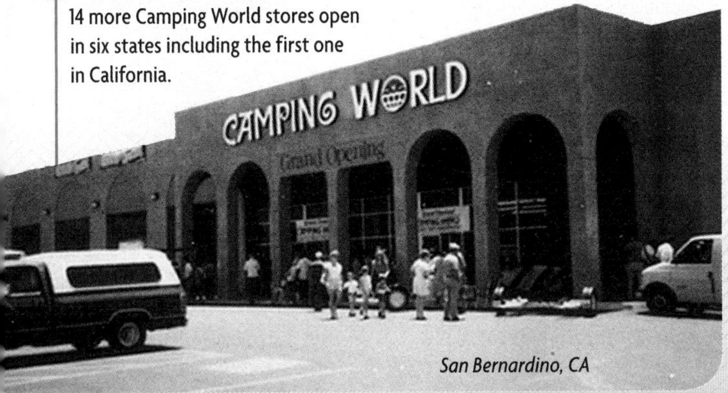

San Bernardino, CA

1984

Good Sam launches Emergency Road Service to help stranded RVers. Over its 32-year history, Roadside Assistance has aided more than 2 million RV travelers.

One Big, Happy Good Sam Family

The Good Sam Club offers more than camping discounts to its members. Club members have the chance to take part in group activities by joining state, or provincial chapters, and by attending Samborees. Members provide thousands of hours of volunteer labor annually for charitable causes, including annual Cleanup Days, Adopt-A-Highway and Adopt-A-Park programs. Members help each other through the Standby Sams, and exchange advice and information via online forums. Tireless fundraisers, Good Sam chapters have helped support veterans' programs, Ronald McDonald House, and many more. Good Sam members help others as their way to give back to their communities.

Sowega Sam'ers, GA 1973

1996

CampingWorld.com is launched, giving customers the opportunity to shop thousands of RV, camping and outdoor products and accessories online 24/7.

2000

The inaugural Rally opens its gates in Gillette, Wyoming.

1995

Camping World opens its 25th store!

1997

Camping World joins the Affinity Group family of outdoor, travel and RV lifestyle enterprises.

2000-2009

58 additional Camping World retail stores and service centers open in 32 states.

1990 1991 1992 1993 1994 1995 1996 1997 1998 1999 2000 2001 2002

1990-1999

Camping World's nationwide network of retail stores and service centers expands by another 17 locations in 13 states.

1995

The Good Sam Club makes inroads into the fledgling Internet. Today, GoodSamClub.com helps members plan trips, find events, locate Good Sam Parks and so much more.

1994

At Camping World, professional technicians take a new approach to their work with the introduction of the comprehensive RV ProCare Service Program.

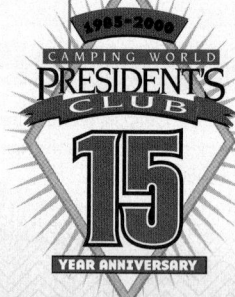

1997

The President's Club grows to 500,000 members who save at least 10% every day on Camping World products and services.

Marcus Lemonis

Carrying the Legacy into the 21st Century and Beyond

As Chairman & CEO of Camping World and Good Sam Enterprises, Marcus Lemonis has been on a mission to take Camping World and the Good Sam Club to the next level. Under his leadership, the number of Camping World SuperCenters has quadrupled, offering RV sales dealerships, expanded service and repair, and over 10,000 products and accessories. Good Sam Club benefits have expanded and membership has risen to a record high of over 1.6 million. No other RV and camping organization or retailer comes close to matching the advantages offered by the two biggest names in the RV lifestyle industry.

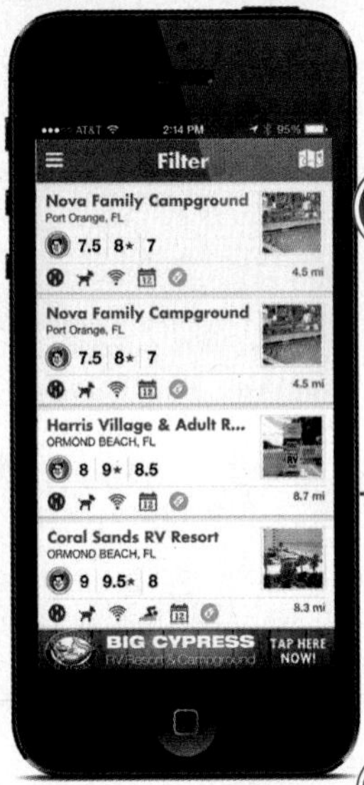

2003 Camping World expands into new and used RV sales at select locations.

2006 Camping World opens its 50th store!

2011 Affinity Group Incorporated becomes Good Sam Enterprises, and the President's Club merges with the Good Sam Club to form the world's largest RV lifestyle organization, with 1.5 million members.

2013 The Good Sam Camping app enables smartphone users to find Good Sam Parks in the palms of their hands. Today, the app can be downloaded on smartphones and tablets on both Apple and Android operating systems.

2013 The *Trailer Life Directory* merges with Woodall's, creating the *Good Sam RV Travel Guide*.

2003 2004 2005 2006 2007 2008 2009 2010 2011 2012 2013 2014 2015

2009 Camping World becomes the title sponsor of NASCAR Camping World Truck Series™ racing.

2013 Camping World opens its 100th store!

2014 The Camping World mobile app launches, offering smartphone users access to products, services, locations and more.

2015 Good Sam debuts RV Parks and Campground Reviews for members, enabling RVers to share their experiences at RV parks on GoodSamClub.com.

The NASCAR Camping World Truck Series™ logo and word mark are used under license by the National Association for Stock Car Auto Racing, Inc. and CWI, Inc.

Note from Marcus—Looking Toward the Future

As we celebrate this milestone in the history of the Camping World and Good Sam Club, I want to thank you, our valued Club members and customers, for the honor of providing you and your family with the benefits, products and services that have helped you make priceless memories while enjoying your RV travels over the last half century. We are proud and honored that you have chosen us as your partners in fun and adventure. As we look beyond this anniversary year, we recommit ourselves to listening to you and seeking out the best ways to help you get the most from your RV lifestyle. We plan on being around for another 50 years and beyond, and look forward to seeing you soon!

Happy Camping!

Marcus Lemonis
Chairman & CEO
Camping World | Good Sam

Good Sam

1966 50 YEARS 2016

Get the Most GOOD SAM CL

Be Sure You're Taking Advantage of these EXCITING CLUB BENEFITS!

SAVE

Savings at Good Sam Parks, Pilot Flying J, Camping World, and more!

- Save 10% on the nightly rate at 2,100+ Good Sam Parks
- Save instantly on fuel at Pilot Flying J
- Save at Camping World—the Club's official RV accessory retailer!
- RV show discounts
- Smile & Save Partner discounts
- Up to 8% instant rebates* at CampingWorld.com

Camping World SuperCenters

- Up to 30% savings on parts and accessories
- Special installation offers
- Hundreds of dollars in coupons
- 25% savings on LP Gas on Tuesdays and Wednesdays
- Free dump station privileges

*Visit CampingWorld.com/buymoresavemore for details.

SUPPORT

Enjoy exclusive pricing on Good Sam Roadside Assistance which protects you while driving your RV and household vehicles.

RV services you can count on

- Special price on Good Sam Roadside Assistance
- Action Line—RV dispute resolution service
- Sam Alerts—RV recall notification service
- Free online RV trip planning
- RV Parking Rights Advisory Council—helping resolve local RV parking restrictions

Easy, quick and FREE! Plan your next trip using the Online Trip Planning service. Get driving directions, trip itineraries, travel guides and points-of-interest along the way. Customized for RVers!

GoodSamClub.com/travel

Not a Member? JOIN TODAY!

out of your
UB MEMBERSHIP!

LEARN

RV tips and more!

- Special member price on a subscription to *MotorHome* or *Trailer Life* magazine
- Free eCommunications with RV tips, member news and more!

CONNECT

Enjoy the RV Community with over 1.6 million members

- Good Sam Events planned across the country
- Local Chapters—friends with similar interests
- Standby Sams—volunteer network

In 2015 Good Sam chapters from across North America celebrated the 20th anniversary of Good Sam Cleanup days by spending the weekend picking up trash around campgrounds, lakes and anywhere in need of a cleanup.

Go to GoodSamClub.com/volunteering to see how you can get involved!

The Philanthropy of Good Sam Club

The Good Sam Club has its roots in the biblical story of the Good Samaritan who offered to help a traveler in need. As part of the club's Samaritan philosophy, Good Sam Club chapters regularly open their hearts and wallets for worthy causes and volunteer for local nonprofits and national organizations such as Adopt-a-Highway and Adopt-a-Park.

Good Sam encourages members to be active stewards of North America's natural resources by always leaving their RV campsites cleaner than when they arrived and volunteering during the club's annual Cleanup Days event. For the past 18 years, thousands of Good Sam members have gathered at public parks, beaches and roadsides during Cleanup Days to pitch in and pick up trash and debris.

Visit any **Camping World SuperCenter**, call **1-866-428-5704** or visit **CampingWorld.com/whyjoin**

From a Single Store in 1966 to a

NATIONWIDE NETWORK

OF OVER 115 SUPERCENTERS!

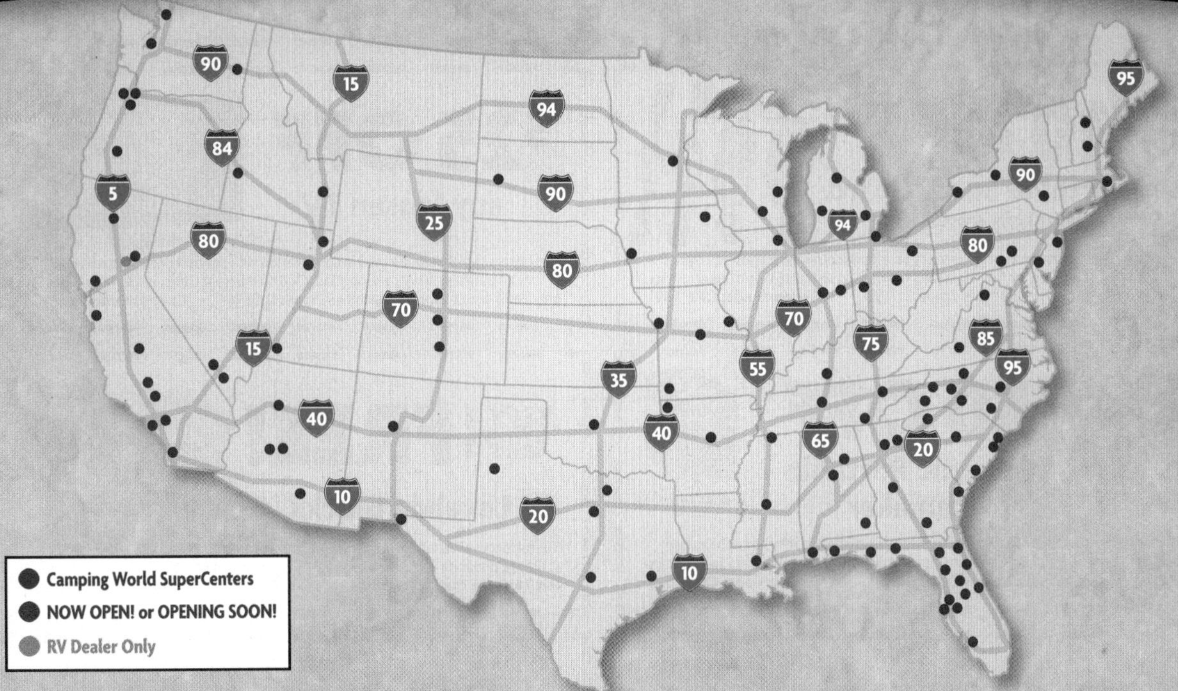

ALABAMA
Calera • Dothan
Anniston
Robertsdale

ARIZONA
Avondale • Flagstaff
Mesa • Tucson

ARKANSAS
Lowell • North Little Rock

CALIFORNIA
Bakersfield • Fresno
La Mirada • Redding
Rocklin • San Bernardino
San Marcos • San Martin
Vacaville • Valencia

COLORADO
Colorado Springs
Golden • Longmont

FLORIDA
Bartow • Cocoa • Ft. Myers
Gulf Breeze • Jacksonville
Kissimmee • Lake City
New Port Richey • Ocala
Panama City • St. Augustine

FLORIDA *(continued)*
Tallahassee • Tampa
Winter Garden

GEORGIA
Byron • Lake Park
Oakwood • Pooler
Woodstock

IDAHO
Boise
Idaho Falls

ILLINOIS
Island Lake

INDIANA
Greenwood
Richmond NOW OPEN!

IOWA
Cedar Falls • Council Bluffs

KENTUCKY
Bowling Green

LOUISIANA
Hammond

MASSACHUSETTS
Berkley

MICHIGAN
Belleville • Grand Rapids
Houghton Lake

MINNESOTA
Rogers

MISSISSIPPI
Olive Branch
Jackson NOW OPEN!

MISSOURI
Columbia • Grain Valley
Springfield
Wentzville OPENING SOON!

NEVADA
Henderson • Las Vegas

NEW HAMPSHIRE
Chichester • Conway

NEW JERSEY
Bridgeport • Lakewood

NEW MEXICO
Albuquerque

NEW YORK
Hamburg • Kingston
Syracuse

NORTH CAROLINA
Asheville • Colfax
Concord OPENING SOON!
Fayetteville
Marion NOW OPEN!
Raleigh • Statesville

OHIO
Akron
Fairfield NOW OPEN!
London NOW OPEN!
Rossford

OKLAHOMA
Oklahoma City

OREGON
Coburg • Hillsboro
Wilsonville • Wood Village

PENNSYLVANIA
Hanover • Harrisburg

SOUTH CAROLINA
Charleston • Columbia
Myrtle Beach *2 Locations!*
Spartanburg

SOUTH DAKOTA
Rapid City

TENNESSEE
Chattanooga • Louisville
Nashville

TEXAS
Anthony • Denton
Ft. Worth • Katy
Lubbock • New Braunfels

UTAH
Draper • Kaysville
St. George

VIRGINIA
Roanoke • Winchester

WASHINGTON
Burlington • Spokane • Tacoma

WISCONSIN
Madison • Saukville

RV DEALER ONLY
Roseville, CA

More SuperCenters Opening in 2016!

Go online to **CampingWorld.com/stores** for updates.

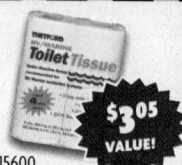

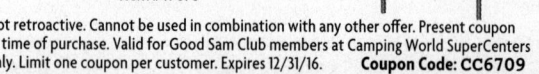

CLUB MEMBERS
SAVE – Over $1,500 in SAVINGS!

25% OFF
Any Dometic or Carefree Awning

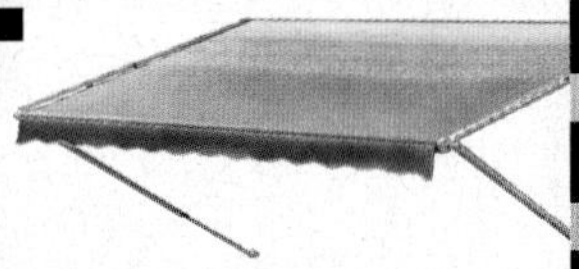

Not retroactive. Cannot be used in combination with any other offer. Present coupon at time of purchase. Valid for Good Sam Club members at Camping World SuperCenters only. Limit one coupon per customer. Expires 12/31/16. **Coupon Code: CC6712**

20% OFF
Any Elements RV Cover

Not retroactive. Cannot be used in combination with any other offer. Present coupon at time of purchase. Valid for Good Sam Club members at Camping World SuperCenters only. Limit one coupon per customer. Expires 8/1/16. **Coupon Code: CC6718**

$10 OFF
Any Electrical Cord of $20 or more

Not retroactive. Cannot be used in combination with any other offer. Present coupon at time of purchase. Valid for Good Sam Club members at Camping World SuperCenters only. Limit one coupon per customer. Expires 12/31/16. **Coupon Code: CC6713**

$15 OFF
Any Bike Rack

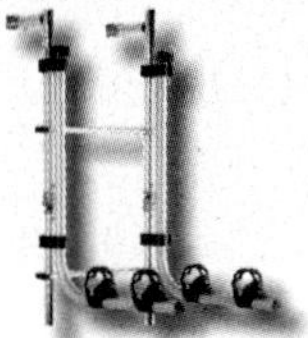

Not retroactive. Cannot be used in combination with any other offer. Present coupon at time of purchase. Valid for Good Sam Club members at Camping World SuperCenters only. Limit one coupon per customer. Expires 12/31/16. **Coupon Code: CC6719**

$10 OFF
Foldable Wagon
Item #74219 or #54756

Not retroactive. Cannot be used in combination with any other offer. Present coupon at time of purchase. Valid for Good Sam Club members at Camping World SuperCenters only. Limit one coupon per customer. Expires 12/31/16. **Coupon Code: CC6714**

$5 OFF
Any Chair of $20 or More

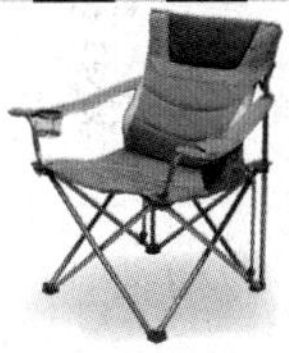

Not retroactive. Cannot be used in combination with any other offer. Present coupon at time of purchase. Valid for Good Sam Club members at Camping World SuperCenters only. Limit one coupon per customer. Expires 12/31/16. **Coupon Code: CC6720**

$75 OFF
Any RDS Fuel Tank

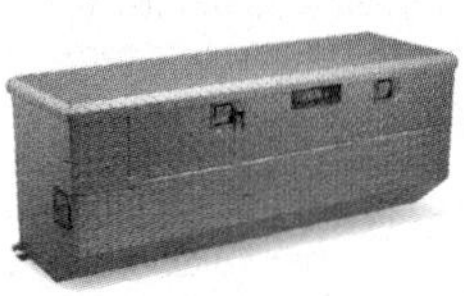

Not retroactive. Cannot be used in combination with any other offer. Present coupon at time of purchase. Valid for Good Sam Club members at Camping World SuperCenters only. Limit one coupon per customer. Expires 12/31/16. **Coupon Code: CC6715**

$10 OFF
Any Grill

Not retroactive. Cannot be used in combination with any other offer. Present coupon at time of purchase. Valid for Good Sam Club members at Camping World SuperCenters only. Limit one coupon per customer. Expires 12/31/16. **Coupon Code: CC6721**

$40 OFF
Any Electric Step

Not retroactive. Cannot be used in combination with any other offer. Present coupon at time of purchase. Valid for Good Sam Club members at Camping World SuperCenters only. Limit one coupon per customer. Expires 12/31/16. **Coupon Code: CC6716**

$30 OFF
Any Generator

Not retroactive. Cannot be used in combination with any other offer. Present coupon at time of purchase. Valid for Good Sam Club members at Camping World SuperCenters only. Limit one coupon per customer. Expires 12/31/16. **Coupon Code: CC6722**

$20 OFF
Flojet RV Waste Pump
Item #26125

Not retroactive. Cannot be used in combination with any other offer. Present coupon at time of purchase. Valid for Good Sam Club members at Camping World SuperCenters only. Limit one coupon per customer. Expires 12/31/16. **Coupon Code: CC6717**

BUY 1 GET 1 FREE!
Double Fridge Bars

$6.99 VALUE!

Item #70079

Not retroactive. Cannot be used in combination with any other offer. Present coupon at time of purchase. Valid for Good Sam Club members at Camping World SuperCenters only. Limit one coupon per customer. Expires 12/31/16. **Coupon Code: CC6723**

CAMPING WORLD PROCARE 50 Years of Expert RV Service!

Your #1 SOURCE for RV PARTS, MAINTENANCE & SERVICE REPAIRS | NATIONWIDE NETWORK OF SERVICE CENTERS

WE OFFER A VARIETY OF SERVICES FOR ALL TYPES OF RVS:

45 POINT INSPECTION #989013
Ideal service for a complete RV physical to identify what is working well and what requires attention.

WHEEL BEARING PACKS
Single Axle #989914 Double Axle #989915
Triple Axle #989916
Recommended annually to prevent bearing and brake failure.

WATER HEATER SERVICE #989035
Recommended annually to prolong the life of the storage tank and keep it operating efficiently.

FURNACE SERVICE #989034
Annual inspections and service will help keep your furnace operating safely and efficiently.

RUBBER ROOF PREVENTATIVE MAINTENANCE #989008
One of the most expensive RV repairs can be avoided with an annual inspection, cleaning and UV treatment of your rubber roof.

GENERATOR OIL CHANGE
Gas #989009 Diesel #989016
Manufacturers recommend this service every 75 operating hours or 12 months to maintain trouble-free operation and long life.

GAS GENERATOR SERVICE #989037
Manufacturers recommend this service every 75 operating hours or 12 months to maintain trouble-free operation and long life.

MOTORIZED & TOWABLE ANNUAL SERVICE PACKAGES
Includes service on LP system, refrigerator, water heater and battery plus exterior inspection. Towable package includes bearing pack. Packages with generator service also available for motorized or towable RVs.

WATER SYSTEM CHECK #989789
Recommended annually to prevent water system failures.

RV ORIENTATION #989031
Just bought a previously owned RV and want to know how it operates? Let us show you how!

AIR CONDITIONER SERVICE #989038
Air conditioners operate more efficiently and perform better with the coils cleaned and filters changed annually.

WINTERIZATION PACKAGES
Basic #987002 Complete #987003 Deluxe #987004
Prior to Winter storage, make sure to winterize for enjoyment next Spring.

REFRIGERATOR SERVICE #989036
Routine inspections for optimal air flow and burner/flue cleaning can prolong the life of your refrigerator and keep it operating efficiently.

RV SPA† PACKAGES
We're your cleaning professionals! Exterior and interior cleaning and detailing to keep your RV looking sharp.

EXTENDED WARRANTY SERVICE
Repair or replace awnings, appliances, electronics and more!

LP INSPECTION SERVICE #989033
Annual inspections and pressure checks are recommended to help ensure safe travels.

SLIDEOUT MAINTENANCE SERVICE
Single #9890022 Double #9890023 Triple #9890024
Quad #9890025 Full #9890026
Annual inspections are recommended to maintain trouble-free operation and long life. Includes slideout inspection and lubrication of seals and slide mechanism.

For service details and pricing, go to **CampingWorld.com/procare** or visit your nearest SuperCenter.

CAMPING WORLD Since 1966 **COLLISION CENTERS**

Preferred & Endorsed by America's Leading Insurance Companies

COME SEE US FOR A **FREE ESTIMATE!**

SERVICES: Collision Repair • Windshield Replacement • Interior Remodeling • Aluminum Skin Replacement Sidewall Repair/Replacement • Hail, Wind & Sand Damage Repair • Custom Painting & Graphics • **AND MORE!**

Visit **CampingWorldCollision.com** today!

Service & Repair Price Guarantee: We'll beat any competitor's installation, service or repair price. The installation, service or repair must be for identical work. Competitor's written estimate may not be more than 30 days old. We reserve the right to inspect the vehicle and to verify the competitor's estimate amount. Guarantee applies to labor only. Installation fees shown cover labor charges for standard installation. Some installations require additional material and labor charges and are quoted upon inspection. A standard supply charge is added to each work order.

Workmanship Guarantee: Installation guaranteed as long as you own your vehicle. Service work and collision repair guaranteed for 12 months. Some exclusions apply. See store for additional details.

Treat Your Tires Right

Keep your tires protected with Good Sam Roadside Assistance

In a recent study, Good Sam Roadside Assistance discovered that 40 percent of auto and RV disablements are tire related. To help get their members back on the road after a flat, Good Sam Roadside Assistance plans include an essential benefit—Flat Tire Service.

If a Good Sam Club member gets a flat tire while out on the road, Good Sam Roadside Assistance will dispatch a service technician to come out to replace the flat tire with an inflated spare. And because many motorhomes don't travel with spare tires, Good Sam Roadside Assistance maintains a nationwide tire delivery network. If a member needs a replacement tire for their RV, Good Sam Roadside will make arrangements whenever possible to purchase a brand name tire(s) through their network of providers, have it delivered to the disablement location and installed on the spot! Good. Sam Roadside Assistance will take care of the delivery, and members handle the cost of tires, mounting, parts and labor.

Service is available 24 hours a day, and if the appropriate tire isn't available, Good Sam Roadside Assistance will tow the vehicle to the nearest professional service center. No other Roadside Assistance service offers a network that can "bring the shop to you."

Other benefits include:

- Coverage for RVs and autos, even motorcycles and boat trailers
- Coverage for member, spouse and dependent children
- Unlimited distance towing to the nearest service center
- Battery jumpstarts, fuel/fluid delivery, locksmith service

Even with proper tire care, one never knows what the road may bring. Having a tire replacement service as part of a roadside assistance plan can minimize the burden on a trip and ensure peace of mind. It's always better to be safe than sorry, so Good Sam Roadside Assistance has put together some tips to prevent tire problems in the future

Under Pressure

Unlike passenger-car tires, where the maximum inflation pressure on the sidewall should never be exceeded, the pressure figure on the sidewall of a light or medium-duty truck tire is the minimum pressure necessary to carry the maximum stated load. In other words, if a tire reads "Max Load single: 3650 lbs at 65 psi cold" then 65 psi is the minimum cold-air inflation pressure necessary to carry the maximum load figure. Some RVers may be inclined to simply inflate such a tire to 65 psi—but unless that tire is carrying its maximum load, all this will result in is a rough ride.

In fact, tire manufacturers like Goodyear and Michelin publish load/inflation tables online that indicate how much weight a tire can carry based on inflation pressure. Therefore, it is recommended that you first weigh your coach loaded and ready for travel (including passenger weight, fuel, freshwater, supplies, etc.) to determine the amount of air necessary to carry your load.

Axle Weight and Tire Pressure

It's best to use individual wheel scales, giving you weight figures at each corner, but even a typical platform scale allows for weighing the front and rear axles separately. While you may find that you need to inflate the front and rear tires to different pressures for their different loads, it is critical that tire pressures remain the same across an axle (even if weight differs from side-to-side) to ensure safe handling. It's also vital to continue monitoring tire performance on the road.

Even stored motorhomes are susceptible to tire air-pressure loss.

Tires can lose 1 psi per month, and about 1 psi for every 10-degree F drop in ambient temperature, which is why tire manufacturers recommend that you check it at least monthly.

Tire pressure should always be checked when the tires are cold and not driven for more than 1 mile. If you must check tire pressure when the tires are warm, allow for an increase in air pressure.

Avoid Excessive Flex in Your RV Tires

Any time an under-inflated tire is run at normal highway speeds, the excessive flex builds heat that can damage the inner liner, casing and outer sidewall of the tire. According to guidelines published by the Rubber Manufacturers Association, any tire that has been run at less than 80 percent of the recommended air pressure for the load it is carrying should be inspected for possible damage. What's more, when one tire in a dual configuration is underinflated, the other tire can be overloaded and should be inspected for damage as well.

Incidentally, the improper use of leveling blocks can cause damage similar to that created by overloading and under inflation. When using leveling blocks, make sure that they are wider than the tire's tread and longer than its footprint. In the case of rear duals, make sure both tires are supported equally.

Numbers Game

Besides load and inflation, RVers should become familiar with the numbers molded into the tire's sidewalls. You need to concern yourself with size, load ratings, load index/speed symbol and the DOT number that indicates the week and year the tire was built.

Let's start with size. A typical Class A motorhome tire would be a 275/70R22.5. Here, "275" is the cross-section width of the tire, measured at its widest part (not the tread) and expressed in millimeters; "70" is the aspect ratio, also expressed in millimeters. The aspect ratio indicates the height of the sidewall relative to the cross-section width; in this instance, the sidewall is 70 percent as tall as the cross-section is wide. "R" indicates radial, and 22.5 is the rim diameter.

As we noted, air pressure and load-carrying capacity go hand-in-hand, so the two figures are displayed together on the sidewall. Again, a typical example might read, "Max load single: 3640 lbs at 65 psi cold; Max load dual: 3415 lbs at 65 psi cold." Note the tire in question is capable of carrying more load as a single-tire application than it is when paired with another tire; there is a logical reason for this, and it has to do with road crown and heat.

Load Index

As you know, almost every road is built with a crown (curvature) to promote water runoff. While on a crowned road, it is easy to see that the inner tires are carrying more load than the outers. Also, the proximity of dual tires makes them run hotter than single tires. For both reasons, tire manufacturers reduce the load-carrying rating of tires in dual configuration to prevent overloading.

The load index reflects the maximum load ratings of the tire (discussed above) and is expressed in an alphanumeric manner. It may appear something like "143/141L." In this instance, 143 represents the maximum load for a single tire, 141 for dual tires. The letter is the speed symbol, representing the maximum speed that the tire is rated for. The letter L, for example, is a common speed symbol for a Class A motorhome tire and indicates a maximum speed of about 75 mph.

If the letter is lower than that (K, for example), the top speed is only 69 mph. If you are driving faster than the maximum speed rating for the tire, you are exceeding that tire's design limit—and inviting disaster. Keeping your speed within a safe margin is crucial for tire health.

Five-Year Life Span

Finally, remember that even though you may only put 5,000 miles a year on your coach/truck tires, it is likely that your tires will "time out" before they wear out.

This is where those last four digits of the DOT number on the sidewall come in. The first two figures indicate the week the tire was made. The second two indicate its year of manufacture. So, if the last four numbers read "5004," it translates to a tire built in the 50th week of 2004.

At the end of five years of service, you should have your tires closely inspected, regardless of miles they have traveled. Many tire manufacturers recognize seven years as the age at which a tire should be replaced (including the spare) regardless of its apparent condition.

Follow these tips for a safe trip and make sure to purchase a Good Sam Roadside Assistance membership for ultimate peace of mind on the road.

ESP Has Got You Covered

Don't rely on warranties—let the Good Sam Extended Service Plan pay your repair bills

The Good Sam Extended Service Plan is a policy that YOU own, not the dealer or manufacturer. Among the valuable benefits offered:

- **ESP pays for your repairs—at any repair facility***
- **Parts and labor are covered**
- **Pay as you go, not all at once**
- **Travel benefits such as hotel, meals and rental car reimbursement**
- **Lock in rates from 3-7 years on new policies**
- **Multiple deductible options**
- **Free 22-point RV inspections**
- **Adds value to your vehicle—transferable if you sell**

Don't let a mechanical breakdown on your RV put a dent in your travel budget. Get the protection that will enable you to overcome these setbacks without worry.

After all, your RV is your home away from home, and there are many things that can malfunction, including refrigerators, air conditioners, water pumps, slide-out controls and awnings, not to mention the engine, the transmission and all the associated mechanical parts. Oftentimes, it can be a hassle to submit claims and deal with warranty administrators. Third party shops can also be difficult to work with, overcharge customers and provide poor work. Good Sam Extended Service Plan (ESP) will alleviate the burden, save you time and money, and create a hassle-free experience.

Good Sam ESP is better than a warranty. It is mechanical breakdown insurance that will be there for you. It is the only RV plan backed by an A+ rated insurance underwriter and therefore complies with stringent insurance regulations and will be there to pay your claims. To date, Good Sam ESP has paid out more than $90 million in claims to Good Sam customers.

ESP also boasts a unique alliance of Preferred Providers around the country to take care of you and your RV. Made up of 2,000+ providers, the alliance is only available to Good Sam members. So the next time you have a mechanical breakdown, call ESP first. ESP will help match you to the closest qualified repair facility. The providers offer a minimum 10 percent discount to all Good Sam ESP members, accept direct payment from Good Sam for covered repairs and stand behind their work.

Two partners in ESP's Preferred Provider Network, Camping World and AAMCO, now offer disappearing deductibles to ESP customers. Camping World has over 100 locations and offers Good Sam ESP members $50 off their deductible when they take their rigs in for repair on covered coach components. There are also exclusive member-only discounts offered by AAMCO. With over 750 locations, AAMCO not only repairs transmissions, but also hundreds of specialized RV mechanical components. You can save up to $100 off your deductible at select AAMCO locations.

*Less deductible. All program benefits are subject to limitations set forth in the current terms and conditions. ESP is available to U.S. residents only. Designed for the Good Sam Club by Affinity Brokerage, LLC. Vehicles qualifying for coverage include RVs that are 15 years old or newer; motorhomes with less than 80,000 miles; and cars, trucks and SUVs that are 15 years old or newer with less than 100,000 miles.

Contact Us Today!

866-457-7351 • GoodSamESP.com/RVGuide

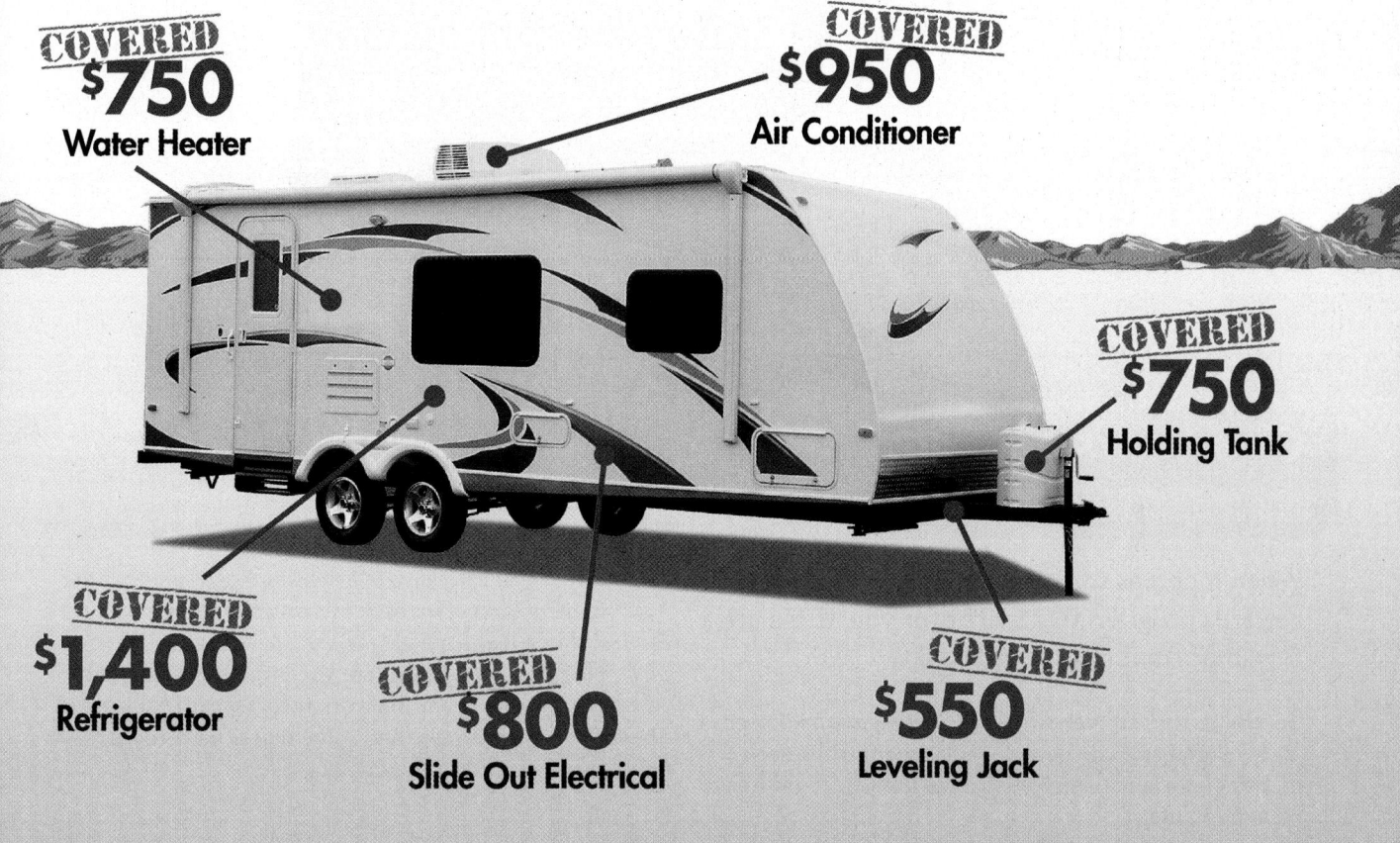

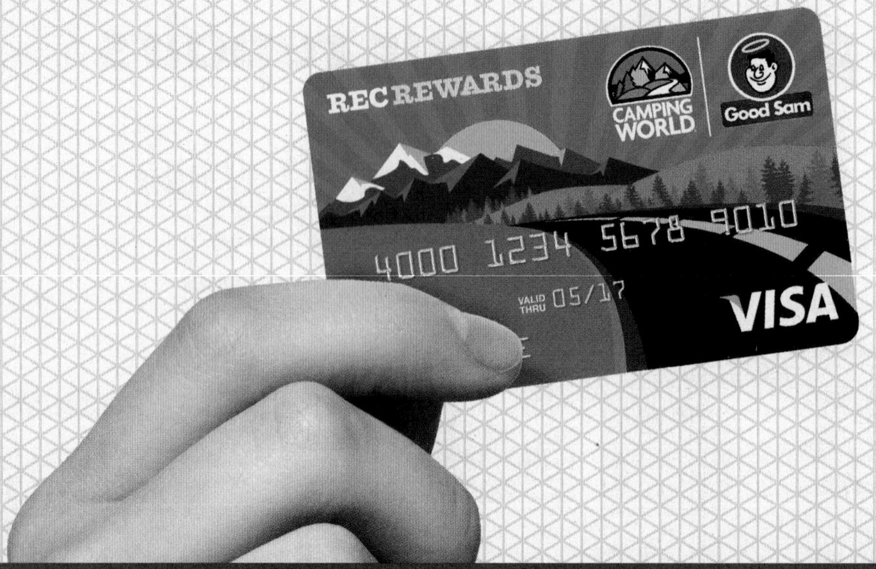

Give Yourself Credit

The Good Sam|Camping World Visa® fits your lifestyle

When it comes to choosing the credit card rewards program that's right for you, there are a few important questions to ask:

1 **What's the interest rate if you carry a balance?** Keep in mind that if you pay your balance off in full each month, there are no interest charges, but you can still earn rewards points.

2 **Is there an annual fee?** If there is, make sure that the value of your rewards points exceeds the annual fee.

3 **What kind of rewards are you interested in?** There are some programs that strictly offer cash back, travel rewards or merchandise and some that offer cardholders a choice of rewards for their points.

If you're like most people, you probably have more than one credit card in your wallet. We all use credit cards for different reasons—from financing larger purchases to enjoying the convenience of a no-hassle cash alternative. Whatever the reason, it's important to make sure that the credit cards you use provide you with the most benefit for your specific spending habits.

We're all familiar with credit card programs geared towards airline and hotel travel, many of which require an annual fee to participate. While even the most dedicated RVer doesn't restrict all of their travel to RVing, they likely rack up more miles on the road than in the air and more nights in their rig than a hotel.

For RVers, the Good Sam|Camping World Visa® with REC REWARDS was designed to reward you for doing what you love...camping. Cardholders earn points on every purchase, including extra points for purchases on Good Sam products and services at Camping World and at private campgrounds throughout the United States and Canada*.

REC REWARDS points add up fast and can be redeemed for Good Sam memberships, Camping World gift cards, and even gas, restaurant and retail gift cards. Cardholders can also redeem points for cash back as a statement credit. All this and NO ANNUAL FEE!*

To apply for the Good Sam|Camping World Visa® and start earning REC REWARDS, please visit www.GoodSamCampingWorldVisa.com or call toll-free 1-844-271-2591**

*Standard APR of 24.99%, 19.99% and 13.99% based on Prime Rate and your credit worthiness. Balance Transfer and Cash Advance APR of 25.99% based on Prime Rate. Minimum interest charge is $2.00 per credit.

**Offer subject to credit approval. For information about the rates, fees other costs and the reward program rules (including point accrual rate, bonus award points, etc.) and benefits associated with the use of this credit card program please visit http://www.comenity.net/goodsamcampingworld for complete terms and conditions.

The Good Sam|Camping World Visa® and Visa Signature® cards are issued by Comenity Capital Bank, pursuant to license from Visa® U.S.A. Inc. VISA is a registered trademark of Visa International Service Association and used under license.

6 Facts to Keep You Protected

Get the lowdown on Good Sam TravelAssist and roam without a worry

Hundreds of miles from home, your trip takes an unexpected turn. Your back goes out...your fever spikes...you fall mountain biking...your chest develops a sharp pain...

Many members have shared similar experiences when accidents, injuries and illnesses have interrupted their travels. One thing they all agree on: while being sick is always unwelcome, a medical emergency when traveling is 10 times worse. The worries just seem to multiply: not only concerns about your health, but also the costs, logistics and impact to your family.

Be ready for such medical emergencies with Good Sam TravelAssist — your action plan for medical emergencies away from home. As a member, TravelAssist is available to help you and your family 24/7, anywhere in the world.

The facts below clarify coverage—and highlight just how valuable the benefits are:

1 TravelAssist provides benefits your health insurance typically does not. Medical evacuation, travel companion benefits, vehicle return home: health insurance policies rarely cover any of these. But TravelAssist does, saving you thousands of dollars in unexpected expenses.

2 Membership is assured regardless of medical history. Membership in TravelAssist is available to everyone, no matter your age.

3 TravelAssist is available worldwide. Emergencies can happen anywhere: TravelAssist covers you in the USA and anyplace else in the world—whether you're traveling for business or pleasure, by car, RV, airplane or cruise ship.

4 Full benefits also apply to your family. Membership extends to your spouse and any dependent children under 25 years of age.

5 TravelAssist offers incredible value. Other companies offer more limited programs but with higher prices—as much as four times more than TravelAssist.

6 Your satisfaction is guaranteed. If you decide the coverage is not exactly what you want, notify TravelAssist within thirty days to get a full refund (pro-rated thereafter).

Get protected today.

Call 888-633-6457 or visit GoodSamTravelAssist.com

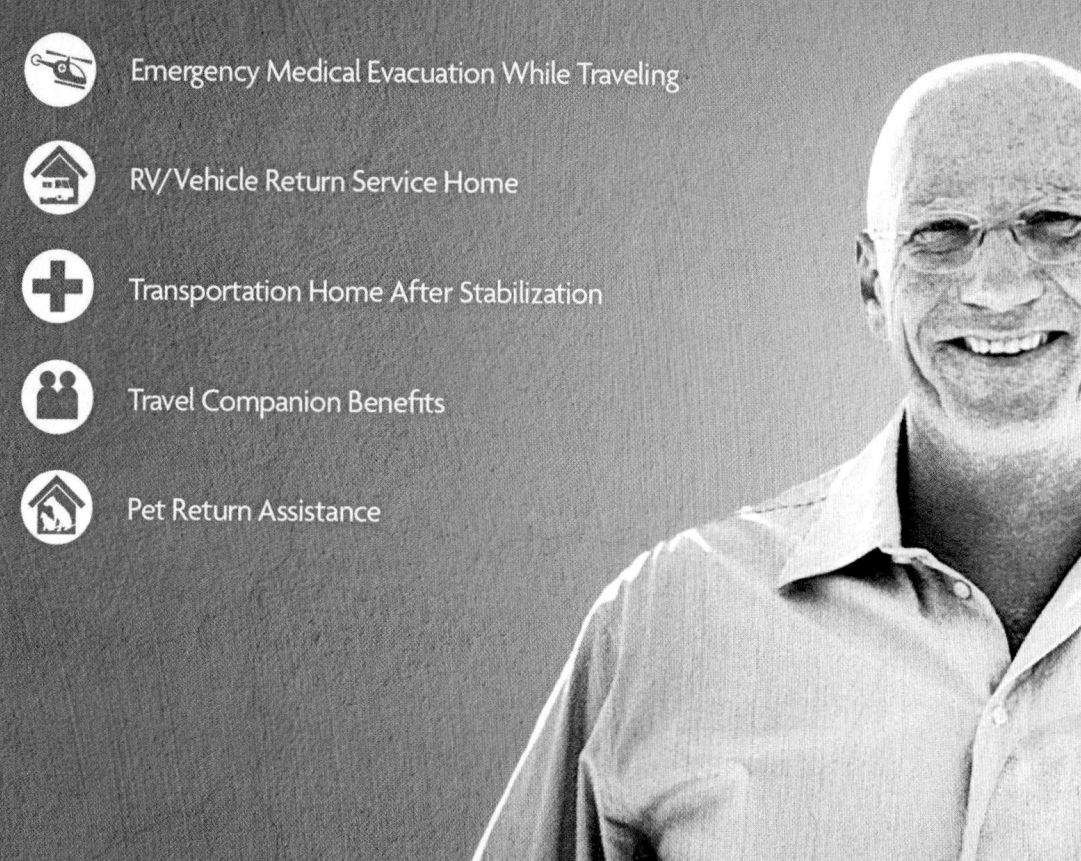

A Practical Guide to Financing Your RV

Don't lose sleep over getting the funds for your home on wheels

Thinking of buying a new or pre-owned RV? Preparing prior to even beginning to shop is key. Armed with a solid understanding of the financing process, you will be better positioned to drive away with your dream RV while working within your budget.

Pay Cash or Finance?

If you have the means, it may be tempting to avoid monthly payments and purchase your RV with cash. However, that's not necessarily the most beneficial option.

Cash buyers sometimes mistakenly believe they're saving money by avoiding interest payments. However, consider the loss of earning power from the money you put into an RV. For example, any income derived from liquidating an asset may incur a capital-gains tax. Or, if your money is in a bank certificate of deposit (CD) that has not yet matured, you may incur a penalty for early withdrawal.

With affordable interest rates and flexible payment options, taking out an RV loan may be a more prudent option depending on your particular situation and goals. Financing your RV frees up cash that might otherwise be spent on a cash purchase. Financing might even allow you to purchase a larger RV than if you paid with cash.

Determine Your Price Range

The easiest way to help determine how much you can spend on an RV is to subtract all monthly expenses from your monthly income. Doing this will help you estimate the amount of money that you can afford to spend each month.

There are many websites that offer online tools to help you calculate the loan amount and monthly payments, including the Good Sam Finance Center. Simply go to www.goodsamfinancecenter.com and click on the "Loan Calculator" link. You can find the Good Sam Finance Center's current interest rates and request a custom rate quote.

Loan Options

Financing an RV is easier than ever with flexible payment plans and loan terms up to 20 years when financing over $50,000. For those who consider their RV as their full-time residence, there are loan options for full-time RVers that meet the stricter federal guidelines, but not all lenders offer full-timer RV loans, so be sure to ask.

Be Prepared and Get Pre-Approved

Having a loan approval in hand before you start RV shopping helps make the process more efficient. Many finance companies offer free quotes and no application fees, so it's a safe start to your purchasing process. Once pre-approved, you'll know exactly how much you can afford to spend at the dealership or with a private party seller.

Whether you purchase from a dealership or a private party or are looking to refinance, now is a good time to check out how Good Sam can help you. For the Good Sam Finance Center's current interest rates and to apply for pre-approval, go to the Good Sam Finance Center at www.goodsamfinancecenter.com or call toll-free 800-444-1476 and a loan specialist will be happy to assist you and answer your questions.

RV FINANCING PACKAGES **TO FIT YOUR NEEDS!**

Now is the time...

Purchase a new or pre-owned RV or refinance your existing RV loan with competitive rates. Good Sam Finance Center has experienced RV associates ready to provide fast, convenient, and flexible service to make the process hassle-free so you can focus on enjoying your RV.

Thinking of Purchasing...

Did you know that Good Sam Finance Center offers financing for private party and dealer purchases? Whether you are purchasing an RV from your neighbor, dealer down the street or across the country, we have the RV financing you may need.

Thinking of Refinancing...

If you'd like to take advantage of the current interest rates and the potential to reduce your monthly payments, refinancing your existing RV loan may make financial sense - get the ball rolling today!

Are you a Full-Timer?

Good Sam Finance Center offers financing to purchase or refinance the perfect RV to call home.

Good Sam
RV Loans

CALL **1-800-444-1476**

CLICK **GoodSamRVLoans.com**

Coverage Concerns

Do you have the right insurance protection for your RV?

For many RVers, the answer to the above question has been "NO." Out of convenience, many RVers add their RV to the same policy that covers their automobiles. Your auto insurer may offer RV coverage, but is it the right coverage?

Under an auto policy, most insurance companies don't cover all of the components of an RV. In fact, two out of three of the largest insurance companies consider items like plumbing, refrigeration and dining equipment to be personal property that should be covered under a homeowner's policy. Unfortunately, homeowner's insurance policies limit coverage on property away from the main home. So what does this mean?

If you've insured your RV on your auto policy and are counting on your homeowner's to cover the rest, consider this: without the right RV coverage, you could be faced with paying two deductibles, not all of the loss being covered, and possible premium increases on both your auto and homeowner's policies if your RV is involved in an accident.

RV specialty insurance companies offer benefits and coverage options designed to meet the unique needs of your RV, like:

+ Personal Belongings Coverage
+ Permanent Attachments Coverage
+ Optional Full Replacement Cost Coverage
+ Emergency Expense Allowance
+ Full Timer's Liability
+ Vacation Liability

As the largest RV insurance agency in the world, the Good Sam Insurance Agency truly understands the needs of RVers. From the protection options you need to helping you find a qualified repair facility in the event of a claim, we'll help you design the optimum protection plan to fit your needs.

For more information or to obtain a quote
Call 888-736-3512 and mention savings code TD-B2 for the best rate

Wellness on the Road

Let Good Sam Life & Health Solutions help give you greater peace of mind and soundness of body

+ **Does your health insurance take into account your RV lifestyle?**

+ **Is your policy compatible with the adventurous road you've taken?**

If you have a Good Sam Life & Health Solutions product, the answer to both questions is probably "yes." Indeed, the Good Sam Club's array of insurance programs is tailored for people like you: RV travelers who'd rather think about what's around the next corner than worry about their health.

Here are some of the great programs:

Good Sam Cancer Care Insurance Plan*
Provides cash benefits if you're caught in a battle with cancer.

Long Term Care Insurance
Keep more control of your health care & financial decisions with a special long-term care insurance plan for Good Sam Club Members.

Medicare Supplemental Insurance*
Gives you protection against today's medical bills while protecting your freedom of choice among doctors who accept Medicare at the same time.

Secure Start Term Life Insurance Plan*
Life insurance coverage for your children, grandchildren, godchildren, nieces and nephews between the ages of 6 months and 17 years.

Major Medical Insurance
The largest selection of Major Medical plans from the leading health insurance companies.

Transportation Accidental Death Insurance*
The $5,000 No-Cost-To-You member benefit is an important safety net when you're using your RV or at a campground. Add the increased benefit for an even stronger layer of protection when you're traveling in your everyday life.

Good Sam Discount Card
Keep more money in your wallet with special discounts on prescription drugs, eyeglasses, contact lenses, hearing aids or even diabetes products.

*These policies have exclusions and limitations. For costs and complete details of the coverage please call 866-477-4401 or visit GSCInsurance.com

For more information
Visit GSCInsurance.com or Call 866-477-4401

GS Events RV Shows: One-Stop RV Shopping

Explore new RVs, the latest gadgets and accessories at a show near you

RV and outdoor enthusiasts across the nation continue to choose the open road for leisure travel and vacations. For shoppers in search of the best deal on a new RV, a GS Events RV show is the perfect place to start.

GS Events continues to lead the industry in producing high-quality consumer RV shows across the county. GS Events provides one location where current and potential RVers can receive the education and assistance they need to make the right buying decision. Entertainment is also thrown into the mix, creating a fantastic shopping experience.

These shows host a variety of dealers that display hundreds of RVs for comparison-shopping at each event. The hands-on experience of browsing different units at a show gives consumers a first-hand opportunity to see different sizes, floorplans and amenities to meet their budget. Additionally, the events showcase innovative technology and environmentally friendly options to ensure that today's RVers are prepared to hit the open road.

The GS Events team understands that RV trips provide a less costly means of travel, regardless of duration or destination. RV trips also enable families to spend more quality time together.

Every day, informative seminars hosted by industry experts provide vital information to RVers, allowing even the least experienced RVer to be road-ready after just one show. Attendees can have their questions about RV maintenance, insurance plans, campgrounds, RV parks and resorts, and more answered in person.

In addition to new RVs, daily seminars and entertainment, GS Events RV shows give attendees the opportunity to interact with fellow RV enthusiasts and browse new products, including innovative kitchen accessories, patio décor, space-saving gadgets, clothing, pet-care items and much more.

In the fall of 2015, GS Events introduced the Great American RV Show series with events in Atlantic City, New Jersey; Colorado Springs, Colorado; Conyers, Georgia; and Prior Lake, Minnesota. In 2016, GS Events plans to host over 20 RV-centric shows across the country.

Why come to an RV show?

- **An average of 63% of attendees attend a GS Events show looking for an RV**
- **76% of attendees say the show was beneficial to their buying decision**
- **81% of attendees find the seminars helpful to their overall RVing experience and lifestyle**

800-848-6247 • GSEvents.com

Make the most of your RV lifestyle with Good Sam's family of publications

Are you looking for the latest RV models, travel destinations and how-to articles? Look no further than *MotorHome* and *Trailer Life* magazines and the annual *RV Buyers Guide*, published by Good Sam Enterprises. Members of the Good Sam Club can take advantage of discounted annual subscription rates exclusively for members. RV enthusiasts can buy these widely respected publications on newsstands, subscribe to the print or digital editions, and purchase single issues or annual subscriptions on mobile apps for Android, Apple and Kindle tablets.

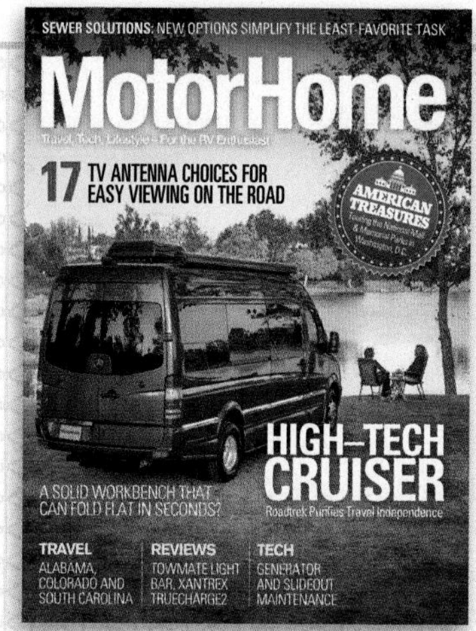

MotorHome

For 48 years, *MotorHome* has been the trusted source for technical, travel and lifestyle information for savvy coach owners. Each month, *MotorHome* delivers the latest news about Class A, B and C motorhomes, as well as expert coach and product reviews, hands-on technical features and intriguing travel destinations, campgrounds and RV resorts. With a subscription, *MotorHome* readers also receive the annual *Guide to Dinghy Towing*, an indispensable resource for selecting and accessorizing towed vehicles.

Good Sam member subscriptions:
www.GoodSamClub.com/MHoffer
866-799-4084

Apple App Store, Google Play & Kindle apps - search for:
MotorHome Mag

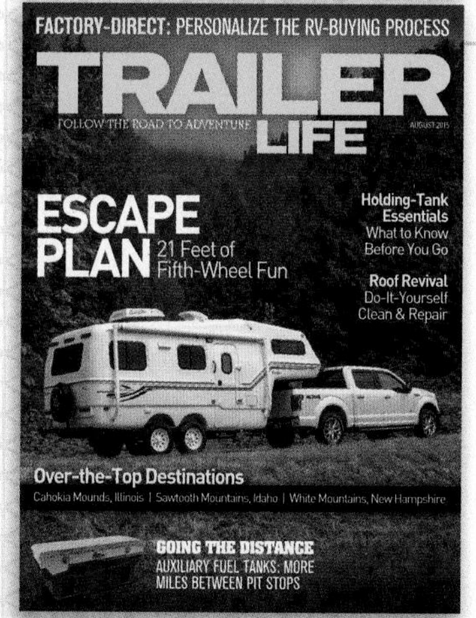

Trailer Life

Celebrating its 75th anniversary in 2016, America's bestselling RV magazine covers travel trailers, fifth-wheels, folding trailers, truck campers and small motorhomes, along with must-see RV destinations. *Trailer Life* sets the standard for objective RV testing and puts the latest products through the paces. RV authorities offer guidance on installations, repairs and upgrades and answer questions on a wide range of technical topics. Subscribers also receive the yearly *Towing Guide*, packed with up-to-date tow ratings and tips for selecting a suitable tow vehicle.

Good Sam member subscriptions:
www.GoodSamClub.com/TLoffer
or 866-799-4038

Apple App Store, Google Play & Kindle apps - search for:
Trailer Life Mag

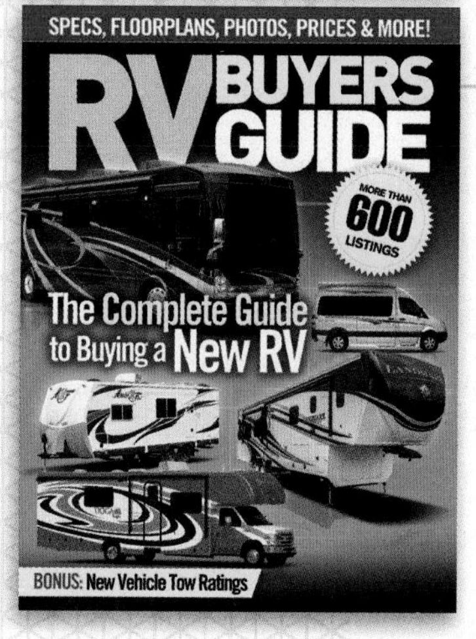

RV Buyers Guide

For readers researching their next RV purchase, the annual *RV Buyers Guide* is an invaluable resource, packed with timely information on more than 500 new RVs of all types and sizes. Compiled by the *Trailer Life* and *MotorHome* staff, each listing is accompanied by a photo, floorplan and specifications that include measurements, capacities, amenities and the approximate base retail price. Motorhome listings include specs on engines, transmissions and chassis, and towable listings cover important trailer weights and ratings to help buyers match their RV to appropriate tow vehicles.

RV Buyers Guide: Look for the 2016 RV Buyers Guide at:
newsstands and Camping World SuperCenters

Stay on Course with Good Sam

5 navigation tools to guide you across North America

Maneuver through North America like a pro with an array of navigation tools from Good Sam. Choose a place to stay from one of our 2,100-plus Good Sam Parks, then use one of our aids to design a smart trip that takes into account your travel preferences, gas budget and vehicle specifications. Chances are, you'll arrive on time with some great memories of your travels along the way.

1 Good Sam Camping App

Use your smartphone or tablet to find your way around. Download the Good Sam Camping app on your Android or Apple iOS and filter your searches to include campgrounds based on "Pets OK," "Swimming," "Internet," "50 Amps" and "Open All Year." Find the Good Sam Park of your dreams, then get driving directions from your current location. Smartphone users can touch the number in each listing and call the park for reservations.

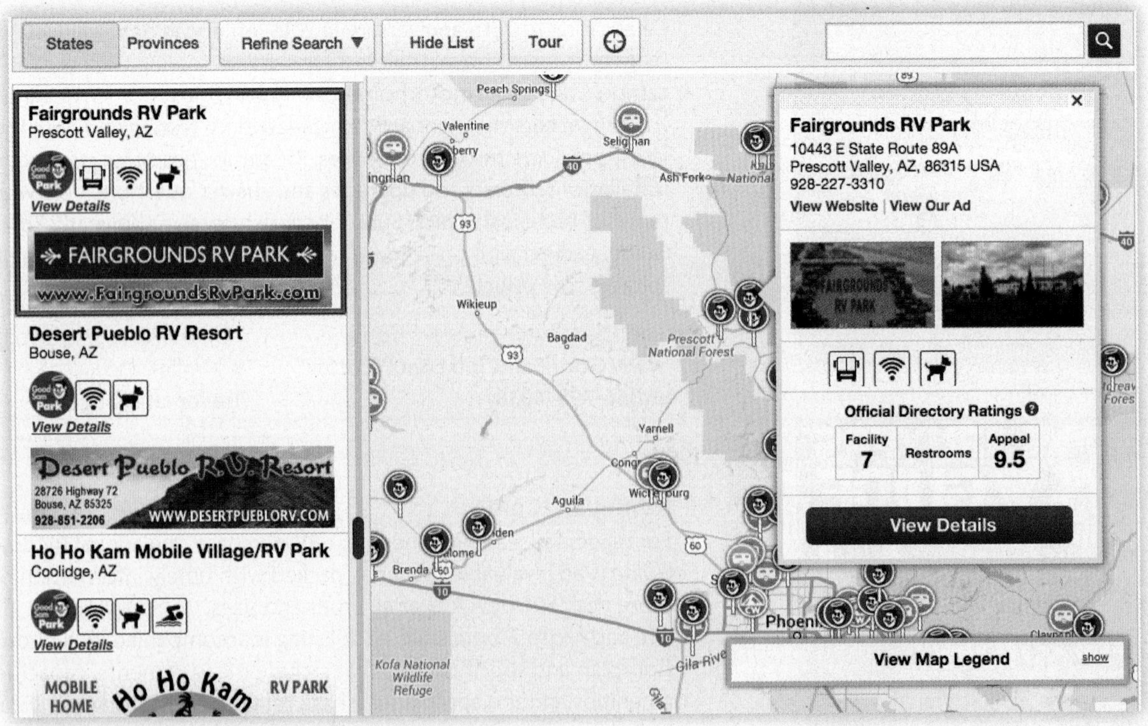

2 Map View

Can't decide where to stay? GoodSamClub.com's Map View Feature shows the locations of RV parks in the area that you're visiting. From the Plan a Trip tab, click Map View and enter your destination in the upper right-hand field. Good Sam Parks are represented by pins bearing our smiling mascot. Nearby Camping World SuperCenters, likewise, appear with the distinctive blue "CW" icon. Filter for parks that suit your preference, then click on the icon that strikes your interest for detailed information, including ratings and amenities.

3 Good Sam Trip Planner

Use GoodSamClub.com to create a detailed route to your location. Powered by Rand McNally, the Good Sam Trip Planner maps out travel itineraries and displays locations of Good Sam Parks and Camping World SuperCenters along the way.

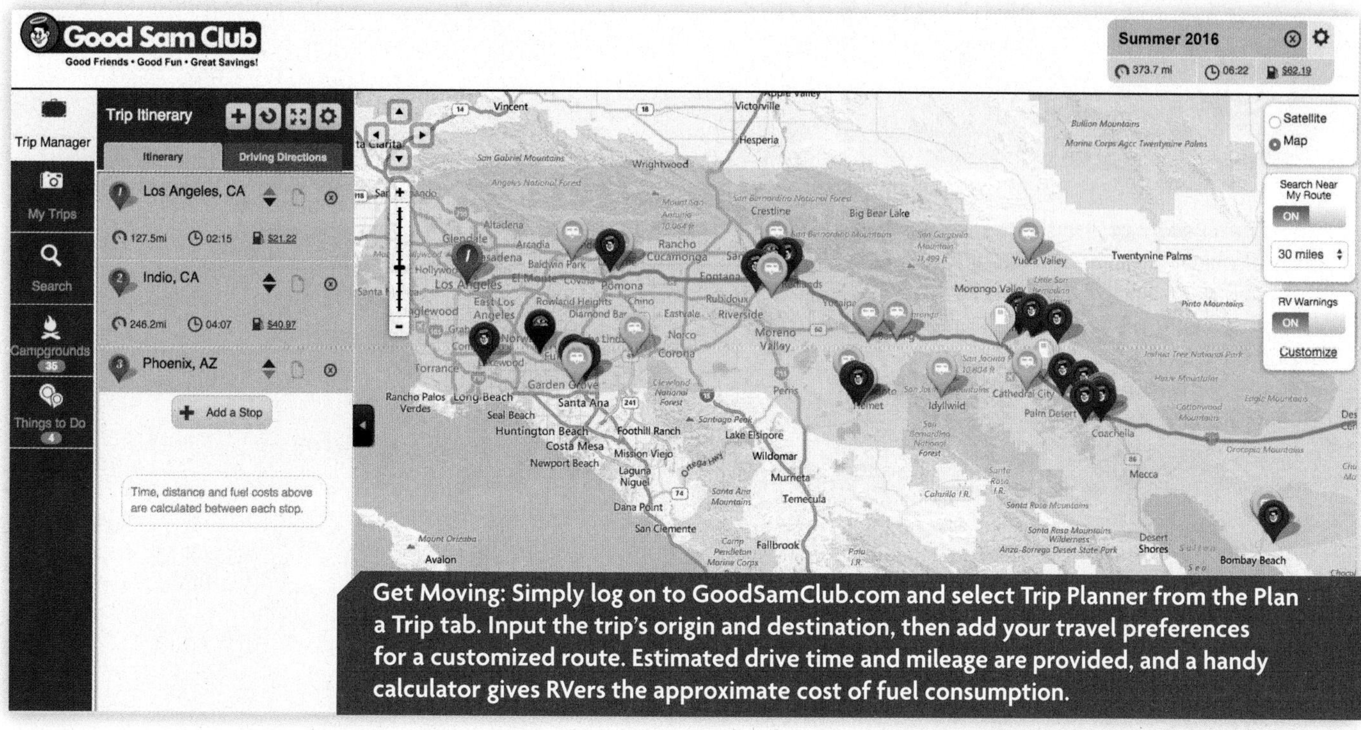

Get Moving: Simply log on to GoodSamClub.com and select Trip Planner from the Plan a Trip tab. Input the trip's origin and destination, then add your travel preferences for a customized route. Estimated drive time and mileage are provided, and a handy calculator gives RVers the approximate cost of fuel consumption.

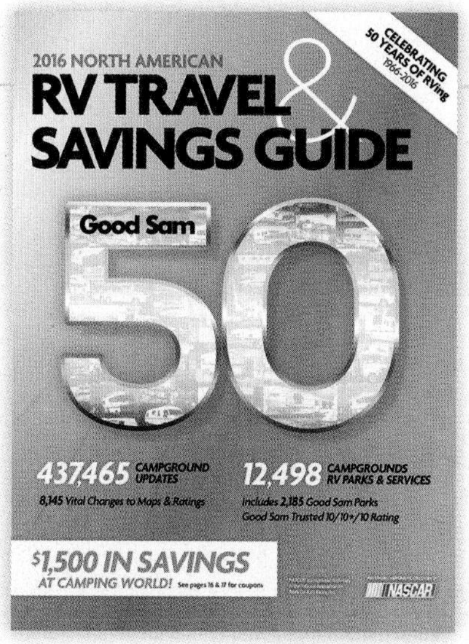

4 Good Sam RV Travel & Savings Guide Campground Information Pages

Consult the mother of all RV travel guides—the one you're holding in your hands. In the Campground Information pages of this book, peruse the *Good Sam RV Travel & Savings Guide's* 12,500 RV parks, campgrounds and services, including 2,100-plus Good Sam parks. Find the amenities that suit your interests, and make sure that the park's 10/10★/10 ratings are up to snuff. Consult the full-color maps of each state and province for locations of Good Sam Parks. The *2016 Good Sam RV Travel & Savings Guide* also includes lifestyle tips, travel articles and money-saving offers.

5 Good Sam RV Road Atlas

Prefer hard copy to computer screens? Good Sam has collaborated with Rand McNally to publish the *Good Sam RV Road Atlas*, an easy-to-read, large-scale print atlas sold through Camping World. Open the spiral-bound book to the color map of the state or Canadian province you're visiting and find the pins indicating Good Sam Parks, Camping World SuperCenters and Pilot Flying J Travel Centers. Consult the Listing Index to find parks alphabetically by state and city to hone your search.

Camping Under the Halo

Follow the smiling face to find a Good Sam Park that's right for you

Good Sam Parks carry on the traditions of quality and savings that have sustained our brand for 50 years. Each one of the 2,100-plus Good Sam Parks in our network offers a 10 percent discount* to members along with minimum standards of quality found nowhere else in the industry.

Located across North America, Good Sam Parks come in all shapes and sizes. These independently owned and operated RV parks range from low-key, family-owned getaways to high-end resorts with ample amenities. With 1.6 million members, Good Sam is adding new parks regularly to meet the growing demand. You can bet that there are Good Sam Parks to meet your RVing preferences.

All Good Sam Parks must have a minimum 5/7/5 Good Sam Rating to qualify for inclusion in the Good Sam RV Park & Resort Network. (See page 158 for a full explanation of the Good Sam Rating System.)

To receive the discount, simply show your Good Sam membership card when you check in. The discount will be deducted from the regular nightly RV rate and is available 365 days a year with no blackout dates.

Find Good Sam Parks by visiting GoodSamClub.com, GoodSamCamping.com or perusing the pages of this directory. Just look for the smiling face of our haloed mascot. Each Good Sam Park listing in this directory contains the park's rating along with prices and facility information, including pet restrictions and Wi-Fi access.

*Note that the discount can't be applied to long-term rates or combined with group or other discounts.

Share Your RV Park Experience

Let your voice be heard – RV travelers can now post reviews about their experiences at RV parks across North America

Our new RV Park and Campground Reviews on GoodSamClub.com lets members share information about their RV park stays, from favorite campsites and amenities to what to see and do in the area. The online review form lets you write about your RV camping experiences and assign one- to five-star overall scores.

After being screened for inappropriate content, each approved review will appear on the park's information page, and the park's average star rating will be displayed next to Good Sam's Triple Rating. By posting your feedback, you're helping fellow RV travelers make decisions about where to stay.

Be among the first to share your experiences and write a review on GoodSamClub.com. Posting a review is easy. Just follow the step-by-step instructions below.

Use the Find A Campground search to find the park you want to review

Click on the park's information page

Go to the Review tab and start sharing!

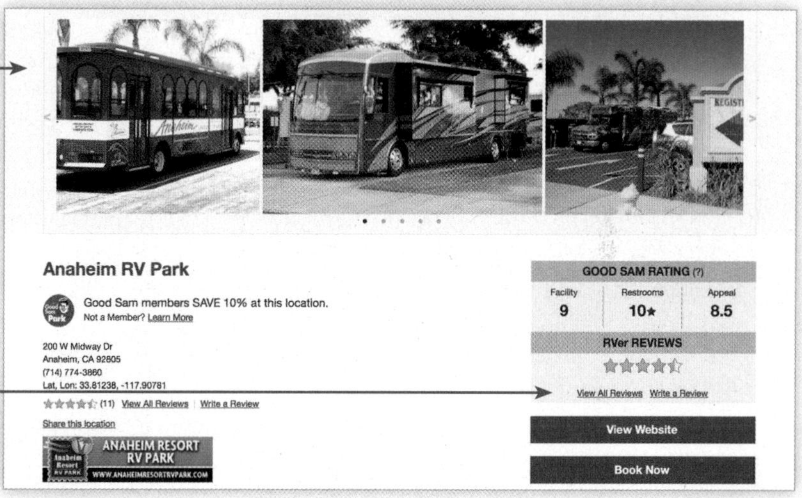

RVExplorer48

Reviews: 1
Helpful Reviews: 0

GOOD SAM MEMBER

Date of Stay: June, 2015

★★★★★ *Overall Rating*
★★★★★ *Facility Rating*
★★★★★ *Restroom Rating*
★★★★★ *Appeal Rating*

My sons and I stayed here to visit Disneyland this summer. it was WONDERFUL and we LOVED it. The staff was very nice and went out of their way for us. The facilities we clean, well maintained and nice. The proximity to the park was the best. We took the bus over. It was so close we came back for lunch and then went back until close. And the added bonus was you could see the park fireworks from the rv park pool!!! We watched the fireworks in the pool the first night before we went to the parks. The park was very family friendly. We had a blast and would go back in a heartbeat. Plus the price was such a great deal.

Get Social With Good Sam

Pull into Good Sam's nonstop online RV gathering

Good Sam's online community is like an RV rally that never ends. Join other RV travelers in this nonstop get-together to learn about tech tips, share photos of a recent RV adventure or simply post a review about your latest RV park experience (see accompanying article). Get the skinny about RV destinations, share some RV advice and make new friends—all without leaving your home on wheels.

So find an RV-related Facebook post, tweet, pin or blog article that piques your interest or start a conversation of your own. Join the online rally that never rests.

FACEBOOK

Click the thumbs-up button on the Good Sam Club page and join the fun on Facebook. Over 200,000 users have "liked" Good Sam's Facebook page, and that number is growing. RVers and club members frequent the page to join the discussions on topics posted by Good Sam, such as "Throwback Thursday" and "Washing and cleaning your motorhome."

Followers share travel photos, swap RV advice and post impressions about the places they've camped. When you see a post you like, click on the Share link to post it on your own timeline or a friend's. Be sure to check out the Tech Tuesday posts for tips on RV troubleshooting and maintenance, and Throwback Thursday to see what RVing was like in decades past.

facebook.com/thegoodsamclub

BLOG

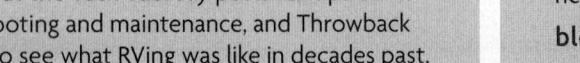

The Good Sam Camping Blog posts daily articles about RV-friendly destinations, RV-lifestyle issues, technical topics and trip ideas from a team of seasoned RVers. This is the place to get the latest RV tech tips or learn how to keep the kids occupied during long stretches on the road. Bloggers also post about Good Sam products, benefits and services to help members have more fun and save money on the road. Users can comment about blog articles, click on the Facebook, Pinterest and Twitter buttons to share posts, and subscribe to receive email alerts about new blog posts.

blog.goodsam.com

TWITTER

Take flight on Twitter, the popular microblogging service that enables users to express themselves with photos and text—as long as the posts don't exceed 140 characters. Use a smartphone or tablet to tweet about your RV experiences on the go or link to an article from another site. With Twitter, you can exchange messages with friends and follow other users—and even get tweets from the Good Sam Club.

twitter.com/thegoodsamclub

PINTEREST

Pin your favorite RV park. Pinterest.com is the social media site that functions like a virtual bulletin board. Users "pin" pictures of things they like to their own "board"—a special pin button can be installed on your browser, enabling you to pin anything you find on the Internet. As with Facebook, users can "like" an item from another board or re-pin it to their own board. Users also can follow members who have similar interests. Use Pinterest to create an on-the-fly scrapbook of your next RV outing or simply share favorite treats or trip ideas on your online board.

pinterest.com/goodsamclub

Arizona's Cactus League caters to RVing baseball fans

By Lynn Seldon

Around March every year, legions of baseball fans motor to Arizona for baseball's annual rite of spring—Cactus League spring training. Since the late-1940s, when the Cleveland Indians and New York Giants (before becoming the San Francisco Giants) first went west to the warm desert sun, attending ballgames in the Cactus League has been a popular pastime—and RVers have become a vital strand in this colorful tapestry of baseball fandom. Today, with 15 Major League Baseball teams playing in 10 unique stadiums in central Arizona, the Cactus League is bigger than ever.

From late-February to early-April, game day experiences in the Cactus League can be quite different from regular season games. Though some teams and games do sell out, spring training generally means RV-friendly parking, smaller crowds, and lower parking, ticket and concession prices. Visitors enjoy more player interaction, along with the kind of intimate baseball experience that fans won't experience in Major League games in the likes of venerable Yankee Stadium and other big league parks.

Baseball stadiums are concentrated in the Valley of the Sun, including the big towns of Phoenix, Scottsdale, Tempe and Mesa. In contrast to many stadiums in Florida's Grapefruit League, the distances between Cactus League ballparks are typically short.

Most stadium complexes sit adjacent to practice fields, where die-hard fans can often catch veterans and future stars taking batting and infield practice. These fields remain a secret to most visitors, who typically only attend the games (most of which take place in the afternoon). A few of night games give savvy fans the opportunity to take in a day-night doubleheader.

Many Cactus League stadiums also host Minor League Baseball and Arizona Fall League games, so even after spring training has ended, fans can still enjoy action play in these world-class facilities. Both Minor League and Fall League games offer opportunities to see rising stars before they make it to the majors.

Of course, campgrounds abound all around the area, and Cactus League ballparks and teams are particularly welcoming to RVers. Along with easy RV parking at many stadium complexes, public transportation and frequent trolleys or other shuttles make it easy to reach stadiums near and far. See RV park listings for information about nearby RV parks.

Here's an overview of Arizona's 10 Cactus League stadiums and what to expect:

1 Maryvale Baseball Park
Phoenix, AZ
Milwaukee Brewers

One of the oldest ballparks in the Cactus League, classic Maryvale Stadium is situated in a neighborhood where Brewers fans, brats and beer are

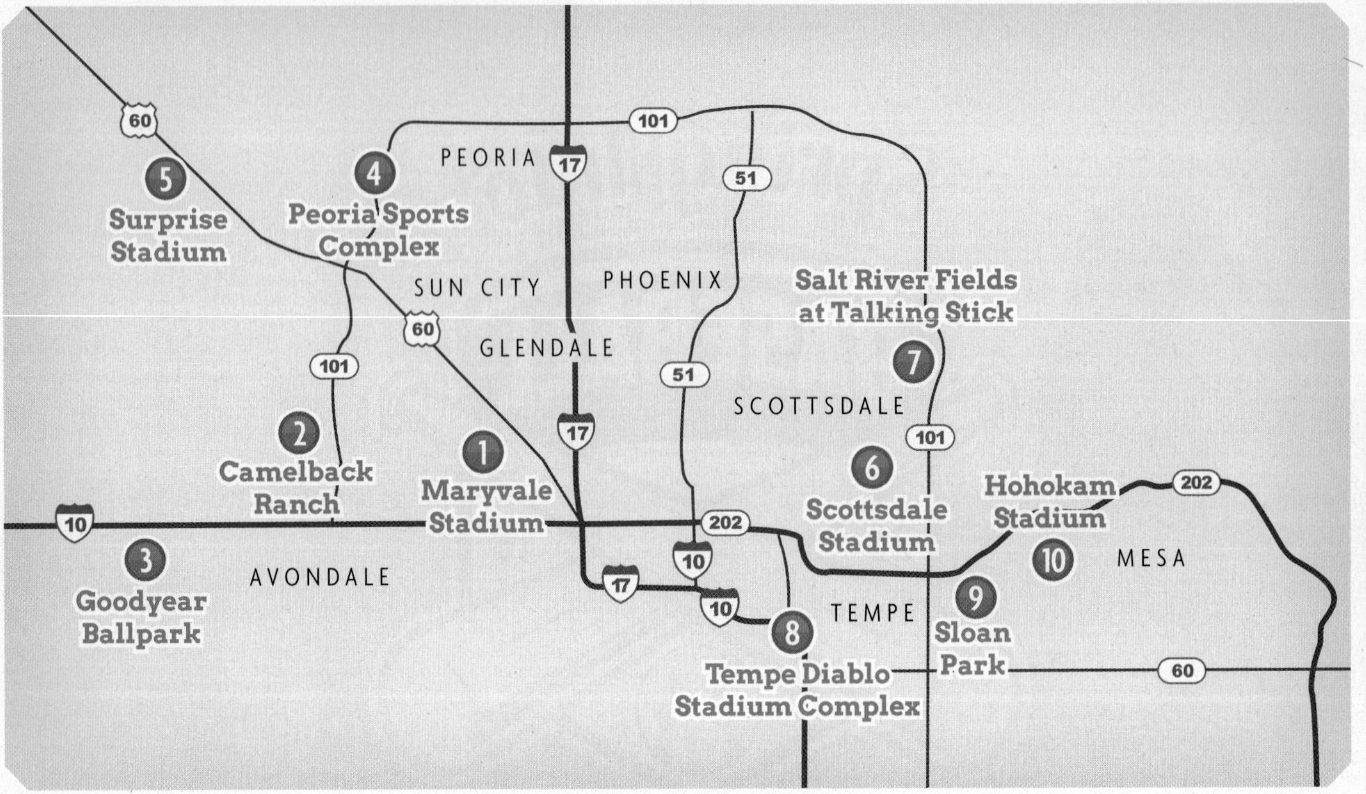

a spring staple. Intimate seating and a lush outfield berm means there's not a bad seat in the house—and the shaded concourse is the perfect place to head for a brat and brew. Reached by Valley Metro Light Rail Service, the stadium is close to bustling downtown Phoenix proper.

2 Camelback Ranch

Glendale, AZ

Chicago White Sox & Los Angeles Dodgers

Sprawling Camelback Ranch is situated just off Loop 101 from Glendale's popular Westgate Entertainment District. Opened in 2009, the two-team Sonoran Desert-inspired facility features 12 full practice fields and three half-fields, an orange grove, water features, a river, and a fully stocked lake between the White Sox and Dodgers facilities. Fans will love the life-sized Tommy Lasorda bobblehead doll, the mini-version of the iconic DodgerVision scoreboard, and famed Dodger Dogs and Vienna Beef Chicago Dogs. Those attending practice in the morning will want to check out two specific practice fields, built to the same dimensions of Dodger Stadium and U.S. Cellular Field, respectively.

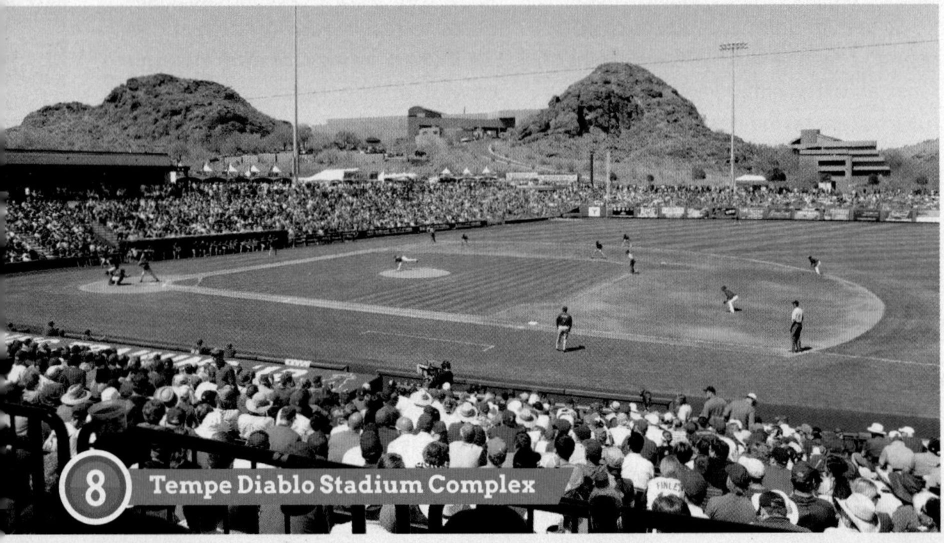

8 Tempe Diablo Stadium Complex

3 Goodyear Ballpark

Goodyear, AZ

Cincinnati Reds & Cleveland Indians

The Reds and Indians both moved spring training from Florida to Arizona and they now share Cactus League games and practice at the modern Goodyear Ballpark complex. Each team has six full practice fields. Highlights of a Goodyear Ballpark game include the largest kids zone in the Cactus League, plus Skyline Chili and Bertman Ballpark Mustard as tasty nods to Cincinnati and Cleveland, respectively.

4 Peoria Sports Complex

Peoria, AZ

San Diego Padres & Seattle Mariners

Built more than 20 years ago, the groundbreaking Peoria Sports Complex was Arizona's first two-team spring training facility. Several phases of improvements are ushering in a new era at this long-time favorite spring destination. Additional seating, a new

team shop, and new patio area and pavilion have led to record-setting attendance, while improved food offerings led to a 33 percent increase in concession sales in 2015—including more than 50,000 tasty sausages and hot dogs.

5 Surprise Stadium
Surprise, AZ
Kansas City Royals & Texas Rangers

Located less than 30 miles northwest of downtown Phoenix, Surprise Stadium helped lead the Cactus League into the 21st century. Loyal Royals and Rangers fans love the open nature of the entire ballpark, including great site lines from any seat and a wide concourse, where barbecue cuisine is a popular choice for fans from both cities.

6 Scottsdale Stadium
Scottsdale, AZ
San Francisco Giants

Located in the heart of downtown, the current Scottsdale Stadium has been the spring home of the San Francisco Giants since 1982. Baseball fans can take advantage of free downtown parking (lots fill up quickly), and free trolley and shuttle service make it easy to catch a Giants game. The always-bustling Charro Lodge overlooks right field and serves up more than two-dozen varieties of beer, while a smoker cranks out pulled pork and brisket sandwiches. The stadium is also the home of the Arizona Fall League Hall of Fame and the Scottsdale Sports Hall of Fame.

7 Salt River Fields at Talking Stick
Scottsdale, AZ
Arizona Diamondbacks & Colorado Rockies

One of the Cactus League's newest and largest complexes, Salt River Fields at Talking Stick is the only spring training destination situated on Native American land. Noted for its attendance records, the ballpark features some of the most spectacular mountain backdrops in all of baseball. Game day highlights on hot days might include quaffing one of 20-plus craft beers from Arizona and Colorado breweries.

8 Tempe Diablo Stadium Complex
Tempe, AZ
Los Angeles Angels

Located just blocks from two major freeways, and also accessible by shuttle from Tempe's downtown, Tempe Diablo Stadium sits in the shadows of stunning nearby mountains. The complex features varied practice fields anchored by the main stadium, which was named Gene Autry Field after the former Angels owner passed away in 1999. Tasty highlights include piled-high nachos served in a mini Angels batting helmet, microbrews in the Tempe Tap Room and Angelo's Italian Ice.

9 Sloan Park
Mesa, AZ
Chicago Cubs

The Chicago Cubs opened Sloan Park in 2014 to rave reviews, thanks to its Wrigley Field feel and modern amenities. Ballpark food is a tasty highlight here, thanks to Chicago-style deep-dish pizza, Chicago dogs, food trucks and more. Revel on the huge party deck or unroll a blanket on the sprawling outfield berm. After the game, Mesa Riverview Park, and an adjacent shopping and dining complex, await fans.

10 Hohokam Stadium
Mesa, AZ
Oakland Athletics

Built back in 1997 in the heart of Mesa, but undergoing major renovations before the 2015 spring training season, Hohokam Stadium now features the largest HD scoreboard display in the Cactus League, plus all new seats and seating areas—including a berm. It remains a classic spring training venue, but with modern amenities—like Ike's Sandwiches (an Oakland-area favorite).

For Cactus League information visit, **www.cactusleague.com**

NASCAR -across- AMERICA

6 speedways that roll out the welcome mat for RVing race fans

By Lynn Seldon

It's easy to spot fans of the National Association for Stock Car Auto Racing on America's highways. Just look for the RVs adorned with stickers that bear the numbers of NASCAR drivers. It's likely that these RV travelers are headed to another big-time NASCAR race weekend to cheer on their favorite cars.

By many parameters, NASCAR racing is America's pastime. With an estimated fan base of 75 million (about a third of the nation's adult population), NASCAR is the No. 1 spectator sport in the nation. Each NASCAR Sprint Cup Series event draws an average attendance of about 100,000 fans.

For the uninitiated, the Sprint Cup Series is considered NASCAR's top racing series. Some die-hard fans travel the nation to attend each of the 30-plus Sprint events held in a dozen states from coast to coast between February and November. Others make do with a handful of races at tracks in one region. The winner of the Sprint Cup is determined by a point system based on finishing placement and laps led.

But Sprint competition isn't the only game in town. The NASCAR Xfinity Series and Camping World Truck Series are among the NASCAR events that keep tracks busy throughout the year. Indeed, the geographical diversity of NASCAR competition provides lots of opportunities for adventurous RVers to attend races in a variety of environments. Regardless of the type of competition, race weekends see hundreds of RVs converging on tracks.

At many venues, RVing fans enjoy perks like camping in areas adjacent to the track, including the coveted infield. And there are even more upsides to the NASCAR-RV marriage. "Did you ever wonder why so many race fans take recreational vehicles to the race and why they seem to have more fun than everyone else?" asks Jay Ahuja, author of *Speed Dreams*, a guide to NASCAR travel. As he sees it, the answer lies in the camaraderie between RVers, the great seats on RV roofs, and the ability to beat the crowds to races (often a day or more in advance) and wait out post-race traffic—all with the comforts of home.

Exciting NASCAR racing in great places has made for a travel combination that's hard to beat. Just start your RV's engine—but leave the speeding to the NASCAR drivers.

The following tracks stand out for their RV accommodations. Visit the website of each track to make reservations or get information about opening times, prices and camping. (This list is by no means comprehensive—check with www.NASCAR.com to find RV-friendly tracks throughout North America.)

Charlotte Motor Speedway

For many racing fans, North Carolina's Charlotte Motor Speedway is the ultimate NASCAR travel destination. Nestled in the very heart of the motorsports industry, the speedway annually hosts three major Sprint Cup Series race weekends. However, it's not just the races that make Charlotte so special.

During racing season, weekends in the Speedway feature concerts, pre-race show stunts and a state-fair-type fan area (Fan Fest) near the main entrance. And with more than 6,000 affordable camping spaces within sight of the track—as well as popular infield RV sites—it's convenient for RVers.

As a bonus, virtually every major team shop—from Hendrick Motorsports to Roush Fenway Racing to Richard Childress Racing—is located within a short drive of the speedway. The speedway offers tours that start right from the track, as well as trips to downtown Charlotte to experience the NASCAR Hall of Fame. Fans can partake in ride-along and drive programs in real NASCAR vehicles reaching speeds as high as 160 miles per hour on the fabled track.
www.charlottemotorspeedway.com

Daytona International Speedway

Daytona International Speedway in Florida is famed for the Daytona 500, but racing lives here year-round. Track tours and shopping for the latest NASCAR apparel at the Pit Shop are among the highlights of race weekends.

The infield at Daytona International Speedway is the ultimate place for RV camping during race weekend. Between heats, the Sprint Fanzone provides a great place for fans to peak into NASCAR Sprint Cup Series garages, dine in the Budweiser Bistro, attend driver Q&A's, and enjoy lots of other activities and displays.

Daytona International Speedway is undergoing a $400 million Daytona Rising renovation project that will see all-new amenities throughout the track. It's scheduled for completion in early 2016, well ahead of the year's NASCAR racing season.
www.daytonainternationalspeedway.com

Watkins Glen International

Located in the beautiful Finger Lakes region of upstate New York, Watkins Glen International gives fans a NASCAR experience that is as beautiful as it is exciting. When fans aren't enjoying the action of the track, they can take in the views of majestic Lake Seneca.

Starting at 6 a.m. on the Wednesday of race week, the rolling hills of legendary Watkins Glen quickly turn into stand-alone communities made up of dedicated, well-traveled race fans. Because the facility is one of only two "road" courses (the other is Sonoma) on the Sprint circuit, several options with varying amenities exist for those camping at the track.

In recent years, reserved camping for the Cheez-It 355 race has completely sold out, prompting the historic venue to expand its infield Pit Road RV Camping, complete with 50-amp electric and water hook-ups. Located inside the track behind the pit terrace grandstands, these sites provide proximity to the paddock, pit lane and infield activity.
www.theglen.com

Michigan International Speedway

Campers will love the multitude of offerings at Michigan International Speedway. Choose from an array of 10 campgrounds with a total of 9,000 sites both in the infield and in areas surrounding the track. In fact, the Speedway comprises the largest registered campground in the entire state of Michigan.

Opposite page: Campers overlooking the Iowa Speedway. Below: Fireworks over the Michigan International Speedway.

Surrounded by lots of trees and lakes, Michigan International Speedway provides a pleasant environment for race fans to enjoy socializing, relaxing and listening to live music between races. Race weekends in June and August are timed for summer vacation, and many repeat RVers say it's like experiencing NASCAR in a national park.
www.mispeedway.com

Iowa Speedway

Known as the "Fastest Short Track on the Planet," the Rusty Wallace-designed Iowa Speedway provides unique race weekends for seasoned fans and newcomers alike. RVers looking for epic RV parking during race events should look no further than the Blue Ox Campgrounds, sponsored by the manufacturer of towing products. Overlooking turns three and four, the campground is a welcome place to the many team owners, fans and drivers who make racetracks their home for more than 30 event weekends a year.

The lot opens at noon on Thursday before each race weekend, and guests are invited to stay until noon on the day following the race. The two-tiered trackside campground overlooks the track, and RVers are drawn to the ease and affordability of camping within earshot of the world's greatest drivers.

The Iowa Speedway offers RV campers six- or 10-race tickets and access to the concourse, display areas and the popular Infield Fan Walk. The Fan Walk affords the opportunity for fans to get up close to the action. Each camper also receives two designated parking passes for the camping unit and the tow vehicle or companion unit. RVers receive the same benefits as season ticket holders, as well as promotional items from many sponsors and partners. It's the ultimate heartland racing venue.
www.iowaspeedway.com

Sonoma Raceway

Combining NASCAR excitement with world-class vintages is a tasty possibility in California, thanks to Sonoma Raceway. Situated in the heart of wine country in proximity to 400-plus wineries, Sonoma Raceway has more than 1,600 campsites at six campgrounds. Guests can enjoy outdoor movies or live music from Wonderbread 5 in Club 7. Keep your eyes peeled for the GoPro Prize Patrol, which roams the area giving out goodies.

All campers receive weekend ticket discounts, early campsite arrival and late departure. Cold Pit access is available on Friday and Saturday. When you're not enjoying the action on the track, you can relax and take in views of the surrounding vineyards.
www.racesonoma.com

Top: Iowa Speedway action. Below, left: Camping at the Sonoma Raceway. Below: Rooftop viewing at the Daytona International Speedway.

NASCAR Camping

See the races at these top NASCAR tracks (in blue), and stay at the nearby RV parks listed below each venue

TALLADAGA SUPERSPEEDWAY

Country Court RV Park
Anniston, AL

Lakeside Landing Marina & RV Resort
Pell City, AL

PHOENIX INTERNATIONAL RACEWAY

Cotton Lane RV & Golf Resort
Goodyear, AZ

Desert Shadows RV Resort
Phoenix, AZ

Desert's Edge RV The Purple Park
Phoenix, AZ

Destiny Phoenix RV Resorts
Goodyear, AZ

Leaf Verde RV Resort
Buckeye, AZ

Phoenix Metro RV Park
Phoenix, AZ

Pueblo El Mirage Golf & RV Resort
El Mirage, AZ

Estrella Valley MH & RV Park, Buckeye, AZ

Sunflower RV Resort
Surprise, AZ

AUTO CLUB SPEEDWAY

Shady Oasis Kampground
Victorville, CA

KERN COUNTY RACEWAY PARK

A Country RV Park
Bakersfield, CA

Bakersfield River Run RV Park, Bakersfield, CA

Bakersfield RV Resort
Bakersfield, CA

DAYTONA INTERNATIONAL SPEEDWAY

Beverly Beach Camptown RV Resort
Flagler Beach, FL

Bulow RV Resort
Flagler Beach, FL

Daytona Beach RV Resort
Port Orange, FL

Flagler By the Sea Campground
Flagler Beach, FL

Harris Village & Adult RV Park LLC
Ormond Beach, FL

Highbanks Marina & Campresort
Debary, FL

New Smyrna Beach RV Park
New Smyrna Beach, FL

Orange City RV Resort
Orange City, FL

Nova Family Campground
Daytona Beach, FL

Sugar Mill Ruins Travel Park, LLC
New Smyrna Beach, FL

Twelve Oaks RV Resort
Sanford, FL

City Of Florida City Campsite & RV Park, Florida City, FL

Gold Coaster RV Resort and Manufactured Home Community, Homestead, FL

Larry & Penny Thompson Campground
Miami, FL

Pine Isle Park
Homestead, FL

The Boardwalk RV Resort
Homestead, FL

ATLANTA MOTOR SPEEDWAY

Atlanta South RV Park
McDonough, GA

IOWA SPEEDWAY

Kellogg RV Park
Kellogg, IA

Newton KOA
Newton, IA

INDIANAPOLIS MOTOR SPEEDWAY

Lake Haven Retreat
Indianapolis, IN

S & H Campground
Greenfield, IN

KENTUCKY SPEEDWAY

Follow the River RV Resort
Florence, IN

KANSAS SPEEDWAY

Walnut Grove RV Park
Merriam, KS

STAFFORD MOTOR SPEEDWAY

Oak Haven Family Campground
Wales, MA

DOVER INTERNATIONAL SPEEDWAY

Holiday Park Campground
Greensboro, MD

MICHIGAN INTERNATIONAL SPEEDWAY

Greenwood Acres Family Campground
Jackson, MI

Apple Creek Campground & RV Park
Grass Lake, MI

Holiday RV Campground
Grass Lake, MI

CHARLOTTE MOTOR SPEEDWAY

Camping at Charlotte Motor Speedway
Charlotte, NC

Carowinds Camp Wilderness Resort
Charlotte, NC

Glenwood Acres RV Park
Concord, NC

LEE USA SPEEDWAY

Great Bay Camping LLC
Newfields, NH

Tidewater Campground LP
Hampton, NH

Wakeda Campground LLC
Hampton Falls, NH

Exeter Elms Family Campground
Exeter, NH

NEW HAMPSHIRE MOTOR SPEEDWAY

Twin Tamarack Family Camping & RV Resort
Meredith, NH

Crown Point Campground
Strafford, NH

Newfound RV Park
Bridgewater, NH

Pine Hollow Campground
Weirs Beach, NH

LAS VEGAS MOTOR SPEEDWAY

Arizona Charlie's Boulder RV Park
Las Vegas, NV

Duck Creek RV Park
Las Vegas, NV

Hitchin' Post RV Park
Las Vegas, NV

Las Vegas RV Resort
Las Vegas, NV

Riviera RV Park
Las Vegas, NV

WATKINS GLEN INTERNATIONAL

Camp Bell Campground
Corning, NY

Ferenbaugh Campground
Corning, NY

Cool Lea Camp
Alpine, NY

Warren W Clute Memorial Park
Watkins Glen, NY

LAKE COUNTY SPEEDWAY

Heritage Hills RV Park
Thompson, OH

POCONO RACEWAY

Four Seasons Campgrounds
Scotrun, PA

Mountain Vista Campground
Stroudsburg, PA

Pocono Vacation Park
Stroudsburg, PA

Lehigh Gorge Campground
White Haven, PA

BRISTOL MOTOR SPEEDWAY

Lakeview RV Park
Bristol, TN

Rocky Top Campground & RV Park,
Kingsport, TN

TEXAS MOTOR SPEEDWAY

Northlake Village RV Park
Roanoke, TX

The Vineyards Campground & Cabins
Grapevine, TX

RICHMOND INTERNATIONAL RACEWAY

Americamps RV Resort
Ashland, VA

Kosmo Village Campground
Glen Allen, VA

Pampered Pets

How to keep your four-legged travel companions happy and comfortable

By Rene Agredano

Human beings aren't the only mammals that love hitting the road. According to some studies, close to 50 percent of RV travelers camp with pets, and that number will only grow as more RVers discover the joys of journeying with their four-legged companions.

Most pets are great travelers, but before planning that big RV trip with Fido, consider your pet's suitability for the road. Is your pet hampered by age or mobility? Have you plotted an itinerary that takes into account your pet's unique needs?

The following tips will enhance your RV getaways for years to come. Because most pet-owning RVers travel with canines, our recommendations are unabashedly dog-centric, but even cat owners will find useful hints. Just be sure to research specific travel concerns for felines—the same goes for birds, reptiles and other non-mammal pets that travel with you.

1 Check in with the Vet

A pre-departure vet exam can spot potential health problems and ensure that your pet is current on core vaccines required by pet-friendly establishments. Parvovirus, distemper, rabies and bordetella inoculations are the most common, but your vet may recommend others to protect against geographically specific conditions like leptospirosis and Lyme disease. Pets with chronic immune-system illnesses like cancer can apply for vaccine waivers. File all of these records in the RV, because vaccination certificates are often required, especially at international border crossings.

2 Update Dog ID Info on the Go

Abrupt events like thunderstorms often cause pets to flee. Consider purchasing a GPS locator tag that lets you track your dog's movements on a smartphone. Other electronic pet ID devices enable you to update your pet's location details on the go, such as your RV park name and campsite number. The information gets stored in the cloud and on a compact USB drive that hangs from a collar, allowing anyone who finds your dog to read its info on a computer.

3 Create a Pet-Friendly Home on Wheels

Familiarize your pet with the RV by placing their toys, feeding station, bedding and crate in a safe, cozy spot. Prepare for daily walks by keeping leashes, collars and a portable water bowl by the door. Hopefully, your adventures will be injury-free, but be prepared with a good pet first-aid kit that includes tick removal kits, vet bandages and a muzzle. Camping World stores carry many of the pet travel accessories that you'll need for your RV adventures.

4 Choose the Right Chow

Feeding time can be tricky on the road, especially if your pet eats an uncommon food. Consider transitioning to a more common one at least three weeks before leaving. Dehydrated pet food is helpful too; it's made on the spot with hot water, takes up less space and weighs less than cans.

5 Avoid Motion Sickness and Boredom

Pets and people alike get carsick. Acclimate your pet to vehicle motion with progressively longer RV trips around your neighborhood. Some pets will need anti-nausea prescription medication, but another good option is a "calming cap" device that works like a horse blinder; it goes over

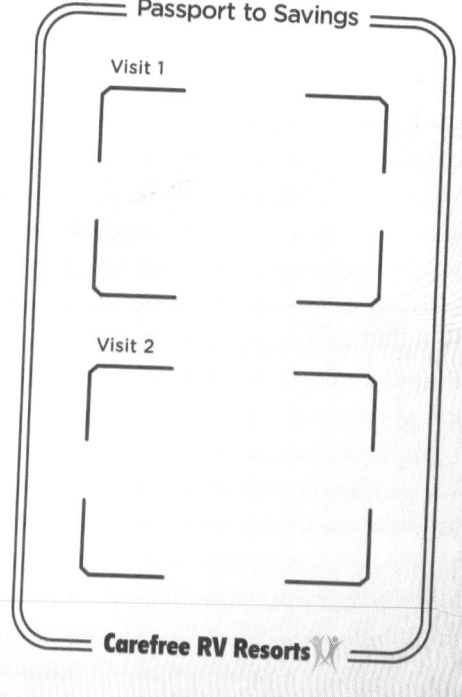

FLORIDA

Clearwater & Gulf Coast

Dunedin
800-345-7504
2920 Alt 19 N
Dunedin, 34698

Homosassa River
800-471-3722
10200 W Fishbowl Dr
Homosassa, 34448

Marco Naples
239-774-1259
100 Barefoot Williams Rd
Naples, 34113

Rainbow Village
727-536-3545
11911 66th St
Largo, 33773

Bradenton & Sarasota

Ellenton Gardens
941-722-0341
7310 US Hwy 301 N
Ellenton, 34222

Horseshoe Cove
800-291-3446
5100 60th St E
Bradenton, 34203

Pleasant Lake
941-756-5076
6633 53rd Ave E
Bradenton, 34203

Sun-N-Fun
800-843-2421
7125 Fruitville Rd
Sarasota, 34240

Vista del Lago
941-755-5680
801 53rd Ave W
Bradenton, 34207

Florida Keys

Pelican
305-289-0011
59151 Overseas Hwy
Marathon, 33050

Riptide
305-852-8481
97680 Overseas Hwy
Key Largo, 33037

San Pedro
305-289-0011
87401 Old Hwy
Islamorada, 33036

North Tampa

Baker Acres
813-782-3950
7820 Wire Rd
Zephyrhills, 33540

Blue Jay
352-567-9678
38511 Wilds Rd
Dade City, 33525

Citrus Hill
352-567-6045
9267 US Hwy 98
Dade City, 33525

Glen Haven
813-782-1856
37251 Chancey Rd
Zephyrhills, 33541

Grove Ridge
352-523-2277
10721 US Hwy 98
Dade City, 33525

Majestic Oaks
813-783-7518
3751 Laurel Valley Blvd
Zephyrhills, 33542

Rainbow Village
813-782-5075
4150 Lane Rd
Zephyrhills, 33541

Red Oaks
352-793-7117
5551 SW 18th Terrace
Bushnell, 33513

Settler's Rest
813-782-2003
37549 Chancey Rd
Zephyrhills, 33541

Spanish Main
813-986-2415
12110 Spanish Main Tr
Thonotosassa, 33592

Southern Charm
813-783-3477
37811 Chancey Rd
Zephyrhills, 33541

Sweetwater
813-788-7513
37647 Chancey Rd
Zephyrhills, 33541

Waters Edge
813-783-2708
39146 Otis Allen Rd
Zephyrhills, 33540

Orlando & Central Florida

Big Tree
863-494-7247
2626 NE Hwy 70
Arcadia, 34266

Central Park
863-422-5322
1501 W Commerce Ave
Haines City, 33844

Daytona Beach
386-761-2663
4601 S. Clyde Morris Blvd
Port Orange, 32129

Kissimmee South
863-424-1286
3700 US Hwy 17-92
Davenport, 33837

Lakeland
888-622-4115
900 Old Combee Rd
Lakeland, 33805

Mill Creek
407-847-6288
2775 Michigan Ave
Kissimmee, 34744

Shell Creek
941-639-4234
35711 Washington Loop Rd
Punta Gorda, 33982

Tropical Palms
800-647-2567
2650 Holiday Tr
Kissimmee, 34746

CALIFORNIA

Indian Wells
760-347-0895
47-340 Jefferson St
Indio, 92201

TEXAS

Austin Lone Star
800-284-0206
7009 South I-35
Austin, 78744

Sandy Lake
972-242-6808
1915 Sandy Lake Rd
Carrollton, 75006

Travelers World
800-755-8310
2617 Roosevelt Ave
San Antonio, 78214

Treetops
817-467-7943
1901 W Arbrook Blvd
Arlington, 76015

MASSACHUSETTS

Campers Haven
508-398-2811
184 Old Wharf Rd
Dennis Port, 02639

NEW JERSEY

Long Beach
609-698-5684
30 Route 72
Barnegat, 08005

Shady Pines
609-652-1516
443 South 6th Ave
Galloway Township, 08205

NORTH CAROLINA

Fort Tatham
828-586-6662
175 Tathams Creek Rd
Sylva, 28779

ONTARIO, CANADA

Arran Lake
519-934-1224
53 Concession 12 W
Allenford, N0H 1A0

Craigleith
519-599-3840
496875 Grey Rd 2
Clarksburg, N0H 1J0

Deer Lake
705-789-3326
85 Hutcheson Beach Rd
Huntsville, P1H 1N4

Grand Oaks
905-772-3713
107 Haldimand Hwy 54
Cayuga, N0A 1E0

Hidden Valley
519-426-5666
61 Mole Side Rd
Normandale, N0E 1W0

Lafontaine
705-533-2961
240 Lafontaine Rd E
Tiny, L9M 0S2

Lake Avenue
613-476-4990
37 Lake Avenue Ln
Cherry Valley, K0K 1P0

Pickerel Park
613-373-2812
665 South Shore Rd
Napanee, K7R 3K7

Sherkston Shores
800-263-8121
490 Empire Rd
Sherkston, L0S 1R0

Silver Birches
519-243-2480
9537 Army Camp Rd
Lambton Shores, N0N 1J3

Trailside
705-378-2844
105 Blue Lake Rd
Seguin, P2A 0B2

Willow Lake
519-446-2513
14 Willow Lake Private Rd
Scotland, N0E 1R0

Willowood
519-736-3201
4610 Essex County Rd 18
Amherstburg, N9V 2Y7

Woodland Lake
519-347-2315
6710 Line 46
Bornholm, N0K 1A0

Carefree RV Resorts

your dog's head and tones down visual disturbances that cause anxiety. When you're finally on the road, chew toys and frequent bathroom breaks can help minimize anxiety.

6 Know the Rules

Visit the listings section of this Guide (starting after the magazine section) or log on to www.GoodSamCamping.com for pet restrictions at the RV parks you're considering for your trip. If you seek more detailed information, always call and ask before visiting. If you are allowed to bring a commonly prohibited breed, like a pit bull, Doberman or Rottweiler, go the extra mile to be an great canine citizen.

7 Enjoy Dog Days at the Park

Many RV parks now have dog parks, and some even include obstacles and play apparatus for your furry passengers. For the most freedom to roam, visit during off-peak hours. Bring your own water bowls to avoid contagious diseases like the canine flu, which are spread through common drinking areas. Observe common courtesy at the dog park; clean up after your pet and make sure it plays nicely with others. Back at the RV, fast cleanups are easy when you keep dry dog shampoos and moist towelettes in the RV, but stock extra towels for the occasional bath and grooming session. Many RV parks have dog wash stations just for furry guests.

8 Consistency is Key

Dogs thrive on routine, so try to maintain a consistent schedule of regular activities like feeding, walking and playtime. If your dog is in good shape, summertime swimming holes are great for extra exercise, but play it safe with a canine floatation jacket for peace of mind in unfamiliar waters. If bad weather keeps you inside the rig, interactive doggy "brain games" can engage a bored pet.

9 Keep Cool

Humans don't wear fur coats in July, but that's what our dogs must endure during the heat of summer. Shield all pets from hot temperatures, and remember that older canines and dogs with darker hair are more vulnerable to summer heat. Canine cooling jackets and cooling bandanas are widely available to help dogs stay comfortable in hot weather.

10 Watch Out for Critters

Supervise dogs carefully so that they don't have dangerous encounters with wild animals like coyotes and porcupines. Unfortunately, smaller pests like fleas and ticks are a little

Preferred Pampered Pet Parks

Indian Wells Carefree RV Resorts
Indio, CA

Dunedin Carefree RV Resort & the Blue Moon Inn
Dunedin, FL

Emerald Coast RV Beach Resort
Panama City Beach, FL

Ocala Sun RV Resort
Ocala, FL

Sun-N-Fun Carefree RV Resort
Sarasota, FL

Whittington Woods Campground At Benton
Whittington, IL

Deer Creek Valley RV Park LLC
Topeka, KS

Normandy Farms Family Camping Resort
Foxboro, MA

Indian Rock RV Park
Jackson, NJ

Lake George RV Park
Lake George, NY

By the Lake RV Park Resort
Ardmore, OK

harder to spot, but they're easy to keep away from your pet and RV with eco-friendly repellants like citronella sprays, cedar oil and food-grade diatomaceous earth. Should you discover a parasitic hitchhiker, use a flea comb or tick removal tool to pull them out and away from the skin.

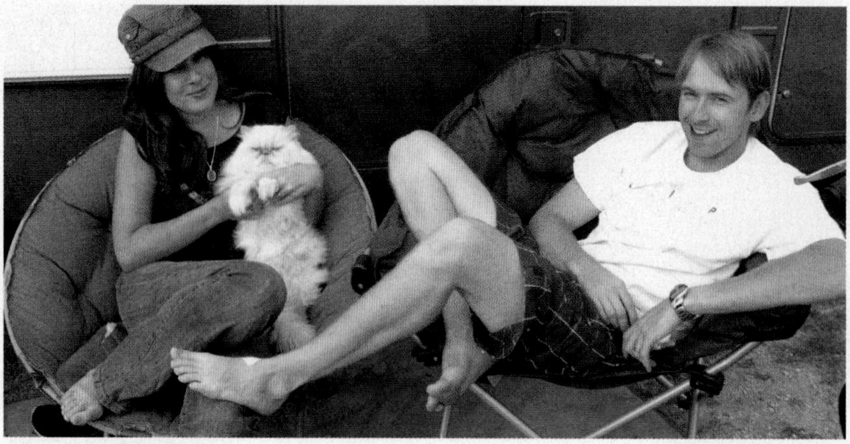

11 Ban the Barking

Dog barking is a major annoyance to RV park neighbors, but a few simple exercises can put a stop to it. For example, if your dog gets anxious when you leave the RV, start daily training sessions that have you coming and going from your RV while gradually extending your away times. Just don't leave your pet unattended too long, because even well-behaved dogs will bark at outside noises. Other good tools include pheromone collars with calming scents and anti-anxiety music composed especially for dogs.

12 Look for Parks that Pamper Your Pets

Treat your pet to a fabulous camping experience by staying at one of the Preferred Pampered Pet Parks on the previous page. Many of the parks on this list offer perks like dog runs, dog washing stations and dog walking services. Some of the parks even conduct pet parades during special holidays. Take time now to plan a road trip with your pet for meaningful memories that last a lifetime.

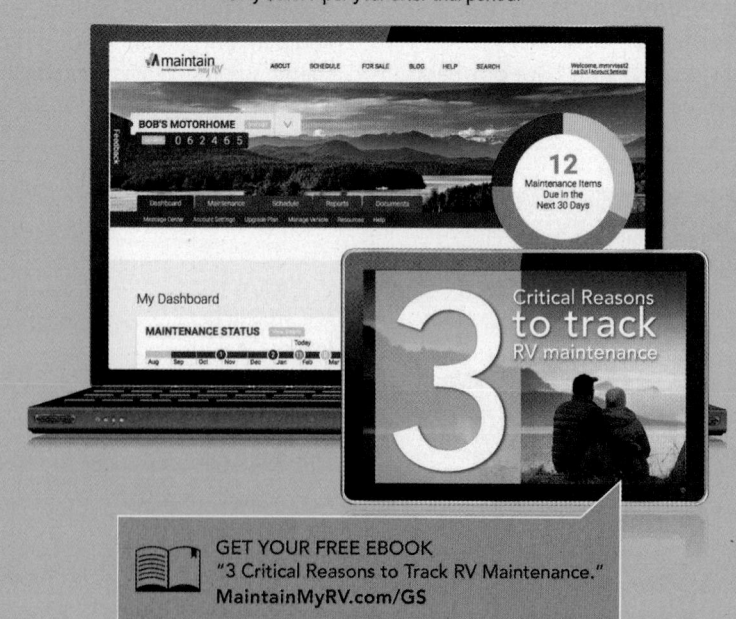

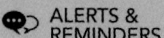

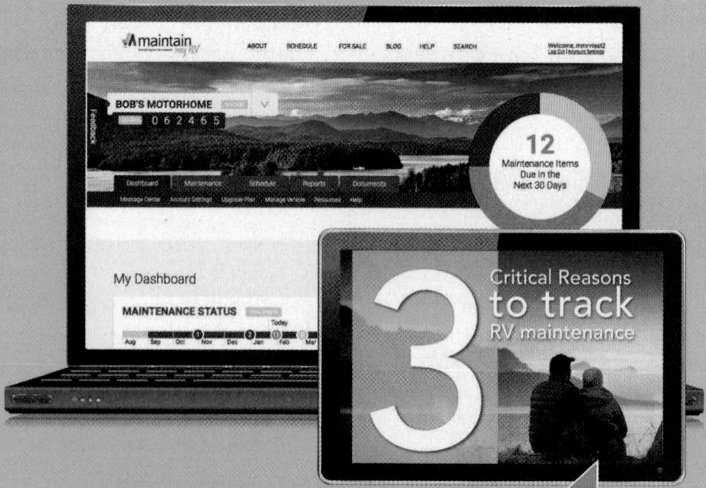

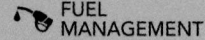

RV INFORMATION FORM

Form C-1 #2016

Finding the Right RV Fit

By Kristopher Bunker

Choosing the right RV for your needs is your best bet for an enjoyable camping experience

PLEASE SELECT YOUR APPROPRIATE RV:

☐ CLASS A	☐ CLASS C	☐ FIFTH-WHEEL	☐ POP-UP CAMPER
☐ CLASS B	☐ TRAVEL TRAILER	☐ TRUCK CAMPER	☐ SURV

Much like buying a new home, selecting the proper RV type to fit your needs is a bit more complex than choosing the cabinet colors and/or kitchen appliances. An RV combines all the amenities of home, along with an automotive drivetrain (motorhomes) or a mobile platform (trailers and truck campers). In order to deliver memorable experiences and a truck full of happy campers, it's important to understand the differences between RV types.

The best place to begin: what's in your driveway right now? If you already have a suitable tow vehicle and aren't averse to pulling a trailer, a towable may be the right choice for you. Or, if you'd rather pilot a single rig down the highway, a motorhome is the way to go.

Other things to consider when choosing an RV type are whether you'll be traveling alone or with your family, how long you'll be on the road (an extended weekend or RVing full time) and if you'll be taking along any pets.

Determining which RV is right for you is a decidedly personal decision. Although any RV type is a great way to enjoy the company of friends and family while experiencing the great outdoors, each of the following RV categories offers its own list of pros and cons. Also included are models available at Camping World (note, check the store you are visiting to verify that the model you're seeking is in stock).

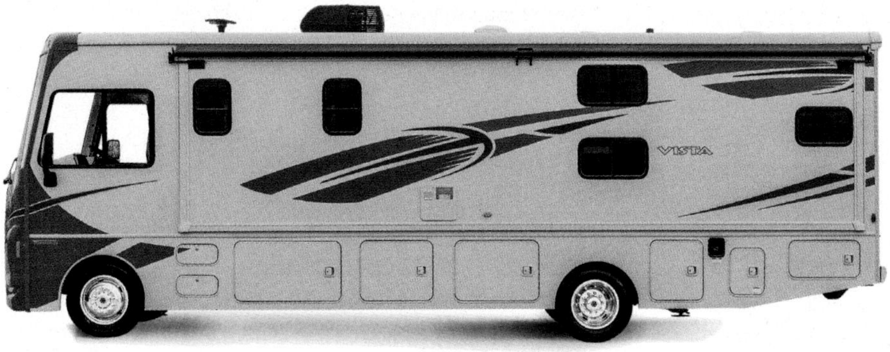

WINNEBAGO VISTA 31BE

AVAILABLE AT CAMPING WORLD

The Vista may be Winnebago's most affordable Class A gas-powered motorhome, but you'd never know it from the impressive list of offerings. The family-friendly 31BE can sleep up to seven, sporting a full-wall slide with bunks and an available StudioLoft bed. The roomy walk-through bath offers private master-bedroom access, while a one-piece fiberglass roof and powered patio awning are also standard. Families can even enjoy movie night under the stars thanks to the available outdoor entertainment center.

CLASS A MOTORHOMES

When you hear the word "motorhome," a Class A is likely the first image that comes to mind. Class A's are the large, breadbox-shaped motorized RVs that require a small learning curve for operation, as the steering column is sometimes even with, or slightly ahead of, the front axles (think bus drivers). If that sounds intimidating, don't feel daunted. These coaches are fun to drive, and are tough to beat in terms of all the amenities that are included.

Class A's begin at the factory as rolling chassis with the drivetrain and steering wheel in place. From there, the coachmaker essentially builds the entire length of the walls and roof, meaning there is a bit of wiggle room for floorplan variety. Gas-driven Class A's generally feature the engine up front, while the often larger, more robust diesel motorhomes are generally known as "pushers" due to the power plant residing out back (there are a few exceptions, of course). Class A's can range from about 20-45 feet in length, and can cost from $100,000 to upward of $2 million (custom bus conversions), depending on the size and configuration.

That price range is easily justified, as a Class A is typically outfitted with just about everything you would want in a home on wheels: multiple slideouts, a spacious galley, larger bed configurations, solid-surface countertops and a bathroom with separate toilet and shower facilities (sometimes even two). As with all motorhomes, unless you tow a dinghy vehicle, traveling the surrounding area necessitates completely breaking camp, though you undoubtedly will be doing so in style.

WINNEBAGO TRAVATO 59K AVAILABLE AT CAMPING WORLD

Built on the Ram ProMaster chassis and available standard with a 280-hp 3.6-liter gas engine, the Travato Class B is the perfect ride for adventurers who enjoy the freedom of an easy-to-maneuver motorhome. Optional bike carrier and kayak racks further attest to its thrill-seeking roots, and the available 100-watt solar-panel battery charger is ideal for camping off the grid. Inside, twin beds and a fold-down, space-saving bathroom washbasin are among the highlights, while the galley features a microwave, two-burner range and a refrigerator.

CLASS B MOTORHOMES

Also known as camping van conversions, Class B's are manufactured on van chassis, meaning they are easier to drive for first-timers due to increased visibility, size and the fact that many drivers have experience behind the wheel of a similarly handling vehicle (a small cargo- or even a larger mini-van). As such, B's tend to be much more nimble than their larger counterparts, and can deliver mileage that rivals or even outperforms many tow vehicles. The van chassis are modified slightly for RV purposes, often stretched longer and taller for a more usable area. And perhaps the greatest asset of owning a Class B is the fact they can be used as everyday commuters or, if not, they can be stored in your driveway with little in the way of modifications to the existing structure.

The trade-off, of course, is space: a smaller platform means tighter quarters. For a traveling couple, however, that may be just the ticket. Bathrooms tend to be of the portable or wet variety (that is, either a cassette toilet, or lav in the shower), and sleeping accommodations are generally limited to two-four very intimate occupants. That's not to say Class B's don't have the amenities that make RVing so exciting; they still include a galley, and the seating in the "living area" can often be reconfigured from travel mode to a more inviting, relaxation-type atmosphere. Class B's aren't cheap—they can easily crawl past the $100,000 mark—but you're essentially getting a travel vehicle and a recreational vehicle wrapped into one package.

THOR MOTOR COACH FREEDOM ELITE 22FE
AVAILABLE AT CAMPING WORLD

The Freedom Elite 22FE Class C motorhome offers many thoughtful features often reserved for larger Class A coaches, but in a much more compact package. The eye-catching 24-footer boasts aluminum running boards and plentiful exterior storage, plus an impressive 8,000-pound-rated hitch receiver perfect for towing a boat or off-pavement vehicles. A power patio awning with integrated LED lights helps keep the adventure churning until well after dark, while the interior can easily sleep four to five, including a cozy bedroom retreat at the rear.

CLASS C MOTORHOMES

These are the coaches you see with cabover sleeping areas, much like on some 18-wheeler rigs, in a much more friendly looking package. Class C's combine the easy driving of a Class B (though not quite as nimble) with the large living of a Class A (though not quite as wide open, except for the larger Super C's, which feature living arrangements that will have buyers double-checking they aren't in a Class A).

Class C motorhomes begin life as a full-size van cab and frame, to which the manufacturer adds the floor, roof and walls. Depending on size, a Class C can offer the same amenities as a Class A motorhome, and the familiar chassis is a tremendous lure to those entering (or who already are established) in the RV lifestyle. Plus, with the growing popularity of diesel-based Sprinter-type chassis, Class C's are more effectively bridging the gap between A's and C's, bringing even better gas mileage without sacrificing livability space. Prices for a conventional Class C generally start at around $70,000, though some of the aforementioned Super C's can reach $250,000 before all is said and done.

TRAVEL TRAILERS

Travel trailers are easily one of the most common RVs on the road, and why not? They're often towable by a vehicle already in your driveway (a proposition that can save you a cool $60,000), and users aren't required to completely break camp when they want to explore the countryside (leave the trailer at the RV park and hit the road in the tow vehicle).

Travel trailers start at about 12 feet in length, and can make their way to 40-plus feet in a hurry. The main thing here is to make sure your tow vehicle can handle the weight; many dealers will quote dry weights on the trailers, while neglecting to mention that water, fuel and cargo can add on the pounds quickly. When in doubt, consider these easy calculations: water weighs approximately 8.6 pounds per gallon (don't forget the water heater), while LPG weighs 4.2 pounds per gallon. Throw in camp chairs, clothes, an AC generator, firewood, etc., and it's easy to see how dry weight can be a deceptive concept.

A travel trailer houses all you need to spend your time away from it all: a full galley, a workable bathroom, a dedicated living area, and exterior pass-through storage for odds and ends. A couple of slideouts can really open up the interior, so manufacturers tend to include them in travel trailer configurations. Prices start at around $12,000, and can reach the upper $60s in more luxurious configurations. Remember to allow for trailer-break controls and weight-distribution/sway bars in your budget.

JAYCO WHITE HAWK 27DSRL AVAILABLE AT CAMPING WORLD

With a spacious rear-living-room floorplan, the White Hawk 27DSRL is a great trailer for entertaining. The dinette, sofa bed and even rear recliners all provide a great view of the mid-coach entertainment center, with the galley, cold drinks and snacks just a few steps away. The single, sturdy 36-inch-wide ram-driven slideout should withstand even the most rigorous touchdown celebrations, but if you need to take the festivities outside, a deluxe 18-foot LED-illuminated awning, exterior TV brackets and dual outside speakers should help ease the agony of defeat.

STARCRAFT 16RB AVAILABLE AT CAMPING WORLD

The compact 16RB is a smartly appointed hybrid trailer with an unloaded vehicle weight (uvw) of less than 2,600 pounds, making it towable by the truck, van or SUV that's likely already in the driveway. The trailer offers sleeping for up to seven, thanks to dual pop-out beds, a convertible dinette and a sofa, and the dry bathroom means you'll have all the comforts of home. Other niceties include a fridge, microwave, two-burner cooktop and range, in addition to heated bunk mats and a 12-foot electric awning.

POP-UP CAMPERS

Sure, it may only be a step above sleeping on the hard ground—but it's an important step. All kidding aside, these campers have also taken great strides since the old Colemans of the 1960s. Pop-ups, or folding-camping trailers, come in hybrid (canvas-walled) or even clamshell varieties, and their worth is so much more than dirt-free living. Pop-ups can be outfitted with more amenities than the typical camping family can shake a stick at, from soft beds to refrigerators to stoves to—hooray!—toilets and showers. Some even come with holding tanks, though the majority still stick to the tried-and-true jerry cans for storing waste- and gray-water.

And the towing—oh my, the towing! This is the ideal vehicle with which to learn the art of towing: lane changes, backing in, sharp turns, etc. Because the RV is compacted for travel, it's easy to forget there is a trailer behind you, and the effect on gas mileage, while still apparent, is miniscule when compared to larger trailers.

But perhaps most importantly, sleeping under the stars with your little ones—in a mosquito-free environment with a fluffy mattress and bathroom facilities at hand—make the pop-up worth its weight in gold. Prices typically range from $5,000 to about $15,000.

FOREST RIVER ROCKWOOD FOLDING CAMPER

AVAILABLE AT CAMPING WORLD

A folding camping trailer doesn't necessarily mean a tent trailer. Pop-ups like the Forest River Rockwood A122S seen here utilize an A-frame design for all hard walls. The trailer's unloaded vehicle weight (uvw) is less than 2,000 pounds, and it measures a mere 5 feet tall when in travel mode, making towing a snap. Inside, a refrigerator, three-burner stove, microwave and optional cassette toilet make former tent campers relish their decision to upgrade, as do the comfy quilted-top bed, exterior RV-Que grill and loads of available storage.

FIFTH-WHEELS

Consider fivers the "Class A" of the trailering sect. These are typically the more luxurious trailers, with a raised front (or sometimes rear) section that can be configured as a private bedroom with attached bath or even a home-theater section for entertainment.

Much like with Class A's, fifth-wheel manufacturers tend to outfit these trailers with top-of-the-line appointments, from flooring to TVs to residential appliances. There is also a wide selection of more affordable fivers, offering the convenience of the dual-level floorplan without all the costly add-ons.

The main concern (if you could call it that) with piloting a fiver is the need for a "saddle" in the bed of the pickup tow vehicle (alas, no van option here). These saddles often necessitate drilling holes into the truck bed, and can also occupy some much-needed cargo space, not to mention the fact that they can be quite heavy and difficult to remove when you're not RVing.

All gripes aside, consider a fifth-wheel to offer the luxury of a Class A with the ability to explore in your favorite pickup without breaking camp. Prices start at about $20,000, and can reach up to $200,000 in some of the larger, custom-made units.

JAYCO EAGLE HT 27.5RKDS

AVAILABLE AT CAMPING WORLD

Designed to be towed by a properly equipped half-ton truck, the 27.5RKDS is a dual-slide fiver with an impressive amount of space that even allows for a walk-around queen bed and linen/wardrobe/dresser unit in the master bedroom. The living area offers an open floorplan with an amidships entertainment center, sofa bed and recliner. Outside, you'll find a few surprises like a nifty six-in-one side-wall-mounted hookup convenience center, plus a high-gloss fiberglass exterior in addition to a fully enclosed and heated underbelly.

TRUCK CAMPERS

What a journey this segment has made in recent years. Whereas in days past, a pickup camper was little more than a shell covering the bed of a truck, today's campers offer full kitchens, bathrooms, bedrooms and even slideouts.

Though the floor of the camper is limited to the footprint of the pickup, camper manufacturers have designed the floorplans to utilize the space over the bedrails, above the truck cab and everything in between.

There are automatic jacks available to make on- and off-loading the campers a bit more manageable, but we wouldn't recommend raising the camper off the bed in camp as a regular practice. Besides, with a camper, you're likely driving a truck you're already accustomed to. Sure, the suspension may be a bit different (there are aftermarket air springs for this) and the mileage may suffer, but the freedom of a truck camper is readily apparent—especially when you consider they add very limited length to your RV combo, and can go just about anywhere your truck can (with proper height clearance, of course). Prices typically start around $8,000, while some of the more-outfitted rigs can run up to $60,000.

PALOMINO CAMPERS

AVAILABLE AT CAMPING WORLD

A pickup camper can essentially go wherever the truck can, making the Palomino Backpack Edition a popular choice among hunters, fishermen and other RVing adventure-seekers. The SS-1251 is a soft-side camper that pops up using an electric lift, revealing a fully appointed interior that can easily accommodate three to four RVers. A galley, lav and storage areas make this camper a smart choice, especially considering it weighs less than 1,800 pounds dry. Other helpful features include a battery-charging station, LED interior lighting and a large 55-inch one-piece door.

KEYSTONE CARBON TOY HAULER

AVAILABLE AT CAMPING WORLD

Keystone has designed its popular Carbon toy haulers to deliver adventurous RVers luxurious living at an affordable price point. The Carbon 377 delivers in spades, offering a 12-foot garage area, 30-gallon on-board fuel station and rugged 8-foot-tall ramp door, in addition to a king bed up front, island-kitchen layout and impressive loft with a twin bed. More sleeping positions are available via the electric bed with dual opposing sofas in the garage. Plus, a separate garage lav means the dirt stays out of the main living area.

SURVS

Sport-Utility Recreational Vehicles, or toy haulers, are perhaps the most aggressively expanding segment of the RV industry, and have been for some years now. These handy vehicles are available in motorhome varieties of all types (even a handful of Class B's), in addition to travel-trailer, fifth-wheel and, yes, truck-camper footprints.

Generally, an SURV features a garage in the rear of the vehicle with tie-downs for hauling off-road vehicles, motorcycles, snowmobiles and the like (trailer weight limits apply). Some hobbyists even use the area to dabble in their various pursuits. The garage area is typically separated from the living area, which does necessitate a bit of a compromise when it comes to livability area. However, remove those adult toys and the garage often features a second living or sleeping area, often outfitted with fold-down beds, a dining table and/or an additional entertainment center. Some even offer a separate bathroom in the garage area, while still others include an on-board fuel station that can be topped off at the gas station, and used to fuel those wheeled toys for off-pavement pursuits without having to travel back to civilization.

But these aren't only garages on wheels—some can offer residential-type appointments and atmosphere in the front living area.

Prices start around $20,000 for a travel trailer, and can work their way above and beyond the top of the Class A price range.

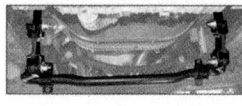

CAMPING INFORMATION FORM — Form C-2 #2016

FINDING THE RIGHT SITE By Kristopher Bunker

All RVs are not created equal—neither are the campgrounds at which we stay

Please select appropriate box:

☑ Big-Rig Friendly	☐ 30-Day Stay	☐ Pet Friendly
☐ 50-Amp Power	☑ Family Friendly	☐ ATV Friendly

Once you've selected your new RV and become familiar with its operations, it's time to hit the open road. And, at the end of each day, you need to have an RV park at which to park your home on wheels. As eager as you may be to crack open this guide and simply pick the first park on your route, it should be noted that all RV parks are not the same. Just as different lifestyles necessitate different RV types, those very same RV types may necessitate a different type of campground.

Your best bet is to call ahead and discuss your situation with the park owners or camp host. Although that may not always be possible due to last-minute changes of plans, doing so whenever you can will ensure a pleasant experience the majority of the time, and will help eliminate that sinking feeling when you are turned away at the gate or can't stay at a particular campground for whatever reason.

Following are some of the more common restrictions you may encounter on occasion. They are by no means implemented at every camping spot, but are put in place at the park's discretion, based on space, patrons, funding and regulations.

SIZE MATTERS

First and foremost, consider the type of RV you're piloting. Larger Class A and Class C motorhomes, as well as longer fifth-wheels and travel trailers, are simply going to need more space. You also need to consider the slideouts; the sites need to be wide enough (and with minimal foliage) to accommodate them. Overhead clearance also needs to be taken into account. Tree limbs, power lines, light poles and archway structures are included on the list of the usual suspects.

The owners of larger, longer RVs have every right to enjoy off-the-grid camping at a secluded Bureau of Land Management (BLM) site, and may even be able to do so the majority of the time. However, common sense dictates they should probably look for campgrounds and/or resorts with larger spaces.

When it comes to site size, each park's campground information will include a description of the campground's sites, the number of RV spaces, surface preparation, and width and length of pull-through and back-in sites. For more information, see #12 in How to Use This Travel Guide, page 163.

POWER AT THE POLE

Many of today's newer, pricier rigs have been outfitted with dual air-conditioners, a washer/dryer and cutting edge home-theater technology. In order to make the most of your RV's potential, it may not make sense to head for an off-the-beaten-path campground, or even some of the older mom-and-pop campgrounds. You can almost bet they won't have 50-amp shorepower at the campsite.

That means that even if you can squeeze your rig into a site, all the gadgetry you paid extra for won't be operable, as it requires a much larger power draw. There are 50/30 adapters available for such a situation, but we recommend a clean power source that's designed to accept your RV's capacity, especially if you plan on an extended stay. In the long run, you'll have a much more enjoyable trip.

Each campground's listing will include the minimum and maximum type of electrical receptacle found at the RV sites (15, 20, 30 or 50 amp). See #12 in How to Use This Travel Guide, page 163.

TIME LIMITS

If you're planning on staying a while, check with management about the maximum-stay policy. Some parks have a two-week limit, some have a 30-day limit and others even allow full-time living. It's never fun to be asked to leave before you'd planned, and that can easily be avoided with a quick pre-stay conversation.

Each park's campground information will include information about seasonal stay sites. See #13 in How to Use This Travel Guide, page 163.

AGE OF INNOCENCE

Many of the larger resorts across the country won't accept an RV that's older than 10 years (and yes, that includes your immaculate, completely made-over vintage Airstream). Not knowing this ahead of time can be frustrating, so plan accordingly.

Listings will indicate if an RV park enforces vehicle age restrictions. See #22 in How to Use This Travel Guide, page 164.

SOUNDS OF SILENCE

It's a wonderful feeling when your 3-year-old daughter belts out "Let it Go" along with your exterior entertainment system's speakers every night. But for your neighbors, who may not enjoy the musical stylings of the latest Disney movie, not so much. And, be sure to heed the campground's restrictions on AC generator use. You also want to make sure that the park allows children—55+ parks, for example, allow only campers who are 55 years and up in age.

Look for "age restrictions" in the listing to make sure your kids are allowed. For general policies regarding noise, contact the RV park.

PARK PLACE AND TOY BOXES

Anybody towing a trailer of any size (or a dinghy vehicle) should inquire about the park's tow-vehicle policy. Is there enough room at the site for your tow vehicle or dinghy? Or, is there ample parking nearby, so the inevitable trip back to the truck doesn't take half the morning?

Plus, if you plan on having visitors, be sure to check with the park; some charge day-use fees for occupants who have guests. These are generally very reasonable, and when you consider all the amenities the visitors will have access to, the fees are a downright bargain.

Another thing to watch for is the park's policy on off-loading motorized vehicles, like motorcycles and ATVs. Many have restrictions on these because the park doesn't want the vehicles buzzing around the campsites.

Consult the description of sites in the park's campground information to ensure space is available for your vehicle combination. See #12 in How to Use This Travel Guide, page 163. You should also contact the RV park with questions about guests and ATVs. Look at the bottom of each listing for the Web address, email and phone number to get more info on the park.

Remember, these restrictions may seem limiting and unreasonable to some, but they are often made with the best intentions of pleasing the majority of RVers. The good news is there are enough potential camping spots for everybody; if a particular park turns you away at the gate, there's likely another down the road that will be more than happy with your business.

4 Fantastic RV Grill Recipes by Nina Fussing

Fire up great flavors for meat eaters and veggie lovers alike

Sriracha Honey Chicken Wings ©Nina Fussing

RV barbecues bring family and friends together for freshly cooked food under an open sky. Dazzle your hungry guests on your next outing with this foodie-approved grill fest.

These recipes highlight how you only need one trick, or special ingredient, to take a dish from good to out-of-this-world great. Your guests will think you spent hours working on something that really only took you minutes to make. Be sure to hit the nearest farmers market to get the freshest ingredients for your cookout.

Sriracha Honey Chicken Wings

Serves 6-8 as an appetizer
Total cooking time: 5 minutes prep, 1 hour marinade, 18-20 minutes grilling

Grilled chicken wings are a classic starter. The secret to good wings is the marinade, and this one combines spicy Sriracha sauce with just the right amount of sweetness to create a finger-licking-good flavor. Whenever we've served these, our wings have received compliments all-around with requests to share the "secret" recipe, created by Stephanie Le.

Ingredients:

2 pounds of chicken wings, skin on
½ cup Sriracha sauce
4 tablespoons soy sauce
4 tablespoons honey
2 tablespoons rice vinegar
2 tablespoons olive oil
4 teaspoons toasted sesame oil
4 cloves garlic, crushed

Directions:

1 To make the special marinade, combine the last seven ingredients (Sriracha sauce, soy sauce, honey, rice vinegar, olive oil, toasted sesame oil and garlic) in a bowl and whisk to mix. Set aside half of the marinade to use for basting.

2 Place the chicken wings in a large 1-gallon resealable plastic bag. Pour the remaining marinade over the chicken wings, press any air out of the bag and close it up. Then massage the wings around to thoroughly coat them (note, you can also just pour the marinade over the wings in a dish, but I find that using the plastic bag is a snazzy trick that gets much better marinating results). Put the closed bag into the fridge and let it sit for 1 hour.

3 Remove the chicken wings from the bag and discard the marinade.

4 Preheat the grill and brush it with oil. Once the grill is hot, turn the temperature down to medium and place the wings meat-side down on the grill. Cook for 18-20 minutes, turning the wings over every 3-5 minutes to get even cooking on both sides. Every time you turn the wings, brush them with the reserved marinade for extra tastiness.

5 Once cooked, remove the chicken wings and get busy eating! The wings are absolutely delicious, but you can also serve them with ranch or blue-cheese dressing dip if you like.

Dry-Rubbed Gourmet Moist Grilled Ribs

Serves 4

Total cooking time: 5 minutes prep, 1 hour marinade, 40 minutes grilling

The secret solution is easier than you think. Last year, hubby had the brilliant idea to use a smoking trick called the "Texas Crutch," which basically involves braising the meat in moisture on the grill for 30 minutes. By combining this with a good dry-rub, we've created a rib recipe that is both tasty and fall-off-the-bone tender moist.

Dry Rub Ingredients:

You can use a store-brought dry rub if you like, but if you want something amazing, this is one of the best pork dry rubs we've ever tasted. The sugar creates an incredible crispy crust and the spice adds the perfect taste counterpoint.

½ cup white sugar
½ cup brown sugar
½ cup paprika
¼ cup onion powder
2 tablespoons powdered ginger
2 tablespoons dried oregano
2 tablespoons cayenne (add more if you want extra spice)
2 tablespoons black pepper

Mix all ingredients together and your dry rub is ready.

Ribs Ingredients:

1 rack of pork ribs (any kind)
2 tablespoons prepared mustard
1 cup dry rub
1 cup water, chicken stock or apple juice (for the braise)

Directions:

1. Rub 1 tablespoon of the mustard onto the front side of the ribs until completely covered (the mustard adds taste and serves as a "glue" for the dry rub). Sprinkle a good amount of dry rub over the mustard and pat it down. Turn the ribs over and do the same thing with the mustard and dry rub on the backside. Cover the ribs with plastic wrap and let them sit with the rub for 1 hour.

2. Preheat the grill. When hot, place the ribs meat-side down on the grill for 5 minutes until they are browned and have nice grill-marks. Turn the ribs over and do the same thing on the other side. This initial step creates a yummy "crust" on the ribs without burning them.

3. Prepare a large foil packet using heavy-duty aluminum foil. Place the ribs inside the foil, meat-side up and pour 1 cup of braise liquid (water, chicken stock or apple juice) into the bottom. Close the packet tightly by crimping together the top (make sure there's nothing leaking out) and place the entire packet back on the grill. Turn the grill down to medium, close the lid and let the ribs cook for an additional 30 minutes. This is the "crutch" trick that will braise the meat slowly and keep it moist.

4. When the crutch is done, take the packet off the grill, remove the meat and place the ribs back on the grill under high heat for an additional 5 minutes of cooking on each side. This step will remove excess moisture from the meat and leave you with the perfect grill/moist balance. When done, remove the ribs from the grill, allow the meat to rest for 3-5 minutes, and then slice them up and enjoy!

Dry-Rubbed Gourmet Moist Grilled Ribs ©Nina Fussing

Grilled Portobello Mushroom Burger with Basil-Garlic Aioli

Serves 4

Total cooking time: 5 minutes prep, 15 minutes marinade, 8 minutes grilling

Looking for something special to serve your vegetarian friends? Portobello mushrooms are the perfect answer. Meaty yet tender, they can be grilled in just 8 minutes and require no special prep except for a quick 15-minute marinade. Add in a tasty topping and you'll create a veggie burger that even your meat-loving friends will drool over.

Our "secret sauce" here is a basil-garlic aioli. When basil is in season, it's one of our all-time favorites and it's so good that we end up using it on just about everything. Not only is basil-garlic aioli a topping for portobello mushrooms, it's an excellent dip for veggies and a super-tasty topping for meat burgers (it pairs particularly well with chicken and lamb). This sauce is what "makes" this recipe and my advice is to make extra 'cause you're going to want it.

Basil-Garlic Aioli Ingredients (makes 1 cup):

1 cup mayonnaise
24 basil leaves, thinly sliced
3 large cloves of garlic, chopped or crushed
Juice of 1 lemon
salt to taste

Directions:

1 Cut basil into thin strips and either finely chop the garlic or crush it with a garlic press. Whisk all the ingredients together, cover with plastic wrap and put the aioli mixture into the refrigerator for at least 1 hour to allow flavors to develop.

Marinated/Grilled Portobello Mushroom Ingredients:

4 large portobello mushrooms
¼ cup balsamic vinegar
¼ cup olive oil
2 cloves of garlic, crushed
1 teaspoon dried thyme
1 teaspoon dried oregano
salt and pepper

Directions:

1 Whisk together the balsamic vinegar, olive oil, garlic, thyme, oregano, and salt and pepper to create the marinade.

2 Place the portobello mushrooms in a 1-gallon resealable plastic bag and pour the marinade into the bag. Close the bag and carefully massage/distribute the marinade around the mushrooms. Leave to marinate for at least 15 minutes.

Grilled Portobello Mushroom Burger ©Nina Fuss

3 Preheat the grill. When hot, place the mushrooms cap-side down on the grill. Grill for 4 minutes. Turn the mushrooms over and grill another 4 minutes on the other side. You can use the last few minutes to grill/heat your burger buns too.

4 Slather the burger buns with the aioli and layer the grilled mushrooms with whatever extra toppings you like. I find red onions, tomatoes and salad greens (especially salad greens with a little bite like spinach or arugula) go well, but any topping with do. Enjoy.

Grilled Peach Salad with Balsamic Honey Drizzle ©Nina Fussing

Grilled Peach Salad with Balsamic Honey Drizzle

Peaches are one of our favorite fruits, and when they are in season, peaches are oh-so-amazingly good. This recipe takes only 5 minutes to make and is so easy it's almost silly, but the salad is so tasty you'll think it came from a five-star restaurant.

The secret is quickly grilling the peaches to bring out their sugar, and pairing that fruit with spicy arugula, salty goat cheese and a sweet balsamic drizzle. The resulting combo is amazing. Serve this summer delight with your favorite grilled meat, or just have it as a refreshing afternoon meal.

Serves 4
Total cooking time: 5 minutes prep, 4 minutes grilling

Balsamic Honey Drizzle Ingredients:
⅓ cup balsamic vinegar
2 tablespoons honey

Directions:

1. Bring the balsamic vinegar to a boil over medium heat in a small pan and let it boil/reduce for about 2 minutes. This step intensifies the flavor of the balsamic. Take the pan off the heat and stir in 2 tablespoons of honey. Leave to cool.

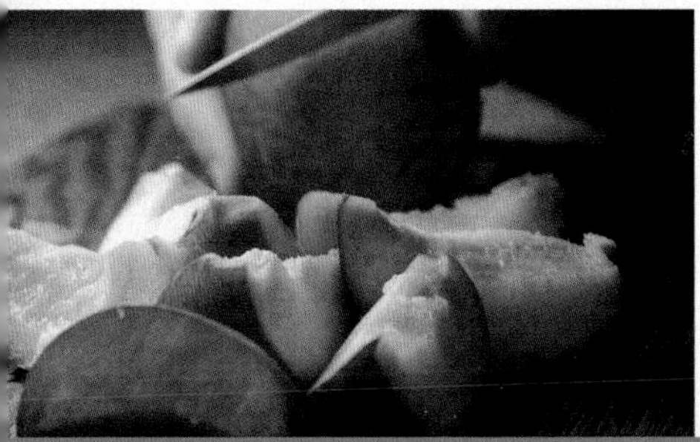

Peach Salad Ingredients:
4 ripe peaches
1 7-ounce bag of arugula salad
6 slices prosciutto ham (can omit for vegetarians)
¼ cup crumbled goat cheese
2 tablespoons walnuts, chopped
Olive oil (to dress)

Directions:

1. Cut the peaches into six wedges each (cut in half, remove the stone and then cut each half into three wedges).

2. Heat up the grill and brush the rack with oil. Place peach wedges face down on the grill for 1 minute until they get nice grill-marks on the first side. Turn them over and grill for another 1 minute on the other wedge face. If peaches are very ripe/soft you may only need to grill 30 seconds on each side. Take the peaches off the grill.

3. Place arugula salad in a large salad bowl. Drizzle 2 tablespoons of olive oil onto the salad and toss until well mixed.

4. Distribute salad into four plates or bowls. Arrange prosciutto ham, grilled peaches, goat cheese and walnuts on top of the salad. Drizzle everything with the balsamic honey drizzle. Eat and enjoy!

Fun, Families and CAMPING

Keep the whole crew happy and entertained on your next getaway

After countless weekend getaways and dozens of family vacations in our RV, we're absolutely convinced there's no better way to travel with children. The RV allows us to discover new places and have amazing adventures, while at the same time enjoying the comforts of home.

There's no such thing as a one-size-fits-all family vacation. The secret to planning your family's perfect outing lies in finding a great destination, an amazing campsite, awe-inspiring activities and rejuvenating relaxation that works for the whole gang.

Sounds like a tall order, right? Well, here are five steps that will help make your next RV vacation magical and memorable.

Choose the Perfect Campground

The best thing about traveling by RV is that you can go just about anywhere in this big, beautiful country. However, that can be a little overwhelming too. Think about what type of vacation you want. Does your family want to relax on a beach or escape into the mountains? Would you prefer to be near a downtown with shopping and restaurants or far away from the hustle and bustle of activity? Is your family happiest kayaking and hiking, or do they love water parks, boardwalks and amusement rides? Maybe you are looking to explore a bit of history by visiting battlefields and monuments. Once you know the type of location you want, then you can narrow down your campground options.

Next, think about campground amenities and activities. Some campgrounds offer packed activity schedules and loads of kid-friendly play options. Make sure that the campground you choose has everything that is important to your family. We rarely stay at a campground without a pool and a playground because that is what thrills our little campers. Movie nights, pottery painting, mini golf and splash pads—there are campgrounds out there that offer it all, and one will definitely provide the perfect setting for your family vacation.

Before you make any reservations, pour over the campground's ratings in this guide and read all the information you can about the region surrounding this RV park. Make sure you focus on the details that matter to your family. If you are traveling in a popup trailer without a bathroom, you might want to pay particular attention to the rating for restrooms and showers. If that score isn't important to you, then hone in on the score for facilities. We love full-service campgrounds with lots of recreational options for our kids, so that is what we search for in the guide. We also adore staying at campgrounds that are surrounded by natural beauty. The visual appearance score helps us determine whether a campground will provide the beautiful scenery we crave.

Find the Perfect Campsite

Even after you've found the perfect campground, your planning isn't done. We highly recommend calling to make your reservations instead of using an online system. Why? Because you need to communicate exactly what type of site will make this your best family vacation ever.

Do you love being right near the playground so your kids can play 24/7? Is it important to be tucked away in a quiet spot so that your little ones can go to bed at a reasonable hour? A waterfront site might be heaven for some families and a nightmare for others. Are there any rules regarding quiet hours? Is this park popular mong families? We always ask to be far away from any main roads because we don't want to be worried about traffic while our boys are riding their bikes.

Make a list of your ideal campsite features and then call to reserve your spot. Don't book a reservation until you're absolutely certain the campsite is the perfect one for your family.

Arrive with Happy Campers

Depending on the duration of your trip, you might want to spend some time preparing for the vehicle ride. Road trips are phenomenal experiences for kids, and with a little planning, everyone can enjoy the drive instead of dreading it.

Healthy, individually packaged snacks will keep kids happy without causing them to bounce off the walls. Trail mix, raisins and hummus with carrots are some our favorites, and then we also throw in a couple of special treats here and there. Lollipops offer you a great bang for your buck, because they last a good long time and give you a bit of desperately needed peace and quiet.

If your kids need a break from the DVDs and tablets, consider making a little activity packet for each child. There are tons of free printables available online, and we particularly like the bingo boards that include road signs, RV models and license plates. Don't forget to reach back into your own childhood and teach the kids classics like I Spy and 20 Questions. They'll love these old-fashioned games, we promise.

Plan the Perfect Activities

A great family vacation is all about balancing kid activities with adult activities and excitement with relaxation. We never plan more than one excursion on any given day, and we are always on the lookout for places that will delight every member of the family.

Hiking, kayaking, swimming and fishing are fun, active ways to experience the great outdoors. Want to ramp up the excitement? Throw in some zip lining, parasailing or four-wheeling. Your kids will have a blast and you might feel younger than you have in ages.

Here's another important tip: Get out and see the sites early in the morning, and then return to enjoy the campground amenities during the afternoon. This way you will avoid the crowds and vacation burnout.

Create Family Campground Rituals

One of the reasons our kids love camping so much is that they look forward to the many campground traditions we've established over the years. They know they're guaranteed camp store ice cream, unlimited trips to the playground and stories around the fire at night. We also keep certain games, like Spot It! Gone Camping, in the RV and only play them when traveling.

Our boys also adore the cartoons they get to watch in the morning when they wake up before quiet hours are over at 8 a.m. Your family may want to completely unplug during a campground stay, but we choose to dole out the Wi-Fi and DVDs in small doses throughout a trip. Movie nights are a great way to end an active day. Make it just a little more special by cooking s'mores over the fire before hitting play.

Planning the perfect family RV vacation starts with finding the destination, the campground and the campsite that will suit your family the best. After you have reservations, make sure you plan activities that will be enjoyable for everyone in the family. Finally, make family time at the campground count. Simple family traditions are the ones your kids will remember and cherish forever. And that is the whole point, right?

Jeremy and Stephanie Puglisi are the founders of the RV Family Travel Atlas podcast and blog. They spend over 40 nights a year in their RV traveling with their three young sons, sharing their experiences as they explore the new golden age of RVing.

Family Fun in the Northwest

In the majestic Pacific Northwest, families can follow in the footsteps of Lewis and Clark, wallow in natural hot springs, descend into canyons formed from thousands of years of geological history and watch beloved Old Faithful fire off like a rocket engine. With its clean, green, offbeat towns and cities where cars take a back seat to bicycles, at every turn the Pacific Northwest triumphs the environment and the arts: it's the perfect antidote to today's digital world.

Washington

Boasting eight national parks, 68 state parks and Puget Sound's 2,500 miles of shoreline, Washington State offers myriad adventures. The forested slopes of Mount Rainier provide plenty of outdoor thrills and wildlife watching opportunities. Parents can decompress and let children run free on the San Juan Islands or pop in to Seattle's Pike Place Market. The Cascades and Olympic National Park hold their own among awe-inspiring attractions.

RECOMMENDED FAMILY CAMPING PARKS
WASHINGTON

Columbia Sun RV Resort
Kennewick, WA

Family Fun in the Southwest

There are some things that you just can't replicate in a classroom: climbing inside a 1,000- year-old cave dwelling, hiking among ancient sequoia trees or through a petrified forest, descending into a 2.7-mile-wide, 550-foot-deep meteor crater and contemplating prehistoric and alien life forms. For families that seek adventure and natural wonders, the Southwest's primal landscapes will beguile, transfix and make the heart flutter. Children can embrace their inner cowboy as they climb aboard the Grand Canyon Railway, saddle up at a dude ranch or watch the gunslingers at Tombstone.

Arizona

Arizona is an otherworldly land that feels plucked straight from a child's imagination. At every turn surreal wonders define the moment. There are giant meteor craters, bizarre rock formations, ancient cliff dwellings, gigantic shaggy cacti at Saguaro National Park and the preternaturally beautiful and eternally photogenic Camelback Mountain. Children and teens will redefine their concept of "awesome" at Grand Canyon National Park.

RECOMMENDED FAMILY CAMPING PARKS
ARIZONA

Black Canyon Ranch RV Resort
Black Canyon City, AZ
Pleasant Harbor RV Resort
Peoria, AZ
Sentinel Peak RV Park
Tucson, AZ

California

With its mild climate, iconic national parks and glittering cityscapes, it's no wonder California is hailed as the quintessential family road trip. Yosemite National Park is a fantasia of deep rivers, ancient sequoia trees, plunging waterfalls and stellar recreation. Within easy reach of San Francisco, children are star-struck by the cavorting seals and migrating California gray whales at Point Reyes National Seashore. Head south for Disneyland, SeaWorld, Universal Studios and more family-friendly destinations.

RECOMMENDED FAMILY CAMPING PARKS
CALIFORNIA

Anaheim RV Park
Anaheim, CA
Newport Dunes Waterfront Resort & Marina
Newport Beach, CA
Campland On the Bay
San Diego, CA
Mission Bay RV Resort
San Diego, CA
Santee Lakes Recreation Preserve
Santee, CA

Family Fun in the Midwest

From Michigan's Upper Peninsula to the fantastical caves and Badlands of South Dakota, the Midwest's national and state parks offer every family recreational activity conceivable, including hiking, swimming, backpacking, fishing, rafting and dune surfing. In quaint towns, Main Streets awash with pastel-painted diners, kitschy souvenir shops and ice-cream parlors give way to sandy beaches or wooded forests and offer an idyllic throwback to the traditional American family vacations. Whether it is biking through open plains or hiking through parks steeped in Native American history, the Midwest is a timeless land.

Wisconsin

Idyllic and innocent, Wisconsin captures the hearts and minds of young children. With bright yellow tractors and red barns, cherry pies served by the roadside and picturesque lighthouses that watch over 19th-century villages, Wisconsin is a world of timeless pleasures. At the state's two national parks and 64 state parks, children can explore mystical forests, build sandcastles on pristine beaches and swim in cobalt blue lakes. A rite of passage for Midwestern families, the Wisconsin Dells, the "Waterpark Capital of the World," offers thrills and spills.

RECOMMENDED FAMILY CAMPING PARKS
WISCONSIN

Westward Ho RV Resort & Campground
Fond Du Lac, WI
Jellystone Park Warrens
Warrens, WI

Family Fun in the South Central U.S.

The South Central U.S. promises adventure at every turn, from the rugged Ozark Mountains to the rolling Mississippi River to the sprawling Great Plains. Explore one-of-a-kind museums, celebrated halls of fame and quaint towns before heading underground for serious spelunking. Plan to attend a Texas rodeo or marvel at a towering arch. It's all here in the middle of America.

Arkansas

Explore primeval forests and lakes in the northern Arkansas Ozarks, but don't miss what lies beneath: more than 2,000 caves, with several offering tours. Check out the Arkansas Inland Maritime Museum in Little Rock, the Arkansas Sports Hall of Fame and Heifer Village. Head to Hot Springs, home to fun history and fun on Lake Hamilton and Lake Ouachita.

RECOMMENDED FAMILY CAMPING PARKS
ARKANSAS

Catherine's Landing At Hot Springs
Hot Springs, AR

Missouri

Take the family out to the ballgame at Busch Stadium and visit the St. Louis Cardinals Hall of Fame Museum, a shrine for any baseball fan. Take a ride over the city's Gateway Arch—a symbol of the gateway leading to the West—then go west for Kansas City, where thick steaks and a rich Old West heritage await. Travel southwest to Branson for rousing shows and captivating museums.

RECOMMENDED FAMILY CAMPING PARKS
MISSOURI

Mark Twain Landing
Monroe City, MO
Basswood Resort
Platte City, MO

Oklahoma

Welcome to the authentic Old West, home of countless legendary cowboys. Experience a real rodeo at the Freedom Rodeo and Old Cowhand Reunion or the Will Rogers Memorial Rodeo. Visit Indian heritage sites scattered throughout the state, and travel west on the Chisholm Trail, a major route for cattle drives. Catch the beat on the Rhythm and Routes Oklahoma Music Trail, and then drive along historic Route 66.

RECOMMENDED FAMILY CAMPING PARKS — OKLAHOMA

Marval Resort
Gore, OK

Texas

Everything's bigger in Texas. Start in the Panhandle Plains and see the world's largest windmill collection at the American Wind Power Center. Central Texas Hill Country flourishes with cultural diversity, while warm beaches await you on the Gulf Coast. Visit Fort Worth to witness a larger-than-life cattle drive, and time your visit for the State Fair of Texas in Dallas in the fall. Head south to San Antonio, home of the Alamo.

RECOMMENDED FAMILY CAMPING PARKS — TEXAS

La Hacienda RV Resort
Austin, TX
Summit Vacation & RV Resort
Canyon Lake, TX
Medina Highpoint Resort
Medina, TX
Pecan Park Riverside RV & Cabins
San Marcos, TX
Lonestar Yogi
Waller, TX

Family Fun in the Northeast

The Northeast is home to a multitude of surprises, from the towering mountains and robust rivers of Canada to the heart-pounding roar of racecar engines in Indiana. Discover world-class museums, big cities steeped in history, serene primeval forests and some of the most pristine beaches in the world. Don't forget a stroll along the boardwalk for authentic saltwater taffy. Stunning views, quirky roadside attractions and rugged coastlines make the Northeast region memorable.

Maine

The Pine Tree State is a nature lover's paradise, with 92 miles of the Allagash River rushing through massive forests. Start your journey where the Appalachian Trail begins; enjoy moose watching, rugged hiking and inland water adventures. Quaint seafaring villages, superb lobster eateries and historical lighthouses are scattered along the Atlantic coast. Set aside a day to explore Acadia National Park, a refuge of untamed wilderness.

RECOMMENDED FAMILY CAMPING PARKS — MAINE

Wagon Wheel RV Resort & Campground
Old Orchard Beach, ME
Wild Acres RV Resort & Campground
Old Orchard Beach, ME
Saco/Old Orchard Beach KOA
Saco, ME

New Hampshire

Behold those stunning views atop Mt. Washington Auto Road, which ascends the highest peak in New England. More exceptional scenery is found along the Kancamagus Highway. Chug down to Conway and experience the golden age of transportation along the Conway Scenic Railroad, and then head south to beautiful Hampton Beach. By the same token, Lake Winnipesaukee is a perennial vacation paradise.

RECOMMENDED FAMILY CAMPING PARKS — NEW HAMPSHIRE

Friendly Beaver Campground
New Boston, NH

Massachusetts

From the shores of Cape Cod to Salem, home of the infamous 17th-century Witch Trials, to the cultural cities of Cambridge and Boston, eastern Massachusetts is brimming with history and mystery. Amble along bluffs, beaches and dunes on the Atlantic Coast, and then walk historic trails in its cities. To the east, the Berkshires offer outdoor sporting events plus excellent museums, live theater and music festivals.

RECOMMENDED FAMILY CAMPING PARKS — MASSACHUSETTS

Peters Pond RV Resort
Sandwich, MA

New York

Get back to nature in the scenic Adirondack Mountains and frolic in Lake George. Central New York state features the International Boxing Hall of Fame and the Northeast Classic Car Museum. Head south to experience hippie-infused charms in Woodstock before escaping to the Hudson Valley for rolling vales, romantic rivers and quaint towns. True to its larger-than-life reputation, New York bursts with family-friendly activities.

Recommended Family Camping Parks New York

Jellystone Park™ at Birchwood Acres
Ellenville, NY
Jellystone Park™ of Western New York
North Java, NY

New Jersey

Atlantic City is quintessential New Jersey, with its famous boardwalk, saltwater taffy and Steel Pier amusement park jutting over the Atlantic Ocean. Cape May and Ocean City also beckon lovers of boardwalks. Head northwest to Camden to see the Battleship New Jersey Museum and Memorial. Go on a hike in the Pine Barrens, and Teach kids about history and science at the Thomas Edison National Historical Park in West Orange.

Recommended Family Camping Parks New Jersey

Lake Laurie RV Resort & Campground
Cape May, NJ
Seashore Campsites & RV Resort
Cape May, NJ
Big Timber Lake RV and Camping Resort
Cape May Court House, NJ
Driftwood RV Resort & Campground
Clermont, NJ

Pennsylvania

Pittsburgh was forged in the steel industry and today sports kid-friendly museums galore. Philadelphia shines as the beacon of democracy and boasts a treasure-trove of educational attractions. But the fun really starts beyond the big cities. Lancaster County will teach family members of all ages about the "plain" lifestyle of the Amish. Don't forget Hersheypark, where visitors can enjoy fun rides and learn how chocolate is made.

Recommended Family Camping Parks Pennsylvania

Gettysburg Campground
Gettysburg, PA
Yogi At Shangri-La
Milton, PA
Lake In Wood Resort
Narvon, PA
Bear Run Campground
Portersville, PA
Otter Lake Camp-Resort
Stroudsburg, PA

Ontario

Discover adventure in Thunder Bay at the Blue Point Amethyst Mine, Fort William Historical Park, and Founders' Museum and Pioneer Village. Take Canada's most scenic route along Lake Superior to Sault Ste. Marie, one of the oldest settlements in North America. Ottawa is teeming with museums, parks and family-friendly attractions while Toronto is unparalleled in big-city thrills.

Recommended Family Camping Parks Ontario

Sherkston Shores Carefree RV Resort
Port Colborne, ON

Indiana

Start your engines and cruise to Indianapolis, home of the Indy 500 as well as the Indianapolis Motor Speedway Hall of Fame Museum. Switch tracks at the French Lick Scenic Railway, and then take a slower trip as you motor over the many covered bridges and serene highways in Indiana's countryside. Classic college towns like Bloomington—home of Indiana University—and Notre Dame's South Bend will get you in the spirit for the big game.

RECOMMENDED FAMILY CAMPING PARKS — INDIANA

Ceraland Park
Columbus, IN
S & H Campground
Greenfield, IN
Lake Rudolph Campground & RV Resort
Santa Claus, IN

Ohio

Wander Stan Hywet Hall and Gardens, a stately manor house in Akron. Experience the simple life in Ohio Amish Country with backroad tours, fun shopping and an Amish musical. Dayton is the home of aviation, featuring the Wright Brothers Memorial, Wright Cycle Company, Huffman Prairie Flying Field and National Museum of the U.S. Air Force. Feel the beat of the Rock 'n' Roll Hall of Fame in Cleveland, then head over to Cincinnati USA!, a world-class amusement park.

RECOMMENDED FAMILY CAMPING PARKS — OHIO

Indian Creek RV & Camping Resort
Geneva-On-The-Lake, OH

Michigan

Michigan boasts more than 3,200 miles of shoreline along the Great Lakes, providing breathtaking sand dunes to climb and miles of pristine beaches to traverse. Hit the water for kayaking, canoeing, fishing and boating. Waterfalls abound here, and you'll discover more lighthouses than in any other state. Compelling destinations like Mackinac Island and Holland will bring out the kid in you.

RECOMMENDED FAMILY CAMPING PARKS — MICHIGAN

Myers Lake Campground
Byron, MI
Hidden Ridge RV Resort
Hopkins, MI

Family Fun in the Southeast

America's Southeast is home to gentle hospitality and larger-than-life attractions. On the Atlantic Coast, stroll across windswept dunes and soak in the history of pirates and pivotal naval battles. Hit the Gulf Coast for rollicking fishing trips and superb seafood. Inland, you'll discover that sophisticated cities compete with down-home towns for your attention. Premier shopping locations entice, and world-class amusement parks beg to be explored. Enjoy a glass of handcrafted Kentucky bourbon while the kids play. These are the elements of true Southern life.

Maryland

Called "Little America," Maryland encapsulates this country's spirit, from lighthouses and beaches to military conflicts spanning the Revolutionary War, Civil War and both world wars. Check out naval history in Annapolis, and then hop aboard the Western Maryland Scenic Railroad. Decipher clues at the National Cryptologic Museum before celebrating all things Edgar Allan Poe in the bustling town of Baltimore.

RECOMMENDED FAMILY CAMPING PARKS — MARYLAND

Holiday Park Campground
Greensboro, MD
Castaways RV Resort & Campground
Ocean City, MD
Frontier Town RV Resort & Campground
Ocean City, MD
Fort Whaley RV Resort & Campground
Whaleyville, MD
Ramblin' Pines Family Campground & RV Park
Woodbine, MD

Virginia

Explore Virginia, home of Colonial Williamsburg and Thomas Jefferson's Monticello. Quaint fishing villages and berry farms dot the shores of Chesapeake Bay. Central Virginia is considered the "birthplace of black capitalism," and the city of Richmond preserves several pivotal historic events. The vast Shenandoah Valley stretches 200 miles along the mountains; take the scenic Blue Ridge Parkway to catch stunning valley vistas.

Recommended Family Camping Parks — Virginia

Cherrystone Family Camping Resort
Cheriton, VA
Gwynn's Island RV Resort & Campground
Gwynn, VA
Lake Ridge RV Resort
Hillsville, VA
New Point RV Resort
New Point, VA
North Landing Beach RV Resort & Cottages
Virginia Beach, VA

Tennessee

Relish the diversity of nature in Great Smoky Mountains National Park, where waterfalls, misty valleys and abundant wildlife thrive. Nashville boasts the Country Music Hall of Fame and Museum, RCA Studio B and the Grand Ole Opry. Walk the Memphis sidewalks to discover historic Beale Street and the Stax Museum of American Soul Music.

Recommended Family Camping Parks — Tennessee

River Plantation RV Park Inc
Pigeon Forge, TN

North Carolina

More than 300 miles of barrier-island beaches make up a coastline where wild horses run free, battleships loom offshore and mysterious shipwrecks call out to intrepid divers. Discover the vibrant culture of the Piedmont region, and then race to the Charlotte Motor Speedway. History and great food flourish side-by-side in Winston-Salem, and family-friendly museums thrive in the Triangle, made up of Raleigh, Durham and Chapel Hill.

Recommended Family Camping Parks — North Carolina

Yogi In the Smokies
Cherokee, NC
Frisco Woods Campground
Frisco, NC
Lanier's Campground
Surf City, NC

South Carolina

Delightful coastal views and pristine beaches beckon in the Palmetto State. Escape to one of the local islands for recreation and rejuvenation, and then venture out to the bustling towns of Myrtle Beach or Charleston. History comes alive at Fort Sumter National Monument, which preserves the Civil War's opening battle. Nature and history live side-by-side in the Blue Ridge Mountains.

Recommended Family Camping Parks — South Carolina

The Campground At James Island County Park
Charleston, SC
Willowtree RV Resort & Campground
Longs, SC
Lakewood Camping Resort
Myrtle Beach, SC
Myrtle Beach KOA
Myrtle Beach, SC
Myrtle Beach Travel Park
Myrtle Beach, SC
Ocean Lakes Family Campground
Myrtle Beach, SC
Pirateland Family Camping Resort
Myrtle Beach, SC

Georgia

Nature calls in the Peach State. In the north, the Chattahoochee National Forest and Amicalola Falls State Park will leave you breathless. Head south to Atlanta, where you'll discover the World of Coca-Cola museum and Stone Mountain Park, home to the world's largest high-relief sculpture. Airplane buffs can fly over to Warner Robins to see the Museum of Aviation, and then motor to the Atlantic coast for Savannah's preserved streetscapes. Make a getaway at Tybee Island.

RECOMMENDED FAMILY CAMPING PARKS
GEORGIA

Georgia State Parks & Historic Sites
Cartersville, GA

Mississippi

The Magnolia State is steeped in blues music, rock 'n' roll and spirits of the past. Visit Tupelo, the birthplace of Elvis Presley; sing the blues at the Delta Blues Museum or catch a local blues act. Learn the heritage of the Choctaw Indians on their reservations. Ghosts are rumored to roam the Pines regions, just ask the locals about recent sightings. On the Gulf Coast, places like Gulfport and Biloxi serve up delicious seafood that will please the most finicky eater.

RECOMMENDED FAMILY CAMPING PARKS
MISSISSIPPI

Yogi On the Lake
Pelahatchie, MS

Florida

It's a small world in Orlando, home of Walt Disney World, the Wizarding World of Harry Potter and more. Miami proffers Art Deco splendor, while, to the south, Key West exudes the mystique of Hemingway; take a picture with the kids at the southernmost point in the continental United States. Naples provides world-class shopping, and the Fort Myers area has world-class beaches. Go wild at the Ringling Museum of Art in Sarasota.

RECOMMENDED FAMILY CAMPING PARKS
FLORIDA

Grand Lake RV & Golf Resort
Citra, FL
Camp Gulf
Destin, FL
Disney's Fort Wilderness Resort & Campground
Lake Buena Vista, FL
Orange City RV Resort
Orange City, FL
Emerald Coast RV Beach Resort
Panama City Beach, FL
Riverside RV Resort & Campground
Port Charlotte, FL

Snowbird Destinations

- Make a Latitude Adjustment -

Dodge the Snowdrifts and Steer for Your Spot in the Sun

By Jeremy and Stephanie Puglisi

Many retired and semi-retired folks in Canada and the Northern United States grow weary of hunkering down through the long, cold winter months. It's no wonder that these restless souls yearn to turn the RV ignition and set a course for warmer locales.

For millions of snowbirds, the RV lifestyle offers the perfect way to escape from the ice and inclement weather while maintaining freedom and flexibility of travel. Today's Sun Belt campgrounds come in a wide variety, from rustic getaways to upscale resorts. Whether you want a quiet, slow-paced respite or a scenic luxury retreat with a jam-packed roster of activities, there is a perfect campsite waiting for you in the Sun Belt.

Questions to Ask When Choosing a Location

1 **Do you want to kick back and relax or stay active?**
Some people are looking to spend the winter months reading and recharging on the beach or by a pool. Others want organized golf outings and book clubs. Think about your ideal activity level and look for an area that will match your expectations.

2 **Do you want to be close to a downtown area?**
If you enjoy fine dining, shopping and museums, look for a campground close to a city or arts district.

3 **Do you want to go for walks on the beach or hikes in the mountains?**
There are snowbird communities in the coastal regions of the East and the mountains of the West. What is your ideal home away from home?

4 **Do you want sunshine and consistent warmth, or do you still want to experience seasonal changes?**
Some snowbirds are happy to head to southern Florida where they barely have to worry about putting on a sweater. Others prefer places farther north like Myrtle Beach, South Carolina, where the temperatures get a bit cooler. Determine your tolerance for temperature fluctuations.

Once you have decided on your ideal location, it is time to choose the perfect campground. This travel guide, along with the Good Sam website and mobile app, has all the tools you need to find a sun-drenched winter escape right for your needs.

Start by consulting our list of Snowbird Parks on the following pages. Then look at each park's individual listing in the Campground Information section of this book. You can also find online reviews of some of these parks on GoodSamClub.com or GoodSamCamping.com.

One of the best parts of the RV lifestyle is the flexibility to experience all of the great options this country has to offer. Where you choose to winter this year may become a return destination, or you might choose a new adventure for the next snowbird season.

Wherever your RV dreams lead you, enjoy every mile of the journey. You have earned it.

Get more snowbird tips and insights at: **GoodSamCamping.com/Snowbird**

California

Surfing, movie stars and New Age gurus often come to mind when people think of California. The truth, however, is more complex. World-class golf courses, stunning national parks, white sandy beaches and incredible desert landscapes abound.

Snowbirds flock to the Golden State for its diverse terrain, high temperatures and abundance of year-round outdoor activities. Palm Springs and the Coachella Valley in particular are popular roosting spots, offering a rich assortment of RV parks and resorts across a wide array of budgets.

① Central Coast

Strung between the bursting cityscapes of Southern California and the laid-back vibes of San Francisco Bay is the Golden State's best kept secret—the Central Coast. Speedy Highway 101 links the City by the Bay with Hollywood in about six hours of driving, but take the scenic route instead. Hop on U.S. Highway 1, which hugs the meandering Pacific coastline, and pencil in a few days worth of aimless exploring while enjoying one of the country's most scenic drives. Don't miss the cliff-side city Big Sur, massive Monterey Aquarium and historic Santa Barbara.

Featured Snowbird RV Resorts

California Central Coast

Pismo Sands RV Park
Oceano, CA

Vines RV Resort
Paso Robles, CA

Wine Country RV Resort
Paso Robles, CA

② Southern California

Battling boredom certainly isn't a problem in Southern California, where the attraction-rich cities of Los Angeles and San Diego anchor a region-wide spirit of world-class fun and adventure. Think Disneyland, Six Flags Magic Mountain, Universal Studios, SeaWorld, the San Diego Zoo and Knott's Berry Farm. And when you're done with thrills and ready for frills, head for Rodeo Drive in Beverly Hills, the TCL Chinese Theatre in Hollywood or the sparkling ocean-front beaches of Malibu west of downtown L.A. There's no end to SoCal's red carpet of incredible sights, attractions and family-friendly activities.

Featured Snowbird RV Resorts

Southern California

Trailer Rancho RV Park
Encinitas, CA

Golden Village Palms RV Resort - Sunland
Hemet, CA

Indian Waters RV Resort & Cottages
Indio, CA

Shadow Hills RV Resort
Indio, CA

Newport Dunes Waterfront Resort & Marina
Newport Beach, CA

Oceanside RV Park
Oceanside, CA

Emerald Desert RV Resort - Sunland
Palm Desert, CA

Los Angeles KOA
Pomona, CA

Mission Bay RV Resort
San Diego, CA

Santee Lakes Recreation Preserve
Santee, CA

Pechanga RV Resort
Temecula, CA

③ Desert

East of the City of Angels and San Diego the landscape of Southern California comes alive with surreal vigor. Stark and punishing desert landscapes dotted with dust-blown scrub, rocky mountains, craggy canyons and epic national parks makes the entire southeast quadrant of the Golden State a boon for adventure buffs. Hikers, bikers and nature photographers won't want to miss Joshua Tree National Park, Anza-Borrego Desert State Park and the landlocked Salton Sea. If you're a golf nut, there's no better place on the planet than Palm Springs, home to more than 130 courses in the immediate area.

Featured Snowbird RV Resorts

California Desert

The Springs At Borrego RV Resort & Golf Course
Borrego Springs, CA

Caliente Springs Resort
Desert Hot Springs, CA

Sam's Family Spa
Desert Hot Springs, CA

Sands RV & Golf Resort
Desert Hot Springs, CA

Sky Valley Resort
Desert Hot Springs, CA

Rio Bend RV & Golf Resort
El Centro, CA

Indian Wells Carefree RV Resorts
Indio, CA

Outdoor Resort Indio
Indio, CA

Needles Marina RV Park
Needles, CA

Pirate Cove Resort
Needles, CA

Fountain Of Youth Spa RV Resort
Niland, CA

Twentynine Palms Resort: RV Park-Cottages-Golf
Twentynine Palms, CA

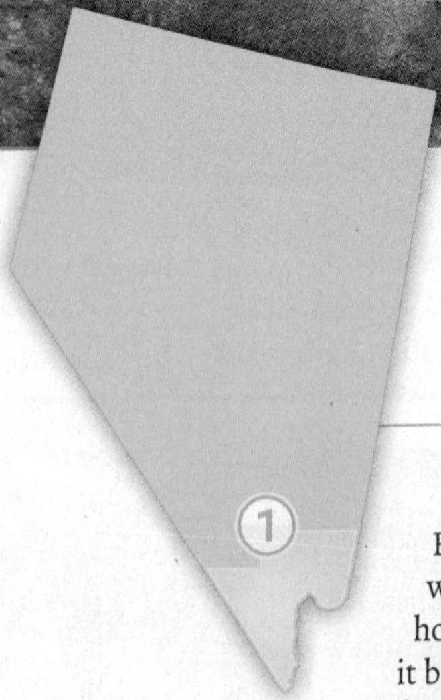

NEVADA

Strike gold on your next visit to the Silver State. Choose between rollicking Las Vegas or the stark rock canyons beyond of the Strip. You won't run out of things to do in this sunny spot in the Southwest.

1 SOUTHERN NEVADA

Break out of Las Vegas for an afternoon or weekend getaway and you'll quickly discover how much more southern Nevada has going for it beyond casinos and magic shows. Sun-drenched desert vistas filled with rocky canyons and rolling foothills abound, making this one of the most visually striking regions in the entire country. Of course, the Hoover Dam is no slouch either when it comes to attractions; just don't miss making a stop at nearby Boulder City when you're en route. Founded to house Hoover Dam construction workers, the town offers unique insight into this marvel of the industrial age.

FEATURED SNOWBIRD RV RESORTS

SOUTHERN NEVADA

HITCHIN' POST RV PARK
Las Vegas, NV

LAKESIDE CASINO & RV RESORT
Pahrump, NV

NEVADA TREASURE RV RESORT
Pahrump, NV

WINE RIDGE RV RESORT & COTTAGES
Pahrump, NV

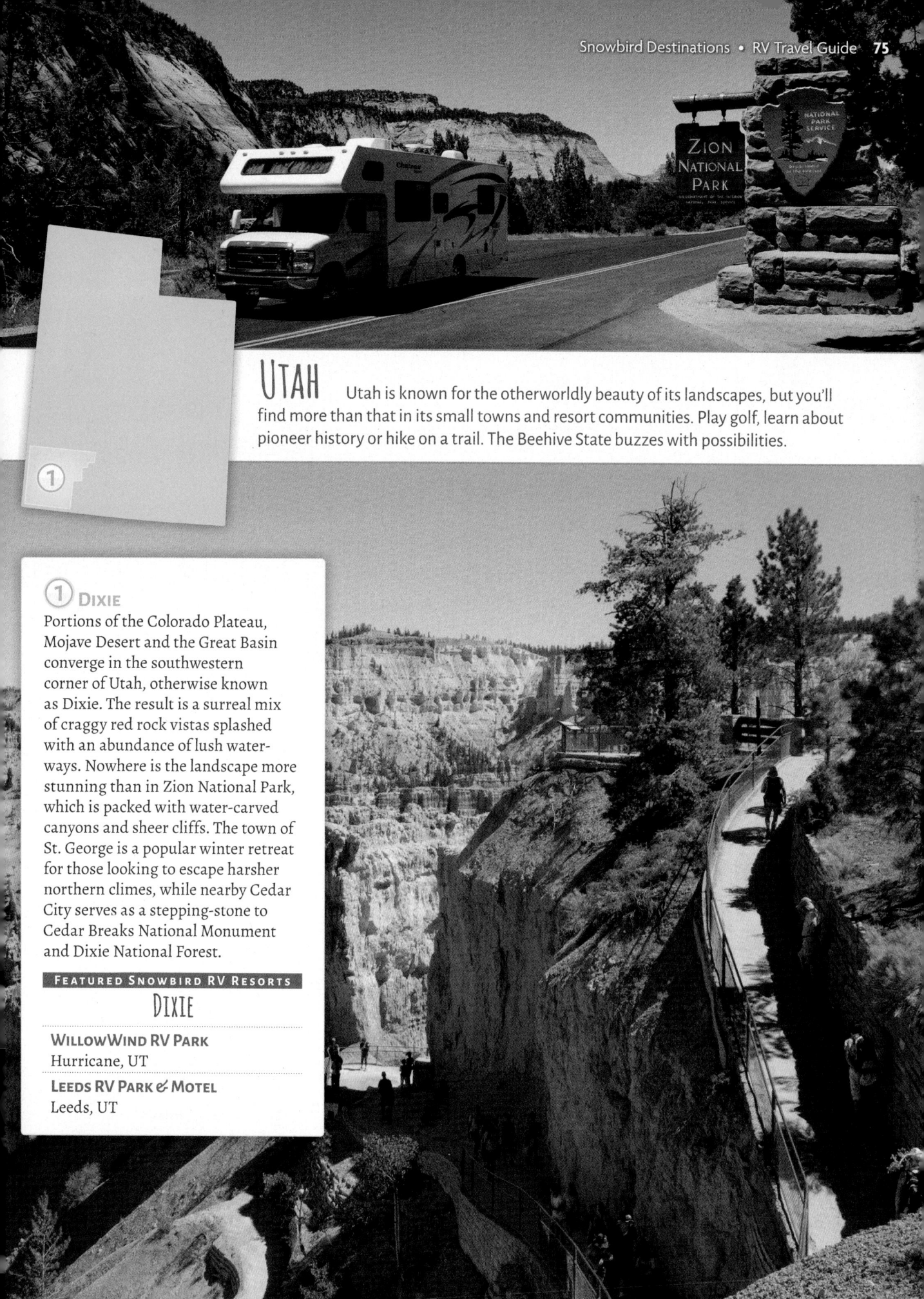

Utah

Utah is known for the otherworldly beauty of its landscapes, but you'll find more than that in its small towns and resort communities. Play golf, learn about pioneer history or hike on a trail. The Beehive State buzzes with possibilities.

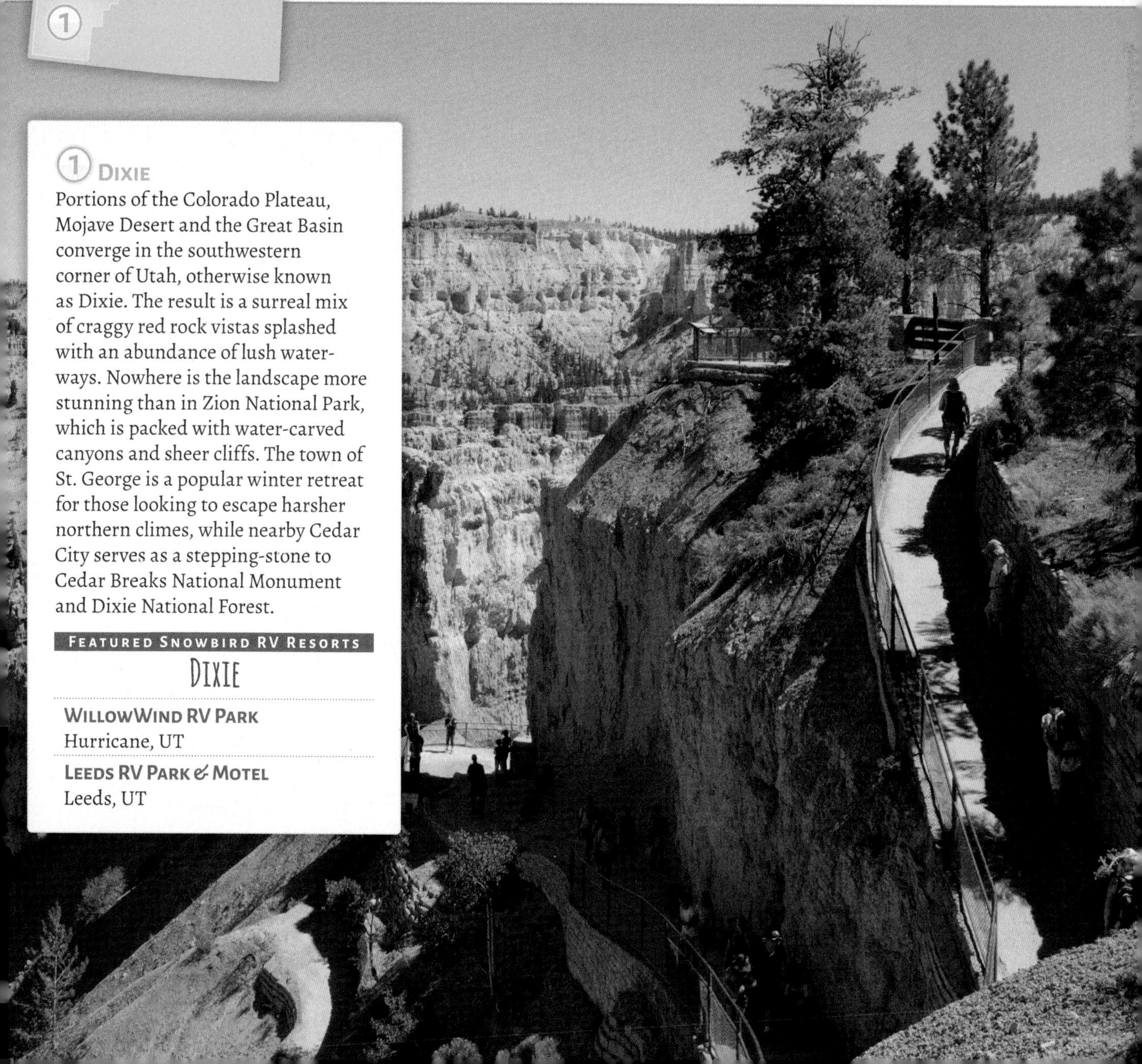

1 Dixie

Portions of the Colorado Plateau, Mojave Desert and the Great Basin converge in the southwestern corner of Utah, otherwise known as Dixie. The result is a surreal mix of craggy red rock vistas splashed with an abundance of lush waterways. Nowhere is the landscape more stunning than in Zion National Park, which is packed with water-carved canyons and sheer cliffs. The town of St. George is a popular winter retreat for those looking to escape harsher northern climes, while nearby Cedar City serves as a stepping-stone to Cedar Breaks National Monument and Dixie National Forest.

Featured Snowbird RV Resorts

Dixie

WillowWind RV Park
Hurricane, UT

Leeds RV Park & Motel
Leeds, UT

ARIZONA

Arizona is the place where snowbirds can walk in the footsteps of old-time cowboys, tee-off at award-winning PGA golf courses and float down the mighty Colorado River. Spectacular landscapes dominated by picturesque mesas and buttes bake under powerfully hot temperatures, so visitors will want a thirst for the sun and an eye for otherworldly desert vistas. Amenities for Snowbirds and traveling vacationers are spread all across the state, making it a treat to roam and explore.

1 Western Arizona

The mighty Colorado River serves as Arizona's de facto western coastline, snaking its way south from the Hoover Dam to the old frontier town of Yuma. In between lies a smorgasbord of treasured small towns. Explore a fully preserved mining town in Castle Dome, visit the infamous Yuma Territorial Prison (once the most notorious jailhouse in the old Wild West) or open-up on a stretch of the original Route 66. Just don't forget your sunscreen—this is one of the hottest regions in the country, with Yuma holding the Guinness World Record as the sunniest spot on earth.

FEATURED SNOWBIRD RV RESORTS

Western Arizona

Desert Gold RV Resort
Brenda, AZ

Vista Del Sol RV Resort
Bullhead City, AZ

88 Shades RV Park
Quartzsite, AZ

Holiday Palms RV Park
Quartzsite, AZ

Blue Sky RV Resort
Yuma, AZ

Del Pueblo RV Park and Tennis Resort
Yuma, AZ

Desert Holiday RV Resort
Yuma, AZ

Fortuna de Oro RV Resort
Yuma, AZ

Sun Vista RV Resort
Yuma, AZ

Sundance RV Resort
Yuma, AZ

Villa Alameda RV Resort
Yuma, AZ

Westwind RV & Golf Resort
Yuma, AZ

② Greater Phoenix

Dusty desert vistas full of sun-soaked badlands and craggy canyons ring the scenic outer edges of Greater Phoenix, a massive metropolitan area home to everything from Wild West-themed walking tours to major league sporting events to world-class attractions and festivals. It's no wonder this is one of the fastest growing cities (and states) in the country, as well as one of the most popular destinations on the continent for winter-weary northern snowbirds. Rustic backcountry environs and laid-back outer suburbs perfectly balance the lively downtown core, making this an ideal landing spot for those with a diverse palette of interests and tastes.

Featured Snowbird RV Resorts

Greater Phoenix

La Hacienda RV Resort
Apache Junction, AZ

Sunrise RV Resort
Apache Junction, AZ

Superstition Sunrise RV Resort
Apache Junction, AZ

Distant Drums RV Resort
Camp Verde, AZ

Verde River RV Resort & Cottages
Camp Verde, AZ

Pueblo El Mirage Golf & RV Resort
El Mirage, AZ

Eagle View RV Resort At Fort McDowell
Fort McDowell, AZ

Arizonian RV Resort
Gold Canyon, AZ

Canyon Vistas RV Resort & Superstition Views Resort
Gold Canyon, AZ

Gold Canyon RV & Golf Resort
Gold Canyon, AZ

Superstition Views Resort & Canyon Vistas RV Resort
Gold Canyon, AZ

Apache Wells RV Resort
Mesa, AZ

Good Life RV Resort
Mesa, AZ

Mesa Regal RV Resort
Mesa, AZ

Sun Life RV Resort
Mesa, AZ

Towerpoint Resort
Mesa, AZ

Val Vista Village RV Resort
Mesa, AZ

Valle Del Oro RV Resort
Mesa, AZ

Pleasant Harbor RV Resort
Peoria, AZ

Desert Shadows RV Resort
Phoenix, AZ

Phoenix Metro RV Park
Phoenix, AZ

Sunflower RV Resort
Surprise, AZ

③ South Central Arizona

Ghost towns, cacti and craggy desert foothills make a drive through the outlands of south central Arizona akin to stepping into your own classic Wild West film. Set up camp in the buzzing desert metropolis of Tucson or the vibrant border city of Nogales farther south and go for a deep dive into the region's rich tapestry of quintessentially Southwest terrain, which stretches as far as the eye can see in every direction. Don't miss the Old West towns of Bisbee and Tombstone, where guided tours reanimate the rough-and-tumble days of high noon gunfights and rollicking saloon smashups.

Featured Snowbird RV Resorts

South Central Arizona

Casa Grande RV Resort & Cottages
Casa Grande, AZ

High Chaparral RV Park
Casa Grande, AZ

Palm Creek Golf & RV Resort
Casa Grande, AZ

Ho Ho Kam RV Park/Mobile Village
Coolidge, AZ

Desert Gardens RV Park
Florence, AZ

Valley Of the Sun RV Resort
Marana, AZ

Mission View RV Resort
Tucson, AZ

Rincon Country East RV Resort
Tucson, AZ

Rincon Country West RV Resort
Tucson, AZ

Far Horizons Tucson Village RV Resort
Tucson, AZ

New Mexico

The Land of Enchantment rolls out the red carpet for snowbirds seeking beautiful desert vistas, rich Native American history and compelling slices of Americana. Find desert bliss in the rugged landscapes of New Mexico.

1 Southwest New Mexico

The heart of Southwest New Mexico is Las Cruces, a 400-year-old frontier settlement that bursts with the kind of rich cultural diversity only a bubbling borderlands region is capable of delivering. Mexican and American ways of life have crossed paths and coexisted here for centuries, resulting in a wealth of intricately layered cuisine and art. Outdoorsy types can dive into Gila National Forest (spanning 3.3 million acres), City of Rocks State Park or Rock Hound State Park. Over in Silver City, explore the old Wild West while walking in the footsteps of legends like Billy the Kid and Geronimo.

Featured Snowbird RV Resorts

Southwest New Mexico

A Deming Roadrunner RV Park
Deming, NM

Little Vineyard RV Park
Deming, NM

Elephant Butte Lake RV Resort
Elephant Butte, NM

Sunny Acres RV Park
Las Cruces, NM

2 Central New Mexico

Feel the enchantment of a region that encompasses New Mexico's largest city as well as some fantastic small towns and stunning public lands. Start in Albuquerque, where the 850-year-old Sky City beckons visitors to learn the history of the region's Acoma people. While in town, grab a seat at a local Mexican restaurant, where fire-roasted green chiles add bold flavors to time-honored dishes. Explore the Sandia and Manzano Mountains to the east, and then cool off at Chochiti Lake, which has been described as "heaven with a zip code." Las Lunas is a charming small town that serves as a stop on the region's commuter railroad, the New Mexico Rail Runner Express.

Featured Snowbird RV Resorts

Central New Mexico

American RV Park
Albuquerque, NM

3 Southeast New Mexico

Toward the southeast, several attractions highlight the rugged mountains and sprawling deserts that characterize this region. Marvel at the vast sea of dunes at White Sands National Monument; follow the trails that wind through the Sacramento and Guadalupe mountains; and land in Roswell, a magnet for UFO aficionados. Seeking cooler air? Go underground at Carlsbad Caverns National Park.

Featured Snowbird RV Resorts

Southeast New Mexico

Town & Country RV Park
Roswell, NM

Texas

Everything is bigger in Texas, including the menu for snowbird destinations. Find a remote getaway near Big Bend National Park, or head for the Gulf Coast, where bustling centers like Houston and Galveston promise a good time. Or follow the highways to Hill Country or the Plains for music, down-home cuisine and authentic cowboy culture.

① Big Bend

Rugged, wild, open frontier still stretches across vast swathes of west Texas, otherwise known as Big Bend Country. The legendary Rio Grande, the punishing Chihuahuan Desert and the incomparable Big Bend National Park dominate the region, making this is a boon for outdoors enthusiasts and nature photographers. The borderland city of El Paso dates to 1581 and offers a mix of casual, open-air history alongside some of the best museums in the state. This is largely undeveloped country though, so pack your hiking boots and wide-angle lens and go exploring.

Featured Snowbird RV Resorts

Big Bend

Big Bend Resort & Adventures RV Park
Terlingua, TX

② Hill Country

Hill Country is the heart and soul of Texas, living on the edge of a guitar string that never seems to stop vibrating. Austin, the Lone Star State's capital, is the driving musical force for the entire region, but wander into any small town or far-flung community here and you'll find great live music in abundant (and oftentimes impromptu) supply. In spring, the rolling karst-formed hills that define the area burst with wildflowers, making trips to Enchanted Rock, Hill Country State Natural Area and Bastrop State Park a sightseeing extravaganza. In San Antonio, which straddles a number of different regions, don't miss River Walk and the Alamo.

Featured Snowbird RV Resorts

Hill Country

La Hacienda RV Resort
Austin, TX

Oak Forest RV Park
Austin, TX

Parkview Riverside RV Park
Concan, TX

Medina Highpoint Resort
Medina, TX

Hill Country Cottage and RV Resort
New Braunfels, TX

③ Prairies and Lakes

The Dallas and Fort Worth Metroplex anchor the Prairies and Lakes region of Texas, offering a big-city smorgasbord of world-class attractions, entertainment venues and dining options. Don't miss Six Flags Hurricane Harbor or the Fort Worth Zoo if you're traveling with kids. Farther afield, a landscape dotted with lakes, ranchland and small towns awaits exploration at a decidedly slower pace. Waco, Gonzales and La Grange are must-visits for history buffs. Dinosaur Valley State Park is another popular draw, giving visitors the chance to literally walk in the footprints of prehistoric dinosaurs.

Featured Snowbird RV Resorts

Prairies and Lakes

The Vineyards Campground & Cabins
Grapevine, TX

Colorado Landing RV Park
La Grange, TX

4 Piney Woods

Thick, coniferous forests full of pine, hickory and oak trees dominate the eastern edges of Texas, further underscoring the incredible geological diversity of the Lone Star State. Davy Crockett National Forest and Angelina National Forest offer an abundance of hiking, hunting and fishing opportunities, while Big Thicket National Preserve is a remarkable spot for bird-watching and canoeing. Visit Nacogdoches (which dates back 10,000 years) to explore the oldest city in the state. Huntsville, Jacksonville, Longview and Kilgore are popular landing spots for visitors seeking a mix of small-town charm and big vacation fun.

Featured Snowbird RV Resorts

Piney Woods

Rayford Crossing RV Resort
The Woodlands, TX

5 Gulf Coast

Think of Texas and you're likely to envision vistas replete with sun-soaked desert hills, rolling prairie plains and craggy red-rock canyons. It's easy to overlook the Lone Star State's 600-plus miles of Gulf Coast shoreline, which are full of white sandy beaches and dotted with lively seaside towns. Houston, Galveston and Corpus Christi are the primary centers of attention, activity and attraction here, along with the longest undeveloped barrier island in the world—Padre Island National Seashore. Don't miss NASA's Lyndon B. Johnson Space Center (Houston), the Texas State Aquarium (Corpus Christi) and the amusement rides at Pleasure Pier (Galveston).

Featured Snowbird RV Resorts

Gulf Coast

Houston West RV Park
Brookshire, TX

Colonia Del Rey RV Park
Corpus Christi, TX

Hatch RV Park
Corpus Christi, TX

Dellanera RV Park
Galveston, TX

Kenwood RV Resort
La Feria, TX

Mustang Hollow Campground
Mathis, TX

Island RV Resort
Port Aransas, TX

Texas Lakeside RV Resort
Port Lavaca, TX

Ancient Oaks RV Park
Rockport, TX

⑥ South Texas Plains

More than 300 days of sunshine a year and an incredible slate of world-class attractions make the South Texas Plains one of the most popular landing spots for winter escapists. San Antonio bursts with possibilities, including the Alamo, Six Flags Fiesta Texas, the San Antonio Zoo and SeaWorld. Most of the region is undeveloped borderland, showcasing a hearty fusion of Mexican and American culture. History buffs will revel in exploring old Spanish missions and tiny rustic towns, while nature enthusiasts will find themselves drawn to the Rio Grande Valley, where sweeping views and an abundance of wildlife make for incredible vacation snapshots.

Featured Snowbird RV Resorts

South Texas Plains

Casa Del Valle RV Resort
Alamo, TX

Alsatian RV Resort & Golf Club
Castroville, TX

Vip-La Feria RV Park
La Feria, TX

Bentsen Grove Resort MHP
Mission, TX

Bentsen Palm Village RV Resort
Mission, TX

Admiralty RV Resort
San Antonio, TX

Blazing Star Luxury RV Resort
San Antonio, TX

Stone Creek RV Park
San Antonio, TX

Travelers World Carefree RV Resort
San Antonio, TX

Pecan Park Riverside RV & Cabins
San Marcos, TX

Snow To Sun RV Resort
Weslaco, TX

ARKANSAS

Steaming hot springs, rugged mountains and crystal creeks and lakes characterize the Natural State's appealing features. Arkansas doesn't carry the same snowbird cachet as Florida and Arizona, but the RVers who spend their winters here like it that way—they don't want their carefree paradise spoiled by flocks of sun seekers. Find out for yourself, but don't let the cat out of the bag.

(1) OUACHITAS

The Ouachitas is a region in west-central Arkansas that contains the eponymous mountain range and national forest. Visitors will find numerous mountain-biking and horseback-riding trails, in addition to the Ouachita National Recreation Trail, a hiker's paradise that traverses an impressive 223 miles across the region. After a long hike, visitors should seek out Hot Springs National Park, which includes historical Bathhouse Row, offering patrons a glimpse into the past and even a chance to submerge themselves in the soothing thermal waters. Nearby Lake Ouachita is known as the "Striped Bass Capital of the World," and is also a prime destination for scuba diving.

FEATURED SNOWBIRD RV RESORTS

OUACHITAS

CATHERINE'S LANDING AT HOT SPRINGS
Hot Springs, AR

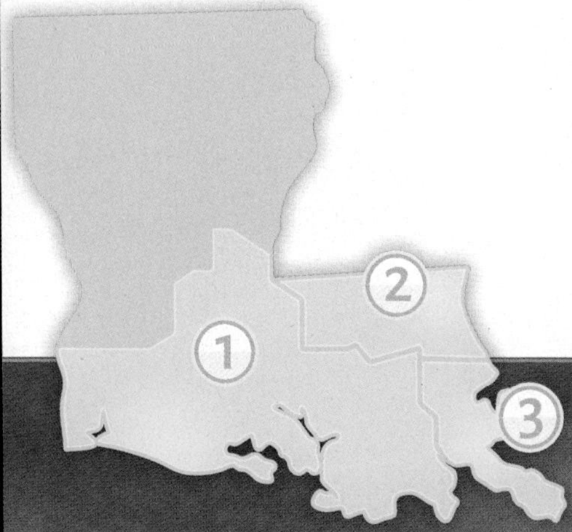

LOUISIANA

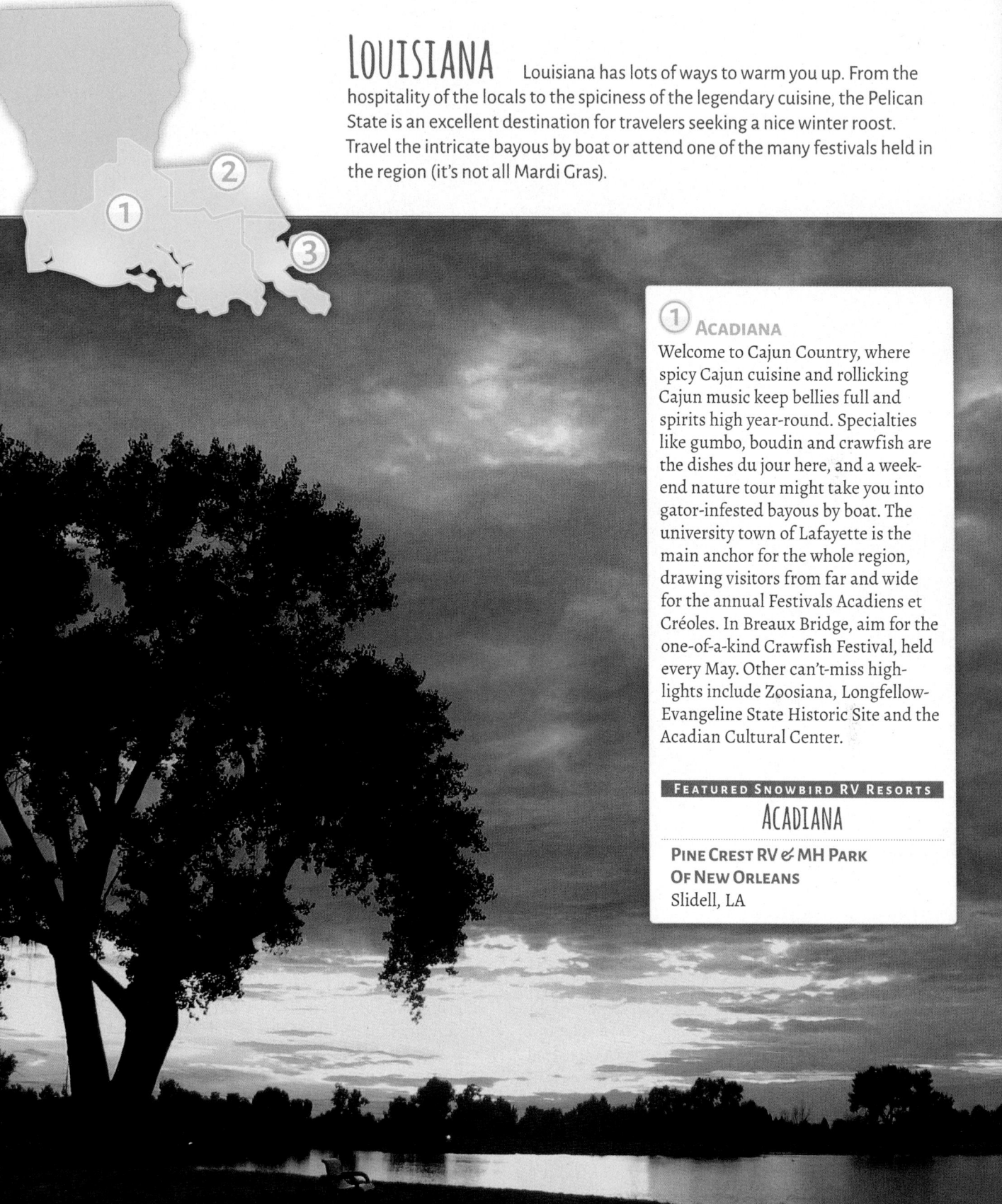

Louisiana has lots of ways to warm you up. From the hospitality of the locals to the spiciness of the legendary cuisine, the Pelican State is an excellent destination for travelers seeking a nice winter roost. Travel the intricate bayous by boat or attend one of the many festivals held in the region (it's not all Mardi Gras).

1 Acadiana

Welcome to Cajun Country, where spicy Cajun cuisine and rollicking Cajun music keep bellies full and spirits high year-round. Specialties like gumbo, boudin and crawfish are the dishes du jour here, and a weekend nature tour might take you into gator-infested bayous by boat. The university town of Lafayette is the main anchor for the whole region, drawing visitors from far and wide for the annual Festivals Acadiens et Créoles. In Breaux Bridge, aim for the one-of-a-kind Crawfish Festival, held every May. Other can't-miss highlights include Zoosiana, Longfellow-Evangeline State Historic Site and the Acadian Cultural Center.

Featured Snowbird RV Resorts

ACADIANA

Pine Crest RV & MH Park Of New Orleans
Slidell, LA

② Florida Parishes

You can thank the 19th-century yellow fever outbreaks in lower Louisiana for the modern-day popularity of the Florida Parishes. The Parishes' abundance of fresh air and natural mineral springs were seen as a common-sense elixir for those needing to escape from the fever-plagued coastal cities, and these areas have remained a treasured point of escape for Louisiana locals ever since. Start in historic Baton Rouge and dive head first into a cityscape full of museums, art galleries and guided walking tours. Don't miss the River Road African American Museum, Old State Capitol and LSU Campus. Then go exploring abroad.

③ Greater New Orleans

A weekend in Greater New Orleans might be a lifetime anywhere else. The city whose unofficial motto is "Let the Good Times Roll!" certainly lives up to its reputation, offering a bottomless wellspring of fantastic food, incredible music, scintillating nightlife and a diffusion of rich worldly cultures that has to be seen (and tasted) to believe. Dance your way from Jackson Square to the French Quarter, stroll through the Audubon Zoological Gardens and be sure to tag along on a guided food tour or two. Outside the city limits, explore a treasure trail of historic, fully restored plantation homes.

Featured Snowbird RV Resorts

Florida Parishes

Lakeside RV Park
Livingston, LA

Featured Snowbird RV Resorts

Greater New Orleans

Jude Travel Park Of New Orleans
New Orleans, LA

MISSISSIPPI

Mississippi makes the most out of it's snowbird status. From rollicking casinos to superb seafood restaurants, the state serves up a great time for travelers seeking sun and fun.

1 Gulf Coast

More than 60 miles of sparkling Gulf of Mexico shoreline snake their way along Mississippi's scenic southern coast, stringing together a litany of world-class beaches anchored by an array of quaint seaside towns. But that's not all. Along for the laid-back, beachcomber-vibe ride is a collection of glittering casino resorts that offer shiny changes of pace when you're tired of surfing, sun tanning or deep-sea fishing. This region was battered hard by Hurricane Katrina in 2005 and in many ways is still in recovery mode, but the idyllic beaches, great weather and world-class casinos keep the crowds coming.

FEATURED SNOWBIRD RV RESORTS

GULF COAST

Bay Hide Away RV Park & Campground
Bay St Louis, MS

Gulf Haven Campground
Gulfport, MS

Sun Roamers RV Resort
Picayune, MS

ALABAMA

Sweet home Alabama will welcome you with open arms. Go for a stroll on the banks of a legendary river or walk the quaint streets of classic Southern towns. Wherever you go, you'll be greeted with that legendary Southern hospitality.

1 Gulf Coast

Alabama's Gulf Coast combines tropical white-sand beaches with Southern hospitality...all with a fraction of the crowds generally found in neighboring Florida. Gulf Shores and Orange Beach combine for 32 miles of Gulf of Mexico beauty, offering the perfect spot for relaxing and soaking up some sun. Miles of hiking trails, endless waterways for canoeing and top-notch golf opportunities abound. Or, visitors can dance the night away in Mobile, which is home to the oldest Mardi Gras celebration in the U.S. Dauphin Island features world-class birdwatching and the Dauphin Island Sea Lab, while Fairhope offers boutiques, art galleries and panoramic views of the bay.

2 River Heritage

History pours from almost every nook and cranny in southern Alabama's River Heritage region. From Civil War-era battle cries to Civil Rights Movement rallying cries a century later, the region is synonymous with names like Rosa Parks and Martin Luther King Jr. Today, the area is bursting with museums and interpretive centers, including the Rosa Parks Museum, National Voting Rights Museum and Selma To Montgomery Trail National Historic Trail. For a dose of family fun, don't miss Adventureland Theme Park and the Montgomery Zoo.

Featured Snowbird RV Resorts

Gulf Coast

Lake Osprey RV Resort
Elberta, AL

Heritage Motorcoach Resort & Marina
Orange Beach, AL

Featured Snowbird RV Resorts

River Heritage

Deer Run RV Park
Troy, AL

FLORIDA

From the Panhandle to the Florida Keys, the Sunshine State's coasts are lined with stunning golf courses, eclectic beach towns and an array of miscellaneous museums, attractions and theme parks that have something for every taste, pace or disposition. Scuba dive one day, ride roller coasters the next and cruise the Everglades the day after that—Florida is an endless adventure.

① Florida Panhandle

Florida's panhandle is famous for its white-sand beaches and barrier islands on the Gulf of Mexico. As a result, it's also a major spring-break attraction for college students, so plan accordingly. The area is home to an extensive amount of history, with influences from Spanish, Native American, French and English evident in the architecture and culture. Pensacola Beach is home to Quietwater Óeach Boardwalk, which offers visitors retail shops, restaurants, nightclubs and a large stage where concerts are held throughout the year. For a more natural experience, Falling Waters State Park and Florida Caverns State Park allow visitors to view the power of water first-hand.

Featured Snowbird RV Resorts

Florida Panhandle

Carrabelle Beach RV Resort
Carrabelle, FL

Camp Gulf
Destin, FL

Live Oak Landing
Freeport, FL

Navarre Beach Campground
Navarre, FL

② North Florida

They say the farther north you go in Florida, the farther south you get. From Tallahassee to Gainesville to Jacksonville, the Dixie spirit and down-to-earth charm of the American South is stronger here than anywhere else in the state. But this is also home to the largest collection of natural springs in the world, as well as a stunning abundance of freshwater rivers and well-groomed backcountry trails—so be sure to pack your swimming trunks and hiking boots. Don't miss St. Augustine (the oldest continuously occupied European-settled city in the country) for a chance to visit Ponce de León's Fountain of Youth.

Featured Snowbird RV Resorts

North Florida

Grand Lake RV & Golf Resort
Citra, FL

Rock Crusher Canyon RV Resort
Crystal River, FL

Gulf Coast RV Resort
Inglis, FL

Orange City RV Resort
Orange City, FL

Daytona Beach RV Resort
Port Orange, FL

Williston Crossings RV Resort
Williston, FL

3 Central Florida

Space Age launch pads, sky-high roller coasters, world-class beaches and championship golf courses make Central Florida a gateway to nonstop, year-round fun. Tour Cape Canaveral and the Kennedy Space Center to see how men were put on the moon, then buckle in for an adrenaline ride or two yourself with stops at theme parks like Walt Disney World, Universal Studios Florida and Busch Gardens. If you're traveling with kids, then Disney's Animal Kingdom (dedicated entirely to conservation and currently the largest Disney park in the world), SeaWorld Orlando and Legoland are musts.

Featured Snowbird RV Resorts

Central Florida

Belle Parc RV Resort
Brooksville, FL

Blueberry Hill RV Resort
Bushnell, FL

Red Oaks Carefree RV Resort
Bushnell, FL

Tampa East RV Resort
Dover, FL

Rainbow RV Resort
Frostproof, FL

Three Lakes RV Resort
Hudson, FL

Tropical Palms Carefree RV Resort
Kissimmee, FL

Lakeland RV Resort
Lakeland, FL

Rainbow Village Carefree RV Resort
Largo, FL

Yankee Traveler RV Park
Largo, FL

Camelot RV Park, Inc
Malabar, FL

Hide A Way RV Resort
Ruskin, FL

Tampa South RV Resort
Ruskin, FL

Wekiva Falls Resort
Sanford, FL

Vero Beach Kamp, Inc.
Sebastian, FL

Buttonwood Bay RV Resort & Manufactured Home Community
Sebring, FL

Outback RV Resort At Tanglewood
Sebring, FL

The Great Outdoors RV, Nature & Golf Resort
Titusville, FL

Happy Days RV Park
Zephyrhills, FL

Southern Charm Carefree RV Resort
Zephyrhills, FL

④ South Florida

If you can't decide on where to set up camp in South Florida, just throw all of your major options into a hat and pick one at random—any one of Tampa Bay, Miami, Palm Beach, Sarasota, Fort Lauderdale, Port St. Lucie or Fort Myers will do just fine. The embarrassment of riches is overwhelming, and you won't have to stray very far to find yourself on a soft, sandy beach astride crystal-clear tropical waters. At the extreme southern tip, head for the incomparable Florida Keys for some of the best boating, fishing, snorkeling and scuba diving in the country.

Featured Snowbird RV Resorts

South Florida

Craig's RV Park
Arcadia, FL

Cross Creek RV Resort
Arcadia, FL

Little Willie's RV Resort
Arcadia, FL

Arbor Terrace RV Resort
Bradenton, FL

Horseshoe Cove Carefree RV Resort
Bradenton, FL

Big Cypress RV Resort
Clewiston, FL

Kissimmee South Carefree RV Resort
Davenport, FL

Paradise Island RV Resort
Fort Lauderdale, FL

Groves RV Resort
Fort Myers, FL

Shady Acres RV Park
Fort Myers, FL

Siesta Bay RV Resort
Fort Myers, FL

Indian Creek RV Resort and Manufactured Housing Community
Fort Myers Beach, FL

Red Coconut RV Park
Fort Myers Beach, FL

Road Runner Travel Resort
Fort Pierce, FL

Gold Coaster RV Resort and Manufactured Home Community
Homestead, FL

The Boardwalk RV Resort
Homestead, FL

Boyd's Key West Campground
Key West, FL

Whisper Creek RV Resort
La Belle, FL

Jolly Roger
Marathon, FL

Aztec RV Resort
Margate, FL

North Lake Estates RV Resort
Moore Haven, FL

Club Naples RV Resort
Naples, FL

Lake San Marino RV Resort
Naples, FL

Naples Motorcoach Resort & Boat Club
Naples, FL

Naples RV Resort
Naples, FL

Brighton RV Resort
Okeechobee, FL

Silver Palms RV Resort
Okeechobee, FL

Riverside RV Resort & Campground
Port Charlotte, FL

Sun N Shade RV Park
Punta Gorda, FL

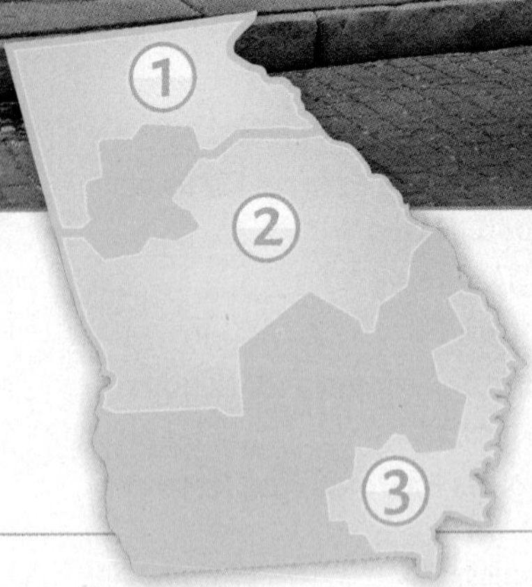

GEORGIA

The Peach State beckons visitors to enjoy warm weather with Southern flair. Tour Civil War sites, savor architectural gems in Savannah or feel rhythm and blues in Macon. Stroll remote beaches on the Atlantic Coast or walk the corridors of legendary antebellum mansions.

1 Historic High Country

Comprised of 17 counties, this quaint northwestern region of Georgia enables visitors to experience the scenic beauty on a driving, walking, bicycling or riding trail. RVers can also travel back in time with a stop at a Civil War battlefield or a Native American village. Museums, shops and art galleries are aplenty, and you're never more than two hours from Atlanta, Chattanooga or Birmingham, making the High Country a great easy-access day trip from the big city. Pine Mountain Gold Museum & Scenic Railroad is a must-stop for families with little ones, while various bed and breakfasts throughout the region are ideal for a romantic getaway for two. Regional offerings include wine, handmade furniture and, of course, mouth-watering fruits and vegetables.

Featured Snowbird RV Resorts

Historic High Country

Best Holiday Trav-L-Park
Chattanooga, TN

② Classic Heartland

The midlands of Georgia are home to a region rich with history, bursting with incredible Southern food and brimming with original antebellum homesteads. With all of its Deep South heritage, it's easy to see why this is known as the Classic Heartland of the Peach State, and anyone with a penchant for small, laid-back communities will feel right at home here. Don't miss Madison (once named the "No. 1 small town in America"), Macon (home of the annual Cherry Blossom Festival) and Augusta (location of the famous Masters golf tournament, held each spring).

Featured Snowbird RV Resorts

Classic Heartland

Fair Harbor RV Park
Perry, GA

③ Coastal

Georgia's historic Atlantic coastline is a treasure trail of idyllic seaside towns and communities, many of which date back through the centuries to an era of high-seas swashbuckling and shattered shipwrecks. Today, Savannah's still-cobbled streets remain the main attraction for history buffs and anyone on the hunt for a slice of classic Southern style, architecture and charm. Nature enthusiasts won't want to miss taking a guided boat tour of Okefenokee Swamp (the largest black-water swamp in North America) or a jaunt out to super-quiet Cumberland Island National Seashore (where access is restricted to 300 visitors per day).

Featured Snowbird RV Resorts

Coastal

Coastal Georgia RV Resort
Brunswick, GA

River's End Campground & RV Park
Tybee Island, GA

South Carolina

Savor big-city charm in the heart of Charleston, then go explore some of the interesting outlying areas like Kiawah Island. You'll see the South in a new light after visiting this corner of Dixie.

1 Grand Strand

South Carolina's Grand Strand, more commonly referred to as the Myrtle Beach area, has been a favorite destination of vacationers for decades. The area is essentially 60 miles of pristine, sandy beaches in a relatively tropical climate, spurring *Southern Living* magazine to declare it the "Favorite Beach Town." Families will enjoy Ripley's Aquarium and the NASCAR Racing Experience, while those looking for a bit of culture should visit Brookgreen Gardens or the Horry County Museum. Live entertainment awaits around nearly every corner, including venues like the Alabama Theatre and Carolina Opry. Local seafood is a must-eat, and the area golf courses are second to none.

Featured Snowbird RV Resorts

Grand Strand

Willowtree RV Resort & Campground
Longs, SC

Apache Family Campground & Pier
Myrtle Beach, SC

Lakewood Camping Resort
Myrtle Beach, SC

Myrtle Beach KOA
Myrtle Beach, SC

Myrtle Beach Travel Park
Myrtle Beach, SC

Ocean Lakes Family Campground
Myrtle Beach, SC

Pirateland Family Camping Resort
Myrtle Beach, SC

② Greater Charleston

Charleston's historic downtown is perched on a scenic peninsula surrounded by the Ashley and Cooper rivers, which flow smoothly into the Atlantic Ocean. Coupled with the city's great food and requisite dosage of genuine Southern hospitality, it's more than enough to make the Greater Charleston region a popular landing spot for out-of-town visitors who are hankering for a taste of Civil War history and world-renowned grits. Outside of the city, head for the Isle of Palms, Kiawah Island or Seabrook Island for an even slower pace and access to some of the best beaches in the area.

③ Hilton Head

Visiting Hilton Head Island is like entering another world. Accessible by the William Hilton Parkway, this island paradise boasts world-class restaurants, the charming Harbour Town and intriguing coves and inlets that inspire explorers. Nine miles of bike paths lead eager travelers to beautiful stops, and fishing charters will help you catch the big one. Relax on the beach and watch million-dollar yachts navigate the harbor, or go golfing on one of the many award-winning courses, including the George Fazio Golf Course, created by the revered designer. Shopaholics will find lots of stores and boutiques for souvenirs and more.

Featured Snowbird RV Resorts

Greater Charleston

Oak Plantation Campground, LP
Charleston, SC

The Campground At James Island County Park
Charleston, SC

Featured Snowbird RV Resorts

Hilton Head

Hilton Head Harbor RV Resort & Marina
Hilton Head Island, SC

North Carolina

North Carolina offers a range of snowbirding opportunities from classic small Southern towns to beachside resorts. Pick a spot and relax in the slow pace that has made the South famous.

① Piedmont

The Piedmont region of North Carolina is basketball country, home to the famed NCAA North Carolina Tar Heels and Duke Blue Devils. But you don't have to understand the subtle nuances of a pick-and-roll to enjoy this section of central North Carolina, home to such crowd-pleasers as Asheboro (North Carolina Zoological Park), Hillsborough (famous for music festivals), High Point (known as the "Furniture Capital of the World") and Concord (home of the Charlotte Motor Speedway, which hosts three major NASCAR races). Raleigh, Charlotte, Winston-Salem and Durham all steep their big-city roots in Southern hospitality, and offer everything from great dining to fine arts to a dynamite night life.

② Coastal Plain

We've all heard of the Outer Banks region of North Carolina's Coastal Plains, and with good reason. The white-sand beaches are central to prime surfing spots, world-famous Hatteras lighthouse and historically significant events (on display at the Wright Brothers National Memorial in Kitty Hawk). But dig a little deeper, and you'll discover so much more, including historic sites on Beaufort, Fort Bragg in Fayetteville, wild horses at Corolla and championship golf courses at Ocean Isle Beach. Nearby Holden Beach was named one of the 38 Best American Beaches and rated 9th out of all United States beaches, in the Family Beach Category by *National Geographic's Traveler,* and visitors throughout the region will easily find world-class fishing, hang-gliding, scuba diving and snorkeling opportunities.

Featured Snowbird RV Resorts

Piedmont

Fayetteville RV Resort & Cottages
Wade, NC

Featured Snowbird RV Resorts

Coastal Plain

Raleigh Oaks RV Resort & Cottages
Four Oaks, NC

WHERE DO YOU SUN RV?

Amazing locations coast to coast!

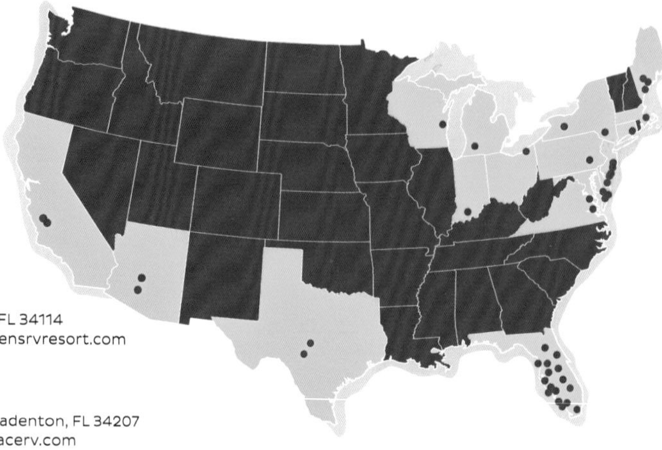

ARIZONA

PHOENIX AREA

Lost Dutchman MH & RV Resort | Active 55+
11050 E. Apache Trail • Apache Junction, AZ 85120
(800) 220-2081 • lostdutchmanarizona.com

Palm Creek Golf & RV Resort | Active 55+
1110 N. Henness Road • Casa Grande, AZ 85122
(877) 695-5146 • palmcreekgolf.com

CALIFORNIA

PASO ROBLES

Vines RV Resort | All Age
88 Wellsona Road • Paso Robles, CA 93446
(877) 820-0940 • vinesrvresort.com

Wine Country RV Resort | All Age
2500 Airport Road • Paso Robles, CA 93446
(866) 550-2117 • winecountryrvresort.com

CONNECTICUT

MYSTIC/STONINGTON

Seaport | All Age
45 Campground Road • Old Mystic, CT 06372
(877) 817-5696 • seaportcampground.com

DELAWARE

REHOBOTH BEACH

Sea Air Village | All Age
19837 Sea Air Ave. • Rehoboth Beach, DE 19971
(888) 534-3037 • seaairvillage.com

FLORIDA

CENTRAL FLORIDA AREA

Buttonwood Bay | Active 55+
10001 U.S. 27 South • Sebring, FL 33876
(800) 355-0646 • buttonwoodbay.com

North Lake Estates | Active 55+
12044 E. SR78 • Moore Haven, FL 33471
(877) 690-2739 • northlakeestatesrvresort.com

Rainbow RV Resort | Active 55+
700 County Road 630A • Frostproof, FL 33843
(877) 701-9107 • rainbowresortrv.com

Rock Crusher Canyon RV Resort | All Age
237 S. Rock Crusher Rd. • Crystal River, FL 34429
(877) 722-7875 • rockcrushercanyon.com

DAYTONA BEACH AREA

Orange City RV | All Age
2300 East Graves Ave. • Orange City, FL 32763
(877) 691-2916 • orangecityrvresort.com

FORT MYERS AREA

Groves | All Age
16175 John Morris Rd. • Ft. Myers, FL 33908
(888) 723-2278 • grovesrv.com

Indian Creek | Active 55+
17340 San Carlos Blvd. • Ft. Myers Beach, FL 33931
(888) 726-6358 • 4indiancreek.com

Siesta Bay | Active 55+
19333 Summerlin Rd. • Ft. Myers, FL 33908
(877) 817-5710 • siestabay.com

GAINESVILLE/OCALA AREA

Grand Lake RV & Golf | All Age
18545 NW 45th Ave. Rd. • Citra, FL 32113
(888) 723-1030 • grandlakeresort.com

HOMESTEAD/MIAMI AREA

Goldcoaster | All Age
34850 S.W. 187Th Ave. • Homestead, FL 33034
(888) 445-9056 • goldcoasterrv.com

NAPLES AREA

Club Naples | All Age
3180 Beck Blvd. • Naples, FL 34114
(800) 640-1896 • clubnaplesrv.com

Lake San Marino | Active 55+
1000 Wiggins Pass Rd. • Naples, FL 34110
(877) 669-1972 • lakesanmarino.com

Naples RV | All Age
8230 Collier Blvd. • Naples, FL 34114
(877) 676-8917 • naplesgardensrvresort.com

TAMPA AREA

Arbor Terrace | All Age
405-57th Avenue, West • Bradenton, FL 34207
(800) 205-9908 • arborterracerv.com

Blueberry Hill | All Age
6233 Lowery St. • Bushnell, FL 33513
(800) 236-5504 • blueberryhillrvresort.com

Tampa East | All Age
4630 McIntosh Rd. • Dover, FL 33527
(877) 818-6170 • tamparvresort.com

Three Lakes | All Age
10354 Smooth Water Dr. • Hudson, FL 34667
(877) 819-9502 • threelakesrvresort.com

INDIANA

SANTA CLAUS

Lake Rudolph Campground & RV Resort | All Age
78 North Holiday Blvd. • Santa Claus, IN 47579
(888) 929-7010 • lakerudolph.com

MAINE

OLD ORCHARD BEACH/PORTLAND AREA

Saco/Old Orchard Beach KOA | All Age
814 Portland Road • Saco, ME 04072
(800) 562-1886 • oldorchardbeachkoa.com

Wagon Wheel | All Age
3 Old Orchard Rd. • Old Orchard Beach, ME 04064
(866) 305-0051 • wagonwheelrvresort.com

Wild Acres | All Age
179 Saco Ave. • Old Orchard Beach, ME 04064
(866) 493-1313 • wildacresrvresort.com

MARYLAND

OCEAN CITY AREA

Castaways RV Resort & Campground | All Age
12550 Eagles Nest Road • Berlin, MD 21811
(888) 733-9497 • castawaysrvoc.com

BERLIN AREA

Fort Whaley RV Resort & Campground | All Age
11224 Dale Road • Whaleyville, MD 21872
(888) 322-7717 • frontiertown.com/fort-whaley/

Frontier Town RV Resort & Campground | All Age
8428 Stephen Decatur Hwy • Berlin, MD 21811
(800) 228-5590 • frontiertown.com/frontier-town/

MASSACHUSETTS

CAPE COD AREA

Peters Pond | All Age
185 Cotuit Rd. • Sandwich, MA 02563
(877) 700-1280 • peterspond.com

MICHIGAN

WEST MICHIGAN AREA

Hidden Ridge | All Age
2306 12th St. • Hopkins, MI 49328
(888) 726-3931 • hiddenridgerv.com

NEW JERSEY

CAPE MAY AREA

Big Timber Lake | All Age
116 Swainton-Goshen Rd.
Cape May Court House, NJ 08210
(800) 206-3232 • bigtimberlake.com

Driftwood | All Age
1955 Route 9 • Clermont, NJ 08210
(800) 647-8714 • driftwoodcampingresorts.com

Lake Laurie | All Age
669 Route 9 • Cape May, NJ 08204
(877) 666-7035 • lakelaurie.com

Seashore | All Age
720 Seashore Road • Cape May, NJ 08204
(877) 817-5697 • seashorecampsites.com

NEW YORK

CATSKILL MOUNTAINS AREA

Jellystone Park™ at Birchwood Acres | All Age
85 Martinfeld Road • Greenfield Park, NY 12435
(888) 726-7804 • nyjellystone.com

NIAGARA FALLS/BUFFALO AREA

Jellystone Park™ of Western New York | All Age
5204 Youngers Road • North Java, NY 14113
(800) 582-9135 • wnyjellystone.com

OHIO

GENEVA ON THE LAKE

Indian Creek | All Age
4710 Lake Road East • Geneva on the Lake, OH 44041
(888) 726-7802 • indiancreekresort.com

PENNSYLVANIA

LANCASTER AREA

Lake in Wood | All Age
576 Yellow Hill Rd. • Narvon, PA 17555
(877) 371-2426 • lakeinwoodcampground.com

TEXAS

AUSTIN AREA

La Hacienda RV Resort | All Age
5220 Hudson Bend Rd • Austin, TX 78734
(888) 378-7275 • lahaciendarvpark.com

SAN ANTONIO AREA

Blazing Star Luxury RV Resort | All Age
1120 West Loop 1604 N • San Antonio, TX 78251
(800) 207-1188 • blazingstarresort.com

VIRGINIA

CHESAPEAKE BAY AREA

Gwynn's Island | All Age
551 Buckchase Rd. • Gwynn, VA 23066
(888) 723-2535 • gwynnsislandrvresort.com

New Point | All Age
846 Sand Bank Rd. • New Point, VA 23125
(877) 681-9597 • newpointcampground.com

WISCONSIN

FOND DU LAC AREA

Westward Ho | All Age
N5456 Division Rd. • Glenbeulah, WI 53023
(866) 361-9917 • westwardhocampresort.com

Sun RV Resorts | Sun RV Resorts

Finding the Right Snowbird Park

Consider your options when choosing a snowbird landing zone

Finding the ideal snowbird destination can be a daunting task. From the beautiful Florida coast to the striking deserts of Arizona, there are hundreds of wonderful Sun Belt options.

But once you have done the hard work and pinpointed your perfect winter escape, the planning isn't over yet. You still have to find the right RV park. The good news is that there are plenty of options in the most popular snowbird destinations, no matter your tastes or preferences. Here are the most important points to consider as you narrow down your snowbird search.

City or Country?

You may have decided that you want to be in the Tucson area. Or maybe you have chosen an east coast location like Myrtle Beach. In popular snowbird destinations such as these, there are RV parks right in the middle of the bustling cities. These parks will put you within walking distance of theaters, restaurants and shopping. However, you can also position yourself a little bit outside of the city boundaries if you would like to have access to all the city attractions while enjoying more picturesque scenery.

Busy or Peaceful?

Do you want an RV park with nonstop activities and recreational opportunities? Or maybe the sound of golf carts and scheduled get-togethers are not really your thing. Make sure that you research the pace of life at a park before you choose it as your snowbird destination.

Large or Small?

Whether an RV park is in the middle of the city or out in the country, the size will certainly affect the atmosphere there. If you like larger social gatherings and the opportunity to interact with lots of people from different locations, then choose one of the parks with hundreds of sites. If you enjoy smaller groups and want the chance to connect with a smaller community, there are plenty of snowbird parks with just a few dozen residents.

Whether you want a large and active community in the country, or a small park in the middle of the city, the perfect snowbird destination is waiting for you. So first identify your ideal environment, and then find an RV park to match it. Then make your reservation and drive.

Snowbird Preflight Checklist: Consult this list before you leave

After you've found the snowbird nest of your dreams, get ready to fly south. Here is a checklist of some of the most important items that will need your attention before departure

- ☐ Arrange for a trusted friend or family member to inspect the house you left behind on a regular basis.
- ☐ Hire a local business to take care of snow and ice removal.
- ☐ Suspend all newspaper delivery, cable service and Internet.
- ☐ Forward your mail with the Good Sam Mail Service: www.goodsammailservice.com
- ☐ Set up online pay for as many monthly bills as possible.
- ☐ Renew all identification and registration documents before departure.
- ☐ Double-check all carbon monoxide and smoke detectors in your house.
- ☐ Schedule a landscaping company and cleaning service to freshen up the house a few days before your arrival home in the spring. There are even some companies that will stock your refrigerator and pantry.
- ☐ If you're snowbirding with a pet, make sure that you've taken the necessary steps to ensure that your four-legged friend stays happy and healthy (see Pamper Your Pet on the Road, page 48).
- ☐ Notify family and friends about your travel plans and make sure they have your contact info.

Photo Credits

Kenny Braun .... p. 81
Emily & Mark Fagan .... p. 76
Dave G. Houser .... p. 72, 73, 75
Joe Lee .... p. 87
George Ostertag .... p. 83
Mary Zalmanek .... p. 74, 77, 78, 90, 91
Getty Images/iStockphoto .... p. 80, 81, 84, 85, 86, 88, 89, 94, 95, 96
Georgia Department of Economic Development .... p. 92, 93
New Mexico Tourism Department .. p. 79
Texas Tourism Department .... p. 82
Visit Mississippi .... p. 87

RV Trips of a Lifetime: FOOD LOVERS

EDITORIAL TRAVELS FROM EAST TO WEST

On these trips, you'll experience local specialties that will take your taste buds to new and exciting places. You're bound to find a stop that will satisfy your appetite.

Maine

Go on a lobster crawl

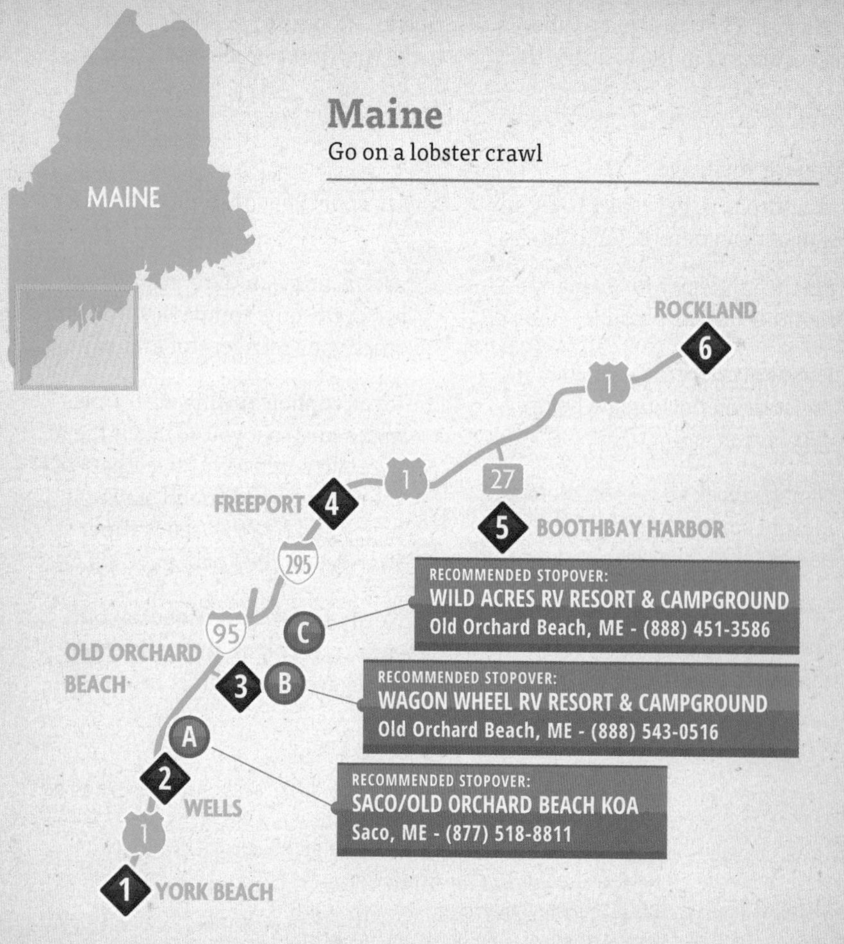

Do you crave crustaceans? Maine's coast arguably boasts the finest lobsters in the world. Take this tour of the rugged shore for succulent seafood straight out of the Atlantic.

Drive 145.4 miles, 3 hours

1 YORK BEACH
STARTING POINT

It's no secret, the world's finest lobsters come from Maine, and the best of the best can be found at York Beach. The Beach Plum Lobster Farm, voted "Best Lobster Rolls" at the 2014 Seafood Festival, is more a roadside stand, but the food is excellent. Select your crustacean from a "live" tank to cook yourself, or order lobster to go (cracked and packaged) with a side of steamed clams.

2 WELLS
11.9 MILES, 23 MINUTES

This little village by the sea is known as the "Friendliest Town in Maine," and after dining at one of their affable restaurants, you're sure to agree. Don't miss Varano's Italian Restaurant for authentic antipasto, zuppa, pasta and pesce, all served with an Italian twist. The Maine Diner cooks up "World Famous Food Like Grandma Used to Make," including their famous Lobster Pie featured on the Food Network's "Diners, Drive-Ins and Dives."

RECOMMENDED STOPOVERS

A SACO/OLD ORCHARD BEACH KOA
Saco, ME - (877) 518-8811

3 OLD ORCHARD BEACH
22.1 MILES, 23 MINUTES

Enjoy laid-back meals in this beach-side town with over 40 restaurants to choose from. The Fried Clam is a no-frills seafood shack with ample portions of fried (not greasy) clams, chicken fingers and pickles. The Landmark is a seafood lover's paradise featuring local lobster, fried clams, fresh haddock and panko-fried scallops. For an elegant dinner out, it's Joseph's by the Sea, with romantic views and memorable meals.

RECOMMENDED STOPOVERS

B WAGON WHEEL RV RESORT & CAMPGROUND
Old Orchard Beach, ME - (888) 543-0516

C WILD ACRES RV RESORT & CAMPGROUND
Old Orchard Beach, ME - (888) 451-3586

4 FREEPORT
31.7 MILES, 35 MINUTES

Freeport should be your "Maine" dining destination for everything from haute cuisine to quaint chowder houses. You'll find lots of places to eat near the shores of scenic Casco Bay. Azure Café offers a taste of Italy on the coast of Maine with high-quality classic Italian entrees and a seafood grill featuring an Italian twist. Buck's Naked BBQ and Steakhouse splashes barbecue on everything—ribs, brisket, pulled pork, chicken wings, even Brussel sprouts—and it's so delicious you'll happily lick your fingers in front of company.

5 BOOTHBAY HARBOR
39.7 MILES, 48 MINUTES

Shipbuilding and sailing vessels are synonymous with Boothbay Harbor, a quaint New England fishing village providing fresh seafood, and the best places in town to watch the boats in the harbor. The Lobster Dock is a rustic jewel not to be missed, featuring a wide assortment of exceptional seafood like Maine chowder, oysters, scallops and shrimp. Their famous lobster roll is served with sweet butter or mayo.

6 ROCKLAND
40 MILES, 51 MINUTES

This outstanding oceanfront town is full of surprises, and Primo Restaurant is one such restaurant, providing diners with the ultimate farm-to-table experience. What's on the menu has been raised or grown on the restaurant's farm, giving the chef an opportunity to offer a seasonal and ever-changing menu to tantalize the taste buds. Dine here for a nice change of pace.

Massachusetts
Get hooked on Cape Cod cuisine

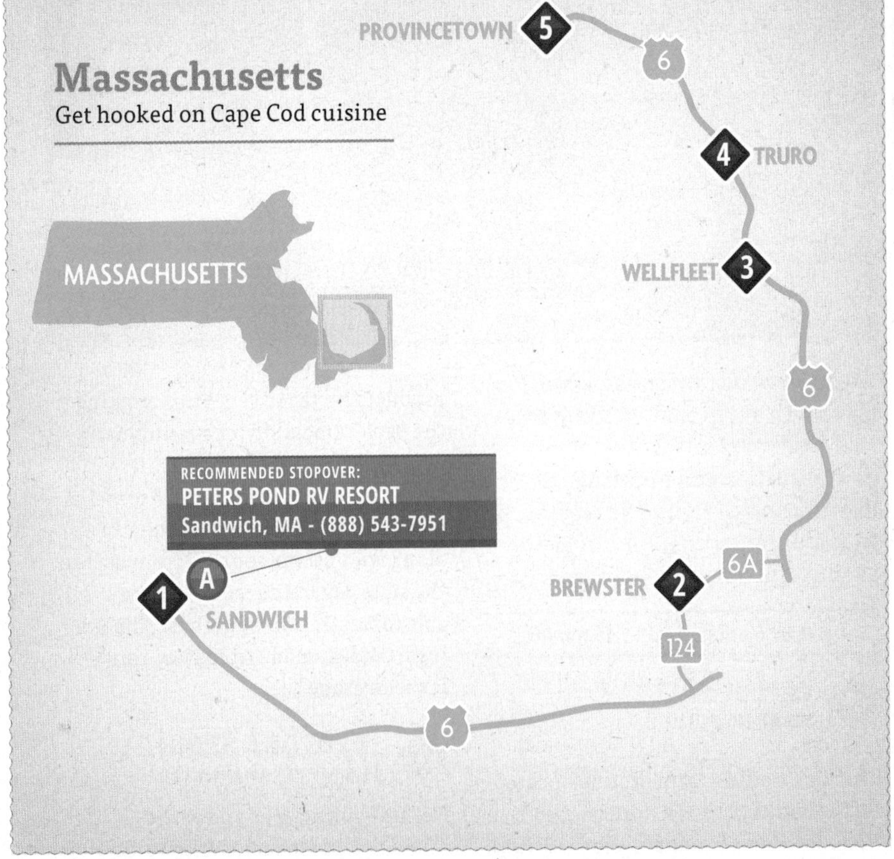

Follow an unforgettable route around New England's iconic vacation destination. Drink in the charming Bay State scenery, and then sample seafood delights from lobster to oysters.

Drive 64.7 miles, 2 hours, 19 minutes

1 SANDWICH
STARTING POINT

This village is a seafood lover's delight. Check out Seafood Sam's, a serve-yourself clam shack right on the canal with the best fried seafood around featuring fried shrimp, clams, scallops, haddock and huge red lobsters served eight different ways. Drop anchor at Captain Scott's Seafood Restaurant for fantastic food like pan-fried smelts, heavenly lobster bisque and a seafood pot pie that equates to comfort food.

RECOMMENDED STOPOVERS

A PETERS POND RV RESORT
Sandwich, MA - (888) 543-7951

2 BREWSTER
31.4 MILES, 35 MINUTES

The Brewster Fish House has been called the best restaurant on the Cape and rated in the top 50 by Zagat. With artful entrees served fresh in a contemporary manner, this is a place that rivals the best that even Boston has to offer. The menu will entice with peekytoe crab cakes, sea scallops, caviar, slate grilled tuna, seared Scottish Atlantic salmon and lemon sole.

3 WELLFLEET
17 MILES, 28 MINUTES

This National Seashore town is famous for oysters, but take time to slurp up other regional seafood too. Mac's Shack serves up an abundance of good food and fun including fish tacos and an outstanding raw bar. Make plans to have a whale of a good time at Moby Dick's restaurant where the grilled seafood melts in your mouth and the classic fried platters are pure Cape Cod.

4 TRURO
5.5 MILES, 8 MINUTES

This crown jewel of the Cape Cod National Seashore has so many great dining places that it presents a dining dilemma. Hands down, the best fish and chips in town is at Murphy's Fish and Chips Eatery, where fresh flaky fish are fried to crispy perfection. Blackfish Restaurant is a hidden gem, with seafood always on the menu. Try the fresh tuna Bolognese, panko-crusted sole and an order of Massachusetts fried oysters.

5 PROVINCETOWN
10.8 MILES, 17 MINUTES

From down-home cooking to haute cuisine, Provincetown delivers on dining pleasure. Local 186 is all about the beef with almost a dozen burgers to choose from, or build your own from locally sourced beef, lamb or turkey with house-made condiments, bringing out the flavors. Slip out to Jimmy's Hideaway, an upscale supper club that's a favorite of locals and visitors alike, for delightful food, cozy ambience and quality service; Jimmy's is a winner of two Trip Advisor Certificates of Excellence.

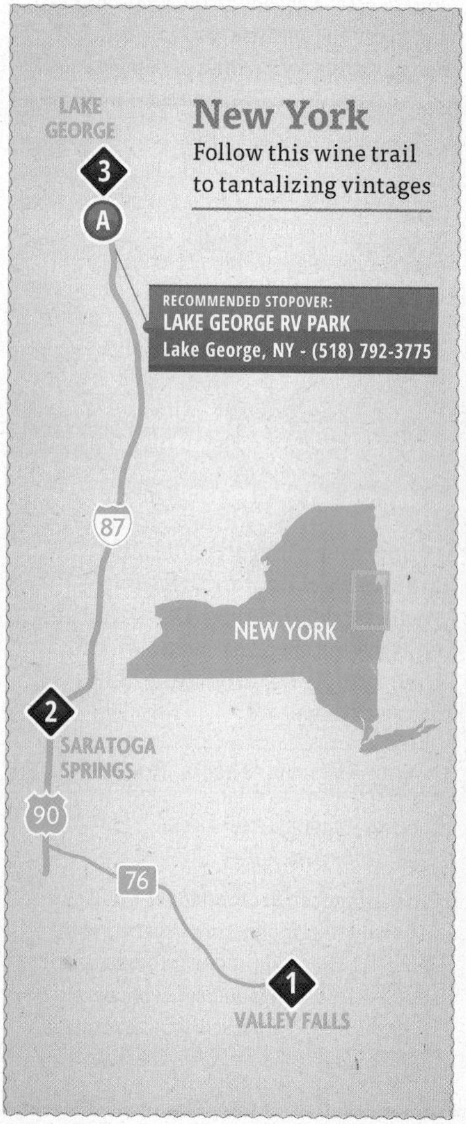

New York
Follow this wine trail to tantalizing vintages

Go on the hunt for great wine flavors in a trip that encompasses laid-back agricultural communities and bustling resort destinations. Along the way, stop in a spot renowned for horse racing and natural springs.

Drive 69.5 miles, 1 hour, 15 minutes

1 VALLEY FALLS
STARTING POINT

This rich, rolling farm ground, located on the banks of the pastoral Hoosic River, has been producing agricultural products for three centuries, making it the perfect location for a family farm winery. Amorici Vineyard crafts vinos from estate-grown grapes—Aromella, Fontenac, Kay Gray and Marquette—along with others sourced from within the state. Over a dozen wines are available for tasting and purchase, including a Cayuga made from New York's favorite grape.

2 SARATOGA SPRINGS
21.6 MILES, 31 MINUTES

Natural-spring spas and world-renowned horse racing may bring you here, but spend a day winery hopping, and you'll have a new appreciation for local vinos. Halfmoon Cellars crafts several Old-World classic wines and pairs them with chocolate or cheese; the Saratoga Winery has a downhome rustic vibe with unpretentious wine names like Torched Cherry Bomb, Saratoga Spitfire and Hillbilly Mountain Mash; Thirsty Owl Outlet & Wine Garden is located on the shores of Cayuga Lake with a roster of more than 20 wines to choose from.

3 LAKE GEORGE
47.9 MILES, 44 MINUTES

This quaint Adirondack town has it all: unique shopping, delectable food and a steamboat cruise. Visitors can shop in town or hike the trails that follow the shores of this world-famous destination. When it's time to unwind and soak up the local ambience, head for the Adirondack Winery. Over two dozen wines are crafted here, running the gamut from traditional grape varietals to fruit-infused vinos to Port-style dessert wines. Tasting possibilities include the standard offering, an upgraded session for two, a premium wine tasting, or a group session for eight or more. If you feel the urge to wander, check out more wineries on the state's newest trail, the Upper Hudson Valley Wine Trail.

RECOMMENDED STOPOVERS

A LAKE GEORGE RV PARK
Lake George, NY
(518) 792-3775

No beach trip is complete without a boardwalk snack, from greasy cheesesteak to sweet taffy. Nosh on sugary and salty treats, and then burn off the calories with a stroll along the shore. You'll feel like a kid again as you dive into rich Jersey fare.

Drive 127.3 miles, 2 hours, 17 minutes

1 POINT PLEASANT
STARTING POINT

The sun, the sea, the sand—what more could you ask for, except maybe a cold brew and something to nosh on? That's where Jenks North Inlet Bar comes in, a relaxing beach bar secluded on the Point Pleasant inlet so you never have to leave the beach for a meal or a drink. Jenks offers signature cocktails and cold craft beers you can enjoy with sliders, wings or fried seafood.

2 SEASIDE HEIGHTS
10.6 MILES, 22 MINUTES

The best cheesesteaks can be found at Steaks Unlimited, an institution in the area that serves up eight hearty steak options. Go traditional with an original cheesesteak, or spice it up with a buffalo chicken cheesesteak. Maybe a Seaside Tony is more your style, topped with the restaurant's original deep-fried cheese balls.

3 ATLANTIC CITY
61.7 MILES, 56 MINUTES

No boardwalk stroll would be complete without the saltwater taffy—a boardwalk tradition. Fralinger's Salt Water Taffy is the taffy you remember—soft,

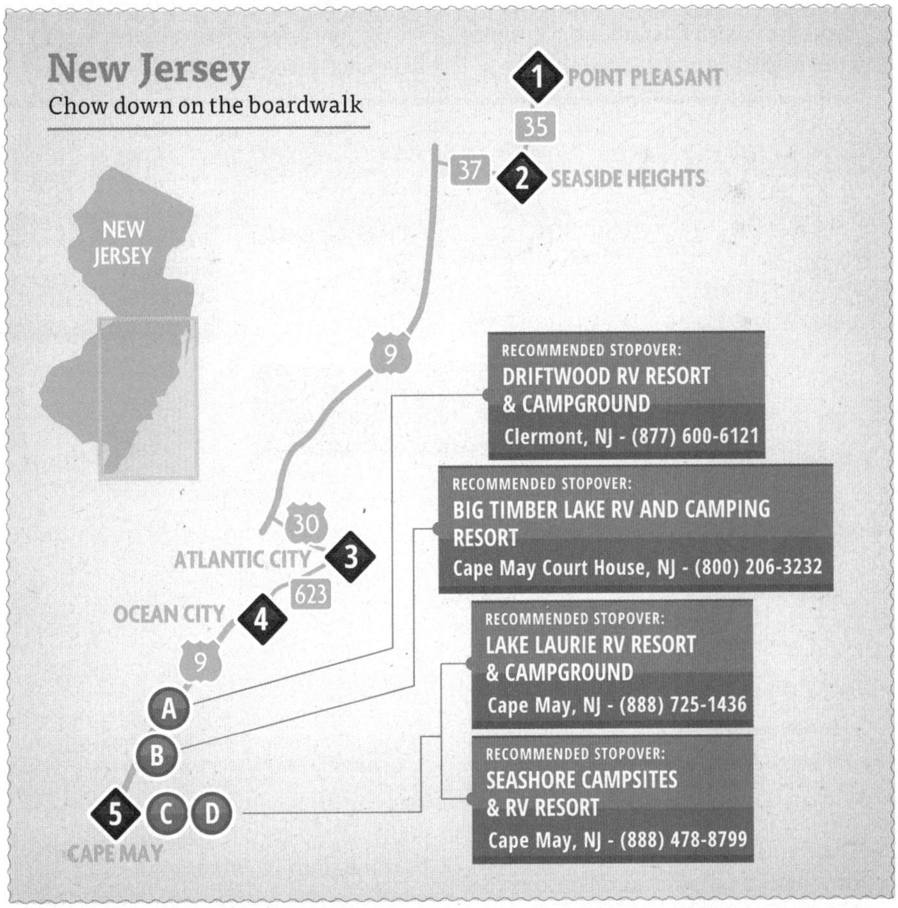

creamy, tasty and chewy—in a rainbow of colors and a variety of flavors including banana, molasses, peppermint and root beer. Taffy is also available with filled centers, chocolate-sealed and sugar-free.

4 OCEAN CITY
19.9 MILES, 23 MINUTES

Ocean City routinely ranks high when travel publications compile their lists of top family-friendly beaches. Its boardwalk is one of the most beloved spots in America, with two amusement parks and endless food choices. Kohr Brothers Frozen Custard is the ultimate Ocean City boardwalk food, available in a variety of flavors like vanilla, chocolate, mint and peanut butter.

5 CAPE MAY
35.1 MILES, 36 MINUTES

While walking the beach in Cape May, drop in for lunch at Zoe's Beachfront Eatery. Menu items include turkey and beef roasted from scratch, along with homemade pancakes, muffins and a variety of tasty omelets. Then head down the road a bit with a couple of cool destinations in mind. Sea Shell Ice Cream offers huge sundaes and tasty cones. Cool Scoops is a 1950s-themed ice cream parlor offering more than 30 delicious flavors.

RECOMMENDED STOPOVERS

A DRIFTWOOD RV RESORT & CAMPGROUND
Clermont, NJ - (877) 600-6121

B BIG TIMBER LAKE RV AND CAMPING RESORT
Cape May Court House, NJ
(800) 206-3232

C LAKE LAURIE RV RESORT & CAMPGROUND
Cape May, NJ - (888) 725-1436

D SEASHORE CAMPSITES & RV RESORT
Cape May, NJ - (888) 478-8799

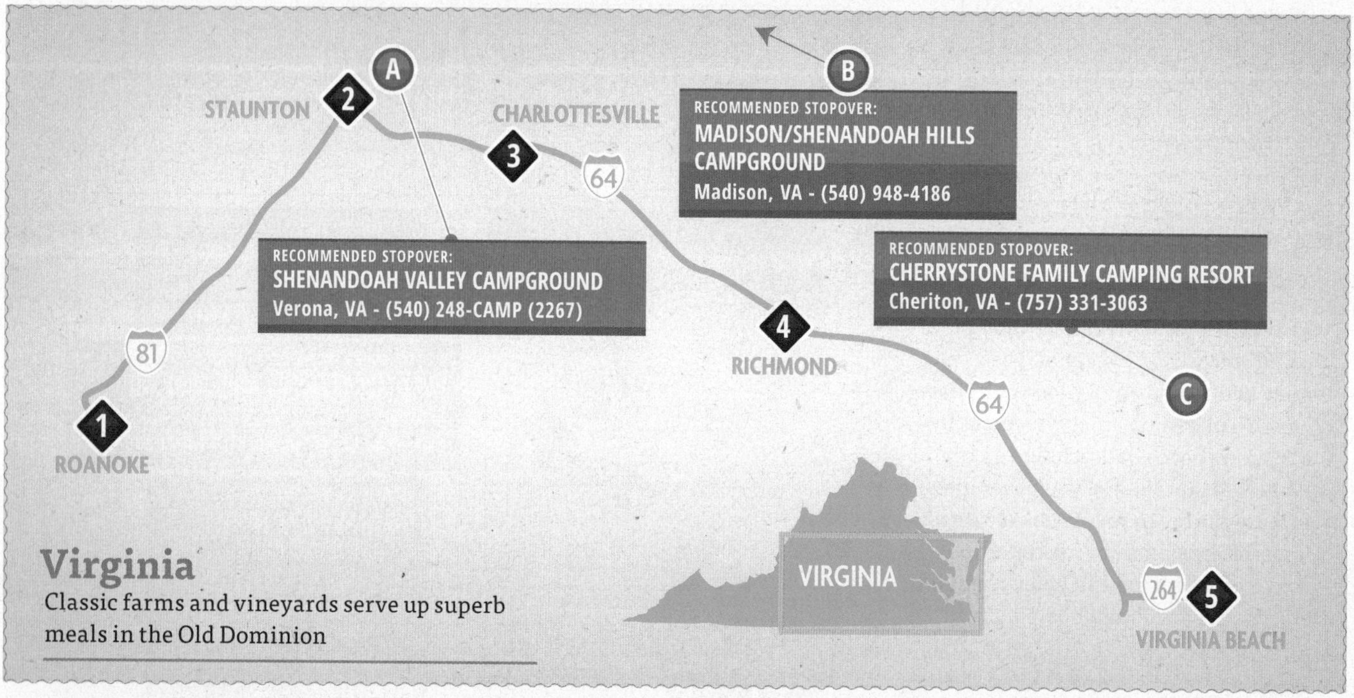

Virginia
Classic farms and vineyards serve up superb meals in the Old Dominion

Take your choice between downhome dishes and trendy treats. From farmers market produce to artisanal dishes, you'll love what Virginia has to offer.

Drive 301.6 miles, 5 hours, 54 minutes

1 ROANOKE
STARTING POINT

"Virginia is for Lovers," especially wine and beer lovers, and with six wineries and three microbreweries in Roanoke, libations are easily available. Close to town, *willkommen* to AmRhein's Wine Cellars, crafting great wines with a German flair. Down the road a bit, wind down, stay and play at Beliveau Estate Winery, offering great wine and quiet times. Roanoke also has several brewers that craft superb beverages.

2 STAUNTON
86.9 MILES, 1 HOUR, 38 MINUTES

Staunton is a well-kept foodie secret, where "farm-to-fork" is the real deal and neighborhood restaurants proudly feature locally grown or raised ingredients on their menus. Head downtown and shop organic at Cranberry's Grocery & Eatery, and then visit the farmers market for locally raised produce, poultry and meats you can craft into dinner. Rather dine out? Consider Zynodoa Restaurant, where each day's menu is based on the local harvest.

RECOMMENDED STOPOVERS

A SHENANDOAH VALLEY CAMPGROUND
Verona, VA - (540) 248-CAMP(2267)

3 CHARLOTTESVILLE
38.7 MILES, 51 MINUTES

Fine wines are a hallmark of the nation's fifth-largest wine-producing state, and Charlottesville is situated right in the heart of wine country, which boasts the Monticello Wine Trail—the largest concentration of wineries (over 30) in the state. Stately Jefferson Vineyards, named after President Thomas Jefferson, produces quality wines from Jefferson's superior Virginia soil. Check out the only thatched-roofed winery building in the U.S. at First Colony Winery and enjoy a glass of their estate reserve Chardonnay.

RECOMMENDED STOPOVERS

B MADISON/SHENANDOAH HILLS CAMPGROUND
Madison, VA - (540) 948-4186

4 RICHMOND
70.4 MILES, 1 HOUR, 20 MINUTES

Saveur magazine calls the capital of the Old Dominion, the "next great American food city," where artisanal dishes have a uniquely Virginian flair. With more than 550 restaurants located here, it's difficult not to find a spot-on dining experience. Try the Roosevelt, which has a 1930s vibe with meals that are comfortably Southern but made with a modern twist. Amuse Restaurant, on the other hand, will entertain your taste buds with inventive cuisine served in a charming atmosphere.

5 VIRGINIA BEACH
105.6 MILES, 2 HOURS, 5 MINUTES

Located at the mouth of the Chesapeake Bay, Virginia Beach has a vibrant restaurant scene that promises plenty of foodie surprises like lavender ice cream, homemade sweet potato biscuits and hearty Brunswick stew. It's also a culinary hub for freshly caught seafood from the Atlantic and the bay, offering flavorful options like barbecued shrimp, fresh-baked clams, crab lollipops and an array of oyster tastings.

RECOMMENDED STOPOVERS

C CHERRYSTONE FAMILY CAMPING RESORT
Cheriton, VA - (757) 331-3063

The jury is still out on which sauce makes for the most authentic South Carolina barbecue, but two ingredients are for sure—pork and heat. Slow-cooked for hours, the succulent meat you'll find on this trip through the heart of barbecue country guarantees a mouth-watering good time. Bring a napkin!

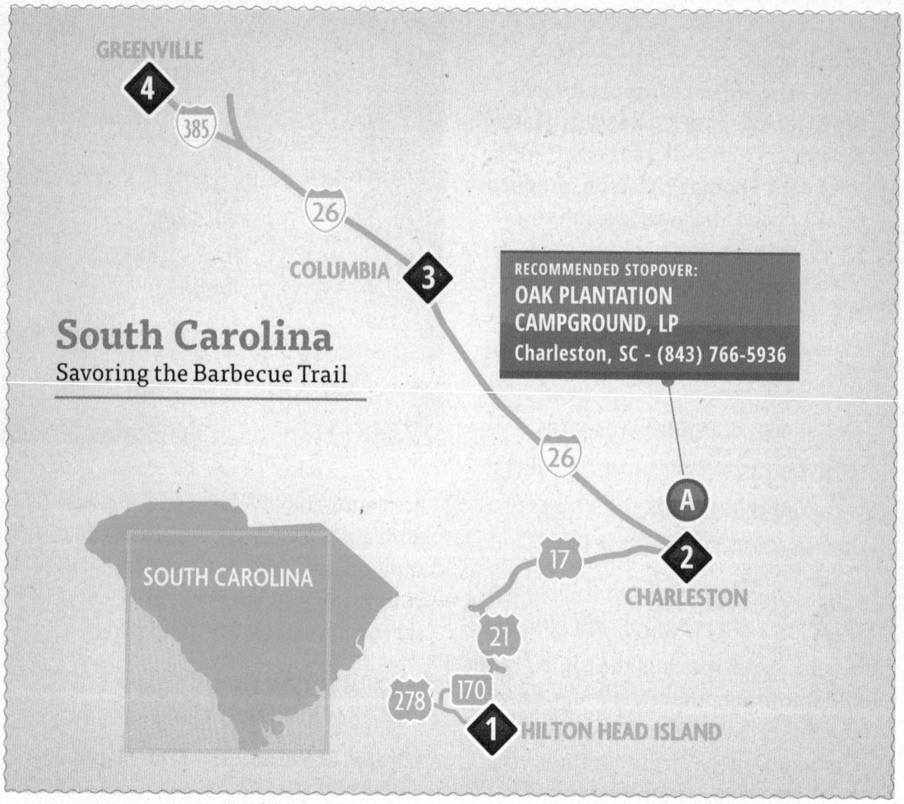

Drive 322.8 miles, 4 hours, 47 minutes

1 HILTON HEAD ISLAND
STARTING POINT

Known best as a beach resort with long stretches of pristine white sand, your first thought dining out in Hilton Head Island will probably be fresh seafood. You wouldn't be wrong—fresh oysters at the Old Oyster Factory or a high-end affair at Red Fish are singular experiences—but don't skimp on trying out a little low-country barbecue after a day in the sun. Bullies BBQ is a low-key joint, specializing in Carolina-style pulled pork, which simmers and smokes for over 14 hours.

2 CHARLESTON
104.6 MILES, 1 HOUR, 54 MINUTES

Savor barbecue made with love. At the Swig & Swine, the kitchen staff uses high-quality hickory, oak and other hardwoods to infuse the meat with just the right flavor. "Low and slow" could be their motto, and the customer wins with succulent barbecue plates like pulled pork and beef brisket, along with an array of barbecue sandwiches that includes smoked turkey and homemade sausage. Enjoy your meal with a wide variety of appetizers and salads, and then wash it all down with a tantalizing selection of craft beers.

RECOMMENDED STOPOVERS

A OAK PLANTATION CAMPGROUND, LP
Charleston, SC - (843) 766-5936

3 COLUMBIA
114.8 MILES, 1 HOUR, 32 MINUTES

Choose a side in the ongoing debate about which sauce makes for authentic South Carolina barbecue at Little Pigs in Columbia. Tomato, mustard and vinegar-based sauces are available at this traditional buffet-style restaurant, alongside never-ending plates of sides, from collard greens and macaroni and cheese to tomato pie. The Palmetto Pig on Devine Street, Southern Belly BBQ and Maurice's Piggie Park BBQ also make the list for best in town, so make a day of it.

4 GREENVILLE
103.4 MILES, 1 HOUR, 21 MINUTES

In a town chock full of barbecue restaurants, it's the "leanest butt" that wins the most accolades. If the lines out the door didn't give it away, a trip to Henry's Smokehouse is a must in Greenville. Twelve hours of slow cooking and a time-honored hand-pulling technique yield the incredibly tender meat that sets this smokehouse apart. Especially popular at lunch, Henry's Smokehouse is the perfect place to try traditional fare in an informal setting. For barbecue of a different stripe, dinner at the upscale Smoke on the Water or the innovative and tangy sauces at Bucky's Bar-B-Q should do the trick.

Northern Florida

Florida's panhandle is a paradise for lovers of seafood

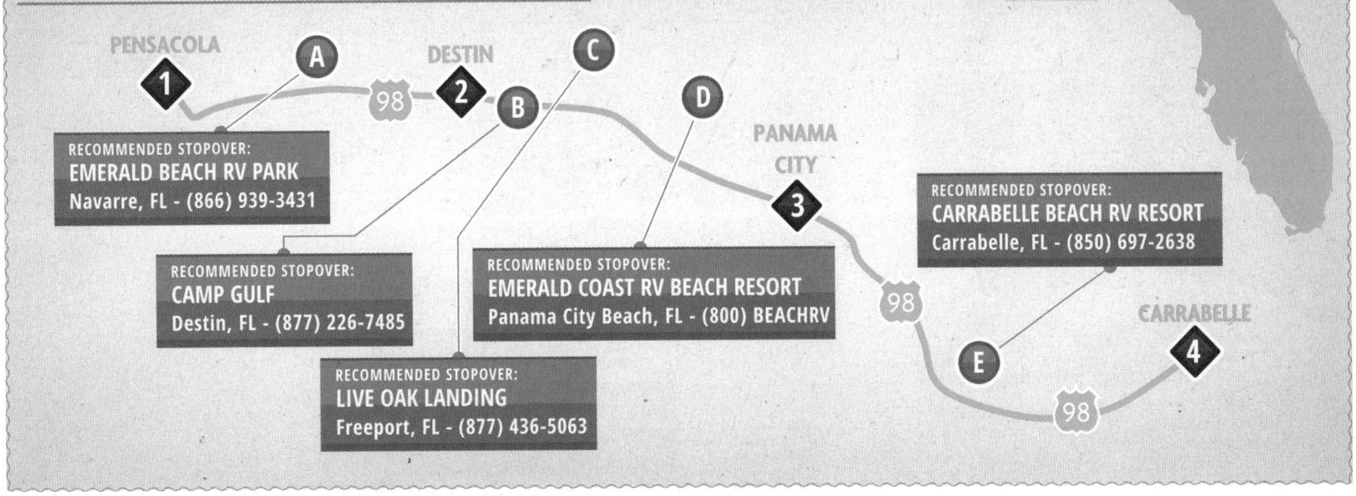

This strip of the Gulf Coast offers a lot more than beachcombing and beautiful views of the ocean. Sink your teeth into legendary seafood offerings and find out why Florida's panhandle is a food lover's favorite.

Drive 185.6 miles, 3 hours, 53 minutes

1 PENSACOLA
STARTING POINT

An Irish pub may seem out of place in sunny Pensacola, but once you set foot in McGuire's Irish Pub, you'll feel right at home with its delicious Celtic cuisine. Savor the 18-cent bean soup, or enjoy their crab cakes or fish and chips. No pub visit would be complete without hearty beer to chase down the vittles. Choose from a wide selection of fine brews on tap.

RECOMMENDED STOPOVERS

A EMERALD BEACH RV PARK
Navarre, FL - (866) 939-3431

2 DESTIN
47.8 MILES, 1 HOUR, 5 MINUTES

For one of the finest and most unique dining experiences in Destin, look no further than the Beach Walk Café at Henderson Park Inn. Enjoy waterfront dining on the secluded beach while watching a gorgeous Emerald Coast sunset. Choose from a variety of innovative entrees featuring fresh seafood, steaks, chops and venison, all cooked to perfection. It's a feast for your eyes and your appetite.

RECOMMENDED STOPOVERS

B CAMP GULF
Destin, FL - (877) 226-7485

C LIVE OAK LANDING
Freeport, FL - (877) 436-5063

3 PANAMA CITY
56 MILES, 1 HOUR, 9 MINUTES

Panama City offers an eclectic array of restaurants serving up everything from fusion cuisine to Spanish, African and Caribbean dishes touched with Cuban flourishes. All are guaranteed to make your mouth water and your taste buds sing. Uncle Ernie's Bayfront Grill & Brew House offers a casual atmosphere with fine dining, live entertainment, craft beers and great sunsets.

RECOMMENDED STOPOVERS

D EMERALD COAST RV BEACH RESORT
Panama City Beach, FL - (800) BEACHRV

4 CARRABELLE
81.8 MILES, 1 HOUR, 39 MINUTES

Unpretentious describes Carrabelle's laid-back vibe, and this national fishing destination is the place to sample seafood at its best. First stop is the Fisherman's Wife Restaurant for flavorful fish dished up in sizable portions at a great value. The unassuming Pearle Restaurant may look like a dive, but looks can be deceiving—the seafood is "fresh off the boat."

RECOMMENDED STOPOVERS

E CARRABELLE BEACH RV RESORT
Carrabelle, FL - (850) 697-2638

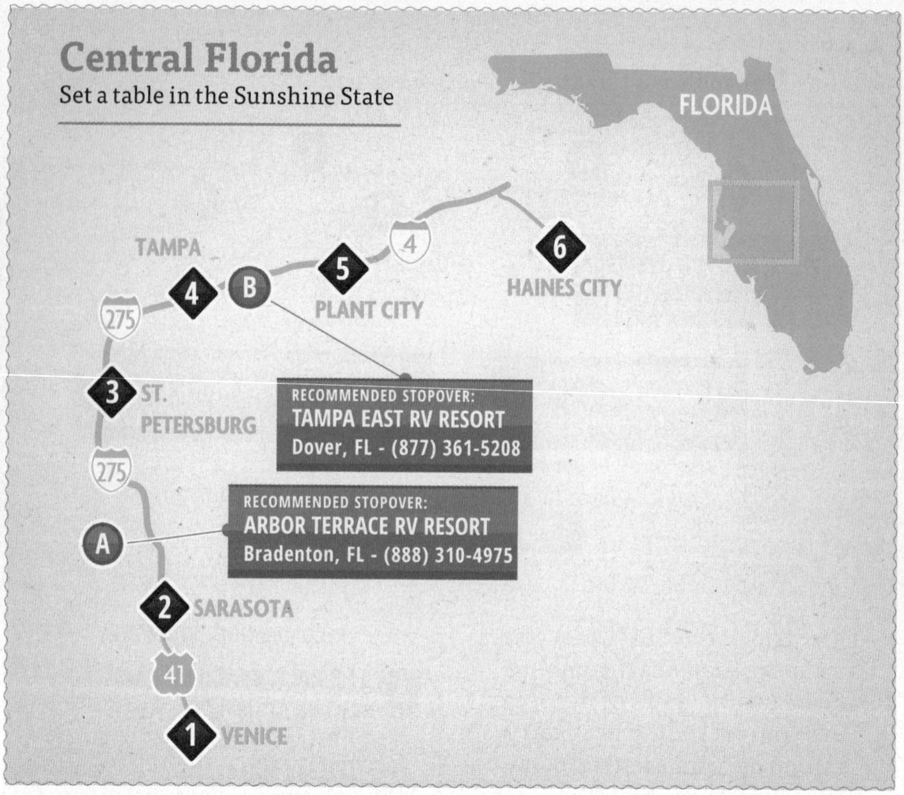

From seafood to farm-fresh produce to succulent steaks, Central Florida is a movable feast. Start at the Gulf Coast for prime seafood, then move inland where strawberries and prime cuts await hungry travelers.

Drive 172 miles, 3 hours, 28 minutes

1 VENICE
STARTING POINT

With its relaxing Mediterranean vibe, Venice appropriately conjures images of charming beaches, tranquil waters, quaint shops and delicious food. This "Paradise on the Gulf" has several authentic Italian restaurants, but locals rave about Cassariano Italian Eatery, with its amazing balance of hearty bistro flavors served in a contemporary Italian cuisine style.

RECOMMENDED STOPOVERS

A ARBOR TERRACE RV RESORT
Bradenton, FL - (888) 310-4975

2 SARASOTA
23.7 MILES, 40 MINUTES

Eclectic eateries abound in this circus town, and Painter's Palate is the big top of fun, providing a delightfully hip vibe with extraordinary food with an Asian fusion twist. This hidden gem has a vast selection of dishes that promise to "bring beauty to your belly," from the delectable mahi-mahi in a tangy mango sauce to the beef tenderloin, with a stunning mushroom and tangerine sauce.

3 ST. PETERSBURG
38.3 MILES, 59 MINUTES

The "Sunshine City" is home to a thriving restaurant scene, but nothing beats a grouper sandwich on the beach in the St. Petersburg sunshine. Kick back on the patio at Guppy's on the Beach and enjoy a fresh grouper sandwich served picatta style with a lemon caper beurre blanc sauce. Dockside Dave's offers a grouper sandwich (voted Best Grouper in the South by *Southern Living* magazine) served six different ways. Gussie up for dinner (or not) at the landmark Hurricane Seafood Restaurant.

RECOMMENDED STOPOVERS

B TAMPA EAST RV RESORT
Dover, FL - (877) 361-5208

4 TAMPA
23.9 MILES, 31 MINUTES

Treasure awaits food lovers in Tampa, and that includes the city's signature sandwich, the Cuban. Brocato's Sandwich Shop serves up a massive Cuban sandwich featuring succulent roast pork that melts in your mouth, along with Genoa salami, sliced ham and imported Swiss cheese, all piled on fresh-baked Cuban bread. Aguila Sandwich Shop offers a hearty Cuban sandwich with thinly sliced ham, shredded roast pork, tangy Swiss cheese and a side of salsa picante.

5 PLANT CITY
46.5 MILES, 39 MINUTES

What an apt name for the place known as the "Winter Strawberry Capital of the World," which is home to almost 3,000 farms and nurseries. The Florida Strawberry Festival takes you back to a time when fairs and festivals brought members of the community together to celebrate the harvest. If you miss the spring festival, don't despair: these sweet, juicy fresh-from-the-farm beauties are available from December through April.

6 HAINES CITY
39.6 MILES, 39 MINUTES

Welcome to the heart of Florida, where life bustles and people-watching is a sport, especially at one of the most popular steak houses in town, Manny's Original Chophouse. Mouth-watering steaks cooked to perfection, chargrilled and generously seasoned, served with hot, yeasty rolls, an endless salad and a side dish of your choice. Save room for Key lime pie.

Louisiana

Hit Highway 90 for classic Pelican State fare

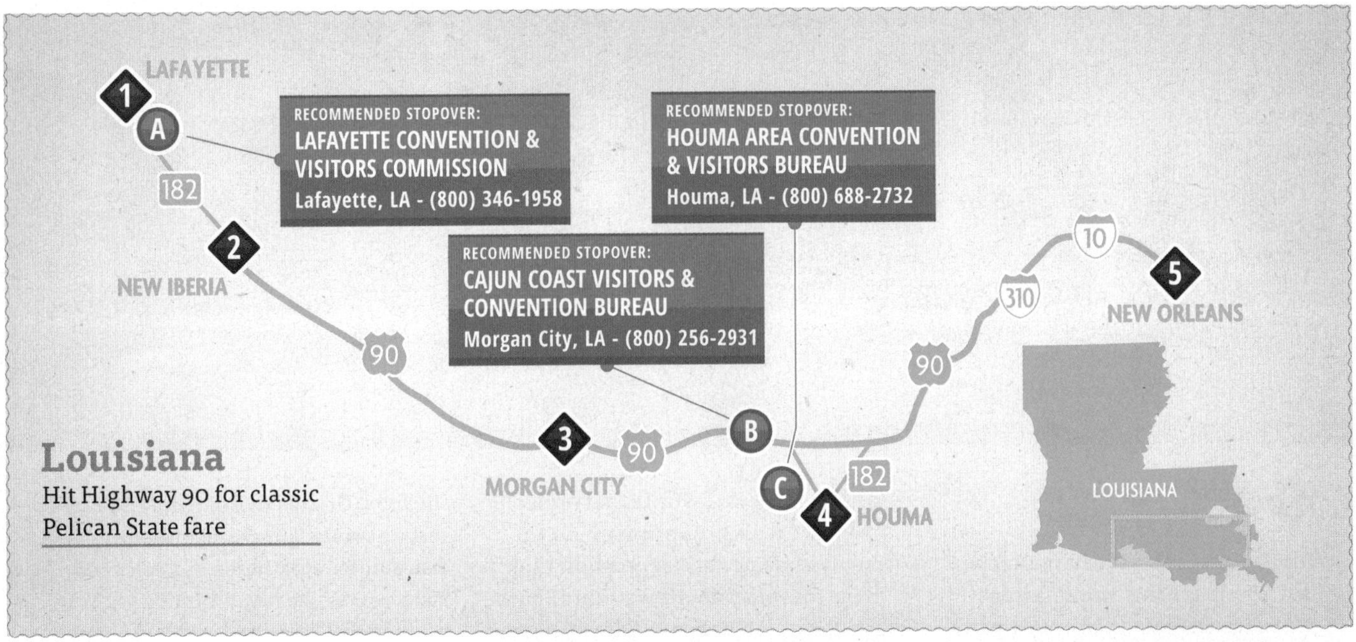

Like the high temperatures of the region's climate, the spicy sauces and seasoning of Cajun-style cooking are found nowhere else on the planet. From New Iberia, home to world-famous Tabasco sauce, to Houma's crawfish etoufee, you'll savor the sizzling flavors.

Drive 165.6 miles, 2 hours, 46 minutes

1 LAFAYETTE
STARTING POINT

Known as Hub City because of the many roads that converge there, Lafayette resides in the very heart of Acadiana, which explains why Cajun cuisine is a passion here. Louisiana Crawfish Time features fresh local seafood, expertly boiled and seasoned; the crawfish are impeccably spiced, but not for the faint of heart. Po'boys are awesomely stuffed, and the staff is knowledgeable. Bon Temps Grill is a Cajun foodies dream specializing in swamp-edge cuisine like Bon Temps Sausage, Blackened Chicken, Crawfish Pot Pie—even barbecue Alligator—and all of the dishes have that melding of flavors that say, "Cajun."

RECOMMENDED STOPOVERS

A LAFAYETTE CONVENTION & VISITORS COMMISSION
Lafayette, LA - (800) 346-1958

2 NEW IBERIA
24 MILES, 29 MINUTES

This Queen City of the Bayou Teche is also home to that world-famous pepper sauce—McIlhenny Company Tabasco. A trip to Avery Island is a hot pick among visitors, and the first stop is a tour of the pepper sauce factory to see how Tabasco is made. Experience nature Louisiana-style at Jungle Gardens, which features 170 acres of tropical beauty. Take an afternoon Tabasco Food Tour and delight in Cajun cuisine while soaking up the culture and savoring that down-home Southern atmosphere, but remember, reservations are required.

3 MORGAN CITY
49.8 MILES, 47 MINUTES

Local restaurants here know how to serve up the perfect Cajun and Creole dishes. Pull up a chair at Rita Mae's Kitchen for tasty local catfish with fresh cornbread and white beans, or order a bowl of seafood gumbo and a sausage po' boy to enjoy in the homey, laid-back atmosphere. Morgan's Restaurant is a local favorite that prides itself on Creole/Cajun home cooked family-style buffets, or order off the menu for some mouth-watering Southern dishes. Atchafalaya Café dishes out authentic Creole and Cajun food like the Bayou Pasta with fried shrimp in a crawfish cream sauce.

RECOMMENDED STOPOVERS

B CAJUN COAST VISITORS & CONVENTION BUREAU
Morgan City, LA - (800) 256-2931

4 HOUMA
34.6 MILES, 37 MINUTES

Dine where the locals eat, soak up the atmosphere, and revel in authentic Creole and Cajun dishes. Bayou Delight Restaurant cooks up some of the best fried chicken around, along with boudin balls, fried crab claws and tasty alligator, all served in their quaint dining room. A 12-foot stuffed 'gator stands by to greet you at Boudreau & Thibodeau's Cajun Cookin' Seafood Restaurant, but that huge impression will soon be replaced by the outstanding food. Grab a bowl of corn-and-crab bisque before launching into the crawfish etoufee smothered in a spicy red sauce, or try the restaurant's signature seafood platter served with a creamy crawfish sauce.

RECOMMENDED STOPOVERS

C HOUMA AREA CONVENTION & VISITORS BUREAU
Houma, LA - (800) 688-2732

5 NEW ORLEANS
57.2 MILES, 53 MINUTES

NOLA, the Crescent City, the Big Easy—New Orleans may go by a lot of names, but regardless of the moniker, foodies know this is the home of Creole and Cajun cooking. Charcoal's Gourmet Burger Bar isn't your ordinary burger joint: Here, a burger can be crafted from venison, buffalo, elk, antelope, salmon or akaushi-kobe, with ample sides and specialty cocktails. Tableau at Le Petit Theatre marries understated elegance with exceptional French Creole dishes to provide a depth of flavors with a twist.

Michigan serves up a smorgasbord of foodie experiences for adventurous eaters. Start this tour with some brew in Frankenmuth, then end it in the sweet spot of Traverse City, the "Cherry Capital of the World."

Drive 305.1 miles, 4 hours, 45 minutes

1 FRANKENMUTH
STARTING POINT

Willkommen to Frankenmuth, Michigan's Little Bavaria, where German hospitality is always in season and fun is just around the corner. Festivals abound here; there's the Winter Beer Festival, the Bavarian Festival and, of course, Oktoberfest. However, the main event each year is the World Expo of Beer, held the third weekend of May. Sample nearly 300 different brews from around the world and enjoy savory German cuisine.

RECOMMENDED STOPOVERS

A BRONNER'S CHRISTMAS WONDERLAND
Frankenmuth, MI - (989) 652-9931

B YOGI BEAR'S JELLYSTONE PARK CAMP-RESORT
Frankenmuth, MI - (989) 652-6668

2 GAYLORD
144.5 MILES, 1 HOUR, 53 MINUTES

This "Alpine village" may be located in Michigan, but its heart is in Germany. Gaylord celebrates its heritage every year with two festivals: In February, the Alpenfrost is held to celebrate the heart of the winter season with an ice fishing derby, snow sculpture events and a Frosty 5K run. Summer brings more family fun when the town transforms into an Alpine village during Alpenfest, with a carnival, parades, the burning of the Boogg and lots of food.

3 MACKINAW CITY
58.2 MILES, 47 MINUTES

Mackinaw City is a famed resort village that boasts beautiful views of the Mackinac Bridge and Mackinac Island, and it's home to some exceptional fudge shops. The Murdick family opened the first fudge shop on Mackinac Island in 1887, and Aaron Murdick's Fudge still uses those original, decadent fudge recipes in its Mackinaw City Store. On nearby Mackinac Island, JoAnn's Fudge crafts 29 different flavors.

4 PETOSKEY
36.2 MILES, 45 MINUTES

Named one of America's best small towns, Petoskey has an abundance of local shops and delightful eateries located in the historic gaslight district. For breakfast or lunch, it's Julienne Tomatoes Deli & Bakery, where the food is fresh, made from quality ingredients and served in a charming dining room. A hearty meal may be had at the Polish Kitchen serving up authentic cuisine like kielbasa, pierogi and schnitzel in great portions at an excellent value.

5 TRAVERSE CITY
66.2 MILES, 1 HOUR, 20 MINUTES

The "Cherry Capital of the World" annually hosts the National Cherry Festival, one of the top-10 annual festivals in the country, according to *USA Today*. Held the first week of July, the National Cherry Festival attracts over half a million people each year. Take a guided orchard tour for an up-close look at the cherry industry, and sample the newest in cherry products, like jams, jellies, salsa, turnovers, strudels, pies and wine.

Wisconsin's Door County is known for its beautiful landscapes and dramatic coastal scenery, but visitors would be wise to put down the camera and check out what's on the table. You'll discover cuisine that ranges from farm-fresh produce to artisanal cheese.

Drive 137.3 miles, 2 hours, 55 minutes

1 STURGEON BAY
STARTING POINT

This Door County community is home to a classic farmers market where locals meet to trade gossip as they peruse the harvest. Regional fare includes locally made maple syrup, cheese and bratwurst, along with organically grown herbs, fruits and vegetables. There are plenty of fresh-baked pastries, homemade jams and jellies, and freshly baked cakes and pies to satisfy any sweet tooth.

2 EGG HARBOR
17.2 MILES, 22 MINUTES

Egg Harbor offers the best in artisan cheese and wine in a quaint one-stop package. Harbor Ridge Winery features only uncommon Wisconsin cheeses—those made in small vats with distinctive flavors and aromas that pair superbly with the handcrafted wines. With over a dozen vintages to choose from, you're sure to find one that appeals to your tastes.

RECOMMENDED STOPOVERS

A RUSTIC TIMBERS DOOR COUNTY CAMPING
Egg Harbor, WI - (920) 868-3151

3 ELLISON BAY
19.8 MILES, 31 MINUTES

Nestled in the woods of Door County, Wickman House delivers on the promise of farm-fresh-to-table cuisine. Local produce, seafood, and grass-fed meats comprise the menu with innovative dishes that fit well with the rustic yet upscale atmosphere and friendly vibe of the restaurant. Craft cocktails mixed with fresh ingredients will hit the spot, and the bar menu features old favorites.

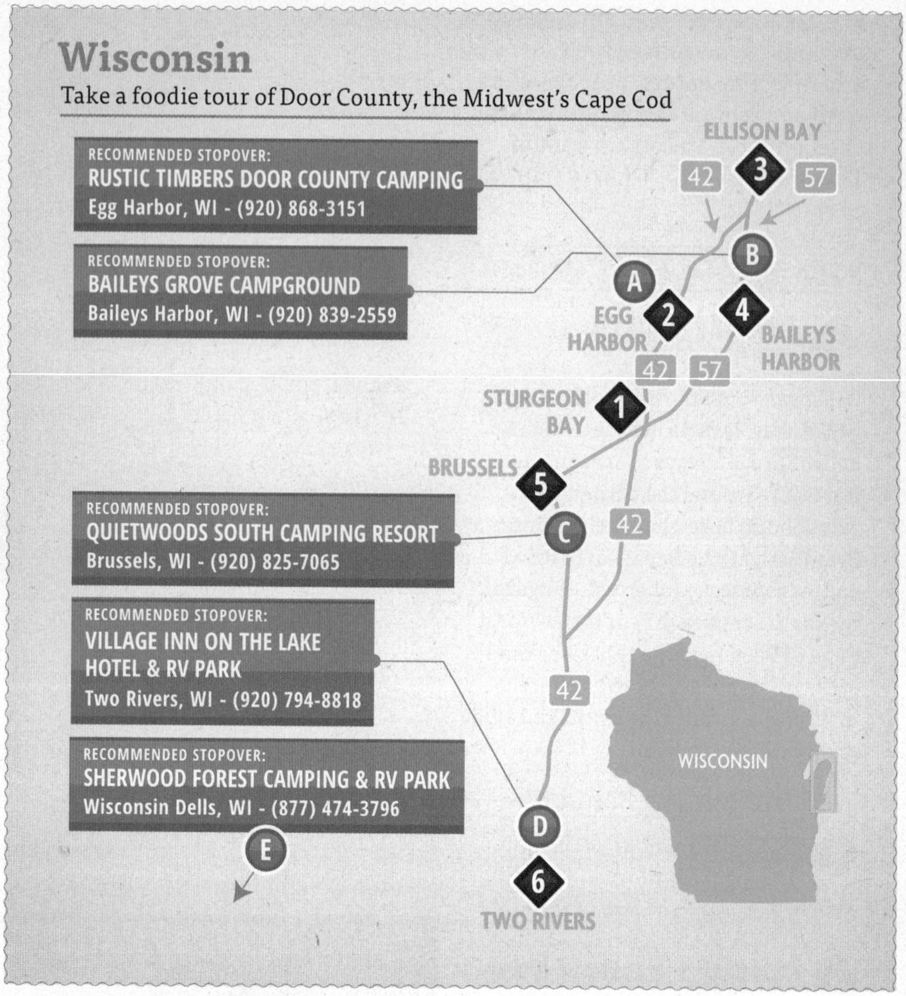

4 BAILEYS HARBOR
14.3 MILES, 20 MINUTES

This Lake Michigan town is the foremost fishing destination on the lake, and after a day of angling, nothing goes down better than fresh seafood. Residents head for Harbor Fish Market & Grille with a view of the lake, and local perch and white fish on the menu, along with fresh Atlantic salmon and crab legs. Mark your travel calendars for the traditional New England

Lobster Boil held every Wednesday and Friday, and on weekends. It's a must-attend event for folks who enjoy succulent crustaceans.

RECOMMENDED STOPOVERS

B BAILEYS GROVE CAMPGROUND
Baileys Harbor, WI - (920) 839-2559

5 BRUSSELS
37.4 MILES, 46 MINUTES

Celebrate the Old Country during Belgian Days, held every July in the town that bears the name of the European nation's capital. Enjoy Belgian cuisine, Old World customs and several events to benefit charity. Attendees can indulge in pies, trippe, potato jutt, booyah and burgers. And yes, there will be Belgian waffles. Not feeling hungry? Belgian music and dance will be performed.

RECOMMENDED STOPOVERS

C QUIETWOODS SOUTH CAMPING RESORT
Brussels, WI - (920) 825-7065

6 TWO RIVERS
48.6 MILES, 56 MINUTES

If you're the kind of fisherman who loves a good fight on the end of the line, then Carp Fest is for you. Held every June, Carp Fest features food, drinks, live music, and the Wisconsin Carp catch-and-release fishing tournament, where world-class carp fishermen angle for a spot on Team USA and the chance to fish in the World Carp Championship.

RECOMMENDED STOPOVERS

D VILLAGE INN ON THE LAKE HOTEL & RV PARK
Two Rivers, WI - (920) 794-8818

E SHERWOOD FOREST CAMPING & RV PARK
Wisconsin Dells, WI - (877) 474-3796

Influenced by Germans, Mexicans, cowboys and more, the cuisine you'll encounter on this route through Texas' picturesque Hill Country is sure to surprise you. Steer-sized steaks abound, but it's the Tex-Mex dishes, innovative barbecue and international offerings that will keep your taste buds hungry for more.

Drive 196.6 miles, 3 hours, 59 minutes

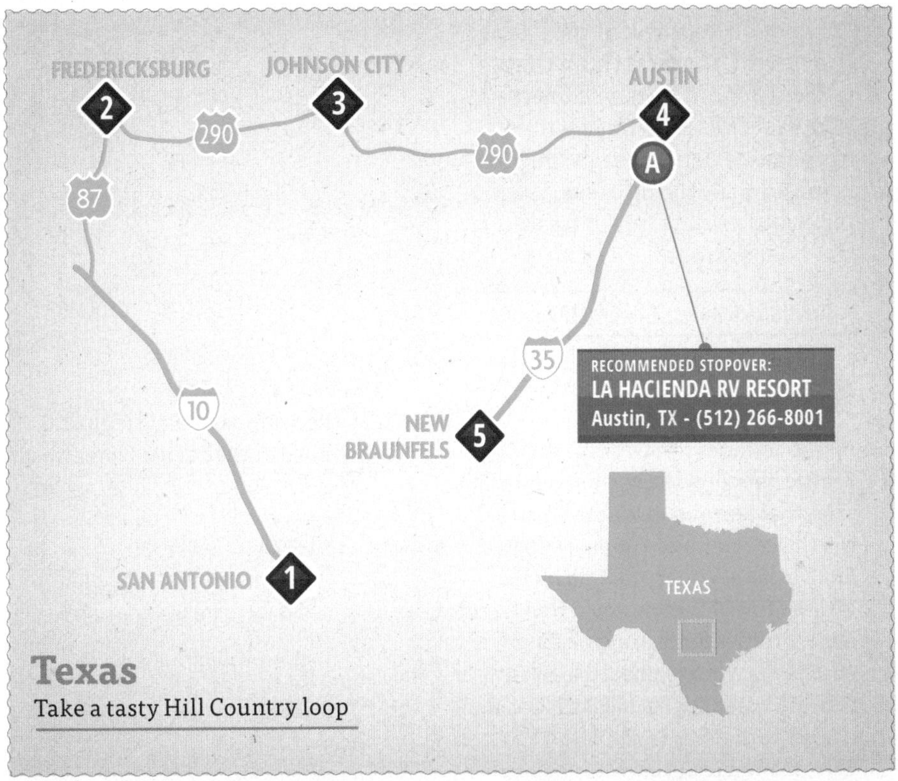

Texas
Take a tasty Hill Country loop

1 SAN ANTONIO
STARTING POINT

The home of the Alamo has long served as a crossroads of culture, and there is no better way to understand a place than through its food. In San Antonio, that means Tex-Mex, a fusion of American and Mexican styles and tastes that has come to define the city's cuisine. The Tex-Mex offerings in this bustling city here are strong, with institutions like the 60-year-old Casa Rio and innovative newbie Acenar attracting locals and visitors alike.

2 FREDERICKSBURG
70.1 MILES, 1 HOUR, 1 MINUTE

The proud German heritage in the region is preserved through attractions like the Pioneer Museum and the Sauer-Beckmann Living History Farm, but if you really want to trace the old-European traditions all the way to modern day, you'll have to do it at the dinner table. Auslander Restaurant on

East Main Street offers a wide-variety of German beers, schnitzels and wursts. Save room for apple strudel at the historic Der Lindenbaum.

3 JOHNSON CITY
30.2 MILES, 30 MINUTES

At the Hye Market Restaurant and Tasting Room, you can talk shop with one of the neighbors while sipping bourbon distilled right in town. This is also the heart of the burgeoning Texas wine scene, so the try-before-you-buy mentality will come in handy as you discover your favorite local grape. So belly up to the bar, chat with the locals and enjoy bold new flavors.

4 AUSTIN
47.9 MILES, 52 MINUTES

Juan in a Million, Torchy's Tacos and Polvos hold their own in the Tex-Mex department, and La Barbecue and County Line on the Hill are barbecue favorites, but it's Austin's global flair that keeps visitors coming back. Indeed, the city's food offerings reflect the ecclectic culture of the Lone Star State's capital city. Try a Creole breakfast at the Cherrywood Coffeehouse, followed by French-inspired classics for lunch at Epicerie Café & Grocery. Top it off with dinner at the popular East Side King Asian-fusion food truck for some truly wild flavor combinations.

RECOMMENDED STOPOVERS

A LA HACIENDA RV RESORT
Austin, TX - (512) 266-8001

5 NEW BRAUNFELS
48.4 MILES, 40 MINUTES

Visit in November to experience the 10-day Wurstfest, a must-see celebration of the city's Bavarian heritage. Sausages, beer and live music are the main draws here, but be sure to stay for the surprisingly entertaining polka dance contest. The family-owned New Braunfels Smokehouse is another Texas institution that doubles as both a wholesale business and popular restaurant.

When foodies think of the Pacific Northwest, the first thing that comes to mind might be Seattle's Pike Place Market, but a whole universe of delicious possibilities is found in outlying areas, from pick-your-own farms to fresh-off-the-boat seafood.

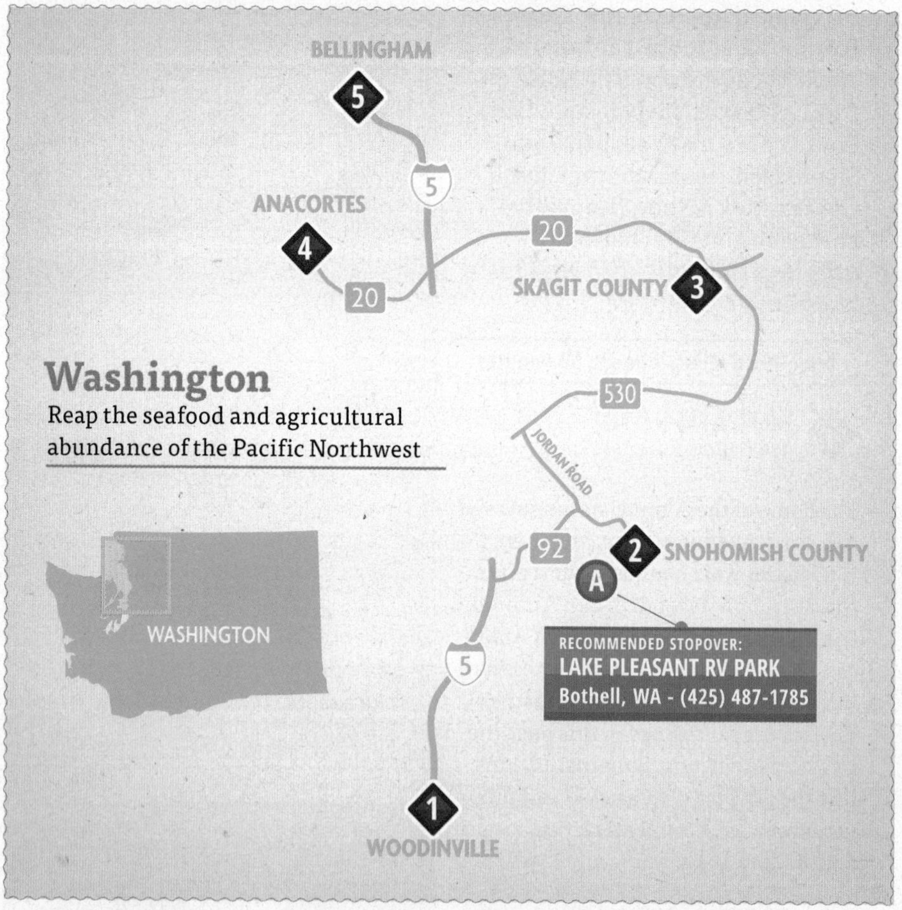

Drive 254.6 miles, 7 hours, 39 minutes

1 WOODINVILLE
STARTING POINT

Just 30 minutes from downtown Seattle, Woodinville hosts several wineries that serve up distinctive Pacific Northwest vintages. From the Chateau Ste. Michelle Winery to Ambassador Wines of Washington, you'll find lots of opportunities for tastings and purchases. For a hearty meal to pair with your wine, take a trip to Pike Place Market in nearby Seattle. Explore 9 acres of fresh produce, great seafood, quality meats, fresh cheese and more.

RECOMMENDED STOPOVERS

A LAKE PLEASANT RV PARK
Bothell, WA - (425) 487-1785

2 SNOHOMISH COUNTY
48.3 MILES, 1 HOUR, 31 MINUTES

Libations abound in Snohomish County, where you can choose from five wineries, five breweries and two local distilleries. Wine lovers can enjoy local wines at Columbia Winery, Quilceda Creek Vintners, Silver Lake Winery, Alai Wines and Dubindil Winery, all close by and specializing in the distinct fruit-forward wines of Washington. Beer lovers can quaff a brew at Redhook Brewery, Skookum Brewery, Lazy Boy Brewing, Black Raven Brewing Company, or Mac & Jack's Brewing. Dry County Distillery and Skip Rock Distillers offer vodka, gin and whiskey.

3 SKAGIT COUNTY
94.4 MILES, 3 HOURS, 9 MINUTES

Skagit County is an agricultural delight with more than 90 different crops and 1,500 acres of tulip, daffodil and iris bulbs—more than anywhere else in the country. Skagit Valley also produces more strawberries, raspberries, and red potatoes than anywhere else in Wash-

ington. Get out and explore this fertile valley by visiting local farms, u-picks and farmers markets for organic veggies, fruit, honey, eggs, dairy and fresh flowers.

4 ANACORTES
71.2 MILES, 2 HOURS, 13 MINUTES

Located on Fidalgo Island, Anacortes is a fishing town where "fresh" means caught today by local fishing boats and "slow" promotes clean and fair fishing practices for sustainable food. For fresh-caught seafood to prepare on your own, visit Black Rock Seafood or Puget Sound Prawns, or head to the other side of the bay and visit Blau Oyster Company, Taylor Shellfish Farm and Skagit's Own Fish Market, which also offers lunch.

5 BELLINGHAM
40.7 MILES, 46 MINUTES

Get away to Whatcom County, home to a bevy of pick-your-own berry farms growing some of the most delicious berries (blueberries, raspberries, strawberries and blackberries) in the Pacific Northwest. For a u-pick experience in a natural, no frills setting, visit Barbie's Berries with strawberries, raspberries, blackberries and blueberries. Boxx Berry Farm offers more than just fruit; select from fresh produce, abundant flowers, thick jams and wonderful preserves. Bellingham Country Gardens beckons harvesters with everything from beets to strawberries to onions. Pick some flowers to complete your trip.

RV Trips of a Lifetime: ON THE WILD SIDE

EDITORIAL TRAVELS FROM WEST TO EAST

Take a recreational vehicle trip on the wild side. The North American itineries found on the following pages will quicken your pulse and push your adrenaline to new heights.

Southern California

Discover golden shores in the Golden State

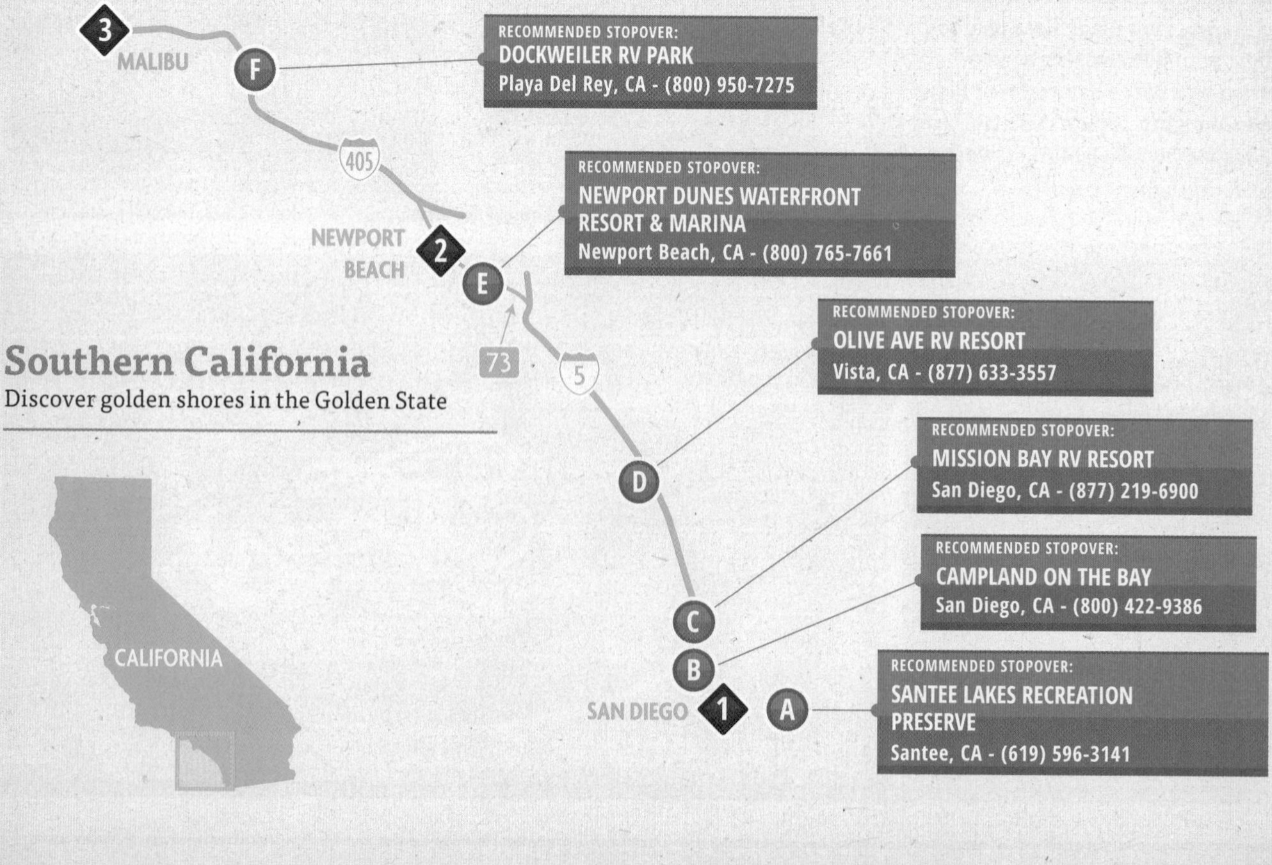

Follow the coast with this great SoCal beach trip. From San Diego to Malibu, there's no shortage of stellar shores for beachcombers, surfers or scenery lovers.

Drive 156.1 miles, 2 hours, 36.1 minutes

1 SAN DIEGO
STARTING POINT

Known as "America's Finest City," San Diego offers year-round sunshine, gorgeous coastline and pristine beaches that are wonders to explore. Mission Beach is the iconic California beach community, with plenty of sandy shores, boardwalks, shops and amusements. Coronado's beach has been voted one of the best beaches in the world for family fun. La Jolla Shores is "the Jewel" of San Diego, with its gentle waves and exceptional views.

RECOMMENDED STOPOVERS

A SANTEE LAKES RECREATION PRESERVE
Santee, CA - (619) 596-3141

B CAMPLAND ON THE BAY
San Diego, CA - (800) 422-9386

C MISSION BAY RV RESORT
San Diego, CA - (877) 219-6900

D OLIVE AVE RV RESORT
Vista, CA - (877) 633-3557

2 NEWPORT BEACH
90.6 MILES, 1 HOUR, 15 MINUTES

Welcome to California's oceanside retreat, with picturesque beaches, unspoiled coastlines, continuous sunshine and plenty of azure water. For fun-in-the-sun, Newport Beach has the largest recreational harbor on the west coast, with opportunities for swimming, surfing, bodyboarding, fishing, yachting, boating and kayaking.

RECOMMENDED STOPOVERS

E NEWPORT DUNES WATERFRONT RESORT & MARINA
Newport Beach, CA - (800) 765-7661

3 MALIBU
65.5 MILES, 58 MINUTES

This beautiful beachfront town, stretching more than 27 miles along the Pacific Ocean, is home to Hollywood stars, yoga-loving sun worshipers and world-class board riders. Surfrider Beach, designated as the first World Surfing Reserve, had a huge impact on the surfing culture of the 1960s and continues to be recognized as the best place in the world for summertime "point" surf.

RECOMMENDED STOPOVERS

F DOCKWEILER RV PARK
Playa Del Rey, CA - (800) 950-7275

Nevada

Hit the tables in Vegas, then hit the water in America's largest reservoir

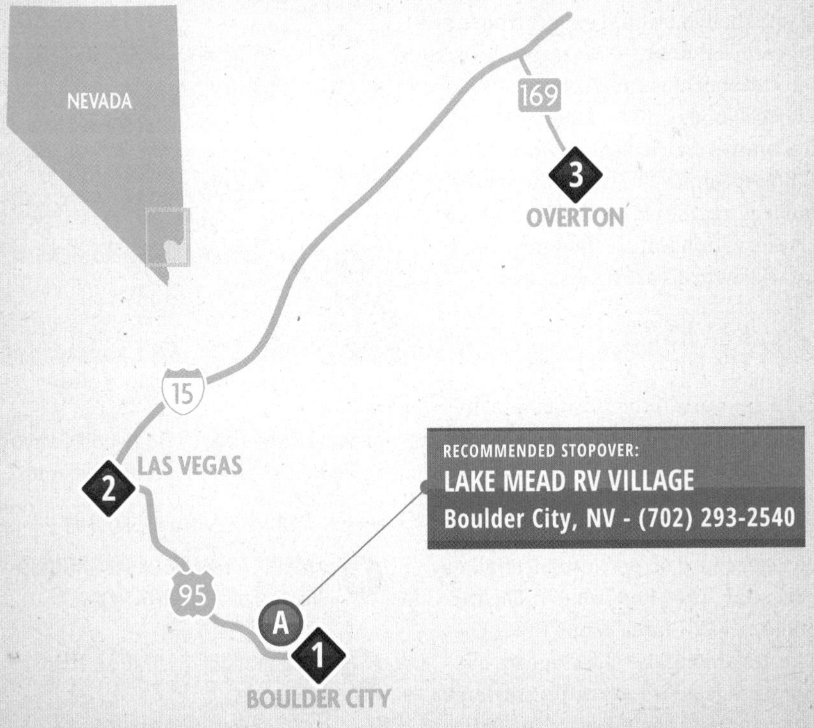

You'll want to go all in on this desert excursion. From the Hoover Dam to Vegas' glitz and glam to laid-back living under the sun, Nevada's personality radiates as you explore the truly unique landscapes.

Drive 89.8 miles, 1 hour, 47 minutes

1 BOULDER CITY
STARTING POINT

One of America's great landmarks, Hoover Dam should be on everyone's bucket list. Thankfully, it's just minutes from your door with a stop in this small desert city. Take a tour of the dam or drive the nearby Mike O'Callaghan–Pat Tillman Memorial Bridge across the river for spectacular views of this testament to American ingenuity. Before you go sightseeing, be sure to spend time downtown eyeing the boutiques on Main Street, and visit the Memorial to the Hoover Dam Dead.

RECOMMENDED STOPOVERS

A **LAKE MEAD RV VILLAGE**
Boulder City, NV - (702) 293-2540

2 LAS VEGAS
26.4 MILES, 36 MINUTES

Few cities buzz with as much energy as Vegas. It's straight to the Strip for neon lights, over-the-top shows and bustling gaming tables in the most extravagant hotels and casinos in the world. With dozens to choose from, you won't have any trouble finding an open table, but make sure to inquire about the discounted dinner and entertainment specials that many venues offer gamers. Catch the renowned nighttime fountain show at the Bellagio or the volcano show at the Mirage.

3 OVERTON
63.4 MILES, 1 HOUR, 11 MINUTES

This enclave on the north shore of Lake Mead is an ideal jumping-off point to explore the country's largest reservoir and the rugged, desert landscape that surrounds it. Created by backflow from the Hoover Dam, Lake Mead has countless coves and inlets that beckon canoe or kayak enthusiasts. Travel back in time as you walk on Overton Beach, once home to a Native American community. Check out the Lost City Museum, featuring reconstructions of homes built by the Puebloan Indians.

Missouri

Go fishing for fun in great lakes and great towns

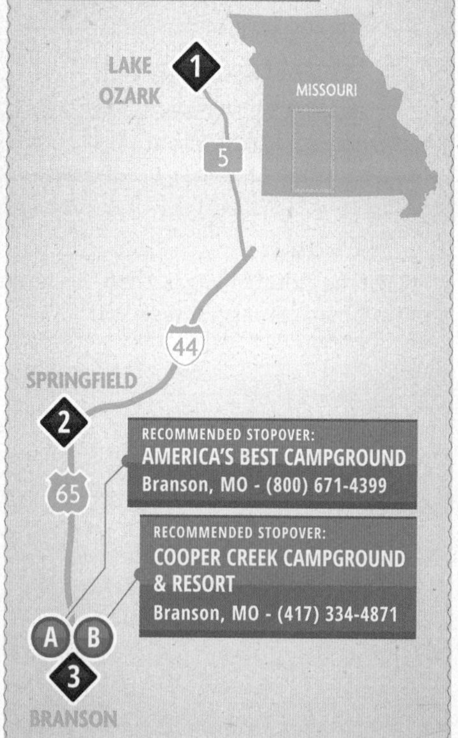

Experience Missouri's natural beauty and casual charm in a trip that offers both easy-going lake life and one-of-a-kind entertainment. Between Lake Ozark's world-class fishing, Springfield's Americana history and Branson's "family-friendly Las Vegas" style, touring the Show Me state is a romp you won't soon forget.

Drive 143.7 miles, 2 hours, 17 minutes

1 LAKE OZARK
STARTING POINT

The top lake destination in the state is a water sports wonderland. The town's namesake body of water offers up to nearly 1,200 miles of shoreline for boating and fishing adventures. Head out on a sightseeing cruise with Leisure Lake Charters or hire Big Ed's Guide Service to show you the hidden banks and eddies where the bass are hiding. The lake region also is home to 16 world-class golf courses that highlight the dramatic natural surroundings.

2 SPRINGFIELD
98.8 MILES, 1 HOUR, 33 MINUTES

This city-on-the-rise has all the charisma that you would expect from a pivotal stop on Route 66. Start by checking out the boutiques and eclectic, handcrafted goods for sale along the stretch of Commercial Street known as the "C-Street Stroll." See the outdoors without leaving the city at the Springfield Conservation Nature Center, where the Ozark environs are on display.

3 BRANSON
44.9 MILES, 44 MINUTES

Calling yourself the "Live Entertainment Capital of America" makes for big expectations, but for 25 years, visitors know that Branson lives up to the hype. With more theater seats than Broadway, you can count on performances all day, every day. The Shoji Tabuchi Theatre and Andy Williams' Moon River Theatre are among the most lauded, but every stage offers something different. Take a break from the glitz and glam of downtown by exploring the rugged beauty of the nearby Dogwood Canyon, Table Rock Lake or Lake Taneycomo.

RECOMMENDED STOPOVERS

A **AMERICA'S BEST CAMPGROUND**
Branson, MO - (800) 671-4399

B **COOPER CREEK CAMPGROUND & RESORT**
Branson, MO - (417) 334-4871

Long a haven for outlaws and outcasts, the Outer Banks area is now a favorite destination for history buffs and nature lovers. This 130-mile stretch of barrier islands means plentiful sand, surf and solitude. Thankfully, the locals now are a lot more welcoming than the pirates who used to call these waters home.

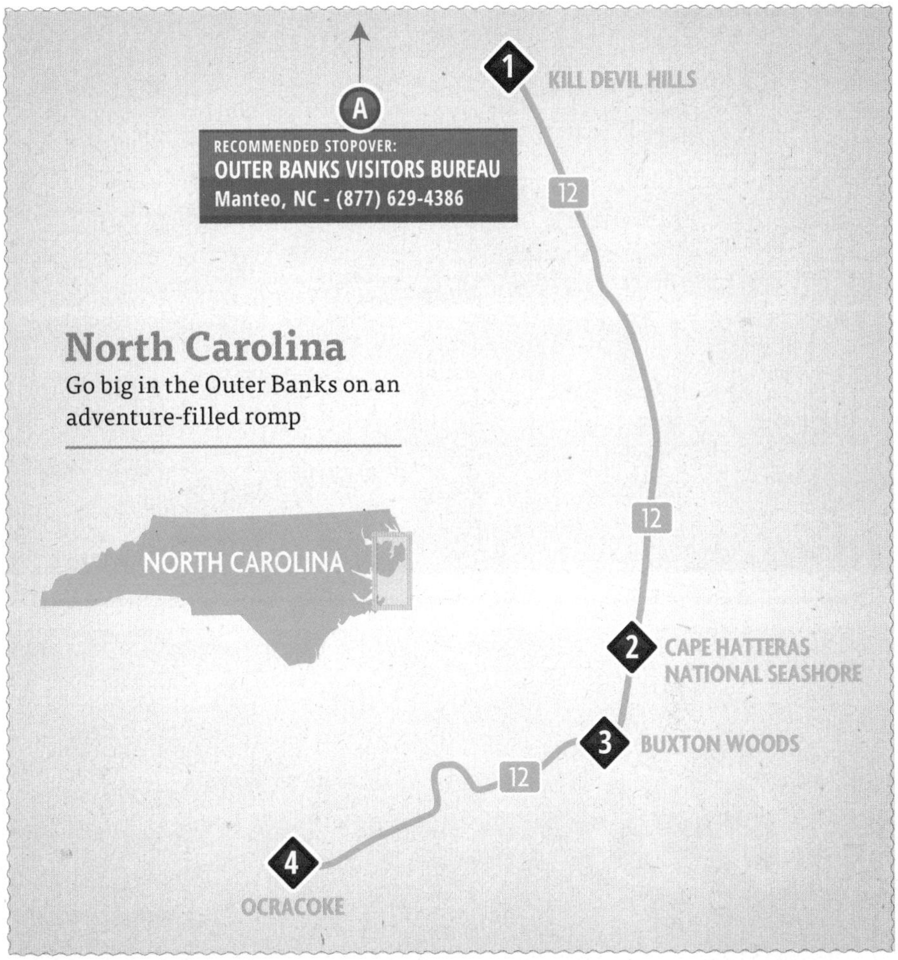

Drive 85.3 miles, 2 hours, 16 minutes

1 KILL DEVIL HILLS
STARTING POINT

One of the great achievements of American ingenuity took flight among these hills and is celebrated at the Wright Brothers National Memorial. Wander among the tools and models that brought powered flight to life at the visitors center before touring the hangars and hilltops of the four flight routes the Brothers followed. Workshops, guided tours and family activities are available all year.

RECOMMENDED STOPOVERS

A OUTER BANKS VISITORS BUREAU
Manteo, NC - (877) 629-4386

2 CAPE HATTERAS NATIONAL SEASHORE
46.2 MILES, 52 MINUTES

Despite boasting the tallest brick lighthouse in the country, the rough tides off the coast have bested many ships, giving this area the nickname "the Graveyard of the Atlantic." A visit to the Museum of the Sea, adjacent to the iconic Cape Hatteras Lighthouse, offers insights into the region's maritime history. Pack a picnic and spend the rest of the day enjoying your own secluded spot along the miles of shoreline.

3 BUXTON WOODS
11.7 MILES, 18 MINUTES

With miles of beaches to draw you in, it's easy to overlook the maritime forests that flourish on the Outer Banks. The Buxton Woods offer an alternative to the surf, with ponds, marshes and pine trees found along a network of trails. One easy access point is just past the Cape Hatteras Lighthouse in the town of Buxton—hike all 7 miles and you'll be rewarded with stunning views of the ocean from atop massive dunes. Red-tailed foxes, deer and bald eagles call these rustic paths home, so be on the lookout.

4 OCRACOKE
27.4 MILES, 1 HOUR, 16 MINUTES

The last island in the Outer Banks can only be reached by ferry, but it's more than worth the trip. Ocracoke Village is an artist's hamlet with a bustling gallery and nightlife scene. Local bands perform regularly, and sunset cocktails overlooking Silver Lake Harbor are a must. Make sure to visit the Pony Pen, where Ocracoke's distinctive wild horses are on display. Walk Ocracoke's 16 miles of undeveloped beaches.

OBX
marks the spot
Treasure comes in many forms on the OBX. The same place that inspired the Wright Brothers' first flight and the country's first National Seashore at Cape Hatteras, now marks the spot for a host of world class adventures. Set-up camp on the Outer Banks!
The Outer Banks
877-629-4386 | OuterBanksSoul.com

Maryland

Take a trip from the doorstep of the nation's capital to a legendary Atlantic hotspot

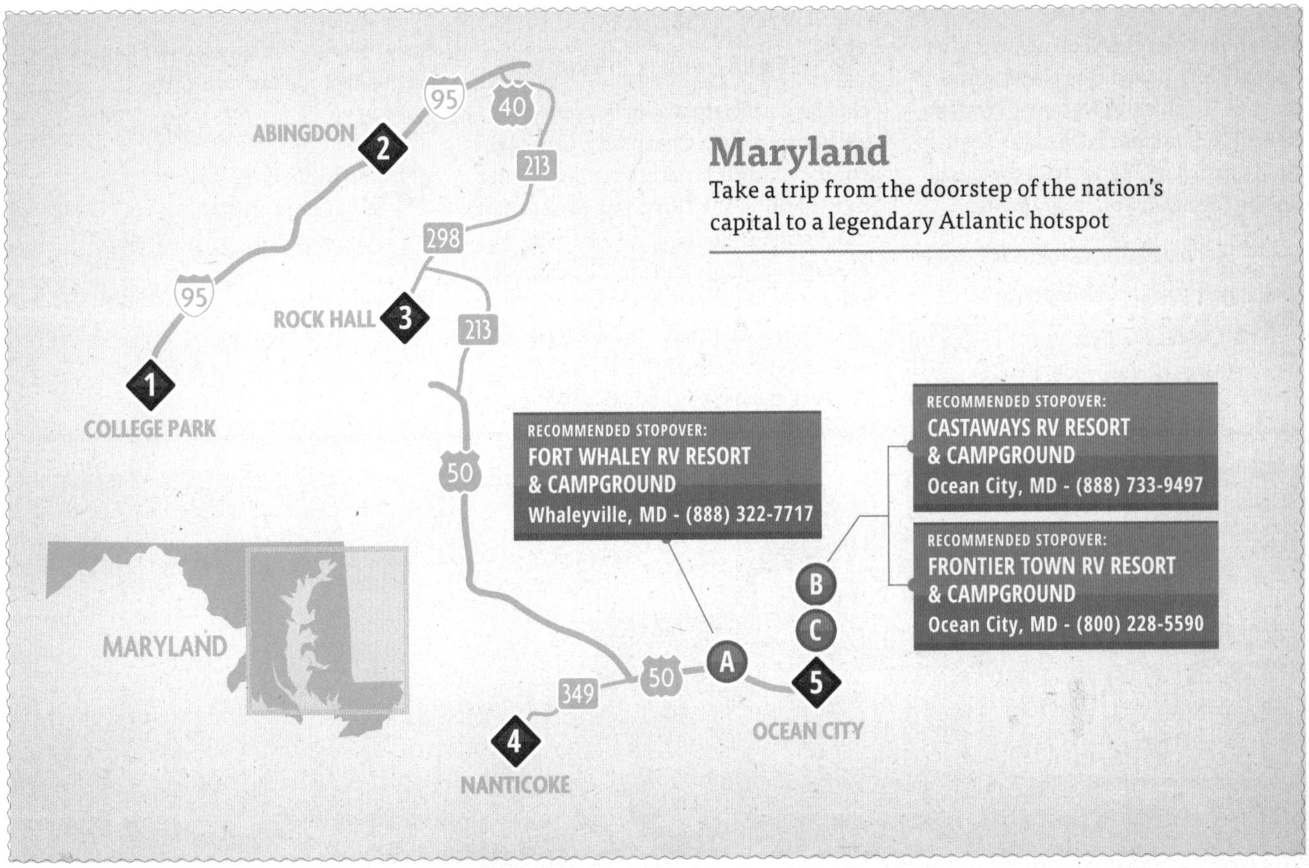

From some of the East Coast's most diverse cities to one of its most iconic boardwalks, this trip combines the best the Mid-Atlantic has to offer. Explore the Washington Mall, Baltimore's charming harbor and Ocean City's bustling boardwalk, all while staying out of the fray in bayside communities. The Chesapeake never felt so welcoming.

Drive 304.2 miles, 5 hours, 35 minutes

1 COLLEGE PARK
STARTING POINT

This Beltway city is the perfect launch pad for exploring Washington D.C. Getting to D.C. is a breeze—a 30-minute drive or metro ride will get you to the Mall, so day trips and quick visits are easy to plan. Try the monuments and museums during the day and one of the city's innovative new seasonal restaurants for dinner.

2 ABINGDON
55.8 MILES, 49 MINUTES

Nestled on the shores of the Chesapeake Bay, this town gives you the opportunity you divide your time between rural life, seaside adventures and day trips to Baltimore. Step back in time on a visit to nearby Jerusalem Mill Village or the Anita C. Leight Estuary Center at Otter Point Creek. For dinner, head to the Inner Harbor neighborhood in nearby Baltimore to dine on the famous steamed blue crabs while taking in a sunset over the Bay.

3 ROCK HALL
87.6 MILES, 1 HOUR, 28 MINUTES

Staying true to its small harbor town roots, Rock Hall is the perfect place to enjoy the laid-back lifestyle of Bayside life. Known as the "Pearl of the Chesapeake," the area features delicious casual dining and relaxing forays into the outdoors. For birdwatchers, the Eastern Neck National Wildlife Refuge is a great place to spot migratory water birds, from herons to tundra swans. After you've worked up an appetite exploring the outdoors, retire to one of dockside restaurants for fresh off-the-boat seafood. Better yet, book a reservation for one of the many charter boats that leave from the marina for a chance to catch your own seafood.

4 NANTICOKE
110.8 MILES, 2 HOURS, 13 MINUTES

With a secluded beach and small-town vibe, Nanticoke is a great place to disappear from it all for a while. Bordered by the Chesapeake Forest Lands, the area is also primed for hiking, biking and bird watching. Known for its hunting and fishing opportunities as well, the rich, old-wood forest draws outdoors people from across the region. Photographers can check off a bucket-list opportunity by making the 90-minute drive to Blackwater National Wildlife Refuge, a tidal marsh world-renowned for its flora and fauna. It's a top destination for nature photographers.

RECOMMENDED STOPOVERS

A **FORT WHALEY RV RESORT & CAMPGROUND**
Whaleyville, MD - (888) 322-7717

5 OCEAN CITY
50 MILES, 1 HOUR, 5 MINUTES

No Maryland trip would be complete without a stop in Ocean City. One of the country's most quintessential summer destinations, it's also home to one of its most famous boardwalks. Packing delicious food, shops and amusement rides into the most exciting 3 miles you'll find on the east coast, the OC boardwalk is one of a kind. Fun late nights are easy to come by, but try waking early to enjoy the spectacular sunrises on the Atlantic horizon.

RECOMMENDED STOPOVERS

B **CASTAWAYS RV RESORT & CAMPGROUND**
Ocean City, MD - (888) 733-9497

C **FRONTIER TOWN RV RESORT & CAMPGROUND**
Ocean City, MD - (800) 228-5590

New England charm meets rugged wilderness in this trip through the most scenic parts of the Granite State. Scale the slopes of majestic Mount Washington then enjoy a hot cup of tea in one of the quaint towns.

Drive 112 miles, 2 hours, 19 minutes

1 NORTH CONWAY
STARTING POINT

Gateway to the White Mountains, North Conway offers up more than its fair share of outdoors excitement. In winter, head to Wildcat Mountain Resort for some of the Northeast's best ski trails. The nearby Moat Mountain Smoke House and Brewing Co. can handle all of your après-ski needs. In warmer months, hikers can take the trail to the top of Mount Washington, the Northeast's tallest peak. Drive the Mount Washington Auto Road that winds its way to the eastern summit or ride the Cog Railway that ascends the west side. Both routes deliver spectacular vistas without demanding a rugged, backcountry hike.

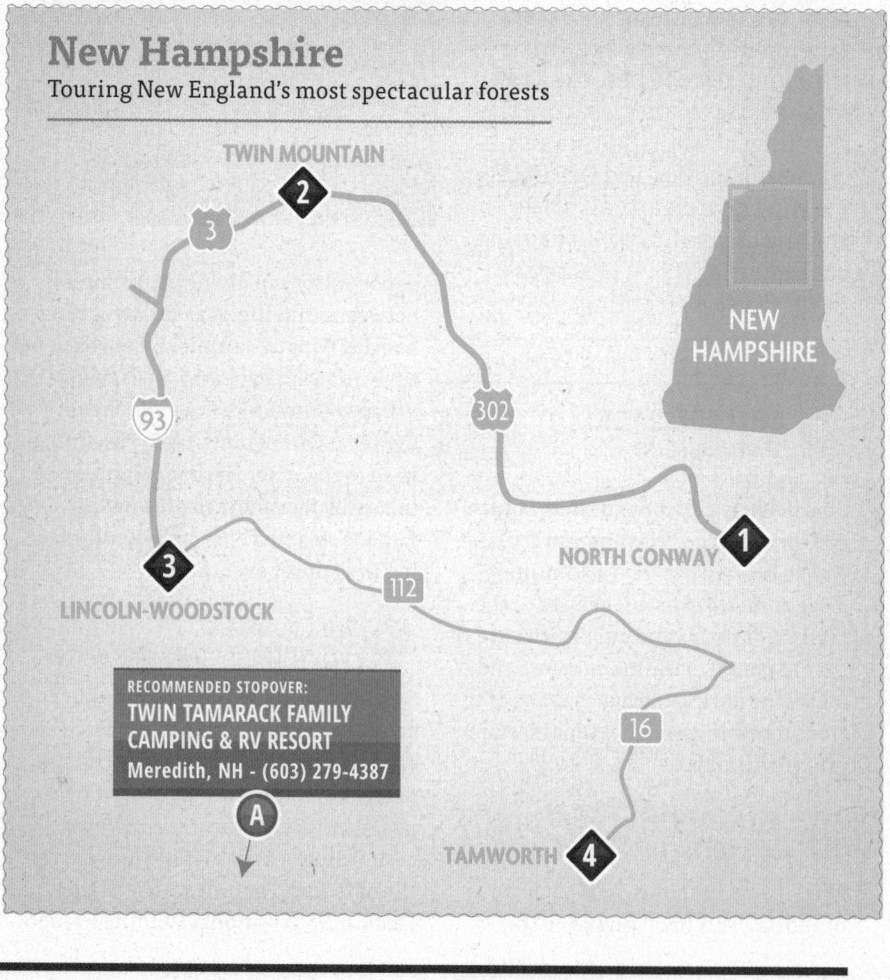

2 TWIN MOUNTAIN
35.1 MILES, 44 MINUTES

Another four-season destination, this tiny hamlet serves up trails for hiking and biking, wildlife sightings and bird watching galore. Bald Mountain and Sugarloaf are two nearby trails that top out with stunning views of the White Mountains, and at two and three miles, respectively, they're comfortable routes for most visitors. Try a visit to Echo Lake in Franconia Notch State Park to catch a glimpse of both the moose and peregrine falcons that call it home. You can't beat visiting in autumn, when the trees put on one of the most vibrant, colorful displays of foliage imaginable.

3 LINCOLN-WOODSTOCK
52.1 MILES, 54 MINUTES

This is a great jumping-off point for family adventure. Your only struggle will be packing it all in. Start your day at the Lost River Gorge and Boulder Caves, where you'll discover pristine waterfalls and underground pools. The nighttime lantern tours are also exceptional. Next, plot a course through the winding forests abutting the picturesque Pemigewasset River on the Hobo Railroad. The historic ride is considered one of the best attractions for kids in the region.

4 TAMWORTH
24.8 MILES, 41 MINUTES

Nestled between the state's lake and mountain districts, Tamworth offers the serene setting and quaint New England charm that has long made it popular among artists and poets. In summertime, make sure to visit the Barnstormers, the oldest summer repertory theater in the country, for a unique collection of performances. A quick hike to Mount Chocorua—said to be the most photographed mountain in America—serves up spectacular views of the Whites, lakes and fall foliage that make the Tamworth area so magnificent.

RECOMMENDED STOPOVERS

A TWIN TAMARACK FAMILY CAMPING & RV RESORT
Meredith, NH - (603) 279-4387

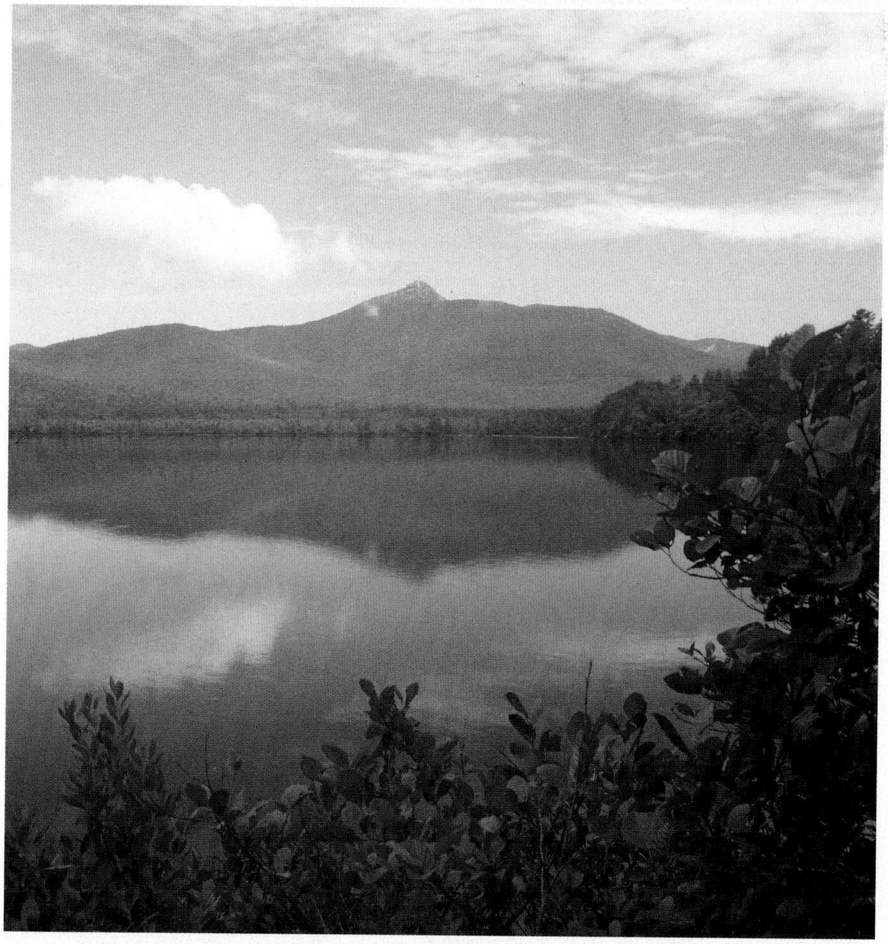

RV Trips of a Lifetime:
LIVING HISTORY

EDITORIAL TRAVELS FROM EAST TO WEST

Don't rely only on dusty history books to experience North America's past. Instead, get out on the road and discover the continent's famous museums, preserved buildings and historic landmarks in person.

Pennsylvania
Five historic hotspots that span centuries of American history

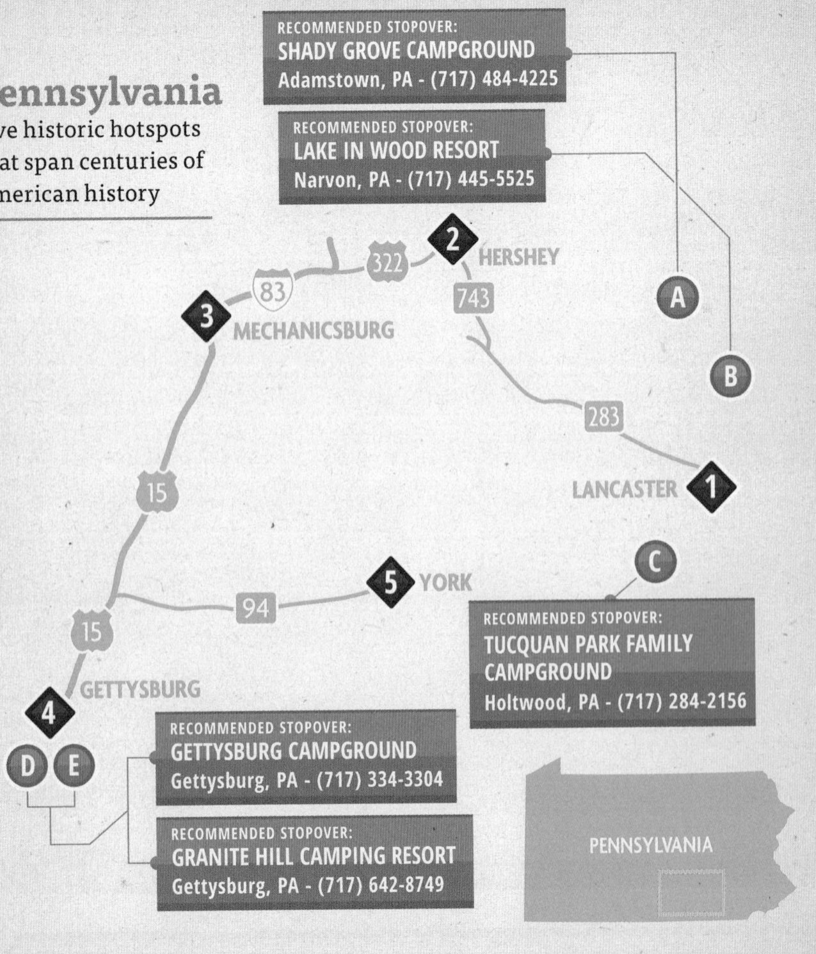

History buffs can have it all on this trip through several eras of America's past. Whether you spend time learning about Amish craftsmanship in Lancaster, the influence of the railroads in Mechanicsburg or the process of making chocolate in Hershey, you won't find a trip that better illustrates how America was built from the ground up.

Drive 113 miles, 2 hours, 16 minutes

1 LANCASTER
STARTING POINT

Ease your way into this trip with a return to the simple life. Amish country is on full display in Lancaster, where horse and buggy rides are easy to come by and windmills dot the horizon. Start at the farms along Old Philadelphia Pike for a buggy tour that winds through the countryside. The drivers will answer all of your questions about the life and history of the centuries-old community. The Amish Farm and House offers a more hands-on approach to the culture: tour a traditional home, working farm, blacksmith shop and one-room school.

RECOMMENDED STOPOVERS

A SHADY GROVE CAMPGROUND
Adamstown, PA - (717) 484-4225

B LAKE IN WOOD RESORT
Narvon, PA - (717) 445-5525

C TUCQUAN PARK FAMILY CAMPGROUND
Holtwood, PA - (717) 284-2156

2 HERSHEY
30.6 MILES, 36 MINUTES

Satisfy your sweet tooth at the "Sweetest Place on Earth." Hershey's Chocolate World has just about everything you'll need for your visit from rides, attractions, restaurants and, of course, dessert. Take the Chocolate Tour to learn more about the company's history and how chocolate is made. Then don a hairnet and apron while you step inside the assembly line and create your very own bar! Spend the afternoon exploring HersheyPark, the amusement theme park with a roller coaster, a Ferris wheel and more.

3 MECHANICSBURG
20.8 MILES, 23 MINUTES

Another era of American history comes alive in this charming small town. The railroad arrived in the mid-19th century and brought with it trade, jobs and money—many of the town's original buildings now house museums to this era of industrial boom. The Stationmaster's House offers a glimpse into family life during the period. The Mechanicsburg Museum Association is housed in the original Passenger's Station beside the tracks, and guided tours and special exhibits are available.

4 GETTYSBURG
31.2 MILES, 32 MINUTES

There are few names more synonymous with American history than Gettysburg. The stories here are so epic and important that you shouldn't skip on the orientation program at the Gettysburg National Military Park. It's a great place to learn the context and background of the war's turning point, and it's easy to arrange tours of the battlefield by car, bike, horseback or foot. For a truly memorable experience, take a private tour with one of the park's expert guides. Spring through fall, many of the restored soldier's encampments are open to the public, and living historians in Civil War garb adopt roles from private to general.

RECOMMENDED STOPOVERS

D GETTYSBURG CAMPGROUND
Gettysburg, PA - (717) 334-3304

E GRANITE HILL CAMPING RESORT
Gettysburg, PA - (717) 642-8749

5 YORK
30.4 MILES, 45 MINUTES

Lauded as an "architectural museum," the city is home to four different historic districts, encompassing three centuries of American history. You'll see plenty of significant buildings by exploring the city on your own, but for a more intimate look, the guided tours of downtown's Colonial Complex highlight the private and public life of residents in the 18th century through exhibits and living-history demonstrations. The brand new Steam into History attraction features a replica of the Civil War steam locomotive that carried President Lincoln to deliver the Gettysburg address. This elegant iron horse takes visitors for regular rides.

Georgia
Sherman's March to the Sea

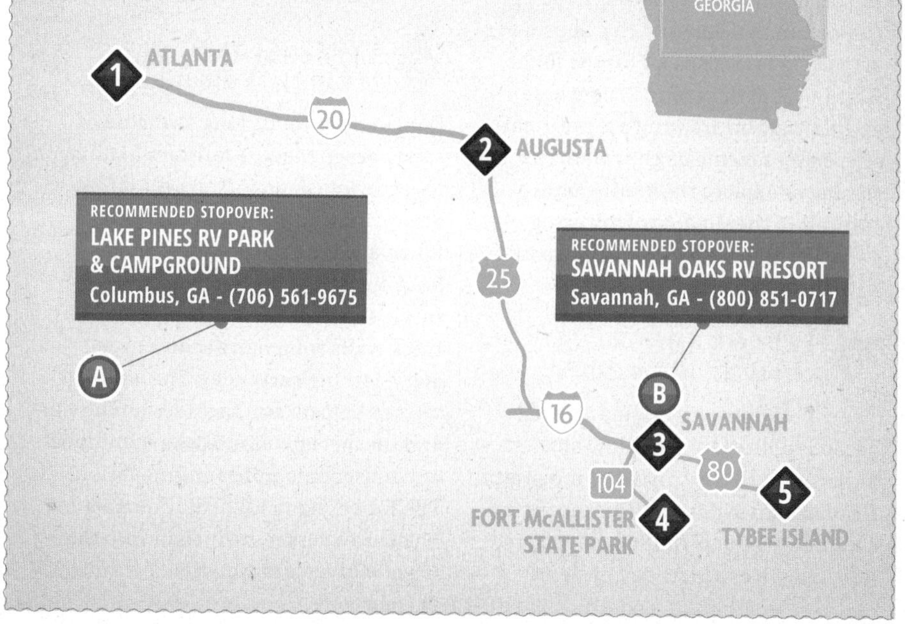

General William Tecumseh Sherman's legacy is controversial, but his Civil War victories were decisive. He marched across Georgia, scorching the earth as he went and effectively ending the South's hope of victory. This trip, from the Oakland Cemetery in Atlanta to the beaches of Tybee Island, follows Sherman's route through the most relevant and revitalized cities in the state.

Drive 344.5 miles, 7 hours, 16 minutes

1 ATLANTA
STARTING POINT

Forever immortalized in "Gone with the Wind," the reality of Atlanta's destruction wasn't very romantic. Thankfully, after being burned to the ground, the capital city has been renewed as a bustling and vibrant cultural hub. To learn more, head to

the historic Buckhead neighborhood, where the Atlanta History Center showcases an extensive Civil War exhibition. It also offers tours of historic homes and farms. Less than a mile from the heart of downtown, the Oakland Cemetery offers a singular look at the war's consequences—nearly 3,000 Confederate troops are buried there. From its hilltop location, you'll see sculptures hidden among the grounds' magnolia trees when you're not taking in stunning views of the city's growing skyline.

RECOMMENDED STOPOVERS

A LAKE PINES RV PARK & CAMPGROUND
Columbus, GA - (706) 561-9675

2 AUGUSTA
148.5 MILES, 2 HOURS, 39 MINUTES

As the second-oldest city in Georgia, Augusta has grown into a vibrant town with a compelling historic district, unique restaurants and splendid views of the Savannah River. Delve into the past at the Magnolia Cemetery, resting place for 300 soldiers and seven generals. Then stroll the banks of the Savannah River, where you'll find locally grown produce, fresh-baked goodies, locally roasted coffee and regional artisans. You can also hop on the Patriot Riverboat for a tour down the historic waterway, or browse the Morris Museum of Art. When it's time to eat, check out the many restaurants that serve up cuisine steeped in local tradition. Nosh on mile-high layered cakes at the Boll Weevil Restaurant.

3 FORT MCALLISTER STATE PARK
148.7 MILES, 3 HOURS, 21 MINUTES

On a bluff overlooking the Ogeechee River, the best-preserved earthwork forts of the Confederacy remain as a testament to one of the final battles of the Civil War. Explore the walls and bombproof interiors of the structures, built into the hills themselves, where soldiers were able to hold off Union gun ships from multiple attacks. Sherman's arrival signaled the end for the fortifications, but the grounds now hold an information area and recreational site. Enjoy a picnic on the riverbank, go fishing or explore the 3-mile nature trail, all in the shadow of towering oaks that stood when the park was a battleground.

4 SAVANNAH
30.4 MILES, 46 MINUTES

The cobblestone streets, manicured gardens and weeping willow-shaded parks made this historic city too pretty for Sherman to destroy. Instead, upon capturing the port in 1864, he "offered" it to Lincoln as a birthday present. Today, it stands as the largest National Historic Landmark district in the country and a must-see destination. First, explore River Street, where music pours from venues and street performers. Try the famous Bernie's Oyster Bar or the pralines at Savannah Sweets for an authentic taste of the city. The old cotton mills and iron works have been turned into the boutiques and galleries that define the city's new Bohemian flare, keeping one of the country's classic towns truly timeless.

RECOMMENDED STOPOVERS

B SAVANNAH OAKS RV RESORT
Savannah, GA - (800) 851-0717

5 TYBEE ISLAND
16.9 MILES, 30 MINUTES

Known more for its long stretches of sandy beach than its military history, this barrier island just 18 miles from Savannah is full of surprises. Fort Pulaski was a Confederate stronghold until Union soldiers used newly invented rifle cannons to pierce the thick walls from more than a mile away, forcing surrender. The landmark victory helped turn the tides on the war and the fort now stands as a monument and museum to military innovation. The Tybee Island Light Station and Museum offers more insight into the island's diverse occupants.

Unearth the Smoky Mountains' past on this trip filled with eclectic adventures. From classic muscle cars to historic warbirds to curios from the past, this journey will make you see Tennessee in a whole new way.

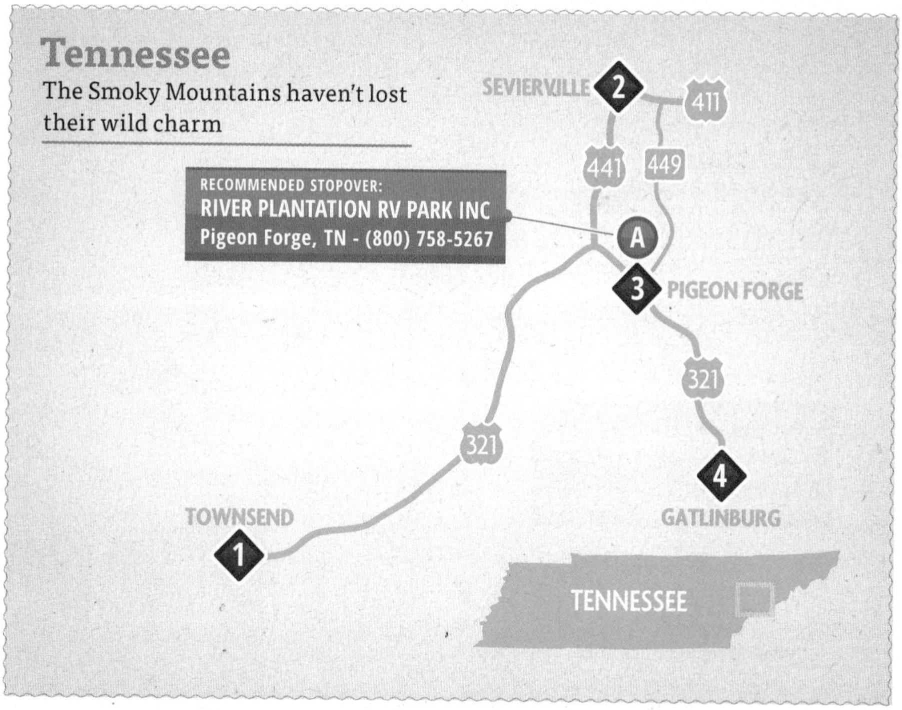

Drive 35.1 miles, 57 minutes

1 TOWNSEND
STARTING POINT

Nestled in the foothills of the Great Smoky Mountains, Townsend is a mecca for bluegrass music lovers, with two annual festivals devoted to the traditional musical art form. The Townsend Spring Festival and Old Timer's Day is held each May, and the Fall Heritage Festival is celebrated each September, but the music never stops here, thanks to sunset music events, hot jam sessions and seasonal concerts throughout the year.

2 SEVIERVILLE
20.9 MILES, 33 MINUTES

Get your motor running and head out on the highway to Sevierville, home of Floyd Garrett's Muscle Car Museum. Garret was an expert on high-performance vehicles in the 1960s and '70s, and today his museum focuses on rare and unusual cars with over 5,000 autos in the collection—90 of them are muscle car bad boys. Touch down at the Tennessee Museum of Aviation, a living museum with superbly restored airworthy warbirds that provides frequent flight demonstrations.

3 PIGEON FORGE
6.5 MILES, 12 MINUTES

Recognized as one of the world's best theme parks, Dollywood has it all: 50 rides and attractions, along with a coal-fired steam engine train to take you around the park. You can also catch a wave at Dollywood's Splash Country Water Adventure Park, where more than 23 water slides and rides await visitors. Head indoors to cool down and take in a live musical show that's sure to make you smile.

RECOMMENDED STOPOVERS

A RIVER PLANTATION RV PARK INC
Pigeon Forge, TN - (800) 758-5267

4 GATLINBURG
7.7 MILES, 12 MINUTES

Discover true Southern charm when you stroll the streets of Gatlinburg. The 8-mile Great Smoky Arts and Crafts Loop in the village is packed with one-of-a-kind craft shops, galleries and studios. Shopaholics are advised to wear comfy shoes, because there are over 500 stores and galleries waiting for you to search for treasure. Be sure to check out the Salt and Pepper Shaker Museum, Hollywood Star Cars Museum and Ripley's Aquarium of the Smokies, which serves as a home for rays, penguins and sharks. The Swarm exhibit features eels, mice and more.

Arkansas

Soak in the history of gangsters, presidents and stagecoach riders

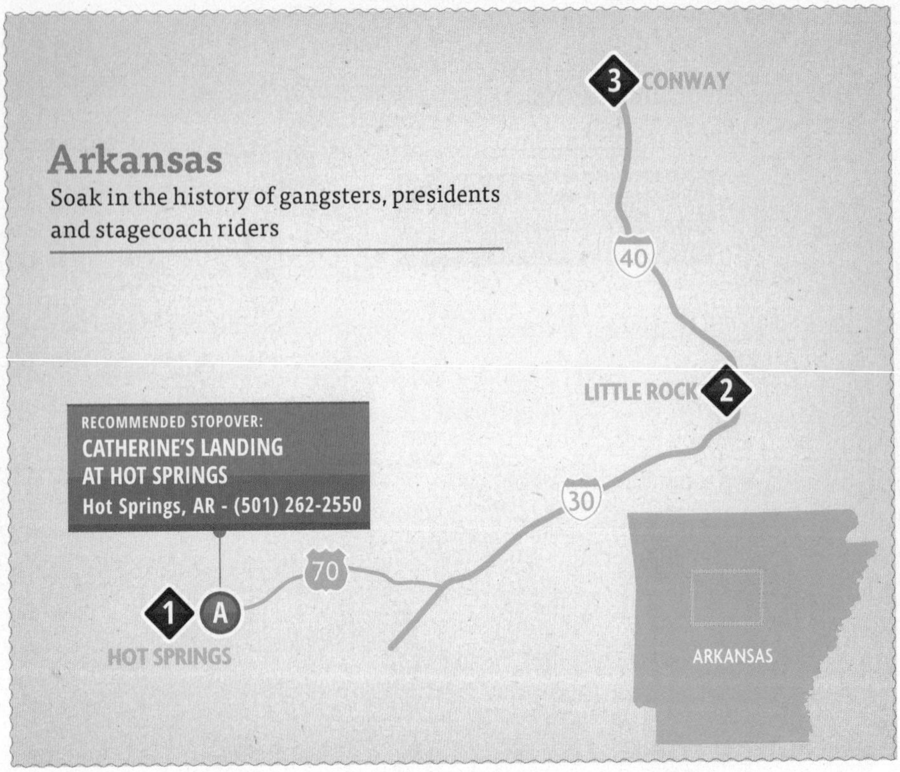

Tour the eclectic cities that once lured gangsters and future presidents. After a dip in medicinal hot springs, take a trip to the state capital, Little Rock, where a presidential library awaits your inspection. Finish your trip in Conway, where a legendary trail meets a pioneering mail route.

Drive 85.3 miles, 1 hour, 20 minutes

1 HOT SPRINGS
STARTING POINT

Located in the Ouachita Mountains, "Spa City" welcomes travelers to relax and refresh in the thermal mineral waters that have made this town legendary. Numerous spas and bathhouses proffer thermal baths and soaks amid the steamy vapors for soothing relief of pains and tension. The hot water is also pumped into several hotels. Once you're feeling up to snuff, it's time to check out those bad boys at the Gangster Museum of America. Get an inimitable look into the Roaring '20s and the rough-and-tumble '30s, including the mobsters and gangsters who gambled their time away in Hot Springs, including Al "Scarface" Capone, Owney "The Killer" Madden and Charles "Lucky" Luciano. The museum exhibits antique slot machines as well as weapons carried by the gangsters.

RECOMMENDED STOPOVERS

A CATHERINE'S LANDING AT HOT SPRINGS
Hot Springs, AR - (501) 262-2550

2 LITTLE ROCK
54.6 MILES, 52 MINUTES

History is at home in Little Rock, and the William J. Clinton Presidential Center lets you enjoy it all. Explore the many exhibits for an up-close look at the day-to-day operations of the Clinton White House. The Presidential Library is a treasure-trove of memorabilia relating to our 42nd president. Watch the Clinton inauguration from 1993 and follow the presidential timeline through both terms, then visit a full-scale replica of the Oval Office and Cabinet Room before a quick look at the presidential limousine. Delve into nature at the 33-acre Riverfront Park, located on the banks of the Arkansas River, before a trip into the William E. Clark Presidential Park Wetlands.

3 CONWAY
30.7 MILES, 28 MINUTES

Conway is home to Arkansas' first settlers, thanks to river access and new trade routes. Many of these are now designated as Heritage Trails. Cadron Settlement Park provides a glimpse into pioneer life with the two-story replica of an 18th-century blockhouse, originally used as a residence, tavern, trading post and protection against the Cherokee Indians. Walk a part of the Cherokee Trail of Tears, the route hundreds of Native Americans took during their forced trek to Indian Territory. The legendary Butterfield Overland Mail Route also ran through the area.

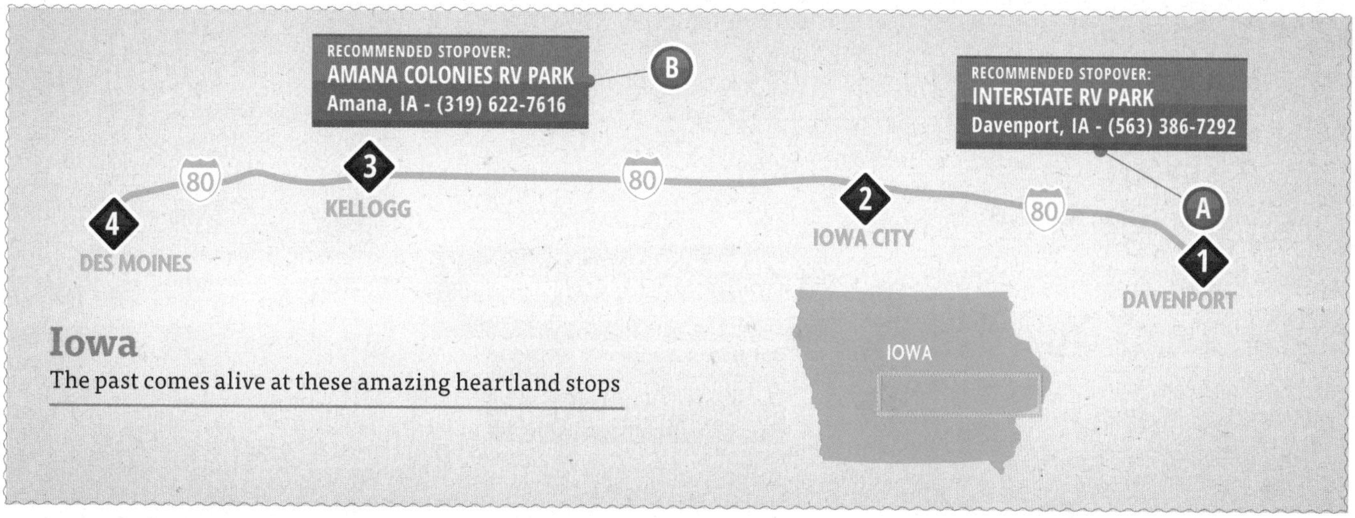

Iowa

The past comes alive at these amazing heartland stops

Prairie history comes alive on this history-filled route through the heartland. From Davenport's state-of-the-art museums to the political history on display in Iowa City and Des Moines, the Hawkeye State impresses with its old-meets-new mentality and unending Midwestern charm.

Drive 175.6 miles, 2 hours, 32 minutes

1 DAVENPORT
STARTING POINT

For nearly 150 years, the Putnam Museum has been a centerpiece of Davenport's downtown culture. Founded as a natural history museum, it is now one of the country's finest immersive, educational experiences. Adults and kids will delight in the hands-on approach to science, technology and nature on display in the numerous exhibitions. The Skybridge, stretching from Second Avenue right up to the Mississippi River waterfront, offers unparalleled views of the river and a must-see nighttime light show. Round out the day with a river sunset cruise on an authentic paddleboat to truly capture the historic feel of this riverside city.

RECOMMENDED STOPOVERS

A INTERSTATE RV PARK
Davenport, IA - (563) 386-7292

2 IOWA CITY
56.5 MILES, 52 MINUTES

A gateway to America's cultural and political past, Iowa City has it all. The historic downtown district is home to a vibrant, creative scene, with street musicians, artists and novelists honing their crafts and performing and lecturing on a regular basis. The University of Iowa is to thank for this, and even a quick stroll around town—from the beautiful Oakland Cemetery to the pedestrian mall—is enough to understand the small town, high-minded balance that the college town strikes. The Herbert Hoover Presidential Museum in nearby West Branch is a source of great pride for the community and does an excellent job of detailing Hoover's life and global influence.

RECOMMENDED STOPOVERS

B AMANA COLONIES RV PARK
Amana, IA - (319) 622-7616

3 KELLOGG
75.5 MILES, 1 HOUR, 3 MINUTES

With a population of only about 600, this town is an easy place to overlook. However, the Kellogg Historical Museum, which encompasses a large part of the downtown area, will leave history buffs in awe. The main museum building is in the Simpson Hotel, which includes accurately preserved bedrooms, laundries, playrooms and more. There is also an extensive research library and archive in the building—be sure to look through the historic newspapers for headlines noting the railroad's arrival in town.

4 DES MOINES
43.6 MILES, 37 MINUTES

A historical trip through Iowa wouldn't be complete without visiting Living History Farms just outside of Des Moines. This 500-acre estate is an interactive museum with working Indian and pioneer farms and re-enactments of prairie life. Head into Des Moines for a visit to the Capitol building, the epicenter of state politics and first stop on many presidential campaigns. The guided tours are excellent and, if you're brave enough, you'll have the chance to climb the narrow, winding steps to the top of the building's massive dome. In the evening, take a stroll along the Principal Riverwalk, a pedestrian pathway that winds its way through landscaped public spaces as it connects many of the city's walking and biking trails.

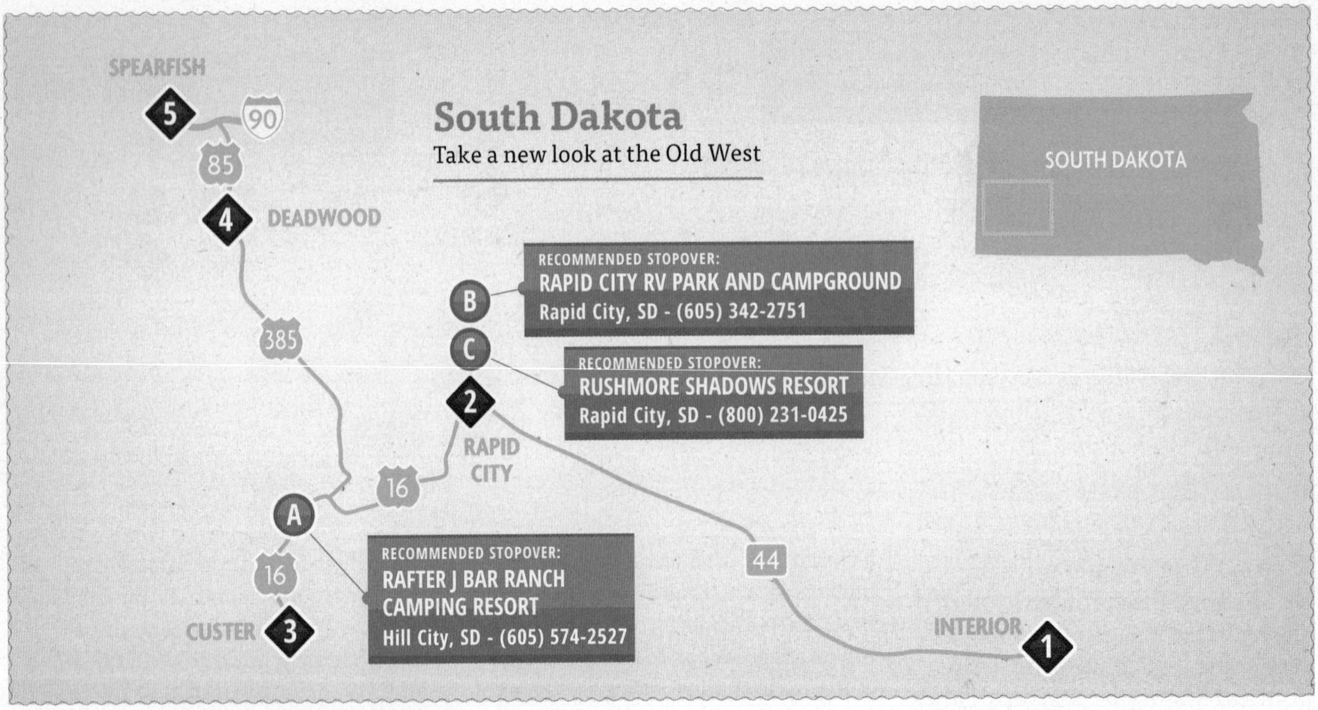

Explore the rugged land that lured Native Americans and Western pioneers alike. From the Badlands to the bad guys of the Old West, South Dakota never fails to inspire.

Drive 187.3 miles, 2 hours, 55 minutes

1 INTERIOR
STARTING POINT

The Lakota called this area "mako sica" (land that makes you sick), but this tiny town is the gateway to Badlands National Park, perhaps North America's most surreal public land. The rugged vistas of this region are stunning, with eroded buttes, spires and pinnacles that give the landscape an otherworldly feel. Badlands National Park has the largest protected mixed grass prairie in the U.S. and is home to an abundance of wildlife, including jackrabbits, ferrets, bison and bighorn sheep. It also contains one of the richest fossil beds of ancient mammals in the world.

2 RAPID CITY
75.5 MILES, 1 HOUR, 11 MINUTES

Here is an adventure set in stone and Rapid City provides the ultimate launching point for the Mount Rushmore National Memorial experience. This awe-inspiring granite mountaintop features 60-foot sculptures of four American presidents: George Washington, Thomas Jefferson, Theodore Roosevelt and Abraham Lincoln. Glean fascinating facts about this year-round destination at the Lincoln Borglum Museum, devoted to the stories behind the creation of this larger-than-life monument. Take a breezy stroll along the Avenue of Flags, where 50 states and six territories are represented; plan to be on hand at the end of the day for the breathtaking lighting ceremony of the mountain.

RECOMMENDED STOPOVERS

A RAFTER J BAR RANCH CAMPING RESORT
Hill City, SD - (605) 574-2527

B RAPID CITY RV PARK AND CAMPGROUND
Rapid City, SD - (605) 342-2751

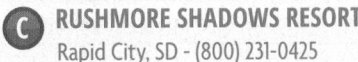

C RUSHMORE SHADOWS RESORT
Rapid City, SD - (800) 231-0425

3 CUSTER
40.7 MILES, 50 MINUTES

Custer offers more than rugged views and crisp mountain air: It's home to Custer State Park, where the rumble of more than 1,300 bison can be heard as they pound their way down into the valley for the annual Buffalo Roundup. Take it slow and cruise the Peter Norbeck Scenic Byway for dramatic views of the Black Hills, or get up close and personal on Wildlife Loop Road. Visit the awe-inspiring Crazy Horse Memorial, over 60-plus years in the making. The sculpture-in-progress of the Lakota warrior depicts him sitting astride his horse with an outstretched hand.

4 DEADWOOD
55.9 MILES, 1 HOUR, 13 MINUTES

Deadwood is a rough-and-tumble Old West town where anything can happen. Wyatt Earp, Calamity Jane, Poker Alice and Wild Bill Hickok strolled these streets in the late 1800s in search of adventure; follow in their footsteps as gunslingers re-enact shootouts on Main Street. Witness the trial of

Jack McCall, the poker player charged with the murder of Wild Bill Hickok. Tour the 100-year-old Broken Boot Gold Mine, then explore the Historic Fairmont Hotel, where ghosts are said to roam. Pay your respects at Mount Moriah Cemetery, better known as Boot Hill, where Wild Bill, Calamity Jane and Potato Creek Johnny were all laid to rest—with their boots on.

5 SPEARFISH
15.2 MILES, 21 MINUTES

Spearfish offers a variety of adventures for outdoor enthusiasts; fly fishing is "reel-in" in these parts, home to one of the best populations of wild rainbow trout in the Black Hills (averages size is 29 feet) while fishermen can also net walleye, trout and largemouth bass in local streams and lakes. Spearfish Canyon is a hiker's paradise with several trails offering rustic canyon views or massive limestone cliffs. In the winter, don't miss Community Caves with their frozen waterfalls; Iron Creek is lined with summer wildflowers; the day is darker at 11th Hour Gulch, which gets only one hour of sunlight every 24 hours, and Devils Bathtub is the local's favorite canyon hike.

A true multicultural crossroads, New Mexico has a bit of everything. From Santa Fe's stylish arts district to the lakeside activities at Elephant Butte and Las Cruces' Green Chile Trail, this trip combines food, history and culture in an unforgettable desert landscape.

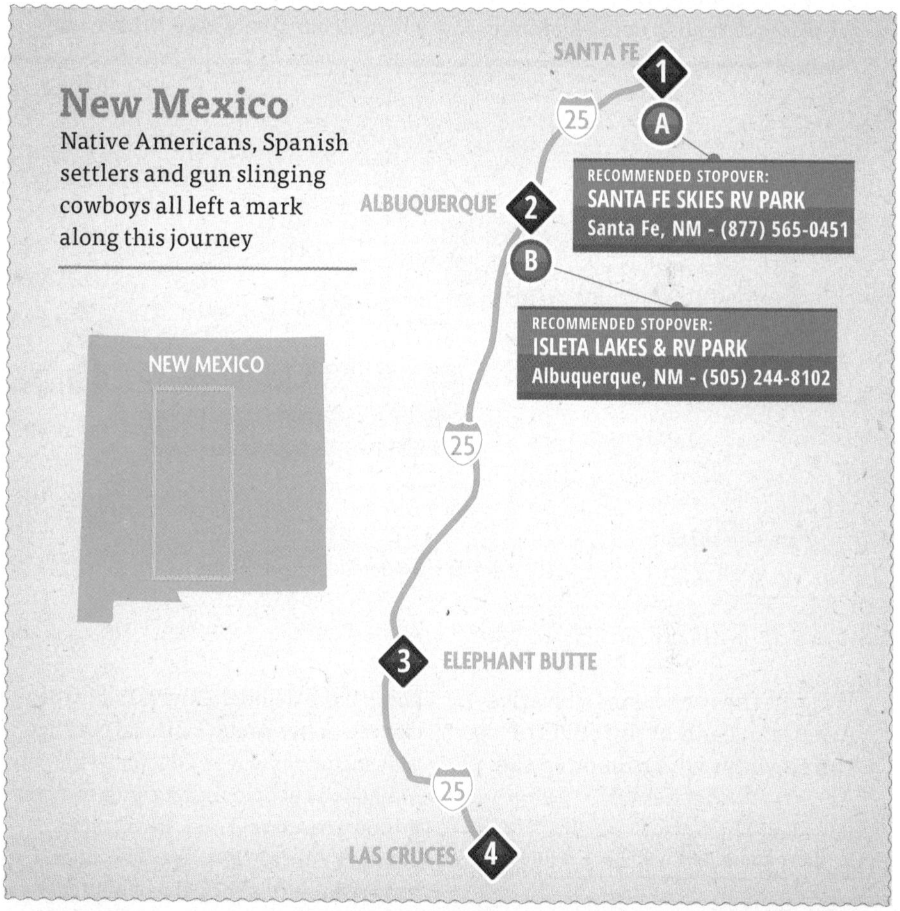

Drive 290.4 miles, 4 hours, 1 minute

1 SANTA FE
STARTING POINT

Regarded as one of the finest cultural getaways in the country, Santa Fe boasts perfect weather, a well-established gallery and museum scene, and dozens of one-of-a-kivnd boutiques. Start at the Georgia O'Keeffe Museum, featuring the work of the country's most famous female artist. Then take a guided tour of the historic downtown plaza, which highlights the singular Spanish architecture that gives the city its unforgettable style.

RECOMMENDED STOPOVERS

A SANTA FE SKIES RV PARK
Santa Fe, NM - (877) 565-0451

2 ALBUQUERQUE
63.4 MILES, 56 MINUTES

As one of the oldest cities in the U.S., Albuquerque serves up authentic Southwest experiences at every turn. Spanish heritage is on display in the Old Town neighborhood, where the adobe buildings, flamenco music and spicy cuisine captivate visitors. Known for its red clay pottery, the Isleta Pueblo just outside town offers a fascinating glimpse into Native American and missionary life in the region. For thrill seekers, a visit to the annual Albuquer-

que International Balloon Fiesta in October is a sight to behold.

RECOMMENDED STOPOVERS

B ISLETA LAKES & RV PARK
Albuquerque, NM - (505) 244-8102

3 ELEPHANT BUTTE
145.5 MILES, 1 HOUR, 55 MINUTES

All manner of watersports is at your fingertips in this lakeside refuge. Part of the largest state park in New Mexico, the reservoir holds a number of state fishing records, so this might be your chance to land the big one. Not in a competitive spirit? You can still sail or kayak all the nooks and crannies of the 200-plus miles of shoreline. Keep an eye out for the pelicans that dot the shoreline—this is one of the best places to see them in the Southwest.

4 LAS CRUCES
81.5 MILES, 1 HOUR, 10 MINUTES

With 350 days of sunshine annually, you're all but guaranteed to have the weather on your side while you explore the numerous offerings in what has been called a "dream town" for visitors. Burger buffs will be happy to know that Las Cruces is a stop on the Green Chile Cheeseburger Trail, a statewide string of bars and restaurants serving a Southwestern version of the famous sandwich. North of the city on State Road 52, you'll find a series of ghost towns and abandoned churches that tell the compelling story of the area's wild and woolly boomtown days.

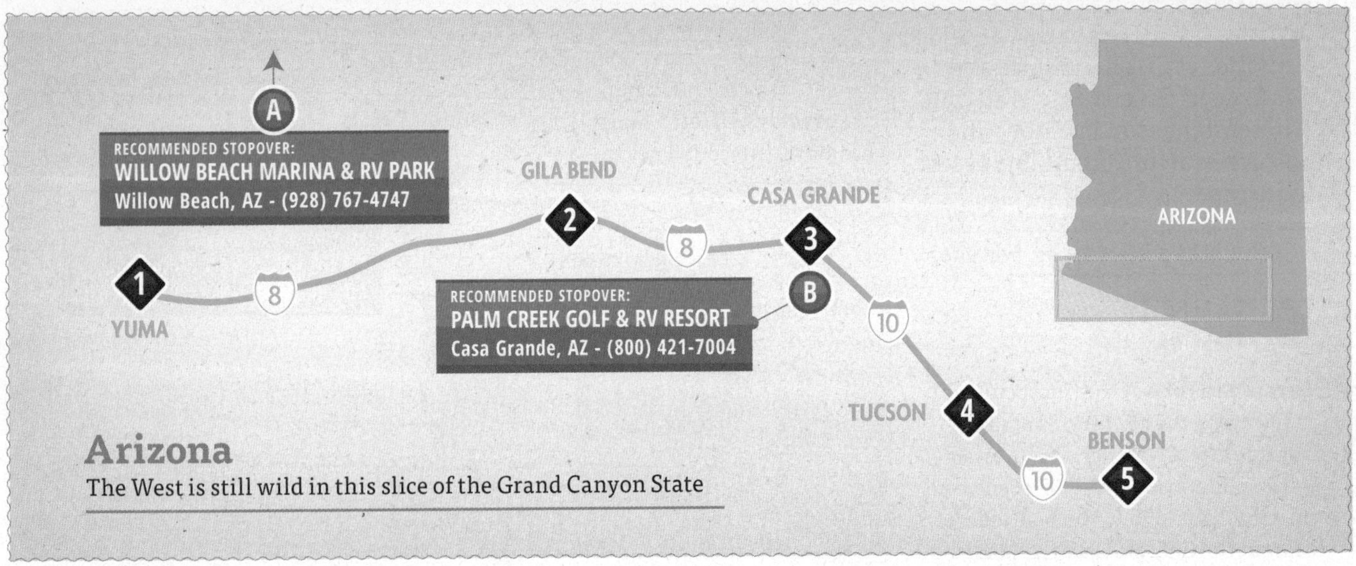

Arizona
The West is still wild in this slice of the Grand Canyon State

Walk in the moccasins of Native Americans and in the boots of the cowboys who inhabited the Arizona wilderness.

Drive 294.8 miles, 4 hours, 5 minutes

1 YUMA
STARTING POINT

For centuries, all roads led to Yuma, which once served as a key crossing point of the Colorado River. Today the city celebrates a multicultural heritage that encompasses the Cocopah—an indigenous people—along with miners, military personnel and the intrepid pioneers who settled here. This once-busy river port is the perfect winter retreat for snowbirds, offering excellent golf courses, birding expeditions, fishing opportunities, hiking trails and plenty of museums to visit.

RECOMMENDED STOPOVERS

A WILLOW BEACH MARINA & RV PARK
Willow Beach, AZ - (928) 767-4747

2 GILA BEND
116.2 MILES, 1 HOUR, 30 MINUTES

Gila Bend is the home of the Painted Rock Petroglyph Site and gateway to the Sonoran Desert National Monument. There are hundreds of petroglyphs that were etched on the rocks by prehistoric people centuries ago; the site is breathtaking in its scope and history. The rocks also are adorned by writings left by settlers passing through. The nearby Sonoran Desert is made up of three mountain ranges and an extensive saguaro cactus forest; outfitters in the area provide hiking and equestrian trails. Take a horseback tour of the area with Corral West Horse Adventures, which also offers fun-filled wagon rides.

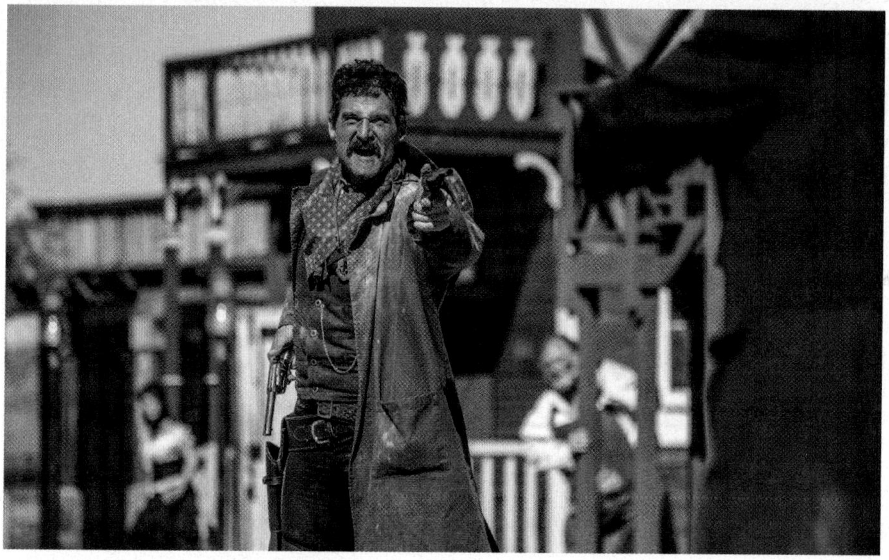

3 CASA GRANDE
63.8 MILES, 55 MINUTES

Casa Grande (Great House) is home to one of the largest prehistoric ruins in North America. The region's early inhabitants, the Hohokams, constructed an elaborate system of irrigation canals and developed widespread trading networks throughout the region. However, the purpose of this ancient walled compound and four-story house-like structure remains a mystery. The Casa Grande Ruins National Monument features paved walkways and trails that lead to the site's most important areas, along with ranger-guided tours of the ruins.

RECOMMENDED STOPOVERS

B PALM CREEK GOLF & RV RESORT
Casa Grande, AZ - (800) 421-7004

4 TUCSON
67.9 MILES, 57 MINUTES

Tucson is still home to a Wild West shootout, but this one doesn't involve cowboys or guns—it's all about the cars. Each January, the USA Raceway hosts drivers from around the country for a six-race series that kicks off with an open practice, followed by daily events for late models, modifieds and X-mods. Race into the past at Old Tucson, a filming location that served as the backdrop for up to 300 Western-themed shows and movies, including the 1956 film, "Gunfight at the O.K. Corral." You can take a tour, ride on a stagecoach and witness a simulated gunfight at high noon.

5 BENSON
46.9 MILES, 43 MINUTES

Benson was a hub in the development of southwestern transportation and connection on the Butterfield Overland Trail, the first overland transcontinental mail by stagecoach route. At 2,800 miles, it was the world's longest stagecoach line. Also making a stop in the town was the Pony Express, which provided unprecedented speed in delivering the mail. Locals pay tribute to this dashing chapter in history each October with the Butterfield Overland Stage Days and Rodeo. Kartchner Caverns State Park is another attraction.

RV Trips of a Lifetime: PICTURE PERFECT

EDITORIAL TRAVELS FROM WEST TO EAST

From towering glaciers to lush forests to sparkling ocean shores, these trips serve up great views in abundance. Just make sure that your camera has enough memory to capture them all.

Alaska

Glaciers, mountains and wildlife compete for your attention on the Kenai Peninsula

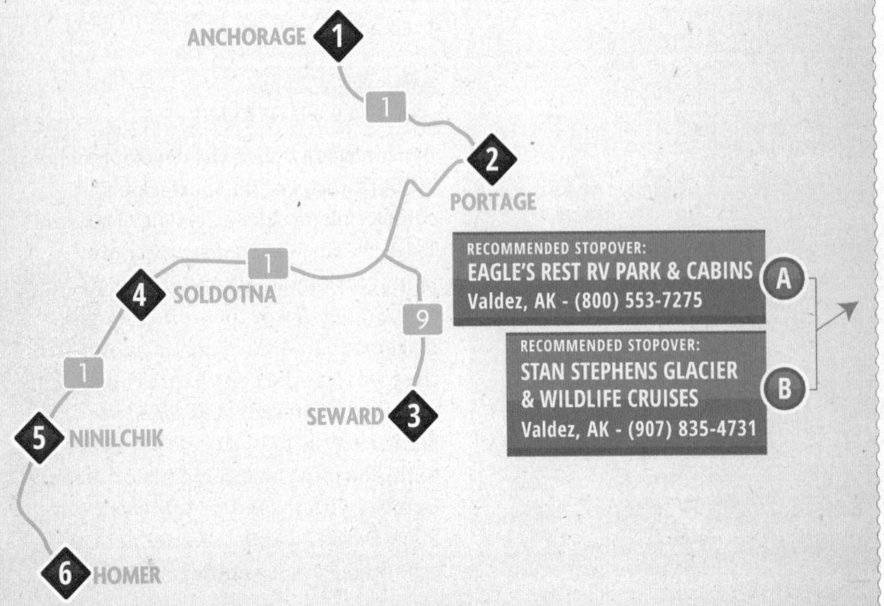

Dramatic landscapes are surpassed only by the sightings of wildlife on this trip through Alaska's playground. Bring your camera and binoculars for some spectacular sightseeing.

DRIVE 312 MILES, 6 HOURS, 27 MINUTES

1 ANCHORAGE
STARTING POINT

This hip metropolitan area is home to a bustling art scene. The Alaska Center for the Performing Arts houses three complexes for award-winning musicals, theater and cultural venues. Take a flightseeing tour by helicopter for a bird's-eye view of Anchorage's wild backyard. If terra firma is more your thing, amble along scenic trails for spectacular views of Denali National Park to the north, Prince William Sound and Kenai Fjords National Park to the south, and Chugach State Park right in Anchorage. Take an afternoon trip on one of the bike paths in the park, or pack a picnic basket and set out on one of its many hiking trails.

RECOMMENDED STOPOVERS

A **EAGLE'S REST RV PARK & CABINS**
Valdez, AK - (800) 553-7275

B **STAN STEPHENS GLACIER & WILDLIFE CRUISES**
Valdez, AK - (907) 835-4731

2 PORTAGE
55.8 MILES, 1 HOUR, 5 MINUTES

This Alaskan town was destroyed in the 1964 Good Friday earthquake; what remains today are ruins from several buildings and a "ghost forest" of trees killed by the salt water that flooded the land on that fateful day. The Portage Glacier may be receding, but blue icebergs can still be seen up close on the Portage Glacier Cruise. This is one of Alaska's most visited attractions, and more than 100 feet of the icebergs extend down into the lake with spectacular hanging glaciers visible on the mountainside.

3 SEWARD
83.5 MILES, 1 HOUR, 36 MINUTES

As one of Alaska's oldest communities, this seaside village is treated to views of the towering Kenai Mountains filling the skyline and the dramatic Kenai Fjords luring boating enthusiasts. Immerse yourself in salmon fishing, sailing, hiking and kayaking on Resurrection Bay, with its secluded coves and tidewater caves. Grab your camera and explore Kenai Fjords National Park, which provides the best wildlife views in the state. Lace up your hiking boots and follow a 5-mile coastal trail in Caines Head State Recreation Area, then reach out and touch an iceberg at Exit Glacier.

4 SOLDOTNA
94.3 MILES, 1 HOUR, 59 MINUTES

The party never ends near the Kenai River, with the Frozen River Fest kicking off in the winter and the Kenai River Festival highlighting the summer. Outdoor activities include fishing for rainbow trout and all five varieties of Pacific salmon (some weighing in at 85 pounds), guided canoeing, rafting and float trips, along with hiking, birding, hunting and camping. The Kenai National Wildlife Refuge consists of almost 2 million rugged acres of ice fields, glaciers, boreal forests, alpine areas, mountain tundra, wetlands, lakes and rivers inhabited by wildlife.

5 NINILCHIK
41 MILES, 56 MINUTES

Originally settled by Russian immigrants, Ninilchik retains much of its Old World charm, with the local Russian Orthodox Church perched grandly atop a bluff overlooking Cook Inlet and what remains of the original settlement. Traces of this community still exist, including fir log cabins and the area's first Russian schoolhouse. Clamming is a family event, and razor clams are the prize. Take your time when you savor these golden-brown treasures, which boast oval shells that range from 3 to 10 inches long.

6 HOMER
37.4 MILES, 51 MINUTES

Known as the Halibut Fishing Capital of the World, Homer is also called "the End of the Road" because it's surrounded by rugged wilderness on three sides and the Pacific Ocean on the other. Despite its apparent remoteness, this is one of the most vibrant artist communities in Alaska; more than 35 established artists, along with numerous galleries and world-class artistic events, can be found in nearby Halibut Cove, which is tucked away in Kachemak Bay State Park. Whether a novice fisherman or a seasoned angler, casting a rod from Homer Spit is a thrill. Hop a chartered fishing boat for the chance to reel an infamous white halibut.

Journey from cosmopolitan Vancouver to the rugged interior of British Columbia. From modern skyscrapers to towering mountains, this trip redefines the meaning of "town and country."

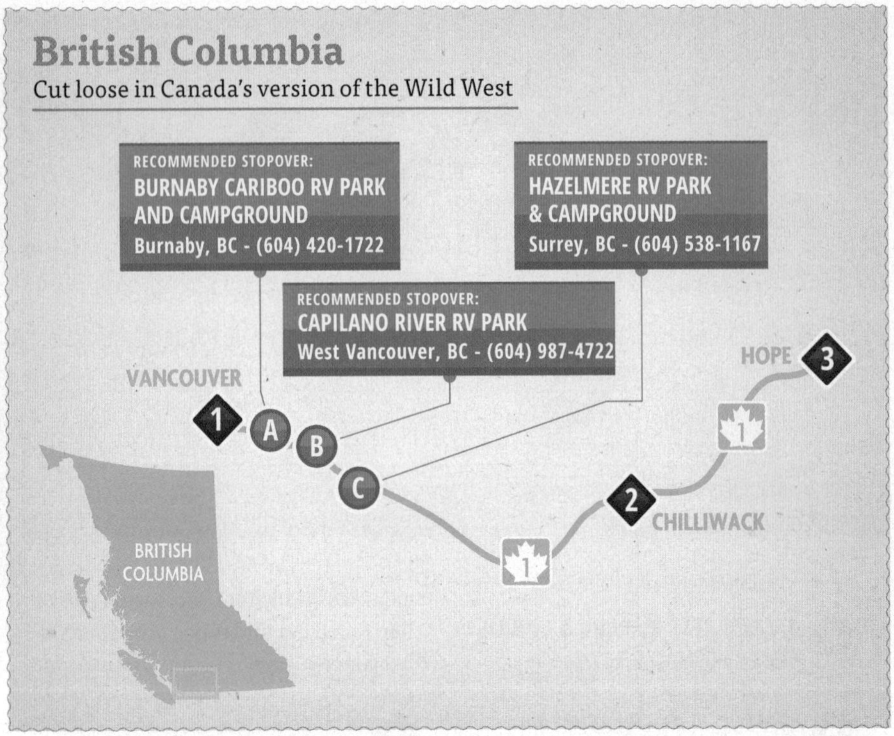

Drive 97.4 miles, 1 hour, 55 minutes

1 VANCOUVER
STARTING POINT

Vancouver is a world-class city full of contrasts. Experience its sophisticated side at the Vancouver Art Gallery and Orpheum Theatre, and then hit the historic neighborhood of Gastown. You can overlook the mountains and the ocean from high upon the cliffs at the UBC Museum of Anthropology, renowned for a collection that includes more than a half-million archaeological artifacts in-house. Take a day trip outside the city and step out for a long stroll across the Capilano Suspension Bridge, which stretches 450 feet across the Capilano River.

RECOMMENDED STOPOVERS

A BURNABY CARIBOO RV PARK AND CAMPGROUND
Burnaby, BC - (604) 420-1722

B CAPILANO RIVER RV PARK
West Vancouver, BC - (604) 987-4722

C HAZELMERE RV PARK & CAMPGROUND
Surrey, BC - (604) 538-1167

2 CHILLIWACK
62.5 MILES, 1 HOUR, 14 MINUTES

Set among the Cascade Mountains in the Fraser Valley, Chilliwack has some of the richest farmland in Canada, with over 900 farms located nearby. Take the self-guided Circle Farm Tour and enjoy down-home food, fun and hospitality from more than a dozen farms and agritourism businesses. The town recalls days of old at the Atchelitz Threshermens Association Pioneer Village, which boasts a general store, blacksmith shop and antique tractors. Hike and bike on the Trans Canada Trail as it winds through the Chilliwack River Valley and on up to Cultus Lake, home to the Pygmy Sculpin fish, found nowhere else in the world.

3 HOPE
34.9 MILES, 41 MINUTES

Located between the Coast Mountains and Cascade Mountain Range, Hope is the "Gold Gem of British Columbia," an outdoor enthusiasts' paradise surrounded by a diverse landscape, hundreds of trails and intriguing parks. Explore the spectacular B.C. wilderness at Coquihalla Canyon Provincial Park, known for the Othello Railway Tunnels, which were bored through granite mountains and can now be explored on foot. Travel "where no human should venture"—Hell's Gate. Climb aboard a gondola, where you'll be suspended above 200 million gallons of churning water on one of the most thrilling passages on the Fraser River.

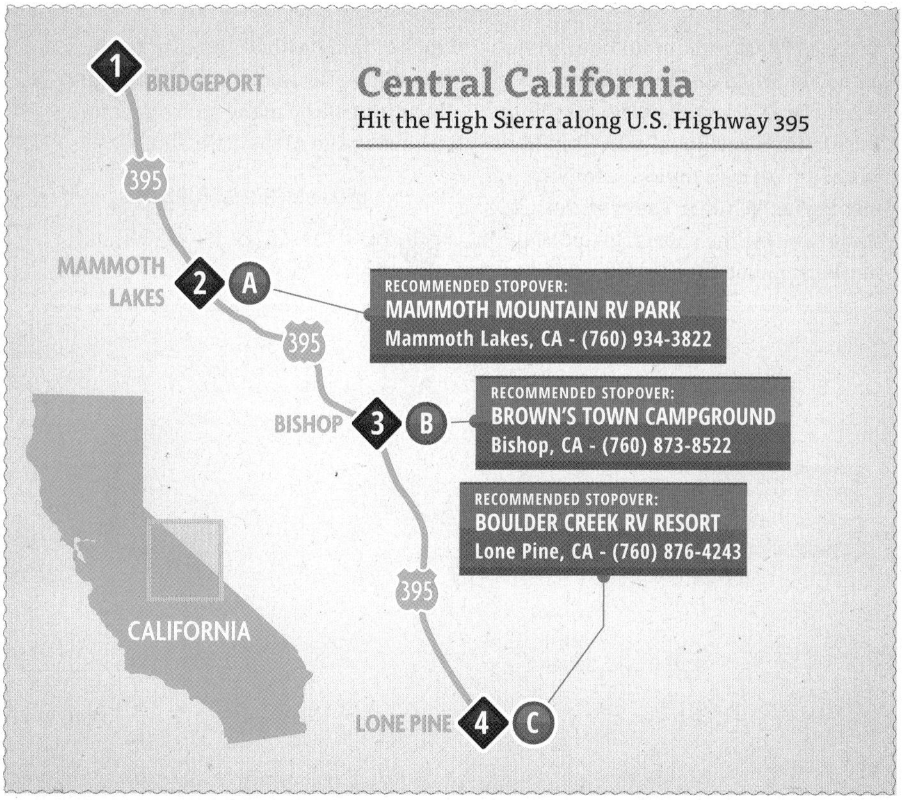

You'll discover lots of great views as you cruise beautiful U.S Highway 395, which follows the formidable High Sierra as the mountain range thrusts into the sky to the west. Equally impressive are the small towns found along the way, which offer recreation and history in equal doses. Take your time as you discover the treasures of the Golden State running parallel to the Nevada border.

Drive 154.2 miles, 2 hours, 28 minutes

1 BRIDGEPORT
STARTING POINT

Come to play and plan to stay for a while in this unspoiled natural playground surrounded by pristine lakes, rivers, streams and hot springs. Bridgeport is famous for world-class trout fishing, hiking, horseback riding, trophy mule deer hunting, and more than 500 miles of cross-country skiing, snowshoeing, snowmobiling and dogsledding. Adventure awaits at the Bridgeport Reservoir, where watersports, mountaineering and bird watching are favorite activities. Don't miss the authentic gold rush ghost town of Bodie, frozen in time and boasting a legendary curse.

2 MAMMOTH LAKES
54.2 MILES, 54 MINUTES

Welcome to Mammoth Lakes, a year-round recreational paradise that receives over 400 inches of snow during the winter, providing it with one of the longest skiing seasons in the country. Abundant snow makes it easy to hit the slopes and enjoy snowboarding, sledding, ice climbing, ice fishing and ice skating, but summer offers its own pleasures: fishing for natural golden trout, canoeing, kayaking, golfing, horseback riding, rock climbing, mountaineering and zip lining. For more adventure, grab a ride on the Scenic Gondola for panoramic views atop Mammoth Mountain.

RECOMMENDED STOPOVERS

A MAMMOTH MOUNTAIN RV PARK
Mammoth Lakes, CA - (760) 934-3822

3 BISHOP
42.1 MILES, 41 MINUTES

Known as the "small town with the big backyard," Bishop is located in the heart of the spectacular Eastern Sierra. Outdoor enthusiasts can enjoy a hike among some of the oldest living trees in the world at the Ancient Bristlecone Pine Forest. Fish for the area's famous trout in a rushing stream or head to one of the greatest rock climbing sites in California, maybe the world: the Gorge. Photographers and artists will delight in the scenery and breathtaking views at Cardinal Village Resort, located at the bottom of Bishop Creek Canyon. Stand in awe of Native American petroglyphs, and then take to the mountain back roads for a scenic motor tour around the area.

RECOMMENDED STOPOVERS

B BROWN'S TOWN CAMPGROUND
Bishop, CA - (760) 873-8522

4 LONE PINE
57.9 MILES, 53 MINUTES

"Where the Real West Becomes the Reel West" is the slogan of Lone Pine, a film mecca established in 1920 and utilized for Westerns, space epics and historical adventure films. The Lone Pine Film History Museum is a treasure-trove of movie props, cars, costumes and memorabilia used in more than 700 films, over 100 TV episodes and innumerable commercials, all shot on location here and in the surrounding Alabama Hills. Discover the most famous characters associated with this town, where "Gunga Din," "How the West Was Won," "Bad Day at Black Rock" and "Iron Man" were filmed; it's a must-see for any moviegoer. While in the area, set aside some time for the short trip up Whitney Portal Road for the self-guided tour of "Movie Road." The route gives travelers a firsthand look at shooting locations of the many motion pictures filmed in the Alabama Hills.

RECOMMENDED STOPOVERS

C BOULDER CREEK RV RESORT
Lone Pine, CA - (760) 876-4243

These northern landscapes vary from rugged wilderness to towering city skylines—who could ask for more? Recharge your batteries with an escape to Northern Arizona's vacation sanctuaries.

Drive 200.9 miles, 2 hours, 53 minutes

1 FLAGSTAFF
STARTING POINT

This bustling college town moves on its feet with over 50 miles of non-motorized pathways for walkers, runners, hikers and bikers. You'll find these trails in urban areas, meadows, grasslands, canyons and nearby forests. Brookbank Trail is perfect for solitude and reflection; Arizona Trail in the Walnut Canyon National Monument passes by curved canyon walls and cliff dwellings for some of the most beautiful yet isolated wilderness in the state. The Arizona Snowbowl provides the ultimate in skiing and snowboarding.

RECOMMENDED STOPOVERS

A GRAND CANYON RAILWAY RV PARK
Williams, AZ - (800) 843-8724

2 SEDONA
32.7 MILES, 49 MINUTES

You'll see red in Sedona—red rock buttes, spires and monoliths created by wind and water erosion over millions of years. Native Americans believed these formations held mystical properties. Enjoy a panoramic view of these magical rocks from a hot air balloon or take an explorative hike up the monolith of your choice. Cathedral Rock is awe-inspiring and seems to exude a soul-soothing energy that has drawn spiritual visitors for centuries.

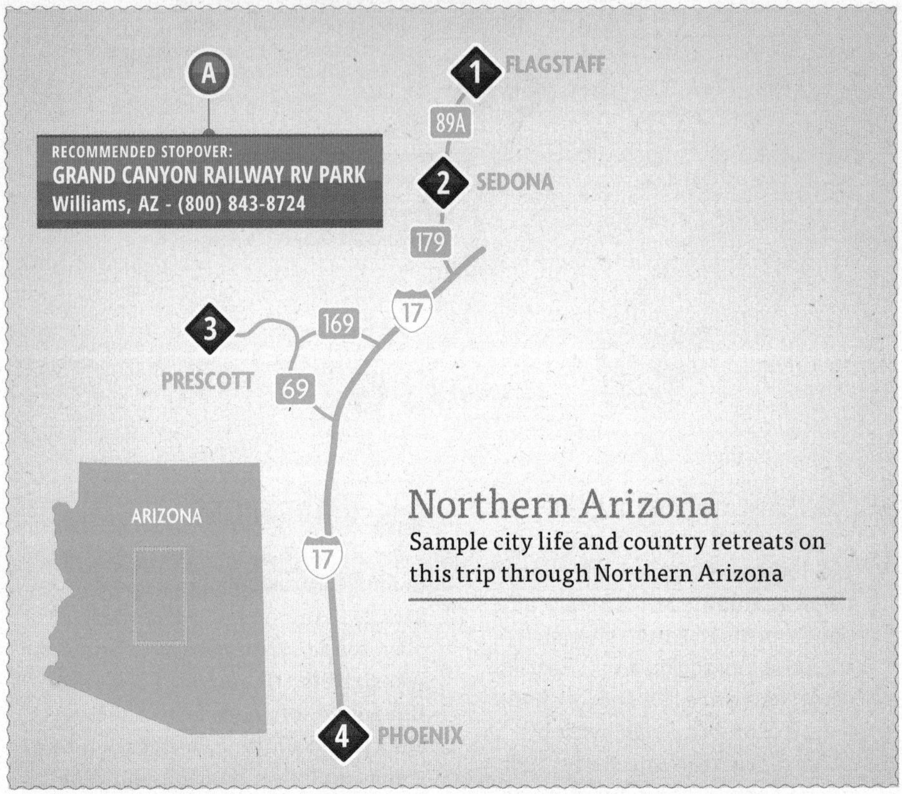

Northern Arizona
Sample city life and country retreats on this trip through Northern Arizona

3 PRESCOTT
68.5 MILES, 1 HOUR, 13 MINUTES

Prescott has so much to offer, it's no wonder it was voted "Travelers' Choice" by TripAdvisor as one of the "10 Destinations on the Rise" in the U.S. The downtown historical district retains the feel of a bygone era, with intrigu-

ing museums, Victorian homes and Old Western saloons. The Sharlot Hall Museum tells the story of Prescott and its founders by offering a glimpse into life in the Wild West during the late 1800s. Stroll down Whiskey Row, a one-block area that housed over 40 saloons at one time.

4 PHOENIX
99.7 MILES, 1 HOUR, 31 MINUTES

Explore one of America's sunniest cities. Walk the trails at the Desert Botanical Garden to learn more about the plants, people and wildlife of the Sonoran Desert. The Heard Museum of American Indian Art and History emphasizes Southwestern cultures and offers a better understanding into the ways of indigenous peoples. Saddle up for a real western horseback ride, reserve a wagon ride, complete with a cookout, or catch some family entertainment—1880s style—at Rawhide Western Town and Steakhouse.

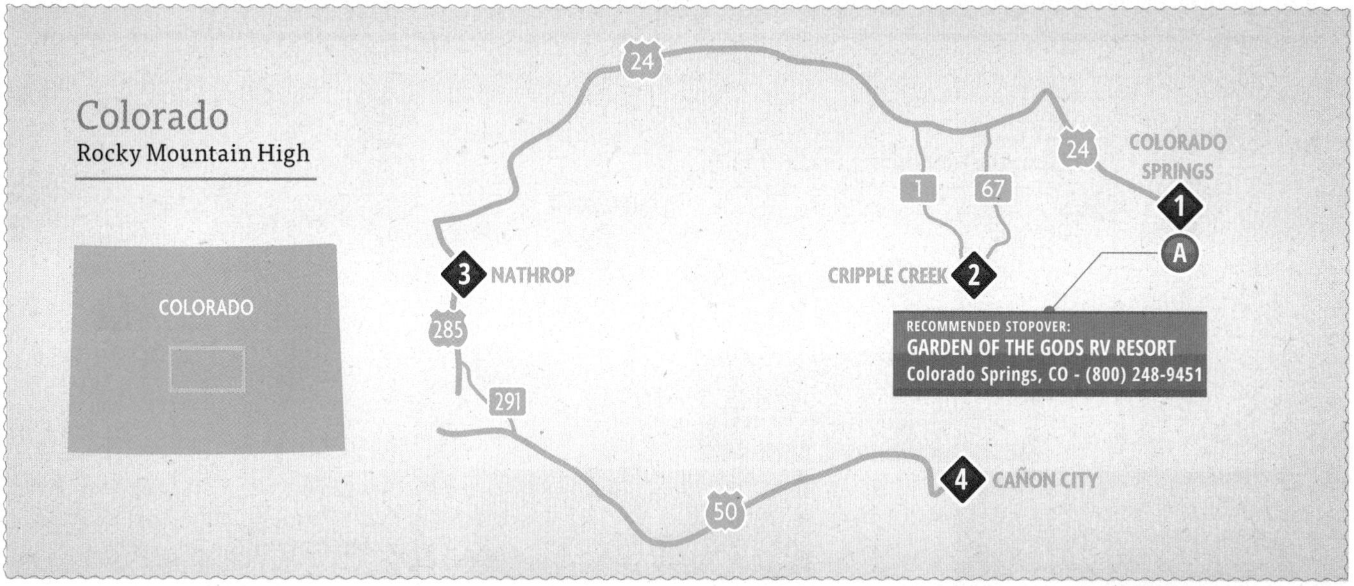

Experience the heights of Olympians and follow the trails of Gold Rush treasure seekers. This trip will show you a side of Colorado that remains as beautiful as it is wild.

Drive 202 miles, 3 hours, 11 minutes

1 COLORADO SPRINGS
STARTING POINT

Colorado Springs is composed of artists, historians, high-flying military personnel and Olympians who call this individualistic western city "home." Learn what it takes to fly with the best at the U.S. Air Force Academy and find out what's required for cadets to earn their wings. Don't miss the all-faith Cadet Chapel, designed with 17 awe-inspiring spires that soar into the sky. Come back down to earth at the U.S. Olympic Training Center, where aspiring champions hone their skills in state-of-the-art facilities. Take the 45-minute tour of the complex, which includes the Olympic Visitor Center.

RECOMMENDED STOPOVERS

A GARDEN OF THE GODS RV RESORT
Colorado Springs, CO - (800) 248-9451

2 CRIPPLE CREEK
44.9 MILES, 1 HOUR

Relive the Gold Rush era in Cripple Creek, home to one of the largest gold strikes in U.S. history. Here, you'll discover how 8,000 miners extracted more than 22 million ounces of gold from 500 mines to produce 30 regional millionaires. Descend 1,000 feet below ground for a first-hand look at the Mollie Kathleen Mine. Discover mining machines and equipment used during the Rush at Victor's Gold Camp Ag and Mining Museum, then it's all aboard the Cripple Creek and Victor Narrow Gauge Railroad for a trip through historic mining country.

3 NATHROP
79.8 MILES, 1 HOUR, 35 MINUTES

Nathrop serves as a tranquil basecamp for a slew of outdoors adventures. To the west, several historic structures preserve the history of St. Elmo, one of Colorado's most intriguing ghost towns. In its Gold Rush heyday, this area boasted 150 mines. Stop in the St. Elmo General Store for everything from antiques to yard art. After a busy day of hiking or off-roading, soak in the soothing Mount Princeton Hot Springs, where therapeutic waters bubble out of the ground at 135 degrees. At the nearby town of Salida, Captain Zipline offers high-flying aerial adventures for every member of the family.

4 CAÑON CITY

77.3 MILES, 1 HOUR, 26 MINUTES

Cañon City offers turn-of-the-century architecture and a comfortable Western atmosphere. Here, you can pull up your cowboy boots and mosey downtown for a walking tour featuring 40 turn-of-the-century historical buildings. Visit the Museum of Colorado Prisons for a look back at 140 years of prison life. Check out working and living conditions, isolation cells and the hangman's noose, then learn about the infamous prisoners who were held here. Take a nighttime ghost tour to learn about the city's legendary past and find out who haunts the historic Hotel St. Cloud. For a more "spiritual" experience, check out ghost tours at the Abbey, a former monastery.

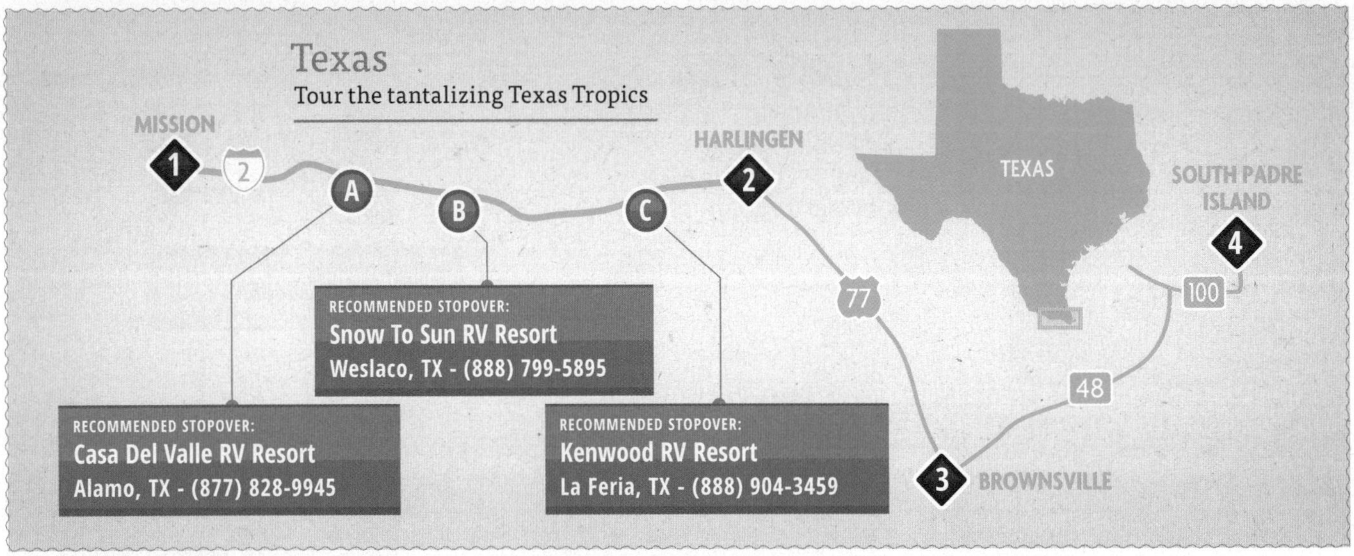

Texas' Lower Rio Grande Valley offers up singular outdoors adventures, natural beauty and more than its fair share of fun. Bird and butterfly sightings, rugged wilderness regions and long stretches of shoreline guarantee that you can see it all on a visit to the border.

Drive 98.3 miles, 1 hour, 42 minutes

1 MISSION

STARTING POINT

Known as the nation's "butterfly capital," a visit to the Lower Rio Grande Valley in October means a trip to the annual Texas Butterfly Festival, when the hundreds of species that call the region home are on full display. Special viewing stations, private garden tours and educational hikes are available through the National Butterfly Center, and a photo contest offers up cash prizes for the best shot.

RECOMMENDED STOPOVERS

A CASA DEL VALLE RV RESORT
Alamo, TX - (877) 828-9945

B SNOW TO SUN RV RESORT
Weslaco, TX - (888) 799-5895

C KENWOOD RV RESORT
La Feria, TX - (888) 904-3459

2 HARLINGEN

42.3 MILES, 39 MINUTES

In this charming town, a host of boutiques and art galleries line Jackson Street, as do larger-than-life murals that have brought acclaim to the local art scene. Birders will delight at the opportunity to see rare avians like the green jay and Altamira oriole from viewing stations in the Hugh Ramsey Nature Park or Laguna Atascosa National Wildlife Refuge. These spots also offer hikes and river trips through moss-covered woodlands.

3 BROWNSVILLE
27.9 MILES, 27 MINUTES

Tropical and green, the Texas coast is a magnet for outdoors adventurers. The Historic Battlefield Trail, Monte Bella Mountain Bike Trail and Belden Trail make for excellent hiking and biking opportunities within minutes of downtown Brownsville. For an off-the-beaten-path approach, try the Resaca de la Palma State Park, where miles of trails wind through native scrub brush, grasslands and pine.

4 SOUTH PADRE ISLAND
28.1 MILES, 36 MINUTES

Home to the ultimate Texas beach scene, 34-miles of white sand await visitors in South Padre Island. You could spend your whole visit lounging on one of the most pristine beaches in the Gulf of Mexico, but since the island is only a half-mile wide, many attractions, restaurants and bars are just a quick walk from where you planted your beach umbrella. Try and hook the big one on a deep-sea charter.

Stellar beach towns beckon RV travelers to a Sunshine State joy ride. Pack the sunscreen, because you'll be spending lots of time outdoors when you're not dining in one of the area's fine restaurants.

Drive 71.8 miles, 1 hour, 32 minutes

1 PORT CHARLOTTE
STARTING POINT

Visitors will delight in the 165 miles of waterways located here, making Port Charlotte the perfect destination for aquatic fun. Cast your line at Charlotte Harbor Flats Fishing and take the opportunity to hook redfish, snook and tarpon. The harbor beckons for exploration by scuba divers and snorkelers, but if you prefer to stay above the surface, you can rent a canoe or kayak for some enjoyable downtime on the water. Set sail on an evening cruise to witness dolphins frolicking in the water and the sun dipping below the horizon. It's a great way to end the day.

RECOMMENDED STOPOVERS

A RIVERSIDE RV RESORT & CAMPGROUND
Port Charlotte, FL - (800) 795-9733

B SUN N SHADE RV PARK
Punta Gorda, FL - (941) 639-5388

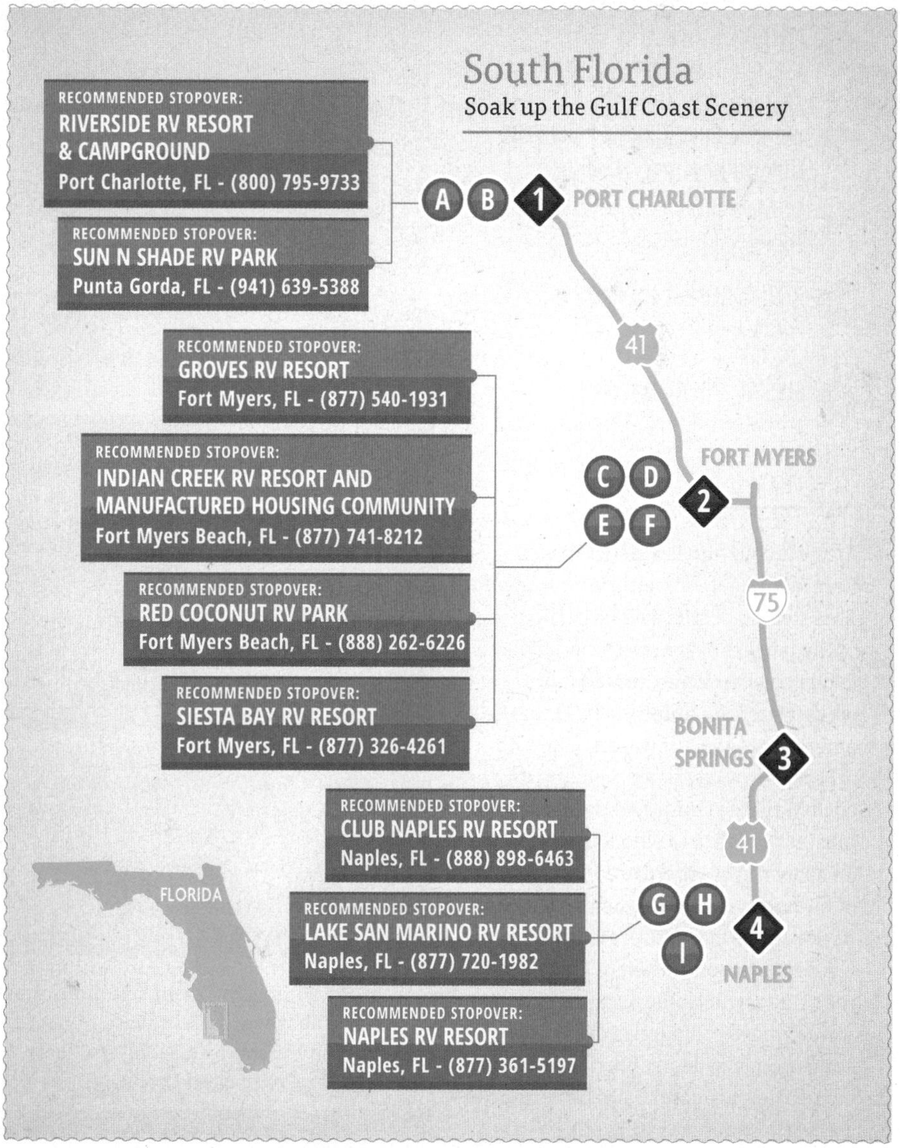

2 FORT MYERS
29 MILES, 40 MINUTES

Visit Fort Myers' charming River District and stroll through shops and boutiques before you embark on a fishing charter or go parasailing over the water. Get close to nature at the Six Mile Cypress Slough Preserve, with over 3,400 acres of wetlands that invite explorers to amble along the boardwalk for great views of the local wildlife. Situated on 20 lush acres, the Edison and Ford Winter Estates are stunning, with several historical buildings to explore, including both Main Houses and the Edison Botanic Research Laboratory. At the Edison and Ford Museum, travel with the "vagabonds" as they camped their way through Florida in a 1918 Model T camper.

RECOMMENDED STOPOVERS

C GROVES RV RESORT
Fort Myers, FL - (877) 540-1931

D INDIAN CREEK RV RESORT AND MANUFACTURED HOUSING COMMUNITY
Fort Myers Beach, FL - (877) 741-8212

E RED COCONUT RV PARK
Fort Myers Beach, FL - (888) 262-6226

F SIESTA BAY RV RESORT
Fort Myers, FL - (877) 326-4261

3 BONITA SPRINGS
28.9 MILES, 29 MINUTES

Kick off your shoes and head for Barefoot Beach Preserve County Park. This stretch of shore is the definition of the perfect beach, with sugar white sands you can sink your toes into while watching dolphins frolic in the emerald green Gulf waters. Then it's off to Estero Bay for an amazing day with Manatee Guides, certified Florida master naturalists who will take you on a kayaking adventure into the world of manatee, dolphins and turtles. Step back in time at the Everglades Wonder Gardens, one of the last of Florida's roadside attractions, but now getting a much-needed upgrade to be more educational and family-friendly. See butterflies, alligators and pink flamingos in their natural habitat.

4 NAPLES
13.9 MILES, 23 MINUTES

Naples is the crown jewel of southwestern Florida, a region that's often referred to as the Paradise Coast. Take a stroll in a community that evokes Old Florida as well as today's sophisticated Sunshine State. Enjoy a 1-mile walking tour through Old Naples and see the history of the region come to life; discover where the general store was located, what happened to the first movie theater and where the grand Naples Hotel originally stood. Learn about the well-to-do city founders, including the Briggs, Haldemans and DuPonts.

RECOMMENDED STOPOVERS

G CLUB NAPLES RV RESORT
Naples, FL - (888) 898-6463

H LAKE SAN MARINO RV RESORT
Naples, FL - (877) 720-1982

I NAPLES RV RESORT
Naples, FL - (877) 361-5197

Mississippi

Linger on the shores of the Magnolia State

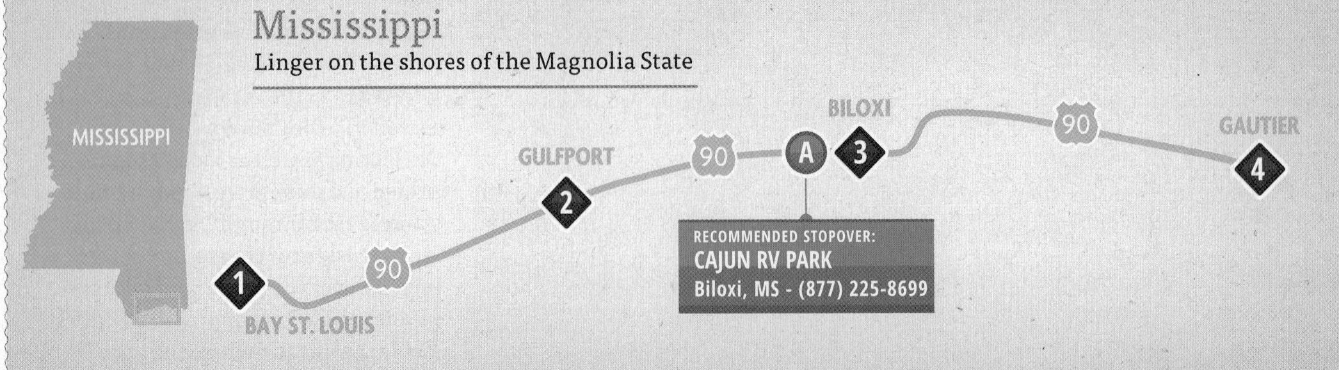

The Magnolia State has many claims to fame—a superb waterfront, unforgettable cooking and warm Southern hospitality. This route along the scenic Highway 90 will treat you to all those qualities and more as you explore the laid-back communities that define Southern living.

Drive 54 miles, 1 hour, 7 minutes

1 BAY ST. LOUIS
STARTING POINT

Having a main drag called Beach Boulevard should say it all. If you have any trouble finding a stretch of sand and warm water in this bayside hamlet, you're doing something wrong. A walking tour of the Creole cottages and 19th-century homes that make up the historic Old Town is a great introduction to the town's laid-back Southern lifestyle. Stop at the hip Blind Tiger restaurant for shrimp and cocktails, or relax in the welcoming "living room-like" atmosphere of the Mockingbird Café.

2 GULFPORT
17.8 MILES, 24 MINUTES

Let the good times roll right on the beach at the famed Island View Casino, where slots, poker and craps await gamers. Check the casino calendar ahead of time, as top musical performers regularly take the stage of the View Showroom. You can easily wander back and forth between the near 7 miles of white sand beaches and the gaming room floor, so don't hesitate to take a break from the tables and enjoy dinner and a sunset out by the dunes.

For adrenaline junkies, check out the Smokin' the Sound speed boat races, which roar into town every spring.

3 BILOXI
20 MILES, 20 MINUTES

Sport fishermen flock to Biloxi year-round for a chance to reel in the big one, and one of the many charter boats that leave the marina will help you hook a sea trout, mackerel or even a shark. After a morning on the water, try your luck at the Beau Rivage Resort and Casino, a well-known landmark and the tallest building in Mississippi. Between hot hands, check out the singular Ohr-O'Keefe Museum of Art, which was designed by famed architect Frank Gehry. The collection includes abstract impressionist pottery from George E. Ohr, known locally as "the Mad Potter of Biloxi."

RECOMMENDED STOPOVERS

A CAJUN RV PARK
Biloxi, MS - (877) 225-8699

4 GAUTIER
16.2 MILES, 23 MINUTES

Home to the wetlands and bayous of the Pascagoula River, Gautier has something for everyone. From birding among the endangered seabirds at the Sandhill Crane National Wildlife Refuge to enjoying an afternoon guided kayaking tour of the bayous with Eco-Tours of South Mississippi, the outdoorsman in you will be busy. Next, challenge yourself to some championship golf at the Hickory Hill Country Club, a course designed to highlight the natural beauty of the area. The Mississippi National Golf Club challenges golfers as it winds through the area's lush surroundings.

From Toronto to Niagara Falls, this journey serves up the best Ontario has to offer. Toronto is one of the world's great cities, with dozens of neighborhoods just waiting to be explored. Niagara Falls, one of the world's great natural wonders, needs even less of an introduction. With the artist's haven of Hamilton in between, this memorable trip truly has it all.

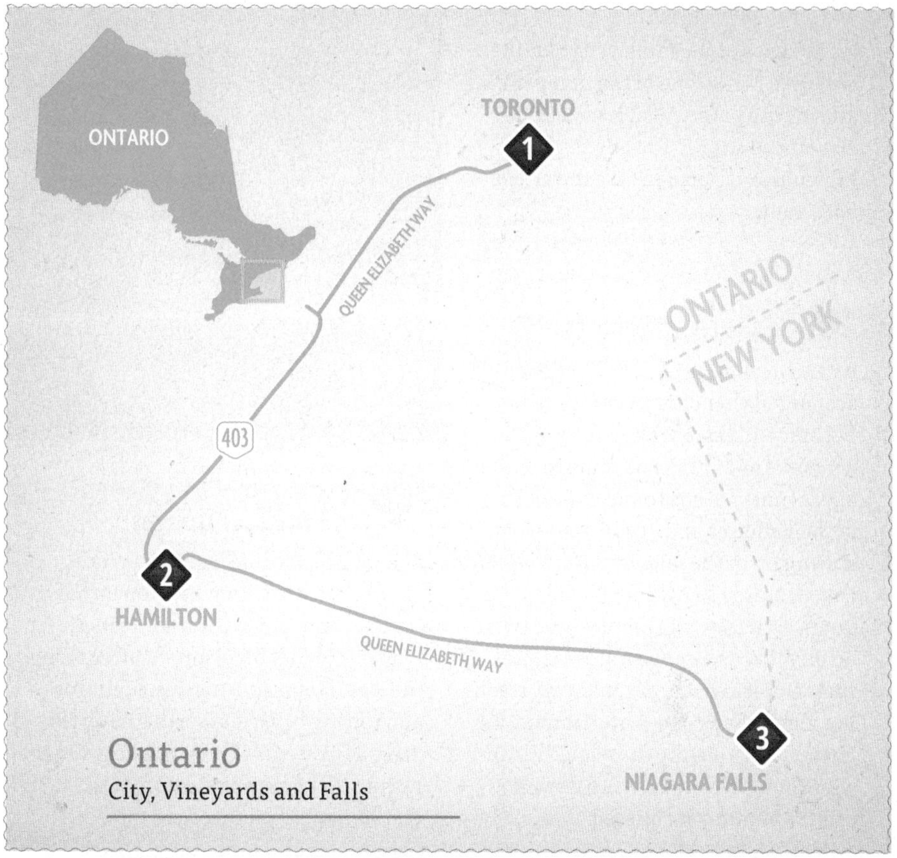

Drive 88.2 miles, 1 hour, 43 minutes

1 TORONTO
STARTING POINT

Recognized as the most multicultural city on the planet, you won't be wanting for things to see and do in this metropolis. Each neighborhood has something to offer, but start your visit by exploring the historic Old Town's St. Lawrence Market Complex, where farmers sell local produce, restaurants abound and craftsmen display all manner of handmade goods. Take an afternoon ferry ride to Toronto Island for

great views of the famed city skyline, and then tackle one of the many hiking and biking paths. Visitors who ride elevator to the CN Tower's 1,136-foot-high observation deck are rewarded with stellar views.

2 HAMILTON
42.8 MILES, 52 MINUTES

As an alternative to the established scenes in other cities, Hamilton has become a grassroots hub for artists across Canada. Take advantage of the opportunity to see some of the best at the galleries and events that have sprung up in the James St. North Arts District. Also known for its many outdoors activities, the picturesque twist on city life that exploring the shores of Lake Ontario by canoe or kayak, strolling along the serene waterfront in the harbor, and touring the waterfalls in the Stoney Creek and Ancaster areas offers shouldn't be missed.

3 NIAGARA FALLS
45.4 MILES, 51 MINUTES

The world's most famous waterfall makes for a thrilling last stop on this trip, but the scenic Queen Elizabeth Way has plenty of beauty to offer along the way. Home to wineries, orchards and rolling hills, it's worth giving the drive a little extra time for photos or a picnic. Make sure to stop off at Niagara-on-the-Lake, a picturesque 19th-century village that takes great pride in its history. It's also the heart of the wine region, and many tours and tastings are organized in town. Of course, no visit is complete without the falls themselves, a wondrous sight. Hornblower Cruises offers boat trips into the gorge, where you'll be overwhelmed by the mist and thunderous roar of the water. The Journey Behind the Falls provides an up-close look at the spectacle.

10 Facilities | **10★** Restrooms & Showers | **10** Visual Appearance

10/10★/10 Parks A roundup of RV parks that have earned flawless ratings

The parks in the following list have earned perfect 10/10★/10 Good Sam Ratings by earning top marks in amenities, cleanliness, and environment and appearance ("Win the Numbers Game" on page 158 for an explanation of the trusted Good Sam Rating System). Our traveling consultants have ensured that each of these parks have met or exceeded every point in our criteria. Parks below are listed by city, state and province, followed by non-Good Sam Parks.

Lake Osprey RV Resort, Elberta, Alabama

This stunning RV resort is located on the north shore of the Alabama Gulf coastland and built for the true outdoor enthusiast. With a golf resort right next door, Lake Osprey is designed for high-end RVs but not restricted to Class A's. There's a beautiful, large pool and spa along with two lakes.

Windemere Cove RV Resort, Langston, Alabama

RV lot sales, as well as overnight rentals, are available in this beautiful gated RV resort. Located on Lake Guntersville, Windemere has a private boat launch and pier. Guests can also gather around the community rock fire pit, relax in the clubhouse or swim in the saltwater pool.

Heritage Motorcoach Resort & Marina, Orange Beach, Alabama

This unique Gulf Coast motor coach resort and boating destination has pristine beaches, a saltwater marina, infinity pool, coach houses, paved streets, gas lamps, huge shade trees, ample fishing and great golf. You will not want to leave.

Superstition Sunrise RV Resort, Apache Junction, Arizona

This is Apache Junction's top 55+ resort. Enjoy indoor and outdoor pools, spa, hair salon, massage therapist, cabana, pickleball courts, Wi-Fi, satellite and more. So much to do and see in the Valley of the Sun! Come for a visit and stay for the lifestyle.

Black Canyon Ranch RV Resort, Black Canyon City, Arizona

You are warmly welcomed to Black Canyon Ranch RV Resort. Only a mile from Interstate 17 and 25 miles north of Phoenix, Black Canyon City is a quaint Arizona mining town. "The Ranch" is far enough from 1-17 to be free from traffic noise but close enough for a quick trip to Phoenix or Flagstaff.

Moon River RV Resort, Bullhead City, Arizona

This RV resort is located in a quiet country setting, but convenient to state highway 95, Interstate 40 and the exciting attractions along the beautiful Colorado River, which offers kayaking, fishing, boating and wakeboarding. It's just five minutes from Avi Casino and 15 minutes from Laughlin, Nevada, casinos.

Vista Del Sol RV Resort, Bullhead City, Arizona

A 55+ gated, active adult retirement community and RV resort, Vista Del Sol is within striking distance of a number of natural and man-made attractions. Serviced by the Laughlin/Bullhead Airport, this resort features a heated pool, rec hall and exercise room.

Distant Drums RV Resort, Camp Verde, Arizona

Located in the central Verde Valley region of Arizona, Distant Drums is minutes away from many great national parks and attractions like Cliff Castle Casino, Sedona Red Rock Country, Montezuma National Monument, Tuzigoot National Monument, Verde Canyon Railroad and many more.

Palm Creek Golf & RV Resort, Casa Grande, Arizona

Palm Creek has been described as "Disneyland for adults" because the resort so effectively pairs world-class amenities with a vibrant social network of active, friendly adults. Master your swing on the par-three golf course, take part in a stained glass workshop and relax by the pool.

Sundance 1 RV Resort, Casa Grande, Arizona

Located just 45 miles from Phoenix and 65 miles from Tucson in the city of Casa Grande, Sundance 1 RV Resort is close to modern health facilities, large shopping malls, theaters, fine dining, golf courses and major grocery chains. The resort offers horseshoes, shuffleboard, cards, darts and other activities for all guests.

Pueblo El Mirage Golf & RV Resort, El Mirage, Arizona

This truly is a luxury snowbird resort. This country club and RV resort is a 55+ gated community just minutes from Phoenix. It's full of big-rig sites and park models to rent or purchase. Enjoy the 18-hole golf course/pro shop/restaurant/lounge/pool/spa and more.

Eagle View RV Resort at Fort McDowell, Fort McDowell, Arizona

Guests here can experience serenity and solitude nestled along the Verde River. Located in the Valley of the Sun, it's only minutes away from We-Ko-Pa Golf Club, art festivals and auto auctions. Enjoy boating and fishing at nearby lakes and a free shuttle to Fort McDowell Casino.

Gold Canyon RV & Golf Resort, Gold Canyon, Arizona

Check out this luxury golf and RV resort. Experience a community of natural beauty from the Sonoran Desert to countless activities and amenities. It's a 55+ active adult retirement community that is an energetic and beautiful place and redefines active adult living and RVing.

Apache Wells RV Resort, Mesa, Arizona

Enjoy an invigorating game of tennis on one of the lighted courts or a fun game of bridge in the rec room. Don't forget our pool and spa for relaxation after long drives. High-speed Internet in the computer room will help you stay touch with family and friends.

Good Life RV Resort, Mesa, Arizona

Guest can enjoy a wide range of activities, including fun dancing events, a great pool, a game under lighted tennis/shuffleboard courts, nearby shopping and restaurants, and a short distance to fabulous golf courses. A new dog park will keep your furry traveling companions happy.

Mesa Regal RV Resort, Mesa, Arizona

This resort has it all: four outdoor pools and spa, and computer and fitness centers. Also available are in-house beauty/barber shops, massage therapy, a travel agency, five lighted tennis courts, batting/driving cages, water volleyball, bocce ball, pickleball and much more.

Sun Life RV Resort, Mesa, Arizona

This is one of the best locations to see and do it all. Try casinos, golfing, bowling, museums, sports stadiums, shopping, restaurants and local hiking. The social director has a full schedule of activities/events, like ever popular dancing in the Grand Ballroom.

Desert Shadows RV Resort, Phoenix, Arizona

Feel at home in a beautiful, well-manicured resort in North Phoenix. A friendly, tranquil place with all the amenities you may want. Close to golf, restaurants and sporting events.

Desert's Edge RV—The Purple Park, Phoenix, Arizona

Stay at this award-winning RV resort in Phoenix. Desert's Edge welcomes guests of all ages to enjoy the Purple Park Experience—one you will not soon forget. Conveniently located on the north side of Phoenix. Guests say, "friendly staff, easy access, good Wi-Fi and nicest park around."

Far Horizons Tucson Village RV Resort, Tucson, Arizona

Welcome to Tucson and a friendly RV community designed for vacationers age 55 and better. From your doorstep, walk, ride or drive to nearby outdoor adventures, scenic attractions, golf, shopping, dining, arts and culture. Enjoy a full slate of on-property activities.

Rincon Country East RV Resort, Tucson, Arizona

Near the fascinating city of Tucson, Rincon County East RV Resort boasts world-class facilities and a helpful, friendly staff. Sit by the pool or join the wide range of activities. The resort opens up a new world for guests seeking the best that Arizona has to offer.

Rincon Country West RV Resort, Tucson, Arizona

Whether you want to relax and restore yourself after a long journey or jump into a community bustling with activities, you'll be at home at Rincon West Resort in Tucson—a comfortable, historical world-class destination that for centuries has offered visitors a warm environment.

Del Pueblo RV Park and Tennis Resort, Yuma, Arizona

This is a new, up-to-date family owned and operated 55+ RV resort. Included is a large, centrally located recreation center, convenient to all lots, as well as a separate neighborhood center with its own pool and Jacuzzi, card room, barbecue site and laundry and shower facilities.

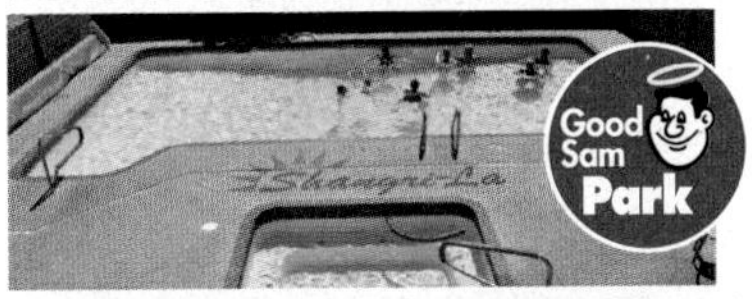

Shangri-La RV Resort, Yuma, Arizona

Family owned and operated over 30 years, it's just getting better! With the absolute best hospitality, facilities and value, come and see for yourself why Shangri-La has been rated a perfect 10/10★/10. You deserve the best, and you'll find it at Shangri-La.

Westwind RV & Golf Resort, Yuma, Arizona

More than a resort—a lifestyle! A nine-hole golf course meanders throughout the resort, giving you a chance to hone your swing on unique, executive fairways with well-manicured greens and lush landscaping. It's an ideal place to retire or vacation with great mountain views.

Ozarks RV Resort on Table Rock Lake, Blue Eye, Arkansas

Located on a peninsula on Table Rock Lake, the Ozarks RV Resort puts you right where the action is. Guests will find themselves located between Eureka Springs, with its quaint shops and tourist attractions, and Branson, Missouri, a mecca of entertainment and shopping.

Catherine's Landing at Hot Springs, Hot Springs, Arkansas

Catherine's Landing sits on a mile of pristine lake frontage 10 minutes away from Hot Springs' historic downtown bathhouses. Relax on 400 acres of lush surroundings with great views, superb amenities and easy access to local attractions. It's the ultimate RV escape.

The Springs at Borrego RV Resort & Golf Course, Borrego Springs, California

Located in the magnificent Anza-Borrego Desert State Park, the Springs at Borrego RV Resort & Golf Course features lush amenities amid the rugged beauty of the California desert. This world-class RV experience has spacious RV sites and a host of recreational activities.

Indian Waters RV Resort & Cottages, Indio, California

Indian Waters RV Resort and Cottages is located in the heart of the Palm Springs area. New ownership has renovated the property, adding cottages, a second pool, lighted pickleball courts, 50-amp service and city sewer service to all sites, enhanced Wi-Fi and "makeover" for the clubhouse.

Jackson Rancheria RV Park, Jackson, California

Unwind in this luxurious RV resort, which is nestled in a secluded forest setting, or take a short ride via 24-hour shuttle to the thrilling Jackson Rancheria Casino. Relax with ample amenities between day trips to Jackson and areas beyond.

Emerald Desert RV Resort—Sunland, Palm Desert, California

Stay at the most luxurious RV resort in Palm Desert. In this gated enclave, guests can work out at the state-of-the-art fitness center, swim and soak in two pools/spas, and test their skills at the putting greens and billiards room. Take advantage of RV storage and dog-run area.

Redding Premier RV Resort, Redding, California
Enjoy California's stellar West Coast. A great place to start is Redding, home to the Premier RV Resort, which offers something for everyone. Get wet at the Water Works Park or Shasta Lake, or try your luck at the Win-River Casino. Shasta Caverns will thrill you with its rock formations.

Pechanga RV Resort, Temecula, California
Nestled in the picturesque hills of Temecula Wine Country, the award-winning Pechanga RV Resort offers guests endless opportunities for excitement, relaxation and fun. Wine tasting, casino, golf, Historic Old Town and more await adventurous RV travelers. The RV resort features a heated pool and whirlpool for relaxation.

Tiger Run RV Resort, Breckenridge, Colorado
Full-service RV luxury awaits visitors to Tiger Run Resort in Breckenridge. Enjoy the spectacular location and savor the accommodations. Located between the Swan and Blue rivers and sheltered by the Tenmile Mountain Range, it's the ultimate getaway.

Royal View @ Royal Gorge Campground, Canon City, Colorado
Family adventures abound here along with spectacular views. Indeed, this full-service camp resort can make your next Colorado vacation worry-free. Enjoy the large, heated pool, hot showers, clubroom, game room, mini golf and much more.

Mesa Verde RV Resort, Mancos, Colorado
Nestled in the sage and pinion country of Southwest Colorado, Mesa Verde RV Resort is simply the best-rated resort in the area. First-rate amenities and a dedicated and friendly staff will help make your stay enjoyable.

Aces High RV Park, East Lyme, Connecticut
Conveniently located off Interstate 95, Aces High RV Park sits on 93 acres of land, with its own large, trout-stocked pond, two other ponds, a pool and brand-new big-rig sites that offer cable, sewer, water and electric. You'll feel like you're far away from civilization while being just minutes from town.

Cross Creek RV Resort, Arcadia, Florida
Cross Creek RV Resort is a first-class, gated RV park. Each site is at least 40 feet by 75 feet, with 100-amp electric, paved parking for two cars and a large patio. Most of the sites at Cross Creek are rented annually, as the residents enjoy the "non-transient" nature of the resort.

Gulf Waters RV Resort, Fort Myers Beach, Florida
Experience the Sunshine State at its best at this resort, which offers weekend or seasonal camping. Own your own spacious site, belly up to the tiki bar, jump into the swimming pool or take a swing at the tennis courts.

Crystal Lake RV Resort, Naples, Florida
Savor the views of Crystal Lake as you settle into this luxurious RV resort. But don't let the waters entrance you. There's also great RV resort living, heated pools and three spas. Take in the sights and shops of Naples or stroll along miles of beaches.

Naples Motorcoach Resort & Boat Club, Naples, Florida
Own your own piece of Florida's "Paradise Coast" at Naples Motorcoach Resort. The resort offers large RV sites, upscale amenities, a grand clubhouse and canal lots with direct access to the Gulf of Mexico. Find your own "place in the sun" as one of the privileged owners at this resort.

The Great Outdoors RV, Nature & Golf Resort, Titusville, Florida
Reserve an RV site on a lake and enjoy the views of nature. The concrete pads and 50-amp service will accommodate your needs, and the pools and golf course will keep you busy. With special sections just for custom-built RV ports, this resort is something special.

Williston Crossings RV Resort, Williston, Florida
At Williston Crossings RV Resort, you just might lose track of time. Take in a stroll through the beautiful grounds or simply relax in the park reading your favorite book. All lots are well appointed to meet the needs of RV owners.

Cajun Palms RV Resort, Henderson, Louisiana

Travel deep into the heart of Cajun Country for a first-class resort in the midst of a tropical paradise. The friendly staff will make you feel at home with family-oriented entertainment and fun. Relax by the side of the pool or cruise around the 40-acre grounds.

Coushatta Luxury RV Resort At Red Shoes Park, Kinder, Louisiana

This is Louisiana's best bet for RV travelers. Enjoy 2,850 slots, 70 table games, six restaurants and a stellar RV resort with furnished chalets, two nightclubs, supervised childcare, a teen arcade, award-winning championship golf course and more.

A+ Motel & RV Park, Lake Charles, Louisiana

A+ is centrally located near Calcasieu "Big" Lake and other great fishing and hunting destinations. You'll also find casinos, horse racing and the Creole Nature Trail. Stay at one of 134 all-concrete RV sites with picnic tables, 50/30-amp hookups with cable and Wi-Fi at each site, stocked fishing and more.

Paragon Casino RV Resort, Marksville, Louisiana

A world of choices opens up for guests at Paragon Casino RV Resort. Relax in the luxurious RV park, which boasts a kids' playground and spacious lodge with a large pool, or take the short walk to the luxurious resort, where you can take to the greens or relax in the spa.

Cape Cod Campresort & Cabins, East Falmouth, Massachusetts

The rolling terrain of southwestern Cape Cod serves as the setting for this stunning resort. Take a dip in one of the three pools, the adult-only Jacuzzi or swim with the family at the beach. Enjoy the resort's own private lake and turn the kids loose on the playground.

Normandy Farms Family Camping Resort, Foxboro, Massachusetts

Nestled in the woods between Cape Cod and Boston lies an RV resort that has been a family tradition for four decades. Come spring, summer or fall, you can relax and enjoy a peaceful setting or participate in one of the many resort activities.

Pine Acres Family Camping Resort, Oakham, Massachusetts

Is there anything better than lakeside camping under towering pines? You'll find this and more at Pine Acres Family Camping Resort on Lake Dean. Nestled in the heart of New England, Pine Acres boasts full amenities, including a resort-style pool, kids' splash zone and adult spa.

Little River Casino RV Park, Manistee, Michigan

Little River Casino Resort has an RV park designed with all the comforts of home. Pull-through and back-in sites are available, along with clean restrooms and shower facilities, high-speed Wi-Fi, access to the hotel pool, sauna and fitness center and a dog run and walking trail.

Petoskey Motorcoach Resort, Petoskey, Michigan

The Petoskey Motorcoach Resort sets the standard for quality and beauty. Located in northern Michigan along Lake Michigan's shoreline, the resort features a grand lodge, tennis, Wi-Fi, pool, spa and saunas. Nearby, golf, fine dining and beaches beckon visitors.

Traverse Bay RV Resort, Traverse City, Michigan

Traverse Bay Motorcoach and RV Resort Community is a gorgeous, laid-back and affordable haven for luxury-seeking RVers. Located near a majestic Great Lake bay and surrounded by beaches, it's a wonderful retreat.

Grand Casino Hinckley RV Resort, Hinckley, Minnesota

Open year-round, the Grand Casino Hinckley RV Resort boasts 24-hour security, shuttle service to the casino, full hookups and sites as long as 60 feet. Hit the gambling tables or lay out a meal on the many picnic tables. Take a dip in the pool, or organize a group outing with fellow RVers.

Big Creek RV Park, Annapolis, Missouri

Although this was the ARVC Small Park of the Year winner, management puts the focus on guests, not awards. Take a dip in the relaxing pool, participate in the famous "duck" races, play in the arcade room or simply participate in the many planned activities. The park has private showers.

Mark Twain Landing, Monroe City, Missouri

This is the gateway to a wealth of boating, hunting, fishing and historical sightseeing pleasures. Golfers are in for a real treat, as Monroe City boasts two of the finest nine-hole golf courses in the entire region. The facilities include everything to make your stay a relaxed and pleasant experience.

Chipmunk Crossing RV Park, West Plains, Missouri

Located in the heart of the Ozarks, this RV resort sits in a quiet, rural setting that's worth the drive. Enjoy mostly shaded sites with picnic tables, a catch-and-release pond and recreation hall. Management cultivates an atmosphere that is both people-friendly and animal-friendly.

Las Vegas RV Resort, Las Vegas, Nevada

RVers expect only the best in Las Vegas, and Las Vegas RV Resort delivers. With beautiful resort-style amenities and state-of-the-art facilities, you can count on a quality stay. The resort boasts large pull-through sites, a lavish pool and gorgeous mountain views.

LVM Resort, Las Vegas, Nevada

LVM Resort puts guests close to the excitement of Las Vegas. But if you'd prefer to relax, you can chill out amid the lush tropical landscaping of this exclusive Class A resort. Moments away from world-class entertainment, shopping, dining and sporting events, guests can enjoy a secure environment.

Lakeside Casino & RV Resort, Pahrump, Nevada

Lakeside Casino & RV Resort offers a heated swimming pool and hot tub, kayaks, paddleboats, fishing, nine-hole Frisbee golf, pingpong and horseshoes. Swim in the lake lagoon or relax on the sandy beach under a cabana. Go gambling with the latest video and slot machines.

Nevada Treasure RV Resort, Pahrump, Nevada

Find vacation gold at Nevada Treasure RV Resort. World-class amenities and affordable rates combine to make the perfect RV escape. The perfectly manicured grounds and paved landscaped big-rig sites make it an ideal place for RVing.

Wine Ridge RV Resort & Cottages, Pahrump, Nevada

Less than an hour from the Vegas Strip, Wine Ridge RV Resort & Cottages is one of the most beautiful destination RV resort and lodging experiences in the Southwest. It's all new, all first class, and all at great value for you and your family.

Sparks Marina RV Park, Sparks, Nevada

Sparks Marina RV Park has fishing and swimming, and boasts 204 level sites, including 122 spacious pull-through sites. Connect to full hookups with 30/50-amp service, with a large clubhouse, fitness equipment and hot tub. The resort is adjacent to Outlets at Sparks.

Angel Fire Resort, Angel Fire, New Mexico

This family-friendly destination in the southern Rockies is open year-round. Partake in zip line adventures, mountain biking, fishing, great golf and many other fun-filled activities. Enjoy the heated pool, pickleball facilities and putting greens.

Skyway Camping Resort Inc., Ellenville, New York

Just a couple of hours north of New York City and nestled in the foothills of the Catskill Mountains, Skyway Camping Resort transports you to the splendor of nature, where cool mountain breezes and a scenic setting replace the complexities of city and suburban life.

Black Bear Campground Inc., Florida, New York

Tour the big city, then sleep in the country. Black Bear makes camping complete with outstanding amenities that includes rental cabins and NYC tours (in season). The campground is near West Point, the New York Renaissance Faire and Woodbury Common Premium Outlets.

The Villages at Turning Stone, Verona, New York

The Villages at Turning Stone offer recreational fun, championship golf, superb dining, full-service gaming, rejuvenating spas and headline entertainment. The excitement of Turning Stone is always close by, with great gambling and fabulous entertainment.

Raleigh Oaks RV Resort & Cottages, Four Oaks, North Carolina
This RV resort has over 150 RV Sites—both back-in and pull-thrus—with full hookups, including water, sewer, 30/50-amp electric, cable TV and Wi-Fi. Amenities include two swimming pools, spa, pickleball courts, fitness center, 18 private bath suites, two laundry facilities, dog park and club/rally room.

The Great Outdoors RV Resort, Franklin, North Carolina
The park is surrounded by the Great Smoky Mountains and the Blue Ridge Parkway. It is conveniently located off of Highway 441, about two hours north of Atlanta, an hour south of Asheville and close to Cherokee. Stay in big-rig sites within a wooded setting.

Fayetteville RV Resort & Cottages, Wade, North Carolina
Don't miss out on staying at this awesome RV resort when you are visiting or working in the Fort Bragg/Fayetteville area. For the military, the Fayetteville RV Resort is the perfect solution for short-term and long-term housing. Book your RV site and take advantage of the weekly/monthly/seasonal rates.

Cross Creek Camping Resort, Columbus, Ohio
The resort is 20 minutes north of Columbus on Interstate 71, exit 131. It's close to world-famous Columbus Zoo, Ohio State University and Muirfield, and next to Alum Creek Marina. Check out more than 120 restaurants and Polaris Fashion Place a mere 10 minutes away.

Evergreen Park RV Resort, Mount Eaton, Ohio
Located in the heart of Ohio's Amish Country, Evergreen Park RV Resort is a modern RV getaway that has a heated and enclosed pool, game room and shuffleboard. Extra-large pull-through sites accommodate the longest rigs.

Autumn Lakes, Sunbury, Ohio
Thirty minutes north of downtown Columbus, this RV resort is a short drive to the Columbus Zoo, the kid-friendly Center of Science and Industry, Ohio State University and Amish Country. Get pampered at the day spa, or enjoy the catering lodge.

WinStar RV Park, Thackerville, Oklahoma
Nestled in the southern Oklahoma foothills, WinStar RV Park offers lodging accommodations that are conveniently located next to the WinStar World Casino. Hit the golf course, set the kids loose at the playground, relax in the spa or go swimming in the pool.

Seven Feathers RV Resort, Canyonville, Oregon
Seven Feathers has all the ingredients for a rejuvenating RV trip. Relax on your RV site's patio, enjoy the heated pool and spa, workout in a state-of-the-art fitness room, use computers in the library lounge or meet friends and indulge in the Seven Feathers Hotel and Casino Resort.

Olde Stone Village RV Park, McMinnville, Oregon
Tree-lined streets and soft grassy knolls are just part of the appeal of Olde Stone Village, McMinnville Oregon's premier RV resort and community. The resort offers easy access to highways, as well as McMinnville's shops, restaurants, scenic vineyards and historic attractions.

Pacific Shores Motorcoach Resort, Newport, Oregon
Whether taking a leisurely stroll on the beach or a refreshing dip in one of two heated swimming pools, three saunas and two Jacuzzis, or relaxing by the cozy clubhouse fireplace, Pacific Shores offers the ultimate in luxury accommodations and service.

Hee Hee Illahee RV Resort, Salem, Oregon
Situated in the heart of the Willamette Valley, this resort offers a wide array of tourist attractions. Guests can stay and enjoy the seasonal outdoor pool, and the clubhouse offers a spa, fitness center, meeting and game rooms and kitchen.

Bend/Sisters Garden RV Resort, Sisters, Oregon
Find a home away from home at Bend/Sisters Garden RV Resort. Discover luxurious camping cabins and fully furnished cottages. Park your RV in a fully appointed site. Boasting full amenities and ample outdoor recreation, this resort is an ideal destination for families.

Casey's Riverside RV Park, Westfir, Oregon

Get a taste of lush, verdant Oregon at Casey's Riverside RV Park. Sitting on the banks of the Willamette River, guests can enjoy kayaking, canoeing, fishing, hiking or just relaxing in one of the peaceful riverside hammocks. Casey's is friendly, beautiful and heavenly.

Pheasant Ridge RV Resort, Wilsonville, Oregon

Find out why Pheasant Ridge RV Resort is a top-rated RV destination. Close to Portland, the coast, wine country, shopping and many Pacific Northwest attractions, this upscale RV facility sits on 45 wooded acres overlooking the Willamette Valley.

Shenango Valley RV Park, Sharon, Pennsylvania

From quiet, wooded sites backed up to the stream, to the convenience of concrete patios and pull-through sites, Shenango Valley RV Park serves up camping your way. The pet-friendly campsites are a minimum 40 feet wide and 75 feet in length.

Smoky Bear Campground, Gatlinburg, Tennessee

Nestled near Smoky Mountains National Park in beautiful east Tennessee, this park has it all. Come back to great amenities after a beautiful day of hiking or having a family picnic in the Great Smoky Mountains. You can just relax around the campsite.

Twin Creek RV Resort, Gatlinburg, Tennessee

Family owned and operated since 1984, you'll enjoy the peace and beauty of camping with all the comforts and conveniences of a full-service accommodation. Just imagine going to sleep with the sound of a rippling stream just outside your window.

Two Rivers Landing RV Resort, Sevierville, Tennessee

This is a luxury RV resort, featuring large, fully landscaped concrete sites on the banks of the beautiful French Broad River. Relax in the well-appointed clubhouse, and then enjoy being close to all the major attractions of this compelling region.

K.E. Bushman's Camp, Bullard, Texas

K.E. Bushman's Camp offers four gazebo barbecue and campfire areas, private bathhouses with all-inclusive shower suites and restrooms, free Wi-Fi Internet access and an all-season pool and hot tub. The RV resort is a short stroll from the Kiepersol Estates, a food and wine destination.

Mill Creek Ranch Resort, Canton, Texas

Seconds away from the world-famous First Monday Trade Days and Free State Bluegrass Festival, Mill Creek Ranch Resort boasts two pools, a spa, a playground, fishing, biking, paddleboats, a large gift shop, big-rig friendly sites, and cottage rentals and sales.

Alsatian RV Resort & Golf Club, Castroville, Texas

Enjoy indoor and outdoor dining, along with cocktails, serenity spa, luxurious casitas, lovely garden pavilion, live music, infinity pool, golf, fitness room, walk path, concrete roads and pads and much more.

Galveston Island RV Resort, Galveston, Texas

This newly constructed RV resort is located on the scenic West End of Galveston Island, away from the crowds but still close to the beaches and convenient to the many attractions of the city of Galveston. This new RV resort offers top-quality amenities and beautiful natural surroundings.

Jamaica Beach RV Resort, Galveston, Texas

Jamaica Beach RV Resort is one of Galveston Island's newest RV parks. Located just past the beautiful city of Jamaica Beach, this resort is right across the street from the beach and has an unobstructed view of the Galveston Bay area and the Gulf of Mexico.

Shallow Creek RV Resort, Gladewater, Texas

Shallow Creek RV Resort is nestled in the Piney Woods of east Texas. The park offers 63 oversized RV sites. Amenities include cable TV, wireless Internet access and a 5,000-square-foot clubhouse with full kitchen. Cool off in the pool during the toasty east Texas summer.

San Jacinto Riverfront RV Park, Highlands, Texas

Located less than 20 miles east of downtown Houston, this peaceful and quiet park sits high on the riverbank, with a serene view of the famous San Jacinto Monument, where Texas' independence was won in 1836. The 33-acre park features more than 300 full-hookup RV pads.

Advanced RV Resort, Houston, Texas

Located near the intersection of South Beltway 8 and Highway 288, just 12 miles south of downtown Houston, Advanced RV Resort features cable TV, Wi-Fi, hot tub, heated pool, laundry room and rec building. Directly accessible is Tom Bass Regional Park.

Katy Lake RV Resort, Katy, Texas

Katy Lake RV Resort is a full-service, adult-only RV resort. In addition to RV spaces, the resort has six furnished luxury park models available for rent. Amenities include free Wi-Fi and DirecTV, an activity center, two indoor TV viewing areas, one outdoor TV viewing area, a lighted water fountain, exercise room, walking/jogging trail, dog park and walk-in pool with hot tub.

Buckhorn Lake Resort, Kerrville, Texas

Located in the heart of Texas Hill Country, guests will find everything they'd expect from a top-rated RV resort. Designed with large rigs and rallies in mind with an 8,000-square-foot event center, the resort accommodates both large and small groups for rallies and gatherings.

Johnson Creek RV Resort & Park, Kerrville, Texas

Voted the No. 1 small RV resort in Texas, this RV resort and park is nestled in a pecan orchard in the Texas Hill Country along the Johnson Creek. The park exit is off Interstate 10 and sets back off Highway 27. Enjoy the natural beauty, along with views of wildlife.

Rio Bonito RV & Cabin, Liberty Hill, Texas

Rio Bonito RV resort in Texas sits on 14 acres along the river and is easily accessible to Austin, Cedar Park, Round Rock, Georgetown and Leander. Rio Bonito provides a quiet, peaceful camping environment and is the perfect getaway to Texas Hill Country, with fishing, tubing, swimming, biking, relaxing and more.

Fernbrook Park, Longview, Texas

Sitting on 35 acres, Fernbrook Park is the perfect place to relax and explore the east Texas Piney Woods. Enjoy a serene country setting, walking trails, saltwater pool, disc golf, manicured FHU sites, clean home-style bathrooms and laundry facilities.

Bentsen Palm Village RV Resort, Mission, Texas

Lush landscapes and exotic wildlife define this south Texas destination. Bentsen Palm Village RV Resort is surrounded by 3,000 acres of state and federally protected parks, miles of hiking and bike trails, kayaking and other attractions.

Forest Retreat RV Park, New Caney, Texas

Experience Houston camping at its finest. Forest Retreat is convenient to the Kingswood/Humble area and all the best of the greater Houston area. Relax in a serene country setting with walking trails, a saltwater pool, home-style bathrooms and laundry facilities.

Texas Lakeside RV Resort, Port Lavaca, Texas

Located just north of Rockport and 1 mile off of State Highway 35, this is a brand-new, privately owned, gated luxury RV resort. Boasting the largest big-rig sites, the park's amenities include a crystal-clear pool and hot tub, and a paved walking track around the lake.

Northlake Village RV Park, Roanoke, Texas

Enjoy quiet country living near Dallas. Beautiful sites with paved patios and easy access, close to all that DFW has to offer. Only 3 minutes to Texas Motor Speedway and 15 minutes to Fort Worth and Denton. Book your reservations now for a short or long term stay.

Oak Creek RV Park, Weatherford, Texas

Oak Creek RV Park in Weatherford provides guests with high-quality facilities and superior service. RVers staying in the 120 spacious sites enjoy free Wi-Fi and cable TV. A spacious reception hall is great for gatherings, and the pool and hot tub will help you unwind.

Rayford Crossing RV Resort, The Woodlands, Texas
Rayford Crossing RV Resort boasts superior service and total tranquility. The park has a heated pool and spa, Wi-Fi, a great clubhouse, an exercise room, game room, beautiful bathhouses and concrete sites. An on-site activity director and rally facilities keep the good times rolling.

Mountain Valley RV Resort, Heber City, Utah
The highest-rated park in Utah, this family-friendly resort, just off Highway 40 in Heber City, is open year round and sheltered by the stunning Rocky Mountains of the Heber Valley. Guests can enjoy the absolute best in full-service RV lifestyle and accommodations.

Spokane RV Resort at Deer Park Golf Club, Deer Park, Washington
Spokane RV Resort is surrounded by a rolling 18-hole golf course, fresh air, views of the nearby mountains, gorgeous sunsets and a quiet ambiance. RVers can enjoy one of the spacious paved sites with full hookups, including 50-amp service and Wi-Fi. A large heated swimming pool and hot tub are available.

Columbia Sun RV Resort, Kennewick, Washington
Guests at this RV resort have access to both the countryside and nearby city. The region has beautiful weather year round. The park is centrally located, just minutes from Interstate 82. Nearby are 160 wineries, 67 miles of paved trails, three minor league sports teams, four waterfront parks and more.

North Spokane RV Campground, Spokane, Washington
North Spokane RV Campground caters to RVers seeking an overnight stay or long-term vacation. Located just minutes from downtown Spokane, this resort is within walking distance to shopping, entertainment and dining. The beautifully landscaped resort is only a short drive to some of the region's finest outdoor recreation areas.

Bissell's Hideaway Resort, Pelham, Ontario
With camping, cottages and cabins, a water park, resort amenities and facilities for group events, Bissell's Hideaway Resort is the ideal place for a fun-filled family vacation. Activities include an arcade, walk-in pool, playground, paddleboats, and basketball and volleyball courts.

Camping Alouette - Parkbridge, Saint-Mathieu-De-Beloeil, Quebec
With a beautiful year-round view, Alouette is situated between Mont-Saint-Hilaire and Mont-Saint-Bruno. The resort offers full-service seasonal and overnight voyager sites with limited service in the winter.

Camping La Cle Des Champs RV Resort, Saint-Philippe, Quebec
Within 20 minutes of this fine resort sits downtown Montreal and a fun casino. The bilingual staff will greet you with a smile and help you plan your visit. Relax at the newly renovated pool and plan trips to fascinating nearby attractions.

Bella Terra of Gulf Shores, Gulf Shores, Alabama
Bella Terra is the Emerald Coast's premier luxury outdoor RV resort, ideally located minutes from the sugar-white beaches of Gulf Shores and Orange Beach, Alabama and Perdido Key, Florida. This tranquil, tropical retreat sits on approximately 40 acres of land with a 9-acre centerpiece lake. The resort's 6,000-square-foot clubhouse features a movie theater and fitness center.

Sugar Sands RV Resort, Gulf Shores, Alabama
Sugar Sands RV Resort harkens back to the simpler time of family sightseeing, with all the modern conveniences. The craftsman-style coastal architecture is reminiscent of early-20th-century beach destinations, where new friends can gather under the awning and share memories.

Superstition Lookout RV Resort, Apache Junction, Arizona
Whether you're looking for a permanent place to call home, a winter getaway destination or just an overnight stay, you will feel welcomed, relaxed and comfortable. These communities are the place for you.

Queen Valley RV Resort, Queen Valley, Arizona
Queen Valley RV Resort is an extended-stay adult park in the heart of the Superstition Mountains. Boasting fresh air and beautiful views, Queen Valley RV Resort offers an 18-hole golf course along with nearby hiking trails, ATV trails and four-wheel-drive areas. Park models are available, along with planned activities and pickleball.

Outdoor Resort Palm Springs, Cathedral City, California
Enjoy a comfortable stay in the heart of the Coachella Valley, minutes away from excellent entertainment and recreation. It's a completely self-contained, five-star resort with golf, tennis, swimming, fitness center, restaurants and convenience store.

Motorcoach Country Club, Indio, California
Boasting sweeping views of the Santa Rosa and La Quinta mountains, this unique Motorcoach Country Club provides an exclusive experience to its guests. Enjoy private lots, ample golf, waterfront lots with boat docks and a mile-long navigable waterway.

Outdoor Resort Indio, Indio, California
It's the ultimate Class A experience. Take the plunge into the creatively designed activities, or relax amid superb amenities. Bask in the warmth of Indio's winter sun for a snowbird vacation that you won't forget.

Pueblo South/Colorado City KOA, Colorado City, Colorado
Planning a trip to the Pueblo area? This park is in a mountain setting yet just minutes from the city. Enjoy the heated pool or adult-only hot tub, work out in the fitness center, play a game of mini-golf or join in the planned activities, barbecues, breakfasts and dessert socials. Groups are welcome.

Outdoor Resorts/Chokoloskee Island, Chokoloskee, Florida
At Outdoor Resorts/Chokoloskee Island, guests can relax and enjoy a private tropical island retreat surrounded by clear Gulf waters. Boasting a marina, this paradise is also a sport fishing destination. Relish the three pools, sauna, whirlpools, tennis courts, boat rentals, and bait and tackle shop.

Cypress Trail RV Resort, Fort Myers, Florida
Enjoy RV living at a fraction of the price. Off Interstate 75, you'll experience excellent RV fun: clubhouse/fitness room, pool/hot tub, tennis and pickleball courts, and fishing at the lake—even a nature preserve. Great shopping and dining are nearby. Included are great interior roads, RV storage, a self-service RV wash and more.

RiverBend Motorcoach Resort, La Belle, Florida
RiverBend covers more than 120 acres, has four lakes and boasts three preserved wooded conservation areas. With a boat launch, boat slips and access to the Gulf of Mexico and Atlantic Ocean via the Okeechobee Waterway, it's a boater's paradise.

Disney's Fort Wilderness Resort & Campground, Lake Buena Vista, Florida
Disney's Fort Wilderness Resort & Campground evokes the timeless beauty of the American frontier, with deer, rabbits, ducks and armadillos roaming the resort's 750 acres of pine and cypress forest. Discover charming woodland trails, a pristine beach, spectacular pool areas and rip-roarin' entertainment at this picturesque backcountry retreat.

Emerald Coast RV Beach Resort, Panama City Beach, Florida
Treat yourself to a stay at a spectacular RV resort. The luxurious beach resort sits on several beautifully manicured acres in the heart of Panama City. Beautiful beaches lapped by warm ocean water will make you want to extend your stay indefinitely.

Beach Rose RV Park, Salisbury Beach, Massachusetts
Beach Rose RV Park is the closest private campground to the Atlantic Ocean at Salisbury Beach. Enjoy Wi-Fi, gated security, 50 big-rig sites, full-hookup sites, top-notch laundry facilities, cable TV, paved roads and an enclosed dog run. The great city of Boston is just a short train ride away.

Vacation Station RV Resort, Ludington, Michigan
As the name implies, Vacation Station is your first and only stop for family fun. Enjoy the great outdoors and then savor a great meal at one of the nearby restaurants. Shopping in town is great, and the resort is just minutes from Michigan beaches.

Silver Creek RV Resort, Mears, Michigan
Great family vacation memories are made at Silver Creek RV Resort. Walk the beautiful Lake Michigan beaches, climb the shifting sand dunes, take in the nearby tourist attractions or simply relax and enjoy the park's fabulous amenities. It's a great place for the whole family.

Harbortown RV Resort, Monroe, Michigan
Take your family to the go-kart park or visit the Henry Ford Museum during your stay at this top-rated resort. Lots of trees, a beautiful pond and creek at the family golf center, landscaped grounds and family-friendly campground amenities make it a great place for the whole family.

Soaring Eagle Hideaway RV Park, Mount Pleasant, Michigan
Open April through October, this park's sites each include a cement pad, grill and fire pit. Also included is a camp stove and wireless Internet. Have fun in the game room, on the beach or in the swimming area. The campground also has a clean bathhouse and showers.

Duck Creek RV Resort, Muskegon, Michigan
The RV resort is conveniently located next to Michigan's Adventure Amusement Park between the lakefront towns of Muskegon and Whitehall. Guests can enjoy Lake Michigan beaches, boating, fishing, golf, summer festivals, museums and amusement park thrills. The resort includes a heated pool and rec hall.

Petoskey KOA RV & Cabin Resort, Petoskey, Michigan
Let your dreams come true at the Petoskey RV Resort at Bay Harbor. See the local wildlife as you stroll along the walking paths or hone your swing on the resort's nine-hole greens. With so many great amenities and opportunities for fun, you'll feel like a kid again.

South Haven Sunny Brook RV Resort, South Haven, Michigan
Sunny Brook RV Resort offers luxury as well as an ownership opportunity. Hang out at the 6,000-square-foot clubhouse, or take a dip in the heated pool and hot tub. There's also a fitness room, game room, free Wi-Fi and a 5-acre lake.

Prairie View RV Park & Campground, Granite Falls, Minnesota
Located 3 miles south of Granite Falls, Prairie's Edge Casino Resort boasts everything you need for the ultimate RV getaway. RVers can enjoy all the comforts of home at the well-appointed campground.

Polson Motorcoach & RV Resort, Polson, Montana
Attain the very best in luxury RV resort living. This elite Class A resort community is nestled in the heart of Montana's Flathead Lake region. In addition to great amenities, the park boasts stellar views of Flathead Lake and the Mission Mountains. Best of all, the staff will help you customize your own luxury lifestyle.

Chautauqua Lake KOA, Dewittville, New York
Chautauqua Lake KOA offers a complete Chautauqua Lake camping experience with plenty of fun activities to enjoy right there, including a heated swimming pool, playground, basketball, volleyball, horseshoes, a game room, nature trails, a book and video library and many more fun amenities.

Triple R Camping Resort & Trailer Sales, Franklinville, New York
This is a family-run, pet-friendly facility welcoming everyone to try the Triple R experience. Triple R Camping Resort & Trailer Sales prides itself in being the cleanest, most service oriented facility in the country, with onsite RV service and a well stocked RV parts store.

Lake George RV Park, Lake George, New York
Lake George RV Park added a state-of-the-art dog park for the campers' canine friends along with the bike trails, heated swimming pools, arcades and a fishing pond for the kids to enjoy. Work out at the fitness center, sit in an air-conditioned movie theater and enjoy great live professional entertainment.

Branches of Niagara Campground and Resort, Niagara Falls, New York
Located on Grand Island, Branches of Niagara Campground is a perfect location to enjoy the outdoors with your family in a spacious RV site. Guests can sit on the shore of an 8-acre scenic lake, go fishing, launch a boat or even take a ride on our zip line. It's only 10 minutes from the American Falls State Park and the border with Canada.

Watkins Glen/Corning KOA Camping Resort, Watkins Glen, New York
Stay at one of the spacious RV sites in a park located in the fabulous Finger Lakes region of New York. The Watkins Glen KOA Campground offers amenities that include the ever-popular indoor heated pool and spa, as well as a fitness center, camp and gift store. There's an open pavilion and meeting and conference room.

Mountain Falls Luxury Motorcoach Resort, Lake Toxaway, North Carolina

Situated in the majestic Blue Ridge Mountains, this luxury resort has tranquil lakes, fabulous waterfalls and pristine nature trails in proximity to the property. Guests can dive right into the outdoor activities, from canoeing to rafting, hiking and fishing to motorcycling.

Choctaw Casino Resort KOA, Durant, Oklahoma

Join family and friends for good times and lasting memories in this award-winning RV resort. With all the comforts and amenities that make a top-rated RV Park, Choctaw KOA RV Park features 12-foot-by-80-foot pull-through sites, 50-amp service and free Wi-Fi.

Lake-In-Wood Resort, Narvon, Pennsylvania

Explore covered bridges and Amish country. With an atmosphere straight out of a fairy tale, the whole family will love the resort's scenic grounds and unique rentals. Cool down at the pool, get creative with planned activities or have a meal at the Gnome Cafe.

Hilton Head Harbor RV Resort & Marina, Hilton Head Island, South Carolina

Enjoy a scenic waterside resort with landscaped sites and concrete pads. Dine on a fine meal at the Sunset Grille after chartering a boat at the marina. Beautiful beaches and premier golf are just minutes away. RV lots are also for sale at this top-rated resort.

Hilton Head Island Motorcoach Resort, Hilton Head Island, South Carolina

Located on 50 acres of woodland on a dream island off the South Carolina coast, Hilton Head delivers an unbeatable RV experience. Relax amid live oaks dripping with Spanish moss, palms, ferns and flowering shrubs. Guests can enjoy golf, restaurants, bike paths and beaches.

WillowTree RV Resort & Campground, Longs, South Carolina

Unwind in a spacious RV site in a family- and pet-friendly environment. With the theme "Peaceful, Easy Camping," the park puts guests in the right state of mind. The park is minutes from the beach and features the Summit Slide and a 36-acre lake.

Ocean Lakes Family Campground, Myrtle Beach, South Carolina

Situated on more than 300 acres along 1 mile of white, sandy beach, the Ocean Lakes Family Campground boasts a 2-acre recreation area with its own pool area with sun decks, a game center and miniature golf course with a fisherman's wharf theme.

Anchor Down RV Resort, Dandridge, Tennessee

Located on beautiful Douglas Lake, Anchor Down RV Resort's luxurious amenities include 175 spacious sites, lakefront and lake view sites, concrete pad, free Wi-Fi Internet access and bathhouse with private bathrooms.

Llano Grande Lake Park Resort & Country Club MHP, Mercedes, Texas

Llano Grande Resort is a 55+ active adult community located in Mercedes, the Queen City of the marvelous Rio Grande Valley, surrounded by citrus groves and palm trees in a beautiful, tropical setting. The park is a world away from the cares of city life, yet freeway close to all that makes southern Texas the destination of choice for many travelers.

Fisherman's Cove Tent & Trailer Park, Kincardine, Ontario

Fisherman's Cove Tent and Trailer Park sits on 250 acres with approximately 500 sites in the RV park. The resort is nestled in a wonderful forest that is a home to birds, deer and many other forms of wildlife. The resort features a 9,300-square-foot clubhouse with an indoor pool.

Woodland Park, Sauble Beach, Ontario

This tranquil park is situated in a setting surrounded by beautiful hills and trees. Park grounds are beautifully landscaped and maintained in pristine condition for guests. It's the closest park to downtown Sauble Beach and a five-minute walk to one of Canada's top-rated beaches.

KOA Bas-St-Laurent Campground, Saint-Mathieu-De-Rioux, Quebec

Explore the eastern St. Lawrence area and stay in the warmer climate of this bilingual resort. There's a swimmable lake with dock, boat rentals, playground and jumping pillow. Check out the heated pool, spa, splash pad, rec building and fitness equipment.

Win the Numbers Game

Read an RV park's Good Sam Ratings before planning to stay there

Before you make reservations at an RV park, check out its Good Sam rating. These three simple numbers serve as a report card that evaluates an RV park's overall quality.

The first number in the rating grades a campground's facilities, the second number rates cleanliness of restrooms and showers, and the third rates environment and visual appearance. Each number is based on a scale from 1 to 10, with 10 being the highest score.

For each of the three ratings categories, a campground may receive 1 point, a half-point or no points. A small percentage of campgrounds attain the coveted 10/10★/10 rating, meaning top marks in every category (see our list of perfect parks on page 145). A park must receive a minimum 5/7/5 rating and meet specific minimum requirements within each category to qualify as a Good Sam Park.

Each campground's rating is determined by a Good Sam Review Team. These highly trained RVers travel thousands of miles each year to personally inspect and rate private RV parks and campgrounds. In all, 34 teams crisscrossed North America throughout 2015 in preparation for the 2016 edition, making unannounced visits to the RV park and taking a complete tour of each facility to compile their reports.

Over the years, the directory's editors and inspectors have used feedback from RVers and individual professionals to hone our ratings system. We believe this evaluation tool accurately gauges a campground's level of quality. If you're curious about how we determine our ratings, try it for yourself at the next RV park you visit. The ratings guidelines on the following three pages are identical to those used by our review teams. Use these guidelines to see how our results compare with your findings.

If you have any suggestions, email us at: **info@goodsamfamily.com**

Good Sam RATED 10/10★/10

RATED 10/10★/10

RATING CATEGORIES

Facilities: Evaluates the level of development of RV sites, hookups, recreation, swimming, security, laundry services, interior roads, registration area and Internet access.

Restrooms and Showers: Rates the cleanliness and physical characteristics of toilets, walls, showers, sinks/counters/mirrors and floor. If a park achieves a full point in each of the above, it receives a star (★) that indicates exceptionally clean restrooms. Also rated are restrooms' interior construction, odor, supplies, number of facilities, interior appearance, exterior appearance and location as it relates to park sites.

Visual Appearance: Appraises the park's setting and site layout, function and identification of signage, overall exterior building maintenance, noise, trash disposal, litter and debris around the grounds and sites, and appearance of the grounds, sites and entrance area.

CAMPGROUNDS & RV PARKS

A full point should be awarded in a category only if the amenity is outstanding.
If not best in each category, rate down 1/2 point.

DEFINTION OF ALL-WEATHER SURFACE: *Unpaved surface that is constructed of crushed concrete, crushed stone, crushed shell, brick or gravel, compacted materials,* ***deep enough*** *that does not create mud during rainfall or kicks up dust in dry conditions.*

	0 Points	1/2 point	1 point
______	**INTERIOR ROADS (Assessing roads used by overnight RV's in park.) :**		
	Grass, dirt, pine needles, sand or gravel/dirt. Narrow, steep or hazardous. In poor condition (potholes, ruts, or tree roots.)	Gravel, stone, shell or highly compacted sand or all weather surface. Reasonably mud/dust free with good drainage and the surface is in good condition and/or less than 12' wide. 14' overhead clearance across the full width of the road.	Paved (asphalt, concrete, or chip seal) or all-weather roads professionally constructed with good drainage and the surface is in superior condition (very few potholes or cracks in surface pavement). That is dust/mud free. Roads have adequate maneuverability. Roads are a minimum 12' wide for one-way, or 18' for two-way. 14' overhead clearance across the full width of the road.
______	**REGISTRATION (Assessing how customers register, check in and pay for sites):**		
	Self-service registration or part-time staff. Unsheltered outside pay window for office and registration, or no office exists. No registration procedure for off-hours.	Part-time staff with regular posted hours of business. Enclosed office in residence or sheltered outside pay window. Signage clearly directs where to register. Registration procedure for off-hours.	Separate business office with full time staff and regular posted hours of business. Signage clearly directs where to register. Registration procedures for off-hours.
______	**SITES (An assessment of RV site construction, preparation and drainage.):**		
	Greater than 50% of sites not level. Undesignated or unidentifiable sites with no prepared surface. Poor site drainage that may create mud/dust buildup in adverse weather conditions.	Greater than 50% of sites are level and have easy access. Clearly designated or identifiable sites with a graded prepared surface of gravel, grass, dirt, shell, or all-weather surface in reasonable condition. Site drainage that is reasonably dust free of mud/dust buildup in adverse weather conditions.	100 % of sites have easy access and 14' overhead clearance. Clearly designated or identifiable sites with paved (asphalt, concrete, or chip seal) or All-weather surface professionally constructed with good drainage and the surface is in good condition that is dust/mud free. Minimal leveling needed for RV.
______	**HOOKUPS (An assessment of water, electric and sewer hookups, pedestals and dump stations. Tent sites excluded):**		
	Less than 50% of sites have water and electric hookups. Sub-standard, non-professional water, sewer or electric hookups. Hookups in poor condition. No dump station.	Greater than 50% of sites with 30 amp electric service and water hookups professionally constructed and in very good condition. Dump station in good repair with faucet, hose, capped receptacle and surrounding catch basin located within the park.	Underground utilities with all hookups professionally constructed and in good repair. 100% full hookups, no dump station required OR majority of sites with full hookups and remaining sites having water and electricity plus a dump station with faucet, hose, capped receptacle and surrounding basin available within the park. All hookups on driver's side. Majority of overnight/short term sites have electric receptacles with 30 or 50 amp service, with a minimum of 25% having 50 amps.

FULL	W	S	E

______ **RECREATION (circle applicable items, bold items = major):**

No Minors/No Majors	Two Items with a Minimum of One Major	Four Items with a Minimum of Two Majors

Badminton, basketball, bicycle rentals, **billiard room (min. 2 tables), boat marina**, boat dock, boat rentals, **bocce ball, bounce pillow**, children's activities, **driving range, exercise room (enclosed, min. 200 sq. ft. w/varied equipment)**, fishing, **Frisbee golf, game room (enclosed, min. 200 sq. ft. w/varied equipment), golf, horseback riding**, horseshoes, ladder ball, **lawn bowling, lawn chess**, mini-golf (non-professional construction), **mini-golf (professionally constructed)**, nature trails, **outdoor games (any 3 outdoor games = 1 major)**, paddle boats, pavilion (min. 200 sq. ft.), pedal carts, **pickle ball**, planned activities, playground, pool room (one table), **putting green, rec hall (enclosed min. 500 sq. ft.), sauna**, shuffleboard court, **shuffleboard courts (2 or more)**, softball, **splash pad, tennis**, things to see and do nearby, **tourist attraction (owned by and adjacent to park)**, volleyball, **wading pool, water slide, water umbrella, whirlpool (spa or hot tub)**.

Other minors:______________________________ **Other majors (Director approval required):**______________________________

	0 Points	1/2 point	1 point
______	**SWIMMING:**		
	Poorly maintained swimming pool or designated swimming area.	Well-maintained above ground pool or designated, well-maintained beach area on lake, river or ocean.	Well maintained in-ground swimming pool. Fence and concrete around pool in excellent condition.
______	**SECURITY:**		
	Park not enclosed. No daytime staff. No public or private phone available for emergency use.	Park partially enclosed by a man-made or natural boundary with part-time or daytime staff on site. Lighted office area. Emergency phone available but not posted.	Park fully enclosed by a man made or natural boundary including a controlled access gate. If there is no controlled access gate, staff resides or is present in the park 24/7. Emergency phone or night staff location is posted at the office and/or in park brochure. The area around the office, restrooms and laundry are well lighted.
______	**LAUNDRY:**		
	Outside location or laundry equipment located inside only one restroom. Area and washers/dryers are not clean and/or not operational. Washers/Dryers have excessively worn appearance. Only 1 washer and 1 dryer for the entire park.	Machines operational but require some minor cleaning and/or maintenance. Minimum of 2 washers and 2 dryers (25 sites or less OK for 1 washer/1 dryer). Excessively worn appearance. Area needs some minor cleaning or attention. Semi-enclosed location or incomplete interior construction.	Commercial quality washers/dryers clean and all are operational, in superior condition with very little wear and tear with a minimum of 2 washers and 2 dryers. Fully enclosed clean facility, finished interior construction with vinyl or tiled floors and painted or tiled walls. Must have a folding table and a hanging rack (or hooks).

______ **SERVICES (circle applicable items, bold items = major):**

No Minors/No Majors	Any Two Items	Four Items with a Minimum of Two Majors

Arrange appointments (e.g. for doctor, dentist, hair dresser, nail salon, pet grooming, restaurant reservations, RV repair, tour show tickets, veterinarian, other_______), ATM Machine, boat storage, BBQ at site, **car rentals, cable/TV service (25+ channels)**, cable/TV service (less than 25 channels), **church services (in season), cocktail lounge, complimentary breakfast (daily)**, dog run (fenced), **dog park**, DVD rentals, **entertainment, fax/copy service**, fire rings, **firewood, fishing guides, golf cart rentals, groceries, guest services (minimum of 3 to list), horse corral**, ice, library/book exchange, LP bottles only, **LP gas (metered)**, mail delivery, **newspaper (delivered free to site weekdays)**, newspaper available, patios, **personal escort to site, pet boarding, pet grooming, public phone available 24/7, rental units, restaurant, RV storage (secured)**, RV storage (unsecured), **RV supplies**, RV wash (self-service at site), **shuttle service**, snack bar, **Staffed RV wash (on site), spa services, table at site, trash pickup at site (daily).**

Other minors:______________________________ **Other majors (Director approval required):**______________________________

	0 Points	1/2 point	1 point
______	**INTERNET ACCESS:**		
	Office or pay phone access or no internet access.	Minimum of 25% of overnight sites have at least one of the following: Wi-Fi, a designated central hot spot, or 2 or more central modem hookups (DSL or phone).	Minimum of 50% of available sites have WiFi.

______ **TOTAL RATING**

MUST HAVE 5 POINTS OVERALL TO QUALIFY FOR GOOD SAM PARK MEMBERSHIP.

RESTROOMS & SHOWERS

A full point should be awarded in a category only if the amenity is outstanding.
If not best in each category, rate down 1/2 point.

	0 Points	1/2 point	1 point
		CLEANLINESS	
■ ____ **TOILETS:**	Cleaning required on interior/exterior surfaces and/or exterior pedestals on all or most toilets. Or multiple toilet seats cracked or missing.	Clean interior and most or all toilets are fully operational. Cleaning is required on some interior/exterior surfaces and/or exterior pedestals. No cracked or missing toilet seats.	Clean interior/exterior surfaces and/or exterior pedestals and all are fully operational. No cracked or missing toilet seats.
■ ____ **SHOWERS:**	Showers have unacceptable amount of dirt, mildew, or soap buildup on floors, walls, shower curtains or around drains. Shower floor mats have unacceptable dirt or grime underneath them.	Showers have some dirt, mildew or soap buildup on floors, walls, shower curtains or around drains. Shower floor mats have some dirt or grime underneath them.	All showers are clean and free of dirt, mildew and soap buildup on floors, walls, shower curtains and around drains. Shower floor mats have no dirt or grime underneath them.
■ ____ **FLOORS:**	Floors have unacceptable amount of dirt, mildew, litter or insects.	Floors have some dirt, mildew, litter or insects.	Floors clean and free of dirt, mildew, litter and insects.
■ ____ **WALLS:**	Unacceptable amount of dirt, mildew, insects or webs on walls, ceilings, light fixtures, vents, dividers or window sills.	Have some dirt, mildew, insects or webs on walls, ceilings, light fixtures, vents, dividers, window sills or doors.	Clean and free of mildew, insects and webs on walls, ceilings, light fixtures, vents, dividers, window sills and doors.
■ ____ **SINKS/COUNTERS/MIRRORS/HARDWARE:**	Unacceptable amount of dirt, mildew, or soap buildup on sinks, counters, hardware or mirrors.	Have some dirt, mildew or soap buildup on sinks, counters or hardware. Mirrors require cleaning.	Clean and free of dirt, mildew and soap buildup. Clean mirrors.
		PHYSICAL CHARACTERISTICS	
____ **INTERIOR CONSTRUCTION:**	No doors/curtains on toilet or shower stalls. Dividers between toilets, showers or dressing rooms are curtains or an unpainted porous surface. Incomplete construction on interior walls or ceilings. Non-professional utility installation. Cold water only in showers or sinks. Semi-enclosed restrooms or not fully enclosed.	Fully enclosed restrooms. Privacy in toilets and shower areas. Toilet stalls have lockable doors. No dressing rooms. Painted partitions for shower walls. Dividers between toilets and dressing rooms have a solid, water resistant surface. Concrete block, plaster, painted, wallpapered, or marlite-type walls. Floors are concrete (bare, painted or un-sealed stain) or carpeted. Counters or shelves for toiletries are unpainted, or no counters or shelves for toiletries. Professional utility installation. Hot water in sinks and showers.	Hardware, fixtures, & construction of professional quality. Privacy in toilets, showers & dressing rooms with clothes hooks and seating and toilet stall doors must be solid material and lockable. Adequate electrical outlets conveniently located. Hot water in sinks and showers. **FLOORS:** Surface of ceramic tile (no missing tile or grout) or vinyl floor covering, or epoxy painted or sealed concrete. **WALLS:** Surface of ceramic tile (no missing tiles or grout) Formica-type, fiberglass, cultured marble (minimum 3' high for all). **SHOWERS:** Surface of ceramic tile (no missing tiles or grout), Formica-type, fiberglass, cultured marble, stainless steel. No exposed plumbing. **COUNTERS, SHELVES FOR TOILETRIES:** Surface of ceramic tile (no missing tile or grout), Formica-type, cultured marble, Corian, stainless steel, glass or shelac wood.
____ **SUPPLIES/ODOR FREE:**	No venting or odor is noticeable. No paper products or trash disposal.	Minimum open air venting that is sufficient to keep room odor free, or no access to switch for power venting. Toilet paper available, but no hand drying materials available. Free of trash with adequate trash disposal containers.	Power exhaust fans or AC run continuously during peak hours (6am-10pm) or they are available on demand (switch or motion sensor only). Odor free. Toilet paper and hand drying materials available and are in proper supply. Free of trash with clean and adequate trash disposal containers.
____ **AMOUNT OF FACILITIES (Men & Women):**			
		PARKS WITH LESS THAN 100% FULL HOOKUPS	
	One toilet & one shower for entire park.	Minimum of 2 showers & 2 toilets each for men & women (or 2 showers, 1 toilet & 1 urinal for men).	Minimum of 3 showers & 3 toilets each for men & women (or 3 showers, 2 toilets & 1 urinal for men).

	MAIN		SATELLITE	
	MEN	WOMEN	MEN	WOMEN
TOILETS				
SHOWERS				

	0 Points	1/2 point	1 point
		PARKS WITH 100% FULL HOOKUPS	
	One toilet & one shower for entire park.	Minimum of 1 shower & 1 toilet each for men & women.	Minimum of 2 showers & 2 toilets each for men & women (or 2 showers, 1 toilet & 1 urinal for men).
____ **EXTERIOR APPEARANCE AND CONDITION BATHROOM BUILDINGS:**	Non-professional construction. Building exterior, doorways and windows require major repair or painting or needs web removal or cleaning or roof and gutters require major repair. Walkways around buildings are unsafe and require major repair.	Semi-professionally construction. Building exterior, doorways and windows require some cleaning or web removal or painting or minor repair. Roof and gutters require some minor repair. Walkways around buildings safe but require some minor repair.	Professional construction (skirting required if off ground). Building exterior is well maintained including doorways and windows, clean in appearance, free of webs and in good repair. No repairs required to roof or gutters. Walkways around buildings, safe and no repair required.
____ **INTERIOR APPEARANCE:**	Needs remodeling or overall repair. Excessive hard water deposits, pitting, rusting, chipping or cracking of dividers, hardware, vents, sinks or toilets. Floor surface in poor condition with excessive cracks, missing tiles or chips. Excessive graffiti. Poor lighting throughout the restroom. No lighting in shower stalls.	Adequate appearance but has some hard water deposits, pitting, rusting, chipping or cracking of vents, dividers, hardware, sinks or toilets. Floor surface in fair condition with some cracks, missing tiles or chips. Some minor graffiti throughout the restroom and shower stalls.	Superior appearance with no hard water deposits, pitting, rusting, chipping or cracking of vents, dividers, hardware, sinks or toilets. Floor surface in superior condition without cracks, missing tiles or chips. No graffiti. Well lighted throughout the restroom and shower stalls.

____ **TOTAL RATING**

MUST HAVE 1 POINT IN 4 OUT OF 5 OF THESE ■ AREAS, AND 7 POINTS TOTAL TO QUALIFY FOR GOOD SAM PARK MEMBERSHIP.

VISUAL APPEARANCE/ ENVIRONMENTAL QUALITY

A full point should be awarded in a category only if the amenity is outstanding. If not best in each category, rate down 1/2 point.

	0 Points	1/2 point	1 point
______	**FUNCTION & IDENTIFICATION OF SIGNAGE AND ENTRANCE TO PARK (Assessing sign and entrance to access the park.):**		
	Entrance is difficult to see. Access into or out of the park is dangerous. No sign or sign difficult to identify, poorly maintained or difficult to read. Not illuminated and not readable at night.	Entrance is clearly visible with safe access into and out of park. Sign that is well-maintained, easily seen and read from distance and at night, illuminated by street lights or reflective material.	Entrance is clearly visible with safe wide easy access in and out of park. Well maintained professional quality sign that is easily seen and read from distance and is illuminated with flood lights or back lights.
______	**APPEARANCE OF ENTRANCE AREA (An assessment of the area and frontage extending 50' each side of entrance way):**		
	Park entrance is not landscaped, or landscaping is minimal and/or poorly maintained with excessive litter or roadside debris is present.	Park entrance is reasonably landscaped with a ground cover (grass, decorative rock or bark) **plus one of the following**: trees, shrubs, flowers, landscaping timbers, or ornamental vegetation appropriate to climate, free of most litter and/or roadside debris and well-maintained.	Park entrance has an invitingly landscaped appearance with a ground cover (grass, decorative rock or bark) **Plus at least two of the following:** trees, shrubs, flowers, landscaping timbers, or ornamental vegetation appropriate to climate, free of litter and roadside debris and carefully manicured.
______	**APPEARANCE OF PARK GROUNDS (An assessment of common areas excluding RV Sites):**		
	Common areas (non-campsite) of park sporadically landscaped or poorly landscaped. Not maintained or overgrown with weeds or other vegetation.	Landscaping of common areas (non-campsite) is consistent throughout the park, includes a ground cover (grass, gravel, decorative rock or bark), and a **limited quantity** of trees, shrubs, flowers, landscaping timbers, or ornamental vegetation appropriate to climate. Landscaping is well-maintained (grass mowed, leaves raked, trees trimmed).	Landscaping of common areas (non-campsite) is consistent throughout the park, includes a ground cover (grass, gravel, decorative rock or bark), and a **significant** quantity of trees, shrubs, flowers, landscaping timbers, or ornamental vegetation appropriate to climate. Landscaping is carefully manicured (trees and plants trimmed and pruned, grass is mowed, edged and weeded, leaves raked; no grass, weeds or ground cover growing or creeping onto RV parking area).
______	**APPEARANCE OF SITES (An assessment of overnight RV sites only):**		
	Sites not landscaped or poorly or minimally landscaped, or unmaintained (overgrown with weeds or other vegetation).	Site landscaping is consistent throughout the park in all overnight-type sites. Landscaping is regularly scheduled and maintained (grass mowed or between regular cuttings, leaves raked, trees trimmed). And includes a ground cover (grass, gravel, pavement, decorative rock or bark) **plus one of the following:** trees, shrubs, flowers, landscaping timbers, privacy screens, or ornamental vegetation appropriate to climate.	Site landscaping is consistent throughout the park in all overnight-type sites and includes a ground cover (grass, gravel, pavement, decorative rock or bark) and **at least two of the following:** trees, shrubs, flowers, landscaping timbers, privacy screens, ornamental vegetation appropriate to climate, patio, table or fire pit (all in good condition). Landscaping shows evidence of constant maintenance and is carefully manicured (trees and plants trimmed and pruned, grass is mowed, edged and weeded, leaves raked; no grass, weeds or ground cover growing or creeping onto RV sites).
______	**LITTER AND DEBRIS AROUND PARK GROUNDS AND SITES, INCLUDING FIRE PITS (An assessment of litter and debris around entire park and sites):**		
	Park grounds area around buildings and/or sites (including fire pits) are littered with refuse, clutter, or debris. Seasonal or long term sites are in view of overnight sites and have an unacceptable amount of refuse, clutter & debris.	Park grounds area around buildings and/or sites (including fire pits) are reasonably free of refuse, clutter, or debris. Seasonal or long term sites are in view of overnight sites are reasonably free of refuse, clutter & debris.	Park grounds area around buildings and/or sites (including fire pits) and RV's are free of all refuse, clutter and debris. Seasonal or long term sites are in view of overnight sites are free of refuse, clutter & debris.
______	**OVERALL EXTERIOR BUILDING MAINTENANCE (An assessment of all buildings except bathroom buildings:**		
	Buildings including doorways and windows require major repair or painting or web removal or cleaning or maintenance. Roof and gutters require major repair. Walkways around buildings are unsafe and require major repair.	Some or all buildings including doorways and windows require some cleaning or web removal or painting or minor repair. Roof and gutters require some minor repair. Walkways around buildings safe but require some minor repair.	All buildings including doorways and windows, clean in appearance, free of webs and in good repair. No repair required to roof or gutters. Walkways around buildings, safe and no repair required.
______	**TRASH DISPOSAL:**		
	No trash receptacles or trash receptacles overflowing. Receptacles not regularly emptied.	Trash receptacles of ample capacity, well maintained, regularly emptied, located more than 500' from 50% of overnight sites.	Trash pickup at site daily and/or receptacles of ample capacity, well-maintained, regularly emptied, located less than 500' from 50% of overnight sites.
______	**NOISE:**		
	Park is located in flight path of nearby major airport or active military airstrip. It borders an active railroad track, interstate or heavily traveled major highway or industrial or commercial area which results in frequent, major noise pollution.	Park is close enough to one of the following: airport, active railroad track, interstate or heavily traveled major highway or industrial or commercial area which results in occasional, moderate noise pollution.	Park is distant enough from one of the following: airport, active railroad tracks, interstate or other heavily traveled major highways, industrial or commercial areas which results in minimal noise pollution. People are able to converse in a normal tone of voice.
______	**PARK SETTING:**		
	Park and sites have no natural or man-made visual barrier that shield park from commercial, industrial, or residential surroundings on all four sides and is a major detraction from the parks setting.	Park and sites are shielded from commercial, industrial or residential surroundings by a manmade or natural visual barrier on at least two sides and has some impact on the parks setting.	Park and sites are shielded from commercial or industrial or residential surroundings by a manmade or natural visual barrier on all four sides and does not detract the parks setting.
______	**SITE LAYOUT:**		
	Greater than 50% of sites have side-by-side hookups or sites measure less than 20' between RV parking space from pedestal to pedestal, perpendicular to the site. Entry and exit into and from the site is difficult with some obstacles such as rocks or trees.	Less than 50% of sites have side-by-side hookups. Distance between majority of parking space from pedestal line to pedestal line, perpendicular to the site is minimum of 20'. Entry and exit into and from the site allows easy access but with some obstacles such as rocks or trees.	No side-by-side hookups. All sites measure greater than 30' between parking space from pedestal line to pedestal line, perpendicular to the site. Entry and exit into and from the site allows easy access with minimum obstacles such as rocks or trees.
______	**TOTAL RATING**		

GS-21

MUST HAVE 5 POINTS OVERALL TO QUALIFY FOR GOOD SAM PARK MEMBERSHIP.

How to Use This Travel Guide

A guide to help you get the most of your 2016 Good Sam RV Travel & Savings Guide

To help you get the most out of your ***2016 Good Sam RV Travel & Savings Guide***, the editors have split the publication into two major sections. **The glossy, magazine section** in the front of the book with travel features, lifestyle insights and how-to guides that will help you enjoy your RV travels. Refer to the table of contents on page 2 for the magazine section. **The campground information section**, printed on lighter paper, lists RV parks and campgrounds throughout North America.

The campground information section is organized alphabetically, first by U.S. state, then by Canadian provinces. Within each state and province, the listing information is alphabetized by town. Each town name is followed by map-grid coordinates and the appropriate county name. **The map grid coordinate (a letter and a number, such as A1)** refers to coordinates on the maps found at the beginning of each state or province. County information is often helpful when weather alerts occur while you're traveling. Each campground is listed by town.

Welcome Sections & Spotlights

Each state and province in the campground information section includes the Welcome Section: At least one page of travel information that includes climate, trivia, travel and tourism contact information, and topography. Many states and provinces also feature a series of Spotlights, which feature local points of interest. **For a complete list of spotlights, refer to page 176 in the magazine section.**

Special Sections

Don't miss the Yellow Pages at the back of the Travel Guide for RV and travel-related services. Also just before the Yellow Page section, you'll find our Seasonal Stay section and our list of Military Parks, for active and retired military campers.

How We Get Our Campground Information

Good Sam consultants make personal inspections of privately-owned RV parks and campgrounds each year. This year, 35 teams traveled in their RVs across North America, rating and inspecting parks so that you'll know what to expect before you get there. **Read more about our rating system on page 158** in the magazine section. We proudly display our consultant teams' names at the front of every state and province.

How To Read Our Campground Information

For 2016, we have basic information for thousands of campgrounds, including the park name, our rating (for privately owned parks only), phone and physical location (driving directions are only provided for public parks). You will find expanded listings which have more detail, and are outlined below. We also list dealers, services and attractions (or travel & tourism locations). These will include physical location, basic information and a description of the location.

1. Town Name: This indicates the campground's location. If the campground isn't located in a municipality, we list the nearest town. This campground information also includes "See also" lines, which provide helpful listings of towns within a 30-mile radius of a major metropolitan area.

2. Map Coordinates: The letter and number next to a town correspond to the coordinates on the state/provincial map noted at the top of the page. To find a town, draw straight lines from the number at the top and the letter at the sides of the map. The town is near the point of intersection.

3. County Name: Shows the county in which that town is located.

4. Directional Arrow: Indicates facility's location relative to the town. An arrow pointing straight up shows that the facility is due north of the town.

5. Facility Name: The name of the facility.

6. Good Sam Park Logo: Indicates parks that offer the 10% discount to Good Sam Club members on an overnight stay for two people in one recreational vehicle. You must present a valid Good Sam Club membership card at the time of registration. Learn more about the Good Sam RV Park & Resort Network in the magazine section page 38.

7. Triple Digit Rating: We rate privately owned campgrounds in three categories: Development of Facilities, Cleanliness & Construction of Restrooms and Showers, and Visual Appearance & Environmental Quality. If no rating appears, we didn't rate the park. See page 158 for more information on our exclusive triple-digit rating system.

8. Type Of Facility & Management: Classifies parks into several unique categories to help RVers envision the park setting before arrival. These classifications and a summary of their definitions are:

RV Resort: Designs and caters to larger RVs and has highly developed grounds.

RV Park: Includes formal site and grounds development and is primarily designed for RVs.

Campgrounds: Usually located in a rural or natural setting, with less formal grounds and site development; accepts tents as well as RVs.

RV Spaces: A handful of RV spaces reserved for overnight travelers, and often has few, if any, additional facilities or amenities.

To give us feedback about our listings, email us at:
TravelGuideComments@GoodSamFamily.com

Membership Resort: Primary business is selling memberships to consumers and less than 10 sites are available for overnight RVers.

RV Area in Mobile Home Park: A designated area for RVs within a mobile home park.

Condo Park: A condo park sells its sites to individuals then reserves the right to rent out the sites when not in use by owner.

Public Campground: Campgrounds with camping sites open to the public that are owned and operated by a government agency, includes state, national, city parks, etc.

9. Directions: Beginning with the nearest highway exit or major intersection, you may locate the facility by following the directions and mileage. Note: (L), (R), and (E) denote whether the facility entrance is to the left, right, or end of the road respectively.

10. Special Info: Unique information provided by park owners who want you to know about special features and offers at their park. These individualized messages are highlighted in yellow and give you a little extra nugget of information not found in our standardized listing information.

11. Interior Roads: Unless "poor" is noted, the condition and surface of the interior roads is fair to good. Note: When the primary interior roads are paved, yet those leading to the sites are gravel, we label them as paved/gravel. When interior roads are a mixture of gravel and dirt, we label them as gravel/dirt.

12. Description Of Sites: Site description includes total number of RV spaces, surface preparation at most sites (paved, all weather, gravel, grass or dirt), hookup information, width and length of pull-thru sites and back-ins, etc.

Big Rig: We also indicate here if sites accept Big Rigs. A Big Rig designation is only offered to parks which have 25% or more of sites that meet this criteria: minimum of 14-ft. overhead clearance, 12-foot-wide roads (1-way), 50-amp full hookup sites, sites that are a minimum of 24 ft. by 60 ft., and adequate site access. Parks without a Big Rig designation may still have a few such sites. Call ahead for availability with all parks.

Side-by-Side Hookups: Indicates that the configuration of some hookups may create space limitations for slide outs, as you could be close to your neighbor.

Full Hookups: Indicates sites that have all three: water, electric and sewer. If the hookups are not full, we indicate how many sites have at least water (W), electric (E), and sewer (S). We also note the minimum and maximum type of electrical receptacles that will be found at sites (15, 20, 30, or 50 amps). We only list the availability of 50-amp receptacles when at least 25% of the sites have them. The type of receptacle doesn't guarantee exact amperage or voltage.

13. Seasonal Stay Sites: Tells if a park makes its sites available to RVers for an extended stay. For more detailed information, check out the Seasonal Stay Section at the back of the Travel Guide.

14. Tent Sites: Indicates tent sites are available at the campground.

15. Rental Units: Indicates the number of rental units available at the park.

16. Internet Access: Wifi $ indicates an extra charge not included in the nightly rate. WiFi indicates locations that provide overnight RVers with access to the Internet wirelessly from over 150 ft. or more. WiFi Hotspot indicates that WiFi is available at a central location, such as a rec hall.

17. Basic Facilities: This includes store, laundry, etc. A ($) after the facilities (e.g., showers ($) indicates an extra charge not included in the overnight rate listed.

18. Recreation (Rec): Notes the types of recreational facilities the campground offers. This listing can include swimming, fishing, shuffleboard and playground.

19. Pet Information: Pet Restrictions are noted when they apply, such as breed (B), quantity (Q) or size (S). If pets are not allowed at all, No Pets will appear. Pet $ indicates the park charges extra for pets. Note: Call ahead to ask for the park's specific pet policy and limitations.

20. Partial Handicapped Access: Indicates the park has been adapted in one or more ways to accommodate RVers/campers with disabilities. This listing may include showers with benches and handrails, wheelchair-accessible sinks and toilets, wide doorways with no curbs or steps, wheelchair ramps, signs on buildings and/or hiking trails printed in Braille, TDD equipment, etc. If you or a family member has special needs, please call ahead to determine the type of services/facilities available. This indication does not mean the park

Anatomy of Our Listing

1. Town Name
2. Map Coordinates
3. County Name
4. Directional Arrow
5. Facility Name
6. Good Sam Park Logo
7. Ratings
8. Type of Facility & Management
9. Directions

TARPON SPRINGS – A3 *Pinelas*

Viewpoint RV Park

Ratings: 9/9.5★/9.5 (Campground)
From jct I-10 and I-5: Go 5 N on I-5 to Exit 23, Go 1/2 W on Green Valley Road (R).

10. Special Information

ENJOY THE SPACE COAST'S BEST!
Enjoy activities galore in the beautiful setting of the Cocoa Beach Area! Visit Kennedy Space Center. Enjoy the Atlantic Ocean Beaches or just relax at one of our beautiful sites. Our RV Resort is near all area attractions.

11. Interior Roads
12. Description of Sites
13. Seasonal Stay Sites
14. Tent Sites
15. Rental Units
16. Internet Access
17. Basic Facilities
18. Recreation
19. Pet Information
20. Partial Handicap Access
21. Age Restrictions
22. RV Age Restrictions
23. 2015 Rates
24. Eco-Friendly
25. Seasonality

FAC: paved/gravel rds. (200 spaces). 100 Avail: 50 paved, 50 gravel, patios, 20 pull-thrus (30 x 60), back-ins (30 x 60), some side by side hkups, 90 full hkups, 10 W, 10 E (30/50 amps) seasonal sites, cable, WiFi, tent sites. Rentals. Dump, mobile sewer, laundry, groc, LP gas, fire rings, firewood, restaurant, controlled access. **REC:** Gulf of Mexico: fishing, marina, golf, shuffleboard, playground, rec open to public. Pets OK, partial handicap access. Age restrict may apply. Big rig sites, RV age restrict, 28 day max stay, eco-friendly. 2015 rates: $25 - $50. Disc: AAA, military. Nov 1 to May 30. No reservations.
AAA Approved

26. Contact Information
27. Advertiser Reference

(888) 123-4567 Lat : 12.34567 , Lon: -89.87654
123 Main Street, Tarpon Springs, FL 12345
viewpointrvp@gmail.com
www.viewpointrvp.com
See ad page 65

is ADA compliant.

21. Age Restrictions: Parks with this designation usually cater to 55+ guests. Children are usually restricted. Call the park for details.

22. RV Age Restrictions: Parks with this designation may have an RV Age restriction. Call the park for details.

23. Rates, Credit Cards & Discounts: Rates are listed as minimum to maximum, for two adults in one RV, in effect at the time of inspection in 2015. Rates include any additional fees that may typically be found at the site such as air conditioning, TV service and heating. Rates and discounts are shown as a guideline only. They can change without notice. Call for the most current information. (NA) indicates that rates aren't available at the time of publication. This information is deemed accurate but is not guaranteed. Unless "no cc" is noted; credit cards are accepted. Call park for credit card policies.

24. Eco-Friendly: Identifies parks that meet our Eco-Friendly standards. See page 163 for more information.

25. Season: Indicates opening and closing dates for seasonal parks. Otherwise, facilities are open year round.

26. Contact Info: Easy, at-a-glance information gives you everything you need to contact and reserve a site at the park.

27. Advertiser Reference: This line will refer you to the specific page for the listed campground's advertisement(s).

Special Notes & Misc. Info

Cancellations: Policies regarding canceling reservations vary with each campground. Remember to ask what that policy is when making a reservation.

Toilets? Showers? Unless otherwise noted, all campgrounds have flush toilets and hot showers. If only pit toilets are available, the listing will note pit toilet. If the restroom and showers are coin operated, the listing will indicate it with a ($) in the listing. If the Restroom Rating is NA, this indicates that restrooms are not available at the facility. If the Restroom Rating is UI, this means that the restrooms could not be inspected by our consultants during the time of the visit.

Rates And Discounts: All information about rates and discounts are deemed accurate at the time of inspectors' visit in 2015. These are not guaranteed. Please call ahead for detailed, up-to-date information.

The Preferred Location Logo: Indicates locations that meet certain criteria and invest in providing consumers more information about their business; earning them a check mark next to their listing.

Name in Red: Indicates Good Sam Parks that meet certain criteria and invest in providing consumers more information about their business.

Advertisers Want Your Business

The basic listings in this Travel Guide are provided at no charge to the business owner. Any campground that meets our minimum requirements receives a listing. Many campground owners want to tell you more about their campground than the listing includes. These campgrounds have purchased advertising for that purpose. You'll see their ad reference at the bottom of their listing (e.g., See ad page 111). These ads can be a great help to you in choosing where to stay because they describe the special features and uniqueness of that campground. Please remember to tell them you saw them in this Travel Guide!

Abbreviation Key

Corps	Corps of Engineers-managed
CR	county road
E	east
Elev	elevation
expwy	expressway
FAC	facilities & sites available at location
FM Rd	farm-to-market road
FR	forest road
frntg	frontage
fwy	freeway
hkups	hookups
hwy	highway
I-(#)	interstate (followed by number)
jct	junction
LP	liquid propane
MHP	mobile home park
mi	mile
MP	mile post
N	north; NE = northeast; NW = northwest
Natl	national
NF	national forest
pk	park
pkwy	parkway
PR	provincial road
prov	provincial
QEW	Queen Elizabeth Way
REC	recreation available at location
RR	rural route
rte	route
S	south; SE = southeast; SW = southwest
SR	state route
St	street
St/Ste	saint or sainte
tpke	turnpike
TCH	Trans-Canada Highway
US-(#)	United States Highway (followed by a No.)
UI	uninspected
W	west
yd	yard
yr	year

Comment utiliser ce guide

Aide-mémoire pour vous aider à utiliser pleinement votre guide de voyage 2016 Good Sam

Afin d'en faciliter la consultation, ce **guide de voyage 2016 Good Sam** est séparé en deux grandes sections. La première adopte un **style magazine**. Imprimée sur papier glacé, elle se trouve au début du guide et présente différents articles et conseils utiles aux propriétaires de VR en voyage. Une table des matières se trouve à la page 2 de cette section. La deuxième correspond à la **section camping**. Elle est imprimée sur papier plus fin et répertorie les parcs pour VR et les terrains de camping d'Amérique du Nord.

La section camping est organisée par ordre alphabétique, d'abord par État américain, puis par province canadienne. Pour chaque État ou province, l'information sur les campings est classée alphabétiquement par nom de ville, lequel est suivi de coordonnées et du nom du comté ou de la région où cette ville se trouve. **Les coordonnées, composées d'une lettre et d'un chiffre (p. ex. A1)**, se rapportent à la grille cartographique apparaissant au début de chaque État ou province. L'indication du comté ou de la région est souvent utile lorsque des alertes météo surviennent et que vous êtes sur la route.

Introduction et endroits à découvrir

Chaque État et province fait l'objet d'une introduction dans la section camping. Celle-ci contient au moins une page de renseignements utiles au voyageur (climat et topographie, faits généraux, coordonnées des bureaux de tourisme, etc.). Des lieux phares et points d'intérêt locaux sont aussi présentés pour bon nombre d'États et de provinces. **On peut trouver la liste complète de ces endroits à découvrir à la page 176 de la section magazine.**

Sections spéciales

À la fin du guide, vous trouverez des pages jaunes présentant des services liés aux voyages et aux VR. Ces pages sont précédées d'une section sur les parcs et terrains permettant un séjour saisonnier, de même qu'une liste de parcs réservés aux campeurs militaires en service actif ou retraités.

Comment les renseignements sur les campings sont obtenus

Chaque année, nos représentants vont inspecter des parcs et terrains de camping privés qui accueillent des VR. Cette année, 35 équipes ont parcouru l'Amérique du Nord en VR afin d'évaluer les sites pour que vous sachiez à quoi vous attendre. **Consultez la page 158 de notre section magazine pour en savoir plus sur notre système de pointage.** Le nom de nos représentants est donné au début du répertoire propre à chaque État et province.

Comment utiliser le guide

Notre publication 2016 fournit les renseignements de base de milliers de campings : leur nom, leur qualité (pointage attribué aux sites privés seulement), leur numéro de téléphone et leur emplacement exact (indications routières fournies pour les parcs publics seulement). Des descriptifs viennent ajouter de nombreux détails (structure expliquée ci-après). Le guide répertorie aussi les vendeurs de VR, de même que les principaux services et attraits touristiques du coin (avec leur emplacement, des renseignements de base et une description sommaire).

1. **Localité :** Endroit où se trouve le camping (ou localité la plus proche). Signale aussi pour les grandes villes une liste des localités se trouvant dans un rayon de 50 km (mention *See also*).
2. **Coordonnées cartographiques :** Lettre et chiffre indiquant où se trouve la localité sur la carte de l'État ou de la province fournie au début de la partie. La localité est à proximité de l'intersection imaginaire que vous pouvez dessiner entre la lettre (axe vertical) et le chiffre (axe horizontal).
3. **Comté :** Comté (ou région) où se trouve cette localité.
4. **Flèche :** Emplacement du camping par rapport à la localité. Par exemple, une flèche pointant vers le haut indique que le camping est vers le nord.
5. **Nom :** Nom du camping présenté.
6. **Logo Good Sam :** Sur présentation d'une carte Good Sam valide au moment de l'inscription, vous obtiendrez un rabais de 10 % sur le prix journalier (deux adultes, un VR). Reportez-vous à la page 38 de la section magazine pour plus de détails sur le réseau Good Sam.
7. **Pointage :** Les campings privés sont évalués sur trois grands aspects : installations disponibles, propreté générale et qualité des installations sanitaires, apparence visuelle et environnement. Les campings sans pointage n'ont pas été visités par nos évaluateurs. Notre méthode d'évaluation exclusive en trois points est expliquée en détail à la page 158.
8. **Type d'installation/modèle de gestion :** Catégories permettant aux propriétaires de VR de se faire une idée de chaque site. Les catégories sont définies ainsi :

   RV Resort/Centre pour VR : Installations conçues pour accueillir de gros VR et offrant de nombreux aménagements et services adaptés.

   RV Park/Parc pour VR : Site doté d'une infrastructure et d'aménagements conçus principalement pour les VR.

   Campgrounds/Terrain de camping : Site généralement situé en milieu rural ou naturel comptant une infrastructure et des aménagements limités et accueillant aussi bien les VR que les tentes.

   RV Spaces/Espaces pour VR : Espaces réservés aux VR, qui peuvent s'y stationner pour la nuit. Installations et services le plus souvent absents ou très limités.

   Membership Resort/Centre avec abonnement : Site vendant des abonnements et n'offrant au maximum qu'une dizaine d'espaces pour la nuit aux VR.

Vous avez des commentaires sur ce guide? Écrivez-nous à TravelGuideComments@GoodSamFamily.com

RV Area in Mobile Home Park/Parc de maisons mobiles : Espace réservé aux VR dans un parc de maisons mobiles.

Condo Park/Espaces en copropriété : Site où des espaces sont vendus à des particuliers, avec possibilité pour le camping de louer cet espace lorsque le propriétaire ne l'occupe pas.

Public Campground/Camping public : Sites ouverts à la population et gérés par une instance gouvernementale (province, État, pays, municipalité, etc.).

9. Indications routières : Trajet à suivre à partir de la sortie d'autoroute ou de la grande intersection la plus proche pour se rendre sur les lieux. L=entrée du site sur la gauche (*left*); R=entrée à droite (*right*); E=entrée au bout du chemin (*end*).

10. Infos supplémentaires : Espace en jaune où le propriétaire du site peut indiquer des éléments particuliers, des offres spéciales ou des renseignements supplémentaires jugés utiles.

11. Voies carrossables : À moins de trouver la mention *poor*, l'état et le revêtement des chemins à l'intérieur du site sont adéquats. La mention *paved/gravel* indique que les chemins principaux sont pavés mais font place au gravier pour les emplacements de camping. La mention *gravel/dirt* indique que les chemins sont de gravier ou de terre battue.

12. Description du site : Comprend le nombre total d'espaces pour VR, la description des emplacements (majoritairement pavés, sur gravillons, sur gravier, sur l'herbe ou sur terre battue), l'info sur les branchements, l'ombre disponible, la dimension des emplacements avec entrée directe (*pull-thru*) et à reculons (*back-in*), etc.

Big Rig/Gros VR : Site où au moins 25 % des espaces peuvent accommoder les gros VR (dégagement en hauteur de plus de 4 m, routes larges d'au moins 3,6 m en sens unique, branchement complet sur 50 ampères, dimensions minimales de 7,5 m x 18 m, accès aisé). Un site sans cette mention peut quand même avoir quelques espaces convenant aux gros VR. Téléphoner pour vérifier.

Side-by-Side Hookups/Branchement partagé : Emplacements où l'espace est réduit autour du branchement, si bien qu'il peut être difficile d'utiliser les extensions coulissantes du VR ou qu'il faut s'attendre à être collé sur un voisin.

Full Hookups/Branchement complet : Site où on peut se brancher à la fois sur l'eau (W – *Water*), l'électricité (E – *Electricity*) et les égouts (S – *Sewer*). Sinon, le nombre d'emplacements offrant chacun des trois branchements possibles est indiqué à côté de la lettre correspondante. L'ampérage minimum et maximum offert est également précisé (15, 20, 30 ou 50 ampères). L'ampérage à 50 ampères est indiqué seulement si au moins 25 % des emplacements le fournissent. L'ampérage et la tension fournis ne peuvent être garantis.

13. Séjour saisonnier : Indique si des emplacements sont offerts aux VR pour un séjour prolongé (*seasonal/extended stay*). Lisez notre section sur les séjours saisonniers à la fin du guide de voyage pour plus de détails.

14. Tentes : Indique si des espaces sont prévus expressément pour les tentes.

15. En location (rentals) : Indique ce qui peut être loué sur place.

16. Accès Internet : Indique si l'accès Internet sans fil s'accompagne d'un supplément (*Wifi $*), s'il est inclus dans le prix journalier et offert dans un rayon d'au moins 45 m (*WiFi*), ou s'il est offert dans un endroit précis, p. ex. la salle communautaire (*WiFi Hotspot*).

17. Installations de base : Installations et services offerts (boutique, buanderie, douche, etc.). Le symbole $ indique qu'il faut payer un supplément pour en profiter.

18. Activités récréatives (REC) : Installations et activités récréatives offertes sur le site (p. ex. nage, pêche, jeu de palets, terrain de jeu, etc.).

19. Animaux de compagnie : Indique si les animaux sont acceptés (*Pets OK*), si des restrictions s'appliquent (B=breed/race; Q=quantity/nombre; S=size/taille), s'ils sont interdits (*No Pets*) et s'il faut payer un supplément pour leur présence ($). Il est recommandé de téléphoner pour s'informer au préalable des politiques et restrictions en vigueur pour les animaux de compagnie.

20. Accès partiel aux handicapés : Indique que certains aménagements ont été faits pour accueillir les personnes handicapées sur le site (p. ex. douches avec banc et rampe, éviers et toilettes pour handicapés, portes larges sans marche ni bordure, rampes d'accès pour fauteuils roulants, affichage en braille, appareils ATS, etc.). La mention *Partial Handicapped Access* ne garantit aucunement la conformité à la loi ADA sur les handicapés. Téléphoner pour vérifier les installations et services exacts disponibles.

Structure d'un article

1. Localité
2. Coordonnées cartographiques
3. Comté
4. Flèche
5. Nom
6. Logo Good Sam
7. Pointage
8. Type d'installation/modèle de gestion
9. Indications routières

TARPON SPRINGS – A3 *Pinelas*

Viewpoint RV Park

Good Sam Park

Ratings: 9/9.5★/9.5 (Campground)

From jct I-10 and I-5: Go 5 N on I-5 to Exit 23, Go 1/2 W on Green Valley Road (R).

10. Infos supplémentaires

ENJOY THE SPACE COAST'S BEST!

Enjoy activities galore in the beautiful setting of the Cocoa Beach Area! Visit Kennedy Space Center. Enjoy the Atlantic Ocean Beaches or just relax at one of our beautiful sites. Our RV Resort is near all area attractions.

11. Voies carrossables
12. Description du site
13. Séjour saisonnier
14. Tentes
15. En location
16. Accès Internet
17. Installations de base
18. Activités récréatives
19. Animaux de compagnie
20. Accès partiel aux handicapés
21. Restrictions d'âge
22. Restriction âge des VR
23. Tarification 2015
24. Site vert
25. Saison

FAC: paved/gravel rds. (200 spaces). 100 Avail: 50 paved, 50 gravel, patios, 20 pull-thrus (30 x 60), back-ins (30 x 60), some side by side hkups, 90 full hkups, 10 W, 10 E (30/50 amps) seasonal sites, cable, WiFi, tent sites. Rentals. Dump, mobile sewer, laundry, groc, LP gas, fire rings, firewood, restaurant, controlled access. **REC:** Gulf of Mexico: fishing, marina, golf, shuffleboard, playground, rec open to public. Pets OK, partial handicap access. Age restrict may apply. Big rig sites, RV age restrict, 28 day max stay, eco-friendly. 2015 rates: $25 - $50. Disc: AAA, military. Nov 1 to May 30. No reservations.

AAA Approved

26. Coordonnées générales
27. Voir l'annonce

(888) 123-4567 Lat : 12.34567 , Lon: -89.87654
123 Main Street, Tarpon Springs, FL 12345
viewpointrvp@gmail.com
www.viewpointrvp.com
See ad page 65

21. Restrictions d'âge : En général, les sites portant cette mention se spécialisent dans la clientèle de l'âge d'or et limitent l'accès aux enfants. Téléphoner pour plus de détails.

22. Restriction âge des VR : Les sites portant cette mention n'acceptent pas les VR d'un certain âge. Téléphoner pour plus de détails.

23. Tarification, cartes de crédit et rabais : Tarif minimum-maximum (pour deux adultes avec un VR) qui était en vigueur au moment de l'inspection en 2015 (peut changer sans préavis). Les suppléments (p. ex. pour l'air climatisé, la télé et le chauffage) sont inclus dans le tarif maximum. Téléphoner pour confirmer les prix et rabais en vigueur. La mention *NA* indique que la grille de prix n'était pas disponible au moment de la publication. À moins de trouver la mention *no cc*, les cartes de crédit sont acceptées. Téléphoner pour connaître les politiques concernant les cartes de crédit.

24. Site vert (Eco-Friendly) : Indique que le site respecte les normes environnementales détaillées à la page 166.

25. Saison : Date d'ouverture et de fermeture du site lorsqu'il est saisonnier. L'absence d'information indique un site ouvert à l'année. La mention *Limited facilities Winter* indique que l'accès aux toilettes, au branchement et/ou à la décharge est limité en hiver. Téléphoner au préalable pour vérifier les services disponibles.

27. Coordonnées générales : Tous les renseignements requis pour communiquer avec les responsables du site et réserver une place.

28. Voir l'annonce (See ad) : Donne la page où on peut trouver la publicité du site, le cas échéant.

Renseignements divers

Annulations : Les politiques concernant l'annulation des réservations varient d'un site à l'autre. Pensez à vous informer au moment de réserver.

Toilettes et douches : Sauf mention contraire, tous les campings ont des toilettes à chasse d'eau et l'eau chaude pour les douches. La mention *pit toilets* signifie qu'il y a uniquement des toilettes sèches, et le symbole $ indique qu'il faut payer pour accéder aux toilettes et aux douches. La mention *NA* dans le pointage pour la catégorie des installations sanitaires signifie que le site n'offre pas de toilettes. La mention *UI* indique que notre représentant n'a pas été en mesure d'inspecter les toilettes lors de sa visite.

Tarification et rabais : Les renseignements sur la tarification et les rabais étaient exacts au moment de la visite de nos inspecteurs en 2015, mais sont sujets à changement et ne peuvent être garantis. Il est recommandé de téléphoner pour confirmer au préalable les tarifs et offres en vigueur et obtenir tout détail supplémentaire à cet égard.

Sceau de vérification : Crochet indiquant que ce camping respecte certains critères de qualité et de transparence vis-à-vis de ses clients.

Nom en rouge : Sites du réseau Good Sam qui respectent certains critères définis et qui prennent soin de renseigner leurs clients sur leur entreprise.

Nos annonceurs espèrent vous voir!

L'inscription de base dans notre guide de voyage est offerte gratuitement aux propriétaires des sites de camping qui répondent à nos critères. Cependant, beaucoup sont désireux de vous en dire plus sur ce qu'ils ont à offrir, et ont donc acheté de la publicité dans notre guide. Un renvoi à leurs annonces se trouve à la fin de leurs entrées respectives, après la mention *See ad on page 111*. Ces annonces peuvent vous aider à choisir un lieu de séjour en vous faisant connaître les particularités et avantages d'un site. Dans ce cas, n'hésitez pas à faire savoir au camping choisi que c'est leur annonce dans notre guide qui vous a convaincu!

Tableau des abréviations

Corps	Corps of Engineers (géré par le Corps des ingénieurs de l'armée américaine)
CR	county road (route de comté)
E	est
Elev	elevation (altitude)
expwy	expressway (voie express)
FAC	facilities (installations et emplacements offerts sur le site)
FM Rd	farm-to-market road (route en milieu rural)
FR	forest road (route en milieu forestier)
frntg	frontage (voie de desserte)
fwy	freeway (voie rapide à accès limité)
hkups	hookups (branchements)
hwy	highway (autoroute)
I-(#)	interstate (route inter-États, avec son numéro)
jct	junction (intersection)
LP	liquid propane (propane liquide)
MHP	mobile home park (parc de maisons mobiles)
mi	mile (1 mille ≈ 1,6 km)
MP	mile post (borne routière)
N	nord; NE = nord-est; NW = nord-ouest
Natl	national
NF	national forest (réserve forestière)
pk	park (parc)
pkwy	parkway (route de plaisance)
PR	provincial road (route provinciale)
prov	provincial
QEW	Queen Elizabeth Way (autoroute QEW, en Ontario)
REC	activités récréatives offertes sur le site
RR	rural route (chemin de campagne)
rte	route
S	sud; SE = sud-est; SW = sud-ouest
SR	state route (route d'État)
St	street (rue)
St/Ste	saint ou sainte
tpke	turnpike (autoroute à péage)
TCH	Trans-Canada Highway (autoroute Transcanadienne)
US-(#)	United States Highway (autoroute nationale américaine, avec son numéro)
UI	uninspected (non inspecté)
W	west (ouest)
yd	yard (longueur : 1 yard ≈ 0,9 m; superficie : 1 yard ≈ 0,8 m^2)
yr	year (année)

Rules of the Road & Towing Laws

An at-a-glance guide to state and provincial laws pertaining to RVs and automobiles

	Size Limits				Towing		Riding				Equipment						Cell Phone	
	Width	Trailer Length	Motorhome Length	Height	2-vehicle Combined Length	Triple Towing	In Pickup Camper	In Fifth-Wheel Trailer	In Travel Trailer	Overnight Parking in State Rest Areas	Weight of Trailer Requiring Brakes	Breakaway Switch	Safety Chain	Flares / Reflective Signs	Fire Extinguisher in RV	Lights Required ON	Voice Calling	Text Messaging
AK	8 ½'	40'	45'	14'	75'	•	•			•	5000	•[2]	•	•	NS	1000[14]	•	•
AL	8 ½'	40'	45'	13 ½'	65'		•			P	3000	•[2]	•	•	23	500[11,12]	•[1,24]	
AR	8 ½'	43 ½'	45'	13 ½'	65'	•				•	1500	•[2]	•	•	NS	500[11,12]	•[1,24]	
AZ	8'-8 ½'	40'	45'	13 ½'	65'	•	•	•	•	•[15]	3000[10]	•[2]	NS	NS	NS	500	•[1]	•[1]
CA	8 ½'	40'	45'[1]	14'	65'		•[17,20]	•[17,20]		P	1500[10]	•	•	•	•	1000[11]	•[1,24,25]	
CO	8 ½'	NS	45'	13 ½'	60'[1]		•			P	3000[10]	•	•	•	•	1000	•[24]	
CT	8 ½'	40'	45'	13 ½'	65'		•				4000[10]	NS	NS	•	NS	500[11,12]		
DC	8'	NS	40'	13 ½'	55'	•	•				NS	•	•	•	NS	500		
DE	8 ½'	40'	45'	13 ½'	65'		•			P	4000		•	•	NS	1000[11]		
FL	8 ½'	40'	45'	13 ½'	65'	NO	•			P	3000[10]	•	•	•	•	•[11]	•[25]	
GA	8 ½'	NS	NS	13 ½'	60'	NO	•[21]				1500	NS	•	•	•	500[11,12]	•[1,24]	
HI	9'	NS	45'	14'	65'	NO	•[19]				3000[10]	•[2]	•	NS	NS	•[12]		
IA	8 ½'	53'	45'	13 ½'	65'	70'	•	•	•		3000	•	•	•	NS	500[11]	•[1,24]	
ID	8 ½'	48'	45'	14'	75'	•	•			P	1500	•	NS	NS	NS	500	•[1]	
IL	8 ½'	45'	45'	13 ½'	60'	60'[1]	•				3000[10]	•[2]	•[1]	•	NS	1000[11]		
IN	8 ½'	40'	45'	13 ½'	60'	65'	•	•	•	•	3000[10]	•	•	•	NS	500	•[24]	
KS	8 ½'	NS	45'	14'	65'	70'	•[19]	•[19]	•[19]	P	[1,8]	•	•	•	23	1000[11]	•[1,24]	
KY	8 ½'	NS	45'	13 ½'	65'	65'	•			NS	3000[7]	•	•	•	•	•[28]	•[1,24]	
LA	8 ½'	40'	45'	14'	70'	70'	•			P	3000	•[2]	•[3]	•	NS	500[11]	•[1,24]	
MA	8 ½'	40'	45'	13 ½'	60'	NO	•			•[15]	10000	NS	•	NS	NS	•[11,12]	•[24]	
MD	8 ½'	40'	40'	13 ½'	55'	NO	•	•	•	P	3000	•[7]	•	•	•	1000[11]		
ME	8 ½'	48'	45'	13 ½'	65'	NO				P	3000	NS	•	NS	NS	1000[11,12]	•[24]	
MI	8 ½'	45'	45'	13 ½'	75'	60'	•	•	•	P	3000	•[3]	•	•	NS	500[12]	•[1,24]	
MN	8 ½'	45'	45'	13 ½'	75'	60'	•	•	•	P	3000[10]	•[3]	•	•	NS	500[11,12]	•[1,24]	
MO	8 ½'[1]	NS	45'	14'[1]	65'[1]	•[1]	•	•	•	•	NS	NS	•	NS	NS	500[11,12]	•	•[1,24]
MS	8 ½'	40'	45'	13 ½'	53'	•	NO	NO	NO	NO	2000	•	•	•	NS	500	•[1]	•[1,24]
MT	8 ½'[1]	NS	55'	14'	75'	70'	•	•		P	3000[27]	•	•	•	NS	500[11,12]	•[1]	•[1]
NC	8 ½'	35'	45'	13 ½'	60'	NO	•	•	•	P	4000	NS	•	NS	NS	400[11]	•[1,24]	
ND	8 ½'	53'	50'	14'	75'	75'	•	•		•	3000	•	•	•	NS	1000[11]	•[24]	
NE	8 ½'	40'	45'	14 ½'	65'	65'	•	•	•	NO	3000	•[2]	•	•	NS	500	•[1]	
NH	8 ½'	48'	45'	13 ½'	NS	NO	NO	NO	NO	NO	3000	NS	•	NS	NS	1000[11,12]		
NJ	8'[1]	40'	40'	13 ½'	50'[1]	NO	•	•	NO	P	3000	•	•	•	NS	500[11]		
NM	8 ½'	40'	45'	14'[1]	65'	•	•			P	3000	NS	•	•	NS	500[12]	•[1,24]	•
NV	8 ½'	NS	45'	14'	70'	•[1]	•			•[16]	3000	NS	•	NS	NS	1000[12]		
NY	8 ½'[1]	48'	45'	13 ½'	65'	NO	•			P	1000[5]	NS	•	NS	NS	1000[11,12]	•[25]	
OH	8 ½'	40'	45'	13 ½'	65'	65'	•			NO	2000	•	•	NS	NS	1000[11]	•[1,24]	
OK	8 ½'	40'	45'	13 ½'	65'	65'	•			•	3000	•	•	•	NS	1000[11,12]	•[24]	•
OR	8 ½'	45'	45'	14'	65'[1]	NO	•	•[17,20]	NO	•[16]	NS	NS	•	NS	NS	1000	•[24,25]	

	Size Limits				Towing		Riding				Equipment						Cell Phone	
	Width	Trailer Length	Motorhome Length	Height	2-vehicle Combined Length	Triple Towing	In Pickup Camper	In Fifth-Wheel Trailer	In Travel Trailer	Overnight Parking in State Rest Areas	Weight of Trailer Requiring Brakes	Breakaway Switch	Safety Chain	Flares / Reflective Signs	Fire Extinguisher in RV	Lights Required ON	Voice Calling	Text Messaging
PA	8 ½'[1]	NS	45'	13 ½'	60'	NO		•[17, 20]		NO	3000[7, 10]	•	•	•	•	1000[11, 12, 29]	•	
RI	8 ½'	NS	40'	13 ½'	60'	NO	•			•	4000	•	NS	•	NS	500[11]	•[1, 24]	
SC	8 ½'	48'	45'	13 ½'	NS	NO	•			P	3000	•	•	•	•	500[11, 12]	•	•[1]
SD	8 ½'	53'	45'	14'[1]	80'	75'[1]	•	•[17, 20]		P[16]	3000	•	•	•	•	200[12]	•[1, 24]	•
TN	8 ½'	40'	45'	13 ½'	65'	65'	•	NO	NO	•	1500	•[2]	•	•	•	200[12]	•[1, 24]	
TX	8 ½'	NS	45'	14'	65'	65'	•	NO	NO	P[16]	4500	•[2]	•	•	NS	1000	•[1, 24, 25]	•[1]
UT	8 ½'	40'	45'	14'	61'	65'[1]	•	NO	NO	P[16]	2000	•[2]	•	•	•	1000[11]	•[24]	
VA	8 ½'	45'	45'	13 ½'	65'	NO	•	NO	NO	P	3000	•[2]	•	NS	NS	500[11]	•[1, 24]	
VT	8 ½'	46'	46'	13 ½'	68'	NO	•	NO	NO	NO	3000	•[2]	•	•	•	500[11, 12]		
WA	8 ½'	NS	46'	14'	75'	NO	•	NO	NO	•[16]	3000	•[2]	•	•	•	1000[12]		
WI	8 ½'	48'	40'	13 ½'	60'[1]	60'[1]	•	•[1]		NO	3000	NS	•	NS	NS		•[1, 24]	
WV	8 ½'	40'	45'	13 ½'	65'	NO	•	•		NO	3000[7]	•	•	•	NS	500[11]		
WY	8 ½'	45'	60'	14'	85'	85'	•			P	[8]	NS	•[8]	NS	NS	1000[11, 12]	•[1]	
CANADA:																		
AB	2.6m	12.5m	13m	3.85m	20m	55'	•	NS	NS	NS	2000[6]	•[5]	•[9]	NS	•	150m		
BC	2.6m	12.5m	12.5m	4.15m	20m	NS	NS	NS	NS	NS	1400kg[6]	•[5]	•	•	NS	150m[12]		
MB	2.6m	12.5m	12.5m	4.15m	21.5m	20m	•	NS	NS	•	910kg	NS	•	•[2]	NS	60m[12]		
NB	2.6m	12.5m	12.5m	4.15m	23m	NS	•	NS	NS	P	1350kg	•[2]	•	•	NS	150m		
NL	2.6m	12.5m	12.5m	4.2m	23m	NS	•	•	•	•	NS	•[22]	•	• 4	•[22]	150m[12]		
NS	2.6m	12.5m	12.5m	4.15m	23m	72'	•	NS	NS	NS	1800kg	•	•	•	•	•[13]		
NT	3.2m	NS	12.5m	4.2m	21m	NS	•	NS	NS	NS	1360kg[6]	•	•	NS	NS	•[13]		
ON	2.6m	12.5m	12.5m	4.15m	23m	NS	•	NS	NS	NS	1360kg	NS	•	NS	NS	150m[12]		
PE	2.6m	12.5m	16.2m	4.5m	25m	NS	•	•	•	P	1500kg	NS	•	NS	NS	150m[13]		
QC	2.6m	12.5m	12.5m	4.15m	23m	NS	•[18]	NS	NS	P	1300kg[6]	•[9]	•[9]	•[26]	NS	•[11]		
SK	2.6m	12.5m	12.5m[1]	4.15m	23m	•	•	•	•[1]	NS	1360kg	NS	•	NS	NS	•[12]		
YT	2.6m	16.15m	26m	4.2m	26m	NS	•	•	NS	P	910kg	•	•	•	NS	•[13]		

! **NOTE**: The regulations in the table above may have changed since the publication date. Please call state or provincial motor vehicle agencies for up-to-date rules and complete details. Information is based on the latest available data.

- • Indicates "yes" item is permitted or required
- NS Indicates "not specified"
- P Indicates "as posted"
- 1 Some exceptions
- 2 Required if weight is more than 3000 lbs; IL: 3700 kg
- 3 Required if weight is more than 6000 lbs
- 4 Required if gross weight is more than 2500 kg
- 5 Or required if gross weight (laden) is 3000 lbs (1350 kg in Canada)
- 6 Or required if the gross weight of the trailer is more than half the unladen weight of the vehicle
- 7 Or required if the gross vehicle weight is greater than 40% of the motorhome; or if the trailer weight exceeds 40% of the tow vehicle weight
- 8 Not required, but must be able to stop within 40 feet at 20 mph
- 9 Two safety chains or breakaway switch required on trailers
- 10 Laden weight noted (gross weight of the trailer plus the cargo)
- 11 Required when wipers are in continuous use
- 12 Required 30 min. before sunset and 30 min. after sunrise
- 13 Headlights or time running lights required at all times
- 14 Required when speeds exceed 45 mph on designated highways
- 15 Prohibited where posted
- 16 12-hour limit; WA: 8-hour limit; TX: 24-hour limit; NV: 18-hour limit; SD: 3-hour limit
- 17 Safety glass in windows required
- 18 With approved safety belt
- 19 Must be 14 years of age or older; HI: 13+ years; WI: 12+ years
- 20 If passenger can communicate with driver and exits can be opened from both exterior and interior
- 21 Must have free access to drive compartment
- 22 Only if required by CSA at time of manufacturer
- 23 Suggested but not required
- 24 Restrictions apply for minor drivers and/or newer drivers, or under certain conditions such as school zones, etc.
- 25 Permitted only if "hands free"
- 26 Required if RV is wider than 2 meters.

Note: Child safety restraints are required in ALL states and provinces. For more details, contact the motor vehicle agency of the state or province you plan to visit.

Bridge, Tunnel and Ferry Restrictions

A roundup of recreational vehicle restrictions in major travel corridors

LP Gas Prohibited

Alaska and British Columbia: Propane tanks on RVs must be turned off while the vehicle is on a ferry. Terminal agents will seal bottled gas containers prior to boarding. Small portable containers of fuel (5 gallons or less and limited to 2 containers) must be properly sealed, labeled with owner's name for ID and stored by Alaska Marine Highway System (AMHS) officials while en route. For more information, visit www.ferrytravel.com/alaskarv.htm.

Maryland/Baltimore: LP gas containers in excess of 10 pounds per container are prohibited on the I-95 tunnels of Baltimore Harbor and Fort McHenry. Smaller containers are allowed in quantities of no more than 10 pounds. An alternate route for RVs with propane is over the Francis Scott Key Bridge on I-695.

Massachusetts/Boston Harbor: LP gas is prohibited in the Callahan, Prudential and Dewey Square tunnels.

New Jersey/New York: LP gas is prohibited in the Holland Tunnel between Manhattan and Jersey City; the lower level of the George Washington Bridge Expressway (I-95 South) between Manhattan and Fort Lee; and in the Lincoln Tunnel between Manhattan and Weehawken.

New York: LP gas is prohibited in the Holland Tunnel between Manhattan and Jersey City; in the lower level of the George Washington Bridge Expressway (I-95 South) between Manhattan and Fort Lee; and in the Lincoln Tunnel between Manhattan and Weehawken. In addition, LP gas is prohibited between Manhattan and Brooklyn in the Brooklyn Battery Tunnel and between Manhattan and Queens in the Queens Midtown Tunnel.

Texas: LP gas is restricted in the Washburn Tunnel between Pasadena and Galena Park on the Houston Ship Channel. Vehicles are limited to a maximum of two 7½-gallon containers (30 pounds gas each) or one 10-gallon container (40 pounds of gas) of DOT (ICC) approved type, with shutoff valve at discharge opening. Valve must be closed when in tunnel. LP gas as vehicle fuel is prohibited.

Virginia: RVs may cross the Hampton Roads Bridge Tunnel, the Chesapeake Bay Bridge Tunnel and the Norfolk-Portsmouth Tunnel provided that the LP tanks don't exceed two 45-pound capacity tanks or two permanently mounted containers with a maximum total capacity of 200 pounds. Tanks must be completely shut off and securely attached.

Washington: Regulations require that you shut off and tag all propane tanks prior to boarding, unless they are the primary fuel source for your vehicle. Any number of full or empty tanks of propane may be transported in a vehicle, provided that the total weight does not exceed one hundred pounds (water weight equivalent).

Canada: In most provinces, the law dictates that all appliances and pilot lights must be turned off and cylinder valves closed while traveling.

Quebec: An RV can transport a maximum of two bottles of flammable gas each with a capacity of 46 liters (12 US gal./54 lbs.) through tunnels and bridge-tunnels.

Trailers Not Permitted

California: Contact the California Highway Patrol before entering a snow area; depending on conditions, chains may be required and pulling trailers may be prohibited. Trailers also may be barred due to high winds, blowing sand, etc. RVs over 20 feet long may experience difficulty in negotiating hairpin turns on State Highway 89.

Connecticut: Trailers are not permitted on the Wilbur Cross and Merritt parkways. Trailers are prohibited from the Connecticut River ferry between Chester and Hadlyme.

Illinois: Trailers are not permitted on boulevards in and around Chicago. If traveling from Illinois to Iowa, route around the bridge between Fulton, IL and Clinton, IA.

Iowa: Trailers are prohibited on the bridge between Clinton, Iowa and Fulton, Illinois.

Massachusetts: Trailers are not permitted on Memorial Drive in Cambridge and Storrow Drive in Boston along the Charles River.

Montana: On Going-to-the-Sun Road in Glacier National Park, all vehicles and combinations of vehicles over 21 feet long and 8 feet wide (including mirrors) are prohibited between Avalanche Campground and the Rising Sun picnic area parking. Vehicles over 10 feet in height may have clearance issues with rock overhangs driving west from Logan Pass to the Loop.

New Jersey: Vehicles longer than 55 feet aren't allowed on the New Jersey Garden State Parkway. Call 908-247-0900 for specific towing regulations for the New Jersey Turnpike or other roads.

New York: Motorhomes and trailers are not permitted on the Taconic State Parkway. Trailers are not permitted on most parkways.

Ferries: Many ferry lines charge extra for RVs. Ask about surcharges before you reserve your space on the ferry. Know your RV's height, length and width, including trailers, overhangs and towed vehicles. Most vessels can accommodate vehicles up to 60-feet in length. An additional premium may be charged for RVs that exceed the standard width rate of 8 feet, 5 inches, with the mirrors folded in.

Note! This summary isn't all-inclusive—it's limited only to the busiest bridges, tunnels and ferries in North America. For more details consult the Road and Highway information numbers on page page 171

Road and Highway Information Numbers

Information about the road/highway conditions in the state/province you're visiting

United States

	511*	Telephone	Website
AK	•	907-456-7623	511.alaska.gov
AL		334-242-6356	dot.state.al.us
AR		501-569-2374	arkansashighways.com
AZ	•	888-411-7623	az511.com
CA	•	916-445-7623	dot.ca.gov
CO	•	303-639-1111	cotrip.org
CT		800-443-6817	ct.gov/dot
DC		202-673-6813	ddot.dc.gov
DE		800-652-5600	deldot.net
FL	•		fl511.com
GA	•	404-635-8000	dot.ga.gov
IA	•	800-288-1047	511ia.org
ID	•	888-432-7623	511.idaho.gov
IL		800-452-4368	idot.illinois.gov
IN		800-261-7623	in.gov/dot
KS	•	800-585-7623	ksdot.org
KY	•	866-737-3767	511.ky.gov
LA	•		511la.org
MA	•	617-374-1234	state.ma.us/eotc
MD	•	800-327-3125	chart.state.md.us
ME	•	866-282-7578	511maine.gov
MI		800-381-8477	michigan.gov/mdot
MN	•	800-542-0220	511mn.org
MO		800-222-6400	modot.mo.gov
MS	•	601-987-1211	mdot.ms.gov
MT	•	800-226-7623	mdt.mt.gov/travinfo
NC	•	877-511-4662	ncdot.gov/travel
ND	•	866-696-3511	dot.nd.gov
NE	•	800-906-9069	511.nebraska.gov
NH		866-282-7579	nh.gov/dot/traveler
NJ	•	800-336-5875	state.nj.us/njcommuter
NM	•	800-432-4269	dot.state.nm.us
NV	•	877-687-6237	nevadadot.com
NY	•	800-847-8929	thruway.state.ny.us
OH		614-644-7031	buckeyetraffic.org
OK		888-425-2385	dps.state.ok.us
OR	•	800-977-6368	tripcheck.com
PA	•	215-567-5678	dot.state.pa.us
RI		401-222-2450	dot.ri.gov
SC	•		dot.state.sc.us
SD	•	866-697-3511	sddot.com
TN	•	800-342-3258	tdot.state.tn.us/travel.htm
TX	•	800-452-9292	dot.state.tx.us
UT	•	800-492-2400	utahcommuterlink.com
VA	•	800-578-4111	virginiadot.org
VT	•	800-429-7623	vtrans.vermont.gov
WA	•	800-695-7623	wsdot.wa.gov/traffic
WI	•	800-762-3947	dot.state.wi.us
WV	•	877-982-7623	wvdot.com
WY	•	307-772-0824	dot.state.wy.us

Canada

	511*	Telephone	Website
AB	•	855-391-9743	511.alberta.ca
BC	•	800-550-4997	drivebc.ca
MB	•	866-626-4862	manitoba511.ca
NB	•	800-561-4063	www2.gnb.ca
NL		709-729-2300	tw.gov.nl.ca
NS	•	888-423-3233	novascotia.ca/tran
NT		867-920-8771	dot.gov.nt.ca
ON	•	800-268-4686	mto.gov.on.ca
PE	•	855-241-2680	gov.pe.ca
QC	•	888-355-0511	quebec511.info
SK		888-335-7623	roadinfo.telenium.ca
YT	•	867-667-5811	511yukon.ca

! *State or province uses #511 for traffic and road information. 511 service applies only to the state or province from which the call is made.

Fishing Licenses

State and provincial fees for the traveling angler

United States

Fishing fees and regulations in the United States are overseen by various governing bodies within each of the 50 states. These offices vary and may be listed as departments of natural resources, conservation, games and parks, or fish and wildlife. Use the contact information below for more information.

	Temporary Visitor Pass		Annual Resident	Annual Visitor	Annual Sr. Resident		Phone Number
	Days	Price			Min. Age	Resident	
AK	1 | 3 | 7 | 14	$20 | $35 | $55 | $80	$24	$145	60	Free	907-465-4100
AL	7	$27.85	$12.85	$49.40	65	Free	334-242-3465
AR	3 | 7	$16 | $25	$10.50	$50	65	$10.50 Life	800-364-4263
AZ	1	$20	$37	$55	70	Free	602-942-3000
CA	1 | 2 | 10	$15.12 | $23.50 | $47.01	$47.01		62	$517 Life	916-445-0411
CO	1 | 2	$9 | $14	$26	$56	64	$1	303-297-1192
CT	3	$22	$28	$55	65	Free	860-424-3000
DE	7	$12.50	$8.50	$20	65	Free	302-739-9910
FL	3 | 7	$17 | $30	$17	$47	65	Free	850-488-4676
GA	3	$20	$9	$45	65	Free	770-918-6400
IA	1 | 3 | 7	$10.50 | $17.50 | $32	$19	$41	65	$52.50 Life	515-281-5918
ID	1	$12.75	$25.75	$98.25	65	$11.75	208-334-3700
IL	3	$16	$15	$31.50	65	$7.75	217-782-6302
IN	1 | 7	$9 | $20	$17	$35	64	$3	317-232-4200
KA	5	$22.50	$20.50	$42.50	65	$11.50	620-672-5911
KY	1 | 7 | 15	10, 30, 40	$20	$50	65	$5	800-858-1549
LA	1	$5	$9.50	$60	60	$5	225-765-2800
MA	3	$23.50	$27.50	$37.50	70	Free	617-626-1500
MD	3 | 7	Varies	$20.50	$30.50 min.	65	$5	877-620-8367
ME	1 | 3 | 7 | 15	$11 | $23 | $43 | $47	$25	$64	70	$8	207-287-8000
MI	1 | 3	$10 | $30	$26	$76	65	$11	517-373-1204
MN	1 | 3 | 7 | 14	$12 | $32 | $38 | $48	$22	$45	90	not needed	888-646-6367
MO	1	$7	$12	$42	65	Free	573-751-4115
MS	1 | 3	$8 | $15	$32	$50	65	$5 Life	601-432-2400
MT	2 | 10	$25 | $53.50	$16	$70	62	$8	406-444-2535
NC	10	$18	$20	$36	65	$15 Life	919-707-0010
ND	3 | 10	$25 | $35	$16	$45	65	$5	701-328-6300
NE	1 | 3	$8.50 | $26.50	$27.50	$59.50	69	$5	402-471-0641
NH	1 | 3 | 7	$15 | $28 | $35	$35	$53	68	Free	603-271-2461
NJ	2 7	$9 $19.50	$22.50	$34	65 70	$12.50 Free	609-292-2965
NM	1 | 5	$12 | $24	$25	$56	65 | 70	$8 | Free	505-476-8000
NV	1	$18 + $7 additional days	$29	$69	65	$13	775-688-1500
NY	1 | 7	$10 | $28	$25	$50	70	$5	518-402-8845
OH	1 | 3	$11 | $19	$19	$40	66	$10	614-265-6565

	Temporary Visitor Pass		Annual Resident	Annual Visitor	Annual Sr. Resident		Phone Number
	Days	Price			Min. Age	Resident	
OK	1 | 6	$15 | $35	$25	$55	65	$15	405-521-2739
OR	1 | 2 | 3 4 | 7	$16.75 | $31.50 | $46.25 $58 | $59.75	$33	$106.25	70	$15	800-720-6339
PA	1 | 3 | 7	$26.70 | $26.70 | $34.70	$21.70	$51.70	65	$10.70	717-705-7800
RI	3	$16	$18	$35	65	Free	401-789-0281
SC	14	$11	$10	$35	64	$9	803-734-3886
SD	1 | 3	$18 | $39	$30	$69	65	$14	605-223-7660
TN	3 10	$20.50 no trout-$40.50 all $30.50 no trout-61.50 all	$34	$50 no trout, $99 all	65	$50 Life	615-781-6500
TX	1	$16	$30-$40	$58-$68	65	$12-$22	800-792-1112
UT	3 | 7	$24 | $40	$34	$75	65	$25	801-538-4700
VA	5	$21	$23	$47	65	$9	804-367-1000
VT	1 | 3 | 7	$20 | $22 | $30	$25	$50	65	$50 Life	802-241-3700
WA	1 | 2 | 3	$20.15 | $28.95 | $35.55	$29.50	$84.50	70	$7.50	360-902-2200
WI	1 | 4 | 15	$10 | $24 | $28	$20	$50	65	$7	888-936-7463
WV	1	$3	$19	$37	65	Free	304-558-2754
WY	1	$14	$24	$92	65	Free	307-777-4600

Canada

Fishing in Canada is governed by provincial, territorial and federal law. A non residential fishing license is required for every territory or province where you plan to fish. Special fishing permits are required for fishing in national parks and can be purchased at the park site. Prices listed in Canadian dollars.

	Temporary Visitor Pass		Annual Resident	Annual Visitor	Annual Sr. Resident		Phone Number
	Days	Price			Min. Age	Resident	
AB	1 | 5	$26.63 | $47.63	$25.66	$70.90	65	Free	780-944-0313
BC	1 | 8	20 | $36* or $50**	$36	$55* or $80**	65	$5	250-387-9771
MB	NA	NA	$13.94	$32.59* or $57.12**	65	Free	204-945-6640
NB	3 | 7	$30 | $41	$18.00	$64.00	65	$15.00	506-453-3826
NL	NA	NA	$17	$53	65	$11.05	709-772-2643
NS	1 | 7	$12.71 | $33.72	$26.73	$61.37	65	$6.57	902-424-3664
NT	3	$15* or $30**	$10	$20* or $40**	65	Free	867-873-0638
NU	3	$15* or $30**	$10	$20* or $40**	65	Free	867-979-8000
ON	1 | 8	$27.27**| $57.80**	$33.72	$54.03* or $81.57**	65	Free	800-667-1940
PE	5	$5 Family	$10	$10	60	Free	902-368-4683
QC	1 | 3 | 7	$13.35 | $29.41 | $45.22	$20.96	$67.55	65	$16.61	418-644-6513
SK	3	$29.44* or $39.25**	$29.44	$58.87* or $78.51**	65	Free	800-567-4224
YT	1 | 6	$10 | $15* or $20**	$15	$25* or $35**	65	Free	867-667-5721

! ***Canadians who reside outside of the province. **Non-Canadians**

★ Playing to Win ★

Reap the physical and psychological benefits of sporting activities at RV parks

Article and photos by James and Stefany Adinaro

Just because we aren't all jocks doesn't mean we have to miss out on the fitness benefits of playing sports. Indeed, the definition of sport is being broadened all the time, and RV parks are paying attention. Many parks cater to sporty RVers by offering activities or tournaments bound to whet your competitive appetite. And because most campground sports are geared around socializing, not skill, even the average Joe (or Josie) can participate.

The Thrill of Victory

There is an overwhelming amount of research on the benefits of engaging in sports in all stages of life. First, there's the obvious physical activity benefit. You can lower your disease risk, including cardiovascular disease, diabetes, cancer and hypertension. Second, there are mental health benefits. Engaging in sports helps depression, increases self-esteem and reduces chronic stress. Since sporting activities typically involve socializing, you'll build relationships and make lifelong friends. And being social might actually add years to your life, according to research.

Read below for some examples of common campground sports, along with each sport's physical requirements and benefits. Then check the RV park listings to find the appropriate sporting opportunities at your next destination.

Pickleball

Pickleball is one of the fastest-growing sports around, and no wonder. It's played on a court that's the same size as a doubles badminton court, and players wield paddles that are smaller than tennis racquets but larger than pingpong paddles. As in tennis, the object is to hit the ball over the net, delivering a shot that lands inbounds but can't be returned by the opponent. Although the playing area is smaller than a tennis court, Pickleball does require moderate physical strain. Sign up for a doubles or singles tournament.

Tennis

While anyone can grab a racquet and volley with a friend without much difficulty, participating in a tennis tournament requires a higher level of skill. And while tennis is physically demanding, having good technique is what wins tournaments. Tennis can be a great sport for RVers since the equipment requirements are minimal, and a racquet fits easily into even the tiniest Class B. Tennis courts at RV parks are easy to find, and many even rent out racquets. After just one game of intense hitting, running and serving, you can be confident that you just got a great full-body workout.

Golf

Over the past decade, golf's popularity has soared. Many campgrounds and RV resorts cater specifically to this demographic, offering driving ranges, putting greens, and even full courses with tournament and league play. Golf is a difficult game of accuracy that will test not only your skill but also your patience; thankfully, many courses offer lessons. If you're dedicated to learning this often-vexing game, you'll be rewarded with great scenery, ample camaraderie and the health benefits of walking between holes.

Horseshoes

When it comes to campground games, horseshoes is an all-time classic. I bet we've all heard that distinctive tlink! sound at a campground or two. It's easy to grasp the basics. In official tournaments, a game is played to 40 points and requires a surprising amount of physical exertion. If you end up playing 50 innings, that's like throwing about 250 pounds of horseshoes a distance of almost a mile.

The authors traveled across America's West in their mototorhome seeking sporting fun at RV parks.

Shuffleboard

Even though it's a simple game, shuffleboard takes a surprising amount of strategy. Players take turns using long poles, called "cues," to slide discs across a court, attempting to land in marked zones to score points, while also knocking the discs of opponents out to keep them from scoring. Shuffleboard can be played at all ability levels. Don't "drink the tang" or let your "biscuit" end up in the "kitchen." No clue what any of that means? Join the next shuffleboard tournament at your campground and find out.

You might also consider water volleyball and bocce ball, both of which are offered at many RV parks. It's never too late to pick up a new sport or hobby and to make new friends.

James and Stefany Adinaro are RVing fitness professionals who work to promote a more health-conscious RV lifestyle.

SPOTLIGHT INDEX

We've taken the time to shine a Spotlight on some of the great RVing spots across North America. Check out our Spotlight features at the front of many state and provincial sections. Here's where you'll find them.

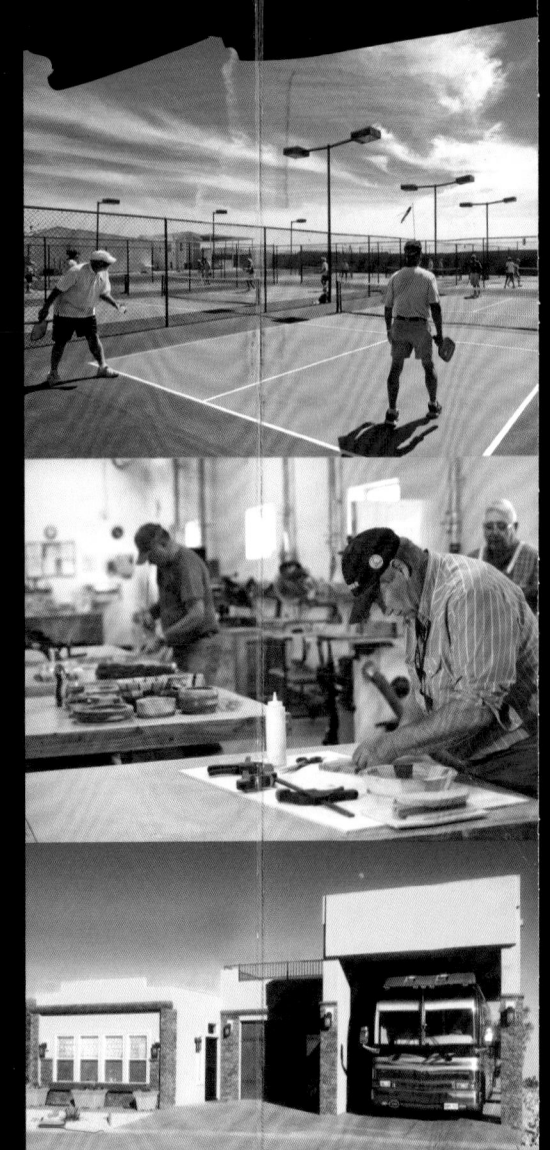

CAL AM RESORTS
ARIZONA RV & SNOWBIRD RESORTS

2016 CAL-AM CONCERT SERIES

NEIL SEDAKA

THE CHARLIE DANIELS BAND

DUBLIN'S IRISH TENORS & THE CELTIC LADIES

JAY AND THE AMERICANS

THE FAB FOUR THE ULTIMATE TRIBUTE

MALLORY LEWIS & LAMBCHOP

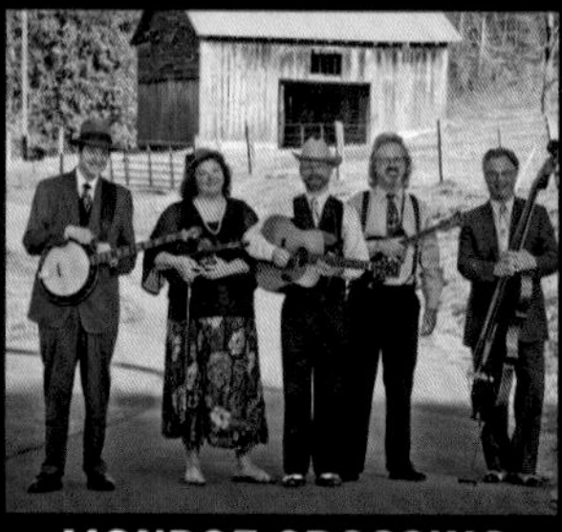

MONROE CROSSING

CAL-AM.COM/RESORTS

CAL AM RESORTS

JANUARY

MALLORY LEWIS & LAMBCHOP
JANUARY 5: VAL VISTA VILLAGE
JANUARY 6: SUNDANCE (YUMA)

JAY AND THE AMERICANS
JANUARY 27: GOOD LIFE
JANUARY 28: FORTUNA DE ORO (YUMA)

FEBRUARY

THE FAB FOUR THE ULTIMATE TRIBUTE
FEBRUARY 8: SUNFLOWER
FEBRUARY 9: CANYON VISTAS
FEBRUARY 10: SUN LIFE

MONROE CROSSING
FEBRUARY 23: TOWERPOINT
FEBRUARY 24: SUNFLOWER
FEBRUARY 25: FORTUNA DE ORO (YUMA)

MARCH

THE CHARLIE DANIELS BAND
7:30PM ONLY
MARCH 1: MESA REGAL
MARCH 2: VALLE DEL ORO
MARCH 3: VALLE DEL ORO

DUBLIN'S IRISH TENORS & THE CELTIC LADIES
MARCH 8: MESA REGAL
MARCH 9: VALLE DEL ORO

NEIL SEDAKA
7:30PM ONLY
MARCH 15: VALLE DEL ORO
MARCH 16: VALLE DEL ORO

SHOWTIMES

4:00 & 7:30PM

PRICING

Neil Sedaka,
The Charlie Daniels Band
Residents $60 - 65 - 70
Guest $70 - 75 - 80

Jay And The Americans,
The Fab Four The Ultimate Tribute,
Dublin's Irish Tenors & The Celtic Ladies
Residents $35 - 40 - 50
Guests $45 - 50 - 60

Mallory Lewis & Lambchop,
Monroe Crossing
Residents $15 - 20 - 25
Guest $20 - 25 - 30

Canyon Vistas	Mesa Regal	Sun Life	Sunflower	Val Vista Village	Valle Del Oro	Good Life	Towerpoint	Fortuna de Oro	Sundance
480.648.1001	480.981.5118	480.219.6737	623.583.9374	480.832.2550	480.984.5076	480.641.9925	480.854.8180	928.366.1274	928.305.3509

Getty Images/iStockphoto

WELCOME TO Alabama

DATE OF STATEHOOD	WIDTH: 190 MILES (305 KM)	PROPORTION OF UNITED STATES
DEC. 14, 1819	LENGTH: 330 MILES (531 KM)	1.38% OF 3,794,100 SQ MI

Alabama exudes the essence of the Deep South, evoking images of antebellum mansions, quaint country lanes and time-honored Southern traditions. You will find that and more here, including a world-class golf trail, a timeless football tradition and white-sand Gulf beaches rich with recreation opportunities.

Learn

The state capital of Montgomery was also the first capital of the Confederate States of America. Take a tour of the city to see the Greek Revival capitol building where Jefferson Davis took the oath of office as President of the Confederate States of America in 1861. Also in town, you'll find the Dexter Avenue Church where Dr. Martin Luther King presided for six years in his only full-time pastorate. Make sure to check out the Rosa Parks Museum, dedicated to the Civil Rights movement. Closer to the Alabama River, the Hank Williams Museum honors the country-music icon who moved to Montgomery when he was 14 years old and performed his first songs here.

Shipbuilding transformed antebellum Mobile into a modern city, and its most famous product, the battleship USS Alabama, earned nine Battle Stars in World War II. The vessel maintains a permanent berth at Battleship Park. Guarding the entrance to Mobile Bay, Civil War forts Gaines and Morgan still stand and are administered by the National Park Service.

In 1950, the United States Army chose Huntsville as its Ordnance Guided Missile Center; northern Alabama town soon earned the monicker, "Rocket City." Today, the U.S. Space & Rocket Center is "Earth's largest space museum," taking visitors from the very beginning of space exploration to exhibits that offer visions of the future. A Saturn V moon rocket highlights the 1,500 permanent objects on display.

Play

Alabama is justly famous for its pristine white-sand beaches on the Gulf of Mexico. In the central Alabama town of Tuscaloosa, college football is king, and each fall the University of Alabama "rolls" out its Crimson Tide. The Appalachian Mountains to the north are still formidable enough to host the country's southernmost ski resort east of New Mexico. Over the eons, the Little River has carved gorges 700 feet deep to create the most impressive canyon scape in the Southeast. The Sipsey Wilderness calls itself the "Land of 1,000 Waterfalls," and it is underselling the count.

Alabama's Robert Trent Jones Golf Trail features several golf courses across the state; bring your clubs and tee off world-famous links. If you prefer fishing to fairways, the Alabama Bass Trail leads

Top 3 Tourism Attractions:
1) U.S. Space and Rocket Center
2) Talladega Superspeedway
3) Cheaha State Park

Nickname: Yellowhammer State

State Flower: Camellia

State Bird: Yellowhammer

People: Hank Aaron, baseball player; Nat King Cole, singer; Helen Keller, author; Hank Williams, singer, songwriter and musician

Major Cities: Birmingham, Montgomery (capital), Mobile, Huntsville, Tuscaloosa

Topography: Coastal Plains near the Gulf, hills near the central and northern areas

Climate: Humid, subtropical; monthly average temps from 91.5° to -30°; Extremes: 112° to –27°

The Alabama Bureau of Tourism & Travel
©JeffreyGreenberg@aol.com

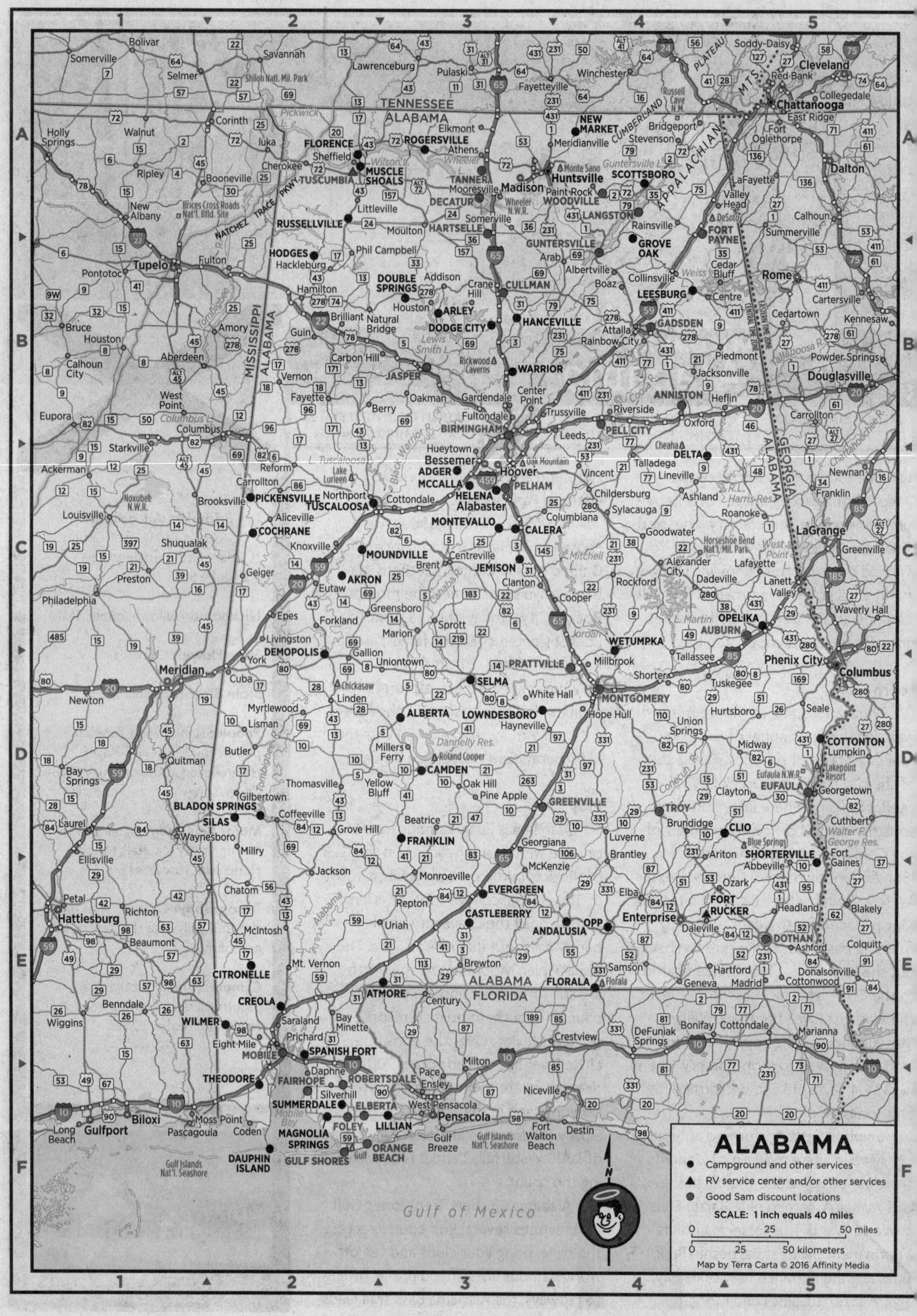
ALABAMA
Campground and other services
RV service center and/or other services
Good Sam discount locations
SCALE: 1 inch equals 40 miles
0 25 50 miles
0 25 50 kilometers
Map by Terra Carta © 2016 Affinity Media
Gulf of Mexico

you on an odyssey for the Big One. The Alabama Scenic River Trail covers 631 miles for paddling and casting on the country's longest single-state water trail.

More than two of every three Alabama acres is covered in woodlands, and that provides shelter for some 400 species of birds along the state's many birding trails. Eight trails have been mapped out for birders; make sure not to miss Lake Guntersville State Park, a winter nesting site for bald eagles. The lake is also Alabama's largest water impoundment, with 69,000 acres of prime largemouth bass fishing.

The Huntsville Botanical Garden has 112 acres of beautiful gardens connected by walking paths. Alabama Bureau of Tourism & Travel

Experience

The first Mardi Gras in the United States was celebrated in Mobile in 1703—15 years before there even was a New Orleans. Nowadays, Carnival season begins in November, with exclusive parties and balls that roar through Twelfth Night on January 6. Every day for two weeks, leading up to actual Mardi Gras day, a parade takes place in Mobile.

When it comes to football, Alabama is legendary. There are many storied college football rivalries, but none can top the gridiron match-up between the two largest public universities in Alabama, the University of Alabama's Crimson Tide and Auburn's Tigers. The two sides traditionally clash every Thanksgiving weekend in the Iron Bowl, a highly charged game that grabs the attention of the sports world.

Taste

When it comes to sweet treats, Moon Pies are an Alabama tradition. Earl Mitchell developed the graham cracker, marshmallow and chocolate confection in 1917 as a snack for coal miners. Today, Tossing Moon Pies during Mardi Gras parades is a tradition in Mobile. The state's largest Moon Pie Eating Contest is staged in McCalla every Labor Day.

TRAVEL & TOURISM

Alabama Tourism Department
800-ALABAMA, 334-242-4169
www.alabama.travel

Alabama Mountain Lakes Tourist Association
800-648-5381
www.northalabama.org

Historic Chattahoochee Commission
334-687-9755
www.chattahoocheetrace.com

Visit Montgomery County
877-789-6904
www.visitmontgomery.com

Southeast Alabama Trails Tourism Association
334-794-4093
www.southeastalabamatrails.com

Tenn-Tom Tourism Association
662-328-3286
www.tenntom.org

Tour East Alabama
www.toureastalabama.com

OUTDOOR RECREATION

Alabama Dept. of Conservation & Natural Resources, Game & Fish Division
334-242-3465
www.dcnr.state.al.us

Sunbelt Golf Corporation
800-949-4444
www.rtjgolf.com

SHOPPING

Boaz Shopper's Paradise
800-SHOP-BOAZ

Mountain Top Flea Market
800-535-2286

Quintard Mall
256-831-4180
www.shopquintardmall.com

Rue's Antique Mall and Deli
334-735-3125

Featured Good Sam Parks

ALABAMA

Good Sam Park

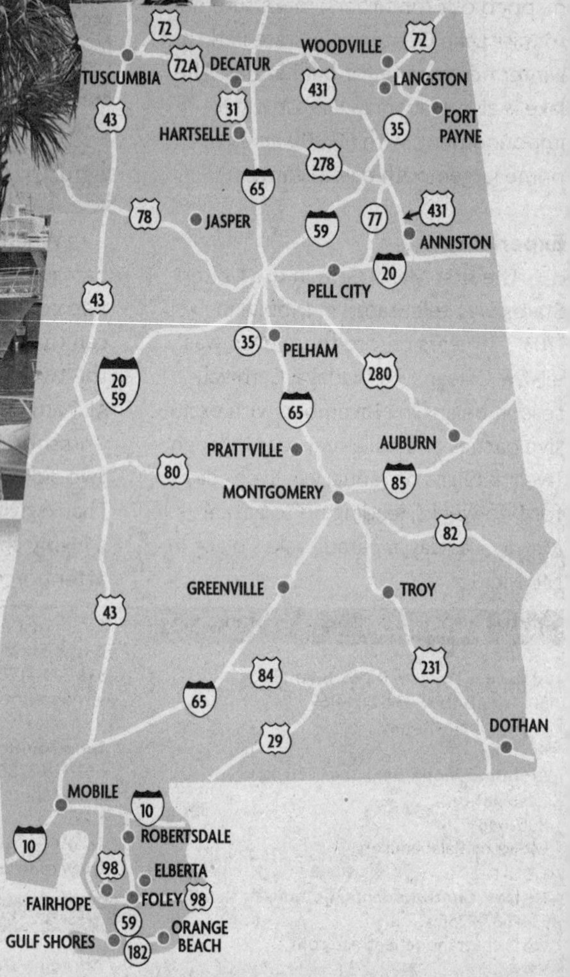

When you stay with Good Sam, you can expect the highest degree of cleanliness and friendliness, and better yet, you get 10% off campground fees.

If you're not already a Good Sam member you can purchase your membership at one of these locations:

ANNISTON
Country Court RV Park
(256)835-2045

AUBURN
Auburn RV Park At Leisure Time Campground
(334)821-2267
Eagles Landing RV Park
(334)821-8805

DECATUR
Point Mallard Campground
(256)341-4826

DOTHAN
Cherry Blossom RV & MH Park
(334)792-3313

ELBERTA
Lake Osprey RV Resort
(251)545-4940

FAIRHOPE
Driftwood RV Park
(251)928-8233

FOLEY
Johnny's Lakeside RV Resort
(251)970-3773

FORT PAYNE
Wills Creek RV Park LLC
(256)845-6703

GREENVILLE
Sherling Lake Park & Campground
(334)382-3638

GULF SHORES
Island Retreat RV Park
(251)967-1666

HARTSELLE
Quail Creek RV Resort
(256)784-5033

JASPER
Sleepy Holler Campground
(205)483-7947

LANGSTON
Windemere Cove RV Resort
(256)228-3010

MOBILE
Bay Palms RV Resort
(251)873-4700
I-10 Kampground
(251)653-9816
I-65 RV Campground
(800)287-3208
Shady Acres Campground
(251)478-0013

MONTGOMERY
Capital City RV Park
(877)271-8026
The Woods RV Park & Campground
(334)356-1887

ORANGE BEACH
Heritage Motorcoach Resort & Marina
(800)730-7032

PELHAM
Birmingham South Campground
(205)664-8832

PELL CITY
Lakeside Landing Marina & RV Resort
(205)525-5701

PRATTVILLE
Kountry Air RV Park
(334)365-6861

ROBERTSDALE
Azalea Acres RV Park
(251)947-9530
Hilltop RV Park
(251)960-1129

TROY
Deer Run RV Park
(334)566-6517

TUSCUMBIA
Heritage Acres RV Park
(256)383-7368

WOODVILLE
Parnell Creek RV Park
(256)508-7308

For more Good Sam Parks go to listing pages

Getty Images/iStockphoto

SPOTLIGHT AL

AUBURN-OPELIKA

A cozy town meets crazy football fandom in 'Bama

With its collection of tidy tree-lined streets, family-owned shops and small-town football traditions, it's easy to see why the cozy little city of Auburn is known as "The Loveliest Village on the Plains." Along with its nearby sister city of Opelika (together they form a combined metropolitan area with a population of of roughly 150,000 people), this hidden gem in eastern Alabama is a treat for anyone on the hunt for a dose of real American nostalgia.

Nestled into the smooth, rolling flatlands of the western Piedmont Plains—midway between Montgomery, Alabama, and Columbus, Georgia—the Auburn and Opelika area is known for its historic homes, raucous college football traditions, great outdoor parks and incredible golf courses.

Start in Auburn with a slice of college life. In Auburn, the university and its football team, the Auburn Tigers, rule the roost.

The Auburn and Opelika area is known for its historic homes, raucous college football traditions, great outdoor parks and incredible golf courses.

College Life

The sprawling (and incredibly historic) Auburn University campus is conveniently situated in the center of town and boasts its own impressive historic district. Revivalist architecture dating from the 1850's buffer the borders of gorgeous Samford Park, with the can't-miss highlights including the University Chapel, Samford Hall and Hargis Hall. Anyone with an eye for architecture, whether trained or untrained, will enjoy a stroll here.

If it's football season (late August to early January) a stop at the country's 10th largest on-campus football stadium, Jordan-Hare, for a Tigers game is a must. On Fridays prior to home games, anyone interested in soaking up the quintessential college football experience can take a free campus tour that includes a pre-game locker room tour. During the game, the Cafe Jordan-Hare offers a chance to dine on the 50-yard line with unparalleled views of the action on the field.

After the game (especially after a Tigers' win), football fans converge at nearby Toomer's Corner.

Named after the family-owned diner and drugstore first established in 1896 at the intersection of College Street and Magnolia Avenue, Toomer's Corner is the place where locals gather to celebrate big wins. The diner still stands and operates today, and no trip to Auburn would be complete without stopping for a taste of its famous lemonade and a freshly made sandwich. After Tigers' victories, fans drape the trees and streets surrounding Toomer's Corner with hundreds of rolls of toilet paper, a quirky tradition dating back to the early 1970's.

Toomer's Corner store serves up lemonade and hot dogs. Auburn and Opelika Tourism

Peaking at Alabama's Past

Bookending your exploration of Auburn University should be a stop at the campus' Jule Collins Smith Museum, which is home to more than 2,000 works of fine art, both traditional and contemporary. The collections are regarded as one of the finest in Alabama, so this is a must for art lovers.

Next on the itinerary, venture just a few miles down the road to the east, where the even smaller city of Opelika offers even more history and small-town charm with its buffet of mom and pop shops, cafes and restaurants.

Opelika's quaint downtown is a treat to stroll and window shop. Start at the Promenade and the Lee County Courthouse, a striking neoclassical building dating to 1896 (and still serving as the county's courthouse today). Nearby, the Northside Historic District is comprised of remarkable and fully restored turn-of-the-century homes built in classic Victorian styles. Informative walking tours of the area can be arranged through the Opelika Tourism Bureau and are highly recommended for history buffs.

A similar attraction can be found just a few miles to the west of Auburn and Opelika. The Loachapoka Historic District is home to 14 antebellum-era homes, two churches dating to the 1840's, a 100-year old schoolhouse and an informative museum showcasing the history of Lee County.

Once you've familiarized yourself with history and attractions, Auburn and Opelika also offers a rich selection of parks and lakes to enjoy year round.

Kiesel Park offers 124-acres of renowned walking and hiking trails, while Chewacla State Park features a 26-acre lake for seasonal boating and swimming. The delightfully named Hickory Dickory Park is a great picnic area and includes playgrounds for children of all ages. For anglers looking to reel in some fresh catch, the Lee County Public Fishing Lake in central Opelika offers 130-acres of fantastic fishing.

For More Information

Auburn and Opelika Tourism Bureau
866-880-8747
www.aotourism.com

Alabama Tourism Department
800-ALABAMA
www.alabama.travel

Alabama Bureau of Tourism & Travel

DECATUR

Meet history at every corner of a town forged in the Civil War

Throughout its history, the small city of Decatur in northern Alabama has been anything but forgettable. Founded in 1820 as a scrappy backcountry ferry crossing, it was soon transformed—almost overnight—with the arrival of the railroad and major industry. The burgeoning settlement expanded and the population boomed. The first glimmers of a city on the rise began to emerge. Then, during the Civil War, Decatur's place on the map and its all-important railroad junction ensured it would be fiercely fought over.

The city, miraculously, was rebuilt—even as two separate plagues of remorseless yellow fever tore through the rebuilding efforts. Today, clusters of perfectly preserved Victorian-era bungalows that were constructed during the city's rebirth still dot its two historic districts.

History Lover's Paradise

There's just no denying it: This is a town for history buffs. So much so that the town has both an Old Decatur Historic District and a New/Albany Decatur Historic District—you can visit both in one stroll. Stop at the Decatur Visitor Center at the center of town beforehand to pick up some self-guided tour maps of each district. One of the major highlights is the Blue & Gray Museum of North Alabama.

When it's time to jump back into the present day and unwind with a bit of family fun, head for Point Mallard Park. In fact, if you're traveling with children, you can absolutely plan to spend more than a few days here, as the park is, in fact, home to a water park, 18-hole golf course, driving range, ice skating complex and batting cage area. Hiking trails and biking trails ring the park.

Civil War Re-enactments

As far as major events go, the Battle for Decatur is a must. Held over Labor Day weekend each year, this Civil War re-enactment is free and open to the public. In addition to battle re-enactments, it includes a re-created walk-through Civil War camp with displays of authentic equipment. Narrated tours are offered at various points during the weekend by Civil War guides.

For More Information

Decatur-Morgan County Convention and Visitors Bureau
256-350-2028
www.decaturcvb.org

Alabama Tourism Department
800-252-2262
www.alabama.travel

GULF SHORES/ORANGE BEACH

Sand and sun rule this laid-back Gulf Coast town

Something incredible happens when you arrive at the white sandy beaches and cozy waterfront towns of Alabama's southern Gulf Coast: The outside world melts away, and only a landscape of sun-soaked relaxation and adventure remains. More than 50 miles from the nearest big city in the state (Mobile), and essentially surrounded by water on three sides, it's easy to slip straight into vacation mode here, where history dances with recreation and the hustle and bustle of city life are nowhere to be found.

Once a little-known hidden gem, this sparkling beachfront region is now a go-to getaway destination for families from far and wide. It's no surprise why—32 miles of soft sandy beaches rim the region's coastal edges, offering an inexhaustible supply world-class fishing, scuba diving, boating, swimming, kayaking, hiking and guided wildlife tours for outdoors enthusiasts. And when you're done with the big skies, big horizons and big beaches for the day, there's the small town of Gulf Shores and the even smaller town of Orange Beach to explore, as well as a slew of eclectic attractions all within easy reach no matter where on the coast you're calling home.

Most will find themselves centered around the area known to locals as Pleasure Island, where you'll find the triple crown cluster: Gulf Shores, Orange Beach and Gulf State Park. From here, a series of short and easy day trips further west to Fort Morgan, Fort Gaines, Bon Secour National Wildlife Refuge and Little Dauphin Island are popular and recommended for visitors of all ages and backgrounds.

Hit the Beach

The town of Orange Beach is particularly inviting. With a population of roughly 5,000 year-round residents, it's the type of charming beachfront community that's easy to imagine only existing in movies. A handful of main streets string together a picturesque village dotted with ice cream parlors, family-owned stores, and delightful mom and pop restaurants. It also offers the easiest access to Wolf Bay, Bay La Launch, Bayou Saint John and Perdido Bay.

When it's time to stray from the quaint streets and shops of Orange Beach and Gulf Shores, set your sights on Gulf State Park. Nestled snuggly between Gulf Shores and Orange Beach, it bursts with a generous mix of protected beaches, well-maintained wildlife trails, public tennis courts, a state-of-the-art zipline center and even an 18-hole championship golf course. Freshwater anglers can drop their lines into 900-acre Lake Shelby, and saltwater anglers can cast their lines straight off the pier into the Gulf of Mexico.

A few miles westward, Bon Secour National Wildlife Refuge offers 7,000 acres of lush protected park space that annually attracts more than 100,000 visitors. Like Gulf State Park, it's a well-balanced blend of beaches and scrub forest, making it popular with hikers, bird-watchers (the refuge is a migratory bird stopover in spring and fall) and anglers. Celebrity park dwellers include loggerhead sea turtles, red foxes, armadillos and more than 370 distinct species of birds.

Wild Animals and Living History

Quaint small towns and water sports aren't the only things going on around the Gulf Coast, though. History buffs and families travelling with children are well served with attractions like Fort Morgan, Fort Gaines, the Orange Beach Indian and Sea Museum, the Gulf Shores Museum, the Alabama Gulf Coast Zoo and Adventure Island.

> Fort Morgan and Fort Gaines are definite must-visit attractions. Bracketing either side of the entry to Mobile Bay, each one is a window back in time.

Fort Morgan and Fort Gaines are definite must-visit attractions. Bracketing either side of the entry to Mobile Bay—like a pair of hardened, concrete teeth—each site stands as a window back in time to the early 19th century, when the region was a place of battle and brinkmanship. On-site museums, exhibits and guided tours tell the stories of each fort as they played witness to moments from four major wars, including the War of 1812, the Battle of Mobile Bay and the Spanish-American War.

For more light-hearted fare, the Alabama Gulf Coast Zoo and nearby Adventure Island are both big hits for visitors of all ages. More than 500 animals, including lions and tigers, call the zoo home. The major highlight is the elevated observation deck that allows for great vantage points and unobstructed views of some of the most exotic animals in the world. Meanwhile, at Adventure Island, thrilling rides and activities like laser tag, go-kart racing and miniature golf offer a nice change of pace. The highlight here is a massive five-story volcano that "erupts" at various scheduled times each day.

Alabama's Gulf Coast has something for everyone. Buzzing with great activities, fun adventures and gorgeous beaches, the region is well worth a visit.

For More Information

Alabama Gulf Coast
800-745-SAND
www.gulfshores.com

Alabama Travel
800-ALABAMA
www.alabama.travel

 See map page 2

SPOTLIGHT
AL
Getty Images/iStockphoto
TROY
Savor small-town Americana in this quaint community

Classic small-town ambiance and charm are on full display in Troy, Alabama. From its walkable downtown core—full of historic buildings and fantastic antique shops clustered around a timeless town square—to its buffet of picturesque "Heart of Dixie" landscapes that stretch for hundreds of miles in every direction, Troy is a spot that's easy to overlook but difficult to forget.

Located in the southeastern corner of the state and at the confluence of U.S. Routes 231 and 29, Troy sits a relatively short distance away from a pair of major cities, making spontaneous day trips easy and painless. Montgomery, 50 miles to the north, is less than an hour's drive away, while Columbus, 88 miles to the northeast in neighboring Georgia, is less than a two-hour drive away.

If you were passing through Troy in its early days, you would have found its location just as central as it is today. However, there's a good chance you would have been stuck scratching your head, trying to figure out where, exactly, you were. Known first as Deer Stand Hill in the 1830s, the settlement was then later called Zebulon. Later still it was known as Centreville. To further confound things, at one point the county seat (then Monticello) was shifted to the community we now know as Troy.

Walk Through Troy's Past

Today, finding and visiting this idyllic Alabama township is, of course, far easier. And when you first arrive, you'll no doubt find yourself drawn to its historic downtown core. With a traditional old town square serving as the hub, the downtown area is dotted with a mix of eclectic museums, art galleries and family-owned restaurants.

For a dash of history, swing by the Pioneer Museum of Alabama. Housed on a massive 35-acre complex, it's home to 20 heritage buildings, more than 18,000 artifacts and a "living history" farmstead. The site features vivid displays and immersive walk-through exhibits that tell the history of Troy and Alabama from pioneer times through the Civil War to the turn of the century. Live folk demonstrations occur daily.

Sweet Southern Air

When it's time to catch some fresh air and stretch your legs, you can follow the locals to Pike County Lake, a popular nearby spot for a picnic, hike or an afternoon of fishing. Closed for renovations and restocking the last two years, the lake is scheduled to reopen summer 2016. Troy University's Arboretum botanical garden is another popular draw, and an entire day can easily be spent exploring its blooming displays and 2.5-mile natural swamp trail. But if you're visiting Troy for the first time, do yourself a favor and hop on the Heart of Dixie Trail to see southern Alabama's gorgeous landscapes by horseback.

For More Information

Troy Alabama
334-670-2283
www.troyal.gov/visiting

Alabama Tourism Department
800-ALABAMA
www.alabama.travel

Alabama

CONSULTANTS

Henry & Anne Goldman

ADGER — C3 *Jefferson*

BURCHFIELD BRANCH PARK (Public Corps) From I-20 (exit 86), N 24.5 mi on CR-59 to Lock 17 Rd/CR-54, W 6.3 mi on Lock 17 Rd/CR-54 to Bankhead Rd, W 2 mi on Bankhead Rd (E). 2015 rates: $16 to $24. (205)497-9828

AKRON — C2 *Hale*

JENNINGS FERRY (Public Corps) From town, E 5.3 mi on SR-14, follow signs (E). 2015 rates: $22. (205)372-1217

ALBERTA — D3 *Wilcox*

DANNELLY LAKE/CHILATCHEE CREEK (Public Corps) From town, SE 9 mi on CR-29 to access rd, E 2 mi, follow signs (E). 2015 rates: $20 to $22. Mar 1 to Sep 2. (334)573-2562

ALEXANDER CITY — C4 *Tallapoosa*

WIND CREEK (State Pk) From Jct of US-280 & Hwy 63, S 4.3 mi on Hwy 63 to Hwy 128, E 1.5 mi (R). 2015 rates: $18 to $24. (205)329-0845

ANDALUSIA — E4 *Covington*

A SWEET HOME ALABAMA CAMPGROUND & RV PARK Ratings: 8/7/8 (RV Park) From Jct of US Hwy 84 & US 29N (In town), N 6 mi on US 29N to CR-59 (Point A Rd), W 2.3 mi to Conecuh Cove Rd, S 0.2 mi to Sailboat Rd (R). **FAC:** Paved rds. 25 paved, 16 pull-thrus (45 x 60), back-ins (35 x 45), 25 W, 25 E (30/50 amps), cable, WiFi, tent sites, dump, mobile sewer, laundry, LP bottles, fire rings, firewood. **REC:** Point A Lake: swim, fishing, playground. Pet restrict 2015 rates: $22 to $26.
(334)388-0342 Lat: 31.37653, Lon: -86.51237
25882 Sailboat Rd, Andalusia, AL 36421
theshac@shacrvpark.com
www.shacrvpark.com

ANNISTON — B4 *Calhoun*

CAMPGROUND OF OXFORD **Ratings: 7/9.5★/7** (RV Park) 2015 rates: $35 to $38. (256)241-2295 20 Garrett Circle, Anniston, AL 36207

COUNTRY COURT RV PARK
Ratings: 5/NA/5.5 (RV Park) From Jct of I-20 & US 431 (Exit 191), N 0.3 mi on US 431 to US 78, W 2.4 mi on US 78 (R). **FAC:** Paved rds. (46 spaces). Avail: 20 gravel, 20 pull-thrus (24 x 60), 20 full hkups (30/50 amps), seasonal sites, cable, WiFi. Pets OK. No tents. Big rig sites, 2015 rates: $27 to $30. No CC.
(256)835-2045 Lat: 33.61771, Lon: -85.76218
3459 US 78E, Anniston, AL 36207
countrycourtrvpark@live.com
See ad this page, 4.

Looking for a new or used RV? Camping World is America's largest retailer of RVs. Click CampingWorld.com or visit SuperCenters nationwide.

Travel Services

CAMPING WORLD OF ANNISTON As the nation's largest retailer of RV supplies, accessories, services and new and used RVs, Camping World is committed to making your total RV experience better. RV Accessories: (888)204-9015. **SERVICES:** RV, tire, RV appliance, staffed RV wash, restrooms, RV Sales. RV supplies, LP, dump, emergency parking, RV accessible. waiting room. Hours: 8am to 6pm. ATM.
(888)873-2216 Lat: 33.61435, Lon: -85.77309
2772 US Hwy 78 E, Suite 2, Anniston, AL 36207
www.campingworld.com

ARLEY — B3 *Winston*

HIDDEN COVE OUTDOOR RESORT **Ratings: 7.5/6/8.5** (Membership Pk) 2015 rates: $36 to $44. (800)405-6188 687 CR 3919, Arley, AL 35541

ATHENS — A3 *Limestone*

NORTHGATE RV-TRAVEL PARK **Ratings: 3/NA/6** (RV Park) 2015 rates: $25. (256)232-8800 1757 Hwy 31 N, Athens, AL 35613

ATMORE — E3 *Escambia*

LITTLE RIVER STATE FOREST (FORMERLY CLAUDE D. KELLEY SP) (State Pk) From jct I-65 & Hwy 21: Go 12 mi N on Hwy 21. 2015 rates: $20 to $22. (251)862-2511

MAGNOLIA BRANCH WILDLIFE RESERVE **Ratings: 6/7/7** (RV Park) 2015 rates: $25 to $30. (251)446-3423 24 Big Creek Road, Atmore, AL 36502

AUBURN — C5 *Lee*

A SPOTLIGHT Introducing Auburn-Opelika's colorful attractions appearing at the front of this state section.

AUBURN RV PARK AT LEISURE TIME CAMPGROUND
Ratings: 7/10★/8 (Campground) From Jct of I-85 & US-29 (Exit 51), S 0.2 mi on US-29 (R). Note: Turn right just after Hampton Inn, follow signs.

NEAR AUBURN UNIVERSITY I-85 EXIT 51
Easy on-off Interstate access. Only RV park in the Auburn city limits that is privately owned. Lg, wide, Big Rig friendly, pull thrus & shady quiet sites avail. Game Day shuttle. Wi-Fi & cable www.rvauburn.com or 334-821-2267

FAC: Paved/gravel rds. (90 spaces). 70 Avail: 30 paved, 40 gravel, 28 pull-thrus (24 x 70), back-ins (24 x 60), 70 full hkups (30/50 amps), seasonal sites, cable, WiFi, tent sites, rentals, laundry, LP gas. Pets OK. Partial handicap access. Big rig sites, eco-friendly, 2015 rates: $26 to $36. Disc: AAA, military.
AAA Approved
(334)821-2267 Lat: 32.55367, Lon: -85.51044
2670 S College St, Auburn, AL 36832
info@rvauburn.com
www.rvauburn.com
See ad pages 12, 4.

CHEWACLA (State Pk) From Jct of I-85 & US-29 (exit 51), S 0.2 mi on US-29 to Shell Toomer Pkwy, E 1.7 mi (E). 2015 rates: $28.25. (334)887-5621

EAGLES LANDING RV PARK
Ratings: 8/10★/10 (RV Park) From Jct I-85 & Hwy 29/147 (Exit 51), N 1.5 mi on Hwy 29/147 to Hwy 267 (University Dr), W 1 mi on Hwy 267 to Wire Rd, SW 1 mi on Wire Rd (R). **FAC:** Gravel rds. (59 spaces). 49 Avail: 18 paved, 31 gravel, 23 pull-thrus (30 x 60), back-ins (30 x 60), 49 full hkups (30/50 amps), seasonal sites, cable, WiFi, rentals, dump, laundry, LP gas, firewood. **REC.** Pets OK. No tents. Big rig sites, eco-friendly, 2015 rates: $35 to $55. Disc: military.
(334)821-8805 Lat: 32.58262, Lon: -85.51929
1900 Wire Road, Auburn, AL 36832
info@eagleslandingrv.com
eagleslandingrv.com
See ad this page, 4.

Explore America's Top RV Destinations! Turn to the Spotlight articles in our State and Province sections to learn more.

Things to See and Do

AUBURN-OPELIKA TOURISM BUREAU Home of Auburn University. Robert Trent Jones Golf Trail. Restaurants, shopping, nightlife, arts and culture. Hours Monday thru Friday. RV accessible. Restrooms. Hours: 8am to 5pm. No CC.
(866)880-8747 Lat: 32.60845, Lon: -85.46747
714 East Glenn Avenue, Auburn, AL 36830
johnwild@aotourism.com
www.aotourism.com
See ad page 6 (Spotlight Auburn-Opelika).

From fishing along the Cape to boating on the Great Lakes, we've put the Spotlight on North America's most popular travel destinations. Turn to the Spotlight articles in our State and Province sections to learn more.

AUBURN RV PARK
at LEISURE TIME CAMPGROUND
(334) 821-2267
PHONE ANSWERED 24/7
2670 South College St. Auburn, AL 36832
Daily, Weekly and Monthly Rates Available
Cabin Rentals Available
Adjacent to I-85 for easy Interstate Access
Next Door to the Auburn Softball Complex
& Auburn Links Golf Course
Heated and Cooled
Full Hookups 30/50 Amp
Cable and Good WiFi
Restrooms & Showers
Laundry and Ice
Gameday Shuttle
Mobile Onsite Repair
Big Rigs Welcome
NOW OFFERING RV STORAGE
ATLANTA
AUBURN UNIVERSITY
I-85 EXIT 51
MONTGOMERY
RV PARK
Water Front Sites
Pull-thru Sites easy-on/off Interstate
TIGER TRANSIT
Gameday Shuttle
Cabin Rentals Available
Convenient to Auburn University
Big Rig Friendly
The Auburn RV Experience
See listing Auburn, AL
www.auburnrv.com
Good Sam Park
AAA APPROVED
WOODALL'S
AARP
FAMILY MOTOR COACH ASSOC.
PET FRIENDLY

BIRMINGHAM — B3 *Jefferson*

BIRMINGHAM See also Calera, Helena, Jasper, McCalla, Pelham, Pell City & Warrior.

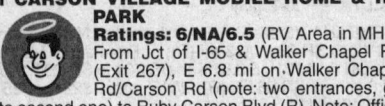

CARSON VILLAGE MOBILE HOME & RV PARK
Ratings: 6/NA/6.5 (RV Area in MHP) From Jct of I-65 & Walker Chapel Rd (Exit 267), E 6.8 mi on Walker Chapel Rd/Carson Rd (note: two entrances, go to second one) to Ruby Carson Blvd (R). Note: Office is in Plaza. CAUTION: Some sites have steep access & deep drainage ditches on roads. **FAC:** Paved rds. (170 spaces). Avail: 47 gravel, patios, back-ins (30 x 80), 47 full hkups (30/50 amps), seasonal sites, cable, laundry, groc, LP bottles, restaurant. **REC.** Pet restrict(B/Q). No tents. Big rig sites, 2015 rates: $30.
(205)854-0059 Lat: 33.65998, Lon: -86.71937
400 North Carson Rd, Birmingham, AL 35215
carsonvillage@towermgmt.com
carsonvillagemhp.com

HOOVER RV PARK
(Public) From Jct of I-459 & Hwy 150 (Exit 10), E 0.3 mi on Hwy 150 to Stadium Trace, S 1.9 mi (L). Follow RV Parking Signs. **FAC:** Paved rds. 142 paved, 142 pull-thrus (20 x 45), mostly side by side hkups, 142 full hkups (30/50 amps), cable, WiFi, dump. Pets OK. No tents. 2015 rates: $32 to $36.
(866)466-8378 Lat: 33.20128, Lon: -86.50884
100 Ben Chapman Drive, Hoover, AL 35244
www.hooveral.org
See ad this page.

BLADON SPRINGS — D2 *Choctaw*

BLADON SPRINGS (State Pk) From jct US 43 & US 84: Go 25 mi on US 84 E, then turn S on CR 6 traveling approx 4 mi to park. 2015 rates: $20 to $23. (251)754-9207

CALERA — C3 *Shelby*

ROLLING HILLS RV PARK **Ratings: 6/6.5/5.5** (RV Park) 2015 rates: $28. (205)668-6893 521 Hwy 304, Calera, AL 35040

Travel Services

CAMPING WORLD OF CALERA As the nation's largest retailer of RV supplies, accessories, services and new and used RVs, Camping World is committed to making your total RV experience better. RV Accessories: (855)209-5030. **SERVICES:** RV, RV appliance, MH mechanical, staffed RV wash, restrooms, RV Sales. RV supplies, LP, dump, emergency parking, RV accessible. waiting room. Hours: 8am to 6pm. No CC.
(888)828-6391 Lat: 33.09549, Lon: -86.46331
730 George Roy Parkway, Calera, AL 35040
CampingWorldofBirmingham.com

CAMDEN — D3 *Wilcox*

DANNELLY LAKE/EAST BANK CAMPGROUND/MILLER'S FERRY CAMPGROUND (Public Corps) From Camden, W 11 mi on Hwy 28 to corps access rd, follow signs (E). 2015 rates: $20 to $22. (334)682-4191

ROLAND COOPER (State Pk) From Jct of SR-10 & CR-43, NE 5 mi on CR-43, follow signs (L). 2015 rates: $13.52 to $26. (334)682-4050

CASTLEBERRY — E3 *Conecuh, Escambia*

COUNTRY SUNSHINE CAMPGROUND **Ratings: 1.5/8★/5** (Campground) 2015 rates: $21 to $23.50. (251)966-5540 3876 Cleveland Ave, Castleberry, AL 36432

CITRONELLE — E2 *Mobile*

CITRONELLE LAKEVIEW RV PARK (CITY PARK) (Public) From jct US 45 & Hwy 96: Go 5 mi W on Hwy 96 to Citronelle Lakeside Park entrance, then 3 mi S. Pit toilets. 2015 rates: $22 to $24. (251)866-9647

CLIO — D5 *Barbour*

BLUE SPRINGS (State Pk) From Jct of SR-10 & SR-51, E 7 mi on SR-10 (R). 2015 rates: $19 to $25. (334)397-4875

COCHRANE — C2 *Pickens*

COCHRANE (Public Corps) From Aliceville, S 10 mi on Hwy-17, W on Perry Long Rd (E). 2015 rates: $16 to $18. (205)373-8806

COTTONTON — D5 *Russell*

BLUFF CREEK PARK (Public Corps) From Jct of US-431 & SR-165, W 25 mi on SR-165 (E). 2015 rates: $24 to $48. Mar to Nov. (334)855-2746

CREOLA — E2 *Mobile*

MOBILE COUNTY RIVER DELTA MARINA CAMPGROUND (Public) From Jct of I-65 & Sailor Rd (exit 22), N 200 ft on Exit Rd to Dead Lake Rd, E 4.1 mi on Dead Lake Rd, follow signs (L). 2015 rates: $18. (251)574-2266

CULLMAN — B3 *Cullman*

CULLMAN CAMPGROUND
Ratings: 7/9★/8.5 (Campground) From Jct of I-65 & SR-157 (exit 310), W 1.5 mi on SR-157 to campground rd (CR-1184), S 0.5 mi, follow signs (L). **FAC:** Paved/gravel rds. 75 gravel, 67 pull-thrus (25 x 75), back-ins (25 x 50), 67 full hkups (30/50 amps), WiFi, dump, laundry, LP gas, firewood. **REC:** pond, fishing, playground. Pet restrict(B). Partial handicap access, no tents. Big rig sites, eco-friendly, 2015 rates: $23 to $25. Disc: AAA, military.
AAA Approved
(256)734-5853 Lat: 34.21444, Lon: -86.90426
220 County Road 1185, Cullman, AL 35057
campgroundscullm@bellsouth.net
See ad this page.

DAUPHIN ISLAND — F2 *Mobile*

DAUPHIN ISLAND CAMPGROUND
(Public) From Jct of I-10 (Exit 17A) & Hwy 193: Go 27 1/2 mi S on Hwy 193 to Bienville Ave, then 2 mi E (R). **FAC:** Paved rds. 152 grass, 8 pull-thrus (20 x 50), back-ins (30 x 60), some side by side hkups, 98 full hkups, 54 W, 54 E (30/50 amps), WiFi Hotspot, tent sites, dump, laundry, groc, firewood, controlled access. **REC:** Gulf of Mexico: swim, fishing, playground. Pets OK. Partial handicap access. Big rig sites, 2015 rates: $36 to $43.
(251)861-2742 Lat: 30.25004, Lon: -88.07981
109 Bienville Blvd, Dauphin Island, AL 36528
campground@dauphinisland.org
www.dauphinisland.org/camping
See ad page 14.

Find it fast! To locate a town on a map, follow these easy instructions: Look for the map grid code after the town heading in the listing section and match it to the letters and numbers on the map borders. Draw a line horizontally from the letter and vertically from the number. You'll find the town near the intersection of the two lines.

See listing Cullman, AL

DECATUR — A3 *Morgan*

JAY LANDINGS MARINA & RV PARK
Ratings: 7.5/8/6.5 (Campground) From Jct of Hwy 31 & Hwy 20/Alt 72, W 2.3 mi on Hwy 20 (R). **FAC:** Paved/gravel rds. 35 gravel, 7 pull-thrus (25 x 40), back-ins (25 x 50), 35 full hkups (30/50 amps), WiFi, laundry, LP gas. **REC:** Tennessee River: swim, fishing. Pet restrict(Q). No tents. Eco-friendly, 2015 rates: $31 to $40. Disc: military.
(256)350-4722 Lat: 34.37154, Lon: -87.00688
1600 Highway 20 W, Decatur, AL 35601
info@jaylandingsrvpark.com
www.jaylandingsrvpark.com
See ad this page.

The RVers' Guide to NASCAR - We'll give you the inside track on how to get high-speed thrills at major NASCAR venues. Turn to the front of the Guide to get the most out of North America's most thrilling sporting event.

POINT MALLARD CAMPGROUND
Ratings: 9/9★/8.5 (Public) From Jct of I-65 & Hwy 20/US-AL72 (exit 340), W 3.2 mi on Hwy 20/US-AL72 (across Tennessee River Bridge) to Jct with US-31, S 1.8 mi on US-31/Hwy 20/US-AL72 to Church St (2nd light past Tennessee River Bridge), SE 3.5 mi (E). Move to left lane as you approach bridge. **FAC:** Paved/gravel rds. 233 gravel, 24 pull-thrus (25 x 60), back-ins (25 x 50), 233 full hkups (30/50 amps), WiFi, tent sites, dump, laundry, groc, LP gas, firewood, restaurant. **REC:** pool $, wading pool, Tennessee River: fishing, golf, playground, rec open to public. Pets OK. Partial handicap access. Big rig sites, 2015 rates: $21.92. No reservations.
(256)341-4826 Lat: 34.57574, Lon: -86.93392
2600-C Pt Mallard Dr SE, Decatur, AL 35601
jrlowman@decatur-al.gov
www.pointmallardpark.com
See ad pages 7 (Spotlight Decatur), 4.

We rate what RVers consider important.

TVA/MALLARD CREEK-WHEELER LAKE (Public) From Jct of I-65 & SR-20 (US-72 Alt), NW 19.5 mi on SR-20 to Spring Creek Rd, N 3.75 mi (R). 2015 rates: $17 to $26. Feb 1 to Nov 30. (256)280-4390

DELTA — C4 *Clay*

CHEAHA (State Pk) From Lineville, N 17 mi on SR-49 to SR-281, W 3 mi (R); or From Jct of I-20 & US-431 (exit 191), S 3.6 mi on US-431 to SR-281, SW 13.3 mi on SR-281S (R). 2015 rates: $22 to $25. (205)488-5111

DEMOPOLIS — D2 *Greene, Marengo*

FORKLAND PARK (Public Corps) From town, N 9 mi on Hwy 43, W 1 mi on gravel rd (E). 2015 rates: $11 to $22. (334)289-5530

FOSCUE CREEK PARK (Public Corps) From Jct of US-80W & Maria Ave exit, N 2 mi on Maria Ave (R). 2015 rates: $22 to $24. (334)289-5535

DODGE CITY — B3 *Cullman*

BIG BRIDGE CAMPGROUND (Public) From Jct of I-65 & Hwy 69 (exit 299), SW 7.4 mi on Hwy 69, NE 6.6 mi on County Road 222 (R). (256)287-0440

DOTHAN — E5 *Houston*

CHERRY BLOSSOM RV & MH PARK
Ratings: 7.5/9.5★/8.5 (RV Park) From Jct of Ross Clark Cir & US-231S, S 1.5 mi on US-231S (R). At South of Town. **FAC:** Paved rds. (86 spaces). Avail: 72 grass, 25 pull-thrus (25 x 70), back-ins (36 x 60), some side by side hkups, 72 full hkups (30/50 amps), cable, WiFi, laundry. **REC.** Pets OK. No tents. Big rig sites, eco friendly, 2015 rates: $32 to $40. Disc: AAA, military.
AAA Approved
(334)792-3313 Lat: 31.16722, Lon: -85.40249
4100 S Oates (Hwy 231 S), Dothan, AL 36301
Cherryblossomrvpark@outlook.com
www.cherryblossomrv.com
See ad this page, 4.

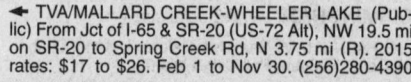

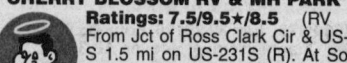

OTHAN (CONT)

Travel Services

➔ **CAMPING WORLD OF DOTHAN** As the nation's largest retailer of RV supplies, accessories, services and new and used RVs, Camping World is committed to making your total RV experience better. RV Accessories: (866)999-0330. **SERVICES:** RV, RV appliance, staffed RV wash, estrooms, RV Sales. RV supplies, LP, dump, emergency parking, RV accessible. waiting room. Hours: 8 am - 6 pm.
334-792-5537 Lat: 31.218961, Lon: -85.431892
2691 Ross Clark Circle SW, Suite 2, Dothan, AL 36301
www.CampingWorldofDothan.com

OUBLE SPRINGS — B3 *Winston*

➔ CORINTH RECREATION AREA (Natl Forest) From town: Go 5 mi E on US 278, then go 3 mi S on CR 57 (at church) to entrance. 2015 rates: $17 to $25. Mar 11 to Oct 13. (205)489-3165

ELBERTA — F2 *Baldwin*

➔ JELLYSTONE PARK **Ratings: 7/7/6** (RV Park) 2015 rates: $34 to $42. (251)986-3566 12160 Wortel Rd, Elberta, AL 36530

➔ **LAKE OSPREY RV RESORT**
Ratings: 10/10★/10 (RV Resort) From Jct of I-10 & Exit 44 (SR-59), S 18.7 mi to US 98, E 8.2 mi to CR-95, S 1.2 mi (L). RV type restrictions: No travel trailers.

RV & GOLF LUXURY DESTINATION

Take the road to a place you won't want to leave...a destination, luxury RV Resort on the North Shore of the Alabama Gulf Coast. Enjoy golf, fishing, clubhouse, pool, tiki bar and more. Come for a visit and stay all year!

FAC: Paved rds. 98 paved, patios, back-ins (45 x 85), 98 full hkups (30/50 amps), cable, WiFi, laundry. **REC:** pool, whirlpool, Lake Osprey: fishing, golf. Pet restrict(B/Q). Partial handicap access, no tents. Big rig sites, RV age restrict, eco-friendly, 2015 rates: $40 to $55. Disc: AAA.
(251)545-4940 Lat: 30.24049, Lon: -87.32725
12054 Gateway Drive, Elberta, AL 36530
lakeosprey@robertsresorts.com
www.lakeosprey.com
See ad pages 3 (Welcome Section), 4 & Snowbird Destinations in Magazine Section.

EUFAULA — D5 *Barbour*

➔ **LAKE EUFAULA CAMPGROUND**
Ratings: 8.5/9★/8.5 (RV Park) (From Columbus) Int of Hwy 280 & Hwy 431 (Martin Luther King Jr Pky), S 44.9 mi on Hwy 431(Martin Luther King Pky), to W Chewalla Creek Dr, W .04 mi on W Chewalla Creek Dr (L). **FAC:** Gravel rds. (61 spaces). Avail: 41 grass, 32 pull-thrus (25 x 45), back-ins (25 x 35), mostly side by side hkups, 41 full hkups (30/50 amps), seasonal sites, WiFi, tent sites, rentals, laundry, groc, fire rings, firewood. **REC:** pool, Lake Eufaula: fishing. Pet restrict(B/Q). Eco-friendly, 2015 rates: $27 to $30. Disc: military.
(334)687-4425 Lat: 31.54420, Lon: -85.09150
151 West Chewalla Creek Drive, Eufaula, AL 36027
Info@lakeeufaulacampground.com
www.lakeeufaulacampground.com
See ad this page.

➔ LAKEPOINT RESORT (State Pk) From Jct of US-82W & US-431, N 6 mi on US-431 (R). 2015 rates: $19 to $28. (334)687-6026

➔ WHITE OAK CREEK PARK (Public Corps) From town, S 8 mi on US-431 to Hwy 95, SE 4 mi (L). 2015 rates: $24 to $48. (334)687-3101

SAVE! Over $1,000 in coupons can be found at the front of the Guide!

EVERGREEN — E3 *Conecuh*

➔ OWASSA LAKESIDE RV PARK **Ratings: 3/5.5/6** (Campground) 2015 rates: $32. (251)578-0976 108 Owassa Circle, Evergreen, AL 36401

FAIRHOPE — F2 *Baldwin*

➔ COASTAL HAVEN RV PARK **Ratings: 6/9.5★/8** (RV Park) 2015 rates: $40. (251)990-9011 10151 CR 32, Fairhope, AL 36532

➔ **DRIFTWOOD RV PARK**
Ratings: 6.5/8/7.5 (RV Park) From Jct of I-10 & US 98 (Exit 35), S 16.7 mi on US 98, E 1.3 mi on US 98 (R); or From Jct of Hwy 59 & US 98 (in Foley, AL), W 11.3 mi on US 98 (L). **FAC:** Gravel rds. 51 Avail: 1 paved, 50 grass, 51 pull-thrus (30 x 70), 51 full hkups (30/50 amps), WiFi, laundry, LP gas. **REC.** Pet restrict(B). No tents. Big rig sites, RV age restrict, 2015 rates: $27. Disc: military.
(251)928-8233 Lat: 30.42087, Lon: -87.86391
9318 US Hwy 98, Fairhope, AL 36532
driftwoodrvpk@mchsi.com
www.driftwoodrvparkalabama.com
See ad this page, 4.

➔ **WALES WEST RV RESORT & LIGHT RAILWAY**
Ratings: 9/9.5★/7 (RV Park) W-bnd: From Jct US 98 & Hwy 59 (in Foley), N5.0 mi on Hwy 59 to CR-32, W 5.3 mi to CR-9, N 2.3 mi (R); E-bnd: From Jct of I-10 & Hwy 59 (Exit 44), S 13.7 mi on Hwy 59 to CR-32, W 2.3 mi to CR-9, N 2.3 mi (R). **FAC:** Gravel rds. (82 spaces). 47 Avail: 37 gravel, 10 grass, patios, 37 pull-thrus (30 x 70), back-ins (22 x 27), 47 full hkups (30/50 amps), cable, WiFi, tent sites, laundry, LP gas. **REC:** heated pool, whirlpool, Lake Victoria: swim, fishing, playground. Pet restrict(B/Q). Partial handicap access. Big rig sites, RV age restrict, eco-friendly, 2015 rates: $32 to $40. Disc: military.
(888)569-5337 Lat: 30.503509, Lon: -87.790440
13670 Smiley Street, Silverhill, AL 36576
enquiries@waleswest.com
www.waleswest.com
See ad page 16.

Things to See and Do

➔ **WALES WEST LIGHT RAILWAY** Full size train that has special events throughout the year for visitors. RV accessible. Restrooms. Hours: call.
(888)569-5337 Lat: 30.30212, Lon: -87.47589
13670 Smiley St, Silverhill, AL 36576
enquiries@waleswest.com
See ad page 16.

FLORALA — E4 *Covington*

➔ FLORALA (State Pk) From Jct of US-331 & SR-54 (East edge of town), S 0.2 mi on US-331 to 3rd Ave, W 0.5 mi on 3rd Ave, follow signs (L). 2015 rates: $23 to $29. (800)ALAPARK

FLORENCE — A2 *Colbert, Lauderdale*

FLORENCE See also Muscle Shoals, Rogersville, Russellville & Tuscumbia.

➔ MCFARLAND PARK (CITY PARK) (Public) From Jct of US-43/US-72 & Hwy 20, W 0.1 mi on Hwy 20 (L). 2015 rates: $10 to $18. Apr 1 to Nov 30. (205)760-6416

VETERANS MEMORIAL PARK (CITY PARK) (Public) From jct US 43, US 72 & Hwy 133: Go 3 mi S on Hwy 133. (At the N end of Wilson Dam). 2015 rates: $14.

FOLEY — F2 *Baldwin*

➔ ANCHORS AWEIGH RV RESORT **Ratings: 9.5/8.5/9** (RV Park) 2015 rates: $36 to $40. (251)971-6644 19814 County Road 20 S, Foley, AL 36535

➔ BEACH EXPRESS RV PARK **Ratings: 7.5/10★/6.5** (RV Park) 2015 rates: $35. (251)970-7277 22225 US Hwy 98, Foley, AL 36535

➔ BLUEGRASS RV PARK **Ratings: 5.5/8/6** (RV Park) 2015 rates: $40. (251)971-1874 21403 Hwy 98, Foley, AL 36535

➔ **JOHNNY'S LAKESIDE RV RESORT**
Ratings: 9.5/10★/8.5 (RV Park) N-bnd: From Jct of Hwy 98 & Hwy 59 (in Foley), N 3.4 mi on Hwy 59 (R); or S-bnd: From Jct of I-10 & Hwy 59 (exit 44), S 15 mi on Hwy 59 (L). **FAC:** Paved rds. (194 spaces). Avail: 149 paved, patios, 82 pull-thrus (24 x 62), back-ins (30 x 60), 149 full hkups (30/50 amps), cable, WiFi, rentals, laundry, LP gas. **REC:** pool, Fountain Lake: fishing, playground. Pet restrict(B/Q). Partial handicap access, no tents. Big rig sites, 2015 rates: $40 to $45.
(251)970-3773 Lat: 30.45551, Lon: -87.68698
15810 State Hwy 59 North, Foley, AL 36535
johnnyslakesideresort@yahoo.com
www.johnnyslakesidervresort.com
See ad this page, 4.

➔ MAGNOLIA FARMS RV PARK **Ratings: 6.5/10★/8** (RV Park) 2015 rates: $30. (251)928-7335 13381 Lipscomb Road, Foley, AL 36535

FORT PAYNE — A4 *DeKalb*

➔ DESOTO (State Pk) From Jct of I-59 & CR-35 (exit 218), E 4.5 mi on CR-35 (passing thru town) to CR-89, N 5 mi (L). 2015 rates: $28.50 to $31.50. (256)845-5075

➔ LITTLE RIVER RV PARK & CAMPGROUND **Ratings: 5/6/5.5** (RV Park) 2015 rates: $25 to $27. (256)619-2267 1357 Co. Rd. 261, Fort Payne, AL 35967

➔ **WILLS CREEK RV PARK LLC**
Ratings: 7.5/10★/9 (RV Park) From Jct of I-59 & SR-35 (Exit 218), W 0.2 mi on SR-35 to Airport Rd, N 1.6 mi (L). **FAC:** Gravel rds. (44 spaces). Avail: 34 gravel, 30 pull-thrus (30 x 70), back-ins (30 x 60), 34 full hkups (30/50 amps), seasonal sites, cable, WiFi, tent sites, rentals, dump, laundry, LP gas, firewood. **REC:** Wills Creek: fishing. Pet restrict(B). Eco-friendly, 2015 rates: $27 to $29. Disc: military.
(256)845-6703 Lat: 34.45875, Lon: -85.73441
1310 Airport Rd W, Fort Payne, AL 35968
info@willscreekrvpark.com
www.willscreekrvpark.com
See ad this page, 4.

FORT RUCKER — E4 *Dale*

FORT RUCKER See also Clio, Dothan, Ozark & Troy.

Things to See and Do

➔ **US ARMY AVIATION MUSEUM** One of the world's largest helicopter collections from the Wright Flyer to the AH-64 Apache helicopter. Dynamic life-size dioramas. Vietnam memorial (honoring aviation personnel). Gift shop & by appointment only, research library. Partial handicap access. Restrooms. Hours: Call.
(888)276-9286 Lat: 31.32196, Lon: -85.71035
bldg 6000 Novosel Street, Fort Rucker, AL 36362
avnmuseum@ala.net
www.armyaviationmuseum.org
See ad page 16.

FRANKLIN — D3 *Monroe*

CLAIBORNE LAKE/ISAAC CREEK PARK (Public Corps) From Monroeville, N 8 mi on SR-41 to CR-17, W 10 mi, follow signs (E). 2015 rates: $20 to $22. (251)282-4254

GADSDEN — B4 *Etowah*

NOCCALULA FALLS CAMPGROUND
Ratings: 8.5/9★/9 (Public) From Jct of I-59 & Rte 211 (Noccalula Falls/exit 188), E 2 mi on Noccalula Rd (R). **FAC:** Paved/gravel rds. 126 paved, 6 pull-thrus (25 x 70), back-ins (24 x 40), 75 full hkups, 51 W, 51 E (30/50 amps), cable, WiFi, tent sites, rentals, dump, laundry, fire rings, firewood. **REC:** pool, Noccalula Falls: playground. Pet restrict(B). Partial handicap access. Big rig sites, 28 day max stay, 2015 rates: $18 to $24. Disc: military.
(256)543-7412 Lat: 34.04219, Lon: -86.02062
1600 Noccalula Rd, Gadsden, AL 35904
campground@cityofgadsden.com
www.cityofgadsden.com

RIVER COUNTRY CAMPGROUND **Ratings: 8.5/9/8.5** (RV Park) 2015 rates: $36 to $42. (256)543-7111 one River Road, Gadsden, AL 35901

GREENVILLE — D3 *Butler*

SHERLING LAKE PARK & CAMPGROUND
Ratings: 7/7.5/10 (Public) From Jct of I-65 (Exit 130) & SR-185: Go 2.25 mi N on SR-185, then 1.2 mi N on Braggs Rd. SR-263 (L). Note: Do not follow GPS coordinates last two miles on Braggs Rd, follow these directions and signs. **FAC:** Paved rds. 41 paved, 23 pull-thrus (35 x 70), back-ins (35 x 45), 30 full hkups, 11 W, 11 E (30/50 amps), WiFi, tent sites, dump, firewood. **REC:** Sherling Lake: fishing, playground. Pets OK. Partial handicap access. Big rig sites, 2015 rates: $25 to $28. No CC.
(334)382-3638 Lat: 31.89648, Lon: -86.67069
4397 Braggs Road, Greenville, AL 36037
sherlinglake@cityofgville.com
www.greenville-alabama.com
See ad this page, 4.

GROVEOAK — A4 *DeKalb*

BUCK'S POCKET (State Pk) From Jct of US-431 & SR-227(in Guntersville), N 21 mi on SR-227 to CR-402, N 1 mi to Jct with CR-50 & CR-19, continue N 2 mi on CR-19 (L). CAUTION: Low water crossing (possible flooding), steep, winding entry road to park. 2015 rates: $15 to $22. (256)659-2000

GULF SHORES — F2 *Baldwin*

A SPOTLIGHT Introducing Gulf Shores colorful attractions appearing at the front of this state section.

GULF SHORES See listings at Dauphin Island, Elberta, Fairhope, Foley, Lillian, Magnolia Springs, Mobile, Orange Beach, Robertsdale & Summerdale.

BAY BREEZE RV ON THE BAY Ratings: 7.5/9★/8.5 (RV Park) From Jct of SR-59 & SR-180 (Fort Morgan Rd), W 6.8 mi on SR-180 to Bay Breeze Pkwy, N 0.2 mi (R). **FAC:** Gravel rds. 25 gravel, patios, back-ins (20 x 50), accepts full hkup units only, 25 full hkups (30/50 amps), WiFi, rentals, laundry. **REC:** Mobile Bay: swim, fishing. Pets OK. No tents. Eco-friendly, 2015 rates: $32 to $48. No CC. (251)540-2362 Lat: 30.25230, Lon: -87.79813 1901 Bay Breeze Parkway, Gulf Shores, AL 36542 baybreeze@gulftel.com www.baybreezerv.com

BELLA TERRA OF GULF SHORES
Ratings: 10/10★/10 (Condo Pk) From Jct of I-10 & Hwy 59 (Exit 44) S 15 mi on SR-59 to Foley Beach Expressway SE 10 mi to Brinks Willis Rd, W 0.25 mi (L) Note: Class A only. **FAC:** Paved rds. 120 paved, patios, 24 pull-thrus (50 x 75), back-ins (50 x 75), accepts full hkup units only, 120 full hkups (30/50 amps), cable, WiFi, laundry, LP bottles, controlled access. **REC:** heated pool, wading pool, whirlpool, Lake Bella Terra: fishing. Pet restrict(B/Q). Partial handicap access, no tents. Big rig sites, RV age restrict, eco-friendly, 2015 rates: $34 t $95.
(866)417-2416 Lat: 30.34790, Lon: -87.65999
101 Via Bella Terra, Foley, AL 36535
rentals@bellaterrarvresort.com
www.bellaterrarvresort.com
See ad this page.

DOC'S RV PARK **Ratings: 8/8.5★/7.5** (R\ Park) 2015 rates: $35. (251)968-4511 17595 State Hwy 180, Gulf Shores, AL 36542

GULF BREEZE RV RESORT **Ratings: 10/9/7.5** (RV Park) 2015 rates: $35. (251)968-8462 1980 Oak Rd W, Gulf Shores, AL 36542

GULF CAMPGROUND (State Pk) From Jct o SR-59 & SR-182, E 2.1 mi on SR-182 to CR-2, N 0.5 mi (R). NOTE: Max stay 14 days except Nov 1 thr Mar 31, 36 sites max stay 14 days all year. 201 rates: $31 to $41. (800)252-7275

ISLAND RETREAT RV PARK
Ratings: 9/9★/7 (RV Park) From Jc of SR-59 & SR-180 (Fort Morgan Rd), W 1.6 mi on SR-180 (R). **FAC:** Paved rds (173 spaces). Avail: 167 paved, patios 17 pull-thrus (30 x 100), back-ins (30 x 60), 167 full hkups (30/50 amps), cable, WiFi laundry, LP gas, fire rings, firewood. **REC:** pool, playground. Pet restrict(B). Partial handicap access, nc tents. Big rig sites, eco-friendly, 2015 rates: $35 to $38. Disc: military.
(251)967-1666 Lat: 30.25751, Lon: -87.71367
18201 State Hwy 180 (Ft Morgan Rd), Gulf Shores AL 36542
islandretreat@gulftel.com
www.islandretreatrv.com
See ad this page, 4.

LAZY LAKE RV PARK **Ratings: 4/7.5/4** (Campground) 2015 rates: $30. (251)968-7875 18950 Olc Plash Isl Rd, Gulf Shores, AL 36547

LUXURY RV RESORT **Ratings: 9/8/8** (RV Park) 2015 rates: $40. (251)948-5444 590 Gulf Shores Parkway, Gulf Shores, AL 36542

RV Park ratings you can rely on!

Take an RV Trip of a Lifetime! Check out trip ideas at the front of the Guide - you'll find something for the history buff, the food lover or even your wild side!

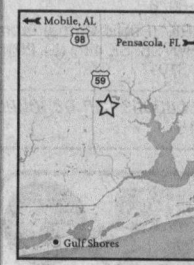

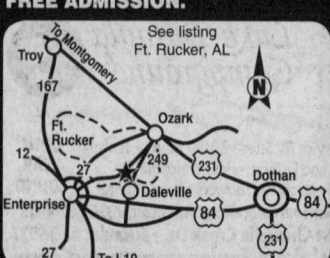

Perdido
A M
Resort LLC
TAKE SHELTER IN OUR COVE
· 56 Full Hookup RV Sites · Wi-Fi and Cable TV
· Swimming Pool · White Sand Picnic Area
· 3 Bedroom, 2-1/2 Bath
Fully Equipped Townhouse
· Playground · Clubhouse · General Store
· 24 Deep Water Marina Slips · Fishing Pier
· Coin Laundry · Horseshoes · Social Activities
Good Sam Park
Good Sam RATED 9/9★/9
13770 RIVER ROAD
PENSACOLA, FL 32507
(850) 492-7304
www.theperdidoresort.com
See listing Perdido Key, FL

GULF SHORES (CONT)

MAGNOLIA SPRINGS RV HIDEAWAY & GOLF
Ratings: 7.5/9★/8.5 (RV Park) From Jct of Hwy 59 & US 98 (in Foley), W 5.3 mi on US 98 to second CR 49 (in Magnolia Springs), S 2 mi on CR 49 (R). **FAC:** Paved/gravel rds. (61 spaces). 51 Avail: 26 paved, 25 gravel, patios, 1 pull-thrus (25 x 60), back-ins (25 x 55), 51 full hkups (30/50 amps), WiFi, tent sites, laundry, firewood. **REC:** golf, shuffleboard. Pet restrict(B/Q). Partial handicap access. Big rig sites, RV age restrict, eco-friendly, 2015 rates: $32. Disc: military.
(251)965-6777 Lat: 30.381, Lon: -87.76806
10831 Magnolia Springs Hwy, Foley, AL 36535
hideaway@gulftel.com
www.magnoliaspringsgolf.com
See ad page 16.

SOUTHPORT CAMPGROUNDS **Ratings: 4/5.5/4.5** (Campground) 2015 rates: $25 to $28. (251)968-6220 108 Waterway W Blvd, Gulf Shores, AL 36542

SUGAR SANDS RV RESORT **Ratings: 10/10★/10** (RV Resort) 2015 rates: $48. (251)968-2223 5343 Roscoe Rd, Gulf Shores, AL 36542

SUN-RUNNERS RV PARK **Ratings: 4.5/5.5/6** (RV Park) 2015 rates: $35. (251)955-5257 19480 Co. Rd 8, Gulf Shores, AL 36542

WALES WEST RV RESORT & LIGHT RAILWAY
Ratings: 9/9.5★/7 (RV Park) W-bnd: From Jct Hwy 182 & Hwy 59 (in Gulf Shores), N 19.9 mi on Hwy 59 to CR-32, W 5.3 mi to CR-9, N 2.3 mi (R); E-bnd: From Jct of I-10 & Hwy 59 (Exit 44), S 13.7 mi on Hwy 59 to CR-32, W 2.3 mi to CR-9, N 2.3 mi (R). **FAC:** Gravel rds. (82 spaces). 47 Avail: 37 gravel, 10 grass, patios, 37 pull-thrus (30 x 70), back-ins (22 x 27), 47 full hkups (30/50 amps), cable, WiFi, tent sites, laundry, LP gas. **REC:** heated pool, whirlpool, Lake Victoria: swim, fishing, marina, playground. Pet restrict(B). Partial handicap access. Big rig sites, RV age restrict, eco-friendly, 2015 rates: $32 to $40.
(888)569-5337 Lat: 30.30212, Lon: -87.47589
13670 Smiley St., Silver Hill, AL 36576
enquiries@waleswest.com
www.waleswest.com
See primary listing at Fairhope and ad page 16.

Thank You to our active and retired military personnel. A dedicated section of Military Listings for places to camp can be found at the back of the Guide.

GUNTERSVILLE — B4 *Marshall*

LAKE GUNTERSVILLE (State Pk) From Jct of US-431 & SR-227, NE 7 mi on SR-227 to park access rd, N 1 mi (L). 2015 rates: $20 to $22. (256)571-5455

SEIBOLD CAMPGROUND
Ratings: 5.5/7.5/7.5 (Campground) From jct US 431 & Hwy 79: Go 1 mi N on Hwy 79. **FAC:** Paved rds. (136 spaces). Avail: 66 gravel, back-ins (40 x 60), 66 W, 66 E (30/50 amps), seasonal sites, tent sites, dump, mobile sewer, controlled access. **REC:** pool, Lake Guntersville: fishing, playground. Pets OK. 2015 rates: $22 to $27. Mar 1 to Oct 31.
(256)582-0040 Lat: 34.43553, Lon: -86.24843
54 Seibold Creek Rd, Guntersville, AL 35976
seiboldcampground@charter.net
See ad this page.

HANCEVILLE — B3 *Cullman*

COUNTRY VIEW RV PARK, LLC **Ratings: 4/5.5/5.5** (RV Park) 2015 rates: $32. (256)352-4678 15959 Al Hwy 91, Hanceville, AL 35077

HARTSELLE — A3 *Morgan*

QUAIL CREEK RV RESORT
Ratings: 8/9★/8.5 (RV Resort) From Jct of I 65 & CR 55 (Exit 322): Go 0.5 mi E on CR 55, then 1.8 mi N on CR 27 (Mount Zion Rd), then 1 mi E on Nat Key Rd, then 0.3 mi S on Quail Creek Dr (R).

NORTH ALABAMA'S NEWEST RESORT
"Welcome Home" to Quail Creek whether it's your first or return stay. Our promise to treat you so many ways, you're bound to like one of them as you rest or play at the foothills of the Appalachian Mountains.

FAC: Gravel rds. 12 gravel, 12 pull-thrus (34 x 95), 12 full hkups (30/50 amps), WiFi, tent sites, rentals. **REC:** pool, pond, fishing, golf, playground, rec open to public. Pets OK. Big rig sites, eco-friendly, 2015 rates: $30. Disc: AAA, military.
(256)784-5033 Lat: 34.23309, Lon: -86.51827
233 Quail Creek Drive, Hartselle, AL 35640
stay@qcresort.com
www.qcresort.com
See ad pages 14, 4.

Enjoy shopping over 10,000 RV products at great prices, at CampingWorld.com.

HELENA — C3 *Shelby*

CHEROKEE CAMPGROUND **Ratings: 7/7.5/8.5** (Campground) 2015 rates: $30 (205)428-8339 2800 Hwy 93, Helena, AL 35080

HODGES — B2 *Franklin*

HORSESHOE BEND CAMPGROUND (Public) From town, W 14 mi on Hwy 24 to CR-88, S 2 mi to CR-16, E 4 mi to Horseshoe Bend Rd, W 2 mi (R). 2015 rates: $7.50 to $15. Apr 1 to Oct 30. (877)367-2232

HOPE HULL — D4 *Montgomery*

HOPE HULL See also Lowndesboro, Montgomery, Prattville & Wetumpka.

HUNTSVILLE — A3 *Madison*

DITTO LANDING MARINA CAMPGROUND (Public) From Jct of US-431 & US-231, S 7 mi on US-231 to Hobbs Island Rd, N 2 mi (R). 2015 rates $19 to $22. (256)883-9420

MONTE SANO (State Pk) From Jct of US-231 & US-431/Governors Dr, E 3.6 mi on US-431S/Governors Dr to Monte Sano Blvd, N 2.5 mi to Nolen Dr, E 1 mi (L). Caution: Some steep & switchback entry roads. 2015 rates: $19 to $28 (256)534-6589

U.S. SPACE & ROCKET CENTER CAMPGROUND **Ratings: 5.5/6.5/6** (Campground) 2015 rates: $18 to $20. (256)830-4987 1 Tranquilty Base Huntsville, AL 35805

JASPER — B3 *Walker, Winston*

CLEAR CREEK RECREATION AREA (Natl Pk) From Jct of SR 5 & SR 195, N 4 mi on Hwy 195 to Fall City Rd, NE 8 mi on Fall City Rd (L). 2015 rates $15 to $37.80. Mar 13 to Nov 1. (205)384-4792

SLEEPY HOLLER CAMPGROUND
Ratings: 7/8/7.5 (Campground) From Jct of Hwy 78 & Industrial Pky (Exit 65), N 3.6 mi on Industrial Pky to Hwy 5 (second traffic light), E 3.2 mi to Buttermilk Rd (caution light), S 0.9 mi on Buttermilk Rd (L), (Do not use GPS). **FAC:** Gravel rds. (130 spaces). 75 Avail: 40 gravel, 35 grass, 60 pull-thrus (18 x 60), back-ins (20 x 60), 75 full hkups (30/50 amps), seasonal sites, WiFi, laundry, LP gas. **REC:** Campground Lake: fishing. Pet restrict(B). Partial handicap access, no tents. Eco-friendly, 2015 rates: $25 to $35. Disc: military. No CC.
(205)483-7947 Lat: 33.48412, Lon: -87.10747
174 Sleepy Holler Circle, Cordova, AL 35550
www.sleepyhollercampgroundal.com
See ad this page, 4.

Say you saw it in our Guide!

JEMISON — C3 *Chilton*

MINOOKA PARK RV CAMPGROUND (Public) From Jct of I-65 & CR-42 (Exit 219), W 3.8 mi on CR-42 to Jct of CR-42 & Hwy 31, N 3.9 mi on Hwy 31 to CR-146, E 1.8 mi on CR-146 (L). 2015 rates: $20 to $23. (205)312-1376

PEACH QUEEN CAMPGROUND
Ratings: 7/7.5/8 (Campground) From Jct of I-65 & Exit 219, E 0.5 mi on exit rd (R). **FAC:** Gravel rds. (54 spaces). Avail: 36 grass, 36 pull-thrus (24 x 60), 36 full hkups (30/50 amps), seasonal sites, WiFi, tent sites, laundry, LP gas, fire rings, firewood. **REC:** pool, Shades Lake: fishing. Pets OK. Partial handicap access. Big rig sites, 2015 rates: $28 to $35. Disc: AAA, military.
AAA Approved
(205)688-2573 Lat: 32.98198, Lon: -86.68341
12986 County Road 42, Jemison, AL 35085
peachqueenrvpark@centurylink.net
www.peachqueencampground.com
See ad this page.

LANETT — C5 *Chambers*

AMITY CAMPGROUND (Public Corps) From town, N 7 mi on CR-212 to CR-393, E 0.5 mi (E). 2015 rates: $16 to $28. Mar 16 to Sep 8. (334)499-2404

LANGSTON — A4 *Jackson*

NORTHSHORE CAMPGROUND AT THE BIG ROCK **Ratings: 6/NA/7.5** (Campground) 2015 rates: $27. (256)582-3367 6845 S Sauty Rd, Langston, AL 35755

SOUTH SAUTY CREEK RESORT
Ratings: 6/8★/6 (Campground) From Jct US 431 & Hwy 227: Go 12 mi S on Hwy 227 (Hwy 227 turns N), then 6-1/2 mi N on S Sauty Rd (L). **FAC:** Paved/gravel rds. (86 spaces). Avail: 36 gravel, back-ins (24 x 60), 36 W, 36 E (30/50 amps), seasonal sites, WiFi Hotspot, tent sites, rentals, dump, mobile sewer, groc, fire rings, restaurant. **REC:** pool, Lake Gunterville: swim, fishing, marina. Pets OK. 2015 rates: $22.
(256)582-3367 Lat: 34.51506, Lon: -86.11020
6845 S Sauty Rd, Langston, AL 35755
southsautycafe@yahoo.com
www.southsautyresort.com
See ad opposite page.

WINDEMERE COVE RV RESORT
Ratings: 10/10★/10 (Condo Pk) From Jct of US 431 & Hwy 227 (Guntersville), go 12 mi E on Hwy 227, then at Jct of Hwy 227 & S. Sauty Rd (CR-67) continue going E 8 mi on CR-67 (R) Please note: RVs 26' or more. **FAC:** Paved rds. 106 paved, patios, 3 pull-thrus (40 x 80), back-ins (40 x 80), 106 full hkups (30/50 amps), WiFi, laundry, controlled access. **REC:** pool, Lake Guntersville: fishing. Pet restrict(Q). Partial handicap access, no tents. Big rig sites, RV age restrict, eco-friendly, 2015 rates: $24 to $55.
(256)228-3010 Lat: 34.32045, Lon: -86.05209
10174 County Rd 67, Langston, AL 35755
windemerecove@aol.com
www.windemerecove.com
See ad opposite page, 4.

LEESBURG — B4 *Cherokee*

CEDAR POINT CAMPGROUND **Ratings: 7.5/8.5★/5.5** (Campground) 2015 rates: $25 to $35. (256)526-8110 2510 Hwy 411 S, Leesburg, AL 35983

LILLIAN — F3 *Baldwin*

LOST BAY KOA **Ratings: 8/7/7** (Campground) 2015 rates: $33 to $58. (251)961-1717 11650 CR 99, Lillian, AL 36549

LOWNDESBORO — D3 *Lowndes*

WOODRUFF LAKE/PRAIRIE CREEK CAMPGROUND (Public Corps) From Jct of US-80 & CR-23 (milepost 108.6), N 3 mi on CR-23 to CR-40, W 3.5 mi (R). 2015 rates: $20 to $24. (334)418-4919

MAGNOLIA SPRINGS — F2 *Baldwin*

SOUTHWIND RV PARK **Ratings: 6/8★/7.5** (RV Park) 2015 rates: $25. (251)988-1216 12821 CR-9N, Foley, AL 36535

MCCALLA — C3 *Tuscaloosa*

TANNEHILL IRONWORKS HISTORICAL STATE PARK (Public) From Jct of I-59 & Bucksville (exit 100), SE 2.5 mi on Tannehill Parkway to Eastern Valley Rd, W 200 ft (L); or From Jct of I-459 & Eastern Valley Rd (exit 1), W 7.2 mi on Eastern Valley Rd (L). 2015 rates: $16 to $26. (205)477-5711

MOBILE — E2 *Baldwin*

MOBILE See also Creola, Dauphin Island, Evergreen, Fairhope, Foley, Magnolia Springs, Robertsdale, Spanish Fort, Summerdale, Theodore & Wilmer.

BAY PALMS RV RESORT
Ratings: 8.5/7.5/8.5 (RV Park) From Jct of SR-193 & SR-188, N 0.4 mi on SR-193 (L). **FAC:** Paved rds. 104 Avail: 70 paved, 34 gravel, patios, 12 pull-thrus (34 x 65), back-ins (30 x 60), accepts full hkup units only, 104 full hkups (30/50 amps), cable, WiFi, dump, laundry, LP gas, firewood, controlled access. **REC:** pool, playground. Pet restrict(B). Partial handicap access, no tents. Big rig sites, eco-friendly, 2015 rates: $39. Disc: military.
(251)873-4700 Lat: 30.22051, Lon: -88.06431
15440 Dauphin Island Parkway, Coden, AL 36523
BayPalmsRV@yahoo.com
www.baypalmsrvresort.com
See ad this page, 4.

CHICKASABOGUE PARK & CAMPGROUND (Public) From Jct of I-65 & Hwy 158 (exit 13), Hwy 158 W 0.1 to Hwy 213, S 2.2 mi to Whistler, E 0.7 mi to Aldock Rd, N 1 mi, follow signs (E). 2015 rates: $15 to $18. (251)574-2267

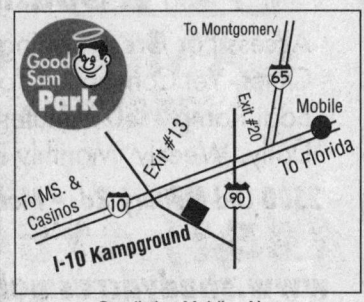

I-10 KAMPGROUND
Ratings: 7/8/7.5 (Campground) From Jct of I-10 & Theodore Dawes Rd (Exit 13), S 0.5 mi on Theodore Dawes Rd (L). **FAC:** Paved/gravel rds. (100 spaces). Avail: 40 gravel, 40 pull-thrus (20 x 60), 40 full hkups (30/50 amps), cable, WiFi Hotspot, tent sites, laundry, LP gas. **REC:** pool. Pets OK. Partial

MOBILE (CONT)

I-10 KAMPGROUND (CONT)
handicap access. Big rig sites, eco-friendly, 2015 rates: $25. Disc: AAA, military.
(251)653-9816 Lat: 30.55831, Lon: -88.19182
6430 Theodore Dawes Rd, Theodore, AL 36582
See ad pages 19, 4.

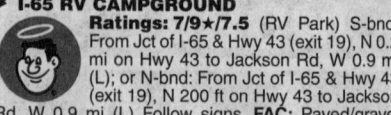

I-65 RV CAMPGROUND
Ratings: 7/9★/7.5 (RV Park) S-bnd: From Jct of I-65 & Hwy 43 (exit 19), N 0.2 mi on Hwy 43 to Jackson Rd, W 0.9 mi (L); or N-bnd: From Jct of I-65 & Hwy 43 (exit 19), N 200 ft on Hwy 43 to Jackson Rd, W 0.9 mi (L) Follow signs. **FAC:** Paved/gravel rds. (87 spaces). Avail: 11 gravel, patios, 11 pull-thrus (30 x 90), 11 full hkups (30/50 amps), seasonal sites, WiFi, tent sites, dump, laundry, LP gas. **REC.** Pet restrict(B). Partial handicap access. Big rig sites, 2015 rates: $33. Disc: military.
(800)287-3208 Lat: 30.87320, Lon: -88.05476
730 Jackson Rd, Creola, AL 36525
sales@I65rvcampground.com
www.i65rvcampground.com
See ad pages 19, 4.

JOHNNY'S RV RESORT **Ratings: 8/9★/7.5** (RV Park) 2015 rates: $35. (251)653-7120 6171 Hwy 90 W, Theodore, AL 36590

PAYNE'S RV PARK **Ratings: 6.5/7.5/8** (RV Park) 2015 rates: $27.25. (251)653-1034 7970 Bellingrath Rd, Theodore, AL 36582

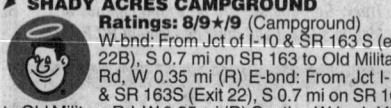

SHADY ACRES CAMPGROUND
Ratings: 8/9★/9 (Campground) W-bnd: From Jct of I-10 & SR 163 S (exit 22B), S 0.7 mi on SR 163 to Old Military Rd, W 0.35 mi (R) E-bnd: From Jct I-10 & SR 163S (Exit 22), S 0.7 mi on SR 163 to Old Military Rd, W 0.35 mi (R) Caution W-bnd: After tunnel, exit 22B from left ln. **FAC:** Paved rds. 92 gravel, 9 pull-thrus (25 x 85), back-ins (25 x 75), some side by side hkups, 92 full hkups (30/50 amps), WiFi, dump, laundry, LP gas. **REC:** Dog River: fishing. Pet restrict(B). Partial handicap access, no tents. Big rig sites, RV age restrict, eco-friendly, 2015 rates: $26. Disc: military.
(251)478-0013 Lat: 30.62771, Lon: -88.09512
2500 Old Military Road, Mobile, AL 36605
dogriver13@aol.com
www.shadyacresmobile.com
See ad this page, 4.

MONTEVALLO — C3 *Bibb*

BRIERFIELD IRONWORKS HISTORICAL PARK (Public) From Jct of SR-25 & SR-119 (downtown Montevallo), S 7 mi on SR-25 to CR-62, S 0.4 mi (L). 2015 rates: $12 to $20. (205)665-1856

MONTGOMERY — D4 *Montgomery*

CAPITAL CITY RV PARK
Ratings: 9/10★/10 (RV Park) From Jct of I-85 & East Blvd (Exit 6), NW 4.4 mi on East Blvd to Hwy 231, N 2.6 mi to Old Wetumpka Hwy (CR-111), E 0.1 mi (R) From NW of Montgomery or From Jct of I-65 & Hwy 152 (Northern Blvd) Exit 173, NE 6.5 mi on Hwy 152 to Hwy 231N, N 2.8 mi on Hwy 231 to Old Wetumpka Hwy (CR-111), E 0.1 mi (R). **FAC:** All weather rds. (89 spaces). Avail: 64 paved, patios, 64 pull-thrus (35 x 65), 64 full hkups (30/50 amps), seasonal sites, cable, WiFi, dump, laundry. **REC:** Talapoosa River: fishing, playground. Pets OK. Partial handicap access, no tents. Big rig sites, eco-friendly, 2015 rates: $30 to $35. Disc: AAA, military.
(877)271-8026 Lat: 32.27157, Lon: -86.12365
4655 Old Wetumka Parkway, Montgomery, AL 36110
mjashcraft@bellsouth.net
www.capitalcityrvpark.net
See ad this page, 4.

MONTGOMERY SOUTH RV PARK & CABINS
Ratings: 8/9★/8.5 (RV Park) From Jct I-65 & Tyson/Pintlala Rd (Exit 158), E 0.5 mi to Venable Rd, N 1 mi on Venable Rd (L). **FAC:** Gravel rds. 33 gravel, 31 pull-thrus (40 x 65), back-ins (40 x 50), 33 full hkups (30/50 amps), WiFi, rentals, laundry, LP gas. **REC.** Pets OK. Partial handicap access, no tents. Big rig sites, eco-friendly, 2015 rates: $26 to $36. Disc: AAA military.
(334)284-7006 Lat: 32.20527, Lon: -86.40858
731 Venable, Hope Hull, AL 36043
jimthornton@hotmail.com
www.montgomerysouthrvpark.com
See ad this page.

Get the Facts! Essential tips and travel info can be found in the Welcome Section at the beginning of each State/Province.

THE WOODS RV PARK & CAMPGROUND
Ratings: 7.5/8.5★/9.5 (RV Park) From Jct of I-65 & US 80/82 (exit 168) E 0.1 mi (one block) on US 80/82 to Sassafras Cir. (R); or From US 231 N & US 80/82, W 5 mi on US 80/82 to Sassafras Cir (L). **FAC:** Gravel rds. (105 spaces). Avail: 93 gravel, patios, 93 pull-thrus (30 x 80), 93 full hkups (30/50 amps), seasonal sites, cable, WiFi, tent sites, dump laundry, LP gas, fire rings, firewood. **REC:** pond, fishing, playground. Pets OK. Partial handicap access Big rig sites, RV age restrict, eco-friendly, 2015 rates $30. Disc: military.
(334)356-1887 Lat: 32.32544, Lon: -86.33126
4350 Sassafras Circle, Montgomery, AL 36105
shanajirik@yahoo.com
www.woodsrvpark.com
See ad this page, 4.

WOODRUFF LAKE/GUNTER HILL CAMPGROUND (Public Corps) From Jct of I-65 & exit 167 (Hwy 80), W 9 mi on Hwy 80 to CR-7, N, follow signs (L). 2015 rates: $18 to $24. Mar 1 to Oct 31. (334)872-9554

MOUNDVILLE — C2 *Hale, Tuscaloosa*

MOUNDVILLE ARCHAEOLOGICAL PARK (Public) From Jct of US-82 & Hwy 69, S 15 mi on Hwy 69 (R). 2015 rates: $12. (205)371-2234

MUSCLE SHOALS — A2 *Colbert*

TVA/WILSON DAM RESERVATION-LOWER ROCKPILE (Public) From Southside Wilson Dam, W 0.5 mi on Hwy 133 (TVA Reservation Rd), N 0.5 mi, follow signs (L). 2015 rates: $17 to $26. (800)882-5263

NEW MARKET — A4 *Madison*

SHARON JOHNSTON PARK (Public) North on Memorial Parkway, right on Winchester, left on Coleman Rd. 2015 rates: $15 to $18. (256)379-2868

OPELIKA — C5 *Lee*

A SPOTLIGHT Introducing Opelika's colorful attractions appearing at the front of this state section.

OPELIKA (CONT)

→ LAKESIDE RV PARK
Ratings: 6.5/7★/7 (Campground) From Jct of I-85 & US-280 (exit 62), E 4.5 mi on US-280 (L). **FAC:** Gravel rds. (58 spaces). Avail: 43 gravel, 35 pull-thrus (40 x 80), back-ins (50 x 80), 43 full hkups (30/50 amps), seasonal sites, cable, WiFi, tent sites, laundry, firewood. **REC:** pond, playground. Pet restrict(B). Partial handicap access. Big rig sites, eco-friendly, 2015 rates: $35. Disc: military. No CC.
(334)705-0701 Lat: 32.62685, Lon: -85.27966
5664 US Hwy 280E, Opelika, AL 36804
www.lakesidervparkopelikaal.com
See ad page 11.

↘ SPRING VILLA CAMPGROUND (Public) From Jct of I-85 & SR-169, SE 4 mi on SR-169 to CR-148, E 1 mi (R). 2015 rates: $10. (334)705-5552

OPP — E4 *Covington*

↑ FRANK JACKSON (State Pk) From Jct of US-331/US 84/Hwy 12, N 0.7 mi on US 331, W 1.0 mi on Opine Rd, N 0.2 mi on Jerry Adams Dr. (L). 2015 rates: $24 to $30. (334)493-6988

ORANGE BEACH — F2 *Baldwin*

↗ BUENA VISTA COASTAL RV RESORT **Ratings: 9/9.5★/10** (Condo Pk) 2015 rates: $65 to $135. (251)980-1855 23601 Perdido Beach Blvd., Orange Beach, AL 36561

→ HERITAGE MOTORCOACH RESORT & MARINA
Ratings: 10/10★/10 (Condo Pk) From Jct of I-10 & AL 59 (Exit 44), S 15.3 mi on AL 59 to Foley Beach Expy, E 14 mi on Foley Beach Expy to AL 180 (Canal Rd), E 5.8 mi on AL 180 (Canal Rd) (R). Note: Class A Motorhomes only. **FAC:** Paved rds. (79 spaces). Avail: 10 paved, patios, back-ins (30 x 70), accepts self-contain units only, 10 full hkups (30/50 amps), cable, WiFi, laundry, controlled access. **REC:** pool, whirlpool, Gulf of Mexico: fishing. Pets OK. Partial handicap access, no tents. Big rig sites, RV age restrict, 2015 rates: $80 to $140.
(800)730-7032 Lat: 30.298963, Lon: -87.533208
28888 Canal Road, Orange Beach, AL 36561
Rentals@heritageorangebeach.com
www.heritageorangebeach.com
See ad pages 8 (Spotlight Gulf Shores/Orange Beach), 4 & Snowbird Destinations in Magazine Section.

PELHAM — C3 *Shelby*

↓ BIRMINGHAM SOUTH CAMPGROUND
Ratings: 9/10★/8.5 (Campground) From Jct of I-65 & CR-52 (exit 242), W 0.6 mi on CR-52 to CR-33, N 300 ft (R). **FAC:** Paved/gravel rds. (102 spaces). 47 Avail: 40 paved, 7 gravel, patios, 47 pull-thrus (30 x 65), 47 full hkups (30/50 amps), seasonal sites, WiFi, tent sites, rentals, dump, laundry, groc, LP gas, fire rings, firewood. **REC:** heated pool, playground. Pets OK. Partial handicap access. Big rig sites, RV age restrict, eco-friendly, 2015 rates: $38 to $46. Disc: military.
(205)664-8832 Lat: 33.28596, Lon: -86.80717
222 Hwy 33, Pelham, AL 35124
bscampground@aol.com
See ad pages 13, 4.

↗ OAK MOUNTAIN (State Pk) From Jct of I-65 & SR-119 (exit 246), W 300 ft on SR-119 to state park rd, S 2 mi to entrance, NE 6 mi (E). 2015 rates: $24 to $30. (205)620-2527

PELL CITY — B4 *St Clair*

↓ LAKESIDE LANDING MARINA & RV RESORT
Ratings: 8.5/8.5★/8 (RV Park) From Jct of I-20 & US-231 (exit 158), S 6 mi on US-231 (L). **FAC:** Paved/gravel rds. (193 spaces). 151 Avail: 93 gravel, 58 grass, patios, 112 pull-thrus (24 x 65), back-ins (30 x 60), 151 full hkups (30/50 amps), seasonal sites, cable, WiFi, tent sites, dump, laundry, groc, LP gas, firewood, restaurant. **REC:** Logan Martin Lake: swim, fishing, marina, rec open to public. Pets OK. Partial handicap access. Big rig sites, 2015 rates: $30 to $55. Disc: military. ATM, no reservations.
(205)525-5701 Lat: 33.52845, Lon: -86.29144
4600 Martin St South, Cropwell, AL 35054
loganmartin.lake@gmail.com
lakeloganmartin.com
See ad this page, 4.

PICKENSVILLE — C2 *Pickens*

→ PICKENSVILLE CAMPGROUND (Public Corps) From Jct Hwy 388 & W Lock and Dam Rd, W 0.6 mi on W Lock and Dam Rd, L 0.1 mi on Camp Rd (E). 2015 rates: $20 to $24. (205)373-6328

PRATTVILLE — D4 *Autagua*

→ AUTAUGA CREEK LANDING RV CAMPGROUND Ratings: 3.5/NA/5 (Campground) From Jct I-65 (Exit 179) & Hwy 82/W6: Go 1 mi W to Hwy 82, then 2 mi S on Hwy 82; then 1 1/2 mi S on Hwy 31, then 3 mi W on Cty Rd 4 (R). **FAC:** Gravel rds. (46 spaces). Avail: 33 grass, back-ins (25 x 50), 33 full hkups (30/50 amps), seasonal sites, WiFi Hotspot, tent sites, rentals, firewood. **REC:** Autauga Creek: fishing. Pet restrict(B). 2015 rates: $25 to $35. Disc: military.
(334)361-3999 Lat: 32.25674, Lon: -86.27621
951 Langford Ct, Prattville, AL 36067
nora10100@yahoo.com
www.autaugacreekrv.com

← KOUNTRY AIR RV PARK
Ratings: 8.5/9★/8.5 (Campground) W-bnd: From jct of I-65 & US 82 (exit-179), W 14.9 mi on US 82 (L); or E-bnd: From Centerville East 46.3 mi on US 82 (R). **FAC:** Gravel rds. 35 gravel, 27 pull-thrus (30 x 75), back-ins (20 x 60), some side by side hkups, 35 full hkups (30/50 amps), WiFi, rentals, laundry, LP gas, firewood. **REC:** pool, playground. Pet restrict(B). Big rig sites, RV age restrict, eco-friendly, 2015 rates: $28 to $45. Disc: military.
(334)365-6861 Lat: 32.51504, Lon: -86.592695
2133 Hwy 82 west, Prattville, AL 36067
kountryairrvpark@hotmail.com
www.kountryairrv.com
See ad this page, 4.

ROBERTSDALE — F2 *Baldwin*

↗ AZALEA ACRES RV PARK
Ratings: 8/10★/10 (RV Park) From Jct of I-10 & CR-64 (Wilcox Rd, exit 53), S 0.1 mi on CR-64 to Wilcox Rd, S 0.5 mi to Patterson Rd, E 0.5 mi on Patterson Rd to Glass Rd (L), 0.3 mi down Glass Rd (R).

THE GULF COAST'S BEST KEPT SECRET
Peaceful country setting with lots of room for even the biggest rigs. NO RIG TOO BIG! Beautiful beaches, outlet shopping, Pensacola & Mobile just minutes away. The Naval Museum, USS Alabama, Casinos & great dining nearby.

FAC: Paved/gravel rds. 66 Avail: 19 paved, 47 grass, patios, 46 pull-thrus (46 x 92), back-ins (37 x 65), 66 full hkups (30/50 amps), WiFi, laundry, LP gas, firewood. **REC.** Pet restrict(B/Q). Partial handicap access, no tents. Age restrict may apply, big rig sites, eco-friendly, 2015 rates: $28 to $35. Disc: military.
(251)947-9530 Lat: 30.62443, Lon: -87.60613
27450 Glass Rd, Robertsdale, AL 36567
azalea.acres@gulftel.com
www.azaleaacresrvpark.com
See ad pages 9 (Spotlight Gulf Shores/Orange Beach), 4.

↗ HILLTOP RV PARK
Ratings: 7.5/7.5★/7 (RV Park) From Jct of I-10 & CR-64 (Wilcox Rd, exit 53), S 0.8 mi on CR-64 (L). **FAC:** Paved/gravel rds. 87 Avail: 31 gravel, 56 grass, 58 pull-thrus (28 x 85), back-ins (30 x 65), 87 full hkups (30/50 amps), WiFi, laundry, LP gas. **REC.** Pet restrict(B/Q). Partial handicap access, no tents. Big rig sites, eco-friendly, 2015 rates: $26 to $27. Disc: AAA.
(251)960-1129 Lat: 30.62594, Lon: -87.62501
23420 CR-64, Robertsdale, AL 36567
Kimcolcord@gmail.com
hilltoprvpark.com
See ad this page, 4.

→ RIVERSIDE RV RESORT **Ratings: 9/9★/7.5** (RV Park) 2015 rates: $35 to $40. (251)945-1110 25625 Water Rapids Rd, Robertsdale, AL 36567

↗ WILDERNESS RV PARK
Ratings: 8.5/8★/8 (RV Park) From I-10 (exit 53) & CR 64: Go S 1/4 mi on CR 64, then turn left on Patterson Rd for 1.3 mi. (Ignore GPS). **FAC:** Gravel rds. (74 spaces). Avail: 64 grass, 64 pull-thrus (25 x 65), 64 full hkups (30/50 amps), WiFi, laundry, LP gas. **REC:** pool. Pet restrict(Q). Partial handicap access, no tents. Big rig sites, eco-friendly, 2015 rates: $29 to $33.
(251)960-1195 Lat: 30.61870, Lon: -87.61132
24280 Patterson Rd, Robertsdale, AL 36567
wildernessrv@gulftel.com
www.wildernessrvpark.com
See ad this page.

Travel Services

← CAMPING WORLD OF ROBERTSDALE As the nation's largest retailer of RV supplies, accessories, services and new and used RVs, Camping World is committed to making your total RV experience better. RV Accessories: (888)445-5990. **SERVICES:** RV, tire, RV appliance, MH mechanical, staffed RV wash, restrooms, RV Sales. RV supplies, LP, dump, emergency parking, RV accessible. waiting room. Hours: 8am to 6pm.
251-947-9910 Lat: 30.534835, Lon: -87.70835
21282 Hwy 59 South, Robertsdale, AL 36567
www.CampingWorldofSouthAlabama.com

ROGERSVILLE — A3 *Lauderdale, Lawrence*

← JOE WHEELER (State Pk) From Jct of US-72 & SR-207, W 1.5 mi on US-72 to park rd, S 3 mi (L). 2015 rates: $22 to $25. (256)247-1184

↓ WHEELER RESERVATION CAMPGROUND (State Pk) From jct US 72 & Hwy 101: Go 3-1/2 mi S on Hwy 101 (just before crossing dam). 2015 rates: $22 to $25. (256)386-2560

RUSSELLVILLE — A2 *Franklin*

← ELLIOTT BRANCH CAMPGROUND (Public) From town, W 14 mi on Hwy 24 to CR-88, S 1.5 mi to Elliott Branch Rd, E 0.5 mi (E). 2015 rates: $7.50 to $15. Mar 15 to Oct 15. (877)367-2232

← PINEY POINT CAMPGROUND (Public) From town, W 18 mi on Hwy 24 to CR-16, S 8 mi to CR-4, S 1.2 mi to CR-37, S 3 mi, cross dam (L). 2015 rates: $7.50 to $15. Mar 15 to Oct 15. (877)367-2232

↑ SLICKROCK CAMPGROUND (Public) From town, W 13 mi on Hwy 24 to CR-33, N 2.3 mi (L). 2015 rates: $7.50 to $15. Mar 15 to Nov 15. (877)367-2232

SCOTTSBORO — A4 *Jackson*

← GOOSEPOND COLONY (Public) From Jct of US-72 & SR-79, S 1 mi on SR-79 (L). Follow signs. 2015 rates: $25 to $30. (800)268-2884

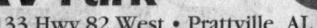

SELMA — D3 *Dallas*

DANNELLY LAKE/SIX MILE CREEK PARK (Public Corps) From town, S 9 mi on Hwy 41 to CR-139, W 1 mi (L). 2015 rates: $20. (334)875-6228

PAUL M. GRIST SP (State Pk) From town: Go 15 mi N on Hwy 22. 2015 rates: $22 to $25. (334)872-5846

SHORTERVILLE — E5 *Henry*

HARDRIDGE CREEK (Public Corps) From Jct Hwy 10 & CR-97, N 6 mi on CR-97 (E). 2015 rates: $24 to $52. Mar 6 to Sep 28. (334)585-5945

SILAS — D2 *Choctaw*

SERVICE PARK (Public Corps) From town, W 4 mi on Hwy 84 (R). 2015 rates: $22. Mar 15 to Dec 15. (251)753-6935

SPANISH FORT — E2 *Baldwin*

BLAKELEY (State Pk) From jct I-10 & US 98: Go N 1 mi on Hwy 98 to Hwy 31, then N 4/5 mi to Hwy 225, follow signs. 2015 rates: $6. (251)626-5581

MEAHER SP (State Pk) 2015 rates: $34. (251)626-5529

SUMMERDALE — F2 *Baldwin*

EMMAUS MOTORCOACH & RV RESORT **Ratings: 6.5/7.5/8.5** (RV Park) 2015 rates: $32 to $38. (251)989-9888 23051 Cty Rd 38, Summerdale, AL 36580

ESCAPEES RAINBOW PLANTATION **Ratings: 8.5/7.5/7.5** (RV Park) 2015 rates: $26.50. (251)988-8132 14301 County Rd 28, Summerdale, AL 36580

TALLADEGA — C4 *Talladega*

TALLADEGA See also Anniston, Delta, Heflin & Pell City.

LOGAN LANDING RV RESORT & CAMPGROUND **Ratings: 8/7/8** (Condo Pk) 2015 rates: $34 to $38. (888)564-2671 1036 Paul Bear Bryant Rd, Alpine, AL 35014

TANNER — A3 *Lime Stone*

SWAN CREEK COMMUNITY (MHP)
Ratings: 7/7.5/8 (RV Area in MHP) From I-65 (Exit 347) & Brownsferry Rd: Go 1 3/4 W on Brownsferry Rd, then 1 1/2 mi s on Hwy 31 (L). **FAC:** Paved rds. (380 spaces). 15 Avail: 8 paved, 7 gravel, patios, 15 pull-thrus (30 x 65), 15 full hkups (30/50 amps), seasonal sites, WiFi, tent sites, laundry. **REC:** playground. Pet restrict(B). Partial handicap access. Big rig sites, eco-friendly, 2015 rates: $30.
(256)355-5392 Lat: 34.70758, Lon: -86.95499
10420 US Hwy 31 Lot 67, Tanner, AL 35671
swancreek@towermgnt.com
www.towerrvparks.com

THEODORE — F2 *Mobile*

PECAN GROVE MOTORHOME RV PARK **Ratings: 6/NA/9** (Campground) 2015 rates: $30. (251)973-1013 10420 Dauphin Island Pkwy, Theodore, AL 36582

TROY — D4 *Pike*

A SPOTLIGHT Introducing Troy's colorful attractions appearing at the front of this state section.

DEER RUN RV PARK
Ratings: 9.5/10★/9.5 (Campground) In Montgomery, From Jct of I 85 & Hwy 271 (Taylor Rd), S 4.9 mi on Hwy 271 to Jct of Hwy 271 (Taylor Rd) & Hwy 231, S 31.8 mi on Hwy 231 to CR 1124, W .01 mi (R) or From Troy, Jct of Hwy 231 & Hwy 29, N 6.3 mi on Hwy 231 to CR-1124, W .01 mi on CR-1124 (R).

2011 - 12 TOP 100 PARK WITH DAY SPA
Manicured park with 45' concrete F/H/U pull thrus surrounded by tall pines and springfed lakes. Offering onsite spa services including facials, peels, massage therapy, hair color, and manicures/pedicures.

FAC: Gravel rds. 86 paved, 81 pull-thrus (30 x 65), back-ins (30 x 65), 86 full hkups (30/50 amps), cable, WiFi, laundry, LP gas, firewood. **REC:** pool, pond, fishing. Pets OK. Partial handicap access, no tents. Big rig sites, RV age restrict, eco-friendly, 2015 rates: $33. Disc: military.
(334)566-6517 Lat: 31.893388, Lon: -86.010072
25629 US Hwy 231, Troy, AL 36081
lagshands@yahoo.com
www.deerrunrvpark.com
See ad pages 10 (Spotlight Troy), 4 & Snowbird Destinations in Magazine Section.

HEART OF DIXIE TRAIL RIDE, LLC **Ratings: 7/9★/7** (Campground) 2015 rates: $25. (334)670-0005 4162 County Road 7708 (Needmore Rd), Troy, AL 36081

Travel Services

THE SPA AT DEER RUN Hair Salon, Spa, Pedicures, Manicures, Waxing, Facials, Peels, Massage Therapy, Organic Color. **SERVICES:** Restrooms. RV accessible. Hours: By Appointment.
(334)492-2977 Lat: 31.53476, Lon: -86.00616
25629 U S Hwy 231, Troy, AL 36081
lagshands@yahoo.com
www.deerrunrvpark.com
See ad page 10 (Spotlight Troy).

TUSCALOOSA — C2 *Tuscaloosa*

HOLT LAKE/DEERLICK CREEK (Public Corps) From Jct of I-59/I-20 & US-82, W 4 mi on US-82 to Rice Mine Rd (CR-30), NE 3 mi to CR-87, NE 3 mi to CR-42, E 3 mi to CR-89, S 3 mi (E). 2015 rates: $22. Mar 1 to Nov 28. (205)759-1591

LAKE LURLEEN (State Pk) From Jct of I-59/I-20 & US-82W (exit 73), NW 12.1 mi on US-82W to CR-21, N 2.5 mi to Lk Lurleen Rd, N 2 mi (E); or From Jct of I-59/I-20 & SR-69 (exit 71B), N 5 mi on SR-69 to US-82W, W 5.3 mi to CR -21, N 2.5 mi to Lk Lurleen Rd, N 2 mi (E). 2015 rates: $22 to $28. (205)339-1558

SUNSET TRAVEL PARK **Ratings: 6.5/7.5/5** (RV Park) 2015 rates: $29 to $32. (205)553-9233 5001 Jvc Rd E., Cottondale, AL 35453

TUSCUMBIA — A2 *Colbert*

HERITAGE ACRES RV PARK
Ratings: 7/9.5★/8.5 (Campground) From Jct of US 72 & US 43 (In Tuscumbia), W 2.5 mi on US 72 to Neil Morris Rd, S 0.25 mi (L). **FAC:** Gravel rds. (61 spaces). Avail: 41 gravel, 4 pull-thrus (30 x 90), back-ins (30 x 60), 41 full hkups (30/50 amps), seasonal sites, cable, WiFi, dump, laundry, LP gas. Pet restrict(B/Q). Partial handicap access, no tents. Big rig sites, eco-friendly, 2015 rates: $29 to $32. Disc: AAA, military.
(256)383-7368 Lat: 34.71025, Lon: -87.71089
1770 Neil Morris Rd, Tuscumbia, AL 35674
heritageacresrv@comcast.net
www.heritageacresrvpark.com
See ad this page, 4.

WARRIOR — B3 *Blount*

RICKWOOD CAVERNS (State Pk) From Jct of I-65 & SR-160 (exit 284), W 0.2 mi on SR-160 to CR-8, N 2.5 mi to Rickwood Caverns Rd, E 1.3 mi (R); or From Jct of I-65 & CR-5 (exit 289), W 0.6 mi on CR-5 to Rickwood Caverns Rd/CR 4, S 2.3 (L). 2015 rates: $20 to $23. (205)647-9692

WETUMPKA — C4 *Elmore*

FORT TOULOUSE/JACKSON PARK (Public Corps) From Jct of I-65 & Hwy 231, N 10 mi on Hwy 231 to Ft Toulouse Rd, W 2.5 mi (E). 2015 rates: $15. (334)567-3002

WILMER — E2 *Mobile*

ESCATAWPA HOLLOW CAMPGROUND (Campground) (Rebuilding) 2015 rates: $25. (251)649-4233 15551 Moffett Rd (Hwy 98), Wilmer, AL 36587

WOODVILLE — A4 *Jackson*

CATHEDRAL CAVERNS SP (State Pk) From Huntsville: Take Hwy 72 E to Hwy 63, then right until you see the Cathedral Caverns rock sigh. Turn left & follow signs. Pit toilets. 2015 rates: $13. (256)728-8193

PARNELL CREEK RV PARK
Ratings: 9/8.5★/9 (RV Park) From Jct of I-65 (Exit 340B) & I-565, E 21.3 mi on I-565 to US-72, E 24.4 mi to Parnell Circle, S 0.1 mi (L). Mile Marker 125. **FAC:** Gravel rds. (46 spaces). Avail: 36 gravel, 22 pull-thrus (24 x 55), back-ins (20 x 50), 27 full hkups, 9 W, 9 E (30/50 amps), seasonal sites, cable, WiFi, tent sites, rentals, dump, mobile sewer, laundry, groc, LP gas, firewood. **REC:** pool, Parnell Creek: fishing, playground. Pets OK. Partial handicap access. Big rig sites, eco-friendly, 2015 rates: $27 to $32.
(256)508-7308 Lat: 34.61335, Lon: -86.23478
115 Parnell Circle, Woodville, AL 35776
parnellcreekrvpark@yahoo.com
www.parnellcreekrvpark.com
See ad pages 18, 4.

Getty Images/iStockphoto

WELCOME TO Alaska

DATE OF STATEHOOD JAN. 3, 1959	WIDTH: 2,261 MILES (3,639 KM) LENGTH: 1,420 MILES (2,285 KM)	PROPORTION OF UNITED STATES 17.54% OF 3,794,100 SQ MI

A land of pure, merciless and epic natural beauty, Alaska defies hyperbole. The self-styled "Final Frontier" boasts a glacier that's bigger than Delaware, king salmon that exceed 70 pounds and humpbacks whales as long as 50 feet.

Alaska is home to the highest peak in North America (Mount McKinley), the nation's largest national forest (Tongass) and America's largest state park (Wood-Tikchik). It's also where the U.S.'s most powerful earthquake struck in 1964 (9.2 on the Richter scale), causing two mammoth chunks of earth to fissure and plummet 20 feet within seconds. Alaska has long been the definitive (and transformative) journey for intrepid travelers who seek the "call of the wild."

Every town in Alaska nudges up against dramatic wilderness where, in the shadows of vast mountain ranges, grizzly bears gorge on salmon plucked from deep-churning waters and moose and caribou irreverently preen for wide-eyed tourists. The time warp city of Anchorage, established as a railroad construction port in 1914, serves as the gateway to the region's bleak but beautiful, stark but stunning landscape. State capital Juneau the only state capital with no road system borders the 140 glaciers that define the Juneau Icefield and provides access to the storied Mendenhall Glacier.

Learn

When U.S. Secretary of State William Seward bought Alaska from Russia for two cents an acre in 1867, the territory deemed nothing more than a wilderness was given the dubious moniker of "Seward's Folly." The critics couldn't have been more wrong. When gold was discovered in the 1890s, 30,000 prospectors converged on the region. Within decades, Alaska became a billion dollar cash cow for the U.S. economy.

In December 1941, Japan bombed Pearl Harbor and ushered in the Pacific Theater of World War II. Just 36 miles

Top 3 Tourism Attractions:
1) Denali National Park
2) Glacier Bay National Park
3) Alaska Native Heritage Center

Nickname: The Last Frontier

State Flower: Forget-me-not

State Bird: Willow Ptarmigan

People: Michelle Johnson, actress; Lisa Murkowski, senator; Curt Schilling, baseball pitcher

Major Cities: Anchorage, Fairbanks, Juneau (capital), Sitka, Ketchikan

Topography: Pacific and Arctic mountain systems, central plateau and Arctic Slope or coastal plain

Climate: Long, cold winters and short, cool summers; Northern Alaska has Arctic climate

Getty Images/iStockphoto

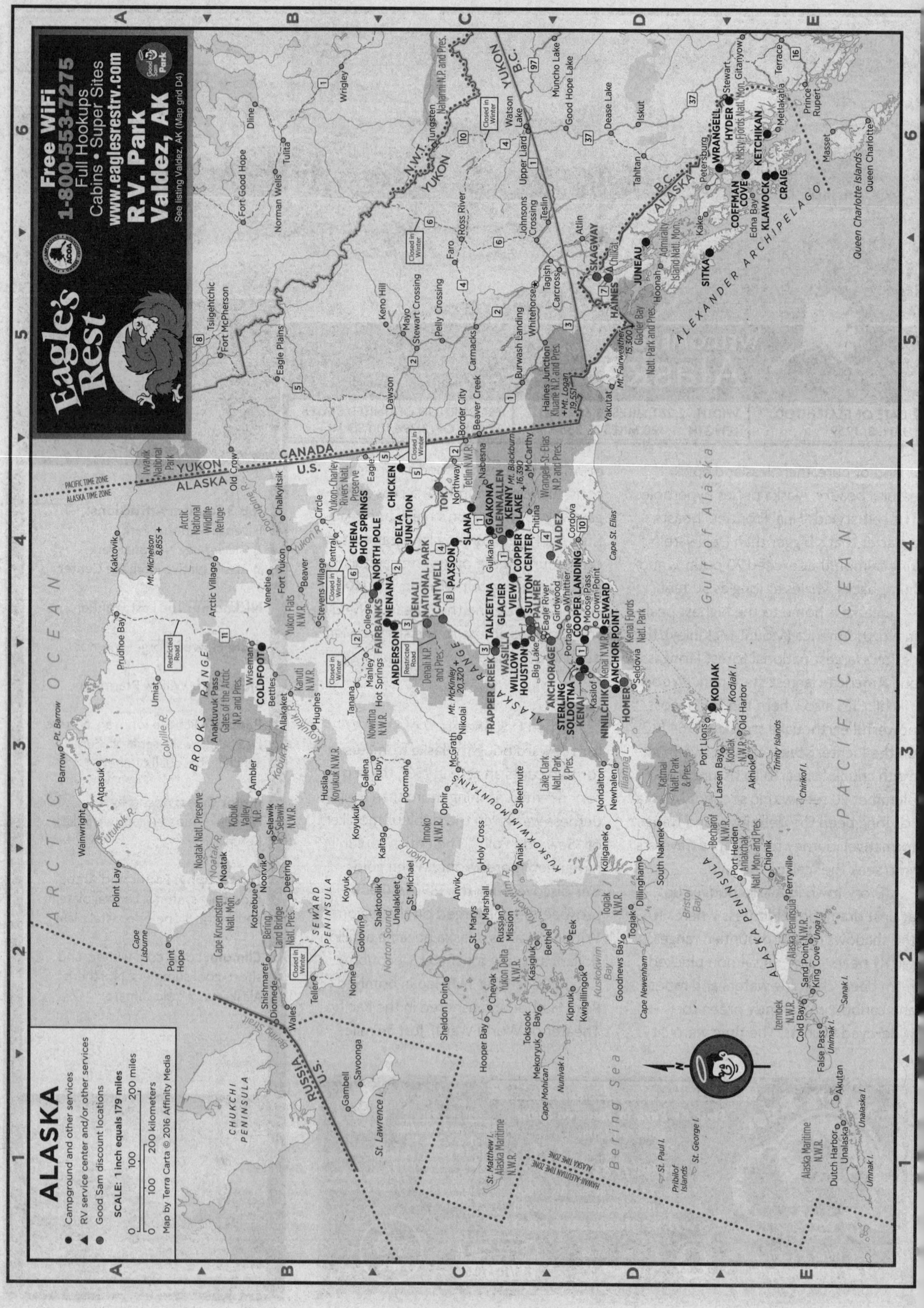
ALASKA
● Campground and other services
▲ RV service center and/or other services
● Good Sam discount locations
SCALE: 1 inch equals 179 miles
0 100 200 miles
0 100 200 kilometers
Map by Terra Carta © 2016 Affinity Media
Eagle's Rest
Free WiFi
1-800-553-7275
Full Hookups
Cabins • Super Sites
www.eaglesrestrv.com
R.V. Park
Valdez, AK
See listing Valdez, AK (Map grid D4)
ARCTIC OCEAN
PACIFIC OCEAN
Gulf of Alaska
Bering Sea
BROOKS RANGE
ALASKA RANGE
KUSKOKWIM MOUNTAINS
SEWARD PENINSULA
ALASKA PENINSULA
ALEXANDER ARCHIPELAGO
CHUKCHI PENINSULA
RUSSIA
U.S.
CANADA
YUKON
ALASKA
N.W.T.
B.C.
PACIFIC TIME ZONE
ALASKA TIME ZONE
HAWAII-ALEUTIAN TIME ZONE
Closed in Winter
Restricted Road
COLDFOOT
CHENA HOT SPRINGS
NORTH POLE
FAIRBANKS
NENANA
ANDERSON
DELTA JUNCTION
CHICKEN
TOK
DENALI NATIONAL PARK
CANTWELL
PAXSON
SLANA
GAKONA
GLENNALLEN
KENNY LAKE
COPPER CENTER
VALDEZ
TALKEETNA
TRAPPER CREEK
WASILLA
WILLOW
HOUSTON
GLACIER VIEW
SUTTON
PALMER
ANCHORAGE
COOPER LANDING
SEWARD
STERLING
SOLDOTNA
KENAI
NINILCHIK
ANCHOR POINT
HOMER
KODIAK
SKAGWAY
HAINES
JUNEAU
SITKA
WRANGELL
HYDER
COFFMAN COVE
KETCHIKAN
KLAWOCK
CRAIG
Mt. McKinley 20,320
Mt. Logan 19,551
Mt. Blackburn 16,390
Mt. Fairweather 15,300
Mt. Michelson 8,855

separated the U.S.'s most western port (in Alaska) from Siberia. On February 6, 1942, in direct response to the Japanese threat to North America's west coast, U.S. Congress and President Roosevelt approved the construction of the 1,422-mile Alaska Highway. Completed in just over eight months by 3,000 U.S. soldiers (grueling conditions claimed the lives of around 200 men), the road's length continues to fluctuate as engineers attempt to address the highway's deadly curves and precipitous drops. Alaska was admitted to the union in 1959. In 1968, a huge oil and gas reservoir (twice the size of any other field in North America) was discovered near Prudhoe Bay, leading to the development, in 1977, of the $8 billion Trans-Alaska Pipeline.

Play

It's an exhilarating four- to five-hour drive from Anchorage to Mount McKinley National Park, a 4-million-acre wilderness area and a national preserve. The park's cinematic landscape bran dishes stark tundra, gorgeous alpine rivers, lush boreal forests and breathtaking glaciers. The massif of Mount McKinley (generally referred to by its native Athabascan name, "Denali"), stands at 20,320 feet, an awesome presence despite omnipresent cloud cover. The country's largest national park (bigger than Switzerland), Wrangell-St. Elias National Park distills the essence

See listing Valdez, AK

of Alaska. Getting there is certainly no mean feat 60 miles on a bone-shaking gravel road but any discomfort subsides in an instant in the presence of the 18,008-foot-tall Mount St. Elias.

Exit Glacier near Seward and Matanuska Glacier State Recreation Site are popular among tour groups operating out of downtown Anchorage.

Topping the list of non-glacier attractions, meanwhile, is Chugach State Park, which spans nearly a half -a-million acres and sits just minutes from downtown Anchorage. With campgrounds, in-park glaciers of its own, ancient ice fields, preserved ocean shorelines and a cluster of premiere hiking trails, this is among Anchorage's top attractions for outdoors enthusiasts of all ages. The park is particularly popular among anglers and wildlife viewers, as well as nature photographers taking advantage of its excellent views of the Chugach Mountain.

When you're done exploring the outdoors, head inside and explore the collections of the Anchorage Museum and the Alaska Heritage Museum, two of the city's premiere must-visit points of interest for history buffs. The former is the largest museum in the state and tells the story of Alaska from the Ice Age to modern times through a series of interactive exhibits containing a mix of historical artifacts and displays of indigenous artwork. The Alaska Heritage Museum, meanwhile, is a massive private collection whose highlights include an in-depth exploration of the Alaskan Gold Rush and a two-thirds scale stagecoach.

The smallest national park in Alaska,

See listing Skagway, AK

Kenai provides sanctuary to more than 20 species of seabirds, including clown-faced puffins, large numbers of bald eagles and peregrine falcons, 10 species of marine mammals and 27 land mammals, including moose, black bears, wolverines and coyotes. The copper-mining communities of McCarthy and Kennicott testify to the state's human history and elucidate the traditional life cycles of an Alaskan bush community. In Klondike Gold Rush National Historical Park, a three- to four-day hike along the Chilkoot Trail traces the journey taken by gold-prospectors in 1898, from the Alaskan panhandle up over the Chilkoot Pass into Canada.

Experience

December to March in Chatanika or along the Gilmore Trail is prime time to experience the aurora borealis. Mid-January, Anchorage's Folk Festival presents more than 120 singers, dancers and storytellers. In Fairbanks, late February, the World Ice Art Championships ranks as one of the largest ice-sculpting competitions and exhibitions on the planet, featuring over 100 ice artists from 50 countries. In early August, the nine-day Tanana Valley State Fair features baby shows, talent competitions, hula-hoop challenges, watermelon-eating contests, antique-tractor pulls, hayrides and barn dances. In December, the Anchorage International Film Festival, North America's northernmost independent film festival, screens 100 films in various theaters in town.

Taste

Over the last decade, Alaska has experienced a culinary renaissance. In the snug town of Fox, 20 minutes outside Fairbanks, erstwhile brewery Silver Gulch (www.silvergulch.com) has extended its repertoire to feature well-executed dishes including zesty halibut tacos, seafood pasta alfredo and beer-braised ribs. The best breakfast spot in Anchorage, Snow City Café (www.snowcitycafe.com) serves crowd pleasers such as the tundra scramble (with reindeer) and sockeye smoked-salmon.

- STAY A WHILE -

Explore Fairbanks

With the midnight summer sun shining nearly 24 hours a day, Fairbanks is bursting with energy and things to do. Pan for gold, float the Chena River, mingle with reindeer, cool off in an ice museum, take a refreshing hike, look for wildlife, or be inspired by art galleries, museums and historic sites.

During the aurora season, August 21-April 21, you have a great chance to see the shimmering light of the aurora borealis along with other activities and events unveiled during the winter.

Fairbanks is the gateway to Denali, Interior and Arctic Alaska. Denali National Park is two hours away; the Arctic Circle is a six-hour drive; villages without road access, refuges and parks are a short flight away.

Make the Morris Thompson Cultural and Visitors Center your first stop in Fairbanks. Not only beautiful but informative, the Center has brochures, maps, free WiFi and telephone, and local walking and driving tours. Serving as the regional visitor facility, the friendly and knowledgeable staff can answer all your questions. The free 9,000-square-foot exhibit hall features outstanding displays and dioramas showcasing Interior Alaska's people, wildlife, landscapes and seasons. Enjoy free films and programs on Alaska's natural and cultural history. The Center also has an artisans' workshop, a planning area for outdoor excursions and an Alaska Geographic Store.

Once a gold rush boomtown, now called the "Golden Heart City," visitors find Fairbanks inviting, engaging and awe-inspiring—the heart of the last frontier. For more information, visit explorefairbanks.com or call 907-456-5774.

- STAY A WHILE -

Alaska Campground Owner's Association

The Alaska Campground Owner's Association (ACOA) represents campgrounds throughout Alaska and is a member-owned non-profit. Our vision is to provide outdoor hospitality excellence to the camping public in Alaska.

The Alaska RV park and campground members of ACOA are generally privately owned, and each Alaskan campground is as unique as its owner! Wherever you are in Alaska, you are never far from an ACOA campground. Because of the variety of members and services offered, we can meet the needs of campers from all backgrounds. We understand that you are looking for your own unique Alaska traveling experience and strive to fulfill your expectations.

Are you looking for a peaceful camping site by a lake or near a glacier? A park with the conveniences of the city? Access to local tourist activities? Our parks can accommodate your traveling style, whether you are traveling in a motorhome, fifth-wheel, pop-up or tent camping. Many of our members also offer room and cabin rentals. We can meet many of your other traveling needs as well. While there may be other camping choices in Alaska, ACOA members offer amenities such as Shower and Laundry Facilities, Wi-Fi and Dial-up Modem access, Cable Television, Dining, Gift and Convenience Shops, Local Information and Activity Booking, and much more.

TRAVEL & TOURISM

Alaska Travel Industry Association
www.travelalaska.com

Anchorage Convention and Visitors Bureau
907-276-4118, 800-478-1255
www.anchorage.net

Fairbanks Convention and Visitors Bureau
800-327-5774, 907-456-5774
www.explorefairbanks.com

Haines Convention and Visitors Bureau
907-766-2234, 800-458-3579
www.haines.ak.us

Homer Chamber of Commerce
907-235-7740
www.homeralaska.org

Juneau Convention and Visitors Bureau
www.traveljuneau.com

Kenai Visitor & Convention Bureau
907-283-1991
www.visitkenai.com

Ketchikan Visitors Bureau
907-225-6166, 800-770-3300
www.visit-ketchikan.com

Skagway Convention & Visitors Bureau
907-983-2854
www.skagway.com

Tok Alaska Chamber of Commerce
907-883-5775
www.tokalaskainfo.com

Valdez CVB
907-835-4636
www.valdezalaska.org

Greater Wasilla Chamber of Commerce
907-376-1299
www.wasillachamber.org

OUTDOOR RECREATION

Alaska Hike Search
www.alaskahikesearch.com

Alaska State Parks
www.dnr.state.ak.us-parks

Fishing and Licensing Div. Alaska Dept. of Fish and Game
www.adfg.state.ak.us

SHOPPING

Alaska Mint
800-770-6468
www.alaskamint.com

Oomingmak
907-272-9225
www.qiviut.com

Raven Eagle Gifts
888-461-8726
www.raveneaglegifts.com

AK

Featured Good Sam Parks

ALASKA/YUKON

Good Sam Park

When you stay with Good Sam, you can expect the highest degree of cleanliness and friendliness, and better yet, you get 10% off campground fees.

If you're not already a Good Sam member you can purchase your membership at one of these locations:

ALASKA

ANCHORAGE
Anchorage Ship Creek RV Park
(907)277-0877
Creekwood Inn Motel & RV Park
(907)258-6006

CANTWELL
Cantwell RV Park
(800)940-2210

DENALI NATIONAL PARK
Denali Rainbow Village RV Park & Motel
(907)683-7777
Denali RV Park & Motel
(800)478-1501

FAIRBANKS
River's Edge RV Park & Campground
(907)474-0286
Riverview RV Park
(888)488-6392

GLENNALLEN
Northern Nights Campground & RV Park
(907)822-3199

HAINES
Haines Hitch-Up RV Park Inc
(907)766-2882
Oceanside RV Park
(907)766-2437

HOMER
Baycrest RV Park
(907)435-7995
Oceanview RV Park
(907)235-3951

KENAI
Beluga Lookout Lodge & RV Park
(907)283-5999
Diamond M Ranch Resort
(907)283-9424

NINILCHIK
Alaskan Angler RV Resort & Cabins
(800)347-4114
All Seasons Campground
(907)567-3396

PALMER
Mountain View RV Park
(907)745-5747

SKAGWAY
Garden City RV Park
(866)983-2378

TOK
Tok RV Village & Cabins
(907)883-5877

TRAPPER CREEK
Trapper Creek Inn & RV Park
(907)733-2302

VALDEZ
Eagle's Rest RV Park & Cabins
(800)553-7275

WASILLA
Big Bear RV Park
(907)745-7445

YUKON

CARMACKS
Carmacks Hotel & RV Park
(867)863-5221

TESLIN
Yukon Motel & Lakeshore RV Park
(867)390-2089

WHITEHORSE
Caribou RV Park
(867)668-2961
Hi Country RV Park
(877)458-3806

For more Good Sam Parks go to listing pages

ANCHORAGE

A sophisticated outpost on the Last Frontier

There's good reason why Alaska is often called The Last Frontier. Vast tracts of untamed wilderness still dominate its rugged tundra landscape, while small coastal communities and even smaller stepping-stone outposts string the state together across a quilt of rocky mountain ranges, jagged fjords, ancient glacial ice flows and dense taiga forests.

This is wild country, to be sure. Yet it's also one of the most richly rewarding vacation spots in the country, and any proper exploration of its bottomless well of natural treasures is best begun at the state's unofficial doorstep: Anchorage.

Tucked snugly at the end of gorgeous Cook Inlet, the city of Anchorage is one of the few areas in Alaska that's directly accessible by air (including major airlines), water (including cruise ship transfers and state ferries), railroad and well-maintained year-round highways. It's also the only place in Alaska where all of the comfort and amenity of big city life exists alongside easy access to some of the country's most stunning environments. Explore glaciers by lunch, kayak with orcas by dinner, dine on gourmet seafood by sunset and enjoy world-class entertainment by bedtime. It's just par for the course.

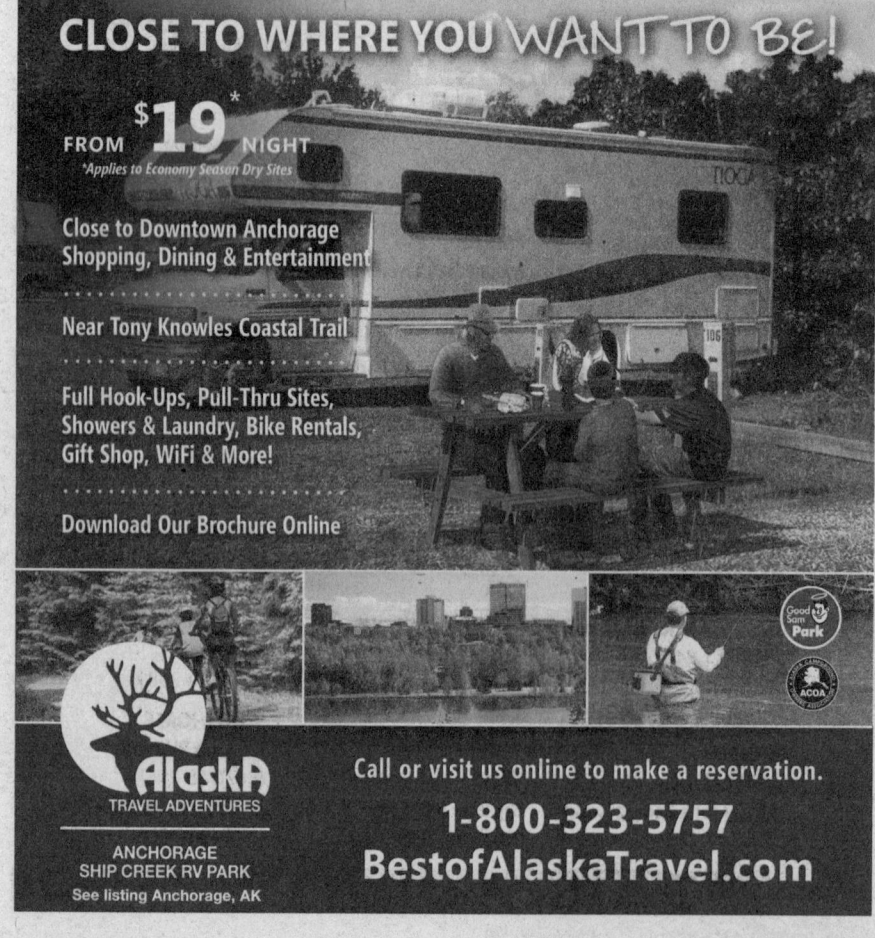

City Life, Alaska Style

The city itself is communal in feel and the downtown area is an easily walkable district teeming with locally owned and operated restaurants, shops, outfitters and tour companies. Far south of the Arctic Circle, protected by the Chugach Mountains and warmed by Pacific Rim ocean currents, the climate is mild and the city is generally spared from extreme cold. Nevertheless, dress in layers and arrive prepared, as weather conditions can shift quickly.

Of course, outdoor action is the name of the game here, and Anchorage has it all. Ice climbing, white-water rafting, paragliding, mountain biking, kayaking, zip lining, skiing, snowboarding and heli-skiing options abound for the more adrenaline-prone adventure seekers.

For More Information

Anchorage Convention & Visitors Bureau
907-276-4118
www.anchorage.net

Alaska Travel Industry Association
800-862-5275
www.travelalaska.com

Getty Images/iStockphoto

FAIRBANKS

Discover vacation gold in this shimmering city

Alaska's wild, rugged weather and rocky mountain landscapes are on full display in the hardy northern city of Fairbanks, where echoes of the Gold Rush and pioneering Arctic expeditions still feature prominently in city's cultural ethos.

Located deep in the Alaskan interior, the state's second-largest city is known mostly for its proximity to Denali National Park (home to Mount McKinley), its surreal northern light displays and its somewhat extreme climate. Summers are defined by long arctic days that burn brightly with up to 22 hours of sunlight, while winters play witness to temperatures that can drop to an exhilarating -60 and beyond.

But there's more to Fairbanks than meets the eye, and there's a reason more than 100,000 people call this unique and pleasantly remote northern gem home.

City on the Frontier

The city center is situated between the picturesque banks of the Tanana River and the Chena River. This pair of meandering navigable waterways once funneled early gold prospecting traffic and supplies into the region. In those days, it was little more than a turn-of-the-century trading post.

Today, visitors arrive by way of the George Parks Highway (Interstate A-4, Alaska Route 3) to find a surprisingly frenetic cityscape that is home to an eclectic mix of local shops and restaurants.

History buffs will be in their element here, as a diverse collection of museums is scattered throughout the area. The Museum of the North at the centrally located University of Alaska is widely regarded as one of the finest in the entire state, but a variety of other collections also warrant considerable exploration, including the Ice Museum, the Pioneer Air Museum, the Fountainhead Antique Auto Museum and the Fairbanks Children's Museum. Pioneer Park in the center of Fairbanks is a must-visit for families, as it blends the town's Golf Rush history with theme rides.

The real appeal up here, though, is found outside the city limits and under a clear blue sky. Hiking even a few minutes from the city center finds you in rugged, wild backcountry that's teeming with moose, caribou, Dall sheep and, of course, grizzly bears—so keep your eyes peeled.

Lace up your hiking boots, make sure your camera is charged and don't forget your binoculars—you never know what you'll see or find on a day spent exploring the area's vast network of trails and nearby state parks.

Adrenaline junkies have their pick of the activity litter: opportunities to go kayaking, river rafting, snowmobiling and alpine skiing are in vast supply. Those looking for a more laid-back experience can soak in natural hot springs, hit the links in one of three golf courses, or cast their lures on a chartered fishing trip.

Delightful Day Trips

The Chena River State Recreation Area (30 minutes to the east of Fairbanks) and Denali National Park and Preserve (2 hours to the southwest) are the most popular destinations for day-trips and wilderness escapes.

The latter is home to iconic Mount McKinley, which towers over the entire region at a height of 20,322 feet, making it the tallest peak in North America. Partially restricted to various types of traffic, Denali is best explored by way of a guided tour or shuttle bus service. These can be found at the park's main visitor entrance, which also features a wide range of shopping, dining and camping options. Expect to spend some time here—the park spans more than six million acres and includes some of the most breathtaking trails, rivers, lakes and sweeping alpine vistas in the state.

By contrast, the Chena River State Recreation Area is the perfect place for a quick getaway, given its proximity to the city. Short, scenic hikes and bubbling public hot springs are visitor favorites, and the park's bounty of regularly stocked fishing ponds are a major draw for anglers with a taste for fresh rainbow trout or Arctic grayling.

In July, the city celebrates itself with a weeklong event called Fairbanks Golden Days. Live music, antique cars and special activities fill the historic downtown core before culminating in the annual Golden Days Parade.

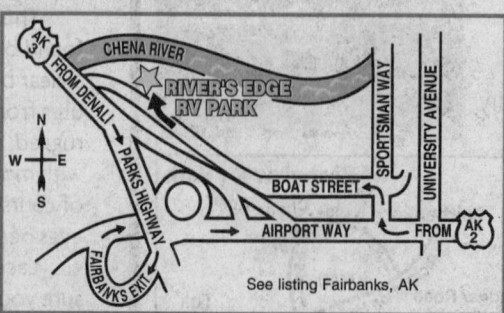

For More Information

Fairbanks Convention and Visitor's Bureau
800-327-5774
www.explorefairbanks.com

Alaska Travel Industry Association
800-862-5275
www.travelalaska.com

Getty Images/iStockphoto

KENAI PENINSULA

Cut loose in the Last Frontier's vast playground

There's a reason this 15,000-square-mile slice of scenic Southern Alaska is known as the state's unofficial "playground." A surprisingly mild climate, an abundance of state parks and proximity to large urban centers like Anchorage make the Kenai Peninsula a natural base of operations to sample the best of everything Alaska has to offer.

Cook Inlet, the Gulf of Alaska and Prince William Sound border the peninsula on three sides, while a land bridge in Chugach National Forest anchors the Kenai to the Alaskan mainland just south of Anchorage. Many will find themselves entering the Kenai via this land bridge and along the Seward Highway, a National Scenic Byway that features incredible coastal views as it snakes alongside Turnagain Arm toward the rocky Chugach Mountains.

Once on the peninsula, first-time visitors will find a mesmerizing landscape home to a high concentration of glaciers, ice fields, mountain ranges, dense taiga forests, glassy alpine lakes, crystal clear rivers and a slate of charming coastal fishing communities.

Chartered cruises offering close-up views of calving glaciers and migrating whales operate year-round. Vast networks of well-maintained trails blanket the peninsula from coast to coast. Opportunities to kayak, canoe, river-raft, zip-line, heli-ski and ice-climb abound. Wild moose, caribou and Dall sheep dot the landscape. Floating in the background (and sneaking into your photos) of any coastal view will be harbor seals, sea lions and belugas.

This is Alaska at your fingertips, plain and simple.

Cruising the Coast

Start your exploring and peninsula-hopping in the north and work your way south to the town of Homer. Along the way, you'll pass through a series of quaint villages and communities that are well worth stopping for a bite, a bit of shopping and a bit of on-foot exploring. Sterling, Kenai, Nikiski, Kasilof, Ninilchik, Anchor Point, Halibut Cove and Seldovia all dot the peninsula's scenic western coast, and each one sports precisely the kind of authentic small-town charm one would expect.

In Homer, striking views of Kachemak Bay, white-capped mountain peaks and the iconic Homer Spit greet visitors. Trendy coffee shops, gourmet cafes and a wide array of art galleries make this small town of 5,000 a surprisingly vibrant place to visit. The Homer Spit is a 4.5-mile long sliver of beach jutting out into Kachemak Bay that buzzes with activity during the summer.

Opposite the bay from Homer lies Kachemak Bay State Park, home to dozens of campsites, hundreds of hiking trails and a craggy coast of coves that are popular with kayakers.

As you circle back and head north on the Peninsula, branch off to the east and turn south at Moose Pass. Arriving in Seward, you'll find yourself on the peninsula's rocky, mountainous, glacier-dominated eastern coast.

Seward sits on the shores of Resurrection Bay and in the foothills of the Kenai Mountains. Its harbor buzzes with activity—cruise ships, fishing charters, tour boats and sailing expeditions all arrive and depart here. Eclectic shops, cafes and restaurants aptly service a non-stop throng of visitors.

If you're traveling to Kenai from the Lower 48, the Alaska Marine Highway will transport you via ferry from Bellingham, Washington, to Whittier, Alaska, which sits on the doorstep of the peninsula. From here, it's less than two hours south to Seward.

Sea Life on Display

The Alaska SeaLife Center, found at the town's southern edge, is one of the most popular attractions in the entire state of Alaska. Part research center, part animal rehabilitation center and part visitor center, it provides an opportunity to learn about the region's marine life and biodiversity through a series of interactive tours and displays.

The most popular attraction in Seward, however, isn't located in town. Seward serves as the gateway to nearby Kenai Fjords National Park, home to Exit Glacier, the Harding Ice Field and a jaw-dropping concentration of wildlife. Some roads and trails meander into the park from Seward, offering road access to its primary points of interest. But the best way to explore this natural treasure is by guided boat tour. These offer the best views of calving ice sheets slipping into icy turquoise waters, as well as migrating whales and native sea lions.

> The Alaska SeaLife Center, found at Seward's southern edge, is an opportunity to learn about the region's marine life and biodiversity through tours and displays.

The Kenai is also a world-renowned location for fishing. Four species of salmon—including 100-pound King Salmon—stream by the hundreds of thousands into Kenai's bays, rivers and lakes during the summer months. Seward is an especially good location to hop aboard a professionally guided fishing charter, but excellent opportunities for both freshwater and saltwater fishing trips abound across the peninsula.

If you're searching for a way to explore the very best of Alaska, then look no further than the Kenai Peninsula's premium concentration of incredible scenery, national attractions and down-to-earth communities.

For More Information

Kenai Visitor and Convention Bureau
907-283-1991
www.visitkenai.com

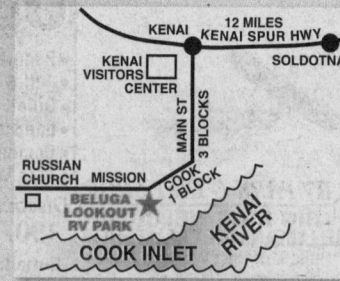

Alaska Travel Industry Association
800-862-5275
www.travelalaska.com

VALDEZ

Make this fun-filled port a basecamp to adventure

Ringed by stunning snow-capped mountain peaks and sitting on the doorstep to spectacular Prince William Sound, the small coastal town of Valdez in sunny southern Alaska is renowned for its state parks, big glaciers and vibrant alpine atmosphere.

From plundering eclectic antique shops and exploring the pioneering history of this one-time Gold Rush outpost, to paddling alongside massive icebergs and hiking across the tops of ancient glaciers, this is a destination for seekers of family-friendly variety and adventure.

Today, most will find themselves arriving in Valdez from Anchorage, a drive that can be made in about six hours via the Richardson Highway. At the turn of the century, scrappy prospectors traveling north to the Alaskan gold fields arrived by way of the town's waterfront, and even more than one hundred years later the small harbor still finds itself as the undisputed heart of Valdez. It's from here that the town center expands backward, with a handful of streets offering local food, shopping and adventure-activity outfitters.

Valdez Adventures

Day cruises to Columbia Glacier, which sits 25 miles east of Valdez, are among the town's most popular activities. Columbia is the second-largest tidewater glacier in the world and sports a front face that's as tall as a football field is long—it's a must-visit and includes a stunning boat journey.

Day cruises to Columbia Glacier, which sits 25 miles east of Valdez, are among the town's most popular activities.

But the area is easily explored on foot as well. The Mineral Creek Trailhead is just a few blocks from the town center and winds its way to abandoned mining ruins deep in the thick boreal forest, and the Shoup Bay Trail follows the coastline of Port Valdez, offering unparalleled views of nearby glaciers.

For those who like to get out on the water for their exploring, kayak rentals can be found in town, and the abundance of protected coves, inlets and fjords make the coast an idyllic place to paddle.

State Park aficionados will be in their element. Shoup Bay State Marine Park, Sawmill Bay State Marine Park, Jack Bay Marine Park, Blueberry Lake State Recreation Site and Worthington Glacier State Recreation Area all make for great day trips.

At Shoup Bay State Marine Park (only five miles southwest of Valdez), visitors will find a surreal landscape left behind in the wake of receding Shoup Glacier. A brackish lagoon, fresh tidal river and an abundance of exotic waterfowl (including eagles, terns and kittiwake) call the bay home.

Going Cruising

To the west, Sawmill Bay State Marine Park is a popular anchoring spot for charters and cruises. Towering 4,000-foot cliffs rim the bay, which teems with harbor seals, sea otters and wild bears. Campers will enjoy setting up shop on the island in the middle of the inlet at Jack Bay State Marine Park, and anglers will want to cast their lures for fresh rainbow trout in Blueberry Lake State Recreation Area. Slightly further afield (29 miles north of Valdez) Worthington Glacier State Recreation Area offers a chance to hike along the outer rim of Worthington Glacier.

For More Information

Valdez Convention and Visitors Bureau
907-835-INFO
www.valdezalaska.org

Alaska Travel Industry Association
800-862-5275
www.travelalaska.com

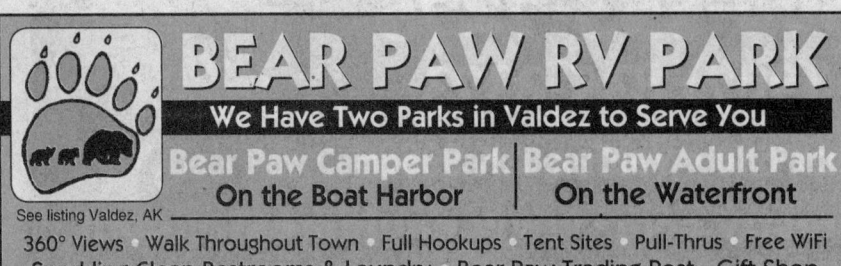

VIEW 18 GLACIERS FROM OUR FRONT PORCH
Good Sam Park
Eagle's Rest
RV Park & Cabins
Park Amenities
• Super Sites • 30/50 Amp
• Pull-Thrus • Cable TV
• 24-Hr Gas Station
• Full Service Convenience Store & Car Wash
• Fish Cleaning Station
• Freezing Facilities (August)
• Lawn Games
• Big Laundromat
• Wash Rigs at Sites
Tour Ticket Office Located in Park:
• Glacier & Wildlife Cruises
• Fishing Charters
• Sight-Seeing & Helicopter Tours
"Stay With Us and Be a Part of Our Family"
250
218
188
Good Sam RATED 8.5/10★/9.5
First RV Park in Town on Right
Reservations:
1-800-553-7275
or (907) 835-2373
P.O. Box 610 • Valdez, AK 99686
FREE Wi-Fi
ALASKA CAMPGROUND OWNERS ASSOCIATION ACOA
E-mail: info@eaglesrestrv.com • www.eaglesrestrv.com
See listing Valdez, AK
Real Value, Real Easy.

Alaska

CONSULTANTS

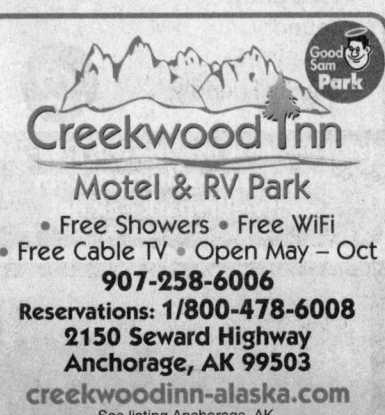

Craig & Debbie Rice

ANCHOR POINT — D3 *Kenai Peninsula*

KYLLONEN RV PARK **Ratings: 6/7.5★/7.5** (RV Park) 2015 rates: $32.50 to $39.50. May 15 to Sep 8. (907)235-7762 74160 Anchor River Beach Rd, Anchor point, AK 99556

ANCHORAGE — D4 *Anchorage*

A SPOTLIGHT Introducing Anchorage's colorful attractions appearing at the front of this state section.

ANCHORAGE See also Girdwood, Palmer, Wasilla & Willow.

ANCHORAGE SHIP CREEK RV PARK
Ratings: 7/9.5★/7.5 (RV Park) From Jct of Glenn Hwy (5th Ave) & Ingra St, N 0.3 mi on Ingra St to 1st Ave, W 500 ft (L). **FAC:** Gravel rds. 130 gravel, 4 pull-thrus (18 x 60), back-ins (15 x 45), 130 full hkups (30 amps), WiFi, tent sites, dump, laundry. **REC:** rec open to public. Pets OK. Partial handicap access. 2015 rates: $19 to $59. May 1 to Sep 30.
(907)277-0877 Lat: 61.22169, Lon: -149.86906
150 N Ingra St, Anchorage, AK 99501
shipcreek@bestofalasktravel.com
www.bestofalaskatravel.com
See ad pages 30 (Spotlight Anchorage), 29.

Tell them you saw them in this Guide!

CENTENNIAL CAMPER PARK (Public) From jct Seward Hwy 1 & Glenn Hwy 1 (Downtown Anchorage): Go 4-1/2 mi E on Glenn Hwy 1, then 1/4 mi S on Muldoon Rd, then 1 block E on Boundry Ave, then 3/4 mi N on Frontage Rd. 2015 rates: $25. May 15 to Sep 30. (907)343-6986

CHUGACH/EAGLE RIVER CAMPGROUND (State Pk) On Glenn Hwy at MP-12.6. 2015 rates: $15. May 15 to Sep 15. (907)694-7982

CREEKWOOD INN MOTEL & RV PARK
Ratings: 7/9.5★/7.5 (RV Park) From Jct of Glenn Hwy & Seward Hwy, S 0.8 mi on Seward Hwy (Gambell St) (R). **FAC:** Gravel rds. 50 gravel, 6 pull-thrus (25 x 45), back-ins (15 x 40), accepts self-contain units only, 50 full hkups (30/50 amps), cable, WiFi, rentals, dump, laundry, groc. **REC.** Pets OK. 2015 rates: $46. May 1 to Oct 31.
(907)258-6006 Lat: 61.20107, Lon: -149.86876
2150 Seward Highway, Anchorage, AK 99503
information@creekwoodinn-alaska.com
http://creekwoodinn-alaska.com/
See ad this page, 29.

GOLDEN NUGGET RV PARK **Ratings: 8/9.5★/9.5** (RV Park) 2015 rates: $42 to $48. (907)333-2012 4100 Debarr Rd, Anchorage, AK 99508

MONTANA CREEK CAMPGROUND (Public) From Jct Talkeetna Spur Rd & Parks Hwy, S 3 mi on Parks Hwy to MP 96.5 (L). 2015 rates: $20 to $45. May 15 to Sep 15. (877)475-2267

Things to See and Do

ALASKA CAMPGROUND OWNERS ASSOCIATION ACOA represents RV Parks and Campgrounds throughout Alaska that provide outdoor hospitality services to campers visiting the State. No CC.
(866)339-9082
PO Box 111005/Acoa, Anchorage, AK 99511-1005
info@alaskacampgrounds.net
www.alaskacampgrounds.net
See ad page 28 (Welcome Section).

ANDERSON — C4 *Denali*

RIVERSIDE PARK (CITY PARK) (Public) From jct Parks Hwy 3 & Anderson Rd: Go 6 mi W on Clear/Anderson Rd. 2015 rates: $12 to $15. (907)582-2500

TATLANIKA TRADING COMPANY & RV PARK **Ratings: 6/7/8.5** (Campground) 2015 rates: $25. May 25 to Sep 15. (907)582-2341 mile 276 Parks Hwy, Nenana, AK 99760

We appreciate your business!

CANTWELL — C4 *Denali*

CANTWELL RV PARK
Ratings: 6.5/10★/9 (RV Park) From Jct of Parks Hwy (Mile 210) & Denali Hwy, W 0.3 mi on Denali Hwy (R). **FAC:** All weather rds. 70 gravel, 58 pull-thrus (22 x 60), back-ins (18 x 30), 41 W, 70 E (30 amps), WiFi, tent sites, rentals, dump, laundry, groc, fire rings, firewood. **REC.** Pets OK. Partial handicap access. 2015 rates: $27.50 to $30.50. Disc: AAA, military. May 20 to Sep 10.
(800)940-2210 Lat: 63.39190, Lon: -148.91074
.3 Mi Cantwell Station Rd, Cantwell, AK 99729
cantwellrvpark@ak.net
www.cantwellrvpark.com
See ad pages 38, 29.

CHENA HOT SPRINGS — B4 *Fairbanks North Star Borough*

CHENA RIVER SRA/TORS TRAIL (State Pk) On Chena Hot Springs Rd at MP-39. 2015 rates: $10. May 21 to Sep 15. (907)451-2695

CHICKEN — C4 *Southeast Fairbanks*

CHICKEN CREEK RV PARK **Ratings: 4.5/9.5★/7** (Campground) 2015 rates: $18 to $40. May 15 to Sep 15. (907)883-5081 mp 66.8 Taylor Highway, Chicken, AK 99732

CHICKEN GOLD CAMP & OUTPOST **Ratings: 5.5/NA/7.5** (Campground) Pit toilets. 2015 rates: $16 to $36. May 15 to Sep 20. (520)413-1480 1/4 Mile Airport Road, Chicken, AK 99732

WEST FORK CAMPGROUND (BLM) (State Pk) From town: Go 19 mi S on the Taylor Hwy 5. Pit toilets. 2015 rates: $10. (907)883-5121

COFFMAN COVE — E6 *Prince of Wales-Outer Ketchikan Census Area*

OCEANVIEW RV PARK **Ratings: 2.5/5.5/6.5** (Campground) 2015 rates: $30. May 1 to Sep 30. (907)329-2032 116 Zarembo Drive, Coffman Cove, AK 99918

COLDFOOT — B3 *Yukon Koyukuk*

MARION CREEK (BLM) (Public) From town: Go 5 mi N on Dalton Hwy. Pit toilets. 2015 rates: $8. (907)474-2200

COOPER LANDING — D4 *Kenai Peninsula*

KENAI PRINCESS RV PARK **Ratings: 8.5/8.5/8.5** (RV Park) 2015 rates: $40. May 20 to Sep 15. (907)595-1425 17238 Frontier Circle, Cooper Landing, AK 99572

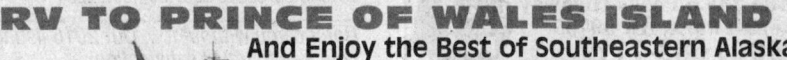

COOPER LANDING (CONT)

KENAI RIVERSIDE CAMPGROUND & RV PARK/B & B **Ratings: 5/8/7.5** (Campground) 2015 rates: $27 to $35. May 21 to Sep 1. (888)536-2478 16918 Sterling Hwy, Cooper Landing, AK 99572

COPPER CENTER — C4 *Valdez Cordova*

KLUTINA SALMON CHARTERS & CAMPGROUND **Ratings: 5/NA/6.5** (Campground) Pit toilets. 2015 rates: $29. Jun 1 to Aug 20. (907)822-3991 mile Post 101 Old Richardson Hwy, Copper Center, AK 99573

SQUIRREL CREEK REC SITE (State Pk) On Richardson Hwy, at milepost 79.5. Pit toilets. 2015 rates: $15. Jun 15 to Sep 15. (907)822-5608

CRAIG — E6 *Prince of Wales-Outer Ketchikan Census Area*

RAIN COUNTRY RV PARK **Ratings: 3.5/5.5/6** (RV Park) 2015 rates: $34. May 1 to Sep 30. (907)826-3632 js Drive, Craig, AK 99921

DELTA JUNCTION — C4 *Southeast Fairbanks*

BIG DELTA STATE HISTORICAL PARK (State Pk) From town: Go 14 mi N on Richardson Hwy 26 to Milepost 274.5, then NE on Rika's Rd. 2015 rates: $5. Jun 15 to Sep 15. (907)451-2695

CLEARWATER REC SITE (State Pk) On AK Hwy at MP-1415. 2015 rates: $10. Jun to Sep. (907)451-2695

DELTA REC SITE (State Pk) On Richardson Hwy at MP-267. 2015 rates: $10. Jun to Sep. (907)451-2695

DONNELLY CREEK REC SITE (State Pk) On Richardson Hwy at MP-238. 2015 rates: $10. 907-269-8400

FIELDING LAKE SRS (State Pk) From Jct of SR-2 & Richardson Hwy, SW 200.5 mi on Richardson Hwy/SR-4, follow signs. Jun 15 to Sep 15. (907)451-2695

We rate what RVers consider important.

HARDING LAKE SRA (State Pk) On Richardson Hwy at MP-321.4. 2015 rates: $10. Jun 15 to Sep 15. (907)451-2695

QUARTZ LAKE CAMPGROUND (State Pk) On Richardson Hwy at MP-277.8 to Quartz Lake Rd, N 2.5 mi (E). 2015 rates: $10. Jun 15 to Sep 15. (907)451-2695

DENALI NATIONAL PARK — C4 *Denali*

DENALI GRIZZLY BEAR RESORT **Ratings: 6.5/8/8.5** (Campground) 2015 rates: $25 to $40. May 20 to Sep 12. (866)583-2696 231.1 Parks Hwy, Denali National Park, AK 99755

DENALI NP (SAVAGE RIVER CAMPGROUND) (Natl Pk) From Hwy 3: Go 12 mi W on Park Rd from entrance: Register first at Visitor Center (1/2 mi on Park Rd). 2015 rates: $22 to $28. (907)683-2294

DENALI NP (TEKLANIKA RIVER CAMPGROUND) (Natl Pk) From Hwy 3: Go 29 mi W on Park Rd from entrance. Register first at Visitor Center (1/2 mi on Park Rd). 2015 rates: $16. (907)683-2294

DENALI RAINBOW VILLAGE RV PARK & MOTEL

Ratings: 6/9★/6 (RV Park) N-bnd on Parks Hwy at MP 238.6 (R). **FAC:** Gravel rds. 61 gravel, 32 pull-thrus (20 x 55), back-ins (20 x 40), mostly side by side hkups, 21 full hkups, 40 W, 40 E (30/50 amps), WiFi, tent sites, rentals, showers $, dump, laundry, groc, fire rings, firewood, restaurant. **REC.** Pets OK. Partial handicap access. 2015 rates: $40 to $44. Disc: military. May 15 to Sep 20.
(907)683-7777 Lat: 63.74765, Lon: -148.89937
mile 238.6 Parks Hwy, Denali National Park, AK 99755
denalirainbow@mtaonline.net
www.denalirv.com
See ad this page, 29.

DENALI RV PARK & MOTEL

Ratings: 7/10★/9.5 (RV Park) On Parks Hwy at MP-245.1 Northbound: (L). **FAC:** Gravel rds. 90 gravel, 10 pull-thrus (21 x 60), back-ins (19 x 40), 69 full hkups, 21 W, 21 E (30 amps), WiFi, rentals, showers $, dump, laundry. **REC.** Pets OK. No tents. 2015 rates: $44 to $52. Disc: AAA, military. May 20 to Sep 10.
(800)478-1501 Lat: 63.82120, Lon: -148.98711
mile 245.1 Parks Hwy, Denali National Park, AK 99755
stay@denalirvparkandmotel.com
www.denalirvparkandmotel.com
See ad this page, 29.

DENALI/RILEY CREEK (Natl Pk) From Healy, 5.12 mi on AK Hwy 3 (R). Entrance fee required ($5). 2015 rates: $22 to $28. (907)683-2294

Don't camp without it ... Our 2016 listings are your key to travel satisfaction.

FAIRBANKS — B4 *Burrough, Fairbanks, North Star*

FAIRBANKS AREA MAP

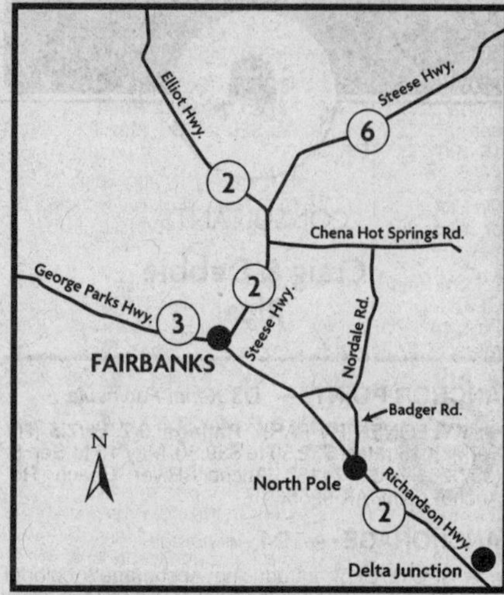

For more detail and a broader overview, please see our full-color state map at the front of the Alaska state section.

Symbols on map indicate towns within a 60 mile radius of Fairbanks where campgrounds are listed. Check listings for more information.

See also Delta Junction & North Pole.

FAIRBANKS (CONT)

A SPOTLIGHT Introducing Fairbanks' colorful attractions appearing at the front of this state section.

CHENA RIVER SRA/ROSEHIP CAMPGROUND (State Pk) On Chena Hot Springs Rd at MP-27. 2015 rates: $10. (907)451-2695

CHENA RIVER WAYSIDE (State Pk) From Jct of Richardson Hwy (Hwy 2) & Lawrence Rd, E 2.6 mi to entrance (L). 2015 rates: $20 to $30. May 15 to Sep 15. (907)455-8881

LOWER CHATANIKA/OLNES POND (State Pk) On Elliott Hwy at MP-10.5. Note: Park not maintained or managed. Pit toilets. 2015 rates: $10. Jun 15 to Sep 15. (907)451-2695

LOWER CHATANIKA/WHITEFISH CAMPGROUND (State Pk) On Elliott Hwy at MP-11. Note: Park not maintained or managed. Pit toilets. 2015 rates: $15. Jun 15 to Sep 15. (907)451-2695

RIVER'S EDGE RV PARK & CAMPGROUND
Ratings: 8.5/10★/9.5 (RV Park) E-bnd: From Jct of AK Hwy 3 & Fairbanks exit (East Airport Way), E 0.5 mi on Airport Way to Sportsman Way, N 50 ft to Boat St, W 0.3 mi (R); or W-bnd: From Jct of AK Hwy 3 & University Ave, N 0.8 mi on University Ave to Airport Way, W 0.25 mi to Sportsman Way, N 50 ft to Boat St, W 0.3 mi (R). **FAC:** All weather rds. 167 gravel, 82 pull-thrus (25 x 60), back-ins (25 x 35), 115 full hkups, 52 W, 52 E (30/50 amps), WiFi, tent sites, rentals, dump, laundry, restaurant. **REC:** Chena River: fishing. Pets OK. Partial handicap access. Big rig sites, 2015 rates: $40 to $51. Disc: military. May 25 to Sep 12.
(907)474-0286 Lat: 64.83944, Lon: -147.83411
4140 Boat Street, Fairbanks, AK 99709
rvpark@riversedge.net
www.riversedge.net
See ad pages 32 (Spotlight Fairbanks), 29.

RIVERVIEW RV PARK
Ratings: 8/10★/9.5 (RV Park) N-bnd: From Jct of Richardson Hwy 2 & Badger Rd (North Pole exit), NE 8.5 mi on Badger Rd (R); or S-bnd: From Jct of Richardson Hwy 2 & Badger Rd (SE of Fairbanks), E 2.7 mi on Badger Rd (L). **FAC:** Gravel rds. 160 gravel, 115 pull-thrus (25 x 60), back-ins (25 x 60), 158 full hkups, 2 W, 2 E (30/50 amps), cable, WiFi, tent sites, dump, laundry. **REC:** Chena River: fishing. Pet restrict(B/Q). Partial handicap access. Big rig sites, 2015 rates: $36 to $48. Disc: military. May 15 to Sep 15.
(888)488-6392 Lat: 64.83259, Lon: -147.51562
1316 Badger Rd, North Pole, AK 99705
riverview@gci.net
www.riverviewrvpark.net
See ad pages 31 (Spotlight Fairbanks), 29.

TANANA VALLEY CAMPGROUND **Ratings: 5.5/6.5/7** (Campground) From Jct of A2 Steese Hwy & College Rd (E of town), N 2.2 mi on College Rd (R); or From Jct of A3 Mitchell Expressway & Giest Rd (W of town), E 1.5 mi on Geist Rd to University Ave, N 0.5 mi to College Rd, E 1.7 mi (L). **FAC:** Gravel rds. 30 gravel, 3 pull-thrus (30 x 42), back-ins (35 x 42), 20 E (30 amps), WiFi, tent sites, dump, laundry, firewood. **REC.** Pets OK. Partial handicap access. 2015 rates: $20 to $26. May 15 to Sep 15.
AAA Approved
(907)456-7956 Lat: 64.51846, Lon: -147.45533
1800 College Road, Fairbanks, AK 99709
info@fairbankscampgroundandrvpark.com
www.fairbankscampgroundandrvpark.com

UPPER CHATANIKA RIVER REC SITE (State Pk) On Steese Hwy at MP-39. Pit toilets. 2015 rates: $13. Jun 15 to Sep 15. (907)456-1104

Things to See and Do

EXPLORE FAIRBANKS Morris Thompson Cultural & Visitors Center in downtown Fairbanks has information on Fairbanks, Denali, Interior & Arctic Alaska and cultural/historical exhibits. Visitor info, trip planning, RV parking, book-gift shop, handicap access. Partial handicap access. RV accessible. Restrooms. Hours: Summer 8am to 9pm Winter 8am to 5pm. ATM, no CC.
(800)327-5774 Lat: 64.84515, Lon: -147.71314
101 Dunkel Street, Fairbanks, AK 99701
info@explorefairbanks.com
www.explorefairbanks.com
See ad page 27 (Welcome Section).

GAKONA — C4 *Valdez Cordova*

GAKONA ALASKA RV PARK **Ratings: 7/4.5/7.5** (Campground) 2015 rates: $28 to $33. (907)822-3550 milepost 4.25 Tok Cutoff, Gakona, AK 99586

GRIZZLY LAKE CAMPGROUND **Ratings: 3.5/5/7** (Campground) 2015 rates: $15 to $20. May 15 to Sep 15. (907)822-5214 mile 53 Tok Cuffoff, Gakona, AK 99586

GLACIER VIEW — C4 *Matanuska Susitna*

GRAND VIEW CAFE & RV CAMPGROUND **Ratings: 7.5/9.5★/8** (RV Park) 2015 rates: $19 to $35.50. May 25 to Sep 15. (907)746-4480 mp 109.7 Glenn Hwy, Glacier View, AK 99674

GLENNALLEN — C4 *Valdez Cordova*

DRY CREEK REC SITE (State Pk) On Richardson Hwy, at milepost 117.5. 2015 rates: $15. Jun 15 to Sep 15. (907)822-5608

LAKE LOUISE REC AREA (State Pk) From town, W 20 mi on Glenn Hwy, N 15 mi on Lake Louise Rd., MP 160. 2015 rates: $15. Jun 15 to Sep 15. (907)441-7575

NORTHERN NIGHTS CAMPGROUND & RV PARK
Ratings: 5.5/9.5★/9 (Campground) From Jct of Glenn Hwy & Richardson Hwy, W 600 yds on Glenn Hwy (R). **FAC:** Gravel rds. 24 gravel, 16 pull-thrus (30 x 70), back-ins (25 x 55), 5 full hkups, 19 W, 19 E (30 amps), WiFi, tent sites, rentals, showers $, dump, fire rings, firewood. **REC.** Pets OK. 2015 rates: $42. Disc: military. May 15 to Sep 15. No CC.
(907)822-3199 Lat: 62.06465, Lon: -145.29202
mile Post 188.7 Glenn Hwy, Glennallen, AK 99588
nncrvpark1989@gmail.com
www.northernnightscampground.com
See ad this page, 29.

SLIDE MOUNTAIN CABINS & RV PARK **Ratings: 6/9★/8.5** (Campground) 2015 rates: $15 to $25. (907)822-3883 mile 135 Glenn Highway, Glennallen, AK 99588

SOURDOUGH CREEK CAMPGROUND (BLM) (State Pk) From town: Go 32 mi N on Richardson Hwy 4 to mile 147.6. Pit toilets. 2015 rates: $12. (907)822-3217

TOLSONA WILDERNESS RV PARK & CAMPGROUND
Ratings: 7.5/8.5★/9.5 (Campground) From town, W 15 mi on Glenn Hwy (SR-1) to MP-173, N 3/4 mi on private road (E). **FAC:** Gravel rds. 80 gravel, 14 pull-thrus (18 x 60), back-ins (24 x 50), 46 W, 46 E (30/50 amps), WiFi, tent sites, showers $, dump, laundry, groc, fire rings, firewood. **REC:** Tolsona Creek: fishing. Pets OK. Partial handicap access. 2015 rates: $35 to $45. Disc: AAA, military. May 20 to Sep 10. No CC.
AAA Approved
(907)822-3865 Lat: 62.06187, Lon: -145.58006
mile 173 Glenn Hwy, Glennallen, AK 99588
camp@tolsona.com
www.tolsona.com
See ad this page.

HAINES — D5 *Haines*

CHILKAT (State Pk) From town, S 7 mi on Mud Bay Rd (E). Pit toilets. 2015 rates: $10. May 15 to Sep 15. (907)766-2292

CHILKOOT LAKE REC SITE (State Pk) On Lutak Rd at MP-10 (E) Note: 35' RV Size Limit. Pit toilets. 2015 rates: $10. May 15 to Oct 15. (907)465-4563

HAINES HITCH-UP RV PARK INC
Ratings: 7/10★/10 (RV Park) From Jct of 2nd Ave & Main St, W 0.5 mi on Main St (L); or From Jct of Haines Hwy & Main St (road forks), E 0.2 mi on Main St (R). **FAC:** All weather rds. 92 grass, 20 pull-thrus (25 x 60), back-ins (25 x 45), 92 full hkups (30/50 amps), cable, WiFi, laundry. Pet restrict(B). No tents. 2015 rates: $38 to $50. May 15 to Sep 15.
(907)766-2882 Lat: 59.23562, Lon: -135.45985
851 Main St, Haines, AK 99827
info@hitchuprv.com
www.hitchuprv.com
See ad this page, 29.

Find it fast! To locate a town on a map, follow these easy instructions: Look for the map grid code after the town heading in the listing section and match it to the letters and numbers on the map borders. Draw a line horizontally from the letter and vertically from the number. You'll find the town near the intersection of the two lines.

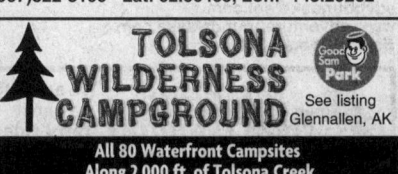

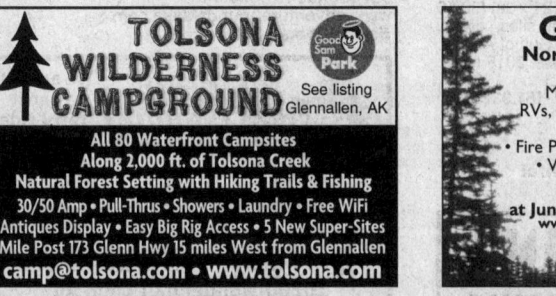

HAINES (CONT)

OCEANSIDE RV PARK
Ratings: 7/9.5★/8 (RV Park) In town, at Jct of Main St & Front St, N 100 ft on Front St (R). **FAC:** Gravel rds. 23 gravel, back-ins (14 x 50), 23 full hkups (30 amps), cable, WiFi $, tent sites, showers $, laundry, fire rings, firewood. **REC:** Lynn Canal. Pets OK. Partial handicap access. 2015 rates: $25 to $38. Disc: AAA, military.
(907)766-2437 Lat: 59.14150, Lon: -135.26494
14 Front St, Haines, AK 99827
greatview@oceansiderv.com
www.oceansiderv.com
See ad pages 39, 29.

HOMER — D3 *Kenai Peninsula*

BAYCREST RV PARK
Ratings: 7.5/10★/9.5 (RV Park) On Sterling Hwy at MP 169. **FAC:** Paved rds. 47 gravel, back-ins (25 x 55), 47 full hkups (30 amps), WiFi, tent sites, showers $, laundry, groc, LP gas, fire rings, firewood, restaurant. **REC:** Kachemak Bay. Pets OK. 2015 rates: $45. May 15 to Oct 1. ATM.
(907)435-7995 Lat: 59.39483, Lon: -151.38356
3425 Sterling Hwy, Homer, AK 99603
baycrestrvpark@gmail.com
www.baycrestrvpark.com
See ad this page, 29.

DEEP CREEK SRA (State Pk) From town, S 0.5 mi on Sterling Hwy (R). 2015 rates: $10. May 1 to Sep 30. (907)262-5581

DRIFTWOOD INN & RV PARK **Ratings: 6.5/9/7.5** (RV Park) 2015 rates: $34 to $75. (907)235-8019 135 W Bunnell Ave, Homer, AK 99603

HERITAGE RV PARK
Ratings: 8/10★/9 (RV Park) From Jct of Seward Hwy & Lake St (Town Center), S 4 mi on Seward Hwy (Homer Spit Rd) (L). **FAC:** Gravel rds. 107 gravel, 24 pull-thrus (30 x 45), back-ins (35 x 45), 107 full hkups (50 amps), WiFi, tent sites, laundry, fire rings, firewood. **REC:** Kachemak Bay on Gulf of Alaska and Homer Spit Fishing Hole: fishing. Pets OK. Partial handicap access. Big rig sites, 2015 rates: $68. May 15 to Sep 15.
(907)226-4500 Lat: 59.36677, Lon: -151.26628
3550 Homer Spit Rd, Homer, AK 99603
heritagervpark@alaska.net
www.alaskaheritagervpark.com
See ad this page.

HOMER SPIT CAMPGROUND **Ratings: 5.5/6.5/6** (Campground) 2015 rates: $30 to $50. May 15 to Sep 15. (907)235-8206 4535 Homer Spit Rd, Homer, AK 99603

NINILCHIK STATE REC AREA (State Pk) From town, S 60 mi on Sterling Hwy, follow signs. Pit toilets. 2015 rates: $10. May 1 to Oct 30. (907)262-5581

OCEANVIEW RV PARK
Ratings: 7.5/10★/9.5 (RV Park) S-bnd: In town at 455 Sterling Hwy (R). **FAC:** Paved rds. 100 gravel, 25 pull-thrus (21 x 40), back-ins (21 x 38) (30/50 amps), cable, WiFi, tent sites, dump, laundry. **REC:** Kachemak Bay of the Gulf of Alaska. Pet restrict(Q). Partial handicap access. 2015 rates: $25 to $59. Disc: military. May 1 to Oct 1.
(907)235-3951 Lat: 59.38502, Lon: -151.33211
455 Sterling Hwy, Homer, AK 99603
camp4fun@gci.net
www.oceanview-rv.com
See ad pages 33 (Spotlight Kenai Peninsula), 29.

SPORTMAN'S SUPPLY & RV PARK
Ratings: 5.5/9★/5.5 (Campground) From Jct of Homer Spit Rd & Freight Dock Rd, E 150 yds on Freight Dock Rd (L). **FAC:** Paved rds. 10 gravel, back-ins (20 x 65), 10 full hkups (30 amps), WiFi, showers $, laundry, groc, LP bottles, firewood. **REC:** Kachemak Bay: fishing. Pets OK. No tents. 2015 rates: $40. Apr 1 to Oct 1.
(907)235-2617 Lat: 59.36409, Lon: -151.26000
1114 Freight Dock, Homer, AK 99603
mlpierce@ptialaska.net
See ad this page.

STARISKI REC SITE (State Pk) On Sterling Hwy at milepost 151. 2015 rates: $10. May 15 to Oct 15. (907)522-8368

HOUSTON — C4 *Matanuska Susitna*

LITTLE SUSITNA RIVER CAMPGROUND (CITY PARK) (Public) On George Parks Hwy 3 at MP 57.5. Pit toilets. 2015 rates: $15. May 25 to Sep 7. (907)892-6869

RIVERSIDE CAMPER PARK **Ratings: 6.5/9.5★/7.5** (RV Park) 2015 rates: $30. May 15 to Sep 30. (907)892-9020 mile 57.7 Parks Hwy, Houston, AK 99694

HYDER — E6 *North Coast Inland, Prince of Wales*

CAMP RUN-A-MUCK **Ratings: 4/5/6.5** (Campground) 2015 rates: $20 to $38. May 15 to Oct 1. (250)636-9006 990 Hyder Ave, Hyder, AK 99923

JUNEAU — D5 *Juneau*

SPRUCE MEADOW RV PARK
Ratings: 8/10★/10 (Campground) From Juneau Ferry Terminal, E (right) 1.6 mi on Glacier Hwy to roundabout at roundabout, north onto Mendenhall Loop Rd, go 2.1 mi on Mendenhall Loop Rd (L). **FAC:** All weather rds. 30 Avail: 30 all weather, back-ins (30 x 45), 30 full hkups (30 amps), WiFi, tent sites, laundry, fire rings, firewood. **REC.** Pet restrict(Q). Partial handicap access. 2015 rates: $36 to $38. Apr 15 to Oct 1.
(907)789-1990 Lat: 58.24210, Lon: -134.36287
10200 Mendenhall Loop Rd, Juneau, AK 99801
spruce@juneaurv.com
www.juneaurv.com
See ad this page.

Things to See and Do

ADVENTURE BOUND ALASKA Cruise by waterfalls & through ice floes en route to Sawyer glaciers. Whales, bears, mountain goats & eagles are common sights.

Adventure Bound Alaska cruises provide incredible up-close views of the best a fjord can offer-touch rock walls, get splashed by a cascading waterfall, weave through icebergs. Family owned & operated & Coast Guard inspected.

Restrooms, food. Hours: 7 am to 6 pm. Adult fee: $160.
(907)463-2509 Lat: 58.17964, Lon: -134.24574
76 Egan Dr, Juneau, AK 99802
advboundak@aol.com
www.adventureboundalaska.com
See ad page 37.

KENAI — D3 *Kenai Peninsula*

A SPOTLIGHT Introducing the Kenai Peninsula's colorful attractions appearing at the front of this state section.

BELUGA LOOKOUT LODGE & RV PARK
Ratings: 8/10★/8.5 (RV Park) From Jct of Kenai Spur Hwy & Main St (not Main St Loop), S 0.2 mi on Main St to Cook Ave, W 0.1 mi (E). **FAC:** Gravel rds. 65 gravel, 40 pull-thrus (20 x 40), back-ins (18 x 30), 65 full hkups (30/50 amps), cable, WiFi, tent sites, rentals, laundry, fire rings, firewood. **REC:** Kenai River/Cook Inlet: fishing. Pets OK. 2015 rates: $45 to $75. Disc: AAA, military. May 15 to Sep 20.
AAA Approved
(907)283-5999 Lat: 60.33069, Lon: -151.15876
929 Mission Ave, Kenai, AK 99611
belugarv@belugalookout.com
www.belugalookout.com
See ad pages 34 (Spotlight Kenai Peninsula), 29.

CAPTAIN COOK/DISCOVERY CAMPGROUND (State Pk) On Kenai Spur at MP-39 (E). 2015 rates: $10. May 15 to Oct 15. (907)262-5581

DIAMOND M RANCH RESORT
Ratings: 8.5/10★/10 (RV Park) From Jct of Sterling Hwy (in Soldotna) & Kalifornsky Beach Rd, W 5.5 mi on Kalifornsky Beach Rd (R). **FAC:** All weather rds. 77 gravel, 32 pull-thrus (36 x 70), back-ins (36 x 60), 77 full hkups (30/50 amps), WiFi, tent sites, rentals, dump, laundry, fire rings, firewood. **REC:** playground. Pets OK. Partial handicap access. Big rig sites, 2015 rates: $39 to $76. Disc: military.
(907)283-9424 Lat: 60.51505, Lon: -151.19067
48500 Diamond M Ranch, Kenai, AK 99611
stay@diamondmranch.com
www.diamondmranchresort.com
See ad pages 33 (Spotlight Kenai Peninsula), 28 (Welcome Section), 29.

KENNY LAKE — C4 *Valdez Cordova*

KENNY LAKE RV PARK & CAMPGROUND **Ratings: 6/7.5/7.5** (Campground) 2015 rates: $15 to $30. May 1 to Sep 30. (907)822-3313 mile 7.2 Edgerton Hwy, Kenny Lake, AK 99573

KETCHIKAN — E6 *Ketchikan Gateway*

CLOVER PASS RESORT **Ratings: 6/5.5/5.5** (Campground) 2015 rates: $34 to $39. May 1 to Sep 30. (907)247-2234 708 N. Point Higgins Rd, Ketchikan, AK 99901

SETTLERS COVE REC SITE (State Pk) Ferry to Ketchikan, on Tongass Rd at MP-18N (E) Note: 35' RV size limit. 2015 rates: $10. May 15 to Sep 15. (907)465-4563

Things to See and Do

ALASKA'S INTER-ISLAND FERRY AUTHORITY Explore Prince of Wales Island by car or RV with daily ferry service between Ketchikan & Hollis. POW has 1,200 miles of roads linking Hollis, Klawock, hydaburg, Craig, Coffman Cove & Thorne Bay. Fishing, camping, wildlife. Partial handicap access. RV accessible. Restrooms, food. Hours: 8am to 4pm - 7 days weekly.
(866)308-4848 Lat: 55.35461, Lon: -131.69346
3501 Tongass Ave, Ketchikan, AK 99921
reservations@interislandferry.com
www.interislandferry.com
See ad page 37.

KLAWOCK — E6 *Prince of Wales-Outer Ketchikan Census Area*

LOG CABIN RESORT & RV PARK **Ratings: 5/8.5★/7.5** (Campground) 2015 rates: $29. May 1 to Sep 30. (800)544-2205 6655 Big Salt Lake Road, Klawock, AK 99925

KODIAK — D3 *Kokiak Island*

BUSKIN RIVER REC SITE (State Pk) South of town, on W Rezanof at mile 4.5. 2015 rates: $10. May 15 to Sep 15. (907)486-6339

AK

NENANA — C4 *Denali*

NENANA RV PARK & CAMPGROUND **Ratings: 5/9.5★/7** (Campground) 2015 rates: $15 to $29.50. May 15 to Sep 30. (907)832-5230 210 E. 4th St, Nenana, AK 99760

NINILCHIK — D3 *Kenai Peninsula*

ALASKAN ANGLER RV RESORT & CABINS
Ratings: 9/10★/9 (RV Park) S-bnd: From Jct of Sterling Hwy & Kingsley Rd (MP-135.4), E 100 yds on Kingsley Rd (L). **FAC:** All weather rds. 58 Avail: 58 all weather, back-ins (24 x 60), 48 full hkups, 10 W, 10 E (50 amps), WiFi, tent sites, rentals, showers $, dump, laundry, LP gas, firewood. **REC:** Kenai River: fishing, rec open to public. Pets OK. Big rig sites, 2015 rates: $38 to $49. Disc: military. May 1 to Sep 15.
(800)347-4114 Lat: 60.04494, Lon: -151.66662
15640 Kingsley Rd, Ninilchik, AK 99369
aarvresort@yahoo.com
www.alaskabestrvpark.com
See ad this page, 34 (Spotlight Kenai Peninsula), 29, 27 (Welcome Section).

ALL SEASONS CAMPGROUND
Ratings: 7/8/7.5 (Campground) From Jct of Sterling Hwy & Oil Well Rd, E 3.2 mi on Oil Well Rd (L). **FAC:** Gravel rds. 52 gravel, 11 pull-thrus (18 x 40), back-ins (16 x 40), 52 full hkups (30 amps), WiFi, tent sites, rentals, laundry, firewood. **REC.** Pets OK. Partial handicap access. 2015 rates: $36 to $42. Disc: military. May 1 to Sep 1. No CC.
(907)567-3396 Lat: 60.01431, Lon: -151.35587
63960 Oil Well Rd, Ninilchik, AK 99639
asc@allseasonsalaska.com
www.allseasonsalaska.com
See ad this page, 29.

REEL 'EM INN & COOK INLET CHARTERS **Ratings: 6/9.5★/8** (Campground) 2015 rates: $36. May 15 to Sep 1. (907)567-7335 65910 Oil Well Dr, Ninilchik, AK 99639

Things to See and Do

AFISHUNT CHARTER Chartering fishing expeditions for Halibut and Salmon spanning the entire Kenai Peninsula. May 1 to Sep 15. RV accessible. Hours: 6am-6pm.
(877)234-7486 Lat: 60.04494, Lon: -151.66662
15640 Kingsley Road, Ninilchik, AK 99639
aarvresort@yahoo.com
www.afishunt.com
See ad this page, 34 (Spotlight Kenai Peninsula), 27 (Welcome Section).

NORTH POLE — C4 *Fairbanks North Star*

"C" LAZY MOOSE **Ratings: 5/9★/8** (Campground) 2015 rates: $38 to $42. May 1 to Sep 30. (907)488-8141 milepost 315, Salcha, AK 99714

CHENA LAKE RECREATION AREA (Public) From Jct of Richardson Hwy (Hwy 2) & Laurance Rd, E 2.6 mi to entrance (L). 2015 rates: $20. (907)488-1655

How much will it all cost? Use this as a guide: Rates shown are the minimum and maximum for two adults in one RV at the time of inspection (excluding any additional fees for items not at the site). Remember, these rates serve as guidelines only. It's always best to call ahead for the most current rate information.

Things to See and Do

SANTA CLAUS HOUSE Christmas ornaments, Alaskan gifts, apparel, toys & collectibles, espresso & homemade fudge. Mail cards & letters for North Pole postmark. Santa & Mrs. Claus available for photos. Extended summer hours. Partial handicap access. RV accessible. Restrooms, food. Hours: 8am to 8pm summer.
(800)588-4078 Lat: 64.75513, Lon: -147.34359
101 St Nicholas Dr, North Pole, AK 99705
info@santaclaushouse.com
www.santaclaushouse.com
See ad this page, 38.

PALMER — C4 *Matanuska Susitna*

CHUGACH/EKLUTNA CAMPGROUND (State Pk) From town, 13 mi NE. 2015 rates: $10. May 15 to Sep 15. (907)345-5014

FINGER LAKE (State Pk) From town, W 4 mi on Palmer-Wasilla Hwy to Trunk Rd, N 1 mi to Bogart Rd, W 1 mi (L). Pit toilets. 2015 rates: $15. May 15 to Sep 15. (907)745-4800

FOX RUN CAMPGROUND & RV PARK Ratings: 5.5/6/7 (Campground) From Jct of Parks Hwy & Glenn Hwy, NE 0.5 mi on Glenn Hwy to MP-36.3 (L). **FAC:** Gravel rds. 40 gravel, 12 pull-thrus (20 x 60), back-ins (24 x 50), some side by side hkups, 22 full hkups, 7 W, 18 E (30/50 amps), WiFi $, tent sites, dump, laundry, groc, firewood. **REC:** Matanuska Lake: fishing, rec open to public. Pets OK. Partial handicap access. 2015 rates: $31.99 to $35.99. Disc: AAA, military.
AAA Approved
(907)745-6120 Lat: 61.33112, Lon: -149.13836
4466 S. Glenn Hwy, Palmer, AK 99645
foxrunrv@mtaonline.net
www.foxrunlodgealaska.com

KING MOUNTAIN STATE REC SITE (State Pk) From town, E 29 mi on Glenn Hwy (R). 2015 rates: $15. May 15 to Sep 15. (907)746-4644

MOUNTAIN VIEW RV PARK
Ratings: 7.5/10★/9.5 (RV Park) From Jct of Glenn Hwy 1 & Old Glenn Hwy, S 2.8 mi on Old Glenn Hwy (Arctic Ave) to Smith Rd, E 0.5 mi to Smith Rd & Smith Rd extension, S 0.3 mi on Smith Rd (L). **FAC:** Gravel rds. (106 spaces). Avail: 80 grass, 75 pull-thrus (22 x 60), back-ins (18 x 50), 80 full hkups (30 amps), seasonal sites, WiFi, tent sites, dump, laundry, LP gas, firewood. **REC.** Pets OK. Partial handicap access. 2015 rates: $34. Disc: military.
(907)745-5747 Lat: 61.35694, Lon: -149.01579
1405 N Smith Rd, Palmer, AK 99645
starr1@mtaonline.net
www.mtviewrvpark.com
See ad pages 28 (Welcome Section), 29.

TOWN & COUNTRY RV PARK **Ratings: 6/7.5/7.5** (RV Park) 2015 rates: $25 to $30. (907)746-6642 1150 Town & Country Lane, Palmer, AK 99645

PAXSON — C4 *Valdez Cordova*

PAXSON LAKE (BLM) (Public) On Richardson Hwy 4 at milepost 175. 2015 rates: $12. (907)822-3217

TANGLE LAKES (BLM) (State Pk) From town: Go 21.7 mi W on Denali Hwy 8. Pit toilets. 2015 rates: $12. (907)822-3217

SEWARD — D4 *Kenai Peninsula*

MILLER'S LANDING **Ratings: 6/5.5/7.5** (Campground) 2015 rates: $26 to $36. Apr 15 to Sep 15. (866)541-5739 13890 Beach Drive, Seward, AK 99664

STONEY CREEK RV PARK **Ratings: 7.5/8.5/7.5** (RV Park) 2015 rates: $36 to $41. May 15 to Sep 15. (877)437-6366 13760 Leslie Place, Seward, AK 99664

WATERFRONT PARK (Public) In town, at Jct of 4th Ave & Ballaine Ave. 2015 rates: $15 to $30. (907)224-4055

Things to See and Do

ALASKA SEALIFE CENTER The Alaska SeaLife Center is Alaska's only public aquarium. Experience, explore and discover the unique marine world of puffins, harbor seals, Stellar sea lions, giant Pacific octopus and more. Partial handicap access. RV accessible. Restrooms, food. Hours: Summer 9AM-9PM, Winter 10AM-5PM. Adult fee: $20.
(888)378-2525 Lat: 60.10025, Lon: -149.44060
301 Railway, Seward, AK 99664
visit@alaskasealife.org
www.alaskasealife.org
See ad page 28 (Welcome Section).

SITKA — D5 *Sitka*

SITKA SPORTSMAN'S ASSOCIATION RV PARK **Ratings: 4/5.5/7** (Campground) 2015 rates: $30. (800)750-4712 5211 Halibut Point Rd, Sitka, AK 99835

SKAGWAY — D5 *Haines, Skagway*

GARDEN CITY RV PARK
Ratings: 5.5/10★/8 (RV Park) S-bnd: At Jct of 15th St & State St (R). **FAC:** Gravel rds. 76 gravel, 25 pull-thrus (20 x 50), back-ins (18 x 40), 76 full hkups (30 amps), WiFi, tent sites, showers $, laundry. Pets OK. Partial handicap access. 2015 rates: $40.50. May 15 to Sep 15.
(866)983-2378 Lat: 59.27728, Lon: -135.18330
15th and E State St., Skagway, AK 99840
gcrv@aptalaska.net
www.gardencityrv.com
See ad pages 26 (Welcome Section), 29.

PULLEN CREEK RV PARK **Ratings: 5.5/6.5/6.5** (Campground) 2015 rates: $30 to $40. May 15 to Sep 15. (907)983-2768 501 Congress Way, Skagway, AK 99840

SLANA — C4 *Valdez Cordova*

HART D RANCH DOUBLETREE RV PARK **Ratings: 4.5/9.5★/9** (Campground) 2015 rates: $28 to $38. (907)822-3973 1/2 Mi Nabesna Rd, Slana, AK 99586

SOLDOTNA — D3 *Kenai Peninsula*

ANCHOR RIVER SRA (State Pk) In town, W 0.5 mi on Sterling Hwy at MP 157 (R). Pit toilets. 2015 rates: $10. May 1 to Sep 30. (907)262-5581

RV Park ratings you can rely on!

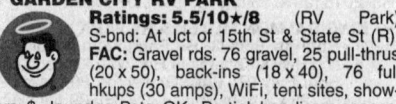

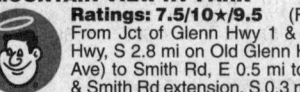

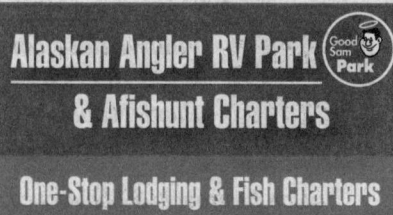

SOLDOTNA (CONT)

CENTENNIAL CAMPGROUND (Public) From jct Kenai Spur Rd & Hwy 1 (Sterling Hwy Mile Post 94.2): Go 2 mi S on Hwy 1, then 500 feet W on Kalifornsky, then 1/4 mi N on Centennial Park Rd. Pit toilets. (907)262-1337

CLAM GULCH (State Pk) From town, S 25 mi on Sterling Hwy, follow signs. MP-117. 2015 rates: $10. May to Oct. (907)262-5581

CROOKED CREEK REC SITE (State Pk) From town, S 14 mi on Sterling Hwy to Coho Loop, N 2 mi (R). 2015 rates: $10. May 15 to Oct 15. (907)262-5581

EDGE WATER RV PARK **Ratings: 6.5/8.5★/7** (RV Park) 2015 rates: $35 to $40. May 15 to Aug 31. (907)262-7733 48798 Funny River Rd, Soldotna, AK 99669

JOHNSON LAKE SRA (State Pk) On Sterling Hwy at MP-110. Note: 35' RV size limit. 2015 rates: $10. (907)262-5581

KENAI NATIONAL WILDLIFE REFUGE (HIDDEN LAKE CAMPGROUND) (Natl Pk) From town: Go 22 mi E on Sterling Hwy to milepost 72.5, then 14-1/2 mi S on Skilak Rd. 2015 rates: $10. (907)262-7021

KENAI NATIONAL WILDLIFE REFUGE (UPPER SKILAK LAKE) (Natl Pk) From town: Go 22 mi E on Sterling Hwy to milepost 72.5, then 8 mi S on Skilak Rd. 2015 rates: $5 to $10. (907)262-7021

KING SALMON MOTEL & RV PARK
Ratings: 6/9★/8 (RV Park) From Jct of Sterling Hwy & Kenai Spur Hwy, W 0.7 mi on Kenai Spur Hwy (R). **FAC:** Gravel rds. 39 gravel, 22 pull-thrus (28 x 60), back-ins (30 x 36), 39 full hkups (30/50 amps), WiFi, tent sites, rentals, showers $, dump, laundry, restaurant. Pets OK. Big rig sites, 2015 rates: $35. May 15 to Sep 15. no reservations.
(907)262-5857 Lat: 60.29743, Lon: -151.04188
35546-A Kenai Spur Hwy, Soldotna, AK 99669
ksalmon@alaska.com
www.bestwesternalaska.com/hotels/best-western-king-salmon-motel
See ad page 41.

KLONDIKE RV PARK & CABINS
Ratings: 8/10★/10 (RV Park) From Jct of Sterling Hwy & Funny River Rd, E. 0.2 mi on Funny River Rd (R) Call for extended season openings. **FAC:** All weather rds. 35 Avail: 35 all weather, 4 pull-thrus (30 x 60), back-ins (30 x 50), 35 full hkups (30/50 amps), WiFi, laundry. Pets OK. No tents. Big rig sites, 2015 rates: $36 to $50. May 1 to Sep 10.
(907)262-6035 Lat: 60.28452, Lon: -151.04623
48665 Funny River Rd, Soldotna, AK 99669
manager@klondikervpark.com
www.klondikervpark.com
See ad this page.

Say you saw it in our Guide!

MORGANS LANDING SRA (State Pk) On Sterling Hwy at MP-85. 2015 rates: $10. May 15 to Oct 15. (907)262-5581

SWIFTWATER CAMPGROUND (Public) From jct Kenai Spur Rd & Hwy 1 (Sterling Hwy Mile Post 94.2): Go 500 feet on Hwy 1, then 1/2 mi E on E Redoubt Ave, then 1/4 mi S on Swiftwater Park Rd. (907)262-1337

STERLING — D3 *Kenai Peninsula*

ALASKA CANOE & CAMPGROUND **Ratings: 6.5/7/7.5** (Campground) 2015 rates: $20 to $30. May 1 to Sep 30. (907)262-2331 35292 Sterling Hwy, Sterling, AK 99672

BINGS LANDING REC SITE (State Pk) On Sterling Hwy at MP-79. 2015 rates: $10. May 15 to Oct 15. (907)262-5581

IZAAK WALTON (State Pk) From town, S 1 mi on Hwy 1 (Sterling Hwy) to Izaak Walton State Park Rd (MP-81), W 0.25 mi (E). 2015 rates: $10. May 15 to Oct 30. (907)262-5581

MOOSE RIVER RV PARK **Ratings: 4/7.5/7.5** (Campground) 2015 rates: $30. May 1 to Oct 1. (907)260-7829 33190 Sterling Hwy, Sterling, AK 99672

SUTTON — C4 *Matanuska Susitna*

PINNACLE MOUNTAIN RV PARK & CAFE **Ratings: 4.5/7.5/5** (Campground) 2015 rates: $20 to $25. (907)746-6531 mile 70 Glenn Hwy, Sutton, AK 99674

TALKEETNA — C4 *Matanuska Susitna*

DENALI/LOWER TROUBLESOME (State Pk) From Talkeentna cutoff, N 40 mi on Parks Hwy(L). 2015 rates: $10. (907)745-3975

TALKEETNA CAMPER PARK **Ratings: 5.5/8.5/7.5** (RV Park) 2015 rates: $35 to $40. May 1 to Sep 30. (907)733-2693 mile 13.7 Talkeetna Spur, Talkeetna, AK 99676

TALKEETNA RV PARK & BOAT LAUNCH **Ratings: 4/5.5/7** (Campground) 2015 rates: $25. May 1 to Sep 30. (907)733-2604 21889 S. "f" St, Talkeetna, AK 99676

TOK — C4 *Southeast Fairbanks*

EAGLE TRAIL REC SITE (State Pk) On Tok Cutoff at MP-109.5. 2015 rates: $15. (907)883-3686

MOON LAKE REC SITE (State Pk) On AK Hwy at MP-1332. 2015 rates: $15. Jun 15 to Sep 15. (907)883-3686

PORCUPINE CREEK REC SITE (State Pk) 2015 rates: $15. Jun 15 to Sep 15. (907)822-3973

SOURDOUGH CAMPGROUND & BREAKFAST CAFE Ratings: 7/10★/10 (Campground) From Jct of Alaska Hwy & Glenn Hwy 1 (Tok Cutoff Rd), S 1.7 mi on Glenn Hwy/Tok Cutoff Rd (R) Note: Facilities may be limited in early & late season. **FAC:** All weather rds. 60 gravel, 25 pull-thrus (30 x 80), back-ins (30 x 45), 23 full hkups, 26 W, 36 E (20/30 amps), WiFi Hotspot, tent sites, dump, laundry, restaurant. **REC.** Pets OK. 2015 rates: $35 to $45. Disc: AAA, military. Apr 15 to Sep 15.
AAA Approved
(907)883-5543 Lat: 63.18698, Lon: -143.00225
1 Prospector Way, Tok, AK 99780
sourdoughcampground@outlook.com
www.sourdoughcampground.com

THREE BEARS OUTPOST **Ratings: 3.5/6.5/6.5** (Campground) 2015 rates: $22.99 to $27.99. May 15 to Sep 15. (907)883-5370 1313.3 Alaska Hwy, Tok, AK 99780

TOK RIVER REC SITE (State Pk) On AK Hwy at MP-1309. Note: 60' RV site limit. Pit toilets. 2015 rates: $15. Jun 15 to Sep 15. (907)451-2705

TOK RV VILLAGE & CABINS
Ratings: 9/10★/10 (RV Park) N-bnd on AK Hwy at MP-1313.4 (R). **FAC:** All weather rds. 154 Avail: 154 all weather, 128 pull-thrus (24 x 60), back-ins (20 x 35), 101 full hkups, 53 W, 53 E (30/50 amps), WiFi, tent sites, rentals, dump, laundry, LP gas, fire rings, firewood. **REC.** Pets OK. Partial handicap access. Big rig sites, 2015 rates: $32.15 to $52.75. Disc: AAA, military. Apr 15 to Sep 30.
AAA Approved
(907)883-5877 Lat: 63.33503, Lon: -142.96435
1313.4 Mile Alaska Hwy, Tok, AK 99780
camp@tokrv.net
www.tokrv.net
See ad pages 25 (Welcome Section), 29, 1483 (YT Map).

TUNDRA LODGE & RV PARK
Ratings: 6/9★/8.5 (RV Park) From Jct of AK Hwy & Tok Cutoff Rd (Glenn Hwy), N 1 mi on AK Hwy (R).

BEST VALUE ALONG ALASKA HIGHWAY...
In the center of Tok. Large secluded forested full hookup sites. Onsite cocktail lounge with friendly family. Owned and operated. Walking distance. Great food "Fast Eddy's" for breakfast, lunch & dinner.
FAC: Gravel rds. 54 gravel, 36 pull-thrus (30 x 70), back-ins (18 x 40), 30 full hkups, 24 W, 24 E (30/50 amps), WiFi Hotspot, tent sites, dump, laundry, fire rings. **REC.** Pets OK. Partial handicap access. 2015 rates: $20 to $35. May 15 to Sep 15.
(907)883-7875 Lat: 63.20322, Lon: -143.01050
1315 Mile Alaska Hwy, Tok, AK 99780
tundrarv@aptalaska.net
www.tokalaska.com/tundra.html
See ad this page.

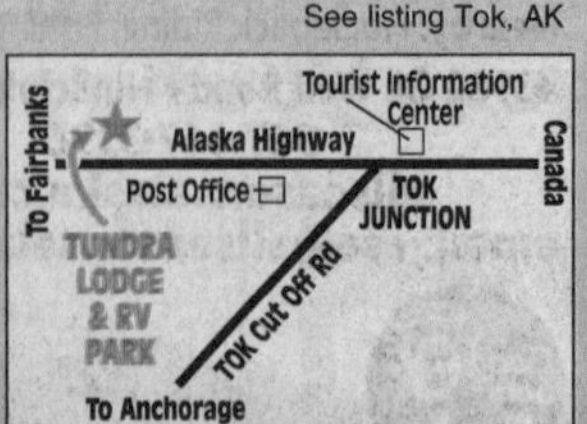

AK

TRAPPER CREEK — C3 *Matanuska Susitna*

DENALI SP/BYERS LAKE (State Pk) On Parks Hwy, at MP 147. Note: RV size limit is 35' or smaller. 2015 rates: $10. May 15 to Sep 15. (907)745-3975

DENALI VIEWPOINT NORTH (State Pk) On Parks Hwy, at MP 162.7. 2015 rates: $10. (907)745-3975

TRAPPER CREEK INN & RV PARK
Ratings: 8/10★/8.5 (Campground) On Parks Hwy (Hwy 3) at MP-114.8 at service station. Northbound: (R). **FAC:** Gravel rds. 31 gravel, 9 pull-thrus (21 x 60), back-ins (15 x 30), 18 full hkups (50 amps), WiFi, tent sites, rentals, showers $, dump, laundry, groc, LP gas, fire rings, restaurant. **REC.** Pets OK. Partial handicap access. 2015 rates: $20 to $35.
(907)733-2302 Lat: 62.18845, Lon: -150.13957
Mp 114.8 Parks Hwy, Trapper Creek, AK 99683
reservations@trappercrkinn.com
www.trappercreekinn.com
See ad opposite page, 29.

VALDEZ — D4 *Nia, Valdez Cordova*

A SPOTLIGHT Introducing Valdez's colorful attractions appearing at the front of this state section.

ALLISON POINT (State Pk) From town, E 6 mi on Richardson Hwy to Dayville Rd, W 5 mi (R) Dry camp site with overnight & day use parking. 2015 rates: $15. May 15 to Sep 15. (907)835-2282

BAYSIDE RV PARK **Ratings: 8/10★/9** (RV Park) 2015 rates: $27 to $40. May 1 to Sep 8. (888)835-4425 230 E. Egan Dr, Valdez, AK 99686

BEAR CREEK CABINS & RV PARK **Ratings: 6/7/7.5** (RV Park) 2015 rates: $31. May 25 to Sep 12. (907)835-2723 3181 Richardson Hwy, Valdez, AK 99686

BEAR PAW ADULT PARK
Ratings: 6.5/10★/8.5 (RV Park) From Jct of Richardson Hwy & Meals Ave, S 0.1 mi on Meals Ave to Harbor Dr, E 150 ft to check in location (L).

LOCATED IN DOWNTOWN VALDEZ
You'll find us on Prince William Sound by the small boat harbor conveniently close to boat tours, restaurants & gift shops. Valdez AK is one of the most beautiful areas in the world. 5 spectacular glaciers for your viewing.

FAC: Gravel rds. 32 gravel, back-ins (20 x 40), 28 full hkups, 4 W, 4 E (30 amps), cable, WiFi, tent sites, dump, laundry, firewood. **REC:** Prince William Sound. Pets OK. Age restrict may apply, 2015 rates: $45. May 1 to Sep 25.
(907)835-2530 Lat: 61.07500, Lon: -146.21537
300 Wyatt Way, Valdez, AK 99686
bearpaw@valdezak.net
www.bearpawrvpark.com
See ad page 35 (Spotlight Valdez).

BEAR PAW CAMPER PARK
Ratings: 7/10★/8.5 (RV Park) From Jct of Richardson Hwy & Meals Ave, S 0.1 mi on Meals Ave to N Harbor Dr, E 150 ft (L). **FAC:** Gravel rds. 70 gravel, 19 pull-thrus (20 x 60), back-ins (20 x 40), 62 full hkups, 8 W, 8 E (30 amps), cable, WiFi, dump, laundry, firewood. **REC.** Pets OK. Partial handicap access, no tents. 2015 rates: $40. May 1 to Sep 25.
(907)835-2530 Lat: 61.12748, Lon: -146.349800
101 North Harbor Drive, Valdez, AK 99686
bearpaw@valdezak.net
www.bearpawrvpark.com
See ad page 35 (Spotlight Valdez).

EAGLE'S REST RV PARK & CABINS
Ratings: 8.5/10★/9.5 (RV Park) From Jct of Richardson Hwy & Pioneer Dr, W 50 ft on Pioneer Dr (R).

SPECTACULAR SCENERY-FABULOUS FISHIN
Surrounded by glaciers, Eagle's Rest offers true Big Rig amenities in the heart of Valdez. The only Good Sam Park in Valdez. Fish, hike, or sit and watch the eagles soar. Be part of our family.

FAC: All weather rds. 184 Avail: 184 all weather, 92 pull-thrus (25 x 80), back-ins (22 x 40), 184 full hkups (30/50 amps), cable, WiFi, tent sites, rentals, dump, laundry, groc, LP gas, fire rings, firewood, restaurant. **REC.** Pets OK. Partial handicap access. Big rig sites, 2015 rates: $37 to $49. Disc: military. May 15 to Sep 15.
(800)553-7275 Lat: 61.05965, Lon: -146.20763
139 E Pioneer, Valdez, AK 99686
info@eaglesrestrv.com
www.eaglesrestrv.com
See ad pages 1483 (YT Map), 36 (Spotlight Valdez), 29, 24 (AK Map), 23 (Welcome Section) & RV Trips of a Lifetime & ad page 133 in Magazine Section.

VALDEZ GLACIER CAMPGROUND (CITY PARK) (Public) From jct Richardson Hwy (Milepost O) & Airport Rd: Go 1-1/2 mi N on Airport Rd. 2015 rates: $21 to $25. (907)835-2282

Things to See and Do

STAN STEPHENS GLACIER & WILDLIFE CRUISES Discover the Glaciers & Wildlife of Prince William Sound from Valdez. Tours feature Columbia or Meares Glac[illegible]. Daily departures.

WILDLIFE-GLAC[illegible]S-LOCAL LORE
Explore the calm waters of Prince William Sound from Valdez to Columbia or Meares Glacier. View seals, sea otters, sea lions, whales, porpoise & marine birdlife. Travel with the local experts - at home in Valdez since 1971.

May 15 to Sep 15. partial handicap access. RV accessible. Restrooms, food. Hours: 8am to 7pm. Adult fee: $125 to $160.
(907)835-4731 Lat: 61.12647, Lon: -146.35007
112 North Harbor Drive, Valdez, AK 99686
info@stephenscruises.com
www.stanstephenscruises.com
See ad page 26 (Welcome Section) & RV Trips of a Lifetime in Magazine Section.

WASILLA — C4 *Matanuska Susitna*

ALASKAN TRAILS RV & CAMPER PARK, LLC **Ratings: 5.5/5.5/4.5** (RV Park) 2015 rates: $27. (907)376-5504 6570 W. Parks Hwy, Wasilla, AK 99623

BIG BEAR RV PARK
Ratings: 9/10★/10 (RV Park) From Jct of Parks Hwy (SR-3) & Trunk Rd, S 500 ft on Trunk Rd to E Fireweed Rd, W 0.8 mi to Church St, SW 0.1 mi (R). **FAC:** All weather rds. 51 Avail: 51 all weather, 33 pull-thrus (20 x 60), back-ins (24 x 45), 24 full hkups, 13 W, 27 E (30/50 amps), WiFi, tent sites, rentals, dump, laundry, LP gas, fire rings, firewood. **REC:** playground. Pets OK. Partial handicap access. Big rig sites, 2015 rates: $25 to $36. Disc: military.
(907)745-7445 Lat: 61.56125, Lon: -149.29221
2010 S Church St, Palmer, AK 99645
bigbear@mtaonline.net
www.bigbearrv.net
See ad pages 25 (Welcome Section), 29.

BIG LAKE NORTH REC SITE (State Pk) From town, W 15 mi on Parks Hwy to Big Lake Rd, S 3 mi (E). 2015 rates: $15. May 15 to Sep 15. (907)746-4644

BIG LAKE SOUTH REC SITE (State Pk) From town, W 15 mi on Parks Hwy to Big Lake Rd, S 5 mi (E). 2015 rates: $15. May 15 to Sep 15. (907)745-3975

ROCKY LAKE REC SITE (State Pk) From town, W 15 mi on Parks Hwy to Big Lake Rd to Beaver Lake Rd, N 1 mi (L). 2015 rates: $15. May 15 to Sep 15. (907)745-3975

WILLOW — C4 *Matanuska Susitna, Willow*

MAT-SU RV PARK & CAMPGROUND **Ratings: 7.5/10★/8** (RV Park) 2015 rates: $20 to $35. May 1 to Sep 30. (907)495-6300 47442 S Yancey, Willow, AK 99688

MONTANA CREEK CAMPGROUND **Ratings: 4.5/NA/8.5** (Campground) Pit toilets. 2015 rates: $28 to $50. May 15 to Sep 1. (907)733-5267 mile 96.5 Parks Hwy, Willow, AK 99688

NANCY LAKE REC AREA/SOUTH ROLLY LAKE (State Pk) After MP 67.3, follow rd 6.5 mi to lake. 2015 rates: $10. May 15 to Sep 15. (907)745-3975

SUSITNA LANDING AND CAMPGROUND **Ratings: 5.5/5/8** (RV Park) 2015 rates: $12 to $24. (907)495-7700 14400 W Susitna Landing Rd, Willow, AK 99688

WILLOW CREEK CAMPGROUND (State Pk) From town, N on Parks Hwy to MP 70.8(L). Pit toilets. 2015 rates: $10. May 15 to Sep 15. (907)745-3975

WRANGELL — D6 *Wrangell*

SHOEMAKER RV PARK (CITY PARK) (Public) From ferry dock: Go 4-9/10 mi E on Zimouia Hwy. Pit toilets. 2015 rates: $15 to $25. (907)874-2444

Find it fast! To locate a town on a map, follow these easy instructions: Look for the map grid code after the town heading in the listing section and match it to the letters and numbers on the map borders. Draw a line horizontally from the letter and vertically from the number. You'll find the town near the intersection of the two lines.

 See map page 45

Arizona Office of Tourism

WELCOME TO Arizona

DATE OF STATEHOOD	WIDTH: 310 MILES (500 KM)	PROPORTION OF UNITED STATES
FEB. 14, 1912	LENGTH: 400 MILES (645 KM)	3.00% OF 3,794,100 SQ MI

You'd expect that a state wouldn't need to try hard when it's home to one of the seven natural wonders of the world. The Grand Canyon, with its iconic views, transcendental hiking and 2-billion-year history carved in stone is Arizona's crowning jewel. But when you take a road trip to Arizona, wonders hit you hard and fast. The red rocks of Sedona, the sandstone buttes of Monument Valley, the hirsute cacti of Saguaro National Park, the famed silhouette of Camelback Mountain and the earth's best-preserved meteorite crater compete aggressively for attention.

On the Colorado River, the Art Deco Hoover Dam, an awe-inspiring feat of engineering and design genius, straddles the border of Arizona and Nevada. Sunny skies and a holistic vibe seduce health conscious vacationers to Scottsdale's exclusive spas and resorts. It's hardly love at first sight, but Phoenix, the fifth-largest city in the U.S., soon works its magic with 200-plus golf courses, no-nonsense western charm and unexpected cultural élan in the form of an opera, a symphony, dynamic

Top 3 Tourism Attractions:
1) The Grand Canyon
2) Saguaro National Park
3) Navajo Nation

Nickname: Grand Canyon State

State Flower: Flower of Saguaro Cactus

State Bird: Cactus Wren

People: Geronimo, leader of Apache Indians; Linda Ronstadt, singer; Cesar Estrada Chavez, union leader

Major Cities: Phoenix (capital), Mesa, Chandler, Tucson, Flagstaff

Topography: Ponderosa Pine forest in northern Colorado Plateau and desert in the South

Climate: South is dry climate; temps from 106° in July in Yuma to 14° in Flagstaff in January

Arizona Office of Tourism

ARIZONA
Campground and other services
RV service center and/or other services
Good Sam discount locations
SCALE: 1 inch equals 52 miles
0 30 60 miles
0 30 60 kilometers
Map by Terra Carta © 2016 Affinity Media
ONE WEEK STARTS AT $99
SOME RESTRICTIONS APPLY
4 Resorts in Sunny Arizona
RobertsResorts.com
866-787-2754
UTAH
ARIZONA
NEVADA
CALIFORNIA
NEW MEXICO
U.S.A.
MEXICO
PACIFIC TIME ZONE
MOUNTAIN TIME ZONE
St. George
LITTLEFIELD
Mesquite
Las Vegas
Henderson
Boulder City
TEMPLE BAR MARINA
MEADVIEW
WILLOW BEACH
KATHERINE
Laughlin
BULLHEAD CITY
FORT MOHAVE
MOHAVE VALLEY
Needles
TOPOCK
LAKE HAVASU CITY
KINGMAN
GOLDEN VALLEY
PEACH SPRINGS
Yucca
WIKIEUP
PARKER
QUARTZSITE
BRENDA
EHRENBERG
Blythe
BOUSE
HOPE
SALOME
Harcuvar
Wenden
YUMA
Somerton
San Luis
San Luis Río Colorado
TACNA
WELLTON
DATELAND
Gila Bend
GILA BEND
AJO
LUKEVILLE
PAGE
MARBLE CANYON
JACOB LAKE
Fredonia
Kanab
Colorado City
GRAND CANYON NATIONAL PARK
Grand Canyon Village
TUSAYAN
Vermillion Cliffs National Monument
Grand Canyon-Parashant National Monument
SELIGMAN
ASH FORK
WILLIAMS
FLAGSTAFF
BELLEMONT
Humphreys Peak 12,633
MUNDS PARK
MORMON LAKE
HAPPY JACK
SEDONA
CORNVILLE
COTTONWOOD
PRESCOTT VALLEY
PRESCOTT
DEWEY
CAMP VERDE
CORDES JUNCTION
CORDES LAKES
CONGRESS
WICKENBURG
BLACK CANYON CITY
CAVE CREEK
PAYSON
SURPRISE
EL MIRAGE
SUN CITY
PEORIA
Glendale
LITCHFIELD PARK
GOODYEAR
PHOENIX
SCOTTSDALE
FORT MCDOWELL
FOUNTAIN HILLS
MESA
TEMPE
CHANDLER
GOLD CANYON
APACHE JUNCTION
QUEEN VALLEY
TONOPAH
BUCKEYE
AVONDALE
ROOSEVELT
GLOBE
MARICOPA
CASA GRANDE
FLORENCE
COOLIDGE
ELOY
PICACHO
ARIZONA CITY
MARANA
TUCSON
BENSON
ST. DAVID
TOMBSTONE
AMADO
SIERRA VISTA
HUACHUCA CITY
PATAGONIA
BISBEE
Nogales
Douglas
Agua Prieta
WILLCOX
SAFFORD
CLIFTON
KAYENTA
CHINLE
FORT DEFIANCE
WINSLOW
JOSEPH CITY
HOLBROOK
SNOWFLAKE
OVERGAARD
SHOW LOW
HON-DAH
SPRINGERVILLE
Petrified Forest National Park
Saguaro National Park
Organ Pipe Cactus N.M.
Cabeza Prieta N.W.R.
Kofa N.W.R.

 See map page 45

theaters and two excellent museums: the Phoenix Art Museum and the Heard Museum. Tucson revels in its Hispanic heritage while vibrant Flagstaff, the quintessential university town, provides the launch pad for the Grand Canyon. Surrounded by national forests and red rock buttes and mesas, stunning Sedona has defined itself as a sanctum for New Age thinkers and retirees.

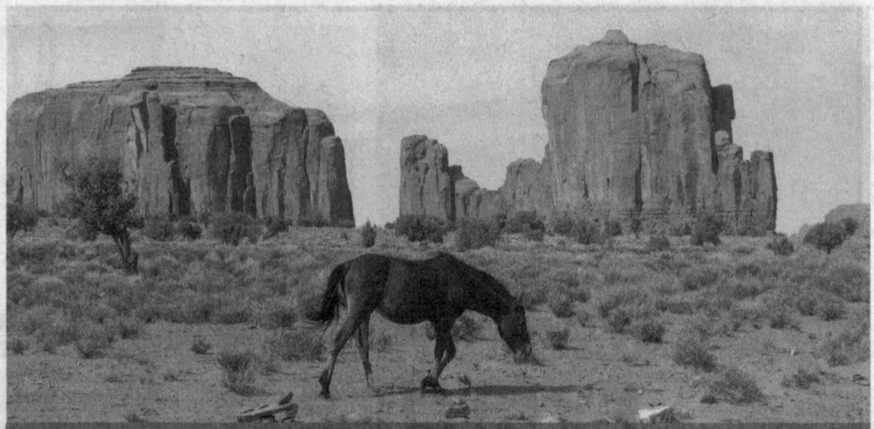

A lone horse wanders Monument Valley Navajo Tribal Park. Getty Images/iStockphoto

Learn

It was a Spanish Franciscan friar, on a quest to find the mythical Seven Cities of Gold in 1539, who first explored the area that is now Arizona. More fortune seekers followed, but the Spaniards ultimately established a settlement for missionary purposes. Following the Mexican War in 1848, most of Arizona ceded to the U.S.; the remaining southern territory was added in 1853 with the Gadsden Purchase. It wasn't until the early 20th century that mining yielded promised riches. Known as the "Copper State," copper mining formed Arizona's premier industry until the 1950s.

Ancestral Puebloans (formerly called Anasazis), Sinagua and Hohokam tribes built villages on mesas, in valleys and in the steep cliff walls of deep canyons. The cliff dwellings and ancient pueblo ruins of national monuments such as Canyon de Chelly, Montezuma Castle, Navajo, Wupatki and Tonto reveal Arizona's 10,000-year-old human history.

In 1912, Arizona achieved statehood, the last of the 48 coterminous U.S. states to be admitted to the union. In the 1920s, sunshine and cloudless skies became the state's most important resource, as "lungers," (a person suffering from tuberculosis) visited the state to recuperate in the dry desert air. After World War II, with the advent of refrigeration and air conditioning, Arizona experienced a population boom. Soon enough, the state's nascent tourist industry cottoned on and began to pitch Arizona as the perfect winter escape for the country's chilly northern denizens.

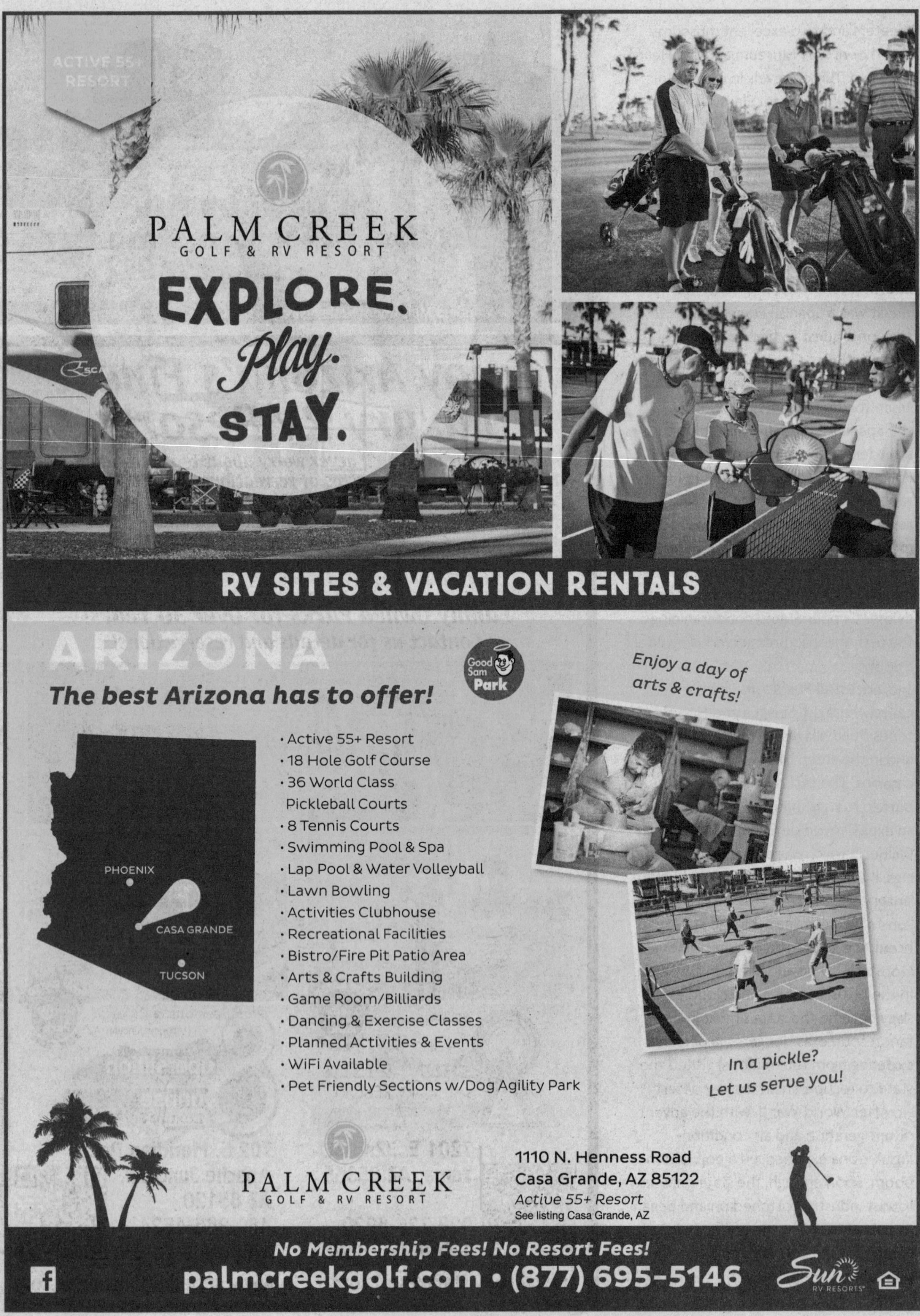
ACTIVE 55+ RESORT
PALM CREEK
GOLF & RV RESORT
EXPLORE.
Play.
STAY.
RV SITES & VACATION RENTALS
ARIZONA
The best Arizona has to offer!
Good Sam Park
PHOENIX
CASA GRANDE
TUCSON
• Active 55+ Resort
• 18 Hole Golf Course
• 36 World Class Pickleball Courts
• 8 Tennis Courts
• Swimming Pool & Spa
• Lap Pool & Water Volleyball
• Lawn Bowling
• Activities Clubhouse
• Recreational Facilities
• Bistro/Fire Pit Patio Area
• Arts & Crafts Building
• Game Room/Billiards
• Dancing & Exercise Classes
• Planned Activities & Events
• WiFi Available
• Pet Friendly Sections w/Dog Agility Park
Enjoy a day of arts & crafts!
In a pickle? Let us serve you!
PALM CREEK
GOLF & RV RESORT
1110 N. Henness Road
Casa Grande, AZ 85122
Active 55+ Resort
See listing Casa Grande, AZ
No Membership Fees! No Resort Fees!
palmcreekgolf.com • (877) 695-5146
Sun RV RESORTS

Play

There is perhaps no better place for a road trip than Arizona. With 22 national parks and 31 state parks, Arizona is home to some of the nation's most extraordinary landscapes. These range from vast desert punctuated with giant cactus to gaping canyons, inverted mountains, meteor craters and ancient ruins steeped in myth and legend. With its epic scale and majesty, the Grand Canyon's multihued rocks and labyrinthine canyons provide hiking adventures that are out of this world.

A compelling wilderness, Vermilion Cliffs National Monument has been inhabited for more than 12,000 years, as evidenced by the ruins and petroglyphs found throughout the plateau. A worthy detour from the Grand Canyon's North Rim, the Wave is arguably the most psychedelic rock formation in the nation. Privately owned, but open to the public, Meteor Crater is a national natural landmark; a gigantic hole, 2.4 miles in circumference and more than 550 feet deep, is the result of a meteor that struck the earth some 50,000 years ago, about the same time that woolly mammoths roamed eastern Arizona.

Bridging the state line between Arizona and Utah, Monument Valley is named for the colossal sandstone buttes and monoliths that tower above an expansive sagebrush landscape. Walnut Canyon's numerous cliff dwellings, built between 1125 and 1250 by the Sinagua people, nestle among the canyon's natural limestone overhangs, just 10 miles east of Flagstaff. A paved 1-mile loop trail that begins a short walk from the visitor center links many of Walnut Canyon's most fascinating structures.

Experience

In February, Scottsdale's Arabian Horse Show draws the world's most revered horse trainers and breeders. Around 2,000 Arabians and Half-Arabians compete for $500,000 in prize money and star in horse skills demonstrations and riding seminars. In Gold Canyon, at the end of February, the Arizona Renaissance Festival is one of the largest period-themed events in

Monoliths loom on the horizon in Monument Valley. Getty Images/iStockphoto

- STAY A WHILE -

Benson Visitor Center

Amid picturesque river valley views, agreeable weather and the Home of Kartchner Caverns State Park, the City of Benson is ideally situated along Interstate 10 as the Gateway to Cochise County in Southeast Arizona.

Founded in 1880 prior to Arizona's mining boom, Benson developed as a stopping point for the Butterfield Overland Stage mail delivery route. Soon thereafter, the Southern Pacific Railroad came into Benson and continued to serve the area until 1997, when the line was purchased by the Union Pacific Railroad.

The City of Benson's culture is ingrained with the Old West and our traditional railroad heritage. The Benson Visitor Center Train Depot, located at 249 East Fourth Street in the heart of Benson's historic downtown, is a beautiful replica railroad depot using many of the same architectural features as the original depot that was built over a century ago.

The City of Benson is proud of their designation as the Home of Kartchner Caverns State Park. Located on 550 acres at the foothills of the Whetstone Mountains just south of Benson on State Highway 90, Kartchner Caverns State Park offers picnicking, camping, hiking, walking and the magnificent still-living caverns.

The San Pedro Golf Course, owned and operated by the City of Benson, is an 18-hole championship course. The front nine meanders through mesquite groves along the San Pedro River, while the back nine plays through natural canyons with significant elevation changes. San Pedro is pure golf played in an all-natural setting, free from man-made obstructions.

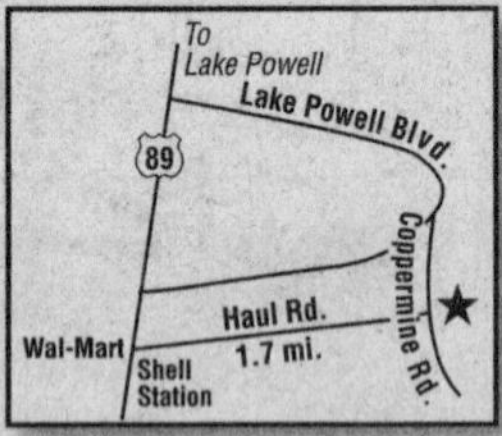

See listing Page, AZ

See listing Benson, AZ

the U.S., attracting more than 250,000 visitors each year. A custom 30-acre village provides the setting for costumed re-enactments, full armor jousting competitions, dancing and more than 200 craft shops.

In April, in Scottsdale, the Scottsdale Culinary Festival is the most established food festival in the nation, drawing some 50,000 visitors each year with gourmet food booths, wine tastings, celebrity chef presentations, competitions and child-friendly festivities. Late June, the World's Oldest Rodeo (also known as Prescott Frontier Days) has been held since 1888. The eight-day event features an elite rodeo competition, the ever-enduring Rodeo Dance and the colorful Prescott Frontier Days Parade.

Lake Havasu's London Bridge
Image courtesy of the Arizona Office of Tourism

Taste

In Phoenix, Beckett's Table (www.beckettstable.com) serves highly praised seasonal dishes in a delightful farmhouse decorated with wooden furniture, exposed ceilings and bunches of centerpiece herbs on each table. A veteran of Arizona's upscale dining scene, the multi-award-winning Vincent on Camelback (www.vincentsoncamelback.com) now has a James Beard Foundation Award under its belt. Flavorful Southwest dishes, including lobster chimichanga draped in a basil beurre blanc, are executed with French flair. From October through May, Vincent's Saturday market serves casual fare, including wood-fired thin-crust pizzas. In Flagstaff, Coppa Café (www.

coppacafe.net) sources the freshest ingredients from local ranches ("Kelly Beef" from Prescott and "Niman Ranch" steak frites), farms and orchards to create elegant yet simple dishes served in a welcoming, Europhile setting.

TRAVEL & TOURISM

Arizona Office of Tourism
602-364-3700, 866-275-5816
www.arizonaguide.com

Flagstaff CVB
800-379-0065
www.flagstaffarizona.org

Grand Canyon Chamber of Commerce
844-638-2901
www.grandcanyonchamber.com

City of Glendale
623-930-2000
www.glendaleaz.org

Kingman Visitors Center
866-427-RT66
www.gokingman.com

Visit Mesa
800-283-6372
www.visitmesa.com

Visit Phoenix
877-CALLPHX
www.visitphoenix.com

Scottsdale CVB
800-782-1117
www.scottsdalecvb.com

Sedona Chamber of Commerce Visitor Information Center
800-288-7336
www.sedonachamber.com

Surprise CVB
623-583-0692
www.surpriseregionalchamber.com

Tempe CVB
480-894-8158
www.tempecvb.com

Visit Tucson
800-638-8350
www.visittucson.org

Visit Yuma
800-293-0071
www.visityuma.com

- STAY A WHILE -

Arizona State Parks

Explore Arizona's great outdoors—even without a tent or RV! Camping Cabins at three Arizona State Parks offer secure shelter with beds, heating, cooling and electricity. Just bring your own bedding and cookware. Camping Cabins are easily accessible by car and feature modern restrooms and showers nearby. Meals are simple with picnic tables and charcoal BBQ grills. Bring bedding and cookware.

Get away from the sizzling temperatures and make a splash at one of our State Parks. Cool down and relax by swimming, water-skiing, boating, canoeing, fishing or kayaking. Wherever your adventure takes you, we hope to see you exploring at one of our Arizona State Parks. Although there are many things you can experience at a State Park, here are the top picks of some fun things to do with your family.

The Top 10 things to do in the State Parks:
1) Canoeing or kayaking at Dead Horse Ranch State Park (Cottonwood)
2) Experience a Cabin at Lyman Lake State Park (St. Johns)
3) Hike the picturesque trails at Red Rock State Park (Sedona)
4) Catch a big one fishing at Roper Lake State Park (Safford)
5) Boating/Waterskiing at Lake Havasu State Park (Lake Havasu City)
6) Enjoying an Evening Concert at Catalina State Park (Tucson)
7) Historic Fourth of July Event at Tubac Presidio State Historic Park (Tubac)
8) Tour a Historic Home at Oracle State Park (Oracle) or Riordan Mansion State Historic Park (Flagstaff) or Ancient Indian Sites at Homolovi State Park (Winslow)
9) Go back in time at Fort Verde State Historic Park (Camp Verde) or Jerome State Historic Park (Jerome)
10) Dragonfly Walk/Hike at Boyce Thompson Arboretum State Park (Superior)

Make a camping or RV reservation at AZStateParks.com or call 520-586-2283. For more information on each park and to create your adventure, visit AZStateParks.com.

For information about all 28 Arizona State Parks, the Trails and Off-Highway Vehicle Programs and State Historic Preservation Office call 602-542-4174 (outside of the Phoenix metro area call toll-free 800-285-3703). Campsite reservations can be made online at AZStateParks.com or by calling the Reservation Call Center at 520-586-2283. Open 7 days a week, from 8 a.m. to 5 p.m. MST. Follow @AZStateParks on Twitter and Facebook.

OUTDOOR RECREATION

Arizona Game & Fish Dept.
602-942-3000
www.azgfd.com

Arizona Golf Association
602-944-3035

SHOPPING

Arizona Mills
480-491-7300
www.arizonamillsmall.com

Foothills Mall
520-219-0650
www.shopfoothillsmall.com

Metrocenter Mall Phoenix
www.metrocentermall.com

Old Town Artisans
520-623-6024
www.oldtownartisans.com

Downtown/Old Town Scottsdale
480-994-2787
www.experiencescottsdale.com

Featured Good Sam Parks

ARIZONA

Good Sam Park

When you stay with Good Sam, you can expect the highest degree of cleanliness and friendliness, and better yet, you get 10% off campground fees.

If you're not already a Good Sam member you can purchase your membership at one of these locations:

APACHE JUNCTION
La Hacienda RV Resort
(480)982-2808
Meridian RV Resort
(866)770-0080
Sunrise RV Resort
(877)573-1168
Superstition Sunrise RV Resort
(800)624-7027
VIP RV Resort
(480)983-0847
Weaver's Needle RV Resort
(480)982-3683

BENSON
Butterfield RV Resort
(800)863-8160

BLACK CANYON CITY
Black Canyon Ranch RV Resort
(623)374-9800

BRENDA
3 Dreamers RV Park
(928)859-4145
Black Rock RV Village
(928)927-4206
Desert Gold RV Resort
(800)927-2101

BULLHEAD CITY
Colorado River Oasis Resort
(928)763-4385
Moon River RV Resort
(928)788-6666
Vista Del Sol RV Resort
(888)347-0230

CAMP VERDE
Distant Drums RV Resort
(928)554-8000
Verde River RV Resort & Cottages
(928)202-3409
Zane Grey RV Park
(928)567-4320

CASA GRANDE
Casa Grande RV Resort & Cottages
(520)421-0401
High Chaparral RV Park
(520)466-5076
Palm Creek Golf & RV Resort
(800)421-7004

COOLIDGE
Ho Ho Kam RV Park/ Mobile Village
(520)723-3697
Indian Skies RV Resort
(520)723-7831

DEWEY
Orchard Ranch RV Resort
(928)772-8266

EHRENBERG
Arizona Oasis RV Resort
(928)923-8230
River Breeze RV Park & OHV Resort
(928)923-7483

EL MIRAGE
Pueblo El Mirage Golf & RV Resort
(623)299-4949

ELOY
Las Colinas RV Park
(520)836-5050
Silverado RV Resort (formerly Desert Valley RV Park)
(866)502-4700

FLAGSTAFF
Black Barts RV Park
(928)774-1912
Greer's Pine Shadows RV Park
(928)526-4977
J & H RV Park
(928)526-1829

FLORENCE
Desert Gardens RV Park
(520)868-3800

FORT MCDOWELL
Eagle View RV Resort At Fort McDowell
(480)789-5310

FORT MOHAVE
Snowbird RV Resort
(928)768-7141

GOLD CANYON
Arizonian RV Resort
(520)463-2978
Canyon Vistas RV Resort & Superstition Views Resort
(888)940-8989
Gold Canyon RV & Golf Resort
(888)349-4172
Superstition Views Resort & Canyon Vistas RV Resort
(888)940-8989

GOLDEN VALLEY
Adobe RV Park
(928)565-3010

GOODYEAR
Cotton Lane RV & Golf Resort
(888)907-7223
Destiny Phoenix RV Resorts
(888)667-2454

KINGMAN
Blake Ranch RV Park
(928)757-3336

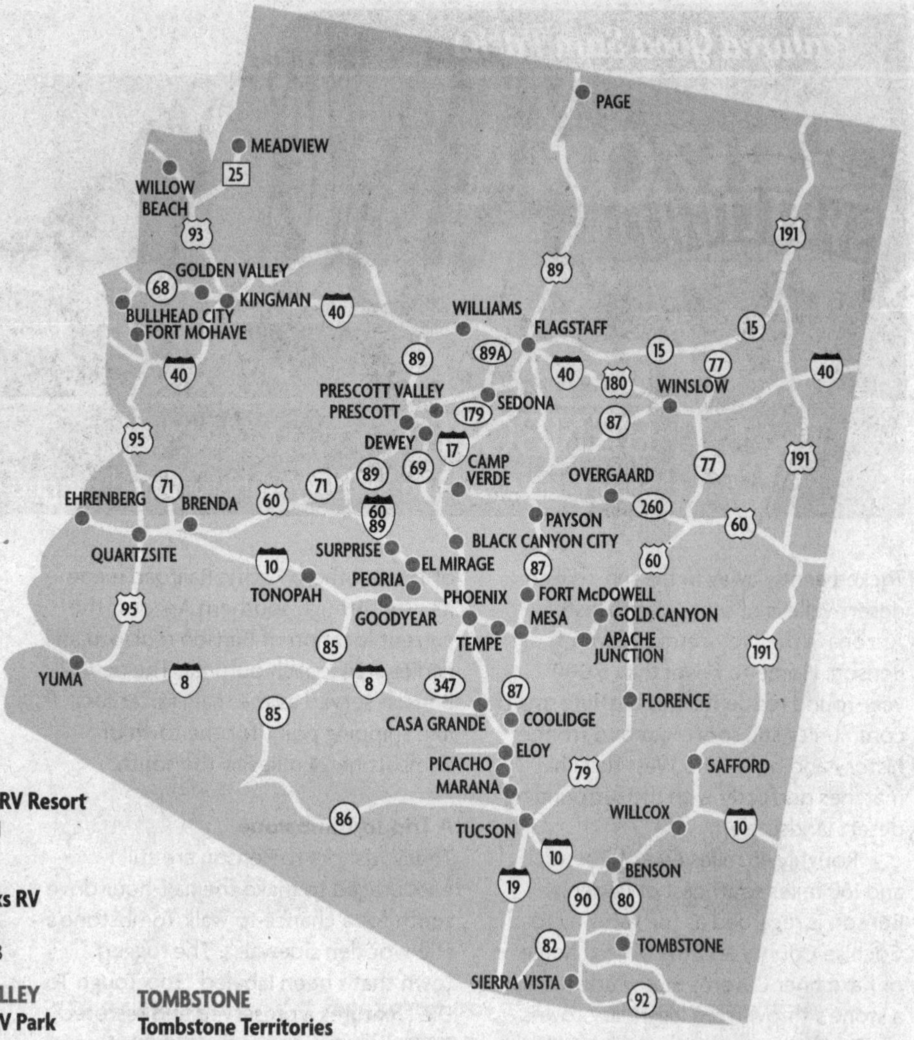

MARANA
Valley Of the Sun RV Resort
(520)682-3434

MEADVIEW
Meadview RV Park
(928)564-2662

MESA
Apache Wells RV Resort
(888)940-8989
Good Life RV Resort
(888)940-8989
Green Acres RV Park
(480)964-5058
Mesa Regal RV Resort
(800)845-4752
Silver Sands RV Resort
(480)984-6731
Sun Life RV Resort
(888)940-8989
Towerpoint Resort
(888)940-8989
Val Vista Village RV Resort
(888)940-8989
Valle Del Oro RV Resort
(888)940-8989
Venture Out At Mesa
(480)832-0200
Western Acres
(480)986-1158

OVERGAARD
Elk Pines RV Resort
(928)535-3833

PAGE
Page Lake Powell Campground
(928)645-3374

PAYSON
Payson Campground and RV Resort
(928)472-2267

PEORIA
Pleasant Harbor RV Resort
(800)475-3272

PHOENIX
Desert Shadows RV Resort
(800)595-7290
Desert's Edge RV-The Purple Park
(623)587-0940
Phoenix Metro RV Park
(623)582-0390
Pioneer RV Resort
(800)658-5895
Royal Palm RV Resort/MHC
(602)943-5833

PICACHO
Picacho Peak RV Resort
(520)466-7841

PRESCOTT
Point Of Rocks RV Campground
(928)445-9018

PRESCOTT VALLEY
Fairgrounds RV Park
(928)227-3310

QUARTZSITE
88 Shades RV Park
(800)457-4392
Holiday Palms RV Park
(800)635-5372
Quail Run RV Park
(928)927-8810
The Scenic Road RV Park
(928)927-6443

SAFFORD
Lexington Pines Resort LLC
(928)428-7570

SEDONA
Rancho Sedona RV Park
(888)641-4261

SIERRA VISTA
Sierra Vista Mobile Home Village & RV Park
(520)459-1690

SURPRISE
Sunflower RV Resort
(623)583-0100

TEMPE
Apache Palms RV Park
(480)966-7399

TOMBSTONE
Tombstone Territories RV Park
(520)457-2584

TONOPAH
Saddle Mountain RV Park
(623)386-3892

TUCSON
Crazy Horse Campgrounds
(800)279-6279
Far Horizons Tucson Village RV Resort
(800)480-3488
Mission View RV Resort
(800)444-8439
Prince Of Tucson RV Park
(800)955-3501
Rincon Country East RV Resort
(520)886-8431
Rincon Country West RV Resort
(520)294-5608
Sentinel Peak RV Park
(520)495-0175
Western Way RV Resort
(800)292-8616

WILLCOX
Grande Vista MH & RV Park
(520)384-4002
Magic Circle RV Park
(520)384-3212
Sagebrush RV Park
(520)384-2872

WILLIAMS
Canyon Gateway RV Park
(888)635-0329
Grand Canyon Railway RV Park
(800)843-8724

WILLOW BEACH
Willow Beach Marina & RV Park
(928)767-4747

WINSLOW
Meteor Crater RV Park
(800)478-4002

YUMA
Blue Sky RV Resort
(877)367-5220
Caravan Oasis RV Resort
(928)342-1480
Cocopah Bend RV & Golf Resort
(800)537-7901
Del Pueblo RV Park and Tennis Resort
(928)341-2100
Desert Holiday RV Resort
(928)344-4680
Fortuna de Oro RV Resort
(928)342-5051
Shangri-La RV Resort
(928)342-9123
Sun Vista RV Resort
(800)423-8382
Sundance RV Resort
(928)342-9333
Villa Alameda RV Resort
(928)344-8081
Westwind RV & Golf Resort
(928)342-2992

For more Good Sam Parks go to listing pages

 See map page 45

Arizona Office of Tourism

BENSON

Enter a gateway into Wild West history and rugged country

Tucked gently away in the sun-soaked desert valleys of scenic southeastern Arizona is the picturesque town of Benson. Home to fewer than 5,000 year-round residents, this bustling small community still sports a proud frontier history and bold Wild West flair that matches perfectly with the surrounding desert landscape.

Roughly 45 miles east of Tucson and 160 miles southeast of Phoenix, Benson is regarded as the gateway to Cochise County and the official home of Kartchner Caverns State Park. It's also a stone's throw from legendary towns like Tombstone, surreal museums like Gammons Gulch, and one-of-a-kind attractions like Cochise Stronghold. Add it all up and you have one of the most compelling small towns in the country.

Founded in 1880 as construction of the Southern Pacific Railroad made its way through southern Arizona, the current location of Benson replaced an earlier stagecoach outpost. The new Benson served as the main rail access and shipping point for the town of Tombstone 24 miles to the south.

A Trip to Tombstone

Today, visitors to Benson are still encouraged to make the half-hour drive south for a chance to walk Tombstone's still-wooden sidewalks. The rugged town that's been labeled "Too Tough To Die" features a preserved and restored 1880s-era street as well as reenactments of the O.K. Corral gunfight.

Rounding out the major historical sites is Cochise Stronghold, a protected woodland lying 33 miles east of Benson, and once the home of Apache Chief Cochise.

Going Underground

South of Benson, in the foothills of the Whetstone Mountains, is the crown jewel of Cochise County: Kartchner Caverns State Park. Home to a massive network of caves and luminous limestone caverns, this is one of Arizona's most popular natural attractions. The highlights are the Throne Room and the Big Room, as well as the mud flats, Rotunda Room, Strawberry Room and Cul-de-sac Passage.

For More Information

Benson Visitor Center
520-586-4293
www.bensonvisitorcenter.com

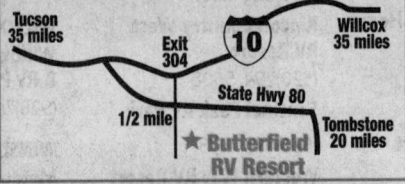

Arizona Office of Tourism
866-275-5816
www.arizonaguide.com

Slaven Gujic

SPOTLIGHT

AZ

GOLD CANYON

Mine vacation memories in a stellar destination

Ghost towns, gold mines, unsolved mysteries and an abundance of incredible desert golf courses are the main attractions in aptly named Gold Canyon, a small, laid-back community located on the eastern outskirts of Greater Phoenix. Visitors searching for a spot with great history, fantastic natural environments to explore and easy access to big city amenities will find Gold Canyon ideally situated in sunny central Arizona.

This is a popular destination for winter-weary northern snowbirds who annually flock to Gold Canyon in droves, nearly doubling its population of 10,000. It's easy to see why. The town enjoys nearly 300 days of sunshine each year and sits on the doorstop of the scenic Superstition Mountains and massive Tonto National Forest, making it a picturesque and recreation-rich hotspot. Dramatic views and mesmerizing vistas extend in every direction. This is the perfect place to set up a tent or park the RV and go exploring.

Of course, in Gold Canyon, exploring is no new trend. Since the late 19th century, the town has been a popular spot for miners, pioneers and even tourists traveling along the Apache Trail. That attraction gained a big boost when Jacob Waltz (a German immigrant, known as the "Deutchman") allegedly discovered a gold mine somewhere in the Superstition Mountains. The legend is that before he died in 1891, he only shared the location of the mine with one other person. Ever since, tourists and optimistic prospectors have been descending on Gold Canyon to try their hand at locating the legendary "Lost Dutchman Gold Mine."

Searching for Treasure

Today, Lost Dutchman State Park is the closest visitors will come to getting their hands on Waltz's mysterious treasure. But the park is a treasure all its own. It makes for a great day trip or for a weekend getaway, and is brimming with well-maintained hiking trails, interpretive nature trails, campgrounds and picnic areas. In spring, visitors are treated to bursts of wild flowers that carpet the desert floor.

From the park, trails lead into Tonto National Forest, where well-preserved cliff dwellings from as early as the 13th century can be toured.

From Gold to Greens

Finally, there are the golf courses. If you're a golfer, no exploration of Gold Canyon would be complete without a stop or two at one of the area's renowned courses. Dinosaur Mountain and Sidewinder at Gold Canyon Golf Resort are among the most popular, featuring striking valley views and multi-level greens. Mountainbrook Golf Course, the Superstition Mountain Golf Community and the 9-hole course at Gold Canyon RV Ranch are also conveniently located and offer a nice variety of landscapes and difficulty levels. As golfing is among the region's most popular activities, it's best to call ahead to inquire about tee time availability and reservations.

For More Information

Gold Canyon
866-996-4222
www.goldcanyon.net

Visit Arizona
866-275-5816
www.visitarizona.com

Golf in Arizona's Gold Canyon. Getty Images

SUPERSTITION VIEWS
AT CANYON VISTAS
CAL AM HOMES
Casita + Carport + RV Pad & Hookups
$ 99,900
POPULAR OPTIONS
RV Garage or Port | Observation Deck | Garage
BEAUTIFUL CUSTOM CASITAS, HUNDREDS OF AMENITIES!
55 + Community | State of the Art Fitness Center | Pickleball
Massage Therapy | Hiking Club | Lighted Tennis Courts
Golfing Club/Putting Green | Shuffleboard Courts | Swimming Pool
888.269.4271
shellyb@cal-am.com
LESS THAN 60
BUILDABLE SITES REMAIN
6601 E. US Hwy 60 • Gold Canyon, AZ • 85118
www.SuperstitionViewsHomes.com
Good Sam Park
See listing Mesa, AZ

GRAND CANYON

Get an eyeful of America's favorite National Park

The crown jewel of American tourism is, without question, the Grand Canyon. Sweeping panoramic vistas—brushed with pastels of tawny orange and rust red at high noon, to soft mauve and glowing midnight blue at sunset—make it one of the most breathtaking natural attractions in the world. An abundance of campgrounds, RV parks and visitor amenities make stopping here both easy and profoundly rewarding, so be sure to set aside ample time in your Grand Canyon itinerary for some proper exploring.

> Check out the Grand Canyon IMAX Theater, a six-story screen that provides spine-tingling views of the canyon and its geological history.

The heart of Grand Canyon tourism is the South Rim Village, about a 90-minute drive north from Flagstaff. Here, the canyon runs a mile deep, spans 10 miles across and separates the South Rim from the lesser visited North Rim. Far below, the iconic Colorado River snakes its way westward to Lake Mead and the

Make a grand trip
Grander
STAY BY THE HISTORIC WILLIAMS DEPOT
Surround yourself with history and the modern comforts of the premiere RV park in the Grand Canyon region. Grand Canyon Railway RV Park is just a short walk from historic Route 66 and downtown Williams. Stay in this quaint mountain town in a Ponderosa pine forest setting just over 60 miles from the canyon. Make your stay even more memorable with a ride aboard the vintage Grand Canyon Railway, which departs daily.
» ULTRA-CLEAN AND MAINTAINED WITH PRIDE
» 124 EXTRA-WIDE SPACES, 50 AMP
» PULL-THROUGHS & BUDDY SPACES
» CABLE TV, FREE WIRELESS INTERNET ACCESS
» LAUNDRY FACILITIES AND CLEAN SHOWERS
» CONVENIENCE STORE & PET RESORT
» BASKETBALL, VOLLEYBALL COURTS, HORSESHOES, FITNESS TRAIL
» INDOOR SWIMMING POOL & HOT TUB
» JUST 2 BLOCKS FROM ROUTE 66
» ONLY ALL-PAVED PARK IN REGION
» OPEN ALL YEAR
CALL 1-800-THE-TRAIN OR VISIT THETRAIN.COM FOR RATES AND PACKAGE OPTIONS
Grand Canyon Railway RV Park
601 W. Franklin Ave., Williams, AZ 86046
Certificate of Excellence
2014 WINNER
Good Sam Park
GRAND CANYON
Railway & Hotel
EST. 1901
See listing Williams, AZ

Desert bighorn sheep navigate the region's rough terrain. NPS

Arizona-Nevada border.

Upon arrival at the South Rim, visitors will find a surprisingly vibrant little community, complete with its own small airport and railway service. Mysteriously, the average stay here for most visitors is only about 12 hours. But with so much to see and do, be sure to stray from the pack and spend at least a few days exploring the canyon's stunning array of trails and lookout points.

Goin' South

As you approach the South Rim, be sure to stop at the National Geographic Visitor Center first, before you make your way into the Village. Here you'll find information on lodging and South Rim attractions, as well as have the chance to sign up for National Geographic-led canyon tours. This is also the home of the Grand Canyon IMAX Theater, a six-story screen that provides spine-tingling views of the canyon and its geological history.

At the South Rim Village head straight to Mather Point for your first look at the Grand Canyon, and then go exploring. A free shuttle bus system makes getting around easy and cost-efficient. Be sure to hop on and hop off at Yavapai Point (home to Yavapai Observation Station), Kolb Studio (scenic lookout and rest house), the Powell Memorial, Hopi Point, Pima Point (where the sounds of river rapids far below reach the canyon rim) and Hermit's Rest (nationally protected stone building designed by Mary Colter).

Hikers will have their pick of the litter, with Bright Angel Trail, Tonto Trail, South Kaibab Trail and Hermit Trail each descending down into the canyon for unparalleled views. Hikes can be self-guided, Ranger-led, or done on the back of a mule.

Northern Rim

On the opposite bank of the canyon, the North Rim offers a similar selection of activities and amenities but is decidedly less popular due in part to its remoteness. Even though it's just 10 miles from the South Rim—as the crow flies—those wishing to visit both rims face a five-hour drive each way to do so. The North Rim is also closed to vehicles throughout the winter months (October 15 to May 15 each year). Winter hikers require valid backcountry permits.

For many, the smaller crowds found at the North Rim and its remoteness only add to its appeal. The North Rim Village offers a variety of lodging, shopping and dining options, as well as information on park trails, sights and free Ranger-led programs.

Be sure to make your way to Bright Angel Point, Point Imperial and Cape Royal. At Bright Angel Point, you'll be treated to some of the most iconic views and vantage points of the canyon, making for fantastic photos. Point Imperial is the highest point on the North Rim and offers stunning views of the Painted Desert (desert badlands) and Marble Canyon (where the Grand Canyon opens dramatically to take on its "grand" stature). And at Cape Royal lookout you'll find some of the best sunrise and sunset views of the canyon, as well as views of the Desert View Watchtower, Angels Window and Unkar Delta.

Further afield, Desert View (25 miles to the east of the South Rim Village) and Grand Canyon West (118 miles east of Las Vegas) are two popular visitor centers that offer a myriad of trails and attractions for tourists.

Desert View is home to the 70-foot Desert View Watchtower, the Tusayan Museum and an interpretive trail that winds through 800-year-old Tusayan ruins. Just a 45-minute drive east of the South Rim Village, this is an easy and highly recommended stop.

Grand Canyon West, for its part, is most popular with those traveling from Las Vegas. Operated by the native Hulapai people, the main attractions are Eagle Point, Guano Point, Hulapai Ranch and the world-famous Skywalk—a horseshoe shaped all-glass bridge that juts 70 feet out from the side of the canyon more than 4,000 feet above the canyon floor. Shuttle buses, guided tours and interpretive hikes are available to make exploring the Grand Canyon West area fun and easy.

Wherever you stop to explore this national natural treasure, be sure to set aside lots and lots of time. Hike to the canyon floor, picnic on the canyon rim and watch as the setting sun paints the canyon walls in bold new colors.

For More Information

Grand Canyon National Park
928-638-7888
www.nps.gov/grca

Arizona Office of Tourism
866-275-5816
www.arizonaguide.com

Getty Images/iStockphoto

METEOR CRATER/WINSLOW

Set a course for the site of one of the greatest collisions on Earth

The history of Meteor Crater, of course, started with a bang. A big bang. More than 50,000 years ago, several hundred thousand tons of space rock traveling 26,000 miles per hour crashed into the high desert plains of what is now northern Arizona. When the massive plume of dust and smoke settled (300 million tons of rock were displaced by the impact), a crater spanning more than 4,000 feet across and descending nearly 600 feet deep was left behind.

Located 44 miles east of Flagstaff and 186 miles north of Phoenix, this natural attraction and the nearby town of Winslow are found on Interstate 40, making this an easy destination.

Cosmic Crash

When you arrive at Meteor Crater you'll find yourself at the main Visitors Center, a state-of-the-art complex that's home to an interactive discovery center, 80-seat theater, air-conditioned indoor viewing areas and signups for guided crater rim tours.

Check out the interactive Visitor Discover Center, where guest-controlled computer simulators, Apollo astronaut training exhibits, asteroid samples and a 1,400-pound fragment from the impact are on display.

Head outside and take an eye-opening, jaw-dropping peek at the real thing. A series of self-guided observation paths weave their way around part of the crater for breathtaking views.

Such a Fine Sight to See...

Winslow, of course, is a pop culture icon for two big reasons. One, for its location on part of a stretch of historic Route 66. And two, for its mention in the famous Eagles' song, "Take It Easy."

The key line from the song—"Well I'm standin' on a corner in Winslow, Arizona, such a fine sight to see/It's a girl my Lord, in a flatbed Ford, slowin' down to take a look at me"—has inspired untold thousands of tourists to stop and stand for a photo op on the most famous corner in rock and roll history. The site has even been transformed into "Standin' On The Corner Park," home to official photo ops and quirky Route 66 memorabilia.

For More Information

Meteor Crater Enterprises
800-289-5898
www.meteorcrater.com

Arizona Office of Tourism
866-275-5816
www.arizonaguide.com

QUARTZSITE

Wheel and deal in this bustling desert bazaar

On the surface, the small footprint community of Quartzsite is just another sleepy western Arizona town that's nestled in the vast expanses of the sprawling Sonoran Desert. Home to less than 4,000 permanent residents and sitting 128 miles west of Phoenix, it offers a modest selection of amenities, heaping doses of down-to-earth charm and easy access to nearby natural attractions, including the Colorado River just 18 miles to the west.

But in winter, however, something incredible happens—the population swells from just fewer than 4,000 to upwards of one million, as visitors from around the world descend on the town for eight major gem and mineral trade shows.

Showtime!

The tradition dates back to 1965 and now encompasses eight major trade shows, including the Quartzsite Sports, Vacation and RV Show and the Tyson Wells Rock and Gem Show. Running in January and February, these events draw thousands of vendors and hundreds of thousands of visitors to town for one of the world's largest open-air flea markets. Tables and tents full of not only rare rocks and gems but also everything from camping gear and RV equipment to hand-made leather jackets and custom-made furniture make this a bargain hunter's dream.

The Sports, Vacation and RV Show is particularly popular. Billed as "the largest gathering of RVers in the world," visitors will find every conceivable piece of equipment, upgrade or RV contraption they can think of here.

Quartzsite's Wild Side

January and February aren't the only times of year to visit Quartzsite. The surrounding Sonoran landscape is a giant playground for outdoor recreation, with a bevy of dedicated hiking, biking and ATV trails.

The town is also near Kofa National Wildlife Refuge, Cibola National Wildlife Refuge, Imperial National Wildlife Refuge and Palm Canyon.

To the north of Quartzsite, hikers can explore an area once used by General George S. Patton as a training ground for his U.S. Army troops during World War II.

For More Information

Quartzsite Business Chamber of Commerce
928-927-9321
www.quartzsitebusinesschamber.com

Arizona Office of Tourism
866-275-5816
www.arizonaguide.com

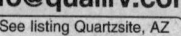

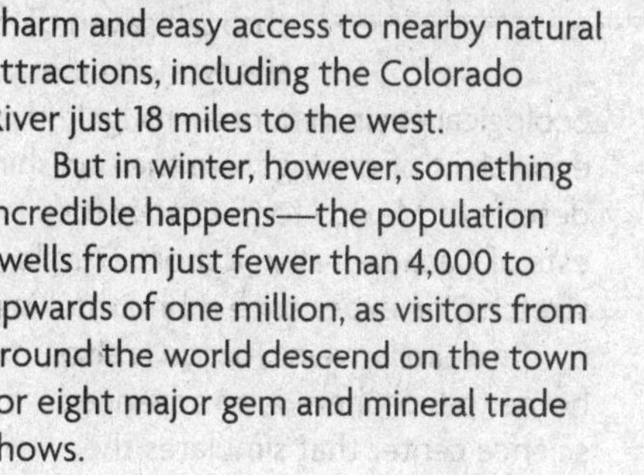

Getty Images/iStockphoto

SPOTLIGHT

TUCSON

Discover compelling urban charms in the Sonoran Desert

Nestled in the Sonoran Desert and surrounded by five sun-soaked mountain ranges, the surprising city of Tucson is a welcome change of pace from more hectic destinations like Phoenix, 115 miles to the northwest. With just over half-a-million residents, this is now the 32nd largest city in the country, and its selection of world-class dining, lodging, shopping and entertainment options reflect that.

When it comes to activities and entertainment, no matter where your interests lie or what you feel in the mood for on any given day, Tucson has a wide range of choices. From state-of-the-art science education centers and unique open-air museums to breathtaking natural environments and family-friendly attractions like Reid Park Zoo, this is the perfect place to set up camp. And with 360 days of annual sunshine each year, it doesn't matter when you plan your visit.

> With 360 days of annual sunshine each year, it doesn't matter when you plan your visit to Tucson.

Tucson's legendary Fox Theatre.
Arizona Office of Tourism

The Call of the Wild

Start with the great outdoors. As impressive as the city of Tucson is, it's no match for the landscapes surrounding it. The only problem you'll face is narrowing down your choices. Saguaro National Park, Catalina State Park, Sabino Canyon Recreation Area and Colossal Cave Mountain Park all sit within easy driving distance of the downtown core.

Nearby Mount Lemmon is an absolute must-visit. It's the southernmost ski area in the country, so skiers and snowboarders will be in their element, but it's the Mt Lemmon National Scenic Byway that's the real attraction here. A drive from the valley floor to the 9,157-foot summit includes passing through seven of the world's nine ecological environments—roughly the equivalent of driving from the punishing deserts of Mexico to the rocky forests of Canada—all in a short 27-mile stretch. The experience is breathtaking.

In a similar vein, Tucson is also home to Biosphere 2, an advanced science center that simulates the earth's complete biosphere in a closed, controlled system. It was recently named by Time Life Books as one of the 50 Wonders of the World. Man-made oceans, rainforests, deserts and forests exist in a self-sufficient artificial environment. Guided tours are led by

scientists who guide guests deep into the rich upper biomes and the complex technical underbelly of the project.

For families traveling with children, the Arizona-Sonora Desert Museum and the Reid Park Zoo make for great day trips.

The former is a unique fusion of zoo, natural history museum, art gallery, aquarium and botanical garden. More than three-quarters of the Arizona-Sonora Desert Museum is outdoors, so this is the perfect way to blend the experience with some open-air recreation. Two miles of walkable paths weave through more than 20 acres of Sonoran Desert habitats, showcasing 230 animal species and 1,200 types of plants.

Meanwhile, at the 24-acre Reid Park Zoo, visitors can not only view a range of exotic animals but also engage in a series of educational activities. Keeper chats, giraffe encounters, camel rides and the in-park zoo train are among the highlights.

Kids will also love Funtasticks Family Fun Park (home to laser-tag, go-karts, bumper boats and mini golf), the Children's Museum (11,000 square feet of interactive exhibits) and Old Tucson (where gunfights of the Wild West are brought to life with fun live performances).

Art, Arizona Style

Of course, any rewarding stopover in Tucson means spending some time in the city itself. And that means a whirlwind of art.

Cited as a "mini-mecca for the arts" by the *Wall Street Journal*, Tucson has established itself as one of the nation's leading arts and cultural heritage centers. The downtown core is home to 35 art galleries, more than 30 museums and 215 performance groups.

A mountain lion in the Reid Park Zoo.
Arizona Office of Tourism

If you're an art lover, be sure to take in a show or two at famous Fox Theatre (a restored 1930's era movie "palace"), a performance from the Tucson Symphony Orchestra (founded in 1929) and a guided docent-led tour through the Tucson Museum of Art.

When you're done exploring for the day, settle in for a night for gourmet dining and relaxation. Home more than half-a-million people, this thriving modern city is packed with international cuisine options, mega-complex shopping centers and a host of world-class casinos.

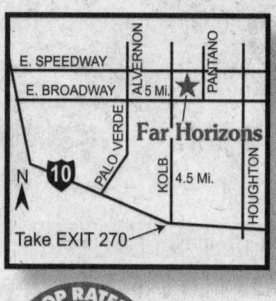

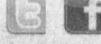

From its stunning ring of mountain ranges to its robust industry of arts and entertainment, Tucson is a premier destination that finds itself all too often overlooked. For tourists seeking a place to escape and explore, that makes it just perfect. Full of big city amenities and home to great outdoor adventures, this bustling cityscape still feels more like a laid-back community than a major American city on the rise.

If exercise and relaxation occupy the top of your travel list, consider dropping into Oro Valley, just 30 minutes to the north of Tucson. Fitness buffs will enjoy the wide choices of world-class cycling, swimming, golf and hiking trails. Nearby Catalina State Park features an equestrian center along with lots of hiking opportunities. Every Saturday, the Oro Valley Farmers market sells locally grown fruits and veggies for travelers eager to stock their pantries.

Can't get enough of the rugged desert country? Make a visit to Tucson Mountain Park, 20,000 acres of rugged landscape dotted with cactus and threaded with 62 miles of non-motorized shared-use trails. Located just 20 minutes to the west of the city, the park is one of the largest natural resource areas owned and managed by a local government in the United States, and visitors will find no end to the recreation opportunities in this stunning area. Enjoy breathtaking views at Gates Pass overlook, and then study the interpretive displays and historic structures. Picnic and wildlife-watching opportunities abound throughout the park, so pack a basket and set aside some time—it's worth an afternoon or a day.

If you'd prefer to see the rugged Arizona wilderness without a tough hike, the Sabino Canyon Trail, northwest of town, is the answer. Ride on a comfortable tram for a 45-minute, 3.8-mile tour into the foothills of the Santa Catalina Mountains. With nine stops, you'll have lots of opportunities to take pictures of spectacular landscapes and local wildlife, including javelina, roadrunners, white-tailed deer and more. Evening rides are available.

For More Information

Tucson Visitor Center
800-638-8350
www.visittucson.org

Arizona Office of Tourism
866-275-5816
www.arizonaguide.com

A stream flows through Lower Bear Canyon near Tucson. Arizona Office of Tourism

© Greater Phoenix CVB—Jill Richards

VALLEY OF THE SUN

This region shines with an array of fun-filled attractions

Veteran snowbirds and seasoned Southwesterners know that there's lots to do in the "Valley of the Sun," the 20 or so communities that make up this desert valley destination. The valley offers a multitude of activities for visitors from all walks of life. Scattered among the bigger cities of Phoenix, Glendale, Scottsdale and Mesa, travelers will find charming small communities with as much to offer as their more bustling neighbors.

Go back to the beginning and see what the valley's earliest inhabitants left behind. Deer Valley Rock Art Center near Sun City is operated by Arizona State University's Department of Anthropology and is dedicated to preserving more than 1,500 petroglyphs—some of which were created as long as 10,000 years ago by pre-Archaic, Archaic, Hohokam and Patayan people.

Arizona's stunning natural beauty is the star of Wickenburg in the High Sonoran Desert. Resting adjacent to the mostly underground Hassayampa River in Wickenburg, kids will choose their own adventure at the Arthur L. Johnson Visitor Center. The interactive displays inside are just the start; outside, where the river comes to the surface, a diverse ecological world awaits visitors. Explore the Hassayampa River Preserve on a trail walk, either self-guided or led by a knowledgeable docent. Keen observers will spot lizards like the rare Gilbert's skink darting in the underbrush.

> In Carefree, the night sky reveals its starry splendor over the granite hills. Local stargazing tours are offered to folks eager to learn about the constellations.

When the sun sets in the west, the town of Carefree in the east is the place to be. The night sky reveals its starry splendor over the granite hills and, if you prefer some assistance in spotting Ursa Minor, local stargazing tours are offered in Carefree as well as other areas of the valley.

Forest Fun

The rugged forests that shoulder the valley to the north are havens for lovers of the great outdoors. McDowell Mountain Regional Park offers several outdoor programs when weather permits, including sunset hikes that culminate under the light of the full moon. There are more than 40 miles of multi-use trails suited for mountain biking, horseback riding and hiking. The park's nature center hosts several activities for young visitors, too. Kids can become junior rangers, engage in nature-craft activities and even watch the center's resident reptiles enjoy a noon meal.

NEW
Eagle View RV Resort
At Fort McDowell, Arizona
Asah gweh Oou-o
FREE Wi-Fi
AN OASIS IN THE VALLEY OF THE SUN
Scottsdale Area
Great Rates
Free Breakfast Pastries
5 Restaurants at Fort McDowell Casino
Boats & RV Storage
Dog Park
Discounts to We Ko Pa Golf Club
Internet Hardwire Available at Certain Sites
State of the Art Fitness Center
Basketball, Pickle-Ball, Bocci Ball & Badminton Court
Close to 4 Major Spring League Ballparks
Minutes to Mayo Clinic
TOP RATED Good Sam Park FOR 2016
FORT MCDOWELL RV RESORT
Asah gweh Oou-o
EAGLE VIEW
Good Sam RATED 10/10★/10
9605 N . Fort McDowell Rd., Fort McDowell, AZ 85264
www.eagleviewrvresort.com
480.789.5310
See listing Fort McDowell, AZ

A Scottsdale golf course winds through the desert. Getty Images/iStockphoto

Views from Sanctuary Resort in Paradise Valley
© Greater Phoenix CVB

Spot Javelina, coyotes and other wildlife as you explore.

Despite Arizona's arid reputation, fishermen will be pleased to learn that rainbow trout can be found year-round north of Mesa in the Salt River, below Saguaro Lake, where the water stays a cool 65 degrees. Bass fishing in the valley is equally challenging and satisfying. Apache Lake, along with Saguaro and Canyon Lake are home to robust populations of largemouth bass and yellow bass. Each lake provides space for shoreline fishing as well as dock and ramp access.

Despite Arizona's arid reputation, fishermen will be pleased to learn that rainbow trout can be found year-round north of Mesa in the Salt River.

Golf is a major draw for avid players and fans of the sport; besides hosting a handful of professional tours, the region boasts nearly 200 courses, including many municipal greens and high-end courses that are open daily. Whether you hit a few at Superstition Springs Golf Club in the East, or at Dove Valley Ranch in the West, there's a course for every skill level.

Journey to the Past

Escape the heat of the valley with a trip into one or more of the area's great museums. The world of music is captured and displayed at the Musical Instrument Museum in Phoenix. More than a place to see, this tuneful museum is place where visitors can also play instruments from around the globe, such as the Southeast Asian gamelan, and where they can enjoy concerts, workshops and classes.

A quieter museum experience can be found at the Scottsdale Museum of

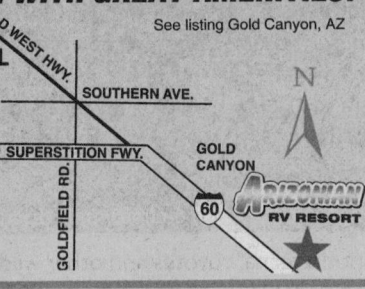

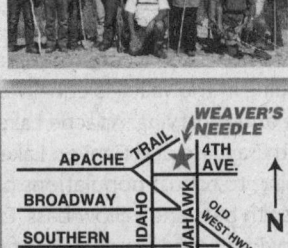

Contemporary Art. Traveling and permanent exhibits showcase the beauty and creativity of everyday objects and elegant pieces.

If the Wild West is what you saddle up for, then visit the Pioneer Living History Museum, west of Cave Creek, where more than 20 preserved structures such as a bakery, cabins and even an opera house help recreate life for settlers in the mid-19th century. In addition to authentic architecture, the museum hosts demonstrations and even battle reenactments. Also offered are self-guided tours of the village and military camps. Check out the restored jailhouse, home to several artifacts including a gun rack, rolltop desk and bunks for inmates.

Fans of TV westerns need to take in the sights at the Superstition Mountain Museum, where a barn famous for its role in the classic "The Rifleman" now sits alongside other historic pieces, including the Elvis Memorial Chapel—so named for its role in the movie "Charro," starring Elvis Presley. The museum's prehistoric Indian exhibit displays Hohokam and Salado artifacts, including bowls, awls, arrowheads, stone hammers, axe heads and shell pendants. Visitors will also see an exhibit dedicated to the legend of the Dutchman's Lost Mine. In the same vein, gold ore and other stones are on display at the goeological exhibit.

North of Phoenix lies the ruin of a town that was born from gold-rush fever. Stanton was founded as Antelope Station and was the site of large gold deposits discovered in the mid-1860s. Near the turn of the century, Stanton was a bustling town with resident miners and businesses such as a stamp mill, hotel and boarding house. But when the gold ran dry, the town was abandoned. Now visitors can wander through well-preserved buildings that are part of an operating RV park.

For More Information

Greater Phoenix Convention and Visitors Bureau
877-CALLPHX
www.visitphoenix.com

Arizona Office of Tourism
866-275-5816
www.arizonaguide.com

Scottsdale South Bridge. Getty Images/iStockphoto

Sedona Chamber of Commerce Tourism Bureau

VERDE VALLEY/SEDONA

Take a breather in green valleys and rugged landscapes

When the thought of scraping ice off your windshield makes you shiver, it's time to pack the RV with plenty of shorts and sunscreen and head out to a place where the daytime temperatures in the winter rarely drop below 60. In Sedona and Camp Verde, both in Arizona's Verde Valley, you'll find a warm climate along with lots of shopping, golf, art and loads of sightseeing opportunities.

> Great beasts of the wild have a home in Camp Verde's Out of Africa Wildlife Park. Get close to bears and tigers.

Sentinals of Stone

When you arrive in Sedona, you'll be amazed at the beauty of your surroundings. The area's red rocks reach for the sky and loom like guards watching over the city. Wake every morning to a warm cup of coffee and see this view out your window.

Awaken your Spirit

For decades, people have been coming to Sedona for spiritual awakenings. This Mecca for artists, healers and spiritual guides has made the area the place to go for personal enrichment. The red rock formations that encompass the town bring a peaceful feeling to all who view them. Visit one of Sedona's spas for a day of relaxation or simple pampering. Hike into the red rock temples and find one of the many "vortex sites" that circle the town. These enhanced-energy sites facilitate prayer and create the potential for spiritual renewal.

Even if you don't believe in this sort of thing, you certainly won't be able to deny the special beauty and energy of Sedona. Hike or bike into Oak Creek Canyon, where you'll find more than 100 trails from challenging to simple. Imagine watching the sunrise while floating under a beautifully colored hot air balloon that's riding a thermal. If you'd like a little more speed, take a tour in a jeep or on an ATV. Each brings with it a different style, taste and experience.

Fodder for Photographers

Sedona sits in the heart of the Coconino National Forest, home to Oak Creek Canyon, which some visitors have described as the smaller cousin of the Grand Canyon. Clean the lens on your camera and pack a few extra SD cards because you won't want to miss a single shot from the breathtaking vistas on the scenic drive through the park. Drive along the switchbacks of this national forest and experience diverse landscapes from ponderosa pines and mountain lakes to the amazing red rock formations of Sedona itself.

When you get back to Sedona, you'll want to see and photograph all of the rock formations that make this place famous. Most of those formations have been named over the years. You'll want to capture the sunrise on Coffee Pot Rock, or watch as an Eagle flies over Doe Mountain. Stand on Airport Mesa at mid-day and get a bird's eye view of the area. From here, you can see nearly all the formations, including Steam Boat

Devils Bridge in Sedona. Sedona Chamber of Commerce Tourism Bureau

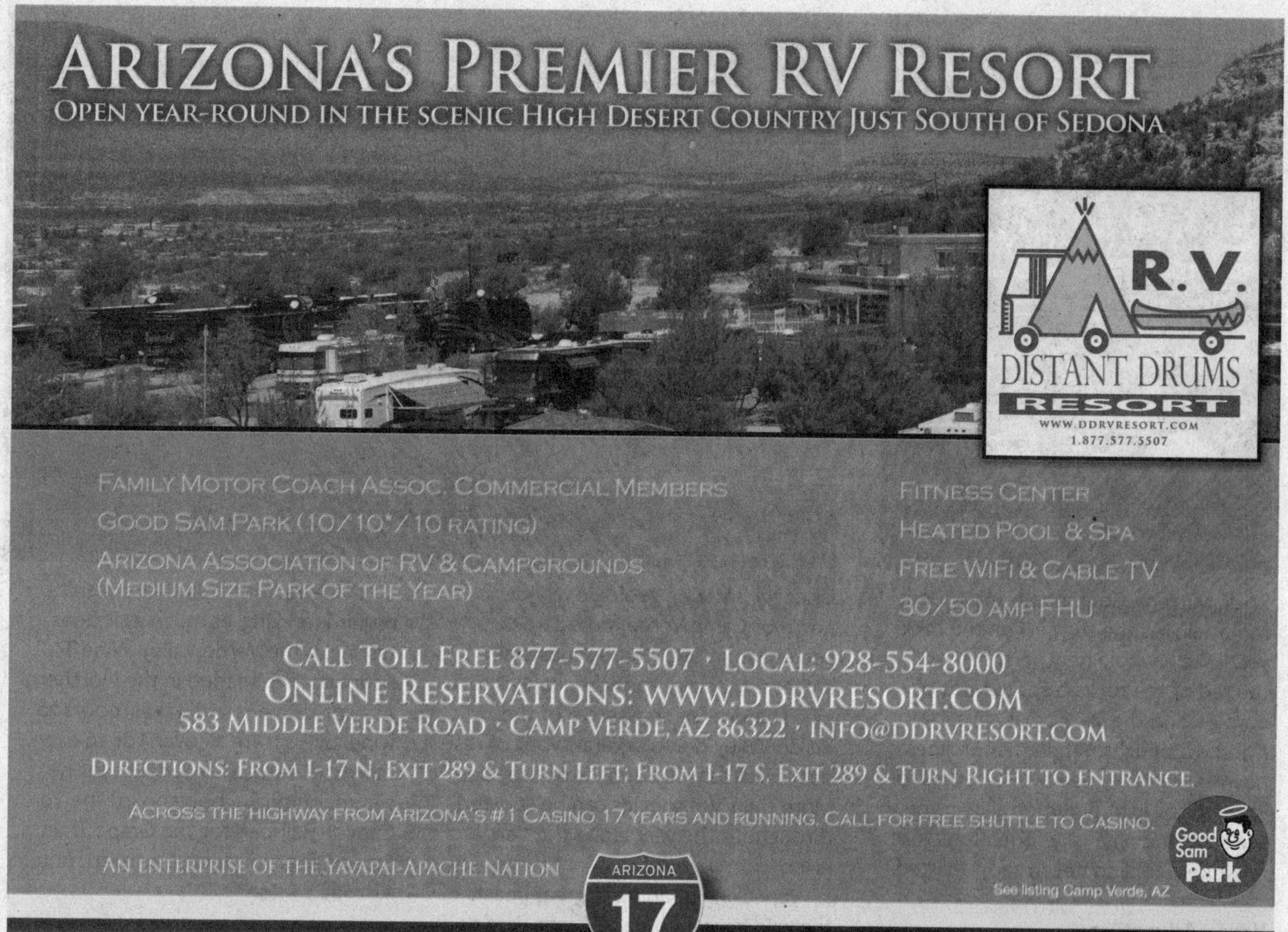
ARIZONA'S PREMIER RV RESORT
OPEN YEAR-ROUND IN THE SCENIC HIGH DESERT COUNTRY JUST SOUTH OF SEDONA
R.V.
DISTANT DRUMS
RESORT
WWW.DDRVRESORT.COM
1.877.577.5507
FAMILY MOTOR COACH ASSOC. COMMERCIAL MEMBERS
GOOD SAM PARK (10/10*/10 RATING)
ARIZONA ASSOCIATION OF RV & CAMPGROUNDS (MEDIUM SIZE PARK OF THE YEAR)
FITNESS CENTER
HEATED POOL & SPA
FREE WIFI & CABLE TV
30/50 AMP FHU
CALL TOLL FREE 877-577-5507 · LOCAL: 928-554-8000
ONLINE RESERVATIONS: WWW.DDRVRESORT.COM
583 MIDDLE VERDE ROAD · CAMP VERDE, AZ 86322 · INFO@DDRVRESORT.COM
DIRECTIONS: FROM I-17 N, EXIT 289 & TURN LEFT; FROM I-17 S, EXIT 289 & TURN RIGHT TO ENTRANCE.
ACROSS THE HIGHWAY FROM ARIZONA'S #1 CASINO 17 YEARS AND RUNNING. CALL FOR FREE SHUTTLE TO CASINO.
AN ENTERPRISE OF THE YAVAPAI-APACHE NATION
ARIZONA
17
Good Sam Park
See listing Camp Verde, AZ

CLIFF CASTLE CASINO
Come see why we've been voted the number 1 casino in Arizona for 17 years in a row.
Just across I-17 from Distant Drums RV Resort.
• Newest, most popular slot machines
• Live Blackjack and Poker
• Kids Quest Supervised Daycare
• Shake, Rattle & Bowl
• Four restaurants offering casual to upscale dining
CLIFF CASTLE
CASINO · HOTEL
The Perfect Place to Play.
cliffcastlecasinohotel.com
800.381.7568 | I-17, Exit 289 · Camp Verde
VOTED No. 1

Montezuma's Castle in Verde Valley.
Arizona Tourism/Edward_Bottomley

A pine tree grows next to red rocks near Sedona. Getty Images/iStockphoto

Rock, Mittens, Cockscomb and Munds Mountain. As the sun sets on the rocks, you'll see a whole new perspective; the red of the rocks turns to hues of purples, and the sky comes alive in a fire show of light. When the sun goes down, an entirely new world comes to life. Limited light pollution allows you to see stars and night sky formations that most people didn't even know existed.

Verde Adventures

Outdoor enthusiasts will discover lots of opportunities to boat or kayak down the Verde River. Camp Verde's location on the downstream end of the valley makes it the only access point to Fossil Creek. Here, a spring feeds a stream at the rate of 20,000 gallons per minute.

Discover amazing geologic wonders north of Camp Verde to Red Rock Secret Mountain, where sandstone arches and secret spots beckon visitors.

The diverse ecosystem of the Verde Valley draws several types of resident birds as well as migratory species. More than 300 species can be spotted throughout the year along the Verde River.

Speaking of animals, great beasts of the wild have a home in Camp Verde's Out of Africa Wildlife Park, where visitors take a safari-style tour that puts them close to the animals, including giraffes, bears, tigers and wolves. Shows and interactive sessions are also offered at the 104-acre park.

High rollers and occasional gamblers can try their luck at Cliff Castle Casino Hotel, home to nearly 700 slot machines and plenty of card tables. At Fort Verde State Historic Park, history and adventure meet: Let the kids earn Junior Ranger status and learn more about the site's use by U.S. Army troops in the late 19th century. Take advantage of great weather when you're at Camp Verde by fishing, paddle boating and enjoying a hayride at Arizona Equestrian Connection.

One Arizona trail that doesn't require trekking, as much as it does tasting, is the Verde Valley Wine Trail. Four wineries nestled in the Northern Arizona canyons open their doors to wine lovers from all over. For an even more memorable experience in the summer months, hop aboard the Verde Canyon Railroad for the Grape Train Escape as an immersive introduction to Arizona wines.

Ancient Indian Ruins

The abundant fish and wildlife, water and moderate temperatures year-round are what have always made this area desirable for human occupation. Long before the hot air balloons and ATV tours, the ancient Anasazi called this area of Arizona home. In the beautiful red rocks around the region, visitors can find numerous ruins from a Pre-Columbian Society.

Most of the ruins are not accessible by foot, but information can be found on them at the Red Rock Ranger District. Montezuma's Cliff Castle in Verde Valley is a stunning example of ingenuity and skill of the ancient builders. Take your time as you explore the legacies of the region's first inhabitants.

For More Information

Sedona Verde Valley Tourism Council
877-GoSVVTC
www.sedona-verdevalley.com

Arizona Office of Tourism
866-275-5816
www.arizonaguide.com

AZ

Yuma Visitors Bureau

YUMA

History meets nature in this perennial resort

Nature, history, arts and the great outdoors collaborate in Yuma to delight visitors from all walks of life. Not just for snowbirds or retirees, Yuma offers fun for young and old, active and leisurely alike. This thriving city rests on the banks of the Colorado River, once a site of exploration by Spanish adventurers and later a city of swift passage to California for settlers eager to find riches during the Gold Rush.

In modern-day Yuma, the unique geography calls to outdoor enthusiasts. Enjoy a night under the stars at Kofa National Wildlife Refuge, and look out for the park's treasured residents, desert bighorn sheep. Enjoy a cool morning hike along the Palm Canyon Trail and bring your binoculars or camera to spot more of the desert's diverse inhabitants.

Birdwatchers are happy to know that upwards of 400 species live or migrate to the waterways surrounding the city. Sites like East Wetlands restoration area and Mittry Lake welcome geese, teal, kites and even bald eagles.

Hunting enthusiasts can pursue limited seasonal opportunities to bag doves, elk and small game, and among other species. The Arizona Game And Fish Department welcomes inquiries and provides detailed information on permissible hunting in the state.

Fed by the River

Yuma's proximity to the Colorado River and several lakes makes it a great destination for boaters and water-loving adventurers. On the Arizona side of Imperial Dam, Martinez Lake gives visitors a chance to go kayaking, canoeing or fishing by boat. On a hot day, you can relax and enjoy a lazy ride down the Colorado River on an inner tube for as little as an hour, or as long as three hours, depending on where you launch.

Largemouth, smallmouth and striped bass make their homes in many of the hidden lakes and water channels created when the dam was constructed. Drop a line in Squaw Lake or Ferguson Lake, or in the Colorado River channel. Board a paddleboat sternwheeler for a chance to see the landscape slide by as you travel down the river.

Explore Yuma's historic downtown, where Main Street once marked the end of the Gila Trail. The oldest buildings date to the 1920s; flooding prior to the 20th century took its toll on the adobe structures that populated the city, often turning them back into mud. In downtown Yuma, stop in at the

Clouds reflected on the Colorado River near Yuma. Yuma Visitors Bureau

Yuma Art Center and visit the recently restored Ocean-to-Ocean Bridge.

The outlaw past of Yuma remains preserved at Yuma Territorial Prison State Historic Park. Though open for just over three decades, the prison's reputation as a tough place for criminals to do time remains.

Yuma's Quartermaster Depot is the birthplace of Southwestern military outposts that were established between 1864 and 1884. The 10-acre park hosts U.S. Army warehouses used to store goods for those posts, and it also features exhibits on the engineering projects that brought irrigation water to the desert valley.

The Castle Dome Mines Museum pays tribute to the mining boom and the town that sprang up as a result. This recreated "ghost town" is a collection of nearly 24 buildings surrounded by the Kofa National Wildlife Refuge. Each structure acts as a freestanding museum, decorated and outfitted with period artifacts. Take a self-guided hike through the mining district and enjoy the area's desert beauty.

Nearby Somerton is home to the Cocopah Museum and Cultural Center, a tribute to the Cocopah, or River People, who thrived along the lower Colorado River for more than 3,000 years. Across the state line in Bard, California, vintage automobiles inspire nostalgia at the Cloud Museum.

Soaring Over Yuma

Escape the confines of gravity in a hot-air balloon trip during the winter season and drift over farmland and desert to watch the sunrise over the Gila Mountains. Catch a race at the Cocopah Speedway or take the family to Wild River Family Entertainment Center, where arcade games and billiards share space with laser tag and karaoke.

Little ones will have a blast at Stewart Vincent Wolfe Memorial Playground, designed by local children, and built by volunteers. The park features a dragon slide and a kid-size Old West town. Meet a herd of dromedary camels and 25 other species of animals at Wild World Zoo and Camel Farm.

For More Information

Yuma Visitor Information Center
800-293-0071
www.visityuma.com

Arizona Office of Tourism
866-275-5816
www.arizonaguide.com

Arizona

CONSULTANTS

Northern Arizona

Randy & Debbie Block

Southern Arizona

Alan & Teresa Breuer

AJO — E2 *Pima*

AJO HEIGHTS RV PARK
Ratings: 8.5/9★/10 (RV Park) From Jct of MP-40 & Hwy 85, S 0.3 mi on Hwy 85 (L); or From center of town (Plaza), N 1.9 mi on Hwy 85 (R). **FAC:** All weather rds. 40 Avail: 40 all weather, patios, 6 pull-thrus (28 x 50), back-ins (30 x 50), accepts full hkup units only, 40 full hkups (30/50 amps), cable, WiFi, dump, laundry. **REC.** Pet restrict(B/Q). No tents. 2015 rates: $28 to $34. Disc: AAA. Oct 1 to May 1. No CC.
(520)387-6796 Lat: 32.39326, Lon: -112.87187
2000 N Ajo-Gila Bend Hwy, Ajo, AZ 85321
ajoheights@gmail.com
www.ajorvparks.com

BELLY ACRES RV PARK
Ratings: 6/7.5★/8.5 (RV Park) From Jct of MP-40 & Hwy 85, S 0.3 mi on Hwy 85 (L); or from center of town (Plaza), N 1.9 mi on Hwy 85 (R). **FAC:** All weather rds. (35 spaces). Avail: 33 gravel, patios, 17 pull-thrus (20 x 45), back-ins (18 x 40), 33 full hkups (30/50 amps), seasonal sites, cable, WiFi, showers $, dump, laundry, LP gas. **REC.** Pets OK. No tents. 2015 rates: $25. Disc: AAA.
(520)387-5767 Lat: 32.39416, Lon: -112.87184
2030 N Hwy 85, Ajo, AZ 85321
kord62@yahoo.com
www.bellyacresrvpark.com
See ad this page.

LA SIESTA MOTEL & RV RESORT **Ratings: 7/6.5/8.5** (RV Park) 2015 rates: $30. (520)387-6569 2561 N Ajo-Gila Bend Hwy, Ajo, AZ 85321

SHADOW RIDGE RV RESORT
Ratings: 8/9★/8.5 (RV Park) N-bnd: From Plaza (center of town), N 0.8 mi on Hwy 85 (L); S-bnd: From Jct of Hwy 85 & MP 40, S 1.5 mi (R). **FAC:** All weather rds. (125 spaces). Avail: 105 gravel, patios, 62 pull-thrus (22 x 45), back-ins (25 x 34), accepts full hkup units only, 105 full hkups (30/50 amps), seasonal sites, cable, WiFi, tent sites, laundry. **REC.** Pets OK. Partial handicap access. 2015 rates: $27.50. Disc: AAA.
(520)387-5055 Lat: 32.37551, Lon: -112.87243
431 N 2nd Ave (Hwy 85), Ajo, AZ 85321
jmmherd@hotmail.com
www.shadowridgerv.com

Check out those views! From awe-inspiring redwood giants to the soaring towers of the Golden Gate Bridge, we've put the Spotlight on North America's most popular travel destinations. Turn to the Spotlight articles in our State and Province sections to learn more.

AMADO — E4 *Santa Cruz*

DE ANZA RV RESORT
Ratings: 10/9★/10 (RV Park) S-bnd: From Jct of I-19 & Arivaca Rd (Exit 48), S 1.5 mi on East Frontage Rd (L); N-bnd: From Jct of I-19 & Agualinda Rd (Exit 42), N 2 mi on East Frontage Rd (R). Elev 3200 ft. **FAC:** Paved rds. 130 Avail: 130 all weather, patios, 16 pull-thrus (30 x 70), back-ins (35 x 55), accepts full hkup units only, 130 full hkups (30/50 amps), cable, WiFi, rentals, laundry, firewood, restaurant, controlled access. **REC:** heated pool, whirlpool, shuffleboard. Pet restrict(Q). Partial handicap access, no tents. Big rig sites, eco-friendly, 2015 rates: $36 to $44. Disc: AAA.
(520)398-8628 Lat: 31.70562, Lon: -111.06379
2869 E Frontage Rd, Amado, AZ 85645
info@deanzarvresort.com
www.deanzarvresort.com
See ad page 86.

MOUNTAIN VIEW RV RANCH **Ratings: 7/8/8** (RV Park) 2015 rates: $29. (520)398-9401 2843 E Frontage Rd, Amado, AZ 85645

APACHE JUNCTION — D3 *Maricopa, Pinal*

APACHE JUNCTION See also Chandler, Coolidge, Florence, Gold Canyon, Mesa, Phoenix, Queen Valley, Scottsdale & Tempe.

BUDGET RV PARK
Ratings: 6.5/7.5/8 (RV Park) From Jct of Hwy 60 & Tomahawk Rd (exit 197), N 1 mi on Tomahawk Rd to Old West Highway, E 0.6 mi to Cortez Rd, S 0.1 mi (R). **FAC:** Paved rds. (176 spaces). Avail: 100 all weather, patios, back-ins (24 x 43), 100 full hkups (30/50 amps), seasonal sites, WiFi, laundry. **REC.** Pet restrict(Q). No tents. 2015 rates: $25.
(480)982-5856 Lat: 33.39697, Lon: -111.52046
2024 S Cortez Rd, Apache Junction, AZ 85119
See ad page 44 (Welcome Section).

CAREFREE MANOR RV RESORT **Ratings: 8.5/7.5/9** (RV Park) 2015 rates: $30. (480)982-4008 1615 N Delaware Dr, Space 57, Apache Junction, AZ 85120

CHEROKEE VILLAGE MH & RV PARK **Ratings: 8.5/5/6** (RV Park) 2015 rates: $45. (480)986-4132 10540 E Apache Trail, Apache Junction, AZ 85120

COUNTRYSIDE RV RESORT **Ratings: 8.5/9.5★/7.5** (Membership Pk) 2015 rates: $38. (800)405-6188 2701 S Idaho Rd, Apache Junction, AZ 85119

GOLDEN SUN RV RESORT **Ratings: 9.5/8.5/9** (RV Park) 2015 rates: $39. (800)405-6188 999 W Broadway Ave, Apache Junction, AZ 85120

IRONWOOD MOBILE HOME PARK **Ratings: 10/8.5/9.5** (RV Area in MHP) 2015 rates: $50. (480)982-3413 1280 N Ironwood Dr, Apache Junction, AZ 85120

LA HACIENDA RV RESORT
Ratings: 9.5/10★/9.5 (RV Resort) From Jct of US Hwy 60 & Ironwood Dr (exit 195), N 200 yds on Ironwood Dr to 28th, W 250 ft (L). **FAC:** Paved rds. (280 spaces). Avail: 45 gravel, patios, back-ins (34 x 54), 45 full hkups (30/50 amps), seasonal sites, cable, WiFi, laundry, controlled access. **REC:** heated pool, whirlpool, shuffleboard. Pet restrict(B/Q). Partial handicap access, no tents. Age restrict may apply, RV age restrict, eco-friendly, 2015 rates: $44.
(480)982-2808 Lat: 33.38900, Lon: -111.56585
1797 W 28th Ave, Apache Junction, AZ 85120
info@lahaciendarv.com
www.lahaciendarv.com
See ad pages 69 (Spotlight Valley of the Sun), 52 & Snowbird Destinations in Magazine Section.

Are you using a friend's Guide? Want one of your own? Call 877-209-6655.

LOST DUTCHMAN
(State Pk) From Jct of US 60 & S Idaho Rd (AZ-88), N 1.9 mi on S Idaho to N Apache Trail, NE 5 mi (R). **FAC:** Paved rds. 70 paved, 42 pull-thrus (25 x 80), back-ins (25 x 50) (30/50 amps), tent sites, dump, fire rings. **REC:** rec open to public. Pets OK. Partial handicap access. 14 day max stay, 2015 rates: $25 to $30. Disc: military.
(480)982-4485 Lat: 33.464206, Lon: -111.481962
6109 N Apache Trail, Apache Junction, AZ 85119
www.azstateparks.com
See ad page 49 (Welcome Section).

MERIDIAN MOBILE HOME PARK **Ratings: 8.5/9★/7.5** (RV Area in MHP) 2015 rates: $35. (480)982-1193 351 N Meridian Rd, Apache Junction, AZ 85120

MERIDIAN RV RESORT
Ratings: 10/10★/9.5 (RV Resort) From Jct of US-60 & Signal Butte Rd, (exit 193), N 0.5 mi on Signal Butte Rd to Southern Ave, E 1 mi to Meridian, N 0.2 mi (R). **FAC:** Paved rds. (254 spaces). Avail: 154 all weather, patios, back-ins (32 x 40), 154 full hkups (30/50 amps), seasonal sites, WiFi, rentals, laundry. **REC:** heated pool, whirlpool. Pet restrict(B/Q). Partial handicap access, no tents. Age restrict may apply, RV age restrict, eco-friendly, 2015 rates: $49. Disc: AAA, military.
(866)770-0080 Lat: 33.39782, Lon: -111.58005
1901 S Meridian, Apache Junction, AZ 85120
info@meridianrvresort.com
www.meridianrvresort.com
See ad this page, 52.

MESA APACHE JUNCTION KOA **Ratings: 7.5/7.5/8.5** (Campground) 2015 rates: $38. (480)982-4015 1540 S Tomahawk Rd, Apache Junction, AZ 85119

PACIFIC MOBILE MANOR **Ratings: 9/8.5★/8.5** (RV Area in MHP) 2015 rates: $35. (480)373-9790 10220 E Apache Trail, Apache Junction, AZ 85120

SHADY REST MH/RV COMMUNITY **Ratings: 8/7/8.5** (RV Area in MHP) 2015 rates: $35. (480)986-6997 11435 E Apache Trail, Apache Junction, AZ 85120

SHIPROCK RV RESORT **Ratings: 10/10★/9.5** (RV Park) 2015 rates: $50. (480)505-1300 1700 W Shiprock St, Apache Junction, AZ 85120

SIERRA DEL SAGUARO/MHP **Ratings: 8.5/6.5/8** (RV Park) 2015 rates: $35. (480)982-2444 1855 W Southern, Apache Junction, AZ 85120

SIERRA LEONE MOBILE HOME PARK **Ratings: 9.5/8.5★/10** (RV Area in MHP) 2015 rates: $35. (480)982-5962 1804 W Teepee St #95, Apache Junction, AZ 85120

STACEY ACRES ESTATES (FORMALLY - ZIM'S TRAILER PARK) **Ratings: 5.5/7/7** (RV Park) 2015 rates: $25. (480)600-2734 475 N Ocotillo, Apache Junction, AZ 85120

SUNDOWNER MH & RV PARK **Ratings: 7.5/6.5/6** (RV Area in MHP) 2015 rates: $40. (480)982-2521 105 N Delaware, Apache Junction, AZ 85120

SUNRISE RV RESORT
Ratings: 10/9.5★/10 (RV Resort) From Jct of US Hwy 60 & Ironwood Dr (exit 195), N 1.4 mi on Ironwood Dr to Broadway, E 0.1 mi (R).

PREMIER ADULT RV RESORT DESTINATION
Welcome to Sunrise RV Resort, a 55+ active adult RV community offering 5-star amenities, including 34 acres of natural beauty, recreational activities and relaxation for your instant comfort.

FAC: Paved rds. (501 spaces). Avail: 138 all weather,

APACHE JUNCTION (CONT)

SUNRISE RV RESORT (CONT)
patios, back-ins (35 x 55), 138 full hkups (30/50 amps), seasonal sites, cable, WiFi, rentals, laundry, controlled access. **REC:** heated pool, whirlpool, shuffleboard. Pet restrict(B/Q). Partial handicap access, no tents. Age restrict may apply, RV age restrict, eco-friendly, 2015 rates: $37 to $40.
(877)573-1168 Lat: 33.40682, Lon: -111.56092
1403 W Broadway Ave, Apache Junction, AZ 85120
sunrise@robertsresorts.com
www.robertsresorts.com
See ad pages 46 (Welcome Section), 45 (AZ Map), 52 & Snowbird Destinations in Magazine Section.

SUPERSTITION LOOKOUT RV RESORT **Ratings: 10/10★/10** (RV Park) 2015 rates: $35. (480)982-2008 1371 E 4th Ave, Apache Junction, AZ 85119

SUPERSTITION SUNRISE RV RESORT
Ratings: 10/10★/10 (RV Resort) From Jct of US Hwy 60 & Ironwood Dr (exit 195), N 0.5 mi on Ironwood Dr to Southern Ave, W 1 mi to Meridian Rd, N 0.6 mi (L).

APACHE JUNCTION'S BEST 55+ RESORT!
Welcome! Enjoy indoor & outdoor pools, spa, hair salon, massage therapist, cabana, pickleball, bocce ball, computer club and more. So much to see and do in the Valley of the Sun! Come for a visit & stay for the lifestyle.

FAC: Paved rds. (1119 spaces). Avail: 250 all weather, patios, back-ins (33 x 48), 250 full hkups (30/50 amps), seasonal sites, cable, WiFi, laundry, controlled access. **REC:** heated pool, whirlpool, shuffleboard. Pet restrict(Q). Partial handicap access, no tents. Age restrict may apply, big rig sites, eco-friendly, 2015 rates: $30 to $50. Disc: AAA. No CC.
(800)624-7027 Lat: 33.40206, Lon: -111.58125
702 S Meridian Rd, Apache Junction, AZ 85120
info@superstitionsunrise.com
www.superstitionsunrise.com
See ad opposite page, 52, 47 (Welcome Section) & Snowbird Destinations in Magazine Section.

VIP RV RESORT
Ratings: 8.5/9★/9 (RV Park) From Jct of US Hwy 60 & Ironwood Dr (Exit 195), N 1.8 mi on Ironwood Dr (R). **FAC:** Paved rds. (128 spaces). Avail: 41 all weather, patios, back-ins (30 x 45), 41 full hkups (30/50 amps), seasonal sites, WiFi, laundry. **REC:** shuffleboard. Pet restrict(B/Q). Partial handicap access, no tents. Age restrict may apply, eco-friendly, 2015 rates: $32. Disc: AAA. No CC. AAA Approved
(480)983-0847 Lat: 33.41203, Lon: -111.56219
401 S Ironwood Drive, Apache Junction, AZ 85120
Waymary60@msn.com
www.viprvresort.com
See ad pages 75, 52.

WEAVER'S NEEDLE RV RESORT
Ratings: 10/10★/9 (RV Park) From Jct of US Hwy 60 & Tomahawk Rd (exit 197), N 1.7 mi on Tomahawk Rd (L). **FAC:** Paved rds. (400 spaces). Avail: 200 all weather, patios, back-ins (30 x 40), 200 full hkups (30/50 amps), seasonal sites, WiFi, laundry. **REC:** heated pool, whirlpool, shuffleboard. Pet restrict(B/Q). Partial handicap access, no tents. Age restrict may apply, eco-friendly, 2015 rates: $39.
(480)982-3683 Lat: 33.41214, Lon: -111.52808
250 S Tomahawk Rd, Apache Junction, AZ 85119
weaversneedle@yahoo.com
www.weaversneedle.com
See ad pages 68 (Spotlight Valley of the Sun), 52.

Like Us on Facebook.

WICKIUP HOME COMMUNITY **Ratings: 7/7/7** (RV Area in MHP) 2015 rates: $35. (480)982-6604 2015 East Old West Highway, Apache Junction, AZ 85119

ARIZONA CITY — D3 *Pinal*

QUAIL RUN RV RESORT
Ratings: 9.5/9.5★/10 (RV Park) From Jct of I-10 & Sunland Gin Rd (exit 200): Go south 3.6 mi on Sunland Gin Rd to Santa Cruz Blvd, W 0.7 mi to Park (R) Santa Cruz changes to Amado Blvd. Call for GPS directions (Monthly reservations only). **FAC:** Paved rds. (324 spaces). Avail: 124 gravel, patios, back-ins (32 x 50), accepts full hkup units only, 124 full hkups (30/50 amps), seasonal sites, cable, WiFi $, rentals, laundry. **REC:** heated pool, whirlpool, shuffleboard. Pet restrict(B/Q). Partial handicap access, no tents. Age restrict may apply, eco-friendly, 2015 rates: $419 monthly.
(800)301-8114 Lat: 32.75300, Lon: -111.68212
14010 S Amado Blvd, Arizona City, AZ 85123
quailrunrv@aol.com
www.quailrunrvresort.com
See ad page 80.

ASH FORK — B3 *Yavapai*

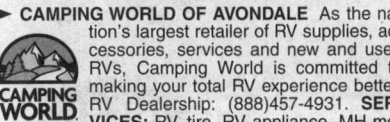

INTERSTATE 40 GRAND CANYON RV PARK
Ratings: 7.5/8.5★/7 (RV Park) From Jct of I-40 & Exit 144, N 0.5 mi on Old Rt 66 to 8th St, E 0.2 Mi on 8th St. (L). Elev 5100 ft. **FAC:** Gravel rds. 47 gravel, 40 pull-thrus (30 x 50), back-ins (20 x 40), some side by side hkups, 24 full hkups, 23 W, 23 E (30/50 amps), WiFi, tent sites, rentals, showers $, dump, laundry, LP gas. **REC.** Pet restrict(Q). Eco-friendly, 2015 rates: $35 to $40. Disc: AAA, military.
(928)220-8993 Lat: 35.22211, Lon: -112.49184
783 S Old Route 66, Ash Fork, AZ 86320
Interstate40gcrv@gmail.com
www.gcrvpark.com
See ad this page.

AVONDALE — D3 *Maricopa*

Travel Services

CAMPING WORLD OF AVONDALE As the nation's largest retailer of RV supplies, accessories, services and new and used RVs, Camping World is committed to making your total RV experience better. RV Dealership: (888)457-4931. **SERVICES:** RV, tire, RV appliance, MH mechanical, engine/chassis repair, staffed RV wash, restrooms, RV Sales. RV supplies, RV accessible. waiting room. Hours: 8am to 6pm.
623-239-3337 Lat: 33.45988, Lon: -112.28304
10255 W. Papago Freeway, Avondale, AZ 85301
CampingWorldofAvondale.com

BELLEMONT — B3 *Coconino*

Travel Services

CAMPING WORLD OF BELLEMONT/FLAGSTAFF As the nation's largest retailer of RV supplies, accessories, services and new and used RVs, Camping World is committed to making your total RV experience better. RV Accessories: (888)883-6440. Elev 7100 ft. **SERVICES:** RV appliance, MH mechanical, restrooms, RV Sales. RV supplies, emergency parking, RV accessible. waiting room. Hours: 8am to 6pm.
928-226-2864 Lat: 35.22899, Lon: -111.81039
9147 E. Bellemont Road, Bellemont, AZ 86015
ebabbitt@campingworld.com
CampingworldofFlagstaff.com

BENSON — E4 *Cochise*

A SPOTLIGHT Introducing Benson's colorful attractions appearing at the front of this state section.

BENSON I-10 RV PARK **Ratings: 6/7.5/5.5** (RV Park) 2015 rates: $38. (800)599-0081 840 N Ocotilllo Rd, Benson, AZ 85602

Tell them you saw them in this Guide!

BENSON KOA Ratings: 7.5/8.5★/7.5 (Campground) From Jct of I-10 & Ocotillo St (exit 304), N 0.6 mi on Ocotillo St to Four Feathers Ln, E 0.3 mi (L). Elev 3580 ft. **FAC:** Gravel rds. (103 spaces). Avail: 97 gravel, 59 pull-thrus (24 x 45), back-ins (24 x 50), 81 full hkups, 16 W, 16 E (30/50 amps), seasonal sites, WiFi, tent sites, rentals, dump, laundry, groc, LP gas, fire rings, firewood. **REC:** heated pool, whirlpool, playground. Pet restrict(B/Q). 2015 rates: $40 to $42. AAA Approved
(800)562-6823 Lat: 31.98739, Lon: -110.30177
180 W Four Feathers, Benson, AZ 85602
kyungkim27@yahoo.com
www.koa.com/where/az/03133.htm

BUTTERFIELD RV RESORT
Ratings: 10/10★/9.5 (RV Park) From Jct of I-10 & Ocotillo Ave (exit 304), go S 0.6 mi on Ocotillo Ave/past Safeway shopping center to 3rd entrance on (L). Elev 3580 ft. **FAC:** Paved rds. (173 spaces). Avail: 24 paved, 139 all weather, 24 pull-thrus (30 x 55), back-ins (30 x 50), 163 full hkups (30/50 amps), seasonal sites, WiFi, rentals, laundry, LP gas. **REC:** heated pool, whirlpool. Pet restrict(B/Q). Partial handicap access, no tents. Eco-friendly, 2015 rates: $38. Disc: AAA, military. AAA Approved
(800)863-8160 Lat: 31.96720, Lon: -110.30677
251 S Ocotillo Ave, Benson, AZ 85602
info@rv-resort.com
http://www.rv-resort.com/
See ad pages 54 (Spotlight Benson), 52.

COCHISE TERRACE RV RESORT **Ratings: 9.5/9.5★/9** (RV Park) 2015 rates: $27.78 to $36.09. (520)720-0911 1030 S Barrel Cactus Ridge, Benson, AZ 85602

KARTCHNER CAVERNS
(State Pk) From Jct of I-10 & Hwy 90 (exit 302) S 9 mi on Hwy 90 (R). Elev 4700 ft. **FAC:** Paved rds. 62 paved, 16 pull-thrus (20 x 60), back-ins (24 x 35), 62 W, 62 E (30/50 amps), tent sites, dump. **REC:** rec open to public. Pets OK. Partial handicap access. 14 day max stay, 2015 rates: $25. Disc: military.
(520)586-2283 Lat: 31.83566, Lon: -110.34367
3330 State Highway 90, Benson, AZ 85602
www.azstateparks.com
See ad page 49 (Welcome Section).

PATO BLANCO LAKES RV RESORT
Ratings: 9/9.5★/8.5 (RV Park) From Jct of I-10 & Pomerene Rd (Exit 306) S 0.1 mi on Pomerene Rd to 4th St, W 0.7 mi to County Rd, N 0.3 mi to Pearl St, W 500 ft (R). Elev 3580 ft. **FAC:** All weather rds. 105 Avail: 105 all weather, patios, 10 pull-thrus (35 x 60), back-ins (35 x 55), 105 full hkups (30/50 amps), cable, WiFi, rentals, dump, laundry, LP gas. **REC:** heated pool, whirlpool, pond, fishing. Pets OK. Partial handicap access, no tents. Age restrict may apply, big rig sites, RV age restrict, eco-friendly, 2015 rates: $38. Disc: AAA, military.
(520)586-8966 Lat: 31.97142, Lon: -110.28841
635 E Pearl St, Benson, AZ 85602
patoblancolakes@rnsmte.com
www.patoblancolakes.com
See ad this page.

RED BARN CAMPGROUND **Ratings: 2.5/6/4** (Campground) 2015 rates: $21 to $23. (520)586-2035 711 N Madison, Benson, AZ 85602

SAN PEDRO RESORT COMMUNITY
Ratings: 10/8.5★/9.5 (RV Park) From Jct of I-10 & Ocotillo St (exit 304), S 0.5 mi on Ocotillo St to Bus 10, E 0.9 mi to SR-80, S 1.3 mi (R). Elev 3600 ft. **FAC:** Paved rds. (270 spaces). Avail: 50 all weather, patios, 30 pull-thrus (30 x 55), back-ins (30 x 40), accepts full hkup units only, 50 full hkups (30/50 amps), seasonal sites, cable, WiFi $, laundry. **REC:** heated pool, whirlpool. Pet restrict(B/Q). No

Check our family camping destinations article in the front of the Guide highlighting the best places to camp in every state and province.

BENSON (CONT)

SAN PEDRO RESORT (CONT)
tents. Age restrict may apply, RV age restrict, eco-friendly, 2015 rates: $33.
(520)586-9546 Lat: 31.94832, Lon: -110.28600
1110 South Hwy 80, Benson, AZ 85602
managers@sanpedrorv.com
www.sanpedrorv.com
See ad page 77.

VALLEY VISTA RV RESORT **Ratings: 8/8.5/8.5** (Membership Pk) 2015 rates: $30. (520)720-0024 1060 South Hwy 80, Benson, AZ 85602

Things to See and Do

BENSON VISITOR CENTER Information center for attractions, shopping & things to see & do in the Benson area. Elev 3500 ft. Restrooms. Hours: 9am to 4pm. No CC.
(520)586-4293 Lat: 31.96809, Lon: -110.29501
249 E 4th St, Benson, AZ 85602
Info@bensonvisitorcenter.com
www.bensonvisitorcenter.com
See ad page 50 (Welcome Section).

BUTTERFIELD RV RESORT OBSERVATORY University grade Observatory open year-round. Free Nightly showings of the heavens and beyond. Elev 3600 ft. No CC.
(800)863-8160 Lat: 31.96732, Lon: -110.30699
251 S Ocotillo Ave, Benson, AZ 85602
info@rv-resort.com
See ad page 54 (Spotlight Benson).

BISBEE — E5 *Cochise*

DESERT OASIS CAMPGROUND
Ratings: 7/9★/8.5 (Campground) From Jct of Hwy 92 & US 80, SE 4.5 mi on Hwy 80 to Double Adobe Rd, E 3.1 mi (R). Elev 4209 ft. **FAC:** Paved/gravel rds. (28 spaces). Avail: 20 gravel, 19 pull-thrus (45 x 90), back-ins (45 x 100), 20 full hkups (30/50 amps), seasonal sites, WiFi Hotspot, tent sites, rentals, LP bottles, controlled access. **REC:** pool, whirlpool. Pets OK. Age restrict may apply, eco-friendly, 2015 rates: $25 to $35. Disc: AAA, military. Nov 1 to Apr 30.
(520)979-6650 Lat: 31.45837, Lon: -109.77684
5311 W Double Adobe Rd, Mcneal, AZ 85617
Campatdo@yahoo.com
http://www.campatdo.com
See ad this page.

Subscribe to Trailer Life Magazine. For a subscription, call 800-825-6861.

DOUBLE ADOBE CAMPGROUND & SHOTGUN SPORTS **Ratings: 6.5/8.5★/8** (RV Park) 2015 rates: $25 to $35. (520)364-4000 5057 W Double Adobe Rd, Mcneal, AZ 85617

QUEEN MINE RV PARK **Ratings: 5/8.5★/8** (RV Park) 2015 rates: $30. (520)432-5006 473 N Dart Rd, Bisbee, AZ 85603

TURQUOISE VALLEY GOLF, RESTAURANT & RV **Ratings: 7.5/9★/8.5** (RV Park) 2015 rates: $27.50. (520)432-3091 1794 W Newell St, Naco, AZ 85620

BLACK CANYON CITY — C3 *Yavapai*

BLACK CANYON CITY KOA **Ratings: 7.5/6.5/7** (Campground) 2015 rates: $35 to $39.50. (800)562-5314 19600 E St Joseph Rd, Black Canyon City, AZ 85324

BLACK CANYON RANCH RV RESORT
Ratings: 10/10★/10 (RV Park) N-bnd: From Jct of I-17 & Exit 242 (W over Fwy to Old Black Canyon Hwy), N 1.3 mi (L); or S-bnd: From Jct of I-17 & Exit 244, S 1 mi on S Old Black Canyon Hwy (R). **FAC:** Paved rds. (107 spaces). Avail: 70 all weather, patios, 11 pull-thrus (30 x 50), back-ins (30 x 50), 70 full hkups (30/50 amps), seasonal sites, cable, WiFi, rentals, laundry. **REC:** heated pool, whirlpool. Pet restrict(B/Q). No tents. Eco-friendly, 2015 rates: $45.
(623)374-9800 Lat: 34.07164, Lon: -112.15262
33900 S Old Black Canyon Hwy, Black Canyon City, AZ 85324
Manager@blackcanyonranchrv.com
http://www.blackcanyonranchrv.com
See ad this page, 883, 52 & Family Camping in Magazine Section.

BOUSE — C1 *La Paz*

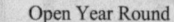

DESERT PUEBLO RV RESORT
Ratings: 7.5/8.5★/7.5 (RV Park) From Jct of Hwy 95 and Hwy 72, E 15 mi on Hwy 72 (R). **FAC:** Gravel rds. (92 spaces). Avail: 32 gravel, patios, 8 pull-thrus (24 x 50), back-ins (24 x 40), 32 full hkups (30/50 amps), seasonal sites, WiFi, tent sites, rentals, laundry, LP gas. **REC.** Pets OK. Age restrict may apply, eco-friendly, 2015 rates: $30.
(928)851-2206 Lat: 33.91752, Lon: -113.99444
28726 Highway 72, Bouse, AZ 85325
dprvresort@gmail.com
www.desertpueblorv.com

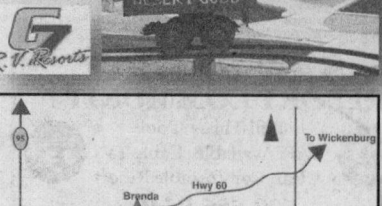

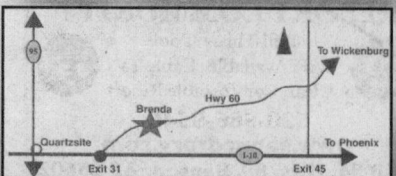

AZ

BRENDA — C1 *La Paz*

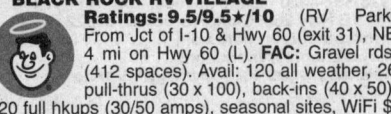

BLACK ROCK RV VILLAGE
Ratings: 9.5/9.5★/10 (RV Park) From Jct of I-10 & Hwy 60 (exit 31), NE 4 mi on Hwy 60 (L). **FAC:** Gravel rds. (412 spaces). Avail: 120 all weather, 26 pull-thrus (30 x 100), back-ins (40 x 50), 120 full hkups (30/50 amps), seasonal sites, WiFi $, rentals, laundry, LP gas, restaurant. **REC:** heated pool, whirlpool, shuffleboard. Pet restrict(B/Q). No tents. Eco-friendly, 2015 rates: $31 to $39. ATM.
(928)927-4206 Lat: 33.68009, Lon: -113.94547
46751 E Hwy 60, Salome, AZ 85348
manager@blackrockrv.com
www.blackrockrv.com
See ad pages 94, 52.

BRENDA RV RESORT
Ratings: 9/9.5★/8.5 (RV Park) From Jct of I-10 & Hwy 60 E (exit 31), NE 3.8 mi on Hwy 60 (L); or W-bnd: From Jct of I-10 & Exit 45 (Vicksburg Rd), N 7 mi on Vicksburg Rd to Hwy 60, SW 10.2 mi (R). **FAC:** All weather rds. (204 spaces). Avail: 20 all weather, 10 pull-thrus (30 x 60), back-ins (25 x 55), 20 full hkups (30/50 amps), seasonal sites, WiFi, laundry, LP gas. **REC.** Pet restrict(B/Q). No tents. Big rig sites, eco-friendly, 2015 rates: $27.
(877)927-5249 Lat: 33.67787, Lon: -113.95332
46251 E Hwy 60, Salome, AZ 85348
brendarvresort@g7rvresorts.com
www.g7rvresorts.com
See ad page 94.

DESERT GOLD RV RESORT
Ratings: 10/9.5★/10 (RV Park) From Jct of I-10 & Hwy 60 E (exit 31), NE 4 mi on Hwy 60 E (R); or W-bnd: From Jct of I-10 & Exit 45 (Vicksburg Rd), N 7 mi on Vicksburg Rd to Hwy 60, SW 10 mi (L). **FAC:** Paved rds. (550 spaces). Avail: 125 all weather, patios, 25 pull-thrus (25 x 70), back-ins (35 x 50), 125 full hkups (30/50 amps), seasonal sites, WiFi, rentals, laundry, LP gas. **REC:** heated pool, whirlpool. Pet restrict(B/Q). Partial handicap access, no tents. Big rig sites, eco-friendly, 2015 rates: $32. Disc: AAA.
(800)927-2101 Lat: 33.67869, Lon: -113.94677
46628 E Hwy 60, Salome, AZ 85348
desertgoldrvresort@g7rvresorts.com
www.g7rvresorts.com
See ad opposite page, 94, 52 & Snowbird Destinations in Magazine Section.

GATEWAY RANCH RV RESORT **Ratings: 7/7.5★/7** (RV Park) 2015 rates: $25. (928)927-7770 44660 S Ave 42 E, Salome, AZ 85348

WAGON WEST RV PARK **Ratings: 6/8★/9** (RV Park) 2015 rates: $27.50. Oct 15 to Apr 15. (928)927-7077 50126 Hwy 60, Salome, AZ 85348

3 DREAMERS RV PARK
Ratings: 8/9.5★/8 (RV Park) From Jct of I-10 & Hwy 60E (Exit 31), NE 11.1 mi on Hwy 60, at MP 42.5 (R) or W-bnd: From Jct of I-10 & Exit 45 (Vicksburg Rd), N 7 mi on Vicksburg Rd to Hwy 60, SW 3 mi (L) Do not use address for GPS. **FAC:** Paved/gravel rds. 50 Avail: 50 all weather, 10 pull-thrus (30 x 75), back-ins (35 x 50), 50 full hkups (30/50 amps), WiFi, tent sites, rentals, dump, laundry, LP gas. **REC:** playground. Pet restrict(B/Q). Big rig sites, eco-friendly, 2015 rates: $32.
AAA Approved
(928)859-4145 Lat: 33.70647, Lon: -113.82067
54000 Hwy 60, Salome, AZ 85348
info@dreamersrvpark.com
www.dreamersrvpark.com
See ad this page, 52.

BUCKEYE — D2 *Maricopa*

ESTRELLA VALLEY MH & RV PARK
Ratings: 3/NA/5 (RV Park) From Jct of I-10 & Cotton Lane (Exit 124), S 4 mi on Cotton Lane to CR-85, W 9.9 mi on CR-85 (L). **FAC:** Paved rds. (99 spaces). Avail: 22 gravel, patios, back-ins (28 x 40), 22 full hkups (30/50 amps), seasonal sites, laundry. **REC.** Pets OK. No tents. 2015 rates: $20. No CC.
(623)386-1268 Lat: 33.37011, Lon: -112.57677
941 E Monroe Ave, Buckeye, AZ 85326
See ad page 44 (Welcome Section).

LEAF VERDE RV RESORT
Ratings: 9.5/10★/8.5 (RV Park) E-bnd: From Jct of I-10 & Exit 114 (Miller Rd), S 0.3 mi to Durango St, E 1.4 mi (Durango St becomes Yuma Rd) to Apache Rd, S 0.3 mi on Apache Rd (R); or W-bnd: From Jct of I-10 & Exit 117 (Watson Rd), S 0.6 mi on Watson Rd to Yuma Rd, W 1 mi to Apache Rd, S 0.3 mi (R) note: Do not follow GPS.

FAMILY OWNED FOR OVER 30 YEARS!
Leaf Verde RV Resort earned an all around "A" grade in the GuestRated satisfaction surveys of RV parks and campgrounds; Honored with "ARIZONA PARK OF THE YEAR" by the Arizona Association of RV Parks and Campgrounds.

FAC: Paved rds. (377 spaces). Avail: 367 gravel, 253 pull-thrus (24 x 75), back-ins (28 x 60), 367 full hkups (30/50 amps), seasonal sites, WiFi $, dump, laundry, LP gas. **REC:** heated pool, shuffleboard. Pet restrict(B/Q). Partial handicap access, no tents. Big rig sites, eco-friendly, 2015 rates: $34. Disc: military.
AAA Approved
(623)386-3132 Lat: 33.43180, Lon: -112.57349
1500 S Apache Rd, Buckeye, AZ 85326
reservations@leafverde.com
www.leafverde.com
See ad page 91.

BULLHEAD CITY — B1 *Mohave*

COLORADO RIVER OASIS RESORT
Ratings: 10/10★/9.5 (RV Park) From Jct of Hwy 95 & Bullhead City Pkwy (Laughlin Bridge), S 3.4 mi on Hwy 95 (R). **FAC:** All weather rds. 28 Avail: 28 all weather, patios, back-ins (30 x 45), 28 full hkups (30/50 amps), cable, WiFi, rentals, dump, laundry. **REC:** pool, whirlpool, Colorado River: fishing. Pet restrict(B/Q). No tents. Big rig sites, eco-friendly, 2015 rates: $35 to $55. Disc: military.
(928)763-4385 Lat: 35.12665, Lon: -114.57882
1641 Highway 95, Bullhead City, AZ 86442
info@coloradoriveroasis.com
www.coloradoriveroasis.com
See ad this page, 52.

DAVIS CAMP RV PARK (MOHAVE COUNTY PARK) (Public) From jct Bullhead Pkwy (Casino Bridge) & Hwy 68: Go 1/2 mi N on Hwy 68 to milepost 250. 2015 rates: $15 to $25. (877)757-0915

FIESTA RV RESORT **Ratings: 9/9★/8.5** (RV Park) 2015 rates: $25. (800)982-1750 3190 Hwy 95, Bullhead City, AZ 86442

Use our handy Snowbird Destinations guide in the front of the Guide to find RV-friendly destinations throughout the Sunbelt.

MOON RIVER RV RESORT
Ratings: 10/10★/10 (RV Park) From Jct of Hwy 95 & Boundary Cone Rd, W 200 yds on Boundary Cone Rd (R); or From SR 68 & Hwy 95, (Laughlin Bridge), S 15.2 mi on Hwy 95 to Boundary Cone Rd, W 200 yds (R). Note: GPS users please call. **FAC:** All weather rds. (89 spaces). Avail: 50 all weather, 22 pull-thrus (30 x 76), back-ins (30 x 56), 50 full hkups (30/50 amps), seasonal sites, WiFi, laundry, groc. **REC:** pool. Pet restrict(B/Q). No tents. Big rig sites, eco-friendly, 2015 rates: $36 to $39. Disc: military.
AAA Approved
(928)788-6666 Lat: 34.96852, Lon: -114.60345
1325 Boundary Cone Rd, Mohave Valley, AZ 86440
info@moonriverresort.com
www.moonriverresort.com
See ad this page, 52.

PALMS RIVER RESORT
Ratings: 9.5/9★/10 (RV Park) From Jct of Hwy 95 & Hwy 155, S 20 mi on Hwy 95 to Needles Hwy/River Rd, N 3 mi on Needles Hwy/River Rd (R). No Pop-up Trailers. **FAC:** Paved rds. (184 spaces). Avail: 51 all weather, 23 pull-thrus (45 x 80), back-ins (40 x 80), accepts full hkup units only, 51 full hkups (30/50 amps), WiFi, rentals, laundry, groc, LP gas, firewood, controlled access. **REC:** pool, wading pool, whirlpool, Colorado River: swim, fishing, golf, playground. Pet restrict(B). Partial handicap access. Big rig sites, RV age restrict, eco-friendly, 2015 rates: $33 to $40. Disc: AAA, military.
(760)326-0333 Lat: 34.88409, Lon: -114.64516
4170 Needles Hwy, Needles, CA 92363
reservations@palmsriverresort.com
www.palmsriverresort.com
See primary listing at Needles, CA and ad page 200.

RIDGEVIEW RV RESORT-SUNRISE RESORTS **Ratings: 8.5/8.5★/8.5** (Membership Pk) 2015 rates: $30. (800)392-8560 775 Bullhead Pkwy, Bullhead City, AZ 86429

RIVER CITY RV PARK **Ratings: 8.5/9★/8.5** (RV Park) 2015 rates: $21. (928)754-2121 2225 Merrill Ave, Bullhead City, AZ 86442

RIVERSIDE ADVENTURE TRAILS **Ratings: 8/8★/7.5** (Membership Pk) 2015 rates: $20. (928)763-8800 4750 Hwy 95, Bullhead City, AZ 86426

SILVER CREEK RV PARK
Ratings: 7/8.5★/7.5 (RV Park) From Jct of Hwys 95 & Bullhead City Pkwy (Laughlin Bridge), S 4.5 mi on Hwy 95 to Silver Creek Rd, E 0.7 mi to Goldrush Rd, S 500 ft (R). **FAC:** Paved/gravel rds. (140 spaces). Avail: 30 gravel, 25 pull-thrus (25 x 55), back-ins (25 x 50), 30 full hkups (30/50 amps), seasonal sites, cable, laundry, groc.

BULLHEAD CITY (CONT)

SILVER CREEK RV PARK (CONT)
REC: heated pool. Pet restrict(B/Q). No tents. 2015 rates: $27.13. Disc: AAA.
(928)763-2444 Lat: 35.11168, Lon: -114.57231
1515 Gold Rush Rd, Bullhead City, AZ 86442
silvercrkrvpark@yahoo.com
See ad page 79.

VISTA DEL SOL RV RESORT
Ratings: 10/10★/10 (RV Resort) From Jct of Hwy 95 & Bullhead Pkwy (Casino Bridge), Go S 8.7 mi on Hwy 95 to Bullhead Pkwy, then NE 1.1 mi to Camino Real, then E 2 blocks to Sierra Santiago, then N 4 blocks on Sierra Santiago (N) Note: Resort scheduled to open early 2015.

VISTA DEL SOL - YOU'RE AT HOME HERE
A 55+ gated, active adult retirement community and RV Resort. Located in Bullhead City, AZ, the resort is within striking distance of a number of natural and man-made attractions. Serviced by the Laughlin/Bullhead Airport.

FAC: Paved rds. 89 Avail: 89 all weather, back-ins (40 x 80), 89 full hkups (30/50 amps), WiFi, laundry, controlled access. **REC:** heated pool, whirlpool. Pets OK. Partial handicap access, no tents. Age restrict may apply, big rig sites, eco-friendly, 2015 rates: $39. No reservations.
(888)347-0230 Lat: 35.06531, Lon: -114.56924
3249 Felipe Dr, Bullhead City, AZ 86442
Delliot@robertsresorts.com
www.robertsresorts.com
See ad pages 46 (Welcome Section), 45 (AZ Map), 52 & Snowbird Destinations in Magazine Section.

CAMP VERDE — C3 *Yavapai*

DISTANT DRUMS RV RESORT
Ratings: 10/10★/10 (RV Resort) From Jct of I-17 & exit 289 (Montezuma Castle), NW 200 yards on Montezuma Castle Rd (L). Elev 3278 ft.

COME ENJOY CLEAN QUIET RV RESORT
Distant Drums RV Resort just south of Sedona, across the freeway from Cliff Castle Casino. Full hookups, cable TV, spotless private showers, laundry room, heated pool & jacuzzi, exercise room & full event center. FREE WI-FI.

FAC: Paved rds. 190 paved, patios, 10 pull-thrus (22 x 77), back-ins (35 x 44), 190 full hkups (30/50 amps), cable, WiFi, dump, laundry, LP gas. **REC:** heated pool, whirlpool. Pets OK. Partial handicap access, no tents. Big rig sites, eco-friendly, 2015 rates: $36 to $44. Disc: AAA, military.
(928)554-8000 Lat: 34.61356, Lon: -111.86389
583 W Middle Verde Rd, Camp Verde, AZ 86322
info@ddrvresort.com
www.distantdrumsrvresort.com
See ad pages 71 (Spotlight Verde Valley), 52 & Snowbird Destinations in Magazine Section.

KRAZY K RV PARK **Ratings: 7/8.5★/6.5** (RV Park) 2015 rates: $22 to $36. (928)567-0565 2075 N. Arena del Loma, Camp Verde, AZ 86322

RANCHO VERDE RV PARK **Ratings: 7/9★/9** (RV Park) 2015 rates: $34 to $42. (928)567-7037 1488 W Horseshoe Bend Dr, Camp Verde, AZ 86322

VERDE RIVER RV RESORT & COTTAGES
Ratings: 7.5/8/8 (RV Resort) From jct Hwy 260 & Horseshoe Bend Dr: Go N 1 mi on Horseshoe Bend Dr. Elev 3300 ft.

SEDONA/NORTHERN AZ LOCATION
Easy I-17 access, exit #287, 100 HUGE, level RV sites, 50+ cottages, 1400 ft Verde River front, pool, spa, fitness center, new private bath suites, free LD phone, WiFi and Cable TV. 3000 fl elev for year-round family fun.

FAC: Paved/gravel rds. (175 spaces). Avail: 10 gravel, 10 pull-thrus (30 x 60), accepts full hkup units only, 10 full hkups (30/50 amps), seasonal sites, WiFi $, rentals, dump, laundry. **REC:** pool, whirlpool, Verde River: shuffleboard, playground. Pet restrict(B). Partial handicap access, no tents. 2015 rates: $30 to $40.
(928)202-3409 Lat: 34.59953, Lon: -111.88461
1472 W Horseshoe Bend Dr, Camp Verde, AZ 86322
See ad pages 72 (Spotlight Verde Valley), 52 & Snowbird Destinations in Magazine Section.

ZANE GREY RV PARK
Ratings: 8/10★/10 (RV Park) From Jct of I-17 & Hwy 260 (Exit 287), E 8 mi on Hwy 260 across Clear Creek Bridge (0.2 mi E of MM 227) (L). Note: Adults only please. Do not use GPS for directions. Elev 3200 ft. **FAC:** Gravel rds. 67 gravel, 11 pull-thrus (30 x 60), back-ins (30 x 65), accepts full hkup units only, 67 full hkups (30/50 amps), WiFi, laundry, LP gas. **REC:** West Clear Creek: fishing. Pet restrict(B/Q). No tents. Big rig sites, eco-friendly 2015 rates: $42.
(928)567-4320 Lat: 34.51665, Lon: -111.77455
4500 E Hwy 260, Camp Verde, AZ 86322
info@zanegreyrvpark.com
www.zanegreyrvpark.com
See ad pages 72 (Spotlight Verde Valley), 52.

Don't miss out on great savings - find over $1,000 in Camping World coupons at the front of the Guide!

Things to See and Do

CLIFF CASTLE CASINO Casino offering slot machines, table games, Bingo, restaurants, bowling alley, Kid's Quest, hotel rooms, helicopter tours, entertainment and adjacent RV Park. Elev 3278 ft. partial handicap access. RV accessible. Restrooms. ATM.
(928)567-7900 Lat: 34.6066539, Lon: 111.86236329
555 Middle Verde Road, Camp Verde, AZ 86322
general@cliffcastlecasino.net
http://www.cliffcastlecasinohotel.com/
See ad page 71 (Spotlight Verde Valley).

We appreciate your business!

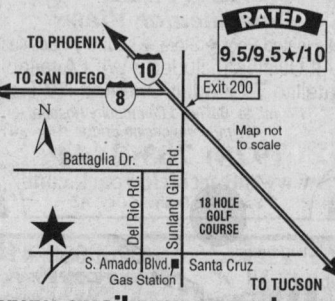

CASA GRANDE — D3 *Pinal*

CASA GRANDE See also Arizona City, Coolidge, Eloy, Florence and Picacho.

CASA GRANDE RV RESORT & COTTAGES
Ratings: 10/10★/9.5 (RV Park) From Jct of I-10 and Pinal Rd (Exit 185) S 5 mi on Pinal Rd to Rodeo Rd, E 300ft (R).

BEST RV RESORT VALUE IN CENTRAL AZ
Easy I-10 access: AZ #185 Hwy 387/Pinal Rd. Excellent long term rates! Fitness center, 2 pools, 4 pickleball, 8 stunning pro billiard tables, free waffle breakfast M-F, dinners 3/nts week, free WiFi, Great Group facilities.

FAC: Paved rds. (350 spaces). Avail: 325 all weather, patios, 14 pull-thrus (30 x 50), back-ins (30 x 50), accepts full hkup units only, 325 full hkups (30/50 amps), seasonal sites, WiFi, rentals, laundry. **REC:** heated pool, whirlpool, shuffleboard, playground. Pets OK. No tents. Big rig sites, eco-friendly, 2015 rates: $33. Disc: AAA, military. Nov 1 to Apr 30.
(520)421-0401 Lat: 32.92311, Lon: -111.7546
195 W Rodeo Rd, Casa Grande, AZ 85122
info@casagrandervresort.com
www.casagrandervresort.com
See ad pages 67 (Spotlight Valley of the Sun), 52, inside back cover & Snowbird Destinations in Magazine Section.

CASITA VERDE RV RESORT **Ratings: 9.5/9★/10** (RV Park) 2015 rates: $45. (520)836-9031 2200 N Trekell Rd, Casa Grande, AZ 85122

COTTONWOOD COVE **Ratings: 5/NA/5.5** (RV Area in MHP) 2015 rates: $30 to $35. (520)836-2528 426 W Cottonwood Ln #37, Casa Grande, AZ 85122

DESERT GARDENS RV PARK
Ratings: 10/9.5★/10 (RV Park) From Casa Grande & N-bnd: Jct I-10 & Exit 104; Go E 9.9 mi on SR-287(Florence Blvd exit) then turn N on SR-287/SR-87 for 8.6 mi, then E on SR-287 for 8.1 mi, merges onto SR-79 for 4.2 mi to park (R) Note: No popups or Pickup campers. **FAC:** All weather rds. (266 spaces). Avail: 166 all weather, back-ins (60 x 70), accepts full hkup units only, 166 full hkups (30/50 amps), seasonal sites, WiFi $, laundry, controlled access. **REC:** heated pool, whirlpool. Pet restrict(B/Q). Partial handicap access, no tents. Age restrict may apply, big rig sites, eco-friendly, 2015 rates: $45 to $50. Oct 1 to Apr 30. No CC.
(520)868-3800 Lat: 32.96353, Lon: -111.33957
9668 N Hwy 79, Florence, AZ 85132
desertgardens@cgmailbox.com
www.desertgardensrvpark.com
See primary listing at Florence and ad page 84.

FIESTA GRANDE RV RESORT **Ratings: 9/9★/10** (RV Park) 2015 rates: $43. (888)934-3782 1511 E Florence Blvd, Casa Grande, AZ 85122

FOOTHILLS WEST RV RESORT **Ratings: 8/8.5★/9.5** (RV Park) 2015 rates: $42. (520)836-2531 10167 N Encore Dr, Casa Grande, AZ 85122

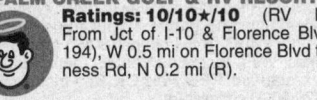

HIGH CHAPARRAL RV PARK
Ratings: 9/9.5★/7.5 (RV Park) From Jct of I-10 & Exit 200 (Sunland Gin Rd), S 3 mi on Sunland Gin Rd to Battaglia Rd, E 1.2 mi (R).

STAY WITH US-YOU'LL BE GLAD YOU DID
Whether you like golf and fine dining or roughing it on mountain trails, we are close to all the main attractions. Centrally located between Greater Phoenix and Tucson. Come stay at one of the friendliest parks in Arizona!

FAC: Paved rds. (172 spaces). Avail: 121 all weather, patios, 72 pull-thrus (36 x 60), back-ins (30 x 50), some side by side hkups, accepts full hkup units only, 121 full hkups (30/50 amps), seasonal sites, WiFi $, dump, laundry. **REC:** heated pool, whirlpool, shuffleboard. Pet restrict(B/Q). No tents. Age restrict may apply, big rig sites, eco-friendly, 2015 rates: $30. Disc: AAA.
AAA Approved
(520)466-5076 Lat: 32.76116, Lon: -111.64968
7575 W Battaglia Rd, Casa Grande, AZ 85193
Highchaparralrvpark@live.com
www.highchaparralrvpark.com
See ad this page, 52 & Snowbird Destinations in Magazine Section.

LEISURE VALLEY RV RESORT **Ratings: 9/8.5★/8** (RV Park) 2015 rates: $29. (800)993-9449 9985 N Pinal Ave, Casa Grande, AZ 85122

PALM CREEK GOLF & RV RESORT
Ratings: 10/10★/10 (RV Resort) From Jct of I-10 & Florence Blvd (exit 194), W 0.5 mi on Florence Blvd to Henness Rd, N 0.2 mi (R).

EXPERIENCE AN ARIZONA OASIS
Gorgeous mountain views with lush greens and fairways await you for a round of 18-holes. Situated between Phoenix and Tucson, you'll enjoy country club living with over 165 activities like pickleball, crafts, tennis and more!

FAC: Paved rds. (1888 spaces). Avail: 954 all weather, patios, 25 pull-thrus (16 x 100), back-ins (40 x 50), accepts full hkup units only, 954 full hkups (30/50 amps), seasonal sites, cable, WiFi $, rentals, laundry, restaurant, controlled access. **REC:** heated pool, whirlpool, golf, shuffleboard. Pet restrict(B/Q). Partial handicap access, no tents. Age restrict may apply, eco-friendly, 2015 rates: $34 to $61. Disc: AAA, military.
AAA Approved
(800)421-7004 Lat: 32.88423, Lon; -111.70441
1110 N Henness Rd, Casa Grande, AZ 85122
info@palmcreekgolf.com
www.palmcreekgolf.com
See ad pages 48 (Welcome Section), 1463 (Welcome Section), 52 & RV Trips of a Lifetime, Snowbird Destinations in Magazine Section.

RANCHO DEL SOL MHP
Ratings: 3/NA/4.5 (RV Area in MHP) From Jct of I-10 & Florence Blvd (exit 194), W 3.5 mi on Florence Blvd to Trekell Rd, N 2.5 mi (L). **FAC:** Paved rds. (76 spaces). Avail: 16 gravel, patios, back-ins (35 x 50), 16 full hkups (30/50 amps), seasonal sites, laundry. Pets OK. No tents. 2015 rates: $24. No CC.
(520)421-0310 Lat: 32.91542, Lon: -111.74009
2175 N Trekell Rd, Casa Grande, AZ 85222
See ad page 44 (Welcome Section).

SUNDANCE 1 RV RESORT
Ratings: 10/10★/10 (RV Resort) From Jct of I-10 & Pinal Ave (exit 185), S 7.3 mi on Pinal Ave to Cottonwood, W 1 mi to Thornton Rd, N 0.2 mi (L); or From Jct of I-8 & Thornton Rd (Exit 172), N 5 mi on Thornton Rd (L). **FAC:** Paved rds. (707 spaces). Avail: 186 all weather, patios, 13 pull-thrus (39 x 55), back-ins (40 x 50), accepts full hkup units only, 186 full hkups (30/50 amps), seasonal sites, cable, WiFi $, rentals, laundry, controlled access. **REC:** heated pool, whirlpool, shuffleboard. Pet restrict(B/Q). Partial handicap access, no tents. Age restrict may apply, eco-friendly, 2015 rates: $24.43 to $39.
(520)426-9662 Lat: 32.8977, Lon: -111.77521
1703 N Thornton Rd, Casa Grande, AZ 85122
fun@sundance1rv.com
www.sundance1rv.com
See ad this page.

SUNSCAPE ESTATES RV PARK COOPERATIVE
Ratings: 10/9★/9 (RV Park) From Jct of I-10 & exit 194 (SR 287/Florence Blvd), E 6.9 mi on SR 287 to Eleven Mile Corner Rd, S 1.3 mi to Sunscape Way, E 0.9 mi (R) Gated property reservations required. **FAC:** Paved rds. (504 spaces). Avail: 25 all weather, patios, back-ins (30 x 60), 25 full hkups (30/50 amps), seasonal sites, WiFi $, laundry, LP gas, controlled access. **REC:** heated pool, whirlpool, shuffleboard. Pets OK. No tents. Age restrict may apply, RV age restrict, 2015 rates: $25 to $37.
(520)723-9533 Lat: 32.86135, Lon: -111.55650
1083 E Sunscape Way, Casa Grande, AZ 85194
reservations@sunscapervresort.com
www.sunscapervresort.com
See ad opposite page.

VAL VISTA RV PARK **Ratings: 9.5/8.5★/9** (RV Park) 2015 rates: $33. (520)836-7800 16680 W Val Vista Blvd, Casa Grande, AZ 85122

Join the flock and head south during the winter. Use our handy Snowbird guide in the front of the Guide to find RV-friendly destinations throughout the Sunbelt. Snowbird Destinations features the top Snowbird roosts and lists great Campgrounds in compelling areas.

CASA GRANDE (CONT)

Things to See and Do

PALM CREEK GOLF & RV RESORT This a player friendly executive-styled course that meanders through the property and features well-manicured greens and lush landscaping highlighted by two lakes & a creek that crosses the fairway on the 9th hole. Partial handicap access. Restrooms, food. Hours: 9 am to 5 pm.
(800)421-7004 Lat: 32.88427, Lon: -111.70515
1110 N Henness Rd, Casa Grande, AZ 85122
info@palmcreekgolf.com
www.palmcreekgolf.com
See ad page 48 (Welcome Section).

CAVE CREEK — C3 *Maricopa*

CAVE CREEK RECREATION AREA (MARICOPA COUNTY PARK) (Public) From jct I-17 (exit 223) & Carefree Hwy: Go 5 mi E on Carefree Hwy, then 1-1/2 mi N on 32nd St. 2015 rates: $12 to $40. (623)465-0431

CHANDLER — D3 *Maricopa*

HACIENDA SOLANO RESORT **Ratings: 8/8/8** (RV Park) 2015 rates: $35. (480)963-3477 15606 S Gilbert Rd, Chandler, AZ 85225

CHINLE — A5 *Apache*

CANYON DE CHELLY/COTTONWOOD (Natl Pk) From Jct of Hwy 191 & Rte 7 (in Chinle), E 2.5 mi on Rte 7 to visitor center, follow signs (E). 2015 rates: $14 to $50. (928)674-2106

CLIFTON — D5 *Greenlee*

NORTH CLIFTON RV PARK (CITY PARK) (Public) From Historic Railroad Station: Go 300 ft N on US 191, then turn E on Zorilla St, then go 100 ft to Frisco Ave, then 1/2 mi N on Frisco Ave. 2015 rates: $19. (928)865-9064

CONGRESS — C2 *Yavapai*

NORTH RANCH RV ESCAPEES **Ratings: 6.5/8.5★/9** (Membership Pk) 2015 rates: $26.50. (928)427-3657 30625 Hwy 89, Mp 264, Congress, AZ 85332

COOLIDGE — D3 *Pinal*

HO HO KAM RV PARK/MOBILE VILLAGE
Ratings: 10/8.5★/8 (RV Area in MHP) From N Jct of Hwys 87 & 287, S 2.9 mi on Hwys 87/287 (L).

CLOSE TO ALL THE ARIZONA FUN!
Located halfway between Phoenix and Tucson. Home of the Casa Grande Ruins National Monument. Coolidge offers easy access to professional sports, car races, ballet, symphony, concerts and major universities.

FAC: Paved rds. (202 spaces). Avail: 93 all weather, patios, back-ins (25 x 45), accepts full hkup units only, 93 full hkups (30/50 amps), seasonal sites, WiFi, laundry. **REC:** heated pool, whirlpool, shuffleboard. Pet restrict(B/Q). Partial handicap access, no tents. Age restrict may apply, eco-friendly, 2015 rates: $35.
(520)723-3697 Lat: 32.96107, Lon: -111.52390
1925 S Arizona Blvd, Coolidge, AZ 85128
Hohokam@westcoastmhp.com
www.hohokamrvpark.com
See ad pages 81, 52 & Snowbird Destinations in Magazine Section.

INDIAN SKIES RV RESORT
Ratings: 9.5/8.5★/8.5 (RV Resort) From N Jct of Hwys 87 & 287, S 2.5 mi on Hwy 87/287 (R). **FAC:** Paved rds. (326 spaces). Avail: 210 gravel, patios, 57 pull-thrus (30 x 75), back-ins (28 x 45), 210 full hkups (30/50 amps), seasonal sites, WiFi, rentals, laundry, LP bottles. **REC:** heated pool, whirlpool, shuffleboard. Pet restrict(B). No tents. Age restrict may apply, eco-friendly, 2015 rates: $33 to $39. Disc: military.
(520)723-7831 Lat: 32.96626, Lon: -111.52537
1050 S Arizona Blvd, Coolidge, AZ 85128
info@indianskiesrvresort.com
www.indianskiesrvresort.com
See ad pages 81, 52.

CORDES JUNCTION — C3 *Yavapai*

CORDES JCT MOTEL, RV PARK, 50'S DINER BACKSEAT BAR
Ratings: 8/8.5★/8 (RV Park) From Jct I-17 and Hwy 69 (exit 262): At traffic circle, go E onto Cordes Lake Rd, then S for 1 block on Stagecoach Trail, then E for 1 Block on Hitching Post Way (I). **FAC:** Gravel rds. (20 spaces). Avail: 15 gravel, 10 pull-thrus (25 x 35), back-ins (25 x 40), 15 full hkups (30/50 amps), seasonal sites, WiFi, tent sites, rentals, dump, laundry, LP gas, restaurant. **REC.** Pets OK. Eco-friendly, 2015 rates: $26.50. Disc: military.
(928)632-5186 Lat: 34.32587, Lon: -112.11619
19780 E. Hitching Post Way, Cordes Lakes, AZ 86333
Motelrvpark@comspeed.net
www.motelrvpark.com
See primary listing at Cordes Lakes and ad this page.

QUAIL RIDGE RV PARK
Ratings: 8/9.5★/9.5 (RV Park) From jct I-17 & S Hwy 69 (exit 262), NW 0.75 mi on Hwy 69, S 100 yds across median to Frontage Rd, SE 0.1 mi (R). **FAC:** Gravel rds. (35 spaces). Avail: 30 all weather, 30 pull-thrus (35 x 65), accepts full hkup units only, 30 full hkups (30/50 amps), seasonal sites, WiFi, tent sites, dump, laundry. **REC:** playground. Pet restrict(B/Q). Big rig sites, eco-friendly, 2015 rates: $42.
(928)227-1919 Lat: 34.33685, Lon: -112.13204
18825 E Copper Star Rd, Mayer, AZ 86333
quailridgerv@yahoo.com
www.quailridgervpark.com
See primary listing at Cordes Lakes and ad this page.

CORDES LAKES — C3 *Yavapai*

CORDES JCT MOTEL, RV PARK, 50'S DINER BACKSEAT BAR
Ratings: 8/8.5★/8 (RV Park) From Jct I-17 and Hwy 69 (Exit 262): At traffic circle, Go E onto Cordes Lakes Rd, then S for 1 block on Stagecoach Trail, then E for 1 block on Hitching Post Way (L). **FAC:** Gravel rds. (20 spaces). Avail: 15 gravel, 10 pull-thrus (25 x 35), back-ins (25 x 40), 15 full hkups (30/50 amps), seasonal sites, WiFi, tent sites, rentals, dump, laundry, LP gas, restaurant. **REC.** Pets OK. Eco-friendly, 2015 rates: $26.50. Disc: military.
(928)632-5186 Lat: 34.32587, Lon: -112.11619
19780 E. Hitching Post Way, Cordes Lakes, AZ 86333
Motelrvpark@comspeed.net
www.motelrvpark.com
See ad this page.

QUAIL RIDGE RV PARK
Ratings: 8/9.5★/9.5 (RV Park) From Jct of I-17 & S Hwy 69 (Exit 262), NW 0.75 mi on Hwy 69, S 100 yds across median to Frontage Rd, SE 0.1 mi (R). **FAC:** Gravel rds. (35 spaces). Avail: 30 all weather, 30 pull-thrus (35 x 65), accepts full hkup units only, 30 full hkups (30/50 amps), seasonal sites, WiFi, tent sites, dump, laundry. **REC:** playground. Pet restrict(B/Q). Big rig sites, eco-friendly, 2015 rates: $42.
(928)227-1919 Lat: 34.33685, Lon: -112.13204
18825 E Copper Star Road, Mayer, AZ 86333
quailridgerv@yahoo.com
www.quailridgervpark.com
See ad this page.

CORNVILLE — C3 *Yavapai*

PAGE SPRINGS RESORT- SUNRISE RESORT **Ratings: 5/8/6.5** (Membership Pk) 2015 rates: $35. (928)634-4309 1951 N. Page Springs Rd, Cornville, AZ 86325

COTTONWOOD — C3 *Yavapai*

DEAD HORSE RANCH
(State Pk) From Jct of US-89A & SR-260, NW 0.6 mi on US-89A to (Historic 89A) Main St, NW 1.4 mi to N 10th St, NE 0.8 mi (R). Elev 3300 ft. **FAC:** Paved rds. 109 paved, patios, 33 pull-thrus (30 x 65), back-ins (30 x 40), 109 W, 109 E (30/50 amps), tent sites, rentals, dump, fire rings. **REC:** Verde River: fishing, playground, rec open to public. Pets OK. Partial handicap access. 14 day max stay, 2015 rates: $25 to $30. Disc: military.
(928)634-5283 Lat: 34.75308, Lon: -112.022116
675 Dead Horse Ranch Rd, Cottonwood, AZ 86326
www.azstateparks.com
See ad page 49 (Welcome Section).

RIO VERDE RV PARK
Ratings: 6/8★/6.5 (RV Park) From Jct of Hwy 260 & Hwy 89A, NE 1 mi on Hwy 89A (R). **FAC:** Gravel rds. 68 gravel, patios, back-ins (30 x 45), some side by side hkups, 68 full hkups (30/50 amps), cable, WiFi, tent sites, laundry, LP gas. **REC:** Verde River: fishing. Pets OK. 2015 rates: $35.
(928)634-5990 Lat: 34.72170, Lon: -111.98984
3420 E Sr 89A, Cottonwood, AZ 86326
info@rioverdervpark.com
www.rioverdervpark.com
See ad this page.

TURQUOISE TRIANGLE RV PARK
Ratings: 6/8★/7.5 (RV Park) From Jct of Hwy 89A & Hwy 260, E 0.25 mi on Hwy 89A (R). **FAC:** Gravel rds. (63 spaces). Avail: 15 gravel, back-ins (27 x 50), some side by side hkups, 15 full hkups (30/50 amps), seasonal sites, cable, WiFi, laundry. **REC.** Pet restrict(B/Q). No tents. 2015 rates: $30 to $35. No CC.
(928)634-5294 Lat: 34.72119, Lon: -111.99907
2501 E Sr 89A, Cottonwood, AZ 86326
www.turquoisetrianglervpark.com
See ad this page.

VERDE VALLEY **Ratings: 8.5/8/9.5** (Membership Pk) 2015 rates: $35. (877)877-0704 6400 Thousand Trails, Sp #16, Cottonwood, AZ 86326

DATELAND — D2 *Yuma*

DATELAND PALMS VILLAGE **Ratings: 2.5/7/7** (RV Park) 2015 rates: $18 to $19. (928)454-2772 1737 S Ave 64 E, Dateland, AZ 85333

OASIS RV PARK AT AZTEC HILLS Ratings: 6.5/8.5★/9 (RV Park) E-bnd: From Jct of I-8 & Exit 67, S 0.25 mi on exit rd to frntg rd, E 2.2 mi to sign, S 0.5 mi on park rd (E) or W-bnd: From Jct of I-8 & Exit 73, S 200 yds on exit rd to frntg rd, W 4 mi to sign, S 0.5 mi on Park Rd (E). **FAC:** Gravel rds. 38 gravel, patios, 16 pull-thrus (30 x 60), back-ins (30 x 50), 35 full hkups, 3 W, 3 E (30/50 amps), WiFi $, rentals, laundry, LP gas. **REC:** heated pool. Pet

We rate what RVers consider important.

RV Park ratings you can rely on!

To get the most out of your Guide, refer to the Table of Contents in the front of the book.

AZ

ATELAND (CONT)

OASIS RV PARK AT AZTEC HILLS (CONT)
estrict(Q). No tents. Big rig sites, eco-friendly, 2015 ates: $25. No CC.
928)454-2229 Lat: 32.80521, Lon: -113.50733
401 S Ave 66E, Dateland, AZ 85333
asisrvpark@hughes.net

EWEY — C3 *Yavapai*

ORCHARD RANCH RV RESORT
Ratings: 10/9★/10 (RV Park) From Jct of I-17 & Hwy 169 (Exit 278), W 15.1 mi on Hwy 169 to SR 69 (in Dewey), NW 3.2 mi (R). Elev 4700 ft. **FAC:** Paved rds. (430 spaces). Avail: 300 all weather, 300 pull-thrus (31 x 50), accepts full hkup units only, 300 ull hkups (30/50 amps), seasonal sites, cable, WiFi $, rentals, laundry, LP gas. **REC:** heated pool, whirlpool, shuffleboard. Pet restrict(B/Q). No tents. Age estrict may apply, eco-friendly, 2015 rates: $35. Disc: AAA.
928)772-8266 Lat: 34.56875, Lon: -112.26939
1250 E Hwy 69, Dewey, AZ 86327
orchardpark@cableone.net
www.orchardrvresort.com
See ad pages 94, 52.

EHRENBERG — D1 *La Paz*

ARIZONA OASIS RV RESORT
Ratings: 9/9.5★/9.5 (RV Park) From Jct of I-10 & Exit 1 (Parker/Ehrenberg), N 0.25 mi on Poston Rd to Ehrenberg/Parker Hwy, W 0.3 mi (R). **FAC:** Gravel rds. 160 gravel, patios, 104 pull-thrus (32 x 55), back-ins (32 x 50), 160 full hkups (30/50 amps), cable, WiFi, tent sites, rentals, laundry, restaurant. **REC:** heated pool, whirlpool, Colorado River: swim, fishing. Pets OK. Partial handicap access. Big rig sites, eco-friendly, 2015 rates: $40 to $55. Disc: AAA.
(928)923-8230 Lat: 33.60612, Lon: -114.52386
50238 Ehrenberg/Parker Hwy, Ehrenberg, AZ 85334
vmcdonald@rvoasis.com
www.rvoasis.com
See ad this page, 52.

RIVER BREEZE RV PARK & OHV RESORT
Ratings: 9.5/9.5★/10 (RV Park) From Jct of I-10 & Exit 1, N 0.25 mi on Access Rd to Ehrenberg/Parker Hwy, W 600 ft (R). **FAC:** Paved rds. (94 spaces). 67 Avail: 37 paved, 30 grass, 37 pull-thrus (40 x 62), back-ins (40 x 60), 67 full hkups (30/50 amps), seasonal sites, cable, WiFi $, tent sites, rentals, laundry, LP gas. **REC:** heated pool, whirlpool, Colorado River: fishing. Pets OK. Big rig sites, eco-friendly, 2015 rates: $39.50 to $50.64.
(928)923-7483 Lat: 33.60673, Lon: -114.52282
50202 Ehrenberg/Parker Hwy, Ehrenberg, AZ 85334
fun@riverbreezerv.com
www.riverbreezerv.com
See ad this page, 52.

EL MIRAGE — C3 *Maricopa*

PUEBLO EL MIRAGE GOLF & RV RESORT
Ratings: 10/10★/10 (RV Resort) From Jct of I-10 & Dysart Rd (Exit 129), N 6.9 mi on Dysart Rd to Olive Ave, E 1 mi to El Mirage Rd, N 1.5 mi (R); or From Jct of I-10 & Loop 101 (Exit 133), N 9 mi on Loop 101 to Olive Ave (Exit 9), W 3.8 mi to El Mirage Rd, N 1.5 mi (R). Note: 26' min length.

LUXURY SNOWBIRD RESORT
Our Country Club & RV Resort is a 55+ gated community just mins. from Phoenix. Full of Big Rig Sites/Park Models to Rent or Purchase a Home. Enjoy our 18 Hole Golf Course/Pro Shop/Restaurant/Lounge/Pool/Spa & more.

FAC: Paved rds. (1075 spaces). Avail: 475 all weather, patios, 15 pull-thrus (39 x 100), back-ins (39 x 50), accepts full hkup units only, 475 full hkups (30/50 amps), seasonal sites, WiFi $, rentals, laundry, restaurant, controlled access. **REC:** heated pool, whirlpool, pond, golf, shuffleboard. Pet restrict(B/Q). Partial handicap access, no tents. Age restrict may apply, big rig sites, eco-friendly, 2015 rates: $27 to $61.
(623)299-4949 Lat: 33.58799, Lon: -112.32334
11201 N El Mirage Rd, El Mirage, AZ 85335
info@robertsresorts.com
www.robertsresorts.com
See ad pages 46 (Welcome Section), 45 (AZ Map), 52 & Snowbird Destinations in Magazine Section.

ELOY — D3 *Pinal*

LAS COLINAS RV PARK
Ratings: 10/9★/9.5 (RV Park) From Jct of I-10 & Exit 200 (Sunland Gin Rd): Go N on Sunland Gin Rd for .5 mi to Redd Rd (First St), turn W on Redd Rd, go 300 ft (L). **FAC:** Paved rds. (150 spaces). Avail: 100 all weather, patios, 3 pull-thrus (32 x 70), back-ins (30 x 45), accepts full hkup units only, 100 full hkups (30/50 amps), seasonal sites, WiFi, laundry. **REC:** heated pool, whirlpool, shuffleboard. Pet restrict(B/Q). Partial handicap access, no tents. Age restrict may apply, big rig sites, eco-friendly, 2015 rates: $38.15. Disc: AAA. No CC. AAA Approved
(520)836-5050 Lat: 32.81531, Lon: -111.67354
7136 Sunland Gin Rd, Eloy, AZ 85131
lascolinas55@yahoo.com
www.lascolinasrvresort.com
See ad pages 81, 52.

SILVERADO RV RESORT (FORMERLY DESERT VALLEY RV PARK)
Ratings: 9.5/9★/9.5 (RV Park) From Jct of I-10 & Toltec Rd (exit 203): Go N for .5 mi on Toltec Rd, turn W on Tonto Rd for .5 mi in to Park. **FAC:** Paved rds. (350 spaces). Avail: 300 gravel, patios, 20 pull-thrus (60 x 120), back-ins (30 x 60), accepts full hkup units only, 300 full hkups (30/50 amps), seasonal sites, cable, WiFi, laundry, controlled access. **REC:** heated pool, whirlpool, shuffleboard. Pets OK. Partial handicap access, no tents. Age restrict may apply, big rig sites, RV age restrict, eco-friendly, 2015 rates: $34. Disc: AAA. No CC.
(866)502-4700 Lat: 32.78527, Lon: -111.62777
4555 W Tonto Rd, Eloy, AZ 85131
info@silveradorvresort.com
www.silveradorvresort.com
See ad pages 81, 52.

FLAGSTAFF — B3 *Coconino*

FLAGSTAFF See also Ash Fork, Mormon Lake, Munds Park, Sedona, Williams & Winslow.

BLACK BARTS RV PARK
Ratings: 5.5/10★/6.5 (RV Park) From Jct of I-40 & exit 198 (Butler), go SE 0.25 mi on Butler (L). Elev 7000 ft. **FAC:** Paved/gravel rds. (174 spaces). Avail: 124 gravel, patios, 80 pull-thrus (25 x 50), back-ins (20 x 37), 124 full hkups (30/50 amps), seasonal sites, tent sites, dump, laundry, restaurant. **REC:** rec open to public. Pets OK. Eco-friendly, 2015 rates: $36.50. Disc: AAA, military. AAA Approved
(928)774-1912 Lat: 35.19263, Lon: -111.61714
2760 E Butler, Flagstaff, AZ 86004
blackbartsrv@gmail.com
www.blackbartssteakhouse.com
See ad this page, 52.

FLAGSTAFF-GRAND CANYON KOA **Ratings:** 8/8/7.5 (Campground) 2015 rates: $34 to $75. (928)526-9926 5803 N Hwy 89, Flagstaff, AZ 86004

FORT TUTHILL COUNTY PARK (Public) From Jct of I-17 & Exit 337, W 200 yards, follow signs to park (E). 2015 rates: $17 to $22. May 1 to Oct 1. (928)679-8000

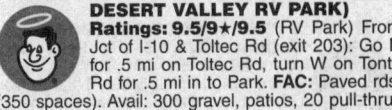

FLAGSTAFF (CONT)

GREER'S PINE SHADOWS RV PARK
Ratings: 8/NA/7.5 (RV Park) From Jct of I-40 & Exit 201, NW 0.4 mi on Country Club Dr to US-89N, NE 1.7 mi on US-89N (L) Note: Follow signage to Page, AZ. Elev 7000 ft. **FAC:** Paved/gravel rds. (80 spaces). Avail: 15 gravel, 13 pull-thrus (20 x 50), back-ins (20 x 40), some side by side hkups, 15 full hkups (30/50 amps), seasonal sites, WiFi, laundry. **REC.** Pet restrict(Q). No tents. Eco-friendly, 2015 rates: $36.40. Disc: military. No CC.
(928)526-4977 Lat: 35.24114, Lon: -111.57014
7101 US 89N, Flagstaff, AZ 86004
www.greerspineshadowsrvpark.com
See ad pages 83, 52.

J & H RV PARK
Ratings: 9/10★/10 (RV Park) From Jct of I-40 & Exit 201 (Page-Grand Cyn exit), go N 0.25 mi on exit rd to N Hwy 89, turn NE 3 mi on US 89 (R) No motorcycles. Elev 7000 ft.

EXPLORE THE GRAND CANYON FROM HERE!
Central location for exploring the Grand Canyon and Sedona. Our warm hospitality and humor have helped us attain the prestigious "National Park of the Year" award. Come enjoy our fun park in the cool hills of Flagstaff, AZ.

FAC: All weather rds. (50 spaces). Avail: 25 all weather, patios, 22 pull-thrus (25 x 55), back-ins (30 x 40), 25 full hkups (30/50 amps), seasonal sites, cable, WiFi, laundry. **REC:** rec open to public. Pet restrict(B). No tents. Age restrict may apply, eco-friendly, 2015 rates: $49.50. May 1 to Oct 20.
(928)526-1829 Lat: 35.25339, Lon: -111.55618
7901 North U.s. Highway 89, Flagstaff, AZ 86004
jhrvpark@aol.com
www.flagstaffrvparks.com
See ad pages 83, 52.

KIT CARSON RV PARK **Ratings: 3/6/4** (Campground) 2015 rates: $36. (928)774-6993 2101 W Route 66, Flagstaff, AZ 86001

Visit Camping World on your RV travels to stock up on accessories and supplies while on the road. Find the nearest SuperCenter at CampingWorld.com

Things to See and Do

BLACK BARTS STEAKHOUSE Steakhouse Saloon and Musical Revue featuring local entertainment. Elev 7000 ft. RV accessible Restrooms, food. Hours: 5:30pm to 10pm.
(928)779-3142 Lat: 35.19233, Lon: -111.61725
2760 E Butler Ave, Flagstaff, AZ 86004
info@blackbartssteakhouse.com
www.blackbartssteakhouse.com
See ad page 83.

FLORENCE — D3 *Pinal*

DESERT GARDENS RV PARK
Ratings: 10/9.5★/10 (RV Park) From Jct of Hwy 79 & SR-287, S 4.2 mi on Hwy 79 (R) Note: No popups or Pick up campers.

AN OASIS IN THE SONORAN DESERT!
Designed to promote a natural, healthy and active lifestyle. Desert Gardens is a popular AZ RV resort with RV lot rentals and RV lot co-op ownership. Room to roam - Super-sized lots.

FAC: All weather rds. (266 spaces). Avail: 166 all weather, back-ins (60 x 70), accepts full hkup units only, 166 full hkups (30/50 amps), seasonal sites, WiFi $, laundry, controlled access. **REC:** heated pool, whirlpool. Pet restrict(B/Q). Partial handicap access, no tents. Age restrict may apply, big rig sites

Say you saw it in our Guide!

AZ

FLORENCE (CONT)

DESERT GARDENS RV PARK (CONT)
eco-friendly, 2015 rates: $45 to $50. Oct 1 to Apr 30. No CC.
(520)868-3800 Lat: 32.96353, Lon: -111.33957
9668 N Hwy 79, Florence, AZ 85132
desertgardens@cgmailbox.com
www.desertgardensrvpark.com
See ad opposite page, 52 & Snowbird Destinations in Magazine Section.

RANCHO SONORA RV PARK
Ratings: 9/9★/9.5 (RV Park) From Jct of Hwy 79 & SR-287 (on S side of town), S 4.3 mi on Hwy 79 (R). MP 128. **FAC:** Gravel rds. (77 spaces). Avail: 57 gravel, patios, 2 pull-thrus (22 x 55), back-ins (45 x 60), accepts full hkup units only, 49 full hkups, 8 W, 8 E (30/50 amps), seasonal sites, WiFi, rentals, dump, laundry, LP gas. **REC:** heated pool, whirlpool, rec open to public. Pet restrict(Q). No tents. Big rig sites, eco-friendly, 2015 rates: $40.
(800)205-6817 Lat: 32.96233, Lon: -111.33758
9160 N Hwy 79, Florence, AZ 85132
linda@ranchosonora.com
www.ranchosonora.com
See ad opposite page.

FORT DEFIANCE — B5 *Apache*

WHEATFIELDS LAKE (Public) From town, N 43 mi on Rte 12 (E) Navajo fishing & boat permits required. You will cross AZ/NE border several times. Pit toilets. 2015 rates: $15 to $25. (928)871-6451

FORT MCDOWELL — D3 *Maricopa*

FORT MCDOWELL See also Apache Junction, Gold Canyon, Mesa, Scottsdale & Tempe.

EAGLE VIEW RV RESORT AT FORT MCDOWELL
Ratings: 10/10★/10 (RV Park) From Jct of SR-87 (Beeline Hwy) & N Fort McDowell Rd, S 0.4 mi on N Fort McDowell Rd (E).

THE RESORT DESTINATION FOR ALL AGES
Serenity & solitude nestled along the Verde River. Yet only minutes away from We-Ko-Pa Golf Club, art festivals and auto auctions. Boating & fishing at nearby lakes and free shuttle to Ft. McDowell Casino.

FAC: Paved rds. (150 spaces). Avail: 140 paved, back-ins (30 x 69), accepts full hkup units only, 140 full hkups (30/50 amps), seasonal sites, cable, WiFi, laundry, restaurant. **REC:** heated pool, whirlpool, golf. Pet restrict(B). No tents. Big rig sites, eco-friendly, 2015 rates: $37 to $54. Disc: AAA, military.
(480)789-5310 Lat: 33.57389, Lon: -111.67469
9605 N Fort Mcdowell Rd, Fort Mcdowell, AZ 85264
eagleview@fmyn.com
www.eagleviewrvresort.com
See ad pages 66 (Spotlight Valley of the Sun), 52 & Snowbird Destinations in Magazine Section.

Things to See and Do

FORT MCDOWELL CASINO Just minutes away from Scottsdale and Mesa Fort McDowell Resort and destination offers incredible variety of gaming options, fine dining, golf and world class entertainment.
www.FortMcDowellCasino.com. Partial handicap access. RV accessible. Restrooms, food. ATM.
(800)843-3678 Lat: 33.58246, Lon: -111.67877
10424 N Fort Mcdowell Rd, Fort Mcdowell, AZ 85264
www.fortmcdowellcasino.com
See ad page 66 (Spotlight Valley of the Sun).

WE-KO-PA GOLF Honored as one of the the Best Resort Courses by Golfweek magazine, We-Ko-Pa is designed by golf course veterans Bill Coore, Ben Crenshaw and Scott Miller. A daily fee golf facility with two 18-hole courses. Restrooms, food.
(480)836-9000 Lat: 33.57857, Lon: -111.68576
18200 E Toh Vee Circle, Fort Mcdowell, AZ 85264
See ad page 66 (Spotlight Valley of the Sun).

FORT MOHAVE — B1 *Mohave*

SNOWBIRD RV RESORT
Ratings: 8/9★/8 (RV Park) From Jct of SR-68 & SR 95 (Laughlin Bridge), S 13 mi on SR 95 to Joy Ln, E 0.2 mi on Joy Ln (R). **FAC:** Paved rds. (124 spaces). Avail: 34 gravel, patios, 30 pull-thrus (18 x 50), back-ins (16 x 48), 34 full hkups (30/50 amps), seasonal sites, WiFi Hotspot, tent sites, laundry. **REC:** pool, whirlpool, golf. Pet restrict(B/Q) $. Big rig sites, eco-friendly, 2015 rates: $30. Disc: AAA. No CC.
(928)768-7141 Lat: 34.99660, Lon: -114.59479
1600 Joy Ln, Fort Mohave, AZ 86426
snowbird@mohavebb.com
www.sbrvresort.com
See ad pages 79, 52.

FOUNTAIN HILLS — D3 *Maricopa*

MCDOWELL MOUNTAIN REGIONAL PARK (MARICOPA COUNTY PARK) (Public) From jct Scottsdale Rd & Shea Blvd: Go 12 mi E on Shea Blvd, then 4 mi N on Saguaro Blvd, then 4 mi E on McDowell Mtn. Rd. 2015 rates: $25. (480)471-0173

GILA BEND — D2 *Maricopa*

GILA BEND KOA (FORMERLY KNOW AS AUGIE'S QUAIL TRAIL RV PARK)
Ratings: 7.5/8.5★/9 (RV Park) From Jct of I-8 & Butterfield Trail (exit 119), N 1 mi on Butterfield Trail (Bus 8) (R); or From Jct of SR-85 & Bus 8, SE 1 mi on Bus 8 (L). **FAC:** All weather rds. (132 spaces). Avail: 102 gravel, 55 pull-thrus (50 x 90), back-ins (50 x 90), accepts full hkup units only, 102 full hkups (30/50 amps), seasonal sites, WiFi, tent sites, laundry. **REC.** Pet restrict(B/Q). Big rig sites, eco-friendly, 2015 rates: $30.
(928)683-2850 Lat: 32.93798, Lon: -112.68084
800 Butterfield Trail, Gila Bend, AZ 85337
www.koa.com/campgrounds/gila-bend
See ad this page.

GLOBE — D4 *Gila*

APACHE GOLD RV PARK
Ratings: 8.5/9★/7.5 (RV Park) From Jct of US-70 & US-60 (in Globe), E 6.3 mi on US-70, Milepost 259 (L). From Jct Hwy 77 & Hwy 70: Go 4 mi E on US 70. Elev 3500 ft. **FAC:** Paved rds. (60 spaces). Avail: 40 paved, patios, 40 pull-thrus (21 x 60), mostly side by side hkups, 40 full hkups (30/50 amps), seasonal sites, WiFi, tent sites, laundry, groc, LP gas, restaurant. **REC:** heated pool, whirlpool, golf. Pets OK. Partial handicap access. Eco-friendly, 2015 rates: $25.
(928)475-7800 Lat: 33.35648, Lon: -110.66725
Milepost 259, San Carlos, AZ 85550
crystallemke@agcr.us
www.apachegoldcasinoresort.com
See ad this page.

GILA COUNTY RV PARK
(RV Spaces) From West jct Hwy 88 & US 60: Go 3-1/2 mi E on US 60, then 100 yards E on Maple, then 50 yards N on Tebbs. (No showers). **FAC:** Gravel/dirt rds. (24 spaces). 21 Avail: 15 gravel, 6 dirt, back-ins (18 x 36), 15 full hkups, 6 W, 6 E (30/50 amps), seasonal sites, WiFi, tent sites, pit toilets, dump. Pet restrict 2015 rates: $25 to $35. AAA Approved
(800)436-8083 Lat: 33.39382, Lon: -110.78720
201 W Cottonwood, Globe, AZ 85501
www.gilamini.com
See ad page 51 (Welcome Section).

GOLD CANYON — D3 *Pinal*

A SPOTLIGHT Introducing Gold Canyon's colorful attractions appearing at the front of this state section.

GOLD CANYON See also Apache Junction, Chandler, Mesa, Phoenix, Queen Valley & Tempe.

ARIZONIAN RV RESORT
Ratings: 9.5/10★/9.5 (RV Resort) From Jct of US Hwy 60 & Goldfield Rd (Exit 198), E 9.2 mi on Hwy 60 (L).

ENJOY THIS SONORAN DESERT RESORT!
Hundreds of miles of ATV and hiking trails right out our back gate. Big rig friendly. Live entertainment, pickle ball, fitness center, pool and spa await you. Near shopping, restaurants, medical facilities & attractions.

FAC: Paved rds. (350 spaces). Avail: 280 gravel, patios, back-ins (40 x 50), 280 full hkups (30/50 amps), seasonal sites, WiFi, laundry. **REC:** heated pool, whirlpool, golf, shuffleboard. Pet restrict(B/Q). Partial handicap access, no tents. Age restrict may apply, eco-friendly, 2015 rates: $39.
(520)463-2978 Lat: 33.30003, Lon: -111.39457
15976 East US Hwy 60, Apache Junction, AZ 85118
arizonianresort@yahoo.com
www.arizonianresort.com
See ad pages 68 (Spotlight Valley of the Sun), 52 & Snowbird Destinations in Magazine Section.

CANYON VISTAS RV RESORT & SUPERSTITION VIEWS RESORT
Ratings: 10/10★/9.5 (RV Resort) From Jct Hwy 88 & US 60: Go E 4.9 mi on US 60 for 4.9 mi.

2 RESORTS IN 1 LOCATION 10/10*/9.5
Nestled at base of Superstition Mts. for quiet morning walks, bike rides or keep in shape in our fitness center. Meet friends for a round at our Pitch & Putt Golf Course. Enjoy a cool drink & desert breeze under the veranda!

FAC: Paved rds. (634 spaces). Avail: 350 all weather, patios, back-ins (40 x 50), accepts full hkup units only, 350 full hkups (30/50 amps), seasonal sites, WiFi, laundry. **REC:** heated pool, whirlpool, shuffleboard. Pet restrict(B/Q). Partial handicap access, no tents. Age restrict may apply, RV age restrict, eco-friendly, 2015 rates: $55. ATM, no CC.
(888)940-8989 Lat: 33.36141, Lon: -111.47491
6601 E US Hwy 60, Gold Canyon, AZ 85118
cap121E@cal-am.com
http://www.cal-am.com/resorts/resorts_details.php?resorts_id=9&search=quick
See ad pages 56 (Spotlight Gold Canyon), 52 & Cal Am Insert & Snowbird Destinations in Magazine Section.

GOLD CANYON RV & GOLF RESORT
Ratings: 10/10★/10 (RV Resort) From Jct of E US Hwy 60 & Goldfield exit (end of freeway), E 3.4 mi on Hwy 60 at mm 202 (R).

LUXURY GOLF AND RV RESORT
Experience a community of natural beauty from the Sonoran Desert to countless activities and amenities. A 55+ active adult retirement community is an energetic and beautiful place that redefines active adult living and RVing.

FAC: Paved rds. (754 spaces). Avail: 200 all weather, patios, back-ins (38 x 50), 200 full hkups (30/50 amps), seasonal sites, cable, WiFi, rentals, laundry, controlled access. **REC:** heated pool, whirlpool, golf, shuffleboard. Pet restrict(Q). Partial handicap access, no tents. Age restrict may apply, RV age restrict, eco-friendly, 2015 rates: $48 to $56. No CC.
(888)349-4172 Lat: 33.35672, Lon: -111.46861
7151 E US Hwy 60, Gold Canyon, AZ 85118
gc@robertsresorts.com
www.robertsresorts.com
See ad pages 46 (Welcome Section), 52, 45 (AZ Map) & Snowbird Destinations in Magazine Section.

SUPERSTITION VIEWS RESORT & CANYON VISTAS RV RESORT
Ratings: 10/10★/9.5 (RV Resort) From Jct Hwy 88 & US 60: Go E 4.9 mi on US 60 for 4.9 mi.

FOR THE RV'ER WHO WANTS IT ALL...
Our highly customizable casitas offer available RV garages, ports and pads, in addition to rooftop sunset decks. The included amenities are next door at Canyon Vistas RV Resorts with overnight stays available.

FAC: Paved rds. (634 spaces). Avail: 350 all weather, patios, back-ins (40 x 50), accepts full hkup units only, 350 full hkups (30/50 amps), seasonal sites, WiFi, laundry. **REC:** heated pool, whirlpool, shuffleboard. Pet restrict(B/Q). Partial handicap access. Big

Like Us on Facebook.

GOLD CANYON (CONT)

SUPERSTITION VIEWS RESORT (CONT)
rig sites, RV age restrict, eco-friendly, 2015 rates: $55. ATM, no CC.
(888)940-8989 Lat: 33.36141, Lon: -111.47491
6601 E US Hwy 60, Gold Canyon, AZ 85118
reservations@cal-am.com
http://www.cal-am.com/resorts/resorts_details.php?resorts_id=30
See ad pages 56 (Spotlight Gold Canyon), 52 & Cal Am Insert & Snowbird Destinations in Magazine Section.

GOLDEN VALLEY — B1 *Mohave*

ADOBE RV PARK
Ratings: 7.5/9.5★/9.5 (RV Park) From Jct of I-40 & US 93 (Exit 48), W 3.5 mi on US 93 to AZ-68, W 4.4 mi on AZ-68 (toward Laughlin, NV) to Adobe Rd (Maverick Country Store), N 600 ft to West Apache Way, E 0.1 mi (R). Elev 2800 ft. **FAC:** Paved rds. (75 spaces). Avail: 25 gravel, 4 pull-thrus (32 x 54), back-ins (32 x 56), 25 full hkups (30/50 amps), seasonal sites, WiFi $, dump, laundry. **REC.** Pet restrict(B/Q). Partial handicap access, no tents. Big rig sites, eco-friendly, 2015 rates: $25. No CC.
(928)565-3010 Lat: 35.22343, Lon: -114.19763
4950 West Apache Way, Golden Valley, AZ 86413
adobervpark@hotmail.com
www.adobervpark.com
See ad this page, 52.

TRADEWINDS RV PARK **Ratings: 8/9.5★/9** (RV Park) 2015 rates: $31.73. (928)565-5115 152 S Emery Park Rd, Golden Valley, AZ 86413

GOODYEAR — D3 *Maricopa*

COTTON LANE RV & GOLF RESORT
Ratings: 9.5/10★/9.5 (RV Park) From Jct of I-10 & Cotton Ln (exit 125), S 0.7 mi on N Citrus Rd to Van Buren St, E 0.5 mi (L). **FAC:** Paved rds. (438 spaces). Avail: 338 gravel, patios, 40 pull-thrus (24 x 70), back-ins (47 x 60), 338 full hkups (30/50 amps), seasonal sites, WiFi $, laundry. **REC:** heated pool, whirlpool, golf. Pet restrict(B/Q). Partial handicap access, no tents. Age restrict may apply, RV age restrict, eco-friendly, 2015 rates: $34. Disc: AAA, military.
(888)907-7223 Lat: 33.45139, Lon: -112.43271
17506 W Van Buren, Goodyear, AZ 85338
cottonlaneoffice@yahoo.com
www.arizonarvresorts.com
See ad pages 65 (Spotlight Valley of the Sun), 52.

Park policies vary. Ask about the cancellation policy when making a reservation.

DESTINY PHOENIX RV RESORTS
Ratings: 10/9.5★/10 (RV Park) E-bnd: From Jct of I-10 & Exit 123, S 0.7 mi on N Citrus Rd (R), or W-bnd: From Jct of I-10 & Exit 125, S 0.8 mi on Sarival Rd to Van Buren, W 2 mi to N Citrus Rd, N 0.1 mi (L).

SNEAK AWAY TO YOUR 2ND HOME TODAY!
Come explore the Arizona lifestyle with us. Enjoy nearby, Nascar racing, NFL games, antique & exotic car auction and many activities right at the park. Come stay a day, a week or months and enjoy our many amenities.

FAC: Paved rds. (284 spaces). Avail: 219 paved, patios, 103 pull-thrus (30 x 50), back-ins (30 x 45), 219 full hkups (30/50 amps), seasonal sites, WiFi $, laundry, LP gas, controlled access. **REC:** heated pool, whirlpool, shuffleboard. Pet restrict(B/Q). Partial handicap access, no tents. Big rig sites, RV age restrict, eco-friendly, 2015 rates: $28 to $43. Disc: AAA, military.
(888)667-2454 Lat: 33.45166, Lon: -112.44509
416 N Citrus Rd, Goodyear, AZ 85338
phoenix@destinyrv.com
www.destinyrv.com
See ad pages 92, 52.

GRAND CANYON NATIONAL PARK — B3 *Coconino*

A SPOTLIGHT Introducing Grand Canyon's colorful attractions appearing at the front of this state section.

GRAND CANYON NATIONAL PARK See also Ash Fork, Flagstaff, Grand Canyon, Jacob Lake, Page, Sedona, Tusayan, Williams & Winslow.

GRAND CANYON TRAILER VILLAGE INC (Natl Pk) From Jct of I-40 & Hwy 64, N 60 mi on Hwy 64 to S entrance, follow signs (L). 2015 rates: $36. (303)297-2757

GRAND CANYON/DESERT VIEW (Natl Pk) From Jct of US-89 & AZ Rte 64 (at Cameron), NW 33 mi on AZ Rte 64 (R). Entrance fee required. 2015 rates: $12. May 15 to Oct 15. (928)638-7888

GRAND CANYON/MATHER (Natl Pk) From Jct of I-180 & SR-64, N 30 mi on SR-64 to entrance station, continue N 3 mi to Mather Camp Rd, E 0.2 mi, follow signs. Entrance fee required. Reservations strongly recommended. For reservations call 1-800-365-2267 from April to November. 2015 rates: $18. (928)638-7851

GRAND CANYON/NORTH RIM (Natl Pk) From Jct of US-89 Alt. & Hwy 67 (N entrance), S 43 mi on Hwy 67 (E). NOTE: Reservations and entrance fee required. For reservations call 1-800-444-6777. 2015 rates: $18 to $25. May 15 to Oct 31. (800)365-2267

GREEN VALLEY — E4 *Pima*

GREEN VALLEY RV RESORT **Ratings: 9.5/8.5/9** (RV Park) 2015 rates: $40. (520)625-3900 19001 S Richfield Ave, Green Valley, AZ 85614

HAPPY JACK — C3 *Coconino*

CLINT'S WELL RESORT- SUNRISE RESORTS **Ratings: 4.5/8★/6** (Membership Pk) 2015 rates: $30. May 1 to Oct 31. (928)477-2299 291 Forest Hwy 3, Happy Jack, AZ 86024

HAPPY JACK LODGE & RV RESORT **Ratings: 7.5/7/8.5** (RV Park) 2015 rates: $34. (928)477-2805 292 S Forest Hwy 3, Happy Jack, AZ 86024

HOLBROOK — B4 *Navajo*

HOLBROOK/PETRIFIED FOREST KOA **Ratings: 8.5/8.5★/8.5** (Campground) 2015 rates: $32 to $40. (800)562-3389 102 Hermosa Ave, Holbrook, AZ 86025

OK RV PARK
Ratings: 6.5/9★/8.5 (RV Park) From Jct of I-40 & Navajo Blvd (exit 286), go NE 1/2 mi on Bus I-40 (Navajo Blvd), then turn W on Buzzard Blvd (R). Elev 5000 ft. **FAC:** Paved/gravel rds. (112 spaces). Avail: 91 gravel, patios, 91 pull-thrus (20 x 108), 91 full hkups (30/50 amps), seasonal sites, cable, WiFi, tent sites, laundry. **REC.** Pet restrict(B/Q). Partial handicap access. Eco-friendly, 2015 rates: $29 to $34. Disc: AAA, military.
AAA Approved
(928)524-3226 Lat: 34.91921, Lon: -110.15411
1576 Roadrunner Rd, Holbrook, AZ 86025
okrvpk@cableone.net
www.okrvpk-llc.com
See ad this page.

HON-DAH — C5 *Navajo*

HON-DAH RV PARK **Ratings: 7/7/8.5** (RV Park) 2015 rates: $31.55. (928)369-7400 1 Hwy 73, Pinetop, AZ 85935

HOPE — C2 *La Paz*

RAMBLIN' ROADS RV PARK **Ratings: 7/8/9** (RV Park) 2015 rates: $27.75. (928)859-3187 60655 E US Hwy 60, Salome, AZ 85348

HUACHUCA CITY — E4 *Cochise*

MOUNTAIN VIEW RV PARK
Ratings: 8.5/9★/8.5 (RV Park) From Jct of Hwys 90 (Huachuca Blvd) & 82, S 0.5 mi on Hwy 90 (R). (Note: Behind RV City Dealership). Elev 4700 ft. **FAC:** Paved rds. (81 spaces). Avail: 61 gravel, patios, 57 pull-thrus (25 x 60), back-ins (21 x 40), 61 full hkups (30/50 amps), seasonal sites, WiFi, laundry. **REC.** Pet restrict(B). No tents. Big rig sites, eco-friendly, 2015 rates: $25 to $32.
(520)456-2860 Lat: 31.68252, Lon: -110.35307
99 W Vista Ln, Huachuca City, AZ 85616
mtviewrvpark@aol.com
www.mountainviewrvpark.com

QUAIL RIDGE RV RESORT **Ratings: 6.5/8.5★/9** (RV Park) 2015 rates: $13. (520)456-9301 2207 N Yucca Dr, Huachuca City, AZ 85616

AZ

JACOB LAKE — A3 *Coconino*

KAIBAB CAMPER VILLAGE **Ratings: 3.5/NA/8** (Campground) Pit toilets. 2015 rates: $36. May 14 to Oct 15. (928)643-7804 jacob Lake-Forest Rd 461, Jacob Lake, AZ 86022

JOSEPH CITY — B4 *Navajo*

CHOLLA LAKE COUNTY PARK (Public) From Jct of I-40 & Exit 277, E 1 mi on Exit 277 (E). 2015 rates: $10 to $13. (928)288-3717

KATHERINE — B1 *Mohave*

LAKE MEAD NRA/KATHERINE LANDING CAMPGROUND (Natl Pk) From Jct of SR-95 & SR-68, N 1 mi on SR-68 to Katherine Rd, W 3.1 mi (E). 2015 rates: $10. (928)754-3245

KAYENTA — A4 *Navajo*

KAYENTA See also Monument Valley, UT.

NAVAJO NAT'L MONUMENT (Natl Pk) From town, SW 19 mi on Hwy 160 to Hwy 564, N 10 mi (E). (928)672-2700

KINGMAN — B1 *Mohave*

BLAKE RANCH RV PARK
Ratings: 9/10★/9.5 (RV Park) From Jct of I-40 & Blake Ranch Rd (exit 66), N 0.2 mi on Blake Ranch Rd (E). Note: Do Not Use GPS. Elev 4300 ft. **FAC:** Paved rds. (58 spaces). Avail: 38 all weather, 25 pull-thrus (30 x 65), back-ins (30 x 68), 38 full hkups (30/50 amps), seasonal sites, WiFi, dump, laundry, groc, LP gas. **REC.** Pet restrict(Q). Partial handicap access, no tents. Big rig sites, eco-friendly, 2015 rates: $25 to $29. Disc: AAA.
(928)757-3336 Lat: 35.18013, Lon: -113.78823
9315 E Blake Ranch Road, Kingman, AZ 86401
lonerider@blakeranchrv.com
www.blakeranchrv.com
See ad opposite page, 52.

FORT BEALE RV PARK **Ratings: 8.5/9.5★/7.5** (RV Park) 2015 rates: $30. (928)753-3355 300 Metcalfe Road, Kingman, AZ 86401

HUALAPAI MOUNTAIN PARK (Public) From Jct of I-40 & Exit 51 (Stockton Hill Rd becomes Hualapai Mountain Rd), S 15 mi on Hualapai Mnt Rd (R). 2015 rates: $15 to $25. (928)681-5700

KINGMAN KOA Ratings: 8.5/10★/9 (Campground) W-bnd: From Jct of I-40 & Andy Devine Ave (Exit 53), NE 0.6 mi on Andy Devine Ave (US 66E) to Airway Ave, W 0.9 mi on Airway Ave to N Roosevelt, N 0.6 mi (R). Elev 3200 ft. **FAC:** Paved/gravel rds. 84 gravel, 84 pull-thrus (23 x 50), some side by side hkups, 69 full hkups, 15 W, 15 E (30/50 amps), cable, WiFi, tent sites, rentals, dump, laundry, groc, LP gas, firewood. **REC:** heated pool, whirlpool, playground. Pet restrict(B/Q). Big rig sites, 2015 rates: $36 to $45. Disc: military.
(800)562-3991 Lat: 35.23401, Lon: -114.01797
3820 N Roosevelt, Kingman, AZ 86409
kingmankoa@gmail.com
http://www.kingmankoa.com/

SUNRISE RV PARK Ratings: 6.5/9.5★/8 (RV Park) From Jct of I-40 & Exit 53 (Andy Devine), SW 0.25 mi on Andy Devine to Michael, NW 500 ft on Michael to McDonald, NE 500 ft (L). **FAC:** Paved rds. (46 spaces). Avail: 15 gravel, patios, 8 pull-thrus (20 x 60), back-ins (24 x 60), 15 full hkups (30/50 amps), seasonal sites, WiFi, laundry. **REC.** Pet restrict(B/Q). No tents. 2015 rates: $36. Disc: AAA. AAA Approved
(928)753-2277 Lat: 35.21655, Lon: -114.01366
3131 Macdonald Ave, Kingman, AZ 86401
sunriserv@frontiernet.net
www.sunriservpark.com

ZUNI VILLAGE RV PARK Ratings: 6.5/9.5★/7.5 (RV Park) From Jct of I-40 & US 66 (Andy Devine Ave/Exit 53), NE 0.6 mi on US 66 to Airway Ave, W 0.6 mi (L). Elev 3200 ft. **FAC:** All weather rds. (130 spaces). Avail: 19 gravel, 19 pull-thrus (30 x 60), accepts self-contain units only, 19 full hkups (30/50 amps), seasonal sites, cable, WiFi, dump, laundry, LP gas. **REC.** Pet restrict(B/Q). Partial handicap access, no tents. Big rig sites, 2015 rates: $38.20. Disc: AAA.
AAA Approved
(866)887-9864 Lat: 35.22506, Lon: -114.01380
2840 Airway Ave, Kingman, AZ 86409
zunirv@frontiernet.net

LAKE HAVASU CITY — C1 *Mohave*

CAMPBELL COVE RV RESORT
Ratings: 9.5/9.5★/8.5 (RV Park) From Jct of US 95 & Industrial Blvd, W 0.4 mi on Industrial Blvd. (R). **FAC:** Paved/gravel rds. (122 spaces). 100 Avail: 72 paved, 28 gravel, 15 pull-thrus (20 x 70), back-ins (20 x 45), 100 full hkups (30/50 amps), seasonal sites, cable, WiFi $, laundry. **REC:** heated pool, whirlpool. Pet restrict(B/Q). No tents. Big rig sites, eco-friendly, 2015 rates: $35 to $42. Disc: military.
(928)854-7200 Lat: 34.49477, Lon: -114.35602
1523 Industrial Blvd, Lake Havasu City, AZ 86403
rvpi@campbellcovervresort.com
www.campbellcovervresort.com

CAT-TAIL COVE
(State Pk) From Jct of Hwy 95 & London Bridge Rd, S 14.5 mi on Hwy 95 (between MP-167 & 168) to Cat Tail Cove Rd, SW 0.5 mi (E). **FAC:** Paved rds. 61 paved, patios, 6 pull-thrus (18 x 40), back-ins (22 x 40), 61 W, 61 E (30/50 amps), tent sites, dump, fire rings. **REC:** Lake Havasu: swim, fishing. Pets OK. Partial handicap access. 2015 rates: $28. Disc: military.
(928)855-1223 Lat: 34.35429, Lon: -114.16703
PO Box 1990, Lake Havasu City, AZ 86405
www.azstateparks.gov
See ad page 49 (Welcome Section).

CRAZY HORSE CAMPGROUNDS **Ratings: 8.5/5.5/7** (Campground) 2015 rates: $40 to $60. (928)855-4033 1534 Beachcomber Blvd, Lake Havasu City, AZ 86403

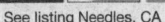

DJ'S RV PARK Ratings: 9.5/9★/8 (RV Park) N-bnd: From Jct of Hwy 95 & McCulloch Blvd (in town), N 4.5 mi on Hwy 95 (L); or S-bnd: From Jct of I-40 & Hwy 95 (exit 9), S 15 mi on Hwy 95 (R). **FAC:** Paved rds. (99 spaces). Avail: 40 all weather, back-ins (22 x 60), 40 full hkups (30/50 amps), seasonal sites, WiFi, laundry. **REC:** heated pool. Pet restrict(B/Q). No tents. Eco-friendly, 2015 rates: $35. AAA Approved
(928)764-3964 Lat: 34.53851, Lon: -114.35394
3501 Hwy 95N, Lake Havasu City, AZ 86404
info@djsrvpark.com
www.djsrvpark.com

LAKE HAVASU CITY (CONT)

HAVASU FALLS RV RESORT **Ratings: 10/10★/9** (RV Park) 2015 rates: $40 to $44. (928)764-0050 3493 Hwy 95 N, Lake Havasu City, AZ 86404

ISLANDER RV RESORT **Ratings: 10/10★/9.5** (RV Park) 2015 rates: $56 to $89. (928)680-2000 751 Beachcomber Blvd, Lake Havasu City, AZ 86403

LAKE HAVASU/WINDSOR BEACH (State Pk) From Jct of I-40 & Hwy 95, S 20 mi on Hwy 95 to Industrial Blvd, follow signs (R). Entrance fee required. **FAC:** Paved rds. 47 gravel, 3 pull-thrus (20 x 60), back-ins (12 x 30) (50 amps), tent sites, dump, fire rings. **REC:** Lake Havasu: swim, fishing, rec open to public. Pets OK. Partial handicap access. 14 day max stay, 2015 rates: $30 to $35. Disc: military.
(928)855-2784 Lat: 34.48922, Lon: -114.35551
699 London Bridge Rd, Lake Havasu City, AZ 86403
www.azstateparks.com
See ad page 49 (Welcome Section).

PIRATE COVE RESORT
Ratings: 8.5/9★/8.5 (RV Park) From the Jct of AZ Hwy 95 & McCulloch Blvd, N 10.5 on Az Hwy 95 to I 40, W 18.6 mi to Park Moabi Rd(exit 153),N 0.6 mi (L). **FAC.** (157 spaces). 145 Avail: 21 paved, 124 gravel, 11 pull-thrus (24 x 46), back-ins (24 x 4), some side by side hkups, 134 full hkups (30/50 amps), seasonal sites, WiFi, tent sites, rentals, showers $, dump, mobile sewer, laundry, groc, LP bottles, firewood, restaurant, controlled access. **REC:** Colorado River: swim, fishing, marina, playground, rec open to public. Pet restrict(B/Q) $. Partial handicap access. RV age restrict, eco-friendly, 2015 rates: $45 to $55. ATM.
(866)301-3000 Lat: 34.72768, Lon: -114.51261
100 Park Moabi Rd, Needles, CA 92363
Piratecoveresort.com
See primary listing at Needles, CA and ad page 87.

PROSPECTORS RV RESORT Ratings: 9/9★/8.5 (RV Park) From Jct of AZ 95 & London Bridge Rd, SW 1.3 mi on London Bridge Rd (L). **FAC:** Paved rds. 108 gravel, patios, back-ins (30 x 60), 108 full hkups (30/50 amps), cable, WiFi $, laundry. **REC:** heated pool, whirlpool. Pet restrict(B) $. No tents. Big rig sites, 2015 rates: $39.
AAA Approved
(928)764-2000 Lat: 34.56047, Lon: -114.37070
4750 London Bridge Road, Lake Havasu City, AZ 86404
infoaz@prospectorsresort.com
www.prospectorsresort.com

SAM'S BEACHCOMBER RESORT (RV Resort) (Rebuilding) 2015 rates: $55. (928)453-1550 601 Beachcomber Blvd, Lake Havasu City, AZ 86403

LAKE POWELL — A3 *Coconino*

LAKE POWELL See also Flagstaff, Page AZ & Kanab, St. George UT.

LITCHFIELD PARK — D3 *Maricopa*

WHITE TANK MOUNTAINS REGIONAL PARK (Public) From Jct of I-17 & Dunlap Ave, W 20 mi on Dunlap Ave/Olive; or From Jct of I-10 & Cotton Ln, N 7 mi on Cotton Ln to Olive, W 4 mi (E). Entrance fee required. 2015 rates: $12 to $30. (623)935-2505

LITTLEFIELD — A2 *Mohave*

VIRGIN RIVER GORGE (Public) From St George, UT, SW 20 mi on I-15 to Cedar Pockets exit, follow signs (L). 2015 rates: $8. (435)688-3200

LUKEVILLE — E2 *Pima*

ORGAN PIPE CACTUS (Natl Pk) From Jct I-10 & AZ-85, S 110 mi to Lukeville, AZ (E). 2015 rates: $12. (520)387-6849

We appreciate your business!

MARANA — D4 *Pima*

A BAR A RV PARK **Ratings: 5/7/6.5** (RV Park) 2015 rates: $25. (520)682-4332 9015 W Tangerine Farms Rd, Marana, AZ 85658

VALLEY OF THE SUN RV RESORT
Ratings: 10/9.5★/9 (RV Park) From Jct of I-10 & Marana Rd (exit 236), S 0.7 mi on Sandario Rd (R).

NEAR TUCSON, CASINO, GOLF & MORE!
Great Value, great prices, great people. Our goal is to make your stay in the area a pleasant and memorable one. Park model sales available. Enjoy the Arizona lifestyle with us!

FAC: All weather rds. (121 spaces). Avail: 111 all weather, patios, 19 pull-thrus (30 x 70), back-ins (35 x 70), accepts full hkup units only, 111 full hkups (30/50 amps), seasonal sites, WiFi $, laundry, LP gas. **REC:** heated pool, whirlpool. Pet restrict No tents. Big rig sites, eco-friendly, 2015 rates: $34.50 to $40. Disc: AAA, military.
(520)682-3434 Lat: 32.45086, Lon: -111.21729
13377 N Sandario Rd, Marana, AZ 85653
admin@votsaz.com
www.valleyofthesunrv.com
See ad pages 62 (Spotlight Tucson), 52 & Snowbird Destinations in Magazine Section.

MARBLE CANYON — A3 *Coconino*

GLEN CANYON NRA/LEES FERRY (Natl Pk) From Jct of US-89 & US-89A, NE 16 mi on US-89A to park access rd, N 5 mi (L). 2015 rates: $12. (928)355-2319

MARICOPA — D3 *Pinal*

WILD WEST RANCH & RV RESORT Ratings: 6.5/8★/8.5 (RV Park) From Jct of I-8E & AZ 84 (Exit 151), N 5 mi on AZ 84 (R); or From Jct of I-10E & Queen Creek Rd (Exit 164), W 28 mi on Queen Creek Rd (becomes John Wayne Parkway) (E). **FAC:** Gravel rds. (150 spaces). Avail: 125 gravel, 31 pull-thrus (32 x 50), back-ins (32 x 60), 125 full hkups (30/50 amps), seasonal sites, WiFi, dump, laundry,

We rate what RVers consider important.

MARICOPA (CONT)

WILD WEST RANCH & RV RESORT (CONT)
LP gas. **REC:** shuffleboard. Pets OK. No tents. Big rig sites, 2015 rates: $25. No CC.
AAA Approved
(520)858-5035 Lat: 32.87518, Lon: -112.04927
860 S John Wayne Parkway, Maricopa, AZ 85139
info@wildwestrvresort.com
www.wildwestrvresort.com

MEADVIEW — B1 *Mohave*

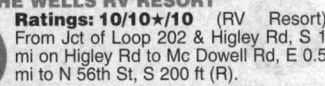

MEADVIEW RV PARK
Ratings: 7/8★/8 (RV Park) From Jct of US 93 & milepost 42/Pierce Ferry Rd, go E 34.5 mi on Pierce Ferry Rd (R). Elev 3494 ft. **FAC:** Gravel rds. 32 gravel, 2 pull-thrus (39 x 75), back-ins (30 x 50), 32 full hkups (30/50 amps), WiFi, tent sites, rentals, showers $, laundry, LP gas, fire rings, firewood. **REC.** Pets OK. Eco-friendly, 2015 rates: $25 to $27.50. Disc: AAA, military.
(928)564-2662 Lat: 35.94115, Lon: -114.08596
28100 N Pierce Ferry Rd, Meadview, AZ 86444
Rvpark@citlink.net
http://www.rv-park.com/
See ad opposite page, 52.

MESA — D3 *Maricopa, Pinal*

MESA See also Apache Junction, Buckeye, Chandler, Fort McDowell, Gold Canyon, Goodyear, Peoria, Phoenix, Queen Valley, Sun City, Surprise & Tempe.

AMBASSADOR DOWNS/MHP **Ratings: 8.5/8/6.5** (RV Area in MHP) 2015 rates: $42. (480)964-8315 2345 E Main St, Mesa, AZ 85213

APACHE WELLS RV RESORT
Ratings: 10/10★/10 (RV Resort) From Jct of Loop 202 & Higley Rd, S 1 mi on Higley Rd to Mc Dowell Rd, E 0.5 mi to N 56th St, S 200 ft (R).

PREMIER MESA RESORT 10/10*/10
Enjoy with friends invigorating game of tennis on our lighted courts or on shuffleboard courts or a fun game of bridge don't forget our pool & spa. High speed internet in the computer room-to keep in touch with family/friends
FAC: Paved rds. (320 spaces). Avail: 88 all weather, patios, back-ins (32 x 45), accepts full hkup units only, 88 full hkups (30/50 amps), seasonal sites, WiFi, laundry, LP bottles. **REC:** heated pool, whirlpool, shuffleboard. Pet restrict(B/Q). No tents. Age restrict may apply, eco-friendly, 2015 rates: $39.
(888)940-8989 Lat: 33.46424, Lon: -111.71028
2656 N 56th St, Mesa, AZ 85215
reservations@cal-am.com
http://www.cal-am.com/resorts/resorts_details.php?resorts_id=4&search=quick
See ad pages 56 (Spotlight Gold Canyon), 52 & Cal Am Insert & Snowbird Destinations in Magazine Section.

ARIZONA ACRES RESORT/MHP **Ratings: 8.5/7.5/8** (RV Area in MHP) 2015 rates: $40. (480)986-0220 9421 E Main St, Mesa, AZ 85207

County names help you follow the local weather report.

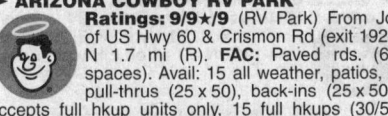

ARIZONA COWBOY RV PARK
Ratings: 9/9★/9 (RV Park) From Jct of US Hwy 60 & Crismon Rd (exit 192), N 1.7 mi (R). **FAC:** Paved rds. (60 spaces). Avail: 15 all weather, patios, 2 pull-thrus (25 x 50), back-ins (25 x 50), accepts full hkup units only, 15 full hkups (30/50 amps), seasonal sites, WiFi, rentals, laundry, controlled access. **REC.** Pet restrict(B). No tents. Age restrict may apply, eco-friendly, 2015 rates: $40 to $50.
(480)986-3333 Lat: 33.41170, Lon: -111.61492
139 S Crismon Rd, Mesa, AZ 85208
AzCowboyRvPark@gmail.com
www.arizonacowboy.com
See ad this page.

ARIZONA MAVERIK FAMILY RV PARK **Ratings: 5.5/7/7** (RV Park) 2015 rates: $35 to $40. (480)354-3700 201 S Crismon, Mesa, AZ 85208

AZTEC RV PARK LLC **Ratings: 9.5/10★/9.5** (RV Park) 2015 rates: $45. (855)832-2700 4220 E Main St, Mesa, AZ 85205

DESERAMA MHP & RV PARK **Ratings: 8/7.5★/8** (RV Park) 2015 rates: $38. (480)964-8850 2434 E Main St - Manager's Office, Mesa, AZ 85213

DESERT VISTA RV RESORT **Ratings: 9.5/NA/9.5** (RV Park) 2015 rates: $48. (480)663-3383 124 S. 54th St, Mesa, AZ 85206

DOLLBEER MH & RV RANCH **Ratings: 8.5/8★/7.5** (RV Park) 2015 rates: $25. (480)986-1514 8421 E Main St, Mesa, AZ 85207

GOOD LIFE RV RESORT
Ratings: 10/10★/10 (RV Resort) From Jct of US Hwy 60 & Val Vista Rd (exit 184), N 2 mi on Val Vista Rd to Main St, W 0.2 mi (L).

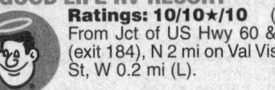

CENTRAL LOCATION RV RESORT10/10*/10
Guest enjoy a wide range of activities-fun dancing events-great pool-a game under lighted tennis/shuffleboard courts-shopping-restaurants and a short distance to fabulous golf courses. A new dog park for your pet!
FAC: Paved rds. (1156 spaces). Avail: 400 all weather, patios, back-ins (30 x 42), accepts full hkup units only, 400 full hkups (30/50 amps), seasonal sites, WiFi, laundry, controlled access. **REC:** heated pool, whirlpool, shuffleboard. Pet restrict(B/Q). Partial handicap access, no tents. Age restrict may apply, big rig sites, eco-friendly, 2015 rates: $46. Disc: AAA. ATM.
AAA Approved
(888)940-8989 Lat: 33.41476, Lon: -111.75791
3403 E Main St, Mesa, AZ 85213
goodlife@cal-am.com
http://www.cal-am.com/resorts/resorts_details.php?resorts_id=26&search=quick
See ad pages 56 (Spotlight Gold Canyon), 52 & Cal Am Insert & Snowbird Destinations in Magazine Section.

GREEN ACRES RV PARK
Ratings: 9/9★/8 (RV Park) From Jct of US Hwy 60 (Superstition Fwy) & Dobson Rd, N 2 mi on Dobson Rd to Main St, W 500 ft (R). **FAC:** Paved rds. 65 Avail: 65 all weather, patios, back-ins (20 x 42), accepts full hkup units only, 65 full hkups (30/50 amps), cable, WiFi, laundry. **REC:** pool, whirlpool. Pet restrict(B/Q). No tents. Eco-friendly, 2015 rates: $42. Disc: AAA, military.
(480)964-5058 Lat: 33.41487, Lon: -111.87518
2052 W Main, Mesa, AZ 85201
greenacresrvpark@aol.com
www.greenacresrvparkmesa.com
See ad this page, 52.

Refer to the Table of Contents in front of the Guide to locate everything you need.

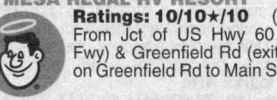

M & M BUDGET RV PARK
Ratings: 7/NA/7 (RV Area in MHP) From Jct of AZ-202 & exit 13, S 0.3 mi on AZ-87/Country Club Dr to E McKellips Rd, E 0.9 mi on E McKellips Rd (L). **FAC:** Paved rds. (240 spaces). Avail: 100 gravel, patios, back-ins (35 x 60), 100 full hkups (30/50 amps), seasonal sites, restrooms only, laundry. **REC:** heated pool, whirlpool, playground. Pets OK. Big rig sites, 2015 rates: $30. No CC.
(480)461-6000 Lat: 33.451538, Lon: -111.826847
320 E Mckellips Rd, Mesa, AZ 85201
See ad page 44 (Welcome Section).

MESA DUNES RV & MHP **Ratings: 9/7.5/8.5** (RV Park) 2015 rates: $45. (866)575-6468 7807 E Main St, Mesa, AZ 85207

MESA REGAL RV RESORT
Ratings: 10/10★/10 (RV Resort) From Jct of US Hwy 60 (Superstition Fwy) & Greenfield Rd (exit 185), N 2 mi on Greenfield Rd to Main St, E 0.4 mi (L).

PREMIER MESA RESORT 10/10*/10
Enjoy...our 4 outdoor pools & spa-computer & fitness centers. Plus in-house beauty/barber shops-massage therapy-travel agency-5 lighted tennis courts-batting/driving cages-water volleyball-bocce ball-pickle ball & much more!
FAC: Paved rds. (2005 spaces). Avail: 800 all weather, patios, back-ins (35 x 45), accepts full hkup units only, 800 full hkups (30/50 amps), seasonal sites, WiFi, laundry. **REC:** heated pool, whirlpool, shuffleboard. Pet restrict(B/Q). No tents. Age restrict may apply, eco-friendly, 2015 rates: $45. Disc: AAA. ATM.
(800)845-4752 Lat: 33.41571, Lon: -111.72971
4700 E Main, Mesa, AZ 85205
reservations@cal-am.com
http://www.cal-am.com/resorts/resorts_details.php?resorts_id=15&search=quick
See ad pages 56 (Spotlight Gold Canyon), 52 & Cal Am Insert & Snowbird Destinations in Magazine Section.

MESA SPIRIT RV RESORT **Ratings: 9.5/10★/9.5** (RV Resort) 2015 rates: $59 to $79. (877)924-6709 3020 E Main St, Mesa, AZ 85213

MONTE VISTA VILLAGE RESORT **Ratings: 9/9.5★/9.5** (RV Resort) 2015 rates: $53. (800)435-7128 8865 E Baseline Rd, Mesa, AZ 85209

ORANGEWOOD SHADOWS RV RESORT **Ratings: 9.5/9.5★/9.5** (RV Park) 2015 rates: $45. (800)826-0909 3165 E University Dr, Mesa, AZ 85213

PALM GARDENS MHC & RV PARK **Ratings: 9.5/9★/9.5** (RV Area in MHP) 2015 rates: $40. (480)832-0290 2929 E. Main St, Mesa, AZ 85213

PARK PLACE COMMUNITY RESORT **Ratings: 8/7.5/7** (RV Park) 2015 rates: $33. (480)830-1080 306 S Recker Rd, Mesa, AZ 85206

SILVER SANDS RV RESORT
Ratings: 7/8★/7 (RV Park) From Jct of US Hwy 60 & Ellsworth Rd (exit 191), N 1.5 mi on Ellsworth Rd to Broadway Rd, E 500 ft (L). **FAC:** Paved rds. (178 spaces). Avail: 100 gravel, patios, back-ins (30 x 45), 100 full hkups (30/50 amps), seasonal sites, WiFi Hotspot, laundry. **REC:** heated pool, whirlpool, shuffleboard. Pet restrict(B/Q). No tents. Age restrict may apply, big rig sites, 2015 rates: $35. Disc: AAA, military. No CC.
(480)984-6731 Lat: 33.40834, Lon: -111.63074
9252 E Broadway Rd, Mesa, AZ 85208
silversandsrvresort@hotmail.com
www.silversandsrvmesa.com
See ad this page, 52.

SILVERIDGE RV RESORT **Ratings: 9/10★/9** (RV Resort) 2015 rates: $50. (800)354-0054 8265 E Southern Ave, Mesa, AZ 85209

RV Park ratings you can rely on!

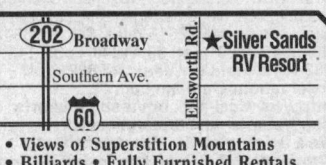

MESA (CONT)

➔ **SUN LIFE RV RESORT**
Ratings: 10/10★/10 (RV Resort) From Jct of Hwy 60 & Higley Rd (exit 186), N 2.5 mi on Higley Rd to University Dr, W 0.2 mi (L).

PERFECT SNOWBIRD LOCATION 10/10*/10
Best location to see & do it all...casinos-golfing-bowling-museums-sports stadiums-shopping-restaurants-local hiking. Social director has a full schedule of activities/events like ever popular-dancing in the Grand Ballroom!

FAC: Paved rds. (761 spaces). Avail: 235 all weather, patios, back-ins (32 x 45), accepts full hkup units only, 235 full hkups (30/50 amps), seasonal sites, WiFi, laundry, restaurant, controlled access. **REC:** heated pool, whirlpool, shuffleboard. Pet restrict(B/Q). Partial handicap access, no tents. Age restrict may apply, big rig sites, eco-friendly, 2015 rates: $22.50 to $45. ATM.
(888)940-8989 Lat: 33.42001, Lon: -111.72228
5055 E University Dr, Mesa, AZ 85205
reservations@cal-am.com
http://www.cal-am.com/resorts/resorts_details.php?resorts_id=17&search=quick
See ad pages 56 (Spotlight Gold Canyon), 52 & Cal Am Insert & Snowbird Destinations in Magazine Section.

➔ THE RESORT **Ratings: 9/9.5★/9.5** (RV Resort) 2015 rates: $50. (866)386-1101 1101 S Ellsworth Rd, Mesa, AZ 85208

➔ **TOWERPOINT RESORT**
Ratings: 10/9.5★/10 (RV Resort) From Jct of US Hwy 60 & Higley Rd (exit 186), N 2 mi on Higley Rd to Main St, W 0.4 mi (R).

LUXURY MESA RESORT 10/9.5*/10
Endless activities-silversmithing-woodworking-cards-games-sewing-concerts-chapel services-Bible studies-tennis/shuffleboard courts-swimming-dancing (square & round) all winter long. Relax in our 2 large therapy pools & more.

FAC: Paved rds. (1112 spaces). Avail: 287 all weather, patios, back-ins (30 x 50), accepts full hkup units only, 287 full hkups (30/50 amps), seasonal sites, WiFi, laundry, restaurant. **REC:** heated pool, whirlpool, shuffleboard. Pet restrict(B/Q). Partial handicap access, no tents. Age restrict may apply, big rig sites, eco-friendly, 2015 rates: $21to $43. Disc: AAA. ATM.
(888)940-8989 Lat: 33.41905, Lon: -111.72572
4860 E Main St, Mesa, AZ 85205
towerpoint@cal-am.com
http://www.cal-am.com/resorts/resorts_details.php?resorts_id=25&search=quick
See ad pages 56 (Spotlight Gold Canyon), 52 & Cal Am Insert & Snowbird Destinations in Magazine Section.

↑ USERY MOUNTAIN REC AREA (Public) From Jct of US-60 & Ellsworth/Usery Pass Rd (exit 191), N 7.5 mi (R). Entrance fee required. 2015 rates: $8 to $30. (480)984-0032

↑ **VAL VISTA VILLAGE RV RESORT**
Ratings: 10/10★/9.5 (RV Resort) From Jct of US Hwy 60 & Val Vista Dr (exit 184), N 2.3 mi on Val Vista Dr (R). Note: No Pickup campers.

VILLAGE FOR VACATIONERS 10/10*/9.5
Stay with us in our RV resort or a new beautiful manufactured home (for sale or rent) deluxe RV super sites w/gas BBQs and privacy fence or invite family/friends to enjoy a vacation home (fully furnished) to rent or purchase.

FAC: Paved rds. (1498 spaces). Avail: 498 all weather, patios, 61 pull-thrus (32 x 82), back-ins (30 x 40), accepts full hkup units only, 498 full hkups (30/50 amps), seasonal sites, WiFi, laundry, controlled access. **REC:** heated pool, whirlpool, shuffleboard. Pet restrict(B/Q). No tents. Age restrict may apply, big rig sites, eco-friendly, 2015 rates: $45 to $85. ATM.
(888)940-8989 Lat: 33.41940, Lon: -111.75340
233 N Val Vista Dr, Mesa, AZ 85213
reservations@cal-am.com
http://www.cal-am.com/resorts/resorts_details.php?resorts_id=2&search=quick
See ad pages 56 (Spotlight Gold Canyon), 52 & Cal Am Insert & Snowbird Destinations in Magazine Section.

➔ **VALLE DEL ORO RV RESORT**
Ratings: 10/10★/9.5 (RV Resort) From Jct of US Hwy 60 & Ellsworth Rd (exit 191), N 0.1 mi on Ellsworth Rd (L).

STAY & PLAY WITH US 10/10*/9.5
Enjoy our 2 pools & 2 spas-premier fitness center-fantastic wood shop-tennis courts-bocce ball-softball field & dancing. Join a hiking/biking club-ceramics-stained glass, computer class or enjoy discount at local golf courses

FAC: Paved rds. (1761 spaces). Avail: 487 all weather, patios, back-ins (35 x 50), accepts full hkup units only, 487 full hkups (30/50 amps), seasonal sites, WiFi, laundry, controlled access. **REC:** heated pool, whirlpool, shuffleboard. Pet restrict(B/Q). Partial handicap access, no tents. Age restrict may apply, big rig sites, eco-friendly, 2015 rates: $59. ATM.
(888)940-8989 Lat: 33.38885, Lon: -111.63307
1452 S Ellsworth Rd, Mesa, AZ 85209
reservations@cal-am.com
http://www.cal-am.com/resorts/resorts_details.php?resorts_id=16&search=quick
See ad pages 56 (Spotlight Gold Canyon), 52 & Cal Am Insert & Snowbird Destinations in Magazine Section.

➔ **VENTURE OUT AT MESA**
Ratings: 9.5/9.5★/10 (Condo Pk) From Jct of Hwy 60 & Greenfield Rd (exit 185), N 2 mi on Greenfield Rd to Main St, E 0.8 mi (R). **FAC:** Paved rds. (1769 spaces). Avail: 20 paved, patios, 10 pull-thrus (30 x 70), back-ins (30 x 65), accepts full hkup units only, 20 full hkups (30/50 amps), seasonal sites, WiFi Hotspot, rentals, laundry, controlled access. **REC:** heated pool, whirlpool, shuffleboard. No pets. No tents. Age restrict may apply, big rig sites, eco-friendly, 2015 rates: $27.50 to $60.
(480)832-0200 Lat: 33.41493, Lon: -111.72347
5001 E Main, Mesa, AZ 85205
Desk@ventureoutrvresort.com
www.ventureoutrvresort.com
See ad pages 88, 52.

➔ VIEWPOINT RV & GOLF RESORT **Ratings: 9.5/8.5/10** (RV Park) 2015 rates: $65. (480)373-8700 8700 E University Dr, Mesa, AZ 85207

➔ **WESTERN ACRES**
Ratings: 8.5/9.5★/8.5 (RV Area in MHP) From Jct of US Hwy 60 & Crismon Rd (Exit 192), N 2 mi on Crismon Rd to E Apache Trail, W 0.2 mi, E 0.1 mi (R). **FAC:** Paved rds. (180 spaces). Avail: 29 all weather, patios, 12 pull-thrus (25 x 35), back-ins (25 x 35), some side by side hkups, accepts full hkup units only, 29 full hkups (30/50 amps), seasonal sites, WiFi, laundry. **REC:** shuffleboard, playground. Pet restrict(B/Q). Partial handicap access, no tents. Eco-friendly, 2015 rates: $31.12. No CC.
(480)986-1158 Lat: 33.41485, Lon: -111.61742
9913 East Apache Trail, Mesa, AZ 85207
westernacre@yahoo.com
www.western-acres.com
See ad pages 68 (Spotlight Valley of the Sun), 52.

Travel Services

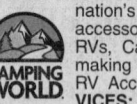

➔ **CAMPING WORLD STORE OF MESA** As the nation's largest retailer of RV supplies, accessories, services and new and used RVs, Camping World is committed to making your total RV experience better. RV Accessories: (888)481-1974. **SERVICES:** RV, RV appliance, restrooms, RV Sales. RV supplies, LP, emergency parking, RV accessible. waiting room. Hours: 8am to 6pm.
480-964-6616 Lat: 33.41553, Lon: -111.78377
2222 E. Main Street, Mesa, AZ 85213
efernandez@campingworld.com
www.campingworldofmesa.com

Things to See and Do

➔ **CAL AM PROPERTIES** AZ Premier RV Resorts - 12 Locations, Mesa, Surprise, Gold Canyon & Yuma. No CC.
(888)940-8989
www.cal-am.com/resorts
See ad page 56 (Spotlight Gold Canyon) & CalAm Insert.

MOHAVE VALLEY — B1 *Mohave*

↓ **CROSSROADS RV PARK**
Ratings: 8/8.5★/9 (RV Park) From Jct of Hwy 95 & Boundary Cone Rd (Rd to Oatman), E 3.7 mi on Boundary Cone Rd (L). **FAC:** Paved rds. 136 gravel, patios, 128 pull-thrus (30 x 50), back-ins (30 x 50), 136 full hkups (30/50 amps), WiFi, laundry, LP gas. **REC.** Pet restrict(B/Q). No tents. Age restrict may apply, big rig sites, eco-friendly, 2015 rates: $30.
(928)768-3303 Lat: 34.97522, Lon: -114.53425
3299 Boundary Cone Rd, Mohave Valley, AZ 86440
Reservations@crossroadsrvspace.com
www.crossroadsrvspace.com

↓ SPIRIT MOUNTAIN RV PARK **Ratings: 4.5/8/7** (RV Park) 2015 rates: $25. (928)346-1225 8545 S Highway 95, Mohave Valley, AZ 86440

MORMON LAKE — B3 *Coconino*

↓ **MORMON LAKE LODGE & RV PARK & CAMPGROUND Ratings: 5/7.5/6.5** (RV Park) From Jct of I-17 & Mary Lake Rd turnoff, go 23 mi on LK Rd to Mormon Lake Village Rd, then SW 7 mi (L). Elev 7200 ft. **FAC:** Gravel rds. 74 gravel, 74 pull-thrus (18 x 60), mostly side by side hkups, 74 full hkups (30/50 amps), tent sites, rentals, showers $, laundry, groc, LP gas, firewood, restaurant. **REC:** pond, Lake Mormon: playground. Pets OK. Partial handicap access. 2015 rates: $44. Disc: AAA.
AAA Approved
(928)354-2227 Lat: 34.91165, Lon: -111.46779
1991 Mormon Lake Rd, Mormon Lake, AZ 86038
mllres@skycasters.net
www.mormonlakelodge.com

MUNDS PARK — B3 *Coconino*

← MUNDS PARK RV RESORT **Ratings: 9/10★/10** (RV Park) 2015 rates: $32 to $36. Apr 1 to Oct 31. (928)286-1309 17550 Munds Ranch Rd., Munds Park, AZ 86017

OVERGAARD — C4 *Navajo*

➔ **ELK PINES RV RESORT**
Ratings: 8.5/9★/9 (RV Park) From Jct of Hwy 260 & SR-277, E 3.1 mi on Hwy 260 (L). Between MM-308 & 309. Elev 6500 ft. **FAC:** Paved rds. 68 gravel, back-ins (30 x 50), 68 full hkups (30/50 amps), WiFi $, showers $, laundry. **REC.** Pet restrict(B/Q) $. No tents. Big rig sites, eco-friendly, 2015 rates: $38. Apr 1 to Oct 31.
(928)535-3833 Lat: 34.39100, Lon: -110.53803
2256 Hwy 260, Overgaard, AZ 85933
info@elkpinesrvresort.com
www.elkpinesrvresort.com
See ad pages 96, 52.

↗ HEBER RV RESORT **Ratings: 7.5/8.5★/9** (RV Park) 2015 rates: $36. (928)535-4004 3065 Hwy 277 N, Overgaard, AZ 85933

PAGE — A3 *Coconino*

↓ **PAGE LAKE POWELL CAMPGROUND**
Ratings: 8.5/8.5★/8.5 (RV Park) From Jct of Hwy 89 & Haul Rd (Walmart), go E 1.7 mi on Haul Rd to Coppermine Rd, cross Coppermine Rd to entrance (E). Note: Call if using GPS. Elev 4300 ft. **FAC:** Paved/gravel rds. 105 gravel, 24 pull-thrus (23 x 40), back-ins (30 x 38), 71 full hkups, 34 W, 34 E (30/50 amps), cable, WiFi, tent sites, dump, laundry, groc, LP gas. **REC:** heated pool, whirlpool, playground. Pets OK. Big rig sites, eco-friendly, 2015 rates: $24 to $31.
(928)645-3374 Lat: 36.90156, Lon: -111.45299
849 S Coppermine Rd, Page, AZ 86040
cgmanager@baits.com
www.pagecampground.com
See ad pages 50 (Welcome Section), 52.

↖ WAHWEAP LODGE & MARINA/RV PARK (LAKE POWELL) **Ratings: 8/8/9** (RV Park) 2015 rates: $49. (800)528-6154 100 Lake Shore Dr, Page, AZ 86040

PARKER — C1 *La Paz*

↑ BLUE WATER RV PARK **Ratings: 8/8.5★/7.5** (RV Park) 2015 rates: $35. (928)669-2433 1001 Bluewater Dr, Parker, AZ 85344

↑ **BUCKSKIN MOUNTAIN**
(State Pk) From Jct of Hwys 62 & 95, N 10.5 mi on Hwy 95, at N Jct of Bus 95 & Hwy 95 (L). **FAC:** Paved rds. 68 paved, patios, 8 pull-thrus (20 x 65), back-ins (27 x 45), 15 full hkups, 53 W, 53 E (30 amps), WiFi Hotspot, tent sites, dump, groc, firewood, restaurant. **REC:** Colorado River: swim, fishing, playground, rec open to public. Pets OK. Partial handicap access. 14 day max stay, 2015 rates: $30 to $33.
(928)667-3231 Lat: 34.25557, Lon: -114.16204
5476 North US Hwy 95, Parker, AZ 85344
www.azstateparks.com
See ad page 49 (Welcome Section).

↑ BUCKSKIN MOUNTAIN/RIVER ISLAND UNIT (State Pk) From town, N 11 mi on SR-95 (L). Entrance fee required. 2015 rates: $30. (928)667-3386

↑ CASTLE ROCK SHORES RESORT **Ratings: 7/7/6.5** (RV Park) 2015 rates: $35 to $50. (928)667-2344 5220 Hwy 95, Parker, AZ 85344

AZ

PARKER (CONT)

LA PAZ COUNTY PARK (Public) From North city limits: Go 8 mi N on Hwy-95. 2015 rates: $16 to $25. (928)667-2069

RIVER ISLAND

(State Pk) From Jct of Hwys 62 & 95, N 12 mi on Hwy 95 (L). **FAC:** Paved rds. 37 paved, patios, 19 pull-thrus (50 x 65), back-ins (50 x 65), 29 W, 29 E (30/50 amps), tent sites, dump. **REC:** Colorado River: swim, fishing, rec open to public. Pets OK. Partial handicap access. 14 day max stay, 2015 rates: $25 to $28. Disc: military.
(928)667-3386 Lat: 34.25345, Lon: -114.13859
5200 N Hwy 95, Parker, AZ 85344
www.azstateparks.com
See ad page 49 (Welcome Section).

PATAGONIA — E4 *Santa Cruz*

PATAGONIA LAKE

(State Pk) From Jct of I-19 & Hwy 82, NE 12 mi on Hwy 82 to Patagonia Rd, W 4 mi (E). Elev 3750 ft. **FAC:** Paved rds. 105 paved, 105 W, 105 E (30/50 amps), tent sites, dump, groc, fire rings, firewood, controlled access. **REC:** Patagonia Lake: swim, fishing, rec open to public. Pets OK. Partial handicap access. 15 day max stay, 2015 rates: $25 to $28. Disc: military.
(520)287-6965 Lat: 31.48822, Lon: -110.85372
400 Patagonia Lake Rd, Patagonia, AZ 85624
www.azstateparks.com
See ad page 49 (Welcome Section).

PAYSON — C3 *Gila*

OX BOW ESTATES RV PARK **Ratings: 6/5.5/7.5** (RV Park) 2015 rates: $40. (800)520-5239 962 W Oxbow Trail, Payson, AZ 85541

PAYSON CAMPGROUND AND RV RESORT

Ratings: 9/10★/10 (RV Park) From Jct of Hwy 87 & Hwy 260, go E 0.7 mi on Hwy 260 (L). Elev 5000 ft.

COOL REFRESHING MOUNTAIN AIR

Enjoy the fabulous cool nights and beautiful sky blue days in this Arizona mountain resort along with some of the most beautiful ponderosa pines anywhere. Escape to the scenery. You are cordially invited to stay with us!

FAC: Paved/gravel rds. (109 spaces). Avail: 75 gravel, 26 pull-thrus (15 x 50), back-ins (30 x 50), 71 full hkups, 4 W, 4 E (30/50 amps), seasonal sites, WiFi, tent sites, dump, laundry, firewood. **REC:** heated pool, playground. Pets OK. Eco-friendly, 2015 rates: $35 to $40. Disc: AAA, military.
AAA Approved
(928)472-2267 Lat: 34.24264, Lon: -111.31019
808 E Hwy 260, Payson, AZ 85541
info@paysoncampground.com
www.paysoncampground.com
See ad this page, 52.

PEACH SPRINGS — B2 *Mohave*

GRAND CANYON CAVERNS RV PARK & CAMPGROUND

Ratings: 6.5/8.5★/8 (Campground) From Jct of Historic Rt 66 & Diamond Creek Rd (in town of Peach Springs), n 11 mi (R). **FAC:** Gravel rds. 50 gravel, 50 pull-thrus (30 x 55), 50 W, 50 E (30/50 amps), WiFi Hotspot, tent sites, rentals, dump, laundry, groc, fire rings, firewood, restaurant. **REC:** pool, playground, rec open to public. Pets OK. Eco-friendly, 2015 rates: $30.
(928)422-4565 Lat: 35.52889, Lon: -113.23110
Mile Marker 115 Route 66, Peach Springs, AZ 86434
info@gccaverns.com
www.gccaverns.com
See ad page 86.

We shine "Spotlights" on interesting cities and areas.

PEORIA — D3 *Maricopa*

LAKE PLEASANT (Public) From Jct of I-17 & SR-74 (Carefree Hwy), W 15 mi on SR-74 (R). Entrance fee required. 2015 rates: $17 to $25. (928)501-1710

PLEASANT HARBOR RV RESORT

Ratings: 9.5/9.5★/9.5 (RV Park) From Jct of I-17 & Carefree Hwy (Exit 223B), W 8 mi on Carefree Hwy to 87th Ave, N 1.8 mi (L).

WELCOME TO PLEASANT HARBOR!

On the shores of Lake Pleasant, just outside of Phoenix metro is the best kept secret in Arizona. Enjoy boating, fishing, swimming, skiing, scuba, sailing, hiking, kayaking and parasailing. Families & Snowbirds love it here!

FAC: Paved rds. (254 spaces). Avail: 126 gravel, 4 pull-thrus (31 x 70), back-ins (25 x 45), 126 full hkups (30/50 amps), seasonal sites, WiFi, tent sites, dump, laundry, groc, LP gas, restaurant, controlled access. **REC:** heated pool, whirlpool, Lake Pleasant: swim, fishing, marina, shuffleboard, rec open to public. Pet restrict(Q) $. Partial handicap access. Big rig sites, eco-friendly, 2015 rates: $39 to $52. Disc: military.
(800)475-3272 Lat: 33.84732, Lon: -112.24911
8708 W Harbor Blvd, Peoria, AZ 85383
reservations@mwdaz.com
www.pleasantharbor.com
See ad pages 67 (Spotlight Valley of the Sun), 52 & Family Camping, Snowbird Destinations in Magazine Section.

SUNDIAL RV PARK

Ratings: 3.5/NA/5 (RV Park) From Jct of 101 Loop & Grand Ave (Exit 11), SE 3 mi on Grand Ave to 75th Ave, N 0.2 mi to W. Hatcher Rd, W 20 ft (L). **FAC:** Paved rds. (103 spaces). Avail: 60 gravel, patios, back-ins (35 x 50), 60 full hkups (30/50 amps), seasonal sites, laundry. Pets OK. No tents. 2015 rates: $20.
(623)979-1921 Lat: 33.57021, Lon: -112.22134
9250 N 75th Ave, Peoria, AZ 85345
See ad page 44 (Welcome Section).

TURF SOARING RV PARK

(RV Spaces) From Jct of I-17 and Carefree Fwy/74: Go W on Carefree Fwy/74 for 6-1/2 mi: turn S on Lake Pleasant Pkwy for 1/2 mi, turn. Park on Right on paved road. **FAC:** Paved rds. (40 spaces). Avail: 10 gravel, patios, 2 pull-thrus (25 x 70), back-ins (25 x 40), 10 full hkups (30/50 amps), seasonal sites, tent sites, dump, laundry. Pets OK. 2015 rates: $27 to $34.
AAA Approved
(623)566-5960 Lat: 33.79792, Lon: -112.24767
8720 W Carefree Hwy, Peoria, AZ 85383
royc@pleasantvalleyairport.com
www.turfsoaringrvpark.com
See ad page 51 (Welcome Section).

VALLEY OF THE SUN RV PARK **Ratings: 5/6.5/6** (RV Park) 2015 rates: $32. (623)334-1977 8955 NW Grand Ave, Peoria, AZ 85345

PHOENIX — D3 *Maricopa, Pinal*

PHOENIX AREA MAP

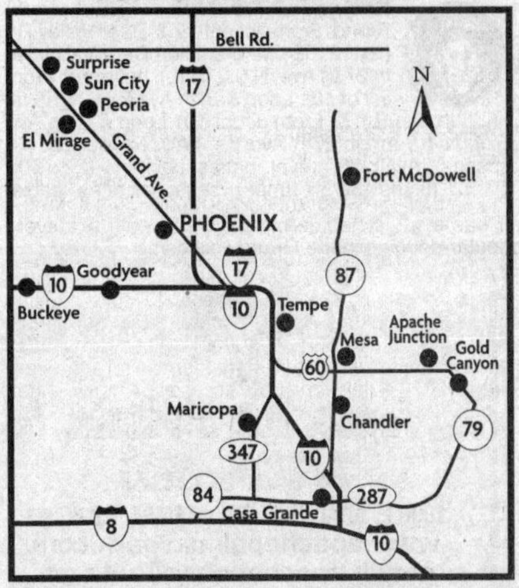

Symbols on map indicate towns within a 40 mile radius of Phoenix where campgrounds are listed. Check listings for more information.

See also Apache Junction, Buckeye, Casa Grande, Chandler, El Mirage, Fort McDowell, Gold Canyon, Goodyear, Maricopa, Mesa, Peoria, Sun City, Surprise & Tempe.

COVERED WAGON RV PARK **Ratings: 8/7.5★/8** (RV Park) 2015 rates: $32 to $42. (602)242-2500 6540 N Black Canyon Hwy #53, Phoenix, AZ 85017

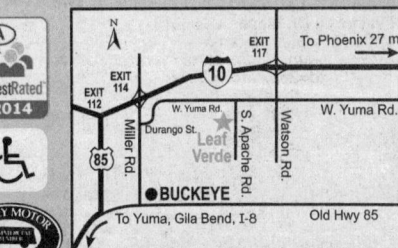

PHOENIX (CONT)

DESERT SANDS RV PARK

Ratings: 6.5/8.5★/8 (RV Park) S-bnd: From Jct of I-17 & Deer Valley Rd (Exit 215B), W 0.2 mi on Deer Valley Rd to 27 th Ave, N 0.2 mi (L); or N-bnd: From Jct of 101 Loop & 27th Ave Exit, N 1.5 mi on 27th Ave (L); or From Jct of 101 Loop & 27th Ave Exit, N 1.5 mi on 27th Ave (L). **FAC:** Paved rds. (70 spaces). Avail: 50 gravel, patios, back-ins (22 x 50), 50 full hkups (30/50 amps), seasonal sites, cable, WiFi $. **REC:** pool. Pet restrict(B). No tents. Big rig sites, 2015 rates: $50. Disc: AAA, military.
AAA Approved
(623)869-8186 Lat: 33.68721, Lon: -112.11778
22036 N 27th Ave, Phoenix, AZ 85027
desertsandsrvpark@yahoo.com
www.desertsandsrv.com

Heading South? We have lots of Snowbird Destination ideas to explore at the front of the Guide.

DESERT SHADOWS RV RESORT

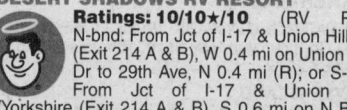

Ratings: 10/10★/10 (RV Park) N-bnd: From Jct of I-17 & Union Hills Dr (Exit 214 A & B), W 0.4 mi on Union Hills Dr to 29th Ave, N 0.4 mi (R); or S-bnd From Jct of I-17 & Union Hills Dr/Yorkshire (Exit 214 A & B), S 0.6 mi on N Black Canyon Hwy/Frontage Rt to Union Hills Dr, W 0.4 mi to 29th Ave, N 0.4 mi (R).

FEEL AT HOME WITH US!

A beautiful resort in North Phoenix. A friendly, tranquil place with all the amenities you may want. Close to golf, restaurants & sporting events. We hope you will choose to visit soon.

FAC: Paved rds. (638 spaces). Avail: 238 all weather, patios, 26 pull-thrus (30 x 80), back-ins (30 x 45), accepts full hkup units only, 238 full hkups (30/50 amps), seasonal sites, WiFi $, laundry. **REC:** heated pool, whirlpool, shuffleboard. Pet restrict(B/Q). Partial handicap access, no tents. Big rig sites, eco-friendly, 2015 rates: $47 to $69.
(800)595-7290 Lat: 33.65968, Lon: -112.12146
19203 N 29th Ave, Phoenix, AZ 85027
info@phoenixrvresorts.com
www.phoenixrvresorts.com
See ad this page, 52 & Snowbird Destination in Magazine Section.

DESERT'S EDGE RV-THE PURPLE PARK

Ratings: 10/10★/10 (RV Park) S-bnd: From Jct of I-17 & Deer Valley Rd/Exit 215B (N side of Phoenix), E 0.1 mi on Deer Valley to 23rd Ave, N 0.4 mi on 23rd Ave to Williams Dr, W 0.1 mi (R); or N-bnd: I-17 & Deer Valley/Rose Garden (Exit 215A), E 0.1 mi on Rose Garden to 23rd Ave, N 0.9

PHOENIX (CONT)

DESERT'S EDGE RV-THE (CONT)
mi to Williams Dr, W 0.1 mi (R). **FAC:** Paved rds. 203 Avail: 203 all weather, patios, 14 pull-thrus (25 x 50), back-ins (30 x 60), accepts full hkup units only, 203 full hkups (30/50 amps), WiFi, laundry, LP gas. **REC:** heated pool, whirlpool, playground. Pet restrict(B). No tents. Big rig sites, eco-friendly, 2015 rates: $45 to $75.
(623)587-0940 Lat: 33.69139, Lon: -112.11060
2398 W Williams Dr, Phoenix, AZ 85027
info@desertsedgerv.com
www.desertsedgerv.com
See ad opposite page, 52.

LEAF VERDE RV RESORT
Ratings: 9.5/10★/8.5 (RV Park) From Jct of I-10 & I-17 in Phoenix, Go 21 mi W on I-10 to Exit 117 (Watson Rd), S 0.6 mi on Watson Rd to Yuma Rd, W 1 mi to Apache Rd, S 0.3 mi (R) note: Do not follow GPS. **FAC:** Paved rds. (377 spaces). Avail: 367 gravel, 253 pull-thrus (24 x 75), back-ins (28 x 60), 367 full hkups (30/50 amps), seasonal sites, WiFi $, dump, laundry, LP gas. **REC:** heated pool, shuffleboard. Pet restrict(B/Q). Partial handicap access. Big rig sites, eco-friendly, 2015 rates: $34. Disc: military.
(623)386-3132 Lat: 33.43180, Lon: -112.57349
1500 S Apache Rd, Buckeye, AZ 85326
reservations@leafverde.com
www.leafverde.com
See primary listing at Buckeye and ad page 91.

PARADISE VALLEY RANCH **Ratings: 6/6.5/8.5** (RV Park) 2015 rates: $34. (602)992-3140 16005 N 32nd St, Phoenix, AZ 85032

PHOENIX METRO RV PARK
Ratings: 10/10★/9.5 (RV Park) From Jct of 101 & I-17, N 1 mi on I-17 to Deer Valley Rd/Rose Garden (Exit 215), N 0.7 mi on N Black Canyon Hwy/E Frontage Rd (R). Call If using GPS.

YOUR HOME AWAY FROM HOME!
Escape to our gorgeous, mountainous northwest Phoenix setting and enjoy spectacular sunrises and sunsets from our convenient location. Near Mayo Clinic, area attractions, restaurants and sporting events. Welcome Home!

FAC: Paved rds. (310 spaces). Avail: 100 all weather, back-ins (30 x 43), 100 full hkups (30/50 amps), seasonal sites, WiFi, laundry. **REC:** heated pool, whirlpool, shuffleboard. Pet restrict(B/Q). Partial handicap access, no tents. Age restrict may apply, eco-friendly, 2015 rates: $37 to $75. Disc: AAA, military.
(623)582-0390 Lat: 33.69343, Lon: -112.11235
22701 N Black Canyon Hwy, Phoenix, AZ 85027
info@phoenixmetrorvpark.com
www.phoenixmetrorvpark.com
See ad this page, 52 & Snowbird Destinations in Magazine Section.

PIONEER RV RESORT
Ratings: 9.5/9.5★/8.5 (RV Resort) From Jct of I-17 & Pioneer Rd exit (225), NW 0.3 mi on Pioneer Rd (L). **FAC:** Paved rds. (583 spaces). Avail: 313 gravel, patios, 46 pull-thrus (25 x 50), back-ins (25 x 40), accepts full hkup units only, 313 full hkups (30/50 amps), seasonal sites, WiFi $, laundry. **REC:** heated pool, whirlpool, shuffleboard. Pet restrict(B/Q). Partial handicap access, no tents. Age restrict may apply, big rig sites, RV age restrict, eco-friendly, 2015 rates: $37.40. Disc: AAA.
(800)658-5895 Lat: 33.82114, Lon: -112.14690
36408 N Black Canyon Hwy, Phoenix, AZ 85086
pioneerofficestaff@yahoo.com
www.arizonarvresorts.com
See ad pages 65 (Spotlight Valley of the Sun), 52.

PLEASANT HARBOR RV RESORT
Ratings: 9.5/9.5★/9.5 (RV Park) From Jct of I-10 & I-17, Go N 23.7 mi on I-17, then Carefree Hwy (Exit 223B), W 8 mi on Carefree Hwy to 87th Ave, N 1.8 mi (L). **FAC:** Paved rds. (254 spaces). Avail: 126 gravel, 4 pull-thrus (31 x 40), back-ins (25 x 45), 126 full hkups (30/50 amps), seasonal sites, WiFi, tent sites, dump, laundry, groc, LP gas, restaurant, controlled access. **REC:** heated pool, whirlpool, Lake Pleasant: marina, shuffleboard, rec open to public. Pet restrict(Q) $. Partial handicap access. Big rig sites, eco-friendly, 2015 rates: $39 to $52.
(800)475-3272 Lat: 33.84732, Lon: -112.24911
8708 W Harbor Blvd, Peoria, AZ 85383
reservations@mwdaz.com
www.pleasantharbor.com
See primary listing at Peoria and ad page 67 (Spotlight Valley of the Sun).

ROYAL PALM RV RESORT/MHC
Ratings: 9/9★/9.5 (RV Area in MHP) From Jct of I-10 & I-17, N 6.5 mi on I-17 (Exit 207) to Dunlap Ave, E 0.8 mi (L) Note: Reservations required. **FAC:** Paved rds. (425 spaces). Avail: 125 gravel, patios, back-ins (32 x 42), accepts full hkup units only, 125 full hkups (30/50 amps), seasonal sites, WiFi $, laundry, controlled access. **REC:** heated pool, whirlpool. Pet restrict(B/Q). No tents. Age restrict may apply, eco-friendly, 2015 rates: $33.85.
(602)943-5833 Lat: 33.56957, Lon: -112.10299
2050 West Dunlap Ave, Phoenix, AZ 85021
royalpalm@continentalcommunities.com
www.continentalcommunities.com
See ad opposite page, 52.

Things to See and Do

ARIZONA STATE PARKS From pine forests to awe inspiring desert vistas, something for everyone. Over 27 parks. Contact parks for their detailed information. No CC.
(602)542-1993 Lat: 33.41305, Lon: -111.71506
1300 W Washington St, Phoenix, AZ 85007
www.azstateparks.com
See ad page 49 (Welcome Section).

PICACHO — D3 *Pinal*

PICACHO PEAK
(State Pk) From Jct of I-10 & Exit 219, W 0.7 mi on E Picacho Peak Rd, S 1 mi on State Park Rd (E). **FAC:** Paved rds. 85 paved, 20 pull-thrus (25 x 75), back-ins (25 x 60), 85 E (30/50 amps), WiFi $, tent sites, dump, fire rings. **REC:** rec open to public. Pets OK. Partial handicap access. 14 day max stay, 2015 rates: $25. Disc: military. Sep 12 to May 24. No CC.
(520)466-3183 Lat: 32.645952, Lon: -111.401153
picacho Peak Road, Picacho, AZ 85141
www.azstateparks.com
See ad page 49 (Welcome Section).

PICACHO PEAK RV RESORT
Ratings: 10/10★/9.5 (RV Park) From Jct of I-10 & exit 219, exit to S Frontage Rd., SE 0.5 mi (R). **FAC:** Paved rds. (312 spaces). Avail: 252 all weather, patios, 77 pull-thrus (31 x 50), back-ins (40 x 50), accepts full hkup units only, 252 full hkups (30/50 amps), seasonal sites, WiFi $, rentals, laundry, LP gas, controlled access. **REC:** heated pool, whirlpool, shuffleboard. Pet restrict(B/Q). Partial

PICACHO (CONT)

PICACHO PEAK RV RESORT (CONT)
handicap access, no tents. Age restrict may apply, big rig sites, eco-friendly, 2015 rates: $31. Disc: AAA. **(520)466-7841 Lat: 32.64093, Lon: -111.38468 17065 E Peak Lane, Picacho, AZ 85141 picachopeakrv@aol.com www.picachopeakrv.com**
See ad pages 80, 52.

Like Us on Facebook.

← PICACHO/TUCSON NORTHWEST KOA **Ratings: 7.5/9.5★/9** (Campground) 2015 rates: $36.79. Sep 1 to Apr 30. (520)466-2966 18428 S Picacho Hwy, Picacho, AZ 85241

Enjoy the scenery as you travel North America. We exclusively rate campgrounds for their visual appearance and environmental quality, and represent their score, 1 through 10, as the third rating in our Triple Rating System.

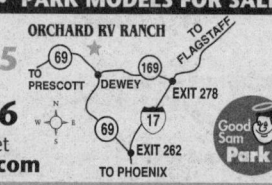

PRESCOTT — C3 *Yavapai*

↑ POINT OF ROCKS RV CAMPGROUND
Ratings: 7/8.5★/9 (Campground) From Jct of SR-89 & SR-69, N 4 mi on SR-89N (R); or From Jct of SR-89A & SR-89, S 2.7 mi on SR-89 (L). Note: Call if using GPS. Between Milepost 316 & 317. Elev 5240 ft. **FAC:** Gravel rds. (96 spaces). Avail: 60 gravel, 4 pull-thrus (22 x 40), back-ins (35 x 35), 60 full hkups (30 amps), seasonal sites, WiFi, laundry, groc. **REC.** Pet restrict(B/Q). No tents. Eco-friendly, 2015 rates: $33.50. Disc: military. **(928)445-9018 Lat: 34.59530, Lon: -112.42618 3025 N State Route 89, Prescott, AZ 86301 www.pointofrockscampground.com**
See ad this page, 52.

↑ WATSON LAKE PARK (Public) From town, N 3.7 mi on Hwy 89, follow signs (R). Campground closed Tuesday, Wednesday, and Thursday nights. 2015 rates: $15. Apr 1 to Sep 30. (928)777-1100

↑ WILLOW LAKE RV & CAMPING PARK **Ratings: 6.5/8.5★/8** (Campground) 2015 rates: $30. (928)445-6311 1617 Heritage Park Road, Prescott, AZ 86301

PRESCOTT VALLEY — C3 *Yavapai*

→ FAIRGROUNDS RV PARK
Ratings: 8.5/NA/9.5 (RV Park) From Jct of SR-89A & Roberts Rd, E 2.1 mi on 89A to Yavapai County Fairgrounds, S 0.2 mi (L). Elev 5040 ft. **FAC:** Paved rds. (153 spaces). Avail: 123 all weather, patios, 63 pull-thrus (45 x 70), back-ins (45 x 60), 123 full hkups (30/50 amps), seasonal sites, cable, WiFi $, laundry, LP gas. **REC.** Pet restrict(B/Q). No tents. Big rig sites, eco-friendly, 2015 rates: $30. Disc: AAA. **(928)227-3310 Lat: 34.64778, Lon: -112.28305 10443 East Hwy 89A, Prescott Valley, AZ 86315 fairgroundsrv@cableone.net www.fairgroundsrvpark.com**
See ad this page, 52.

QUARTZSITE — C1 *La Paz*

A SPOTLIGHT Introducing Quartzsite's colorful ttractions appearing at the front of this state section.

QUARTZSITE See also Bouse, Brenda, Ehren-erg & Salome.

AMERI-CAN TRAILS RV PARK **Ratngs: 6/9.5★/7.5** (RV Park) 2015 rates: $25 to $35. 928)927-5733 310 N Central Blvd, Quartzsite, AZ 5346

ARIZONA SUN RV RESORT **Ratings: 7/9★/8.5** RV Park) 2015 rates: $35.87 to $45.12. Oct 1 to Apr . (928)927-5057 715 E Quail Trail, Quartzsite, AZ 5346

B-10 RV PARK & CAMPGROUND **Ratngs: 4.5/7.5/6.5** (Campground) 2015 rates: $25.50 o $45.10. Oct 1 to Mar 31. (928)927-4393 615 W Main St, Quartzsite, AZ 85346

DESERT GARDENS INTERNATIONAL RV & MHP **Ratings: 5.5/7/6** (RV Park) 2015 rates: $30. 928)927-6361 1240 Acacia Blvd, Quartzsite, AZ 85346

HASSLER'S RV PARK Ratings: 6/7.5/7.5 (RV Park) From Jct of I-10 & Exit 19, N 0.3 mi on Riggles Ave to Main St, W 1.3 mi on Main St (R). **FAC:** Gravel rds. (115 spaces). Avail: 25 gravel, patios, 25 pull-thrus (28 x 55), 25 full hkups (30/50 amps), seasonal sites, WiFi Hotspot, showers $, laundry. **REC.** Pet restrict(B/Q). Partial handicap access. 2015 rates: $20 to $35. No CC.
928)927-6950 Lat: 33.66621, Lon: -114.22348
400 W Main St, Quartzsite, AZ 85346
hasslersrvpark@yahoo.com
www.hasslersrvpark.com

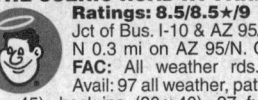

HOLIDAY PALMS RV PARK
Ratings: 8/9.5★/7.5 (RV Park) From Jct of I-10 & Bus Loop 10 (exit 19), W 1.4 mi on Bus Loop 10 (L). **FAC:** Paved rds. (243 spaces). Avail: 143 all weather, 14 pull-thrus (25 x 55), back-ins (30 x 50), accepts self-contain units only, 143 full hkups (30/50 amps), seasonal sites, WiFi, laundry, LP bottles. **REC:** whirlpool, shuffleboard. Pet restrict(B/Q). No tents. Eco-friendly, 2015 rates: $32. Disc: AAA.
(800)635-5372 Lat: 33.66587, Lon: -114.22256
355 W Main, Quartzsite, AZ 85346
holidaypalmsrvpark@g7rvresorts.com
www.g7rvresorts.com
See ad opposite page, 52 & Snowbird Destinations in Magazine Section.

KOFA MOUNTAIN RV PARK **Ratings: 7/8.5★/8.5** (RV Park) 2015 rates: $34. (928)927-6778 170 N Central Blvd, Quartzsite, AZ 85346

LA PAZ VALLEY RV PARK **Ratings: 5.5/NA/7.5** (RV Park) 2015 rates: $20. Oct 15 to May 1. (928)927-9754 52301 Century Dr, Quartzsite, AZ 85346

QUAIL RUN RV PARK
Ratings: 8.5/10★/8.5 (RV Park) From Jct of I-10 & Quartzsite Blvd (Exit 17), N 0.2 mi on Quartzsite Blvd to Bus Loop 10, E 1.4 mi on Bus Loop 10 to Central Blvd, N 0.9 mi (L). **FAC:** Paved rds. 168 Avail: 168 all weather, patios, 88 pull-thrus (30 x 70), back-ins (40 x 60), 168 full hkups (30/50 amps), WiFi, showers $, laundry. **REC:** rec open to public. Pet restrict(B/Q). Partial handicap access, no tents. Big rig sites, eco-friendly, 2015 rates: $25 to $34.
(928)927-8810 Lat: 33.67998, Lon: -114.21742
918 N Central Blvd, Quartzsite, AZ 85346
info@quailrv.com
www.quailrv.com
See ad pages 61 (Spotlight Quartzsite), 52.

SHADY LANE RV COURT
Ratings: 7/9★/8 (RV Park) From Jct of Hwy 95 & Bus I-10, N 0.2 mi on Hwy 95 (R). **FAC:** Gravel rds. (111 spaces). Avail: 66 gravel, patios, 30 pull-thrus (30 x 60), back-ins (30 x 45), some side by side hkups, 66 full hkups (30/50 amps), seasonal sites, WiFi, showers $, laundry. **REC:** shuffleboard. Pet restrict(Q). No tents. Big rig sites, 2015 rates: $23 to $33. Oct 1 to Apr 1. No CC.
(928)927-6844 Lat: 33.67001, Lon: -114.21686
185 N Central Blvd, Quartzsite, AZ 85346
http://www.shadylanervcourt.com
See ad opposite page.

SPLIT RAIL RV PARK **Ratings: 5.5/6.5/6.5** (RV Park) 2015 rates: $20 to $30. Oct 1 to May 1. (928)927-5296 1258 N Central Blvd/N Hwy 95, Quartzsite, AZ 85346

TEWS & DATE PALM RV PARK
(RV Park) (Seasonal Stay Only) From Jct of I-10 & US 95 (exit 17) Go 1/4 mi N on US 95, then 3/4 mi E on W Main St, then 1.5 N on N Moon Mtn Ave (L) Note: Accepts reservations for monthly, seasonal and annual only. **FAC:** Paved/gravel rds. (98 spaces). Patios, accepts self-contain units only, seasonal sites, WiFi, laundry. **REC.** Pet restrict(B/Q). Big rig sites, eco-friendly, Disc: military. No CC.
(928)927-8929 Lat: 33.685937, Lon: -114.225673
1360 N Moon Mtn Ave, Quartzsite, AZ 85346
tewsinquartzsite@tds.net
http://www.tewsrv.com/
See ad page 61 (Spotlight Quartzsite).

THE SCENIC ROAD RV PARK
Ratings: 8.5/8.5★/9 (RV Park) From Jct of Bus. I-10 & AZ 95/N. Central Blvd, N 0.3 mi on AZ 95/N. Central Blvd (L). **FAC:** All weather rds. (180 spaces). Avail: 97 all weather, patios, 38 pull-thrus (30 x 45), back-ins (30 x 40), 97 full hkups (30/50 amps), seasonal sites, WiFi, laundry. **REC.** Pet restrict(B/Q). No tents. Age restrict may apply, eco-friendly, 2015 rates: $28. Disc: AAA. Oct 1 to Apr 30. No CC.
(928)927-6443 Lat: 33.67459, Lon: -114.21806
480 N Central Blvd, Quartzsite, AZ 85346
info@thescenicroad.com
www.thescenicroad.com
See ad pages 61 (Spotlight Quartzsite), 52.

88 SHADES RV PARK
Ratings: 8/9★/7.5 (RV Park) From Jct of I-10 & Bus Loop 10 (exit 17), NE 0.8 mi on Bus Loop 10 (R); or From Jct of US-95/Hwy 95 & Bus Loop 10, W 0.45 mi on Bus Loop 10 (L). **FAC:** All weather rds. (230 spaces). Avail: 30 all weather, 25 pull-thrus (25 x 50), back-ins (25 x 40), 30 full hkups (30/50 amps), seasonal sites, WiFi, laundry, LP bottles. **REC:** whirlpool, shuffleboard. Pet restrict(B/Q). No tents. Eco-friendly, 2015 rates: $29. Disc: AAA, military.
(800)457-4392 Lat: 33.66410, Lon: -114.22579
575 W Main St, Quartzsite, AZ 85346
88shades@passionright.com
http://www.88shadesquartzsitervpark.com/
See ad this page, 52 & Snowbird Destinations in Magazine Section.

QUEEN VALLEY — D3 *Pinal*

QUEEN VALLEY RV RESORT **Ratings: 10/10★/10** (RV Park) 2015 rates: $42. (520)463-2300 50 West Oro Viejo Dr, Queen Valley, AZ 85118

ROOSEVELT — C4 *Gila*

TONTO (INDIAN POINT CAMPGROUND) (Natl Forest) From jct Hwy 88 & Hwy 188: Go 10 mi NW on Hwy 188, then 2 mi E on FR 60, then 2 mi S on FR 661. Tonto Creek crossing may be impassable at times Jan thru Apr. Pit toilets. 2015 rates: $6. (928)467-3200

SAFFORD — D5 *Graham*

LEXINGTON PINES RESORT LLC
Ratings: 9/9.5★/9.5 (RV Park) W-bnd: From Jct of US-191 & US-70, W 1.2 mi on US-70 (L); or E-bnd: From Jct of Hwy 70 & 20th St, E .01 mi on Hwy 70 (R). Note: Behind Auto Zone. Elev 2900 ft. **FAC:** Paved rds. (200 spaces). Avail: 24 all weather, patios, back-ins (30 x 50), 24 full hkups (30/50 amps), seasonal sites, cable, WiFi, laundry. **REC:** shuffleboard. Pet restrict(B/Q). No tents. Age restrict may apply, RV age restrict, eco-friendly, 2015 rates: $30.
(928)428-7570 Lat: 32.83464, Lon: -109.72665
1535 Thatcher Blvd, Safford, AZ 85546
manager@lexingtonpinesresort.com
www.lexingtonpinesresort.com
See ad pages 51 (Welcome Section), 52.

ROPER LAKE
(State Pk) From Jct of US 70 & US 191, S 5.3 mi to Roper Lake Rd, E 1 mi (E). Elev 3130 ft. **FAC:** Paved rds. 50 paved, 6 pull-thrus (25 x 45), back-ins (25 x 45), 45 W, 45 E (30/50 amps), tent sites, rentals, dump, fire rings. **REC:** Roper Lake: swim, fishing, rec open to public. Pets OK. Partial handicap access. 14 day max stay, 2015 rates: $25. Disc: military.
(928)428-6760 Lat: 32.758624, Lon: -109.707456
101 E Roper Lake Rd, Safford, AZ 85546
www.azstateparks.com
See ad page 49 (Welcome Section).

SAFFORD RV RESORT
Ratings: 9/8.5★/7 (RV Park) From Jct of US-70/W Thatcher Blvd & S 20th Ave, SE 1.5 mi on S 20th Ave to Golf Course Rd, SW 0.3 mi (L). Elev 2950 ft. **FAC:** Paved rds. (92 spaces). Avail: 32 all weather, patios, 4 pull-thrus (24 x 55), back-ins (24 x 50), 32 full hkups (30/50 amps), seasonal sites, cable, WiFi, laundry. **REC:** heated pool, whirlpool. Pets OK. Eco-friendly, 2015 rates: $25.
(928)792-2277 Lat: 32.81474, Lon: -109.73417
2075 W Golf Course Rd, Safford, AZ 85546
Saffordrvresort@hotmail.com
www.saffordrvpark.com
See ad this page.

SALOME — C2 *La Paz*

DESERT PALMS RV RESORT
Ratings: 10/9.5★/10 (RV Park) E-bnd: From Jct of I-10 & US Hwy 60 (Exit 31) NE 25 mi to Salome Rd, S 0.3 mi on Salome Rd to Harquahala Rd, SW 0.75 mi (R); or W-bnd: From Jct of I-10 W & Salome Rd (Exit 81), NW 30 mi on Salome Rd to Harquahala Rd, SW 0.75 (R). **FAC:** Paved rds. (330 spaces). Avail: 150 all weather, patios, 15 pull-thrus (20 x 70), back-ins (40 x 55), 150 full hkups (30/50 amps), seasonal sites, WiFi $, laundry. **REC:** heated pool, whirlpool, golf. Pet restrict(B/Q). Partial handicap access, no tents. Age restrict may apply, eco-friendly, 2015 rates: $36.
(928)859-2000 Lat: 33.76429, Lon: -113.61072
39258 Harquahala Rd, Salome, AZ 85348
desertpalmsrv@yahoo.com
www.desertpalmsrv.com
See ad this page.

SALOME KOA **Ratings: 8/7.5★/8** (RV Park) 2015 rates: $32.31 to $37.70. (928)859-4639 64812 Harcuvar Dr, Salome, AZ 85348

SCOTTSDALE — D3 *Maricopa*

EAGLE VIEW RV RESORT AT FORT MCDOWELL
Ratings: 10/10★/10 (RV Park) From Jct of AZ-101 LOOP S & SR-87 (Beeline Hwy) Go NE 12.9 mi on SR-87, then 0.4 mi S on N Fort McDowell Rd (E). **FAC:** Paved rds. (150 spaces). Avail: 140 paved, back-ins (30 x 69), accepts full hkup units only, 140 full hkups (30/50 amps), seasonal sites, cable, WiFi, laundry, restaurant. **REC:** heated pool, whirlpool, golf. Pet restrict(B). Big rig sites, eco-friendly, 2015 rates: $37 to $54. Disc: AAA, military.
(480)789-5310 Lat: 33.57389, Lon: -111.67469
9605 N Fort Mcdowell Rd, Fort Mcdowell, AZ 85264
eagleview@fmyn.com
www.eagleviewrvresort.com
See primary listing at Fort McDowell and ad page 66 (Spotlight Valley of the Sun).

Tell them you saw them in this Guide!

SCOTTSDALE (CONT)

Things to See and Do

CAREFREE RV RESORTS Enjoy parks in California, Texas, Florida, North Carolina, New Jersey, Massachusetts & Ontario, Canada. Park models also available for sale at many parks. Hours: 8am to 5pm.
www.carefreervresorts.com
See Carefree Tab.

SEDONA — C3 *Coconino, Yavapai*

SEDONA See also Camp Verde, Cottonwood, Flagstaff & Munds Park.

LO LO MAI SPRINGS **Ratings: 8.5/9★/8** (Campground) 2015 rates: $37 to $55. (928)634-4700 11505 E Lolomai Rd, Cornville, AZ 86325

RANCHO SEDONA RV PARK
Ratings: 8/10★/10 (RV Park) From Jct of I-17 & SR-179, N 14 mi on SR-179 to Schnebly Hill Rd, NE 0.25 mi (at 9th Roundabout), NE 0.25 mi (L). Elev 4300 ft. **FAC:** All weather rds. 84 gravel, patios, back-ins (30 x 40), accepts full hkup units only, 84 full hkups (30/50 amps), cable, WiFi, laundry. **REC:** fishing. Pets OK $. No tents. Big rig sites, eco-friendly, 2015 rates: $35 to $71. Disc: AAA. AAA Approved
(888)641-4261 Lat: 34.86530, Lon: -111.75897
135 Bear Wallow Lane, Sedona, AZ 86336
info@ranchosedona.com
www.ranchosedona.com
See ad this page, 52.

SELIGMAN — B2 *Yavapai*

SELIGMAN/ROUTE 66 KOA
Ratings: 8/9.5★/8 (Campground) From Jct of I-40 & Historic Rte 66 (exit 123), NE 1.2 mi on Historic Rte 66 (L). Elev 5250 ft. **FAC:** Gravel rds. 56 gravel, 56 pull-thrus (30 x 70), 29 full hkups, 27 W, 27 E (30/50 amps), WiFi, tent sites, rentals, dump, laundry, groc, LP gas, firewood. **REC:** pool, playground. Pet restrict(B). Big rig sites, 2015 rates: $32 to $46.
(800)562-4017 Lat: 35.32269, Lon: -112.85578
801 E Hwy 66, Seligman, AZ 86337
seligmankoa@seligmankoa.com
www.campaz.net
See ad this page.

SHOW LOW — C4 *Navajo*

FOOL HOLLOW LAKE RECREATION AREA (State Pk) From Jct US 60 & Hwy 260, W 2 mi on Hwy 260 to Old Linden Rd, E 0.6 mi (L) Follow signs. Elev 6300 ft. **FAC:** Paved rds. 123 paved, patios, back-ins (30 x 40), 92 W, 63 S, 92 E (30/50 amps), tent sites, dump, fire rings. **REC:** Fool Hollow Lake: swim, fishing, playground, rec open to public. Pets OK. Partial handicap access. 14 day max stay, 2015 rates: $30. Disc: military.
(928)537-3680 Lat: 34.26332, Lon: -110.07629
1500 N Fool Hollow Lake, Show Low, AZ 85901
www.azstateparks.com
See ad page 49 (Welcome Section).

SHOW LOW LAKE PARK (Public) From Jct of SR-77 & US-60, W 0.8 mi on US-60 to SR-260, S 5 mi to Show Low Lake Rd, E 1 mi, follow signs (L). 2015 rates: $16 to $28. (928)537-4126

VENTURE IN RV RESORT **Ratings: 8.5/9.5/9.5** (RV Park) 2015 rates: $38. May 1 to Nov 1. (928)537-4443 270 N Clark Rd, Rte 260, Show Low, AZ 85901

WALTNER'S RV RESORT **Ratings: 6/8/7** (RV Park) 2015 rates: $30. May 1 to Oct 15. (928)537-4611 4800 S 28th St, Show Low, AZ 85901

WHITE MOUNTAIN RESORT- SUNRISE RESORT **Ratings: 7/7.5★/6.5** (Membership Pk) 2015 rates: $30. May 1 to Oct 15. (928)535-5978 1876 Hwy 260 Mp 317, Show Low, AZ 85901

SIERRA VISTA — E4 *Cochise*

SIERRA VISTA See also Benson, Huachuca City, Tombstone and Willcox.

MOUNTAIN VISTA MH & RV COMMUNITY
Ratings: 4.5/7/4.5 (RV Park) From W Jct of Hwy 90 & Buffalo Soldier Trail (East gate-Fort Huachuca), E 0.3 mi on Fry Blvd to Carmichael Ave, S 0.6 mi (R). Elev 4610 ft. **FAC:** Paved/gravel rds. (160 spaces). Avail: 49 grass, 49 pull-thrus (28 x 60), accepts full hkup units only, 49 full hkups (30/50 amps), seasonal sites, cable, WiFi, laundry. Pet restrict(B) $. Partial handicap access, no tents. Big rig sites, 2015 rates: $22. No reservations.
(520)452-0500 Lat: 31.54792, Lon: -110.29970
700 S Carmichael Ave, Sierra Vista, AZ 85635
See ad page 44 (Welcome Section).

SIERRA VISTA MOBILE HOME VILLAGE & RV PARK
Ratings: 9.5/8.5★/9 (RV Resort) From the Jct of AZ-90 S and E Fry Blvd, Go E 2.6 mi on AZ-90 (R). **FAC:** Paved rds. 33 gravel, patios, 8 pull-thrus (25 x 55), back-ins (25 x 50), 33 full hkups (30/50 amps), cable, WiFi, laundry. **REC:** heated pool, whirlpool, playground. Pet restrict(B/Q). Eco-friendly, 2015 rates: $30. No CC.
(520)459-1690 Lat: 31.54783, Lon: -110.22002
733 S Deer Creek Lane, Sierra Vista, AZ 85635
Managersvmhv@aol.com
www.svmobilehomepark.com
See ad this page, 52.

SNOWFLAKE — C4 *Navajo*

PUTTER'S PARADISE RV PARK **Ratings: 8/8.5★/8.5** (RV Park) 2015 rates: $35. (928)536-2127 2085 W. Snowflake Blvd (Hwy 277), Snowflake, AZ 85937

SPRINGERVILLE — C5 *Apache*

CASA MALPAIS RV PARK
Ratings: 7/8.5★/8 (RV Park) From Jct US 60 (W Main St) & Bus 180 (Mountain Ave at only Stoplight in Town): go 1-1/4 mi W on US 60 (L). Elev 6000 ft. **FAC:** Gravel rds. 58 gravel, 24 pull-thrus (25 x 66), back-ins (30 x 50), 58 full hkups (30/50 amps), WiFi, laundry. **REC.** Pet restrict(B). No tents. Big rig sites, eco-friendly, 2015 rates: $28. Disc: AAA
(928)333-4632 Lat: 34.15037, Lon: -109.29704
272 W Main St, Springerville, AZ 85938
casamalpais@frontiernet.net
www.arizona-rim-country-rv-parks.com
See ad this page.

LYMAN LAKE
(State Pk) From Jct of US 180 & US 191, g S 11.4 mi on US 180/191, then E 1.6 mi (R) Elev 6000 ft. **FAC:** Paved rds. 61 paved, pull-thrus (30 x 100), back-ins (30 x 100), 38 W, 13 S 38 E (30/50 amps), tent sites, rentals, dump, fir rings, firewood. **REC:** Lyman Lake: swim, fishing, re open to public. Pets OK. Partial handicap access. 1 day max stay, 2015 rates: $27 to $30. Disc: military May 15 to Oct 15. No CC.
(928)337-4441 Lat: 34.363418, Lon: -109.386234
state Highway 81, St Johns, AZ 85936
www.azstateparks.com
See ad page 49 (Welcome Section).

ST DAVID — E4 *Cochise*

ST DAVID RV RESORT A WESTERN HORIZON PROPERTY **Ratings: 7/8.5★/8.5** (Membership Pk 2015 rates: $42. (520)720-4140 801 S Lee St, Sain David, AZ 85630

SUN CITY — D3 *Maricopa*

SUN CITY See also El Mirage, Goodyear, Phoe nix, Peoria & Surprise.

PARADISE RV RESORT **Ratings: 8.5/9.5★/9.** (Membership Pk) S-bnd: From Jct of I-17 & 101 Loop (Exit 215A), W 7 mi on 101 Loop to Union Hills Dr (Exi 15), W 3.5 mi (R); or N-bnd: From Jct of I-10 (E or W & 101 Loop (Exit 133), N 14 mi on 101 Loop to Unior Hills Dr (Exit 15), W 3.5 mi (R). **FAC:** Paved rds. (95 spaces). Avail: 130 gravel, patios, back-ins (38 x 55) 130 full hkups (30/50 amps), seasonal sites, WiF Hotspot, laundry, restaurant, controlled access **REC:** heated pool, whirlpool, shuffleboard. Pet re strict(B/Q). Partial handicap access, no tents. Age restrict may apply, big rig sites, 2015 rates: $46. AAA Approved
(800)405-6188 Lat: 33.65361, Lon: -112.29482
10950 W Union Hills Dr, Sun City, AZ 85373
paradise_rv@equitylifestyle.com
www.RVontheGo.com

SURPRISE — C3 *Maricopa*

DONORMA RV PARK
Ratings: 5/9★/5 (RV Park) From Jct of Hwy 60 (Grand Ave) & Greenway Rd, N 100 ft or Greenway Rd (across RR tracks) to Santa Fe Dr, W (left) 0.1 mi to Norma Ln (R). **FAC:** Paved/gravel rds. (61 spaces). Avail: 58 gravel, patios, 6 pull-thrus (20 x 45), back-ins (20 x 45), some side by side hkups, accepts self-contain units only, 58 full hkups (30/50 amps), seasonal sites, WiFi $, laundry, LP gas. **REC.** Pet restrict(B/Q). No tents.

SURPRISE (CONT)

DONORMA RV PARK (CONT)
Age restrict may apply, RV age restrict, 2015 rates: $39.50 to $43.50.
(623)583-8195 Lat: 33.62617, Lon: -112.33260
15637 Norma Ln (Office), Surprise, AZ 85378
donormarvpark@gmail.com
http://www.donormarv.com/
See ad page 69 (Spotlight Valley of the Sun).

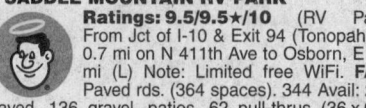

SUNFLOWER RV RESORT
Ratings: 9.5/10★/10 (RV Resort) N-bnd: From Jct of I-10 & 101 Loop (Exit 133), N 12.5 mi on the 101 Loop to Bell Rd (Exit 14), W 5.6 mi on Bell Rd to N El Mirage Rd, S 0.3 mi (L); or S-bnd: From Jct of I-17 & 101 Loop (Exit 285), W 8 mi on 101 Loop to Bell Rd (Exit 14), W 5.6 mi on to El Mirage Rd, S 0.3 mi (L). Min. length 22 ft.

FUN IN THE SUN RESORT 9.5/10*/10
Sunflower offers endless activities and outstanding amenities amid intimate surroundings. Choose from hundreds of activities, classes and clubs to find the event just for you. Close to great shopping-restaurants-local events.

FAC: Paved rds. (1139 spaces). Avail: 229 gravel, patios, 30 pull-thrus (24 x 100), back-ins (35 x 55), 229 full hkups (30/50 amps), seasonal sites, WiFi, dump, laundry, restaurant, controlled access. **REC:** heated pool, whirlpool, shuffleboard. Pet restrict(B/Q). Partial handicap access, no tents. Age restrict may apply, eco-friendly, 2015 rates: $29 to $59. ATM.
(623)583-0100 Lat: 33.63384, Lon: -112.32458
16501 N El Mirage Rd, Surprise, AZ 85378
reservations@cal-am.com
http://www.cal-am.com/resorts/resorts_details.php?resorts_id=14&search=quick
See ad pages 56 (Spotlight Gold Canyon), 52 & Cal Am Insert & Snowbird Destinations in Magazine Section.

TACNA — D1 *Yuma*

COPPER MOUNTAIN RV PARK **Ratings: 6.5/9★/7** (RV Park) 2015 rates: $20. (928)750-6652 39886 E. County 9 1/2 St, Tacna, AZ 85352

TEMPE — D3 *Maricopa*

APACHE PALMS RV PARK
Ratings: 9/9.5★/8.5 (RV Park) From Jct of I-10 & US Hwy 60, E 3.5 mi on US Hwy 60, to Loop 101 N (Exit 176B), N 1 mi to Broadway Rd (Exit 53), 0.5 mi on Price Rd Frontage Rd to Apache Blvd, W 1 mi (R). **FAC:** Paved rds. 80 Avail: 80 all weather, patios, 8 pull-thrus (16 x 70), back-ins (24 x 42), accepts full hkup units only, 80 full hkups (30/50 amps), cable, WiFi, laundry. **REC:** heated pool, whirlpool. Pet restrict(B/Q) $. No tents. Big rig sites, eco-friendly, 2015 rates: $37 to $42. Disc: AAA, military.
AAA Approved
(480)966-7399 Lat: 33.41471, Lon: -111.90687
1836 E Apache Blvd, Tempe, AZ 85281
apachepalms@aol.com
www.apachepalmsrvpark.com
See ad pages 92, 52.

TEMPLE BAR MARINA — B1 *Mohave*

LAKE MEAD NRA/TEMPLE BAR (Natl Pk) From Jct of US-93 & Temple Bar Rd, NE 26 mi on Temple Bar Rd CR-148, follow signs (R). 2015 rates: $10. (928)767-3211

TOMBSTONE — E4 *Cochise*

STAMPEDE RV PARK **Ratings: 4/7.5★/4** (RV Park) 2015 rates: $29 to $31. (520)457-3738 18 W Allen, Tombstone, AZ 85638

TOMBSTONE RV PARK & CAMPGROUND
Ratings: 7.5/8.5★/9 (RV Park) From Jct of Hwy 82 & SR-80, S 1.7 mi on SR-80 (R). Elev 4350 ft. **FAC:** Gravel rds. (83 spaces). Avail: 63 gravel, 38 pull-thrus (24 x 45), back-ins (24 x 50), 63 full hkups (30/50 amps), seasonal sites, WiFi, tent sites, rentals, laundry, LP gas. **REC:** pool, playground. Pets OK. Eco-friendly, 2015 rates: $33.25. Disc: AAA.
(520)457-3829 Lat: 31.73036, Lon: -110.07935
1475 N Hwy 80, Tombstone, AZ 85638
Tombstonervparkcg@gmail.com
http://www.tombstonervparkandcampground.com
See ad this page.

TOMBSTONE TERRITORIES RV PARK
Ratings: 10/9.5★/10 (RV Park) From Jct of I-10 & AZ Hwy 90 (Exit 302), go S on AZ-90 for 19 mi to AZ-82, turn E on to AZ-82, go 7.8 mi (L). Elev 4500 ft. **FAC:** Paved rds. (102 spaces). Avail: 90 all weather, patios, 90 pull-thrus (40 x 80), 90 full hkups (30/50 amps), seasonal sites, cable, WiFi, tent sites, rentals, laundry, LP gas. **REC:** heated pool, whirlpool, swim, shuffleboard. Pet restrict(B/Q). Partial handicap access. Big rig sites, eco-friendly, 2015 rates: $20 to $35. Disc: AAA, military.
(520)457-2584 Lat: 31.72107, Lon: -110.22435
2111 E Hwy 82, Tombstone, AZ 85616
info@tombstoneterritories.com
www.tombstoneterritories.com
See ad pages 49 (Welcome Section), 52.

WELLS FARGO RV PARK **Ratings: 6/9★/7** (RV Park) 2015 rates: $35. (520)457-3966 215 E Fremont, Tombstone, AZ 85638

We rate what RVers consider important.

TONOPAH — D2 *Maricopa*

SADDLE MOUNTAIN RV PARK
Ratings: 9.5/9.5★/10 (RV Park) From Jct of I-10 & Exit 94 (Tonopah), S 0.7 mi on N 411th Ave to Osborn, E 0.2 mi (L) Note: Limited free WiFi. **FAC:** Paved rds. (364 spaces). 344 Avail: 208 paved, 136 gravel, patios, 62 pull-thrus (36 x 60), back-ins (32 x 60), 344 full hkups (30/50 amps), seasonal sites, WiFi $, rentals, laundry, LP gas. **REC:** heated pool, shuffleboard. Pet restrict(B/Q). Partial handicap access, no tents. Big rig sites, eco-friendly, 2015 rates: $32. Disc: AAA.
(623)386-3892 Lat: 33.48713, Lon: -112.73337
40902 W Osborn Rd, Tonopah, AZ 85354
info@saddlerv.com
www.saddlemountainrvpark.com
See ad pages 92, 52.

TOPOCK — C1 *Mohave*

ROUTE 66 GOLDEN SHORES RV PARK
Ratings: 7.5/8.5★/7.5 (RV Park) From Jct of I-40 & Oatman/Topock Hwy (exit 1), Go 5 mi N on Oatman/Topock Hwy, then 3/4 mi W on Powell Lake Rd (L). **FAC:** Gravel rds. 30 gravel, patios, 3 pull-thrus (30 x 60), back-ins (35 x 60), 30 full hkups (30/50 amps), WiFi, tent sites, dump, laundry, fire rings, firewood. **REC.** Pets OK. 2015 rates: $28.
(928)788-1001 Lat: 34.778382, Lon: -114.491927
13021 Waterreed Way, Topock, AZ 86436
Mgr@goldenshores.info
www.route66goldenshores.com
See ad this page.

TUCSON — E4 *Pima*

A SPOTLIGHT Introducing Tucson's colorful attractions appearing at the front of this state section.

TUCSON See also Amado, Green Valley & Marana.

ADVENTURE BOUND CAMPING RESORTS-TUCSON CACTUS COUNTRY **Ratings: 8.5/8.5★/8.5** (RV Park) 2015 rates: $32 to $43. (520)574-3000 10195 S Houghton Rd, Tucson, AZ 85747

Things change ... last year's rates serve as a guideline only.

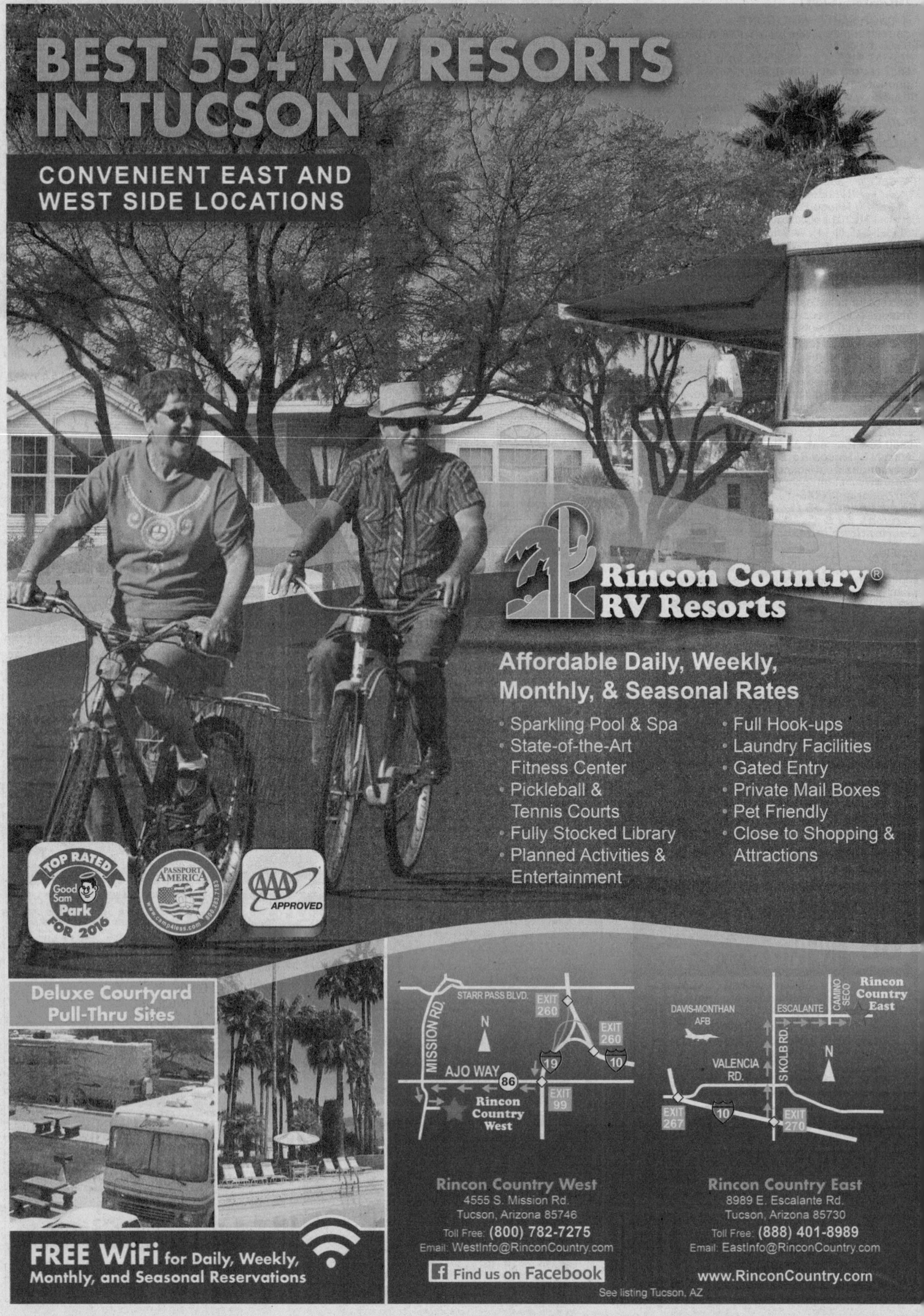
BEST 55+ RV RESORTS IN TUCSON
CONVENIENT EAST AND WEST SIDE LOCATIONS
Rincon Country® RV Resorts
Affordable Daily, Weekly, Monthly, & Seasonal Rates
• Sparkling Pool & Spa
• State-of-the-Art Fitness Center
• Pickleball & Tennis Courts
• Fully Stocked Library
• Planned Activities & Entertainment
• Full Hook-ups
• Laundry Facilities
• Gated Entry
• Private Mail Boxes
• Pet Friendly
• Close to Shopping & Attractions
TOP RATED Good Sam Park FOR 2016
PASSPORT AMERICA
AAA APPROVED
Deluxe Courtyard Pull-Thru Sites
FREE WiFi for Daily, Weekly, Monthly, and Seasonal Reservations
STARR PASS BLVD.
MISSION RD.
AJO WAY
86
EXIT 260
EXIT 99
19
10
N
Rincon Country West
DAVIS-MONTHAN AFB
ESCALANTE
CAMINO SECO
S KOLB RD.
VALENCIA RD.
EXIT 267
EXIT 270
Rincon Country East
Rincon Country West
4555 S. Mission Rd.
Tucson, Arizona 85746
Toll Free: (800) 782-7275
Email: WestInfo@RinconCountry.com
Rincon Country East
8989 E. Escalante Rd.
Tucson, Arizona 85730
Toll Free: (888) 401-8989
Email: EastInfo@RinconCountry.com
Find us on Facebook
www.RinconCountry.com
See listing Tucson, AZ

TUCSON (CONT)

CATALINA
(State Pk) From Jct of I-10 & W Tangerine Rd, E 13.5 mi on W Tangerine Rd to N Oracle Rd, S 0.4 mi on N Oracle Rd. (L). Elev 2650 ft. **FAC:** Paved rds. 120 paved, 95 W, 95 E (30/50 amps), tent sites, dump. **REC.** Pets OK. Partial handicap access. 14 day max stay, 2015 rates: $25 to $30. Disc: military.
(520)628-5798 Lat: 32.416777, Lon: -110.937581
11570 N Oracle Rd, Tucson, AZ 85737
www.azstateparks.com
See ad page 49 (Welcome Section).

CRAZY HORSE CAMPGROUNDS
Ratings: 8.5/8.5★/9.5 (RV Park) From Jct of I-10 & Craycroft Rd (Exit 268) take Frontage Rd to Craycroft Rd, N 1/4 mi on Craycroft Rd (L) Note: GPS not recommended. Call for directions.

SAME LOW PRICE YEAR-ROUND!
Monthly rate only $11/day plus tax. Minutes from Gem Shows, downtown & many attractions. Come relax in the recreation hall with your friends & neighbors. Pet friendly. Call for a complete list of our amenities and discounts.

FAC: All weather rds. (208 spaces). Avail: 178 gravel, patios, 146 pull-thrus (20 x 55), back-ins (18 x 50), accepts full hkup units only, 178 full hkups (30/50 amps), seasonal sites, WiFi, laundry, LP gas. **REC:** pool. Pet restrict(B/Q) $. No tents. Eco-friendly, 2015 rates: $30.50 to $32.50. Disc: AAA.
AAA Approved
(800)279-6279 Lat: 32.13072, Lon: -110.87533
6660 S Craycroft Rd., Tucson, AZ 85756
crazyhorservpark@gmail.com
www.crazyhorservcampgrounds.com
See ad pages 100, 52.

CRESCENT MANOR MH VILLAGE
Ratings: 6.5/NA/8.5 (RV Area in MHP) Wbnd: From Jct of I-10 and Miracle Mile (Exit 255) 0.2 mi on ramp to Miracle Mile, E 0.7 mi to Flowing Wells, N 1.5 mi to Prince, E 1.7 mi.(L) Ebnd: From Jct of I-10 & Ruthrauff (exit 252) 0.4 mi on ramp to Ruthrauff, E. 2.3 mi to Flowing Wells, S. 1 mi to Prince, 0.3 mi (L) Do not use GPS. **FAC:** Paved rds. (131 spaces). Avail: 23 gravel, patios, back-ins (40 x 60), accepts full hkup units only, 23 full hkups (30 amps), seasonal sites, laundry. **REC:** heated pool, shuffleboard. Pet restrict(B/Q). No tents. Age restrict may apply, 2015 rates: $30. No CC.
(520)887-4452 Lat: 32.27263, Lon: -110.99096
1150 W Prince Road, Tucson, AZ 85705
crescentmanor@continentalcommunities.com
www.continentalcommunities.com
See ad page 92.

DESERT PUEBLO MHP & RV PARK
Ratings: 9/8.5★/10 (RV Park) From Jct of I-19 & I-10 (Exit 260), S 1.5 mi on I-19 to Ajo Way (Exit 99), W 0.3 mi on Ajo Way (R). **FAC:** Paved rds. (421 spaces). Avail: 77 all weather, patios, back-ins (45 x 60), 77 full hkups (30/50 amps), seasonal sites, laundry, controlled access. **REC:** heated pool, whirlpool, shuffleboard. Pet restrict(Q). No

A campground rating is based on ALL facilities available at the park.

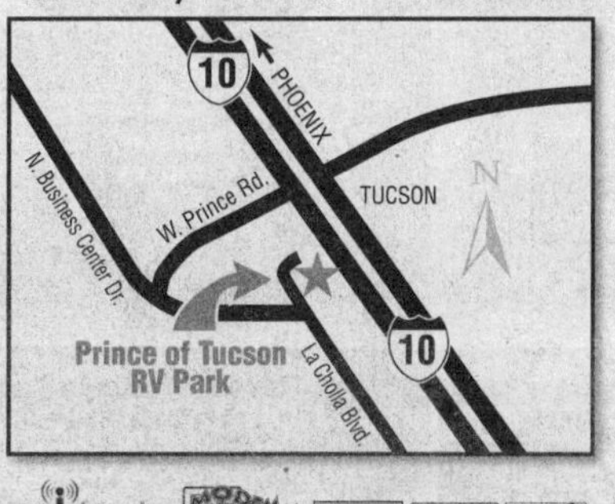

TUCSON (CONT)

DESERT PUEBLO MHP & RV PARK (CONT) tents. Age restrict may apply, big rig sites, eco-friendly, 2015 rates: $25.85. No CC.
(520)889-9557 Lat: 32.17875, Lon: -110.99215
1302 W Ajo Way, Tucson, AZ 85713
office@desertpueblo.com
www.desertpueblo.com
See ad page 64 (Spotlight Tucson).

DESERT TRAILS RV PARK
Ratings: 9/9★/9 (RV Park) From Jct of I-10 & I-19 (Exit 260), S 1.5 mi on I-19 to Ajo Way (Exit 99), W 8.5 mi on Ajo Way to San Joaquin Rd, N 2.5 mi (R) Note: Do not follow GPS directions. **FAC:** All weather rds. 244 gravel, 20 pull-thrus (22 x 45), back-ins (25 x 50), 244 full hkups (30/50 amps), WiFi, laundry. **REC:** heated pool, whirlpool. Pet restrict(B). No tents. Age restrict may apply, RV age restrict, 2015 rates: $29 to $33.
(520)883-8340 Lat: 32.17941, Lon: -111.14790
3551 S San Joaquin Rd, Tucson, AZ 85735
deserttrailsrvpark@msn.com
www.deserttrailsrvpark.com
See ad this page.

New to RVing? Be sure to check out the all the great articles on getting the most out of your RV, at the front of the Guide.

FAIRVIEW MANOR **Ratings: 7.5/8.5★/8** (Membership Pk) 2015 rates: $36. (520)888-1502 3115 North Fairview Ave #3, Tucson, AZ 85705

FAR HORIZONS TUCSON VILLAGE RV RESORT
Ratings: 10/10★/10 (RV Park) From Jct of I-10 & Kolb Rd (Exit 270), N 9 mi on Kolb Rd to Speedway, E 1 mi to Pantano Rd, S 0.5 mi (R).

ONLY MINUTES FROM DOWNTOWN TUCSON..
Step out of your RV and walk, ride your bike, or drive to nearby outdoor adventure, scenic attractions, outstanding golf, shopping, dining, and the arts. Experience spectacular mountain views, desert sunrises and sunsets.

FAC: Paved rds. (514 spaces). Avail: 40 paved, 153 all weather, patios, back-ins (36 x 47), accepts full hkup units only, 193 full hkups (30/50 amps), seasonal sites, cable, WiFi, rentals, laundry, controlled access. **REC:** heated pool, whirlpool, shuffleboard. Pets OK. No tents. Age restrict may apply, big rig sites, eco-friendly, 2015 rates: $31 to $51. Disc: AAA, military.
(800)480-3488 Lat: 32.22802, Lon: -110.82414
555 N Pantano Rd, Tucson, AZ 85710
vacation@tucsonvillage.com
www.tucsonvillage.com
See ad pages 63 (Spotlight Tucson), 52, 120 (CA Map) & Snowbird Destinations in Magazine Section.

GILBERT RAY CAMPGROUND (Public) From Jct of Hwy 86 & Kinney Rd, N 5 mi on Kinney Rd to McCain Loop Rd, W 0.5 mi (L). 2015 rates: $20. (520)877-6000

JUSTINS DIAMOND J RV PARK
Ratings: 6.5/NA/9 (RV Park) From Jct I-19 & I-10 (Exit 260), S 1.5 mi on I-19 to Ajo Way (Hwy 99), W 7.9 mi on Ajo Way to San Joaquin Rd, N 2.8 mi (R). **FAC:** Paved rds. (138 spaces). Avail: 100 gravel, 18 pull-thrus (33 x 55), back-ins (34 x 55), accepts full hkup units only, 100 full hkups (30/50 amps), seasonal sites, WiFi, rentals, laundry. **REC.** Pet restrict(B/Q). No tents. Big rig sites, eco-friendly, 2015 rates: $29. No CC.
(520)883-6706 Lat: 32.18100, Lon: -111.15068
3451 S San Joaquin Rd, Tucson, AZ 85735
www.diamondjrvpark.com

MISSION VIEW RV RESORT
Ratings: 10/9.5★/10 (RV Park) From Jct of I-10 & I-19 (Exit 260), S 8.5 mi on I-19 to San Xavier Loop Rd (Exit 92), E 1.4 mi on San Xavier Loop Rd (L). Note: No tent trailers. **FAC:** Paved rds. (342 spaces). Avail: 267 all weather, patios, back-ins (36 x 50), accepts full hkup units only, 267 full hkups (30/50 amps), seasonal sites, WiFi, rentals, laundry. **REC:** heated pool, whirlpool, shuffleboard. Pet restrict(B/Q). No tents. Age restrict may apply, eco-friendly, 2015 rates: $25 to $38. No CC.
(800)444-8439 Lat: 32.11721, Lon: -110.97208
31 West Los Reales, Tucson, AZ 85756
missionviewrv@aol.com
www.missionviewrv.com
See ad pages 97, 52 & Snowbird Destinations in Magazine Section.

PIMA COUNTY FAIRGROUNDS & RV PARK
Ratings: 6.5/8.5★/8 (RV Park) From Jct of I-10 & Houghton Rd (Exit 275), S 1 mi on Houghton Rd to Brekke, N 0.2 mi (L). **FAC:** Paved/gravel rds. 400 Avail: 53 paved, 347 gravel, 53 pull-thrus (20 x 60), back-ins (25 x 70), accepts full hkup units only, 205 full hkups, 195 W, 195 E (30/50 amps), WiFi, dump, laundry, restaurant. **REC:** rec open to public. Pets OK. Partial handicap access, no tents. Big rig sites, eco-friendly, 2015 rates: $20. Sep 15 to Mar 30. ATM.
(520)762-9100 Lat: 32.04851, Lon: -110.77380
11300 S Houghton Rd, Tucson, AZ 85747
rvoffice@pimacountyfair.com
www.pimacountyfair.com
See ad page 99.

PRINCE OF TUCSON RV PARK
Ratings: 10/9.5★/9 (RV Park) From Jct of I-10 & Prince Rd (Exit 254), Go W 0.2 mi on Prince Rd to stop sign, (do not turn onto frontage Rd) then S 0.1 mi on Business Center Dr, (L). **FAC;** Paved rds. 176 Avail: 176 all weather, patios, 42 pull-thrus (24 x 70), back-ins (25 x 45), some side by side hkups, accepts full hkup units only, 176 full hkups (30/50 amps), WiFi, dump, laundry. **REC:** heated pool, whirlpool, shuffleboard. Pet restrict(B/Q). No tents. Big rig sites, eco-friendly, 2015 rates: $28.25.
(800)955-3501 Lat: 32.27146, Lon: -111.01092
3501 N Freeway, Tucson, AZ 85705
princeoftucson@comcast.net
www.princeoftucsonrvpark.com
See ad pages 99, 52.

RINCON COUNTRY EAST RV RESORT
Ratings: 10/10★/10 (RV Park) From Jct of I-10 & Kolb Rd (exit 270), N 5 mi on Kolb Rd to Escalante Rd, E 2.5 mi (L).

VOTED ARIZONA'S BEST 2 YRS IN A ROW
Located near many attractions Tucson has to offer; Kartcher Caverns, Saguaro National Park, Arizona Desert Museum. Come enjoy our sunshine, hospitality & experience the resort you bought the RV for in the first place.

FAC: Paved rds. (460 spaces). Avail: 55 paved, patios, back-ins (30 x 45), accepts full hkup units only, 55 full hkups (30/50 amps), seasonal sites, cable, WiFi, rentals, laundry, controlled access. **REC:** heated pool, whirlpool, shuffleboard. Pet re-

TUCSON (CONT)

RINCON COUNTRY EAST RV RESORT (CONT)
strict(B/Q). Partial handicap access, no tents. Age restrict may apply, RV age restrict, eco-friendly, 2015 rates: $49 to $53. Disc: AAA.
AAA Approved
(520)886-8431 Lat: 32.17878, Lon: -110.80155
8989 E Escalante Rd, Tucson, AZ 85730
eastinfo@rinconcountry.com
www.rinconcountry.com
See ad pages 98, 52, 45 (AZ Map) & Snowbird Destinations in Magazine Section.

RINCON COUNTRY WEST RV RESORT
Ratings: 10/10★/10 (RV Resort) From Jct of I-10 & I-19 (exit 260), S 1.5 mi on I-19 to Ajo Way (exit 99), W 1 mi to Mission Rd, S 0.5 mi (L).

EXPERIENCE RESORT RV LIVING
Located near shopping, restaurants and all that Tucson has to offer. This 55+ gated community hosts an abundance of amenities including 2 fitness centers, WiFi & all the comforts you would expect from a world class resort.

FAC: Paved rds. (1083 spaces). Avail: 24 paved, 329 all weather, patios, 24 pull-thrus (22 x 57), back-ins (35 x 50), accepts full hkup units only, 353 full hkups (30/50 amps), seasonal sites, cable, WiFi, rentals, laundry, controlled access. **REC:** heated pool, whirlpool, shuffleboard. Pet restrict(B/Q). Partial handicap access, no tents. Age restrict may apply, RV age restrict, eco-friendly, 2015 rates: $53 to $59. Disc: AAA.
AAA Approved
(520)294-5608 Lat: 32.16873, Lon: -111.00249
4555 S Mission Rd, Tucson, AZ 85746
westinfo@rinconcountry.com
www.rinconcountry.com
See ad pages 98, 52, 45 (AZ Map) & Snowbird Destinations in Magazine Section.

SENTINEL PEAK RV PARK
Ratings: 9/NA/9 (RV Park) From the Jct of I-10 & Exit 257, Merge onto N Freeway St, then W 0.4 mi on W Speedway Blvd, then S 0.1 mi on N Grande Ave (L). **FAC:** Paved rds. 23 paved, 3 pull-thrus (30 x 60), back-ins (32 x 60), 23 full hkups (30/50 amps), WiFi, restrooms only, laundry, controlled access. **REC:** heated pool. Pets OK. Big rig sites, eco-friendly, 2015 rates: $38 to $59.
(520)495-0175 Lat: 32.228154, Lon: -110.988893
450 N Grande Ave, Tucson, AZ 85745
info@sentinelpeakrv.com
www.sentinelpeakrv.com
See ad pages 99, 52 & Family Camping in Magazine Section.

TRA-TEL TUCSON RV PARK **Ratings: 7/8★/7** (RV Park) 2015 rates: $27. (520)888-5401 2070 W Ft Lowell Rd, Tucson, AZ 85705

TUCSON LAZYDAYS KOA **Ratings: 10/9★/9.5** (RV Resort) 2015 rates: $24 to $49. (520)799-3701 5151 S Country Club Rd, Tucson, AZ 85706

VOYAGER RV RESORT **Ratings: 9/9.5★/8.5** (RV Park) 2015 rates: $26 to $55. (800)405-6188 8701 S Kolb Rd, Tucson, AZ 85756

WESTERN WAY RV RESORT
Ratings: 9.5/9.5★/10 (RV Park) From Jct of I-19 & I-10 (Exit 260), S 1.5 mi on I-19 to Ajo Way (Exit 99), W 5 mi on Ajo Way to Kinney Rd, N 1.5 mi to Western Way Cir, SW 500 ft (R). **FAC:** Paved rds. (300 spaces). Avail: 84 gravel, patios, back-ins (33 x 45), accepts self-contain units only, 84 full hkups (30/50 amps), seasonal sites, WiFi, dump, laundry. **REC:** heated pool, whirlpool, shuffleboard. Pet restrict(B/Q). Partial handicap access, no tents. Age restrict may apply, eco-friendly, 2015 rates: $51.36.
(800)292-8616 Lat: 32.18515, Lon: -111.09227
3100 S Kinney Rd, Tucson, AZ 85713
Reservations@wwrvresort.com
www.wwrvresort.com
See ad pages 99, 52.

WHISPERING PALMS RV PARK **Ratings: 7/8/7.5** (RV Park) 2015 rates: $25. (520)888-2500 3445 N Romero Rd, Tucson, AZ 85705

WISHING WELL RV PARK **Ratings: 6.5/8.5★/6** (RV Park) 2015 rates: $28. (520)825-3361 16100 N Oracle Rd, Tuscon, AZ 85739

Travel Services

CAMPING WORLD OF TUCSON As the nation's largest retailer of RV supplies, accessories, services and new and used RVs, Camping World is committed to making your total RV experience better. RV Accesories: (866)298-1029. **SERVICES:** Tire, RV appliance, MH mechanical, engine/chassis repair, restrooms, RV Sales. RV supplies, dump, emergency parking, RV accessible. waiting room. Hours: 8am to 6pm.
(888)546-1417 Lat: 32.176007, Lon: -110.917790
4700 S. Palo Verde Road, Tucson, AZ 85714
jgeringer@campingworld.com
www.campingworld.com

TUSAYAN — B3 *Coconino*

GRAND CANYON CAMPER VILLAGE **Ratings: 5.5/7/6** (Campground) 2015 rates: $46 to $56. (928)638-2887 549 Camper Village Lane, Tusayan, AZ 86023

Things to See and Do

GRAND CANYON IMAX THEATER & NATIONAL GEOGRAPHIC VISITOR CENTER In only 34 minutes, viewers will discover 4,000 years of Grand Canyon history in this IMAX film presentation. Also on site; National Park Pass Sales, Pink Jeep Tours, free maps and tourist information. Elev 7000 ft. partial handicap access. RV accessible. Restrooms, food. Hours: 8am to 10pm. Adult fee: $12.50. ATM.
(928)638-2468 Lat: 35.97454, Lon: -112.12633
450 State Route 64, Tusayan, AZ 86023
Group2@ngvccanyon.com
www.explorethecanyon.com
See ad page 57 (Spotlight Grand Canyon).

WELLTON — D1 *Yuma*

ARROWHEAD RV PARK **Ratings: 8.5/8.5★/7.5** (RV Park) 2015 rates: $32. (928)785-3971 30115 Wellton-Mohawk Dr, Wellton, AZ 85356

SUN COUNTRY RV PARK **Ratings: 5.5/7.5★/5** (RV Park) 2015 rates: $24. (928)785-4072 10321 Fresno St, Wellton, AZ 85356

TIER DROP RV PARK Ratings: 8.5/7.5/7.5 (RV Park) From Jct of I-8 & Avenue 29 E (Exit 30), N 25 ft on Avenue 29 to E County Rd 11th St, W 0.75 mi (R). **FAC:** Paved/gravel rds. (250 spaces). Avail: 60 gravel, patios, 60 pull-thrus (25 x 50), 60 full hkups (30/50 amps), seasonal sites, WiFi, laundry. **REC:** heated pool, whirlpool, shuffleboard. Pet restrict(B). No tents. Big rig sites, eco-friendly, 2015 rates: $27.
AAA Approved
(928)785-9295 Lat: 32.66370, Lon: -114.15481
28320 E Co 11th St, Wellton, AZ 85356
tierdroprv@aol.com
www.tierdroprvpark.com

WENDEN — C2 *La Paz*

ALAMO LAKE
(State Pk) From the city of Wenden, go north 38 miles on Alamo Dam Road to reach Alamo Lake State Park. **FAC:** Paved rds. 99 paved, 5 pull-thrus (22 x 45), back-ins (22 x 40), 19 full hkups, 80 W, 80 E (30/50 amps), tent sites, dump, groc, firewood. **REC:** Alamo Lake: fishing, rec open to public. Pets OK. 2015 rates: $22 to $25. Disc: military.
(928)669-2088 Lat: 34.234158, Lon: -113.552799
35211 Cunningham Pass Rd, Wenden, AZ 85357
www.azstateparks.gov
See ad page 49 (Welcome Section).

WICKENBURG — C2 *Maricopa, Mohave*

COUNTRY CLUB PARK **Ratings: 8/8★/9.5** (RV Area in MHP) 2015 rates: $35. (928)684-2110 1855 W Wickenburg Way, Wickenburg, AZ 85390

DESERT CYPRESS RV & MH PARK **Ratings: 9/8.5★/9.5** (RV Area in MHP) 2015 rates: $36. (928)684-2153 610 Jack Burden Rd, Space 33, Wickenburg, AZ 85390

HORSPITALITY RV PARK
Ratings: 9/9.5★/10 (RV Park) From Jct of US-60/89 & SR-93, SE 2 mi on Hwys 60/89/93, between MP-112 & 113 (R). **FAC:** Paved rds. (100 spaces). Avail: 50 all weather, patios, 7 pull-thrus (20 x 100), back-ins (30 x 55), 50 full hkups (30/50 amps), seasonal sites, WiFi, tent sites, dump, laundry, LP gas, firewood. **REC.** Pet restrict(B). Eco-friendly, 2015 rates: $28 to $38. Disc: AAA, military.
(928)684-2519 Lat: 33.95275, Lon: -112.70964
51802 US Hwy 60-89, Wickenburg, AZ 85390
Horspitality@hotmail.com
www.horspitality.com
See ad this page.

WIKIEUP — C2 *Mohave*

BURRO CREEK BLM (Public) From town, N 55 mi on Hwy 93 to Burro Creek Rd, W 1.25 mi (R). 2015 rates: $14. (928)718-3700

HIDDEN OASIS RV PARK **Ratings: 7/8.5★/7.5** (RV Park) 2015 rates: $20. (928)765-2439 17653 S Hwy 93, Wikieup, AZ 85360

WILLCOX — E5 *Cochise*

CHIRICAHUA NAT'L MON/BONITA CANYON (Natl Pk) From town, SE 34 mi on Hwy 186 to Hwy 181, E 3 mi (L). 2015 rates: $12. (520)824-3560

GRANDE VISTA MH & RV PARK
Ratings: 8.5/8.5★/8.5 (RV Park) From Jct of I-10 & Rex Allen Dr (exit 340), go S 0.5 mi on Rex Allen Dr, turn W on Prescott Ave, go 500 ft (L). Elev 4200 ft. **FAC:** All weather rds. (57 spaces). Avail: 36 all weather, 36 pull-thrus (23 x 55), accepts self-contain units only, 36 full hkups (30/50 amps), seasonal sites, WiFi, tent sites, rentals, dump,

Remember, ratings are based on ALL available facilities.

WILLCOX (CONT)

GRANDE VISTA MH & RV PARK (CONT)
laundry. **REC.** Pet restrict(B). Eco-friendly, 2015 rates: $31. Disc: AAA, military.
(520)384-4002 Lat: 32.26238, Lon: -109.83405
711 North Prescott Ave, Willcox, AZ 85643
granderv@hotmail.com
www.grandevistarvpark.com
See ad pages 101, 52.

LIFESTYLE RV RESORT
Ratings: 9/8.5★/8 (RV Park) E-bnd: From Jct of I-10 & Exit 336, SE 4 mi on Bus I-10/Haskell Ave (L); or W-bnd: From Jct of I-10 & Exit 344, SW 4 mi on Bus I-10/Haskell Ave (R). Elev 4200 ft. **FAC:** All weather rds. (65 spaces). Avail: 60 all weather, 21 pull-thrus (19 x 65), back-ins (20 x 35), accepts full hkup units only, 60 full hkups (30/50 amps), seasonal sites, cable, WiFi, tent sites, rentals, laundry, restaurant. **REC:** heated pool, whirlpool, rec open to public. Pets OK. Big rig sites, eco-friendly, 2015 rates: $32. Disc: AAA.
(520)384-3303 Lat: 32.26045, Lon: -109.82781
622 N Haskell Ave, Willcox, AZ 85643
lifestylerv@gmail.com
www.lifestylervresortaz.com
See ad page 101.

MAGIC CIRCLE RV PARK
Ratings: 9/9★/8.5 (Campground) From Jct of I-10 & Ft Grant Rd (exit 340), NW 0.1 mi on Ft Grant Rd to Virginia Ave (left at Super 8 Motel), W 0.1 mi (E). Elev 4200 ft. **FAC:** All weather rds. (59 spaces). Avail: 57 all weather, 43 pull-thrus (32 x 55), back-ins (35 x 46), accepts full hkup units only, 57 full hkups (30/50 amps), seasonal sites, cable, WiFi, tent sites, dump, laundry, LP gas. **REC:** playground. Pets OK. Big rig sites, eco-friendly, 2015 rates: $33. Disc: AAA, military.
(520)384-3212 Lat: 32.26447, Lon: -109.84633
700 N Virginia Ave, Willcox, AZ 85643
magic1@vtc.net
www.magiccirclerv.com
See ad pages 101, 52.

SAGEBRUSH RV PARK
Ratings: 7.5/9★/7 (RV Park) From the Jct of I-10 & Exit 336, Go E 3.3 mi to Lewis Rd, W 100 ft (R). Elev 4200 ft. **FAC:** Paved rds. (63 spaces). Avail: 31 gravel, 11 pull-thrus (20 x 150), back-ins (20 x 70), accepts full hkup units only, 31 full hkups (30/50 amps), seasonal sites, WiFi, laundry. **REC.** Pets OK. No tents. Eco-friendly, 2015 rates: $25 to $28.
(520)384-2872 Lat: 32.24434, Lon: -109.83922
200 West Lewis St, Willcox, AZ 85643
info@sagebrushrvpark.com
www.sagebrushrvpark.com
See ad pages 101, 52.

WILLIAMS — B3 *Coconino*

CANYON GATEWAY RV PARK
Ratings: 7.5/10★/8 (RV Park) From Jct of I-40 & Grand Canyon Blvd (exit 163), N 650 ft on Grand Canyon Blvd (R). Elev 7000 ft. **FAC:** Gravel rds. (101 spaces). Avail: 91 gravel, 53 pull-thrus (20 x 60), back-ins (20 x 45), 91 full hkups (30/50 amps), seasonal sites, WiFi, tent sites, dump, laundry, groc. **REC.** Pet restrict(Q). Partial handicap access. Big rig sites, eco-friendly, 2015 rates: $33 to $39. Disc: AAA, military.
(888)635-0329 Lat: 35.26284, Lon: -112.19315
1060 N Grand Canyon Blvd, Williams, AZ 86046
canyongatewayrvpark@yahoo.com
www.grandcanyonrvparks.com
See ad pages 59 (Spotlight Grand Canyon), 52.

CANYON MOTEL & RV PARK Ratings: 9/8.5★/9 (RV Park) From Jct of I-40 & Hwy 64/Bus I-40 (exit 165), S 1 mi on Bus I-40 to Rodeo Rd, NW 50 ft (R). Elev 7000 ft. **FAC:** All weather rds. 47 gravel, 29 pull-thrus (30 x 70), back-ins (25 x 60), 47 full hkups (30/50 amps), cable, WiFi, tent sites, rentals, laundry, groc, firewood. **REC:** heated pool, playground. Pets OK. Partial handicap access. Big rig sites, eco-friendly, 2015 rates: $35.99 to $44.99. Disc: AAA, military.
AAA Approved
(928)635-9371 Lat: 35.25719, Lon: -112.17078
1900 E Rodeo Rd/Route 66, Williams, AZ 86046
thecanyonmotel@aol.com
www.thecanyonmotel.com

CIRCLE PINES KOA **Ratings: 9/9.5★/8** (Campground) 2015 rates: $33.75 to $50.75. Apr 1 to Oct 31. (800)562-9379 1000 Circle Pines Rd, Williams, AZ 86046

GRAND CANYON RAILWAY RV PARK
Ratings: 10/10★/9 (RV Park) From Jct of I-40 & Grand Canyon Blvd (exit 163), S 0.3 mi on Grand Canyon Blvd to Franklin Ave, SW 0.2 mi (L). Elev 6800 ft.

ALL ABOARD GRAND CANYON NATL PARK
Take the historic train into Grand Canyon National Park without having to worry about navigating through the busy local roadways. Park your RV in the clean mountain air in Williams, just two blocks away from Route 66.

FAC: Paved rds. 124 paved, 73 pull-thrus (30 x 65), back-ins (30 x 56), 124 full hkups (30/50 amps), cable, WiFi, rentals, laundry, groc, restaurant. **REC:** heated pool, whirlpool, playground. Pets OK. Partial handicap access, no tents. Big rig sites, eco-friendly, 2015 rates: $39.99 to $44.99. Disc: AAA, military. ATM.
AAA Approved
(800)843-8724 Lat: 35.25157, Lon: -112.19410
601 W Franklin Ave, Williams, AZ 86046
info@thetrain.com
www.thetrain.com
See ad pages 58 (Spotlight Grand Canyon), 52 & RV Trips of a Lifetime in Magazine Section.

GRAND CANYON/WILLIAMS KOA **Ratings: 8/8.5/7** (Campground) 2015 rates: $35 to $56. (800)562-5771 5333 N Hwy 64, Williams, AZ 86046

RAILSIDE RV RANCH & CABIN RESORT
Ratings: 7.5/9.5★/8 (RV Park) From Jct of I-40 & Grand Canyon Blvd (Exit 163), S 0.1 mi on Grand Canyon Blvd to Rodeo Rd, E 0.6 mi (L). Elev 7000 ft. **FAC:** All weather rds. 96 gravel, 67 pull-thrus (25 x 65), back-ins (25 x 55), 96 full hkups (30/50 amps), cable, WiFi, tent sites, rentals, dump, laundry, LP gas. **REC:** whirlpool, playground. Pets OK. Partial handicap access. Big rig sites, eco-friendly, 2015 rates: $36.95 to $39.95. Disc: AAA, military.
AAA Approved
(928)635-4077 Lat: 35.25918, Lon: -112.17977
877 E Rodeo Rd, Williams, AZ 86046
reservations@railsiderv.com
www.railsiderv.com
See ad this page.

Things to See and Do

GRAND CANYON RAILWAY Grand Canyon Railway offers train trips from Williams to the Grand Canyon on trains that made their first journey in 1901. Elev 6800 ft. RV accessible. Restrooms, food. ATM.
(800)843-8724 Lat: 35.25157, Lon: -112.1941
235 N Grand Canyon Blvd, Williams, AZ 86046
info@thetrain.com
www.thetrain.com
See ad page 58 (Spotlight Grand Canyon).

Shop at Camping World and SAVE with over $1,000 of coupons. Check the front of the Guide for yours!

GRAND CANYON RAILWAY PET RESORT Pet Resort has 28 spacious rooms for dogs & 16 comfortable condos for cats. Elev 7000 ft. RV accessible. Restrooms. Hours: 8am to 8pm.
(800)843-8724 Lat: 35.25157, Lon: -112.1941
601 W Franklin, Williams, AZ 86046
info@thetrain.com
www.thetrain.com
See ad page 58 (Spotlight Grand Canyon).

WILLOW BEACH — B1 *Mohave*

WILLOW BEACH MARINA & RV PARK
Ratings: 9/9.5★/9 (Campground) From Jct of US 93 & Willow Beach Rd (between Mile Marker 14 & 15), NW 4.2 mi on Willow Beach Rd (E).

WILLOW BEACH ADVENTURES START HERE
A premier location for your favorite outdoor activity on the Colorado River, close to Hoover Dam and Las Vegas. Whether hiking, rafting, or fishing, enjoy the desert sun year 'round as you explore 235 miles of shoreline.

FAC: Paved rds. (29 spaces). Avail: 27 paved, patios, 20 pull-thrus (32 x 70), back-ins (32 x 65), 27 full hkups (30/50 amps), WiFi, tent sites, dump, laundry, groc, firewood, restaurant. **REC:** Lake Mohave/Colorado River: swim, fishing, marina. Pets OK. Big rig sites, eco-friendly, 2015 rates: $35. Disc: AAA, military.
(928)767-4747 Lat: 35.87029, Lon: -114.66007
25804 N Willow Beach Rd, Willow Beach, AZ 86445
willowbeachmarina@gmail.com
http://www.willowbeachharbor.com
See ad pages 744 (Spotlight Las Vegas), 52 & RV Trips of a Lifetime in Magazine Section.

WINSLOW — B4 *Navajo*

A SPOTLIGHT Introducing Winslow's colorful attractions appearing at the front of this state section.

HOMOLOVI (State Pk) From Jct of I-40 & AZ 87, go N 1.9 mi on AZ 87, then SE 0.9 mi on State Park Rd (E). 2015 rates: $25. (928)289-4106

MCHOOD PARK (Public) From town, S 1.5 mi on SR-87 to SR-99, E 5 mi (L). (928)289-5714

METEOR CRATER RV PARK
Ratings: 9/10★/10 (RV Park) From Jct of I-40 & Meteor Crater Rd (exit 233), go S 100 yds on Meteor Crater Rd (R). (Do not use GPS). Elev 5300 ft.

SEE THE BEST METEOR CRATER ON EARTH
Visit the best preserved meteor crater impact site on earth! RV park guests receive coupons for Meteor Crater admission, plus coupons for food and other area attractions. A great location for overnight or exploring the area.

FAC: All weather rds. (72 spaces). Avail: 65 all weather, 65 pull-thrus (30 x 60), 40 full hkups, 25 W, 25 E (30/50 amps), seasonal sites, WiFi, tent sites, dump, laundry, groc, controlled access. **REC.** Pet restrict(B/Q). Partial handicap access. Big rig sites, eco-friendly, 2015 rates: $30 to $35. Disc: AAA, military. ATM.
AAA Approved
(800)478-4002 Lat: 35.10517, Lon: -111.03237
I-40 Exit 233, Winslow, AZ 86047
Rvpark@meteorcrater.com
www.meteorcrater.com
See ad pages 60 (Spotlight Meteor Crater Winslow), 52.

Things to See and Do

METEOR CRATER The best preserved meteor impact site on earth, where Apollo astronauts trained. Interactive learning center, Subway restaurant, gift shop & rock shop. Open all year, summer hours 7am to 7pm. Elev 5300 ft. partial handicap access. RV accessible. Restrooms, food. Hours: 8am to 5pm. Adult fee: $18. ATM.
(928)289-2362 Lat: 35.03292, Lon: -111.02272

WINSLOW (CONT)

METEOR CRATER (CONT)
I-40, Exit 233, Meteor Crater Road, Winslow, AZ 86047
info@meteorcrater.com
www.meteorcrater.com
See ad page 60 (Spotlight Meteor Crater Winslow).

YUMA — D1 *Yuma*

A SPOTLIGHT Introducing Yuma's colorful attractions appearing at the front of this state section.

➔ ARABY ACRES RV RESORT **Ratings: 8.5/9.5★/9.5** (RV Park) 2015 rates: $53. (800)405-6188 6649 E 32nd St, Yuma, AZ 85365

➔ ARIZONA SANDS RV PARK **Ratings: 6.5/9.5★/8.5** (RV Park) 2015 rates: $33. (928)726-0160 5510 E 32nd St, Yuma, AZ 85365

➔ ARIZONA WEST RV PARK **Ratings: 9.5/9.5★/9** (RV Park) 2015 rates: $30. (928)726-1481 6825 E 32nd Street, Yuma, AZ 85365

➔ **BLUE SKY RV RESORT**
Ratings: 9.5/9.5★/9.5 (RV Resort) From Jct of I-8 & Fortuna Rd (exit 12), S 50 ft on Fortuna Rd to S Frontage Rd, W 0.8 mi (L). **FAC:** Paved rds. (252 spaces). 32 Avail: 8 paved, 24 gravel, patios, 8 pull-thrus (24 x 70), back-ins (30 x 50), 32 full hkups (30/50 amps), seasonal sites, cable, WiFi $, rentals, laundry. **REC:** heated pool, whirlpool, shuffleboard. Pet restrict(B/Q) $. Partial handicap access. Big rig sites, eco-friendly, 2015 rates: $40 to $50. Disc: military.
(877)367-5220 Lat: 32.401217, Lon: -114.272343
10247 S Frontage Rd, Yuma, AZ 85365
managerbluesky@yahoo.com
http://www.blueskyyuma.com/
See ad pages 78, 883, 74 (Spotlight Yuma), 52 & Snowbird Destinations in Magazine Section.

➔ BONITA MESA RV RESORT **Ratings: 9/9.5★/9** (RV Park) From Jct of I-8 & exit 12 (Fortuna Rd), N on Fortuna Rd to Frntg rd, W 1.5 mi (R). **FAC:** Paved rds. (470 spaces). Avail: 200 all weather, patios, back-ins (30 x 50), 200 full hkups (30/50 amps), seasonal sites, WiFi Hotspot, laundry. **REC:** heated pool, whirlpool, shuffleboard. Pet restrict(B/Q). Partial handicap access, no tents. Eco-friendly, 2015 rates: $37.50. Disc: AAA.
AAA Approved
(928)342-2999 Lat: 32.67159, Lon: -114.47103
9400 N Frontage Rd, Yuma, AZ 85365
bonitamesa@aol.com
www.bonitamesa.com

➔ CACTUS GARDENS RV RESORT **Ratings: 9/8.5★/8.5** (RV Park) 2015 rates: $40 to $47. (800)405-6188 10657 S Ave 9E, Yuma, AZ 85365

⬇ CAPRI RV RESORT **Ratings: 8/9★/7** (RV Park) 2015 rates: $35. (800)405-6188 3380 S 4th Ave, Yuma, AZ 85365

➔ **CARAVAN OASIS RV RESORT**
Ratings: 9.5/9★/9.5 (RV Park) From Jct of I-8 & Exit 12 (Fortuna Rd), N on Fortuna Rd to Frntg Rd, W 0.2 mi (R). **FAC:** Paved rds. (550 spaces). Avail: 200 gravel, patios, 27 pull-thrus (28 x 60), back-ins (42 x 56), 200 full hkups (30/50 amps), seasonal sites, WiFi $, rentals, laundry. **REC:** heated pool, whirlpool, shuffleboard. Pets OK. Partial handicap access, no tents. Big rig sites, eco-friendly, 2015 rates: $42. Disc: AAA, military.
(928)342-1480 Lat: 32.67127, Lon: -114.44962
10500 N Frontage Rd, Yuma, AZ 85365
caravan@caravanoasisresort.com
www.caravanoasisresort.com
See ad pages 74 (Spotlight Yuma), 52.

Traveling with a Fido? Many campground listings indicate pet-friendly amenities and pet restrictions.

➔ CAREFREE VILLAGE RESORT **Ratings: 10/10★/9.5** (RV Resort) 2015 rates: $45. (800)987-0567 3900 Ave 8 1/2 E, Yuma, AZ 85365

➔ **COCOPAH BEND RV & GOLF RESORT**
Ratings: 9.5/9.5★/10 (RV Park) From Jct of I-8 & Winterhaven/4th Ave (CA Exit 172), Go S 1/2 mi on 4th Ave (I-8 Bus Loop) then Go W 2-1/4 mi on 1st St, then Go S 1/4 mi on Ave C, then go W 1-1/2 mi on Riverside Dr, then go N 3/4 mi on Strand Ave, (E). **FAC:** Paved rds. (800 spaces). Avail: 375 all weather, patios, back-ins (35 x 50), 375 full hkups (30/50 amps), seasonal sites, cable, WiFi Hotspot, laundry, groc, restaurant, controlled access. **REC:** heated pool, whirlpool, Colorado River: fishing, golf, shuffleboard, rec open to public. Pet restrict(B/Q). Partial handicap access, no tents. Big rig sites, eco-friendly, 2015 rates: $43.
(800)537-7901 Lat: 32.73416, Lon: -114.69114
6800 S Strand Ave, Yuma, AZ 85364
reservations@cocopahrv.com
www.cocopahrv.com
See ad this page, 52.

⬇ **DEL PUEBLO RV PARK AND TENNIS RESORT**
Ratings: 10/10★/10 (RV Park) Jct of I-8 & Ave 3E (exit 3), S 5.2 mi on Ave 3E (R). **FAC:** Paved rds. (478 spaces). Avail: 398 all weather, patios, 30 pull-thrus (40 x 90), back-ins (40 x 55), 398 full hkups (30/50 amps), seasonal sites, cable, WiFi, laundry. **REC:** heated pool, whirlpool, shuffleboard. Pet restrict(Q). Partial handicap access, no tents. Age restrict may apply, big rig sites, eco-friendly, 2015 rates: $49. Oct 1 to May 1.
(928)341-2100 Lat: 32.61330, Lon: -114.58139
14794 S. Ave 3E, Yuma, AZ 85365
info@delpueblorv.com
www.delpueblorv.com
See ad this page, 52 & Snowbird Destinations in Magazine Section.

⬇ **DESERT HOLIDAY RV RESORT**
Ratings: 10/10★/9 (RV Park) From Jct of I-8 & 4th Ave (Exit 172 in CA), S 4 mi on 4th Ave to 4th Ave Extension, S 0.6 mi (L). **FAC:** Paved rds. (225 spaces). Avail: 100 all weather, patios, 5 pull-thrus (25 x 70), back-ins (30 x 40), 100 full hkups (30/50 amps), seasonal sites, WiFi, rentals, laundry. **REC:** heated pool, whirlpool, shuffleboard. Pet restrict(Q). Partial handicap access, no tents. Age restrict may apply, eco-friendly, 2015 rates: $29.95 to $39.95.
(928)344-4680 Lat: 32.66141, Lon: -114.62442
3601 S 4th Ave, Yuma, AZ 85365
rvdesertholiday@yahoo.com
www.rvdesertholiday.com
See ad opposite page, 52 & Snowbird Destinations in Magazine Section.

Find it Fast! Use our alphabetized index of campgrounds and parks.

➔ DESERT PARADISE RV RESORT **Ratings: 9/8.5★/9** (RV Park) 2015 rates: $38. (800)405-6188 10537 S Ave 9E, Yuma, AZ 85365

➔ **EL PRADO ESTATES RV PARK**
Ratings: 6/NA/7 (RV Park) From Jct of I-8 & US 95, E 4.5 mi on US 95 (L). **FAC:** Paved rds. (125 spaces). Avail: 40 gravel, patios, back-ins (20 x 40), 40 full hkups (30/50 amps), seasonal sites, WiFi Hotspot, laundry. Pet restrict(B/Q). No tents. 2015 rates: $18 to $25. No CC.
(928)726-4006 Lat: 32.69936, Lon: -114.52795
6200 E Hwy 95, Yuma, AZ 85365
See ad this page.

➔ FOOTHILL VILLAGE RV RESORT **Ratings: 8.5/8/8.5** (RV Park) 2015 rates: $38. (800)405-6188 12705 E S Frontage Rd, Yuma, AZ 85367

➔ **FORTUNA DE ORO RV RESORT**
Ratings: 9.5/9.5★/9 (RV Resort) From Jct of I-8 & Foothills Blvd (exit 14), N 50 ft on Foothills Blvd to N frntg rd, E 0.6 mi (L).

A PLACE TO CALL HOME!
Fill your days with fun! With over 1200 sites, a 9-hole golf course and on-site restaurant, you won't have to leave your car to enjoy this 5-star resort. Located in the foothills of Yuma, AZ with lakes and casinos nearby.

FAC: Paved rds. (1294 spaces). Avail: 794 gravel, patios, 34 pull-thrus (30 x 50), back-ins (34 x 50), 794 full hkups (30/50 amps), seasonal sites, WiFi, laundry, LP bottles, restaurant. **REC:** heated pool, whirlpool, golf, shuffleboard. Pet restrict(B/Q). Partial handicap access, no tents. Age restrict may apply, eco-friendly, 2015 rates: $40. ATM.
(928)342-5051 Lat: 32.66831, Lon: -114.39853
13650 N Frontage Rd, Yuma, AZ 85367
valariew@cal-am.com
http://www.cal-am.com/resorts/resorts_details.php?resorts_id=31&search=quick
See ad pages 56 (Spotlight Gold Canyon), 52 & Cal Am Insert & Snowbird Destinations in Magazine Section.

Check out those views! From awe-inspiring redwood giants to the soaring towers of the Golden Gate Bridge, we've put the Spotlight on North America's most popular travel destinations. Turn to the Spotlight articles in our State and Province sections to learn more.

Sun Vista RV RESORT
"WHERE THE FUN NEVER SETS!"
FITNESS CENTER
TWO STORIES OF FUN
Gated Resort, Endless Activities, Full Amenities, Craft Building, Café, Indoor/ Outdoor Pools & Jacuzzis, Driving Cages and Putting Green, Walking Path Two Story Fitness Center, Casino and Mexico Tours, Massage Therapy, Beauty Salon, RC Car Tracks, Bocce Ball, Internet Friendly And Much Much More!
The Finest 55+ Resort In Western Arizona
Pull-Thrus Available
PICKLEBALL
INDOOR POOL
OUTDOOR POOL
YUMA
ARABY RD.
I-8
Exit 7
Exit 9
PHOENIX
32nd ST
AVE 7E
AVE 8E
SUN VISTA RV RESORT
EXERCISE ROOM
Family Owned Park for Over 30 Years!
SHUFFLEBOARD
TOP RATED Good Sam Park FOR 2016
Good Sam RATED 9.5/10★/10
AAA
WiFi
Sun Vista RV Resort
7201 East 32nd Street • Yuma, AZ 85365
1-800-423-8382 928-726-8920 FAX 928-726-1629
www.sunvistarvresort.com
See listing Yuma, AZ

YUMA (CONT)

FRIENDLY ACRES RV PARK
Ratings: 9/9★/9 (RV Park) From Jct of I-8 & 4th Ave (Exit 172 in CA), go S 1-1/4 mi on 4th Ave to 8th St, then go W 1-1/2 mi on 8th St (L). **FAC:** Paved rds. (300 spaces). Avail: 70 gravel, patios, 10 pull-thrus (20 x 80), back-ins (32 x 45), 70 full hkups (30/50 amps), seasonal sites, WiFi Hotspot, laundry, controlled access. **REC:** heated pool, whirlpool, shuffleboard. Pet restrict(B/Q). No tents. Age restrict may apply, eco-friendly, 2015 rates: $27. Oct 1 to May 1.
(928)783-8414 Lat: 32.71304, Lon: -114.65430
2779 W 8th St, Yuma, AZ 85364
friendlyacresrvpark@gmail.com
www.friendly-acres.com
See ad page 74 (Spotlight Yuma).

GILA MOUNTAIN RV PARK Ratings: 8.5/8.5★/8.5 (RV Park) 2015 rates: $30. (928)342-1310 12325 S Frontage Rd, Yuma, AZ 85367

LAS QUINTAS OASIS RV RESORT Ratings: 10/9.5★/9.5 (RV Park) 2015 rates: $41. (928)305-9005 10442 N Frontage Rd, Yuma, AZ 85365

MESA VERDE RV RESORT **Ratings: 9/8.5★/8** (RV Park) 2015 rates: $39. (800)405-6188 3649 S 4th Ave, Yuma, AZ 85365

RIVER FRONT RV PARK **Ratings: 7/7.5/7** (RV Park) 2015 rates: $25 to $28. Oct 1 to Jun 1. (928)783-5868 2300 Water St, Yuma, AZ 85364

ROLLE'S LYNDA VISTA RV PARK Ratings: 7/8.5★/7 (RV Park) From Jct of I-8 & 16th St (Exit 2), W 2.5 mi on 16th St to Ave B, N 1.5 mi to W 5th St, W 0.25 mi (R). **FAC:** Paved/gravel rds. (110 spaces). Avail: 40 grass, patios, back-ins (30 x 40), some side by side hkups, 40 full hkups (30 amps), seasonal sites, WiFi, laundry. **REC:** heated pool. Pet restrict(Q). Partial handicap access, no tents. Age restrict may apply, eco-friendly, 2015 rates: $26.33. Disc: AAA. No CC.
AAA Approved
(928)782-9009 Lat: 32.71852, Lon: -114.65660
2900 W 5th St, Yuma, AZ 85364
lyndavistarvpark@gmail.com
http://www.yumarvcommunity.com/

SHADY ACRES MH & RV PARK
Ratings: 8/8.5★/7 (RV Park) From Jct of I-8 & 4th Ave (Exit 172 in CA), S 0.7 mi on 4th Ave to W 3rd St, W .7 mi (R). **FAC:** Paved rds. (155 spaces). 69 Avail: 50 gravel, 19 grass, back-ins (20 x 50), 69 full hkups (30/50 amps), seasonal sites, cable, WiFi, laundry. **REC:** heated pool, whirlpool. Pets OK. No tents. Age restrict may apply, eco-friendly, 2015 rates: $32. No CC.
(928)783-9431 Lat: 32.72367, Lon: -114.63605
1340 W. 3rd Street, Yuma, AZ 85364
Manager@shadyacresyuma.com
http://westernm.com/Shady%20Acres/
See ad page 103.

SHANGRI-LA RV RESORT
Ratings: 10/10★/10 (RV Park) From Jct of I-8 & Exit 12 (Fortuna Rd), N on Fortuna Rd to frntg rd, W 0.4 mi (R). Note: Do not use GPS. **FAC:** Paved rds. (301 spaces). Avail: 151 all weather, patios, 18 pull-thrus (30 x 90), back-ins (30 x 45), 151 full hkups (30/50 amps), seasonal sites, cable, WiFi, laundry, LP gas. **REC:** heated pool, whirlpool, shuffleboard. Pet restrict(B/Q). Partial handicap access, no tents. Big rig sites, eco-friendly, 2015 rates: $35.95 to $47.95. Disc: AAA, military.
(928)342-9123 Lat: 32.67127, Lon: -114.45050
10498 N Frontage Rd, Yuma, AZ 85365
info@shangrilarv.com
www.shangrilarv.com
See ad pages 103, 52.

SOUTHERN MESA RV PARK **Ratings: 8.5/8/8.5** (RV Park) 2015 rates: $46. (928)726-5167 18540 S Ave 3E, Yuma, AZ 85365

SUN VISTA RV RESORT
Ratings: 9.5/10★/10 (RV Resort) W-bnd: From Jct of I-8 & Exit 9 (Ave 8 1/2 E), W 0.7 mi on N Frontage Rd to 32nd St (Bus 8), W 0.9 mi (L); or E-bnd: From Jct of I-8 & Araby Rd (exit 7), S 0.5 mi on Araby Rd to 32nd St (Bus 8), E 0.6 mi (R).

RESORT LIVING AT ITS BEST IN YUMA!
Welcome! Enjoy indoor & outdoor pools, jacuzzis, 2-story fully equipped fitness center, pickleball, bocce ball, salon, massage therapy, cafe, computer room & so much more. Come enjoy resort living at its finest in Yuma, AZ.

FAC: Paved rds. (1226 spaces). Avail: 285 gravel, patios, 4 pull-thrus (30 x 60), back-ins (34 x 48), 285 full hkups (30/50 amps), seasonal sites, cable, WiFi $, laundry, LP bottles, restaurant, controlled access. **REC:** heated pool, whirlpool, shuffleboard. Pet restrict(Q). Partial handicap access, no tents. Age restrict may apply, eco-friendly, 2015 rates: $47. Disc: AAA. ATM.
AAA Approved
(800)423-8382 Lat: 32.66974, Lon: -114.51026
7201 E 32nd St, Yuma, AZ 85365
funtimes@sunvistarvresort.com
www.sunvistarvresort.com
See ad pages 105, 52, 47 (Welcome Section) & Snowbird Destinations in Magazine Section.

SUNDANCE RV RESORT
Ratings: 9.5/9.5★/9.5 (RV Park) From Jct of I-8 & Foothills Blvd (exit 14), N 50 ft on Foothills Blvd to N Frontage Rd, E 0.3 mi (L).

THE MOST FUN IN THE SUN!
Resort is located in the scenic Foothills area of Yuma, Arizona where the beauty of the desert can be enjoyed while still close to shopping, medical facilities and a brief drive to old Mexico.

FAC: Paved rds. (457 spaces). Avail: 157 gravel, patios, back-ins (30 x 40), 157 full hkups (30/50 amps), seasonal sites, cable, WiFi, laundry. **REC:** heated pool, whirlpool, shuffleboard. Pet restrict(B/Q). Partial handicap access, no tents. Age restrict may apply, eco-friendly, 2015 rates: $32.50 to $37.50.
(928)342-9333 Lat: 32.66895, Lon: -114.40320
13502 N Frontage Rd, Yuma, AZ 85367
Nancyb@cal-am.com
http://www.cal-am.com/resorts/resorts_details.php?resorts_id=32
See ad pages 56 (Spotlight Gold Canyon), 52 & Cal Am Insert & Snowbird Destinations in Magazine Section.

SUNI SANDS RV RESORT **Ratings: 8.5/8.5★/7.5** (RV Park) 2015 rates: $39. (800)405-6188 1960 E 32nd St, Yuma, AZ 85365

Heading to a privately owned park? Be sure to read how our inspection team rated it in the Guide "How to Use This Travel Guide" section.

VILLA ALAMEDA RV RESORT
Ratings: 9.5/10★/10 (RV Park) From Jct of I-8 & Ave 3E (exit 3), Go 1-1/4 mi S on Ave 3E, then 2 mi E on 32nd St (Bus 8), then 1/2 mi S on Ave 5E (L); or From Jct of I-8 & Araby Rd (Exit 7), Go 1/2 mi S on Araby Rd, then 1-1/2 mi W on 32nd St (Bus 8), then 1/2 mi S on Ave 5E (L). **FAC:** Paved rds. (302 spaces). Avail: 151 gravel, patios, back-ins (33 x 52), 151 full hkups (30/50 amps), seasonal sites, cable, WiFi, laundry. **REC:** heated pool, whirlpool, shuffleboard. Pet restrict(B/Q). Partial handicap access, no tents. Age restrict may apply, eco-friendly, 2015 rates: $33. No CC.
(928)344-8081 Lat: 32.66280, Lon: -114.54618
3547 S Ave 5E, Yuma, AZ 85365
villaalamedarv@aol.com
www.villaalamedarvresort.com
See ad pages 73 (Spotlight Yuma), 52 & Snowbird Destinations in Magazine Section.

WESTWIND RV & GOLF RESORT
Ratings: 10/10★/10 (RV Park) From Jct of I-8 & Fortuna Rd (exit 12), S 50 ft on Fortuna Rd to S Frontage Rd, W 1 mi (L) Do not use GPS.

MORE THAN A RESORT - A LIFESTYLE!
Our nine hole par 3 golf course meanders throughout our resort. This is a unique, executive course with well-manicured greens and lush landscaping. An ideal place to retire or vacation, with great mountain views.

FAC: Paved rds. (1150 spaces). Avail: 550 all weather, patios, back-ins (30 x 45), 550 full hkups (30/50 amps), seasonal sites, cable, WiFi $, rentals, laundry, restaurant, controlled access. **REC:** heated pool, whirlpool, golf, shuffleboard. Pet restrict(B/Q). No tents. Age restrict may apply, eco-friendly, 2015 rates: $29.95 to $50. Disc: AAA. ATM.
AAA Approved
(928)342-2992 Lat: 32.66957, Lon: -114.46294
9797 E 32nd St, Yuma, AZ 85365
info@westwindrvgolfresort.com
www.westwindrvgolfresort.com
See ad pages 104, 178, 52 & Snowbird Destinations in Magazine Section.

WINDHAVEN RV PARK Ratings: 8/8.5★/7.5 (RV Park) From Jct of I-8 & Ave 8 1/2 E (Exit 9), S 100 yds on Ave 8 1/2 E to E 32nd St, W 1.9 mi (R). **FAC:** Paved rds. (136 spaces). Avail: 50 gravel, patios, 5 pull-thrus (22 x 50), back-ins (27 x 40), 50 full hkups (30/50 amps), seasonal sites, WiFi Hotspot, laundry. **REC:** heated pool, whirlpool, shuffleboard. Pets OK. Partial handicap access, no tents. Big rig sites, 2015 rates: $35. Disc: AAA.
AAA Approved
(928)726-0284 Lat: 32.67024, Lon: -114.51991
6580 E 32nd St, Yuma, AZ 85365
windhavenyuma@yahoo.com
http://www.windhavenrvpark.com/

YUMA MESA RV PARK Ratings: 6.5/5/5 (RV Park) 2015 rates: $28. (928)344-3369 5990 E 32nd St, Yuma, AZ 85365

Your neighbor just told you about a great little campground in Kentucky M what was the name of it again? The "Find-it-Fast" index in the back of the Guide can help. It's an alphabetical listing, by state, of every private and public park in the Guide.

Arkansas Dept. of Parks and Tourism

WELCOME TO Arkansas

DATE OF STATEHOOD	WIDTH: 239 MILES (385 KM)	PROPORTION OF UNITED STATES
JUNE 15, 1836	LENGTH: 261 MILES (420 KM)	1.40% OF 3,794,100 SQ MI

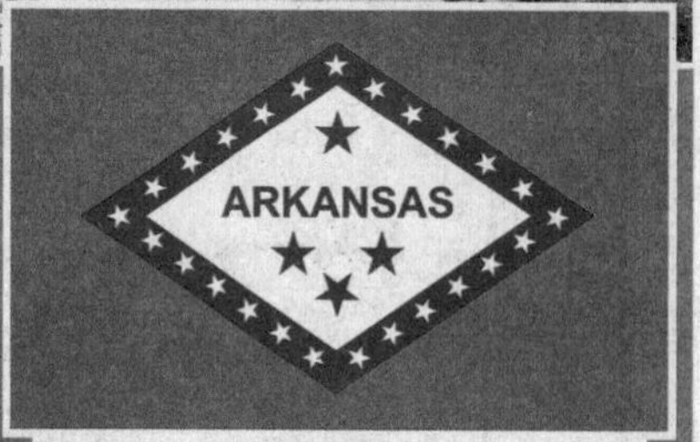

President Bill Clinton achieved something that singer Johnny Cash, military leader Douglas MacArthur, movie star Alan Ladd and baseball great Brooks Robinson could never do—elevate the profile of his home state of Arkansas into the national consciousness. Now everyone knows that it is "Arkan-saw" and not "Ar-kansas," a matter so important it was decided by an act of the legislature in the 1880s.

Learn

Civil War battlefields at Pea Ridge and Prairie Grove have been preserved to tell the tale of Union forces that held control of the land west of the Mississippi River against the Confederate Army. A century later, Little Rock Central High School played a pivotal role in school desegregation, and the Gothic schoolhouse has been declared a National Historic Site with galleries and interactive exhibits.

Bill Clinton selected the state capital of Little Rock as the site for his Clinton Presidential Center, and the modern building that cantilevers over the Arkansas River has become the nucleus for a 32-block revitalization of the River Market District. In the state's northwest corner, Bentonville is known as the headquarters of the Walmart store chain. The Walton family has given back here with the first major art museum of the 21st century: the Crystal Bridges Museum of American Art, which chronicles the American experience through art. You can also find the Walmart Museum, which is housed in founder Sam Walton's original store, and chronicles the retailer's rise from local merchant to global powerhouse.

The National Trust for Historic Preservation touts the Victorian resort town of Eureka Springs as one of the country's "Distinctive Destinations." The town's unique stone buildings are anchored on Ozark Mountain hillsides and connected by winding staircases.

Top 3 Tourism Attractions:
1) Crystal Bridges Museum of American Art
2) Boyhood Home of Johnny Cash
3) Clinton Presidential Center

Nickname: The Natural State

State Flower: Apple Blossom

State Bird: Mockingbird

People: Johnny Cash, singer; Bill Clinton, president; Douglas MacArthur, general

Major Cities: Little Rock (capital), Fort Smith, Fayetteville, Springdale, Jonesboro

Topography: Eastern Delta and prairie; southern lowland forests and northwestern highlands that include the Ozark plateaus

Climate: Four distinct seasons; mostly mild climate year round; hot and humid in late summer

See listing Bentonville, AR

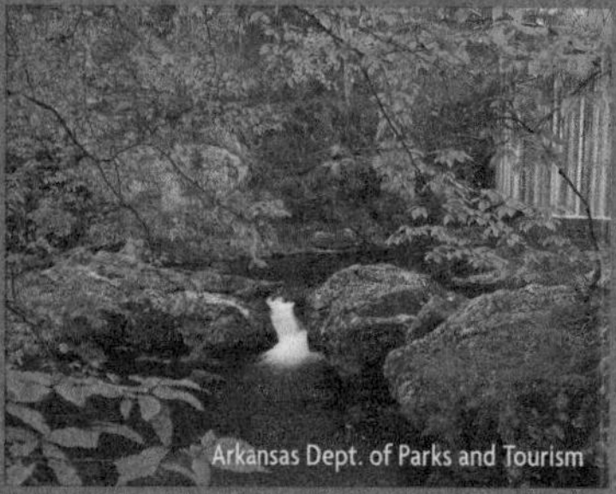
Arkansas Dept. of Parks and Tourism

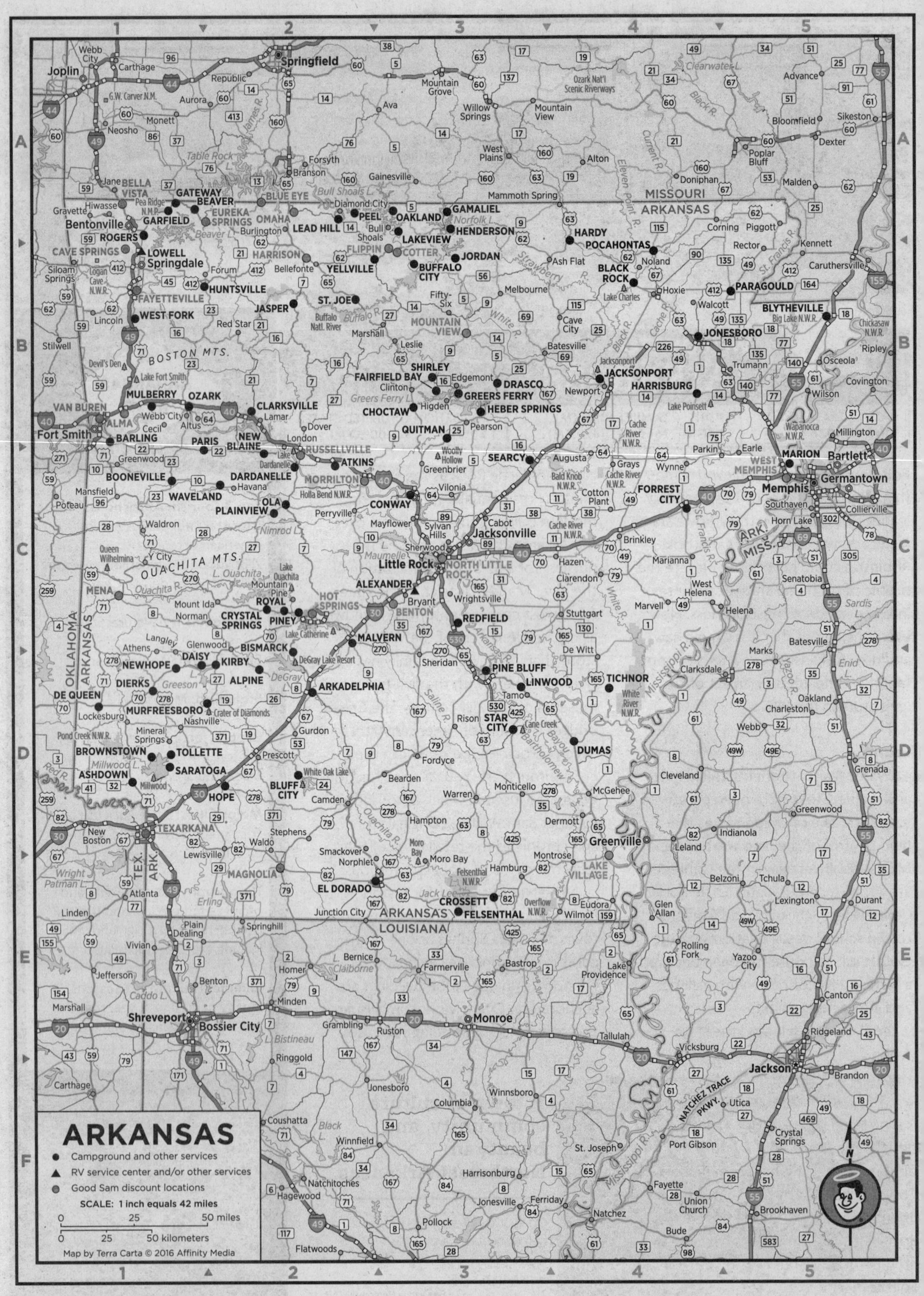
ARKANSAS
Campground and other services
RV service center and/or other services
Good Sam discount locations
SCALE: 1 inch equals 42 miles
0 25 50 miles
0 25 50 kilometers
Map by Terra Carta © 2016 Affinity Media
MISSOURI
ARKANSAS
OKLAHOMA
TEX.
ARK.
LOUISIANA
ARK. MISS.
Springfield
Joplin
Little Rock
Memphis
Shreveport
Jackson
BELLA VISTA
GATEWAY
BEAVER
EUREKA SPRINGS
GARFIELD
ROGERS
LOWELL
Springdale
FAYETTEVILLE
HUNTSVILLE
WEST FORK
HARRISON
LEAD HILL
OMAHA
DIAMOND CITY
PEEL
OAKLAND
GAMALIEL
HENDERSON
LAKEVIEW
FLIPPIN
COTTER
YELLVILLE
BUFFALO CITY
JORDAN
ST. JOE
JASPER
MOUNTAIN VIEW
HARDY
POCAHONTAS
BLACK ROCK
PARAGOULD
BLYTHEVILLE
JONESBORO
JACKSONPORT
HARRISBURG
SHIRLEY
FAIRFIELD BAY
DRASCO
GREERS FERRY
HEBER SPRINGS
CHOCTAW
QUITMAN
SEARCY
VAN BUREN
ALMA
Fort Smith
MULBERRY
OZARK
CLARKSVILLE
BARLING
PARIS
NEW BLAINE
RUSSELLVILLE
ATKINS
DARDANELLE
BOONEVILLE
WAVELAND
MORRILTON
CONWAY
OLA
PLAINVIEW
MARION
WEST MEMPHIS
FORREST CITY
Jacksonville
NORTH LITTLE ROCK
ALEXANDER
BENTON
MENA
ROYAL
HOT SPRINGS
CRYSTAL SPRINGS
PINEY
REDFIELD
MALVERN
BISMARCK
DAISY
KIRBY
NEWHOPE
ALPINE
DIERKS
DE QUEEN
ARKADELPHIA
PINE BLUFF
LINWOOD
TICHNOR
MURFREESBORO
STAR CITY
DUMAS
BROWNSTOWN
TOLLETTE
SARATOGA
ASHDOWN
HOPE
BLUFF CITY
TEXARKANA
MAGNOLIA
EL DORADO
CROSSETT
FELSENTHAL
LAKE VILLAGE

Now known as an arts mecca, the entire downtown is listed on the National Register of Historic Places.

Play

Arkansas has been promoting itself as "The Natural State" since the 1970s, but Americans have known about its natural wonders since before statehood in 1836. The land around Hot Springs was the first ever set aside by the United States government to be protected and preserved. Those were the territorial days of 1832. Today, eight of the historic bathhouses in "America's Spa" are still operational.

Two mountain ranges, the Ouachitas and the Ozarks, fold across the northern and western tiers of the state and give rise to seven national parks and 52 state parks. The Crater of Diamonds State Park in the Ouachitas is the only place in the world where visitors can dig for diamonds—and 70,000 of the gems have been found over the years, including North America's largest, a 40.23-carat stone.

The Buffalo River is America's first national river, protected back in 1972 for its scenic route through limestone bluffs. In addition to fishing and wildlife watching, outfitters stand ready to lead rafting trips down the Buffalo. At Blanchard Springs Caverns in the Ozarks, the Forest service operates its only developed cave system, with tours through huge underground chambers.

Experience

Food and music, music and food. You'll find both celebrated with zest in Arkansas. Local farmers in Hope held their first Watermelon Festival in 1926 to recognize the harvest of a 136-pound melon, and today, the fruit is feted in a free, four-day event.

The Ozarks town of Mountain View is renowned for its folklore collections at the Ozark Folk Center, which operates as a living-history state park. About any time, you can wander into an impromptu "pickin" in the downtown area. Since 1963, musicians have gathered here each April for the Arkansas Folk Festival.

- STAY A WHILE -

Bentonville

Once known primarily as a corporate town, Bentonville, Arkansas, has boomed as a leisure travel spot since the opening of Crystal Bridges Museum of American Art in 2011. Housing the largest collection of American art anywhere in the world, Crystal Bridges is home to iconic works like Norman Rockwell's Rosie the Riveter and Andy Warhol's Dolly. The museum has no admission for the permanent collection, no parking fee and is open every day except Tuesdays.

In 2013, the city welcomed the 21c Museum Hotel, a contemporary art museum couched with an ultra-modern lodging property and award-winning restaurant, the Hive. Bentonville's culinary scene is comprised of James Beard-nominated chefs, Food & Wine magazine winners, and a fun assortment of pubs, breweries and food trucks.

Bentonville's newest attraction is the Scott Family Amazeum, a family-centric museum that engages visitors of all ages through a climbable tree canopy, a homestead cabin and farm, chocolate laboratory and much more. Other popular attractions include the Walmart Museum, which is an interactive museum that traces the history of Walmart Stores, Inc. This museum is also home to the popular Spark Café, a 1950's soda shop and ice cream parlor, as well as a working five and dime store.

Travelers should also visit the Museum of Native American History in west Bentonville that is home to a giant mammoth skeleton and incredible indigenous pottery. The Peel Mansion and Heritage Gardens is another must-see. This late 1800's Italianate mansion offers tours and has a fun gift shop.

TRAVEL & TOURISM

Arkansas Department of Parks & Tourism
501-682-7777, 1-800-NATURAL
www.arkansas.com

Arkansas Delta Byways
870-972-2803
www.deltabyways.com

Arkansas's Great Southwest Recreational Association
870-777-7500, 800-223-4673
www.agsw.org

Arkansas's Land of Legends Travel Association
870-536-8742
www.thelandoflegends.com

Arkansas River Valley Tri-Peaks Region
479-498-2321
www.arvtripeaks.com

Arkansas's South Tourism Association
870-866-4060
www.arkansassouth.com

Diamond Lakes Association
501-321-1700
www.hotsprings.org

Greers Ferry Lake/ Little Red River Association
888-490-4357
www.greersferrylake.org

Heart of Arkansas Travel Association
501-370-3209, 501-835-3399
www.heartofarkansas.com

Little Rock CVB
800-844-4781
www.littlerock.com

Northwest Arkansas Tourism Association
479-521-5776
www.northwestarkansas.org

Ozark Gateway Tourist Council
870-793-9316, 800-264-0316
www.ozarkgateway.com

Ozark Mountain Region
870-404-2741
www.ozarkmountainregion.com

Western Arkansas's Mountain Frontier
479-883-2996
www.visitwestarkansas.com

OUTDOOR RECREATION

Arkansas Game & Fish Commission
800-364-4263
www.agfc.com

Natural State Golf Trail
866-2-GOLF-AR
www.NaturalStateGolfTrail.com

SHOPPING

Arkansas Craft Guild Gallery
www.arkansascraftguild.org

Arlington Mall
www.arlingtonhotel.com

River Market, Little Rock
www.rivermarket.info

AR

Featured Good Sam Parks

ARKANSAS

Good Sam Park

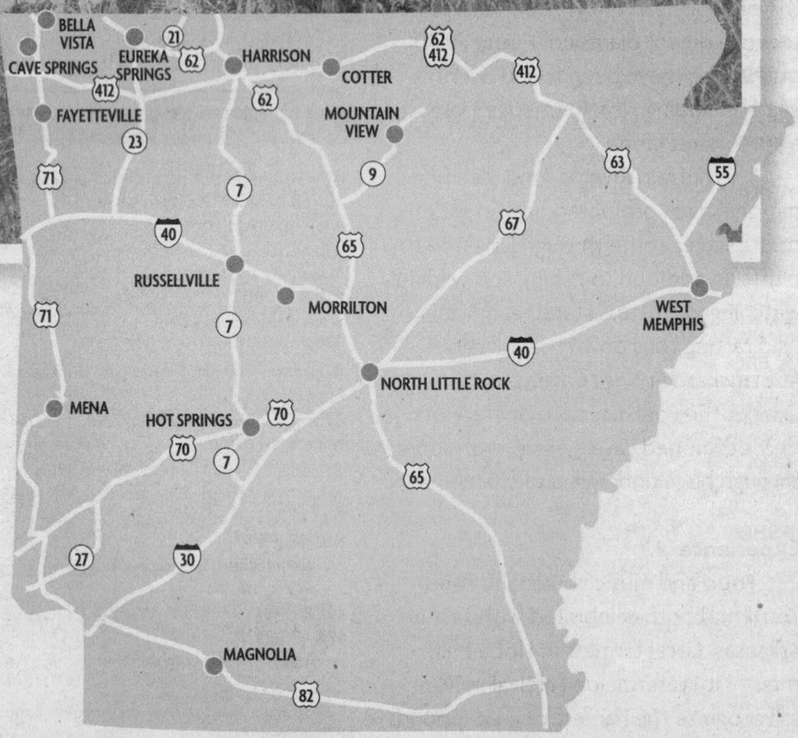

When you stay with Good Sam, you can expect the highest degree of cleanliness and friendliness, and better yet, you get 10% off campground fees.

If you're not already a Good Sam member you can purchase your membership at one of these locations:

BELLA VISTA
Bella Vista Village RV Park
(479)855-8075

CAVE SPRINGS
The Creeks Golf & RV Resort
(479)248-1000

COTTER
Denton Ferry RV Park & Resort
(870)435-7275

EUREKA SPRINGS
Kettle Campground, Cabins & RV Park
(479)253-9100
Wanderlust RV Park
(479)253-7385

FAYETTEVILLE
Southgate RV Park Of Fayetteville
(479)442-2021

HARRISON
Harrison Village Campground & RV Park
(870)743-3388
Parkers RV Park
(870)743-2267

HOT SPRINGS
Catherine's Landing At Hot Springs
(501)262-2550
Cloud Nine RV Park
(501)262-1996

MAGNOLIA
Magnolia RV Park, LLC
(870)562-2908

MENA
Iron Mountain
(870)389-6560

MORRILTON
Morrilton I40/107 RV Park
(501)354-8262

MOUNTAIN VIEW
Ozark RV Park
(870)269-2542

NORTH LITTLE ROCK
Downtown Riverside RV Park
(501)340-5312

RUSSELLVILLE
Ivy's Cove RV Retreat
(479)280-1662
Outdoor Living Center RV Park
(800)828-4307

WEST MEMPHIS
Tom Sawyer's RV Park
(870)735-9770

For more Good Sam Parks go to listing pages

Arkansas

CONSULTANTS

Gary & Sherry Wilcox

ALMA — B1 *Crawford*

CLEAR CREEK (Public Corps) From town, S 5.2 mi on Hwy 162 to Kibler Rd/cnty rd, E 3.6 mi (E). 2015 rates: $10 to $16. (479)632-4882

CRABTREE RV PARK **Ratings: 5/8★/4.5** (RV Park) 2015 rates: $25.02 to $27.02. (479)632-0909 405 Heather Ln, Alma, AR 72921

FORT SMITH-ALMA RV PARK
Ratings: 9.5/9★/8 (Campground) From Jct of I-40 & US-71 (exit 13), N 2.3 mi on US-71 (L); or From Jct of I-540/I-49 & Exit 24 (Rudy/SR-282), E 0.5 mi on SR-282 to US-71, S 1 mi (R). **FAC:** Paved rds. (58 spaces). 52 Avail: 5 paved, 47 gravel, 39 pull-thrus (18 x 70), back-ins (18 x 40), mostly side by side hkups, 39 full hkups, 13 W, 13 E (30/50 amps), seasonal sites, cable, WiFi, tent sites, rentals, dump, laundry, groc, fire rings. **REC:** pool, pond, fishing, playground. Pet restrict(B). 2015 rates: $36.35 to $50.
(479)632-2704 Lat: 35.52231, Lon: -94.22349
3539 N US-71, Alma, AR 72921
See ad page 112.

ALPINE — D2 *Clark*

ALPINE RIDGE (Public Corps) From Jct of I-30 & Exit 73/Hwy 8, W 19 mi on Hwy 8 to Fendley Rd (in Alpine), N 9 mi (E). 2015 rates: $12 to $18. (870)246-5501

ARKADELPHIA — D2 *Clark*

ARKADELPHIA CAMPGROUND & RV PARK **Ratings: 8/9★/7** (Campground) 2015 rates: $32. (870)246-4922 221 Frost Road, Arkadelphia, AR 71923

DE GRAY LAKE RESORT (State Pk) From Jct of I-30 & SR-7 (exit 78), N 5 mi on SR-7 to park entrance rd, NW 1 mi (L). 2015 rates: $19. (501)865-5810

EDGEWOOD (Public Corps) From Jct of I-30 & Exit 78/Hwy 7, N 6 mi on Hwy 7 to Edgewood Rd, W 2 mi (E). 2015 rates: $12 to $24. Mar 1 to Oct 31. (870)246-5501

IRON MOUNTAIN (Public Corps) From Jct of I-30 & Exit 78/Hwy 7, N 2.5 mi on Hwy 7 to Skyline Dr, W 2.5 mi to Iron Mountain Rd, N to park (E). 2015 rates: $12. Mar 1 to Nov 30. (870)246-5501

ASHDOWN — D1 *Little River*

BEARD'S BLUFF (Public Corps) From town, E 12.5 mi on AR-32 to CR-196, N 1 mi (E). 2015 rates: $10 to $15. (870)388-9556

MILLWOOD (State Pk) From Jct of US-71 & SR-32, E 9 mi on SR-32 (L). 2015 rates: $19 to $30. (870)898-2800

OCP - MILLWOOD LANDING RESORT **Ratings: 8.5/9★/9** (Membership Pk) 2015 rates: $10. (866)888-1655 596 Hwy 317, Ashdown, AR 71822

ATKINS — C2 *Pope*

SWEEDEN ISLAND PARK (Public Corps) From town, S 15 mi on Hwy 105 (L). Pit toilets. 2015 rates: $10 to $16. (479)968-5008

BARLING — B1 *Sebastian*

SPRINGHILL (Public Corps) From town, N 1.6 mi on Hwy 59 (R). 2015 rates: $10 to $20. (479)452-4598

Check the air pressure on your tires and inflate any that are lower than the pressure recommended in the owner's manual. Properly inflated tires can increase fuel efficiency by 3.3 percent.

BEAVER — A1 *Lawrence*

BEAVER RV PARK & CAMPGROUND (Public) From Jct of Hwy 62 W & Hwy 187 E (10 mi W. of Eureka Springs), E 4.3 mi on Hwy 187 E to Golden Gate Road (in town) N 500'. 2015 rates: $25 to $35. Apr 1 to Oct 31. (479)253-5469

BELLA VISTA — A1 *Benton*

BELLA VISTA VILLAGE RV PARK
Ratings: 8/9.5★/8.5 (RV Park) N-bnd & S-bnd (in Bella Vista): From Int US-71 & Mercy Way, go E .3 mi on Mercy Way, to Blowing Springs Rd, go E, .3 mi to RV Park (L). **FAC:** Paved rds. 64 paved, patios, back-ins (25 x 50), 36 full hkups, 28 W, 28 E (30/50 amps), cable, WiFi, tent sites, dump, laundry. **REC:** Blowing Springs. Pets OK. Partial handicap access. 14 day max stay, 2015 rates: $33.
(479)855-8075 Lat: 36.44115, Lon: -94.22869
700 Blowing Spring Rd., Bella Vista, AR 72714
www.bellavistapoa.com
See ad this page, 110.

BENTON — C3 *Saline*

I-30 RV PARK **Ratings: 7/8.5/7** (RV Park) 2015 rates: $37.50 to $39.50. (501)778-1244 19719 I-30, Benton, AR 72015

JB'S RV PARK & CAMPGROUND
Ratings: 5.5/8★/7.5 (Campground) From Jct of I-30 & Exit 106, SE 0.2 mi to Rte 67, NE (left) 0.1 mi to J.B. Baxley Rd, SE 0.1 mi (R). **FAC:** Gravel rds. (45 spaces). Avail: 31 gravel, 22 pull-thrus (30 x 150), back-ins (30 x 50), 22 full hkups, 9 W, 9 E (30/50 amps), seasonal sites, tent sites, dump, laundry, firewood. **REC:** pond, fishing. Pet restrict(B). Big rig sites, 2015 rates: $24 to $28. No CC.
(501)778-6050 Lat: 34.48095, Lon: -92.72022
8601 J.b. Baxley Rd., Benton, AR 72015
jlhaddox@aol.com
www.jbsrvpark.com
See ad page 114.

BENTONVILLE — A1 *Benton*

BENTONVILLE See also Beaver, Cave Springs, Eureka Springs, Fayetteville, Garfield, Lowell, Rogers, Springdale; Anderson, MO.

Things to See and Do

VISIT BENTONVILLE North West Arkansas tourism info for the city of Bentonville. RV accessible. Restrooms. Hours: 9am to 6pm (Mon to Sat) no CC.
(479)271-9153 Lat: 36.37245, Lon: -94.20879
104 E. Central, Bentonville, AR 72712
Courtney@visitbentonville.com
www.visitbentonville.com
See ad page 107 (Welcome Section).

BISMARCK — D2 *Hot Spring*

ARLIE MOORE (Public Corps) From town, S 2.3 mi on Hwy 7 to Arlie Moore Rd (CR-254), W 2 mi (E). 2015 rates: $10 to $18. (870)246-5501

BLACK ROCK — B4 *Lawrence*

LAKE CHARLES (State Pk) From town, NW 8 mi on US-63 to Hwy 25, S 6 mi (R). 2015 rates: $19 to $30. (870)878-6595

BLUE EYE — A2 *Carroll*

OZARKS RV RESORT ON TABLE ROCK LAKE
Ratings: 10/10★/10 (Condo Pk) From Jct of US-65 & SR-86, W 11.6 mi on SR-86 to SR-13/21, S 1.1 mi to SR-311 (straight thru Blue Eye), E 4.9 mi to entrance sign, E 1.2 mi (R). Call for RV restrictions. **FAC:** Paved rds. (164 spaces). Avail: 64 paved, patios, back-ins (34 x 65), 64 full hkups (30/50 amps), seasonal sites, WiFi, laundry, controlled access. **REC:** heated pool, whirlpool, Table Rock Lake: fishing, golf. Pet restrict(Q). Partial handicap access, no tents. Big rig sites, 2015 rates: $45 to $65.
(888)749-7396 Lat: 36.48460, Lon: -93.30688
1229 CR-663, Oak Grove, AR 72660
Ozarksrvresort@verizon.net
www.ozarksrvresortontablerocklake.com
See ad page 688.

BLUFF CITY — D2 *Nevada*

WHITE OAK LAKE (State Pk) From Jct of SR-24 & SR-299 (in Bluff City), S 100 yds on SR-299 to SR-387, SE 2 mi (L). 2015 rates: $19 to $24. (870)685-2748

BLYTHEVILLE — B5 *Mississippi*

SHEARIN'S RV PARK **Ratings: 3.5/NA/5** (RV Park) 2015 rates: $35. (870)763-4858 2953 N US Hwy 61, Blytheville, AR 72315

BOONEVILLE — C1 *Logan*

BOONEVILLE MUNICIPAL PARK (Public) From Jct of AR-23 & AR-10, E 4.5 blks on AR-10 (L). 2015 rates: $15 to $17.50. (479)675-3811

BROWNSTOWN — D1 *Sevier*

PARALOMA LANDING (Public Corps) From town, E 3 mi on Hwy 234 to Jackson Rd, S 2 mi (E). Pit toilets. 2015 rates: $8 to $11. (870)898-3343

WHITE CLIFFS (Public Corps) From town, S 4 mi on Rte 317 (E). Pit toilets. 2015 rates: $15 to $21. (870)898-3343

BULL SHOALS — A3 *Marion*

BULL SHOALS-WHITE RIVER (State Pk) From Mountain Home, N 6 mi on SR-5 to SR-178, W 8 mi (L). 2015 rates: $19 to $30. (870)445-3629

DAM SITE (Public Corps) From town, SE 1 mi on Hwy 178 (L). 2015 rates: $18. Apr 1 to Sep 30. (870)445-7166

CAVE SPRINGS — B1 *Benton*

THE CREEKS GOLF & RV RESORT
Ratings: 7.5/9★/10 (RV Park) From Jct of I-540 & Hwy 264 (Exit 78), W 5 mi on Rte 264 to Rte 112, S 1.1 mi (R). **FAC:** Paved/gravel rds. (60 spaces). Avail: 50 paved, patios, 30 pull-thrus (28 x 77), back-ins (28 x 74), 50 full hkups (30/50 amps), seasonal sites, cable, WiFi, dump, LP gas, restaurant. **REC:** golf. Pets OK. No tents. Big rig sites, RV age restrict, 2015 rates: $45.
(479)248-1000 Lat: 36.24545, Lon: -94.23905
1499 S Main Street, Cave Springs, AR 72718
reservations@nwarvresort.com
www.nwarvresort.com
See ad pages 117, 110.

Things to See and Do

THE CREEKS GOLF & RV RESORT Creeks Golf Course. RV accessible. Restrooms, food. Hours: 7am to 8pm. Adult fee: $33 to $42.
(479)248-1000 Lat: 36.24545, Lon: -94.23905
1499 S. Main Street, Cave Springs, AR 72718
cpmurray@yahoo.com
www.creeksgolf.com
See ad page 117.

CHOCTAW — B3 *Van Buren*

CHOCTAW (Public Corps) From Clinton, S 5 mi on US-65 to Hwy 330, E 3.5 mi (R). 2015 rates: $14 to $20. May 15 to Oct 30. (501)745-8320

CLARKSVILLE — B2 *Johnson*

SPADRA (Public Corps) From Jct of I-40 & Hwy 103, S 2 mi on Hwy 103 (E). 2015 rates: $10 to $18. (479)968-5008

CONWAY — C3 *Faulkner, Perry*

CONWAY See also Morrilton, Little Rock & North Little Rock.

CONWAY (CONT)

FOREST LAKE ESTATES MH AND RV COMMUNITY Ratings: 4.5/NA/5.5 (Campground) From Jct of I-40 & Dave Ward Dr (Exit 129), W 4.1 mi on Dave Ward Dr to McNutt Rd, S 0.2 mi (R). **FAC:** Paved rds. (197 spaces). Avail: 27 gravel, patios, back-ins (27 x 53), 27 full hkups (30/50 amps), WiFi Hotspot. **REC:** pond, fishing, playground. Pet restrict(B/Q). No tents. 2015 rates: $30.
(501)329-2240 Lat: 35.06592, Lon: -92.49413
1001 Mcnutt Rd. #1000, Conway, AR 72034
forestlake@towermgmt.com
www.towerrvparks.com

WOOLLY HOLLOW (State Pk) From Jct of US-65 & SR-285, E 6 mi on SR-285 (L). 2015 rates: $30. (501)679-2098

COTTER — B3 *Baxter*

DENTON FERRY RV PARK & RESORT
Ratings: 8.5/9.5★/9.5 (RV Park) From Jct of Hwy 62/412 & Denton Ferry Rd/S Hwy 62B (W side of Cotter), N 0.5 mi on Denton Ferry Rd (L). **FAC:** All weather rds. 44 Avail: 44 all weather, 27 pull-thrus (30 x 65), back-ins (30 x 65), 44 full hkups (30/50 amps), WiFi, rentals, laundry, LP gas, firewood. **REC:** White River: fishing. Pet restrict(B). Partial handicap access, no tents. Big rig sites, 2015 rates: $28 to $34. Disc: AAA, military.
(870)435-7275 Lat: 36.29259, Lon: -92.52139
740 Denton Ferry Rd., Cotter, AR 72626
bill@dentonrv.com
www.dentonrv.com
See ad pages 115, 110.

CROSSETT — E3 *Ashley*

CROSSETT RV PARK & CAMPGROUND (CROSSETT PORT AUTH) (Public) From town: Go 8 mi W on US 82. 2015 rates: $16. (870)364-6136

CRYSTAL SPRINGS — C2 *Garland*

CRYSTAL SPRINGS (Public Corps) From Jct of US-7 & US-270, W 15 mi on US-270 to park access rd, N 3 mi, follow signs (E). 2015 rates: $10 to $20. (501)991-3390

DAISY — D1 *Pike*

DAISY (State Pk) From Jct SR-84 & US-70 (in Kirby), W 6 mi on US-70 (L). 2015 rates: $19 to $24. (870)398-4487

SELF CREEK/JIM WYLIE (Public Corps) From town, W 1.5 mi on US-70 (L). 2015 rates: $10 to $15. (870)285-2151

DARDANELLE — C2 *Yell*

MOUNT NEBO (State Pk) From Jct Hwy 22 & Hwy 155, 7 mi W on Hwy 155 (E). Caution: Trailers over 15 ft should not attempt zig zag mountainous climb to park. 2015 rates: $19. (479)229-3655

RIVERVIEW (Public Corps) From town, NW 0.75 mi on Second St, adjacent to Dardanelle Power House (E). Pit toilets. 2015 rates: $10 to $18. Mar 1 to Oct 31. (479)968-5008

DE QUEEN — D1 *Sevier*

BELLAH MINE (Public Corps) From town, N 7 mi on US-71 to Bellah Mine Rd, W 5 mi, follow signs (E). 2015 rates: $10 to $25. (870)584-4161

PINE RIDGE (Public Corps) From town, N 3 mi on US-71 to De Queen Lake Rd, W 5.5 mi to Rink Rd, N 1.5 mi (E). 2015 rates: $9 to $15. (870)584-4161

Nobody said it was easy being a 10. And our rating system makes it even tougher.

DIERKS — D1 *Howard*

BLUE RIDGE (Public Corps) From town, N 3 mi on Hwy 70 to Hwy 4, N 4 mi, W on Blue Ridge Rd. follow signs (E). 2015 rates: $8 to $12. (870)286-2346

DRASCO — B3 *Cleburne*

CHEROKEE REC AREA (Public Corps) From town, W 7.5 mi on Hwy 92 to Brownsville, S 4.5 mi (E). 2015 rates: $18 to $20. Mar 1 to Oct 31. (501)362-2416

HILL CREEK (Public Corps) From town, W 12 mi on Hwy 92 to Hwy 225, NW 3 mi to paved access rd, S 2 mi (E). 2015 rates: $14 to $17. May 15 to Sep 15. (870)948-2419

DUMAS — D4 *Arkansas, Desha*

PENDLETON BEND PARK (Public Corps) From town, NE 10.5 mi on US-165 to AR-212, E 2 mi (E). 2015 rates: $16 to $19. (870)548-2291

WILBUR D MILLS PARK (Public Corps) From town, N 10.5 mi on US-165 to AR-212, E 5 mi (E). 2015 rates: $16. Feb 27 to Nov 1. (870)548-2291

EL DORADO — E2 *Union*

MORO BAY (State Pk) From Warren, SW 29 mi on US-63 (L). 2015 rates: $19 to $24. (870)463-8555

EUREKA SPRINGS — A2 *Carroll*

EUREKA SPRINGS See also Beaver, Garfield, Lowell, Springdale, Cassville, MO, Eagle Rock, MO.

DAM SITE LAKE PARK (Public Corps) From town, W 4.8 mi on US-62 to Hwy 187, S 2.5 mi (L). 2015 rates: $18 to $25. Apr 1 to Oct 30. (479)253-5828

DAM SITE RIVER (BEAVER LAKE) (Public Corps) From town, W 9 mi on US-62 to Hwy 187, S 2.5 mi (E). 2015 rates: $20 to $23. Apr 1 to Oct 31. (479)253-9865

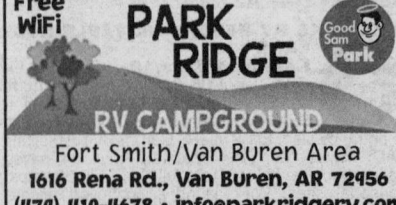

KETTLE CAMPGROUND, CABINS & RV PARK
Ratings: 8/9.5★/8.5 (Campground) From Jct of US-62 & SR-23S, E 2.9 mi on US-62 (L). **FAC:** Paved/gravel rds. (47 spaces). Avail: 40 gravel, 10 pull-thrus (26 x 70), back-ins (26 x 40), 18 full hkups, 22 W, 22 E (30/50 amps), seasonal sites, WiFi $, tent sites, rentals, dump, mobile sewer, laundry, LP gas, fire rings, firewood. **REC:** pool, playground. Pets OK. Big rig sites, 2015 rates: $26 to $30. Disc: military.
(479)253-9100 Lat: 36.39627, Lon: -93.70579
4119 E Van Buren, Eureka Springs, AR 72632
kettleinfo@cox.net
www.KettleCampground.net
See ad this page, 110.

LAKE LEATHERWOOD CITY PARK (Public) From north Jct Hwy 23 & US 62: Go 3-1/4 mi NW on US 62, then 1-1/2 mi N on entry road. (Not suitable for Big Rigs). 2015 rates: $12 to $25. Mar 1 to Nov 30. (479)253-7921

STARKEY (Public Corps) From town, W 2.5 mi on US-62 to Hwy 187, SW 4.2 mi to CR-2176 (Mundel Rd), W 4.3 mi (E). 2015 rates: $18 to $21. May 1 to Sep 8. (479)253-5866

WANDERLUST RV PARK
Ratings: 9.5/9.5★/9.5 (RV Park) From Jct of US-62 & SR-23S, E 2 mi on US-62 to Passion Play Rd, N 0.5 mi (L). **FAC:** All weather rds. (91 spaces). Avail: 81 all weather, 50 pull-thrus (27 x 65), back-ins (27 x 40), some side by side hkups, 81 full hkups (30/50 amps), seasonal sites, WiFi, tent sites, rentals, dump, laundry. **REC:** pool. Pet restrict(B). Big rig sites, 2015 rates: $35.
(479)253-7385 Lat: 36.39771, Lon: -93.71383
468 Passion Play Road, Eureka Springs, AR 72632
Wanderlustrvpark@gmail.com
www.wanderlustrvpark.com
See ad this page, 110.

FAIRFIELD BAY — B3 *Van Buren*

FAIRFIELD BAY MARINA & RV PARK (Public) From Jct of US-65 & SR-16, E 1.8 mi on SR-16 to Burnt Ridge Rd, E 7.7 mi to SR-330, S 1.4 mi (R). 2015 rates: $12 to $17. (501)884-6029

FAYETTEVILLE — B1 *Washington*

SOUTHGATE RV PARK OF FAYETTEVILLE
Ratings: 5.5/8★/8 (RV Park) N-bnd: From Jct of I-540/I-49 (Exit 60), 1/8 mi E to stoplight, 3/4 mi N on 71 S (L) S-bnd Jct of I-540/I-49:Take US Hwy 71 (Exit 61), E 1/8 mi to stoplight, then 3/4 mi N on 71B (L). **FAC:** Gravel rds. (50 spaces). 42 Avail: 7 paved, 35 gravel, 30 pull-thrus (30 x 70), back-ins (20 x 38), 42 full hkups (30/50 amps), seasonal sites, cable, WiFi, laundry. **REC.** Pets OK. Partial handicap access, no tents. Big rig sites, RV age restrict, 2015 rates: $35. Disc: military. No CC.
(479)442-2021 Lat: 36.03810, Lon: -94.16773
2331 S. School Ave., Fayetteville, AR 72701
southgatervpark.com
See ad this page, 110.

FELSENTHAL — E3 *Union*

GRAND MARAIS (UNION COUNTY PARK) (State Pk) From jct Hwy 129 & Hwy 129B: Go 1 mi NE on Hwy 129B, then 3-1/2 mi W on CR 30. 2015 rates: $21 to $30. (870)943-2930

FLIPPIN — B3 *Marion*

BLUE HERON RV CAMPGROUND & RESORT **Ratings: 6.5/8★/7.5** (RV Park) 2015 rates: $30 to $33. (870)453-4678 150 Blue Heron Dr, Flippin, AR 72634

WHITE RIVER CAMPGROUND & CABINS
Ratings: 7/7.5/7.5 (Campground) From Jct of US 62 E & BR 62, E 0.6 mi on BR 62 to White River Trail, N 0.3 mi on White River Trail (L). **FAC:** Gravel rds. 59 gravel, 42 pull-thrus (35 x 50), back-ins (35 x 40), 59 full hkups (30/50 amps), cable, WiFi, tent sites, rentals, dump, laundry, groc, fire rings, firewood. **REC:** White River: fishing, playground. Pets OK. Big rig sites, 2015 rates: $27 to $35. Disc: AAA, military.
(870)453-2299 Lat: 36.26827, Lon: -92.54946
258 White River Trail, Flippin, AR 72634
Whiterivercampground@gmail.com
www.whiterivercampgroundcabins.com

AR

FORREST CITY — C4 *St Francis*

VILLAGE CREEK (State Pk) From Jct of I-40 & Hwy 284 (exit 242), N 13 mi on Hwy 284 (R). 2015 rates: $19 to $30. (870)238-9406

FORT SMITH — B1 *Crawford*

FORT SMITH See also Alma, Barling, Mulberry, Ozark, Van Buren, Gore, OK; Sallisaw, OK;.

GAMALIEL — A3 *Baxter*

GAMALIEL (Public Corps) From Mountain Home, E 9 mi on Hwy 62/412 to Hwy 101, N 5 mi to CR-42, SE 3 mi (E). 2015 rates: $18 to $19. Apr 1 to Oct 31. (870)467-5680

GARFIELD — A1 *Benton*

LOST BRIDGE NORTH (Public Corps) From Jct of US-62 & SR-127, SE 6.1 mi on SR-127 (follow 127 spur) to Marina Rd, E into park (E). 2015 rates: $20 to $35. Apr 1 to Sep 29. (479)359-3312

LOST BRIDGE SOUTH (Public Corps) From town, SE 5 mi on SR-127 (E). 2015 rates: $17 to $20. May 1 to Sep 29. (479)359-3755

GATEWAY — A1 *Benton*

INDIAN CREEK (Public Corps) From town, E 3 mi on Hwy 62 to Indian Creek Rd (E). 2015 rates: $18. May 1 to Sep 29. (479)253-5866

GREERS FERRY — B3 *Cleburne*

DEVILS FORK (Public Corps) From Jct of AR-16 & AR-92, N 0.5 mi on AR-16 (L). 2015 rates: $17 to $22. Mar 15 to Oct 30. (501)825-8618

MILL CREEK (Public Corps) From town, SW 2 mi on AR-16 to AR-92, W 0.5 mi to Mill Creek Rd, N 3 mi (E). Pit toilets. 2015 rates: $12. May 15 to Sep 15. (501)362-2416

NARROWS CAMPGROUND (Public Corps) From town, W 2 mi on Hwy 16/92 (R). 2015 rates: $17 to $19. May 15 to Sep 15. (501)825-7602

SHILOH (Public Corps) From town, SE 3 mi on AR-110 (E). 2015 rates: $14 to $19. May 15 to Sep 15. (501)362-2416

SUGAR LOAF (Public Corps) From town, SW 2 mi on Hwy 16 to Hwy 92, W 1 mi to SR-337, W 1 mi (E). 2015 rates: $14 to $19. May 15 to Sep 15. (501)654-2267

HARDY — A4 *Sharp*

HARDY CAMPER PARK (CITY PARK) (Public) From west jct US 62 & US 63: Go 1/4 mi E on US 62/63, then 2 blocks S on Spring St. 2015 rates: $20. (870)856-2356

HARRISBURG — B4 *Poinsett*

LAKE POINSETT (State Pk) From Jct of SR-14 & SR-163 (E of Harrisburg), S 3 mi on SR-163 (L). 2015 rates: $12 to $24. (870)578-2064

HARRISON — B2 *Boone*

HARRISON See also Blue Eye, Cotter, Flippin, Jasper, Omaha and Yellville.

HARRISON VILLAGE CAMPGROUND & RV PARK
Ratings: 10/10★/9 (Campground) From Jct of US-65 & 7 (in town), S 3.5 mi on US-65 (R); or E-bnd: From Jct of US-412 & US-62, E 7 mi on 412/62 to US-65, S 9 mi (R); or N-bnd: From Jct of US 412/62 & US-65, go N 1.5 mi on US 65 (L). **FAC:** All weather rds. (76 spaces). Avail: 72 all weather, 66 pull-thrus (24 x 75), back-ins (22 x 50), mostly side by side hkups, 32 full hkups, 40 W, 40 E (30/50 amps), seasonal sites, cable, WiFi, tent sites, dump, laundry, LP gas, fire rings, firewood. **REC:** pool. Pet restrict(B/Q). Partial handicap access. 2015 rates: $24 to $29.83.
(870)743-3388 Lat: 36.20508, Lon: -93.06013
2364 Hwy 65 S, Harrison, AR 72601
harrisonvillage@yahoo.com
www.harrisonvillagervpark.com
See ad this page, 110.

PARKERS RV PARK
Ratings: 9/10★/10 (RV Park) From Jct of US-62/US-412 & US-65 (N of Harrison), S 1.3 mi on US-65 (R). **FAC:** Paved rds. (41 spaces). Avail: 36 all weather, 6 pull-thrus (30 x 65), back-ins (30 x 65), 36 full hkups (30/50 amps), seasonal sites, cable, WiFi, laundry, LP gas. **REC.** Pets OK. Partial handicap access, no tents. Big rig sites, RV age restrict, 2015 rates: $26.50. Disc: AAA, military.
(870)743-2267 Lat: 36.28275, Lon: -93.16611
3629 Hwy 65 N, Harrison, AR 72601
parkersrv@eritter.net
www.parkersrvinc.com
See ad this page, 110.

HEBER SPRINGS — B3 *Cleburne*

DAM SITE (GREERS FERRY) (Public Corps) From town, N 3 mi on SR-25 (L). 2015 rates: $14 to $22. Mar 15 to Oct 30. (501)362-5233

HEBER SPRINGS (Public Corps) From town, W 2 mi on Hwy 110 to park access rd, N 0.5 mi (E). 2015 rates: $14 to $20. Mar 15 to Oct 30. (501)250-0485

JOHN F KENNEDY (Public Corps) From town, NE 4 mi on Hwy 25 to access rd, E 1 mi, follow signs (E). 2015 rates: $17 to $22. Mar 15 to Oct 30. (501)250-0481

OLD HWY 25 (Public Corps) From town, NE 7 mi on Hwy 25 to Hwy 25S, W 3 mi (E). 2015 rates: $14 to $20. May 15 to Oct 30. (501)250-0483

HENDERSON — A3 *Baxter*

HENDERSON REC. AREA (COE-NORFORK LAKE) (Public Corps) From jct Hwy-101 & US-62: Go 1/4 mi S off US-62. 2015 rates: $18 to $20. May 1 to Sep 30. (870)488-5282

HOPE — D2 *Hempstead*

FAIR PARK RV PARK (Public) From Jct of I-30 & Rte 278 (exit 30), SE 0.3 mi on Rte 278 to Rte 278B, SE 1.1 mi to Rte 67, W 0.2 mi to Rte 174, S 0.3 mi to Park Dr, W 0.1 mi (E). 2015 rates: $15. (870)777-7500

HOT SPRINGS — C2 *Garland*

CATHERINE'S LANDING AT HOT SPRINGS
Ratings: 10/10★/10 (Campground) From Jct of US 270 & AR 128 (Exit 7), W 0.3 mi on AR 128 (Carpenter Dam Rd) to Shady Grove Rd, SE 1.7 mi (Do not use GPS) (R).

LAKESIDE LUXURY
Located on Lake Catherine, Catherine's Landing features RV Sites, RVC Resort Cottages & Yurts, community lodge, private boat ramp, pontoon boat, kayak & canoe rentals, walking trails, disc golf course & a new Zip Line course!

FAC: Paved rds. 118 paved, patios, 53 pull-thrus (32 x 80), back-ins (32 x 62), 118 full hkups (30/50 amps), cable, WiFi, rentals, dump, laundry, LP gas, fire rings, firewood. **REC:** heated pool, Lake Catherine: fishing, playground. Pets OK. Partial handicap access, no tents. Big rig sites, 2015 rates: $39 to $54.
(501)262-2550 Lat: 34.45161, Lon: -93.00056
1700 Shady Grove Rd., Hot Springs, AR 71901
catherineslanding@rvcoutdoors.com
www.rvcoutdoors.com/catherines-landing/
See ad this page, 110 & Family Camping, RV Trips of a Lifetime, Snowbird Destinations in Magazine Section.

CLOUD NINE RV PARK
Ratings: 8.5/9.5★/9.5 (RV Park) W-bnd: From Jct of I-30 & US-70 (Exit 111), W 12.5 mi to Cloud Nine Dr - exit Left (L); or E-bnd: From Jct of US-70-270 E Bypass, E 5.5 mi on Hwy 70 to Cloud Nine Dr (R) (1 mi past rest area). **FAC:** Paved rds. (45 spaces). Avail: 30 gravel, 15 pull-thrus (38 x 70), back-ins (30 x 55), 30 full hkups (30/50 amps), seasonal sites, WiFi, tent sites, dump, laundry. **REC.** Pets OK. Big rig sites, eco-friendly, 2015 rates: $25.
(501)262-1996 Lat: 34.54313, Lon: -92.88271
136 Cloud Nine Drive, Hot Springs, AR 71901
cloudninervpark@aol.com
www.cloudninervpark.com
See ad page 110.

HOT SPRINGS NATIONAL PARK KOA **Ratings: 9.5/9.5★/8.5** (Campground) 2015 rates: $35 to $75. (501)624-5912 838 Mc Clendon Road, Hot Springs National Park, AR 71901

HOT SPRINGS/GULPHA GORGE CAMPGROUND (Natl Pk) From Jct of Hwy 70 & 70B (E of town), N 0.25 mi on 70B, follow signs (L). 2015 rates: $10 to $24. (501)620-6743

J & J RV PARK
Ratings: 7.5/9★/7.5 (RV Park) E-bnd: From Jct of US-270B/70B & SR-7, E 4 mi on US-70B at exit 4 (R) or W-bnd: From Jct of I 30 & 70 W, 25 mi on 70B W to exit 3 (Magic Springs Dr exit), first left over freeway, E (left) 0.5 mi on access road (R). **FAC:** Paved rds. 46 gravel, 17 pull-thrus (30 x 70), back-ins (26 x 40), 46 full hkups (30/50 amps), cable, WiFi, laundry. **REC:** playground. Pets OK. Partial handicap access, no tents. Big rig sites, 2015 rates: $35. No CC.
(501)321-9852 Lat: 34.50833, Lon: -93.01000
2000 E Grand Ave, Hot Springs, AR 71901
janice@jjrvpark.com
www.jjrvpark.com
See ad this page.

LAKE HAMILTON RV RESORT **Ratings: 8.5/8.5★/7** (RV Park) 2015 rates: $25 to $45. (866)767-9996 3027 Albert Pike, Hot Springs National Park, AR 71913

LAKE OUACHITA (State Pk) From Jct of US-270 & SR-227, N 12 mi on SR-227 (E). For reservations call 1-800-264-2441. 2015 rates: $12 to $30. (501)767-9366

TREASURE ISLE RV PARK **Ratings: 6/UI/5** (Campground) 2015 rates: $28 to $35. (501)767-6852 205 Treasure Isle Rd #99, Hot Springs, AR 71913

Park owners want you to be satisfied with your stay. Get to know them.

Keep one Guide at home, and one in your RV! To purchase additional North American Edition copies, call 877-209-6655.

HOT SPRINGS (CONT)

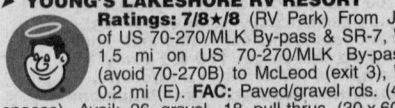

YOUNG'S LAKESHORE RV RESORT
Ratings: 7/8★/8 (RV Park) From Jct of US 70-270/MLK By-pass & SR-7, W 1.5 mi on US 70-270/MLK By-pass (avoid 70-270B) to McLeod (exit 3), W 0.2 mi (E). **FAC:** Paved/gravel rds. (46 spaces). Avail: 26 gravel, 18 pull-thrus (30 x 60), back-ins (25 x 50), some side by side hkups, 26 full hkups (30/50 amps), seasonal sites, cable, WiFi, tent sites, rentals, dump, laundry, LP gas, fire rings, firewood. **REC:** Lake Hamilton: fishing. Pet restrict(B/Q). Partial handicap access. Big rig sites, 2015 rates: $34.50. Disc: AAA, military.
(800)470-7875 Lat: 34.47044, Lon: -93.09467
1601 Lakeshore Dr, Hot Springs, AR 71913
www.rvhotsprings.com
See ad page 113.

HUNTSVILLE — B2 *Madison*

WITHROW SPRINGS (State Pk) From Jct of SR-412 & SR-23, N 5 mi on SR-23 (L). 2015 rates: $30. (479)559-2593

JACKSONPORT — B4 *Jackson*

JACKSONPORT (State Pk) In town, NW 0.25 mi on AR-69S (L). 2015 rates: $24. (870)523-2143

JASPER — B2 *Newton*

DOGWOOD SPRINGS CAMPGROUND/RESORT **Ratings: 7/7/7.5** (Campground) 2015 rates: $27 to $29. (870)446-2163 hwy 7 @ Dogwood Lane, Jasper, AR 72641

JONESBORO — B4 *Craighead*

CRAIGHEAD FOREST PARK (Public) From jct US 63 (exit 44) & Hwy 1B: Go 1 block S on Hwy 1B, then 1 mi W on Parker Rd, then 2 mi S on Culberhouse St (Hwy 141) to Forest Park Dr. (R). 2015 rates: $20. (870)933-4604

PERKINS RV PARK **Ratings: 4.5/NA/5.5** (RV Park) 2015 rates: $25. (870)897-5700 1821 E Parker Rd, Jonesboro, AR 72404

JORDAN — B3 *Izard*

JORDAN PARK (Public Corps) From town, SE 12 mi on Hwy 5 to Hwy 177, E 5 mi to CR-64, N 3 mi (E). 2015 rates: $9 to $18. (870)499-7223

KIRBY — D2 *Pike*

KIRBY LANDING (Public Corps) From town, W 2.5 mi on US-70 to park access rd, SW 1.5 mi (E). 2015 rates: $16 to $32. (870)285-2151

LAKE VILLAGE — E4 *Chicot*

CHICOT COUNTY PARK (Public) From Jct of Hwy 65 & Hwy 82 E 5.2 mi on Hwy 82 to CR 403 Levee Rd (just before Mississippi River Bridge) N 1.3 mi to Lake Hall Rd SW 3 mi (L). 2015 rates: $20 to $30. (870)265-3500

LAKE CHICOT (State Pk) From Jct of US-82 & US-65, N 4 mi on US-65 to SR-257, E 4 mi to SR-144, NE 4 mi (R). For reservations call (800)264-2430. 2015 rates: $19 to $30. (870)265-5480

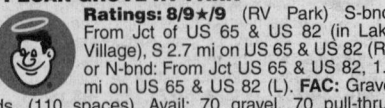

PECAN GROVE RV PARK
Ratings: 8/9★/9 (RV Park) S-bnd: From Jct of US 65 & US 82 (in Lake Village), S 2.7 mi on US 65 & US 82 (R); or N-bnd: From Jct US 65 & US 82, 1.7 mi on US 65 & US 82 (L). **FAC:** Gravel rds. (110 spaces). Avail: 70 gravel, 70 pull-thrus (35 x 75), 70 full hkups (30/50 amps), seasonal sites, cable, WiFi, tent sites, rentals, laundry, groc, firewood. **REC:** Lake Chicot: fishing, playground. Pet restrict(B). Big rig sites, 2015 rates: $30 to $32. Disc: AAA, military.
AAA Approved
(870)265-3005 Lat: 33.29582, Lon: -91.27629
3768 Highway 82 & 65 South, Lake Village, AR 71653
info@pecangrove.net
www.turnoninn.com
See ad this page.

LAKEVIEW — A3 *Baxter, Marion*

LAKEVIEW (Public Corps) From town, N 1 mi on Hwy 178 to Boat Dock Rd, N 1.5 mi (E). 2015 rates: $18 to $54. (870)431-8116

LEAD HILL — A2 *Boone*

LEAD HILL (Public Corps) From town, N 4 mi on Hwy 7 (E). 2015 rates: $18 to $54. Apr 1 to Oct 31. (870)422-7555

TUCKER HOLLOW (Public Corps) From town, NW 7.5 mi on Hwy 14 to Hwy 281, N 3 mi (E). 2015 rates: $20. May 1 to Sep 30. (870)436-5622

LINWOOD — D3 *Jefferson*

RISING STAR (Public Corps) From Pine Bluff, S 7.8 mi on US-65 to Blankinship Rd (in Linwood), N 3.5 mi (E). 2015 rates: $19. Mar 1 to Oct 31. (870)534-0451

LITTLE ROCK — C3 *Pulaski*

LITTLE ROCK See also Benton, Bryant, Conway & North Little Rock.

MAUMELLE PARK (Public Corps) From Jct of I-430 & Hwy 10 (exit 9), W 2.6 mi on Hwy 10 to Pinnacle Valley Rd, N 2.1 mi (E). 2015 rates: $22 to $26. (501)868-9477

Our rating system isn't just tough, it's thorough. We know the kinds of things that are important to you — like clean restrooms and showers, attractive, secure, well-tended grounds, and extras like swimming pools. We give the first rating for development of facilities, the second for cleanliness and physical characteristics of restrooms and showers, and the third for visual appearance.

LOWELL — B1 *Benton*

Travel Services

CAMPING WORLD OF LOWELL As the nation's largest retailer of RV supplies, accessories, services and new and used RVs, Camping World is committed to making your total RV experience better. RV Accessories: (800)582-2701. **SERVICES:** Staffed RV wash, restrooms, RV Sales. RV supplies, LP, RV accessible. waiting room. Hours: 8 am - 7 pm.
(888)540-8764 Lat: 36.256023, Lon: -94.148316
317 North 6th Place, Lowell, AR 72745
CampingWorldofLowell.com

MAGNOLIA — E2 *Columbia*

MAGNOLIA RV PARK, LLC
Ratings: 8/10★/10 (RV Park) S-Bnd: Jct of US-82 & US-371, S .5 mi on US-371 to W University, R .5 mi (R) N-Bnd: Jct of US-371 & US-82B, N 1.6 mi on US-371 to W University, L .5 mi (R). **FAC:** Gravel rds. 30 gravel, 13 pull-thrus (30 x 80), back-ins (30 x 55), 30 full hkups (30/50 amps), cable, WiFi, tent sites, dump, laundry, LP gas. **REC:** pond, fishing, playground. Pets OK. Big rig sites, eco-friendly, 2015 rates: $35 to $50. No CC.
(870)562-2908 Lat: 33.29061, Lon: -93.256421
1399 W University, Magnolia, AR 71753
Info@magnoliarvpark.net
www.magnoliarvpark.net
See ad this page, 110.

MALVERN — C2 *Hot Spring*

LAKE CATHERINE (State Pk) From Jct of I-30 & SR-171 (exit 97), N 12 mi on SR-171 (E). For reservations call (800)264-2422. 2015 rates: $19 to $30. (501)844-4176

MARION — C5 *Crittenden*

MEMPHIS KOA **Ratings: 9/9★/8** (RV Park) 2015 rates: $39 to $55. (870)739-4801 7037 I-55, Marion, AR 72364

MENA — C1 *Polk*

IRON MOUNTAIN
Ratings: 7.5/9★/9.5 (Campground) From W Jct of US-270 & US-71, S 12.5 mi on US-71 (L). **FAC:** Paved rds. 110 gravel, patios, 55 pull-thrus (24 x 65), back-ins (24 x 65), 110 full hkups (30/50 amps), WiFi, tent sites, rentals, laundry, firewood. **REC:** playground. Pets OK. Partial handicap access. 2015 rates: $22.10.
(870)389-6560 Lat: 34.52525, Lon: -94.32408
106 Iron Mountain Lane, Mena, AR 71953
chris@cmausa.org
cmausa.org/iron-mountain/
See ad this page, 110.

QUEEN WILHELMINA (State Pk) From Jct of SR-88 & US 71/59, W 13 mi on SR-88 (L). 2015 rates: $19. (479)394-2693

SHADOW MOUNTAIN RV PARK Ratings: 8.5/8★/6.5 (Campground) From W Jct of US-71 & SR-88 (in town), S 5.9 mi on US-71 (R). **FAC:** Paved/gravel rds. 64 Avail: 58 gravel, 6 grass, 50 pull-thrus (20 x 60), back-ins (20 x 40), 42 full hkups, 19 W, 19 E (30/50 amps), WiFi, tent sites,

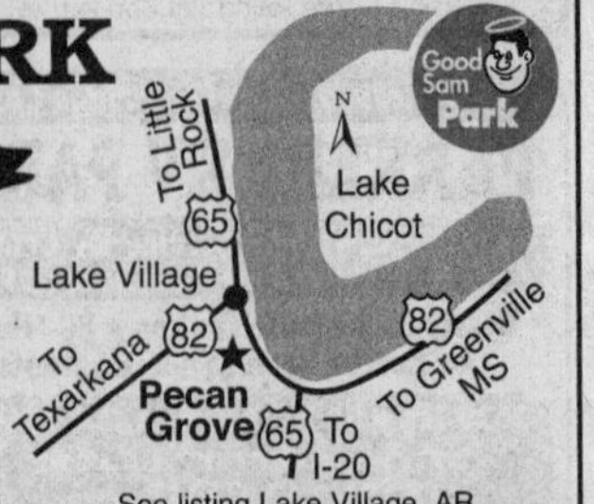

MENA (CONT)

SHADOW MOUNTAIN RV PARK (CONT) rentals, dump, laundry, fire rings, firewood. **REC:** pool, pond, fishing, playground. Pets OK. 2015 rates: $18 to $35. No CC.
(479)394-6099 Lat: 34.53844, Lon: -94.31574
3708 Hwy 71 South, Mena, AR 71953
ronanddarline@localnet.com
www.shadowmountaincampground.com

MORRILTON — C2 *Conway*

MORRILTON I40/107 RV PARK
Ratings: 7.5/9★/9 (Campground) From Jct of I-40 & Hwy 95 (exit 107), N 1/10 mi. on Hwy 95, immediate left (into gas station) (E). **FAC:** All weather rds. (54 spaces). Avail: 30 all weather, 30 pull-thrus (30 x 55), 30 full hkups (30/50 amps), seasonal sites, WiFi, tent sites, rentals, dump, laundry, groc, firewood. **REC:** playground. Pets OK. 2015 rates: $30. Disc: military.
(501)354-8262 Lat: 35.17755, Lon: -92.74904
30 Kamper Lane, Morrilton, AR 72110
jj@morriltonrvpark.com
www.morriltonrvpark.com
See ad this page, 110.

PETIT JEAN (State Pk) From Jct of I-40 & SR-9 (exit 108), S 9 mi on SR-9 to SR-154, W 12 mi (R). 2015 rates: $19 to $30. (501)727-5441

TOAD SUCK CHEROKEE PARK (Public Corps) From Jct of I-40 & Hwy 95, S to Hwy 64, follow signs (E). 2015 rates: $18 to $20. (501)329-2986

MOUNT IDA — C2 *Montgomery*

BIG FIR (Public Corps) From town, N 6 mi on Hwy 27 to Hwy 188, E 8 mi (E). Pit toilets. 2015 rates: $10 to $20. (501)767-2101

DENBY POINT (Public Corps) From town, E 9 mi on US-270 to Ouachita Shores Pkwy, N 1 mi, follow signs (E). 2015 rates: $16 to $20. (870)867-4475

JOPLIN REC AREA (Public Corps) From town, E 11 mi on US-270 to Mountain Harbor Rd, N 3 mi (E). 2015 rates: $10 to $16. (501)767-2108

LITTLE FIR (Public Corps) From town, NE 7 mi on SR-27 to Hwy 188, E 9 mi (E). 2015 rates: $12 to $18. (501)767-2101

TOMPKINS BEND (Public Corps) From town, E 10.7 mi on US-270 to Shangri La Dr., N 2.4 mi (E). 2015 rates: $10 to $20. (501)767-2108

MOUNTAIN HOME — A3 *Baxter*

BIDWELL POINT PARK (Public Corps) From town, E 9 mi on US-62/412 to AR-101, N 2 mi, over bridge, E on access rd (R). 2015 rates: $18 to $20. May 1 to Sep 30. (870)467-5375

CRANFIELD PARK (Public Corps) From town NE 5 mi on Hwy 62 to Cranfield Rd, N 2 mi (L). 2015 rates: $18 to $20. Apr 1 to Oct 31. (870)492-4191

DAM-QUARRY CAMPGROUND (COE - NORFORK LAKE) (Public Corps) From jct US 62 & Hwy 5: Go 11 mi SE on Hwy 5 to Salesville, then 2 mi E on Hwy 177 to Norfork Dam. 2015 rates: $18 to $20. (870)499-7216

PANTHER BAY (Public Corps) From town, E 9 mi on US-412/Hwy 62 to Hwy 101, N 1 mi (R). Pit toilets. 2015 rates: $9 to $18. Apr 1 to Sep 30. (870)425-2700

ROBINSON POINT (Public Corps) From town, E 9 mi on US-421/Hwy 62 to Robinson Point Rd (CR-279), S 3 mi (E). 2015 rates: $18 to $40. Apr 1 to Oct 31. (870)492-6853

MOUNTAIN VIEW — B3 *Stone*

ANGLERS HOLIDAY MOUNTAIN RESORT **Ratings: 8/8.5/8** (Membership Pk) 2015 rates: $30. Mar 15 to Nov 15. (800)395-7108 473 Swinging Bridge Rd, Mountain View, AR 72560

OZARK RV PARK
Ratings: 8.5/9.5★/9.5 (Campground) N-bnd: Jct of SR-5/9/14, N 0.5 mi on SR14 to E Webb, W 0.7 mi to Park Ave, N 0.4 mi (L); S-bnd: Jct of SR-5/9/14, N of town, S 5 mi on SR9 to SR382, W 0.2 mi to Roper, SW 0.5 mi to Park Ave, N 0.1 mi (L); E-bnd: Jct of 65/66, E 27 mi on 66 to Peabody, N 500' to Webb, E 150' to Park Ave, N 0.4 mi (L). **FAC:** Gravel rds. (76 spaces). Avail: 56 all weather, 21 pull-thrus (24 x 60), back-ins (24 x 45), 52 full hkups, 4 W, 4 E (30/50 amps), seasonal sites, cable, WiFi, tent sites, rentals, dump, laundry, fire rings, firewood. **REC.** Pet restrict(B). 2015 rates: $24 to $28. Mar 1 to Nov 30.
(870)269-2542 Lat: 35.87908, Lon: -92.11608
1022 Park Ave., Mountain View, AR 72560
www.ozarkrvpark.com
See ad this page, 110.

SYLAMORE CREEK CAMP **Ratings: 6.5/5.5/7** (Campground) 2015 rates: $20 to $30. (870)585-2326 214 Sylamore Creek Rd., Mountain View, AR 72560

WHITEWATER BLUEGRASS RV PARK **Ratings: 5/5.5/7.5** (Campground) 2015 rates: $19 to $23. Mar 1 to Oct 31. (870)269-8047 108 East Webb St., Mountain View, AR 72560

MULBERRY — B1 *Crawford, Franklin*

VINE PRAIRIE (Public Corps) From town, S 1.7 mi on Hwy 917 to access rd (E). 2015 rates: $10 to $20. (479)667-2129

MURFREESBORO — D1 *Pike*

COWHIDE COVE (Public Corps) From town, N 9 mi on Hwy 27 to Laurel Creek Rd., W 1.4 mi, S 1.8 mi CR-77 (E). 2015 rates: $13 to $15. Mar 1 to Nov 30. (870)285-2151

CRATER OF DIAMONDS (State Pk) From town, SE 2 mi on Hwy 301, follow signs (R). 2015 rates: $30. (870)285-3113

LAUREL CREEK (Public Corps) From town, N 10 mi on SR-27 to access rd, W 5 mi (E). Pit toilets. 2015 rates: $5. Mar 1 to Oct 31. (877)444-6777

NARROWS DAM (Public Corps) From town, N 6 mi on Hwy 19 to access rd, NW 0.5 mi (E). 2015 rates: $10 to $18. (870)285-2151

PARKER CREEK (Public Corps) From town, N 6 mi on Hwy 19, NW (across dam) 3 mi on Beacon Hill/Parker Creek Rd. 2015 rates: $10 to $16. Mar 1 to Dec 15. (870)285-2151

NEW BLAINE — C2 *Logan*

SHOAL BAY PARK ON LAKE DARDANELLE (Public Corps) From town, N 2 mi on Hwy 197 to access rd (E). 2015 rates: $16 to $20. Mar 1 to Oct 31. (479)938-7335

NEWHOPE — D1 *Pike*

STAR OF THE WEST (Public Corps) From town, E 2.8 mi on US-70, at bridge (R). Pit toilets. 2015 rates: $5. (870)285-2151

NORTH LITTLE ROCK — C3 *Pulaski*

BURNS PARK CAMPGROUND (Public) W-bnd I-40 (Exit 150): .3 mi on ramp to SR-176 (Military Dr), L .3 mi on SR-176 to Burns Park Dr, R .6 mi on Burns Park Dr (R) E-bnd I-40 (Exit 150): .2 mi on ramp to SR-176 (Military Dr), R .1 mi on SR-176 to Burns Park Dr, R .6 mi on Burns Park Dr (R). 2015 rates: $18 to $20. (501)771-0702

DOWNTOWN RIVERSIDE RV PARK
Ratings: 7.5/8★/7 (Public) W-bnd I-30 (Exit 141B): S .6 mi on N Cypress St to Riverfront Dr, L .06 mi to S Locust Dr (R) E-bnd I-30 (Exit 141B): N .1 mi on ramp to US-70, R .3 mi on US-70 to Riverfront Dr, R .4 mi to S Locust Dr (L). **FAC:** Paved rds. 61 gravel, 14 pull-thrus (40 x 100), back-ins (20 x 50), some side by side hkups, 61 full hkups (50 amps), WiFi, dump, laundry, controlled access. **REC:** Arkansas River. Pets OK. No tents. Big rig sites, 2015 rates: $22 to $30. Disc: AAA, military.
(501)340-5312 Lat: 34.75233, Lon: -92.26153
250 S Locust St., North Little Rock, AR 72114
rvpark@northlittlerock.org
www.downtownriversidervpark.com
See ad pages 116, 110.

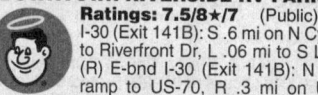

NORTH LITTLE ROCK (CONT)

KOA LITTLE ROCK NORTH **Ratings: 9/8.5★/7** (Campground) 2015 rates: $49.57. (501)758-4598 7820 Kampground Way, North Little Rock, AR 72118

TRAILS END RV PARK **Ratings: 6/4.5/6** (RV Park) 2015 rates: $36. (501)851-4594 14223 Stricklin Cove, North Little Rock, AR 72118

WILLOW BEACH (Public Corps) From town, SE 2.5 mi on US-165 to Col. Maynard Rd, S 3 mi to Blue Heron, W 1 mi, follow signs (R). 2015 rates: $19. (501)961-1332

Travel Services

CAMPING WORLD OF NORTH LITTLE ROCK As the nation's largest retailer of RV supplies, accessories, services and new and used RVs, Camping World is committed to making your total RV experience better. RV Sales: (888)615-6178. **SERVICES:** RV appliance, staffed RV wash, restrooms, RV Sales. RV supplies, LP, RV accessible. Hours: 8am - 6pm.
(888)686-5038 Lat: 34.784026, Lon: -92.139666
9801 Diamond Drive, North Little Rock, AR 72117
CampingWorldofNorthLittleRock.com

OAKLAND — A3 *Marion*

OAKLAND PUBLIC USE AREA (Public Corps) From town, SW 8 mi on Hwy 202 (E). 2015 rates: $19 to $38. May 1 to Sep 30. (870)431-5744

OZARK ISLE (Public Corps) From town, SW 10 mi on Hwy 202 (E). 2015 rates: $9 to $16. May 1 to Oct 31. (870)431-5744

OLA — C2 *Yell*

QUARRY COVE (Public Corps) From town, E 7 mi on Hwy 60 to access rd (E). 2015 rates: $14 to $32. (479)272-4233

OMAHA — A2 *Boone, Carroll*

CRICKET CREEK (Public Corps) From town, N 4 mi on Hwy 65 to Hwy 14, W 5.9 mi (E). 2015 rates: $21. Apr 1 to Sep 14. (870)426-3331

OZARK VIEW RV PARK **Ratings: 7.5/9★/10** (Campground) 2015 rates: $32. (870)715-0131 18412 Old Hwy 65, Omaha, AR 72662

OZARK — B1 *Franklin, Johnson*

AUX ARC (Public Corps) From Ozark, S 1.5 mi on Hwy 23 to Hwy 309, E 1 mi (L). 2015 rates: $10 to $20. (479)667-1100

PARAGOULD — B5 *Greene*

CROWLEY'S RIDGE (State Pk) From Jct of SR-141 & SR-168 (in town), E 0.25 mi on SR-168 (R). 2015 rates: $19. (870)573-6751

Directional arrows indicate the campground's position in relation to the nearest town.

PARIS — C1 *Logan*

MT MAGAZINE/CAMERON BLUFF CAMPGROUND (State Pk) From town, S 17 mi on Hwy 309 (E). 2015 rates: $27 to $30. (479)963-8502

PEEL — A2 *Marion*

BUCK CREEK REC. AREA (COE-BULL SHOALS LAKE) (Public Corps) 5 mi N on Hwy-125 (free ferry). 2015 rates: $14 to $38. May 1 to Sep 30. (870)425-2700

HIGHWAY 125 (Public Corps) From town, NW 14 mi on Hwy 14 to Hwy 125, N 13 mi (R). 2015 rates: $19 to $20. Apr 1 to Oct 31. (870)436-5711

PINE BLUFF — D3 *Jefferson*

SARACEN TRACE RV PARK (Public) From Jct of US-79 & US-65 (in town), E 1.25 mi on US-65B (avoid Loop 530) to Convention Center Dr, N 2 mi (beyond golf course) (E); or From Jct of US-65 & US-65B (E of town), N 3.4 mi on US-65B to Convention Center Dr, N 2 mi (beyond golf course) (E). 2015 rates: $14. (870)534-0711

PINEY — C2 *Garland*

PINEY BAY (Public Corps) From town, W 3.7 mi on US-64 to SR-359, N 3.5 mi (L). 2015 rates: $16 to $20. Mar 1 to Oct 31. (479)885-3029

PLAINVIEW — C2 *Yell*

CARTER COVE (Public Corps) From town, SE 3 mi on Hwy 60 to access rd, S 1 mi (E). 2015 rates: $14 to $32. (479)272-4983

COUNTY LINE (Public Corps) From town, E 6 mi on Hwy 60 to access rd (E). 2015 rates: $16 to $18. Mar 1 to Oct 31. (479)272-4945

RIVER ROAD (Public Corps) From town, E 8.5 mi on Hwy 60 to Hwy 7, S 0.25 mi (R). 2015 rates: $13 to $32. (479)272-4835

SUNLIGHT BAY (Public Corps) From town, W 0.25 mi on Hwy 28 to Sunlight access rd, S 2 mi (R). 2015 rates: $14 to $32. (479)272-4234

POCAHONTAS — B4 *Randolph*

DAVIDSONVILLE (State Pk) From Jct of US-62 & SR-166, S 9 mi on SR-166 (E); or From Jct of US-63 & SR-361, N 6 mi on SR-361 (R). 2015 rates: $19 to $24. (870)892-4708

QUITMAN — B3 *Cleburne*

COVE CREEK (Public Corps) From town, NW 3 mi on Hwy 16 to access rd, right (E). 2015 rates: $14 to $19. May 15 to Sep 15. (501)362-2416

REDFIELD — C3 *Jefferson*

TAR CAMP (Public Corps) From town, E 6 mi on River Rd, follow signs (E). 2015 rates: $9 to $19. Mar 1 to Oct 31. (501)397-5101

ROGERS — A1 *Benton, Carroll, Rogers*

ROGERS See also Cave Springs, Garfield & Springdale.

HORSESHOE BEND EAST (Public Corps) From Jct of US-62/I-546 & SR-94, E 7.5 mi on SR-94/New Hope Rd.(E). 2015 rates: $16 to $50. Apr 1 to Oct 30. (479)925-2561

MONTE NE FAMILY CAMPGROUND RV PARK & CABINS Ratings: 5.5/7.5/7 (RV Park) From Jct of I-49 & Exit 83 (New Hope Rd/Hwy 94E), E 7 mi on New Hope Rd/Hwy 94E, E 2 mi on Hwy 94E (Do not take 94S) (R). **FAC:** Gravel rds. 81 gravel, 12 pull-thrus (20 x 134), back-ins (20 x 67), 71 full hkups, 10 W, 10 E (30/50 amps), WiFi, tent sites, rentals, dump, laundry, firewood. **REC:** Beaver Lake: fishing, playground. Pets OK. 2015 rates: $25.
(479)925-1265 Lat: 36.29489, Lon: -94.05029
15039 E Highway 94, Rogers, AR 72758
campgroundreservations@yahoo.com
monteneatbeaverlake.com

PRAIRIE CREEK (Public Corps) From Jct of US-62 & SR-12, E 4 mi on SR-12 to North Park Rd, N into park (E). 2015 rates: $16 to $32. Apr 1 to Oct 31. (501)925-3957

ROCKY BRANCH (Public Corps) From town, E 11 mi on Hwy 12 to SR-303, NE 4.5 mi to paved access road (E). 2015 rates: $20 to $21. May 1 to Oct 30. (479)925-2526

ROYAL — C2 *Garland*

BRADY MOUNTAIN (Public Corps) From town, W 2 mi on US-270 to SH 926, N 6 mi (E). 2015 rates: $14 to $18. Mar 1 to Oct 1. (501)760-1146

RUSSELLVILLE — C2 *Pope*

IVY'S COVE RV RETREAT
Ratings: 9/9.5★/10 (RV Park) From Jct of I-40 & SR 331 (Exit 84) E 0.4 mi on SR 331 (R). **FAC:** All weather rds. 25 Avail: 25 all weather, 14 pull-thrus (30 x 60), back-ins (30 x 58), 25 full hkups (30/50 amps), cable, WiFi, dump, laundry, fire rings, firewood. **REC.** Pet restrict(B). Partial handicap access, no tents. Big rig sites, 2015 rates: $34 to $36. Disc: AAA.
(479)280-1662 Lat: 35.28353, Lon: -93.08375
321 Bradley Cove Rd., Russellville, AR 72802
dmi@ivyscove.com
www.ivyscove.com
See ad this page, 110.

LAKE DARDANELLE (State Pk) From Jct of I-40 & SR-7 (exit 81) to Aspen Rd, W (left) 0.1 mi on Aspen Rd to Rte 7, S 0.1 mi to SR 326, W 5.5 mi (R). 2015 rates: $19 to $30. (479)967-5516

OLD POST ROAD (Public Corps) From Jct of I-40 & Hwy 7, S 6 mi on Hwy 7 to Old Post Rd, W 2 mi (E). 2015 rates: $20. (501)968-7962

RUSSELLVILLE (CONT)

OUTDOOR LIVING CENTER RV PARK
Ratings: 7/9★/9.5 (RV Park) W-bnd: From Jct of I-40 & SR-7 (exit 81) to Aspen Rd, W (left) 0.1 mi to Rte 7, N 0.2 mi (L); or E-bnd: From Jct of I-40 & SR-7 (Exit 81), N 0.3 mi on SR-7 (L). **FAC:** Paved/gravel rds. (50 spaces). Avail: 26 gravel, 16 pull-thrus (20 x 60), back-ins (20 x 60), 26 full hkups (30/50 amps), seasonal sites, cable, WiFi, tent sites, dump, laundry, LP bottles. **REC.** Pets OK. Partial handicap access. 2015 rates: $37 to $40.
(800)828-4307 Lat: 35.31097, Lon: -93.13919
10 Outdoor Ct., Russellville, AR 72802
Olcrvpark@hotmail.com
www.olcrvpark.com
See ad opposite page, 110.

SARATOGA — D1 *Hempstead*

SARATOGA LANDING (Public Corps) From town, S 1 mi on Hwy 32 to Hwy 234, W 1 mi (E). Pit toilets. 2015 rates: $5. Mar 1 to Oct 31. (870)898-3343

SEARCY — C3 *White*

WHITNEY LANE RV PARK
Ratings: 5/NA/7.5 (RV Park) From Jct of Hwy 67/167 (exit 46), E .7 mi on SR 36 (E Race Ave/W Wilbur Mills Ave) to Whitney Lane(L) .8 mi (R). **FAC:** Gravel rds. (85 spaces). Avail: 55 gravel, patios, 55 pull-thrus (25 x 65), mostly side by side hkups, 55 full hkups (30/50 amps), seasonal sites, WiFi, laundry, LP gas. **REC:** Little Red River: fishing. Pet restrict(B/Q). No tents. Big rig sites, 2015 rates: $30.
(501)230-8000 Lat: 35.24269, Lon: -91.66643
597 Whitney Lane, Kensett, AR 72082
Monamcf01@gmail.com
www.whitneylanervpark.com
See ad this page.

SHIRLEY — B3 *Van Buren*

GOLDEN POND R.V. PARK **Ratings: 7.5/8.5★/8** (RV Park) 2015 rates: $28. (501)723-8212 241 Hwy 330 S., Shirley, AR 72153

SPRINGDALE — B1 *Benton, Washington*

SPRINGDALE See also Cave Springs, Rogers & Siloam Springs.

HICKORY CREEK (Public Corps) From Jct of US-71 & SR-264, E 4.5 mi on SR-264 to Cow Face Rd, S 1 mi to Hickory Creek Rd, E 1 mi (R). 2015 rates: $21. Apr 1 to Oct 30. (479)750-2943

PILGRIMS REST RV PARK Ratings: 5.5/7.5★/7 (RV Park) From Jct of I-540 & Hwy 412 (Exit 72), E 13.5 mi on Hwy 412 to Hickory Flatt Rd (CR-97), N 0.3 mi (L). Caution: Steep gravel drive at entrance. **FAC:** Gravel rds. 37 gravel, 30 pull-thrus (26 x 64), back-ins (26 x 40), 37 full hkups (30/50 amps), WiFi, tent sites, dump, laundry, firewood. **REC.** Pets OK. 2015 rates: $24.
(479)789-7152 Lat: 36.18512, Lon: -93.96840
21225 Hickory Flatt Road, Springdale, AR 72764
pilgrimsrestrvpark.com

WAR EAGLE (Public Corps) From town, E 14 mi on SR-412 to Knob Hill Loop (CR-389), N 2.1 mi, follow signs (L). For reservations call (877)444-6777. 2015 rates: $20. May 1 to Sep 8. (479)636-1210

ST JOE — B2 *Searcy*

BUFFALO NATIONAL RIVER (TYLER BEND CAMPGROUND) (Public) From town: Go 3 mi S on US 65, then 3 mi W on access road. 2015 rates: $16. (877)444-6777

STAR CITY — D3 *Lincoln*

CANE CREEK (State Pk) From Jct of US-425 & SR-293 (in town), E 5 mi on SR-293 (L). 2015 rates: $19 to $24. (870)628-4714

TEXARKANA — D1 *Miller*

SUNRISE RV PARK **Ratings: 9/9.5★/9.5** (RV Park) 2015 rates: $35. (870)772-0751 8225 Camper Lane, Texarkana, AR 71854

TICHNOR — D4 *Desha*

MERRISACH LAKE (Public Corps) From town, S 10 mi on Tichnor Balcktop Rd to Merrisach Lake Ln, W 1 mi (E). 2015 rates: $11 to $19. (870)548-2291

NOTREBES BEND (COE-ARKANSAS POST RIVER AREA) (Public Corps) From town: Go 10 mi S on County Road, then follow signs 6-1/2 mi SW & SE on paved access road. 2015 rates: $19. Mar 1 to Oct 27. (870)548-2291

TOLLETTE — D1 *Howard*

COTTONSHED LANDING (Public Corps) From town, W 4 mi on CR-332 to access rd (E). 2015 rates: $13 to $15. (870)898-4533

VAN BUREN — B1 *Crawford*

OVERLAND RV PARK
Ratings: 5.5/7/5 (RV Park) From Jct of I-40 & SR-59 (exit 5), S 0.1 mi on SR-59 (move to left lane) to Access Rd (behind Motel 6), E 500' (E). **FAC:** Gravel rds. 50 gravel, 30 pull-thrus (20 x 55), back-ins (20 x 30), 50 full hkups (30/50 amps), cable, WiFi, laundry. **REC.** Pets OK. No tents. 2015 rates: $31. No CC.
(479)471-5474 Lat: 35.46071, Lon: -94.35335
1716 1/2 Fayetteville Hwy, Van Buren, AR 72956

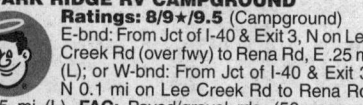

PARK RIDGE RV CAMPGROUND
Ratings: 8/9★/9.5 (Campground) E-bnd: From Jct of I-40 & Exit 3, N on Lee Creek Rd (over fwy) to Rena Rd, E .25 mi (L); or W-bnd: From Jct of I-40 & Exit 3, N 0.1 mi on Lee Creek Rd to Rena Rd, E .25 mi (L). **FAC:** Paved/gravel rds. (56 spaces). Avail: 40 gravel, 31 pull-thrus (25 x 65), back-ins (28 x 45), some side by side hkups, 40 full hkups (30/50 amps), seasonal sites, cable, WiFi, tent sites, dump, laundry, firewood. **REC:** Lee Creek: fishing, playground. Pets OK. Big rig sites, 2015 rates: $33 to $35.
(479)410-4678 Lat: 35.46693, Lon: -94.38724
1616 Rena Rd., Van Buren, AR 72956
parkridge4rvfun@aol.com
www.parkridgerv.com
See ad page 112.

WAVELAND — C2 *Yell*

OUTLET AREA (Public Corps) From town, S 1 mi on Hwy 309 to access rd, W l mi to Blue Mountain Dam, follow signs (E). For reservations call (877)444-6777. 2015 rates: $16 to $36. Mar 1 to Oct 30. (479)947-2101

WAVELAND PARK (Public Corps) From town, S 1 mi on Hwy 309 to paved cnty rd, W 1 mi, follow signs. Pit toilets. 2015 rates: $16 to $18. Mar 1 to Oct 30. (479)947-2102

Treat your pet to a fabulous camping experience by staying at one of the Pampered Pet Parks featured in the front of the Guide. Many of the parks on this list offer perks like dog runs, dog washing stations and dog walking services. Some of the parks even conduct pet parades during special holidays.

WEST FORK — B1 *Washington*

DEVIL'S DEN (State Pk) From Jct of US-71 & SR-170, SW 18 mi on SR-170 (R). Trailers longer than 26' use caution on ARK-74. For reservations call (800)264-2417. 2015 rates: $15 to $30. (479)761-3325

WEST MEMPHIS — C5 *Crittenden*

WEST MEMPHIS See also Marion & Memphis, TN.

TOM SAWYER'S RV PARK
Ratings: 8.5/10★/10 (RV Park) From Jct of I-40 (exit 280) & ML King Dr, or From Jct of I-55 (exit 4) & ML King Dr, S 2.5 mi on ML King Dr (becomes South Loop Dr) to 8th St, S 0.2 mi over Levy (L).
STAY ON THE MIGHTY MISSISSIPPI
Enjoy watching river traffic from your site! Long, level, concrete, full service pull-thrus on the unspoiled Arkansas Banks of the Mississippi River. Minutes from both I-40 & I-55 as well as downtown Memphis.
FAC: All weather rds. 37 paved, 63 all weather, 82 pull-thrus (30 x 130), back-ins (30 x 60), 100 full hkups (30/50 amps), WiFi, tent sites, laundry, firewood, controlled access. **REC:** Mississippi River: fishing. Pet restrict(B). Big rig sites, 2015 rates: $25 to $45.
(870)735-9770 Lat: 35.12999, Lon: -90.16714
1286 S 8th St, West Memphis, AR 72301
tomsawyersrvpark@gmail.com
tomsawyersrvpark.com
See ad pages 1089, 110.

YELLVILLE — B2 *Marion*

BUFFALO NATL RIVER/BUFFALO POINT (Natl Pk) From town, S 14 mi on AR-14 to AR-268, E 3 mi (E) For reservations call (877)444-6777. 2015 rates: $22. Mar 13 to Nov 15. (870)449-4311

Did you know we sent 35 husband-wife RVing teams out this year to scour North America, rating and inspecting RV parks and campgrounds? You can rest easy when you read our listings, knowing we've already been there.

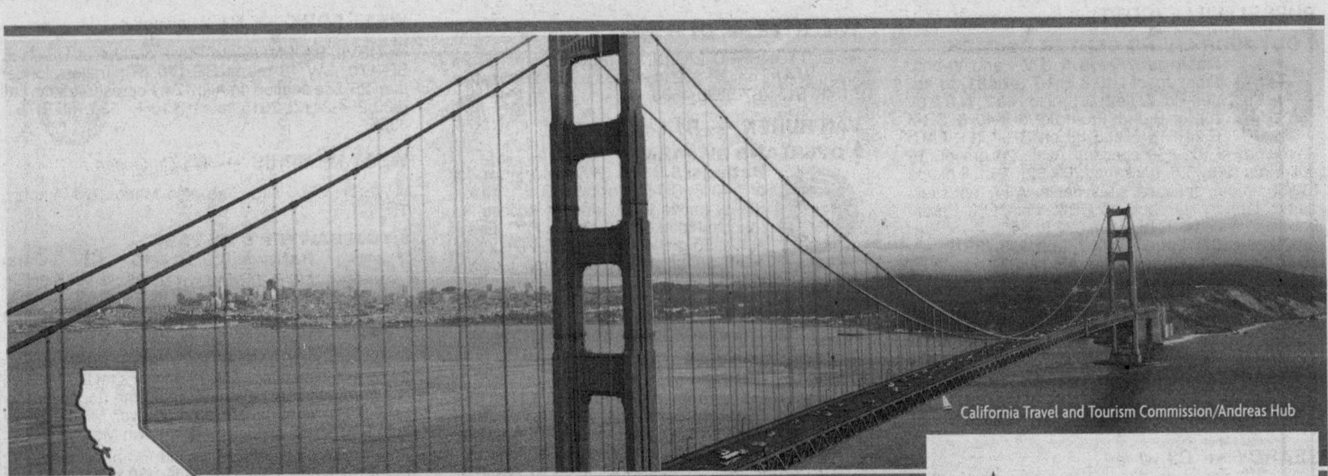
California Travel and Tourism Commission/Andreas Hub

WELCOME TO California

DATE OF STATEHOOD SEPT. 9, 1850	WIDTH: 250 MILES (400 KM) LENGTH: 770 MILES (1,240 KM)	PROPORTION OF UNITED STATES 4.31% OF 3,794,100 SQ MI

For centuries, travelers have felt California's magnetic allure. It's easy to see why. The California that lies beneath the sanitized Hollywood script is a stunning, productive, powerful and diverse state. There are misty redwood forests, scorched deserts that erupt with wildflowers in spring, hundreds of miles of scenic coastline, bucolic wine towns, a robust festival calendar and a host of world-renowned cities.

There's out-there Hollywood, with its movie moment touchstones, San Diego's passionate embrace of every life-affirming moment, Los Angeles, ever glossy, global and optimistic, and trend kick-starter San Francisco. To round it out, California is home to Yosemite, Death Valley and Joshua Tree national parks.

History

In 1847, during the Mexican-American War, Mexico surrendered to John C. Frémont and California became a U.S. territory. Shortly after, the discovery of gold by James W. Marshall at Sutter's Mill compelled a wave of settlers to go west in search of a new gilded life. In 1850, California became the 31st state. The third-largest state in size (after Alaska and Texas) and boasting abundant farmland, California leads the nation in agricultural production.

In the early 20th century, when unrestrained mining, logging and oil-drilling threatened to undermine California's natural wonders, pioneering environmentalists, including John Muir and the Sierra Club, inspired the creation of national and state parks that, today, draw visitors from across the world. In 1964, California eclipsed New York state as the most populous state in the nation. In 2011, 27 percent of California's population was foreign-born, which is double the U.S. percentage.

Play

Carved by massive glaciers some 3 million years ago, Yosemite National Park (a UNESCO World Heritage

Top 3 Tourism Attractions:
1) Disneyland Park
2) Golden Gate Bridge
3) The Hollywood Sign

Nickname: Golden State

State Flower: Golden Poppy

State Bird: California Valley Quail

People: Julia Child, chef; Leonardo DiCaprio, actor; Joe DiMaggio, baseball player; Robert Frost, poet; Jeff Gordon, race car driver; Jack London, author; Sally K. Ride, first American woman in space

Major Cities: Los Angeles, San Diego, San Jose, San Francisco, Fresno, (Sacramento, capital)

Topography: 800-mile mountainous coastline; fertile central valley; east—Sierra Nevada; southern desert basins; north—rugged mountains

Climate: Moderate on coasts; desert temps in the interior; mountain temps in the high sierras

California Travel and Tourism Commission/Andreas Hub

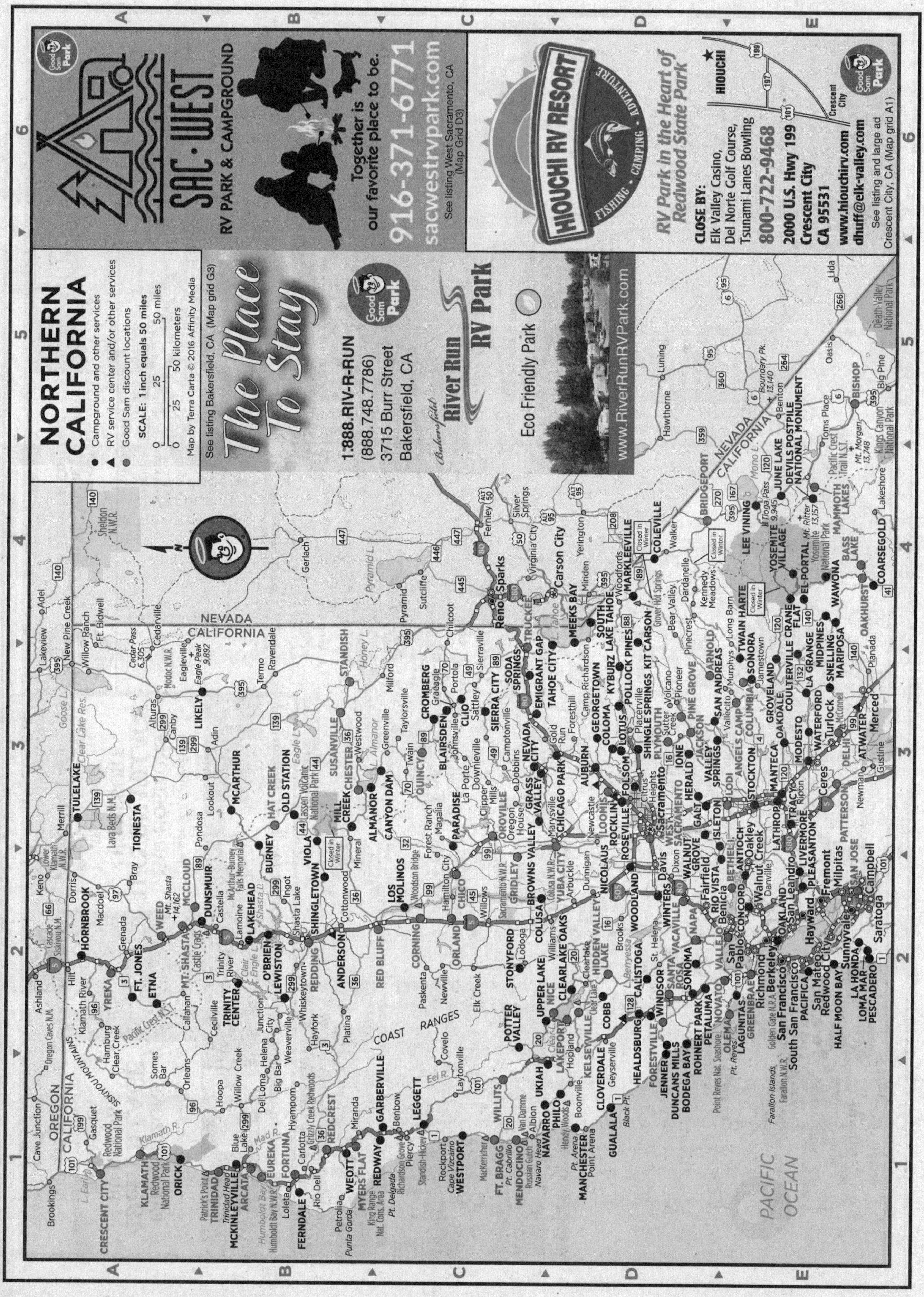
NORTHERN CALIFORNIA
Campground and other services
RV service center and/or other services
Good Sam discount locations
SCALE: 1 inch equals 50 miles
Map by Terra Carta © 2016 Affinity Media
SAC·WEST
RV PARK & CAMPGROUND
Together is our favorite place to be.
916-371-6771
sacwestrvpark.com
See listing West Sacramento, CA (Map Grid D3)
See listing Bakersfield, CA (Map grid G3)
The Place To Stay
1.888.RIV-R-RUN
(888.748.7786)
3715 Burr Street
Bakersfield, CA
River Run RV Park
Eco Friendly Park
www.RiverRunRVPark.com
HIOUCHI RV RESORT
FISHING · CAMPING · ADVENTURE
RV Park in the Heart of Redwood State Park
CLOSE BY:
Elk Valley Casino,
Del Norte Golf Course,
Tsunami Lanes Bowling
800-722-9468
2000 U.S. Hwy 199
Crescent City
CA 95531
www.hiouchirv.com
dhuff@elk-valley.com
See listing and large ad
Crescent City, CA (Map grid A1)
PACIFIC OCEAN
OREGON
CALIFORNIA
NEVADA

SOUTHERN CALIFORNIA
Campground and other services
RV service center and/or other services
Good Sam discount locations
SCALE: 1 inch equals 54 miles
0 25 50 miles
0 25 50 kilometers
Map by Terra Carta © 2016 Affinity Media
SEE LOS ANGELES METRO MAP FOR ENLARGEMENT OF BOXED AREA
THE BEACH IN YOUR BACKYARD!
Campland on the Bay
RVing · Tent Camping · Watersports
Mission Bay, San Diego
See listing San Diego, CA (Map grid K4)
1-800-4-BAY-FUN
www.campland.com
ENJOY a healthy dose of NATURE... Without leaving Civilization!
Every Amenity
Big Rigs
Cottages
Natural Beauty
Golf
Recreation
Free WiFi
Pets Welcome
In California's Wine & Gold Country:
FAR HORIZONS
49er VILLAGE
RV RESORT
Plymouth, CA
See listing Plymouth, CA (Map grid D3)
800-339-6981
www.49ervillage.com
In beautiful Arizona:
FAR HORIZONS
TUCSON VILLAGE
RV RESORT
Tucson, AZ
See listing Tucson, AZ (Map grid E4)
800-480-3488
www.tucsonvillage.com
TOP RATED Good Sam Park FOR 2016
Good Sam Park
Good Sam RATED 10/10★/10
INDIAN WATERS
RV RESORT & COTTAGES
See listing Indio, CA (Map grid J5)
"...A Classic Beauty."
47202 Jackson St. • Indio, CA 92201
760-342-8100
www.IndianWatersRVResort.com

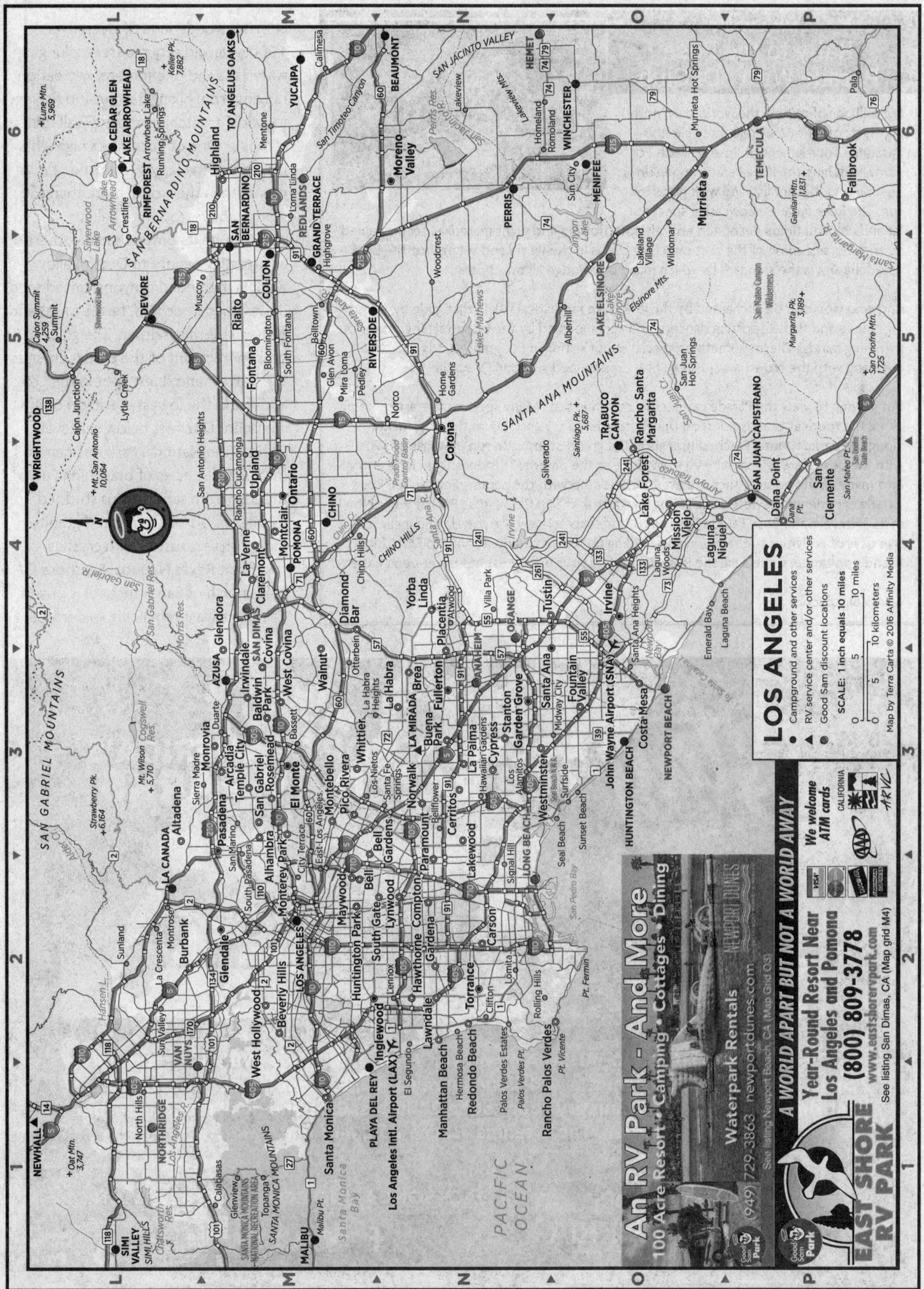
LOS ANGELES
Campground and other services
RV service center and/or other services
Good Sam discount locations
SCALE: 1 inch equals 10 miles
0 5 10 miles
0 5 10 kilometers
Map by Terra Carta © 2016 Affinity Media
An RV Park - And More
100 Acre Resort • Camping • Cottages • Dining
Waterpark Rentals
(949) 729-3863 newportdunes.com
See listing Newport Beach, CA (Map Grid O3)
A WORLD APART BUT NOT A WORLD AWAY
EAST SHORE RV PARK
Year-Round Resort Near Los Angeles and Pomona
(800) 809-3778
www.eastshorervpark.com
See listing San Dimas, CA (Map grid M4)
We welcome ATM cards

CA

- STAY A WHILE -

Rally to the Rose Parade With SOI Club

For millions of people the world over, nothing starts off the New Year quite like the Pasadena Tournament of Roses Parade. For many, watching the Rose Parade in person is high on their bucket list, and with good reason: The Rose Parade, showcasing spectacular and colorful floats decorated entirely with flowers and plant materials, accompanied by trick horses, some of the best marching bands in the world and set against the blue Pasadena sky, is the standard by which many of us judge all other parades.

And who wouldn't be enchanted by the jewel-like fantastical floats that glide by, spouting smoke and flame, sporting dancers, and accompanied by the bone-rattling drums of marching bands? There's something special about sitting in the grandstands and cheering along with the crowd that just can't be experienced via your TV screen.

But getting to view the Parade can seem a daunting task. Many spectators start camping along the route at exactly noon on December 31st to try and secure the best location along the parade route. Purchasing seats in the grand-stands can run upwards of $90, with the best seats selling out well in advance of the parade. This doesn't include entry into many of the popular ancillary events associated with the parade. For the full Rose Parade experience, however, one might take a look at SOI Club's Rose Parade Rally. Now in its 35th year, the Rose Parade Rally has prime seats to view the parade and includes five days of activities to the key events leading up to the parade. Thanks to SOI Club's friendly volunteers, checking the Rose Parade off your bucket list has never been easier.

www.soiclub.com

Site) is a wonderland of deep rivers, 3,000-year-old sequoia trees, plunging waterfalls and phenomenal recreation ranging from hiking, rafting and fishing to wildlife watching and big-wall rock climbing. One of Yosemite's highlights is El Capitan, the largest exposed granite monolith in the world, more than 350 stories above Yosemite Valley.

Despite its ominous name, there's an arresting beauty to Death Valley with its multihued canyons, tinted sand dunes, mudstone hills, fertile oases and 200-square-mile saltpan. The graben (a sunken fragment of the Earth's crust) is the hottest and driest spot in the U.S. and marks the lowest elevation on the continent (282 feet below sea level). Joshua Tree National Park was named for the tall species of branching yucca that rise from sandy plains studded by piles of outsize pink-hued granite monoliths encrusted with crystals.

Point Reyes National Seashore (37 miles north of San Francisco) is one of California's last remaining wilderness

CA

beaches, refuge to seals and migrating California gray whales. Point Reyes affords an excellent network of hiking trails for day hikes and backpacking.

Experience

With a mild climate year round, California's festival calendar is robust and varied. In August, the Outside Lands Music and Arts Festival, held at Golden Gate Park in San Francisco, draws some of the world's top artists. In mid-July, Death Valley is the setting for the Badwater Ultramarathon, a grueling 135-mile race across Death Valley. Runners are undeterred by the fact that the hottest temperature ever recorded was at Furnace Creek: 134 degrees Fahrenheit, reached on July 10, 1913.

In early October, the Savor the Central Coast Festival, one of the most fashionable events on California's food and wine calendar, takes place around Paso Robles, San Luis Obispo and Pismo Beach. In Southern California, Santa Barbara, Los Angeles and San Diego buzz year-round with celebrations and events. Pasadena's Rose Parade boasts more than a century of celebrating the New Year with flower-bedecked floats.

Taste

California cuisine is revered for its celebration of garden fresh ingredients and its triumph of all things local. California produces most of the nation's fresh produce, not to mention more than 90 percent of the nation's winemaking grapes. It's also home to twice as many breweries as any other state.

If you want to improvise in Napa, you don't need a reservation to experience the convivial Bistro Don Giovanni (www.bistrodongiovanni.com), which serves mouthwatering Italian classics, including traditional Neapolitan pizzas, "Mama Concetta's meatballs," and piquant Chicken Diavolo. In the early 1980s, it was Rubio's Fresh Mexican Grill (www.rubios.com) that raised the humble fish taco from street snack to cult status. These days Rubio's is a popular chain, but the original location in Pacific Beach gets as close to the authentic recipe as you'll find anywhere.

TRAVEL & TOURISM

California Travel and Tourism Commission
800-862-2543, 916-444-4429
www.visitcalifornia.com

Anaheim-Orange County CVB
714-765-8888
www.anaheim411.org

Big Sur Chamber of Commerce
831-667-2100

Bishop Chamber of Commerce
760-873-8405
www.bishopvisitor.com

Calaveras Visitors Bureau
800-225-3764, 209-736-0049

Catalina Island Chamber of Commerce and Visitors Bureau
310-510-1520

Chico Chamber of Commerce
800-852-8570, 530-891-5556

Fresno City and County Convention & Visitors Bureau
800-788-0836, 559-233-0836

Lake Tahoe Visitors Authority
800-288-2463, 530-544-5050

Los Angeles CVB
800-228-2452, 213-689-8822
www.lacvb.com

Mammoth Lakes Visitors Bureau
888-GO-MAMMOTH, 760-934-2712
www.visitmammoth.com

Monterey Peninsula
831-649-1770
www.montereyinfo.org

Napa Valley CVB
707-226-7459
www.napavalley.com

Palm Springs CVB
800-417-3529, 760-770-9000

San Diego CVB
619-232-3101
www.sandiego.org

San Francisco Travel
415-391-2000
www.sanfrancisco.travel

San Jose CVB
888-SAN-JOSE, 408-977-0900
www.sanjose.org

Santa Barbara Conference & Visitors Bureau
805-966-9222, 800-549-5133
www.santabarbaraca.com

Sonoma Valley Visitors Bureau
707-996-1090
www.sonomavalley.com

Ventura Visitors and Convention Bureau
800-333-2989 or 805-648-2075

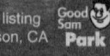

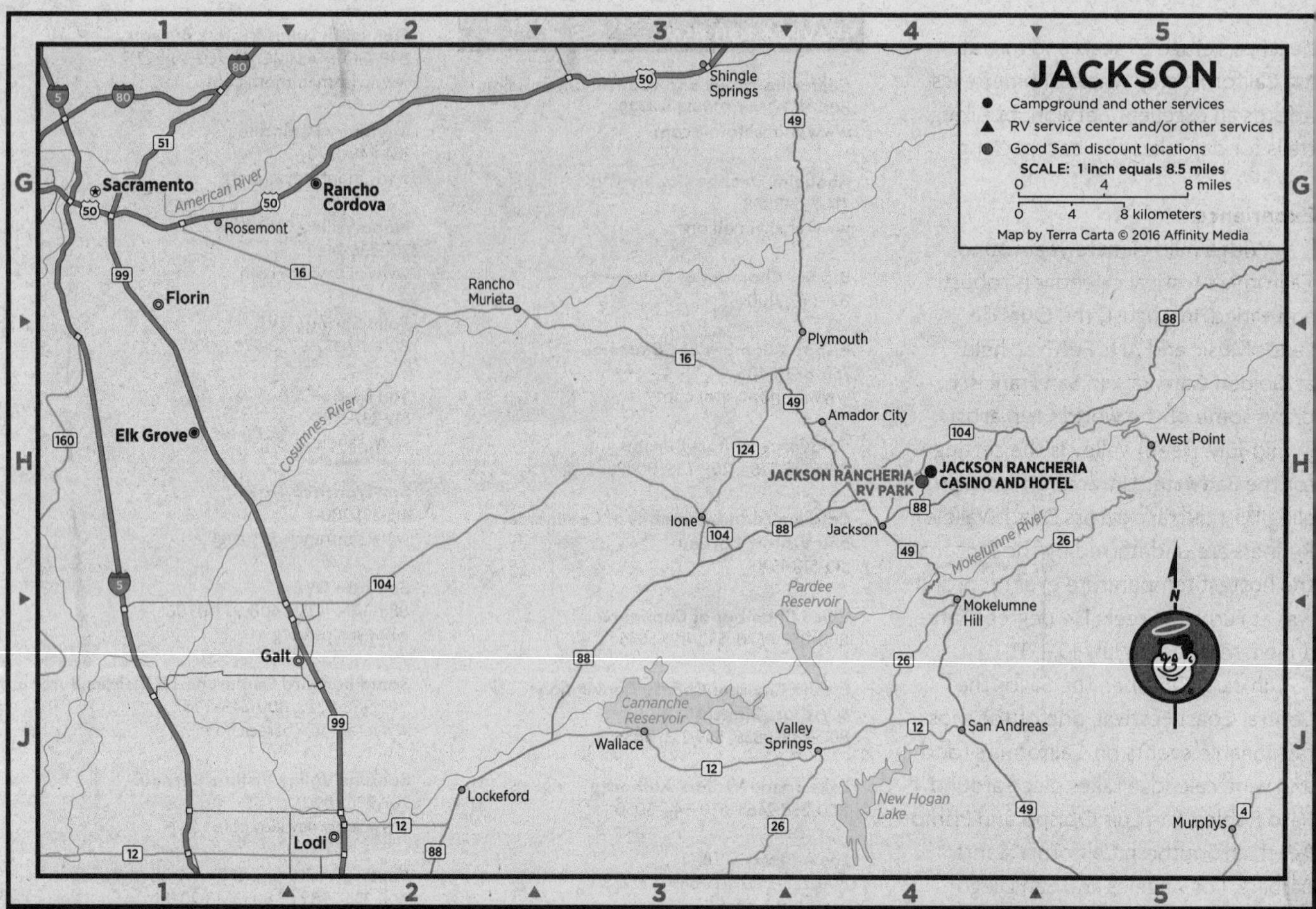
JACKSON
Campground and other services
RV service center and/or other services
Good Sam discount locations
SCALE: 1 inch equals 8.5 miles
0 4 8 miles
0 4 8 kilometers
Map by Terra Carta © 2016 Affinity Media
Sacramento
Rancho Cordova
Rosemont
American River
Shingle Springs
Florin
Rancho Murieta
Plymouth
Elk Grove
Cosumnes River
Amador City
West Point
JACKSON RANCHERIA RV PARK
JACKSON RANCHERIA CASINO AND HOTEL
Ione
Jackson
Mokelumne River
Pardee Reservoir
Mokelumne Hill
Galt
Camanche Reservoir
Wallace
Valley Springs
San Andreas
Lockeford
New Hogan Lake
Lodi
Murphys

Featured Good Sam Parks

SOUTHERN CALIFORNIA

When you stay with Good Sam, you can expect the highest degree of cleanliness and friendliness, and better yet, you get 10% off campground fees.

If you're not already a Good Sam member you can purchase your membership at one of these locations:

ANAHEIM
Anaheim RV Park
(714)774-3860

BLYTHE
Riviera RV Resort and Marina
(855)922-5350

BORREGO SPRINGS
The Springs At Borrego RV Resort & Golf Course
(866)330-0003

CHULA VISTA
Chula Vista RV Resort and Marina
(800)770-2878

DESERT HOT SPRINGS
Caliente Springs Resort
(760)329-8400
Desert Springs Spa & RV Park
(760)329-1384
Sands RV & Golf Resort
(760)251-1030
Sky Valley Resort
(760)329-2909

EL CENTRO
Rio Bend RV & Golf Resort
(760)352-7061

ESCONDIDO
Champagne Lakes RV Resort
(760)749-7572

HEMET
Golden Village Palms RV Resort - Sunland
(866)225-6320

INDIO
Indian Waters RV Resort & Cottages
(760)342-8100
Indian Wells Carefree RV Resorts
(760)347-0895
Shadow Hills RV Resort
(760)360-4040

LAKESIDE
Rancho Los Coches RV Park
(800)630-0448

NEEDLES
Desert View RV Resort
(760)326-4000
Needles Marina RV Park
(760)326-2197
Palms River Resort
(760)326-0333
Pirate Cove Resort
(866)301-3000

NEWPORT BEACH
Newport Dunes Waterfront Resort & Marina
(800)765-7661

NILAND
Fountain Of Youth Spa RV Resort
(760)354-1340

NORTHRIDGE
Walnut RV Park
(800)868-2749

OCEANSIDE
Oceanside RV Park
(760)722-4404

ORANGE
Orangeland RV Park
(714)633-0414

PALM DESERT
Emerald Desert RV Resort - Sunland
(866)226-9001

SAN DIEGO
Campland On the Bay
(800)422-9386
La Pacifica RV Resort
(619)428-4411
Mission Bay RV Resort
(877)219-6900

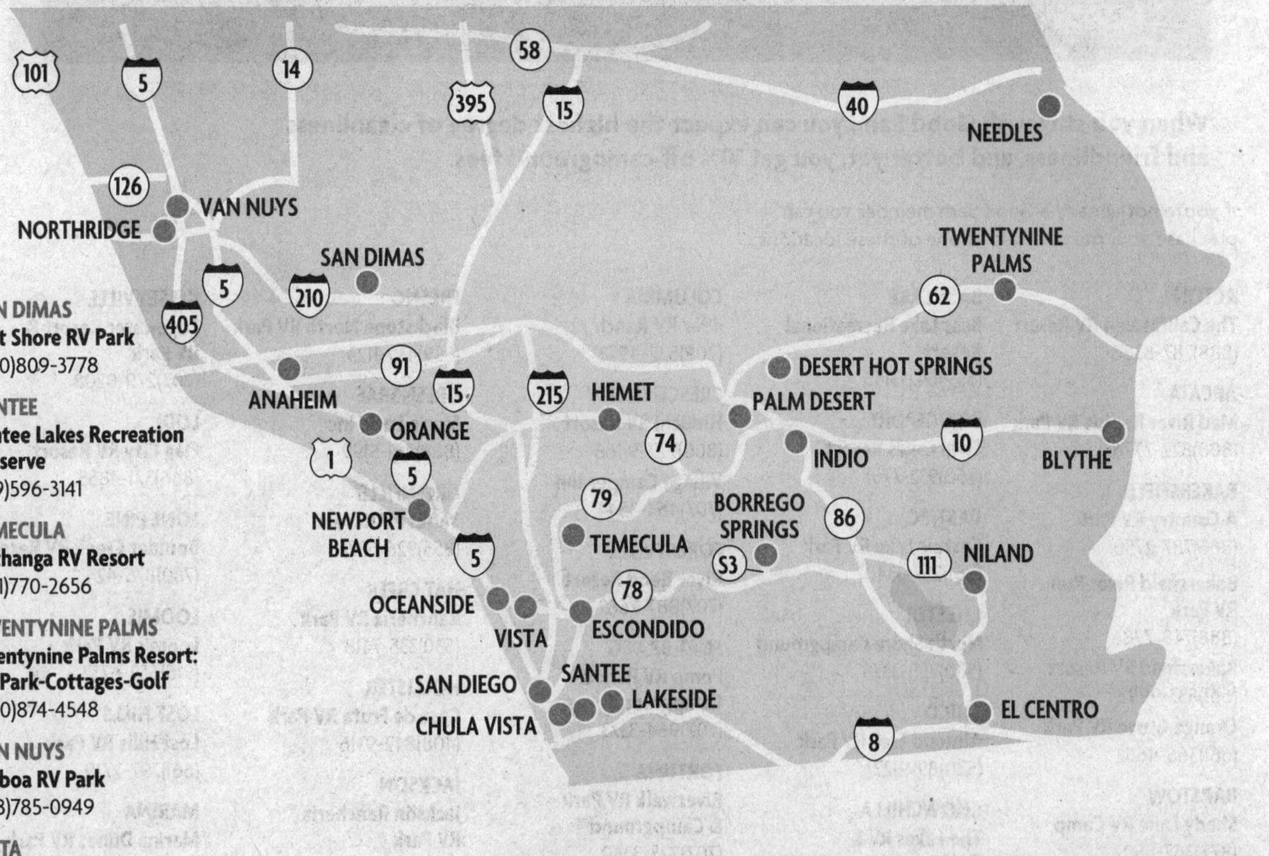

SAN DIMAS
East Shore RV Park
(800)809-3778

SANTEE
Santee Lakes Recreation Preserve
(619)596-3141

TEMECULA
Pechanga RV Resort
(951)770-2656

TWENTYNINE PALMS
Twentynine Palms Resort: RV Park-Cottages-Golf
(800)874-4548

VAN NUYS
Balboa RV Park
(818)785-0949

VISTA
Olive Ave RV Resort
(877)633-3557

For more Good Sam Parks go to listing pages

Featured Good Sam Parks

NORTHERN & CENTRAL CALIFORNIA

Good Sam Park

When you stay with Good Sam, you can expect the highest degree of cleanliness and friendliness, and better yet, you get 10% off campground fees.

If you're not already a Good Sam member you can purchase your membership at one of these locations:

ACTON
The Californian RV Resort
(888)787-8386

ARCATA
Mad River Rapids RV Park
(800)822-7776

BAKERSFIELD
A Country RV Park
(866)787-2750

Bakersfield River Run RV Park
(888)748-7786

Bakersfield RV Resort
(661)833-9998

Orange Grove RV Park
(661)366-4662

BARSTOW
Shady Lane RV Camp
(877)367-8502

BASS LAKE
Bass Lake Recreational Resort
(559)642-3145

BRIDGEPORT
Twin Lakes Resort
(760)932-7751

CASTAIC
Castaic Lake RV Park
(661)257-3340

CHESTER
North Shore Campground
(530)258-3376

CHICO
Almond Tree RV Park
(530)899-1271

CHOWCHILLA
The Lakes RV & Golf Resort
(866)665-6980

COLUMBIA
49er RV Ranch
(209)532-4978

CRESCENT CITY
Hiouchi RV Resort
(800)722-9468

Village Camper Inn
(707)464-3544

FORESTVILLE
River Bend Resort
(707)887-7662

FORT BRAGG
Pomo RV Park & Campground
(707)964-3373

FORTUNA
Riverwalk RV Park & Campground
(707)725-3359

FRESNO
Blackstone North RV Park
(559)439-1123

GREENBRAE
Marin Park, Inc
(888)461-5199

GREENFIELD
Yanks RV Resort
(855)926-5778

HAT CREEK
Rancheria RV Park
(530)335-7418

HOLLISTER
Casa de Fruta RV Park
(408)842-9316

JACKSON
Jackson Rancheria RV Park
(800)822-WINN

KELSEYVILLE
Edgewater Resort & RV Park
(707)279-0208

LODI
Flag City RV Resort
(866)371-4855

LONE PINE
Boulder Creek RV Resort
(760)876-4243

LOOMIS
Loomis RV Park
(916)652-6737

LOST HILLS
Lost Hills RV Park
(661)797-2719

MARINA
Marina Dunes RV Park
(831)384-6914

CA

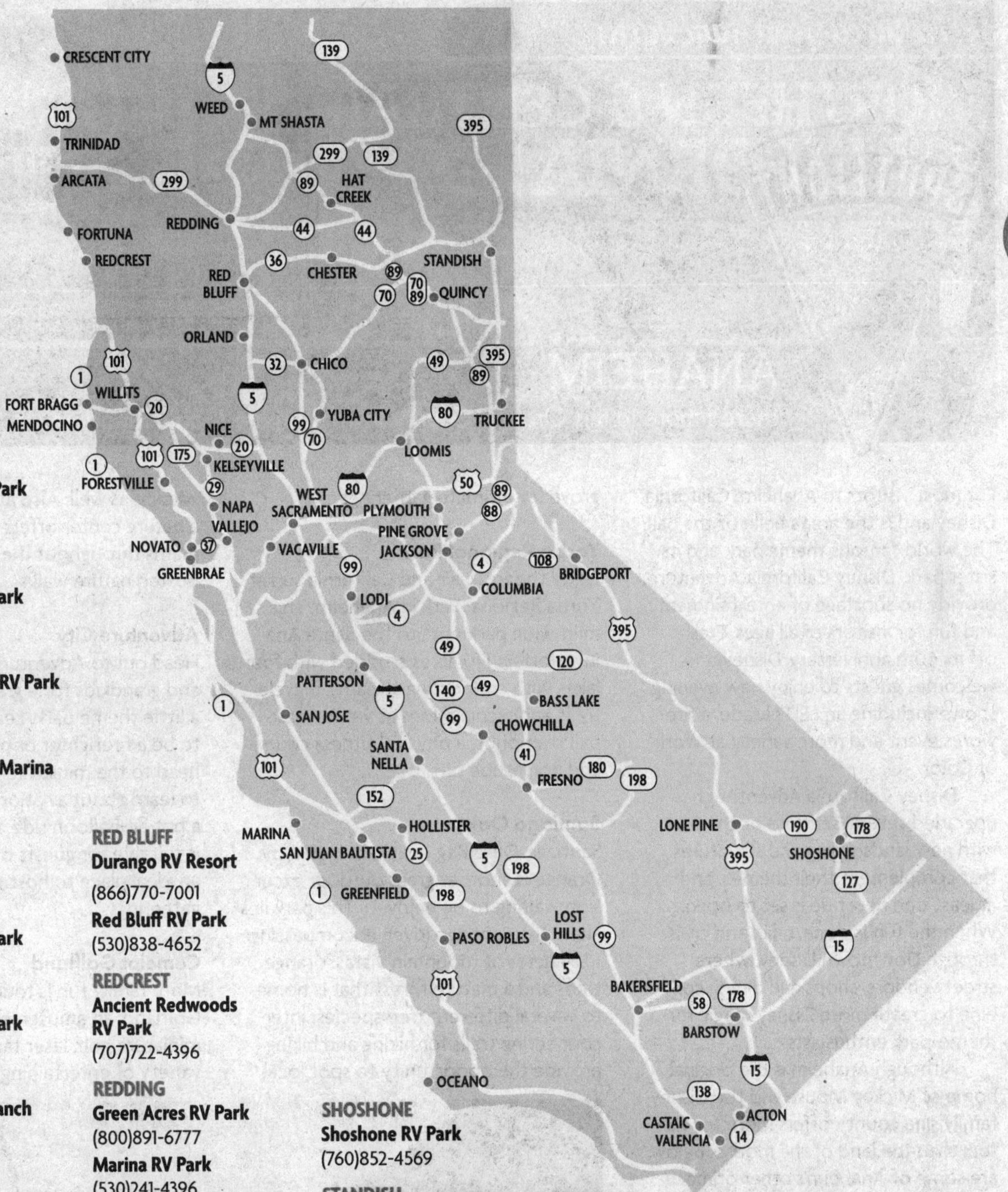

MENDOCINO
Caspar Beach RV Park & Campground
(707)964-3306

MOUNT SHASTA
Abrams Lake RV Park
(530)926-2312

NAPA
Napa Valley Expo RV Park
(707)253-4900

NICE
Aurora RV Park & Marina
(707)274-5531

NOVATO
Novato RV Park
(800)733-6787

OCEANO
Pismo Sands RV Park
(800)404-7004

ORLAND
Old Orchard RV Park
(530)865-5335

PASO ROBLES
Paso Robles RV Ranch
(805)237-8685
Vines RV Resort
(888)710-6552
Wine Country RV Resort
(888)713-0819

PATTERSON
Kit Fox RV Park
(209)892-2638

PINE GROVE
Gold Country Campground Resort
(209)296-4650

PLYMOUTH
Far Horizons 49er Village RV Resort
(800)339-6981

QUINCY
Pioneer RV Park
(530)283-0769

RED BLUFF
Durango RV Resort
(866)770-7001
Red Bluff RV Park
(530)838-4652

REDCREST
Ancient Redwoods RV Park
(707)722-4396

REDDING
Green Acres RV Park
(800)891-6777
Marina RV Park
(530)241-4396
Mountain Gate RV Park
(800)404-6040
Redding Premier RV Resort
(888)710-8450
Redding RV Park
(530)241-0707

SAN JOSE
Coyote Valley RV Resort
(866)376-5500

SAN JUAN BAUTISTA
Betabel RV Park
(800)278-7275

SANTA NELLA
Santa Nella RV Park
(888)826-3105

SHOSHONE
Shoshone RV Park
(760)852-4569

STANDISH
Days End RV Park
(530)254-1094

TRINIDAD
Emerald Forest Of Trinidad
(707)677-3554
Sounds Of the Sea RV Park & Spa
(707)677-3271

TRUCKEE
Coachland RV Park
(530)587-3071
Truckee River RV Park
(530)448-4650

VACAVILLE
Midway RV Park
(707)446-7679
Vineyard RV Park
(866)447-8797

VALENCIA
Valencia Travel Village
(661)257-3333

VALLEJO
Tradewinds RV Park Of Vallejo
(707)643-4000
Vallejo MH Community & RV Park
(707)310-8480

WEED
Trailer Lane RV Park
(530)938-4554

WEST SACRAMENTO
Sac-West RV Park and Campground
(916)371-6771

WILLITS
Golden Rule RV Park
(707)459-2958

YUBA CITY
Travelhome Park
(530)674-8910

For more Good Sam Parks go to listing pages

Anaheim/Orange County Visitor and Convention Bureau

ANAHEIM

There's more to this Orange County town than the Magic Kingdom

For most visitors to Anaheim, California, Disneyland is the area's belle of the ball. The world-famous theme park and its sister park, Disney California Adventure, provide no shortage of entertainment and fun for visitors of all ages. Fresh off its 60th anniversary, Disneyland welcomes guests to enjoy new evening shows, including an LED parade, a fireworks event and more variety at World of Color.

Disney California Adventure has upgraded several sections of the park with new landscaping and structures that complement their themes, and at least one new ride is set to open. When the fun is done, relax and cruise through Downtown Disney, where street vendors, shops and dining combine to create more Disney magic for theme-park enthusiasts.

Although Anaheim is the original home of Mickey Mouse and the Disney family, the county offers more for visitors than the land of the mouse. Below are some of Anaheim's other prime attractions.

Packing District

Downtown Anaheim pays homage to the area's historic citrus-packing industry at the Anaheim Packing District, a collection of refurbished historic structures that now house restaurants. The district's two main buildings are the Packard Building and car showroom (built 1925) and the Anaheim Citrus Packing House (built 1919). In addition to more than 20 dining spots and live music on the weekends, the Packing District offers a community kitchen and a backyard with an adjoining orange grove for intimate gatherings.

Yorba Regional Park

Enjoy the fresh air and California sun at Yorba Regional Park in Anaheim. This mile-wide park next to the Santa Ana River offers 140 acres studded with four lakes with connecting streams, bicycle trails and picnic tables as well as baseball diamonds, a physical fitness course and horseshoe pits.

Santiago Oaks

Santiago Oaks Regional Park in nearby Orange is another great outdoor excursion waiting to be enjoyed. This park lies along the Santiago River, encompassing 1,269 acres of mountain vistas, orange trees and a mature forest that is home to several different tree species. Interconnecting trails for hiking and biking provide the opportunity to spot local wildlife as well. Also at Santiago Oaks, a nature center offers exhibits and pro grams throughout the year, including hosted nature walks.

Adventure City

Head out to Adventure City with kids and grandkids for a great deal of fun in a little theme park. Learn what it's like to be a firefighter or police officer, the head to the miniature airport terminal to learn about aviation and take off in a hot-air-balloon ride. Adventure City is suitable for guests of all ages and is an ideal place to host group and family gatherings.

Camelot Golfland

More family fun is found at Camelot Golfland, an amusement complex with miniature golf, laser tag, bumper boats variety of entertaining rides and games

The Sawdust Art and Craft Festival offers year-round events celebrating local creativity
Anaheim/Orange County Visitor and Convention Bureau

Choose one or two activities or spend the afternoon experiencing everything inside the walls of this castle of fun.

Anaheim Hills Golf Course
Anaheim Hills Golf Course offers a tranquil respite from the busy streets and amusement parks for golfers who want to enjoy the pleasant scenery while working on their swing. Anaheim Hills is a par-71 course dotted with trees and nestled against a quintessential California hillside.

Anaheim Farmers Market
Eat fresh and local at Anaheim Farmers Market, held downtown in conjunction with a craft fair on Thursday afternoons. Local farmers bring their wares for tasting and selling, and artisans tempt shoppers with handmade treasures. Grab a snack from one of over a dozen quick dining establishments selling treats like artisan breads, tamales and kettle corn.

Anaheim Arts
The Sawdust Art and Craft Festival offers year-found exhibits and events for lovers of painting and sculpture. Take a class or peruse a gallery of creative works from local artists. The Bowers Museum in nearby Santa Ana displays everything from Native American artifacts to modern art. Special exhibits for children keep kids engaged.

Ramon Peralta Adobe Historic Site
The Spanish influence on Southern California lives on at the Ramon Peralta Adobe Historic Site. Set on land that once was part of the Rancho Santiago de Santa Ana, the Peralta Adobe houses a museum that features the history of the Santa Ana Canyon, from the time of the earliest Spanish explorers in the late 1700s to the present day. Artifacts excavated on-site are displayed, along with a room furnished in the period style and photographs of the region's early settlers.

Muzeo Museum
Art, culture and innovation combine to enthrall visitors to Muzeo Museum and Cultural Center. In addition to three traveling exhibitions each year, Muzeo displays a wide variety of art and photography themes that provide deep insights into nature, community history, societal trends and more. The adjacent Heritage Center features a reading room in addition to historical documents that are available for research purposes.

SwingIt Trapeze
If you, or a family member, have ever dreamed of running away with the circus, SwingIt Trapeze will train you—or at least provide a taste of the acrobatic life. SwingIt provides trapeze and acrobatic classes by trained professionals, satisfying the high-flying daredevil in all of us.

For More Information

Anaheim/Orange County Visitor and Convention Bureau
855-405-5020
www.anaheimoc.org

California Travel and Tourism Commission
877-225-4367
www.visitcalifornia.com

Vega Photography

BAKERSFIELD

Rock to the Bakersfield sound and savor Basque dishes

At the southern edge of California's Central Valley, Bakersfield has forged its own path through industry and the arts. In addition to a history of successful oil production and agriculture, the city is the birthplace of a singular country-music style known as the Bakersfield Sound. The Bakersfield Sound Museum traces the phenomenon's roots to the 1950s and 1960s, displaying artifacts from musical legends like Merle Haggard, Red Simpson and Buck Owens.

Buck Owens' Crystal Palace is a modern icon of Bakersfield entertainment and the music hall today still offers live music and a museum with memorabilia, guitars and suits from the entertainer's private collection.

Bakersfield is also home to the largest collection of Basque restaurants in the U.S. Don't pass up a chance to taste cuisine from this European community. Good luck choosing from the iconic Noriega Restaurant and Hotel, Wool Growers, Pyrenees Café or any other of the half-dozen establishments serving up traditional dishes. Satisfy a sweet tooth at Dewar's Candy Shop, where taffy has been served for more than 100 years, and where patrons sidle up to an old-fashioned soda fountain for floats and shakes mixed with house-made ice cream.

Bakersfield is home to the largest collection of Basque restaurants in the U.S. Don't pass up a chance to taste cuisine from this European community.

The city's early history and the industry that helped it grow are popular exhibits at the Kern County Museum. The museum's Pioneer Village houses more than 50 historic structures and exhibits on 16 acres, an ideal spot for self-guided learning and discovery. Black Gold: The Oil Experience is an interactive exhibit that invites visitors of all ages to learn firsthand about Bakersfield's primary industry, while the Lori Brock Children's Discovery Center caters to the youngest of explorers with youth-centric displays like Kid City and Safari Art.

Bakersfield Back in Time

Travel further back in time to learn Bakersfield's prehistoric past at

Farmers cultivate rich soil in the Bakersfield foothills. Bakersfield CVB

Buck Owens Crystal Palace. Wiladene Sawyer

the Buena Vista Museum of Natural History. In addition to permanent displays focusing on ancient geology and cultures, the museum hosts fossil digs, rock art tours and geology field trips. View the beauty of the night sky over Bakersfield at the William M. Thomas Planetarium. Located at Bakersfield College, the planetarium offers weekly shows to the public.

Present-day flora and fauna that make their home in Kern County are the residents of the California Living Museum, and Bakersfield's 14-acre zoo. Native animals such as bighorn sheep, raptors, mule deer and mountain lions are among the dozens of creatures sought out by visitors year-round.

Wind Wolves Preserve is where ecologically diverse habitats merge into one 93,000-acre site. Elk, California condors, kit foxes and other native species make their home here. Visitors can take full-moon hikes and blackout hikes to discover how nocturnal creatures live and thrive in their habitats. The preserve also offers outdoor movie evenings for families to enjoy in the shadow of San Emigdio Canyon.

Despite its roughneck reputation, Bakersfield has built a thriving arts community. The city's downtown Arts District is home to theater and concert venues as well as organizations that support and encourage production and display of multiple art forms. A clean-air trolley runs through the district, allowing visitors to tour galleries and shops, and stop for a concert or show at their leisure.

The Bakersfield Museum of Art showcases California artists and their work as well as offering community education and opportunities like summer camps and traveling presentations. Innovative twists on classic themes are the focus of many pieces at the Younger Gallery of Contemporary and Functional Art, which is overseen by the Arts Council of Kern. Metro Galleries presents works in pottery, sculpture and mixed media from artists at varying stages in their careers who represent California and the West Coast.

Peacocks and More

Treat the younger members of your family to an afternoon at Hart Memorial Park, where resident peacocks wander around and where visitors take advantage of soccer fields, lakes, trails and the Kern River. The Kern River Golf Course, adjacent to the park, welcomes the public to hit a few on its manicured greens nestled against the Southern Sierra Nevada.

Learn more about the region's agriculture on a stop at Murray Family Farms. The farm invites visitors on group tours that include hayrides and picking your own fruit, as well as a petting zoo and a giant pillow to jump on. Specialty tours share the day-to-day activities that happen on a working family farm. Find some fun inside Camelot Park, a family entertainment center with an arcade, miniature golf, go-karts and bumper boats. Satisfy your need for speed at Kern County Raceway Park, which features regular Saturday night races.

When the water is flowing through Kern Canyon, hop on a raft and experience whitewater thrills, or take a more relaxed trip in a kayak. Pan for gold along the shoreline or soar over the desert landscape on a paragliding adventure. Ernst Quarries, next to Sharktooth Hill, is a prime spot for digging up ancient treasures left by long-ago residents of the region.

For More Information

Bakersfield Convention and Visitors Bureau
866-425-7353
www.visitbakersfield.com

California Travel and Tourism Commission
877-225-4367
www.visitcalifornia.com

Getty Images/Purestock

BORREGO SPRINGS

Take a rugged desert retreat in this capital of calm

Borrego Springs in scenic southeastern California is a gem of immense seclusion, somehow massive in its smallness and remoteness. Home to fewer than 4,000 year-round residents, it sits tucked in the highly accessible western corner of the punishing Sonoran Desert and finds itself almost completely surrounded by Anza-Borrego Desert State Park—California's largest state park—which sprawls across more than 600,000 acres of sagebrush and desert hardpan.

There's no question about it: If you're chasing a chance to escape from the big city and soak in rugged desert landscapes, Borrego Springs is where you want to be.

From the center of town, the nearest traffic light is 50 miles away. On an average summer day, the temperature is best described as blistering, with the town often being listed as the hottest place in the country. And at night visitors are treated to one of the rarest natural treasures of all: mesmerizing darkness. Look no further than the town's Dark Sky Community status, a classification awarded by the International Dark Sky Association, which is dedicated to minimizing worldwide light pollution. With its massive and undeveloped state park backyard providing a picture-perfect buffer, Borrego Springs is one of only 10 communities in the world to receive the Dark Sky Community honor.

Beating it to Borrego

From a sightseeing perspective, half the fun is found simply in getting here. For most visitors, that will mean making the journey east from either Los Angeles or San Diego. The trip shouldn't take more than three hours, and watching the terrain transform as you move inland from the smooth and sweeping landscapes of coastal California to the ragged and mesmerizing vistas of the majestic Sonoran Desert, is a hard-to-top experience. Somewhere near the halfway mark of your drive you'll begin cruising through Anza-Borrego Desert State Park, and find yourself greeted by sweeping panoramic views of myriad near-and-far mountain ranges: the Bucksnorts, the Santa Rosas, the Jacumbas, the Vallecitos and the Pinyons.

Soon you'll pass the final lonely traffic light of your inbound journey. From here, the theme of trekking deeper and deeper into remote desert backcountry will climax with your arrival in the surprising, utterly charming and very tiny town of Borrego Springs.

The history of Borrego Springs,

High rock walls entice explorers at Anza-Borrego.
Getty Images/iStockphoto

Colorful barrel cacti in the hot desert sun. Getty Images/iStockphoto

California, is long yet charmingly sporadic. The first recorded appearance of Europeans here wasn't until 1772, when members of the San Diego Presidio were moving up through Coyote Canyon in search of deserters. But it was another hundred years before the area begin to be settled by pioneering cattle ranchers. Even then, growth was slow. The first working water well wasn't completed until 1926, and it was only then that any significant degree of farming was able to take root. The first paved roads and electricity appeared during World War II. Soon after the war, the Borrego Springs we know today began to emerge, leveraging its location in Anza-Borrego Desert State Park.

And what a park it is. Recreation hounds and nature buffs will be in their element. Hundreds upon hundreds of miles of well-marked trails wind their way through and around the park, with dozens of trailheads near the town center. Hiking, mountain biking, horseback riding and overnight backpacking trips are among the most popular activities in the park.

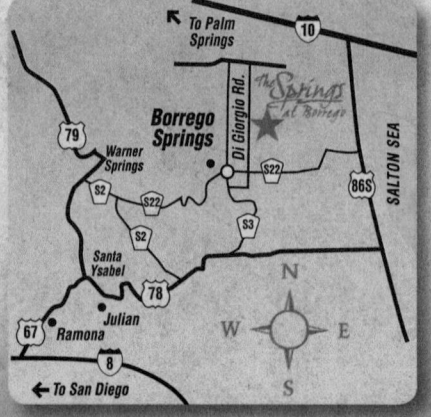

> Borrego Springs is one of only 10 communities in the world to receive the Dark Sky Community honor.

Flowers and Fantastic Views

Despite its desert terrain, Anza-Borrego Desert State Park is renowned for its diversity of flower and plant life, so be sure to stop at the park's main visitor center, where you can stroll through an onsite botanical garden that showcases a wide variety of desert fauna species.

One hour away to the northeast, nature buffs will also want to pay a visit to the Salton Sea State Recreation Area. Hugging the eastern shores of the Salton Sea—the final watery remains of prehistoric Lake Cahuilla—the recreation area is home to 1,400 campsites, multiple boat ramps, five distinct beach areas, myriad hiking trails and a park ranger-staffed visitor center that offers a full schedule of programs, presentations and lecture series throughout the summer months.

Finally, for a blend of the great outdoors and a dash of the surreal, be sure to head into the foothills surrounding Borrego Springs while keeping your eyes peeled for massive metallic monsters bursting out of the dusty desert ground. More than 130 large metal sculptures guard the landscapes around Borrego Springs, with many of them in the Galleta Meadows area. Begun as a free public art project, the sculptures were inspired by a mix of prehistoric creatures and dinosaurs that once roamed the same foothills hundreds of millions of years ago.

For More Information

Borrego Springs Chamber of Commerce and Visitors Bureau
800-559-5524
www.borregospringschamber.com

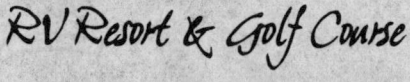

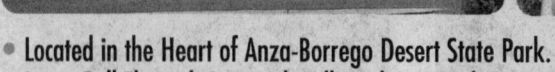

California Travel and Tourism Commission
877-225-4367
www.visitcalifornia.com

GOLD COUNTRY

Mine vacation memories at this treasure-rich destination

Walk in the footsteps of America's great fortune seekers on a trip through California's Gold Country. The state's central region, from Oakhurst to the Sierra Nevada Mountains, is filled with rich finds of Gold Rush history and legend.

Madera County, the southernmost point of Gold Country, welcomes visitors to explore sites rich with prehistory. The Fossil Discovery Center displays fossilized remains of sabre-toothed cats, mammoths and other ancient species that roamed the region. Stop at the Yosemite Mountain Sugar Pine Railroad and hop on board the Logger, a steam-powered train that transports riders for four miles along Yosemite Park's south gate, in the shadow of the Sierra National Forest.

The soil and climate of Madera County yield prized produce, such as wine, grapes and pomegranates. The fruits of the local farmers' efforts are showcased at local cellars and wineries—jump on the Madera Wine Trail to taste the bounty of the region.

Expansive Mariposa County is the original site of 11 additional California counties, and it remains the largest of the state's original 27 counties. This penchant for grandness extends to guests of Mariposa County, who can explore museums and history centers like the California State Mining and Mineral Museum that share the story of the Gold Rush and its impact on the region. Historic buildings remain intact in several small towns, including Coulterville. A stunning natural treasure, Yosemite National Park sits in Mariposa County, and it continues to draw nature lovers for birding, wildflower viewing, skiing and more.

Frontier life is a centerpiece of the Tuolumne County seat, the city of Sonora. The Wild West characters—gamblers, outlaws, miners and painted ladies—have left a lasting mark on the town built by the Gold Rush. Ride a stagecoach in Columbia and visit historic buildings that are still in service in the town of Groveland. Stanislaus National Forest reveals itself to be an ideal spot for fishing, boating, hiking and even panning for gold.

The Wild West characters—gamblers, outlaws, miners and painted ladies—have left a lasting mark on the town built by the Gold Rush.

Fabulous Frogs

Mark Twain, pen name of Samuel Clemens, wrote about a famous jumping frog in Calaveras County, where the state's Gold Rush was born and where towns from the era still stand. Hike into caves speckling the limestone cliffs, or stop in at a local winery for a taste of the region's best vintages. Get your heart racing on a Stanislaus river rafting trip, then wind down with a calming sunset fishing trip.

Amador County lies at the heart of Gold Country, and it speaks to the hearts of visitors who love to seek out antique treasures and trek deep into the earth via gold mines and caves. Thrill seekers climb cliffs or mountain bike through rolling hills, while laidback types will enjoy fishing in streams and lakes or playing a round of golf on manicured greens. See how Amador's early inhabitants lived on a trip to Indian Grinding Rock Historic State Park, and then quench your thirst at a local wine tasting.

California's capital city is the seat of Sacramento County, which also is the gateway to numerous adventures. Traveling to Lake Tahoe takes visitors through the town of Folsom, famous for more than just its prison. The first railroad west of the Mississippi was laid here, and Folsom Lake welcomes watersport enthusiasts for boating and skiing. Folsom and Lake Natoma are bordered by several miles of biking trails. In the heart of Sacramento, stop by Sutter's Fort to learn more about the history of the city.

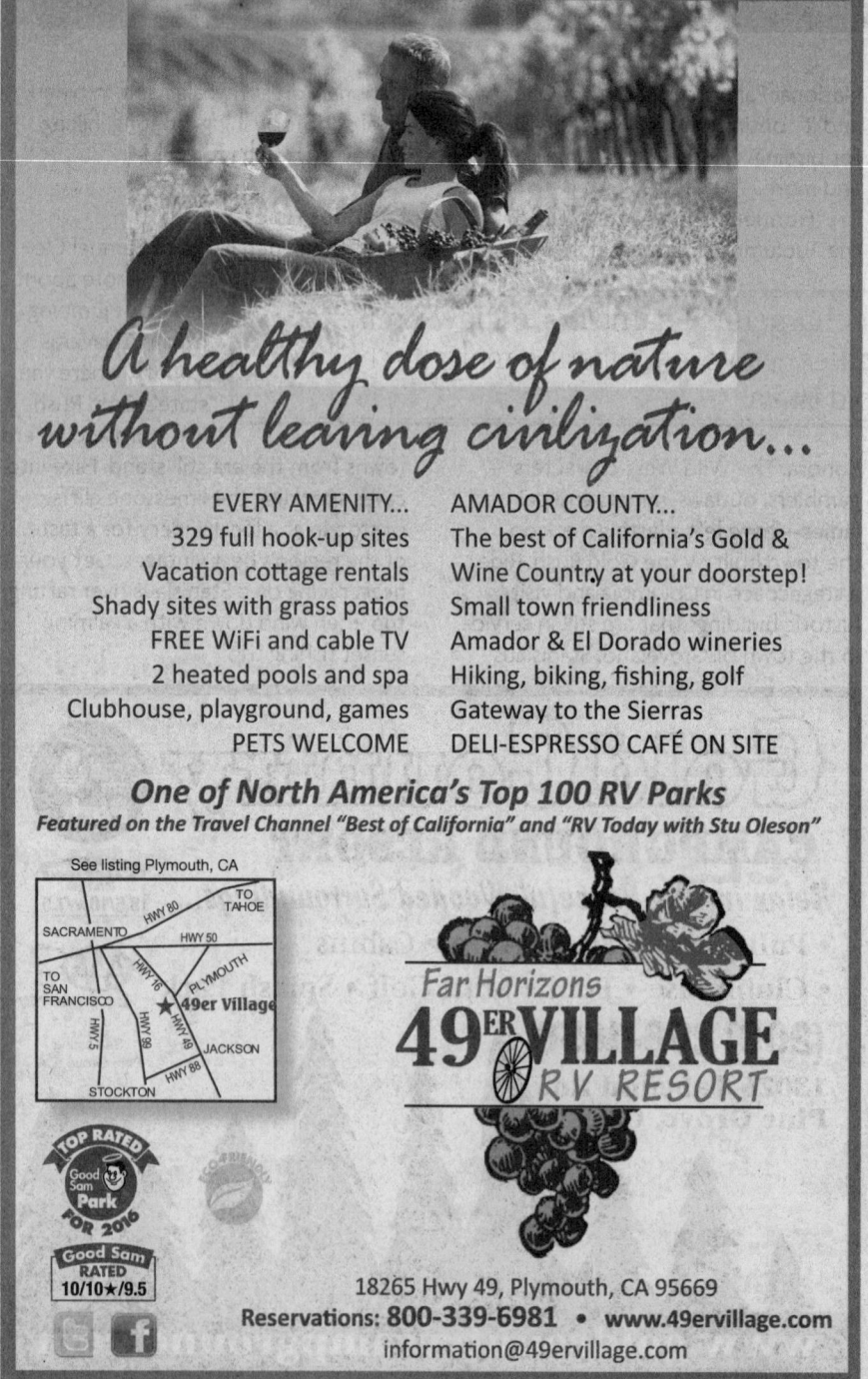

East of Sacramento, El Dorado County includes South Lake Tahoe and its enticing blue water, where skiing and whitewater rafting are just two of the many aquatic activities available to guests. Peruse art galleries and sign up for a tee time at a local public golf course, then pop into a museum where the region's past is impeccably preserved.

The Super Sierra Nevada

The prize of Placer County is the Sierra Nevada, from the valley to the peaks and including Lake Tahoe. Once home to native tribes, Mexican settlers and gold miners, Placer County's history is dotted with war, fortune and industry. Now the towns of Placer County draw visitors in to enjoy muscle cars on cruise nights, see original works of creativity on art walks, and enjoy music festivals and fairs.

The state's richest gold mine is a well-preserved part of Nevada County's history, as are historic downtown structures in the communities of Grass Valley and Nevada City. Tahoe National Forest and Malakoff Diggins State Historic Park attract hundreds of visitors each year with scenic hiking trails and meandering rivers.

Brave adventurers will get a kick out of a llama-assisted wilderness pack trip. Take a boat out on the South Yuba River and drop a line in for some great fishing. Railroad lovers should see the Nevada County Narrow Gauge Railroad and Transportation Museum, where historic Engine No. 5 makes its home.

Sierra County, the northernmost county in Gold Country, is a nature lover's paradise. In the heart of the northern Sierra Nevadas, creeks and rivers, forest meadows and freshwater marshes are preserved for generations to come. The Lakes Basin is a mountainous destination for off-road vehicle riding, hiking and kayaking.

For More Information

Gold Country Visitors Association
800-225-3764
www.calgold.org

California Travel and Tourism Commission
877-225-4367
www.visitcalifornia.com

LOS ANGELES

Shine with the stars or go off the beaten path in eclectic LA

Home to film stars, fashion icons and sports titans, Los Angeles is a patchwork of communities that oozes with cinema history, high and low culture and diverse recreation. Mix it up on a trip to the City of Angels with visits to hidden treasures alongside the more famous landmarks.

> Don't miss Griffith Park, a vast, mountainous civic jewel that's larger than New York's Central Park.

Hurray for Hollywood

If movies move you, the Hollywood Museum is four stories of history in stunning exhibits like Marilyn Monroe's dress, Rocky's boxing gloves and more. The museum, located in the Max Factor building, preserves 10,000 pieces of movie-making history. Jazz lovers have a home in Hollywood, at Loews Hollywood during their Sunday brunch, or at the Catalina Jazz Club.

While in the neighborhood, find out who's playing in the Hollywood Bowl. This 18,000-seat outdoor amphitheater has hosted acts ranging from the Beatles to Barbara Streisand. Nestled in a canyon, the venue's distinctive band shell and fine acoustics draw music lovers from across the world.

Nearby, CBS Studio Center anchors Studio City, once known as Laurelwood. Actors, musicians and writers flock to this creative destination, where El Paradiso is among the landmarks. The prefabricated aluminum home was built in 1964 and considered futuristic at the time.

To the southwest, Century City is the birthplace of the movie business, beginning as the backlot of 20th Century Fox studios. Now the area is a city within a city, the site of commerce and enterprise. But it's also home to the Annenberg Space for Photography, home to images reflecting the human condition. The museum's philanthropy is the basis for themes in many of the collections.

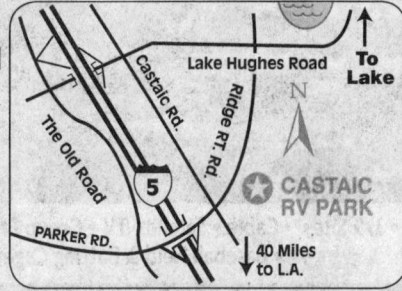

Beverly—Hills, That Is

Revisit Hollywood's Golden Age on a tour of Beverly Hills, home to some of the most famous stars of the silver screen. The Academy of Motion Picture Arts and Sciences is here, and visitors can peruse galleries in the lobby and on the building's fourth floor. The Saban Theatre is an art deco treasure that hosts live productions with an emphasis on Judaism and the arts.

Tired of all the tinsel? Sip a spot of tea at the American Tea Room in Beverly Hills. Once just a tea retailer, the business opened its full-service tearoom for guests who also enjoy accompanying sweet treats including traditional petits fours. Afterward, wander through the Rose Garden at Beverly Gardens Park, where several varieties of the fragrant blooms are grown and displayed.

A hidden retreat in Beverly Hills supplies guests with a taste of the good life at Virginia Robinson Gardens. This six-acre estate is on the National Register of Historic Places. Make an appointment to get away from the hustle and bustle and enjoy the regal surroundings there.

The Hollywood Bowl hosts outdoor concerts. Visit California/Robert Holmes

Cruise Culver City

One of LA's rising jewels, Culver City boasts even more movie history as the home of Metro Goldwyn Mayer/ Sony Pictures and the site of films such as "The Wizard of Oz" and "Gone With the Wind." Aviation pioneer Howard Hughes opened his aircraft plant here in the 1940s as well.

Retreat to a less urban setting at the Baldwin Hills Scenic Overlook, a 511-foot peak that's accessed by concrete stairs or hiking trails. The visitor center features exhibits on the site's history. See up-and-coming actors in a performance at the Kirk Douglas Theatre, housed in a movie palace built in 1947 with a well-preserved exterior.

See how the magic is made on a Sony Pictures Studio Tour on a week-

Dusk at the Griffith Observatory. California Travel and Tourism Commission/Andreas Hub

day. Each tour is unique, but chances are you'll find yourself on a game-show stage, the site where Dorothy followed the yellow brick road to see the wizard, and more.

Peek behind the Iron Curtain at the Wende Musuem and Archive of the Cold War. The influence and eventual collapse of communism in the former Soviet Union is captured in more than 75,000 artifacts from East Germany and former Eastern Bloc countries.

Outdoors, LA Style

Spend a lovely California day outside on a stroll down the North Valleyheart Riverwalk. This 1.9-mile stretch along the Los Angeles River leads visitors past Great Toad Gate, Rattlesnake Wall and Butterfly Garden. More shade grows over the Rainforest Trail in Fryman Canyon Park in the eastern Santa Monica Mountains. The short (one-mile) trail ends at a gully covered by foliage, and it connects with the Dearing Mountain Trail; the latter leads to an outlook point on Mulholland Drive.

Stroll the beach in Santa Monica, located where State Route 1 turns into Interstate 10 and heads east. The iconic Santa Monica Pier offers rides, games and stunning views of the Los Angeles coast. The recreational opportunities are here for one and all. Surf, swim, paddleboard or just spend an afternoon sightseeing.

Outdoor enthusiasts are bound to venture out to Echo Park, not far from Dodge Stadium. They'll also enjoy a day paddleboating on Echo Park Lake, or gearing up for a hearty hike up the Baxter Street Stairs. The 231-step climb shows off great views of LA, including the Hollywood sign.

Don't miss Griffith Park, a vast, mountainous civic jewel that's larger than New York's Central Park and boasts several hiking trails along with stunning views of the sprawling Los Angeles basin. The centerpiece is the Griffith Observatory, which tells the story of our universe with compelling interactive displays.

For More Information

Los Angeles Tourism
888-733-6952
www.discoverlosangeles.com

California Travel and Tourism Commission
877-225-4367
www.visitcalifornia.com

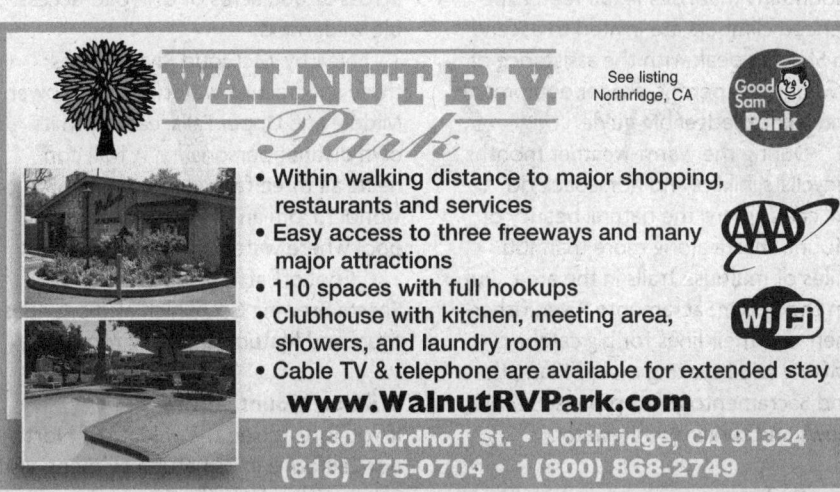

Getty Images/iStockphoto

MOUNT SHASTA

Northern California's iconic peak offers up fun

Mount Shasta is a family-friendly destination that offers world-class skiing, rafting and kayaking—to name just a few popular activities. This region has been home to native peoples, European settlers, gold miners and timber barons.

In the winter, cross-country skiing, downhill skiing and snowboarding bring adventurers to the area's namesake, a single peak in the Cascade chain of mountains that rises 14,180 feet. Experienced climbers are invited to ascend to Shasta's peak with the assistance of a wilderness permit, proper equipment and a knowledgeable guide.

During the warm-weather months, bicyclists, hikers and horseback riders can explore the natural beauty of Mount Shasta along more than 100 miles of multiuse trails in the area. Out on the upper Sacramento River, fishermen cast their lines for big catches. Rafting and kayaking on the Klamath and Sacramento rivers promise scenic views and thrilling whitewater.

Terrific Tours

Take in more of the sights around Mount Shasta on a scenic tour. Several vista points along the slopes of the volcano offer stellar views of the Sacramento River Canyon, the Eddy Mountain and nearby Mount Lassen. If you've got an all-wheel-drive vehicle, venture down Sand Flat Road, which winds through rare red-fir forests before looping back to the highway.

Take your sturdy 4x4 for a spin at the Chappie-Shasta OHV Area, which offers elevations ranging from 600 to 5,000 feet. The diverse terrain stretches across 52,000 acres of off-road-accessible wilderness.

Nearby, McCloud River boasts three spectacular waterfalls: the Lower, Middle and Upper Falls, each with its own distinct personality. A trail connects all three falls; see the natural wonder from an overlook or from a pool where water collects.

Cool off after the tour at Mt. Shasta Brewing Co., which also provides tours and features a tasting room.

Wild on Mount Shasta

If you long to see the wildlife of Northern California in its natural element, visit Shasta Valley Wildlife Area and gaze at pronghorn antelope, coyote, porcupine and several species of game birds, including quail and dove.

Take a guided tour of Lake Shasta Caverns, situated more than 800 feet above Lake Shasta. Paved walkways, stairs and guardrails help visitors safely navigate this subterranean wonderland. Pay an independent visit to Barnum Cave or Pluto's Cave, which were formed by lava.

For More Information

Mt. Shasta Visitors Bureau
530-926-4865
www.visitmtshasta.com

California Travel and Tourism Commission
877-225-4367
www.visitcalifornia.com

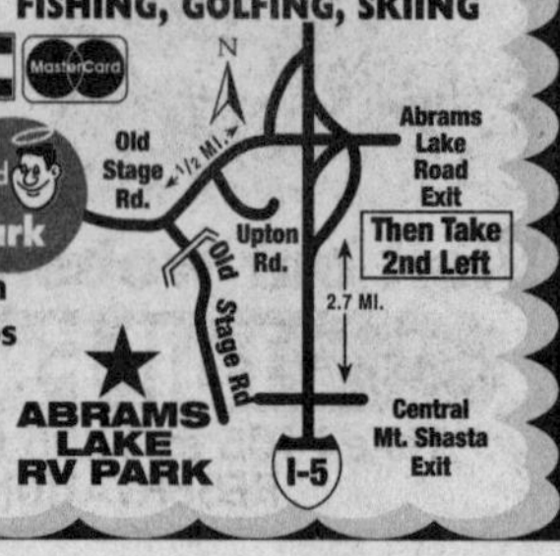

Getty Images/iStockphoto

NORTHCOAST & THE GIANT REDWOODS

Walk among giants in a spectacularly wooded wonderland

Rich biodiversity and towering natural wonders lie at the heart of California's North Coast. Outdoor lovers find paradise among giant redwoods and on hiking trails along coastal cliffs.

The Del Norte Region boasts the Bandon Marsh National Wildlife Refuge, a tidal salt marsh that is home to shorebirds, waterfowl, salmon, bald eagles and brown pelicans. Overlooks allow visitors to see the wildlife without disturbing them. Birdwatchers enjoy spotting sandpipers, plovers, falcons and the rare ruff.

Native residents of the region, the Yurok Tribe, invite visitors to see the Klamath River on an exhilarating jet-boat tour. The tour takes riders 45 miles up the Klamath, and tour guides tell passengers about the history of the river, the people and the wildlife that have made the waterway their home. Bear, otters, elk and golden eagles are often spotted on this exciting trip.

In the heart of Redwood National and State Parks, the Trees of Mystery tours teach visitors about the forest and the legends that have grown alongside these ancient giants. The Skytrail gondolas transport riders through the high canopy for a bird's-eye view of the park's most famous residents, including the Brotherhood Tree, a 297-foot-tall natural wonder that's more than 2,000 years old.

Humboldt County is home to the Avenue of Giants. The stretch of U.S. Highway 101 takes travelers to hiking trails and memorial groves as well as prized fishing spots and swimming holes along the Eel River. On the coast, Humboldt Bay, Trinity River and Trinidad Harbor beckon visitors for kayaking, boating and rafting. See how the winds have shaped this part of the California coast at Ma-le'l Dunes, where sand dunes meet forest and wetlands. The pedestrian-only destination can be explored during daylight hours only.

Looking for fun after dark? Then try your luck at Elk Valley Casino, which features slots, bingo, blackjack and poker. If you're not the gambling type, go for a strike at Tsunami Bowling.

Make a Splash

Enjoy a day or two on the water in Lake County, where California's largest freshwater lake is open for fishing or boating. Clear Lake is also one of the oldest lakes in North America. Boat tours are available for birding, wildlife spotting and photography opportunities. Soak up the California sun in a variety of other ways; spend the morning on a manicured golf course, then take an afternoon horseback ride through vineyards or along forest trails. Clear Lake's volcanic field invites rock hounds to scour for minerals and semiprecious stones.

Marin County combines small-town charm with big adventure. Downtown San Rafael offers a mix of Victorian architecture and ethnic flavors. Visit Art Works Downtown or the farmers market, or just marvel at City Plaza's water wall fountain. In Larkspur, riders of the Golden Gate Ferry take in views of Mount Tamalpais, Angel Island and the Golden Gate Bridge. The culture of Marin's ancient residents is preserved in exhibits at the Marin Museum of the American Indian in Novato, along with Olompali State Historic Park. Novato City Hall resides in a former Presbyterian church, built in 1896.

Kayak through Pacific whitewater in Mendocino County, and trek the Fern Canyon scenic trail system in Van Damme State Park. The park's Pygmy Forest is the home of mature cypress and pine trees ranging in size from 6 inches to 8 feet tall. Ride into history on the Skunk Train, a scenic railway that runs over 30 trestles suspended above mountain streams and passes redwood forests and mountain meadows along its journey into the Noyo River Canyon.

See how the sun sustains life at the Solar Living Institute, a 12-acre renewable energy and sustainable-living site that includes a biodiesel fueling station, organic garden and classic cars that now serve as planter boxes.

California Vintages

Vineyards are the destination *du jour* in Sonoma County, and it's not surprising considering the region's fame as a producer of extraordinary varietals. More than 400 wineries call Sonoma home, and they open their doors to thousands of tourists each year. Visit the Green Music Center and Wells Fargo Center for the Arts to taste the culture that grows in the region.

Families enjoy trips to Sonoma County where the ocean and forests meet, and Charles M. Schulz—the creator of "Peanuts"—has a museum in his honor. Sonoma TrainTown invites rail fans of all ages to enjoy a remarkable scale railroad, and everyone can enjoy outdoor fun at Spring Lake Regional Park. The Environmental Discovery Center, located at the park, connects visitors with the natural world.

For More Information

Humboldt County Convention and Visitors Bureau
800-346-3482
www.redwoods.info

California Travel and Tourism Commission
877-225-4367
www.visitcalifornia.com

Redwoods in the mist off of Highway 101. Getty Images/iStockphoto

Getty Images/iStockphoto

PALM SPRINGS

Find fun and culture in SoCal's favorite desert getaway

'alm Springs is an eclectic cocktail of :alifornia cultures and attitudes. The ;unny SoCal town is a desert oasis that's)een home to both 1ative peoples and nodern Hollywood egends. It is equal)arts desolate)eauty and modern ıesthetics, and you'll find plenty to ›xplore both inside and out.

Situated 100 miles east of Los \ngeles, Palm Springs seamlessly blends :he trendy sophistication of the City of Angels with the vibrant sensibility of ;outhwestern desert culture.

'alm Springs' Past

f native history appeals to you, learn about the area's earliest inhabitants at the Agua Caliente Cultural Museum. The Agua Caliente, a band of Cahuilla Indians, made the present-day Palm Springs region their home and built their society around the mineral springs that fed the land. The museum's exhibits tell the stories of the Agua Caliente culture, way of life and role in the development of the region.

> In Cahuilla Canyon Country, hikers can gaze in wonder at California fan palms rising above rocky landscapes.

The modern-day history of Palm Springs is shared by the Palm Springs Historical Society, which conducts several tours of the city for visitors eager to see how Hollywood's elite lived when not working under the lights.

Tour guests can also visit the McCallum Adobe, built in 1884 by the area's first European-American settler, John McCallum. It sits adjacent to the Cornelia White House, built in 1893 of recycled railroad ties. A museum and cultural center display items relating to early life in the city.

A tour of the historic O'Donnell House introduces guests to the story of one-time owner Thomas O'Donnell and his contributions to the valley region. Exhibits also chronicle challenges faced

Palm Springs Aerial Tramway.
Getty Images

SANDS RV & GOLF RESORT
California's Greater Palm Springs Area
Good Sam Park
Affordable Luxury - Where the FUN Shines All Year Long!
At the beautiful Sands RV & Golf Resort in California's Coachella Valley, you'll find yourself warmed by gentle California sunshine just minutes above Palm Springs—and surrounded by the majestic scenery of the San Jacinto Mountains and San Gorgonio Wilderness. Enjoy excellent recreational opportunities, the best in quality RV resort accommodations, golfing at our executive nine-hole golf course, and clubhouse activities just minutes from the glamour, fun, and excitement that makes the Greater Palm Springs area world-famous.
You'll find plenty of planned activities to keep you entertained when you're away from the golf course, including the latest additions to our Sport Complex, Pickle Ball and Bocce Ball courts. The Oasis Hall in our beautiful and spacious clubhouse provides a generous area for dances, dinners and entertainment. And for the dog lovers, our resort is known for having one of the best enclosed grass Dog Parks. Whether you're a first-time visitor or a long-term resident who travels year after year to reside at our beautiful resort, you'll find there's always something fun and entertaining going on with our full activities schedule!
16400 Bubbling Wells Road • Desert Hot Springs CA 92240
866.559.7298 • www.cal-am.com/resorts
CAL AM RESORTS
See listing Desert Hot Springs, CA

Frank Sinatra's historic Palm Springs residence. Palm Springs Bureau of Tourism

y the city's founding families.

Ruddy's General Store Museum is private collection of retail items from he 1930s and 1940s. Young visitors can earn what a trip into town might have een like, and older guests will enjoy eminiscing about items they once saw their own homes as children.

The Palm Springs Art Museum ombines modern and contemporary works with traditional Native American art in a setting that astounds and delights the senses. Photography from Ansel Adams, sculptures from Alexander Calder and paintings by Pablo Picasso are just a few of the treasures that reside in this world-class collection. The museum's Architecture and Design Center showcases historic buildings and mid-century modernist homes like those found throughout the city.

Hiking the Desert

In Cahuilla Canyon Country, hikers can gaze in wonder at stately California fan palms rising above rocky landscapes and growing on the banks of streams. Rock formations give way to perennial creeks, and a sighting of the area's bighorn sheep is a rare treat. The canyon trading post provides maps and guidelines for hiking in a safe and respectful manner. In the Coachella Valley Preserve, Willis Palms Trail leads to a virtual palm oasis. Nearly 200 bird species roost in the area, and observant visitors might catch a glimpse of the Coachella fringe-toed lizard, a protected species.

Challenge yourself on the South Lykken Trail, which rises in elevation from 560 feet to more than 1,400 feet. The hike is roughly three and a half miles and treats visitors to stunning views of Palm Springs, the Coachella Valley and Tahquitz Canyon.

Established in 1938, the Moorten Botanical Garden preserves desert flora from the region. Take a guided walk through this "living museum" to see plants along with ancient fossils, pioneer artifacts and geological exhibits.

Play Time in Palm Springs

Enjoy a cool desert morning at one of Palm Springs' verdant golf courses, where seasonal rates and public accessibility invite players to tee off amid desert splendor year-round. Choose from 18 or 27 holes on courses designed by masters like John Fought and Gary Player.

Step off the green and see Palm Springs from the sky on a biplane tour. This special treat puts guests in the seat of a vintage aircraft for aerial tours of the desert oasis and surrounding landscapes. Equally enjoyable is a land-based trek through Palm Springs on horseback. Local stables offer trail rides through mountain and canyon passes, as well as ranch rides.

Laidback family fun is the goal at local hangouts like Ruth Hardy Park and Demuth Park. Both parks have public tennis courts as well as a children's play area, and Demuth features baseball diamonds and batting cages. Palm Springs Swim Center invites sunbaked visitors to cool off in its Olympic-sized swimming pool, which is open year-round. Wet 'n Wild in Palm Springs is a daredevil's dream with water slides and a wave pool to keep the kids busy.

Take home a piece of Palm Springs from retailers that do business in the trendy El Paseo Shopping District. This collection of home décor boutiques, art galleries and gift shops offers something for everyone.

Salty Sojourn

Palm Springs has no shortage of day-trip possibilities, and a short drive south will take you to the Salton Sea, an eerily beautiful lake that keeps visitors coming back again and again.

Created by an engineering accident when the Colorado River breached a canal in 1905, the Salton Sea is an anomaly. It is so massive that in some places you can't see the other shore because of the curvature of the Earth. Only Death Valley is farther below sea level, and the shimmering heat waves rising off the desert floor add to the mirage effect. The approach alone is worth the trip. Luckily, the sea lies on the Pacific flyway and attracts an astounding 400 varieties of migrating birds each winter.

Outdoor diners make a toast. Palm Springs Bureau of Tourism

Exploring a canyon by jeep. Palm Springs Bureau of Tourism

The communities that have formed on the water's edge are some of the more resilient and interesting anywhere in the country.

Desert Wine

Wine lovers will enjoy satisfying sips at famed Spencer's Restaurant, where watching the sunset from the mountainside patio truly enhances the experience. Get a musical blast from the past with your appetizers at Purple Room Restaurant and Stage, where dinner comes with a live show and a plateful of history.

Palm Springs is a veritable wellspring of creativity, and the array of independent shops featuring one-of-a-kind pieces of furniture, accessories and more will provide an interesting browsing experience for lovers of great design. A safe bet is the Palm Springs Art Museum, home to a stellar collection of oustanding original art.

Cool Coachella

Take a short trip down to Coachella Valley to enjoy a true oasis in the Thousand Palms Oasis Preserve. This spot of respite features a visitor center and offers guided hikes along 25 miles of trails that wind through hundreds of acres of desert wilderness.

If you've got a day to spare, the Mojave National Preserve, a three-hour drive north, is just as refreshing an escape from urban life.

Before gold fever struck California, the Mojave Desert was home to Chemehuevi and Mojave tribes who lived on the flora and fauna of the valley. Petroglyphs remain, along with tools, artifacts and pictographs throughout the preserve, telling the story of the clans who lived there.

For an epic experience, take a scenic drive down Essex Road, Canyon Road and Black Canyon Road; they lead to stopping points like Rock Spring and adjacent wayside exhibits that detail the history of the Mojave tribe and the U.S. Army presence during the early days of U.S. settlement. At the north end of Black Canyon, get your hiking boots on and explore Hole-in-the-Wall, a cluster of rhyolite cliffs riddled with holes and hollow spaces.

If you just want to relax, you'll be pleasantly surprised. The average winter temperature is 77 degrees and the

Palm Springs Art Museum.
Palm Springs Bureau of Tourism

Chic shopping in Palm Springs. Palm Springs Bureau of Tourism

warm days cool off to starry nights. The Coachella Valley is like no other, and there's a lot more to the area than the glitz and glamour of Palm Springs.

Coachella Valley History

Make sure you save time to visit the Coachella Valley History Museum, a repository of the area's colorful past that's much more than a collection of artifacts. It's home to a historic 1909 local schoolhouse and the world's only Date Museum. Browse the displays and learn more about the area's earliest settlers, the Cahuilla and Chemehuevi tribes, as well as the history of the local railroad industry and agriculture. A trip to the museum wouldn't be complete without a walk through the variety of gardens, including the Japanese Garden, Geissler Rose Garden and the Jardin del Deierto.

Desert Homes to the Stars

One of the allures for visitors to Palm Springs is the abundance of mid-century modern residential architecture that dots the landscape around town. From simple dwellings to sprawling single-story mansions, Palm Springs has long served as a blank canvas for architects eager to experiment with new designs. Among the hallmarks of this design style are ample glass, clean lines, and the use of both natural and manufactured resources. Much of the architecture was influenced by the rugged desert landscape, and for residents, comfort and style were paramount.

One of the most famous of these structures is the home of Frank Sinatra, who came to town in 1947 after having signed a lucrative contract with MGM. Working with architect Roger Williams, the crooner requested a Georgian-style mansion. The architect pursuaded Ol' Blue Eyes to go with a structure that harmonized with the stark desert surroundings. When the house was completed, architectural history was made.

Sinatra's 4,500-square-foot Twin Palms house features four bedrooms, seven bathrooms and a piano-shaped swimming pool. Ample patio space and shady overhangs make the home an ideal place to entertain guests during warm desert days and nights. The house was often the site of furious spats between Sinatra and his wife, fellow movie star Ava Gardner; one of the sinks has a crack from a campagne bottle that Sinatra hurled at her.

Today, the house can be rented out for corporate events and parties. Take a drive by the house and get a sense of Hollywood star power for yourself. While in the neighborhood, discover the houses of the Hollywood glitterati who followed Sinatra's lead and discovered glamor in the desert.

For More Information

Palm Springs Visitors Center
800-347-7746
www.visitpalmsprings.com

California Travel and Tourism Commission
877-225-4367
www.visitcalifornia.com

Getty Images/iStockphoto

SAN DIEGO

California's vacation mecca entrances beach combers and history buffs alike

The storied history of San Diego is only part of its charm; taken with the multicultural legacy and cosmopolitan cultural attractions, this seaside destination satisfies visitors who seek a day at the beach, a stroll through a timeless shopping district or a jaunt to a museum.

Seemingly endless stretches of beach await adventurous visitors, and its two fantastic bays—Mission Bay and San Diego Bay—offer seemingly endless water recreation.

> Located on San Diego Bay, the Maritime Museum of San Diego is a collection of ships that sailed the coast from California's early days to the Cold War.

Historic Old Town

Start at the beginning. Visit Old Town San Diego State Historic Park in the heart of the city to experience the heritage of early San Diego. This neighborhood truly provides a connection to the past.

Learn about life in the Mexican and

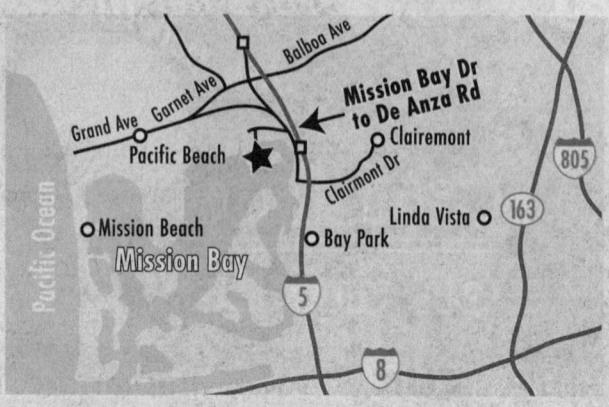

early American periods of 1821 to 1872. Even today, life moves more slowly in this part of San Diego, where the hustle and bustle of visitors is balanced with history and fiestas. Look into yesteryear and see how converging cultures transformed San Diego from a Mexican pueblo to an American settlement.

The core of restored original historic buildings is complemented by reconstructed sites, along with early 20th-century buildings designed in the same vein. The Historic Plaza remains a gathering place for community events and historic activity. Five original adobe buildings are part of the historic park, which includes museums, unique retail shops and several restaurants.

Equally significant in the development of San Diego is the city's history as a military port and shipping hub. Located on San Diego Bay aboard the *Berkley*, a century-old steam ferry, the Maritime Museum of San Diego offers a look into the region's seafaring past. Moored nearby are vintage ships that sailed the coast from the state's

The Balboa Park Botanical Garden.
Getty Images/iStockphoto

early days all the way to the Cold War. Among the ships in the collection is a replica of the *San Salvador*, which sailed into San Diego Bay in 1542 and was captained by explorer Juan Rodriguez Cabrillo. Roam the museum's galleries and marvel at the intricate models of famous ships. You can even take a tour of San Diego harbor in a vintage craft with a helpful guide at the helm.

See where faith and frontier came together in Mission Basilica San Diego de Alcala, California's first Mission Church. The mission was founded in 1769; today, it still serves an active congregation. Over the years, it has been renovated to resemble its 18th-century grandeur.

Balboa Park

You won't be in San Diego long before you learn the directions to Balboa Park. These 1,200 acres were officially declared a park in 1868. But you won't find meandering paths with strollers and parasols. Once a scrub mesa inhabited by rattlesnakes, the park was transformed into an elegant showcase of architecture, landscaping and culture. In 1915, San Diego used Balboa Park to put on the Panama-California Exposition, becoming the smallest city to attempt a world's fair.

Balboa Park also boasts the Spreckels Organ Pavilion, one of the world's largest outdoor pipe organs. The grand instrument was donated to the park in 1914, and today guests enjoy weekly free concerts on Sundays. The organ houses 4,530 pipes ranging in size from as small as a pencil to as large as 32 feet tall.

The Botanical Building and Lily Pond in Balboa Park form a welcome oasis on sweltering days. Here, more than 2,100 plants flourish, including ferns, orchids, palms and seasonal flower displays. Nearby is the San Diego Natural History Museum, with dozens of permanent displays and continuously rotating exhibits that showcase the earth's biological and geological past and present.

Mission Basilica San Diego de Alcala. Getty Images/iStockphoto

Hit the Beach

San Diego's celebrated coastline provides virtually unlimited entertainment and recreation, from surfing to shell collecting to exploring sandy beaches. Shell Beach Tide Pools, at the south end of Scripps Park in La Jolla, is a collection of tide pools that reveal their tiny inhabitants at extremely low tides; nearby Seal Rock Reserve is a popular spot for seals and sea lions to sun themselves, taking in as many fascinated stares from tourists as they do the afternoon rays.

The La Jolla Cove is the ideal spot for relaxing water recreation such as kayaking, snorkeling and diving. This calm stretch of water is also a protected home for leopard sharks, rays and yellowtail. Rent a kayak and explore the La Jolla Sea Caves within a 75-million-year-old sandstone cliff. Once used by smugglers to bring immigrants to America, most of the caves are only accessible from the water.

San Diego's celebrated coastline provides virtually unlimited entertainment and recreation, from surfing to shell collecting to exploring sandy beaches.

In the San Diego-La Jolla Underwater Park, four distinct habitats are visible here—rocky reefs, kelp beds, sand flats and underwater canyons—which are revealed more fully through snorkeling or scuba diving. Get an up-close look at more marine wildlife in Birch Aquarium, part of the Scripps Institution of Oceanography. Here, guests can get to know the residents of a tide pool through interactive exhibits, and watch aquarium staff feed the many residents, including a loggerhead sea turtle.

Further south, view the coastline from on high at Sunset Cliffs Natural Park. Sunset Cliffs runs along Point Loma peninsula's western shore and offers ocean views as well as glimpses of cliff formations, caves and an intertidal area.

Head out into the open ocean for a day of dolphin or whale watching with any of several tour companies. Gray whales, humpback and fin whales, and blue whales travel through these waters at different times during the year.

Slip a little shopping into your busy schedule at Seaport Village. This collection of shopping, dining and entertainment establishments satisfies a plethora of tastes and appetites. You'll hear everything from classic rock and pop standards to traditional Greek music.

Little Italy is a source of cultural pride in San Diego. This community celebrates and preserves its heritage as an enclave that supports residents and businesses who make their home here. Food, music and film are celebrated annually, and its landmark structures are well preserved.

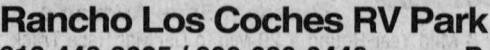

The town's center may have shifted, but the importance of the military never disappeared. San Diego

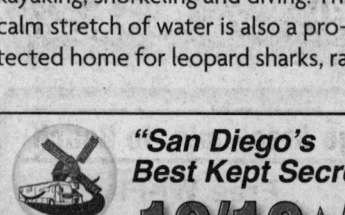

Surfers on the La Jolla coastline. Getty Images/iStockphoto

boasts one of the largest concentrations of fighting forces on the globe. The city is the principal port of America's Pacific Fleet.

Ship Ahoy!

If you're interested in U.S. naval history, you can experience life aboard the *USS Midway*, anchored in the San Diego harbor. The largest ship in the world when she was put to sea in 1945, more than 225,000 sailors served on the aircraft carrier until it was decommissioned in 1991. The *USS Midway* is now the country's most-visited naval ship museum, with 29 restored aircraft and two flight simulators to allow landlubbers a chance to "ride" in a fighter jet cockpit.

Across San Diego Bay is Coronado Island, the base for the North Island Naval Air Station and its elite corps of Navy SEALS. The Hotel del Coronado, playground of movie stars and the rich and famous, is also here. The island's sparkling white sand beaches are perennially ranked among the finest in the nation. Just up the coast along Mission Bay is SeaWorld, a marine theme park filled with thrilling exhibits, shows and demonstrations of sea life.

Unlike other major cities that seem to be in a hurry to build bigger and gaudier office towers, a chunk of downtown San Diego still lingers in the late 1800s. These three- and four-story Victorian buildings are congregated in a 16-block area called the Gaslamp Quarter. This is where San Diego shops during the day and parties at night. Festivals and events are a staple of the Quarter, including Taste of Gaslamp, ShamROCK on St. Patrick's Day, a Mardi Gras celebration and the Street Scene Music Festival.

A block away from the Gaslamp Quarter is Petco Park, home field to Major League Baseball's San Diego Padres. Sculpted from native sandstone and stucco, the ballpark features a grassy slope beyond the left field wall where fans can watch big leaguers for a great price. On non-game days, it's open as a public park.

Tasty Tacos

Can't decide between San Diego's many seafood and Mexican specialty restaurants for dinner? Seek out Oscar's Mexican Seafood. It's ranked as the No. 13 restaurant in the country in Yelp's first-ever ranking of the best restaurants reviewed on its website. Oscar's is a classic local hole-in-the-wall taco shop, and it would go unnoticed, if not for the crowds outside waiting for spicy shrimp and surf and turf tacos.

And never come to San Diego without your dog. North Ocean Beach, also known as Dog Beach, is the second largest leash-free beach in America, with 38 acres of sand. Hundreds of tail-wagging canines visit Dog Beach every week to frolic in sand and sun.

Off to the Races

Just north of San Diego on Interstate 5, Del Mar offers great horse racing action. Advertised as the place where "the surf meets the turf," the Del Mar Thoroughbred Club caters of horse-racing enthusiasts just a short distance from the Pacific Ocean. Lay down your bets on a fast horse and watch the action as it circles the track.

For More Information

San Diego Convention and Visitors Bureau
619-236-1212
www.sandiego.org

California Travel and Tourism Commission
877-225-4367
www.visitcalifornia.com

Getty Images/iStockphoto

SAN FRANCISCO

Peer beneath the surface of the City by the Bay

The ring of cable car bells and the sound of foghorns on the bay are synonymous with legendary San Francisco. But there's much more to this metropolis than the Golden Gate Bridge and Alcatraz Island.

Founded more than 200 years ago, the iconic city's cultural treasures and rolling landscapes have made it a favorite travel destination for over a century. Stay at one of the many RV parks located just outside the city, then take the area's mass transit into its legendary neighborhoods.

> Some tours will take visitors up the winding Lombard Street, which climbs the steep terrain in a distinctive serpentine pattern.

Cosmos and Culture

Explore the mysteries of the planet at the California Academy of Sciences, where far-away galaxies, dense rainforests and deep-ocean creatures are brought to life through stunning displays. Step into the Kimball Natural History Museum to learn about the planet's past, present and future evolution, then visit the Exploratorium at Pier 15 for more remarkable hands-on exhibits in science and art.

Fans of Mickey Mouse must make time for the Walt Disney Family Museum, which chronicles the life and work of the creator of the eponymous media empire. Special exhibits highlight Disney's love of trains and Hollywood glamour portraiture.

The Chinese immigrants who helped build San Francisco are recognized in the Chinese Historical Society of America. Exhibits detail the hardships and triumphs of Chinese in America, and personal narratives and compelling artifacts shed light on this influential immigrant culture.

Fine art finds its way into the halls of the de Young-Legion of Honor museums, where special exhibitions range from tapestries to costumes to rare porcelain. Permanent collections include European sculpture, Greek and Roman antiquities, and graphic arts.

See how the cable car became an icon of San Francisco at the Cable Car Museum, which chronicles the vehicle's colorful history from its first run in 1873 to the present day. Preserved cable

CA

The towering rotunda of the San Francisco Palace of Fine Arts. Getty Images/iStockphoto

cars, mechanical displays and more are part of the museum experience.

The city's steep, winding streets are legendary in their own right. Some tours will take visitors up the winding Lombard Street, which climbs the steep terrain in a distinctive serpentine pattern.

Confront your fear of heights by taking a trip to the top of the Coit Tower, which rises from the top of Telegraph Hill. The observation deck provides a 360-degree view outside, and intricate murals are painted on the inside of the tower's base.

Timeless Japanese tradition lives on in the Japanese Tea Garden in Golden Gate Park. Created as an exhibit for the 1894 California Midwinter International Exposition, it remains the oldest public Japanese garden in the U.S. The 5-acre park includes a teahouse that overlooks a tranquil pond and the surrounding landscape.

The Conservatory of Flowers at Golden Gate Park encompasses hundreds of aquatic, tropical and potted plants. Visitors can thrill at the aquascapes—underwater gardens—and walk paths that wind through vibrant displays. The expansive Victorian-era greenhouse hosts several special exhibits throughout the year.

To the north, the Golden Gate National Recreation Area incorporates units on both sides of the Golden Gate Bridge along 60 miles of bay and ocean shoreline. The park was cobbled together from a menagerie of outdated government properties that included forts, a prison, and an airfield. The total area of the urban park is more than twice the size of San Francisco and its surrounding county.

Deep Roots

The city's connection to ocean trade is the focus of the San Francisco Maritime National Historical Park, where Pacific Coast maritime history is displayed in a collection of exhibits and historic ships. Square-riggers, paddle-wheelers and steamers are moored side by side at Hyde Street Pier. The park surrounds Aquatic Park Cove, where sailboats and other non-motorized boats can cruise the famous harbor.

The city's religious roots go deep, and Mission Dolores—first named Mission San Francisco de Asisi in 1776—is the oldest original intact mission chapel in California. It's also the oldest building in the city. The cemetery and gardens remain intact, and both reflect the history of native peoples and early settlers. Guided tours are available to the public.

Cute, sometimes friendly and always entertaining, sea lions are the stars of the Sea Lion Center, which is managed by the city's Aquarium of the Bay. Free programs educate visitors about the importance of preserving and protecting sea lion populations and their habitats.

San Francisco is known for quirky characters, and the denizens of The San Francisco Dungeon fit the bill. This mix of live-actor shows, a scary boat ride and spooky storytelling about the early days of the city might have you jumping out of your seat.

The Haas-Lilienthal House is a hallmark of San Francisco heritage; the home's original owner was a prominent businessman whose family legacy includes denim magnate Levi Strauss. The Queen Anne-style home is the only period residence in the city open to the public for touring and exemplifies Victorian life for upper-class citizens.

Harvest from the Sea

Fisherman's Wharf, with it shops and restaurants, is one of the busiest tourist destinations anywhere, but is worth the visit if only for the Dungeness crab. The season for one of the West Coast's most commercially important crustaceans doesn't open until November, with a celebration along Fisherman's Wharf. Dodging the passenger ferries to Alcatraz Island, an active fishing fleet still brings fresh seafood from the seas to the dock for the "catch of the day" specials.

San Francisco Sweets

You've probably tasted the delicious chocolate with "Ghirardelli" on the label, but did you know why these morsels are packaged in square shapes? The answer lies in the chocolate factory established in 1852 by Italian immigrant Domenico "Domingo" Ghirardelli. The fantastic flavors created by the chocolatier drew sugar addicts from across the city, and today, the chocolate continues to be sold in Ghirardelli Square, which also boasts restaurants and shops.

A ship sails under the Golden Gate Bridge. San Francisco Travel Association

For More Information

San Francisco Travel
415-391-2000
www.sanfrancisco.travel

California Travel and Tourism Commission
877-225-4367
www.visitcalifornia.com

Getty Images/iStockphoto

SANTA BARBARA

Discover Golden State treasures in this Central Coast gem

Lying on the Central California coast between the Pacific Ocean and the Santa Ynez Mountains, the dazzling city of Santa Barbara charms visitors from across the world. The town exudes a blend of stylish elegance and laid-back California cool that's found nowhere else on the planet.

Architectural styles here are as varied as the recreational opportunities. Visit the Santa Barbara County Courthouse to see a California-Spanish style structure in fine form. Unique features like the distinctive wooden gate and detailed tile work throughout the interior make it a standout. The Mural Room and the Observation Tower are not to be missed when visiting the courthouse.

Dating back to 1786, Old Mission Santa Barbara is often called the Queen of the Missions. Self-guided and docent-led tours of the mission, which is home to a community of Franciscan friars, include visits to landscaped gardens, the mission museum, the church and the mission's historic cemetery.

> During migration season, lucky visitors will see large whale pods traveling through the open ocean.

Gaze at lotus blossoms floating in peaceful waters at Ganna Walska Lotusland, a 37-acre estate and botanical garden that houses more than 3,000 plants from all over the globe. The property also features a Japanese garden, a horticultural clock and topiary animals. Lotusland is a public garden in a residential neighborhood, therefore, reservations are required.

The Santa Barbara Zoo welcomes animal lovers to visit with its dozens of residents. See 146 species of animals, many of which are exhibited in open, natural habitats. Popular animals include the western lowland gorilla, African lion and Humboldt penguin. The zoo offers evening and overnight safaris behind-the-scenes for enthusiastic guests.

Orange tile roofs adorn many of the buildings in Santa Barbara. Getty Images/iStockphoto

Santa Barbara by the Sea

Stroll Santa Barbara's Waterfront, where dining, shopping and wine tasting lure visitors off the promenade. Walk along State Street and window shop for trendy clothes, beautiful antiques and marvelous works of art.

The Santa Barbara Museum of Natural History Sea Center on Stearns Wharf showcases interactive exhibits that focus on marine life and the human impact on the marine ecosystem. Nearby, the Santa Barbara Maritime Museum is dedicated to education, history and community involvement through presentations like the Marine Science Program, tall-ship tours and family kayak races.

Catch a wave or watch the sun set over the surf at Shoreline Park, which runs along the coast and includes a children's play area. During migration season, lucky visitors will see whale pods traveling through the open ocean. Take a charter cruise from Santa Barbara Harbor to enjoy a sunset dinner or a whale-watching excursion.

In downtown Santa Barbara, the Reagan Ranch Center showcases items and multimedia presentations devoted to the 40th president. Reagan spent 25 years at nearby Rancho del Cielo, also known as the "Western White House."

Scenic Santa Barbara

See the best of the city and its surroundings on the Santa Barbara Scenic Drive. Stunning architecture and ocean views reward motorists.

Enjoy the outdoors on a hike of the Jesusita Trail, a 7-mile round trip that thrills dedicated hikers with views of spring wildflowers and waterfalls. Cold Spring Trail passes small waterfalls as well. Hiking around Santa Barbara invites stunning views of the landscape, and many weary walkers seek refreshment inside Cold Spring Tavern. This 1860s-era structure originally served as a waystation for stagecoach travelers heading over the San Marcos Pass. Also on the property is the Ojai Jail, built in 1873 and donated to the property's owners when the Ojai sheriff retired.

Santa Barbara has a hot art scene, and temperatures rise to their highest at Santa Barbara Art Glass. Visitors can make their own creations in private glassblowing classes with the assistance of talented instructors. If you'd rather leave it to the professionals, one-of-a-kind pieces are available for purchase.

> Architectural styles in this Pacific Coast city are as varied as the recreational opportunities for visitors.

The Old West comes to life at the Carriage and Western Art Museum. Displays of antique Western tack gear and stagecoaches sit alongside saddles once used by Will Rogers, Clark Gable and Jimmy Stewart.

The Spanish-style Lobero Theatre is an architectural treasure that puts on plays and concerts, and showcases vintage architecture. Whether you stop in for a show or just want to look around, this theater always entertains.

Little ones can get their adventure on and adults can enjoy a relaxing afternoon at Kids' World at Alameda Park. The expansive playground caters to children ranging in age from 2 to 12. Across the street, the memorial garden at Alice Keck Park offers self-guided tours that help grown-ups to recharge their batteries.

The life of early Spanish settlers is re-created at El Presidio de Santa Barbara. This state historic park is nestled downtown and preserves the remains of the last Spanish fortress built in Central California, which dates to 1782. Two adobe buildings still stand, and several parts are open for visitors to explore on self-guided tours. Reconstructed rooms show how Presidio officers, soldiers and their families once lived.

For More Information

Visit Santa Barbara
800-676-1266
www.santabarbaraca.com

California Travel and Tourism Commission
877-225-4367

Visit Temecula

TEMECULA

Ride a balloon and pour a glass in this SoCal getaway

Come to Southern California's wine country. Temecula, located just 60 miles north of San Diego, has a year-round climate that's perfect for outdoor activities or indoor fun.

Wine Country

As soon as you arrive in Temecula, located in the hills east of Orange County, you'll be hard-pressed not to see a grape vine. Temecula has a climate that's ideal for growing grapes, with cool, foggy mornings that give way to warm, sun-kissed afternoons and clear, crisp, star-filled nights. There are over 30 wineries waiting for you to experience award-winning varietals. No matter what your taste, Temecula Valley Wineries can accommodate your palate. You'll find Merlot, Cabernet Sauvignon, Cabernet Franc, Petit Verdot and even Gewurztraminer.

Visiting a winery in Temecula is more than just buying a bottle of award-winning wine. You need to do it for the experience. Each winery is unique in its atmosphere, architecture and, of course, wine. For instance, you can visit a winery that's housed in Snow White's Cottage or another located on a rolling estate where you'll feel wrapped in robes of luxury. Temecula's wineries are as unique as each grape that comes off the vine.

Self-guided wine tours will help you find all the wineries from the comfort of your own vehicle. Find a designated driver if you plan to imbibe.

Hot Air Balloons

Hot air balloons are fun to watch from the ground, but riding in one is something unlike any other form of transportation. Some companies in Temecula offer hot air balloon rides. Each excursion typically takes about 60 to 75 minutes and they are offered seven days a week all year round, weather permitting.

If you happen to be visiting Temecula around the first week of June, make sure you check out the Temecula Balloon and Wine Festival. Every morning of the festival there's a balloon launch. Get there early, because they take off around 6:30 a.m.

Old Town Temecula

Take a stroll through Old Town Temecula and you'll find a variety of things to do. Quaint antique shops, specialty shops and art galleries are just a few of the ways to spend an afternoon. Be sure to stop by the Temecula Farmers Market to pick up some fresh herbs or homemade baked goods.

Outdoor Activities

If you're in search of that ever-elusive large-mouth bass, you won't want to pass up a trip to the Vail Lake Resort. Reputed to be California's No. 1 place to find largemouth bass, the lake is situated on 11,000 acres and offers year-round outdoor activities.

Brought your bike? Ride the 110 miles of cycling trails in the area.

Toasting vintages in the Monte de Oro Winery. Jake Ashcraft

For More Information

Visit Temecula Valley
888-363-2852
www.visittemeculavalley.com

California Travel and Tourism Commission
877-225-4367
www.visitcalifornia.com

PECHANGA
RV RESORT

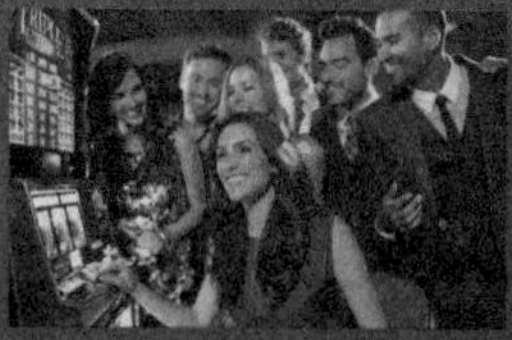

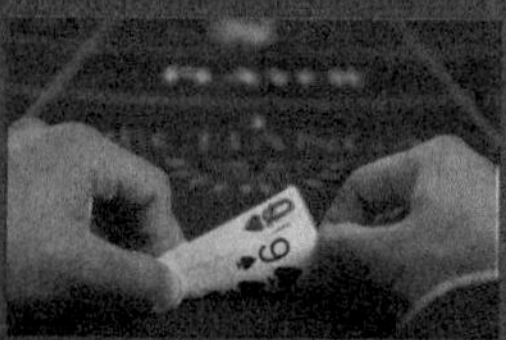

California

CONSULTANTS

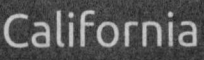

Northern California
Frank & Linda Mintken

Central California
Jim & Chris Mays

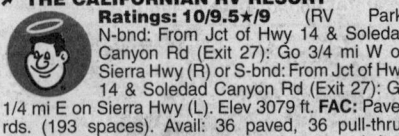

Southern California
Mike & Mary Lou Dillon

ACTON — H4 *Los Angeles, Valencia*

ACTON KOA Ratings: 5.5/7.5/7 (Campground) From Jct of Hwy 14 and Soledad Canyon Rd (Exit 11): Go 8.5 mi E on Soledad Canyon Rd (L). **FAC:** Gravel/dirt rds. (79 spaces). Avail: 46 dirt, 9 pull-thrus (15 x 60), back-ins (15 x 34), 46 full hkups (30/50 amps), seasonal sites, WiFi, tent sites, laundry, groc, LP gas, fire rings. **REC:** whirlpool, shuffleboard, playground, rec open to public. Pets OK. Partial handicap access. Eco-friendly, 2015 rates: $45 to $57. Disc: AAA, military.
AAA Approved
(661)268-1214 Lat: 34.43776, Lon: -118.26565
7601 Soledad Canyon Rd, Acton, CA 93510
info@acton-koa.com
www.acton-koa.com

THE CALIFORNIAN RV RESORT
Ratings: 10/9.5★/9 (RV Park) N-bnd: From Jct of Hwy 14 & Soledad Canyon Rd (Exit 27): Go 3/4 mi W on Sierra Hwy (R) or S-bnd: From Jct of Hwy 14 & Soledad Canyon Rd (Exit 27): Go 1/4 mi E on Sierra Hwy (L). Elev 3079 ft. **FAC:** Paved rds. (193 spaces). Avail: 36 paved, 36 pull-thrus (25 x 60), 36 full hkups (30/50 amps), seasonal sites, cable, WiFi, laundry, groc, LP gas, controlled access. **REC:** heated pool, whirlpool. Pet restrict(B/Q). Partial handicap access, no tents. Big rig sites, eco-friendly, 2015 rates: $42. Disc: AAA, military.
AAA Approved
(888)787-8386 Lat: 34.486545, Lon: -118.143256
1535 W. Sierra Hwy., Acton, CA 93510
info@calrv.com
www.calrv.com
See ad pages 192, 128.

ADELANTO — H4 *San Bernardino*

ADELANTO RV PARK **Ratings: 7/8.5/8** (RV Park) 2015 rates: $33.33. (877)246-5554 11301 Airbase Rd / Air Expressway, Adelanto, CA 92301

AGUANGA — J5 *Riverside*

CLEVELAND (DRIPPING SPRINGS CAMPGROUND) (Natl Forest) From town: Go 8 mi S on Hwy-79. Pit toilets. 2015 rates: $15. (858)673-6180

RANCHO CALIFORNIA RV RESORT **Ratings: 9.5/9.5★/10** (Condo Pk) 2015 rates: $55 to $75. (951)767-1788 45525 Hwy 79 S., Aguanga, CA 92536

ALMANOR — B3 *Plumas*

PG & E/FEATHER RIVER/COOL SPRINGS CAMPGROUND (Public) From Jct of Hwys 147 & 89, NW 5 mi on Hwy 89 to Butt Lake Rd, SW 5 mi (R). Pit toilets. 2015 rates: $16. (916)386-5164

ANAHEIM — N3 *Orange*

ANAHEIM See also Azusa, Chino, Huntington Beach, Long Beach, Los Angeles, Newport Beach, Orange & Placentia.

ANAHEIM HARBOR RV PARK Ratings: 8.5/9.5★/6.5 (RV Park) From Jct of I-5 & Harbor Blvd (Exit 110), N 0.3 mi on Harbor Blvd (L). **FAC:** Paved rds. (195 spaces). Avail: 63 paved, patios, back-ins (14 x 40), 63 full hkups (30/50 amps), seasonal sites, cable, WiFi, tent sites, laundry. **REC:** heated pool, playground. Pets OK. Partial handicap

ANAHEIM (CONT)

ANAHEIM HARBOR RV PARK (CONT)
access. RV age restrict, 2015 rates: $32 to $65. Disc: AAA, military.
AAA Approved
(888)835-6495 Lat: 33.82064, Lon: -117.91612
1009 S Harbor Blvd, Anaheim, CA 92805
info@anaheimharborrvpark.com
www.anaheimharborrvpark.com

ANAHEIM RV PARK
Ratings: 9/10★/8.5 (RV Park) S-bnd: From Jct of I-5 & Ball Rd exit, E 0.8 mi on Ball Rd to Anaheim Blvd, S 0.3 mi to Midway, W 0.1 mi (L); or N-bnd: From Jct of I-5 & Harbor Blvd exit, N 100 ft on Harbor Blvd to Ball Rd, E 0.5 mi to Anaheim Blvd, S 0.3 mi to Midway, W 0.1 mi (L).

CAMPING IN MICKEY'S BACKYARD!
We are so close to Mickey's backyard, you can watch the fireworks right from your RV or take a shuttle to Disney from the park! Long, wide sites for any size rig. FREE Wi-Fi! Our friendly staff will make you feel at home!

FAC: Paved rds. (108 spaces). Avail: 98 paved, patios, 17 pull-thrus (20 x 70), back-ins (22 x 45), 98 full hkups (30/50 amps), seasonal sites, cable, WiFi, tent sites, laundry. **REC:** heated pool, whirlpool. Pet restrict(B). Partial handicap access. RV age restrict, eco-friendly, 2015 rates: $52 to $86. Disc: AAA, military.
AAA Approved
(714)774-3860 Lat: 33.81238, Lon: -117.90781
200 W Midway Dr, Anaheim, CA 92805
info@anaheimrvpark.com
www.anaheimrvpark.com
See ad pages 131 (Spotlight Anaheim), 126 & Family Camping in Magazine Section.

CANYON RV PARK **Ratings: 7.5/5.5/7.5** (RV Park) 2015 rates: $60. (714)637-0210 24001 Santa Ana Canyon Rd, Anaheim, CA 92808

PONDEROSA TRAVEL TRAILER PARK **Ratings: 6/6/6.5** (RV Park) 2015 rates: $39 to $59. (714)634-3390 2337 S Manchester Ave, Anaheim, CA 92802

ANDERSON — B2 *Shasta*

Travel Services

CAMPING WORLD OF ANDERSON/REDDING
As the nation's largest retailer of RV supplies, accessories, services and new and used RVs, Camping World is committed to making your total RV experience better. RV Accessories: (855)631-8963. **SERVICES:** RV, tire, RV appliance, staffed RV wash, restrooms, RV Sales. RV supplies, LP, emergency parking, RV accessible. Hours: 8am to 6pm. No CC.
(888)740-1875 Lat: 40.767029, Lon: -122.317376
3700 Automall Drive, Anderson, CA 96007
www.campingworldofredding.com

ANGELS CAMP — E3 *Calaveras*

ANGELS CAMP RV & CAMPING RESORT
Ratings: 9.5/9.5★/10 (Campground) From Jct of Hwy 49 & Hwy 4, S 2.6 mi on Hwy 49 (L). **FAC:** Paved rds. 84 Avail: 20 paved, 64 gravel, 53 pull-thrus (24 x 70), back-ins (24 x 40), 84 full hkups (30/50 amps), WiFi, tent sites, rentals, dump, laundry, groc, LP gas, fire rings, firewood. **REC:** pool, playground. Pet restrict(B/Q) $. Partial handicap access. 2015 rates: $37 to $53. Disc: AAA, military.
AAA Approved
(209)736-0404 Lat: 38.04390, Lon: -120.52215
3069 Hwy 49 South, Angels Camp, CA 95222
angelscampresort@sbcglobal.net
www.angelscamprv.com
See ad page 220.

FROGTOWN RV PARK (Public) From Jct of Hwy 49 & Hwy 4, S 1.2 mi on Hwy 49 to Gun Club Road, E 0.4 mi (E) (Not open to overnight RV'ers during May). 2015 rates: $22. (209)736-2561

GLORYHOLE REC AREA/BIG OAK CAMPGROUND (Public) From town, S 3 mi on Hwy 49 (R). 2015 rates: $18 to $22. (209)536-9094

GLORYHOLE REC AREA/IRONHORSE CAMPGROUND (Public) From town, S 3 mi on Hwy 49 (R). 2015 rates: $18 to $22. (209)536-9094

ANGELUS OAKS — M6 *San Bernardino*

SAN BERNARDINO NATIONAL FOREST (SAN GORGONIO CAMPGROUND) (State Pk) From town: Go 8-1/2 mi E on Hwy 38. 2015 rates: $26 to $52. (909)382-2790

Say you saw it in our Guide!

ANTIOCH — E2 *Contra Costa*

CONTRA COSTA COUNTY FAIR RV PARK (Public) From Jct of SR-4 & Exit 26B (Auto Center Dr), N 0.8 mi on Auto Center Dr to W 10th St, E 0.3 mi to fair entrance, S 200 ft on entry rd (L). 2015 rates: $20. (925)757-4400

ARCATA — B1 *Humboldt*

MAD RIVER RAPIDS RV PARK
Ratings: 9.5/9.5★/9.5 (RV Park) From Jct of US-101 & SR-299, N 0.2 mi on US-101 to Giuntoli Ln/Janes Rd Exit 716B, W 0.3 mi on Janes Rd (L).

WE ACCOMMODATE ANY SIZE RV!
Enjoy walks on nearby ocean beaches. Easy access to 101. Large meeting room, arcade for kids, free Wifi. Close to Humboldt State, Eureka, & the Redwoods.

FAC: Paved rds. (92 spaces). Avail: 43 paved, patios, 29 pull-thrus (28 x 63), back-ins (35 x 60), accepts full hkup units only, 43 full hkups (30/50 amps), seasonal sites, cable, WiFi, dump, laundry, groc. **REC:** heated pool, whirlpool, playground. Pets OK. Partial handicap access, no tents. Big rig sites, 2015 rates: $38 to $47. Disc: AAA, military.
AAA Approved
(800)822-7776 Lat: 40.90165, Lon: -124.08883
3501 Janes Rd, Arcata, CA 95521
stay@madriverrv.com
www.madriverrv.com
See ad pages 182, 128.

ARNOLD — D3 *Calaveras*

CALAVERAS BIG TREES (State Pk) From town, NE 4 mi on Hwy 4 (R). 2015 rates: $20 to $35. (209)795-2334

GOLDEN PINES RV RESORT & CAMPGROUND
Ratings: 9/10★/8.5 (Campground) From Jct of Hwys 49 & 4, E 25.2 mi on Hwy 4 (L). Elev 5200 ft. **FAC:** Paved rds. (57 spaces). 27 Avail: 14 paved, 13 gravel, 5 pull-thrus (16 x 40), back-ins (16 x 36), 27 full hkups (20/30 amps), seasonal sites, WiFi $, tent sites, rentals, showers $, dump, laundry, LP gas, firewood. **REC:** heated pool, playground. Pet restrict(B/Q). Partial handicap access. 29 day max stay, 2015 rates: $40 to $45. Disc: AAA.
AAA Approved
(209)795-2820 Lat: 38.29659, Lon: -120.28525
2869 Golden Torch Drive, Arnold, CA 95223
camping.goldenpines@gmail.com
www.goldenpinesresort.com

AROMAS — F2 *San Benito*

MONTEREY VACATION RV PARK
Ratings: 7/10★/8.5 (RV Park) N-bnd: From Jct of US-101 & Hwy 156W: Go 7 mi N on US-101 (R); or S-bnd: From Jct of US-101 & Hwy 156E: Go 2-1/2 mi S on US-101 to San Juan Rd (exit 342), then E over the overpass and return to US-101 N-bnd, then 3/4 mi north on US-101(R). **FAC:** Paved rds. (88 spaces). Avail: 15 gravel, 15 pull-thrus (23 x 33), 15 full hkups (30 amps), seasonal sites, WiFi, laundry, LP gas. **REC.** Pet restrict(B/Q) $. No tents. Eco-friendly, 2015 rates: $35 to $40.
(831)726-9118 Lat: 36.862407, Lon: -121.614149
1400 Hwy 101, Aromas, CA 95004
See ad page 196.

ARROYO GRANDE — G2 *San Luis Obispo*

LOPEZ LAKE REC AREA (Public) From Jct of US-101 & Grand Ave exit, E 0.9 mi on Grand Ave to Huasna Rd/Lopez Dr, SE 10 mi, follow signs (E). 2015 rates: $23 to $38. (805)788-2381

AUBURN — D3 *Placer*

AUBURN GOLD COUNTRY RV PARK Ratings: 8.5/9★/9 (RV Park) From Jct of I-80 & (Bell Rd) Exit 123, NW 2.9 mi on Bell Rd to SR-49, N 0.2 mi to Rock Creek Rd, E 0.1 mi to KOA Way, N 0.1 mi (R). **FAC:** Paved rds. (66 spaces). Avail: 40 paved, patios, 10 pull-thrus (32 x 60), back-ins (25 x 45), 40 full hkups (30/50 amps), seasonal sites, WiFi, tent sites, rentals, dump, laundry, LP gas, firewood. **REC:** heated pool, whirlpool, pond, fishing, playground. Pet restrict(B/Q). Big rig sites, 2015 rates: $37 to $59.
(530)885-0990 Lat: 38.94775, Lon: -121.09515
3550 Koa Way, Auburn, CA 95602
mgr@auburnrvpark.com
www.auburnrvpark.com

Everyone wants to be noticed. Tell your RV Park that you found them in the this Guide.

The Place To Stay
Bakersfield
River Run
RV Park
• 122 Spaces
• Wireless Internet
• Across the River from Yokuts Park
• Easy access to the Kern River Parkway - Bicycle or walk to local attractions from 30 miles of recreational paths along the river
• Close to Local Attractions, Hotels, Restaurants & Stores
• Easy Hwy. 99 Access
• Swimming Pool & Spa
• Grass & Trees at all Sites
• 2 Laundry & Shower Facilities
• Propane & Convenience Store
• Rec Room
• Fitness Room
• Conference Room
• Group Discounts
• Kitchen & B.B.Q. for Groups
Buck Owens Blvd
Rosedale Hwy
Hwy 178
Gibson St.
River Run RV Park
Burr St.
Oak Street
99
www.RiverRunRVPark.com
1.888.RIV-R-RUN
(888.748.7786)
3715 Burr Street
Bakersfield, CA
Eco Friendly Park
Good Sam Park
Bakersfield's Premier Park Built for Today's RVer
See listing Bakersfield, CA

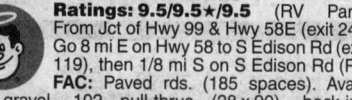

AZUSA — M3 *Los Angeles*

CARAVAN MOBILE HOME PARK
(RV Spaces) From Jct of I 210 & Exit 40 (Azusa Ave exit), S 0.3 mi on S Azusa Ave to W Gladstone St, W 0.4mi (L). **FAC:** Paved rds. (120 spaces). Avail: 13 paved, no slide-outs, 5 pull-thrus (12 x 45), back-ins (14 x 42), 13 full hkups (30/50 amps), laundry. **REC:** pool. Pet restrict(B). No tents. RV age restrict, 2015 rates: $20. No CC.
(626)334-2306 Lat: 34.11406, Lon: -117.91439
600 W. Gladstone St, Azusa, CA 91702
See ad page 141 (Spotlight Los Angeles).

BAKERSFIELD — G3 *Kern*

A SPOTLIGHT Introducing Bakersfield's colorful attractions appearing at the front of this state section.

BAKERSFIELD See also Lake Isabella, Rosedale & Tehachapi.

A COUNTRY RV PARK
Ratings: 10/10★/9 (RV Park) From Jct of Hwy 99 & Hwy 58: Go 6 mi E on Hwy 58 to Fairfax Rd, then 1/4 mi S on Fairfax Rd (R). **FAC:** Paved rds. (120 spaces). Avail: 20 paved, patios, 20 pull-thrus (25 x 65), 20 full hkups (30/50 amps), seasonal sites, cable, WiFi, tent sites, laundry, groc, LP gas, controlled access. **REC:** pool, whirlpool. Pet restrict(B). Partial handicap access. Big rig sites, eco-friendly, 2015 rates: $38. Disc: AAA, military.
(866)787-2750 Lat: 35.349673, Lon: -118.932431
622 S Fairfax Rd, Bakersfield, CA 93307
acntryrvprk@aol.com
www.acountryrvpark.com
See ad pages 168, 128.

BAKERSFIELD RIVER RUN RV PARK
Ratings: 10/10★/9 (RV Park) From Jct of Hwy 99 & Hwy 58 W/Rosedale Hwy (Exit 26): Go 1/2 mi W on Hwy 58 to Gibson St, then 1/4 mi S on Gibson St to Burr St, then 1/4 mi E on Burr St (E).

THE PLACE TO STAY
Newer park centrally located, walk to many of Bakersfield's finest restaurants, attractions and hotels. Enjoy our sites with lots of grass and large patios. The wide roads and big sites makes it easy for the largest RVs.

FAC: Paved rds. (121 spaces). Avail: 71 all weather, patios, 31 pull-thrus (24 x 60), back-ins (30 x 40), 71 full hkups (30/50 amps), seasonal sites, cable, WiFi, dump, laundry, groc, LP gas. **REC:** pool, whirlpool, Kern River (seasonal). Pet restrict(B/Q) $. Partial handicap access, no tents. Big rig sites, 28 day max stay, eco-friendly, 2015 rates: $33 to $59.
AAA Approved
(888)748-7786 Lat: 35.378573, Lon: -119.047051
3715 Burr St, Bakersfield, CA 93308
info@riverrunrvpark.com
www.riverrunrvpark.com
See ad opposite page, 128, 134 (Spotlight Bakersfield), 119 (CA Map).

BAKERSFIELD RV RESORT
Ratings: 10/10★/9.5 (RV Park) From Jct of Hwy 99 & White Lane (exit 21): Go 100 ft W on White Lane to Wible Road, then 1/2 mi S on Wible Rd (R).

ENJOY LUXURY IN CENTRAL CA
Luxury, style, and comfort COMBINE to make us the ideal stop on your travels, with exceptional amenities and superior customer service. Enjoy our onsite restaurant, Crest Bar & Grill, during your stay.

FAC: Paved rds. 215 Avail: 215 all weather, patios, 88 pull-thrus (30 x 65), back-ins (30 x 50), 215 full hkups (30/50 amps), cable, WiFi, laundry, groc, LP gas, restaurant, controlled access. **REC:** heated pool, whirlpool. Pet restrict(B/Q). Partial handicap access, no tents. Big rig sites, 28 day max stay, eco-friendly, 2015 rates: $44. Disc: military.
(661)833-9998 Lat: 35.308642, Lon: -119.039610
5025 Wible Rd, Bakersfield, CA 93313
info@bakersfieldrvresort.com
www.bakrv.com
See ad pages 169, 128.

BAKERSFIELD RV TRAVEL PARK
Ratings: 8/8.5/5 (RV Park) From Jct of Hwy 99 & Hwy 58E: Go 7 mi E on Hwy 58E to Hwy 184 (Weedpatch Hwy), then 1/8 mi N on Hwy 184 to E Brundage Ln, then 1/4 mi E on E Brundage Ln (R). **FAC:** Paved rds. (100 spaces). Avail: 20 paved, patios, 10 pull-thrus (18 x 72), back-ins (18 x 36), 20 full hkups (30/50 amps), seasonal sites, cable, WiFi, tent sites, dump, laundry. **REC:** pool. Pet restrict(B). Partial handicap access. Big rig sites, eco-friendly, 2015 rates: $33.50. Disc: AAA, military.
AAA Approved
(661)366-3550 Lat: 35.354280, Lon: -118.909184
8633 E Brundage Ln, Bakersfield, CA 93307
info@bakersfieldrvtravelpark.com
www.bakersfieldrvtravelpark.com

BEAR MOUNTAIN RV RESORT **Ratings: 5/4.5/6** (RV Park) 2015 rates: $27. (661)834-3811 16501 S. Union Ave, Bakersfield, CA 93307

BUENA VISTA AQUATIC REC AREA (Public) From Jct of I-5 & Hwy 119 (Exit 244), W 1.6 mi on Hwy 119 to Hwy 43, S 2.7 mi (E). Entrance fee required. 2015 rates: $28 to $40. (661)868-7050

KERN RIVER COUNTY PARK (Public) From town, E 8 mi on Hwy 178 to Lake Ming Rd exit, follow signs (R). 2015 rates: $12 to $24. (661)868-7000

ORANGE GROVE RV PARK
Ratings: 9.5/9.5★/9.5 (RV Park) From Jct of Hwy 99 & Hwy 58E (exit 24): Go 8 mi E on Hwy 58 to S Edison Rd (exit 119), then 1/8 mi S on S Edison Rd (R). **FAC:** Paved rds. (185 spaces). Avail: 110 gravel, 102 pull-thrus (28 x 90), back-ins (28 x 65), 102 full hkups, 8 W, 8 E (30/50 amps), seasonal sites, cable, WiFi, dump, laundry, LP gas. **REC:** pool, playground. Pets OK. Partial handicap access, no tents. Big rig sites, 21 day max stay, eco-friendly, 2015 rates: $30 to $42. Disc: AAA, military.
AAA Approved
(661)366-4662 Lat: 35.341833, Lon: -118.879139
1452 S Edison Rd, Bakersfield, CA 93307
ogrvp@orangegrovervpark.com
www.orangegrovervpark.com
See ad this page, 128.

SMOKE TREE RV PARK **Ratings: 7.5/6.5/5** (RV Park) 2015 rates: $30. (661)832-0433 4435 Hughes Lane, Bakersfield, CA 93304

SOUTHLAND RV PARK **Ratings: 8/7.5/6.5** (RV Park) From Jct of Hwy 99 & Hwy 119 (Taft Hwy/exit 18): Go 1/4 mi E on Hwy 119 (Taft Hwy) to Southland Ct, then 1/8 mi S on Southland Ct (E). **FAC:** Paved rds. (93 spaces). Avail: 10 paved, patios, 10 pull-thrus (20 x 54), 10 full hkups (30/50 amps), seasonal sites, cable, laundry. **REC:** pool, whirlpool. Pet restrict Partial handicap access, no tents. Eco-friendly, 2015 rates: $38. Disc: AAA, military.
AAA Approved
(877)834-4868 Lat: 35.266210, Lon: -119.019184
9901 Southland Court, Bakersfield, CA 93307
southlandrvpark@gmail.com

Travel Services

CAMPING WORLD OF BAKERSFIELD As the nation's largest retailer of RV supplies, accessories, services and new and used RVs, Camping World is committed to making your total RV experience better. RV Dealership: (888)808-1451. **SERVICES:** RV, tire, RV appliance, MH mechanical, staffed RV wash, restrooms, RV Sales. RV supplies, LP, emergency parking, RV accessible. waiting room. Hours: 8am to 6pm.
661-833-9797 Lat: 35.304481, Lon: -119.038863
5500 Wible Road, Bakersfield, CA 93313
bherron@campingworld.com
campingworldofbakersfield.com

Things to See and Do

BUCK OWENS' CRYSTAL PALACE Steak House Restaurant with Live Theater entertainment and dance floor. Features Country Music Museum, Country Store, and Buck Owens memorabilia. Open for Sunday Brunch. Closed Mondays. Partial handicap access. RV accessible. Restrooms, food. Hours: Tue-Sat 5-10 pm, Sunday 9:30 am-2 pm.
(661)328-7560 Lat: 35.38568, Lon: -119.04220
2800 Buck Owens Blvd, Bakersfield, CA 93308
reservations@buckowens.com
www.buckowens.com
See ad page 134 (Spotlight Bakersfield).

County names are provided after the city names. If you're tracking the weather, this is the information you'll need to follow the reports.

CREST BAR & GRILL Restaurant with bar area serving breakfast, lunch and dinner. Catering for groups. Delivery of meals to RV sites. Partial handicap access. RV accessible. Restrooms, food. Hours: 7am to 9pm.
(661)833-9998 Lat: 35.308642, Lon: -119.039610
5025 Wible Rd, Bakersfield, CA 93313
info@bakersfieldrvresort.com
www.bakersfieldrvresort.com
See ad page 169.

Use our handy Snowbird Destinations guide in the front of the Guide to find RV-friendly destinations throughout the Sunbelt.

GATEWAY TO THE DESERT
A Country RV Park
Family Owned - Where You'll Feel at Home
Bakersfield
Good Sam RATED 10/10★/9
Good Sam Park
FREE WIFI
Snowbirds Welcome!
• Wi-Fi • 2 Bathhouse & Laundry • Exercise Room • Pool and Spa
• 120 RV Spaces • 102 Pull-Thrus 25' X 65' • 30/50 Amps • Paved Roads
• Grass at Most Sites • Clubhouse • Large Grassy Areas • Dog Run
• Metered Propane • Concrete Pads
622 So. Fairfax Rd., Bakersfield, CA
1-866-787-2750
(661) 363-6412
E-mail: acntryrvprk@aol.com
To San Francisco
To Sacramento
To Paso Robles
46
99
58
58
Stockdale Hwy.
5
To Mojave
Fairfax Rd.
To Los Angeles
A Country RV Park
See listing Bakersfield, CA

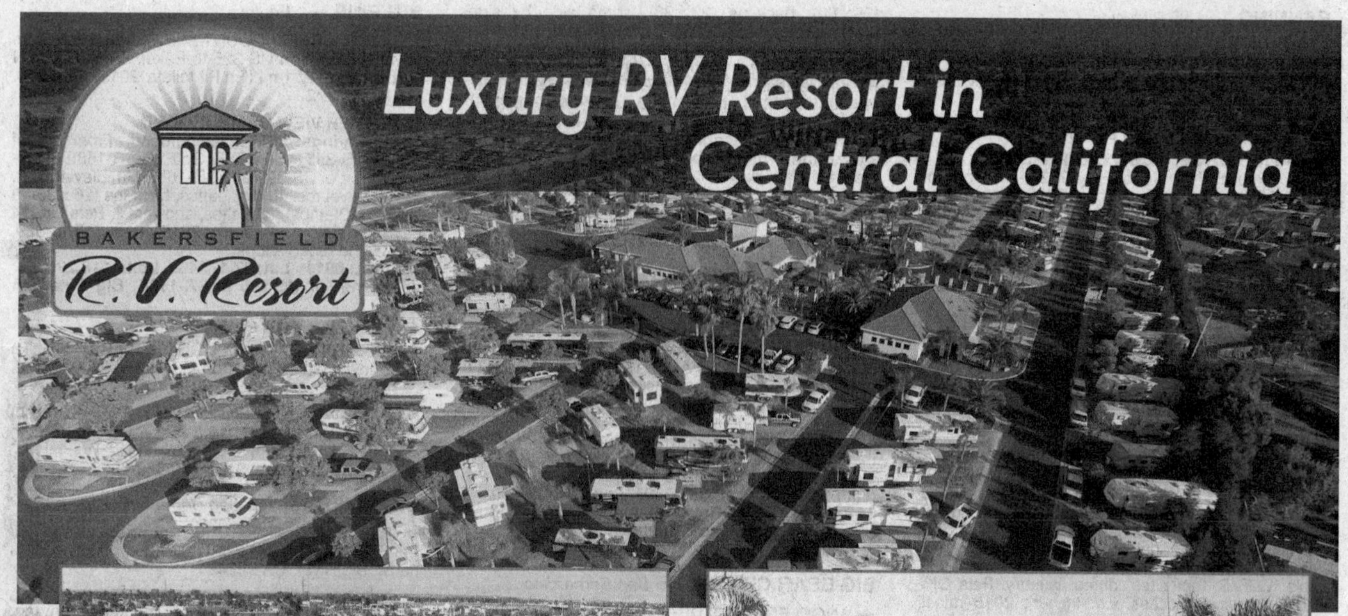
Luxury RV Resort in
Central California
BAKERSFIELD
R.V. Resort

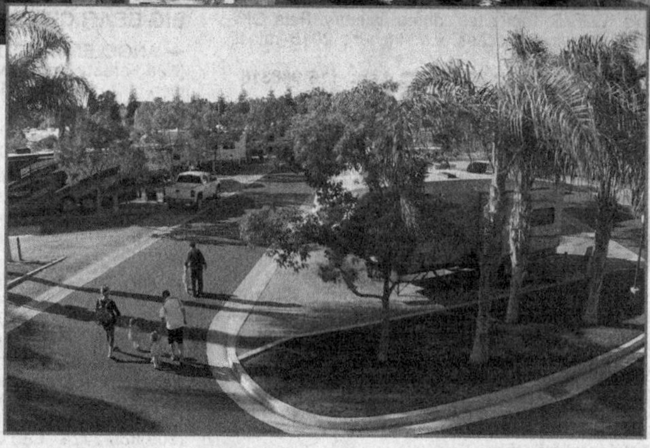

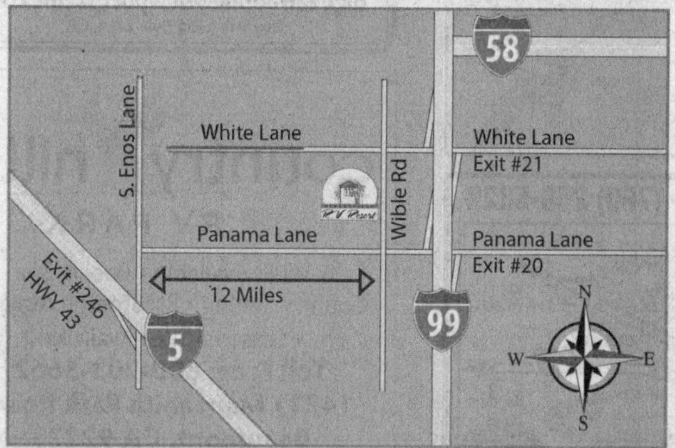
58
S. Enos Lane
White Lane
Wible Rd
White Lane
Exit #21
Panama Lane
Panama Lane
Exit #20
12 Miles
Exit #246
HWY 43
5
99
N
W
E
S

CA

BANNING — J5 *Riverside*

BANNING STAGECOACH KOA **Ratings: 8.5/9/8.5** (Campground) 2015 rates: $44 to $49.50. (800)562-4110 1455 S San Gorgonio Ave, Banning, CA 92220

BARSTOW — H4 *San Bernardino*

CALICO GHOST TOWN CAMPGROUND (Public) From Jct of Hwy 58 & I-15: Go 8 mi NE on I-15 to Ghost Town Rd (Exit 191), then 3-1/2 mi N on Ghost Town Rd (L). Elev 2938 ft. **FAC:** Paved rds. 265 dirt, 23 pull-thrus (20 x 50), back-ins (30 x 40), 64 full hkups, 20 W, 60 E (30/50 amps), tent sites, rentals, showers $, dump. **REC:** rec open to public. Pets OK $. Partial handicap access. 14 day max stay, 2015 rates: $37 to $47.
(800)862-2542 Lat: 34.94337, Lon: -116.86667
36600 Ghost Town Rd, Yermo, CA 92398
calicotown@parks.sbcounty.gov
http://cms.sbcounty.gov/parks/activities/camping.aspx
See ad page 123 (Welcome Section).

SHADY LANE RV CAMP
Ratings: 6.5/8.5/8 (Campground) From Jct of I-15 & Old Hwy 58 (Exit 186): Go 1 mi W on Old Hwy 58 to Soap Mine Rd, then 1/10 mi S on Soap Mine Rd (L). **FAC:** Gravel rds. (35 spaces). Avail: 23 gravel, patios, 13 pull-thrus (20 x 60), back-ins (20 x 40), 23 full hkups (30/50 amps), seasonal sites, cable, WiFi $, tent sites, dump, laundry. Pets OK. Partial handicap access. Eco-friendly, 2015 rates: $35 to $39. No CC.
(877)367-8502 Lat: 34.912323, Lon: -116.988316
36445 Soap Mine Rd, Barstow, CA 92311
See ad this page, 128.

BASS LAKE — E4 *Madera*

BASS LAKE RECREATIONAL RESORT
Ratings: 9.5/8/8.5 (RV Park) From jct Hwy 49 & Hwy 41: Go 3 mi N on Hwy 41, then 3-3/4 mi S on Road 222 (winding road), then 2-1/4 mi SE on Road 274 (R). Elev 3980 ft. **FAC:** Paved rds. (159 spaces). Avail: 89 gravel, 10 pull-thrus (20 x 40), back-ins (24 x 60), 89 full hkups (30/50 amps), seasonal sites, cable, WiFi, tent sites, rentals, laundry, LP gas. **REC:** pool, playground. Pet restrict(Q). Partial handicap access. Big rig sites, 14 day max stay, eco-friendly, 2015 rates: $66.
(559)642-3145 Lat: 37.323594, Lon: -119.554711
39744 Rd 274, Bass Lake, CA 93604
rvatbasslake@sti.net
basslake-rvresort.com
See ad this page, 128.

BEAUMONT — N6 *Riverside*

COUNTRY HILLS RV PARK
Ratings: 9/8/7 (RV Park) From Jct of Hwy I-10 & Beaumont Ave (exit94), S 3.6mi on Beaumont Ave to 1st St,E 0.5 mi to Michigan Ave, S 0.6 mi on Michigan Ave which becomes Manzanita Park Rd, S 0.6mi (E). **FAC:** Gravel rds. (85 spaces). Avail: 45 all weather, patios, 12 pull-thrus (25 x 60), back-ins (23 x 38), some side by side hkups, 35 full hkups (20/50 amps), seasonal sites, WiFi, rentals, showers $, dump, laundry, controlled access. **REC:** pool, whirlpool, playground. Pets OK $. RV age restrict, eco-friendly, 2015 rates: $33 to $36.
(951)845-5919 Lat: 33.90882, Lon: -116.96811
14711 Manzanita Park Rd, Beaumont, CA 92223
Countryhills@newportpacific.com
www.countryhillsrv.com
See ad this page.

BETHEL ISLAND — E2 *Contra Costa*

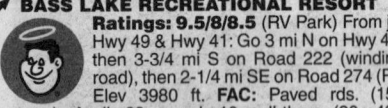

SUGAR BARGE RV RESORT AND MARINA
Ratings: 9/8.5★/9.5 (RV Park) From Jct of SR-160 & SR-4, E 3.5 mi on SR-4 to Cypress Rd, E 3.7 mi to Bethel Island Rd, N 1.4 mi to Gateway Rd, E 0.9 mi to Piper Rd, N 0.3 mi to Sugar Barge Rd (rd 300 ft after St sign), E 0.3 mi (E). **FAC:** Paved rds. 114 Avail: 11 gravel, 103 grass, patios, back-ins (28 x 42), 114 full hkups (30 amps), WiFi, tent sites, rentals, dump, laundry, LP gas, firewood, restaurant, controlled access. **REC:** heated pool, Franks Tract/Delta: fishing, marina, playground. Pets OK. Partial handicap access. 2015 rates: $39.50 to $41.50.
(800)799-4100 Lat: 38.02598, Lon: -121.61390
1440 Sugar Barge Rd, Bethel Island, CA 94511
rvsugarbarge@comcast.net
www.sugarbarge.com

BIG BEAR CITY — H5 *San Bernardino*

ANGELES (COLDBROOK CAMPGROUND) (Natl Forest) From town: Go 1-3/4 mi W on Hwy-18, then 1/2 mi S on Tulip Lane. 2015 rates: $12. (909)383-5588

BIG BEAR LAKE — H5 *San Bernardino*

BIG BEAR LAKE MWD RV PARK (Public) From Jct of Hwys 38 & 18 (south shore of the lake), E 3.9 mi on Hwy 18 (Big Bear Blvd) to Lakeview Dr, N 0.1 mi (R). 2015 rates: $30 to $40. May 1 to Oct 31. (909)866-5796

BIG BEAR MOBILE ESTATES AND RV RESORT
Ratings: 8/7.5/7.5 (RV Resort) From Jct of Hwy 38 and Hwy18, E 4 mi on Hwy 18 to Big Bear Blvd. N 0.6 mi to Alden Rd, S 200 (E). **FAC:** Paved rds. 18 paved, back-ins (25 x 42), 18 full hkups (30/50 amps), cable, WiFi, laundry. **REC:** pool. Pets OK. RV age restrict, 2015 rates: $50.
(909)866-7774 Lat: 34.24291, Lon: -116.90837
547 Alden Rd, Big Bear Lake, CA 92315
bigbearmobile@newportpacific.com
www.bigbearmobileestates.com
See ad this page.

HOLLOWAY'S RV PARK & MARINA **Ratings: 6/9.5/7.5** (RV Park) 2015 rates: $50 to $60. (800)448-5335 398 Edgemoor Road, Big Bear Lake, CA 92315

Like Us on Facebook.

BIG PINE — F4 *Inyo*

BAKER CREEK COUNTY PARK (Public) From town, N 0.5 mi on US-395 to Baker Creek Rd (at N end of town), W 1 mi (E). Pit toilets. 2015 rates: $10. (760)878-0272

GLACIER VIEW CAMPGROUND
Ratings: 1/5/5 (Campground) From Jct of US-395 & SR-168E: Go E on SR-168E at corner of US-395 and SR-168E (R). Elev 4000 ft. **FAC:** Gravel rds. 40 dirt, patios, back-ins (26 x 36), 9 W, 9 E (30 amps), tent sites, showers $. Pets OK. 14 day max stay, eco-friendly, 2015 rates: $15 to $20. No CC, no reservations.
(760)872-6911 Lat: 37.173469, Lon: -118.290204
se Corner of US-395 & SR-168E, Big Pine, CA 93513
See ad opposite page.

GLACIER VIEW(INYO COUNTY PARK) (Public) From town: Go 1/2 mi N on US-395 at jct Hwy-168. 2015 rates: $10. (760)872-6911

TINNEMAHA CREEK COUNTY PARK (Public) From Independence, N 19.5 mi on US-395 to Fish Springs Rd, W 0.5 mi to Tinnemaha Rd, W 2 mi (R). Pit toilets. 2015 rates: $10. (760)878-0272

BIG RIVER — H6 *San Bernardino*

BIG RIVER RV PARK **Ratings: 7.5/7/8** (RV Park) 2015 rates: $34 to $41. (760)665-9359 1 Marina St, Big River, CA 92242

RIO DEL SOL RV HAVEN **Ratings: 6.5/7.5/7.5** (Campground) 2015 rates: $40 to $50. (760)665-2981 7905 Rio Vista Dr, Big River, CA 92242

BIG SUR — F1 *Monterey*

BIG SUR CAMPGROUND & CABINS **Ratings: 5/9★/8** (Campground) 2015 rates: $65 to $80. (831)667-2322 47000 Hwy 1, Big Sur, CA 93920

FERNWOOD RESORT CAMPGROUND Ratings: 3.5/6.5/6.5 (Campground) From jct Hwy 1 & Hwy 68: Go 27-1/2 mi S on Hwy 1 (1-1/2 mi S of Big Sur) (R). **FAC:** Dirt rds. 30 dirt, back-ins (18 x 30), 30 W, 30 E (30 amps), tent sites, rentals, showers $, dump, laundry, groc, fire rings, firewood, restaurant. **REC:** Big Sur River: swim, rec open to public. Pets OK $. 28 day max stay, eco-friendly, 2015 rates: $65. Disc: AAA, military. ATM, no CC.
AAA Approved
(831)667-2422 Lat: 36.26053, Lon: -121.79245
47200 Hwy 1, Big Sur, CA 93920
www.fernwoodbigsur.com

PFEIFFER BIG SUR (State Pk) From Carmel, S 26 mi on Hwy 1 (L). 2015 rates: $35 to $50. (831)667-3100

RIVERSIDE CAMPGROUND Ratings: 5/5/7.5 (Campground) From jct Hwy 1 & Hwy 68: Go 26 mi S on Hwy 1 (R). **FAC:** Dirt rds. 12 gravel, back-ins (20 x 40), 12 W, 12 E (20 amps), WiFi, tent sites, rentals, showers $, laundry, fire rings, firewood. **REC:**

BIG SUR (CONT)

RIVERSIDE CAMPGROUND (CONT)
Big Sur River: swim. Pet restrict(Q) $. 2015 rates: $55 to $60.
AAA Approved
(831)667-2414 Lat: 36.26705, Lon: -121.80411
47020 Hwy 1, Big Sur, CA 93920
www.riversidecampground.com

BISHOP — E5 *Inyo, Mono*

BROWN'S MILLPOND CAMPGROUND
Ratings: 3.5/6.5/7.5 (Campground) From Jct of Hwy 6 & US-395: Go 4-1/2 mi N on Hwy 395 to Ed Powers Rd, then 1/4 mi S to Sawmill Rd, then 1 mi W (L). Elev 4200 ft. **FAC:** Gravel rds. 72 dirt, back-ins (27 x 54), 19 W, 19 E (30 amps), tent sites, showers $, laundry, fire rings, firewood. **REC:** McGee Creek: rec open to public. Pets OK. Partial handicap access. 14 day max stay, eco-friendly, 2015 rates: $25 to $30. Mar 1 to Oct 31. No CC.
(760)873-5342 Lat: 37.374309, Lon: -118.493713
230 Sawmill Rd, Bishop, CA 93514
campmillpond@aol.com
www.brownscampgrounds.com
See ad this page.

BROWN'S TOWN CAMPGROUND
Ratings: 5/8/7.5 (Campground) From Jct of US-6 & US-395: Go 3 mi S on US-395 to Schober Ln, then 1/8 mi W on Schober Ln (L). Elev 4137 ft. **FAC:** Paved/dirt rds. 47 dirt, 10 pull-thrus (22 x 40), back-ins (24 x 36), 47 W, 47 E (30 amps), cable, tent sites, showers $, dump, laundry, groc, fire rings, firewood. **REC:** playground. Pets OK. Partial handicap access. 14 day max stay, eco-friendly, 2015 rates: $30. Mar 1 to Nov 30.
(760)873-8522 Lat: 37.346299, Lon: -118.396187
20 Schober Lane, Bishop, CA 93514
www.brownscampgrounds.com
See ad this page & RV Trips of a Lifetime in Magazine Section.

Set a destination for family fun! Check our family camping destinations article highlighting the best places to camp in every state and province. Find a great destination, then select one of the family-friendly campgrounds listed by region.

HIGHLANDS RV PARK
Ratings: 8/9★/8.5 (RV Park) From Jct of US-6 & US-395: Go 1 mi N on US-395 to N Sierra Hwy (R). Elev 4140 ft. **FAC:** Paved rds. 103 paved, patios, 50 pull-thrus (20 x 55), back-ins (20 x 55), 103 full hkups (30/50 amps), cable, WiFi, dump, laundry, LP gas. **REC:** Bishop Creek. Pets OK. No tents. Eco-friendly, 2015 rates: $43.
(760)873-7616 Lat: 37.376197, Lon: -118.414922
2275 N Sierra Hwy, Bishop, CA 93514
www.highlandsrvpark.com
See ad this page.

HORTON CREEK BLM (Public) From town, NW 8.5 mi on US-395 to Round Valley Rd, W 5 mi (L). Donations accepted. Pit toilets. 2015 rates: $5. May 1 to Oct 30. (760)872-5000

J DIAMOND MOBILE RANCH **Ratings: 6.5/7.5/6** (Campground) 2015 rates: $25 to $35. (760)872-7341 771 N Main St, Bishop, CA 93514

KEOUGH'S HOT SPRINGS
Ratings: 5.5/7/7.5 (RV Park) From Jct of US-395 & US-6: Go 8 mi S on US-395 to Keough Hot Springs Rd, then 1 mi W on Keough Hot Springs Rd (E). Elev 4350 ft. **FAC:** Gravel/dirt rds. 19 Avail: 10 grass, 9 dirt, 1 pull-thrus (24 x 57), back-ins (20 x 40), 11 W, 11 E (20/30 amps), WiFi, tent sites, rentals, showers $, fire rings, firewood. **REC:** heated pool $, whirlpool, rec open to public. Pet restrict(Q). 14 day max stay, 2015 rates: $33.
(760)872-4670 Lat: 37.253555, Lon: -118.374905
800 Keough's Hot Springs Rd, Bishop, CA 93514
www.keoughshotsprings.com
See ad this page.

PLEASANT VALLEY COUNTY PARK (Public) From Jct of US-6 & US-395, NW 7 mi on US-395 to Pleasant Valley Rd, N 1 mi (R). Pit toilets. 2015 rates: $10. (760)873-5577

BLAIRSDEN — C3 *Plumas*

LITTLE BEAR RV PARK **Ratings: 7.5/8.5★/8** (Campground) 2015 rates: $33 to $36. Apr 15 to Oct 28. (530)836-2774 102 Little Bear Rd, Blairsden, CA 96103

Tell them you saw them in this Guide!

PLUMAS-EUREKA (State Pk) From Jct of SR-89 & CR-A14, SW 5.5 mi on CR-A14 (L). For reservations call 1-800-444-7275. 2015 rates: $35. May 24 to Sep 29. (916)836-2380

BLYTHE — J6 *Riverside*

DESTINY RV RESORTS-MCINTYRE CAMPGROUND
Ratings: 6.5/5.5/6.5 (Campground) From Jct of I-10 & Intake Blvd (Exit 241), S 7 mi on Intake Blvd (L). **FAC:** Paved/dirt rds. (222 spaces). Avail: 19 grass, 11 pull-thrus (22 x 55), back-ins (20 x 40), some side by side hkups, 11 full hkups, 8 W, 8 E (30/50 amps), seasonal sites, WiFi $, tent sites, dump, mobile sewer, LP gas. **REC:** Colorado River: swim, fishing, marina, rec open to public. Pet restrict(B). Partial handicap access. RV age restrict, 2015 rates: $21.64 to $39.64. Disc: AAA.
(760)922-8205 Lat: 33.51597, Lon: -114.56555
8750 Peter D. Mcintyre Ave, Blythe, CA 92225
mcintyre@destinyrv.com
www.destinyrv.com
See ad this page.

HIDDEN BEACHES RIVER RESORT **Ratings: 6/8★/7.5** (RV Park) 2015 rates: $30 to $42. (760)922-7276 6951 Sixth Ave, Blythe, CA 92225

MAYFLOWER COUNTY PARK (Public) From town, N 3.5 mi on State Hwy 95 to 6th Ave, E 3 mi to the Colorado River Rd, N 0.5 mi (E). 2015 rates: $20 to $30. (760)922-4665

RIVIERA RV RESORT AND MARINA
Ratings: 9/9★/8 (RV Resort) E-bnd: From Jct of I-10 & Riviera Dr (Exit 243), E 0.1 mi on Riviera Dr (L); or W-bnd: From Jct of I-10 & Riviera Dr (Exit 243) (CA Agriculture Stn), E 0.5 mi on Riviera Dr (L) Note: DO NOT USE GPS. **FAC:** Paved rds. 175 Avail: 5 gravel, 170 grass, 60 pull-thrus (32 x 55), back-ins (20 x 54), mostly side by side hkups, 175 full hkups (30/50 amps), cable, WiFi, tent sites, rentals, dump, laundry, groc, LP gas, firewood, controlled access. **REC:** pool, whirlpool, Colorado River: swim, fishing, marina, playground, rec open to public. Pet restrict(B). Partial handicap access. RV age restrict, eco-friendly, 2015 rates: $39.11 to $61.11. ATM.
AAA Approved
(855)922-5350 Lat: 33.60380, Lon: -114.53583
500 Riviera Drive, Blythe, CA 92225
info@rivierarvresort.com
www.rivierarvresort.com
See ad this page, 126.

BODEGA BAY — D2 *Sonoma*

BODEGA BAY RV PARK
Ratings: 8.5/10★/9.5 (RV Park) From Jct of SR-1 & Bay Hill Rd (1.2 mi N of town), NW 100 ft on SR-1 (L). **FAC:** Paved rds. (68 spaces). Avail: 66 gravel, 26 pull-thrus (29 x 62), back-ins (24 x 40), accepts full hkup units only, 53 full hkups,

BODEGA BAY (CONT)

BODEGA BAY RV PARK (CONT)
13 W, 13 E (30/50 amps), seasonal sites, cable, WiFi, dump, laundry, restaurant. **REC:** Bodega Bay: fishing. Pets OK. Partial handicap access, no tents. Big rig sites, eco-friendly, 2015 rates: $44 to $46. Disc: AAA, military.
AAA Approved
(707)875-3701 Lat: 38.34068, Lon: -123.04906
2001 Hwy 1, Bodega Bay, CA 94923
www.bodegabayrvpark.com
See ad page 171.

DORAN BEACH PARK (Public) From Jct of Hwy 1 & Doran Pk Rd, S 1 mi on Doran Pk Rd, follow signs (R). For reservations call (707)565-CAMP. 2015 rates: $32. (707)875-3540

SONOMA COAST STATE BEACH/BODEGA DUNES (State Pk) From town, N 0.5 mi on Hwy 1 (L). 2015 rates: $35. (707)875-3483

SONOMA COAST STATE BEACH/WRIGHTS BEACH (State Pk) From town, N 6 mi on Hwy 1 (L). 2015 rates: $35 to $45. (707)875-3483

WESTSIDE PARK (Public) From Jct of Hwy 1 & Eastshore Rd, exit onto Bay Flat Rd, W 2 mi (L). For reservations call (707)565-CAMP. 2015 rates: $32. (707)875-3540

BONITA — K5 *San Diego*

SWEETWATER SUMMIT COUNTY PARK (Public) From Jct of I-5 & I-805 (exit 31), S 20 mi on I-805 to Bonita Rd (exit 7C), E 4 mi to San Miguel Rd (do not cross bridge), continue 2 mi to entrance (L). 2015 rates: $29 to $33. (877)565-3600

BORON — H4 *Kern*

ARABIAN RV OASIS
Ratings: 6/6/5 (RV Park) From Hwy 58 & Boron Ave (Exit 199): Go 1/4 mi S on Boron Ave (R). Elev 2550 ft.

BETWEEN MOJAVE AND BARSTOW
Stop over in Boron and eat where the Astronauts eat when they return from Space. While you're here, visit the New Air Museum, the Borax Visitor Center (one of the largest open pit mines in the world) and the Boron Museum.

FAC: Paved rds. (52 spaces). Avail: 30 gravel, patios, 12 pull-thrus (25 x 80), back-ins (25 x 40), 30 full hkups (30/50 amps), seasonal sites, WiFi, dump, laundry. Pets OK. Eco-friendly, 2015 rates: $26.
(760)762-5008 Lat: 35.004831, Lon: -117.65024
12401 Boron Ave, Boron, CA 93516
See ad this page.

BORREGO SPRINGS — J5 *San Diego*

ANZA-BORREGO PALM CANYON (State Pk) From Jct of CR-S3 & CR-S22 (in town), W 2 mi on CR-S22/Palm Canyon Dr (R). 2015 rates: $20 to $35. (800)444-7275

BLU IN PARK RV RESORT AND CAFE **Ratings: 6.5/10★/7.5** (RV Park) 2015 rates: $45 to $55. (760)561-1370 2189 Hwy 78, Borrego Springs, CA 92004

PALM CANYON HOTEL AND RV RESORT
Ratings: 8/8★/8.5 (RV Park) From Jct of Hwy 78 & S-3, N 11.5 mi on S-3 to S-22, W 1.6 mi (L). **FAC:** Paved rds. 85 dirt, 33 pull-thrus (22 x 70), back-ins (22 x 40), 85 full hkups (30 amps), WiFi $, rentals, laundry, LP gas, restaurant. **REC:** heated pool, whirlpool. Pet restrict(B/Q). Partial handicap access, no tents. RV age restrict, eco-friendly, 2015 rates: $45 to $55.
(760)767-5341 Lat: 33.25642, Lon: -116.39828
221 Palm Canyon Drive, Borrego Springs, CA 92004
stay@palmcanyonrvresort.com
www.highwaywestvacations.com

THE SPRINGS AT BORREGO RV RESORT & GOLF COURSE
Ratings: 10/10★/10 (RV Resort) From Jct of Hwys S-3 & S-22 (in town), E 0.5 mi on Hwy S-22 to Di Giorgio Rd, N 0.6 mi (R). **FAC:** Paved rds. 163 paved, patios, 90 pull-thrus (35 x 60), back-ins (40 x 70), 163 full hkups (30/50 amps), cable, WiFi, rentals, dump, laundry, LP gas, firewood, controlled access. **REC:** heated pool, whirlpool, Golf Lake: fishing, golf, playground. Pet restrict(Q). Partial handicap access, no tents. Big rig sites, RV age restrict, eco-friendly, 2015 rates: $29 to $108. Disc: military.
(866)330-0003 Lat: 33.26626, Lon: -116.36526
2255 Digiorgio Road, Borrego Springs, CA 92004
danwright@springsatborrego.com
www.springsatborrego.com
See ad pages 136 (Spotlight Borrego Springs), 126 & Snowbird Destinations in Magazine Section.

BOULDER CREEK — F1 *Santa Cruz*

REDWOODS/BIG BASIN (State Pk) From Santa Cruz, N 14 mi on SR-9 to SR-236 (at Boulder Creek), NW 9 mi (R). 2015 rates: $35. (831)338-8860

BOULEVARD — K5 *San Diego*

THE OAKS AT SACRED ROCKS RV PARK AND CAMPGROUND **Ratings: 9/9★/8** (Campground) 2015 rates: $37. (619)766-4480 1331 Shasta Way, Boulevard, CA 91905

BRIDGEPORT — D4 *Mono*

BRIDGEPORT RESERVOIR RV PARK & MARINA **Ratings: 6.5/8.5★/7.5** (Campground) 2015 rates: $30 to $34. Apr 1 to Oct 31. (760)932-7001 1845 Hwy 182, Bridgeport, CA 93517

PARADISE SHORES RV PARK **Ratings: 6/8.5★/7.5** (RV Park) 2015 rates: $34. Apr 15 to Nov 5. (760)932-7735 2399 Hwy 182, Bridgeport, CA 93517

TWIN LAKES RESORT
Ratings: 7/7.5/7 (Campground) From the intersection of Hwy 395 and Twin Lakes Rd: Go 11 miles W on Twin Lakes Rd (R) Note: Office is at second sign for park. Elev 7126 ft. **FAC:** Paved/gravel rds. 20 dirt, back-ins (22 x 45), 20 full hkups (30/50 amps), WiFi Hotspot, tent sites, rentals, showers $, laundry, groc, LP gas, fire rings, firewood. **REC:** Lower Twin Lake: swim, fishing, marina, playground. Pets OK. Eco-friendly, 2015 rates: $29 to $40. Disc: military. Apr 15 to Nov 15.
(760)932-7751 Lat: 38.1719, Lon: -119.3322
10316 Twin Lakes Rd, Bridgeport, CA 93517
misti@twinlakeresort.com
www.twinlakeresort.com
See ad this page, 128.

VIRGINIA CREEK SETTLEMENT **Ratings: 3/6/5** (Campground) From Jct of Hwy 182 & US-395: Go 5-1/4 mi S on US-395 (R). Elev 6800 ft. **FAC:** Paved/gravel rds. 3 gravel, no slide-outs, WiFi Hotspot, tent sites, rentals, showers $, fire rings, firewood, restaurant. **REC:** Virginia Creek: fishing. Pets OK $. 2015 rates: $18. Disc: AAA. Mar 1 to Nov 1. No CC, no reservations.
AAA Approved
(760)932-7780 Lat: 38.187791, Lon: -119.206263
70847 Hwy 395, Bridgeport, CA 93517
info@virginiacrksettlement.com
www.virginiacreeksettlement.com

WILLOW SPRINGS MOTEL & RV PARK **Ratings: 4/8★/8.5** (RV Park) 2015 rates: $35 to $55. Apr 24 to Oct 31. (760)932-7725 70970 Hwy 395, Bridgeport, CA 93517

BROWNS VALLEY — C3 *Yuba*

COLLINS LAKE RECREATION AREA **Ratings: 6.5/7/7.5** (Campground) 2015 rates: $42 to $58. (800)286-0576 7530 Collins Lake Rd, Browns Valley, CA 95918

BUELLTON — H2 *Santa Barbara*

FLYING FLAGS RV RESORT & CAMPGROUND **Ratings: 9/10★/8.5** (RV Park) 2015 rates: $32 to $98. (805)688-3716 180 Avenue of Flags, Buellton, CA 93427

BURNEY — B3 *Plumas, Shasta*

BURNEY See Also Hat Creek, McArthur & Shingletown.

MCARTHUR BURNEY FALLS MEMORIAL (State Pk) From Jct of SR-299 & SR-89, N 6 mi on SR-89 (L). 2015 rates: $15 to $35. (530)335-2777

PG & E/PIT RIVER/CASSEL CAMPGROUND (Public) From Jct of Hwys 299 & 89, E 2 mi on Hwy 299 to Cassel Rd, S 3.6 mi (L). Pit toilets. 2015 rates: $20. (916)386-5164

CALISTOGA — D2 *Napa*

BOTHE-NAPA VALLEY (State Pk) From town, N 5 mi on SR-29 (L). Reservations strongly recommended. 2015 rates: $35. (800)942-4575

CALISTOGA RV PARK
(Public) From Jct of SR-128 & 29, NE 0.4 mi on SR-29 (Lincoln Ave) to Fairway, NW 0.3 mi to N Oak St, NE 500 ft (L). **FAC:** Paved rds. 69 gravel, 32 pull-thrus (30 x 70), back-ins (18 x 40), some side by side hkups, accepts full hkup units only, 24 full hkups, 45 W, 45 E (30/50 amps), WiFi, dump. Pets OK $. Partial handicap access, no tents. 14 day max stay, 2015 rates: $37 to $55.
(707)942-5221 Lat: 38.58518, Lon: -122.58423
1601 N. Oak Street, Calistoga, CA 94515
info@CalistogaRVpark.org
www.calistogarvpark.org
See ad this page.

CANYON DAM — C3 *Plumas*

PG & E/FEATHER RIVER/ROCKY POINT CAMPGROUND (Public) From Jct of Hwys 147 & 89, NW 5 mi on Hwy 89. Pit toilets. 2015 rates: $22.94 to $45.88. (916)386-5164

CAPITOLA — F1 *Santa Cruz*

NEW BRIGHTON STATE BEACH (State Pk) From Jct of Hwy 1 & Park Ave (exit 456/frntg rd), W 0.5 mi on frntg rd (R). 2015 rates: $35 to $50. (831)464-6329

CARDIFF-BY-THE-SEA — J4 *San Diego*

SAN ELIJO STATE BEACH (State Pk) From Jct of I-5 & Encinitas Blvd exit (Exit 41B), W 0.75 mi on Encinitas Blvd to US-101(1st St), S 2 mi (R). 2015 rates: $35 to $70. (760)753-5091

Tell your RV Campground that you found them in this Guide.

CARLSBAD — J4 *San Diego*

SOUTH CARLSBAD (State Pk) From Jct of I-5 & Palomar Airport Rd (Exit 47), W on Palomar Airport Rd to Carlsbad Blvd, S 3 mi (R). For reservations call 1-800-444-7275. 2015 rates: $35 to $50. (760)438-3143

TRAILER RANCHO RV PARK
Ratings: 7.5/9.5★/6.5 (RV Park) From Jct of Carlsbad Village Dr & I-5,(San Diego Freeway) S 6 mi on I-5 (San Diego Freeway) to La Costa Ave (exit 44), W 0.5 mi on La Costa Ave to N Vulcan Ave, S 0.5 mi (L). **FAC:** Paved rds. (83 spaces). Avail: 50 all weather, patios, back-ins (28 x 36), 50 full hkups (30/50 amps), seasonal sites, WiFi, laundry. **REC.** Pet restrict(B/Q). Partial handicap access, no tents. RV age restrict, 2015 rates: $50.
(760)753-2741 Lat: 33.07549, Lon: -117.30527
1549 N Vulcan Ave, Encinitas, CA 92024
trailerrancho@prodigy.net
www.goodsamcamping.com.s3.amazonaws.com/gsparks/840000652/index.html
See primary listing at Encinitas and ad page 153 (Spotlight San Diego).

CARMEL — F1 *Monterey*

CARMEL BY THE RIVER RV PARK **Ratings: 7.5/10★/9.5** (RV Park) 2015 rates: $60 to $85. (831)624-9329 27680 Schulte Rd, Carmel, CA 93923

SADDLE MOUNTAIN RV PARK & CAMPGROUND **Ratings: 6.5/7/8.5** (RV Park) 2015 rates: $60 to $90. (831)624-1617 27625 Schulte Rd, Carmel, CA 93923

CARPINTERIA — H3 *Santa Barbara*

CARPINTERIA STATE BEACH (State Pk) From Jct of US-101 & Casitas Pass exit (Exit 86A), SW 0.1 mi on exit rd to Carpinteria St, N 0.1mi to Palm, W 0.5 mi (E). Advance Reservations Recommended. 2015 rates: $50 to $65. (800)444-7275

CASTAIC — H3 *Los Angeles*

CASTAIC LAKE RV CAMPGROUND (Public) From Jct of I-5 & Lake Hughes Rd exit (exit 176B), E 1.5 mi on Lake Hughes Rd to 2nd park entrance, cross lake bridge, follow signs (L). 2015 rates: $20. (661)257-4050

CASTAIC LAKE RV PARK
Ratings: 8.5/10★/8 (RV Park) From Jct of N-bnd I-5 & Parker Rd. (Exit 176A): Go 1/4 mi E on Parker Rd/becomes Ridge Route Rd (R); From Jct of S-Bnd I-5 & Lake Hughes Rd (Exit 176): Go 1/2 mi S on The Old Rd, then 1/2 mi E on Parker Rd/becomes Ridge Route Rd (R).

5 MINUTES TO SIX FLAGS * FREE WIFI
35 minutes to Universal Studios & Hollywood. Newly renovated sites. Easy access pull thrus. Grass sitting area and fire pits. Store with groceries, beverages, pet supplies and RV supplies. Propane.

FAC: Paved rds. (103 spaces). Avail: 15 paved, patios, 15 pull-thrus (27 x 60), 15 full hkups (30/50 amps), seasonal sites, cable, WiFi, dump, laundry, groc, LP gas, fire rings, firewood. **REC:** heated pool, whirlpool, playground. Pet restrict(B/Q). Partial handicap access, no tents. Big rig sites, eco-friendly, 2015 rates: $50 to $53. Disc: AAA, military.
AAA Approved
(661)257-3340 Lat: 34.491688, Lon: -118.616590
31540 Ridge Route Rd, Castaic, CA 91384
castaicrvprk@earthlink.net
castaiclakervpark.com
See ad pages 139 (Spotlight Los Angeles), 128.

CATHEDRAL CITY — J5 *Riverside*

OUTDOOR RESORT PALM SPRINGS
Ratings: 10/10★/10 (Condo Pk) From Jct of I-10 & Bob Hope Dr (Exit 130), S 0.3 mi on Bob Hope Dr to Ramon Rd, W 2.1 mi (L). **FAC:** Paved rds. (1213 spaces). Avail: 200 paved, patios, back-ins (35 x 65), accepts self-contain units only, 200 full hkups (30/50 amps), seasonal sites, cable, WiFi $, laundry, groc, restaurant, controlled access. **REC:** heated pool, whirlpool, golf. Pet restrict(Q) $. Partial handicap access, no tents. Big rig sites, RV age restrict, 2015 rates: $41 to $84.
(800)843-3131 Lat: 33.81509, Lon: -116.44833
69411 Ramon Rd, Cathedral City, CA 92234
reservations1@orps.com
www.outdoorresortpalmsprings.com
See ad page 147 (Spotlight Palm Springs).

PALM SPRINGS OASIS RV RESORT **Ratings: 8.5/9★/7.5** (RV Resort) 2015 rates: $49 to $55. (800)680-0144 36100 Date Palm Dr, Cathedral City, CA 92234

CEDAR GLEN — L6 *San Bernardino*

SAN BERNADINO NATIONAL FOREST (NORTH SHORE CAMPGROUND) (State Pk) From town: Go 1-1/2 mi N on Hwy-173, then 1/4 mi E on Hospital Rd (CR-3N41). 2015 rates: $22 to $46. (909)337-6399

CEDAR GROVE — F3 *Fresno, Tulare*

KINGS CANYON NATIONAL PARK (CANYON VIEW) (Natl Pk) From the village: Go 1/2 mi E on Hwy 180. 2015 rates: $35 to $40. May 20 to Sep 29. (559)565-3341

KINGS CANYON/MORAINE CAMPGROUND (Natl Pk) From Cedar Grove Ranger Station, E 1 mi on Hwy 180 (L). 2015 rates: $18. (559)335-2856

KINGS CANYON/SENTINEL (Natl Pk) At Cedar Grove Ranger Station on Hwy 180 (E). 2015 rates: $18. (559)335-2856

KINGS CANYON/SHEEP CREEK CAMPGROUND (Natl Pk) From Cedar Grove Ranger Station, W 0.5 mi on Hwy 180 (R). 2015 rates: $18. (559)335-2856

CHERRY VALLEY — J5 *Riverside*

BOGART PARK (RIVERSIDE COUNTY) (Public) From jct Hwy 60 & I-10: Go 3/4 mi E on I-10, then 2-1/4 mi N on Beaumont Ave, then 3/4 mi E on Brookside Ave, then 1 mi N on Cherry Ave. 2015 rates: $10 to $12. (951)845-3818

Heading to a privately owned park? Be sure to read how our inspection team rated it in the Guide "How to Use This Travel Guide" section.

CHESTER — B3 *Plumas, Tehama*

LASSEN NF (CHERRY HILL CAMPGROUND) (Natl Forest) From town: Go 11-1/2 mi W on Hwy-36, then 20 mi SW on Hwy-32, then 6 mi E on CR-91422. Pit toilets. 2015 rates: $14. May 1 to Oct 31. (530)257-2151

MARTIN'S RV PARK (RV Spaces) From jct SR-89/SR-36 Go 2mi NE on SR-36 then rt on Martin Way (L). Elev 4500 ft. **FAC:** Gravel rds. (14 spaces). Avail: 12 grass, 1 pull-thrus (15 x 40), back-ins (15 x 35), some side by side hkups, accepts full hkup units only, 12 full hkups (30/50 amps), seasonal sites, cable, WiFi, rentals, dump. Pet restrict(B/Q). 2015 rates: $31. No CC.
(530)258-2407 Lat: 40.30554, Lon: -121.23190
443 Martin way, Chester, CA 96020
diannemartin@ronmartinrealty.com

NORTH SHORE CAMPGROUND
Ratings: 7/9.5★/7.5 (RV Park) E-bnd: Jct of SR-36 & 89 (at Chester), NE 4.6 mi on SR-36 (R); or W-bnd: From Jct of SR-36 & CR-A13, W 2.9 mi on SR-36 (L). **FAC:** Paved/gravel rds. (136 spaces). Avail: 101 gravel, 101 full hkups (20/30 amps), seasonal sites, WiFi Hotspot, dump, mobile sewer, laundry, groc, LP gas, fire rings, controlled access. **REC:** Lake Almanor: swim, fishing. Pets OK. 2015 rates: $40 to $56. May 1 to Oct 1. No CC.
(530)258-3376 Lat: 40.31136, Lon: -121.18942
541 Catfish Beach Rd., Chester, CA 96020
info@northshorecampground.com
www.northshorecampground.com
See ad pages 189, 128.

CHICAGO PARK — D3 *Nevada*

ORCHARD SPRINGS RESORT **Ratings: 4.5/6/7** (Campground) 2015 rates: $39. (530)346-2212 19085 Larsen Rd, Chicago Park, CA 95712

CHICO — C2 *Butte*

ALMOND TREE RV PARK
Ratings: 9.5/10★/9 (RV Park) From Jct of SR-99 & SR-32 (SE of town/Exit 389), N 3.7 mi on SR-99 to Eaton Rd, SW 0.2 mi to Esplanade, SE 0.4 mi (L). **FAC:** Paved rds. 42 gravel, patios, 26 pull-thrus (25 x 65), back-ins (25 x 60), accepts self-contain units only, 42 full hkups (30/50 amps), cable, WiFi, dump, laundry, groc. **REC:** pool. Pets OK. Partial handicap access, no tents. Big rig sites, 2015 rates: $43. Disc: AAA, military.
AAA Approved
(530)899-1271 Lat: 39.76880, Lon: -121.87062
3124 Esplanade Ave, Chico, CA 95973
rvpark@chico.com
www.chico.com/rvpark
See ad this page, 128.

CHINO — M4 *San Bernardino*

PRADO REGIONAL PARK
(Public) From Jct of Hwy 91 & Hwy 71 exit, N 3.7 mi on Hwy 71 to Euclid Ave (Hwy 83), NE 1 mi (R). Minimum 2 ngts stay on weekends. **FAC:** Paved rds. 75 paved, patios, 58 pull-thrus (25 x 60), back-ins (25 x 40), 75 full hkups (20/50 amps), tent sites, showers $, dump, laundry, fire rings, firewood, controlled access. **REC:** Prado Lake:

CHINO (CONT)

PRADO REGIONAL PARK (CONT)
fishing, golf, playground, rec open to public. Pet restrict(Q) $. Big rig sites, RV age restrict, 14 day max stay, 2015 rates: $35 to $45.
(909)597-4260 Lat: 33.94618, Lon: -117.65157
16700 S Euclid Ave, Chino, CA 91708
www.sbcountyparks.com
See ad page 123 (Welcome Section).

CHOWCHILLA — F2 *Madera*

ARENA RV PARK
Ratings: 5.5/7/6.5 (RV Park) From Jct of Hwy 99 & Hwy 233 (Robertson Blvd exit 170): Go 1/4 mi W on Hwy 233 to Chowchilla Blvd, then 1/4 mi S on Chowchilla Blvd (L). **FAC:** Paved/gravel rds. (38 spaces). Avail: 25 grass, 12 pull-thrus (18 x 55), back-ins (24 x 40), 25 full hkups (30/50 amps), seasonal sites, WiFi, tent sites, dump, laundry. Pet restrict(Q). Eco-friendly, 2015 rates: $28 to $42.
(559)665-1752 Lat: 37.123801, Lon: -120.255200
203 S Chowchilla Blvd, Chowchilla, CA 93610
arenarvparkmanager@outlook.com
www.arenarvpark.net
See ad page 183.

THE LAKES RV & GOLF RESORT
Ratings: 10/10★/9.5 (RV Resort) From Jct of Hwy 99 & E Robertson Blvd (Exit 170): Go 1-1/4 mi E on Robertson Blvd (R).

GOLF FOR 2 INCL WITH YOUR STAY!
The Lakes RV & Golf Resort is in California's Heartland. Close to Hwy 99 an easy drive to SF, Napa, Yosemite, Tahoe & Monterey. Tranquil lakes, refreshing pool & spa. Complimentary golf for two. Big Rigs welcome.
FAC: Paved rds. (87 spaces). Avail: 81 paved, patios, 18 pull-thrus (30 x 77), back-ins (26 x 54), accepts full hkup units only, 81 full hkups (30/50 amps), seasonal sites, cable, WiFi, dump, laundry, restaurant, controlled access. **REC:** heated pool, whirlpool, golf. Pet restrict(Q). Partial handicap access, no tents. Big rig sites, eco-friendly, 2015 rates: $40 to $60. Disc: AAA.
(866)665-6980 Lat: 37.12714, Lon: -120.22880
5001 E Robertson, Chowchilla, CA 93610
thelakesrv@yahoo.com
www.thelakesrv.com
See ad this page, 128.

Things to See and Do

PHEASANT RUN GOLF CLUB 18 hole championship golf course Par 72. RV accessible. Restrooms, food. Hours: 7am to 5pm.
(559)665-3411 Lat: 37.12547, Lon: -120.23061
19 Clubhouse Dr, Chowchilla, CA 93610
See ad this page.

THE FINAL ROUND Breakfast, lunch and dinner served daily. Outdoor, wood fire pizza oven. RV accessible. Restrooms, food. Hours: 7am to 9pm.
(559)744-7000 Lat: 37.12549, Lon: -120.23061
19 Clubhouse Dr, Chowchilla, CA 93610
See ad this page.

CHULA VISTA — K4 *San Diego*

CHULA VISTA RV RESORT AND MARINA
Ratings: 10/10★/9.5 (RV Park) From Jct of I-5 & J St (exit 7B), W 500 ft on J St (becomes Marina Pkwy), continue 0.5 mi on Marina Pkwy to Sandpiper Way, W 0.2 mi (L).

NESTLED ON BEAUTIFUL SAN DIEGO BAY
On San Diego Bay, surrounded by landscaped parks & its own marina. Amenities include a general store, boutique, picnic area w/barbeques, swimming pool & spa, laundry, club rooms & adjacent water-front restaurants.
FAC: Paved rds. 237 paved, patios, 54 pull-thrus (20 x 62), back-ins (20 x 52), 237 full hkups (30/50 amps), cable, WiFi, laundry, groc, LP gas, restaurant, controlled access. **REC:** heated pool, whirlpool, San Diego Bay: fishing. Pet restrict(B/Q) $. Partial handicap access, no tents. RV age restrict, eco-friendly, 2015 rates: $61 to $80. Disc: AAA. ATM.
AAA Approved
(800)770-2878 Lat: 32.62691, Lon: -117.10480
460 Sandpiper Way, Chula Vista, CA 91910
info@chulavistarv.com
www.chulavistarv.com
See ad pages 155 (Spotlight San Diego), 126.

SAN DIEGO METROPOLITAN KOA **Ratings: 9/10★/8.5** (RV Park) 2015 rates: $49 to $90. (800)562-9877 111 North 2nd Ave, Chula Vista, CA 91910

CLEAR LAKE — D2 *Lake*

CLEAR LAKE See also Hidden Valley Lake, Kelseyville, Lakeport, Nice & Upper Lake.

CLEARLAKE OAKS — D2 *Lake*

M & M CAMPGROUND (Public) From Water District & Hwy 20, L on I-5 to Stubbs Island (E). 2015 rates: $15. (707)349-0866

CLIO — C3 *Plumas*

CLIO'S RIVERS EDGE RV PARK **Ratings: 8.5/9★/9** (RV Park) 2015 rates: $36 to $50. Apr 15 to Oct 15. (530)836-2375 3754 Hwy 89, Clio, CA 96106

We give campgrounds one rating for amenities, a second for restrooms and a third for visual appearance and environmental quality. That's the Triple Rating System.

CLOVERDALE — D2 *Sonoma*

CLOVERDALE CITRUS FAIR
(Public) From Jct of US-101 & Citrus Fair Dr exit (S of town), exit Fwy W to stop light, W 300 ft (straight across intersection) on Citrus Fair Dr (R). After 5pm or on weekends, check phone numbers on Washington Street gate. **FAC:** Paved rds. 40 paved, patios, 6 pull-thrus (12 x 35), back-ins (20 x 60), mostly side by side hkups, 4 full hkups, 36 W, 36 E (20/50 amps), WiFi, tent sites, dump. Pets OK. Partial handicap access. 14 day max stay, 2015 rates: $25.
(707)894-3992 Lat: 38.27353, Lon: -122.68046
1 Citrus Fair Drive, Cloverdale, CA 95425
citrus@sonic.net
www.cloverdalecitrusfair.org
See ad this page.

CLOVERDALE/HEALDSBURG KOA CAMPING RESORT Ratings: 8.5/8.5/7.5 (Campground) From Jct of US-101 & Citrus Fair Dr, exit E to Asti Rd, N 0.6 mi to First St (changes to Crocker Rd), E 0.8 mi to River Rd, S 3.7 mi to Asti Ridge Rd, E 1.3 mi (E). Winding Rds. (During summer months, use Asti Exit). **FAC:** paved/gravel rds. (82 spaces). Avail: 62 gravel, 6 pull-thrus (15 x 40), back-ins (15 x 50), mostly side by side hkups, 62 full hkups (30/50 amps), seasonal sites, WiFi $, tent sites. Rentals, dump, laundry, groc, LP gas, firewood. **REC:** heated pool, whirlpool, pond, fishing, playground. Pet restrict(B). Partial handicap access. Big rig sites, eco-friendly, 2015 rates: $55 to $70.
AAA Approved
(707)894-3337 Lat: 38.77647, Lon: -122.96157
1166 Asti Ridge Rd, Cloverdale, CA 95425
clovkoa@sonic.net
www.winecountrykoa.com

RUSSIAN RIVER RV **Ratings: 8/8.5★/8.5** (RV Park) 2015 rates: $38 to $43. (800)405-6188 33655 Geysers Rd, Cloverdale, CA 95425

COALINGA — G2 *Fresno*

SOMMERVILLE RV PARK **Ratings: 6.5/6/5.5** (RV Park) 2015 rates: $41. (559)935-0711 41191 S Glenn Ave, Coalinga, CA 93210

COARSEGOLD — E4 *Madera*

YOSEMITE SOUTH/COARSEGOLD KOA **Ratings: 7.5/6/7** (RV Park) 2015 rates: $47 to $78. (559)683-7855 34094 Hwy 41, Coarsegold, CA 93614

COBB — D2 *Lake*

JELLYSTONE RV PARK & CAMP RESORT **Ratings: 8/6.5/7.5** (RV Park) 2015 rates: $36 to $45. (707)928-4322 14117 Bottle Rock Rd, Cobb, CA 95426

Had a great stay? Let us know by emailing us travelguidecomments@goodsamfamily.com

COLEVILLE — D4 *El Dorado*

COLEVILLE/WALKER KOA **Ratings: 8/10★/7.5** (RV Park) 2015 rates: $35 to $45. Mar 1 to Nov 30. (530)495-2255 110437 US Hwy 395, Coleville, CA 96107

COLOMA — D3 *El Dorado*

AMERICAN RIVER RESORT **Ratings: 7/7.5/7.5** (Campground) 2015 rates: $45. (530)622-6700 6019 New River Rd, Coloma, CA 95613

COLOMA RESORT **Ratings: 7.5/9★/8.5** (RV Park) 2015 rates: $41 to $49. (800)238-2298 6921 Mt Murphy, Coloma, CA 95613

FOLSOM LAKE SRA/PENINSULA (State Pk) From Jct of Hwy 49 & Rattlesnake Bar Rd, W 9 mi on Rattlesnake Bar Rd (E). 2015 rates: $28 to $33. (916)988-0205

COLTON — M5 *San Bernardino*

RECHE CANYON MOBILE ESTATE & RV PARK **Ratings: 8.5/8/7.5** (RV Park) 2015 rates: $45 to $50. (909)825-4824 2751 Reche Canyon Rd, Colton, CA 92324

COLUMBIA — E3 *Tuolumne*

MARBLE QUARRY RV PARK
Ratings: 8/7.5/7.5 (Campground) From Jct of Hwy 49 & Parrotts Ferry Rd (Columbia exit), N 1.5 mi on Parrotts Ferry Rd to Columbia St, E 0.5 mi to Jackson/Yankee Hill Rd, E 0.3 mi(R). **FAC:** Paved/gravel rds. (70 spaces). Avail: 64 gravel, 6 pull-thrus (20 x 60), back-ins (15 x 40), 64 full hkups (30/50 amps), seasonal sites, WiFi, tent sites, rentals, dump, laundry, groc, LP gas, fire rings, firewood. **REC:** pool, playground. Pets OK. Partial handicap access. Eco-friendly, 2015 rates: $40 to $52. Disc: AAA, military.
AAA Approved
(866)677-8464 Lat: 38.03519, Lon: -120.39302
11551 Yankee Hill Rd, Columbia, CA 95310
info@marblequarry.com
www.marblequarry.com
See ad this page.

TUTTLETOWN REC AREA/ACORN (Public) From town, N 8 mi on Hwy 49 to Reynolds Fairy Rd (access rd), W 2 mi (E). 2015 rates: $16 to $20. (209)536-9094

TUTTLETOWN REC AREA/MANZANITA (Public) From town, N 8 mi on Hwy 49 to Reynolds Fairy Rd (acess rd), W 2 mi (E). 2015 rates: $16 to $20. (209)536-9094

49ER RV RANCH
Ratings: 8/9★/9 (RV Park) From Jct of Hwy 49 & Parrotts Ferry Rd (Columbia exit), N 1.5 mi on Parrotts Ferry Rd to Columbia St (follow camping signs), NE 0.4 mi to Pacific St, W 1 blk to Italian Bar Rd, N 0.5 mi (R). **FAC:** Paved rds. (55 spaces). Avail: 45 gravel, 1 pull-thrus (20 x 60), back-ins (23 x 48), accepts full hkup units only, 45 full hkups (30/50 amps), seasonal sites, cable, WiFi, dump, laundry, groc, LP gas, firewood. **REC.** Pets OK. No tents. Big rig sites, eco-friendly, 2015 rates: $40 to $49. Disc: AAA, military.
AAA Approved
(209)532-4978 Lat: 38.04347, Lon: -120.39869
23223 Italian Bar Rd, Columbia, CA 95310
stay@49rv.com
www.49rv.com
See ad pages 220, 128.

Find it Fast! Use our alphabetized index of campgrounds and parks.

COLUSA — C2 *Colusa*

COLUSA COUNTY FAIRGROUNDS (Public) W-bnd: From Jct of SR-20 & SR-45 (in town), W 0.7 mi on SR-20 (L); or E-bnd: From Jct of I-5 & SR-20, E 7.9 mi on SR-20 (R). Register at office on side next to SR-20. 2015 rates: $10 to $20. (530)458-2641

COLUSA SACRAMENTO RIVER SRA (State Pk) From Jct of I-5 & Hwy 20 (exit 578), E 9 mi on Hwy 20 (becomes 10th St), follow signs (E). 2015 rates: $15 to $25. (530)458-4927

CONCORD — E2 *Contra Costa*

SUNNY ACRES MOBILE HOME PARK AND RV PARK
(RV Spaces) From jct Hwy 4 & I-680: Go 3-1/2 mi S on I-680 to Gregory Lane/Pleasant Hill exit, then 2-1/4 mi E on Monument Blvd, then 1 block S on Systron, then 1/4 mi S on San Miguel. **FAC:** Paved rds. (80 spaces). Avail: 10 paved, 2 pull-thrus (20 x 45), back-ins (20 x 40), 10 full hkups (30/50 amps), seasonal sites, WiFi Hotspot, laundry. **REC:** heated pool. Pet restrict(Q). No tents. 2015 rates: $41. No CC.
(925)685-7048 Lat: 37.96245, Lon: -122.02962
1080 San Miguel, Concord, CA 94518
See ad this page.

CORNING — C2 *Tehama*

CORNING RV PARK **Ratings: 5.5/9★/7** (Campground) 2015 rates: $30. (530)824-2200 4720 Barham Ave, Corning, CA 96021

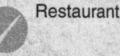

HERITAGE RV PARK
Ratings: 9.5/9.5★/9 (RV Park) From Jct of I-5 & Corning Rd Exit 631 (CR-A9), exit to E side of freeway to CR-99 W, S 300 ft (L). Through Heritage Square entrance. **FAC:** Paved rds. (87 spaces). Avail: 47 gravel, 40 pull-thrus (22 x 70), back-ins (20 x 40), accepts full hkup units only, 47 full hkups (30/50 amps), seasonal sites, WiFi, laundry, LP gas. **REC:** pool. Pets OK. Partial handicap access, no tents. Big rig sites, eco-friendly, 2015 rates: $30 to $38.
(530)824-6130 Lat: 39.92682, Lon: -122.19622
975 Hwy 99W, Corning, CA 96021
heritagervparkcorning@gmail.com
www.heritagervcorning.com
See ad this page.

THE RV PARK AT ROLLING HILLS
Ratings: 7/9.5★/9.5 (Campground) From jct of I-5 & Exit 628 (cross to West side of fwy) W on Liberal Ave, then 1/2 mi S on Everett Freeman Way (R). **FAC:** Paved rds. 72 gravel, 72 pull-thrus (25 x 80), accepts full hkup units only, 72 full hkups (30/50 amps), WiFi, showers $, laundry. Pets OK. Partial handicap access. Big rig sites, eco-friendly, 2015 rates: $28.
530-528-3586 Lat: 39.8728, Lon: -122.2024
2655 Everett Freeman Way, Corning, CA 96021
www.rollinghillscasino.com/hotels/rv-park/
See ad page 176.

WOODSON BRIDGE RV PARK **Ratings: 6/6/6.5** (RV Park) 2015 rates: $32 to $40. (530)839-2151 25433 South Ave, Corning, CA 96021

WOODSON BRIDGE SRA (State Pk) From Jct of I-5 & South Ave (Exit 630), E 6 mi on South Ave (L); or From Jct of E Hwy 99 & South Ave, W 3 mi on South Ave (R). 2015 rates: $28. (530)839-2112

Things to See and Do

OLIVE PIT Tasting bars for olives, wine, beer and much more plus burgers & a cafe. Partial handicap access. RV accessible. Restrooms, food. Hours: 7am to 7pm.
(800)654-8374 Lat: 39.92844, Lon: -122.19642
2156 Solano St., Corning, CA 96021
orders@olivepit.com
www.olivepit.com
See ad this page.

ROLLING HILLS CASINO Gaming Machines & Restaurant. Hours: 24 hour.
(888)331-6400 Lat: 39.87406, Lon: -122.20216
2655 Everett Freeman Way, Corning, CA 96021
info@rollinghillscasino.com
www.rollinghillscasino.com
See ad page 176.

SEVILLANO LINKS John Daly Signature, 18 hole golf course. RV accessible. Restrooms. Hours: 7am to 9pm.
Lat: 39.87406, Lon: -122.20216
2655 Everett Freeman Way, Corning, CA 96021
See ad page 176.

TIMBER'S STEAKHOUSE Timber's Steakhouse is the perfect place for a special dinner. Restrooms. Hours: 5pm to 10pm. No CC.
Lat: 39.87406, Lon: -122.20216
2655 Everett Freeman Way, Corning, CA 96021
See ad page 176.

Had a great stay? Let us know by emailing us travelguidecomments@goodsamfamily.com

COULTERVILLE — E3 *Mariposa*

BAGBY RECREATION AREA (Public) From town, N 15 mi on Hwy 49 at Lake McClure (E). 2015 rates: $22 to $32. (209)378-2521

HORSESHOE BEND (Public) From Jct of Hwys 49 & 132, W 3 mi on Hwy 132 (L). For reservations call 1-800-468-8889. 2015 rates: $15. (209)378-2521

CRANE FLAT — E4 *Mariposa*

YOSEMITE/CRANE FLAT (Natl Pk) From Groveland, W 33 mi SR-120 (R). Entrance fee required. 2015 rates: $26. Jul 12 to Oct 13. (209)372-0200

CRESCENT CITY — A1 *Del Norte, Humboldt*

CRESCENT CITY See also Eureka, Fort Bragg, Fortuna, Klamath, Manchester & Trinidad.

BAYSIDE RV PARK **Ratings: 6/8.5★/5.5** (RV Park) 2015 rates: $30 to $35. (707)464-9482 750 Hwy 101 S, Crescent City, CA 95531

CRESCENT CITY REDWOODS KOA Ratings: 8/9★/8.5 (Campground) From Jct of US-199 & US-101, N 1 mi on US-101 (R). **FAC:** Gravel rds. 41 Avail: 5 gravel, 36 grass, 21 pull-thrus (20 x 60), back-ins (20 x 40), 27 full hkups, 14 W, 14 E (30/50 amps), cable, WiFi, tent sites, rentals, dump, laundry, groc, LP gas, firewood. **REC:** playground. Pets OK. 2015 rates: $38 to $65. Disc: AAA, military. Mar 1 to Nov 15.
AAA Approved
(800)562-5754 Lat: 41.82115, Lon: -124.14512
4241 US Hwy 101 N, Crescent City, CA 95531
info@crescentcitykoa.com
www.crescentcitykoa.com

DEL NORTE COAST REDWOODS (State Pk) From city center, S 7 mi on US-101 to park entrance rd, E 2.5 mi, follow signs (R). 2015 rates: $35. (707)465-2146

HARBOR RV ANCHORAGE **Ratings: 6/8.5★/4.5** (RV Park) 2015 rates: $38. (707)464-1724 159 Starfish Way, Crescent City, CA 95531

HIOUCHI RV RESORT
Ratings: 8.5/9.5★/9.5 (RV Park) From Jct of US-101 & US-199, NE 5.3 mi on US-199 (L). **FAC:** Paved rds. (120 spaces). Avail: 90 gravel, patios, 82 pull-thrus (35 x 60), back-ins (30 x 60), 90 full hkups (30/50 amps), seasonal sites, cable, WiFi, tent sites, rentals, showers $, dump, laundry. **REC:** pond. Pet restrict(Q). Partial handicap access. Big rig sites, eco-friendly, 2015 rates: $33 to $49.
AAA Approved
(800)722-9468 Lat: 41.79348, Lon: -124.07177
2000 US Hwy 199, Crescent City, CA 95531
dhuff@elk-valley.com
www.hiouchirv.com
See ad pages 143 (Spotlight Northcoast and the Giant Redwoods), 128, 119 (CA Map).

JEDEDIAH SMITH REDWOODS (State Pk) From Jct of US-101 & US-199 (exit 197), E 6 mi on US-199 (R). 2015 rates: $35. (707)465-7335

SHORELINE RV PARK (Public) From Jct US-101 & Front St (S end of downtown), SE 0.1 mi on US-101 to Sunset Circle, SW 500 ft (E). 2015 rates: $22 to $33. (707)464-2473

SUNSET HARBOR RV PARK **Ratings: 7.5/8.5/7.5** (RV Park) 2015 rates: $28. (707)464-3423 205 King St, Crescent City, CA 95531

We rate what RVers consider important.

THE REDWOODS RV RESORT Ratings: 6/7/8 (RV Park) N-bnd: From Jct of US Hwy 101 & Hwy 199, N 4 mi on US Hwy 101 (R); or S-bnd: From Jct of US Hwy 101 & Hwy 197, S 1 mi on US Hwy 101 (L). **FAC:** Gravel rds. 65 gravel, 17 pull-thrus (20 x 60), back-ins (20 x 50), 61 full hkups, 4 W, 4 E (30/50 amps), WiFi, tent sites, rentals, showers $, dump, laundry, LP gas, fire rings, firewood. **REC:** playground. Pet restrict(B/Q). 2015 rates: $32 to $52. Disc: AAA, military.
AAA Approved
(707)487-7404 Lat: 41.86641, Lon: -124.13989
6701 Highway 101 N, Crescent City, CA 95531
info@redwoodsrv.com
www.redwoodsrv.com

VILLAGE CAMPER INN
Ratings: 8/9★/9 (Campground) N-bnd: From Jct of US-101 & Parkway Dr/Exit 791, (N edge of town), E 0.1 mi on Washington Ave to Parkway Dr, NE 0.5 mi (R); or S-bnd: From Jct of US-101 & Washington Blvd (N edge of town), cross over fwy to E side & Parkway Dr, NE 0.1 mi (R). **FAC:** Paved rds. (135 spaces). Avail: 70 gravel, patios, 12 pull-thrus (21 x 60), back-ins (25 x 50), 70 full hkups (30/50 amps), seasonal sites, cable, WiFi, tent sites, dump, laundry, fire rings, firewood. **REC.** Pets OK. Big rig sites, eco-friendly, 2015 rates: $40.50. Disc: AAA, military.
AAA Approved
(707)464-3544 Lat: 41.77362, Lon: -124.18248
1543 Parkway Dr, Crescent City, CA 95531
vcirvpk@aol.com
www.villagecamperinn.com
See ad this page, 128.

Things to See and Do

DEL NORTE GOLF CLUB 9 Hole Golf Course, Driving Range, Putting Green, Bar & Snack Bar. Partial handicap access. RV accessible. Restrooms, food. Hours: 8am to 6pm. Adult fee: $26 to $36.
(707)458-3214 Lat: 41.49672, Lon: -124.05709
130 Club Dr, Crescent City, CA 95531
www.elk-valley.com
See ad pages 143 (Spotlight Northcoast and the Giant Redwoods), 119 (CA Map).

ELK VALLEY CASINO Blackjack, Poker, Bingo, Slots. Partial handicap access. RV accessible. Restrooms, food. Hours: 24 hours.
(707)464-1020 Lat: 41.76135, Lon: -124.15894
2500 Holland Hill Rd, Crescent City, CA 95531
elkvalleycasino.com
See ad pages 143 (Spotlight Northcoast and the Giant Redwoods), 119 (CA Map).

CROMBERG — C3 *Plumas*

GOLDEN COACH RV PARK **Ratings: 7/8.5/7** (Campground) 2015 rates: $29. May 1 to Oct 31. (530)836-2426 59704 Hwy 70, Cromberg, CA 96103

DAGGETT — H5 *San Bernardino*

DESERT SPRINGS RV PARK **Ratings: 5.5/5.5/5.5** (Campground) 2015 rates: $30. (760)254-2000 34805 Daggett-Yermo Rd, Daggett, CA 92327

DANA POINT — J4 *Orange*

DOHENY BEACH (State Pk) From Jct of PCH & Dana Point Harbor Dr, W 0.8 mi on Dana Point Harbor Dr (L). 2015 rates: $35 to $60. (949)496-6172

RV Park ratings you can rely on!

DEATH VALLEY — F5 *Inyo*

BOULDER CREEK RV RESORT
Ratings: 9.5/9★/9 (RV Park) From Jct of Hwy 267, Hwy 374 & Hwy 190: Go SW 50 mi on Hwy 190, then NW 40 mi on SR-136, then S 2.6 mi on US-395 (L). Elev 3700 ft. **FAC:** Paved rds. (109 spaces). Avail: 78 gravel, 64 pull-thrus (33 x 60), back-ins (25 x 50), 78 full hkups (30/50 amps), seasonal sites, WiFi, tent sites, rentals, laundry, groc, LP gas, fire rings, firewood. **REC:** heated pool, whirlpool, playground. Pets OK. Partial handicap access. Big rig sites, 28 day max stay, eco-friendly, 2015 rates: $40. Disc: AAA, military.
(760)876-4243 Lat: 36.543175, Lon: -118.046786
2550 S Hwy 395, Lone Pine, CA 93545
bouldercreekrv@yahoo.com
www.bouldercreekrvresort.com
See primary listing at Lone Pine and ad page 191.

NEVADA TREASURE RV RESORT
Ratings: 10/10★/10 (RV Resort) From Jct of CA 190 & CA 127: Go S 1/4 mi on CA 127, then E 23 mi on Ash Meadow Rd/Stateline Rd (Bell Vista Rd in NV), then W 4-3/4 mi on N Leslie St (R). Elev 2699 ft. **FAC:** Paved rds. (202 spaces). Avail: 167 paved, patios, back-ins (36 x 50), 167 full hkups (30/50 amps), seasonal sites, WiFi, laundry, LP gas, restaurant, controlled access. **REC:** heated pool, whirlpool, rec open to public. Pets OK. Partial handicap access, no tents. Big rig sites, eco-friendly, 2015 rates: $40 to $60. Disc: AAA.
(800)429-6665 Lat: 36.30349, Lon: -116.01604
301 West Leslie St, Pahrump, NV 89060
frontdesk@nvtreasure.com
www.nvtreasure.com
See primary listing at Pahrump, NV and ad page 746 (Spotlight Pahrump).

DELHI — E3 *Merced*

MERCED RIVER RV RESORT
Ratings: 9/9.5★/8.5 (RV Park) From Jct of Hwy 99 & Collier Rd exit, W 0.2 mi on Collier Rd to Campground Rd, S 0.8 mi (E). **FAC:** Gravel rds. (100 spaces). 30 Avail: 10 gravel, 20 grass, 10 pull-thrus (24 x 72), back-ins (22 x 60), some side by side hkups, accepts full hkup units only, 30 full hkups (30/50 amps), seasonal sites, WiFi, dump, laundry, LP gas. **REC:** pool, Merced River: fishing. Pet restrict(Q). No tents. Eco-friendly, 2015 rates: $35. Disc: AAA, military.
(209)634-6056 Lat: 37.40070, Lon: -120.74580
7765 Campground Rd, Delhi, CA 95315
mercedrv@hotmail.com
www.campingfriend.com/mercedriverrvresort
See ad this page.

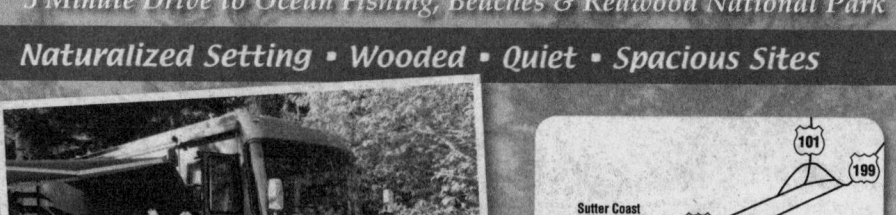

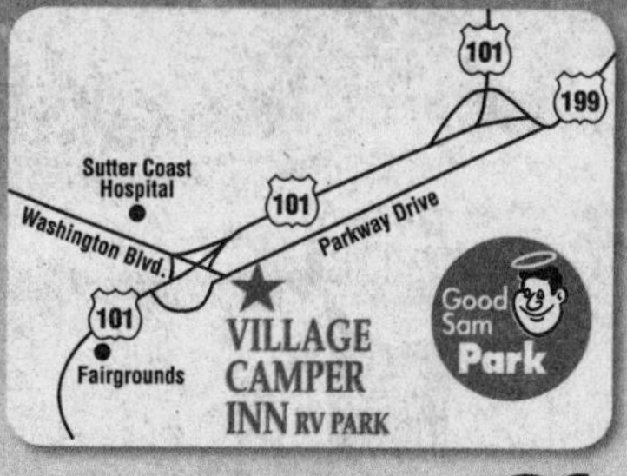

DESCANSO — K5 *San Diego*

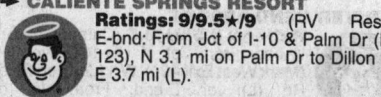

↑ OAKZANITA SPRINGS **Ratings: 7/8/7** (Membership Pk) 2015 rates: $48 to $56. (800)405-6188 11053 Hwy 79, Descanso, CA 91916

DESERT HOT SPRINGS — J5 *Riverside*

→ **CALIENTE SPRINGS RESORT**
Ratings: 9/9.5★/9 (RV Resort) E-bnd: From Jct of I-10 & Palm Dr (Exit 123), N 3.1 mi on Palm Dr to Dillon Rd, E 3.7 mi (L).

EVERY"BODY" LOVES OUR WATER
Come experience the most amazing natural hot water pools and spas around in our 55+ gated community. Family owned and operated we specialize in warm weather, relaxation, friendly faces, and fun activities. Also: GOOD WIFI.

FAC: Paved rds. (679 spaces). 200 Avail: 10 gravel, 190 dirt, patios, 4 pull-thrus (28 x 52), back-ins (33 x 55), 200 full hkups (30/50 amps), seasonal sites, cable, WiFi $, rentals, laundry, controlled access. **REC:** heated pool, whirlpool, golf, shuffleboard. Pet restrict(B/Q). Partial handicap access, no tents. Big rig sites, RV age restrict, eco-friendly, 2015 rates: $50 to $59. Disc: AAA.
(760)329-8400 Lat: 33.92611, Lon: -116.43606
70-200 Dillon Rd, Desert Hot Springs, CA 92241
info@calientesprings.com
www.calientesprings.com
See ad pages 148 (Spotlight Palm Springs), 126 & Snowbird Destinations in Magazine Section.

↘ CATALINA SPA & RV RESORT **Ratings: 8.5/8/8.5** (Membership Pk) 2015 rates: $45. (760)329-4431 18-800 Corkhill Rd, Desert Hot Springs, CA 92241

↘ DESERT POOLS RV RESORT **Ratings: 9/8.5★/8.5** (RV Resort) 2015 rates: $45. Oct 1 to Apr 30. (760)251-6555 70405 Dillon Rd, Desert Hot Springs, CA 92241

↘ **DESERT SPRINGS SPA & RV PARK**
Ratings: 7.5/9★/7.5 (RV Park) From Jct of I-10 & Palm Dr (Exit 123), N 3.4 mi on Palm Dr to Dillon Rd, E 3.5 mi to Johnson Rd, S 0.1 mi (R). **FAC:** Paved/gravel rds. (84 spaces). Avail: 35 dirt, 6 pull-thrus (30 x 50), back-ins (33 x 40), 35 full hkups (30/50 amps), seasonal sites, WiFi Hotspot, tent sites, rentals, laundry, controlled access. **REC:** heated pool, whirlpool. Pet restrict(B/Q). Age restrict may apply, RV age restrict, eco-friendly, 2015 rates: $45 to $50. Disc: AAA.
(760)329-1384 Lat: 33.92255, Lon: -116.44290
17325 Johnson Rd, Desert Hot Springs, CA 92241
hhh1689@gmail.com
www.desertspringsrvpark.com
See ad pages 149 (Spotlight Palm Springs), 126.

↘ **SAM'S FAMILY SPA**
Ratings: 9.5/9★/9 (RV Park) From Jct of I-10 & Palm Dr (exit 123), N 3 mi on Palm Dr to Dillon Rd, E 4.2 mi (R). **FAC:** Paved rds. (350 spaces). Avail: 175 all weather, patios, back-ins (32 x 45), 175 full hkups (30/50 amps), seasonal sites, WiFi $, tent sites, rentals, laundry, groc. **REC:** heated pool, whirlpool, playground, rec open to public. Pets OK. Partial handicap access. Big rig sites, RV age restrict, 2015 rates: $50.
(760)329-6457 Lat: 33.92488, Lon: -116.42535
70875 Dillon Rd, Desert Hot Springs, CA 92241
samsfamilyspa@aol.com
www.samsfamilyspa.com
See ad page 145 (Spotlight Palm Springs) & Snowbird Destinations in Magazine Section.

↘ **SANDS RV & GOLF RESORT**
Ratings: 10/9.5★/9.5 (RV Park) From Jct of I-10 & Palm Dr (Exit 123), N 3 mi on Palm Dr to Dillon Rd, E 1 mi to Bubbling Wells Rd, N 0.2 mi (R).

LUXURY RV LIVING, WIFI & GOLF
Premiere RV resort in the Palm Springs area. Enjoy our beautifully maintained golf course and amenities. Good Sam "Top Rated Park"! Abundant activities for you, or run your pets in one of our two leash free, grassy dog parks!

FAC: Paved rds. (507 spaces). Avail: 250 all weather, back-ins (30 x 46), 250 full hkups (30/50 amps), seasonal sites, cable, WiFi, rentals, laundry, controlled access. **REC:** heated pool, whirlpool, pond, golf, shuffleboard. Pet restrict(B/Q). Partial handicap access, no tents. Age restrict may apply, RV age restrict, eco-friendly, 2015 rates: $42 to $49.
(760)251-1030 Lat: 33.92861, Lon: -116.48438
16400 Bubbling Wells Road, Desert Hot Springs, CA 92240
stay@sandsrvresort.com
www.sandsrvresort.com
See ad pages 146 (Spotlight Palm Springs), 126 & Cal Am Insert & Snowbird Destinations in Magazine Section.

→ **SKY VALLEY RESORT**
Ratings: 9.5/9.5★/9 (RV Resort) E-bnd: From Jct of I-10 & Palm Dr (Exit 123), N 3.1 mi on Palm Dr to Dillon Rd, E 8.5 mi (R); W-bnd: From Jct of I-10 & Dillon Rd, NW 18.6 mi on Dillon Rd (L).

SUN, FUN, & FRIENDS
We are famous for our natural hot springs pools and spas but RVers keep coming back because of our community. Amazing resort amenities and so close to Palm Springs; if you are bored here it is your own fault.

FAC: Paved rds. (891 spaces). 100 Avail: 4 gravel, 96 dirt, patios, 6 pull-thrus (32 x 50), back-ins (30 x 50), 100 full hkups (30/50 amps), seasonal sites, cable, WiFi $, rentals, dump, laundry, groc, restaurant, controlled access. **REC:** heated pool, whirlpool, pond, shuffleboard. Pet restrict(B/Q). Partial handicap access, no tents. RV age restrict, eco-friendly, 2015 rates: $50 to $59.
(760)329-2909 Lat: 33.90341, Lon: -116.35998
74-711 Dillon Rd, Desert Hot Springs, CA 92241
info@skyvalleyresort.com
www.rvwell.com
See ad pages 148 (Spotlight Palm Springs), 126 & Snowbird Destinations in Magazine Section.

Things to See and Do

↘ **SAM'S FAMILY SPA RESORT AND MOTEL** 13 Motel units, refrigerators in all rooms plus color satellite TV, doubles & queens, some with kitchen. Pool views & sun decks. Adult fee: $85 to $165.
(760)329-6457 Lat: 33.92325, Lon: -116.42522
70875 Dillon Rd, Desert Hot Springs, CA 92241
samsfamilyspa@aol.com
www.samsfamilyspa.com
See ad page 145 (Spotlight Palm Springs).

DEVILS POSTPILE NATIONAL MONUMENT — E4 *Madera*

← DEVILS POSTPILE NAT'L MON (Natl Pk) From Jct of Hwys 395 & 203, W 9 mi on Hwy 203 to Minerate Summit, W 8 mi follow signs (E). CAUTION: Narrow mountain road. 2015 rates: $14. Jun 29 to Sep 1. (760)934-2289

DEVORE — L5 *San Bernardino*

↑ **GLEN HELEN REGIONAL PARK**
(State Pk) From Jct of I-15 Glen Helen Parkway, N 0.5 mi on Glen Helen Pkwy to Glen Helen Park Rd, W 0.1 mi (R). **FAC:** Paved rds. 66 paved, 13 pull-thrus (25 x 40), back-ins (25 x 40), 20 full hkups (20/30 amps), tent sites, showers $. **REC:** pool $, Glen Helen: fishing, playground. Pets OK. RV age restrict, 2015 rates: $35.
(909)887-7540 Lat: 34.20869, Lon: -117.40953
2555 Glen Helen Pkwy, San Bernardino, CA 92407
www.sbcountyparks.com
See ad page 123 (Welcome Section).

DUNCANS MILLS — D2 *Sonoma*

→ **CASINI RANCH FAMILY CAMPGROUND Ratings: 6.5/5.5/6.5** (Campground) From Jct of SR-1 & SR-116, NE 3.8 mi on SR-116 to Moscow Rd, E 0.7 mi (L). **FAC:** Paved/gravel rds. 200 grass, patios, 28 pull-thrus (22 x 50), back-ins (30 x 60), 36 full hkups, 164 W, 164 E (20/30 amps), cable, WiFi Hotspot, tent sites, rentals, dump, mobile sewer, laundry, groc, LP gas, firewood, controlled access. **REC:** Russian River: fishing, playground. Pet restrict(B) $. 2015 rates: $45 to $55. ATM.
AAA Approved
(707)865-2255 Lat: 38.46051, Lon: -123.04514
22855 Moscow Rd, Duncans Mills, CA 95430
info@casiniranch.com
www.casiniranch.com

DUNSMUIR — B2 *Siskiyou*

↑ CASTLE CRAGS (State Pk) From Jct of I-5 & Castle Creek Rd, W 0.5 mi on Castle Creek Rd (R). 2015 rates: $15 to $25. (530)235-2684

EARP — H6 *San Bernardino*

↑ EMERALD COVE RESORT **Ratings: 7.5/7/8.5** (Membership Pk) 2015 rates: $50. (866)663-2727 2715 Parker Dam Rd, Earp, CA 92242

↑ RIVERLAND RESORT **Ratings: 8/6/7.5** (RV Park) 2015 rates: $55 to $77. (760)663-3733 3401 Parker Dam Rd, Earp, CA 92242

↓ RIVERVIEW MOBILE HOME & RV PARK, LLC **Ratings: 6.5/8/7.5** (RV Park) 2015 rates: $35 to $40. (760)665-9953 47 Parker Dam Rd, Hwy 62, Earp, CA 92242

EL CAJON — K5 *San Diego*

↗ **CIRCLE RV RESORT - SUNLAND**
Ratings: 10/9/7.5 (RV Park) From Jct of I-8 & Greenfield Dr (Exit 20 A or B), N 100 ft on Greenfield Dr to Main St, E 0.2 mi (R). **FAC:** Paved rds. (165 spaces). Avail: 50 all weather, patios, 8 pull-thrus (18 x 65), back-ins (24 x 40), 50 full hkups (30/50 amps), seasonal sites, cable, WiFi $, dump, laundry, LP gas. **REC:** heated pool, whirlpool. Pet restrict(B/Q) $. Partial handicap access, no tents. RV age restrict, eco-friendly, 2015 rates: $45 to $69. Disc: AAA, military.
(866)226-2747 Lat: 32.81577, Lon: -116.91542
1835 E Main st, El Cajon, CA 92021
circlerv@sunlandrvresorts.com
www.circlerv.com

→ **OAK CREEK RV RESORT - SUNLAND**
Ratings: 10/9.5★/7.5 (RV Park) E-bnd: From Jct of I-8 & Lake Jennings Rd (Exit 23/Olde Hwy 80), E 2.5 mi on Olde Hwy 80 to Oak Creek Rd, N 100 ft (L); or W-bnd: From Jct of I-8 & Harbison Canyon/Dunbar Ln (Exit 27), N 100 ft on Alpine Bl to Olde Hwy 80, W 1.4 mi to Oak Creek Rd, N 100 ft (L). **FAC:** Paved rds. (120 spaces). Avail: 34 paved, patios, 3 pull-thrus (18 x 70), back-ins (20 x 40), 34 full hkups (30/50 amps), seasonal sites, cable, WiFi, laundry, LP gas. **REC:** heated pool, whirlpool. Pet restrict(B/Q) $. Partial handicap access, no tents. RV age restrict, eco-friendly, 2015 rates: $38 to $68. Disc: AAA.
(866)225-6164 Lat: 32.85711, Lon: -116.84330
15379 Oak Creek Rd, El Cajon, CA 92021
oakcreekrv@sunlandrvresorts.com
www.oakcreekrv.com

↗ **VACATIONER RV PARK - SUNLAND**
Ratings: 10/9.5★/5.5 (RV Park) From Jct of I-8 & Greenfield Dr (Exit 20 A or B), N 100 ft on Greenfield Dr to Main St, W 0.5 mi (L). **FAC:** Paved rds. 147 Avail: 147 all weather, patios, 13 pull-thrus (27 x 67), back-ins (22 x 40), 147 full hkups (30/50 amps), cable, WiFi $, dump, laundry, LP gas, controlled access. **REC:** heated pool, whirlpool. Pet restrict(B/Q) $. Partial handicap access, no tents. RV age restrict, eco-friendly, 2015 rates: $45 to $77. Disc: AAA, military.
(866)226-8998 Lat: 32.80682, Lon: -116.92299
1581 E Main St, El Cajon, CA 92021
vacationerrv@sunlandrvresorts.com
www.vacationerrv.com

EL CENTRO — K5 *Imperial*

↘ DESERT TRAILS RV PARK & GOLF COURSE **Ratings: 9/9/8.5** (RV Park) 2015 rates: $37 to $45. (760)352-7275 225 Wake Ave, El Centro, CA 92243

← **RIO BEND RV & GOLF RESORT**
Ratings: 10/9★/9 (RV Resort) From Jct of I-8 & Hwy 86 (Imperial Ave), W 8 mi on I-8 to Drew Rd (Exit 107), S 0.4 mi (R).

MORE THAN A RESORT - A LIFESTYLE!
Whether it's inspiration or relaxation that you seek, our landscaped sites, first class amenities, pleasing climate & good old fashioned western hospitality make our resort a clear choice as your premier resort destination.

FAC: Paved rds. (500 spaces). Avail: 210 all weather, 23 pull-thrus (28 x 50), back-ins (30 x 50), 210 full hkups (30/50 amps), seasonal sites, cable, WiFi, rentals, laundry, LP gas, restaurant. **REC:** heated pool, whirlpool, Drew Lake: fishing, golf, shuffleboard. Pet restrict(B/Q). Partial handicap access, no tents. Age restrict may apply, RV age restrict, eco-friendly, 2015 rates: $38 to $70. Disc: AAA. ATM.
AAA Approved
(760)352-7061 Lat: 32.76540, Lon: -115.69423
1589 Drew Rd, El Centro, CA 92243
info@riobendrvgolfresort.com
www.riobendrvgolfresort.com
See ad opposite page, 104, 126 & Snowbird Destinations in Magazine Section.

↓ VACATION INN RV PARK **Ratings: 6/7/5** (RV Park) 2015 rates: $20. (800)328-6289 2015 Cottonwood Circle, El Centro, CA 92243

EL PORTAL — E4 *Mariposa*

← INDIAN FLAT RV PARK **Ratings: 4.5/6.5/6.5** (Campground) 2015 rates: $37 to $42. (209)379-2339 10008 Hwy 140, El Portal, CA 95318

CA

EMIGRANT GAP — C3 *Placer, Shasta*

PG & E/DONNER SUMMIT AREA/LAKE SPAULDING CAMPSITE (Public) From Jct of I-80 & Hwy 20 (exit 161), W 2 mi on Hwy 20 (R). Pit toilets. 2015 rates: $20. Jun 1 to Sep 30. (916)386-5164

PG & E/DONNER SUMMIT AREA/LODGEPOLE (Public) From Jct of I-80 & Yuba Gap (exit160), S 1.5 mi on access rd/Yuba Gap exit (follow rt fork) (E). Pit toilets. 2015 rates: $25. (916)386-5164

SNOWFLOWER **Ratings: 6.5/8.5/8** (Membership Pk) 2015 rates: $48 to $62. (800)405-6188 41776 Yuba Gap Dr, Emigrant Gap, CA 95715

ENCINITAS — J4 *San Diego*

TRAILER RANCHO RV PARK
Ratings: 7.5/9.5★/6.5 (RV Park) From Jct of I-5 & La Costa Ave (Exit 44), W 0.5 mi on La Costa Ave to N Vulcan Ave, S 0.5 mi (L).

VISITING THE SAN DIEGO AREA?
We are located in a quiet residential area minutes to the beach. Enjoy great surfing, miles of sandy beaches, gentle ocean breezes and beautiful sunsets. Visit us for a comfortable and enjoyable stay.

FAC: Paved rds. (83 spaces). Avail: 50 all weather, patios, back-ins (28 x 36), 50 full hkups (30/50 amps), seasonal sites, WiFi, laundry. **REC.** Pet restrict(B/Q). Partial handicap access, no tents. RV age restrict, 2015 rates: $50.
(760)753-2741 Lat: 33.07549, Lon: -117.30527
1549 N Vulcan Ave, Encinitas, CA 92024
trailerrancho@jandhmgt.com
www.goodsamcamping.com.s3.amazonaws.com/gsparks/840000652/index.html
See ad page 153 (Spotlight San Diego) & Snowbird Destinations in Magazine Section.

ESCONDIDO — J4 *San Diego*

ALL SEASONS RV PARK **Ratings: 9/9★/8** (RV Park) 2015 rates: $38. (760)749-2982 30012 Hwy 395, Escondido, CA 92026

CHAMPAGNE LAKES RV RESORT
Ratings: 8.5/9★/9 (Campground) From Jct of I-15 & Old Hwy 395 (exit 43), S 0.8 mi on Hwy 395 (L). **FAC:** Paved rds. (140 spaces). Avail: 30 paved, back-ins (30 x 45), 30 full hkups (30/50 amps), seasonal sites, WiFi $, tent sites, dump, mobile sewer, laundry, groc, LP gas, controlled access. **REC:** pool, Eagle Lake: fishing, playground, rec open to public. Pet restrict(B) $. Partial handicap access. RV age restrict, eco-friendly, 2015 rates: $45.
AAA Approved
(760)749-7572 Lat: 33.27535, Lon: -117.15138
8310 Nelson Way, Escondido, CA 92026
info@champagnelakesrvresort.com
www.champagnelakesrvresort.com
See ad this page, 126.

ESCONDIDO RV RESORT - SUNLAND
Ratings: 9.5/10★/8 (RV Park) From Jct of I-15 & El Norte Pkwy, E 0.1 mi on El Norte Pkwy to Seven Oakes Rd, N 100 ft (R). **FAC:** Paved rds. (125 spaces). Avail: 55 paved, patios, back-ins (24 x 50), 55 full hkups (30/50 amps), seasonal sites, cable, WiFi $, laundry, LP gas. **REC:** heated pool, whirlpool. Pet restrict(B/Q) $. Partial handicap access, no tents. RV age restrict, eco-friendly, 2015 rates: $49 to $90. Disc: AAA.
(866)226-2661 Lat: 33.14682, Lon: -117.10222
1740 Seven Oakes Road, Escondido, CA 92026
escondidorv@sunlandrvresorts.com
www.escondidorv.com

ETNA — A2 *Siskiyou*

MOUNTAIN VILLAGE RV PARK **Ratings: 7/9★/7.5** (RV Park) 2015 rates: $29. (877)386-2787 30 Commercial Way, Etna, CA 96027

EUREKA — B1 *Humboldt*

EUREKA KOA **Ratings: 8.5/8/7.5** (Campground) 2015 rates: $28 to $47. (707)822-4243 4050 N Hwy 101, Eureka, CA 95503

REDWOOD ACRES FAIRGROUNDS (Public) N-bnd: From Jct of US-101 & Harris St (S end of town), E 3 mi on Harris St (R); or S-bnd: From Jct of US-101 & V St (N edge of town), S 0.3 mi on V St to Myrtle Ave, SE 0.4 mi to Harrison Ave, S 1.2 mi to Harris St (unmarked), E 0.5 mi (R). Note: Gate closes 10pm, Park only accepts RVs 2005 and newer. 2015 rates: $35. (707)445-3037

SAMOA BOAT RAMP (Public) From Hwy 101, exit Hwy 255W (exit 713) to Samoa Peninsula, S 5 mi on New Navy Base, follow signs (L). 2015 rates: $20. (707)445-7652

SHORELINE RV PARK
Ratings: 8/9.5★/7 (RV Park) N-bnd: From Jct of Hwy 101 & V St (in Eureka), N 0.1 mi on US-101 to next exit (unmarked), E 0.1 mi on unmarked exit & thru Circle K (N) S-bnd: From Jct of Hwy 101 & V St (in Eureka), E 0.1 mi on V St to US-101, N 0.1 mi on US-101 to next exit (unmarked), E 0.1 mi on unmarked exit & thru Circle K (N). **FAC:** Paved rds. 59 paved, 45 pull-thrus (26 x 74), back-ins (26 x 46), accepts full hkup units only, 59 full hkups (30/50 amps), cable, WiFi, dump, laundry. Pet restrict(B) $. Partial handicap access, no tents. Big rig sites, eco-friendly, 2015 rates: $32 to $45.
(707)443-2222 Lat: 40.80363, Lon: -124.14343
2600 6th St, Eureka, CA 95501
reservations@shorelinervpark.com
www.shorelinervpark.com
See ad this page.

FAWNSKIN — H5 *San Bernardino*

SAN BERNARDINO NATIONAL FOREST (GROUT BAY CAMPGROUND) (PICNIC SITE ONLY) (State Pk) From town: Go 1/2 mi S on Hwy-38. Pit toilets. (909)382-2790

SAN BERNARDINO NF (HANNA FLATS CAMPGROUND) (Natl Forest) From town: Go 2-1/2 mi NW on CR-3N/14, then 1/2 mi NW on FR-3N/14. Pit toilets. 2015 rates: $26 to $54. May 2 to Oct 26. (909)382-2790

FELTON — F1 *Santa Cruz*

COTILLION GARDENS RV PARK
Ratings: 8/8.5/8.5 (RV Park) From Jct of Hwy 17 & Mt Hermon Rd (Felton exit): Go 3-1/2 mi W on Mt Hermon Rd to Graham Hill Rd, then 1/4 mi W on on Graham Hill Rd to Hwy 9, then 1/2 mi S on Hwy 9 to Old Big Trees Rd, then 1/4 mi E on Old Big Trees Rd (E). Caution: Max 36 ft RV length & RVs not allowed on Hwy-9 from Santa Cruz. **FAC:** Paved rds. (80 spaces). Avail: 65 gravel, patios, 2 pull-thrus (20 x 48), back-ins (18 x 40), 39 full hkups, 26 W, 26 E (20/30 amps), seasonal sites, cable, WiFi, tent sites, rentals, dump, groc, fire rings, firewood. **REC:** heated pool, Toll House Creek: playground. Pet restrict(B). Partial handicap access. RV age restrict, 14 day max stay, eco-friendly, 2015 rates: $57 to $64. Disc: military.
AAA Approved
(831)335-7669 Lat: 37.034636, Lon: -122.060486
300 Old Big Trees Rd, Felton, CA 95018
cotilliongardensrvpark@gmail.com
www.santacruzrvpark.com

REDWOODS/HENRY COWELL (State Pk) From Jct of SR-9 & Graham Hill Rd, SE 2.5 mi on Graham Hill Rd (R). 2015 rates: $35. (831)335-4598

SANTA CRUZ REDWOODS RV RESORT **Ratings: 7.5/9/9** (Campground) 2015 rates: $55 to $85. (831)335-8312 4980 Hwy 9, Felton, CA 95018

SMITHWOODS RV PARK-(MHP) **Ratings: 8/6.5/7.5** (Campground) 2015 rates: $52 to $79. (831)335-4321 4770 Hwy 9, Felton, CA 95018

FERNDALE — B1 *Humboldt*

HUMBOLDT COUNTY FAIRGROUNDS (Public) From Jct of US-101 & Hwy 1 (Fernbridge, exit 621), SW 5 mi on Hwy 1 to Van Ness St, W 0.25 mi (L). 2015 rates: $10 to $25. (707)786-9511

FOLSOM — D3 *Sacramento*

FOLSOM LAKE SRA/BEALS POINT CAMPGROUND (State Pk) From Jct of Hwy 80 & Douglas Blvd E (exit 103A), E 5 mi on Douglas Blvd to Auburn-Folsom Rd, S 2 mi (L). 2015 rates: $48. (916)988-0205

FORESTVILLE — D2 *Sonoma*

RIVER BEND RESORT
Ratings: 8.5/9★/8.5 (Campground) W-bnd: From Jct of US-101/River Rd (Mark West Exit 494), W 11.2 mi on River Rd (L); or E-bnd: From Jct of SR-116/River Rd (at E end of Guerneville SR-116 turns S over Russian River Bridge), E 4.2 mi on River Rd (R). **FAC:** Paved rds. (88 spaces). Avail: 68 gravel, 3 pull-thrus (17 x 50), back-ins (20 x 30), 57 full hkups, 11 W, 11 E (30/50 amps), seasonal sites, WiFi, tent sites, dump, laundry, groc, LP gas, fire rings, firewood. **REC:** wading pool, Russian River: swim, fishing, playground. Pet restrict(B) $. Partial handicap access. Eco-friendly, 2015 rates: $50 to $60. Disc: military.
(707)887-7662 Lat: 38.50475, Lon: -122.94186
11820 River Road, Forestville, CA 95436
info@riverbendresort.net
www.riverbendresort.net
See ad pages 220, 128.

Follow the arrow. The arrow in each listing indicates where the facility is located in relation to the listed town.

Take an RV Trip of a Lifetime!

Check out our itineraries for the Food Lover, Living History, Picture Perfect and On the Wild Side! These once-in-a-lifetime journeys are required fun for RVers of all ages.

Browse the RV Trips of a Lifetime, with routes and handy maps, in the front of this Guide.

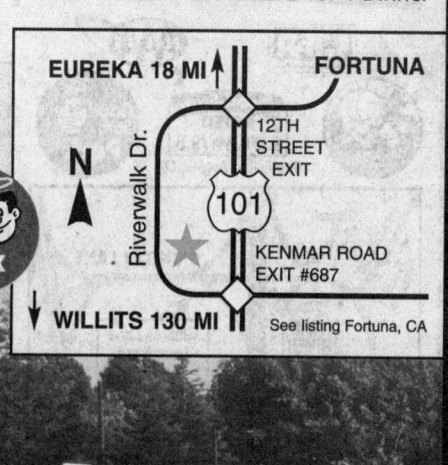

MAD RIVER RAPIDS

RV PARK

One of the North Coast's Highest Rated Parks

Beautifully Landscaped
Paved Sites & Streets
Pull-Thrus (no RV too long)
Full Hookups (30-50 amps)
Complete Mini Mart
Cable TV • Video Rentals
Heated Pool & Spa
Jogging Trail • Playground
Deluxe Laundry & Shower Facilities
Basketball • Horseshoes
Table Tennis • Video Arcade
Free High Speed Internet

Large Meeting Room
Groups & Clubs Welcome!

Lot's to do and see. . .
Ocean & Beach Access (2 mi)
Ferndale, Victorian Village (25 mi)
Golf Courses (7 mi)
Fishing (freshwater & ocean) (9 mi)
Ancient Redwood Forests (23 mi)

7 miles north of Eureka

CTPA California Trailer Parks Assn
Go Camping America!
Good Sam RATED 9.5/9.5★/9.5
See listing Arcata, CA
Good Sam Park

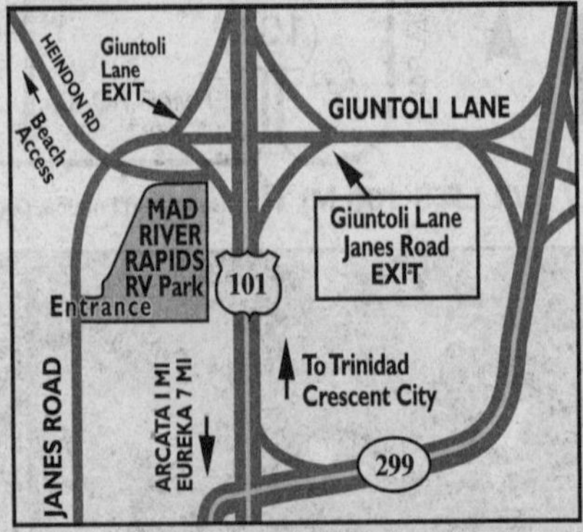

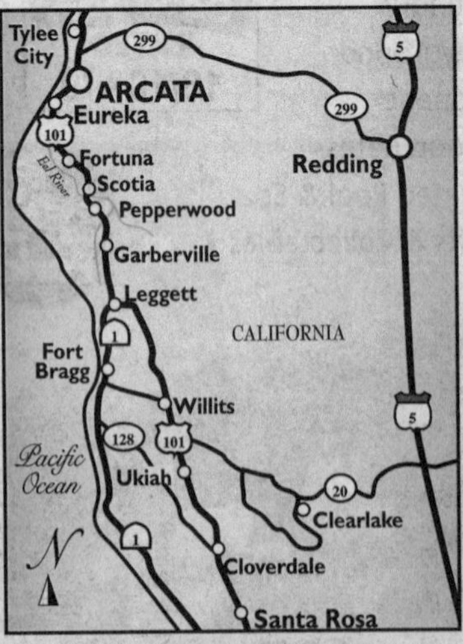

RESERVATIONS SUGGESTED (800) 822-7776

3501 Janes Rd. • Arcata, CA 95521 707-822-7275
www.madriverrv.com

FORT BRAGG — C1 *Mendocino*

MACKERRICHER (State Pk) From N end of town, N 3 mi on SR-1 (L). 2015 rates: $25 to $35. (707)937-5804

POMO RV PARK & CAMPGROUND
Ratings: 8.5/10★/10 (RV Park) From Jct of SR-20 & SR-1, S 1 mi on SR-1 to Tregoning Ln, E 0.1 mi (E).

NICEST PARK ON THE MENDOCINO COAST!
17 wooded acres-secluded large individual sites-paved roads-clean restrooms-RV supplies & convenience items. Group area-meeting room-tent area-fishing-diving-Skunk Train-Botanical Gardens near by. Quiet.

FAC: Paved rds. 96 gravel, 6 pull-thrus (25 x 60), back-ins (30 x 60), 74 full hkups, 22 W, 22 E (30/50 amps), cable, WiFi, tent sites, showers $, dump, laundry, LP gas, fire rings, firewood. **REC.** Pets OK $. Big rig sites, eco-friendly, 2015 rates: $43 to $45. No CC. AAA Approved
(707)964-3373 Lat: 39.40455, Lon: -123.80663
17999 Tregoning, Fort Bragg, CA 95437
www.pomorv.com
See ad this page, 195, 128, 144 (Spotlight Northcoast and the Giant Redwoods).

Average site width and length are indicated in many campground listings to give you an idea of how much room and privacy you can expect.

FORT JONES — A2 *Siskiyou*

KLAMATH NF (INDIAN SCOTTY CAMPGROUND) (Natl Forest) From town: Go 18 mi W on CR-7F01 (Scott River Rd), then 1/4 mi SW on FR-44N45. Pit toilets. 2015 rates: $10. May 15 to Oct 31. (530)842-6131

FORTUNA — B1 *Humboldt*

REDWOODS/GRIZZLY CREEK (State Pk) From Jct of Hwy 101 & exit SR-36, E 17 mi on SR-36 (R). 2015 rates: $35. (707)777-3683

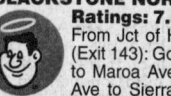

RIVERWALK RV PARK & CAMPGROUND
Ratings: 10/10★/9 (Campground) From Jct of US-101 & Kenmar Rd/Riverwalk Dr (Exit 687), W 0.2 mi on Riverwalk Dr (R). **FAC:** Paved rds. 89 paved, 54 pull-thrus (25 x 60), back-ins (25 x 50), 89 full hkups (30/50 amps), cable, WiFi, tent sites, rentals, dump, laundry, groc, LP gas, firewood. **REC:** heated pool, whirlpool, playground. Pet restrict(B). Partial handicap access. Big rig sites, eco-friendly, 2015 rates: $38 to $48. Disc: AAA, military.
(707)725-3359 Lat: 40.57625, Lon: -124.15082
2189 Riverwalk Dr, Fortuna, CA 95540
riverwalkrv@gmail.com
www.riverwalkrvpark.com
See ad pages 181, 128.

FRESNO — F3 *Fresno*

FRESNO See also Chowchilla, Friant, Hanford, Kingsburg, Madera, Piedra, Tulare & Visalia.

Don't take any chances when it comes to cleanliness. We rate campground restrooms and showers for cleanliness and physical characteristics such as supplies and appearance.

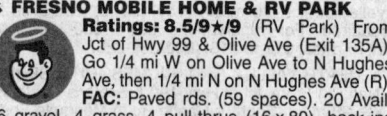

BLACKSTONE NORTH RV PARK
Ratings: 7.5/9.5★/8.5 (RV Park) From Jct of Hwy 99 & W. Herndon Ave (Exit 143): Go 7 mi E on W. Herndon Ave to Maroa Ave, then 1/4 mi S on Maroa Ave to Sierra Ave, then 1/4 mile E on Sierra Ave to N Blackstone Ave, then 1/4 mi N on N Blackstone Ave (R).

1 1/2 HOUR TO YOSEMITE OR SEQUOIA
North Fresno's finest RV Park. Big Rig Friendly. Located within easy reach of shopping & restaurants. 50' 65' shaded pull thru's. Full hook ups 30/50 amp. Clean restrooms w/HOT showers. Free Wifi. Reservations recommended.

FAC: Paved rds. (94 spaces). Avail: 85 paved, patios, 18 pull-thrus (55 x 65), back-ins (45 x 58), 85 full hkups (30/50 amps), seasonal sites, cable, WiFi, dump, laundry. Pet restrict(B). Partial handicap access, no tents. Big rig sites, eco-friendly, 2015 rates: $43. Disc: AAA, military.
AAA Approved
(559)439-1123 Lat: 36.831857, Lon: -119.790035
6494 N Blackstone Ave, Fresno, CA 93710
office@blackstonenorthrvpark.com
www.blackstonenorthrvpark.com
See ad this page, 128.

FRESNO MOBILE HOME & RV PARK
Ratings: 8.5/9★/9 (RV Park) From Jct of Hwy 99 & Olive Ave (Exit 135A): Go 1/4 mi W on Olive Ave to N Hughes Ave, then 1/4 mi N on N Hughes Ave (R). **FAC:** Paved rds. (59 spaces). 20 Avail: 16 gravel, 4 grass, 4 pull-thrus (16 x 80), back-ins (32 x 30), 20 full hkups (30/50 amps), seasonal sites, WiFi, laundry. **REC:** pool. Pet restrict(B/Q). No tents. Eco-friendly, 2015 rates: $45. Disc: AAA, military.
(559)264-3122 Lat: 36.760073, Lon: -119.835219
1362 N Hughes Ave, Fresno, CA 93728
fresnomhp@msn.com
www.fresnomobilehomeandrv.com
See ad this page.

CA

FRESNO (CONT)

PG & E/KINGS RIVER AREA/TRAPPER SPRINGS (Public) From Jct of Hwy 168 & Dinkey Creek Rd (exit 1), E 12.5 mi on Dinkey Creek Rd to McKinley Grove Rd, E 14.1 mi to Courtright Rd, N 7.5 mi (R). Pit toilets. 2015 rates: $24. (916)386-5164

Travel Services

CAMPING WORLD OF FRESNO As the nation's largest retailer of RV supplies, accessories, services and new and used RVs, Camping World is committed to making your total RV experience better. **SERVICES:** Staffed RV wash, RV Sales, RV supplies, LP. Hours: 8am - 6pm.
(559)400-7348 Lat: 36.679732, Lon: -119.744867
3672 South Maple Avenue, Fresno, CA 93725
www.campingworld.com

FRIANT — F3 *Fresno*

MILLERTON LAKE SRA (State Pk) From Fresno, NE 20 mi on Hwy 41 to SR-145, E 7 mi (E). 2015 rates: $30 to $50. (559)822-2332

FURNACE CREEK — F5 *Inyo*

DEATH VALLEY NATL PK/FURNACE CREEK (Natl Pk) From Jct of SR-127 & Hwy 190 (Death Valley Jct), E 30 mi on Hwy 190 (L). Entrance fee required. For reservations call 1-800-365-CAMP. 2015 rates: $12 to $18. (800)365-2267

DEATH VALLEY NATL PK/MESQUITE SPRING (Natl Pk) From Jct of Hwy 190 & Scotty's Castle Rd, NW 28 mi on Scotty's Castle Rd to Mesquite Spring Rd, W 2 mi (E). Entrance fee required. 2015 rates: $12. (760)786-2331

DEATH VALLEY NATL PK/SUNSET CAMPGROUND (Natl Pk) From Jct of Hwy 190 & Campground Rd, E 0.25 mi on Campground Rd (L). Entrance fee required. 2015 rates: $12. Oct 1 to Apr 30. (760)786-2331

DEATH VALLEY NATL PK/TEXAS SPRING (Natl Pk) From Jct of Hwy 190 & Campground Rd, E 0.25 mi on Campground Rd (E). Entrance fee required. 2015 rates: $14. Oct 1 to Apr 30. (760)786-3247

GALT — D3 *Sacramento*

GALT MOBILE ESTATES **Ratings: 4.5/5.5/5.5** (RV Area in MHP) 2015 rates: $39. (209)745-3010 820 N. Lincoln Way, Galt, CA 95632

GARBERVILLE — C1 *Humboldt*

BENBOW KOA **Ratings: 9.5/9/9.5** (RV Park) 2015 rates: $35 to $90. (707)923-2777 7000 Benbow Dr, Garberville, CA 95542

RICHARDSON GROVE (State Pk) From town, S 7 mi on US-101 (R). 2015 rates: $35 to $45. (707)247-3318

GAVIOTA — H2 *Santa Barbara*

GAVIOTA (State Pk) 1 mi NW on US-101. (805)968-1033

GEORGETOWN — D3 *El Dorado*

ELDORADO NF (STUMPY MEADOWS CAMPGROUND) (Natl Forest) From town: Go 18 mi E on CR-12N29 (Georgetown Wentworth Springs Rd). Pit toilets. 2015 rates: $19. Apr 18 to Oct 13. (530)333-4312

GIANT FOREST — F3 *Tulare*

SEQUOIA NATIONAL PARK (DORST CREEK CAMPGROUND) (Natl Pk) From town: Go 12 mi N on Generals Hwy. 2015 rates: $22. Jun 17 to Sep 8. (800)365-3341

SEQUOIA NATIONAL PARK (LODGEPOLE CAMPGROUND) (Natl Pk) From town: Go 4 mi N on Generals Hwy. 2015 rates: $22. May 20 to Sep 29. (559)565-3341

Say you saw it in our Guide!

GILROY — F2 *Santa Clara*

GILROY See also Aromas, Hollister, Morgan Hill, Marina, Moss Landing & San Juan Baustista.

GILROY GARLIC USA RV PARK **Ratings: 9/9/7.5** (RV Park) 2015 rates: $49 to $55. (408)848-8081 650 Holloway Rd, Gilroy, CA 95020

GLENDALE — H4 *Los Angeles*

Things to See and Do

SOI MOTORHOME CLUB The SOI Motorhome Club is an international club dedicated to fun and friendship conducting rallies and tours throughout North America and Overseas. Partial handicap access. Restrooms. Hours: 8am to 5pm.
(209)815-1837 Lat: 34.2345615, Lon: -118.257102
3550 Foothill Blvd, Glendale, CA 91214
paul@soiclub.com
http://www.soiclub.com/
See ad page 118 (Welcome Section).

GOLD RUN — D3 *Placer*

DUTCH FLAT RV RESORT **Ratings: 4.5/7/6** (RV Park) 2015 rates: $34. (530)389-8924 55 Canyon Creek Rd, Gold Run, CA 95717

GOLETA — H3 *Santa Barbara*

EL CAPITAN STATE BEACH (State Pk) From town, N 10 mi on US-101 (L). 2015 rates: $35. (805)968-1033

REFUGIO STATE BEACH (State Pk) From town, N 15 mi on SR-101 to Refugio State Beach exit (Exit 120), W 0.2 mi on state beach service rd (L). 2015 rates: $35 to $55. (805)968-1033

GORMAN — H3 *Los Angeles*

ANGELES NATIONAL FOREST (LOS ALAMOS CAMPGROUND) (Natl Pk) From I-5 (Hungry Valley, exit 221): Go S on Old Hwy 99 to Pyramid Lake entrance. 2015 rates: $18. (626)574-1613

PYRAMID LAKE RV RESORT Ratings: 8/6/6 (RV Park) From Jct of I-5 & Smokey Bear Rd (Exit 195): Go 1/8 mi E on Smokey Bear Rd to Copco Ave, then 1 mi N on Copco Ave (E). Elev 3000 ft. **FAC:** Paved rds. 117 gravel, patios, 50 pull-thrus (21 x 61), back-ins (20 x 50), 117 full hkups (30/50 amps), WiFi, tent sites, rentals, laundry, LP gas, fire rings, controlled access. **REC:** pool, whirlpool, playground. Pet restrict(B/Q). Partial handicap access. 28 day max stay, eco-friendly, 2015 rates: $42 to $44. Disc: AAA, military.
AAA Approved
(661)248-0100 Lat: 34.722273, Lon: -118.798360
45100 Copco Ave., Gorman, CA 93243
info@pyramidlakerv.com
www.pyramidlakerv.com

GRAEAGLE — C3 *Plumas*

GRAEAGLE See also Blairsden, Clio, Cromberg, Portola, Sierra City & Quincy.

MOVIN' WEST RV PARK (MHP) **Ratings: 6/8.5★/8.5** (RV Park) 2015 rates: $36 to $39. May 1 to Oct 21. (530)836-2614 305 Johnsville, Graeagle, CA 96103

SIERRA SPRINGS TRAILER RESORT **Ratings: 4/4.5/5.5** (RV Park) 2015 rates: $30. Apr 1 to Oct 31. (530)836-2747 70099 Hwy 70, Graeagle, CA 96103

GRAND TERRACE — M5 *San Bernardino*

TERRACE VILLAGE RV PARK **Ratings: 9/9/8** (RV Park) 2015 rates: $50. (909)783-4580 21900 Barton Road #170, Grand Terrace, CA 92313

GRANT GROVE — F3 *Fresno, Tulare*

KINGS CANYON/AZALEA CAMPGROUND (Natl Pk) From N end of town, N 0.5 mi on SR-180 (L). 2015 rates: $18. (559)335-2856

KINGS CANYON/CRYSTAL SPRINGS (Natl Pk) From town, N 0.5 mi on Grant Grove Village (R). Big rigs not recommended. 2015 rates: $18 to $35. (209)335-2856

KINGS CANYON/SUNSET (Natl Pk) From Grant Grove Village, N 0.2 mi on Grant Grove Village Rd (L). 2015 rates: $18. (209)335-2856

GRASS VALLEY — C3 *Nevada*

NEVADA COUNTY FAIRGROUNDS (Public) From Jct of SR-49 & SR-20, W 500 ft on SR-20 to Mill St exit, S 200 ft on Mill St to McCourtney Rd, W 0.6 mi to Gate 4 (R); or E-bnd: From Jct of SR-20 & McCourtney Rd exit (500 ft prior to Jct of SR-49 & SR-20), SW 0.6 mi on McCourtney Rd to Gate 4 (R). Call first for availability. 2015 rates: $27 to $35. (530)273-6217

GREENBRAE — E2 *Marin*

MARIN PARK, INC
Ratings: 8.5/9.5★/7.5 (RV Park) N-bnd: From Jct of US-101 & Exit 450A (Lucky Dr), N 0.1 mi on frntg rd (R); or S-bnd: From Jct of US-101 & Exit 450A (Lucky Dr), W 300 ft on Fifer Ave to Tamal Vista Blvd, S 0.2 mi to Wornum, E 0.1 mi on Wornum (under Fwy) to Redwood Hwy (Frntg Rd), N 0.3 mi (R). **FAC:** Paved rds. (86 spaces). Avail: 63 gravel, back-ins (17 x 50), accepts full hkup units only, 63 full hkups (30/50 amps), seasonal sites, cable, WiFi, dump, laundry. **REC:** heated pool. Pet restrict(Q). No tents. Big rig sites, eco-friendly, 2015 rates: $75 to $90.
AAA Approved
(888)461-5199 Lat: 37.94111, Lon: -122.51518
2140 Redwood Hwy, Greenbrae, CA 94904
marinrvpark@hotmail.com
www.marinrvpark.com
See ad pages 158 (Spotlight San Francisco), 128.

GREENFIELD — F2 *Monterey*

YANKS RV RESORT
Ratings: 10/10★/9 (RV Resort) From jct Hwy 101 & Thorne Rd (Exit 295): Go 1/10 mi E on Livingston Rd (E). **FAC:** Paved rds. 80 paved, patios, 74 pull-thrus (32 x 70), back-ins (30 x 50), 80 full hkups (30/50 amps), cable, WiFi, dump, laundry, groc, LP gas, controlled access. **REC:** heated pool, whirlpool. Pet restrict(B/Q). Partial handicap access. Big rig sites, eco-friendly, 2015 rates: $44 to $64.
(855)926-5778 Lat: 36.342459, Lon: -121.254156
40399 Livingston Rd, Greenfield, CA 93927
info@yanksrvresort.com
www.yanksrvresort.com
See ad pages 195, 128.

GRIDLEY — C2 *Butte*

GRIDLEY INN & RV PARK
Ratings: 8/9.5★/8.5 (RV Park) From Jct of SR-99 & SR-20, N 17 mi on SR-99 to center of Gridley (across from Taco Bell) (R). **FAC:** Gravel rds. 46 gravel, 1 pull-thrus (24 x 64), back-ins (24 x 50), some side by side hkups, accepts full hkup units only, 46 full hkups (30/50 amps), cable, WiFi, laundry. **REC:** pool, whirlpool. Pets OK $. Partial handicap access, no tents. Big rig sites, eco-friendly, 2015 rates: $35. Disc: AAA, military.
AAA Approved
(877)846-4520 Lat: 39.35943, Lon: -121.68735
1490 Hwy 99, Gridley, CA 95948
gridleyinnrv@sbcglobal.net
www.gridleyinnrv.com
See ad this page.

GROVELAND — E3 *Tuolumne*

MOCCASIN POINT RECREATION AREA (Public) From Jct of Hwys 120 & 49 (Chinese Camp), SE 6.2 mi on Hwy 120/49 to Jacksonville Rd exit, N 100 ft (R). 2015 rates: $22 to $41. (209)852-2396

YOSEMITE LAKES **Ratings: 6/8★/6.5** (Membership Pk) 2015 rates: $43 to $52. (800)533-1001 31191 Hardin Flat Rd, Groveland, CA 95321

YOSEMITE PINES RV RESORT Ratings: 8/7.5/6.5 (Campground) E bnd: From Jct of Hwy 120 & Old Hwy 120 (east of town), S (right turn) 1.3 mi on Old Hwy 120 (L). Elev 2800 ft. **FAC:** Paved/gravel rds. (181 spaces). Avail: 159 grass, 4 pull-thrus (20 x 60), back-ins (22 x 42), 96 full hkups, 63 W, 63 E (30/50 amps), seasonal sites, WiFi, tent sites, rentals, dump, laundry, groc, LP gas, fire rings, firewood. **REC:** heated pool, playground. Pet restrict(Q). Partial handicap access. Eco-friendly, 2015 rates: $38 to $56. Disc: AAA, military.
AAA Approved
(209)962-7690 Lat: 37.82576, Lon: -120.19562
20450 Old Hwy 120, Groveland, CA 95321
yosemite@yosemitepinesrv.com
www.yosemitepinesrv.com

YOSEMITE RIDGE RESORT **Ratings: 6/8★/7.5** (RV Park) 2015 rates: $40. (800)706-3009 7589 Hwy 120, Groveland, CA 95321

YOSEMITE/HODGDON MEADOW (Natl Pk) From Groveland, E 25 mi on SR-120, follow signs (L). Camp located at park entrance. Entrance fee required. 2015 rates: $26. (209)372-0200

GROVER BEACH — H2 *San Luis Obispo*

LE SAGE RIVIERA RV PARK **Ratings: 4.5/9/7.** (RV Park) 2015 rates: $40 to $55. (805)489-5506 31 N. Hwy 1, Grover Beach, CA 93433

Like Us on Facebook.

GUALALA — D1 *Mendocino*

↓ GUALALA POINT (SONOMA COUNTY REG PARK) (Public) From town: Go 1 mi S on Hwy-1. 2015 rates: $32. (707)785-2377

HALF MOON BAY — E2 *San Mateo*

← HALF MOON BAY STATE BEACH (State Pk) From Hwy 1 in town: Go 1/2 mi W on Kelly Ave. 2015 rates: $37 to $65. (650)726-8819

↓ PELICAN POINT RV PARK **Ratings: 7/7.5/5.5** (RV Park) 2015 rates: $53 to $58. (650)726-9100 1001 Miramontes Point Rd, Half Moon Bay, CA 94019

HANFORD — F3 *Kings*

↓ BEL AIR RV & MH COMMUNITY **Ratings: 5.5/NA/7** (RV Park) 2015 rates: $35 to $50. (559)582-9692 10954 Hanford Armona Rd, Hanford, CA 93230

HAT CREEK — B3 *Shasta*

↓ HAT CREEK HEREFORD RANCH RV PARK & CAMPGROUND **Ratings: 7/8★/8.5** (Campground) 2015 rates: $35. Apr 15 to Oct 15. (530)335-7171 17855 Doty Rd, Hat Creek, CA 96040

↓ **RANCHERIA RV PARK**

Ratings: 8/9★/8 (RV Park) S-bnd: From Jct of SR-89 & SR-299, S 16 mi on SR-89 (R); or N-bnd: From Jct of SR-89 & SR-44, N 5.7 mi on SR-89 (L). Elev 3600 ft. **FAC:** Paved rds. 65 gravel, 21 pull-thrus (25 x 75), back-ins (25 x 65), 65 full hkups (30/50 amps), WiFi, tent sites, rentals, laundry, groc, LP gas, fire rings, firewood, restaurant. **REC:** pond, fishing. Pets OK. Partial handicap access. Big rig sites, eco-friendly, 2015 rates: $42.

(530)335-7418 Lat: 40.74076, Lon: -121.46939
15565 Black Angus Lane, Hat Creek, CA 96040
rancheriarv593@gmail.com
www.rancheriarvpark.com
See ad this page, 128.

Things to See and Do

↓ **THE COOKHOUSE** Great home cooked breakfast, lunch & dinner. Elev 3600 ft. Restrooms, food. Hours: Call for hours. ATM.

(800)346-3430 Lat: 40.740706, Lon: -121.46998
15565 Black Angus Lane, Hat Creek, CA 96040
rancheriarv@gmail.com
www.rancheriarvpark.com
See ad this page.

HEALDSBURG — D2 *Sonoma*

↑ ALEXANDER VALLEY RV PARK & CAMPGROUND **Ratings: 6/8/9** (Campground) 2015 rates: $50. Mar 15 to Nov 15. (800)640-1386 2411 Alexander Valley Rd, Healdsburg, CA 95448

HEMET — N6 *Riverside*

← CASA DEL SOL RV RESORT **Ratings: 9/10★/8** (RV Park) 2015 rates: $55. (888)925-2516 2750 W Acacia Ave, Hemet, CA 92545

Thank you for being one of our best customers!

← **GOLDEN VILLAGE PALMS RV RESORT - SUNLAND**

Ratings: 10/10★/9 (RV Resort) From Jct of Hwys 74/79 (Florida Ave) & Sanderson Ave, W 0.2 mi on Florida Ave (R).

WELCOME TO YOUR HOME AWAY FROM HOME

Golf, golf, golf! On-site resort events, classes, tours, ballroom dancing, BBQs & more. Putting green, fitness center, heated pools/spas, poolside bar, shuffleboard. Large groups welcome. Top Rated! Largest RV resort in CA.

FAC: Paved rds. (1000 spaces). Avail: 40 paved, 710 all weather, patios, 40 pull-thrus (30 x 90), back-ins (32 x 44), 750 full hkups (30/50 amps), seasonal sites, cable, WiFi $, rentals, laundry, controlled access. **REC:** heated pool, whirlpool, shuffleboard. Pet restrict(B/Q) $. Partial handicap access, no tents. RV age restrict, eco-friendly, 2015 rates: $45 to $90. Disc: AAA, military.

(866)225-6320 Lat: 33.74900, Lon: -117.01190
3600 W Florida Ave, Hemet, CA 92545
goldenrv@sunlandrvresorts.com
www.goldenvillagepalms.com
See ad this page, 126 & Snowbird Destinations in Magazine Section.

← HEMET RV RESORT **Ratings: 9/9★/6.5** (RV Park) 2015 rates: $37. (951)925-5812 235 S Lyon Ave, Hemet, CA 92543

HERALD — D3 *Sacramento*

↗ RANCHO SECO RECREATIONAL AREA **Ratings: 7.5/7/8.5** (Campground) 2015 rates: $30. (209)748-2318 14440 Twin Cities Rd, Herald, CA 95638

HESPERIA — H4 *San Bernardino*

← **DESERT WILLOW RV RESORT**

Ratings: 9.5/9★/7.5 (RV Park) From I-15 & Main St (Exit 143): Go 2/10 mi W, then 50 feet N on Cataba Rd (L). Elev 3300 ft. **FAC:** Paved rds. (173 spaces). Avail: 25 gravel, patios, 25 pull-thrus (35 x 87), mostly side by side hkups, 25 full hkups (30/50 amps), seasonal sites, cable, WiFi, laundry, LP gas, controlled access. **REC:** heated pool, whirlpool. Pet restrict(B/Q). Partial handicap access, no tents. Big rig sites, RV age restrict, eco-friendly, 2015 rates: $40.

(760)949-0377 Lat: 34.427885, Lon: -117.38673
12624 Main St, Hesperia, CA 92345
colleen@desertwillowrv.com
www.desertwillowrv.com

→ HESPERIA LAKE PARK (Public) From Jct of I-15 & Main St/Arrowhead Lake Rd, E 9.5 mi on Main St/Arrowhead Lake Rd (L). 2015 rates: $35 to $50. (760)244-5488

Tell them you saw them in this Guide!

↘ **MOJAVE RIVER FORKS REGIONAL PARK**

(Public) From Jct of I-15 & Phelan/Main St exit: Go 7 mi E on Main St to Arrowhead Lake Rd, then 5-1/2 mi SE on Arrowhead Lake Rd to SR 173, then 1 mi E on SR 173 (R). Elev 3500 ft. **FAC:** Paved/gravel rds. 25 gravel, 8 pull-thrus (20 x 40), back-ins (20 x 40), 25 full hkups (15/30 amps), tent sites, dump, fire rings. **REC:** rec open to public. Pets OK $. 14 day max stay, 2015 rates: $25 to $40.

(760)389-2322 Lat: 34.3301758, Lon: -117.267795
17891 Ca Hwy 173, Hesperia, CA 92345
parks@parks.sbcounty.gov
www.sbcountyparks.com
See ad page 123 (Welcome Section).

HIDDEN VALLEY LAKE — D2 *Lake*

→ **HIDDEN VALLEY LAKE RV PARK/CAMPGROUND**

Ratings: 5/8.5/8.5 (RV Park) From Jct of Hwy 29 & Hartmann Rd (in town), E 0.1 mi on Hartmann Rd to Hidden Valley Lake Rd, N 1 mi (L). **FAC:** Paved rds. 18 gravel, 2 pull-thrus (30 x 64), back-ins (20 x 40), 18 full hkups (30/50 amps), dump, groc, restaurant. **REC:** golf, playground. Pets OK. Partial handicap access, no tents. 14 day max stay, eco-friendly, 2015 rates: $20 to $40. No CC.

(707)987-3138 Lat: 38.79909, Lon: -122.55135
19234 Hidden Valley Lake Rd, Hidden Valley Lake, CA 95467
info@hvla.com
www.hvla.com

HOLLISTER — F2 *Santa Clara*

↘ **BOLADO PARK EVENT CENTER & CAMPGROUND**

(Public) From San Benito St and 4th St: Go 2 mi S to Union Rd, then 1-1/2 mi E to Airline Hwy, then 8 miles SE (R). **FAC:** Paved/dirt rds. (43 spaces). 42 Avail: 11 paved, 31 dirt, 8 pull-thrus (24 x 60), back-ins (24 x 60), 32 full hkups, 10 W, 5 E (30/50 amps), tent sites, dump, controlled access. **REC:** golf, rec open to public. Pet restrict(B/Q). Partial handicap access. Big rig sites, 2015 rates: $35. ATM.

(831)628-3421 Lat: 36.766564, Lon: -121.301949
9000 Airline Hwy, Tres Pinos, CA 95075
rvcamping@boladoparkeventcenter.com
boladoparkeventcenter.com
See ad this page.

How can you tell whether you're traveling in the right direction? The arrow in each listing denotes the compass direction of the facility in relation to the listed town. For example, an arrow pointing straight up indicates that the facility is located due north from town. An arrow pointing down and to the right indicates that the facility is southeast of town.

HOLLISTER (CONT)

CASA DE FRUTA RV PARK
Ratings: 9.5/10★/8 (RV Park) From Jct of 4th St & San Benito St (Hwy 156B): Go 5 mi N to Jct of Hwy 156B & Hwy 156, then 3-1/2 mi N on Hwy 156 to Jct of Hwy 156 & Hwy 152 (Pacheco Pass Hwy), then 1-1/2 mi N on Hwy 152 to Casa de Fruta Pkwy Exit, then E to Frontage Rd, then 1/2 mi N on Frontage Rd (R).

FAMILY FUN AND ENTERTAINMENT
Surrounded by the gently sloping hills of Pacheco Pass Valley, Casa de Fruta has delighted and refreshed travelers for 100 years! Come renew your spirit among the hills and trees. Visit our website www.CasadeFruta.com

FAC: Paved rds. (250 spaces). Avail: 226 paved, 100 pull-thrus (22 x 45), back-ins (24 x 46), mostly side by side hkups, 226 full hkups (30/50 amps), seasonal sites, WiFi, tent sites, rentals, dump, laundry, groc, LP gas, firewood, restaurant. **REC:** pool, wading pool, Pacheco Creek: playground. Pet restrict(Q) $. Partial handicap access. Eco-friendly, 2015 rates: $40 to $45. ATM.
AAA Approved
(408)842-9316 Lat: 36.99448, Lon: -121.37793
10031 Pacheco Pass Hwy, Hollister, CA 95023
rvandinn@casadefruta.com
www.casadefruta.com
See ad this page, 128.

HOLLISTER HILLS STATE VEHICULAR RECREATION AREA (State Pk) From town: Go 6 mi S on Cienega Rd. 2015 rates: $10. (831)637-3874

Things to See and Do

CASA DE FRUTA FRUIT STAND California fresh fruit, dried fruit & nuts, local vegetables, gift packs and mail order. Partial handicap access. RV accessible. Restrooms, food. Hours: 7am to 9pm.
(408)842-9316 Lat: 36.98862, Lon: -121.38252
10021 Pacheco Pass Hwy, Hollister, CA 95023
info@casadefruta.com
www.casadefruta.com
See ad this page.

CASA DE FRUTA PLAZA 24-Hour Chevron Plaza & Casa de Burrito Food Mart. Partial handicap access. RV accessible. Restrooms, food. Hours: Gas 24 Hr/Casa de Burrito 10am-8pm. ATM.
(408)842-9316 Lat: 36.98862, Lon: -121.38252
10021 Pacheco Pass Hwy, Hollister, CA 95023
info@casadefruta.com
www.casadefruta.com
See ad this page.

CASA DE FRUTA RESTAURANT & BAKERY Open 24 Hours featuring Kobe burgers, charbroiled steaks and homemade desserts. Partial handicap access. RV accessible. Restrooms, food. Hours: Open 24 Hrs.
(408)842-9316 Lat: 36.98862, Lon: -121.38252
10021 Pacheco Pass Hwy, Hollister, CA 95023
info@casadefruta.com
www.casadefruta.com
See ad this page.

The RVers' Guide to NASCAR helps RV travelers get the most out of North America's most thrilling sporting event. Turn to the front of the Guide and we'll give you the inside track on how to get high-speed thrills at major NASCAR venues.

CASA DE FRUTA SWEET SHOP & COFFEE BAR Fresh baked pastries, espresso bar, homemade pies, ice cream and gelato with mix-ins, fudge, chocolates and gift items. Partial handicap access. RV accessible. Restrooms, food. Hours: 7am to 7pm.
(408)842-9316 Lat: 36.99448, Lon: -121.37793
10021 Pacheco Pass Hwy, Hollister, CA 95023
info@casadefruta.com
www.casadefruta.com
See ad this page.

CASA DE FRUTA TRAIN & VENETIAN CAROUSEL & MINING SLUICE Model Train Ride, Pan Mining Sluice, Double Decker Venetian Carousel. Partial handicap access. RV accessible. Restrooms, food. Hours: Fri-Sun 11am to 6:30pm Weather Permit. Adult fee: $4. ATM.
(408)842-9316 Lat: 36.99448, Lon: -121.37793
10021 Pacheco Pass Hwy, Hollister, CA 95023
info@casadefruta.com
www.casadefruta.com
See ad this page.

CASA DE FRUTA WINE & DELI Wine tasting room, gourmet sandwiches, award-winning wines, deli trays. Partial handicap access. RV accessible. Restrooms, food. Hours: 8:30am to 7pm.
(408)842-9316 Lat: 36.98862, Lon: -121.38252
10021 Pacheco Pass Hwy, Hollister, CA 95023
info@casadefruta.com
www.casadefruta.com
See ad this page.

HORNBROOK — A2 *Siskiyou*

BLUE HERON RV PARK **Ratings: 7.5/9.5★/9** (RV Park) 2015 rates: $40 to $59. (530)475-3270 6930 Copco, Hornbrook, CA 96044

HUNTINGTON BEACH — O3 *Orange*

HUNTINGTON BY THE SEA RV RESORT Ratings: 8.5/8/6 (RV Park) From Jct of Pacific Coast Hwy & Hwy 39/Beach Blvd, S 0.5 mi on Pacific Coast Hwy to Newland St, E 100 ft (L). **FAC:** Paved rds. (92 spaces). Avail: 46 paved, patios, 27 pull-thrus (20 x 50), back-ins (20 x 50), 46 full hkups (30/50 amps), seasonal sites, cable, WiFi, laundry. **REC:** heated pool, whirlpool. Pet restrict(B/Q). Partial handicap access, no tents. RV age restrict, 2015 rates: $58 to $89. Disc: AAA.
AAA Approved
(800)439-3486 Lat: 33.64492, Lon: -117.98083
21871 Newland St, Huntington Beach, CA 92646
hbtsea@hotmail.com

SUNSET VISTA RV PARK (Public) From jct I-405 & Hwy 39: Go 5-1/2 mi S on Hwy 39, then 3/4 mi NE on Pacific Coast Hwy (Hwy 1). 2015 rates: $60. (714)536-5286

IDYLLWILD — J5 *Riverside*

IDYLLWILD COUNTY PARK (Public) From Jct of SR-243 & Riverside Cnty Playground, W 0.5 mi on Riverside Cnty Playground (E). Reservations strongly recommended. 2015 rates: $20. (951)659-2656

IDYLLWILD RV RESORT & CAMPGROUND **Ratings: 7.5/9★/8** (RV Park) 2015 rates: $45 to $54. (951)659-4137 24400 Canyon Trail, Idyllwild, CA 92549

MOUNT SAN JACINTO/IDYLLWILD CAMPGROUND (State Pk) From Jct of I-215 & I-10 (exit 40A), E 21 mi on I-10 to SR-243 (8th St, exit 100), S 28 mi (R). 2015 rates: $20 to $25. (951)659-2607

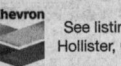

MOUNT SAN JACINTO/STONE CREEK (State Pk) From town, N 6 mi on State Hwy 243 (R). Pit toilets. 2015 rates: $20. (951)659-2607

INDEPENDENCE — F4 *Inyo*

GOODALE CREEK BLM (Public) From town, N 16 mi on US-395 to Aberdeen Cut-off Rd, W 2 mi (R). Donations accepted. Pit toilets. 2015 rates: $5. Apr 15 to Nov 30. (760)872-4881

INDEPENDENCE CREEK COUNTY PARK (Public) From Jct of US-395 & Market St, W 0.5 mi on Market St to Creek Rd, 2.5 mi (R). Pit toilets. 2015 rates: $10. (760)878-0272

TABOOSE CREEK COUNTY PARK (Public) From Jct of US-395 & Taboose Creek Rd (14 mi N of Independence), W 2.5 mi on Taboose Creek Rd (L). Pit toilets. 2015 rates: $10. (760)878-0272

INDIO — J5 *Riverside*

INDIAN WATERS RV RESORT & COTTAGES
Ratings: 10/10★/10 (RV Resort) From Jct of I-10 & Golf Center Pky (Exit 144): Go SW 0.9 mi on Golf Center Pkwy to Hwy 111, then W 0.3 mi to Jackson St, then S 0.7 mi (L).

PALM SPRINGS AREA BEST RESORT VALUE
Top Rated Resort 10/10/10! Excellent long-term rates! Gated. Private bath suites, grassy or desert sites, fitness center, 2 pools, spa, free LD phones, large group room w/kitchen, free waffle breakfast M-F, Free WiFi.

FAC: Paved rds. 265 paved, 15 pull-thrus (26 x 60), back-ins (35 x 48), 265 full hkups (50 amps), WiFi, rentals, dump, laundry, controlled access. **REC:** heated pool, whirlpool, pond, shuffleboard. Pets OK. Partial handicap access, no tents. RV age restrict, eco-friendly, 2015 rates: $39 to $69. Disc: AAA, military.
(760)342-8100 Lat: 33.70674, Lon: -116.21637
47202 Jackson St, Indio, CA 92201
info@iwrvr.com
www.indianwatersrvresort.com
See ad pages 150 (Spotlight Palm Springs), 126, 120 (CA Map) & ad inside back cover & Snowbird Destinations in Magazine Section.

INDIAN WELLS CAREFREE RV RESORTS
Ratings: 10/9★/9 (RV Park) From Jct of I-10 & Jefferson St (Exit 139), S 2.7 mi on Jefferson St (L).

INDIAN WELLS CAREFREE RV RESORT!
This sun-filled, fun-filled Palm Springs area resort is set in the foothills with breathtaking views of the Santa Rosa Mountains. It's your gateway to golf, art galleries, shops and everything that makes this area a favorite!

FAC: Paved rds. (349 spaces). Avail: 199 paved, 80 pull-thrus (20 x 70), back-ins (20 x 60), some side by side hkups, 199 full hkups (30/50 amps), seasonal sites, cable, WiFi, rentals, laundry. **REC:** heated pool, whirlpool, shuffleboard. Pets OK. No tents. RV age restrict, eco-friendly, 2015 rates: $46 to $90. Disc: AAA.
(760)347-0895 Lat: 33.70396, Lon: -116.26833
47-340 Jefferson St, Indio, CA 92201
indianwells@carefreervresorts.com
www.carefreervresorts.com
See ad pages 202, 126 & Pampered Pets, Snowbird Destinations in Magazine Section.

JOSHUA TREE/COTTONWOOD SPRING (Natl Pk) From Jct of I-10 & Joshua Tree Park exit, N 7 mi (R). Entrance fee required. 2015 rates: $15. (760)367-7511

MOTORCOACH COUNTRY CLUB
Ratings: 10/10★/10 (Condo Pk) From Jct of I-10 & Jefferson St (Exit 139), S 3 mi on Jefferson St to Ave 48, E 0.5 mi (R). Note: Class A Motorcoach only-Min. 30 ft. **FAC:** Paved rds. (400 spaces). Avail: 100 paved, patios, back-ins (35 x 63), 100 full hkups (50 amps), cable, WiFi $, laundry, restaurant, controlled access. **REC:** heated pool, whirlpool, Waterway: golf. Pet restrict(Q). Partial handicap access, no tents. Big rig sites, RV age restrict, 2015 rates: $90 to $184.
(888)277-0789 Lat: 33.69980, Lon: -116.26005
80501 Avenue 48, Indio, CA 92201
dschultz@drminternet.com
www.motorcoachcountryclub.com
See ad page 150 (Spotlight Palm Springs).

Subscribe to MotorHome Magazine Questions? Change of address? Call 800-678-1201.

INDIO (CONT)

OUTDOOR RESORT INDIO
Ratings: 10/10★/10 (Condo Pk) From Jct of I-10 & Jefferson St (Exit 139), S 3 mi on Jefferson St to Ave 48, E 0.3 mi (L). Class A Motorhomes only - Minimum 34 ft. Note: Minimum length of stay may apply. **FAC:** Paved rds. (419 spaces). Avail: 100 paved, patios, back-ins (30 x 60), accepts full hkup units only, 100 full hkups (50 amps), seasonal sites, cable, WiFi $, laundry, restaurant, controlled access. **REC:** heated pool, whirlpool, pond, golf. Pet restrict(Q). Partial handicap access, no tents. Big rig sites, RV age restrict, 2015 rates: $65 to $121.
(800)892-2992 Lat: 33.70010, Lon: -116.26232
80-394 Avenue 48, Indio, CA 92201
info@orindio.com
www.orindio.com
See ad page 149 (Spotlight Palm Springs) & Snowbird Destinations in Magazine Section.

SHADOW HILLS RV RESORT
Ratings: 9.5/9.5★/9 (RV Park) From Jct of I-10 & Jefferson St (Exit 139), N 0.25 mi on Jefferson St (L).

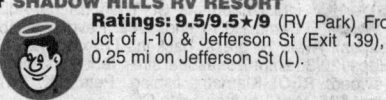

EXPERIENCE THE COACHELLA VALLEY
Looking to relax and enjoy clear skies, beautiful sunsets, and panoramic mountain views? You'll find it all here at Shadow Hills RV Resort. We are a Family Owned and Operated Resort, perfect for enjoying the Palm Springs Area

FAC: Paved rds. (120 spaces). 113 Avail: 99 paved, 14 grass, patios, 1 pull-thrus (25 x 96), back-ins (28 x 42), 113 full hkups (30/50 amps), seasonal sites, WiFi, tent sites, dump, laundry, LP gas, controlled access. **REC:** heated pool, whirlpool, pond, fishing, shuffleboard. Pet restrict(Q) $. Partial handicap access. RV age restrict, eco-friendly, 2015 rates: $37.50 to $62.50. Disc: AAA.
(760)360-4040 Lat: 33.75423, Lon: -116.27004
40655 Jefferson Street, Indio, CA 92203
info@shadowhillsrvresort.com
www.shadowhillsrvresort.com
See ad pages 202, 126 & Snowbird Destinations in Magazine Section.

Things to See and Do

MOTORCOACH COUNTRY CLUB GOLF COURSE Open only to owners and resort guests, private, challenging 9 hole par 3 golf course offers lush greens, sand traps and water. Partial handicap access. Restrooms, food. Hours: 12pm to 5:00 pm. No CC.
(888)277-0789 Lat: 33.6998, Lon: -116.26005
80-501 Avenue 48, Indio, CA 92201
dschultz@drminternet.com
www.motorcoachcountryclub.com
See ad page 150 (Spotlight Palm Springs).

IONE — D3 *Amador*

LAKE CAMANCHE NORTH **Ratings: 4.5/6/7.5** (Campground) 2015 rates: $28 to $34. (866)763-5121 2000 Camanche Rd, Ione, CA 95640

PARDEE LAKE RECREATION INC. Ratings: 6/7.5/8 (Campground) From Jct of Hwy 88 & Jackson Valley Rd, S 3 mi on Jackson Valley Rd to Buena Vista Rd, S 2.6 mi to Stony Creek Rd, N 1 mi (R). **FAC:** Paved rds. 190 Avail: 12 paved, 178 dirt, back-ins (24 x 45), 12 full hkups (30/50 amps), tent sites, dump, laundry, LP gas, firewood, restaurant, controlled access. **REC:** pool, Lake Pardee: fishing, marina. Pet restrict(B) $. 14 day max stay, eco-friendly, 2015 rates: $22 to $32. Feb 17 to Nov 6.
AAA Approved
(209)772-1472 Lat: 38.28151, Lon: -120.86893
4900 Stony Creek Rd, Ione, CA 95640
pardeelakerecreation.com

ISLETON — D3 *Sacramento*

DELTA SHORES RESORT & MARINA **Ratings: 7/7.5/6** (Membership Pk) 2015 rates: $25. (916)777-5577 601 Brannan Island Rd, Isleton, CA 95641

LIGHTHOUSE RESORT & MARINA **Ratings: 8/7.5/7** (Membership Pk) 2015 rates: $15 to $21. (916)777-5901 151 Brannan Island Rd, Isleton, CA 95641

SACRAMENTO RIVER-DELTA BAY KOA **Ratings: 8/9.5★/8** (RV Park) 2015 rates: $41.76 to $46.40. (916)777-5588 922 W Brannan Island Rd, Isleton, CA 95641

VIEIRA'S RESORT MHP **Ratings: 7/8.5★/6** (Campground) 2015 rates: $37 to $40. (916)777-6661 15476 State Hwy 160, Isleton, CA 95641

We appreciate your business!

JACKSON — D3 *Amador*

JACKSON RANCHERIA RV PARK
Ratings: 10/10★/10 (RV Resort) From Jct of Hwy 49 & Hwy 88 (in Jackson), E 2.5 mi on Hwy 88 to Dalton Rd, N 0.9 mi (L).

STAY AND PLAY AT JACKSON RANCHERIA
Welcome to Northern California's newest full service RV park. Located in a natural forest setting & only a short ride on the free 24 hr shuttle to the casino! Free WI-FI, a beautiful clubhouse for groups, huge pool & 2 spas.

FAC: Paved rds. 100 paved, 30 pull-thrus (35 x 60), back-ins (35 x 45), 100 full hkups (30/50 amps), cable, WiFi, dump, laundry, groc, LP gas, restaurant. **REC:** heated pool, whirlpool. Pet restrict(Q). Partial handicap access, no tents. Big rig sites, 14 day max stay, eco-friendly, 2015 rates: $45 to $55. Disc: AAA.
(800)822-WINN Lat: 38.37568, Lon: -120.73648
11407 Dalton Rd, Jackson, CA 95642
contactus@jacksoncasino.com
www.jacksoncasino.com
See ad pages 212, 128, 122 (Welcome Section), 124 (CA Featured Map).

Things to See and Do

JACKSON RANCHERIA CASINO & HOTEL Casino, Restaurants, General Store & Gas Station. Partial handicap access. RV accessible. Restrooms, food. Hours: Open 24 hours. ATM.
(800)822-WINN Lat: 38.38734, Lon: -120.73703
12222 New York Ranch Rd, Jackson, CA 95642
contactus@jacksoncasino.com
www.jacksoncasino.com
See ad pages 212, 122 (Welcome Section), 124 (CA Featured Map).

JAMUL — K5 *San Diego*

PIO PICO **Ratings: 9/8.5★/8** (Membership Pk) 2015 rates: $54 to $58. (800)405-6188 14615 Otay Lakes Rd, Jamul, CA 91935

JENNER — D2 *Sonoma*

FORT ROSS STATE HISTORIC PARK (State Pk) From town: Go 10 mi N on Hwy 1. Dirt road access. 2015 rates: $15. (707)847-3286

SALT POINT (State Pk) From town: Go 20 mi N on Hwy-1. 2015 rates: $35. (707)847-3221

STILLWATER COVE REGIONAL PARK (Public) From town, N 16 mi on Hwy 1 (R). For reservations call (707)565-CAMP. 2015 rates: $32. (707)847-3245

JOSHUA TREE NATIONAL PARK — J5
San Bernardino

JOSHUA TREE/INDIAN COVE (Natl Pk) From I-10 to Hwy 62, E 39 mi to Indian Cove Rd (7 mi W of Twentynine Palms), S 3 mi (E). For reservations call 1-800-365-CAMP. 2015 rates: $15. (760)362-4367

JOSHUA TREE/JUMBO ROCK (Natl Pk) From Jct of I-10 & Hwy 62, E 45 mi on Hwy 62 to Twentynine Palms, S 4 mi on Utah Trail (L). Sharp left, 8 mi uphill. Entrance fee required. Pit toilets. 2015 rates: $10. (760)367-7511

JULIAN — J5 *San Diego*

AGUA CALIENTE COUNTY PARK (Public) From Jct of Hwy S-2 & Agua Caliente Springs Rd, SE 0.5 mi on Agua Caliente Springs Rd (E). 2015 rates: $24 to $33. Sep to May. (877)565-3600

BUTTERFIELD RANCH RESORT **Ratings: 6.5/5/6.5** (RV Park) 2015 rates: $35. (760)765-1463 14925 Great Southern Overland Stage Rte, Julian, CA 92036

CUYAMACA RANCHO/GREEN VALLEY (State Pk) From Jct I-8 & Descanso Rd, NE 1 mi on Descanso Rd to Hwy 79, N 4 mi (L). 2015 rates: $30. (760)765-0755

CUYAMACA RANCHO/PASO PICACHO CAMPGROUND (State Pk) From Jct of I-8 & SR-79 (exit 40), N 15 mi on SR-79 (L). 2015 rates: $30. (760)765-0755

LAKE CUYAMACA (Public) From Jct of I-8 & Hwy 79 (exit 40), N 12 mi on Hwy 79 (R). 2015 rates: $20 to $30. (760)765-0515

PINEZANITA TRAILER RANCH **Ratings: 6.5/9★/8** (Campground) 2015 rates: $31. (760)765-0429 4446 Hwy 79, Julian, CA 92036

STAGECOACH TRAILS RV PARK Ratings: 7.5/8/8.5 (RV Park) From Jct of Hwy 78 & Hwy S-2 (east of Julian), S 4 mi on Hwy S-2 (R). **FAC:** Paved/gravel rds. (280 spaces). Avail: 278 gravel, 100 pull-thrus (22 x 50), back-ins (20 x 50), some side by side hkups, 278 full hkups (30 amps), WiFi Hotspot, tent sites, rentals, laundry, groc, LP gas, firewood. **REC:** heated pool, shuffleboard, rec open to public. Pets OK $. Partial handicap access. RV age restrict, 2015 rates: $35. Disc: AAA.
(760)765-3765 Lat: 33.06087, Lon: -116.42688
7878 Great Southern Overland Stage Rte of 1849(S-2), Julian, CA 92036
stagecoachrv@gmail.com
www.stagecoachtrails.com

VALLECITO COUNTY PARK (Public) From Jct of Hwy S-2 & Agua Caliente Springs Rd, N 4.5 mi on S-2 (L). 2015 rates: $22. Sep to May. (877)565-3600

WILLIAM HEISE COUNTY PARK (Public) From Jct of Hwy 79 & Pine Hills Rd (1 mi W of town), S 2 mi on Pine Hills Rd to Frisius Rd, E 2 mi (R). 2015 rates: $24 to $29. (877)565-3600

CA

JUNE LAKE — E4 *Mono*

GRANT LAKE RESORT **Ratings: 3.5/7/4.5** (Campground) 2015 rates: $20 to $23. Apr 25 to Oct 15. (760)648-7964 1 Grant Lake Rd, June Lake, CA 93529

PINE CLIFF RESORT Ratings: 5/7/7 (Campground) From Jct of US-395 & Hwy 158 (S Loop entrance): Go 1 mi SW on Hwy 158 to North Shore Dr, then 1/2 mi W on North Shore Dr to Pine Cliff Rd, then 1/2 mi SW on Pine Cliff Rd (R). Elev 7500 ft. **FAC:** Gravel/dirt rds. (135 spaces). Avail: 122 dirt, patios, 17 pull-thrus (20 x 45), back-ins (16 x 32), some side by side hkups, 107 full hkups, 15 W, 15 E (20 amps), seasonal sites, tent sites, rentals, showers $, dump, laundry, groc, LP gas, fire rings, firewood. **REC:** June Lake: swim, fishing, playground. Pet restrict(Q) $. Partial handicap access. 2015 rates: $25 to $33. Apr 15 to Oct 31. ATM, no CC.
AAA Approved
(760)648-7558 Lat: 37.797892, Lon: -119.075705
1 Pine Cliff Rd, June Lake, CA 93529
www.pinecliffresort.net

SILVER LAKE RESORT **Ratings: 6/8.5/8** (RV Park) 2015 rates: $36. Apr 29 to Oct 17. (760)648-7525 6957 Hwy 158, June Lake, CA 93529

KELSEYVILLE — D2 *Lake*

CLEAR LAKE (State Pk) From Jct of US-101 & SR-20 (Exit 555B), E 13 mi on SR-20 to SR-29, S 8 mi to Soda Bay Rd, E 6 mi (L). 2015 rates: $30 to $45. (707)279-4293

EDGEWATER RESORT & RV PARK
Ratings: 9/8.5★/8.5 (RV Park) S-bnd: From Jct of SR-29 (RVs not permitted on SR-175) & Kelseyville/Merritt Rd exit (W of town), N 3.3 mi on Merritt Rd (changes to Gaddy Ln) to Soda Bay Rd, E (Right Turn) 2.8 mi (L); or N-bnd: From Jct of SR-29 & SR-281 (Soda Bay Rd), NW 8.9 mi on Soda Bay Rd (L). **FAC:** Gravel rds. 58 dirt, back-ins (25 x 35), mostly side by side hkups, 58 full hkups (30/50 amps), cable, WiFi, tent sites, rentals, laundry, groc, fire rings, firewood. **REC:** heated pool, Clear Lake: swim, fishing. Pets OK $. 2015 rates: $45. Disc: AAA.
AAA Approved
(707)279-0208 Lat: 39.00159, Lon: -122.79288
6420 Soda Bay Road, Kelseyville, CA 95451
business@edgewaterresort.net
www.edgewaterresort.net
See ad pages 174, 128.

KERNVILLE — G4 *Kern, Tulare*

CAMP JAMES Ratings: 5.5/8.5/8.5 (RV Park) From Jct of Kernville Rd & Sierra Way: Go 1/2 mi N on Sierra Way (L). Elev 2730 ft. **FAC:** Paved/dirt rds. (68 spaces). Avail: 54 dirt, patios, back-ins (36 x 50), 15 full hkups, 39 W, 39 E (30/50 amps), seasonal sites, WiFi, tent sites, rentals, showers $, dump, fire rings, firewood, controlled access. **REC:** Kern River: swim, fishing. Pet restrict(B/Q) $. Partial handicap access. Eco-friendly, 2015 rates: $42 to $48. ATM, no CC.
AAA Approved
(760)376-6119 Lat: 35.762693, Lon: -118.421595
13801 Sierra Way, Kernville, CA 93238
campjamesrv@gmail.com
www.campjames.net

CAMP KERNVILLE **Ratings: 6/8/8** (RV Area in MHP) 2015 rates: $40 to $60. (760)376-2345 24 Sirretta St, Kernville, CA 93238

FRANDY PARK CAMPGROUND Ratings: 5.5/5.5/5.5 (Campground) From Jct Hwy 178 & Hwy 155: Go NW 11 mi on Hwy 155 (R). Elev 2700 ft. **FAC:** Gravel/dirt rds. 92 dirt, 12 pull-thrus (20 x 60), back-ins (26 x 40), 16 W, 16 E (30/50 amps), WiFi Hotspot, tent sites, showers $, dump, firewood. **REC:** Kern River: swim, fishing. Pet re-

We rate what RVers consider important.

KERNVILLE (CONT)

FRANDY PARK CAMPGROUND (CONT)
strict(B/Q) $. 13 day max stay, eco-friendly, 2015 rates: $37 to $100. Disc: military.
(760)376-6483 Lat: 35.754794, Lon: -118.421328
11252 Kernville Rd, Kernville, CA 93238
camping@frandy.net
www.frandy.net

RIVERNOOK CAMPGROUND **Ratings: 5.5/4.5/7.5** (Campground) 2015 rates: $40 to $45. (760)376-2705 14001 Sierra Way, Kernville, CA 93238

KING CITY — F2 *Monterey*

CIUDAD DEL REY
Ratings: 7.5/7/6.5 (RV Park) From Jct of US-101 & Wild Horse Rd exit: Go 100 ft W on Wild Horse Rd to Mesa Verde Rd, then 2/10 mi N on Mesa Verde Rd (L). **FAC:** Paved rds. (38 spaces). Avail: 18 gravel, 5 pull-thrus (22 x 50), back-ins (22 x 40), 18 full hkups (30/50 amps), seasonal sites, cable, WiFi $, tent sites, rentals, showers $, dump, laundry, groc, LP gas, firewood, restaurant. **REC:** heated pool, playground. Pet restrict(Q). Eco-friendly, 2015 rates: $35 to $45. Disc: AAA, military. ATM.
AAA Approved
(831)385-4828 Lat: 36.188693, Lon: -121.075255
50620 Mesa Verde Rd, King City, CA 93930
See ad this page.

SAN LORENZO PARK (Public) From Jct of US-101 & Broadway exit, W (left at stoplight) 0.2 mi on Broadway (L). 2015 rates: $32 to $42. (831)385-5964

Things to See and Do

WILD HORSE CAFE Cafe serving breakfast, lunch and dinner. Partial handicap access. RV accessible. Restrooms, food. Hours: 6:30 AM to 9 PM. ATM.
(831)385-4312 Lat: 36.188693, Lon: -121.075255
50640 Mesa Verde Rd, King City, CA 93930
See ad this page.

KINGSBURG — F3 *Fresno, King, Tulare*

CLUB ROYAL OAK
Ratings: 8.5/9.5★/9 (RV Park) From Jct of Hwy 99 & Sierra St (Hwy 201/Exit 112): Go 2-3/4 mi E on Sierra St (Ave 400) to Road 28, then S on Road 28, then 1/4 mi E, then 1/4 mi S (E). **FAC:** Paved rds. (100 spaces). Avail: 85 grass, 23 pull-thrus (32 x 100), back-ins (50 x 80), 23 full hkups, 62 W, 62 E (30/50 amps), seasonal sites, WiFi $, tent sites, dump, mobile sewer, laundry, LP gas, fire rings, firewood, controlled access. **REC:** Kings River (seasonal): swim, fishing, marina, rec open to public. Pet restrict(B/Q) $. Partial handicap access. Big rig sites, eco-friendly, 2015 rates: $40 to $80. Disc: AAA, military.
(559)897-0351 Lat: 36.510724, Lon: -119.507573
39700 Road 28, Kingsburg, CA 93631
clubroyaloak@yahoo.com
www.clubroyaloak.com

RIVERLAND RV RESORT **Ratings: 7/6/4** (RV Park) 2015 rates: $34 to $55. (559)897-5166 38743 Hwy 99, Kingsburg, CA 93631

KIT CARSON — D4 *Amador*

ELDORADO (CAPLES LAKE CAMPGROUND) (Natl Forest) 1/4 mi W on CR-10N20, then 6 mi NE on Hwy-88. Pit toilets. 2015 rates: $24. (209)295-4251

ELDORADO (WOODS LAKE CAMPGROUND) (Natl Forest) From town: Go 1/4 mi on CR 10N20, then 10 mi NE on Hwy 88, then 1-1/4 mi S on CR 10N01. Pit toilets. 2015 rates: $24. Jun 15 to Oct 15. (209)295-4251

KLAMATH — A1 *Del Norte*

CAMPER CORRAL RIVER BEACH RESORT **Ratings: 8.5/10★/10** (Campground) 2015 rates: $35 to $50. Apr 1 to Nov 1. (800)701-7275 18151 Hwy 101, Klamath, CA 95548

CHINOOK RV RESORT Ratings: 5.5/7.5/5 (RV Park) From Jct of US 101 & Terwer Valley Rd/SR-169 (Exit 769), W 1.75 mi on US 101 (L). **FAC:** Gravel rds. 70 grass, 50 pull-thrus (20 x 50), back-ins (23 x 40), mostly side by side hkups, 70 full hkups (30/50 amps), WiFi, tent sites, laundry, groc, LP gas, firewood. **REC:** Klamath River: fishing. Pets OK. 2015 rates: $35 to $40.
AAA Approved
(866)482-3511 Lat: 41.54328, Lon: -124.05160
17465 Hwy 101 S, Klamath, CA 95548
stephen-peach@thegrid.net
chinookrvresort.com

GOLDEN BEAR RV PARK **Ratings: 4.5/6.5/5.5** (Campground) 2015 rates: $35. (707)482-3333 17581 Hwy 101 S, Klamath, CA 95548

KAMP KLAMATH Ratings: 5.5/7.5/7.5 (Campground) From Jct of US 101 & Exit 768 (Klamath Beach Rd), W 2 mi on Klamath Beach Rd (R). **FAC:** Gravel rds. (46 spaces). 40 Avail: 24 gravel, 16 grass, 11 pull-thrus (25 x 70), back-ins (30 x 50), some side by side hkups, 31 full hkups, 9 W, 9 E (30 amps), seasonal sites, cable, WiFi, tent sites, dump, LP gas, fire rings, firewood. **REC:** Klamath River: fishing, playground. Pets OK. 2015 rates: $34.50. Disc: AAA, military.
AAA Approved
(866)KLAMATH Lat: 41.53069, Lon: -124.05223
1661 W Klamath Beach Rd, Klamath, CA 95548
kampklamath@msn.com
www.kampklamath.com

KLAMATH RIVER RV PARK
Ratings: 7.5/9.5★/9 (RV Park) From Jct of Hwy 101 & Exit 768/W Klamath Beach Rd (South of Klamath Bridge), W 1.0 mi on Klamath Beach Rd (R) Caution: Do not turn R on Klamath Beach Rd (Rd dead ends). **FAC:** Paved/gravel rds. 104 grass, 6 pull-thrus (20 x 55), back-ins (20 x 60), 104 full hkups (30 amps), WiFi $, tent sites, laundry, fire rings, firewood. **REC:** Klamath River: fishing, playground. Pets OK. Eco-friendly, 2015 rates: $42 to $44. Apr 15 to Nov 1.
AAA Approved
(707)482-2091 Lat: 41.51593, Lon: -124.03894
700 W Klamath Beach Rd, Klamath, CA 95548
info@klamathriverrv.com
klamathriverrv.com
See ad this page.

RV Park ratings you can rely on!

MYSTIC FOREST RV PARK
Ratings: 7.5/9.5★/7.5 (RV Park) From Jct of US-101 & SR-169 (Exit 769), stay on 101, N 4.4 mi on US-101 (L). **FAC:** Paved/gravel rds. (30 spaces). Avail: 28 grass, 17 pull-thrus (18 x 50), back-ins (25 x 50), 28 full hkups (20/30 amps), seasonal sites, WiFi, tent sites, rentals, laundry, groc, fire rings, firewood. **REC:** playground. Pets OK. Partial handicap access. Eco-friendly, 2015 rates: $34. Disc: AAA, military.
AAA Approved
(707)482-4901 Lat: 41.57650, Lon: -124.07418
15875 US Hwy 101, Klamath, CA 95548
tcam@hughes.net
www.mysticforestrv.com
See ad this page.

REDWOOD RV PARK
Ratings: 5.5/7/7 (Campground) From jct US-101 & Terwer Valley Rd/SR-169 (Exit 769), exit W 1 1/2 mi on 169 turning into Chapmans St. Then (L) on Adler Camp Rd to end. **FAC:** Paved rds. (30 spaces). Avail: 26 grass, back-ins (15 x 40), 26 full hkups (20/30 amps), seasonal sites, tent sites, dump, firewood. **REC:** Klamath: fishing. Pets OK. 2015 rates: $35. May 1 to Nov 1. No CC.
AAA Approved
(707)482-0657 Lat: 41.4775, Lon: -123.93733
145 Alder Camp Rd., Klamath, CA 95548
tsangrey@yuroktribe.nsn.us
www.redwoodrvpark.com
See ad this page.

RIVERSIDE RV PARK
Ratings: 7.5/8.5★/7.5 (Campground) From jct US-101 & Terwer Valley Rd/SR-169 (Exit 769), W 2 mi on US 101 (L). **FAC:** Paved rds. 45 paved, 35 pull-thrus (15 x 70), back-ins (15 x 35), 45 full hkups (20/30 amps), cable, WiFi, tent sites, laundry. **REC:** Klamath River: fishing. Pets OK. 2015 rates: $30. Jun 1 to Nov 1.
AAA Approved
(707)482-0657 Lat: 41.54272, Lon: -124.05076
17505 Hwy 101, Klamath, CA 95548
tsangrey@yuroktribe.nsn.us
www.riversidervparkklamath.com
See ad this page.

KYBURZ — D3 *El Dorado*

ELDORADO (CHINA FLAT CAMPGROUND) (Natl Forest) From town: Go 2-1/2 mi S on FR 11N40. Pit toilets. 2015 rates: $18. May 17 to Oct 7. (530)622-5061

ELDORADO (SAND FLAT CAMPGROUND) (Natl Forest) From town: Go 8 mi S on US 50. Pit toilets. 2015 rates: $18. May 16 to Oct 6. (530)622-5061

LA CANADA — L2 *Los Angeles*

ANGELES NATIONAL FOREST (HORSE FLATS CAMPGROUND) (Natl Pk) From jct I-210 & Hwy 2 (exit 2) (Angeles Crest Hwy): Go 29 mi NE on Hwy 2, then 2-1/2 mi W on FR 3N17, then 1/2 mi S on FR 3N17D (Horse Flats Rd). Pit toilets. 2015 rates: $12. (818)899-1900

LA GRANGE — E3 *Stanislaus, Tuolumne*

BARRETT COVE (Public) From Jct of Hwy 132 & Merced Falls Rd, S 3 mi on Merced Falls Rd to Ranchito Dr, E 1 mi (E). 2015 rates: $22 to $32. (209)378-2521

BLUE OAKS REC AREA (Public) From Jct of Hwy 132 & CR-J59 (La Grange Rd), N 8 mi on La Grange Rd to Bonds Flat Rd, S 1 mi (L). 2015 rates: $30 to $41. (209)852-2396

FLEMING MEADOWS REC AREA (Public) From Jct of Hwy 132 & CR-J59 (La Grange Rd), N 8 mi on CR-J59 to Bonds Flat Rd, S 3.2 mi (L). 2015 rates: $35 to $41. (209)852-2396

Our travel services section will help you find services that you'll find handy in your travels.

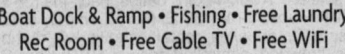

LA HONDA — E2 *San Mateo*

PORTOLA REDWOODS (State Pk) From Jct of Hwy 35 & Alpine Rd exit, W 3 mi on Alpine Rd to Portola State Park Rd, S 3 mi (E). Steep & winding rds to park. 2015 rates: $35. (650)948-9098

LA MESA — K5 *San Diego*

SAN DIEGO RV RESORT-SUNLAND
Ratings: 10/9.5★/7.5 (RV Park) E-bnd: From Jct of I-8 & Lake Murray Blvd (Exit 11), SW 200 ft on Lake Murray Blvd to Alvarado Rd, E 0.5 mi (R); or W-bnd: From Jct of I-8 & Fletcher Pkwy exit, W 360 yds on Fletcher Pkwy (across I-8) to Alvarado Rd, W 0.4 mi (L). **FAC:** Paved rds. (172 spaces). Avail: 72 paved, patios, 2 pull-thrus (25 x 70), back-ins (25 x 40), 72 full hkups (30/50 amps), seasonal sites, cable, WiFi $, laundry, LP gas. **REC:** heated pool, whirlpool. Pet restrict(B/Q) $. Partial handicap access, no tents. RV age restrict, eco-friendly, 2015 rates: $40 to $90. Disc: AAA.
(866)225-6358 Lat: 32.77195, Lon: -117.03912
7407 Alverado Rd, La Mesa, CA 91942
sandiegorv@sunlandrvresorts.com
www.sdrvresort.com

LA MIRADA — N3 *Los Angeles*

Travel Services

CAMPING WORLD OF LA MIRADA As the nation's largest retailer of RV supplies, accessories, services and new and used RVs, Camping World is committed to making your total RV experience better. **SERVICES:** RV, tire, RV appliance, staffed RV wash, restrooms. RV supplies, emergency parking, RV accessible. waiting room. Hours: 8am to 6pm.
714-522-8400 Lat: 33.87504, Lon: -118.012642
14900 S Firestone Blvd, La Mirada, CA 90638
www.campingworld.com

LA QUINTA — J5 *Riverside*

LAKE CAHUILLA PARK (Public) From Jct of I-10 & Monroe Ave (exit 142), S 7.5 mi on Monroe Ave to Ave 58, W 2.5 mi (R). Note: Call park for availability from May 4 to Oct 7. 2015 rates: $15 to $35. (760)564-4712

LAGUNITAS — E2 *Marin*

SAMUEL P TAYLOR (State Pk) From Jct of US-101 & Sir Francis Drake Blvd exit (Exit 450B), W 16 mi on Sir Francis Drake Blvd (L); or From Jct of US-1 & Sir Francis Drake Blvd at Olema, E 6 mi on Sir Francis Drake Blvd (R). 2015 rates: $35 to $50. (415)488-9897

LAKE ALMANOR — B3 *Plumas*

LAKE ALMANOR See also Chester and Lake Almanor East Shore.

LAKE ALMANOR EAST SHORE — B3 *Plumas*

LAKE COVE RESORT & MARINA (RV Spaces) From jct Hwy-89 & Hwy-147: Go 3 mi N on Hwy-147. Elev 4500 ft. **FAC:** Paved/gravel rds. (20 spaces). Avail: 11 paved, back-ins (25 x 45), accepts full hkup units only, 11 full hkups (20/30 amps), seasonal sites, WiFi Hotspot, laundry, fire rings. **REC:** Lake Almanor: swim, fishing, marina. Pets OK. No tents. 2015 rates: $35 to $40.
AAA Approved
(530)284-7697 Lat: 40.21507, Lon: -121.06707
3584 State Highway 147, Lake Almanor, CA 96137

LAKE ARROWHEAD — L6 *San Bernardino*

SAN BERNARDINO NATIONAL FOREST (GREEN VALLEY CAMPGROUND) (State Pk) From town: Go 10 mi E on Hwy-18, then 5 mi NE on Green Valley Rd (Green Valley). 2015 rates: $22 to $46. May 2 to Nov 2. (909)382-2600

SAN BERNARDINO NF (CRAB FLATS CAMPGROUND) (Natl Forest) From town: Go 10 mi E on Hwy-18, then 8 mi N on CR (Green Valley). Pit toilets. 2015 rates: $20 to $22. May 9 to Nov 2. (909)382-2790

LAKE ELSINORE — O5 *Riverside*

CLEVELAND (BLUE JAY CAMPGROUND) (Natl Forest) From town: Go 12 mi W on Hwy-74, then 7-1/2 mi NW on FR-3S04, then 1 mi S on FR-6S05. Pit toilets. 2015 rates: $20. (858)673-6180

CLEVELAND (EL CARISO CAMPGROUND) (Natl Forest) From town: Go 12 mi W on Hwy-74. Pit toilets. 2015 rates: $15. (858)673-6180

CRANE LAKESIDE MH PARK & RV RESORT **Ratings: 7.5/7.5/8** (RV Park) 2015 rates: $45. (951)678-2112 15980 Grand Ave, Lake Elsinore, CA 92530

LA LAGUNA RESORT & BOAT LAUNCH (Public) From Jct of US-91 & US-15 (Exit 96), S 15 mi on US-15 to Central St, S 3 mi (E). 2015 rates: $25 to $35. (951)471-1212

LAKE ELSINORE MARINA & RV RESORT **Ratings: 6/7/6.5** (Campground) 2015 rates: $35 to $45. (800)328-6844 32700 Riverside Drive, Lake Elsinore, CA 92530

LAKE PARK RV RESORT & MOTEL
Ratings: 8/8/8 (RV Park) From Jct of I-15 & Hwy 74 (Central Ave), SW 1,000 ft on Hwy 74 (Central Ave) to Collier Ave, NW 0.5 mi to Riverside Dr, SW 2 mi (L). Maximum length 42'. **FAC:** Paved rds. (200 spaces). Avail: 50 all weather, 8 pull-thrus (30 x 80), back-ins (28 x 32), 50 full hkups (30/50 amps), seasonal sites, WiFi, rentals, laundry. **REC:** pool, Lake Elsinore: fishing. Pet restrict(B). Partial handicap access, no tents. RV age restrict, eco-friendly, 2015 rates: $35.
(951)674-7911 Lat: 33.67776, Lon: -117.37218
32000 Riverside Drive (Hwy74), Lake Elsinore, CA 92530
lakeparkrv2012@gmail.com
www.lakeparkrvresort.com
See ad this page.

LAKE HUGHES — H4 *Los Angeles*

ELIZABETH LAKE COUNTRY CLUB (RV Park) (Rebuilding) (661)347-0537 42505 Ranch Club Rd., Lake Hughes, CA 93532

LAKE ISABELLA — G4 *Kern*

HAVEN RV PARK **Ratings: 5.5/8/6** (Campground) 2015 rates: $25 to $35. (760)478-4310 6950 Lake Isabella Blvd, Lake Isabella, CA 93240

LAKE ISABELLA RV RESORT **Ratings: 8/7.5/7.5** (RV Park) 2015 rates: $37. (760)379-2046 11936 Hwy 178, Lake Isabella, CA 93240

LAKE ISABELLA/KERN RIVER KOA **Ratings: 7.5/7.5/7** (Campground) 2015 rates: $41.40 to $50.40. (800)562-2085 15627 Hwy 178, Weldon, CA 93283

LAKE MORENA VILLAGE — K5 *San Diego*

LAKE MORENA COUNTY PARK (Public) From San Diego, E 46 mi on I-8 to Buckman Spgs Rd (exit 51), S 4 mi to Oak Dr, W 3 mi to Lake Morena Dr (R). 2015 rates: $22 to $27. (877)565-3600

LAKE SAN ANTONIO — G2 *Monterey*

LAKE SAN ANTONIO REC AREA/NORTH SHORE (Public) N-bnd: From Jct of Hwy 101 & Exit 252, Jolon Rd (G-18), NW 9.3 mi on Jolon Rd (G-18) to New Pleyto Rd, S 1.8 mi (E); or S-bnd: From Jct of Hwy 101 & Jolon Rd exit (G-14), S 22.8 mi on Jolon Rd to Lockwood (G-18/go straight), S 6.3 mi to New Pleyto Rd, S 1.8 mi (E). 2015 rates: $28 to $40. (831)755-4895

LAKE SHASTA — B2 *Shasta*

LAKE SHASTA See also Lakehead, Lewiston, O'Brien, Redding & Shasta Lake.

Everyone wants to be noticed. Tell your RV Park that you found them in the this Guide.

LAKE TAHOE — D3 *El Dorado*

LAKE TAHOE AREA MAP

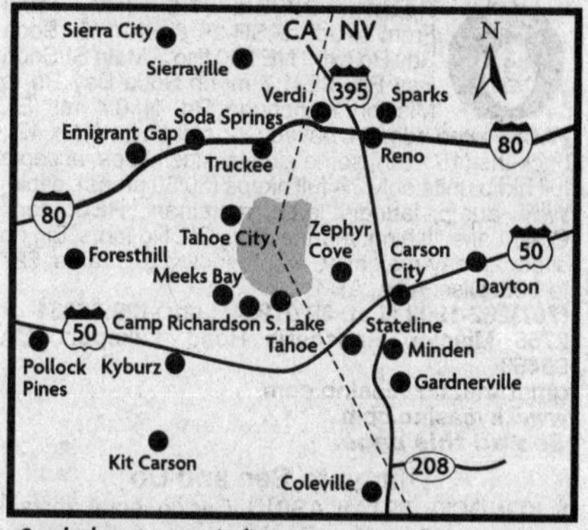

Symbols on map indicate towns within a 50 mile radius of Lake Tahoe where campgrounds are listed. Check listings for more information.

In CA, see also Camp Richardson, Coleville, Emigrant Gap, Foresthill, Kit Carson, Kyburz, Meeks Bay, Pollock Pines, Sierra City, Sierraville, Soda Springs, South Lake Tahoe, Tahoe City & Truckee.

In NV, see also Carson City, Dayton, Gardnerville, Minden, Reno, Sparks, Stateline, Verdi & Zephyr Cove.

LAKEHEAD — B2 *Shasta*

ANTLERS RV PARK & CAMPGROUND **Ratings: 6.5/5.5/6.5** (Campground) 2015 rates: $25 to $41.65. (800)642-6849 20682 Antlers Rd, Lakehead, CA 96051

DONEY CREEK LAKESHORE VILLA RV PARK **Ratings: 5.5/5.5/4.5** (RV Park) 2015 rates: $38. (530)238-8688 20672 Lakeshore Dr, Lakehead, CA 96051

LAKEHEAD CAMPGROUND & RV PARK **Ratings: 7/6.5/7** (RV Park) 2015 rates: $27 to $33. (530)238-8450 20999 Antlers, Lakehead, CA 96051

SHASTA LAKE RV RESORT & CAMPGROUND
Ratings: 5.5/5/6 (Campground) From Jct of I-5 & Antlers Rd/Lakeshore Dr (Exit 702), exit to W side of Fwy to Lakeshore Dr, S 1.3 mi (R). **FAC:** Paved/gravel rds. 50 Avail: 25 gravel, 25 dirt, 37 pull-thrus (18 x 50), back-ins (18 x 50), 50 full hkups (20/30 amps), WiFi Hotspot, tent sites, laundry, groc, firewood. **REC:** pool, Shasta Lake: fishing, playground. Pet restrict(B/Q) $. 14 day max stay, 2015 rates: $33.
AAA Approved
(800)374-2782 Lat: 40.87376, Lon: -122.38939
20433 Lakeshore Drive, Lakehead, CA 96051
shastarv@aol.com
www.shastalakerv.com

Don't miss the best part! Look in the front of most state sections for articles that focus on areas of special interest to RVers. These "Spotlights" tell you about interesting tourist destinations you might otherwise miss.

LAKEPORT — D2 *Lake County*

KONOCTI VISTA RV PARK
Ratings: 9.5/8.5★/7.5 (RV Park) From N Jct of SR-29 & SR-175 (Soda Bay Rd exit), NE 200 ft to S Main St/Soda Bay Rd, SE 1.7 mi on Soda Bay Rd to Mission Rancheria Rd, N 0.4 mi (E). **FAC:** Paved rds. 74 paved, 32 pull-thrus (15 x 42), back-ins (15 x 36), some side by side hkups, accepts full hkup units only, 74 full hkups (30/50 amps), cable, WiFi, dump, laundry, groc, restaurant. **REC:** pool, Clear Lake: fishing, marina. Pets OK. No tents. Big rig sites, 28 day max stay, eco-friendly, 2015 rates: $27 to $38. Disc: AAA. ATM.
(707)262-1900 Lat: 39.01964, Lon: -122.88864
2755 Mission Rancheria Road, Lakeport, CA 95453
gmartinez@kvcasino.com
www.kvcasino.com
See ad this page.

Things to See and Do

KONOCTI VISTA CASINO Casino, hotel, restaurant & marina. Partial handicap access. RV accessible. Restrooms, food. Hours: 24 hours. ATM.
(707)262-1900 Lat: 39.0195, Lon: -122.88736
2755 Mission Rancheria Rd, Lakeport, CA 95453
kvplayers@konocti-vista-casino.com
www.kvcasino.com
See ad this page.

LAKESIDE — K5 *San Diego*

LAKE JENNINGS CAMPGROUND (Public) From Jct of I-8 & Lake Jennings Park Rd, NW 0.3 mi on Lake Jennings Park Rd to Harritt Rd, N 0.4 mi to Bass Dr, E 0.7 mi (E). 2015 rates: $33 to $39. (619)390-1623

RANCHO LOS COCHES RV PARK
Ratings: 10/10★/9 (RV Park) From Jct of I-8 & Los Coches Rd (Exit 22), N 0.5 mi on Los Coches Rd to Hwy 8 Bus, E 0.4 mi (L) Do Not Use GPS. **FAC:** Paved rds. (134 spaces). Avail: 48 all weather, patios, 5 pull-thrus (22 x 55), back-ins (20 x 40), 48 full hkups (30/50 amps), seasonal sites, cable, WiFi $, tent sites, rentals, dump, laundry. **REC:** heated pool, whirlpool, Los Coches Creek. Pet restrict(B). Partial handicap access. RV age restrict, eco-friendly, 2015 rates: $39 to $48. Disc: AAA.
(800)630-0448 Lat: 32.83638, Lon: -116.90037
13468 Hwy 8 Bus, Lakeside, CA 92040
ranchorvpark@yahoo.com
www.rancholoscochesrv.com
See ad pages 154 (Spotlight San Diego), 126.

LANCASTER — H4 *Los Angeles*

ANTELOPE VALLEY FAIRGROUNDS RV PARK
(Public) From Jct of Hwy 14 & Ave H: Go 3/4 mi W on Ave H to 30th St W, then 1/2 mi N to Ave G8, then 1/4 mi E to Gate 6 (R). **FAC:** Paved rds. 62 paved, 22 pull-thrus (21 x 60), back-ins (21 x 50), 62 full hkups (30/50 amps), WiFi. Pets OK. No tents. 21 day max stay, 2015 rates: $20 to $25.
(661)206-0427 Lat: 34.725613, Lon: -118.176721
2551 West Ave G8 (Gate 6), Lancaster, CA 93536
pat@avfair.com
www.avfair.com
See ad this page.

CRESTVIEW MH COMMUNITY (RV Spaces) From Jct Hwy 14 & Ave I: Go 3mi E on Ave I (R). **FAC:** Paved rds. (14 spaces). Avail: 7 dirt, back-ins (20 x 40), 7 full hkups (30/50 amps), seasonal sites, laundry. **REC:** pool, playground. Pets OK. 2015 rates: $20.
(661)942-3487 Lat: 34.704308, Lon: -118.104027
1449 East Ave I, Lancaster, CA 93535
crestview@towermgt.com

SADDLEBACK BUTTE (State Pk) From the Jct of Hwy 14 & Ave J (Exit 43), E 20 mi on East Ave J (R). 2015 rates: $20. (661)946-6092

Travel Services

ANTELOPE VALLEY FORD Ford Dealership. Chassis service, all makes & models of RVs. **SERVICES:** MH mechanical, engine/chassis repair, restrooms. Waiting room. Hours: 8:00am to 5:00pm.
(661)949-3686 Lat: 34.67000, Lon: -118.15088
1155 Auto Mall Drive, Lancaster, CA 93534
Flyingmj1@aol.com
www.avford.com
See ad page 192.

Things to See and Do

ANTELOPE VALLEY FAIRGROUNDS Antelope Valley Fairgrounds is a multi-purpose, year-round facility used for education and entertainment including buildings of various sizes, an outdoor pavilion, a waterfall display and BBQ areas. Partial handicap access. RV accessible. Restrooms. ATM.
(661)948-6060 Lat: 34.725613, Lon: -118.176721
2551 West Ave H Ste 102, Lancaster, CA 93536
wendy@avfair.com
avfair.com
See ad this page.

LATHROP — E3 *San Joaquin*

DOS REIS PARK (Public) From Jct of I-5 & Lathrop Rd, (Exit 463) Lathrop Rd onto Manthey Rd (frntg rd), N 0.3 mi to Dos Reis Rd, W 1.4 mi (R). 2015 rates: $25. (209)953-8800

LEE VINING — E4 *Mono*

LUNDY LAKE (Public) From Jct of US-395 & SR-120, W 3.5 mi on SR-120 (E). 2015 rates: $5 to $20. Apr 15 to Oct 15. (760)932-5231

MONO VISTA RV PARK **Ratings: 6.5/9.5/7.5** (RV Park) 2015 rates: $29 to $35. Apr 1 to Oct 31. (760)647-6401 57 Beaver's Ln, Lee Vining, CA 93541

YOSEMITE/TUOLUMNE MEADOWS (Natl Pk) From Jct of SR-120 & Tioga Pass Rd, E 39 mi on Tioga Pass Rd (R). Entrance fee required. 2015 rates: $26. Jul 12 to Sep 27. (209)372-0200

YOSEMITE/WHITE WOLF (Natl Pk) From Jct of SR-120 & Tioga Pass Rd, E 15 mi on Tioga Pass Rd (L). Entrance fee required. 2015 rates: $18. Jul 1 to Sep 14. (209)372-0200

LEGGETT — C1 *Mendocino*

REDWOODS RIVER RESORT & CAMPGROUND Ratings: 6.5/8/7 (RV Park) N-bnd: From Jct of US-101 & SR-1, N 6.6 mi on US-101/0.3 mi beyond World Famous Tree House (L); or S-bnd: 4.5 mi S of Piercy on US-101 (R). **FAC:** Gravel/dirt rds. 38 Avail: 7 gravel, 31 dirt, 8 pull-thrus (26 x 64), back-ins (20 x 50), 31 full hkups, 7 W, 7 E (30 amps), WiFi, tent sites, dump, laundry, groc, fire rings, firewood. **REC:** heated pool, Eel River: fishing, playground. Pet restrict(B/Q) $. 2015 rates: $42 to $52. Disc: AAA, military.
AAA Approved
(707)925-6249 Lat: 39.91961, Lon: -123.76648
75000 Hwy 101, Leggett, CA 95585
redwoodsriverresort@gmail.com
www.redwoodriverresort.com

STANDISH-HICKEY (State Pk) From town, N 1.5 mi on Hwy 101 (L). 2015 rates: $35. (707)925-6482

LEMON COVE — F3 *Tulare*

HORSE CREEK CAMPGROUND (Public Corps) From town, E 6 mi on SR-198 (L). 2015 rates: $20 to $40. (559)597-2301

LEMON COVE VILLAGE RV PARK **Ratings: 7/9★/7.5** (RV Park) 2015 rates: $43 to $48. (559)370-4152 32075 Sierra Dr, Lemon Cove, CA 93244

LEWISTON — B2 *Trinity*

OLD LEWISTON BRIDGE RV RESORT
Ratings: 6.5/8.5/7.5 (Campground) From Jct of SR-299 & Trinity Dam Blvd (30.7 mi W of I-5/Redding), NW 5.7 mi on Trinity Dam Blvd to Rush Creek Rd (immediately past bridge), SW 0.8 mi (L). **FAC:** Gravel rds. (52 spaces). Avail: 42 paved, back-ins (30 x 45), mostly side by side hkups, 42 full hkups (20/30 amps), seasonal sites, WiFi Hotspot, tent sites, laundry, groc, LP gas, fire rings, firewood. **REC:** Trinity River: fishing. Pet restrict(B). Eco-friendly, 2015 rates: $30.
AAA Approved
(530)778-3894 Lat: 40.70915, Lon: -122.81241
8460 Rush Creek Rd, Lewiston, CA 96052
olb@snowcrest.net
www.lewistonbridgerv.com
See ad this page.

LIKELY — A3 *Lassen*

LIKELY PLACE GOLF COURSE AND RESORT Ratings: 7.5/9★/8 (RV Park) From Jct of US-395 & CR-64 (in town), E 1.5 mi on CR-64 (R). Elev 4500 ft. **FAC:** Paved/gravel rds. (55 spaces). Avail: 52 gravel, 40 pull-thrus (25 x 80), back-ins (30 x 60), 42 full hkups, 10 W, 10 E (30/50 amps), seasonal sites, WiFi Hotspot, tent sites, rentals, dump, laundry, restaurant. **REC:** golf, rec open to public. Pet restrict(B). Partial handicap access. Big rig sites, 2015 rates: $25 to $32. Disc: AAA, military.
AAA Approved
(530)233-4466 Lat: 41.23015, Lon: -120.47430
1255 Likely Place, Likely, CA 96116
rvgolf@hdo.net
www.likelyplace.com

LIVERMORE — E2 *Alameda*

DEL VALLE PARK (Public) From Jct of Hwy 580 & N Livermore Ave exit (Exit 52), S 1.5 mi on Livermore Ave through town (becomes Tesla Rd outside of town) to Mines Rd, S 3.5 mi to Del Valle Rd, S 4 mi (E). 2015 rates: $25 to $45. (888)327-2757

Got a different point of view? We want to know. Rate the campgrounds you visit using the rating guidelines located in front of this Guide, then compare your ratings to ours.

LODI — E3 *San Joaquin*

FLAG CITY RV RESORT
Ratings: 10/10★/9 (RV Park) From Jct of I-5 & SR 12, E 0.2 mi on SR 12 to Star St, S 500 ft to Banner St, E 0.1 mi (R). **FAC:** Paved rds. (180 spaces). Avail: 115 paved, patios, 115 pull-thrus (28 x 60), 115 full hkups (30/50 amps), seasonal sites, cable, WiFi, laundry, groc, LP gas. **REC:** pool, whirlpool. Pets OK $. Partial handicap access, no tents. Big rig sites, eco-friendly, 2015 rates: $54. Disc: AAA, military.
AAA Approved
(866)371-4855 Lat: 38.11420, Lon: -121.38995
6120 W Banner Rd, Lodi, CA 95242
info@flagcityrvresort.com
www.flagcityrvresort.com
See ad pages 216, 128.

STOCKTON DELTA KOA **Ratings: 8.5/7/6.5** (Campground) 2015 rates: $45 to $75. (209)369-1041 14900 W Hwy 12, Lodi, CA 95242

WESTGATE LANDING (SAN JOAQUIN COUNTY PARK) (Public) From jct I-5 & Hwy 12 (exit 485): Go 5 mi W on Hwy 12, then 1 mi N. 2015 rates: $20. (209)953-8800

LOMA MAR — E2 *San Mateo*

SAN MATEO COUNTY MEMORIAL PARK (Public) From Jct of Hwy 1 & Pescadero Rd, E 9.5 mi on Pescadero Rd (R). 2015 rates: $25 to $40. (650)879-0238

LOMPOC — H2 *Santa Barbara*

JALAMA BEACH PARK (Public) From Jct of Hwy 246 & Hwy 1, S 4.2 mi on Hwy 1 to Jalama Rd, SW 14 mi (E). 2015 rates: $20 to $30. (805)736-3504

RIVER PARK RV CAMPGROUND (Public) From Jct of Hwys 1 & 246: Go 1/2 mi E on Hwy 246 (L). 2015 rates: $20. (805)875-8034

Wasn't that a beautiful campground you visited ten years ago? But can you remember where it was? Use our "Find-it-Fast" index, located in the back of the Guide. It's an alphabetical list, by state, of every private and public park and campground in the Guide.

LONE PINE — F4 *Inyo*

BOULDER CREEK RV RESORT
Ratings: 9.5/9★/9 (RV Park) From Jct of US-395 & SR-136: Go 2.6 mi S on US-395 (L). Elev 3700 ft.

GREAT FOR OUTDOOR ENTHUSIASTS
Fish, Boat, Hike, 4-Wheel, Trail Ride, Star Gaze. Horse Corral, Dog Park & Dog Day Care. Mt Whitney, Ghost Towns, Fish Hatchery, Alabama Hills, Movie Locations, Film Museum, Manzanar. All while staying in a beautiful Park.

FAC: Paved rds. (109 spaces). Avail: 78 gravel, 64 pull-thrus (33 x 60), back-ins (25 x 50), 78 full hkups (30/50 amps), seasonal sites, WiFi, tent sites, rentals, laundry, groc, LP gas, fire rings, firewood. **REC:** heated pool, whirlpool, playground. Pets OK. Partial handicap access. Big rig sites, 28 day max stay, eco-friendly, 2015 rates: $40. Disc: AAA, military.
AAA Approved
(760)876-4243 Lat: 36.543175, Lon: -118.046786
2550 S Hwy 395, Lone Pine, CA 93545
bouldercreekrv@yahoo.com
www.bouldercreekrvresort.com
See ad this page, 128 & RV Trips of a Lifetime in Magazine Section.

DIAZ LAKE (Public) From Jct of US-395 & SR-136, S 1 mi on US-395 (R). 2015 rates: $10. (760)873-5577

PORTAGEE JOE COUNTY PARK (Public) From Jct of US-395 & Whitney Portal Rd, W 0.5 mi on Whitney Portal Rd to Tuttle Creek Rd, turn left (R). Pit toilets. 2015 rates: $10. (760)878-0272

TUTTLE CREEK BLM (Public) From Jct of I-395 & Whitney Portal Rd, W 3.5 mi on Whitney Portal Rd to Horseshoe Meadows Rd, S 1.5 mi (E). Donations accepted. Pit toilets. 2015 rates: $5. (760)872-4881

Things to See and Do

LONE PINE CAR WASH Self-serve car wash with motor home bays. Elev 3700 ft. Hours: 24 hour. No CC.
Lat: 36.60326, Lon: -118.06285
415 S Main St, Lone Pine, CA 93545
See ad this page.

LONG BEACH — N2 *Los Angeles*

LONG BEACH See also Anaheim, Huntington Beach, Los Angeles, Newport Beach, Orange.

ARBOR MOBILE VILLAGE
Ratings: 5.5/8/5 (RV Park) From Jct of I-405 & Long Beach Blvd exit, N 1.6 mi on Long Beach Blvd to Arbor St, E 0.1 mi (R). Maximum length 37'. **FAC:** Paved rds. (60 spaces). 10 Avail: 5 paved, 5 dirt, patios, 4 pull-thrus (30 x 60), back-ins (18 x 25), 10 full hkups (30/50 amps), WiFi Hotspot, laundry. **REC.** Pets OK. Partial handicap access, no tents. Age restrict may apply, RV age restrict, 2015 rates: $35.
(562)422-3666 Lat: 33.84367, Lon: -118.19067
300 E Arbor St, Long Beach, CA 90805
arbor@towermgmt.com
www.arbormhc.com

GOLDEN SHORE RV RESORT
Ratings: 9.5/9.5★/8 (RV Park) From Jct of I-405 & I-710, S 3.8 mi on I-710 (veer left to Downtown) to Golden Shore Exit, S 0.3 mi on Golden Shore (R). **FAC:** Paved rds. (80 spaces). Avail: 60 dirt, back-ins (22 x 40), 60 full hkups (30/50 amps), seasonal sites, WiFi $, laundry, firewood, controlled access. **REC:** heated pool, whirlpool. Pet restrict(B/Q) $. Partial handicap access, no tents. RV age restrict, eco-friendly, 2015 rates: $55 to $68.
(800)668-3581 Lat: 33.76476, Lon: -118.20280
101 Golden Shore, Long Beach, CA 90802
gsrvresort@goldenshorerv.com
www.goldenshorerv.com

LOOMIS — D3 *Placer*

LOOMIS RV PARK
Ratings: 7/8/7.5 (Campground) From Jct of I-80 & Exit 109 (Sierra College Blvd), N 0.6 mi on Sierra College Blvd to Taylor Rd, NE 0.1 mi (R). **FAC:** Paved/gravel rds. (79 spaces). Avail: 14 gravel, 12 pull-thrus (19 x 60), back-ins (19 x 30), 14 full hkups (30/50 amps), seasonal sites, cable, WiFi Hotspot, dump, laundry, LP gas. **REC:** pool, play-

Making campground reservations? Remember to ask about the cancellation policy when making your reservation.

CA

See listing Lone Pine, CA

LOOMIS (CONT)

LOOMIS RV PARK (CONT)
ground. Pet restrict(B/Q). Big rig sites, eco-friendly, 2015 rates: $45. Disc: AAA.
(916)652-6737 Lat: 38.81274, Lon: -121.20343
3945 Taylor Rd, Loomis, CA 95650
Tami.lo@starmanagement.com
loomisrvpark.com
See ad this page, 128.

LOS ANGELES — M2 *Los Angeles*

A SPOTLIGHT Introducing Los Angeles' colorful attractions appearing at the front of this state section.

LOS ANGELES See also Anaheim, Azusa, Castaic, Gorman, Long Beach, Malibu, Northridge, Playa Del Rey, Pomona, San Dimas, Santa Paula, Valencia, Van Nuys & Vista.

CARAVAN MOBILE HOME PARK
(RV Spaces) From Jct of I-5 & I-10, E 12.6 mi on I-10 to I-605, N 5.6 mi to I-210, E 3 mi to exit 40 (Azusa Ave exit) S 0.3 mi on S Azusa Ave to W Gladstone St, W 0.4mi (L). **FAC:** Paved rds. (120 spaces). Avail: 13 paved, no slide-outs, 5 pull-thrus (12 x 38), back-ins (14 x 42), 13 full hkups (30/50 amps), laundry. **REC:** pool. Pet restrict(B). RV age restrict, 2015 rates: $20. No CC.
(626)334-2306 Lat: 34.11406, Lon: -117.91439
600 W Gladstone St, Azusa, CA 91702
See primary listing at Azusa and ad page 141 (Spotlight Los Angeles).

LOS BANOS — F2 *Merced*

SAN LUIS RESERVOIR SRA/BASALT (State Pk) From Jct of I-5 & Hwy 152 (Exit 403B), W 6 mi on Hwy 152, follow Basalt Area signs (L). For reservations call 1-800-444-7275. 2015 rates: $30 to $35. (209)826-1197

LOS MOLINOS — C2 *Tehama*

HUNTERS RESORT **Ratings: 5.5/9★/7** (Campground) 2015 rates: $40. (530)527-5293 10675 Bryne Ave, Los Molinos, CA 96055

Do you know how to read each part of a listing? Check the How to Use This Campground Guide in the front.

LOST HILLS — G3 *Kern*

LOST HILLS RV PARK
Ratings: 8.5/10★/8.5 (Campground) From jct I-5 & Hwy 46 (Exit 278): Go 1/4 mi W on Hwy 46 to Warren St, then 1/8 mi S on Warren St (E). **FAC:** Gravel rds. (55 spaces). Avail: 49 gravel, patios, 49 pull-thrus (33 x 45), 49 full hkups (30/50 amps), seasonal sites, WiFi, tent sites, rentals, dump, laundry, groc, LP gas. **REC:** pool, playground. Pet restrict(B) $. Partial handicap access. Eco-friendly, 2015 rates: $43 to $48. Disc: military.
(661)797-2719 Lat: 35.614172, Lon: -119.659331
14831 Warren Street, Lost Hills, CA 93249
info@losthillsrvpark.com
www.losthillsrvpark.com
See ad this page, 128.

LOTUS — D3 *El Dorado*

PONDEROSA RESORT **Ratings: 7.5/7.5/7.5** (Membership Pk) 2015 rates: $42 to $62. (800)405-6188 7291 Hwy 49, Lotus, CA 95651

MADERA — F3 *Madera*

COUNTRY LIVING RV PARK **Ratings: 6/5.5/5.5** (RV Area in MHP) 2015 rates: $20 to $30. (559)674-5343 2169 West Kennedy St, Madera, CA 93637

MALIBU — M1 *Los Angeles, Ventura*

LEO CARRILLO (State Pk) From town, N 13 mi on PCH 1 (R). 2015 rates: $10 to $45. (310)457-8143

MALIBU BEACH RV PARK **Ratings: 8/9/8.5** (Campground) 2015 rates: $40 to $190. (800)622-6052 25801 Pacific Coast Hwy, Malibu, CA 90265

Our rating system isn't just tough, it's thorough. We know the kinds of things that are important to you — like clean restrooms and showers, attractive, secure, well-tended grounds, and extras like swimming pools. We give the first rating for development of facilities, the second for cleanliness and physical characteristics of restrooms and showers, and the third for visual appearance.

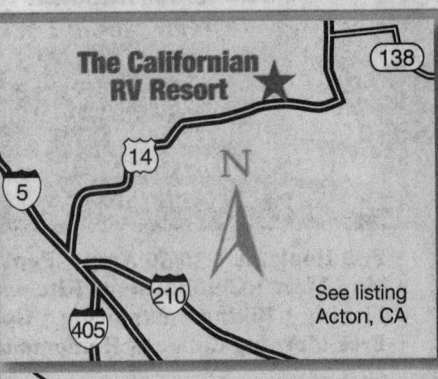

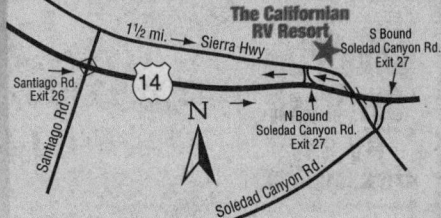

Thank you for being one of our best customers!

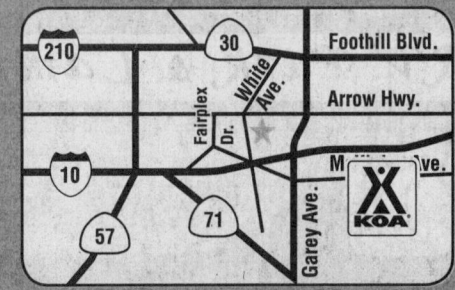

MAMMOTH LAKES — E4 *Madera, Mono*

MAMMOTH LAKES See also Bishop, June Lake & Lee Vining.

BROWN'S OWENS RIVER CAMPGROUND
Ratings: 3/8★/6 (Campground) From Jct of US-395 & Hwy 203 (Mammoth Lakes exit): Go 5-1/4 mi S on US-395 to Benton Crossing Rd, then 6-3/4 mi E on Benton Crossing Road (R). Elev 7000 ft. **FAC:** Gravel rds. 92 grass, 11 pull-thrus (30 x 50), back-ins (40 x 50), tent sites, rentals, showers $, groc, fire rings, firewood. **REC:** Owens River: fishing. Pets OK. Partial handicap access. 2015 rates: $28. Apr 24 to Oct 1. No CC.
(760)920-0975 Lat: 37.694685, Lon: -118.758601
benton Crossing Rd, Mammoth Lakes, CA 93546
www.brownscampgrounds.com
See ad page 171.

CAMP HIGH SIERRA (Public) From Jct of SR-203/395 & Lake Mary Rd, N 1 mi on Lake Mary Rd (L). Caution: Winding, dirt road. 2015 rates: $30 to $40. May 25 to Sep 5. (800)626-6684

CROWLEY LAKE BLM (Public) From Jct of US-395 & Crowley Lake Dr, N 5.5 mi (L). Donations accepted. Pit toilets. 2015 rates: $5. Apr 15 to Oct 31. (760)872-4881

MAMMOTH MOUNTAIN RV PARK
Ratings: 7.5/8.5/7.5 (RV Park) From Jct of US-395 & Hwy 203: Go 2-1/2 mi W on Hwy 203 (L). Elev 7825 ft. **FAC:** Paved/gravel rds. 154 Avail: 105 paved, 49 dirt, 5 pull-thrus (20 x 40), back-ins (24 x 40), mostly side by side hkups, 49 full hkups, 105 W, 105 E (30/50 amps), cable, WiFi, tent sites, rentals, dump, laundry, LP gas, fire rings, firewood. **REC:** heated pool, whirlpool, playground. Pet restrict(B/Q) $. Partial handicap access. 28 day max stay, eco-friendly, 2015 rates: $42 to $52.
(760)934-3822 Lat: 37.64557, Lon: -118.95996
2667 Main Street, Mammoth Lakes, CA 93546
info@mammothrv.com
www.mammothrv.com
See ad this page & RV Trips of a Lifetime in Magazine Section.

MCGEE CREEK RV PARK **Ratings: 5/7/8** (RV Park) 2015 rates: $30 to $35. Apr 20 to Oct 5. (760)935-4233 110 Mcgee Creek Rd, Mammoth Lakes, CA 93546

MANCHESTER — D1 *Mendocino*

MANCHESTER (State Pk) From town, N 1 mi on Hwy 1 to Kinny Rd, W 1 mi (R). Pit toilets. 2015 rates: $25. (707)882-2463

MANCHESTER BEACH/MENDOCINO COAST KOA **Ratings: 8.5/9★/9.5** (Campground) 2015 rates: $45 to $65. (800)562-4188 44300 Kinney Road, Manchester, CA 95459

MANTECA — E3 *San Joaquin*

CASWELL MEMORIAL PARK (State Pk) From Jct of Hwy 99 & Austin Rd (Exit 240), S 6 mi on Austin Rd (E). 2015 rates: $30. (209)599-3810

FRENCH CAMP RV PARK RESORT & GOLF COURSE **Ratings: 9/9★/9.5** (RV Park) 2015 rates: $41 to $49.50. (209)234-1544 3919 E French Camp Rd, Manteca, CA 95336

TURTLE BEACH **Ratings: 5.5/9★/7.5** (Membership Pk) 2015 rates: $42. (800)405-6188 703 E Williamson Rd, Manteca, CA 95337

MARINA — F1 *Monterey*

MARINA DUNES RV PARK
Ratings: 8.5/9★/9 (RV Park) From Jct of Hwy 1 & Reservation Rd (Exit 410): Go 200 ft W on Reservation Rd to Dunes Dr, then 3/10 mi N (R). **FAC:** Paved rds. 65 gravel, patios, back-ins (28 x 45), 61 full hkups, 4 W, 4 E (30/50 amps), cable, WiFi, tent sites, dump, laundry, LP gas, firewood. **REC:** playground. Pet restrict(Q). Partial handicap access. Eco-friendly, 2015 rates: $55 to $75. Disc: AAA, military.
AAA Approved
(831)384-6914 Lat: 36.701989, Lon: -121.803274
3330 Dunes Dr, Marina, CA 93933
info@marinadunesrv.com
www.marinadunesrv.com
See ad pages 196, 128.

MARIPOSA — E4 *Mariposa*

MARIPOSA FAIRGROUNDS (Public) From No. Jct of Hwys 140 & 49, S 1.5 mi on Hwy 49 (L). 2015 rates: $30 to $35. (209)966-2432

MARKLEEVILLE — D4 *Alpine*

GROVER HOT SPRINGS (State Pk) From Jct of Hwy 89 & Hot Springs Rd, W 4 mi on Hot Springs Rd (R). For reservations call 1-800-444-7275. 2015 rates: $35. (530)694-2248

INDIAN CREEK (BLM) (Public) From town: Go 3 mi S on Hwy 89. 2015 rates: $20 to $32. (702)885-6000

PG & E/CARSON PASS/LOWER BLUE LAKE (Public) From Jct of Hwys 89 & 88, W 2.5 mi on Hwy 88 to Blue Lakes Rd, S 12 mi (L). Pit toilets. 2015 rates: $23. May 31 to Oct 15. (916)386-5164

PG & E/CARSON PASS/UPPER BLUE LAKE (Public) From Jct of Hwys 89 & 88, W 2.5 mi on Hwy 88 to Blue Lakes Rd, S 11 mi (L). Pit toilets. 2015 rates: $23. May 31 to Oct 1. (916)386-5164

PG & E/CARSON PASS/UPPER BLUE LAKE DAM (Public) From Jct of Hwys 89 & 88, W 2.5 mi on Hwy 88 to Blue Lakes Rd, S 12 mi (R). Pit toilets. 2015 rates: $23. May 30 to Oct 15. (916)386-5164

MCARTHUR — B3 *Lassen*

INTER-MOUNTAIN FAIR OF SHASTA COUNTY (Public) From Jct of SR-299 & CR-A19, E 0.1 mi on SR-299 to Grove St (follow signs) (L). 2015 rates: $20 to $25. Apr 1 to Oct 31. (530)336-5694

MCCLOUD — A2 *Siskiyou*

MCCLOUD (DANCE COUNTRY) RV RESORT
Ratings: 7.5/8★/9 (RV Park) From Jct of SR-89 & Squaw Valley Rd (unmarked, at McCloud Reservoir/McCloud Downtown turnoff), S 200 ft on Squaw Valley Rd (L). Elev 3200 ft. **FAC:** Paved rds. 130 Avail: 22 paved, 1 gravel, 107 grass, 5 pull-thrus (20 x 56), back-ins (20 x 48), 106 full hkups, 24 W, 24 E (30/50 amps), cable, WiFi, tent sites, rentals, dump, laundry, firewood. **REC:** pond. Pet restrict(B). Partial handicap access. Big rig sites, eco-friendly, 2015 rates: $33 to $44.
(530)964-2252 Lat: 41.25044, Lon: -122.13593
480 Hwy 89, Mccloud, CA 96057
info@mccloudrvpark.com
www.mccloudrvpark.com

MCKINLEYVILLE — B1 *Humboldt*

WIDOW WHITE CREEK RV PARK **Ratings: 5/4.5/6** (Campground) 2015 rates: $30 (707)839-1137 1085 Murray Rd, Mckinleyville, CA 95519

MECCA — J5 *Riverside*

SALTON SEA SRA/HEADQUARTERS CAMP (State Pk) From Jct of Hwys 195 & 111, S 11 mi on Hwy 111 (R). 2015 rates: $20 to $30. (760)393-3052

MEEKS BAY — D4 *El Dorado*

D L BLISS (State Pk) From Jct of SR-28 & SR-89, S 17 mi on SR-89 (L). For reservations call 1-800-444-7275. 2015 rates: $35 to $45. May 15 to Sep 15 (530)525-7277

EMERALD BAY (State Pk) From Jct of 50 & SR-89, N 8 mi on SR-89 (R). 2015 rates: $35 (916)541-3030

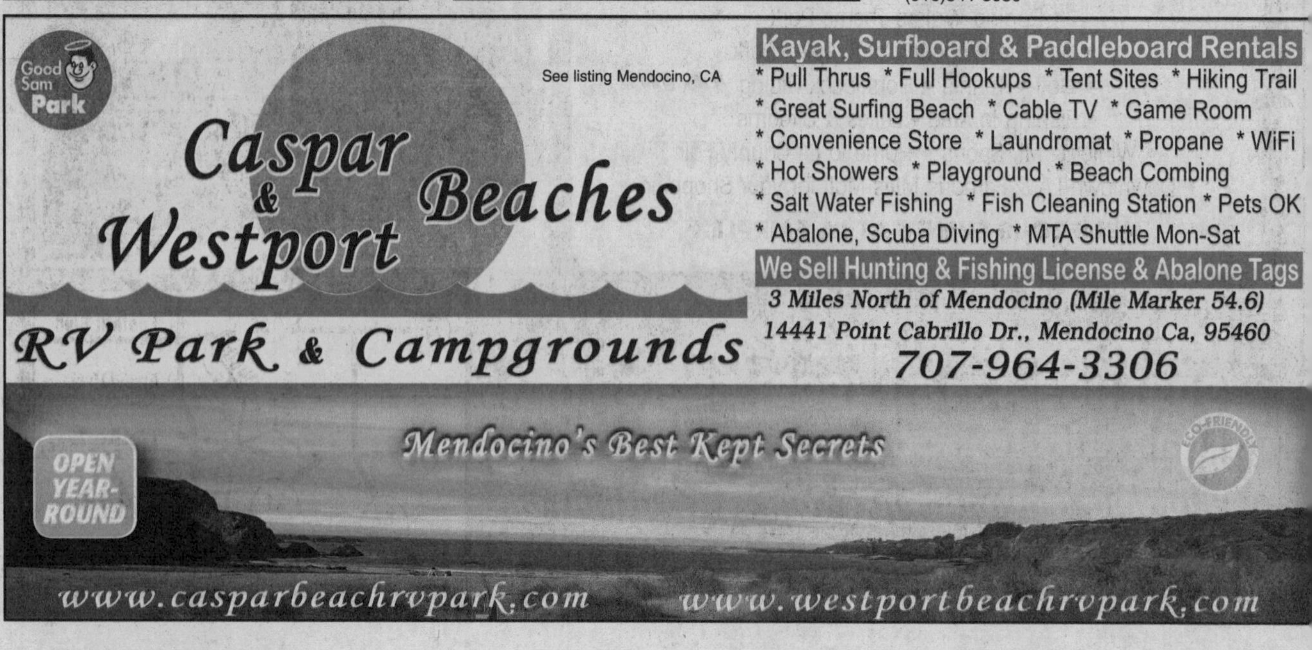

MEEKS BAY (CONT)

LAKE TAHOE BASIN MGMT. UNIT-USFS (MEEKS BAY CAMPGROUND) (Natl Forest) In town, off Hwy 89. 2015 rates: $27 to $29. May 15 to Oct 18. (877)326-3357

MENDOCINO — C1 *Mendocino*

CASPAR BEACH RV PARK & CAMPGROUND
Ratings: 7.5/8.5★/8.5 (Campground) From Jct of SR-1 & SR-20 (at Ft Bragg), S 4 mi on SR-1 to Pt Cabrillo Dr (at S end of Caspar Creek Bridge, 3.5 mi N of Mendocino), W 0.7 mi (L). **FAC:** Gravel rds. 52 Avail: 10 paved, 25 gravel, 17 grass, 19 pull-thrus (18 x 50), back-ins (18 x 40), some side by side hkups, 40 full hkups, 12 W, 12 E (20/30 amps), WiFi, tent sites, showers $, dump, laundry, groc, LP gas, fire rings, firewood. **REC:** Pacific Ocean: swim, playground. Pets OK $. Eco-friendly, 2015 rates: $35 to $44.
(707)964-3306 Lat: 39.35947, Lon: -123.81561
14441 Pt Cabrillo Rd, Mendocino, CA 95460
casparbeach@comcast.net
www.casparbeachrvpark.com
See ad opposite page, 128.

RUSSIAN GULCH (State Pk) From town, N 2 mi on Hwy 1 (L). 2015 rates: $35. (707)937-5804

VAN DAMME (State Pk) From town, S 3 mi on Hwy 1 (L). For reservations call 1-800-444-7572. 2015 rates: $25 to $35. (707)937-5804

MENIFEE — O6 *Riverside*

WILDERNESS LAKES **Ratings: 9.5/8/7.5** (Membership Pk) 2015 rates: $55. (800)405-6188 30605 Briggs Rd, Menifee, CA 92584

MIDPINES — E4 *Mariposa*

YOSEMITE-MARIPOSA KOA **Ratings: 9/8.5/8.5** (Campground) 2015 rates: $50 to $65. Mar 15 to Oct 25. (209)966-2201 6323 Hwy 140, Midpines, CA 95345

MILL CREEK — B3 *Tehama*

CHILDS MEADOW RESORT
Ratings: 6/7/6.5 (Campground) From jct Hwy 89 (Lassen Peak Hwy) & Hwy 89/36: Go 5 mi E on Hwy 89/36. Elev 5000 ft. **FAC:** Paved/gravel rds. 24 gravel, 8 pull-thrus (24 x 60), back-ins (24 x 60), 24 full hkups (30/50 amps), WiFi Hotspot, tent sites, rentals, dump, laundry, fire rings, firewood, restaurant. **REC.** Pets OK. Big rig sites, 2015 rates: $30.
(888)595-3383 Lat: 40.36063, Lon: -121.49365
41500 Highway 36 E, Mill Creek, CA 96061
VisitUs@childsmeadowresort.com
See ad this page.

Like Us on Facebook.

Things to See and Do

CHILDS MEADOW MOTEL & RESTAURANT
Full service restaurant serving breakfast, lunch & dinner. Next to the Motel. May 1 to Sep 30. partial handicap access. Restrooms, food. Hours: 7am to 9pm.
(888)595-3383 Lat: 40.36063, Lon: -121.49365
41500 Hwy 36 E, Mill Creek, CA 96061
visitus@childsmeadowresort.com
https://plus.google.com/107269448476129629591/about?gl=us&hl=en
See ad this page.

MOJAVE — H4 *Kern*

RED ROCK CANYON (State Pk) From town, NE 25 mi on Hwy 14 (L). Pit toilets. 2015 rates: $25. (661)946-6092

Time and rates don't stand still. Remember that last year's rates serve as a guideline only. Call ahead for the most current rate information.

SIERRA TRAILS RV PARK
Ratings: 7/7.5/7 (Campground) From Hwy 58 (exit 167): Go 2 mi N on Hwy 14 to California City Blvd (Exit 73), then go E to an immediate turn N onto State Hwy 14 Frontage Rd East, then go 1/4 mi N on State Hwy Frontage Rd East (L). Elev 2750 ft. **FAC:** Gravel/dirt rds. (70 spaces). Avail: 25 dirt, patios, 7 pull-thrus (25 x 70), back-ins (25 x 55), 18 full hkups, 7 W, 7 E (30 amps), seasonal sites, WiFi Hotspot, tent sites, dump, laundry. **REC:** heated pool. Pet restrict(B/Q). Eco-friendly, 2015 rates: $40. Disc: AAA, military.
AAA Approved
(760)373-4950 Lat: 35.129620, Lon: -118.119368
21282 Hwy 14, Mojave, CA 93501
See ad this page.

MONTEREY — F1 *Monterey*

MONTEREY See also Aromas, Big Sur, Carmel, Marina, Moss Landing, Morgan Hill & Watsonville.

Tell them you saw them in this Guide!

CA

Nobody takes to the road like we do. In many listings we tell you the surface type and condition of interior campground roads.

We've listened to thousands of RVers like you, so we know exactly how to rate campgrounds. Got feedback? Call us!877-209-6655

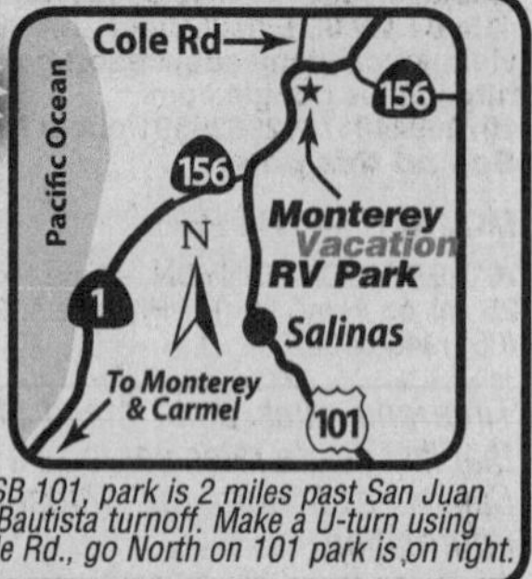

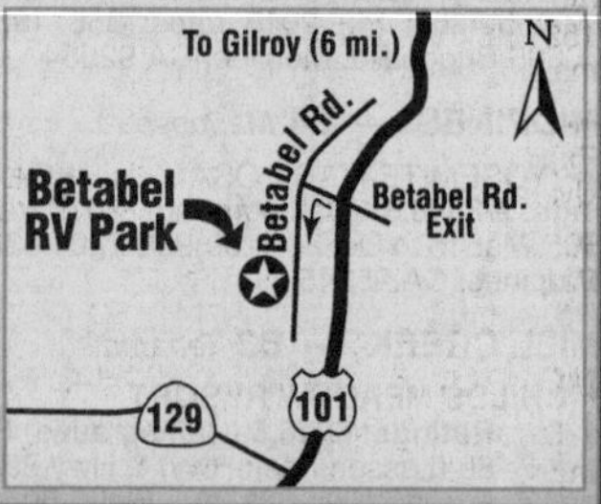

MONTEREY (CONT)

MONTEREY COUNTY FAIR & EVENTS CENTER RV PARK (Public) From Jct of Hwy 1 & Casa Verde exit: Go 3/10 mi SE on Casa Verde to Fairground Rd, then 200 ft NE to Gate 6 (R) Note: Reservations suggested. **FAC:** Paved/dirt rds. (56 spaces). 48 Avail: 28 paved, 20 dirt, back-ins (18 x 45), mostly side by side hkups, 48 full hkups (30/50 amps), WiFi, laundry, controlled access. Pet restrict(Q). Partial handicap access, no tents. 28 day max stay, 2015 rates: $50. Disc: military. ATM.
(831)717-7167 Lat: 36.594985, Lon: -121.861804
2004 Fairground Rd, Gate 6, Monterey, CA 93940
info@montereycountyfair.com
www.montereycountyfair.com
See ad opposite page.

VETERANS MEMORIAL PARK (CITY PARK) (Public) In town, from jct Pacific St & Jefferson Dr: Go 1 mi up narrow, winding Jefferson Dr. 2015 rates: $30. (831)646-3865

MORGAN HILL — F2 *Santa Clara*

MAPLE LEAF RV PARK Ratings: 8.5/8/6 (RV Park) From Jct of Hwy 101 & Tennant Ave: Go 1 mi W on Tennant Ave to Monterey Rd, then 3/4 mi S on Monterey Rd (L). **FAC:** Paved rds. (190 spaces). Avail: 62 paved, patios, 49 pull-thrus (20 x 62), back-ins (22 x 42), 62 full hkups (30/50 amps), seasonal sites, WiFi, dump, laundry, groc, LP gas. **REC:** heated pool, whirlpool. Pet restrict(B) $. Partial handicap access, no tents. Eco-friendly, 2015 rates: $45. Disc: AAA.
AAA Approved
(408)776-1818 Lat: 37.105362, Lon: -121.631376
15200 Monterey Rd, Morgan Hill, CA 95037
mapleaf@garlic.com

MORGAN HILL **Ratings: 5/4.5/5** (Membership Pk) 2015 rates: $60 to $63. (800)405-6188 12895 Uvas Rd, Morgan Hill, CA 95037

UVAS PINES RV PARK **Ratings: 4.5/4.5/8** (RV Park) 2015 rates: $45. (408)779-3417 13210 Uvas Rd, Morgan Hill, CA 95037

MORRO BAY — G2 *San Luis Obispo*

BAY PINES TRAVEL TRAILER PARK **Ratings: 8/8.5/7.5** (RV Park) 2015 rates: $36. (805)772-3223 1501 Quintana Rd, Morro Bay, CA 93442

CYPRESS MORRO BAY RV & MHP **Ratings: 6.5/9.5★/8.5** (RV Park) 2015 rates: $40 to $44. (805)772-2515 1121 Main St, Morro Bay, CA 93442

MONTANA DE ORO (State Pk) From Jct Hwy 101 & Los Osos Valley Rd (exit 200), W 9 mi on Los Osos Valley Rd to Pecho Valley Rd, S 3 mi (L). Pit toilets. 2015 rates: $20 to $25. (805)528-0513

MORRO BAY (State Pk) From town, S 1 mi on Main St (state park rd) (L). 2015 rates: $35 to $50. (805)772-2560

We make finding the perfect campground easier. Just use the "Find-it-Fast" index in the back of the Guide. It's a complete, state-by-state, alphabetical listing of our private and public park listings.

MORRO DUNES Ratings: 8.5/8.5/8.5 (RV Park) From Jct of Hwy 1 & Rte 41 (Atascadero exit): Go 1/2 mi W on Atascadero Rd (L).

ONLY STEPS AWAY FROM THE BEACH
From golfing to surfing, sunbathing to wine tasting, whether you're looking for excitement or relaxation it's here in Morro Bay. We have the only pull thru sites in town. A short drive to Hearst Castle.

FAC: Paved rds. 152 Avail: 152 all weather, 35 pull-thrus (20 x 48), back-ins (30 x 40), 152 full hkups (30/50 amps), cable, WiFi, tent sites, dump, laundry, groc, LP bottles, fire rings, firewood. **REC:** Morro Bay: swim. Pet restrict(Q) $. Partial handicap access. 14 day max stay, eco-friendly, 2015 rates: $36 to $44.
(805)772-2722 Lat: 35.378893, Lon: -120.861511
1700 Embarcadero, Morro Bay, CA 93442
morrodunes@sbcglobal.net
www.morrodunes.com
See ad this page.

MORRO STRAND RV PARK **Ratings: 5.5/6.5/6** (RV Park) 2015 rates: $38 to $59. (800)799-6030 221 Atascadero Rd, Morro Bay, CA 93442

MORRO STRAND STATE BEACH (State Pk) From Jct SR-41 & SR-1, N 2 mi on SR-1 to Yerba Buena Rd, W 0.3 mi (L). NOTE: Vehicle maximum length 24 ft. 2015 rates: $35. (805)772-2560

RANCHO COLINA RV PARK **Ratings: 7.5/9/6.5** (RV Park) 2015 rates: $42. (805)772-8420 1045 Atascadero Rd, Morro Bay, CA 93442

Travel Services

MORRO DUNES RV REPAIR RV Repairs. **SERVICES:** RV, RV appliance, restrooms. RV storage. **TOW:** RV. RV supplies, dump, RV accessible. Hours: 8:30am to 5pm.
(805)772-2722 Lat: 35.378893, Lon: -120.861511
1700 Embarcadero, Morro Bay, CA 93442
See ad this page.

MOSS LANDING — F1 *Monterey*

MOSS LANDING KOA EXPRESS **Ratings: 7.5/7.5/7** (RV Park) 2015 rates: $68.50 to $78.50. (800)562-3390 7905 Sandholdt Rd, Moss Landing, CA 95039

MOUNT SHASTA — A2 *Siskiyou*

A SPOTLIGHT Introducing Mount Shasta's colorful attractions appearing at the front of this state section.

MOUNT SHASTA See also McCloud, Shasta Lake, Weed & Yreka.

ABRAMS LAKE RV PARK Ratings: 8/NA/8 (RV Area in MHP) From Jct of I-5 & SR-89, N 4.3 mi on I-5 to Abrams Lake Rd (exit 741), W 0.3 mi to N Old Stage Rd (through underpass to left), S 0.4 mi (R). Elev 3700 ft. **FAC:** Paved rds. (32 spaces). 27 Avail: 24 gravel, 3 dirt, 13 pull-thrus (24 x 65), back-ins (24 x 50), some side by side hkups, accepts full hkup units only, 27 full hkups (30/50 amps), seasonal sites, cable, WiFi, dump, laundry. **REC:** pond. Pet restrict(B). No tents. Big rig sites, eco-friendly, 2015 rates: $33.
(530)926-2312 Lat: 41.33725, Lon: -122.35399
2601 N Old Stage Road, Mount Shasta, CA 96067
abramslake@hotmail.com
See ad pages 142 (Spotlight Mount Shasta), 128.

CHATEAU SHASTA MOBILE HOME & RV PARK **Ratings: 3.5/5.5/5** (RV Park) 2015 rates: $25. (530)926-3279 704 S Old Stage Rd #25, Mount Shasta, CA 96067

LAKE SISKIYOU CAMP RESORT LLC **Ratings: 7/8/8** (Campground) 2015 rates: $35. Apr 1 to Oct 31. (530)926-2618 4239 W.a. Barr Rd, Mount Shasta, CA 96067

MT. SHASTA KOA **Ratings: 8.5/9/7.5** (Campground) 2015 rates: $39 to $46. (800)562-3617 900 N Mt Shasta Blvd, Mount Shasta, CA 96067

MOUNTAIN CENTER — J5 *Riverside*

HURKEY CREEK COUNTY PARK (Public) From Jct of SR-243 & SR-74, SE 4 mi on SR-74 (L). 2015 rates: $20. (951)659-2050

LAKE HEMET CAMPGROUND (Public) From Jct of I-215 & SR-74 (Exit 15), E 36 mi on SR-74 (R). 2015 rates: $25 to $30. (951)659-2680

MCCALL MEMORIAL PARK (Public) From jct Hwy 79 & Hwy 74: Go 17-1/2 mi E on Hwy 74, then N on McCall Park Rd. 2015 rates: $17. (951)659-2311

MYERS FLAT — B1 *Humboldt*

GIANT REDWOODS RV AND CAMP Ratings: 8/9★/8.5 (Campground) N-bnd: From Jct of US-101/Myers Flat (Exit 656), exit to Ave of Giants, N 0.2 mi to Myers Ave, SW 0.4 mi (E); or S-bnd: From Jct of US-101/Myers Flat, exit to Ave of Giants, NW 100 ft to Myers Ave, SW 0.4 mi (E) (Caution: Do not use Boy Scout Rd). **FAC:** Gravel rds. 53 Avail: 32 gravel, 16 grass, 5 dirt, 33 pull-thrus (18 x 50), back-ins (20 x 40), 13 full hkups, 40 W, 40 E (30/50 amps), cable, WiFi, tent sites, dump, laundry, groc, fire rings, firewood. **REC:** wading pool, South Fork Eel River: swim, fishing, playground. Pet restrict(B) $. Partial handicap access. Eco-friendly, 2015 rates: $42 to $45. Disc: AAA.
(707)943-9999 Lat: 40.26247, Lon: -123.87744
400 Myers Ave, Myers Flat, CA 95554
reservations@giantredwoodsrv.com
www.giantredwoodsrv.com
See ad this page.

NAPA — D2 *Napa*

NAPA VALLEY EXPO RV PARK Ratings: 9/10★/9.5 (Public) From Jct of SR-12/121 & SR-29, N 1.4 mi on SR-29/121 to SR-121/Imola Ave, E 1.4 mi to Soscol Ave/SR-121, N 0.6 mi to Silverado Trail/SR-121, N 0.5 mi (L). **FAC:** Paved rds. 28 paved, 18 pull-thrus (30 x 75), back-ins (30 x 75), 28 full hkups (50 amps), WiFi, dump, laundry. **REC.** Pet restrict(Q). Partial handicap access, no tents. 28 day max stay, 2015 rates: $50. Disc: AAA, military.
AAA Approved
(707)253-4900 Lat: 38.29610, Lon: -122.27583
601 Silverado Trail, Napa, CA 94559
rstockwell@napavalleyexpo.com
www.napavalleyexpo.com
See ad pages 198, 128.

SKYLINE WILDERNESS PARK (Public) From jct Hwy 12 & Hwy 29: Go 1-1/2 mi N on Hwy 29, then 2-1/2 mi E on Imola Ave (exit 16). 2015 rates: $50 to $75. (707)252-0481

Things to See and Do

NAPA VALLEY EXPO Napa Town & Country Fair, Napa Fermentation Supplies & Bingo Emporium. Restrooms. Hours: 9am to 5pm. Adult fee: $35.
(707)253-4900 Lat: 38.29543, Lon: -122.27649
575 3rd St, Napa, CA 94559
rstockwell@napavalleyexpo.com
www.napavalleyexpo.com
See ad page 198.

NAVARRO — C1 *Mendocino*

NAVARRO RIVER REDWOODS (PAUL M. DEMMICK CAMPGROUND) (State Pk) From jct Hwy-1 & Hwy-128: Go 8 mi E on Hwy-128. Pit toilets. (707)895-3141

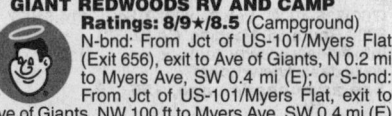

Got something to tell us? We welcome your comments and suggestions regarding the ratings for a particular campground, or our rating system in general. Please email them to: travelguidecomments@goodsamfamily.com

NEEDLES — H6 *San Bernardino*

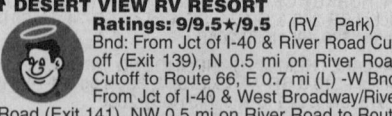

DESERT VIEW RV RESORT
Ratings: 9/9.5★/9.5 (RV Park) E Bnd: From Jct of I-40 & River Road Cutoff (Exit 139), N 0.5 mi on River Road Cutoff to Route 66, E 0.7 mi (L) -W Bnd: From Jct of I-40 & West Broadway/River Road (Exit 141), NW 0.5 mi on River Road to Route 66, W 0.6 mi (R). **FAC:** Paved/gravel rds. 66 Avail: 66 all weather, patios, 37 pull-thrus (30 x 60), back-ins (30 x 76), 66 full hkups (30/50 amps), WiFi, laundry, LP gas. **REC:** heated pool. Pet restrict(B/Q). Partial handicap access, no tents. Big rig sites, RV age restrict, eco-friendly, 2015 rates: $35. Disc: AAA, military.
(760)326-4000 Lat: 34.86889, Lon: -114.64027
5300 Route 66, Needles, CA 92363
info@desertviewrv.com
www.desertviewrv.com
See ad opposite page, 126.

MOJAVE NATIONAL PRESERVE/HOLE-IN-THE-WALL (Natl Pk) From Jct of I-40 & Essex Rd (exit 100), N 10 mi on exit rd to Jct with Black Canyon Rd, N 10 mi on Black Canyon Rd., follow signs (R). Pit toilets. 2015 rates: $12. (760)733-4040

NEEDLES KOA **Ratings: 7/8/8.5** (Campground) 2015 rates: $31.95. (800)562-3407 5400 Route 66, Needles, CA 92363

NEEDLES MARINA RV PARK
Ratings: 8.5/9.5★/7.5 (RV Park) W-bnd: From Jct of I-40 & J St (Exit 142), N (right) 0.1 mi on J St to Broadway, W (left at flashing light) 0.7 mi (over overpass) to Needles Hwy, NE (right) 0.5 mi thru 4 way stop. (L); E-bnd: From Jct of I-40 & W Broadway (Exit 141), NE (left) 1 mi on Broadway (thru 4 way stop), NE 0.5 mi (L). **FAC:** Paved/gravel rds. 157 Avail: 90 gravel, 11 grass, 56 dirt, patios, 60 pull-thrus (20 x 45), back-ins (25 x 40), 157 full hkups (30/50 amps), WiFi $, tent sites, rentals, dump, laundry, controlled access. **REC:** heated pool, whirlpool, Colorado River: swim, fishing, marina. Pet restrict(Q) $. Partial handicap access. Big rig sites, RV age restrict, eco-friendly, 2015 rates: $38 to $40. Disc: military.
(760)326-2197 Lat: 34.84788, Lon: -114.60652
100 Marina Dr, Needles, CA 92363
www.needlesmarinapark.com
See ad opposite page, 126 & Snowbird Destinations in Magazine Section.

SAVE! Over $1,000 in coupons can be found at the front of the Guide!

PALMS RIVER RESORT
Ratings: 9.5/9★/10 (RV Park) From Jct of I 40 & W. Broadway (Exit 141), N 3 mi on Needles Hwy/River Rd (R). No Pop-up Trailers. **FAC:** Paved rds. (184 spaces). Avail: 51 all weather, 23 pull-thrus (45 x 80), back-ins (40 x 80), accepts full hkup units only, 51 full hkups (30/50 amps), WiFi, rentals, laundry, groc, LP gas, firewood, controlled access. **REC:** pool, wading pool, whirlpool, Colorado River: swim, fishing, playground. Pet restrict(B). Partial handicap access, no tents. RV age restrict, eco-friendly, 2015 rates: $33 to $40. Disc: AAA, military.
(760)326-0333 Lat: 34.88409, Lon: -114.64516
4170 Needles Hwy, Needles, CA 92363
reservations@palmsriverresort.com
www.palmsriverresort.com
See ad pages 200, 126.

PIRATE COVE RESORT
Ratings: 8.5/9★/8.5 (RV Park) From Jct of I-40 & US-95S-(South), E 9.5 mi on I-40 to Park Moabi Rd (Exit 153), N 0.6 mi (L).

AN OASIS ON THE COLORADO RIVER
Rated TOP BEACH RV PARK by Good Sam. A Pirate themed first-class destination located along the Colorado River and Route 66. In addition to its General Store & Restaurant we feature Waterfront RV Sites and miles of Off-Roading

FAC: All weather rds. (157 spaces). 145 Avail: 21 paved, 124 gravel, 11 pull-thrus (24 x 46), back-ins (24 x 46), some side by side hkups, 134 full hkups (30/50 amps), seasonal sites, WiFi, tent sites, rentals, showers $, dump, mobile sewer, laundry, groc, LP bottles, firewood, restaurant, controlled access. **REC:** Colorado River: swim, fishing, marina, playground, rec open to public. Pet restrict(B/Q) $. Partial handicap access. RV age restrict, eco-friendly, 2015 rates: $45 to $55. ATM.
(866)301-3000 Lat: 34.72768, Lon: -114.51261
100 Park Moabi Rd, Needles, CA 92363
piratecoveresort.com
See ad pages 87, 126 & Snowbird Destinations in Magazine Section.

NEVADA CITY — C3 *Nevada*

MALAKOFF DIGGINS STATE HISTORICAL PARK (State Pk) From town: Go 6 mi N on Hwy-49, then 7 mi on Tyler-Foote Crossing Rd, then 5 mi on Lake City Rd, then 3 mi on N. Bloomfield Rd. (N. Bloomfield) (Caution: steep, gravel road). 2015 rates: $35. (530)265-2740

NEWBERRY SPRINGS — H5 *San Bernardino*

NEWBERRY MOUNTAIN RV PARK
Ratings: 6.5/7.5/5.5 (RV Park) From Jct of I 40 & Fort Cady Rd (Exit 23): Go 1/4 mi S on Fort Cady Rd to National Trails Hwy, then 1/4 mi W on National Trails Hwy (R). Elev 2800 ft. **FAC:** Gravel rds. (20 spaces). Avail: 18 gravel, 9 pull-thrus (40 x 50), back-ins (39 x 42), 18 full hkups (30/50 amps), seasonal sites, WiFi Hotspot $, tent sites, laundry, LP gas. **REC:** pool, pond, Newberry Pond: fishing. Pet restrict(Q). Big rig sites, eco-friendly, 2015 rates: $39. Disc: AAA, military.
(760)257-0066 Lat: 34.81476, Lon: -116.61664
47800 National Trails Hwy, Newberry Springs, CA 92365
newberrymountainrvpark@yahoo.com
www.newberryrvpark.com

NEWHALL — H3 *Los Angeles*

Travel Services

CAMPING WORLD STORE OF NEWHALL/VALENCIA As the nation's largest retailer of RV supplies, accessories, services and new and used RVs, Camping World is committed to making your total RV experience better. RV Accessories: (800)235-3337. **SERVICES:** RV, tire, RV appliance, engine/chassis repair, restrooms, RV Sales. RV supplies, LP, dump, RV accessible. Hours: 8:00am - 6:00pm. No CC.
661-255-9220 Lat: 34.380663, Lon: -118.569699
24901 W Pico Canyon Rd, Newhall, CA 91381
www.campingworld.com/stores

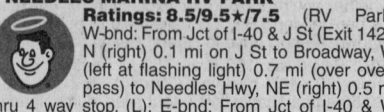

We appreciate your business!

NEWPORT BEACH — O3 *Orange*

NEWPORT DUNES WATERFRONT RESORT & MARINA

Ratings: 9.5/9.5★/9 (RV Park) From Jct of Pacific Coast Hwy (Hwy 1) & Jamboree Rd exit, N 0.2 mi on Jamboree Rd to Back Bay Dr, W 0.1 mi (L); or From Jct of I-405 & Jamboree Rd exit (in Irvine), S 5 mi on Jamboree Rd to Back Bay Dr, W 0.1 mi (L).

LUXURIOUS WATERFRONT RESORT

Newport Dunes Waterfront Resort surrounds its own beach and lagoon connected to the Pacific Ocean. Featuring our deluxe beachfront cottages. We are close to Disneyland! Come and stay a day, a week, or a few months!

FAC: Paved rds. (377 spaces). 287 Avail: 5 paved, 282 dirt, 8 pull-thrus (24 x 80), back-ins (24 x 40), 287 full hkups (30/50 amps), seasonal sites, WiFi, tent sites, rentals, laundry, groc, LP bottles, fire rings, firewood, restaurant, controlled access. **REC:** heated pool, whirlpool, Newport Bay: swim, playground, rec open to public. Pet restrict(B/Q) $. Partial handicap access. RV age restrict, eco-friendly, 2015 rates: $64 to $350. Disc: military. ATM.
(800)765-7661 Lat: 33.61480, Lon: -117.89670

NEWPORT BEACH (CONT)

NEWPORT DUNES WATERFRONT (CONT)
1131 Back Bay Drive, Newport Beach, CA 92660
info@newportdunes.com
www.newportdunes.com
See ad pages 164, 132 (Spotlight Anaheim), 126, 119 (CA Map) See ad back cover & Family Camping, RV Trips of a Lifetime, Snowbird Destinations in Magazine Section.

Things to See and Do

BACK BAY BISTRO The Back Bay Bistro offers affordable waterfront dining and an award winning menu. Open for lunch and dinner. Partial handicap access. RV accessible. Food. Hours: 11am to 10pm. ATM.
(949)729-1144 Lat: 33.61486, Lon: -117.89222
1131 Back Bay Dr, Newport Beach, CA 92660
info@backbaybistronewportbeach.com
See ad page 164.

NICE — D2 *Lake*

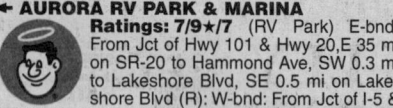

AURORA RV PARK & MARINA
Ratings: 7/9★/7 (RV Park) E-bnd: From Jct of Hwy 101 & Hwy 20,E 35 mi on SR-20 to Hammond Ave, SW 0.3 mi to Lakeshore Blvd, SE 0.5 mi on Lakeshore Blvd (R): W-bnd: From Jct of I-5 & SR-20, W 45mi on SR-20 thru Nice (take center turn lane left) to Lakeshore Blvd, W 0.2 mi on Lakeshore Blvd (L). **FAC:** Paved/gravel rds. 56 Avail: 12 paved, 18 gravel, 26 grass, 16 pull-thrus (22 x 75), back-ins (18 x 35), 56 full hkups (30/50 amps), cable, WiFi, tent sites, laundry. **REC:** Clear Lake. Pets OK. 28 day max stay, eco-friendly, 2015 rates: $30 to $45.
(707)274-5531 Lat: 39.12088, Lon: -122.85671
2985 Lakeshore Blvd, Nice, CA 95464
Mike@enjoyourpark.com
www.EnjoyOurPark.com
See ad this page, 128.

NICOLAUS — D3 *Sutter*

LAKE MINDEN **Ratings: 7/8.5★/8** (Membership Pk) 2015 rates: $41. (800)405-6188 1256 Marcum Rd, Nicolaus, CA 95659

NILAND — J6 *Imperial*

BASHFORD'S HOT MINERAL SPA RV PARK **Ratings: 8.5/7.5/7** (RV Park) 2015 rates: $37.50. Oct 15 to May 15. (760)354-1315 10590 Hot Mineral Spa Rd, Niland, CA 92257

FOUNTAIN OF YOUTH SPA RV RESORT
Ratings: 10/9★/9 (RV Resort) From Jct of Hwy 111 & Hot Mineral Spa Rd (14 mi N of Niland), E 1.5 mi to Spa Rd, SE 1 mi (L). **FAC:** All weather rds. (850 spaces). Avail: 400 all weather, back-ins (25 x 60), some side by side hkups, 400 full hkups (30/50 amps), cable, WiFi $, tent sites, rentals, dump, laundry, groc, LP gas, restaurant, controlled access. **REC:** heated pool, whirlpool, shuffleboard. Pets OK. Partial handicap access. Big rig sites, RV age restrict, eco-friendly, 2015 rates: $34 to $54. Disc: AAA.
(760)354-1340 Lat: 33.39796, Lon: -115.66265
1500 Spa Rd, Niland, CA 92257
foyresort@yahoo.com
www.foyspa.com
See ad pages 149 (Spotlight Palm Springs), 126 & Snowbird Destinations in Magazine Section.

GLAMIS NORTH HOT SPRINGS RESORT **Ratings: 8.5/8/8.5** (RV Resort) 2015 rates: $40 to $90. Oct 17 to Apr 30. (760)354-1010 10595 Hot Mineral Spa Rd, Niland, CA 92257

Find 'em fast. Our advertisers often include extra information or provide a detailed map in their ads to help you find their facilities quickly and easily.

NORTHRIDGE — L1 *Los Angeles*

WALNUT RV PARK
Ratings: 8/9.5★/7.5 (RV Park) From Jct of I-405 & Nordhoff exit (Exit 69), W 4.5 mi on Nordhoff (L) (Maximum Length 40 ft). **FAC:** Paved rds. (114 spaces). Avail: 10 all weather, back-ins (26 x 42), 10 full hkups (30/50 amps), seasonal sites, WiFi, laundry. **REC:** heated pool. Pet restrict(B/Q) $. No tents. RV age restrict, eco-friendly, 2015 rates: $65. Disc: AAA.
AAA Approved
(800)868-2749 Lat: 34.23515, Lon: -118.55082
19130 Nordhoff St, Northridge, CA 91324
walnutrvpark@yahoo.com
www.walnutrvpark.com
See ad pages 141 (Spotlight Los Angeles), 126.

NOVATO — E2 *Marin*

NOVATO RV PARK
Ratings: 9/10★/9.5 (RV Park) From Jct of US-101 & Atherton Ave/San Marin Dr exit, E 300 ft on Atherton Ave to Armstrong Ave, S 0.1 mi (L). **FAC:** Paved rds. (69 spaces). Avail: 49 gravel, patios, 8 pull-thrus (22 x 45), back-ins (22 x 45), accepts full hkup units only, 49 full hkups (30/50 amps), seasonal sites, cable, WiFi, dump, laundry, groc. **REC:** pool. Pets OK. Partial handicap access, no tents. Big rig sites, eco-friendly, 2015 rates: $71 to $80. Disc: AAA, military.
AAA Approved
(800)733-6787 Lat: 38.11585, Lon: -122.56369
1530 Armstrong Ave, Novato, CA 94945
novatorvp@aol.com
www.novatorvpark.com
See ad pages 216, 128.

O'BRIEN — B2 *Shasta*

HOLIDAY HARBOR SHASTA LAKE RESORT & MARINA **Ratings: 6/6/7** (Campground) 2015 rates: $36. Apr 1 to Nov 1. (800)776-2628 20061 Shasta Caverns Rd, Obrien, CA 96070

OAK HILLS — H4 *San Bernardino*

OAK HILLS RV VILLAGE
Ratings: 6.5/8.5★/5 (RV Park) From Jct of Hwy 395 & I-15: Go 3 mi S on I-15 to Oak Hills Rd Exit, then 1/10 mi NE on Caliente Rd (L). Elev 4072 ft. **FAC:** Paved rds. (31 spaces). Avail: 10 gravel, patios, 3 pull-thrus (20 x 60), back-ins (30 x 40), 10 full hkups (30/50 amps), seasonal sites, WiFi, laundry. **REC.** Pet restrict(B/Q) $. Partial handicap access, no tents. Eco-friendly, 2015 rates: $31 to $34.
(760)949-1716 Lat: 34.365002, Lon: -117.431868
6238 Caliente Rd, Oak Hills, CA 92344
oakhillsrvpark@aol.com
www.oakhillsrvpark.com

OAKDALE — E3 *Stanislaus, Tuolumne*

WOODWARD RESERVOIR (Public) From Jct of SR-120 & CR-J14, N 4 mi on CR-J14 (R). 2015 rates: $20 to $25. (209)847-3304

OAKHURST — E4 *Madera*

HIGH SIERRA RV PARK-MHP
Ratings: 6.5/7.5★/6 (RV Park) From jct of Hwy 41 & Rd 426 (Crane Valley Rd): Go 1/4 mi S on Rd 426 to Golden Oak Dr (stoplight), then go 1/4 mi E on Golden Oak Dr (E). Elev 2600 ft. **FAC:** Paved/gravel rds. 29 gravel, 2 pull-thrus (20 x 50), back-ins (20 x 40), mostly side by side hkups, 23 full hkups, 6 W, 6 E (30/50 amps), cable, WiFi, tent sites, rentals, dump, laundry, LP gas, fire rings, firewood. **REC:** Fresno River (Seasonal): swim, fishing. Pet restrict(B/Q). Partial handicap access. 28 day max stay, eco-friendly, 2015 rates: $26 to $54. Disc: AAA military.
AAA Approved
(559)683-7662 Lat: 37.331674, Lon: -119.647046
40389 Hwy 41, Oakhurst, CA 93644
camping@highsierrarv.com
www.highsierrarv.com

We rate what RVers consider important.

SIERRA MEADOWS RV PARK **Ratings: 8/7.5/7** (RV Park) From Jct Hwy 41 & Hwy 4 (in Oakhurst): Go 2-1/2 mi NW on Hwy 49 to Harmon Ln, then 1/4 mi N on Harmony Ln to Opah Dr, the 2-3/4 mi N on Opah Dr (R). **FAC:** Paved rds. (4 spaces). 44 Avail: 24 paved, 20 grass, 29 pull-thru (40 x 60), back-ins (25 x 35), 44 full hkups (30/5 amps), seasonal sites, WiFi, laundry, restauran **REC:** heated pool, whirlpool, golf, playground, re open to public. Pets OK. No tents. Big rig sites eco-friendly, 2015 rates: $32 to $50. Disc: AAA, mil tary.
(800)642-7448 Lat: 37.36542, Lon: -119.69900
46516 Opah Dr, Ahwahnee, CA 93601
proshop@sierrameadows.com
www.sierrameadows.com

OAKLAND — E2 *Alameda*

OAKLAND See also Bethel Island, Concord Greenbrae, Half Moon Bay, Pacifica & San Fran cisco.

ANTHONY CHABOT FAMILY CAMP REGIONA PARK (Public) E-bnd: From Hwy 13 to Redwood R exit (Exit 1), E & S 7.5 mi on Redwood Rd to Marcie Gate (R); or W-bnd: From Hwy 580 to Castro Valle Blvd exit (Exit 37), W 1 mi on Castro Valley Blvd t Redwood Rd, NW 5 mi to Marciel Gate (L). 201 rates: $20 to $28. (888)327-2757

OCEANO — H2 *San Luis Obispo*

COASTAL DUNES RV PARK (Public) S-Bnd From Jct of Hwy 101 & Pismo Beach exit (Dollive Hwy 1), S 2.5 mi on Hwy 1 (L); or N-bnd: From Jct o Hwy 101 N & Grand exit, W 2.7 mi on Grand to Hw 1, S 0.5 mi (L). 2015 rates: $23 to $38. (805)781-490

PISMO SANDS RV PARK
Ratings: 10/9.5★/8.5 (RV Park N-bnd: From Jct of US-101 & Grand Av (Hwy 227): Go 1/2 mi W on Grand Ave t Halcyon Rd, then 1-1/2 mi S on Halcyo Rd to Cienaga St (Hwy 1), then 3/4 mi W on Cienaga St (L); or S-bnd: From Jct of US-101 & Halcyon Rd: Go 1-1/2 mi S on Halcyon Rd to Cienag St (Hwy 1), then 3/4 mi W on Cienaga St (L).

GOOD TIMES AWAIT AT PISMO SANDS
New Deluxe Rental Cabins * Watch the kids "play" o our wooden ship structure * Grab a cappuccino meet new friends on our patio area * enjoy our spar kling pool & Spa * Visit our store & gift shop * It a awaits you.

FAC: Paved rds. (133 spaces). Avail: 103 paved, 8 pull-thrus (24 x 70), back-ins (22 x 42), accepts self contain units only, 103 full hkups (30/50 amps), sea sonal sites, cable, WiFi, rentals, dump, laundry, LP gas, firewood, controlled access. **REC:** heated pool whirlpool, playground. Pet restrict(Q). Partial hand icap access, no tents. Big rig sites, eco-friendly, 201 rates: $55 to $59. Disc: military.
(800)404-7004 Lat: 35.097802, Lon: -120.606513
2220 Cienaga St., Oceano, CA 93445
manager@pismosands.com
www.pismosands.com
See ad pages 206, 128 & Snowbird Destinations in Magazine Section.

PISMO STATE BEACH/OCEANO (State Pk From town, S 2 mi on Hwy 1 to Pier Ave, W 2 blks (R) 2015 rates: $25 to $50. (805)473-7220

OCEANSIDE — J4 *San Diego*

➔ GUAJOME COUNTY PARK (Public) From Jct of I-5 & Mission Ave (exti 53), E 7 mi on Mission Ave (L). 2015 rates: $29. (877)565-3600

OCEANSIDE RV PARK
Ratings: 9/9★/8 (RV Park) From Jct of I-5 & Oceanside Blvd (exit 52), W 0.5 mi on Oceanside Blvd to S. Coast Hwy, S 0.1 mi across railway track-4th Entrance (L). **FAC:** Paved rds. 139 paved, patios, 33 pull-thrus (20 x 45), back-ins (22 x 40), 139 full hkups (30 amps), cable, WiFi, tent sites, dump, laundry, LP gas, controlled access. **REC:** heated pool, whirlpool. Pet restrict(B/Q) $. RV age restrict, eco-friendly, 2015 rates: $54 to $88. Disc: AAA.
(760)722-4404 Lat: 33.18222, Lon: -117.36663
1510 S Coast Hwy, Oceanside, CA 92054
oceansidervpark@yahoo.com
www.oceansidervpark.com
See ad this page, 126, 155 (Spotlight San Diego) & Snowbird Destinations in Magazine Section.

PARADISE BY THE SEA RV RESORT **Ratings: 10/10★/8.5** (RV Park) 2015 rates: $60 to $115. (760)439-1376 1537 S Coast Hwy, Oceanside, CA 92054

OCOTILLO WELLS — J5 *San Diego*

LEAPIN' LIZARD RV RANCH
Ratings: 6.5/9.5★/9 (RV Park) From Jct of Hwy 78 & Split Mtn Rd, S 0.1 mi on Split Mtn Rd to Kunkler Ln, W 300 yds (L). **FAC:** Gravel/dirt rds. (60 spaces). Avail: 20 dirt, back-ins (30 x 50), 20 full hkups (30/50 amps), seasonal sites, WiFi, rentals, laundry, controlled access. **REC:** playground. Pet restrict(Q). Partial handicap access, no tents. RV age restrict, 2015 rates: $30 to $35. Oct 1 to Jun 1. No CC.
(760)767-4526 Lat: 33.14010, Lon: -116.13566
5929 Kunkler Ln, Borrego Springs, CA 92004
reservation@leapinlizardrvranch.com
www.leapinlizardrvranch.com
See ad this page.

OJAI — H3 *Ventura*

➔ CAMP COMFORT (Public) From Jct of Hwy 33 (Ojai Ave) & Creek Rd, S 2 mi on Creek Rd (L). 2015 rates: $40. (805)654-3951

LOS PADRES (WHEELER GORGE CAMPGROUND) (Natl Forest) From jct Hwy-150 & Hwy-33: Go 8 mi NW on Hwy-33. Pit toilets. 2015 rates: $23. (805)640-1977

OLD STATION — B3 *Lassen*

➔ LASSEN VOLCANIC NATIONAL PARK (BUTTE LAKE) (Natl Pk) From jct Hwy-89/44 & Hwy-44 (Feather Lake Hwy): Go 10 mi E on Hwy-44, then 5 mi S on Halls Flat Rd. 2015 rates: $10 to $16. Jun 5 to Oct 26. (530)595-6121

OLEMA — E2 *Marin*

OLEMA CAMPGROUND
Ratings: 7.5/8★/7.5 (RV Park) From Jct of SR-1 & Sir Francis Drake Blvd (in town), N 0.2 mi on SR-1 (L). **FAC:** Paved/gravel rds. 80 gravel, back-ins (20 x 50), mostly side by side hkups, 26 full hkups, 54 W, 54 E (30/50 amps), WiFi, tent sites, dump, mobile sewer, laundry, LP gas, fire rings, firewood. **REC:** shuffleboard, playground. Pet restrict(B). 14 day max stay, 2015 rates: $53 to $63. ATM, no CC.
AAA Approved
(415)663-8106 Lat: 38.04409, Lon: -122.78994
10155 Hwy 1, Olema, CA 94950
ed@olemacampground.com
www.olemacampground.com
See ad this page.

ORANGE — N4 *Orange*

ORANGELAND RV PARK
Ratings: 10/10★/8.5 (RV Park) S-bnd: From Jct of I-5 & Katella Ave (exit 109A), E 2 mi on Katella Ave to W Struck Ave, SE 150 ft (R).

MINUTES TO DISNEYLAND
We are in the heart of Orange County within walking distance of the Honda Center, Angel Stadium, movies, dining and more. Take our shuttle to Disneyland, pick fresh oranges at your site or just relax in the pool and spa.

FAC: Paved rds. (195 spaces). Avail: 101 paved, patios, 19 pull-thrus (26 x 50), back-ins (22 x 50), 101 full hkups (30/50 amps), seasonal sites, WiFi, dump, laundry, groc. **REC:** heated pool, whirlpool, shuffleboard, playground. Pet restrict(B/Q) $. Partial handicap access, no tents. RV age restrict, eco-friendly, 2015 rates: $65 to $80. Disc: AAA. ATM.
AAA Approved
(714)633-0414 Lat: 33.80474, Lon: -117.86956
1600 W Struck Ave, Orange, CA 92867
orangelandrvpark@yahoo.com
www.orangeland.com
See ad pages 165, 126.

OREGON HOUSE — C3 *Yuba*

LAKE OF THE SPRINGS RV **Ratings: 8/6/8** (Membership Pk) 2015 rates: $48 to $53. (800)405-6188 14152 French Town Road, Oregon House, CA 95962

ORICK — A1 *Humboldt*

PRAIRIE CREEK REDWOODS (State Pk) From town, N 3 mi on US-101 to Davison Rd, W 4 mi (L). 2015 rates: $35. (707)488-2039

➔ PRAIRIE CREEK REDWOODS (GOLD BLUFFS BEACH CAMPGROUND) (State Pk) From town: Go 3 mi N on US-101, then 7 mi W on Davidson Rd/Fern Canyon(caution: graded, dirt road). 2015 rates: $35. (707)464-6101

ORLAND — C2 *Glenn*

OLD ORCHARD RV PARK
Ratings: 6.5/8.5★/6.5 (RV Park) From Jct of I-5 & Exit 619 (SR-32, Chico-Black Butte Lake), W 0.3 mi on Rd 200 (unmarked) to Rd HH, N 0.1 mi (R). **FAC:** Paved/gravel rds. (52 spaces). Avail: 37 gravel, 37 pull-thrus (22 x 60), 23 full hkups, 14 W, 14 E (30/50 amps), seasonal sites, WiFi, tent sites, dump, laundry. Pet restrict(B/Q). Partial handicap access. Big rig sites, 2015 rates: $15 to $26. Disc: AAA, military.
AAA Approved
(530)865-5335 Lat: 39.75384, Lon: -122.20842
4490 County Road H H, Orland, CA 95963
See ad pages 202, 128.

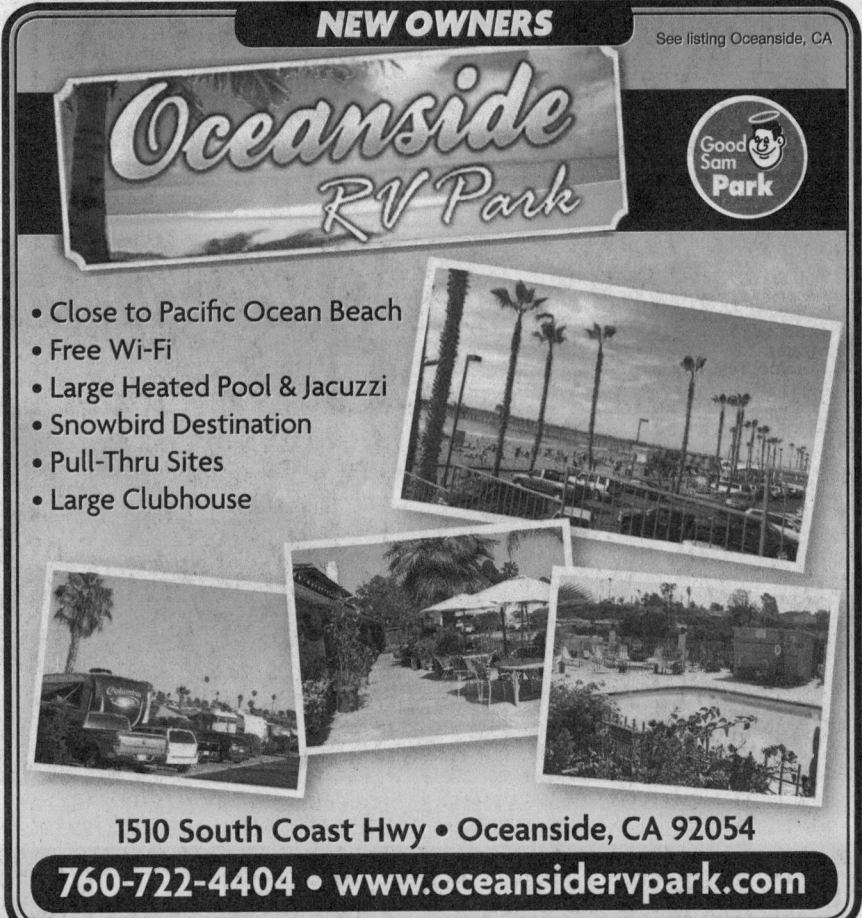

THE PARKWAY RV RESORT & CAMPGROUND
Ratings: 9/10★/9 (RV Park) From Jct of I-5 & SR-32, Exit 619 (Orland/Chico), W 0.5 mi on Rd 200 (Newville Rd) (R). **FAC:** Paved/gravel rds. (86 spaces). 66 Avail: 40 gravel, 26 grass, 40 pull-thrus (46 x 74), back-ins (23 x 40), mostly side by side hkups, 40 full

ORLAND (CONT)

THE PARKWAY RV RESORT (CONT) hkups, 26 W, 26 E (30/50 amps), seasonal sites, WiFi, tent sites, dump, laundry, groc. **REC:** pool, playground. Pets OK. Big rig sites, eco-friendly, 2015 rates: $33.50 to $36.50. Disc: AAA.
(530)865-9188 Lat: 39.75554, Lon: -122.21671
6330 County Road 200, Orland, CA 95963
info@theparkwayrv.com
www.theparkwayrv.com
See ad page 201.

OROVILLE — C3 *Butte*

FEATHER FALLS KOA & CASINO
Ratings: 10/9★/9.5 (RV Park) From Jct of Hwy 70 & Ophir Rd, E 3.3 mi on Ophir Rd (L). **FAC:** Paved rds. 43 paved, patios, 24 pull-thrus (29 x 55), back-ins (29 x 50), accepts full hkup units only, 43 full hkups (30/50 amps), cable, WiFi, laundry, groc, LP gas, fire rings, firewood, restaurant. **REC:** heated pool, whirlpool, playground. Pet restrict(B). Partial handicap access, no tents. Big rig sites, eco-friendly, 2015 rates: $37 to $75.
(800)562-5079 Lat: 39.46503, Lon: -121.51811
3 Alverda Drive, Oroville, CA 95966
kamp@koafeatherfallscasino.com
www.featherfallscasino.com
See ad this page.

LAKE OROVILLE SRA/BIDWELL CANYON (State Pk) From Jct of SR-70 & SR-162 (exit 46), E 7 mi on SR-162 to Kelly Ridge Rd, N 0.5 mi to Arroyo Dr, follow signs (E). 2015 rates: $45. (530)538-2218

LAKE OROVILLE SRA/LOAFER CREEK UNIT SRA (State Pk) From Jct of SR-70 & SR-162 (exit 46), E 8 mi on SR-162 (L). 2015 rates: $25 to $35. Apr to Sep. (530)538-2217

RIVER REFLECTIONS RV PARK & CAMPGROUND
Ratings: 7.5/7.5/7.5 (Campground) From Jct of SR-70 & SR-162 (at Oroville), S 1.6 mi on SR-70 to Pacific Heights Rd, NW 0.1 mi (L). **FAC:** Paved rds. 78 Avail: 10 paved, 68 gravel, 18 pull-thrus (30 x 70), back-ins (30 x 70), 71 full hkups, 7 W, 7 E (30/50 amps), WiFi, tent sites, rentals, dump, laundry, fire rings, firewood. **REC:** Feather River: swim, fishing. Pet restrict(B). Big rig sites, 2015 rates: $45 to $50.
(530)533-1995 Lat: 39.47915, Lon: -121.57757
4360 Pacific. Heights Rd, Oroville, CA 95965
information@rvparkresorts.com
www.rvparkresorts.com
See ad this page.

SEACLIFF STATE BEACH (State Pk) From Jct of Hwy 1 & State Park Dr (Seacliff Beach exit), SW 0.4 mi on State Park Dr (E). 2015 rates: $55 to $65. (831)685-6442

Things to See and Do

FEATHER FALLS CASINO Slots, Table Games Poker, Buffet & Shows. Partial handicap access. RV accessible. Restrooms, food. Hours: Open 24 hour. ATM.
(530)533-3885 Lat: 39.46503, Lon: -121.51811
#3 Alverda Dr, Oroville, CA 95966
www.featherfallscasino.com
See ad this page.

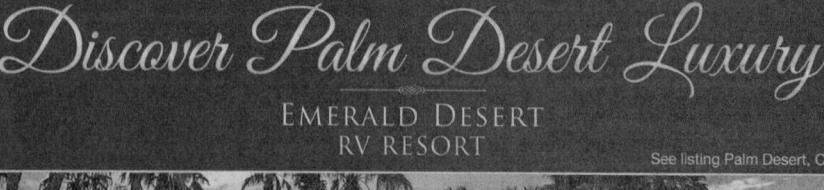

OXNARD — H3 *Ventura*

EVERGREEN RV PARK **Ratings: 6/8/7** (RV Park) 2015 rates: $55. (805)485-1936 2135 N Oxnard Blvd, Oxnard, CA 93036

PT MUGU/BIG SYCAMORE CANYON (State Pk) From town, S 14 mi on PCH 1 (L). For reservations call 1-800-444-7275. 2015 rates: $45. (310)457-8143

PT MUGU/THORNHILL BROOM BEACH (State Pk) From town, S 10 mi on PCH 1 (R). For reservations call 1-800-444-7275. Pit toilets. 2015 rates: $35. (818)880-0350

PACIFICA — E2 *San Mateo*

SAN FRANCISCO RV RESORT Ratings: 7.5/8.5/6 (RV Park) From Jct of Hwy 1 S & Manor-Palmetto Dr (Exit 507): Go 1/4 mi S on Palmetto Dr (R) (Caution: Do not take Hwy 35 from I-280 N due to steep downhill grade). **FAC:** Paved rds. (151 spaces). Avail: 83 paved, patios, 32 pull-thrus (15 x 60), back-ins (15 x 45), 64 full hkups (30/50 amps), seasonal sites, cable, WiFi Hotspot, dump, laundry, LP gas. **REC:** heated pool, whirlpool, playground. Pet restrict(B/Q). Partial handicap access, no tents. Eco-friendly, 2015 rates: $65 to $102.
AAA Approved
(650)355-7093 Lat: 37.646377, Lon: -122.492216
700 Palmetto Ave, Pacifica, CA 94044
SanFranciscoRV@equitylifestyle.com
www.rvonthego.com

PALM DESERT — J5 *Riverside*

EMERALD DESERT RV RESORT - SUNLAND
Ratings: 10/10★/10 (RV Park) From Jct of I-10 & Cook St (Exit 134), S 0.9 mi on Cook St to Frank Sinatra Dr, E 1 mi to El Dorado (L).

THE CROWN JEWEL OF THE DESERT
The most luxurious RV resort in Palm Desert! State-of-the-art fitness center, 2 pools/spas, putting greens, rv storage, billiards room, dog-run area, resort villas, newly renovated clubhouse, tv lounge. Gated. Top rated 10!

FAC: Paved rds. (255 spaces). Avail: 105 paved, patios, 8 pull-thrus (30 x 100), back-ins (30 x 45), 105 full hkups (30/50 amps), seasonal sites, cable, WiFi $, rentals, laundry, controlled access. **REC:** heated pool, whirlpool. Pet restrict(B/Q) $. Partial handicap access, no tents. RV age restrict, eco-friendly, 2015 rates: $98. Disc: AAA.
(866)226-9001 Lat: 33.77283, Lon: -116.33842
76000 Frank Sinatra Dr, Palm Desert, CA 92211
info@emeralddesert.com
www.emeralddesert.com
See ad opposite page, 126 & Snowbird Destinations in Magazine Section.

THOUSAND TRAILS - PALM SPRINGS **Ratings: 9.5/8.5/7.5** (Membership Pk) 2015 rates: $69. Sep 15 to May 15. (800)328-6226 77-500 Varner Rd, Palm Desert, CA 92211

PALM SPRINGS — J5 *Riverside*

A SPOTLIGHT Introducing Palm Spring's colorful attractions appearing at the front of this state section.

PALO VERDE — J6 *Imperal*

OXBOW BLM (Public) From town, S 3 mi on Hwy 78, E on gravel rd btwn mileposts 77 & 78, 0.75 mi to Colorado River (E). Pit toilets. 2015 rates: $15. (928)317-3200

PALOMAR MOUNTAIN — J5 *San Diego*

PALOMAR MOUNTAIN/DOANE VALLEY (State Pk) From town, E on State Hwy 76 to CR-S6, N 7 mi to CR-S7, W 3 mi (E) For reservations call 1-800-274-7275. 2015 rates: $30. (760)742-3462

PARADISE — C3 *Butte, Plumas*

PG & E/FEATHER RIVER/PHILBROOK (Public) From Jct of Elliot Rd & Skyway, N 27.3 mi on Skyway to Humbug Summit Rd, NE 1.9 mi to Philbrook Rd, E 3.1 mi (R). Pit toilets. 2015 rates: $16. (916)386-5164

PARKER DAM — H6 *San Bernardino*

BIG BEND RESORT **Ratings: 7/7.5/7.5** (RV Park) 2015 rates: $44 to $49. (760)663-3755 501 Parker Dam Rd, Parker Dam, CA 92267

ECHO LODGE RESORT **Ratings: 6.5/6.5/7.5** (RV Park) 2015 rates: $64 to $69. (760)663-4931 451 Parker Dam Rd, Parker Dam, CA 92267

RIVER LODGE RESORT **Ratings: 6.5/6/6** (RV Park) 2015 rates: $35 to $50. (760)663-4934 675 N Parker Dam Road, Parker Dam, CA 92267

Don't camp without it ... Our 2016 listings are your key to travel satisfaction.

PASO ROBLES — G2 *San Luis Obispo*

LAKE NACIMIENTO RESORT (Public) From Jct of Hwy 101 & 24th St (Hwy 46E exit), W 16.2 mi on 24th St (Becomes Nacimiento Lake Rd)/G14 (L). (805)238-3256

LAKE SAN ANTONIO REC AREA/SOUTH SHORE (Public) From Jct of Hwy 101 & Exit 252 (SR-G18), W 0.1 mi on G18 (Jolon Rd) to G19 (Nacimiento Lake Dr), SW 11.7 mi to G14 (Interlake Rd), N 8 mi to San Antonio Rd, NE 2 mi (E). 2015 rates: $28 to $40. (831)755-4895

PASO ROBLES RV RANCH
Ratings: 8.5/8/7.5 (Campground) From Jct of US-101 & Hwy 46E: Go 3 mi N on US-101 to Exline Rd Exit (N-bnd left lane exit), then 200 ft S on Stockdale Rd (R) (Note: Entry turn is before Exline Rd). **FAC:** Paved rds. (67 spaces). Avail: 36 gravel, 30 pull-thrus (22 x 60), back-ins (24 x 35), mostly side by side hkups, 36 full hkups (30/50 amps), seasonal sites, WiFi, laundry, LP gas, fire rings, firewood. **REC:** pool. Pet restrict(B). Partial handicap access, no tents. Big rig sites, eco-friendly, 2015 rates: $49.50 to $55.
(805)237-8685 Lat: 35.681529, Lon: -120.697893
398 Exline Rd, Paso Robles, CA 93446
pasoroblesrvranch101@gmail.com
See ad this page, 128.

VINES RV RESORT
Ratings: 10/9.5★/7.5 (RV Resort) From jct US 101 & Hwy 46E: Go N 4 mi on US 101 to Wellsona Rd (R), then 200 ft on Wellsona Rd (L).

WINE AND UNWIND AT THE VINES
Vines RV Resort offers elegant living, excellent customer service and luxury amenities with modern comforts. We are situated in the heart of Wine Country on the central coast of California - stay a day, a week or a month!

FAC: Paved rds. (125 spaces). Avail: 113 paved, patios, 19 pull-thrus (26 x 72), back-ins (26 x 50), 113 full hkups (30/50 amps), seasonal sites, WiFi, rentals, laundry, groc. **REC:** heated pool, whirlpool. Pet restrict(Q). Partial handicap access, no tents. Big rig sites, RV age restrict, eco-friendly, 2015 rates: $50 to $89. Disc: AAA, military.
(888)710-6552 Lat: 35.696436, Lon: -120.695270
88 Wellsona Rd, Paso Robles, CA 93446
vines@suncommunities.com
www.vinesrvresort.com
See ad pages 204, 1463 (Welcome Section), 128 & Snowbird Destinations in Magazine Section.

WINE COUNTRY RV RESORT
Ratings: 9.5/10★/8.5 (RV Resort) From Jct of Hwy 101 & Hwy 46E: Go 2-1/4 mi E on Hwy 46E to Airport Rd, then 2/10 mi N on Airport Rd (R).

WINE COUNTRY RV RESORT
Experience Paso Robles wine region with over 170 wine tasting rooms, golf courses, beaches and lakes, shopping and fine dining! Relax in our heated pool and spas, play some billiards or enjoy numerous planned activities.

FAC: Paved rds. (161 spaces). 151 Avail: 81 paved, 70 gravel, 33 pull-thrus (24 x 80), back-ins (25 x 54), 151 full hkups (30/50 amps), seasonal sites, cable, WiFi, rentals, mobile sewer, laundry, groc, LP gas. **REC:** heated pool, whirlpool, playground. Pet restrict(B/Q). Partial handicap access, no tents. Big rig sites, eco-friendly, 2015 rates: $52 to $93. Disc: AAA, military.
(888)713-0819 Lat: 35.648137, Lon: -120.640381
2500 Airport Rd, Paso Robles, CA 93446
winecountry@suncommunities.com
www.winecountryrvresort.com
See ad pages 204, 1463 (Welcome Section), 128 & Snowbird Destinations in Magazine Section.

Exclusive! According to our research, restroom cleanliness is of the utmost concern to RVers. Of course, you knew that already. The cleanest campgrounds have a star in their restroom rating!

Get a tune-up. Routine maintenance can up fuel efficiency by 4 percent, while fixing more serious problems can improve efficiency up to 40 percent.

CA

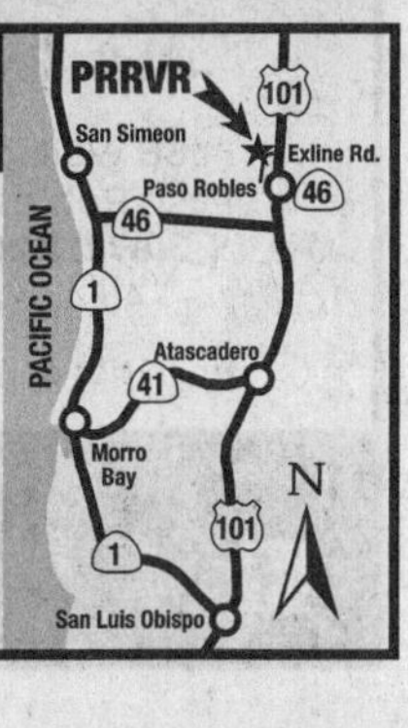

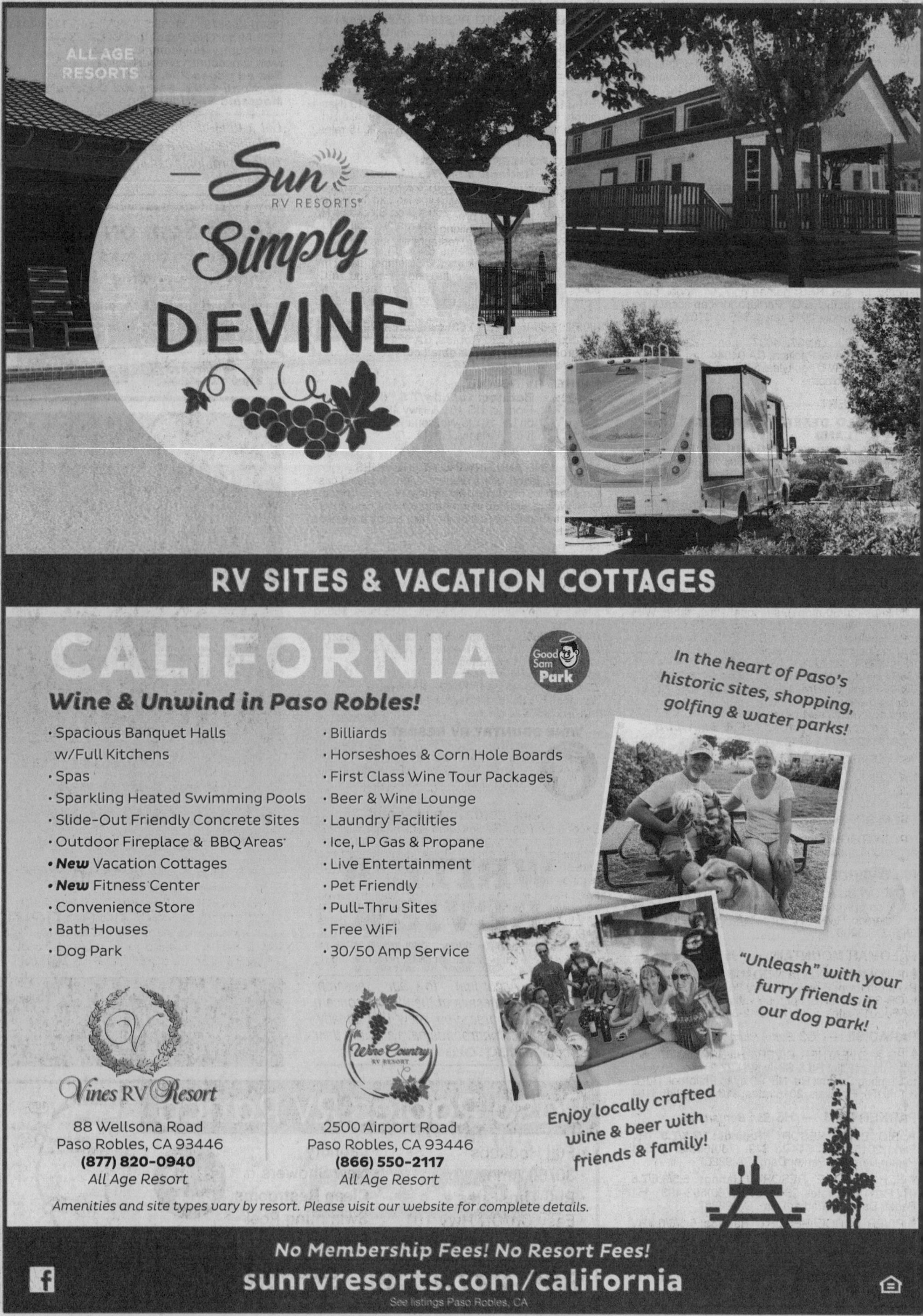
ALL AGE RESORTS
Sun RV RESORTS®
Simply DEVINE
RV SITES & VACATION COTTAGES
CALIFORNIA
Good Sam Park
Wine & Unwind in Paso Robles!
In the heart of Paso's historic sites, shopping, golfing & water parks!
• Spacious Banquet Halls w/Full Kitchens
• Spas
• Sparkling Heated Swimming Pools
• Slide-Out Friendly Concrete Sites
• Outdoor Fireplace & BBQ Areas
• New Vacation Cottages
• New Fitness Center
• Convenience Store
• Bath Houses
• Dog Park
• Billiards
• Horseshoes & Corn Hole Boards
• First Class Wine Tour Packages
• Beer & Wine Lounge
• Laundry Facilities
• Ice, LP Gas & Propane
• Live Entertainment
• Pet Friendly
• Pull-Thru Sites
• Free WiFi
• 30/50 Amp Service
"Unleash" with your furry friends in our dog park!
Vines RV Resort
88 Wellsona Road
Paso Robles, CA 93446
(877) 820-0940
All Age Resort
Wine Country RV RESORT
2500 Airport Road
Paso Robles, CA 93446
(866) 550-2117
All Age Resort
Enjoy locally crafted wine & beer with friends & family!
Amenities and site types vary by resort. Please visit our website for complete details.
No Membership Fees! No Resort Fees!
sunrvresorts.com/california
See listings Paso Robles, CA

PATTERSON — E3 *Stanislaus*

FRANK RAINES PARK (STANISLAUS COUNTY PARK) (Public) From jct I-5 & Del Puerto Canyon Rd (exit 434): Go 17 mi W on Del Puerto Canyon Rd. (209)525-6750

KIT FOX RV PARK
Ratings: 8.5/10★/9 (RV Park) From Jct of I-5 & Exit 434 (Sperry Av), E 0.2 mi on Sperry Av to Rogers Rd, N 0.3 mi (R). **FAC:** Paved rds. (151 spaces). Avail: 91 gravel, patios, 13 pull-thrus (20 x 70), back-ins (21 x 36), 91 full hkups (30/50 amps), seasonal sites, WiFi, laundry, LP gas. **REC:** playground. Pet restrict(B). Partial handicap access, no tents. Eco-friendly, 2015 rates: $36 to $41. Disc: AAA, military.
AAA Approved
(209)892-2638 Lat: 37.46890, Lon: -121.17692
240 Rogers Rd, Patterson, CA 95363
kitfoxrvpark@yahoo.com
www.kitfoxrvpark.com
See ad pages 220, 128.

PERRIS — N6 *Riverside*

LAKE PERRIS-SRA LUISENO CAMPGROUND (State Pk) From Jct of I-215 & Ramona Expwy, E 2.5 mi on Ramona Expwy to Lake Perris Dr, N 1 mi (E). 2015 rates: $25 to $45. (800)444-7275

MEADOWBROOK RV PARK **Ratings: 7/9.5★/8.5** (Membership Pk) 2015 rates: $35. (951)943-7233 26734 Peach St, Perris, CA 92570

PESCADERO — E2 *San Mateo*

SANTA CRUZ NORTH COSTANOA KOA **Ratings: 8/7/8** (Campground) 2015 rates: $69 to $101. (650)879-7302 2001 Rossi Rd, Pescadero, CA 94060

PETALUMA — D2 *Sonoma*

SAN FRANCISCO NORTH/PETALUMA KOA **Ratings: 9.5/10★/10** (Campground) 2015 rates: $29.95 to $77. (800)992-2267 20 Rainsville Rd, Petaluma, CA 94952

PHILO — D1 *Mendocino*

HENDY WOODS (State Pk) From town, NW 2 mi on Hwy 128 to Philo-Greenwood Rd, SW 0.5 mi (L). 2015 rates: $45. (707)895-3141

PIEDRA — F3 *Fresno*

CHOINUMNI PARK (Public) From Jct of SR-180 & Piedra Rd, NE 5 mi on Piedra Rd to Trimmer Springs Rd, E 4 mi to Pine Flat Rd, S 0.25 mi (R). 2015 rates: $18. (559)600-3004

ISLAND PARK (Public Corps) From town, NE 8 mi on Trimmer Springs Rd (R). 2015 rates: $20 to $30. (559)787-2589

TRIMMER CAMPGROUND (Public Corps) From Jct of Pine Flat Rd & Trimmer Springs Rd, NE 15 mi on Trimmer Springs Rd (R). 2015 rates: $20. (559)787-2589

PINE GROVE — D3 *Amador*

GOLD COUNTRY CAMPGROUND RESORT
Ratings: 8.5/10★/7.5 (Campground) From Jct of Hwy 49 & Hwy 88, E 9.5 mi on Hwy 88 to Tabeaud Rd, S 0.8 mi (L). **FAC:** Paved/gravel rds. 80 gravel, 12 pull-thrus (25 x 50), back-ins (25 x 50), 80 full hkups (30/50 amps), WiFi, tent sites, rentals, dump, laundry, groc, LP bottles, fire rings, firewood. **REC:** heated pool, playground. Pet restrict(Q). Big rig sites, eco-friendly, 2015 rates: $35 to $64. Disc: AAA, military.
AAA Approved
(209)296-4650 Lat: 38.39635, Lon: -120.64344
13026 Tabeaud Rd, Pine Grove, CA 95665
info@goldcountrycampground.com
www.goldcountrycampground.com
See ad pages 137 (Spotlight Gold Country), 128.

INDIAN GRINDING ROCK STATE HISTORIC PARK (State Pk) From Jackson, E 10 mi on Hwy 88 to Pine-Grove/Volcano Rd, N 2 mi (L). 2015 rates: $25. (209)296-7488

PINE VALLEY — K5 *San Diego*

CLEVELAND (LAGUNA CAMPGROUND) (Natl Forest) From I-8 (Sunrise Hwy, exit 47): Go 14 mi N on CR S1 (Sunrise Hwy), then 1/10 mi S on CR J31B. 2015 rates: $22. (853)673-6180

PIRU — H3 *Ventura*

LAKE PIRU RECREATION AREA (Public) From Jct of I-5 & Hwy 126, W 12 mi on Hwy 126 to Main St, N 7 mi, follow signs (E). 2015 rates: $22 to $44. (805)521-1500

PISMO BEACH — G2 *San Luis Obispo*

PISMO BEACH See also Grover Beach, Morro Bay, Oceano, Santa Margarita & Santa Maria.

HOLIDAY RV PARK **Ratings: 8.5/7.5/6** (RV Park) 2015 rates: $44 to $56. (800)272-3672 100 S Dolliver St, Pismo Beach, CA 93449

PISMO COAST VILLAGE RV RESORT
Ratings: 9.5/9/8.5 (RV Park) N-bnd: From Jct of US-101 & Price St: Go 75 ft N on Price St to Ocean View Rd, then 1/10 mi W to Dolliver St (US-1), then 1/2 mi S (R); or S-bnd: From Jct of US-101 & Dolliver St (Pismo Beach exit): Go 9/10 mi S on Dolliver St (R).

A UNIQUE RV PARADISE ON THE OCEAN
Relax to the sound of the surf, scent of the salt air, and the feel of an ocean breeze. This award winning resort is located within walking distance from downtown Pismo Beach shopping, restaurants, and the famous Pismo Pier.

FAC: Paved rds. 400 Avail: 400 all weather, back-ins (26 x 45), 400 full hkups (30/50 amps), cable, WiFi, laundry, groc, LP gas, fire rings, firewood, restaurant, controlled access. **REC:** heated pool, wading pool, Pacific Ocean: swim, playground. Pet restrict(B/Q). Partial handicap access, no tents. Big rig sites, 29 day max stay, eco-friendly, 2015 rates: $47 to $64. ATM.
(888)782-3224 Lat: 35.134770, Lon: -120.637282
165 S Dolliver St, Pismo Beach, CA 93449
rv@pismocoastvillage.com
www.pismocoastvillage.com
See ad page 207.

PISMO SANDS RV PARK
Ratings: 10/9.5★/8.5 (RV Park) N-bnd: From Jct of US-101 & Grand Ave (Hwy 227): Go 1/2 mi W on Grand Ave to Halcyon Rd, then 1-1/2 mi S on Halcyon Rd to Cienaga St (Hwy 1), then 3/4 mi W on Cienaga St (L); or S-bnd: From Jct of US-101 & Halcyon Rd: Go 1/2 mi S on Halcyon Rd to Cienaga St, then 3/4 mi W on Cienaga St (L). **FAC:** Paved rds. (133 spaces). Avail: 103 paved, 84 pull-thrus (24 x 70), back-ins (22 x 42), accepts self-contain units only, 103 full hkups (30/50 amps), seasonal sites, cable, WiFi, rentals, dump, laundry, LP gas, firewood, controlled access. **REC:** heated pool, whirlpool, playground. Pet restrict(Q). Partial handicap access. Big rig sites, eco-friendly, 2015 rates: $55 to $59. Disc: AAA, military.
(800)404-7004 Lat: 35.097802, Lon: -120.606513
2220 Cienaga St, Oceano, CA 93445
manager@pismosands.com
www.pismosands.com
See primary listing at Oceano and ad page 206.

Wasn't that a beautiful campground you visited ten years ago? But can you remember where it was? Use our "Find-it-Fast" index, located in the back of the Guide. It's an alphabetical list, by state, of every private and public park and campground in the Guide.

CA

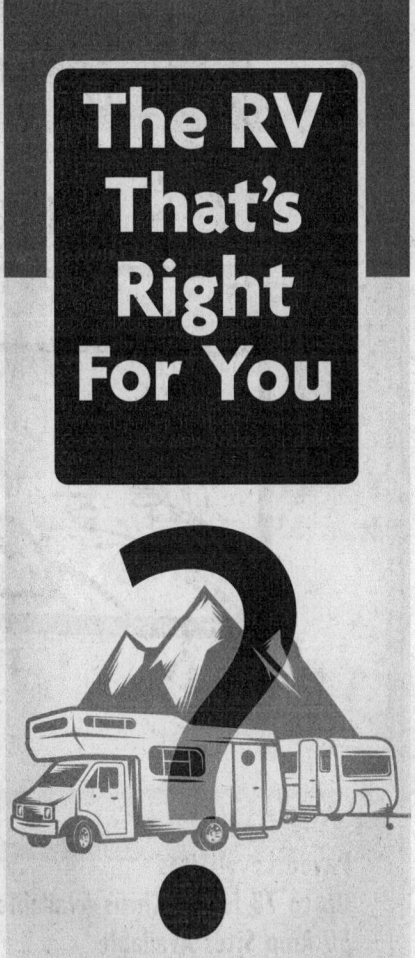

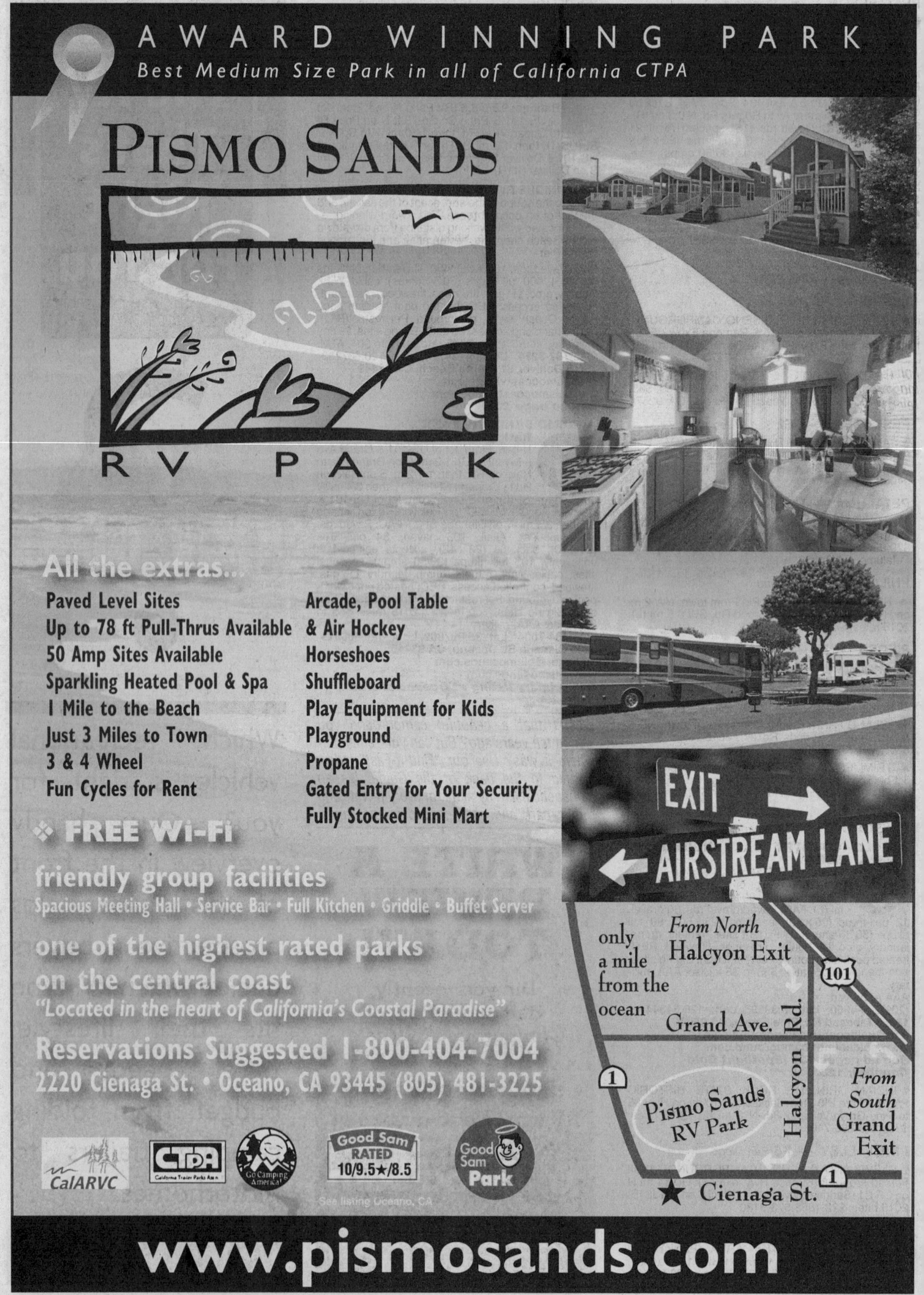
AWARD WINNING PARK
Best Medium Size Park in all of California CTPA
PISMO SANDS
RV PARK
EXIT
AIRSTREAM LANE
All the extras...
Paved Level Sites
Up to 78 ft Pull-Thrus Available
50 Amp Sites Available
Sparkling Heated Pool & Spa
1 Mile to the Beach
Just 3 Miles to Town
3 & 4 Wheel
Fun Cycles for Rent
Arcade, Pool Table
& Air Hockey
Horseshoes
Shuffleboard
Play Equipment for Kids
Playground
Propane
Gated Entry for Your Security
Fully Stocked Mini Mart
FREE Wi-Fi
friendly group facilities
Spacious Meeting Hall • Service Bar • Full Kitchen • Griddle • Buffet Server
one of the highest rated parks on the central coast
"Located in the heart of California's Coastal Paradise"
Reservations Suggested 1-800-404-7004
2220 Cienaga St. • Oceano, CA 93445 (805) 481-3225
only a mile from the ocean
From North Halcyon Exit
101
Grand Ave.
Halcyon Rd.
1
Pismo Sands RV Park
From South Grand Exit
Cienaga St.
CalARVC
CTPA
Go Camping America!
Good Sam RATED 10/9.5★/8.5
Good Sam Park
See listing Oceano, CA
www.pismosands.com

PLAYA DEL REY — M1 *Los Angeles*

DOCKWEILER RV PARK
(Public) From Jct of I-405 & I-105, W 2.5 mi on I-105 to end of Fwy-becoming Imperial Hwy, continue W 1.9 mi on Imperial Hwy to Vista del Mar (Entrance to RV park at state beach entrance). **FAC:** Paved rds. 117 paved, patios, back-ins (20 x 42), 117 full hkups (30/50 amps), dump, laundry, fire rings, controlled access. **REC:** Pacific Ocean: swim, fishing. Pet restrict(Q) $. Partial handicap access, no tents. RV age restrict, 21 day max stay, 2015 rates: $55 to $69. Feb 1 to Jan 1.
(800)950-7275 Lat: 33.93113, Lon: -118.43506
12001 Vista Del Mar, Playa Del Rey, CA 90293
http://reservations.lacounty.gov
See ad page 141 (Spotlight Los Angeles) & RV Trips of a Lifetime in Magazine Section.

PLEASANTON — E2 *Alameda*

THE FAIR PARK RV
(Public) From Jct of I-680 & Exit 26 (Bernal Ave), E 0.3 mi on Bernal to Valley Ave, N 0.2 mi to Gate 12 (R). Reservations Recommended. **FAC:** Paved rds. 176 Avail: 137 gravel, 39 grass, 13 pull-thrus (20 x 80), back-ins (20 x 40), 176 full hkups (30/50 amps), WiFi, laundry, restaurant. **REC:** golf. Pets OK. No tents. 21 day max stay, 2015 rates: $30 to $50.
(925)426-7600 Lat: 37.66185, Lon: -121.89259
4501 Pleasanton Ave, Pleasanton, CA 94566
frontdesk@alamedacountyfair.com
www.thefairparkrv.com
See ad page 158 (Spotlight San Francisco).

Follow the arrow. The arrow in each listing indicates where the facility is located in relation to the listed town.

PLYMOUTH — D3 *Amador*

FAR HORIZONS 49ER VILLAGE RV RESORT
Ratings: 10/10★/9.5 (RV Park) From Sacramento: From Jct of Hwy 50 & Hwy 16 (Jackson Rd) :Go 30 miles SE on Hwy 16 (Jackson Rd) (to intersection Hwy 16 & Hwy 49)-(which turns into Hwy 49) continue E 1.8 mi on Hwy 49 (L).

We offer 329 spacious, shady sites on tree-lined streets designed to accommodate even the largest rigs. All sites are equipped with full hookups, including water, sewer, electricity (30 or 30/50 amp) and cable TV.

FAC: Paved rds. (275 spaces). Avail: 240 paved, patios, 17 pull-thrus (27 x 50), back-ins (30 x 50), accepts full hkup units only, 240 full hkups (30/50 amps), seasonal sites, cable, WiFi, rentals, dump, laundry, groc, LP bottles, firewood, restaurant. **REC:** heated pool, whirlpool, pond, fishing, shuffleboard, playground. Pets OK. Partial handicap access, no tents. Big rig sites, eco-friendly, 2015 rates: $43 to $80.
(800)339-6981 Lat: 38.47507, Lon: -120.85041
18265 Hwy 49, Plymouth, CA 95669
information@49ervillage.com
www.49ervillage.com
See ad pages 138 (Spotlight Gold Country), 128, 120 (CA Map).

Say you saw it in our Guide!

Things to See and Do

CAFE AT THE PARK Deli-Espresso Cafe - continental breakfast, sandwiches, salads & wine, beer, soft drinks, shakes, malts,floats & ice cream. Partial handicap access. RV accessible. Restrooms, food. Hours: 8am to 7pm.
(209)245-6983 Lat: 38.47491, Lon: -120.85031
18265 Hwy 49, Plymouth, CA 95669
cafe@49ervillage.com
www.49ervillage.com
See ad page 138 (Spotlight Gold Country).

POLLOCK PINES — D3 *El Dorado*

ELDORADO (WOLF CREEK CAMPGROUND) (Natl Forest) From town: Go 8-1/2 mi E on US 50, then 16-1/2 mi N on FR 3 (Ice House Rd), then 3-1/2 mi W on FR 12N52. Pit toilets. 2015 rates: $22. May 23 to Sep 1. (530)644-6048

GHOST MOUNTAIN RANCH-COLORADO RIVER ADVENTURES **Ratings: 7/7/7.5** (Membership Pk) 2015 rates: $30. (530)644-2204 5560 Badger Hill Road, Pollock Pines, CA 95726

CA

POLLOCK PINES (CONT)

SLY PARK RECREATION AREA (Public) From Jct of Hwy 50 & Sly Park Rd (exit 60), S 5 mi on Sly Park Rd (L). Pit toilets. 2015 rates: $30 to $45. (530)295-6810

POMONA — M4 *Los Angeles*

LOS ANGELES KOA
Ratings: 10/10★/8 (RV Park) W-bnd: From I-10 & Garey Ave onto Orangegrove, SW under Fwy 300 ft to McKinley, NW 0.6 mi to White Ave, N 0.8 mi (R); or E-bnd: From Jct of I-10 & White Ave, N 1.4 mi on White Ave (R). E-bnd or W-bnd: From Jct of I-210 & Fruit St (Exit 48), S 2 mi on Fruit St (becomes White Ave) (L).

HOME OF THE LOS ANGELES FAIRPLEX
Set against the backdrop of the beautiful San Gabriel Mtns, enjoy year round camping in a safe & serene environment. Our friendly, helpful KOA staff is ready to assist you at any time.

FAC: Paved rds. (182 spaces). Avail: 122 paved, 122 pull-thrus (18 x 55), 122 full hkups (30/50 amps), seasonal sites, WiFi, rentals, dump, laundry, groc, restaurant. **REC:** pool, whirlpool, golf. Pet restrict(B/Q). Partial handicap access, no tents. RV age restrict, 2015 rates: $53.35 to $62.80. ATM.
(888)562-4230 Lat: 34.08981, Lon: -117.76391
2200 N White Ave, Pomona, CA 91768
koa@fairplex.com
www.fairplex.com
See ad page 193 & Snowbird Destinations in Magazine Section.

Like Us on Facebook.

PORTERVILLE — G3 *Tulare*

SUCCESS LAKE/TULE CAMPGROUND (Public Corps) Freeway 99: Take the highway 190 exit east to the park (8 miles east of Porterville). 2015 rates: $20 to $30. (877)444-6777

POTRERO — K5 *San Diego*

POTRERO COUNTY PARK (Public) From town, E 1 mi on Hwy 94 to Potrero Valley Rd to Potrero Park Rd, E 1 mi (E). 2015 rates: $22 to $27. (877)565-3600

POTTER VALLEY — C2 *Lake, Mendocino*

PG & E/SAN JOAQUIN RIVER/TROUT CREEK (Public) From Jct of Eel River Rd & E Potter Valley Rd, E 6.5 mi on Eel River Rd (R). Pit toilets. 2015 rates: $16. (916)386-5164

QUINCY — C3 *Plumas*

PG & E/FEATHER RIVER/HASKINS VALLEY (Public) From Jct of Hwy 70 & Bucks Lake Rd, SW 16.5 mi on Bucks Lake Rd (R). Pit toilets. 2015 rates: $22.94. May 1 to Oct 31. (916)386-5164

PIONEER RV PARK
Ratings: 9/10★/9.5 (RV Park) E-bnd: From Jct SR-70/SR-89 & Fairground Rd (in town), N 0.1 mi on Fairground Rd to Pioneer Rd, E 0.1 mi (E). Elev 3400 ft. **FAC:** Paved rds. (62 spaces). Avail: 54 paved, 37 pull-thrus (30 x 70), back-ins (30 x 48), accepts full hkup units only, 54 full hkups (30/50 amps), seasonal sites, WiFi, showers $, dump, laundry, LP gas. **REC.** Pet restrict(B). No tents. Big rig sites, eco-friendly, 2015 rates: $36. Disc: military.
(530)283-0769 Lat: 39.93658, Lon: -120.91299
1326 Pioneer Rd, Quincy, CA 95971
info@pioneerrvpark.com
www.pioneerrvpark.com
See ad this page, 128.

Tell them you saw them in this Guide!

RAMONA — J5 *San Diego*

DOS PICOS COUNTY PARK (Public) From Jct of SR-67 & Mussey Grade Rd, SE 1 mi on Mussey Grade Rd to Dos Picos Rd, E 0.2 mi (E). 2015 rates: $24 to $29. (877)565-3600

RED BLUFF — C2 *Tehama*

DURANGO RV RESORT
Ratings: 10/10★/9.5 (RV Resort) From Jct of I-5 & Antelope Blvd (Exit 649), W 0.1 mi on Antelope Blvd to Belle Mill Rd, N 0.1 mi to East Ave, NE 0.1 mi (L). **FAC:** Paved rds. (174 spaces). Avail: 154 paved, patios, 118 pull-thrus (35 x 85), back-ins (35 x 75), accepts full hkup units only, 154 full hkups (30/50 amps), seasonal sites, cable, WiFi, dump, laundry, groc, LP gas, controlled access. **REC:** heated pool, whirlpool, Sacramento River. Pet restrict(B). Partial handicap access, no tents. Big rig sites, eco-friendly, 2015 rates: $43 to $58. Disc: AAA, military.
(866)770-7001 Lat: 40.18317, Lon: -122.22939
100 Lake Ave, Red Bluff, CA 96080
reservations@durangorvresorts.com
www.durangorvresorts.com
See ad this page, 128.

LAKE RED BLUFF RECREATION AREA/SYCAMORE GROVE CAMPGROUND (Public Corps) From Jct of I-5 & Hwy 99 (Lassen Park, exit 649), E 0.5 mi on Lassen Park to Sale Ln, S 2 mi (E). 2015 rates: $16 to $30. (530)934-3316

RED BLUFF RV PARK
Ratings: 8/9★/9.5 (RV Park) From Jct of I-5 & SR-36E/99S (Antelope Blvd/Lassen Natl Park exit 649), E 0.7 mi on SR-36E/99S to Chestnut, N 0.1 mi (L). **FAC:** Paved/gravel rds. (69 spaces). 44 Avail: 16 paved, 28 gravel, patios, 44 pull-thrus (27 x 65), accepts full hkup units only, 44 full hkups (30/50 amps), cable, WiFi, laundry, LP gas. **REC:** pool. Pets OK. Partial handicap access, no tents. Big rig sites, eco-friendly, 2015 rates: $35. Disc: AAA, military.
(530)838-4652 Lat: 40.18778, Lon: -122.21075
80 Chestnut Ave, Red Bluff, CA 96080
reservations@redbluffrvpark.com
www.redbluffrvpark.com
See ad opposite page, 128.

REDCREST — B1 *Humboldt*

ANCIENT REDWOODS RV PARK
Ratings: 8/9.5★/8.5 (RV Park) N-bnd: From Jct of Hwy 101 & Redcrest Exit 667, N 1.7 mi on Avenue of the Giants (at the Immortal Tree) (R); or S-bnd: From Jct of Hwy 101 & Exit 674 (SR-254) Avenue of the Giants, S 5 mi on Avenue of the Giants (L). **FAC:** Paved rds. 49 paved, 30 pull-thrus (30 x 60), back-ins (30 x 45), accepts full hkup units only, 49 full hkups (30/50 amps), WiFi, laundry, fire rings, firewood. **REC.** Pet restrict(B). Partial handicap access, no tents. Big rig sites, eco-friendly, 2015 rates: $38.50 to $42.25. May 1 to Oct 31.
(707)722-4396 Lat: 40.41702, Lon: -123.96721

We appreciate your business!

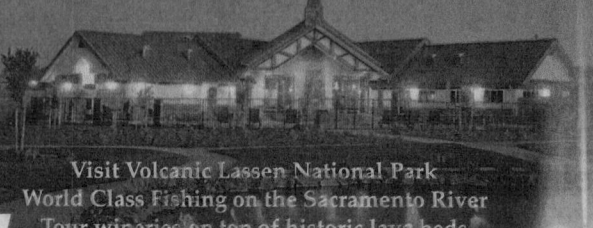

REDCREST (CONT)

ANCIENT REDWOODS RV PARK (CONT)
28101 Avenue Of The Giants, Redcrest, CA 95569
ancientredwoods@gmail.com
www.ancientredwoods.net
See ad pages 144 (Spotlight Northcoast and the Giant Redwoods), 128.

Things to See and Do

THE BURL N' DRIFT NOVELTY SHOP Novelty and gift shop specializing in local manufactured redwood souvenirs and gifts. Also provided a picnic area and stock local wines and beer. RV accessible. Restrooms.
(707)722-4396 Lat: 40.41693, Lon: -123.96431
28101 Ave of the Giants, Redcrest, CA 95569
ancientredwoods@hughes.net
www.ancientredwoods.net
See ad page 144 (Spotlight Northcoast and the Giant Redwoods).

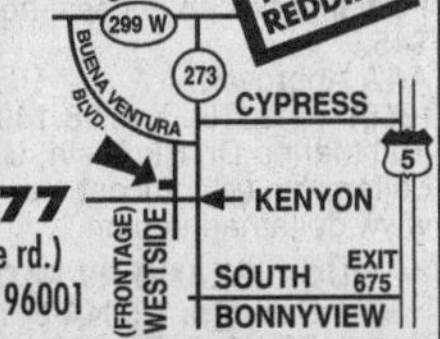

REDDING — B2 Shasta

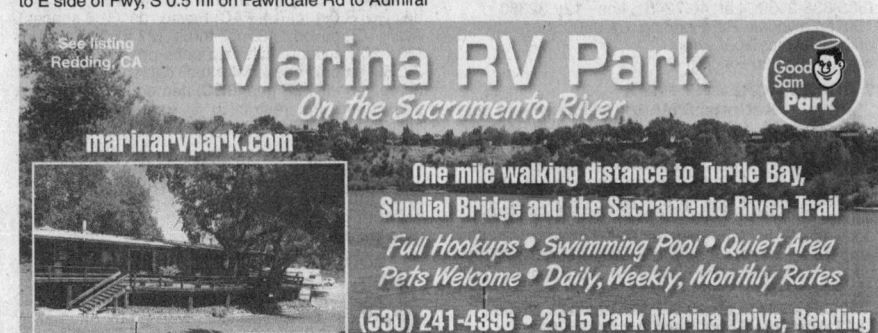

FAWNDALE OAKS RV PARK Ratings: 5/UI/7.5 (RV Park) From Jct of I-5 & Fawndale Rd/Wonderland Blvd exit 689 (10 mi N of town), exit to E side of Fwy, S 0.5 mi on Fawndale Rd to Admiral Way (L). **FAC:** Paved/gravel rds. (27 spaces). Avail: 14 gravel, 6 pull-thrus (28 x 54), back-ins (20 x 40), 14 full hkups (30 amps), seasonal sites, cable, WiFi, tent sites, laundry, groc, LP gas. **REC:** pool, play-

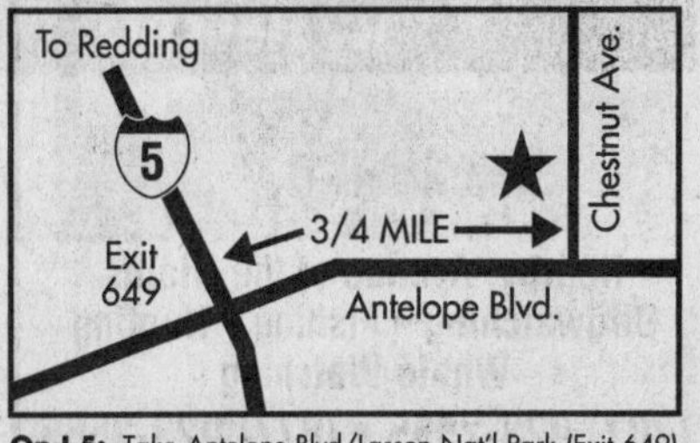

REDDING (CONT)

FAWNDALE OAKS RV PARK (CONT)
ground. Pet restrict(B) $. Partial handicap access. 2015 rates: $27 to $37. Disc: AAA, military. ATM. AAA Approved
(888)838-2159 Lat: 40.72451, Lon: -122.32350
15015 Fawndale Rd, Redding, CA 96003
office@fawndaleoaks.com
www.fawndaleoaks.com

GREEN ACRES RV PARK
Ratings: 9/NA/9 (RV Park) From Jct of I-5 & S Bonnyview Rd/Bechelli Ln/Churn Creek exit 675 (S of town), W 2 mi on S Bonnyview Rd (unmarked) to SR-273, N 1 mi to Kenyon Dr, W 50 ft to Westside Rd, N 300 ft (L). **FAC:** Paved rds. (33 spaces). Avail: 28 paved, patios, back-ins (28 x 60), accepts self-contain units only, 28 full hkups (30/50 amps), seasonal sites, cable, WiFi, laundry. **REC:** pool, shuffleboard. Pet restrict(B). No tents. Big rig sites, 2015 rates: $30.
(800)891-6777 Lat: 40.54509, Lon: -122.38750
4812 Westside Road, Redding, CA 96001
greenacresrvp@gmail.com
www.greenacresrvpark.com
See ad pages 209, 128.

JGW RV PARK
Ratings: 9.5/10★/9.5 (RV Park) From Jct of I-5 & Knighton Rd exit 673 (6 mi S of town), exit to W side of I-5 to Riverland Dr (Frntg Rd), S 2 mi (R). **FAC:** Paved rds. (75 spaces). Avail: 50 paved, 38 pull-thrus (26 x 60), back-ins (26 x 60), some side by side hkups, accepts full hkup units only, 50 full hkups (30/50 amps), seasonal sites, cable, WiFi, laundry, LP gas, fire rings, firewood. **REC:** pool, Sacramento River: fishing. Pets OK. Partial handicap access, no tents. Big rig sites, eco-friendly, 2015 rates: $35 to $47. Disc: AAA, military.
(530)365-7965 Lat: 40.48062, Lon: -122.32066
6612 Riverland Dr, Redding, CA 96002
jgwrvpark@charter.net
www.jgwrvpark.com
See ad page 209.

MARINA RV PARK
Ratings: 8/8/7.5 (RV Park) From Jct of I-5 & SR 44, exit 678 B (Central Redding exit), W 0.8 mi on SR-44 to Exit 1 (Park Marina Dr exit), S 300 ft over Fwy to Park Marina Dr/Butte St, E 0.8 mi on Park Marina Dr (L). **FAC:** Paved rds. (75 spaces). Avail: 36 paved, patios, back-ins (20 x 45), accepts full hkup units only, 35 full hkups, 1 E (20/30 amps), seasonal sites, WiFi, dump, laundry. **REC:** pool, whirlpool, Sacramento River: fishing. Pet restrict(B). No tents. 2015 rates: $27 to $30. No CC.
(530)241-4396 Lat: 40.57589, Lon: -122.37096
2615 Park Marina Dr, Redding, CA 96001
www.marinarvpark.com
See ad pages 209, 128.

Are you using a friend's Guide? Want one of your own? Call 877-209-6655.

MOUNTAIN GATE RV PARK
Ratings: 10/10★/9 (RV Park) From Jct of I-5 & SR-44/SR-299E, N 6.5 mi on I-5 to Mountain Gate/Wonderland Blvd (Old Oregon Trail) exit 687, E 100 ft on Old Oregon Trail (unmarked rd) to Holiday Rd, S 0.4 mi (L). **FAC:** Paved rds. (108 spaces). Avail: 72 paved, 43 pull-thrus (27 x 60), back-ins (30 x 50), accepts full hkup units only, 72 full hkups (30/50 amps), seasonal sites, cable, WiFi, rentals, dump, laundry, LP gas. **REC:** heated pool, whirlpool, playground. Pet restrict(B) $. Partial handicap access, no tents. Big rig sites, eco-friendly, 2015 rates: $29 to $40.
(800)404-6040 Lat: 40.69974, Lon: -122.33963
14161 Holiday Rd, Redding, CA 96003
info@mt-gatervpark.com
www.mt-gatervpark.com
See ad pages 209, 128.

REDDING PREMIER RV RESORT
Ratings: 10/10★/10 (Campground) From Jct of I-5 & Exit 680 (SR-299E/Lake Blvd/Burney-Alturas), W 0.2 mi on Lake Blvd to N Boulder Dr, N 0.1 mi (L). **FAC:** Paved rds. (104 spaces). Avail: 90 paved, patios, 66 pull-thrus (25 x 70), back-ins (25 x 65), accepts full hkup units only, 90 full hkups (30/50 amps), seasonal sites, WiFi, tent sites, rentals, dump, laundry, LP gas. **REC:** pool, playground. Pet restrict(B). Partial handicap access. Big rig sites, eco-friendly, 2015 rates: $43 to $55.
(888)710-8450 Lat: 40.61314, Lon: -122.37035
280 N Boulder Dr, Redding, CA 96003
reddingpremier@msn.com
www.premierrvresorts.com
See ad pages 209, 128.

REDDING RV PARK
Ratings: 10/9.5★/9 (RV Park) From Jct of I-5 & SR-299E (Exit 680), W 0.2 mi on Lake Blvd to Black Marble/Boulder (second stoplight W of I-5, get in inside lane), S 50 ft to Boulder Dr, SE 0.2 mi on Frontage Rd (Boulder Dr) to Campers Ct, S 0.2 mi (L). **FAC:** Paved rds. (107 spaces). Avail: 77 paved, 52 pull-thrus (22 x 67), back-ins (22 x 45), accepts full hkup units only, 77 full hkups (30/50 amps), seasonal sites, cable, WiFi, laundry, groc, LP gas. **REC:** pool. Pets OK. Partial handicap access, no tents. Big rig sites, eco-friendly, 2015 rates: $30 to $36. Disc: AAA, military.
(530)241-0707 Lat: 40.60932, Lon: -122.36398
11075 Campers Ct, Redding, CA 96003
rdgrvpk@juno.com
www.reddingrvpark.com
See ad pages 209, 128.

SACRAMENTO RIVER RV PARK **Ratings: 8.5/6.5/8.5** (RV Park) 2015 rates: $41.80. (530)365-6402 6596 Riverland Dr, Redding, CA 96002

WHISKEYTOWN NRA/BRANDY CREEK (Natl Pk) From Redding, W 8 mi on Hwy 299 to visitor center, W 5 mi(E). Self-contained units only. Entrance fee required. 2015 rates: $7 to $14. (530)242-3412

WHISKEYTOWN NRA/OAK BOTTOM CAMPGROUNDS (Natl Pk) From W-end of town, W 14 mi on SR-299 (L). For reservations call 1-800-365-CAMP. 2015 rates: $20 to $25. (530)359-2269

E2. C5. F1. It's not a cipher; it's our easy-to-use map grid. Draw a line horizontally from the letter, vertically from the number, in the map border. "X" will mark a spot near your destination.

REDLANDS — M6 *San Bernardino*

MISSION RV PARK
Ratings: 7/9★/7.5 (RV Park) From Jct of I-10 & California St (Exit 76), S 0.2 mi on California St to Redlands Blvd, W 0.1 mi (L). **FAC:** Paved rds. (98 spaces). Avail: 76 paved, 10 all weather, patios, back-ins (20 x 40), 86 full hkups (30/50 amps), WiFi Hotspot, dump, laundry. Pet restrict(B/Q). No tents. RV age restrict, eco-friendly, 2015 rates: $40. AAA Approved
(909)796-7570 Lat: 34.06293, Lon: -117.22869
26397 W. Redlands Blvd, Redlands, CA 92373
allthree.conleys@gmail.com
www.missionrvparkca.com

REDWAY — C1 *Humboldt*

DEAN CREEK RESORT
Ratings: 8/6.5/8 (Campground) From Jct of US-101 & Garberville Exit (Exit 642), W 0.1 mi on Garberville Exit to Redwood Dr., S 0.1 mi (R); or S-Bnd: From Eureka, S 60 mi on US-101 to Redway Exit (Exit 642), S 0.1 mi (R). **FAC:** Paved rds. (62 spaces). Avail: 53 gravel, 9 pull-thrus (20 x 70), back-ins (20 x 40), 23 full hkups, 30 W, 30 E (20/30 amps), seasonal sites, cable, WiFi, tent sites, rentals, dump, laundry, groc, fire rings, firewood. **REC:** heated pool, whirlpool, Eel River: fishing, playground. Pets OK. Partial handicap access. 2015 rates: $44 to $46.
(707)923-2555 Lat: 40.14098, Lon: -123.81031
4112 Redwood Drive, Redway, CA 95560
deancrk@humboldt.net
www.deancreekresort.com
See ad this page.

Things to See and Do

DEAN CREEK MOTEL 11 Motel units; kitchens & suites. Restrooms. Hours: 24 hour. Adult fee: $55.
(877)923-2555 Lat: 40.14113, Lon: -123.81026
4112 Redwood Dr, Redway, CA 95560
deancrk@humboldt.net
www.deancreekresort.com
See ad this page.

RIMFOREST — L6 *San Bernardino*

SAN BERNARDINO NF (DOGWOOD CAMPGROUND) (Natl Forest) From town: Go 1/2 mi NE on Hwy-18. 2015 rates: $28 to $33. May 2 to Nov 2. (909)382-2790

RIO VISTA — D2 *Solano*

BRANNAN ISLAND SRA (State Pk) From Jct of SR-12 & SR-160, S 3.5 mi on SR-160 (L). 2015 rates: $25 to $40. (916)777-6671

DELTA MARINA YACHT HARBOR (RV RESORT) Ratings: 7.5/8.5/7.5 (Campground) From Jct of SR-12 & Main St (W end of town, bear rt at downtown Rio Vista), SE 0.4 mi on Main St to Second St, S 0.4 mi on Second St to Marina Dr, E 500 ft (L). **FAC:** Paved rds. 25 paved, 5 pull-thrus (27 x 45), back-ins (18 x 45), 25 full hkups (30/50 amps), cable, WiFi, laundry, LP gas, restaurant. **REC:** Sacramento River: fishing, marina, playground. Pet restrict(B). Partial handicap access, no tents. 2015 rates: $35 to $45.
AAA Approved
(866)774-2315 Lat: 38.14968, Lon: -121.69175
100 Marina Dr, Rio Vista, CA 94571
deltamarina@comcast.net
www.deltamarina.com

DUCK ISLAND RV PARK & FISHING RESORT
Ratings: 7.5/NA/8 (RV Park) From Jct of SR-12 & SR-160, S 0.8 mi on SR-160 (R). **FAC:** Paved rds. (50 spaces). Avail: 25 gravel, patios, back-ins (24 x 36), accepts full hkup units only, 25 full hkups (30/50 amps), seasonal sites, WiFi $, laundry, LP gas, controlled access. **REC:** Sacramento River: fishing. Pet restrict(B) $. Partial hand-

Subscribe to Trailer Life Magazine. For a subscription, call 800-825-6861.

RIO VISTA (CONT)

DUCK ISLAND RV PARK & FISHING (CONT)
icap access, no tents. Big rig sites, eco-friendly, 2015 rates: $40. Disc: AAA, military.
(916)777-6663 Lat: 38.14411, Lon: -121.68455
16814 Hwy 160, Rio Vista, CA 94571
duckislandrvpark@frontiernet.net
www.duckislandrv.com
See ad opposite page.

RIO VIENTO RV PARK **Ratings: 6/9/8** (RV Park) 2015 rates: $40. (925)382-4193 4460 W. Sherman Island Rd, Rio Vista, CA 94571

SANDY BEACH COUNTY PARK
(Public) From Jct of Hwy 12 & Main St, E 0.4 mi on Main St to 2nd St, S 0.5 mi on 2nd St to Beach Dr, E 0.7 mi (R). **FAC:** Paved rds. 41 paved, 41 pull-thrus (25 x 45), 41 W, 41 E (30 amps), tent sites, dump, fire rings, firewood. **REC:** wading pool, Sacramento River: fishing. Pets OK. Partial handicap access. 14 day max stay, 2015 rates: $18 to $30.
(707)374-2097 Lat: 38.08184, Lon: -121.41273
2333 Beach Drive, Rio Vista, CA 94571
www.solanocounty.com
See ad opposite page.

RIVERSIDE — M5 *Riverside*

RANCHO JURUPA PARK (Public) From Jct of Hwy 60 & Rubidioux (exit 50), S 0.6 mi on Rubidioux to Mission Blvd, E 0.8 mi to Crestmore, S 1 mi (E). Reservations strongly recommended. 2015 rates: $25 to $35. (951)684-7032

ROCKLIN — D3 *Placer*

Travel Services

CAMPING WORLD OF ROCKLIN As the nation's largest retailer of RV supplies, accessories, services and new and used RVs, Camping World is committed to making your total RV experience better. **SERVICES:** Tire, RV appliance, MH mechanical, restrooms. RV supplies, emergency parking, RV accessible. waiting room. Hours: 8am to 6pm.
916-632-1023 Lat: 38.799142, Lon: -121.213046
4435 Granite Drive, Rocklin, CA 95677
www.campingworld.com

ROHNERT PARK — D2 *Sonoma*

WINE COUNTRY RV PARK SONOMA **Ratings: 7/8.5/8.5** (RV Park) 2015 rates: $39 to $49. (707)795-9333 7450 Cristobal Way, Rohnert Park, CA 94928

ROSEVILLE — D3 *Placer*

PLACER COUNTY FAIR (Public) From Jct of I-80 & Hwy 65 (Exit 106), N 2 mi on Hwy 65 to Pleasant Grove Blvd, SE 1.4 mi to Washington Blvd, S 1.5 mi to Corporation Yard Rd., W 0.2 mi (Left through Gate J, follow signs) (R). Closed during month of June. 2015 rates: $30. Jul 1 to May 31. (916)786-2023

To get the most out of your Guide, refer to the Table of Contents in the front of the book.

Travel Services

CAMPING WORLD OF ROSEVILLE/SACRAMENTO As the nation's largest retailer of RV supplies, accessories, services and new and used RVs, Camping World is committed to making your total RV experience better. RV Accessories: (888)496-9710. **SERVICES:** RV, RV appliance, restrooms, RV Sales. RV supplies, emergency parking, RV accessible. Hours: 8am to 5pm.
(888)713-3749 Lat: 38.726719, Lon: -121.28668
1039 Orlando Ave, Roseville, CA 95661
CampingWorldofSacramento.com

SACRAMENTO — D3 *Sacramento*

SACRAMENTO See also Auburn, Lodi, Plymouth, Rio Vista, Vacaville & West Sacramento.

CAL EXPO RV PARK
(Public) From Jct of Capitol City Fwy (Bus 80) & Cal Expo/Exposition Blvd exit, E 1.3 mi on Exposition Blvd to Ethan Way, S 0.4 mi (past Gate 12) onto service rd (continuing straight), S 0.1 mi (R). **FAC:** Paved/gravel rds. (177 spaces). 176 Avail: 94 paved, 82 gravel, patios, 77 pull-thrus (22 x 50), back-ins (21 x 35), accepts full hkup units only, 176 full hkups (30/50 amps), WiFi, laundry. **REC:** American River: fishing. Pets OK. Partial hand-

Park policies vary. Ask about the cancellation policy when making a reservation.

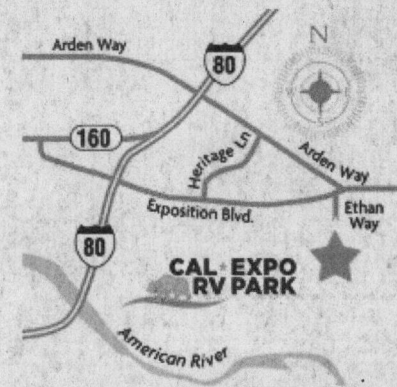

Good Sam Park
See listing Jackson, CA
Play Stay Dine Rancheria Style®
JACKSON RANCHERIA CASINO RESORT
Family Owned & Operated SINCE 1985
JACKSONCASINO.COM • 800-822-WINN
YouTube
Management reserves all rights. Problem Gambling? 1-800-GAMBLER

Stay
AT ONE OF NORTH AMERICA'S
TOP RATED RV PARKS
100 Full hookup spots, 20-30-50 AMP power, Free Cable TV & WiFi, Heated pool & 2 Spas, 24-hour property shuttle , 24-hour surveillance, Pets welcome, Guest BBQ area, Restrooms with showers, Laundry room open 24 hours, Propane available, Horseshoes, Putting green, Table tennis, Bocce ball,
and much more...
JACKSON
RANCHERIA
CASINO RESORT
Family Owned & Operated SINCE 1985
JACKSONCASINO.COM • 800-822-WINN
You Tube
Management reserves all rights. Problem Gambling? 1-800-GAMBLER

SACRAMENTO (CONT)

CAL EXPO RV PARK (CONT)
icap access, no tents. 30 day max stay, 2015 rates: $40.
(916)263-3187 Lat: 38.58672, Lon: -121.422009
1600 Exposition Blvd, Sacramento, CA 95815
rvpark@calexpo.com
www.calexpo.com/attractions/cal-expo-rv-park/
See ad page 211.

SAC-WEST RV PARK AND CAMPGROUND Ratings: 9.5/9.5★/8.5 (RV Park) W-bnd: From W Jct of I-80 & Bus Loop 80, W 0.1 mi on I-80 to W Capital Ave, circle S under fwy on Enterprise Dr to Lake Rd, E 0.1 mi (R): or E-bnd: From Jct of I-80 & W Capital Ave exit, W on exit rd to Enterprise Dr to Lake Rd, E 0.1 mi (R). **FAC:** Gravel rds. (70 spaces). Avail: 50 gravel, patios, 50 pull-thrus (20 x 42), 50 full hkups (30/50 amps), seasonal sites, cable, WiFi, tent sites, rentals, dump, laundry, groc, LP gas, firewood. **REC:** heated pool, pond, fishing, playground. Pets OK. Partial handicap access. Eco-friendly, 2015 rates: $40 to $55.
(916)371-6771 Lat: 38.57312, Lon: -121.57523
3951 Lake Rd, West Sacramento, CA 95691
info@sacwestrvpark.com
www.sacwestrvpark.com
See primary listing at West Sacramento and ad pages 214, 119 (CA Map).

SACRAMENTO SHADE RV PARK (RV Spaces) S-bnd: From Jct of I-80 Business & Fulton Rd, S 0.1 mi on Fulton Rd to Auburn Blvd, SW 1 mi (L); or N-bnd: From Jct of I-80 Business & Marconi Exit, N 0.5 mi on Auburn (frontage rd) (R). **FAC:** Paved rds. (80 spaces). Avail: 10 gravel, patios, back-ins (35 x 40), 10 full hkups (30/50 amps), seasonal sites, cable, WiFi, laundry. **REC:** pool. Pet restrict(B/Q). No tents. 2015 rates: $40.
(916)922-0814 Lat: 38.623616, Lon: -121.41632
2150 Auburn Blvd, Sacramento, CA 95821
sacrv@comcast.net
sacramentoshadervpark.com

Things to See and Do

CAL EXPO HARNESS RACING & SPORTS AND WAGERING CENTER Harness Racing & Sports and Wagering Center. Partial handicap access. Restrooms, food. Hours: 9am to 5pm. ATM.
(877)CALEXPO Lat: 38.35380, Lon: -121.25292
1600 Exposition Blvd, Sacramento, CA 95815
www.calexpo.com
See ad page 211.

CALIFORNIA STATE FAIR State Fair Grounds - Special Events and Concerts. Partial handicap access. Restrooms, food. Adult fee: $7.50 to $25.
(916)263-FAIR Lat: 38.59511, Lon: -121.43444
1600 Exposition Blvd, Sacramento, CA 95852
info@calexpo.com
www.bigfun.org
See ad page 211.

RAGING WATERS Water Park. Restrooms, food. Hours: 11am to 6pm.
(916)924-3747 Lat: 38.59511, Lon: -121.43444
1600 Exposition Blvd, Sacramento, CA 95852
jpinnell@ragingwaters.com
www.ragingwaters.com
See ad page 211.

SAGE — J5 *Riverside*

TUCALOTA SPRINGS RV RESORT & CAMPGROUND **Ratings: 8.5/7.5/7.5** (RV Park) 2015 rates: $45. (951)767-0604 41601 E Benton Rd, Hemet, CA 92544

SALINAS — F2 *Monterey*

LAGUNA SECA RECREATION AREA (Public) From Jct of Hwy 101 & Exit 326B/Monterey Peninsula exit (in Salinas), SW 2.4 mi on S Sanborn Rd (becomes E Blanco Rd) to Hwy 68 (S Main St), S 9.0 mi (R); or From Jct of Hwy 1 & Hwy 68E, E 7 mi on Hwy 68E (L). 16% grade at park. 2015 rates: $30 to $35. (888)588-CAMP

SALINAS/MONTEREY KOA **Ratings: 8.5/7.5/4.5** (RV Park) 2015 rates: $53 to $59. (800)541-0085 8710 Prunedale North Rd, Salinas, CA 93907

SALTON CITY — J5 *Imperial*

SALTON SEA MHP & RV RESORT Ratings: 8.5/7.5/6 (RV Park) From Jct of Hwy 86 & South Marina Dr, E 3 mi on South Marina Dr to Seaview Dr, S 1 mi (R). **FAC:** Paved rds. (307 spaces). Avail: 125 gravel, patios, 110 pull-thrus (20 x 50), back-ins (25 x 38), 125 full hkups (30/50 amps), seasonal sites, WiFi $, tent sites, rentals, laundry. **REC:** heated pool, golf. Pet restrict(B/Q). Partial handicap access. Age restrict may apply, RV age restrict, 2015 rates: $32.
(760)394-4333 Lat: 33.30820, Lon: -115.93010
336 Seaview Drive, Salton City, CA 92275
saltonseamhp@aol.com
www.saltonseamhp.com
See ad this page.

SAN ANDREAS — D3 *Calaveras*

GOLD STRIKE VILLAGE Ratings: 5.5/8.5★/7 (RV Area in MHP) From Jct Hwy 12 & Hwy 49: Go NE 1.5 mi on Hwy 49 to Gold Strike Rd., SE 0.75 mi on Gold Strike Rd (R). **FAC:** Paved/gravel rds. (50 spaces). Avail: 35 gravel, patios, back-ins (22 x 40), 17 full hkups, 18 W, 18 E (30/50 amps), seasonal sites, WiFi Hotspot, dump, laundry, firewood. **REC:** pool, shuffleboard. Pets OK. No tents. 2015 rates: $37. Disc: AAA. No CC.
AAA Approved
(209)754-3180 Lat: 38.22222, Lon: -120.69605
1925 Gold Strike Rd, San Andreas, CA 95249
manager@goldstrikevillage.com
www.goldstrikevillage.com

SAN BERNARDINO — M5 *San Bernardino*

SAN BERNARDINO RV PARK Ratings: 8/9/7 (RV Park) From Jct of I-10 & Tippecanoe/Anderson Exit, N 3.6 mi on Tippecanoe to E 9th St, W 600' (R). **FAC:** Paved rds. (133 spaces). Avail: 33 all weather, patios, 3 pull-thrus (22 x 85), back-ins (20 x 40), 33 full hkups (30/50 amps), seasonal sites, WiFi, rentals, laundry, controlled access. **REC.** Pet restrict(B). Partial handicap access, no tents. RV age restrict, 2015 rates: $35. Disc: AAA.
AAA Approved
(909)381-2276 Lat: 34.11595, Lon: -117.26298
1080 East 9th St, San Bernardino, CA 92410
manager.sbrvpark@gmail.com
www.sanbernardinorvpark.com

Travel Services

CAMPING WORLD OF SAN BERNARDINO As the nation's largest retailer of RV supplies, accessories, services and new and used RVs, Camping World is committed to making your total RV experience better. **SERVICES:** Tire, RV appliance, restrooms. RV supplies, emergency parking, RV accessible. waiting room. Hours: 8am to 6pm.
(909)370-4580 Lat: 34.06035, Lon: -117.28252
151 E Redlands Blvd, San Bernardino, CA 92408
www.campingworld.com

Things to See and Do

SAN BERNARDINO COUNTY REGIONAL PARKS Camp at any of the six scenic parks - from the mountains to the Colorado River. Reserve your spot online.

CAMP IN THE GREAT OUTDOORS
Camp at any of our six scenic parks where you will find lots to do in the great outdoors. We offer a wide variety of programs and events. Reserve online at www.sbcountyparks.com
Partial handicap access. Hours: 9am to 5pm. No CC.
(909)38-PARKS Lat: 34.10130, Lon: -117.27138
www.sbcountyparks.com
See ad page 123 (Welcome Section).

SAN CLEMENTE — J4 *Orange*

SAN CLEMENTE STATE BEACH (State Pk) From town, S 1 mi on I-5 to Avenida Calafia exit (Exit 73), follow signs (L). For reservations call 1-800-444-7275. 2015 rates: $25 to $60. (949)492-3156

SAN ONOFRE SB (SAN MATEO CAMPGROUND) (State Pk) From Jct of I-5 & Christianitos Rd (exit 72), E 1 mi on Christianitos Rd (R). 2015 rates: $25 to $60. (949)492-4872

SAN ONOFRE STATE BEACH (State Pk) From Jct of I-5 & Basilone Rd exit (Exit 71), S 3 mi on Basilone Rd (E). Pit toilets. 2015 rates: $25 to $60. (949)492-4872

We rate what RVers consider important.

SAN DIEGO — K4 *San Diego*

A SPOTLIGHT Introducing San Diego's colorful attractions appearing at the front of this state section.

SAN DIEGO See also Chula Vista, Descanso, El Cajon, Encinitas, Escondido, Imperial Beach, Julian, La Mesa, Lakeside, Oceanside, Ramona, Valley Center & Santee.

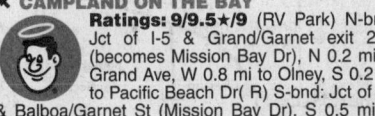

CAMPLAND ON THE BAY

Ratings: 9/9.5★/9 (RV Park) N-bnd: Jct of I-5 & Grand/Garnet exit 23A (becomes Mission Bay Dr), N 0.2 mi to Grand Ave, W 0.8 mi to Olney, S 0.2 mi to Pacific Beach Dr(R) S-bnd: Jct of I-5 & Balboa/Garnet St (Mission Bay Dr), S 0.5 mi to Mission Bay Dr to Grand Ave, follow N-bnd directions (E).

SANDY BEACH ON MISSION BAY

We have our own fabulous beach overlooking Mission Bay! Enjoy our cafe, spas, heated pools, gameroom & market. Year-round activities & entertainment for all ages! New skateboard park! Close to Seaworld & San Diego Zoo.

FAC: Paved rds. 568 paved, 26 pull-thrus (20 x 45), back-ins (18 x 37), some side by side hkups, 405 full hkups, 145 W, 145 E (30 amps), cable, WiFi, tent sites, dump, laundry, groc, LP gas, firewood, controlled access. **REC:** heated pool, whirlpool, Mission Bay: swim, fishing, marina, playground. Pet restrict(B/Q) $. Partial handicap access. Eco-friendly, 2015 rates: $56 to $339.47. Disc: AAA. ATM.
(800)422-9386 Lat: 32.79630, Lon: -117.22390
2211 Pacific Beach Drive, San Diego, CA 92109
reservations@campland.com
www.campland.com
See ad this page, 126, 151 (Spotlight San Diego), 120 (CA Map) See ad back cover & Family Camping, RV Trips of a Lifetime in Magazine Section.

LA PACIFICA RV RESORT

Ratings: 9.5/10★/8 (RV Park) From Jct of I-5 & Dairy Mart Rd (Exit 2), E 0.1 mi on Dairy Mart Rd to San Ysidro Blvd, N 0.1 mi (L).

YOU'LL BE SO WELCOME, STAY AWHILE

Enjoy coastal living or vacationing at La Pacifica RV Park starting at just $595 month or $39 day! Just 10 minutes away from San Diego's clean beaches and close to all of San Diego's many attractions.

FAC: Paved rds. (179 spaces). Avail: 68 paved, patios, 34 pull-thrus (25 x 45), back-ins (25 x 45), some side by side hkups, 68 full hkups (30/50 amps), seasonal sites, cable, WiFi, laundry. **REC:** heated pool, whirlpool. Pet restrict(B/Q). Partial handicap access, no tents. RV age restrict, eco-friendly, 2015 rates: $28 to $38. Disc: AAA, military.
AAA Approved
(619)428-4411 Lat: 32.56095, Lon: -117.06501
1010 W San Ysidro Blvd, San Diego, CA 92173
lapacificarvpark@thomsenproperties.net
www.lapacificarvpark.com
See ad pages 154 (Spotlight San Diego), 126.

MISSION BAY RV RESORT

Ratings: 9/8/8.5 (RV Park) From Jct of I-5 & Clairemont Dr (East Mission Bay Dr/Exit 22), N 0.8 mi on East Mission Bay Dr to De Anza Rd, W 0.1 mi (R).

EXPERIENCE SAN DIEGO, CALIFORNIA

You've already discovered the delights of the RV experience, now its time to enjoy the Mission Bay RV Resort experience! If you see a quiet, clean secure environment with breathtaking location, our resort is for you.

FAC: Paved rds. 260 paved, patios, back-ins (24 x 48), 260 full hkups (30/50 amps), WiFi, laundry, firewood, controlled access. **REC:** Mission Bay: swim, fishing. Pet restrict(B/Q) $. Partial handicap access, no tents. RV age restrict, eco-friendly, 2015 rates: $50 to $95.
(877)219-6900 Lat: 32.79433, Lon: -117.21898
2727 De Anza Road, San Diego, CA 92109
info@missionbayrvresort.com
www.missionbayrvresort.com
See ad pages 152 (Spotlight San Diego), 126 & Family Camping, RV Trips of a Lifetime, Snowbird Destinations in Magazine Section.

SANTA FE PARK & RV RESORT **Ratings: 9/9/7.5** (RV Park) 2015 rates: $61 to $85. (800)959-3787 5707 Santa Fe St, San Diego, CA 92109

County names help you follow the local weather report.

SANTEE LAKES RECREATION PRESERVE

Ratings: 9.5/9.5★/9.5 (Public) From Jct of I-5 (Mission Valley Fwy) & I-15 (Escondido Fwy) N 4.4 mi on I-15 (Escondido Fwy) to Hwy 52, E 5.9mi to Mast Blvd, NE 1.4 mi to Fanita Pkwy, S 0.2 mi (R). **FAC:** Paved rds. 300 Avail: 65 paved, 235 dirt, 111 pull-thrus (26 x 62), back-ins (25 x 60), 300 full hkups (15/50 amps), cable, WiFi, tent sites, rentals, dump, laundry, LP gas, firewood, controlled access. **REC:** heated pool, whirlpool, Santee Lakes: fishing, playground, rec open to public. Pet restrict(Q) $. Partial handicap access. Big rig sites, RV age restrict, 2015 rates: $42 to $52.
(619)596-3141 Lat: 32.84594, Lon: -117.00381
9310 Fanita Parkway, Santee, CA 92071
santeelakes@padre.org
www.santeelakes.com
See primary listing at Santee and ad page 153 (Spotlight San Diego).

Refer to the Table of Contents in front of the Guide to locate everything you need.

SAN DIMAS — M4 *Los Angeles*

EAST SHORE RV PARK

Ratings: 9.5/8.5★/9 (Campground) From Jct of I-10 & Fairplex Dr (exit 44), N 0.5 mi on Fairplex Dr to Via Verde, W 0.6 mi to Camper View Rd, N 0.3 mi (E). **FAC:** Paved rds. (518 spaces). Avail: 138 paved, patios, 15 pull-thrus (33 x 45), back-ins (27 x 50), 138 full hkups (30/50 amps), seasonal sites, cable, WiFi Hotspot, tent sites, dump, laundry, groc, LP gas, fire rings, firewood, controlled access. **REC:** pool, Puddingstone Lake: fishing, playground. Pet restrict $. Partial handicap access. RV age restrict, eco-friendly, 2015 rates: $48 to $58. Disc: AAA. ATM.
AAA Approved
(800)809-3778 Lat: 34.08404, Lon: -117.79150
1440 Camper View Rd, San Dimas, CA 91773
eastshore@linkline.com
www.eastshorervpark.com
See ad pages 192, 126, 121 (CA Map).

RV Park ratings you can rely on!

Got a big rig? Look for listings indicating "big rig sites." These campgrounds are made for you, with 12'-wide roads and 14' overhead clearance. They guarantee that 25% or more of their sites measure 24' wide by 60' long or larger, and have full hookups with 50-amp electricity.

We give you what you want. First, we surveyed thousands of RVers just like you. Then, we developed our exclusive Triple Rating System for campgrounds based on the results. That's why our rating system is so good at explaining the quality of facilities and cleanliness of campgrounds.

SAN FRANCISCO — E2 *San Francisco*

SAN FRANCISCO AREA MAP

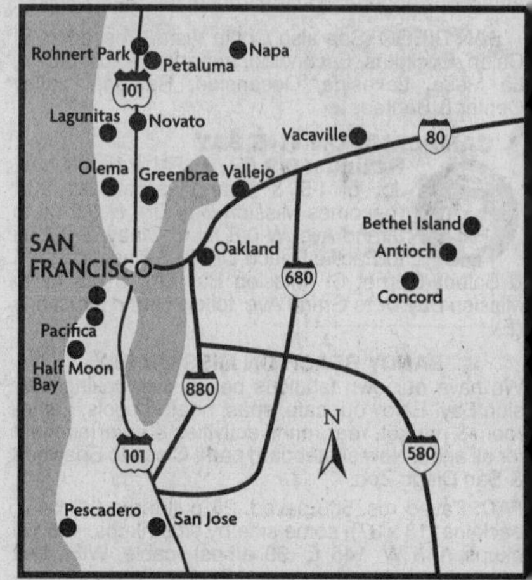

Symbols on map indicate towns within a 50 mile radius of San Francisco where campgrounds are listed. Check listings for more information.

See also Antioch, Bethel Island, Concord, Greenbrae, Half Moon Bay, Lagunitas, Napa, Novato, Oakland, Olema, Pacifica, Pescadero, Petaluma, Rohnert Park, San Jose, Vacaville & Vallejo.

A SPOTLIGHT Introducing San Francisco's colorful attractions appearing at the front of this state section.

↓ CANDLESTICK RV PARK **Ratings: 8/9/6.5** (RV Park) 2015 rates: $84 to $94. (800)888-2267 650 Gilman St, San Francisco, CA 94124

↓ **COYOTE VALLEY RV RESORT**
Ratings: 10/10★/9.5 (RV Resort) From Jct I-280 and Hwy 101: Go 52 miles S on Hwy 101 to Blossom Hill Rd, (exit 378), then 1/2 mile W on Blossom Hill Rd, then 3/4 mile NW on Monterey Rd (R). **FAC:** Paved rds. 127 paved, patios, back-ins (30 x 60), accepts full hkup units only, 127 full hkups (30/50 amps), WiFi, dump, laundry, groc, LP gas. **REC:** heated pool, whirlpool. Pet restrict(B/Q) $. Partial handicap access. Big rig sites, RV age restrict, eco-friendly, 2015 rates: $65 to $80. Disc: AAA.
(866)376-5500 Lat: 37.191388, Lon: -121.713097
9750 Monterey Rd, San Jose, CA 95037
info@coyotevalleyresort.com
www.coyotevalleyresort.com
See primary listing at San Jose and ad page 159 (Spotlight San Francisco).

SAN JACINTO — J5 *Riverside*

↓ REFLECTION LAKE RV PARK & CAMPGROUND **Ratings: 7.5/6.5/6** (Campground) From Jct Hwy 79N & Sanderson Ave, S 4 mi on Sanderson Ave to Cottonwood Ave, W 1.5 mi (L). **FAC:** Paved rds. (119 spaces). Avail: 57 dirt, back-ins (30 x 40), 57 W, 57 E (30 amps), seasonal sites, WiFi, tent sites, showers $, dump, laundry, firewood, controlled access. **REC:** pool, Reflection Lake: fishing, playground, rec open to public. Pet restrict(B) $. RV age restrict, 2015 rates: $29 to $40.
(951)654-7906 Lat: 33.78706, Lon: -117.03283
3440 Cottonwood Ave, San Jacinto, CA 92582
info@reflectionlakerv.com
www.reflectionlakerv.com

SAN JOSE — E2 *Santa Clara*

SAN JOSE See also Gilroy & Morgan Hill.

See listing San Jose, CA

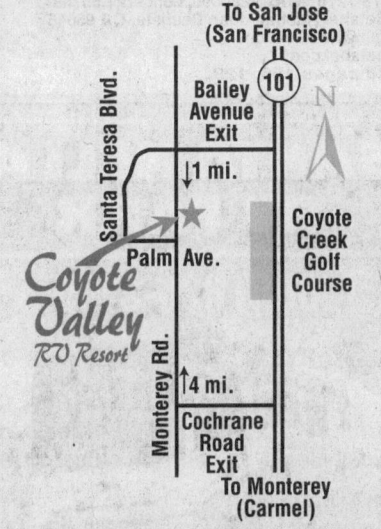

SAN JOSE (CONT)

COYOTE VALLEY RV RESORT

Ratings: 10/10★/9.5 (RV Resort) From Jct of Hwy 101 & Cochrane Rd (Exit 367): Go 3/4 mi W on Cochrane Rd to Monterey Rd, then 4 mi N on Monterey Rd (R).

THE BEST OF BOTH WORLDS

A magnificent valley setting with access to everything in the San Francisco Bay Area. Stay in a 10/10/9.5 rated RV Resort with easy access to the entire Bay Area; including Silicon Valley, Monterey, Carmel & THE City itself.

FAC: Paved rds. 127 paved, patios, back-ins (30 x 60), accepts full hkup units only, 127 full hkups (30/50 amps), WiFi, dump, laundry, groc, LP gas. **REC:** heated pool, whirlpool. Pet restrict(B/Q) $. Partial handicap access, no tents. Big rig sites, RV age restrict, eco-friendly, 2015 rates: $65 to $80. Disc: AAA.
AAA Approved
(866)376-5500 Lat: 37.191388, Lon: -121.713097
9750 Monterey Rd, San Jose, CA 95037
info@coyotevalleyresort.com
www.coyotevalleyresort.com
See ad pages 217, 128, 159 (Spotlight San Francisco).

Things to See and Do

WINCHESTER MYSTERY HOUSE Daily tours-historical, beautiful but bizarre 160 room mansion. RV accessible. Restrooms, food. Hours: 9am to 5pm. Adult fee: $25 to $44. ATM.
(408)247-2000 Lat: 37.31884, Lon: -121.95080
525 S Winchester Blvd, San Jose, CA 95128
info@winchestermysteryhouse.com
www.winchestermysteryhouse.com
See ad page 156 (Spotlight San Francisco).

SAN JUAN BAUTISTA — F2 *San Benito*

BETABEL RV PARK

Ratings: 10/10★/9.5 (RV Park) From Jct of US-101 & Hwy 156: Go 2 mi N on US-101 to Betabel Rd (exit 349), then W across the overpass to Betabel Rd, then 2/10 mi S on Betabel Rd (R).
FAC: Paved rds. (164 spaces). Avail: 25 paved, patios, 19 pull-thrus (24 x 60), back-ins (22 x 50), 25 full hkups (30/50 amps), seasonal sites, WiFi, dump, laundry, groc, LP gas, controlled access. **REC:** heated pool. Pet restrict(B/Q). Partial handicap access, no tents. Big rig sites, RV age restrict, eco-friendly, 2015 rates: $45. Disc: AAA, military.
AAA Approved
(800)278-7275 Lat: 36.90098, Lon: -121.55788
9664 Betabel Rd, San Juan Bautista, CA 95045
manager@betabel.com
www.betabel.com
See ad pages 196, 128.

FREMONT PEAK (State Pk) From jct Hwy 156E & CR G1: Go 11 mi S on CR G1 (San Juan Canyon Rd). Pit toilets. (831)623-4255

MISSION FARM RV PARK INC. **Ratings: 6/7/7.5** (RV Park) 2015 rates: $35. (831)623-4456 400 San Juan-Hollister Rd, San Juan Bautista, CA 95045

SAN JUAN CAPISTRANO — P4 *Orange*

RONALD W. CASPERS WILDERNESS PARK (ORANGE COUNTY PARK) (Public) From jct I-5 (San Diego Fwy) & Hwy 74 (exit 82) (Ortega Hwy): Go 7-1/2 mi E on Hwy 74. 2015 rates: $15 to $21. (949)923-2210

SAN LUIS OBISPO — G2 *San Luis Obispo*

AVILA PISMO BEACH KOA **Ratings: 9/6/8** (Campground) 2015 rates: $56 to $90. (800)562-1244 7075 Ontario Rd, San Luis Obispo, CA 93405

EL CHORRO REGIONAL PARK (Public) From town, N 5 mi on Santa Rosa St/Hwy 1 to Dairy Creek Rd., turn right to entrance (L). Reservation charge & transaction charge ($8/each). 2015 rates: $23 to $38. (805)781-5930

SAN MARCOS — J4 *San Diego*

Travel Services

CAMPING WORLD OF SAN MARCOS As the nation's largest retailer of RV supplies, accessories, services and new and used RVs, Camping World is committed to making your total RV experience better. **SERVICES:** Tire, RV appliance, staffed RV wash, restrooms. RV supplies, LP, RV accessible. waiting room. Hours: 8am to 6pm.
760-471-0645 Lat: 33.138356, Lon: -117.172309
200 Travelers Way, San Marcos, CA 92069
www.campingworld.com

SAN MARTIN — F2 *Santa Clara*

Travel Services

CAMPING WORLD OF SAN MARTIN As the nation's largest retailer of RV supplies, accessories, services and new and used RVs, Camping World is committed to making your total RV experience better. **SERVICES:** Tire, RV appliance, restrooms. RV supplies, emergency parking, RV accessible. waiting room. Hours: 8am to 6pm.
408-683-2807 Lat: 37.092073, Lon: -121.599859
13575 Sycamore Avenue, San Martin, CA 95046
jmartinek@campingworld.com
www.campingworld.com

SAN SIMEON — G2 *Monterey*

SAN SIMEON (State Pk) 5 mi S on Hwy-1. 2015 rates: $35. (805)927-2020

We shine "Spotlights" on interesting cities and areas.

SANTA BARBARA — H3 *Santa Barbara*

CACHUMA RECREATION AREA (Public) From Jct of Hwys 101 & 154, NW 18 mi on Hwy 154 (F Reservable group area. 2015 rates: $23 to $4 (805)686-5055

OCEAN MESA AT EL CAPITAN

Ratings: 9/9/8.5 (RV Resort) From Jct of Hw 101 & El Capitan State Beach Rd (Exit 117 Go: 1/4 mi E on El Capitan State Beach Rd t Calle Real, then 1/2 mi N on Calle Real (R).

CAMPING SANTA BARBARA STYLE

Luxurious RV Resort overlooking El Capitan Stat Beach. Paved RV and Travel Trailer sites with fu hook ups, fire rings and grills. Private tenting sites Swimming Pool and Spa. Free WiFi.

FAC: Paved rds. 80 paved, 32 pull-thrus (33 x 50 back-ins (30 x 45), 80 full hkups (30/50 amps), WiF tent sites, laundry, groc, fire rings, firewood. **REC** heated pool, whirlpool, playground. Pets OK. Partia handicap access. 14 day max stay, eco-friendly, 201 rates: $75 to $95. Disc: AAA, military.
AAA Approved
(866)410-5783 Lat: 34.46557, Lon: -120.02430
100 El Capitan Terrace Lane, Goleta, CA 93117
info@oceanmesa.com
www.oceanmesa.com
See ad page 161 (Spotlight Santa Barbara).

RANCHO OSO **Ratings: 7/7.5/6** (RV Park) 201 rates: $55 to $69. (805)683-5686 3750 Paradise Rc Santa Barbara, CA 93105

SANTA BARBARA SUNRISE RV PARK Ratings: 6/8/5.5 (RV Park) S-bnd: From Jct of US-101 & Hot Springs Rd (Left Lane Exit 94B): Go E and retur to US-101 N-bnd, then 1/4 mi N to Salinas St (Ex 95), then 1/2 block E on Salinas St (L); N-bnd: Fron Jct of US-101 & Salinas St (Exit 95): Go 1/2 block l on Salinas St (L). **FAC:** Paved/gravel rds. 33 grave 4 pull-thrus (20 x 45), back-ins (20 x 45), 33 fu hkups (30/50 amps), WiFi, laundry. Pet restrict(B). N tents. 28 day max stay, eco-friendly, 2015 rates: $6 to $70.
AAA Approved
(805)966-9954 Lat: 34.42213, Lon: -119.66666
516 S Salinas St, Santa Barbara, CA 93103
Santabarbararv@gmail.com
www.santabarbararv.com

SANTA CRUZ — F1 *Santa Cruz*

SANTA CRUZ See also Aromas, Felton, Marina Moss Landing, San Jose, Scotts Valley & Watson ville.

SANTA CRUZ PORT DISTRICT (Public) S-bnd From Jct of Hwy 1 & Soquel Ave, W 0.1 mi (right) o Frontage Rd to Soquel Ave (stay in Left lane), W 0. mi to 7th Ave; N-bnd: From Jct of Hwy 1 & Soquel Av exit, W 0.2 mi on Soquel Ave to 7th Ave, S 1 mi t Brommer Ave, W 0.2 mi (L). 2015 rates: $50 (831)475-3279

SANTA MARGARITA — G2 *San Luis Obispo*

SANTA MARGARITA LAKE (SAN LUIS OBISPC COUNTY PARK) (Public) From town: Go 10 mi SE on Pozo Rd, then E on Santa Margarita Lake Rd. Pi toilets. 2015 rates: $23 to $38. (805)788-2397

SANTA MARGARITA LAKE KOA **Ratings: 7.5/5/7** (Campground) 2015 rates: $50 to $65 (800)562-5619 4765 Santa Margarita Lake Rd, Santa Margarita, CA 93453

SANTA MARIA — H2 *Santa Barbara*

SANTA MARIA PINES RV PARK **Ratings: 5/5.5/5** (RV Park) 2015 rates: $40. (805)928 9534 2210 Preisker Lane, Santa Maria, CA 9345

SANTA NELLA — F2 *Merced*

LOS BANOS WEST I-5 KOA **Ratings: 7.5/9/7.** (Campground) 2015 rates: $32 to $42. (209)826 5542 28485 Gonzaga Rd, Santa Nella, CA 9532

SAN LUIS RESERVOIR SRA/SAN LUIS CREEK (State Pk) From Jct of I-5 & Hwy 152 (Exit 402B), W 7 mi on Hwy 152, follow San Luis Creek signs (E). Pi toilets. 2015 rates: $40 to $45. (209)826-1197

SANTA NELLA RV PARK

Ratings: 8/9★/8.5 (RV Park) From Jct of I-5 & Exit 407 (Santa Nella exit): Go 1/4 mi S on Hwy 33 (R).

OVERNIGHT/LONG TERM STAY

Come stay a day, week or month at our beautifully landscaped park. All sites are pull-thrus/full hookups EZ on EZ off, I-5. Walking distance to restaurants only 1/2 mile to Pea Soup Andersons. Free WiFi cable TV available.

FAC: Paved rds. (56 spaces). Avail: 28 paved, patios 27 pull-thrus (30 x 65), back-ins (30 x 38), 28 ful

SANTA NELLA (CONT)

SANTA NELLA RV PARK (CONT)
hkups (30/50 amps), seasonal sites, WiFi, laundry, LP gas. Pet restrict(B). Partial handicap access, no tents. Big rig sites, eco-friendly, 2015 rates: $30. Disc: AAA, military.
AAA Approved
(888)826-3105 Lat: 37.100661, Lon: -121.016658
13023 State Hwy 33, Santa Nella, CA 95322
santanellarvpark@gmail.com
www.santanellarvpark.com
See ad opposite page, 128.

SANTA PAULA — H3 *Ventura*

KENNEY GROVE PARK (Public) From town, W 2 mi on Hwy 126, E 0.25 mi on Old Telegraph Rd, follow signs (L). 2015 rates: $15 to $20. (805)524-0750

MOUNTAIN VIEW RV PARK
Ratings: 7/NA/8.5 (RV Area in MHP) From Jct of Hwy 126 & Peck Rd (Exit 10): Go 1/4 mi N on Peck Rd to Harvard Blvd, then 1/4 mi E on Harvard Blvd (R). **FAC:** Paved rds. 28 paved, patios, 15 pull-thrus (23 x 61), back-ins (22 x 40), accepts full hkup units only, 28 full hkups (30/50 amps), cable, WiFi. **REC:** whirlpool. Pet restrict(B/Q) $. No tents. Eco-friendly, 2015 rates: $32. Disc: military.
(805)933-1942 Lat: 34.339967, Lon: -119.082433
714 W Harvard Blvd, Santa Paula, CA 93060
mountainview.park@verizon.net
www.rvmtview.com

VENTURA RANCH KOA **Ratings: 7/6/7.5** (RV Park) 2015 rates: $39 to $69. (877)779-8080 7400 Pine Grove Rd, Santa Paula, CA 93060

SANTA ROSA — D2 *Sonoma*

SONOMA COUNTY RV PARK-AT THE FAIRGROUNDS
Ratings: 6.5/8.5★/7 (Public) From Jct of Hwy 101 & CA 12 E, E 0.5 mi on CA 12 E/Bennett Valley, NE 0.6 mi on Bennett Valley to Brookwood, S 0.4 mi to Aston, W 0.1 mi (L) (Note: Closed July 15 to Aug 15 for fair). **FAC:** Gravel rds. 87 gravel, 87 pull-thrus (22 x 70), accepts full hkup units only, 87 full hkups (30/50 amps), WiFi, laundry. Pets OK. No tents. 14 day max stay, 2015 rates: $27 to $35.
(707)293-8410 Lat: 38.42594, Lon: -122.69838
1500 Aston Ave, Santa Rosa, CA 94504
info@sonomacountyfair.com
www.sonomacountyfair.com/rv-park.php
See ad this page.

SPRING LAKE PARK CAMPGROUND (Public) From Jct of SR-101 & SR-12 (Exit 488B), E 3 mi on SR-12 to Hoen Ave, N 2 mi to Newanga Ave (E). For reservations call (707)565-CAMP. 2015 rates: $32. May 1 to Sep 30. (707)539-8092

SUGARLOAF RIDGE (State Pk) From Jct of Hwys 12 & 101, E 7 mi on Hwy 12 to Adobe Canyon Rd, N 3 mi (E). 2015 rates: $35. (707)833-5712

SANTEE — K5 *San Diego*

SANTEE LAKES RECREATION PRESERVE
Ratings: 9.5/9.5★/9.5 (Public) From Jct of Hwy 52 & Mast Blvd, NE 1.4 mi on Mast Blvd to Fanita Pkwy, S 0.2 mi (R).

GREAT FACILITIES AND GREAT LOCATION
Over 190 acres of Parkland! Enjoy the quiet tranquility of the country, and be close enough to visit the many attractions of San Diego County. The perfect location to explore the mountains, deserts, and beaches.

FAC: Paved rds. (300 spaces). 283 Avail: 65 paved, 218 dirt, 111 pull-thrus (26 x 62), back-ins (25 x 60), 283 full hkups (15/50 amps), cable, WiFi, tent sites, rentals, dump, laundry, LP gas, firewood, controlled access. **REC:** heated pool, whirlpool, Santee Lakes: fishing, playground, rec open to public. Pet restrict(Q) $. Partial handicap access. Big rig sites, RV age restrict, 2015 rates: $42 to $52.
(619)596-3141 Lat: 32.84594, Lon: -117.00381
9310 Fanita Parkway, Santee, CA 92071
santeelakes@padre.org
www.santeelakes.com
See ad pages 153 (Spotlight San Diego), 126 & Family Camping, RV Trips of a Lifetime, Snowbird Destinations in Magazine Section.

SCOTTS VALLEY — F1 *Santa Cruz*

SANTA CRUZ RANCH RV RESORT Ratings: 6.5/6.5/7.5 (RV Park) From Jct of Hwy 17 & Scotts Valley/Mt Hermon Rd (Exit 3): Go 1/2 mi NW on Mt Hermon Rd to Scotts Valley Dr, then 3/4 mi NE on Scotts Valley Dr to Disc Dr, then 1/4 mi SE on Disc Dr (L). **FAC:** Paved rds. (97 spaces). Avail: 27 paved, patios, 27 pull-thrus (21 x 45), mostly side by side hkups, 27 full hkups (30 amps), seasonal sites, cable, WiFi, tent sites, laundry, LP gas. **REC.** Pet restrict(B/Q). Partial handicap access. Eco-friendly, 2015 rates: $54 to $78. Disc: military.
AAA Approved
(831)438-1288 Lat: 37.0460, Lon: -122.0149
917 Disc Dr, Scotts Valley, CA 95066
santacruzranch@equitylifestyle.com
www.rvonthego.com

SHASTA LAKE — B2 *Shasta*

SHASTA LAKE See also Lakehead, O'Brien & Redding.

LAKESHORE INN & RV **Ratings: 6/6/5.5** (Campground) 2015 rates: $20 to $37. May 15 to Sep 15. (530)238-2003 20483 Lakeshore Dr, Lakehead, CA 96051

SHAVER LAKE — F3 *Fresno*

CAMP EDISON (Public) From Jct of Hwys 99 & 180, 3.2 mi on Hwy 180 to Hwy 168, E 46.5 mi (R). 2015 rates: $32 to $73. (559)841-3134

SHINGLE SPRINGS — D3 *El Dorado*

PLACERVILLE KOA Ratings: 9/9★/7.5 (Campground) From Jct of US-50 & Exit 39/Shingle Springs Dr, N 100 ft on Shingle Springs Dr to Rock Barn Rd, W 0.5 mi (E). **FAC:** Paved/gravel rds. (77 spaces). Avail: 55 gravel, patios, 44 pull-thrus (24 x 50), back-ins (20 x 38), 26 full hkups, 29 W, 29 E (30/50 amps), seasonal sites, WiFi, tent sites, rentals, dump, laundry, groc, LP gas, firewood. **REC:** pool, whirlpool, pond, fishing, playground. Pet restrict(B). Partial handicap access. Eco-friendly, 2015 rates: $50 to $60. Disc: AAA, military.
AAA Approved
(530)676-2267 Lat: 38.67371, Lon: -120.92344
4655 Rock Barn Rd, Shingle Springs, CA 95682
koa@koa-placerville.com
www.koa-placerville.com

SHINGLETOWN — B2 *Shasta*

MT LASSEN/SHINGLETOWN KOA **Ratings: 9/10★/9** (Campground) 2015 rates: $42 to $64. Apr 1 to Oct 31. (530)474-3133 7749 Koa Rd, Shingletown, CA 96088

SHOSHONE — G5 *Inyo*

SHOSHONE RV PARK
Ratings: 7.5/8★/7.5 (RV Park) From Jct Hwy 178 & Hwy 127: Go 1/2 mi N on Hwy 127 (L). **FAC:** Gravel/dirt rds. (33 spaces). 31 Avail: 24 gravel, 7 grass, 14 pull-thrus (30 x 60), back-ins (25 x 50), some side by side hkups, 31 full hkups (30/50 amps), seasonal sites, WiFi, tent sites, rentals, laundry. **REC:** heated pool, pond. Pets OK. Partial handicap access. Eco-friendly, 2015 rates: $30. Disc: AAA.
AAA Approved
(760)852-4569 Lat: 35.979765, Lon: -116.271374
State Hwy. 127, Shoshone, CA 92384
rvpark@shoshonevillage.com
www.shoshonevillage.com
See ad this page, 128.

Travel Services

CHARLES BROWN GENERAL STORE & GIFT SHOP Vendor of groceries, household and camping supplies, Native American jewelry, gifts, gasoline and propane. **SERVICES:** Restrooms. RV accessible. Hours: 7am to 8:30pm.
(760)852-4123 Lat: 35.974865, Lon: -116.270287
Old State Hwy 127, Shoshone, CA 92384
www.shoshonevillage.com/shoshone-charles-brown-general-store.html
See ad this page.

CROWBAR CAFE & SALOON Western style saloon and full service restaurant with inside and outside dining. **SERVICES:** Restaurant, restrooms. Hours: 8am to 9:30pm.
(760)852-4123 Lat: 35.974718, Lon: -116.270207
Old State Hwy 127, Shoshone, CA 92384
villagecentral@shoshonevillage.com
www.shoshonevillage.com
See ad this page.

SHOSHONE INN Contemporary Seventeen Room Inn with Internet Wireless Access & Telephone. Five rooms offer kitchenettes. **SERVICES:** Restrooms. RV accessible. Hours: 8am to 10pm.
(760)852-4335 Lat: 35.975128, Lon: -116.270332
Old State Hwy 127, Shoshone, CA 92384
inn@shoshonevillage.com
www.shoshonevillage.com/shoshone-inn.html
See ad this page.

Things to See and Do

SHOSHONE MUSEUM Museum preserves and interprets history of local area cultural and natural artifacts. Hours: 8am to 4pm. No CC.
(760)852-4941 Lat: 35.974840, Lon: -116.269914
Old State Hwy 127, Shoshone, CA 92389
See ad this page.

SIMI VALLEY — L1 *Ventura*

OAK PARK (Public) From Jct of Fwy 118 & Collins Dr, exit 19B (W-side of town), W 2 mi on Collins Dr, follow signs (R). 2015 rates: $31. (805)654-3951

SNELLING — E3 *Mariposa*

LAKE MCSWAIN (Public) From Jct of SR-99 & G St (in Merced), NE 20 mi on G St (Snelling Rd) to Hwy 59, (follow signs). 2015 rates: $22 to $34. (209)378-2521

MCCLURE POINT (Public) From Jct of SR-99 & G St (in Merced), NE 20 mi on G St (Snelling Rd) to Hwy 59, E 13 mi (follow signs) (R). 2015 rates: $22 to $32. (209)378-2521

SODA SPRINGS — C3 *Nevada*

CISCO GROVE CAMPGROUND & RV PARK **Ratings: 4.5/7/6** (Campground) 2015 rates: $35 to $41. (530)426-1600 48415 Hampshire Rocks Rd, Soda Springs, CA 95728

SOLVANG — H2 *Santa Barbara*

SOLVANG See also Buellton & Santa Barbara.

SONOMA — D2 *Sonoma*

SONOMA See also Greenbrae, Novato, Petaluma, Rohnert Park, Vacaville & Vallejo.

Keeping pets quiet and on a leash is common courtesy. "Pet Restrictions" which you'll find in some listings refers to limits on size, breed or quantity of pets allowed.

Want to know how we rate? Our campground inspection guidelines are detailed in the front pages of the Guide.

SONORA — E3 *Tuolumne*

SONORA See also Angels Camp, Arnold, Columbia, Groveland, San Andreas & Twain Harte.

MOTHER LODE FAIRGROUNDS - SONORA (Public) From Jct of Hwy 108 (in town) & Hwy 49 (Downtown Sonora Exit), N 1.1 mi on Hwy 49 to Southgate Dr, SE 0.3 mi on Southgate Dr (R). **FAC:** Paved rds. 100 Avail: 20 paved, 80 grass, 20 pull-thrus (15 x 65), back-ins (15 x 60), some side by side hkups, 50 full hkups, 50 W, 50 E (30/50 amps), WiFi, dump. Pets OK. No tents. 14 day max stay, 2015 rates: $30.
(209)532-7428 Lat: 37.97899, Lon: -120.38886
220 Southgate Drive, Sonora, CA 95370
Info@mlfair.com
www.motherlodefair.org
See ad this page.

SOUTH LAKE TAHOE — D4 *El Dorado*

CAMP RICHARDSON RESORT **Ratings: 4/4.5/5** (Campground) 2015 rates: $45. (800)544-1801 1900 Jameson Beach Rd, South Lake Tahoe, CA 96158

CAMPGROUND BY THE LAKE (Public) From Jct of Hwy 50 & Rufus Allen Blvd (in South Lake Tahoe), S 200 yds on Rufus Allen Blvd (E). 2015 rates: $24 to $40. Apr 1 to Oct 31. (530)542-6096

CHRIS HAVEN RV & MH COMMUNITY **Ratings: 6.5/7/5** (Campground) 2015 rates: $40 to $45. (530)541-1895 2030 E St, Space 35, South Lake Tahoe, CA 96150

LAKE TAHOE KOA **Ratings: 6.5/7.5/5** (Campground) 2015 rates: $74 to $108. Apr 1 to Oct 1. (800)562-3477 760 North Hwy 50, South Lake Tahoe, CA 96150

TAHOE VALLEY RV RESORT **Ratings: 8.5/6.5/7.5** (Campground) 2015 rates: $34 to $78. (877)717-8737 1175 Melba Dr, South Lake Tahoe, CA 96150

Things change ... last year's rates serve as a guideline only.

STANDISH — B3 *Lassen*

DAYS END RV PARK
Ratings: 7/9.5★/9 (RV Park) From Jct of US-395 & CR-A3 (in Standish), W 150 ft on CR-A3 (R). Elev 4100 ft. **FAC:** Gravel rds. 27 gravel, 10 pull-thrus (23 x 75), back-ins (27 x 60), accepts full hkup units only, 27 full hkups (30/50 amps), WiFi, laundry. Pets OK. Partial handicap access, no tents. Big rig sites, 2015 rates: $33. Disc: AAA, military. AAA Approved
(530)254-1094 Lat: 40.36568, Lon: -120.42320
718-755 Hwy 395, Standish, CA 96128
daysendrv@hotmail.com
www.daysendrv.com
See ad this page, 128.

STOCKTON — E3 *San Joaquin*

RIVER POINT LANDING MARINA-RESORT **Ratings: 8/9.5★/9.5** (RV Park) 2015 rates: $38 to $60. (209)951-4144 4950 Buckley Cove Way, Stockton, CA 95219

STONYFORD — C2 *Colusa*

MENDOCINO NF (LETTS LAKE CAMPGROUND) (Natl Forest) From town: Go 9 mi W on CR-18N01, then 6 mi SW on FR-18NO1, then 3 mi SE on FR-17N02. Pit toilets. 2015 rates: $12. May 1 to Oct 31. (530)963-3128

STOVEPIPE WELLS VILLAGE — F4 *Inyo*

DEATH VALLEY NATL PK/STOVEPIPE WELLS VILLAGE (Natl Pk) From Furnace Creek, NW 25 mi on Hwy 190 (R). Entrance fee required. 2015 rates: $10. Oct 1 to Apr 30. (760)786-2331

SUSANVILLE — B3 *Lassen*

EAGLE LAKE RV PARK **Ratings: 8/8.5★/7.5** (RV Park) 2015 rates: $36.50 to $38.50. May 15 to Nov 15. (530)825-3133 687-125 Palmetto Way, Susanville, CA 96130

EAGLE LAKE RV RESORT **Ratings: 6.5/8/8** (RV Park) 2015 rates: $30 to $36. May 31 to Nov 1. (530)251-6770 509-725 Stones Rd, Susanville, CA 96130

NORTH EAGLE LAKE BLM (Public) From town, 29 mi on SR-139 to CR-A1, W 1 mi (R). Pit toilets. 2015 rates: $8 to $11. May 15 to Nov 5. (530)257-0456

SUSANVILLE RV PARK
Ratings: 9/9.5★/9 (RV Park) E-bnd: From Jct of SR-36 & SR-139, SE 1.1 mi on SR-36 to E Riverside Dr, NE (left turn) 0.1 mi to Johnstonville Rd (1st left turn), NW 0.1 mi (R); or W-bnd: From Jct of SR-36 & US-395, NW 2.9 mi on SR-36 to E Riverside Dr, NE (right turn) 0.1 mi to Johnstonville Rd (1st left turn), NW 0.1 mi (R). Elev 4200 ft. **FAC:** Paved rds. (101 spaces). Avail: 71 paved, patios, 60 pull-thrus (25 x 60), back-ins (25 x 60), accepts full hkup units only, 71 full hkups (30/50 amps), seasonal sites, cable, WiFi, dump, laundry, LP gas. **REC.** Pet restrict(B). Partial handicap access, no tents. Big rig sites, 2015 rates: $43.15. Disc: AAA, military. AAA Approved
(877)686-7878 Lat: 40.408025, Lon: -120.631723
3075 Johnstonville Rd, Susanville, CA 96130
guestservices@susanvillervpark.com
www.susanvillervpark.com
See ad this page.

TAHOE CITY — D4 *Placer*

SUGAR PINE POINT/GENERAL CREEK (State Pk) From Tahoma, S 1 mi on Hwy 89 (R). 2015 rates $25 to $35. (800)444-7275

TAHOE SRA (State Pk) From town, NE 0.25 mi on Hwy 28 (R). 2015 rates: $35. (530)583-3074

TECOPA — G5 *Inyo*

TECOPA HOT SPRINGS (Public) From Shosone S 5 mi on SR-127, follow signs to campground; or From Jct of I-15 & Hwy 127 (at Baker), N 52 mi on Hwy 127, follow signs to campground. 2015 rates $10. (760)852-4377

TEHACHAPI — G4 *Kern*

MOUNTAIN VALLEY RV PARK **Ratings: 4/7.5/6.5** (Campground) 2015 rates: $30 (661)822-1213 16334 Harris Rd, Tehachapi, CA 93581

TEHACHAPI MTN PARK (Public) From town, S 3 mi on Tucker Rd to Highline Rd, SW 1 mi to Water Canyon Rd, S 3 mi (E). 2015 rates: $18. (661)822-4632

TEMECULA — P6 *Riverside*

PECHANGA RV RESORT
Ratings: 10/10★/10 (RV Resort) From Jct of I-15 & Hwy 79S/Temecula Pkwy), E 0.8 mi on Hwy 79S/Temecula Pkwy) to Pechanga Pkwy, SE 2.1 mi to Pechanga Resort Dr, S 0.25 mi (L).

MINUTES FROM WINE COUNTRY AND GOLF! Nestled in the picturesque hills of Temecula Wine Country, the award-winning Pechanga RV Resort offers guests endless opportunities for excitement, relaxation and fun! Wine tasting, casino, golf, Historic Old Town and more!

FAC: Paved rds. 168 paved, patios, 25 pull-thrus (28 x 55), back-ins (28 x 55), 168 full hkups (30/50 amps), cable, WiFi, dump, laundry, groc, LP gas, restaurant. **REC:** heated pool, whirlpool, golf, rec open to public. Pet restrict(Q) $. Partial handicap access, no tents. RV age restrict, 29 day max stay.

We salute you! Our Military Listings indicate campgrounds for use exclusively by active and retired military personnel.

TEMECULA (CONT)

PECHANGA RV RESORT (CONT)
eco-friendly, 2015 rates: $50 to $105. Disc: AAA. ATM.
AAA Approved
(951)770-2656 Lat: 33.45264, Lon: -117.10373
45000 Pechanga Hwy, Temecula, CA 92592
www.pechangarv.com
See ad pages 163 (Spotlight Temecula), 126 & Snowbird Destinations in Magazine Section.

VAIL LAKE RV RESORT **Ratings: 7.5/7/8.5** (Campground) 2015 rates: $45 to $110. (951)303-0173 38000 Hwy 79 S, Temecula, CA 92592

Your neighbor just told you about a great little campground in Kentucky — what was the name of it again? The "Find-it-Fast" index in the back of the Guide can help. It's an alphabetical listing, by state, of every private and public park in the Guide.

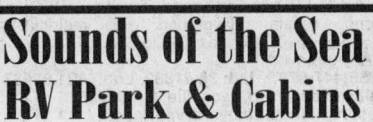

Things to See and Do

PECHANGA CASINO RESORT Use Pechanga Resort and Casino as a base from which to explore the area's wineries. Casino with 15 delectable dining options and 514 luxury suites. Shuttle service from casino to the RV park. Partial handicap access. RV accessible. Restrooms, food. ATM.
(888)732-4264 Lat: 33.45264, Lon: -117.10373
45000 Pechanga Pkwy, Temecula, CA 92589
info@pechanga.com
www.pechanga.com
See ad page 163 (Spotlight Temecula).

THREE RIVERS — F3 *Tulare*

KAWEAH PARK RESORT **Ratings: 8.5/8/8.5** (Campground) 2015 rates: $50 to $55. (559)561-4424 40457 Sierra Dr, Three Rivers, CA 93271

SEQUOIA RV RANCH
Ratings: 8/7.5/8.5 (RV Park) From Jct Hwy 65 & Hwy 198: Go 20-1/4 mi E on Hwy 198, then 2-1/4 mi N on North Fork Dr (R). **FAC:** Paved/gravel rds. 48 gravel, 27 pull-thrus (22 x 60), back-ins (20 x 40), 34 full hkups, 14 W, 14 E (30/50 amps), WiFi, tent sites, rentals, showers $, dump, mobile sewer, laundry, fire rings, firewood. **REC:** North Fork Kaweah River: swim, fishing. Pets OK $. 14 day max stay, eco-friendly, 2015 rates: $38 to $60.
(559)561-4333 Lat: 36.465807, Lon: -118.916287
43490 North Fork Dr, Three Rivers, CA 93271
sequoiarvranch@gmail.com
www.sequoiarvranch.com
See ad this page.

SEQUOIA/LODGEPOLE (Natl Pk) From town, E 18 mi on CA-198 (Gen Hwy) (R); or From Giant Forest Vlg, N 5 mi on CA-198 (R). For reservations call 1-800-365-CAMP. 2015 rates: $22. May 20 to Sep 29. (559)565-3774

SEQUOIA/POTWISHA (Natl Pk) From town, NE 9 mi on SR-198 (E). 2015 rates: $22. (559)565-3134

THREE RIVERS HIDEAWAY Ratings: 5.5/8.5/7 (RV Park) From Jct Hwy 65 & Hwy 198: Go 21-1/2 mi E on Hwy 198 (L). **FAC:** Paved/gravel rds. (20 spaces). Avail: 12 dirt, back-ins (18 x 50), 9 full hkups, 3 W, 3 E (30/50 amps), seasonal sites, WiFi, tent sites, rentals, dump, laundry, fire rings, firewood. **REC:** Kaweah River: swim, fishing. Pets OK. Partial handicap access. 28 day max stay, eco-friendly, 2015 rates: $34 to $44. Disc: military.
AAA Approved
(559)561-4413 Lat: 36.458223, Lon: -118.881101
43365 Sierra Dr, Three Rivers, CA 93271
info@threerivershideaway.com
www.threerivershideaway.com

TIONESTA — A3 *Modoc*

EAGLES NEST RV PARK **Ratings: 3.5/8★/6** (Campground) 2015 rates: $24. Apr 1 to Nov 15. (530)664-2081 634 CR 97A, Tionesta, CA 96134

HAWKS NEST RV & CABINS **Ratings: 7/8.5★/8** (RV Park) 2015 rates: $27. (530)664-3187 200 CR 97A, Tulelake, CA 96134

TRABUCO CANYON — O4 *Orange*

O'NEILL REGIONAL PARK (ORANGE COUNTY PARK) (Public) From jct I-5 & El Toro Rd (exit 91) (CR S18): Go 7 mi NE on El Toro Rd, then 3 mi S on Live Oak Canyon Rd (CR S19). 2015 rates: $20. (949)923-2260

TRACY — E3 *San Joaquin*

CARNEGIE STATE VEHICULAR RECREATION AREA (State Pk) From town: Go 10 mi W on Tesla/Corral Hollow Rd. 2015 rates: $10. (925)447-9027

MOREHEAD PARK Ratings: 5/7.5/7.5 (RV Park) From Jct I-205 & I-5: Go 2-1/2 mi S on I-5, then 1/2 mi W on Kasson Rd, then 3 mi SW on W 11th St (Bus I-205), then 200 yds S on S Chrisman Rd. **FAC:** Paved/gravel rds. (110 spaces). Avail: 10 grass, back-ins (20 x 40), accepts full hkup units only, 10 full hkups (30/50 amps), seasonal sites, WiFi Hotspot, laundry. Pets OK. No tents. 2015 rates: $37.50. Disc: AAA, military.
AAA Approved
(209)835-1455 Lat: 37.73787, Lon: -121.39860
24221 S Chrisman Rd, Tracy, CA 95304
morepark@sbcglobal.net
www.moreheadpark.com

TRINIDAD — B1 *Humboldt*

EMERALD FOREST OF TRINIDAD
Ratings: 7/8/8.5 (Campground) N-bnd: From Jct of US-101 & Exit 728 (Trinidad), W 100 ft to Patricks Point Dr, N 0.7 mi (R); or S-bnd: From Jct of US-101 & Seawood Dr exit (apx 2.5 mi N of Trinidad), exit W 0.2 mi to Patricks Pt Dr, S 1.9 (L). **FAC:** Gravel rds. 47 Avail: 13 gravel, 34 dirt, 13 pull-thrus (18 x 40), back-ins (18 x 35), 36 full hkups, 11 W, 11 E (20/30 amps), cable, WiFi, tent sites, rentals, dump, laundry, groc, LP gas, fire rings, firewood. **REC:** playground. Pet restrict(B). Partial handicap access. 2015 rates: $25 to $45.
(707)677-3554 Lat: 41.07241, Lon: -124.14410
753 Patricks Point Dr, Trinidad, CA 95570
vacation@emeraldforest.ws
www.rvintheredwoods.com
See ad this page, 128.

PATRICKS POINT (State Pk) From town, N 5 mi on Hwy 101 (L). For reservations call 1-800-444-7275. 2015 rates: $35 to $45. (707)677-3570

SOUNDS OF THE SEA RV PARK & SPA
Ratings: 8/9★/10 (RV Park) From Jct of US-101 & Patricks Point State Park Exit/Exit 734, (5 mi N of town), S 1.2 mi on Patricks Point Dr (L). **FAC:** Paved/gravel rds. 52 Avail: 50 gravel, 2 grass, 10 pull-thrus (40 x 110), back-ins (40 x 80), 52 full hkups (30/50 amps), cable, WiFi, rentals, laundry, groc, LP gas, firewood. **REC:** Pacific Ocean. Pet restrict(B). No tents. Big rig sites, eco-friendly, 2015 rates: $35 to $50. Disc: AAA, military. Jan 1 to Oct 31.
AAA Approved
(707)677-3271 Lat: 41.12326, Lon: -124.15578
3443 Patrick's Point Deive, Trinidad, CA 95570
reservations@soundsofthesea.us
www.soundsofthesea.us
See ad this page, 128.

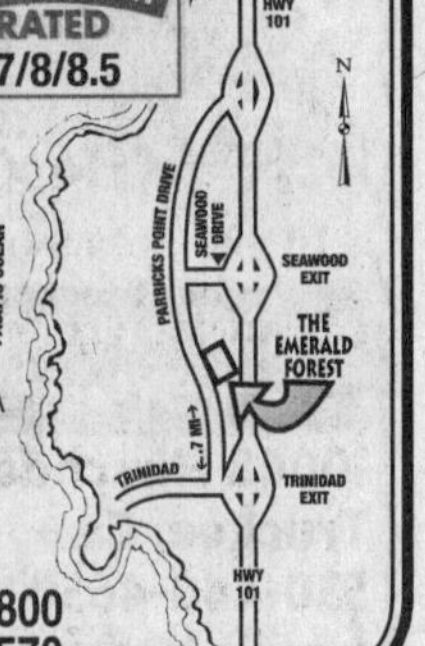

TRINITY CENTER — B2 *Trinity*

TRINITY LAKE KOA **Ratings: 8.5/8.5★/8** (Campground) 2015 rates: $43 to $56. May 1 to Oct 15. (800)562-7706 60260 State Hwy 3, Trinity Center, CA 96091

TRINITY LAKE RESORTS AT PINEWOOD COVE **Ratings: 7/6.5/7** (Campground) 2015 rates: $36 to $46. Apr 15 to Oct 31. (530)286-2201 45110 State Hwy 3, Trinity Center, CA 96091

TRUCKEE — C4 *Nevada, Placer*

COACHLAND RV PARK

Ratings: 9/9.5★/8.5 (RV Park) E-bnd: From E Jct of I-80 & SR-89N (Exit 188A), N 0.1 mi on SR-89N to Pioneer Trail, W 0.1 mi on Pioneer Trail (R); or W-bnd: From Jct of I-80 & Truckee/Sierraville/SR 89 (exit 188), N 0.2 mi on SR 89 to Pioneer Trail, W 0.1 mi on Pioneer Trail (R). Elev 5900 ft. **FAC:** Paved rds. (130 spaces). Avail: 80 paved, 80 pull-thrus (24 x 62), mostly side by side hkups, accepts full hkup units only, 80 full hkups (30/50 amps), seasonal sites, cable, WiFi, dump, laundry, LP gas. **REC:** Seasonal creek: playground. Pets OK. No tents. Big rig sites, eco-friendly, 2015 rates: $39 to $54. Disc: AAA, military.
AAA Approved
(530)587-3071 Lat: 39.33897, Lon: -120.17439
10100 Pioneer Trail #35, Truckee, CA 96161
coachlandrvpark@yahoo.com
www.coachlandrvpark.com
See ad this page, 128.

DONNER MEMORIAL (State Pk) From Jct of Donner Pass Rd (Exit 184) & Hwy 80, W 0.1 mi on Donner Pass Rd (L) Park is closed until August. 2015 rates: $35. (530)582-7892

MARTIS CREEK LAKE/ALPINE MEADOWS CAMPGROUND (Public Corps) I-80 (exit 188B): Go 4 mi S on Hwy 267. Pit toilets. 2015 rates: $18. Apr 25 to Oct 15. (530)587-8113

TRUCKEE RIVER RV PARK

Ratings: 7/9.5★/8.5 (Campground) From jct of I-80 & SR 89 N: Go 6 mi E on I-80 to (Exit 194) Hirschdale Rd, then S .1 mi (R). Elev 5500 ft. **FAC:** Paved rds. 50 paved, patios, back-ins (25 x 45), 50 full hkups (30/50 amps), WiFi, dump, laundry, groc, LP gas, firewood. **REC:** playground. Pets OK. Partial handicap access, no tents. Big rig sites, eco-friendly, 2015 rates: $40. ATM.
(530)448-4650 Lat: 39.38203, Lon: -120.08061
10068 Hirschdale Rd, Truckee, CA 96161
truckeeriverrv@gmail.com
www.truckeeriverrv.com
See ad this page, 128.

TULARE — F3 *Tulare*

SUN & FUN RV PARK

Ratings: 9.5/9/6 (RV Park) From Jct of Hwy 99 & Ave 200 (Exit 83): Go 1/4 mi W on Ave 200 (R). **FAC:** Paved rds. (69 spaces). Avail: 10 paved, patios, 3 pull-thrus (20 x 50), back-ins (20 x 40), some side by side hkups, 10 full hkups (30/50 amps), seasonal sites, cable, WiFi, dump, laundry. **REC:** pool, whirlpool, playground. Pet restrict(B/Q). Partial handicap access, no tents. Eco-friendly, 2015 rates: $37. Disc: AAA, military. No CC.
(559)686-5779 Lat: 36.152991, Lon: -119.334194
1000 E Rankin Ave, Tulare, CA 93274
sun-fun@westernm.com
www.westernm.com
See ad page 183.

Say you saw it in our Guide!

TULELAKE — A3 *Siskiyou*

LAVA BEDS NATL MON/INDIAN WELL CAMPGROUND (Natl Pk) From Tulelake, S 4 mi on Hwy 139, to CR-111, S 4.5 mi on CR-111 to Lava Beds Rd (park entrance), W 18 mi (E) Entrance fee required. 2015 rates: $10. (530)667-2282

TULELAKE-BUTTE VALLEY FAIR RV PARK (Public) From Jct of Hwy 139 & Main St (in Tulelake) S 0.5 mi on Main St, W 0.2 mi on G St (L). 2015 rates: $60 to $125. (530)667-5312

TWAIN HARTE — E3 *Tuolumne*

SUGAR PINE RV PARK & RESORT **Ratings: 7/6/6.5** (Campground) 2015 rates: $42. (209)586-4631 23699 Hwy 108, Twain Harte, CA 95832

TWENTYNINE PALMS — H5 *San Bernardino*

TWENTYNINE PALMS RESORT: RV PARK-COTTAGES-GOLF

Ratings: 9.5/9.5★/8.5 (RV Park) From Jct of Hwy 62 (Twenty Nine Palms Hwy) & Adobe Rd (in town), N 2 mi on Adobe Rd to Amboy Rd, E 0.5 mi to Desert Knoll Ave, N 100 ft (R). **FAC:** Paved rds. (195 spaces). Avail: 150 all weather, 31 pull-thrus (27 x 52), back-ins (28 x 48), 150 full hkups (30/50 amps), seasonal sites, WiFi, tent sites, rentals, laundry, groc, LP gas, firewood. **REC:** heated pool, whirlpool, shuffleboard. Pets OK. Partial handicap access. RV age restrict, eco-friendly, 2015 rates: $38 to $40. Disc: AAA, military.
AAA Approved
(800)874-4548 Lat: 34.16555, Lon: -116.04531
4949 Desert Knoll Ave, Twentynine Palms, CA 92277
info@29palmsresort.com
www.29palmsresort.com
See ad pages 150 (Spotlight Palm Springs), 126 & Snowbird Destinations in Magazine Section.

UKIAH — C1 *Mendocino*

LAKE MENDOCINO (COE) (Public Corps) From jct Hwy 101 & Hwy 20E (exit 555B): Go 2 mi E on Hwy 20. 2015 rates: $8 to $20. (707)462-7581

REDWOOD EMPIRE FAIR RV PARK (Public) From jct Hwy 253 & US 101: Go 4-1/2 mi N on US 101 (N State St Exit), then S on N State St, 0.5 mi. 2015 rates: $25 to $30. (707)462-3884

UPPER LAKE — C2 *Lake*

KELLY'S KAMP **Ratings: 4/7/7.5** (Campground) 2015 rates: $31 to $35. Apr 1 to Oct 31. (707)263-5754 8220 Scotts Valley Rd, Upper Lake, CA 95485

PINE ACRES BLUE LAKE RESORT **Ratings: 6.5/7★/7.5** (Campground) 2015 rates: $33 to $42. (707)275-2811 5328 Blue Lake Road, Upper Lake, CA 95485

Our rating system isn't just tough, it's thorough. We know the kinds of things that are important to you — like clean restrooms and showers, attractive, secure, well-tended grounds, and extras like swimming pools. We give the first rating for development of facilities, the second for cleanliness and physical characteristics of restrooms and showers, and the third for visual appearance.

Like Us on Facebook.

VACAVILLE — D2 *Solano*

MIDWAY RV PARK

Ratings: 8/9★/9 (RV Park) From Jct of I-80 & I-505, N 2.5 mi on I-505 to Midway Rd, E 0.2 mi (L). **FAC:** Paved rds. (64 spaces). Avail: 34 gravel, 34 pull-thrus (23 x 55), accepts full hkup units only, 34 full hkups (30/50 amps), seasonal sites, cable, WiFi, laundry. **REC:** pool, playground. Pet restrict(B). No tents. Eco-friendly, 2015 rates: $48.
(707)446-7679 Lat: 38.41900, Lon: -121.93970
4933 Midway Rd, Vacaville, CA 95688
frank@midwayrvpark.com
midwayrvpark.com
See ad pages 197, 128, 159 (Spotlight San Francisco).

VINEYARD RV PARK

Ratings: 9.5/10★/10 (RV Park) From Jct of I-80 & I-505, N 3.3 mi to Midway Rd, E 0.4 mi (L) or From Jct of I-80 & Midway Rd exit, W 0.1 mi to Midway Rd, W 3 mi (R). **FAC:** Paved rds. (160 spaces). Avail: 130 gravel, patios, 47 pull-thrus (25 x 64), back-ins (25 x 45), 130 full hkups (30/50 amps), seasonal sites, cable, WiFi, tent sites, dump, laundry, LP gas, fire rings, firewood. **REC:** pool, pond, fishing, playground. Pet restrict(B) $. Eco-friendly, 2015 rates: $56 to $58.
AAA Approved
(866)447-8797 Lat: 38.41832, Lon: -121.93687
4985 Midway Rd, Vacaville, CA 95688
reservations@vineyardrvpark.com
www.vineyardrvpark.com
See ad pages 199, 128.

Travel Services

CAMPING WORLD OF VACAVILLE As the nation's largest retailer of RV supplies, accessories, services and new and used RVs, Camping World is committed to making your total RV experience better. RV Accessories: (800)448-1253. **SERVICES:** Tire, RV appliance, MH mechanical, staffed RV wash, restrooms, RV Sales. RV supplies, emergency parking, RV accessible. waiting room. Hours: 8am to 6pm.
(888)691-4581 Lat: 38.390669, Lon: -121.932118
5065 Quinn Road, Vacaville, CA 95688
cyoung@campingworld.com
CampingWorldofVacaville.com

VALENCIA — H3 *Los Angeles*

VALENCIA TRAVEL VILLAGE

Ratings: 9/9/8 (Campground) From Jct of I-5 & Hwy 126 W (Exit 172): Go 1 mi W on Hwy 126 (L).

CLOSEST RV RESORT TO MAGIC MOUNTAIN
Convenient access from I-5. Minutes to Disneyland, Universal Studios, Hollywood, Beaches and Lakes. Excitement, fun, theatrics, surfing and fishing. Or just sit and relax. Quiet country setting. Groups & clubs welcome.

FAC: Paved rds. (379 spaces). Avail: 64 gravel, 64 pull-thrus (24 x 60), 64 full hkups (30/50 amps), seasonal sites, cable, WiFi, dump, mobile sewer, laundry, groc, LP gas, fire rings, firewood. **REC:** heated pool, wading pool, whirlpool, shuffleboard, playground. Pet restrict(B/Q). Partial handicap access, no tents. Big rig sites, eco-friendly, 2015 rates: $50. Disc: AAA, military. ATM.
AAA Approved
(661)257-3333 Lat: 34.454555, Lon: -118.507655
27946 Henry Mayo Dr (Hwy 126), Castaic, CA 91384
reservations@valenciatravelvillagellc.com
www.valenciatravelvillagellc.com
See ad pages 140 (Spotlight Los Angeles), 128.

A campground rating is based on ALL facilities available at the park.

VALLEJO — E2 *Solano*

SOLANO COUNTY FAIRGROUNDS RV PARK (Public) From I-80, go W on 37 to Fairgrounds Dr, turn L at ramp, 2nd light. Or from I-80 go E on 37 (R) at ramp, next light, turn L at main entrance. 2015 rates: $30. Apr 1 to Oct 31. (707)551-2007

TRADEWINDS RV PARK OF VALLEJO
Ratings: 8/9★/7.5 (RV Park) W-bnd (to San Fran): From Jct of I-780 & I-80, W 0.25 mi on I-80 to Magazine St exit, sharp rt immediately after exit for 600 ft on Lincoln Rd/W service rd (L). See our San Francisco ad for E-bnd/I-80 directions (L). **FAC:** Paved rds. (78 spaces). Avail: 28 gravel, patios, 13 pull-thrus (19 x 52), back-ins (22 x 35), accepts full hkup units only, 28 full hkups (30/50 amps), seasonal sites, cable, WiFi $, laundry. **REC:** playground. Pet restrict(B). Partial handicap access, no tents. 2015 rates: $39 to $42. Disc: AAA, military.
AAA Approved
(707)643-4000 Lat: 38.08628, Lon: -122.23321
239 Lincoln Rd West, Vallejo, CA 94590
tradewindsrv@sbcglobal.net
www.tradewindsrvpark.net
See ad pages 157 (Spotlight San Francisco), 128.

VALLEJO MH COMMUNITY & RV PARK
Ratings: 6.5/8★/6 (RV Area in MHP) From Jct of I-80 & SR-37, W 1 mi on SR-37 to SR-29 (Napa/Sonoma Blvd Exit), S 0.1 mi on SR-29 to Lewis Brown, E 0.2 mi to Broadway St, S 0.4 mi (R). **FAC:** Paved rds. (203 spaces). 30 Avail: 15 paved, 15 gravel, patios, 10 pull-thrus (24 x 45), back-ins (26 x 38), accepts full hkup units only, 30 full hkups (30/50 amps), seasonal sites, WiFi $, laundry. Pet restrict No tents. 2015 rates: $40.
(707)310-8480 Lat: 38.13380, Lon: -122.25258
1867 Broadway St, Vallejo, CA 94589
manager@vallejorvpark.com
www.vallejorvpark.com
See ad pages 216, 128.

VALLEY CENTER — J5 *San Diego*

WOODS VALLEY KAMPGROUND & RV PARK, LLC **Ratings: 6.5/6.5/7.5** (Campground) 2015 rates: $33 to $45. (760)749-2905 15236 Woods Valley Rd, Valley Center, CA 92082

VALLEY SPRINGS — D3 *Calaveras*

ACORN WEST (COE-NEW HOGAN LAKE) (Public Corps) From jct Hwy 12 & Hwy 26: Go 1 mi S on Hwy 26, then 2-1/2 mi E on Hogan Dam Rd. 2015 rates: $16 to $20. (209)772-1343

LAKE CAMANCHE SOUTH **Ratings: 6.5/NA/8** (RV Park) 2015 rates: $47.50 to $52.50. (866)763-5121 11700 Wade Lane, Valley Springs, CA 95252

NEW HOGAN LAKE (Public Corps) From S end of town, S 0.75 mi on Hwy 26 to Hogan Dam Rd, E 0.75 mi (R). For reservations call 1(877)444-6777. 2015 rates: $14 to $20. (209)772-1343

OAK KNOLL CAMPGROUND (COE - NEW HOGAN LAKE) (Public Corps) From jct Hwy 12 & Hwy 26: Go 1 mi S on Hwy 26, then 2-1/2 mi E on Hogan Dam Rd. 2015 rates: $14. Apr 1 to Sep 30. (209)772-1343

VAN NUYS — L1 *Los Angeles*

BALBOA RV PARK
Ratings: 8/10★/7 (RV Park) From Jct of US-101 & Balboa Blvd (Exit 21), N 2.8 mi on Balboa Blvd (R); or From Jct of I-405 & Roscoe Blvd (Exit 68), W 1.7 mi on Roscoe Blvd to Balboa Blvd, S 0.7 mi (L). **FAC:** Paved rds. (192 spaces). Avail: 130 all weather, patios, 6 pull-thrus (26 x 60), back-ins (18 x 32), some side by side hkups, 130 full hkups (30/50 amps), seasonal sites, cable, WiFi, laundry. **REC.** Pet restrict(B). Partial handicap access, no tents. RV age restrict, eco-friendly, 2015 rates: $65.
(818)785-0949 Lat: 34.21121, Lon: -118.49930
7740 Balboa Blvd, Van Nuys, CA 91406
info@balboarvpark.com
www.balboarvpark.com
See ad pages 139 (Spotlight Los Angeles), 126.

VENTURA — H3 *Ventura*

EMMA WOOD BEACH NORTH (State Pk) From US-101 exit State Beaches (Exit 72), N 0.25 mi on Old US-1/Pacific Coast Hwy (L). 2015 rates: $30. (805)968-1033

FARIA BEACH PARK (Public) From Jct of US-101 & State Beaches exit (Exit 72), N 6 mi on Old US-1/Pacific Coast Hwy (L). 2015 rates: $32 to $53. (805)654-3951

FOSTER PARK (Public) From Jct of Hwy 33 & Casitas Vista Rd, W 0.4 mi on Casitas Vista Rd (R). 2015 rates: $20 to $34. (805)654-3951

HOBSON BEACH PARK (Public) From Jct of US-101 & State Beaches, exit 72 (Pacific Coast Hwy), N 7 mi on Old US-101/Pacific Coast Hwy (L). 2015 rates: $32 to $48. (805)654-3951

LAKE CASITAS RECREATION AREA (Public) From jct Hwy 101 & Hwy 33: Go 11 mi N on Hwy 33, then 3 mi W on Hwy 150, then S on Santa Ana Rd. (805)649-2233

RINCON PARKWAY (Public) From US-101 & State Beaches (exit 72), N 6.5 mi on Old US-101/Pacific Coast Hwy (R). 2015 rates: $28. (805)654-3951

VENTURA BEACH RV RESORT **Ratings: 10/10★/7** (RV Park) 2015 rates: $60 to $95. (805)643-9137 800 W Main St., Ventura, CA 93001

VICTORVILLE — H4 *San Bernardino*

MOJAVE NARROWS COUNTY REGIONAL PARK
(Public) From Jct of I-15 & Bear Valley Rd: Go 4 mi E on Bear Valley Rd to Ridgecrest Rd, then 2-1/2 mi N on Ridgecrest Rd (L). Elev 2850 ft. **FAC:** Paved rds. 38 paved, 7 pull-thrus (50 x 55), back-ins (30 x 50), 38 full hkups (30/50 amps), tent sites, dump, firewood, controlled access. **REC:** Horse Lake: fishing, playground, rec open to public. Pets OK $. Partial handicap access. 14 day max stay, 2015 rates: $25 to $40.
(877)387-2757 Lat: 34.50748, Lon: -117.27299
18000 Yates Rd, Victorville, CA 92392
parks@parks.sbcounty.gov
www.sbcountyparks.com
See ad page 123 (Welcome Section).

SHADY OASIS KAMPGROUND
Ratings: 6.5/6/6.5 (Campground) From Jct of I-15 & Second Stoddard Wells Rd (Exit 154) Go 1/4 mi S (R). Elev 2996 ft. **FAC:** Paved/dirt rds. (120 spaces). 71 Avail: 27 paved, 44 dirt, 50 pull-thrus (22 x 70), back-ins (25 x 40), some side by side hkups, 42 full hkups, 29 W, 29 E (30/50 amps), seasonal sites, WiFi Hotspot, tent sites, rentals, dump, laundry, groc, LP gas. **REC:** playground. Pets OK. 2015 rates: $35 to $40. Disc: AAA.
AAA Approved
(760)245-6867 Lat: 34.55102, Lon: -117.28983
16530 Stoddard Wells Rd, Victorville, CA 92395
shadyoasisvv@yahoo.com
shadyoasis.tripod.com
See ad this page.

VIOLA — B3 *Shasta*

LASSEN VOLCANIC NATIONAL PARK (MANZANITA LAKE) (Natl Pk) From town: Go 6 mi E on Hwy-44, then 3/4 mi E on Lassen Park Rd. 2015 rates: $10 to $18. May 22 to Nov 30. (530)595-6121

LASSEN VOLCANIC NATIONAL PARK (SUMMIT LAKE) (Natl Pk) From town: Go 6 mi E on Hwy-44, then 12 mi E/NE/SE on Lassen Park Rd. 2015 rates: $10 to $18. Jun 27 to Sep 30. (530)595-4444

VISALIA — F3 *Tulare*

COUNTRY MANOR RV & MH COMMUNITY
Ratings: 9/9/8 (RV Area in MHP) From Jct of Hwy 99 & SR-198 (Exit 97): Go 3-1/2 mi E on SR-198 to Akers St exit, then S on Akers St to W Noble Ave, then 1 mi E on W Noble Ave to S Chinowth St, then 1/4 mi S on S Chinowth St (L). **FAC:** Paved rds. (127 spaces). Avail: 27 paved, patios, back-ins (24 x 45), 27 full hkups (30/50 amps), seasonal sites, WiFi, laundry. **REC:** pool. Pet restrict(B/Q). Partial handicap access, no tents. Age restrict may apply, RV age restrict, eco-friendly, 2015 rates: $40.
(559)732-8144 Lat: 36.323008, Lon: -119.335807
820 S Chinowth St, Visalia, CA 93277
countrymanor@towermgmt.com
www.countrymanormhc.com

VISALIA SEQUOIA NATIONAL PARK KOA
Ratings: 8.5/9/8.5 (Campground) From Jct of Hwys 99 & 198E: Go 1/2 mi E on Hwy 198E to Plaza Dr, then 1-1/4 mi N on Plaza Dr to Goshen Ave, then 1/2 mi W on Goshen Ave to American Rd (Rd 76), then 1/2 mi N on American Rd (Rd 76) to Ave 308, then 1/4 mi W on Ave 308 (R). **FAC:** Paved/gravel rds. (75 spaces). Avail: 49 gravel, 49 pull-thrus (25 x 60), 42 full hkups, 7 W, 7 E (30/50 amps), seasonal sites, WiFi $, tent sites, rentals, dump, laundry, groc, LP gas, fire rings, firewood. **REC:** heated pool, playground. Pet restrict(B). Big rig sites, eco-friendly, 2015 rates: $42 to $57. Disc: AAA, military.
(800)562-0540 Lat: 36.349307, Lon: -119.406139
7480 Ave 308, Visalia, CA 93291
camp@visaliakoa.com
www.visaliakoa.com
See ad this page.

VISTA — J4 *San Diego*

OLIVE AVE RV RESORT
Ratings: 8.5/9.5★/8 (RV Park) From Jct of N Melrose Dr & Olive Ave, W 450 ft on Olive Ave (R).

MAKE US YOUR "HOME BASE"
Stay a day or a season with us as you explore Southern CA. Central location with easy access to Vista, Carlsbad, Oceanside and Escondido. Enjoy all that San Diego County has to offer. Family oriented. Groups welcome.

FAC: Paved rds. (60 spaces). Avail: 40 paved, 31 pull-thrus (25 x 62), back-ins (36 x 40), 40 full hkups (50 amps), seasonal sites, cable, WiFi, laundry. **REC:** heated pool, whirlpool. Pet restrict(B) $. Partial handicap access, no tents. RV age restrict, eco-friendly, 2015 rates: $40. Disc: military.
(877)633-3557 Lat: 33.20471, Lon: -117.25660
713 Olive Ave, Vista, CA 92083
reservations@oliveavervresort.com
www.oliveavervresort.com
See ad pages 224, 126 & RV Trips of a Lifetime in Magazine Section.

WALNUT GROVE — D3 *Sacramento*

SNUG HARBOR RESORTS LLC **Ratings: 8/8★/9** (RV Park) 2015 rates: $44 to $52. (916)775-1455 3356 Snug Habor Dr, Walnut Grove, CA 95690

WATERFORD — E3 *Stanislaus*

MODESTO RESERVOIR REGIONAL PARK (Public) From Jct of SR-99 & SR-132 (exit 226B), E 35 mi on SR-132 to Reservoir Rd, N 0.5 mi (E). 2015 rates: $10 to $25. (209)874-4283

TURLOCK LAKE SRA (State Pk) From Jct of Hwys 99 & 132, E 14 mi on Hwy 132 to Hickman Rd (CR-J9), S 1 mi to Lake Rd, E 10 mi (L). 2015 rates: $33. (209)874-2056

WATSONVILLE — F1 *Santa Cruz*

PINTO LAKE PARK (Public) N-bnd: From Jct of Hwy 1 & Green Valley Rd, NE 2.5 mi on Green Valley Rd (L); or S-bnd: From Jct of Hwy 1 & Watsonville/Gilroy (Hwy 152) exit, take immediate left (N) onto Green Valley Rd, NE 2 mi (L). 2015 rates: $35. (831)722-8129

SANTA CRUZ/MONTEREY BAY KOA **Ratings: 8.5/7/8** (Campground) 2015 rates: $75 to $102. (831)722-0551 1186 San Andreas Rd, Watsonville, CA 95076

SUNSET (State Pk) From Santa Cruz, S on Hwy 1 to Larkin Valley Rd/San Andreas Rd, W 5 mi on San Andreas Rd to Sunset Beach Rd (R). 2015 rates: $35. (831)763-7063

WAWONA — E4 *Mariposa*

YOSEMITE/WAWONA (Natl Pk) From N end of Wawona, N 1 mi on SR-41 (L). Entrance fee and reservations required. 2015 rates: $26. (209)372-0200

Canada — know the rules, regulations and tips before crossing the border. This is listed at the beginning of the country.

WEED — A2 *Siskiyou*

FRIENDLY RV PARK

Ratings: 7/10★/9 (Campground) From Jct of I-5 and Exit 745 (S Weed), E 0.1 mi on Vista Dr to Black Butte Dr, N 0.1 mi (R). Elev 3500 ft. **FAC:** Paved/gravel rds. 50 Avail: 18 paved, 32 gravel, patios, 20 pull-thrus (32 x 50), back-ins (32 x 40), 50 full hkups (30 amps), cable, WiFi, tent sites, dump, laundry. **REC.** Pets OK. 2015 rates: $33. No CC.
(530)938-2805 Lat: 41.39982, Lon: -122.37817
1800 Black Butte Drive, Weed, CA 96094
friendlyrv@yahoo.com
www.friendlyrvpark.com

HI-LO RV PARK

(RV Spaces) From (N-Bnd) I-5 & Weed Blvd (Exit 747- Central Weed) : Go rt on Weed Blvd .25 mi (R) Note: park on Weed Blvd and register at the motel. **FAC:** Paved rds. 16 paved, no slide-outs, back-ins (20 x 40), mostly side by side hkups, accepts full hkup units only, 16 full hkups (15/30 amps), cable, WiFi, restaurant. Pets OK. 2015 rates: $25.99 to $31.99.
(530)938-2731 Lat: 41.42103, Lon: -122.38408
88 S. Weed Blvd, Weed, CA 96094
hilo@sisdevco.com
www.sisdevco.com
See ad page 142 (Spotlight Mount Shasta).

TRAILER LANE RV PARK

Ratings: 7/9★/7 (RV Park) N-bnd: From Jct of I-5 & US-97, N 0.5 mi on I-5 to N Weed exit (exit 748), exit to E side of Fwy to Edgewood Rd, N 1.2 mi (L); or S-bnd: From Jct of I-5 & US-97/Central Weed/Klamath Falls exit 748, exit to E side of Fwy to Edgewood Rd, N 1.2 mi (L). Elev 3500 ft. **FAC:** Gravel rds. 20 Avail: 10 gravel, 10 grass, 7 pull-thrus (20 x 56), back-ins (15 x 48), 20 full hkups (30/50 amps), WiFi, laundry. **REC.** Pet restrict(B). No tents. Big rig sites, 2015 rates: $33. Disc: AAA. Mar 1 to Nov 15.
(530)938-4554 Lat: 41.43082, Lon: -122.41403
27535 Edgewood Rd, Weed, CA 96094
trailerlane@hotmail.com
www.trailerlane.com
See ad pages 142 (Spotlight Mount Shasta), 128.

Things to See and Do

HI-LO CAFE Locally owned since 1951 - serving breakfast, lunch, dinner, and homemade desserts, all day every day. Restrooms, food. Hours: 7am to 9pm. No CC.
(530)938-2904 Lat: 41.42103, Lon: -122.38408
88 S. Weed Blvd, Weed, CA 96094
hilo@sisdevco.com
www.sisdevco.com
See ad page 142 (Spotlight Mount Shasta).

HI-LO MOTEL Locally owned since 1951 - breathtaking views, comfortable, clean, great prices, local discounts & much more. Hours: 24 hour.
(530)938-2731 Lat: 41.42103, Lon: -122.38408
88 S. Weed Blvd, Weed, CA 96094
hilo@sisdevco.com
See ad page 142 (Spotlight Mount Shasta).

WEOTT — B1 *Humboldt*

HUMBOLDT REDWOODS/ALBEE CREEK CAMPGROUND (State Pk) From town, N 2 mi on Hwy 101 to Mattole Rd, W 5 mi (R). 2015 rates: $35. May 15 to Oct 15. (707)946-2409

HUMBOLDT REDWOODS/BURLINGTON (State Pk) From Jct of US-101 & Weott exit (Ave of the Giants), S 2 mi on Ave of the Giants (L). 2015 rates: $35. (707)946-2409

HUMBOLDT REDWOODS/HIDDEN SPRINGS (State Pk) From town, S 1 mi on Hwy 254 (L). Closed until summer of 2011. 2015 rates: $35. May 1 to Sep 7. (707)946-2409

WEST SACRAMENTO — D3 *Yolo*

CAPITOL WEST RV PARK

(RV Spaces) From Jct of I-80 & Bus I-80 (at West Sacramento), E 1.2 mi on Bus I-80 to Harbor Blvd exit, N 0.3 mi to West Capital Ave, E 0.1 to Glide Ave, N 100 feet (R). **FAC:** Gravel rds. (69 spaces). Avail: 9 gravel, back-ins (24 x 42), accepts full hkup units only, 9 full hkups (30/50 amps), WiFi, laundry. Pets OK. 2015 rates: $40. No CC.
(916)371-6671 Lat: 38.58084, Lon: -121.54472
715 Glide Ave, West Sacramento, CA 95691
info@capitolwestrv.com
www.capitolwestrv.com
See ad page 214.

SAC-WEST RV PARK AND CAMPGROUND

Ratings: 9.5/9.5★/8.5 (Campground) W-bnd: From W Jct of I-80 & Bus Loop 80, W 0.1 mi on I-80 to W Capitol Ave exit, circle S under fwy on Enterprise Dr to Lake Rd, E 0.1 mi (R); or E-bnd: From Jct of I-80 & W Capitol Ave exit, W on exit rd to Enterprise Dr to Lake Rd, E 0.1 mi (R). **FAC:** Paved rds. (70 spaces). Avail: 50 gravel, patios, 50 pull-thrus (20 x 42), some side by side hkups, 50 full hkups (30/50 amps), seasonal sites, cable, WiFi, tent sites, rentals, dump, laundry, groc, LP gas, firewood. **REC:** heated pool, pond, fishing, playground. Pet restrict(B). Partial handicap access. Eco-friendly, 2015 rates: $40 to $55.
(916)371-6771 Lat: 38.57312, Lon: -121.57523
3951 Lake Rd, West Sacramento, CA 95691
info@sacwestrvpark.com
www.sacwestrvpark.com
See ad pages 214, 128, 119 (CA Map).

WESTPORT — C1 *Mendocino*

WESTPORT BEACH

Ratings: 8/8/8 (Campground) From Jct of SR-1 & SR-20, N 18.4 mi on SR-1, 17 mi N of Fort Bragg on SR-1 (L). **FAC:** Gravel rds. 75 grass, 9 pull-thrus (30 x 60), back-ins (30 x 60), mostly side by side hkups, 75 full hkups (30/50 amps), WiFi, tent sites, rentals, showers $, laundry, groc, fire rings, firewood. **REC:** Pacific Ocean: swim, playground. Pets OK $. Partial handicap access. 2015 rates: $56 to $59.
(707)964-2964 Lat: 39.64912, Lon: -123.78215
37700 North Hwy 1, Westport, CA 95488
westportbeachkoa@gmail.com
www.westportbeachrvpark.com
See ad page 194.

WESTPORT-UNION LANDING STATE BEACH (State Pk) From town: Go 1-1/2 mi N on Hwy 1. Pit toilets. 2015 rates: $25. (707)937-5804

WILLITS — C1 *Mendocino*

GOLDEN RULE RV PARK

Ratings: 8/8.5★/8.5 (RV Park) S-bnd: From Jct of US-101 & SR-20W (in Willits), S 7 mi on US-101 to Ridgewood Ranch entrance, W 1.6 mi (L); or N-bnd: From Jct of US-101 & SR-20E (Ukiah), N 8.5 mi on US-101/SR-20 to Ridgewood Ranch entrance, W 1.6 mi (L). **FAC:** Paved rds. 33 gravel, 7 pull-thrus (18 x 55), back-ins (20 x 50), accepts full hkup units only, 33 full hkups (20/30 amps), WiFi Hotspot, laundry. **REC:** pool. Pets OK. No tents. Eco-friendly, 2015 rates: $35. No CC.
(707)459-2958 Lat: 39.31066, Lon: -123.30557
16100 N Hwy 101, Willits, CA 95490
grmv@instawave.net
www.goldenrulervpark.com
See ad this page, 128.

WILLITS (CONT)

WILLITS KOA **Ratings: 9/10★/9.5** (Campground) 2015 rates: $45 to $75. (800)562-8542 1600 Hwy 20, Willits, CA 95490

WINCHESTER — O6 *San Bernardino*

LAKE SKINNER (Public) From Jct of I-15 & Hwy 215 (exit 123), S 3 mi on I-15 to Rancho California Rd (exit 59), E 10 mi (R). For reservations call (800)234-7275. 2015 rates: $15 to $30. (951)926-1541

WINDSOR — D2 *Sonoma*

WINDSOR WINE COUNTRY RV PARK (RV Park) (Not Visited) From jct Hwy 101 & Shiloh Rd: Go .5 mi W on Shiloh Rd, then 2 mi N on Conde Lane (L). **FAC:** Gravel rds. (95 spaces). Avail: 27 gravel, accepts full hkup units only, 27 full hkups (30/50 amps), WiFi, dump, laundry, LP gas. **REC:** heated pool, playground. Pet restrict(B). Big rig sites, eco-friendly, 2015 rates: $35 to $42. No CC, no reservations.
(707)838-4195 Lat: 38.54129, Lon: -122.80468
8225 Conde Ave, Windsor, CA 95492
windsorrvpark@thomsenproperties.net
www.windsorwinecountryrv.com
See ad opposite page.

WINTERHAVEN — K6 *Imperial*

PICACHO STATE RECREATION AREA (State Pk) From I-8 in town: Go 25 mi N on unpaved road. Pit toilets. 2015 rates: $20 to $25. (760)996-2963

PILOT KNOB RV RESORT
Ratings: 7.5/8/7.5 (Membership Pk) From Jct of I-8 & Sidewinder Rd (Exit 164), S 300 ft on Sidewinder Rd to Frontage Rd, W 0.3 mi (L). (Park operates on Arizona time). **FAC:** Gravel rds. (240 spaces). Avail: 10 gravel, patios, 10 pull-thrus (20 x 56), 10 full hkups (30/50 amps), seasonal sites, WiFi $, laundry, controlled access. **REC:** heated pool, whirlpool, shuffleboard. Pets OK. Partial handicap access, no tents. RV age restrict, 2015 rates: $25 to $35. Nov 15 to Apr 30.
(800)370-3707 Lat: 32.74758, Lon: -114.76362
3707 W. Hwy 80, Winterhaven, CA 92283
www.whresorts.com

RIVERS EDGE RV RESORT **Ratings: 8/7.5/7.5** (RV Park) 2015 rates: $30. (760)572-5105 2299 Winterhaven Drive, Winterhaven, CA 92283

SANS END RV PARK **Ratings: 6.5/7/7** (RV Park) 2015 rates: $29. (760)572-0797 2209 Winterhaven Drive, Winterhaven, CA 92283

SENATOR WASH RESERVOIR BLM (Public) From Jct of 4th St & I-8 (exit 172), N 0.25 mi on 4th St to Imperial County Hwy S-24, NE 16 mi (through Indian Reservation) to Senator Wash Rd, W 2.5 mi, (across canal) follow signs (E). Pit toilets. 2015 rates: $15. (928)317-3200

SQUAW LAKE BLM (Public) From town, E 20 mi on SR-24 to Senator Wash Rd, N 4 mi (E). 2015 rates: $15. (928)317-3200

WINTERS — D2 *Solano*

LAKE SOLANO COUNTY PARK (Public) From Jct of I-80 & I-505 (Exit 56), N 15 mi on I-505 to Winters exit, W 4 mi to Pleasant Valley Rd, S 0.25 mi (R). **FAC:** Paved rds. 32 paved, 9 pull-thrus (15 x 65), back-ins (15 x 60), 2 full hkups, 30 W, 30 E (30 amps), tent sites, dump, fire rings, firewood, controlled access. **REC:** wading pool, Putah Creek: playground. Pet restrict(Q) $. Partial handicap access. 14 day max stay, 2015 rates: $18 to $40.
(530)795-2990 Lat: 38.49305, Lon: -122.02833
8685 Pleasant Valley, Winters, CA 95694
www.solanocounty.com/parks
See ad page 222.

WOFFORD HEIGHTS — G4 *Kern*

GREEN HORN MTN COUNTY PARK (Public) From Jct of I-5 & SR-99 (Exit 221), N 20 mi on SR-99 to SR-178 (Exit 26), E 50 mi to SR-155 (thru Wofford Heights & Lake Isabella), W 10 mi (L). Steep, 13% grade. 2015 rates: $18. (760)376-6780

SEQUOIA NF (LIVE OAK CAMPGROUND) (Natl Forest) From town: Go 1/2 mi S on Hwy-155. 2015 rates: $24. (760)379-5646

WOODLAND — D2 *Yolo*

CACHE CREEK CANYON (Public) From Jct of I-505 & SR-16, NW 40 mi on SR-16 (L). 2015 rates: $25. (530)666-8115

YOLO COUNTY FAIR (Public) From Jct of I-5 & Exit 537 (Main St), W 1 mi on Main St to Thomas St, S 0.6 mi on Gum St, SW 0.2 mi (L). 2015 rates: $35. (530)402-2222

YERMO — H5 *San Bernardino*

BARSTOW CALICO KOA **Ratings: 8/8.5★/8.5** (Campground) 2015 rates: $51.89 to $53.89. (760)254-2311 35250 Outer Hwy 15 N, Yermo, CA 92398

Things to See and Do

CALICO GHOST TOWN Authentic Old West mining boom town featuring silver mine, saloon, general store, train ride, shops, gold panning and historical tours. Elev 2938 ft. partial handicap access. RV accessible. Restrooms, food. Hours: 9am to 5pm. Adult fee: $5 to $8. ATM.
(800)862-2542 Lat: 34.94515, Lon: -116.86475
36600 Ghost Town Rd, Yermo, CA 92398
calicotown@parks.sbcounty.gov
cms.sbcounty.gov/parks/Parks/CalicoGhostTown.aspx
See ad page 123 (Welcome Section).

YOSEMITE NATIONAL PARK — E4 *Mariposa*

YOSEMITE NATIONAL PARK AREA MAP

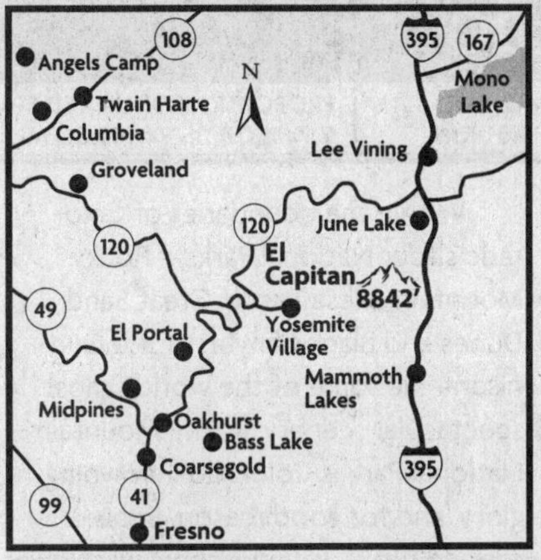

Symbols on map indicate towns within a 60 mile radius of Yosemite National Park where campgrounds are listed. Check listings for more information.

See also Angels Camp, Bass Lake, Coarsegold, Columbia, El Portal, Fresno, Groveland, June Lake, Lee Vining, Mammoth Lakes, Midpines, Oakhurst, Twain Harte & Yosemite Village.

YOSEMITE VILLAGE — E4 *Mariposa*

YOSEMITE/BRIDALVEIL CREEK (Natl Pk) From town, S on Hwy 41 to Chinquapin, E 10 mi to Glacier Point Rd (R). Entrance fee required. 2015 rates: $18. Jul 12 to Sep 21. (209)372-0200

YOSEMITE/LOWER PINES (Natl Pk) In Yosemite Valley, on Yosemite Village loop. Entrance fee and reservations required. 2015 rates: $26. Apr 6 to Nov 2. (209)372-8502

YOSEMITE/NORTH PINES (Natl Pk) In Yosemite Valley, on Yosemite Village loop. Entrance fee and reservations required. 2015 rates: $20. Mar 30 to Nov 2. (209)372-8502

YOSEMITE/UPPER PINES (Natl Pk) In Yosemite Valley, on Yosemite Village loop. Entrance fee and reservations required. 2015 rates: $26. (209)372-8502

YREKA — A2 *Siskiyou*

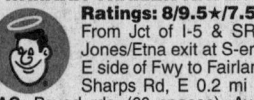

WAIIAKA TRAILER HAVEN
Ratings: 8/9.5★/7.5 (Campground) From Jct of I-5 & SR-3/Exit 773 (Fort Jones/Etna exit at S-end of town), exit to E side of Fwy to Fairlane Rd, N 0.3 mi to Sharps Rd, E 0.2 mi (L). Elev 2600 ft. **FAC:** Paved rds. (60 spaces). Avail: 50 gravel, 50 pull-thrus (22 x 60), 50 full hkups (30/50 amps), seasonal sites, cable, WiFi, tent sites, showers $, laundry, LP gas. **REC:** playground. Pet restrict(B). Eco-friendly, 2015 rates: $38.50. Disc: AAA, military.
(530)842-4500 Lat: 41.70952, Lon: -122.63810
240 Sharps Road, Yreka, CA 96097
waiiakarvpark@gmail.com
www.waiiakarvpark.com
See ad this page.

YREKA RV PARK **Ratings: 7/9.5★/7** (RV Park) 2015 rates: $35 to $39. (530)841-0100 767 Montague Rd, Yreka, CA 96097

YUBA CITY — D3 *Sutter, Yuba*

TRAVELHOME PARK
Ratings: 7.5/9.5★/9 (RV Park) N & E-bnd: From Jct of SR-99 & SR-20, E 0.7 mi on SR-20 to Live Oak Blvd, N 0.4 mi (R); or S-bnd: From Jct of SR-99 & Queens Ave, E 0.7 mi on Queens Ave to Live Oak Blvd, S 0.3 mi (L). **FAC:** Paved rds. (52 spaces). 45 Avail: 40 paved, 5 gravel, patios, 6 pull-thrus (20 x 58), back-ins (30 x 50), accepts full hkup units only, 45 full hkups (30/50 amps), seasonal sites, WiFi, dump, laundry. Pet restrict(B/Q). No tents. Big rig sites, eco-friendly, 2015 rates: $35.
(530)674-8910 Lat: 39.14745, Lon: -121.62006
1257 Live Oak Blvd, Yuba City, CA 95991
travelhomepark@comcast.net
www.travelhomepark.com
See ad this page, 128.

YUBA-SUTTER FAIRGROUNDS RV PARK (Public) From Jct of SR-99 & SR-20, S 1.0 mi on SR-99 to Franklin Ave, E 1.3 mi to Wilbur Ave, S 50 ft, go left into fenced parking lot (L). 2015 rates: $25. (530)674-1280

YUCAIPA — M6 *San Bernardino*

YUCAIPA REGIONAL PARK (Public) From Jct of I-10 & Oak Glen Rd/Live Oak Cyn. Dr. (Exit 85), N 3.5 mi on Oak Glen Rd (L). Elev 2659 ft. **FAC:** Paved rds. 42 paved, patios, 20 pull-thrus (33 x 96), back-ins (30 x 60), 42 full hkups (30/50 amps), tent sites, showers $, dump, firewood, controlled access. **REC:** pool $, pond, swim, fishing, playground, rec open to public. Pets OK. Partial handicap access. Big rig sites, RV age restrict, 14 day max stay, 2015 rates: $40.
(909)790-3127 Lat: 34.04963, Lon: -117.04791
33900 Oak Glen Rd, Yucaipa, CA 92399
www.sbcountyparks.com
See ad page 123 (Welcome Section).

YUCCA VALLEY — H5 *San Bernardino*

JOSHUA TREE/BLACK ROCK CANYON (Natl Pk) From Jct of I-10 & Hwy 62, E 25 mi on Hwy 62 to Yucca Valley, S 5 mi on Joshua Ln (E). For reservations call 1-800-365-CAMP. 2015 rates: $10 to $15. (760)367-3001

YUCCA VALLEY RV PARK Ratings: 6.5/8/6.5 (RV Park) W-bnd: From Jct of Hwys 62 (Twentynine Palms Hwy) & 247 (in town), W 2.4 mi on Hwy 62 (R). Elev 3200 ft. **FAC:** Paved rds. 18 gravel, back-ins (24 x 78), 18 full hkups (30/50 amps), cable, WiFi, tent sites, laundry. Pets OK. Partial handicap access. RV age restrict, 2015 rates: $40. Disc: AAA.
AAA Approved
(760)365-5596 Lat: 34.11744, Lon: -116.45576
55408 29 Palms Hwy, Yucca Valley, CA 92284
pandhi2009@gmail.com
www.yuccavalleyrvpark.net

Colorado Tourism Office

WELCOME TO
Colorado

DATE OF STATEHOOD	WIDTH: 380 MILES (612 KM)	PROPORTION OF UNITED STATES
AUG. 1, 1876	LENGTH: 280 MILES (451 KM)	2.74% OF 3,794,100 SQ MI

With its wild beauty and shifting mountain scenery, Colorado's snowcapped Rocky Mountains loom large in the popular consciousness as a symbol of freedom and adventure.

Its cities, however, tell a more complex story. With its tree-lined boulevards, expansive city parks, eclectic museums and rich architectural heritage, Denver—the Mile-High City—blends Old West ideals with 21st-century savoir-faire. Young and bold, Boulder is the gateway to the Rockies and delivers an adrenaline-infused mountain experience for intrepid hikers, mountain-bikers and skiers.

Colorado Springs—the second biggest city in Colorado—combines sophisticated dining, a healthy climate, mineral springs and an array of outdoor adventures with Gold Rush-era charm. Positioned at more than one mile above sea level, Colorado Springs also provides the launch pad for climbing one of the most awe-inspiring mountains in the U.S., the purple-peaked majesty that is Pikes Peak, which rises 8,000 feet above sea level. There's a curious bourgeois-hip vibe to Telluride, the storied mining town steeped in Wild West history, which lures a diverse brigade of travelers, ranging from the gilded and glamorous (Oprah Winfrey and Oliver Stone are big fans) to ski bums and occasional peddlers of vice.

Within the boundaries of Colorado's four National Parks—Rocky Mountain, Mesa Verde, Great Sand Dunes and Black Canyon of the Gunnison—lie some of the world's most spectacular scenery. Rocky Mountain National Park is Colorado's crowning glory, and for good reason. Snow-capped peaks, kaleidoscopic wildflower meadows, crystalline mountain lakes and cascading waterfalls deliver exhilarating adventures, ranging from hiking, rafting and rock-climbing to biking, skiing, snowboarding and wildlife watching. History and adventure coalesce at Mesa Verde (a UNESCO World Heritage Site), with its 600 mountainside cliff dwellings inhabited long agave by ancestral Puebloans almost 1,000 years ago.

Boasting 30 ski resorts, Colorado gets twice as many ski days as any other state. With a stunning backdrop, glorious terrain and an enchanting Alpine-style village, it's easy to see why Vail consistently ranks as one of the best ski towns in the U.S. During the summer months, you can swap your skis for hiking boots and, where the rivers run through it, trout-fishing opportunities abound.

At the end of August, the Colorado State Fair in Pueblo is a dose of old-fashioned family fun complete with carnival rides, children's parades, funnel cakes and five entertainment stages.

Top 3 Tourism Attractions:
1) Pikes Peak, America's Mountain
2) Red Rocks Park and Amphitheatre
3) Denver Art Museum

Nickname: Centennial State

State Flower: Rocky Mountain Columbine

State Bird: Lark Bunting

People: Tim Allen, actor; Lon Chaney, actor; Jack Dempsey, boxer; Douglas Fairbanks, actor; Al and Bobby Unser, race car drivers

Major Cities: Denver (capital), Colorado Springs, Aurora, Fort Collins, Lakewood

Topography: East—high, dry plains; central—hills to mountains; Rockies—high ranges, broad valleys, deep narrow canyons

Climate: Sunshine and low humidity; snowy, cold winters; summers—warm days, cool nights

Branson Reynolds

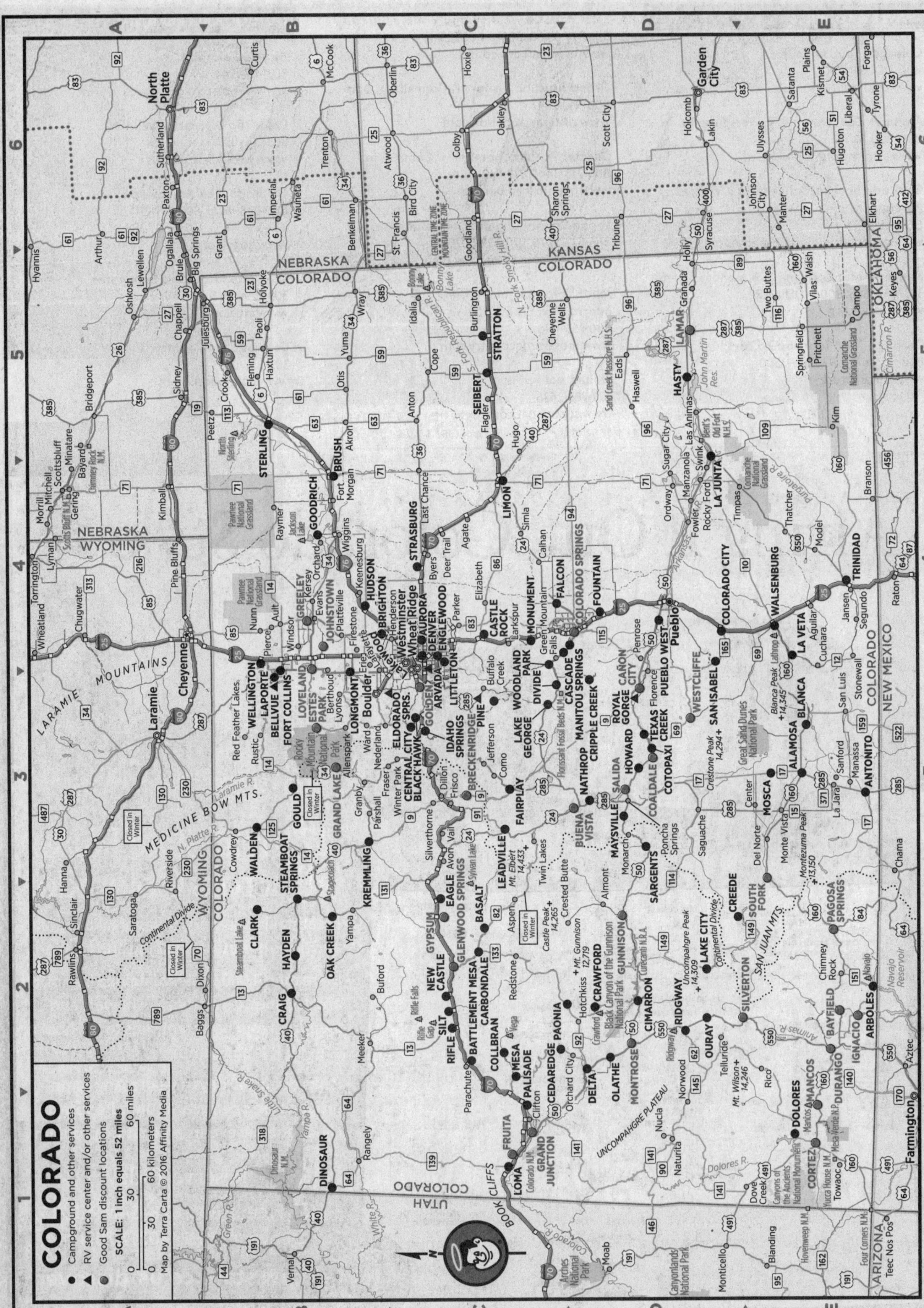
COLORADO
Campground and other services
RV service center and/or other services
Good Sam discount locations
SCALE: 1 inch equals 52 miles
0 30 60 miles
0 30 60 kilometers
Map by Terra Carta © 2016 Affinity Media
NEBRASKA
WYOMING
KANSAS
COLORADO
UTAH
NEW MEXICO
OKLAHOMA
ARIZONA
LARAMIE MOUNTAINS
MEDICINE BOW MTS.
BOOK CLIFFS
UNCOMPAHGRE PLATEAU
SAN JUAN MTS.
Continental Divide
CENTRAL TIME ZONE
MOUNTAIN TIME ZONE
North Platte
Cheyenne
Laramie
Garden City
Farmington
Moab
DENVER
Boulder
Pueblo
COLORADO SPRINGS
FORT COLLINS
GRAND JUNCTION
STERLING
LIMON
LAMAR
LA JUNTA
TRINIDAD
WALSENBURG
ALAMOSA
DURANGO
CORTEZ
MONTROSE
GUNNISON
DELTA
GLENWOOD SPRINGS
LEADVILLE
BUENA VISTA
SALIDA
STEAMBOAT SPRINGS
CRAIG
DINOSAUR
Rocky Mountain National Park
Great Sand Dunes National Park
Black Canyon of the Gunnison National Park
Mesa Verde N.P.
Arches National Park
Canyonlands National Park
Pawnee National Grassland
Comanche National Grassland
Mt. Elbert 14,433
Pikes Peak
Blanca Peak 14,345
Crestone Peak 14,294
Mt. Wilson 14,246
Uncompahgre Peak 14,309
Castle Peak 14,265
Mt. Gunnison 12,719
Montezuma Peak 13,150
Closed in Winter

TRAVEL & TOURISM

Colorado Tourism Office
800-COLORADO
www.colorado.com

Alamosa Convention & Visitors Bureau
800-BLU-SKYS
www.alamosa.org

Colorado Springs Convention & Visitors Bureau
877-745-3773
www.experiencecoloradosprings.com

Denver Metro Convention & Visitors Bureau
303-892-1565, 800-2-DENVER
www.denver.org

Durango Area Tourism Office
800-463-8726, 970-247-3500
www.durango.org

Estes Park Convention and Visitors Bureau
970-577-9900, 800-44-ESTES
www.estesparkcvb.com

Grand Junction Visitors & Convention Bureau
800-962-2547
www.visitgrandjunction.com

Greater Pueblo Chamber of Commerce
800-233-3446, 719-542-1704
www.pueblochamber.org

Logan County Chamber of Commerce
866-522-5070, 970-522-5070
www.logancountychamber.com

Mesa Verde Country Visitor Information Bureau
800-253-1616
www.mesaverdecountry.com

Steamboat Springs
877-783-2628
www.steamboat.com

OUTDOOR RECREATION

Bicycle Colorado
303-417-1544
www.bicyclecolo.org

Colorado Division of Wildlife
303-297-1192
www.wildlife.state.co.us

Colorado Golf Association
800-228-4675, 800-392-2942, 303-366-4653, 303-366-7888
www.cogolf.org

Colorado River Outfitters Assn.
303-229-6075
www.croa.org

Colorado Ski Country USA
303-837-0793
www.coloradoski.com

Featured Good Sam Parks

COLORADO

When you stay with Good Sam, you can expect the highest degree of cleanliness and friendliness, and better yet, you get 10% off campground fees.

If you're not already a Good Sam member you can purchase your membership at one of these locations:

BAYFIELD
Blue Spruce RV Park & Cabins
(888)884-2641

BRECKENRIDGE
Tiger Run RV Resort
(800)895-9594

BUENA VISTA
Arrowhead Point Campground and Cabins
(719)395-2323

CANON CITY
Royal View @ Royal Gorge Campground
(719)275-1900

COLORADO SPRINGS
Fountain Creek RV Park
(719)633-2192

Garden Of the Gods RV Resort
(800)248-9451

Goldfield RV Park
(888)471-0495

CORTEZ
Sleeping Ute RV Park
(800)889-5072

Sundance RV Park LLC
(800)880-9413

DURANGO
Bayfield Riverside RV Park
(970)884-2475

ESTES PARK
Elk Meadow Lodge and RV Resort
(970)586-5342

Manor RV Park
(970)586-3251

Spruce Lake RV Park
(970)586-2889

FRUITA
Monument RV Resort
(970)858-4405

GLENWOOD SPRINGS
Glenwood Canyon Resort
(800)958-6737

GOLDEN
Dakota Ridge RV Resort
(303)279-1625

GRAND JUNCTION
Cruise Inn - Junction West RV Park
(970)245-8531

RV Ranch At Grand Junction
(970)434-6644

GRAND LAKE
Winding River Resort, Inc
(970)627-3215

CO

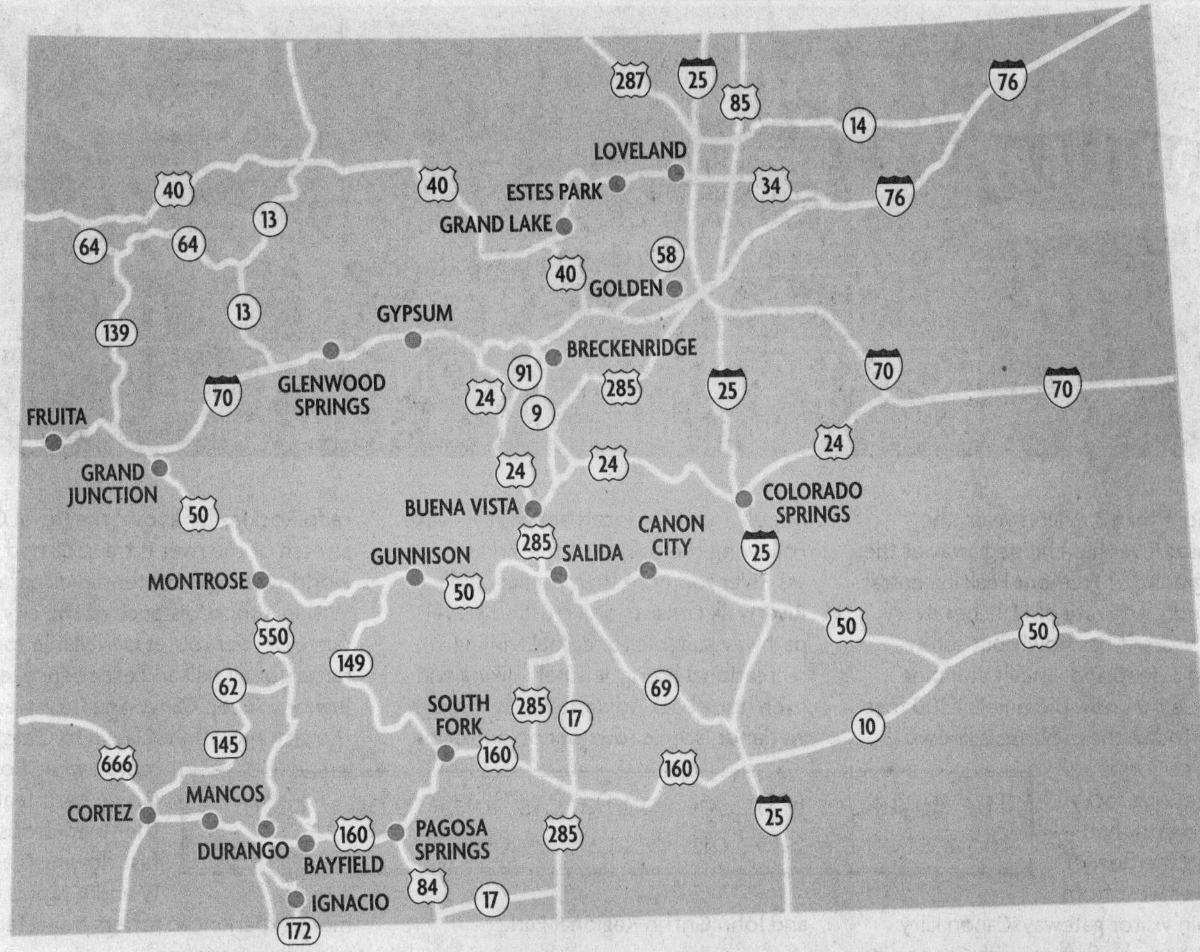

GUNNISON
Mesa Campground & RV Resort
(970)641-3186

GYPSUM
Aunt Sara's River Dance RV Resort
(720)933-9212

IGNACIO
Sky Ute Casino RV Park
(970)563-7777

LOVELAND
Loveland RV Resort
(970)667-1204

MANCOS
Ancient Cedars @ Mesa Verde RV Resort
(844)565-3517

Mesa Verde RV Resort
(800)776-7421

MONTROSE
Cedar Creek RV Park
(877)425-3884

Centennial RV Park & Campground
(970)240-3832

PAGOSA SPRINGS
Pagosa Riverside Campground
(970)264-5874

SALIDA
Four Seasons RV Park
(719)539-3084

SOUTH FORK
South Fork Campground
(719)873-5500

For more Good Sam Parks go to listing pages

Yinghai

SPOTLIGHT

CO

ROYAL GORGE-CANON CITY

Explore a breathtaking gorge or ride the rails of a classic train

For more than 3 million years, the Arkansas River has chipped away at the hard granite of Fremont Peak in central Colorado. At a rate of 12 inches every 2,500 years, it has slowly but surely carved a deep and visually stunning crevasse that now plummets 1,200 feet deep. Today, the crevasse is known as Royal Gorge, a 10-mile-long rocky granite gash that follows the flow of the river west from its main visitor gateway: Canon City.

When you first arrive in Canon City, you'll notice an abundance of incredible turn-of-the-century architecture. The entire downtown core is listed on the National Historic Registry, and a casual stroll through the center of town is an absolute must for first-time visitors.

The city's Riverwalk is another popular spot for locals and visitors alike. Following the course of the Arkansas River for more than 7 miles, the Riverwalk consists of a crushed gravel pathway suitable for casual trolling, recreational hiking, leisurely biking and even horseback riding. It winds through wetlands, scenic rows of cottonwoods and John Griffin Regional Park.

> The Royal Gorge Bridge and Park is home to one of the highest suspension bridges in the country.

Radical Rafting

Of course, the best way to experience the Arkansas River when you're in Canon City or the Royal Gorge area is by strapping on a lifejacket and helmet and jumping in a raft. As temperatures rise, and the snows melt high the Colorado Rockies far above, the Royal Gorge stretch of the river is transformed into a world-class whitewater rapids paradise. Within a short distance of the city, a range of river routes is available for rafters of all skill and experience levels. Bighorn Sheep Canyon lies just west of the city and offers Class II to Class III rapids, while Royal Gorge itself features the steep drops and fast flowing Class IV and V rapids that more experienced rafters travel far and wide to experience.

But if plummeting down raging rivers isn't quite your pace, then plunk yourself knee-deep in some of the slower stretches of the river. A large selection of connected streams and creeks make the area a renowned fly fishing favorite. Trophy sized wild

The Royal Gorge Route Railroad snakes along the bottom of the gorge on the banks of the Arkansas River.
Royal Gorge

Fantastic views dazzle passengers of the Royal Gorge Gondolas. Bkthomson

brown trout are abundant, and a variety of guided fishing trips led by experienced local fisherman are available throughout the season. Hikers, bikers and wildlife watchers will want to head to the Arkansas Headwaters Recreation Area. Well-marked trails weave their way through the park, and visitors can expect to see wild bore, bighorn sheep, elk, bald eagles, antelope and even the odd family of black bears.

When it's time for a change of pace, there's the Royal Gorge Bridge and Park, home to one of the highest suspension bridges in the country. It's also home to a handful of other tourist attractions, such as a scenic gondola ride and the Royal Rush Skycoaster thrill ride.

Riding the Rails

Far less tummy turning (but no less dramatic), the Royal Gorge Route Railroad takes guests on a first-class streamliner train for a ride up through the gorge and along the twisting, winding banks of the tumbling Arkansas River. Various classes of train cars are available to choose from, but the open-air car with panoramic views in every direction is available to passengers.

Of course sometimes there's no substitute for exploring on your own. Skyline Drive is a narrow, one-way paved road that snakes its way to the summit of a high razorback ridge that overlooks the entire surrounding area. The road is narrow and in some parts the terrain on either side drops sharply away, but for careful, confident drivers, the views are worth it. Those who reach the summit are treated to an interpretive display and a chance to view dinosaur footprints that are embedded in the cliff face.

For history buffs, the Royal Gorge Regional Museum is a must visit, as is the Florence Pioneer Museum. At the former, visitors stroll through a historic municipal building completed in 1927 while exploring artifacts that tell the history of the entire Royal Gorge region. Highlights include life-size dinosaur replicas, massive photograph exhibits and an authentic 1860s log cabin. The Florence Pioneer Museum, for its part, is a small collection made up to replicate an old school room, doctor's office and general store.

Of course, before leaving Canon City you should pay a visit to one of the most unusual attractions of all, the Museum of Colorado Prisons. Since its earliest days, Canon City's remote location has made it a natural location for incarceration. The area's history and economy are both significantly tied to the evolution of corrections in the United States, from its wild gun slinging frontier days to the modern era. Today, visitors can explore that history on self-guided audio tours through this very eclectic prison. Exhibits and artifacts are displayed across 32 different prison cells, including confiscated contraband from 1871 to the present day and historic photographs.

For More Information

Royal Gorge Region in Colorado
800-704-6743
www.royalgorgetravel.com

Colorado Tourism Office
800-COLORADO
www.colorado.com

Colorado

CONSULTANTS

Gary & Leesa Palmer

ALAMOSA — E3 *Alamosa*

ALAMOSA KOA **Ratings: 9/9★/8** (Campground) 2015 rates: $33 to $45. May 1 to Oct 15. (800)562-9157 6900 Juniper Ln, Alamosa, CO 81101

ANTONITO — E3 *Conejos*

CANON BONITO RV PARK & FISHERMAN'S CLUB **Ratings: 6/6/8** (Campground) 2015 rates: $30. May 1 to Nov 15. (719)376-2274 6819 CR D5, Antonito, CO 81120

CONEJOS RIVER CAMPGROUND **Ratings: 8/9★/9** (RV Park) 2015 rates: $32 to $36. May 1 to Oct 31. (719)376-5943 26714 Hwy 17, Antonito, CO 81120

MOGOTE MEADOW CABINS AND RV PARK Ratings: 6.5/7/7.5 (Campground) From Jct of US-285 & SR-17, W 5 mi on SR-17 (R). Elev 8038 ft. **FAC:** Gravel rds. 36 gravel, patios, 6 pull-thrus (30 x 80), back-ins (30 x 50), 36 full hkups (30/50 amps), WiFi, tent sites, rentals, dump, laundry, LP gas, firewood. **REC:** playground. Pet restrict(Q). Big rig sites, 2015 rates: $29 to $31. Disc: AAA. May 1 to Nov 15. No CC.
AAA Approved
(719)376-5774 Lat: 37.06338, Lon: -106.09818
34127 State Hwy 17, Antonito, CO 81120
mogotemeadow@hotmail.com
www.colorado-directory.com/mogotemeadows/

ARBOLES — E2 *Archuleta*

NAVAJO
(State Pk) From Jct of US-160 & SR-151, SW 18 mi on SR-151 to CR-982, S 2 mi (E). Entrance fee required. Elev 6100 ft. **FAC:** Paved rds. 82 Avail: 9 paved, 73 gravel, 68 pull-thrus (15 x 80), back-ins (15 x 80), 39 full hkups, 43 E (30/50 amps), tent sites, rentals, showers $, dump, laundry, firewood. **REC:** Navajo Reservoir: swim, fishing, marina. Pets OK. Partial handicap access. Big rig sites, 14 day max stay, 2015 rates: $10 to $24.
(970)883-2208 Lat: 37.00931, Lon: -107.40732
1526 CR-982, Arboles, CO 81121
navajo.park@state.co.us
http://cpw.state.co.us/placestogo/Parks/Navajo
See ad page 228 (Welcome Section).

PINON PARK CAMPGROUND & RV RESORT **Ratings: 5.5/6.5/6.5** (RV Park) 2015 rates: $28 to $30. Apr 1 to Nov 30. (970)883-3636 19 Lazy Lane, Arboles, CO 81121

ARVADA — C3 *Adams, Jefferson*

Travel Services

CAMPING WORLD COLLISION CENTER OF ARVADA Collision Center ONLY. Elev 5850 ft. **SERVICES:** RV, restrooms. Hours: 8am to 5pm.
(303)456-6004 Lat: 39.803583, Lon: -105.06096
5880 W 59th Avenue, Unit A, Arvada, CO 80003
cawright@campingworld.com
www.campingworld.com

AURORA — C4 *Adams, Arapahoe*

CHERRY CREEK
(State Pk) From Jct of I-225 & Parker Rd/SR-83 (exit 4), S 1.2 mi on Parker Rd/SR-83 at Lehigh Ave (R), Entrance fee required. Elev 5550 ft. **FAC:** Paved rds. 130 paved, 61 pull-thrus (30 x 45), back-ins (30 x 45), 100 full hkups (30/50 amps), WiFi, tent sites, showers $, dump, laundry, fire rings, firewood. **REC:** Cherry Creek Reservoir: swim, fishing, marina, playground, rec open to public. Pets OK. Partial handicap access. 14 day max stay, 2015 rates: $16 to $26.
(303)690-1166 Lat: 39.64908, Lon: -104.84253
4201 S Parker Rd, Aurora, CO 80014
cherry.creek.park@state.co.us
http://cpw.state.co.us/placestogo/Parks/cherrycreek
See ad page 228 (Welcome Section).

BASALT — C2 *Eagle, Pitkin*

ASPEN BASALT CAMPGROUND
Ratings: 8/8★/5.5 (RV Park) From Jct of SR-82 & Mile Marker 20 (2 mi E of town), E 0.2 mi on SR-82 to Original Rd, S 500 ft, 1st left (R) Note: Do not follow GPS. Elev 6558 ft. **FAC:** Gravel rds. 68 gravel, 53 pull-thrus (16 x 53), back-ins (16 x 40), mostly side by side hkups, 64 full hkups, 4 W, 4 E (30/50 amps), cable, WiFi, dump, laundry, LP gas. **REC:** heated pool, whirlpool, Roaring Fork: fishing, playground. Pets OK. No tents. 2015 rates: $50. Disc: military.
(970)927-3405 Lat: 39.37326, Lon: -107.07522
20640 Highway 82, Basalt, CO 81621
abcampground@aspensnowmass.com
www.aspensnowmass.com
See ad this page.

BATTLEMENT MESA — C2 *Garfield*

BATTLEMENT MESA RV PARK **Ratings: 3.5/7.5/4.5** (RV Park) 2015 rates: $28. (970)285-9740 95 Eldora Dr, Battlement Mesa, CO 81636

BAYFIELD — E2 *La Plata, San Juan*

BLUE SPRUCE RV PARK & CABINS
Ratings: 8/9.5★/9.5 (RV Park) From Jct of US-160 & CR-501, N 18 mi on CR-501 to CR-500, N 1.7 mi (L) (Cabins are open year 'round). Elev 7829 ft. **FAC:** Gravel rds. 78 gravel, patios, 14 pull-thrus (30 x 60), back-ins (30 x 40), 78 full hkups (30/50 amps), cable, WiFi, rentals, laundry, groc, LP gas, fire rings, firewood. **REC:** playground. Pets OK. No tents. Big rig sites, eco-friendly, 2015 rates: $30 to $40. Disc: military. Apr 15 to Oct 31.
(888)884-2641 Lat: 37.275791, Lon: -107.331314
1875 CR-500, Bayfield, CO 81122
bluespruce@durango.net
www.bluesprucervpark.com
See ad pages 240, 230.

5 BRANCHES CAMPER PARK **Ratings: 6.5/6.5/6** (Campground) 2015 rates: $36. May 15 to Sep 7. (970)884-2582 4677 CR-501A, Bayfield, CO 81122

BELLVUE — B3 *Larimer*

Things to See and Do

LORY STATE PARK CO State Park. Tent camping only. Entrance fee required. Elev 5134 ft. Adult fee: $10 Tent Camping. No CC.
(970)493-1623 Lat: 40.600301, Lon: -105.182122
708 Lodgepole Dr, Bellvue, CO 80512
Lory.Park@State.co.us
www.cpw.state.co.us
See ad page 228 (Welcome Section).

BLACK HAWK — C3 *Gilpin, Jefferson*

BASE CAMP @ GOLDEN GATE CANYON **Ratings: 5/7/7** (Campground) 2015 rates: $38. (303)582-9979 661 Hwy 46, Blackhawk, CO 80422

BLANCA — E3 *Costilla*

BLANCA RV PARK **Ratings: 6.5/6/6** (RV Park) 2015 rates: $30. (719)379-3201 521 Main, Blanca, CO 81123

BOULDER — B3 *Boulder*

BOULDER See also Black Hawk, Brighton, Denver, Estes Park, Golden, Johnstown, Longmont, Loveland & Ward.

BRECKENRIDGE — C3 *Summit*

TIGER RUN RV RESORT
Ratings: 10/10★/10 (RV Resort) From Jct of I-70 & SR-9 (Exit 203), S 6.3 mi on SR-9 (L). Elev 9200 ft.

COLORADO'S BEST KEPT SECRET
Activities of all types are at your doorstep. Hike or bike the scenic trails, test your fishing skills, challenge the slopes. Enjoy all Tiger Run has to offer where imagination is all that limits you! Come & see if you agree!

FAC: Paved rds. 144 paved, patios, 28 pull-thrus (50 x 60), back-ins (40 x 75), 144 full hkups (30/50 amps), cable, WiFi, rentals, laundry, LP gas, fire rings, firewood, controlled access. **REC:** heated pool, whirlpool, Swan and Blue River: fishing, playground. Pet restrict(Q). No tents. Big rig sites, eco-friendly, 2015 rates: $55 to $110. Disc: AAA, military.
(800)895-9594 Lat: 39.53959, Lon: -106.04087
85 Revett Dr, Breckenridge, CO 80424
info@tigerrunresort.com
www.tigerrunresort.com
See ad opposite page, 230.

BRIGHTON — B4 *Adams*

BARR LAKE RV PARK **Ratings: 5.5/6.5/6.5** (RV Park) 2015 rates: $34 to $36. (303)659-6180 17180 E 136th Ave, Brighton, CO 80601

Things to See and Do

BARR LAKE STATE PARK Day use only. No camping. Entrance fee required. Fishing, multi-use trail, boating, bird watching, archery range. Elev 5137 ft. No CC.
(303)659-6005 Lat: 39.56400, Lon: -104.44145
13401 Picadilly Road, Brighton, CO 80603
barr.lake.nature.center@state.co.us
http://cpw.state.co.us/placestogo/parks/BarrLake
See ad page 228 (Welcome Section).

BRUSH — B4 *Morgan*

MEMORIAL PARK CAMPGROUND (Public) From Jct of SR-34 & Cameron St, S .27 mi on Cameron St, right on Ellsworth, left on Jordan Pl (R). 2015 rates: $10. Apr 1 to Oct 15. (970)842-5001

BUENA VISTA — D3 *Chaffee*

ARKANSAS RIVER RIM CAMPGROUND & RV PARK **Ratings: 5.5/7/6.5** (Campground) 2015 rates: $35 to $38. (719)395-8883 33198 US Hwy 24N, Buena Vista, CO 81211

ARROWHEAD POINT CAMPGROUND AND CABINS
Ratings: 8/9.5★/9.5 (Campground) From Jct of US 24 & US 285, N 7.9 mi on US 24 West (L). Elev 8295 ft. **FAC:** Gravel rds. 63 gravel, 15 pull-thrus (30 x 60), back-ins (30 x 50), 44 full hkups, 19 W, 19 E (30/50 amps), WiFi, tent sites, rentals, dump, laundry, groc, LP gas, fire rings, firewood. **REC:** playground. Pet restrict(Q). Big rig sites, eco-friendly, 2015 rates: $38 to $56. Disc: military. Apr 15 to Oct 15.
(719)395-2323 Lat: 38.91155, Lon: -106.18107
33975 U.s. Hwy 24 North, Buena Vista, CO 81211
reservations@arrowheadpointresort.com
www.arrowheadpointresort.com
See ad this page, 230.

MT PRINCETON RV PARK & CABINS **Ratings: 8/10★/8** (RV Park) 2015 rates: $39 to $49. Apr 1 to Nov 30. (719)395-6206 30380 County Rd 383, Buena Vista, CO 81211

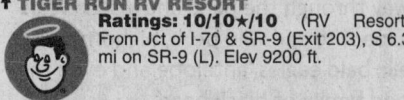

Join Us For the Fabulous Aspen Leaf Season

TIGER RUN RESORT

Colorado's Premier All-Season Resort

OPEN ALL YEAR

- Indoor Pool & Hot Tub
- On Free Bus Route to 4 Major Ski Areas
- Landscaped Sites With Patios
- Luxury Restrooms
- Large Pull-Thru Sites Available
- Nicklaus Golf Course 1/4 mi.
- Lake & Stream Fishing

Good Sam Park

Good Sam RATED 10/10★/10

See listing Breckenridge, CO

Reservations Recommended

For more information please call **1-800-895-9594**

or find us on the web: **www.tigerrunresort.com**

85 Tiger Run Rd.
Breckenridge, Colorado 80424

Sorry, no tents, tent trailers, pop-ups or truck campers. All rigs/trailers must be a minimum of 20'.

BUENA VISTA (CONT)

SNOWY PEAKS RV PARK AND RENTALS **Ratings: 8/8.5/8.5** (RV Park) 2015 rates: $34 to $70. (719)395-8481 30430 US Hwy 24, Buena Vista, CO 81211

CANON CITY — D3 *Fremont*

A SPOTLIGHT Introducing Royal Gorge/Canon City's colorful attractions appearing at the front of this state.

CANON CITY See also Penrose, Royal Gorge, Texas Creek.

CANON CITY RV CAMPGROUND **Ratings: 3.5/5/5** (RV Park) 2015 rates: $30 to $45. (719)275-4576 3120 E Main St, Canon City, CO 81212

ECHO CANYON CAMPGROUND **Ratings: 6/8.5★/7.5** (RV Park) 2015 rates: $34 to $42. May 1 to Sep 30. (866)341-7875 45044 US Hwy 50 West, Canon City, CO 81212

MOUNTAIN VIEW RV RESORT **Ratings: 7.5/9★/8.5** (RV Park) 2015 rates: $42 to $46. Apr 27 to Oct 31. (719)275-0900 45606 Highway 50W, Canon City, CO 81212

PROSPECTORS RV RESORT AT ROYAL GORGE **Ratings: 7.5/7/6.5** (Campground) 2015 rates: $34 to $42. (719)275-2128 43595 Hwy 50 West, Canon City, CO 81212

ROYAL GORGE KOA **Ratings: 8.5/8.5/7** (Campground) 2015 rates: $34 to $54. Apr 15 to Oct 1. (800)562-5689 559 Cr 3A, Canon City, CO 81212

ROYAL VIEW @ ROYAL GORGE CAMPGROUND
Ratings: 10/10★/10 (RV Park) E-bnd: From Jct of US-50 & SR-9, E 500 ft on US-50, between MP-269 & 270 (R); or W-bnd: From Jct of US-50 & Royal Gorge Rd, W 1 mi on US-50 (L). Elev 6238 ft. **FAC:** All weather rds. 48 Avail: 48 all weather, 42 pull-thrus (24 x 65), back-ins (28 x 60), 48 full hkups (30/50 amps), WiFi, tent sites, rentals, showers $, laundry, groc, fire rings, firewood. **REC:** heated pool, playground. Pet restrict(B/Q). Big rig sites, eco-friendly, 2015 rates: $33 to $55. Apr 15 to Oct 1.
(719)275-1900 Lat: 38.49504, Lon: -105.35056
43590 US Hwy 50 W, Canon City, CO 81212
royalviewcg@aol.com
www.royalviewcampground.com
See ad pages 249, 233 (Spotlight Royal Gorge/Canon City), 230.

CARBONDALE — C2 *Garfield, Pitkin*

CARBONDALE/CRYSTAL RIVER KOA **Ratings: 8/8.5/7.5** (Campground) 2015 rates: $42 to $45. Apr 1 to Nov 15. (970)963-2341 7202 Hwy 133, Carbondale, CO 81623

GATEWAY RV PARK
(Public) From Jct of Hwy 133 & Hwy 82: Go W on Hwy 82 1 mi to Satank (CR 106), then go .9 mi (at each Jct, veer left) (L). Elev 6192 ft. **FAC:** Gravel rds. 17 gravel, 6 pull-thrus (24 x 45), back-ins (24 x 35), 12 full hkups, 5 W, 5 E (30 amps), WiFi, tent sites, dump, fire rings. **REC:** Roaring Fork River: fishing. Pets OK. 14 day max stay, 2015 rates: $25 to $35. May 1 to Oct 15.
(970)510-1290 Lat: 39.41558, Lon: -107.22498
640 CR 106, Carbondale, CO 81623
ebrendlinger@carbondaleco.net
www.gateway-rv-park.com
See ad this page.

CASCADE — D4 *El Paso*

LONE DUCK CAMPGROUND Ratings: 8/9★/8 (Campground) From Jct of US-24 & Pikes Peak Hwy, W 2.1 mi on US-24 to Chipita Park/Green Mountain Falls exit, make U-turn, E 0.1 mi on US-24 to first right turn (R). Elev 7507 ft. **FAC:** Gravel rds. 43 Avail: 26 gravel, 17 grass, 5 pull-thrus (18 x 45), back-ins (18 x 35), some side by side hkups, 8 full hkups, 35 W, 35 E (30/50 amps), WiFi, tent sites, rentals, dump, laundry, groc, fire rings, firewood. **REC:** heated pool, pond, fishing, playground, rec open to public. Pets OK. 2015 rates: $36 to $42. Disc: AAA, military. May 1 to Sep 30.
AAA Approved
(719)684-9907 Lat: 38.91788, Lon: -104.98501
8855 W Hwy 24, Cascade, CO 80809
oneloneduck@aol.com
www.loneduckcamp.com

CASTLE ROCK — C4 *Douglas*

YOGI BEARS JELLYSTONE PARK @ LARKSPUR **Ratings: 8.5/8.5/7.5** (Campground) 2015 rates: $43 to $72. (720)325-2393 650 Skyview Lane, Larkspur, CO 80118

CEDAREDGE — C2 *Delta*

ASPEN TRAILS CAMPGROUND **Ratings: 5.5/6.5/7** (RV Park) 2015 rates: $32 to $40. (970)856-6321 19991 Hwy 65, Cedaredge, CO 81413

CENTRAL CITY — C3 *Gilpin*

DENVER WEST/CENTRAL CITY KOA **Ratings: 8/9.5/8.5** (RV Park) 2015 rates: $41 to $50. Apr 15 to Oct 15. (800)562-8613 605 Lake Gulch Road, Central City, CO 80427

CIMARRON — D2 *Gunnison*

BLACK CANYON RV PARK & CAMPGROUND **Ratings: 7.5/7/8** (RV Park) 2015 rates: $30. Apr 1 to Nov 30. (970)249-1147 348 Hwy 50, Cimarron, CO 81220

CLARK — B2 *Routt*

PEARL LAKE
(State Pk) From Steamboat Springs, W 2 mi on US-40 to CR-129, N 23 mi to Pearl Lake Rd, E 2 mi (E). Entrance fee required. Elev 8065 ft. **FAC:** Gravel rds. 36 dirt, tent sites, rentals, restrooms only, fire rings. **REC:** Pearl Lake: fishing, rec open to public. Pets OK. 14 day max stay, 2015 rates: $18. May 1 to Oct 31.
(970)879-3922 Lat: 40.812222, Lon: -107.013333
PO Box 750 - C/O Steamboat Lake, Clark, CO 80428
steamboat.lake@state.co.us
www.parks.state.co.us/parks/pearllake
See ad page 228 (Welcome Section).

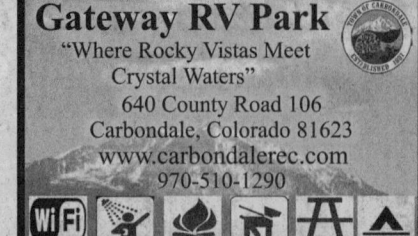

CLARK (CONT)

STEAMBOAT LAKE SRA
(State Pk) From Jct of US-40 & CR-129, N 26 mi on CR-129 (L). Entrance fee required. Elev 8060 ft. **FAC:** Paved rds. 168 gravel, 99 pull-thrus (10 x 50), back-ins (10 x 35), 106 E (30 amps), tent sites, rentals, showers $, dump, laundry, firewood. **REC:** Steamboat Lake: swim, fishing, marina, rec open to public. Pets OK. Partial handicap access. 14 day max stay, 2015 rates: $16 to $22. Jun 1 to Sep 30.
(970)879-3922 Lat: 40.816944, Lon: -107.077500
61105 Rcr 129, Clark, CO 80428
steamboat.lake@state.co.us
www.cpw.state.co.us
See ad page 228 (Welcome Section).

COALDALE — D3 *Fremont*

BIGHORN RV PARK
Ratings: 8.5/9★/8.5 (RV Park) From Jct of US-50 & CR-40: Go W on US-50 .3 mi (R) (Between Mile Post 242 & 243 - 4 mi W of Cotopaxi). Elev 6495 ft. **FAC:** Gravel rds. 23 gravel, 16 pull-thrus (30 x 60), back-ins (30 x 40), 20 full hkups, 3 W, 3 E (30/50 amps), WiFi, tent sites, rentals, dump, laundry, groc, LP gas, firewood. **REC:** heated pool, Arkansas River: fishing, playground. Pet restrict(B). Big rig sites, 2015 rates: $32 to $39. Disc: military. Apr 1 to Nov 1.
(719)942-4266 Lat: 38.215184, Lon: -105.444922
16373 Hwy 50 W, Coaldale, CO 81222
bighornpark@yahoo.com
www.bighornpark.com

CUTTY'S HAYDEN CREEK RV CAMPING & RESORT **Ratings: 7.5/7.5/8** (Campground) 2015 rates: $49 to $60. May 1 to Oct 15. (719)942-4222 3428 Hayden Creek Rd, Coaldale, CO 81222

COLLBRAN — C2 *Mesa*

VEGA
(State Pk) From town, E 6 mi on CR-330E to Vega Reservoir Rd, SE 6 mi (E). Entrance fee required. Elev 8000 ft. **FAC:** Paved/gravel rds. 99 Avail: 60 paved, 39 gravel, patios, back-ins (12 x 30), some side by side hkups, 33 W, 33 E (30/50 amps), tent sites, rentals, showers $, dump, firewood. **REC:** Vega Reservoir: fishing, playground, rec open to public. Pets OK. Partial handicap access. 14 day max stay, 2015 rates: $16 to $20.
(970)487-3407 Lat: 39.267500, Lon: -107.911944
15247 North 64 6/10 Road, Collbran, CO 81624
vega.park@state.co.us
www.cpw.state.co.us
See ad page 228 (Welcome Section).

COLORADO CITY — D4 *Pueblo*

PUEBLO SOUTH/COLORADO CITY KOA **Ratings: 10/10★/10** (RV Park) 2015 rates: $41 to $46. (888)676-3370 9040 I-25 S @ Exit 74, Pueblo, CO 81004

COLORADO SPRINGS — D4 *El Paso*

COLORADO SPRINGS See also Cascade, Falcon, Fountain, Manitou Springs, Monument & Woodland Park.

CHEYENNE MOUNTAIN
(State Pk) From I-25 (Exit 135): Go W on S Academy 2 mi to Hwy 115. Go S on Hwy 115 2 mi. Go W on JL Ranch Heights Rd (L) Note: Pets welcome in developed areas only. Entrance fee required. Elev 6010 ft. **FAC:** Paved rds. 51 paved, 12 pull-thrus (20 x 40), back-ins (20 x 40), some side by side hkups, 51 full hkups (30/50 amps), tent sites, showers $, dump, laundry, fire rings, firewood. **REC:** rec open to public. Pets OK. 14 day max stay, 2015 rates: $24 to $26.
(719)576-2016 Lat: 38.73708, Lon: -104.817774
410 Jl Ranch Heights, Colorado Springs, CO 80926
cheyenne.park@state.co.us
www.cpw.state.co.us
See ad page 228 (Welcome Section).

FOOT OF THE ROCKIES RV RESORT **Ratings: 7/NA/8.5** (RV Park) 2015 rates: $37 to $47. (719)447-0670 53 Resort Pointe, Colorado Springs, CO 80905

FOUNTAIN CREEK RV PARK
Ratings: 8/8.5★/7 (RV Park) From Jct of I-25 & US-24 (exit 141), W 2.7 mi on US-24 to 31st St, N 0.1 mi to Colorado Ave, E 1/4 Blk to Golden Lane Rd, S 300 ft (E). Elev 6077 ft. **FAC:** All weather rds. 90 Avail: 90 all weather, patios, 36 pull-thrus (30 x 60), back-ins (18 x 40), 90 full hkups (30/50 amps), cable, WiFi, rentals, dump, laundry, LP gas. **REC:** Fountain Creek. Pets OK. No tents. Big rig sites, 2015 rates: $41 to $44. Disc: military.
(719)633-2192 Lat: 38.51606, Lon: -104.521969
3023 W Colorado Avenue, Colorado Springs, CO 80904
info@fountaincreekrvpark.com
www.fountaincreekrvpark.com
See ad this page, 230.

GARDEN OF THE GODS RV RESORT
Ratings: 9.5/9.5★/9.5 (RV Park) From Jct of I-25 & US-24 (exit 141), W 2.7 mi on US-24 to 31st St, N 0.1 mi to Colorado Ave, W 0.7 mi (R). Elev 6157 ft.

PIKES PEAK & GARDEN OF THE GODS
Make Garden of the Gods RV Resort the base camp for your Colorado adventure. Beautiful landscaping, 5-star amenities, concierge service, and a location central to natural attractions. Big-rig friendly sites!
FAC: Paved rds. 173 Avail: 6 paved, 167 gravel, patios, 65 pull-thrus (24 x 60), back-ins (24 x 45), 173 full hkups (30/50 amps), WiFi, tent sites, rentals, dump, laundry, LP gas, fire rings, firewood, restaurant. **REC:** heated pool, playground. Pet restrict(B) $. Big rig sites, RV age restrict, eco-friendly, 2015 rates: $42 to $64.
(800)248-9451 Lat: 38.85717, Lon: -104.88499

We appreciate your business!

CO

COLORADO SPRINGS (CONT)

GARDEN OF THE GODS RV RESORT (CONT)
3704 W Colorado Ave, Colorado Springs, CO 80904
GOG@RVCOutdoors.com
www.rvcoutdoors.com/garden-of-the-gods/
See ad pages 237, 230 & RV Trips of a Lifetime in Magazine Section.

GOLDEN EAGLE CAMPGROUND, INC
Ratings: 7.5/8★/7.5 (Campground) From S Jct of I-25 & Academy Blvd (exit 135), W 2 mi on Academy Blvd to SR-115 (Nevada), S 4.8 mi to Rock Creek Canyon Rd, W 1 mi (R). Elev 6350 ft. **FAC:** Gravel rds. 200 gravel, 144 pull-thrus (35 x 60), back-ins (21 x 45), 120 full hkups, 80 W, 80 E (30/50 amps), WiFi, tent sites, dump, laundry, groc, fire rings, firewood. **REC:** Golden Eagle Lakes: fishing, playground. Pets OK. Partial handicap access. Big rig sites, eco-friendly, 2015 rates: $32 to $34.
(719)576-0450 Lat: 38.70516, Lon: -104.84080
710 Rock Creek Canyon Road, Colorado Springs, CO 80926
diana.fruh@goldeneaglecg.com
www.campingincoloradosprings.com
See ad page 237.

GOLDFIELD RV PARK
Ratings: 7.5/9★/7 (RV Park) From Jct of I-25 & US-24 (exit 141), W 2.1 mi on US-24 to 26th St, S 100 ft (L) Please call for Big Rig Availability. Elev 6096 ft. **FAC:** All weather rds. 52 Avail: 52 all weather, 10 pull-thrus (19 x 75), back-ins (19 x 60), some side by side hkups, 52 full hkups (30/50 amps), cable, WiFi, tent sites, rentals, dump, laundry. Pets OK. Big rig sites, 2015 rates: $30 to $40. Disc: AAA, military.
AAA Approved
(888)471-0495 Lat: 38.84494, Lon: -104.86694
411 S 26th Street, Colorado Springs, CO 80904
info@goldfieldrvpark.com
www.goldfieldrvpark.com
See ad pages 236, 230.

MOUNTAINDALE CABINS & RV RESORT **Ratings: 8/9★/9.5** (RV Park) 2015 rates: $41 to $44. (719)576-0619 2000 Barrett Road, Colorado Springs, CO 80926

ROCKY TOP MOTEL & CAMPGROUND **Ratings: 7.5/8★/7** (Campground) 2015 rates: $37. (866)900-9044 10090 W. Hwy 24, Green Mountain Falls, CO 80819

WRANGLER RV RANCH & MOTEL
Ratings: 6/6.5/5.5 (RV Park) From Jct of I-25 & US-24 (exit 139), E 4.5 mi on US-24 (becomes Fountain Blvd) to Powers Blvd, N 2.4 mi to Platte Ave, E 0.4 mi (R); or W-bnd (from Limon): Jct of US-24 & SR-94, W 1.2 mi on US-24, just prior to Powers Blvd (L). Elev 6270 ft. **FAC:** Gravel rds. 95 gravel, 16 pull-thrus (25 x 100), back-ins (25 x 40), 95 full hkups (30/50 amps), WiFi, laundry. Pet restrict(B/Q). No tents. Big rig sites, 2015 rates: $29 to $30.
(719)591-1402 Lat: 38.8338, Lon: -104.71258
6225 E Platte Ave, Colorado Springs, CO 80915
wranglerrvandmotel@yahoo.com
www.wranglerrvpark.com
See ad page 237.

CORTEZ — E1 *Montezuma*

CORTEZ See also Dolores & Mancos.

CORTEZ/MESA VERDE KOA Ratings: 8/9.5★/9 (RV Park) From Jct of US-160 & SR-145, E 0.4 mi on US-160 (R). Elev 6248 ft. **FAC:** Gravel rds. 74 gravel, 59 pull-thrus (24 x 60), back-ins (24 x 35), mostly side by side hkups, 36 full hkups, 38 W, 38 E (30/50 amps), WiFi, tent sites, rentals, dump, laundry, groc, fire rings, firewood. **REC:** heated pool, Denny Lake: fishing, playground. Pet restrict(B). Partial handicap access. Big rig sites, eco-friendly, 2015 rates: $33 to $65. Disc: AAA, military. Apr 1 to Oct 15. ATM.
AAA Approved
(800)562-3901 Lat: 37.21259, Lon: -108.32479
27432 E Hwy 160, Cortez, CO 81321
cortzkoa@fone.net
www.cortezkoa.com

LA MESA RV PARK **Ratings: 6/8.5★/8** (RV Park) 2015 rates: $30 to $40. (505)215-0712 2380 E Main, Cortez, CO 81321

SLEEPING UTE RV PARK
Ratings: 8.5/10★/9 (RV Park) From Jct 160/491:Go S on 160 11 mi (R). Elev 5843 ft. **FAC:** Gravel rds. 76 gravel, 61 pull-thrus (35 x 62), back-ins (35 x 35), 30 full hkups, 46 W, 46 E (30/50 amps), cable, WiFi, tent sites, dump, laundry. **REC:** heated pool, playground. Pets OK. Big rig sites, 2015 rates: $32.95 to $36.25. Disc: AAA, military. Mar 1 to Nov 1.
AAA Approved
(800)889-5072 Lat: 37.20642, Lon: -108.68837
No. 3 Weeminuche Drive, Towaoc, CO 81334
RBROOKER@UTEMOUNTAINCASINO.COM
www.utemountaincasino.com
See ad this page, 230.

SUNDANCE RV PARK LLC
Ratings: 9/10★/9.5 (RV Park) E-Bnd: From Jct of US-160 & US-491, E 1 mi on US-160 (R); or W-Bnd: From Jct of US-160 & SR-145, W 1.3 mi on US-160 (L). Elev 6200 ft. **FAC:** Paved rds. 64 Avail: 64 all weather, 13 pull-thrus (30 x 65), back-ins (30 x 50), 64 full hkups (30/50 amps), cable, WiFi, dump, laundry. **REC.** Pet restrict(Q). No tents. Big rig sites, eco-friendly, 2015 rates: $38. Disc: AAA, military.
(800)880-9413 Lat: 37.34847, Lon: -108.57442
815 E Main, Cortez, CO 81321
sundancervpark@yahoo.com
www.sundancervpark.com
See ad this page, 230.

COTOPAXI — D3 *Fremont*

ARKANSAS RIVER KOA & LOMA LINDA MOTEL **Ratings: 8.5/7.5/7.5** (Campground) 2015 rates: $35 to $62. Apr 1 to Oct 31. (800)562-2686 21435 US-50, Cotopaxi, CO 81223

CRAIG — B2 *Moffat*

CRAIG KOA **Ratings: 8/10★/9** (RV Park) 2015 rates: $44 to $46. Mar 15 to Nov 20. (970)824-5105 2800 E. Hwy 40, Craig, CO 81625

ELKHEAD RESERVOIR
(State Pk) From town, E 6 mi on Hwy 40 to Moffat CR-29, N 5 mi, Entrance fee required. Elev 6300 ft. **FAC:** Gravel rds. 16 grass, back-ins (18 x 60), tent sites, showers $, dump, fire rings. **REC:** Elkhead Reservoir: swim, fishing. Pets OK. Partial handicap access. 14 day max stay, 2015 rates: $16. May 1 to Nov 15. No CC.
(970)276-2061 Lat: 40.4938069, Lon: -107.279026
p.o Box 789, Hayden, CO 81639
yampa.river@state.co.us
www.cpw.state.co.us
See ad page 228 (Welcome Section).

Looking for places the "locals" frequent? Make friends with park owners and staff to get the inside scoop!

CRAWFORD — D2 *Delta*

CRAWFORD
(State Pk) From Jct of Hwy 133 & Hwy 92 (in Hotchkiss), SE 12.3 mi on Hwy 92 (R) (1 mi S of Crawford) Entrance Fee Required. Elev 6600 ft. **FAC:** Gravel rds. 61 Avail: 4 paved, 57 gravel, 33 pull-thrus (20 x 70), back-ins (30 x 60), 45 W, 45 E (30/50 amps), tent sites, showers $, dump, firewood. **REC:** Crawford Reservoir: swim, fishing, playground, rec open to public. Pets OK. Partial handicap access. 14 day max stay, 2015 rates: $16 to $20.
(970)921-5721 Lat: 38.68753, Lon: -107.59540
40468 Hwy 92, Crawford, CO 81415
crawford.park@state.co.us
www.cpw.state.co.us
See ad page 228 (Welcome Section).

CREEDE — D2 *Mineral*

ANTLER'S RIO GRANDE LODGE & RV PARK **Ratings: 8/8.5★/8.5** (RV Park) 2015 rates: $40 to $45. May 15 to Oct 1. (719)658-2423 26222 Hwy 149, Creede, CO 81130

MOUNTAIN VIEWS AT RIVERS EDGE RV RESORT **Ratings: 9.5/10★/10** (RV Resort) 2015 rates: $28 to $43. May 25 to Oct 1. (719)658-2710 539 Airport Rd, Creede, CO 81130

CRIPPLE CREEK — D3 *Teller*

CRIPPLE CREEK HOSPITALITY HOUSE & TRAVEL PARK Ratings: 6/6/6.5 (RV Park) From Jct of SR-67 & B St (W edge of town), N 0.4 mi on B St (E). Elev 9630 ft. **FAC:** Gravel rds. 53 Avail: 33 gravel, 20 grass, 36 pull-thrus (20 x 45), back-ins (20 x 45), 53 full hkups (30/50 amps), WiFi Hotspot, tent sites, dump, laundry. **REC:** playground. Pets OK. 2015 rates: $33 to $36. May 15 to Oct 1.
AAA Approved
(719)689-2513 Lat: 38.451323, Lon: -105.11384
600 N B Street, Cripple Creek, CO 80813
CCHospitalityHouse@icloud.com
www.cchospitalityhouse.com

CRIPPLE CREEK KOA **Ratings: 8/9★/9** (Campground) 2015 rates: $33 to $70. May 23 to Oct 6. (719)689-5647 2576 CR 81, Cripple Creek, CO 80813

EAGLES LANDING RV PARK **Ratings: 6/6.5/5** (RV Park) 2015 rates: $30 to $40. (719)689-2006 202 E May Ave, Cripple Creek, CO 80813

LOST BURRO CAMPGROUND **Ratings: 5/6/7.5** (Campground) 2015 rates: $27 to $46. (719)689-2345 4623 Teller Co Rd 1, Cripple Creek, CO 80813

DELTA — D2 *Delta*

VALLEY SUNSET RV RANCH **Ratings: 8.5/8/6.5** (RV Park) 2015 rates: $25. (970)874-0200 1675 Hwy 92, Delta, CO 81416

Things to See and Do

SWEITZER LAKE STATE PARK CO State Park. Day use only. No camping. Entrance fee required. Elev 4953 ft. Hours: 9am to 5pm. No CC.
(970)874-4258 Lat: 38.716308, Lon: -108.02874
1735 E Rd, Delta, CO 81416
www.cpw.state.co.us
See ad page 228 (Welcome Section).

Did you know we sent 35 husband-wife RVing teams out this year to scour North America, rating and inspecting RV parks and campgrounds? You can rest easy when you read our listings, knowing we've already been there.

DENVER — C4 *Jefferson*

DENVER AREA MAP

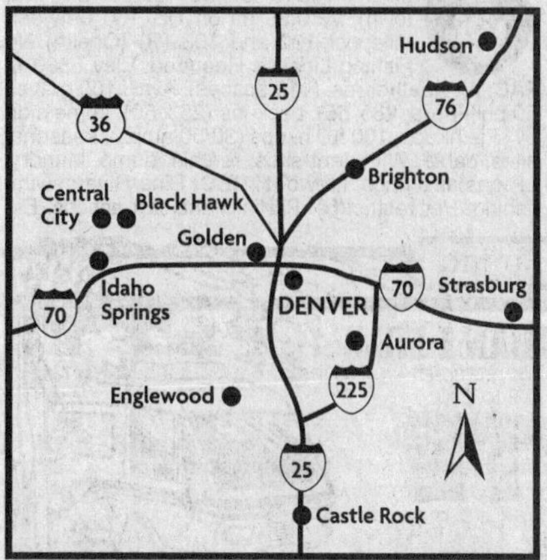

For more detail and a broader overview, please see our full-color state map at the front of the Colorado state section.

Symbols on map indicate towns within a 35 mile radius of Denver where campgrounds are listed. Check listings for more information.

See also Aurora, Black Hawk, Brighton, Castle Rock, Central City, Englewood, Golden, Hudson, Idaho Springs & Strasburg.

PROSPECT PLACE R.V. PARK & CAMPGROUND **Ratings: 7/9★/7.5** (RV Park) 2015 rates: $30 to $32.50. (303)424-4414 11600 W. 44th Ave, Wheat Ridge, CO 80033

Things to See and Do

CASTLEWOOD CANYON STATE PARK CO State Park. Day use only. No camping. Entrance fee required. Elev 6635 ft. No CC.
(303)688-5242 Lat: 39.19464, Lon: -104.44177
2989 S State Hwy 83, Franktown, CO 80116
castlewood.canyon@state.co.us
www.cpw.state.co.us
See ad page 228 (Welcome Section).

Find it Fast! Use our alphabetized index of campgrounds and parks.

COLORADO PARKS & WILDLIFE Colorado's 42 state parks offer some of the highest quality outdoor recreation destinations in the state. See individual park listings for campground information. Elev 5800 ft. partial handicap access. RV accessible. Restrooms. Hours: 8am to 5pm. No CC.
(800)678-2267 Lat: 39.80600, Lon: -104.98755
www.cpw.state.co.us
See ad page 228 (Welcome Section).

DINOSAUR — B1 *Moffat*

DINOSAUR NATIONAL MONUMENT/GATES OF LODORE (Natl Pk) From town, E 54 mi on US-40 to SR-318, NW 72 mi (L). Pit toilets. 2015 rates: $8. (435)781-7700

DIVIDE — C3 *Teller*

MUELLER
(State Pk) From Jct US 24 & Hwy 67, S 3.5 mi on Hwy 67 (E). Entrance fee required. Elev 9600 ft. **FAC:** Paved rds. 110 paved, 80 pull-thrus (14 x 40), back-ins (14 x 40), 110 E (30 amps), tent sites, rentals, pit toilets, dump, laundry, fire rings, firewood. **REC:** pond, fishing, playground, rec open to public. Pets OK. Partial handicap access. 14 day max stay, 2015 rates: $18 to $22. No CC.
(719)687-2366 Lat: 38.89254, Lon: -105.15788
21045 Hwy 67 S, Divide, CO 80814
mueller.park@state.co.us
www.cpw.state.co.us
See ad page 228 (Welcome Section).

DOLORES — E1 *Montezuma*

DOLORES RIVER CAMPGROUND Ratings: 8.5/10★/9 (Campground) From Jct of US-160 & SR-145 (in Cortez), NE 13 mi on SR-145 (R). Elev 6974 ft. **FAC:** All weather rds. 77 Avail: 77 all weather, patios, 21 pull-thrus (30 x 60), back-ins (30 x 50), some side by side hkups, 76 full hkups, 1 W, 1 E (30/50 amps), cable, WiFi, tent sites, rentals, dump, laundry, groc, LP gas, fire rings, firewood. **REC:** Dolores River: fishing, playground. Pet restrict(B). Big rig sites, eco-friendly, 2015 rates: $37. May 1 to Oct 31.
(970)882-7761 Lat: 37.47596, Lon: -108.45500
18680 Hwy 145, Dolores, CO 81323
doloresrivercampground@gmail.com
www.doloresrivercampground.com

DURANGO — E2 *La Plata*

ALPEN-ROSE RV PARK
Ratings: 8.5/10★/9.5 (RV Park) From W Jct of US-160 & US-550, N 6.3 mi on US-550, 2 mi from the N edge of town (L). Elev 6482 ft. **FAC:** All weather rds. 100 gravel, 61 pull-thrus (27 x 70), back-ins (20 x 40), mostly side by side hkups, 100 full hkups (30/50 amps), WiFi, dump, laundry, groc, LP gas, restaurant. **REC:** heated pool, pond, fishing, playground. Pets OK. Partial handicap

DURANGO (CONT)

ALPEN-ROSE RV PARK (CONT)
access, no tents. Big rig sites, 2015 rates: $45 to $51. Disc: AAA, military. Apr 1 to Oct 31.
(877)259-5791 Lat: 37.35053, Lon: -107.85550
27847 Hwy 550 N, Durango, CO 81301
camp@alpenroservpark.com
www.alpenroservpark.com
See ad this page.

BAYFIELD RIVERSIDE RV PARK
Ratings: 9/10★/9 (RV Park) From Jct of US 160 & CR-501 (West edge of town), W 0.25 mi on US 160 between milepost 102 and 103 (R) (Onsite) No Fishing License Required. Elev 6800 ft. **FAC:** All weather rds. (119 spaces). Avail: 100 gravel, 60 pull-thrus (28 x 65), back-ins (25 x 50), some side by side hkups, 100 full hkups (30/50 amps), seasonal sites, cable, WiFi, tent sites, rentals, dump, laundry, LP gas, fire rings, firewood. **REC:** Pine River: swim, fishing. Pet restrict(B). Partial handicap access. Big rig sites, eco-friendly, 2015 rates: $48. Disc: AAA, military.
(970)884-2475 Lat: 37.23018, Lon: -107.60691
41743 US Hwy 160, Bayfield, CO 81122-0919
riversidervparkbayfield@gmail.com
www.pineriverrvcamp.com
See ad pages 239, 230.

DURANGO KOA **Ratings: 9/9.5★/8.5** (Campground) 2015 rates: $33 to $70. May 1 to Oct 15. (800)562-0793 30090 Hwy 160 E, Durango, CO 81303

DURANGO RIVERSIDE RESORT & RV PARK **Ratings: 9/8/8** (RV Park) 2015 rates: $37 to $79. May 1 to Oct 1. (800)351-2819 13391 CR-250, Durango, CO 81301

LIGHTNER CREEK CAMPGROUND **Ratings: 8.5/9.5★/9** (RV Park) 2015 rates: $46 to $51. May 1 to Oct 15. (970)247-5406 1567 CR-207, Durango, CO 81301

UNITED CAMPGROUND OF DURANGO **Ratings: 8.5/9.5★/8.5** (RV Park) 2015 rates: $37 to $47. Apr 15 to Oct 15. (970)247-3853 1322 Animas View Drive, Durango, CO 81301

VALLECITO RESORT
Ratings: 8/9.5★/8.5 (RV Park) From Jct of US-160 & CR-501, N 12.6 mi on CR-501 (R). Elev 7598 ft. **FAC:** Gravel rds. (150 spaces). Avail: 100 gravel, 37 pull-thrus (26 x 80), back-ins (26 x 60), 100 full hkups (30/50 amps), seasonal sites, WiFi, tent sites, rentals, dump, laundry, LP gas, firewood. **REC:** whirlpool, playground. Pet restrict(B/Q). Partial handicap access. Big rig sites, eco-friendly, 2015 rates: $37.95. Disc: military. May 1 to Oct 1.
(970)884-9458 Lat: 37.224517, Lon: -107.345273
13030 County Road 501, Bayfield, CO 81122
info@vallecitoresort.com
www.vallecitoresort.com
See ad this page.

WESTERLY RV PARK
Ratings: 7.5/NA/7.5 (RV Park) From the W. Jct of US 160 and US 550, N 9 mi on US 550 to Trimble Lane, W 0.1 mi to CR 203, N 200 ft (R). Elev 6600 ft. **FAC:** Gravel rds. 25 gravel, 4 pull-thrus (24 x 70), back-ins (30 x 60), 25 full hkups (30/50 amps), WiFi, laundry, fire rings. **REC:** whirl-

Park owners and staff are rightly proud of their business. Let them know how much you enjoyed your stay.

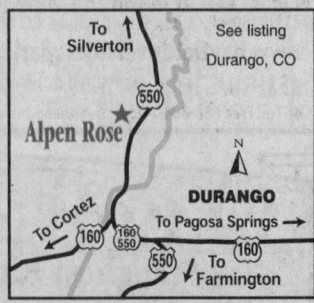

DURANGO (CONT)

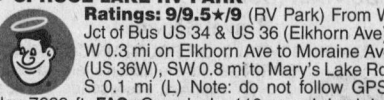

WESTERLY RV PARK (CONT)
pool. Pet restrict(B/Q) $. No tents. Big rig sites, 2015 rates: $37 to $45. Disc: military.
(970)247-1275 Lat: 37.232675, Lon: -107.505320
6440 CR 203, Durango, CO 81301
relax@westerlyrvpark.com
www.westerlyrvpark.com
See ad opposite page.

EAGLE — C2 *Eagle*

SYLVAN LAKE
(State Pk) From Jct of I-70 & Eagle exit (#147), S 1 mi on Main St to West Brush Creek Rd, S 16 mi (road becomes unpaved - stay right at the fork) (R). Entrance fee required. Visitor center. Elev 8500 ft. **FAC:** Gravel rds. 46 gravel, 28 pull-thrus (12 x 36), back-ins (12 x 40), tent sites, rentals, showers $, dump, firewood. **REC:** Sylvan Lake: fishing, rec open to public. Pets OK. 14 day max stay, 2015 rates: $18. May 1 to Oct 1.
(970)328-2021 Lat: 39.579167, Lon: -106.882778
10200 Brush Creek Road, Eagle, CO 81631
sylvan.park@state.co.us
www.cpw.state.co.us
See ad page 228 (Welcome Section).

ELDORADO SPRINGS — B3 *Boulder*

Things to See and Do

ELDORADO CANYON STATE PARK Day use only. Hiking. No camping. Entrance fee required. Elev 6108 ft. No CC.
(303)543-8882 Lat: 39.55509, Lon: -105.17423
9 Kneale Road, Eldorado Springs, CO 80025
eldorado.park@state.co.us
www.cpw.state.co.us
See ad page 228 (Welcome Section).

ENGLEWOOD — C4 *Arapahoe*

FLYING SAUCER RV PARK & STORAGE **Ratings: 5.5/6.5/6.5** (RV Park) 2015 rates: $45. (303)789-1707 2500 W Hampden Ave, Englewood, CO 80110

SOUTH PARK MOBILE HOMES AND RV COMMUNITY
Ratings: 8.5/8.5/8 (RV Park) From Jct of I-25 Hampden Ave/US 285 (exit 201), W 5.3 mi on Hampden Ave/US 285 to Federal Blvd, S 0.1 mi (L) Note: No dogs allowed in park. Elev 5261 ft. **FAC:** Paved rds. 23 Avail: 13 paved, 10 gravel, patios, back-ins (24 x 60), accepts full hkup units only, 23 full hkups (30/50 amps), WiFi Hotspot, laundry. **REC:** heated pool, shuffleboard. No pets. No tents. Age restrict may apply, RV age restrict, eco-friendly, 2015 rates: $40. No CC.
AAA Approved
(303)761-0121 Lat: 39.64989, Lon: -105.02355
3650 S. Federal Blvd #97, Englewood, CO 80110
southparkrvparkreservations@gmail.com
www.southparkmhc.com
See ad page 239.

ESTES PARK — B3 *Larimer*

ELK MEADOW LODGE AND RV RESORT
Ratings: 9/8.5★/8.5 (RV Park) From W Jct of Bus US 34 & US 36 (Elkhorn Ave), W 0.3 mi on Elkhorn Ave to Moraine Ave (US 36 W), SW 1.2 mi to Hwy-66, SW 0.2 mi (R) Note: do not follow GPS. Elev 7750 ft. **FAC:** Gravel rds. 169 gravel, 50 pull-thrus (30 x 60), back-ins (30 x 50), 169 full hkups (30/50 amps), cable, WiFi, tent sites, rentals, laundry, groc, LP gas, fire rings, firewood. **REC:** heated pool, whirlpool, playground, rec open to public. Pet restrict(B/Q). Big rig sites, eco-friendly, 2015 rates: $65. Disc: military. May 1 to Oct 3.
(970)586-5342 Lat: 40.36203, Lon: -105.55320
1665 Co Hwy 66, Estes Park, CO 80517
info@elkmeadowrv.com
www.elkmeadowrv.com
See ad this page, 230.

ESTES PARK CAMPGROUND AT EAST PORTAL (Public) From W Jct of Bus US-34 & US-36 (in town), S 1.6 mi on US-36 to SR-66 (Rocky Mountain Natl Park to W on US-36), SW 3.2 mi on SR-66 (E). Small rigs only. 2015 rates: $30 to $45. May 15 to Oct 15. (800)964-7806

ESTES PARK CAMPGROUND AT MARY'S LAKE (Public) From jct US 34 & US 36: Go 1/2 mi SE on US 36, then 1-1/2 mi S on Hwy 7, then 1-1/2 mi W on Peak View Dr. 2015 rates: $15 to $37. May 15 to Oct 15. (800)679-4570

ESTES PARK KOA **Ratings: 7.5/9★/8** (Campground) 2015 rates: $36 to $67. May 1 to Oct 15. (800)562-1887 2051 Big Thompson Ave, Estes Park, CO 80517

MANOR RV PARK
Ratings: 7/9/8 (RV Park) From E Jct of US-34 & US-36, W 0.2 mi on Bus US-34/US-36 to Riverside Dr (on left in center of town), 3rd light W-bnd, SW 1.5 mi on Riverside Dr (R). Elev 7644 ft. **FAC:** Paved/gravel rds. 115 gravel, patios, 4 pull-thrus (25 x 65), back-ins (25 x 40), 115 full hkups (30/50 amps), cable, WiFi, rentals, laundry, LP bottles, firewood. **REC:** Big Thompson River: fishing, playground. Pet restrict(Q). No tents. Big rig sites, 2015 rates: $55 to $72. Disc: AAA, military. May 15 to Oct 15.
(970)586-3251 Lat: 40.36171, Lon: -105.53824
815 Riverside Dr, Estes Park, CO 80517
alison@trouthavenresorts.com
www.manorrvpark.com
See ad this page, 230.

PARADISE ON THE RIVER RV PARK **Ratings: 6.5/9★/8** (RV Park) 2015 rates: $48 to $62. May 1 to Oct 15. (866)556-3422 1836 State Hwy 66, Estes Park, CO 80517

ROCKY MTN/ASPENGLEN (Natl Pk) From Rocky Mountain National Park entrance, S 0.2 mi on US-34 (L). Entrance fee required. 2015 rates: $20. May 21 to Sep 27. (970)586-1206

ROCKY MTN/GLACIER BASIN (Natl Pk) From town, W 5 mi on Bear Lake Rd (L). Reservations required. Entrance fee required. 2015 rates: $20. May 21 to Sep 7. (970)586-1206

ROCKY MTN/LONGS PEAK (Natl Pk) 9 miles south of Estes Park off of Highway 7. 2015 rates: $20. May 15 to Sep 15. (970)586-1206

ROCKY MTN/MORAINE PARK MUSEUM CAMPGROUND (Natl Pk) From Jct US-34 & US-36, W 5 mi on US-36 (L). Entrance fee required. Pit toilets. 2015 rates: $14 to $20. (970)586-1206

We rate what RVers consider important.

SPRUCE LAKE RV PARK
Ratings: 9/9.5★/9 (RV Park) From W Jct of Bus US 34 & US 36 (Elkhorn Ave), W 0.3 mi on Elkhorn Ave to Moraine Ave (US 36W), SW 0.8 mi to Mary's Lake Rd, S 0.1 mi (L) Note: do not follow GPS. Elev 7622 ft. **FAC:** Gravel rds. 110 gravel, back-ins (40 x 40), 88 full hkups, 22 W, 22 E (30/50 amps), cable, WiFi, rentals, dump, laundry, LP gas, firewood. **REC:** heated pool, whirlpool, Big Thompson River: fishing, playground. Pet restrict(B/Q). No tents. Eco-friendly, 2015 rates: $65. Disc: military. May 1 to Oct 3.
(970)586-2889 Lat: 40.36246, Lon: -105.54265
1050 Mary's Lake Rd, Estes park, CO 80517
info@sprucelakerv.com
www.sprucelakerv.com
See ad this page, 230.

YOGI BEAR'S JELLYSTONE PARK OF ESTES **Ratings: 8/8/7.5** (Campground) 2015 rates: $49 to $59. May 10 to Sep 30. (800)722-2928 5495 US Hwy 36, Estes Park, CO 80517

FAIRPLAY — C3 *Park*

MIDDLEFORK RV RESORT **Ratings: 5.5/6.5/6.5** (RV Park) 2015 rates: $25 to $36. May 1 to Oct 1. (719)836-4857 255 US Hwy 285, Fairplay, CO 80440

FALCON — C4 *El Paso*

FALCON MEADOW RV CAMPGROUND
Ratings: 7/8.5★/8 (RV Park) From Jct of US-24 & Power Blvd (E Edge of Colorado Springs), NE 7.9 mi on US 24 (L). Elev 6800 ft. **FAC:** Gravel rds. 45 gravel, 25 pull-thrus (28 x 60), back-ins (25 x 60), some side by side hkups, 40 full hkups, 5 W, 5 E (30/50 amps), WiFi, tent sites, dump, laundry, groc, LP gas, firewood. **REC:** playground. Pets OK. Partial handicap access. Big rig sites, 2015 rates: $33 to $35.
AAA Approved
(719)495-2694 Lat: 38.92408, Lon: -104.61981
11150 E Hwy 24, Peyton, CO 80831
falconmeadowcg@aol.com
www.falconmeadowrvcampground.com
See ad page 237.

FORT COLLINS — B3 *Larimer*

FORT COLLINS KOA LAKESIDE **Ratings: 9.5/9/9.5** (Campground) 2015 rates: $41 to $93. (800)562-9168 1910 Lakeside Resort Ln, Fort Collins, CO 80524

HORSETOOTH RESERVOIR (LARIMER COUNTY PARK) (Public) From jct I-25 (exit 265) & Hwy 68 (Harmony Rd): Go 7 mi W on Hwy 68, then 1 mi N on CR 19 (Taft Hill Rd), then W on CR 38E. Pit toilets. 2015 rates: $15. (970)619-4570

FOUNTAIN — D4 *El Paso*

COLORADO SPRINGS KOA **Ratings: 9.5/10★/9** (RV Park) 2015 rates: $54. (719)382-7575 8100 Bandley Drive, Fountain, CO 80817

CO

FOUNTAIN (CONT)

Travel Services

CAMPING WORLD OF FOUNTAIN/COLORADO SPRINGS As the nation's largest retailer of RV supplies, accessories, services and new and used RVs, Camping World is committed to making your total RV experience better. RV Accessories: (888)502-3870. Elev 5720 ft. **SERVICES:** RV appliance, MH mechanical, staffed RV wash, restrooms, RV Sales. RV supplies, emergency parking, RV accessible. waiting room. Hours: 8am to 6pm.
(888)539-1869 Lat: 38.73251, Lon: -104.73804
6830 Bandley Drive, Fountain, CO 80817
mlongmire@campingworld.com
www.CampingWorldofColoradoSprings.com

FRUITA — C1 *Mesa*

COLORADO NATL MON/SADDLEHORN CAMPGROUND (Natl Pk) From Jct of I-70 & SR-340, S 3 mi on SR-340 to park entrance, S 4.5 mi (L). Entrance fee required. Note: 40' RV length limit. 2015 rates: $20. (970)858-3617

JAMES M. ROBB - COLORADO RIVER/FRUITA (State Pk) From Jct of I-70 & SR-340 (exit 19), S 0.3 mi (R) Park entrance fee is required. Corn Lake 970-434-3388. Elev 4495 ft. **FAC:** Paved rds. 44 paved, 34 pull-thrus (25 x 60), back-ins (25 x 60), 22 full hkups, 22 W, 22 E (30/50 amps), tent sites, showers $, dump, laundry, fire rings, firewood. **REC:** Colorado River: playground, rec open to public. Pets OK. Partial handicap access. Big rig sites, 14 day max stay, 2015 rates: $13 to $24.
(970)858-9188 Lat: 39.14988, Lon: -108.74145
595 Hwy 340, Fruita, CO 81521
colorado.river.park@state.co.us
www.cpw.state.co.us
See ad page 228 (Welcome Section).

MONUMENT RV RESORT
Ratings: 9.5/10★/8.5 (RV Park) From Jct of I-70 & SR-340 (exit 19), S 0.3 mi on SR-340 (L). Elev 4466 ft. **FAC:** All weather rds. 75 Avail: 75 all weather, 35 pull-thrus (30 x 95), back-ins (30 x 60), some side by side hkups, 60 full hkups, 15 W, 15 E (30/50 amps), cable, WiFi, tent sites, rentals, dump, mobile sewer, laundry, groc, LP gas. **REC:** pool, whirlpool, playground. Pet restrict(B). Big rig sites, eco-friendly, 2015 rates: $31 to $40. Disc: AAA, military.
AAA Approved
(970)858-4405 Lat: 39.14944, Lon: -108.73773
607 Hwy 340, Fruita, CO 81521
monumentrvresort@earthlink.net
www.monumentrvresort.com
See ad opposite page, 230.

GLENWOOD SPRINGS — C2 *Garfield*

AMI'S ACRES CAMPING
Ratings: 6/7/8 (Campground) From Jct of I-70 & Exit 114, W 0.9 mi on N frntg rd (R). Elev 5800 ft. **FAC:** Gravel rds. 46 gravel, 20 pull-thrus (25 x 80), back-ins (25 x 60), 46 full hkups (30/50 amps), WiFi, tent sites, rentals, firewood. **REC.** Pet restrict(B). 2015 rates: $36. Mar 1 to Nov 15.
(970)945-5340 Lat: 39.55790, Lon: -107.29160
50235 Hwy 6, Glenwood Springs, CO 81601
amisacres@yahoo.com
www.amisacrescampground.ws
See ad this page.

GLENWOOD CANYON RESORT
Ratings: 8.5/8.5★/8.5 (RV Park) At Jct of I-70 & No Name Exit 119, S side of exit (E). Elev 5858 ft. **FAC:** Paved/gravel rds. 65 gravel, back-ins (30 x 70), 42 full hkups, 23 W, 23 E (30/50 amps), WiFi, tent sites, rentals, dump, laundry, groc, firewood, restaurant. **REC:** Colorado River: swim, fishing, playground, rec open to public. Pet restrict(B/Q) $. Partial handicap access. Big rig sites, 7 day max stay, eco-friendly, 2015 rates: $48 to $58. Disc: AAA, military. ATM.
AAA Approved
(800)958-6737 Lat: 39.55939, Lon: -107.29356
1308 CR-129, Glenwood Springs, CO 81601
info@glenwoodcanyonresort.com
www.glenwoodcanyonresort.com
See ad this page, 230.

GOLDEN — C3 *Jefferson*

CHIEF HOSA CAMPGROUND (Public) From Jct of I-70 & Exit 253, S 100 ft on Exit Rd (R). 2015 rates: $30 to $32.50. May 1 to Sep 30. (303)526-1324

DAKOTA RIDGE RV RESORT
Ratings: 10/10★/9.5 (RV Park) E-bnd: From Jct of I-70 & US-40 (exit 259), NE 1.5 mi on US-40/Colfax Ave (R); or W-bnd: From Jct of I-70 & US-40 (exit 262), W 1.7 mi on US-40/Colfax Ave (L). Elev 6049 ft. **FAC:** Paved rds. 141 paved, 88 pull-thrus (28 x 70), back-ins (24 x 50), some side by side hkups, 141 full hkups (30/50 amps), WiFi, dump, laundry, LP gas. **REC:** heated pool, whirlpool, playground. Pet restrict(B/Q). Partial handicap access, no

Nobody said it was easy being a 10. And our rating system makes it even tougher.

GOLDEN (CONT)

DAKOTA RIDGE RV RESORT (CONT)
tents. Big rig sites, 2015 rates: $51 to $65. Disc: military.
(303)279-1625 Lat: 39.71952, Lon: -105.20124
17800 W Colfax Ave, Golden, CO 80401
info@dakotaridgerv.com
www.dakotaridgerv.com
See ad pages 239, 230.

GOLDEN CLEAR CREEK RV PARK
(Public) W-bnd: From Jct of I-70 & SR-58 (Exit 265), W 4.5 mi on SR-58 to Washington Ave, S 0.3 mi to 10th St, W 0.5 mi (E)); or E-bnd: From Jct of I-70 & US-40 (Exit 262), SW (left turn) 1 mi on US-40 to US-6, W 3.5 mi to SR-58, NE 0.5 mi to Washington Ave, to 10th St. SE 0.3 (L). Elev 5657 ft. **FAC:** Paved rds. 33 paved, 2 pull-thrus (26 x 45), back-ins (26 x 45), 22 full hkups, 11 W, 11 E (30/50 amps), WiFi, tent sites, dump, laundry. **REC:** Clear Creek: fishing. Pets OK. 2015 rates: $40 to $55.
(303)278-1437 Lat: 39.75327, Lon: -105.23163
1400 10th St, Golden, CO 80401
rv@cityofgolden.net
www.clearcreekrvpark.com
See ad opposite page.

GOLDEN GATE CANYON
(State Pk) From Golden, go W 27 mi on SR-6 N then SR-119 to Gap Rd, E 1 mi (L). Entrance fee required. Elev 9100 ft. **FAC:** Paved rds. 59 paved, 32 pull-thrus (20 x 60), back-ins (20 x 30), 59 E (15 amps), tent sites, rentals, dump, laundry, firewood. **REC:** pond, fishing, rec open to public. Pets OK. Partial handicap access. 14 day max stay, 2015 rates: $6 to $22. No CC.
(303)582-3707 Lat: 39.945833, Lon: -105.572222
92 Crawford Gulch Road, Golden, CO 80403
golden.gate.park@state.co.us
www.cpw.state.co.us
See ad page 228 (Welcome Section).

GOLDEN TERRACE SOUTH RV RESORT **Ratings: 5.5/7.5/6** (RV Park) 2015 rates: $40.85. (800)628-6279 17801 W Colfax Ave, Golden, CO 80401

Each privately owned campground has been rated three times. The first rating is for development of facilities. The second one is for cleanliness and physical characteristics of restrooms and showers. The third is for campground visual appearance and environmental quality.

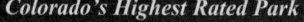

Travel Services

CAMPING WORLD OF GOLDEN/DENVER As the nation's largest retailer of RV supplies, accessories, services and new and used RVs, Camping World is committed to making your total RV experience better. RV Accessories (800)222-6795. Elev 5280 ft. **SERVICES:** RV appliance, staffed RV wash, restrooms, RV Sales. RV supplies, LP, waiting room. Hours: 8am to 6pm.
303-431-0751 Lat: 39.728183, Lon: -105.18035
16000 W Colfax, Golden, CO 80401
www.campingworldofdenver.com

GOODRICH — B4 *Morgan*

JACKSON LAKE
(State Pk) From Jct of I-76 & US-34/CR-39 (exit 66B), N 7.9 mi on CR-39 through Goodrich to RD Y5, W 2.4 mi (E) Entrance Fee Required. Elev 4440 ft. **FAC:** Paved/gravel rds. 260 gravel, 100 pull-thrus (14 x 40), back-ins (15 x 30), 163 E (30/50 amps), tent sites, showers $, dump, laundry, LP bottles, firewood. **REC:** Jackson Lake: swim, fishing, marina, rec open to public. Pets OK. Partial handicap access. 14 day max stay, 2015 rates: $16 to $30. ATM, no CC.
(970)645-2551 Lat: 40.38050, Lon: -104.09188
26363 County Road 3, Orchard, CO 80649
jackson.lake@state.co.us
www.cpw.state.co.us
See ad page 228 (Welcome Section).

GOULD — B3 *Jackson, Larimer*

STATE FOREST (State Pk) From Jct of CR 27 & Hwy 14: Go SE on Hwy 14 6.8 mi. Pit toilets. 2015 rates: $16 to $20. (970)723-8366

GRAND JUNCTION — C1 *Mesa*

GRAND JUNCTION See also Fruita.

CRUISE INN - JUNCTION WEST RV PARK
Ratings: 9/9.5★/9.5 (RV Park) From Jct of I-70 & US-6 (exit 26), W 0.2 mi on US-6/US-50 to 22 Rd, N 0.5 mi (L). Elev 4543 ft. **FAC:** All weather rds. 66 Avail: 66 all weather, 47 pull-thrus (35 x 65), back-ins (40 x 40), 66 full hkups (30/50 amps), cable, WiFi, tent sites, dump, laundry, groc, LP gas, fire rings, firewood. **REC:** playground. Pet restrict(B/Q). Big rig sites, eco-friendly, 2015 rates: $35 to $39.50. Disc: AAA, military.
(970)245-8531 Lat: 39.120153, Lon: -108.645686
793 22 Rd, Grand Junction, CO 81505
info@junctionwestrvpark.com
www.JunctionWestRVPark.com
See ad this page, 230.

GRAND JUNCTION KOA
Ratings: 10/10★/9 (RV Park) E-bnd: From Jct of I-70 & US-50 (exit 26), SE 9 mi on US-50 (R); or W-bnd: From Jct of I-70 & Bus I-70 (exit 37), SW 0.8 mi on Bus I-70 to SR-141 (turn left), S 5.4 mi to US-50, N 3.3 mi (L). Elev 4665 ft. **FAC:** All weather rds. 66 Avail: 66 all weather, 50 pull-thrus (30 x 75), back-ins (25 x 55), some side by side hkups, 66 full hkups (30/50 amps), cable, WiFi, tent sites, rentals, dump, laundry, groc, LP gas, fire rings, firewood. **REC:** heated pool, playground. Pet restrict(B). Partial handicap access. Big rig sites, eco-friendly, 2015 rates: $35 to $52. Disc: AAA, military.
AAA Approved
(800)562-1510 Lat: 39.03550, Lon: -108.52976
2819 Hwy 50, Grand Junction, CO 81503
gjkoa@yahoo.com
www.grandjunctionkoa.com
See ad this page.

MOBILE CITY RV HOME PARK/MHP Ratings: 6/3.5/6 (RV Area in MHP) From Jct of I-70 & US 6 & 50 W (Exit 26), SE 1.5 mi on US 6 & 50 (L). Elev 4541 ft. **FAC:** Gravel rds. 44 gravel, 12 pull-thrus (30 x 60), back-ins (24 x 40), some side by side hkups, 44 full hkups (30/50 amps), cable, WiFi, dump, laundry, LP gas. **REC.** Pet restrict(B). No tents. Big rig sites, 2015 rates: $28.
AAA Approved
(970)242-9291 Lat: 39.09914, Lon: -108.62209
2322 Hwy 6 & 50, Grand Junction, CO 81505
mobilecitygj@gmail.com
www.mobilecityrv.com

MOON DANCE RV PARK **Ratings: 6/8.5/6** (RV Park) 2015 rates: $35 to $45. (970)245-0769 774 23 Rd, Grand Junction, CO 81505

RV RANCH AT GRAND JUNCTION
Ratings: 9.5/10★/9 (RV Park) From Jct of I-70 & Bus I-70 (exit 37), SW 0.6 mi on Bus I-70 to F Rd, W 0.1 mi to Frontage Rd, NE 0.1 mi (L); or From Jct of US-50 & SR-141, N 5.4 mi on SR-141 to Bus I-70/US-6, NE 0.2 mi to F Rd, W 0.1 mi to Frontage Rd, NE 0.1 mi (L). Elev 4722 ft. **FAC:** Paved rds. 127 paved, 40 pull-thrus (24 x 70), back-ins (22 x 42), mostly side by side hkups, 116 full hkups, 11 W, 11 E (30/50 amps), WiFi, tent sites, rentals, dump, laundry, groc, LP gas. **REC:** heated pool, shuffleboard, playground. Pet restrict(B) $. Partial handicap access. Big rig sites, eco-friendly, 2015 rates: $37 to $45. Disc: AAA.
AAA Approved
(970)434-6644 Lat: 39.09407, Lon: -108.45292
3238 E I-70 Bus Loop, Clifton, CO 81520
rvranch@cflane.com
www.rvranchgj.com
See ad this page, 230.

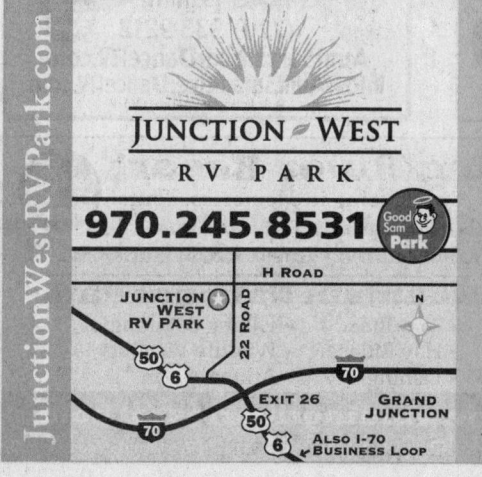

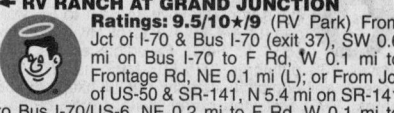

GRAND LAKE — B3 *Boulder, Grand, Larimer*

ELK CREEK CAMPGROUND & RV RESORT **Ratings: 7/9.5★/8** (RV Park) 2015 rates: $40 to $45. May 15 to Oct 15. (970)627-8502 143 CR 48/Golf Course Rd, Grand Lake, CO 80447

ROCKY MTN/TIMBER CREEK (Natl Pk) From town, N 11 mi on Hwy 34 (L). Entrance fee required. Note: 30' RV length maximum. 2015 rates: $14 to $20. (970)586-1206

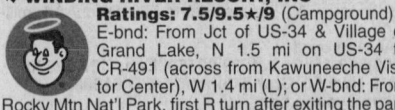

WINDING RIVER RESORT, INC
Ratings: 7.5/9.5★/9 (Campground) E-bnd: From Jct of US-34 & Village of Grand Lake, N 1.5 mi on US-34 to CR-491 (across from Kawuneeche Visitor Center), W 1.4 mi (L); or W-bnd: From Rocky Mtn Nat'l Park, first R turn after exiting the park (CR-491), W 1.4 mi on CR-491 (L). Elev 8650 ft. **FAC:** Gravel rds. 102 gravel, 20 pull-thrus (40 x 60), back-ins (40 x 50), 40 full hkups, 62 W, 62 E (30/50 amps), WiFi, tent sites, rentals, dump, laundry, groc, LP gas, fire rings, firewood. **REC:** North Fork of Colorado River: fishing, playground, rec open to public. Pets OK. Big rig sites, eco-friendly, 2015 rates: $45 to $48. Disc: AAA, military. May 25 to Sep 30.
AAA Approved
(970)627-3215 Lat: 40.27729, Lon: -105.85144
1447 Cr 491, Grand Lake, CO 80447
trailboss@rkymtnhi.com
www.windingriverresort.com
See ad this page, 230.

GREELEY — B4 *Weld*

GREELEY RV PARK
Ratings: 7.5/9★/8 (RV Park) From I-25 Go East on Hwy 34 East, follow the signs that say Hwy 34 East to Ft. Morgan.(L) 1/4 mile east of Hwy 85. Elev 4667 ft. **FAC:** Paved/gravel rds. 178 gravel, 139 pull-thrus (27 x 60), back-ins (27 x 60), accepts self-contain units only, 178 full hkups (30/50 amps), WiFi, tent sites, dump, laundry, groc, LP gas. **REC.** Pet restrict(B). Big rig sites, eco-friendly, 2015 rates: $35. Disc: military.
(970)353-6476 Lat: 40.39300, Lon: -104.67179
501 E 27th Street, Greeley, CO 80631
www.greeleyrvpark.com
See ad this page.

GUNNISON — D2 *Gunnison*

BLUE MESA RECREATIONAL RANCH **Ratings: 8.5/7.5/8** (Membership Pk) 2015 rates: $10. May 1 to Oct 15. (970)642-4150 27601 W. Hwy 50, Gunnison, CO 81230

CURECANTI NATIONAL RECREATION AREA (STEVENS CREEK) (Natl Pk) From town: Go 12 mi W on US 50. Pit toilets. 2015 rates: $12. (970)641-2337

CURECANTI NRA/ELK CREEK CAMPGROUND (Natl Pk) From town, W 16 mi on US-50 (L). 2015 rates: $12 to $18. (970)641-2337

CURECANTI NRA/LAKE FORK (Natl Pk) From town, W 27 mi on US-50 (R). 2015 rates: $12. Apr 1 to Oct 15. (970)641-2337

GUNNISON KOA **Ratings: 8/9.5★/8** (Campground) 2015 rates: $37 to $47. May 1 to Oct 1. (970)641-1358 105 CR-50, Gunnison, CO 81230

GUNNISON LAKESIDE RV PARK & CABINS
Ratings: 8/9★/8.5 (RV Park) From Jct of US-50 & SR-149, W 2.3 mi on US-50 (R). Elev 7477 ft. **FAC:** Gravel rds. 67 gravel, 8 pull-thrus (35 x 100), back-ins (30 x 45), 67 full hkups (30/50 amps), WiFi, tent sites, rentals, showers $, laundry, groc, LP gas, firewood. **REC:** Blue Mesa Reservior: fishing, marina, playground. Pets OK. Big rig sites, eco-friendly, 2015 rates: $38.50 to $43. Disc: AAA, military. May 1 to Oct 15.
AAA Approved
(970)641-0477 Lat: 38.48667, Lon: -107.10244
28357 US Hwy 50, Gunnison, CO 81230
info@gunnisonlakeside.com
www.gunnisonlakeside.com

MESA CAMPGROUND & RV RESORT
Ratings: 8/9.5★/9.5 (Campground) From Jct of US-50 & SR-135, W 4 mi on US-50 (L). Elev 7577 ft. **FAC:** Paved/gravel rds. (100 spaces). Avail: 75 gravel, patios, 25 pull-thrus (25 x 60), back-ins (25 x 50), 75 full hkups (30/50 amps), seasonal sites, WiFi $, tent sites, rentals, dump, laundry, LP gas, firewood. **REC:** playground. Pets OK. Big rig sites, eco-friendly, 2015 rates: $31.95 to $72.95. Apr 15 to Oct 15.
(970)641-3186 Lat: 38.52205, Lon: -106.99049
36128 US Hwy 50, Gunnison, CO 81230
mesarvcampground@gmail.com
www.mesacampground.com
See ad this page, 230.

PALISADES SENIOR R.V. PARK **Ratings: 7.5/9.5★/8** (RV Park) 2015 rates: $35 to $40. May 15 to Sep 22. (970)641-4951 470 N. Third, Gunnison, CO 81230

TALL TEXAN RV PARK & CABINS **Ratings: 7.5/9/8** (RV Park) 2015 rates: $22 to $42. May 1 to Oct 1. (970)641-2927 194 County Rd 11, Gunnison, CO 81230

GYPSUM — C2 *Eagle*

AUNT SARA'S RIVER DANCE RV RESORT
Ratings: 7/9★/8.5 (RV Park) From Jct of I-70 & Gypsum Rd (exit 140), S 0.1 mi on Gypsum Rd to S Frontage Rd, W 2.5 mi (L). Elev 6202 ft. **FAC:** Paved/gravel rds. 45 Avail: 16 paved, 29 gravel, 25 pull-thrus (40 x 65), back-ins (40 x 65), 8 full hkups, 37 W, 37 E (30/50 amps), WiFi, tent sites, dump, mobile sewer, laundry, LP gas, fire rings, firewood. **REC:** Eagle River: swim, fishing. Pets OK. Big rig sites, 2015 rates: $40. Disc: military.
(720)933-9212 Lat: 39.64784, Lon: -107.00223
6700 US Hwy 6, Gypsum, CO 81637
info@auntsarasriverdancerv.com
www.auntsarasriverdancerv.com
See ad this page, 230.

RV Park ratings you can rely on!

HASTY — D5 *Bent*

JOHN MARTIN RES/LAKE HASTY REC. AREA
(State Pk) From Jct of US-50 & CR-24, S 3 mi on CR-24 (E). Entrance fee required. Elev 3750 ft. **FAC:** Paved/gravel rds. 213 gravel, 6 pull-thrus (20 x 64), back-ins (20 x 32), 1 full hkups, 109 W, 109 E (30/50 amps), tent sites, showers $, dump, laundry. **REC:** Lake Hasty: swim, fishing, playground, rec open to public. Pets OK. Partial handicap access. 14 day max stay, 2015 rates: $13 to $20. Apr 1 to Oct 31.
(719)829-1801 Lat: 38.07648, Lon: -102.93904
30703 Rd 24, Hasty, CO 81044
john.martin@state.co.us
http://cpw.state.co.us/placestogo/Parks/JohnMartinReservoir
See ad page 228 (Welcome Section).

LAKEVIEW RV CAMPGROUND **Ratings: 3/5/4** (Campground) 2015 rates: $20. (719)776-9811 31230 CR 24, Hasty, CO 81044

HAYDEN — B2 *Routt*

YAMPA RIVER HEADQUARTERS
(State Pk) From Hayden, W 2 mi on Hwy 40 (follow signs). Entrance fee required. Elev 6300 ft. **FAC:** Gravel rds. 35 gravel, back-ins (25 x 60), 35 E (30/50 amps), tent sites, rentals, dump, laundry, firewood. **REC:** Yampa River: swim, fishing, playground, rec open to public. Pets OK. Partial handicap access. 14 day max stay, 2015 rates: $16 to $25. May 1 to Nov 15.
(970)276-2061 Lat: 40.49184, Lon: -107.30457
6185 W US Hwy 40, Hayden, CO 81639
yampa.river@state.co.us
www.cpw.state.co.us
See ad page 228 (Welcome Section).

HOWARD — D3 *Fremont*

BANDERA'S BUNKHOUSE **Ratings: 6.5/7.5/7.5** (RV Park) 2015 rates: $32. Apr 1 to Sep 15. (719)942-3811 10281 Hwy 50, Howard, CO 81233

SUGARBUSH STORE & CAMPGROUND Ratings: 7/8★/7 (Campground) At E edge of Howard on US-50 at MP 234.5 (L). Elev 6675 ft. **FAC:** Gravel rds. (16 spaces). Avail: 10 gravel, 4 pull-thrus (24 x 50), back-ins (24 x 45), 10 full hkups (30/50 amps), seasonal sites, WiFi, tent sites, dump, laundry, groc, firewood. **REC:** playground. Pet restrict(B). 2015 rates: $33.
(719)942-3363 Lat: 38.255756, Lon: -105.50002
9229 Hwy 50, Howard, CO 81233
info@sugarbushco.com
www.sugarbushCO.com

Take your Guide with you wherever you go! The front section is chock-full of vital reference information and all new 2016 travel editorial you'll want to keep handy all the time.

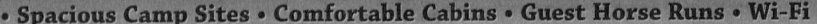

HUDSON — B4 *Weld*

PEPPER POD CAMPGROUND
Ratings: 5/7/6.5 (RV Park) From Jct of I-76 & Exit 31, Exit to Frontage Rd on SE side, SW 0.2 mi on Frontage Rd (L). Elev 4988 ft. **FAC:** Gravel rds. 40 gravel, 30 pull-thrus (30 x 55), back-ins (25 x 40), mostly side by side hkups, 20 full hkups, 20 W, 20 E (30/50 amps), WiFi, tent sites, rentals, dump, laundry, LP gas. **REC.** Pet restrict(Q). Eco-friendly, 2015 rates: $25 to $35. Disc: AAA, military.
(303)536-4763 Lat: 40.07181, Lon: -104.64607
450 5th Ave, Hudson, CO 80642
hudsoncamp@earthlink.net
www.pepperpodcamp.com
See ad opposite page.

IDAHO SPRINGS — C3 *Clear Creek, Gilpin*

COTTONWOOD RV CAMP
Ratings: 5.5/NA/8.5 (RV Park) From Jct of I-70 & SR-103 (exit 240), SW 1.4 mi on SR-103 (L). Elev 7750 ft. **FAC:** Gravel rds. 22 Avail: 18 gravel, 4 grass, back-ins (20 x 60), accepts self-contain units only, 22 full hkups (30/50 amps), cable, WiFi, dump. **REC:** Chicago Creek. Pet restrict(B). No tents. Eco-friendly, 2015 rates: $36. No CC.
(303)567-2617 Lat: 39.72974, Lon: -105.53986
1485 Hwy 103, Idaho Springs, CO 80452
www.cottonwoodrvcolorado.com
See ad this page.

IGNACIO — E2 *La Plata*

SKY UTE CASINO RV PARK
Ratings: 9.5/10★/9.5 (RV Park) From Jct of US 160 & US 550 (E edge of Durango), E 2 mi on US 160 to SR-172, S 17 mi (L) Check in at hotel lobby in casino. Elev 6535 ft. **FAC:** Paved rds. 24 paved, 24 pull-thrus (30 x 60), 24 full hkups (30/50 amps), WiFi, rentals, laundry, restaurant. **REC:** heated pool, whirlpool, playground, rec open to public. Pet restrict(B/Q). Partial handicap access, no tents. Big rig sites, eco-friendly, 2015 rates: $30. Disc: AAA, military. Apr 1 to Dec 31. ATM.
(970)563-7777 Lat: 37.13702, Lon: -107.63209
14324 Hwy 172N, Ignacio, CO 81137
Travis.Garlick@skyutecasino.com
www.skyutecasino.com
See ad pages 239, 230.

SKY UTE FAIRGROUNDS & RV PARK
Ratings: 5.5/8.5/6.5 (RV Park) From Jct of Hwy 172 & Hwy 151 (in Ignacio), E 0.1 mi on CR-151 (R). Elev 6500 ft. **FAC:** Gravel rds. 65 gravel, 65 pull-thrus (25 x 60), 65 full hkups (30/50 amps), WiFi $, tent sites, showers $, dump, laundry. **REC:** Los Pinos River: fishing. Pet restrict(B). Big rig sites, 14 day max stay, 2015 rates: $30.
(970)563-5541 Lat: 37.11378, Lon: -107.63030
200 E Hwy 251, Ignacio, CO 81137
info@skyutefairgrounds.com
www.skyutefairgrounds.com
See ad page 240.

Lend a hand. During the busy season park services are stretched to the max! Please do your best to keep your area "ship-shape".

JOHNSTOWN — B4 *Weld*

RV RETREAT AT JOHNSON'S CORNER
Ratings: 9/8.5★/7 (RV Park) From Jct of I-25 & Exit 254, S 0.2 mi on E frntg rd (L). Elev 5052 ft. **FAC:** Paved rds. 140 gravel, 96 pull-thrus (24 x 60), back-ins (24 x 45), mostly side by side hkups, 140 full hkups (30/50 amps), WiFi, rentals, laundry. **REC:** heated pool, playground, rec open to public. Pet restrict(Q). Partial handicap access, no tents. Big rig sites, eco-friendly, 2015 rates: $38. Disc: AAA, military.
(970)669-8400 Lat: 40.35578, Lon: -104.98074
3618 SE Frontage Rd, Johnstown, CO 80534
info@rvretreatatjohnsonscorner.com
www.rvretreatatjohnsonscorner.com
See ad this page.

KREMMLING — B3 *Grand*

RED MOUNTAIN RV PARK Ratings: 7.5/9★/7.5 (RV Park) From Jct of SR-9 & US-40, E 1 mi on US-40 to 22nd St (at E edge of town), N 0.1 mi (R). Elev 7430 ft. **FAC:** Paved/gravel rds. 45 gravel, 45 pull-thrus (25 x 45), 45 full hkups (30/50 amps), WiFi, tent sites, dump, laundry, LP gas, firewood. **REC:** playground. Pets OK. 2015 rates: $32. Disc: AAA, military.
AAA Approved
(970)724-9593 Lat: 40.05773, Lon: -106.367801
2201 Central Ave, Kremmling, CO 80459
sara@redmtnrvpark.com
www.redmtnrvpark.com

LA JUNTA — D4 *Otero*

LA JUNTA KOA **Ratings: 8.5/9.5★/7.5** (Campground) 2015 rates: $41 to $44. (800)562-9501 26680 W. Hwy 50, La Junta, CO 81050

LA VETA — E4 *Huerfano*

CIRCLE THE WAGONS RV PARK
Ratings: 8/10★/8 (RV Park) From Jct of US 160 & SR 12, S 4.3 mi on SR-12 to 2nd St, W 0.1 mi (R). Elev 6970 ft. **FAC:** Gravel rds. 43 gravel, back-ins (30 x 60), 43 full hkups (30/50 amps), WiFi, tent sites, rentals, dump, laundry. **REC:** Cuchara River. Pets OK. Partial handicap access. Big rig sites, eco-friendly, 2015 rates: $30 to $35. May 1 to Oct 31.
(719)742-3233 Lat: 37.51318, Lon: -105.01182
126 W 2nd St., La Veta, CO 81055
J@circlethewagonsrvpark.com
www.circlethewagonsrvpark.com
See ad this page.

LUCY'S RV PARK **Ratings: 6/7.5★/6.5** (RV Park) 2015 rates: $30. May 1 to Oct 15. (719)742-3252 206 W Grand, La Veta, CO 81055

SAMMIE'S RV PARK & MOTEL **Ratings: 6/5.5/6** (RV Park) 2015 rates: $25. (719)742-5435 124 N Main St, La Veta, CO 81055

LAKE CITY — D2 *Hinsdale*

CASTLE LAKES CAMPGROUND & CABINS **Ratings: 6.5/9★/7.5** (Campground) 2015 rates: $34 to $37. May 24 to Oct 1. (970)944-2622 8201 Hc Rd 30, Lake City, CO 81235

ELKHORN RV RESORT **Ratings: 7/9.5★/8** (RV Park) 2015 rates: $35 to $40. May 15 to Oct 1. (970)944-2920 713 N Bluff, Lake City, CO 81235

HENSON CREEK RV PARK **Ratings: 7/8★/6** (RV Park) 2015 rates: $35. Jun 1 to Oct 1. (970)944-2394 131 S Gunnison Ave, Lake City, CO 81235

HIGHLANDER RV CAMPGROUND, INC **Ratings: 8/9.5★/8.5** (RV Park) 2015 rates: $37. May 15 to Oct 15. (888)580-4636 1245 Cty Rd 30, Lake City, CO 81235

WOODLAKE PARK **Ratings: 7/9.5★/8** (RV Park) 2015 rates: $38. Jun 1 to Oct 1. (800)201-2694 2690 S. Colorado Hwy 149, Lake City, CO 81235

LAKE GEORGE — C3 *Park*

ELEVEN MILE
(State Pk) From town, W 1 mi on US-24 to CR-90, S 6 mi (stay on pavement) to CR-92, S 5 mi (E). Entrance fee required. Elev 8597 ft. **FAC:** Paved/gravel rds. 348 dirt, 50 pull-thrus (25 x 115), back-ins (20 x 85), 52 E (20/30 amps), tent sites, showers $, dump, laundry, fire rings, firewood. **REC:** Eleven Mile Reservoir: fishing, marina, playground, rec open to public. Pets OK. Partial handicap access. 14 day max stay, 2015 rates: $13 to $20.
(719)748-3401 Lat: 38.948475, Lon: -105.526519
4229 CR-92, Lake George, CO 80827
eleven.mile.park@state.co.us
www.cpw.state.co.us
See ad page 228 (Welcome Section).

Things to See and Do

SPINNEY MOUNTAIN STATE PARK Day use only. Fishing and Boating on Reservoir. No Camping. Entrance fee required. Elev 8715 ft. Jun 1 to Sep 30. Hours: 9:00 am - 4:00 pm. No CC.
(719)748-3401 Lat: 39.00511, Lon: -105.37267
4229 CR 92, Lake George, CO 80827
eleven.mile.park@state.co.us
www.cpw.state.co.us
See ad page 228 (Welcome Section).

LAMAR — D5 *Prowers*

COUNTRY ACRES RV PARK & MOTEL **Ratings: 5.5/6.5/7** (RV Park) 2015 rates: $45. (866)336-1031 29151 US-287/385, Lamar, CO 81052

LAMAR SPORTSMAN'S RV PARK & HORSE MOTEL
Ratings: 8.5/8.5★/7.5 (RV Park) From Jct of US 50 & US 287 (W of Lamar), E 3 mi on US 50/287 (L); or W-bnd: From W edge of Lamar, W 3 mi on US 50/287 (R). Elev 3635 ft. **FAC:** Gravel rds. 37 gravel, 37 pull-thrus (30 x 60), 27 full hkups, 10 W, 10 E (30/50 amps), WiFi, tent sites, dump, laundry. **REC:** pool. Pets OK. Big rig sites, 2015 rates: $33 to $42. Disc: military.
(719)336-3623 Lat: 38.51851, Lon: -102.13669
5385 US Hwy 50 West, Lamar, CO 81052
dgomez_lcc207@yahoo.com
www.rvandhorses.com
See ad this page.

LAPORTE — B3 *Larimer*

FORT COLLINS/POUDRE CANYON KOA **Ratings: 7.5/9★/8.5** (Campground) 2015 rates: $40 to $50. May 1 to Oct 1. (800)562-2648 6670 Hwy 287, Laporte, CO 80535

LEADVILLE — C3 *Eagle, Lake*

LEADVILLE RV CORRAL Ratings: 5/7/6 (RV Park) From Jct SR-91 & US 24: Go S on US-24 1.75 mi to 2nd St, go W on 2nd St 300 ft (L). Elev 10109 ft. **FAC:** Gravel rds. (33 spaces). Avail: 21 gravel, 19 pull-thrus (20 x 45), back-ins (20 x 45), 21 full hkups

Say you saw it in our Guide!

CO

LEADVILLE (CONT)

LEADVILLE RV CORRAL (CONT)
(30/50 amps), seasonal sites, cable, WiFi, tent sites, showers $, laundry. Pets OK $. 2015 rates: $35.
(719)486-3111 Lat: 39.24492, Lon: -106.29123
135 West 2nd St, Leadville, CO 80461
info@mountainrvpark.com
www.mountainrvpark.com

← SUGAR LOAFIN RV/CAMPGROUND
Ratings: 6.5/8.5★/7.5 (Campground) From Jct of US-24S & CR-4 (unmarked) (S edge of town at MP-177), NW 3 mi on CR-4, follow signs (R). Elev 9728 ft. **FAC:** Paved/gravel rds. 68 Avail: 13 paved, 55 grass, 8 pull-thrus (30 x 120), back-ins (35 x 50), some side by side hkups, 42 full hkups, 26 W, 26 E (30/50 amps), tent sites, rentals, dump, laundry, groc, LP gas, fire rings, firewood. **REC:** playground. Pets OK. Big rig sites, eco-friendly, 2015 rates: $36 to $45. Disc: AAA, military. May 13 to Oct 1.
(719)486-1031 Lat: 39.249159, Lon: -106.35344
2665 CR 4, Leadville, CO 80461
sugarloafin@sugarloafin.com
www.sugarloafin.com
See ad page 245.

LIMON — C4 *Lincoln*

→ LIMON KOA
Ratings: 8.5/10★/8.5 (RV Park) From Jct of I-70 & Limon exit (exit 361), SW 0.2 mi on Main/US-24 to Colorado, NW 0.2 mi (E). Elev 5368 ft. **FAC:** Gravel rds. 48 gravel, 43 pull-thrus (30 x 60), back-ins (30 x 35), 39 full hkups, 9 W, 9 E (30/50 amps), cable, WiFi, tent sites, rentals, dump, laundry, groc, LP gas. **REC:** heated pool, playground. Pets OK. Big rig sites, eco-friendly, 2015 rates: $30 to $44.
(800)562-2129 Lat: 39.155814, Lon: -103.402584
575 Colorado Ave, Limon, CO 80828
limonkoa@hotmail.com
www.limonkoa.com
See ad this page.

LITTLETON — C4 *Arapahoe*

↓ CHATFIELD
(State Pk) From Jct of SR-470 & Wadsworth Blvd (SR-121), S 1 mi on SR-121 (L); or From Jct of SR-470 & Santa Fe Dr (US-85), S 4.2 mi on US-85 to Titan Rd, W 3.6 mi to Roxborough Park Rd, N 1.5 mi (E) Entrance Fee Required. Elev 5550 ft. **FAC:** Paved rds. 197 paved, 181 pull-thrus (30 x 60), back-ins (30 x 60), 120 full hkups, 77 E (30/50 amps), WiFi, tent sites, showers $, dump, laundry, firewood. **REC:** Chatfield Reservoir: swim, fishing, marina, playground, rec open to public. Pets OK. Partial handicap access. 14 day max stay, 2015 rates: $20 to $26.
(303)791-7275 Lat: 39.53822, Lon: -105.06592
11500 N Roxborough Park Rd, Littleton, CO 80125
chatfield.park@state.co.us
www.cpw.state.co.us
See ad page 228 (Welcome Section).

Things to See and Do

↓ ROXBOROUGH STATE PARK CO State Park. Day use only. No camping. Entrance fee required. Elev 5351 ft. Restrooms. Hours: 8am to 5pm. No CC.
(303)973-3959 Lat: 39.429663, Lon: -105.068657
4751 E Roxborough Dr, Littleton, CO 80125
www.cpw.state.co.us
See ad page 228 (Welcome Section).

LOMA — C1 *Mesa*

↑ HIGHLINE LAKE
(State Pk) From Jct of I-70 & SR-139, N 6 mi on SR-139 to Rd Q, W 1.2 mi to Rd 11.8, N 1 mi (E). Entrance fee required. Elev 4700 ft. **FAC:** Paved rds. 31 grass, 22 pull-thrus (15 x 45), back-ins (15 x 45), 31 W, tent sites, dump, laundry, fire rings, firewood. **REC:** Highline Lake: swim, fishing, playground, rec open to public. Pets OK. Partial handicap access. 14 day max stay, 2015 rates: $16 to $18.
(970)858-7208 Lat: 39.359167, Lon: -108.979444
1800 11.8 Rd, Loma, CO 81524
highline.park@state.co.us
www.cpw.state.co.us
See ad page 228 (Welcome Section).

So you're the one with "pooch" duty? Please make a clean sweep of it! Your fellow RVers will appreciate it!

LONGMONT — B3 *Boulder, Weld*

← ST VRAIN
(State Pk) From Jct of I-25 & SR-119, W 1 mi on SR-119 to CR-7, N until it turns into CR-24 1/2 (R). Entrance fee required. Elev 4830 ft. **FAC:** Paved/gravel rds. 87 Avail: 41 paved, 46 gravel, back-ins (15 x 40), 46 full hkups, 41 E (30/50 amps), tent sites, showers $, dump, fire rings, firewood. **REC:** Blue Heron Reservoir: fishing, rec open to public. Pets OK. Partial handicap access. 14 day max stay, 2015 rates: $22 to $26.
(303)678-9402 Lat: 40.16933, Lon: -104.98800
3785 Weld County Road 24 1/2, Firestone, CO 80504
st.vrain.park@state.co.us
www.cpw.state.co.us
See ad page 228 (Welcome Section).

Travel Services

↗ CAMPING WORLD OF LONGMONT As the nation's largest retailer of RV supplies, accessories, services and new and used RVs, Camping World is committed to making your total RV experience better. RV Accessories: (866)599-4874. Elev 4979 ft. **SERVICES:** RV, tire, RV appliance, MH mechanical, engine/chassis repair, staffed RV wash, restrooms, RV Sales. RV supplies, LP, emergency parking, RV accessible. waiting room. Hours: 8am to 6pm.
970-535-9696 Lat: 40.204551, Lon: -104.97866
4050 Camelot Circle, Longmont, CO 80504
www.campingworld.com

LOVELAND — B3 *Larimer*

→ BOYD LAKE
(State Pk) From Jct of I-25 & US-34 (exit 257B), W 3.4 mi on US-34 to Madison Ave, N 1.5 mi to CR-24E, E 0.7 mi to CR-11C, N 0.3 mi (R). Follow signs. Entrance Fee Required. Elev 5300 ft. **FAC:** Paved rds. 148 paved, 148 pull-thrus (25 x 40), 148 E (30/50 amps), tent sites, dump, laundry, firewood. **REC:** Boyd Lake: swim, fishing, marina, playground, rec open to public. Pets OK. 14 day max stay, 2015 rates: $20.
(970)669-1739 Lat: 40.43313, Lon: -105.04440
3720 N Cr-11C, Loveland, CO 80538
boyd.lake@state.co.us
http://cpw.state.co.us/placestogo/parks/BoydLake
See ad page 228 (Welcome Section).

← CARTER LAKE (LARIMER COUNTY PARK) (Public) From jct I-25 & Hwy 56: Go 9 mi W on Hwy 56, then W on CR 8E. Pit toilets. 2015 rates: $15. (970)619-4570

← CARTER VALLEY CAMPGROUND **Ratings: 6.5/7/7.5** (RV Park) 2015 rates: $35. (970)663-3131 1326 N Carter Lake Rd, Loveland, CO 80537

← FIRESIDE RV PARK & CABINS **Ratings: 6.5/7/8** (RV Park) 2015 rates: $33 to $35. (970)667-2903 6850 W Hwy 34, Loveland, CO 80537

← FLATIRON RESERVOIR (LARIMER COUNTY PARK) (Public) From town: Go 6 mi W on US 34, then 2-1/2 mi S on CR 29E. Pit toilets. (970)619-4570

→ LOVELAND RV RESORT
Ratings: 9.5/8.5★/8.5 (RV Park) From Jct of I-25 & US-34 (Exit 257), W 1 mi on US-34 (R). Elev 5000 ft. **FAC:** Paved rds. 161 gravel, 80 pull-thrus (25 x 60), back-ins (25 x 40), mostly side by side hkups, 153 full hkups, 8 W, 8 E (30/50 amps), WiFi, tent sites, dump, laundry, groc, LP gas. **REC:** heated pool, playground. Pet restrict(B/Q). Big rig sites, eco-friendly, 2015 rates: $38 to $56.93. Disc: AAA, military.
AAA Approved
(970)667-1204 Lat: 40.40789, Lon: -105.01328
4421 E Hwy 34, Loveland, CO 80537
info@lovelandrvresort.com
www.lovelandrvresort.com
See ad this page, 230.

← PINEWOOD LAKE (LARIMER COUNTY PARK) (Public) From jct US 34 & Hwy 29: Go 2 mi S on Hwy 29, then 6-1/2 mi W on CR 18E. Pit toilets. 2015 rates: $15. (970)679-4570

EXCLUSIVE! Every listing includes a special "arrow" symbol. This valuable tool shows you where the facility is located (N, S, E, W, NE, NW, SE, SW) in relation to the town.

LOVELAND (CONT)

RIVERVIEW RV PARK & CAMPGROUND
Ratings: 8/8.5★/8 (RV Park) From Jct of US 34 & I-25 (Exit 257), W 10.8 mi on US 34, 6 mi W of town (L). Elev 5175 ft. **FAC:** Gravel rds. 165 gravel, 42 pull-thrus (25 x 70), back-ins (25 x 50), some side by side hkups, 137 full hkups, 28 W, 28 E (30/50 amps), WiFi, tent sites, rentals, dump, laundry, groc, LP gas, fire rings, firewood. **REC:** Big Thompson River: fishing, playground. Pet restrict(Q). Partial handicap access. Big rig sites, eco-friendly, 2015 rates: $36 to $54. Disc: AAA, military.
(800)447-9910 Lat: 40.41688, Lon: -105.18990
2444 River Rim Rd, Loveland, CO 80537
info@riverviewrv.com
www.riverviewrv.com

MANCOS — E1 *Montezuma*

ANCIENT CEDARS @ MESA VERDE RV RESORT
Ratings: 9/10★/9 (RV Park) From Jct of US-160 & Mesa Verde Natl Pk exit, turn opposite of nat'l park entrance to frntg rd (N side of US-160), E 0.1 mi on frntg rd, follow camping signs (L). Elev 6908 ft. **FAC:** Gravel rds. 47 gravel, 40 pull-thrus (25 x 65), back-ins (20 x 35), 34 full hkups, 13 W, 13 E (30/50 amps), WiFi, tent sites, rentals, dump, laundry, groc, LP gas, fire rings, firewood. **REC:** heated pool, whirlpool, playground. Pets OK. Big rig sites, 2015 rates: $34 to $39. Disc: AAA, military. Mar 15 to Nov 1.
(844)565-3517 Lat: 37.202843, Lon: -108.24224
34979 Hwy 160, Mancos, CO 81328
acmesaverde@outlook.com
www.ancientcedarsmesaverde.com
See ad this page, 230.

MANCOS
(State Pk) From Jct of Hwy 160 & Hwy 184, N 0.5 mi on Hwy 184 to CR-42, E 4 mi to CR-N, W 0.5 mi (L) Entrance fee required. Off season 970-882-2213. Elev 7800 ft. **FAC:** Gravel/dirt rds. 30 gravel, back-ins (15 x 50), tent sites, rentals, pit toilets, dump, fire rings, firewood. **REC:** Jackson Gulch Reservoir: fishing, rec open to public. Pet restrict Partial handicap access. 14 day max stay, 2015 rates: $16.
(970)533-7065 Lat: 37.40031, Lon: -108.27004
42545 County Road N, Mancos, CO 81328
mancos.park@state.co.us
www.cpw.state.co.us
See ad page 228 (Welcome Section).

MESA VERDE RV RESORT
Ratings: 10/10★/10 (RV Park) From Jct of US-160 & SR-184 (in Mancos), W 6.5 mi on US-160 (R); or From Jct of US-160 & Mesa Verde Nat'l Park exit, E 0.75 mi on US-160 (L). Elev 6853 ft. **FAC:** All weather rds. 48 Avail: 48 all weather, 38 pull-thrus (35 x 60), back-ins (24 x 35), 31 full hkups, 17 W, 17 E (30/50 amps), WiFi, tent sites, rentals, dump, laundry, groc, LP gas. **REC:** heated pool, whirlpool, pond, swim, playground. Pet restrict(B). Partial handicap access. Big rig sites, eco-friendly, 2015 rates: $38.95 to $44.95. Disc: AAA, military. Mar 1 to Nov 1.
AAA Approved
(800)776-7421 Lat: 37.33707, Lon: -108.39673
35303 Hwy 160, Mancos, CO 81328
info@mesaverdervresort.com
www.mesaverdervresort.com
See ad pages 238, 230.

Park owners want you to be satisfied with your stay. Get to know them.

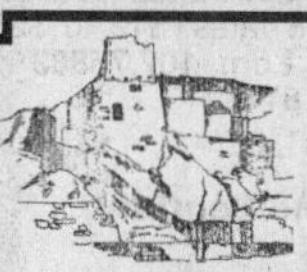

MANITOU SPRINGS — D4 *El Paso*

PIKES PEAK RV PARK & CAMPGROUND Ratings: 6.5/9★/8.5 (RV Park) 2015 rates: $28 to $42. Mar 1 to Oct 31. (719)685-9459 320 Manitou Ave, Manitou Springs, CO 80829

MESA — C2 *Mesa*

GRAND MESA RV PARK **Ratings: 6.5/9/5** (RV Park) 2015 rates: $35. (970)268-5651 11674 Hwy 65, Mesa, CO 81643

MONTROSE — D2 *Montrose*

BLACK CANYON OF THE GUNNISON NM (NPS) (SOUTH RIM) (Natl Pk) From jct US-50 & Hwy-347: Go 6 mi N on Hwy-347. Note: RVs over 35' not recommended. Pit toilets. 2015 rates: $12 to $18. May 30 to Sep 15. (970)641-2337

CEDAR CREEK RV PARK
Ratings: 9/9★/9 (RV Park) From Jct of US-50 & 550, E 1.5 mi on US-50 to Hillcrest Dr, S 0.1 mi to Alley Way, W 0.1 mi (W). Elev 5800 ft. **FAC:** All weather rds. 45 Avail: 45 all weather, 30 pull-thrus (24 x 80), back-ins (22 x 60), some side by side hkups, 28 full hkups, 17 W, 17 E (30/50 amps), cable, WiFi, tent sites, rentals, dump, laundry, LP gas, fire rings, firewood. **REC:** Cedar Creek: playground, rec open to public. Pets OK. Big rig sites, eco-friendly, 2015 rates: $32.50 to $38.50. Disc: AAA, military.
(877)425-3884 Lat: 38.48664, Lon: -107.85936
126 Rose Ln, Montrose, CO 81401
rv@cedarcreekrv.com
www.cedarcreekrv.com
See ad this page, 230.

CENTENNIAL RV PARK & CAMPGROUND
Ratings: 8.5/9.5★/9.5 (RV Park) From Jct of US-50 & US-550, S 11 mi on US-550 (R). Elev 6291 ft. **FAC:** All weather rds. (60 spaces). Avail: 40 all weather, 40 pull-thrus (35 x 90), mostly side by side hkups, 40 full hkups (30/50 amps), seasonal sites, WiFi, tent sites, dump, laundry, LP gas. **REC:** playground. Pet restrict(B). Big rig sites, eco-friendly, 2015 rates: $37 to $40. May 1 to Oct 1.
(970)240-3832 Lat: 38.34258, Lon: -107.78929
23449 US Hwy 550, Montrose, CO 81403
dustin@centennialrvpark.net
www.centennialrvpark.net
See ad this page, 230.

JELLYSTONE PARK OF BLACK CANYON Ratings: 8.5/9/7.5 (RV Park) From Jct of US-50 & US-550, S 9.4 mi on US-550 (R) (NOTE: Entrance is 0.2 mi S of mile post 120 at Vernal Rd). Elev 6300 ft. **FAC:** Gravel rds. 138 gravel, 77 pull-thrus (30 x 70), back-ins (30 x 50), some side by side hkups, 138 full hkups (30/50 amps), WiFi, tent sites, rentals, dump, laundry, LP gas, fire rings, firewood. **REC:** heated pool, whirlpool, shuffleboard, playground, rec open to public. Pets OK. Big rig sites, eco-friendly, 2015 rates: $36 to $54. Disc: AAA, military.
AAA Approved
(970)249-6382 Lat: 38.36168, Lon: -107.80742
22045 S US-550, Montrose, CO 81403
blackcanyonjellystone@gmail.com
www.blackcanyonjellystone.com

KING'S RIVER BEND RV PARK AND CABINS
Ratings: 8/8★/8.5 (RV Park) From Jct of US-50 & US-550, S 3.3 mi on US-550 to Chipeta Rd (turn at Ute Indian Museum, see teepees), NW 0.5 mi to Old Chipeta Trail, N 0.1 mi (L). Elev 5927 ft. **FAC:** All weather rds. 55 Avail: 55 all weather, 10 pull-thrus (35 x 70), back-ins (33 x 50), some side by side hkups, 55 full hkups (30/50 amps), WiFi, tent sites, rentals, laundry, LP gas, fire rings, firewood. **REC:** Uncompahgre River: fishing. Pet restrict(B). Big rig sites, 2015 rates: $36 to $42. Disc: military. Apr 15 to Oct 15. No CC.
(877)249-8235 Lat: 38.44163, Lon: -107.87028
65120 Old Chipeta Trail, Montrose, CO 81403
www.kingsriverbend.com
See ad this page.

MONTROSE/BLACK CANYON KOA **Ratings: 8/9.5★/9.5** (RV Park) 2015 rates: $46.89. (800)562-9114 200 N Cedar Ave, Montrose, CO 81401

MOUNTAIN VILLAGE MHP **Ratings: 3/NA/5** (RV Area in MHP) 2015 rates: $20. (970)249-8314 69905 E Hwy 50 #100, Montrose, CO 81403

MONUMENT — C4 *El Paso*

COLORADO HEIGHTS **Ratings: 8/9★/8.5** (RV Park) 2015 rates: $40 to $50. (719)481-2336 19575 Monument Hill Rd, Monument, CO 80132

MOSCA — E3 *Alamosa*

GREAT SAND DUNES NATL MON/PINYON FLATS (Natl Pk) From Jct of US-160 & Hwy 17, E 15 mi on US-160 to SR-150, N 18 mi (E); or From Jct of US-160 & Hwy 17, N 14 mi on US-160 to County Six Mile Lane, E 20 mi (E). 2015 rates: $20. Apr 1 to Oct 31. (719)378-6300

GREAT SAND DUNES OASIS **Ratings: 6/8/7.5** (RV Park) 2015 rates: $38. Apr 1 to Nov 1. (719)378-2222 7800 Hwy 150 N, Mosca, CO 81146

SAN LUIS LAKES
(State Pk) From Jct of US-160 & Hwy 150 (E of Alamosa), N 13.5 mi on Hwy 150 to Six Mile Ln, W 8 mi (R); or From Jct of Hwy 17 & Six Mile Ln (N edge of Mosca), E 7.9 mi on Six Mile Ln (L) Entrance fee required. Elev 7525 ft. **FAC:** Gravel rds. 51 paved, 40 pull-thrus (40 x 85), back-ins (40 x 60), 51 E (30/50 amps), tent sites, dump, laundry, firewood. **REC:** San Luis Lake: fishing, rec open to public. Pets OK. Partial handicap access. 14 day max stay, 2015 rates: $20. May 1 to Sep 30. No CC.
(719)378-2020 Lat: 37.66682, Lon: -105.73521
county Lane 6 North, Mosca, CO 81146
sanluis.park@state.co.us
www.cpw.state.co.us
See ad page 228 (Welcome Section).

NATHROP — D3 *Chaffee*

CHALK CREEK CAMPGROUND & RV PARK
Ratings: 8/10★/9 (RV Park) From Jct of US-24 & US-285, S 5.3 mi on US-285, in Nathrop (L). Elev 7937 ft. **FAC:** Gravel rds. 57 gravel, 18 pull-thrus (30 x 60), back-ins (30 x 40), 29 full hkups, 28 E (30/50 amps), WiFi, tent sites, rentals, showers $, dump, laundry, groc, LP gas, fire rings, firewood. **REC:** Chalk Creek: swim, fishing, playground. Pet restrict(Q). Big rig sites, eco-friendly, 2015 rates: $41 to $55.
(719)395-8301 Lat: 38.741709, Lon: -106.080414
11430 Cty Rd 197, Nathrop, CO 81236
camp@chalkcreek-campground.com
www.chalkcreek-campground.com
See ad page 236.

Like Us on Facebook.

CO

NEW CASTLE — C2 *Garfield*

ELK CREEK CAMPGROUND **Ratings: 5.5/6/6.5** (Campground) 2015 rates: $45 to $55. May 1 to Nov 1. (970)984-2240 0581 CR-241, New Castle, CO 81647

OAK CREEK — B2 *Routt*

STAGECOACH
(State Pk) From Jct of US-40 & SR-131 (S of Steamboat Springs), S 6.4 mi on SR-131 to CR-14, S 5.3 mi (L); or From Jct of SR-131 & CR-14 (S edge of Oak Creek), N 5 mi on CR-14 (R) Entrance fee required. Elev 7250 ft. **FAC:** Gravel rds. 91 gravel, 39 pull-thrus (25 x 45), back-ins (25 x 35), 65 E (30 amps), tent sites, showers $, dump, fire rings, firewood. **REC:** Stagecoach Reservoir: swim, fishing, marina, rec open to public. Pets OK. Partial handicap access. 14 day max stay, 2015 rates: $10 to $20. No CC.
(970)736-2436 Lat: 40.29015, Lon: -106.86341
25500 CR 14, Oak Creek, CO 80467
stagecoach.park@state.co.us
www.cpw.state.co.us
See ad page 228 (Welcome Section).

OLATHE — D2 *Montrose*

UNCOMPAHGRE RIVER ADULT RV PARK **Ratings: 7.5/9.5★/9.5** (RV Park) 2015 rates: $40. Apr 1 to Nov 1. (970)323-8706 804 S Church Ave, Olathe, CO 81425

OURAY — D2 *Ouray*

FOUR J PLUS ONE PLUS ONE CAMPGROUND **Ratings: 7.5/8/7** (RV Park) 2015 rates: $30 to $36. May 1 to Oct 15. (970)325-4418 790 Oak, Ouray, CO 81427

OURAY KOA **Ratings: 7/8/8** (Campground) 2015 rates: $38 to $53. May 1 to Sep 30. (970)325-4736 225 CR #23, Ouray, CO 81427

OURAY RV PARK **Ratings: 6.5/8/7.5** (RV Park) 2015 rates: $38 to $55. (970)325-4523 1700 N Main, Ouray, CO 81427

UNCOMPAHGRE NF (AMPHITHEATER CAMPGROUND) (Natl Forest) From town: Go 1/2 mi S on US-550, then 1/2 mi E on FR-855. Pit toilets. 2015 rates: $18. May 18 to Sep 30. (970)249-4552

PAGOSA SPRINGS — E2 *Archuleta*

BLANCO RIVER RV PARK **Ratings: 7/9/7.5** (RV Park) 2015 rates: $35 to $45. May 1 to Oct 30. (800)280-9429 97 Leisure Court, Pagosa Springs, CO 81147

BRUCE SPRUCE RANCH **Ratings: 6.5/6/6** (Campground) 2015 rates: $32. May 23 to Oct 15. (970)264-5374 231 CR 648, Pagosa Springs, CO 81147

COOL PINES RV PARK **Ratings: 8.5/8.5/7.5** (RV Park) 2015 rates: $32 to $36. Apr 15 to Oct 1. (855)268-1022 1501 W Hwy 160 #3, Pagosa Springs, CO 81147

HAPPY CAMPER RV PARK **Ratings: 6.5/7/5.5** (RV Park) 2015 rates: $29. (970)731-5822 9260 West Hwy 160, Pagosa Springs, CO 81147

MOUNTAIN LANDING SUITES & RV PARK **Ratings: 6.5/8.5★/8.5** (RV Park) 2015 rates: $40. May 1 to Oct 31. (970)731-5345 345 Piedra Road, Pagosa Springs, CO 81147

Directional arrows indicate the campground's position in relation to the nearest town.

PAGOSA RIVERSIDE CAMPGROUND
Ratings: 8.5/10★/9 (Campground)
From Jct of US-84 & US-160, NE 1.3 mi on US-160 (L) Between mile makers 145 & 146. GPS is not always accurate on address. Elev 7200 ft. **FAC:** Gravel rds. 57 gravel, 24 pull-thrus (35 x 60), back-ins (20 x 35), some side by side hkups, 42 full hkups, 15 W, 15 E (30/50 amps), cable, WiFi, tent sites, rentals, dump, laundry, groc, fire rings, firewood. **REC:** pool, wading pool, San Juan River: fishing, playground, rec open to public. Pets OK. Big rig sites, eco-friendly, 2015 rates: $42 to $47. Disc: AAA, military. Apr 15 to Nov 15.
AAA Approved
(970)264-5874 Lat: 37.28608, Lon: -106.97950
2270 E Hwy 160, Pagosa Springs, CO 81147
info@pagosariverside.com
www.pagosariverside.com
See ad this page, 230.

PAGOSA SPRINGS RV PARK & CABINS **Ratings: 6/7.5★/8.5** (RV Park) 2015 rates: $44. May 1 to Oct 31. (888)724-6727 10 Leisure Court, Pagosa Springs, CO 81147

SPORTMAN'S CAMPGROUND & MOUNTAIN CABINS **Ratings: 7.5/8★/7** (Campground) 2015 rates: $29 to $41. May 15 to Nov 15. (970)731-2300 2095 Taylor Ln, Pagosa Springs, CO 81147

WOLF CREEK RUN MOTOR COACH RESORT **Ratings: 8.5/9.5★/10** (RV Resort) 2015 rates: $55 to $75. May 1 to Oct 13. (970)264-0365 1742 E Hwy 160, Pagosa Springs, CO 81147

PALISADE — C1 *Mesa*

JAMES M. ROBB - COLORADO RIVER STATE PARK/ISLAND ACRES
(State Pk) From Jct I-70 & Exit 47 (5 mi NE of town), exit N to Frontage Rd, E 0.4 mi (E) Park Entrance Fee Required. Elev 4800 ft. **FAC:** Paved rds. 74 gravel, 45 pull-thrus (25 x 50), back-ins (25 x 50), 34 W, 34 S, 74 E (30 amps), tent sites, dump, laundry, fire rings, firewood. **REC:** Colorado River: swim, fishing, playground, rec open to public. Pets OK. Partial handicap access. 14 day max stay, 2015 rates: $13 to $24.
(970)464-0548 Lat: 39.16624, Lon: -108.30150
@ Exit 47/I 70, Palisade, CO 81526
colorado.river.park@stateco.us
www.cpw.state.us.co
See ad page 228 (Welcome Section).

PAONIA — D2 *Delta*

PAONIA
(State Pk) From Jct of Hwy 82 & Hwy 133 (Colorado) in Carbondale, S 46 mi; or From Jct of Hwy 92 & Hwy 133 (through Paonia), N 16 mi. Entrance fee required (For credit card payment, reservations must be made through Reserve America 800-678-2267 - No credit cards accepted at park.) Entrance fee required. Elev 6500 ft. **FAC:** Gravel rds. 13 gravel, back-ins (15 x 30), tent sites, pit toilets, fire rings, firewood. **REC:** North Fork Gunnison River: fishing, rec open to public. Pets OK. 14 day max stay, 2015 rates: $10. May 1 to Oct 1.
(970)921-5721 Lat: 38.91737, Lon: -107.49459
hwy 133, Paonia, CO 81428
crawford.park@state.co.us
http://www.cpw.state.co.us
See ad page 228 (Welcome Section).

You have high expectations, so we point out campgrounds, service centers and tourist attractions with elevations over 2,500 feet.

PINE — B3 *Jefferson*

Things to See and Do

STAUNTON STATE PARK Day use only. Hiking and Fishing. No camping. Entrance fee required. Elev 8877 ft. Jun 1 to Sep 30. No CC.
(303)816-0912 Lat: 39.31050, Lon: -105.23220
11559 Upper Ranch Rd, Pine, CO 80470
staunton.park@state.co.us
www.cpw.state.co.us
See ad page 228 (Welcome Section).

PUEBLO — D4 *Pueblo*

FORTS RV PARK (MHP) **Ratings: 5/8.5★/6.5** (RV Park) 2015 rates: $32 to $35. (719)564-2327 3015 Lake Ave, Pueblo, CO 81004

LAKE PUEBLO
(State Pk) From Jct of I-25 & SR-45/Pueblo Blvd (exit 94), NW 4.6 mi on Pueblo Blvd to SR-96 (Thatcher Ave), W 3.8 mi (R); or From Jct of US-50 & SR-45 (Pueblo Blvd), S 4 mi on Pueblo Blvd to SR-96(Thatcher Ave), W 3.8 mi (R) Park Entrance Fee Required. Elev 5000 ft. **FAC:** Paved rds. 400 paved, 126 pull-thrus (35 x 60), back-ins (35 x 40), 280 E (20/30 amps), tent sites, showers $, dump, LP bottles, firewood. **REC:** Lake Pueblo: swim, fishing, marina, playground. Pets OK. Partial handicap access. 14 day max stay, 2015 rates: $16 to $20. No CC.
(719)561-9320 Lat: 38.25310, Lon: -104.72342
640 Pueblo Reservoir Rd, Pueblo, CO 81005
lake.pueblo.park@state.co.us
www.cpw.state.co.us
See ad page 228 (Welcome Section).

PUEBLO KOA **Ratings: 9/9.5★/8** (RV Park) 2015 rates: $32 to $63. (800)562-7453 4131 I-25 N, Pueblo, CO 81008

PUEBLO WEST — D4 *Pueblo*

HAGGARD'S RV CAMPGROUND **Ratings: 8.5/8.5★/8** (Campground) 2015 rates: $27. (719)547-2101 7910 W Hwy 50, Pueblo West, CO 81007

PUEBLO WEST CAMPGROUND & HORSEMAN'S ARENA **Ratings: 6/7/6** (RV Park) 2015 rates: $25. (719)547-9887 480 E Mcculloch Blvd, Pueblo, CO 81007

RANGELY — B1 *Rio Blanco*

BUCK 'N' BULL RV PARK **Ratings: 7.5/9.5★/7.5** (RV Park) 2015 rates: $30. Apr 1 to Oct 31. (866)675-8335 2811 East Main Street, Rangely, CO 81648

RIDGWAY — D2 *Ouray*

RIDGWAY/DUTCH CHARLIE
(State Pk) From Jct Hwy 62 & US-550 (in town), N 4.5 mi on US-550 (L); or From Jct US-50 & US-550 (in Montrose), S 22.7 mi on US-550 (R) Entrance fee required. Elev 6900 ft. **FAC:** Paved rds. 177 paved, patios, 114 pull-thrus (45 x 60), back-ins (45 x 50), 177 W, 177 E (20/30 amps), tent sites, rentals, showers $, dump, laundry, fire rings, firewood. **REC:** Ridgway Reservoir: swim, fishing, marina, playground, rec open to public. Pets OK. Partial handicap access. 14 day max stay, 2015 rates: $16 to $22.
(970)626-5822 Lat: 38.21374, Lon: -107.73296
28555 Hwy 550, Ridgway, CO 81432
ridgway.park@state.co.us
www.parks.state.co.us/parks/ridgway
See ad page 228 (Welcome Section).

RIDGWAY/PA CO-CHU PUK
(State Pk) From Jct of Hwy 62 & US-550 (in town), N 8.1 mi on US-550 (L); or From Jct of US-50 & US-550 (in Montrose), S 19.1 mi on US-550 (R) Entrance fee required. Elev 6800 ft. **FAC:** Paved rds. 239 paved, patios, 177 pull-thrus (45 x 60), back-ins (45 x 50), 80 full hkups (20/30 amps), tent sites, showers $, laundry, fire rings, firewood. **REC:** Uncompahgre River: swim, fishing, playground, rec open to public. Pets OK. Partial handicap access. 14 day max stay, 2015 rates: $18 to $26.
(970)626-5822 Lat: 38.24560, Lon: -107.75883
28555 Hwy 550, Ridgway, CO 81432
ridgway.park@state.co.us
www.cpw.state.co.us
See ad page 228 (Welcome Section).

RIFLE — C2 *Garfield*

RIFLE FALLS
(State Pk) From town, N 3 mi on SR-13 to SR-325, E 9.8 mi (L). Entrance fee required. Elev 6500 ft. **FAC:** Gravel rds. 20 dirt, 20 pull-thrus (15 x 40), 11 E (30 amps), tent sites, pit toilets, dump, firewood. **REC:** Rifle Gap Reservoir: swim, fishing, rec open to public. Pets OK. Partial handicap

RIFLE (CONT)

RIFLE FALLS (CONT)
access. 14 day max stay, 2015 rates: $16 to $22.
(970)625-1607 Lat: 39.641944, Lon: -107.89000
5775 Hwy 325, Rifle, CO 81650
rifle.gap.park@state.co.us
www.cpw.state.co.us
See ad page 228 (Welcome Section).

RIFLE GAP/HARVEY GAP
(State Pk) From Jct I-70 & Hwy 13, N 3 mi on Hwy 13 to Colorado 325, R 9.8 mi on Colorado 325 to County Road 252, stay on County Road 252 2 mi to County Road 219, R 0.1 mi on County Road 219 Entrance fee required. Elev 6000 ft. **FAC:** Paved/gravel rds. 87 Avail: 50 paved, 37 gravel, 44 pull-thrus (18 x 40), back-ins (16 x 30), some side by side hkups, 36 full hkups, 8 W, 43 E (30/50 amps), tent sites, showers $, dump, fire rings, firewood. **REC:** Rifle Gap Reservoir: swim, fishing, rec open to public. Pets OK. Partial handicap access. 14 day max stay, 2015 rates: $16 to $24.
(970)625-1607 Lat: 39.6521, Lon: -107.7793
5775 Hwy 325, Rifle, CO 81650
rifle.gap.park@state.co.us
www.cpw.state.co.us
See ad page 228 (Welcome Section).

ROYAL GORGE — D3 *Fremont*

A SPOTLIGHT Introducing Royal Gorge/Canon City's colorful attractions appearing at the front of this state.

ROYAL VIEW @ ROYAL GORGE CAMPGROUND
Ratings: 10/10★/10 (RV Park) E-bnd: From Jct of US-50 & SR-9, E 500 ft on US-50, between MP-269 & 270 (R); or W-bnd: From Jct of US-50 & Royal Gorge Rd, W 1 mi on US-50 (L). Elev 6238 ft. **FAC:** All weather rds. 48 Avail: 48 all weather, 42 pull-thrus (24 x 65), back-ins (28 x 60), 48 full hkups (30/50 amps), WiFi, tent sites, rentals, showers $, laundry, groc, fire rings, firewood. **REC:** heated pool, playground. Pet restrict(B/Q). Big rig sites, eco-friendly, 2015 rates: $33 to $55. Apr 15 to Oct 1.
(719)275-1900 Lat: 38.49504, Lon: -105.35056
43590 US Hwy 50 W, Canon City, CO 81212
royalviewcg@aol.com
www.royalviewcampground.com
See primary listing at Canon City and ads this page, 233 (Spotlight Royal Gorge-Canon City).

SALIDA — D3 *Chaffee*

ARKANSAS HEADWATERS/RECREATION AREA
(State Pk) Call for directions (6 campgrounds) to specify campground, or check website. Park Fee is required. Elev 7500 ft. **FAC:** Paved/dirt rds. 74 gravel, 70 pull-thrus (20 x 50), back-ins (15 x 50), accepts self-contain units only, tent sites, pit toilets, fire rings. **REC:** Arkansas River: fishing, rec open to public. Pets OK. 14 day max stay, 2015 rates: $16. No CC.
(719)539-7289 Lat: 38.53780, Lon: -105.99250
307 W Sackett Ave, Salida, CO 81201
ahra@state.co.us
www.cpw.state.co.us
See ad page 228 (Welcome Section).

FOUR SEASONS RV PARK
Ratings: 8/9/8.5 (RV Park) From Jct of US-50 & SR-291 (E end of Salida), E 1.5 mi on US-50 (L). Elev 6900 ft. **FAC:** Paved/gravel rds. 56 gravel, 14 pull-thrus (25 x 60), back-ins (25 x 35), 56 full hkups (30/50 amps), WiFi, rentals, laundry, groc, LP gas. **REC:** Arkansas River: fishing, shuffleboard. Pet restrict(B). No tents. Big rig sites, eco-friendly, 2015 rates: $36 to $69. Disc: AAA.
(719)539-3084 Lat: 38.51031, Lon: -105.96754
4305 E Hwy 50, Salida, CO 81201
fourseasonspark@qwestoffice.net
www.fourseasonsrvresort.com
See ad this page, 230.

HEART OF THE ROCKIES CAMPGROUND **Ratings: 6.5/6.5/7.5** (RV Park) 2015 rates: $28 to $35. (800)317-4052 16105 Hwy 50 W, Salida, CO 81201

SAN ISABEL — D4 *Pueblo*

ASPEN ACRES CAMPGROUND **Ratings: 6.5/8/7.5** (Campground) 2015 rates: $42. May 15 to Nov 1. (719)485-3275 16561 State Highway 165, Rye, CO 81069

SARGENTS — D3 *Saguache*

TOMICHI CREEK TRADING POST **Ratings: 6/7.5/7** (RV Park) 2015 rates: $35 to $40. (970)641-0674 71420 Highway 50, Sargents, CO 81248

SEIBERT — C5 *Kit Carson*

SHADY GROVE CAMPGROUND **Ratings: 5.5/7/6** (RV Park) 2015 rates: $24. (970)664-2218 306 Colorado Ave, Seibert, CO 80834

SILT — C2 *Garfield*

SILT/COLORADO RIVER KOA **Ratings: 9.5/9.5★/9** (RV Park) 2015 rates: $41 to $43. (970)876-4900 629 River Frontage Road, Silt, CO 81652

SILVERTON — E2 *San Juan*

A & B RV PARK **Ratings: 5/8.5★/6.5** (RV Park) 2015 rates: $38. May 1 to Oct 10. (970)387-5347 1445 Mineral, Silverton, CO 81433

RED MOUNTAIN MOTEL RV PARK CABINS & JEEP RENTALS **Ratings: 7/9.5/7.5** (RV Park) 2015 rates: $35 to $38. Jun 1 to Oct 15. (970)387-5512 664 Greene St, Silverton, CO 81433

SILVER SUMMIT RV PARK
Ratings: 7.5/9★/8 (RV Park) From Jct of US-550 & SR-110, N 0.2 mi on SR-110 to E 7th St, E 0.1 mi(R). Elev 9265 ft. **FAC:** Gravel rds. 39 gravel, 1 pull-thrus (25 x 60), back-ins (25 x 60), 39 full hkups (30/50 amps), WiFi, dump, laundry. **REC:** whirlpool. Pets OK. Partial handicap access, no tents. Big rig sites, 2015 rates: $38. Disc: military. May 15 to Oct 15.
AAA Approved
(970)387-0240 Lat: 37.80596, Lon: -107.66697
640 Mineral St, Silverton, CO 81433
silversummitrv@gmail.com
www.silversummitrvpark.com
See ad this page.

SILVERTON LAKES CAMPGROUND **Ratings: 6.5/8★/6** (RV Park) 2015 rates: $35 to $39. May 30 to Oct 1. (970)387-9888 2100 Kendall St, Silverton, CO 81433

SOUTH FORK — E2 *Rio Grande*

ALPINE TRAILS R.V. PARK
Ratings: 8/9★/8.5 (RV Park) From Jct of US160 & SR149, NW 0.2 mi on SR149 to Wharton Rd, go E .01 mi (L). Elev 8230 ft. **FAC:** Gravel rds. 42 gravel, 5 pull-thrus (24 x 60), back-ins (24 x 40), 42 full hkups (30/50 amps), WiFi, tent sites, rentals, dump, laundry, fire rings, firewood. **REC:** Rio Grande River. Pets OK. Big rig sites, eco-friendly, 2015 rates: $28 to $35. May 21 to Sep 21.
(719)873-0261 Lat: 37.401787, Lon: -106.383154
0111 Wharton Rd, South Fork, CO 81154
alpinetrailsrvpark@yahoo.com
www.alpinetrailsrvpark.com
See ad this page.

ASPEN RIDGE RV PARK **Ratings: 7.5/8★/7.5** (RV Park) 2015 rates: $29 to $33. May 10 to Oct 1. (719)873-2248 0700 W Hwy 149, South Fork, CO 81154

SOUTH FORK (CONT)

BLUE CREEK LODGE & RV PARK **Ratings: 6/7/5.5** (RV Park) 2015 rates: $30. May 15 to Oct 1. (719)658-2479 11682 Hwy 149, South Fork, CO 81154

COTTONWOOD COVE RV PARK **Ratings: 7.5/6.5/7.5** (Campground) 2015 rates: $29. May 1 to Nov 1. (719)658-2242 13046 Hwy 149, South Fork, CO 81154

FUN VALLEY RESORT **Ratings: 7.5/7/7** (RV Park) 2015 rates: $29.50. May 23 to Sep 13. (719)873-5566 36000 Hwy 160 W, South Fork, CO 81154

GOOD NIGHTS LONESOME DOVE
Ratings: 6.5/7/8 (Campground) From Jct of US-160 & Hwy 149, SW 6.2 mi on US-160 (R) at mile maker 180. Elev 8454 ft. **FAC:** Gravel rds. 38 grass, back-ins (30 x 60), 38 full hkups (30 amps), WiFi, tent sites, rentals, dump, laundry, firewood. **REC:** whirlpool. Pets OK. 2015 rates: $31 to $37. Disc: AAA, military. May 1 to Nov 1.
(719)873-1072 Lat: 37.60996, Lon: -106.71512
180065 W. Hwy 160, South Fork, CO 81154
goodnightslonesomedove@hotmail.com
www.goodnightslonesomedove.com
See ad page 249.

MOON VALLEY CAMPGROUND **Ratings: 6.5/7/6** (Campground) 2015 rates: $28. May 1 to Nov 1. (719)873-5216 180173 W. Hwy 160, South Fork, CO 81154

RIVERBEND RESORT **Ratings: 7.5/8.5★/7.5** (RV Park) 2015 rates: $34 to $38. May 1 to Nov 7. (800)621-6512 33846 W. Hwy 160, South Fork, CO 81154

SOUTH FORK CAMPGROUND
Ratings: 8/9.5★/8.5 (Campground) From Jct of US-160 & SR-149, E 3.5 mi on US-160 (L). Elev 8180 ft. **FAC:** Gravel rds. 51 gravel, 12 pull-thrus (40 x 60), back-ins (30 x 40), 51 full hkups (30/50 amps), WiFi, tent sites, rentals, dump, laundry, LP bottles, fire rings, firewood. **REC:** Rio Grande River: fishing, playground. Pet restrict(B). Big rig sites, 2015 rates: $29 to $39. May 1 to Oct 1.
(719)873-5500 Lat: 37.67728, Lon: -106.56849
26359 W US-160, South Fork, CO 81154
manager@southforkcampground.com
www.southforkcampground.com
See ad this page, 230.

UTE BLUFF LODGE & RV PARK **Ratings: 8/9★/8** (RV Park) 2015 rates: $27 to $33. May 1 to Oct 31. (800)473-0595 27680 Hwy 160, South Fork, CO 81154

STEAMBOAT SPRINGS — B2 *Routt*

STEAMBOAT SPRINGS KOA **Ratings: 8.5/6.5/7.5** (Campground) 2015 rates: $51.42 to $61.28. (970)879-0273 3603 Lincoln Ave, Steamboat Springs, CO 80487

STERLING — B5 *Logan*

NORTH STERLING
(State Pk) From Jct of I-76 & US-6 (exit 125), W 2.3 mi on Chestnut St (to 3rd Ave, N 0.3 mi to Broadway, W 0.3 mi to 7th Ave/Hwy 37, N 9.3 mi to CR-46, W 2 mi to CR-33, N 0.3 mi, follow signs (L) Entrance fee required. Elev 4000 ft. **FAC:** Paved/gravel rds. 141 gravel, 130 pull-thrus (20 x 50), back-ins (20 x 50), 97 E (30/50 amps), tent sites, showers $, dump, laundry, fire rings, firewood. **REC:** North Sterling Reservoir: swim, fishing, playground, rec open to public. Pets OK. Partial handicap access. 14 day max stay, 2015 rates: $16 to $20.
(970)522-3657 Lat: 40.78945, Lon: -103.26480
24005 County Road 330, Sterling, CO 80751
north.sterling.park@state.co.us
www.cpw.state.co.us
See ad page 228 (Welcome Section).

STRASBURG — C4 *Arapahoe*

DENVER EAST/STRASBURG KOA **Ratings: 9/9★/8** (Campground) 2015 rates: $46 to $60. (800)562-6538 1312 Monroe St, Strasburg, CO 80136

STRATTON — C5 *Kit Carson*

MARSHALL ASH VILLAGE RV PARK **Ratings: 5.5/6/3.5** (RV Park) 2015 rates: $27.27 to $30.42. (719)348-5141 814 Colorado Ave, Stratton, CO 80836

TEXAS CREEK — D3 *Fremont*

SWEET WATER RIVER RANCH **Ratings: 6/7.5/6.5** (RV Park) 2015 rates: $38 to $50. Apr 15 to Oct 15. (719)276-3842 24871 US Highway 50, Texas Creek, CO 81223

TRINIDAD — E4 *Las Animas*

CAWTHON CAMPGROUND & MOTEL **Ratings: 4.5/6/5.5** (RV Park) 2015 rates: $30. (719)846-3303 1701 Santa Fe Trail, Trinidad, CO 81082

SUMMIT RV PARK **Ratings: 5.5/8.5★/5** (RV Park) 2015 rates: $39. (719)846-2251 9800 Santa Fe Drive, Trinidad, CO 81082

TOWER 64 MOTEL & RV PARK
Ratings: 6/UI/6.5 (RV Park) From Jct of I-25 & exit 11, E 100 ft on exit rd to Santa Fe Trail Dr, North 0.25 mi (L). **FAC:** Gravel rds. 12 paved, 12 pull-thrus (24 x 40), 12 full hkups (30/50 amps), WiFi, laundry. **REC.** Pet restrict(B) $. Eco-friendly, 2015 rates: $35 to $45. Disc: AAA, military.
(719)846-3307 Lat: 37.138918, Lon: -104.518562
10301 Sante Fe Trail, Trinidad, CO 81082
rvreservations@tower64.com
http://www.tower64.com/
See ad this page.

TRINIDAD LAKE
(State Pk) From Jct of I-25 & Hwy 12(Exit 13b), W 4 mi on Hwy 12 (L). Entrance fee required. Elev 6300 ft. **FAC:** Paved rds. 73 Avail: 20 paved, 53 gravel, patios, 4 pull-thrus (15 x 45), back-ins (15 x 35), 4 full hkups, 4 S, 37 E (30/50 amps), tent sites, showers $, dump, laundry, firewood. **REC:** Trinidad Lake: fishing, playground, rec open to public. Pets OK. Partial handicap access. 14 day max stay, 2015 rates: $16 to $24.
(719)846-6951 Lat: 37.14554, Lon: -104.57020
32610 Hwy 12, Trinidad, CO 81082
trinidad.lake@state.co.us
www.cpw.state.co.us
See ad page 228 (Welcome Section).

WALDEN — B3 *Jackson*

NORTH PARK CAMPGROUND **Ratings: 6/9/7.5** (Campground) 2015 rates: $32 to $38. May 15 to Nov 15. (970)723-4310 53337 Hwy 14, Walden, CO 80480

STATE FOREST CAMPGROUND/BOCKMAN CAMPGROUND
(State Pk) From town, SE 20.25 mi, E 4 mi on CR-41 (R). Entrance fee required. Elev 9500 ft. **FAC:** Dirt rds. 52 gravel, 13 pull-thrus (30 x 40), back-ins (15 x 50), tent sites, pit toilets, dump. **REC:** Michigan River: fishing. Pets OK. Partial handicap access. 14 day max stay, 2015 rates: $10 to $20.
(970)723-8366 Lat: 40.58616, Lon: -105.97478
56750 Hwy 14, Walden, CO 80480
state.forest@state.co.us
www.cpw.state.co.us
See ad page 228 (Welcome Section).

STATE FOREST CAMPGROUND/RANGER LAKES CAMPGROUND
(State Pk) From Jct of Hwy 287 & Hwy 14, N 75 mi on Hwy 14 (L). Entrance fee required. Elev 9200 ft. **FAC:** Dirt rds. 32 gravel, back-ins (12 x 50), 32 E (30 amps), tent sites, pit toilets, dump. **REC:** Ranger Lakes. Pets OK. Partial handicap access. 14 day max stay, 2015 rates: $10 to $20.
(970)723-8366 Lat: 40.550356, Lon: -106.036731
56750 Hwy 14, Walden, CO 80480
state.forest@state.co.us
www.parks.state.co.us/parks/stateforest
See ad page 228 (Welcome Section).

WALSENBURG — E4 *Huerfano*

LATHROP
(State Pk) From Jct of I-25 & US-160 (Exit 49 or 52), W 4.5 mi on US-160 (R). Entrance fee required. Elev 6400 ft. **FAC:** Paved/gravel rds. 103 Avail: 82 paved, 21 gravel, 77 pull-thrus (15 x 50), back-ins (15 x 40), 103 W, 82 E (30/50 amps), tent sites, showers $, dump, firewood, restaurant. **REC:** Martin Lake: swim, fishing, golf, playground, rec open to public. Pets OK. Partial handicap access. 14 day max stay, 2015 rates: $16 to $20.
(719)738-2376 Lat: 37.60245, Lon: -104.83262
70 County Rd 502, Walsenburg, CO 81089
lathrop.park@state.co.us
http://cpw.state.co.us/placestogo/Parks/lathrop
See ad page 228 (Welcome Section).

WELLINGTON — B4 *Larimer*

FORT COLLINS NORTH/WELLINGTON KOA **Ratings: 9/9★/9** (Campground) 2015 rates: $37 to $50. (800)562-8142 4821 E CR 70, Wellington, CO 80549

WESTCLIFFE — D3 *Custer*

CROSS D BAR TROUT RANCH & CAMPGROUND **Ratings: 4/5/4.5** (Campground) 2015 rates: $29. May 15 to Oct 31. (800)453-4379 2299 CR 328, Westcliffe, CO 81252

GRAPE CREEK RV PARK CAMPGROUND & CABINS
Ratings: 8.5/9.5/10 (RV Park) From Jct of SR-69 & SR-96 (in town), S 1.9 mi on SR-69 (R). Elev 7891 ft. **FAC:** Gravel rds. 34 Avail: 34 all weather, 34 pull-thrus (30 x 60), 34 full hkups (30/50 amps), WiFi, tent sites, rentals, dump, laundry, groc. **REC:** Grape Creek: fishing. Pet restrict(Q). Big rig sites, 2015 rates: $36.99 to $39.99. May 1 to Oct 31.
(719)783-2588 Lat: 38.10822, Lon: -105.46362
56491 Hwy 69, Westcliffe, CO 81252
grapecreekrv@gmail.com
www.grapecreekrv.net
See ad this page.

WOODLAND PARK — C4 *Teller*

BRISTLECONE LODGE **Ratings: 7.5/8.5/8** (RV Park) 2015 rates: $39. (800)600-0399 510 N State Hwy 67, Woodland Park, CO 80863

WOODLAND PARK (CONT)

DIAMOND CAMPGROUND & RV PARK **Ratings: 7.5/8.5★/7** (RV Park) 2015 rates: $36. May 10 to Sep 30. (719)687-9684 900 N Hwy 67, Woodland Park, CO 80863

Replace clogged air filters. A clogged air filter can cut a vehicle's fuel efficiency by 10 percent.

Take time now to plan a road trip with your pet. Read more in our Pampered Pet Parks feature at the front of the Guide.

Take an RV Trip of a Lifetime!

Check out our itineraries for the Food Lover, Living History, Picture Perfect and On the Wild Side! These once-in-a-lifetime journeys are required fun for RVers of all ages.

Browse the RV Trips of a Lifetime, with routes and handy maps, in the front of this Guide.

Know The Rules Of The Road!

RV-related laws in every state and province, including: Fishing licenses, bridge and tunnel restrictions and highway information numbers for every state and province.

Find the Rules in the front of this Guide.

CLEAN RESTROOMS GET A STAR

Campgrounds that receive the maximum 5 points for restroom cleanliness (toilets, showers, floors, walls and sinks/counters/mirrors) are honored with a star beside their total restroom rating. RATED 10/10★/10

CO

Get Social Online with Good Sam

Post, pin or tweet about your RV lifestyle

Drop in at one of our social media stomping grounds on Facebook, Pinterest, Twitter or the Good Sam Camping Blog to mingle with thousands of fellow RVers. Learn about new RV destinations, share some hard-earned RV advice and make new friends — all with a few clicks of the mouse.

Good Sam Camping BLOG
Updated daily with the hottest topics in today's RV world from our team of RVing bloggers.
blog.goodsam.com

FACEBOOK
Click the thumbs-up button on the Good Sam Club page and join the fun with nearly 200,000 users.
facebook.com/thegoodsamclub

PINTEREST
Pin your favorite RV campground, create an on-the-fly scrapbook of your next RV outing or simply share favorite treats or trip ideas on your online board.
pinterest.com/goodsamclub

TWITTER
Tweet about your RV experiences on the go, follow other RVers and even get tweets from the Good Sam Club.
twitter.com/thegoodsamclub

Don't be a wallflower at the social media party. Take the plunge and expand your RV horizons. We'll see you online!

 See map page 253

Getty Images/iStockphoto

WELCOME TO Connecticut

DATE OF STATEHOOD	WIDTH: 70 MILES (113 KM)	PROPORTION OF UNITED STATES
JAN. 9, 1788	LENGTH: 110 MILES (177 KM)	0.15% OF 3,794,100 SQ MI

With its picture-perfect colonial towns, windswept fishing villages and rich maritime traditions, Connecticut is New England's front porch. The nation's third smallest state, Connecticut's history is entwined with the cultural, political and industrial foundation of America. At the ripe old age of 400, Hartford (Connecticut's capital) is one of the oldest cities in the U.S. The city's 19th-century golden age wasn't lost on Mark Twain, who wrote about the city's beauty.

Nowadays, as the headquarters of several major insurance companies, Hartford is known, more prosaically, as the "Insurance Capital of the World."

With its sumptuous yachts, Tudor mansions and Maseratis, the hedge fund capital of Greenwich is serious coin. On the other hand, New Haven has worked hard to cast off its gritty reputation. The city's historic kernel, with its Gothic towers and gracefully aging Victorian homes, now gives way to a clutch of upscale boutiques, sleek martini bars and trailblazing playhouses. In the serene towns of Essex, Litchfield Hills, Mystic and Stonington, antique stores nudge up against 19th-century homes with picket fences.

Learn

One of the six New England states, Connecticut was one of the original 13 colonies. English settlers, dissatisfied by with the shenanigans unfolding at Plymouth Colony, established Connecticut in 1635. Connecticut is known as "The Constitution State" because the tenets of the U.S. Constitution were drawn from the state's first constitution. Originally an agricultural community, in the late 18th century, Eli Whitney's development of the assembly line transformed Connecticut into a major manufacturing center. In 1797, when Whitney began to manufacture weapons in Middletown, the state became the primary supplier of pistols to the U.S. government, which led to Connecticut's other moniker, "the arsenal of democracy."

As with most of Puritan New England, Connecticut's denizens believed that industry not only strengthened an individual's moral fortitude but also enabled the independent colony to pursue its own philosophical ideals. Many great colleges were founded, with Yale University the most significant.

Play

With no striking geographical features and just 2,380 feet at its highest elevation, Connecticut is not typically considered a hot vacation spot. But that couldn't be more wrong. Connecticut boasts 65 state parks and 27 state forests. Studded with towns that bear the imprint of their maritime histories, Connecticut's shoreline is one of the most scenic byways in America. Stonington is home to the only remaining

Top 3 Tourism Attractions:
1) Mystic Seaport
2) Mystic Aquarium
3) Mark Twain House

Nickname: Constitution State

State Flower: Mountain Laurel

State Bird: American Robin

People: Charles Goodyear, inventor of vulcanized rubber; Katherine Hepburn, actress; Harriet Beecher Stowe, abolitionist, humanitarian, author; Noah Webster, dictionary publisher

Major Cities: Bridgeport, New Haven, Hartford (capital), Stamford, Waterbury

Topography: Berkshire Mountains in the Northwest; narrow central lowlands; hilly eastern uplands

Climate: Temperate climate with mild winters and warm summers; coastal regions—cooler summers and warmer winters

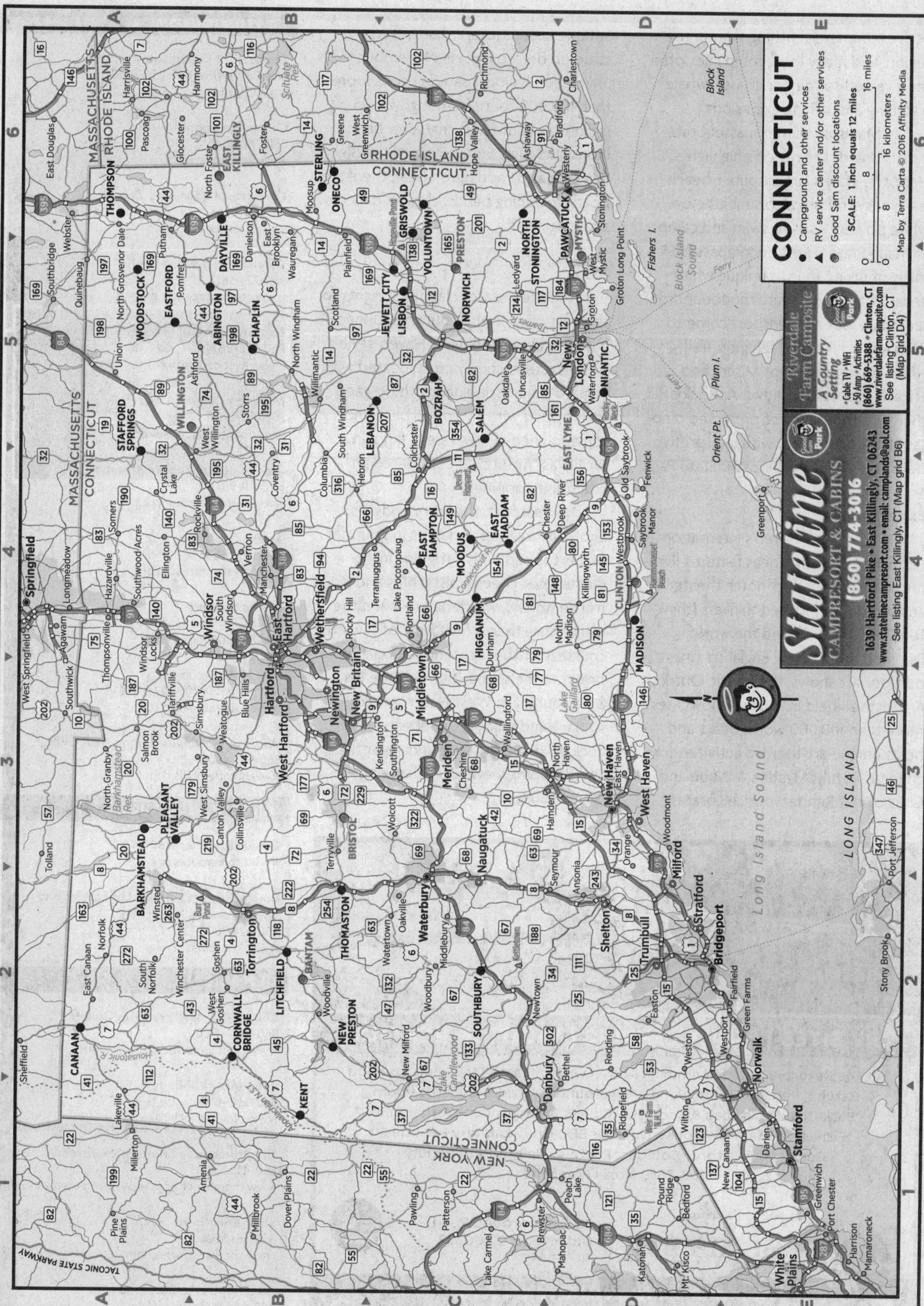
CONNECTICUT
Campground and other services
RV service center and/or other services
Good Sam discount locations
SCALE: 1 inch equals 12 miles
16 miles
16 kilometers
Map by Terra Carta © 2016 Affinity Media
Stateline
CAMPRESORT & CABINS
(860) 774-3016
1639 Hartford Pike • East Killingly, CT 06243
www.statelinecampresort.com • email: camplands@aol.com
See listing East Killingly, CT (Map grid B6)
Riverdale Farm Campsite
A Country Setting
• Cable TV • WiFi
• 50 Amp • Activities
(860) 669-5388 • Clinton, CT
www.riverdalefarmcampsite.com
See listing Clinton, CT
(Map grid D4)

CT

active commercial fishing fleet in the region, and many local companies offer their vessels for dinner cruises, whale watching and fishing excursions.

In Madison, Hammonasset State Park is one of the region's highlights. Here, the state's largest public beach is a wonderful place to sunbathe on white powdery sands, swim and camp. Pachaug State Forest encompasses 54 miles of hiking trails, a unique white cedar swamp and a rare rhododendron sanctuary. But most visitors come to Pachaug to hike the Nehantic Trail, which traverses Mount Misery and affords spectacular views. At Rocky Hill, there are thousands of preserved dinosaur tracks complete with interpretive trails at the 70-acre Dinosaur State Park.

Experience

In June, New Haven's International Festival of Arts and Ideas features live music and dance, top-notch theater and a cadre of inspired thinkers (think Ted Talks) from around the world. Deemed one of New England's finest outdoor art shows, the Mystic Outdoor Art Festival (held in August) showcases more than 100,000 works of art and hosts unique art-themed activities for children. In July, Mystic's Antique and Classic Boat Rendezvous celebrates antique vessels (more than 50) constructed before 1965. In November, Stamford's balloon parade draws more than 100,000 tourists. Along with 25 gigantic helium-filled character balloons, including Elmo, Clifford the Big Red Dog and Paddington Bear, there are floats, marching bands, clowns, dancers and magicians.

Taste

A fair few states claim first rights to the best pizza in the country. Connecticut is no exception. New Haven-style pizza is a thin, chewy crust, coated with tomato sauce, sprinkled with oregano and topped with shredded pecorino romano cheese. Mozzarella (known locally as "mootz") is considered an additional topping.

In Westport, the Tarry Lodge Enoteca Pizzeria specializes in gourmet pizzas topped with intriguing ingredients (goat cheese, pistachios and truffle honey), which have earned the place more than a few "best of" awards courtesy of the local and national food press. At the scuba-themed Dive Bar & Restaurant in West Haven, you can sit back and enjoy a Caribbean-style cocktail or a craft beer and savor the jaw-dropping views over the Long Island Sound.

TRAVEL & TOURISM

Connecticut Commission
888-CT VISIT or 860-256-2800
www.ctvisit.com

Central Regional Tourism
860-787-9640
www.visitctriver.com

Connecticut Beardsley Zoo
203-394-6565
www.beardsleyzoo.com

Connecticut Science Center
860-724-3623
www.ctsciencecenter.org

Eastern Regional Tourism District
860-536-8822
www.mysticcountry.com

Maritime Center at Norwalk
203-852-0700
www.maritimeaquarium.org

Mashantucket Pequot Museum
800-411-9671
www.pequotmuseum.org

Mystic Aquarium
860-572-5955
www.mysticaquarium.org

Mystic Seaport
860-572-0711
www.mysticseaport.org

Visit New Haven
203-777-8550, 800-332-STAY
www.visitNewHaven.com

Western-Northwest Connecticut CVB
860-567-4506
www.litchfieldhills.com

OUTDOOR RECREATION

Connecticut Bike Route
www.ctbikeroutes.org

Connecticut Department of Energy and Environmental Protection
860-424-3000
ww.ct.gov/deep

SHOPPING

Clinton Crossing Premium Outlets
860-664-0700
www.premiumoutlets.com/clinton

Olde Mistick Village
860-536-4941
www.oldemistickvillage.com

The Promenade Shops at Evergreen
860-432-3398
www.thepromenadeshopsatevergreenwalk.com

Shop Westfarms
860-561-3024
www.shopwestfarms.com

The Shoppes at Buckland Hills
860-644-1450
www.theshoppesatbucklandhills.com

Featured Good Sam Parks

CONNECTICUT

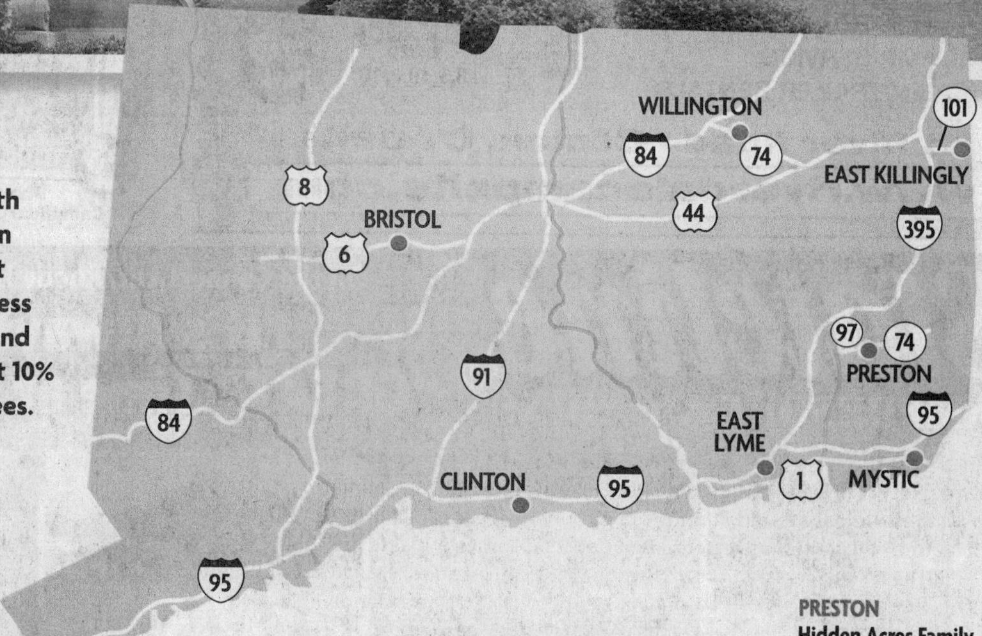

When you stay with Good Sam, you can expect the highest degree of cleanliness and friendliness, and better yet, you get 10% off campground fees.

If you're not already a Good Sam member you can purchase your membership at one of these locations:

BRISTOL
Bear Creek Campground At Lake Compounce
(860)583-3300

CLINTON
Riverdale Farm Campsite
(860)669-5388

EAST KILLINGLY
Stateline Campresort & Cabins
(860)774-3016

EAST LYME
Aces High RV Park
(877)785-8478

MYSTIC
Seaport RV Resort & Campground
(888)472-4189

PRESTON
Hidden Acres Family Campground
(860)887-9633

WILLINGTON
Wilderness Lake Park
(860)684-6352

For more Good Sam Parks go to listing pages

Connecticut

CONSULTANTS

Mark & Wendy Pitts

ABINGTON — B5 *Windham*

MASHAMOQUET BROOK (State Pk) From Jct of US-44 & SR-101, W 1.5 mi on US-44(L). 2015 rates: $14 to $24. Apr 15 to Oct 12. (860)928-6121

Tell them you saw them in this Guide!

ASHFORD — A5 *Windham*

BRIALEE RV & TENT PARK, INC **Ratings: 8/7/7.5** (Campground) 2015 rates: $20 to $62. Apr 1 to Oct 31. (800)303-2267 174 Laurel Ln, Ashford, CT 06278

BANTAM — B2 *Litchfield*

COZY HILLS CAMPGROUND
Ratings: 7.5/8.5/8.5 (Campground) From Hwy 8 and SR 118 (Exit 42), W 4.8 mi on SR 118 to SR 202, W 5 mi (L). **FAC:** Gravel rds. (120 spaces). Avail: 41 dirt, back-ins (25 x 45), 41 W, 41 E (30 amps), seasonal sites, WiFi, tent sites, rentals, dump, mobile sewer, groc, LP gas, fire rings, firewood, restaurant, controlled access. **REC:** pool, pond, fishing, playground. Pet restrict(B/Q). Partial handicap access. Eco-friendly, 2015 rates: $56. Apr 26 to Oct 15.
(860)567-2119 Lat: 41.71507, Lon: -73.26342
1311 Bantam Rd, Bantam, CT 06750
admin@cozyhills.com
www.cozyhills.com

BARKHAMSTED — A3 *Litchfield*

WHITE PINES CAMPSITES **Ratings: 6.5/7.5/6.5** (Campground) 2015 rates: $47 to $59. Apr 14 to Oct 15. (860)379-0124 232 Old North Rd, Barkhamsted, CT 06063

BOZRAH — C5 *New London*

ODETAH CAMPING RESORT **Ratings: 9/9.5★/9** (Campground) 2015 rates: $52 to $73. May 1 to Oct 31. (860)889-4144 38 Bozrah St. Ext, Bozrah, CT 06334

BRISTOL — B3 *Hartford*

BEAR CREEK CAMPGROUND AT LAKE COMPOUNCE
Ratings: 8.5/10★/9.5 (Campground) From Jct I-84 and Rte 229 (exit 31) N 2 mi on Rte 229 and follow signs. **FAC:** All weather rds. 56 Avail: 56 all weather, 56 pull-thrus (25 x 60), some side by side hkups, 56 W, 56 E (30/50 amps), WiFi, tent sites, rentals, dump, laundry, groc, fire rings, firewood, controlled access. **REC:** playground. Pets OK. Partial handicap access. Eco-friendly, 2015 rates: $40 to $60. May 1 to Oct 31. ATM.
(860)583-3300 Lat: 41.6479236, Lon: -72.9094710
186 Enterprise Drive, Bristol, CT 06010
mcordani@lakecompounce.com
www.campbearcreek.com
See ad this page, 255.

Things to See and Do

LAKE COMPOUNCE THEME PARK New England's Theme Park. May 1 to Oct 31. partial handicap access. RV accessible. Restrooms, food. Hours: Call for hours.
(860)583-3300 Lat: 41.6479236, Lon: -72.9094710
186 Enterprise Dr., Bristol, CT 06010
info@lakecompounce.com
www.lakecompounce.com
See ad this page.

CANAAN — A2 *Litchfield*

LONE OAK CAMPSITES **Ratings: 8.5/10★/10** (RV Park) 2015 rates: $57 to $73. Apr 15 to Oct 15. (800)422-2267 360 Norfolk, East Canaan, CT 06024

CHAPLIN — B5 *Windham*

NICKERSON PARK **Ratings: 6.5/7/7.5** (Campground) 2015 rates: $35 to $40. (860)455-0007 1036 Phoenixville Rd, Chaplin, CT 06235

EXCLUSIVE! Military Listings in the back of the Guide indicate campgrounds for use exclusively by active and retired military personnel.

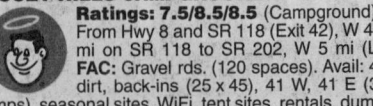

CLINTON — D4 *Middlesex*

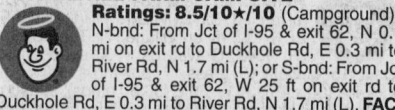

RIVERDALE FARM CAMPSITE
Ratings: 8.5/10★/10 (Campground) N-bnd: From Jct of I-95 & exit 62, N 0.1 mi on exit rd to Duckhole Rd, E 0.3 mi to River Rd, N 1.7 mi (L); or S-bnd: From Jct of I-95 & exit 62, W 25 ft on exit rd to Duckhole Rd, E 0.3 mi to River Rd, N 1.7 mi (L). **FAC:** Paved/gravel rds. (250 spaces). 120 Avail: 20 gravel, 80 grass, 20 dirt, patios, 15 pull-thrus (34 x 60), back-ins (35 x 45), 85 full hkups, 35 W, 35 E (30/50 amps), seasonal sites, cable, WiFi, tent sites, rentals, showers $, dump, mobile sewer, laundry, groc, LP gas, fire rings, firewood, controlled access. **REC:** Hammonasset River: swim, fishing, shuffleboard, playground. Pet restrict(B). Big rig sites, eco-friendly, 2015 rates: $45 to $50. Apr 15 to Nov 1. ATM, no CC.
(860)669-5388 Lat: 41.30788, Lon: -72.58386
111 River Rd, Clinton, CT 06413
riverdalefarmcampsite@comcast.net
www.riverdalefarmcampsite.com
See ad opposite page, 255, 253 (CT Map).

CORNWALL BRIDGE — B2 *Litchfield*

HOUSATONIC MEADOWS (State Pk) From Jct of Rte 4 & Rte 7, N 2 mi on Rte 7 (R). 2015 rates: $17 to $27. May 15 to Sep 30. (860)672-6772

DAYVILLE — B6 *Windham*

HIDE-A-WAY-COVE FAMILY CAMPGROUND **Ratings: 7/6/7** (Campground) 2015 rates: $30. May 1 to Oct 8. (860)774-1128 1060 North Rd, Dayville, CT 06241

EAST HADDAM — C4 *Middlesex*

DEVIL'S HOPYARD (State Pk) From town, E 10 mi on SR-82 (L). Pit toilets. 2015 rates: $14 to $24. Apr 15 to Sep 30. (860)526-2336

WOLF'S DEN FAMILY CAMPGROUND **Ratings: 8/8/8.5** (Campground) 2015 rates: $47. May 1 to Oct 27. (860)873-9681 256 Town St (Rte 82), East Haddam, CT 06423

EAST HAMPTON — C4 *Middlesex*

MARKHAM MEADOWS CAMPGROUND **Ratings: 8/7/7.5** (Campground) 2015 rates: $45. (860)267-9738 7 Markham Rd, East Hampton, CT 06424

NELSON'S FAMILY CAMPGROUND **Ratings: 8/7/7** (Campground) 2015 rates: $47. Apr 16 to Oct 11. (860)267-5300 71 Mott Hill Rd, East Hampton, CT 06424

EAST KILLINGLY — B6 *Windham*

STATELINE CAMPRESORT & CABINS
Ratings: 8.5/9/9 (RV Park) From Jct of I 395 & Rte 101 (Exit 93), E 5 mi on Rte 101 (R).

FINEST FAMILY CAMPING ON CT/RI LINE
Join us for your best-ever family camping experience! We offer many fun filled activities, fully equipped cabins, & spring, summer & fall specials. Reservations taken year round. It's always a GREAT time at Stateline!
FAC: Paved/gravel rds. (241 spaces). 155 Avail: 80 grass, 75 dirt, back-ins (32 x 43), 14 full hkups, 141 W, 141 E (30/50 amps), seasonal sites, cable, WiFi, tent sites, rentals, dump, mobile sewer, laundry, groc, LP gas, fire rings, firewood, controlled access. **REC:** pool, Campground Lake: swim, fishing, playground. Pet restrict(Q) $. Partial handicap access. 2015 rates: $25 to $68. Disc: AAA, military. Apr 15 to Oct 15. ATM.
(860)774-3016 Lat: 41.84802, Lon: -71.79518
1639 Hartford Pike, East Killingly, CT 06243
camplands@aol.com
www.statelinecampresort.com
See ad opposite page, 255, 253 (CT Map).

EAST LYME — D5 *New London*

ACES HIGH RV PARK
Ratings: 10/10★/10 (RV Park) From Jct of I-95 & SR-161 (exit 74), N 3 mi on SR-161 (R). **FAC:** All weather rds. (86 spaces). Avail: 61 all weather, 50 pull-thrus (52 x 80), back-ins (35 x 50), 61 full hkups (30/50 amps), seasonal sites, cable, WiFi, rentals, showers $, dump, laundry, groc, LP gas, fire rings, firewood, controlled access. **REC:** heated pool, pond, swim, fishing, playground. Pets OK. Partial handicap access, no tents. Big rig sites, eco-friendly, 2015 rates: $64 to $69. ATM.
(877)785-8478 Lat: 41.40568, Lon: -72.22517
301 Chesterfield Road, East Lyme, CT 06333
sales@aceshighrvpark.com
www.aceshighrvpark.com
See ad this page, 255.

EASTFORD — A5 *Windham*

CHARLIE BROWN CAMPGROUND INC **Ratings: 7.5/8.5★/8.5** (Campground) 2015 rates: $47.50 to $65. Apr 15 to Oct 13. (877)974-0142 98 Chaplin Rd, Rte 198, Eastford, CT 06242

PEPPERTREE CAMPING **Ratings: 7.5/7/8.5** (Campground) 2015 rates: $35. Apr 1 to Oct 13. (860)974-1439 146 Chaplin Rd, Eastford, CT 06242

GRISWOLD — C6 *New London*

COUNTRYSIDE RV PARK **Ratings: 8.5/7.5/8** (Campground) 2015 rates: $48. May 1 to Oct 10. (860)376-0029 75 Cook Hill Rd, Griswold, CT 06351

HARTFORD — B3 *Hartford*

HARTFORD See also Ashford, Barkhamsted, Bozrah, Bristol, East Haddam, East Hampton, Higganum, Lebanon, Litchfield, Salem, South Windsor, Stafford Springs, Thomaston & Willington.

HIGGANUM — C4 *Middlesex*

LITTLE CITY CAMPGROUND Ratings: 7.5/6/7 (RV Park) From Jct of I-91 & Rte 9 (exit 22S), S 10 mi on Rte 9 to Rte 154 (exit 10), SE 2 mi to Candlewood Hill Rd (just before traffic light), W 3.2 mi to Little City Rd, SW 1 mi (R). **FAC:** Gravel rds. (55 spaces). Avail: 25 grass, back-ins (50 x 60), 5 full hkups, 20 W, 20 E (30/50 amps), seasonal sites, WiFi, tent sites, dump, mobile sewer, laundry, LP bottles, fire rings, firewood. **REC:** pool, pond, fishing, playground. Pet restrict(B). 2015 rates: $36 to $40. May 1 to Oct 1. No CC.
(860)345-8469 Lat: 41.45562, Lon: -72.60570
741 Little City Rd, Higganum, CT 06441
info@campconn.com

JEWETT CITY — C5 *New London*

HOPEVILLE POND (State Pk) (I-395): TAKE EXIT 86, FROM N, GO (L), FROM S, GO (R); FOLLOW HOPEVILLE RD TO Y INTERSECTION, PROCEED TO (R). ENTRANCE IS 1/2 MILE ON (R), OFF RTE 201. 2015 rates: $17 to $27. May 24 to Sep 30. (860)376-0313

KENT — B1 *Litchfield*

MACEDONIA BROOK (State Pk) From Jct of US-7 & SR-341, NW 2 mi on SR-341 to Macedonia Brook Rd, N 2 mi (R). Note: Alcohol-free campground. Pit toilets. 2015 rates: $14 to $24. Apr 15 to Sep 30. (860)927-4100

LEBANON — C5 *New London*

LAKE WILLIAMS **Ratings: 7/7/8** (Campground) 2015 rates: $32.95 to $69.95. Apr 16 to Oct 10. (860)642-7761 1742 Exeter Rd, Lebanon, CT 06249

WATER'S EDGE **Ratings: 8/7/8.5** (Campground) 2015 rates: $45 to $57. Apr 15 to Oct 15. (860)642-7470 271 Leonard Bridge Rd, Lebanon, CT 06249

LISBON — C5 *New London*

ROSS HILL PARK **Ratings: 7.5/7.5/7** (Campground) 2015 rates: $43 to $48. Apr 15 to Oct 31. (860)376-9606 170 Ross Hill Rd, Lisbon, CT 06351

SUNFOX CAMPGROUND **Ratings: 7/8★/8** (Campground) 2015 rates: $34 to $69. Apr 1 to Oct 31. (860)376-1081 15 Kenyon Rd, Lisbon, CT 06351

LITCHFIELD — B2 *Litchfield*

HEMLOCK HILL CAMP-RESORT COOPERATIVE **Ratings: 8/7.5/8** (Campground) 2015 rates: $50 to $56. Apr 25 to Oct 18. (860)567-2267 118 Hemlock Hill Rd, Litchfield, CT 06759

WHITE MEMORIAL FAMILY CAMPGROUND (POINT FOLLY) (Public) From jct Hwy-63 & US-202: Go 2 mi W on Hwy-202, then 1 mi S on Bissell Rd, then .3 mi W on Whitehall Rd. Pit toilets. 2015 rates: $14.50 to $17.50. (860)567-0089

Don't miss a thing! Check out the Table of Contents for everything the Guide has to offer.

MADISON — D4 *New Haven*

HAMMONASSET BEACH (State Pk) From Jct of I-95 & Hammonasset Connecter (exit 62), S 0.5 mi on Hammonasset Connecter (E). 2015 rates: $35 to $45. May 15 to Oct 10. (203)245-1817

MOODUS — C4 *Middlesex*

GRANDVIEW CAMPING RESORT **Ratings: 7.5/9.5★/8.5** (Campground) 2015 rates: $59 to $65. Apr 15 to Oct 31. (860)873-3332 89 North Moodus Rd, Moodus, CT 06469

MYSTIC — D5 *New London*

SEAPORT RV RESORT & CAMPGROUND
Ratings: 9/9.5★/9 (Campground) From Jct of I-95 & Allyn St/Cow Hill Rd (Exit 89), N 1.3 mi on Allyn St/Cow Hill Rd to Gold Star Rd/SR-184, E (Rt turn) 1.5 mi (L).

MARITIME SEAPORTS AND MYSTIC PIZZA
Experience all the charm of a 19th century ship building town with the modern comforts of resort-style living. This all ages resort provides spacious sites with fun features like a heated pool, miniature golf and laser tag!
FAC: All weather rds. (145 spaces). Avail: 126 gravel, 24 pull-thrus (53 x 110), back-ins (53 x 60), 126 W, 126 E (30/50 amps), seasonal sites, cable, WiFi, tent sites, rentals, dump, mobile sewer, laundry, groc, LP gas, fire rings, firewood, controlled access. **REC:** heated pool, pond, fishing, playground, rec open to public. Pet restrict(Q). Partial handicap access. 2015 rates: $44 to $65. Disc: AAA, military. Apr 15 to Oct 31.
AAA Approved
(888)472-4189 Lat: 41.39985, Lon: -71.95905
45 Campground Rd, Old Mystic, CT 06372
seaport@suncommunities.com
www.seaportcampground.com
See ad pages 254 (Welcome Section), 1463 (Welcome Section), 255.

CT

NEW PRESTON — B2 *Litchfield*

LAKE WARAMAUG (State Pk) From town, NW 3 mi on Hwy 45 to North Shore Rd, W 5 mi (R). 2015 rates: $17 to $27. May 23 to Sep 30. (860)868-0220

NIANTIC — D5 *New London*

ROCKY NECK (State Pk) From Jct of I-95 & Rte 156 (exit 72), S 0.5 mi on Rte 156, E .25 mi (R). 2015 rates: $20 to $30. May 1 to Sep 30. (860)739-1339

NORTH STONINGTON — C6 *New London*

MYSTIC KOA **Ratings: 8.5/8.5★/9** (Campground) 2015 rates: $51 to $93. (800)562-3451 118 Pendleton Hill Rd, North Stonington, CT 06359

NORWICH — C5 *New London*

ACORN ACRES **Ratings: 7.5/7/6** (Campground) 2015 rates: $45 to $55. Apr 15 to Oct 13. (860)859-1020 135 Lake Rd, Bozrah, CT 06334

ONECO — B6 *Windham*

RIVER BEND CAMPGROUND **Ratings: 8/9/8** (Campground) 2015 rates: $37 to $51. Apr 13 to Oct 13. (860)564-3440 41 Pond St, Oneco, CT 06373

PAWCATUCK — D6 *New London*

Travel Services

RJ'S DIESEL REPAIR INC Diesel and Gas RV mechanical repairs, emergency mobile road service, ASE Certified. **SERVICES:** Tire, MH mechanical, engine/chassis repair, mobile RV svc, emergency rd svc. RV accessible. Hours: M-F 8-5.
(860)599-3088 Lat: 41.40364, Lon: -71.84600
62 Voluntown Rd, Pawcatuck, CT 06379
rjsdiesel@yahoo.com
www.rjsdiesel.com
See ad this page.

We appreciate your business!

PLEASANT VALLEY — A3 *Litchfield*

AMERICAN LEGION SF (Public) From Jct of Rte 8 & 44, E 5 mi on Rte 44 to Rte 318, E 1 mi to WCenter Hill Rd., N 2 mi (R). 2015 rates: $17 to $27. Apr 10 to Oct 11. (860)379-0922

PRESTON — C5 *New London*

HIDDEN ACRES FAMILY CAMPGROUND
Ratings: 8.5/10★/9 (Campground) From Jct of I-395 & Hwy 164 (Exit 85), S 0.9 mi on Hwy 164 (rt turn) to Palmer Rd (River Ridge Golf Course), SW 1.6 mi to River Rd, W 1.4 mi (R). **FAC:** Paved/gravel rds. (200 spaces). Avail: 73 grass, patios, back-ins (45 x 60), 28 full hkups, 45 W, 45 E (30/50 amps), seasonal sites, WiFi, tent sites, rentals, showers $, dump, mobile sewer, laundry, groc, LP gas, fire rings, firewood, restaurant, controlled access. **REC:** pool, Quinebaug River: swim, fishing, playground. Pet restrict(B). Partial handicap access. 2015 rates: $48 to $58. Disc: military. May 1 to Oct 10.
(860)887-9633 Lat: 41.55354, Lon: -72.01463
47 River Rd, Preston, CT 06365
info@hiddenacrescamp.com
www.hiddenacrescamp.com
See ad this page, 255.

STRAWBERRY PARK RV RESORT **Ratings: 8/8.5/9** (Campground) 2015 rates: $40 to $100. May 1 to Oct 31. (860)886-1944 42 Pierce Rd, Preston, CT 06365

SALEM — C5 *New London*

SALEM FARMS CAMPGROUND Ratings: 8.5/9★/8.5 (Campground) From Jct of Rtes 2 & 11, S 4 mi on Rte 11 to Witch Meadow Rd (exit 5), W 0.5 mi to Alexander Rd, W 0.25 mi (L). **FAC:** Gravel rds. (189 spaces). 49 Avail: 35 gravel, 14 grass, 3 pull-thrus (27 x 48), back-ins (27 x 48), mostly side by side hkups, 49 W, 49 E (30/50 amps), seasonal sites, cable, WiFi, tent sites, rentals, showers $, dump, mobile sewer, laundry, groc, LP bottles, fire rings, firewood, restaurant, controlled access. **REC:** pool, pond, fishing, shuffleboard, playground. Pet restrict(Q). 2015 rates: $42 to $50. Disc: military. May 1 to Oct 13. ATM.
(800)479-9238 Lat: 41.49943, Lon: -72.31784
39 Alexander Rd, Salem, CT 06420
sfcg2003@aol.com
www.salemfarmscampground.com

WITCH MEADOW LAKE FAMILY CAMPGROUND **Ratings: 8.5/8.5★/9.5** (Campground) 2015 rates: $50 to $60. May 1 to Oct 15. (860)859-1542 139 Witch Meadow Rd, Salem, CT 06420

RV Park ratings you can rely on!

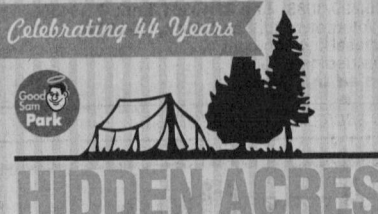

SOUTHBURY — C2 *Fairfield*

KETTLETOWN (State Pk) From Jct of I-84 & SR-67, E 0.1 mi on SR-67 to Kettletown Rd, S 3.5 mi to Georges Hill Rd, W 0.75 mi (L).From Labor Day to Memorial Day, campground is open weekends only. No rigs over 28 ft long. 2015 rates: $17 to $27. May 15 to Sep 30. (203)264-5678

STAFFORD SPRINGS — A4 *Tolland*

MINERAL SPRINGS FAMILY CAMPGROUND **Ratings: 7/6.5/8** (Campground) 2015 rates: $40 to $45. May 1 to Oct 15. (860)684-2993 135 Leonard Rd, Stafford Springs, CT 06076

STERLING — B6 *Windham*

GIBSON HILL RV PARK **Ratings: 4.5/6.5/6** (Campground) 2015 rates: $42 to $46. Apr 8 to Oct 8. (860)564-9996 177 Gibson Hill Rd, Sterling, CT 06377

THOMASTON — B2 *Litchfield*

BLACK ROCK (State Pk) From Jct of I-84 & Rte 8N (exit 38), N 10 mi on Rte 8N to Rte 6W, W 0.5 mi (R). April-May, open weekends only. 2015 rates: $17 to $27. Apr 15 to Sep 30. (860)283-8088

BRANCH BROOK CAMPGROUND **Ratings: 8/8.5★/7.5** (Campground) 2015 rates: $43 to $45. Apr 1 to Nov 1. (860)283-8144 435 Watertown Rd, Thomaston, CT 06787

THOMPSON — A6 *Windham*

WEST THOMPSON LAKE (COE-WEST THOMPSON LAKE) (Public) From jct I-395 (exit 99) & Hwy 200: Go 1 mi W on Hwy 200 to Thompson Center, then 2 mi S on Hwy 193, straight across Hwy 12 at traffic light, then 1/4 mi W on Reardon Rd to Campground Rd. 2015 rates: $15 to $30. May 15 to Sep 12. (860)923-3121

VOLUNTOWN — C6 *New London*

CIRCLE C CAMPGROUND, INC **Ratings: 7.5/7/7** (Campground) 2015 rates: $40 to $55. Apr 15 to Oct 13. (860)564-4534 21 Bailey Pond Rd, Voluntown, CT 06384

NATURES CAMPSITES **Ratings: 7.5/6/7.5** (Campground) 2015 rates: $40 to $48. May 1 to Oct 15. (860)376-4203 96 Ekonk Hill Rd, Voluntown, CT 06384

PACHAUG/GREEN FALLS CAMPGROUND (State Pk) From town, E 2.5 mi on Rte-138 to Forest Park Rd, S 2.5 mi (R). Pit toilets. 2015 rates: $17 to $27. Apr 17 to Sep 30. (860)376-4075

PACHAUG/MOUNT MISERY (State Pk) From town, N 0.6 mi on Rte 49 (L). Pit toilets. 2015 rates: $14 to $24. Apr 15 to Dec 31. (860)376-4075

WILLINGTON — A5 *Tolland*

MOOSE MEADOW **Ratings: 8/10★/7.5** (Campground) 2015 rates: $38 to $57. Apr 19 to Oct 13. (860)429-7451 28 Kechkes Rd, W Willington, CT 06279

Don't miss the best part! Look in the front of most state sections for articles that focus on areas of special interest to RVers. These "Spotlights" tell you about interesting tourist destinations you might otherwise miss.

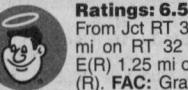

WILDERNESS LAKE PARK
Ratings: 6.5/9.5★/8 (Campground) From Jct RT 32 & I-84 (Exit 70): N 0.05 mi on RT 32 to Village Hill(first right), E(R) 1.25 mi on Village Hill. Turn at sign (R). **FAC:** Gravel rds. (100 spaces). 30 Avail: 15 gravel, 15 grass, 7 pull-thrus (30 x 60), back-ins (30 x 45), 30 W, 30 E (30/50 amps), seasonal sites, WiFi Hotspot, tent sites, rentals, dump, mobile sewer, groc, LP gas, fire rings, firewood. **REC:** Wilderness Lake: swim, fishing, playground. Pets OK. Eco-friendly, 2015 rates: $45. Disc: AAA, military. Apr 1 to Nov 20. No CC.
(860)684-6352 Lat: 41.91863, Lon: -72.28282
150 Village Hill Rd, Willington, CT 06279
crossenray@yahoo.com
www.wildernesslakect.com
See ad this page, 255.

WOODSTOCK — A5 *Windham*

CHAMBERLAIN LAKE CAMPGROUND **Ratings: 6.5/6.5/7.5** (Campground) 2015 rates: $40. Apr 15 to Nov 1. (860)974-0567 1379 Rte 197, Woodstock, CT 06281

Delaware Tourism Office

WELCOME TO Delaware

DATE OF STATEHOOD DEC. 7, 1787	WIDTH: 30 MILES (48 KM) LENGTH: 96 MILES (154 KM)	PROPORTION OF UNITED STATES 0.07% OF 3,794,100 SQ MI

Known as the Small Wonder state, Delaware still manages to pack quite a punch. Generally cast in the role of wallflower to its neighbor states, Delaware brings more to the table than just tax-free shopping and NASCAR. There are pristine, white-sand beaches, charming waterfronts and hillsides dotted with chocolate-box towns. State capital Wilmington balances its industrial dynamism with a love of the outdoors and cultural brio.

Dover may lack urban edge, but its pretty streets lined with row homes harbor eclectic restaurants and curio shops. With its inclusive vibe, Rehoboth is every Delawarian's favorite stretch of sand. Here, classic beachfront hotels nudge up against slick new condos, quaint cottages and tasteful boutiques. Just outside of town, the Tanger Outlets shopping Mecca stretches for two miles along Route 1 and purveys seemingly every brand known to man (with tax-free sales, no less).

Delaware's 28 miles of sandy Atlantic beaches give sweet justification to wile away your time. North of Rehoboth, the town of Lewes is a gem. Founded in 1681 as a Dutch whaling station, Lewes harbors a fascinating clutch of historic sites, eclectic "Ye Olde" stores, fine restaurants and atmospheric inns.

And what would Delaware be without NASCAR? Since "The Monster Mile" opened in 1969, it has hosted the USAC and Verizon IndyCar Series in addition to NASCAR races.

Delaware's regional delicacy is the blue crab. Along the coast and in its cities, hungry travelers can take their pick of fine restaurants and crab shacks that serve up this delicious food.

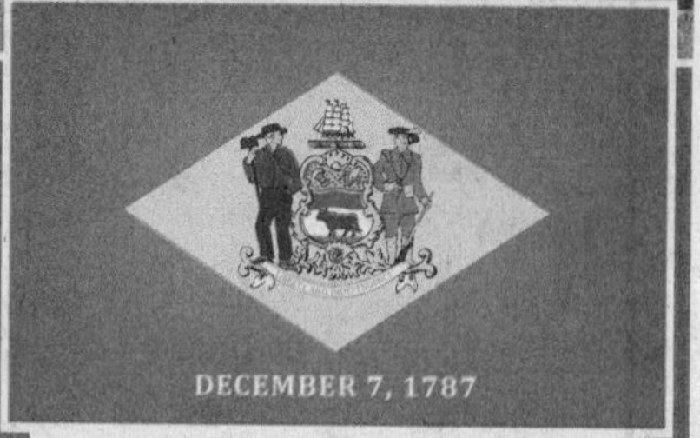

Top 3 Tourism Attractions:
1) Rehoboth Beach
2) Winterthur Museum, Garden and Library
3) Firefly Music Festival

Nickname: Diamond State

State Flower: Peach Blossom

State Bird: Blue Hen Chicken

People: Valerie Bertinelli, actress; Henry Heimlich, surgeon; Howard Pyle, illustrator and writer

Major Cities: Wilmington, Dover (capital), Newark, Middletown, Smyrna

Topography: A level plain with the lowest mean elevation of any state in the nation

Climate: Temperate and humid, with the normal daily mean temperature in Wilmington at 54°

TRAVEL & TOURISM

Delaware Tourism Office
866-284-7483
www.visitdelaware.com

Good Libations Tour
800-233-KENT
www.goodlibationstour.com

Greater Wilmington CVB
800-489-6664, 302-295-2210
www.visitwilmingtonde.com

Kent County Tourism
800-233-KENT, 302-734-1736
www.visitdover.com

Southern Delaware Tourism
800-357-1818, 302-856-1818
www.visitsoutherndelaware.com

OUTDOOR RECREATION

Division of Fish & Wildlife
302-739-4431
www.fw.delaware.gov

SHOPPING

Bargain Bill
302-875-9958
www.bargainbill.com

Christiana Mall
302-731-9815
www.shopchristianamall.com

Delaware Store
302-724-5127
www.delawaremade.com

Dover Mall
302-734-0415
www.dovermall.com

Tanger Outlets and Rehoboth Beach
866-665-8682
www.tangeroutlet.com

DE

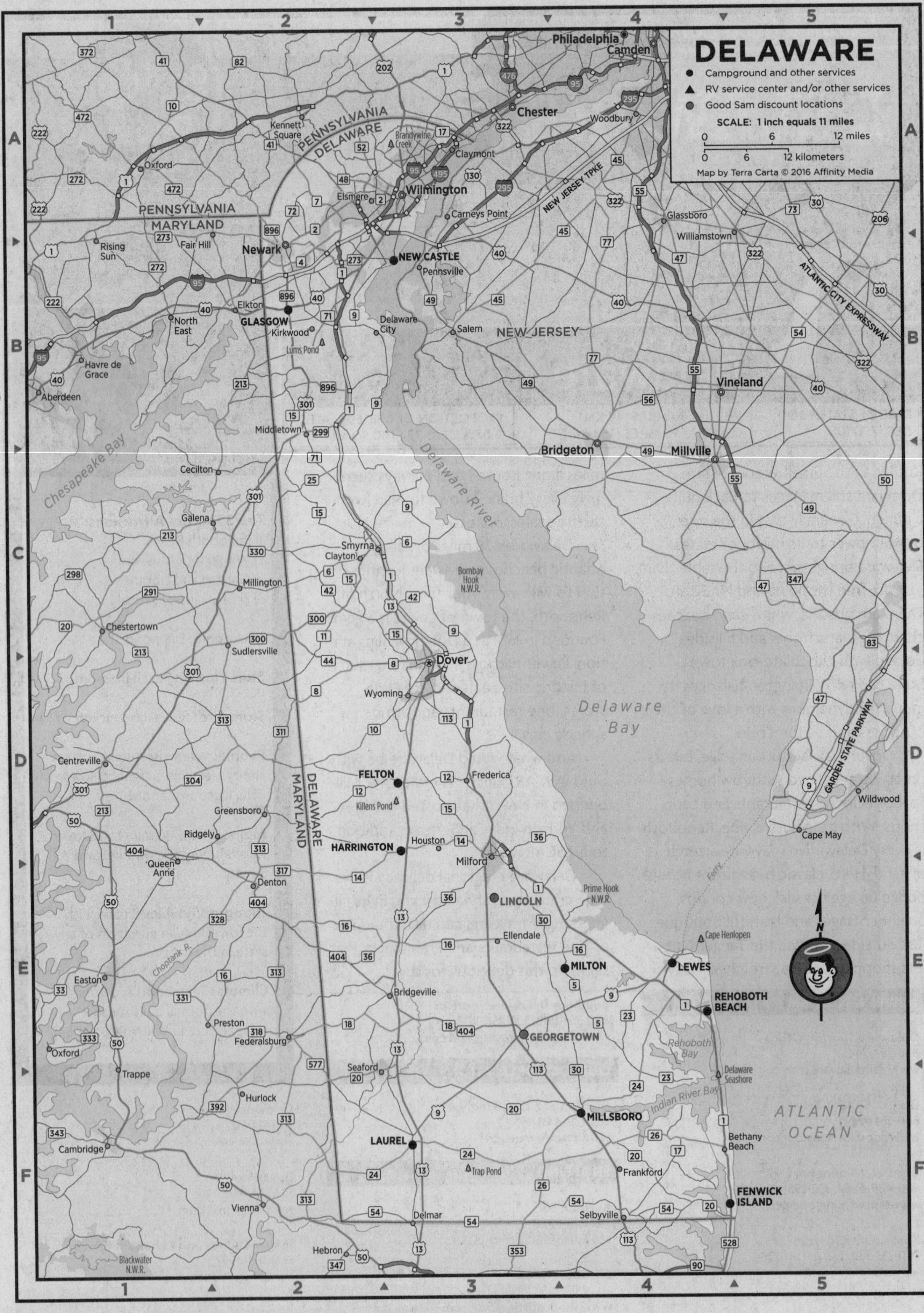
DELAWARE
Campground and other services
RV service center and/or other services
Good Sam discount locations
SCALE: 1 inch equals 11 miles
0 6 12 miles
0 6 12 kilometers
Map by Terra Carta © 2016 Affinity Media
Philadelphia
Camden
Chester
Woodbury
Kennett Square
PENNSYLVANIA
DELAWARE
Brandywine Creek
Claymont
Oxford
Wilmington
Elsmere
Carneys Point
NEW JERSEY TPKE
MARYLAND
Rising Sun
Fair Hill
Newark
NEW CASTLE
Pennsville
Glassboro
Williamstown
ATLANTIC CITY EXPRESSWAY
Elkton
North East
GLASGOW
Kirkwood
Lums Pond
Delaware City
Salem
NEW JERSEY
Havre de Grace
Aberdeen
Vineland
Middletown
Bridgeton
Millville
Chesapeake Bay
Cecilton
Delaware River
Galena
Smyrna
Clayton
Bombay Hook N.W.R.
Millington
Chestertown
Sudlersville
Dover
Wyoming
Delaware Bay
GARDEN STATE PARKWAY
Centreville
FELTON
Frederica
Killens Pond
Wildwood
Greensboro
Ridgely
HARRINGTON
Houston
Milford
Cape May
Queen Anne
Denton
LINCOLN
Prime Hook N.W.R.
Ferry
Choptank R.
Ellendale
Cape Henlopen
Easton
MILTON
LEWES
Bridgeville
REHOBOTH BEACH
Preston
Federalsburg
GEORGETOWN
Rehoboth Bay
Oxford
Trappe
Seaford
Delaware Seashore
Hurlock
Indian River Bay
MILLSBORO
ATLANTIC OCEAN
LAUREL
Bethany Beach
Cambridge
Trap Pond
Frankford
FENWICK ISLAND
Vienna
Delmar
Selbyville
Hebron
Blackwater N.W.R.

Featured Good Sam Parks

DELAWARE

Good Sam Park

When you stay with Good Sam, you can expect the highest degree of cleanliness and friendliness, and better yet, you get 10% off campground fees.

If you're not already a Good Sam member you can purchase your membership at one of these locations:

GEORGETOWN
Homestead Campground
(302)684-4278

LINCOLN
Yogi Bear's Jellystone Park at Delaware Beach
(302)491-6614

For more Good Sam Parks go to listing pages

Delaware

CONSULTANTS

Mark & Wendy Pitts

DOVER — D3 *Kent*

➔ **HOLIDAY PARK CAMPGROUND**
Ratings: 8/9★/8.5 (Campground) From Jct of US 13 (Dupont Hwy) & Hwy 8 (in Dover) W 12.7 mi on Hwy 8 to Hwy 311(in MD), SW 6 mi on Hwy 311/313 to Hwy 314, E 0.3 mi on Hw 314 to Wothers Rd, N 0.2 mi to Boyce Mill Rd, NE 0.7 mi to Drapers Mill Rd, N 2.3 mi (L). **FAC:** Paved/gravel rds. (200 spaces). Avail: 150 dirt, 28 pull-thrus (27 x 60), back-ins (25 x 60), some side by side hkups, 150 W, 150 E (30/50 amps), seasonal sites, cable, WiFi Hotspot, tent sites, rentals, dump, mobile sewer, laundry, groc, LP gas, fire rings, firewood, controlled access. **REC:** pool, Choptank River: fishing, shuffleboard, playground. Pet restrict(B). Eco-friendly, 2015 rates: $38 to $50. Disc: AAA, military. Apr 1 to Nov 15.
(410)482-6797 Lat: 39.00788, Lon: -75.76484
14620 Drapes Mill Rd, Greensboro, MD 21639
holiday@dmv.com
www.holidaypark.com
See primary listing at Greensboro, MD and ad page 589.

FELTON — D3 *Kent*

⬇ KILLENS POND (State Pk) From Jct of US-13 & SR-12, S 2.4 mi on US-13 to Paradise Alley Rd, E 1.7 mi (L). 2015 rates: $20 to $37. Mar 1 to Nov 30. (302)284-4526

FENWICK ISLAND — F4 *Sussex*

⬅ **TREASURE BEACH RV PARK Ratings: 8.5/8.5★/9** (RV Park) E Bnd: From Jct US 113 & SR 17, E 0.8 mi on SR 17 (Church St)to SR 54 (Main St.), S 0.3 mi on SR 54 (becomes Lighthouse Rd.), E 7.8 mi on Lighthouse Rd (L) W Bnd: Jct of SR-1 & SR-54, W 1.8 mi on SR-54 (R). **FAC:** Paved/gravel rds. (1012 spaces). Avail: 152 gravel, 18 pull-thrus (30 x 80), back-ins (30 x 40), 152 full hkups (30/50 amps), cable, WiFi Hotspot, tent sites, dump, laundry, groc, LP gas, firewood, controlled access. **REC:** pool, wading pool, Little Assawoman Bay: playground. Pet restrict Eco-friendly, 2015 rates: $65 to $100. May 1 to Oct 26. ATM.
AAA Approved
(855)380-6174 Lat: 38.46276, Lon: -75.07969
37291 Lighthouse Rd, Selbyville, DE 19975
camping@TBRVPK.com
www.treasurebeachrvpark.com

GEORGETOWN — E3 *Sussex*

➔ **HOMESTEAD CAMPGROUND**
Ratings: 8.5/9★/9.5 (Campground) W Bnd: From Jct of US 9 & SR-1, W 6.5 mi on US 9 to Prettyman Rd, NW1.1 mi (R) E Bnd: US 113 & SR 9, E 5.8 mi on SR 9 to Prettyman Rd, NW 1.1 mi (R). **FAC:** Paved rds. (358 spaces). Avail: 39 grass, 30 pull-thrus (40 x 80), back-ins (30 x 40), 39 full hkups (30/50 amps), seasonal sites, WiFi, tent sites, rentals, dump, mobile sewer, laundry, groc, LP gas, fire rings, firewood. **REC:** pool, pond, fishing, shuffleboard, playground. Pets OK. Big rig sites, 2015 rates: $50 to $60. May 1 to Sep 30.
(302)684-4278 Lat: 38.72841, Lon: -75.30874
25165 Prettyman Rd, Georgetown, DE 19947
homestead@l-realty.com
www.i-realty.com/homestead/gs.html
See ad this page, 261.

GLASGOW — B2 *New Castle*

⬇ LUMS POND (State Pk) From Glasgow (I-95 exit 1A), S 3 mi on SR-896 to SR-71, N 2 mi (L). For reservations call (877)987-2757. 2015 rates: $25 to $37. Mar 1 to Nov 30. (302)368-6989

HARRINGTON — D3 *Kent*

⬅ G & R CAMPGROUND **Ratings: 6/6.5/7.5** (Campground) 2015 rates: $45. (302)398-8108 4075 Gun & Rod Club Rd, Houston, DE 19954

LAUREL — F3 *Sussex*

➔ TRAP POND (State Pk) From Jct of US-13 & SR-24, E 4.7 mi on SR-24 to CR-450, S 0.8 mi (L). 2015 rates: $20 to $37. Mar 1 to Nov 30. (302)875-2392

Replace clogged air filters. A clogged air filter can cut a vehicle's fuel efficiency by 10 percent.

LEWES — E4 *Sussex*

➔ CAPE HENLOPEN (State Pk) From town, E 1 mi on US-9, follow signs (E). For reservations call (877)987-2757. 2015 rates: $25 to $45. Mar 1 to Nov 30. (302)645-8983

⬅ **TALL PINES CAMPGROUND RESORT**
Ratings: 8.5/8.5★/9 (RV Park) From Jct of US 9 & SR-1, W 2.7 mi on US-9 to Sweetbriar Rd, N 50 ft. then immediate left on Log Cabin Hill Rd, W 0.8 mi on Log Cabin Hill Rd (R). **FAC:** Paved rds. (499 spaces). Avail: 22 grass, 5 pull-thrus (26 x 35), back-ins (30 x 40), 22 W, 22 E (50 amps), cable, WiFi, tent sites, rentals, dump, laundry, groc, LP bottles, fire rings, firewood, controlled access. **REC:** pool, pond, fishing, shuffleboard, playground. Pet restrict(B). Partial handicap access. Eco-friendly, 2015 rates: $59 to $63.
(302)684-0300 Lat: 38.73725, Lon: -75.23697
29551 Persimmon Rd, Lewes, DE 19958
tpinfo@tallpines-del.com
www.tallpines-del.com
See ad this page.

LINCOLN — E3 *Sussex*

➔ **YOGI BEAR'S JELLYSTONE PARK AT DELAWARE BEACH**
Ratings: 9/9.5★/10 (Campground) From Jct of US 113 & SR-1 (E of Lincoln), S 6.5 mi on SR-1 (towards beaches) to Brick Granary Rd, Right 0.2 mi (L). **FAC:** Paved/gravel rds. (306 spaces). Avail: 271 gravel, 16 pull-thrus (40 x 65), back-ins (40 x 50), 271 full hkups (30/50 amps), seasonal sites, cable, WiFi, rentals, dump, laundry, groc, fire rings, firewood, controlled access. **REC:** pool, playground. Pet restrict(B/Q). Partial handicap access, no tents. Eco-friendly, 2015 rates: $55 to $70. Apr 1 to Nov 3.
(302)491-6614 Lat: 38.87449, Lon: -75.36021
8295 Brick Granary Rd, Lincoln, DE 19960
camp@delawarejellystone.com
www.delawarejellystone.com
See ad this page, 261.

MILLSBORO — F4 *Sussex*

LEISURE POINT RESORT **Ratings: 9/9.5★/10** (Membership Pk) 2015 rates: $70. Apr 15 to Oct 15. (302)945-2000 25491 Dogwood Ln, Millsboro, DE 19966

THE RESORT AT MASSEY'S LANDING (RV Resort) (Under Construction) **FAC.** 5 paved, 5 pull-thrus (30 x 50), 5 full hkups (30/50 amps). **REC.** No CC, no reservations.
(888)985-1761 Lat: 38.625340, Lon: -75.103807
20628 Long Beach Drive, Millsboro, DE 19930
info@masseyslanding.com
http://www.masseyslanding.com
See ad opposite page.

MILTON — E4 *Sussex*

BRUMBLEY'S FAMILY PARK **Ratings: 6.5/8★/7** (RV Park) 2015 rates: $65. (302)684-5189 25601 Amy's Lane, Milton, DE 19968

NEW CASTLE — B3 *New Castle*

DELAWARE MOTEL & RV PARK (RV Spaces) From jct I-295 & US 13: Go 3-1/2 mi SW on US 13, at the US 40/US 13 split, stay R on US 40, go 50 ft. **FAC:** Gravel rds. 28 gravel, back-ins (24 x 38), 28 full hkups (30/50 amps), laundry. Pet restrict(B). No tents. 2015 rates: $35 to $50.
(302)328-3114 Lat: 39.654886, Lon: -75.618450
235 S Dupont Hwy, New Castle, DE 19720
See ad opposite page.

REHOBOTH BEACH — E4 *Sussex*

BIG OAKS FAMILY CAMPGROUND
Ratings: 9/9★/9 (Campground) S-bnd: From Jct of SR-1 & SR-24 (John Williams Hwy), S 0.7 mi on SR-1 to Munchy Branch Rd (CR 270A), E 1.1 mi to Wolf Neck Rd, N 0.1 mi (L); or N-bnd: From Jct of SR-1 & CR-270 (Wolf Neck Rd), E 0.5 mi on CR-270 (L). **FAC:** Paved/gravel rds. (150 spaces). 75 Avail: 15 grass, 60 dirt, back-ins (23 x 40), 75 full hkups (30/50 amps), seasonal sites, cable, WiFi, tent sites, rentals, dump, laundry, groc, fire rings, firewood. **REC:** pool, shuffleboard, playground. Pet restrict(B). 2015 rates: $61 to $69.50. May 1 to Oct 14. No CC.
(302)645-6838 Lat: 38.73765, Lon: -75.12912
35567 Big Oaks Lane, Rehoboth Beach, DE 19971
campbigoaks@earthlink.net
www.bigoakscamping.com
See ad this page.

DELAWARE SEASHORE (State Pk) From Jct SR-24 and SR-1, S 10.2 mi on SR-1 to Entrance on S side of Indian River Inlet (R). 2015 rates: $25 to $50. (302)539-7202

SEA AIR VILLAGE MANUFACTURED HOME & RV RESORT **Ratings: 7.5/9.5★/9** (RV Area in MHP) 2015 rates: $70 to $75. (888)465-8909 19837 Sea Air Ave., Rehoboth Beach, DE 19971

SAVE! Over 1,000 dollars in coupons can be found at the front of the Guide!

Join the flock and head south during the winter. Use our handy Snowbird guide in the front of the Guide to find RV-friendly destinations throughout the Sunbelt. Snowbird Destinations features the top Snowbird roosts and lists great Campgrounds in compelling areas.

DE

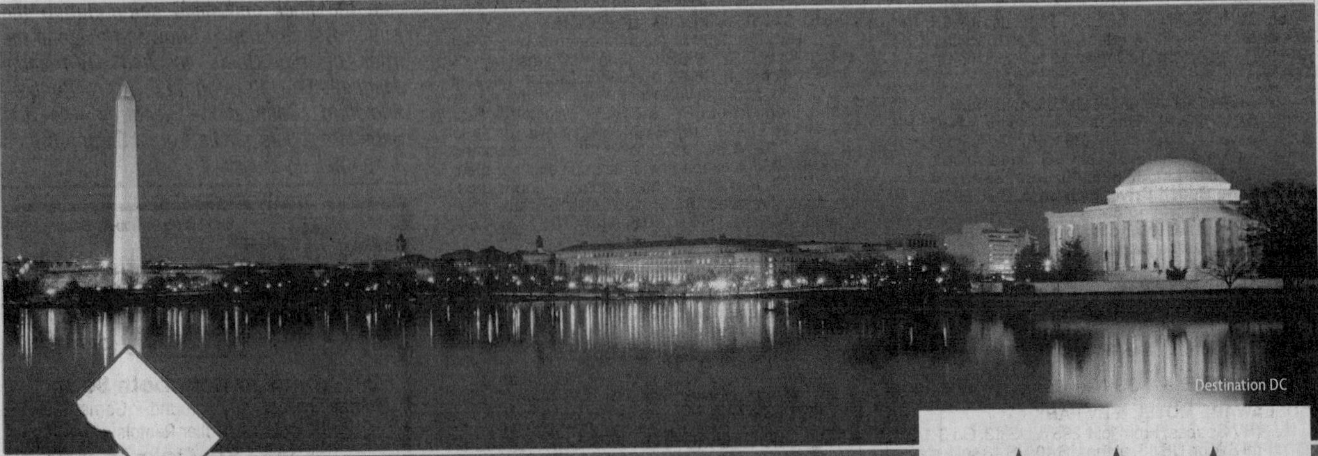

Destination DC

WELCOME TO
District of Columbia

ESTABLISHED JULY 16, 1790	WIDTH: 9 MILES (14 KM) LENGTH: 14 MILES (23 KM)	PROPORTION OF UNITED STATES 0.002% OF 3,794,100 SQ MI

From the resplendent memorials that commemorate Abraham Lincoln and veterans of the Vietnam War to the flag that inspired the "Star Spangled Banner" at the National Museum of American History, Washington's monuments enshrine America's commitment to freedom and democracy. In 1826, Englishman James Smithson donated half a million dollars to foster what he termed a "diffusion of knowledge." The result was Washington's sublime Smithsonian Institution, a collection of 19 world-class museums, including the National Air and Space Museum and the Museum of Natural History.

The official residence for every U.S. president since John Adams, the White House is the nation's spiritual heart, while on Capitol Hill thrusting politicos thrash out legislation, albeit in a dysfunctional fashion. For all its buttoned-up clichés, Washingtonians take pride in their city's dynamic streetscapes awash with elegant restaurants, funky music venues and innovative cultural spaces. The spirit of native son Duke Ellington lingers in the sultry jazz clubs of the Adams Morgan neighborhood, while the Folger Library celebrates the "Bard of Avon" with its venerable Shakespeare research center, which hosts plays, concerts and literary readings. Georgetown speaks to the city's contemporary élan with gorgeous row homes punctuated with stylish boutiques, modern galleries and fashionable brunch spots. And who doesn't love a good cherry blossom festival? From late March, Washington D.C.'s floral rhapsody is one of the world's most spectacular.

History

A federal district rather than a state, the District of Columbia was originally part of the state of Maryland. Located between Virginia and Maryland on the north bank of the Potomac River, President George Washington chose Washington D.C in 1791 as the nation's capital. French architect Pierre Charles L'Enfant designed the city that is now home to all three branches of the federal government. During the War of 1812, British forces invaded the city, leaving a trail of fire and destruction in their wake.

As part of the South, Washington has long been home to a large, proud African American community whose members led the nation when it came to civil rights activism. Slaves owned in Washington were freed nine months before the Emancipation Proclamation of 1863. In the nation's capital, you'll find a touchstone for every seminal moment in American history, including the spot where Martin Luther King Jr. gave his "I Have a Dream" speech on the steps of the Lincoln Memorial, and the Ford Theater where Abraham Lincoln was assassinated in 1865. Much

Top 3 Tourism Attractions:
1) Houses of Government
2) National Monuments
3) Smithsonian Institution

Nickname: The Capitol

State Flower: American Beauty Rose

State Bird: Wood Thrush

People: Carl Bernstein, reporter; Connie Chung, TV anchor; Al Gore, U.S. vice president; John Edgar Hoover, FBI director; Edward "Duke" Ellington, jazz musician

Topography: Situated in the low point of a topographic "bowl" left behind as rivers carved through sediment

Climate: Hot, humid summers; pleasant springs and autumns; mild winters with snowfall averaging less than 20 inches

Destination DC

the chagrin of D.C's residents, the ate doesn't have democratic repre- ntation in the U.S. Senate or the U.S. ouse of Representatives. The Con- itution grants the Congress "exclu- ve jurisdiction" over the district. In e House of Representatives, D.C. is epresented by a delegate whose voting ower is limited.

lay

Not only is Washington one of he nation's greenest cities, within easy each of the cut-and-thrust capital e expansive national parks, forests nd recreation areas. Top of the list, ccupying some 2,100 acres, rustic Rock Creek Park includes Pierce Mill, he Old Stone House (built in 1785), the talianate gardens of Meridian Hill Park, nature center, tennis courts, riding tables, an 18-hole golf course, scenic canoeing along the Potomac River and 5 miles of trails. Officially established n 1965, the National Mall and Memorial Park protect some of the nation's old- est parkland.

The 400-acre Fort Dupont Park preserves six Civil War fortifications that are scattered along the seven-mile paths of the beautifully forested Hiker/Biker Trail. Fort Dupont Park is also a popular place for ice-skating, mountain bike riding, cultural programs (including a summer theater), environmental education and ranger-led Civil War programs. The Theodore Roosevelt Island stands as a tribute to the 26th president, who dedicated much of life to conservation. Accessed via a footbridge from the mainland (cars and bikes are prohibited), Roosevelt's namesake wilderness affords excellent hiking and swimming. Connecting the Potomac and upper Ohio River basins, the Potomac Heritage Trail network traverses the distinctive landscapes of Chesapeake Bay and the Allegheny Highlands.

TRAVEL & TOURISM

Washington, DC Convention & Tourism Corp.
202-789-7000
www.washington.org

Cultural Tourism DC
202-661-7581
www.culturaltourismdc.org

DC Chamber of Commerce
202-347-7201
www.dcchamber.org

DC Commission on the Arts and Humanities
202-724-5613
www.dcarts.dc.gov

DC Visitor Information Center
202-312-1300
www.itcdc.com

Humanities Council of Washington, DC
202-387-8391
www.wdchumanities.org

National Capital Region
202-426-6841
www.nps.gov/nacc

SHOPPING

Georgetown Park
202-298-5577
www.shopatgeorgetownpark.com

Old Post Office Pavilion
202-289-4224
www.oldpostofficedc.com

The Shops at National Place
202-662-1250

DC

District of Columbia

WASHINGTON — C6 *District of Columbia*

WASHINGTON D.C. AREA MAP

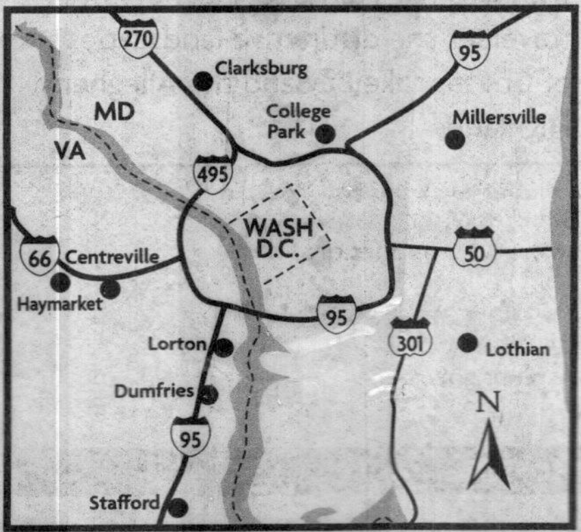

For more detail and a broader overview, please see our full-color state maps at the front of the Maryland & Virginia state sections.

Symbols on map indicate towns within a 30 mile radius of Washington D.C. where campgrounds are listed. Check listings for more information.

In MD, see also Clarksburg, College Park, Lothian & Millersville.

In VA, see also Centreville, Dumfries, Haymarket, Lorton & Stafford.

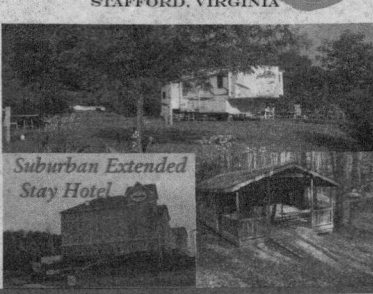

WASHINGTON (CONT)

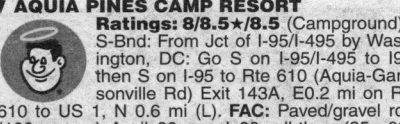

AQUIA PINES CAMP RESORT
Ratings: 8/8.5★/8.5 (Campground) S-Bnd: From Jct of I-95/I-495 by Washington, DC: Go S on I-95/I-495 to I95, then S on I-95 to Rte 610 (Aquia-Garrisonville Rd) Exit 143A, E0.2 mi on Rte 610 to US 1, N 0.6 mi (L). **FAC:** Paved/gravel rds. (100 spaces). Avail: 80 gravel, 80 pull-thrus (25 x 60), 80 full hkups (30/50 amps), seasonal sites, cable, WiFi, tent sites, rentals, dump, laundry, groc, LP gas, firewood. **REC:** pool, playground. Pets OK. Big rig sites, 2015 rates: $45 to $62.
(540)659-3447 Lat: 38.47028, Lon: -77.40011
3071 Jefferson Davis Hwy, Stafford, VA 22554
aquiapines@aol.com
www.aquiapines.com
See primary listing at Stafford, VA and ad opposite page.

Heading South? We have lots of Snowbird Destination ideas to explore at the front of the Guide.

PRINCE WILLIAM FOREST RV CAMPGROUND
Ratings: 8.5/9★/9 (RV Park) From Jct I395 & I95: Go 26 miles S on I95 (exit 152B/Manassas), then 2.5 mi NW on SR-234 (L) Caution: 42' max length. **FAC:** Paved rds. 72 paved, 54 pull-thrus (24 x 45), back-ins (24 x 35), 36 full hkups, 36 W, 36 E (30/50 amps), WiFi, tent sites, dump, laundry, LP gas, firewood. **REC:** pool, playground. Pets OK. Partial handicap access. 14 day max stay, eco-friendly, 2015 rates: $34 to $52.
AAA Approved
(888)737-5730 Lat: 38.60398, Lon: -77.35073
16058 Dumfries Rd., Dumfries, VA 22025
princewilliamrv@racpack.com
www.princewilliamforestrvcampground.com
See primary listing at Dumfries, VA and ad this page.

Had a great stay? Let us know by emailing us travelguidecomments@goodsamfamily.com

Thank You to our active and retired military personnel. A dedicated section of Military Listings for places to camp can be found at the back of the Guide.

CLEAN RESTROOMS GET A STAR

Campgrounds that receive the maximum 5 points for restroom cleanliness (toilets, showers, floors, walls and sinks/counters/mirrors) are honored with a star beside their total restroom rating. RATED 10/10★/10

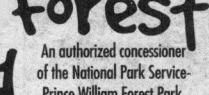

SHADY ACRES
RV & CAMPINGPARK
888-634-4080
www.ShadyAcresFL.com
See listing Fort Myers, FL (Map grid E3)
FLORIDA
Campground and other services
RV service center and/or other services
Good Sam discount locations
SCALE: 1 inch equals 49 miles
0 25 50 miles
0 25 50 kilometers
Map by Terra Carta © 2016 Affinity Media
Riverside RV Resort & Campground
9770 SW CR769 • Arcadia, FL
www.riversidervresort.com
800.795.9733
See listing Port Charlotte (Map Grid D3)
WOODSMOKE
CAMPING RESORT
South Florida's friendliest and most beautiful RV Resort
• Giant Heated Pool
• Jacuzzi • Free WiFi
• Large Clubhouse
• Many Wooded Sites
• 75-80' Concrete Pull-Thrus
19551 South Tamiami Trail (US41)
Fort Myers, FL 33908
(800) 231-5053
woodsmokecampingresort.com
See listing Fort Myers, FL (Map grid E3)
Good Sam Park
SEE CENTRAL FLORIDA MAP FOR ENLARGEMENT OF BOXED AREA
GEORGIA
FLORIDA
ALABAMA
GULF OF MEXICO
ATLANTIC OCEAN
Gulf of Mexico
TALLAHASSEE
JACKSONVILLE
GAINESVILLE
Orlando
Tampa
St. Petersburg
Daytona Beach
Fort Myers
MIAMI
Key West
PENSACOLA
PANAMA CITY

WELCOME TO
Florida

DATE OF STATEHOOD	WIDTH: 361 MILES (582 KM)	PROPORTION OF UNITED STATES
MARCH 3, 1845	LENGTH: 447 MILES (721 KM)	1.73% OF 3,794,100 SQ MI

FL

There's something about Florida that seems just way out there. It's a Magic Kingdom, where a kid's dreams come true. It's the "Sunshine State, where snowbirds search for eternal youth. It's the "Psychic Capital of the World" (that would be a town called Cassadaga), where mystical mavens commune with dead relatives. It's the launch pad for NASA astrophysicists' quest for alien life forms.

Escapism is what Florida is all about. From Miami's piquant Latin culture to the gilded socialites of Palm Beach and the rich wildlife of Everglades National Park, Florida offers exoticism, sophistication and nature at its most primal. You can drive through acres of citrus groves to historic St. Augustine (the oldest European-established settlement and port in the U.S.) or immerse yourself in the bacchanalian spirit of the Keys with a journey on the Margaritaville trail (strictly for fans of Jimmy Buffet).

State capital Tallahassee is a laissez-faire marriage of modern flair and demure Southern charm, while Sarasota is obsessed with a more traditional kind of circus. John Ringling (of Ringling Brothers fame) made Sarasota the winter home for his circus. The Ringling Museum of Art is one of the country's most visited attractions, a showcase for Ringling's lavish Venetian Gothic home, a superb art museum and, of course, a circus museum that sheds insight into life under the big top.

Learn

As legend would have it, when Spanish explorer Ponce de León came ashore in Florida in 1513, he believed Florida's crystalline springs to be the fountains of eternal youth. Given the number of lean, tanned octogenarians jogging along Florida's surf-splashed boulevards, perhaps he was right.

It was Ponce de León who named the state Pascua Florida, or Feast of Flowers, in honor of Spain's Easter celebration. Home to the oldest masonry fort, the oldest public park and the first settlement for free African Americans, St. Augustine (capital of Spanish Florida for 200 years) provides a fascinating insight into the state's Spanish roots. It was in the late 19th century that chilly northern migrants carved out Florida's role as a winter haven.

Thanks to its balmy climate, national parks and gorgeous coastline, not to mention Disney's magic touch, tourism remains Florida's leading industry. Snowbirds flock to the state every winter, and cruise ships regularly visit its harbors. Certainly, it's a befitting place to contemplate "life on the pale blue dot;" for an even more vivid appreciation, there's always the Kennedy Space Center, created in 1962 for the Apollo manned Moon landing program.

Top 3 Tourism Attractions:
1) Walt Disney World
2) Kennedy Space Center
3) Everglades National Park

Nickname: Sunshine State

State Flower: Orange Blossom

State Bird: Mockingbird

People: Bobby Allison, race car driver; Faye Dunaway, actress; Pat Boone, singer; Sidney Poitier, actor; Janet Reno, attorney general

Major Cities: Jacksonville, Miami, Tampa, St. Petersburg, Orlando (Tallahassee, capital)

Topography: Mostly flat with rolling hills in northwest; warm ocean breezes

Climate: North and central—humid and subtropical; south—tropical; rainy season June-September

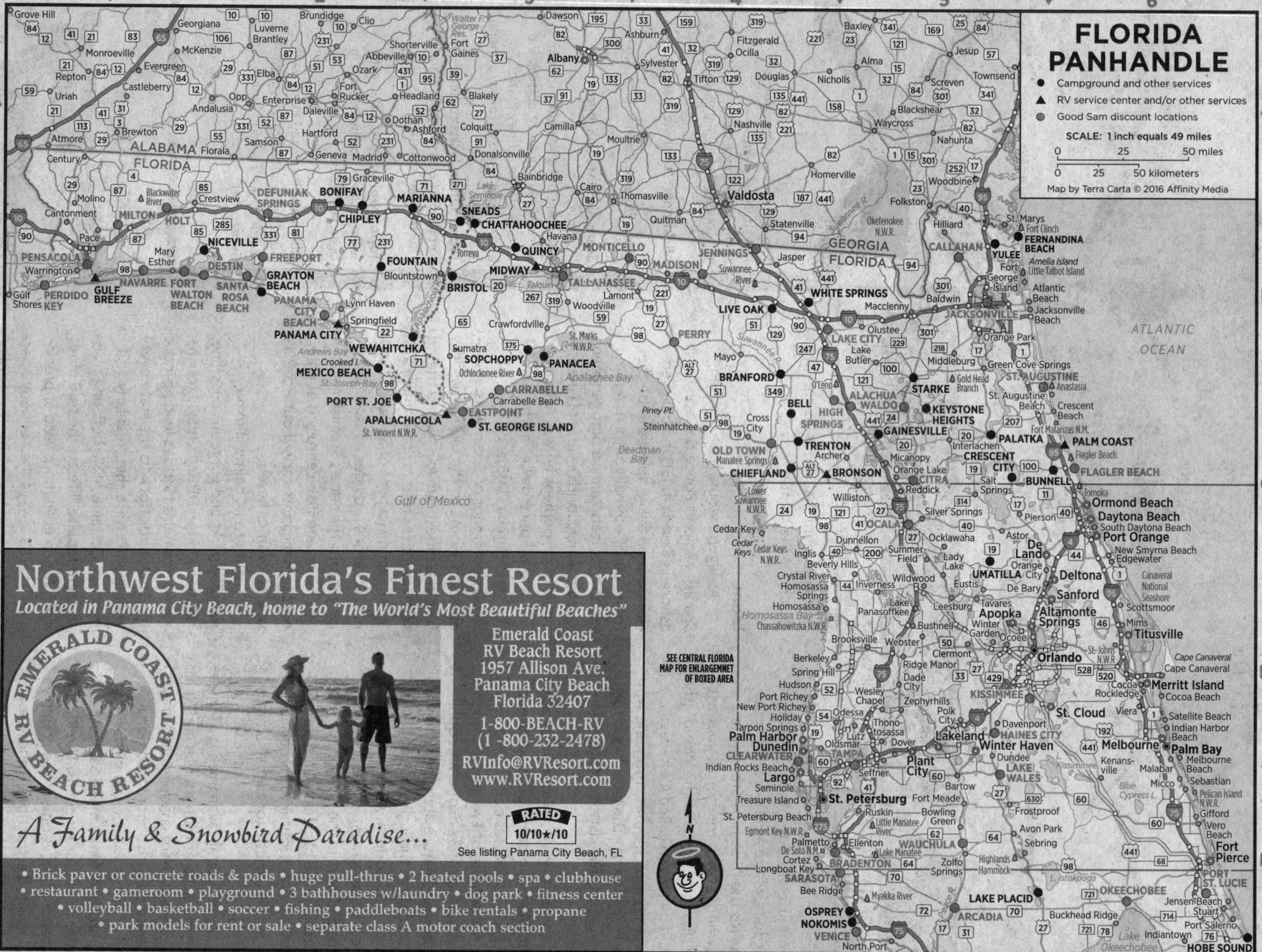
FLORIDA PANHANDLE
● Campground and other services
▲ RV service center and/or other services
● Good Sam discount locations
SCALE: 1 inch equals 49 miles
0 25 50 miles
0 25 50 kilometers
Map by Terra Carta © 2016 Affinity Media
SEE CENTRAL FLORIDA MAP FOR ENLARGEMNET OF BOXED AREA
ATLANTIC OCEAN
Gulf of Mexico
Apalachee Bay
Deadman Bay
ALABAMA
GEORGIA
FLORIDA
PENSACOLA
TALLAHASSEE
JACKSONVILLE
PANAMA CITY
GAINESVILLE
Orlando
St. Petersburg
Valdosta

FL

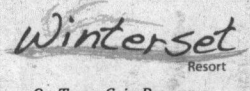

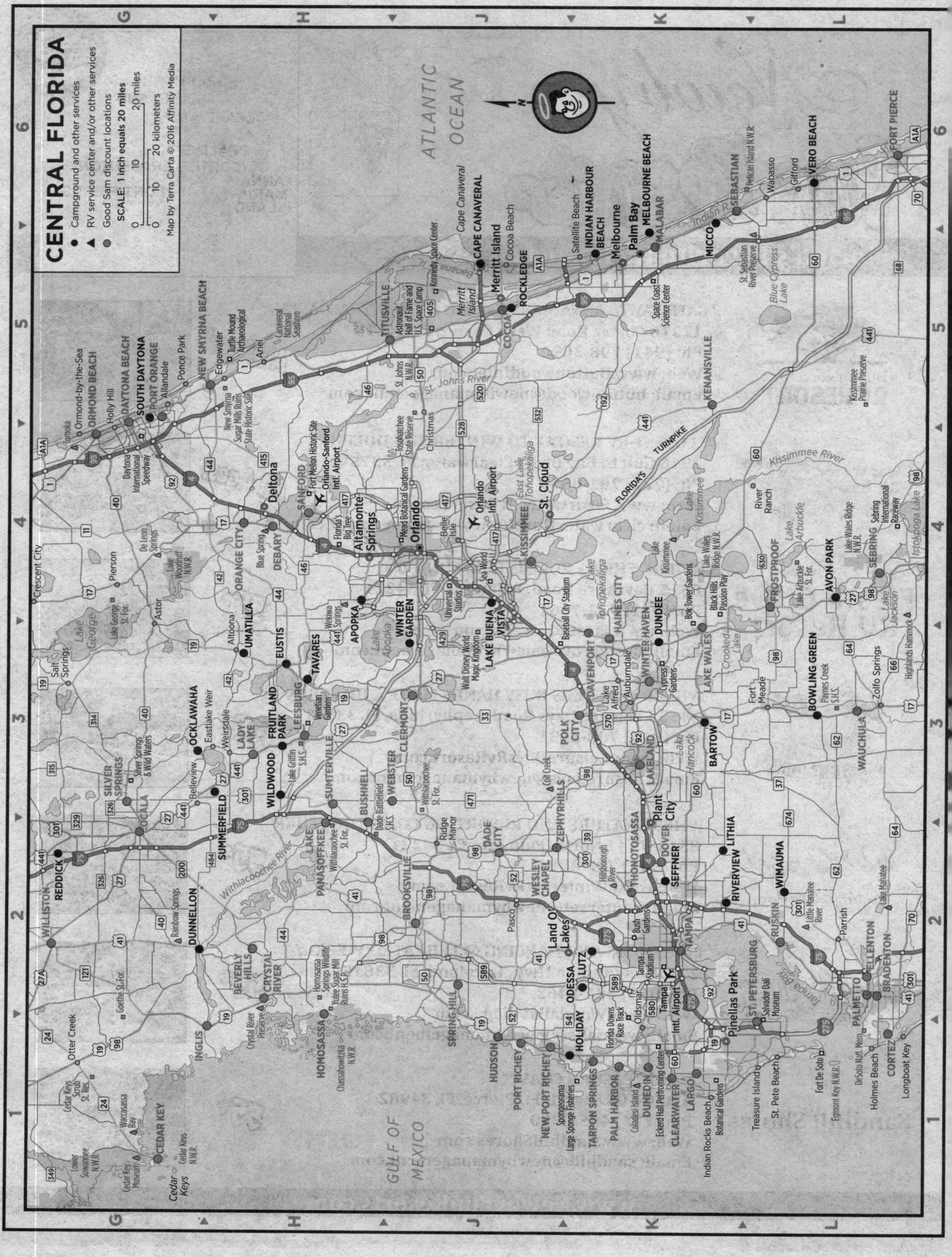
CENTRAL FLORIDA
Campground and other services
RV service center and/or other services
Good Sam discount locations
SCALE: 1 inch equals 20 miles
Map by Terra Carta © 2016 Affinity Media
ATLANTIC OCEAN
GULF OF MEXICO
FLORIDA'S TURNPIKE

A manatee swims the waters of the Everglades. Getty Images/iStockphoto

Play

Florida boasts 171 state parks and mile after golden mile of beach. Humming with alligators, manatees, raccoons and Florida panthers, the Everglades (bisected by Alligator Alley) are Florida's Outback. The state's poster child is the Gulf shore, a dreamscape of indigo waters caressing white sand beaches, which runs the entire length of the panhandle. Here, old-time fun prevails in the form of sandcastle competitions, beach volleyball, shrimp shacks and diving pelicans. For more seclusion, the pristine beaches of Lover's Key State Park lie a few miles south of the more commercialized Fort Myers Beach. One of the region's highlights, the 2,132-acres of pine forest, mangrove swamp, and grassland that form Cayo Costa State Park (off Captiva Island—renowned for its prime sea shelling—provide excellent opportunities for hiking, fishing, kayaking, beach camping and snorkeling.

In Marianna (west of Tallahassee), the Florida Caverns State Park brims with rare and beautiful stalagmite and stalactite formations. You can immerse yourself in nature and history at Fort DeSoto Park (St. Petersburg), which is comprised of 1,136 acres of five interconnected islands, three miles of beach, fishing piers, hiking, cycling and a fort (a registered landmark) complete with four 12-inch seacoast rifled mortars and two six-inch Armstrong rapid-fire rifled guns. On North Key Largo, Crocodile Lake National Wildlife Refuge harbors the single largest population of alligators in the U.S. (500 at the last count).

Experience

In Everglades City, you can taste everything from spiny lobster to a gator tail at the steamy Everglades City Seafood Festival in February (www.evergladesseafoodfestival.com). The largest, most popular (and highly competitive) festival in the state, the Coconut Grove Arts Festival (www.coconutgrovearts fest.com) provides a showcase for 300 respected artists. On Presidents' Day weekend, the South Beach Wine & Food Festival (www.sobewineandfood fest.com) draws foodies from across the nation with a three-day feeding frenzy at various restaurants and tasting events courtesy of the nation's top chefs. Late April, visitors flock in their millions to Fort Lauderdale's glamorous four-mile beach to witness elite military and civilian pilots perform crowd pleasing antics during Air Lauderdale (www.airlauderdale.com).

Taste

With its bounty of fruits and veggies (citrus, avocado, kumquat, star fruit, coconut, Key lime and passion fruit) and fresh seafood infused with Caribbean and Latin flavors, Florida is made for al fresco dining. For a taste of Old Florida, head to Al Capone's erstwhile bootlegging and gambling hangout, Cap's Place Island Restaurant (www.capsplace.com). In Key Biscayne, Jimbo's (www.jimbosplace.com) is something of an institution, a quintessential South Florida watering hole where fisherman, washed-up poets, polo-clad yachters and tourists mix and mingle, buy dollar beers and put the world to rights over a game of boccie ball.

En route to the Keys, follow the revving Harleys to Alabama Jack's (www.alabamajacks.com), a 1950s waterfront bar on two barges where bikers devour conch fritters and chili-cheese fries, survey the river for crocs and jam to live music. The Key lime pie at Key West Key Lime Pie Company (www.keylimepieco.com) comes close to a religious experience.

TRAVEL & TOURISM

Florida Department of Tourism
850-488-5607
www.visitflorida.com

Florida State Chamber of Commerce
850-521-1200
www.flchamber.com

Visit Central Florida
800-828-7655
www.visitcentralflorida.org

Cocoa Beach Area Chamber of Commerce
321-459-2200
www.cocoabeachchamber.com

Daytona Beach Area CVB
www.daytonabeach.com

Emerald Coast CVB
800-322-3319, 850-651-7131
www.destin-fwb.com

Flagler County Chamber of Commerce
800-670-2640
www.visitflagler.org

Florida Keys & Key West Tourist Development Council
800-648-5510
www.fla-keys.com

Greater Fort Lauderdale CVB
800-22-SUNNY
www.sunny.org

Hernando County Tourism Bureau
800-601-4580
www.NaturallyHernando.org

Jacksonville & the Beaches CVB
800-733-2668
www.visitjacksonville.com

Kissimmee CVB
407-944-2400
www.floridakiss.com

Lee County Visitor & Convention Bureau
239-338-3500, 800-237-6444
www.fortmyerssanibel.com

Nature Coast Visitor Information Center, Weeki Wachee Springs State Park
www.visitnaturecoast.com

New Smyrna Beach Visitors Bureau
800-541-9621
www.nsbfla.com

North Florida Regional Chamber of Commerce
904-964-5278
www.bradfordregion.com

Greater Miami CVB
800-933-8448
www.miamiandbeaches.com

Naples, Marco Island, Everglades CVB
800-688-3600
www.paradisecoast.com

Ocala-Marion County VCB
888-FL-OCALA, 352-291-9169
www.ocalamarion.com

Orlando-Orange County CVB
407-363-5872, 800-972-3304
www.orlandoinfo.com

Palm Beach County CVB
800-833-5733
www.palmbeachfl.com

Panama City Beach CVB
800-553-1330, 850-233-5070
www.thebeachloversbeach.com

Pensacola Bay Chamber of Commerce
800-874-1234
www.visitpensacola.com

Sarasota CVB
800-522-9799
www.sarasotafl.org

Tallahassee Area Convention & Visitors Bureau
800-628-2866
www.visittallahassee.com

OUTDOOR RECREATION

Florida Professional Paddlesports Assn.
800-268-0083
www.paddleflausa.com

Florida Fish and Wildlife Conservation Commission
850-488-4676
www.myfwc.com

SHOPPING

Altamonte Mall
407-830-4400
www.altamontemall.com

Governor's Square
850-877-8106
www.governorssquare.com

Largo Mall
727-587-0100
www.largomall.com

The Kennedy Center's Shuttle Launch experience.

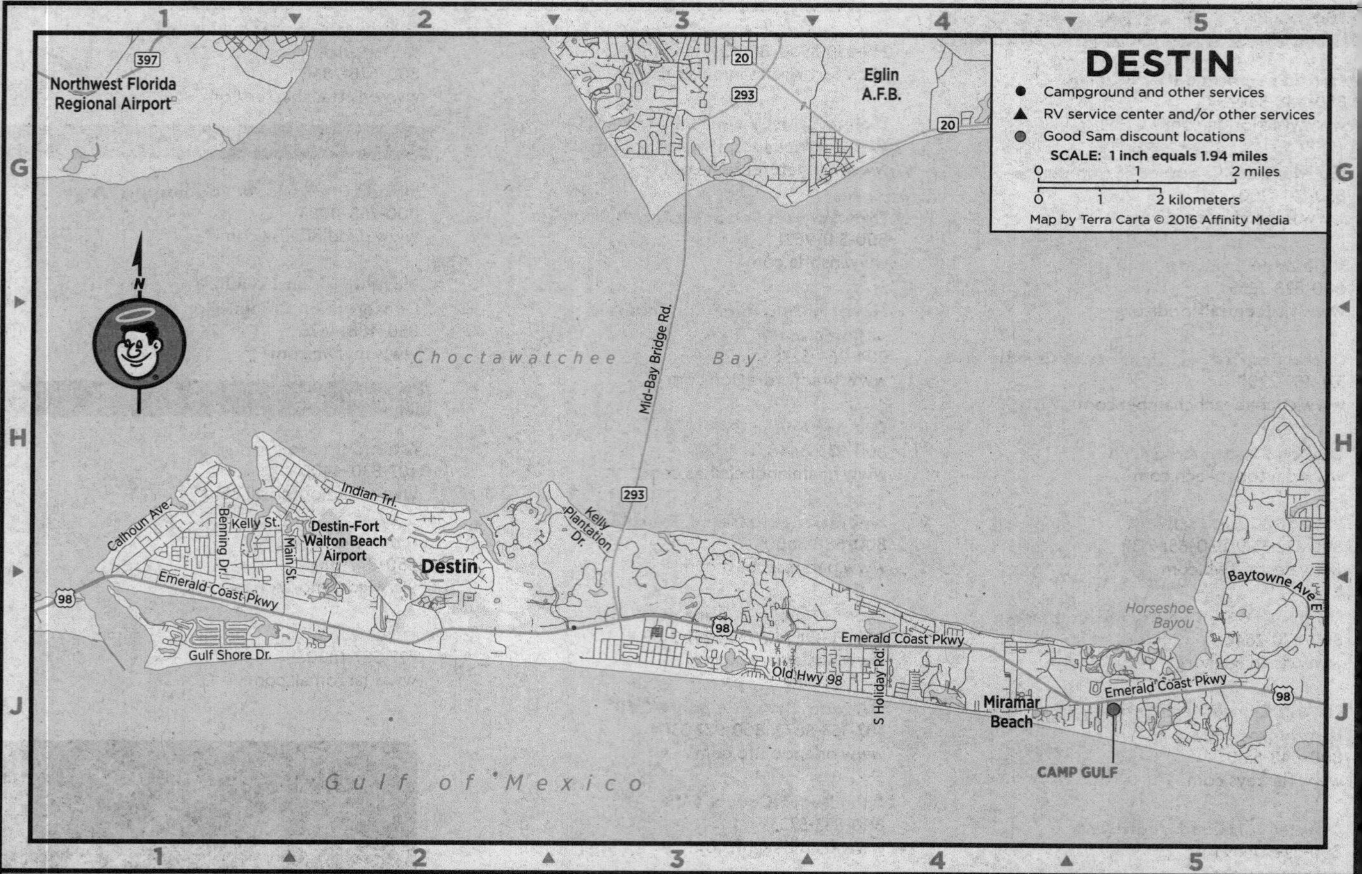
DESTIN
● Campground and other services
▲ RV service center and/or other services
● Good Sam discount locations
SCALE: 1 inch equals 1.94 miles
0 1 2 miles
0 1 2 kilometers
Map by Terra Carta © 2016 Affinity Media
Northwest Florida Regional Airport
Eglin A.F.B.
Choctawatchee Bay
Mid-Bay Bridge Rd.
Indian Trl.
Calhoun Ave.
Kelly St.
Benning Dr.
Main St.
Destin-Fort Walton Beach Airport
Destin
Kelly Plantation Dr.
Emerald Coast Pkwy
Gulf Shore Dr.
Old Hwy 98
S Holiday Rd.
Miramar Beach
Horseshoe Bayou
Baytowne Ave E
CAMP GULF
Gulf of Mexico

See listing Destin, FL
CAMP GULF
TOP RATED Good Sam Park FOR 2016
10/10★/9
DESTIN, FLORIDA
CAMP GULF .com
MORE THAN A GREAT PLACE TO PARK!
877-226-7485

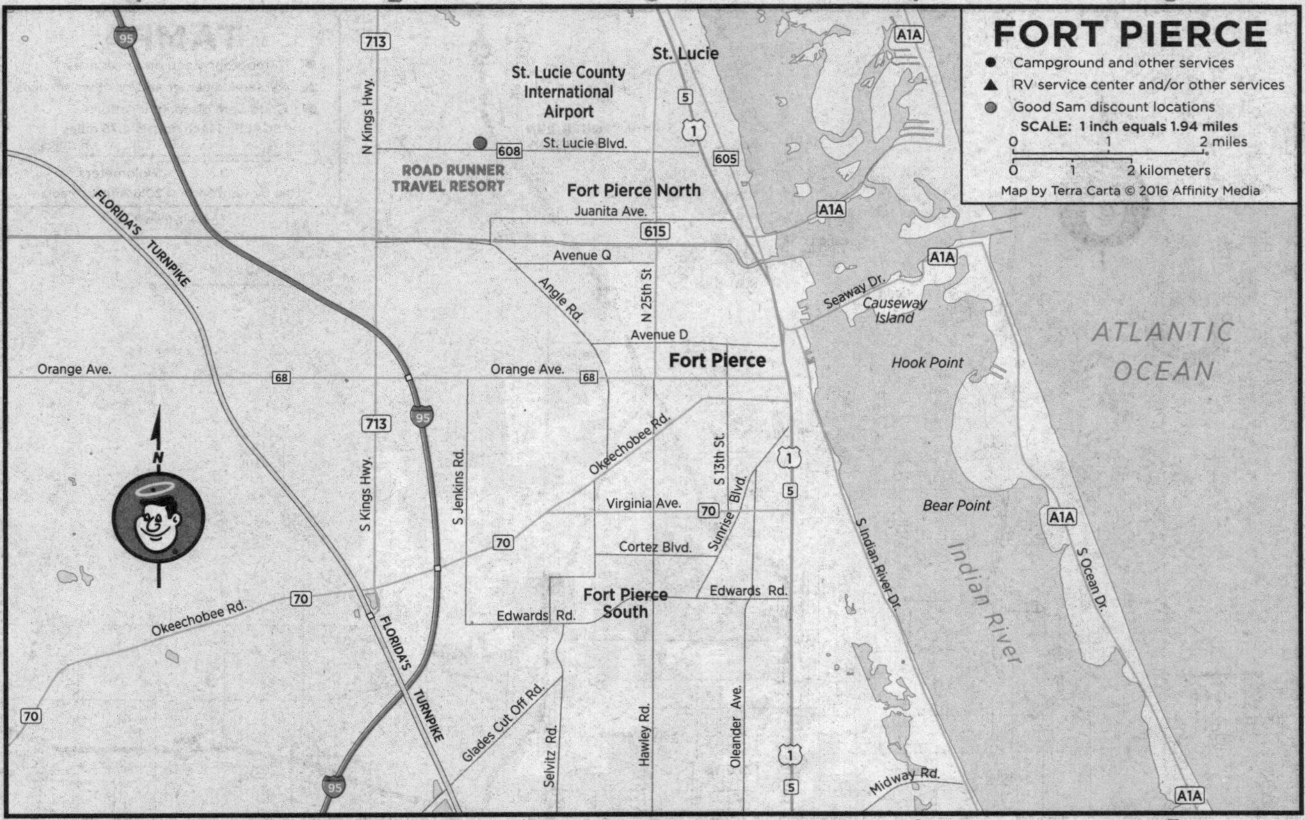

Road Runner Travel Resort
Bike Riding
Pets welcome
Swimming pool
3 hole golf course
Fishing on the lake
One of the country's Top Rated R.V. destinations, offering 452 full hook-up sites with an unbeatable location! Situated on Florida's Treasure Coast, just three miles from the pristine shoreline of the Atlantic Ocean. The friendly atmosphere & nature welcomes you from the moment you arrive. On site you will find an array of amenities, including a heated swimming pool, restaurant, free Wi-Fi area, a three-hole golf course, tennis courts, shuffleboard and a general store with everything you need for your pantry and your R.V.
"Nestled in a beautiful 38 acre Florida Hammock"
Sites
Cabin Suites
Cabins
For Reservations & Information Toll Free: 1-800 833-7108
www.RoadrunnerTravelResort.com

See listing Fort Pierce, FL

FL

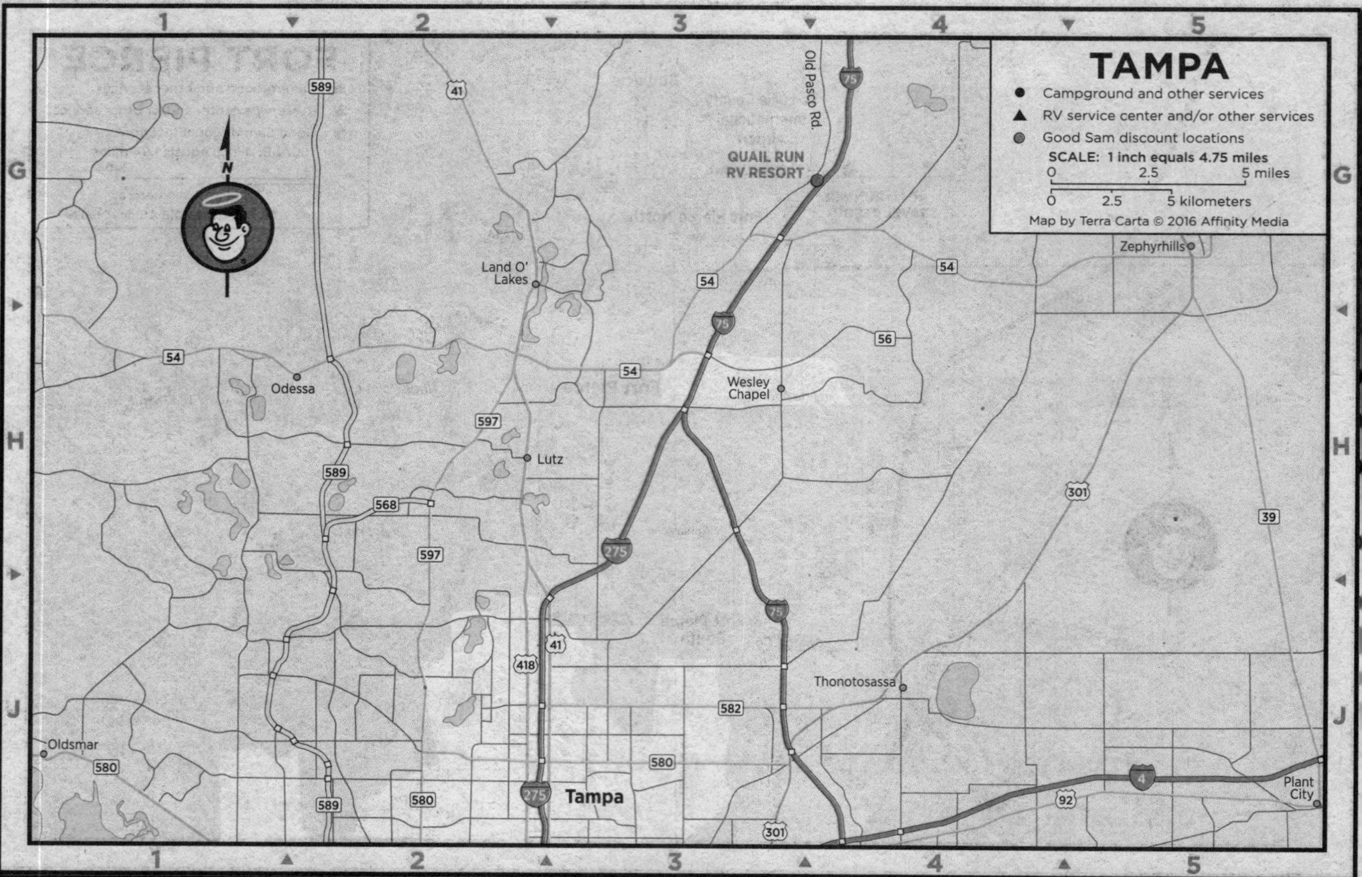
TAMPA
Campground and other services
RV service center and/or other services
Good Sam discount locations
SCALE: 1 inch equals 4.75 miles
0 2.5 5 miles
0 2.5 5 kilometers
Map by Terra Carta © 2016 Affinity Media
QUAIL RUN RV RESORT
Old Pasco Rd.
Zephyrhills
Land O' Lakes
Odessa
Wesley Chapel
Lutz
Thonotosassa
Oldsmar
Tampa
Plant City
1 2 3 4 5
G H J

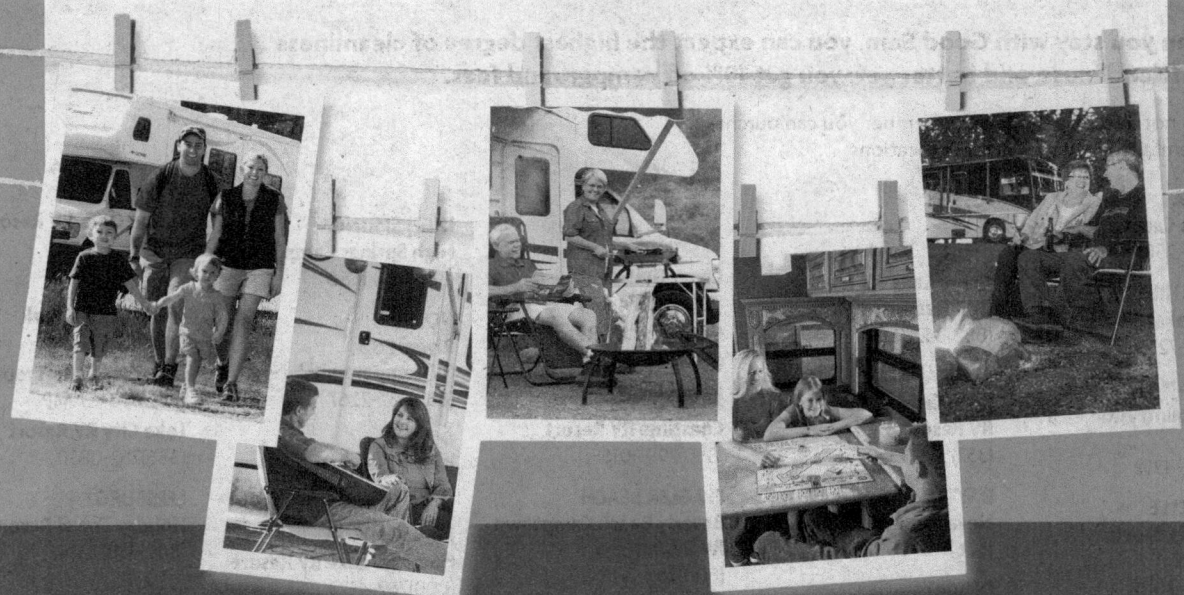

Featured Good Sam Parks

NORTHERN FLORIDA

When you stay with Good Sam, you can expect the highest degree of cleanliness and friendliness, and better yet, you get 10% off campground fees.

If you're not already a Good Sam member you can purchase your membership at one of these locations:

ALACHUA
Travelers Campground
(386)462-2505

BEVERLY HILLS
Sandy Oaks RV Resort
(352)465-7233

CALLAHAN
Kelly's Countryside RV Park
(904)845-4252

CARRABELLE
Carrabelle Beach RV Resort
(850)697-2638
Ho Hum RV Park
(850)697-3926

CEDAR KEY
Cedar Key Sunset Isle RV Park
(800)810-1103

CITRA
Grand Lake RV & Golf Resort
(888)842-9219

CRYSTAL RIVER
Rock Crusher Canyon RV Resort
(352)564-9350

DAYTONA BEACH
Nova Family Campground
(386)767-0095

DEBARY
Highbanks Marina & Campresort
(386)668-4491

DEFUNIAK SPRINGS
Twin Lakes Camp Resort
(850)892-5914

DESTIN
Camp Gulf
(877)226-7485
Geronimo RV Resort
(850)424-6801

EASTPOINT
Coastline RV Resort
(850)799-1016

FLAGLER BEACH
Beverly Beach Camptown RV Resort
(800)255-2706

FORT WALTON BEACH
Destin West RV Resort
(850)200-4533

FREEPORT
Live Oak Landing
(877)436-5063

HIGH SPRINGS
High Springs Campground
(386)454-1688

HOLT
Rivers Edge RV Campground
(850)537-2267

INGLIS
Gulf Coast RV Resort
(352)447-2900

JACKSONVILLE
Flamingo Lake RV Resort
(800)782-4323
Pecan Park RV Resort
(904)751-6770

JENNINGS
Jennings Outdoor Resort Campground
(386)938-3321

LADY LAKE
Grand Oaks RV Resort
(352)750-6300

LAKE CITY
Inn & Out RV Park
(386)752-1648
Lake City Campground
(866)773-CAMP
Lake City RV Resort
(386)752-0830

LEESBURG
Holiday Travel Resort
(800)428-5334

MADISON
Yogi Bear Jellystone Camp Resorts
(850)973-8269

MARIANNA
Alliance Hill RV Resort
(850)688-8561

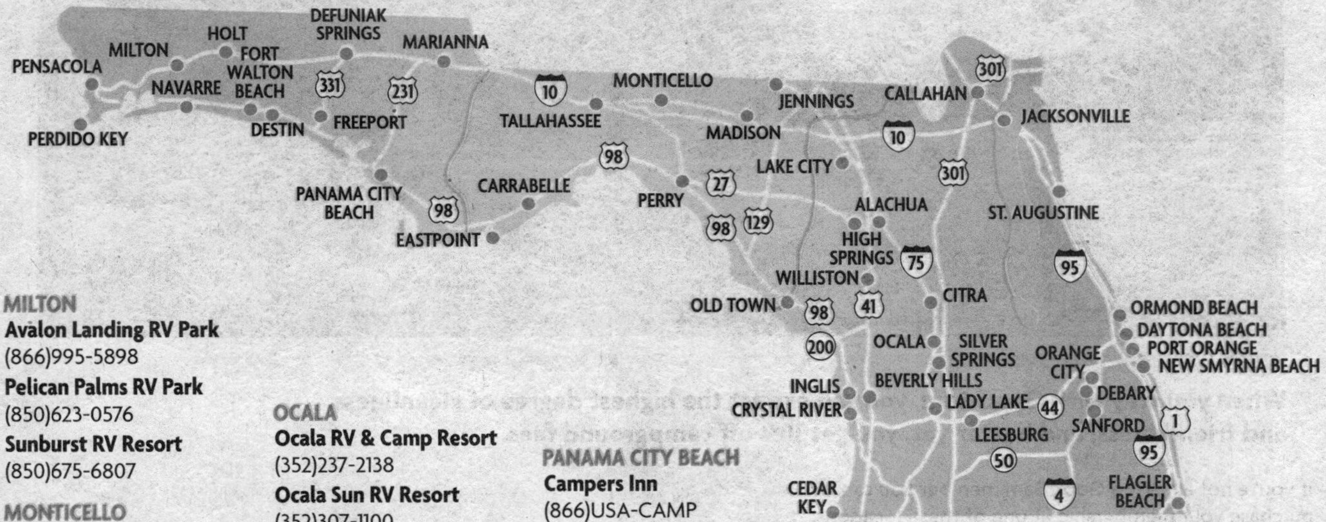

FL

MILTON

Avalon Landing RV Park
(866)995-5898

Pelican Palms RV Park
(850)623-0576

Sunburst RV Resort
(850)675-6807

MONTICELLO

Tallahassee East Campground
(844)997-3890

NAVARRE

Emerald Beach RV Park
(866)939-3431

Navarre Beach Campground
(888)639-2188

Santa Rosa RV Resort
(888)936-4791

NEW SMYRNA BEACH

New Smyrna Beach RV Park
(800)928-9962

Sugar Mill Ruins Travel Park, LLC
(386)427-2284

OCALA

Ocala RV & Camp Resort
(352)237-2138

Ocala Sun RV Resort
(352)307-1100

Wandering Oaks RV Resort
(866)380-6700

OLD TOWN

Lucky Charm RV Park
(352)542-0033

Suwannee River Hideaway
(352)542-7800

ORANGE CITY

Orange City RV Resort
(888)653-1480

ORMOND BEACH

Coral Sands RV Resort
(800)441-1831

Harris Village & Adult RV Park LLC
(386)673-0494

PANAMA CITY BEACH

Campers Inn
(866)USA-CAMP

PENSACOLA

Pensacola Beach RV Resort
(850)438-1266

Pensacola RV Park
(850)944-1734

PERDIDO KEY

A & M Perdido Resort LLC
(877)402-7873

PERRY

Rocky's Campground
(850)584-6600

PORT ORANGE

Daytona Beach RV Resort
(386)761-2663

SANFORD

Twelve Oaks RV Resort
(800)633-9529

SILVER SPRINGS

Silver Springs Campers Garden
(352)236-3700

ST AUGUSTINE

Indian Forest Campground
(904)824-3574

North Beach Camp Resort
(800)542-8316

Stagecoach RV Park Inc
(904)824-2319

TALLAHASSEE

Big Oak RV Park
(850)562-4660

Tallahassee RV Park
(850)878-7641

WILLISTON

Williston Crossings RV Resort
(877)785-4405

For more Good Sam Parks go to listing pages

Featured Good Sam Parks

SOUTHERN FLORIDA

When you stay with Good Sam, you can expect the highest degree of cleanliness and friendliness, and better yet, you get 10% off campground fees.

If you're not already a Good Sam member you can purchase your membership at one of these locations:

ARCADIA
Big Tree Carefree RV Resort
(863)494-7247
Craig's RV Park
(863)494-1820
Cross Creek RV Resort
(863)494-7300
Little Willie's RV Resort
(863)494-2717

BOKEELIA
Tropic Isle RV Park
(239)283-4456

BONITA SPRINGS
Gulf Coast Camping Resort
(239)992-3808

CHOKOLOSKEE
Chokoloskee Island Park
(239)695-2414

CLEWISTON
Big Cypress RV Resort
(863)983-1330

FORT LAUDERDALE
Paradise Island RV Resort
(800)487-7395
Yacht Haven Park & Marina
(800)581-2322

FORT MYERS
Groves RV Resort
(877)540-1931
Seminole Campground
(239)543-2919
Shady Acres RV Park
(888)634-4080
Siesta Bay RV Resort
(877)326-4261
Sunseeker's RV Park
(239)731-1303
Tamiami RV Park
(866)573-2041
Upriver RV Resort
(239)543-3330
Woodsmoke Camping Resort
(800)231-5053

FORT MYERS BEACH
Gulf Waters RV Resort
(239)437-5888
Indian Creek RV Resort and Manufactured Housing Community
(877)741-8212
Red Coconut RV Park
(888)262-6226
San Carlos RV Park and Islands
(239)466-3133

FORT PIERCE
Road Runner Travel Resort
(800)833-7108
Sandhill Shores
(772)465-0990

HALLANDALE
Holiday Park
(954)981-4414

HOMESTEAD
Gold Coaster RV Resort and Manufactured Home Community
(877)466-9758
The Boardwalk RV Resort
(305)248-2487

JUPITER
West Jupiter Camping Resort
(888)746-6073

KEY LARGO
Riptide RV & Motel Carefree RV Resort
(305)852-8481

LA BELLE
The Glades RV Resort
(863)983-8070
Whisper Creek RV Resort
(863)675-6888

MARATHON
Grassy Key RV Park and Resort
(305)289-1606
Jolly Roger
(800)995-1525
Pelican RV Park & Motel Carefree RV Resort
(305)289-0011

MARGATE
Aztec RV Resort
(888)493-2856

MOORE HAVEN
North Lake Estates RV Resort
(877)417-6193

NAPLES
Club Naples RV Resort
(888)898-6463
Crystal Lake RV Resort
(239)348-0017
Lake San Marino RV Resort
(877)720-1982
Marco-Naples Carefree RV Resort
(239)774-1259
Naples Motorcoach Resort & Boat Club
(888)939-3783
Naples RV Resort
(877)361-5197
Rock Creek RV Resort
(239)643-3100

OKEECHOBEE
Brighton RV Resort
(863)357-6644
Silver Palms RV Resort
(888)323-4833

PORT CHARLOTTE
Riverside RV Resort & Campground
(800)795-9733

PORT ST LUCIE
Port St Lucie RV Resort
(772)337-3340

PUNTA GORDA
Shell Creek Carefree RV Resort
(941)639-4234
Sun N Shade RV Park
(941)639-5388

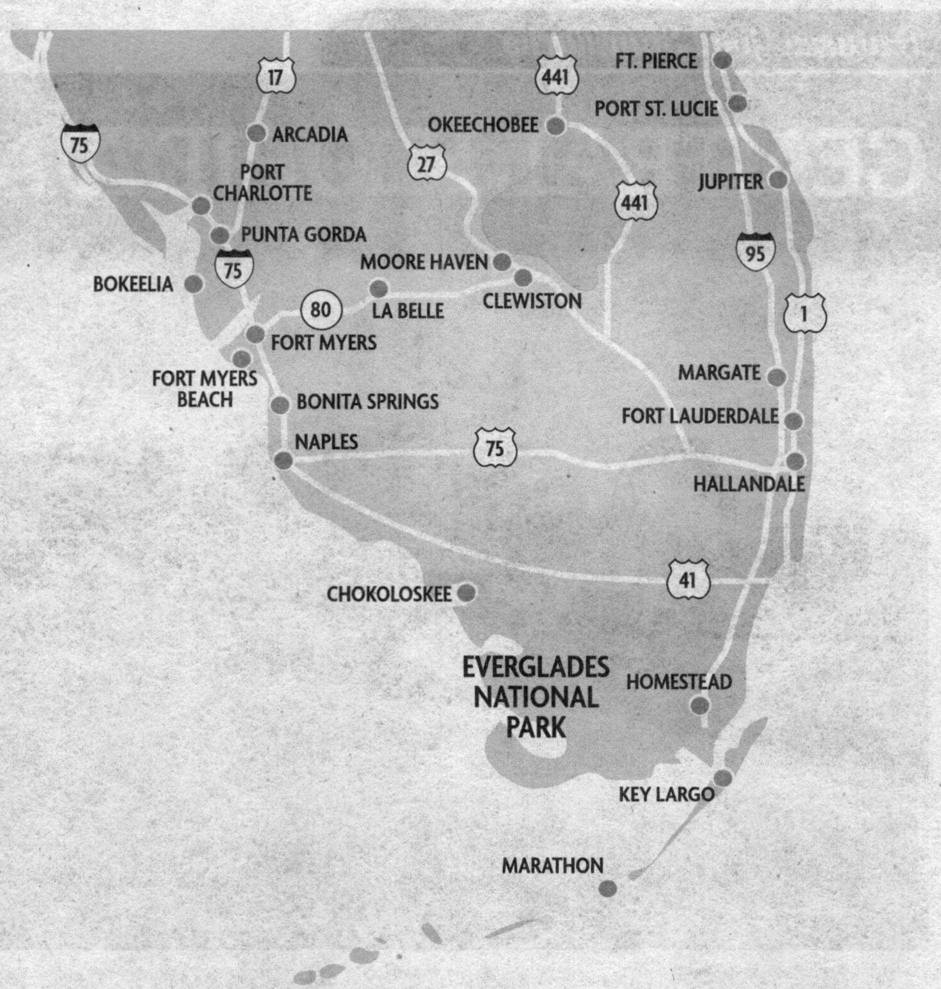

FL

For more Good Sam Parks go to listing pages

Featured Good Sam Parks

CENTRAL FLORIDA

When you stay with Good Sam, you can expect the highest degree of cleanliness and friendliness, and better yet, you get 10% off campground fees.

If you're not already a Good Sam member you can purchase your membership at one of these locations:

BRADENTON
Arbor Terrace RV Resort
(888)310-4975
Horseshoe Cove Carefree RV Resort
(800)291-3446
Vista Del Lago Carefree RV Resort
(941)755-5680

BROOKSVILLE
Belle Parc RV Resort
(352)796-5760

BUSHNELL
Blueberry Hill RV Resort
(888)759-4957
Paradise Oaks RV Resort
(352)793-1823
Red Oaks Carefree RV Resort
(352)793-7117

CLEARWATER
Clearwater RV Resort
(727)791-0550
Travel World RV Park
(727)536-1765

CLERMONT
Outdoor Resorts At Orlando, Inc
(863)424-1407

COCOA
Sonrise Palms Christian RV Park
(321)633-4335

CORTEZ
Buttonwood Inlet RV Resort
(941)798-3090
Holiday Cove RV Resort
(941)251-7809

DAVENPORT
Kissimmee South Carefree RV Resort
(863)424-1286

DOVER
Tampa East RV Resort
(877)361-5208

DUNEDIN
Dunedin Carefree RV Resort & the Blue Moon Inn
(727)784-3719

ELLENTON
Ellenton Gardens Carefree RV Resort
(941)722-0341

FROSTPROOF
Rainbow RV Resort
(888)650-8189

HAINES CITY
Central Park Carefree RV Resort
(863)422-5322

HOMOSASSA
Chassahowitzka River Campground
(352)382-2200
Homosassa River Carefree RV Resort
(352)628-2928
Nature's Resort
(800)301-7880

HUDSON
Three Lakes RV Resort
(888)316-6991

KISSIMMEE
Merry D RV Sanctuary Inc
(800)208-3434
Mill Creek Carefree RV Resort
(407)847-6288
Tropical Palms Carefree RV Resort
(800)647-2567

LAKE PANASOFFKEE
Countryside RV Park
(352)793-8103

LAKELAND
Lakeland RV Resort
(863)687-6146
Valencia Estates
(863)665-1611
Woodall's Mobile Home Village & RV Park
(863)686-7462

LARGO
Rainbow Village Carefree RV Resort
(727)536-3545
Yankee Traveler RV Park
(727)531-7998

MALABAR
Camelot RV Park, Inc
(321)724-5396

NEW PORT RICHEY
Seven Springs Travel Park
(727)376-0000

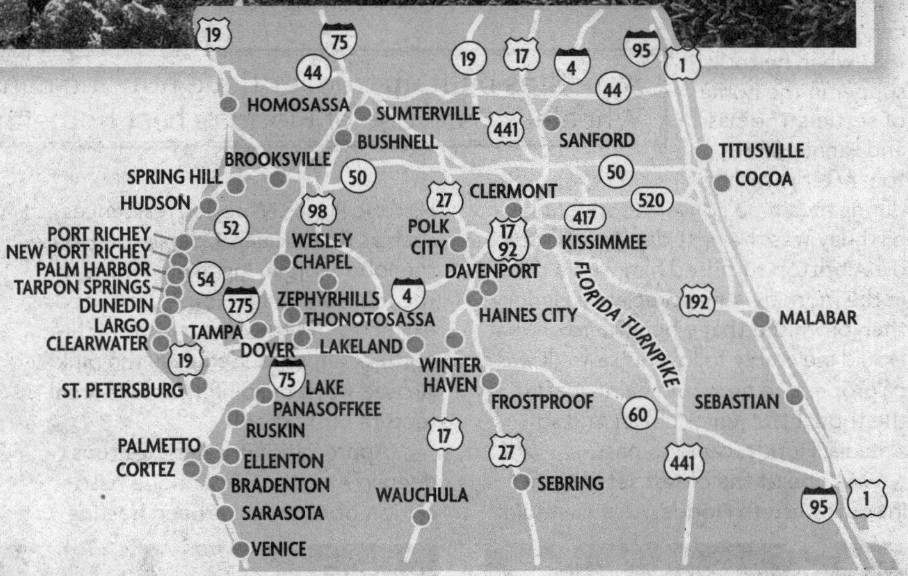

PALM HARBOR
Sherwood Forest RV Park
(727)784-4582

PALMETTO
Fiesta Grove RV Resort
(877)722-7661
Winterset RV Resort
(877)946-8376

POLK CITY
Le Lynn RV Resort
(800)736-0409

PORT RICHEY
Ja-Mar North Travel Park
(727)862-8882

RUSKIN
Hide A Way RV Resort
(800)607-2532
Sun Lake RV Resort
(813)645-7860
Tampa South RV Resort
(813)645-1202

SANFORD
Wekiva Falls Resort
(352)383-8055

SARASOTA
Sarasota Sunny South RV Resort
(941)921-4409

SEBASTIAN
Vero Beach Kamp, Inc.
(877)589-5643
Whispering Palms RV Resort
(800)414-0814

SEBRING
Buttonwood Bay RV Resort & Manufactured Home Community
(888)469-1733
Outback RV Resort At Tanglewood
(888)364-3729
Sebring Gardens RV Community
(863)385-7624

SPRING HILL
Big Oaks RV & Mobile Home Community
(352)799-5533

ST PETERSBURG
Bickley Park
(727)392-3807

SUMTERVILLE
Shady Brook Golf & RV Resort
(352)568-2244

TAMPA
Bay Bayou RV Resort
(813)855-1000
Tampa RV Park
(813)971-3460

TARPON SPRINGS
Hickory Point Mobile Home & RV Park
(727)937-7357

THONOTOSASSA
Happy Traveler RV Park
(813)986-3094

TITUSVILLE
The Great Outdoors RV, Nature & Golf Resort
(321)269-5004
Whispering Pines
(321)267-2081

VENICE
Florida Pines Mobile Home Court
(941)493-0019
Myakka RV Resort
(941)426-5040

WAUCHULA
Crystal Lake Village
(800)661-3582

WESLEY CHAPEL
Beginning Point RV Park
(813)788-2415
Quail Run Resort
(800)582-7084

WINTER HAVEN
Cypress Campground & RV Park
(863)324-7400

ZEPHYRHILLS
Forest Lake Estates R.V. Resort
(813)782-1058
Happy Days RV Park
(813)788-4858
Hillcrest RV Resort
(813)782-1947
Leisure Days RV Resort
(813)788-2631
Ralph's Travel Park
(813)782-8223

For more Good Sam Parks go to listing pages

Visit Florida

SPOTLIGHT FL

ARCADIA

Pie, paddling and citrus greet visitors to this tantalizing Florida getaway

According to local lore, it all began with a birthday cake. A rancher and Baptist preacher named James Madison Hendry was in the process of setting up a sawmill along the Peace River in south central Florida in 1883 when he took supper in the home of settlers Thomas and Fannie Albritton. After revealing during mealtime conversation that his birthday was the next day, young Arcadia Albritton surprised him with a cake in the morning. An appreciative Hendry then promised that when the town that would inevitably follow his sawmill was of proper size he would name it after the thoughtful junior baker. And so Arcadia, Florida, came to pass.

As one of the oldest settlements in southwestern Florida, Arcadia retains the distinctive appearance of its pioneer days. The two- and three-story brick buildings along Oak Street have been herded into the Arcadia Historic District on the National Register of Historic Places. Wooden residences such as the Micajah T. Singleton House, the John Morgan Ingraham House and the Johnson-Smith House are prized as examples of 19th-century folk architecture. On a grander level, the pink Arcade-Koch building will make architecture buffs drool.

> Appetites built up from antique hunting can be sated at Wheeler's Café, one of Florida's best hometown diners.

Appreciation for heritage runs deep in Arcadia. The Antique Association of Arcadia has been hosting Antique Fairs on the fourth Saturday of every month since the 1990s. The fairs are some of the largest in Florida, often drawing thousands of shoppers to pick through the offerings of more than 100 dealers. On non-fair days, two-dozen antique shops line the streets of downtown for browsers to explore. Parking is free and a slice of "Old Florida" is within easy walking range inside a four-block area.

Superb Pie

Appetites built up from a day of antique hunting can be sated at Wheeler's Café, which has been recognized as one of Florida's best authentic hometown diners. Wheeler's has been family-owned and dishing out its famous

Joshua Citrus. Getty Images/iStockphoto

The Desoto County Chamber of Commerce. Ebyabe

FL

MORE ROOM...
to Make Memories
AT CROSS CREEK RV RESORT
TOP RATED
Good Sam Park
FOR 2016

See listing Arcadia, FL

FL

The Peace River north of Arcadia. Ebyabe

The Arcade-Koch building. Ebyabe

peanut butter pie since 1929. Of course, the Shelfer family over at Joshua Citrus can be excused for considering the Wheelers and their 86 years in business as "newcomers." James Shelfer planted his first orange trees along Joshua Creek in 1880 before there was a dream of a town. The marketing mavens at the Florida Department of Agriculture have designated Joshua Citrus a Century Pioneer Family Farm. Today, you can visit the heritage groves and see a Florida packinghouse in operation—don't leave without a glass of trademark strawberry orange juice.

The ranching roots of Arcadia are still very much in evidence with rodeos scheduled through the year at the DeSoto County Fairgrounds, highlighted by "The Granddaddy of 'em All"—the Arcadia All-Florida Championship Rodeo in March. First started in 1928 as a way to raise money for a new American Legion building, the All-Florida is now the premier bull-riding and barrel-racing event in the Sunshine State and a much-anticipated stop for performers of the Professional Rodeo Cowboys Association.

Riding Horses and Boats

You can saddle up your own mounts at Deep Creek Preserve southwest of town, where nine miles of multi-use trails wind through 2,000 acres of freshwater prairie and longleaf pine flatwoods. Once you are through rambling up and over the scrub oak-covered ridges, several local canoe outfitters stand ready to launch you onto the Peace River. Meandering 106 lazy miles towards the Charlotte Harbor estuary, the Peace River has made Arcadia the best place to canoe in the state, according to *Florida Monthly* magazine readers. By the way, those folks you see prowling the banks with their heads down are seeking fossilized shark teeth and prehistoric mammal bones. The Peace River is such a rich ground for fossil hunters that Arcadia took a star turn on the Travel Channel adventure reality show, "Cash & Treasures."

> Settle into a cushion seat of a Peace River Charters airboat and cruise with 450 horsepower behind you.

If paddling languidly past the majestic Peace River cypress trees and water oaks dressed in Spanish moss is too slow for your tastes, settle into an elevated cushion seat of a Peace River Charters airboat and cruise the waters with 450 horsepower behind you. In an hour, you will cover 20 miles of primordial river teeming with of 400 native Florida animal species from Roseate Spoonbills to American alligators. To experience non-natives, visit Lions, Tigers and Bears just north of Arcadia, where unwanted exotic pets and non-releasable wildlife have been given a home on 40 acres of Florida habitat.

Arcadia boosters like to tout their home as the "Best Small Town in Florida." Clearly the reference is to population (less than 7,000) rather than visitor attractions. And it all began with a birthday cake served so many years ago.

For More Information

Discover DeSoto County Tourism Development Council
863-491-7574
www.visitdesoto.com

Florida Department of Tourism
888-735-2872
www.visitflorida.com

SPOTLIGHT

FL

CITRUS COUNTY

Make friends with manatees and bike through small towns

Once you hear the name "Citrus County, Florida," you're likely to envision fields and fields of lush, sun-soaked orange groves set against a sparkling Gulf of Mexico backdrop. You wouldn't be entirely wrong—this idyllic coastal region was once one of the country's largest producers of citrus fruit—but today it's known more as "Water Lover's Florida," meaning it's an ideal spot to kick back, splash in the surf and explore the beachfront.

Twenty different towns, communities and census-designated places are spread across Citrus County's 774 square miles, and visitors can fill entire days hopping from spot to spot exploring the local sights. Set up camp in one of the county's four main population centers—Crystal River, Inverness, Floral City or Homosassa—for the easiest access to the region at large. Each location offers a balance of small-town charm and comfortable amenities such as gourmet restaurants, great entertainment and top-tier tourist attractions.

Crystal River and Homosassa hug the Gulf of Mexico coast, making them picture-perfect spots for water sports enthusiasts and beach bums. The former is buffered by Crystal River Preserve State Park and features a historic downtown village area that's peppered with a collection of heritage homes and buildings. The latter, Homosassa, is really two different twin-sister towns: Homosassa and Homosassa Springs. Each offers visitors access to some of the most picturesque scenery in the county, including the gorgeous freshwater spring from which the towns get their names.

Digging Crystal River's Past

In Crystal River, be sure to visit the nearby Archaeological State Park. Spread across 61 acres of historic ceremonial land that's home to ancient burial mounds and temple platforms, the important Native American complex is one of the longest continuously occupied sites in the country. It's estimated that the site once attracted thousands of people from far and wide.

The town of Inverness is found farther inland, near the banks of Tsala Apopka Lake—an expansive chain of lakes, swamps and marshes that cover more than 60,000 acres. Inverness is the largest community in the county, but with a year-round population of 7,000 people, it remains decidedly down-to-earth and laid-back. The town is particularly popular with cross-country bicyclists. A wide selection of both paved and unpaved biking trails seamlessly connect the town's downtown area with the surrounding wilderness.

A short distance to the south sits Floral City, once the largest settlement in all of Florida. Today, the population tops out at just a few thousand year-round residents, but the entire community is listed in the National Register of Historic Places, making it a treat to stroll and explore for history buffs. The town is renowned for its vast fields of dazzling wildflowers.

A guide holds a young alligator. Visit Florida

For More Information

Visit Citrus County
800-587-6667
www.visitcitrus.com

Florida Department of Tourism
888-735-2872
www.visitflorida.com

FL

Enjoy flats fishing off the coast of Crystal River

Slow down at RV parks with water front views

Savor the food and scenery at Peck's Old Port Cove in Ozello

Ride 46 miles of the Withlacoochee State Trail

DRIVE FAST FOR A FEW MORE MILES.

THEN SLOW DOWN FOR A FEW DAYS.

Paddle crystal clear springs at Three Sisters Springs

See listing Crystal River, FL

FLAGLER COUNTY/PALM COAST

Get in touch with Florida's "quiet side" in a laid-back beachside county

Known as the "quiet side of Florida," Flagler County mixes small-town living with natural wonders. The 571-square-mile area is situated between historic St. Augustine and festive Daytona Beach, and the region is home to 44 nature parks, 10 golf courses and 19 miles of pristine Atlantic shoreline known as the Palm Coast.

Visitors will be drawn to Marineland, a pioneering educational facility where Dolphins and other sealife can be studied up close, or discover nature in a more elemental form at one of the county's state parks and preserves.

A great place to start is at the city of Flagler Beach. Cozy cafes, waterfront restaurants and a stunning stretch of beachfront are what this vintage oceanside community is all about. Plus, when you're ready for a change of pace or a day trip abroad, the likes of Daytona Beach, St. Augustine, Orlando and Jacksonville are all within easy reach. In short, there's a reason why Flagler Beach was once named the coolest small town in America—it offers all of the wonderful perks of small-town bliss with none of the sacrifice of small-town remoteness.

The first thing you'll notice when arriving here are the 19 miles of spacious shoreline. Thousands of years of crushed Coquina shells have given the soft, powdery sand a vibrant cinnamon-colored hue. Kayaking and stand up paddle boarding are among the most popular recreational activities, but generally kicking back beachside is just as highly recommended. If you're visiting in April, however, you'll have a hard time taking your eyes off one of the most mesmerizing natural sights in the world: Turtle nesting season, wherein thousands of baby turtles hatch from their eggs, emerge bleary-eyed from the sand and make their trek to the sea.

Swimming with the dolphins in Marineland. Getty Images/iStockphoto

Outside of the Flagler Beach, the surrounding county boasts a full menu of parks, preserves and recreation areas. At the Betty Steflik Preserve, visitors can walk a boardwalk over coastal scrub and salt marsh. Take a canoe or kayak through the waterways to see plants, birds and animals in their habitat. At Haw Creek Preserve, tucked away in western Flagler County, visitors can roam a 1,005-acre area with cypress oak and hardwood swamp.

Where the Waves Are

Two of the best places to catch some surf, check out sea turtles or go for a seaside stroll are Gamble Rogers Memorial State Recreation Area and Washington Oaks Garden State Park (located about 10 miles to the north of town). The former is perched atop a sand dune sporting spectacular views of the Atlantic Ocean, as well as a boat launch, nature trail and beachfront boardwalk. At Washington Oaks, visitors can stroll through intricately designed floral gardens that are full of exotic plants and are frequented by a stunning range of bird species. The park also features picnic areas, hiking trails and great places to fish.

For More Information

City of Flagler Beach
386-517-2000
www.cityofflaglerbeach.com

Palm Coast and the Flagler Beaches
866-736-9291
www.palmcoastandtheflaglerbeaches.com

See listings Bunnell, Flagler Beach & Palm Coast, FL

FORT MYERS

Edison fans and baseball buffs flock to this snowbird roost

Like the colors of a Gulf Coast sunset, Fort Myers presents a different image to all who visit. The shading begins with the location of the city itself, not on the seacoast but several miles inland along the Caloosahatchee River. While the Fort Myers area enters a vacation planner for beaches, it is really Fort Myers Beach and Sanibel Island that are in play—Fort Myers itself is a river town.

> Both the American League's Minnesota Twins and Boston Red Sox put down stakes in the city to get in shape for the coming Major League Baseball season.

Located two hours from Tampa to the north and Miami to the southeast, Fort Myers is a happy medium between a relaxed coastal town and the bustling city. Tourists will discover a relaxed community that boasts a massive selection of seafood restaurants, top-flight museums and all the amenities of a large metropolitan area. It's also got the laid-back vibe that travelers relish

Beachfront Camping on the Gulf of Mexico...
RED COCONUT
RV PARK LLP
www.redcoconut.com
3001 Estero Blvd.
Fort Myers Beach, FL 33931
1-888-262-6226
See listing Fort Myers Beach, FL
AAA
Good Sam Park

when visiting the Sunshine State. Tourists can stay local and enjoy attractions in town, or venture out to see some of the compelling cities and parks in outlying areas.

City With a Bright Future

Founded in the 1800s, the city enjoyed rapid growth as visitors discovered its friendly climate and natural beauty.

In August 1885, Fort Myers was incorporated—with less than 350 residents. By 1898, the city had become a nationally known winter resort destination with the building of the Royal Palm Hotel. With the opening of the Atlantic Coast Line Railroad, connecting Punta Gorda to Fort Myers in May 1904, access to the Fort Myers area was greatly

Dining in the Bubble Room on Captiva Island. © The Lee County Visitor & Convention Bureau.

FL

See listing Fort Myers, FL

SHADY ACRES
RV & CAMPINGPARK

Good Sam RATED 8.5/9.5★/8.5

Good Sam Park

19370 South Tamiami Trail (US 41 S)
Ft. Myers, FL 33908
Toll Free: (888) 634-4080
Local: (239) 267-8448
Fax: (239) 267-7026
www.ShadyAcresFL.com
camp@shadyacresfl.com
GPS: 26.45804 • 81.83054

- 2 Decks Overlooking the Lake with BBQ
- Heated Pool
- Pool Parties
- Recreation Hall with Free WiFi, Computer Station, Pool Table & TV Lounge
- Café
- Planned Activities
- Dinner/Dances
- Horseshoes
- Shuffleboard
- Bingo • Casino Trips
- Fire Rings • Handicap Site
- Dump Station
- Comfort Station
- Car Wash Area
- Trailer Storage
- Trailer Supplies
- Propane • Laundry

— SISTER PARKS —

1150 Hamilton Ln
P.O. Box 430
Chokoloskee Island, FL 34138
239-695-2414
FAX 239-695-3033
8 Miles S of U.S. 41 on SR 29
manager@chokoloskee.com
www.chokoloskee.com

See listing Chokoloskee, FL

Poinciana trees dazzle with red blossoms. Lee County Visitor & Convention Bureau

improved. The city continued to grow with the construction of the Tamiami Trail Bridge in 1924.

Fort Myers owes much of its fame to inventor Thomas Alva Edison, who thought the native bamboo that grew in abundance along the Caloosahatchee River might be the perfect filament for his incandescent light bulbs. It wasn't, but Edison stayed 45 years anyway and convinced his friend Henry Ford to build a winter retreat in town as well. Today, the Edison and Ford Winter Estates, burnished by 20 acres of botanical gardens, are the most popular attractions in Fort Myers.

That residences should be the area's top draw fits right in with the family-friendly Fort Myers ethos. The Imaginarium Science Center is an innovative blend of hands-on museum discoveries and live creatures cavorting in aquariums and an outdoor lagoon. Even Edison would envy the Discovery Lab exploration station.

Manatee Park on Palm Beach Boulevard is the place to spot the much-loved sea cows. Visitors can watch the creatures swim from three observation decks. The gentle creatures congregate in the river when the Gulf waters slip below 68 degrees in November and don't rise again until March.

Meet the Major Leaguers

About the middle of February, the voices around Fort Myers take on the distinct accents of New England and the Upper Midwest. It is baseball spring training season, and the Minnesota Twins and Boston Red Sox have both trained in Fort Myers since the early 1990s. Currently, the teams get in shape only six miles apart, with the Twins hunkered down in Hammond Stadium and the Red Sox occupying their elaborate Fenway South complex with its replica of Boston's famed Green Monster left-field wall. Fans can catch a Grapefruit

FL

League game in Fort Myers just about any day during the month of March.

If the sun gets too hot, the family can cool off with public ice skating sessions at the nearby Fort Myers Skatium.

Hitting the Waves

For real cooling down, nothing beats a trip on the water. Consider chartering a sailboat or powerboat from the Fort Myers Yacht Basin or riding the waves in a jet boat. Or take your time on a fishing boat, dropping a line into some of America's most productive sport fishing waters. When it comes to real leisure on the water, Fort Myers and surrounding Lee County are home to more than 20 establishments that rent paddleboards, kayaks and other small craft. Adventurous paddlers can set out on the 190-mile Great Calusa Blueway Paddling Trail. With more than 80 access points, the Blueway is conveniently marked with signs and will accommodate any level of paddler. Expect to see Atlantic bottlenose dolphins, manatees, sea turtles and any of 300 common species of birds on your journey as you dip in and out of barrier islands and mangrove-dotted estuaries.

While other southwest Florida towns play up their Gulf of Mexico beaches, Fort Myers offers the languid pace of a historic river town. In its refurbished River District, art galleries, eclectic boutiques and vibrant eateries mingle along brick-lined streets while the Caloosahatchee River ambles past. Monthly art and music walks make the waterfront entertainment district a year-round must-see.

On permanent display in the Historic River District are rows of historic buildings that have been restored and preserved. Perhaps the most interesting structure in Fort Myers is the town's former post office, which now houses the Sidney & Berne Davis Art Center. When it was constructed during the height of the Great Depression in 1933, the federal building was lauded as one of the most attractive post offices in any town the size of Fort Myers in America. Remarkably, it featured 24-hour-a-day open-air lockboxes. Embedded in the building's limestone walls are coral and seashells. As you browse through the world-class art, you'll get a sense of the fascinating, quirky history of Fort Myers.

Centennial Park's Uncommon Friends Statue depicting famous winter residents (from left) Henry Ford, Harvey Firestone and Thomas Edison. © Lee County Visitor & Convention Bureau

Fort Myers Beach fishing pier. Getty Images/iStockphoto

Although a river town, Fort Myers is just a hop away from the famous white powder sand beaches of the Florida Gulf Coast. Short bridges link the mangrove-speckled mainland with San Carlos Island, popular for its restaurants, and busy Fort Myers Beach. Bring lots of sunscreen and a good book for a day at the beach, or walk the shore in search of great scenery.

Do the Sanibel Stoop

A three-mile causeway leads to Sanibel Island, where visitors engage in the time-honored practice known as the "Sanibel Stoop," the best way to gather up the treasures from the sea in one of the best shelling spots in the world. The popular barrier island sports 22 miles of bike paths in addition to its 15 miles of unspoiled beach, and Sanibel's undeveloped mangrove ecosystem is the most expansive in the country. Dog owners will want to point south of Fort Myers to Bonita Springs and one of the few beaches along Florida's 1,380 miles of coastline, where dogs can romp.

Nature lovers flock to the Calusa Nature Center, which spotlights Southwest Florida's natural history along three nature trails and a bird aviary. The center's planetarium brings the solar system to life for visitors.

If that is too much nature, the Fort Myers River District Farmer's Market operates every Thursday under the Caloosahatchee Bridge and brings the natural bounty of Southwest Florida into town.

Bonita Springs

Beyond Fort Myers, several fantastic cities merit exploration. Put Bonita Springs on your list of side trips.

Bonita Springs is situated on the southwest coast of Florida in Lee County near Cape Coral and Fort Myers. Benefiting from a tropical climate, Bonita Springs is located on both the Gulf of Mexico and Estero Bay. The Imperial River flows through the city's downtown district, emptying into Estero Bay.

With "small-town charm and a bright future"—the city's motto—Bonita Springs boasts several alluring beaches as well as cultural art attractions. The Center for the Arts of Bonita Springs hosts local, regional, and national traveling exhibitions as well as offering art classes and multiple community events. The arts organization, which is spread across two campuses, holds the annual Bonita Springs National Arts Festivals in January, February and March in the historic downtown districts. Other local events held by various organizations, such as the Old Fashion Fish Fry and CREW Benefit Concert, keep locals and visitors entertained.

Bonita Beach Park features a swimming area and boardwalk along with picnic shelters and a gazebo. In 2013, *Forbes* ranked Barefoot Beach Preserve Park—one of the last undeveloped barrier islands on Florida's southwest coast—the sixth best beach in the nation. Wildlife lovers and sightseers alike will enjoy Lover's Key State Park, a wildlife haven composed of four barrier islands that feature hiking and biking trails and miles of pristine beaches. Just east of Bonita Springs, visitors will discover the Corkscrew Swamp Sanctuary, a Bald Cypress reserved managed by the National Audubon Society.

Thomas Edison experimenting with electric lamps on his wedding day. Getty Images

Punta Gorda Day Trip

One of the most interesting cities near Fort Myers is Punta Gorda, a town slammed by Hurricane Charley in 2004 and rebuilt into a fun-filled recreation mecca.

The rebirth of Punta Gorda is symbolized by the Harborwalk that hugs the water's edge of the Peace River for more than two miles. In Laishley Park, the concrete walk passes the "Spirit of Punta Gorda" sundial that symbolizes the community's response to Hurricane Charley. Harborwalk links to Fisherman's Village, an upscale waterfront shopping and entertainment complex constructed on a 1928 municipal pier. The Punta Gorda Linear Park traces the former rail bed of the Florida Southern Railroad in the downtown.

> In Fort Myers' refurbished River District, art galleries, eclectic boutiques and vibrant eateries mingle along brick-lined streets while the Caloosahatchee River ambles past.

The Punta Gorda Historical Mural Society rides herd over two dozen public paintings depicting the city's heritage that dates back to the 19th century, when Punta Gorda was the southernmost stop on the railroad. The Society also provides walking tour maps to explore the government seat of Charlotte County. Artifacts and exhibits are presented in the Punta Gorda Atlantic Coast Line Depot, constructed in a Mediterranean Revival style in 1928. The Blanchard House Museum of African American History collection can be found in the former home of sea captain Joseph Blanchard.

Recreation in Punta Gorda points towards the "thin waters" of Charlotte Harbor, which are ideal for small and medium-sized craft and sailboats. Deep sea fishermen need only navigate out past the sheltered harbor waters to reach the prime sport fishing grounds where big silver king tarpon feed. Some 84 percent of the shoreline is preserved land, and the Charlotte Harbor Preserve State Park is Florida's fourth largest state park.

On the shore, Punta Gorda is a whirlwind of activity, beginning with farmer's markets every Saturday and Sunday and Downtown Merchants Gallery Walks the third Thursday of every month. Seafood festivals take place in the spring and fall, and the Peace River National Art Show in March attracts artists from across the country. After a busy day at Punta Gorda, return to Fort Myers and rest up for another day of fun.

For More Information

The Beaches of Fort Myers and Sanibel
800-237-6444
www.fortmyers-sanibel.com

Florida Department of Tourism
888-735-2872
www.visitflorida.com

Getty Images/iStockphoto

FRANKLIN COUNTY

Make memories in Florida's so-called 'Forgotten Coast'

The "Forgotten Coast" of Franklin County is a far cry from Florida's magic kingdoms, glitzy beaches, strip malls and quests for eternal youth. In the Florida Panhandle, along the Gulf of Mexico, the 545-square-mile Franklin County is a haven for wildlife, an unassuming land that likes to keep Florida's "best-kept secrets" all to itself.

Virtually 90 percent of the county falls under the rubric of protected parkland or nature preserve. The community's mammal inventory includes black bears and the elusive Florida panther, while the region's swamps, beaches and waterways entice passionate birdwatchers. Find fun in the form of canoeing along the 100 miles of the Apalachicola River's swamp lands to hiking across pristine white sand beaches or reveling in the small town hospitality of the county's rough diamond towns—Apalachicola, Carrabelle and St. George Island—Franklin is a flashback to sultry "Old Florida."

Small but Perfectly Formed

One of Franklin County's most charming and eclectic towns, the fishing town of Apalachicola (known affectionately as Apalach) was founded by 19th-century cotton and lumber barons. The cobbled streets of the romantic historic district are dotted with hip bistros, arty cafés, eclectic stores and contemporary galleries that lend the town a poise and grace that feels more Nantucket than steamy Florida.

Shifting Sands

Franklin County's 250 miles of magnificent beaches unfurl from Alligator Point to Apalachicola. The St. George Island, a 28-mile-long barrier island of pristine white sand, gently rolling surf, bay forests and salt marshes invite a wealth of recreation including shelling, kayaking, sailing, hiking and swimming. The nine-mile-long St. George Island State Park Beach ranks as the longest beachfront state park in Florida. St. George Island is also home to Cape St. George Lighthouse, a magnet for aspiring young mariners. At the easternmost end of St. Vincent Island, the castaway dreamscape of Tahiti Beach remains true to its name. Reminiscent of a Gauguin painting, this quintessential South Seas paradise can only be accessed by boat, which keeps the tourist footprint pleasingly light. Old Carrabelle beach's magnificent stretch of pure white sand offers superb fishing, especially during the summer and fall. Bald Point State Park beach attracts naturalists with congregations of shorebirds and wading birds, including herons, egrets, American oystercatcher and sandpipers that feed on the shore, shallow water oyster beds and exposed bars.

Wild at Heart

The largest of Florida's three national forests, the Apalachicola National Forest occupies almost 938 square miles—more than half a million acres—of the Panhandle from just west of Tallahassee to the Apalachicola River. Scores of species find refuge in the park's lowlands, pine and oak forests and cypress hammocks including gray and red foxes, coyotes, bats, minks, beavers, red cockaded woodpeckers, alligators, Florida black bears and the elusive Florida panther.

A pristine estuary that pulsates with wildlife, the 246,000 acres of the Apalachicola Bay National Estuarine Research Reserve (the second-largest estuarine research reserve system in the nation) has been deemed a "biological hotspot" due to its 1,300 species of plants, 131 species of fish and 50 species of mammals (including manatees).

For More Information

Franklin County
866-914-2068
www.saltyflorida.com

Florida Department of Tourism
888-735-2872
www.visitflorida.com

Coastline
RV RESORT
The Pristine RV Resort of Florida's Forgotten Coast
TOP RATED Good Sam Park FOR 2016
Good Sam RATED 10/10★/9
See listing Eastpoint, FL
Uniquely positioned right on the coast of the beautiful Apalachicola Bay, Coastline RV Resort offers guests an unobstructed view of St. George Sound, St. George Island, Dog Island, and the spectacular sunrises and sunsets for which Franklin County is known.
• Full Hookups • Swimming Pool
• Gulf View Sites • Fishing • Gift Shop
• Free WiFi • Free Cable • Pet Friendly
• Recreation Building • Bath House
• Full Kitchen • Laundry Facilities
Welcome Snowbirds! Please ask about our snowbird monthly special and save today!
957 Highway 98
Eastpoint, Florida 32328
850-799-1016
stay@coastlinervresort.com
www.coastlinervresort.com

Getty Images/iStockphoto

HENDRY COUNTY

Get your sugar fix and go skydiving in this vibrant town

If you are going to call yourself "America's Sweetest Town," you had better bring the goods. In the case of Clewiston, located in Hendry County, Florida, the proof lies in the massive sugar-cane plantations that can be seen in every direction. The mills of the U.S. Sugar Corporation in Clewiston produce 700,000 metric tons of nature's sweetener each year—more than any other United States manufacturer.

Before the sugar industry exploded, Hendry County was cow country. Namesake Francis Asbury Hendry ran cattle here beginning in the 1850s. He supplied beef to the Confederate Army in the Civil War and eventually fenced in more than 25,000 acres for his 50,000 head of cattle. Hendry was active in Florida state politics and after he died in 1917 the legislature carved out more than 1,000 square miles for a county stretching from the shores of Lake Okeechobee in the north to the edge of the Everglades wetlands in the south. At the time there were fewer than three people per square mile in Hendry County.

> Skydive Spaceland-Clewiston has been dropping first-time skydivers from the skies since 1980s. Turbine aircraft enable up to 23 skydivers to jump on every flight.

It is more crowded than that today in Hendry County, but not by much. The watchword for visitors is still outdoor recreation. Lake Okeechobee, the largest freshwater lake within the borders of a single state in the Lower 48, is famous for its big trophy large-mouth bass fishing. The "Big O" is also a destination for black crappie, speckled perch and bluegill fishermen. On land, hikers and cyclists take to hard-packed and partially paved Lake Okeechobee Scenic Trail (LOST) that circles the lake for 109 miles.

For the Birds

Hendry County is in the heart of the 2,000-mile Great Florida Birding Trail, and the Hendry-Glades Audubon Society oversees Stormwater Treatment Area 5, recognized as one of America's best bird-watching locations. The Society stages the Big "O" Birding Festival every March, in which participants can expect to see well over 100 species of winged critters. At the Devils Garden Bird Park, more than 7,000 acres have been carved from a working ranch of open prairie and wetlands for guided tours to see

The preserved Hendry House, home to the county's founder. Ebyabe

A skydiver in freefall.
Getty Images/iStockphoto

FL

hundreds of Florida wild birds. Public birding and wildlife hotspots include the Spirit of the Wild and Dinner Island Ranch.

For those seeking a bit more adventure in their Hendry County experience, Skydive Spaceland-Clewiston has been dropping first-time skydivers from the skies since 1980s. Turbine aircraft enable up to 23 skydivers to jump on every flight. And if you are looking to churn up some ground-based fun, family-friendly Devils Garden Mud Park trucks in Okeechobee mud by the ton for its obstacle courses and trails. Another fantastic water attraction is the Caloosahatchee River, which runs through much of Hendry County. This waterway is known for the towering leather ferns and stately oaks that line its wild banks. Kayakers and canoe enthusiasts will find lots of possibilities for exploration on this waterway.

While Clewiston, located on the rim of the "Big O," reigns as the metropolis of Hendry County with a population of 7,000, the county seat resides further west in LaBelle, a town platted by Francis Hendry and named for his daughters Laura and Belle. Both communities keep a close watch on the region's history. In LaBelle, history is on display at the Heritage Museum. The Clewiston Museum, meanwhile, is housed in the old offices of the *Clewiston News*. Built in 1928, it is one of the oldest structures in town. A revealing fossil exhibit tells the tale of the area's natural history and videos chronicle the rise of the local sugar industry.

Human habitation in Hendry County traces back long before Francis Hendry and his Florida cows. The culture of the Seminole Tribe of Florida is preserved and celebrated in the Ah-Tah-Thi-Ki Museum, a fully accredited Smithsonian Institution affiliate, in Clewiston. In the Seminole language, "Ah-Tah-Thi-Ki" is a place to remember and learn, which is accomplished with more than 30,000 unique artifacts, including dioramas and one-of-a-kind oral histories. Detailed dioramas include a glimpse of traditional mealtime, in which multiple generations gather around their food. Also included are exhibits on jewelry making.

FL

Sweet Times in Clewiston

Still very much alive are Hendry County celebrations. The Clewiston Sugar Festival has been "raising cane" in April since 1986, reviving a tradition dating back to the 1930s that marks the end of the sugar-cane harvest season. Multi-

The Caloosahatchee River runs through much of Hendry County.
Ebyabe

day festivities include a rodeo, bass tournament and the crowning of Miss Sugar. The last full weekend in February finds Hendry County partying in Barron Park in LaBelle for the Swamp Cabbage Festival. The honoree is the Sabal Palm, the state tree of Florida.

Local trees are chopped down to provide decorations for parade floats, and gourmets nosh on the "Heart of the Palm," the meat of the cabbage palm tree. Palm Hearts won't win any accolades for LaBelle as "America's Sweetest Town," but they sure are an authentic slice of Real Florida cuisine. Fans of palm hearts have compared them to artichoke hearts, and this treat goes well with salads or as deep fried appetizers. Adventurous eaters might just be won over by the taste.

For More Information

Hendry County Tourist Development Council
863-983-7979
www.visithendrycounty.com

Florida Department of Tourism
888-735-2872
www.visitflorida.com

LEVY COUNTY/CEDAR KEY

Go wild in this untamed slice of the Sunshine State

Locals of Levy (Lee-vee) County call this slice of north Florida the Nature Coast. Fully one-fifth of the county is set aside for state and national wildlife areas, and when you poke around the back roads and through the dense hardwood forests, marshes and sandhills, you will find more than two-dozen nature-based recreational sites.

The biggest outdoor playground is the Goethe State Forest, with 53,000 accessible acres across southeastern Levy County. This is horse country (1975 Kentucky Derby winner Foolish Pleasure was a Levy native) and trail riders flock to the Black Prong Equestrian Center. This is the gateway to over 150 miles of hoof-friendly passages through scrubby flatwoods and cypress swamps.

Not all recreational opportunities in Levy County lie above ground. About half of Florida's 400 freshwater springs percolate within the Suwannee River Basin (the river Stephen Foster wrote a song about but never saw). Sometimes the surface sinks right into the aquifer like at Devil's Den Spring, where scuba divers descend 30 feet underground to open dive. Less experienced underwater explorers can snorkel in the springs. Nearby, Blue Grotto is a dive park built into a spacious natural limestone cavern. Snorkeling is also on the menu at Manatee Springs State Park and Fanning Springs State Park—spring water in Levy County is 72 degrees year round.

The best way to explore the nooks and crannies of Florida's Nature Coast is by boat, canoe or kayak. That is the only way to access the Waccasassa Bay Preserve State Park, which preserves 32,000 acres of coastal wilderness on the Gulf of Mexico. The Wekiva River has managed to survive as one of the few pristine riverine systems in Florida, and Henry Beck Park can be used for a launch site onto the Wekiva to paddle down a mapped State Canoe Trail.

Horse trails stretch for miles through Levy County. Levy County Florida

Levy Locals

Although Great Blue Herons, manatees and wild hogs outnumber humans in the area, Levy County homo sapiens have nonetheless made their mark in charming towns that evoke the term "Old Florida." Renowned for its production of peanuts, Williston sits on the eastern edge of the county. The goober—a roasted, boiled, fired and baked peanut—is celebrated the first Saturday of October at the Central Florida Peanut Festival. At the Cedar Lakes Woods and Gardens, more than 50 botanical showcases have been planted amidst the waterfalls of an abandoned 100-year-old lime rock quarry.

Feeling adventurous? Check out the 13 islands that make up the Cedar Keys National Wildlife Refuge. Here, you'll find the fishing village of Cedar Key, which traces its origins back to a United States Army fort in 1839. In 1854, a 28-foot-tall lighthouse was constructed on a 47-foot-high sandhill on Seahorse Key. The sandhill is the highest natural elevation on the Florida Gulf Coast, and the lighthouse still stands. Cedar Key, which takes its name from

Now, this is what Cedar Key is all about!
CEDAR KEY
SUNSET ISLE
RV PARK
& MOTEL
Good Sam Park
Waterfront sites on the bay of the Gulf of Mexico
The finest and friendliest RV park, campground and motel you'll find in the Cedar Key vicinity. That's why RVers keep coming back year after year to visit beautiful Cedar Key and meet friends that do the same. Entertainment frequently and, in the Winter months, featuring some of the best bluegrass music you'll find anywhere.
• Daily and Weekly Prices Include Water, Sewer, Electric, Cable TV
• Sunrise Cottage Rental
• Fishing • Boat Rentals at Cedar Key Marina
• Homemade Deluxe Bar-B-Q
• Home Made Fudge
CLUB HOUSE
CEDAR KEY SUNSET ISLE
RV PARK & MOTEL
11850 SR 24
Cedar Key, Florida 32625
352-543-5375 or 1-800-810-1103
SunsetIsle@CedarKeyRV.com
www.cedarkeyrv.com
See listing Cedar Key, FL

the abundant red cedar that once grew on the shore, was a bit of a boomtown in those days. The Florida Railroad was the first to connect the Atlantic and Gulf Coasts, and its western terminus was Cedar Key.

For generations, the residents of Cedar Key made a living hauling sea trout, redfish and tarpon from the flats around the island. But in 1994, the State of Florida enacted a ban on net fishing that abruptly brought an end to "Old Florida" life. The state did, however, provide resources for Cedar Key watermen to begin aquaculture. Today, the village is the leading clam farming community in the United States. Those clams are put to good use in the traditional seafood restaurants that line the waterfront streets in Cedar Key. The clam chowder at Tony's Seafood Restaurant on 2nd Street has three times scored top honors at the International Clam Chowder competition. If you want to catch your own seafood dinner, drop a line in at the Cedar Key Fishing Pier on Dock Street; many of the town restaurants will be happy to cook up your bounty from the sea.

Deep History

The Cedar Key Historical Society Museum captures the evolution of the Gulf Cost Island community from one of Florida's early important towns to a quaint fishing village and artists' retreat. Over at the Cedar Key State Museum, the collection of shells and Indian artifacts assembled by resident Saint Clair Whitman have been preserved in his 1880s frame house. Human habitation from 1,800 years ago on Cedar Key is interpreted at the Shell Mound Unit of Lower Suwannee National Wildlife Refuge. The mound was created by Eastern Woodland Indians who'd lived here for at least 1,000 years.

For More Information

Levy County Visitors Bureau
877-387-5673
www.visitnaturecoast.com

Florida Department of Tourism
888-735-2872
www.visitflorida.com

FL

Peter W. Cross, VISIT FLORIDA

OKEECHOBEE COUNTY

Have Fun Exploring South Florida's Natural Attractions and Diverse History

Centrally located between Florida's east and west coasts sits Okeechobee County, an area filled with Old Florida beauty and natural wonders. Outdoor activities here include fishing on world-famous Lake Okeechobee, camping on the sweeping grasslands of Kissimmee Prairie Preserve State Park or settling in at one of the beautiful RV camping resorts located throughout the county. There are also lots of trails for hikers, bicyclists and equestrians to enjoy.

Okeechobee County is bordered on the south by Lake Okeechobee and by the Kissimmee River to the west. Surrounded by these historic and pristine waterways, Okeechobee is a serene, rural community with strong historic roots in agriculture, business and recreational water activities. The county's agriculture includes cattle ranching, dairy, citrus production and farming, which are among its oldest industries and still thriving today. The famous catfishing industry of Lake Okeechobee and the recreational fishing for bass, crappie, catfish and more, continues to put Okeechobee on the map.

The Land of Big Water

Lake Okeechobee, the second-largest inland lake in the United States, boasts 730 square miles of majestic freshwater. The name, Okeechobee, given by the Seminole Indians, means "plenty big water," while the word, Kissimmee, is derived from a Calusa Indian word meaning "long water." The Kissimmee River encompasses more than two-dozen lakes in the Kissimmee Chain of Lakes (KCOL), their tributary streams and associated marshes, and the Kissimmee River and floodplain. The basin forms the headwaters of Lake Okeechobee and the Everglades; together they comprise the Kissimmee-Okeechobee-Everglades (KOE) system.

The Everglades is nationally and internationally recognized as one of the world's most unique natural and cultural resources. Lake Okeechobee and the Kissimmee River serve as a direct source of water to the Everglades by way of numerous small tributaries passing out of the lake's southern end.

Anglers will find ample fishing in Lake Okeechobee, which has an average depth of 9 feet. Try fishing from the bank for largemouth bass, bluegill, black crappie and catfish, but if you want to get a trophy fish you might need to venture out a little farther onto the water. Bring your own boat or take advantage of one of the local guide services to help you find a place on the lake where the fish are biting.

For an exciting way to see the lake, try an airboat ride. Unlike conventional motorboats, airboats are flat-bottomed boats that reach high speeds as they skim across the water's surface, giving passengers a thrilling ride. A number of airboat tour companies in Okeechobee County offer ecotours of the area to see Florida wildlife in their natural habitat. Birdwatchers can see various types of waterfowl as well as a growing population of endangered American bald eagles and beautiful blue herons.

County History and Activities

Nearly a century after its founding, Okeechobee remains the only city in Okeechobee County. The wide, inviting downtown streets are courtesy of the Florida East Coast Railway, which planned the town for bigger things long ago. Historical and recreational points of interest include the Battle of Okeechobee State Park, Okeechobee

Pleasure boats docked on Lake Okeechobee. Visit Florida

BRIGHTON
RV RESORT
Enjoy the Natural wonders
of the Real Florida

See listing Okeechobee, FL

A tri-colored heron stalks Lake Okeechobee's shores.
Getty Images/iStockphoto

County Historic Courthouse, Okeechobee City Hall, historical murals throughout downtown, Okeechobee Historical Society Museum & Schoolhouse, Veteran's Memorial Park, the Fishing Pier at Lock 7, Downtown Flagler Park, Okeechobee County Parks & Recreation Facilities, and the Okeechobee County Agri-Civic Center.

A variety of restaurants and quaint eateries highlight the flavor of local specialty foods, which include steak, barbeque, catfish, gator, turtle, swamp cabbage and Seminole Indian traditional pumpkin bread. These items can also be enjoyed at the festivals and events that take place in the community, such as the Okeechobee County Fair, the Taste of Okeechobee and the Speckled Perch Festival. Other events include barbecue contests, art festivals and parades celebrating the rich pioneering spirit of cattle ranching, farming, fishing and the beautiful wildlife of the area.

Okeechobee County invites visitors to come and discover Old Florida's natural attractions.

For More Information

Okeechobee County Tourist Development Council
863-763-3959
www.visitokeechobeecounty.com

Visit Florida
888-735-2872
www.visitflorida.com

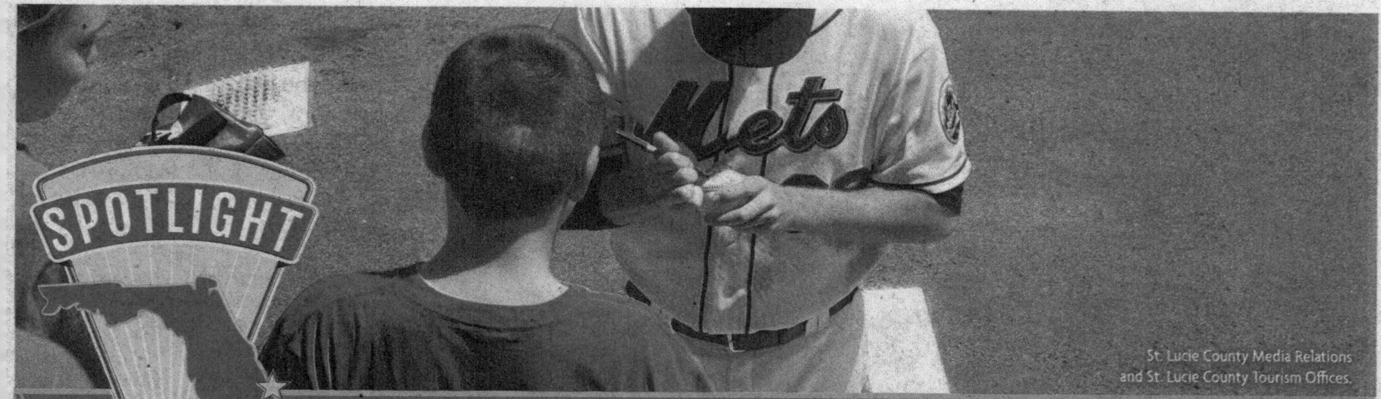

St. Lucie County Media Relations and St. Lucie County Tourism Offices.

ST. LUCIE COUNTY

Make three stops in this enchanting coastal region

Visitors to St. Lucie County will find themselves drawn to its gorgeous coastline, where they'll discover eclectic culture, outdoor escapism and pristine beachfronts. The three cities of the region—Fort Pierce, Port St. Lucie and Hutchinson Island—gems on the Florida stretch known as the Treasure Coast.

> Hutchinson Island has more than 21 miles of Atlantic Ocean beaches and more public access points per square mile than any coastal community in Florida.

Fort Pierce Embraces the Past

Fort Pierce is the county seat. American settlement in the area began in 1838 with the construction of a supply depot named for Lt. Col. Benjamin K. Pierce. Today, the town's efforts to preserve its Spanish-flavored Main Street architecture have been nationally recognized. Local street treasures include the Sunrise Theatre, which opened its doors in 1923. Also notable is the Spanish Colonial-style Arcade Building that was once the town's largest commercial structure.

At the P.P. Cobb General Store & Delicatessen in downtown Fort Pierce, you can shop for old-time candy and regional favorites, much like local farmers and fishermen did when the store was built in 1882. Although the original Fort Pierce burned to the ground in 1843, the site is preserved in a park by the Indian River. Nearby lies a preserved burial mound built by the Ais Indians, who were the first inhabitants of the Treasure Coast.

In 1943, the Naval Combat Demolition Unit training school was created at Fort Pierce to teach maritime commandos who participated in World War II missions. Those first "frogmen" would evolve into the elite U.S. Navy SEAL (Sea, Air, Land) teams. Their amazing story, which features NASA astronaut ocean retrievals and top-secret special operations, is told in the National Navy UDT-SEAL Museum on North Hutchinson Island.

Port of Pleasure

While Fort Pierce embodies the spirit of Old Florida, St. Lucie County's other city, Port St. Lucie, represents boomtown Florida. Port St. Lucie was a fishing camp and farmland in the 1950s; by the 1970s, it was an incorporated town with a few hundred residents; by the 2000s, the population was sprinting toward 200,000. Baseball fans flock to the city when the New York Mets hold spring training in town.

All the modern development has not crowded out nature. Savannas Preserve State Park in Port St. Lucie is the largest and most intact slice of Florida's east coast savanna ecosystem, waiting to be explored across eight miles of trails. The Oxbow Eco-Center offers guided hikes and an environmental learning center and is one of the many places in St. Lucie County to launch a canoe to explore mangrove forests and native plants.

The Heathcote Botanical Gardens began life in the 1980s in a commercial landscape nursery and is now home to more than 100 tropical bonsai trees—more than anywhere else in Florida. The Port St. Lucie Botanical Gardens is an oasis of rose gardens and orchid displays in the heart of the city, where you can often enjoy free jazz concerts.

Hit Hutchinson Island

Hutchinson Island, the barrier island that guards St. Lucie County, has more than 21 miles of Atlantic Ocean beaches and more public access points per square mile than any coastal community in Florida. Not only are the county- and city-owned beaches free to use, but Walton Rocks Beach is one of the few Florida Atlantic Ocean beaches that welcomes your dog.

Golf has become entrenched in St. Lucie County, and the Professional Golfers Association of America has established PGA Village here with courses by top architects like Tom Fazio and Pete Dye. Even nongolfers can appreciate the "good walk spoiled" at the PGA Museum of Golf, where admission is always complimentary.

For More Information

St. Lucie County
800-344-8443
www.visitstluciefla.com

Florida Department of Tourism
888-735-2872
www.visitflorida.com

Road Runner Travel Resort
TOP RATED RV PARK in South Florida – Fort Pierce.
NO COYOTES
BEST PARKS IN AMERICA
AAA
Good Sam Park
"Nestled in a beautiful 38 acre Florida Hammock"
One of the country's Top Rated R.V. destinations, the Road Runner Travel Resort in Ft. Pierce, Florida, offers 452 full hook-up sites with an unbeatable location! Situated on Florida's Treasure Coast, the Road Runner Travel Resort is just three miles from the pristine shoreline of the Atlantic Ocean. The friendly atmosphere at the Road Runner welcomes you from the moment you arrive. On site is a wide array of amenities, including a heated swimming pool, restaurant & grill, free Wi-Fi porch area, a three-hole golf course, tennis courts, shuffleboard and a general store with everything you need for your pantry and your R.V.
Sites
Cabin Suites
Cabins
The Road Runner Travel Resort also offers over 25 cabin accommodations. Each cabin comes beautifully decorated and furnished, fully equipped with dishes, cookware and bedding. The villas are also a great way to get away from it all when you want to "travel light," yet still experience the benefits of an R.V. vacation.
Fishing on the lake
3 hole golf course
Bike Riding
Pets welcome
Swimming pool
Family Owned & Operated!
Toll Free: 1-800 833-7108
For Reservations & Information
Ph: 772-464-0969
Address: 5500 St. Lucie Blvd., Fort Pierce, FL34946
Website: www.RoadrunnerTravelResort.com
Email: info@RoadrunnerResort.com
Florida
See listing Fort Pierce, FL

Visit Tampa Bay

SPOTLIGHT FL

TAMPA

Savor Florida's favorite Gulf Coast stomping ground

As the hub of western Florida's busy and buzzing Gulf Coast region, Tampa serves as the nucleus of a massive metropolitan area, home to the likes of St. Petersburg, Clearwater and Sarasota. It also sits just an hour away from family-friendly major attractions like Disney World, Universal Studios and SeaWorld, making this the perfect place to set up camp and sample the best of Florida piece by piece.

The city's buffet of world-class beaches will quickly draw you in and forever hold your attention.

The first thing to catch your eye in Tampa will largely depend on what kind of visitor you are. If you're an outdoors enthusiast or a water lover, then the city's buffet of world-class beaches will quickly draw you in and forever hold your attention. An annual average of 361 days of sunshine certainly doesn't hurt.

Many of the world's top-rated beaches are found in the immediate area, with all manner of water sports available in spades. Surf, SUP or kayak in the morning, get your tan on in the afternoon and take a sunset cruise or harbor sail in the evening. Most beaches are public, dusted with soft, white sand and serviced by a mouthwatering supply of beachside food trucks, restaurants, pubs and cafes.

The Latin Quarter and More

If you're more content to stroll the streets, relax with a light afternoon drink on an urban cafe patio or dabble in a bit of window-shopping, then you're in luck. Downtown Tampa, the Channel District and Ybor City (Tampa's historic Latin Quarter) are tailor-made for casual on-foot exploration. The city's historic streetcar still operates here—easily connecting downtown with the Channel District and Ybor City—so prepare to explore the city's most eclectic neighborhoods the very same way visitors would have traveled the city in 1892, when the streetcar first appeared on the scene in Tampa.

Ybor City is particularly worth a thorough exploration. Once the center of a thriving cigar manufacturing industry, this historic Latin Quarter buzzes both by day and by night. Before sunset the district is among the most popular spots in the city to grab a bite of gourmet lunch or coffee. Once the

FL

Quail Run R.V. Resort
"No Rig Too Big!
6946 Old Pasco Road, Wesley Chapel, FL 33544
Exit 279 West Off I-75 to SR54 • (813) 973-0999
For Reservations Only: 1-800-582-7084
www.quailrunrv.com • info@quailrunrv.com
Close to Attractions, Restaurants, Shopping and Entertainment!
See listing Wesley Chapel, FL
FREE 70+ CHANNEL CABLE
FREE WI-FI
Selected By BIG RIGS Best Bets
www.big-rigs-rv.com
TOP RATED Good Sam Park FOR 2016
Good Sam RATED 10/9.5★/9.5

A giraffe at the Lowry Park Zoo. Visit Tampa Bay

sun goes down the quarter morphs into a lively hot spot for those on the prowl for great live music and hopping nightclubs. If you're a sports fan, don't miss a stop at the often-overlooked Tampa Baseball Museum, located at the Al Lopez House.

If you're an art or history buff, be sure to make your way to Ybor City Museum State Park at some point. The complex consists of a museum (housed in the historic Ferlita Bakery building), Mediterranean-style botanical garden and a re-created version of a cigar worker's house. The museum offers insight into the history of the Ybor City neighborhood, including its role as a major cigar-manufacturing center. Guided tours are available and each is led by a prominent member of the Ybor City community.

The Tampa Museum of Art and the Tampa Bay History Center are two other must-visits for art and history buffs, while those traveling with small children might want to pay a visit to the Glazer Children's Museum. At the Tampa Museum of Art, a constantly changing set of collections are on display across a range of themed galleries. The museum's permanent exhibits include six galleries of ancient Greek and Roman artifacts.

Art buffs can drive across Tampa Bay to nearby St. Petersburg for a truly surreal experience. The Dali Museum showcases the work of the 20th century's most eccentric artist, along with multimedia exhibits that pay homage to his masterpieces.

The Tampa Bay History Center is an affiliate of the world-famous Smithsonian Institution, which may be all anyone needs to know before walking through the front doors. The museum's exhibits

Golfing at Saddlebrook Resort. Visit Tampa Bay

cover more than 12,000 years of history, specifically focusing on the Florida peninsula. The museum is located in downtown Tampa on the Riverwalk that overlooks the Garrison Channel.

Fishy Family Fun

You won't have to go far when it's time to find some big-time family fun. Start at the Florida Aquarium, which is conveniently located right in downtown Tampa. It features interactive exhibits and activities that allow visitors to walk through re-created swamps, swim with sharks and embark on informative ecotours by catamaran. The aquarium is home to more than 20,000 different animals and also features an outdoor water park for kids.

For an added boost of adrenaline, head a few miles north of downtown Tampa to Busch Gardens, where thrill rides and live shows mix with one of the largest zoos in the country. Busch Gardens sprawls across more than 300 acres, and features five different roller coasters that snake their way around the park, including Falcon's Fury, which drops 300 feet at 60 miles per hour.

Finally there's the Lowry Park Zoo, also located just a few miles north of downtown Tampa. Here, visitors can explore 64 acres of lush, natural habitats, home to more than 1,000 different animals, including elephants, chimpanzees, giraffes, cheetahs and white rhinos. Guests can tour several "free-flight" aviaries full of exotic birds, saddle up for a camel ride, help feed the giraffes and partake in a guided rhino encounter.

Thonotosassa: More Than a Name

After touring Tampa, take a side trip 15 miles northeast to Thonotosassa, a

The Dali Museum exhibits work by the Spanish artist. Visit Tampa Bay

Crowds gather at Skippers Smokehouse. Visit Tampa Bay

town with recreation menu as interesting as its name.

Opportunities for outdoor play abound on the northern fringes of Thonotosassa in places like the Lower Hillsborough Wilderness Preserve and Hillsborough River State Park. Paddling on the unhurried waters of the Hillsborough River is a favorite pastime here, along with explorations along more than 60 miles of forest and cypress swamp trails. Fort Foster State Historic Site, located along the river, is one of two reconstructed Seminole War forts in Florida and is open for visitors. The rough-hewn wooden walls and buildings of this military outpost recreate the conditions that U.S. soldiers faced in 1836, when Seminoles laid seige to the fort and attempted to burn down the bridge crossing the Hillsborough River. The attackers were repelled by musket and cannon fire from the combatants defending the fort.

In the days when there was nothing but wilderness on the shores of Lake Thonotosassa, the Church at Antioch was established in 1854. That pioneer spirit is celebrated each November at Antioch Days with a parade, traditional craft demonstrations and entertainment.

> In Busch Gardens, thrill rides and live shows mix with one of the largest zoos in the country.

While Thonotosassa embodies all things small town, the relaxed way of life belies the fact that the community is close to one of Florida's biggest family-friendly tourist attractions. Dinosaur World in nearby Plant City boasts more than 200 life-size replicas of the "terrible lizards." Visitors can learn about dinosaurs as they walk a path through a lush garden setting.

One place where the old and new of Thonotosassa mingle is Reese's Beach & Fish Camp. Families have gathered here since 1961, and it has recently been given a facelift for fishermen, boaters and swimmers.

For More Information

Visit Tampa Bay
800-448-2672
www.visittampabay.com

Florida Department of Tourism
888-735-2872
www.visitflorida.com

According to the Wall Street Journal, 100 billion plastic shopping bags are consumed in the United States annually. Consider toting your own reusable shopping bags instead of using plastic.

ALACHUA — B3 *Alachua*

TRAVELERS CAMPGROUND
Ratings: 9/8.5★/8 (Campground) From Jct of I-75 & US-441 (exit 399), E 100 ft on US-441 to service rd (April Blvd, Waffle House), N 1 mi (R). **FAC:** Paved rds. (130 spaces). Avail: 60 grass, 42 pull-thrus (30 x 70), back-ins (30 x 70), accepts self-contain units only, 60 full hkups (30/50 amps), seasonal sites, cable, WiFi, tent sites, dump, laundry, groc, LP gas. **REC:** pool, shuffleboard, rec open to public. Pets OK. Partial handicap access. Big rig sites, eco-friendly, 2015 rates: $37.40. Disc: AAA, military. ATM, no CC.
AAA Approved
(386)462-2505 Lat: 29.81820, Lon: -82.51371
17701 April Blvd, Alachua, FL 32615
dreamcamper@juno.com
www.travelerscampground.com
See ad pages 357, 282.

ALVA — D4 *Hendry, Lee*

FRANKLIN LOCK & DAM/W.P. FRANKLIN NORTH (Public Corps) From Jct of SR-31 & SR-78, E 3 mi on CR-78 to N Franklin Lock Rd, follow signs (R). 2015 rates: $30. (239)694-8770

APALACHICOLA — B1 *Franklin*

Things to See and Do

FRANKLIN COUNTY TOURISM DEVELOPMENT COUNCIL Tourism Office. Partial handicap access. No CC.
(850)653-9020 Lat: 29.7272, Lon: -84.9840
info@saltyflorida.com
www.saltyflorida.com
See ad page 305 (Spotlight Franklin County).

APOPKA — H4 *Orange*

ORANGE BLOSSOM KOA **Ratings: 8.5/8.5★/8** (Campground) 2015 rates: $41 to $50. (407)886-3260 3800 W Orange Blossom Trail, Apopka, FL 32712

WEKIWA SPRINGS (State Pk) From Jct of I-4 & SR-434 (exit 94), W 1 mi on SR-434 to Wekiwa Springs Rd, NW 4.9 mi to Park Entrance Rd, follow signs (R) NOTE: There is a $2 per pet per day fee for all pets. 2015 rates: $24. (407)884-2008

ARCADIA — D3 *De Soto*

BIG TREE CAREFREE RV RESORT
Ratings: 8/7.5/8.5 (RV Park) From Jct of US-17 & SR-70, E 1.8 mi on SR-70 (L). **FAC:** Paved rds. (392 spaces). Avail: 55 grass, patios, back-ins (30 x 55), 37 full hkups, 18 W, 18 E (30/50 amps), seasonal sites, WiFi Hotspot, rentals, dump, laundry, LP bottles. **REC:** heated pool, whirlpool, pond, fishing, shuffleboard. Pet restrict(B). Partial handicap access, no tents. Age restrict may apply, RV age restrict, 2015 rates: $33 to $42. Disc: AAA, military.
(863)494-7247 Lat: 27.20914, Lon: -81.83057
2626 NE Hwy 70, Arcadia, FL 34266
bigtree@carefreervresorts.com
www.carefreervresorts.com
See ad this page, 284.

CRAIG'S RV PARK
Ratings: 8.5/9★/8.5 (RV Park) From Jct of SR-70 & US-17, N 6.7 mi on US-17 to NE Cubitis Ave, W 0.1 mi (R).

COUNTRY CAMPING & GREAT BLUEGRASS!
Nestled in the country in SW Florida. Trade the city for quiet country camping. Great rates & home of Bluegrass Jammin' Weekends. Enjoy the climate of Florida's unspoiled heartland & Southern hospitality. Come enjoy the fun!

FAC: Paved rds. (333 spaces). Avail: 172 grass, patios, 25 pull-thrus (30 x 65), back-ins (30 x 50), 172 full hkups (30/50 amps), seasonal sites, cable, WiFi $, dump, laundry, LP gas. **REC:** heated pool, shuffleboard. Pet restrict(B/Q). Partial handicap access, no tents. 2015 rates: $25 to $40. Disc: military.
(863)494-1820 Lat: 27.30908, Lon: -81.81987
7895 NE Cubitis Ave, Arcadia, FL 34266
craigsrvpark@gmail.com
www.craigsrvpark.com
See ad this page, 292 (Spotlight Arcadia), 284 & Snowbird Destinations in Magazine Section.

CROSS CREEK RV RESORT
Ratings: 10/10★/10 (RV Park) From Jct of SR-70 & US-17, N 4.9 mi on US-17 to CR-660, W (L) 100 yds to NE Cubitis Ave, N (R) 0.9 mi (L).

SOUTH FLORIDA PREMIER RV RESORT
Cross Creek is a pristine 10/10*/10 Good Sam rated park. Exceptional living in a gated resort with beautiful landscaping, full amenities and activities. Large RV sites, wide streets, Olympic-size pool and 2 large clubhouses.

FAC: Paved rds. (526 spaces). Avail: 50 paved, patios, back-ins (40 x 75), accepts full hkup units only, 50 full hkups (30/50 amps), seasonal sites, cable, WiFi $, rentals, dump, laundry, LP gas, controlled

ARCADIA (CONT)

CROSS CREEK RV RESORT (CONT)
access. **REC:** heated pool, whirlpool, shuffleboard. Pet restrict(B). Partial handicap access, no tents. Age restrict may apply, big rig sites, eco-friendly, 2015 rates: $57.
(863)494-7300 Lat: 27.29428, Lon: -81.83052
6837 NE Cubitis Ave, Arcadia, FL 34266
info@crosscreekrv.com
www.crosscreekrv.com
See ad pages 290 (Spotlight Arcadia), 284 & Snowbird Destinations in Magazine Section.

LETTUCE LAKE TRAVEL RESORT **Ratings: 8.5/8.5/8.5** (Campground) 2015 rates: $40. (863)494-6057 8644 SW Reese St, Arcadia, FL 34269

LITTLE WILLIE'S RV RESORT
Ratings: 8/9/8.5 (RV Park) From Jct of SR-70 & US-17, N 3.3 mi on US-17 to McKay Rd, W 0.1 mi to NE Cubitis Ave, N 1.3 mi (L).

FRIENDLY AT-HOME RV RESORT
We offer a warm, home atmosphere combined with our many amenities including pool, shuffleboard, clubhouse and regularly scheduled activities at competitive prices. Join us during this season.

FAC: Paved rds. (331 spaces). Avail: 175 grass, patios, 30 pull-thrus (30 x 50), back-ins (30 x 50), 175 full hkups (30/50 amps), seasonal sites, WiFi $, rentals, laundry, fire rings, firewood. **REC:** heated pool, shuffleboard. Pet restrict(B). Partial handicap access, no tents. Age restrict may apply, big rig sites, 2015 rates: $30. Sep 15 to May 15.
(863)494-2717 Lat: 27.28032, Lon: -81.83408
5905 NE Cubitis Ave, Arcadia, FL 34266
staff@littlewilliesrvresort.com
www.littlewilliesrvresort.com
See ad opposite page, 284 & Snowbird Destinations in Magazine Section.

OAK HAVEN MH & RV PARK **Ratings: 8/9.5★/8.5** (RV Park) 2015 rates: $40. (863)494-4578 10307 SW Lettuce Lake Ave, Arcadia, FL 34269

PEACE RIVER CAMPGROUND **Ratings: 8/7/8** (Campground) 2015 rates: $63. (863)494-9693 2998 NW Hwy 70, Arcadia, FL 34266

TOBY'S RV RESORT **Ratings: 8.5/7/8.5** (RV Park) 2015 rates: $24 to $51. (800)405-6188 3550 NE Hwy 70, Arcadia, FL 34266

AVON PARK — L4 *Highlands*

ADELAIDE SHORES RV RESORT **Ratings: 8.5/8.5/8** (RV Area in MHP) 2015 rates: $39. (863)453-2226 2881 US Hwy 27 N, Avon Park, FL 33825

BONNET LAKE CAMPGROUNDS **Ratings: 8.5/UI/7** (RV Park) 2015 rates: $40 to $50. (863)385-3700 2825 SR-17 S, Avon Park, FL 33825

LAKE GLENADA RV & MHP **Ratings: 7/8.5★/6** (RV Park) 2015 rates: $22 to $38. (863)453-7007 2525 US Hwy 27 S, Avon Park, FL 33825

LAKE LETTA RV PARK **Ratings: 6/7.5/7** (RV Park) 2015 rates: $35 to $40. (863)453-7700 2455 S Lake Letta Dr, Avon Park, FL 33825

BAHIA HONDA KEY — F4 *Monroe*

BAHIA HONDA (State Pk) S-bnd: On US-1 (oceanside), at MP-37 (L). 2015 rates: $36. (305)872-2353

BARTOW — K3 *Polk*

GOOD LIFE RV RESORT **Ratings: 9.5/10★/8.5** (RV Park) 2015 rates: $39. (863)537-1971 6815 SR-60E, Bartow, FL 33830

Visit CampingWorld.com where you can get deals on over 10,000 RV and camping related products!

Travel Services

CAMPING WORLD/ DUSTY'S CAMPER WORLD OF BARTOW As the nation's largest retailer of RV supplies, accessories, services and new and used RVs, Camping World is committed to making your total RV experience better. RV Accessories: (800)329-7878. **SERVICES:** RV, RV appliance, MH mechanical, engine/chassis repair, staffed RV wash, RV Sales. RV supplies, LP, emergency parking. Hours: 8am - 6pm.
863-533-2458 Lat: 27.889193, Lon: -81.820519
7400 S.r. 60 East, Bartow, FL 33830
rvinfo@dustysrv.com
CampingWorldofBartow.com

BELL — B3 *Gilchrist*

HART SPRINGS PARK (Public) From Jct of US 19 & SR-26 to CR-232 (in Fanning Springs), E 2 mi on SR-26 to CR-232, N 4 mi to CR-344, W 1 mi (R). 2015 rates: $25. (352)463-3444

BELLE GLADE — D5 *Palm Beach*

BELLE GLADE CAMPGROUND (CITY PARK) (Public) From jct Hwy 80 & Hwy 715: Go 2-1/4 mi N on Hwy 715, then 2 mi W on Torry Rd. (Turn left immediately after crossing bridge.). 2015 rates: $20. (561)996-6322

BEVERLY HILLS — H2 *Citrus*

SANDY OAKS RV RESORT
Ratings: 9.5/10★/9 (RV Park) From Jct of US 41 & CR 491, S 0.7 mi on CR 491 (R). **FAC:** Paved rds. 185 gravel, patios, 32 pull-thrus (30 x 75), back-ins (30 x 50), accepts self-contain units only, 185 full hkups (30/50 amps), cable, WiFi, laundry, LP gas, firewood. **REC:** heated pool. Pet restrict(B). No tents. Eco-friendly, 2015 rates: $36 to $42.
(352)465-7233 Lat: 28.962501, Lon: -82.432173
6760 N Lecanto Hwy (Cr 491), Beverly Hills, FL 34465
info@sandyoaksrvresort.com
www.sandyoaksrvresort.com
See ad this page, 282.

BIG PINE KEY — F4 *Monroe*

BIG PINE KEY FISHING LODGE **Ratings: 8/10★/8** (RV Park) 2015 rates: $63 to $69. (305)872-2351 33000 Overseas Hwy, Big Pine Key, FL 33043

SUNSHINE KEY RV RESORT & MARINA **Ratings: 8/7.5/8** (RV Park) 2015 rates: $72 to $138. (800)405-6188 38801 Overseas Hwy, Big Pine Key, FL 33043

BOKEELIA — D3 *Lee*

TROPIC ISLE RV PARK
Ratings: 7.5/7.5/8.5 (RV Park) From jct Hwy 78 & Hwy 767: Go 5-3/4 mi N on Hwy 767 (L). **FAC:** Paved rds. (146 spaces). Avail: 50 grass, patios, back-ins (35 x 60), 50 full hkups (30/50 amps), cable, WiFi, rentals, dump, laundry, controlled access. **REC:** heated pool, whirlpool, Gulf of Mexico: fishing, shuffleboard. Pets OK. Partial handicap access, no tents. Age restrict may apply, RV age restrict, 2015 rates: $50.
(239)283-4456 Lat: 26.68275, Lon: -82.14949
15175 Stringfellow Rd, Bokeelia, FL 33922
info@tropicislepark.com
www.tropicislepark.com
See ad pages 353, 284.

BONIFAY — E2 *Holmes*

FLORIDA SPRINGS RV RESORT & CAMPGROUND **Ratings: 7.5/9★/8.5** (RV Park) 2015 rates: $34 to $37. (850)258-3110 90 Son In Law Rd, Bonifay, FL 32425

Had a great stay? Let us know by emailing us travelguidecomments@goodsamfamily.com

BONITA SPRINGS — E4 *Lee*

BONITA LAKE RV RESORT **Ratings: 9/8.5/8** (RV Park) 2015 rates: $39 to $58. (239)992-2481 26325 Old 41 Rd, Bonita Springs, FL 34135

GULF COAST CAMPING RESORT
Ratings: 7.5/8.5★/7.5 (RV Park) From jct I-75 (exit 116) & CR-865/Bonita Beach Rd: Go 3/4 mi W on Bonita Beach Rd, then 1 mi N on Imperial St, then 1 mi W on E Terry St, then 3/4 mi N on Old US-41/Tamiami Trail, then 1/4 mi E on Production Circle. (R). **FAC:** Paved rds. (260 spaces). 186 Avail: 2 paved, 184 grass, back-ins (40 x 50), some side by side hkups, 186 full hkups (30/50 amps), WiFi, tent sites, dump, laundry. **REC:** pool, pond, fishing, shuffleboard. Pets OK. Age restrict may apply, RV age restrict, 2015 rates: $55. Oct 1 to May 1.
(239)992-3808 Lat: 26.38475, Lon: -81.80530
24020 Production Circle, Bonita Springs, FL 34135
info@gulfcoastcampingresort.com
www.gulfcoastcampingresort.com
See ad this page, 284.

IMPERIAL BONITA ESTATES MH & RV RESORT
Ratings: 9/9.5★/9 (RV Park) From Jct of I-75 & CR-865 (exit 116/Bonita Beach Rd), W 0.7 mi on CR-865 (Bonita Beach) to Imperial Pkwy, N 0.2 mi to Dean St, E 0.1 mi (L). **FAC:** Paved rds. (307 spaces). Avail: 187 gravel, patios, 30 pull-thrus (30 x 60), back-ins (28 x 50), accepts full hkup units only, 187 full hkups (30/50 amps), WiFi, dump, laundry. **REC:** heated pool, Imperial River: fishing, shuffleboard. Pets OK. Partial handicap access, no tents. Age restrict may apply, big rig sites, 2015 rates: $40 to $65.
(800)690-6619 Lat: 26.33679, Lon: -81.75849
27700 Bourbonniere Dr, Bonita Springs, FL 34135
ibecoop@comcast.net
www.imperialbonitaestates.com
See ad page 326.

SANCTUARY RV RESORT
Ratings: 9.5/9★/9 (RV Resort) From jct I-75 (exit 116) & Bonita Beach Rd: Go 1 mi E on Bonita Beach Rd (L). **FAC:** Paved rds. 185 Avail: 185 all weather, patios, 48 pull-thrus (35 x 85), back-ins (35 x 85), 185 full hkups (30/50 amps), WiFi, laundry, restaurant, controlled access. **REC:** heated pool. Pet restrict(B/Q). Partial handicap access. Big rig sites, RV age restrict, eco-friendly, 2015 rates: $45 to $80.
(239)495-9700 Lat: 26.33179, Lon: -81.72894
13660 Bonita Beach Rd SE, Bonita Springs, FL 34135
info@sanctuaryrvresort.com
www.sanctuaryrvresort.com
See ad this page.

Our inspectors look for the same things you do. Our unique Triple Rating System is based on years of market research, analysis and surveys from RVers like you. One thing you suggested was the need for separate ratings on facility completeness, restroom cleanliness/construction, and visual appearance/environmental quality. So we give three ratings, each based on a scale of 1 to 10, 10 being best and 5 being average. To give you an idea how tough we are, less than 1% of inspected campgrounds receive 10/10/10 ratings.*

BOWLING GREEN — **L3** *Hardee, Polk*

ORANGE BLOSSOM ADULT RV PARK

Ratings: 7/7.5/6.5 (RV Park) From Jct Hwy 62 & US 17: Go N .5 mi on US-17 (L). **FAC:** Paved rds. (185 spaces). Avail: 75 grass, back-ins (24 x 45), 75 full hkups (30/50 amps), seasonal sites, WiFi $, laundry. **REC:** heated pool, shuffleboard. Pet restrict No tents. Age restrict may apply, 2015 rates: $27. No CC.
(863)773-2282 Lat: 27.60109, Lon: -81.82386
2829 US Highway 17 N, Bowling Green, FL 33834
See ad this page.

PIONEER CREEK RV RESORT Ratings: 8/8/7.5 (RV Area in MHP) 2015 rates: $35. (863)375-4343 138 E Broward St, Bowling Green, FL 33834

TORREY OAKS RV & GOLF RESORT Ratings: 8.5/9/9 (Condo Pk) 2015 rates: $40. (863)773-3157 2908 Country Club Dr, Bowling Green, FL 33834

BRADENTON — **L2** *Manatee*

BRADENTON See also Cortez, Palmetto, Ruskin, Sarasota, St Petersburg, Tampa & Venice.

ARBOR TERRACE RV RESORT

Ratings: 7.5/7.5/7.5 (RV Park) From Jct of I-75 (exit 217 A) & SR-70: Go W 7.2 mi on SR-70, then S 0.5 mi on US-41, then E 0.5 mi on 57th Ave W (L).

DISCOVER FLORIDA'S BEST KEPT SECRET
Enjoy a relaxed atmosphere with a variety of on-site amenities and local attractions just minutes from the best beaches on the Gulf Coast. Stay your way with a great selection of spacious RV sites and lovely vacation rentals.

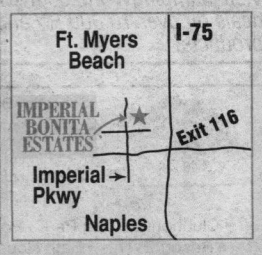

FAC: Paved rds. (376 spaces). Avail: 210 grass, patios, 62 pull-thrus (20 x 60), back-ins (30 x 60),

BRADENTON (CONT)

ARBOR TERRACE RV RESORT (CONT)
some side by side hkups, 210 full hkups (30/50 amps), seasonal sites, WiFi $, dump, laundry. **REC:** heated pool, shuffleboard. Pet restrict(B/Q). No tents. Big rig sites, 2015 rates: $29 to $57. Disc: AAA. AAA Approved
(888)310-4975 Lat: 27.44081, Lon: -82.56654
405 57th Ave W, Bradenton, FL 34207
arborterrace@suncommunities.com
www.arborterracerv.com
See ad opposite page, 275 (Welcome Section), 286, 1463 (Welcome Section) & RV Trips of a Lifetime, Snowbird Destinations in Magazine Section.

HORSESHOE COVE CAREFREE RV RESORT
Ratings: 8.5/8.5★/8.5 (RV Park) From Jct of I-75 (Exit 217) & SR-70: Go W 1.5 mi on SR-70, then N 0.2 mi on 60th St. E/Caruso Rd (L). **FAC:** Paved rds. (476 spaces). 70 Avail: 40 paved, 30 grass, patios, 40 pull-thrus (30 x 60), back-ins (35 x 40), 70 full hkups (30/50 amps), seasonal sites, WiFi, rentals, laundry, controlled access. **REC:** heated pool, whirlpool, Braden River: fishing, shuffleboard. Pet restrict(B/Q). Partial handicap access, no tents. Age restrict may apply, 2015 rates: $35 to $65.
(800)291-3446 Lat: 27.45035, Lon: -82.48586
5100 60Th St E, Bradenton, FL 34203
horseshoecove@carefreervresorts.com
www.carefreervresorts.com
See ad this page, 286 & Snowbird Destinations in Magazine Section.

LAKE MANATEE SRA (State Pk) From Jct I-75 (Exit 220) & SR-64, E 9 mi on SR-64 (L). 2015 rates: $22. (941)741-3028

PLEASANT LAKE CAREFREE RV RESORT
Ratings: 9.5/8/8 (RV Park) From Jct of I-75 (Exit 217) & SR-70: Go W 0.6 mi on SR-70 (R). **FAC:** Paved rds. (340 spaces). Avail: 110 grass, patios, 16 pull-thrus (40 x 50), back-ins (40 x 50), 110 full hkups (30/50 amps), seasonal sites, cable, WiFi, laundry, LP gas, controlled access. **REC:** heated pool, Pleasant Lake: fishing, shuffleboard. Pet restrict(B). Partial handicap access, no tents. Age restrict may apply, 2015 rates: $40 to $60.
(941)756-5076 Lat: 27.44845, Lon: -82.47576
6633 53rd Ave E, Bradenton, FL 34203
pleasantlake@carefreervresorts.com
www.carefreervresorts.com
See ad this page.

Say you saw it in our Guide!

SARASOTA BAY RV PARK
Ratings: 8/8/8.5 (RV Park) From Jct of I-75 (exit 217) & SR-70: Go W 13 mi on SR-70, then W 2 mi on SR-684/Cortez Rd (L). **FAC:** Paved rds. (240 spaces). Avail: 100 paved, patios, back-ins (25 x 55), 100 full hkups (30/50 amps), WiFi, dump, laundry. **REC:** heated pool, whirlpool, Sarasota Bay: fishing, shuffleboard. No pets. No tents. Age restrict may apply, 2015 rates: $45 to $56.
(941)794-1200 Lat: 27.46314, Lon: -82.66993
10777 Cortez Rd W, Bradenton, FL 34210
info@sarabayrvpark.com
www.sarabayrvpark.com
See ad this page.

Want to see what our inspectors see? The exact reproductions of the rating guidelines our inspectors used for this edition of the Guide are printed in the front of the book. Try using them on your next trip to perform your own inspection. Since our rating system is based on objective criteria, we're confident that your ratings will be similar to ours.

TIMBERLANE RV PARK & RESORT
(RV Park) (Too New to Rate) From jct I-75 (exit) and Hwy 64: Go E .5 mi (R). **FAC:** Paved rds. 49 grass, 12 pull-thrus (32 x 65), back-ins (32 x 65), accepts full hkup units only, 49 full hkups (30/50 amps), WiFi. Pet restrict(B/Q). Big rig sites, 2015 rates: $35 to $72. No CC.
(941)896-9744 Lat: 27.487296, Lon: -82.462631
1404 Timber Oak Lane, Bradenton, FL 34211
info@timberlanervpark.com
www.timberlanervpark.com
See ad opposite page.

TROPICAL GARDENS RV PARK **Ratings: 8.5/9★/7.5** (RV Park) 2015 rates: $28 to $55. (941)756-1135 1120 53rd Ave East (Hwy 70), Bradenton, FL 34203

VISTA DEL LAGO CAREFREE RV RESORT
Ratings: 6/NA/7.5 (RV Area in MHP) From jct I-75 (exit 217) & Hwy 70: Go W 7 mi on Hwy 70 (R). **FAC:** Paved rds. (181 spaces). Avail: 16 grass, back-ins (25 x 36), accepts full hkup units only, 16 full hkups (30/50 amps), seasonal sites, WiFi Hotspot. **REC:** heated pool, pond, fishing, shuffleboard. Pet restrict

Check out the travel services section of this Guide to find services that you'll find handy in your travels.

See listing Brooksville, FL

BRADENTON (CONT)

VISTA DEL LAGO CAREFREE (CONT)
Partial handicap access. Age restrict may apply, 2015 rates: $35.
(941)755-5680 Lat: 27.44801, Lon: -82.57053
801 53rd Ave W, Bradenton, FL 34207
vistadellago@carefreervresorts.com
http://www.carefreervresorts.com/rv-parks/florida/vista-del-lago/
See ad pages 327, 286.

➔ WINTER QUARTERS MANATEE RV RESORT **Ratings: 8.5/8/8** (RV Park) 2015 rates: $27 to $75. (800)405-6188 800 Kay Rd NE, Bradenton, FL 34212

BRANFORD — B3 *Bradford, Suwannee*

ELLIE RAY'S RIVER RV RESORT **Ratings: 8/8.5★/9** (RV Park) 2015 rates: $27 to $36. (386)935-9518 3349 NW 110th St., Branford, FL 32008

➔ RIVER RUN CAMPGROUND **Ratings: 4/8★/7** (Campground) 2015 rates: $32. (386)935-6553 2739 U.s. Hwy 27, Branford, FL 32008

BRISTOL — A1 *Liberty*

TORREYA (State Pk) From Jct of S.R. 12 & CR 1641, NW 7 mi on CR 1641 (E). Entrance fee required. 2015 rates: $16. (850)643-2674

BRONSON — B3 *Levy*

Things to See and Do

LEVY COUNTY VISITORS BUREAU Camping & RV sites, swimming in springs, canoe gentle rivers or bike & hike pristine trails await your arrival. Escape to the National Wildlife Refuges where tidal marshes & coastal islands are home to many. Hours: 8am to 5pm. No CC.
(877)387-5673 Lat: 29.452596, Lon: -82.648311
carol@visitnaturecoast.com
www.visitlevy.com
See ad page 313 (Spotlight Levy County/Cedar Key).

Nobody said it was easy being a 10. And our rating system makes it even tougher. Check out 10/10/10 RV parks and campgrounds in the front of the guide.*

BROOKSVILLE — J2 *Hernando*

BELLE PARC RV RESORT
Ratings: 8/9.5★/9.5 (RV Park) From Jct of I-75 (exit 301) & US-98: Go W 9.6 mi on US-98, then N 2.3 mi on US-41 (L).

NEW DEVELOPMENT OPENING IN 2016!
Enjoy Brooksville - a location close to everything the Sunshine State has to offer, yet away from it all in the peace and quiet of Central Florida. Belle Parc offers large sites, free WiFi, a heated pool, lake views and more!

FAC: Gravel rds. 100 gravel, patios, 9 pull-thrus (35 x 60), back-ins (35 x 60), 100 full hkups (50 amps), WiFi, laundry, controlled access. **REC:** heated pool, whirlpool, pond, fishing, shuffleboard. Pet restrict(Q). Partial handicap access, no tents. Big rig sites, 2015 rates: $44 to $66. Disc: AAA.
(352)796-5760 Lat: 28.58613, Lon: -82.37573
11089 Ancient Trail, Brooksville, FL 34601
info@belleparcrvresorts.com
www.belleparcrvresorts.com
See ad opposite page, 286 & Snowbird Destinations in Magazine Section.

CLOVER LEAF FOREST RV RESORT **Ratings: 6.5/8/7.5** (RV Park) 2015 rates: $42 to $47. (352)796-8016 910 N Broad St, Brooksville, FL 34601

➔ HIDDEN VALLEY CAMPGROUND **Ratings: 5/5.5/5.5** (RV Park) 2015 rates: $22. (352)796-8710 22329 Cortez Blvd, Brooksville, FL 34601

BUNNELL — B4 *Flagler*

FLAGLER COUNTY BULL CREEK CAMPGROUND
(Public) From Jct of US-1 & SR-100, W 7 mi on SR-100 to CR-305, S 4 mi to CR-2006, W 3.8 mi (E). **FAC:** Gravel rds. 25 gravel, patios, back-ins (30 x 50), 25 full hkups (30/50 amps), dump, laundry, fire rings, restaurant. **REC:** Crescent Lake: fishing, marina, rec open to public. Pets OK. No tents. Big rig sites, 2015 rates: $20 to $35.
(386)313-4020 Lat: 29.42301, Lon: -81.43522
3861 CR-2006, Bunnell, FL 43522
info@flagercounty.org
www.flaglerparks.com
See ad page 296 (Spotlight Flagler County/Palm Coast).

THUNDER GULCH CAMPGROUND
(Campground) (Not Visited) From the south on I-95 exit 273, (Old 89): Go N on US 1 or; From the north on I-95 take exit 298 (Old 92): Go S om US 1. **FAC:** Gravel rds. 20 grass, back-ins (25 x 65), some side by side hkups, accepts full hkup units only, 20 full hkups (30/50 amps), WiFi, tent sites, laundry, restaurant. Pets OK. 2015 rates: $28.60 to $36. No CC.
AAA Approved
(800)714-8388 Lat: 29.49279, Lon: -81.26579
2551 N State St (US 1), Bunnell, FL 32110
www.thundergulch-campground.com/
See ad page 296 (Spotlight Flagler County/Palm Coast).

Everyone wants to be noticed. Tell your RV Park that you found them in the this Guide.

BUSHNELL — H2 *Sumter*

BLUEBERRY HILL RV RESORT
Ratings: 9.5/10★/8 (RV Park) From Jct of I-75 & SR-48 (Exit 314), E 0.3 mi on SR-48 to Lowery St., S 0.2 mi to entrance (L).

FIND YOUR THRILL AT BLUEBERRY HILL
Unsurpassed amenities like a heated pool and an assortment of gorgeous courts including pickleball, shuffleboard and bocce ball make this resort one-of-a-kind! Experience the pinnacle of luxury RV camping at Blueberry Hill.

FAC: Paved rds. (406 spaces). 248 Avail: 96 paved, 152 grass, 96 pull-thrus (21 x 60), back-ins (45 x 55), accepts full hkup units only, 248 full hkups (50 amps), seasonal sites, WiFi, rentals, dump, laundry, LP gas. **REC:** heated pool, shuffleboard. Pet restrict(B/Q). Partial handicap access, no tents. Big rig sites, 2015 rates: $32 to $45. Disc: AAA, military.
AAA Approved
(888)759-4957 Lat: 28.66534, Lon: -82.13707
6233 Lowery St, Bushnell, FL 33513
blueberryhill@suncommunities.com
www.blueberryhillrvresort.com
See ad this page, 275 (Welcome Section), 286, 1463 (Welcome Section) & Snowbird Destinations in Magazine Section.

According to some studies, almost 50 percent of RVers camp with pets! Find out more about the joys of traveling with your four-legged companions in our Pampered Pet Parks feature at the front of the Guide.

FL

Just Another Ho Hum Day in Paradise
RV Park
Offering a Quiet Environment for Our Guests in a No Children Park
Located Directly on the Gulf of Mexico off Scenic Hwy 98
• Big Rig and Dog Friendly
• All Sites 50/30 Amp
• Free Cable • Free Wi-Fi • Pull-Thrus
• Fishing Pier • Shelling
• Bring Your Boats, Inflatables & Kayaks for Year Round Fun & Unsurpassed Summer Fishing
(850) 697-3926
2132 Hwy 98 E., Carrabelle, FL 32322
www.hohumrvpark.com
Good Sam Park
See listing Carrabelle, FL

BUSHNELL (CONT)

PARADISE OAKS RV RESORT
Ratings: 9.5/10★/9 (RV Park) From the Jct of I-75 (exit 321) & CR 470: Go E 100 ft on CR 470, then S 4.5 mi on CR 475 (R).

WELCOME TO PARADISE IN FLORIDA!
Paradise Oaks is a true RV park community w/first-class RV accommodations: heated pool/spa, at site wifi, best in class bathrooms, large rec hall w/kit, friendly and dedicated staff. Winter Activities galore and so much more!

FAC: Paved rds. (235 spaces). 230 Avail: 18 paved, 212 grass, patios, 18 pull-thrus (25 x 65), back-ins (30 x 65), 230 full hkups (30/50 amps), seasonal sites, WiFi, rentals, dump, laundry, LP gas. **REC:** heated pool, whirlpool, pond, fishing, shuffleboard. Pet restrict(B). No tents. Big rig sites, 2015 rates: $30 to $40. Disc: military.
(352)793-1823 Lat: 28.68838, Lon: -82.11208
4628 CR 475, Bushnell, FL 33513
myparadiseoaks@yahoo.com
www.paradiseoaksrv.com
See ad pages 329, 286.

RED OAKS CAREFREE RV RESORT
Ratings: 7.5/8.5★/7.5 (RV Park) From Jct of I-75 & SR-48 (Exit 314), E 0.3 mi on SR-48 to SW 18th Terrace, 0.3 mi (R).

WELCOME TO RED OAKS CAREFREE RESORT
Let the good times roll...staying at this amazing resort is music to your ears with weekly jam sessions and sing-a-longs. Double your pleasure with two pools, clubhouses and activities galore! We cater to rallies too.

FAC: Paved rds. (910 spaces). 500 Avail: 44 paved, 456 grass, 258 pull-thrus (25 x 60), back-ins (25 x 55), some side by side hkups, 500 full hkups (30/50 amps), seasonal sites, cable, WiFi $, rentals, dump, laundry. **REC:** heated pool, whirlpool, pond, fishing, shuffleboard. Pet restrict(B/Q). Partial handicap access, no tents. Big rig sites, 2015 rates: $37. Disc: AAA, military.
(352)793-7117 Lat: 28.67517, Lon: -82.13484
5551 SW 18th Terrace, Bushnell, FL 33513
redoaks@carefreervresorts.com
www.carefreervresorts.com
See ad pages 329, 286 & Snowbird Destinations in Magazine Section.

SUMTER OAKS RV PARK **Ratings: 7/8★/6.5** (RV Park) 2015 rates: $29. (352)793-1333 4602 CR-673, Bushnell, FL 33513

CALLAHAN — A3 *Nassau*

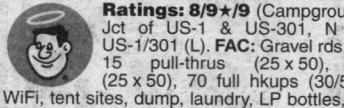

KELLY'S COUNTRYSIDE RV PARK
Ratings: 8/9★/9 (Campground) From Jct of US-1 & US-301, N 7 mi on US-1/301 (L). **FAC:** Gravel rds. 70 grass, 15 pull-thrus (25 x 50), back-ins (25 x 50), 70 full hkups (30/50 amps), WiFi, tent sites, dump, laundry, LP bottles, firewood. **REC:** shuffleboard. Pet restrict(B). Partial handicap access. Big rig sites, 2015 rates: $37.60.
(904)845-4252 Lat: 30.64492, Lon: -81.86980
36065 Kelly's Ln, Callahan, FL 32011
pattie6830@windstream.net
www.kellyscountrysidervpark.com
See ad pages 364, 282.

CAPE CANAVERAL — J5 *Brevard*

JETTY PARK (CANAVERAL PORT AUTH) (Public) From Jct US-1 & SR-528: Go E 8 mi on SR-528, then take the George J King Blvd/Port Canaveral/B Cruises Terminal exit, go N 1.3 mi on George J King Blvd, then continue on Jetty Park Dr (E). 2015 rates: $20 to $49. (321)783-7111

CARRABELLE — B1 *Franklin*

CARRABELLE BEACH RV RESORT
Ratings: 10/9.5★/9 (RV Park) From town Bus Dist, W 1.5 mi on US-98 (R).

NATURE'S SECRET ON FLORIDA COAST
Carrabelle Beach is just an hour from Tallahassee and features RV sites, cottages, lofts with ocean views, community lodge, fitness center, free WiFi, boat rentals and charters at our own Carrabelle Beach Boat Club.

FAC: Paved rds. 80 paved, patios, 34 pull-thrus (30 x 65), back-ins (30 x 40), 65 full hkups (30/50 amps), cable, WiFi, rentals, dump, laundry, groc. **REC:** pool, playground. Pets OK. No tents. Big rig sites, 2015 rates: $42.95. Disc: AAA.
(850)697-2638 Lat: 29.82963, Lon: -84.69135
1843 Hwy 98 W, Carrabelle, FL 32322
carrabellebeach@rvcoutdoors.com
www.rvcoutdoors.com/carrabelle-beach/
See ad this page, 282 & RV Trips of a Lifetime, Snowbird Destinations in Magazine Section.

HO HUM RV PARK
Ratings: 8.5/8.5★/8 (RV Park) From Town Bus District, E 4 mi on US Hwy 98 (R). **FAC:** All weather rds. 60 Avail: 60 all weather, 26 pull-thrus (30 x 70), back-ins (30 x 60), 50 full hkups (30/50 amps), cable, WiFi, dump, laundry. **REC:** Gulf of Mexico: swim, fishing. Pets OK. Partial handicap access, no tents. Big rig sites, eco-friendly, 2015 rates: $29 to $37. Disc: AAA, military.
(850)697-3926 Lat: 29.87129, Lon: -84.61003
2132 Hwy 98E, Carrabelle, FL 32322
www.hohumrvpark.com
See ad opposite page, 282.

SUNSET ISLE RV & YACHT CLUB **Ratings: 7/8★/8** (RV Park) 2015 rates: $48. (850)556-0051 260 Timber Island Rd, Carrabelle, FL 32322

CEDAR KEY — G1 *Levy*

ANGLERS RV CAMPGROUND
Ratings: 8/8★/7.5 (Campground) From Jct of Hwy 19/98 & SR 24 (Otter Creek), W 15 mi on Hwy 24 (R). **FAC:** Gravel rds. 66 grass, patios, 18 pull-thrus (25 x 60), back-ins (25 x 60), some side by side hkups, accepts full hkup units only, 50 full hkups, 16 W, 16 E (30/50 amps), cable, WiFi, tent sites, dump, laundry, LP gas, firewood, controlled access. **REC:** pool. Pet restrict(Q). Partial handicap access. 2015 rates: $25 to $33.
(352)543-6268 Lat: 29.21714, Lon: -82.96823
11951 SW Shiloh Rd, Cedar Key, FL 32625
www.anglersrv.com
See ad page 311 (Spotlight Levy County/Cedar Key).

CEDAR KEY RV RESORT
Ratings: 9.5/9.5★/9.5 (RV Park) From Jct of Hwy 19/98 & SR-24 (Otter Creek), W 15 mi on Hwy 24 to Shiloh Rd, N .01 mi (L). **FAC:** Paved rds. (98 spaces). Avail: 83 paved, patios, 3 pull-thrus (45 x 80), back-ins (45 x 80), accepts self-contain units only, 83 full hkups (30/50 amps), seasonal sites, WiFi, dump, laundry. **REC:** pool. Pets OK. Partial handicap access, no tents. Big rig sites, eco-friendly, 2015 rates: $34 to $44. Disc: AAA, military.
(352)543-5097 Lat: 29.21604, Lon: -82.97051
11980 SW Shiloh Rd, Cedar Key, FL 32625
cedarkeyrvresort@bellsouth.net
www.cedarkeyrvresort.com
See ad this page.

CEDAR KEY SUNSET ISLE RV PARK
Ratings: 8/8.5★/7.5 (RV Park) From Jct of US-19/98 & SR-24 (Ottercreek), W 19 mi on SR-24 (R). **FAC:** Gravel rds. 66 grass, 10 pull-thrus (20 x 50), back-ins (20 x 60), accepts self-contain units only, 66 full hkups (30/50 amps), cable, WiFi, dump, laundry, restaurant. **REC:** Gulf of Mexico: fishing. Pets OK. Partial handicap access, no tents. Big rig sites, eco-friendly, 2015 rates: $36 to $47.
(800)810-1103 Lat: 29.15413, Lon: -83.03049
11850 S.W. Hwy 24, Cedar Key, FL 32625
sunsetisle@cedarkeyrv.com
www.cedarkeyrv.com
See ad pages 312 (Spotlight Levy County/Cedar Key), 282.

CHATTAHOOCHEE — A1 *Gadsden*

TRIPLE C'S CAMPGROUND & RV PARK **Ratings: 8/8★/8** (Campground) 2015 rates: $30 to $38. (850)442-3333 2309 Flat Creek Rd, Chattahoochee, FL 32324

Tell them you saw them in this Guide!

CHIEFLAND — B3 *Levy*

BREEZY ACRES CAMPGROUND Ratings: 7/8.5★/7.5 (Campground) From Jct of Hwy 19/98 & US Alt 27, E 7 mi on US Alt 27 (L). **FAC:** Paved/dirt rds. 50 grass, patios, 20 pull-thrus (30 x 50), back-ins (30 x 50), accepts self-contain units only, 50 full hkups (30/50 amps), WiFi, dump, laundry. **REC.** Pets OK. No tents. 2015 rates: $20. No CC.
(352)493-7602 Lat: 29.47647, Lon: -82.74021
10050 NE 20th Ave, Chiefland, FL 32626

MANATEE SPRINGS (State Pk) From Jct of US-19/98 & SR-320, W 6 mi on SR-320 (E). 2015 rates: $20. (352)493-6072

CHIPLEY — E2 *Washington*

FALLING WATERS SRA (State Pk) From Jct of I-10 & SR-77 (exit 120), S 0.5 mi on SR-77 to SR-77A, E 2 mi (E). 2015 rates: $19.80. (850)638-6130

CHOKOLOSKEE — E4 *Collier*

CHOKOLOSKEE ISLAND PARK
Ratings: 6/9★/7.5 (RV Area in MHP) From Jct of US-41 & SR-29, S 7.4 mi on SR-29 to Demere Ln, W 0.1 mi to Mamie St, SW 200 ft to Hamilton Ln (E).

FLORIDA FISHERMAN'S PARADISE
On FL south Gulf Coast-near 10,000 Islands and Everglades Nat. Park. Fish inside the islands or in the Gulf. Kayak in the mangrove. About 30 minutes to Naples and Marco Island. Tenting, RV sites, rentals and boat marina.

FAC: Paved rds. (53 spaces). 38 Avail: 20 gravel, 18 grass, patios, back-ins (25 x 35), 38 full hkups (20/30 amps), seasonal sites, cable, WiFi Hotspot, tent sites, rentals, dump, laundry, LP bottles. **REC:** Gulf of Mexico: fishing, playground, rec open to public. Pet restrict(B). Partial handicap access. Eco-friendly, 2015 rates: $44.10 to $49. Disc: AAA.
AAA Approved
(239)695-2414 Lat: 25.81429, Lon: -81.36294
1150 Hamilton Lane, Chokoloskee, FL 34138
manager@chokoloskee.com
www.chokoloskee.com
See ad pages 300 (Spotlight Fort Myers), 284.

OUTDOOR RESORTS/CHOKOLOSKEE ISLAND **Ratings: 10/10★/10** (Condo Pk) 2015 rates: $69 to $89. (239)695-3788 150 Smallwood Dr, Hwy 29 S, Chokoloskee, FL 34138

CITRA — B3 *Marion*

GRAND LAKE RV & GOLF RESORT
Ratings: 9.5/9★/9.5 (RV Park) From Jct of I-75 (exit 368) & Hwy 318, E 2.9 mi on Hwy 318, cross over Hwy 441 (L).

CENTRAL FLORIDA LUXURY GOLF RESORT
Combine an RV lifestyle with country club living and Florida's tropical climate for the ultimate getaway. This resort features a 9-hole course, putting green and driving range; a full service restaurant; heated pool and more!

FAC: Paved rds. (457 spaces). 407 Avail: 232 paved, 175 grass, patios, 216 pull-thrus (30 x 90), back-ins (30 x 90), accepts self-contain units only, 337 full hkups, 70 W, 70 E (30/50 amps), seasonal sites, WiFi, rentals, dump, laundry, groc, LP gas, controlled access. **REC:** heated pool, Orange Lake: fishing, golf, shuffleboard. Pets OK. Partial handicap access, no tents. Big rig sites, eco-friendly, 2015 rates: $32 to $42. Disc: AAA, military.
AAA Approved
(888)842-9219 Lat: 29.41931, Lon: -82.20305
18545 NW 45th Avenue Road, Citra, FL 32681
grandlake@suncommunities.com
www.grandlakeresort.com
See ad pages 332, 275 (Welcome Section), 282, 1463 (Welcome Section) & Family Camping, Snowbird Destinations in Magazine Section.

FL

CLEARWATER — K1 *Pinellas*

CLEARWATER See also Dunedin, Holiday, Largo, New Port Richey, Palm Harbor, Port Richey, Ruskin, St Petersburg, Tampa & Tarpon Springs.

➜ CLEARWATER RV RESORT
Ratings: 9/9★/8.5 (RV Park) From Jct of US-19 & SR-60: Go E 0.9 mi on SR-60 (L). **FAC:** Paved rds. (163 spaces). Avail: 75 grass, patios, back-ins (30 x 62), 75 full hkups (30/50 amps), WiFi, dump, laundry, LP gas. **REC:** heated pool, shuffleboard, playground. Pets OK. No tents. Big rig sites, 2015 rates: $41 to $47. Disc: AAA, military.
(727)791-0550 Lat: 27.96232, Lon: -82.71532
2946 Gulf To Bay Blvd, Clearwater, FL 33759
clearwater@newbymanagement.com
www.clearwatertravelresort.net
See ad pages 271 (Welcome Section), 286.

➘ TRAVEL WORLD RV PARK
Ratings: 8.5/8★/7 (RV Park) From Jct of I-275 (Exit 30) & 118 Ave: Go W 3.6 mi on 118 Ave/ SR-296, then N 0.4 mi on US 19 (stay in right lane) on Frontage Rd to 126 Ave, W (U-turn under freeway) to S Frontage Rd, S 200 ft (R). **FAC:** Paved rds. (329 spaces). Avail: 171 grass, patios, 6 pull-thrus (20 x 70), back-ins (30 x 40), 171 full hkups (30/50 amps), seasonal sites, WiFi, dump, laundry, LP gas. **REC:** heated pool, whirlpool, shuffleboard. Pet restrict(B). Partial handicap access, no tents. Age restrict may apply, 2015 rates: $32 to $40. Disc: AAA, military.
AAA Approved
(727)536-1765 Lat: 27.88530, Lon: -82.71709
12400 US 19 N, Clearwater, FL 33764
travelworld@tampabay.rr.com
www.travelworldrvpark.com
See ad this page, 286.

CLERMONT[#] — J3 *Lake, Polk*

↑ CLERBROOK GOLF & RV RESORT **Ratings: 8/8/8.5** (RV Area in MHP) 2015 rates: $33 to $53. (800)405-6188 20005 Hwy 27, Clermont, FL 34715

↓ ELITE RESORTS AT CITRUS VALLEY **Ratings: 9/9★/8.5** (Condo Pk) (352)432-5934 16246 Citrus Parkway, Clermont, FL 34714

↙ LAKE MAGIC RV RESORT **Ratings: 8.5/8★/8.5** (RV Park) 2015 rates: $34 to $67. (800)405-6188 9600 Hwy 192 W, Clermont, FL 34714

We appreciate your business!

CLERMONT (CONT)

OUTDOOR RESORTS AT ORLANDO, INC
Ratings: 9.5/9.5★/9 (Condo Pk) From Jct of US-27 & US-192: Go E 0.8 mi on US-192 (R). **FAC:** Paved rds. (979 spaces). Avail: 41 paved, patios, back-ins (35 x 60), 41 full hkups (30/50 amps), seasonal sites, cable, WiFi Hotspot, rentals, dump, laundry, LP gas, controlled access. **REC:** heated pool, Lake Davenport: fishing, marina, golf, shuffleboard, playground. Pet restrict(B/Q). Partial handicap access, no tents. Big rig sites, 2015 rates: $40 to $50. Disc: AAA, military.
(863)424-1407 Lat: 28.34640, Lon: -81.65746
9000 US Hwy 192, Clermont, FL 34714
leslie@RentWithORO.com
www.RentWithORO.com
See ad pages 383, 286.

THE BEE'S RV RESORT **Ratings: 8.5/9★/7.5** (Membership Pk) 2015 rates: $27 to $42. (352)429-2116 20260 US Hwy 27, Clermont, FL 34715

CLEWISTON — D4 *Hendry, Palm Beach*

BIG CYPRESS RV RESORT
Ratings: 8.5/8.5★/9.5 (RV Park) S-bnd: From Jct of US-27 & SR-80 (W of town), W 2.9 mi on SR-80 to CR-833, S 35.2 mi to Halls Rd, E 0.2 mi (L); or N-bnd: From Jct of I-75 & SR-833 (Exit 49), N 18 mi on SR-833 to Halls Rd, E 0.2 mi (L).

FULL SERVICE RV RESORT & CAMPGROUND
Enjoy the scenic Florida Everglades on the Big Cypress Reservation at the Big Cypress RV Resort & Campground. Full service, pet friendly, swimming pool, cabin rentals and more. One hour from Fort Lauderdale, Naples or Miami.

FAC: Paved rds. 110 Avail: 60 paved, 50 grass, patios, 10 pull-thrus (25 x 60), back-ins (25 x 60), 110 full hkups (30/50 amps), WiFi, tent sites, rentals, dump, laundry, LP bottles, firewood. **REC:** heated pool, whirlpool, shuffleboard. Pet restrict(B). Partial handicap access. Big rig sites, 2015 rates: $40 to $50.
(863)983-1330 Lat: 26.32818, Lon: -80.99539
34950 Halls Rd, Clewiston, FL 33440
bcrvresort@semtribe.com
www.bigcypressrvresort.com
See ad pages 310 (Spotlight Hendry County), 284 & Snowbird Destinations in Magazine Section.

CLEWISTON/LAKE OKEECHOBEE RV PARK **Ratings: 9/9★/8.5** (Campground) 2015 rates: $31 to $36. (863)983-7078 194 CR 720, Clewiston, FL 33440

CROOKED HOOK RV RESORT **Ratings: 7.5/9★/8.5** (Campground) 2015 rates: $39.95. (863)983-7112 51700 E US-27, Clewiston, FL 33440

We rate what RVers consider important.

OKEECHOBEE LANDINGS RV RESORT **Ratings: 8/7.5/7** (RV Park) 2015 rates: $25 to $38. (863)983-4144 420 Holiday Blvd, Clewiston, FL 33440

Things to See and Do

AH-TAH-THI-KI MUSEUM Museum located on the Big Cypress Indian Reservation with tours, lifelike exhibits, rare artifacts & culture of Seminole Indians. See native plants on mile long boardwalk through 60-acres of cypress. Living Native Village. Museum Store. Partial handicap access. RV accessible. Restrooms. Hours: 9am to 5pm. Adult fee: $10.
(877)902-1113 Lat: 26.32541, Lon: -80.99829
34725 W Boundary Rd, Clewiston, FL 33440
carriedilley@semtribe.com
www.ahtahthiki.com
See ad page 310 (Spotlight Hendry County).

BILLIE SWAMP SAFARI Adventure in a Swamp Buggy through Big Cypress Wetland's 2200-acre preserve, or take an Airboat ride. See native wildlife including panthers, bears, bobcats, otters & alligators. Gift Shop & Cafe. Snake & Critters shows. Partial handicap access. RV accessible. Restrooms, food. Hours: 8am to 6pm. Adult fee: $20. ATM.
(863)983-6101 Lat: 26.32239, Lon: -81.05290
30000 Gator Tail Trail, Clewiston, FL 33440
safari@semtribe.com
www.swampsafari.com
See ad page 310 (Spotlight Hendry County).

COCOA — J5 *Brevard*

SONRISE PALMS CHRISTIAN RV PARK
Ratings: 9/9★/8.5 (RV Park) From Jct of I-95 (Exit 201) & SR-520: Go W 0.1 mi on SR-520, then S 1 mi on Tucker Ln (R).

ON FLORIDA'S SPACE COAST
Sonrise Palms is near the new Cocoa Expo Sports Center with easy access to I-95 for shopping, dining, beaches & Kennedy Space Center. Spend the day sunning poolside, fishing or take a stroll to enjoy the scenery & wildlife.

FAC: Paved rds. 96 gravel, patios, back-ins (30 x 60), 83 full hkups, 13 W, 13 E (30/50 amps), WiFi, rentals, dump, laundry, LP gas. **REC:** heated pool, pond, fishing. Pet restrict(B/Q). Partial handicap access, no tents. Big rig sites, 2015 rates: $45 to $50. Disc: AAA, military.
(321)633-4335 Lat: 28.35061, Lon: -80.79176
660 Tucker Ln, Cocoa, FL 32926
sonrisepalmsrvpark@hotmail.com
www.sonrisepalmsrv.com
See ad this page, 286.

RV Park ratings you can rely on!

SONRISE VILLAGE RV RESORT
Ratings: 7.5/9★/7 (RV Park) From Jct of I-95 (Exit 201) & SR-520: Go W 0.1 mi on SR-520, then S 0.5 mi on Tucker Ln (R). **FAC:** Paved rds. 75 grass, patios, 1 pull-thrus (26 x 45), back-ins (26 x 65), 75 full hkups (30/50 amps), WiFi, rentals, laundry, LP gas. **REC:** heated pool. Pet restrict(B/Q). Partial handicap access, no tents. Age restrict may apply, big rig sites, 2015 rates: $50.
(321)631-0305 Lat: 28.35501, Lon: -80.79247
245 Flamingo Drive, Cocoa, FL 32926
sonrisevillagerv@yahoo.com
www.sonrisevillagervresort.com
See ad this page.

Travel Services

CAMPING WORLD OF COCOA As the nation's largest retailer of RV supplies, accessories, services and new and used RVs, Camping World is committed to making your total RV experience better. RV Accessories: (855)244-8916. **SERVICES:** RV, RV appliance, MH mechanical, staffed RV wash, RV Sales. RV supplies, LP. Hours: 8am to 6pm.
(888)825-7549 Lat: 28.359927, Lon: -80.800581
4680 King Street, Cocoa, FL 32754
CampingWorldofCocoa.com

CORTEZ — L1 *Manatee*

BUTTONWOOD INLET RV RESORT
Ratings: 8.5/9.5★/9 (RV Park) From Jct of I-75 (Exit 27) & SR-70: Go W 12 mi on SR-70, then N 1 mi on 75 St, then W 3 mi on Cortez Rd (SR-684) (R). **FAC:** Paved rds. 58 paved, 18 all weather, patios, back-ins (35 x 60), 76 full hkups (30/50 amps), WiFi, dump, laundry. **REC:** heated pool, Gulf of Mexico: fishing. Pet restrict(B/Q). Partial handicap access, no tents. Big rig sites, 2015 rates: $37 to $81. Disc: AAA, military.
(941)798-3090 Lat: 27.46967, Lon: -82.68526
12316 Cortez Rd, Cortez, FL 34215
buttonwood@newbymanagement.com
www.buttonwoodinlet.com
See ad pages 271 (Welcome Section), 286.

HOLIDAY COVE RV RESORT
Ratings: 9.5/10★/9.5 (Condo Pk) From Jct of I-75 (Exit 217) & SR-70: Go W 12 mi on SR-70, then N 1 mi on 75 St., then W 2.8 mi on Cortez Rd (SR-684) (R). **FAC:** Paved rds. (97 spaces). Avail: 17 paved, patios, 2 pull-thrus (32 x 60), back-ins (30 x 50), 17 full hkups (30/50 amps), seasonal sites, WiFi, laundry. **REC:** heated pool, Gulf of Mexico. Pet restrict(Q). Partial handicap access, no tents. Big rig

Look in the Guide to Seasonal Sites to find places you can stay for a month, a season or longer.

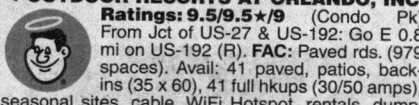

FL

See listing Inglis, FL

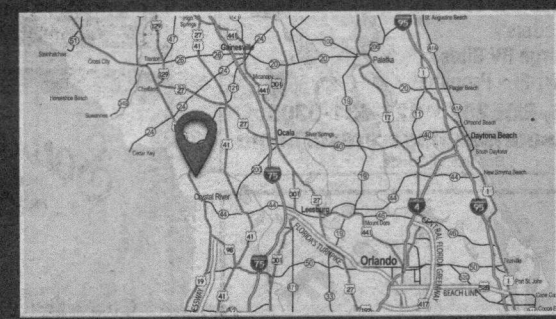

CORTEZ (CONT)

HOLIDAY COVE RV RESORT (CONT)
sites, RV age restrict, 2015 rates: $74 to $135. Disc: AAA.
(941)251-7809 Lat: 27.46972, Lon: -82.68209
11900 Cortez Rd W, Cortez, FL 34215
holidaycoverv@gmail.com
www.holidaycovervinc.com
See ad pages 333, 286.

CRYSTAL RIVER — H2 *Citrus*

← CRYSTAL ISLES RV PARK **Ratings: 8.5/8.5★/8.5** (RV Park) 2015 rates: $30 to $60. (800)405-6188 11419 W Fort Island Trail, Crystal River, FL 34429

↑ **LAKE ROUSSEAU RV PARK**
Ratings: 8.5/8.5★/8 (RV Park) From the Jct of SR-44 & US19, N 6 mi on US19 to CR488, E 3.6 mi to Northcut Ave, N 1.5 mi (L). **FAC:** Paved rds. (120 spaces). Avail: 80 grass, back-ins (30 x 50), some side by side hkups, 80 full hkups (30/50 amps), cable, WiFi, dump, laundry. **REC:** heated pool, Lake Rousseau. Pet restrict(B/Q). Partial handicap access. 2015 rates: $30 to $39. No CC.
(352)795-6336 Lat: 29.019296, Lon: -82.587617
10811 N. Coveview Terrace, Crystal River, FL 34428
lakerousseaurvpark@aol.com
www.lakerousseaurvpark.com
See ad this page.

↑ QUAIL ROOST RV CAMPGROUND **Ratings: 8/8.5★/8** (Campground) 2015 rates: $32. (352)563-0404 9835 N Citrus Ave, Crystal River, FL 34428

↘ **ROCK CRUSHER CANYON RV RESORT**
Ratings: 9.5/9.5★/9 (Condo Pk) From Jct of US-19 & SR-44, E 3.4 mi on SR-44 to Rock Crusher Rd, S 1.6 mi (L); or From Jct of I-75 & SR-44 (exit 329), W 22 mi to CR-490, SW 3.5 mi to Rock Crusher Rd, N 2.1 mi (R).

MYSTICAL MAGICAL MANATEES
This central Florida gem has a state park feel with a fun and relaxing atmosphere perfect for the whole family! Spend some time at the screened-in swimming pool, participate in seasonal activities or explore the local area.

FAC: Paved rds. (391 spaces). Avail: 291 grass, 4 pull-thrus (35 x 80), back-ins (35 x 80), accepts self-contain units only, 291 full hkups (30/50 amps), seasonal sites, cable, WiFi, laundry, controlled access. **REC:** heated pool, whirlpool, playground. Pet restrict(B/Q). Partial handicap access, no tents. Big rig sites, eco-friendly, 2015 rates: $38 to $45.
(352)564-9350 Lat: 28.85579, Lon: -82.53685
237 S Rock Crusher Rd, Crystal River, FL 34429
rockcrusher@suncommunities.com
www.rockcrusherrvpark.com
See ad this page, 1463 (Welcome Section), 275 (Welcome Section), 282 & Snowbird Destinations in Magazine Section.

Park owners want you to be satisfied with your stay. Get to know them.

Things to See and Do

↓ **VISIT CITRUS** Tourism Office. Hours: 9:00 to 5:00. No CC.
(800)587-6667 Lat: 28.8750, Lon: -82.5789
info@visitcitrus.com
www.visitcitrus.com
See ad page 294 (Spotlight Citrus County).

CUDJOE KEY — F4 *Monroe*

→ VENTURE OUT RESORT **Ratings: 9/9★/9.5** (Condo Pk) 2015 rates: $40 to $85. (305)414-8936 701 Spanish Main Dr, Cudjoe Key, FL 33042

DADE CITY — J2 *Pasco*

↓ **BLUE JAY CAREFREE RV RESORT**
Ratings: 6.5/NA/8 (RV Area in MHP) From Jct of US-301 & US-98 South (on South Side of town), SE 0.7 mi on US-98 South (L). **FAC:** Paved/gravel rds. (263 spaces). Avail: 54 grass, patios, back-ins (26 x 40), 54 full hkups (30 amps), seasonal sites, WiFi Hotspot, restrooms only, laundry. **REC:** heated pool, shuffleboard. Pet restrict(B/Q). Partial handicap access, no tents. Age restrict may apply, 2015 rates: $33. No CC.
(352)567-9678 Lat: 28.31772, Lon: -82.17901
38511 Wilds Rd, Dade City, FL 33525
bluejay@carefreervresorts.com
www.carefreervresorts.com
See ad page 406.

↓ **CITRUS HILL CAREFREE RV RESORT**
Ratings: 7/7.5/8 (RV Area in MHP) From Jct of US-301 & US-98 South (on South side of town), SE 4 mi on US-98 (R). **FAC:** Paved rds. (182 spaces). Avail: 45 grass, back-ins (35 x 50), 45 full hkups (30/50 amps), seasonal sites, WiFi $, laundry, controlled access. **REC:** shuffleboard. Pets OK. Partial handicap access, no tents. Age restrict may apply, 2015 rates: $32. Disc: AAA.
(352)567-6045 Lat: 28.29221, Lon: -82.13528
9267 US-98, Dade City, FL 33525
citrushill@carefreervresorts.com
www.carefreervresorts.com
See ad page 406.

Say you saw it in our Guide!

FL

DADE CITY (CONT)

COUNTRY AIRE MANOR **Ratings: 7/7/8** (RV Area in MHP) 2015 rates: $35. (352)523-1228 10249 Wellington Ave, Dade City, FL 33525

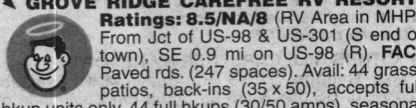

GROVE RIDGE CAREFREE RV RESORT
Ratings: 8.5/NA/8 (RV Area in MHP) From Jct of US-98 & US-301 (S end of town), SE 0.9 mi on US-98 (R). **FAC:** Paved rds. (247 spaces). Avail: 44 grass, patios, back-ins (35 x 50), accepts full hkup units only, 44 full hkups (30/50 amps), seasonal sites, WiFi $, dump, laundry. **REC:** heated pool, shuffleboard. Pet restrict(B). Partial handicap access, no tents. Age restrict may apply, big rig sites, 2015 rates: $32. Disc: AAA.
(352)523-2277 Lat: 28.31378, Lon: -82.17379
10721 US Hwy 98, Dade City, FL 33525
groveridge@carefreervresorts.com
www.carefreervresorts.com
See ad page 406.

MANY MANSIONS RV PARK **Ratings: 7/9★/7** (RV Park) 2015 rates: $18. (800)359-0135 40703 Stewart Rd, Dade City, FL 33525

MORNINGSIDE RV ESTATES **Ratings: 9/8.5★/8.5** (RV Park) 2015 rates: $29 to $35. (352)523-1922 12645 Morning Drive, Dade City, FL 33525

TOWN AND COUNTRY RV RESORT
Ratings: 8.5/8★/8.5 (RV Area in MHP) From jct US 98 & US 301: Go 4-1/4 mi N on US 301 (L). **FAC:** Paved rds. (200 spaces). Avail: 20 grass, patios, back-ins (40 x 60), some side by side hkups, 20 full hkups (30/50 amps), seasonal sites, WiFi, rentals, dump, laundry. **REC:** heated pool, golf, shuffleboard, playground. Pet restrict(B/Q). No tents. Age restrict may apply, RV age restrict, 2015 rates: $25 to $34. No CC.
(352)567-7707 Lat: 28.42010, Lon: -82.19091
18005 US 301, Dade City, FL 33523
townandcountryrvresortfl@gmail.com
www.townandcountryrvresortfl.com
See ad page 335.

TRAVELERS REST RESORT & GOLF COURSE **Ratings: 8.5/8.5★/8.5** (RV Park) 2015 rates: $35. (800)565-8114 29129 Johnson Rd, Dade City, FL 33523

WITHLACOOCHEE RIVER PARK (Public) From Jct US-301/US-98 & River Rd: Go E 2.6 mi on River Rd, then L to stay on River Rd for 1.9 mi, then S 0.2 mi on Auton Rd (L). 2015 rates: $25. (352)567-0264

DAVENPORT — K3 *Polk*

FLORIDA CAMP INN Ratings: 7.5/7.5/7.5 (RV Area in MHP) From Jct of I-4 (exit 55) & US-27: Go N 4.5 mi on US-27 (L). **FAC:** Paved rds. (501 spaces). Avail: 50 grass, 30 pull-thrus (30 x 55), back-ins (30 x 50), 50 full hkups (30/50 amps), seasonal sites, WiFi Hotspot, tent sites, dump, laundry, LP gas. **REC:** heated pool, shuffleboard. Pet restrict 2015 rates: $50.
AAA Approved
(863)424-2494 Lat: 28.29579, Lon: -81.66620
48504 US-27, Davenport, FL 33897
www.floridacampinnrecreationcommunity.com

KISSIMMEE SOUTH CAREFREE RV RESORT
Ratings: 8.5/8/8 (RV Area in MHP) From Jct of I-4 (exit 58) & CR-532: Go E 4.2 mi on CR-532, then SW 4 mi on US 17-92 (L). **FAC:** Paved/gravel rds. (347 spaces). 27 Avail: 20 paved, 7 gravel, patios, 6 pull-thrus (20 x 45), back-ins (20 x 45), 27 full hkups (30/50 amps), seasonal sites, WiFi $, rentals, dump, laundry, LP gas, controlled access. **REC:** heated pool, pond, fishing, shuffleboard. Pet restrict(B). Partial handicap access, no tents. 2015 rates: $32 to $49.
(863)424-1286 Lat: 28.20854, Lon: -81.57444
3700 US Hwy 17-92N, Davenport, FL 33837
kissimmeesouth@carefreervresorts.com
www.carefreervresorts.com
See ad pages 383, 286 & Snowbird Destinations in Magazine Section.

Like Us on Facebook.

MOUSE MOUNTAIN TRAVEL RESORT **Ratings: 8.5/8.5★/7.5** (RV Park) 2015 rates: $38 to $48. (863)424-2791 7500 Osceloa-Polk Line Rd, Davenport, FL 33896

ORLANDO SW/FORT SUMMIT KOA **Ratings: 8.5/8.5★/7.5** (RV Park) 2015 rates: $58 to $70. (863)424-1880 2525 Frontage Rd, Davenport, FL 33837

RAINBOW CHASE RV RESORT **Ratings: 6.5/7.5/6.5** (RV Park) 2015 rates: $33. (863)424-2688 6300 W Lake Wilson Rd, Davenport, FL 33896

THEME WORLD RV RESORT **Ratings: 8/8.5/7** (RV Park) 2015 rates: $48 to $58. (863)424-8362 2727 Frontage Rd, Davenport, FL 33837

DAVIE — E5 *Broward*

DAVIE/FORT LAUDERDALE KOA **Ratings: 8/9.5★/7.5** (RV Park) 2015 rates: $55 to $72. (954)473-0231 3800 SW 142nd Avenue, Davie, FL 33330

DAYTONA BEACH — G5 *Volusia, Brevard, Seminole*

DAYTONA BEACH See also Bunnell, Debary, Flagler Beach, New Smyrna Beach, Orange City, Ormond Beach, Pam Coast, Port Orange, Sanford, South Daytona & Titusville.

DAYTONA/SPEEDWAY KOA **Ratings: 6.5/8.5★/7** (RV Park) 2015 rates: $25 to $100. (386)257-6137 3003 W International Speedway Blvd, Daytona Beach, FL 32124

INTERNATIONAL RV PARK CAMPGROUND **Ratings: 9.5/9★/8.5** (RV Park) 2015 rates: $25 to $50. (386)239-0249 3175 W International Speedway Blvd., Daytona Beach, FL 32124

Wasn't that a beautiful campground you visited ten years ago? But can you remember where it was? Use our "Find-it-Fast" index, located in the back of the Guide. It's an alphabetical list, by state, of every private and public park and campground in the Guide.

CAMPING WORLD

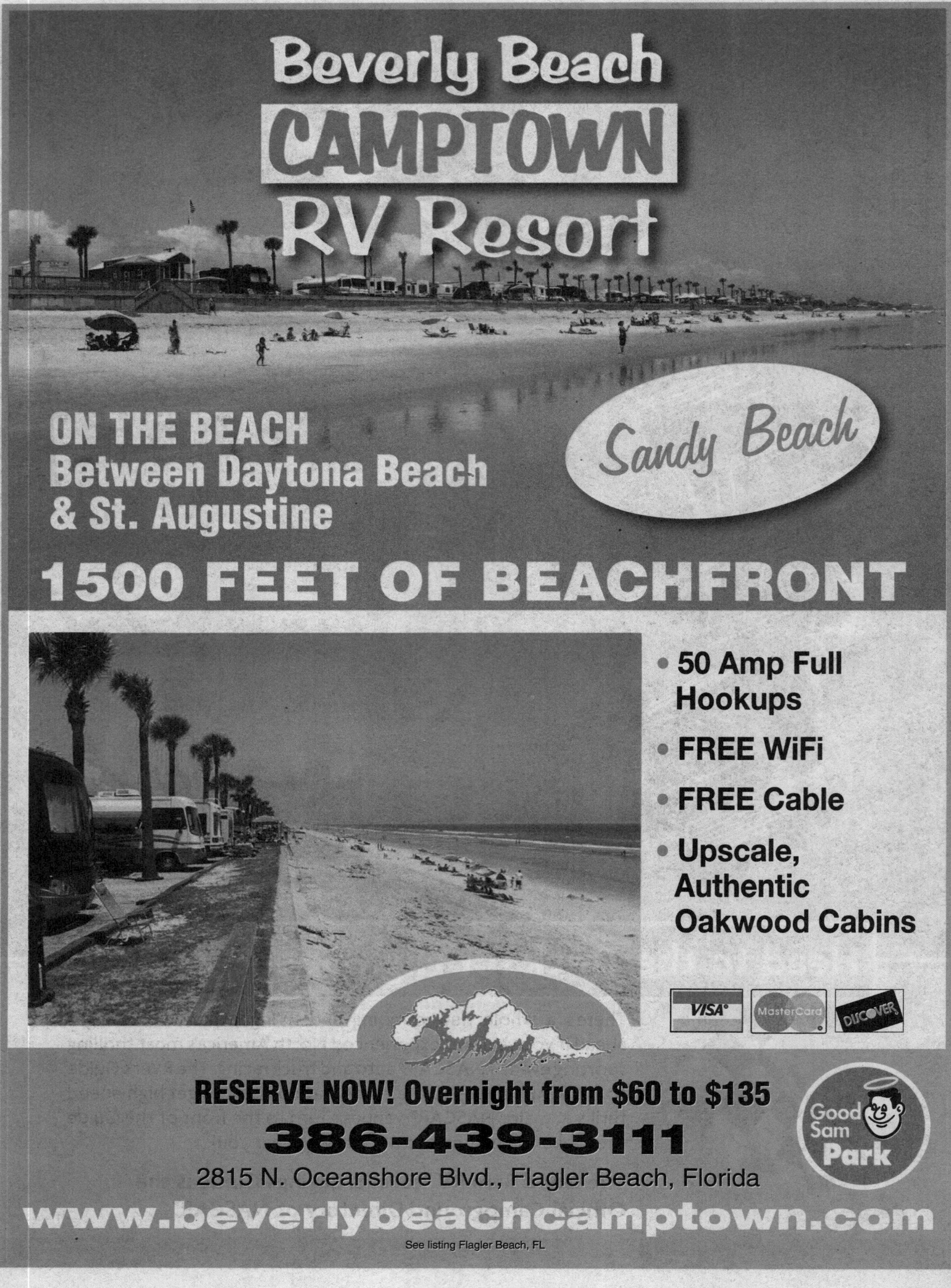
Beverly Beach
CAMPTOWN
RV Resort
ON THE BEACH
Between Daytona Beach
& St. Augustine
Sandy Beach
1500 FEET OF BEACHFRONT
• 50 Amp Full Hookups
• FREE WiFi
• FREE Cable
• Upscale, Authentic Oakwood Cabins
VISA
MasterCard
DISCOVER
RESERVE NOW! Overnight from $60 to $135
386-439-3111
2815 N. Oceanshore Blvd., Flagler Beach, Florida
Good Sam Park
www.beverlybeachcamptown.com
See listing Flagler Beach, FL

Pet friendly with miles of beach for you and your four-legged friends to enjoy the day combing the beach.

- 3 Oceanfront Cabins for Rent
- 2 Laundry Facilities with TVs
- 3 Full Service Bath Houses
- 4 Beach Walkways

See listing Ormond Beach, FL

DAYTONA BEACH (CONT)

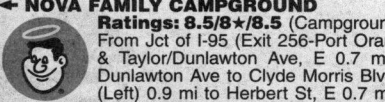

◄ NOVA FAMILY CAMPGROUND
Ratings: 8.5/8★/8.5 (Campground) From Jct of I-95 (Exit 256-Port Orange) & Taylor/Dunlawton Ave, E 0.7 mi on Dunlawton Ave to Clyde Morris Blvd, N (Left) 0.9 mi to Herbert St, E 0.7 mi on Herbert St (R). **FAC:** Paved/gravel rds. (371 spaces). 254 Avail: 204 grass, 50 dirt, 10 pull-thrus (21 x 55), back-ins (21 x 55), 40 full hkups, 105 W, 105 E (30/50 amps), seasonal sites, cable, WiFi, tent sites, rentals, dump, mobile sewer, laundry, groc, LP gas, firewood. **REC:** heated pool, shuffleboard. Pet restrict(B/Q) $. Eco-friendly, 2015 rates: $31 to $69. Disc: AAA. AAA Approved
(386)767-0095 Lat: 29.13451, Lon: -81.01434
1190 Herbert St, Port Orange, FL 32129
friends@novacamp.com
www.novacamp.com
See ad pages 336, 282.

DEBARY — H4 *Volusia*

◄ HIGHBANKS MARINA & CAMPRESORT
Ratings: 9.5/8.5★/8.5 (RV Park) From Jct of I-4 & CR-4162/Dirksen Dr (exit 108), W 2 mi on CR-4162 to US-17/92, N 1.8 mi to Highbanks Rd, W 2.8 mi. (E). **FAC:** Paved rds. (235 spaces). Avail: 56 dirt, patios, 10 pull-thrus (30 x 75), back-ins (24 x 46), accepts self-contain units only, 56 full hkups (30/50 amps), seasonal sites, cable, WiFi $, tent sites, laundry, groc, LP gas, restaurant. **REC:** pool, St John's River: fishing, marina, shuffleboard, rec open to public. Pet restrict(B/Q). Partial handicap access. Big rig sites, eco-friendly, 2015 rates: $45 to $65.
(386)668-4491 Lat: 28.89061, Lon: -81.35384
488 West Highbanks Rd, Debary, FL 32713
info1@campresort.com
www.campresort.com
See ad pages 342, 282.

▼ LAKE MONROE PARK (Public) From town, S 3 mi on US-17/92, follow signs (L). 2015 rates: $22. (386)668-3825

Things to See and Do

◄ SWAMP HOUSE RIVER FRONT GRILL Located at Highbanks Marina & Campresort. Seating for 150 overlooking the beautiful St John's River. Hours: 9:00 am to 10:00 pm.
(386)668-8891 Lat: 28.89089, Lon: -81.35396
488 W Highbanks Rd, Debary, FL 32713
gm@swamphousegrill.com
www.swamphousegrill.com
See ad page 342.

We make finding the perfect campground easier. Just use the "Find-it-Fast" index in the back of the Guide. It's a complete, state-by-state, alphabetical listing of our private and public park listings.

Average site width and length are indicated in many campground listings to give you an idea of how much room and privacy you can expect.

Got a different point of view? We want to know. Rate the campgrounds you visit using the rating guidelines located in front of this Guide, then compare your ratings to ours.

FL

DEERFIELD BEACH — E5 *Broward*

QUIET WATERS PARK (BROWARD COUNTY PARK) (Public) From jct I-95 & SW 10th St: Go 2 mi W on SW 10th St, then 1/2 mi N on Powerline Rd. 2015 rates: $35. (954)357-5100

DEFUNIAK SPRINGS — E2 *Walton*

SUNSET KING LAKE RESORT **Ratings: 9/9★/8.5** (RV Park) 2015 rates: $39. (850)892-7229 366 Paradise Island Dr, Defuniak Springs, FL 32433

TWIN LAKES CAMP RESORT
Ratings: 9/10★/9 (RV Park) From the jct of I10 & US331 (exit 85), Non US331 2 mi. to US331 North, N 3 mi to Holley King Rd, W .5 mi. (E). **FAC:** Gravel rds. 26 grass, 15 pull-thrus (30 x 60), back-ins (30 x 60), 26 full hkups (30/50 amps), cable, WiFi, tent sites, rentals, dump, laundry, groc, firewood. **REC:** heated pool, Holley Lake: playground. Pets OK. 2015 rates: $30 to $50. Disc: military.
(850)892-5914 Lat: 30.77763, Lon: -86.18099
580 Holly King Rd., Defuniak Springs, FL 32433
stay@twinlakescampresort.com
www.twinlakescampresort.com
See ad pages 344, 282.

SPOTLIGHT ON THE SOUTH

Explore America's Top RV Destinations!

Relax on white sandy beaches under palm fronds or get dancing at Mardi Gras; we've put the Spotlight on North America's most popular destinations. Turn to the Spotlight articles in our State and Province sections to learn more.

TwinLakesCampResort.com
Lakeview RV Sites
-New Bathrooms
-New Activity Center
-Big Rig friendly
-Cable TV
-50 Amp
-Pull thrus
& Suites
-Renovated
-Kitchen
-Jacuzzi tubs
Amazing views, Quiet, Peaceful, Secure right off I-10
580 Holley King Road, DeFuniak Springs, Florida
Good Sam Park
(850) 892-5914
Twin Lakes Camp Resort
See listing DeFuniak Springs, FL

DELRAY BEACH — E5 *Palm Beach*

DEL-RATON RV PARK

Ratings: 6.5/NA/7 (RV Park) From Jct of I-95 & Linton Blvd (exit 51), E 1 mi on Linton Blvd to US-1, S 1 mi (R); or From Jct of FL Tpke & Atlantic Ave (exit 81), E 6 mi on Atlantic Ave to US-1, S 3 mi (R) Note: Max 36 ft. **FAC:** Paved rds. (60 spaces). Avail: 59 gravel, patios, 25 pull-thrus (30 x 60), back-ins (22 x 47), accepts full hkup units only, 59 full hkups (30/50 amps), seasonal sites, WiFi, dump, laundry, LP gas, controlled access. **REC.** Pet restrict(B/Q). No tents. 2015 rates: $41 to $45.
(561)278-4633 Lat: 26.42749, Lon: -80.07345
2998 S Federal Hwy (US-1), Delray Beach, FL 33483
delraton@gmail.com
www.delraton.com
See ad this page.

DESTIN — F2 *Okaloosa, Walton*

CAMP GULF

Ratings: 10/10★/9 (RV Park) From Jct of Mid Bay Bridge (SR-293) & US-98, E 5 mi on US-98 (R); or From Jct of Hwy 331 & Hwy 98, W 9 mi on Hwy 98 (L).

YOU CAN'T GET ANY CLOSER THAN THIS!
Beachfront camping, designer outlet shopping, gulf fishing, golfing, great seafood, heated pool, wireless internet, deluxe luxury cabins. 22 new beautiful family-style bathrooms. 877-CAMPGUL(F) 877-226-7485 WWW.CAMPGULF.COM

FAC: Paved rds. 200 paved, patios, 27 pull-thrus (36 x 55), back-ins (35 x 50), 200 full hkups (30/50 amps), cable, WiFi, rentals, dump, laundry, LP gas, controlled access. **REC:** heated pool, Gulf of Mexico: fishing, shuffleboard, playground. Pets OK. Partial handicap access, no tents. Big rig sites, eco-friendly, 2015 rates: $55 to $165. Disc: AAA, military.
(877)226-7485 Lat: 30.37664, Lon: -86.34257
10005 W Emerald Coast Pkwy, Destin, FL 32550
camp@campgulf.com
www.campgulf.com
See ad pages 346, 282, 278 (FL Featured Map) & Family Camping, RV Trips of a Lifetime, Snowbird Destinations in Magazine Section.

DESTIN RECREATION AREA (Public Corps) From jct US 98 & Benning Dr.: Go N on Benning Dr. to the USAIC Reac. Area. 2015 rates: $20 to $24. (805)837-6423

EMERALD COAST RV BEACH RESORT

Ratings: 10/10★/10 (RV Resort) From Hathaway Bridge, W 1.5 mi on US-98 (Panama City Beach Pkwy) to Alison Ave, S 0.25 mi (R). **FAC:** Paved rds. 172 paved, patios, 25 pull-thrus (35 x 70), back-ins (35 x 65), 172 full hkups (30/50 amps), cable, WiFi $, dump, laundry, LP gas, firewood, controlled access. **REC:** heated pool, whirlpool, Emerald Lake: fishing, playground. Pets OK. Partial handicap access, no tents. Big rig sites, 2015 rates: $58 to $82.
(800)BEACHRV Lat: 30.18375, Lon: -85.78699
1957 Allison Ave, Panama City Beach, FL 32407
rvinfo@rvresort.com
www.RVresort.com
See primary listing at Panama City Beach and ad pages 386, 270 (FL Map).

GERONIMO RV RESORT

Ratings: 7.5/10★/9 (RV Park) E-bnd: From Jct of Hwy 98 & SR-293 (Mid Bay Bridge), E 4 mi on US 98 to Geronimo St, S 0.2 mi to Arnett Ln (R); or W-bnd: From Jct of Hwy 98 & US 331, W 11.1 mi on Hwy 98 to Geronimo St, S 0.2 mi to Arnett Ln (R). **FAC:** Paved rds. 34 paved, patios, 5 pull-thrus (30 x 60), back-ins (30 x 60), 34 full hkups (30/50 amps), cable, WiFi, laundry. Pets OK. Partial handicap access, no tents. Big rig sites, 2015 rates: $55 to $70. Disc: AAA, military.
AAA Approved
(850)424-6801 Lat: 30.37844, Lon: -86.36095
75 Arnett Ln, Destin, FL 32550
info@geronimorvresort.com
www.geronimorvresort.com
See ad pages 350, 282.

How much will it all cost? Use this as a guide: Rates shown are the minimum and maximum for two adults in one RV at the time of inspection (excluding any additional fees for items not at the site). Remember, these rates serve as guidelines only. It's always best to call ahead for the most current rate information.

Check out a campground's ad. In it you might find a locator map, photos, and a lot more information about the park to help you find just the right place to stay.

Dispose of old paint, chemicals, and oil properly. Don't put batteries, antifreeze, paint, motor oil, or chemicals in the trash. Use proper toxics disposal sites.

The RV That's Right For You

Which recreational vehicle is right for you? Our handy overview in the front of this Guide helps prospective buyers decide which RV type fits their lifestyle, travel needs and budget, from folding camping trailers to motorhomes.

CAMP
10/10★/9
CAMP GULF .COM
CHOOSE YOUR SITE ONLINE!
877-226-7485

See listing Destin, FL

DESTIN WEST
RV RESORT
Full Service Resort...
Island Style
Good Sam RATED 10/10★/9
Good Sam Park
Discover Northwest Florida's best new Gem on the Emerald Coast. An upscale bay-front resort featuring 54 full-service sites in a luxurious tropical setting with amenities that simply can't be matched.
Reserve your piece of paradise today!
Full-Service Hook-ups
Spacious Sites with Patios
Free Cable TV and Wifi
Restrooms with Showers
Laundry Facilities
Pool & Gulf Beach Access
Family Friendly
Pet Friendly
Accommodates Class A, C & 5th Wheel Coaches
Pull-in & Back-in Sites
Groups & Rallies Welcome
Nearby Attractions:
Gulfarium Marine Park
Water Parks
Water Sports and Golf
Shopping & Dining
Museums & Festivals
www.destinwestrvresort.com
1310 Miracle Strip Pkwy SE
Fort Walton Beach, FL 32548
800-947-0701 850-200-4533
From I-10 take SR 85 South to US Hwy 98 (Miracle Strip Pkwy). Just 1.4 miles East on US Hwy 98.
See listing Fort Walton Beach, FL

See listing Navarre, FL

GERONIMO RV resort

VACATION WITH US IN PARADISE

2 Blocks Walk to the Beach

Short Drive to 7 Golf Courses,
Large Retail & Shopping Centers,
Churches, Restaurants,
Movie Theatre,
Water Park and Deep Sea Fishing

FREE WiFi

Cable TV • 30/50 Amp

- Quiet, Secluded and Private
- Nightly, Weekly, Monthly Rates
- Pets Welcome

Good Sam Park

75 Arnett Lane
Destin, FL 32550
GPS users use Miramar Beach
850-424-6801

See listing Destin, FL

www.geronimorvresort.com

Navarre Beach
Campground
9201 Navarre Pkwy
Navarre, FL 32566
Cabins Rentals
FHU Sites
Heated Pool
Hot Tub
Shuffleboard Court
Fishing Pier
Recreation Hall
Fitness Center
888-639-2188
850-939-2188
camp@NavBeach.com
www.NavBeach.com
Good Sam Park
Legacy
RV RESORTS
You Tube
tripadvisor
See listing Navarre, FL

DESTIN (CONT)

HENDERSON BEACH (State Pk) From town, S 305 ft on Benning Dr to US-98 E, 3 mi on US 98 E to Henderson Beach Rd (R). 2015 rates: $30. (850)837-7550

DOVER — K2 *Hillsborough*

CITRUS HILLS RV PARK **Ratings: 6.5/7.5/8.5** (RV Park) 2015 rates: $30. (813)737-4770 5401 Boca Grande Circle, Dover, FL 33527

TAMPA EAST RV RESORT
Ratings: 9/8/9 (RV Park) From Jct of I-4 (exit 14) & McIntosh Rd: Go S 0.2 on McIntosh Rd (R).

EASY ACCESS TO TAMPA AND ORLANDO
Get a great location near popular Florida attractions like Boston Gardens and Disney World! Spacious and well-maintained, Tampa East has large lots, super sites and extras like heated pools, a hot tub, billiards and petanque.

FAC: Paved rds. (700 spaces). 450 Avail: 20 paved, 430 grass, patios, 208 pull-thrus (30 x 70), back-ins (30 x 60), 426 full hkups, 24 W, 24 E (30/50 amps), seasonal sites, WiFi $, rentals, dump, laundry, LP gas. **REC:** heated pool, whirlpool, pond, fishing, shuffleboard, playground. Pet restrict(B/Q). Partial handicap access, no tents. Big rig sites, 2015 rates: $32 to $55. Disc: AAA, military.
AAA Approved
(877)361-5208 Lat: 28.01934, Lon: -82.24506
4630 Mcintosh Rd, Dover, FL 33527
tampaeast@suncommunities.com.com
www.tamparvresort.com
See ad pages 406, 275 (Welcome Section), 286, 1463 (Welcome Section) & RV Trips of a Lifetime, Snowbird Destinations in Magazine Section.

Travel Services

CAMPING WORLD RV SALES OF DOVER/TAMPA As the nation's largest retailer of RV supplies, accessories, services and new and used RVs, Camping World is committed to making your total RV experience better. RV Accessories: (800)331-3638. **SERVICES:** RV, RV Sales. RV supplies. Hours: 8:00am - 6:00pm. (888)881-4719 Lat: 28.024655, Lon: -82.2446 4811 Mcintosh Road, Dover, FL 33527 www.campingworld.com

DUNDEE — K3 *Polk*

ROYAL OAKS MOBILE HOME PARK AND TRAVEL RESORT Ratings: 7.5/8★/7 (Condo Pk) From Jct of US-27 & SR-542 (Dundee Rd), go W 0.2 mi on SR-542 (R). **FAC:** Paved rds. (167 spaces). Avail: 37 grass, patios, 20 pull-thrus (30 x 45), back-ins (25 x 45), 37 full hkups (30/50 amps), seasonal sites, WiFi, dump, laundry. **REC:** heated pool, whirlpool, shuffleboard. Pet restrict(B/Q). No tents. Age restrict may apply, 2015 rates: $30. Disc: AAA. No CC.
AAA Approved
(863)439-5954 Lat: 28.0189, Lon: -81.63597
1012 Dundee Rd, Dundee, FL 33838
royaloaksmhp@gmail.com
www.royaloaksmhp.com

DUNEDIN — K1 *Pinellas*

DUNEDIN CAREFREE RV RESORT & THE BLUE MOON INN
Ratings: 9.5/9.5★/10 (RV Park) From Jct of Alt US-19 & SR-586 (Curlew Rd): Go N 0.5 mi on Alt US-19 (R). **FAC:** Paved rds. (233 spaces). 79 Avail: 55 paved, 24 gravel, patios, 18 pull-thrus (30 x 60), back-ins (30 x 60), 79 full hkups (30/50 amps), seasonal sites, WiFi, tent sites, dump, laundry, LP gas. **REC:** heated pool, shuffleboard, playground. Pet restrict(B). Partial handicap access. Big rig sites, eco-friendly, 2015 rates: $60 to $75. Disc: AAA, military.
(727)784-3719 Lat: 28.05711, Lon: -82.77418
2920 Bayshore Blvd, Dunedin, FL 34698
dunedinrv@carefreervresorts.com
www.carefreervresorts.com
See ad pages 327, 286 & Pampered Pets in Magazine Section.

DUNNELLON — G2 *Levy*

GOETHE TRAILHEAD RANCH & RV PARK **Ratings: 7.5/9★/8.5** (RV Park) 2015 rates: $35. (352)489-8545 9171 SE Levy County Rd 337, Dunnellon, FL 34431

EASTPOINT — C3 *Franklin*

COASTLINE RV RESORT
Ratings: 10/10★/9 (RV Resort) From the jct of SR 65 and US98, W .3 mi on US 98 (L). **FAC:** All weather rds. 30 Avail: 30 all weather, patios, 10 pull-thrus (35 x 70), back-ins (35 x 70), 30 full hkups (30/50 amps), cable, WiFi, dump, laundry, fire rings. **REC:** pool, Atlantic Ocean: fishing. Pet restrict(B). Partial handicap access. Big rig sites, eco-friendly, 2015 rates: $42 to $54. Disc: military.
(850)799-1016 Lat: 29.7573, Lon: -84.8372
P.O. Box 1064, Eastpoint, FL 32328
stay@coastlinervresort.com
www.coastlinervresort.com
See ad pages 306 (Spotlight Franklin County), 282.

ELLENTON — L2 *Manatee*

ELLENTON GARDENS CAREFREE RV RESORT
Ratings: 8.5/8/7 (RV Area in MHP) From Jct of I-75 (exit 224) & US-301: Go NE 1.1 mi on US-301 (L). **FAC:** Paved rds. (192 spaces). Avail: 47 grass, patios, back-ins (24 x 50), 47 full hkups (30/50 amps), seasonal sites, WiFi Hotspot, dump, laundry. **REC:** heated pool, pond, fishing, shuffleboard. Pet restrict(B/Q). No tents. 2015 rates: $43.
(941)722-0341 Lat: 27.53773, Lon: -82.48873
7310 US Hwy 301 N, Ellenton, FL 34222
ellentongardens@carefreervresorts.com
www.carefreervresorts.com
See ad pages 327, 286.

ESTERO — E4 *Lee*

KORESHAN STATE HISTORIC SITE (State Pk) From Jct of I-75 & CR-850/Corkscrew Rd (exit 123/old exit 19), W 2.2 mi on CR-850/Corkscrew Rd (R). 2015 rates: $26. (239)992-0311

EUSTIS — H3 *Lake*

SOUTHERN PALMS RV RESORT **Ratings: 8.5/8.5★/7.5** (RV Park) 2015 rates: $30 to $41. (800)405-6188 1 Avocado Ln, Eustis, FL 32726

Thank you for being one of our best customers!

EVERGLADES CITY — E4 *Collier*

EVERGLADES ISLE MOTORCOACH RETREAT & MARINA **Ratings: 10/10★/9** (Condo Pk) 2015 rates: $90 to $143. (239)695-2600 803 N. Collier Ave, Everglades City, FL 34139

FERNANDINA BEACH — A4 *Nassau*

FORT CLINCH (State Pk) From Jct of I-95 & SR-A1A (exit 373), E 16 mi on SR-A1A to Atlantic Ave, E 2 mi (L). 2015 rates: $26. (904)277-7274

FIESTA KEY — F4 *Monroe*

FIESTA KEY RV RESORT **Ratings: 7/7/8** (Campground) 2015 rates: $61 to $154. (305)249-1035 70001 Overseas Hwy, Layton, FL 33001

FLAGLER BEACH — B4 *Flagler*

BEVERLY BEACH CAMPTOWN RV RESORT
Ratings: 9/10★/8.5 (RV Park) From Jct of I-95 & SR-100 exit 284, E 3.25 mi on SR-100 to SR-A1A, N 3 mi (R).

1500 FEET OF BEACHFRONT
Come & experience our beautiful beach frontage, 1500 ft! We have clean, air conditioned bathhouses & a complete convenience store. Close to Daytona & St Augustine. Pets & clubs welcome, all sites 30/50.
FAC: Paved rds. 205 Avail: 50 paved, 155 dirt, back-ins (30 x 60), accepts self-contain units only, 205 full hkups (30/50 amps), cable, WiFi, tent sites, rentals, dump, laundry, groc. **REC:** Atlantic Ocean: swim. Pets OK. Partial handicap access. Big rig sites, eco-friendly, 2015 rates: $65 to $185. Disc: AAA, military.
(800)255-2706 Lat: 29.52104, Lon: -81.14767
2815 N Oceanshore Blvd (A1A), Flagler Beach, FL 32136
www.beverlybeachcamptown.com
See ad pages 338, 282, 296 (Spotlight Flagler County/Palm Coast).

BULOW RV RESORT
Ratings: 8.5/7.5★/8.5 (RV Park) From Jct of I-95 & SR-100/exit 284, E 0.1 mi on SR-100 to Old Kings Rd (CR-2001), S 3 mi (L). **FAC:** Paved/gravel rds. 303 grass, 100 pull-thrus (50 x 75), back-ins (50 x 75), some side by side hkups, accepts self-contain units only, 251 full hkups, 52 W, 52 E (30/50 amps), cable, WiFi Hotspot, tent sites, dump, mobile sewer, laundry, LP gas, firewood. **REC:** heated pool, Lake Bulow: fishing. Pets OK. Partial handicap access. Big rig sites, 2015 rates: $36. Disc: AAA, military.
(800)405-6188 Lat: 29.43619, Lon: -81.14486
3345 Old Kings Road South, Flagler Beach, FL 32136
bulow_village_rv@equitylifestyle.com
www.RVontheGo.com
See ad page 296 (Spotlight Flagler County/Palm Coast).

FLAGLER BY THE SEA CAMPGROUND
Ratings: 4/5.5/5.5 (Campground) From Jct of I-95 & SR 100 (exit 284). E 3 mi on SR 100 to A1A, N 4 mi (R). **FAC:** Dirt rds. 10 dirt, back-ins (22 x 50), mostly side by side hkups, accepts self-contain units only, 10 full hkups (30 amps), dump, laundry. **REC:** Atlantic Ocean. Pet restrict(B). 2015 rates: $55 to $70. ATM, no CC, no reservations.
(800)434-2124 Lat: 29.52732, Lon: -81.15090
2982 N Oceanshore Blvd, Flagler Beach, FL 32136
See ad page 296 (Spotlight Flagler County/Palm Coast).

GAMBLE ROGERS MEM REC AREA AT FLAGLER BEACH
(State Pk) From Jct of Hwys 100 & A1A, S 3 mi on Hwy A1A (R). **FAC:** Paved/dirt rds. 34 dirt, back-ins (30 x 40), 34 W, 34 E (30/50 amps), dump, firewood. **REC:** Atlantic Ocean: swim, fishing. Pets OK. Partial handicap access, no tents. 14 day max stay, 2015 rates: $28.
(386)517-2086 Lat: 29.43779, Lon: -81.10903
3100 South A1A, Flagler Beach, FL 32136
gambler@pfl.net
www.floridastateparks.org/gamblerogers/
See ad page 296 (Spotlight Flagler County/Palm Coast).

FLORIDA CITY — F5 *Miami-Dade*

CITY OF FLORIDA CITY CAMPSITE & RV PARK
(Public) From Jct of FL Tpke & Exit 1 (Florida City North/336 th St), W 0.5 mi on 336th St/Davis Pkwy to NW 2nd Ave, N 0.1 mi (R); or From Jct of SR-997/Krome Ave & 312th St/Campbell Dr (in center of Homestead), S 1.6 mi on SR-997/Krome Ave to Davis Pkwy (336th St), W 0.1 mi to NW 2nd Ave, N 0.1 mi (R). **FAC:** Paved rds. (280 spaces). 180 Avail: 20 gravel, 160 grass, back-ins (20 x 35), mostly side by side hkups, 150 full hkups, 30 W, 30 E (30 amps), WiFi Hotspot, tent sites, dump, laundry, LP gas. **REC:** playground. Pet restrict(B/Q). Partial handicap access. 2015 rates: $30. No reservations.
(305)248-7889 Lat: 25.45701, Lon: -80.47912
601 NW 3rd Ave, Florida City, FL 33034
See ad page 360.

FLORIDA KEYS — F4 *Monroe*

FLORIDA KEYS See also Bahia Honda Key, Big Pine Key, Fiesta Key, Islamorada, Key Largo, Key West, Long Key, Marathon & Sugarloaf Key.

FORT LAUDERDALE — E5 *Broward*

KOZY KAMPERS RV PARK
Ratings: 7/9★/7.5 (RV Park) From Jct of FL Tpke & Commercial Blvd (exit 62), E 1 mi on Commercial Blvd (L); or From Jct of I-95 & Commercial Blvd (exit 32), W 2.9 mi on Commercial Blvd (R). **FAC:** Paved rds. (104 spaces). 64 Avail: 9 paved, 55 grass, patios, 7 pull-thrus (16 x 60), back-ins (24 x 43), 64 full hkups (30/50 amps), seasonal sites, WiFi $, dump, laundry. **REC.** Pets OK. No tents. 2015 rates: $39 to $49. Disc: AAA.
(954)731-8570 Lat: 26.18677, Lon: -80.19780
3631 W Commercial Blvd, Fort Lauderdale, FL 33309
info@kozykampers.com
www.kozykampers.com
See ad this page.

NORTH COAST RV PARK & MARINA **Ratings: 3/NA/6.5** (RV Park) 2015 rates: $60. (954)983-2083 4500 Anglers Ave, Fort Lauderdale, FL 33312

PARADISE ISLAND RV RESORT
Ratings: 9/8.5/8 (RV Park) From Jct of I-95 & W Oakland Park Blvd (exit 31), W 0.7 mi on Oakland Park Blvd to NW 21st Ave, S 0.1 mi to 29th Ct (R).

FUN IN THE SUN YEAR ROUND
Four miles from a beautiful beach, famous shopping, finest dining in the world within a few miles. Clean & well maintained Park for your relaxation with heated pool, recreation rooms, exercise equipment, and billiard tables.
FAC: Paved rds. 232 paved, patios, 18 pull-thrus (30 x 61), back-ins (26 x 45), 232 full hkups (30/50 amps), WiFi, dump, laundry. **REC:** heated pool, shuffleboard. Pet restrict(Q). Partial handicap access, no tents. 2015 rates: $40 to $50. Disc: AAA, military.
(800)487-7395 Lat: 26.16350, Lon: -80.17158
2121 NW 29th Ct, Fort Lauderdale, FL 33311
paradiserv@gmail.com
www.paradiserv.com
See ad pages 273 (Welcome Section), 284 & Snowbird Destinations in Magazine Section.

SUNSHINE HOLIDAY MHCC **Ratings: 9/7/7.5** (RV Park) 2015 rates: $35 to $55. (877)327-2757 2802 W Oakland Park Blvd, Oakland Park, FL 33311

TWIN LAKES RV PARK **Ratings: 9/8.5/8** (RV Park) 2015 rates: $40 to $70. (800)327-8182 3055 Burris Rd, Fort Lauderdale, FL 33314

YACHT HAVEN PARK & MARINA
Ratings: 8.5/7.5/8.5 (RV Park) From Jct of I-95 & SR-84 (Exit 25) (Marina Mile Blvd), W 0.1 mi on SR-84 (R). **FAC:** Paved rds. (250 spaces). 200 Avail: 188 paved, 12 gravel, patios, back-ins (25 x 45), some side by side hkups, 200 full hkups (30/50 amps), seasonal sites, WiFi, dump, laundry, controlled access. **REC:** heated pool, New River: fishing, shuffleboard. Pet restrict(B/Q) $. Partial handicap access, no tents. 2015 rates: $35 to $83. Disc: AAA.
AAA Approved
(800)581-2322 Lat: 26.08791, Lon: -80.17221
2323 State Road 84, Fort Lauderdale, FL 33312
yhpm@bellsouth.net
www.yachthavenpark.com
See ad this page, 284.

FORT MYERS — E3 *Lee*

FORT MYERS See also Alva, Bokeelia, Bonita Springs, Estero, Fort Myers Beach, La Belle, Naples, Punta Gorda & St James City.

CYPRESS TRAIL RV RESORT **Ratings: 10/10★/10** (Condo Pk) 2015 rates: $50 to $90. (239)333-3249 5468 Tice Street, Fort Myers, FL 33905

CYPRESS WOODS RV RESORT **Ratings: 9.5/10★/10** (Condo Pk) 2015 rates: $40 to $80. (888)299-6637 5551 Luckett Rd, Fort Myers, FL 33905

We appreciate your business!

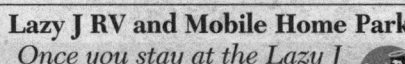

FL

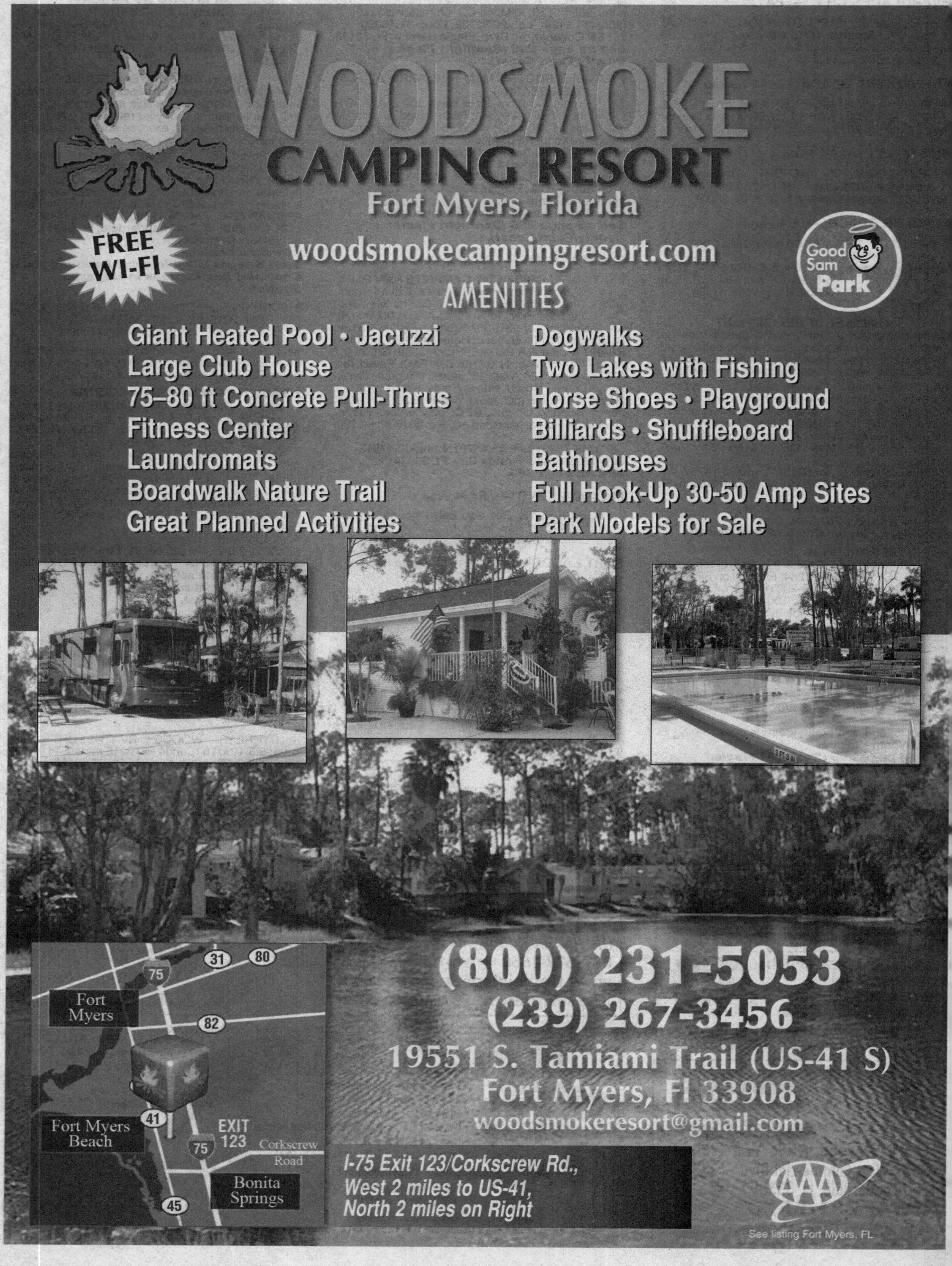
WOODSMOKE
CAMPING RESORT
Fort Myers, Florida
FREE WI-FI
woodsmokecampingresort.com
Good Sam Park
AMENITIES
Giant Heated Pool • Jacuzzi
Large Club House
75–80 ft Concrete Pull-Thrus
Fitness Center
Laundromats
Boardwalk Nature Trail
Great Planned Activities
Dogwalks
Two Lakes with Fishing
Horse Shoes • Playground
Billiards • Shuffleboard
Bathhouses
Full Hook-Up 30-50 Amp Sites
Park Models for Sale
31
80
75
Fort Myers
82
41
Fort Myers Beach
EXIT 123
75
Corkscrew Road
Bonita Springs
45
(800) 231-5053
(239) 267-3456
19551 S. Tamiami Trail (US-41 S)
Fort Myers, Fl 33908
woodsmokeresort@gmail.com
I-75 Exit 123/Corkscrew Rd.,
West 2 miles to US-41,
North 2 miles on Right
AAA
See listing Fort Myers, FL

FORT MYERS (CONT)

FORT MYERS BEACH RV RESORT Ratings: 7/7/7.5 (RV Park) 2015 rates: $44 to $66. (877)570-2267 16299 San Carlos Blvd, Fort Myers, FL 33908

FORT MYERS RV RESORT Ratings: 7.5/7.5/7 (RV Park) 2015 rates: $46.62. (239)267-2141 16800 S Tamiami Tr, Fort Myers, FL 33908

GROVES RV RESORT
Ratings: 8.5/10★/9 (RV Park) From Jct of I-75 & Daniels Pkwy (exit 131), W 5.5 mi on Daniels Pkwy/Cypress Lake Dr to Summerlin Rd, SW 7.2 mi to John Morris Rd, N 0.8 mi (R).

A FAMILY-FRIENDLY TROPICAL PARADISE
Beaches, fishing, shelling and more are just minutes away from this charming Fort Myers resort. Participate in the many planned activities, swim in the heated pool or stay active with a game of horseshoes or shuffleboard!

FAC: Paved rds. (275 spaces). Avail: 43 grass, patios, 21 pull-thrus (30 x 60), back-ins (30 x 50), 43 full hkups (30/50 amps), seasonal sites, WiFi $, tent sites, rentals, dump, laundry. **REC:** heated pool, shuffleboard. Pet restrict(B/Q). Partial handicap access. 2015 rates: $31 to $51. Disc: AAA, military.
AAA Approved
(877)540-1931 Lat: 26.50586, Lon: -81.96786
16175 John Morris Rd, Fort Myers, FL 33908
groves@suncommunities.com
www.grovesrv.com
See ad pages 302 (Spotlight Fort Myers), 275 (Welcome Section), 284, 1463 (Welcome Section) & RV Trips of a Lifetime, Snowbird Destinations in Magazine Section.

LAZY J RV & MOBILE HOME PARK
Ratings: 6.5/8/6 (RV Area in MHP) From jct Hwy 82 & I-75: Go 1-1/2 mi N on I-75(exit 139), then 1/4 mi W on Luckett Rd, then 1/2 mi S on Golden Lake Rd (L). **FAC:** Paved rds. (127 spaces). Avail: 58 grass, patios, back-ins (25 x 80), accepts full hkup units only, 58 full hkups (30/50 amps), seasonal sites, WiFi, rentals, dump, laundry. **REC:** pond, fishing. Pet restrict(B). 2015 rates: $35 to $50.
(239)694-5038 Lat: 26.65389, Lon: -81.80637
1263 Golden Lake Rd, Fort Myers, FL 33905
lazyj.mgr@gmail.com
www.lazyjpark.com
See ad page 353.

ORANGE GROVE MOBILE HOME & RV PARK Ratings: 8/8.5/8 (RV Area in MHP) 2015 rates: $60. (239)694-5534 647 Nuna Ave, Fort Myers, FL 33905

ORANGE HARBOR CO-OP & RV RESORT Ratings: 9/9★/9.5 (RV Area in MHP) 2015 rates: $30 to $70. (239)694-3707 5749 Palm Beach Blvd, Fort Myers, FL 33905

PIONEER VILLAGE RV RESORT Ratings: 8/7.5/7.5 (RV Park) 2015 rates: $36 to $58. (800)405-6188 7974 Samville Rd, North Fort Myers, FL 33917

RAINTREE RV RESORT
Ratings: 9/9.5★/10 (RV Park) S-bnd: From Jct of I-75 & Tuckers Grade Rd (exit 158), W 1 mi on Tuckers Grade Rd to US-41, S 9 mi (L); or N-bnd: From Jct of I-75 & SR-78 (exit 143), W 5.3 mi on SR-78 to Bus US-41, N 2.4 mi to US-41, NW 2.3 mi (R). **FAC:** Paved rds. (340 spaces). 110 Avail: 92 paved, 18 grass, patios, 6 pull-thrus (34 x 60), back-ins (34 x 60), 110 full hkups (30/50 amps), cable, WiFi, dump, laundry, controlled access. **REC:** heated pool, whirlpool, pond, fishing, shuffleboard. Pet restrict(B/Q). Partial handicap access, no tents. Age restrict may apply, big rig sites, eco-friendly, 2015 rates: $60 to $72.
(239)731-1441 Lat: 26.74401, Lon: -81.91631
19250 N Tamiami Trail, North Fort Myers, FL 33903
raintreerv@gmail.com
www.raintreerv.com
See ad page 353.

SEMINOLE CAMPGROUND
Ratings: 8.5/10★/9.5 (RV Park) From Jct Hwy 82 & I-75: Go 5 1/2 mi N on I-75 (exit 143), then 1/4 mi E on Hwy 78 (Bayshore Rd), then 1/4 mi N on Wells Rd, then 1/4 mi W on Triplett Rd (R).

CHARMING "OLD FLORIDA" PARK
Native live Oaks in a natural setting with the Pop Ash Creek adding to the serene landscape. Comfort of full RV hook-ups. Heated pool & free Wi-Fi. A peaceful getaway but close enough to enjoy the Gulf beaches.

FAC: Gravel rds. 145 gravel, patios, 7 pull-thrus (30 x 70), back-ins (30 x 70), 145 full hkups (30/50 amps), WiFi, tent sites, rentals, laundry, LP bottles, fire rings, firewood. **REC:** heated pool, shuffleboard, playground. Pet restrict(Q). Partial handicap access. Big rig sites, 2015 rates: $45 to $50.
(239)543-2919 Lat: 26.71867, Lon: -81.80989
8991 Triplett Rd, N Fort Myers, FL 33917
seminolecampground@gmail.com
www.seminolecampground.com
See ad pages 303 (Spotlight Fort Myers), 284.

SHADY ACRES RV PARK
Ratings: 8.5/9.5★/8.5 (RV Park) From Jct of I-75 N-bnd & Alico Rd (exit 128), W (left) 3 mi on Alico Rd to US-41, S (left) 3 mi (R); or From Jct of I-75 S-bnd & Alico Rd (Exit 128), W (right) 3 mi on Alico Rd to US-41, S (left) 3 mi (R).

RELAX & ENJOY AT SHADY ACRES
Peaceful, relaxing park in a natural Florida setting. Many activities include heated pool, on-site cafe, shuffleboard, dances or karaoke. Located between Fort Myers and Naples for shopping, attractions, casinos, or dining.

FAC: Paved rds. (325 spaces). 262 Avail: 5 paved, 30 gravel, 227 grass, patios, 7 pull-thrus (30 x 50), back-ins (30 x 50), 262 full hkups (30/50 amps), seasonal sites, WiFi $, tent sites, dump, laundry, LP bottles, restaurant. **REC:** heated pool, pond, shuffleboard. Pet restrict(B/Q). Partial handicap access. Eco-friendly, 2015 rates: $42 to $59.
(888)634-4080 Lat: 26.45757, Lon: -81.83121
19370 S Tamiami Trail, Fort Myers, FL 33908
camp@shadyacresfl.com
www.shadyacresfl.com
See ad pages 300 (Spotlight Fort Myers), 284, 268 (FL Map) & Snowbird Destinations in Magazine Section.

SIESTA BAY RV RESORT
Ratings: 9.5/10★/9 (RV Park) From Jct of I-75 & Daniels Pkwy (exit 131), W 5.5 mi on Daniel Pkwy/Cypress Lake Dr to Summerlin Rd, SW 6.6 mi (L).

GET AWAY IN STYLE AT SIESTA BAY
Resort-style vacationing with world class service. Spend a day at the beach or enjoy the active atmosphere of our amenity-packed resort. With so much to do, you'll never want to leave this tropical paradise!

FAC: Paved rds. (836 spaces). Avail: 30 paved, patios, back-ins (37 x 55), accepts full hkup units only, 30 full hkups (30/50 amps), seasonal sites, cable, WiFi $, rentals, laundry. **REC:** heated pool, whirlpool, pond, fishing, shuffleboard. No pets. Partial handicap access, no tents. Age restrict may apply, 2015 rates: $34 to $52. Disc: AAA, military.
AAA Approved
(877)326-4261 Lat: 26.49292, Lon: -81.95935
19333 Summerlin Rd, Fort Myers, FL 33908
siestabay@suncommunities.com
www.siestabay.com
See ad pages 302 (Spotlight Fort Myers), 275 (Welcome Section), 284, 1463 (Welcome Section) & RV Trips of a Lifetime, Snowbird Destinations in Magazine Section.

SUNSEEKER'S RV PARK
Ratings: 8.5/8.5★/8 (RV Park) From Jct Hwy 82 & I-75: Go 6 mi N on I-75 (exit 143), then 6 1/4 mi W on Hwy 78 (Bayshore Rd), then 5 mi N on US 41 (L).

FUN AND FOREVER FRIENDSHIPS!
Sunseekers RV Park makes memories and lifelong friendships the priority. We offer events and activities from dances, theme nights to group trips. All at the lowest comparable park rates in Fort Myers. Something for everyone!

FAC: Paved rds. (224 spaces). Avail: 61 gravel, patios, 2 pull-thrus (25 x 80), back-ins (30 x 50), 61 full hkups (30 amps), seasonal sites, WiFi $, rentals, laundry, controlled access. **REC:** heated pool, shuffleboard. Pet restrict(B/Q). Partial handicap access, no tents. Age restrict may apply, RV age restrict, eco-friendly, 2015 rates: $34. Disc: AAA. Oct 1 to May 1. No CC.
(239)731-1303 Lat: 26.75040, Lon: -81.92062
19701 N Tamiami Trail, North Fort Myers, FL 33903
www.sunseekersrvpark.com
See ad pages 301 (Spotlight Fort Myers), 284.

SWAN LAKE VILLAGE & RV RESORT Ratings: 8/10★/7.5 (RV Area in MHP) 2015 rates: $35 to $45. (239)995-3397 2400 N Tamiami Tr, North Fort Myers, FL 33903

Treat your pet to a fabulous camping experience by staying at one of the Pampered Pet Parks featured in the front of the Guide.

TAMIAMI RV PARK
Ratings: 9/9.5★/8 (RV Park) From N Jct of US-41 & US-41 Bus, S 0.5 mi on US-41 (R). **FAC:** Paved rds. (242 spaces). Avail: 186 grass, patios, back-ins (28 x 47), 186 full hkups (50 amps), seasonal sites, WiFi, dump, laundry. **REC:** heated pool, shuffleboard. Pet restrict(B/Q). Partial handicap access, no tents. 2015 rates: $30 to $34.
(866)573-2041 Lat: 26.70520, Lon: -81.90133
16555-A N Cleveland Ave, North Fort Myers, FL 33903
reservationist@tamiamicommunity.com
www.tamiamicommunity.com
See ad pages 303 (Spotlight Fort Myers), 284.

TICE COURTS & RV PARK
Ratings: 7/7.5★/7 (RV Area in MHP) From Jct of I-75 & SR-80 (exit 141), W 1.7 mi on SR-80 to New York Dr, S 300 ft (L). **FAC:** Paved rds. (104 spaces). Avail: 45 grass, patios, 3 pull-thrus (25 x 50), back-ins (25 x 35), 45 full hkups (30/50 amps), WiFi Hotspot, tent sites, dump, laundry. **REC:** heated pool, shuffleboard. Pet restrict Age restrict may apply, 2015 rates: $36.
(239)694-3545 Lat: 26.66919, Lon: -81.82218
541 New York Dr, Fort Myers, FL 33905
ticecourts@comcast.net
www.ticemobilehomecourt.com
See ad this page.

UPRIVER RV RESORT
Ratings: 9/9.5★/9.5 (RV Park) From Jct of I-75 & SR-78 (exit 143/Bayshore Rd), E 1.6 mi on SR-78 (R).

#1 RV RESORT IN SWFL IS UPRIVER
Upriver offers fun activities for active adults, enjoy our heated pool/spa - newly renovated rec hall/library/billiards rooms. New paved sites for all sized rigs. New boat ramp & the best fishing in FL. Paradise on the water!

FAC: Paved rds. (351 spaces). 226 Avail: 196 paved, 30 grass, patios, 65 pull-thrus (35 x 100), back-ins (32 x 60), 226 full hkups (30/50 amps), cable, WiFi, rentals, dump, laundry, LP gas. **REC:** heated pool, whirlpool, Caloosahatchee River: fishing, golf, shuffleboard. Pet restrict(B/Q). Partial handicap access, no tents. Age restrict may apply, big rig sites, RV age restrict, eco-friendly, 2015 rates: $35 to $79. Disc: AAA, military.
AAA Approved
(239)543-3330 Lat: 26.71156, Lon: -81.78521
17021 Upriver Dr, North Fort Myers, FL 33917
info@upriver.com
www.upriver.com
See ad pages 297 (Spotlight Fort Myers), 284.

WOODSMOKE CAMPING RESORT
Ratings: 9.5/9.5★/9 (RV Park) From Jct of I-75 & Corkscrew Rd (exit 123), W 2 mi on Corkscrew Rd to US-41, N 2 mi (R).

SOUTH FL'S FRIENDLIEST RV RESORT
A beautiful 300-site (many wooded) RV resort w/giant heated pool, whirlpool spa, 75' concrete pull thrus, planned activities, large pavilion, boardwalk nature trail, 5 shuffleboard courts. Park Models for sale. 800-231-5053

FAC: Paved rds. (300 spaces). 160 Avail: 35 paved, 80 gravel, 45 grass, patios, 18 pull-thrus (35 x 75), back-ins (35 x 55), 160 full hkups (30/50 amps), seasonal sites, cable, WiFi, tent sites, rentals, dump, laundry. **REC:** heated pool, whirlpool, Cypress Head Lake: fishing, shuffleboard, playground. Pet restrict(B/Q). Partial handicap access. Big rig sites; eco-friendly, 2015 rates: $53 to $85. Disc: AAA, military.
AAA Approved
(800)231-5053 Lat: 26.45666, Lon: -81.82332

FL

FORT MYERS (CONT)

WOODSMOKE CAMPING RESORT (CONT)
19551 S Tamiami Trail (US 41S), Fort Myers, FL 33908
woodsmokeresort@gmail.com
www.woodsmokecampingresort.com
See ad pages 354, 304 (Spotlight Fort Myers), 284, 268 (FL Map).

Travel Services

CAMPING WORLD FORT MYERS As the nation's largest retailer of RV supplies, accessories, services and new and used RVs, Camping World is committed to making your total RV experience better. RV Accessories: (800)553-9730. **SERVICES:** RV, tire, RV appliance, MH mechanical, engine/chassis repair, staffed RV wash, restrooms, RV Sales. RV supplies, LP, emergency parking, RV accessible. waiting room. Hours: 8:30am to 6:00pm.
(888)751-8930 Lat: 26.66383, Lon: -81.80018
4681 Waycross Rd., Fort Myers, FL 33905
Rhollan@campingworld.com
www.campingworld.com

Things to See and Do

BEACHES OF FORT MYERS & SANIBEL Discover The Beaches of Fort Myers & Sanibel through the new free guidebook from Lonely Planet. Explore naturally preserved islands, white sand beaches, and warm Gulf waters. No CC.
(800)237-6444 Lat: 26.64248, Lon: -81.86945
vcb@leegov.com
www.fortmyers-sanibel.com
See ad page 140 in Magazine Section.

FORT MYERS BEACH — E3 *Lee*

GULF AIR RV RESORT **Ratings: 7/6.5/7.5** (RV Park) 2015 rates: $44 to $66. (877)570-2267 17279 San Carlos Blvd SW, Fort Myers Beach, FL 33931

GULF WATERS RV RESORT
Ratings: 10/10★/10 (Condo Pk) From Hwy 82 & I-75: Go 6 mi S on I-75 (exit 131), then 5-3/4 mi W on Daniels Rd/Cypress Lake Dr, then 5-1/2 mi S on Summerlin Rd, then 100 feet E on Pine Ridge Rd, then 500 feet S on Summerlin Sq Dr (L).
FAC: Paved rds. (319 spaces). Avail: 100 paved, patios, back-ins (30 x 100), accepts full hkup units only, 100 full hkups (30/50 amps), seasonal sites, cable, WiFi, laundry, restaurant, controlled access. **REC:** heated pool, whirlpool, pond, fishing, shuffleboard. Pet restrict(Q). Partial handicap access, no tents. Big rig sites, RV age restrict, eco-friendly, 2015 rates: $46 to $82. Disc: AAA, military.
AAA Approved
(239)437-5888 Lat: 26.49298, Lon: -81.93710
11201 Summerlin Sq. Dr, Fort Myers Beach, FL 33931
info@gulfwatersrv.com
www.gulfwatersrv.com
See ad pages 304 (Spotlight Fort Myers), 284.

INDIAN CREEK RV RESORT AND MANUFACTURED HOUSING COMMUNITY
Ratings: 9/9.5★/9.5 (RV Park) From Jct of I-75 & Daniels Pkwy (exit 131), W 5.5 mi on Daniels Pkwy/Cypress Lake Dr to Summerlin Rd, SW 5.6 mi to San Carlos Blvd, SW 0.25 mi (R).

ESCAPE TO A TRUE TROPICAL PARADISE
Stay at a true gem of the Ft. Myers area with on-site features like three pools, outdoor recreation and unique activities such as ceramics. Enjoy nearby golf courses, shelling and spring training for major league baseball!

FAC: Paved rds. (1432 spaces). Avail: 40 grass, patios, 34 pull-thrus (30 x 60), back-ins (30 x 60), accepts full hkup units only, 40 full hkups (30/50 amps), seasonal sites, cable, WiFi $, rentals, laundry. **REC:** heated pool, whirlpool, pond, fishing, shuffleboard. Pet restrict(B/Q). Partial handicap access, no tents. Age restrict may apply, big rig sites, RV age restrict, eco-friendly, 2015 rates: $37 to $55. Disc: AAA, military.
AAA Approved
(877)741-8212 Lat: 26.48907, Lon: -81.94503
17340 San Carlos Blvd, Fort Myers Beach, FL 33931
indiancreek@suncommunities.com
www.4indiancreek.com
See ad pages 302 (Spotlight Fort Myers), 284, 275 (Welcome Section), 1463 (Welcome Section) & RV Trips of a Lifetime, Snowbird Destinations in Magazine Section.

We rate what RVers consider important.

RED COCONUT RV PARK
Ratings: 7/8.5★/7.5 (RV Park) From Jct of I-75 & Daniels Pkwy (Exit 131), W 5.5 mi on Daniels Pkwy/Cypress Lake Dr to Summerlin Rd, SW 5.6 mi to San Carlos Blvd, S 3 mi to Estero Blvd, SE 1.4 mi (L).

BEACHFRONT CAMPING ON THE GULF
Bask in the warm Florida sun on sugar white beaches. Go fishing, boating or parasailing, kayaking, or play in the gentle waves of the Gulf of Mexico. Enjoy staying in your RV or on-site rentals. Sizzling sunsets!

FAC: Paved/gravel rds. (256 spaces). 176 Avail: 15 paved, 83 gravel, 78 grass, patios, 12 pull-thrus (25 x 52), back-ins (20 x 30), 176 full hkups (30/50 amps), seasonal sites, cable, WiFi, tent sites, rentals, dump, laundry, LP gas, restaurant. **REC:** Gulf of Mexico: swim, shuffleboard. Pet restrict(B/Q) $. Partial handicap access. 2015 rates: $67.71 to $120.99.
AAA Approved
(888)262-6226 Lat: 26.44540, Lon: -81.93588
3001 Estero Blvd, Fort Myers Beach, FL 33931
Info@redcoconut.com
www.redcoconut.com
See ad pages 298 (Spotlight Fort Myers), 284 & RV Trips of a Lifetime, Snowbird Destinations in Magazine Section.

SAN CARLOS RV PARK AND ISLANDS
Ratings: 8.5/9★/9 (RV Park) From Jct of I-75 & Daniels Pkwy (exit 131), W 5.5 mi on Daniels Rd/Cypress Lake Dr to Summerlin Rd, SW 5.6 mi to San Carlos Blvd, S 2 mi (L).

CAMP ON THE WATER'S EDGE
Waterfront camping with big rig sites - 6 premier RV pull-ins. Great wildlife. Planned activities in winter. Extremely friendly. Family owned & operated. Loyal staff. Customer satisfaction is our main goal! Free Wi-Fi.

FAC: Paved rds. (135 spaces). 132 Avail: 6 paved, 126 grass, patios, back-ins (25 x 40), 132 full hkups (30/50 amps), WiFi, tent sites, rentals, dump, laundry, controlled access. **REC:** heated pool, whirlpool, Gulf of Mexico: fishing, shuffleboard. Pet restrict(B/Q). Partial handicap access. Big rig sites, RV age restrict, eco-friendly, 2015 rates: $48 to $115. Disc: AAA, military.
AAA Approved
(239)466-3133 Lat: 26.46811, Lon: -81.95078
18701 San Carlos Blvd, Fort Myers Beach, FL 33931
mail@sancarlosrv.com
www.sancarlosrv.com
See ad pages 299 (Spotlight Fort Myers), 284.

FORT PIERCE — L6 *St Lucie*

FORT PIERCE/PORT ST LUCIE KOA **Ratings: 7/10★/7.5** (RV Park) 2015 rates: $45 to $66. (772)812-7200 1821 Sunny Lane, Fort Pierce, FL 34946

ROAD RUNNER TRAVEL RESORT
Ratings: 9.5/10★/9 (RV Park) From Jct of FL Tpke & SR-713 (exit 152), N 5 mi on SR-713 to CR-608, E 1.2 mi (L); or From Jct of I-95 & Indrio Rd (exit 138), E 3.2 mi on Indrio Rd to SR-713, S 2.5 mi to CR-608 (St Lucie Blvd), E 1.2 mi (L).

ROAD RUNNER TRAVEL RESORT, FLORIDA
East Coast RV resort nestled in a 38-acre natural Florida Hammock. Full-service resort with immaculate facilities, pool, great recreation, restaurant & 3 hole golf course on site. 5 miles from beach & fantastic FL weather.

FAC: Paved rds. (452 spaces). Avail: 275 grass, patios, 14 pull-thrus (30 x 55), back-ins (30 x 55), 275 full hkups (30/50 amps), seasonal sites, WiFi, tent sites, rentals, laundry, groc, LP gas, restaurant, controlled access. **REC:** heated pool, pond, fishing, golf, shuffleboard. Pet restrict(B/Q). Partial handicap access. Big rig sites, eco-friendly, 2015 rates: $33.60 to $46. Disc: AAA, military. ATM.
AAA Approved
(800)833-7108 Lat: 27.48544, Lon: -80.38001
5500 St Lucie Blvd, Fort Pierce, FL 34946
info@roadrunnerresort.com
www.roadrunnertravelresort.com
See ad pages 279 (FL Featured Map), 318 (Spotlight St Lucie County), 284 & Snowbird Destinations in Magazine Section.

It's the law! Rules of the Road and Towing Laws are updated each year. Be sure to consult this chart to find the laws for every state on your traveling route.

SANDHILL SHORES
Ratings: 9/NA/9 (RV Area in MHP) From Jct I-95 (exit 129) & FL-70: Go E 4 mi on FL-70, then S 1.2 mi on US-1 (L).
FAC: Paved rds. (375 spaces). 90 Avail: 30 paved, 20 gravel, 40 grass, back-ins (40 x 60), accepts full hkup units only, 90 full hkups (30/50 amps), WiFi, restrooms only, laundry, controlled access. **REC:** heated pool, shuffleboard. Pet restrict(Q). Age restrict may apply, big rig sites, 2015 rates: $35. Disc: AAA, military. No CC.
(772)465-0990 Lat: 27.40866, Lon: -80.32557
3200 S Hwy 1, Fort Pierce, FL 34982
sandhill@newbymanagement.com
www.sandhillshores.com
See ad pages 271 (Welcome Section), 284.

THE SAVANNAS REC AREA (Public) From Jct of US-1 & Hwy 712, E 1.3 mi on Hwy 712 (L). 2015 rates: $20 to $22. (772)464-7855

TREASURE COAST RV RESORT **Ratings: 10/9.5★/10** (RV Resort) 2015 rates: $42 to $50. (772)468-2099 2550 Crossroads Parkway, Fort Pierce, FL 34945

FORT WALTON BEACH — F2 *Okaloosa*

DESTIN WEST RV RESORT
Ratings: 10/10★/9 (RV Resort) From Jct of US 98 & Santa Rosa Blvd, E 0.3 mi on US 98 (L).

WELCOME TO DESTIN WEST RV RESORT
Nestled on beautiful Okaloosa Island on the Emerald Coast of Northwest Florida. Bayview lots with access to the bay and Gulf of Mexico beaches. Gated resort with bayside in-ground heated pool and full-service lots.

FAC: Paved rds. 54 paved, patios, back-ins (40 x 65), 54 full hkups (30/50 amps), cable, WiFi, laundry, restaurant. **REC:** heated pool, whirlpool, Choctawhatchee Bay. Pets OK. No tents. Big rig sites, eco-friendly, 2015 rates: $97. Disc: military.
(850)200-4533 Lat: 30.39609, Lon: -86.58858
1310 Miracle Strip Parkway SE, Fort Walton Beach, FL 32548
info@destinwestrvresort.com
www.destinwestrvresort.com
See ad pages 348, 282.

PLAYGROUND RV PARK/MHP **Ratings: 7/9★/8** (RV Area in MHP) 2015 rates: $44.52. (850)862-3513 777 N Beal Pkwy, Fort Walton Beach, FL 32547

FOUNTAIN — F3 *Bay*

PINE LAKE RV PARK **Ratings: 8/8.5★/7** (RV Park) From Jct of I H-10 & US-231, S 15 mi on US-231 (L). **FAC:** Paved/dirt rds. (175 spaces). 135 Avail: 10 gravel, 125 grass, 72 pull-thrus (30 x 60), back-ins (30 x 60), accepts self-contain units only, 65 full hkups, 70 W, 40 E (30/50 amps), seasonal sites, WiFi, tent sites, dump, laundry, LP gas. **REC:** Pine Lake: fishing. Pet restrict(B). Big rig sites, 2015 rates: $34.95.
(850)722-1401 Lat: 30.53025, Lon: -85.39575
21036 Hwy 231, Fountain, FL 32438
pinelakerv@gmail.com
www.pinelakerv.com

FREEPORT — F2 *Walton*

LIVE OAK LANDING
Ratings: 9.5/9.5★/10 (RV Park) From Jct of US 331 & CR-3280, E 1.2 mi on CR-3280 to McDaniels Fish Camp Rd, S 0.8 mi (L).

JUST OUTSIDE DESTIN, FLORIDA!
Live Oak Landing is within minutes of the Emerald Coast beaches and features a new screened in Saline Pool, RV sites, Resort cottages, private boat ramp & dock leading strait to Chochtawhatchee Bay, the Gulf, & local rivers!

FAC: Paved rds. 63 paved, patios, 21 pull-thrus (30 x 70), back-ins (30 x 60), 63 full hkups (30/50 amps), WiFi, rentals, dump, laundry, fire rings. **REC:** pool, Choctawhatchee River: playground. Pets OK. No tents. Big rig sites, 2015 rates: $42.99 to $46.99. Disc: AAA, military.
(877)436-5063 Lat: 30.43048, Lon: -86.11936
229 Pitts Ave, Freeport, FL 32439
liveoaklanding@rvcoutdoors.com
www.rvcoutdoors.com/live-oak-landing/
See ad pages 345, 282 & RV Trips of a Lifetime, Snowbird Destinations in Magazine Section.

Take time now to plan a road trip with your pet. Read more in our Pampered Pet Parks feature at the front of the Guide.

FROSTPROOF — L4 *Polk*

RAINBOW RV RESORT
Ratings: 9.5/10★/9.5 (RV Park) From Jct of US 27 & SR-60: Go S 10.2 mi on US 27, then E 0.8 mi on CR-630A (L).

FISHING AND FUN TIMES IN FROSTPROOF
Rainbow Resort is an amenity-packed resort with friendly people and a relaxed atmosphere. Our RV sites have cement pads with space to relax. We also have RV's for rent!

FAC: Paved rds. (499 spaces). 249 Avail: 80 paved, 169 gravel, patios, 13 pull-thrus (40 x 90), back-ins (40 x 80), 249 full hkups (50 amps), seasonal sites, WiFi $, rentals, laundry, controlled access. **REC:** heated pool, whirlpool, pond, fishing, shuffleboard. Pet restrict(Q). Partial handicap access, no tents. Age restrict may apply, big rig sites, 2015 rates: $50. AAA Approved
(888)650-8189 Lat: 27.75560, Lon: -81.57477
700 CR-630A, Frostproof, FL 33843
rainbow@suncommunities.com
www.rainbowresortrv.com
See ad this page, 275 (Welcome Section), 286, 1463 (Welcome Section) & Snowbird Destinations in Magazine Section.

FRUITLAND PARK — H3 *Lake, Leesburg*

LAKE GRIFFIN (State Pk) From town, N 0.5 mi on US-27/441 (R). 2015 rates: $18. (352)360-6760

GAINESVILLE — B3 *Alachua*

PAYNES PRAIRIE STATE PRESERVE (State Pk) From town, N 1 mi on US-441, follow signs (R). 2015 rates: $18. (352)466-3397

Set a destination for family fun! Check our family camping destinations article highlighting the best places to camp in every state and province. Find a great destination, then select one of the family-friendly campgrounds listed by region.

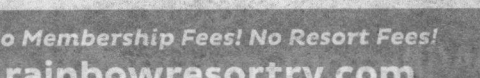

FL

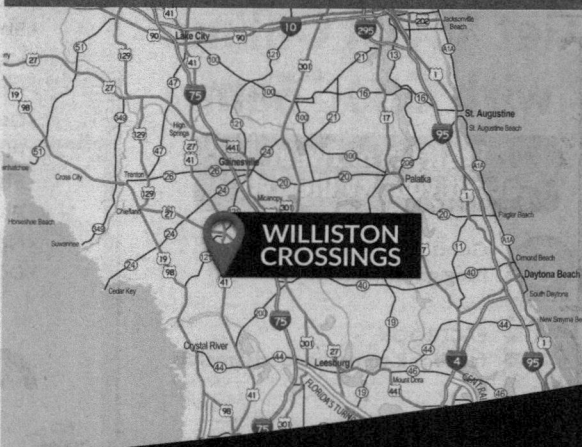

GRAYTON BEACH — F2 *Walton*

GRAYTON BEACH STATE REC AREA (State Pk) From Jct of US-98 & CR-C283, S 1 mi on CR-C283 to SR-30A, E 0.6 mi (R). 2015 rates: $24 to $30. (850)267-8300

GULF BREEZE — F1 *Santa Rosa*

Travel Services

CAMPING WORLD OF GULF BREEZE As the nation's largest retailer of RV supplies, accessories, services and new and used RVs, Camping World is committed to making your total RV experience better. RV Accessories: (800)713-2557. **SERVICES:** RV appliance, staffed RV wash, RV Sales. RV storage. RV supplies, LP, dump. Hours: 8:00am - 5:00pm.
(888)697-8004 Lat: 30.403927, Lon: -86.961284
6242 Gulf Breeze Pkwy, Gulf Breeze, FL 32563
www.campingworld.com

HAINES CITY — K3 *Polk*

CENTRAL PARK CAREFREE RV RESORT
Ratings: 8.5/8.5★/9 (RV Park) From Jct of I-4 (exit 55) & US-27: Go S 7.8 mi on US-27, then W 0.25 mi on Commerce Ave (L). **FAC:** Paved rds. (354 spaces). Avail: 68 grass, patios, 14 pull-thrus (32 x 68), back-ins (30 x 60), 68 full hkups (30/50 amps), seasonal sites, cable, WiFi $, tent sites, laundry, LP bottles. **REC:** heated pool, pond, fishing, shuffleboard. Pet restrict(B/Q). Partial handicap access. Big rig sites, 2015 rates: $33 to $38. Disc: AAA.
(863)422-5322 Lat: 28.11743, Lon: -81.64640
1501 W Commerce Ave, Haines City, FL 33844
centralpark@carefreervresort.com
www.carefreervresorts.com
See ad pages 369, 286.

OAK HARBOR LODGING & RV PARK **Ratings: 6.5/UI/7.5** (RV Park) 2015 rates: $29 to $42. (877)956-1341 10000 Lake Lowery Rd, Haines City, FL 33844

PARADISE ISLAND RV PARK **Ratings: 6.5/7.5/6** (RV Park) 2015 rates: $35 to $40. (863)439-1350 32000 Hwy 27, Haines City, FL 33844

HALLANDALE — E5 *Broward*

HOLIDAY PARK
Ratings: 8.5/8.5/6.5 (RV Area in MHP) From Jct of I-95 & Exit 18 (W. Hallandale Beach Blvd), W 0.3 mi on W. Hallandale Beach Blvd (L). **FAC:** Paved rds. (250 spaces). 138 Avail: 112 paved, 26 grass, patios, back-ins (30 x 35), mostly side by side hkups, 138 full hkups (30/50 amps), seasonal sites, WiFi, laundry. **REC:** heated pool, pond, shuffleboard. Pet restrict(B). No tents. 2015 rates: $35 to $45. Disc: AAA.
(954)981-4414 Lat: 25.98468, Lon: -80.16968
3140 W. Hallandale Beach Blvd, Hallandale, FL 33009
holidaymobileestates@lakeshoremhc.com
www.holidayparksrv.com
See ad this page, 284.

RV Park ratings you can rely on!

HIGH SPRINGS — B3 *Gilchrist*

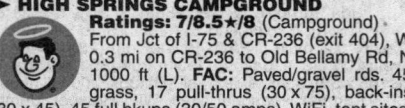

HIGH SPRINGS CAMPGROUND
Ratings: 7/8.5★/8 (Campground) From Jct of I-75 & CR-236 (exit 404), W 0.3 mi on CR-236 to Old Bellamy Rd, N 1000 ft (L). **FAC:** Paved/gravel rds. 45 grass, 17 pull-thrus (30 x 75), back-ins (30 x 45), 45 full hkups (30/50 amps), WiFi, tent sites, dump, laundry, firewood. **REC:** pool. Pets OK. 2015 rates: $30. Disc: AAA, military. No CC.
AAA Approved
(386)454-1688 Lat: 29.87520, Lon: -82.54955
24004 NW Old Bellamy Rd, High Springs, FL 32643
camp@highspringscampground.com
www.highspringscampground.com
See ad this page, 282.

O'LENO (State Pk) From Jct of I-75 & US-441/41 (exit 414), S 5 mi on US-441 to park access rd, E 0.4 mi (L). 2015 rates: $18. (386)454-1853

HOBE SOUND — D5 *Martin*

FLORIDAYS RV PARK Ratings: 5/5/6.5 (RV Park) From jct I-95 (exit 96) & Hwy 708: Go 7 mi E on Hwy 708, then 1 mi N on US 1, then 200 feet E on Porter St. (R). **FAC:** Paved rds. (87 spaces). Avail: 56 gravel, patios, 3 pull-thrus (42 x 70), back-ins (42 x 70), 56 full hkups (30/50 amps), seasonal sites, WiFi, laundry. **REC.** Pets OK. No tents. Big rig sites, 2015 rates: $35.
AAA Approved
(772)546-5060 Lat: 27.07450, Lon: -80.14159
10705 SE Federal Hwy, Hobe Sound, FL 33455
info@floridaysrvpark.com
www.floridaysrvpark.com

JONATHAN DICKINSON (State Pk) N-bnd: From Jct of I-95 & SR-706 (exit 87A), E 4 mi on SR-706 to US-1, N 5.5 mi (L); or S-bnd: From Jct of I-95 & CR-708 (exit 96), E 6.4 mi on SR-708 to US-1, S 3 mi (R). 2015 rates: $26. (772)546-2771

HOLIDAY — K1 *Pasco*

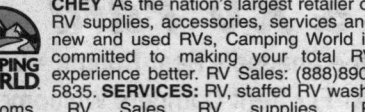

HOLIDAY TRAVEL PARK
(RV Park) (Not Visited) From jct Hwy 595 & US-19: Go S .4 mi on US-19, then E .2 mi on Continental Dr. (L). **FAC.** (613 spaces). Avail: 83 paved, patios, 18 pull-thrus (30 x 60), back-ins (30 x 60), 83 full hkups (30/50 amps), dump, laundry, LP gas. **REC:** heated pool, pond, shuffleboard. Pet restrict Partial handicap access. 2015 rates: $32. No CC, no reservations.
(727)934-6782 Lat: 28.18264, Lon: -82.73727
1622 Aires Dr., Holiday, FL 34690
HolidayTravelPark@aol.com
www.holidaytravelpark.net
See ad this page.

Travel Services

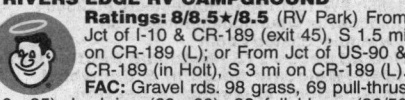

CAMPING WORLD OF HOLIDAY/NEW PORT RICHEY As the nation's largest retailer of RV supplies, accessories, services and new and used RVs, Camping World is committed to making your total RV experience better. RV Sales: (888)890-5835. **SERVICES:** RV, staffed RV wash, restrooms, RV Sales. RV supplies, LP. Hours: 8:00am to 6:00pm.
800-782-1551 Lat: 28.18991, Lon: -82.73965
2112 US Hwy 19, Holiday, FL 34691
www.campingworld.com

HOLLYWOOD — E5 *Broward*

HOLLYWOOD KOA **Ratings: 6/8/7.5** (RV Park) 2015 rates: $45 to $50. (954)983-8225 5931 Polk St, Hollywood, FL 33021

LAKE TRINITY ESTATES RV PARK **Ratings: 7/8.5/8.5** (RV Park) 2015 rates: $32 to $46. (954)962-7400 3300 Pembroke Rd, Hollywood, FL 33021

SEMINOLE PARK **Ratings: 8/8/7.5** (RV Park) 2015 rates: $40 to $50. (954)987-6961 3301 N SR-7, Hollywood, FL 33021

TOPEEKEEGEE YUGNEE/WHISPERING PINES (Public) From Jct of I-95 & Sheridan St (Exit 21), W 0.75 mi to North Park Rd, N 0.1 mi (R). **FAC:** Paved rds. 61 paved, patios, 39 pull-thrus (20 x 50), back-ins (20 x 50), 61 full hkups (50 amps), WiFi, tent sites, dump, laundry, controlled access. **REC:** pool, pond, swim, fishing, marina, playground, rec open to public. Pets OK. Big rig sites, 2015 rates: $30 to $40.
(954)357-8811 Lat: 26.040384, Lon: -80.176064
3300 N Park Rd, Hollywood, FL 33021
typark@broward.org
www.broward.org/parks

HOLT — E1 *Okaloosa*

BLACKWATER RIVER (State Pk) From town, W 10 mi on US-90 to cnty rd (Deaton Bridge Rd), N 3 mi (E). 2015 rates: $20. (850)983-5363

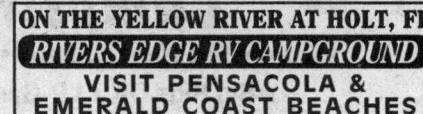

RIVERS EDGE RV CAMPGROUND
Ratings: 8/8.5★/8.5 (RV Park) From Jct of I-10 & CR-189 (exit 45), S 1.5 mi on CR-189 (L); or From Jct of US-90 & CR-189 (in Holt), S 3 mi on CR-189 (L). **FAC:** Gravel rds. 98 grass, 69 pull-thrus (40 x 85), back-ins (60 x 60), 98 full hkups (30/50 amps), WiFi, dump, laundry, LP gas, firewood. **REC:** Yellow River: fishing, playground. Pet restrict(B). No tents. Big rig sites, 2015 rates: $36. Disc: military.
(850)537-2267 Lat: 30.67731, Lon: -86.74894
4001 Log Lake Rd, Holt, FL 32564
riversedgervcamping@gmail.com
http://riversedgerv.co/
See ad this page, 282.

HOMESTEAD — F5 *Miami-Dade*

HOMESTEAD See also Florida City, Key Largo & Miami.

EVERGLADES/LONG PINE KEY (Natl Pk) From Jct of US-1 & SR-9336, SW 10 mi on SR-9336 to park entrance, W 6 mi (E). For reservations call 1-800-365-CAMP. Entrance fee required. 2015 rates: $16. Nov 15 to May 1. (305)242-7873

Check out those views! From awe-inspiring redwood giants to the soaring towers of the Golden Gate Bridge, we've put the Spotlight on North America's most popular travel destinations. Turn to the Spotlight articles in our State and Province sections to learn more.

FL

HOMESTEAD (CONT)

GOLD COASTER RV RESORT AND MANUFACTURED HOME COMMUNITY
Ratings: 8.5/9/8.5 (RV Area in MHP) From S Jct of FL Tpke & US-1, S 0.1 mi on US-1 to SR-9336 (Palm Dr), W 1 mi to SW 187th Ave, S 0.1 mi (R); or From Jct of SR-997 (Old Rte 27) & SR-9336 (Palm Dr), W 1 mi on SR-9336 to SW 187th Ave, S 0.1 mi (R).

COAST TO A JOURNEY OF DISCOVERY
Warm in the winter, breezy in the summer and perfect for your vacation. Relax and soak in the sun-drenched landscape of tropical south Florida. Reserve a quiet RV site and enjoy this resort's many amenities.

FAC: Paved rds. (547 spaces). Avail: 32 grass, patios, back-ins (45 x 80), 32 full hkups (30/50 amps), seasonal sites, WiFi Hotspot, laundry, controlled access. **REC:** heated pool, whirlpool, shuffleboard, playground. Pet restrict(B/Q). Partial handicap access, no tents. Big rig sites, 2015 rates: $50 to $66. Disc: AAA.
AAA Approved
(877)466-9758 Lat: 25.44347, Lon: -80.49385
34850 SW 187th Ave, Homestead, FL 33034
goldcoaster@suncommunities.com
www.goldcoasterrv.com
See ad pages 275 (Welcome Section), 284, 1463 (Welcome Section) & Snowbird Destinations in Magazine Section.

PINE ISLE PARK
Ratings: 7.5/6.5/6 (RV Park) From Jct of Florida Turnpike & SW 288th St Exit 5 (NE of town), E 0.8 mi on SW 288th St to SW 132nd Ave, N 0.2 mi (L). **FAC:** Paved rds. (280 spaces). Avail: 200 grass, patios, 1 pull-thru (35 x 60), back-ins (35 x 50), some side by side hkups, 200 full hkups (30/50 amps), seasonal sites, WiFi Hotspot, dump, laundry. **REC:** heated pool, shuffleboard. Pets OK. No tents. Age restrict may apply, big rig sites, 2015 rates: $40.
(305)248-0783 Lat: 25.50162, Lon: -80.40469
28600 S.W. 132 Ave, Homestead, FL 33033
mdureiko@bellsouth.net
www.campingpineisle.com
See ad this page, 1418 (Welcome Section).

THE BOARDWALK RV RESORT
Ratings: 8.5/8.5/9 (RV Park) From FL Turnpike S (exit 2): Go 1-1/2 mi W on Campbell Dr, then 3/4 mi S on US-1, then 500 feet E on NE 6th Ave (L).

GATEWAY TO EVERGLADES & FL KEYS
Gated RV resort located close to shopping and restaurants. Nearby attractions include Biscayne National Park, Everglades National Park, Pennekamp Coral Reef State Park, Homestead-Miami Speedway, and Coral Castle.

FAC: Paved rds. (310 spaces). Avail: 145 grass, patios, back-ins (30 x 60), 145 full hkups (30/50 amps), WiFi, laundry, groc, controlled access. **REC:** heated pool, shuffleboard, playground. Pet restrict(B). Partial handicap access, no tents. 2015 rates: $42 to $53. Disc: AAA, military.
(305)248-2487 Lat: 25.47142, Lon: -80.46889
100 NE 6th Ave, Homestead, FL 33030
boardwalkrv@gmail.com
www.boardwalkrv.com
See ad pages 273 (Welcome Section), 284 & Snowbird Destinations in Magazine Section.

HOMOSASSA — H2 *Citrus*

CAMP 'N' WATER OUTDOOR RESORT
Ratings: 8.5/8★/8 (RV Park) From Jct US-19 & Hwy 490: Go W 2 mi on Yulee Dr (Hwy 490), then SW .8 mi on Mason Creek Rd, then N .2 mi on Garcia Rd, then SE 0.1 mi on Priest Lane (L). **FAC:** Paved rds. (90 spaces). Avail: 44 grass, patios, 20 pull-thrus (25 x 45), back-ins (25 x 45), some side by side hkups, 44 full hkups (30/50 amps), cable, WiFi, tent sites, rentals, laundry. **REC:** heated pool, Homosassa River: fishing, marina. Pets OK. 2015 rates: $40. Disc: military.
(352)628-2000 Lat: 28.77786, Lon: -82.62368
11465 W Priest Lane, Homosassa, FL 34448
ccampground1@tampabay.rr.com
www.campnwater.com
See ad this page.

CHASSAHOWITZKA RIVER CAMPGROUND
Ratings: 7.5/9★/7.5 (Campground) From Jct Hwy 19 & Hwy 98: Go W 2 mi on Miss Magee Dr (E). **FAC:** Gravel rds. 52 grass, 10 pull-thrus (35 x 50), back-ins (35 x 50), 52 full hkups (30/50 amps), WiFi, tent sites, rentals, dump, laundry, groc, fire rings, firewood. **REC:** Chassahowitzka River: fishing, playground. Pet restrict(Q). Big rig sites, 2015 rates: $33 to $38.
(352)382-2200 Lat: 28.71320, Lon: -82.57625
8600 W Miss Magee Dr, Homosassa, FL 34448
www.chassahowitzkaflorida.com
See ad this page, 286.

The Guide gives you one less thing to worry about. Our directional arrows in service center and tourist attraction listings make them much easier to find.

HOMOSASSA (CONT)

HOMOSASSA RIVER CAREFREE RV RESORT
Ratings: 8.5/8/7.5 (RV Park) From Jct of US-19 & SR-490A, W 0.5 mi on SR-490A to Fish Bowl Dr, SW (left turn at rd fork) (L). **FAC:** Paved rds. (222 spaces). Avail: 122 gravel, patios, 32 pull-thrus (25 x 50), back-ins (30 x 50), some side by side hkups, 122 full hkups (30/50 amps), seasonal sites, cable, WiFi $, tent sites, rentals, laundry, LP gas. **REC:** heated pool, Homossasa Springs: shuffleboard. Pet restrict(B/Q). Partial handicap access. Big rig sites, 2015 rates: $29 to $39. Disc: AAA, military.
(352)628-2928 Lat: 28.79114, Lon: -82.60163
10200 W Fishbowl Dr, Homosassa, FL 34448
homosassariver@carefreervresorts.com
www.carefreervresorts.com
See ad pages 327, 286.

NATURE'S RESORT
Ratings: 8.5/8/8 (RV Park) From Jct of US-19 & Hwy 490A (Halls River Rd), W 1.8 mi on Halls River Rd (R). **FAC:** Paved rds. 310 gravel, patios, back-ins (25 x 52), 310 full hkups (30/50 amps), cable, WiFi, tent sites, rentals, dump, laundry, groc, LP gas, firewood, restaurant. **REC:** heated pool, Halls River: fishing, marina, playground. Pets OK. Partial handicap access. Big rig sites, 2015 rates: $38 to $48.
(800)301-7880 Lat: 28.79806, Lon: -82.60614
10359 W Halls River Rd, Homosassa, FL 34448
naturesresortfla@yahoo.com
www.naturesresortfla.com
See ad this page, 286.

HUDSON — J1 *Pasco*

BARRINGTON HILLS RV RESORT **Ratings: 9/UI/8** (RV Area in MHP) 2015 rates: $30 to $39. (800)405-6188 9412 New York Ave, Hudson, FL 34667

THREE LAKES RV RESORT
Ratings: 9/8.5★/8.5 (RV Park) From Jct of SR-52 & US-19: Go N 4.6 mi on US-19, then E 1.5 mi on Denton Ave (R).

RELAX, YOU'RE ON GULF TIME!
Three Lakes RV Resort offers all of your favorite amenities close to the beautiful Florida Gulf Coast. Our relaxed atmosphere and friendly staff are the secret ingredients to your vacation experience.
FAC: Paved rds. (308 spaces). Avail: 127 paved, patios, back-ins (40 x 65), 127 full hkups (30/50 amps), seasonal sites, WiFi $, rentals, laundry, LP bottles, controlled access. **REC:** heated pool, shuffleboard. Pet restrict(B/Q). No tents. Big rig sites, 2015 rates: $39 to $51. Disc: AAA.
AAA Approved
(888)316-6991 Lat: 28.38970, Lon: -82.64730
10354 Smooth Water Drive, Hudson, FL 34667
threelakes@suncommunities.com
www.threelakesrvresort.com
See ad pages 275 (Welcome Section), 286, 1463 (Welcome Section) & Snowbird Destinations in Magazine Section.

7 OAKS RV PARK **Ratings: 7.5/UI/7.5** (RV Area in MHP) 2015 rates: $32. (727)862-3016 9207 Bolton Ave, Hudson, FL 34667

A campground rating is based on ALL facilities available at the park.

INDIAN HARBOUR BEACH — K5 *Brevard*

LUCKY CLOVER RV & MHP **Ratings: 6.5/NA/7** (RV Area in MHP) 2015 rates: $35. (321)773-3661 635 E Eau Gallie Blvd (SR-518), Melbourne, FL 32937

INGLIS — G1 *Levy*

GULF COAST RV RESORT
Ratings: 9/9★/8.5 (RV Park) From Jct of US-19 & SR-40, S 0.5 mi on US-19 (L).

THE PEACEFUL NATURE COAST AWAITS
Gulf Coast RV Resort provides the perfect getaway for those looking for a tranquil and peaceful setting along the famous Nature Coast of Florida. Enjoy large sites with full hookups, a heated pool and so much more!
FAC: Paved rds. 158 grass, patios, 5 pull-thrus (50 x 60), back-ins (30 x 65), 158 full hkups (30/50 amps), cable, WiFi, dump, laundry, LP gas. **REC:** heated pool, playground. Pet restrict(B). No tents. Big rig sites, 2015 rates: $30 to $35.
(352)447-2900 Lat: 29.01739, Lon: -82.67247
13790 W Foss Groves Path, Inglis, FL 34449
www.gulfcoastrvfl.com
See ad pages 334, 282 & Snowbird Destinations in Magazine Section.

ISLAMORADA — F5 *Monroe*

SAN PEDRO VILLAGE CAREFREE RV RESORT **Ratings: 2.5/NA/7** (RV Park) 2015 rates: $70. (305)289-0011 87401 Old Hwy, Islamorada, FL 33036

JACKSONVILLE — A4 *Duval*

JACKSONVILLE See also Callahan, St Augustine & Yulee, and Kingsland, GA.

It's the law! Rules of the Road and Towing Laws are updated each year. Be sure to consult this chart to find the laws for every state on your traveling route.

FL

PECAN PARK
—RV RESORT—

Jacksonville's Newest RV Resort

Reserve Now! 904.751.6770

Free WiFi & 80+ Cable Channels
All Sites 20, 30, & 50 Amp Service
Large Clubhouse with Kitchen

Rallies Welcome!

Huge PULL THRU Sites

Lakeside Pool

NEW Rec Room & Exercise Facilities

Next To
PECAN PARK
Flea & Farmers' Market

Free Admission Free Parking FREE FUN!!!
www.PecanPark.net

Exit 366 West off I-95
0.2 miles on the left

650 Pecan Park Road, Jacksonville, FL 32218
www.PecanParkRVResort.com

Good Sam Park

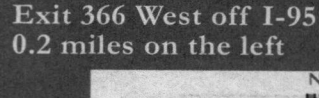

See listing Jacksonville, FL

See listing Jacksonville, FL

FL

JACKSONVILLE (CONT)

COUNTRY OAKS CAMPGROUND & RV PARK
Ratings: 8.5/9★/8.5 (RV Park) From North Jct I-295 & I-95: Go 19 mi N on I-95 (GA exit 1), then 1/4 mi W on St. Mary's Rd. (L). **FAC:** Paved rds. (43 spaces). Avail: 23 gravel, 18 pull-thrus (28 x 60), back-ins (30 x 30), 23 full hkups (30/50 amps), seasonal sites, WiFi, laundry, LP gas, firewood. **REC:** pond, fishing. Pets OK. Partial handicap access, no tents. Big rig sites, 2015 rates: $34.
(912)729-6212 Lat: 30.76032, Lon: -81.65920
6 Carlton Cemetery Rd, Kingsland, GA 31548
www.countryoaksrv.com
See primary listing at Kingsland, GA and ad page 361.

FLAMINGO LAKE RV RESORT
Ratings: 9/9.5★/9.5 (RV Park) From Jct of I-295 & Lem Turner Rd exit 32, W 0.1 mi on Lem Turner Rd to Newcomb Rd, S 100 yds (E).

FLAMINGO LAKE HAS IT ALL
A beautiful park, manicured around a 17 acre lake, pristine seclusion, minutes from beaches, airport & downtown, but you won't want to leave our onsite beach, water toys & restaurant.

FAC: Paved/gravel rds. 288 Avail: 158 paved, 130 gravel, patios, 116 pull-thrus (35 x 60), back-ins (35 x 60), 288 full hkups (30/50 amps), cable, WiFi, dump, laundry, LP gas, restaurant, controlled access. **REC:** heated pool, Flamingo Lake: fishing, playground. Pet restrict(B). Partial handicap access, no tents. Big rig sites, eco-friendly, 2015 rates: $44. Disc: AAA, military. ATM.
AAA Approved
(800)782-4323 Lat: 30.45602, Lon: -81.70847
3640 Newcomb Rd, Jacksonville, FL 32218
customer.service@flamingolake.com
www.flamingolake.com
See ad pages 363, 282.

Like Us on Facebook.

FLEETWOOD MHP RV PARK Ratings: 6/8.5★/7 (RV Area in MHP) From the jct of I-95 & Bowden Rd (exit 345), W 0.2 mi on Bowden Rd to Phillips Hwy (US 1), N 0.2 mi (R). **FAC:** Paved rds. 84 Avail: 15 paved, 69 grass, patios, 11 pull-thrus (27 x 60), back-ins (27 x 50), 84 full hkups (30/50 amps), WiFi, dump, laundry. Pets OK. 2015 rates: $34.
(904)737-4733 Lat: 30.2713, Lon: -81.6218
5001 Phillips Hwy, Jacksonville, FL 32207
fleetwoodrvpark@aol.com

HANNA PARK CAMPGROUND (Public) From Jct of SR-10 (Atlantic Ave) & A1A (Mayport Rd), N 2 mi on A1A (Mayport Rd) until becomes CR-101, N 1 mi to Wonderwood Dr, E 0.1 mi (E). 2015 rates: $33.90. (904)249-4700

LITTLE TALBOT ISLAND (State Pk) From Jct of I-95 & SR-A1A exit 373, E 32.4 mi on SR-A1A (L). 2015 rates: $24. (904)251-2320

PECAN PARK RV RESORT
Ratings: 10/9★/9.5 (RV Park) From Jct of I-95 & Pecan Park Rd Exit 366, W 0.1 mi on Pecan Park Rd (L).

******FROM ORLANDO TO SAVANNAH******
Stay with us at Jacksonville's newest, finest resort! Mins. to Alltel Stadium, airport, Mayo Clinic, & attractions from Orlando to Savannah. Adjacent to flea & farmers market, we offer 183 FHU luxury sites incl. cable & WIFI.

FAC: Paved rds. 183 paved, patios, 183 pull-thrus (40 x 70), accepts self-contain units only, 183 full hkups (30/50 amps), cable, WiFi, dump, laundry, LP gas. **REC:** pool, pond. Pets OK. Partial handicap access, no tents. Big rig sites, 2015 rates: $44. Disc: military.
(904)751-6770 Lat: 30.51741, Lon: -81.63950
650 Pecan Park Rd, Jacksonville, FL 32218
info@pecanpark.net
www.pecanparkrvresort.com
See ad pages 362, 282.

Travel Services

CAMPING WORLD OF JACKSONVILLE As the nation's largest retailer of RV supplies, accessories, services and new and used RVs, Camping World is committed to making your total RV experience better. RV Accessories: (855)277-1218. **SERVICES:** RV, tire, RV appliance, staffed RV wash, RV Sales. RV supplies, LP. Hours: 8:00am - 6:00 pm.
(888)615-8824 Lat: 30.421820, Lon: -81.658268
10101 Interstate Center Drive, Jacksonville, FL 32218
www.campingworld.com

Get the Facts! Essential tips and travel info for can be found in the Welcome Section at the beginning of each State/Province.

Things to See and Do

PECAN PARK FLEA & FARMERS MARKET
North Florida's largest Flea & Farmer's Market. Adjacent to Jacksonville's newest & finest RV Resort, Pecan Park. EZ on/off I-95, Exit 366. Partial handicap access. Hours: 8am to 5pm. No CC.
(904)751-6770 Lat: 30.51618, Lon: -81.63883
614 Pecan Park Rd, Jacksonville, FL 32218
info@pecanpark.net
www.pecanparkrvresort.com
See ad page 362.

JENNINGS — A2 *Hamilton*

JENNINGS OUTDOOR RESORT CAMPGROUND
Ratings: 8.5/8.5★/7.5 (RV Park) From Jct of I-75 & SR-143 (Exit 467), W 0.1 mi on SR-143 (R). **FAC:** Paved rds. 102 paved, patios, 102 pull-thrus (25 x 60), 102 full hkups (30/50 amps), cable, WiFi, dump, laundry, groc, LP gas. **REC:** pool, pond, fishing, shuffleboard, playground. Pets OK. No tents. Big rig sites, 2015 rates: $30 to $35. Disc: AAA.
(386)938-3321 Lat: 30.59244, Lon: -83.12398
2039 Hamilton Ave, Jennings, FL 32053
jor@windstream.net
www.jenningsoutdoorresort.com
See ad pages 439, 282.

JUNO BEACH — D5 *Palm Beach*

JUNO OCEAN WALK RV RESORT
Ratings: 9.5/10★/9.5 (Condo Pk) From Jct of I-95 & Exit 83, Donald Ross Rd, E 4.4 mi on Donald Ross Rd to US 1, N 0.8 mi to Juno Ocean Walk, W 0.2 mi (R). **FAC:** Paved rds. (246 spaces). Avail: 70 paved, patios, back-ins (30 x 50), accepts full hkup units only, 70 full hkups (30/50 amps), seasonal sites, cable, WiFi $, rentals, laundry. **REC:** heated pool, whirlpool, shuffleboard, playground. Pet restrict(Q). Partial handicap access, no tents. Big rig sites, 2015 rates: $35 to $74.96.
(561)622-7500 Lat: 26.89272, Lon: -80.06228
900 Juno Ocean Walk, Juno Beach, FL 33408
jowca-rental@comcast.net
www.junooceanwalkrvresort.com
See ad this page.

JUPITER — D5 *Palm Beach*

WEST JUPITER CAMPING RESORT
Ratings: 9/8.5★/7.5 (Campground) From Jct of I-95 & SR-706/Indian Town Rd (exit 87B), W 5.2 mi on SR-706 to 130th Ave, S (left) 0.25 mi (R); or From Jct of FL Tpke & SR-706/Indian Town Rd (exit 116), W 5 mi on SR-706 to 130th Ave, S (left) 0.25 mi (R). **FAC:** Paved rds. (101 spaces). 91 Avail: 71 paved, 15 gravel, 5 grass, patios, 5 pull-thrus (28 x 50), back-ins (26 x 50), 91 full hkups (30/50 amps), seasonal sites, cable, WiFi, rentals, dump, laundry, groc, LP bottles, fire rings, firewood, controlled access. **REC:** heated pool, pond, fishing, shuf-

JUPITER (CONT)

WEST JUPITER CAMPING (CONT)
fleboard, playground. Pet restrict(B). Partial handicap access, no tents. Eco-friendly, 2015 rates: $30 to $51. Disc: AAA, military.
(888)746-6073 Lat: 26.93954, Lon: -80.23945
17801 130th Avenue N, Jupiter, FL 33478
wjcr@bellsouth.net
www.westjupitercampingresort.com
See ad opposite page, 284.

KENANSVILLE — K5 *Osceola*

LAKE MARIAN PARADISE MARINA & RV RESORT
Ratings: 8/8★/7.5 (RV Park) From Jct US-441 & Hwy 523: Go W 3.25 mi on Hwy 523, then S 0.5 mi on Arnold Rd (E). **FAC:** Paved/gravel rds. (126 spaces). 25 Avail: 12 gravel, 13 grass, 8 pull-thrus (24 x 107), back-ins (22 x 41), some side by side hkups, 25 full hkups (30/50 amps), seasonal sites, WiFi, rentals, dump, laundry, groc, LP gas. **REC:** Lake Marian: fishing, marina, shuffleboard. Pet restrict(B). No tents. Big rig sites, 2015 rates: $33 to $38. Disc: AAA.
AAA Approved
(407)436-1464 Lat: 27.87023, Lon: -81.04365
901 Arnold Rd, Kenansville, FL 34739
lakemarian@embarqmail.com
www.lakemarian.com

KEY LARGO — F5 *Monroe*

CALUSA CAMPGROUND **Ratings: 8.5/10★/8.5** (Condo Pk) 2015 rates: $52 to $95. (305)451-0232 325 Calusa Street, Key Largo, FL 33037

JOHN PENNEKAMP CORAL REEF (State Pk) S-bnd: On US-1 at MP-102.5 (L). 2015 rates: $32. (800)326-3521

KEY LARGO KAMPGROUND & MARINA **Ratings: 8/8/9** (Condo Pk) 2015 rates: $65 to $90. (305)451-1431 101551 Overseas Hwy, Key Largo, FL 33037

KEYS PALMS RV RESORT
(RV Resort) (Not Visited) S-bnd: On US-1 at MM 104 (R). **FAC:** Paved rds. 30 Avail: 30 all weather, patios, 8 pull-thrus (25 x 70), back-ins (25 x 70), accepts full hkup units only, 30 full hkups (30/50 amps), cable, WiFi, laundry, groc, controlled access. **REC:** pool, whirlpool, Gulf of Mexico: fishing. Pet restrict Partial handicap access. Big rig sites, 2015 rates: $125.
(855)786-6104 Lat: 25.14680, Lon: -80.39523
104200 Overseas Hwy, Key Largo, FL 33037
www.keyspalmsrvresort.com
See ad this page.

KINGS KAMP, RV, TENT & MARINA **Ratings: 5.5/9★/7** (Campground) 2015 rates: $50 to $75. (305)451-0010 103620 Overseas Hwy, Key Largo, FL 33037

RIPTIDE RV & MOTEL CAREFREE RV RESORT
Ratings: 7/8★/7.5 (RV Park) S-bnd: On US 1 at MP 97 (R). **FAC:** Paved rds. 38 gravel, patios, back-ins (25 x 40), some side by side hkups, 38 full hkups (30/50 amps), cable, WiFi, tent sites, rentals, dump, laundry. **REC:** Gulf of Mexico: swim, fishing, shuffleboard. Pet restrict(B/Q). Partial handicap access. 2015 rates: $53 to $93. Disc: AAA, military.
(305)852-8481 Lat: 25.07628, Lon: -80.46124
97680 Overseas Hwy, Key Largo, FL 33037
riptide@carefreervresorts.com
www.carefreervresorts.com
See ad opposite page, 284.

KEY WEST — F4 *Monroe*

KEY WEST See also Bahia Honda Key, Big Pine Key, Cudjoe Key, Fiesta Key, Islamorada, Key Largo, Long Key, Marathon & Sugarloaf Key.

BLUEWATER KEY RV RESORT **Ratings: 9.5/9.5★/10** (Condo Pk) S-bnd: On US-1 at MP-14.5 (L). **FAC:** Paved rds. (81 spaces). Avail: 66 paved, patios, back-ins (35 x 75), accepts full hkup units only, 66 full hkups (30/50 amps), cable, WiFi, laundry, controlled access. **REC:** heated pool, Bluewater Bay: fishing. Pet restrict(Q). Partial handicap access, no tents. Big rig sites, 2015 rates: $84 to $175.
AAA Approved
(305)745-2494 Lat: 24.62358, Lon: -81.60033
2950 US Hwy 1, Key West, FL 33040
bluekeyrv@aol.com
www.bluewaterkey.com

Our travel services section will help you find services that you'll find handy in your travels.

BOYD'S KEY WEST CAMPGROUND
Ratings: 8.5/8.5/9.5 (Campground) From Jct of US-1 & 3rd St at MP-5, S 0.2 mi on 3rd St to MacDonald Ave/Maloney Ave, E 0.3 mi (L). **FAC:** Paved rds. (203 spaces). 163 Avail: 35 gravel, 25 grass, 103 dirt, patios, back-ins (24 x 44), 163 full hkups (30/50 amps), seasonal sites, cable, WiFi, tent sites, dump, laundry, groc, firewood, controlled access. **REC:** heated pool, Atlantic Ocean: fishing. Pet restrict(B). Partial handicap access. 2015 rates: $55 to $126. ATM.
AAA Approved
(305)294-1465 Lat: 24.57111, Lon: -81.73372
6401 Maloney Ave, Key West, FL 33040
info@boydscampground.com
www.boydscampground.com
See ad this page & Snowbird Destinations in Magazine Section.

Things to See and Do

BIG PINE KEY & FLORIDA LOWER KEYS FL
Keys campground & RV facilities range from small properties with basic amenities to waterfront campground resorts, inc heated pools, hot tubs, onsite laundries, gift/con stores, marina/docking facilities & restaurants. Busy in winter.
DOESN'T GET MORE LOW KEY THAN THIS
Talk about truth in advertising. No crowds. No Noise. And unlimited biking, hiking, camping and kayaking. Big Pine Key and the Lower Keys is exactly as the name implies.
no CC.
(800)USA-ESCAPE Lat: 24.669071, Lon: -81.347563
webeditor@fla-keys.com
www.fla-keys.com/lowerkeys
See ad Magazine Section page 141.

KEYSTONE HEIGHTS — B3 *Clay*

MIKE ROESS GOLD HEAD BRANCH (State Pk) From Jct of SR-100 & SR-21, NE 6 mi on SR-21 (R). 2015 rates: $20. (352)473-4701

KISSIMMEE — J4 *Osceola*

KISSIMMEE See also Clermont, Davenport, Haines City, Lake Buena Vista, Orlando, Polk City, Sanford, Titusville & Winter Haven.

FL

KISSIMMEE (CONT)

↗ BOGGY CREEK RESORT & RV PARK **Ratings: 8/7.5/7** (Campground) 2015 rates: $40 to $45. (407)348-2040 3705 Big Bass Rd, Kissimmee, FL 34744

← **DISNEY'S FORT WILDERNESS RESORT & CAMPGROUND**
Ratings: 10/10★/10 (Campground) From Jct I-4 (Exit 64) & US-192: Go W 0.75 mi on US-192 then N 1 mi on World Dr (R). **FAC:** Paved rds. 709 paved, 90 all weather, back-ins (35 x 60), 709 full hkups, 90 W, 90 E (30/50 amps), cable, WiFi, tent sites, rentals, dump, laundry, groc, restaurant, controlled access. **REC:** heated pool, whirlpool, Bay Lake: fishing, playground. Pets OK $. Partial handicap access. Big rig sites, 2015 rates: $69 to $145. Disc: AAA. ATM.
(407)939-7723 Lat: 28.3933, Lon: -81.55524
4510 N Fort Wilderness Trail, Lake Buena Vista, FL 32830
disneyworlddisney.go.com/resorts/campsites-at-fort-wilderness-resort/
See primary listing at Lake Buena Vista and ad page 384.

← GREAT OAK RV RESORT **Ratings: 8/7.5/7** (RV Area in MHP) 2015 rates: $35. (407)396-9092 4440 Yowell Rd, Kissimmee, FL 34746

↓ **MERRY D RV SANCTUARY INC**
Ratings: 8/8★/8 (Campground) From Jct of Florida Tpke (exit 249) & Osceola Pkwy: Go W 2.6 mi on Osceola Pkwy, then S 6.2 mi on John Young Pkwy, then S 6.8 mi on Pleasant Hill Rd (L). **FAC:** Paved rds. 121 Avail: 60 gravel, 61 dirt, patios, 34 pull-thrus (40 x 75), back-ins (45 x 65), 121 full hkups (30/50 amps), cable, WiFi, tent sites, dump, laundry, LP gas, controlled access. **REC:** pond, fishing, shuffleboard. Pet restrict(B/Q). Partial handicap access. Big rig sites, 2015 rates: $38.
(800)208-3434 Lat: 28.16347, Lon: -81.43984
4261 Pleasant Hill Rd, Kissimmee, FL 34746
reservation@merryd.com
www.merryd.com
See ad pages 385, 286.

↗ **MILL CREEK CAREFREE RV RESORT**
Ratings: 7.5/7.5/6 (RV Area in MHP) From Jct of FL Turnpike (Exit 249) & Osceola Parkway: Go W 0.5 mi on Osceola Pkwy, then S 0.7 mi on Michigan Ave. (L). **FAC:** Paved rds. (156 spaces). 30 Avail: 10 grass, 20 dirt, patios, back-ins (25 x 45), some side by side hkups, 30 full hkups (30/50 amps), seasonal sites, WiFi Hotspot, laundry, LP gas. **REC:** heated pool, shuffleboard. Pet restrict(B/Q). No tents. 2015 rates: $34.
(407)847-6288 Lat: 28.32835, Lon: -81.39101
2775 Michigan Ave, Kissimmee, FL 34744
millcreek@carefreeresorts.com
www.carefreervresorts.com
See ad pages 383, 286.

← **ORANGE GROVE CAMPGROUND**
Ratings: 8.5/8/8 (Campground) From Jct of I-4 (Exit 68) & SR 535: Go S 3.5 mi, then E 2.7 mi on US-192, then N 1 mi on Old Vineland Rd (R). **FAC:** Paved rds. (201 spaces). 141 Avail: 4 paved, 111 gravel, 16 grass, 10 dirt, patios, 3 pull-thrus (24 x 66), back-ins (25 x 45), 141 full hkups (30 amps), WiFi, tent sites, dump, laundry, LP gas. **REC:** pool, shuffleboard. Pet restrict(B/Q). Partial handicap access. 2015 rates: $31 to $34. Disc: AAA.
AAA Approved
(407)396-6655 Lat: 28.31641, Lon: -81.46420
2425 Old Vineland Rd, Kissimmee, FL 34746
info@ogcrvpark.com
www.ogcrvpark.com
See ad page 365.

← ORLANDO/KISSIMMEE KOA **Ratings: 8.5/10★/9** (RV Park) 2015 rates: $59 to $81. (407)396-2400 2644 Happy Camper Place, Kissimmee, FL 34746

← SHERWOOD FOREST RV RESORT **Ratings: 8.5/8.5/8** (RV Park) 2015 rates: $47 to $85. (800)405-6188 5300 W Irlo Bronson Hwy, Kissimmee, FL 34746

← **TROPICAL PALMS CAREFREE RV RESORT**
Ratings: 9/9.5★/9.5 (RV Resort) From Jct of I-4 (exit 64) & US-192: Go E 1.5 mi on US-192, then S 0.5 mi on Holiday Trail (E).

FAR FROM ORDINARY, NEAR THE MAGIC
Tropical Palms located within 5 miles of the world's most popular theme parks, water parks, can accommodate anything from a tent trailer to the biggest RV. Kick back and relax in our heated pool, playground, fishing and more.

FAC: Paved rds. (559 spaces). 335 Avail: 210 paved, 125 grass, patios, 202 pull-thrus (30 x 55), back-ins (35 x 62), 288 full hkups, 47 W, 47 E (30/50 amps), WiFi, tent sites, rentals, dump, laundry, groc, LP gas, controlled access. **REC:** heated pool, pond, fishing, shuffleboard, playground. Pet restrict(Q). Partial handicap access. Big rig sites, 2015 rates: $30 to $85. Disc: AAA. ATM.
AAA Approved
(800)647-2567 Lat: 28.32559, Lon: -81.51653
2650 Holiday Trail, Kissimmee, FL 34746
TropicalPalms@carefreervresorts.com
www.tropicalpalmsresortfl.com
See ad pages 383, 286 & Snowbird Destinations in Magazine Section.

Travel Services

← **CAMPING WORLD OF KISSISSMMEE/ORLANDO** As the nation's largest retailer of RV supplies, accessories, services and new and used RVs, Camping World is committed to making your total RV experience better. RV Accessories: (800)327-9153. **SERVICES:** RV, tire, RV appliance, staffed RV wash, restrooms, RV Sales. RV supplies, LP, RV accessible. waiting room. Hours: 8:00am to 6:00pm.
(888)837-7751 Lat: 28.333024, Lon: -81.490498
5175 W. Irlo Bronson Hwy, Kissimmee, FL 34746
dtouchton@cwrvs.com
www.campingworld.com

LA BELLE — D4 *Glades*

← AQUA ISLES MOBILE HOME & RV RESORT **Ratings: 8.5/8.5/8.5** (RV Area in MHP) 2015 rates: $45. (863)675-2331 900 Aqua Isle Blvd, La Belle, FL 33935

← GRANDMA'S GROVE RV PARK **Ratings: 7.5/8/8** (RV Park) 2015 rates: $30 to $35. (863)675-2567 2250 Sr 80 W, La Belle, FL 33935

↗ MEADOWLARK SHORES RV PARK **Ratings: 7.5/7/7.5** (RV Park) 2015 rates: $30. (863)675-0006 1880 Williams Rd, Moore Haven, FL 33471

→ ORTONA LOCK & DAM/ORTONA SOUTH (Public Corps) From town, E 8 mi on SR 80 to Dalton Ln, N 1 mi (E). 2015 rates: $30. (863)675-8400

← RIVERBEND MOTORCOACH RESORT **Ratings: 10/10★/10** (Condo Pk) 2015 rates: $90 to $112. (866)787-4837 5800 West SR-80, La Belle, FL 33935

→ **THE GLADES RV RESORT**
Ratings: 9/8/9 (RV Park) From Jct of SR-80 & SR-29, E 13 mi on SR-80 (L).

JUST MINUTES FROM LAKE OKEECHOBEE
Centrally located on the Caloosahatchee River between LaBelle & Clewiston. 500 acres, 328 LARGE full-hookup sites, 9-hole golf course, marina, pool, cabin rentals & lots of room to relax & enjoy our peaceful Florida setting.

FAC: Paved rds. (328 spaces). Avail: 192 gravel, patios, back-ins (45 x 70), 192 full hkups (30/50 amps), seasonal sites, WiFi $, rentals, dump, laundry, restaurant. **REC:** heated pool, Caloosahatchee River: fishing, marina, golf, shuffleboard. Pet restrict(B). Partial handicap access, no tents. Big rig sites, eco-friendly, 2015 rates: $40 to $45. Disc: AAA, military.
AAA Approved
(863)983-8070 Lat: 26.77723, Lon: -81.22821
1682 Indian Hills Dr, Moore Haven, FL 33471
info@thegladesresort.com
www.thegladesresort.com
See ad pages 309 (Spotlight Hendry County), 284.

↑ **WHISPER CREEK RV RESORT**
Ratings: 9.5/10★/9.5 (RV Park) From Jct of SR-80 & SR-29, N 1.8 mi on SR-29 (L).

THE ULTIMATE 55+ RV RESORT
Our family owned and operated resort is 1 mile N of the historic town of LaBelle. Celebrating 27 seasons in our renovated resort. Enjoy small town living with little traffic. Centrally located to most FL attractions.

FAC: Paved rds. (473 spaces). Avail: 184 grass, patios, back-ins (50 x 60), 184 full hkups (30/50 amps), seasonal sites, cable, WiFi, laundry. **REC:** heated pool, pond, fishing, shuffleboard. Pet restrict(Q). Partial handicap access, no tents. Age restrict may apply, big rig sites, eco-friendly, 2015 rates: $35 to $40. Disc: military.
(863)675-6888 Lat: 26.78713, Lon: -81.43482
1887 North State Rd 29, La Belle, FL 33935
whispercreek@whispercreek.com
www.whispercreek.com
See ad pages 308 (Spotlight Hendry County), 284 & Snowbird Destinations in Magazine Section.

Things to See and Do

→ **THE GLADES RV, GOLF & MARINA RESORT** Championship length par-36 9-hole golf course with water features, natural landscaping & a grill at the 19th hole. Open to the public. Restrooms, food. Hours: Call for tee times. Adult fee: $11 to $30.
(863)983-8464 Lat: 26.76863, Lon: -81.22736
1682 Indian Hills Dr, Moore Haven, FL 33471
info@thegladesresort.com
www.thegladesresort.com
See ad page 309 (Spotlight Hendry County).

→ **THE GLADES RV, MARINA & GOLF RESORT** The Marina sits on the Caloosahatchee River, which is the intercoastal waterway connecting the Atlantic Ocean & the Gulf of Mexico. Private boat launch for park guests, accommodates watercraft up to 58 feet. Pump-out station available. Partial handicap access. Restrooms, food. Hours: 8am to 6pm. Adult fee: $1 to $10 per foot.
(863)983-8070 Lat: 26.76863, Lon: -81.22736
1682 Indian Hills Dr, Moore Haven, FL 33471
info@thegladesresort.com
www.thegladesresort.com
See ad page 309 (Spotlight Hendry County).

LADY LAKE — H3 *Lake*

↑ BLUE PARROT RV RESORT **Ratings: 8.5/8/8** (RV Park) 2015 rates: $37.10. (352)753-2026 40840 CR-25, Lady Lake, FL 32159

→ **GRAND OAKS RV RESORT**
Ratings: 8.5/10★/10 (RV Resort) From the jct of US 441/27 (in Lady Lake) & Griffin Ave, E 2.5 mi on Griffin Ave (L). **FAC:** Paved rds. 35 paved, 10 all weather, patios, 35 pull-thrus (35 x 85), back-ins (35 x 65), 45 full hkups (30/50 amps), WiFi, laundry, fire rings, restaurant. **REC:** pond, rec open to public. Pets OK. Big rig sites, eco-friendly, 2015 rates: $45 to $55.
(352)750-6300 Lat: 28.94313, Lon: -81.89752
3525 Griffin Ave, Lady Lake, FL 32159
info@grandoaksrv.com
www.grandoaksrv.com
See ad this page, 282.

← RECREATION PLANTATION **Ratings: 9/9★/9** (RV Park) 2015 rates: $50. (800)448-5646 609 Hwy 466, Lady Lake, FL 32159

LAKE BUENA VISTA — J4 *Lake, Polk*

↖ **DISNEY'S FORT WILDERNESS RESORT & CAMPGROUND**
Ratings: 10/10★/10 (Campground) From Jct I-4 (exit 64) & US-192: Go W 0.75 mi on US-192, then N 1 mi on World Dr (R).

DISNEY SAYS IT ALL
Disney's Fort Wilderness Resort & Campground—in the middle of the Walt Disney World Resort magic. Visit disneyworldcamping.com or call 407-939-2267.

FAC: Paved rds. 709 paved, 90 all weather, back-ins (35 x 60), 709 full hkups, 90 W, 90 E (30/50 amps), cable, WiFi, tent sites, rentals, dump, laundry, groc, LP gas, restaurant, controlled access. **REC:** heated pool, whirlpool, Bay Lake: fishing, playground. Pets OK $. Partial handicap access. Big rig sites, 2015 rates: $69 to $145. Disc: AAA. ATM.
(407)939-7723 Lat: 28.39330, Lon: -81.55524

SAVE! Over $1,000 in coupons can be found at the front of the Guide!

LAKE BUENA VISTA (CONT)

DISNEY'S FORT WILDERNESS (CONT)
4510 N. Fort Wilderness Trail, Lake Buena Vista, FL 32830
disneyworld.disney.go.com/resorts/campsites-at-fort-wilderness-resort/
See ad page 384 & Family Camping in Magazine Section.

LAKE CITY — A3 *Columbia*

INN & OUT RV PARK
Ratings: 7/8★/7.5 (RV Park) From Jct of I-75 & US-90 exit 427, E 0.25 mi on US-90 (R). **FAC:** Paved rds. 95 Avail: 8 gravel, 87 grass, 60 pull-thrus (25 x 70), back-ins (25 x 50), 87 full hkups (30/50 amps), cable, WiFi, rentals, dump, laundry, groc, LP gas. Pets OK. Partial handicap access, no tents. Big rig sites, 2015 rates: $34.95. Disc: AAA, military. ATM.
(386)752-1648 Lat: 30.17951, Lon: -82.68190
3010 W Hwy 90, Lake City, FL 32055
info@inandoutrvpark.com
www.inandoutrvpark.com
See ad this page, 282.

LAKE CITY CAMPGROUND
Ratings: 8.5/9★/8 (Campground) From Jct of I-75 & I-10, E 5.5 mi on I-10 to US-441 (exit 303), N 1 mi (R). **FAC:** Paved/gravel rds. 40 Avail: 25 paved, 15 grass, 40 pull-thrus (25 x 70), 40 full hkups (30/50 amps), cable, WiFi, tent sites, dump, laundry, groc, LP gas, fire rings, firewood. **REC:** pool, pond, fishing, shuffleboard, playground. Pets OK. Partial handicap access. Big rig sites, 2015 rates: $34 to $36. Disc: AAA.
(866)773-CAMP Lat: 30.25697, Lon: -82.63701
4743 N. US 441, Lake City, FL 32055
lakecitycampground@yahoo.com
www.lakecitycampground.com
See ad this page, 282.

LAKE CITY RV RESORT
Ratings: 7.5/8.5★/8 (RV Park) From Jct of I-10 & US-441 (exit 303), N 0.1 mi on US-441 (L). **FAC:** Gravel rds. 67 Avail: 20 gravel, 47 grass, patios, 67 pull-thrus (30 x 66), 67 full hkups (30/50 amps), cable, WiFi, rentals, laundry, LP gas. **REC:** pond, fishing. Pet restrict(B/Q). No tents. Big rig sites, 2015 rates: $36.
(386)752-0830 Lat: 30.24320, Lon: -82.64083
3864 N US Hwy 441, Lake city, FL 32055
info@lakecityrvresort.com
www.lakecityrvresort.com
See ad pages 368, 282.

Travel Services

CAMPING WORLD OF LAKE CITY As the nation's largest retailer of RV supplies, accessories, services and new and used RVs, Camping World is committed to making your total RV experience better. RV Accessories: (855)208-1279. **SERVICES:** RV, tire, RV appliance, MH mechanical, staffed RV wash, restrooms, RV Sales. RV supplies, LP, waiting room. Hours: 8:00 - 6:00.
(888)890-1722 Lat: 30.175074, Lon: -82.686803
530 SW Florida Gateway Dr., Lake City, FL 32024
www.campingworld.com

Our rating system isn't just tough, it's thorough. We know the kinds of things that are important to you — like clean restrooms and showers, attractive, secure, well-tended grounds, and extras like swimming pools. We give the first rating for development of facilities, the second for cleanliness and physical characteristics of restrooms and showers, and the third for visual appearance.

Nobody said it was easy being a 10. And our rating system makes it even tougher. Check out 10/10/10 RV parks and campgrounds in the front of the guide.*

Thank You to our active and retired military personnel. A dedicated section of Military Listings for places to camp can be found at the back of the Guide.

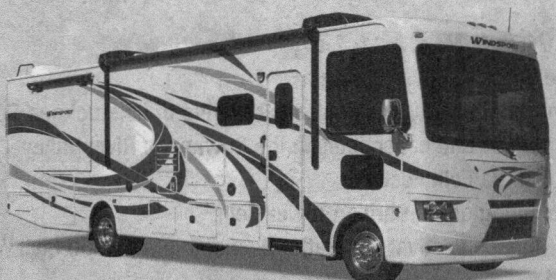

FL

Clubhouse with Commercial Kitchen

Good Sam Park

- Located at the Crossroads of Florida (I-10 & I-75)
- Spacious Shaded or Open Sites
- Long Pull-Thrus, Paved Sites
- Big Rigs & Pets Welcome
- 30/50 Amp Service, Laundry
- Special Rates for Sports Fans & Rallies
- FREE Cable TV, FREE WiFi Internet

New Owner/New Attitude!

Fun Activities in Lake City

- Explore the Santa Fe River Springs
- Tube the mystical beauty and cool, clear waters of Ichetucknee Springs
- Shop for antiques and collectibles in the Suwannee River Valley
- Attend the Florida Folk Festival
- Enjoy the chiming of the Carillon Tower Bells
- Attend the Olustee Festival and Battle Reenactment – 1700 Civil War Reenactors
- Navigate the Class III Rapids of Big Shoals State Park
- Experience Alligator Lake which is on the Great Florida Birding Trail

I-10, Exit 303, 2 Miles East of I-75

3864 North US Highway 441 • Lake City, Florida 32055

www.lakecityrvresort.com

LAKE OKEECHOBEE — D4 *Okeechobee*

LAKE OKEECHOBEE AREA MAP

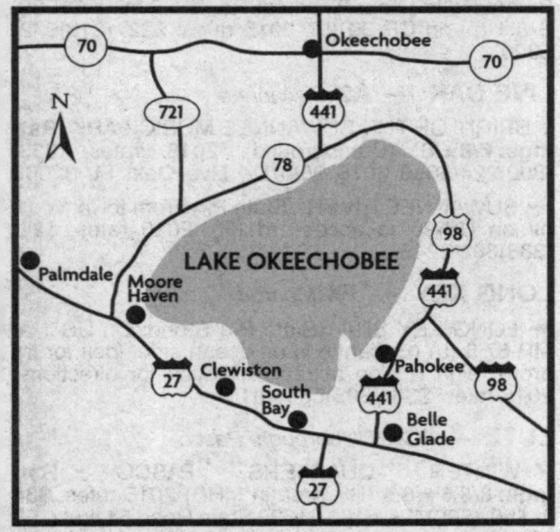

For more detail and a broader overview, please see our full-color state map at the front of the Florida state section.

Symbols on map indicate towns within a 30 mile radius of Lake Okeechobee where campgrounds are listed. Check listings for more information.

See also Belle Glade, Clewiston, Moore Haven, Okeechobee, Pahokee, Palmdale & South Bay.

LAKE PANASOFFKEE — H2 *Sumter*

COUNTRYSIDE RV PARK
Ratings: 7.5/10★/8.5 (RV Park) From Jct of I-75 (exit 321) & Hwy 470: Go NW 0.25 mi on Hwy 470, then SW 0.5 mi on CR-489 (L). **FAC:** Paved rds. (72 spaces). Avail: 29 grass, patios, 10 pull-thrus (45 x 56), back-ins (45 x 56), some side by side hkups, 26 full hkups, 3 W, 3 E (30/50 amps), WiFi, tent sites, dump, laundry. **REC:** shuffleboard. Pet restrict(B). Partial handicap access. Age restrict may apply, RV age restrict, 2015 rates: $30. No CC.
(352)793-8103 Lat: 28.75524, Lon: -82.11595
741 CR-489, Lake Panasoffkee, FL 33538
countrysidervparkfl@yahoo.com
www.countrysiderrvparkfl.com
See ad this page, 286.

Tell them you saw them in this Guide!

LAKE PANASOFFKEE I-75 KOA **Ratings: 8.5/8/7.5** (Campground) 2015 rates: $32. (352)793-2051 190 CR-488, Lake Panasoffkee, FL 33538

LAKE PLACID — D4 *Highlands*

CAMP FLORIDA RESORT **Ratings: 9.5/9★/9.5** (RV Resort) 2015 rates: $39 to $49. (863)699-1991 100 Shoreline Dr, Lake Placid, FL 33852

SUNSHINE RV RESORT **Ratings: 9/UI/8.5** (RV Park) 2015 rates: $32 to $39. (863)465-4815 303 SR-70E, Lake Placid, FL 33852

LAKE WALES — K3 *Polk*

CAMP 'N AIRE RV RESORT **Ratings: 8/8/8** (RV Park) 2015 rates: $30. (863)638-1015 15860 Hwy 27, Lake Wales, FL 33859

CAMP MACK'S RIVER RESORT **Ratings: 8/7/7** (Condo Pk) 2015 rates: $36 to $41. (800)243-8013 14900 Camp Mack Rd, Lake Wales, FL 33898

CAPERNAUM INN CHRISTIAN RV PARK **Ratings: 6/9★/8.5** (RV Park) 2015 rates: $25 to $30. (863)439-1080 3500 Canal Rd, Lake Wales, FL 33898

LAKE KISSIMMEE (State Pk) From Jct of US-27 & SR 60, E 9.5 mi on SR-60 to Boy Scout Rd, N 3.5 mi to Camp Mack Rd, E 5.1 mi (R); or From Jct of Florida's Tnpk and SR-60, NW 40 mi to Boy Scout Rd, N 3.5 mi to Camp Mack Rd, E 5.1 mi (R). 2015 rates: $20. (863)696-1112

LAKE WALES RV & CAMPSITES
Ratings: 9/8.5★/8 (RV Park) From Jct of US-27 & SR-60: Go S 3.3 mi on US-27 (R). **FAC:** Paved rds. (122 spaces). Avail: 45 grass, 15 pull-thrus (30 x 60), back-ins (20 x 35), some side by side hkups, 45 full hkups (30/50 amps), seasonal sites, WiFi, tent sites, dump, laundry. **REC:** pool, pond, fishing, shuffleboard. Pet restrict(B/Q). Partial handicap access. Age restrict may apply, 2015 rates: $38 to $45. Disc: AAA.
(863)638-9011 Lat: 27.85213, Lon: -81.58671
15898 Hwy 27, Lake Wales, FL 33859
lwcgfl@yahoo.com
www.lakewalescampgroundrvresort.com
See ad this page.

THE HARBOR RV RESORT & MARINA **Ratings: 8.5/7.5/7** (RV Area in MHP) 2015 rates: $24 to $45. (863)696-1194 10511 Monroe Ct, Lake Wales, FL 33898

LAKE WORTH — E5 *Palm Beach*

JOHN PRINCE PARK CAMPGROUND (Public) From Jct of I-95 & exit 63 (6th Ave S Lake Worth), W 1.5 mi on 6th Ave S to Congress Ave, S 0.2 mi (L); or From Jct of FL Tpke & Lake Worth Rd exit, E 5 mi on Lake Worth Rd to Congress Ave, S 0.5 mi (L). 2015 rates: $25.65 to $30. (561)582-7992

LAKELAND — K3 *Polk*

LAKELAND See also Dover, Polk City, Seffner, Thonotosassa, Winter Haven & Zephyrhills.

LAKELAND RV RESORT
Ratings: 9/9★/8.5 (RV Park) From Jct of I-4 (E-bnd) & SR-33 (exit 33): Go E 0.4 mi on SR-33, then N 0.25 mi on Old Combee Rd (R); or From Jct of I-4 (W-bnd) & Exit 33: Go N 0.7 mi on Socrum Loop Rd, then E 0.4 mi on Old Combee Rd (L).

WELCOME TO LAKELAND CAREFREE RESORT
An extraordinary getaway with all the extras! This prime location is only 30 minutes to the fun and excitement of Orlando or Tampa with easy access to I-4. It's your beautiful oasis amid all the great fun of Central Florida.

FAC: Paved rds. (230 spaces). 100 Avail: 50 paved, 50 grass, patios, 50 pull-thrus (35 x 80), back-ins (35 x 65), 100 full hkups (30/50 amps), seasonal sites, WiFi Hotspot, dump, laundry, LP gas, controlled access. **REC:** heated pool, whirlpool, pond, fishing,

Check our family camping destinations article in the front of the Guide highlighting the best places to camp in every state and province.

We appreciate your business!

LAKELAND (CONT)

LAKELAND RV RESORT (CONT)
shuffleboard. Pet restrict(B/Q). No tents. Big rig sites, 2015 rates: $38. Disc: AAA, military.
(863)687-6146 Lat: 28.11044, Lon: -81.93998
900 Old Combee Rd, Lakeland, FL 33805
lakelandrv@carefreervresorts.com
www.carefreervresorts.com
See ad pages 369, 286 & Snowbird Destinations in Magazine Section.

LE LYNN RV RESORT
Ratings: 9.5/8.5★/8.5 (RV Park) From jct. I-4 & SR-559 (exit 44): Go N 3 mi on SR-559 (L). **FAC:** Paved rds. (370 spaces). Avail: 220 paved, patios, 10 pull-thrus (25 x 66), back-ins (34 x 60), 220 full hkups (30/50 amps), seasonal sites, WiFi $, dump, laundry, LP gas. **REC:** pool, Little Lake Agnes: fishing, shuffleboard. Pet restrict(B/Q). Partial handicap access, no tents. Big rig sites, 2015 rates: $32 to $34. No CC.
(800)736-0409 Lat: 28.16321, Lon: -81,80183
1513 SR-559, Polk City, FL 33868
See primary listing at Polk City and ad page 369.

SANLAN RV & GOLF RESORT **Ratings: 8.5/8/8.5** (RV Park) 2015 rates: $25 to $51. (863)665-1726 3929 US-98 S, Lakeland, FL 33812

VALENCIA ESTATES
Ratings: 7.5/9★/7.5 (RV Area in MHP) From Jct Hwy 570 & US 98: Go N 1/2 mi on US-98 (L). **FAC:** Paved rds. (135 spaces). Avail: 35 grass, back-ins (25 x 45), 35 full hkups (30/50 amps), WiFi Hotspot, laundry. **REC:** pool, shuffleboard. Pet restrict(Q). Partial handicap access. Age restrict may apply, RV age restrict, 2015 rates: $45. No CC.
(863)665-1611 Lat: 28.00999, Lon: -81.90665
3325 Highway 98S, Lakeland, FL 33803
See ad pages 369, 286.

WOODALL'S MOBILE HOME VILLAGE & RV PARK
Ratings: 7.5/NA/8 (RV Area in MHP) From Jct of I-4 (Exit 28) & US 92/Memorial Blvd: Go E 2 mi on Memorial Blvd, then S 1 mi on Wabash Ave, then W 0.1 mi on New Tampa Hwy (R). **FAC:** Paved rds. (380 spaces). Avail: 125 grass, 4 pull-thrus (30 x 50), back-ins (30 x 40), accepts full hkup units only, 125 full hkups (30/50 amps), seasonal sites, WiFi, dump, laundry. **REC:** heated pool, shuffleboard. Pets OK. No tents. Age restrict may apply, 2015 rates: $45. Disc: AAA, military. No CC.
(863)686-7462 Lat: 28.04143, Lon: -81.99204
2121 New Tampa Hwy, Lakeland, FL 33815
woodalls@newbymanagement.com
www.woodallsvillage.com
See ad pages 271 (Welcome Section), 286.

LANTANA — E5 *Palm Beach*

PALM BEACH TRAVELER PARK **Ratings: 9/8/8** (RV Park) 2015 rates: $45 to $65. (561)967-3139 6159 Lawrence Rd, Lake Worth, FL 33462

LARGO — K1 *Pinellas*

INDIAN ROCKS TRAVEL PARK
Ratings: 7.5/7.5/8 (RV Park) From Jct of US-19Alt & SR-688 (Ulmerton Rd): Go W 2.9 mi on SR-688, then N 0.2 mi on Vonn Rd (R). **FAC:** Paved rds. (175 spaces). Avail: 40 grass, patios, back-ins (30 x 50), 40 full hkups (30/50 amps), cable, WiFi, showers $, dump, laundry, LP gas. **REC:** heated pool, shuffleboard. No pets. No tents. 2015 rates: $40.
(727)595-2228 Lat: 27.88301, Lon: -82.81884
12121 Vonn Rd, Largo, FL 33774
www.indianrockstravelpark.com
See ad this page.

LEE'S TRAVEL PARK **Ratings: 7/7/7** (RV Park) 2015 rates: $25 to $40. (727)536-2050 1610 S Belcher Rd, Largo, FL 33771

RAINBOW VILLAGE CAREFREE RV RESORT
Ratings: 9.5/9.5★/8 (RV Park) From Jct I-275 (Exit 31) & Hwy 688/Ulmerton: Go W 4 mi on Hwy 688, then S 3/4 mi on 66th St (L). **FAC:** Paved rds. (307 spaces). 102 Avail: 82 gravel, 20 grass, patios, 5 pull-thrus (30 x 50), back-ins (30 x 45), 102 full hkups (30/50 amps), seasonal sites, WiFi $, laundry. **REC:** heated pool, shuffleboard. Pet restrict(B). Partial handicap access, no tents. Age restrict may apply, big rig sites, 2015 rates: $44. Disc: AAA, military.
(727)536-3545 Lat: 27.88060, Lon: -82.72802
11911 66th St N, Largo, FL 33773
rainbowlargo@carefreervresorts.com
www.carefreervresorts.com
See ad pages 327, 286 & Snowbird Destinations in Magazine Section.

YANKEE TRAVELER RV PARK
Ratings: 9.5/10★/8.5 (RV Park) From Jct US-19 & Hwy 688 (Ulmerton Rd): Go W 2 mi on Ulmerton Rd (L).

BEST RV PARK IN CENTRAL FLORIDA
Centrally located between Clearwater-St Petersburg-Tampa and minutes to the beaches! Beautiful landscaping-heated pool-free WiFi-new private bathrooms & extensive activities. Perfect anytime of the year. Come Stay & Play!

FAC: Paved rds. (211 spaces). Avail: 21 gravel, patios, back-ins (25 x 60), 21 full hkups (30/50 amps), seasonal sites, WiFi, dump, laundry, LP gas. **REC:** heated pool, whirlpool, pond, shuffleboard. Pet restrict Partial handicap access, no tents. Age restrict may apply, big rig sites, 2015 rates: $34 to $40.
(727)531-7998 Lat: 27.89361, Lon: -82.75691
8500 Ulmerton Rd, Largo, FL 33771
info@yankeetraveler.net
www.yankeetraveler.net
See ad pages 332, 286 & Snowbird Destinations in Magazine Section.

LEESBURG — H3 *Lake, Sumter*

HOLIDAY TRAVEL RESORT
Ratings: 9/9★/8 (RV Park) From Jct of I-75 & SR-44 (Exit 329 Wildwood), E 12 mi on SR-44 to US-27, S 2.8 mi to SR-33, W 0.5 mi (R) or From Jct of FL Tnpk & SR-470 (Exit 296), E 3 mi on SR-470 to SR-33, N 1 mi (L). **FAC:** Paved rds. (935 spaces). Avail: 200 gravel, 200 pull-thrus (35 x 65), accepts self-contain units only, 200 full hkups (30/50 amps), seasonal sites, cable, WiFi Hotspot, dump, laundry, LP gas, controlled access. **REC:** heated pool, whirlpool, Big Lake Harris: fishing, marina, shuffleboard, playground. Pets OK. Partial handicap access, no tents. Big rig sites, 2015 rates: $42. Disc: AAA, military.
AAA Approved
(800)428-5334 Lat: 28.75658, Lon: -81.88581
28229 CR-33, Leesburg, FL 34748
www.holidaytravelresort.com
See ad opposite page, 282.

RIDGECREST RESORT COMMUNITY
Ratings: 9/8.5★/8 (RV Area in MHP) From Jct of FL Tpke & US-27 (Leesburg-Clermont exit 285), N 8.2 mi on US-27 (L); or From I-75 exit 329 (Wildwood), E 12 mi on Rte 44 to Rte 27S, S 5.5 mi (R). **FAC:** Paved rds. (301 spaces). 77 Avail: 14 paved, 63 grass, 6 pull-thrus (25 x 55), back-ins (25 x 40), accepts self-contain units only, 71 full hkups, 6 W, 6 E (30/50 amps), seasonal sites, WiFi Hotspot, dump, laundry, LP gas. **REC:** heated pool, whirlpool, shuffleboard. Pet restrict(B/Q). No tents. Big rig sites, 2015 rates: $29. No reservations.
(866)787-1504 Lat: 28.72793, Lon: -81.86402
26125 US Hwy 27, Leesburg, FL 34748
funatridgecrest@embarqmail.com
www.ridgecrestresortcommunity.com
See ad this page.

We rate what RVers consider important.

LITHIA — K2 *Hillsborough*

ALAFIA RIVER (State Pk) From town, S 0.9 mi on Bryant Rd to Lithia Pinecrest Rd, E 1.5 mi to CR-39, S 5.1 mi on CR-39 (L). 2015 rates: $22. (813)672-5320

LIVE OAK — A2 *Suwannee*

SPIRIT OF THE SUWANNEE MUSIC PARK **Ratings: 8/8★/8** (Campground) 2015 rates: $33. (800)224-5656 3076 95th Dr, Live Oak, FL 32060

SUWANNEE RIVER (State Pk) From town, W 13 mi on US-90 to access rd (R). 2015 rates: $22. (386)362-2746

LONG KEY — F4 *Monroe*

LONG KEY SRA (State Pk) S-bnd: On US-1 at MP-67.5 (L) (Entrance is on ocean side, look for lrg brown sign & stop at ranger station for directions. 2015 rates: $36. (305)664-4815

LUTZ — K2 *Hillsborough, Pasco*

WINTER QUARTERS PASCO **Ratings: 8/8.5★/8.5** (RV Area in MHP) 2015 rates: $34 to $50. (800)405-6188 21632 State Road 54, Lutz, FL 33549

MADISON — A2 *Madison*

DEERWOOD INN & MADISON CAMPGROUND
Ratings: 6/6.5/7 (Campground) From Jct of I-10 & SR-53 (exit 258), S 0.25 mi on SR-53 (R). **FAC:** Gravel/dirt rds. 77 gravel, 75 pull-thrus (36 x 60), back-ins (25 x 50), mostly side by side hkups, 43 full hkups, 32 W, 32 E (30/50 amps), WiFi Hotspot, dump, laundry. **REC:** pool, shuffleboard. No pets. No tents. 2015 rates: $25 to $30.
AAA Approved
(850)973-2504 Lat: 30.39229, Lon: -83.35553
155 SW Old St. Augustine Rd, Madison, FL 32340
reservations@deerwoodinn.com
www.deerwoodinn.com

Relax on white sandy beaches under palm fronds or get dancing at Mardi Gras; we've put the Spotlight on North America's most popular destinations. Turn to the Spotlight articles in our State and Province sections to learn more.

See listing Leesburg, FL

FL

FLORIDA'S ONLY
Yogi Bear Park
Good Sam Park
Come Enjoy Our New Lazy River
Located on I-10 at Exit 258
Near the Center of the State.
Great Destination
Yet on the Way Everywhere!
Water Features Now Open
See listing Madison, FL
JELLYSTONE PARK™
Yogi Bear's
CAMP-RESORTS
TM & © Hanna-Barbera
Madison, Florida
1051 SW Old St. Augustine Rd.
I10 & Exit 258 • Madison, FL 32340
• 30 & 50 amp sites • Long Pull-Thrus
• Large, spacious sites • Big Rigs Welcome
• Group Camping • We cater to Snowbirds!
• Lakeside RV sites available
• We recommend calling ahead of time (they fill up fast!)
WiFi
1-800-347-0174 • www.jellystonefla.com

MADISON (CONT)

YOGI BEAR JELLYSTONE CAMP RESORTS
Ratings: 9/9.5★/9 (RV Park) From Jct of I-10 (exit 258) & SR-53, S 0.2 mi on SR-53 to St. Augustine Rd, W 0.5 mi (L). **FAC:** Gravel rds. 175 gravel, 77 pull-thrus (35 x 60), back-ins (30 x 50), accepts self-contain units only, 120 full hkups, 52 W, 52 E (30/50 amps), WiFi, tent sites, rentals, dump, mobile sewer, laundry, groc, LP gas, fire rings, firewood, controlled access. **REC:** pool, Ragans Lake: fishing, playground, rec open to public. Pets OK. Partial handicap access. Big rig sites, eco-friendly, 2015 rates: $40 to $55. Disc: AAA.
AAA Approved
(850)973-8269 Lat: 30.39611, Lon: -83.36816
1051 SW Old St Augustine Rd, Madison, FL 32340
yogibearfl@embarqmail.com
www.yogicampingflorida.com
See ad opposite page, 282.

MALABAR — K5 *Brevard*

CAMELOT RV PARK, INC
Ratings: 9/9.5★/9 (RV Park) From Jct of I-95 (exit 173) & SR-514 (Malabar Rd): Go E 4.2 mi on Malabar Rd, then S 0.3 mi on US-1 (R).

MELBOURNE & PALM BAY AREA
15 minutes to the ocean! Our area has much to see & do! Come have fun! Camelot has a variety of activities so you can meet new friends. Whether you want to relax or be busy-it's here! Come enjoy your stay at Camelot!

FAC: Paved rds. (177 spaces). 150 Avail: 50 paved, 100 gravel, patios, 25 pull-thrus (20 x 60), back-ins (35 x 50), some side by side hkups, 150 full hkups (30/50 amps), cable, WiFi, laundry, LP gas, controlled access. **REC:** heated pool, Indian River Lagoon: fishing, shuffleboard. Pet restrict(B). Partial handicap access, no tents. Big rig sites, 2015 rates: $36 to $40.
(321)724-5396 Lat: 28.00009, Lon: -80.56114
1600 S US-1, Malabar, FL 32950
camelot@camelotrvpark.com
www.camelotrvpark.com
See ad this page, 286 & Snowbird Destinations in Magazine Section.

ENCHANTED LAKES ESTATES & RV RESORT **Ratings: 6/5/7** (RV Park) 2015 rates: $35 to $40. (321)723-8847 750 Malabar Rd, Malabar, FL 32950

MARATHON — F4 *Monroe*

GRASSY KEY RV PARK AND RESORT
Ratings: 10/NA/10 (RV Park) S-bnd: On US-1 at MP 58.7, Gulfside (R). **FAC:** All weather rds. 38 Avail: 38 all weather, 8 pull-thrus (30 x 62), back-ins (30 x 50), accepts full hkup units only, 38 full hkups (30/50 amps), cable, WiFi, laundry. **REC:** heated pool, Gulf of Mexico: fishing. Pet restrict(B/Q). No tents. Big rig sites, 2015 rates: $50 to $160.
(305)289-1606 Lat: 24.76501, Lon: -80.94814
58671 Overseas Hwy (US-1), Marathon, FL 33050
paradise@grassykeyrvpark.com
www.grassykeyrvpark.com
See ad this page, 284.

JOLLY ROGER
Ratings: 8/10★/8 (RV Park) S-bnd: On US-1 at MP-59.5 (R). **FAC:** Paved rds. 162 Avail: 142 grass, 20 dirt, patios, 34 pull-thrus (25 x 60), back-ins (24 x 44), 162 full hkups (30/50 amps), cable, WiFi, tent sites, rentals, laundry. **REC:** heated pool, Gulf of Mexico: swim, fishing. Pet restrict(Q). Partial handicap access. 2015 rates: $60 to $91.
(800)995-1525 Lat: 24.76965, Lon: -80.94196
59275 Overseas Hwy, Marathon, FL 33050
email@jrtp.com
www.jrtp.com
See ad this page, 284 & Snowbird Destinations in Magazine Section.

PELICAN RV PARK & MOTEL CAREFREE RV RESORT
Ratings: 7.5/8.5/7.5 (RV Park) From the Jct of US 1 and CR-905 in Key Largo, S 47 mi to MP 59 (R). Note: Max. length 35'. **FAC:** Paved rds. (85 spaces). Avail: 11 gravel, patios, back-ins (25 x 38), 10 full hkups, 1 W, 1 E (30/50 amps), seasonal sites, cable, WiFi, rentals, dump, laundry. **REC:** heated pool, Gulf of Mexico: fishing. Pet restrict(B/Q). Partial handicap access, no tents. 2015 rates: $65 to $95. Disc: military.
(305)289-0011 Lat: 24.76878, Lon: -80.94250
59151 Overseas Hwy, Marathon, FL 33050
pelicanrv@carefreervresorts.com
www.carefreervresorts.com
See ad pages 364, 284.

MARGATE — E5 *Broward*

AZTEC RV RESORT
Ratings: 9.5/10★/10 (Condo Pk) From Jct of I-95 & Exit 36 (SR-814, W. Atlantic Blvd), W 5 mi on SR-814 (W. Atlantic Blvd) to US 441 (SR-7), S 0.6 mi to Aztec Blvd, E 0.4 mi (E); or From Jct of Florida Turnpike & Exit 62 (SR-870, NW 56th St), E 0.5 mi on SR-870 (NW 56th St) to US 441 (SR-7), N 2.7 mi to Aztec Blvd, E 0.4 mi (E). **FAC:** Paved rds. 645 paved, patios, back-ins (35 x 90), accepts full hkup units only, 645 full hkups (50 amps), WiFi Hot-spot, laundry, controlled access. **REC:** heated pool, whirlpool, shuffleboard. Pets OK. Partial handicap access, no tents. Big rig sites, 2015 rates: $49 to $129.
(888)493-2856 Lat: 26.22608, Lon: -80.20185
1 Aztec Blvd, Margate, FL 33068
info@aztecrvresort.com
www.aztecrvresort.com
See ad pages 352, 284 & Snowbird Destinations in Magazine Section.

Don't miss a thing! Check out the Table of Contents for everything the Guide has to offer.

MARIANNA — E3 *Jackson*

ALLIANCE HILL RV RESORT
Ratings: 9.5/10★/9 (RV Park) From the jct of I 10 (exit 142) & SR 71, S on SR 71 7.2 mi. to CR 278 (Alliance Rd), E. 1.3 mi. (R). **FAC:** Paved rds. 30 Avail: 30 all weather, patios, 5 pull-thrus (30 x 80), back-ins (40 x 70), accepts full hkup units only, 30 full hkups (30/50 amps), WiFi, laundry, controlled access. **REC:** pool. Pets OK. Age restrict may apply, big rig sites, RV age restrict, 2015 rates: $36.
(850)688-8561 Lat: 30.6166, Lon: -85.1333
639 Plymouth Loop, Marianna, FL 33428
robtglen@aol.com
www.alliancehill.com
See ad pages 374, 282.

ARROWHEAD CAMPSITES **Ratings: 5/6/5** (Campground) 2015 rates: $33. (800)643-9166 4820 Hwy 90E, Marianna, FL 32446

FLORIDA CAVERNS (State Pk) From Jct of Hwy 90 & SR-166, N 3 mi on SR-166 (L). 2015 rates: $20. (850)482-9598

Our rating system isn't just tough, it's thorough. We know the kinds of things that are important to you — like clean restrooms and showers, attractive, secure, well-tended grounds, and extras like swimming pools. We give the first rating for development of facilities, the second for cleanliness and physical characteristics of restrooms and showers, and the third for visual appearance.

FL

Alliance Hill RV Resort

RV Park Community in North Florida

Good Sam Park

Alliance Hill provides top-quality amenities to create a natural, outdoor way of life for you while living in our safe and comfortable, gated Community:

- Luxury Clubhouse
- Swimming Pool
- Nature At Its Most Beautiful
- All New Park & Facilities
- Close Enough for Convenience
- Far Enough to Be Serene
- A Great Place to Retire

- Double-Wide Lots in Relaxed, Quiet, Natural Setting
- 30-Amp and 50-Amp Service
- Sewer, Water and Electric Allowance
- New Community Center
- TV Lounge with Wide-Screen Cable TV
- Wi-Fi and Internet Access
- Laundry Facilities
- Restrooms & Showers
- Sewing, Quilting and Arts & Crafts
- Kitchen Facilities • Picnic Tables
- Grilling Areas
- Woodland Nature Walking Paths
- Close to Good Fshing

DOG PARK

639 Plymouth Loop
Marianna, FL 33428
(850) 545-4928

www.alliancehill.com

Good Sam RATED 9.5/10★/9

See listing Marianna, FL

MELBOURNE — K5 *Brevard*

WICKHAM PARK (Public) From Jct of I-95 & Exit 191 (Wickham Rd), E 8.4 mi on Wickham Rd to Parkway Dr, E 0.5 mi (R). NOTE: N-bnd follow Exit 72 E to Wickham Rd. 2015 rates: $15 to $19. (321)255-4307

MELBOURNE BEACH — K5 *Brevard*

MELBOURNE BEACH MOBILE PARK **Ratings: 4.5/UI/6** (RV Area in MHP) 2015 rates: $45. (321)723-4947 2670 So. A1A, Melbourne Beach, FL 32951

OUTDOOR RESORTS/MELBOURNE BEACH **Ratings: 8.5/9★/9.5** (Condo Pk) 2015 rates: $37 to $72. (321)724-2600 214 Horizon Ln, Melbourne Beach, FL 32951

MEXICO BEACH — F3 *Bay*

RUSTIC SANDS RESORT CAMPGROUND **Ratings: 7/5.5/7** (Campground) 2015 rates: $48. (850)648-5229 800 N 15th St, Mexico Beach, FL 32456

MIAMI — E5 *Miami-Dade*

MIAMI See also Florida City, Hallandale, Hollywood & Homestead.

LARRY & PENNY THOMPSON CAMPGROUND
(Public) From Jct of FL Tpke & SW 184th St (exit 13), W 1.1 mi on 184th St (Eureka) (R). **FAC:** Paved rds. 240 paved, 8 pull-thrus (35 x 70), back-ins (35 x 50), 240 full hkups (30/50 amps), WiFi, tent sites, dump, laundry. **REC:** heated pool, pond, fishing. Pet restrict Partial handicap access. Big rig sites, 2015 rates: $33.90.
(305)232-1049 Lat: 25.60126, Lon: -80.39480
12451 SW 184th St, Miami, FL 33177
l&pcampground@miamidade.gov
www.miamidade.gov/parks/larry-penny.asp
See ad this page.

MIAMI EVERGLADES RESORT **Ratings: 8.5/10★/9.5** (Campground) 2015 rates: $35 to $69. (305)233-5300 20675 SW 162 Ave, Miami, FL 33187

MICCO — K5 *Brevard*

BREEZEWAY TRAILER & RV PARK
Ratings: 4.5/NA/6.5 (RV Park) From Jct Hwy 505 & US-1: Go N 3 mi on US-1 (L). **FAC:** Gravel rds. (43 spaces). Avail: 15 grass, 5 pull-thrus (28 x 50), back-ins (28 x 50), accepts full hkup units only, 15 full hkups (30/50 amps), WiFi Hotspot, dump, laundry. **REC:** Indian River: fishing. Pet restrict(B). No tents. Age restrict may apply, 2015 rates: $31.
(772)664-5073 Lat: 27.866554, Lon: -80.496241
8860 US Hwy 1, Micco, FL 32976
info@breezewaytrailerpark.com
www.breezewaytrailerpark.com
See ad this page.

MIDWAY — A1 *Gadsden*

Travel Services

CAMPING WORLD OF MIDWAY/TALLAHASSEE As the nation's largest retailer of RV supplies, accessories, services and new and used RVs, Camping World is committed to making your total RV experience better. RV Accessories (800)446-3199. **SERVICES:** RV, tire, RV appliance, MH mechanical, staffed RV wash, restrooms, RV Sales. RV supplies, LP, emergency parking, RV accessible. waiting room. Hours: 8:00am to 6:00pm.
(888)506-0375 Lat: 30.50063, Lon: -84.45085
31300 Blue Star Hwy, Midway, FL 32343
www.campingworld.com

MILTON — E1 *Santa Rosa*

AVALON LANDING RV PARK
Ratings: 9/10★/9 (RV Park) From Jct of IH10 & SR 281 (Avalon Blvd Exit 22), S 0.4 mi on SR 281 (L). **FAC:** Paved rds. 79 paved, 8 pull-thrus (30 x 60), back-ins (30 x 60), 79 full hkups (30/50 amps), cable, WiFi, dump, laundry, LP gas. **REC:** pool, Escambia Bay: fishing. Pet restrict(B/Q). Partial handicap access, no tents. Big rig sites, eco-friendly, 2015 rates: $37 to $43. Disc: AAA.
(866)995-5898 Lat: 30.52509, Lon: -87.08662
2444 Avalon Blvd, Milton, FL 32583
contact@avalonlandingrvpark.com
www.avalonlandingrvpark.com
See ad pages 390, 282.

CEDAR PINES RV CAMPGROUND
Ratings: 6/7.5★/7 (Campground) From Jct of I-10 & CR 89 (Ward Basin Rd) exit 28, N on CR 89 (Ward Basin Rd) 2.9 mi to US-90, W 1.9 mi to Hwy 87, N 4.5 mi (R). **FAC:** Gravel rds. 40 grass, patios, 33 pull-thrus (28 x 60), back-ins (28 x 60), 40 full hkups (30/50 amps), cable, dump, laundry. **REC:** pool. Pet restrict(B/Q). No tents. Big rig sites, 2015 rates: $32 to $35. Disc: military.
(850)623-8869 Lat: 30.68221, Lon: -87.05351
6436 Robie Rd, Milton, FL 32570
info@cedarpines.com
www.cedarpines.com
See ad page 387.

GULF PINES KOA **Ratings: 9.5/9.5★/9** (RV Park) 2015 rates: $44 to $57. (888)562-4258 8700 Gulf Pines Dr, Milton, FL 32583

PELICAN PALMS RV PARK
Ratings: 8.5/8.5★/8 (RV Park) From Jct of I-10 & CR-191 (exit 26/old exit 8), S 0.1 mi on CR-191 (L). **FAC:** Gravel rds. 49 grass, 23 pull-thrus (25 x 50), back-ins (25 x 50), 49 full hkups (30/50 amps), WiFi, tent sites, dump, laundry, LP gas. **REC:** pool, pond. Pets OK. Big rig sites, eco-friendly, 2015 rates: $34. Disc: AAA, military.
AAA Approved
(850)623-0576 Lat: 30.57004, Lon: -87.02941
3700 Garcon Point Rd, Milton, FL 32583
pprvp@aol.com
www.pelicanpalmsrvpark.com
See ad pages 387, 282.

SUNBURST RV RESORT
Ratings: 8.5/8.5★/8.5 (RV Resort) From the jct of US90 & SR87, N on SR87 14.9 mi. to CR178, W .7 mi to Horne Rd, N .7 mi (L). **FAC:** All weather rds. 50 paved, back-ins (25 x 45), 50 full hkups (30/50 amps), WiFi, rentals, dump, laundry, LP gas, fire rings. **REC:** pool. Pets OK. 2015 rates: $35. No CC.
(850)675-6807 Lat: 30.84486, Lon: -87.0636
2375 Horn Road, Milton, FL 32570
info@sunburstrvresort.com
www.sunburstrvresort.com
See ad pages 391, 282.

How can we make a great Travel Guide even better? We ask YOU! Please share your thoughts with us. Drop us a note and let us know if there's anything we haven't thought of.

MONTICELLO — A2 *Jefferson*

A CAMPERS WORLD
Ratings: 6/8.5★/7.5 (Campground) From Jct of I-10 & Hwy 19 (exit 225), N 0.2 mi on Hwy 19 to campground rd, W 0.25 mi (L). **FAC:** Gravel rds. 29 gravel, 23 pull-thrus (22 x 60), back-ins (22 x 60), 29 full hkups (30/50 amps), WiFi Hotspot, laundry. **REC:** pool. Pets OK. No tents. 2015 rates: $31 to $33. No CC, no reservations.
(850)997-3300 Lat: 30.47816, Lon: -83.89466
397 Campground Rd, Lamont, FL 32336

TALLAHASSEE EAST CAMPGROUND
Ratings: 8/8.5★/7.5 (Campground) From Jct of I-10 & US-19 (exit 225), S 0.5 mi on US-19 to 158B, W 2 mi to Hwy 259, N 0.5 mi to access rd, E 0.25 mi (E). **FAC:** Gravel rds. 66 Avail: 29 gravel, 19 grass, 18 dirt, 66 pull-thrus (32 x 60), 58 full hkups, 8 W, 8 E (30/50 amps), WiFi Hotspot, tent sites, rentals, dump, laundry, groc, LP gas. **REC:** pool, Lake Catherine: fishing, playground. Pets OK. Big rig sites, 2015 rates: $37 to $42. Disc: AAA.
(844)997-3890 Lat: 30.47766, Lon: -83.91598
346 Koa Rd, Monticello, FL 32344
tallahasseeeastcampground@gmail.com
www.TallahasseeEastCampground.com
See ad pages 403, 282.

MOORE HAVEN — D4 *Glades*

M R.V. RESORT **Ratings: 7.5/9★/7** (RV Park) 2015 rates: $37.50. (863)946-6616 17192 US Hwy 27, Moore Haven, FL 33471

NORTH LAKE ESTATES RV RESORT
Ratings: 9.5/9.5★/9.5 (RV Park) From Jct of US-27 & SR-78 (1 mi N of Moore Haven), NE 11 mi on SR-78 (R); or From Jct of SR-70 & US-441/98 (Okeechobee), S 3 mi on US-441/98 to SR-78, SW 23 mi (L).

MINUTES FROM LAKE OKEECHOBEE
A lovely resort that offers the perfect getaway. Minutes from the largest freshwater lake in Florida, this fisherman's paradise offers stunning amenities onsite, so you will always have something to enjoy.

FAC: Paved rds. (273 spaces). Avail: 42 paved, patios, back-ins (34 x 50), 42 full hkups (30/50 amps), seasonal sites, WiFi, rentals, laundry, restaurant. **REC:** heated pool, pond, fishing, shuffleboard. Pet restrict(B). Partial handicap access, no tents. Age restrict may apply, 2015 rates: $35 to $42. Disc: AAA, military.
AAA Approved
(877)417-6193 Lat: 26.98526, Lon: -81.09855

RV Park ratings you can rely on!

FL

MOORE HAVEN (CONT)

NORTH LAKE ESTATES RV RESORT (CONT)
12044 East State Rd 78, Moore Haven, FL 33471
northlake@suncommunities.com
www.northlakeestatesrvresort.com
See ad pages 275 (Welcome Section), 284, 1463 (Welcome Section) & Snowbird Destinations in Magazine Section.

NAPLES — E4 *Collier*

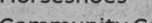

➔ **CLUB NAPLES RV RESORT**
Ratings: 9/10★/9 (RV Park) From Jct of I-75 & SR-951 (Exit 101), S 0.2 mi on SR-951 to Beck Blvd, E 1 mi (R).

NIGHTLIFE AND NATURE IN NAPLES
Surrounded by nature preserves and just minutes from the excitement of Naples - have it all at Club Naples!From swimming and shuffleboard to petanque and planned activiities, you're sure to have an unforgettable experience.

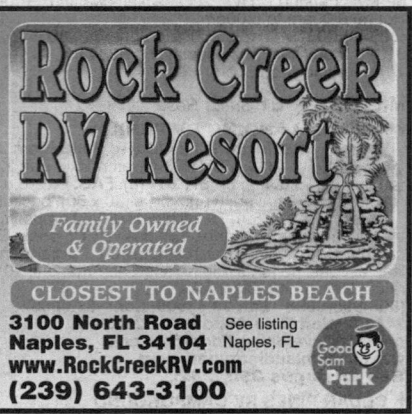

FAC: Paved rds. (305 spaces). 124 Avail: 12 paved, 112 grass, patios, 12 pull-thrus (20 x 60), back-ins

NAPLES (CONT)

CLUB NAPLES RV RESORT (CONT)
(28 x 40), accepts full hkup units only, 124 full hkups (30/50 amps), seasonal sites, cable, WiFi, rentals, dump, laundry, LP gas. **REC:** heated pool, whirlpool, shuffleboard. Pet restrict(B/Q). Partial handicap access, no tents. 2015 rates: $41 to $54. Disc: AAA, military.
AAA Approved
(888)898-6463 Lat: 26.15447, Lon: -81.66979
3180 Beck Blvd, Naples, FL 34114
clubnaples@suncommunities.com
www.clubnaplesrv.com
See ad opposite page, 275 (Welcome Section), 284, 1463 (Welcome Section) & RV Trips of a Lifetime, Snowbird Destinations in Magazine Section.

COLLIER-SEMINOLE (State Pk) From Jct of US-41 & SR-84, SE 15 mi on US-41 (R). 2015 rates: $22. (239)394-3397

Enjoy shopping over 10,000 RV products at great prices, at CampingWorld.com.

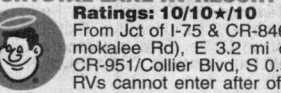

CRYSTAL LAKE RV RESORT
Ratings: 10/10★/10 (Condo Pk) From Jct of I-75 & CR-846 (exit 111/Immokalee Rd), E 3.2 mi on CR-846 to CR-951/Collier Blvd, S 0.5 mi (L) Note: RVs cannot enter after office hours unless prior arrangements are made. Minimum 25' RV length.

CRYSTAL LAKE 10/10*/10 RATED
Providing the utmost service in RV resort rentals & sales and is most sought-after RV destination. Located in SW FL, Crystal Lake has something for everyone; beaches, shopping, fine dining, sports & entertainment for all ages

FAC: Paved rds. (490 spaces). Avail: 100 paved, patios, back-ins (40 x 80), accepts full hkup units only, 100 full hkups (30/50 amps), seasonal sites, cable, WiFi, rentals, dump, laundry, controlled access. **REC:** heated pool, whirlpool, Crystal Lake: fishing, shuffleboard. Pet restrict(Q). Partial handicap access, no tents. Big rig sites, eco-friendly, 2015 rates: $40 to $90.
(239)348-0017 Lat: 26.26494, Lon: -81.68756
14960 Collier Blvd, Naples, FL 34119
crystalrealty@mindspring.com
www.crystallakervresort.com
See ad opposite page, 284.

Say you saw it in our Guide!

ENDLESS SUMMER RV PARK **Ratings: 6.5/7/6.5** (RV Area in MHP) 2015 rates: $46.80 to $52. (239)643-1511 2 Tina Lane, Naples, FL 34104

HOLIDAY MANOR **Ratings: 8/7.5/8.5** (RV Park) 2015 rates: $30. (239)774-4474 1185 Henderson Creek Dr, Naples, FL 34114

The RVers' Guide to NASCAR helps RV travelers get the most out of North America's most thrilling sporting event. Turn to the front of the Guide and we'll give you the inside track on how to get high-speed thrills at major NASCAR venues.

NAPLES (CONT)

LAKE SAN MARINO RV RESORT
Ratings: 9/9★/8.5 (RV Park) From Jct of I-75 & CR- 846/ Immokalee Rd (Exit 111), W 3.5 mi on CR-846/ Immokalee Rd to US-41, N 1.5 mi to CR-888 (Wiggins Pass Rd), E 0.2 mi (R).

LIVE LIFE AT YOUR PACE IN NAPLES
A great location in Naples combined with a relaxed atmosphere equals your road to the good life! Cool off in the sparkling pool, fish at the lake or keep it social with a game of shuffleboard, petanque or horseshoes.

FAC: Paved rds. (407 spaces). Avail: 209 grass, patios, back-ins (25 x 50), accepts full hkup units only, 209 full hkups (30/50 amps), seasonal sites, WiFi, rentals, dump, laundry. **REC:** heated pool, Swan Lake: fishing, shuffleboard. Pet restrict(B/Q). Partial handicap access, no tents. Age restrict may apply, 2015 rates: $36 to $52. Disc: AAA, military. AAA Approved
(877)720-1982 Lat: 26.29435, Lon: -81.79815
1000 Wiggins Pass Rd, Naples, FL 34110
lakesanmarino@suncommunities.com
www.lakesanmarino.com
See ad pages 376, 275 (Welcome Section), 284, 1463 (Welcome Section) & RV Trips of a Lifetime, Snowbird Destinations in Magazine Section.

MARCO-NAPLES CAREFREE RV RESORT
Ratings: 7/8/7 (RV Park) From Jct of I-75 & Collier Blvd (CR-951) (Exit 101), S 7 mi on Collier Blvd (CR-951) to US-41, N 1.3 mi (L). **FAC:** Paved rds. (305 spaces). 70 Avail: 4 paved, 5 gravel, 61 grass, patios, 26 pull-thrus (25 x 60), back-ins (25 x 45), accepts full hkup units only, 70 full hkups (30/50 amps), seasonal sites, WiFi, rentals, dump. **REC:** heated pool, shuffleboard. Pets OK. Partial handicap access, no tents. Age restrict may apply, eco-friendly, 2015 rates: $50 to $52. Disc: AAA, military.
(239)774-1259 Lat: 26.07227, Lon: -81.71578
100 Barefoot Williams Rd, Naples, FL 34113
marconaples@carefreervresorts.com
www.carefreervresorts.com
See ad pages 327, 284.

NAPLES MOTORCOACH RESORT & BOAT CLUB
Ratings: 10/10★/10 (Condo Pk) From Jct of I-75 & Collier Blvd (CR-951/Exit 101), S 7 mi on Collier Blvd/CR-951 to US 41, SE 0.7 mi (R).

LUXURY MOTORCOACH RESORT
Naples Motorcoach Resort sets the standard for quality & beauty in FL. Located on the SW Coast w/direct access to the Gulf. Enjoy the clubhouse, theater, tennis, hot tubs & pools. Discover nearby fishing, golf & shopping.

FAC: Paved rds. 184 paved, patios, back-ins (38 x 90), accepts full hkup units only, 184 full hkups (50 amps), cable, WiFi $, laundry, controlled access. **REC:** heated pool, whirlpool, Henderson Creek: fishing. Pet restrict(B/Q) $. Partial handicap access, no tents. Big rig sites, RV age restrict, eco-friendly, 2015 rates: $39 to $124. Disc: AAA, military.
(888)939-3783 Lat: 26.05563, Lon: -81.68922
13300 Tamiami Trail E, Naples, FL 34114
info@naplesmotorcoachresort.com
www.naplesmotorcoachresort.com
See ad pages 377, 284 & Snowbird Destinations in Magazine Section.

Wasn't that a beautiful campground you visited ten years ago? But can you remember where it was? Use our "Find-it-Fast" index, located in the back of the Guide. It's an alphabetical list, by state, of every private and public park and campground in the Guide.

NAPLES RV RESORT
Ratings: 8/10★/8.5 (RV Park) From Jct of I-75 & Collier Blvd (Exit 101), S 4.5 mi on Collier Blvd to Grand Lely Blvd, W/U-turn back to Collier Blvd, N 0.5 mi (R).

THE FRIENDLIEST RV RESORT IN NAPLES
Naples RV Resort is nestled among trees, immersing you in a tropical experience. Head out to the beach or relax by the pool. We have RV sites and vacation rentals available.

FAC: Paved rds. (161 spaces). Avail: 129 grass, patios, 20 pull-thrus (25 x 60), back-ins (22 x 40), some side by side hkups, accepts full hkup units only, 129 full hkups (30/50 amps), seasonal sites, cable, WiFi, rentals, dump, laundry, LP gas. **REC:** heated pool, shuffleboard. Pet restrict(B/Q). Partial handicap access, no tents. RV age restrict, eco-friendly, 2015 rates: $45 to $60. Disc: AAA, military.
AAA Approved
(877)361-5197 Lat: 26.10275, Lon: -81.68580
8230 Collier Blvd, Naples, FL 34114
naples@suncommunities.com
www.naplesgardensrvresort.com
See ad pages 376, 275 (Welcome Section), 284, 1463 (Welcome Section) & RV Trips of a Lifetime, Snowbird Destinations in Magazine Section.

NAPLES/MARCO ISLAND KOA **Ratings: 8/8/8** (Campground) 2015 rates: $45 to $95. (800)562-7734 1700 Barefoot Williams Rd, Naples, FL 34113

NEAPOLITAN COVE RV RESORT **Ratings: 9.5/NA/9.5** (RV Park) 2015 rates: $50 to $83. (239)793-0091 3790 Tamiami Tr-E, Naples, FL 34112

PARADISE POINTE RV RESORT **Ratings: 9/8.5/8.5** (RV Park) 2015 rates: $70 to $75. (239)793-6886 14500 E Tamiami Trail, Naples, FL 34114

PELICAN LAKE MOTORCOACH RESORT
Ratings: 9.5/10★/10 (Condo Pk) From Jct of I-75 & Collier Blvd (exit 101), S 9.2 mi on Collier Blvd (CR-951) (L) Note: Class A motorhomes 26 ft or larger only. **FAC:** Paved rds. (289 spaces). Avail: 100 paved, patios, back-ins (55 x 95), accepts full hkup units only, 100 full hkups (50 amps), seasonal sites, cable, WiFi Hotspot, laundry, controlled access. **REC:** heated pool, whirlpool, Pelican Lake: fishing, shuffleboard. Pet restrict(Q). Partial handicap access, no tents. Big rig sites, 2015 rates: $60 to $145.
(800)835-4389 Lat: 26.03330, Lon: -81.69625
4555 Southern Breeze Dr, Naples, FL 34114
pelicanlakeinfo@aol.com
www.pelicanlakemotorcoachresort.com
See ad page 377.

ROCK CREEK RV RESORT
Ratings: 9/9★/9 (RV Park) From Jct of I-75 & Golden Gate Pkwy (Exit 105), W 2 mi on Golden Gate Pkwy to Hwy 31/Airport Pulling Rd, S 2.4 mi to North Rd, W 100 yds on North Rd (L). **FAC:** Paved rds. (237 spaces). 110 Avail: 100 paved, 10 gravel, patios, 5 pull-thrus (25 x 70), back-ins (30 x 60), accepts full hkup units only, 110 full hkups (30/50 amps), seasonal sites, cable, WiFi, rentals, laundry. **REC:** heated pool, Rock Creek. Pets OK. Partial handicap access, no tents. Big rig sites, 2015 rates: $40 to $68.
(239)643-3100 Lat: 26.14531, Lon: -81.76820
3100 North Rd, Naples, FL 34104
rc@rockcreekrv.com
www.rockcreekrv.com
See ad pages 376, 284.

SILVER LAKES RV RESORT & GOLF CLUB
Ratings: 9.5/10★/10 (Condo Pk) From Jct of I-75 & Collier Blvd (CR-951/Exit 101), S 9 mi on Collier Blvd (CR-951) (L) Note: 25' minimum length RV. **FAC:** Paved rds. (551 spaces). Avail: 251 paved, patios, 13 pull-thrus (50 x 100), back-ins (40 x 80), accepts full hkup units only, 251 full hkups (30/50 amps), seasonal sites, cable, WiFi Hotspot, laundry, controlled access. **REC:** heated pool, whirlpool, Silver Lake: fishing, golf, shuffleboard. Pet restrict(B/Q). Partial handicap access, no tents. Big rig sites, 2015 rates: $45 to $89.
(800)843-2836 Lat: 26.03859, Lon: -81.69960
1001 Silver Lakes Blvd, Naples, FL 34114
silverlkes@aol.com
www.silverlakesrvresort.com
See ad page 377.

Things to See and Do

SILVER LAKES GOLF CLUB Challenging 9-Hole Executive Golf Course within Silver Lake RV Resort. The 2 par-4's & 7 par-3's are available to all owners and renters. Many golf events. Cart useage. Partial handicap access. Restrooms. Hours: 7am to 8pm. Adult fee: $16. No CC.
(800)843-2836 Lat: 26.03859, Lon: -81.69960
1001 Silver Lakes Blvd, Naples, FL 34114
silverlkes@aol.com
www.silverlakesrvresort.com
See ad page 377.

NAVARRE — F1 *Santa Rosa*

EMERALD BEACH RV PARK
Ratings: 10/10★/9.5 (RV Park) E-bnd: From the Jct of US 87 & US 98, E 1 mi on US 98 (R); W-bnd: From entrance to Hurlburt Field (US Army Installation) & US 98, W 9 mi on US 98 (past park entrance) to Navarre Sound Circle, U-turn if possible or S onto Navarre Sound Circle & back to Hwy 98, E 0.1 mi (R).

BEST OF SNOWBIRD & FAMILY CAMPING!
Private beach, pier, kayaks, 24/7 gym off site, activities. 1.5 miles from the Gulf. EMERALD BEACH RV PARK is one of the highest rated GS parks in the US. Great reviews on TripAdvisor!

FAC: Paved rds. 76 paved, patios, 37 pull-thrus (37 x 60), back-ins (25 x 60), 76 full hkups (30/50 amps), cable, WiFi, dump, laundry, LP gas. **REC:** pool, Santa Rosa Sound: swim. Pet restrict(B/Q). No tents. Big rig sites, 2015 rates: $49 to $75. Disc: AAA.
(866)939-3431 Lat: 30.40477, Lon: -86.85124
8885 Navarre Pkwy, Navarre, FL 32566
info@emeraldbeachrvpark.com
www.emeraldbeachrvpark.com
See ad pages 345, 282 & RV Trips of a Lifetime in Magazine Section.

NAVARRE BEACH CAMPGROUND
Ratings: 9.5/10★/9 (Campground) From Jct of Hwy 87 & US-98, E 2 mi on US-98 (R).

ENJOY THE WATER AND SHADE
Located in the middle of the beautiful Emerald Coast white beaches and activities and shopping galore. Great cabins and pool area.

FAC: Paved/gravel rds. 116 Avail: 16 paved, 94 gravel, 6 grass, patios, 43 pull-thrus (30 x 60), back-ins (32 x 40), 116 full hkups (30/50 amps), cable, WiFi, tent sites, rentals, dump, laundry, LP gas, controlled access. **REC:** heated pool, whirlpool, Santa Rosa Sound: swim, shuffleboard, playground. Pets OK. Partial handicap access. Big rig sites, 2015 rates: $49 to $85. Disc: AAA, military.
(888)639-2188 Lat: 30.40943, Lon: -86.83785
9201 Navarre Parkway, Navarre, FL 32566
info@navbeach.com
www.navbeach.com
See ad pages 351, 282 & Snowbird Destinations in Magazine Section.

SANTA ROSA RV RESORT
Ratings: 10/10★/9 (RV Park) From the Jct of IH & SR-87, go S 16 mi on SR-87 to dead end at Hwy 98, W 0.1 mi (L). **FAC:** Paved rds. 88 paved, patios, 7 pull-thrus (30 x 80), back-ins (30 x 60), accepts full hkup units only, 88 full hkups (30/50 amps), cable, WiFi, laundry, LP gas. **REC:** pool, Santa Rosa Sound. Pet restrict(B). No tents. Big rig sites, eco-friendly, 2015 rates: $45 to $98. No CC.
(888)936-4791 Lat: 30.40170, Lon: -86.87336
8315 Navarre Pkwy, Navarre, FL 32566
info@santarosarvresort.com
www.santarosarvresort.com
See ad pages 349, 282.

NEW PORT RICHEY — J1 *Pasco*

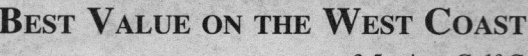

ORCHID LAKE RV RESORT **Ratings: 9/10★/8.5** (RV Area in MHP) From Jct of US 19 & SR-54: Go N 4.7 mi on US 19, then E 2.5 mi on Ridge Rd, then S 0.5 mi on Little Rd, then W 0.25 mi on Arevee Dr (E). **FAC:** Paved rds. (465 spaces). Avail: 100 gravel, patios, back-ins (30 x 50), some side by side hkups, 100 full hkups (30/50 amps), WiFi, laundry. **REC:** heated pool, Orchid Lake: fishing, shuffleboard. No pets. Partial handicap access, no

NEW PORT RICHEY (CONT)

ORCHID LAKE RV RESORT (CONT)
tents. Age restrict may apply, 2015 rates: $38. Disc: AAA.
AAA Approved
(727)847-1925 Lat: 28.27408, Lon: -82.67898
8225 Arevee Drive, New Port Richey, FL 34653
terry.wells47@yahoo.com
orchidlakervresort.com

➔ SEVEN SPRINGS TRAVEL PARK
Ratings: 9/7.5/8 (RV Park) From Jct of US-19 & SR-54: Go E 3.3 mi on SR-54, then NE 0.2 mi on Old County Rd 54 (L). **FAC:** Paved rds. (220 spaces). Avail: 70 gravel, patios, back-ins (30 x 65), 70 full hkups (30/50 amps), seasonal sites, WiFi $, dump, laundry, LP gas, controlled access. **REC:** pool, pond, fishing, shuffleboard. No pets. Partial handicap access, no tents. Age restrict may apply, big rig sites, 2015 rates: $37. No CC.
(727)376-0000 Lat: 28.21758, Lon: -82.68102
8039 Old County Road 54, New Port Richey, FL 34653
joe@sevenspringsrvpark.com
www.sevenspringsrvpark.com
See ad opposite page, 286.

NEW SMYRNA BEACH — G5 *Volusia*

← NEW SMYRNA BEACH RV PARK
Ratings: 9/9.5★/9 (RV Park) S-bnd: From Jct of I-95 & SR-44 (exit 249A), E 3 mi on SR-44 to Mission Drive (becomes Old Mission Rd), S 1.3 mi (R); or N-bnd: From Jct of I-95 & CR-442 (exit 244), E 0.9 mi on CR-442 to Old Mission Rd, N 3 mi (L). **FAC:** Paved/dirt rds. (291 spaces). 161 Avail: 36 grass, 125 dirt, 140 pull-thrus (25 x 65), back-ins (25 x 65), accepts self-contain units only, 161 full hkups (30/50 amps), seasonal sites, cable, WiFi, tent sites, laundry, LP gas. **REC:** heated pool, shuffleboard, playground. Pet restrict(Q). Big rig sites, 2015 rates: $35 to $43. Disc: AAA.
AAA Approved
(800)928-9962 Lat: 28.99652, Lon: -80.94326
1300 Old Mission Rd, New Smyrna Beach, FL 32168
beachcamp@beachcamp.net
www.beachcamp.net
See ad pages 336, 282.

← SUGAR MILL RUINS TRAVEL PARK, LLC
Ratings: 9/9★/8.5 (RV Park) From Jct of I-95 & SR-44 exit 249A, E 2.8 mi on SR-44 to Mission Drive (becomes Old Mission Rd), S 1 mi (R). **FAC:** Gravel rds. (225 spaces). Avail: 100 dirt, 50 pull-thrus (25 x 60), back-ins (25 x 60), some side by side hkups, accepts self-contain units only, 100 full hkups (30/50 amps), seasonal sites, cable, WiFi, dump, laundry, groc, LP gas, controlled access. **REC:** heated pool, Turnbull Creek: fishing, shuffleboard, playground. Pet restrict(B). Partial handicap access, no tents. Eco-friendly, 2015 rates: $30.95 to $39.95.
(386)427-2284 Lat: 29.00134, Lon: -80.94003
1050 Old Mission Rd, New Smyrna Beach, FL 32168
sugarmillruinscampground@gmail.com
www.sugarmillruinsrvpark.com/
See ad this page, 282.

NICEVILLE — F2 *Okaloosa*

➔ FRED GANNON ROCKY BAYOU SRA (State Pk) From Jct of I-10 & SR-85, S 14 mi on SR-85 to SR-20 (in Niceville), E 3 mi (L). 2015 rates: $16. (850)833-9144

NOKOMIS — D3 *Sarasota*

➔ ROYAL COACHMAN RV RESORT **Ratings: 9/9★/9** (RV Resort) 2015 rates: $44 to $83. (800)405-6188 1070 Laurel Rd E, Nokomis, FL 34275

OAKLAND PARK — E5 *Broward*

↑ EASTERLIN PARK (Public) From Jct of I-95 & Commercial Blvd, W 0.5 mi on Commercial Blvd to Powerline Rd, S 1.5 mi to NW 38th St, W 1 blk across railroad tracks (L). **FAC:** Paved rds. 55 gravel, back-ins (20 x 40), 45 full hkups, 6 W, 6 E (30/50 amps), WiFi Hotspot, tent sites, dump, fire rings. **REC:** pond, playground, rec open to public. Pet restrict(Q). Partial handicap access. 2015 rates: $30 to $40.
(954)357-5190 Lat: 26.17351, Lon: -80.15806
1000 NW 38th St, Oakland Park, FL 33309
easterlinpark@broward.org
www.broward.org/parks

OCALA — G2 *Marion*

← HOLIDAY TRAV-L-PARK RV RESORT **Ratings: 8/8★/7** (RV Park) 2015 rates: $36.75. (800)833-2164 4001 W Silver Springs Blvd, Ocala, FL 34482

↖ OAK TREE VILLAGE CAMPGROUND & MHP
Ratings: 7.5/8/6 (Campground) From Jct of I-75 & US-27 exit 354, W 0.2 mi on US-27 to driveway, N 0.3 mi (R). **FAC:** Poor paved/dirt rds. (187 spaces). Avail: 137 grass, 137 pull-thrus (25 x 60), some side by side hkups, accepts self-contain units only, 70 full hkups, 67 W, 67 E (30 amps), seasonal sites, WiFi, dump, laundry. **REC:** pool, shuf-

Don't camp without it ... Our 2016 listings are your key to travel satisfaction.

Are you using a friend's Guide? Want one of your own? Call 877-209-6655.

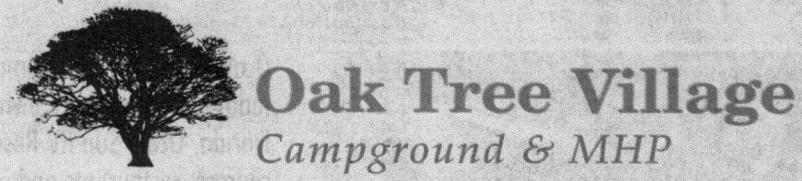

OCALA SUN
RV Resort

Explore Sunny Central Florida

Ocala Sun is a resort community designed to fulfill every wish of today's discerning RV owner. Conveniently located in sunny central Florida, Ocala Sun RV Resort is within minutes of numerous golf courses, restaurants and other attractions.

- 175 Spacious Full Hookup Sites • 50 Amp • Big Rig Friendly
- Large Clubhouse with Community Room, Kitchen, Sparkling Clean Private Showers/Baths • Laundry Facilities
- Heated Outdoor Pool & Spa
- Outdoor Recreation and Picnic Area • Numerous Walking Trails
- 65+ Channel Cable TV & WiFi included free at all sites
- Pet Friendly with Fenced Dog Run Area
- A Secure Community with Entry Gate & Perimeter Privacy fence
- Full Activities & Events Calendar with Lots of Fun for Everyone
- Professional, Helpful & Friendly Staff
- Onsite Coach Detail

STAFFED 24/7

2559 SW Hwy 484 • Ocala, Florida 34473
Phone: (352) 307-1100
Toll Free: (877) 809-1100
www.ocalasunrvresort.com

Hwy Exit # 341

Good Sam RATED 9/10★/9.5

Good Sam Park

See listing Ocala, FL

OCALA (CONT)

OAK TREE VILLAGE CAMPGROUND (CONT)
fleboard, playground. Pet restrict(B). No tents. 2015 rates: $28 to $32.
AAA Approved
(352)629-1569 Lat: 29.20855, Lon: -82.18887
4039 NW Blichton Rd, Ocala, FL 34475
manager@oaktreevillageocala.com
www.oaktreevillageocala.com
See ad page 379.

OCALA RV & CAMP RESORT
Ratings: 8.5/8.5★/7 (Campground) From Jct of I-75 & SR-200 (Exit 350), W 300 ft on SR-200 to SW 38th Ave (beside Cracker Barrel), N 0.1 mi to stop, E 0.5 mi on 38th Ave (L). **FAC:** Paved/dirt rds. (291 spaces). Avail: 166 dirt, 166 pull-thrus (25 x 50), accepts self-contain units only, 166 full hkups (30/50 amps), seasonal sites, cable, WiFi, tent sites, dump, laundry, LP gas, firewood. **REC:** heated pool, wading pool, pond, shuffleboard, playground. Pet restrict(B/Q). Partial handicap access. Big rig sites, 2015 rates: $30 to $36. Disc: AAA.
(352)237-2138 Lat: 29.15648, Lon: -82.18621
3200 SW 38th Ave, Ocala, FL 34474
ocalarvcampresort@yahoo.com
www.rvcampocala.com
See ad pages 379, 282.

OCALA SUN RV RESORT
Ratings: 9/10★/9.5 (RV Resort) From Jct of I-75 & SR-484 (Exit 341), W 0.5 mi on SR-484 (R).

SPEND A NIGHT OR A LIFETIME!
Ocala Sun RV Park. Set smack dab in the center of the "Winner's Circle" of destinations, including Daytona Beach, Crystal River, Gainesville & Orlando, the town of Ocala offers easy access to it all!

FAC: Gravel rds. 171 grass, 60 pull-thrus (30 x 60), back-ins (30 x 60), accepts self-contain units only, 171 full hkups (50 amps), cable, WiFi, dump, laundry, LP gas, controlled access. **REC:** heated pool, whirlpool, shuffleboard. Pet restrict(Q). Partial handicap access, no tents. Big rig sites, eco-friendly, 2015 rates: $34 to $44. Disc: AAA, military.
(352)307-1100 Lat: 29.02729, Lon: -82.16729
2559 SW Hwy 484, Ocala, FL 34473
info@ocalasunrvresort.com
www.ocalasunrvresort.com
See ad opposite page, 282 & Pampered Pets in Magazine Section.

WANDERING OAKS RV RESORT
Ratings: 8/8.5★/8 (RV Resort) From Jct of I-75 & SR-326 (Exit 358), E 2.2 mi on SR-326 (R). **FAC:** Paved rds. 85 grass, 40 pull-thrus (45 x 100), back-ins (45 x 100), accepts self-contain units only, 85 full hkups (30/50 amps), cable, WiFi, dump, laundry, LP gas, firewood. **REC.** Pet restrict(B). No tents. Age restrict may apply, big rig sites, eco-friendly, 2015 rates: $34.
(866)380-6700 Lat: 29.25764, Lon: -82.15498
1860 W Hwy 326, Ocala, FL 34475
info@wanderingoaksrv.com
www.wanderingoaksrv.com
See ad this page, 282.

WILD FRONTIER RV PARK Ratings: 9/8/7.5 (Condo Pk) 2015 rates: $34. (352)629-3540 3101 Nw 16th Ave, Ocala, FL 34475

OCKLAWAHA — G3 *Marion*

LAKE IN THE FOREST RESORT **Ratings: 8/7.5★/8** (Campground) 2015 rates: $40. (877)LIFESOK 19175 SE 44th St, Ocklawaha, FL 32179

ODESSA — K2 *Hillsborough*

SILVER DOLLAR GOLF & TRAP CLUB RESORT **Ratings: 8.5/8★/8** (Membership Pk) 2015 rates: $25 to $60. (800)405-6188 12515 Silver Dollar Drive, Odessa, FL 32726

OKEECHOBEE — D4 *Glades, Okeechobee*

BIG LAKE LODGE & RV PARK **Ratings: 4.5/6/6.5** (RV Park) 2015 rates: $40 to $55. (863)763-4638 8680 Hwy 441 S.e., Okeechobee, FL 34974

BRIGHTON RV RESORT
Ratings: 8/8.5/9 (RV Park) From jct US 441 & Hwy 70:Go 16 mi W on Hwy 70, then 13 mi S on SR 721 (R).

A NATURAL WONDER OF REAL FLORIDA
Newly renovated RV Resort with cabins, RV sites, 24-hr store, salon & day spa, & pool. Swim, fish or walk along the lakefront. Spend evenings in nearby Seminole Brighton Casino with slots, bingo, poker & Josiah's Restaurant.

FAC: Paved rds. (56 spaces). Avail: 50 paved, back-ins (40 x 75), 50 full hkups (30/50 amps), seasonal sites, WiFi, rentals, dump, laundry, groc, LP bottles. **REC:** heated pool, rec open to public. Pet restrict(B/Q). Partial handicap access. 2015 rates: $35 to $40. Disc: AAA, military. ATM.
(863)357-6644 Lat: 27.04331, Lon: -81.06901
14685 Reservation Rd, Okeechobee, FL 34974
reservation@semtribe.com
www.brightonrvresort.com
See ad pages 315 (Spotlight Okeechobee County), 284 & Snowbird Destinations in Magazine Section.

GRACIOUS RV PARK **Ratings: 6.5/5.5/7** (RV Park) 2015 rates: $36. (863)763-6200 6500 Highway 441 SE, Okeechobee, FL 34974

OKEECHOBEE KOA KAMPGROUND & GOLF COURSE **Ratings: 9/10★/9** (RV Park) 2015 rates: $54 to $85. (863)763-0231 4276 US Hwy 441 S, Okeechobee, FL 34974

SILVER PALMS RV RESORT
Ratings: 9.5/10★/10 (Condo Pk) From Jct of US-441 & SR 70, S 4 mi on US-441 (R).

Fun. It's in Our Nature.
Silver Palms RV Resort, just minutes from Lake Okeechobee, features full hookup sites, large clubhouse, gym, pool, sport courts, activities, and 16 acres of wetlands and wildlife preserve. RV lot sales and rentals available.

FAC: Paved rds. (364 spaces). 199 Avail: 100 paved, 99 grass, patios, 16 pull-thrus (40 x 90), back-ins (40 x 75), accepts full hkup units only, 199 full hkups (30/50 amps), seasonal sites, WiFi, laundry, LP gas, controlled access. **REC:** heated pool, whirlpool,

FL

OKEECHOBEE (CONT)

SILVER PALMS RV RESORT (CONT)
pond, fishing, shuffleboard. Pet restrict(Q). Partial handicap access, no tents. Big rig sites, RV age restrict, eco-friendly, 2015 rates: $38 to $115. Disc: AAA, military.
(888)323-4833 Lat: 27.20633, Lon: -80.83060
4143 U.s. Hwy 441 S, Okeechobee, FL 34974
reservations@silverpalmsrv.com
www.silverpalmsrv.com
See ad pages 381, 284 & Snowbird Destinations in Magazine Section.

TAYLOR CREEK RESORT RV PARK **Ratings: 5.5/6/6** (RV Park) 2015 rates: $40 to $60. (863)763-4417 2730 Hwy 441 SE, Okeechobee, FL 34974

WATER'S EDGE MOTOR COACH & RV RESORT
Ratings: 9/NA/10 (RV Park) From Jct of SR-70 & SR-710 (E of town), E 5.7 mi on SR-710 to CR-15A, S 0.9 mi to US 441, E 11.3 mi (R); or From Jct of SR-76 & SR-710 in Indiantown, W 11.5 mi on SR-76 to US 441, N 5.3 mi (L). **FAC:** Paved rds. (30 spaces). Avail: 24 paved, patios, back-ins (35 x 65), accepts full hkup units only, 24 full hkups (30/50 amps), seasonal sites, WiFi, controlled access. **REC:** pool, Lake Okeechobee Rim Canal: fishing, shuffleboard. Pet restrict(B/Q). Partial handicap access, no tents. Big rig sites, RV age restrict, 2015 rates: $35 to $60. Disc: AAA, military.
AAA Approved
(863)357-5757 Lat: 27.14581, Lon: -80.69471
12766 Hwy 441 SE, Okeechobee, FL 34974
watersedgerv@innisfree.com
www.okeechobeervpark.com
See ad page 381.

ZACHARY TAYLOR RV RESORT **Ratings: 8.5/9★/8.5** (Campground) 2015 rates: $25.50 to $50. (863)763-3377 2995 US Highway 441 SE, Okeechobee, FL 34974

Things to See and Do

OKEECHOBEE COUNTY TOURISM DEVELOPMENT COUNCIL Okeechobee County is on the North shore of Lake Okeechobee, 2nd largest freshwater lake in US. Over 5000 campsites in the county. Local events include annual festivals, PRCA rodeos & a sportsman's paradise. Call for information. Hours: 8am to 5pm. No CC.
(863)763-3959 Lat: 27.26574, Lon: -80.85575
tourism@co.okeechobee.fl.us
www.visitokeechobeecounty.com
See ad page 316 (Spotlight Okeechobee County).

Heading South? We have lots of Snowbird Destination ideas to explore at the front of the Guide.

OLD TOWN — B2 *Dixie*

LUCKY CHARM RV PARK
Ratings: 9/9.5★/9 (RV Park) From Jct of US 19/98 & SR-349, N 4 mi on SR-349 (R). **FAC:** Gravel rds. 67 Avail: 67 all weather, 60 pull-thrus (40 x 150), back-ins (40 x 80), 67 full hkups (30/50 amps), cable, WiFi, laundry, fire rings. **REC:** pool, whirlpool, shuffleboard. Pets OK. Partial handicap access, no tents. Age restrict may apply, big rig sites, RV age restrict, eco-friendly, 2015 rates: $32.
(352)542-0033 Lat: 29.66054, Lon: -82.98350
4114 NE Hwy 349 N, Old Town, FL 32680
luckycharmrvpark@gmail.com
www.luckycharmrvpark.com
See ad this page, 282.

OLD TOWN CAMPGROUND Ratings: 7/8.5★/8 (Campground) From Jct of 19/98, US-27A & CR-349, S 2 mi on CR-349 (L). **FAC:** Gravel rds. 47 grass, 14 pull-thrus (40 x 80), back-ins (40 x 80), 29 full hkups, 18 W, 18 E (30/50 amps), cable, WiFi Hotspot, dump, laundry, LP bottles, firewood. **REC.** Pets OK. Partial handicap access, no tents. Big rig sites, eco-friendly, 2015 rates: $27. Disc: AAA, military. No CC.
(888)950-2267 Lat: 29.56943, Lon: -82.98395
2241 SE 349 Hwy, Old Town, FL 32680
oldtowncampground@gmail.com
www.oldtowncampground.com

New to RVing? Be sure to check out the all the great articles on getting the most out of your RV, at the front of the Guide.

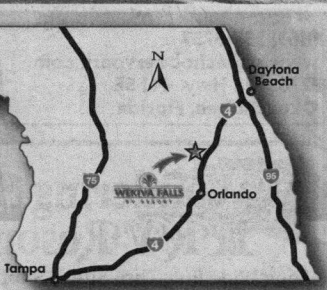

OLD TOWN (CONT)

SUWANNEE RIVER HIDEAWAY
Ratings: 9/8★/9 (Campground) From Jct of US 19/98/27A & SR-349, S 3 mi on SR-349 to CR-346 A, E 1 mi (R). **FAC:** Gravel rds. (84 spaces). Avail: 59 grass, patios, 25 pull-thrus (35 x 60), back-ins (35 x 60), 34 full hkups, 25 W, 25 E (30/50 amps), seasonal sites, cable, WiFi, tent sites, dump, laundry, firewood. **REC:** pool, Suwannee River: fishing. Pets OK. Partial handicap access. Big rig sites, 2015 rates: $30 to $34. Disc: AAA.
AAA Approved
(352)542-7800 Lat: 29.55426, Lon: -82.96749
1218 SE 346 Hwy, Old Town, FL 32680
camping@riverhideaway.com
www.riverhideaway.com
See ad opposite page, 282.

YELLOW JACKET RV RESORT **Ratings: 9/10★/9** (RV Resort) 2015 rates: $34 to $49. (352)542-8365 55 SE 503 Ave, Old Town, FL 32680

ORANGE CITY — H4 *Volusia*

BLUE SPRING (State Pk) 2 mi W of Orange City - off US-17-92. (386)775-3663

CLARK FAMILY CAMPGROUND Ratings: 8/8.5/8 (Campground) From Jct of I-4 & SR-472 (exit 114), W 1.5 mi on SR-472 to Minnesota Ave, SW 0.2 mi (L). **FAC:** Gravel rds. (190 spaces). Avail: 145 dirt, patios, 47 pull-thrus (20 x 55), back-ins (20 x 55), mostly side by side hkups, accepts self-contain units only, 80 full hkups, 20 W, 20 E (30/50 amps), WiFi $, tent sites, dump, laundry, groc, LP gas, firewood. **REC:** pool, pond, playground, rec open to public. Pet restrict(B). 2015 rates: $25 to $55. Disc: military.
AAA Approved
(866)953-3358 Lat: 28.96944, Lon: -81.28778
1440 E Minnesota Ave, Orange City, FL 32763
info@clarkfamilycampground.com
www.clarkfamilycampground.com

ORANGE CITY RV RESORT
Ratings: 9.5/9★/8 (RV Park) From Jct of I-4 & SR-472 (exit 114), W 0.3 mi on SR-472 to CR-4101, S 0.75 mi to Graves Ave, E 0.1 mi (R).

NEAR THE BEST FLORIDA ATTRACTIONS
From Daytona to Disney World, you can have the best of Florida at your doorstep! Conveniently located between Daytona and Orlando, enjoy roomy sites with great amenities like a heated pool and spa, billiards and more!

FAC: Paved/gravel rds. (344 spaces). 244 Avail: 46 paved, 57 gravel, 104 grass, 37 dirt, 20 pull-thrus (25 x 55), back-ins (25 x 55), accepts self-contain units only, 244 full hkups (30/50 amps), seasonal sites, cable, WiFi, tent sites, rentals, dump, laundry, LP gas. **REC:** heated pool, wading pool, whirlpool, shuffleboard. Pet restrict(B). Partial handicap access. 2015 rates: $34 to $44. Disc: AAA, military.
AAA Approved
(888)653-1480 Lat: 28.94777, Lon: -81.26356
2300 E Graves Ave, Orange City, FL 32763
orangecityrv@suncommunities.com
www.orangecityrvresort.com
See ad pages 332, 275 (Welcome Section), 282, 1463 (Welcome Section) & Family Camping, Snowbird Destinations in Magazine Section.

Driving a big rig? Average site width and length measurements tell you which campgrounds can accommodate your wide load.

ORLANDO — J4 *Orange, Osceola, Seminole, Lake, Polk*

ORLANDO AREA MAP

Symbols on map indicate towns within a 45 mile radius of Orlando where campgrounds are listed. Check listings for more information.

See also Apopka, Clermont, Cocoa, Davenport, Debary, Dundee, Eustis, Haines City, Kissimmee, Lake Buena Vista, Leesburg, Orange City, Polk City, Sanford, St Cloud, Tavares, Titusville, Umatilla, Winter Garden & Winter Haven.

BILL FREDERICK PARK AT TURKEY LAKE (Public) From Jct of I-4 (exit 75B) & SR-435/Kirkman Rd-N: Go N 1.5 mi on Kirkman Rd, then W 1.5 mi on Conroy Rd, then N 0.9 mi Hiawassee Rd. (R). 2015 rates: $13.33 to $20.44. (407)246-4486

DISNEY'S FORT WILDERNESS RESORT & CAMPGROUND
Ratings: 10/10★/10 (Campground) From Jct I-4 (Exit 64) & US-192: Go W 0.75 mi on US-192, then N 1 mi on World Dr (R). **FAC:** Paved rds. 709 paved, 90 all weather, back-ins (35 x 60), 709 full hkups, 90 W, 90 E (30/50 amps), cable, WiFi, tent sites, rentals, dump, laundry, groc, restaurant, controlled access. **REC:** heated pool, whirlpool, Bay Lake: fishing, playground. Pets OK $. Partial handicap access. Big rig sites, 2015 rates: $69 to $145. Disc: AAA. ATM.
(407)939-7723 Lat: 28.3933, Lon: -81.55524
4510 N. Fort Wilderness Trail, Lake Buena Vista, FL 32830
disneyworld.disney.go.com/resorts/campsites-at-fort-wilderness-resort/
See primary listing at Lake Buena Vista and ad page 384.

Like Us on Facebook.

MOSS PARK (Public) From Jct of Hwy 528 & SR-15, S 2.5 mi on SR-15 to Moss Park Rd, N 4.5 mi (E) Note: No alcohol allowed in park. 2015 rates: $15 to $23. (407)254-6840

ORLANDO S.E./LAKE WHIPPOORWILL KOA **Ratings: 8.5/8★/7.5** (Campground) 2015 rates: $48 to $70. (407)277-5075 12345 Narcoossee Rd, Orlando, FL 32832

OUTDOOR RESORTS AT ORLANDO, INC
Ratings: 9.5/9.5★/9 (Condo Pk) From jct I-4 (exit 64B) & US-192: Go W 7.9 mi on US-192 (L). **FAC:** Paved rds. (979 spaces). Avail: 41 paved, patios, back-ins (35 x 60), 41 full hkups (30/50 amps), seasonal sites, cable, WiFi Hotspot, rentals, dump, laundry, LP gas, controlled access. **REC:** heated pool, Lake Davenport: fishing, marina, golf, shuffleboard, playground. Pet restrict(B/Q). Partial handicap access, no tents. Big rig sites, 2015 rates: $40 to $50. Disc: AAA, military.
(863)424-1407 Lat: 28.34640, Lon: -81.65746
9000 US Hwy 192, Clermont, FL 34714
leslie@RentWithORO.com
www.RentWithORO.com
See primary listing at Clermont and ad this page.

Nobody takes to the road like we do. In many listings we tell you the surface type and condition of interior campground roads.

FL

See listing Lake Buena Vista, FL

ORMOND BEACH — G4 *Flagler, Volusia*

CORAL SANDS RV RESORT
Ratings: 8.5/8.5★/8 (RV Resort) From the Jct of I-95 & US40/Granada Blvd (Exit 268) E 4.1 mi on US40/Granada Blvd to SRA1A, N 2 mi (R). **FAC:** All weather rds. 31 gravel, back-ins (20 x 40), accepts full hkup units only, 31 full hkups (30/50 amps), WiFi, rentals, laundry. **REC:** heated pool, Atlantic Ocean. Pets OK. No tents. 2015 rates: $55 to $88. Disc: military. ATM.
(800)441-1831 Lat: 29.317592, Lon: -81.052521
1047 Ocean Shore Blvd, Ormond Beach, FL 32176
reservation@coralsandsinn.com
www.coralsandsinn.com
See ad pages 340, 282.

HARRIS VILLAGE & ADULT RV PARK LLC
Ratings: 8/9★/8.5 (RV Park) From Jct of I-95 & US-1 (exit 273), S 2.5 mi on US-1 (R). **FAC:** Paved rds. (30 spaces). 24 Avail: 10 paved, 14 grass, patios, 4 pull-thrus (30 x 60), back-ins (25 x 50), 24 full hkups (30/50 amps), cable, WiFi, dump, laundry. **REC.** Pet restrict(B/Q). Partial handicap access, no tents. Age restrict may apply, big rig sites, eco-friendly, 2015 rates: $49.95. Disc: AAA, military.
(386)673-0494 Lat: 29.31034, Lon: -81.10130
1080 N US-1, Ormond Beach, FL 32174
harrisvillage@aol.com
www.harrisvillage.com
See ad pages 341, 282.

TOMOKA BASIN GEOPARK (State Pk) From Jct of US-1 & SR-40, E 0.5 mi on SR-40 to Beach St, N 3 mi (R). CAUTION: Max height 11ft, length 34 ft. 2015 rates: $24. (386)676-4050

OSPREY — D3 *Sarasota*

OSCAR SCHERER (State Pk) From Jct of US-41 & SR-681, N 1.6 mi on US-41 (R). 2015 rates: $26. (941)483-5956

PAHOKEE — D5 *Palm Beach*

PAHOKEE CAMPGROUND & MARINA
Ratings: 7.5/7.5/8 (Campground) From jct S Hwy 715 & N US-441: Go 100 ft N on US-441, then 1 blk W on S Lake Ave (E). **FAC:** Paved rds. (118 spaces). Avail: 112 grass, back-ins (30 x 50), 112 full hkups (30/50 amps), WiFi Hotspot, tent sites, dump, laundry, restaurant. **REC:** pool, Lake Okeechobee: fishing, marina. Pets OK $. Partial handicap access. 2015 rates: $30. Disc: military.
(561)924-7832 Lat: 26.82502, Lon: -80.66639
190 North Lake Avenue, Pahokee, FL 33476
marina&campground@cityofpahokee.com
www.cityofpahokee.com
See ad this page.

PALATKA — B4 *Putnam*

RODMAN (COE - LAKE OCKLAWAHA) (Public Corps) From jct Hwy 20 & Hwy 19: Go 12 mi S on Hwy 19, then 2 mi W on Rodman Dam Rd. Pit toilets. 2015 rates: $12 to $22. (386)326-2846

PALM COAST — B4 *Flagler*

Things to See and Do

PALM COAST AND THE FLAGLER BEACHES Comprehensive area information. Hours: 9am to 5pm. No CC.
(800)670-2640 Lat: 29.47481, Lon: -81.20827
20 Airport Road, Suite B, Palm Coast, FL 32164
jaffy@flaglerchamber.org
http://www.palmcoastandtheflaglerbeaches.com
See ad page 296 (Spotlight Flagler County/Palm Coast).

PALM HARBOR — K1 *Pinellas*

BAY AIRE RV PARK **Ratings: 7/7.5/6.5** (RV Park) 2015 rates: $40 to $65. (727)784-4082 2242 Alt US-19, Palm Harbor, FL 34683

CLEARWATER-TARPON SPRINGS RV CAMPGROUND **Ratings: 7.5/8/6** (Campground) 2015 rates: $45. (877)420-2267 37061 US-19N, Palm Harbor, FL 34684

SHERWOOD FOREST RV PARK
Ratings: 7.5/8.5★/8 (RV Park) From Jct of Alt US-19 & SR-584 (Tampa Rd): Go S 100 ft on Alt US-19 (R). **FAC:** Paved rds. (106 spaces). Avail: 49 grass, patios, back-ins (30 x 45), 49 full hkups (30/50 amps), seasonal sites, WiFi, laundry. **REC:** heated pool, pond, fishing. Pet restrict(B/Q). Partial handicap access, no tents. Big rig sites, 2015 rates: $40 to $65. Disc: AAA.
AAA Approved
(727)784-4582 Lat: 28.06702, Lon: -82.77018
175 Alt 19S, Palm Harbor, FL 34683
sherwoodrv@aol.com
www.sherwoodrvresort.com
See ad pages 332, 286.

PALMDALE — D4 *Glades*

FISHEATING CREEK OUTPOST (Public) From jct Hwy 29 & US 27: Go 1 mi N on US 27. 2015 rates: $29. (863)675-5999

SABAL PALM RV RESORT **Ratings: 8/7.5/8** (RV Park) 2015 rates: $35. (863)675-1778 1947 Main Ave N, Palmdale, FL 33944

PALMETTO — L2 *Manatee*

FIESTA GROVE RV RESORT
Ratings: 9/9★/8 (RV Park) From Jct of I-75 (Exit 228) & I-275: Go W 2 mi on I-275, then N 0.7 mi on US-41, then W 0.5 mi on Bayshore Rd (R). **FAC:** Paved rds. (220 spaces). 80 Avail: 65 paved, 15 grass, patios, back-ins (30 x 60), 65 full hkups, 15 W, 15 E (50 amps), seasonal sites, WiFi, dump, laundry. **REC:** heated pool, shuffleboard. Pet restrict(B/Q). No tents. Age restrict may apply, big rig sites, 2015 rates: $30 to $39. Disc: AAA, military. No CC.
(877)722-7661 Lat: 27.59222, Lon: -82.54510
8615 Bayshore Rd, Palmetto, FL 34221
fiestagrove@newbymanagement.com
www.fiestagroverv.com
See ad pages 271 (Welcome Section), 286.

FISHERMANS COVE RV RESORT **Ratings: 6.5/7.5/6.5** (RV Park) 2015 rates: $30 to $50. (941)729-3685 100 Palmview Rd, Palmetto, FL 34221

FROG CREEK RV RESORT & CAMPGROUND **Ratings: 8.5/8/8.5** (Campground) 2015 rates: $40 to $55. (941)722-6154 8515 Bayshore Rd, Palmetto, FL 34221

TERRA CEIA VILLAGE RV RESORT **Ratings: 8.5/8.5★/8.5** (RV Park) 2015 rates: $29 to $39. (800)405-6188 9303 Bayshore Dr, Palmetto, FL 34221

Tell them you saw them in this Guide!

WINTERSET RV RESORT
Ratings: 9/9★/8 (RV Park) From Jct of I-275 (Exit 2) & US-41: Go N 0.4 mi on US-41 (L). **FAC:** Paved rds. (237 spaces). Avail: 65 grass, patios, back-ins (30 x 70), 65 full hkups (30/50 amps), seasonal sites, WiFi, dump, laundry. **REC:** heated pool, Frog Creek: fishing, shuffleboard. Pet restrict(B/Q). No tents. Age restrict may apply, big rig sites, 2015 rates: $30 to $39. Disc: AAA, military.
(877)946-8376 Lat: 27.59056, Lon: -82.54118
8515 US Hwy 41 N, Palmetto, FL 34221
winterset@newbymanagement.com
www.wintersetrvresort.com
See ad pages 271 (Welcome Section), 286.

PANACEA — B1 *Wakulla*

HOLIDAY CAMPGROUND **Ratings: 8.5/8.5★/7.5** (Campground) 2015 rates: $36.75. (850)984-5757 14 Coastal Hwy, Panacea, FL 32346

PANAMA CITY — F2 *Bay*

Travel Services

CAMPING WORLD OF PANAMA CITY As the nation's largest retailer of RV supplies, accessories, services and new and used RVs, Camping World is committed to making your total RV experience better. RV Accessories: (855)890-0281. **SERVICES:** RV Sales. RV supplies, LP. Hours: 8:00 - 6:00.
(888)804-5063 Lat: 30.191104, Lon: -85.713355
4100 W. 23rd Street, Panama City, FL 32405
www.campingworld.com

PANAMA CITY BEACH — F2 *Bay*

CAMPERS INN
Ratings: 9/9★/6 (Campground) W-bnd: From Hathaway Bridge, W 0.25 mi on US-98 to C-3031 (Thomas Dr), S 7 mi (R); or E-bnd: From Jct of US-98 & C-3033, E 0.7 mi on C-3033 to Hwy 392 (Thomas Dr), SE 2 mi (L). **FAC:** Paved rds. 115 Avail: 88 paved, 27 grass, patios, 11 pull-thrus (20 x 65), back-ins (30 x 40), some side by side hkups, accepts self-contain units only, 115 full hkups (30/50 amps), cable, WiFi, tent sites, dump, laundry, groc, LP gas, controlled access. **REC:** pool, wading pool, Grand Lagoon: shuffleboard, playground. Pets OK. Partial handicap access. Big rig sites, eco-friendly, 2015 rates: $44.95 to $54.95. Disc: AAA. ATM.
AAA Approved
(866)USA-CAMP Lat: 30.17072, Lon: -85.79302
8800 Thomas Dr, Panama City Beach, FL 32408
manager@campersinn.net
www.campersinn.net
See ad pages 387, 282.

Subscribe to Trailer Life Magazine. For a subscription, call 800-825-6861.

Northwest Florida's Finest Resort

Located in Panama City Beach, home to "The World's Most Beautiful Beaches"

A Family & Snowbird Paradise...

Treat yourself to the best RV Resort destination in North Florida. Experience the most luxurious, cleanest and friendliest resort with spotless grounds & facilities and friendly, helpful staff who treat you like family. Free coffee, free Beach Shuttle in summer and fabulous weekend buffets!

Ask About Our Introductory Offer

Emerald Coast
RV Beach Resort
1957 Allison Ave.
Panama City Beach
Florida 32407

1-800-BEACH-RV
(1 -800-232-2478)

RVInfo@RVResort.com
www.RVResort.com

RATED
10/10★/10

See listing
Panama City Beach, FL

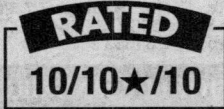

Brick paver or concrete roads & pads • huge pull-thrus • 2 heated pools • spa • clubhouse restaurant • gameroom • playground • 3 bathhouses w/laundry • dog park • fitness center volleyball • basketball • soccer • fishing • paddleboats • bike rentals • propane park models for rent or sale • separate class A motor coach section

PANAMA CITY BEACH (CONT)

EMERALD COAST RV BEACH RESORT
Ratings: 10/10★/10 (RV Resort) From Hathaway Bridge, W 1.5 mi on US-98 (Panama City Beach Pkwy) to Alison Ave, S 0.25 mi (R).

A FAMILY & SNOWBIRD PARADISE
Treat yourself to the best RV Resort destination in North Florida. Experience the most luxurious, cleanest & friendliest resort with spotless grounds & facilities & friendly helpful staff who treat you like family.
FAC: Paved rds. 242 paved, patios, 25 pull-thrus (35 x 70), back-ins (35 x 65), 172 full hkups (30/50 amps), cable, WiFi $, dump, laundry, LP gas, firewood, controlled access. **REC:** heated pool, whirlpool, Emerald Lake: fishing, shuffleboard, playground. Pet restrict(B). Partial handicap access, no tents. Big rig sites, 2015 rates: $67 to $92.
AAA Approved
(800)BEACHRV Lat: 30.18375, Lon: -85.78699
1957 Allison Ave, Panama City Beach, FL 32407
rvinfo@rvresort.com
www.RVResort.com
See ad opposite page, 270 (FL Map) & Family Camping, Pampered Pets, RV Trips of a Lifetime in Magazine Section.

PANAMA CITY BEACH RV RESORT Ratings: 9/9.5★/9 (RV Park) From Jct of US 98 & Thomas Rd, S 3.5 mi on Thomas Rd to CR 392, E 0.3 mi (L). **FAC:** Paved rds. 69 paved, patios, 14 pull-thrus (35 x 80), back-ins (35 x 60), 69 full hkups (50 amps), cable, WiFi, laundry, controlled access. **REC:** heated pool. Pet restrict(Q). No tents. Big rig sites, 2015 rates: $57 to $74.
(866)637-3529 Lat: 30.13759, Lon: -85.74749
4702 Thomas Dr, Panama City Beach, FL 32408
info@panamacityrvresort.com
www.panamacityrvresort.com

PINEGLEN MOTORCOACH & RV PARK **Ratings: 7.5/9★/8.5** (RV Park) 2015 rates: $45 to $58. (850)230-8535 11930 Panama City Beach Parkway, Panama City Beach, FL 32407

RACCOON RIVER RESORT **Ratings: 7/7.5/7** (RV Park) 2015 rates: $40 to $63. (877)234-0181 12209 Hutchinson Blvd, Panama City Beach, FL 32407

ST ANDREWS SRA (State Pk) From Jct of US-98 & Hwy 3031, S 3.5 mi on Hwy 3031 to Thomas Dr, E 0.25 mi (E). 2015 rates: $28. (850)233-5140

PEMBROKE PINES — E5 *Broward*

CB SMITH PARK (Public) From Jct of I-75 & Pine Blvd, E 1 mi on Pine Blvd to Flamingo Rd, N 0.5 mi (L). **FAC:** Paved rds. 83 paved, back-ins (10 x 40), 83 full hkups (30/50 amps), WiFi, dump, laundry, controlled access. **REC:** pond, fishing, playground, rec open to public. Pet restrict(Q) $. Partial handicap access, no tents. 2015 rates: $30 to $40.
(954)357-5170 Lat: 26.014306, Lon: -80.312194
900 N Flamingo Rd, Pembroke Pines, FL 33028
cbsmithpark@broward.org
www.broward.org/parks

PENSACOLA — F1 *Escambia*

BIG LAGOON (State Pk) From jct Hwy 292 & Hwy 292A: Go 2 mi E on Hwy 292A. 2015 rates: $20. (850)492-1595

DRIFTERS RV PARK **Ratings: 7/8.5★/7.5** (RV Park) 2015 rates: $30. (850)484-2488 9110 Untreiner Rd, Pensacola, FL 32534

GULF ISLANDS NATIONAL SEASHORE (FORT PICKENS) (Natl Pk) From jct US-98 & Hwy-399: Go 15 mi SW on Hwy-399 & Ft. Pickens Rd. 2015 rates: $20 to $30. (850)934-2622

PENSACOLA BEACH RV RESORT
Ratings: 10/10★/9 (RV Resort) From Jct of US 98 & Pensacola Beach Blvd, E 2.2 mi on Pensacola Beach Blvd (becomes Via De Luna Dr at Fort Pickens Rd) (L). **FAC:** Paved rds. 72 paved, patios, 1 pull-thrus (30 x 60), back-ins (30 x 60), accepts full hkup units only, 72 full hkups (30/50 amps), cable, WiFi, laundry. **REC:** pool, Santa Rosa Sound: swim, shuffleboard. Pets OK. Partial handicap access, no tents. Big rig sites, 2015 rates: $65 to $125. Disc: military.
(850)438-1266 Lat: 30.33473, Lon: -87.13560
17 Via De Luna Dr., Pensacola, FL 32561
info@pensacolabeachrvresort.com
www.pensacolabeachrvresort.com
See ad pages 388, 282 & RV Trips of a Lifetime in Magazine Section.

Reducing your speed to 55 mph from 65 mph may increase your fuel efficiency by as much as 15 percent; cut it to 55 from 70, and you could get a 23 percent improvement.

PENSACOLA RV PARK
Ratings: 8/9.5★/9 (RV Park) From the Jct of IH 10 & Pine Forest Rd (Exit 7), S 0.1 mi on Pine Forest Rd to Wilde Lake Blvd., W (past the hotels & large church), 0.5 mi (L). **FAC:** Gravel rds. 67 gravel, patios, 16 pull-thrus (34 x 80), back-ins (34 x 70), 67 full hkups (30/50 amps), cable, WiFi, laundry, LP bottles. **REC:** pond, fishing, rec open to public. Pet restrict(B/Q). Partial handicap access, no tents. Big rig sites, 2015 rates: $38. Disc: AAA, military.
(850)944-1734 Lat: 30.51950, Lon: -87.32617
3117 Wilde Lake Blvd, Pensacola, FL 32526
info@pensacolarvpark.com
www.pensacolarvpark.com
See ad pages 389, 282.

FL

Pensacola RV Park
Good Sam Park
FREE WiFi
PARK AMENITIES:
• 23 Large Pull-Thru Sites
• Pet Friendly/2 Dog Runs
• WiFi Throughout the Park
• Kitchen Facilities
• Laundromat
• 30/50 Amp Hookup at Each Site
• Cable TV
NEARBY ACTIVITIES:
• Naval Aviation Museum
• Historical Downtown District
• Civic Center Concerts
• Deep Sea Fishing
• Stock Car Racing
• Fairgrounds
• Shopping
• Restaurants
• Golf
QUIET
DISCOUNTS:
Good Sam
First Responders
U.S. Military
3117 Wilde Lake Blvd.
Pensacola, FL 32526
(850) 944-1734
See listing Pensacola, FL
10
E-Bnd Exit 7A
W-Bnd Exit 7
Wilde Lake Blvd.
.7 mi.
10
PENSACOLA RV PARK
Pine Forest Rd.
N
www.pensacolarvpark.com

See listing Milton, FL
Less than 5 miles to Pensacola
Relaxing View
ROCKWOOD
Good Sam RATED 9/10★/9
Middle of Nowhere
Close to Everything
Walmart & Dining
10 Minutes
Airport, Mall & Hospitals
15 Minutes
Gulf Beaches
25 -30 Minutes
AVALON LANDING
RV PARK
75 Sites All Full Hookups
50, 30 & 20 Amp
Cable TV * Free WiFi(e-mail/light surfing)
Propane * Laundry
Clean Restrooms w/Showers(ADA)
Big Rigs - up to 45'
Long Pull-Thru Sites
Daily, Weekly
Monthly Rates
Pet Friendly
Late Night Check-In & After Hours Arrivals
Private Saltwater Fishing Bridge/Pier
(No Fishing Lic. Req)
2444 Avalon Blvd. (Hwy #281)
Milton, FL 32583
I-10 * Exit #22
South 1/2 mile
Easy Interstate Access
27 Waterfront Sites
Pull-in & Back-in
Private Boat Ramp
10% Off Daily Rates w/valid Good Sam or Active Duty Military
GPS - N 30° 31' 58.1"
W 87° 05' 22.9"
850-995-5898
Good Sam Park
Kayaking & Canoeing
Rental or Bring your Own
AvalonLandingRVPark.com
E-Mail : Contact@AvalonLandingRVPark.com

PERDIDO KEY — F1 *Escambia*

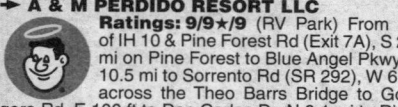

A & M PERDIDO RESORT LLC
Ratings: 9/9★/9 (RV Park) From Jct of IH 10 & Pine Forest Rd (Exit 7A), S 2.5 mi on Pine Forest to Blue Angel Pkwy, S 10.5 mi to Sorrento Rd (SR 292), W 6 mi across the Theo Barrs Bridge to Gongora Rd, E 100 ft to Don Carlos Dr, N 0.1 mi to River Rd, W 0.1 mi (R). **FAC:** Paved rds. 56 gravel, 13 pull-thrus (29 x 80), back-ins (30 x 75), accepts full hkup units only, 56 full hkups (30/50 amps), cable, WiFi, laundry, LP gas. **REC:** pool, Intercostal Waterway: marina, shuffleboard, playground. Pet restrict(B). Partial handicap access, no tents. Big rig sites, 2015 rates: $57 to $110. Disc: AAA, military.
(877)402-7873 Lat: 30.31132, Lon: -87.42855
13770 River Rd., Pensacola, FL 32507
frontdesk@theperdidoresort.com
www.theperdidoresort.com
See ad pages 17, 282.

PERRY — B2 *Jefferson, Taylor*

PERRY KOA **Ratings: 8/8.5★/7.5** (RV Park) 2015 rates: $34 to $38. (850)584-3221 3641 So. Byron Butler Pkwy, Perry, FL 32348

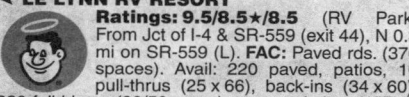

ROCKY'S CAMPGROUND
Ratings: 7/9.5★/7 (Campground) From the Jct of US 19 & US 98, W 4.5 mi on US 98 (L). **FAC:** Gravel rds. 47 grass, 9 pull-thrus (30 x 80), back-ins (30 x 60), some side by side hkups, 47 full hkups (30/50 amps), WiFi, laundry, groc. **REC.** Pets OK. Partial handicap access, no tents. Big rig sites, 2015 rates: $35.
(850)584-6600 Lat: 30.08448, Lon: -83.65833
5175 W US 98, Perry, FL 32348
See ad this page, 282.

POLK CITY — K3 *Polk*

LE LYNN RV RESORT
Ratings: 9.5/8.5★/8.5 (RV Park) From Jct of I-4 & SR-559 (exit 44), N 0.3 mi on SR-559 (L). **FAC:** Paved rds. (370 spaces). Avail: 220 paved, patios, 10 pull-thrus (25 x 66), back-ins (34 x 60), 220 full hkups (30/50 amps), seasonal sites, WiFi $, dump, laundry, LP gas. **REC:** pool, Little Lake Agnes: fishing, shuffleboard. Pet restrict(B/Q). Partial handicap access, no tents. Big rig sites, 2015 rates: $32 to $34. No CC.
(800)736-0409 Lat: 28.16321, Lon: -81.80183
1513 SR-559, Polk City, FL 33868
See ad pages 369, 286.

POMPANO BEACH — E5 *Broward*

BREEZY HILL **Ratings: 8.5/7.5/7.5** (RV Park) 2015 rates: $42 to $77. (866)340-0649 800 NE 48th St, Pompano Beach, FL 33064

HIGHLAND PINES RV RESORT Ratings: 8.5/7.5/7.5 (RV Park) From Jct of I-95 & Sample Rd (exit 39), E 1 mi on Sample Rd to Dixie Hwy (Rte 811), N 1 mi to 48th St, W 0.3 mi (R). **FAC:** Paved rds. (420 spaces). Avail: 220 paved, patios, back-ins (20 x 34), 220 full hkups (30/50 amps), seasonal sites, WiFi $, dump, laundry. **REC:** heated pool, shuffleboard. Pet restrict(B). Partial handicap access, no tents. 2015 rates: $45 to $50.
AAA Approved
(954)421-5372 Lat: 26.29013, Lon: -80.11226
875 NE 48th St, Deerfield Beach, FL 33064
highlandpines@bellsouth.net
www.florida-rv-parks.net

HIGHLAND WOODS RV RESORT **Ratings: 7/9.5★/7.5** (RV Park) 2015 rates: $42 to $77. (866)340-0649 800 NE 48th St, Pompano Beach, FL 33064

PORT CHARLOTTE — D3 *De Soto*

HARBOR LAKES RV RESORT **Ratings: 9/9/9** (RV Park) 2015 rates: $35 to $69. (800)405-6188 3737 El Jobean Rd, Port Charlotte, FL 33953

MYAKKA RIVER MOTORCOACH RESORT **Ratings: 10/9.5★/10** (RV Resort) 2015 rates: $90 to $120. (941)740-2599 14100 Myakka Ave, Port Charlotte, FL 33953

RIVERSIDE RV RESORT & CAMPGROUND
Ratings: 10/10★/9.5 (RV Park) From Jct of I-75 & CR-769 (Exit 170), NE 4.5 mi on CR-769/Kings Hwy (R).

A TRUE RV RESORT ON THE PEACE RIVER
You will love our quiet country setting, friendly helpful staff, sparkling facilities & outstanding planned activities! Enjoy our 2 heated pools, riverfront piers & boat ramp. Big rig & pet friendly. Nearby new Super Walmart!
FAC: Paved rds. (499 spaces). Avail: 449 all weather, patios, 5 pull-thrus (35 x 70), back-ins (45 x 80), 449 full hkups (30/50 amps), seasonal sites, cable, WiFi, tent sites, dump, laundry, groc, LP gas, fire rings, firewood, controlled access. **REC:** heated pool, whirlpool, Peace River: fishing, shuffleboard, playground. Pets OK. Partial handicap access. Big rig sites,

Shop at Camping World and SAVE with over $1,000 of coupons. Check the front of the Guide for yours!

FL

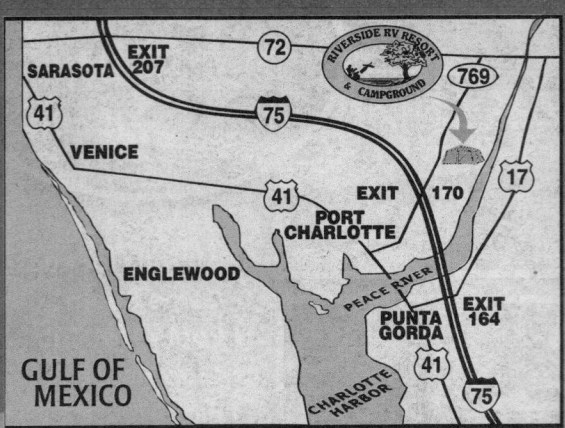

See listing Port Charlotte, FL

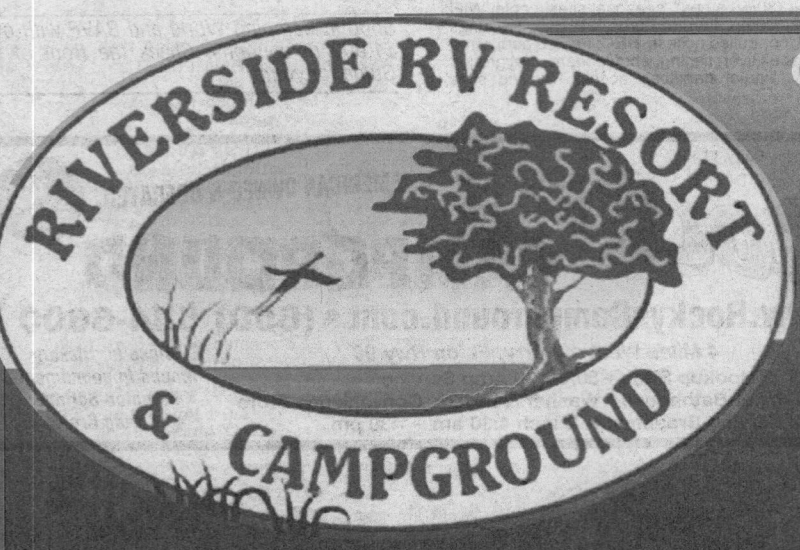

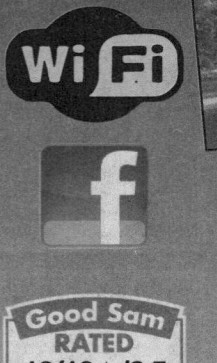

PORT CHARLOTTE (CONT)

RIVERSIDE RV RESORT & CAMP- (CONT)
eco-friendly, 2015 rates: $42 to $58. Disc: AAA, military.
AAA Approved
(800)795-9733 Lat: 27.07961, Lon: -82.01331
9770 SW Cr-769 Kings Hwy, Arcadia, FL 34269
riverside@desoto.net
www.riversidervresort.com
See ad opposite page, 268 (FL Map), 284 & Family Camping, RV Trips of a Lifetime, Snowbird Destinations in Magazine Section.

PORT ORANGE — G5 *Volusia*

DAYTONA BEACH KOA **Ratings: 8/7.5★/8** (RV Park) 2015 rates: $25 to $100. (386)767-9170 3520 S Nova Rd, Port Orange, FL 32129

DAYTONA BEACH RV RESORT
Ratings: 9.5/10★/8.5 (RV Park) From Jct of I-95 (exit 256) & SR 421, E 2 mi on SR 421 to Clyde Morris Blvd, N 1 mi (R).

DAYTONA BEACH CAREFREE RESORT
The world's most famous beach, International Speedway, and Orlando attractions nearby—it's what great vacations are made of! Enjoy all the excitement and then relax in a peceful, family-friendly resort.

FAC: Paved rds. 176 grass, 15 pull-thrus (28 x 70), back-ins (28 x 55), accepts self-contain units only, 176 full hkups (30/50 amps), cable, WiFi $, tent sites, dump, laundry, LP gas. **REC:** heated pool, wading pool, shuffleboard. Pet restrict(B). Partial handicap access. Big rig sites, 2015 rates: $44 to $49.
(386)761-2663 Lat: 29.13384, Lon: -81.02809
4601 S Clyde Morris Blvd, Port Orange, FL 32129
dbcampground@cfl.rr.com
www.carefreervresorts.com
See ad pages 336, 282 & Snowbird Destinations in Magazine Section.

ROSE BAY TRAVEL PARK **Ratings: 9/8.5/7** (RV Park) 2015 rates: $25 to $45. (386)767-4308 5200 S. Nova Rd, Port Orange, FL 32127

PORT RICHEY — J1 *Pasco*

JA-MAR NORTH TRAVEL PARK
Ratings: 8.5/9.5★/9 (RV Park) From Jct of SR-52 & US-19: Go S 0.5 mi on US-19, then W 0.2 mi on San Marco Dr. (E). **FAC:** Paved rds. (353 spaces). Avail: 202 grass, patios, back-ins (35 x 57), 202 full hkups (30/50 amps), seasonal sites, WiFi Hotspot, laundry. **REC:** heated pool, pond, fishing, shuffleboard. Pet restrict(B). Partial handicap access, no tents. Age restrict may apply, 2015 rates: $35. No CC.
(727)862-8882 Lat: 28.324078, Lon: -82.701649
6650 San Marco Dr, Port Richey, FL 34668
jamartravelparks@aol.com
www.ja-mar-travelpark.com
See ad this page, 286.

JA-MAR TRAVEL PARK
Ratings: 8/9★/8 (RV Area in MHP) From Jct of SR-52 & US-19: Go S 0.8 mi on US-19 (R). **FAC:** Paved rds. (396 spaces). 245 Avail: 60 paved, 185 grass, patios, back-ins (30 x 50), 245 full hkups (30/50 amps), seasonal sites, WiFi Hotspot, laundry. **REC:** heated pool, pond, fishing, shuffleboard. Pet restrict(B). Partial handicap access, no tents. Age restrict may apply, 2015 rates: $49. Disc: AAA. No CC.
(727)863-2040 Lat: 28.31982, Lon: -82.69937
11203 US-Hwy 19-N, Port Richey, FL 34668
jamartravelparks@aol.com
www.ja-mar-travelpark.com
See ad this page.

OAK SPRINGS RV RESORT **Ratings: 7.5/7/8** (RV Area in MHP) 2015 rates: $36. (727)863-5888 10521 Scenic Dr, Port Richey, FL 34668

SUNCOAST RV RESORT **Ratings: 6.5/6.5/6.5** (RV Park) 2015 rates: $40. (727)842-9324 9029 US-19, Port Richey, FL 34668

SUNDANCE LAKES RV RESORT **Ratings: 8/8/7** (RV Park) 2015 rates: $38. (727)862-3565 6848 Hachem Dr, Port Richey, FL 34668

PORT ST JOE — F3 *Gulf*

ST JOSEPH PENINSULA (State Pk) From town, E 2 mi on US-98 to C-30, S 10 mi to Cape San Blas Rd (C-30E), N 11 mi (E). 2015 rates: $24. (850)227-1327

PORT ST LUCIE — D5 *St Lucie*

MOTORCOACH RESORT ST. LUCIE WEST
Ratings: 9.5/10★/10 (Condo Pk) From Jct of I-95 & St Lucie Blvd (Exit 121), E 0.3 mi on St Lucie Blvd to NW Peacock Blvd, N 1.3 mi (L) Note: Class A Motorhomes only. **FAC:** Paved rds. (400 spaces). Avail: 150 paved, patios, back-ins (30 x 80), accepts full hkup units only, 150 full hkups (30/50 amps), seasonal sites, cable, WiFi Hotspot, laundry, controlled access. **REC:** heated pool, whirlpool, pond, fishing, golf. Pet restrict(Q). Partial handicap access, no tents. Big rig sites, 2015 rates: $35 to $100.
(772)336-1135 Lat: 27.33262, Lon: -80.40221
800 NW Peacock Blvd, Port St Lucie, FL 34986
mrslw@comcast.net
www.motorcoachresortstluciewest.com
See ad this page.

PORT ST LUCIE RV RESORT
Ratings: 9.5/9★/8 (RV Park) From Jct of I-95 & Gatlin Blvd (exit 118), E 3 mi on Gatlin Blvd to Port St Lucie Blvd, NE 5.9 mi to US-1, N 0.5 mi to Jennings Rd, E 0.1 mi (R); or From Jct of FL Tpke & Port St Lucie Blvd (exit 142), E 4 mi on Port St Lucie Blvd to US-1, N 0.5 mi to Jennings Rd, E 0.1 mi (R). **FAC:** Paved rds. (117 spaces). Avail: 107 paved, patios, 4 pull-thrus (24 x 66), back-ins (24 x 57), 107 full hkups (30/50 amps), seasonal sites, cable, WiFi, laundry. **REC:** heated pool. Pet restrict(Q). Partial handicap access, no tents. 2015 rates: $48. Disc: AAA.
(772)337-3340 Lat: 27.27584, Lon: -80.28770
3703 SE Jennings Rd, Port St Lucie, FL 34952
portstluciervresort@juno.com
www.portstluciervresort.com
See ad this page, 284.

PSL VILLAGE RV RESORT **Ratings: 6.5/8.5★/7** (RV Park) 2015 rates: $35 to $45. (772)337-0333 3600 SE Mariposa Ave, Port St Lucie, FL 34952

PUNTA GORDA — D3 *Charlotte*

ALLIGATOR PARK **Ratings: 10/9★/8.5** (Condo Pk) 2015 rates: $20.65 to $40.35. (941)639-7000 6400 Taylor Rd #112, Punta Gorda, FL 33950

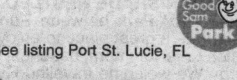

Traveling with a Fido? Many campground listings indicate pet-friendly amenities and pet restrictions.

FL

PUNTA GORDA (CONT)

GULF VIEW RV RESORT **Ratings: 9/8.5/8.5** (RV Park) 2015 rates: $32 to $62. (800)405-6188 10205 Burnt Store Rd, Punta Gorda, FL 33950

PUNTA GORDA RV RESORT
Ratings: 8.5/8.5★/8 (RV Park) From Jct of I-75 & US-17 (Exit 164), W 2 mi on US-17 (S-bnd) to US-41, S 4 mi to Rio Villa Dr, W 200 ft to Baynard Dr, S 0.1 mi (R). **FAC:** Paved rds. (223 spaces). Avail: 54 grass, 4 pull-thrus (25 x 50), back-ins (26 x 50), accepts full hkup units only, 54 full hkups (30/50 amps), cable, WiFi $, laundry, groc. **REC:** heated pool, whirlpool, Alligator Creek: fishing, shuffleboard. Pets OK. Partial handicap access, no tents. 2015 rates: $38 to $54. Disc: military.
(941)639-2010 Lat: 26.90549, Lon: -82.03975
3701 Baynard Dr, Punta Gorda, FL 33950
puntagordarv@earthlink.net
www.pgrvresort.com
See ad this page.

SHELL CREEK CAREFREE RV RESORT
Ratings: 8.5/8/9 (RV Park) From Jct of I-75 & US-17 (exit 164), N 4.2 mi on US-17 to CR-764/Washington Loop Rd, NE 4.2 mi (L). **FAC:** Paved rds. (239 spaces). Avail: 37 grass, patios, 2 pull-thrus (30 x 60), back-ins (30 x 50), 37 full hkups (30/50 amps), seasonal sites, WiFi $, rentals, laundry, LP bottles. **REC:** heated pool, whirlpool, Shell Creek: fishing, shuffleboard. Pet restrict(B). Partial handicap access, no tents. Age restrict may apply, 2015 rates: $32 to $41. Disc: AAA, military.
(941)639-4234 Lat: 26.97531, Lon: -81.89527
35711 Washington Loop Rd, Punta Gorda, FL 33982
shellcreek@carefreervresorts.com
www.carefreervresorts.com
See ad pages 327, 284.

SUN N SHADE RV PARK
Ratings: 8/8/8.5 (Campground) From Jct of I-75 & CR-762/Tuckers Grade Rd (Exit 158), W 1 mi on CR-762 to US-41, S 3.4 mi (L) Note: Watch for tall American flag.

SUN-N-SHADE NESTLED IN COUNTRY
Peaceful RV Park between Punta Gorda and Fort Myers, FL - a great place to enjoy all that Florida has to offer. Entertainment, beaches, shopping, nature all nearby. We welcome traveling RVers, 6/6 and yearly residents.

FAC: Paved rds. (191 spaces). Avail: 116 grass, patios, back-ins (30 x 60), 116 full hkups (30/50 amps), seasonal sites, WiFi $, dump, laundry. **REC:** heated pool, pond, fishing, shuffleboard. Pet restrict(Q). Partial handicap access, no tents. 2015 rates: $30 to $35.
(941)639-5388 Lat: 26.81390, Lon: -81.95707
14880 Tamiami Trail, Punta Gorda, FL 33955
sun_n_shade@hotmail.com
www.sunnshade.com
See ad pages 273 (Welcome Section), 284 & RV Trips of a Lifetime, Snowbird Destinations in Magazine Section.

WATER'S EDGE RV RESORT OF PUNTA GORDA **Ratings: 8/8.5/8.5** (Condo Pk) 2015 rates: $27 to $46. (800)637-9224 6800 Golf Course Blvd, Punta Gorda, FL 33982

QUINCY — A1 *Gadsden*

BEAVER LAKE CAMPGROUND **Ratings: 6/8.5★/7** (Campground) 2015 rates: $38. (850)856-9095 133 Kneeology Way, Quincy, FL 32351

REDDICK — G2 *Athens*

OCALA NORTH RV PARK **Ratings: 8/8★/8** (RV Park) 2015 rates: $32 to $36. (877)267-8737 16905 NW Hwy 225, Reddick, FL 32686

RIVERVIEW — K2 *Hillsborough*

HIDDEN RIVER TRAVEL RESORT **Ratings: 8.5/8.5★/8.5** (RV Park) 2015 rates: $39 to $47. (813)677-1515 12500 Mc Mullen Loop, Riverview, FL 33569

RICE CREEK RV RESORT **Ratings: 7.5/7.5/8** (RV Area in MHP) 2015 rates: $39. (813)677-6640 10719 Rice Creek Dr, Riverview, FL 33578

ROCKLEDGE — J5 *Brevard*

SPACE COAST RV RESORT **Ratings: 9/8.5/8.5** (Campground) 2015 rates: $56. (321)636-2873 820 Barnes Blvd, Rockledge, FL 32955

RUSKIN — L2 *Hillsborough*

HAWAIIAN ISLES RV RESORT/MHP **Ratings: 8.5/8★/8.5** (RV Area in MHP) 2015 rates: $39. (813)645-1098 4054 Aloha Blvd, Ruskin, FL 33570

HIDE A WAY RV RESORT
Ratings: 8.5/8.5★/9 (RV Park) From Jct of I-75 (exit 240) & SR-674: Go W 2.9 mi on SR-674, then S 2.6 mi on US-41, then E 0.7 mi on Chaney Dr (E). **FAC:** Paved rds. (405 spaces). Avail: 146 gravel, patios, 10 pull-thrus (30 x 45), back-ins (40 x 60), 146 full hkups (30/50 amps), seasonal sites, WiFi, dump, laundry, LP gas. **REC:** heated pool, Little Manatee River: fishing, shuffleboard. Pet restrict(B/Q). Partial handicap access, no tents. Big rig sites, 2015 rates: $32 to $41. Disc: AAA. AAA Approved
(800)607-2532 Lat: 27.68973, Lon: -82.45593
2206 Chaney Dr, Ruskin, FL 33570
hideawayrv@hotmail.com
Myhideawayrv.com
See ad pages 323 (Spotlight Tampa), 286 & Snowbird Destinations in Magazine Section.

MANATEE RV PARK **Ratings: 8/8★/8** (RV Area in MHP) 2015 rates: $37. (813)645-7652 6302 US-41 S, Ruskin, FL 33570

SUN LAKE RV RESORT
Ratings: 8/8★/8 (RV Park) From Jct of I-75 (Exit 240) & SR-674: Go W 1.0 mi on SR-674, then S 0.5 mi on 27th St SE, then E 0.3 mi on 14th Ave SE (L). **FAC:** Paved rds. (49 spaces). Avail: 30 grass, patios, 18 pull-thrus (25 x 50), back-ins (40 x 60), some side by side hkups, 30 full hkups (30/50 amps), seasonal sites, WiFi $, tent sites, dump, laundry. **REC:** pool, Sun Lake: fishing. Pet restrict(Q). Age restrict may apply, big rig sites, 2015 rates: $36. Disc: AAA.
(813)645-7860 Lat: 27.70636, Lon: -82.39371
3006 14th Ave SE, Ruskin, FL 33570
sunlakerv@aol.com
See ad this page, 286.

Slow down. For most vehicles, fuel efficiency begins to drop rapidly at 60 mph. Driving within the speed limit can improve fuel efficiency by up to 23 percent.

TAMPA SOUTH RV RESORT
Ratings: 9/10★/8.5 (RV Park) From Jct of I-75 (exit 240) & SR-674: Go W 2.9 mi on SR-674, then S 2 mi on US-41 (L).

WATERFRONT CLOSE TO TAMPA
Need a great place to stay in the Tampa area? Look no further TAMPA SOUTH welcomes all RVs. Right on the Little Manatee River's open waterway to Tampa Bay & the Gulf, it's an easy drive to all Central Florida's attractions.

FAC: Paved rds. (121 spaces). Avail: 53 gravel, patios, 51 pull-thrus (30 x 50), back-ins (30 x 50), 53 full hkups (30/50 amps), seasonal sites, WiFi, dump, laundry, LP gas. **REC:** heated pool, Little Manatee River: fishing, shuffleboard. No pets. Partial handicap access, no tents. Big rig sites, RV age restrict, 2015 rates: $45 to $65. Disc: AAA.
(813)645-1202 Lat: 27.69643, Lon: -82.45934
2900 S US Hwy 41, Ruskin, FL 33570
tampasouthrv@yahoo.com
www.tampasouthrvresort.com
See ad pages 319 (Spotlight Tampa), 286 & Snowbird Destinations in Magazine Section.

SANFORD — H4 *Seminole, Volusia*

TWELVE OAKS RV RESORT
Ratings: 8.5/8.5★/8 (RV Park) From Jct of I-4 & Sanford/Mt Dora exit (exit 101C/SR-46), W 2 mi on SR-46 (R). **FAC:** Paved rds. (247 spaces). Avail: 80 gravel, patios, 20 pull-thrus (25 x 70), back-ins (30 x 50), accepts full hkup units only, 80 full hkups (30/50 amps), WiFi Hotspot, dump, laundry, LP gas. **REC:** pool, pond, shuffleboard. Pet restrict(B/Q). Partial handicap access, no tents. Age restrict may apply, big rig sites, 2015 rates: $43. Disc: military.
(800)633-9529 Lat: 28.81237, Lon: -81.37153
6300 Sr 46 W, Sanford, FL 32771
info@twelveoaksrvresort.com
www.twelveoaksrvresort.com
See ad this page, 282.

WEKIVA FALLS RESORT
Ratings: 9/9★/9 (Campground) From Jct of I-4 (exit 101C) & SR-46: Go W 5.5 mi on SR-46, then S 1.4 mi on Wekiva River Rd (L).

ONE PARK, TWO SEASONS
Wekiva Falls features full hook up sites and modern amenities close to nature. Enjoy swimming in our spring or heated pool, canoeing on the Wekiva River, planned activities in the clubhouse and so much more!

FAC: Paved/gravel rds. (817 spaces). Avail: 569 grass, patios, back-ins (40 x 60), 569 full hkups (30/50 amps), seasonal sites, cable, WiFi $, tent sites, laundry, groc, LP gas, controlled access. **REC:** heated pool, Wekiva River: swim, fishing, shuffleboard, playground, rec open to public. Pet restrict(B). Partial handicap access. Big rig sites, 2015 rates: $44 to $49. Disc: AAA, military.
(352)383-8055 Lat: 28.79477, Lon: -81.42585
30700 Wekiva River Rd, Sorrento, FL 32776
info@wekivafallsresort.com
www.wekivafalls.com
See ad pages 382, 286 & Snowbird Destinations in Magazine Section.

SANTA ROSA BEACH — F2 *Walton*

RV @ THE RANCH **Ratings: 6/9★/8** (RV Park) 2015 rates: $40. (850)208-3114 613 S County Road Hwy 393, Santa Rosa Beach, FL 32459

SANTA ROSA BEACH (CONT)

← TOPSAIL HILL PRESERVE (State Pk) From Jct of US-331 & US-98, W 5.7 mi on US-98 to CR-30A, SE 0.4 mi on CR-30A (R). 2015 rates: $24 to $42. (850)267-8330

SARASOTA — D3 *Sarasota*

↘ MYAKKA RIVER (State Pk) From Jct of I-75 & SR-72 (exit 205/old exit 37), E 8.7 mi on SR-72 (L). 2015 rates: $26. (941)361-6511

↓ **SARASOTA SUNNY SOUTH RV RESORT**
Ratings: 9/10★/8.5 (RV Park) From Jct of I-75 (Exit 205) & SR-72/Clark Rd: Go W 4.7 mi on SR-72 to US 41, then S 1.4 mi on US-41, then E 0.1 mi on Doud St (R). **FAC:** Paved rds. (84 spaces). Avail: 63 gravel, patios, back-ins (35 x 60), 63 full hkups (30/50 amps), seasonal sites, cable, WiFi, laundry. **REC:** heated pool. Pets OK. Partial handicap access, no tents. Age restrict may apply, big rig sites, 2015 rates: $45 to $65.
(941)921-4409 Lat: 27.24228, Lon: -82.50486
2100 Doud St, Sarasota, FL 34231
info@srqsunnysouth.com
www.sarasotasunnysouth.com
See ad this page, 286.

→ **SUN-N-FUN CAREFREE RV RESORT**
Ratings: 9.5/9.5★/9.5 (RV Park) From Jct of I-75 (exit 210) & SR-780: Go E 1.1 mi on SR-780/Fruitville Rd (L).

SARASOTA'S BEST RV RESORT
Great camping with all amenities & endless fun. Huge swimming pool, 18 shuffleboard courts, mini golf, pro horseshoe courts, hot tubs, billiard room, lawn boules, lighted tennis courts, 10 acre fishing lake & much more.

FAC: Paved rds. (1519 spaces). 600 Avail: 135 gravel, 465 grass, patios, 60 pull-thrus (30 x 60), back-ins (35 x 60), 600 full hkups (30/50 amps), seasonal sites, cable, WiFi, tent sites, rentals, dump, laundry, LP gas, restaurant, controlled access. **REC:** heated pool, wading pool, whirlpool, Lake Ibis: fishing, shuffleboard, playground. Pet restrict(Q). Partial handicap access. Big rig sites, 2015 rates: $53 to $85. Disc: AAA.
(941)371-2505 Lat: 27.33893, Lon: -82.42682
7125 Fruitville Rd, Sarasota, FL 34240
gweir@sunnfunfl.com
www.sunnfunfl.com
See ad page 327 & Pampered Pets in Magazine Section.

← **TURTLE BEACH CAMPGROUND AT TURTLE BEACH PARK**
(Public) From Jct I-75 (Exit 205) & Clark Rd: Go W 4 mi on Clark Rd, continue W 1.8 mi on Sticking Point Rd, then S 2.5 mi on Midnight Pass Rd (R). **FAC:** Paved rds. 39 gravel, back-ins (20 x 45), 39 full hkups (30/50 amps), WiFi, tent sites, laundry, controlled access. **REC:** Gulf of Mexico: swim, fishing, playground, rec open to public. No pets. 2015 rates: $32 to $60.
(941)349-3839 Lat: 27.22022, Lon: -82.51558
8862 Midnight Pass Rd, Sarasota, FL 34242
turtlebeachcampground@scgov.net
scgov.net/turtlebeachcampground
See ad this page.

SEBASTIAN — K6 *Indian River*

↓ LONG POINT REC & CAMPING PARK (Public) From Sebastian Inlet, N 1.5 mi on Hwy A1A (L); or from town, S 14 mi on Hwy A1A (R). 2015 rates: $28. (321)952-4532

↓ SEBASTIAN INLET (State Pk) S-Bnd: From Jct of I-95 & exit 180 (in Melbourne), E 11 mi on Hwy 192 to A1A, S 18 mi to State Rec Area (R); or N-Bnd: From Jct of US-1 & SR-510 (in Wabasso), E 2.6 mi on SR-510 to A1A, N 7 mi (L). 2015 rates: $28. (321)984-4852

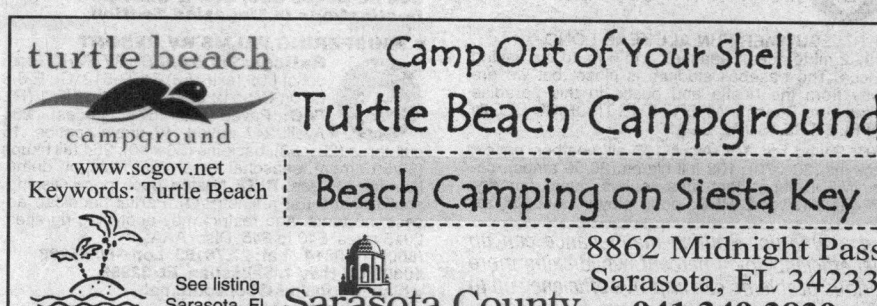

SEBASTIAN (CONT)

↑ VERO BEACH KAMP, INC.
Ratings: 9/9.5★/9 (RV Park) From Jct of I-95 (Exit 156) & CR-512: Go E 2.4 mi on CR-512, then S 5.8 mi on CR-510, then N 0.4 mi on US-1 (R).

SUMMER FUN ALL YEAR LONG
Only 2 mi to ocean beaches and 5 mi to the fishing mecca. The baseball stadium is close, but we are away from the hustle and bustle in this paradise called Vero Beach - WHERE THE TROPICS BEGIN ON FL'S TREASURE COAST

FAC: Paved rds. 105 Avail: 105 all weather, patios, back-ins (30 x 70), 105 full hkups (30/50 amps), cable, WiFi Hotspot, tent sites, rentals, dump, laundry, LP gas, firewood. **REC:** pool, playground. Pet restrict(B). Partial handicap access. Big rig sites, 2015 rates: $46 to $61. Disc: AAA.
(877)589-5643 Lat: 27.75450, Lon: -80.43652
8850 N US Hwy-1, Sebastian, FL 32958
verobeachkamp@yahoo.com
www.verobeachkamp.com
See ad pages 395, 286 & Snowbird Destinations in Magazine Section.

Get a tune-up. Routine maintenance can up fuel efficiency by 4 percent, while fixing more serious problems can improve efficiency up to 40 percent.

↓ WHISPERING PALMS RV RESORT
Ratings: 9/9.5★/8.5 (RV Park) From Jct of I-95 (exit 156) & CR-512: Go E 6.6 mi on CR-512 then S 2 mi on US-1 (R). **FAC:** Paved rds. (571 spaces). 264 Avail: 247 paved, 17 gravel, patios, 15 pull-thrus (28 x 53), back-ins (30 x 40), 264 full hkups (30/50 amps), seasonal sites, WiFi Hotspot, dump, laundry, LP gas. **REC:** heated pool, pond, fishing, shuffleboard. Pet restrict(B/Q). Partial handicap access, no tents. Age restrict may apply, big rig sites, 2015 rates: $40 to $45. Disc: AAA.
(800)414-0814 Lat: 27.78163, Lon: -80.45238
10305 US Hwy 1, Sebastian, FL 32958
whisperingpalms@bellsouth.net
www.whisperingpalmsrv.com
See ad pages 395, 286.

SEBRING — L4 *Highlands*

↓ BUTTONWOOD BAY RV RESORT & MANUFACTURED HOME COMMUNITY
Ratings: 9.5/9★/9.5 (RV Area in MHP) From Jct of US-27 & SR 98/66: Go S 1 mi on US-27 (R).

PRIME FISHING COUNTRY IN SEBRING
Great weather, a friendly atmosphere and an impressive amenity package make this resort a premier vacation destination. Features include a boat ramp, two heated pools, 210' fishing pier, outdoor recreation and more!

FAC: Paved rds. (533 spaces). 150 Avail: 45 paved, 105 gravel, patios, back-ins (30 x 50), 150 full hkups (30/50 amps), seasonal sites, WiFi $, rentals, laundry. **REC:** heated pool, Lake Josephine: fishing, shuffleboard. Pet restrict(B/Q). Partial handicap access, no tents. Age restrict may apply, big rig sites, 2015 rates: $26 to $56. Disc: AAA.
AAA Approved
(888)469-1733 Lat: 27.40730, Lon: -81.41724
10001 US 27 S, Sebring, FL 33876
buttonwoodbay@suncommunities.com
www.buttonwoodbay.com
See ad pages 275 (Welcome Section), 286, 1463 (Welcome Section) & Snowbird Destinations in Magazine Section.

↓ HIGHLAND OAKS RV RESORT **Ratings: 6/8/6.5** (RV Park) 2015 rates: $35. (863)655-1685 7001 Old Plantation Ave, Sebring, FL 33876

← HIGHLANDS HAMMOCK (State Pk) From Jct of US-27-98 & CR-634, W 4 mi on CR-634 (E). 2015 rates: $22. (941)386-6094

↓ LAKE JOSEPHINE RV RESORT **Ratings: 7.5/6.5/6.5** (RV Area in MHP) 2015 rates: $42 to $48. (863)655-0925 10809 US Hwy 27 S, Sebring, FL 33876

↑ OUTBACK RV RESORT AT TANGLEWOOD
Ratings: 9/9★/9.5 (RV Park) From Jct of US-27 & CR-634A: Go N 0.7 mi on US-27 (L).

CENTRAL FLORIDA PREMIER RV RESORT
Live the ultimate Florida lifestyle at Outback RV Resort (ages 40+). Amenity Highlights: 2 clubhouses, fishing, horseshoes, pickle ball, shuffleboard, tennis, huge swimming pool with water volleyball, and more.

FAC: Paved rds. (151 spaces). 147 Avail: 31 paved, 116 grass, patios, back-ins (50 x 85), 147 full hkups (30/50 amps), seasonal sites, cable, WiFi, rentals, dump, laundry, controlled access. **REC:** heated pool, pond, fishing, shuffleboard. Pet restrict(B/Q). Partial handicap access, no tents. Age restrict may apply, big rig sites, 2015 rates: $38 to $73.
(863)402-1501 Lat: 27.51860, Lon: -81.50798
3000 Tanglewood Pkwy, Sebring, FL 33872
Tammy.Martin@hometownamerica.com
www.OutbackRvResort.com
See ad this page, 286 & Snowbird Destinations in Magazine Section.

← SEBRING GARDENS RV COMMUNITY
Ratings: 7/8★/7.5 (RV Park) From Jct of US-27 & Alt CR-634 (Flare Rd): Go W 0.3 mi on Flare Rd, then S 0.1 mi on Brunns Rd S(L). **FAC:** Paved rds. (62 spaces). Avail: 30 grass, patios, 7 pull-thrus (25 x 65), back-ins (25 x 50), 30 full hkups (30/50 amps), seasonal sites, WiFi, dump, laundry.

To get the most out of your Guide, refer to the Table of Contents in the front of the book.

SEBRING (CONT)

SEBRING GARDENS RV (CONT)
REC: pond, shuffleboard. Pet restrict(B). No tents. Big rig sites, 2015 rates: $28. No CC.
(863)385-7624 Lat: 27.48296, Lon: -81.48562
1920 Brunns Rd, Sebring, FL 33872
sebringgardens@gmail.com
See ad opposite page, 286.

SEBRING GROVE RV RESORT **Ratings: 7.5/6/5** (RV Park) 2015 rates: $48. (863)382-1660 4105 US-27 S, Sebring, FL 33870

SUNNY PINES RV & MHP **Ratings: 8.5/9★/6.5** (RV Park) 2015 rates: $42. (863)385-4144 1200 US 27 N, Sebring, FL 33870

WHISPERING PINES VILLAGE **Ratings: 7.5/8/5.5** (RV Park) 2015 rates: $45. (863)385-8806 2323 Brunns Rd, Sebring, FL 33872

SEFFNER — K2 *Hillsborough*

LAZYDAYS RV RESORT
Ratings: 10/9★/8.5 (RV Park) From Jct of I-75 & I-4: Go E 1 mi on I-4 (exit 10) to CR-579, then N 0.1 mi on CR-579 (L).

TAMPA'S MOST BELOVED RV PARK
Everyone's welcome at our 300 site resort where you are treated to exceptional amenities and a fun-filled atmosphere. Our activities director can keep you busy or you can just relax at our screened and heated pool and spa.

FAC: Paved rds. 299 paved, patios, back-ins (30 x 45), 299 full hkups (30/50 amps), cable, WiFi, dump, laundry, LP gas, restaurant. **REC:** heated pool, whirlpool, playground. Pets OK. Partial handicap access, no tents. Big rig sites, 2015 rates: $25 to $51. Disc: military.
AAA Approved
(866)456-7015 Lat: 28.01285, Lon: -82.30348
6210 County Rd 579, Seffner, FL 33584
campground@lazydays.com
www.lazydays.com/rvcampground
See ad page 407.

Travel Services

LAZYDAYS SALES & SERVICE RV Sales & Service. **SERVICES:** RV, RV appliance, engine/chassis repair, restrooms, RV Sales. RV supplies, emergency parking, waiting room. Hours: 9am to 5pm. ATM.
(813)246-4333 Lat: 28.00638, Lon: -82.30848
6130 Lazydays Blvd, Seffner, FL 33584
www.lazydays.com
See ad page 407.

SILVER SPRINGS — G3 *Marion*

LAKE WALDENA RESORT **Ratings: 8/8.5★/9** (Campground) 2015 rates: $40. (800)748-7898 13582 East Hwy 40, Lot#300, Silver Springs, FL 34488

SILVER SPRINGS CAMPERS GARDEN
Ratings: 9/8.5★/7 (RV Park) From Jct of I-75 & SR-40 (Exit 352), E 8 mi on SR-40 Across from Silver Spring and Wild Waters (L). **FAC:** Paved rds. (199 spaces). Avail: 88 paved, patios, 88 pull-thrus (25 x 60), accepts self-contain units only, 88 full hkups (30/50 amps), cable, WiFi, dump, laundry, LP gas. **REC:** heated pool, shuffleboard. Pet restrict(B). No tents. Big rig sites, 2015 rates: $30.
(352)236-3700 Lat: 29.21953, Lon: -82.05614
3151 NE 56th Ave, Silver Springs, FL 34488
silverspringsrvpark@gmail.com
www.silverspringsrvpark.com
See ad pages 381, 282.

THE SPRINGS RV RESORT **Ratings: 7.5/8.5★/8.5** (RV Park) 2015 rates: $36. (352)236-5250 2950 NE 52nd Ct, Silver Springs, FL 34488

WHISPERING PINES RV PARK **Ratings: 7/9.5★/8.5** (RV Park) 2015 rates: $28. (352)625-1295 1700 NE 115th Ave, Silver Springs, FL 34488

WILDERNESS RV RESORT AT SILVER SPRINGS Ratings: 9.5/9.5★/9.5 (Condo Pk) From jct I-75 & Hwy 326 (Exit 358): Go E 9 mi on Hwy 326 to US 40, then E 3 mi (L). **FAC:** Paved rds. (412 spaces). Avail: 138 paved, 48 pull-thrus (40 x 63), back-ins (40 x 60), 138 full hkups (30/50 amps), seasonal sites, cable, WiFi, dump, laundry, groc, LP bottles, controlled access. **REC:** heated pool, whirlpool, Ocklawaha River: fishing, shuffleboard. Pet restrict(B/Q). No tents. Big rig sites, 2015 rates: $40.50 to $44.50. Disc: AAA, military.
AAA Approved
(352)625-1122 Lat: 29.21446, Lon: -81.98204
2771 NE 102nd Ave Rd, Silver Springs, FL 34488
reservations@wildernessrvresort.net
www.wildernessrvresort.net

SNEADS — A1 *Gadsden, Jackson*

THREE RIVERS SRA (State Pk) From town, N 2 mi on SR-271 (R). 2015 rates: $16. (850)482-9006

SOPCHOPPY — B1 *Wakulla*

OCHLOCKONEE RIVER (State Pk) From Jct of SR-375 & US-319, S 4 mi on US-319 (L). 2015 rates: $18. (850)962-2771

SOUTH BAY — E4 *Palm Beach*

SOUTH BAY RV CAMPGROUND (Public) From Jct of US-27 & SR-80 in South Bay, N 1.5 mi on US-27 (R). 2015 rates: $21 to $22. (561)992-9045

SOUTH DAYTONA — G5 *Volusia*

DAYTONA RV PARK & TROPICAL GARDENS **Ratings: 7/8★/7** (RV Park) 2015 rates: $39.50. (386)304-8680 2430 S Nova Rd, South Daytona, FL 32119

SPRING HILL — J2 *Hernando, Pasco*

BIG OAKS RV & MOBILE HOME COMMUNITY
Ratings: 8/8★/7 (RV Area in MHP) From Jct of US-19 & Hwy 578 (County Line Rd), go E 11 mi on Hwy 578 then S 2.5 mi on US-41 (L). **FAC:** Paved rds. 115 grass, patios, 12 pull-thrus (30 x 60), back-ins (25 x 55), 115 full hkups (30/50 amps), WiFi, dump, laundry, LP gas. **REC:** heated pool, shuffleboard. Pets OK. No tents. Age restrict may apply, 2015 rates: $35. No CC.
(352)799-5533 Lat: 28.39970, Lon: -82.48167
16654 US-41, Spring Hill, FL 34610
bigoakspark@hotmail.com
www.bigoakspark.com
See ad this page, 286.

HOLIDAY SPRINGS RV RESORT **Ratings: 8/8.5/8.5** (RV Park) 2015 rates: $35 to $38. (352)683-0034 138 Travel Park Dr, Spring Hill, FL 34607

TOPICS RV COMMUNITY **Ratings: 6/7/8** (RV Area in MHP) 2015 rates: $36 to $43. (800)405-6188 13063 County Line Rd, Spring Hill, FL 34609

ST AUGUSTINE — B4 *St Johns*

ANASTASIA SRA (State Pk) From Jct of US-1 & SR-312, E 2.5 mi on SR-312 to SR-AIA, N 1.5 mi (R). 2015 rates: $28. (904)461-2033

FAVER-DYKES (State Pk) From town: Go 15 mi S on US-1. 2015 rates: $9 to $11. (904)794-0997

INDIAN FOREST CAMPGROUND
Ratings: 7/8.5★/8.5 (RV Park) From Jct of I-95 & SR-207 (exit 311), NE 2.1 mi on SR-207 (L). **FAC:** Gravel rds. 105 grass, 40 pull-thrus (30 x 75), back-ins (30 x 55), 86 full hkups, 19 W, 19 E (30/50 amps), WiFi, dump, laundry, LP gas. **REC:** pond, fishing. Pets OK. Partial handicap access, no tents. Big rig sites, eco-friendly, 2015 rates: $38 to $43. Disc: AAA, military.
AAA Approved
(904)824-3574 Lat: 29.85131, Lon: -81.35895
1505 SR-207, St Augustine, FL 32086
www.indianforestcampground.com
See ad pages 401, 282.

NORTH BEACH CAMP RESORT
Ratings: 9/8.5★/9 (Campground) From Jct of Bus US-1 & SR-A1A, N 4 mi on SR-A1A (L).

OCEAN OUT FRONT & RIVER OUT BACK!
Sunrise on the ocean, sunset on the river, a bit of Olde Florida in between! From spectacular ocean sunrises to river sunset vistas and endless stars at night, here's your ticket to the best camping vacation ever!

FAC: Gravel rds. 150 gravel, 26 pull-thrus (40 x 90), back-ins (40 x 60), accepts self-contain units only, 150 full hkups (30/50 amps), cable, WiFi, tent sites, dump, laundry, groc, LP bottles, controlled access. **REC:** heated pool, whirlpool, Atlantic Ocean: shuffleboard, playground. Pet restrict(B/Q). Partial handicap access. Big rig sites, eco-friendly, 2015 rates: $47 to $85. Disc: AAA, military.
AAA Approved
(800)542-8316 Lat: 29.95217, Lon: -81.30484
4125 Coastal Hwy (SR A1A), St Augustine, FL 32084
NBCR@bellsouth.net
www.northbeachcamp.com
See ad pages 400, 282.

ST AUGUSTINE BEACH KOA KAMPGROUND RESORT **Ratings: 8.5/8/7** (RV Park) 2015 rates: $63.71 to $78.71. (800)562-4022 525 West Pope Road, St Augustine, FL 32080

ST JOHNS RV PARK **Ratings: 7/8.5★/7** (Campground) From Jct of I-95 & SR-207 (exit 311), E 0.1 mi on SR-207 (L). **FAC:** Paved/gravel rds. (60 spaces). Avail: 37 gravel, 15 pull-thrus (30 x 70), back-ins (25 x 60), some side by side hkups, 15 full hkups, 7 W, 7 E (30/50 amps), seasonal sites, cable, WiFi Hotspot, dump, laundry. **REC:** pond. Pet restrict(B). Partial handicap access, no tents. Big rig sites, 2015 rates: $30. Disc: AAA, military.
AAA Approved
(904)824-9840 Lat: 29.83230, Lon: -81.37794
2493 SR-207, St Augustine, FL 32086
www.stjohnsfleamarket.com

STAGECOACH RV PARK INC
Ratings: 8/9★/8 (RV Park) From Jct of I-95 & SR-16 (exit 318), W 0.2 mi on SR-16 to Toms Rd, S 0.1 mi to CR 208, W 0.2 mi (L). **FAC:** Gravel rds. 80 grass, 60 pull-thrus (40 x 60), back-ins (40 x 60), 80 full hkups (30/50 amps), cable, WiFi, dump, laundry, LP gas. **REC.** Pet restrict(B). Partial handicap access, no tents. Big rig sites, 2015 rates: $45 to $49. Disc: AAA, military.
AAA Approved
(904)824-2319 Lat: 29.91940, Lon: -81.42218
2711 CR 208, St Augustine, FL 32092
stagecoachrvpark@bellsouth.net
www.stagecoachrv.net
See ad pages 399, 282.

THE FOUNTAINS OF ST AUGUSTINE
(RV Resort) (Under Construction) From the jct. of I-95 & SR 16 (exit 318), E 0.5 mi on SR 16 to Inman Rd., N 0.2 mi (R). **FAC:** Paved rds. 241 paved, 241 full hkups (30/50 amps). **REC.** Pets OK. Big rig sites.
(904)365-5600 Lat: 29.90368, Lon: -81.39174
3800 Inman Road, St Augustine, FL 32084
info@thefountainsofstaugustine.com
TheFountainsofStAugustine.com
See ad page 398.

Travel Services

CAMPING WORLD OF ST AUGUSTINE As the nation's largest retailer of RV supplies, accessories, services and new and used RVs, Camping World is committed to making your total RV experience better. RV Accessories: (866)450-4740. **SERVICES:** RV, tire, RV appliance, staffed RV wash, restrooms, RV Sales. RV supplies, LP, emergency parking, waiting room. Hours: 9am to 6pm. ATM.
888-650-6347 Lat: 29.925596, Lon: -81.414229
600 Outlet Mall Blvd. Suite 102, St Augustine, FL 32084
www.campingworld.com

Things to See and Do

OLD TOWN TROLLEY Old Town Trolley Tours is the best way to see the city, highlighting the best St. Augustine Attractions, with 23 stops and more than 100 points of interest. No CC.
(844)367-5584 Lat: 29.8448, Lon: -81.2777
http://www.trolleytours.com/st-augustine/
See ad page 401.

Our inspectors look for the same things you do. Our unique Triple Rating System is based on years of market research, analysis and surveys from RVers like you. One thing you suggested was the need for separate ratings on facility completeness, restroom cleanliness/construction, and visual appearance/environmental quality. So we give three ratings, each based on a scale of 1 to 10, 10 being best and 5 being average. To give you an idea how tough we are, less than 1% of inspected campgrounds receive 10/10/10 ratings.*

OPEN ALL YEAR
FREE WI-FI
CABLE TV
STAGECOACH RV PARK INC.
See listing St Augustine, FL
• Outlet Malls 1/2 Mile • Pull-Thru Sites
• Close To Tourist Attractions & PGA World Golf Village
• Camping World Close By
(904) 824-2319 • 877-824-2319
Good Sam Park
www.stagecoachrv.net
stagecoachrvpark@bellsouth.net

CAMP
with the ocean out your front door
and the river out your back door
North Beach
CAMP RESORT
www.northbeachcamp.com
NBCR@bellsouth.net
4125 COASTAL HWY. (A-1-A)
NORTH BEACH, ST. AUGUSTINE, FL 32084
800-542-8316
See listing St. Augustine, FL
Good Sam Park
WIRELESS INTERNET
Good Sam RATED
9/8.5★/9
AAA

ST GEORGE ISLAND — B1 *Franklin*

➔ ST GEORGE ISLAND (State Pk) Cross the bridge to St George Island & go East. 2015 rates: $24. (850)927-2111

ST JAMES CITY — E3 *Lee*

⬆ PINE ISLAND RESORT KOA **Ratings: 8.5/8/8.5** (RV Park) 2015 rates: $37 to $65. (800)405-6188 5120 H Stringfellow Rd, St James City, FL 33956

ST PETERSBURG — L1 *Pinellas*

ST PETERSBURG See also Bradenton, Clearwater, Dunedin, Largo, Palmetto, Ruskin & Tampa.

⬇ **BICKLEY PARK**
Ratings: 8.5/8.5★/8.5 (RV Park) From Jct of I-275 (Exit 28) & SR-694: Go W 7.7 mi on SR-694/Gandy Blvd, then S 1.1 mi on Seminole Blvd (R). **FAC:** Paved rds. (152 spaces). Avail: 11 paved, 60 all weather, patios, back-ins (27 x 58), 71 full hkups (30/50 amps), seasonal sites, WiFi, laundry. **REC:** heated pool. Pets OK. Partial handicap access, no tents. Age restrict may apply, big rig sites, 2015 rates: $60 to $98.
(727)392-3807 Lat: 27.82318, Lon: -82.78834
5640 Seminole Blvd, Seminole, FL 33772
bickleypark@bickleypark.com
BickleyPark.com
See ad this page, 286.

➚ ROBERTS MH & RV RESORT **Ratings: 8.5/UI/8.5** (RV Area in MHP) 2015 rates: $35 to $50. (727)577-6820 3390 Gandy Blvd, St Petersburg, FL 33702

➘ ST PETERSBURG/MADIERA BEACH KOA **Ratings: 8.5/8/8** (Campground) 2015 rates: $43 to $110. (727)392-2233 5400 95th St N, St Petersburg, FL 33708

STARKE — B3 *Bradford*

⬇ STARKE KOA **Ratings: 9.5/9★/8** (RV Park) 2015 rates: $36.75 to $46.75. (800)562-8498 1475 S Walnut St, Starke, FL 32091

SUGARLOAF KEY — F4 *Monroe*

⬆ LAZY LAKES RV RESORT **Ratings: 8/7/7.5** (RV Park) 2015 rates: $30 to $100. (305)745-1079 311 Johnson Rd, Sugarloaf Key, FL 33042

➘ SUGARLOAF KEY WEST KOA **Ratings: 9/9★/9** (Campground) 2015 rates: $84.50 to $102. (305)745-3549 251 Sr 939, Summerland Key, FL 33042

SUMMERFIELD — H3 *Marion*

➔ SOUTHERN OAKS RV RESORT **Ratings: 9/9.5★/8** (RV Park) 2015 rates: $38. (352)347-2550 14140 SE US Hwy 441, Summerfield, FL 34491

Travel Services

⬇ **CAMPING WORLD OF SUMMERFIELD/OCALA**
As the nation's largest retailer of RV supplies, accessories, services and new and used RVs, Camping World is committed to making your total RV experience better. RV Accessories; (855)244-8917. **SERVICES:** RV Sales. RV supplies, LP. Hours: 8:00am - 6:00pm.
(888)795-1707 Lat: 29.15153, Lon: -82.12312
14200 South US Hwy 441, Summerfield, FL 34491
www.campingworld.com

SUMTERVILLE — H3 *Sumter*

⬆ **SHADY BROOK GOLF & RV RESORT**
Ratings: 7.5/8/9 (RV Park) From Jct of I-75 and CR-470 (exit 321), E 2.5 mi on CR-470 to US-301, N 0.5 mi to entrance (L). **FAC:** Paved rds. (172 spaces). Avail: 100 grass, 5 pull-thrus (45 x 75), back-ins (40 x 60), 100 full hkups (50 amps), seasonal sites, WiFi Hotspot, dump, laundry. **REC:** golf. Pets OK. Partial handicap access, no tents. Big rig sites, 2015 rates: $32 to $37. Disc: AAA.
(352)568-2244 Lat: 28.75648, Lon: -82.06170
178 N US 301, Sumterville, FL 33585
shadybrookrvandgolf@aol.com
shadybrookrvandgolf.com
See ad pages 402, 286.

SUNRISE — E5 *Broward*

⬅ **MARKHAM PARK & RANGE** (Public) From Jct of US-441 & SR-84, W 11 mi on SR-84 to entrance across from Weston Rd (R). **FAC:** Paved rds. 88 paved, 8 pull-thrus (15 x 40), back-ins (15 x 40), 88 full hkups (30/50 amps), WiFi, tent sites, dump, fire rings, firewood. **REC:** pool, pond, fishing, playground, rec open to public. Pets OK $. Big rig sites, 14 day max stay, 2015 rates: $30 to $40.
(954)357-8868 Lat: 26.126278, Lon: -80.360750
16001 W SR-84, Sunrise, FL 33326
markhampark@broward.org
www.broward.org/parks

Keep one Guide at home, and one in your RV! To purchase additional North American Edition copies, call 877-209-6655.

Heading to a privately owned park? Be sure to read how our inspection team rated it in the Guide "How to Use This Travel Guide" section.

FL

TALLAHASSEE — A1 *Leon*

BIG OAK RV PARK
Ratings: 8/8.5★/8 (RV Park) From Jct of I-10 & US-27 (exit 199), N 2.5 mi on US-27 (L). **FAC:** Paved/gravel rds. (156 spaces). Avail: 117 gravel, patios, 41 pull-thrus (30 x 65), back-ins (30 x 60), 117 full hkups (30/50 amps), seasonal sites, cable, WiFi, dump, laundry, LP gas. **REC.** Pets OK. No tents. Big rig sites, eco-friendly, 2015 rates: $41 to $49. Disc: military.
(850)562-4660 Lat: 30.50881, Lon: -84.33741
4024 N Monroe St, Tallahassee, FL 32303
bigoakrvpark@gmail.com
www.bigoakrv.com
See ad pages 405, 282.

LAKESIDE TRAVEL PARK **Ratings: 5/8★/5** (RV Park) 2015 rates: $35. (850)574-5998 6401 W Tennessee St, Tallahassee, FL 32304

TALLAHASSEE RV PARK
Ratings: 9/9★/9 (RV Park) From Jct of I-10 & US-90 (exit 209A) W 0.5 mi on US-90 (R).

SOUTHERN HOSPITALITY AT ITS FINEST!
We have been under the same great ownership for over 10 years! Our Welcome Bear invites you to come in to our rustic recreation room where you can relax and watch cable TV, work on your laptop, read or just sit a spell.

FAC: Paved rds. 66 Avail: 26 gravel, 40 grass, 59 pull-thrus (20 x 60), back-ins (20 x 60), 66 full hkups (30/50 amps), cable, WiFi, dump, laundry. **REC:** pool. Pet restrict(B/Q). Partial handicap access, no tents. Eco-friendly, 2015 rates: $46. Disc: AAA.
AAA Approved
(850)878-7641 Lat: 30.48298, Lon: -84.17054
6504 Mahan Dr, Tallahassee, FL 32308
manager@tallahasseervpark.com
www.tallahasseervpark.com
See ad pages 404, 282.

Our inspectors look for the same things you do. Our unique Triple Rating System is based on years of market research, analysis and surveys from RVers like you. One thing you suggested was the need for separate ratings on facility completeness, restroom cleanliness/construction, and visual appearance/environmental quality. So we give three ratings, each based on a scale of 1 to 10, 10 being best and 5 being average. To give you an idea how tough we are, less than 1% of inspected campgrounds receive 10/10/10 ratings.*

How much will it all cost? Use this as a guide: Rates shown are the minimum and maximum for two adults in one RV at the time of inspection (excluding any additional fees for items not at the site). Remember, these rates serve as guidelines only. It's always best to call ahead for the most current rate information.

Know The Rules Of The Road!

At-a-glance Rules of the Road table shows RV-related laws in every state and province, including: fishing licenses, bridge and tunnel restrictions and highway information numbers for every state and province.

Find the Rules in the front of this Guide.

Get Social Online with Good Sam

Post, pin or tweet about your RV lifestyle

Drop in at one of our social media stomping grounds on Facebook, Pinterest, Twitter or the Good Sam Camping Blog to mingle with thousands of fellow RVers. Learn about new RV destinations, share some hard-earned RV advice and make new friends — all with a few clicks of the mouse.

Good Sam Camping BLOG
Updated daily with the hottest topics in today's RV world from our team of RVing bloggers.
blog.goodsam.com

FACEBOOK
Click the thumbs-up button on the Good Sam Club page and join the fun with nearly 200,000 users.
facebook.com/thegoodsamclub

PINTEREST
Pin your favorite RV campground, create an on-the-fly scrapbook of your next RV outing or simply share favorite treats or trip ideas on your online board.
pinterest.com/goodsamclub

TWITTER
Tweet about your RV experiences on the go, follow other RVers and even get tweets from the Good Sam Club.
twitter.com/thegoodsamclub

Don't be a wallflower at the social media party. Take the plunge and expand your RV horizons. We'll see you online!

Tallahassee East Campground

Good Sam Park

See listing Monticello, FL

Camp Here for Great Nature and Relaxation

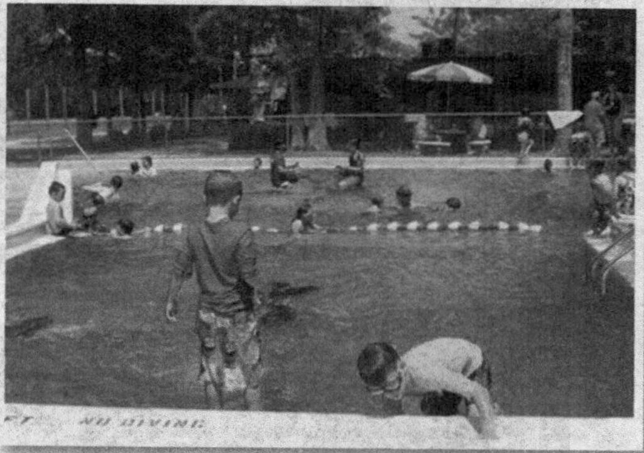

We have all pull-through sites. Individual cabins and cottages are also available with plenty of park amenities close by.

We offer a complimentary breakfast and deserts/ coffee in the afternoon. We are a pet friendly park. We have a fishing pond and plenty of room for a nice walk. Enjoy nearby Wacissa River and Wakulla Springs State Park. We are located only 4 hours from Orlando area attractions.

• 30/50 Amp • 100' Max Length • Lounge
• Tent Spaces • Pool • Propane

Wacissa River

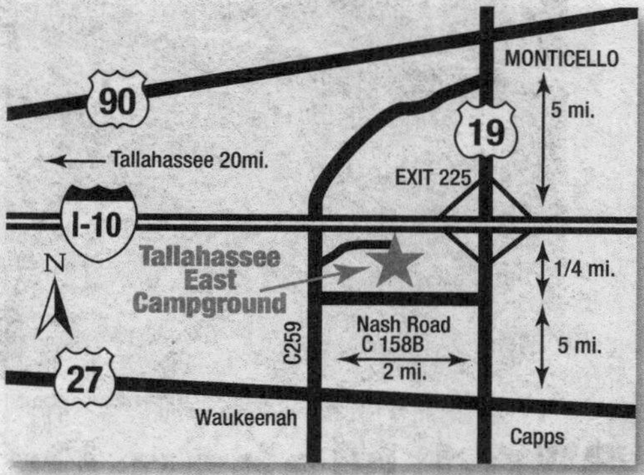

346 KOA Road • Monticello, FL 32344

850-997-3890

www.TallahasseeEastCampground.com

FL

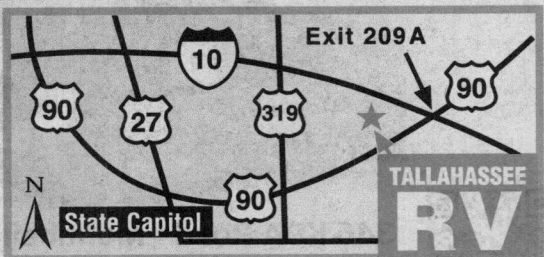

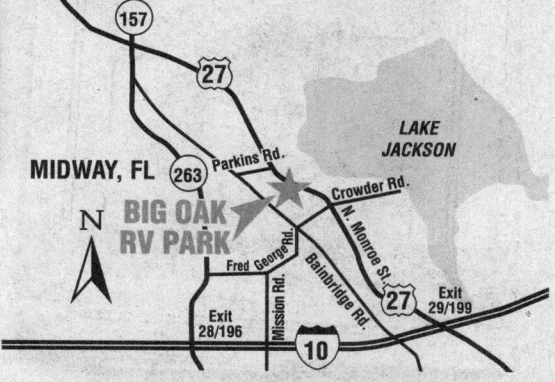

TAMPA — K2 *Hillsborough*

TAMPA See also Clearwater, Dade City, Dover, Dunedin, Largo, Riverview, Ruskin, Seffner, St Petersburg, Thonotosassa, Wesley Chapel & Zephyrhills.

What will it cost to catch a salmon in Alaska? State-by-state fishing license information is listed in the front section of the Guide.

Know the name? Then you can use our special "Find-it-Fast" index to locate your campground on the map. The index arranges private and public campgrounds alphabetically, by state. Next to the name, you'll quickly find the name of the town the park is in, plus the Listing's page number.

BAY BAYOU RV RESORT

Ratings: 9/10★/9 (RV Park) From Jct of I-275 (exit 47) & SR-580/Hillsborough Ave: Go W 10.8 mi, then N 0.5 mi on Country Way Blvd, then W 0.75 mi on Memorial Hwy (L).

PREMIER WATERFRONT RESORT IN TAMPA
Natural surroundings on Double Branch Creek just minutes from Tampa and Clearwater's top attractions and Gulf beaches. Bay Bayou offers deluxe facilities and amenities with a friendly staff to assist you.

FAC: Paved rds. (274 spaces). 173 Avail: 99 gravel, 74 grass, patios, back-ins (40 x 60), accepts full hkup units only, 173 full hkups (30/50 amps), seasonal sites, cable, WiFi, dump, laundry, LP gas, controlled access. **REC:** heated pool, whirlpool, Double Branch Creek: fishing, shuffleboard. Pet restrict(B/Q). Partial handicap access, no tents. Big rig sites, RV age restrict, 2015 rates: $43 to $66. Disc: AAA, military.
(813)855-1000 Lat: 28.02971, Lon: -82.63068
8492 Manatee Bay Dr, Tampa, FL 33635
info@baybayou.com
www.baybayou.com
See ad pages 322 (Spotlight Tampa), 286.

TAMPA RV PARK

Ratings: 6.5/8.5★/6.5 (RV Park) From Jct of I-275 & SR-582 (Exit 51), E 0.2 mi on SR-582 (Fowler Ave) to US-41, S 0.7 mi on US-41 (Nebraska Ave) to E Bougainvillea Ave, W 250 ft (L). **FAC:** Gravel rds. 86 grass, patios, 16 pull-thrus (20 x 50), back-ins (20 x 50), 86 full hkups (30/50 amps), WiFi, dump, laundry. Pet restrict(B/Q). No tents. Big rig sites, 2015 rates: $33.
(813)971-3460 Lat: 28.04323, Lon: -82.45219
10314 N Nebraska Ave, Tampa, FL 33701
info@tamparvpark.com
www.tampa-rv-park-camp-nebraska.com
See ad pages 323 (Spotlight Tampa), 286.

TARPON SPRINGS — K1 *Pinellas*

HICKORY POINT MOBILE HOME & RV PARK

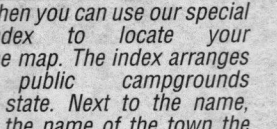

Ratings: 6/7.5/7.5 (Campground) From N Jct US-19 & US 19A: Go SW 1 m on US 19Alti, then W 2 mi on Anclote Blvd, then SE 0.1 m on Anclote Rd/Seminole St (R). **FAC:** Paved/dirt rds. (64 spaces). Avail: 46 gravel, 11 pull-thrus (20 x 50),

TARPON SPRINGS (CONT)

HICKORY POINT MOBILE HOME (CONT)
back-ins (20 x 50), 46 full hkups (30/50 amps), seasonal sites, WiFi, tent sites, dump, laundry. **REC:** Ancolte River: fishing. Pet restrict(B). 2015 rates: $40 to $65. Disc: AAA.
AAA Approved
(727)937-7357 Lat: 28.17063, Lon: -82.78138
1181 Anclote Rd, Tarpon Springs, FL 34689
info@hickorypointmhp.com
www.hickorypointmhp.com
See ad this page, 286.

TAVARES — H3 *Lake*

FISHERMAN'S COVE GOLF & RV RESORT, INC. **Ratings: 9/8.5★/7.5** (RV Park) 2015 rates: $39 to $49. (352)343-1233 3950 N Eichelberg Rd, Tavares, FL 32778

THONOTOSASSA — K2 *Hillsborough*

HAPPY TRAVELER RV PARK
Ratings: 8/8.5★/8.5 (RV Park) From Jct of I-75 (exit 265) & Fowler Ave: Go E 0.5 mi on Fowler Ave (R).

CLOSE TO BUSCH GARDENS
Happy Traveler provides a shady site with 24/7 security. NEW management means NEW ideas, NEW amenities, NEW fun. Best choice to access all Tampa Bay has to offer - 1/2 mile from I-75 with easy access to Moffit & VA Hospitals.

FAC: Paved rds. (224 spaces). 175 Avail: 75 grass, 100 dirt, back-ins (30 x 50), 175 full hkups (30/50 amps), seasonal sites, cable, WiFi, dump, laundry, LP gas. **REC:** heated pool. Pet restrict(Q). No tents. Big rig sites, 2015 rates: $26 to $36. Disc: AAA.
AAA Approved
(813)986-3094 Lat: 28.05324, Lon: -82.33915
9401 E Fowler Ave, Thonotosassa, FL 33592
htrvpk@aol.com
www.happytravelerrvpark.com
See ad pages 321 (Spotlight Tampa), 286.

HILLSBOROUGH RIVER (State Pk) From Jct of US-301 & SR-54, S 7 mi on US-301 (R). 2015 rates: $24. (813)987-6771

SOUTHERN AIRE RV RESORT **Ratings: 7.5/7.5/8** (RV Park) 2015 rates: $34. (813)986-1596 10511 Florence Ave, Thonotosassa, FL 33592

SPANISH MAIN CAREFREE RV RESORT
Ratings: 8/8★/7.5 (RV Area in MHP) From Jct of I-4 (Exit 10) & CR-579: Go N 3.9 mi on CR-579, to Florence Ave, W 0.1 mi on Florence Ave (R); or From Jct of I-75 (Exit 265) & SR-582: Go E 0.5 mi on SR-582/Fowler Ave, then N 1.5 mi on US-301 (R). **FAC:** Paved rds. (331 spaces). Avail: 150 dirt, patios, 7 pull-thrus (30 x 60), back-ins (30 x 50), 150 full hkups (30/50 amps), seasonal sites, WiFi $, laundry. **REC:** heated pool, pond, fishing, shuffleboard, playground. Pet restrict(B/Q). Partial handicap access, no tents. Big rig sites, 2015 rates: $33. Disc: AAA, military.
(813)986-2415 Lat: 28.06399, Lon: -82.30539
12110 Spanish Main Resort Trail, Thonotosassa, FL 33592
spanishmain@carefreervresorts.com
www.carefreervresorts.com
See ad opposite page.

TITUSVILLE — H5 *Brevard*

CAPE KENNEDY KOA **Ratings: 7.5/8/6.5** (Campground) 2015 rates: $34 to $45. (321)269-7361 4513 W Main St, Mims, FL 32754

CHRISTMAS RV PARK **Ratings: 7.5/7.5/6** (RV Park) 2015 rates: $40 to $45. (407)568-5207 25525 E Colonial Dr, Christmas, FL 32709

MANATEE HAMMOCK PARK (Public) From Jct of I-95 & SR-50 (exit 215), E 3.3 mi on SR-50 to US-1, S 3.7 mi (L). 2015 rates: $25. (321)264-5083

SEASONS IN THE SUN RV RESORT **Ratings: 9/10★/8.5** (RV Park) From Jct of I-95 (exit 223) & SR-46: Go W 0.4 mi on SR-46 (L). **FAC:** Paved rds. (232 spaces). 175 Avail: 100 paved, 75 gravel, back-ins (34 x 65), 175 full hkups (30/50 amps), seasonal sites, cable, WiFi, dump, laundry, LP gas, controlled access. **REC:** heated pool, whirlpool, pond, fishing, shuffleboard. Pets OK. Partial handicap access, no tents. Big rig sites, 2015 rates: $35 to $48. Disc: AAA.
AAA Approved
(877)687-7275 Lat: 28.66588, Lon: -80.87805
2400 Seasons in the Sun Blvd, Titusville, FL 32754
seasonsinthesnrv@aol.com
www.seasonsinthesunrv.com

THE GREAT OUTDOORS RV, NATURE & GOLF RESORT
Ratings: 10/10★/10 (Condo Pk) From Jct of I-95 (exit 215) & SR-50: Go W 0.5 mi on SR-50 (Cheney Hwy) to entrance rd (L).

STAY A NIGHT OR A LIFETIME!
Near Florida's premier attractions - Kennedy Space Center, Orlando theme parks, Daytona racing, cruise terminals & casinos. Enjoy onsite 18 hole golf course, tennis, swimming, fishing and much more.

FAC: Paved rds. (600 spaces). Avail: 100 paved, patios, back-ins (40 x 80), 100 full hkups (30/50 amps), seasonal sites, WiFi $, dump, laundry, LP gas, restaurant, controlled access. **REC:** heated pool, whirlpool, pond, fishing, golf, shuffleboard. Pet restrict(Q). Partial handicap access, no tents. Big rig sites, 2015 rates: $50 to $65.
(321)269-5004 Lat: 28.55026, Lon: -80.86089
125 Plantation Dr, Titusville, FL 32780
info@tgoresort.com
www.tgoresort.com
See ad pages 408, 286 & Snowbird Destinations in Magazine Section.

WHISPERING PINES
Ratings: 8/9★/8 (RV Area in MHP) From Jct I-95 (exit 215) & Hwy 50: Go E 3 mi on Hwy 50 (Cheney Hwy) (R). **FAC:** Paved rds. (200 spaces). 63 Avail: 30 gravel, 33 grass, patios, back-ins (26 x 50), 63 full hkups (30/50 amps), seasonal sites, WiFi Hotspot, laundry. **REC:** shuffleboard. Pet restrict No tents. Age restrict may apply, 2015 rates: $35. Disc: AAA. No CC.
(321)267-2081 Lat: 28.55719, Lon: -80.80255
359 Cheney Hwy, Titusville, FL 32780
whisperingpines55@gmail.com
mywhisperingpines.com
See ad this page, 286.

WILLOW LAKES RV & GOLF RESORT **Ratings: 8.5/8/9** (Condo Pk) 2015 rates: $34 to $55. (321)269-7440 2852 Willow Lakes Lane, Titusville, FL 32796

TRENTON — B3 *Gilchrist*

FOR VETS@OTTER SPRINGS (Public) From Jct of US-19 & SR-26 (Fanning Springs): E 2 mi on SR-26 to CR-232, N 1.7 mi to 70th St (Otter Springs Rd), W 1 mi (R). 2015 rates: $24. (800)883-9107

UMATILLA — H3 *Lake*

OLDE MILL STREAM RV RESORT **Ratings: 8.5/9★/8** (RV Resort) 2015 rates: $29 to $39. (800)449-3141 1000 N Central Ave, Umatilla, FL 32784

Our rating system isn't just tough, it's thorough. We know the kinds of things that are important to you — like clean restrooms and showers, attractive, secure, well-tended grounds, and extras like swimming pools. We give the first rating for development of facilities, the second for cleanliness and physical characteristics of restrooms and showers, and the third for visual appearance.

VENICE — D3 *Sarasota*

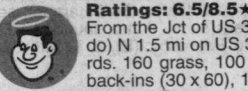

FLORIDA PINES MOBILE HOME COURT
Ratings: 8/9.5★/8 (RV Area in MHP) From Jct of I-75 (exit 193) & Jacaranda Blvd: Go S 4 mi on Jacaranda Blvd, then N 0.5 mi on SR-776 (R). **FAC:** Paved rds. (130 spaces). Avail: 30 paved, patios, back-ins (45 x 65), 30 full hkups (30/50 amps), seasonal sites, cable, WiFi, laundry. **REC:** pond, fishing, shuffleboard. No pets. No tents. Age restrict may apply, big rig sites, 2015 rates: $36 to $49. Disc: AAA. No CC.
AAA Approved
(941)493-0019 Lat: 27.04838, Lon: -82.40494
150 Satulah Cir, Venice, FL 34293
http://www.goodsamcamping.com.s3.amazonaws.com/gsparks/731000284/index.html
See ad this page, 286.

MYAKKA RV RESORT
Ratings: 8.5/8.5★/8 (RV Park) From Jct of I-75 (Exit 191) & River Rd: Go SE 5 mi on River Rd, then S 0.8 mi on US-41(R). **FAC:** Paved rds. (83 spaces). Avail: 56 gravel, patios, back-ins (30 x 45), 56 full hkups (30/50 amps), seasonal sites, cable, WiFi, tent sites, dump, laundry, LP gas. **REC:** heated pool, Myakka River. Pets OK. 2015 rates: $55 to $75.
(941)426-5040 Lat: 27.04699, Lon: -82.28883
10400 S. Tamiami Tr, North Port, FL 34287
www.myakkarv.com
See ad this page, 286.

County names help you follow the local weather report.

RAMBLERS REST RESORT **Ratings: 9/10★/8.5** (RV Area in MHP) 2015 rates: $39 to $77. (800)405-6188 1300 N River Rd, Venice, FL 34293

VERO BEACH — L6 *Indian River, St Lucie*

MIDWAY ESTATES/MHP **Ratings: 7/NA/7** (RV Area in MHP) 2015 rates: $35. (772)567-2764 1950 S US Hwy 1, Vero Beach, FL 32962

SUNSHINE TRAVEL RV RESORT **Ratings: 9/9★/8.5** (RV Park) 2015 rates: $35 to $55. (800)405-6188 9455 108th Ave, Vero Beach, FL 32967

Find it fast! To locate a town on a map, follow these easy instructions: Look for the map grid code after the town heading in the listing section and match it to the letters and numbers on the map borders. Draw a line horizontally from the letter and vertically from the number. You'll find the town near the intersection of the two lines.

WALDO — B3 *Alachua*

DIXIELAND MUSIC & RV PARK
Ratings: 6.5/8.5★/8.5 (RV Park) From the Jct of US 301 & SR 24 (in Waldo) N 1.5 mi on US 301 (L). **FAC:** Gravel rds. 160 grass, 100 pull-thrus (30 x 80), back-ins (30 x 60), 160 full hkups (30/50 amps), WiFi, dump, LP gas, controlled access. **REC.** Pets OK. Big rig sites, eco-friendly, 2015 rates: $35. No CC.
(352)468-3988 Lat: 29.81603, Lon: -82.16884
17500 US Hwy 301, Waldo, FL 32694
dixielandmusicpark@gmail.com
www.dixielandmusicpark.net
See ad page 357.

We appreciate your business!

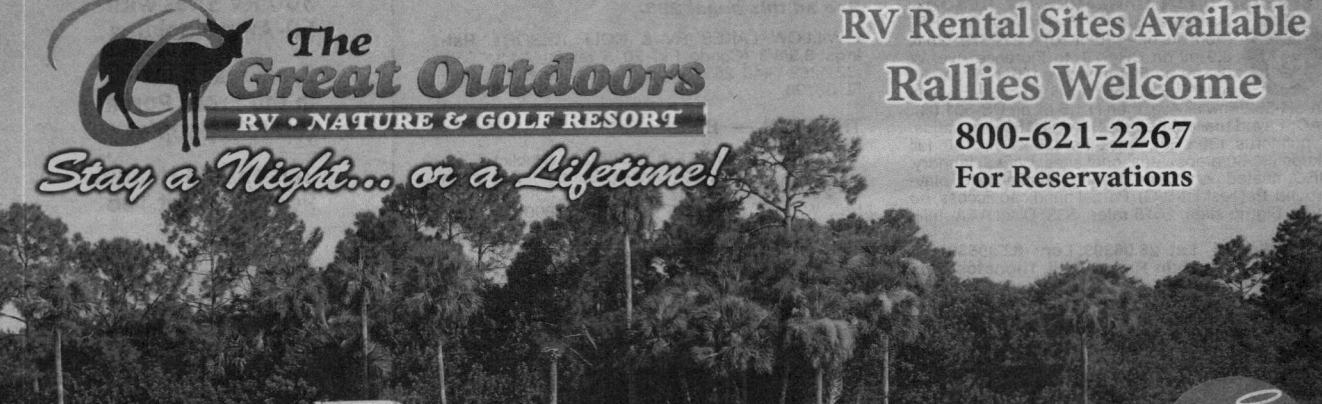

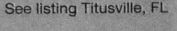

WAUCHULA — L3 *Hardee*

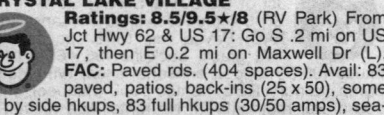

↑ **CRYSTAL LAKE VILLAGE**
Ratings: 8.5/9.5★/8 (RV Park) From Jct Hwy 62 & US 17: Go S .2 mi on US 17, then E 0.2 mi on Maxwell Dr (L). **FAC:** Paved rds. (404 spaces). Avail: 83 paved, patios, back-ins (25 x 50), some side by side hkups, 83 full hkups (30/50 amps), seasonal sites, WiFi Hotspot, rentals, laundry, controlled access. **REC:** heated pool, whirlpool, pond, fishing, shuffleboard. Pet restrict(B). Partial handicap access, no tents. Age restrict may apply, RV age restrict, 2015 rates: $30 to $35.
(800)661-3582 Lat: 27.58667, Lon: -81.81701
237 Maxwell Dr, Wauchula, FL 33873
crystallakevillage@hardeemail.com
crystallake-village.com
See ad opposite page, 286.

↓ PEACE RIVER THOUSAND TRAILS **Ratings: 7.5/8.5/6.5** (Membership Pk) 2015 rates: $35 to $45. (800)405-6188 2555 US Hwy 17 South, Wauchula, FL 33873

WEBSTER — J3 *Sumter*

→ FLORIDA GRANDE MOTORCOACH RESORT **Ratings: 10/10★/9.5** (Condo Pk) 2015 rates: $35 to $46. (352)569-1169 9675 SE 49th Terrace, Webster, FL 33514

← **SUNSHINE VILLAGE MH/RV RESORT**
Ratings: 8/9★/8 (RV Park) From Jct of CR 478 & CR 471: Go S 0.3 mi on CR 471, then W 0.6 mi on W Central Ave (L). **FAC:** Paved rds. (128 spaces). Avail: 44 grass, back-ins (50 x 80), 44 full hkups (30/50 amps), WiFi $, laundry. **REC:** heated pool, shuffleboard. Pet restrict(B/Q). Partial handicap access, no tents. Age restrict may apply, big rig sites, 2015 rates: $44. Disc: AAA. No CC.
(352)793-8626 Lat: 28.60990, Lon: -82.06724
2236 SE 100 Lane, Webster, FL 33597
office@sunshinevillageflorida.com
www.sunshinevillageflorida.com
See ad this page.

WESLEY CHAPEL — J2 *Pasco*

→ **BEGINNING POINT RV PARK**
Ratings: 7/8.5/7 (RV Park) From Jct I-75 (exit 279) and SR-54: Go E 6 mi on SR-54 (R). **FAC:** All weather rds. (48 spaces). Avail: 47 grass, patios, 10 pull-thrus (35 x 60), back-ins (30 x 50), accepts full hkup units only, 47 full hkups (30/50 amps), seasonal sites, WiFi, laundry. **REC:** heated pool. Pet restrict No tents. Big rig sites, 2015 rates: $30.
AAA Approved
(813)788-2415 Lat: 28.21922, Lon: -82.26483
4205 Lado Dr, Wesley Chapel, FL 33543
BeginningPoint@mberling.com
beginning-point-rv-park.com
See ad this page, 286.

← **QUAIL RUN RESORT**
Ratings: 10/9.5★/9.5 (RV Park) From Jct of I-75 (exit 279) & SR-54: Go W 0.5 mi on SR-54 then N 2 mi on Old Pasco Rd (R).

NO RIG TOO BIG
Nestle into our friendly country setting. Enjoy our rec hall, exercise room, pool & fun activities. Fabulous shopping & restaurants close by. NEW SUPER SIZED BIG RIG SITES with concrete pads & patios. Your Home Away from Home

FAC: Paved rds. (292 spaces). Avail: 148 paved, 94 all weather, patios, 39 pull-thrus (35 x 70), back-ins (35 x 55), 242 full hkups (30/50 amps), seasonal sites, cable, WiFi, dump, laundry, groc, LP gas, controlled access. **REC:** heated pool, pond, fishing, shuffleboard. Pet restrict(B/Q). Partial handicap access, no tents. Age restrict may apply, big rig sites, RV age restrict, 2015 rates: $42 to $55. Disc: AAA.
(800)582-7084 Lat: 28.25814, Lon: -82.34162
6946 Old Pasco Rd, Wesley Chapel, FL 33544
info@quailrunrv.com
www.quailrunrv.com
See ad pages 320 (Spotlight Tampa), 286, 280 (FL Featured Map).

WEST PALM BEACH — D5 *Palm Beach*

← **LION COUNTRY SAFARI KOA**
Ratings: 9/9.5★/9 (Campground) From Jct of I-95 & Southern Blvd (exit 68/SR-80), W 15.5 mi on Southern Blvd to Lion Country Safari Rd, N (right) 2 mi (E). Note: Max 40 ft. **FAC:** Paved rds. (211 spaces). Avail: 201 dirt, patios, 152 pull-thrus (30 x 50), back-ins (24 x 45), 201 full hkups (30/50 amps), seasonal sites, WiFi, tent sites, rentals, laundry, groc, LP gas, controlled access. **REC:** heated pool, shuffleboard, playground. Pet restrict(B/Q). Partial handicap access. Big rig sites, 2015 rates: $68 to $74. Disc: AAA. ATM.
(561)793-9797 Lat: 26.71411, Lon: -80.31819
2000 Lion Country Safari Rd, Loxahatchee, FL 33470
koa@lioncountrysafari.com
www.lioncountrysafari.com
See ad page 277 (Welcome Section).

← VACATION INN RESORT OF THE PALM BEACHES **Ratings: 9/10★/10** (Condo Pk) 2015 rates: $35 to $66. (561)848-6170 6500 N. Military Trl, West Palm Beach, FL 33407

Things to See and Do

← **LION COUNTRY SAFARI** A 245 acre wild animal preserve with over 800 wild animals roaming free within inches of your vehicle. Visit Safari World Amusement Park with giraffe feeding, carousel, animals, gift shop, restaurant & more. Partial handicap access. RV accessible. Restrooms, food. Hours: 9:30 am to 5:30 pm. Adult fee: $31.50. ATM.
(561)793-1084 Lat: 26.71339, Lon: -80.32249
2003 Lion Country Safari Rd, Loxahatchee, FL 33470
sales@lioncountrysafari.com
www.lioncountrysafari.com
See ad page 277 (Welcome Section).

WEWAHITCHKA — F3 *Gulf*

↑ DEAD LAKES STATE RECREATION AREA (State Pk) From jct Hwy-71 & Hwy-22: Go 4 mi N on Hwy-71. 2015 rates: $10 to $50. (850)639-2702

WHITE SPRINGS — A3 *Columbia, Hamilton*

↓ KELLY'S RV/MH PARK **Ratings: 7/7.5★/7.5** (RV Area in MHP) 2015 rates: $30.27. (866)355-9600 142 Nw Kelly Ln, White Springs, FL 32096

↑ STEPHEN FOSTER FOLK CULTURE CENTER (State Pk) From Jct of I-75 & SR-136 (exit 439), E 3 mi on SR-136 to US-41, N 0.1 mi (L). 2015 rates: $20. (386)397-2733

WILDWOOD — H3 *Sumter*

→ THOUSAND PALMS RV RESORT **Ratings: 9/9★/8.5** (RV Park) 2015 rates: $30 to $55. (321)284-4910 6545 W State Rd 44, Lake Panasoffkee, FL 33538

← THREE FLAGS RV RESORT **Ratings: 9/9★/8** (Membership Pk) 2015 rates: $38. Nov 1 to May 1. (800)405-6188 1755 E Sr. Rd 44, Wildwood, FL 34785

WILLISTON — G2 *Marion*

→ **WILLISTON CROSSINGS RV RESORT**
Ratings: 10/10★/10 (RV Resort) S-bnd: From Jct of I-75 & CR-121/Williston Rd (Exit 382), SW 15 mi on CR-121/Williston Rd to US 27/41, S 0.3 mi to US 27/Alt 27, SE 0.4 mi to NE 5th St, N 0.2 mi (R); or N-bnd: From Jct of I-75 & US 27 (Exit 354) NW 21 mi on US 27 to NE 5th St, N 0.2 mi (R).

NORTHERN FLORIDA'S BEST KEPT SECRET
Our one week campers wind up staying all year! Williston Crossings offers a pristine 135 acre paradise complete with large, paved sites, a lively social scene, onsite amenities, free WiFi and cable TV, and so much more!

FAC: Paved rds. 455 paved, patios, 35 pull-thrus (35 x 100), back-ins (40 x 70), accepts full hkup units only, 455 full hkups (30/50 amps), cable, WiFi, laundry, LP gas, controlled access. **REC:** heated pool, Williston Crossing Lake: fishing, shuffleboard, playground. Pet restrict(Q). Partial handicap access, no tents. Big rig sites, eco-friendly, 2015 rates: $39.95 to $54.95. Disc: AAA.
(877)785-4405 Lat: 29.40038, Lon: -82.43993
410 NE 5th St, Williston, FL 32696
info@willistoncrossingrv.com
www.willistoncrossingrv.com
See ad pages 358, 282 & Snowbird Destinations in Magazine Section.

WIMAUMA — L2 *Hillsborough*

↓ LITTLE MANATEE RIVER STATE RECREATION AREA (State Pk) From jct Hwy 674 & US 301: Go 5 mi S on US 301, then W on Lightfoot Rd. 2015 rates: $22. (813)671-5005

WINTER GARDEN — J3 *Orange*

← **STAGE STOP CAMPGROUND Ratings: 6.5/7.5/7** (Campground) From Jct FL Tpk (exit 267) & Hwy 50: Go W 2.5 mi on Hwy 50 (L). **FAC:** Paved rds. (248 spaces). Avail: 158 grass, patios, back-ins (35 x 50), mostly side by side hkups, 158 full hkups (30/50 amps), WiFi Hotspot, tent sites, dump, laundry. **REC:** pool, shuffleboard, playground. Pet restrict(Q). Partial handicap access. 2015 rates: $32. Disc: AAA.
AAA Approved
(407)656-8000 Lat: 28.55064, Lon: -81.59929
14400 W Colonial Dr, Winter Garden, FL 34787
stagestop@centurylink.net
Stagestopcampground-fl.embarqspace.com

← WINTER GARDEN RV RESORT **Ratings: 8/8.5★/7** (RV Area in MHP) 2015 rates: $42 to $55. (800)405-6188 13905 W Colonial Dr, Winter Garden, FL 34787

Travel Services

→ **CAMPING WORLD STORE OF WINTER GARDEN** As the nation's largest retailer of RV supplies, accessories, services and new and used RVs, Camping World is committed to making your total RV experience better. RV Accessories: (855)277-1220. **SERVICES:** RV, tire, RV appliance, MH mechanical, staffed RV wash, RV Sales. RV supplies, LP, emergency parking. Hours: 8am to 6pm.
(888)720-7146 Lat: 28.551366, Lon: -81.562121
12201 W Colonial Dr. Sr 50, Winter Garden, FL 34787
www.campingworld.com

FL

WINTER HAVEN — K3 *Polk*

→ **CYPRESS CAMPGROUND & RV PARK**
Ratings: 9/9★/8 (RV Park) From Jct of US-27 & SR-540: Go W 1 mi on SR-540 (L). **FAC:** Paved rds. (191 spaces). Avail: 15 gravel, patios, 10 pull-thrus (30 x 60), back-ins (25 x 55), 15 full hkups (30/50 amps), seasonal sites, cable, WiFi, rentals, dump, laundry, LP gas, controlled access. **REC:** heated pool, shuffleboard, playground. Pet restrict(B). Partial handicap access, no tents. Big rig sites, 2015 rates: $33 to $48. Disc: military.
(863)324-7400 Lat: 27.9781501, Lon: -81.650746
7400 Cypress Gardens Blvd, Winter Haven, FL 33884
info@cypresscampground.com
www.cypresscampground.com
See ad pages 410, 286.

→ EAST HAVEN RV PARK **Ratings: 8/9★/7.5** (RV Park) 2015 rates: $40. (863)324-2624 4320 Dundee Rd, Winter Haven, FL 33884

→ HAMMONDELL CAMPSITES **Ratings: 7.5/7.5/7.5** (RV Area in MHP) 2015 rates: $40. (863)324-5775 5601 Cypress Gardens Rd, Winter Haven, FL 33884

YULEE — A4 *Nassau*

→ HORNE LAKE RV PARK **Ratings: 8/8.5★/7** (RV Park) 2015 rates: $37.50. (800)628-9953 77219 Hance Pkwy, Yulee, FL 32097

How much will it all cost? Use this as a guide: Rates shown are the minimum and maximum for two adults in one RV at the time of inspection (excluding any additional fees for items not at the site). Remember, these rates serve as guidelines only. It's always best to call ahead for the most current rate information.

ZEPHYRHILLS — J2 *Pasco*

BAKER ACRES CAREFREE RV RESORT
Ratings: 8.5/NA/8 (RV Park) From Jct of US-301 & CR 54 (on N side of town): Go E 0.25 mi on CR 54, then N 1.3 mi on Wire Rd (R). **FAC:** Paved rds. (353 spaces). Avail: 60 grass, back-ins (25 x 45), accepts full hkup units only, 60 full hkups (30/50 amps), seasonal sites, WiFi $, dump, laundry. **REC:** heated pool, shuffleboard. Pets OK $. No tents. 2015 rates: $33. Disc: military.
(813)782-3950 Lat: 28.27120, Lon: -82.17949
7820 Wire Rd Lot 1, Zephyrhills, FL 33540
bakeracres@carefreervresorts.com
www.carefreervresorts.com
See ad page 406.

FOREST LAKE ESTATES R.V. RESORT
Ratings: 9/8.5★/8.5 (RV Park) From N-bnd Jct US-301 & SR-54: Go 3 mi E on SR 54-E (R). **FAC:** Paved rds. (274 spaces). Avail: 194 grass, patios, back-ins (32 x 45), accepts full hkup units only, 194 full hkups (30/50 amps), WiFi, laundry, LP bottles. **REC:** heated pool, whirlpool, pond, fishing, shuffleboard. Pet restrict Partial handicap access, no tents. Age restrict may apply, 2015 rates: $32.
(813)782-1058 Lat: 28.25312, Lon: -82.13520
41219 Hockey Dr, Zephyrhills, FL 33540
forestlakerv@tampabay.rr.com
http://www.forestlake-estates.com/rv.html
See ad this page, 286.

GLEN HAVEN CAREFREE RV RESORT
Ratings: 8.5/8/8 (RV Park) From S Jct of SR-54 & US-301: Go S 1.8 mi on US-301, then W 0.6 mi on Chancey Rd (R). **FAC:** Paved rds. (218 spaces). Avail: 50 grass, patios, back-ins (35 x 50), 50 full hkups (30/50 amps), seasonal sites, WiFi $, dump, laundry. **REC:** heated pool, whirlpool, shuffleboard. Pet restrict(B). Partial handicap access, no tents. Age restrict may apply, 2015 rates: $37. Disc: military.
(813)782-1856 Lat: 28.20943, Lon: -82.19946
37251 Chancey Rd, Zephyrhills, FL 33541
glenhaven@carefreervresorts.com
www.carefreervresorts.com
See ad page 406.

HAPPY DAYS RV PARK
Ratings: 8.5/7.5★/8.5 (RV Park) From Jct of US-301 & SR-54: Go W 1.25 mi on SR-54, then S 0.3 mi on Allen Rd (R). **FAC:** Paved rds. (292 spaces). Avail: 130 grass, back-ins (30 x 60), 130 full hkups (30/50 amps), seasonal sites, WiFi $, rentals, dump, laundry. **REC:** heated pool, shuffleboard. Pet restrict(B/Q). No tents. Age restrict may apply, big rig sites, 2015 rates: $33. Disc: AAA, military.
(813)788-4858 Lat: 28.22399, Lon: -82.20536
4603 Allen Rd, Zephyrhills, FL 33541
info@rvhappydays.com
www.happy-days-rv-park.com
See ad this page, 286 & Snowbird Destinations in Magazine Section.

HILLCREST RV RESORT
Ratings: 8/8★/8.5 (RV Park) From Jct of US-301 & SR-54: Go W 1 mi on SR-54, then S 0.5 mi on Lane Rd (R). **FAC:** Paved rds. (502 spaces). Avail: 146 grass, back-ins (35 x 65), 146 full hkups (30/50 amps), seasonal sites, WiFi Hotspot, dump, laundry. **REC:** heated pool, whirlpool, shuffleboard. Pet restrict(B/Q). No tents. Age restrict may apply, big rig sites, 2015 rates: $32.
(813)782-1947 Lat: 28.22183, Lon: -82.19697
4421 Lane Rd, Zephyrhills, FL 33541
hillcrestrv@verizon.net
hillcrestrvresortfl.com
See ad this page, 286.

LEISURE DAYS RV RESORT
Ratings: 8/8.5★/8 (RV Park) From Jct of I-75 (Exit 279) & SR-54: Go E 6.8 mi on SR-54, then S 0.1 mi on CR-579 (Morris Bridge Rd) (L). **FAC:** Paved rds. (240 spaces). Avail: 40 grass, back-ins (30 x 50), 40 full hkups (50 amps), WiFi, dump, laundry, LP bottles. **REC:** heated pool, shuffleboard. Pet restrict(B/Q). No tents. Age restrict may apply, 2015 rates: $36. Disc: AAA, military.
(813)788-2631 Lat: 28.21597, Lon: -82.24529
34533 Leisure Days Drive, Zephyrhills, FL 33541
leisuredays@newbymanagement.com
www.leisuredaysrvresort.com
See ad pages 271 (Welcome Section), 286.

MAJESTIC OAKS CAREFREE RV RESORT
Ratings: 8/8.5★/9 (RV Park) From Jct of US-301 & SR-54: Go S 2 mi on US-301, then E 1.5 mi on Chancey Rd (L). **FAC:** Paved rds. (252 spaces). Avail: 90 grass, patios, back-ins (40 x 72), 90 full hkups (30/50 amps), seasonal sites, WiFi Hotspot, laundry. **REC:** heated pool, shuffleboard. Pet restrict(B). Partial handicap access, no tents. Age restrict may apply, big rig sites, RV age restrict, 2015 rates: $32. Disc: military.
(813)783-7518 Lat: 28.21221, Lon: -82.16151
3751 Laurel Valley Blvd, Zephyrhills, FL 33542
majesticoaks@carefreervresorts.com
www.carefreervresorts.com
See ad page 406.

ZEPHYRHILLS (CONT)

↓ PALM VIEW GARDENS RV RESORT **Ratings: 7.5/7.5/7.5** (RV Area in MHP) 2015 rates: $32. (813)782-8685 3331 Gall Blvd, Zephyrhills, FL 33541

← RAINBOW VILLAGE CAREFREE RV RESORT
Ratings: 9/9.5★/8.5 (RV Area in MHP) From Jct of US-301 & SR-54: Go W 0.8 mi on SR-54, then S 0.8 mi on Lane Rd (L). **FAC:** Paved rds. (382 spaces). Avail: 32 grass, patios, back-ins (30 x 55), 32 full hkups (30/50 amps), seasonal sites, cable, WiFi $, rentals, dump, laundry. **REC:** heated pool, shuffleboard. Pet restrict(B). Partial handicap access, no tents. Age restrict may apply, big rig sites, 2015 rates: $34. Disc: AAA.
(813)782-5075 Lat: 28.21825, Lon: -82.19619
4150 Lane Rd, Zephyrhills, FL 33541
rainbowvillage@carefreervresorts.com
www.carefreervresorts.com
See ad page 406.

← RALPH'S TRAVEL PARK
Ratings: 7.5/7.5/6.5 (RV Park) From S Jct of US-301 & SR-54: Go W 2.5 mi on SR-54 (L). **FAC:** Paved rds. (385 spaces). Avail: 75 grass, patios, 15 pull-thrus (16 x 45), back-ins (16 x 40), some side by side hkups, 75 full hkups (30/50 amps), seasonal sites, WiFi Hotspot, dump, laundry. **REC:** pool, pond, shuffleboard. Pet restrict(B). No tents. 2015 rates: $31. Disc: AAA. No CC.
(813)782-8223 Lat: 28.21859, Lon: -82.24739
34408 State Rd. 54 West, Zephyrhills, FL 33543
ralphs33543@aol.com
ralphstravelpark.net
See ad opposite page, 286.

Each privately owned campground has been rated three times. The first rating is for development of facilities. The second one is for cleanliness and physical characteristics of restrooms and showers. The third is for campground visual appearance and environmental quality.

↓ SETTLER'S REST CAREFREE RV RESORT
Ratings: 6.5/8★/8 (RV Park) From S Jct of US-301 & SR-54: Go S 1.8 mi on US-301, then W 0.5 mi on Chancey Rd (R). **FAC:** Paved rds. (379 spaces). Avail: 30 grass, back-ins (30 x 50), 30 full hkups (30/50 amps), seasonal sites, WiFi, laundry. **REC:** shuffleboard. Pets OK. No tents. Age restrict may apply, 2015 rates: $32. Disc: military. No CC.
(813)782-2003 Lat: 28.20854, Lon: -82.19503
37549 Chancey Rd, Zephyrhills, FL 33541
settlersrest@carefreervresorts.com
Carefreervresorts.com
See ad page 406.

↓ SOUTHERN CHARM CAREFREE RV RESORT
Ratings: 8.5/8/8.5 (RV Park) From S Jct of US-301 & SR-54: Go S 1.8 mi on US-301, then W 0.3 mi on Chancey Rd (R). **FAC:** Paved rds. (497 spaces). Avail: 47 grass, patios, back-ins (35 x 50), accepts full hkup units only, 47 full hkups (30/50 amps), seasonal sites, WiFi $, dump, laundry. **REC:** heated pool, whirlpool, shuffleboard. Pet restrict(B). Partial handicap access, no tents. Age restrict may apply, big rig sites, 2015 rates: $32. Disc: AAA, military.
(813)783-3477 Lat: 28.20851, Lon: -82.19100
37811 Chancey Rd, Zephyrhills, FL 33541
southerncharm@carefreervresorts.com
www.carefreervresorts.com
See ad page 406 & Snowbird Destinations in Magazine Section.

↓ SWEETWATER CAREFREE RV RESORT
Ratings: 8/8/8 (RV Park) From Jct of SR-54 & US-301: Go S 1.8 mi on US-301, then W 0.4 mi on Chancey Rd (R). **FAC:** Paved rds. (289 spaces). Avail: 50 grass, patios, back-ins (30 x 50), accepts full hkup units only, 50 full hkups (30/50 amps), seasonal sites, WiFi $, laundry. **REC:** heated pool, shuffleboard. Pet restrict(B). No tents. Age restrict may apply, 2015 rates: $33. Disc: AAA, military.
(813)788-7513 Lat: 28.20841, Lon: -82.19347
37647 Chancey Rd, Zephyrhills, FL 33541
sweetwater@carefreervresorts.com
www.carefreervresorts.com
See ad page 406.

↑ WATERS EDGE CAREFREE RV RESORT
Ratings: 8/9★/8 (RV Park) From north Jct of US-301 & Hwy 54: Go E 0.25 mi on Hwy 54, then N 1.5 mi on Wire Rd, then E 0.7 mi on Otis Allen Rd (R). **FAC:** Paved rds. (217 spaces). Avail: 75 grass, patios, back-ins (30 x 45), 75 full hkups (30/50 amps), seasonal sites, WiFi $, laundry. **REC:** heated pool, shuffleboard. Pet restrict(B). Partial handicap access, no tents. Age restrict may apply, 2015 rates: $33. Disc: military.
(813)783-2708 Lat: 28.27097, Lon: -82.16862
39146 Otis Allen Rd, Zephyrhills, FL 33540
watersedge@carefreervresorts.com
www.carefreervresorts.com
See ad page 406.

← ZEPHYR PALMS RV PARK **Ratings: 7.5/8/6.5** (RV Park) 2015 rates: $38. (813)782-5610 35120 SR-54 W, Zephyrhills, FL 33541

Our rating system isn't just tough, it's thorough. We know the kinds of things that are important to you — like clean restrooms and showers, attractive, secure, well-tended grounds, and extras like swimming pools. We give the first rating for development of facilities, the second for cleanliness and physical characteristics of restrooms and showers, and the third for visual appearance.

FL

ralph daniel photography, inc

WELCOME TO
Georgia

DATE OF STATEHOOD	WIDTH: 254 MILES (409 KM)	PROPORTION OF UNITED STATES
JAN. 2, 1788	LENGTH: 320 MILES (515 KM)	1.57% OF 3,794,100 SQ MI

Georgia, the quintessential Southern belle, is the largest state east of the Mississippi River. It's a land of intriguing contradictions, where parochial towns nestle in the shadows of soaring cityscapes and, on any given Sunday, pastors rally their flocks in white steeple churches while aspiring entrepreneurs (Georgia is a hotbed for start-up companies) tap on their Macs over a latte in Starbucks. Atlanta, the shiny state capital, was dubbed the city "Too Busy To Hate" during the 1960s and it remains ever proud of its native son, Martin Luther King Jr.

Twenty-first-century Atlanta is a thriving metropolis, boasting world-class attractions, including the World of Coca-Cola, Centennial Olympic Park, the Fernbank Museum of Natural History and the world's largest aquarium. Sassy Savannah, with her spellbinding antebellum architecture draped in Spanish moss, preserves her raw beauty and grace without sacrificing her passion for decadent pleasures. Savannah is one of the nation's most bewitching cities, a blend of stately charm, old-fashioned elegance and timeless rituals. Between the Appalachian Mountains of North Georgia and the lowlands and marshes of the Atlantic coast, Georgia offers a wealth of outdoor attractions, including monuments that speak of Civil War lore, a "Gone with the Wind" trail and mile after mile of parkland and Atlantic coastline.

> At the Atlanta Beer Fest, you can sample up to 150 beers from local breweries such as SweetWater, Red Brick and Wild Heaven.

Learn

The youngest of the 13 former English colonies, Georgia was founded in 1732. By the mid-19th century, Georgia

Top 3 Tourism Attractions:
1) Georgia Aquarium
2) World of Coca-Cola
3) Centennial Olympic Park

Nickname: Peach State

State Flower: Cherokee Rose

State Bird: Brown Thrasher

People: Ray Charles, musician; Amy Grant, singer; Martin Luther King, Jr., civil rights leader; Jackie Robinson, baseball player; Trisha Yearwood, singer

Major Cities: Atlanta (capital), Augusta, Columbus, Savannah, Athens

Topography: North to northeast—Blue Ridge Mountains; Central—Piedmont Plateau; south–coastal plain and coastal flatlands

Climate: Humid, subtropical climate with most of the state having mild winters and hot summers

Georgia Department of Economic Development

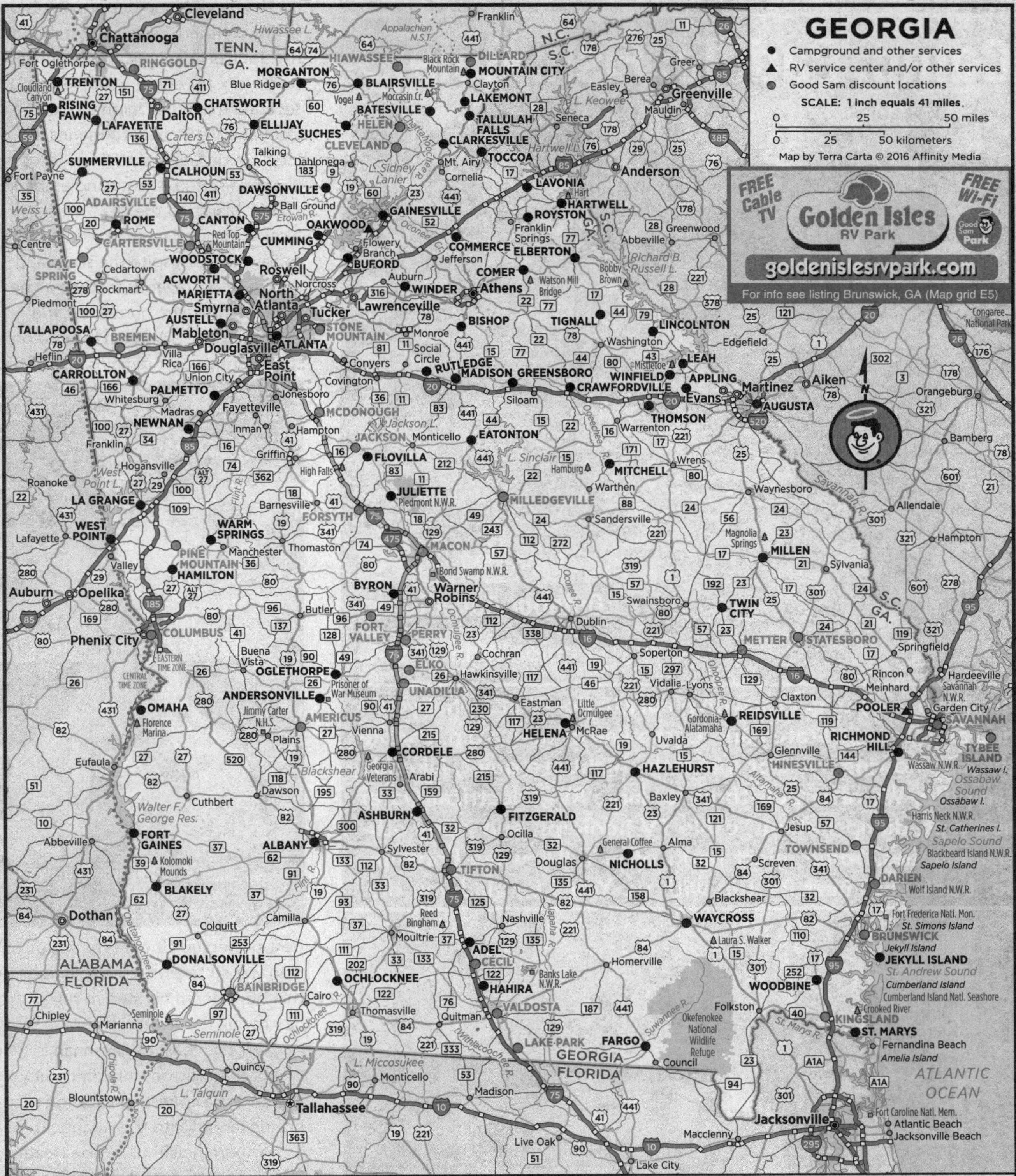
GEORGIA
Campground and other services
RV service center and/or other services
Good Sam discount locations
SCALE: 1 inch equals 41 miles
0 25 50 miles
0 25 50 kilometers
Map by Terra Carta © 2016 Affinity Media
FREE Cable TV
Golden Isles RV Park
FREE Wi-Fi
Good Sam Park
goldenislesrvpark.com
For info see listing Brunswick, GA (Map grid E5)

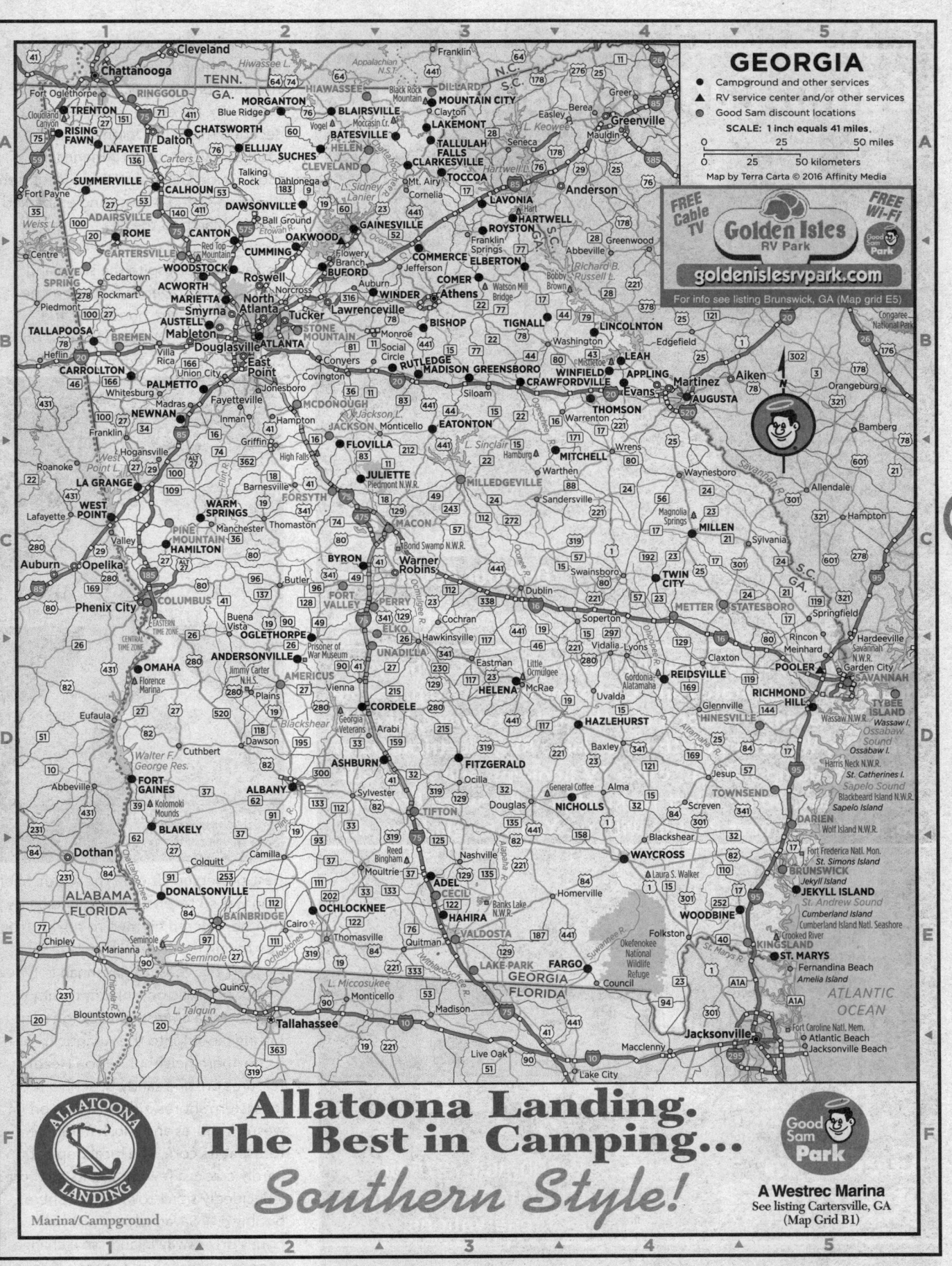

had the largest number of plantations of any southern state and symbolized the South's economic dependence on slavery. In February 1861, Georgia seceded from the Union to join the Confederate States of America. In 1864, Union General William Tecumseh Sherman seized Atlanta and embarked on his "March to the Sea," leaving in his wake a conflagration all the way to Savannah. Despite the slings and arrows of outrageous fortune—the Yankee onslaught, hurricanes and earthquakes—Savannah located on the Atlantic coast remains one of the

Museum of Aviation at Robins Air Force Base in Warner Robins
Georgia Department of Economic Development

best-preserved cities in the south. Sherman was so taken by the splendid city that he ordered his men to refrain from destroying the town.

Off the coast of Savannah is Tybee Island, an idyllic oceanfront community that is a cherished vacation secret. Jutting far out into the Atlantic (like its northern neighbor, Hilton Head), it features pristine sandy beachfront on its eastern shores, tidal marshes on its western shores and a lush maritime forest at its core. The local population hardly cracks a few thousand, so there's a decidedly small-town atmosphere, but big city Savannah sits just half-hour's drive away inland, so a change of pace is always just a stone's throw away. It's easy to see why regional locals consider this one of the best places to vacation or simply escape for a day trip.

Considered the "Song and Soul of the South," Macon hosts an eclectic musical heritage, beautiful antebellum buildings and an impressive Civil War history. The confederate army set up a hospital for its soldiers here, and the city also was home to a prison holding captured Union soldiers. Take a tour of the Cannonball House, a restored home that was struck by a cannonball during Stoneman's Raid. End your stay in Macon with a walk along the river and city streets filled with eateries, boutiques and music venues.

Play

Within Georgia's 11 national parks, there are more than 300 archeological sights and 18 endangered species. One of the world's largest intact freshwater ecosystems, the 353,981-acre Okefenokee National Wildlife Refuge, was established in 1937 and is one of the region's highlights. The fertile swamp is home to as many as 15,000 alligators, 234 bird species, 49 types of mammal and 60 amphibian species in addition to the endangered red-cockaded woodpecker, wood storks and indigo snakes. Trails lead visitors to amazing habitats and viewpoints.

- STAY A WHILE -

Camping at Georgia State Parks

Whether you are a first-time camper or an experienced backpacker, Georgia's state parks have a campsite for you. Forty-one parks offer more than 2,700 campsites, including tent-only areas, RV pull-thru sites, primitive camping and group camping areas.

There is nothing more enjoyable than the adventure of spending an evening under the stars. And there is no better place to do it than the campgrounds of Georgia State Parks. With so many unspoiled locations around the state, you're sure to find one that's close to home and close to your budget, too.

Georgia has 18 significant historic sites and historic parks. There are many opportunities for both adult and family volunteers to become involved with a local historic site. Volunteers dress up in period clothing and serve as hosts to help interpret the history of the Revolutionary or Civil War, plantation life or even the gentle times of the Victorian period. Other volunteers serve behind the scene to catalog and archive historic artifacts or assist as museum docent volunteers to offer visitors information and education opportunities. Volunteers can serve on a one-time or extended basis.

Experience

Beginning in late February, St. Patrick's Day celebrations in Savannah are the second largest in the U.S., drawing more than 300,000 people. All summer long, Atlanta keeps the mercury rising with a comprehensive lineup of festivities ranging from Independence Day fireworks at Stone Mountain Park to the National Black Arts Festival, a celebration of emerging and established Black artists; previous attendees included Maya Angelou, Charles Dutton and Spike Lee.

At the Atlanta Beer Fest, you can sample up to 150 beers from local breweries such as SweetWater, Red Brick and Wild Heaven while you enjoy live music from two main stages. The Grant Park Summer Shade festival is a two-day visual arts extravaganza. One of Atlanta's largest music festivals, Music Midtown, is held every year at Piedmont Park and attracts big-name artists including Eminem, Jack White, John Mayer, Lana Del Rey and Gregg Allman.

GA

TRAVEL & TOURISM

Georgia Dept. of Economic Development
800-VISIT GA
www.exploregeorgia.org

Albany Area Chamber of Commerce
800-475-8700, 229-434-8700
www.albanyga.com

Athens CVB
800-653-0603, 706-357-4430
www.visitathensga.com

Atlanta CVB
404-521-6600
www.atlanta.net

Augusta Metropolitan CVB
800-726-0243
www.augustaga.org

Brunswick-Golden Isles Chamber of Commerce
912-265-0620, 800-933-COAST
www.bgivb.com

Columbus CVB
706-322-1613, 800-999-1613
www.columbusga.com

Georgia State Parks & Historic Sites
404-656-2770
www.gastateparks.org

Historic Chattahoochee Commission
706-845-8440

Jekyll Island Welcome Center
912-635-3636
www.jekyllisland.com

Macon CVB
800-768-3401
www.maconga.org

Savannah CVB
877-savannah
www.savannahvisit.com

OUTDOOR RECREATION

Georgia Dept. of Natural Resources
404-656-3500
www.gadnr.org

Georgia Golfing
800-864-7275
www.golfgeorgia.org

Georgia Hunting
www.georgiawildlife.com/hunting

SHOPPING

Antiques & Crafts Unlimited Mall
706-655-2468
www.acum.org

Lane Packing
800-27-PEACH
www.lanesouthernorchards.com

North Georgia Premium Outlets
706-216-3609
www.premiumoutlets.com/northgeorgia

Lenox Square
317-636-1600
www.simon.com/mall/lenox-square

Tanger Outlet Centers
336-292-3010
www.tangeroutlets.com

Featured Good Sam Parks

GEORGIA

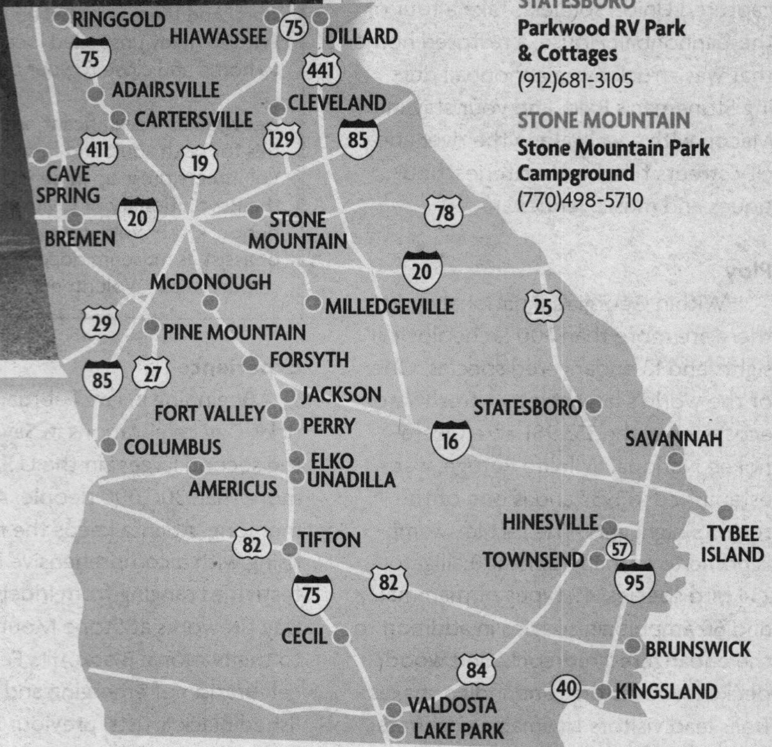

When you stay with Good Sam, you can expect the highest degree of cleanliness and friendliness, and better yet, you get 10% off campground fees.

If you're not already a Good Sam member you can purchase your membership at one of these locations:

ADAIRSVILLE
Harvest Moon RV Park
(770)773-7320

AMERICUS
Brickyard Plantation Golf Club & RV Park
(229)874-1234

BREMEN
Yogi Bears Jellystone Park-Camp Resort
(404)855-2778

BRUNSWICK
Coastal Georgia RV Resort
(912)264-3869
Golden Isles RV Park
(912)261-1025

CARTERSVILLE
Allatoona Landing Marine Resort & Campground
(770)974-6089

CAVE SPRING
Cedar Creek RV & Outdoor Center
(706)777-3030

CECIL
Cecil Bay RV Park
(229)794-1484

CLEVELAND
Leisure Acres Campground
(706)865-6466
Yonah Mountain Campground
(706)865-6546

COLUMBUS
Lake Pines RV Park & Campground
(706)561-9675

DILLARD
River Vista Mountain Village
(888)850-7275

ELKO
Twin Oaks RV Park
(478)987-9361

FORSYTH
L & D RV Park
(478)994-5401

FORT VALLEY
Perry Ponderosa Park
(478)825-8030

HIAWASSEE
Bald Mountain Camping Resort
(706)896-8896

HINESVILLE
Happy Campers RV Park
(912)876-6881

JACKSON
Forest Glen Mobile Home & RV Park
(770)228-3399

KINGSLAND
Country Oaks Campground & RV Park
(912)729-6212

LAKE PARK
Eagles Roost RV Resort
(229)559-5192

MCDONOUGH
Atlanta South RV Park
(770)957-2610

MILLEDGEVILLE
Scenic Mountain RV Park & Campground
(478)454-1013

PERRY
Crossroads Travel Park
(478)987-3141
Fair Harbor RV Park
(478)988-8844

PINE MOUNTAIN
Pine Mountain an RVC Outdoor Destination
(706)663-4329

RINGGOLD
Battlefield Campground & RV Park
(706)937-4166

SAVANNAH
Biltmore RV Park
(912)236-4065
Red Gate Campground & RV Park
(912)272-8028
Savannah Oaks RV Resort
(800)851-0717

STATESBORO
Parkwood RV Park & Cottages
(912)681-3105

STONE MOUNTAIN
Stone Mountain Park Campground
(770)498-5710

TIFTON
Pines RV Park
(229)382-3500

TOWNSEND
Lake Harmony RV Park and Campground
(888)767-7864
McIntosh Lake RV Park
(912)832-6215

TYBEE ISLAND
River's End Campground & RV Park
(800)786-1016

UNADILLA
Southern Trails RV Resort
(478)627-3254

VALDOSTA
River Park RV Park
(229)244-8397
Valdosta Oaks RV Park
(229)247-0494

For more Good Sam Parks go to listing pages

Getty Images/iStockphoto

ATLANTA

Navigate the Peach State's diverse capital city like a native

There's no denying it—Atlanta, Georgia, is massive. It sprawls across a gigantic geographic area and just keeps growing and growing. But don't rush to judgment here, as guidebook labels can be traps and collective wisdom can be misleading. This large and bustling cityscape is best viewed as an eclectic collection of five distinct, much smaller neighborhoods—Downtown, Midtown, Westside, Eastside and Buckhead—which are all strung together by Peachtree Street. Embrace this nuanced view of Atlanta and you'll be well on your way to enjoying an insider's understanding of "The City Too Busy to Hate."

If you're like most visitors you'll find yourself starting in Downtown. This is the hub of all major happenings about town, including home games for the NFL's Atlanta Falcons (at the Georgia Dome) and the NBA's Atlanta Hawks (at Philips Arena). This is also where you'll find Centennial Olympic Park, a 21-acre oasis in the heart of the city full of green spaces, dotted with water fountains and supported by an informative visitor center. Built to commemorate the 1996 Summer Olympic Games, the park now serves as a scenic hub for attractions like the Georgia Aquarium, CNN Studio Tours and the World of Coca-Cola Museum.

The Georgia Aquarium is the largest in the western hemisphere and a must-visit for all ages. Home to massive whale sharks, elegant belugas and a playful group of bottlenose dolphins, this cutting-edge facility also features an extravagant Broadway-style show, in which actors and dolphins perform incredible acrobatic feats. At the World of Coca-Cola, visitors can sample more than 60 different products while exploring the fascinating history of the world's most iconic soda, while a trip behind the scenes at CNN includes an hourlong guided tour of the newsroom and high-tech control room.

Atlanta's Georgia Aquarium is the biggest aquarium in the world. Getty Images/iStockphoto

Take a Bite Out of Southern Culture

Over in Midtown, arts and culture come to life. Take a stroll through Piedmont Park before heading to the High Museum of Art, a groundbreaking museum that was the first in the world to showcase items on loan from Paris' legendary Louvre. After exploring galleries of classic and contemporary works, head to one of Midtown's world-renowned gourmet restaurants for dinner, then catch a show at the Atlanta Symphony Orchestra.

Westside Atlanta is a shopper's paradise and a food-lover's dream come true. Head to Roman-inspired Atlantic Station to plunder your way around a neighborhood-sized, open-air shopping center that's so big it has its own ZIP code. For a mouth-watering food tour (professionally guided or otherwise), beeline it for the Design District, also known as West Midtown. This area has rapidly transformed from an industrial hub into a hip and trendy spot for young professionals, resulting in a fantastic food scene.

Serious shopaholics will also find themselves in the lap of luxury with a trip to the neighborhood of Buckhead, perhaps the wealthiest spot in all of Atlanta. Sporting a wealth of high-end retail outlets, the area is the part-time home of Sir Elton John, and is renowned for its megamansions and overt opulence.

When it's time to let your hair

down, shift your focus to Eastside Atlanta. This artsy and trendy neighborhood is the place to find live street music and impromptu public art projects. It's also home to iconic Turner Field (home of the Atlanta Braves, where you can catch Major League Baseball games) and Zoo Atlanta. Those traveling with children will definitely want to make a stop at the zoo, which is home to a daily slate of interactive keeper-led wildlife shows, as well as a petting zoo for kids.

Look at Atlanta's Past

Finally, for history buffs, Atlanta is home to a vast collection of eclectic museums and sites. Three in particular are can't-miss: Martin Luther King Jr. National Historic Site, Jimmy Carter Presidential Library and Museum and the Atlanta History Center.

The Jimmy Carter Presidential Library and Museum is worthy of a visit if only for its spectacular views of the city. Perched on a hilltop high above the downtown core, it offers panoramic views of the city far below. The museum showcases items from Jimmy Carter's presidency and his Nobel Peace Prize, as well as an exact replica of the Oval Office, which makes for a surreal walk-through.

Atlanta's Historic Old Fourth Ward Park. Getty Images/iStockphoto

At the Martin Luther King Jr. National Historic Site, visitors can explore the life and incredible accomplishments of Atlanta's most notable and distinguished citizen. Guests can pay their respects at Dr. King's gravesite.

For More Information

Atlanta CVB
800-285-2682
www.atlanta.net

Georgia Department of Economic Development
800-847-4842
www.exploregeorgia.org

Getty Images/iStockphoto

COLUMBUS

Ride the rapids or walk Civil War museums in this eclectic city

Columbus, sitting on the eastern banks of the Chattahoochee River on the Georgia-Alabama border, is a classic American river town. In the 1800s, that meant sending bales of cotton and textiles from local mills down to Apalachicola, Florida, and into the Gulf of Mexico. Today, that means strolling down the nationally acclaimed 15-mile Chattahoochee RiverWalk or riding the Whitewater Express, a 2.5-mile run of rapids through town that is the longest urban whitewater course in the world.

Recreation draws lots of fun-seeking visitors, but Columbus has not forgotten its past. Columbus has grown to be the second largest city in Georgia, so it makes sense that the Columbus Museum, an American art and regional history depository, is the second-largest museum in the Peach State as well. Founded in 1953, the collection now comprises more than 14,000 items and admission is always free.

War and Peace

The city's rich industrial heritage from the 19th century is the inspiration for Heritage Park on Broadway, where granite pools recreate the tumbling waters of the Chattahoochee, which once provided power for mills and factories. Across the street, the Historic Columbus Foundation conducts tours of its Heritage Corner, which features the 1850s Italianate-style Rankin House and the Walker Peters Langdon House, both of which date to the early 1800s. Also nearby is the Coca-Cola Space Science Center, with simulated missions, hands-on exhibits, and shows and demonstrations in the Omnisphere Theater. The Mead Observatory opens once a month for the public to come and gaze at the stars like a trained astronomer.

The Columbus Black History Museum and Archives highlights the contribution of the African American community to the city, including Horace King, who directed the building of the Columbus City Bridge while still constricted to slavery. King purchased his freedom in 1846 and eventually engineered lattice truss bridges at major crossings of the Chattahoochee River. The museum's music collection is particularly strong, with the archives of Gertrude "Ma" Rainey, the Mother of the Blues, and of savant slave "Blind Tom" Bethune, who became internationally famous in the 19th century as a composer and musician.

Since 1918, the fortunes of Columbus have traveled in lockstep with Fort Benning, which occupies 182,000 acres on the city's southern doorstep. Fort Benning is home to the United States Army Infantry and more than 120,000 active military personnel. A self-guided driving tour will lead to 35 destinations inside the Main Post, which has been rebranded the "Home of the Maneuver Center of Excellence." Admission is free and pets are allowed to tour as well. On Legacy Way, where the city meets the base, the National Infantry Museum and Soldier Center honors the American foot soldier from the days of the War of Independence to the nation's longest war in Afghanistan. At the National Civil War Naval Museum on Victory Drive, you can see the CSS Jackson, the largest surviving Confederate warship, as well as artifacts from both sides in the battle for supremacy of the coast during the War Between the States.

Columbus Culture

Civilian pursuits thrive in Columbus as well. The Columbus Symphony Orches-

Browsing vendors' wares during Columbus Market Days. Columbus, GA CVB tra, organized in 1855 by Herman S. Saroni as the second orchestra in the United States after the New York Philharmonic, performs out of the state-of-the-art RiverCenter for the Performing Arts. Also making appearances at the RiverCenter is the Columbus Ballet, featuring students at the Columbus State University Dance Conservatory. The sumptuous stage at the Springer Opera House has been designated the State Theatre of Georgia. When it opened in 1871, the Springer was considered by traveling troupes to be the finest theater between New York City and New Orleans.

When it's time to get outside in Columbus, you can enjoy passive recreation like birdwatching in the urban jungle or strolling through the display gardens in the Columbus Botanical Garden outside the historic 1890s Adams Farmhouse. The Oxbow Meadows Environmental Learning Center takes advantage of a hardwood wetland in a bend in the Chattahoochee River to introduce visitors to the city's small mammals, birds and turtles. A special Tree Top Trail can be accessed for $5.

Columbus has also made it easy for geocachers to explore the city with 32 caches hidden along the Chattahoochee RiverWalk. Complete a grid sheet created by the Convention & Visitors Bureau and return it to the center to receive a bronze, silver or gold coin. Bikers and hikers will want to explore the Fall Line Trace, an 11-mile Rails-to-Trails project that has converted abandoned Norfolk Southern Railroad tracks into a scenic asphalt pathway.

And what about that Whitewater Express through the center of town? Those rapids can reach up to 13,000 cubic feet per second in volume.

For More Information

Columbus Convention and Visitors Bureau
800-999-1613
www.visitcolumbusga.com

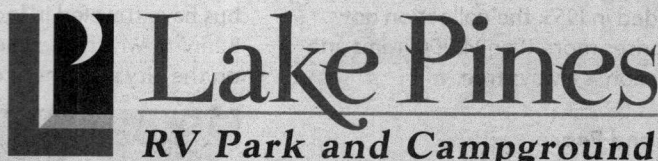

Georgia Department of Economic Development
800-VISIT-GA
www.exploregeorgia.org

MACON

Experience the song and soul of the South

Located near the geographic center of Georgia, Macon boasts a rich past. Native Americans made the region home more than 17,000 years ago, and the 1600s and 1700s saw waves of settlers putting down roots. Today, living history abounds on the streets of Macon, with 14 designated historic districts and more than 6,000 structures nominated for the National Register of Historic Places.

Macon Music

Nothing makes Maconites prouder than their musical heritage. Jazz vocalist Lena Horne began her career with City Hall youth choir performances in the 1930s; the Reverend Pearly Brown, blind from birth and the last of America's great street blues singers, began arriving from his hometown of Americus by bus in the 1940s to play his guitar with a cup attached; native son Richard Wayne Penniman—better known as Little Richard—redefined rock and roll in the 1950s; Otis Redding, "The Mad Man from Macon," became the 1960s' seminal soul artist; and the Allman Brothers honed Southern Rock here in the 1970s.

You can still walk in the footsteps of musical Macon giants in places like Grant's Lounge, the Original Home of Southern Rock, and the Big House, a Tudor Revival mansion on Vineville Avenue where the Allman Brothers lived from 1970 through 1973.

Touring History

Seeking more traditional touring? The Hay House on Georgia Avenue is often called the "Palace of the South" for its 18,000 square feet and stunning Antebellum-era Italian Renaissance architecture. Builder William Butler Johnston, a prosperous merchant, oversaw the Confederate treasury.

Macon blends its historical roots with outdoor recreation on the 11-mile Ocmulgee Heritage Trail, Middle Georgia's only riverside trail and park system. A life-size bronze statue of Otis Redding resides trailside.

Macon also preserves the African American experience with more than 20 historic and cultural sites.

For More Information

Visit Macon
800-768-3401
www.maconga.org

Georgia Department of Economic Development
800-VISIT-GA
www.exploregeorgia.org

Getty Images/iStockphoto

SAVANNAH

Seductive Southern charm welcomes visitors to a centuries-old city

In 1887, a girl named Florence Martus showed up at the Savannah port and began waving at the passengers in arriving ships. During the day, the 19-year-old resident waved a piece of cloth; at night she brandished a lantern. She did not stop waving until 1931, and legend has it she never missed a ship. The statue Waving Girl, designed by Felix de Weldon, was placed in Emmet Park along the Savannah River in 1972.

The town, built on old-fashioned Southern charm, is still the same one that Florence symbolized so many years ago.

> No visit to the "Hostess City of the South" is complete without sampling the city's innovative take on traditional Southern food.

City of Squares

British settler James Oglethorpe founded the town in 1733. Oglethorpe laid out his town in 24 public squares, and the visionary grids set the stage for a downtown district that has thrived for 300 years.

The port of entry for Savannah's leafy public squares is the Visitor Center, which occupies the yards of the former Central of Georgia Railway. From here, guided tours in open-air trolleys and horse-drawn carriages launch into the downtown area, which has put strict limits on commercial development. The rare building that rises above eight stories is usually obscured by the live oaks draped in Spanish moss that grow in the squares.

Many downtown buildings—67 in fact—have been rescued by the Savannah College of Art and Design and put to use for the school's vibrant urban campus. The streets of the 2.5-mile Historic District are an outdoor classroom for American architecture, from the Regency design of the Owens-Thomas House on Oglethorpe Square to the French Gothic spires of the Cathedral of St. John the Baptist on Lafayette Square. The Telfair Museum of Art was the first public art museum in the South when a mansion on Telfair Square was transformed to gallery space in 1884.

Forsyth Park in Savannah, Georgia. Getty Images/iStockphoto

History and Charm

There is so much history dripping from the balconies overlooking Savannah's squares that a tour of the city practically transports visitors back in time. Visit Johnson Square and tour the Christ Episcopal Church that occupies one corner. At more than 280 years old, this is considered the "Mother Church" of Georgia. On Madison Square, you'll find the Green-Meldrim House, which became the Civil War Union headquarters for General William Tecumseh Sherman following his scorched earth "March to the Sea" through the Confederacy in 1864. On Reynolds Square, the Pink House is as old as the country itself.

The Colonial Park Cemetery on Oglethorpe Avenue dates back to colonial times, with the victim of Savannah's first dueling death in 1740 interred here. The Bonaventure Cemetery, located on the eastern edge of downtown overlooking the Wilmington River, took a star turn in both the book and movie adaptation of Midnight in the Garden of Good and Evil. It is equal parts sacred burial ground and Gothic sculpture garden.

Beyond the City Limits
History buffs will want to drift from Savannah over to Cockspur Island to see Fort Pulaski, which was built by the Confederate army to defend the city. The fort was considered impregnable to smooth bore cannon, but during the Civil War, the walls were breached by the Union Army, with the world's first rifled cannon reaching their target from four miles offshore. Fort Pulaski National Monument is on the way to Tybee Island, which is known affectionately as "Savannah's Beach."

Savanah Vittles
No visit to the "Hostess City of the South" is complete without sampling the city's innovative take on traditional Southern food. Indulge in everything from international gourmet dinners to quick casual bites of coastal cuisine. Culinary adventures await visitors on nearly every square. You'll also find great spots along the honeycomb of iron bridges and staircases that make up Factors Walk, a converted cotton exchange on brick-lined River Street.

And it's still possible to be greeted by the waving girl of lore from while you're riding on the deck of a steamboat in the Savannah River. Savannah Riverboat Cruises has been running sightseeing and dinner entertainment cruises on restored paddle wheelers since 1991.

The boats give passengers a taste of 19th-century travel, when paddlewheelers propelled people and cargo up and down the Savannah River. Enjoy live performances, drinks and fine dining as the city's fantastic skyline drifts into view. Groups can schedule special events, from weddings to reunions.

For More Information

Visit Savannah
877-SAVANNAH
www.visitsavannah.com

Georgia Department of Economic Development
800-VISIT-GA
www.exploregeorgia.org

Savannah's famous Oglethorpe Square. Getty Images/iStockphoto

GA

Georgia

CONSULTANTS

Ken & Kathy Wente

ACWORTH — B2 *Bartow, Cherokee, Cobb*

CLARK CREEK NORTH (Public Corps) From Jct of I-75 & Exit 278, NW 2 mi on Glade Rd, follow signs (L). 2015 rates: $30. May 15 to Sep 7. (678)721-6700

MCKINNEY CAMPGROUND (Public Corps) From Jct of I-75 & Exit 278, NE 3 mi on Glade Rd to Kings Camp Rd, W 1 mi, follow signs (E). 2015 rates: $26 to $30. (678)721-6700

OLD HWY 41 #3 (Public Corps) From Jct of I-75 & exit 278, NW 1 mi to Hwy 92, left 1 mi to Hwy 293, follow signs (E). 2015 rates: $26 to $60. May 15 to Sep 7. (678)721-6700

PAYNE CAMPGROUND (Public Corps) From Jct of I-75 & Hwy 92 (exit 277), N 2 mi on Hwy 92 to Kellogg Crk Rd, NE 3 mi (R). 2015 rates: $26 to $60. Mar 27 to Sep 7. (678)721-6700

ADAIRSVILLE — A1 *Bartow*

HARVEST MOON RV PARK
Ratings: 8/9★/8 (RV Park) From Jct of I-75 (exit 306) & Hwy 140: Go 1/4 mi W on Hwy 140, then 1/4 mi S on Poplar Springs Rd (R). **FAC:** Paved/gravel rds. (77 spaces). Avail: 30 gravel, 21 pull-thrus (35 x 90), back-ins (35 x 70), 30 full hkups (30/50 amps), seasonal sites, cable, WiFi, laundry, LP gas. **REC:** pool. Pet restrict(B/Q). Partial handicap access, no tents. Big rig sites, 2015 rates: $36.50. Disc: AAA, military.
(770)773-7320 Lat: 34.37450, Lon: -84.91673
1001 Poplar Springs Rd, Adairsville, GA 30103
harvmoon@bellsouth.net
www.harvestmoonrvpark.com
See ad pages 426, 416.

ADEL — E3 *Colquitt, Cook*

REED BINGHAM
(State Pk) From Jct of I-75 & SR-37 (Exit 39) W 5.5 mi on SR-37 to Evergreen Church Rd, N 0.3 mi to Reed Bingham Rd, W 0.9 mi (E). Entrance fee required. **FAC:** Paved rds. 46 gravel, 23 pull-thrus (40 x 50), back-ins (40 x 50), 19 full hkups, 27 W, 27 E (30/50 amps), tent sites, dump, laundry, fire rings, firewood. **REC:** Reed Bingham Lake: swim, fishing, playground, rec open to public. Pet restrict(Q). Partial handicap access. 14 day max stay. 2015 rates: $25 to $38. Disc: military.
(800)864-PARK Lat: 31.161633, Lon: -83.538933
542 Reed Bingham Rd, Adel, GA 31620
www.gastateparks.org
See ad page 414 (Welcome Section).

ALBANY — D2 *Dougherty*

ALBANY RV RESORT **Ratings: 7.5/9★/9** (RV Park) 2015 rates: $32 to $36. (866)792-1481 1202 Liberty Expressway SE, Albany, GA 31705

THE PARKS AT CHEHAW CAMPGROUND (Public) From Jct of US-19 & SR-91, NE 1.3 mi on SR-91 (L). 2015 rates: $20 to $28. (229)430-5277

AMERICUS — D2 *Sumter*

BRICKYARD PLANTATION GOLF CLUB & RV PARK
Ratings: 7.5/9.5★/8.5 (RV Park) From Jct of I-75 (Exit 101) & Hwy 280: Go 24 mi W on Hwy 280 (R). **FAC:** Gravel rds. 48 Avail: 24 gravel, 24 grass, 48 pull-thrus (35 x 70), 48 full hkups (30/50 amps), WiFi Hotspot, laundry. **REC:** golf, rec open to public. Pets OK. Partial handicap access, no tents. Big rig sites, 2015 rates: $40.
(229)874-1234 Lat: 32.00314, Lon: -84.11077
1619 US Hwy 280 E, Americus, GA 31709
bpgcdeb@sowega.net
www.brickyardgolfclub.com
See ad pages 412 (Welcome Section), 416.

Things to See and Do

BRICKYARD PLANTATION GOLF CLUB 27-hole golf course, 2 PGA pros, driving range, senior activities Wed & Fri, snack bar. Open to public all year. Closed Thanksgiving & Christmas. Golf clinics & lessons. Partial handicap access. Food. Hours: M-Sat 8am to 6pm, Sun 12:30pm to 6pm. Adult fee: $15.
(229)874-1234 Lat: 32.00536, Lon: -84.11317
1619 US 280 East, Americus, GA 31709
bpgcdeb@sowega.net
www.brickyardgolfclub.com
See ad page 412 (Welcome Section).

ANDERSONVILLE — D2 *Sumter*

CITY CAMPGROUND (Public) From jct Hwy 49 & Hwy 228: Go 1/4 mi W on Hwy 228, then 1 block S to Monument, then 1 block W (follow signs). 2015 rates: $18. (229)924-2558

APPLING — B4 *Columbia*

MISTLETOE
(State Pk) From Jct of I-20 & SR-150 (Exit 175), N 7.8 mi on Hwy 150 to Mistletoe Rd, W 3 mi (E). Parking fee required. **FAC:** Paved/gravel rds. 92 gravel, patios, 32 pull-thrus (25 x 60), back-ins (25 x 60), 92 W, 92 E (30/50 amps), tent sites, rentals, dump, laundry, fire rings, firewood. **REC:** Clarks Hill Lake: swim, fishing, playground, rec open to public. Pet restrict(Q). Partial handicap access. 14 day max stay, 2015 rates: $27 to $32. Disc: military.
(800)864-PARK Lat: 33.643283, Lon: -82.385200
3725 Mistletoe Rd, Appling, GA 30802
www.gastateparks.org
See ad page 414 (Welcome Section).

WILDWOOD PARK (Public) From Jct of US Hwy 221 & SR-47 (in Pollards Corner), NW 1.6 mi on SR-47 (R). 2015 rates: $20. (706)541-0586

ASHBURN — D3 *Turner*

WANEE LAKE GOLF & RV RESORT **Ratings: 5.5/7.5/6.5** (RV Park) 2015 rates: $30. (229)567-CAMP 3821 Ga Hwy 112W, Ashburn, GA 31714

ATLANTA — B2 *Cobb, Fulton*

ATLANTA AREA MAP

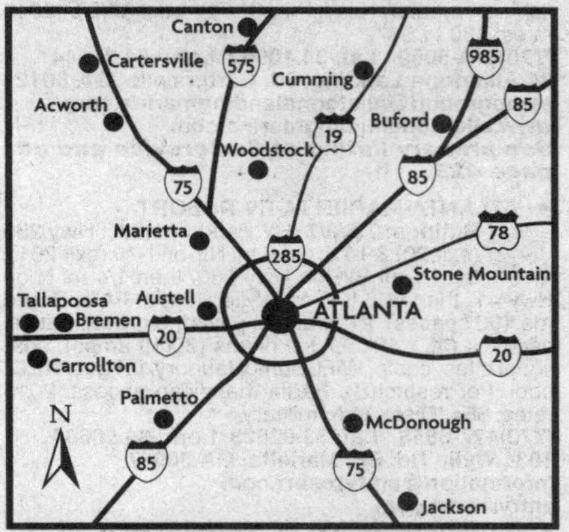

For more detail and a broader overview, please see our full-color state map at the front of the Georgia state section.

Symbols on map indicate towns within a 40 mile radius of Atlanta where campgrounds are listed. Check listings for more information.

See also Acworth, Austell, Bremen, Buford, Canton, Carrollton, Cartersville, Cumming, Jackson, Marietta, McDonough, Palmetto, Stone Mountain, Tallapoosa & Woodstock.

GA

ALLATOONA LANDING MARINE RESORT & CAMPGROUND
Ratings: 9/9★/8.5 (Campground) From Jct I-285 & I-75: Go 24 mi N on I-75 (exit 283), then 2 mi E on Allatoona Rd (L). **FAC:** Paved rds. 99 paved, 14 pull-thrus (30 x 60), back-ins (30 x 45), 20 full hkups, 79 W, 79 E (30/50 amps), cable, WiFi, tent sites, rentals, dump, mobile sewer, laundry, LP gas, fire rings, firewood, controlled access. **REC:** pool, Lake Allatoona:

ATLANTA (CONT)

ALLATOONA LANDING MARINE (CONT)
fishing, marina, playground. Pet restrict(B). 2015 rates: $30 to $47.
(770)974-6089 Lat: 34.10903, Lon: -84.71144
24 Allatoona Landing Rd, Cartersville, GA 30121
campground@allatoonalandingmarina.com
www.allatoonalandingmarina.com
See primary listing at Cartersville and ad page 425.

ATLANTA-MARIETTA RV RESORT
Ratings: 7.5/8/7 (RV Park) From Jct Hwy 285 (exit 20) & I-75: Go 5 mi NE on I-75 (exit 261), then 1 mi SW on Hwy 280, then 1/4 mi N on Hwy 41, then 500 ft E on Wylie Rd (R). **FAC:** Paved rds. (62 spaces). 27 Avail: 22 paved, 5 gravel, patios, back-ins (26 x 40), 27 full hkups (30/50 amps), seasonal sites, cable, WiFi, dump, laundry, LP gas. **REC:** pool. Pet restrict(B). Partial handicap access. 2015 rates: $54. Disc: AAA, military.
(770)427-6853 Lat: 33.92823, Lon: -84.50684
1031 Wylie Rd. SE, Marietta, GA 30067
Information@amrvresort.com
amrvresort.com
See primary listing at Marietta and ad this page.

FOREST GLEN MOBILE HOME & RV PARK
Ratings: 7.5/8★/6.5 (RV Park) From jct I-75 (exit 237A) & Hwy 285/407: Go 32 mi S on I-75 (exit 205), then1/4 mi W on Hwy 16, then 500 ft S on Windy Lane Circle, then 1/2 mi E on Forest Glen Rd, then 500 ft S on Entrance Rd (E). **FAC:** Paved rds. (148 spaces). Avail: 44 paved, 42 pull-thrus (22 x 50), back-ins (22 x 50), 44 full hkups (30/50 amps), seasonal sites, WiFi Hotspot, laundry. **REC:** pool. Pet restrict(B). 2015 rates: $30.
(770)228-3399 Lat: 33.25707, Lon: -84.09341
218 Glade Road, Jackson, GA 30233
See primary listing at Jackson and ad this page.

RV Park ratings you can rely on!

AUGUSTA — B4 *Richmond*

HERITAGE RV PARK
Ratings: 5.5/NA/7 (RV Park) From Jct I-20 (exit 194) & Hwy 383: Go 1/2 mi S on Hwy 383 (Dyess Parkway), then 1 mi E on Wrightsboro Rd (L). **FAC:** Gravel rds. (105 spaces). Avail: 55 gravel, patios, back-ins (30 x 50), 55 full hkups (30/50 amps), seasonal sites, WiFi. Pet restrict(B). No tents. 2015 rates: $35.
(706)863-3333 Lat: 33.47053, Lon: -82.11390
3863 Wrightsboro Road, Augusta, GA 30909
hmhc@aol.com
www.heritagervpark.com
See ad this page.

AUSTELL — B2 *Cobb*

SWEETWATER CREEK RV RESERVE
(Campground) (Too New to Rate) From Jct I-20 (exit44) & Hwy 6 (Thornton Road): Go 1-1/4 mi NW on Hwy 6, then 1 mi N on Maxham Rd, then 1/2 mi W on Old Alabama, then 500 ft NW on Love St, then 1/4 mi NE on Wren Circle (R). **FAC:** Paved rds. (48 spaces). Avail: 38 grass, 2 pull-thrus (26 x 60), back-ins (30 x 45), 38 full hkups (30/50 amps), seasonal sites. **REC.** Pets OK. Big rig sites, 2015 rates: $45 to $55.
(404)218-1100 Lat: 33.81260, Lon: -84.63437
2558 Wren Circle, Austell, GA 30168
reservations@sweetwatercreekrv.com
http://sweetwatercreekrv.com
See ad this page.

BAINBRIDGE — E2 *Decatur*

FLINT RIVER RV PARK
Ratings: 8/8.5★/7 (RV Park) From Jct of US 27 & Hwy 97 (Shotwell/Bainbridge): Take Shotwell exit, then 500 ft W on Hwy 97, then 1/4 mi S on Shotwell (L). **FAC:** Gravel rds. (85 spaces). 55 Avail: 50 gravel, 5 grass, 34 pull-thrus (35 x 110), back-ins (35 x 40), 55 full hkups (30/50 amps), seasonal sites, cable, WiFi, tent sites, dump, laundry, LP gas, firewood. **REC:** pool, playgroun[d]. Pets OK. Big rig sites, 2015 rates: $36 to $40.
(229)246-5802 Lat: 30.89877, Lon: -84.58886
801 W. Shotwell St, Bainbridge, GA 39819
davidbrantly@hotmail.com
www.flintriverrvpark.com
See ad this page.

Say you saw it in our Guide!

BATESVILLE — A3 *Batesville, Rabun, White*

SUGAR MILL CREEK RV RESORT Ra[t]ings: 6.5/6.5/8 (Campground) 2015 rates: $30 [to] $35. (706)947-0162 4960 Laurel Lodge Rd, Clarke[s]ville, GA 30523

BISHOP — B3 *Oconee*

PINE LAKE CAMPGROUND **Ratings: 7.5/9★/**[…] (Campground) 2015 rates: $32 to $35. (706)76[…]5486 5540 High Shoals Rd (Hyw 186), Bishop, G[A] 30621

BLAIRSVILLE — A2 *Union*

POTEETE CREEK (UNION COUNTY PARK) (Public) From jct US-19/129 & Hwy-325: Go 3-1/2 [mi] W on Hwy-325, then follow signs 1 mi E on coun[ty] road. 2015 rates: $18 to $25. Apr 1 to Oct 1[…] (706)439-6103

TRACKROCK CAMPGROUND & CABINS **Ra[t]ings: 8.5/8★/8** (Campground) 2015 rates: $28 [to] $40. (706)745-2420 141 Trackrock Camp Rd, Blair[s]ville, GA 30512

VOGEL
(State Pk) From Jct of US 76 & US 129, S 1[…] mi on US 129 (R). Parking fee required. CAU[…]TION: Several tight turn arounds. Elev 2640 f[t]. **FAC:** Paved rds. 85 gravel, patios, 14 pull-thru[s] (18 x 45), back-ins (18 x 30), 85 W, 85 E (30/5[0] amps), tent sites, rentals, dump, laundry, groc, fi[re] rings, firewood. **REC:** Trahlyta Lake: swim, fishing, playground, rec open to public. Pet restrict(Q). Partia[l] handicap access. 14 day max stay, 2015 rates: $2[…] to $30. Disc: military.
(800)864-PARK Lat: 34.765883, Lon: -83.92541
405 Vogel State Park Rd, Blairsville, GA 30512
www.gastateparks.org
See ad page 414 (Welcome Section).

Dispose of old paint, chemicals, and o[il] properly. Don't put batteries, antifreeze, pain[t], motor oil, or chemicals in the trash. Us[e] proper toxics disposal sites.

BLAKELY — D1 *Early*

KOLOMOKI MOUNDS
(State Pk) From Jct of 27 Bus & SR-62, N on 27 Bus 1.2 mi to First Kolomoki Rd, N 4.4 mi (R) Entrance fee required. **FAC:** Paved rds. 24 gravel, patios, 10 pull-thrus (30 x 70), back-ins (30 x 60), 24 W, 24 E (30 amps), tent sites, dump, laundry, fire rings, firewood. **REC:** Lake Kolomoki: swim, fishing, playground, rec open to public. Pets OK. Partial handicap access. 14 day max stay, 2015 rates: $24 to $26. Disc: military.
(800)864-PARK Lat: 31.468633, Lon: -84.948533
205 Indian Mounds Rd, Blakely, GA 39823
www.gastateparks.org
See ad page 414 (Welcome Section).

BREMEN — B1 *Carroll, Haralson*

YOGI BEARS JELLYSTONE PARK-CAMP RESORT
Ratings: 9.5/9.5/9 (Campground) From Jct of I-20 (Exit 9) & Waco Rd: Go 1 mi N on Waco Rd, then 3/4 mi W on US-78/SR-8, then 1/4 mi SW on King St (L). **FAC:** Paved rds. (89 spaces). Avail: 50 gravel, 36 pull-thrus (25 x 80), back-ins (25 x 40), 50 full hkups (30/50 amps), seasonal sites, cable, WiFi, tent sites, rentals, laundry, fire rings, firewood, controlled access. **REC:** pool, pond, fishing, playground, rec open to public. Pets OK. Partial handicap access. Big rig sites, 2015 rates: $38 to $41. Disc: military. ATM.
(404)855-2778 Lat: 33.70208, Lon: -85.19664
106 King Street, Bremen, GA 30110
info@gajellystone.com
www.gajellystone.com
See ad opposite page, 416.

BRUNSWICK — E5 *Glynn*

BLYTHE ISLAND REGIONAL PARK CAMPGROUND (Public) From Jct of I-95 (Exit 29) & US 17: Go 1/2 mi W on US 17, then 2-3/4 mi NE on Hwy 303 (R). 2015 rates: $36.63. (800)343-7855

COASTAL GEORGIA RV RESORT
Ratings: 10/10★/9.5 (RV Park) From the Jct of I-95 (Exit 29) & US 17/US 82: Go 1/2 mi W on US 17/US-82, then 1/4 mi S on US 17 S, then 1/2 mi SE on Martin Palmer Dr (E).

NEWEST RV RESORT NEAR S. GA COAST!
Bring the family & enjoy our amenities! Minutes from golf, beaches & historical sites. Have a cookout at the enclosed or open air pavilion, enjoy fun in the sun at our pool, cruise the lake in paddleboats or do some fishing.

FAC: Paved rds. (105 spaces). Avail: 65 paved, patios, 60 pull-thrus (35 x 75), back-ins (35 x 60), 65 full hkups (30/50 amps), seasonal sites, cable, WiFi, laundry, LP gas, firewood. **REC:** pool, Lake Earl: fishing, playground. Pet restrict(B). Partial handicap access, no tents. Big rig sites, 2015 rates: $40. Disc: military.
(912)264-3869 Lat: 31.13377, Lon: -81.58249
287 South Port Parkway, Brunswick, GA 31523
coastalgarv@att.net
www.coastalgarvresort.com
See ad pages 428, 416 & Snowbird Destinations in Magazine Section.

GOLDEN ISLES RV PARK
Ratings: 8/7.5/6.5 (Campground) From Jct of I-95 (Exit 29) & US Hwy 82/17: Go 1/2 mi W on US Hwy 82/17, then 1/4 mi N on GA 303 (L).

ENJOY BRUNSWICK & THE GOLDEN ISLES!
Country cooking buffet at Fran's Place. Beautiful beaches, historic sites, water park & cruise ship. Golf, fish & sightsee. Affordable family fun! Come relax by the pool or a campfire! Free WIFI! and 63 ch cable TV.

FAC: Paved/gravel rds. (165 spaces). Avail: 125 dirt, 96 pull-thrus (28 x 60), back-ins (28 x 45), 115 full hkups, 10 W, 10 E (30/50 amps), seasonal sites, cable, WiFi, tent sites, dump, laundry, LP gas, firewood, restaurant. **REC:** pool, playground. Pets OK. Partial handicap access. Big rig sites, 2015 rates: $34 to $36. Disc: military.
(912)261-1025 Lat: 31.14542, Lon: -81.57653
7445 Blythe Island Hwy, Brunswick, GA 31523
goldenislesrv@bellsouth.net
www.goldenislesrvpark.com
See ad this page, 413 (GA Map), 416.

Did you know we sent 35 husband-wife RVing teams out this year to scour North America, rating and inspecting RV parks and campgrounds? You can rest easy when you read our listings, knowing we've already been there.

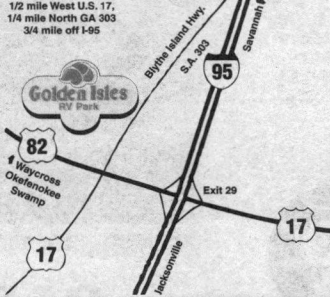

GA

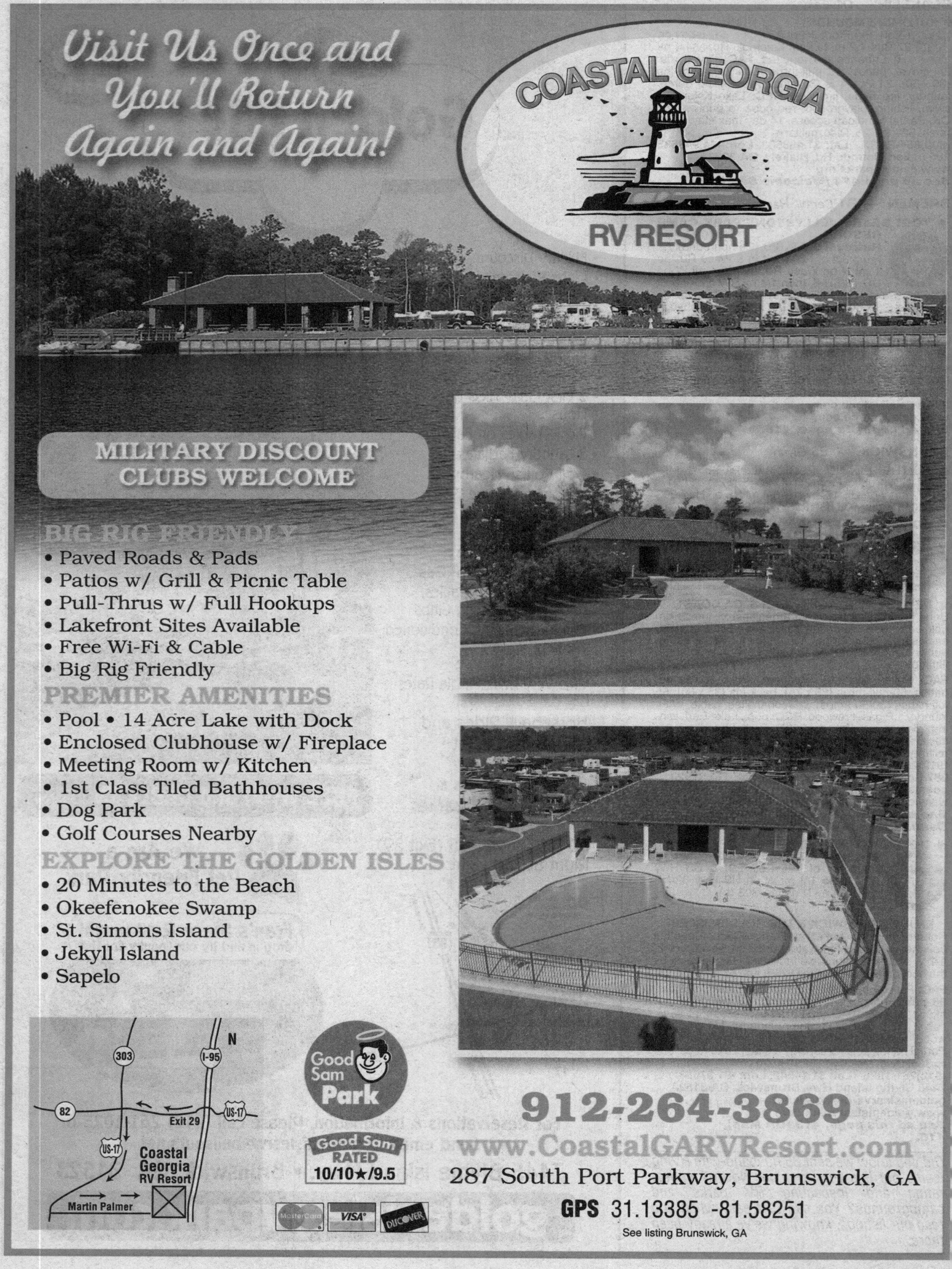
Visit Us Once and You'll Return Again and Again!
COASTAL GEORGIA
RV RESORT
MILITARY DISCOUNT
CLUBS WELCOME
BIG RIG FRIENDLY
• Paved Roads & Pads
• Patios w/ Grill & Picnic Table
• Pull-Thrus w/ Full Hookups
• Lakefront Sites Available
• Free Wi-Fi & Cable
• Big Rig Friendly
PREMIER AMENITIES
• Pool • 14 Acre Lake with Dock
• Enclosed Clubhouse w/ Fireplace
• Meeting Room w/ Kitchen
• 1st Class Tiled Bathhouses
• Dog Park
• Golf Courses Nearby
EXPLORE THE GOLDEN ISLES
• 20 Minutes to the Beach
• Okeefenokee Swamp
• St. Simons Island
• Jekyll Island
• Sapelo
N
303
I-95
82
Exit 29
US-17
US-17
Coastal Georgia RV Resort
Martin Palmer
Good Sam Park
Good Sam RATED
10/10★/9.5
VISA
DISCOVER
912-264-3869
www.CoastalGARVResort.com
287 South Port Parkway, Brunswick, GA
GPS 31.13385 -81.58251
See listing Brunswick, GA

BRUNSWICK (CONT)

Things to See and Do

FRAN'S PLACE RESTAURANT Full service restaurant, serving breakfast & lunch, featuring country cooking & special menu items. RV accessible. Restrooms, food. Hours: 8am to 9am and 11am to 2pm weekdays.
(912)262-9663 Lat: 31.14438, Lon: -81.57933
7445 Blythe Island Hwy, Brunswick, GA 31523
goldenislesrv@bellsouth.net
www.goldenislesrvpark.com
See ad page 427.

THREE OAKS FARM 50 acre equine facility. Boarding, lessons, horseback riding, horse sales/leasing. Specializing in Hunter Jumpers, Dressage & Western trail rides on beach & forest. Carriage rides. Riding on Jekyll & St. Simons beaches. Open all year.
(912)635-9000 Lat: 31.17022, Lon: -81.58803
332 Oyster Rd, Brunswick, GA 31523
http://www.threeoaksfarm.org
See ad page 427.

BUFORD — B2 *Gwinnett, Hall*

BLUE RIDGE CAMPGROUND **Ratings: 5/7.5/6** (Campground) 2015 rates: $39 to $43. (678)482-0332 7000 Lanier Islands Parkway, Buford, GA 30518

SHOAL CREEK (Public) From Jct of 985 & Hwy 20 (exit 4), W 4 mi on Hwy 20 to Peachtree Industrial Blvd, N 2 mi to Shadburn Ferry Rd, NW 3 mi (E). 2015 rates: $34 to $43. (678)482-0332

SHOAL CREEK CAMPGROUND **Ratings: 6/7/7** (Campground) 2015 rates: $39 to $43. (678)482-0332 6300 Shadburn Ferry Rd, Buford, GA 30518

BYRON — C2 *Houston, Peach*

INTERSTATE CAMPGROUND **Ratings: 6.5/4.5/4.5** (Campground) 2015 rates: $25. (888)817-0906 305 Chapman Rd, Byron, GA 31008

Travel Services

CAMPING WORLD OF BYRON/MACON As the nation's largest retailer of RV supplies, accessories, services and new and used RVs, Camping World is committed to making your total RV experience better. RV Accessories: (888)204-9976. **SERVICES:** RV, RV appliance, staffed RV wash, self RV wash, restrooms, RV Sales. RV supplies, LP, emergency parking, RV accessible. Hours: 8am to 6pm.
(888)716-5436 Lat: 32.652742, Lon: -83.745104
225 W.e. Green Jr. Parkway, Byron, GA 31008
www.campingworld.com

CALHOUN — A1 *Gordon*

CALHOUN, GEORGIA KOA **Ratings: 8/6.5/6** (Campground) 2015 rates: $30 to $42. (706)629-7511 2523 Redbud Rd NE, Calhoun, GA 30701

CANTON — A2 *Cherokee*

SWEETWATER CAMPGROUND (Public Corps) From Jct of I-75 & Hwy 20 (exit 290), E 11 mi on Hwy 20 to Field's Chapel Rd, S 1.4 mi (E). 2015 rates: $26 to $60. Mar 20 to Sep 7. (678)721-6700

CARROLLTON — B1 *Carroll*

JOHN TANNER (Public) From town, W 6 mi on Hwy 16 to Tanner Beach Rd, follow signs S 0.6 mi (E); or From Jct of I-20 (Exit 11) & US 27, S 0.4 mi on John Tanner Park Dr to Bowden Jct Rd, W 3.1 mi to SR-16, S 1.5 mi to Rte 224 (Tanner Beach Rd), W 0.6 mi (R). 2015 rates: $30. (770)830-2222

CARTERSVILLE — B1 *Bartow*

ALLATOONA LANDING MARINE RESORT & CAMPGROUND
Ratings: 9/9★/8.5 (Campground) From Jct of I-75 (exit 283) & Emerson-Allatoona Rd: Go 2 mi E on Allatoona Rd (L).

ALLATOONA LANDING MARINE RESORT
Offers a lakeside experience for the traveling RVer to come & fish, relax, or visit many attractions in the area. We're near Barnsley Gardens, Kennesaw Mountain Nat'l Battlefield, Etowah Indian Mounds & more. A Good Sam Park.

FAC: Paved rds. 99 paved, 14 pull-thrus (30 x 60), back-ins (30 x 45), 20 full hkups, 79 W, 79 E (30/50 amps), cable, WiFi, tent sites, rentals, dump, mobile sewer, laundry, LP gas, fire rings, firewood, controlled access. **REC:** pool, Lake Allatoona: fishing, marina, playground. Pet restrict(B). 2015 rates: $30 to $47. Disc: military.
(770)974-6089 Lat: 34.10903, Lon: -84.71144
24 Allatoona Landing Rd, Cartersville, GA 30121
campground@allatoonalandingmarina.com
www.allatoonalandingmarina.com
See ad pages 425, 416, 413 (GA Map).

MCKASKEY CREEK CAMPGROUND (Public Corps) From Jct of I-75 & Hwy 20 (exit 290), E 0.2 mi on Hwy 20 to Hwy 20 Spur, SE 2 mi to McKasky Crk Rd, E 1 mi (E). 2015 rates: $26 to $30. Mar 27 to Sep 7. (678)721-6700

RED TOP MOUNTAIN (State Pk) From Jct of I-75 & Red Top Mountain Rd (Exit 285), E 2 mi on Red Top Mountain Rd (E). Entrance fee required. CAUTION: Narrow winding roads. **FAC:** Paved rds. 92 gravel, patios, 12 pull-thrus (40 x 60), back-ins (30 x 50), 92 W, 92 E (30/50 amps), WiFi Hotspot, tent sites, rentals, dump, fire rings, firewood, restaurant. **REC:** Allatoona Lake: swim, fishing, marina, playground, rec open to public. Pets OK. Partial handicap access. 14 day max stay, 2015 rates: $20 to $35. Disc: military.
(800)864-7275 Lat: 34.142950, Lon: -84.706700
50 Lodge Rd SE, Cartersville, GA 30121
www.gastateparks.org
See ad page 414 (Welcome Section).

Things to See and Do

GEORGIA STATE PARKS & HISTORIC SITES A division of the Georgia Dept of Natural Resources. State parks, campgrounds, historic sites, golf courses, and events. Open all year. Hours: 8:30am to 4pm. Adult fee: $5. No CC.
(800)864-7275 Lat: 34.14295, Lon: -84.70670
781 Red Top Mountain Rd. SE, Cartersville, GA 30121
georgiastateparks.org
See ad page 414 (Welcome Section) & Family Camping In Magazine Section.

CAVE SPRING — B1 *Floyd*

CEDAR CREEK RV & OUTDOOR CENTER
Ratings: 7.5/9★/7.5 (Campground) From Jct of US 27 & US 411: Go 7 mi W on US 411 (R). **FAC:** Gravel rds. (62 spaces). Avail: 57 gravel, 10 pull-thrus (24 x 54), back-ins (27 x 35), 57 full hkups (30/50 amps), seasonal sites, WiFi, tent sites, rentals, laundry, LP gas, fire rings, firewood. **REC:** Cedar Creek: fishing, rec open to public. Pets OK. Partial handicap access. 2015 rates: $29 to $35.
(706)777-3030 Lat: 34.13313, Lon: -85.30828
6770 Cave Spring Rd SW, Cave Spring, GA 30124
camp@bigcedarcreek.com
www.bigcedarcreek.com
See ad this page, 416.

CECIL — E3 *Cook*

CECIL BAY RV PARK
Ratings: 6/8★/7 (RV Park) From Jct of I-75 (Exit 32) & Old Coffee Rd, W 0.1 mi on Old Coffee Rd (R).

OVERSIZED PULL-THRU'S
The park that can accommodate all RVs. You can spread out and enjoy our very wide & long pull-thru sites. Easy ON & OFF for the overnight traveler, yet convenient for those that want to stay longer.

FAC: Gravel rds. (104 spaces). Avail: 80 gravel, 80 pull-thrus (40 x 62), 72 full hkups, 8 W, 8 E (30/50 amps), seasonal sites, WiFi, tent sites, dump, laundry. **REC:** pond, fishing. Pets OK. Partial handicap access. Big rig sites, 2015 rates: $31. Disc: military.
(229)794-1484 Lat: 31.04404, Lon: -83.39869
1787 Old Coffee Rd, Cecil, GA 31627
winco5@windstream.net
www.cecilbayrv.com
See ad pages 439, 416.

CHATSWORTH — A1 *Gilmer, Murray*

FORT MOUNTAIN (State Pk) From Jct US 411 & Hwy 52: Go 7-1/4 mi E on Hwy 52 (L) CAUTION: Steep, narrow, winding Rd, uphill for 7 miles. Parking fee required. Elev 2639 ft. **FAC:** Paved rds. 62 gravel, 32 pull-thrus (35 x 60), back-ins (35 x 60), 62 W, 62 E (30 amps), tent sites, rentals, dump, laundry, fire rings, firewood. **REC:** Fort Mt Lake: swim, fishing, playground, rec open to public. Pets OK. Partial handicap access. 14 day max stay, 2015 rates: $27 to $32. Disc: military.
(800)864-PARK Lat: 34.760916, Lon: -84.707166
181 Fort Mountain Park Rd, Chatsworth, GA 30705
www.gastateparks.org
See ad page 414 (Welcome Section).

WOODRING CAMPGROUND (Public Corps) From town, S 13 mi on US-411 to SR-136, E 0.75 mi to 4-way intsec (Old US-411), N 5 mi to SR-282, E 5 mi, follow signs (R). 2015 rates: $22 to $28. Apr 3 to Oct 31. (706)276-6050

CLARKESVILLE — A3 *Habersham*

MOCCASIN CREEK (State Pk) From town, W 12 mi on US 76 to SR-197, S 3.6 mi; or From Clarkesville, N 20 mi on Hwy 197 (R). Parking fee required. **FAC:** Paved rds. 54 gravel, patios, 8 pull-thrus (25 x 50), back-ins (25 x 32), 54 W, 54 E (20/30 amps), tent sites, dump, laundry, fire rings, firewood. **REC:** Lake Burton: fishing, playground, rec open to public. Pets OK. Partial handicap access. 14 day max stay, 2015 rates: $29 to $32. Disc: military.
(800)864-PARK Lat: 34.847100, Lon: -83.588900
3655 Hwy 197, Clarkesville, GA 30523
www.gastateparks.org
See ad page 414 (Welcome Section).

CLEVELAND — A2 *Habersham, Hall, Lumpkin, White*

JENNY'S CREEK CAMPGROUND **Ratings: 4/5.5/6.5** (Campground) 2015 rates: $28 to $35. (706)865-6955 4542 Hwy 129 N, Cleveland, GA 30528

LEISURE ACRES CAMPGROUND
Ratings: 8.5/8.5★/7.5 (Campground) S-bnd: From Cleveland, From Jct of US 129 & Hwy 115: Go 3-3/4 mi S on US-129, then 1/2 mi W on Westmoreland Rd (L); N-bnd: From Clermont, From Jct of US 129 & Hwy 254: Go 2-3/4 N on US 129 then 1/2 mi W on Westmoreland Rd (L). **FAC:** Gravel rds. (94 spaces). Avail: 54 gravel, 29 pull-thrus (25 x 60), back-ins (25 x 45), 54 full hkups (30/50 amps), seasonal sites, WiFi, dump, laundry, LP gas, fire rings, firewood. **REC:** pool, wading pool, pond, fishing, playground. Pet restrict(B). Partial handicap access, no tents. Big rig sites, 2015 rates: $36 to $50. Disc: AAA, military.
(706)865-6466 Lat: 34.53684, Lon: -83.76715
3840 Westmoreland Rd, Cleveland, GA 30528
info@leisureacrescampground.com
www.leisureacrescampground.com
See ad pages 432, 416.

TURNER CAMPSITES **Ratings: 5/7/6** (Campground) 2015 rates: $30 to $36. (706)865-4757 142 Turner Campsite Rd, Cleveland, GA 30528

YONAH MOUNTAIN CAMPGROUND
Ratings: 8/8.5★/7 (Membership Pk) From Jct US 129 & Hwy 75: Go 3-3/4 mi N on Hwy 75 (R). **FAC:** Paved/gravel rds. (109 spaces). 99 Avail: 92 gravel, 7 grass, 5 pull-thrus (35 x 60), back-ins (25 x 50), 99 full hkups (30/50 amps), seasonal sites, WiFi Hotspot, tent sites, laundry, LP gas, fire rings, firewood. **REC:** pool, pond, fishing, playground. Pet restrict(B). Partial handicap access. 2015 rates: $38 to $45. Disc: military.
(706)865-6546 Lat: 34.64765, Lon: -83.73565
3678 Helen Hwy, Cleveland, GA 30528
Frontoffice@yonahcampground.com
www.yonahcampground.com
See ad pages 432, 416.

COLUMBUS — C1 *Muscogee*

A SPOTLIGHT Introducing Columbus's colorful attractions appearing at the front of this state section.

Our rating system isn't just tough, it's thorough. We know the kinds of things that are important to you — like clean restrooms and showers, attractive, secure, well-tended grounds, and extras like swimming pools. We give the first rating for development of facilities, the second for cleanliness and physical characteristics of restrooms and showers, and the third for visual appearance.

Refer to the Table of Contents in front of the Guide to locate everything you need.

Like Us on Facebook.

GA

COLUMBUS (CONT)

→ **LAKE PINES RV PARK & CAMPGROUND**
Ratings: 9/8.5★/9 (Campground)
N-S: From Jct of I-185 (Exit 10 East on I-185) & US-80, E 9.5 mi on US-80 (between MM 12 & 13) to Garrett Rd, S 0.1 mi (L) E-W: From Jct of US 280 & US 80, E 15 mi on US 80 (between MM 12 & 13) to Garrett St, S on Garrett St 0.1 mi (L).

49 YEARS OF SOUTHERN HOSPITALITY!
Family owned & operated since 1967. Minutes from historic sites, art & history museums, unique dining, antiquing & shopping, whitewater rafting, hiking & biking. See visitcolumbusga.com for 51 reasons to spend a week or two!

FAC: Gravel rds. (112 spaces). 87 Avail: 77 gravel, 10 grass, 31 pull-thrus (27 x 60), back-ins (27 x 30), 87 full hkups (30/50 amps), seasonal sites, WiFi, tent sites, rentals, dump, laundry, LP gas, firewood. **REC:** pool, pond, fishing, playground. Pet restrict(B). Big rig sites, 2015 rates: $37 to $40.
(706)561-9675 Lat: 32.53804, Lon: -84.82728
6404 Garrett Rd, Columbus, GA 31820
info@lakepines.net
www.lakepines.net
See ad pages 420 (Spotlight Columbus), 416 & RV Trips of a Lifetime in Magazine Section.

Things to See and Do

→ **LAKE PINES EVENT CENTER** Specializing in weddings, family reunions, clubs, special meetings & gatherings. Restrooms.
(706)561-9675 Lat: 32.53812, Lon: -84.82727
6404 Garrett Rd, Columbus, GA 31820
info@lakepineseventcenter.com
www.lakepineseventcenter.com
See ad page 420 (Spotlight Columbus).

COMER — B3 *Oglethorpe*

↘ **WATSON MILL BRIDGE**
(State Pk) From town, S 3 mi on Hwy 22 to Watson Mill Rd, E 3.3 mi (E). Caution: Low branches, narrow internal roads, tight turns. Parking fee required. **FAC:** Paved rds. 31 gravel, patios, 18 pull-thrus (20 x 50), back-ins (20 x 40), 31 W, 31 E (30/50 amps), tent sites, dump, laundry, fire rings, firewood. **REC:** South Fork River: fishing, playground, rec open to public. Pets OK. Partial handicap access. 14 day max stay, 2015 rates: $25 to $29. Disc: military.
(800)864-PARK Lat: 34.025000, Lon: -83.074983
650 Watson Mill Rd, Comer, GA 30629
www.gastateparks.org
See ad page 414 (Welcome Section).

COMMERCE — B3 *Jackson*

↓ GEORGIA RV PARK **Ratings: 5.5/7/7** (Campground) 2015 rates: $25 to $30. (706)335-5535 5473 Mt Olive Rd, Commerce, GA 30529

CORDELE — D2 *Crisp*

↓ CORDELE KOA KAMPGROUND **Ratings: 8.5/9★/8** (Campground) 2015 rates: $36 to $46. (800)562-0275 373 Rockhouse Rd E, Cordele, GA 31015

← **GEORGIA VETERANS**
(State Pk) From Jct of I-75 & US 280 (Exit 101): Go 9-1/4 mi W on US 280 (L). **FAC:** Paved rds. 77 gravel, patios, 38 pull-thrus (40 x 65), back-ins (40 x 65), 77 W, 77 E (30 amps), tent sites, rentals, dump, laundry, fire rings, firewood, restaurant. **REC:** Lake Blackshear: swim, fishing, marina, golf, playground, rec open to public. Pets OK. Partial handicap access. 14 day max stay, 2015 rates: $35 to $65. Disc: military.
(800)864-PARK Lat: 31.968020, Lon: -83.912300
2459 U.s. Hwy 280 W, Cordele, GA 31015
www.gastateparks.org
See ad page 414 (Welcome Section).

Tell them you saw them in this Guide!

CRAWFORDVILLE — B3 *Taliaferro*

↑ **A.H. STEPHENS**
(State Pk) From Jct of I-20 & Hwy 22 (exit 148): Go 2 mi N Hwy 22, then 1 mi E on US 278, then 1/2 mi N on Monument St (Crawfordville), Follow signs (E). Caution: 12' 10" overhead clearance; alternate route available if necessary. Call for directions. Parking fee required. **FAC:** Paved rds. 40 gravel, 10 pull-thrus (22 x 70), back-ins (25 x 45), 22 W, 40 E (30/50 amps), tent sites, rentals, dump, laundry, fire rings, firewood. **REC:** Lake Buncombe: fishing, playground, rec open to public. Pets OK. Partial handicap access. 14 day max stay, 2015 rates: $23 to $28. Disc: military.
(800)864-PARK Lat: 33.563483, Lon: -82.897156
456 Alexander St NW, Crawfordville, GA 30631
www.gastateparks.org
See ad page 414 (Welcome Section).

CUMMING — B2 *Forsyth*

→ BALD RIDGE CREEK (Public Corps) From town, N 2.5 mi on GA-400 to exit 16 (Pilgrim Mill Rd), S 3 mi on Sinclair Shores Rd to Bald Ridge Rd, E follow signs (E). 2015 rates: $20 to $30. Apr 2 to Sep 30. (770)889-1591

← BOLDING MILL CAMPGROUND (Public Corps) From town, SW 5 mi on Hwy 53 to Sardis Rd, N 0.5 mi to Chestatee Rd, follow signs (E). 2015 rates: $12 to $30. Mar 15 to Sep 30. (770)534-6960

↘ SAWNEE (Public Corps) From town, E 4 mi on Buford Dam Rd (L). 2015 rates: $18 to $30. Apr 2 to Sep 30. (770)887-0592

↗ SHADY GROVE (Public) From Jct of GA-400 & CSR-306 (exit 17), N 1 mi on CSR-306 to Hwy 369, E 2 mi to Shady Grove Rd, follow signs (E). 2015 rates: $26 to $28. Mar 30 to Nov 8. (770)205-6849

↓ **TWIN LAKES RV PARK**
Ratings: 5.5/NA/7 (RV Park) From Jct of Hwy 400 (exit 13) & Hwy 141, Go 500 ft W on Hwy 141, then 1 mi SW on Hwy 9, then 1/4 mi W on Lake Rd (E). **FAC:** Paved/gravel rds. (130 spaces). Avail: 45 gravel, 7 pull-thrus (25 x 50), back-ins (25 x 60), 30 full hkups, 15 W, 15 E (30/50 amps), seasonal sites, WiFi, dump, LP gas. **REC:** Twin Lakes: fishing. Pets OK. No tents. Big rig sites, 2015 rates: $30 to $35. No CC.
(770)887-4400 Lat: 34.16316, Lon: -84.19444
3300 Shore Drive, Cumming, GA 30040
www.twinlakes-rvpark.com
See ad page 426.

DARIEN — D5 *McIntosh*

↖ **CATHEAD CREEK RV PARK**
Ratings: 7/8.5★/7 (Campground)
From Jct of I-95 (Exit 49) & SR 251, Go 3 mi NW on SR 251, becomes Cox Rd (R). **FAC:** Gravel rds. 24 grass, 15 pull-thrus (25 x 90), back-ins (30 x 50), 22 full hkups, 2 W, 2 E (30/50 amps), cable, WiFi, tent sites, dump, laundry, fire rings, firewood. **REC:** pond, fishing, rec open to public. Pet restrict(Q). Big rig sites, 2015 rates: $30. Disc: military.
(912)437-2441 Lat: 31.42470, Lon: -81.48864
1288 Cox Road S.w, Townsend, GA 31331
www.catheadcreekrvpark.com
See ad this page.

↖ **INLAND HARBOR RV PARK Ratings: 6.5/8/8.5** (RV Park) From Jct of I-95 (exit 49) & GA 251: Go 1/4 mi E on GA 25 (R). **FAC:** Paved rds. (50 spaces). Avail: 40 paved, 40 pull-thrus (27 x 60), 40 full hkups (30/50 amps), seasonal sites, cable, WiFi, laundry. **REC.** Pet restrict(B/Q). No tents. Big rig sites, 2015 rates: $30. Disc: AAA. No CC.
AAA Approved
(912)437-6172 Lat: 31.39277, Lon: -81.44618
13566 Ga Highway 251, Darien, GA 31305
www.inlandharborrvpark.com

Thank you for using our 2016 Guide. Now you have all the latest information about RV parks, campgrounds and RV resorts across North America!

DAWSONVILLE — A2 *Dawson, Forsyth*

↑ **AMICALOLA FALLS**
(State Pk) From Jct Hwy 53 & Hwy 9: Go 10 mi NE Hwy 9, then 15 mi W on Hwy 52 (R) Half-way between Elijay & Dahlonega. Parking fee required. CAUTION: 25 degree grade to campsites, not recommended for RVs over 30'. Elev 2800 ft. **FAC:** Paved rds. 25 gravel, patios, 1 pull-thrus (40 x 70), back-ins (40 x 70), 25 W, 25 E (30/50 amps), WiFi Hotspot, tent sites, rentals, dump, laundry, fire rings, firewood, restaurant. **REC:** Little Amicalola Creek: fishing, playground, rec open to public. Pets OK $. Partial handicap access. 14 day max stay, 2015 rates: $25 to $28. Disc: military.
(800)864-PARK Lat: 34.562652, Lon: -84.247627
280 Amicalola Falls State Park Rd, Dawsonville, GA 30534
www.gastateparks.org
See ad page 414 (Welcome Section).

→ WARHILL (Public) From Jct of Hwy 53 & Hwy 400, SE 1.8 mi SH-53, E 3.75 mi SH 318. Cash only, self registration. 2015 rates: $16. Mar 20 to Oct 3. (706)344-3646

DILLARD — A3 *Rabun*

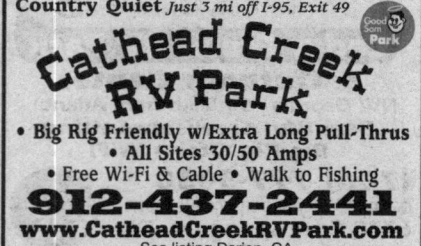

→ **RIVER VISTA MOUNTAIN VILLAGE**
Ratings: 9.5/9★/10 (Condo Pk)
From Jct US 441 & Hwy 246: Go 1 mi E on Hwy 246 (R). **FAC:** Paved rds. (143 spaces). 93 Avail: 7 paved, 86 gravel, 30 pull-thrus (35 x 60), back-ins (35 x 60), 93 full hkups (30/50 amps), seasonal sites, cable, WiFi, rentals, laundry, LP gas. **REC:** heated pool, whirlpool, Mud Creek: fishing, playground. Pets OK. Partial handicap access, no tents. Big rig sites, 2015 rates: $30 to $60. Disc: military.
(888)850-7275 Lat: 34.98759, Lon: -83.36545
960 Hwy 246, Dillard, GA 30537
relax@rivervistarvresort.com
www.rvmountainvillage.com
See ad this page, 416.

DONALSONVILLE — E1 *Seminole*

↓ FINS & FEATHERS CAMPGROUND AT LAKE SEMINOLE **Ratings: 5/8/9** (RV Park) 2015 rates: $30 to $35. (229)861-2279 8065 Hwy 374, Donalsonville, GA 39845

↓ **SEMINOLE**
(State Pk) From Jct of US 84 & SR-39, S 16 mi on SR-39 to SR-253, E 0.3 mi (R). Entrance fee required. **FAC:** Paved rds. 46 gravel, 43 pull-thrus (20 x 50), back-ins (20 x 35), 46 W, 46 E (30 amps), tent sites, rentals, dump, laundry, fire rings, firewood. **REC:** Lake Seminole: swim, fishing, playground, rec open to public. Pet restrict(Q). Partial handicap access. 14 day max stay, 2015 rates: $26 to $30. Disc: military.
(800)864-PARK Lat: 30.805016, Lon: -84.879200
7870 State Park Dr, Donalsonville, GA 39845
www.gastateparks.org
See ad page 414 (Welcome Section).

EATONTON — B3 *Putnam*

→ LAWRENCE SHOALS PARK (GEORGIA POWER) **Ratings: 6.5/8/9** (Campground) 2015 rates: $20. Feb 25 to Oct 4. (706)485-5494 123 Wallace Dam Rd, Eatonton, GA 31024

→ OCONEE SPRINGS PARK (Public) From Jct of US-441 & Hwy 16, E 10 mi on Hwy 16 to Oconee Springs Rd, S 1.5 mi to Rockville Rd, SE 3.5 mi (L). 2015 rates: $22.40. (706)485-8423

ELBERTON — B3 *Elbert*

↘ **BOBBY BROWN**
(State Pk) From town, E 11 mi on SR-72 to Bobby Brown State Park Rd, SE 7 mi (E). Parking fee required. **FAC:** Paved rds. 61 gravel, 4 pull-thrus (25 x 45), back-ins (25 x 35), 61 W, 61 E (30 amps), tent sites, dump, laundry, fire rings. **REC:** Clarks Hill Lake: swim, fishing, playground, rec open to public. Pets OK. Partial handicap access. 14 day max stay, 2015 rates: $25 to $28. Disc: military. Mar 15 to Sep 15.
(800)864-PARK Lat: 33.978500, Lon: -82.588100
2509 Bobby Brown State Park Rd, Elberton, GA 30635
www.gastateparks.org
See ad page 414 (Welcome Section).

↗ **RICHARD B. RUSSELL**
(State Pk) From Jct of SR-77 & SR-17, N 1.2 mi on SR-77 to Ruckersville Rd, E 7.8 mi (R) 35' maximum length RV (parking fee required). **FAC:** Paved rds. 28 gravel, 6 pull-thrus (30 x 60), back-ins (30 x 40), 28 W, 28 E (30 amps), WiFi, tent sites, rentals, dump, laundry, fire rings, firewood, restaurant. **REC:** Russell Lake: swim, fishing, golf, playground, rec open to public. Pets OK. Partial handicap access. 14 day max stay, 2015 rates: $27 to $32. Disc: military.

ELBERTON (CONT)

RICHARD B. RUSSELL (CONT)
(800)864-PARK Lat: 34.179833, Lon: -82.764333
2650 Russell State Park Dr, Elberton, GA 30635
www.gastateparks.org
See ad page 414 (Welcome Section).

ELKO — C3 *Houston*

TWIN OAKS RV PARK
Ratings: 9/9★/8.5 (RV Park) From Jct of I-75 (exit 127) & GA 26: Go 500 ft E on GA 26 (L). **FAC:** Gravel rds. (70 spaces). Avail: 50 gravel, patios, 38 pull-thrus (30 x 90), back-ins (30 x 60), 50 full hkups (30/50 amps), seasonal sites, WiFi, rentals, dump, laundry, LP gas, firewood. **REC:** pool, whirlpool. Pets OK. No tents. Big rig sites, 2015 rates: $40.
(478)987-9361 Lat: 32.33598, Lon: -83.76465
305 Ga Hwy 26 E, Elko, GA 31025
info@twinoaksrvpark.com
www.twinoaksrvpark.com
See ad pages 434, 416.

ELLIJAY — A2 *Gilmer*

DOLL MOUNTAIN CAMPGROUND (Public Corps) From town, S 9 mi on Hwy 411 to GA-136, E 9.1 mi to Harris Branch Rd., W 1.5 mi CAUTION: Steep entrance road. 2015 rates: $22 to $28. Apr 3 to Oct 31. (706)276-4413

PLUM NELLY CAMPGROUND
Ratings: 6/7/5.5 (Campground) From Jct US 76 & Hwy 515: Go 3-1/2 mi S on Hwy 515 (R). **FAC:** Gravel rds. (32 spaces). Avail: 17 gravel, 17 pull-thrus (35 x 60), 17 full hkups (30/50 amps), seasonal sites, WiFi, tent sites, rentals, dump, laundry, fire rings. **REC:** pond, fishing, playground. Pet restrict(B). Partial handicap access. 2015 rates: $25 to $30.
(706)698-7586 Lat: 34.63994, Lon: -84.50109
15828 Highway 515 S, Ellijay, GA 30536
plumnellycampground@yahoo.com
www.plumnellycampground.com
See ad this page.

FARGO — E4 *Charlton*

STEPHEN C. FOSTER
(State Pk) From town, S 1 mi on US 441 to Jct of US 441 & SR-177, NE 18 mi on Georgia Hwy 177 (E). Entrance fee required. **FAC:** Paved rds. 64 grass, 8 pull-thrus (30 x 50), back-ins (30 x 45), 64 W, 64 E (30 amps), tent sites, rentals, dump, laundry, fire rings, firewood, controlled access. **REC:** Okefenokee Swamp: fishing, marina, playground, rec open to public. Pets OK. Partial handicap access. 14 day max stay, 2015 rates: $28 to $35. Disc: military.
(800)864-PARK Lat: 30.8269500, Lon: -82.3621000
17515 Georgia Hwy 177, Fargo, GA 31631
www.gastateparks.org
See ad page 414 (Welcome Section).

FITZGERALD — D3 *Ben Hill*

PAULK PARK RV PARK & CAMPGROUND (Public) From Jct of US Hwy 129/90 & Main St (in town), S 0.6 mi on Main St to W Roanoke Dr, W 0.4 mi to Perry House Rd, S 1.2 mi to Paulk Park Rd, W 0.3 mi (L). 2015 rates: $20. (800)386-4642

FLOVILLA — C2 *Butts*

INDIAN SPRINGS
(State Pk) S-bnd: From Jct of I-75 & SR-16 (Exit 205), E 7.5 mi on SR-16 to Merge with SR 42, continue W on SR 42 6.2 mi (R); or N-bnd: From Jct of I-75 & SR-42 (Exit 188), NE 15 mi on SR-42 (L). Entrance fee required. **FAC:** Paved rds. 60 gravel, patios, 2 pull-thrus (23 x 60), back-ins (25 x 60), 60 W, 60 E (20/30 amps), WiFi Hotspot, tent sites, rentals, dump, laundry, fire rings, firewood, controlled access. **REC:** McIntosh Lake: swim, fishing, playground, rec open to public. Pets OK. Partial handicap access. 14 day max stay, 2015 rates: $27 to $30. Disc: military.
(800)864-PARK Lat: 33.247433, Lon: -83.923450
678 Lake Clark Rd, Flovilla, GA 30216
www.gastateparks.org
See ad page 414 (Welcome Section).

FOLKSTON — E4 *Charlton*

OKEFENOKEE RV PARK **Ratings: 5.5/8★/6** (Campground) 2015 rates: $20. (912)496-2220 252 Bowery Ln, Homeland, GA 31537

TRADERS HILL PARK (Public) From town, S 5 mi on Hwy 121, E 1.5 to stop sign (E). 2015 rates: $20. (912)496-3412

FORSYTH — C2 *Monroe*

FORSYTH KOA Ratings: 8/7.5/7.5 (Campground) From Jct of I-75 (exit 186) & Juliette Rd, E 0.3 mi on Juliette Rd to Frntg Rd, N 0.5 mi (R). **FAC:** Paved/gravel rds. (131 spaces). 61 Avail: 36 paved, 25 gravel, 49 pull-thrus (24 x 62), back-ins (20 x 40), 50 full hkups, 11 W, 11 E (30/50 amps), seasonal sites, cable, WiFi $, tent sites, rentals, dump, laundry, groc, LP gas, firewood. **REC:** pool, pond, KOA Pond: fishing, playground. Pets OK. Partial handicap access. 2015 rates: $31 to $33.
AAA Approved
(478)994-2019 Lat: 33.03771, Lon: -83.92596
414 S Frontage Rd, Forsyth, GA 31029
ke123@msn.com
www.koa.com/where/ga/10101.htm

L & D RV PARK
Ratings: 7.5/9★/8 (RV Park) From Jct of I-75 (Exit 185) & Hwy 18: Go 2-1/2 mi E on Hwy 18 (R). **FAC:** Paved rds. 30 Avail: 21 gravel, 9 grass, 15 pull-thrus (22 x 60), back-ins (22 x 35), 24 full hkups, 6 W, 6 E (30/50 amps), WiFi, tent sites, dump, laundry, firewood. **REC:** pool. Pets OK. 2015 rates: $23 to $28. Disc: military.
(478)994-5401 Lat: 33.02757, Lon: -83.86998
1655 Dames Ferry Rd, Forsyth, GA 31029
ldrv@bellsouth.net
rvparkforsythga.com
See ad this page, 416.

FORT GAINES — D1 *Clay*

COTTON HILL (Public Corps) From town, N 7 mi on SR-39, follow signs (L). 2015 rates: $26 to $52. (229)768-3061

FORT VALLEY — C2 *Houston, Peach*

PERRY PONDEROSA PARK
Ratings: 6.5/9★/7 (Campground) From Jct of I-75 (Exit 142) & GA 96: Go 1/4 mi E on GA 96 (L). **FAC:** Paved/gravel rds. (60 spaces). 35 Avail: 20 grass, 15 dirt, 30 pull-thrus (25 x 55), back-ins (25 x 55), 35 full hkups (30/50 amps), seasonal sites, WiFi, laundry, LP gas. **REC:** shuffleboard, playground. Pets OK. No tents. 2015 rates: $32 to $35. Disc: AAA. No CC.
(478)825-8030 Lat: 32.54694, Lon: -83.73919
13841 Hwy 96 E, Fort Valley, GA 31030
See ad pages 434, 416.

GAINESVILLE — A2 *Hall*

DON CARTER
(State Pk) From Clarks Bridge Rd, go S on N. Browning Bridge Rd. At the "Y" take the left fork and go 1/2 mi to park entrance (L). **FAC:** Paved/gravel rds. 44 gravel, 44 W, 44 E (30/50 amps), tent sites, rentals, dump, laundry, controlled access. **REC:** Lake Lanier: swim, fishing, playground, rec open to public. Pets OK. Partial handicap access. 14 day max stay, 2015 rates: $25 to $29. Disc: military.
(800)864-7275 Lat: 34.38762, Lon: -83.74646
5000 N. Browning Bridge Rd, Gainesville, GA 30506
www.gastateparks.org
See ad page 414 (Welcome Section).

DUCKETT MILL (Public Corps) From town, W 5 mi on Hwy 53 to Duckett Mill Rd, S 2 mi (E). 2015 rates: $20 to $30. Apr 2 to Sep 8. (770)532-9802

OLD FEDERAL (Public Corps) From town, N 7 mi on McEver Rd to Jim Crow Rd, W 3 mi (E). 2015 rates: $12 to $30. Apr 2 to Sep 30. (770)967-6757

RIVER FORKS PARK AND CAMPGROUND (Public) SE of town, Jct I-985 & Hwy 53 (Exit 16) NW 2.6 mi on Hwy 53 to McEver Rd, N 1.8 mi on McEver Rd to SR-369, W 0.5 mi on SR-369 (R). Call park for exact pricing. 2015 rates: $30. Mar 1 to Dec 31. (770)531-3952

Tell them you saw them in this Guide!

GREENSBORO — B3 *Greene, Oconee*

LAKE OCONEE/GREENSBORO KOA **Ratings: 8.5/7.5/8** (Campground) 2015 rates: $35 to $70. (706)453-4505 2541 Carey Station Rd, Greensboro, GA 30642

OLD SALEM PARK (GEORGIA POWER) **Ratings: 6/8.5/8.5** (Campground) 2015 rates: $20. Mar 1 to Sep 30. (706)467-2850 1530 Old Salem Rd, Greensboro, GA 30642

PARK'S FERRY PARK (GEORGIA POWER) **Ratings: 6/8/8.5** (Campground) 2015 rates: $20. Apr 27 to Sep 13. (706)453-4308 1491 Parks Mill Rd, Greensboro, GA 30642

HAHIRA — E3 *Lowndes*

CAIN'S CREEKSIDE RV PARK **Ratings: 5.5/8★/8** (RV Park) 2015 rates: $40. (229)794-9416 6143 US Hwy 41 North, Hahira, GA 31632

HAMILTON — C1 *Harris*

BLANTON CREEK PARK (GEORGIA POWER) **Ratings: 6/8/9** (Campground) 2015 rates: $20. Mar 1 to Sep 2. (706)643-7737 1001 Lick Skillet Rd, Hamilton, GA 31811

HARTWELL — A3 *Hart*

HART STATE OUTDOOR RECREATION AREA
(State Pk) From Jct of I-85 & SR-77 (Exit 177), S 14 mi on SR-77 to US 29N (in town), SE 1 mi to Ridge Rd, E 1 mi to entrance rd (L) Parking fee required. **FAC:** Paved rds. 62 gravel, patios, 17 pull-thrus (20 x 45), back-ins (20 x 45), 5 full hkups, 57 W, 57 E (30/50 amps), WiFi Hotspot, tent sites, dump, laundry, fire rings, firewood. **REC:** Lake Hartwell: swim, fishing, playground, rec open to public. Pets OK. Partial handicap access. 14 day max stay, 2015 rates: $25 to $28. Disc: military. Mar 15 to Sep 15.
(800)864-PARK Lat: 34.37612, Lon: -82.91023
330 Hart Park Rd, Hartwell, GA 30643
www.gastateparks.org
See ad page 414 (Welcome Section).

MILLTOWN (Public Corps) From town, N 4 mi on SR-51 to New Prospect Rd, E 4 mi, follow signs to park (R). 2015 rates: $10. May 1 to Sep 6. (888)893-0678

PAYNE'S CREEK (Public Corps) From town, N 7 mi on Hwy 51 to CR-301, W 5 mi (R). 2015 rates: $24 to $52. May 1 to Sep 7. (888)893-0678

WATSADLER (Public Corps) From town, N 5 mi on US-29, follow signs (L). 2015 rates: $26 to $52. (888)893-0678

HAZLEHURST — D4 *Jeff Davis*

TOWNS BLUFF PARK (Public) S-bnd: From Jct of US 221 & SR 56 (in Uvalda), S 6.1 mi on US 221 to Uvalda Landing Rd, E 0.1 mi to River Rd, E 0.5 mi (R); or N-bnd: From Jct of US 341 & US 221 (in Hazelhurst), N 5.3 mi on US 221 to Uvalda Landing Rd, E 0.1 mi to River Rd, E 0.5 mi (R). 2015 rates: $22. (912)379-9303

HELEN — A2 *Habersham, Lumpkin, White*

HELEN See also Batesville, Blairsville, Cleveland & Hiawassee.

CHEROKEE CAMPGROUND **Ratings: 5/6/7** (Campground) 2015 rates: $25. (888)878-2268 45 Bethel Rd, Sautee Nacoochee, GA 30571

Looking for a new or used RV? Camping World is America's largest retailer of RVs. Click CampingWorld.com or visit SuperCenters nationwide.

GA

HELEN (CONT)

➔ CREEKWOOD RESORT
Ratings: 7.5/8.5★/9.5 (RV Park) From Jct of SR-356 & SR-17/75, NE 5.8 mi on SR-356 (R). **FAC:** Paved rds. 17 paved, back-ins (30 x 60), 17 full hkups (30/50 amps), cable, WiFi, rentals, laundry, fire rings, firewood. **REC:** Creek Walk. Pet restrict(B/Q). Partial handicap access, no tents. Big rig sites, 2015 rates: $34.50 to $50.60.
(706)878-2164 Lat: 34.74948, Lon: -83.66819
5730 Hwy 356, Sautee Nacoochee, GA 30571
creekwoodresort@windstream.net
www.creekwoodresort.com
See ad this page.

ENOTA MOUNTAIN RETREAT
Ratings: 8/9.5★/9.5 (Campground) From Jct Hwy 75/17 & Hwy 356: Go 10 3/4 mi N on Hwy 75/17, then 2 1/2 mi W on Hwy 180 (L). Elev 3200 ft. **FAC:** Gravel rds. 31 paved, patios, 3 pull-thrus (30 x 50), back-ins (30 x 40), 31 full hkups (30/50 amps), WiFi, tent sites, rentals, dump, laundry, groc, fire rings, firewood. **REC:** whirlpool, Soapstone Creek: fishing, playground, rec open to public. Pets OK. Partial handicap access. 2015 rates: $34 to $39.
(706)896-9966 Lat: 34.83783, Lon: -83.77019
1000 Highway 180, Hiawassee, GA 30546
enota@enota.com
www.enota.com
See ad this page.

UNICOI
(State Pk) From Jct of SR-75 & SR-356, E 1.5 mi on SR-356 (L). Parking fee required. **FAC:** Paved rds. 72 gravel, patios, back-ins (14 x 30), 23 full hkups, 49 W, 49 E (30/50 amps), WiFi Hotspot, tent sites, rentals, dump, laundry, fire rings, firewood, restaurant. **REC:** Lake Unicoi: swim, fishing, playground, rec open to public. Pet restrict(Q). Partial handicap access. 14 day max stay, 2015 rates: $38 to $65. Disc: military.
(800)864-PARK Lat: 34.723033, Lon: -83.722300
1788 Hwy 356, Helen, GA 30545
www.gastateparks.org
See ad page 414 (Welcome Section).

HELENA — D3 *Telfair*

LITTLE OCMULGEE
(State Pk) From Jct of US 280 & US 319/441, N 0.5 mi on US 319/441 (L). Parking fee required. **FAC:** Paved rds. 54 gravel, 12 pull-thrus (20 x 50), back-ins (17 x 40), 54 W, 54 E (30/50 amps), cable, WiFi Hotspot, tent sites, rentals, dump, laundry, fire rings, firewood, restaurant. **REC:** pool, Little Ocmulgee Lake: swim, fishing, golf, playground, rec open to public. Pets OK. 14 day max stay, 2015 rates: $35. Disc: military.
(800)864-PARK Lat: 32.095150, Lon: -82.889666
hwy 441, Mc Rae, GA 31055
www.gastateparks.org
See ad page 414 (Welcome Section).

The RVers' Guide to NASCAR helps RV travelers get the most out of North America's most thrilling sporting event. Turn to the front of the Guide and we'll give you the inside track on how to get high-speed thrills at major NASCAR venues.

HIAWASSEE — A2 *Towns*

BALD MOUNTAIN CAMPING RESORT
Ratings: 9/9★/9 (Campground) From E Jct of US 76 & Hwy 288: Go 1/4 mi SW on Hwy 288, the 3-1/2 mi S on Fodder Creek Rd (L). **FAC:** Paved rds. (300 spaces). 180 Avail: 7 paved, 173 gravel, 47 pull-thrus (30 x 100), back-ins (30 x 70), 180 full hkups (30/50 amps), seasonal sites, cable, WiFi, tent sites, rentals, dump, laundry, LP gas, fire rings, firewood. **REC:** pool, Mountain Lake: fishing, shuffleboard, playground. Pet restrict(B). Partial handicap access. Big rig sites, 2015 rates: $39.50 to $44.50. Apr 1 to Oct 31.
(706)896-8896 Lat: 34.89177, Lon: -83.77051
751 Gander Gap Rd, Hiawassee, GA 30546
www.baldmountainpark.com
See ad this page, 416.

GEORGIA MOUNTAIN FAIRGROUNDS (Public) From Jct of US-76 & SR-75 (W side of town), W 1 mi on US-76 (R). 2015 rates: $24 to $35. (706)896-4191

RIVER BEND RV PARK & CAMPGROUND **Ratings: 6/8★/8** (Campground) 2015 rates: $32 to $34. (706)896-1415 2626 Streak Hill Rd, Hiawassee, GA 30546

HINESVILLE — D5 *Liberty*

HAPPY CAMPERS RV PARK
Ratings: 6.5/NA/7.5 (RV Park) From jct I-95 (exit 87) & Hwy 17: Go 12 miles SW on Hwy 17, then 5 miles SW on Hwy 196/Leroy Coffer Hwy, then 9 miles W on Hwy 84/E Oglethorpe Hwy, then W on Kacey Dr, then N on S Main St, then W on Glenn Bryant Rd, then S on Kelly Dr (R). **FAC:** Paved rds. 12 Avail: 6 gravel, 6 grass, back-ins (30 x 70), accepts full hkup units only, 12 full hkups (30/50 amps), WiFi, rentals, laundry, LP bottles. **REC.** Pet restrict(Q). Big rig sites, 2015 rates: $36. Disc: military. AAA Approved
(912)876-6881 Lat: 31.481859, Lon: -81.373130
1125 Kelly Drive, Hinesville, GA 31313
happyacresinfo@gmail.com
www.happycampersga.com
See ad pages 437, 416.

JACKSON — B2 *Butts*

FOREST GLEN MOBILE HOME & RV PARK
Ratings: 7.5/8★/6.5 (RV Park) From Jct of I-75 (exit 205) & Hwy 16: Go 1/4 mi W on Hwy 16, then 500 ft S on Windy Lane Circle, then 1/2 mi E on Forest Glen Rd, then 500 ft S on Entrance Rd (E). **FAC:** Paved rds. (148 spaces). Avail: 44 paved, 42 pull-thrus (22 x 50), back-ins (22 x 50), 44 full hkups (30/50 amps), seasonal sites, WiFi Hotspot, laundry. **REC:** pool. Pet restrict(B). No tents. 2015 rates: $30.
(770)228-3399 Lat: 33.25707, Lon: -84.09341
218 Glade Rd, Jackson, GA 30233
See ad pages 426, 416.

HIGH FALLS
(State Pk) From Jct of I-75 & High Falls Rd (Exit 198), E 1.5 mi on High Falls Rd (L). Entrance fee required. **FAC:** Paved rds. 107 gravel, patios, 20 pull-thrus (30 x 75), back-ins (30 x 50), 107 W, 107 E (30/50 amps), WiFi Hotspot, tent sites, rentals, dump, laundry, fire rings, firewood. **REC:** pool $, High Falls Lake: fishing, playground, rec open to public. Pets OK. Partial handicap access. 14 day max stay, 2015 rates: $27 to $35. Disc: military.
(800)864-PARK Lat: 33.128333, Lon: -84.020533
76 High Falls Park Dr, Jackson, GA 30233
www.gastateparks.org
See ad page 414 (Welcome Section).

JEKYLL ISLAND — E5 *Glynn*

JEKYLL ISLAND CAMPGROUND (Public) From Jct of I-95, US-17/82 & SR-520 (exit 29), NE 5.4 mi on US-17/SR-520 to Jekyll Island Causeway, SE 6.6 mi to Jekyll Island gate, continue 0.5 mi to N Beachview Dr, N 4.5 mi (L). Entrance fee required (Reservations Recommended). 2015 rates: $29 to $38. (866)658-3021

JULIETTE — C2 *Monroe*

DAMES FERRY PARK (GEORGIA POWER) **Ratings: 5/7.5/8.5** (Campground) 2015 rates: $20. Mar 1 to Oct 31. (478)994-7945 9546 Hwy 87, Juliette, GA 31046

KINGSLAND — E5 *Camden*

➔ COUNTRY OAKS CAMPGROUND & RV PARK
Ratings: 8.5/9★/8.5 (RV Park) From Jct of I-95 & St Marys Rd (exit 1): Go 1/4 W mi on St Marys Rd (L). **FAC:** Paved rds. (43 spaces). Avail: 23 gravel, 18 pull-thrus (28 x 60), back-ins (30 x 30), 23 full hkups (30/50 amps), seasonal sites, WiFi, laundry, LP gas, firewood. **REC:** pond, fishing. Pets OK. Partial handicap access, no tents. Big rig sites, 2015 rates: $34.
(912)729-6212 Lat: 30.76032, Lon: -81.65920
6 Carlton Cemetery Rd, Kingsland, GA 31548
www.countryoaksrv.com
See ad pages 361, 416.

JACKSONVILLE N/ST MARY'S KOA **Ratings: 8/8/7** (Campground) 2015 rates: $40 to $45. (800)562-5220 2970 Scrubby Bluff Rd, Kingsland, GA 31548

KIKI RV PARK **Ratings: 6.5/NA/5** (RV Park) 2015 rates: $33. (912)673-7336 1135 E King Ave (SR 40), Kingsland, GA 31548

LAKE PARK — E3 *Lowndes*

EAGLES ROOST RV RESORT
Ratings: 9/9.5★/8 (Campground) From Jct of I-75 (Exit 5) & Hwy 376: Go 200 ft E on Hwy 376, then 1/2 mi S on Mill Store Rd (L). **FAC:** Paved/gravel rds. (111 spaces). 101 Avail: 50 paved, 51 dirt, 101 pull-thrus (26 x 60), 101 full hkups (30/50 amps), seasonal sites, WiFi, tent sites, dump, laundry, LP gas. **REC:** pool, shuffleboard, playground. Pets OK. Partial handicap access. Big rig sites, 2015 rates: $33.45 to $42.95. Disc: AAA, military.
(229)559-5192 Lat: 30.66882, Lon: -83.21207
5465 Mill Store Rd, Lake Park, GA 31636
camp@eaglesroostresort.com
www.eaglesroostresort.com
See ad pages 439, 416.

Travel Services

CAMPING WORLD OF LAKE PARK As the nation's largest retailer of RV supplies, accessories, services and new and used RVs, Camping World is committed to making your total RV experience better. RV Accessories: (855)862-0600. **SERVICES:** RV, restrooms, RV Sales. RV supplies, LP, dump, emergency parking, RV accessible. Hours: 8am to 6pm.
(888)697-3430 Lat: 30.67651, Lon: -83.22102
5244 Jewel Futch Rd, Lake Park, GA 31636
www.campingworld.com

LAKEMONT — A3 *Rabun*

RIVER FALLS AT THE GORGE **Ratings: 7.5/8.5★/7** (Membership Pk) 2015 rates: $29 to $69. (706)754-0292 32 US 441, Lakemont, GA 30552

LAVONIA — A3 *Franklin*

SUNSET CAMPGROUND **Ratings: 4/5.5/5.5** (Campground) 2015 rates: $24 to $28. (706)356-8932 17139 Hwy 17 (Appalachian Foothills Parkway), Martin, GA 30557

TUGALOO
(State Pk) From Jct of I-85 & SR-17 (Exit 173), S 1.2 mi on SR-17 to SR-59, E 1.2 mi to SR-328, N 3.9 mi to park rd, SE 1.6 mi (E). CAUTION: Narrow internal roads, sharp curves, low branches. Parking fee required. **FAC:** Paved rds. 113 gravel, patios, 25 pull-thrus (18 x 60), back-ins (18 x 60), 113 W, 113 E (30 amps), WiFi Hotspot, tent sites, rentals, dump, laundry, fire rings, firewood, controlled access. **REC:** Lake Hartwell: swim, fishing, playground, rec open to public. Pets OK. Partial handicap access. 14 day max stay, 2015 rates: $25 to $35. Disc: military.
(800)864-PARK Lat: 34.499100, Lon: -83.078100
1763 Tugaloo State Park Rd, Lavonia, GA 30553
www.gastateparks.org
See ad page 414 (Welcome Section).

LEAH — B4 *Columbia*

PETERSBURG (Public Corps) From town, NE 8 mi on US-221 to cnty rd, N 1 mi (E). For reservations call 1-877-444-6777. 2015 rates: $18 to $26. Feb 27 to Nov 28. (706)541-9464

RIDGE ROAD CAMPGROUND (Public Corps) From town, S 1 mi on Hwy 47 to Ridge Rd, E 5 mi (E). For reservations call 1-877-444-6777. 2015 rates: $18 to $52. Mar 27 to Sep 26. (706)541-0282

LINCOLNTON — B4 *Lincoln*

CLAY HILL CAMPGROUND (Public Corps) From town, S 8 mi on Hwy 43 to Clay Hill rd, E 2 mi (E). For reservations call 1-877-444-6777. 2015 rates: $18 to $20. Mar 13 to Sep 30. (706)359-7495

ELIJAH CLARK
(State Pk) From Jct of I-20 & Hwy 78 (Exit 172), NW 2 mi on Hwy 78 to Hwy 43, N 19 mi to Lincolnton (US 378), NE 7 mi (L). Parking fee required. **FAC:** Paved rds. 165 gravel, 60 pull-thrus (20 x 80), back-ins (20 x 40), 165 W, 165 E (30 amps), tent sites, rentals, dump, laundry, fire rings, firewood, controlled access. **REC:** Thurmond Lake: swim, fishing, playground, rec open to public. Pets OK. Partial handicap access. 14 day max stay, 2015 rates: $25 to $28. Disc: military.
(800)864-PARK Lat: 33.842983, Lon: -82.397600
2959 Mccormick Hwy, Lincolnton, GA 30817
www.gastateparks.org
See ad page 414 (Welcome Section).

HESTERS FERRY (Public Corps) From town, N 13 mi on Elberton Hwy to Hwy 44, E 4 mi to Cnty Rd, follow signs (L). For reservations call 1-877-44-6777. 2015 rates: $16 to $18. (706)359-2746

MACON — C3 *Bibb*

A SPOTLIGHT Introducing Macon's colorful attractions appearing at the front of this state section.

LAKE TOBESOFKEE RECREATION AREA-ARROWHEAD (Public) From Jct of I-475 & US 80 (Exit 3) W on US 80 4.9 mi to Columbus Rd, NE on Columbus Rd 0.8 mi to Arrowhead Rd, N on Arrowhead Rd 0.7 mi (E). 2015 rates: $22 to $25. (478)474-8770

LAKE TOBESOFKEE RECREATION AREA-CLAYSTONE (Public) From Jct of I-475 & Hwy 74 (Exit 5), W on Hwy 74 0.8 mi to Moseley Dixon Rd, SW on Moseley Dixon Rd 1.8 mi (L). 2015 rates: $22 to $25. (478)474-8770

SAFE HAVEN RV PARK
Ratings: 5.5/8.5★/5.5 (RV Park) From jct I-75 (exit 160 northbound; 160A southbound) & Hwy 247/41: Go 1/4 mi S on Hwy 247/41, then 1/4 mi E on Glendale Ave, then 1/4 mi N on Glendale Circle (E). **FAC:** Paved rds. (15 spaces). Avail: 10 gravel, 10 pull-thrus (30 x 60), 10 full hkups (30/50 amps), seasonal sites, WiFi, rentals, laundry. Pets OK. Big rig sites, 2015 rates: $25.
(478)420-0775 Lat: 32.79277, Lon: -83.66894
1294 Glendale Ave, Macon, GA 31206
admin@safehavenrvpark.com
www.safehavenrvpark.com
See ad this page.

TOBESOFKEE REC AREA (Public) From Jct of Exit 5 (Hwy 74) & I-475, W .8 mi on Hwy 74 to Mosley Dixon Rd, W 2 mi (L). 2015 rates: $22 to $25. (478)474-8770

MADISON — B3 *Morgan*

COUNTRY BOY'S RV PARK **Ratings: 5.5/8.5★/5.5** (Campground) 2015 rates: $35. (706)342-1799 2750 Eatonton Rd (Hwy 441), Madison, GA 30650

MARIETTA — B2 *Cobb*

ATLANTA-MARIETTA RV RESORT
Ratings: 7.5/8/7 (RV Park) From Jct I-75 (Exit 261) & Hwy 280 (Delk Rd): Go 1 mi SW on Hwy 280, then 1/4 mi N on Hwy 41, then 500 ft E on Wylie Rd (R). **FAC:** Paved rds. (62 spaces). 27 Avail: 22 paved, 5 gravel, patios, back-ins (26 x 40), 27 full hkups (30/50 amps), seasonal sites, cable, WiFi, dump, laundry, LP gas. **REC:** pool. Pet restrict(B). Partial handicap access, no tents. 2015 rates: $54. Disc: AAA, military.
(770)427-6853 Lat: 33.92823, Lon: -84.50684
1031 Wylie Rd SE, Marietta, GA 30067
information@amrvresort.com
amrvresort.com
See ad page 426.

MCDONOUGH — B2 *Henry*

ATLANTA SOUTH RV PARK
Ratings: 8.5/8.5★/6.5 (RV Park) From Jct of I-75 & Jodeco Rd (exit 222-Flippen): Go 1/4 mi W on Jodeco Rd, then 1 block S on Feucht Dr, then 1/2 mi E on Mt Olive Rd (E).

ONE OF THE SOUTH'S FINEST PARKS!
Easy On/Off from I-75 (exit 222). Just 30 minutes from Downtown Atlanta & near many of Georgia's most popular attractions. After sightseeing, relax by the pool and enjoy our amenities. A Fun & Friendly place to stay.

FAC: Paved/gravel rds. (140 spaces). Avail: 80 gravel, 80 pull-thrus (20 x 50), 80 full hkups (30/50 amps), seasonal sites, WiFi, tent sites, rentals, dump, laundry, LP gas, fire rings, firewood. **REC:** pool, playground. Pet restrict(B). Partial handicap access. 2015 rates: $36 to $49. Disc: AAA, military.
(770)957-2610 Lat: 33.48016, Lon: -84.22193
281 Mt Olive Rd, Mcdonough, GA 30253
atlrvresort@gmail.com
www.atlantasouthrvresort.com
See ad pages 424, 416.

METTER — C4 *Candler*

BEAVER RUN RV PARK
Ratings: 8.5/9.5★/8.5 (Campground) From Jct of I-16 (Exit 111) & Excelsior Church Rd, Go 1/4 mi S on Excelsior Church Rd (R). **FAC:** Gravel rds. (62 spaces). Avail: 40 gravel, 40 pull-thrus (31 x 100), 40 full hkups (30/50 amps), seasonal sites, WiFi, tent sites, rentals, dump, laundry, LP gas, fire rings, firewood. **REC:** Mirror Lake: swim, fishing, playground. Pet restrict(B). Partial handicap access. Big rig sites, eco-friendly, 2015 rates: $32 to $35.
(912)685-2594 Lat: 32.33401, Lon: -81.95462
22321 Excelsior Church Rd, Metter, GA 30439
camp@beaverrunrvpark.com
www.beaverrunrvpark.com
See ad page 437.

MILLEDGEVILLE — C3 *Baldwin*

SCENIC MOUNTAIN RV PARK & CAMPGROUND
Ratings: 8/8.5★/8 (RV Park) From Jct GA 22 & GA 441 By-Pass (GA 29): Go 7 mi S on 441 By-Pass, then 1/4 mi N on Bus 441 (GA 243) (R).

HISTORIC HEARTLAND'S HIDDEN GEM
Pet friendly campground. Large sites to accommodate big rigs, 5 fishing ponds, 112 wooded acres, swimming pool and hiking trails. Open year round. Just S of Historic Milledgeville, 12 mi from Lake Sinclair, 30 mi from Macon.

FAC: Paved rds. (59 spaces). Avail: 39 gravel, 6 pull-thrus (30 x 90), back-ins (45 x 45), 39 full hkups (30/50 amps), seasonal sites, cable, WiFi, tent sites, rentals, laundry, LP gas, firewood. **REC:** pool, whirlpool, pond, fishing. Pets OK. Big rig sites, 2015 rates: $20 to $44. Disc: military.
AAA Approved
(478)454-1013 Lat: 33.02898, Lon: -83.23576
2686 Irwinton Road, Milledgeville, GA 31061
Info@Scenicmountainrv.com
www.scenicmountainrv.com
See ad pages 421 (Spotlight Macon), 416.

MILLEN — C4 *Jenkins*

MAGNOLIA SPRINGS
(State Pk) From Jct of US 25 & Hwy 23 (in town), N 5 mi on US 25 (R). Parking fee required. **FAC:** Paved rds. 26 gravel, 6 pull-thrus (40 x 60), back-ins (25 x 50), 26 W, 26 E (30/50 amps), tent sites, rentals, dump, laundry, fire rings, firewood, controlled access. **REC:** pool $, Magnolia Springs Lake: fishing, playground, rec open to public. Pets OK. Partial handicap access. 14 day max stay, 2015 rates: $26 to $30. Disc: military.
(800)864-PARK Lat: 32.873333, Lon: -81.96133
1053 Magnolia Springs Dr, Millen, GA 30442
www.gastateparks.org
See ad page 414 (Welcome Section).

We rate what RVers consider important.

MITCHELL — C4 *Glascock*

HAMBURG
(State Pk) From town, S 2 mi on Hwy 102 to Hamburg/Agricola Rd, NW 4 mi (L) Parking fee required. **FAC:** Paved rds. 30 gravel, 7 pull-thrus (20 x 80), back-ins (20 x 40), 30 W, 30 E (30/50 amps), tent sites, dump, laundry, fire rings, firewood. **REC:** Lake Hamburg: fishing, playground, rec open to public. Pets OK. Partial handicap access. 14 day max stay, 2015 rates: $25 to $28. Disc: military. Mar 15 to Nov 30.
(800)864-PARK Lat: 33.206966, Lon: -82.778400
6071 Hamburg State Park Rd, Mitchell, GA 30820
www.gastateparks.org
See ad page 414 (Welcome Section).

MORGANTON — A2 *Fannin*

WHISPERING PINES CAMPGROUND & RV PARK **Ratings: 5.5/7/5** (RV Park) 2015 rates: $24 to $39. (706)374-6494 290 Whispering Pines Rd, Morganton, GA 30560

MOUNTAIN CITY — A3 *Rabun*

BLACK ROCK MOUNTAIN
(State Pk) From Jct of SR-441 & SR-76, N 2.9 mi on SR-441 to Black Rock Mtn Rd, W 3 mi (E). Caution: Last 3 mi are steep and winding, interior roads also winding with sharp curves (max RV length 25'). Parking fee required. Elev 3640 ft. **FAC:** Paved rds. 44 gravel, 1 pull-thrus (25 x 60), back-ins (18 x 40), 44 W, 44 E (30 amps), tent sites, rentals, dump, laundry, fire rings, firewood. **REC:** Black Rock Lake: fishing, playground, rec open to public. Pets OK. Partial handicap access. 14 day max stay, 2015 rates: $27 to $30. Disc: military. Mar 16 to Nov 30.
(800)864-PARK Lat: 34.917240, Lon: -83.403730
3085 Black Rock Mountain Pkwy, Mountain City, GA 30562
GeorgiaStateParks.org/BlackRockMountain
See ad page 414 (Welcome Section).

GA

NEWNAN — B1 *Coweta*

CHATTAHOOCHEE BEND
(State Pk) From Newman, Hwy 34-W to Thomas Powers Rd (R). Go 5.5 mi to Flatrock Rd (R), 1 mi to park entrance. **FAC:** Paved rds. 35 paved, 9 pull-thrus (30 x 55), back-ins (30 x 45), 35 W, 35 E (30/50 amps), tent sites, dump, laundry, fire rings, firewood. **REC:** Chattahoochee River: fishing, playground, rec open to public. Pets OK. Partial handicap access. 14 day max stay, 2015 rates: $25 to $28. Disc: military.
(800)864-7275 Lat: 33.429722, Lon: -84.989548
425 Bobwhite Way, Newnan, GA 30263
www.gastateparks.org
See ad page 414 (Welcome Section).

NICHOLLS — D4 *Coffee*

GENERAL COFFEE
(State Pk) From Jct of US 441 & SR-32 (in town), E 6 mi on SR-32 (L). Parking fee required. **FAC:** Paved/gravel rds. 40 gravel, 40 pull-thrus (20 x 60), 40 W, 40 E (30/50 amps), WiFi Hotspot, tent sites, rentals, dump, laundry, fire rings, firewood. **REC:** wading pool, 17 Mile River: fishing, playground, rec open to public. Pets OK. Partial handicap access. 14 day max stay, 2015 rates: $24 to $26. Disc: military.
(800)864-7275 Lat: 31.509300, Lon: -82.755116
46 John Coffee Rd, Nicholls, GA 31554
www.gastateparks.org
See ad page 414 (Welcome Section).

Check out a campground's ad. In it you might find a locator map, photos, and a lot more information about the park to help you find just the right place to stay.

OAKWOOD — B2 *Hall*

Travel Services

CAMPING WORLD OF OAKWOOD/ATLANTA
As the nation's largest retailer of RV supplies, accessories, services and new and used RVs, Camping World is committed to making your total RV experience better. RV Accessories: (888)396-0334. **SERVICES:** RV, RV appliance, engine/chassis repair, staffed RV wash, restrooms, RV Sales. RV supplies, LP, emergency parking, RV accessible. Hours: 8 am to 6 pm.
(888)798-5989 Lat: 34.222776, Lon: -83.87131
4696 Smithson Blvd, Oakwood, GA 30566
www.campingworld.com

OCHLOCKNEE — E2 *Thomas*

SUGAR MILL RV PARK **Ratings: 6.5/7/6.5** (RV Park) 2015 rates: $28.20. (229)227-1451 4857 Mcmillan Rd, Ochlocknee, GA 31773

OGLETHORPE — D2 *Macon*

WHITEWATER CREEK PARK (MACON COUNTY PARK) (Public) From jct Hwy 26 & Hwy 49/128: Go 6-1/4 mi N on Hwy 128 or Hwy 128 Bypass. 2015 rates: $17. (478)472-8171

OMAHA — D1 *Stewart*

FLORENCE MARINA
(State Pk) From Jct of Hwy 27 & Rt 1 (in Lumpkin): Go 1/4 mi N on Rt 1, then 15 mi W on Hwy 39C (E). Entrance fee required. **FAC:** Paved rds. 43 Avail: 9 paved, 34 gravel, 20 pull-thrus (22 x 50), back-ins (16 x 45), 43 full hkups (30/50 amps), tent sites, rentals, laundry, fire rings, firewood. **REC:** pool, Lake Walter F George: fishing, marina, playground, rec open to public. Pets OK. Partial handicap access. 14 day max stay, 2015 rates: $32. Disc: military.
(800)864-7275 Lat: 32.089666, Lon: -85.043266
218 Florence Rd, Omaha, GA 31821
www.gastateparks.org
See ad page 414 (Welcome Section).

PALMETTO — B2 *Coweta*

SOUTH OAKS MOBILE HOME & RV COMMUNITY
Ratings: 4.5/NA/4.5 (RV Area in MHP) From Jct of I-85 (exit 56) & Collinsworth Road: Go 200 ft N on Collinsworth Rd, then 1/4 mi E on Tingle Lane (L). **FAC:** Paved rds. (310 spaces). 140 Avail: 135 paved, 5 grass, 4 pull-thrus (18 x 60), back-ins (35 x 60), some side by side hkups, 140 full hkups (30/50 amps), seasonal sites, dump. **REC:** Justa Stream: playground. Pet restrict(B). No tents. Big rig sites, 2015 rates: $35. No CC.
(770)463-3070 Lat: 33.50457, Lon: -84.63689
240 Tingle Lane, Palmetto, GA 30268
See ad page 426.

PERRY — C2 *Houston, Peach*

PERRY See also Elko, Fort Valley, Macon & Unadilla.

RV Park ratings you can rely on!

BOLAND'S PERRY OVERNIGHT PARK **Ratings: 4/4.5/4** (RV Park) 2015 rates: $22 to $25. (478)987-3371 800 Perimeter Rd, Perry, GA 31069

CROSSROADS TRAVEL PARK
Ratings: 8/8.5/8 (RV Park) From Jct of I-75 & US-341 (exit 136), W 0.2 mi on US-341/Sam Nunn Blvd (L). **FAC:** Paved rds. (72 spaces). Avail: 49 paved, 33 pull-thrus (26 x 50), back-ins (30 x 40), 49 full hkups (30/50 amps), seasonal sites, cable, WiFi, tent sites, dump, laundry, LP gas. **REC:** pool, playground. Pets OK. Partial handicap access. Big rig sites, 2015 rates: $37. Disc: military.
AAA Approved
(478)987-3141 Lat: 32.47372, Lon: -83.74663
1513 Sam Nunn Blvd, Perry, GA 31069
crossroadstravelpark@gmail.com
www.crossroadstravelpark.com
See ad this page, 416.

FAIR HARBOR RV PARK
Ratings: 8.5/10★/8.5 (RV Park) From Jct of I-75 (exit 135) & GA 127: Go 1/4 mi W on GA 127 (R). **FAC:** Paved rds. (170 spaces). Avail: 70 gravel, 60 pull-thrus (28 x 60), back-ins (28 x 60), 70 full hkups (30/50 amps), seasonal sites, cable, WiFi, tent sites, rentals, dump, laundry, LP gas, firewood. **REC:** pond, fishing, playground. Pets OK. Partial handicap access. Big rig sites, 2015 rates: $39 to $49. Disc: AAA, military.
(478)988-8844 Lat: 32.44752, Lon: -83.75840
515 Marshallville Rd, Perry, GA 31069
info@GaCampground.com
www.GaCampground.com
See ad this page, 416.

PINE MOUNTAIN — C1 *Harris, Meriwether, Troup*

FD ROOSEVELT
(State Pk) From Jct of US 27 & SR-190, E 3 mi on SR-190 (R). Entrance fee required. **FAC:** Paved/gravel rds. 109 gravel, 24 pull-thrus (20 x 40), back-ins (16 x 30), 109 W, 109 E (30/50 amps), tent sites, rentals, dump, laundry, fire rings, firewood, controlled access. **REC:** pool $, Lake Delano: fishing, playground, rec open to public. Pets OK. Partial handicap access. 14 day max stay, 2015 rates: $25 to $28. Disc: military.
(800)864-PARK Lat: 32.837533, Lon: -84.81516
2970 Hwy 190E, Pine Mountain, GA 31822
www.gastateparks.org
See ad page 414 (Welcome Section).

PINE MOUNTAIN AN RVC OUTDOOR DESTINATION
Ratings: 8.5/9★/8.5 (RV Park) From Jct I-85 S (exit 21) & I-185: Go S on I-185 (exit 42), then 8 mi S on US 27 (R).

Right outside Callaway Gardens, take your ideal natural environment and mix it with your favorite hotel experience, and you have Pine Mountain RV Resort, an RVC Outdoor Destination.

FAC: Paved/gravel rds. (202 spaces). 172 Avail: 87 paved, 85 gravel, 156 pull-thrus (30 x 70), back-ins (30 x 60), 159 full hkups, 13 W, 13 E (30/50 amps), seasonal sites, cable, WiFi, tent sites, rentals, dump, laundry, LP gas, fire rings, firewood. **REC:** pool, whirlpool, pond, playground. Pets OK. Partial handicap access. Big rig sites, eco-friendly, 2015 rates: $39.99 to $49.99.
(706)663-4329 Lat: 32.87412, Lon: -84.87070
8804 Hamilton Rd/Hwy 27, Pine Mountain, GA 31822
pinemountain@rvcoutdoors.com
http://www.rvcoutdoors.com/pine-mountain/
See ad this page, 416.

POOLER — D5 *Chatham*

Travel Services

CAMPING WORLD OF POOLER/SAVANNAH
As the nation's largest retailer of RV supplies, RV accessories, services and new and used RVs, Camping World is committed to making your total RV experience better. RV Accessories: (866)793-8880. **SERVICES:** RV, tire, RV appliance, MH mechanical, staffed RV wash, restrooms, RV Sales. RV supplies, LP, dump, emergency parking, RV accessible. waiting room. Hours: 8am to 6pm.
(888)552-1394 Lat: 32.109525, Lon: -81.235305
129 Continental Blvd., Pooler, GA 31322
cfuller@cwrvs.com
www.campingworld.com

REIDSVILLE — D4 *Tattnall*

GORDONIA - ALATAMAHA
(State Pk) From Jct of SR-57 & US 280 (in town), W 0.4 mi on US 280 (R). Parking fee required. **FAC:** Paved/gravel rds. 29 gravel, 3 pull-thrus (30 x 60), back-ins (30 x 50), 5 full hkups, 24 W, 24 E (30/50 amps), WiFi Hotspot, tent sites, rentals, dump, fire rings, firewood. **REC:** Gordonia Lake: fishing, golf, playground, rec open to public. Pets OK. Partial handicap access. 14 day max stay, 2015 rates: $19 to $30. Disc: military.
(800)864-PARK Lat: 32.082340, Lon: -82.122740
322 Park Lane, Hwy 280 W, Reidsville, GA 30453
www.gastateparks.org
See ad page 414 (Welcome Section).

RICHMOND HILL — D5 *Bryan*

FORT MCALLISTER
(State Pk) From Jct I-95 & Hwy 144 (Exit 90): Go 6-1/2 mi SE on Hwy 144, then 4 mi E on Spur Rte 144, follow signs (E) Entrance fee required. **FAC:** Paved rds. 65 dirt, 49 pull-thrus (30 x 80), back-ins (30 x 60), 65 W, 65 E (20/30 amps), tent sites, rentals, dump, laundry, fire rings, firewood, controlled access. **REC:** Ogeechee River: swim, fishing, playground, rec open to public. Pets OK. Partial handicap access. 14 day max stay, 2015 rates: $32. Disc: military. No CC.
(800)864-PARK Lat: 31.888583, Lon: -81.200883
3894 Fort Mcallister Rd, Richmond Hill, GA 31324
www.gastateparks.org
See ad page 414 (Welcome Section).

KOA SAVANNAH SOUTH **Ratings: 8.5/8.5/8** (Campground) 2015 rates: $43.50. (912)756-3396 4915 Hwy 17 S, Richmond Hill, GA 31324

We shine "Spotlights" on interesting cities and areas.

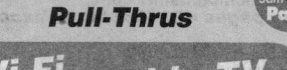

RINGGOLD — A1 *Catoosa*

BATTLEFIELD CAMPGROUND & RV PARK
Ratings: 8/9.5★/7.5 (Campground) From Jct of I-75 (exit 350) & Hwy 2: Go 1/4 mi W on Hwy 2/Battlefield Pkwy, then 500 ft N on Koa Blvd (E).

CHATTANOOGA'S NEWEST RV PARK
/4 mi off I-75 (exit 350). An easy on/off and minutes o Chattanooga. Sparkling new secure facilities. The est place to stay when you visit the area. 50 AMP full ook-ups that are Long & Spacious.

FAC: Paved/gravel rds. (109 spaces). Avail: 79 gravel, 50 pull-thrus (25 x 60), back-ins (24 x 45), 39 full kups, 40 W, 40 E (30/50 amps), seasonal sites, able, WiFi, tent sites, rentals, dump, laundry, LP gas, fire rings, firewood. **REC:** playground. Pet restrict(B). Partial handicap access. Big rig sites, 2015 ates: $39 to $43. Disc: AAA, military.
706)937-4166 Lat: 34.92928, Lon: -85.15740
99 Koa Blvd, Ringgold, GA 30736
nfo@battlefieldrvpark.com
www.battlefieldrvpark.com
See ad pages 1080, 416.

RISING FAWN — A1 *Dade*

CLOUDLAND CANYON
(State Pk) From Jct I-59 & SR-136 (exit 11), SE 5.9 mi on SR-136 (L) Note: Parking fee required. **FAC:** Paved rds. 72 gravel, patios, 5 pull-thrus (30 x 50), back-ins (30 x 35), 72 W, 72 E 20/30 amps), tent sites, rentals, dump, laundry, fire ings, firewood. **REC:** Daniel's Creek: fishing, golf, playground, rec open to public. Pets OK. Partial handicap access. 14 day max stay, 2015 rates: $25 o $30. Disc: military.
800)864-PARK Lat: 34.817676, Lon: -85.488366
22 Cloudland Canyon Park Rd, Rising Fawn, GA 30738
www.gastateparks.org
See ad page 414 (Welcome Section).

ROME — A1 *Floyd*

COOSA RIVER CAMPGROUND AT LOCK & DAM PARK (Public) From Jct of US-411 & US-27S, S 3.4 mi on US-27S to Walker Mtn Rd, changes to Blacks Bluff Rd, W 3.2 mi to Lock & Dam Rd, N 0.2 mi (E). 2015 rates: $22 to $24. (706)234-5001

ROYSTON — A3 *Hart, Franklin*

VICTORIA BRYANT
(State Pk) From Jct of I-85 & SR-51 (Exit 160), S 10 mi on SR-51 to SR-145, S 1.2 mi to US 29, E 1 blk to SR-327, N 1 mi (L). Parking fee required. **FAC:** Paved rds. 27 paved, patios, 8 pull-thrus (30 x 80), back-ins (30 x 50), 27 W, 27 E (30 amps), tent sites, dump, laundry, fire rings, firewood, controlled access. **REC:** pool $, wading pool, pond, swim, fishing, golf, playground, rec open to public. Pets OK. Partial handicap access. 14 day max stay, 2015 rates: $26 to $40. Disc: military.
(800)864-PARK Lat: 34.296750, Lon: -83.160716
1105 Bryant Park Rd, Royston, GA 30662
www.gastateparks.org
See ad page 414 (Welcome Section).

RUTLEDGE — B3 *Morgan*

HARD LABOR CREEK
(State Pk) From Jct of I-20 & Exit 105, N 4.9 mi thru Rutledge (E) Parking fee required. **FAC:** Paved rds. 46 gravel, patios, 6 pull-thrus (40 x 80), back-ins (40 x 60), 46 W, 46 E (30/50 amps), tent sites, rentals, dump, laundry, fire rings, firewood. **REC:** Lake Brantley: swim, fishing, golf, playground, rec open to public. Pets OK. Partial handicap access. 14 day max stay, 2015 rates: $26 to $32. Disc: military.
(800)864-PARK Lat: 33.664333, Lon: -83.606500
5 Hard Labor Creek Rd, Rutledge, GA 30663
www.gastateparks.org
See ad page 414 (Welcome Section).

SAVANNAH — D5 *Chatham*

A SPOTLIGHT Introducing Savannah's colorful attractions appearing at the front of this state section.

SAVANNAH See also Richmond Hill, Rincon & Tybee Island; Hardeeville, SC, Hilton Head Island, SC.

Pamper Your Pet on the Road - turn to our Pampered Pet Parks feature at the front of the Guide for great tips and advice when traveling with pets.

GA

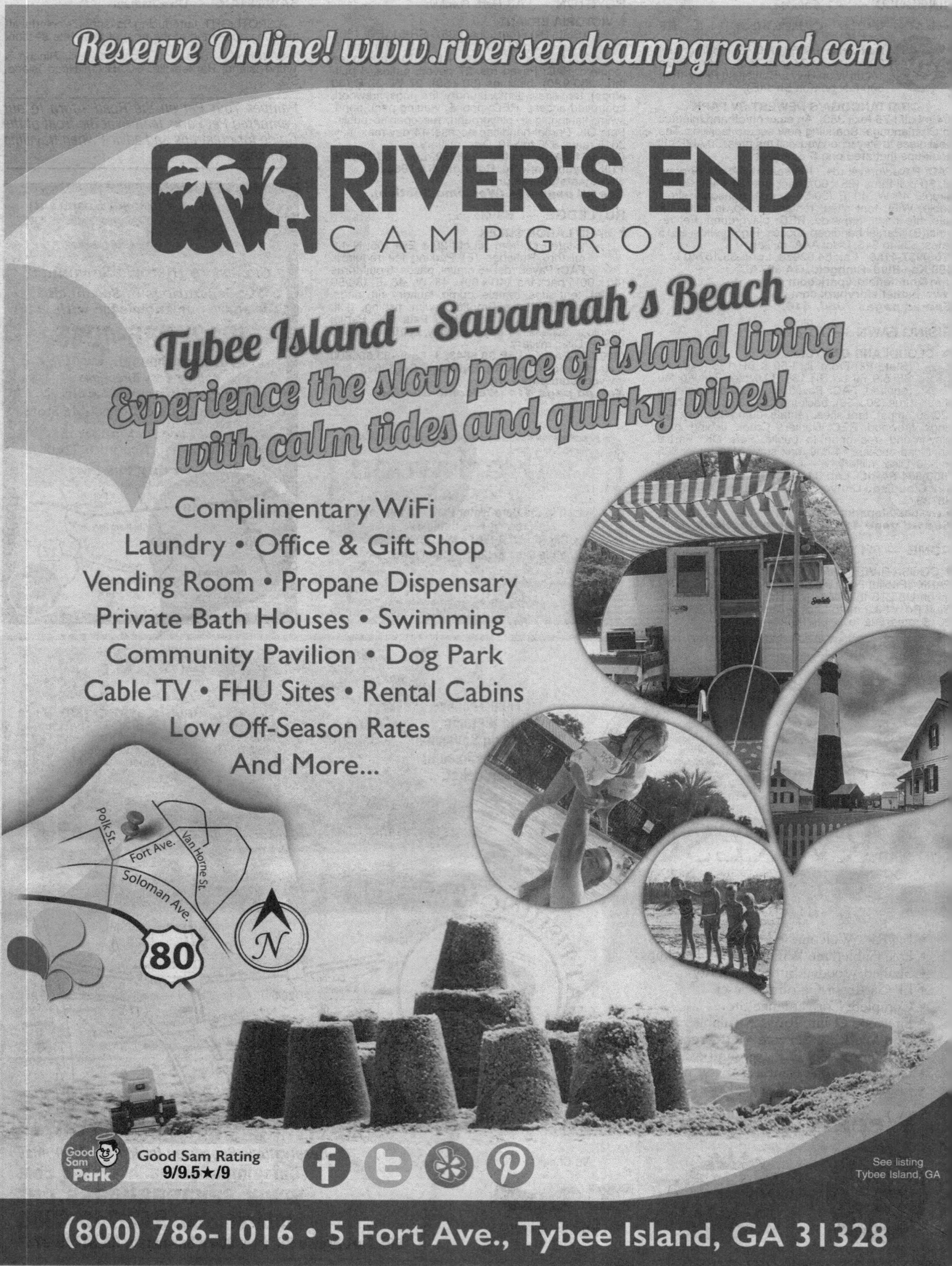
Reserve Online! www.riversendcampground.com
RIVER'S END
CAMPGROUND
Tybee Island - Savannah's Beach
Experience the slow pace of island living
with calm tides and quirky vibes!
Complimentary WiFi
Laundry • Office & Gift Shop
Vending Room • Propane Dispensary
Private Bath Houses • Swimming
Community Pavilion • Dog Park
Cable TV • FHU Sites • Rental Cabins
Low Off-Season Rates
And More...
Polk St.
Fort Ave.
Van Horne St.
Soloman Ave.
80
N
Good Sam Park
Good Sam Rating
9/9.5★/9
See listing
Tybee Island, GA
(800) 786-1016 • 5 Fort Ave., Tybee Island, GA 31328

SAVANNAH (CONT)

BILTMORE RV PARK
Ratings: 5.5/NA/8 (RV Park) From Jct I-95 & I-16: Go 5 mi E on I-16 (exit 162), then 1-1/2 mi S on Chatham Pkwy, then 1/2 mi SW on US 17 (Ogeechee Rd) (L) Closed Sunday. **FAC:** Paved rds. (38 spaces). 33 Avail: 25 gravel, 8 grass, 5 pull-thrus (25 x 60), back-ins (25 x 60), accepts full hkup units only, 33 full hkups (30/50 amps), seasonal sites, WiFi Hotspot, firewood. **REC:** rec open to public. Pet restrict(Q). No tents. Big rig sites, 2015 rates: $38 to $40.
(912)236-4065 Lat: 32.04469, Lon: -81.17985
4707 Ogeechee Rd, Savannah, GA 31405
Info@biltmorerv.com
www.biltmorerv.com
See ad pages 435, 416.

RED GATE CAMPGROUND & RV PARK
Ratings: 8/8.5★/7.5 (RV Park) From Jct of I-95 & I-16: Go 5 mi E on I-16 (Exit 162), then 2-1/4 mi S on Chatham Pkwy, then 500 ft W on Red Gate Farms Trail (R). **FAC:** Paved/gravel rds. 30 gravel, 10 pull-thrus (30 x 60), back-ins (30 x 60), some side by side hkups, 24 full hkups, 6 W, 6 E (30/50 amps), WiFi, dump, laundry, firewood. **REC:** pool, pond, fishing, playground. Pets OK. No tents. Big rig sites, 2015 rates: $40 to $55. Disc: military.
(912)272-8028 Lat: 32.04152, Lon: -81.16544
136 Red Gate Farm Trail, Savannah, GA 31405
theredgaterv@gmail.com
www.redgatecampground.com
See ad pages 423 (Spotlight Savannah), 416.

SAVANNAH OAKS RV RESORT
Ratings: 7.5/8.5★/7.5 (Campground) From Jct of I-95 (exit 94) & SR 204: Go 2-1/2 mi W on SR 204 (L). **FAC:** Paved/gravel rds. (139 spaces). 99 Avail: 21 paved, 78 gravel, 76 pull-thrus (24 x 60), back-ins (24 x 60), 86 full hkups, 13 W, 13 E (30/50 amps), seasonal sites, cable, WiFi, rentals, dump, laundry, groc, LP gas, controlled access. **REC:** pool, Ogeechee River: fishing, playground. Pets OK. Partial handicap access, no tents. Big rig sites, 2015 rates: $44 to $49. Disc: AAA.
(800)851-0717 Lat: 32.025745, Lon: -81.31976
805 Fort Argyle Rd Hwy 204, Savannah, GA 31419
campinginsavannah@yahoo.com
www.savannahoaks.net
See ad pages 435, 416 & RV Trips of a Lifetime in Magazine Section.

SKIDAWAY ISLAND
(State Pk) From Jct of I-95 & SR-204 (Exit 94), E 10.6 mi on SR-204 to Spur 204, SE 6.8 mi on Spur 204 to park gate (L). Parking fee required. **FAC:** Paved rds. 87 gravel, 87 pull-thrus (40 x 110), 17 full hkups, 70 W, 70 E (30/50 amps), WiFi Hotspot, tent sites, rentals, dump, laundry, fire rings, firewood. **REC:** playground, rec open to public. Pets OK. Partial handicap access. 14 day max stay, 2015 rates: $26 to $45. Disc: military.
(800)864-7275 Lat: 31.942400, Lon: -81.052333
52 Diamond Causeway, Savannah, GA 31411
www.gastateparks.org
See ad page 414 (Welcome Section).

ST MARYS — E5 *Camden*

CROOKED RIVER
(State Pk) N-bnd: From Jct of I-95 & St Marys Rd (Exit 1), E 5.1 mi on St Marys Rd to Charlie Smith Sr Hwy, N 4 mi (R). Entrance fee required. **FAC:** Paved rds. 62 gravel, 21 pull-thrus (35 x 60), back-ins (35 x 50), 62 W, 62 E (30 amps), tent sites, rentals, dump, laundry, fire rings, firewood, controlled access. **REC:** Crooked River: fishing, playground, rec open to public. Pets OK. Partial handicap access. 14 day max stay, 2015 rates: $25 to $28. Disc: military.
(800)864-PARK Lat: 30.840650, Lon: -81.560867
6222 Charlie Smith, Sr. Hwy, Saint Marys, GA 31558
www.gastateparks.org
See ad page 414 (Welcome Section).

STATESBORO — C4 *Bulloch*

PARKWOOD RV PARK & COTTAGES
Ratings: 9/9★/8.5 (RV Park) From Jct of I-16 & US-301(Exit 116): Go 8 3/4 mi N on US 301 (R). From Jct of US 301 & US 301 Bypass: Go 6 mi SW On US 301 Bypass, then 1/4 mi S on US 301 (L). **FAC:** Paved rds. (48 spaces). Avail: 28 grass, 28 pull-thrus (30 x 80), 28 full hkups (30/50 amps), seasonal sites, cable, WiFi, tent sites, rentals, laundry, LP gas. **REC:** pool. Pet restrict(B). Big rig sites, 2015 rates: $35 to $40.
(912)681-3105 Lat: 32.41204, Lon: -81.80400
12188 US Hwy 301 S, Statesboro, GA 30458
parkwood@parkwoodrv.com
www.parkwoodrv.com
See ad pages 435, 416.

STONE MOUNTAIN — B2 *DeKalb, Gwinett*

STONE MOUNTAIN PARK CAMPGROUND
Ratings: 8.5/8/8.5 (Campground) From Jct of I-285 & Hwy 78 (Stone Mtn Fwy, Exit 39B): Go 7-1/2 mi E on Hwy 78, then follow signs to Exit #8 (E).

FAMILY FUN IN THE GREAT OUTDOORS
Georgia's most popular attraction features a wide variety of activities for the whole family. Located on 3,200 acres of natural beauty, you'll discover interactive family adventure, historical sites, and fun annual events.

FAC: Paved rds. (385 spaces). Avail: 335 gravel, 20 pull-thrus (25 x 50), back-ins (40 x 55), 206 full hkups, 129 W, 129 E (30/50 amps), seasonal sites, cable, WiFi, tent sites, rentals, dump, laundry, groc, LP gas, fire rings, firewood, restaurant, controlled access. **REC:** pool, Stone Mountain Lake: fishing, golf, playground, rec open to public. Pets OK. Partial handicap access. Big rig sites, 2015 rates: $33 to $69.50.
(770)498-5710 Lat: 33.81969, Lon: -84.113329
4003 Stonewall Jackson Dr., Stone Mountain, GA 30083
campground@stonemountainpark.com
www.stonemountainpark.com
See ad pages 418 (Spotlight Atlanta), 416.

Things to See and Do

STONE MOUNTAIN PARK Outdoor entertainment & recreation on 3300 acres of family fun including a riverboat, railroad, summit skyride, crossroads, an 1870 town, treehouse challenge, ride the Duck & see the world's largest laser show spectacular. RV accessible. Restrooms, food. Hours: 8am to 8pm. Adult fee: $29.95. ATM.
(800)317-2006 Lat: 33.81969, Lon: -84.13329
generalinfo@stonemountainpark.com
www.stonemountainpark.com
See ad page 418 (Spotlight Atlanta).

SUCHES — A2 *Union*

WILDCAT LODGE & CAMPGROUND **Ratings: 5/7.5/7** (Campground) 2015 rates: $40. (706)973-0321 7475 Georgia Hwy 60, Suches, GA 30572

SUMMERVILLE — A1 *Chattooga*

JAMES H (SLOPPY) FLOYD
(State Pk) From Jct of US 27 & Sloppy Floyd Lake Rd (4 mi S of town), SW 3 mi on Sloppy Floyd Lake Rd (E). Caution: Steep, narrow roads. **FAC:** Paved rds. 25 gravel, patios, 9 pull-thrus (30 x 60), back-ins (30 x 38), 25 W, 25 E (30/50 amps), tent sites, rentals, dump, laundry, fire rings, firewood. **REC:** James H Floyd State Park Lakes: fishing, playground, rec open to public. Pets OK. Partial handicap access. 14 day max stay, 2015 rates: $26 to $30. Disc: military.
(800)864-7275 Lat: 34.439933, Lon: -85.337250
2800 Sloppy Floyd Lake Rd, Summerville, GA 30747
www.gastateparks.org
See ad page 414 (Welcome Section).

TALLAPOOSA — B1 *Haralson*

BIG OAK RV PARK **Ratings: 5/8.5★/6.5** (RV Park) 2015 rates: $20 to $23. (770)574-5522 1179 Hwy 100, Tallapoosa, GA 30176

TALLULAH FALLS — A3 *Rabun*

TALLULAH GORGE
(State Pk) From Jct of US 441 & Main St (in town), N 0.6 mi on US 441 to Jane Hurt Yarn Dr, E 0.2 mi (R). Parking fee required. **FAC:** Paved rds. 50 gravel, 9 pull-thrus (20 x 60), back-ins (20 x 40), 50 W, 50 E (30/50 amps), tent sites, dump, laundry, fire rings, firewood, controlled access. **REC:** Tallulah Falls Lake: swim, fishing, playground, rec open to public. Pets OK. Partial handicap access. 14 day max stay, 2015 rates: $40. Disc: military.
(800)864-7275 Lat: 34.74294, Lon: -83.39618
338 Jane Hurt Yarn Dr, Tallulah Falls, GA 30573
www.gastateparks.org
See ad page 414 (Welcome Section).

THOMASVILLE — E2 *Thomas*

THOMASVILLE See also Ochlocknee.

THOMSON — B4 *McDuffee*

BIG HART CAMPGROUND (Public Corps) From Jct of I-20 & US-78, N 8 mi on US-78 to Russell Landing Rd, E 4 mi (E). 2015 rates: $24 to $26. Mar 27 to Sep 26. (706)595-8613

RAYSVILLE CAMPGROUND (Public Corps) From town, W 5 mi on Hwy 78 to GA-43, N 6.8 mi (L). 2015 rates: $20 to $24. Mar 1 to Oct 30. (706)595-6759

TIFTON — D3 *Tift*

I75 RV PARK
Ratings: 5/8.5/7 (RV Park) From Jct I75 (Exit 61) & Omega Rd: Go 500 ft W on Omega Rd, then 500 ft S on Casseta Rd (L). **FAC:** Gravel rds. 13 gravel, patios, 13 pull-thrus (30 x 60), 13 full hkups (30/50 amps), cable, WiFi, tent sites, laundry. Pets OK. Partial handicap access. Big rig sites, 2015 rates: $27.
(229)392-0808 Lat: 31.43648, Lon: -83.52700
15 Casseta Rd, Tifton, GA 31793
info@I75RVPark.com
www.I75rvpark.com
See ad this page.

PINES RV PARK
Ratings: 6/9★/7 (RV Park) From Jct of I-75 (Exit 61) & Omega Rd: Go 500 ft W on Omega Rd, then 1/4 mi S on Casseta Rd (R).

PULL-THRU'S & BEST RATES ON I-75
We are the "RIGHT CHOICE." The park on your "RIGHT", off Casseta Rd in Tifton. Easy On/Off from I-75 (exit 61). Choose shade or sun sites. The BEST PARK IN THE AREA. Restaurants & shopping nearby.

FAC: Gravel rds. (40 spaces). Avail: 28 gravel, 28 pull-thrus (25 x 60), 28 full hkups (30/50 amps), seasonal sites, cable, WiFi, tent sites, laundry, firewood. **REC.** Pets OK. Partial handicap access. Big rig sites, 2015 rates: $27. Disc: AAA, military. No CC.
(229)382-3500 Lat: 31.43972, Lon: -83.52823
18 Casseta Rd, Tifton, GA 31793
contactus@pinesrvparki75.com
pinesrvparki75.com
See ad pages 438, 416.

TIFTON KOA **Ratings: 6.5/7/6.5** (RV Park) 2015 rates: $33 to $40. (229)386-8441 4632 Union Rd, Tifton, GA 31794

TIGNALL — B3 *Wilkes*

BROAD RIVER CAMPGROUND (Public Corps) From town, N 19 mi on Hwy 79 (L). For reservations call 1-877-444-6777. 2015 rates: $20 to $60. Apr 1 to Sep 7. (706)359-2053

Say you saw it in our Guide!

TOCCOA — A3 *Stephens*

TOCCOA RV PARK

Ratings: 4/6/7 (Campground) From Jct I-85 (Exit 173) & Hwy 17: Go 13 mi N on Hwy 17/17A, then 3-1/4 mi E on Oak Valley Rd (R). **FAC:** Gravel rds. (46 spaces). 38 Avail: 19 gravel, 19 grass, 20 pull-thrus (25 x 50), back-ins (25 x 40), 37 full hkups, 1 W, 1 E (30/50 amps), seasonal sites, WiFi, tent sites, dump, laundry. **REC:** playground. Pet restrict(B). 2015 rates: $12 to $15. No CC.
(706)886-2654 Lat: 34.58060, Lon: -83.24039
3494 Oak Valley Rd, Toccoa, GA 30577
See ad this page.

Know how to keep your four-legged travel companions happy and comfortable? Check out our Pampered Pet Parks feature at the front of the Guide.

TOWNSEND — D5 *McIntosh*

LAKE HARMONY RV PARK AND CAMPGROUND

Ratings: 8.5/9.5★/8.5 (Campground) From Jct of I-95 (exit 58) & Hwy 57: Go 1/2 mi W on Hwy 57 (L). **FAC:** Gravel rds. (49 spaces). Avail: 29 dirt, 27 pull-thrus (25 x 60), back-ins (25 x 50), 29 full hkups (30/50 amps), seasonal sites, cable, WiFi, laundry, LP gas, fire rings, firewood, controlled access. **REC:** Lake Harmony: swim, fishing, shuffleboard. Pets OK. Partial handicap access, no tents. Big rig sites, 2015 rates: $34.50. Disc: AAA, military.
AAA Approved
(888)767-7864 Lat: 31.53692, Lon: -81.45537
1088 Lake Harmony Dr. SW, Townsend, GA 31331
info@lakeharmonypark.com
www.lakeharmonypark.com
See ad this page, 416.

MCINTOSH LAKE RV PARK

Ratings: 7/9★/7.5 (Campground) From Jct I-95 (Exit 58) & Hwy 57: Go 3/4 mi W on Hwy 57 (L). **FAC:** Gravel rds. (38 spaces). 28 Avail: 1 gravel, 27 grass, 26 pull-thrus (33 x 60), back-ins (25 x 50), 28 full hkups (30/50 amps), seasonal sites, cable, WiFi, dump, laundry, fire rings, firewood. **REC:** McIntosh Lake: fishing. Pet restrict(B). No tents. Big rig sites, 2015 rates: $28. Disc: AAA, military.
AAA Approved
(912)832-6215 Lat: 31.53830, Lon: -81.45771
1093 Mcintosh Lake Ln SW, Townsend, GA 31331
mcintoshlake@gmail.com
www.mcintoshlakervpark.com
See ad this page, 416.

TRENTON — A1 *Dade*

LOOKOUT MOUNTAIN/CHATTANOOGA WEST KOA **Ratings: 8.5/8.5/7.5** (Campground) 2015 rates: $34 to $50. (800)562-1239 930 Mountain Shadows Dr, Trenton, GA 30752

TWIN CITY — C4 *Emanuel*

GEORGE L SMITH

(State Pk) From Jct US 80 & Hwy 23 (in town): Go 3-1/2 mi S on Hwy 23, the 1-3/4 mi E on George L. Smith Park Rd (E) Entrance fee required. **FAC:** Paved rds. 25 gravel, patios, 7 pull-thrus (40 x 80), back-ins (40 x 50), 25 W, 25 E (30/50 amps), tent sites, rentals, dump, laundry, fire rings, firewood. **REC:** Old Parrish Pond: fishing, playground, rec open to public. Pets OK. Partial handicap access. 14 day max stay, 2015 rates: $30. Disc: military.
(800)864-PARK Lat: 32.544717, Lon: -82.125400
371 George L Smith State Park Rd, Twin City, GA 30471
www.gastateparks.org
See ad page 414 (Welcome Section).

TYBEE ISLAND — D5 *Chatham*

RIVER'S END CAMPGROUND & RV PARK

Ratings: 9/9.5★/9 (Public) From Jct I-95 (Exit 94) & Hwy 204: Go 10 mi E on Hwy 204, then 8 mi N on Harry Truman Parkway, then 15-1/2 mi E on US 80E, then 1/4 mi N on Polk St, then 500 ft E on Fort Ave (L).

TYBEE ISLAND, GA * SAVANNAH'S BEACH
A place for all seasons. Sandy beaches, great fishing & history at every turn. Walking distance to beach & 16 mi to historic Savannah. Enjoy Tybee Time under our live oak canopy. See our website for detailed rate guide.

FAC: Paved/gravel rds. (87 spaces). Avail: 82 gravel, 30 pull-thrus (20 x 45), back-ins (20 x 40), 75 full hkups, 7 W, 7 E (30/50 amps), cable, WiFi, tent sites, rentals, dump, laundry, LP gas, fire rings, firewood. **REC:** pool. Pet restrict(Q). Partial handicap access. 2015 rates: $44 to $99. Disc: AAA, military. ATM.
(800)786-1016 Lat: 32.02274, Lon: -80.85020
5 Fort Ave, Tybee Island, GA 31328
riversend@cityoftybee.org
www.riversendcampground.com
See ad pages 436, 416 & Snowbird Destinations in Magazine Section.

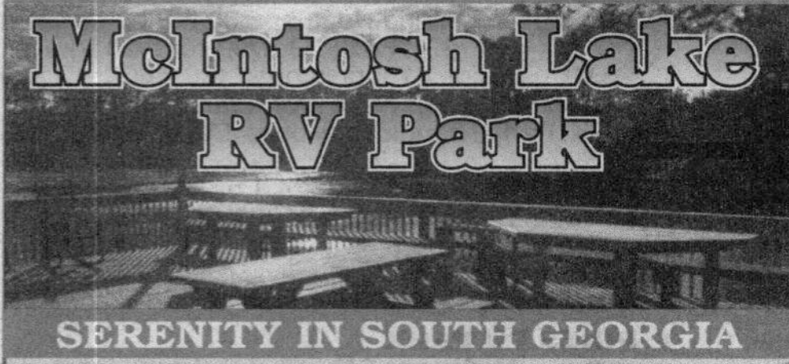

UNADILLA — D2 *Dooly*

↓ SOUTHERN TRAILS RV RESORT
Ratings: 6.5/7.5/5.5 (Membership Pk) From Jct I-75 (Exit 121) & Hwy 41: Go 1/4 mi E on Hwy 41, then 1/4 mi S on Speeg Rd, then 1/2 mi SW on E Railroad St (Arena Rd) (L). **FAC:** Gravel rds. (191 spaces). 161 Avail: 141 gravel, 20 grass, 114 pull-thrus (20 x 50), back-ins (20 x 45), some side by side hkups, 103 full hkups, 58 W, 58 E (30/50 amps), seasonal sites, WiFi Hotspot, tent sites, dump, laundry, LP gas. **REC:** pool, pond, fishing, playground. Pets OK. 2015 rates: $20 to $30. Disc: AAA. No CC.
(478)627-3254 Lat: 32.24037, Lon: -83.73928
2690 Arena Rd, Unadilla, GA 31091
info@southerntrailsresort.com
www.southerntrailsresort.com
See ad opposite page, 416.

VALDOSTA — E3 *Lowndes*

VALDOSTA See also Cecil & Lake Park.

How can you tell whether you're traveling in the right direction? The arrow in each listing denotes the compass direction of the facility in relation to the listed town. For example, an arrow pointing straight up indicates that the facility is located due north from town. An arrow pointing down and to the right indicates that the facility is southeast of town.

← RIVER PARK RV PARK
Ratings: 7.5/9.5★/8.5 (RV Park) From Jct of I-75 (Exit 18) & SR 133: Go 1/4 mi W on SR 133 (R). **FAC:** Paved rds. (118 spaces). Avail: 57 paved, 57 pull-thrus (25 x 70), 57 full hkups (30/50 amps), seasonal sites, cable, WiFi, tent sites, dump, laundry. Pets OK. Big rig sites, 2015 rates: $30 to $34.
(229)244-8397 Lat: 30.84753, Lon: -83.33459
1 Suwanee Dr, Valdosta, GA 31602
info@riverparkvaldosta.com
www.riverparkvaldosta.com
See ad opposite page, 416.

Like Us on Facebook.

← VALDOSTA OAKS RV PARK
Ratings: 5/8★/6 (RV Park) From Jct I-75 (Exit 22) & Hwy 41: N-Bnd, Go 1/4 mi W on Hwy 41 to Citgo, then 1/4 mi N on N Valdosta Rd (E); S-Bnd (Exit 22) continue straight 1/4 mi N on Valdosta Rd (E). **FAC:** Paved/gravel rds. (76 spaces). Avail: 56 gravel, 56 pull-thrus (35 x 60), accepts full hkup units only, 56 full hkups (30/50 amps), seasonal sites, cable, WiFi, tent sites, laundry. Pet restrict(Q). Big rig sites, 2015 rates: $32. Disc: military.
(229)247-0494 Lat: 30.53906, Lon: -83.21601
4630 N Valdosta Rd, Valdosta, GA 31602
winco5@windstream.net
www.valdostaoaksrv.com
See ad this page, 416.

GA

WARM SPRINGS — C2 *Meriwether*

RAMSEY RV PARK **Ratings: 3.5/5/5** (Campground) 2015 rates: $19 to $20. (706)655-2480 5153 White House Pkwy (Hwy 85 Alt N), Warm Springs, GA 31830

WAYCROSS — E4 *Ware*

LAURA S WALKER
(State Pk) From Jct of US 82 & SR-177, S 2 mi on SR-177 (R). Parking fee required. **FAC:** Paved rds. 44 gravel, patios, 5 pull-thrus (20 x 60), back-ins (20 x 45), 44 W, 44 E (30 amps), tent sites, dump, laundry, fire rings, firewood. **REC:** Laura S. Walker Lake: fishing, golf, playground, rec open to public. Pets OK. Partial handicap access. 14 day max stay, 2015 rates: $25 to $30. Disc: military.
(800)864-PARK Lat: 31.143466, Lon: -82.214533
5653 Laura Walker Rd, Waycross, GA 31503
www.gastateparks.org
See ad page 414 (Welcome Section).

WEST POINT — C1 *Troup*

R SHAEFER HEARD PARK (Public Corps) From town, N 4 mi on US-29, follow signs (L). 2015 rates: $24 to $56. (706)645-2404

WINDER — B2 *Barrow*

FORT YARGO
(State Pk) From Jct I-85 & Hwy 53 (Exit 129): Go 11 mi S on Hwy 53, then 3/4 mi S on Hwy 81 (in town), follow signs (L) Parking fee required. **FAC:** Paved rds. 40 gravel, patios, 5 pull-thrus (20 x 50), back-ins (20 x 35), 40 W, 40 E (20/30 amps), tent sites, rentals, dump, laundry, fire rings, firewood. **REC:** Lake Yargo: swim, fishing, playground, rec open to public. Pets OK. Partial handicap access. 14 day max stay, 2015 rates: $28 to $32. Disc: military.
(800)864-PARK Lat: 33.984083, Lon: -83.732916
210 South Broad St, Winder, GA 30680
www.gastateparks.org
See ad page 414 (Welcome Section).

WINFIELD — B4 *Columbia*

WINFIELD (Public Corps) From Jct of I-20 & Hwy 150, NE 8 mi on Hwy 150 to Winfield Rd, N 3.5 mi (Left at intersection). For reservations call 1-877-444-6777. 2015 rates: $26. Mar 27 to Sep 26. (706)541-0147

Slow down. For most vehicles, fuel efficiency begins to drop rapidly at 60 mph. Driving within the speed limit can improve fuel efficiency by up to 23 percent.

WOODBINE — E5 *Camden*

WALKABOUT CAMP & RV PARK **Ratings: 7/8★/7** (RV Park) 2015 rates: $35 to $38. (912)729-4110 742 Old Still Rd, Woodbine, GA 31569

WOODSTOCK — B2 *Cherokee*

VICTORIA (Public Corps) From Jct of I-575 & Old Alabama Rd (exit 7), W 3 mi on Old Alabama Rd to Bells Ferry Rd, N 4 mi to Victoria Landing Dr, W 3 mi (R). 2015 rates: $26 to $30. Mar 27 to Oct 4. (678)721-6700

Travel Services

CAMPING WORLD STORE OF WOODSTOCK/ATLANTA As the nation's largest retailer of RV supplies, accessories, services and new and used RVs, Camping World is committed to making your total RV experience better. RV Accessories: (888)396-0335. **SERVICES:** RV, RV appliance, engine/chassis repair, staffed RV wash, restrooms, RV Sales. RV supplies, LP, RV accessible. Hours: 8am to 6pm.
(888)711-8231 Lat: 34.088942, Lon: -84.531262
505 Parkway 575, Woodstock, GA 30188
www.campingworld.com

Getty Images/iStockphoto

WELCOME TO Idaho

DATE OF STATEHOOD	WIDTH: 305 MILES (491 KM)	PROPORTION OF UNITED STATES
JULY 3, 1890	LENGTH: 479 MILES (771 KM)	2.20% OF 3,794,100 SQ MI

"Spud State," "Gem State" or "Little Ida," these are hardly worthy monikers for a state of such epic natural beauty. With more running white water than any other state (3,100 miles), serrated snowcapped mountains that seem to follow your every move, haunting volcanic landscapes and ethereal glacial lakes, Ernest Hemingway—Idaho's most famous denizen—hit the nail on the head when he remarked, "A lot of state, this Idaho, that I didn't know about."

Boise, Idaho's state capital, is a sleeper hit if ever there was one. Nudging up against wild foothills, the former gold rush mining center is blazing its own trail as a vibrant metropolis that combines cosmopolitan élan with a convivial vibe.

Recreation is big in this state. With swathes of high desert dappled with sage, white-water rivers that plummet through Rocky Mountain canyons, glorious snowy mountain peaks and aspen groves framed by a big, blue sky, Idaho is an outdoor enthusiast's heaven. For adrenaline seekers, rafting the Salmon River's deep rolling 100-mile Middle Fork is a rite of passage. The river runs through 20,000 square miles of untamed backcountry.

Arguably more rugged and wild than any national park (in large part because it's not one) and with only 700,000 visitors annually (compared to 4.1 million annually for Yosemite), the 756,000-acre Sawtooth National Recreation Area is every traveler's "own private Idaho." Over 700 miles of trails encompass four mountain ranges.

Another highlight is Nez Perce Park, the only national park celebrating a people instead of a place. Comprising 38 historical sites, the park follows the 1,170-mile route taken by the Nez Perce people as they fled U.S. Cavalry.

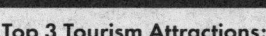

Top 3 Tourism Attractions:
1) Craters of the Moon National Monument and Preserve
2) Shoshone Falls
3) Hells Canyon National Recreation Area

Nickname: Gem State

State Flower: Syringa

State Bird: Mountain Bluebird

People: Gutzon Borglum, sculptor of Mount Rushmore; Sarah Palin, governor; Sacagawea, Shoshone interpreter; Picabo Street, ski racer

Major Cities: Boise (capital), Nampa, Meridian, Idaho Falls, Pocatello

Topography: South—Snake River plains; central—mountains and canyon gorges; north—subalpine

Climate: Diverse climate influenced by Pacific Ocean weather patterns; north receives more rain than south

TRAVEL & TOURISM

Idaho Division of Tourism Development
800-VISIT-ID, 208-334-2470
www.visitidaho.org

Boise CVB
800-635-5240
www.boise.org/visitors

Coeur d'Alene
877-782-9232
www.coeurdalene.org

Visit Pocatello
208-479-7659
www.visitpocatello.com

Southern Idaho Tourism
800-255-8946
www.visitsouthidaho.com

OUTDOOR RECREATION

Idaho Department of Fish & Game
208-334-3700
www.fishandgame.idaho.gov

Idaho Golf Association
208-342-4442
www.idahogolfassn.org

Idaho Outfitters and Guides Association
800-847-4843
www.theiga.org

Winter Sports
800-VISIT-ID
www.visitidaho.org/winter

SHOPPING

Boise Towne Square Mall
www.boisetownsquare.com

Cedar Street Bridge Public Market
www.cedarstreetbridge.com

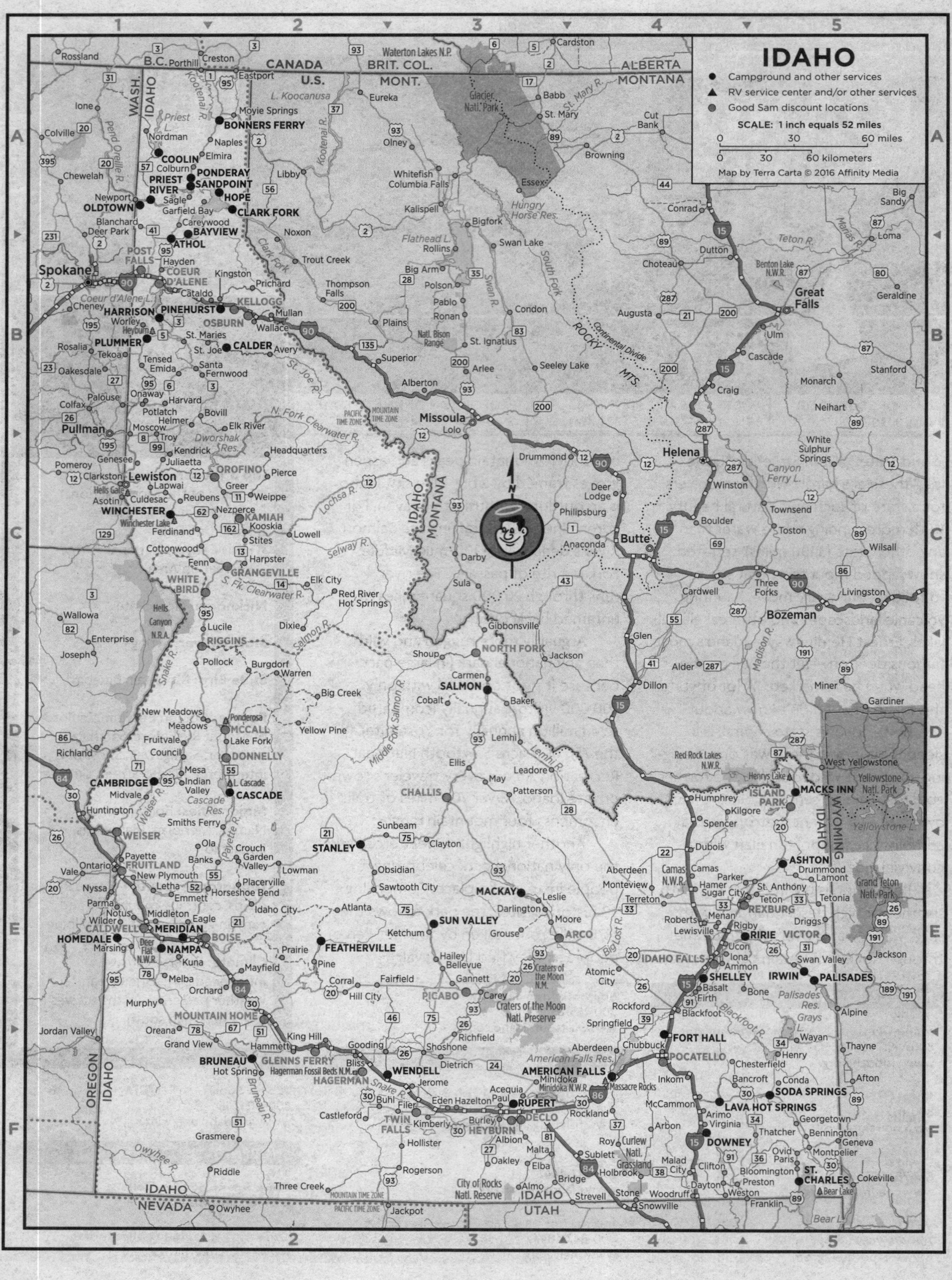
IDAHO
Campground and other services
RV service center and/or other services
Good Sam discount locations
SCALE: 1 inch equals 52 miles
0 30 60 miles
0 30 60 kilometers
Map by Terra Carta © 2016 Affinity Media
CANADA
U.S.
B.C.
BRIT. COL.
MONT.
ALBERTA
MONTANA
WASH.
IDAHO
OREGON
NEVADA
UTAH
WYOMING
Rossland
Porthill
Creston
Eastport
Cardston
Waterton Lakes N.P.
Glacier Natl. Park
Babb
St. Mary
Cut Bank
Browning
Eureka
L. Koocanusa
Moyie Springs
BONNERS FERRY
Naples
Nordman
COOLIN
Colburn
Elmira
PRIEST RIVER
PONDERAY
SANDPOINT
HOPE
CLARK FORK
OLDTOWN
Newport
Sagle
Garfield Bay
Blanchard
Deer Park
Carevwood
BAYVIEW
ATHOL
Ione
Colville
Chewelah
Libby
Olney
Whitefish
Columbia Falls
Essex
Kalispell
Bigfork
Hungry Horse Res.
Conrad
Big Sandy
Flathead L.
Rollins
Swan Lake
Noxon
Trout Creek
Dutton
Loma
Teton R.
Choteau
Benton Lake N.W.R.
Spokane
POST FALLS
Hayden
COEUR D'ALENE
Kingston
Prichard
Thompson Falls
Big Arm
Polson
Pablo
Ronan
Condon
Augusta
Great Falls
Geraldine
Cheney
Cataldo
HARRISON
PINEHURST
KELLOGG
Mullan
Wallace
OSBURN
Worley
Heyburn
Plains
Natl. Bison Range
St. Ignatius
Ulm
Cascade
Stanford
Rosalia
PLUMMER
Tekoa
St. Maries
St. Joe
CALDER
Avery
Superior
Arlee
Seeley Lake
Craig
Monarch
Oakesdale
Tensed
Emida
Santa
Fernwood
Alberton
Continental Divide
ROCKY MTS.
Neihart
Colfax
Palouse
Onaway
Harvard
Potlatch
Helmer
Bovill
Elk River
Missoula
Lolo
Pullman
Moscow
Troy
Dworshak Res.
N. Fork Clearwater R.
Headquarters
Kendrick
Juliaetta
Genesee
PACIFIC TIME ZONE
MOUNTAIN TIME ZONE
Helena
White Sulphur Springs
Drummond
Pomeroy
Clarkston
Lewiston
Lapwai
OROFINO
Pierce
Greer
Weippe
Hells Gate
Asotin
Culdesac
Reubens
Deer Lodge
Winston
Canyon Ferry L.
WINCHESTER
Winchester Lake
Nezperce
KAMIAH
Kooskia
Lochsa R.
Philipsburg
Boulder
Townsend
Ferdinand
Stites
Lowell
Anaconda
Butte
Toston
Wilsall
Cottonwood
Harpster
Selway R.
Darby
Fenn
GRANGEVILLE
Elk City
Sula
Three Forks
Livingston
WHITE BIRD
S. Fk. Clearwater R.
Red River Hot Springs
Cardwell
Bozeman
Wallowa
Hells Canyon N.R.A.
Lucile
Dixie
Salmon R.
Gibbonsville
Enterprise
Joseph
RIGGINS
NORTH FORK
Shoup
Jackson
Glen
Madison R.
Pollock
Burgdorf
Warren
Carmen
SALMON
Alder
Dillon
Miner
Big Creek
Cobalt
Baker
Gardiner
New Meadows
Meadows
Ponderosa
MCCALL
Lake Fork
Yellow Pine
Middle Fork Salmon R.
Lemhi
Lemhi R.
Red Rock Lakes N.W.R.
Richland
Fruitvale
Council
DONNELLY
Ellis
May
Leadore
Henrys Lake
West Yellowstone
Yellowstone Natl. Park
CAMBRIDGE
Mesa
Indian Valley
L. Cascade
CASCADE
CHALLIS
Patterson
Humphrey
ISLAND PARK
MACKS INN
Midvale
Cascade Res.
Kilgore
Huntington
Smiths Ferry
Sunbeam
Spencer
Yellowstone L.
WEISER
Payette R.
Clayton
Dubois
Ola
STANLEY
Crouch
Garden Valley
Lowman
Banks
Payette
FRUITLAND
Ontario
Vale
New Plymouth
Obsidian
Aberdeen
Camas N.W.R.
Camas
ASHTON
Drummond
Lamont
Letha
Emmett
Placerville
Horseshoe Bend
Sawtooth City
MACKAY
Monteview
Hamer
Parker
St. Anthony
Nyssa
Parma
Notus
Wilder
Middleton
Eagle
Idaho City
Atlanta
Leslie
Darlington
Terreton
Sugar City
Teton
REXBURG
Tetonia
Grand Teton Natl. Park
CALDWELL
MERIDIAN
BOISE
SUN VALLEY
Ketchum
Moore
Roberts
Menan
Driggs
HOMEDALE
Marsing
Deer Flat N.W.R.
NAMPA
Kuna
Prairie
FEATHERVILLE
Pine
Grouse
ARCO
Lewisville
Rigby
RIRIE
VICTOR
Hailey
Bellevue
Big Lost R.
IDAHO FALLS
Ucon
Iona
Ammon
Swan Valley
Jackson
Mayfield
Melba
Orchard
Gannett
Craters of the Moon N.M.
Atomic City
SHELLEY
IRWIN
PALISADES
Corral
Fairfield
Hill City
PICABO
Carey
Craters of the Moon Natl. Preserve
Basalt
Firth
Bone
Palisades Res.
Murphy
MOUNTAIN HOME
Rockford
Blackfoot
Grays L.
Alpine
Oreana
Springfield
Jordan Valley
Grand View
King Hill
Richfield
Blackfoot R.
FORT HALL
Wayan
Thayne
Hammett
Gooding
Shoshone
Aberdeen
American Falls Res.
Chubbuck
POCATELLO
Henry
BRUNEAU
GLENNS FERRY
Hot Spring
Hagerman Fossil Beds N.M.
Bliss
Dietrich
AMERICAN FALLS
Minidoka
Minidoka N.W.R.
Massacre Rocks
Chesterfield
HAGERMAN
WENDELL
Jerome
Acequia
Inkom
Bancroft
Conda
SODA SPRINGS
Afton
Bruneau R.
Snake R.
Buhl
Filer
Eden
Hazelton
Paul
RUPERT
McCammon
LAVA HOT SPRINGS
Castleford
TWIN FALLS
Kimberly
Burley
HEYBURN
DECLO
Rockland
Arimo
Virginia
Georgetown
Grasmere
Hollister
Albion
Arbon
DOWNEY
Thatcher
Bennington
Geneva
Owyhee R.
Oakley
Malta
Sublett
Roy
Curlew Natl. Grassland
Holbrook
Malad City
Clifton
Ovid
Paris
Montpelier
Riddle
Rogerson
Elba
Bridge
Bloomington
Preston
ST. CHARLES
Cokeville
Three Creek
City of Rocks Natl. Reserve
Almo
Dayton
Weston
Bear Lake
Owyhee
Jackpot
Strevell
Stone
Woodruff
Snowville
Franklin
Bear L.

Featured Good Sam Parks

IDAHO

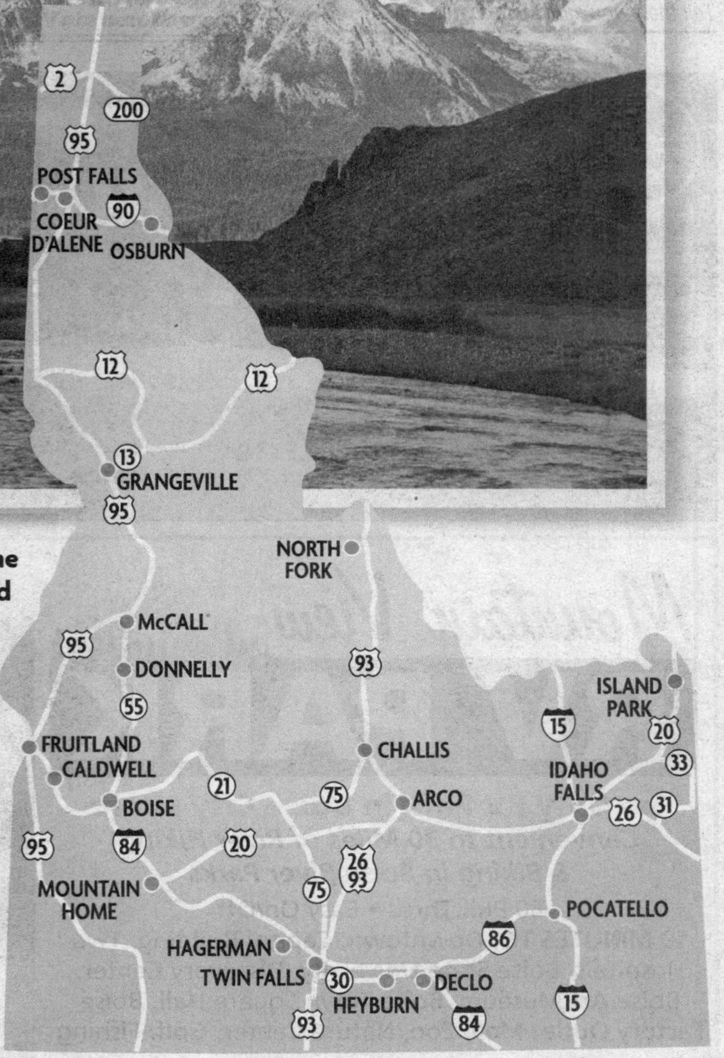

When you stay with Good Sam, you can expect the highest degree of cleanliness and friendliness, and better yet, you get 10% off campground fees.

If you're not already a Good Sam member you can purchase your membership at one of these locations:

ARCO
Mountain View RV Park
(208)527-3707

BOISE
Hi Valley RV Park
(888)457-5959
Mountain View RV Park
(877)610-4141

CALDWELL
Ambassador RV Resort
(888)877-8307
Country Corners RV Park and Campground
(877)474-9826

CHALLIS
Challis Golf Course RV Park
(208)390-9568

COEUR D'ALENE
Alpine Country RV Park
(208)772-4305
Wolf Lodge Campground
(866)664-2812

DECLO
Village Of Trees RV Resort
(208)654-2133

DONNELLY
Chalet RV Park
(208)325-8223

FRUITLAND
Neat Retreat RV Park
(208)452-4324

GRANGEVILLE
Bear Den RV Resort
(208)983-0140

HAGERMAN
Hagerman RV Village
(208)837-4906

HEYBURN
Heyburn Riverside RV Park
(208)431-2977

IDAHO FALLS
Snake River RV Park and Campground
(208)523-3362

ISLAND PARK
RedRock RV and Camping Park
(800)473-3762
Sawtelle Mountain Resort
(208)558-9366

MCCALL
McCall RV Resort
(208)634-5646

MOUNTAIN HOME
Mountain Home RV Park
(208)580-1211

NORTH FORK
Wagonhammer RV & Campground
(208)865-2477

OSBURN
Blue Anchor RV Park
(208)752-3443

POCATELLO
Cowboy RV Park
(208)232-4587

POST FALLS
Suntree RV Park
(208)777-8888

TWIN FALLS
Anderson Camp RV Park
(888)480-9400

For more Good Sam Parks go to listing pages

Idaho

CONSULTANTS

Jim & Chris Mays

Tell them you saw them in this Guide!

AMERICAN FALLS — F4 *Power*

MASSACRE ROCKS (State Pk) From Jct I-86 & Exit 28 N 0.1 mi (E). 2015 rates: $14 to $38. (208)548-2672

ARCO — E3 *Butte*

CRATERS OF THE MOON/LAVA FLOW CAMPGROUND (Natl Pk) From Jct of US-26 & US-20, SW 18 mi on US-20 (L). Entrance fee required. 2015 rates: $6 to $10. (208)527-3257

MOUNTAIN VIEW RV PARK
Ratings: 7.5/9★/9 (RV Park) From Jct of US 20/26 & US 93: Go 1 mi W on US 20/26 & US 93 (L). Elev 5400 ft. **FAC:** Gravel rds. 33 gravel, 33 pull-thrus (51 x 72), 33 full hkups (30/50 amps), WiFi, tent sites, dump, laundry, LP gas, restaurant. **REC:** rec open to public. Pets OK. Partial handicap

Things change ... last year's rates serve as a guideline only.

ARCO (CONT)

MOUNTAIN VIEW RV PARK (CONT)
access. Big rig sites, 2015 rates: $35.50 to $40. Disc: AAA, military.
AAA Approved
(208)527-3707 Lat: 43.62714, Lon: -113.30581
705 W Grand Ave, Arco, ID 83213
info@mountainviewrvarco.com
www.mountainviewrvarco.com
See ad opposite page, 443.

ASHTON — E5 *Fremont*

➔ ASPEN ACRES RV & GOLF RESORT **Ratings: 5.5/7/8** (Campground) 2015 rates: $32.50 to $40. May 15 to Oct 15. (208)652-3524 4179 E 1100 N, Ashton, ID 83420

ATHOL — B1 *Kootenai*

➔ FARRAGUT (State Pk) From Jct of US-95 & SR-54, E 4 mi on SR-54 (E). 2015 rates: $12 to $24. (208)683-2425

↓ RAVENWOOD RV RESORT **Ratings: 4.5/NA/8** (RV Resort) 2015 rates: $35 to $50. May 1 to Sep 30. (208)683-0891 25700 N Pope Rd, Athol, ID 83801

↓ SILVERWOOD RV PARK **Ratings: 5.5/8.5/7.5** (Campground) 2015 rates: $39. May 2 to Sep 30. (208)683-3400 27843 N Hwy 95, Athol, ID 83801

BAYVIEW — A1 *Kootenai*

↑ LAKELAND RV PARK **Ratings: 6/7/7** (Campground) 2015 rates: $35. May 1 to Oct 1. (208)683-4108 20139 E Perimeter Rd, Bayview, ID 83803

BOISE — E1 *Ada*

BOISE See also Caldwell, Meridian & Nampa.

➔ **AMBASSADOR RV RESORT**
Ratings: 10/9.5★/9.5 (RV Park) From Jct I-84 & I-184 (in Boise): Go 20 mi W on I-84, then 3/4 mi E on US 20/26 (exit 29) then 1/8 mi N on Smeed Pkwy (R). **FAC:** Paved rds. (187 spaces). Avail: 102 all weather, patios, 102 pull-thrus (33 x 80), 102 full hkups (30/50 amps), seasonal sites, cable, WiFi, rentals, dump, laundry, LP gas. **REC:** heated pool, wading pool, whirlpool, playground. Pet restrict(B/Q). Partial handicap access, no tents. Big rig sites, eco-friendly, 2015 rates: $35. Disc: AAA, military. ATM.
(888)877-8307 Lat: 43.66439, Lon: -116.64215
615 Smeed Pkwy, Caldwell, ID 83605
ambassador@g7rvresorts.com
www.g7rvresorts.com
See primary listing at Caldwell and ad page 446.

We appreciate your business!

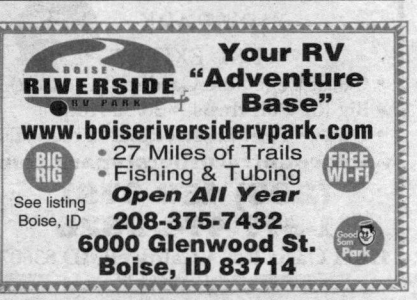

ID

BOISE (CONT)

BOISE RIVERSIDE RV PARK
Ratings: 8/9.5★/8.5 (Campground) From Jct I-84 & SR-55 (exit 46): Go 4 1/2 mi N on SR-55 to US-20/26, then 3 3/4 mi E on US-20/26 to N Glenwood St, then 3/4 mi N on N Glenwood St to Marigold, then 1/4 mi E on Marigold (E). Elev 2600 ft. **FAC:** Gravel rds. (139 spaces). Avail: 63 gravel, patios, 29 pull-thrus (36 x 46), back-ins (21 x 36), 27 full hkups, 36 W, 36 E (30/50 amps), seasonal sites, WiFi, tent sites, rentals, dump, laundry, LP gas. **REC:** Boise River: swim, fishing, rec open to public. Pet restrict(Q). Partial handicap access. Eco-friendly, 2015 rates: $35.24. Disc: military.
(208)375-7432 Lat: 43.65860, Lon: -116.27769
6000 N Glenwood St, Garden City, ID 83714
brrvpark@yahoo.com
www.boiseriversidervpark.com
See ad page 445.

HI VALLEY RV PARK
Ratings: 9.5/9.5★/9 (RV Park) From Jct I-84 & Hwy 55 / Eagle Rd (exit 46) : Go 6 mi N on Hwy 55 / Eagle Rd, then 2 mi E on West State St (Hwy 44), then 1 mi N on Horseshoe Bend Rd (L).

ENJOY THE SIGHTS & SOUNDS OF BOISE
With easy access to Idaho's scenic rivers and mountain valleys, yet next door to the Boise metro area. Hi Valley offers a full range of activities right outside your door. Come and see why guests come back year after year.

FAC: Paved rds. (192 spaces). Avail: 34 gravel, patios, 34 pull-thrus (24 x 70), 34 full hkups (30/50 amps), seasonal sites, cable, WiFi, rentals, dump, laundry, LP gas. **REC:** heated pool, whirlpool, playground. Pet restrict(B/Q). Partial handicap access, no tents. Big rig sites, eco-friendly, 2015 rates: $36. Disc: AAA, military. ATM.
AAA Approved
(888)457-5959 Lat: 43.69797, Lon: -116.31573
10555 Horseshoe Bend Rd, Boise, ID 83714
hivalley@g7rvresorts.com
www.g7rvresorts.com
See ad pages 445, 443.

MOUNTAIN VIEW RV PARK
Ratings: 8/10★/7.5 (RV Park) From Jct I-84 & US 20/26 / Broadway Ave (exit 54): Go 1/8 mi S on Broadway Ave, then 1/2 mi W on Commerce Ave, then 1/4 mi N on S Development Ave, then 1/8 mi E on W Airport Way (L). Elev 2883 ft.

ONLY RV PARK IN BOISE CITY LIMITS
Within 3.4 miles of Bronco Stadium & 4 miles of the State Capitol. We have 60 pull thru service sites w/both 30 & 50 amp: laundry & showers. On-site resident managers ensure safe, clean, well maintained, friendly environment

FAC: Paved rds. (60 spaces). Avail: 25 paved, 25 pull-thrus (20 x 70), 25 full hkups (30/50 amps), seasonal sites, WiFi, dump, laundry. Pet restrict(B/Q). Partial handicap access, no tents. Eco-friendly, 2015 rates: $34.50. Disc: AAA.
AAA Approved
(877)610-4141 Lat: 43.56793, Lon: -116.20437
2040 W Airport Way, Boise, ID 83705
mountainviewrvpark@live.com
www.boiservpark.com
See ad pages 444, 443.

BONNERS FERRY — A2 *Boundary*

BLUE LAKE RV RESORT Ratings: 8.5/9★/6.5 (Campground) From Jct of Hwy 95/Hwy 2 & Ash St: Go 13 mi S on Hwy 95 (MP 498.3) (R). **FAC:** Gravel rds. (37 spaces). Avail: 32 gravel, 13 pull-thrus (45 x 80), back-ins (30 x 45), 16 full hkups, 16 W, 16 E (30/50 amps), seasonal sites, WiFi, tent sites, rentals, dump, laundry, LP gas, fire rings, firewood. **REC:** Blue Lake: swim, fishing. Pet restrict(B). Partial handicap access. Eco-friendly, 2015 rates: $36.75. Apr 1 to Nov 30.
(208)946-3361 Lat: 48.58290, Lon: -116.38582
242 Blue Lake Rd, Bonners Ferry, ID 83847
stay@bluelakervresort.com
www.bluelakervresort.com

IDYL ACRES RV PARK **Ratings: 4/7.5/8** (Campground) 2015 rates: $34. May 1 to Sep 30. (208)267-3629 533817 Hwy 95, Bonners Ferry, ID 83805

TWIN RIVERS CANYON RESORT **Ratings: 4.5/6/7.5** (Campground) 2015 rates: $33 to $36. Apr 1 to Oct 31. (888)258-5952 1823 Twin Rivers Rd, Moyie Springs, ID 83845

BRUNEAU — F2 *Elmore, Owyhee*

BRUNEAU DUNES (State Pk) From Jct of I-84 & So. State Hwy 51, S 17 mi on So State Hwy 51 to Jct State Hwy 78, E 2 mi on State Hwy 78 (R). 2015 rates: $12 to $27. (208)366-7919

BURLEY — F3 *Cassia*

BURLEY See also Declo & Heyburn.

CALDER — B2 *Shoshone*

HUCKLEBERRY FLAT (Public) From town, N 11 mi on US-55 to West Roseberry Rd., W 1.6 mi on W. Roseberry Rd., SW 2.7 mi to Rainbow Point Rd., S 3 mi on W Mountain Rd. Pit toilets. 2015 rates: $14 to $18. May 15 to Oct 15. (208)769-5000

Want to see what our inspectors see? The exact reproductions of the rating guidelines our inspectors used for this edition of the Guide are printed in the front of the book. Try using them on your next trip to perform your own inspection. Since our rating system is based on objective criteria, we're confident that your ratings will be similar to ours.

CALDWELL — E1 *Canyon*

AMBASSADOR RV RESORT
Ratings: 10/9.5★/9.5 (RV Park) From Jct I-84 & US 20/26 (exit 29): Go 3/4 mi E on US 20/26, then 1/8 mi N on Smeed Pkwy (R).

EXCELLENCE IN RV LODGING
Friendly guest service, first-rate amenities & clean facilities ensure that a stay with the Ambassador is one of class & comfort. A perfect home base for all your activities here in the Treasure Valley & Boise.

FAC: Paved rds. (187 spaces). Avail: 102 all weather, patios, 102 pull-thrus (33 x 80), 102 full hkups (30/50 amps), seasonal sites, cable, WiFi, rentals, dump, laundry, LP gas. **REC:** heated pool, wading pool, whirlpool, playground. Pet restrict(B/Q). Partial handicap access, no tents. Big rig sites, eco-friendly, 2015 rates: $35. Disc: AAA, military. ATM.
AAA Approved
(888)877-8307 Lat: 43.66439, Lon: -116.64215
615 Smeed Pkwy, Caldwell, ID 83605
ambassador@g7rvresorts.com
www.g7rvresorts.com
See ad opposite page, 443.

CALDWELL CAMPGROUND & RV PARK
Ratings: 7/9/7 (Campground) From Jct I-84 & Hwy 20/26 (exit 26): Go 1/8 mi E on US 20/26 to Old Hwy 30, then 1/8 mi S on Old Hwy 30 to Town Circle, then 1/4 mi SW on Town Circle (L). **FAC:** Paved/gravel rds. (108 spaces). Avail: 58 gravel, 55 pull-thrus (22 x 65), back-ins (30 x 45), 58 full hkups (30/50 amps), seasonal sites, cable, WiFi, tent sites, dump, laundry, LP gas, fire rings, firewood. **REC:** Bass Lake: fishing, rec open to public. Pet restrict(B). Eco-friendly, 2015 rates: $25.
(888)675-0279 Lat: 43.68556, Lon: -116.68686
21830 Towns Circle #34, Caldwell, ID 83607
info@caldwellrvparkllc.com
www.caldwellcampgroundandrvparkllc.com
See ad opposite page.

CANYON SPRINGS RV RESORT
(RV Resort) (Under Construction) From jct I-84 & US 20/26: Go 1/4 mi W on US 20/26 (L). **FAC:** Paved rds. 136 gravel, patios, 21 pull-thrus (25 x 60), back-ins (25 x 50), 136 full hkups (30/50 amps), cable, rentals, laundry, LP gas. **REC:** Canyon Springs Lake: swim, fishing. Pets OK. Partial handicap access, no tents. Big rig sites, 2015 rates: $33 to $46.
(208)402-6630 Lat: 43.69060, Lon: -116.69813
15255 US 20, Caldwell, ID 83607
stay@canyonspringsRVresort.com
www.canyonspringsrvresort.com
See ad page 445.

COUNTRY CORNERS RV PARK AND CAMPGROUND
Ratings: 7.5/9/9 (Campground) From Jct I-84 & Oasis Rd (exit 17): Go 1/4 mi E Oasis on Rd (R). **FAC:** Gravel rds. (62 spaces). Avail: 10 gravel, 10 pull-thrus (20 x 66), 10 full hkups (30/50 amps), seasonal sites, WiFi, tent sites, laundry, LP gas, firewood. **REC:** pond, fishing. Pet restrict(B/Q). Partial handicap access. Big rig sites, eco-friendly, 2015 rates: $30. Disc: AAA, military.
AAA Approved
(877)474-9826 Lat: 43.80690, Lon: -116.74588
17671 Oasis Rd, Caldwell, ID 83607
manager@countrycornersrvpark.com
www.countrycornersrvpark.com
See ad opposite page, 443.

A campground rating is based on ALL facilities available at the park.

CAMBRIDGE — D1 *Washington*

MCCORMICK PARK (Public) From town, N 28 mi on Hwy 71 to Snake River, follow signs (R). NOTE: 45' RV LENGTH MAXIMUM. 2015 rates: $8 to $16. (208)257-3332

WOODHEAD PARK (Public) From town, S 0.1 mi on SR-82 to SR-350, E 7.5 mi to FR 39, SE 25 mi follow signs (E). 2015 rates: $8 to $16. (208)388-2231

CASCADE — D2 *Valley*

ARROWHEAD RV PARK ON THE RIVER Ratings: 8/9.5★/8.5 (Campground) From Cascade City Center: Go 1/2 mi S on Hwy 55 (R). Elev 4800 ft. **FAC:** Gravel rds. (127 spaces). Avail: 15 gravel, patios, 12 pull-thrus (25 x 80), back-ins (20 x 80), 15 full hkups (30/50 amps), seasonal sites, WiFi, tent sites, rentals, dump, laundry, LP gas, firewood. **REC:** Payette River: fishing, shuffleboard, playground. Pets OK. Partial handicap access. Big rig sites, eco-friendly, 2015 rates: $29. May 1 to Oct 1.
AAA Approved
(208)382-4534 Lat: 44.50273, Lon: -116.02644
955 S Main St, Cascade, ID 83611
arrowheadrv@yahoo.com
www.arrowheadpark.com

BUTTERCUP (Public) From town, N 11 mi on US-55 to W Roseberry Rd (in Donnelly), W 1.6 mi, S 1 mi Rainbow Pt. Rd., W 1.7 to W. Mountain Rd., S 2.25 mi. Pit toilets. 2015 rates: $12 to $28. May 24 to Dec 31. (208)382-6544

LAKE CASCADE (Public) From town, N 11 mi on US-55 to Tamarack Rd (in Donnelly), W 5 mi to Tamarack Falls Store, W to West Mountain Rd, W 3 mi (L). 2015 rates: $10 to $28. (208)382-6544

LAKE CASCADE/SUGARLOAF (State Pk) From town, N 7 mi on US-55 (L). 2015 rates: $12 to $24. (208)382-4258

LAKE CASCADE/VAN WYCK (State Pk) From Jct of SR-55 & Old State Hwy, W 2 mi on Old State Hwy (E). NOTE: Entrance fee required & 32' RV LENGTH MAXIMUM. Pit toilets. 2015 rates: $10.60 to $15.60. May 1 to Oct 20. (208)382-6544

LAKE CASCADE/WEST MOUNTAIN (State Pk) From town, N 11 mi on US-55, W 1.5 mi W Roseberry Rd., SW 2.6 mi Rainbow Point Rd., S W. Mountain Rd. 2.5 mi. 2015 rates: $12 to $26. May 24 to Dec 31. (208)382-6544

WATER'S EDGE RV RESORT **Ratings: 7.5/7.5/7** (Campground) 2015 rates: $30. May 1 to Oct 15. (800)574-2038 620 N Main St, Cascade, ID 83611

CHALLIS — D3 *Custer*

CHALLIS GOLF COURSE RV PARK
Ratings: 5.5/9.5★/7.5 (RV Park) From Jct US 93 & Hwy 75: Go 2-1/4 mi N on US 93, then 1-1/4 mi W on Main (becomes Garden Creek Rd), then 1/8 mi S on Emily Ln (R). Elev 5355 ft. **FAC:** All weather rds. 30 Avail: 30 all weather, 24 pull-thrus (25 x 60), back-ins (40 x 40), 30 full hkups (30/50 amps), WiFi, tent sites, laundry. **REC:** pond, fishing, golf, rec open to public. Pets OK. Partial handicap access. Big rig sites, 2015 rates: $33.02. Apr 15 to Oct 15.
(208)390-9568 Lat: 44.50391, Lon: -114.24709
210 Golf Club Lane, Challis, ID 83226
relax@golfcourserv.com
www.golfcourserv.com
See ad this page, 443.

CHALLIS HOT SPRINGS & RV PARK **Ratings: 6.5/6.5/7** (Campground) 2015 rates: $35.19. (208)879-4442 5025 Hot Springs Rd, Challis, ID 83226

PIONEER MOTEL & RV PARK **Ratings: 5/7.5★/6** (Campground) 2015 rates: $29 to $34. (208)879-6791 220 Hwy 93 S, Challis, ID 83226

ROUND VALLEY RV PARK **Ratings: 6/7.5/5.5** (RV Park) 2015 rates: $36. Mar 1 to Nov 30. (208)879-2393 211 Ramshorn Ln, Challis, ID 83226

CLARK FORK — A2 *Bonner*

RIVER LAKE RV PARK **Ratings: 5.5/8.5★/7** (Campground) 2015 rates: $35. May 1 to Oct 1. (208)266-1115 145 N River Lake Dr, Clark Fork, ID 83811

COEUR D'ALENE — B1 *Kootenai*

COEUR D'ALENE See also Athol, Pinehurst & Post Falls.

ALPINE COUNTRY RV PARK
Ratings: 6/9★/7.5 (RV Park) From Jct US 95 & I-90: Go 10 mi N on US-95 (MP 439.6) (R). **FAC:** Paved/gravel rds. 36 gravel, 25 pull-thrus (42 x 63), back-ins (40 x 90), 25 full hkups, 11 W, 11 E (30/50 amps), WiFi, dump, laundry, groc, LP gas, firewood. **REC.** Pets OK. Partial handicap access, no tents. Big rig sites, 14 day max stay, 2015 rates: $34.95. Apr 15 to Oct 15. ATM.
(208)772-4305 Lat: 47.82968, Lon: -116.77953
17568 N Hwy 95, Hayden Lake, ID 83835
alpine@imaxmail.net
www.nirvpark.com
See ad this page, 443.

BLACKWELL ISLAND RV RESORT **Ratings: 8.5/10★/8.5** (RV Park) 2015 rates: $39.50 to $58.48. Apr 1 to Oct 15. (888)571-2900 800 S Marina Dr, Coeur d'alene, ID 83814

RIVER WALK RV PARK **Ratings: 6/8/5.5** (RV Park) 2015 rates: $40. (208)765-5943 1214 Mill Ave, Coeur D'alene, ID 83814

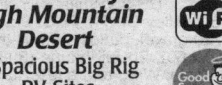

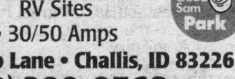

WOLF LODGE CAMPGROUND
Ratings: 7.5/7/8.5 (Campground) From Jct I-90 & Hwy 97 (exit 22): Go 1/8 mi N on Hwy 97, then 1-1/2 mi E on Frontage Rd (L). **FAC:** Gravel rds. (53 spaces). 50 Avail: 12 gravel, 38 grass, 23 pull-thrus (23 x 70), back-ins (30 x 40), 27 full hkups, 23 W, 23 E (30/50 amps), seasonal sites, WiFi, tent

COEUR D'ALENE (CONT)

WOLF LODGE CAMPGROUND (CONT)
sites, rentals, dump, laundry, firewood. **REC:** Wolf Lodge Creek: fishing, shuffleboard, playground. Pets OK. Eco-friendly, 2015 rates: $32 to $40. Disc: military. May 15 to Sep 30.
(866)664-2812 Lat: 47.63113, Lon: -116.61620
12329 E Frontage Rd, Coeur D'alene, ID 83814
info@wolflodgecampground.com
www.wolflodgecampground.com
See ad pages 447, 443.

COOLIN — A1 *Bonner*

INDIAN CREEK UNIT (State Pk) From Jct of SR-57 & Coolin Rd, NE 5.4 mi on Coolin Rd to East Shore Rd, N 11.5 mi (E). Pit toilets. 2015 rates: $18. (208)443-2200

PRIEST LAKE/LIONHEAD CAMPING UNIT (State Pk) From jct US 2 & Hwy 57: Go 22-1/2 mi N on Hwy 57, then 5 mi NE on Dickensheet Rd to Coolin, then 23 mi N on East Shore Rd. Pit toilets. 2015 rates: $12. (208)443-2200

Relax on white sandy beaches under palm fronds or get dancing at Mardi Gras; we've put the Spotlight on North America's most popular destinations. Turn to the Spotlight articles in our State and Province sections to learn more.

DECLO — F3 *Cassia*

VILLAGE OF TREES RV RESORT
Ratings: 8.5/9★/8.5 (Campground) From Jct I-84 & Rupert-Declo Rd (exit 216): Go 1/4 mi N on Rupert-Declo Rd (L). Elev 4200 ft. **FAC:** All weather rds. (84 spaces). Avail: 54 all weather, 54 pull-thrus (30 x 70), 54 full hkups (30/50 amps), seasonal sites, cable, WiFi, tent sites, rentals, dump, laundry, groc, LP gas, firewood, restaurant. **REC:** heated pool, Snake River: fishing, playground. Pet restrict(B). Partial handicap access. Big rig sites, eco-friendly, 2015 rates: $32. Disc: AAA, military. ATM.
AAA Approved
(208)654-2133 Lat: 42.57195, Lon: -113.62503
274 Hwy 25, Declo, ID 83323
nancy@villageoftreesrvresort.com
www.villageoftreesrvresort.com
See ad this page, 443.

Travel Services

TRAVEL STOP 216 C-STORE & RESTAURANT
The Village of Trees RV Resort Travel Stop 216 offers 24 hour Phillips 66 gas & diesel, propane, convenience store, groceries, gift shop, RV supplies and full service grill. Elev 4200 ft. **SERVICES:** restaurant, restrooms. RV storage. RV supplies, LP, dump, emergency parking, RV accessible. Hours: 6 am - 9 pm. ATM.
(208)654-2133 Lat: 42.57195, Lon: -113.62503
274 Hwy 25, Declo, ID 83323
nancy@villageoftreesrvresort.com
www.villageoftreesrvresort.com
See ad this page.

We rate what RVers consider important.

DONNELLY — D2 *Valley*

CHALET RV PARK
Ratings: 7.5/9★/8.5 (Campground) From Donnelly (city center): Go 1/2 mi S on Hwy 55 (L) (MP 131). Elev 4860 ft.

IN THE HEART OF MOUNTAIN RECREATION
This charming park is the perfect getaway to one of Idaho's best recreation areas. Chalet RV Park offers a beautiful wooded setting with full hookups and all the comfort of home. Come and explore or rest, relax and renew!

FAC: Gravel rds. 76 gravel, patios, 12 pull-thrus (22 x 48), back-ins (22 x 42), 76 full hkups (30/50 amps), cable, WiFi, tent sites, dump, laundry. **REC:** Boulder Creek: fishing. Pet restrict(B). 2015 rates: $32. Disc: AAA. May 1 to Oct 1.
AAA Approved
(208)325-8223 Lat: 44.72797, Lon: -116.07477
418 S Hwy 55 (Main St), Donnelly, ID 83615
chalet@grapevine7.com
www.g7rvresorts.com
See ad this page, 443.

DOWNEY — F4 *Bannock*

DOWNATA HOT SPRINGS CAMPGROUND
Ratings: 5/7/7 (Campground) From Jct I-15 & Hwy 40 (Exit 31): Go 2-1/2 mi E on Hwy 40, then 4 mi SE on Hwy 91 (R). Elev 4700 ft. **FAC:** Gravel rds. 49 gravel, 10 pull-thrus (23 x 72), back-ins (20 x 36), 28 W, 44 E (30/50 amps), WiFi, tent sites, rentals, showers $, laundry, fire rings, firewood, restaurant. **REC:** heated pool $, whirlpool, playground, rec open to public. Pet restrict(B). Partial handicap access. 2015 rates: $20 to $30.
AAA Approved
(208)897-5736 Lat: 42.38853, Lon: -112.08860
25900 S Downata Rd, Downey, ID 83234
info@downatahotsprings.com
www.downatahotsprings.com

FEATHERVILLE — E2 *Elmore*

SAWTOOTH NF BAUMGARTNER CAMPGROUND (Natl Forest) From town: Go 10 mi E on Forest Road. Pit toilets. 2015 rates: $10 to $20. May 16 to Oct 15. (208)764-3202

FORT HALL — F4 *Bingham*

BUFFALO MEADOWS RV PARK
Ratings: 7.5/9.5★/7 (RV Park) From Jct I-15 & Simplot Rd (exit 80): Go 1/4 mi W on Simplot Rd (R) (Behind casino). Elev 4525 ft. **FAC:** Paved rds. 37 paved, 37 pull-thrus (23 x 60), 37 full hkups (30/50 amps), WiFi, tent sites, laundry, groc, restaurant. **REC:** rec open to public. Pets OK. Partial handicap access. 2015 rates: $27. ATM.
(208)237-8778 Lat: 43.02524, Lon: -112.41444
I-15, Exit 80, Simplot Rd, Fort Hall, ID 83203
www.shobangaming.com
See ad opposite page.

Things to See and Do

FORT HALL CASINO Multi-Denominational Gaming Machines, Bingo, Live Entertainment, Monthly Promotions. Elev 4525 ft. partial handicap access. RV accessible. Restrooms, food. Hours: 24 Hrs/Day. ATM.
(208)237-8778 Lat: 43.02242, Lon: -112.41285
I-15 Exit 80/Simplot Rd, Fort Hall, ID 83203
www.shobangaming.com
See ad opposite page.

FRUITLAND — E1 *Payette*

NEAT RETREAT RV PARK
Ratings: 8/9.5★/8.5 (RV Park) From Jct I-84 & US-30/E Idaho Ave (exit 376-B) CAUTION: Do not take exit 376-A: Go 1-1/4 mi E on US 30 to US-95/Whitley Dr, then go 3/4 mi N on US-95/Whitley Dr (R). **FAC:** Paved rds. (80 spaces). Avail: 20 gravel, patios, 10 pull-thrus (30 x 75), back-ins (30 x 60), 20 full hkups (30/50 amps), seasonal sites, cable, WiFi, tent sites, dump, laundry, LP gas. **REC.** Pet restrict(B/Q). Partial handicap access. Big rig sites, eco-friendly, 2015 rates: $34.75 to $38.61. Disc: AAA, military.
AAA Approved
(208)452-4324 Lat: 44.03567, Lon: -116.92549
2700 Hwy 95, Fruitland, ID 83619
reserve@neatretreatrvpark.com
www.neatretreatrvpark.com
See ad pages 450, 443.

ID

GLENNS FERRY — F2 *Elmore, Gooding*

CARMELA RV PARK **Ratings: 5/NA/6.5** (RV Park) 2015 rates: $25. (208)366-2313 1294 W Madison Ave, Glenns Ferry, ID 83623

THREE ISLAND CROSSING (State Pk) From Jct of I-84 & Exit 121 (W-bnd) or Exit 120 (E-bnd), exit rd to Commercial (in center of town), S 0.75 mi to Madison Ave, W 1.0 mi (L). 2015 rates: $22 to $43. (208)366-2394

TRAIL BREAK RV PARK & CAMPGROUND
Ratings: 6/9★/7.5 (Campground) From Jct I-84 & I-84 Bus / East 1st Ave (Exit 121): Go 1/4 mi S on East 1st Ave, then 1 mi W on Old Hwy 30 (R). Elev 2569 ft. **FAC:** Gravel rds. 28 gravel, 8 pull-thrus (27 x 65), back-ins (19 x 36), 28 full hkups (30/50 amps), cable, WiFi, tent sites, laundry, fire rings, firewood. **REC.** Pets OK. Eco-friendly, 2015 rates: $30. Disc: AAA, military.
(208)366-7745 Lat: 42.95657, Lon: -115.30774
432 N Bannock St, Box A, Glenns Ferry, ID 83623
mr.huskisson@yahoo.com
www.trailbreakrvpark.com

GRANGEVILLE — C2 *Idaho*

BEAR DEN RV RESORT
Ratings: 8/9.5★/9 (Campground) From Jct US 95 & SR 13: Go 3/4 mi S on US 95 (MP 239) to Fish Hatchery Rd, then 1/8 mi E on Fish Hatchery Rd (R). Elev 3410 ft. **FAC:** Gravel rds. 34 gravel, 21 pull-thrus (26 x 78), back-ins (26 x 78), 34 full hkups (30/50 amps), WiFi, tent sites, rentals, dump, laundry, LP gas, firewood. **REC:** pond, playground. Pet restrict(B/Q). Partial handicap access. Big rig sites, eco-friendly, 2015 rates: $26.50 to $29.50. Disc: AAA, military.
AAA Approved
(208)983-0140 Lat: 45.92385, Lon: -116.14672
20 Fish Hatchery Rd, Grangeville, ID 83530
info@beardenrv.com
www.beardenrv.com
See ad this page, 443.

HAGERMAN — F2 *Gooding*

HAGERMAN RV VILLAGE
Ratings: 8/9/9 (RV Park) From Jct I-84 & US 26 (exit 141) : Go 1/4 mi W on US 26, then 8 mi S on US 30 (R). Elev 2975 ft. **FAC:** Gravel rds. (72 spaces). Avail: 57 gravel, 57 pull-thrus (30 x 75), 57 full hkups (30/50 amps), seasonal sites, WiFi, tent sites, rentals, laundry, LP gas, fire rings. **REC:** playground. Pet restrict(B/Q). Partial handicap access. Big rig sites, eco-friendly, 2015 rates: $30. Disc: military.
(208)837-4906 Lat: 42.82347, Lon: -114.89572
18049 Hwy 30, Hagerman, ID 83332
hagermanrvvillage@yahoo.com
www.hagermanrvvillage.com
See ad this page, 443.

HIGH ADVENTURE RIVER TOURS & RV PARK **Ratings: 4.5/7/8** (Campground) 2015 rates: $36 to $40. (208)837-9005 1211 E 2350 S, Hagerman, ID 83332

THOUSAND SPRINGS RESORT **Ratings: 6/4.5/7.5** (Campground) 2015 rates: $35. (208)837-4987 18734 Hwy 30, Hagerman, ID 83332

HARRISON — B1 *Kootenai*

CITY OF HARRISON CAMPGROUND (Public) In town, S on US-97, follow signs (R). 2015 rates: $35 to $42. May 15 to Sep 15. (208)689-3212

HEYBURN — F3 *Minidoka*

HEYBURN RIVERSIDE RV PARK
Ratings: 5.5/8/9 (Public) From Jct I-84 & Hwy 30 (exit 211): Go 2 mi S on Hwy 30, then 1/4 mi E on 7th St (R). Elev 4150 ft. **FAC:** Paved/gravel rds. (29 spaces). 22 Avail: 2 paved, 20 gravel, patios, 9 pull-thrus (51 x 64), back-ins (51 x 45), 22 full hkups (30/50 amps), WiFi, tent sites. **REC:** Snake River: swim, fishing, rec open to public. Pets OK. Partial handicap access. Big rig sites, 2015 rates: $22 to $23. Disc: military. Mar 1 to Nov 30. No CC.
(208)431-2977 Lat: 42.54665, Lon: -113.75904
1177 7th St, Heyburn, ID 83336
heyburnparks@pmt.org
www.heyburnidaho.org
See ad pages 455, 443.

HOMEDALE — E1 *Owyhee*

SNAKE RIVER RV RESORT **Ratings: 6/8/7.5** (Campground) 2015 rates: $28. (208)337-3744 4030 River Resort Dr, Homedale, ID 83628

HOPE — A2 *Bonner*

BEYOND HOPE RESORT **Ratings: 5.5/6/7** (Campground) 2015 rates: $45. May 15 to Sep 30. (208)264-5251 1267 Peninsula Rd, Hope, ID 83836

ISLAND VIEW RV PARK **Ratings: 5.5/NA/7.5** (Campground) 2015 rates: $45. May 1 to Sep 30. (208)264-5509 1767 Peninsula Rd, Hope, ID 83836

TRESTLE CREEK RV PARK **Ratings: 3.5/NA/6** (Campground) 2015 rates: $36. Apr 1 to Nov 30. (208)264-5894 42303 Hwy 200, Hope, ID 83836

IDAHO FALLS — E4 *Bonneville*

KELLY ISLAND (Public) From town, NE 23 mi on Hwy 26 (L) NOTE: 40' RV LENGTH MAXIMUM. Pit toilets. 2015 rates: $10 to $20. May 15 to Sep 15. (208)589-2561

Remember, ratings are based on ALL available facilities.

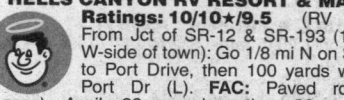

IDAHO FALLS (CONT)

SNAKE RIVER RV PARK AND CAMPGROUND
Ratings: 9/8.5/8.5 (Campground) From Jct I-15 (Exit 119) & US 20 (Grandview Dr): Go 1/8 mi E on US 20 (Grandview Dr) to Lindsay Blvd exit, then 1/2 mi N on Lindsay Blvd (R). Elev 4710 ft. **FAC:** Paved/gravel rds. 110 Avail: 90 gravel, 20 grass, 49 pull-thrus (24 x 72), back-ins (20 x 38), some side by side hkups, 80 full hkups, 30 W, 30 E (30/50 amps), WiFi, tent sites, rentals, dump, laundry, groc, LP gas, fire rings, firewood. **REC:** heated pool, whirlpool, playground. Pets OK. Big rig sites, 2015 rates: $36 to $39.50. Disc: military.
(208)523-3362 Lat: 43.50878, Lon: -112.05312
1440 Lindsay Blvd, Idaho Falls, ID 83402
snakeriverrvpark@hotmail.com
www.snakeriverrvpark.net
See ad opposite page, 443.

SUNNYSIDE ACRES PARK & MHP **Ratings: 6/8/6** (RV Area in MHP) 2015 rates: $32. (208)523-8403 905 W Sunnyside Rd, Idaho Falls, ID 83402

IRWIN — E5 *Bonneville*

HUSKEY'S RESORT **Ratings: 5/7.5/6.5** (Campground) 2015 rates: $27.77 to $32. May 1 to Oct 31. (208)483-3535 3781 Swan Valley Hwy, Irwin, ID 83428

ISLAND PARK — D5 *Fremont*

BUFFALO RUN RV PARK & CABINS Ratings: 6/7.5/7 (Campground) From Jct Hwy 87 & US 20: Go 19 mi S on US 20 (MP 383.5) (L). Elev 6250 ft. **FAC:** Gravel rds. (28 spaces). Avail: 20 gravel, 20 pull-thrus (30 x 65), 20 W, 20 E (30/50 amps), seasonal sites, WiFi, rentals, dump, laundry, fire rings. **REC:** Henry's Fork of Snake River: fishing, rec open to public. Pets OK. No tents. Eco-friendly, 2015 rates: $34. May 15 to Oct 15.
(208)558-7112 Lat: 44.37352, Lon: -111.39545
3402 N Hwy 20, Island Park, ID 83429
buffalorun1@msn.com
www.buffaloruncampground.com

REDROCK RV AND CAMPING PARK
Ratings: 8.5/10★/10 (RV Park) From Jct US 20 and Red Rock Rd (MP 398): Go 5 mi W on Red Rock Rd (R). Elev 6600 ft.

ESCAPE THE CROWDS & STAY AT REDROCK
In just 20 minutes, you'll leave the crowds behind without losing the beauty you enjoy in The Park! Discover why we're the #1 Rated Good Sam Park anywhere around Yellowstone. Make your Reservation request today online!

FAC: Paved/gravel rds. 54 gravel, 46 pull-thrus (32 x 60), back-ins (45 x 42), 54 full hkups (30/50 amps), WiFi, tent sites, dump, laundry, groc, fire rings, firewood, controlled access. **REC:** Henry's Lake: swim, fishing, playground, rec open to public. Pet restrict(B). Partial handicap access. Big rig sites, eco-friendly, 2015 rates: $50 to $54. May 1 to Sep 25.
(800)473-3762 Lat: 44.60362, Lon: -111.41644
3707 Red Rock Rd, Island Park, ID 83429
office@redrockrvpark.com
www.redrockrvpark.com
See ad pages 722, 1349, 443.

SAWTELLE MOUNTAIN RESORT
Ratings: 8/8/8 (Campground) From Jct US 20 & Sawtelle Peak Rd (MP 394.5): Go 1/8 mi W on Sawtelle Peak Rd (R). Elev 6470 ft. **FAC:** Paved rds. (60 spaces). Avail: 37 gravel, 23 pull-thrus (18 x 65), back-ins (15 x 45), 37 full hkups (30/50 amps), seasonal sites, WiFi Hotspot, tent sites, rentals, laundry, fire rings, firewood. **REC:** heated pool, whirlpool, playground, rec open to public. Pets OK. Partial handicap access. 2015 rates: $36. Disc: AAA, military. May 15 to Oct 15.
AAA Approved
(208)558-9366 Lat: 44.52291, Lon: -111.32917
4133 Quakie Ln, Island Park, ID 83429
reservations@sawtellemountainresort.com
www.sawtellemountainresort.com
See ad this page, 443.

Find it Fast! Use our alphabetized index of campgrounds and parks.

KAMIAH — C2 *Idaho*

KAMIAH/CLEARWATER VALLEY KOA **Ratings: 7/5.5/6** (Campground) 2015 rates: $29.89 to $45.89. (208)935-2556 4243 Hwy 12, Kamiah, ID 83536

LONG CAMP RV PARK
Ratings: 7/8.5★/9 (Campground) From Jct SR 13 & US 12 (W of Kooskia): Go 6 mi NW on US 12 (MP 68) (L). **FAC:** Gravel rds. (22 spaces). 20 Avail: 16 gravel, 4 grass, patios, 1 pull-thrus (24 x 60), back-ins (24 x 45), some side by side hkups, 20 full hkups (30/50 amps), seasonal sites, WiFi, tent sites, rentals, laundry, fire rings, firewood. **REC:** Middle Fork of the Clearwater River: swim, fishing. Pets OK. Big rig sites, eco-friendly, 2015 rates: $23.50 to $33.50. No CC.
(208)935-7922 Lat: 46.21693, Lon: -116.00669
4192 Hwy 12, Kamiah, ID 83536
longcamprvpark@gmail.com
www.longcamprvpark.com
See ad this page.

KELLOGG — B2 *Shoshone*

CRYSTAL GOLD MINE & RV PARK
Ratings: 6/NA/7.5 (Campground) From Jct I-90 & Division St (exit 51): Go 1/8 mi N on Division St, then 1-1/4 mi E on Cameron Ave/Silver Valley Rd (L). **FAC:** Paved/gravel rds. (21 spaces). Avail: 14 paved, 2 pull-thrus (27 x 90), back-ins (27 x 66), accepts self-contain units only, 14 full hkups (30/50 amps), seasonal sites, dump, fire rings, firewood. **REC:** Montgomery Creek: rec open to public. Pets OK. No tents. Eco-friendly, 2015 rates: $27. Disc: AAA, military.
(208)783-4653 Lat: 47.53835, Lon: -116.09069
51931 Silver Valley Rd., Kellogg, ID 83837
crystalgoldmine1881@gmail.com
www.goldmine-idaho.com

LAVA HOT SPRINGS — F4 *Bannock, Carribou*

LAVA HOT SPRINGS KOA **Ratings: 6/9/7** (Campground) 2015 rates: $31.95 to $113.95. Mar 1 to Oct 31. (208)776-5295 100 Bristol Park Lane, Lava Hot Springs, ID 83246

MARYS PLACE RV CAMPGROUND **Ratings: 6/7.5/7.5** (Campground) 2015 rates: $30 to $49. May 15 to Sep 7. (208)776-5026 300 Bristol Park Lane, Lava Hot Springs, ID 83246

LEWISTON — C1 *Nez Perce*

LEWISTON See also Lewiston; Clarkston, WA, Pullman, WA.

CLEARWATER RIVER CASINO & RV PARK **Ratings: 5.5/8.5/5.5** (Campground) 2015 rates: $10 to $27. Jun 1 to Oct 31. (208)298-1400 17500 Nez Perce Rd, Lewiston, ID 83501

Do you know how to read each part of a listing? Check the How to Use This Campground Guide in the front.

HELLS CANYON RV RESORT & MARINA
Ratings: 10/10★/9.5 (RV Park) From Jct of SR-12 & SR-193 (15th St, W-side of town): Go 1/8 mi N on SR-193 to Port Drive, then 100 yards west on Port Dr (L). **FAC:** Paved rds. (48 spaces). Avail: 38 paved, patios, 38 pull-thrus (32 x 64), 38 full hkups (30/50 amps), seasonal sites, WiFi, laundry, groc. **REC:** heated pool, whirlpool, Snake River: fishing, marina. Pets OK. Partial handicap access, no tents. Big rig sites, 2015 rates: $33.39 to $44.43. Disc: AAA, military.
(509)758-6963 Lat: 46.420830, Lon: -117.069998
1550 Port Drive, Clarkston, WA 99403
hellscanyonrvpark@gmail.com
www.hellscanyon.net
See primary listing at Clarkston, WA and ad page 1265 (Spotlight Hells Canyon).

HELLS GATE (State Pk) From Jct of US-12 & Snake River Ave, S 3.7 mi on Snake River Ave. 2015 rates: $12 to $29. (208)799-5015

Things to See and Do

VISIT LEWIS CLARK VALLEY Visitor Information Center for Lewiston & Hells Canyon area. Partial handicap access. RV accessible. Restrooms. Hours: 11am to 4pm. No CC.
(509)758-7489 Lat: 46.41806, Lon: -117.01292
415 Main St, Lewiston, ID 83501
info@visitlcvalley.com
www.visitlcvalley.com
See ad page 1244 (Welcome Section).

MACKAY — E3 *Custer*

JOSEPH T. FALLINI CAMPGROUND (FORMERLY MACKAY RESERVOIR BLM) (Public) From town, N 6 mi on US-93 (L). Pit toilets. 2015 rates: $14 to $16. (208)879-6200

MACKS INN — D5 *Fremont*

HENRY'S LAKE (State Pk) From Jct of US-20 & SR-87, S 1.2 mi on US-20 to Henry Lake Rd (MP 401), W 2 mi (E). 2015 rates: $20 to $29. (888)922-6743

ID

MCCALL — D2 *Valley*

MCCALL CAMPGROUND & RV PARK **Ratings: 7/9.5★/6** (Campground) 2015 rates: $35. Apr 1 to Oct 1. (208)634-5165 190 Krahn Ln, Mccall, ID 83638

MCCALL RV RESORT
Ratings: 9.5/10★/10 (RV Resort) From Jct of Hwy 55 (East Lake St) & Hwy 55 (3rd St): Go 1-1/2 mi S on Hwy 55 to Deinhard Ln, then 1/2 mi NW on Deinhard Ln to Mission St, then 1/4 mi S on Mission St to Scott St, then 1/8 mi W on Scott St (E). Elev 5067 ft.

TRULY THE PINNACLE OF IDAHO RVING
This luxurious mountain setting is the perfect retreat & ideal summer destination for fishing, hiking, rafting & sightseeing all at your back door. Enjoy peace & serenity at one of the highest rated parks in Northwest Idaho.

FAC: Paved rds. (105 spaces). 90 Avail: 32 paved, 58 gravel, patios, 55 pull-thrus (45 x 75), back-ins (30 x 70), 90 full hkups (30/50 amps), seasonal sites, cable, WiFi, rentals, dump, laundry, LP gas. **REC:** heated pool, whirlpool, North Fork of Payette River: fishing, playground, rec open to public. Pets OK. Partial handicap access, no tents. Big rig sites,

RV Park ratings you can rely on!

MCCALL (CONT)

MCCALL RV RESORT (CONT)
eco-friendly, 2015 rates: $39 to $47. Disc: AAA, military. ATM.
AAA Approved
(208)634-5646 Lat: 44.89600, Lon: -116.10629
200 Scott St, Mccall, ID 83638
mccallrvresort@g7rvresorts.com
www.g7rvresorts.com
See ad this page, 443.

➔ PONDEROSA (State Pk) From Jct of SR-55 & 3rd/Railroad St, follow signs (E). 2015 rates: $24 to $31. (208)634-2164

MERIDIAN — E1 *Ada*

← BOISE MERIDIAN KOA RV RESORT **Ratings: 9.5/10★/9** (Campground) 2015 rates: $36.97 to $39.89. (866)988-7003 184 W Pennwood, Meridian, ID 83642

Travel Services

CAMPING WORLD OF MERIDIAN/BOISE As the nation's largest retailer of RV supplies, accessories, services and new and used RVs, Camping World is committed to making your total RV experience better. RV Accessories: (208)888-4241. **SERVICES:** RV, tire, RV appliance, MH mechanical, staffed RV wash, restrooms, RV Sales. RV supplies, LP, emergency parking, RV accessible. waiting room. Hours: 8:00 - 6:00.
(888)717-5294 Lat: 43.590126, Lon: -116.412428
1580 W Overland Road, Meridian, ID 83642
www.campingworld.com

MOUNTAIN HOME — E2 *Elmore*

FORT RUNNING BEAR RV RESORT **Ratings: 6.5/5.5/6** (Campground) 2015 rates: $30. May 1 to Sep 30. (208)653-2494 ctc Deluxe #784/25094 Little Camas Reservoir Rd, Mountain Home, ID 83647

MOUNTAIN HOME KOA **Ratings: 7/9/6** (Campground) 2015 rates: $35. (208)587-5111 220 E Tenth North St, Mountain Home, ID 83647

Find it fast! To locate a town on a map, follow these easy instructions: Look for the map grid code after the town heading in the listing section and match it to the letters and numbers on the map borders. Draw a line horizontally from the letter and vertically from the number. You'll find the town near the intersection of the two lines.

➔ **MOUNTAIN HOME RV PARK**
Ratings: 10/10★/9.5 (RV Park) From Jct I-84 & Hwy 51/American Legion Blvd (Exit 95): Go 1/2 mi S on Hwy 51/American Legion Blvd (L). Elev 3200 ft.

THE NEWEST G7 RV RESORTS PARK
Beautifully landscaped quiet, spacious park! Enjoy 90 ft concrete pull-thrus w/50/100 amps, Free WIFI, cable TV & lush green lawns. Minutes from golf, hunting, fishing, bird watching, water sports and winter sports too!

FAC: Paved rds. (93 spaces). Avail: 68 paved, patios, 44 pull-thrus (32 x 90), back-ins (30 x 35), 68 full hkups (30/50 amps), seasonal sites, cable, WiFi, dump, laundry, LP gas. **REC:** heated pool, whirlpool, playground. Pet restrict(B). Partial handicap access, no tents. Big rig sites, eco-friendly, 2015 rates: $35. Disc: AAA, military.
AAA Approved
(208)580-1211 Lat: 43.13105, Lon: -115.67274
2295 American Legion Blvd, Mountain Home, ID 83647
mountainhome@g7rvresorts.com
www.g7rvresorts.com
See ad pages 444, 443.

NAMPA — E1 *Canyon, Owyhee*

GARRITY RV PARK **Ratings: 7/9/5.5** (Campground) 2015 rates: $24. (877)442-9090 3515 Garrity Blvd, Nampa, ID 83687

LEAH'S LANDING
Ratings: 9/NA/6.5 (RV Park) From Jct I-84 & N Franklin Blvd (exit 36): Go 1/8 mi S on N Franklin Blvd to 3rd Ave, then 1/2 mi W on 3rd Ave to 8th St/Madison Ave, then 1/2 mi NW on 8th St/Madison Ave (E). Elev 2560 ft. **FAC:** Paved rds. (90 spaces). Avail: 45 paved, patios, back-ins (30 x 60), accepts self-contain units only, 45 full hkups (30/50 amps), seasonal sites, cable, WiFi, restrooms only, laundry. **REC:** heated pool, whirlpool. Pets OK. Partial handicap access, no tents. Age restrict may apply, big rig sites, 2015 rates: $33.74. No CC.
(208)867-7393 Lat: 43.59913, Lon: -116.56379
1606 North Irene Dr, Nampa, ID 83687
kerri.snowqueen@gmail.com
www.leahslanding.net
See ad this page.

MASON CREEK RV PARK **Ratings: 5.5/7.5/6.5** (Campground) 2015 rates: $26.10. (208)465-7199 807 North Franklin Blvd, Nampa, ID 83687

Say you saw it in our Guide!

NORTH FORK — D3 *Lemhi*

JOSEPHINE'S PIZZA AND RV PARK **Ratings: 5.5/8.5★/8** (Campground) 2015 rates: $20. May 1 to Nov 30. (208)865-2476 2570 Hwy 93 N, North Fork, ID 83466

THE VILLAGE AT NORTH FORK **Ratings: 5.5/9★/7.5** (Campground) 2015 rates: $25 to $27. (208)865-7001 2046 Hwy 93 N, North Fork, ID 83466

WAGONHAMMER RV & CAMPGROUND
Ratings: 8/10★/10 (RV Park) S-bnd: From US 93 (in North Fork): Go 2 mi S on Hwy 93 (R) (MP 324) or N-bnd: From US 93 & Hwy 28 (in Salmon): Go 18 mi N on Hwy 93 (L) (MP 324). Elev 3650 ft. **FAC:** Gravel rds. 49 Avail: 19 gravel, 30 grass, 15 pull-thrus (25 x 80), back-ins (35 x 80), 12 full hkups, 37 W, 37 E (30/50 amps), WiFi, tent sites, rentals, dump, laundry, fire rings, firewood. **REC:** Salmon River: swim, fishing. Pets OK. Partial handicap access. Big rig sites, eco-friendly, 2015 rates: $29 to $32. Apr 25 to Nov 10.
(208)865-2477 Lat: 45.38465, Lon: -113.96165
1826 Hwy 93 N, North Fork, ID 83466
wagonhammerrv@gmail.com
www.wagonhammercampground.com
See ad pages 454, 443.

OLDTOWN — A1 *Bonner*

➔ ALBENI COVE (Public Corps) From town, E 3 mi on 4th St (E). 2015 rates: $20. May 9 to Sep 12. (208)437-3133

OROFINO — C2 *Clearwater*

← **CLEARWATER CROSSING RV PARK**
Ratings: 8.5/9.5★/8 (Campground) From Jct US 12 & Hwy 7 (Michigan Ave): Go 1/8 mi N on Hwy 7 (Michigan Ave) to Riverfront Rd, then 1/16 mi NW on Hwy 7 (Riverfront Rd) (L) Note: Entry is through Hardware store parking lot. **FAC:** Paved rds. (50 spaces). 44 Avail: 5 paved, 39 gravel, patios, 5 pull-thrus (24 x 50), back-ins (24 x 40), 44 full hkups (30/50 amps), seasonal sites, cable, WiFi, tent sites, laundry. **REC:** Clearwater River: swim, fishing. Pets OK. Partial handicap access. 2015 rates: $25 to $33.33.
(208)476-4800 Lat: 46.47999, Lon: -116.25775
500 Riverfront Rd, Orofino, ID 83544
rv@clearwatercrossingrvpark.com
www.clearwatercrossingrvpark.com

DENT ACRES (COE - DWORSHAK RESERVOIR) (Public Corps) From jct US-12 & Hwy-7: Go 1 block N (across bridge) & 1 block W on Hwy-7, then 17 mi N on paved & gravel county road, then 2 mi W on access road. 2015 rates: $10 to $18. Apr 11 to Dec 14. (208)476-1255

OROFINO (CONT)

DWORSHAK/FREEMAN CREEK CAMPGROUND (State Pk) From town: Go 14 mi NW on Hwy 7 to Cavendish, then 10 mi E on county road. Follow signs. 2015 rates: $12 to $24. (208)476-5994

OSBURN — B2 *Shoshone*

BLUE ANCHOR RV PARK
Ratings: 6.5/9.5★/8.5 (Campground) From Jct I-90 & N Third St (exit 57, Osburn): Go 1/4 mi S on N Third St to W Mullan Ave, then go 1/2 mi W on W Mullan Ave (R). Elev 2500 ft. **FAC:** Paved rds. 45 gravel, 26 pull-thrus (27 x 60), back-ins (20 x 40), 45 full hkups (30/50 amps), cable, WiFi, tent sites, laundry. **REC.** Pets OK. Big rig sites, eco-friendly, 2015 rates: $30. Disc: military. Apr 15 to Oct 15.
(208)752-3443 Lat: 47.50809, Lon: -116.00578
300 W Mullan Ave, Osburn, ID 83849
www.blueanchorrv.com
See ad opposite page, 443.

PALISADES — E5 *Bonneville*

PALISADES CABINS & RV **Ratings: 4/7/7.5** (Campground) 2015 rates: $26. May 1 to Oct 1. (208)351-0511 3804 Swan Valley Hwy, Irwin, ID 83428

PICABO — E3 *Blaine*

PICABO RV PARK
Ratings: 5.5/9★/7 (Campground) From Jct of US 26/US 93 & US 20: Go 7 mi W on US 20 (L). Elev 4839 ft. **FAC:** Gravel rds. 17 gravel, 5 pull-thrus (39 x 66), back-ins (39 x 50), 17 W, 17 E (30/50 amps), WiFi, dump, groc, LP gas, fire rings, firewood. **REC:** Silver Creek: fishing, rec open to public. Pets OK. 2015 rates: $25 to $40.
(208)309-3349 Lat: 43.30822, Lon: -114.06934
18915 Hwy 20, Picabo, ID 83348
info@picaboangler.com
www.picaborvpark.com

PINEHURST — B2 *Shoshone*

BY THE WAY CAMPGROUND **Ratings: 6/6.5/6** (Campground) 2015 rates: $25. (208)682-3311 907 N Division St, Pinehurst, ID 83850

PLUMMER — B1 *Benewah*

HEYBURN (State Pk) From Jct of US-95 & SR-5, E 6 mi on SR-5 (L). 2015 rates: $12 to $29. (208)686-1308

POCATELLO — F4 *Bannock*

POCATELLO See also Fort Hall & Lava Hot Spring.

BANNOCK COUNTY EVENT CENTER (Public) From jct I-15 & Bus 15 / Pocatello Creek Rd (exit 71): Go 1/4 mi E on Pocatello Creek Rd, then 1-1/2 mi N on Olympus Dr, then 1/2 mi W on E. Chubbuck Rd, then 1/2 mi S on Fairgrounds Dr (E). Elev 4750 ft. **FAC:** Gravel rds. 117 grass, back-ins (20 x 30), 117 W, 117 E (30/50 amps), WiFi, tent sites, dump. **REC:** pond, swim, fishing, playground, rec open to public. Pets OK. 2015 rates: $25. X no CC, no reservations.
(208)237-1340 Lat: 42.91150, Lon: -112.43204
10588 Fairgrounds Rd., Pocatello, ID 83201
jamiep@bannockcounty.us
www.bannockcounty.us

COWBOY RV PARK
Ratings: 7.5/9.5★/9 (RV Park) From Jct I-15 & 5th Ave (Exit 67): Go 3/4 mi N on 5th Ave, then 1/4 mi N on Barton Rd (R). Elev 4500 ft. **FAC:** Paved rds. (71 spaces). Avail: 45 paved, patios, 10 pull-thrus (25 x 60), back-ins (25 x 40), 45 full hkups (30/50 amps), seasonal sites, WiFi, dump, laundry. **REC:** playground, rec open to public. Pet restrict(B/Q). Partial handicap access, no tents. Big rig sites, eco-friendly, 2015 rates: $39.59.
(208)232-4587 Lat: 42.84971, Lon: -112.42031
845 Barton Rd, Pocatello, ID 83204
cowboy.rvpark@gmail.com
www.cowboyrvidaho.com
See ad this page, 443.

FLAMINGO MANUFACTURED HOUSING COMMUNITY
Ratings: 5/8/5 (RV Area in MHP) From Jct I-15 & 5th Ave (exit 67): Go 1/4 mi SE on 5th Ave, then 1/4 mi E on Samuel (L). Elev 4500 ft. **FAC:** Paved rds. 10 dirt, patios, back-ins (25 x 44), laundry. **REC:** playground. Pets OK. No tents. 2015 rates: $35. No CC, no reservations.
(208)232-1325 Lat: 42.83818, Lon: -112.40242
1002 Samuel St #145, Pocatello, ID 83204
flamingo@towermgmt.com
www.towerrvparks.com

PONDERAY — A1 *Bonner*

SANDPOINT RV PARK **Ratings: 5.5/8/4.5** (Campground) 2015 rates: $37. (208)627-8287 1180 Fontaine Dr, Ponderay, ID 83852

POST FALLS — B1 *Kootenai*

COEUR D'ALENE RV RESORT
Ratings: 9/9★/9 (RV Park) From Jct I-90 & Hwy 41 (Exit 7): Go 1/4 mi N on Hwy 41 to E Mullan Ave, then 1 mi W on E Mullan Ave (L). **FAC:** Paved rds. (190 spaces). Avail: 100 gravel, patios, 89 pull-thrus (30 x 72), back-ins (30 x 54), 100 full hkups (30/50 amps), seasonal sites, cable, WiFi, dump, laundry, LP gas. **REC:** heated pool, whirlpool, playground. Pet restrict(B/Q) $. Partial handicap access, no tents. Big rig sites, eco-friendly, 2015 rates: $41 to $43. Disc: AAA, military.
(208)773-3527 Lat: 47.71564, Lon: -116.91235
2652 E Mullan Ave, Post Falls, ID 83854
coeurd39alenervpark@yahoo.com
www.cdarvpark.com

SUNTREE RV PARK
Ratings: 9/8.5/7.5 (RV Park) From Jct I-90 & Pleasant View Rd (exit 2): Go 1/8 mi N on Pleasant View Rd to 5th Ave, then 1/8 mi E on 5th Ave to Idahline Rd, then 1/8 mi S on Idahline Rd (L).

ALWAYS THE LOWEST RATE IN THE AREA!
We're in the heart of North Idaho's recreational mecca. EZ on EZ off I-90. Park under the shade of our beautiful trees, enjoy our heated pool & hot tub. Post Falls has everything to make your family's visit one to remember.

FAC: Paved/gravel rds. (81 spaces). Avail: 50 gravel, 30 pull-thrus (20 x 76), back-ins (26 x 40), 50 full hkups (30/50 amps), seasonal sites, WiFi, tent sites, dump, laundry. **REC:** heated pool, whirlpool. Pets OK. Eco-friendly, 2015 rates: $35 to $41. Disc: AAA, military.
AAA Approved
(208)777-8888 Lat: 47.71046, Lon: -116.99557
350 N Idahline Rd, Post Falls, ID 83854
info@suntreervpark.com
www.suntreervpark.com
See ad pages 447, 443.

PRIEST RIVER — A1 *Bonner*

PRIEST RIVER See also Sandpoint & Newport, WA.

PRIEST RIVER REC AREA (Public Corps) From town, E 0.5 mi on US-2 (R). 2015 rates: $18. May 9 to Sep 12. (208)437-3133

RILEY CREEK REC AREA (Public Corps) From town, W 0.1 mi on US-2 to Riley Creek Rd, S 1.5 mi (E). 2015 rates: $25. May 9 to Sep 26. (208)437-3133

REXBURG — E4 *Madison*

THOMPSON RV PARK **Ratings: 5/8.5★/6** (Campground) 2015 rates: $25. May 15 to Oct 15. (208)356-6210 4844 S Hwy 191, Rexburg, ID 83440

WAKESIDE LAKE RV PARK
Ratings: 7/8.5/8.5 (Campground) From Jct US-20 & BYU Idaho/Rexburg exit (Exit 332): Go 1/4 mi W on University, then 1 mi S on South 12th St (R). Elev 4840 ft. **FAC:** Gravel rds. 31 gravel, 31 pull-thrus (36 x 70), 31 full hkups (30/50 amps), WiFi, rentals, dump, laundry, fire rings, firewood. **REC:** Rainbow Lake: swim, fishing, playground, rec open to public. Pets OK. No tents. Big rig sites, 2015 rates: $28 to $38. Apr 1 to Oct 31.
(208)356-3681 Lat: 43.79390, Lon: -111.81924
2245 South 2000 West, Rexburg, ID 83440
wakesidelakerv@gmail.com
www.wakesidelakerv.com
See ad this page.

Nobody takes to the road like we do. In many listings we tell you the surface type and condition of interior campground roads.

Things to See and Do

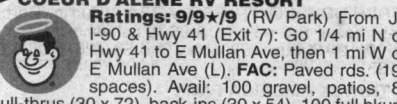

THE CABLE FACTORY Cable wakeboard park with standup paddle board and kayak rentals, stocked fishing and swimming from sandy beach on lakefront. Elev 4840 ft. Jun 1 to Sep 30. Hours: 12 pm to 9 pm M-F, 9 am to 9 pm Sat-Sun.
(208)356-3681 Lat: 43.79112, Lon: -111.82097
2245 S 2000 W, Rexburg, ID 83440
rexburgcablefactory@gmail.com
www.ridecablefactory.com
See ad this page.

RIGGINS — D1 *Idaho*

RIGGINS See also White Bird.

CANYON PINES RV RESORT
Ratings: 7.5/9.5★/10 (Campground) US 95, MP 185.5: 9 mi S of Riggins (R). **FAC:** Paved rds. (54 spaces). Avail: 42 gravel, 13 pull-thrus (30 x 70), back-ins (30 x 55), 42 W, 42 E (30/50 amps), seasonal sites, WiFi, tent sites, dump, mobile sewer, laundry, groc, LP gas, fire rings, firewood. **REC:** Little Salmon: fishing, playground. Pets OK. Partial handicap access. Eco-friendly, 2015 rates: $31.
(208)628-4006 Lat: 45.29321, Lon: -116.35768
159 Barn Rd, Pollock, ID 83547
info@canyonpinesrv.com
www.canyonpinesrv.com

RIVERSIDE RV PARK **Ratings: 3/NA/5** (Campground) 2015 rates: $25. (208)628-3698 1208 S Main St, Riggins, ID 83549

RIRIE — E5 *Jefferson*

HEISE HOT SPRINGS RV CAMP **Ratings: 7/5/8.5** (Campground) 2015 rates: $27 to $32. Apr 15 to Oct 15. (208)538-7944 5130 E Heise Rd, Ririe, ID 83443

MOUNTAIN RIVER RANCH SPORTSMAN'S RV PARK & CAMPGROUND **Ratings: 6/7.5/8** (Campground) 2015 rates: $35. May 15 to Oct 15. (208)538-7337 64 N 5050 E, Ririe, ID 83443

7 N RANCH **Ratings: 3.5/7.5/8** (Campground) 2015 rates: $32. Apr 15 to Oct 15. (208)538-5097 5109 7N Ranch Rd, Ririe, ID 83443

RUPERT — F3 *Minidoka*

LAKE WALCOTT (State Pk) From town: Go 11 mi NE on Hwy 24. 2015 rates: $20 to $29. (208)436-1258

SALMON — D3 *Lemhi*

SALMON See also North Fork.

BUDDY'S RV PARK **Ratings: 5.5/5.5/6** (RV Park) 2015 rates: $30. (208)756-3630 609 River Front Dr, Salmon, ID 83467

CENTURY 2 CAMPGROUND & RV PARK Ratings: 6/6.5/7 (Campground) From Jct of US 93 & Hwy 28: Go 1/8 mi N on US 93 (R). Elev 3960 ft. **FAC:** Paved/gravel rds. 19 gravel, 9 pull-thrus (23 x 55), back-ins (20 x 40), 19 full hkups (30/50 amps), WiFi, tent sites, rentals, dump, laundry, firewood. **REC:** Salmon River: fishing. Pets OK. 2015 rates: $31 to $34. Disc: AAA. May 1 to Nov 1.
AAA Approved
(208)756-2063 Lat: 45.18177, Lon: -113.89645
603 Hwy 93 N (Riverfront Dr), Salmon, ID 83467
century2campground@gmail.com
www.century2campground.com

HEALD'S HAVEN RV & CAMPGROUND **Ratings: 5.5/7.5/7** (Campground) 2015 rates: $22. Jun 1 to Oct 1. (208)756-3929 22 Heald Haven Dr, Salmon, ID 83467

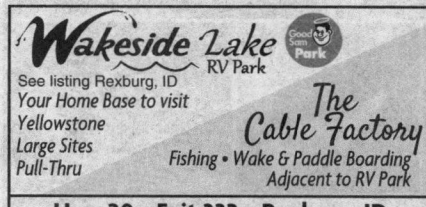

SALMON (CONT)

SALMON RIVER RV PARK **Ratings: 5.5/8★/6** (RV Park) 2015 rates: $25 to $35. (208)894-4549 111 Whitetail Dr, Salmon, ID 83467

SANDPOINT — A1 *Bonner*

SANDPOINT See also Athol, Bonners Ferry, Clark Fork & Hope.

BONNER COUNTY FAIRGROUNDS CAMPGROUND Ratings: 6/7.5/6.5 (Campground) From Jct US-95/US-2 & SR-200: Go 1/2 mi W on Schweitzer Cutoff Rd, then 1/8 mi N on Boyer Rd (L). **FAC:** Paved rds. (33 spaces). Avail: 32 paved, back-ins (24 x 36), 1 full hkups, 31 W, 31 E (30/50 amps), seasonal sites, WiFi, tent sites, dump. **REC:** playground, rec open to public. Pets OK. Partial handicap access. 14 day max stay, eco-friendly, 2015 rates: $25. ATM.
AAA Approved
(208)263-8414 Lat: 48.31152, Lon: -116.55718
4203 N Boyer Rd, Sandpoint, ID 83864
bcfair@intermaxnetworks.com
http://bonnercounty.us/fairgrounds/

EDGEWATER RESORT-BEST WESTERN **Ratings: 6.5/9.5★/4.5** (Campground) 2015 rates: $30 to $55. (208)263-3194 56 Bridge St, Sandpoint, ID 83864

ROUND LAKE (State Pk) From Jct of US-2 & US-95 (in Sandpoint), S 10 mi on US-95 to Dufort Rd, W 2 mi (L). 2015 rates: $12 to $27. (208)263-3489

SPRINGY POINT REC AREA (Public Corps) From town, S 2 mi on US-95 to Lakeshore Dr, W 3 mi (R). 2015 rates: $20. May 9 to Sep 26. (208)437-3133

TRAVEL AMERICA PARK
Ratings: 6.5/8/7 (Campground) From Jct US 2 & US 95 : Go 5 1/2 mi S on US 95 (MP 468.5) (R). **FAC:** Gravel rds. (76 spaces). Avail: 60 grass, 60 pull-thrus (30 x 60), 38 full hkups, 22 W, 22 E (30/50 amps), seasonal sites, WiFi, tent sites, dump, laundry, groc, LP gas, firewood. **REC.** Pet restrict(B). Partial handicap access. Big rig sites, eco-friendly, 2015 rates: $25. ATM.
(208)263-6522 Lat: 48.20363, Lon: -116.56641
468800 Hwy 95, Sagle, ID 83860
See ad this page.

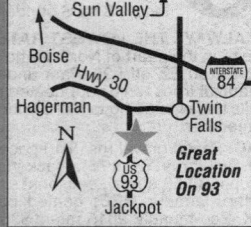

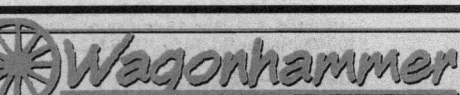

SHELLEY — E4 *Bingham*

NO BINGHAM COUNTY PARK (Public) From Jct I-15 & Exit 108, E on Fir 1.3 mi (R). 2015 rates: $16 to $20. May 1 to Sep 30. (208)357-1895

Travel Services

CAMPING WORLD OF SHELLEY/IDAHO FALLS As the nation's largest retailer of RV supplies, accessories, services and new and used RVs, Camping World is committed to making your total RV experience better. RV Accessories (844)654-6171. **SERVICES:** MH mechanical, RV Sales. RV supplies, LP, dump. Hours: 8 am to 6 pm.
(888)578-9820 Lat: 43.387649, Lon: -112.119693
480 N. State Street, Shelley, ID 83274
www.campingworld.com

SODA SPRINGS — F5 *Caribou*

CARIBOU COUNTY PARK (Public) From town N 12 mi on SR-34 to Blackfoot River Rd, E 0.5 mi (L). (208)547-4324

ST CHARLES — F5 *Bear Lake*

BEAR LAKE (State Pk) From town, S 6 mi on Hwy 89 to N Beach Rd, E 11 mi, follow signs (R). 2015 rates: $12 to $23. (208)945-2565

BEAR LAKE NORTH RV PARK & CAMPGROUND **Ratings: 6/6.5/7** (Campground) 2015 rates: $30. (208)945-2941 220 N Main St, St Charles ID 83272

STANLEY — E2 *Custer*

ELK MOUNTAIN RV RESORT **Ratings: 6/8/6.5** (Campground) 2015 rates: $25. May 15 to Oct 15 (208)774-2202 12655 Hwy 21, Stanley, ID 83278

SMILEY CREEK LODGE Ratings: 5.5/6.5/6.5 (Campground) From Ketchum: Go 36 mi N on Hwy 75 (L); or From Stanley: Go 22 mi S on Hwy 75 (R) (MP 166). Elev 7400 ft. **FAC:** Gravel rds. (33 spaces) Avail: 31 grass, back-ins (27 x 45), mostly side by side hkups, 23 full hkups, 2 W, 8 E (30 amps), seasonal sites, WiFi Hotspot, tent sites, rentals, dump, laundry, groc, LP gas, restaurant. **REC:** Smiley

Nobody said it was easy being a 10. And our rating system makes it even tougher.

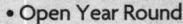

STANLEY (CONT)

SMILEY CREEK LODGE (CONT)
Creek/Salmon River: fishing. Pets OK. Eco-friendly, 2015 rates: $26 to $34. May 1 to Sep 30.
(877)774-3547 Lat: 43.90708, Lon: -114.79666
16546 N Highway 75, Sawtooth City, ID 83278
smileycreek@ruralnetwork.net
www.smileycreeklodge.com

TORREY'S BURNT CREEK INN & RV PARK **Ratings: 5/6.5/7** (Campground) 2015 rates: $28. Apr 1 to Nov 1. (208)838-2313 hc 67 Box 725, Stanley, ID 83278

SUN VALLEY — E3 *Custer*

THE MEADOWS RV PARK Ratings: 6/8.5★/6.5 (Campground) From Jct of Hwy 75 & Broadway Run: Go 1 mi S on Broadway Run (MP 124.8) (L). Elev 5670 ft. **FAC:** Paved rds. (45 spaces). Avail: 35 paved, 35 pull-thrus (20 x 60), mostly side by side hkups, 35 full hkups (30/50 amps), seasonal sites, WiFi, laundry. Pet restrict(B). No tents. Eco-friendly, 2015 rates: $35 to $40.
(208)726-5445 Lat: 43.63448, Lon: -114.35389
13 Broadway Run, Ketchum, ID 83340
www.themeadowsinketchum.com

TWIN FALLS — F3 *Jerome, Twin Falls*

TWIN FALLS See also Hagerman & Wendell.

ANDERSON CAMP RV PARK
Ratings: 8.5/9★/7.5 (Campground) From Jct I-84 & Hwy 50 (Exit 182): Go 1/8 mi N on Hwy 50, then 1/2 mi E on Tipperary Rd (L). Elev 3747 ft.

ENJOY A PLEASANT RELAXING STAY!
Whether it's a large group or single family we have pools to relax by, a water slide for the young at heart and a challenging 18-hole miniature golf course. We have lots of Green Space, Cabins, & quiet areas to rest & renew.

FAC: Gravel rds. (90 spaces). Avail: 65 gravel, 65 pull-thrus (30 x 60), 65 full hkups (30/50 amps), seasonal sites, WiFi, tent sites, rentals, dump, laundry, groc, LP gas, firewood. **REC:** heated pool, playground, rec open to public. Pets OK. Partial handicap access. Big rig sites, 2015 rates: $32. Disc: AAA, military. ATM.
AAA Approved
(888)480-9400 Lat: 42.57735, Lon: -114.28989
1188 East 990 South, Eden, ID 83325
info@andersoncamp.com
www.andersoncamp.com
See ad opposite page, 443.

NAT-SOO-PAH HOT SPRINGS & CAMPGROUND **Ratings: 6.5/7/7.5** (Campground) 2015 rates: $20. May 1 to Sep 2. (208)655-4337 2738 E 2400 N, Twin Falls, ID 83301

OREGON TRAIL CAMPGROUND **Ratings: 7/9★/6** (Campground) 2015 rates: $35. (208)733-0853 2733 Kimberly Rd, Twin Falls, ID 83301

TWIN FALLS / JEROME KOA **Ratings: 8.5/8.5/6** (Campground) 2015 rates: $35 to $50. Mar 1 to Oct 31. (800)562-4169 5431 US Hwy 93, Jerome, ID 83338

TWIN FALLS 93 RV PARK
Ratings: 7.5/9★/9 (RV Park) From Jct I-84 & US 93 (exit 173): Go 3-1/2 mi S on US 93 to Alternate US 93, then 5.3 mi W on Alternate US 93/4100 N, then continue on Alternate US 93 2-1/2 mi S to merge with US 93, then continue 1/2 mi S on US 93 (L). Elev 3745 ft. **FAC:** Gravel rds. 29 gravel, 29 pull-thrus (24 x 67), 29 full hkups (30/50 amps), WiFi, dump, laundry, LP gas, firewood. **REC:** whirlpool. Pet restrict(B/Q). No tents. Big rig sites, eco-friendly, 2015 rates: $37 to $39. Disc: military.
(208)326-5092 Lat: 42.55415, Lon: -114.57399
2404 Jorden Ln, Filer, ID 83328
93rvpark@filertel.com
www.twinfalls93rvpark.com
See ad opposite page.

Travel Services

ANDERSON CAMP FULL SERVICE STOP Located at Jct I-84 and Hwy 50 (Exit 182). Full service: gasoline, diesel & propane for vehicles of any size, convenience store and restaurant. Elev 4150 ft. **SERVICES:** restrooms. LP, dump, emergency parking, RV accessible. Hours: 8am to 9pm. ATM.
(888)480-9400 Lat: 42.57735, Lon: -114.28989
1188 East 990 South, Eden, ID 83325
info@andersoncamp.com
www.andersoncamp.com
See ad opposite page.

VICTOR — E5 *Teton*

TETON VALLEY RV PARK
Ratings: 9/9.5★/8.5 (Campground) From Jct Hwy 33 & Hwy 31 (in Victor): Go 3/4 mi SW on Hwy 31 (R). Elev 6200 ft. **FAC:** Gravel rds. (60 spaces). 54 Avail: 33 gravel, 21 grass, 29 pull-thrus (36 x 66), back-ins (24 x 50), some side by side hkups, 40 full hkups, 14 W, 14 E (30/50 amps), seasonal sites, WiFi, tent sites, rentals, dump, laundry, fire rings, firewood. **REC:** heated pool, playground. Pet restrict(Q). Big rig sites, eco-friendly, 2015 rates: $43 to $59. Disc: AAA, military. May 1 to Oct 15.
(208)787-2647 Lat: 43.59849, Lon: -111.12611
1208 Hwy 31, Victor, ID 83455
tvcampground@silverstar.com
www.tetonvalleycampground.com
See ad page 1344.

WALLACE — B2 *Shoshone*

WALLACE See also Kellogg & Osburn.

WEISER — E1 *Washington*

WEISER See also Fruitland; Vale, OR & Huntington, OR.

COVE BLM (Public) From Jct of SR-51 & SR-78, W 7 mi on SR-78, NE 1.1 mi on Cottonwood Rd. Pit toilets. 2015 rates: $12. (208)384-3300

MONROE CREEK CAMPGROUND & RV PARK
Ratings: 6.5/8/8.5 (Campground) From N Jct US-95 & Bus US-95: Go 1 1/2 mi N on US-95 (N of town MP 84.6) (R). **FAC:** Gravel rds. (53 spaces). Avail: 44 gravel, 36 pull-thrus (22 x 66), back-ins (33 x 36), 11 full hkups, 31 W, 31 E (30/50 amps), seasonal sites, WiFi Hotspot, tent sites, dump, mobile sewer, laundry, LP bottles, firewood. **REC:** Monroe Creek: fishing, playground. Pet restrict(Q). Eco-friendly, 2015 rates: $27. Disc: AAA, military.
(208)549-2026 Lat: 44.27062, Lon: -116.94501
822 Hwy 95, Weiser, ID 83672
monroecreek@gmail.com
www.monroecreek.com
See ad this page.

WENDELL — F3 *Gooding*

INTERMOUNTAIN MOTOR HOMES & RV CAMP **Ratings: 5.5/7.5/8.5** (Campground) 2015 rates: $24. Mar 1 to Nov 1. (208)536-2301 1894 Frontage Rd N, Box 381, Wendell, ID 83355

Did you know we sent 35 husband-wife RVing teams out this year to scour North America, rating and inspecting RV parks and campgrounds? You can rest easy when you read our listings, knowing we've already been there.

WHITE BIRD — C1 *Idaho*

HELLS CANYON JET BOAT TRIPS & LODGING
Ratings: 6/6/7.5 (Campground) From Jct US 95 & White Bird Exit (mp 223): Go 1/4 mi E on White Bird Exit Rd to Old Hwy 95, then 1 mi SW on Old Hwy 95 (R). **FAC:** Gravel rds. 14 Avail: 9 gravel, 5 grass, back-ins (33 x 38), 14 full hkups (30/50 amps), WiFi, tent sites, rentals, LP bottles, fire rings. **REC:** Salmon River: swim, fishing, rec open to public. Pets OK. 2015 rates: $30. Disc: AAA, military.
AAA Approved
(800)469-8757 Lat: 45.75177, Lon: -116.32021
3252 Waterfront Dr, White Bird, ID 83554
jetboat@killgoreadventures.com
www.killgoreadventures.com

SWIFTWATER RV PARK
Ratings: 7/8.5★/8.5 (Campground) From Jct US 95 & Old Hwy 95: Go 1/2 mi NW on Old Hwy 95 (L). **FAC:** Gravel rds. (24 spaces). 21 Avail: 13 gravel, 8 grass, 8 pull-thrus (15 x 60), back-ins (21 x 50), mostly side by side hkups, 1 full hkups, 20 W, 20 E (30/50 amps), seasonal sites, WiFi, tent sites, dump, mobile sewer, laundry, firewood. **REC:** Salmon River: swim, fishing. Pets OK. Eco-friendly, 2015 rates: $25 to $27. Disc: military.
(208)839-2700 Lat: 45.74373, Lon: -116.32481
3154 Salmon River Ct, White Bird, ID 83554
anna@swiftwaterrv.com
www.swiftwaterrv.com
See ad this page.

WINCHESTER — C1 *Lewis*

WINCHESTER LAKE (State Pk) From Jct of US-95 & US-95 ALT, SW 1 mi on US-95 Alt to Camas St, W 0.25 mi (L). 2015 rates: $12 to $38. (208)924-7563

Find out more about the joys of traveling with your four-legged companions in our Pampered Pet Parks feature at the front of the Guide.

ID

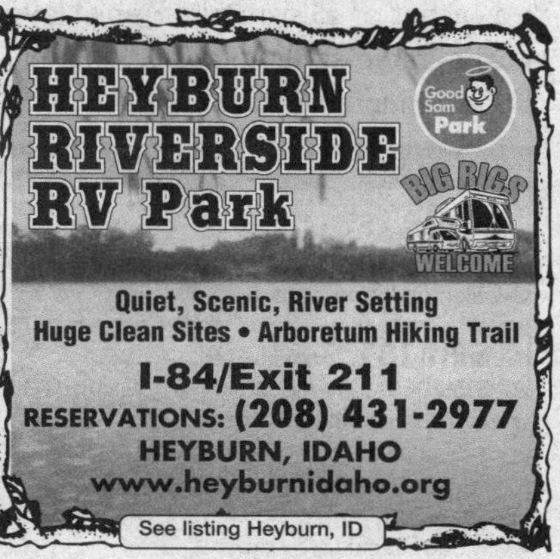

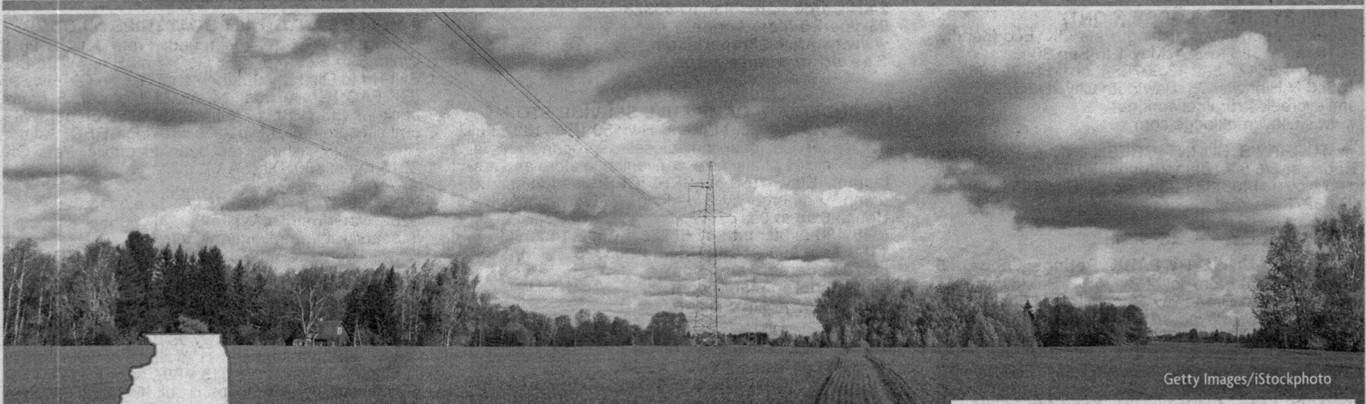

Getty Images/iStockphoto

DATE OF STATEHOOD	WIDTH: 210 MILES (340 KM)	PROPORTION OF UNITED STATES
DEC. 3, 1818	LENGTH: 395 MILES (629 KM)	1.53% OF 3,794,100 SQ MI

ILLINOIS

It's easy to see why Illinois is considered to be America's beating heart. The birthplace of poet Carl Sandburg and Ronald Reagan, home to Abraham Lincoln and Ernest Hemingway, Illinois is pure Americana. From hot dogs (or "red hots") that are deemed culinary icons to a town called Metropolis named in honor of Superman and fecund swamp lands that resemble a Louisiana bayou, Illinois is a land of endless surprise. Illinois is also home to Chicago, the "City of Broad Shoulders" that soars skyward from the Midwest prairies.

Each year, millions of tourists pay homage to the city's pioneering architecture, feel the raw energy of the downtown Loop, marvel at the Impressionist paintings at the Art Institute and wander through hip neighborhoods lined with gorgeous brownstones. Further afield, in Oak Park, Hemingway's "wide laws and narrow minds" give way to a cachet of 25 signature Frank Lloyd Wright Prairie-style homes. Springfield, Illinois' diminutive state capital (not to be confused with the Springfield where Homer Simpson resides) takes pride of place on Historic Route 66, a gaudy trail of mom and pop outposts, kitsch motels, neon diners, vintage gas stations and drive-in movie theaters which, almost a century later, still capture the imagination, the freedom of motion and the essence of the American spirit.

While Chicago's glass and steel monoliths steal the glory, the surrounding landscape is a natural beauty in its own right. There are five scenic byways that lead you to stunning lakes, prairies and acres and acres of farmland (including Amish Country, centered around the town of Arthur). And there's hiking, biking and horseback riding through more than 50 state parks and myriad wildlife and nature centers. Starved Rock National Park is the region's highlight, with 13 miles of trails meandering through trees and canyons.

The Illinois River offers more languid pursuits in the form of fishing (including ice fishing) and boating.

Top 3 Tourism Attractions:
1) The Magnificent Mile
2) SkyDeck Chicago-Willis Tower
3) Shedd Aquarium

Nickname: Prairie State

State Flower: Violet

State Bird: Cardinal

People: Jack Benny, comedian; Walt Disney, founder of Disneyland; Harrison Ford, actor; Ronald Reagan, 40th president; Florenz Ziegfeld, Broadway impresario

Major Cities: Chicago, Aurora, Rockford, Joliet, Naperville (Springfield, capital)

Topography: Prairie and fertile land throughout with open hills in the southern region

Climate: Temperate climate with cold, snowy winters and hot, wet summers

TRAVEL & TOURISM

Illinois Office of Tourism
800-2-CONNECT
www.enjoyillinois.com

Central Illinois Tourism Dev. Office
217-525-7980
www.visitcentralillinois.com

Chicago Convention and Tourism Bureau
312-567-8500
www.choosechicago.com

Northern Illinois Tourism Development Office
815-547-3740
www.visitnorthernillinois.com

Southernmost Illinois Tourism Bureau
618-833-9928, 800-248-4373
www.southernmostillinois.com

The Tourism Bureau of Southwestern Illinois
618-397-1488, 800-442-1488
www.thetourismbureau.org

Western Illinois Tourism Dev. Office
309-837-7460
www.visitwesternillinois.info

OUTDOOR RECREATION

Illinois Dept. of Natural Resources
217-782-6302
nr.state.il.us

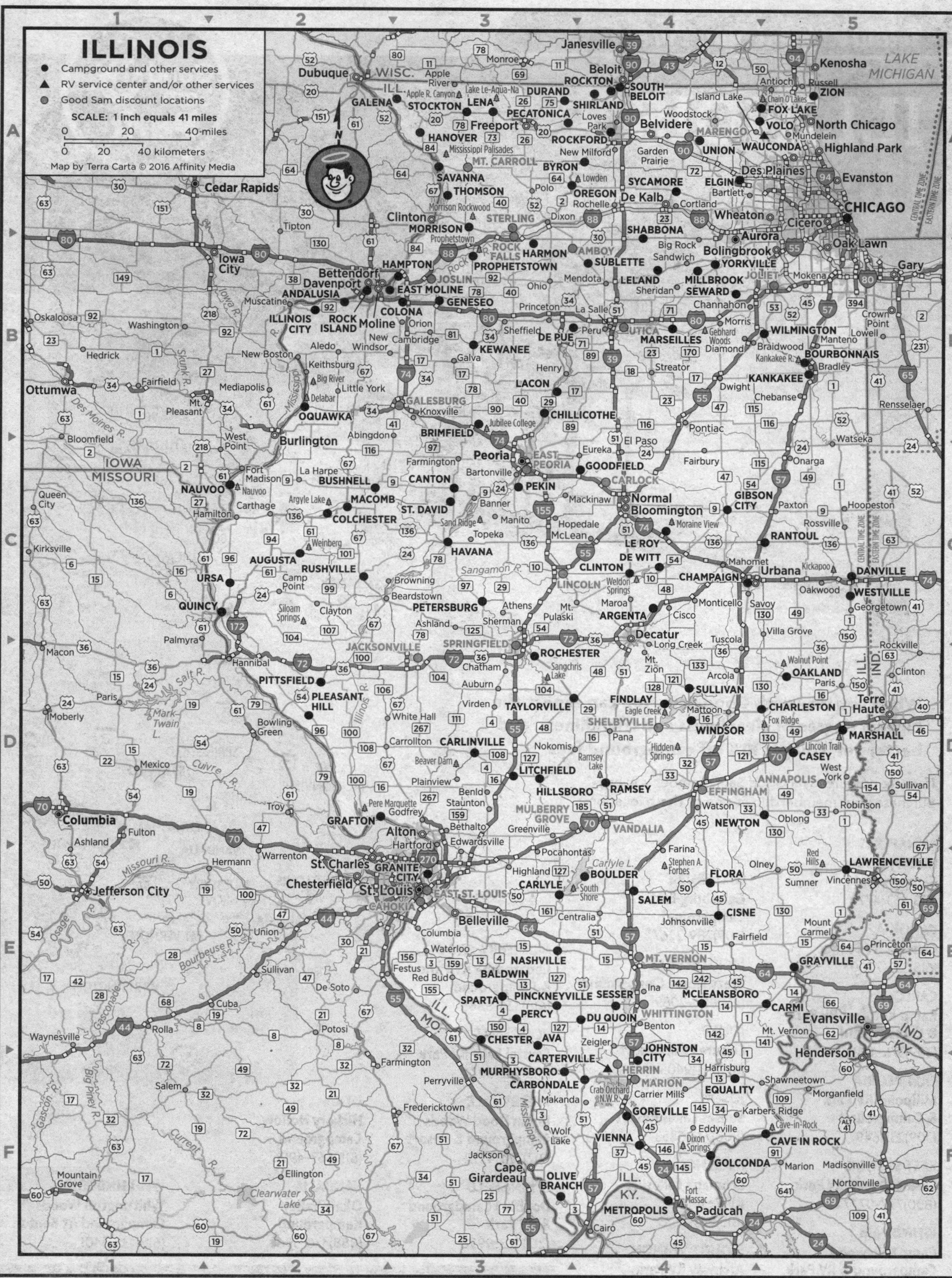
ILLINOIS
Campground and other services
RV service center and/or other services
Good Sam discount locations
SCALE: 1 inch equals 41 miles
0 20 40 miles
0 20 40 kilometers
Map by Terra Carta © 2016 Affinity Media
LAKE MICHIGAN
WISC.
ILL.
IOWA
MISSOURI
IND.
KY.
MO.
CENTRAL TIME ZONE
EASTERN TIME ZONE
Janesville
Beloit
Kenosha
Dubuque
GALENA
STOCKTON
LENA
DURAND
ROCKTON
SOUTH BELOIT
SHIRLAND
PECATONICA
Freeport
ROCKFORD
Belvidere
ZION
FOX LAKE
VOLO
North Chicago
WAUCONDA
Highland Park
HANOVER
SAVANNA
THOMSON
MT. CARROLL
BYRON
OREGON
SYCAMORE
De Kalb
ELGIN
Des Plaines
Evanston
CHICAGO
Cedar Rapids
Clinton
MORRISON
STERLING
ROCK FALLS
SHABBONA
Wheaton
Aurora
Cicero
Oak Lawn
Iowa City
HAMPTON
Bettendorf
Davenport
JOSLIN
PROPHETSTOWN
HARMON
AMBOY
SUBLETTE
LELAND
Bolingbrook
YORKVILLE
MILLBROOK
SEWARD
JOLIET
Gary
ANDALUSIA
EAST MOLINE
GENESEO
ROCK ISLAND
Moline
COLONA
ILLINOIS CITY
KEWANEE
DE PUE
UTICA
MARSEILLES
WILMINGTON
BOURBONNAIS
KANKAKEE
Ottumwa
GALESBURG
OQUAWKA
Burlington
LACON
CHILLICOTHE
BRIMFIELD
Peoria
EAST PEORIA
GOODFIELD
CARLOCK
NAUVOO
BUSHNELL
CANTON
PEKIN
Normal
Bloomington
GIBSON CITY
MACOMB
COLCHESTER
ST. DAVID
HAVANA
LE ROY
DE WITT
RANTOUL
AUGUSTA
RUSHVILLE
URSA
CLINTON
LINCOLN
CHAMPAIGN
Urbana
DANVILLE
WESTVILLE
QUINCY
PETERSBURG
ARGENTA
Decatur
JACKSONVILLE
SPRINGFIELD
ROCHESTER
PITTSFIELD
PLEASANT HILL
TAYLORVILLE
FINDLAY
SULLIVAN
OAKLAND
CHARLESTON
Terre Haute
SHELBYVILLE
WINDSOR
MARSHALL
CARLINVILLE
LITCHFIELD
HILLSBORO
RAMSEY
CASEY
EFFINGHAM
ANNAPOLIS
Columbia
GRAFTON
Alton
MULBERRY GROVE
VANDALIA
NEWTON
Jefferson City
St. Charles
GRANITE CITY
Chesterfield
St. Louis
EAST ST. LOUIS
CAHOKIA
CARLYLE
BOULDER
SALEM
FLORA
LAWRENCEVILLE
Belleville
CISNE
MT. VERNON
NASHVILLE
GRAYVILLE
BALDWIN
SPARTA
PINCKNEYVILLE
SESSER
WHITTINGTON
MCLEANSBORO
CARMI
Evansville
PERCY
DU QUOIN
CHESTER
AVA
CARTERVILLE
HERRIN
JOHNSTON CITY
Henderson
MURPHYSBORO
CARBONDALE
MARION
EQUALITY
GOREVILLE
VIENNA
CAVE IN ROCK
GOLCONDA
Cape Girardeau
OLIVE BRANCH
METROPOLIS
Paducah
Mississippi R.
Illinois R.
Missouri R.

IL

Featured Good Sam Parks

ILLINOIS

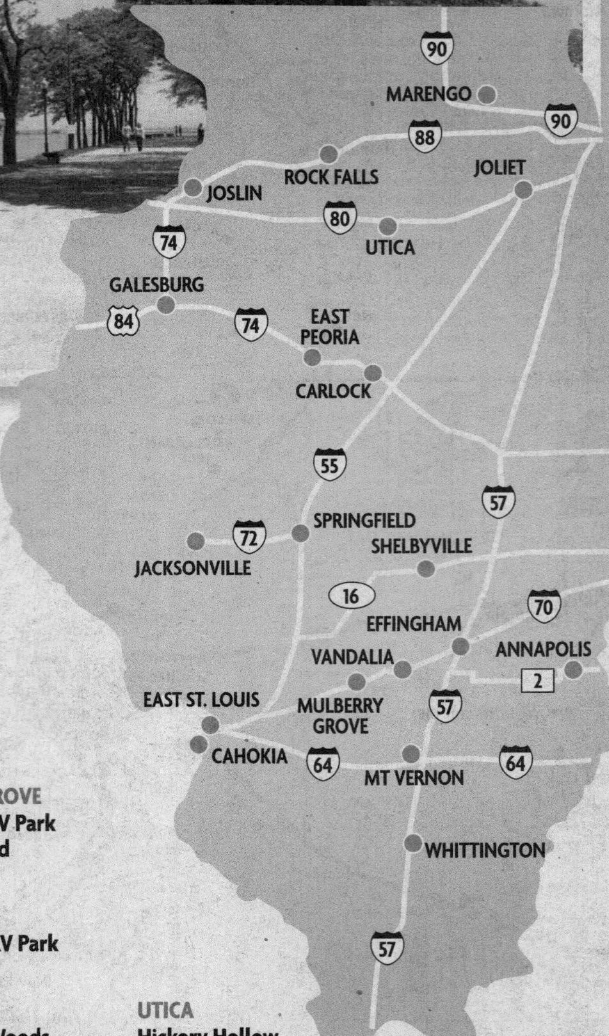

When you stay with Good Sam, you can expect the highest degree of cleanliness and friendliness, and better yet, you get 10% off campground fees.

If you're not already a Good Sam member you can purchase your membership at one of these locations:

ANNAPOLIS
Hickory Holler Campground
(618)563-4779

CAHOKIA
Cahokia RV Parque
(618)332-7700

CARLOCK
Kamp Komfort RV Park & Campground
(309)376-4411

EAST PEORIA
Millpoint RV Park & Campground
(309)231-6497

EAST ST LOUIS
Casino Queen RV Park
(800)777-0777

EFFINGHAM
Camp Lakewood Campground & RV Park
(217)342-6233

GALESBURG
Galesburg East Campground
(309)289-2267

JACKSONVILLE
Crazy Horse Campground
(217)886-2089

JOLIET
Leisure Lake Resort
(815)741-9405

JOSLIN
Sunset Lakes Resort
(800)747-5253

MARENGO
Lehman's Lakeside RV Resort
(815)923-4533

MOUNT VERNON
Archway RV Park
(618)244-0399

MULBERRY GROVE
Cedarbrook RV Park & Campground
(618)326-8865

ROCK FALLS
Crystal Lake RV Park
(815)622-5974

SHELBYVILLE
Robin Hood Woods Campground & Resort
(217)774-4222

SPRINGFIELD
Double J Campground & RV Park
(217)483-9998

UTICA
Hickory Hollow Campground
(815)667-4996

VANDALIA
Okaw Valley Kampground
(888)470-3968

WHITTINGTON
Whittington Woods Campground At Benton
(618)435-3401

For more Good Sam Parks go to listing pages

Illinois

CONSULTANTS
Ed & Susan DeWitt

AMBOY — B3 *Lee*

GREEN RIVER OAKS CAMPING RESORT **Ratings: 7.5/7.5/8** (Campground) 2015 rates: $50. Apr 15 to Oct 15. (815)857-2815 1442 Sleepy Hollow Rd, Amboy, IL 61310

MENDOTA HILLS CAMPGROUND, LLC
Ratings: 8.5/9★/9 (Campground) From Jct US 30 & US 52: Go 6-1/2 mi S on US 52 (R). **FAC:** Gravel rds. (172 spaces). Avail: 40 grass, 7 pull-thrus (40 x 70), back-ins (40 x 60), 40 full hkups (30/50 amps), seasonal sites, WiFi, tent sites, rentals, dump, mobile sewer, laundry, groc, fire rings, firewood, restaurant. **REC:** Bass Lake: swim, fishing, playground. Pets OK. 2015 rates: $38. Apr 15 to Oct 15. ATM.
(815)849-5930 Lat: 41.67308, Lon: -89.27748
642 US Rt 52, Amboy, IL 61310
mendotahillscamp@aol.com
www.mendotahillscampground.com

O'CONNELL'S YOGI BEAR JELLYSTONE PARK CAMP RESORT **Ratings: 9/9.5★/9** (Campground) 2015 rates: $45 to $60. May 2 to Oct 19. (800)405-6188 970 Green Wing Rd, Amboy, IL 61310

PINE VIEW CAMPGROUND **Ratings: 7.5/6/9** (Campground) 2015 rates: $29. Apr 15 to Oct 15. (815)857-3964 1273 Sleepy Hollow Rd, Amboy, IL 61310

ANDALUSIA — B2 *Rock Island*

ANDALUSIA SLOUGH (COE-MISSISSIPPI RIVER REC AREAS-MUSCATINE AREA) (Public Corps) From town: Go 4 mi W on Hwy 92 (follow signs). Pit toilets. 2015 rates: $4. May 15 to Oct 15. (563)263-7913

ANNAPOLIS — D5 *Crawford*

HICKORY HOLLER CAMPGROUND
Ratings: 7/9★/9.5 (Campground) From Jct of I-70 & Exit 147 (SR-1), S 19 mi on SR-1 to E 2000th Ave (CR-2), W 4.2 mi (R). **FAC:** Gravel rds. (89 spaces). Avail: 50 gravel, 35 pull-thrus (25 x 60), back-ins (25 x 45), some side by side hkups, 42 full hkups, 8 W, 8 E (30/50 amps), seasonal sites, WiFi, tent sites, dump, mobile sewer, laundry, LP gas, fire rings, firewood. **REC:** Lake Guyer: fishing, playground. Pets OK. Big rig sites, eco-friendly, 2015 rates: $21 to $30.
(618)563-4779 Lat: 39.13984, Lon: -87.76245
9876 E 2000th Ave, West York, IL 62478
tj3dguyer@gmail.com
www.crosstiescm.org
See ad pages 482, 458.

ARGENTA — C4 *Macon*

FRIENDS CREEK CONSERVATION AREA (Public) From Jct of I-72 & exit 156, S 0.2 mi on exit Rd to CR-18, W 2 mi to 2300N, N 1.2 mi (R). 2015 rates: $10 to $18. May 1 to Nov 1. (217)423-7708

AUGUSTA — C2 *Schuyler*

WEINBERG-KING STATE FISH & WILDLIFE AREA (State Pk) From town, E 3 mi on SR-101 (L). Pit toilets. 2015 rates: $8 to $18. (217)392-2345

AVA — E3 *Jackson*

SHAWNEE NATIONAL FOREST (JOHNSON CREEK CAMPGROUND) (Natl Pk) From town: Go 4 mi S on Hwy-151. 2015 rates: $10 to $18. Mar 15 to Dec 15. (618)687-1731

BALDWIN — E3 *Randolph*

K-RIVER MOTEL & CAMPGROUND **Ratings: 5.5/NA/8** (Campground) 2015 rates: $20 to $25. (618)785-2564 7797 Route 154, Baldwin, IL 62217

BENTON — E4 *Franklin, Williamson*

BENTON KOA
Ratings: 8.5/8★/8.5 (Campground) From Jct of I-57 & Hwy 14 (exit 71), E 1/4 mi on Hwy 14 to first traffic light (Duquoin St), N 1-1/4 mi (R). **FAC:** Gravel rds. (66 spaces). Avail: 62 gravel, 23 pull-thrus (28 x 98), back-ins (25 x 55), some side by side hkups, 28 full hkups, 34 W, 28 S, 34 E (30/50 amps), seasonal sites, cable, WiFi, tent sites, rentals, dump, laundry, groc, LP gas, fire rings, firewood. **REC:** pool, pond, fishing, playground, rec open to public. Pet restrict(B). Partial handicap access. Big rig sites, 2015 rates: $25 to $39.
(618)439-4860 Lat: 38.00720, Lon: -88.91785
1500 N Duquoin St, Benton, IL 62812
bentonkoa@bentonkoa.com
koa.com/campgrounds/BENTON
See ad this page.

GUN CREEK REC AREA (Public Corps) From town, N 6 mi on I-57 to Rte 154, W 0.25 mi to park access rd, S 0.5 mi to Gun Creek Trail, L on Gun Creek Trail/Larry Foster Pkwy, R on Golf Course Rd, .5 mi to park entrance. 2015 rates: $16 to $24. Mar 13 to Nov 29. (618)724-2493

NORTH SANDUSKY CAMPGROUND (Public Corps) From Jct of Rte 57 & Rte 154, W 4 mi on Rte 154 to Rend City Rd, S 1 mi (E). 2015 rates: $16 to $24. Mar 27 to Nov 1. (618)724-2493

SOUTH MARCUM CAMPGROUND (Public Corps) From Jct of Rte 37N & Petroff Rd, W 0.5 mi on Petroff Rd to Duquoin St, N 2 mi to Rend City Rd, N 0.5 mi (E). 2015 rates: $12 to $40. Mar 27 to Nov 1. (618)724-2493

SOUTH SANDUSKY CAMPGROUND (Public Corps) From Jct of I-57 & SR-14, W 2.5 mi on SR-14 to Rend City Rd, N 4 mi (R). 2015 rates: $12 to $24. Mar 27 to Nov 1. (618)724-2493

BOULDER — E4 *Clinton*

BOULDER RECREATION AREA (Public Corps) From town, E 7 mi on Rte 50 to Boulder Rd, N 6 mi (L). 2015 rates: $16 to $32. Apr 15 to Oct 14. (618)594-5253

COLES CREEK REC AREA (Public Corps) From town, E 7 mi on Rte 50 to Boulder-Ferrin Rd, N 4 mi, follow signs (L). 2015 rates: $16 to $32. May 1 to Sep 29. (618)594-5253

BOURBONNAIS — B5 *Kankakee*

KANKAKEE RIVER (State Pk) From town, NW 8 mi on SR-102, follow signs (L). 2015 rates: $25 to $35. (815)933-1383

BRIMFIELD — B3 *Peoria*

JUBILEE COLLEGE (State Pk) From town, E 4 mi on US-150, follow signs (L). 2015 rates: $20 to $30. Apr 15 to Nov 1. (309)446-3758

BUSHNELL — C2 *McDonough*

TIMBERVIEW LAKES CAMPGROUND **Ratings: 6.5/5.5/5.5** (Campground) 2015 rates: $30. Apr 15 to Oct 15. (309)772-3609 23200 N 2000 Rd, Bushnell, IL 61422

BYRON — A4 *Ogle*

LAKE LOUISE CAMPGROUND **Ratings: 8.5/7.5/6.5** (Campground) 2015 rates: $37 to $47. Apr 1 to Oct 31. (815)234-8483 8840 No. II Route 2, Byron, IL 61010

CAHOKIA — E3 *St Clair*

CAHOKIA RV PARQUE
Ratings: 8.5/9★/7 (RV Park) From Jct of I-255 & SR-157 (exit 13), W 2 mi on SR-157 to SR-3, N 500 ft (L). **FAC:** Paved/gravel rds. (119 spaces). Avail: 45 paved, patios, 24 pull-thrus (25 x 50), back-ins (25 x 55), 33 full hkups, 12 W, 12 E (30/50 amps), WiFi, tent sites, rentals, dump, laundry, LP gas, firewood, restaurant. **REC:** pool, pond, fishing, playground. Pet restrict(B) $. Partial handicap ac-

IL

CAHOKIA (CONT)

CAHOKIA RV PARQUE (CONT)
cess. Big rig sites, eco-friendly, 2015 rates: $36. Disc: AAA, military.
AAA Approved
(618)332-7700 Lat: 38.57372, Lon: -90.18631
4060 Mississippi Ave, Cahokia, IL 62206
cahokiarvparque@hotmail.com
www.cahokiarvpark.com
See ad pages 701, 458.

Things to See and Do

SAWMILL BBQ Located next to Cahokia RV Parque. Serving hickory smoked barbeque. Partial handicap access. RV accessible. Restrooms, food. Hours: 11am to 8pm Mon - Sat.
(618)332-3000 Lat: 38.56476, Lon: -90.17853
4060 Mississippi Ave (Rt 3), Cahokia, IL 62206
sawmillbbq@yahoo.com
cahokiarvparque.com
See ad page 701.

CANTON — C3 *Fulton*

RICE LAKE STATE FISH & WILDLIFE AREA (State Pk) From Jct of US-9 & US-24, S 2.5 mi on US-24 (L). Pit toilets. 2015 rates: $10 to $18. (309)647-9184

CARBONDALE — F4 *Williamson*

CRAB ORCHARD LAKE (Public) From Jct of I-57 & SR-13, E 9 mi on SR-13 (R). 2015 rates: $10 to $25. May 1 to Oct 31. (618)985-4983

GIANT CITY (State Pk) From Jct of US-51 & Makanda Rd, E 2.5 mi on Makanda Rd, follow signs (E). 2015 rates: $20 to $30. (618)457-4836

LITTLE GRASSY LAKE CAMPGROUND & MARINA **Ratings: 5/4.5/5.5** (Campground) 2015 rates: $15 to $35. Mar 15 to Nov 25. (618)457-6655 788 Hidden Bay Lane, Makanda, IL 62958

CARLINVILLE — D3 *Macoupin*

BEAVER DAM (State Pk) From Jct of Rte 108 & Carlinville-Shipman Rd (in town), S 8 mi on Carlinville-Shipman Rd, follow signs (R). 2015 rates: $20 to $30. (217)854-8020

CARLOCK — C4 *McLean*

KAMP KOMFORT RV PARK & CAMPGROUND
Ratings: 8.5/9★/9 (Campground) From Jct of I-74 & CR-53 (Exit 120): Go W 3/4 mi on CR-53, then N 1 mi on 600 East Rd (L). **FAC:** All weather rds. (74 spaces). Avail: 39 all weather, 35 pull-thrus (35 x 70), back-ins (24 x 65), 39 full hkups (30/50 amps), WiFi, tent sites, dump, LP gas, fire rings, firewood. **REC:** pool, playground. Pets OK. Partial handicap access. Big rig sites, eco-friendly, 2015 rates: $36. Apr 1 to Oct 31.
(309)376-4411 Lat: 40.58775, Lon: -89.15153
21408 N 600 East Rd, Carlock, IL 61725
kampkomfort@dtnspeed.net
www.kampkomfortcampground.com/
See ad this page, 458.

CARLYLE — E3 *Clinton*

DAM WEST REC AREA (Public Corps) From town, N 0.5 mi on SR 127 to William Rd, E 0.5 mi (L). 2015 rates: $18 to $52. Apr 1 to Oct 31. (618)594-4410

ELDON HAZLET RECREATION AREA (State Pk) From N Jct of US-50 & SR-127, N 2.9 mi on SR-127 to Hazlet Park Rd, E 0.9 mi to CR-1860E, E 1.4 mi (E). 2015 rates: $18 to $35. (618)594-3015

HICKORY SHORES RESORT **Ratings: 5/4.5/5** (RV Park) 2015 rates: $20 to $35. (618)749-5288 21925 Dove Lane, Carlyle, IL 62231

MCNAIR CAMPGROUND (LAKE CARLYLE-CORP OF ENGINEERS) (Public Corps) From jct Hwy-127 & US-50: Go 1 mi E on US-50. 2015 rates: $16 to $32. (618)594-2484

SOUTH SHORE (State Pk) From town, E 3 mi on Hwy 50 (L). Pit toilets. 2015 rates: $8. (618)594-3015

CARMI — E5 *White*

BURRELL PARK CAMPGROUND (Public) From Jct of I-64 & SR-1 (exit 130), S 13 mi on SR-1 to SR-14, W 0.2 mi to 6th St, N 0.3 mi to Stewart St, W 2 mi (L). 2015 rates: $14. Apr 15 to Oct 15. (618)382-2693

CARTERVILLE — F4 *Williamson*

Travel Services

KAMPER'S SUPPLY RV supplies, parts & service. **SERVICES:** RV appliance, MH mechanical, restrooms, RV Sales. RV supplies, emergency parking, RV accessible. waiting room. Hours: 9am to 5pm.
(618)985-6959 Lat: 37.746135, Lon: -89.083517
400 W Plaza Dr, Carterville, IL 62918
shirley@camperssupply.com
www.kamperssupply.com
See ad page 463.

CASEY — D5 *Clark*

CASEY KOA KAMPGROUND **Ratings: 8.5/9.5★/9** (Campground) 2015 rates: $37.95 to $47.59. Mar 1 to Nov 1. (800)562-9113 1248 E 1250 Rd, Casey, IL 62420

CAVE IN ROCK — F5 *Hardin*

CAVE-IN-ROCK (State Pk) From Jct of Hwys 146 & 1, S 2 mi on Hwy 1 (L). 2015 rates: $20 to $30. (618)289-4325

CHAMPAIGN — C4 *Champaign*

CHAMPAIGN See also Gibson City, Mahomet & Rantoul.

D & W LAKE RV PARK **Ratings: 7/9.5★/9** (Campground) 2015 rates: $25. (217)356-3732 411 W Hensley Rd, Champaign, IL 61822

CHARLESTON — D5 *Coles*

FOX RIDGE (State Pk) From Jct of SR-16 & SR-130, S 7 mi on SR-130 (R). 2015 rates: $20 to $30. (217)345-6416

CHESTER — E3 *Randolph*

RANDOLPH COUNTY STATE REC AREA (State Pk) From Jct of SR-3 & 150, E 3 mi on SR-150, follow signs (L). 2015 rates: $18. (618)826-2706

CHICAGO — A5 *Cook*

CHICAGO AREA MAP

Symbols on map indicate towns within a 50 mile radius of Chicago where campgrounds are listed. Check listings for more information.

In IL, see also Bourbonnais, Fox Lake, Joliet, Marengo, Millbrook, Volo, Wilmington, Yorkville & Zion.

In IN, see also Cedar Lake, Chesterton & Portage.

HIDE-A-WAY LAKES
Ratings: 7/7.5/6.5 (Campground) From Jct US 34 & Hwy 47: Go S 1 mi on Hwy 47, then E 2 mi on Van Emmon Rd (L); OR From Jct US 71 & Hwy 47: Go E 3 mi on Hwy 71 (L). **FAC:** Gravel rds. (400 spaces). 200 Avail: 50 gravel, 150 grass, 40 pull-thrus (40 x 65), back-ins (40 x 50), some side by side hkups, 100 full hkups, 100 W, 100 E (30/50 amps), seasonal sites, WiFi, tent sites, dump, laundry, groc, LP bottles, fire rings, firewood, controlled access. **REC:** Fox River: fishing, playground, rec open to public. Pets OK. Big rig sites, 2015 rates: $30 to $35.
(630)553-6323 Lat: 41.65741, Lon: -88.43170
8045 Van Emmon Rd., Yorkville, IL 60560
hideawaylakes@hotmail.com
www.hideawaylakes.com
See primary listing at Yorkville and ad page 460.

Like Us on Facebook.

CHILLICOTHE — B3 *Peoria*

CHILLICOTHE RV & RECREATION AREA
Ratings: 8/10★/10 (RV Park) N-bnd: From Jct I-474/SR-6 & Hwy 29: Go N 12 mi on Hwy 29 (L); or S-bnd: From Jct I-180 & I-80: Go S 11 mi on I-80, then S 22-1/3 mi on Hwy 29 to Santa Fe Railroad Viaduct (R) Note: Use "20026 IL-29" if using GPS. **FAC:** Paved rds. (131 spaces). Avail: 23 gravel, patios, 12 pull-thrus (40 x 70), back-ins (40 x 60), 23 full hkups (30/50 amps), seasonal sites, WiFi, dump, mobile sewer, LP gas, fire rings, firewood, controlled access. **REC:** Lake Chillicothe: swim, fishing, shuffleboard, playground. Pets OK. Partial handicap access, no tents. Big rig sites, RV age restrict, 14 day max stay, eco-friendly, 2015 rates: $27 to $38. Apr 1 to Oct 15.
(309)274-2000 Lat: 40.33749, Lon: -89.486845
20205 Route 29 N, Chillicothe, IL 61523
craltd@frontier.com
http://www.chillirecrv.com/
See ad opposite page.

CISNE — E4 *Wayne*

SAM DALE LAKE STATE FISH & WILDLIFE AREA (State Pk) From Jct of US-45 & CR-161 (in Cisne), W 8 mi on CR-161 to CR-700, N 1 mi, follow signs (L). Pit toilets. 2015 rates: $18. (618)835-2292

CLINTON — C4 *DeWitt*

WELDON SPRINGS (State Pk) From town, E 1 mi on SR-10 to cnty park access rd, S 1 mi, follow signs (R). 2015 rates: $10 to $20. (217)935-2644

COLCHESTER — C2 *McDonough*

ARGYLE LAKE (State Pk) From Jct of SR-67 & SR-136, W 7 mi on SR-136 to Argyle Lake Rd, N 2 mi (R). 2015 rates: $18 to $30. (309)776-3422

COLONA — B3 *Henry*

INDIAN TRAILS @ COLONA'S SCOTT FAMILY PARK (Public) From Jct I-80 & Hwy 6 (exit 9): Go E 1 mi on Hwy 6, then N 1 mi on Green River Rd, then W 100 yds on Poppy Garden Rd. 2015 rates: $30 to $35. (309)949-2128

DANVILLE — C5 *Vermilion*

KICKAPOO (State Pk) From I-74 (exit 206), N 2.1 mi on New Town Rd, follow signs (R). 2015 rates: $20 to $30. (217)442-4915

DE PUE — B4 *Bureau*

LAKE DE PUE CITY PARK (Public) From center of town: Go 2 blocks S on Lake St. Apr 15 to Oct 31. (815)447-2177

DE WITT — C4 *DeWitt*

CLINTON LAKE-MASCOUTIN STATE RECREATION COMPLEX (State Pk) From jct Hwy-54 & CR-14: Go 2 mi S on CR-14. 2015 rates: $20 to $35. (217)935-8722

We've listened to thousands of RVers like you, so we know exactly how to rate campgrounds. Got feedback? Call us!877-209-6655

DU QUOIN — E4 *Perry*

DU QUOIN STATE FAIR CAMPGROUND (Public) From jct Hwy-152 & US-51: Go 2-1/4 mi S on US-51. During fair, enter through Gate 3 off US-51; Off-season, enter through Main Gate. 2015 rates: $20. (618)542-9373

DURAND — A3 *Winnebego*

SUGAR SHORES RV RESORT **Ratings: 8.5/8.5/8.5** (Membership Pk) 2015 rates: $45. Apr 15 to Oct 15. (815)629-2568 9938 W Winslow, Durand, IL 61024

EAST MOLINE — B3 *Rock Island*

LUNDEEN'S LANDING **Ratings: 5.5/6/6.5** (Campground) 2015 rates: $25. Apr 1 to Oct 31. (309)496-9956 2119 Barstow Rd, East Moline, IL 61244

EAST PEORIA — C3 *Tazewell*

MILLPOINT RV PARK & CAMPGROUND
Ratings: 6.5/8/8 (Campground) From Jct I-74 & Hwy 116 (Exit 95): Go 5 mi E on Hwy 116, then 3-1/2 mi N on Hwy 26, then 3/4 mi W on Millpoint Rd. (R). Due to flooding in 2015, Good Sam Enterprises was unable to inspect this park's facilities. Ratings are from previous year's Guide. **FAC:** Gravel rds. (83 spaces). Avail: 80 gravel, 17 pull-thrus (60 x 75), back-ins (60 x 75), 80 full hkups (30/50 amps), seasonal sites, WiFi, tent sites, fire rings, firewood. **REC:** Illinois River: swim, fishing, playground. Pets OK. Big rig sites, 2015 rates: $18 to $30. Disc: military.
(309)231-6497 Lat: 40.75653, Lon: -89.55780
310 Ash Lane, East Peoria, IL 61611
dwb600@gmail.com
See ad pages 464, 458.

SPINDLER CAMPGROUND (Public) From Jct of I-74 & SR-116 (exit 95B), N 4 mi on Hwy 150 to access rd 7, W 500 ft (R). 2015 rates: $21 to $30. (309)699-3549

EAST ST LOUIS — E3 *St Clair*

EAST ST LOUIS See also Cahokia & Granite City.

CASINO QUEEN RV PARK
Ratings: 9.5/9/8.5 (RV Park) W-bnd: From Jct of I-55/70 & Exit 2A (3rd St), S 0.3 mi on 3rd St to River Park Dr, W 0.4 mi (L); or E-bnd: From Jct of I-55/64/70 (at bridge, on MO side), E 1.5 mi on I-55/64/70 over bridge to 4th St (bus exit), NE 0.4 mi on exit rd to River Park Dr, W 0.5 mi (L). **FAC:** Paved rds. 140 paved, 140 pull-thrus (27 x 70), 140 full hkups (30/50 amps), WiFi, dump, laundry, groc, restaurant. **REC:** heated pool, playground. Pets OK. Partial handicap access, no tents. Big rig sites, 2015 rates: $55. Disc: AAA. Apr 1 to Sep 30. ATM.
(800)777-0777 Lat: 38.626198, Lon: -90.168560
200 South Front St, East St Louis, IL 62201
queen@casinoqueen.com
www.casinoqueen.com
See ad pages 701, 458.

Tell them you saw them in this Guide!

Things to See and Do

CASINO QUEEN Casino Queen - overlooking the Gateway Arch and conveniently located just minutes from dtwn St. Louis & Busch Stadium. Casino, hotel, restaurants, and RV park. Partial handicap access. RV accessible. Restrooms, food. Hours: 8am to 6am.
(800)777-0777 Lat: 38.626198, Lon: -90.168560
200 S Front St, East St Louis, IL 62201
queen@casinoqueen.com
www.casinoqueen.com
See ad page 701.

EFFINGHAM — D4 *Effingham*

CAMP LAKEWOOD CAMPGROUND & RV PARK
Ratings: 8/9.5★/9.5 (Campground) From Jct of I-70/57 & Exit 162; Turn R (at bottom of ramp) Go to Rickelman Av. Turn L follow signs 2 mi to campground. (L). **FAC:** Gravel rds. (65 spaces). Avail: 50 gravel, 43 pull-thrus (27 x 60), back-ins (24 x 45), some side by side hkups, 50 full hkups (30/50 amps), seasonal sites, WiFi, tent sites, rentals, dump, laundry, groc, LP gas, fire rings, firewood. **REC:** Lake Pauline: fishing, playground. Pets OK. Partial handicap access. Big rig sites, eco-friendly, 2015 rates: $33 to $34.50. Disc: AAA, military.
(217)342-6233 Lat: 39.11957, Lon: -88.54980
1217 W Rickelmann, Effingham, IL 62401
camp@camplakewoodcampground.com
www.camplakewoodcampground.com
See ad this page, 458.

ELGIN — A4 *Kane*

BURNIDGE FOREST PRESERVE/PAUL WOLFF (Public) From Jct I-90, take the Randall Rd. exit. Go S to Big Timber Rd., approximately 1 mi. Turn right (west) onto Big Timber Rd. until you reach entrance for park, approximately 1.2 mi. Pit toilets. 2015 rates: $10 to $25. May 1 to Oct 31. (630)444-1200

EQUALITY — F4 *Saline*

SALINE COUNTY STATE FISH & WILDLIFE AREA (State Pk) From Jct of SR-13 & SR-142, SE 1 mi on SR-142 to cnty rd, S 5 mi, follow signs (R). Pit toilets. 2015 rates: $8. (618)276-4405

FAIRMONT CITY — E3 *St Clair*

SAFARI RV PARK
Ratings: 4/7/3.5 (RV Park) N-bnd: Jct I-55 & US Hwy 203/Collinsville/Fairmont City (Exit 4): Go S 100 yards, then E 2 mi on Collinsville Rd. (R) S-bnd: Jct I-55 & Hwy 111 (Exit 6): Go E 300 yards on Hwy 111, then S 1/4 mi on Collinsville Rd. (R). **FAC:** Paved/gravel rds. (70 spaces). 15 Avail: 3 paved, 12 gravel, back-ins (20 x 50), 15 full hkups (30/50 amps), WiFi, laundry. Pet restrict(B). 2015 rates: $25.
(618)271-0955 Lat: 38.655700, Lon: -90.097358
5100 Collinsville Road, Fairmont City, IL 62201
Safarirv@charter.net
www.safarirvparkstl.com
See ad page 701.

We appreciate your business!

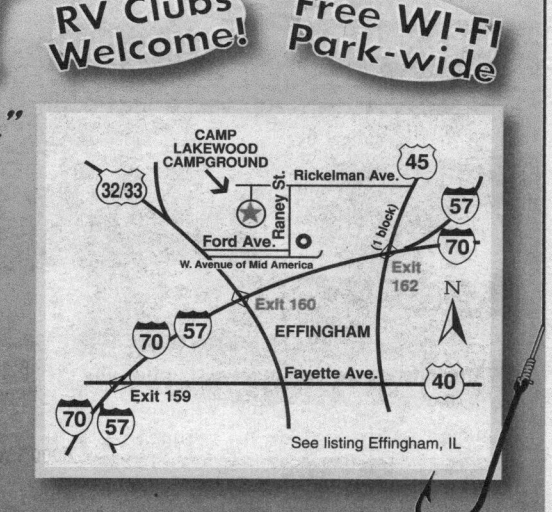

FINDLAY — D4 *Shelby*

EAGLE CREEK (State Pk) From Jct of Hwy 16 & Rte 128, N 10 mi on Rte 128 to Findlay Rd, E 4 mi to park access rd, S 2 mi (E). 2015 rates: $20 to $30. (217)756-8260

LONE POINT REC AREA (Public Corps) From town, S 2.8 mi on Findlay Concrete Hwy to unmarked rd, E 0.5 mi to unmarked rd, S 0.8 mi to unmarked rd, E 0.5 mi to unmarked rd, S 0.5 mi (E). 2015 rates: $16 to $32. May 14 to Sep 7. (217)774-3951

FLORA — E4 *Clay*

CHARLEY BROWN PARK (Public) From Jct of Hwy 50 & Rte 45, W 1 mi on Hwy 50 to cnty rd, S 0.75 mi to 2nd cnty rd, W 1 mi (L). 2015 rates: $15. May 15 to Nov 15. (618)662-8313

FOX LAKE — A5 *Lake*

CHAIN-O-LAKES (State Pk) From Jct of US-12 & Wilmot Rd, N 2 mi on Wilmot Rd (R). 2015 rates: $12 to $35. (847)587-5512

GALENA — A3 *Jo Daviess*

PALACE CAMPGROUND Ratings: 8.5/8.5★/8 (Campground) W-bnd: From Jct US-20 & Main St: Go W 2 mi on US-20 (R); or; E-bnd: From Jct SR-84W & US-20: Go SE 2 mi on US-20 (L) Note: Must be 21 or older or w/parent to stay in any site at this park. **FAC:** Paved/gravel rds. 95 gravel, 8 pull-thrus (30 x 50), back-ins (22 x 40), 50 full hkups, 30 W, 45 E (30/50 amps), WiFi, tent sites, rentals, dump, laundry, fire rings, firewood. **REC:** heated pool, wading pool, playground. Pets OK. Eco-friendly, 2015 rates: $24 to $35. Disc: AAA, military. Apr 1 to Nov 1. AAA Approved
(815)777-2466 Lat: 42.434736, Lon: -90.449436
11357 Rte 20 W, Galena, IL 61036
palace@palacecampground.com
www.palacecampground.com

GALESBURG — B3 *Knox*

GALESBURG EAST CAMPGROUND
Ratings: 9/9.5★/9 (Campground) From Jct I-74 & US-150 (Exit 54): Go E 1/2 mi on US-150 (L). Note: Do not use GPS, follow blue camping signs. **FAC:** Gravel rds. (60 spaces). Avail: 49 gravel, 39 pull-thrus (30 x 60), back-ins (30 x 60), 49 full hkups (30/50 amps), seasonal sites, WiFi, tent sites, rentals, dump, laundry, groc, LP gas, fire rings, firewood. **REC:** heated pool, pond, fishing, playground. Pets OK. Partial handicap access. Big rig sites, eco-friendly, 2015 rates: $34 to $38. Apr 1 to Oct 31.
(309)289-2267 Lat: 40.908171, Lon: -90.234963
1081 US Hwy 150 E, Knoxville, IL 61448
galesburgeastcampground@gmail.com
www.galesburgeastcampground.com
See ad this page, 458.

We rate what RVers consider important.

GENESEO — B3 *Henry*

GENESEO CAMPGROUND
Ratings: 9/9/9.5 (Campground) From Jct of I-80 & IL-82 (Exit 19) follow blue camping signs 4 mi thru town to campground; or carefully follow these directions, From Jct I-80 & IL-82 (Exit 19): Go N 1-1/4 mi on IL-82, then continue N 1/2 mi on Oakwood Ave, then W 1/4 mi on Exchange St, then N 2 mi on IL-82/College St (R) No car GPS. **FAC:** Gravel rds. 62 gravel, 59 pull-thrus (28 x 65), back-ins (28 x 55), 40 full hkups, 22 W, 22 E (30/50 amps), WiFi, tent sites, rentals, dump, laundry, groc, LP gas, fire rings, firewood. **REC:** pool, Hennepin Canal: fishing, playground. Pets OK. Big rig sites, eco-friendly, 2015 rates: $22 to $31. Apr 1 to Oct 31.
(309)944-6465 Lat: 41.483673, Lon: -90.157073
22978 Il Hwy 82, Geneseo, IL 61254
w6465@geneseo.net
www.campingfriend.com/geneseocampground
See ad this page.

GIBSON CITY — C4 *Ford*

SOUTH PARK MUNICIPAL CAMPGROUND (Public) From jct IL47/54/9: Go E one block. 2015 rates: $12. (217)784-5872

GOLCONDA — F4 *Pope*

DIXON SPRINGS (State Pk) From Jct of I-24 & SR-146 (exit 16), E 12 mi on SR-146 (L). 2015 rates: $18. (618)949-3394

GOODFIELD — C4 *Woodford*

TIMBERLINE CAMPGROUND **Ratings: 8.5/8.5★/7.5** (Campground) 2015 rates: $36 to $44. (309)965-2224 1467 Timberline Drive, Goodfield, IL 61742

GOREVILLE — F4 *Johnson*

FERNE CLYFFE (State Pk) From town, S 1 mi on SR-37 (R). 2015 rates: $20 to $30. (618)995-2411

GRAFTON — D2 *Jersey*

PERE MARQUETTE (State Pk) From Jct of SR-3 & SR-100, W 5 mi on SR-100, follow signs (R). 2015 rates: $20 to $30. (618)786-3323

GRANITE CITY — E3 *Madison*

GRANITE CITY KOA **Ratings: 8.5/9.5★/7.5** (Campground) 2015 rates: $41.50 to $47.50. Apr 1 to Nov 1. (618)931-5160 3157 W Chain of Rocks Rd, Granite City, IL 62040

HORSESHOE LAKE (State Pk) From jct I-270 & Hwy 111: Go 4 mi S on Hwy 111. Pit toilets. 2015 rates: $8. May 1 to Sep 30. (618)931-0270

GRAYVILLE — E5 *White*

HILLTOP CAMPGROUND (Public) From Jct of I-64 & Hwy 1 (exit 130), N 1.5 mi on Hwy 1 to North St, E 4 blks to Water St, S 0.25 mi to Walnut St, E 1 blk to Oxford St, S 0.25 mi, follow signs (E). 2015 rates: $10. (618)375-3671

HAMPTON — B3 *Carroll*

FISHERMAN'S CORNER NORTH REC AREA (Public Corps) From Jct of I-80 & SR-84, SW 1 mi on SR-84 (R). 2015 rates: $20. May 1 to Oct 24. (815)259-3628

HANOVER — A3 *Jo Daviess*

BLANDING LANDING (COE - LOCK & DAM 11) (Public Corps) From Hwy-84 in town: Go 7 mi W on Blanding Rd, follow signs. 2015 rates: $10 to $14. May 1 to Oct 24. (563)582-0881

HARMON — B3 *Lee*

GREEN RIVER STATE WILDLIFE AREA (State Pk) From town: Go 6 mi N on hwy 26, then follow signs W on blacktop road. 2015 rates: $8. (815)379-2324

HAVANA — C3 *Fulton, Mason*

ANDERSON LAKE CONSERVATION AREA (State Pk) From town, NE 11 mi on SR-100 (L). Pit toilets. 2015 rates: $8. (309)759-4484

HERRIN — F4 *Williamson*

FOUR SEASONS CAMPGROUND
Ratings: 7/7.5★/8.5 (Campground) From Jct of I-57 & Exit 59 (Herrin St), W 4 mi on Herrin St to N Third St, N 1mi on N Third St/E Carroll St (L). **FAC:** Gravel rds. (37 spaces). Avail: 32 gravel, 12 pull-thrus (45 x 65), back-ins (45 x 60), 32 full hkups (30/50 amps), seasonal sites, WiFi, dump, laundry, LP gas, fire rings. **REC:** pond, fishing. Pets OK. No tents. Big rig sites, 2015 rates: $25.
(618)942-2069 Lat: 37.80121, Lon: -89.03046
721 E Carroll St, Herrin, IL 62948
rvpark4@gmail.com
www.rvparkfourseasons.com

HILLSBORO — D3 *Montgomery*

SHERWOOD FOREST (Public) From Jct of SR-16 & SR-127 (in town), N 0.4 mi on SR-16/SR-127 to Seward St, E 100 ft to Main St, S around square to N Main, N 1.6 mi to CR-1275N, E 1.4 mi (E). 2015 rates: $25 to $35. Apr 1 to Oct 31. (217)532-5211

ILLINOIS CITY — B2 *Rock Island*

BLANCHARD ISLAND (COE-MISSISSIPPI RIVER REC AREAS-MUSCATINE AREA) (Public Corps) From town: Go 6 mi W on Hwy 92/New Boston Rd, follow signs. Pit toilets. 2015 rates: $4. (563)263-7913

According to some studies, almost 50 percent of RVers camp with pets! Find out more in our Pampered Pet Parks feature at the front of the Guide.

JACKSONVILLE — D3 *Morgan*

CRAZY HORSE CAMPGROUND
Ratings: 8/9★/9.5 (Campground) From Jct of I-72 & (Exit 68) Morton Ave (Old Hwy 36), N 0.6 mi on Old 36 to Mobil Rd, N 5 mi to Hacker Rd, W 3 mi (L). **FAC:** Gravel rds. (103 spaces). Avail: 33 gravel, 11 pull-thrus (50 x 60), back-ins (50 x 55), 33 full hkups (30/50 amps), seasonal sites, WiFi, tent sites, rentals, showers $, dump, laundry, groc, LP gas, fire rings, firewood, restaurant. **REC:** pond, swim, fishing, playground. Pets OK. Partial handicap access. Big rig sites, eco-friendly, 2015 rates: $38 to $41. Apr 1 to Oct 31. ATM.
(217)886-2089 Lat: 39.81942, Lon: -90.18249
2113 Crazy Horse Rd, Ashland, IL 62612
camp@crazyhorsecamp.com
www.crazyhorsecamp.com
See ad pages 466, 458.

JOHNSTON CITY — F4 *Williamson*

ARROWHEAD LAKE CAMPGROUND (Public) From Jct of I-57 & Exit 59(Broadway), E 2 mi on Broadway (thru town) to entrance rd (L). 2015 rates: $12 to $23. (618)983-3535

JOLIET — B5 *Will*

LEISURE LAKE RESORT
Ratings: 9.5/9★/9.5 (Membership Pk) S-bnd: From Jct I-55 & IL-59 (Exit 251): Go W 0.1 mi on Seil Rd, then S 2 mi on Frontage Rd (R) or N-bnd: From Jct I-55 & US 52 (Exit 253): Go W 0.5 mi on US 52 (Jefferson St), then S 1 mi on IL-59 (Cottage St), then W 0.1 mi on Seil Rd,then S 2 mi on Frontage Rd (R). **FAC:** Gravel rds. (265 spaces). Avail: 175 paved, patios, 18 pull-thrus (35 x 70), back-ins (35 x 60), 155 full hkups, 20 W, 20 E (30/50 amps), seasonal sites, WiFi, dump, mobile sewer, laundry, LP gas, fire rings, firewood, controlled access. **REC:** pool, Leisure Lake: swim, fishing, playground. Pets OK. Partial handicap access, no tents. Big rig sites, eco-friendly, 2015 rates: $50. Mar 1 to Nov 30.
(815)741-9405 Lat: 41.48433, Lon: -88.20124
21900 SW Frontage Rd, Joliet, IL 60404
info@leisurelakeresort.com
www.leisurelakeresort.com
See ad opposite page, 458.

RV PARK AT HOLLYWOOD CASINO JOLIET
Ratings: 8.5/9.5★/9 (RV Park) From Jct I-80 & IL-7 (exit 130A): Go S 1 mi on IL-7 (Larkin Ave S), then W 1-1/2 mi on US-6 (L). Follow signs thru casino parking lot. **FAC:** Paved rds. 80 paved, patios, 17 pull-thrus (45 x 70), back-ins (40 x 50), 80 W, 80 E (30/50 amps), WiFi Hotspot, dump, laundry, restaurant. **REC:** rec open to public. Pets OK. Partial handicap access, no tents. 2015 rates: $35 to $45. Apr 15 to Oct 15.
(815)744-9400 Lat: 41.48333, Lon: -88.14554
777 Hollywood Blvd, Joliet, IL 60434
www.hollywoodcasinojoliet.com

"Full hookups" in a campground listing means there are water, electric and sewer hookups at the sites.

JOSLIN — B3 *Rock Island*

SUNSET LAKES RESORT
Ratings: 9.5/8★/10 (RV Park) From Jct of I-88 & SR-92 (Exit 6): Go E 1 mi on Hwy 92, then 1/2 mi S on 290th St (L). **FAC:** Paved rds. 268 Avail: 143 paved, 125 gravel, patios, 36 pull-thrus (35 x 55), back-ins (38 x 60), 120 full hkups, 148 W, 148 E (30/50 amps), WiFi $, tent sites, rentals, dump, laundry, groc, fire rings, firewood, restaurant, controlled access. **REC:** pool, Sunset Lake: fishing, shuffleboard, playground. Pets OK. Partial handicap access. Big rig sites, eco-friendly, 2015 rates: $43.12 to $80. Apr 11 to Oct 19. ATM.
(800)747-5253 Lat: 41.549030, Lon: -90.216112
3333 290th St North, Hillsdale, IL 61257
info@sunsetlakesresort.com
www.sunsetlakesresort.com
See ad this page, 458, 459.

KANKAKEE — B5 *Kankakee*

KANKAKEE SOUTH KOA **Ratings: 8.5/8★/8** (Campground) 2015 rates: $40. Apr 1 to Oct 31. (815)939-4603 425 E 6000 S Rd, Chebanse, IL 60922

KEWANEE — B3 *Henry*

FRANCIS PARK (Public) From town, E 4 mi on US 34, follow signs (L). 2015 rates: $6. (309)852-0511

JOHNSON/SAUK TRAIL (State Pk) From town, N 5 mi on SR-78 to park access rd; or From Jct of I-80 (exit 33) & SR-78, S 5 mi on SR-78 (L). 2015 rates: $18 to $40. (309)853-5589

LA SALLE — B4 *La Salle*

LA SALLE See also Marseilles & Utica.

LACON — B3 *Marshall*

MARSHALL STATE FISH & WILDLIFE AREA (State Pk) From Jct of Hwys 17 & 26, S 5 mi on Hwy 26, follow signs (R). 2015 rates: $18. (309)246-8351

LAWRENCEVILLE — E5 *Lawrence*

RED HILLS (State Pk) From Jct of SR-1 & US-50, W 8 mi on US-50, follow signs (L). 2015 rates: $20 to $30. Apr to Nov. (618)936-2469

LE ROY — C4 *McLean*

MORAINE VIEW (State Pk) From Jct of I-74 & Rte. 21, N 5.6 mi to CR-36, E 2 mi, follow signs (R). 2015 rates: $20 to $40. (309)724-8032

LELAND — B4 *La Salle*

HI-TIDE BEACH & CAMPGROUND **Ratings: 8.5/10★/9** (Campground) 2015 rates: $48 to $50. Apr 15 to Oct 15. (815)495-9032 4611 E 22nd Rd, Leland, IL 60531

LENA — A3 *Stephenson*

LAKE LE-AQUA-NA (State Pk) From Jct of Hwy 73 & US-20, N 5.75 mi on Hwy 73 to Lake Rd, W 2.1 mi on Lake Rd (L). 2015 rates: $20. (815)369-4282

LENA KOA **Ratings: 9/9/8** (Campground) 2015 rates: $39.95 to $48.95. Apr 1 to Nov 1. (815)369-2612 10982 W Hwy 20, Lena, IL 61048

LINCOLN — C3 *Logan*

CAMP A WHILE
Ratings: 6.5/8.5★/8.5 (Campground) S-bnd: From Jct I-55 & Bus-55 (Exit 133): Go S 2-1/2 mi on Bus-55, then N 7/10 mi on Nicholson Rd (L) or N-bnd: From Jct I-55 & Lincoln Pkwy (Exit 123): Go N 6 mi on Lincoln Pkwy, then N 7/10 mi on Nicholson Rd (L). **FAC:** All weather rds. (20 spaces). Avail: 18 all weather, 6 pull-thrus (21 x 60), back-ins (21 x 56), 7 full hkups, 11 W, 11 E (30/50 amps), seasonal sites, WiFi, tent sites, showers $, dump, laundry, fire rings. **REC:** playground. Pets OK. Partial handicap access. Eco-friendly, 2015 rates: $20 to $40. Disc: military. Apr 1 to Oct 31. No CC.
(217)732-8840 Lat: 40.17536, Lon: -89.35893
1779-1250th Avenue, Lincoln, IL 62656
lincolncampawhile@gmail.com

LITCHFIELD — D3 *Montgomery*

KAMPER KOMPANION RV PARK **Ratings: 6.5/8.5/7.5** (RV Park) 2015 rates: $34 to $37. Mar 1 to Dec 31. (217)324-4747 18388 E Frontage Rd, Litchfield, IL 62056

MACOMB — C2 *McDonough*

KILJORDAN MEADOWS MH COMMUNITY & RV PARK Ratings: 4/NA/8 (RV Area in MHP) From Hwy 110/IL 336 & US136: Go E 2 mi on US136/W Jackson, then cross RR tracks and1/2mi N onto US136/67S, then at 2nd 4-way stop, E 2 mi on E. Jackson (R). **FAC:** Paved rds. 22 paved, patios, back-ins (35 x 70), 22 full hkups (30/50 amps). **REC:** playground. Pet restrict(B). Big rig sites, 2015 rates: $20.
(309)837-2883 Lat: 40.45859, Lon: -90.64843
1601 E. Jackson St., Macomb, IL 61455
kiljordan@towermgmt.com
www.kiljordanmeadowsmhc.com

SPRING LAKE PARK CAMPGROUND (CITY PARK) (Public) From west jct US 136 & US 67: Go 4 mi N on US 67, then 2 mi W on CR N1500. (Spring Lake Park Rd). 2015 rates: $10 to $15. (309)833-2052

MARENGO — A4 *McHenry*

LEHMAN'S LAKESIDE RV RESORT
Ratings: 9.5/10★/9 (RV Park) From Jct I-90 & US-20 (Marengo exit): Go N 1 mi on US-20, then W 3 mi on Harmony Rd (L). **FAC:** Paved rds. (162 spaces). Avail: 68 all weather, 50 pull-thrus (50 x 70), back-ins (50 x 75), 46 full hkups, 22 W, 22 E (30/50 amps), seasonal sites, WiFi, tent sites, dump, mobile sewer, laundry, groc, LP bottles, fire rings, firewood. **REC:** Lehman's Lake: swim, fishing, playground. Pets OK. Partial handicap access. Big rig sites, eco-friendly, 2015 rates: $38 to $48.
(815)923-4533 Lat: 42.174213, Lon: -88.578605
19609 Harmony Rd, Marengo, IL 60152
lehmanslakeside@aol.com
www.lehmanrv.com
See ad this page, 458.

MARION — F4 *Williamson*

MARION CAMPGROUND & RV PARK
Ratings: 7/9.5★/9 (RV Park) From Jct of I-57 & Exit 53, E 0.1 mi on W Main St to 7th St, N (left) 0.1 mi (R). **FAC:** Gravel rds. (58 spaces). Avail: 40 gravel, 27 pull-thrus (30 x 60), back-ins (28 x 50), some side by side hkups, 40 full hkups (30/50 amps), seasonal sites, cable, WiFi, laundry, firewood. **REC:** playground. Pets OK. Partial hand-

Follow the arrow. The arrow in each listing indicates where the facility is located in relation to the listed town.

MARION (CONT)

MARION CAMPGROUND & RV (CONT)
icap access, no tents. Big rig sites, 2015 rates: $28 to $34.
(618)997-3484 Lat: 37.732684, Lon: -88.954884
119 N 7th St, Marion, IL 62959
julie@marioncampground.com
www.marioncampground.com
See ad page 463.

MARSEILLES — B4 *La Salle*

GLENWOOD RV RESORT
Ratings: 7.5/7★/7.5 (Campground) At I-80 & CR-15 (Exit 97): Go S 3-1/2 mi on CR-15, then E 1/2 mi on Rt 6 (Bluff St) to 4 way stop sign, then N 1/4 mi on Wilson to entrance (R). **FAC:** Paved/gravel rds. (501 spaces). 151 Avail: 21 gravel, 130 grass, 2 pull-thrus (38 x 80), back-ins (38 x 80), some side by side hkups, 14 full hkups, 137 W, 137 E (30 amps), seasonal sites, WiFi Hotspot, tent sites, rentals, dump, mobile sewer, fire rings, firewood, restaurant, controlled access. **REC:** pool, pond, swim, playground. Pets OK. 2015 rates: $36 to $45. Disc: AAA. No CC.
AAA Approved
(815)795-6000 Lat: 41.33057, Lon: -88.70911
551 Wilson St, Marseilles, IL 61341
info@glenwoodrvresort.com
www.glenwoodrvresort.com
See ad page 467.

ILLINI (State Pk) From Jct of I-80 & Marseilles exit/CR-15, S 4 mi on CR-15 (L). 2015 rates: $10 to $30. (815)795-2448

MARSHALL — D5 *Clark*

LINCOLN TRAIL (State Pk) From Jct of I-70 & SR-1 (exit 147), S 5 mi on SR-1, follow signs (R). 2015 rates: $10 to $20. (217)826-2222

MILL CREEK PARK CAMPGROUND (CLARK COUNTY PARK) (Public) From jct I-70 (exit 147) & Hwy 1: Go 1 mi S on Hwy 1, then 3/4 mi W on US 40, then 7 mi NW on Lincoln Heritage Tr. 2015 rates: $12 to $24. (217)889-3901

MCLEANSBORO — E4 *Hamilton*

HAMILTON COUNTY CONSERVATION AREA (State Pk) From town, E 8 mi on Rte 14 to park access rd, S 1 mi, follow signs (E). 2015 rates: $20 to $30. (618)773-4340

METROPOLIS — F4 *Massac*

FORT MASSAC (State Pk) From Jct of I-24 & US-45 (exit 37), W 2.5 mi on US-45 (L). 2015 rates: $10 to $20. (618)524-4712

MILLBROOK — B4 *Cook, Kendall*

YOGI BEAR'S JELLYSTONE PARK CAMP RESORT Ratings: 9.5/6/9.5 (RV Park) From Jct SR-47 & SR-71: Go SW 6 mi on SR-71, then N 1.2 mi on Millbrook Rd (R). **FAC:** Paved rds. (367 spaces). Avail: 219 paved, 2 pull-thrus (30 x 65), back-ins (40 x 70), 55 full hkups, 164 W, 164 E (30/50 amps), seasonal sites, WiFi, tent sites, rentals, dump, laundry, groc, LP gas, firewood, controlled access. **REC:** pool, wading pool, whirlpool, pond, fishing, playground. Pets OK $. Partial handicap access. Big rig sites, eco-friendly, 2015 rates: $51 to $55.
AAA Approved
(800)438-9644 Lat: 41.593120, Lon: -88.542753
8574 Millbrook Rd, Millbrook, IL 60536
info@jellystonechicago.com
www.jellystonechicago.com

MORRISON — A3 *Whiteside*

MORRISON ROCKWOOD (State Pk) From Jct of US-30 & SR-78, N 1 mi on SR-78 to Damen Rd, E 1.5 mi to Crosby Rd, N 0.5 mi (E). 2015 rates: $20. (815)772-4708

MOUNT CARROLL — A3 *Carroll*

TIMBER LAKE RESORT
Ratings: 8/7.5/9.5 (Campground) From Jct US 52 & IL 40: Go E 2.3 mi on IL 40, then S 1.2 mi on Black Oak Rd (L). **FAC:** Paved/gravel rds. (140 spaces). 46 Avail: 32 paved, 14 gravel, 3 pull-thrus (35 x 70), back-ins (30 x 55), 32 full hkups, 14 W, 14 E (30/50 amps), seasonal sites, tent sites, rentals, dump, laundry, LP gas, firewood. **REC:** pool, Timber Lake: fishing, shuffleboard, playground. Pet restrict(Q). Partial handicap access. Big rig sites, eco-friendly, 2015 rates: $40 to $66. Apr 15 to Nov 10. ATM.
(800)485-0145 Lat: 42.051538, Lon: -89.939094
8216 Black Oak Rd, Mount Carroll, IL 61053
info@timberlakeresort.com
www.timberlakeresort.com
See ad this page.

MOUNT VERNON — E4 *Jefferson*

ARCHWAY RV PARK
Ratings: 7.5/9.5★/8 (RV Park) Jct I-57 & IL Hwy-15 (Exit 95): Go 3/4 mi W on IL Hwy-15/Broadway St (R). **FAC:** Gravel rds. 42 gravel, 42 pull-thrus (24 x 65), mostly side by side hkups, 36 full hkups, 6 W, 6 E (30/50 amps), WiFi, tent sites, rentals, dump, laundry, LP gas. **REC:** playground. Pets OK. Partial handicap access. Big rig sites, eco-friendly, 2015 rates: $35.
(618)244-0399 Lat: 38.312921, Lon: -88.965569
4810 Broadway, Mount Vernon, IL 62864
justsidsinc@gmail.com
www.Archwayrvpark.com
See ad this page, 458.

MULBERRY GROVE — D3 *Bond*

CEDARBROOK RV PARK & CAMPGROUND
Ratings: 10/9.5★/9.5 (Campground) From Jct of I-70 & Mulberry Grove/Keyesport Rd (EXIT 52), S 1 mi on Mulberry Grove/Keyesport Rd (R). **FAC:** All weather rds. (89 spaces). Avail: 15 all weather, 10 pull-thrus (22 x 80), back-ins (32 x 40), 10 full hkups, 5 W, 5 E (50 amps), seasonal sites, WiFi, tent sites, rentals, dump, mobile sewer, laundry, groc, LP gas, fire rings, firewood. **REC:** pool, Lake Howard: fishing, playground. Pets OK. Big rig sites, eco-friendly, 2015 rates: $34. Disc: AAA, military. Apr 1 to Oct 31.
AAA Approved
(618)326-8865 Lat: 38.90683, Lon: -89.28458
1109 Mulberry Grove Rd, Mulberry Grove, IL 62262
cedarbrookrvpark@msn.com
www.cedarbrookrvpark.com
See ad this page, 458.

TIMBER TRAILS CAMPGROUND **Ratings: 6/5.5/9** (Campground) 2015 rates: $34. Apr 1 to Nov 15. (618)326-8264 1276 Matts Lane, Mulberry Grove, IL 62262

MURPHYSBORO — F3 *Jackson*

LAKE MURPHYSBORO (State Pk) From Jct of SR-149 & SR-127, W 3.5 mi on SR-149 (R). 2015 rates: $10 to $20. (618)684-2867

NASHVILLE — E3 *Washington*

WASHINGTON COUNTY CONSERVATION AREA (State Pk) From Jct of I-64 & SR-127 (exit 50), S 8 mi on SR-127, follow signs (L). 2015 rates: $20 to $30. (618)327-3137

NAUVOO — C2 *Hancock*

NAUVOO (State Pk) From Jct of Hwy 96 & US-136, N 11 mi on Hwy 96, follow signs (R). 2015 rates: $20 to $30. (217)453-2512

NEWTON — D5 *Jasper*

SAM PARR STATE FISH & WILDLIFE AREA (State Pk) From town, NE 3 mi on SR-33 (L). Pit toilets. 2015 rates: $18. (618)783-2661

OAKLAND — D5 *Coles, Douglas*

HEBRON HILLS CAMPING **Ratings: 6/7.5★/7.5** (Campground) 2015 rates: $16 to $22. May 15 to Oct 15. (217)346-3385 14349 N Co Rd 2350E, Oakland, IL 61943

WALNUT POINT (State Pk) From town, N 1 mi on Hwy 3 (becomes Hwy 7), N 2 mi, follow signs (L). 2015 rates: $10 to $30. (217)346-3336

OLIVE BRANCH — F3 *Alexander*

HORSESHOE LAKE CONSERVATION AREA (State Pk) From S end of town, SE 2 mi on SR-3, follow signs (R). 2015 rates: $8 to $20. May 1 to Oct 31. (618)776-5689

OQUAWKA — B2 *Henderson*

BIG RIVER SF (State Pk) From town, S 4 mi on cnty rd (R). Pit toilets. 2015 rates: $8. (309)374-2496

DELABAR (State Pk) From town, N 1 mi on cnty rd (L) (Must obtain permit from park staff upon arrival). 2015 rates: $14 to $18. (309)374-2496

HENDERSON COUNTY STATE CONSERVATION AREA (State Pk) From town: Go 4 mi S on Hwy 164. Pit toilets. 2015 rates: $8. (309)374-2496

OREGON — A3 *Ogle*

HANSEN'S HIDE AWAY RANCH & FAMILY CAMPGROUND Ratings: 7/9★/8 (Campground) From Jct Hwy 64 & Hwy 2: Go S 3/4 mi on Hwy 2, then W 3-1/2 mi on Pines Rd (CR- 6), then S 1-1/2 mi on Ridge Rd, then W 3/4 mi on Harmony Rd (L). **FAC:** Gravel rds. (54 spaces). Avail: 10 grass, 10 pull-thrus (30 x 60), some side by side hkups, 10 W, 10 E (30 amps), WiFi Hotspot, tent sites, dump, mobile sewer, firewood. **REC:** Lake Liz: swim, playground, rec open to public. Pets OK. Eco-friendly, 2015 rates: $24. Apr 15 to Nov 1. No CC.
(815)732-6489 Lat: 41.974345, Lon: -89.420097
2916 South Harmony Rd, Oregon, IL 61061
www.hansenshideawaycampground.com

LAKE LADONNA FAMILY CAMPGROUND **Ratings: 5.5/8.5/8** (Campground) 2015 rates: $40. Apr 15 to Oct 15. (815)732-6804 1302 S Harmony Rd, Oregon, IL 61061

LOWDEN (State Pk) From Jct of Hwy 64 & River Rd, N 2 mi on River Rd (L). 2015 rates: $10 to $20. (815)732-6828

WHITE PINES FOREST (State Pk) From town, W 8 mi on W Pines Rd, follow signs (R) (Call during Mar-Apr for ground conditions). 2015 rates: $10. May to Oct. (815)946-3717

PECATONICA — A3 *Winnebago*

PECATONICA RIVER FOREST PRESERVE (Public) From Jct of US-20 & SR-70, NW 12 mi on SR-70 to Judd Rd, S 1.5 mi, follow signs (R). Pit toilets. 2015 rates: $8 to $15. (815)877-6100

PEKIN — C3 *Tazewell*

SPRING LAKE FISH & WILDLIFE AREA (State Pk) From town, N 2 mi on CR-16 to CR-21, W 3 mi (E). Pit toilets. 2015 rates: $8. (309)968-7135

PEORIA — C3 *Peoria*

MT HAWLEY RV PARK (MHP)
Ratings: 4.5/NA/7.5 (RV Area in MHP) From Jct of SR-6 & SR-40 (Exit 6): Go S 1 mi on SR-40/Knoxville Ave (R). **FAC:** Paved rds. (90 spaces). Avail: 14 paved, patios, back-ins (25 x 60), 14 full hkups (30/50 amps), seasonal sites. Pets OK. No tents. 2015 rates: $30. No CC.
(309)692-2223 Lat: 40.74554, Lon: -89.60861
8327 N Knoxville Ave, Peoria, IL 61615
See ad this page.

PERCY — E3 *Perry*

LAKE CAMP-A-LOT **Ratings: 6.5/7/6.5** (Campground) 2015 rates: $18. (618)497-2972 13541 Community Lakes Road, Percy, IL 62272

PETERSBURG — C3 *Menard*

LINCOLN'S NEW SALEM STATE HISTORIC SITE-CAMPGROUND (State Pk) From Jct of SR-125 & SR-97, N 13.2 mi on SR-97 (L). 2015 rates: $10 to $30. (217)632-4000

PINCKNEYVILLE — E3 *Perry*

PYRAMID (State Pk) From Jct of SR-154 & SR-13, S 6 mi on SR-13 to Pyatt Black Top, W 2.75 mi, follow signs (R). Pit toilets. 2015 rates: $6 to $8. (618)357-2574

PITTSFIELD — D2 *Pike*

YOGI BEAR'S JELLYSTONE PARK AT PINE LAKES **Ratings: 9.5/8.5★/8.5** (Campground) 2015 rates: $26 to $50. Apr 15 to Nov 15. (217)285-6719 1405 Lakeview Heights, Pittsfield, IL 62363

PLEASANT HILL — D2 *Pike*

GREAT RIVER ROAD CAMPGROUND (CITY PARK) (Public) From Hwy 96 & S Main St: Go 1/2 mi S on S Main St. to Campground Rd. 2015 rates: $10. Apr 1 to Oct 31. (217)734-2113

PROPHETSTOWN — B3 *Whiteside*

PROPHETSTOWN SRA (State Pk) From Jct of Hwys 78 & 172, E 0.25 mi on Hwy 172 (L). 2015 rates: $20 to $30. May 1 to Oct 30. (815)537-2926

QUINCY — C2 *Adams*

DRIFTWOOD CAMPGROUND Ratings: 8.5/7.5/8.5 (Campground) From Jct of I-172 & Broadway (Exit 14), W 4.5 mi on Broadway (Staying in left lane, do not go over bridge) to Bonansinga Dr, N 1.6 mi (R) Caution: Do not use Cedar St, low bridge. **FAC:** Paved rds. (37 spaces). Avail: 24 paved, patios, 2 pull-thrus (36 x 100), back-ins (25 x 55), 20 full hkups, 4 W, 4 E (30/50 amps), seasonal sites, WiFi, tent sites, dump, laundry, fire rings, firewood. **REC:** pool, playground. Pets OK. Big rig sites, eco-friendly, 2015 rates: $19 to $28. Disc: AAA, military. No CC.
(217)222-7229 Lat: 39.960029, Lon: -91.414427
2300 Bonansinga Dr, Quincy, IL 62305
info@rvquincy.com
rvquincy.com

RV Park ratings you can rely on!

See listing Peoria, IL

SILOAM SPRINGS (State Pk) From Jct of SR-24 & CR-2950E, S 10 mi on CR-2950E; or From Jct SR-104 & CR-2873E, N 6 mi on CR-2873E, follow signs (R). 2015 rates: $20. (217)894-6205

RAMSEY — D4 *Fayette*

RAMSEY LAKE (State Pk) From Jct of I-70 & US-51 (exit 63), N 12 mi on US-51, follow signs (L). 2015 rates: $20. (618)423-2215

RANTOUL — C5 *Champaign*

PRAIRIE PINES CAMPGROUND (Public) From Jct of I-57 & US-136 (exit 250), E 1.6 mi on US-136 to US-45, S 2 mi to Chandler Rd, E 1 mi on Chandler/S Perimeter Rds (L); or From Jct of I-74 & US-45 (exit 184), N 10.4 mi on US-45 to Chandler Rd, E 1 mi (L) (No Water Nov-Mar). 2015 rates: $25. (217)893-0438

ROCHESTER — D3 *Christian, Sangamon*

SANGCHRIS LAKE (State Pk) From Jct of I-55 & Hwy 29 (exit 96A), S 5 mi on Hwy 29 to Walnut, S 5 mi to New City, E 3 mi (E); or N-bnd: From Jct of I-55 & Rte 104 (exit 82), W 5 mi on Rte 104, follow signs. 2015 rates: $10 to $20. Apr 1 to Jan 16. (217)498-9208

ROCK FALLS — B3 *Whiteside*

CRYSTAL LAKE RV PARK
Ratings: 8/10★/7.5 (RV Park) Jct of I-88 & IL-40: Go 1.5 mi N on IL-40, then 1 mi E on Hwy-30, then 0.5 mi N on Industrial Park Rd, then 0.5 W on East 17th St straight into park (E). **FAC:** All weather rds. 42 Avail: 42 all weather, patios, 9 pull-thrus (55 x 65), back-ins (55 x 65), 42 full hkups (30/50 amps), WiFi, dump, groc, fire rings, firewood, controlled access. **REC:** Crystal Lake: swim, rec open to public. Pets OK. Partial handicap access, no tents. Big rig sites, eco-friendly, 2015 rates: $45. Apr 15 to Oct 1.
(815)622-5974 Lat: 41.76601, Lon: -89.67114
600 East 17th street, Rock Falls, IL 61071
crystallake11@comcast.net
crystallake1.com
See ad this page, 458.

Park owners want you to be satisfied with your stay. Get to know them.

LEISURE LAKE CAMPGROUND INC. **Ratings: 5/7.5/7** (Campground) 2015 rates: $26 to $28. Apr 1 to Oct 15. (815)626-0005 2304 French St, Rock Falls, IL 61071

ROCK ISLAND — B2 *Rock Island*

ROCK ISLAND/QUAD CITIES KOA
Ratings: 9/9/9.5 (Campground) From Jct of I-280 & SR-92 (exit 11A): Go S 1-1/2 mi on SR-92, then E 500 ft on 78th Ave/SR-92 (Andalusia Rd Exit), then E 1 mi on 78th Ave (L). **FAC:** Gravel rds. (150 spaces). Avail: 85 gravel, 22 pull-thrus (27 x 100), back-ins (25 x 40), 80 full hkups, 5 W, 5 E (30/50 amps), seasonal sites, cable, WiFi, tent sites, rentals, dump, laundry, groc, LP gas, fire rings, firewood, controlled access. **REC:** heated pool, whirlpool, Camelot Lakes: fishing, playground. Pets OK. Partial handicap access. Big rig sites, eco-friendly, 2015 rates: $30 to $60.
(800)787-0605 Lat: 41.443565, Lon: -90.598045
2311 78th Ave W, Rock Island, IL 61201
info@rockislandkoa.com
www.rockislandkoa.com
See ad this page.

Travel Services

CUMMINS CENTRAL POWER Distributor for Cummins and Onan products with diesel engines, products & service. **SERVICES:** Tire, RV appliance, MH mechanical, engine/chassis repair, mobile RV svc, emergency rd svc, restrooms. **TOW:** RV, auto. RV supplies, LP, emergency parking, RV accessible. waiting room. Hours: Mon-Fri: 7 am - Midnight, Sat:7am-3:30pm.
(309)787-4300 Lat: 41.442609, Lon: -90.627243
7820 42nd St. W, Rock Island, IL 61204
See ad page 732.

IL

ROCKFORD — A4 *Winnebago*

BLACKHAWK VALLEY CAMPGROUND **Ratings: 7.5/9.5★/8.5** (Campground) 2015 rates: $30 to $35. Apr 15 to Oct 15. (815)874-9767 6540 Valley Trail Rd, Rockford, IL 61109

ROCK CUT (State Pk) From Jct of I-90 & Riverside Blvd exit, W 3 mi on Riverside Blvd to Forest Hills Rd, N 3.3 mi to SR-173, E 1 mi, follow signs (L). 2015 rates: $20 to $25. (815)885-3311

ROCKTON — A4 *Winnebago*

HONONEGAH FOREST PRESERVE (Public) From Jct of SR-251 & Hononegah Rd, W 2 mi on Hononegah Rd (L). Pit toilets. 2015 rates: $8 to $10. Apr 16 to Nov 19. (815)877-6100

RUSHVILLE — C2 *Schuyler*

SCHUY-RUSH PARK (Public) Jct of Hwy 24 & Hwy 67: Go 2 mi S on Hwy 67, turn W on CR 190 E. 2015 rates: $6 to $12. (217)322-6628

SALEM — E4 *Marion*

STEPHEN A FORBES (State Pk) From Jct of I-57 & US-50 (Salem exit), E 17 mi on US-50 to Omega Iuka Rd, N 7 mi, follow signs (R). 2015 rates: $10 to $30. (618)547-3381

SAVANNA — A3 *Carroll*

MISSISSIPPI PALISADES (State Pk) From Jct US-52 & SR-84, N 2 mi on SR-84, follow signs (R). 2015 rates: $10 to $30. May 1 to Oct 31. (815)273-2731

SESSER — E4 *Franklin*

WAYNE FITZGERRELL REC AREA (State Pk) From Jct of I-57 & Rte 154 (exit 77), W 1 mi on Rte 154 (R). 2015 rates: $20 to $30. (618)629-2320

SEWARD — B4 *Winnebago*

SEWARD BLUFFS FOREST PRESERVE (Public) From Jct of US-20 & SR-70, W 13 mi on US-20 to Pecatonica Rd, S 1 mi to Comly Rd, W 0.5 mi, follow signs (R). Pit toilets. 2015 rates: $10 to $20. Apr 16 to Nov 19. (815)877-6100

SHABBONA — B4 *DeKalb*

SHABBONA RECREATION AREA (State Pk) From town, S 0.75 mi on Shabbona Rd, follow signs (R). 2015 rates: $25 to $35. (815)824-2106

SHELBYVILLE — D4 *Shelby*

COON CREEK REC AREA (Public Corps) From town, S 2.8 mi on Findlay Concrete Hwy to cnty rd, W 0.2 mi to unmarked rd, S 1.7 mi (E). 2015 rates: $18 to $48. May 7 to Oct 11. (217)774-3951

LITHIA SPRINGS REC AREA (Public Corps) From town, E 3.2 mi on SR-16 to cnty rd, N 2.1 mi to unmarked rd, W 1.4 mi (E). 2015 rates: $18 to $36. Apr 16 to Oct 24. (217)774-3951

OPOSSUM CREEK REC AREA (Public Corps) From town, N 3.4 mi on SR-128 to CR-1650, E 0.9 mi to unmarked rd, S 0.5 mi to unmarked rd, E 1.2 mi (E). 2015 rates: $16 to $32. May 14 to Sep 7. (217)774-3951

ROBIN HOOD WOODS CAMPGROUND & RESORT

Ratings: 9/8.5★/9.5 (Campground) From Jct Hwy 128 & Hwy 16: Go 4-1/2 mi E on Hwy 16 (L). **FAC:** Gravel rds. (200 spaces). Avail: 50 gravel, patios, 15 pull-thrus (30 x 70), back-ins (30 x 60), 30 full hkups, 20 W, 20 E (30/50 amps), seasonal sites, WiFi, tent sites, rentals, dump, mobile sewer, laundry, groc, LP gas, fire rings, firewood. **REC:** pool, pond, fishing, playground. Pets OK. Partial handicap access. Big rig sites, eco-friendly, 2015 rates: $30 to $35. Apr 1 to Oct 31.
(217)774-4222 Lat: 39.405331, Lon: -88.742510
2151 State Highway 16, Shelbyville, IL 62565
info@robinhoodwoods.com
www.robinhoodwoods.com
See ad this page, 458.

SHIRLAND — A4 *Winnebago*

SUGAR RIVER FOREST PRESERVE (Public) From Jct of SR-70 & SR-75, E 8 mi on SR-75 to Harrison Rd, N 1.2 mi to Shirland Rd, E 0.5 mi to Boswell Rd, N 1 mi to Forest Preserve Rd, W 2 mi, follow signs (L). 2015 rates: $10 to $17. Apr 16 to Nov 19. (815)877-6100

SOUTH BELOIT — A4 *Winnebago*

PEARL LAKE **Ratings: 7/9.5★/8.5** (Campground) 2015 rates: $50. May 1 to Oct 15. (815)389-1479 1220 Dearborn Ave, South Beloit, IL 61080

SPARTA — E3 *Randolph*

WORLD SHOOTING & RECREATIONAL COMPLEX (State Pk) From jct Hwy 154 & Hwy 4: Go 4-1/2 mi N on Hwy 4, then 3 mi W on CR 18. 2015 rates: $10 to $25. (618)295-2700

SPRINGFIELD — D3 *Sangamon*

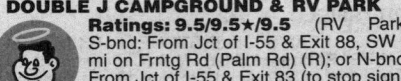

DOUBLE J CAMPGROUND & RV PARK

Ratings: 9.5/9.5★/9.5 (RV Park) S-bnd: From Jct of I-55 & Exit 88, SW 2 mi on Frntg Rd (Palm Rd) (R); or N-bnd: From Jct of I-55 & Exit 83 (to stop sign), W 0.3 mi to Frntg Rd, N 2.5 mi (L). Do Not Use GPS. **FAC:** All weather rds. (120 spaces). Avail: 104 gravel, 104 pull-thrus (29 x 100), 104 full hkups (30/50 amps), seasonal sites, WiFi, tent sites, laundry, groc, LP gas, fire rings, firewood. **REC:** pool,

SPRINGFIELD (CONT)

DOUBLE J CAMPGROUND & RV (CONT)
playground. Pets OK. Big rig sites, eco-friendly, 2015 rates: $43. Disc: military.
(217)483-9998 Lat: 39.658036, Lon: -89.649824
9683 Palm Rd, Chatham, IL 62629
camping@doublejcampground.com
www.doublejcampground.com
See ad opposite page, 458.

ILLINOIS STATE FAIRGROUNDS (State Pk) From jct I-55 & I-72: Go 2 mi W on SR 97, then 1 mi N on 5th St, then 1/4 mi E on Taintor Rd, then 1/8 mi N on Natural Resources Way (Rates change during Fair). 2015 rates: $25. Apr 1 to Oct 31. (217)524-9894

RIVERSIDE PARK CAMPGROUND (Public) From Jct I-55 & S Sherman Blvd., S 3 mi (Reservations accepted May 1-Oct 31). 2015 rates: $25 to $30. May 1 to Oct 31. (217)753-0630

SPRINGFIELD KOA **Ratings: 9/8/8.5** (Campground) 2015 rates: $30 to $45. Apr 1 to Nov 1. (217)498-7002 4320 Koa Rd, Rochester, IL 62563

ST DAVID — C3 *Fulton*

FULTON COUNTY CAMPING & REC AREA (Public) From town, SW 1.5 mi on SR-100 (L). Entrance fee required. 2015 rates: $15 to $18. (309)668-2931

STERLING — A3 *Whiteside*

CROW VALLEY CAMPGROUND **Ratings: 7/7/8** (Campground) 2015 rates: $30. Apr 15 to Oct 15. (815)626-5376 23807 Moline Rd, Sterling, IL 61081

STOCKTON — A3 *Jo Daviess*

APPLE RIVER CANYON (State Pk) From Jct of US-20 & Hwy 78, N 6 mi on Hwy 78 to E Canyon Rd, W 4 mi (L). Pit toilets. 2015 rates: $8 to $18. May 1 to Nov 1. (815)745-3302

SUBLETTE — B4 *Lee*

WOODHAVEN LAKES **Ratings: 9/8.5★/9.5** (Membership Pk) 2015 rates: $10. (815)849-5209 499 Lamoille, Amboy, IL 61310

SULLIVAN — D4 *Moultrie*

FORREST W BO WOOD REC AREA (Public Corps) From Jct of SR-32 & SR-121, S 2.6 mi on SR-32 to access rd, W 0.5 mi (E). 2015 rates: $18 to $40. Apr 16 to Oct 24. (217)774-3951

SYCAMORE — A4 *DeKalb*

SYCAMORE RV RESORT **Ratings: 8.5/7/6.5** (Campground) 2015 rates: $32 to $36. (815)895-5590 375 E North Ave, Sycamore, IL 60178

TAYLORVILLE — D3 *Christian*

LAKE TAYLORVILLE (Public) From Jct of SR-48 & SR-29, SE 2 mi on SR-29 to Lake Dr, SW 50 yds to Lake Shore Dr, NW 0.5 mi, follow signs (L). 2015 rates: $20. Apr 1 to Oct 31. (217)824-5606

THOMSON — A3 *Carroll*

THOMSON CAUSEWAY (Public Corps) From town, E 0.5 mi on Main St to Lewis Ave, S 0.25 mi (E). 2015 rates: $20. May 1 to Oct 24. (815)259-3628

UNION — A4 *McHenry*

CHICAGO NORTHWEST KOA KAMPGROUND **Ratings: 9/9★/9.5** (Campground) 2015 rates: $34 to $54. Apr 15 to Oct 13. (815)923-4206 8404 S Union Rd, Union, IL 60180

URSA — C2 *Adams*

BEAR CREEK (COE - LOCK & DAM 21) (Public Corps) From jct Hwy 96 & CR 2150: Go 3 mi W on CR 2150, then 2-1/2 mi N on CR 500E, then 2-1/2 mi W on CR 2400N, then 1 mi W over levee on gravel road. Pit toilets. 2015 rates: $4. (217)228-0890

UTICA — B4 *La Salle*

HICKORY HOLLOW CAMPGROUND
Ratings: 9/9.5★/9.5 (RV Park) From Jct I-80 & Hwy 178 (Utica exit 81): Go N 20 ft on Hwy 178, then W 1/2 mi on Frontage Rd (R). **FAC:** Paved/gravel rds. 83 Avail: 13 paved, 70 gravel, 38 pull-thrus (25 x 80), back-ins (25 x 60), 61 full hkups, 22 W, 22 E (30/50 amps), WiFi, tent sites, rentals, dump, laundry, groc, fire rings, firewood. **REC:** pool, playground. Pets OK. Partial handicap access. Big rig sites, eco-friendly, 2015 rates: $35 to $38. Apr 1 to Nov 1.
(815)667-4996 Lat: 41.36078, Lon: -89.01708
757 N 3029 Rd, Utica, IL 61373
hichol7@hotmail.com
www.hickoryhollowcg.com
See ad this page, 458.

KOA LA SALLE-PERU **Ratings: 8.5/7.5/8** (Campground) 2015 rates: $35 to $45. Apr 1 to Oct 31. (815)667-4988 756 N 3150th Road, Utica, IL 61373

STARVED ROCK (State Pk) From Jct of I-80 & Rte 178, S 4 mi on Rte 178 to Rte 71, E 2 mi, follow signs (R). 2015 rates: $25 to $35. (815)667-4726

VANDALIA — D4 *Fayette*

OKAW VALLEY KAMPGROUND
Ratings: 8.5/8.5★/8.5 (Campground) From Jct of I-70 & US-40 (Exit 68), E 0.2 mi on US-40 to Boley Dr (frntg rd), W 0.1 mi (R). **FAC:** Gravel rds. (54 spaces). Avail: 44 gravel, 14 pull-thrus (26 x 75), back-ins (26 x 45), 15 full hkups, 29 W, 29 E (30/50 amps), seasonal sites, WiFi, tent sites, rentals, dump, laundry, groc, LP gas, fire rings, firewood. **REC:** pool, pond, fishing, playground, rec open to public. Pets OK. Big rig sites, 2015 rates: $34. Disc: AAA, military.
(888)470-3968 Lat: 38.976879, Lon: -89.004176
1341 East 1655 Avenue, Brownstown, IL 62418
reservations@okawvalley.com
www.okawvalley.com
See ad this page, 458.

VIENNA — F4 *Johnson*

SHAWNEE NATIONAL FOREST (BUCK RIDGE CAMPGROUND) (Natl Pk) From town: Go 7 mi NW on I-24, then 3 mi E on Tunnel Hill Blacktop. Follow signs. Pit toilets. 2015 rates: $5. Mar 15 to Dec 15. (618)253-7114

VOLO — A5 *Lake*

FISH LAKE BEACH CAMPING RESORT **Ratings: 9/8.5★/8** (Campground) 2015 rates: $30 to $48. May 1 to Oct 15. (847)546-2228 32223 North US Hwy 12, Volo, IL 60073

WAUCONDA — A5 *Lake*

Travel Services

CAMPING WORLD OF WAUCONDA/CHICAGO As the nation's largest retailer of RV supplies, accessories, services and new and used RVs, Camping World is committed to making your total RV experience better. RV Accessories: (866)599-4876. **SERVICES:** RV, RV appliance, MH mechanical, staffed RV wash, restrooms, RV Sales. RV supplies, LP, dump, emergency parking, RV accessible. Hours: 8:00 - 6:00.
(888)858-3826 Lat: 42.276968, Lon: -88.194371
27794 N. Darrell Road, Wauconda, IL 60084
jtreptow@campingworld.com
www.campingworld.com

WESTVILLE — C5 *Vermilion*

FOREST GLEN PRESERVE (VERMILION COUNTY PARK) (Public) From jct I-74 & Hwy 1: Go 5 mi S on Hwy 1, then 7 mi E on CR 5. 2015 rates: $15 to $20. (217)662-2142

WHITTINGTON — E4 *Franklin*

WHITTINGTON WOODS CAMPGROUND AT BENTON
Ratings: 9/9.5★/10 (Campground) From Jct of I-57 & SR-154 (exit 77), E 0.25 mi on SR-154 to SR-37, S 0.25 mi (R). **FAC:** Gravel rds. 99 gravel, 22 pull-thrus (25 x 70), back-ins (20 x 50), 80 full hkups, 19 W, 19 E (30/50 amps), WiFi, rentals, dump, laundry, groc, LP gas, fire rings, firewood. **REC:** pool, playground. Pets OK. Partial handicap access, no tents. Big rig sites, eco-friendly, 2015 rates: $34 to $37. No CC.
(618)435-3401 Lat: 38.07038, Lon: -88.91567
14297 State Highway 37, Whittington, IL 62897
whittingtonwoodscampground@gmail.com
www.whittingtonwoodscampground.com
See ad pages 459, 458 & Pampered Pets in Magazine Section.

WILMINGTON — B5 *Will*

DES PLAINES STATE FISH & WILDLIFE AREA (State Pk) From I-55 (exit 241): Go 1 mi W. Pit toilets. 2015 rates: $8. Apr 15 to Oct 15. (815)423-5326

FOSSIL ROCK RECREATION AREA Ratings: 5/7.5/7 (Campground) From Jct I-80 & I-55: Go S 13 mi on I-55 (Exit 236), then E 1/4 mi on Hwy 113, then N 2 mi on Frontage Rd (R). **FAC:** Poor gravel rds. (93 spaces). Avail: 10 gravel, 2 pull-thrus (33 x 52), back-ins (40 x 53), some side by side hkups, 10 full hkups (30/50 amps), seasonal sites, WiFi, tent sites, dump, mobile sewer, fire rings, firewood, controlled access. **REC:** pond, swim, fishing, playground. Pets OK. Partial handicap access. 2015 rates: $30. Disc: military.
AAA Approved
(815)476-6784 Lat: 41.30112, Lon: -88.21292
24615 W Strip Mine Rd, Wilmington, IL 60481
wpavey@zemanmhc.com
www.zemanmhc.com

WINDSOR — D4 *Shelby*

WOLF CREEK (State Pk) From town, N 6 mi on Rte 32 to CH-4, W 3.8 mi to park access rd, S 2.2 mi (Showers closed Nov 1-May 1). 2015 rates: $20 to $30. (217)459-2831

YORKVILLE — B4 *Kendall*

HIDE-A-WAY LAKES
Ratings: 7/7.5/6.5 (Campground) From Jct US 34 & Hwy 47: Go S 1 mi on Hwy 47, then E 2 mi on Van Emmon Rd (L); or From Jct Hwy 47 & US 71: Go E 3 mi on Hwy 71, then S 1 mi on Van Emmon Rd, turn (L) at sign. **FAC:** Gravel rds. (400 spaces). 200 Avail: 50 gravel, 150 grass, 40 pull-thrus (40 x 65), back-ins (40 x 50), 100 full hkups, 100 W, 100 E (30/50 amps), seasonal sites, WiFi, tent sites, dump, mobile sewer, laundry, groc, LP bottles, fire rings, firewood, controlled access. **REC:** Fox River: fishing, golf, playground, rec open to public. Pets OK. Eco-friendly, 2015 rates: $30 to $35.
(630)553-6323 Lat: 41.646660, Lon: -88.409934
8045 Van Emmon Rd, Yorkville, IL 60560
hideawaylakes@hotmail.com
www.hideawaylakes.com
See ad page 460.

Say you saw it in our Guide!

IL

ZION — A5 *Lake*

↖ ILLINOIS BEACH (State Pk) Hwy 173 to Rte 41, R to Wadsworth Rd, L. Wadsworth will dead end into park. 2015 rates: $20 to $25. (847)662-4811

Directional arrows indicate the campground's position in relation to the nearest town.

Getty Images/iStockphoto

WELCOME TO Indiana

DATE OF STATEHOOD DEC. 11, 1816	WIDTH: 140 MILES (225 KM) LENGTH: 270 MILES (435 KM)	PROPORTION OF UNITED STATES 0.96% OF 3,794,100 SQ MI

Indiana is a land that invites contemplation. There are Tibetan temples in Bloomington, horse-drawn buggies clip-clopping down the lanes of Shipshewana in Amish country and an unlikely treasure trove of modern architecture in the small town of Columbus. Then there's Indiana's moniker, the "Hoosier State." Few locals can give you a direct answer, but the most espoused theory about the origin of the name is that when early frontiersmen knocked on a door, they would be met with the response "Who's here?" or "Hoosier."

Indiana has spawned pop idols (Michael Jackson), literary legends (Kurt Vonnegut) and movie icons (James Dean). State capital Indianapolis has more to it than just the Indy 500. The self-proclaimed "Amateur Sports Capital of the World" is home to a world-class inventory of sports facilities. Despite its jock image, when it comes to the arts, Indy is a class act. The city boasts a dynamic lineup of stage productions from emerging theater and dance companies, while the impressive Museum of Art showcases a superb collection of European art, including works by Turner and the post-Impressionists.

Indiana's century-old park system is the fourth largest in the nation. From the marshlands and rolling hillsides of Northern Indiana to the caverns and limestone bluffs of the south, Indiana is a state of compelling natural beauty. There are 24 state parks, 13 state forests, 14 nature preserves and nine reservoirs where you can swim, hike, sail, float, fish and dive.

Top 3 Tourism Attractions:
1) Indianapolis Motor Speedway
2) Indiana Dunes State Park
3) Amish Acres

Nickname: Hoosier State

State Flower: Peony

State Bird: Cardinal

People: Larry Bird, basketball player; James Dean, actor; Virgil "Gus" Grissom, second American astronaut in space; Michael Jackson, singer; David Letterman, comedian; Kurt Vonnegut, writer

Major Cities: Indianapolis (capital), Fort Wayne, Evansville, South Bend, Hammond City

Topography: Hilly southern region; fertile rolling plains in central region; flat north; dunes along Lake Michigan

Climate: Humid continental climate, with cool winters and warm, wet summers

TRAVEL & TOURISM

Indiana Office of Tourism Development
800-677-9800
www.visitindiana.com

Amish Country-Elkhart County CVB
800-250-4827
www.amishcountry.org

Anderson-Madison County VCB
765-643-5633, 800-533-6569
www.heartlandspirit.com

Bloomington-Monroe County CVB
812-334-8900, 888-333-0088
www.visitbloomington.com

Brown County Convention & Visitors Bureau
800-313-0842
www.browncounty.com

Clark-Floyd Counties CVB
812-282-6654, 800-552-3842
www.sunnysideoflouisville.org

Visit Indianapolis
800-323-INDY
www.visitindy.com

Visit South Bend Mishawaka
800-519-0577
www.visitsouthbend.com

Terre Haute CVB
800-366-3043
www.terrehaute.com

OUTDOOR RECREATION

Indiana Parks and Recreation Association
www.inpra.org

SHOPPING

Amish Backroads
www.backroads.org

Borkholder Dutch Village
www.borkholder.com

Edinburgh Premium Outlets
www.premiumoutlets.com-edinburgh

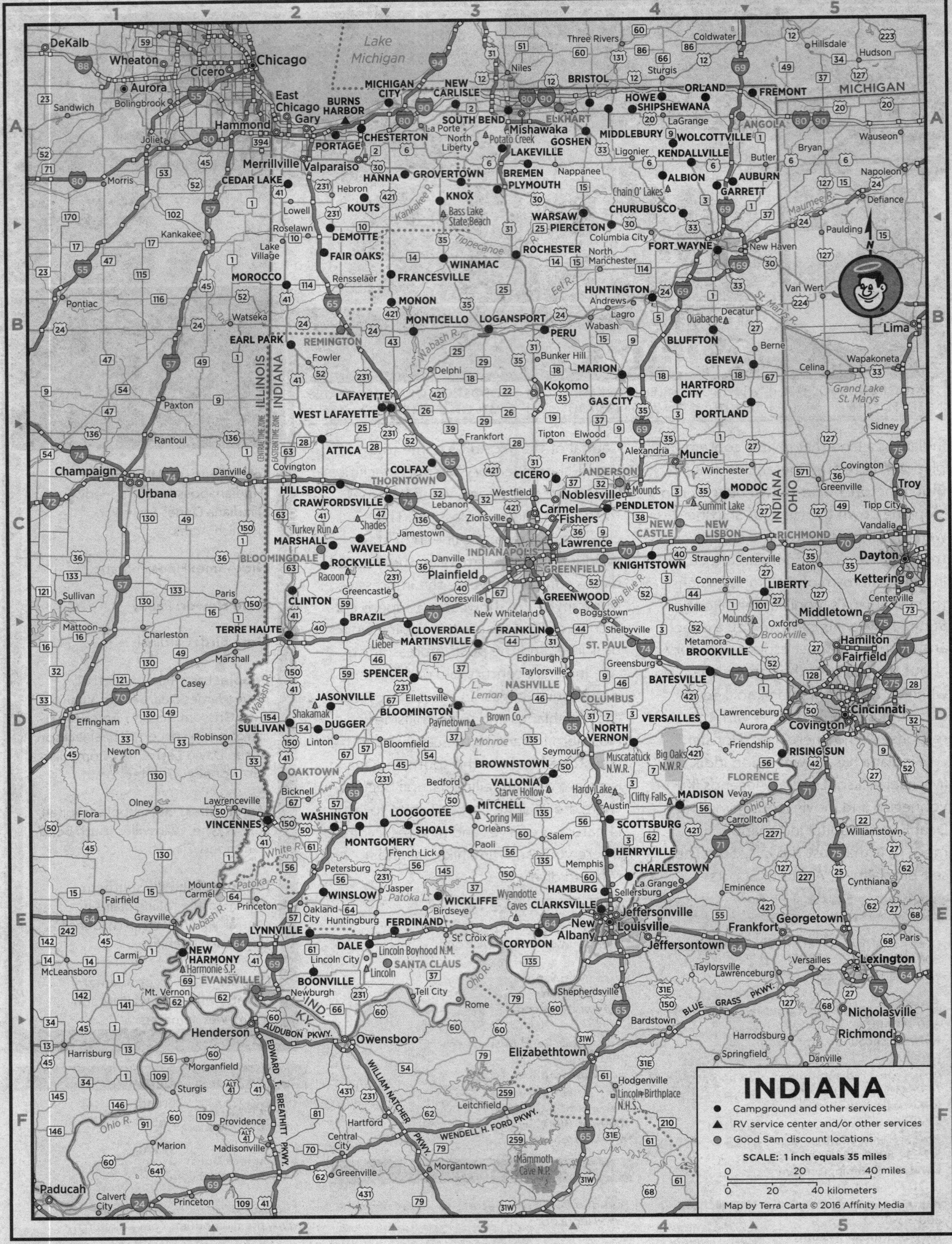

INDIANA
Campground and other services
RV service center and/or other services
Good Sam discount locations
SCALE: 1 inch equals 35 miles
0 20 40 miles
0 20 40 kilometers
Map by Terra Carta © 2016 Affinity Media
Lake Michigan
MICHIGAN
ILLINOIS
INDIANA
OHIO
KY.
IND.
CENTRAL TIME ZONE
EASTERN TIME ZONE
Chicago
Gary
Hammond
MICHIGAN CITY
NEW CARLISLE
SOUTH BEND
Mishawaka
ELKHART
BRISTOL
HOWE
ORLAND
FREMONT
SHIPSHEWANA
ANGOLA
MIDDLEBURY
GOSHEN
WOLCOTTVILLE
KENDALLVILLE
ALBION
AUBURN
GARRETT
FORT WAYNE
PORTAGE
CHESTERTON
BURNS HARBOR
Valparaiso
Merrillville
CEDAR LAKE
HANNA
GROVERTOWN
BREMEN
PLYMOUTH
LAKEVILLE
KOUTS
KNOX
WARSAW
PIERCETON
CHURUBUSCO
DEMOTTE
FAIR OAKS
WINAMAC
ROCHESTER
FRANCESVILLE
MOROCCO
MONON
MONTICELLO
LOGANSPORT
PERU
HUNTINGTON
BLUFFTON
GENEVA
EARL PARK
REMINGTON
MARION
HARTFORD CITY
Kokomo
GAS CITY
PORTLAND
LAFAYETTE
WEST LAFAYETTE
ATTICA
Muncie
COLFAX
THORNTOWN
CICERO
ANDERSON
Noblesville
MODOC
HILLSBORO
CRAWFORDSVILLE
Carmel
Fishers
PENDLETON
NEW CASTLE
NEW LISBON
RICHMOND
MARSHALL
WAVELAND
BLOOMINGDALE
ROCKVILLE
INDIANAPOLIS
Lawrence
GREENFIELD
KNIGHTSTOWN
Plainfield
CLINTON
GREENWOOD
LIBERTY
BRAZIL
TERRE HAUTE
CLOVERDALE
MARTINSVILLE
FRANKLIN
ST. PAUL
BROOKVILLE
SPENCER
NASHVILLE
COLUMBUS
BATESVILLE
JASONVILLE
BLOOMINGTON
SULLIVAN
DUGGER
NORTH VERNON
VERSAILLES
RISING SUN
OAKTOWN
BROWNSTOWN
VALLONIA
FLORENCE
MADISON
WASHINGTON
LOOGOOTEE
MITCHELL
VINCENNES
SHOALS
MONTGOMERY
SCOTTSBURG
HENRYVILLE
CHARLESTOWN
WINSLOW
WICKLIFFE
HAMBURG
CLARKSVILLE
Jeffersonville
New Albany
Louisville
FERDINAND
LYNNVILLE
DALE
CORYDON
NEW HARMONY
SANTA CLAUS
BOONVILLE
EVANSVILLE
Henderson
Owensboro
Elizabethtown
Lexington
Cincinnati
Covington
Dayton
Hamilton
Fairfield
Champaign
Urbana
Paducah

Featured Good Sam Parks

INDIANA

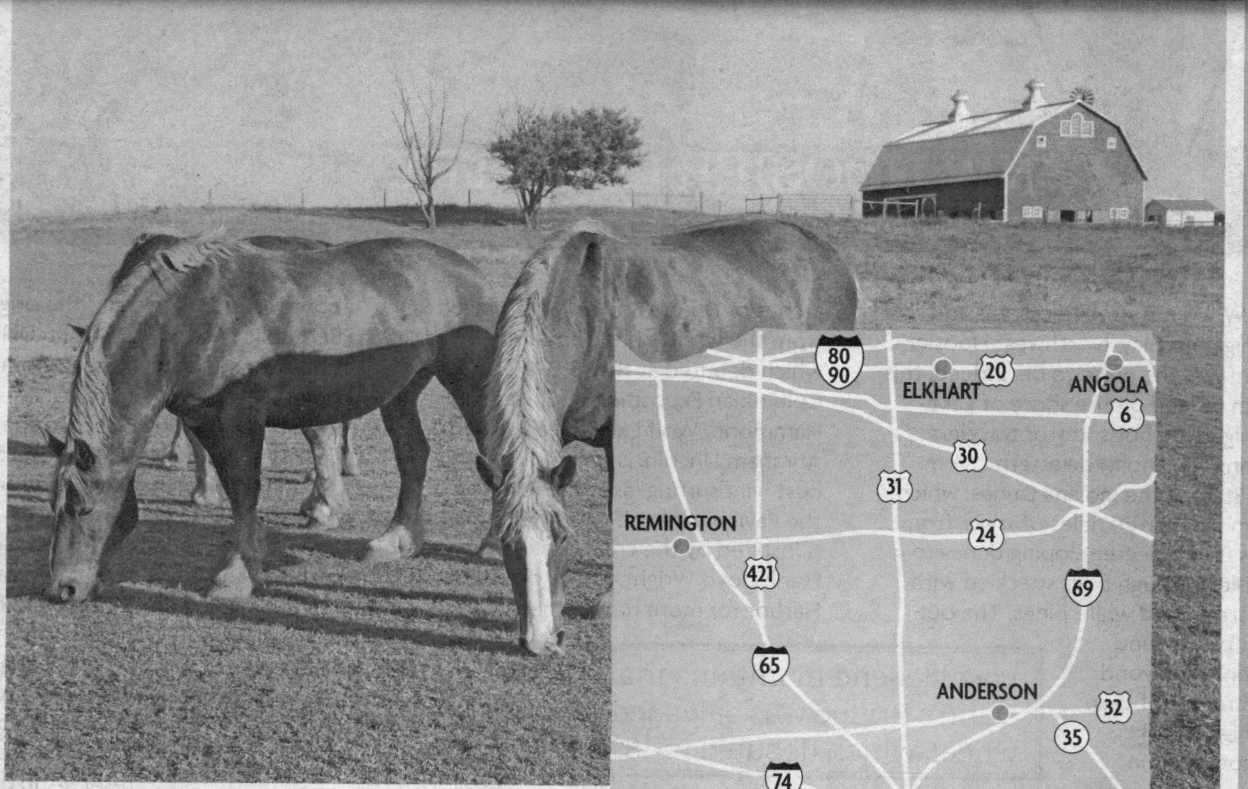

When you stay with Good Sam, you can expect the highest degree of cleanliness and friendliness, and better yet, you get 10% off campground fees.

If you're not already a Good Sam member you can purchase your membership at one of these locations:

ANDERSON
Timberline Valley RV Resort
(765)378-5909

ANGOLA
Circle B RV Park
(260)665-5353

COLUMBUS
Ceraland Park
(812)377-5849
Columbus Woods-N-Waters Kampground
(800)799-3928

ELKHART
Elkhart Campground
(574)264-2914

EVANSVILLE
Vanderburgh 4-H Center
(812)867-6217

FLORENCE
Follow the River RV Resort
(812)427-3330

GREENFIELD
S & H Campground
(317)326-3208

NASHVILLE
The Last Resort RV Park & Campground
(812)988-4675
Westward Ho Campground
(812)988-0008

OAKTOWN
New Vision RV Park
(812)745-2125

REMINGTON
Caboose Lake Campground
(219)261-3828

RICHMOND
Grandpa's Farm
(765)962-7907

ST PAUL
Hidden Paradise Campground
(765)525-6582

For more Good Sam Parks go to listing pages

IN

Indiana Tourism

NW HOOSIER COUNTRY

From big-time dunes to small-town dining, this slice of Indiana has it all

When it is time for Illinois and Michigan to play, Northwest Hoosier Country is the place to be. Indeed, this swath of land on the shore of Lake Michigan is a hot spot for travelers seeking fun and Midwestern charm.

Start at the Indiana Dunes, which has more than 70 miles of trails, from hikes up 40-degree sloping dunes to rambles through bogs speckled with tamaracks and white pines. The outdoor playground continues beyond the breezes of Lake Michigan. Broken Wagon Bison in Hobart, with ample RV parking, runs wagon tours out to meet more than 70 of America's largest land mammals. At Pinhook Bog, a floating boardwalk snakes through blueberry bushes and sphagnum mosses.

Wander Along the Water

On Lake Michigan, Dunn's Bridge County Park offers boat and kayak access to the Kankakee River. Local legend maintains that the steel for the arches of Dunn's Bridge was salvaged from the world's first Ferris wheel, which debuted at the 1893 World's Columbian Exposition in Chicago. In Hammond, Wolf Lake, often visited by Abraham Lincoln, is one of America's best windsurfing lakes. The canopy of the Pavilion at Wolf Lake Memorial Park is inspired by the creations of architect Frank Lloyd Wright. Check out Burns Harbor for more fun on the water.

Local legend maintains that the steel for the arches of Dunn's Bridge was salvaged from the world's first Ferris wheel, which debuted in 1893 in Chicago.

At Taltree Arboretum & Gardens in Valparaiso, formal gardens have been carved out of ancient prairie with 3 miles of delightful trails. The showstopper is the Railway Garden, where model trains steam across handmade wooden trestles.

Good Times in Small Towns

The small towns of Hoosier Country by the Great Lakes are content to let the hurried pace of notoriety shine elsewhere. The classic Midwestern downtown streetscape of Chesterton attracts artists whose work graces the Chesterton Art Center. Porter, located on the Little Calumet River, is known for its abundance of restaurants.

Northwest Hoosier Country also dishes out the big-city amenities. Hammond, the region's major city, once fielded teams in both the National Football League and the National Basketball League. The town's gangsters were big-league as well—you can learn about Hoosier native and the original FBI "Public Enemy No. 1," John Dillinger at his own museum in the Indiana Welcome Center.

On Lake Michigan, board the Ameristar Casino Hotel East Chicago, a floating casino that keeps the action going with 56,000 square feet of gaming. Try your luck with 1,700 slot machines and close to 60 table games. Stay the night at the 288-room hotel on board. In Michigan City's marina, the Blue Chip Casino Hotel Spa boards 24 hours a day and reserves 10,000 square feet for a luxury spa.

And save a bit of that flavored oil for the perfect popcorn. Native Hoosier Orville Redenbacher bought his first corn seed plant near Valparaiso in the 1950s, and the city has been saluting the man who made horn-rimmed glasses and bow ties trendy since 1979. The Popcorn Festival has expanded into a weeklong procession of events each September. And while you are in town, stop by and visit the Hoosier Bat Company for a tour of the nation's third-oldest baseball bat manufacturer.

For More Information

South Shore CVA
219-989-7979
www.southshorecva.com

Indiana Office of Tourism Development
800-677-9800
www.in.gov/visitindiana

IN

Indiana

CONSULTANTS

Joe & Rita Comer

ALBION — A4 *Noble*

CHAIN O'LAKES (State Pk) From town, S 5 mi on SR-9 (L). 2015 rates: $7.63 TO $90. (260)636-2654

ANDERSON — C4 *Madison*

MOUNDS (State Pk) From town, E 2.5 mi on Hwy 232 (L). 2015 rates: $12 to $29. (765)642-6627

TIMBERLINE VALLEY RV RESORT
Ratings: 9/9.5★/10 (RV Park) From Jct of I-69 & Hwy 32 (exit 234), W 2.8 mi on Hwy 32 to CR 300 E, N 0.5 mi to E CR-75 N, E 0.25 mi (L) Note: N-bnd exit 34, stay right, continue up ramp to the Jct of State Rd 32.

A QUIET VALLEY SURROUNDED BY NATURE
Something for everyone! Spacious sites, 80 acres, the first jump pad, free Wi-Fi, river access, trails, RVs, cabins, groups and close to the city with all it has to offer. Minutes to the Casino and Indianapolis.

FAC: Paved/gravel rds. (129 spaces). 95 Avail: 65 gravel, 30 grass, 28 pull-thrus (35 x 100), back-ins (30 x 60), 95 full hkups (30/50 amps), seasonal sites, WiFi, tent sites, rentals, dump, laundry, groc, LP gas, fire rings, firewood. **REC:** White River: swim, fishing, playground. Pet restrict(B). Partial handicap access. Big rig sites, eco-friendly, 2015 rates: $33 to $41.
(765)378-5909 Lat: 40.11715, Lon: -85.61034
3230 E CR-75 N, Anderson, IN 46017
timberlinecamp@sbcglobal.net
www.timberlinecampground.com
See ad pages 477, 471.

ANGOLA — A4 *Steuben*

CAMP SACK-IN **Ratings: 4.5/6.5/7** (Campground) 2015 rates: $29. Apr 15 to Oct 15. (260)665-5166 8740 E 40 S, Angola, IN 46703

CAPTAIN CARL'S FAMOUS BUCK LAKE RANCH **Ratings: 4.5/5.5/8** (Campground) 2015 rates: $25 to $30. Apr 15 to Oct 15. (260)665-6699 2705 W Buck Lake Rd, Angola, IN 46703

CIRCLE B RV PARK
Ratings: 8.5/9★/9 (RV Park) From Jct of I-69 & US-20 (exit 348), W 2 mi on US-20 (L). **FAC:** Paved/gravel rds. (330 spaces). 95 Avail: 50 gravel, 45 grass, patios, 25 pull-thrus (25 x 65), back-ins (30 x 60), 50 full hkups, 45 W, 45 E (30/50 amps), seasonal sites, WiFi, tent sites, rentals, dump, laundry, groc, LP gas, fire rings, firewood, controlled access. **REC:** Hogback Lake: swim, fishing, playground. Pet restrict(Q). Partial handicap access. Big rig sites, eco-friendly, 2015 rates: $31 to $37. Disc: AAA.
AAA Approved
(260)665-5353 Lat: 41.63451, Lon: -85.08717
5251 US Hwy 20 W, Angola, IN 46703
info@circlebpark.com
www.circlebpark.com
See ad this page, 471.

MILLER'S HAPPY ACRES **Ratings: 6.5/5.5/5.5** (Campground) 2015 rates: $30 to $35. Apr 15 to Oct 31. (260)665-9843 1940 S 300 W, Angola, IN 46703

POKAGON (State Pk) From Jct of I-69 & exit 154, W on exit 154, follow signs (E). Guest rooms available. Entrance fee required. 2015 rates: $10 to $40. (260)833-2012

ATTICA — C2 *Fountain*

SUMMERS-CARROLL CAMPGROUND **Ratings: 5.5/5/6.5** (Campground) 2015 rates: $28. Apr 20 to Oct 20. (765)762-2832 5509 N 200 E, Attica, IN 47918

AUBURN — A4 *DeKalb*

FIRESIDE RESORT **Ratings: 4.5/8.5★/6.5** (RV Park) 2015 rates: $24 to $34. (260)925-6747 5612 CR-11A, Auburn, IN 46706

BATESVILLE — D4 *Ripley*

INDIAN LAKES/BATESVILLE KOA **Ratings: 7.5/8/8** (RV Park) 2015 rates: $42 to $51. Apr 1 to Nov 7. (800)405-6188 7234 E State Rd 46, Batesville, IN 47006

BLOOMINGDALE — C2 *Parke*

PEACEFUL WATERS CAMPGROUND AND CABINS
Ratings: 6/9★/8 (Campground) From jct US 36 & US 41: Go 3-3/4 mi N on US 41 (R). **FAC:** Gravel rds. 59 gravel, 15 pull-thrus (30 x 50), back-ins (50 x 60), some side by side hkups, 2 full hkups, 57 W, 57 E (30/50 amps), WiFi, tent sites, rentals, dump, fire rings, firewood. **REC:** pond, fishing, playground. Pets OK. Partial handicap access. 2015 rates: $25 to $35. Disc: military. Apr 25 to Nov 1.
(765)592-6458 Lat: 39.81658, Lon: -87.23631
3325 N Hwy 41, Bloomingdale, IN 47832
peaceful.waters@hotmail.com
www.peacefulwaterscampground.com
See ad this page.

BLOOMINGTON — D3 *Monroe*

JELLYSTONE PARK AT LAKE MONROE **Ratings: 9.5/9.5★/9** (RV Park) 2015 rates: $39 to $63. May 1 to Oct 26. (812)824-3322 9396 S Strain Ridge Rd, Bloomington, IN 47401

LAKE MONROE VILLAGE **Ratings: 9/10★/8.5** (Campground) 2015 rates: $50 to $60. (812)824-2267 8107 S Fairfax Rd, Bloomington, IN 47401

PAYNETOWN SRA/MONROE LAKE (Public) From Jct of SR-46 & SR-446, S 7 mi on SR-446 (R). Entrance fee required. 2015 rates: $12 to $40. (812)837-9546

BLUFFTON — B4 *Wells*

MENDENHALL RV & MOBILE HOME PARK
Ratings: 3/NA/7 (RV Area in MHP) From Jct of SR-1 & SR-124, E 0.8 mi on SR-124 (L). **FAC:** Gravel rds. 14 Avail: 1 paved, 13 gravel, 8 pull-thrus (20 x 50), back-ins (20 x 40), mostly side by side hkups, 14 full hkups (30/50 amps). **REC.** Pets OK. No tents. Big rig sites, 2015 rates: $30. No CC.
(260)824-5365 Lat: 40.74254, Lon: -85.15749
3427 E State Rd 124 (PO Box 351), Bluffton, IN 46714
menden@adamswells.com

OUABACHE (State Pk) From town, E 2 mi on Hwy 124 to Hwy 201, S .75 mi to SH-316, SE .5 mi. 2015 rates: $12 to $55. (260)824-0926

BOONVILLE — E2 *Warrick*

SCALES LAKE PARK (WARRICK COUNTY PARK) (Public) From Jct of I-64 & Hwy 61 (exit 39), S 10 mi on Hwy 61 to Hwy 62, E 0.5 mi to Walnut St, E 0.2 mi to Park Lane Dr, N 0.5 mi (L). 2015 rates: $13 to $26. (812)897-6200

BRAZIL — D2 *Clay*

FALLEN ROCK RV PARKE & CAMPGROUND **Ratings: 6.5/9.5★/9** (RV Park) 2015 rates: $25 to $35. Apr 1 to Nov 5. (765)672-4301 8816 S Fallen Rock Rd, Brazil, IN 47834

BREMEN — A3 *Marshall*

PLA-MOR CAMPGROUND **Ratings: 7/6.5/7** (Campground) 2015 rates: $25 to $30. Apr 15 to Oct 15. (574)546-3665 2162 US Hwy 6, Bremen, IN 46506

BRISTOL — A4 *Elkhart*

EBY'S PINES RV PARK & CAMPGROUND
Ratings: 8.5/8.5★/8.5 (RV Park) From Jct of I-80/90 Toll Rd & SR 15 (Bristol exit), SW 1.5 mi on SR 15 to SR 120, E 3.4 mi (R). **FAC:** Paved/gravel rds. (280 spaces). 190 Avail: 75 gravel, 115 grass, 70 pull-thrus (30 x 60), back-ins (30 x 45), some side by side hkups, 29 full hkups, 161 W, 161 E (30/50 amps), seasonal sites, WiFi $, tent sites, rentals, dump, laundry, groc, LP gas, fire rings, firewood, controlled access. **REC:** heated pool, pond, fishing, shuffleboard, playground. Pets OK. Partial handicap access. RV age restrict, 2015 rates: $34 to $48. Apr 1 to Oct 1.
(574)848-4583 Lat: 41.72502, Lon: -85.74841
14583 SR-120, Bristol, IN 46507
camp@ebyspines.com
www.ebyspines.com
See ad this page.

BROOKVILLE — D4 *Franklin, Union*

BROOKVILLE LAKE (State Pk) From town, N 7 mi on Hwy 101 (L). 2015 rates: $30 to $90. (765)647-2657

BROWNSTOWN — D3 *Jackson*

JACKSON-WASHINGTON SF (Public) From Business Center: Go 2.5 mi SE of Brownstown. Pit toilets. 2015 rates: $10. (812)358-2160

BURNS HARBOR — A2 *Porter*

Travel Services

CAMP-LAND RV RV Dealership with RV sales, part supplies and repair. **SERVICES:** RV, RV appliance, MH mechanical, engine/chassis repair, restrooms, RV Sales. RV supplies, LP, emergency parking, RV accessible. waiting room. Hours: 9am to 5:30pm.
(219)787-1040 Lat: 41.60519, Lon: -87.11882
1171 Lions Dr, Burns Harbor, IN 46304
sales@camplandrv.com
www.camplandrv.com
See ad page 472 (Spotlight NW Hoosier Country).

CEDAR LAKE — A2 *Lake*

CEDAR LAKE MINISTRIES RV PARK **Ratings: 6/9.5★/8.5** (RV Park) 2015 rates: $22 to $31. Apr 15 to Oct 15. (219)374-5941 8816 W 137th Ave, Cedar Lake, IN 46303

CHARLESTOWN — E4 *Clark*

CHARLESTOWN (State Pk) 7 miles East on Hwy 62, straight through stoplight, one more mile-gate is on the right. 2015 rates: $12 TO $55. (812)256-5600

CHESTERTON — A2 *Porter*

INDIANA DUNES (State Pk) From Jct of I-94 & SR-49, N 2 mi on SR-49 (E). 2015 rates: $16 to $65. (219)926-1952

SAND CREEK CAMPGROUND **Ratings: 6/8.5/6.5** (Campground) 2015 rates: $35 to $50. Apr 15 to Oct 15. (219)926-7482 1000 N 350 E, Chesterton, IN 46304

CHURUBUSCO — A4 *Whitley*

BLUE LAKE RESORT CAMPGROUND **Ratings: 6.5/7.5/7.5** (Campground) 2015 rates: $33 to $39. Apr 15 to Oct 15. (260)693-2265 5453 N Blue Lake Rd, Churubusco, IN 46723

CICERO — C3 *Hamilton*

WHITE RIVER CAMPGROUND (Public) From Jct of SR-37 & SR-32 (in Nobleville), N 6.3 mi on SR-37 to Strawtown Rd, W 1.2 mi (L). 2015 rates: $15 to $30. Apr 15 to Oct 31. (317)770-4430

CLARKSVILLE — E4 *Clark*

↑ ADD-MORE CAMPGROUND **Ratings: 5.5/6.5/8** (Campground) 2015 rates: $32 to $37. (812)283-4321 2411 Addmore Lane, Clarksville, IN 47129

↓ **LOUISVILLE METRO KOA**
Ratings: 7.5/10★/7.5 (RV Park) From Jct of I-65 & Stansifer Ave (exit 1), W 50 ft on Stansifer Ave to Marriott Dr, S 0.3 mi (L). N-bnd: Stay on exit ramp until you reach Stansifer Ave. **FAC:** Paved rds. (108 spaces). Avail: 78 paved, 26 pull-thrus (18 x 60), back-ins (18 x 35), 78 full hkups (30/50 amps), seasonal sites, cable, WiFi, tent sites, rentals, dump, laundry, groc, LP gas, fire rings. **REC:** playground. Pets OK. Partial handicap access. 2015 rates: $42 to $48.
(812)282-4474 Lat: 38.27924, Lon: -85.75462
900 Marriott Dr, Clarksville, IN 47129
louisvillenorthcamp@gmail.com
www.louisvillemetrokoa.com
See ad page 521.

CLINTON — C2 *Vermillion*

← HORSESHOE LAKES RV CAMPGROUND **Ratings: 7.5/7/7.5** (Membership Pk) 2015 rates: $39 to $51. Apr 22 to Oct 19. (765)832-2487 12962 S CR 225 W, Clinton, IN 47842

CLOVERDALE — D3 *Putnam*

↙ CAGLES MILL LAKE/LIEBER SRA (State Pk) From town, SW 5 mi on Hwy 42 to Hwy 243, N 1 mi (E). 2015 rates: $10 to $75. (765)795-4576

↑ CLOVERDALE RV PARK **Ratings: 7/8.5/7.5** (Campground) 2015 rates: $30 to $35. (765)795-3294 2789 E CR-800 S, Cloverdale, IN 46120

COLFAX — C3 *Clinton*

↑ BROADVIEW LAKE CAMPGROUND **Ratings: 6.5/6.5/7.5** (Campground) 2015 rates: $26 to $28. Apr 15 to Oct 15. (765)324-2622 4850 South Broadview Rd, Colfax, IN 46035

COLUMBUS — D4 *Bartholomew*

↘ **CERALAND PARK**
Ratings: 8/9★/9.5 (RV Park) Jct I-65 & Walesboro Rd (Exit 64), E 6.4 mi on 450S to US 31, N 2.0 mi on US 31 to State Rd 46, E 1.5 mi on State Rd 46 to CR525 E, S .07 mi on CR525 E (L). **FAC:** Paved/gravel rds. 325 gravel, 12 pull-thrus (25 x 70), back-ins (25 x 60), 112 full hkups, 213 W, 213 E (30/50 amps), WiFi, tent sites, rentals, dump, laundry, groc, fire rings, firewood, restaurant, controlled access. **REC:** pool, wading pool, pond, fishing, shuffleboard, playground, rec open to public. Pets OK. Partial handicap access. Big rig sites, 2015 rates: $32 to $40. Apr 1 to Oct 31.
(812)377-5849 Lat: 39.16237, Lon: -85.81384
3989 South 525 East, Columbus, IN 47203
ceraland@ceraland.org
www.ceraland.org
See ad pages 477, 471 & Family Camping in Magazine Section.

↙ **COLUMBUS WOODS-N-WATERS KAMPGROUND**
Ratings: 8.5/9.5★/8.5 (Campground) From Jct of I-65 & SR-58 (exit 64), W 1/4th mi on SR-58 to CR-300 W, S 1 mi (L). **FAC:** Gravel rds. (137 spaces). Avail: 107 gravel, 16 pull-thrus (40 x 60), back-ins (25 x 45), 22 full hkups, 85 W, 85 E (30/50 amps), seasonal sites, WiFi, dump, laundry, groc, LP gas, fire rings, firewood. **REC:** heated pool, pond, fishing, playground. Pets OK. Partial handicap access, no tents. Big rig sites, 2015 rates: $35 to $37. Disc: military.
(800)799-3928 Lat: 39.12045, Lon: -85.96658
8855 S 300 W, Columbus, IN 47201
woodsnwaters@bcremc.net
www.columbuswoodsnwaters.com
See ad this page, 471.

Directional arrows indicate the campground's position in relation to the nearest town.

CORYDON — E3 *Harrison, Crawford*

← HARRISON-CRAWFORD STATE FOREST (State Pk) From Jct of I-64 & SR-135 (exit 105), S 2 mi on SR-135 to SR-62, W 10 mi to SR-462, S 2 mi (E). 2015 rates: $15. (812)738-7694

← O'BANNON WOODS (State Pk) From jct Hwy-135 & Hwy-62: Go 7 mi W on Hwy-62, then 1 mi S on Hwy-462. 2015 rates: $10.49 TO $32. (812)738-8232

CRAWFORDSVILLE — C2 *Montgomery*

↑ CRAWFORDSVILLE KOA KAMPGROUND **Ratings: 9/8/8.5** (Campground) 2015 rates: $27 to $55. (765)362-4190 1600 Lafayette Rd, Crawfordsville, IN 47933

← SUGAR CREEK CAMPGROUND & CANOE RENTALS **Ratings: 6.5/6/7.5** (Campground) 2015 rates: $32 to $35. (765)362-5528 841 W 83 North, Crawfordsville, IN 47933

DALE — E2 *Spencer*

↓ LINCOLN (State Pk) From Jct of I-64 & US-231 (exit 57), S 8 mi on US-231 to SR-162, E 2 mi (R). Entrance fee required. 2015 rates: $6.12 to $38.76. (812)937-4710

DEMOTTE — B2 *Jasper*

↓ LAKE HOLIDAY CAMP-RESORT **Ratings: 6.5/8/5.5** (Campground) 2015 rates: $44 o $49. Apr 1 to Oct 31. (219)345-3132 11780 W SR-10, Demotte, IN 46310

DUGGER — D2 *Sullivan*

↓ GREENE-SULLIVAN SF (State Pk) From town: Go 2 mi S on Hwy-159. Pit toilets. (812)648-2810

EARL PARK — B2 *Benton*

← EARL PARK REST AREA (CITY PARK) (Public) From jct US-41/52 & Seventh St (550N): Go 1/2 mi W on Seventh St. 2015 rates: $15. (219)474-6108

ELKHART — A3 *Elkhart*

↑ **ELKHART CAMPGROUND**
Ratings: 9/10★/9 (Campground) From Jct of Toll Rd 80/90 & SR-19 (exit 92), N 0.25 mi on SR-19 to CR-4E, E 0.75 mi (R). **FAC:** Paved/gravel rds. (278 spaces). Avail: 238 grass, 238 pull-thrus (30 x 70), 180 full hkups, 58 W, 58 E (30/50 amps), seasonal sites, cable, WiFi, tent sites, rentals, dump, laundry, groc, LP gas, fire rings, firewood. **REC:** heated pool, playground. Pets OK. Partial handicap access. Big rig sites, eco-friendly, 2015 rates: $25 to $42. Disc: AAA, military. Apr 1 to Nov 1.
AAA Approved
(574)264-2914 Lat: 41.73844, Lon: -85.95911
25608 CR-4 E, Elkhart, IN 46514
elkcampground@yahoo.com
www.elkhartcampground.com
See ad this page, 471.

EVANSVILLE — E2 *Vanderburgh, Warrick*

↙ BURDETTE PARK (Public) From Jct of Hwy 62/Lloyd Expressway & Red Bank Rd, S 3.2 mi on Red Bank Rd (becomes Nurrenburn) (R). 2015 rates: $17 to $25. (812)435-5602

↑ **VANDERBURGH 4-H CENTER**
Ratings: 6.5/8/6.5 (Campground) From Jct of I-64 & Hwy 41 S (Exit 25A), S 5.3 mi to Boonville-New Harmony Rd, W 0.2 mi (L). **FAC:** Gravel rds. 41 gravel, 16 pull-thrus (17 x 80), back-ins (30 x 45), mostly side by side hkups, 41 full hkups (30/50 amps), cable, WiFi, tent sites, dump, laundry, fire rings. **REC:** pond, fishing, playground. Pets OK. 2015 rates: $25 to $35.
(812)867-6217 Lat: 38.09172, Lon: -87.56296
201 E. Boonville-New Harmony Rd, Evansville, IN 47725
info@vanderburgh4hcenter.com
www.vanderburgh4hcenter.com
See ad this page, 471.

Like Us on Facebook.

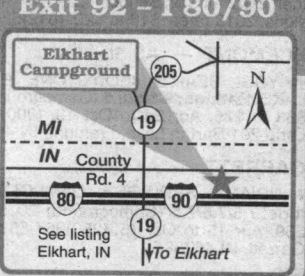

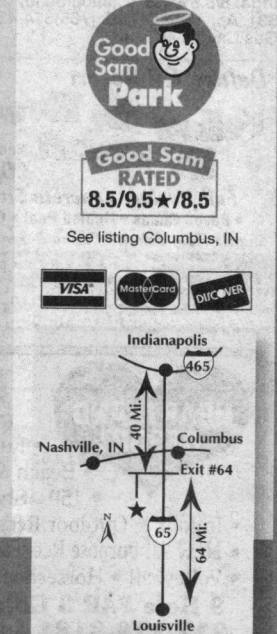

FAIR OAKS — B2 *Jasper*

OAK LAKE FAMILY CAMPGROUND & RV PARK **Ratings: 8/9★/8** (Campground) 2015 rates: $34 to $39. Apr 15 to Oct 15. (219)306-8223 5310 E 900 N, Fair Oaks, IN 47943

FERDINAND — E3 *Dubois*

FERDINAND SF (State Pk) From jct Hwy-162 & Hwy-264: Go 5 mi NE on Hwy-264. (812)367-1524

FLORENCE — D5 *Switzerland*

FOLLOW THE RIVER RV RESORT **Ratings: 9.5/9.5/10** (RV Park) From Jct of I-71 & (Kentucky SR 1039) Exit 55, N 6 mi on SR 1039, W 1 mi on (Indiana SR 156) (R). **FAC:** Paved/gravel rds. 159 paved, patios, 55 pull-thrus (40 x 85), back-ins (40 x 75), 159 full hkups (30/50 amps), WiFi, laundry, LP gas, fire rings, firewood. **REC:** heated pool, pond, fishing, playground. Pets OK. Partial handicap access, no tents. Big rig sites, eco-friendly, 2015 rates: $38 to $49.
(812)427-3330 Lat: 38.78279, Lon: -84.98149
12273 Markland Town Rd, Florence, IN 47020
info@followtheriverrvresort.com
www.followtheriverrvresort.com
See ad this page, 471.

FORT WAYNE — B4 *Allen*

JOHNNY APPLESEED CAMPGROUND (Public) From Jct I-69 & Coldwater Rd, S 1.4 mi on Coldwater Rd to Coliseum Blvd, E 0.5 mi on Coliseum Blvd to Parnell Ave, S 0.25 mi (L). 2015 rates: $18. Apr 15 to Oct 31. (260)427-6720

FRANCESVILLE — B3 *Pulaski*

ACORN OAKS CAMPGROUND **Ratings: 4/6/7** (Campground) 2015 rates: $21 to $23. (219)567-2524 16614 W Sr 114, Francesville, IN 47946

FRANKLIN — D3 *Johnson*

JOHNSON COUNTY PARK & RECREATION AREA (Public) From jct Hwy 144/Hwy 44 & US 31: Go 3 mi S on US 31, then 3-1/2 mi W on Hwy 252, then 2-1/2 mi S on Schoolhouse Rd (CR 550S), follow signs. 2015 rates: $16 to $20. (812)526-6809

FREMONT — A5 *Steuben*

YOGI BEAR'S JELLYSTONE PARK-BARTON LAKE **Ratings: 9/8.5/8.5** (Campground) 2015 rates: $33 to $75. Apr 24 to Oct 19. (800)375-6063 140 Lane 201 Barton Lake, Fremont, IN 46737

GARRETT — A4 *DeKalb*

INDIAN SPRINGS CAMPGROUND **Ratings: 7.5/7.5/7.5** (Campground) 2015 rates: $30 to $39. Apr 15 to Oct 15. (260)357-5572 981 CR 64, Garrett, IN 46738

GAS CITY — B4 *Grant*

MAR-BROOK CAMPGROUND **Ratings: 8/8.5★/7.5** (Campground) 2015 rates: $25 to $31. Apr 15 to Oct 15. (765)674-4383 6690 E 600 S, Gas City, IN 46933

GENEVA — B5 *Adams*

AMISHVILLE USA CAMPGROUND **Ratings: 5.5/6.5/8** (Campground) 2015 rates: $20 to $32. Apr 1 to Oct 31. (260)589-3536 844 E 900 S, Geneva, IN 46740

GOSHEN — A4 *Elkhart*

GOSHEN See also Bremen, Bristol, Elkhart, Middlebury, Shipshewana & South Bend.

ELKHART COUNTY FAIRGROUNDS (Public) From S Jct of SR 15 & US 33, E 0.6 mi on US 33 to Monroe St (left turn) 0.8 mi (R). 2015 rates: $20 to $27. (574)533-3247

GREENFIELD — C4 *Hancock*

HEARTLAND RESORT **Ratings: 8/7/8** (Campground) W-bnd: From Jct of I-70 & SR-9 (exit 104), N 0.4 mi on SR-9 to 300N, W 4 mi (L); or E-bnd: From Jct of I-70 & Mt Comfort Rd (exit 96), N 0.4 mi on Mt Comfort Rd to 300 N, E 4.3 mi (R). **FAC:** Paved/gravel rds. (290 spaces). Avail: 150 gravel, 60 pull-thrus (30 x 60), back-ins (30 x 40), 75 full hkups, 75 W, 75 E (30/50 amps), seasonal sites, WiFi, tent sites, dump, laundry, LP gas, fire rings, firewood. **REC:** heated pool, Sugar Creek: fishing, golf, playground. Pets OK. Partial handicap access. Big rig sites, 2015 rates: $35 to $39. Disc: military.
(317)326-3181 Lat: 39.82740, Lon: -85.83297
1613 W 300 N, Greenfield, IN 46140
jsalisjr@aol.com
www.heartlandresort.com
See ad this page.

INDIANAPOLIS KOA **Ratings: 8.5/9.5★/8** (Campground) 2015 rates: $39 to $75. Mar 1 to Nov 15. (317)894-1397 5896 W 200N, Greenfield, IN 46140

S & H CAMPGROUND **Ratings: 8.5/8.5★/8** (Campground) From Jct I-70 (Exit 104) & IN-9: Go S 1.5 mi on IN-9, W 4.25 mi on McKenzie Rd (W CR-100 N) (L).

MAKING FAMILY MEMORIES SINCE 1968
Open year around, S & H Campground accommodates camping styles from tents to big rigs. All age attractions include a Family Fun Park, mini-golf, pool, drive-in theater, fishing modern amenities, and a weekend restaurant.

FAC: Paved/gravel rds. (360 spaces). 200 Avail: 175 gravel, 25 grass, 30 pull-thrus (24 x 48), back-ins (24 x 45), 125 full hkups, 75 W, 75 E (30/50 amps), seasonal sites, WiFi, tent sites, rentals, dump, mobile sewer, laundry, groc, LP gas, fire rings, firewood, restaurant. **REC:** pool, Sugar Creek: fishing, playground. Pets OK. Partial handicap access. 2015 rates: $25 to $45. Disc: AAA, military.
(317)326-3208 Lat: 39.79832, Lon: -85.85059
2573 W 100 N, Greenfield, IN 46140
reservations@sandhcampground.com
www.sandhcampground.com
See ad this page, 471 & Family Camping in Magazine Section.

Travel Services

S & H RV SERVICE & PARTS CENTER Onsite RV repairs and upgrades at campgrounds. 10% Good Sam/AAA discounts on parts and service. **SERVICES:** Tire, RV appliance, MH mechanical, mobile RV svc, emergency rd svc, staffed RV wash, restrooms. Rentals. **TOW:** RV, auto. RV supplies, LP, dump, emergency parking, RV accessible. Hours: 9am to 9 pm.
(317)326-3208 Lat: 39.79832, Lon: -85.85059
2573 W 100 N, Greenfield, IN 46140
reservations@sandhcampground.com
www.shservicecenter.com
See ad this page.

Tell them you saw them in this Guide!

GREENWOOD — C3 *Johnson*

Travel Services

CAMPING WORLD GREENWOOD/INDIANAPOLIS As the nation's largest retailer of RV supplies, accessories, services and new and used RVs, Camping World is committed to making your total RV experience better. RV Accessories: (800)255-7620. **SERVICES:** RV, RV appliance, MH mechanical, staffed RV wash, restrooms, RV Sales. RV supplies, LP, emergency parking, RV accessible. waiting room. Hours: 8:00am - 6:00pm.
(888)680-9465 Lat: 39.610376, Lon: -86.076163
303 Sheek Road, Greenwood, IN 46143
www.campingworld.com

GROVERTOWN — A3 *Starke*

EZ KAMP **Ratings: 6/7.5/6.5** (RV Park) 2015 rates: $30 to $35. Apr 1 to Oct 31. (574)867-5267 9415 E 500 N Rd, Grovertown, IN 46531

HAMBURG — E4 *Clark*

DEAM LAKE SRA (Public) From town, E 6 mi on Hwy 60, follow signs (L); or From Hamburg, NW 8 mi on Hwy 60, follow signs (R). Entrance fee required. 2015 rates: $12 to $46. (812)246-5421

HANNA — A3 *La Porte*

LAST RESORT CAMPGROUND **Ratings: 7.5/8/6.5** (Campground) 2015 rates: $33 to $42. Apr 1 to Nov 1. (219)797-CAMP 4707 W 1300 S, Hanna, IN 46340

HARTFORD CITY — B4 *Blackford*

WILDWOOD OUTDOOR ESCAPE **Ratings: 7.5/8/7** (Campground) 2015 rates: $31 to $39. Apr 15 to Oct 15. (765)348-2100 520 W 300 N, Hartford City, IN 47348

HENRYVILLE — E4 *Clark*

CLARK SF (Public) From town: Go 1 mi N on US-31. Pit toilets. 2015 rates: $12. (812)294-4306

Want to know how we rate? Our campground inspection guidelines are detailed in the front pages of the Guide.

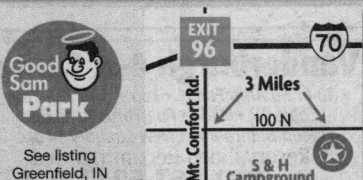

HILLSBORO — C2 *Fountain*

CHARLAROSE LAKE & CAMPGROUND Ratings: 6.5/6.5/8.5 (Campground) From Jct of I-74 & SR-25 (exit 25), S 1 mi on SR-25 to US-136, W 1.3 mi to Mountain Rd, S 0.2 mi to 300S, W 1 mi (R). **FAC:** Paved/gravel rds. (92 spaces). 37 Avail: 9 gravel, 28 grass, 2 pull-thrus (26 x 60), back-ins (26 x 50), mostly side by side hkups, 8 full hkups, 29 W, 29 E (20/30 amps), seasonal sites, dump, laundry, LP gas, fire rings, firewood. **REC:** Lake Charlarose: fishing, shuffleboard, playground. Pet restrict(B). No tents. 2015 rates: $22 to $25. Apr 1 to Nov 1.
(765)234-7286 Lat: 40.08297, Lon: -87.11090
3204 E 300S, Hillsboro, IN 47949
charlarose@hotmail.com
www.charlarose.com

HOWE — A4 *LaGrange*

GRAND VIEW BEND **Ratings: 6/8/8** (Membership Pk) 2015 rates: $15 to $30. Apr 15 to Oct 15. (574)575-5927 4630 N 100 E, Howe, IN 46746

TWIN MILLS RV RESORT **Ratings: 7.5/7/8** (RV Park) 2015 rates: $37 to $44. Apr 15 to Nov 1. (260)562-3212 1675 W SR-120 (West State Road), Howe, IN 46746

HUNTINGTON — B4 *Huntington*

CAMP TIMBER LAKE **Ratings: 8/7.5/8** (Campground) 2015 rates: $24 to $31. (260)672-3251 1740 E 675 N, Huntington, IN 46750

J.E. ROUSH LAKE (State Pk) From town: Go 1-1/2 mi S on Hwy 5. Pit toilets. (260)468-2165

SALAMONIE LAKE (State Pk) From town, S 9 mi on SR-105 (cross the Salamonie Reservoir), W 0.1 mi on park access rd/Lost Bridge West Rd (R). 2015 rates: $10 to $29. (260)468-2125

INDIANAPOLIS — C3 *Indianapolis, Marion*

INDIANAPOLIS See also Anderson, Cicero & Pendleton.

INDIANA STATE FAIRGROUNDS (Public) From Jct of I-465N & SR-31 (Meridian St), S 7.2 mi on SR-31 to 38th St, E 2 mi (L); or From Jct of I-70 & Keystone (exit 85B), N 2 mi on Keystone to 38th St, W 0.9 mi (R). 2015 rates: $20 to $30. (317)927-7503

INDY LAKES CAMPGROUND
Ratings: 7/9★/7 (Campground) From Jct of I-465 & SR 37 (exit 4), S 2.3 mi on SR 37 to Southport Rd, W 1.8 mi (L). **FAC:** Paved/gravel rds. 51 Avail: 25 paved, 26 gravel, patios, back-ins (30 x 60), 51 full hkups (30/50 amps), WiFi, tent sites, rentals, laundry, groc, firewood, controlled access. **REC:** Le An Wa Lake: fishing, rec open to public. Pet restrict(B). Big rig sites, RV age restrict, 2015 rates: $30.
(317)888-6006 Lat: 39.66309, Lon: -86.22815
4001 W Southport Rd, Indianapolis, IN 46217
camping@indylakes.com
www.indylakes.com

LAKE HAVEN RETREAT
Ratings: 7.5/9★/7.5 (Campground) From Jct of I-465 & Hwy 37 (Exit 4), S 1.5 mi on Hwy 37, E on W. Edgewood Ave, then immediately turn again S (R). **FAC:** Paved/gravel rds. (138 spaces). Avail: 78 gravel, 78 pull-thrus (28 x 65), mostly side by side hkups, 78 full hkups (30/50 amps), seasonal sites, cable, WiFi, tent sites, dump, laundry, fire rings, firewood. **REC:** Fishing Lake: fishing, playground. Pets OK. Partial handicap access. Big rig sites, RV age restrict, 2015 rates: $31. Disc: military.
(317)783-5267 Lat: 39.67817, Lon: -86.19492
1951 W Edgewood Ave, Indianapolis, IN 46217
info@lakehavenretreat.com
www.lakehavenretreat.com
See ad this page.

JASONVILLE — D2 *Clay, Green, Sullivan*

SHAKAMAK (State Pk) From Jct of SR-59 & SR-48, W 4 mi on SR-48 (L). 2015 rates: $7.63 TO $29. (812)665-2158

KENDALLVILLE — A4 *LaGrange, Noble*

BIXLER LAKE CAMPGROUND (Public) From Jct of US-6 & SR-3, E 1.3 mi on US-6 to Fair St, S 0.3 mi to Wayne St, E 500 ft to Park Ave, S 0.3 mi to Lake Park Dr, E 0.2 mi (L) Follow signs. 2015 rates: $15 to $38. Apr 30 to Oct 15. (260)242-6898

Don't miss a thing! Check out the Table of Contents for everything the Guide has to offer.

KNIGHTSTOWN — C4 *Henry*

YOGI BEAR'S JELLYSTONE PARK CAMP-RESORT **Ratings: 8/8/8.5** (Campground) 2015 rates: $37 to $50. Apr 1 to Oct 31. (800)446-9644 5964 South SR-109, Knightstown, IN 46148

KNOX — A3 *Starke*

BASS LAKE STATE BEACH AND CAMPGROUND (Public) From town, S 5 mi on US-35 to IN-10, E 3.4 mi (R). 2015 rates: $30 to $40. May 1 to Oct 31. (574)772-3382

KOUTS — A2 *Porter*

DONNA JO CAMPGROUND Ratings: 3/6/6 (Campground) From Jct Hwy 8 & Hwy 49: Go 3-1/2 S on Hwy 49, then 1-1/2 mi E on CR 1125 S, then 1-1/2 S on CR 350 E (L). **FAC:** Dirt rds. (75 spaces). Avail: 55 grass, 7 pull-thrus (30 x 50), back-ins (30 x 40), 30 full hkups, 25 W, 25 E (15/30 amps), seasonal sites, tent sites, laundry, fire rings, firewood. **REC:** pond, fishing, playground. Pets OK. 2015 rates: $36.50. May 1 to Nov 1. No CC.
AAA Approved
(219)766-2186 Lat: 41.24846, Lon: -86.99638
1255 S Co Rd 350E, Kouts, IN 46347
www.donnajocampground.com

LAFAYETTE — B3 *Tippecanoe*

WOLFE'S LEISURE TIME CAMPGROUND **Ratings: 6/6.5/6** (Campground) 2015 rates: $25 to $30. (765)589-8089 7414 Old Sr 25 North, Lafayette, IN 47905

LAKEVILLE — A3 *St Joseph*

MAPLE RIDGE CAMPGROUND **Ratings: 6.5/6.5/7** (Campground) 2015 rates: $29 to $36. Apr 15 to Oct 15. (574)784-8532 65777 Maple Rd, Lakeville, IN 46536

POTATO CREEK (State Pk) From Jct of SR-23 & SR-4, E 4 mi on SR-4 (L). 2015 rates: $12 to $32. (574)656-8186

LIBERTY — C5 *Union*

WHITEWATER MEMORIAL (State Pk) From Jct of US-27 & SR-101, S 1.5 mi on SR-101 (R). Entrance fee required. 2015 rates: $10 to $29. (765)458-5565

IN

LOGANSPORT — B3 *Cass*

FRANCE PARK (Public) From town, W 4 mi on US-24 (L). 2015 rates: $18 to $25. (574)753-2928

LOOGOOTEE — E2 *Daviess, Martin*

WEST BOGGS PARK (DAVIESS-MARTIN COUNTY) (Public) From Jct of US-50 & US-231, N 4.1 mi on US-231 (L). 2015 rates: $27 to $40. (812)295-3421

LYNNVILLE — E2 *Warrick*

LYNNVILLE RV PARK
(Public) From Jct of I-64 & SR-61 (exit 39), N 0.1 mi on SR-61 to SR-68, W 1.5 mi (R). **FAC:** Paved/gravel rds. 39 gravel, 9 pull-thrus (24 x 60), back-ins (24 x 50), some side by side hkups, 23 full hkups, 16 W, 16 E (30/50 amps), tent sites, dump, fire rings, firewood. **REC:** Lynnville Park Lake: fishing, playground. Pets OK. Partial handicap access. 2015 rates: $18 to $22. X no CC.
(812)922-5144 Lat: 38.19400, Lon: -87.32472
405 Sr 68W, Lynnville, IN 47619
lynnvillepk@frontier.com
See ad this page.

MADISON — D4 *Jefferson*

CLIFTY FALLS (State Pk) From town, W 1 mi on SR-56/62 (R). 2015 rates: $7.63 TO $50. (812)273-8885

MADISON CITY (Public) From Jct of Hwys 421 & 56 (Jefferson St), S 0.2 mi on Jefferson St to Vaughn Dr, E 0.2 mi (R). 2015 rates: $25. Apr 1 to Oct 31. (812)265-8333

MARION — B4 *Grant*

SPORTS LAKE CAMPING RESORT **Ratings: 6.5/7/6** (Campground) 2015 rates: $27 to $33. May 1 to Oct 1. (765)998-2558 7230 East 400 S, Marion, IN 46953

MARSHALL — C2 *Parke*

TURKEY RUN (State Pk) From Jct of US-41 & SR-47, E 1.8 mi on SR-47 (L). Entrance fee required. 2015 rates: $12 to $29. (765)597-2635

Had a great stay? Let us know by emailing us travelguidecomments@goodsamfamily.com

MARTINSVILLE — D3 *Monroe, Morgan*

MORGAN-MONROE SF (State Pk) From Jct of Hwy 37 & Old 37 access rd, S 3 mi on Old 37 access rd to forest entrance, E 4.5 mi (L). Pit toilets. 2015 rates: $6 to $16. (765)342-4026

MICHIGAN CITY — A3 *La Porte*

MICHIGAN CITY CAMPGROUND **Ratings: 8.5/9★/8** (Campground) 2015 rates: $37 to $45. (219)872-7600 1601 N US Hwy 421, Michigan City, IN 46360

MIDDLEBURY — A4 *Elkhart, Lagrange*

ELKHART COUNTY MIDDLEBURY KOA
Ratings: 9/8.5/8 (RV Park) From Jct of I-80/I-90 Toll Rd & SR-13 (Middlebury, Exit 107) S 1.5 mi on SR-13 (R), from Jct SR-120 & SR-13, N 0.1 on SR-13 (L). **FAC:** Paved/gravel rds. (99 spaces). 95 Avail: 3 paved, 80 gravel, 12 grass, 58 pull-thrus (30 x 70), back-ins (30 x 40), some side by side hkups, 60 full hkups, 35 W, 35 E (30/50 amps), seasonal sites, cable, WiFi, tent sites, rentals, dump, laundry, groc, LP gas, fire rings, firewood. **REC:** heated pool, pond, fishing, playground. Pets OK. Partial handicap access. Big rig sites, eco-friendly, 2015 rates: $40 to $85. Disc: military. Apr 1 to Oct 31. ATM.
(800)562-5892 Lat: 41.72793, Lon: -85.68373
52867 SR-13, Middlebury, IN 46540
kamp@middleburykoa.com
www.middleburykoa.com
See ad this page.

MITCHELL — D3 *Lawrence*

SPRING MILL (State Pk) From Jct of SR-37 & SR-60, E 3 mi on SR-60 (L). 2015 rates: $10 to $29. (812)849-3534

MODOC — C4 *Randolph*

KAMP MODOC FAMILY CAMPGROUND AND PLAY LAKE **Ratings: 7.5/8/7** (Campground) 2015 rates: $33 to $35. Apr 15 to Oct 15. (765)853-5290 9773 S 800 W, Modoc, IN 47358

MONON — B3 *White*

DREAM ACRES **Ratings: 5.5/5/6** (Campground) 2015 rates: $25. Apr 15 to Oct 15. (219)253-8224 2746 E Sr 16, Monon, IN 47959

MONTGOMERY — E2 *Daviess*

MONTGOMERY REC PARK (Public) From Jct of Hwy 50/150 & First St, N 0.3 mi on First St to Park St (cross RR tracks), E 0.4 mi (L). 2015 rates: $20 to $24. Apr 15 to Oct 15. (812)486-3255

MONTICELLO — B3 *White*

IDEAL BEACH RV RESORT
Ratings: 8/7.5/8 (RV Park) From Jct of US-24 & 6th St (W Shafer Dr), N 3.5 mi on Shafer Dr (L). **FAC:** Paved/gravel rds. (128 spaces). Avail: 116 gravel, 116 pull-thrus (40 x 60), 53 full hkups, 63 W, 63 E (30/50 amps), seasonal sites, cable, WiFi $, tent sites, rentals, dump, laundry, groc, LP gas, fire rings, firewood, controlled access. **REC:** heated pool, wading pool, playground. Pet restrict(Q). Partial handicap access. Big rig sites, 2015 rates: $28 to $58. Disc: AAA, military. May 22 to Sep 8.
(574)583-4141 Lat: 40.79493, Lon: -86.78049
2882 North West Shafer Dr, Monticello, IN 47960
www.indianabeach.com
See ad this page.

INDIANA BEACH RV RESORT
Ratings: 7/7/8 (Campground) From Jct of US-24 & Sixth St (W Shafer Dr), N 3.3 mi on Sixth St (L). **FAC:** Paved/gravel rds. (873 spaces). 595 Avail: 300 gravel, 295 grass, 300 pull-thrus (25 x 55), back-ins (25 x 55), mostly side by side hkups, 270 full hkups, 325 W, 325 E (30/50 amps), seasonal sites, cable, WiFi $, tent sites, rentals, dump, laundry, groc, LP gas, fire rings, firewood, controlled access. **REC:** Lake Shafer: fishing, playground. Pet restrict(Q). Partial handicap access. 2015 rates: $22 to $45. Disc: AAA, military. May 1 to Oct 31. ATM.
(574)583-4141 Lat: 40.79219, Lon: -86.77885
2732 NW Schafer Drive, Monticello, IN 47960
www.indianabeach.com
See ad this page.

LOST ACRES R.V. PARK **Ratings: 7/6/7.5** (RV Park) 2015 rates: $35. May 1 to Oct 31. (574)583-5198 3148 N 400 E, Monticello, IN 47960

We appreciate your business!

MONTICELLO (CONT)

Things to See and Do

INDIANA BEACH AMUSEMENT RESORT Amusement park, beach, shops, restaurants & water park. Call for hours. May 15 to Sep 7. RV accessible. Restrooms, food. Hours: Call for hours. Adult fee: $31.95.
(574)583-4141 Lat: 40.79175, Lon: -86.77399
5224 E Indiana Beach Rd, Monticello, IN 47960
info@indianabeach.com
www.indianabeach.com
See ad opposite page.

MOROCCO — B2 *Newton*

WILLOW SLOUGH STATE FISH & WILDLIFE AREA (State Pk) From jct US-41 & CR-275S: Go 2 mi W on CR-275S. (219)285-2704

NASHVILLE — D3 *Brown*

BILL MONROE MEMORIAL MUSIC PARK & CAMPGROUND **Ratings: 5/5.5/5.5** (Campground) 2015 rates: $27 to $32. May 1 to Nov 1. (812)988-6422 5163 Sr 135 N, Morgantown, IN 46160

BROWN COUNTY (State Pk) From Jct of SR-135N & SR-46W, SW 2.2 mi on SR-46W (L). RVs use west gate. Entrance fee required. 2015 rates: $6.12 to $38.76. (812)988-6406

THE LAST RESORT RV PARK & CAMPGROUND
Ratings: 8/9.5★/8.5 (Campground) From Jct of I-65 & SR-46 (exit 68), W 14 mi on SR-46 (R). **FAC:** Paved/gravel rds. (110 spaces). Avail: 92 gravel, 18 pull-thrus (21 x 50), back-ins (22 x 36), some side by side hkups, 73 full hkups, 19 W, 19 E (30/50 amps), seasonal sites, cable, WiFi, tent sites, rentals, laundry, groc, fire rings, firewood. **REC:** pool, playground. Pets OK. Eco-friendly, 2015 rates: $28 to $46. Disc: AAA. Apr 1 to Nov 1.
AAA Approved
(812)988-4675 Lat: 39.19586, Lon: -86.20509
2248 SR-46 East, Nashville, IN 47448
camp@browncountycampgrounds.com
www.browncountycampgrounds.com
See ad opposite page, 471.

WESTWARD HO CAMPGROUND
Ratings: 7/8/6.5 (RV Park) From Jct of I-65 & SR-46W (Exit 68), W 11.2 mi on SR-46W (L). **FAC:** Gravel rds. (92 spaces). 80 Avail: 5 paved, 75 gravel, 44 pull-thrus (22 x 60), back-ins (24 x 60), mostly side by side hkups, 80 full hkups (30/50 amps), seasonal sites, WiFi, tent sites, rentals, fire rings, firewood. **REC:** pool, pond, fishing. Pets OK. Partial handicap access. 2015 rates: $30 to $35. Disc: AAA, military. Apr 1 to Nov 1.
AAA Approved
(812)988-0008 Lat: 39.18989, Lon: -86.16415
4557 E SR-46, Nashville, IN 47448
www.gowestwardho.com
See ad this page, 471.

YELLOWWOOD SF (Public) From business center: Go 7 mi W on Hwy-46. Pit toilets. 2015 rates: $10 to $40. (812)988-7945

NEW CARLISLE — A3 *St Joseph*

MINI MOUNTAIN CAMPGROUND
Ratings: 7/5.5/6.5 (Campground) From Jct of US-20/US-31 & Hwy 2 (La Porte exit), W 8 mi on Hwy 2/Western Ave (R). **FAC:** Paved/gravel rds. (235 spaces). Avail: 75 gravel, 16 pull-thrus (25 x 60), back-ins (25 x 40), some side by side hkups, 49 full hkups, 26 W, 26 E (30/50 amps), seasonal sites, tent sites, rentals, dump, laundry, groc, LP gas, fire rings, firewood, controlled access. **REC:** heated pool, pond, fishing, playground. Pets OK. 2015 rates: $28 to $30. Disc: military. Apr 1 to Nov 1.
(574)654-3307 Lat: 41.67206, Lon: -86.49600
32351 State Rd 2, New Carlisle, IN 46552
fredmorris50@embarqmail.com
www.minimountaincampgrounds.com
See ad page 482.

NEW CASTLE — C4 *Henry*

CORNERSTONE RETREAT AND FAMILY CAMPGROUND
Ratings: 7.5/9★/8 (Campground) From jct I-70 (exit 123) & SR 3: Go 3/4 mi N on SR 3, then 3/4 mi E on CR 500 S (R). **FAC:** Paved/gravel rds. (100 spaces). Avail: 92 gravel, 7 pull-thrus (35 x 50), back-ins (35 x 45), 19 full hkups, 73 W, 73 E (30/50 amps), seasonal sites, WiFi Hotspot, tent sites, rentals, dump, laundry, groc, LP gas, fire rings, firewood, restaurant, controlled access. **REC:** heated pool, wading pool, pond, fishing, playground. Pets OK. Partial handicap access. Big rig sites, 2015 rates: $30 to $65. Disc: military.
(765)987-8700 Lat: 39.85986, Lon: -85.38825
75 W County Road 500 S, New Castle, IN 47362
admin@cornerstonecampground.com
www.cornerstonecampground.com

SUMMIT LAKE (State Pk) From Jct of SR-3N & US-36, E 4 mi on US-36 to Messick Rd, N 1 mi (E). 2015 rates: $12 TO $29. (765)766-5873

WESTWOOD PARK & CAMPGROUND (Public) From Jct of SR-38 & SR-3, W 2.75 mi on SR-38 to RD 275W, S 2 mi to park access rd, follow signs (L). Pit toilets. 2015 rates: $18 to $24. (765)987-1232

NEW HARMONY — E1 *Posey*

HARMONIE (State Pk) From town, S 4 mi on Hwy 69 to SR-269, W 1 mi (E). 2015 rates: $12 to $95. (812)682-4821

NEW LISBON — C4 *Henry*

NEW LISBON FAMILY CAMPGROUND
Ratings: 7.5/7.5/7.5 (Campground) From Jct of I-70 & Wilbur Wright Rd (exit 131), S 0.4 mi on Wilbur Wright Rd to CR-600S, E 0.4 mi (L). **FAC:** Gravel rds. (165 spaces). Avail: 20 gravel, 20 pull-thrus (22 x 90), 20 full hkups (30 amps), seasonal sites, WiFi, rentals, dump, laundry, groc, LP gas, fire rings, firewood, controlled access. **REC:** New Lisbon Lake: swim, fishing, playground. Pet restrict(B). No tents. 2015 rates: $29. Disc: AAA, military. Mar 1 to Nov 30. No CC.
AAA Approved
(765)332-2948 Lat: 39.84655, Lon: -85.25364
6888 E CR-600S, Straughn, IN 47387
gr6888@aol.com
www.nlcamp.com
See ad this page.

NORTH VERNON — D4 *Jennings*

MUSCATATUCK COUNTY PARK (Public) From Jct of US-50 & Hwy 7/3, S 1.3 mi on Hwy 7/3 (R). 2015 rates: $11 to $24. (812)346-2953

OAKTOWN — D2 *Knox*

NEW VISION RV PARK
Ratings: 7/7.5★/9 (RV Park) From Jct of US-50 & US-41 (N side of Vincennes), N 13 mi on N US-41 (R); or From Jct of US-41 & St Hwy 58, S 6.6 mi on US-41 (L). **FAC:** Gravel rds. 39 gravel, 16 pull-thrus (36 x 65), back-ins (36 x 45), 39 full hkups (30/50 amps), WiFi, tent sites, laundry, LP gas, fire rings, firewood. **REC:** Vision Lake: fishing, playground. Pets OK. Big rig sites, 2015 rates: $24 to $26. Disc: military.
(812)745-2125 Lat: 38.87422, Lon: -87.43491
13552 N US Hwy 41, Oaktown, IN 47561
mitch@newvisionrvpark.com
www.newvisionrvpark.com
See ad pages 482, 471.

ORLAND — A4 *Steuben*

MANAPOGO PARK **Ratings: 8/9★/7.5** (Campground) 2015 rates: $40 to $45. Apr 15 to Oct 1. (260)833-3902 5495 W 760 N, Orland, IN 46776

PENDLETON — C4 *Madison*

GLOWOOD CAMPGROUND **Ratings: 4.5/5/7.5** (Campground) 2015 rates: $25 to $30. (317)485-5239 9384 W 700 S, Pendleton, IN 46064

PERU — B3 *Miami*

HONEY BEAR HOLLOW FAMILY CAMPGROUND
Ratings: 7/9.5★/7.5 (Campground) From Jct of US-24 & US-31, N 1.3 mi on US-31 to CR-200N, W 1.2 mi (R). **FAC:** Gravel rds. (98 spaces). 61 Avail: 51 gravel, 10 grass, 22 pull-thrus (30 x 50), back-ins (30 x 50), some side by side hkups, 5 full hkups, 56 W, 56 E (30/50 amps), seasonal sites, WiFi Hotspot, tent sites, rentals, dump, mobile sewer, laundry, groc, LP gas, fire rings, firewood. **REC:** pool, pond, fishing, playground. Pets OK. Eco-friendly, 2015 rates: $24 to $28. Disc: AAA, military.
(765)473-4342 Lat: 40.79516, Lon: -86.15291
4252 W 200 N, Peru, IN 46970
tylewr@yahoo.com
See ad this page.

MISSISSINEWA LAKE STATE RESERVOIR (State Pk) From Jct of Main/Bus SR-24 & Broadway/SR-19 (in town), S 6 mi on SR-19 to SR-500S, E 2.9 mi (L). Entrance fee required. 2015 rates: $12 to $29. (765)473-6528

PIERCETON — B4 *Kosciusko*

YOGI BEAR'S JELLYSTONE PARK CAMP-RESORT **Ratings: 8/8.5/8.5** (Campground) 2015 rates: $39 to $60. May 13 to Sep 15. (574)594-2124 1916 N 850 E, Pierceton, IN 46562

PLYMOUTH — A3 *Marshall*

HIDDEN LAKE PARADISE CAMPGROUND **Ratings: 5/6/6.5** (Campground) 2015 rates: $24. Apr 21 to Oct 7. (574)936-2900 12589 Rose Rd, Plymouth, IN 46563

YOGI BEAR'S JELLYSTONE PARK PLYMOUTH **Ratings: 8/7.5/8** (RV Park) 2015 rates: $45. May 2 to Sep 30. (574)936-7851 7719 Redwood Rd, Plymouth, IN 46563

PORTAGE — A2 *Porter*

YOGI BEAR'S JELLYSTONE PARK CAMP-RESORT **Ratings: 7.5/8.5/7** (Campground) 2015 rates: $45 to $56. May 15 to Sep 30. (219)762-7757 5300 Old Porter Rd, Portage, IN 46368

PORTLAND — B5 *Jay*

FOX LAKE CAMPGROUND **Ratings: 6/5.5/7** (Campground) 2015 rates: $18 to $33. Apr 15 to Oct 15. (260)335-2639 7424 South 300 E, Portland, IN 47371

REMINGTON — B2 *Jasper*

CABOOSE LAKE CAMPGROUND
Ratings: 8.5/9.5★/8 (RV Park) From Jct of I-65 & US-24 (exit 201), E 0.1 mi on US-24 (R).

MAKING FAMILY FUN AFFORDABLE
Beautiful RV sites on a 20-acre spring fed stocked lake. Perfect 75' overnight pull-thrus or stay longer in NW Indiana. Enjoy our SUMMER BEACH FAMILY FUN ZONE with 35' Water Slide, Water Wars, Bumper Boats, and Inflatables.

FAC: Gravel rds. (125 spaces). Avail: 105 gravel, 43 pull-thrus (30 x 75), back-ins (35 x 60), some side by side hkups, 105 full hkups (30/50 amps), seasonal sites, WiFi, tent sites, rentals, dump, laundry, groc, LP gas, fire rings, firewood, controlled access. **REC:** Caboose Lake: swim, fishing, playground, rec open to public. Pet restrict(B). Partial handicap access. Big rig sites, 2015 rates: $38. Disc: military.
(219)261-3828 Lat: 40.76555, Lon: -87.11518
3657 W US-24, Remington, IN 47977
camp@cabooselake.com
www.cabooselake.com
See ad pages 473 (Spotlight NW Hoosier Country), 471.

Everyone wants to be noticed. Tell your RV Park that you found them in the this Guide.

IN

 See map page 470

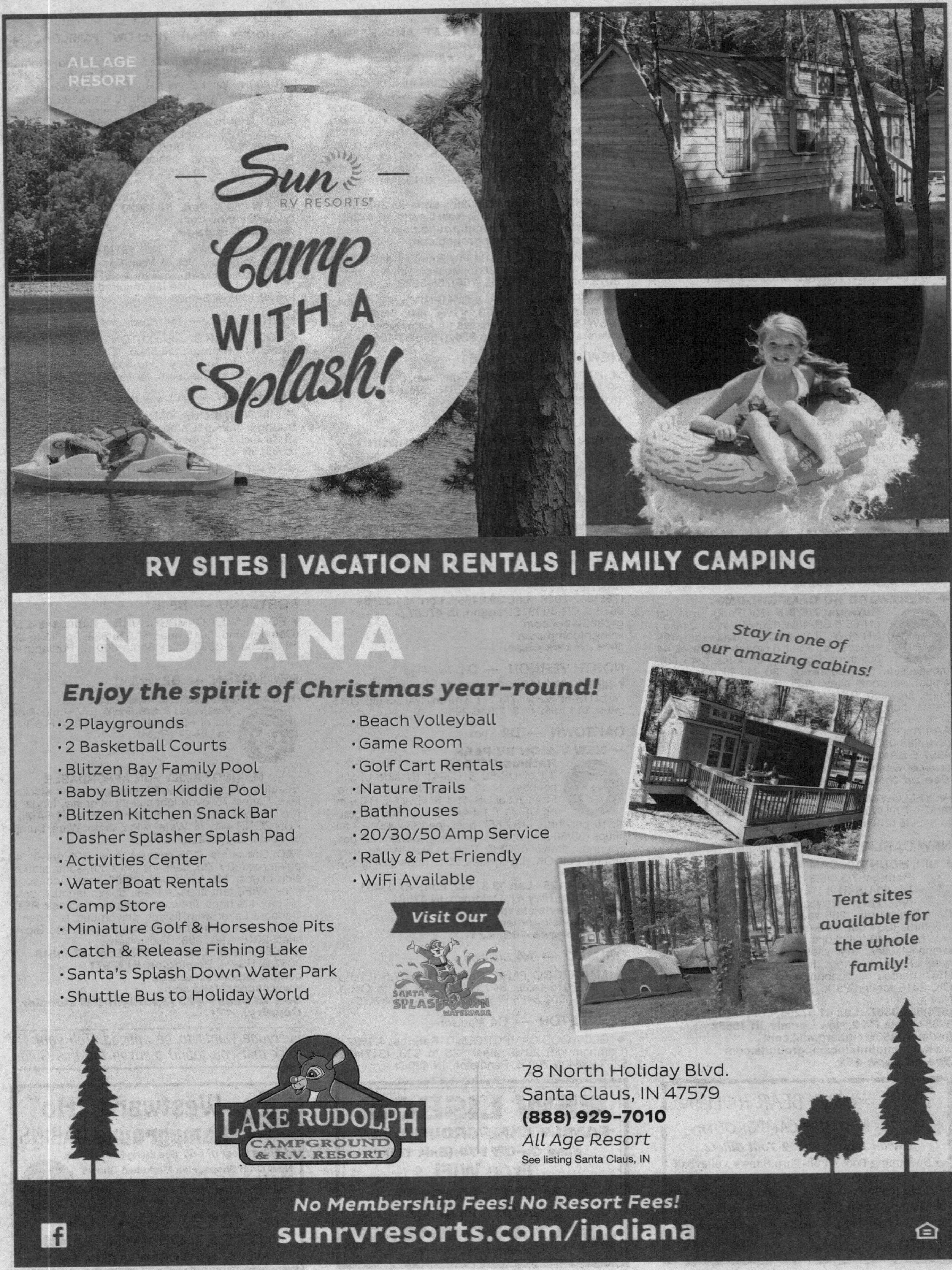

ALL AGE RESORT
Sun RV RESORTS®
Camp WITH A Splash!
RV SITES | VACATION RENTALS | FAMILY CAMPING
INDIANA
Enjoy the spirit of Christmas year-round!
• 2 Playgrounds
• 2 Basketball Courts
• Blitzen Bay Family Pool
• Baby Blitzen Kiddie Pool
• Blitzen Kitchen Snack Bar
• Dasher Splasher Splash Pad
• Activities Center
• Water Boat Rentals
• Camp Store
• Miniature Golf & Horseshoe Pits
• Catch & Release Fishing Lake
• Santa's Splash Down Water Park
• Shuttle Bus to Holiday World
• Beach Volleyball
• Game Room
• Golf Cart Rentals
• Nature Trails
• Bathhouses
• 20/30/50 Amp Service
• Rally & Pet Friendly
• WiFi Available
Stay in one of our amazing cabins!
Visit Our
SANTA'S SPLASH DOWN WATERPARK
Tent sites available for the whole family!
LAKE RUDOLPH CAMPGROUND & R.V. RESORT
78 North Holiday Blvd.
Santa Claus, IN 47579
(888) 929-7010
All Age Resort
See listing Santa Claus, IN
No Membership Fees! No Resort Fees!
sunrvresorts.com/indiana

REMINGTON (CONT)

Things to See and Do

➜ **SUMMER BEACH FAMILY FUN ZONE** 35' Hippo Slide, Bumper Boats, Inflatable Slides, Water Wars, Jumpshot, Water Inflatables, and Dunk Tank. A day-cation located at Caboose Lake Campground. Jun 1 to Aug 31. partial handicap access. RV accessible. Restrooms, food. Hours: 11am to 5pm Sun-Th,11am to 7pm Fri-Sat. Adult fee: $15 day.
(219)261-3828 Lat: 40.76555, Lon: -87.11518
3657 West US 24, Remington, IN 47977
camp@cabooselake.com
www.cabooselake.com
See ad page 473 (Spotlight NW Hoosier Country).

RICHMOND — C5 *Wayne*

ARROWHEAD CAMPGROUND **Ratings: 9/10★/10** (RV Park) From Jct of I-70 & US 40 (Indiana exit 156) go E 1mi on US 40, go N 1.5 mi on OH 320 onto OH 121 N for 8.5 mi to Thomas Rd, go W on Thomas 1 mi (L). **FAC:** All weather rds. (131 spaces). Avail: 26 gravel, patios, 10 pull-thrus (35 x 70), back-ins (30 x 40), 26 full hkups (30/50 amps), seasonal sites, WiFi Hotspot, tent sites, rentals, dump, laundry, LP gas, fire rings, firewood. **REC:** pool, pond, fishing, playground. Pet restrict(B). Big rig sites, eco-friendly, 2015 rates: $39 to $49. Apr 15 to Nov 1.
(937)996-6203 Lat: 39.94380, Lon: -84.74400
1361Thomas Rd, New Paris, OH 45347
patmcc@arrowhead-campground.com
www.arrowhead-campground.com
See primary listing at New Paris, OH and ad page 899.

DEER RIDGE CAMPING RESORT Ratings: 8.5/7.5/8 (Campground) From Jct of I-70 & SR-227 (exit 153), S 0.1 mi on SR-227 to Smyrna Rd, E 0.5 mi (L). **FAC:** Gravel rds. (62 spaces). Avail: 40 gravel, 6 pull-thrus (25 x 80), back-ins (25 x 50), 40 full hkups (30/50 amps), seasonal sites, WiFi Hotspot, tent sites, laundry, groc, LP gas, fire rings, firewood. **REC:** heated pool, pond, fishing, playground. Pets OK. 2015 rates: $32 to $41. Disc: AAA, military. May 1 to Oct 31.
AAA Approved
(765)939-0888 Lat: 39.86586, Lon: -84.85122
3696 Smyrna Rd, Richmond, IN 47374
deerridg@aol.com
www.deerridgecampingresort.com

GRANDPA'S FARM **Ratings: 9/8.5★/9.5** (Campground) From Jct of I-70 & SR-227 (exit 153), N 2 mi on SR-227 (L). **FAC:** Paved/gravel rds. (95 spaces). Avail: 65 gravel, 19 pull-thrus (30 x 70), back-ins (30 x 50), 25 full hkups, 40 W, 40 E (30/50 amps), seasonal sites, WiFi, tent sites, dump, laundry, groc, LP gas, fire rings, firewood. **REC:** heated pool, whirlpool, White Water River: fishing, playground. Pets OK. Big rig sites, eco-friendly, 2015 rates: $28 to $32. Disc: AAA, military. Apr 1 to Nov 1.
(765)962-7907 Lat: 39.88841, Lon: -84.84026
4244 State Road 227 N, Richmond, IN 47374
gpasfarm@aol.com
www.grandpasfarmcamp.com
See ad this page, 471.

RICHMOND KOA KAMPGROUND **Ratings: 8.5/9.5★/8.5** (Campground) 2015 rates: $30 to $65. Mar 15 to Nov 1. (765)962-1219 3101 Cart Rd, Richmond, IN 47374

Travel Services

CAMPING WORLD OF RICHMOND As the nation's largest retailer of RV supplies, accessories, services and new and used RVs, Camping World is committed to making your total RV experience better. **SERVICES:** RV, restrooms, RV Sales. RV supplies, RV accessible. Hours: 8am to 7pm.

(765)966-8361 Lat: 39.85905, Lon: -84.91678
2250 Williamsburg Pike, Richmond, IN 47374
www.campingworld.com

RISING SUN — D5 *Ohio*

LITTLE FARM ON THE RIVER RV PARK CAMPING RESORT **Ratings: 9/8.5★/9** (RV Park) 2015 rates: $34 to $40. (812)438-4500 1343 E Bellview Lane, Rising Sun, IN 47040

ROCHESTER — B3 *Fulton*

LAKEVIEW CAMPGROUND **Ratings: 6/6.5/8.5** (Campground) 2015 rates: $30 to $34. Apr 15 to Oct 15. (574)353-8114 7781 E 300 N, Rochester, IN 46975

ROCKVILLE — C2 *Parke*

➜ CECIL M HARDEN LAKE/RACCOON SRA (State Pk) From Jct of US-36 & US-41, E 9 mi on US-36 (R). 2015 rates: $10 to $40. (765)344-1412

ROCKVILLE LAKE PARK (Public) From Jct of US 41 & US 36, E 0.5 mi on US 36 to Erie St., N 0.4 mi to Stark St, E 0.2 mi to Marshall Rd., NE 1.2 mi (L). 2015 rates: $15 to $35. Apr 1 to Oct 25. (765)569-6541

SANTA CLAUS — E2 *Spencer*

LAKE RUDOLPH CAMPGROUND & RV RESORT
Ratings: 9.5/9.5★/9.5 (RV Park) From Jct of I-64 & SR-162 (exit 63), S 7.2 mi on SR-162 to SR 245 (Holiday Blvd.), N 0.2 mi (R).

CAMPING AND CHRISTMAS COMBO
Yule have a great time a Lake Rudolph where it's always Christmas! Enjoy spacious RV sites and vacation rentals with amenities like miniature golf and free shuttle rides to Holiday World and Splashin' Safari right next door!

FAC: Paved rds. 188 Avail: 116 paved, 72 gravel, patios, 3 pull-thrus (30 x 60), back-ins (30 x 60), 188 full hkups (30/50 amps), WiFi, tent sites, rentals, dump, laundry, groc, LP gas, fire rings, firewood, controlled access. **REC:** pool, wading pool, Lake Rudolph: fishing, playground. Pets OK. Partial handicap access. Big rig sites, 2015 rates: $30 to $64. May 1 to Oct 31. ATM.
(888)349-9733 Lat: 38.12176, Lon: -86.92204
78 N Holiday Blvd, Santa Claus, IN 47579
lakerudolph@suncommunities.com
www.lakerudolph.com
See ad opposite page, 1463 (Welcome Section) & Family Camping in Magazine Section.

SCOTTSBURG — E4 *Scott*

➜ HARDY LAKE (State Pk) From Jct of I-65 & Hwy 256, E 7 mi on Hwy 256 to N Sunnyside Rd., N 4 mi (E). 2015 rates: $10 to $45. (812)794-3800

➜ YOGI BEAR'S JELLYSTONE PARK CAMP-RESORT AT RAINTREE LAKE **Ratings: 8.5/9★/8.5** (Campground) 2015 rates: $36 to $60. (812)752-4062 4577 W SR-56, Scottsburg, IN 47170

SHIPSHEWANA — A4 *LaGrange*

RIVERSIDE CAMPGROUND **Ratings: 2.5/4.5/7.5** (Campground) 2015 rates: $25. May 15 to Oct 15. (260)562-3742 5910 N 450 W, Shipshewana, IN 46565

SHIPSHEWANA CAMPGROUND NORTH PARK & AMISH LOG CABIN LODGING Ratings: 5.5/8.5/8 (RV Park) At Jct of SR-120 & SR-5, SW corner. **FAC:** Gravel rds. 55 Avail: 44 gravel, 11 grass, 11 pull-thrus (30 x 60), back-ins (30 x 50), some side by side hkups, 14 full hkups, 38 W, 41 E (30/50 amps), WiFi, tent sites, rentals, dump, fire rings, firewood. **REC.** Pets OK. Partial handicap access. Big rig sites, 2015 rates: $34 to $40. Disc: AAA, military. Apr 1 to Oct 31.
(260)768-7770 Lat: 41.72590, Lon: -85.58233
5970 North State Rd 5, Shipshewana, IN 46565
shipshewanacampgroundnorth@yahoo.com
www.shipshewanacampgroundnorth.com

SHIPSHEWANA CAMPGROUND SOUTH Ratings: 7/9★/8 (RV Park) From Jct of SR-20 & SR-5, N 0.5 mi on SR-5 (R). **FAC:** Gravel rds. 165 Avail: 146 gravel, 19 grass, 107 pull-thrus (25 x 75), back-ins (30 x 40), 130 full hkups, 6 W, 35 E (30/50 amps), WiFi, tent sites, dump, laundry, firewood. **REC.** Pets OK. Partial handicap access. Big rig sites, eco-friendly, 2015 rates: $26 to $40. Disc: military. May 1 to Oct 15.
(260)768-4669 Lat: 41.66229, Lon: -85.57999
1105 S Van Buren, Shipshewana, IN 46565
south@amish.org
www.amish.org

SHOALS — E3 *Martin*

➜ MARTIN SF (State Pk) From business center: Go 4 mi E on US-50. Pit toilets. (812)247-3491

SOUTH BEND — A3 *St Joseph*

SPAULDING LAKE CAMPGROUND LLC
Ratings: 8/9★/9 (Campground) From Jct of I-80/90 (IN Toll Rd) & IN 933, exit 77(Changes to M 51 in Michigan), N 6 mi on IN 933/MI 51 to Bell Rd, E 1 mi to 17th St, S 1 block to Bell Rd, E 1 mi (L). **FAC:** Gravel rds. 120 grass, 44 pull-thrus (30 x 60), back-ins (30 x 40), some side by side hkups, 120 full hkups (30/50 amps), WiFi, tent sites, laundry, fire rings, firewood. **REC:** Spaulding Lake: swim, fishing, playground. Pets OK. Big rig sites, eco-friendly, 2015 rates: $32. Apr 1 to Oct 31. No CC.
(269)684-1393 Lat: 41.79405, Lon: -86.21507
33524 Bell St, Niles, MI 49120
Spauldingcampground@yahoo.com
www.spauldinglake.com
See primary listing at Niles, MI and ad this page.

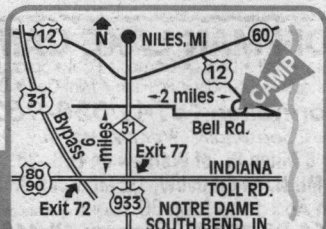

SPENCER — D3 *Owen*

➔ MCCORMICK'S CREEK (State Pk) From town, E 2 mi on Hwy 46, follow signs (L). 2015 rates: $6.12 to $38.76. (812)829-2235

➔ OWEN-PUTNAM SF (Public) From town: Go 5 miles W on Hwy 46, then 1 mile N on Fish Creek Rd. Pit toilets. 2015 rates: $10 to $40. (812)829-2462

ST PAUL — D4 *Decatur*

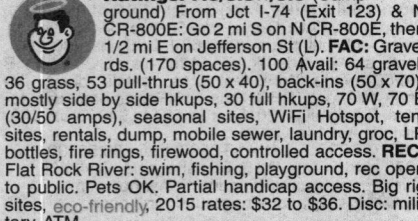

HIDDEN PARADISE CAMPGROUND
Ratings: 7.5/8.5★/8.5 (Campground) From Jct I-74 (Exit 123) & N CR-800E: Go 2 mi S on N CR-800E, then 1/2 mi E on Jefferson St (L). **FAC:** Gravel rds. (170 spaces). 100 Avail: 64 gravel, 36 grass, 53 pull-thrus (50 x 40), back-ins (50 x 70), mostly side by side hkups, 30 full hkups, 70 W, 70 E (30/50 amps), seasonal sites, WiFi Hotspot, tent sites, rentals, dump, mobile sewer, laundry, groc, LP bottles, fire rings, firewood, controlled access. **REC:** Flat Rock River: swim, fishing, playground, rec open to public. Pets OK. Partial handicap access. Big rig sites, eco-friendly. 2015 rates: $32 to $36. Disc: military. ATM.
(765)525-6582 Lat: 39.42318, Lon: -85.62453
802 East Jefferson St, St Paul, IN 47272
www.hiddenparadise.info
See ad pages 477, 471.

➚ THORNTREE LAKE RV PARK **Ratings: 6/8★/9.5** (RV Park) 2015 rates: $25 to $28. (317)604-9261 7306 N. Old US Hwy 421, St Paul, IN 47272

SULLIVAN — D2 *Sullivan*

➚ SULLIVAN COUNTY PARK & LAKE (Public) From Jct of US-41 & W Washington St, E 1.8 on W Washington St to Foley St, N 0.25 mi (E). Entrance fee required. 2015 rates: $13 to $27. Mar 1 to Oct 31. (812)268-5537

TERRE HAUTE — D2 *Vigo*

FOWLER PARK (VIGO COUNTY) (Public) From jct I-70 & US 41: Go 7 mi S on US 41. 2015 rates: $18. May 1 to Oct 15. (812)462-3413

HAWTHORN PARK (Public) From jct I-70 W & Hwy 46: Go 3 mi N on Hwy 46, then 1 mi E on US 40, then 1/2 mi N on Stop 10 Rd, then 1/2 mi W. 2015 rates: $12 to $20. May 1 to Oct 15. (812)462-3225

PRAIRIE CREEK PARK (VIGO COUNTY) (Public) From jct I-70 & US 41: Go 11 mi S on US 41, then W on W French Dr. 2015 rates: $20. May 1 to Oct 15. (812)462-3392

➘ TERRE HAUTE KOA KAMPGROUND **Ratings: 8.5/8.5/8.5** (Campground) 2015 rates: $42 to $59. (800)KOA-4179 5995 E Sony Dr, Terre Haute, IN 47802

Don't take any chances when it comes to cleanliness. We rate campground restrooms and showers for cleanliness and physical characteristics such as supplies and appearance.

THORNTOWN — C3 *Boone*

OLD MILL RUN PARK
Ratings: 8.5/7.5/7.5 (Campground) From Jct of I-65 & SR-47 (Exit 146), W 6.5 mi on SR-47 to CR-825W, N 0.8 mi to CR-690N, W 0.3 mi (R). **FAC:** Paved/gravel rds. (321 spaces). Avail: 45 gravel, 45 pull-thrus (45 x 65), 45 full hkups (30/50 amps), seasonal sites, WiFi Hotspot, tent sites, rentals, dump, laundry, groc, LP bottles, firewood, restaurant. **REC:** heated pool, pond, fishing, golf, shuffleboard, playground. Pets OK. Partial handicap access. 2015 rates: $23.50 to $33. Disc: military. Apr 1 to Oct 15.
(765)436-7190 Lat: 40.08227, Lon: -86.37388
8544 W 690 N, Thorntown, IN 46071
oldmill@frontiernet.net
www.oldmillrun.com
See ad this page.

VALLONIA — D3 *Jackson*

➘ STARVE HOLLOW SRA (State Pk) From Jct of US-50 & Hwy 135, S 3 mi on Hwy 135 to CR-310, E 2.5 mi (L). 2015 rates: $10 to $40. (812)358-3464

VERSAILLES — D4 *Ripley*

➔ VERSAILLES (State Pk) From Jct of US-421 & US-50, E 1 mi on US-50 (L). 2015 rates: $12 to $29. (812)689-6424

VINCENNES — E2 *Knox*

➚ OUABACHE TRAILS PARK (Public) S-bnd: From Jct of US-41 & US-50, S 0.1 mi on US-41(turns into 6th St) to Executive Blvd, W 0.5 mi to Oliphaunt Rd, S 0.25 mi to Old Fort Knox Rd, W 0.5 mi (E). 2015 rates: $18. Apr 15 to Oct 15. (812)882-4316

Our rating system isn't just tough, it's thorough. We know the kinds of things that are important to you — like clean restrooms and showers, attractive, secure, well-tended grounds, and extras like swimming pools. We give the first rating for development of facilities, the second for cleanliness and physical characteristics of restrooms and showers, and the third for visual appearance.

WARSAW — A4 *Kosciusko*

HOFFMAN LAKE CAMP
Ratings: 8/9★/6.5 (Campground) From Jct of US-30 & SR-15, W 8 mi on US-30 to CR-800W, N 0.5 mi to CR-300, E 0.5 mi (L). **FAC:** Paved/gravel rds. (175 spaces). 45 Avail: 5 paved, 10 gravel, 30 grass, 5 pull-thrus (26 x 65), back-ins (25 x 50), 17 full hkups, 28 W, 28 E (30/50 amps), seasonal sites, WiFi Hotspot, tent sites, rentals, dump, mobile sewer, laundry, groc, LP gas, fire rings, firewood, controlled access. **REC:** heated pool, Hoffman Lake: fishing, playground. Pet restrict(Q). Partial handicap access. Big rig sites, 2015 rates: $26 to $33. Apr 15 to Sep 30.
(574)858-9628 Lat: 41.27581, Lon: -85.99152
7638 W 300 N, Warsaw, IN 46582
hoffmanlakecamp@msn.com
www.hoffmanlakecamp.com
See ad this page.

➚ PIC-A-SPOT CAMPGROUND **Ratings: 6/NA/7.5** (Campground) Pit toilets. 2015 rates: $24 to $26. Apr 15 to Oct 15. (574)594-2635 6402 E Mckenna Rd, Warsaw, IN 46582

➚ PIKE LAKE CAMPGROUND (CITY PARK) (Public) From business center: Go 1/2 mi N on Hwy-15, then 1/2 mi E on Arthur St. 2015 rates: $28. Apr 15 to Oct 1. (574)269-1439

WASHINGTON — E2 *Daviess*

➘ GLENDALE REC AREA (Public) From Jct of US-50E & CR-550/Sportsman's Rd, S 7.5 mi on Sportsman's Rd (E). 2015 rates: $7 to $11. Apr 1 to Oct 31. (812)644-7711

WAVELAND — C2 *Montgomery*

➔ LAKE WAVELAND (Public) From Jct of SR-59 & SR-47, W 1 mi on SR-47 (R). 2015 rates: $28. Mar 15 to Oct 15. (765)435-2073

➘ SHADES (State Pk) From town, N 3 mi on CR-750W to SR-234, W 1 mi (L). 2015 rates: $7.63 TO $20. Apr 1 to Sep 30. (765)435-2810

WEST LAFAYETTE — B2 *Tippecanoe*

➚ PROPHETSTOWN (State Pk) From I-65, take exit 178 (St Rd 43), south on State Road 43 to Burnett Road, (1/4 mi), left on Burnett Rd to 9th St Road (3/4 mi), right on 9th St Road to Swisher Road (3/4 mi), left on Swisher Road to park entrance (1-1/2 mi). 2015 rates: $12 TO $40. (765)567-4919

WICKLIFFE — E3 *Crawford*

PATOKA LAKE SRA (State Pk) From Jct of SR-145 & SR-164, W 1 mi on SR-164, turn right on Dillard Rd, continue to Patoka Station (L). 2015 rates: $16.21 to $29. (812)685-2464

WINAMAC — B3 *Pulaski*

TIPPECANOE RIVER (State Pk) From town, N 4 mi on US-35 (R). 2015 rates: $10 to $29. (574)946-3213

WINSLOW — E2 *Pike*

➔ PIKE SF (State Pk) From jct Hwy-61 & Hwy-364: Go 3 mi E on Hwy-364. Pit toilets. 2015 rates: $10 to $40. (812)367-1524

WOLCOTTVILLE — A4 *LaGrange*

➔ ATWOOD LAKE CAMPGROUND **Ratings: 6.5/6/7.5** (Campground) 2015 rates: $30 to $35. Apr 15 to Oct 15. (260)854-3079 655 E 800S, Wolcottville, IN 46795

➔ GORDONS CAMPGROUND **Ratings: 7.5/6.5/7.5** (Campground) 2015 rates: $33 to $38. Apr 15 to Oct 15. (260)351-3383 9500 E 600 S Wolcottville, IN 46795

The RV That's Right For You

Which recreational vehicle is right for you? Our handy overview in the front of this Guide helps prospective buyers decide which RV type fits their lifestyle, travel needs and budget, from folding camping trailers to motorhomes.

Getty Images/iStockphoto

WELCOME TO Iowa

DATE OF STATEHOOD	WIDTH: 310 MILES (500 KM)	PROPORTION OF UNITED STATES
DEC. 28, 1846	LENGTH: 199 MILES (320 KM)	1.48% OF 3,794,100 SQ MI

From the baseball diamond immortalized in "Field of Dreams" to antique carousels and iconic farm implements, Iowa is a place where popular culture touchstones and classic Americana are revealed at every turn. The Hawkeye State is where Clint Eastwood charmed Meryl Streep on the bridges of Madison Country, where John Wayne was born in a town called Winterset in 1907 and where "the music died" when Buddy Holly, Richie Valens and J.P. Richardson's plane crashed at Clear Lake in 1959. Apparently, actor William Shatner need not be concerned by his own mortality. According to Star Trek mythology, his alter ego, Captain James T. Kirk, will be born again in March 2228 in the small town of Riverside.

Often quirky, at times surreal, but always hospitable, in Iowa you can visit the world's only pearl button museum, marvel at the sublime architecture of the Des Moines Art Center and feel the balance of power shift, quite literally; campaigns are won and lost in Iowa during the first caucuses of the presidential primaries.

Regardless of the season, elevation-starved Iowans passionately embrace their great outdoors. With 72 state parks, Iowa offers all manner of outdoor activities, from hiking and biking to trout fishing, hunting, camping and canoeing.

When it comes to national parks, one of the state's undisputed highlights is Maquoketa Caves (30 miles south of Dubuque), a prehistoric world of 16 caves, crawl spaces and low hanging rocks enveloped by sheer stone walls. A popular day trip for families from Des Moines (40 miles southeast), Ledges State Park is a picturesque place to picnic and hike the network of steep trails that crisscross sandstone cliffs.

Top 3 Tourism Attractions:
1) Amana Colonies
2) Des Moines Botanical Center
3) Field of Dreams

Nickname: Hawkeye State

State Flower: Wild Rose

State Bird: Eastern Goldfinch

People: Johnny Carson, comedian; William "Buffalo Bill" Cody, Pony Express rider and showman; Herbert Hoover, 31st president; John Wayne, actor

Major Cities: Des Moines (capital), Cedar Rapids, Davenport, Sioux City, Waterloo

Topography: North and central—flat, fertile plains; northeast—rugged hills and cliffs; south—low, rolling hills and ridges

Climate: Located in the humid continental zone with hot summers, cold winters and wet springs

TRAVEL & TOURISM

Iowa Tourism Office
800-345-IOWA or 515-725-3084
www.traveliowa.com

Catch Des Moines
800-451-2625
www.catchdesmoines.com

Travel Dubuque
800-798-8844
www.traveldubuque.com

Eastern Iowa Tourism Association
563-875-7269, 800-891-3482
www.easterniowatourism.org

Historical Society of Iowa
515-281-6258
www.iowahistory.com

Travel Dubuque
800-798-8844
www.traveldubuque.com

Western Iowa Tourism Region
888-623-4232, 712-623-4232
www.visitwesterniowa.com

OUTDOOR RECREATION

Iowa Department of Natural Resources
515-281-5918
www.iowadnr.com

SHOPPING

Amana Colonies
www.amanacolonies.com

Factory Stores of America Outlet Center
www.factorystores.com

Tanger Outlet Center
www.tangeroutlet.com

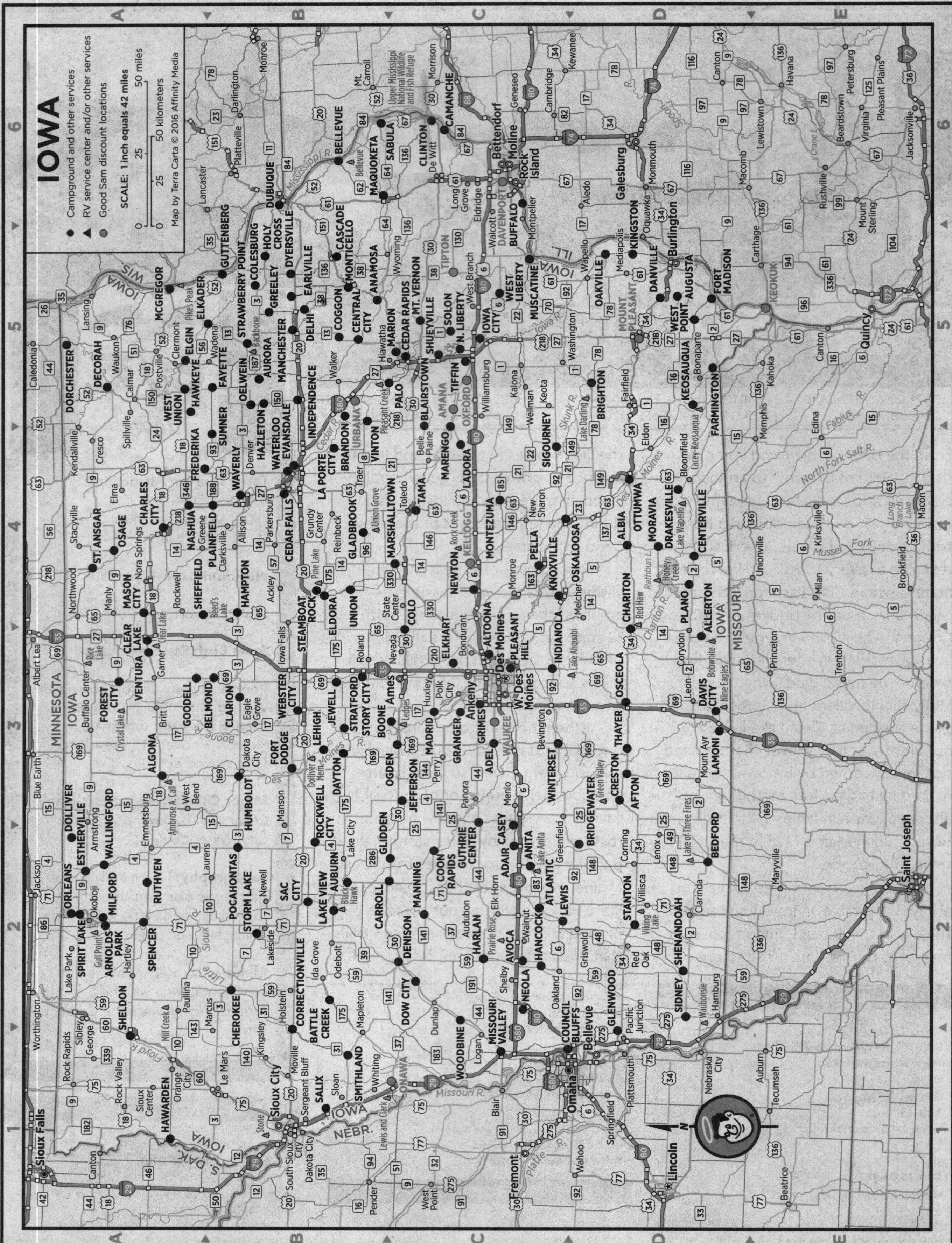
IOWA
Campground and other services
RV service center and/or other services
Good Sam discount locations
SCALE: 1 inch equals 42 miles
0 25 50 miles
0 25 50 kilometers
Map by Terra Carta © 2016 Affinity Media

Featured Good Sam Parks

IOWA

Good Sam Park

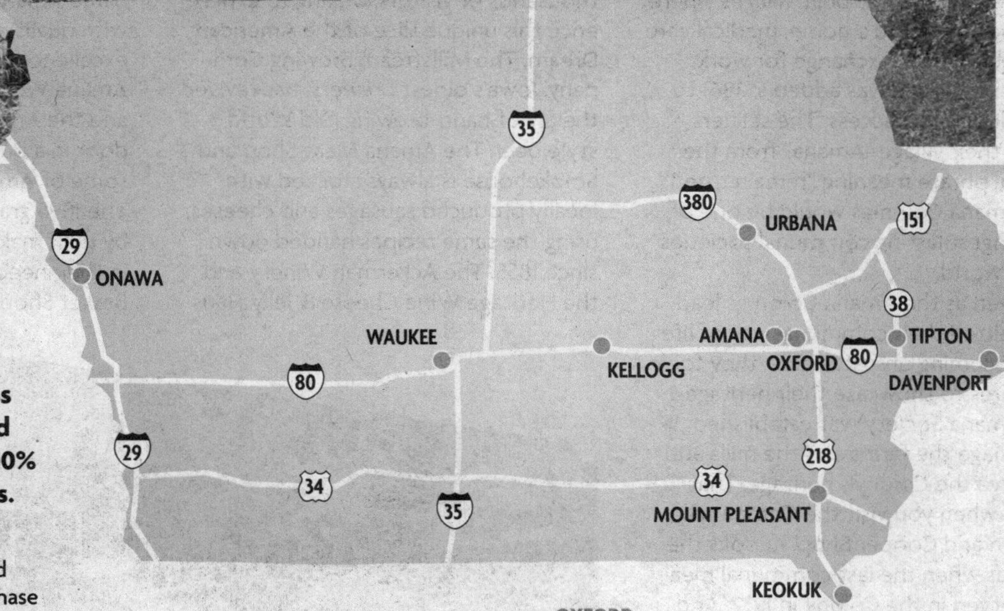

When you stay with Good Sam, you can expect the highest degree of cleanliness and friendliness, and better yet, you get 10% off campground fees.

If you're not already a Good Sam member you can purchase your membership at one of these locations:

AMANA
Amana Colonies RV Park
(319)622-7616

DAVENPORT
Interstate RV Park
(563)386-7292

KELLOGG
Kellogg RV Park
(641)526-8535

KEOKUK
Hickory Haven Campground
(800)890-8459

MOUNT PLEASANT
Crossroads RV Park
(319)385-9737

ONAWA
On-Ur-Wa RV Park
(712)423-1387

OXFORD
Sleepy Hollow RV Park & Campground/MHP
(319)828-4900

TIPTON
Hunt's Cedar River Campground
(563)946-2431

URBANA
Lazy Acres RV Park
(319)443-4000

WAUKEE
Timberline Campground
(515)987-1714

For more Good Sam Parks go to listing pages

Iowa Tourism Office

AMANA COLONIES

Get a taste of Old World craftsmanship in the heartland

Born out of a Utopian Dream, the Amana Colonies were a collection of six communal villages established in Iowa by German settlers. The collective ethos has been replaced by private enterprise, but the villages themselves have been preserved as the legacy of a bygone way of life.

A full community of German religious refugees arrived in eastern Iowa in 1855 and pooled their resources to buy 26,000 acres of bottomland along the Iowa River. They built villages where members received a home, medical care and schooling in exchange for work. A seventh village was added in 1861 to provide railroad access. The settlers called their village "Amana" from the biblical phrase meaning "remain true." The Amana Colonies would be one of the longest lasting communal societies in the world.

Even as the Amana Colonies leaders realized their communal way of life was becoming unsustainable, they took measures to showcase their heritage. The Amana Society was established to manage the farms and the mills and preserve the Colony's heritage. That is why when you visit the Communal Kitchen and Cooper Shop, it looks the same as when the last communal meal was served in the Colony in 1932. And the High Amana General Store smells of homemade soap, dried herbs and kerosene lanterns much as it did in 1858.

Amana Today

Tours begin at the Amana Heritage Museum, where a video explains the idealistic journey from Germany to Iowa and provides an overview of the fertile landscape. The simple but masterfully-constructed meetinghouses, which were built at the center of each village, are on display. These served a vital role to the self-sufficient members of the community. Five different custom tours are available, each focusing on one aspect of life in the Colony.

The Amana food artisans and craftsmen may no longer be working for the community, but they provide insights into this way of life for the thousands of visitors looking to experience this unique slice of the American Dream. The Millstream Brewing Company, Iowa's oldest brewery, has revived the art of hand-brewing Old World-style beer. The Amana Meat Shop and Smokehouse is always stocked with locally produced sausages and cheeses, using the same recipes handed down since 1855. The Ackerman Winery and the Heritage Wine Cheese & Jelly Haus sell award-winning products from the vine in side-by-side shops on Main Street. On busy days, the fresh bread and sweet cinnamon rolls in Hahn's Hearth Oven Bakery sell out before lunchtime.

Working Amana

During the communal era, 39 different jobs were assigned to provide for the needs of each village, which ranged in number from 40 to 100 houses. The name Amana grew to be synonymous with quality and that handcrafted excellence can be purchased in the Amana Woolen Mill on 48th Avenue and the Amana Furniture Shop next door in a building that once produced some of America's finest calico cloth. The 1895 granary has been put to use by quilt makers using heritage fabrics in their needlework. The Broom and Basket Shop uses an old "kicker" broom

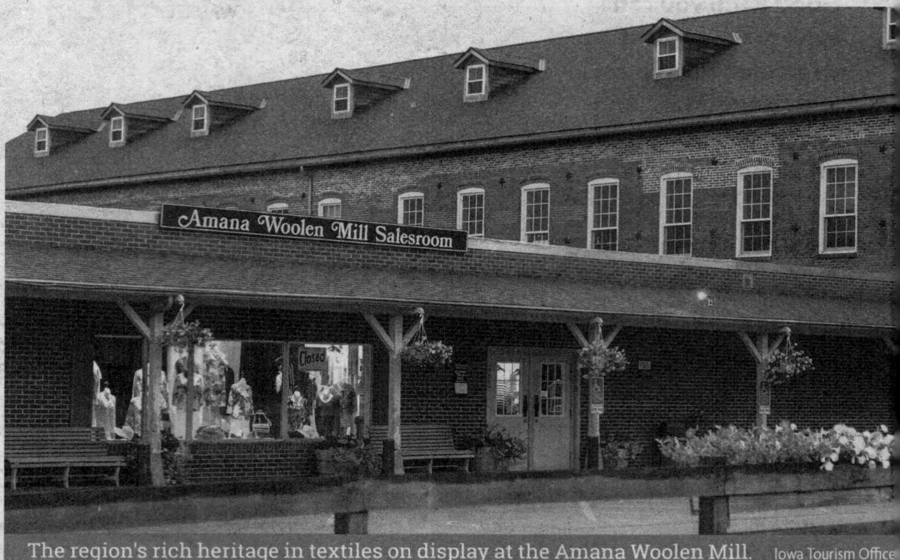

The region's rich heritage in textiles on display at the Amana Woolen Mill. Iowa Tourism Office

winding machine that was used to craft its German Willow baskets and floor sweepers.

Entertainment for the Colonists often meant stage productions with homemade props. The Old Creamery Theatre is the oldest professional theater group in Iowa, having put on its first live performances in 1971. The troupe has been entertaining in the Amana Colonies since 1988, presenting musicals, dramas, comedies and children's shows on the 300-seat Main Stage and the 70-seat Studio Stage every Wednesday through Sunday.

Outdoors, the Kolonieweg, or Colony Way, is a path that wanders past Lily Lake, cropland and pastures as it links Amana, the largest village, and Middle Amana. The Amana Colonies Convention and Visitors Center rents bicycles to ride through the villages; the restored passenger depot serves as the trailhead. Golfers can tee it up at the Amana Colonies Golf Course. Consistently ranked as one of the top public courses in Iowa, the rolling hills not only present a sporty challenge to golfers, but also harbor some of the best wildlife spotting in Amana.

The events calendar in the Amana Colonies is always bursting. Visitors should circle the Maifest, where the celebration of spring takes on a decidedly German flavor with dancing, demonstrations and arts; Oktoberfest where the Burgermeister taps the first keg at the Festhalle Barn and pours free beer until the keg is empty; and Winterfest, where Amana shows off its silly side with the Winter Wreath Toss, the Great Amana Ham-Put and the Best Beard Competition. The best bet is not to stray too far from the open fire chili cookout. In summer, the Hawk A Model A Club summons more than 100 of Henry Ford's best Model A automobiles from five Midwestern states to strut their horsepower on Main Street for Model-A Day.

IA

For More Information

Amana Colonies Visitors Center
800-529-2294
www.amanacolonies.com

Iowa Tourism Office
888-472-6035
www.traveliowa.com

Iowa

CONSULTANTS

Chuck & Alyce Grover

ACKLEY — B4 *Franklin, Hardin*

PRAIRIE BRIDGES PARK (Public) From Jct of St Hwy 20 & SR-S-56, N 0.2 mi on SR-S-56 (L). 2015 rates: $10 to $15. Apr 1 to Nov 1. (641)485-1623

ADAIR — C2 *Adair*

ADAIR CITY PARK (Public) From Jct of I-80 & exit 76, exit N 0.75 mi to Hwy 83 (R). 2015 rates: $15. May 1 to Oct 1. (641)742-3751

ADEL — C3 *Dallas*

DALLAS COUNTY FAIR CAMPGROUNDS (Public) From jct I-80 (exit 110) & US 169: Go 5 mi N on US 169. 2015 rates: $14 to $20. Apr 1 to Nov 1. (515)240-6198

DES MOINES WEST KOA Ratings: 9/10★/9.5 (RV Park) From Jct of I-80 & Exit 106, N 1.5 mi on Dallas County P-58-L Ave (R). Use 3418 L Ave for GPS. **FAC:** Gravel rds. (74 spaces). Avail: 61 gravel, patios, 61 pull-thrus (24 x 70), some side by side hkups, accepts full hkup units only, 61 full hkups (30/50 amps), seasonal sites, cable, WiFi, tent sites, rentals, laundry, groc, LP gas, fire rings, firewood. **REC:** heated pool, pond, fishing, playground. Pets OK. Big rig sites, 2015 rates: $35 to $70. Disc: military. Apr 1 to Oct 31.
(515)834-2729 Lat: 41.54196, Lon: -94.07942
34308 L Ave, Adel, IA 50003
chris@desmoineskoa.com
www.desmoineskoa.com

AFTON — D3 *Union*

THREE MILE REC AREA (Public) From town, N 3 mi on Creamery Rd to 150th St, W 0.5 mi (L). 2015 rates: $10 to $17. (641)347-5100

ALBIA — D4 *Monroe*

MIAMI LAKE PARK (Public) From town, N 2 mi on Hwy 5 to cnty rd, E 0.25 mi, follow signs (R). 2015 rates: $11 to $16. Apr 1 to Nov 1. (641)946-8112

ALGONA — A3 *Kossuth*

AMBROSE A CALL (State Pk) From Jct of US-169 & Call Park Dr, W 2 mi on Call Park Rd (L). Pit toilets. 2015 rates: $9 to $16. Apr 1 to Nov 1. (641)581-4835

SMITH LAKE COUNTY PARK (Public) From Jct of US-18 & US-169, N 3 mi on US-169 (L). 2015 rates: $15. Apr 15 to Oct 31. (515)295-2138

ALLERTON — D3 *Wayne*

BOBWHITE (State Pk) From jct Hwy 40 & Main St (CR J46): Go 1-1/2 mi W on CR J46. 2015 rates: $16. Apr 1 to Dec 1. (641)873-4670

ALTOONA — C3 *Polk*

ADVENTURELAND CAMPGROUND **Ratings: 9.5/7/8.5** (RV Park) 2015 rates: $35 to $45. Apr 1 to Oct 31. (800)532-1286 2600 Adventureland Dr, Altoona, IA 50009

Tell your RV Campground that you found them in this Guide.

GRIFFS VALLEY VIEW RV
Ratings: 7.5/10★/10 (RV Park) From jct I-35 (exit 89) & Corporate Woods: Go 2-3/4 mi E on Corporate Woods Dr, then 1/4 mi N on NE 46th St. (Office located off property at 5200 NE 62nd Ave.) (L). **FAC:** Paved rds. 125 paved, 17 all weather, 21 pull-thrus (40 x 70), back-ins (40 x 60), accepts full hkup units only, 142 full hkups (30/50 amps), WiFi $, laundry, LP gas. **REC:** pond, fishing, playground. Pets OK. Partial handicap access, no tents. Big rig sites, 2015 rates: $30.
(515)967-5474 Lat: 41.67717, Lon: -93.52214
6429 NE 46th St, Altoona, IA 50009
griffieon@msn.com
www.griffsrv.com
See ad this page.

AMANA — C5 *Iowa*

AMANA COLONIES RV PARK
Ratings: 7.5/9.5★/9.5 (Public) From Jct of I-80 & US 151 (Exit 225), N 9.9 mi on US 151 to C St, W 0.5 mi (L). Don't rely on GPS. See map on our ad. Use Good Sam app. **FAC:** Gravel rds. (441 spaces). 426 Avail: 344 gravel, 82 grass, 100 pull-thrus (24 x 80), back-ins (24 x 80), 148 full hkups, 278 W, 278 E (30/50 amps), WiFi, tent sites, dump, laundry, LP gas, fire rings, firewood. **REC:** playground. Pets OK. Partial handicap access. Big rig sites, 2015 rates: $31 to $34. Disc: AAA. Apr 15 to Oct 31.
(319)622-7616 Lat: 41.81396, Lon: -91.87819
3890 C St, Amana, IA 52203
rvamana@amanas.net
www.amanarvpark.com
See ad pages 487 (Spotlight Amana Colonies), 485 & RV Trips of a Lifetime in Magazine Section.

Things to See and Do

AMANA COLONIES CONVENTION & VISITORS BUREAU Located in a restored corn crib, the visitor center provides information about the Amana Colonies; Visitors Guides, maps and brochures for area businesses, including menus for local restaurants. RV accessible. Restrooms. Hours: 9am to 5pm. No CC.
(800)579-2294 Lat: 41.79990, Lon: -91.86796
622 46th Ave, Amana, IA 52203
info@amanacolonies.com
www.amanacolonies.com
See ad page 487 (Spotlight Amana Colonies).

ANAMOSA — B5 *Jones*

WAPSIPINICON (State Pk) From town, S 0.5 mi Elm St. 2015 rates: $6 to $16. (319)462-2761

ANITA — C2 *Cass*

LAKE ANITA (State Pk) From Jct of I-80 & SR-148 (exit 70), S 4.5 mi on SR-148 (R). 2015 rates: $6 to $19. (712)762-3564

ARNOLDS PARK — A2 *Dickinson*

ARNOLDS PARK CITY CAMPGROUND (Public) From Jct of US-71 & Broadway, E on Broadway, to Rohr St (R), entrance on (R). 2015 rates: $25 to $50. May 15 to Sep 1. (712)332-2341

ATLANTIC — C2 *Cass*

CASS COUNTY FAIRGROUNDS CAMPGROUND (Public) From I 80 & US 71/US 6 (Exit 60): Go 6-1/4 mi S on US 71/US 6, then 5 mi W on US 6. 2015 rates: $10 to $15. Apr 1 to Nov 1. (712)254-3203

AUBURN — B2 *Sac*

GRANT PARK (SAC COUNTY PARK) (Public) From jct US-71 & Hwy-175: Go W on US-71/Hwy-175, then 1/2 mi N on CR-D54, then 1/4 mi W. 2015 rates: $10 to $15. Apr 2 to Oct 15. (712)662-4530

AUGUSTA — D5 *Des Moines*

LOWER SKUNK RIVER ACCESS (DES MOINES COUNTY PARK) (Public) From town: Go 1/2 mi E on Skunk River Rd. Pit toilets. 2015 rates: $8 to $15. (319)753-8260

AURORA — B5 *Buchanan*

JAKWAY AREA (BUCHANAN COUNTY PARK) (Public) From town: Go 1-1/2 mi S on CR W45. 2015 rates: $10 to $15. (319)636-3378

AVOCA — C2 *Pottawattamie*

POTTAWATTAMIE COUNTY FAIR CAMPGROUND (Public) From jct I-80 (exit 40) & US 59: Go 1-3/4 mi S on US 59, then 200 yds W on West Lincoln. 2015 rates: $20. (712)482-6220

We rate what RVers consider important.

BATTLE CREEK — B2 *Ida*

CRAWFORD CREEK REC AREA (Public) From Jct of Hwy 175 & CR-L51, S 3.3 mi on CR-L51 (R). 2015 rates: $12 to $17. Apr to Oct. (712)364-3300

BEDFORD — D2 *Taylor*

LAKE OF THREE FIRES (State Pk) From Jct of Hwy 2 & Hwy 49, NE 4 mi on Hwy 49 (L). 2015 rates: $6 to $16. (712)523-2700

BELLEVUE — B6 *Dubuque, Jackson*

BELLEVUE (State Pk) From Jct of US-52 & Hwy 62, S 2.5 mi on US-52 (R). 2015 rates: $6 to $16. Apr 1 to Oct 31. (563)872-4019

PLEASANT CREEK (Public Corps) From town, S 3 mi on US-52, follow signs (L). Pit toilets. 2015 rates: $8. May 15 to Oct 15. (563)872-5782

SPRUCE CREEK PARK (Public) From town, N 2.5 mi on US-52 to 395th Ave, E 0.75 mi (R). 2015 rates: $17 to $20. Apr 1 to Nov 3. (563)652-3783

BELMOND — B3 *Wright*

IOWA RIVER RV PARK (Public) From Jct of US-69 & Main St, S 3 blks on Main St (R). 2015 rates: $10 to $12. Apr 15 to Oct 15. (641)444-3498

BLAIRSTOWN — C4 *Benton*

HANNEN PARK (BENTON COUNTY PARK) (Public) From town: Go 1 mi S on CR-V56, then 3 mi SE on blacktop road. (319)454-6382

BOONE — C3 *Boone*

LEDGES (State Pk) From Jct of SR-30 & SR-17, S 2.8 mi on SR-17 to 250th St, W 3.1 mi (R). 2015 rates: $6 to $11. (515)432-1852

BRANDON — B5 *Buchanan*

LIME CREEK AREA (BUCHANAN COUNTY PARK) (Public) From jct Hwy 150 & Hwy 283: Go 5 mi W on Hwy 283, then 1-1/2 mi NE on CR W17. Pit toilets. 2015 rates: $6 to $12. Apr 15 to Oct 1. (319)636-2617

BRIDGEWATER — D2 *Adair*

MORMAN TRAIL PARK (ADAIR COUNTY PARK) (Public) From jct CR N51 & Hwy 92: Go 1 mi E on Hwy 92, then 1-1/2 mi S on gravel road. Pit toilets. 2015 rates: $6 to $9. (641)743-6450

BRIGHTON — D5 *Washington*

LAKE DARLING (State Pk) From W-end of town, W 3 mi on SR-78/1 (R). 2015 rates: $6 to $19. (319)694-2323

BUFFALO — C6 *Scott*

BUFFALO SHORES CAMPGROUND (Public) From Davenport, W 4 mi on Hwy 22 (L). 2015 rates: $19 to $22. (563)328-3280

BURLINGTON — D5 *Des Moines*

BURLINGTON See also Mount Pleasant.

CAMANCHE — C6 *Clinton*

ROCK CREEK MARINA & CAMPGROUND (CLINTON COUNTY PARK) (Public) From jct I-80 (exit 306) & US 67: Go 14 mi N on US 67, then 1 mi E on 291st St (gravel road). 2015 rates: $12 to $20. (563)847-7202

CARROLL — C2 *Carroll*

SWAN LAKE (State Pk) From Jct of US-30 & US-71, S 2.7 mi on US-71 to 220th St., E 1.4 mi. 2015 rates: $16 to $19. Apr 15 to Oct 15. (712)792-4614

CASCADE — B5 *Dubuque*

FILLMORE RECREATION AREA (DUBUQUE COUNTY PARK) (Public) From town: Go 5 mi E on Hwy 151. 2015 rates: $10 to $16. (563)556-6745

CASEY — C2 *Guthrie*

CASEY CITY PARK (Public) From jct Hwy-25 & I-80: Go 2 mi W on I-80. 2015 rates: $10. May 1 to Oct 1. (641)746-3315

CEDAR FALLS — B4 *Black Hawk*

BLACK HAWK PARK (Public) From Jct of US-218 & SR-58, N 1.3 mi on US-218 to E Lone Tree Rd, W 2.3 mi (E). 2015 rates: $13 to $30. (319)433-7275

GEORGE WYTH MEMORIAL (State Pk) From Jct of Hwys 20 & 218, N 9.8 mi on Hwy 218 to George Wyth Park exit (L). 2015 rates: $6 to $16. Apr 15 to Oct 15. (319)232-5505

Thank you for being one of our best customers!

Travel Services

CAMPING WORLD OF CEDAR FALLS As the nation's largest retailer of RV supplies, accessories, services and new and used RVs, Camping World is committed to making your total RV experience better. RV Accessories: (888)833-3901. **SERVICES:** RV Sales. RV supplies, LP. Hours: 8:00 - 6:00.
(888)673-4757 Lat: 42.467568, Lon: -92.44390
7805 Ace Place, Cedar Falls, IA 50613
www.campingworld.com

CEDAR RAPIDS — C5 *Linn*

CEDAR RAPIDS See also Amana, Mount Vernon, Oxford & Urbana.

MORGAN CREEK CAMPGROUND (LINN COUNTY PARK) (Public) From jct 16th Ave SW & Stoney Point Rd at W edge of town: Go 2 mi N on Stoney Point Rd, then 1/2 mi W on Worcester Rd. 2015 rates: $19. Apr 15 to Oct 15. (319)892-6450

Travel Services

CUMMINS CENTRAL POWER Cummins Central Power is the exclusive distributor for Cummins and Onan products in the Midwest. 12 full service locations in Nebraska, Missouri, Kansas, Iowa, South Dakota, and Illinois support engine and generator customers. **SERVICES:** Engine/chassis repair, emergency rd svc, restrooms. Emergency parking, RV accessible. waiting room. Hours: 7am to 11:59pm, Sat 7am to 3:30pm.
(319)366-7537 Lat: 41.94263, Lon: -91.67778
625 33rd Ave SW, Cedar Rapids, IA 52404
Centralpower@cummins.com
Cumminscentralpower.com
See ad page 732.

TRUCK COUNTRY Store. **SERVICES:** RV, engine/chassis repair, restrooms. **TOW:** RV. Hours: 7am to 1am.
(800)332-6158 Lat: 41.94905, Lon: -91.68053
8415 6th S SW, Cedar Rapids, IA 52406
www.truckcountry.com
See ad opposite page, 1311.

CENTERVILLE — D4 *Appanoose*

ISLAND VIEW CAMPGROUND (Public Corps) From town, N 2.5 mi on SR-5 to CR-29, NW 4 mi to CR-J5T, NE 0.1 mi (L). 2015 rates: $16 to $32. May 1 to Sep 29. (641)647-2079

ROLLING COVE CAMPGROUND (Public Corps) From town, W on Hwy 2 to CR-T14, N 6 mi to CR-J5T, W 2.5 mi to 150 Ave, N 2.5 mi to 435 St, E 1 mi, follow signs (E). May 19 to Sep 2. (641)647-2464

CENTRAL CITY — B5 *Linn*

PINICON RIDGE FLYING SQUIRREL CAMPGROUND (LINN COUNTY PARK) (Public) From town: Go 1 mi N on Hwy 13, then 1/4 mi W on county road. 2015 rates: $19. Apr 15 to Oct 15. (319)892-6450

CHARITON — D3 *Lucas*

RED HAW LAKE (State Pk) From Jct of SR-14 & US-34, E 1 mi on US-34 (R). 2015 rates: $6 to $16. (641)774-5632

CHARLES CITY — A4 *Floyd*

R CAMPGROUND Ratings: 6/7/6.5 (Campground) From Jct US-218 (exit 218) & BUS-218: Go 2 mi N on BUS-218, then 1/4 mi N (cross bridge) on Hwy 18-E, then .8 mi SE on Clark St. (R). **FAC:** Gravel rds. 62 gravel, 41 pull-thrus (41 x 93), back-ins (30 x 83), some side by side hkups, 54 full hkups, 8 W, 8 E (30/50 amps), WiFi, dump, laundry, fire rings, firewood. **REC:** Cedar River: fishing, playground. Pets OK. No tents. Big rig sites, 2015 rates: $26 to $30. No CC.
(641)257-0549 Lat: 43.05873, Lon: -92.66175
1910 Clark St, Charles City, IA 50616
rcamp@fiai.net
www.rcampground.com

CHEROKEE — B2 *Cherokee*

KOSER SPRING LAKE PARK (Public) From Jct of Hwy 59 & Hwy 3, S 3 mi on Hwy 59 to campground, 0.05 mi S of Little Sioux River Bridge (L). 2015 rates: $12 to $20. Apr 15 to Nov 15. (712)225-2715

CLARION — B3 *Wright*

LAKE CORNELIA (Public) From town, E 1 mi on Hwy 3 to CR-R45, N 5 mi (R). 2015 rates: $15 to $20. Apr 15 to Oct 15. (515)532-3185

CLEAR LAKE — A3 *Cerro Gordo*

CLEAR LAKE See Also Forest City.

CLEAR LAKE (State Pk) From Jct of I-35 & Hwy 106 (exit 193), W 1 mi on Hwy 106 to S 8th St, S 1.4 mi to 27th Ave, W 0.5 mi to B35, S 100 ft (R). 2015 rates: $9 to $16. (641)357-4212

OAKWOOD RV PARK
Ratings: 8/8.5★/8 (RV Park) From Jct of I-35 & 4th Ave S (Exit 193), W 1 mi on 4th Ave S to S 8th St, S 1.4 mi to 27th S, W 0.5 mi to S Shore Dr, S 1.2 mi to 240th St, S 300 ft, follow signs (L). Don't rely on GPS. Call for directions. **FAC:** Gravel rds. (98 spaces). Avail: 68 gravel, patios, 62 pull-thrus (45 x 120), back-ins (30 x 55), some side by side hkups, 68 full hkups (30/50 amps), seasonal sites, WiFi, dump, laundry, firewood. **REC:** playground. Pet restrict(B). No tents. Big rig sites, 2015 rates: $30. Apr 15 to Oct 15. No CC.
(641)357-4019 Lat: 43.11120, Lon: -93.41083
5419 240th St, Clear Lake, IA 50428
speakars@cltel.net
www.oakwoodrvpark.net
See ad this page.

CLINTON — C6 *Clinton*

BULGERS HOLLOW REC AREA (Public Corps) From town, N 3 mi on Hwy 67 (R). Pit toilets. 2015 rates: $4. May 15 to Oct 15. (815)259-3628

COGGON — B5 *Linn*

BUFFALO CREEK PARK-WALNUT GROVE CAMPGROUND (Public) From town: Go 1/2 mi W on CR-D62. Pit toilets. 2015 rates: $17. Apr 15 to Oct 15. (319)892-6450

COLESBURG — B5 *Delaware*

TWIN BRIDGES (DELAWARE COUNTY PARK) (Public) From town: Go 5 mi W on Hwy 3. Pit toilets. 2015 rates: $12. May 1 to Nov 1. (563)927-3410

COLO — C3 *Story*

HICKORY GROVE PARK (Public) From town, W 2 mi on US-30 to 680th Ave, S 1 mi on county rd, continues W 0.5 mi (L). 2015 rates: $12 to $20. Apr 1 to Oct 31. (515)232-2516

TWIN ANCHORS CAMPGROUND **Ratings: 6/6.5/6** (Campground) 2015 rates: $17.50 to $24. (641)377-2243 68132 US Highway 30, Colo, IA 50056

COON RAPIDS — C2 *Carroll*

RIVERSIDE PARK (Public) From jct SR 141 & 330th St: Go 1 mi E on 330th, then 1/2 mi N on Walnut St. 2015 rates: $14. Apr 15 to Oct 31. (712)792-4614

CORRECTIONVILLE — B2 *Woodbury*

LITTLE SIOUX PARK (Public) From Jct of US-20 & SR-31, S 2 mi on SR-31 (L). 2015 rates: $15 to $18. May 1 to Oct 31. (712)372-4984

Our travel services section will help you find services that you'll find handy in your travels.

IA

COUNCIL BLUFFS — D1 *Douglas, Pottowattamie*

BLUFFS RUN RV PARK **Ratings: 4/9.5/3.5** (RV Park) 2015 rates: $15 to $40. (800)238-2946 2701 23rd Ave, Council Bluffs, IA 51501

LAKE MANAWA (State Pk) From Jct of I-80 & exit 3, S 1 mi on S Expwy to Hwy 275 & 92, W 1 mi to S 11th St; or From Jct of I-29 & exit 47 to W Hwy 92/275, W 1.5 mi to S 11th St, S 2 blks, follow signs (E). 2015 rates: $6 to $16. (712)366-0220

Travel Services

CAMPING WORLD OF COUNCIL BLUFFS As the nation's largest retailer of RV supplies, accessories, services and new and used RVs, Camping World is committed to making your total RV experience better. RV Accessories: (888)833-4420. **SERVICES:** Tire, RV appliance, MH mechanical, staffed RV wash, RV Sales. RV supplies, LP, dump, RV accessible. waiting room. Hours: 8am to 6pm.
(888)587-6768 Lat: 41.233661, Lon: -95.87493
2802 South 21st Street, Council Bluffs, IA 51501
www.campingworld.com

CRESCO — A4 *Winneshiek*

HARVEST FARM CAMPGROUND **Ratings: 5.5/9/8.5** (Campground) 2015 rates: $33. Apr 1 to Oct 31. (563)883-8562 3690 318th Ave, Cresco, IA 52136

CRESTON — D3 *Adair, Union*

GREEN VALLEY (State Pk) From Jct. of SH25 & Howard St., N .7 mi to W Townline Dr., W .7 mi to Cottonwood Rd., (L). 2015 rates: $9 to $16. Apr 15 to Nov 1. (641)782-5131

MCKINLEY PARK (Public) From jct SH-25 & W Adams St., W .5 mi (L). 2015 rates: $12 to $14. May 15 to Oct 15. (641)782-8220

DANVILLE — D5 *Henry*

GEODE (State Pk) From town, S 2.5 mi on Main St to SR-79, W 3 mi (E). 2015 rates: $11 to $16. (319)392-4601

DAVENPORT — C6 *Scott*

DAVENPORT See also Buffalo.

CLARK'S FERRY (Public Corps) From Davenport, W on Hwy 22 15 mi to Clark's Ferry sign (in Montpelier). 2015 rates: $20. May 1 to Oct 24. (563)381-4043

RV Park ratings you can rely on!

INTERSTATE RV PARK
Ratings: 9/10★/9.5 (Campground) From Jct of I-80 & SR-130 (Exit 292), NW 0.6 mi on SR-130 to Fairmount St, W 0.1 mi (R). Don't rely on GPS. **FAC:** Paved/gravel rds. (100 spaces). Avail: 56 gravel, patios, 49 pull-thrus (24 x 75), back-ins (22 x 50), 49 full hkups, 7 W, 7 E (30/50 amps), seasonal sites, WiFi, dump, laundry, groc, fire rings. **REC:** pool, wading pool, playground. Pet restrict(B). No tents. Big rig sites, 2015 rates: $28 to $40. Disc: AAA, military.
(563)386-7292 Lat: 41.60589, Lon: -90.63126
8448 N. Fairmount St, Davenport, IA 52806
iarvpark@aol.com
www.iowarvpark.com
See ad this page, 485 & see RV Trips of a Lifetime in Magazine Section.

SCOTT COUNTY PARK (Public) From Davenport, N 9 mi on Hwy 61, to Exit 129 (R). 2015 rates: $13 to $21. Apr 15 to Oct 15. (563)285-9656

WEST LAKE PARK (Public) From Jct of I-280 & US-61, W 0.8 mi on US-61 to CR Y-48, N 1 mi (R). 2015 rates: $13 to $21. Apr 15 to Oct 15. (563)328-3280

Travel Services

TRUCK COUNTRY Freightliner/Western Star dealer specializing in service. **SERVICES:** Engine/chassis repair, mobile RV svc, restrooms. Hours: 7am to 1am.
(563)445-5870 Lat: 41.59711, Lon: -90.6142
2350 West 76th Street, Davenport, IA 52806
www.truckcountry.com
See ad pages 488, 1311.

DAVIS CITY — D3 *Decatur*

NINE EAGLES (State Pk) From Jct of US-69 & CR-J66, SE 6 mi on CR-J66 (L). 2015 rates: $6 to $16. (641)442-2855

DAYTON — B3 *Hamilton*

OAK PARK (Public) From town, S 0.4 mi of town center on Hwy 175 (R). 2015 rates: $12. Apr 1 to Sep 30. (515)547-2711

DECORAH — A5 *Winneshiek*

DECORAH MUNICIPAL CAMPGROUND/PULPIT ROCK (Public) From Jct of US-52 & SR-9, N 1 mi on US-52 to Pulpit Rock Rd, E 0.25 mi (R) Holiday rule: minimum 2 night stay. 2015 rates: $13 to $20. Apr 1 to Nov 1. (563)382-9551

SAVE! Over $1,000 in coupons can be found at the front of the Guide!

Travel Services

TRUCK COUNTRY Store. **SERVICES:** RV appliance, engine/chassis repair, mobile RV svc, restrooms. Hours: 7:30am to 5:30pm.
(563)382-6551 Lat: 43.27129, Lon: -91.72701
1653 State Hwy 9, Decorah, IA 52101
darinbohr@truckcountry.com
www.truckcountry.com
See ad pages 488, 1311.

DELHI — B5 *Delaware*

TURTLE CREEK RIVER ACCESS (DELAWARE COUNTY PARK) (Public) From jct US-20 & CR-D-5X: Go 4 mi SE on CR-D-5X, then 4 mi S on CR-X21, then 3 mi E. 2015 rates: $12 to $18. (563)927-3410

DENISON — C2 *Crawford*

YELLOW SMOKE PARK (Public) From town, E 1 mi on US-30 to Yellow Smoke Rd, N 0.5 mi (L). 2015 rates: $18. Apr 15 to Oct 15. (712)263-2748

We rate what RVers consider important.

Know The Rules Of The Road!

At-a-glance Rules of the Road table shows RV-related laws in every state and province, including: fishing licenses, bridge and tunnel restrictions and highway information numbers for every state and province.

Find the Rules in the front of this Guide.

DES MOINES — C3 *Boone, Des Moines, Polk*

DES MOINES AREA MAP

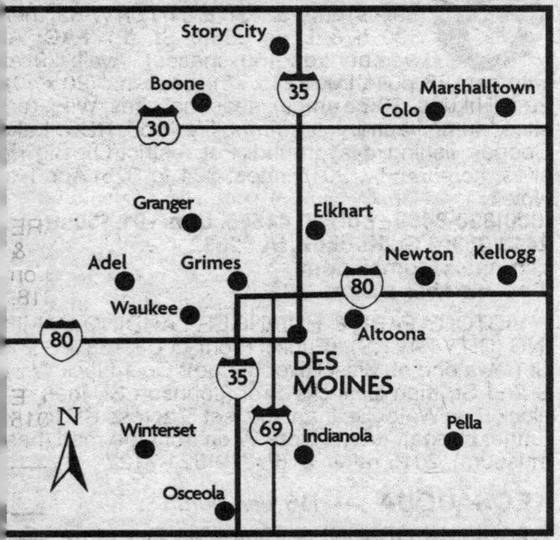

For more detail and a broader overview, please see our full-color state map at the front of the Iowa state section.

Symbols on map indicate towns within a 50 mile radius of Des Moines where campgrounds are listed. Check listings for more information.

See also Adel, Altoona, Boone, Colo, Elkhart, Granger, Grimes, Indianola, Kellogg, Marshalltown, Newton, Osceola, Pella, Story City, Waukee & Winterset.

ACORN VALLEY (Public Corps) From town, N 4 mi on Merle Hay Rd to NW Beaver Dr, W 3.7 mi to NW Coryden Dr (at Natl Weather Service bldg), N 0.5 mi (R). 2015 rates: $18 to $20. May 22 to Sep 7. (515)276-0429

BOB SHETLER REC AREA (Public Corps) From Jct. of I-80 & Hwy 401,N 3.5 mi on Hwy 401, N 2 mi to Beaver Dr, NW 0.5 mi to 78th Ave, E 0.75 mi (E). 2015 rates: $18 to $22. May 1 to Sep 29. (515)276-0873

CHERRY GLEN CAMPGROUND (Public Corps) From Jct of I-35 & Hwy 160 (exit 90), W 3 mi on Hwy 160 to Hwy 415, NW 5.5 mi to 94th Ave, W 0.9 mi (E). 2015 rates: $16 to $24. Apr 15 to Oct 17. (515)964-3792

IOWA STATE FAIR CAMPGROUNDS (Public) From jct I-35/80 & I-235: Go 3-1/2 mi S on I-235, then 1-1/2 mi E on Hwy 163 (University Ave.), then 1/4 mi S on E 30th St (Hwy 46). (Different rates apply during fair). 2015 rates: $20 to $25. (515)262-3111

PRAIRIE FLOWER REC AREA (Public Corps) From town, SE 2.5 mi on Hwy 415 (R). 2015 rates: $18 to $24. May 1 to Oct 24. (515)984-6925

THOMAS MITCHELL PARK (Public) From Jct of I-35 & I-80, E 5 mi on I-80 to exit 143 to 1st Ave., S 1 mi to 8th St, E 4 mi (R). 2015 rates: $13 to $24. Apr 1 to Nov 30. (515)967-4889

WALNUT WOODS (State Pk) From Jct I-35 & 64th Ave, E 0.8 mi to 105th Ave, N 0.7 mi. 2015 rates: $11 to $17. (515)285-4502

Travel Services

CUMMINS CENTRAL POWER Cummins Central Power is the exclusive distributor for Cummins and Onan products in the Midwest. 12 full service locations in Nebraska, Missouri, Kansas, Iowa, South Dakota, and Illinois support engine and generator customers. **SERVICES:** Engine/chassis repair, emergency rd svc, restrooms. Emergency parking, RV accessible. waiting room. Hours: 7am to 11pm.
(515)262-9591 Lat: 41.653868, Lon: -93.593649
1680 NE 51st Ave, Des Moines, IA 50313
Centralpower@cummins.com
Cumminscentralpower.com
See ad page 732.

DOLLIVER — A2 *Emmet*

TUTTLE LAKE (Public) From town, N 1.5 mi on N52 to Hwy A13, E 0.4 mi (L). 2015 rates: $8 to $10. Apr 15 to Nov 15. (712)260-6697

DORCHESTER — A5 *Allamakee*

UPPER IOWA RESORT & RENTAL **Ratings: 6/6.5/8** (Campground) 2015 rates: $22 to $28. (563)568-3263 578 Lonnings Drive, Dorchester, IA 52140

DOW CITY — C2 *Crawford*

NELSON PARK (CRAWFORD COUNTY PARK) (Public) From Jct US-59 & US-30, W 11 mi on US-30 to Nelson Park Rd, NW 4 mi (E). 2015 rates: $12 to $15. (712)643-5426

DRAKESVILLE — D4 *Appanoose, Davis*

LAKE WAPELLO (State Pk) From Jct of US-63 & Hwy 273, W 8 mi on Hwy 273, NW 2.2 mi on Eagle Blvd (L). 2015 rates: $6 to $16. (641)722-3371

DUBUQUE — B6 *Dubuque*

FINLEY'S LANDING (Public) From town, NW 5.3 mi on Hwy 3, NW 6 mi. Sherrill Rd., N 3.2 mi Finley's Landing Rd. 2015 rates: $10 to $16. Apr 15 to Nov 1. (563)556-6745

MASSEY MARINA (DUBUQUE COUNTY PARK) (Public) From town: Go 4 mi SE on US 52, then 7 mi E on Massey Station Rd. 2015 rates: $23. (563)556-6745

MUD LAKE PARK (Public) From Jct of US-3 & Hwy 52, NW 5 mi on Hwy 52 to Mud Lake access rd, E 3 mi (R). 2015 rates: $10 to $16. (563)552-2746

SWISS VALLEY PARK (Public) From town, W 6 mi on US-20 to Swiss Valley Rd, S 3 mi to Whitetop Rd, N 0.25 mi (L). 2015 rates: $10 to $16. Apr 15 to Oct 15. (563)556-6745

Travel Services

TRUCK COUNTRY Corporate Headquaters. **SERVICES:** Restrooms. Hours: 7am to 5pm.
(563)584-2636 Lat: 42.46163, Lon: -90.67216
2099 Southpark Ct, Dubuque, IA 52003
www.truckcountry.com
See ad pages 488, 892, 1311.

TRUCK COUNTRY RV and trailer sales & service center. **SERVICES:** RV, engine/chassis repair, emergency rd svc, guest serv, restrooms. **TOW:** RV. Hours: 7am to 5:30pm.
(563)556-3773 Lat: 42.45215, Lon: -90.67967
2959 Hyw 151/61, Dubuque, IA 52003
www.truckcountry.com
See ad pages 488, 1311.

DYERSVILLE — B5 *Dubuque*

NEW WINE PARK (Public) From town, N 4 mi on Hwy 136, W at sign on Vaske Rd, then 1 mi to New Wine Rd (E). 2015 rates: $10 to $16. Apr 1 to Nov 30. (563)921-3475

EARLVILLE — B5 *Delaware*

TRI STATE RACEWAY & RV PARK **Ratings: 5/4.5/5** (Campground) 2015 rates: $30. Apr 15 to Oct 31. (563)923-2267 2217 270th Ave, Earlville, IA 52041

ELDORA — B4 *Hardin*

PINE LAKE (State Pk) From Jct of SR-175 & CR-S56, NE 1 mi on CR-S56 (E). 2015 rates: $6 to $16. (641)858-5832

ELGIN — A5 *Fayette*

GILBERTSON CONSERVATION EDUCATION AREA (Public) From Jct of US-18 & CR-B64, E 9 mi on CR-B64 (R). 2015 rates: $7 to $12. May 1 to Oct 15. (563)426-5740

ELKADER — B5 *Clayton*

DEER RUN RESORT Ratings: 8.5/9/9 (RV Park) From Jct of Hwy 128 & Hwy 13, S 3 mi on Hwy 13 to S High St, N 0.4 mi (R). Don't rely on GPS. **FAC:** Paved rds. (81 spaces). Avail: 34 paved, patios, back-ins (24 x 75), 34 full hkups (30/50 amps), seasonal sites, WiFi $, rentals, laundry, fire rings, firewood. **REC:** Three Sisters Lake: playground. Pets OK. Partial handicap access, no tents. Big rig sites, eco-friendly. 2015 rates: $35 to $41. Apr 15 to Oct 15.
(563)245-3337 Lat: 42.85237, Lon: -91.39827
501 High St SE, Elkader, IA 52043
www.deerrunresort.net

ELKHART — C3 *Polk*

CHICHAQUA BOTTOMS GREENBELT (Public) From Jct of I-35N & Elkhart exit, E 7.8 mi on 142nd Ave. to NE 72nd, N 1.5 mi (R). 2015 rates: $16 to $22. Apr 1 to Nov 30. (515)967-2596

ESTHERVILLE — A2 *Emmet*

FORT DEFIANCE (State Pk) From Jct of Hwys 4 & 9, W 2 mi on Hwy 9 to county rd, S 1 mi (L). Pit toilets. 2015 rates: $6 to $14. (712)337-3211

We salute you! Our Military Listings indicate campgrounds for use exclusively by active and retired military personnel.

EVANSDALE — B4 *Black Hawk*

DEERWOOD PARK (CITY PARK) (Public) From jct I-380 (exit 70) & River Forest Rd: Go 1 block N on River Forest Rd, then 1/4 mi W on campground road. 2015 rates: $12 to $18. (319)493-0655

FARMINGTON — D5 *Van Buren*

INDIAN LAKE PARK (Public) From Jct of Hwys 218 & 2, W 11 mi on Hwy 2 to Hwy 81, S 0.4 mi (L). 2015 rates: $8 to $18. (319)878-3706

FAYETTE — B5 *Fayette*

VOLGA RIVER SRA (State Pk) From town: Go 4 mi N on Hwy-150, then 2 mi E on gravel road. 2015 rates: $6 to $16. (563)425-4161

FOREST CITY — A3 *Hancock*

PILOT KNOB (State Pk) From town, E 3.4 mi on Hwy 9 to 205th Ave, S 1 mi (L). 2015 rates: $6 to $16. (641)581-4835

FORT DODGE — B3 *Webster*

KENNEDY PARK (Public) From Jct of Hwys 7 & 169, N 2 mi on Hwy 169 to CR-D14, E 2 mi to CR-P56, N 3 mi (L). 2015 rates: $12 to $20. May 1 to Sep 30. (515)576-4258

FORT MADISON — D5 *Lee*

WILSON LAKE PARK (Public) From town, E 3.5 mi on Hwy 2 (L). 2015 rates: $15 to $20. (319)463-7673

FREDERIKA — A4 *Bremer*

ALCOCK PARK (Public) From Jct of US-63 & CR-C16, E 1 mi on CR-C16 to gravel rd, N 0.2 mi (R). 2015 rates: $9 to $12. May 1 to Oct 31. (319)882-4742

GLADBROOK — B4 *Tama*

UNION GROVE (State Pk) From Jct of SR-96 & CR-T47, S 4 mi on CR-T47 to 220th St., W 1 mi (R). 2015 rates: $6 to $14. (641)473-2556

GLENWOOD — D1 *Mills, Pottawattamie*

GLENWOOD LAKE PARK (Public) E edge of town on Hwy 34 (L). Call campground hosts for GPS directions and reservations. 2015 rates: $5 to $22. Mar to Oct. (712)520-7275

GLIDDEN — C2 *Carroll*

DICKSON TIMBER (Public) From town, E 2 mi on US 30 to Velvet Rd., N 5.2 mi on Velvet Rd. to park access rd, N 1 mi (R). Shelter must be reserved. RV sites first come first serve. Pit toilets. 2015 rates: $10. (712)792-4614

RICHEY PARK (Public) From jct SR 30 & CR N58: Go 3 mi N on CR N58. Pit toilets. 2015 rates: $8. Apr 1 to Nov 1. (712)792-4614

GOODELL — A3 *Hancock*

ELDRED SHERWOOD PARK (Public) From town, E 3 mi on CR-B63 to CR-68, N 2.7 mi (L). 2015 rates: $10 to $15. Apr 15 to Oct 15. (641)923-2720

GRANGER — C3 *Polk*

JESTER PARK (POLK COUNTY PARK) (Public) From jct I-80/35 (exit 127) & Hwy 141: Go 7-1/2 mi W on Hwy 141, then 3 mi N on NW 121st St, then 1/2 mi E on NW 118th Ave. 2015 rates: $13 to $24. (515)323-5366

LEWIS A JESTER PARK (Public) From town, E 2 mi on 110 Ave to 121 St, N 1 mi to 118th Ave, W .6 mi, N 1 mi on 128th St. 2015 rates: $13 to $24. Apr 1 to Nov 30. (515)323-5366

GREELEY — B5 *Delaware*

FOUNTAIN SPRINGS (DELAWARE COUNTY PARK) (Public) From town: Go 3 mi NE on gravel county roads, follow signs. Pit toilets. 2015 rates: $15. (563)927-3410

GRIMES — C3 *Polk*

CUTTY'S DES MOINES CAMPING CLUB **Ratings: 8.5/6.5/9** (Membership Pk) 2015 rates: $15. (515)986-3929 2500 SE 37th St, Unit A, Grimes, IA 50111

GUTHRIE CENTER — C3 *Des Moines*

SPRINGBROOK (State Pk) From Jct of SR-44 & SR-25, N 7.5 mi on SR-25 to 160 Rd., E 1 mi (L). 2015 rates: $6 to $16. (641)747-3591

GUTTENBERG — B5 *Clayton*

BOY SCOUT CAMPGROUND (Public) From jct US 52 & Hayden: Go 3 blocks E on Hayden, then 4 blocks N on Third St to the Mississippi River.

IA

HAMPTON — B4 *Franklin*

BEEDS LAKE (State Pk) From Jct of SR-3 & CR-S42, N 1.5 mi on Beeds Lake Rd. 2015 rates: $6 to $16. Apr 1 to Oct 31. (641)456-2047

HANCOCK — C2 *Pottawattamie*

BOTNA BEND PARK (Public) From Jct of I-80 & Hwy 59, S 8 mi on Hwy 59 to Jct Hwy 59 & G-30, W 1.5 mi on G-30 (R). 2015 rates: $15. (712)741-5465

HARLAN — C2 *Cass, Shelby*

PRAIRIE ROSE (State Pk) From town, E 6 mi on SR-44 to M-47, S 3 mi (R). 2015 rates: $6 to $16. (712)773-2701

HAWARDEN — A1 *Sioux*

OAK GROVE PARK (Public) From Jct of Hwy 10 & CR-K18, NE 6 mi on CR-K18 (L). 2015 rates: $16. May 15 to Oct 15. (712)552-1047

HAWKEYE — A5 *Fayette*

GOULDSBURG PARK (Public) From town, N 5 mi on W-14 to Sunset Rd, W 0.5 mi (E). 2015 rates: $7 to $12. (563)425-3613

HAZLETON — B5 *Buchanan*

FONTANA PARK (BUCHANAN COUNTY PARK) (Public) From jct CR C-57 & Hwy 150: Go 1-1/2 mi SW on Hwy 150. 2015 rates: $10 to $15. Apr 15 to Nov 1. (319)636-2617

MORWOOD CAMPGROUND & RESORT **Ratings: 8.5/8.5/9.5** (Campground) 2015 rates: $26 to $34. Apr 15 to Oct 15. (319)636-2422 1865 150th St, Hazleton, IA 50641

HOLY CROSS — B5 *Dubuque*

BANKSTON PARK (DUBUQUE COUNTY PARK) (Public) From town: Go 2 mi E on US 52, then 1-1/2 mi S on Bankston Park Rd. Pit toilets. 2015 rates: $10 to $16. Apr 1 to Nov 1. (563)556-6745

HUMBOLDT — B3 *Humboldt*

FRANK A GOTCH (State Pk) From Jct of I-169 & I-3, S 5 mi on I-169 to CR-49, E 1 mi, N 1 mi on CR-49 to Gotch Park Rd (R). 2015 rates: $10 to $15. Apr 1 to Oct 31. (515)332-5447

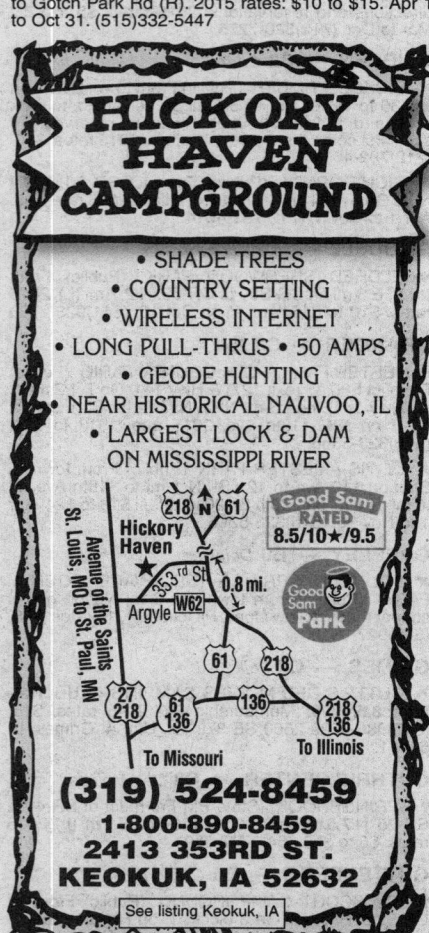

JOE SHELDON PARK (Public) From Jct of US-169 & Hwy 3, W 2 mi on Hwy 3, follow signs (L). 2015 rates: $10 to $15. Apr 1 to Oct 31. (515)332-4087

INDEPENDENCE — B5 *Buchanan*

INDEPENDENCE See also Hazelton, Oelwein & Waterloo.

INDEPENDENCE PARKS & REC RV PARK (Public) From Jct of US 20 & SR 150 (exit 254), N 0.9 mi to 8th St (across bridge), E 500 ft (R). 2015 rates: $18.50 to $19.50. May 1 to Oct 1. (319)440-0472

INDIANOLA — C3 *Warren, Des Moines*

LAKE AHQUABI (State Pk) From Jct of Hwys 69 & 349, W 1 mi on Hwy 349 to 118th Ave, N 1 mi (L). 2015 rates: $6 to $16. (515)961-7101

IOWA CITY — C5 *Johnson*

IOWA CITY See also Amana, Oxford, Tipton & West Liberty.

DAM COMPLEX/LINDER POINT (Public Corps) From Jct of I-80 & exit 244 (Dubuque St), N 2 mi on Dubuque St to West Overlook Rd, E 1 mi (E). 2015 rates: $16 to $26. Apr 15 to Oct 14. (319)338-3543

DAM COMPLEX/WEST OVERLOOK (Public Corps) From Jct of I-80 & exit 244, N 2 mi on exit rd to cnty rd, E 1 mi (L). 2015 rates: $16 to $26. Apr 15 to Oct 15. (319)338-3685

TAILWATER WEST (COE - CORALVILLE LAKE) (Public) From I-80 (exit 244): Go 3 mi N, then follow signs 1-1/2 mi E. 2015 rates: $12 to $20. Apr 15 to Oct 15. (319)338-3543

JEFFERSON — C3 *Boone*

SPRING LAKE (Public) From town, E 7 mi on US-30 to S Ave, N 2.5 mi to 195th St, W 0.5 mi (L). 2015 rates: $8 to $15. (515)386-5674

JEWELL — B3 *Hamilton*

LITTLE WALL LAKE (Public) From Jct of I-35 & SR-175, W 4 mi on SR-175 to US-69, S 1.5 mi (l). 2015 rates: $21 to $25. (515)832-9570

KELLOGG — C4 *Jasper*

KELLOGG RV PARK

Ratings: 6.5/9★/8 (Campground) From Jct of I-80 & SR-224 (Exit 173), N 0.1 mi on SR-224 (R). Register at Phillips 66 station. **FAC:** All weather rds. 38 Avail: 38 all weather, 38 pull-thrus (27 x 85), 28 full hkups, 10 W, 10 E (30/50 amps), WiFi Hotspot, tent sites, dump, laundry, groc, firewood, restaurant. **REC:** playground. Pets OK. Big rig sites, 2015 rates: $25. Apr 1 to Nov 1. ATM.
(641)526-8535 Lat: 41.68493, Lon: -92.90029
1570 Hwy 224 S, Kellogg, IA 50135
www.iowasbestburgercafe.com
See ad this page, 485.

ROCK CREEK (State Pk) From Jct of I-80 & SR-224, N 6 mi on SR-224 to CR-F27, E 3 mi (R). 2015 rates: $6 to $16. (641)236-3722

KEOKUK — E5 *Lee*

CHATFIELD PARK (Public) From town, N 1.5 mi on SR-61/218 to CR-W62 (Argyle Rd), W 1 mi, follow signs (L). Pit toilets. 2015 rates: $10 to $15. Apr to Nov. (319)463-7673

Find out more about the joys of traveling with your four-legged companions in our Pampered Pet Parks feature at the front of the Guide.

HICKORY HAVEN CAMPGROUND

Ratings: 8.5/10★/9.5 (Campground) From Jct of US-27 (Ave of Saints) & W-62: Go E 9 mi on W-62, then 500 ft & L on 353rd St. (L). **FAC:** All weather rds. (50 spaces). Avail: 29 all weather, 23 pull-thrus (24 x 75), back-ins (20 x 40), 29 full hkups (30/50 amps), seasonal sites, WiFi, tent sites, dump, laundry, fire rings, firewood. **REC:** Lake Cooper: fishing, playground. Pet restrict(Q). Big rig sites, eco-friendly, 2015 rates: $24 to $25. Apr 1 to Nov 1.
(800)890-8459 Lat: 40.44555, Lon: -91.45060
2413 353rd St, Keokuk, IA 52632
camphick@gmail.com
See ad this page, 485.

VICTORY PARK & HUBINGER LANDING CAMPING (CITY PARKS) (Public) From jct US 136 & S 2nd St (Iowa end of Miss. River bridge): Go 1 block W on S 2nd St, then 2 blocks S on Johnson St, then 1/2 block E on Water St, then 100 feet S across RR tracks (under bridge), then 1 block W on frontage road (past museum). 2015 rates: $16. (319)524-7122

KEOSAUQUA — D5 *Van Buren*

LACEY-KEOSAUQUA (State Pk) From town, S 1 mi on Hwy 1 (R). 2015 rates: $9 to $16. Apr 10 to Nov 1. (319)293-3502

KINGSTON — D5 *Des Moines*

4TH PUMPING PLANT RECREATION PARK (DES MOINES COUNTY PARK) (Public) From town: Go 6 mi N on Hwy 99, then 5 mi E on Pumping Station Rd. Pit toilets. 2015 rates: $8 to $15. (319)753-8260

KNOXVILLE — C4 *Marion, Story*

ELK ROCK (State Pk) From Hwy 92 in Knoxville, 6 mi N on Hwy 14. From I-80 at Newton, 20 mi S on Hwy 14. 2015 rates: $6 to $16. (641)842-6008

MARION COUNTY PARK (Public) From Jct of Hwy 14 & McKimber St., W 0.5 mi on McKimber St. to Willets Dr, S 0.25 mi (R). 2015 rates: $17 to $20. Apr 3 to Oct 25. (641)828-2214

WHITEBREAST CAMP (Public Corps) From town, W 2 mi on CR-G28 to CR-T15, S 6.8 mi to Hwy S-71, N 2.5 mi (E). 2015 rates: $18. Apr 23 to Sep 27. (641)828-7522

LA PORTE CITY — B4 *Black Hawk, Hardin*

HICKORY HILLS PARK (Public) From Jct of US-218 & CR-D56 (50th St), W 5.1 mi on 50th St to CR-V37 (Dystart Rd), S 1.1 mi (R). 2015 rates: $13 to $25. (319)433-7276

MCFARLANE PARK (Public) From Jct US-218 & Fourth St, 0.6 mi on Fourth St to Bishop Rd, E 2 mi on Bishop Rd to King Rd, N 0.5 (E). 2015 rates: $13 to $27. (319)342-3844

LADORA — C4 *Iowa*

LAKE IOWA (Public) From Jct I-80 & H Ave (exit 211), S 1 mi on H Ave to 230th St, W 1.5 mi to 'G' Ave, follow signs (L). 2015 rates: $9 to $12. (319)655-8465

LAKE VIEW — B2 *Sac*

BLACK HAWK LAKE (State Pk) From town, E 2 mi on Hwy 175, follow signs (R). 2015 rates: $12 to $17. May 1 to Sep 30. (712)657-8712

CAMP CRESCENT (Public) From Jct of Hwy 196 & US 71, W 4.3 mi on US 71 to 3rd St., SW 0.3 mi, follow signs (L). Stay 6 nights, 7th night is free. 2015 rates: $18 to $22. Apr 15 to Oct 1. (712)657-2189

LAMONI — D3 *Decatur*

SLIP BLUFF PARK (Public) From I-35 & Hwy 69 Intchg (exit 4), W 0.3 mi on Hwy 69, N 1 mi on Spruce Rd., E 2 mi on CR-J52, N 1 mi on cnty rd, follow signs (E). 2015 rates: $10 to $15. (641)446-7307

LE MARS — B1 *Plymouth*

WILLOW CREEK CAMPGROUND (Public) From Jct of Hwy 3 & US-75, E 0.8 mi on Hwy 3 to 4th Ave NE, N 0.6 mi (R) (Dump station offsite 0.5 mi). 2015 rates: $18. Apr 15 to Oct 15. (712)546-8360

LEHIGH — B3 *Webster*

BRUSHY CREEK SRA (State Pk) From jct US-169 & Hwy-50: Go 7 mi E on Hwy-50, then 5 mi NE on CR-D46. 2015 rates: $11 to $17. (515)543-8298

DOLLIVER MEMORIAL (State Pk) From town: Go 1-1/4 mi W on Hwy 50, then 1 mi N on CR D33. 2015 rates: $6 to $16. (515)359-2539

LEWIS — C2 *Cass*

COLD SPRINGS (Public) From Jct of US-6 & CR-M56, S 1.75 mi on CR-M56 (R). 2015 rates: $4 to $6. Apr 1 to Oct 31. (712)769-2372

MADRID — C3 *Boone*

SWEDE POINT PARK (Public) From town, W 1 mi on Hwy 210 to QM Ave., N .8 mi, W .5 mi on 322nd Ln. Shelterhouse available by reservation only. 2015 rates: $11 to $17. Apr 15 to Oct 15. (515)353-4237

MANCHESTER — B5 *Delaware*

BAILEY FORD (DELAWARE COUNTY PARK) (Public) From jct US-20 & CR-D-5X: Go 3 mi SE on CR-D-5X. Pit toilets. 2015 rates: $28. (563)927-3410

COFFINS GROVE (DELAWARE COUNTY PARK) (Public) From jct Hwy 13 & CR D-22: Go 2-1/2 mi W on CR D-22, then 1/2 mi W on gravel CR W-69. Pit toilets. May 1 to Oct 30. (563)927-3410

MANNING — C2 *Carroll*

GREAT WESTERN PARK (Public) From jct SR 141 & CR M66: Go 1/4 mi S on M66. 2015 rates: $10 to $12. (712)792-4614

MAQUOKETA — B6 *Jackson*

MAQUOKETA CAVE CAMPGROUND (State Pk) From Town, N 1 mi on US 61, W 6 mi on Caves Rd (E). 2015 rates: $6 to $16. (563)652-5833

MARENGO — C4 *Iowa*

SUDBURY COURT MOTEL & RV PARK **Ratings: 7/9.5★/9.5** (RV Park) 2015 rates: $26.50. (319)642-5411 2211 Highway 6 Trial, Marengo, IA 52301

MARION — C5 *Linn*

SQUAW CREEK PARK (Public) From Jct of US-151 & SR-13, S 1 mi on SR-13 to park access rd (just past Hwy 100), W 0.5 mi (L). 2015 rates: $19 to $30. Apr 15 to Oct 15. (319)892-6450

MARSHALLTOWN — C4 *Marshall*

RIVERVIEW PARK CAMPGROUND (Public) From Jct of SR-14 & Woodland Ave (in town), E 0.1 mi on Woodland Ave (L). 2015 rates: $12 to $17. Apr 15 to Nov 4. (641)754-5715

MASON CITY — A4 *Mitchell*

MASON CITY See also Clear Lake & Forest City.

MARGARET MACNIDER PARK (Public) From Jct of US-65 & 4th St., E 0.7 mi on 4th St. to N Kentucky Ave, N 0.7 mi to Birch Dr, W 0.5 mi (L) Phone disconnected in winter. 2015 rates: $16 to $25. Apr 15 to Oct 15. (641)421-3679

MCGREGOR — A5 *Clayton*

PIKES PEAK (State Pk) From town, SE 3 mi on Hwy 340 to park access rd, S 1 mi (E). 2015 rates: $6 to $16. Apr 15 to Oct 15. (563)873-2341

SPOOK CAVE CAMPGROUND **Ratings: 7.5/7/9** (Campground) 2015 rates: $20 to $33. May 1 to Oct 31. (563)873-2144 13299 Spook Cave Rd, Mc Gregor, IA 52157

MILFORD — A2 *Dickinson*

EMERSON BAY (State Pk) From town: Go 2-1/2 mi N on Hwy 86. 2015 rates: $6 to $19. (712)337-3211

GULL POINT (State Pk) From Jct of US-71 & Hwy 86, N 3 mi on Hwy 86 (R). 2015 rates: $6 to $11. (712)337-3211

MISSOURI VALLEY — C1 *Harrison, Monona*

WILSON ISLAND STATE RECREATION AREA (State Pk) From Jct of I-29 & Hwy 30, W 4 mi on US-30, S 4.6 mi on Desoto Ln, W .9 mi. 2015 rates: $6 to $16. (712)642-2069

MONTEZUMA — C4 *Marion*

DIAMOND LAKE COUNTY PARK (Public) From Jct of US-63 & SR-85, N 1 mi on US-63 (L). 2015 rates: $10 to $17. Apr 25 to Oct 20. (641)623-3191

MONTICELLO — B5 *Jones*

WALNUT ACRES CAMPGROUND **Ratings: 8.5/7.5/8.5** (Campground) 2015 rates: $28 to $35. Apr 15 to Oct 15. (319)465-4665 22128 Hwy 38 N, Monticello, IA 52310

MORAVIA — D4 *Appanoose*

BRIDGEVIEW CAMPGROUND (Public Corps) From town, W 8 mi on Hwy 2 to Hwy 142, N 11 mi (R). 2015 rates: $12 to $18. May 1 to Sep 30. (641)724-3062

BUCK CREEK (Public Corps) From town, N 5 mi on US-5 to CR-J29, NW 4 mi to CR-J5T, NE 2 mi (L). 2015 rates: $16 to $18. May 8 to Sep 29. (641)724-3206

HONEY CREEK (State Pk) From Jct of IA-5 & IA-142, W 8.1 mi on IA-142 to 160th, SE 3.5 mi (L). 2015 rates: $8 to $16. (641)724-3739

HONEY CREEK RESORT (State Pk) From Jct of Hwy 5 & SR-142 (in Moravia), W 5.5 mi on SR-142 to Resort Dr (185th Ave) (L). Campground fee includes four water park passes. 2015 rates: $49. Apr 15 to Oct 15. (877)677-3344

PRAIRIE RIDGE (Public Corps) From town, N 11 mi on SR-5 to SR-142, W 4 mi to cnty rd, S 3 mi, follow signs (E). 2015 rates: $18. May 15 to Sep 15. (641)724-3103

MOUNT PLEASANT — D5 *Henry*

CROSSROADS RV PARK

Ratings: 8/10★/9 (RV Park) From Jct of US 27/218 & US 34 (Exit 42/42B), W 0.4 mi to S Iris St, S 0.2 mi (L); or W-bnd From Jct of US 34 & US 27/218, W 0.4 mi on Bus Hwy 34 (towards town) to S Iris St, S 0.2 mi (L). **FAC:** Gravel rds. 34 gravel, 34 pull-thrus (34 x 90), 34 full hkups (30/50 amps), cable, WiFi, tent sites, dump, laundry, LP gas, fire rings, firewood. **REC:** playground. Pet restrict(B/Q). Partial handicap access. Big rig sites, 2015 rates: $34. Disc: AAA, military.
(319)385-9737 Lat: 40.95789, Lon: -91.52507
708 S Iris St., Mount Pleasant, IA 52641
office@xrdsrv.com
www.xrdsrv.com
See ad this page, 485.

MOUNT VERNON — C5 *Linn*

PALISADES-KEPLER (State Pk) From Jct of SR-1 & US-30, W 3.5 mi on US-30 (L). 2015 rates: $6 to $16. (319)895-6039

MUSCATINE — C5 *Muscatine, Rock Island*

FAIRPORT RECREATION AREA/WILDCAT DEN (State Pk) From town, E 5 mi on SR-22 (R). 2015 rates: $11 to $16. (563)263-4337

SHADY CREEK REC AREA (Public Corps) From town, E 10 mi on US-22 (R). 2015 rates: $20. May 1 to Oct 24. (800)645-0248

WILDCAT DEN (Public) From jct US-61 & Hwy-22: Go 11 mi NE on Hwy-22. 2015 rates: $6 to $9. (563)263-4337

NASHUA — A4 *Chickasaw, Nashua*

CEDAR VIEW PARK (Public) From Jct of SR-346 & Charles City Rd, N 0.2 mi on Charles City Rd (R). 2015 rates: $12 to $15. May 15 to Oct 20. (641)435-4156

NEOLA — C2 *Pottawattamie*

ARROWHEAD PARK (Public) From Jct of I-80 & L-55 (exit 23), SE 1 mi on L-55, follow signs (L). 2015 rates: $15. (712)485-2295

NEWTON — C4 *Jasper*

NEWTON KOA

Ratings: 9/9.5★/9 (RV Park) From Jct of I-80 & Newton exit (Exit 168), NW 0.7 mi on SE Speedway Dr to E 36th St S, (left) S 0.2 mi (E). Hard left turn between church and Barney's. Don't rely on GPS. Call for directions. **FAC:** All weather rds. (68 spaces). Avail: 58 gravel, 36 pull-thrus (24 x 62), back-ins (26 x 60), 36 full hkups, 22 W, 22 E (30/50 amps), seasonal sites, cable, WiFi, tent sites, rentals, dump, laundry, groc, LP gas, fire rings, firewood. **REC:** pool, pond, fishing, playground. Pet restrict(B). Big rig sites, 2015 rates: $27.95 to $41.95. Disc: AAA, military. Apr 1 to Oct 31.
AAA Approved
(641)792-2428 Lat: 41.68498, Lon: -93.01352
1601 E 36th St S, Newton, IA 50208
rollingacres@iowatelecom.net
www.koa.com/campgrounds/newton
See ad page 490.

NORTH LIBERTY — C5 *Johnson*

SUGAR BOTTOM (Public Corps) From town, NE 4 mi on CR-F28 to access rd (E). 2015 rates: $14 to $26. May 1 to Sep 29. (319)338-3543

OAKVILLE — D5 *Louisa*

FERRY LANDING (Public Corps) From town, NE 6 mi on CR-X71 (E). Pit toilets. May 1 to Oct 1. (563)263-7913

OELWEIN — B5 *Fayette*

LAKESHORE RV RESORT & CAMPGROUND
Ratings: 8/9★/9.5 (Membership Pk) From Jct Hwy 150 & Hwy 281: Go 0.6 mi W on Hwy 281 to Q Ave, then right 0.4 mi on Q Ave (R). **FAC:** Gravel rds. (85 spaces). Avail: 20 gravel, 4 pull-thrus (24 x 80), back-ins (25 x 60), 20 full hkups (30/50 amps), seasonal sites, WiFi, dump, laundry, fire rings, firewood. **REC:** Lake Oelwein: swim, fishing, shuffleboard, playground. Pets OK. Partial handicap access, no tents. Big rig sites, 2015 rates: $30. Apr 15 to Oct 15. No CC.
(319)283-5234 Lat: 42.64734, Lon: -91.92329
1418 Q Ave, Oelwein, IA 50662
mail@lakeshoreiowa.com
www.lakeshoreiowa.com

OELWEIN CITY PARK CAMPGROUND (Public) From Jct of Hwys 150 & 281, W 0.3 mi on Hwy 281 (R). 2015 rates: $8 to $14. (319)283-5440

OGDEN — C3 *Boone*

DON WILLIAMS (Public) From Jct of Hwy 30 & CR-P70, N 6.3 mi on CR-P70 (R). 2015 rates: $11 to $16. Apr 1 to Oct 31. (515)353-4237

OKOBOJI — A2 *Dickinson*

OKOBOJI See also Spirit Lake.

ONAWA — C1 *Monona*

LEWIS AND CLARK (State Pk) From Jct of I-29 & Hwy 175, W 1.5 mi on Hwy 175 to Hwy 324, N 1 mi (E). 2015 rates: $6 to $16. (712)423-2829

ON-UR-WA RV PARK

Ratings: 9/10★/10 (RV Park) From Jct of I-29 & SR-175 (exit 112), E 500 ft on SR-175 to 28th St, S 300 ft (L). **FAC:** All weather rds. 44 Avail: 44 all weather, 34 pull-thrus (28 x 100), back-ins (29 x 45), 44 full hkups (30/50 amps), WiFi, tent sites, laundry, LP gas, firewood. **REC.** Pet restrict(B). Partial handicap access. Big rig sites, eco-friendly, 2015 rates: $32 to $36. Disc: military. Mar 15 to Oct 31.
(712)423-1387 Lat: 42.02567, Lon: -96.12615
1111 28th St, Onawa, IA 51040
office@onurwarvpark.com
www.onurwarvpark.com
See ad this page, 485.

ONAWA/BLUE LAKE KOA **Ratings: 8/10★/9** (Campground) 2015 rates: $32 to $40. Apr 15 to Oct 15. (800)562-4182 21788 Dogwood Ave, Onawa, IA 51040

IA

ORLEANS — A2 *Dickinson*

MARBLE BEACH RECREATION AREA (State Pk) From town, N 4 mi on Lake Shore Dr. (R). 2015 rates: $6 to $16. (712)337-3211

OSAGE — A4 *Mitchell*

SPRING PARK (Public) From town, W 2 mi on Hwy 9 to Spring Park Rd, S .5 mi (E). 2015 rates: $5. (641)732-3709

OSCEOLA — D3 *Clarke*

LAKESIDE HOTEL-CASINO RV PARK Ratings: 8.5/NA/8.5 (RV Park) From Jct of I-35 & Exit 34 (Clay St), W 0.2 mi on Clay St. (L). **FAC:** Paved rds. 47 paved, patios, 47 pull-thrus (32 x 80), accepts full hkup units only, 47 full hkups (30/50 amps), cable, WiFi, restaurant. **REC:** heated pool, West Lake: fishing. Pets OK. No tents. Big rig sites, 2015 rates: $20. No CC, no reservations.
AAA Approved
(877)477-5253 Lat: 41.03802, Lon: -93.79735
777 Casino Dr., Osceola, IA 50213
www.affinitygamingllc.com

OSKALOOSA — D4 *Appanoose, Mahaska*

LAKE KEOMAH (State Pk) From Jct. of SR-92 & SR-63, E 6.3 mi on SR-92, S 1.1 mi on Royal Ln. 2015 rates: $6 to $16. (641)673-6975

OTTUMWA — D4 *Wapello*

OTTUMWA PARK (Public) From Jct of US-63 & 34W, S 0.5 mi on Wapello ST (R). 2015 rates: $15. Apr 1 to Oct 31. (641)682-1307

VALLEY VILLAGE MH COMMUNITY Ratings: 4.5/NA/9 (RV Area in MHP) From Jct of Hwy 34 & Hwy 63 (East of town), W 2.2 mi on Hwy 34/63 to traffic circle, S 0.4 mi on Hwy 63 to stoplight at Rabbit Run Rd, SE 1.3 mi (R). **FAC:** Paved rds. (163 spaces). Avail: 60 paved, patios, back-ins (30 x 70), 60 full hkups (30/50 amps), seasonal sites. **REC:** playground. Pet restrict(B/Q). No tents. Big rig sites, 2015 rates: $20. No CC.
(641)682-8481 Lat: 40.98659, Lon: -92.38366
11620 Rabbit Run Rd. Lot 162, Ottumwa, IA 52501
valleyvillage@towermgmt.com
www.valleyvillagemhc.com

OXFORD — C5 *Johnson*

SLEEPY HOLLOW RV PARK & CAMPGROUND/MHP
Ratings: 9/8.5/9.5 (Campground) From Jct of I-80 & SR-W38/Oxford (exit 230), N 500 ft on SR-W38 unmarked (R). **FAC:** Gravel rds. (120 spaces). Avail: 60 gravel, 40 pull-thrus (28 x 65), back-ins (28 x 55), 40 full hkups, 20 W, 20 E (30/50 amps), seasonal sites, WiFi, tent sites, rentals, dump, laundry, groc, LP gas, fire rings, firewood. **REC:** pool, Sleepy Hollow Lake: fishing, playground, rec open to public. Pet restrict(B). Big rig sites, 2015 rates: $29 to $38.
(319)828-4900 Lat: 41.69155, Lon: -91.80237
3340 Blackhawk Ave NW, Oxford, IA 52322
shcamping@southslope.net
www.sleepyhollowia.com
See ad pages 492, 485.

PALO — B5 *Linn*

PLEASANT CREEK SRA (State Pk) From town: Go 4 mi N on CR-W36. 2015 rates: $6 to $16. (319)436-7716

PELLA — C4 *Marion*

HOWELL STATION REC AREA (Public Corps) From Jct of SR-163 & CR-T15, SW 2.8 mi on CR-T15, follow signs (L). 2015 rates: $20. Apr 12 to Oct 28. (641)828-7522

NORTH OVERLOOK CAMP (Public Corps) From town, W 2 mi on CR-G28 to CR-T15, S 2 mi, follow signs (R). 2015 rates: $18. Apr 23 to Sep 27. (641)828-7522

ROBERTS CREEK RECREATION AREA (Public Corps) From town, W 7 mi on CR-G28 (R). 2015 rates: $12 to $20. Apr 3 to Oct 25. (641)627-5507

WALLASHUCK REC AREA (Public Corps) From town, W 4 mi on Hwy-G28, then 0.8 mi S on 190th Ave. 2015 rates: $18. Apr 23 to Sep 27. (641)828-7522

PLAINFIELD — B4 *Bremer*

NORTH CEDAR PARK (Public) From town, E 1 mi on Hwy 188 (L). 2015 rates: $9 to $12. May 1 to Oct 31. (319)882-4742

PLANO — D4 *Monroe*

SOUTH FORK CAMPGROUND, RESORT & MARINA (Public Corps) From town, N 2 mi on SR-142 to CR-J5T, E 2.7 mi to 150th Ave., N 2.6 mi (R). 2015 rates: $12 to $20. Apr 15 to Oct 1. (641)647-2625

PLEASANT HILL — C3 *Polk*

YELLOW BANKS PARK (POLK COUNTY PARK) (Public) From jct US 65 & Vandalia Rd: Go 3 mi E on Vandalia Rd, then turn S on SE 68th St. Follow signs. 2015 rates: $13. Apr 1 to Nov 30. (515)266-1563

POCAHONTAS — B2 *Pocahontas*

POCAHONTAS CITY PARK (Public) From Jct of Hwy 3 & Main St, N 0.3 mi on Main St (R). 2015 rates: $7 to $15. Apr 15 to Oct 15. (712)335-4841

ROCKWELL CITY — B2 *Calhoun*

FEATHERSTONE MEMORIAL PARK (COUNTY PARK) (Public) From Jct of Hwy 20 & CR-N57, N 5.2 mi on CR-N57 (L). 2015 rates: $8. Apr to Oct. (712)297-7131

RUTHVEN — A2 *Palo Alto*

LOST ISLAND HUSTON PARK (Public) From Jct US-18 & 350th Ave, N 2 mi on 350th Ave to 340th St, E 0.5 mi to 355th Ave, N 2 mi to 320th St, W 0.5 mi (L). 2015 rates: $10 to $15. Apr 15 to Oct 15. (712)837-4866

SABULA — B6 *Jackson*

SOUTH SABULA LAKE PARK (Public) Take Hwy 52/64 into Sabula. Go S on Broad St (turns into South Ave). Follow South Ave into park. 2015 rates: $17 to $20. Apr 1 to Oct 31. (563)652-3783

SAC CITY — B2 *Sac*

HAGGE PARK (Public) From town, S 2 mi on CR-M54 to CR-D42, E 0.25 mi (R). 2015 rates: $10 to $15. Apr 1 to Oct 31. (712)662-4530

SALIX — B1 *Woodbury*

BROWN'S LAKE BIGELOW PARK (WOODBURY COUNTY PARK) (Public) From I-29 (Salix exit): Go 2 mi W on county road. 2015 rates: $12 to $18. May 1 to Oct 31. (712)946-7114

SNYDER BEND PARK (Public) From Jct of I-29 & CR-K25 (Salix exit), W 2 mi on CR-K25 to park access rd, S 1.5 mi (L). 2015 rates: $12 to $18. May 1 to Oct 31. (712)946-5622

SHEFFIELD — A4 *Mitchell*

GALVIN MEMORIAL PARK (Public) From Jct US-65 & CR-13, W 1 mi on CR-13, follow signs (L). 2015 rates: $5. May to Sep. (641)892-4718

SHELDON — A1 *Lyon*

HILLS PARK REC AREA (Public) From town, N 0.25 mi on SR-60 (L). 2015 rates: $10 to $15. (712)324-4651

SHENANDOAH — D2 *Page*

PIERCE CREEK REC AREA (Public) From town, N 4 mi on Hwy 59 to 150th St, E 1 mi (L). Pit toilets. 2015 rates: $10 to $15. (712)542-3864

SHUEYVILLE — C5 *Johnson*

SANDY BEACH (COE - CORALVILLE LAKE) (Public Corps) From jct I-380 (Swisher/Shueyville exit) & CR F12: Go 1 mi E on CR F12, then follow signs 4 mi. 2015 rates: $20 to $24. May 1 to Sep 30. (319)338-3543

SIDNEY — D2 *Fremont*

WAUBONSIE (State Pk) From Jct of US-275 & Hwy 2, W 2 mi on Hwy 2 to CH L48, S 0.5 mi (E). 2015 rates: $6 to $16. (712)382-2786

SIGOURNEY — C4 *Marion*

BELVA-DEER REC AREA (Public) From town NE 1.3 mi on Hwy 92, N 4.2 mi on Hwy 149, E 1.8 m on 180th St. 2015 rates: $10 to $18. (641)622-3757

SIOUX CITY — B1 *Plymouth, Woodbury*

SIOUX CITY See also North Sioux City, SD.

STONE (State Pk) From Jct of I-29 & Riverside Blvd, N 5 mi on SR-12 (R). 2015 rates: $6 to $16 (712)255-4698

SMITHLAND — B1 *Woodbury*

SOUTHWOOD CONSERVATION AREA (WOODBURY COUNTY PARK) (Public) From jc Hwy 31 & US 141: Go 1-1/2 mi W on US 141, ther 3/4 mi S & E on gravel road. 2015 rates: $15 to $20 May 1 to Oct 31. (712)889-2215

SOLON — C5 *Johnson*

LAKE MACBRIDE (State Pk) From town, W 5 m on SR-382 to N campground; or W 4 mi on 5th St to S campground (L). 2015 rates: $6 to $16. (319)624-2200

SPENCER — A2 *Clay*

LEACH PARK CAMPGROUND (Public) From S Jct of US-18 & US-71 (S of town), N on US-18/71 to 4th St SE, E 0.2 mi (L); or from N Jct of US-18 & US-71 (N of town), S on US-18/71, over bridge to 4th St SE, E 0.2 mi (L). 2015 rates: $12 to $15. Apr 15 to Oct 15. (712)264-7265

SPIRIT LAKE — A2 *Dickinson*

CENLA RV PARK **Ratings: 8/10★/9** (RV Park) 2015 rates: $32.50 to $34.50. Apr 15 to Oct 15. (712)336-2925 3200 US Hwy 71, Spirit Lake, IA 51360

ST ANSGAR — A4 *Mitchell*

HALVORSON PARK (Public) From Jct of US-218 & Hwy 9, W 10 mi on Hwy 9 to Foothill Ave (St Ansgar sign), N 5 mi (R). 2015 rates: $10 to $16. May 15 to Oct 15. (641)732-5204

STANTON — D2 *Montgomery*

VIKING LAKE (State Pk) From Jct of US-71 & 34, W 4 mi on US-34 to Q Ave, S 0.5 mi to 230th St., E 0.8 mi. 2015 rates: $6 to $16. (712)829-2235

STEAMBOAT ROCK — B4 *Hardin*

PINE RIDGE (Public) From Jct of Hwy 556 & D 35, S .3 mi on Hwy S56, (R). 2015 rates: $10 to $15. Apr 15 to Nov 1. (641)648-4361

STORM LAKE — B2 *Buena Vista*

SUNRISE CAMPGROUND (Public) From Jct US Hwy 71 & Hwy 7/Bus 71: Go 1 1/2 mi W on Hwy 7/Bus 71 (at Lighthouse), then 1/4 mi S on Sunrise Rd (L). 2015 rates: $16 to $25. Apr 1 to Oct 1. (712)732-8023

STORY CITY — B3 *Story*

WHISPERING OAKS RV PARK **Ratings: 6.5/8/9** (Campground) 2015 rates: $25 to $28. (515)733-4663 1011 Timberland Dr, Story City, IA 50248

STRATFORD — B3 *Hamilton*

BELLS MILL PARK (Public) From town, N 3 mi on CR-R21 to CR-D56, E 1.5 mi to park access rd, N 2.5 mi, follow signs (R). 2015 rates: $20. Apr 1 to Nov 30. (515)832-9570

STRAWBERRY POINT — B5 *Clayton*

BACKBONE (State Pk) From town, N 1 mi on CR-W-69 (L). 2015 rates: $6 to $16. (563)924-2000

SUMNER — B4 *Bremer*

NORTH WOODS PARK (Public) From town, N 1.5 mi on CR-V62 (R). 2015 rates: $9 to $12. May 1 to Oct 31. (319)882-4742

TAMA — C4 *Tama*

MESKWAKI CASINO RV PARK Ratings: 8/9.5★/8 (RV Park) From jct US 63 & US 30: Go 4-3/4 mi W on US 30 (behind casino). **FAC:** Paved rds. 50 paved, patios, 50 pull-thrus (30 x 70), accepts full hkup units only, 50 E (30/50 amps), WiFi, tent sites, laundry, restaurant. **REC:** heated pool, whirlpool, rec open to public. Pet restrict(B). Partial handicap access. 2015 rates: $19. ATM.
AAA Approved
(641)484-1439 Lat: 41.99817, Lon: -92.67103
1504 305th St, Tama, IA 52339
Lmorgan@meskwaki.com
www.meskwaki.com

THAYER — D3 *Union*

THAYER LAKE REC AREA (Public) From Jct of 34 & cnty rd, S 0.05 mi on cnty rd to 2nd cnty rd, W 0.7 mi (R). Pit toilets. 2015 rates: $8. (641)782-7111

TIFFIN — C5 *Johnson*

F.W. KENT PARK (JOHNSON COUNTY PARK) (Public) From I-80 (exit 237): Go 1 mi N, then 3-1/2 mi W on US-6. 2015 rates: $20. (319)645-2315

TIPTON — C5 *Cedar*

HUNT'S CEDAR RIVER CAMPGROUND
Ratings: 9/8.5/8 (Campground) From Jct of I-80 & SR-38 (exit 267), N 0.2 mi on SR-38 to Frntg Rd, W 0.7 mi (E). **FAC:** Gravel rds. (156 spaces). Avail: 71 grass, 32 pull-thrus (25 x 60), back-ins (25 x 50), 37 full hkups, 34 W, 34 E (30/50 amps), seasonal sites, WiFi, tent sites, dump, laundry, LP gas, fire rings, firewood. **REC:** pool, Cedar River: fishing, playground. Pet restrict(B). Big rig sites, 2015 rates: $28 to $31. Apr 15 to Oct 15.
(563)946-2431 Lat: 41.64600, Lon: -91.12746
1231 306th St, Tipton, IA 52772
hcrcg95@msn.com
www.friendcamping.com
See ad pages 490, 485.

UNION — B4 *Hardin*

DAISY LONG (Public) From Jct of Hwys 175 & 215, S on Hwy 215 to Union, E 1 mi to SR-D65, N 0.125 mi (L). 2015 rates: $10 to $15. Apr 15 to Nov 1. (641)648-4361

URBANA — B5 *Benton, Linn*

LAZY ACRES RV PARK
Ratings: 8.5/10★/10 (RV Park) From Jct of I-380 & Exit 41 (N of Center Point), E 0.1 mi on 54th St Trail to 32nd Ave, N 0.1 mi (R). Don't rely on GPS. Call for directions. **FAC:** All weather rds. 69 gravel, 54 pull-thrus (75 x 120), back-ins (20 x 80), 52 full hkups, 17 W, 17 E (30/50 amps), WiFi, tent sites, rentals, dump, laundry, groc, LP gas, fire rings, firewood. **REC:** pond, fishing, playground. Pet restrict(B). Partial handicap access. Big rig sites, eco-friendly, 2015 rates: $30 to $33.50. ATM.
(319)443-4000 Lat: 42.23081, Lon: -91.86589
5486 32nd Ave, Center Point, IA 52213
office@lazyacresrv.com
www.lazyacresrv.com
See ad pages 489, 485.

WILDCAT BLUFF (BENTON COUNTY PARK) (Public) From jct Hwy 150 & Hwy 363: Go 1 mi E on Hwy 363 into Urbana, then S on CR W28. 2015 rates: $13. (319)472-3318

VENTURA — A3 *Cerro Gordo*

MCINTOSH WOODS (State Pk) From town: Go 3/4 mi E on US 18, then 1/2 mi S on McIntosh Rd. 2015 rates: $6 to $16. (641)829-3847

VINTON — B5 *Benton*

BENTON CITY-FRY CAMPGROUND (BENTON COUNTY PARK) (Public) From Hwy 150 & 13th St: Go 4-1/2 mi E on 13th St, then follow signs. Pit toilets. 2015 rates: $8 to $12. (319)472-3318

MINNE ESTEMA CAMPGROUND (BENTON COUNTY PARK) (Public) From jct US 218 & Hwy 150: Go 3-1/2 mi N on Hwy 150, then follow signs. Pit toilets. (563)472-3318

RODGERS PARK (BENTON COUNTY PARK) (Public) From town: Go 3 mi W on US-218, then 1 mi N on CR-V61, then 1/4 mi E. 2015 rates: $15. (319)472-4942

WALLINGFORD — A2 *Emmet*

WOLDEN REC AREA (Public) From town, E 3 mi on A-34 (R). 2015 rates: $18 to $20. Apr 15 to Oct 31. (712)867-4422

WATERLOO — B4 *Black Hawk*

WATERLOO See also Hazleton.

BAMBOO RIDGE KOA **Ratings: 9.5/9.5★/9** (RV Park) 2015 rates: $39 to $52. (319)233-3485 4550 Hess Rd, Waterloo, IA 50701

WAUKEE — C3 *Dallas*

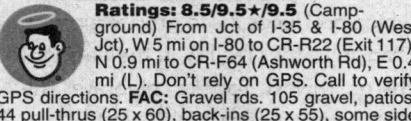

TIMBERLINE CAMPGROUND
Ratings: 8.5/9.5★/9.5 (Campground) From Jct of I-35 & I-80 (West Jct), W 5 mi on I-80 to CR-R22 (Exit 117), N 0.9 mi to CR-F64 (Ashworth Rd), E 0.4 mi (L). Don't rely on GPS. Call to verify GPS directions. **FAC:** Gravel rds. 105 gravel, patios, 44 pull-thrus (25 x 60), back-ins (25 x 55), some side by side hkups, 38 full hkups, 67 W, 67 E (30/50 amps), WiFi, tent sites, rentals, dump, laundry, groc, LP gas, fire rings, firewood. **REC:** pool, playground. Pet restrict(B). Big rig sites, eco-friendly, 2015 rates: $36.50 to $42. Apr 1 to Nov 1.
(515)987-1714 Lat: 41.57954, Lon: -93.87400
31635 Ashworth Rd, Waukee, IA 50263
timberrv@aol.com
www.timberlineiowa.com
See ad pages 490, 485.

WAVERLY — B4 *Bremer*

CEDAR BEND PARK (Public) From Jct of Hwy 3 & 12th St NW (in Waverly), N 2.6 mi on 12th NW (R). 2015 rates: $10 to $15. May 1 to Oct 31. (319)882-4742

WEBSTER CITY — B3 *Hamilton*

BRIGGS WOODS (Public) From Jct of Hwys 520 & 17, S 2 mi on Hwy 17 (L). 2015 rates: $20 to $25. (515)832-9570

RIVERSIDE PARK CITY CAMPGROUND (Public) From Jct of US-20 & Superior St, N 1.3 mi on Superior St to Second St, E 0.1 mi to River St, S 0.05 mi (L). 2015 rates: $12. Apr 15 to Oct 15. (515)832-9193

WEST LIBERTY — C5 *Cedar*

LITTLE BEAR CAMPGROUND **Ratings: 8.5/9.5★/7.5** (Campground) 2015 rates: $27. Apr 15 to Nov 1. (319)627-2676 1961 Garfield Ave, West Liberty, IA 52776

WEST POINT — D5 *Lee*

POLLMILLER PARK (Public) From town, E 0.5 mi on Hwy 103 (R). 2015 rates: $10 to $15. (319)463-7673

WINTERSET — C3 *Madison*

WINTERSET CITY CAMPGROUND & RV PARK (Public) From Jct of Hwys 169 & 92, E 0.5 mi on Hwy 92 to 10th St, S 0.5 mi (E). 2015 rates: $16 to $19. Apr 1 to Nov 1. (515)462-3258

WOODBINE — C2 *Harrison*

WILLOW LAKE (HARRISON COUNTY PARK) (Public) From jct US 30 & CR F20L (Easton Trail): Go 6 mi W on CR F20L (Easton Trail). 2015 rates: $18. Apr 1 to Oct 31. (712)647-2785

Join the flock and head south during the winter. Use our handy Snowbird guide in the front of the Guide to find RV-friendly destinations throughout the Sunbelt. Snowbird Destinations features the top Snowbird roosts and lists great Campgrounds in compelling areas.

We give you what you want. First, we surveyed thousands of RVers just like you. Then, we developed our exclusive Triple Rating System for campgrounds based on the results. That's why our rating system is so good at explaining the quality of facilities and cleanliness of campgrounds.

Each privately owned campground has been rated three times. The first rating is for development of facilities. The second one is for cleanliness and physical characteristics of restrooms and showers. The third is for campground visual appearance and environmental quality.

IA

Getty Images/iStockphoto

WELCOME TO

Kansas

DATE OF STATEHOOD	WIDTH: 417 MILES (645 KM)	PROPORTION OF UNITED STATES
JAN. 29, 1861	LENGTH: 211 MILES (340 KM)	2.17% OF 3,794,100 SQ MI

There's no place like Kansas. With green rolling hills, golden wheat fields and beguiling towns steeped in "Wizard of Oz" mythology, few states instill quite the same feeling of home as Kansas. For all its apple pie pleasures, Kansas's pastoral lands have borne witness to bloody battles over slavery, devastating twisters, Indian skirmishes and shoot-outs courtesy of the Wild West's most infamous gunslingers. But once you take to the road, Kansas captures the imagination and the essence of America's Great Plains.

With eight scenic byways and three historic byways, there are surprising discoveries at every turn. In Hanover, you can visit Hollenberg Station (a National Landmark), built in 1858 to serve as a relay station for the Pony Express. In Hutchinson, the awesome Cosmosphere tells the story of the space race and avails visitors of a space artifact collection surpassed in scope by only the Smithsonian National Air and Space Museum. The aeronautic theme continues in Wichita, one of the leading centers for aircraft manufacture in the U.S., which produces more private aircraft than any other facility in the nation. To the northwest, Topeka celebrates the state's pioneer spirit with world-class museums and attractions.

In the spectacular Smoky Hills region, Kanapolis State Park is one of the region's most breathtaking parks. Mile after mile of scenic trails zigzag through prairies, sandstone bluffs, wooded creeks and canyons, including the foreboding Horsethief Canyon.

It's no surprise that National Geographic deemed Lake Scott State Park one of the country's 50 must-see state parks. An extensive trail system (horseback riding is also allowed) covers 1,020 acres of spectacular wilderness.

Top 3 Tourism Attractions:
1) Old Cowtown Museum
2) Monument Rocks, the Chalk Pyramids
3) Tallgrass Prairie National Preserve

Nickname: Sunflower State

State Flower: Sunflower

State Bird: Western Meadowlark

People: Kirstie Alley, actress; Bob Dole, U.S. senator; Amelia Earhart, first woman to fly solo across the Atlantic Ocean; Dennis Hopper, actor

Major Cities: Wichita, Overland Park, Kansas City, Topeka (capital), Olathe

Topography: East—Hilly Osage plains; central—level prairie and hills; west—high plains

Climate: Humid continental, semi-arid steppe and humid subtropical region; Kansas is one of the windiest states

TRAVEL & TOURISM

Kansas Department of Wildlife, Parks & Tourism
www.travelks.com

Abilene CVB
785-263-2231
www.abileneks.com

Chase County Chamber of Commerce
620-273-8469
www.chasecountychamber.org

Coffey County Chamber of Commerce
620-364-2002
www.coffeycountychamber.com

Kansas City CVB
www.visitkansascityks.com

Russell County CVB
www.russellcoks.org

Topeka Inc.
www.visittopeka.com

Visit Wichita
www.visitwichita.com

OUTDOOR RECREATION

Kansas Dept. of Wildlife & Parks
620-672-5911
www.ksoutdoors.com

SHOPPING

Great Mall of the Great Plains
913-829-6277
www.greatmallgreatplains.com

Kansas Originals Market
877-457-6233
www.kansasoriginals.com

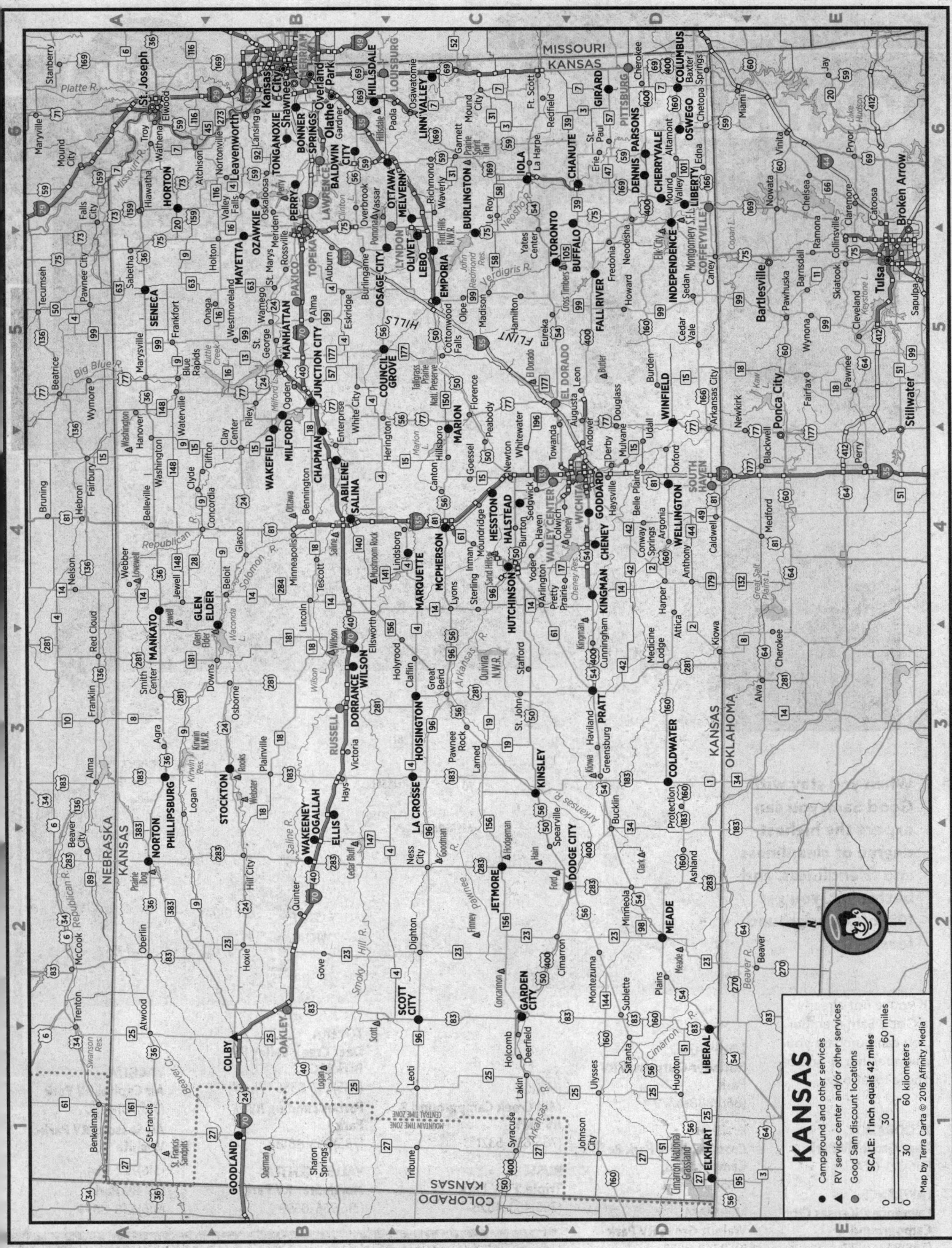
KANSAS
● Campground and other services
▲ RV service center and/or other services
● Good Sam discount locations
SCALE: 1 inch equals 42 miles
0 30 60 miles
0 30 60 kilometers
Map by Terra Carta © 2016 Affinity Media
NEBRASKA
KANSAS
MISSOURI
KANSAS
OKLAHOMA
KANSAS
COLORADO
KANSAS
CENTRAL TIME ZONE
MOUNTAIN TIME ZONE
WICHITA
TOPEKA
Kansas City
MANHATTAN
SALINA
HUTCHINSON
DODGE CITY
GARDEN CITY
LIBERAL
EMPORIA
LAWRENCE
COLBY
GOODLAND

Featured Good Sam Parks

KANSAS

When you stay with Good Sam, you can expect the highest degree of cleanliness and friendliness, and better yet, you get 10% off campground fees.

If you're not already a Good Sam member you can purchase your membership at one of these locations:

EL DORADO
Deer Grove RV Park
(316)321-6272

LAWRENCE
Lawrence / Kansas City Campground
(785)842-3877

LOUISBURG
Rutlader Outpost & RV Park
(866)888-6779

LYNDON
Crossroads RV Park & Campground
(785)221-5482

MERRIAM
Walnut Grove RV Park
(913)262-3023

PAXICO
Mill Creek Campground & RV Park
(785)636-5321

RUSSELL
Triple 'J' RV Park
(785)483-4826

TOPEKA
Deer Creek Valley RV Park LLC
(785)357-8555
Forbes Landing RV Park
(785)862-8818

VALLEY CENTER
North Star RV Park
(316)755-0592

WICHITA
Air Capital RV Park
(316)201-1250
All Seasons RV Park-Wichita
(316)722-1154
USI RV Park
(316)838-8699

For more Good Sam Parks go to listing pages

Frank Lloyd Wright's Allen House

WICHITA AREA

Fly high in the aviation capital of the plains

Wichita, Kansas, has always been a major hub for both business and transportation. In the 1870s, it was a crossroads on the Chisolm Trail; countless head of cattle passed through on their way to market. In 1874, Wyatt Earp was brought in as deputy city marshal to bring order to the cow town.

Later, Wichita became the "Air Capital of the World," and during World War II, four bombers a day were rolling out of its airfield production hangars. Boeing was the major employer, and the city was one of the fastest growing towns in America. Today, Wichita is larger than the next two Sunflower State cities (Overland Park and Kansas City) combined. Aircraft were not the only things taking off in Wichita—Pizza Hut, White Castle and Taco Tico all got their starts here as well.

Today, the town is a hub for history, and the Wichita heritage comes alive in some two-dozen museums around town. The Wichita-Sedgwick County Historical Museum, housed in the gray-stoned Richardsonian Romanesque-styled City Hall building from 1892, is a catch-all for all things Wichita. Old Cowtown is a living-history museum set on 23 acres and is sprinkled with more than 60 restored and re-created buildings. In the revitalized warehouse district of Old Town, the Museum of World Treasures lives up to its name with wonders that include Egyptian mummies and one of the most complete Tyrannosaurus rex skeletons in the world. Stand in awe at the foot of the most ferocious land predator of all time.

The former Municipal Airport, once the fifth busiest in the United States, has been turned over to Kansas Aviation Museum for its displays of pioneering aircraft with roots in Wichita. The Great Plains Transportation Museum is devoted to railroading history, and the grounds at Union Station show off six locomotives along with several other examples of vintage rolling stock. You'll also find museums honoring Kansas firefighters, the Kansas oil industry and Kansas sports.

> Strataca, the Kansas Underground Salt Museum, offers tours 650 feet below ground to a working salt mine.

A penguin swimming in the Sedgwick County Zoo. Sedgewick County Zoo.

Creativity Soars

Art lovers will want to check in on the Wichita Art Museum, which is 100 years old and houses the marquee collection in Kansas with more than 7,000 pieces. The Ulrich Museum of Art on the Wichita State University campus is a depository of modern and contemporary art. The live arts are well represented in the expansive Century II Performing Arts & convention Center that is home to four arts organizations: Wichita Symphony Orchestra, Music Theatre of Wichita, Wichita Grand Opera and Music Theatre for Young People. The restored Orpheum Theatre, designed in 1922 to evoke a romantic Spanish courtyard, hosts more intimate performances.

Wichita supports professional sports in minor-league baseball (the Wingnuts) and hockey (the Thunder), and indoor football (the Force). The 81 Speedway Race Track north of the city sends cars, trucks and motorcycles roaring around a 3/8-mile semi-banked dirt oval track on weekends throughout the year. At the Kansas Star Casino, gamblers can tempt chance with a full range of slot machines, table games and a 13-table poker room.

Wichita's outdoor attractions are as varied as its indoor cultural footprint. Strataca, the Kansas Underground Salt Museum, is truly a one-of-a-kind exploration with tours 650 feet below ground in a working salt mine. Back in the fresh air and sunshine, Botanica, the Wichita Gardens, maintains a prairie oasis with 26 themed gardens entwined with sculptures and gushing fountains. For more naturalistic explorations, the Great Plains Nature Center has carved two miles of fully accessible trails through wetlands and native prairies.

Wild in Wichita

Wichita's favorite family day out is at the Sedgwick County Zoo, one of the 10 largest zoological parks in the nation. More than 3,000 animals make their home here in habitats ranging from Penguin Cove to the Downing Gorilla Forest. Next door, the Sedgwick County Extension Arboretum showcases the nearly 100 trees that are indigenous to south central Kansas.

When Wichita parties—which is often—no one is left out. There are festivals for every taste, from celebrations of yore at the Renaissance Festival, to the Midwest Beerfest and Wingfest, to the annual Wagonmaster's Chili Cookoff. Riverfest is the biggest celebration in Kansas, spreading across nine days with four stages of non-stop music.

The Tallgrass Film Festival has evolved into one of the movie industry's premiere screenings for independent filmmakers. More than 100 feature and short films receive exposure over five days, and films first shown in the Tallgrass lineup have gone on to contend for Academy Awards.

And of course, the "Air Capital of the World" puts on an annual Salute to Aviation. In addition to flyovers of aircraft with Wichita breeding, there are hot-air balloons and paper airplanes From their whimsical designs may come Wichita's next contribution to aviation.

For More Information

Visit Wichita
316-265-2800
www.visitwichita.com

Kansas Department of Commerce, Travel and Tourism
785-296-2009
www.travelks.com

Kansas

CONSULTANTS

Chuck & Alyce Grover

ABILENE — B4 *Dickinson*

COVERED WAGON RV RESORT Ratings: 6.5/7.5/7 (Campground) From jct I-70 (exit 275) & Buckeye St: Go S 2-1/4 mi on Buckeye St. (R). **FAC:** Gravel rds. 44 gravel, 34 pull-thrus (25 x 70), back-ins (25 x 40), some side by side hkups, 39 full hkups, 5 W, 5 E (30/50 amps), cable, WiFi, tent sites, dump, laundry. **REC:** pool, playground. Pets OK. Big rig sites, 2015 rates: $32. Disc: military.
(800)864-4053 Lat: 38.90743, Lon: -97.21412
803 S Buckeye, Abilene, KS 67410
reservations@coveredwagonrvpark.com
coveredwagonrvpark.com

ATCHISON — A6 *Atchison*

WARNOCK (Public) From town, W 1 mi on US-59 to Phillips Rd, S .5 mi on Phillips Rd to 274th Rd, E 0.5 mi (R). Pit toilets. 2015 rates: $10. (913)367-5561

BALDWIN CITY *Douglas*

THE LODGE RV PARK (RV Spaces) From US 59 and US 56: go 3.5 mi W on US 56 (L). **FAC:** All weather rds. 10 Avail: 10 all weather, 3 pull-thrus (24 x 60), back-ins (24 x 50), 10 full hkups (30/50 amps), WiFi Hotspot. **REC.** Pets OK. Big rig sites, 2015 rates: $22 to $25.
(785)594-3900 Lat: 38.782288, Lon: -95.184448
502 Ames, Baldwin City, KS 66006
baldwincitylodge@gmail.com
www.baldwincitylodge.com

BONNER SPRINGS — B6 *Wyandotte*

COTTONWOOD CAMPING RV PARK & CAMPGROUND **Ratings: 4.5/5.5/4** (Campground) 2015 rates: $32 to $36. (913)422-8038 115 S 130th St, Bonner Springs, KS 66012

BUFFALO — D6 *Wilson*

WILSON STATE FISHING LAKE (Public) From Jct of US-75 & SR-39, E .8 mi on Hwy 75/SH-39, (L). Pit toilets. 2015 rates: $7.50 to $8.50. (620)637-2748

BURLINGTON — C5 *Coffey*

JOHN REDMOND/DAMSITE (Public Corps) From town, N 3.5 mi on US-75 to 16th St, W 0.3 mi to Embankment Rd, W 1.2 mi, follow signs (E). 2015 rates: $10 to $15. Apr 1 to Oct 31. (620)364-8613

JOHN REDMOND/RIVERSIDE EAST (Public Corps) From Jct of I-35 & US-75, S 11 mi on US-75 to Embankment Rd, W 1.5 mi, follow signs (E). 2015 rates: $15. May 1 to Sep 30. (620)364-8613

JOHN REDMOND/RIVERSIDE WEST (Public Corps) From town, N 3.5 mi on US-75 to Embankment Rd, W 2.5 mi (across dam) follow signs (R). 2015 rates: $8 to $15. May 1 to Sep 30. (620)364-8613

CHANUTE — D6 *Neosho*

SANTA FE PARK (Public) From town, S 2 mi on Santa Fe Ave (R). 2015 rates: $10. (620)431-5250

CHAPMAN — B4 *Dickinson*

CHAPMAN CREEK RV PARK **Ratings: 6.5/9.5★/7.5** (RV Park) 2015 rates: $32. (785)922-2267 2701 N Marshall Dr, Chapman, KS 67431

CHENEY — D4 *Kingman, Reno, Sedgwick*

CHENEY - EAST SHORE (State Pk) From Jct of US-54 & SR-251, N 5.5 mi on SR-251 (L). 2015 rates: $5 to $35. (316)542-3664

CHENEY - WEST SHORE (State Pk) From Jct of US-54 & SR-251, N 3.5 mi on SR-251 to 21st St, W 2.4 mi (R). 2015 rates: $5 to $35. (316)542-3664

Like Us on Facebook.

CHERRYVALE — D6 *Labette*

CHERRYVALE (Public Corps) From Jct of Hwy 169 & Main St, E 2 mi on Main St to Olive St, S 0.25 mi to Montgomery CR-5000, E 4.5 mi to Big Hill Lake, W 0.75 mi (E). 2015 rates: $17 to $22. Mar 27 to Nov 1. (620)336-2741

TIMBER HILL REC AREA (Public Corps) From Parsons, W 6 mi on Hwy 400 to Dennis-Mound Valley Rd, follow signs (E). Pit toilets. 2015 rates: $8. Mar 29 to Nov 3. (620)336-2741

COFFEYVILLE — D6 *Montgomery*

BUCKEYE MOBILE/RV ESTATES
Ratings: 6.5/9★/7.5 (RV Area in MHP) From S jct of US-169 & US-166: Go 1-1/4 mi W on US-166 (11th Street), then 1 mi N on Buckeye St (L). **FAC:** Gravel rds. 89 gravel, 8 pull-thrus (26 x 65), back-ins (30 x 60), 89 full hkups (30/50 amps), WiFi, rentals, laundry, LP bottles. **REC:** pond, fishing. Pet restrict(B/Q). No tents. Big rig sites, eco-friendly, 2015 rates: $25. Disc: military.
(620)251-2375 Lat: 37.04691, Lon: -95.63843
502 N Buckeye St, Coffeyville, KS 67337
shaffener@aol.com
buckeyemobileestates.com

WALTER JOHNSON PARK (Public) From west jct US 166 & US 169: Go 1-1/4 mi E on US 166/169 (to Old Locomotive/Fairgrounds). 2015 rates: $8 to $15. (620)252-6100

COLBY — B1 *Thomas*

Travel Services

CUMMINS CENTRAL POWER Cummins Central Power is the exclusive distributor for Cummins and Onan products in the Midwest. 12 full service locations in Nebraska, Missouri, Kansas, Iowa, South Dakota and Illinois support engine and generator customers. **SERVICES:** Engine/chassis repair, mobile RV svc, emergency rd svc, restrooms. Emergency parking, RV accessible. waiting room. Hours: 8am to 5pm.
(785)462-3945 Lat: 39.371412, Lon: -101.055865
1880 S Range Ave, Colby, KS 67701
centralpower@cummins.com
www.cumminscentralpower.com
See ad page 732.

COLDWATER — D3 *Comanche*

LAKE COLDWATER (Public) From Jct of US-160 & US-183 (N of town), S 1.5 mi on US-183 to Lake Coldwater Rd, W 1 mi (R). 2015 rates: $12.50 to $22. (620)582-2702

COLUMBUS — D6 *Cherokee*

T & S RV PARK **Ratings: 3/NA/4.5** (Campground) 2015 rates: $20. (620)674-3304 1308 E Hwy 160, Columbus, KS 66725

COUNCIL GROVE — B5 *Morris*

COUNCIL GROVE LAKE/CANNING CREEK COVE (Public Corps) From town, N 1.7 mi on SR-177 to City Lake Rd, NW 3 mi, follow signs (R). 2015 rates: $12 to $22. Apr 1 to Oct 31. (620)767-5195

COUNCIL GROVE LAKE/RICHEY COVE (Public Corps) From town, N 3 mi on SR-177 (L). 2015 rates: $17 to $25. Apr 1 to Oct 31. (620)767-5195

SANTA FE TRAIL (COE - COUNCIL GROVE LAKE) (Public Corps) From west jct Hwy 177 & US 56: Go 1 block W on US 56, then 2-1/2 mi NW on Mission St. 2015 rates: $11 to $22. Apr 15 to Oct 31. (620)767-5195

DENNIS — D6 *Labette*

MOUND VALLEY REC AREA (Public Corps) From Parsons, W 6 mi on Hwy 400 to Dennis-Mound Valley Rd, S 5 mi to Labette CR-19000, W 4 mi (R). 2015 rates: $12 to $20. Mar 27 to Nov 1. (620)336-2741

Tell them you saw them in this Guide!

DODGE CITY — C2 *Ford*

GUNSMOKE RV PARK, INC.
Ratings: 8.5/9.5★/9.5 (RV Park) E-bnd: (W of Town) 0.1 mi before Jct Bus US-50 (Wyatt Earp Blvd) & US-50 (L); or W-bnd: From Jct US-400 & US 56/283: Go .4 mi N on US-283, then 5 mi W on Bus 50 (Wyatt Earp Blvd) (R); or N-bnd: From Jct US-56 & US-283: Go 2 mi N on 2nd Ave, then 3 mi W on Bus US-50 (Wyatt Earp Blvd) (R). Elev 2600 ft. **FAC:** Gravel rds. 89 Avail: 44 gravel, 45 grass, 58 pull-thrus (24 x 80), back-ins (20 x 45), some side by side hkups, 89 full hkups (30/50 amps), cable, WiFi, tent sites, rentals, dump, laundry, groc, fire rings, firewood. **REC:** pool, playground. Pets OK. Partial handicap access. Big rig sites, 2015 rates: $34 to $38. Apr 1 to Oct 31.
(620)227-8247 Lat: 37.75568, Lon: -100.06899
11070 108 Rd, Dodge City, KS 67801
office@gunsmokervpark.com
www.gunsmokervpark.com
See ad this page.

WATER SPORTS CAMPGROUND & RV PARK Ratings: 6/9/5.5 (RV Park) W-bnd: From Jct of By-pass US 56 & Hwy 400 (Trail St), W 3.4 mi on Hwy 400 to Second Ave, S 0.4 mi on Second Ave to Cherry St, E 0.3 mi (E); or N-bnd: From Jct of US 283 (Second Ave) & By-pass US-56/283, N 1.7 mi on Second Ave to Cherry St, E 0.3 mi (E). Or call if questions. Elev 2634 ft. **FAC:** Gravel rds. 84 gravel, 62 pull-thrus (24 x 60), back-ins (20 x 35), 74 full hkups, 10 W, 10 E (30/50 amps), WiFi, tent sites, dump, laundry, groc, LP gas. **REC:** playground. Pets OK. Partial handicap access. 2015 rates: $20 to $25. Disc: AAA, military. AAA Approved
(620)225-8044 Lat: 37.74323, Lon: -100.01310
500 Cherry St., Dodge City, KS 67801
watersportscampground@cox.net
www.watersportscampground.com

DORRANCE — B3 *Russell*

WILSON LAKE/MINOOKA PARK (Public Corps) From Jct of I-70 & Dorrance exit 199 (Hwy 231), N 6 mi on Hwy 231 (E). For reservations call (877)444-6777. 2015 rates: $8 to $40. (785)658-2551

EL DORADO — C5 *Butler*

DEER GROVE RV PARK
Ratings: 7.5/9.5★/9 (RV Park) N-bnd: From Jct I-35 (KS Turnpike) & Exit 71: Go 5.6 mi E on Hwy 254 (Hwy 254 turns into Hwy 54), follow blue camper signs to park (R). S-bnd: From Jct I-35 & Hwy 177 (Exit 92): Go 18 mi S on Hwy 177 to US 54, then W 3 mi (L). **FAC:** Gravel rds. 43 gravel, 18 pull-thrus (25 x 65), back-ins (20 x 45), 43 full hkups (30/50 amps), cable, WiFi, tent sites, laundry, fire rings, firewood. **REC.** Pet restrict(B). Big rig sites, eco-friendly, 2015 rates: $32 to $36. Disc: AAA.
(316)321-6272 Lat: 37.81010, Lon: -96.79176
2873 S.E. US Hwy 54, El Dorado, KS 67042
dongespropertiesllc@hotmail.com
www.deergrovervpark.com
See ad pages 500 (Spotlight Wichita Area), 498.

EL DORADO (State Pk) From jct US 77 & US 54: Go 3 mi E on US 54, then 2 mi N to office. 2015 rates: $7 to $35. (316)321-7180

EL DORADO/BLUESTEM POINT (State Pk) From Jct of US-54 & US-77, E 4.8 mi on US-54 to SR-177, N 4.1 mi (L) Entrance fee required. 2015 rates: $5 to $35. (316)321-7180

EL DORADO/BOULDER BLUFF (State Pk) From Jct of I-35 & US-77, S 0.1 mi on US-77, E 2 mi. Entrance fee required. 2015 rates: $5 to $35. (316)321-7180

EL DORADO/SHADY CREEK (State Pk) From town, E 3 mi on US-54 to Bluestem Dr, N 2 mi to access rd, E 0.2 mi (L). Entrance fee required. 2015 rates: $5 to $35. (316)321-7180

EL DORADO/WALNUT RIVER (State Pk) From Jct of US-54 & US-77, E 3.1 mi on US-54 to Bluestem Rd, N 1.5 mi to Cross Creek, W 1.7 mi (R). Entrance fee required. 2015 rates: $5 to $35. (316)321-7180

KS

ELKHART — D1 *Morton*

PRAIRIE RV PARK & CAR WASH **Ratings: 3/NA/5** (RV Park) 2015 rates: $20. (620)360-1095 e. Point Rock St & Hwy 56, Elkhart, KS 67950

ELLIS — B3 *Ellis*

ELLIS LAKESIDE CAMPGROUND (Public) From Jct of I-70 & Washington St (exit 145), S 7 blks on Washington St to 8th St, E 2 blks (E). 2015 rates: $7 to $15. Apr 15 to Nov 15. (785)726-4812

EMPORIA — C5 *Lyon*

EMPORIA RV PARK **Ratings: 5.5/8.5/4.5** (RV Park) 2015 rates: $30. (620)343-3422 4601 W Hwy 50, Emporia, KS 66801

FALL RIVER — D5 *Greenwood*

DAMSITE (COE - FALL RIVER LAKE) (State Pk) From town: Go 3-1/2 mi W on Hwy 96, then 1-1/2 mi N on Cummings Rd. Follow signs. 2015 rates: $5 to $35. Apr 1 to Oct 30. (620)658-4445

FALL RIVER LAKE/QUARRY BAY AREA (State Pk) From town, W 4 mi on Hwy 400 to Country Rd, N 3 mi (R). 2015 rates: $5 to $35. Apr 15 to Oct 15. (620)637-2213

FALL RIVER LAKE/ROCK RIDGE NORTH (Public Corps) From town, W 6.3 mi on US-400 to CR-19, N 2.5 mi to Chan Cat Rd. E 1.6 mi. Pit toilets. 2015 rates: $9 to $16. Apr 1 to Oct 31. (620)658-4445

FALL RIVER LAKE/SPILLWAY DAMSITE (Public Corps) From town, N on US-400, immediate right turn at Fall River exit follow signs (E). 2015 rates: $10 to $17. Apr 1 to Oct 31. (620)658-4445

FALL RIVER LAKE/WHITEHALL BAY AREA (Public Corps) From town, N on US-400, immediate right turn at Fall River exit, follow signs (E). 2015 rates: $17 to $21. Apr 1 to Oct 30. (620)658-4445

FALL RIVER/FREDONIA BAY AREA (State Pk) From Jct of US-54 & SR-99, S 12 mi on SR-99 to US-400, E 7.7 mi to park access rd (Cummings Rd), N 2.4 mi (E). Entrance fee required. 2015 rates: $5 to $35. Apr 15 to Oct 15. (620)637-2213

NORTH ROCK RIDGE COVE (COE - FALL RIVER LAKE) (Public Corps) From town: Go 3-1/2 mi W on Hwy 96, then 1-1/2 mi N on Cummings Rd. Follow signs. Pit toilets. 2015 rates: $9 to $16. Apr 1 to Oct 31. (620)658-4445

GARDEN CITY — C2 *Finney*

RJ'S RV PARK
Ratings: 7/6/7 (RV Park) From South Jct of US-83 & US-50: Go 1mi E on US-50 (R). Elev 2800 ft. **FAC:** Gravel rds. (61 spaces). Avail: 41 gravel, 41 pull-thrus (24 x 60), mostly side by side hkups, 31 full hkups, 10 W, 10 E (30/50 amps), seasonal sites, cable, WiFi, tent sites, rentals, dump, laundry, groc. **REC:** pool, playground. Pets OK. 2015 rates: $29.
(620)276-8741 Lat: 37.96002, Lon: -100.82188
4100 E Hwy 50, Garden City, KS 67846
See ad this page.

Travel Services

CUMMINS CENTRAL POWER Cummins Central Power is the exclusive distributor for Cummins and Onan products in the Midwest. 12 full service locations in Nebraska, Missouri, Kansas, Iowa, South Dakota and Illinois support engine and generator customers. **SERVICES:** Engine/chassis repair, emergency rd svc, guest serv, restrooms. Emergency parking, RV accessible. waiting room. Hours: 7am to 5pm.
(620)275-2277 Lat: 38.008548, Lon: -100.885131
1285 Acraway St, Garden City, KS 67846
centralpower@cummins.com
www.cumminscentralpower.com
See ad page 732.

We appreciate your business!

GIRARD — D6 *Crawford*

LAKE CRAWFORD (State Pk) From Jct of SR-47 & SR-7 (in town), N 9.3 mi on SR-7 to SR-277, E 0.8 mi (E). Caution: Rapid water crossing at dam during heavy rainfall. 2015 rates: $5 to $35. (620)362-3671

GLEN ELDER — B4 *Mitchell*

GLEN ELDER (State Pk) From Jct of US-24 & SR-128, E 1.1 mi on US-24 (R). Entrance fee required. 2015 rates: $5 to $35. (785)545-3345

GODDARD — D4 *Sedgwick*

LAKE AFTON PARK (Public) From town, S 3 mi on 199th Rd to 39th St S, W 3 mi (L). 2015 rates: $7 to $11. (316)794-2774

GOODLAND — B1 *Sherman*

GOODLAND KOA KAMPGROUND **Ratings: 7/8/8** (Campground) 2015 rates: $29 to $37. Mar 15 to Oct 31. (785)890-5701 1114 E Hwy 24, Goodland, KS 67735

MID AMERICA CAMP INN
Ratings: 6/4/6 (RV Park) From Jct I-70 & Hwy 27 (West Goodland exit 17): Go 1/4 mi S on Hwy 27 (R). Elev 3700 ft. **FAC:** Paved rds. 91 Avail: 81 paved, 10 grass, 91 pull-thrus (35 x 60), 91 full hkups (30/50 amps), cable, WiFi, tent sites, dump, laundry. **REC:** playground. Pets OK. Big rig sites, 2015 rates: $30 to $38.
(785)899-5431 Lat: 39.32393, Lon: -101.72813
2802 Commerce Rd, Goodland, KS 67735
reservations@midamericacamp.com
www.midamericacamp.com
See ad this page.

HALSTEAD — C4 *Harvey*

SPRING LAKE RV RESORT **Ratings: 8.5/4.5/8.5** (Membership Pk) 2015 rates: $26 to $28. (316)835-3443 1308 South Spring Lake Rd., Halstead, KS 67056

HESSTON — C4 *Harvey*

COTTONWOOD GROVE CAMPGROUND Ratings: 2/5/5.5 (Campground) From Jct I-135 (exit 40) & Lincoln Blvd/CR-556: Go 1/4 mi E on CR-556 (E Lincoln Blvd) (L). **FAC:** Gravel rds. 22 gravel, 22 pull-thrus (24 x 45), some side by side hkups, 22 full hkups (30/50 amps), tent sites, dump, laundry. **REC:** Middle Emma Creek: fishing. Pets OK. 2015 rates: $30. No CC.
(620)327-4173 Lat: 38.14465, Lon: -97.41259
1001 E Lincoln Blvd, Hesston, KS 67062
crwalker@cottonwoodgrove.com
www.cottonwoodgrove.com

HILLSDALE — B6 *Miami*

HILLSDALE (State Pk) S-bnd: From Jct of US-169 & 255 St, W 5 mi on 255 St (R); or N-bnd: From Jct of US-169 & SR-68, W 5.5 mi on SR-68 to Osawatomie Rd, N 2.5 mi (L). Entrance fee required. 2015 rates: $5 to $35. Apr 15 to Oct 15. (913)783-4507

Canada — know the rules, regulations and tips before crossing the border. This is listed at the beginning of the country.

HOISINGTON — C3 *Barton*

HOISINGTON RV PARK (Public) From E jct US 281 & K-4: Go 2 blks E on K-4, then 1 blk N on Susank Rd, (behind Activity Center). 2015 rates: $15. (620)653-4311

HORTON — A6 *Brown*

HORTON MISSION LAKE CAMPGROUND (Public) From Jct of Hwys 159 & 73, E 3 blks on Hwy 73 to Wilson Dr, N 0.25 mi (E). 2015 rates: $7 to $10. Apr 1 to Oct 31. (785)486-2324

HUTCHINSON — C4 *Reno*

APPLEWOOD MEADOWS MHP & RV PARK (RV Spaces) From E Jct US-50 & Hwy-61: Go 2.25 mi N on Hwy 61, then .75 mi E on 4th Ave. **FAC:** Paved rds. (35 spaces). Avail: 10 paved, 5 pull-thrus (40 x 90), back-ins (40 x 50), 10 full hkups (50 amps), seasonal sites, WiFi, laundry. Pet restrict(B/Q). No tents. 2015 rates: $30. No CC.
(620)860-4655 Lat: 38.0577, Lon: -97.88894
2214 E 4th Ave, Hutchinson, KS 67501
office@applewoodmeadows.com
www.applewoodmeadows.com

KANSAS STATE FAIR RV PARK (State Pk) From jct KS-61 & E 30th Ave: Go W 2-3/4 mi on 30th Ave, then S 3/4 mi on N Main St, then E 330 yds on 20th Ave. (L). 2015 rates: $20. (620)669-3600

INDEPENDENCE — D6 *Montgomery*

ELK CITY (State Pk) W-bnd: From Jct of US-75 & US-160 (in town), W 1.8 mi on US-160 to Peter Pan rd., N 1 mi to CR-4600, W 2.2 mi to County Park Rd, ; or N-bnd: From Jct of US-75 (from Okla) & US-160, E 0.2 mi on US-160 to Peter Pan Rd., follow above directions. 2015 rates: $5 to $35. Apr 15 to Oct 31. (620)331-6295

IOLA — C6 *Allen*

STORAGE & RV OF IOLA **Ratings: 5/7.5/6** (RV Park) 2015 rates: $25. (620)365-2200 1327 US-54 Hwy, Iola, KS 66749

JETMORE — C2 *Hodgeman*

JETMORE See also Dodge City & Wakeeney.

HORSETHIEF RESERVOIR
(Public) From jct of US-283/Main St & Hwy 156: Go W 9-1/2 mi on Hwy 156 (L). Do not rely on GPS - CALL. **FAC:** Gravel rds. (42 spaces). 32 Avail: 3 paved, 29 gravel, patios, 11 pull-thrus (35 x 120), back-ins (35 x 80), 32 W, 32 E (30/50 amps), tent sites, rentals, dump, groc, fire rings, firewood. **REC:** Horse Thief Reservoir: swim, fishing, playground, rec open to public. Pets OK. Partial handicap access. 14 day max stay, 2015 rates: $9 to $18.
(620)253-8464 Lat: 38.072521, Lon: -100.063510
19005 SW Hwy 156, Jetmore, KS 67854
htr_hobbs@yahoo.com
www.horsethiefres.com
See ad page 501.

JUNCTION CITY — B5 *Geary*

CURTIS CREEK (Public Corps) From Jct of I-70 & US-77, N 5 mi on US-77 to SR-244, W 4 mi to CR-837, N 6 mi (R). 2015 rates: $12 to $18. Apr 15 to Sep 30. (785)238-5714

WEST ROLLING HILLS PARK (Public Corps) From Jct of I-70 & US-77, N 5 mi on US-77 to SR-244, W 3 mi (R). 2015 rates: $12 to $19. Apr 15 to Sep 30. (785)238-5714

How much will it all cost? Use this as a guide: Rates shown are the minimum and maximum for two adults in one RV at the time of inspection (excluding any additional fees for items not at the site). Remember, these rates serve as guidelines only. It's always best to call ahead for the most current rate information.

KANSAS CITY — B6 *Wyandotte*

METROPOLITAN KANSAS CITY AREA MAP

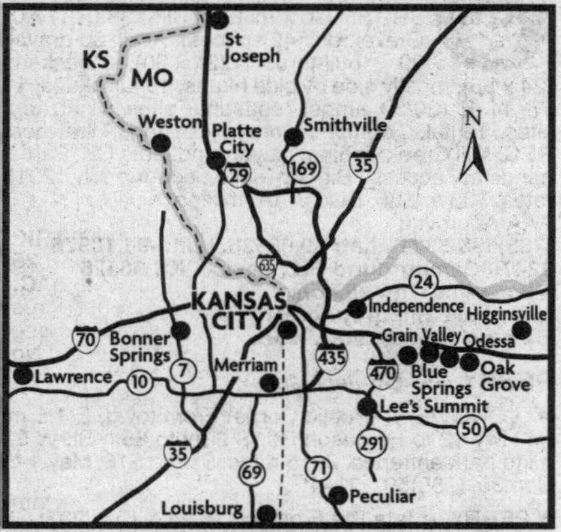

Symbols on map indicate towns within a 40 mile radius of Kansas City where campgrounds are listed. Check listings for more information.

In KS, see also Bonner Springs, Lawrence, Louisburg & Merriam. In MO, see also Blue Springs, Grain Valley, Higginsville, Independence, Lee's Summit, Oak Grove, Odessa, Peculiar, Platte City, Smithville, St Joseph & Weston.

KINGMAN — D4 *Kingman*

KINGMAN STATE FISHING LAKE (State Pk) From Jct of US-54 & SR-14, W 7.8 mi on US-54 to Kingman Lake Rd, N 0.5 mi (L). Pit toilets. 2015 rates: $5 to $35. (620)532-3242

KINSLEY — C3 *Edwards*

FOUR ACES RV PARK **Ratings: 6.5/7.5/7** (Campground) 2015 rates: $30. (620)659-2321 1004 Massachusetts, Kinsley, KS 67547

LA CROSSE — C3 *Rush*

LACROSSE CITY PARK (Public) In town on US-183, E-SIDE, BETWEEN 2ND AND 4TH STREETS. (785)222-2511

LAWRENCE — B6 *Douglas*

CLINTON (State Pk) From Jct of I-70 & 10 Hwy (exit 197), E 3.6 mi on East 10 Hwy to Clinton Pkwy, W 100 ft to E-900 Rd, N 0.2 mi (2nd left to entrance). 2015 rates: $5 to $35. (785)842-8562

LAWRENCE / KANSAS CITY CAMPGROUND **Ratings: 9/10★/9.5** (Campground) From jct I-70 (exit 204) & US-59: Go N 1/2 mi on US-59, then E 1/4 mi on US-24 (R). **FAC:** Gravel rds. (96 spaces). Avail: 70 gravel, patios, 51 pull-thrus (24 x 65), back-ins (21 x 45), some side by side hkups, 61 full hkups, 9 W, 9 E (30/50 amps), seasonal sites, cable, WiFi, tent sites, rentals, dump, laundry, groc, LP gas, fire rings, firewood. **REC:** pool, shuffleboard, playground. Pet restrict(B). Big rig sites, eco-friendly, 2015 rates: $27.50 to $49.50. Disc: AAA, military.
(785)842-3877 Lat: 39.00029, Lon: -95.22891
1473 N. 1800 Rd/Hwy 24/40, Lawrence, KS 66044
camp@kcjellystone.com
www.kcjellystone.com
See ad pages 695, 498.

Don't camp without it ... Our 2016 listings are your key to travel satisfaction.

LEBO — C5 *Osage*

MELVERN LAKE/SUN DANCE PARK (Public Corps) From town, N 3 mi on cnty rd, follow signs (R). Pit toilets. (785)549-3318

LIBERAL — D1 *Seward*

ARKALON RV PARK (Public) From US 54 & US 83: Go 10 mi E on US 54. 2015 rates: $5 to $10. Apr 1 to Oct 31. (620)626-0531

WESTERN STAR RV RANCH Ratings: 7.5/8/8.5 (RV Park) From jct Hwy-54 & Hwy-83: Go E 5 mi on Hwy 54. (R) Note: Do not rely on GPS, call for directions. Elev 2777 ft. **FAC:** All weather rds. 38 Avail: 38 all weather, 30 pull-thrus (30 x 75), back-ins (30 x 75), 38 full hkups (30/50 amps), WiFi, dump, laundry, LP gas. **REC:** whirlpool. Pets OK. Partial handicap access, no tents. Big rig sites, eco-friendly, 2015 rates: $30 to $32.
(888)248-3129 Lat: 37.08326, Lon: -100.83345
13916 Road 7, Liberal, KS 67901

LIBERTY — D6 *Montgomery*

BIG CHIEF RV PARK **Ratings: 4.5/7/4.5** (Campground) 2015 rates: $25. (620)251-8888 2649 N Hwy 169, Liberty, KS 67351

LINN VALLEY — B6 *Linn*

LINN VALLEY LAKES **Ratings: 8.5/5.5/7.5** (Membership Pk) 2015 rates: $10. (913)757-4591 9 Linn Valley Ave., Linn Valley, KS 66040

LOUISBURG — B6 *Miami*

RUTLADER OUTPOST & RV PARK **Ratings: 8/9★/8.5** (Campground) From Jct US-69 South & 335th St (7 mi S of Louisburg): Go 1/2 mi E on 335th St, then 100 ft S on Metcalf Rd (L). **FAC:** Gravel rds. 72 gravel, 24 pull-thrus (27 x 70), back-ins (30 x 60), accepts full hkup units only, 72 full hkups (30/50 amps), WiFi, dump, laundry, groc, LP bottles. **REC:** pond, fishing, playground. Pets OK. Partial handicap access, no tents. Big rig sites, eco-friendly, 2015 rates: $33. Disc: AAA, military.
AAA Approved
(866)888-6779 Lat: 38.51845, Lon: -94.67635
33565 Metcalf Rd., Louisburg, KS 66053
brendah2@rutladeroutpost.com
www.rutladeroutpost.com
See ad pages 695, 498.

LYNDON — C6 *Osage*

LYNDON See also Topeka & Ottawa.

CARBOLYN PARK (Public Corps) From Jct of US-75 & SR-268, N 2 mi on US-75 (R). 2015 rates: $16. May 1 to Sep 30. (785)453-2201

CROSSROADS RV PARK & CAMPGROUND **Ratings: 7/7.5/9** (Campground) From Jct US-75 & SR-31/SR-268: Go .3 mi N on US-75 (L). **FAC:** Gravel rds. 45 gravel, 42 pull-thrus (30 x 65), back-ins (35 x 35), 45 full hkups (30/50 amps), WiFi, tent sites, rentals, laundry, groc, LP gas, firewood. **REC:** pond, fishing, playground. Pets OK. Partial handicap access. Big rig sites, 2015 rates: $32. Disc: military.
(785)221-5482 Lat: 38.644788, Lon: -95.684532
23313 S. US Hwy 75, Lyndon, KS 66451
www.crossroadsrvpark.com
See ad this page, 498.

EISENHOWER (State Pk) From Jct of US-75 & SR-278, W 3 mi on SR-278 (L). 2015 rates: $5 to $35. (785)528-4102

MANHATTAN — B5 *Pottawatomie, Riley*

STOCKDALE CAMPGROUND (Public Corps) From town, N 12 mi on US-24 to CR-895, N 1.5 mi to CR-396, E 2.5 mi (L). 2015 rates: $18. Apr 15 to Oct 31. (785)539-8511

TUTTLE CREEK COVE (Public Corps) From town, N 5 mi on US-24 to KS-13, N 0.2 mi to CR-897S, NW 4 mi (E). 2015 rates: $12 to $18. Apr 15 to Oct 31. (785)539-6523

TUTTLE CREEK/FANCY CREEK (State Pk) From town, N 20 mi on Hwy 24 to park (R). 2015 rates: $5 to $35. (785)539-7941

TUTTLE CREEK/RIVER POND (State Pk) From town, N 5 mi on Hwy 24 to park (R). 2015 rates: $5 to $35. (785)539-7941

TUTTLE CREEK/RIVER POND AREA (State Pk) From Jct of US-24 & SR-177, N 5 mi on W US-24 (Tuttle Creek Blvd) to park access rd (R). Entrance fee required. 2015 rates: $5 to $35. (785)539-7941

MANKATO — A4 *Jewell*

LOVEWELL (State Pk) From Jct of US-36 & K-14, N 8.8 mi on K-14 to unmarked cnty rd (pk access rd), E 4 mi to park access rd, S 0.4 mi (E). 2015 rates: $5 to $35. (785)753-4971

MARION — C4 *Marion*

MARION COUNTY PARK & LAKE (Public) From town, E 2 mi on US-256 to Upland Rd, S 2 mi on Upland Rd to Lakeshore Dr, W 0.5 mi on Lakeshore Dr (E). 2015 rates: $6 to $12. (620)382-3240

MARQUETTE — C4 *Ellsworth*

KANOPOLIS (State Pk) From jct Hwy-14 & Hwy-140: Go 12 mi E on Hwy-140, then 11 mi S onHwy-141. 2015 rates: $5 to $35. (785)546-2565

KANOPOLIS LAKE/HORSETHIEF CANYON (State Pk) From town, W 9 mi on K-4 to K-141, N 5 mi to Venango Rd, W 0.25 to park access rd, NW 0.25 (L). 2015 rates: $5 to $35. (785)546-2565

KANOPOLIS LAKE/LANGLEY POINT (State Pk) From town, W 9 mi on K-4 to K-141, N 4 mi (L). 2015 rates: $5 to $35. (785)546-2565

KANOPOLIS LAKE/RIVERSIDE AREA (Public Corps) From town, W 9 mi on Hwy 4 to Hwy 141, N 3 mi (R). 2015 rates: $6 to $18. (785)546-2294

KANOPOLIS LAKE/VENANGO AREA (Public Corps) From town, NW 8 mi on Hwy 4 to Hwy 141, N 4 mi (L). 2015 rates: $6 to $24. May 1 to Dec 31. (785)546-2294

MAYETTA — B5 *Jackson*

PRAIRIE BAND CASINO RESORT RV PARK **Ratings: 10/9.5★/9** (RV Park) 2015 rates: $31.50. (877)727-4946 12305 150th Rd, Mayetta, KS 66509

MCPHERSON — C4 *McPherson*

MCPHERSON See also Halstead, Hesston, Hutchinson & Wichita.

MCPHERSON RV RANCH & HORSE MOTEL **Ratings: 7/8.5/5.5** (Campground) From Jct I-135 & US-56 (exit 60): Go 0.5 mi W on US-56, then 1.4 mi N on Centennial Dr, then .2 mi E on Northview (L). **FAC:** Gravel rds. (27 spaces). Avail: 14 gravel, 14 pull-thrus (24 x 70), 14 full hkups (30/50 amps), seasonal sites, WiFi, tent sites, laundry, fire rings. **REC:** pond, fishing, playground. Pets OK. Big rig sites, eco-friendly, 2015 rates: $30.
(620)241-5621 Lat: 38.39394, Lon: -97.62487
2201 E Northview Ave., Mcpherson, KS 67460
mcphersonrvranch@yahoo.com
www.mcphersonrvranch.com
See ad this page.

MEADE — D2 *Meade*

CIRCLE-O RV PARK & MOTEL Ratings: 4/4/4.5 (RV Park) From Jct Hwy 23 & US-160/54: Go .3 mi E on US-160/54 (L). **FAC:** Poor gravel/dirt rds. (32 spaces). 24 Avail: 12 gravel, 12 grass, back-ins (22 x 46), some side by side hkups, 12 full hkups, 12 W, 12 E (30/50 amps), seasonal sites, cable, WiFi, dump, laundry. **REC.** Pets OK. No tents. 2015 rates: $20 to $25.
AAA Approved
(620)873-2543 Lat: 37.28574, Lon: -100.33230
700 E Carthage, Meade, KS 67864
kcslate@hotmail.com

MEADE (State Pk) From Jct of US-54 & K-23, SW 13 mi on K-23 (R). 2015 rates: $5 to $35. (620)873-2572

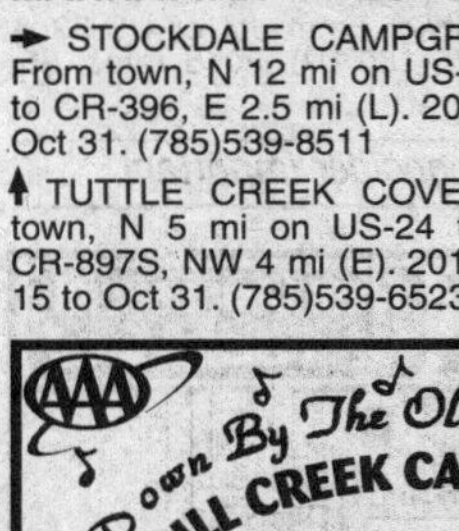

MELVERN — C6 *Osage*

MELVERN LAKE (COE - MELVERN LAKE) (Public) From town: Go 3 mi W on Hwy 31. 2015 rates: $12 to $18. (785)549-3318

MELVERN LAKE/COEUR D'ALENE (Public Corps) From Jct of US-75 & SH-31 exit, S 1.5 mi on SH-31 to Coeur D'Alene Pkwy, NW 1 mi (E). 2015 rates: $12 to $20. May 1 to Sep 30. (785)549-3318

MELVERN LAKE/OUTLET PARK (Public Corps) From Jct of US-75 & SH-31 exit, W 0.25 mi on SH-31 to cut-off rd, NW 0.25 mi to River Pond Pkwy, N 0.5 mi (E). 2015 rates: $18 to $54. Apr 1 to Oct 31. (785)549-3318

MERRIAM — B6 *Johnson*

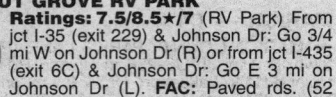

WALNUT GROVE RV PARK
Ratings: 7.5/8.5★/7 (RV Park) From jct I-35 (exit 229) & Johnson Dr: Go 3/4 mi W on Johnson Dr (R) or from jct I-435 (exit 6C) & Johnson Dr: Go E 3 mi on Johnson Dr (L). **FAC:** Paved rds. (52 spaces). Avail: 17 gravel, 7 pull-thrus (24 x 65), back-ins (24 x 45), some side by side hkups, 17 full hkups (30/50 amps), seasonal sites, WiFi, dump, laundry, LP bottles, fire rings, firewood. **REC.** Pets OK. Partial handicap access, no tents. Big rig sites, 2015 rates: $33 to $50. Disc: military. ATM.
(913)262-3023 Lat: 39.0228, Lon: -94.70520
10218 Johnson Dr, Merriam, KS 66203
info@walnutgroverv.com
www.walnutgroverv.com
See ad pages 695, 498.

MILFORD — B5 *Geary*

FARNUM CREEK (Public Corps) From town, S 2 mi on US-77 (R). 2015 rates: $12 to $19. Apr 15 to Sep 30. (785)463-5791

MILFORD (State Pk) From Jct of I-70 & US-77 (exit 295), N 4.5 mi on US-77 to SR-57, W 4.1 mi (L). 2015 rates: $5 to $35. (785)238-3014

NORTON — A2 *Norton*

PRAIRIE DOG (State Pk) W-bnd: From Jct of US-283 & US-36, W 4 mi on US-36 to SR-261, S 1 mi (E); or E-bnd: From Jct of US-36 & SR-383, E 2 mi on US-36 to SR-261, S 1 mi (E). Entrance fee required. 2015 rates: $5 to $35. Apr 15 to Oct 15. (785)877-2953

OAKLEY — B2 *Logan, Thomas*

HIGH PLAINS CAMPING
Ratings: 8/9.5★/7.5 (RV Park) From Jct I-70 & US-83 (exit 70), Go 200 yds S on US-83 (R). Elev 3078 ft. **FAC:** Paved/gravel rds. 52 Avail: 44 gravel, 8 grass, 52 pull-thrus (36 x 70), some side by side hkups, 52 full hkups (30/50 amps), cable, WiFi, tent sites, dump, laundry, groc, LP gas, restaurant. **REC:** pool, whirlpool, rec open to public. Pets OK. Big rig sites, eco-friendly, 2015 rates: $35 to $40. Disc: AAA, military.
AAA Approved
(785)672-3538 Lat: 39.18596, Lon: -100.87113
462 US 83, Oakley, KS 67748
office@highplainscamping.com
www.highplainscamping.com

OGALLAH — B2 *Trego*

CEDAR BLUFF SP (BLUFFTON AREA) (State Pk) From jct I-70 (exit 135) & Hwy 147: Go 13 mi S on Hwy 147. 2015 rates: $5 to $35. (785)726-3212

CEDAR BLUFF SP (PAGE CREEK AREA) (State Pk) From jct I-70 & Hwy-147: Go 19 mi S on Hwy-147, then 4 mi W on countyroad. 2015 rates: $5 to $35. (785)726-3212

Looking for places the "locals" frequent? Make friends with park owners and staff to get the inside scoop!

OLIVET — C5 *Osage*

MELVERN LAKE/ARROW ROCK (Public Corps) From Jct of US-75 & Olivet exit (CR-276), W 1 mi on CR-276 to S Fairlawn Rd, N 1 mi to Arrow Rock Pkwy, W 1 mi (E). 2015 rates: $12 to $18. May 1 to Sep 30. (785)549-3318

OSAGE CITY — B5 *Osage*

MELVERN LAKE/TURKEY POINT (Public Corps) From town, S 8 mi on K-170 to 301st St, E 2 mi to Indian Hills Rd, S 1 mi to Turkey Point Pkwy, S 0.5 mi (E). 2015 rates: $12 to $19. May 1 to Sep 30. (785)549-3318

OSWEGO — D6 *Labette*

HILLSIDE RV PARK **Ratings: 3.5/NA/7.5** (RV Area in MHP) 2015 rates: $20 to $30. (620)795-2471 1108 S Commercial, Oswego, KS 67356

KAMP SIESTA (Public) From Jct of K-96 & Kansas St, N 1 mi on Kansas St to North St, W 1 mi, follow signs (E). 2015 rates: $10. Apr 1 to Oct 31. (620)795-4433

OTTAWA — C6 *Franklin*

ADAMS GROVE (COE-POMONA LAKE) (Public Corps) From town: Go 15 mi W on Hwy 68, then 3 mi W on Hwy 268, then 2 mi N on Lake Rd 1, then 3/4 mi N of dam on lake roads. Pit toilets. 2015 rates: $6. (785)453-2201

HOMEWOOD RV PARK
Ratings: 5.5/9★/7.5 (RV Park) From jct I-35 (exit 176) & Idaho Rd: Go N 1/4 mi on Idaho Rd. (R). **FAC:** Gravel rds. 25 gravel, 10 pull-thrus (24 x 65), back-ins (22 x 50), 25 full hkups (30/50 amps), WiFi, tent sites, dump, laundry, firewood. Pet restrict(B). Partial handicap access. 2015 rates: $25 to $27. No CC.
AAA Approved
(785)242-5601 Lat: 38.53964, Lon: -95.37852
2161 Idaho Rd., Ottawa, KS 66095
homewoodrv@yahoo.com
www.homewoodrvpark.com
See ad this page.

POMONA (State Pk) From Jct of US-75 & SR-268, E 4.4 mi on SR-268 to SR-368, N 1 mi (E). 2015 rates: $5 to $35. (785)828-4933

POMONA LAKE/MICHIGAN VALLEY (Public Corps) From town, E 6.4 mi on SR-268 to Pomona Dam Rd, N 3 mi to Wolf Creek Rd, W 0.1 mi (E). 2015 rates: $12 to $22. May 1 to Sep 30. (785)453-2201

POMONA LAKE/OUTLET PARK (Public Corps) From Jct of US-75 & Rte 268, E 7 mi on Rte 268 to Pomona Dam Rd, N 0.5 mi to 229th St, E 0.25 mi (E). Pit toilets. 2015 rates: $10 to $18. (785)453-2201

POMONA LAKE/WOLF CREEK (Public Corps) From town, N 2 mi on US-75 to Hwy 268, E 6 mi to Pomona Dam Rd, N 2.5 mi to Wolf Creek Pkwy, W 2 mi (E). 2015 rates: $14 to $18. May 1 to Sep 15. (785)453-2201

POMONA LAKE/110 MILE (Public Corps) From Jct of SR-268 & US-75, N 6.7 mi on US-75, follow signs (E). Pit toilets. (785)453-2201

OZAWKIE — B6 *Jefferson*

OLD TOWN (Public Corps) From town, E 1.5 mi on SR-92 (R). 2015 rates: $12 to $17. May 1 to Sep 30. (785)597-5144

PARSONS — D6 *Labette, Neosho*

LAKE PARSONS (Public) From Jct of Main St & 32nd St to Z6000 Rd, W 3 mi to Kiowa Rd, N 2 mi, follow signs (R). 2015 rates: $5 to $12. Apr 1 to Nov 1. (620)421-7031

MARVEL PARK (Public) From Jct of US-59 & US-160, E 0.5 mi on US-160 (R). 2015 rates: $5. (620)421-7000

We rate what RVers consider important.

PAXICO — B5 *Wabaunsee*

MILL CREEK CAMPGROUND & RV PARK
Ratings: 7/9.5★/8 (Campground) From Jct I-70 (Paxico/exit 333) & SR-138: Go 1 mi E on SR-138 (R). **FAC:** Gravel rds. (42 spaces). Avail: 30 gravel, 29 pull-thrus (24 x 90), back-ins (24 x 55), mostly side by side hkups, 19 full hkups, 11 W, 11 E (30/50 amps), seasonal sites, WiFi, tent sites, rentals, dump, laundry, fire rings, firewood. **REC:** Mill Creek: fishing, playground. Pets OK. Partial handicap access. Big rig sites, eco-friendly, 2015 rates: $33 to $35. Disc: AAA, military.
AAA Approved
(785)636-5321 Lat: 39.06526, Lon: -96.16975
22470 Campground Rd., Paxico, KS 66526
Milcreekcg@gmail.com
millcreekcampground.com
See ad pages 503, 498.

PERRY — B6 *Jefferson*

LONGVIEW (Public Corps) From town, E 1.5 mi on Hwy 92 to Ferguson Rd, S 2 mi to 86th St, W 23 mi to park entrance. 2015 rates: $12 to $16. May 1 to Sep 30. (785)597-5144

PERRY (State Pk) From jct US 24 & Hwy 237: Go 4 mi N on Hwy 237. 2015 rates: $5 to $35. (785)246-3449

ROCK CREEK (Public Corps) From town, N 3 mi on Ferguson Rd to 39th St, W 5 mi to Perry Park Dr, N 5 mi to Dam Rd, W 1.5 mi to park entrance. 2015 rates: $12 to $18. May 1 to Sep 30. (785)597-5144

SLOUGH CREEK PARK (Public Corps) From town, N 7 mi on Ferguson Rd to Slough Creek Rd, SW 1.5 mi (E). 2015 rates: $12 to $18. Apr 15 to Oct 15. (785)597-5144

PHILLIPSBURG — A3 *Phillips*

PHILLIPSBURG CAMPGROUND (Public) From Jct of US-36 & Hwy 183, W .5 mi on US-36 (L). 2015 rates: $10. Apr 1 to Oct 31. (785)543-5234

PITTSBURG — D6 *Crawford*

PARKVIEW MH & RV COMMUNITY
Ratings: 7/8.5/9 (RV Area in MHP) From jct US-69/160 & W 20th St: Go .1 mi E on W 20th St. (L). **FAC:** Paved rds. (171 spaces). Avail: 47 gravel, back-ins (35 x 80), 47 full hkups (30/50 amps), seasonal sites, WiFi, laundry. **REC.** Pet restrict(B). Partial handicap access, no tents. Big rig sites, 2015 rates: $30.
(620)232-1030 Lat: 37.42601, Lon: -94.71122
520 W 20th St, Pittsburg, KS 66762
parkview@towermgmt.com
http://parkviewmhc.com/homes.htm

PRATT — D3 *Pratt*

EVERGREEN INN MOTEL & RV PARK **Ratings: 7/8.5/6** (RV Park) 2015 rates: $30 to $35. (800)456-6424 20001 W US-54/400, Pratt, KS 67124

RUSSELL — B3 *Russell*

TRIPLE 'J' RV PARK
Ratings: 7.5/10★/8.5 (RV Park) From Jct I-70 (exit 184) & US-281: Go 500 ft N on US-281 (at Phillips 66 Stn), then 500 ft W on E Edwards Ave. (E). **FAC:** Gravel rds. (68 spaces). Avail: 48 gravel, 48 pull-thrus (24 x 70), some side by side hkups, 48 full hkups (30/50 amps), seasonal sites, cable, WiFi, tent sites, rentals, laundry, fire rings, firewood. **REC:** playground. Pets OK. Big rig sites, 2015 rates: $29 to $32. Disc: AAA, military.
(785)483-4826 Lat: 38.86635, Lon: -98.85729
187 E. Edwards, Russell, KS 67665
triplejrv@ruraltel.net
https://www.triplejrvpark.com
See ad this page, 498.

Are you using a friend's Guide? Want one of your own? Call 877-209-6655.

SALINA — B4 *Saline*

KOA OF SALINA Ratings: 9/10★/7.5 (Campground) From Jct I-70 & 9th St (exit 252): Go 100 ft N on 9th St, then .5 mi W on Diamond Dr. (L). **FAC:** Gravel rds. 63 Avail: 7 paved, 56 gravel, 63 pull-thrus (24 x 70), mostly side by side hkups, 47 full hkups, 16 W, 16 E (30/50 amps), cable, WiFi, tent sites, rentals, dump, laundry, groc, firewood. **REC:** pool, wading pool, pond, fishing, playground. Pet restrict(B). Big rig sites, 2015 rates: $31 to $39. Disc: military.
(785)827-3182 Lat: 38.87775, Lon: -97.62217
1109 W Diamond Dr, Salina, KS 67401
koaofsalina@cox.net
www.koa.com

SCOTT CITY — C2 *Scott*

LAKE SCOTT (State Pk) From Jct of SR-96 & US-83, N 9.7 mi on US-83 to SR-95, NW 3 mi (L). Entrance fee required. 2015 rates: $5 to $35. Apr 10 to Oct 30. (620)872-2061

SENECA — A5 *Nemaha*

STALLBAUMER RV PARK
Ratings: 5.5/9.5★/7.5 (RV Park) From Jct Hwy 63 & US-36 (in town): Go 1.1 mi W on US-36 (North Street) (R) Note: Behind Settle Inn Hotel & Dollar General. **FAC:** Gravel rds. 20 paved, 14 all weather, patios, 20 pull-thrus (24 x 60), back-ins (22 x 45), 34 full hkups (30/50 amps), cable, WiFi, tent sites, dump, laundry. **REC:** pond, fishing. Pets OK. Partial handicap access. Big rig sites, eco-friendly, 2015 rates: $20 to $32. Disc: military.
(785)294-1208 Lat: 39.84171, Lon: -96.07854
1701 North St, Seneca, KS 66538
sstall@rainbowtel.net
www.stallbaumerrvpark.com
See ad this page.

SOUTH HAVEN — D4 *Sumner*

OASIS RV PARK
Ratings: 5/8★/6 (RV Park) From Jct I-35 & US-Hwy 166 (Exit 4): Go 1/2 mi W on US-Hwy 166, then 175 yds N on S. Seneca Rd. (R). **FAC:** Gravel rds. 47 Avail: 47 all weather, 47 pull-thrus (37 x 80), 47 full hkups (30/50 amps), WiFi, tent sites, LP gas. Pets OK. Big rig sites, 2015 rates: $32. Disc: military.
(620)892-5115 Lat: 37.05889, Lon: -97.34679
1592 S Seneca Rd., South Haven, KS 67140
oasisrv@kanokla.net

ST JOHN — C3 *Stafford*

PINE HAVEN RETREAT **Ratings: 3.5/5.5/3.5** (RV Park) 2015 rates: $30. (620)549-3444 217 E US-50, St John, KS 67576

STOCKTON — B3 *Rooks*

ROOKS COUNTY FAIRGROUNDS (CITY PARK) (Public) From jct US 24 & US 183: Go 8-1/2 blocks S on US 183. 2015 rates: $20. (785)425-6703

WEBSTER (State Pk) From Jct of Hwy 183 & Hwy 24, W 8.9 mi on Hwy 24 (L). 2015 rates: $5 to $35. Apr 15 to Oct 15. (785)425-6775

TONGANOXIE — B6 *Leavenworth*

LEAVENWORTH STATE FISHING LAKE (State Pk) From Jct of SR-24 & SR-16, N 3 mi on SR-16 to Hwy 90, W 2 mi (W). Pit toilets. 2015 rates: $5 to $35. (913)845-2665

TOPEKA — B5 *Shawnee*

TOPEKA See also Lawrence, Lyndon, Mayetta & Paxico.

CAPITAL CITY KOA **Ratings: 8.5/10★/8** (Campground) 2015 rates: $35.80 to $49.78. (800)562-4793 1949 SW 49th St, Topeka, KS 66609

DEER CREEK VALLEY RV PARK LLC
Ratings: 10/9.5★/10 (RV Park) From jct I-70 (exit 364B) & Carnahan: Go S 1/4 mi on Carnahan, then E 1/4 mi on 21st St. (L).

TOPEKA'S ONLY LUXURY RV PARK!
Enjoy our level pull thru concrete pads with patios just off I-70. We pamper our pets with a fenced Dog Park, your kids with a heated pool, and you with Wi-Fi, cable and a security access gate. Experience luxury tonight!

FAC: Paved rds. 59 paved, patios, 54 pull-thrus (35 x 95), back-ins (35 x 50), 59 full hkups (30/50 amps), cable, WiFi, dump, laundry, LP gas, controlled access. **REC:** heated pool, playground. Pet restrict(B). Partial handicap access, no tents. Big rig sites, eco-friendly, 2015 rates: $42. Disc: AAA, military.
(785)357-8555 Lat: 39.03068, Lon: -95.63377
3140 SE 21st Street, Topeka, KS 66607
contact@deercreekvalleyrvpark.com
www.deercreekvalleyrvpark.com
See ad pages 506, 498 & Pampered Pets in Magazine Section.

Our Guide to Seasonal Sites will help you find places you can stay for extended periods of time.

FORBES LANDING RV PARK
Ratings: 5.5/9.5★/8 (Campground) From Jct I-470 (Exit 6 & Topeka Blvd): Follow exit ramp directions to SW Topeka Blvd, then go 2-1/4 mi S on SW Topeka Blvd. (L). **FAC:** Gravel rds. 28 gravel, 28 pull-thrus (24 x 65), 28 full hkups (30/50 amps), cable, WiFi, dump. **REC.** Pets OK. Partial handicap access, no tents. Eco-friendly, 2015 rates: $30 to $33. Disc: AAA, military.
AAA Approved
(785)862-8818 Lat: 38.95985, Lon: -95.68562
5932 SW Topeka Blvd., Topeka, KS 66619
info@forbeslandingrvpark.com
www.forbeslandingrvpark.com
See ad this page, 498.

LAKE SHAWNEE CAMPGROUND (SHAWNEE COUNTY) (Public) From I-70 (East Topeka Tnpk exit): Go 1/2 mi SE on 21st St, then 1-1/2 mi S on Croco Rd, then 1/2 mi W on East Edge Rd. 2015 rates: $16 to $20. (785)291-2634

Our rating system isn't just tough, it's thorough. We know the kinds of things that are important to you — like clean restrooms and showers, attractive, secure, well-tended grounds, and extras like swimming pools. We give the first rating for development of facilities, the second for cleanliness and physical characteristics of restrooms and showers, and the third for visual appearance.

KS

• TOPEKA'S FINEST •
DEER CREEK VALLEY
RV PARK
GATED FOR SECURITY
TOP RATED Good Sam Park FOR 2016
Good Sam RATED 10/9.5★/10
See listing Topeka, KS
• All Concrete Roads
• All Sites are 35 x 95 Feet
• All Concrete Sites with 10 x 20 Concrete Patio
• Storm Shelter/Laundry Facility
• Large Enclosed Dog Park
• Heated Swimming Pool
• 30 & 50 Amp • Playground
• Group Meeting Room (10 or more campers)
• 54 Pull-Thru Sites
• 5 Back-Ins
• Free WiFi & Cable TV
3140 SE 21st St. • Topeka, KS • Telephone (785) 357-8555
www.deercreekvalleyrvpark.com
VISA/MASTERCARD/DISCOVER

TORONTO — C5 *Woodson*

CROSS TIMBERS/DAM SITE & HOLIDAY HILL AREA (State Pk) From Jct of US-54 & Hwy 105, S 9 mi on Hwy 105 (L). 2015 rates: $5 to $35. (620)637-2213

CROSS TIMBERS/MANN'S COVE AREA (State Pk) From Jct of US-54 & Hwy 105, S 3.8 mi on Hwy 105 to Hwy 361, SE 2.7 mi (L). 2015 rates: $5 to $35. (620)637-2213

CROSS TIMBERS/TORONTO POINT (State Pk) From Jct of US-54 & SR-105, SE 3.1 mi on SR-105 to Point Rd, S 0.9 mi (E). Entrance fee required. 2015 rates: $5 to $35. (620)637-2213

VALLEY CENTER — C4 *Sedgwick*

NORTH STAR RV PARK
Ratings: 6/8.5/8 (RV Park) From jct I-135 (exit 19) & 101st St: Go 1 mi W on 101st St. (R). **FAC:** Gravel rds. (30 spaces). Avail: 22 gravel, 15 pull-thrus (35 x 70), back-ins (35 x 70), 18 full hkups, 4 W, 4 E (30/50 amps), seasonal sites, WiFi, dump, laundry. **REC:** pool, playground. Pet restrict(B/Q). No tents. Big rig sites, 2015 rates: $29.
(316)755-0592 Lat: 37.86852, Lon: -97.34452
650 W 101st St North, Valley Center, KS 67147
norstar10@earthlink.net
See ad this page, 498.

WAKEENEY — B2 *Trego*

WAKEENEY KOA **Ratings: 7.5/10★/8** (Campground) 2015 rates: $35.50 to $38.50. Mar 15 to Dec 1. (800)562-2761 25027 S. Interstate, Wakeeney, KS 67672

WAKEFIELD — B4 *Clay, Gary*

CLAY COUNTY PARK (Public) From Jct of SR-82 & Dogwood St, S 3 blks on Dogwood St (L). 2015 rates: $16 to $28. Apr 15 to Oct 15. (785)461-5774

SCHOOL CREEK (Public Corps) From town, W 1.4 mi on SR-82 to CR-837, S 7 mi to 2nd Rd, E 4 mi (E). Pit toilets. 2015 rates: $8. (785)238-5714

TIMBER CREEK (Public Corps) From town, E 1.9 mi on SR-82 (E). Pit toilets. 2015 rates: $8. (785)238-5714

WELLINGTON — D4 *Sumner*

WELLINGTON KOA **Ratings: 8.5/10★/8** (Campground) 2015 rates: $39. (800)562-7572 100 South Koa Dr., Wellington, KS 67152

WICHITA — D4 *Sedgwick*

WICHITA See also El Dorado, Halstead, Hesston, South Haven & Valley Center.

AIR CAPITAL RV PARK
Ratings: 9/10★/8.5 (RV Park) From Jct I-135 & 47th St (Exit 1A): Go .2 mi W on 47th St, then 300 ft S on Emporia St (E). **FAC:** Paved rds. 90 paved, 31 pull-thrus (25 x 70), back-ins (25 x 60), 90 full hkups (30/50 amps), cable, WiFi, laundry. **REC:** playground. Pets OK. Partial handicap access, no tents. Big rig sites, eco-friendly, 2015 rates: $44 to $54. Disc: AAA, military.
(316)201-1250 Lat: 37.60778, Lon: -97.33006
609 E 47th St South, Wichita, KS 67216
aircapitalrvpark@yahoo.com
www.aircapital-rvpark.com
See ad pages 500 (Spotlight Wichita Area), 498.

ALL SEASONS RV PARK-WICHITA
Ratings: 8/10★/8.5 (RV Park) W-bnd: From Jct of I-235 & Hwy 54, W 4.4 mi on Hwy 54 to 119th St, N 1 mi to Maple, W 2.25 mi (R); or E-bnd: From Jct of Hwy 54 & 167th St (1 mi E of Goddard), N 1 mi on 167th St to Maple, E 0.75 mi (L). **FAC:** Gravel rds. (48 spaces). Avail: 30 gravel, 30 pull-thrus (24 x 65), mostly side by side hkups, 30 full hkups (30/50 amps), seasonal sites, cable, WiFi, tent sites, dump, laundry, groc, LP gas. **REC:** playground. Pet restrict(B) $. Big rig sites, eco-friendly, 2015 rates: $34 to $37. Disc: AAA.
AAA Approved
(316)722-1154 Lat: 37.67903, Lon: -97.52080
15520 W Maple Street, Goddard, KS 67052
office@allseasonsrvcampground.com
www.allseasonsrvcampground.com
See ad pages 500 (Spotlight Wichita Area), 498.

Take time now to plan a road trip with your pet for meaningful memories that last a lifetime. Read more in our Pampered Pet Parks feature at the front of the Guide.

K & R RV PARK (RV Spaces) From Jct I-35 N-bnd (Exit 45), W to Tollbooth, N 0.9 (After tollbooth) on Southeast Blvd to 31 St, E 0.75 mi on 31 St (R); or S-bnd: From Jct I-35 & Southeast Blvd, N 0.9 mi on Southeast Blvd to 31 St, E 0.75 mi (R). **FAC:** Paved rds. (63 spaces). Avail: 10 grass, patios, 10 pull-thrus (30 x 45), 10 full hkups (50 amps), seasonal sites, WiFi, laundry. Pet restrict(B/Q). No tents. 2015 rates: $30 to $35.
(316)684-1531 Lat: 37.63499, Lon: -97.28973
3200 S. Sotheast Blvd, Wichita, KS 67216
office@kandrrvpark.com
www.kandrrvpark.com

USI RV PARK
Ratings: 8.5/10★/8.5 (RV Park) N-bnd: From Jct I-135 (exit 10-A) & K-96 bypass: Go 1mi E on K-96 bypass, then 300 ft N on Hillside, then .1 mi W on N 33rd St. Or S Bnd: From Jct I-135 (Exit 10) & K-96 bypass: Go 1 mi E on K-96 bypass, then 300 ft N on Hillside, then .1 mi W on N 33rd St (R). **FAC:** All weather rds. (75 spaces). Avail: 42 all weather, 42 pull-thrus (24 x 60), 42 full hkups (30/50 amps), seasonal sites, WiFi, dump, laundry, LP gas. **REC:** playground. Pet restrict(B/Q). No tents. Big rig sites, eco-friendly, 2015 rates: $34 to $50. Disc: military.
(316)838-8699 Lat: 37.74530, Lon: -97.30212
2920 E 33rd St N, Wichita, KS 67219
info@usirvpark.com
www.usirvpark.com
See ad pages 499 (Spotlight Wichita Area), 498.

Travel Services

CUMMINS CENTRAL POWER Cummins Central Power is the exclusive distributor for Cummins and Onan products in the Midwest. 12 full service locations in Nebraska, Missouri, Kansas, Iowa, South Dakota and Illinois support engine and generator customers. **SERVICES:** Engine/chassis repair, mobile RV svc, restrooms. Emergency parking, RV accessible. waiting room. Hours: 7am to 5pm.
(316)838-0875 Lat: 37.776525, Lon: -97.338134
5101 N Broadway St, Wichita, KS 67219
centralpower@cummins.com
www.cumminscentralpower.com
See ad page 732.

WILSON — B3 *Russell*

WILSON LAKE/LUCAS PARK (Public Corps) From Jct of I-70 & SR-232 (exit 206), N 9 mi on SR-232 to access rd, W 2 mi (E). For reservations call (877)444-6777. 2015 rates: $8 to $24. (785)658-2551

WILSON LAKE/SYLVAN PARK (Public Corps) From Jct of I-70 & SR-232 (exit 206), N 10 mi on SR-232 to Hwy 181, E 0.25 mi to access rd (E). For reservations call (877)444-6777. 2015 rates: $10 to $20. (785)658-2551

WILSON SP (HELL CREEK CAMPGROUND) (State Pk) Jct I-70 & Hwy 232: Go 8 miles N on Hwy 232. 2015 rates: $5 to $35. (785)658-2465

WILSON SP (OTOE AREA CAMPGROUND) (State Pk) Jct I-70 & Hwy 232: Go 8 miles N on Hwy 232. 2015 rates: $5 to $35. (785)658-2465

WINFIELD — D5 *Cowley*

WINFIELD FAIRGROUNDS (Public) From Jct of US-77 & SR-160, W 1 mi on SR-160 (L). 2015 rates: $3 to $10. (620)221-5525

Thank you for using our 2016 Guide. Now you have all the latest information about RV parks, campgrounds and RV resorts across North America!

KS

photos by Z

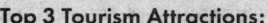

WELCOME TO Kentucky

DATE OF STATEHOOD	WIDTH: 140 MILES (225 KM)	PROPORTION OF UNITED STATES
JUNE 1, 1792	LENGTH: 380 MILES (612 KM)	1.07% OF 3,794,100 SQ MI

Famous Kentucky Bluegrass gets its name from the blue flowers that bloom when the plant is permitted to reach its full height of three feet. The nibbling of the world's finest thoroughbred horses, however, never allows those flowers to emerge in the American state synonymous with racing, immaculate horse farms and mint juleps.

Learn

Daniel Boone led settlers to the Kentucky River in 1775 and started a government in the Colonial wilderness at Fort Boonesborough. Now a state park, the complex of cabins and blockhouses has been recreated to tell the story of pioneer life in Kentucky. So many homesteaders followed Boone's path through the Cumberland Gap that Kentucky became the first state admitted to the Union west of the Allegheny Mountains. Today the Cumberland Gap National Historic Park preserves sections of the Wilderness Road, America's first national highway, along with exhibits and interpretive displays.

At the Kentucky River Museum in Fort Boonesborough, visitors will discover the impact of America's largest network of navigable waterways. For a close-up look at life on Kentucky's most influential river, the paddleboat Belle of Louisville offers tours on America's oldest steam riverboat.

Kentucky was a border state during the Civil War, sending one-tenth of its 1860s population to fight—75,000 on the Union side and 45,000 to wear the colors of the Confederate States of America. There were 453 sites of action here, with the climatic major battle occurring at Perryville, now a state historic site, in the autumn of 1862. Confederate troops carried the day but eventually were forced to abandon Kentucky to the northerners.

Play

Not to be confused with extinct woolly elephants, Mammoth Cave earned its name as the world's longest

Top 3 Tourism Attractions:
1) Mammoth Cave National Park
2) Churchill Downs
3) Shaker Village of Pleasant Hill

Nickname: Bluegrass State

State Flower: Goldenrod

State Bird: Kentucky Cardinal

People: Muhammad Ali, boxer; Kit Carson, scout and Indian agent; Johnny Depp, actor; Abraham Lincoln, 16th president

Major Cities: Louisville, Lexington, Bowling Green, Owensboro, Covington, (Frankfort, capital)

Topography: East—mountains; north central—rolling meadows; south central—flatlands, rolling hills; northwest—coal fields; west—flood plains

Climate: Moderate, humid climate with abundant rainfall; southern and lowlands are slightly warmer than uplands

Kentucky Department of Travel

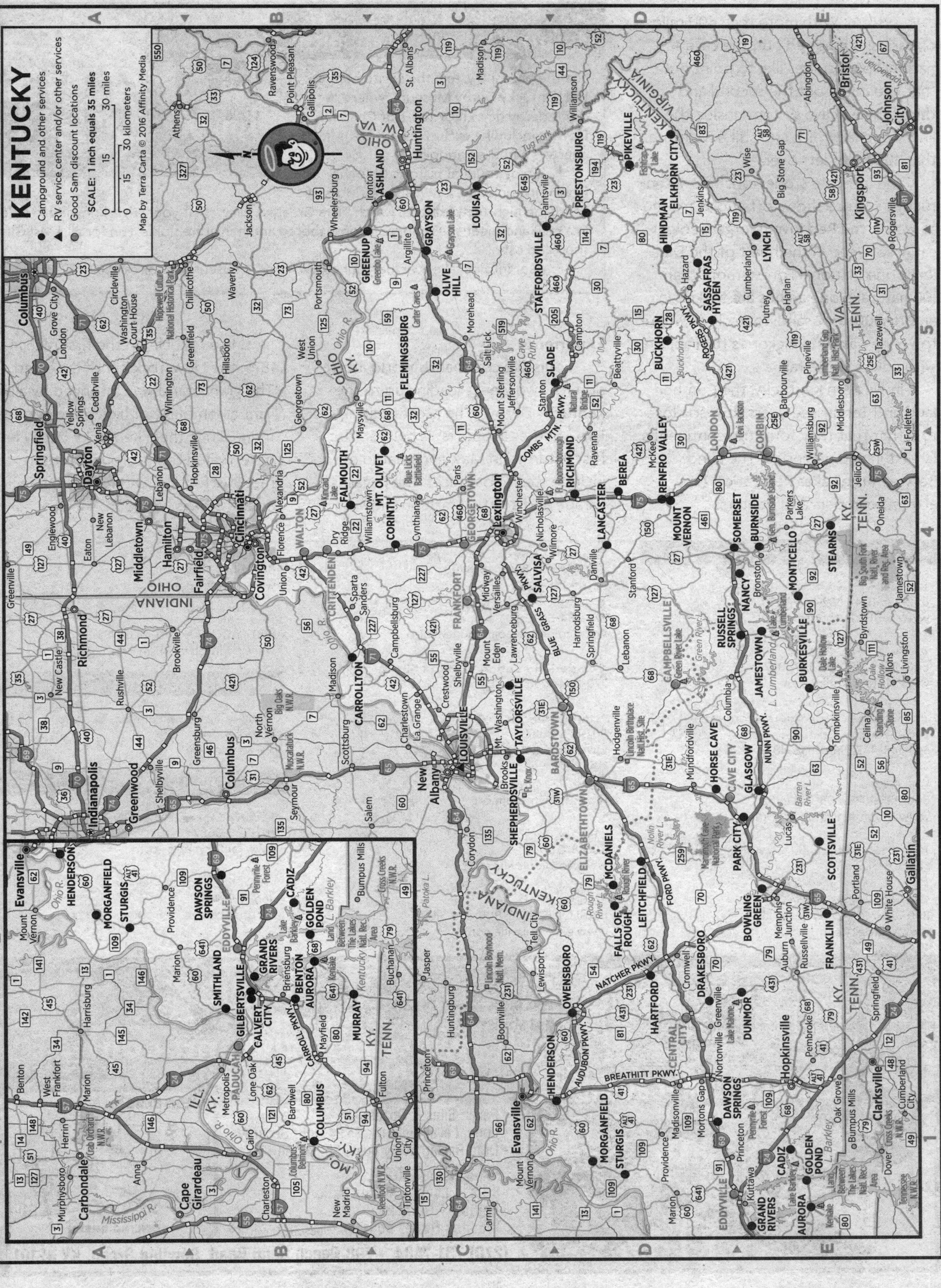
KENTUCKY
Campground and other services
RV service center and/or other services
Good Sam discount locations
SCALE: 1 inch equals 35 miles
0 15 30 miles
0 15 30 kilometers
Map by Terra Carta © 2016 Affinity Media
ASHLAND
GRAYSON
GREENUP
OLIVE HILL
LOUISA
PRESTONSBURG
PIKEVILLE
ELKHORN CITY
STAFFORDSVILLE
HINDMAN
SASSAFRAS
HYDEN
LYNCH
BUCKHORN
SLADE
FLEMINGSBURG
MT. OLIVET
FALMOUTH
CORINTH
WALTON
GEORGETOWN
Lexington
RICHMOND
BEREA
RENFRO VALLEY
LONDON
CORBIN
LANCASTER
MOUNT VERNON
SOMERSET
BURNSIDE
NANCY
MONTICELLO
STEARNS
SALVISA
FRANKFORT
CARROLLTON
TAYLORSVILLE
LOUISVILLE
SHEPHERDSVILLE
BARDSTOWN
ELIZABETHTOWN
RUSSELL SPRINGS
JAMESTOWN
BURKESVILLE
CAMPBELLSVILLE
HORSE CAVE
CAVE CITY
GLASGOW
PARK CITY
SCOTTSVILLE
BOWLING GREEN
FRANKLIN
MCDANIELS
LEITCHFIELD
FALLS OF ROUGH
OWENSBORO
HARTFORD
DRAKESBORO
DUNMOR
CENTRAL CITY
HENDERSON
MORGANFIELD
STURGIS
DAWSON SPRINGS
EDDYVILLE
GRAND RIVERS
AURORA
GOLDEN POND
CADIZ
SMITHLAND
GILBERTSVILLE
CALVERT CITY
BENTON
PADUCAH
MURRAY
COLUMBUS
Cincinnati
Covington
Dayton
Springfield
Columbus
Indianapolis
Evansville
Huntington
Hopkinsville
Clarksville
Kingsport
Bristol
Johnson City
Cape Girardeau
Carbondale

KY

cave system. With more than 400 miles of passages mapped out, the cave's national park guides like to point out that you could put the second and third longest cave systems inside the limestone labyrinth and still have more than 100 miles left over.

The intricate stonework below Kentucky's surface shows off above ground as well in the Red River Gorge Geological Area. Deep in the heart of the Daniel Boone National Forest, more than 100 natural stone arches are tucked in among 300-foot sandstone cliffs, where towering oaks and hickories turn ablaze with colors in the fall.

In western Kentucky, the Cumberland and Tennessee rivers flow so close together that they form the continent's largest inland peninsula. The Land Between the Lakes Recreation Area attracts campers and boaters.

- STAY A WHILE -

Kentucky Derby Museum

See the pageantry, feel the excitement at the Kentucky Derby Museum, where every day is derby day. Enjoy tours of Churchill Downs, including exclusive barn areas, jockey quarters and the paddock.

Enjoy tours of historic Churchill Downs in Louisville, KY. Visit two floors of hands-on high-tech exhibits, watch "The Greatest Race," test your trivia knowledge, ride in a race and meet the resident Thoroughbred and miniature horse. Fun for all ages! Gift shop and cafe.

Get info or take a virtual tour at www.derbymuseum.org or call 502-637-1111.

Experience

Louisville commands world attention for two weeks leading up to the Kentucky Derby. "The Most Exciting Two Minutes in Sports" is held on the first Saturday in May, and related events include steamboat races, the Pegasus Parade and a virtual fashion show of hats. In an article on the first race in 1875, the New York Times reported, "The grandstand was thronged by a brilliant assemblage of ladies and gentlemen." Since then, Kentucky Derby hats have rivaled the thoroughbreds in media attention. Ultimately, the racing action always wins out.

TRAVEL & TOURISM

Kentucky Travel & Tourism
800-225-8747, 502-564-4930
www.kentuckytourism.com

Ashland Area CVB
800-377-6249, 606-329-1007
www.visitashlandky.com

Bardstown-Nelson County Tourist & Convention Commission
502-348-4877, 800-638-4877

Bell County Tourism Commission
800-988-1075, 606-248-2482
www.MountainGateway.com

Belle Plaine Travel Information Center
620-326-5123

Bowling Green Area CVB
800-326-7465, 270-782-0800
www.visitbgky.com

Cave City Tourist Commission
270-773-3131, 800-346-8908

Columbia-Adair County Tourism
270-384-6020
www.columbia-adaircounty.com

Cumberland County Tourism Commission
270-864-2256

Frankfort-Franklin County Tourism
502-875-8687
www.visitfrankfort.com

Kentucky Derby Museum
www.derbymseum.org

Visit Lexington
800-845-3959
www.gotolouisville.com

Louisville CVB
888-LOUISVILLE, 800-626-5646
www.gotolouisville.com

Northern Kentucky CVB
800-STAY-NKY
www.staynky.com

Paducah CVB
800-PADUCAH, 270-443-8783
www.paducah-tourism.org

OUTDOOR RECREATION

Dept. of Fish and Wildlife Resources
800-858-1549
www.fw.ky.gov

SHOPPING

Factory Stores of America
502-868-0682
www.factorystores.com

VF Outlet
866-950-9473
Vfoutlet.com

Featured Good Sam Parks

KENTUCKY

Good Sam Park

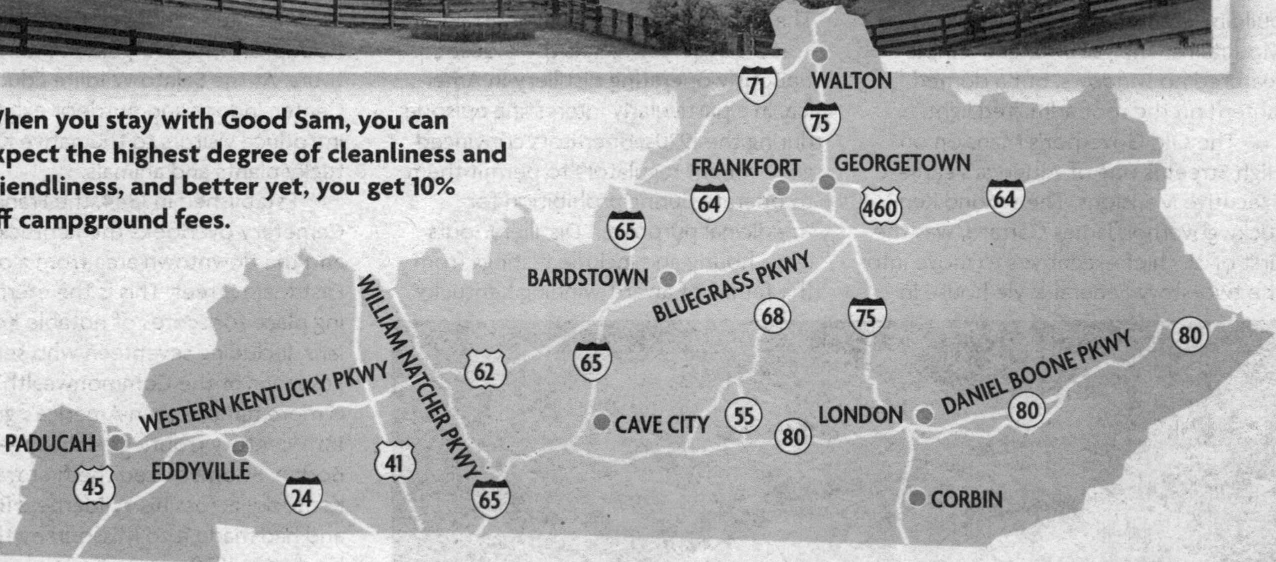

When you stay with Good Sam, you can expect the highest degree of cleanliness and friendliness, and better yet, you get 10% off campground fees.

If you're not already a Good Sam member you can purchase your membership at one of these locations:

BARDSTOWN
White Acres Campground
(502)348-9677

CAVE CITY
Cave Country RV Campground
(270)773-4678

CORBIN
Falls Creek Cabins & Campground
(800)541-7238
Laurel Lake Camping Resort
(606)526-7876

EDDYVILLE
Outback RV Resort
(270)388-4752

FRANKFORT
Elkhorn Campground
(502)695-9154

GEORGETOWN
Whispering Hills RV Park
(502)863-2552

LONDON
Westgate RV Campground
(606)878-7330

PADUCAH
Duck Creek RV Park
(800)728-5109
Fern Lake Campground & RV Park
(270)444-7939

WALTON
Oak Creek Campground
(859)485-9131

For more Good Sam Parks go to listing pages

Getty Images/iStockphoto

FRANKFORT

Pay a visit to the home of bourbon balls, whiskey and Daniel Boone

Frankfort treats visitors with historic architecture and beautiful scenery. Take a trip to the capital of Kentucky for whiskey, candy and trips into America's compelling past.

Beautiful Buildings

Like Lexington and Louisville, its neighbors to the east and west, Frankfort boasts streetscapes that are lined with attractive 19th-century buildings. The Old State Capitol, occupied beginning in 1830, was the first Greek Revival building erected west of the Allegheny Mountains. The government temple featured no windows, but a domed lantern on the roof admitted light.

The Old Governor's Mansion on High Street is one of America's earliest Executive Mansions. The second Kentucky governor, James Garrard, was the first of 35 chief executives to move into the two-story Federal-style house in 1798. So many Bluegrass State politicians resided in the town's north section that it is now known as the Corner in Celebrities Historic District.

Anchoring the district on Wapping Street is the Vest-Lindsey House, which also has roots in the 18th-century. George Graham Vest was a lawyer known for coining the phrase, "a dog is man's best friend," during a trial over a canine killing.

Whiskey and Candy

The local mash house is the Buffalo Trace Distillery, which is the oldest continuously operating distillery in America. In a particularly interesting episode during the 1920s, operators convinced government regulators to permit them to operate during prohibition for "medicinal purposes." Distillery tours leave hourly and include tastings from the family of award-winning Kentucky Straight Bourbon Whiskeys.

Also open for touring is the Rebecca Ruth Candy Factory in downtown Frankfort, started in 1919 by two schoolteachers, Ruth Hanly Booe and Rebecca Gooch. In the 1930s, Booe resuscitated a struggling Depression-era business by blending chocolate and bourbon. "Bourbon Balls" were born.

Outdoors in Frankfort

Frankfort's nature centers beckon. The Buckley Wildlife Sanctuary offers trails across three sections of Kentucky River floodplain with self-guided interpretive tours. At the Salato Wildlife Education Center, indoor and outdoor exhibits introduce visitors to the native Kentucky plants and animals.

Established in 1844, the Frankfort Cemetery overlooks the Kentucky River and the downtown area from a bluff on East Main Street. This is the eternal resting place for scores of notable Kentuckians, including seventeen who served as governor of the Commonwealth. None is more famous than America's greatest 18th-century frontier celebrity—Daniel Boone. Boone blazed the first trails into Kentucky across his Wilderness Road and had made it to Missouri by the time he died in 1820.

Bourbon ages in barrels in a Frankfort distillery. Getty Images/iStockphoto

For More Information

Visit Frankfort
800-960-7200
www.visitfrankfort.com

Kentucky Department of Travel
800-225-8747
www.kentuckytourism.com

• FAMILY OWNED & OPERATED FOR OVER 20 YEARS •

KY

Good Sam Park

Good Sam RATED 10/9.5★/9

See listing Frankfort, KY

FREE WI-FI & CABLE

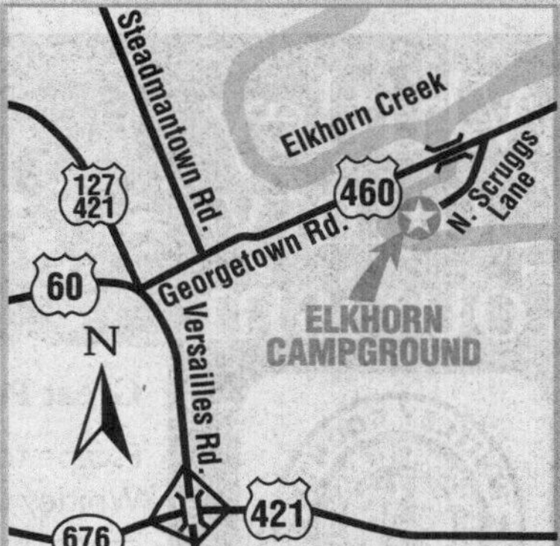

ONLY 10 MI. OR LESS TO:
- Kentucky's Capitol Bldg.
- Major Shopping • Fuel
- Restaurants • Antiques

- Full Hookups • 30/50 Amps • Clean Restrooms/Laundry
- LP Gas • Paved Roads & Sites • Big Rig Friendly
- Sparkling Pool • Mini Golf • Fishing in Elkhorn Creek
- Hand Dipped Ice Cream • Limited Winter Facilities

165 N. Scruggs Lane • Frankfort, KY 40601

(502) 695-9154

www.elkhorncampground.com

Getty Images/iStockphoto

WHITLEY COUNTY/CUMBERLAND FALLS

Discover the forest primeval in Kentucky's beautiful wilderness

When Daniel Boone blazed his lonesome westward trail over the mighty Appalachians and across the scenic Cumberland Gap in the latter half of the 18th century, he reported a landscape full of thick, dense and incredibly diverse forests. Towering oaks, cedars, pines and sycamores thrived side by side, choking out the sun with canopies as thick and lush as an Amazonian rainforest.

Experts think that these types of forests once covered as much as 24 million acres in present-day Kentucky, a state of 26 million acres total. Three hundred years later and the cumulative costs of exploration, homesteading and industrialization have taken their toll. The forests have faded away. Their old-growth and virgin timber has disappeared almost completely from the Bluegrass State.

Luckily there are still a handful of places where visitors can explore the very same ancient forests that Daniel Boone experienced on his westward adventure through this incredible countryside, and Whitley County serves as the region's best gateway for that exploration.

Forest Primeval

The county itself is draped across the Cumberland Mountains and houses a large swath of Daniel Boone National Forest, where the last remnants of Kentucky's prehistoric and incredibly diverse forests still proudly stand.

Because of its mostly wild and all-natural terrain, the county is a popular spot for adventure-seekers, backcountry campers and wildlife photographers.

The Pottsville Escarpment—a craggy line of sandstone cliffs and valleys that form the region's transition from rocky mountains to rolling foothills—carves its way through the county, producing a landscape that's positively packed with dramatic natural features like tumbling waterfalls and massive stone arches. An endless supply of well-marked and well-maintained hiking trails snake their way through the forest, and myriad streams and rivers

An endless supply of well-marked and well-maintained hiking trails snake their way through the forest.

See listing Corbin, KY

The majestic Cumberland Falls.
Getty Images/iStockphoto

Fall landscape in the Cumberland Mountains. Getty Images/iStockphoto

make it easy to explore the forest's 2 million acres by kayak or canoe.

The Red River Gorge Geological Area is a particularly gorgeous portion of the forest. The gorge is renowned for its abundance of archeological dig sites and prehistoric rock shelters, believed to have once been used by nomadic ice age hunters following herds of mastodons and wooly mammoths. If you're short on time or not up for an overnight, rustic camping experience, hop on the Red River Gorge Scenic Byway and explore the area's highlights from the comfort of your recreational vehicle. Don't miss the Gladie Historic Site (a historic logging camp) and the Nada Tunnel (an old steam train passageway).

The undisputed star of the show in Whitley County is, without a doubt, Cumberland Falls. Set within Daniel Boone National Forest itself, Cumberland Falls State Resort Park is home to what locals affectionately refer to as "Niagara of the South."

Cumberland Falls State Resort Park is home to what locals affectionately refer to as "Niagara of the South."

With a wide rock shelf more than 250 million years old, the Cumberland River tumbles over a horseshoe-shaped drop and plummets 65 feet into a large open river basin. At its seasonal peak (when the river is in "flood" status), the width of the falls stretch to upwards of 300 feet, but even at the river's lowest point the falls span a 125-foot half-circle.

Near the falls, the park also houses a Native American museum, which tells the story of the region's earliest inhabitants through a mix of displays, exhibits, special programs and original artifacts. If you're traveling with small children, you'll want to grab a fossil bag from the Cumberland Falls Mining Company. Guests can rinse, sift and clean their bag of fossils at the gemstone flume to reveal their bag's hidden treasure.

Cumberland on Foot

Once you're done ogling the state's most scenic natural attraction and exploring the region's incredible prehistoric history, the park offers lots of opportunities for hiking, camping and fishing. More than 17 miles of marked trails wind their way around the falls area, and more than 50 campsites with full electrical hookups are available for use, while anglers can cast their lures into the Cumberland River, hoping to snag some hefty bass, catfish, panfish and roughfish.

For a unique exploration of the park, saddle up on horseback or buckle into a river raft. The park organizes both guided trail rides and guided rafting expeditions for guests of all ages. Tours are weather-dependent and rafting trips are at the mercy of water levels on the Cumberland River, but otherwise guided outings run from May to September and October yearly.

There are no two ways about it. If you're searching for a quiet, relaxing area to explore to your heart's content, Whitley County is an ideal slice of Kentucky to set your sights on. The fact that it's loaded with old-growth forests and some of the same terrain navigated by legends like Daniel Boone is merely icing on the cake.

KY

For More Information

Whitley County Tourism
606-549-0530
www.whitleycountytourism.com

Kentucky Department of Travel
800-225-8747
www.kentuckytourism.com

Kentucky

CONSULTANTS

David & Donna Harmon

ASHLAND — C6 *Boyd*

ASHLAND See also Grayson, Louisa & Olive Hill.

ASHLAND/HUNTINGTON WEST KOA
Ratings: 8.5/9★/8 (Campground) From Jct of I-64 & SR-67 (Exit 179), N 0.8 mi on SR-67 to E Park Dr, SW 0.1 mi to KOA Ln, W 200 ft (R). **FAC:** Paved/gravel rds. (122 spaces). Avail: 72 gravel, 67 pull-thrus (35 x 75), back-ins (35 x 55), accepts self-contain units only, 72 full hkups (30/50 amps), seasonal sites, WiFi, tent sites, rentals, dump, laundry, groc, LP gas, fire rings, firewood. **REC:** heated pool, pond, playground, rec open to public. Pet restrict(B). Partial handicap access. Big rig sites, eco-friendly, 2015 rates: $39 to $45. Disc: military.
(606)929-5504 Lat: 38.37966, Lon: -82.82001
80 Koa Ln., Argillite, KY 41121
ashlandkoa1@yahoo.com
www.ashlandkoa.com
See ad page 519.

AURORA — B2 *Marshall*

KENLAKE STATE RESORT PARK (State Pk) From Jct of US-68/SR-80 (west end of Tennessee River bridge), N 1200 ft on US-68 (R). 2015 rates: $18 to $29. Apr 1 to Nov 15. (270)474-2211

LAKESIDE CAMPGROUND & MARINA **Ratings: 7.5/5.5/7** (Campground) 2015 rates: $32. Mar 17 to Oct 31. (270)354-8157 12363 US Hwy 68 East, Benton, KY 42025

BARDSTOWN — D3 *Nelson*

MY OLD KENTUCKY HOME (State Pk) From Jct of US-31E & US-150, E 0.5 mi on US-150 to Hwy 49, SE 0.7 mi (R). 2015 rates: $20 to $24. Apr 1 to Oct 31. (800)323-7803

WHITE ACRES CAMPGROUND
Ratings: 6.5/8★/7.5 (Campground) From Jct of Bluegrass Pkwy & US-31 E (exit 21), N 2 mi on US-31E to US-62, W 2.7 mi (R). **FAC:** Gravel rds. (52 spaces). 47 Avail: 24 gravel, 23 grass, 20 pull-thrus (30 x 60), back-ins (30 x 40), mostly side by side hkups, 40 full hkups, 7 W, 7 E (50 amps), seasonal sites, WiFi, tent sites, dump, LP gas, firewood. **REC:** playground. Pets OK. 2015 rates: $33. Disc: AAA.
AAA Approved
(502)348-9677 Lat: 37.80843, Lon: -85.51650
3022 Boston Rd, Bardstown, KY 40004
wcampground@bardstown.com
www.whiteacrescampground.net
See ad this page, 511.

BENTON — B2 *Marshall*

BIG BEAR RESORT CAMPGROUND Ratings: 5/7/7 (Campground) From Jct of Purchase Pkwy & US-68 (Exit 47), S 3.5 mi on US-68 to Big Bear Hwy, E 3.4 mi (L) Do not beyond office. Call for assistance. **FAC:** Poor gravel rds. (73 spaces). Avail: 23 gravel, back-ins (28 x 45), 3 full hkups, 20 W, 20 E (30/50 amps), seasonal sites, cable, WiFi Hotspot, tent sites, rentals, dump, mobile sewer, fire rings, firewood. **REC:** pool, Kentucky Lake: swim, fishing, marina, playground. Pet restrict(B). 2015 rates: $57 to $85. Apr 1 to Oct 31.
AAA Approved
(270)354-6414 Lat: 36.89496, Lon: -88.224558
30 Big Bear Resort Rd, Benton, KY 42025
stay@bigbearkentuckylake.com
bigbearkentuckylake.com

BEREA — D4 *Madison*

OH! KENTUCKY CAMPGROUND Ratings: 6/5/6 (Campground) From Jct of I-75 & SR-21 (exit 76): Go W 0.3 mi on SR-21 (Paint Lick Rd) (R). **FAC:** Gravel rds. (102 spaces). Avail: 60 gravel, 60 pull-thrus (25 x 55), 40 full hkups, 20 W, 20 E (30/50 amps), seasonal sites, WiFi Hotspot, tent sites, dump, laundry, groc, LP gas, fire rings. **REC:** pool, rec open to public. Pets OK. 2015 rates: $30.
(859)986-1150 Lat: 37.56678, Lon: -84.32244
562 Paint Lick Rd, Berea, KY 40403
maelkin@windstream.net
www.ohkentuckycampground.com

BOWLING GREEN — E2 *Warren*

BOWLING GREEN See also Cave City, Dunmor, Franklin, Glasgow, Horse Cave, Park City & Scottsville.

BEECH BEND FAMILY CAMPGROUND
Ratings: 9/9.5★/8 (RV Park) From Jct of I-65 & US-31W (Exit 28), SW 3.6 mi on US-31W (toward South Bowling Green) to Riverview Ave, N 1.8 mi on Riverview Ave to Beech Bend Rd, E 0.5 mi (E). **FAC:** Paved rds. 230 paved, 170 pull-thrus (24 x 60), back-ins (28 x 48), accepts self-contain units only, 214 full hkups, 16 W, 16 E (30 amps), WiFi $, tent sites, dump, laundry, firewood, controlled access. **REC:** pool $, wading pool, Barren River: fishing, rec open to public. Pets OK. Eco-friendly, 2015 rates: $40.
(270)781-7634 Lat: 37.02123, Lon: -86.40219
798 Beech Bend Rd, Bowling Green, KY 42101
beechbendpark@msn.com
www.beechbend.com
See ad page 510 (Welcome Section).

BOWLING GREEN KOA **Ratings: 9/9.5★/8** (Campground) 2015 rates: $41.49 to $59.99. (270)843-1919 1960 Three Springs Rd, Bowling Green, KY 42104

Travel Services

CAMPING WORLD OF BOWLING GREEN As the nation's largest retailer of RV supplies, accessories, services and new and used RVs, Camping World is committed to making your total RV experience better. **SERVICES:** RV, tire, RV appliance, restrooms. RV supplies, LP, dump, emergency parking, RV accessible. waiting room. Hours: 8am to 6pm.
(800)635-3196 Lat: 36.92316, Lon: -86.42271
725 Bluegrass Farms Rd. Ste. 2, Bowling Green, KY 42104
www.campingworld.com

Things to See and Do

BEECH BEND PARK Amusement park with over 40 attractions, including the Kentucky Rumbler wooden coaster, splash lagoon waterpark and raceway with oval track and drag strip. Partial handicap access. Food. Hours: 10am to 8pm. Adult fee: $31.99. ATM.
(270)781-7634 Lat: 37.02123, Lon: -86.40219
798 Beech Bend Rd, Bowling Green, KY 42101
beechbendpark@msn.com
www.beechbend.com
See ad page 510 (Welcome Section).

BEECH BEND RACEWAY Since 1898, NHRA drag racing every Sunday, stock car racing Friday nights; Figure 8 Racing; Beaver Tuesday night drag & oval racing; O'Reilly Saturday night racing. Apr 1 to Dec 15. RV accessible. Restrooms, food. Adult fee: $10 to $15.
(270)781-7634 Lat: 37.02123, Lon: -86.40219
798 Beech Bend Rd, Bowling Green, KY 42101
beechbendpark@msn.com
beechbend.com
See ad page 510 (Welcome Section).

SPLASH LAGOON On the same property as Amusement Park. Giant wave pool, water slides, tiki grill and children's interactive splash pool. Partial handicap access. RV accessible. Restrooms, food. Hours: 10 am to 6pm. Adult fee: $31.99.
(270)781-7634 Lat: 37.02123, Lon: -86.40219
798 Beech Bend Rd, Bowling Green, KY 42101
beechbendpark@msn.com
www.beechbend.com
See ad page 510 (Welcome Section).

Park policies vary. Ask about the cancellation policy when making a reservation.

BUCKHORN — D5 *Perry*

BUCKHORN CAMPGROUND (Public Corps) From town, S 200 yds, follow signs (L). 2015 rates: $20 to $30. May 1 to Sep 29. (606)398-7220

TAILWATER CAMPGROUND (COE-BUCKHORN LAKE) (Public) From jct Hwy 28 & Old Hwy 28: Go 1/2 mi S on Old Hwy 28 (follow signs). (606)398-7220

BURKESVILLE — E3 *Cumberland*

DALE HOLLOW LAKE STATE RESORT PARK (State Pk) From Jct of Hwys 90 & 449, S 4.6 mi on Hwy 449 to Hwy 1206, S 5 mi, follow signs (L). 2015 rates: $21 to $23. Apr 1 to Oct 31. (270)433-7431

SULPHUR CREEK RESORT **Ratings: 7.5/8★/7.5** (Campground) 2015 rates: $35. Apr 1 to Oct 31. (270)433-7200 3622 Sulphur Creek Rd, Burkesville, KY 42717

BURNSIDE — E4 *Pulaski*

GENERAL BURNSIDE (State Pk) From Jct of US-27 & SR-90, S 1.7 mi on US-27 (R). 2015 rates: $19 to $21. Apr 1 to Oct 31. (606)561-4104

LAKE CUMBERLAND RV PARK **Ratings: 9/9★/7.5** (Campground) 2015 rates: $25. (606)561-8222 499 Gibson Ln, Bronston, KY 42518

CADIZ — B2 *Trigg*

HURRICANE CREEK CAMPGROUND (Public Corps) From town, SE 6 mi on Hwy 93 to Hwy 274, S 6 mi (R). 2015 rates: $16 to $22. Apr 25 to Oct 20. (270)522-8821

LAKE BARKLEY STATE RESORT PARK (State Pk) From Jct of US 68/SR 80 & SR-1489, NW 3 mi on SR-1489, N 1.1 mi on Park Road (R). NOTE: Rolling wooded hills. 2015 rates: $17 to $24. Apr 1 to Oct 31. (270)924-1131

PRIZER POINT/KENTUCKY LAKES KOA **Ratings: 8/8.5★/7** (RV Park) 2015 rates: $41 to $82. Mar 15 to Dec 1. (800)548-2048 1777 Prizer Point Rd, Cadiz, KY 42211

CALVERT CITY — B2 *Marshall*

CYPRESS LAKES RV PARK **Ratings: 8/8★/8** (RV Park) 2015 rates: $25. (270)395-4267 30 Cypress Pines Land, Calvert City, KY 42029

KOA I-24/KENTUCKY LAKE DAM/PADUCAH **Ratings: 7.5/8★/8** (Campground) 2015 rates: $39. Mar 15 to Nov 15. (800)562-8540 4793 US Hwy 62, Calvert City, KY 42029

CAMPBELLSVILLE — D3 *Taylor*

GREEN RIVER LAKE (State Pk) From Jct of US-68/SR-70 & SR-55, S 3.5 mi on SR-55 to CR-1061S, S 2 mi (L). 2015 rates: $24 to $30. Apr 1 to Dec 31. (270)465-8255

HEARTLAND CAMPGROUND **Ratings: 7/9★/7.5** (Campground) 2015 rates: $28. (270)789-6886 278 Heartland Drive, Campbellsville, KY 42718

HOLMES BEND (Public Corps) From town center, N 2 mi on Hwy 55 (Campbellsville Rd) to Hwy 551, N 1 mi to Holmes Bend Rd, N 5 mi, follow signs (L). 2015 rates: $17 to $23. Apr 20 to Sep 22. (270)384-4623

PIKES RIDGE (Public Corps) From town, E 4 mi on KY-70 to KY-76, SE 4.8 mi to Pikes Ridge Rd, W 2.5 mi, follow signs (R). Pit toilets. 2015 rates: $15 to $21. Apr 20 to Sep 22. (270)465-6488

SMITH RIDGE (Public Corps) From town, E 1 mi on Hwy 70 to Hwy 372, S 3 mi to County Park Rd, follow signs (R). 2015 rates: $17 to $23. Apr 20 to Sep 22. (270)789-2743

CARROLLTON — B3 *Carroll*

GENERAL BUTLER STATE RESORT PARK (State Pk) From Jct of I-71 & SR-227 (exit 44), N 1.6 mi on SR-227 (L). 2015 rates: $22 to $30. (502)732-4384

2 RIVERS CAMPGROUND Ratings: 8/9.5★/8.5 (RV Park) From Jct I-71 & Exit 44 (SR-227), N 3.6 mi on SR-227 to US-42, W 1.2 mi to 2nd St, N 0.1 mi (L). **FAC:** Paved rds. 33 paved, patios, 18 pull-thrus (40 x 65), back-ins (40 x 65), accepts self-contain units only, 33 full hkups (50 amps), WiFi, tent sites, dump, laundry, fire rings. **REC:** Kentucky & Ohio Rivers: fishing, playground. Pets OK. Partial handicap access. 2015 rates: $35.
AAA Approved
(502)732-4665 Lat: 38.68200, Lon: -85.18546
320 2nd Street, Carrollton, KY 41008
gmcmurry@carrolltonky.net
www.2riverscampground.com

County names help you follow the local weather report.

CAVE CITY — D3 *Barren*

CAVE COUNTRY RV CAMPGROUND
Ratings: 8/10★/9.5 (RV Park) From Jct of I-65 & Hwy 90 (Exit 53), E 0.25 mi on Hwy 90 to Sanders Dr, N 0.25 mi on Sanders Dr to Gaunce Dr, E 0.2 mi (R). **FAC:** All weather rds. 50 gravel, 50 pull-thrus (40 x 65), accepts self-contain units only, 50 full hkups (30/50 amps), WiFi, rentals, laundry, LP gas, fire rings, firewood. **REC.** Pet restrict(Q). Partial handicap access, no tents. Big rig sites, eco-friendly, 2015 rates: $37 to $39. Disc: military.
(270)773-4678 Lat: 37.13496, Lon: -85.96861
216 Gaunce Dr, Cave City, KY 42127
office@cavecountryrv.com
www.cavecountryrv.com
See ad this page, 511.

SINGING HILLS RV PARK
Ratings: 6/8★/8 (Campground) From Jct I-65 & SR-70 (Exit 53), W 2.5 mi on SR-70 (R). **FAC:** Gravel rds. 28 gravel, 21 pull-thrus (20 x 70), back-ins (20 x 40), accepts self-contain units only, 15 full hkups, 13 W, 13 E (30/50 amps), WiFi, tent sites, dump, LP gas, fire rings, firewood. **REC:** pond, fishing, playground. Pets OK. Eco-friendly, 2015 rates: $33 to $37. Disc: military.
(270)773-3789 Lat: 37.13306, Lon: -86.02213
4110 Mammoth Cave Rd., Cave City, KY 42127
ebrown@outdrs.net
www.singinghillsrvpark.com
See ad this page.

YOGI BEAR'S JELLYSTONE PARK CAMP RESORT **Ratings: 8.5/8.5★/9** (Campground) 2015 rates: $38 to $62. (800)523-1854 1002 Mammoth Cave Rd, Cave City, KY 42127

CENTRAL CITY — B3 *Muhlenberg*

WESTERN KENTUCKY RV PARK
Ratings: 6/9.5★/8 (Campground) From Jct of Western Kentucky Pkwy & US-431/SR-70 (Exit 58), S 0.2 mi to SR-604, E 0.2 mi (L). **FAC:** Gravel rds. 50 gravel, 30 pull-thrus (27 x 60), back-ins (30 x 60), accepts self-contain units only, 50 full hkups (30/50 amps), cable, WiFi, dump, LP gas. **REC:** playground. Pets OK. No tents. Big rig sites, 2015 rates: $35. No CC.
(270)757-0345 Lat: 37.28046, Lon: -87.10305
700 Youngstown Rd, Central City, KY 42330
See ad this page.

COLUMBUS — B1 *Hickman*

COLUMBUS-BELMONT (State Pk) From SR-80 in town, N 0.25 mi on Cheatham St, follow signs (L). 2015 rates: $20 to $22. (270)677-2327

CORBIN — E4 *Laurel, Whitley*

CORBIN KOA **Ratings: 8.5/8.5★/8** (Campground) 2015 rates: $41 to $46. (606)528-1534 171 East City Dam Rd, Corbin, KY 40701

CUMBERLAND FALLS STATE RESORT PARK (State Pk) S-bnd: From Jct of I-75 & US-25 (exit 25), SW 7.3 mi on US-25 to Hwy 90, W 7.2 mi (L); or N-bnd: From Jct of I-75 & US-25(exit 15), NW 5.8 mi on US-25 to Hwy 90, W 7.2 mi (L). 2015 rates: $17 to $32. Mar 16 to Nov 14. (606)528-4121

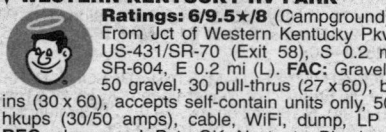

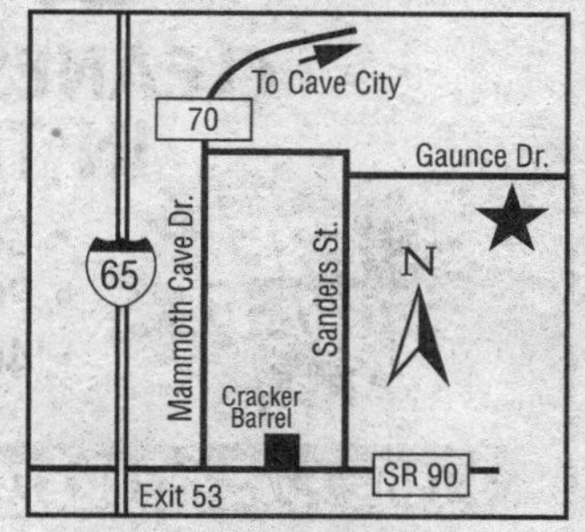

CORBIN (CONT)

DANIEL BOONE NATIONAL FOREST (GROVE BOAT-IN CAMPGROUND) (Natl Pk) From town: Go 5 mi SW on US 25, then 2 mi N on Hwy 1193, then 3-1/2 mi NE on FR 558 to boat ramp. Then 1 mi by private boat on the Laurel River Lake. Pit toilets. May 15 to Sep 15. (606)528-6156

FALLS CREEK CABINS & CAMPGROUND
Ratings: 8/10★/8 (Campground) From the Jct of I-75 & Exit 25 (US-25W): Go W 7.4 mi on US-25W to SR-90, S 1.9 mi (L). **FAC:** Gravel rds. 13 gravel, 6 pull-thrus (40 x 80), back-ins (30 x 50), 6 full hkups, 7 W, 7 E (30/50 amps), WiFi, tent sites, rentals, dump, laundry, fire rings, firewood. **REC:** Falls Creek: rec open to public. Pets OK. Eco-friendly, 2015 rates: $30 to $40. AAA Approved
(800)541-7238 Lat: 36.84181, Lon: -84.25956
1943 Hwy 90, Corbin, KY 40701
fun@ky-rafting.com
www.fallscreekcc.com
See ad pages 515 (Spotlight Whitley County/Cumberland Falls), 511.

LAUREL LAKE CAMPING RESORT
Ratings: 8.5/10★/9.5 (RV Park) From the jct of I 75 & US 25W, SW 4.6 mi on US 25W to SR 1193, W 4.6 mi (R). **FAC:** Gravel rds. 36 gravel, 6 pull-thrus (30 x 80), back-ins (30 x 70), accepts self-contain units only, 36 full hkups (30/50 amps), cable, WiFi, tent sites, rentals, dump, laundry, groc, fire rings, controlled access. **REC:** pond, swim, playground. Pets OK. Big rig sites, 2015 rates: $30 to $40. Apr 1 to Nov 1.
(606)526-7876 Lat: 36.92074, Lon: -84.25977
80 Robert Blair Rd, Corbin, KY 40701
laurellakecamping@gmail.com
www.laurellakecampingresort.com
See ad pages 515 (Spotlight Whitley County/Cumberland Falls), 511.

Things to See and Do

WHITLEY COUNTY TOURISM There's always something to do in Whitley County. No CC.
(606)528-8860 Lat: 32.5111, Lon: -95.8351
www.whitleycountytourism.com
See ad page 514 (Spotlight Whitley County/Cumberland Falls).

CORINTH — C4 *Grant*

THREE SPRINGS CAMPGROUND **Ratings: 6.5/8★/7.5** (Campground) 2015 rates: $30. Mar 15 to Nov 15. (859)823-0185 595 Campground Rd, Corinth, KY 41010

Lend a hand. During the busy season park services are stretched to the max! Please do your best to keep your area "ship-shape".

CRITTENDEN — B4 *Grant*

CINCINNATI SOUTH ROSE GARDEN CAMPGROUND
Ratings: 8.5/9.5★/8 (RV Park) From Jct of I-75 & SR-491 (exit 166), E 0.2 mi on SR-491 to US-25, S 2.6 mi (R). **FAC:** Paved/gravel rds. (100 spaces). Avail: 90 gravel, 62 pull-thrus (28 x 65), back-ins (28 x 40), some side by side hkups, 26 full hkups, 64 W, 64 E (30/50 amps), seasonal sites, WiFi, rentals, dump, laundry, groc, LP gas, fire rings, firewood. **REC:** pool, pond, fishing, playground. Pets OK. No tents. Eco-friendly, 2015 rates: $32 to $35. Mar 1 to Oct 15.
(859)428-2000 Lat: 38.74925, Lon: -84.60307
3315 US 25 (Dixie Hwy), Crittenden, KY 41030
www.cincinnatisouthcampground.com
See ad page 895.

DAWSON SPRINGS — B2 *Christian*

PENNYRILE FOREST STATE RESORT PARK (State Pk) From Jct of Western Ky Pkwy & Hwy 109 (exit 24), S 9.3 mi on SR-109 to Hwy 398, W 2 mi (R). 2015 rates: $17 to $21. Apr 1 to Oct 31. (270)797-3421

DRAKESBORO — B3 *Muhlenberg*

GREGORY LAKE RV PARK **Ratings: 5.5/NA/5** (Campground) 2015 rates: $30. (270)476-9223 430 Gregory Lake Rd, Drakesboro, KY 42337

DUNMOR — B3 *Muhlenberg*

LAKE MALONE CAMPGROUND (State Pk) From Jct of Western Kentucky Pkwy & US-431 (Exit 58), S 16.7 mi on US-431 to SR-973, W 3.1 mi on SR-973 to Conservation Rd (Park Access Rd) (L). 2015 rates: $17 to $21. Mar 15 to Dec 15. (270)657-2858

EDDYVILLE — B2 *Lyon, Trigg*

HOLIDAY HILLS RESORT **Ratings: 7.5/9★/8** (RV Park) 2015 rates: $38. Apr 1 to Nov 1. (800)337-8550 5631 Ky-93 S, Eddyville, KY 42038

INDIAN POINT RV PARK **Ratings: 8.5/8★/7** (Campground) 2015 rates: $32. Apr 1 to Nov 1. (270)388-2730 1136 Indian Hills Trail, Eddyville, KY 42038

OUTBACK RV RESORT
Ratings: 9.5/9★/8.5 (RV Park) From Jct of I-24 & SR-293 (Exit 45), W 0.2 mi on SR-293 to SR-93, S 0.9 mi (L). Note: 40 ft rig plus tow maximum. **FAC:** Paved rds. (88 spaces). Avail: 25 paved, 25 pull-thrus (25 x 65), accepts self-contain units only, 25 full hkups (30/50 amps), seasonal sites, WiFi, laundry, fire rings, firewood. **REC:** pool, playground. Pets OK. Partial handicap access, no tents. Big rig sites, eco-friendly, 2015 rates: $33.50. Apr 1 to Nov 1.
(270)388-4752 Lat: 37.04380, Lon: -88.03138
4481 State Route 93 South, Eddyville, KY 42038
murphysrv2@bellsouth.net
www.murphysrv.com
See ad this page, 511.

So you're the one with "pooch" duty? Please make a clean sweep of it! Your fellow RVers will appreciate it!

ELIZABETHTOWN — D3 *Hardin*

ELIZABETHTOWN CROSSROADS CAMPGROUND
Ratings: 8.5/9★/8.5 (Campground) From Jct of I-65 & US-62 (exit 94), E 0.8 mi on US-62 to Tunnel Hill Rd, N 0.2 mi (L). **FAC:** Gravel rds. 57 gravel, 20 pull-thrus (25 x 55), back-ins (25 x 35), accepts self-contain units only, 25 full hkups, 20 W, 20 E (30/50 amps), cable, WiFi, tent sites, rentals, dump, laundry, LP gas, fire rings, firewood. **REC:** pool, pond, fishing, playground, rec open to public. Pet restrict(B). Eco-friendly, 2015 rates: $28 to $32. Disc: military.
(270)737-7600 Lat: 37.72372, Lon: -85.81611
209 Tunnell Hill Rd, Elizabethtown, KY 42701
etowncg@comcast.net
www.elizabethtowncrossroadscampgroundky.com
See ad this page.

GLENDALE CAMPGROUND **Ratings: 8.5/7.5★/7** (Campground) 2015 rates: $31. (270)369-7755 4566 Sportsman Lake Rd, Elizabethtown, KY 42701

ELKHORN CITY — D6 *Pike*

BREAKS INTERSTATE PARK (Public) From town: Go 8 mi S on Hwy 80, then 2 mi NW on Park Rd. Pit toilets. 2015 rates: $15 to $24. Mar 1 to Dec 2. (800)982-5122

FALLS OF ROUGH — D2 *Grayson*

CAVE CREEK (Public Corps) From town, S 2 mi on Hwy 79 to Hwy 736, E 2 mi, follow signs (R). Pit toilets. 2015 rates: $10 to $14. May 15 to Sep 15. (270)879-4304

ROUGH RIVER DAM STATE RESORT PARK (State Pk) From Jct of Western Kentucky Pkwy & Hwy 79 (Exit 94), N 16.5 mi on Hwy 79 (L). 2015 rates: $12 to $24. Apr 1 to Oct 31. (270)257-2311

FALMOUTH — B4 *Pendleton*

KINCAID LAKE (State Pk) From Jct of SR-22 & SR-159, N 5 mi on SR-159 (R). 2015 rates: $14 to $24. Apr 1 to Oct 31. (859)654-3531

FLEMINGSBURG — C5 *Fleming*

FOX VALLEY REC AREA (Public) S-bnd: From town at Jct of SR-32 & SR-11, SE 5.6 mi on SR-32 to James Rd, E 2 mi (L); or N-bnd: From Jct of I-64 & SR-32 (Exit 137), N 17 mi on SR-32 to James Rd, E 2 mi (L). 2015 rates: $6 to $15. Mar 15 to Oct 31. (606)845-0833

FRANKFORT — C4 *Franklin, Scott, Woodford*

ELKHORN CAMPGROUND
Ratings: 10/9.5★/9 (RV Park) From Jct of I-64 & US-60 (exit 58), NW 2.7 mi on US-60 to US-460, E 2.2 mi to N Scruggs Ln, S 0.1 mi (R). Note: N Scruggs Ln is narrow. **FAC:** Paved rds. (161 spaces). Avail: 125 paved, 26 pull-thrus (25 x 70), back-ins (25 x 70), 64 full hkups, 61 W, 61 E (30/50 amps), seasonal sites, cable, WiFi, tent sites, dump, laundry, groc, LP gas, fire rings, firewood. **REC:** pool, Elkhorn Creek: fishing, playground. Pet restrict(B). Eco-friendly, 2015 rates: $34.
(502)695-9154 Lat: 38.20994, Lon: -84.80109
165 N Scruggs Ln, Frankfort, KY 40601
www.elkhorncampground.com
See ad pages 513 (Spotlight Frankfort), 511.

STILL WATERS CAMPGROUND **Ratings: 3.5/5.5/5** (Campground) 2015 rates: $26. Apr 1 to Oct 31. (502)223-8896 249 Strohmeirer Rd, Frankfort, KY 40601

FRANKLIN — E2 *Simpson*

➡ BLUEGRASS MUSIC RV PARK (Campground) (Rebuilding) 2015 rates: $42. (270)586-5622 2889 Scottsville Rd, Franklin, KY 42135

GEORGETOWN — C4 *Scott*

⬆ **WHISPERING HILLS RV PARK**
Ratings: 9/9.5★/9 (RV Park) From Jct of I-75 & Exit 129 (Cherry Blossom Way), W on Cherry Blossom Way 0.5 mi to US-25, N 1.7 mi to Rogers Gap Rd, E 0.6 mi (R). **FAC:** Paved/gravel rds. (188 spaces). Avail: 177 gravel, 30 pull-thrus (30 x 60), back-ins (30 x 50), accepts self-contain units only, 177 full hkups (30/50 amps), seasonal sites, WiFi, laundry, LP gas, fire rings, firewood. **REC:** pool, pond, fishing, playground. Pets OK. Partial handicap access, no tents. Big rig sites, eco-friendly, 2015 rates: $36 to $45.
(502)863-2552 Lat: 38.30173, Lon: -84.55041
257 Rogers Gap Rd, Georgetown, KY 40324
whisperinghillsrv@yahoo.com
www.whisperinghillsrv.com
See ad pages 520, 511.

GILBERTSVILLE — B2 *Marshall*

⬋ KENTUCKY DAM VILLAGE STATE RESORT PARK (State Pk) From Jct of I 24 & US-62/US-641 (exit 27), S 2.2 mi on US-62/US-641 to SR-282, N 0.5 mi (R). 2015 rates: $12 to $25. Apr 1 to Oct 31. (270)362-4271

⬇ KENTUCKY LAKE RESORT AND RV PARK **Ratings: 5.5/8★/6.5** (RV Park) 2015 rates: $25. (270)362-8652 59 Kentucky Lake Resort Rd, Gilbertsville, KY 42044

GLASGOW — E3 *Barren*

⬇ BARREN RIVER LAKE STATE RESORT PARK (State Pk) From Jct of Cumberland Pkwy & US-31E (exit 11), S 11.3 mi on US-31E (R). 2015 rates: $19 to $29. Apr 31 to Nov 19. (270)646-2151

⬇ THE NARROWS CAMPGROUND (Public Corps) From Glasgow, S 10 mi on Old 31E to Narrows Boat Rd, W 2 mi, follow signs (R). 2015 rates: $22. May 15 to Sep 19. (270)646-3094

GOLDEN POND — B2 *Stewart, Trigg*

⬊ WRANGLERS CAMPGROUND (LBL) (Public) From jct Hwy 94/80/68: Go 5 mi E on Hwy 80/68, then 1 mi S on The Trace Rd, then 5 mi W on Rd 168. 2015 rates: $12 to $40. (270)924-2000

GRAND RIVERS — B2 *Barkley, Lion, Livingston*

⬇ CANAL CAMPGROUND (Public Corps) From town, S 1 mi on Hwy 453, E .7 mi on Canal Campground Rd. 2015 rates: $16 to $29. Mar 27 to Oct 25. (270)362-4840

⬆ EXIT 31 RV PARK **Ratings: 3.5/NA/5** (Campground) 2015 rates: $36. (800)971-1914 708 Complex Rd, Grand Rivers, KY 42045

⬇ HILLMAN FERRY (LBL) NATIONAL RECREATION AREA (Public) From jct I-24 & The Trace (Hwy-453): Go 5 mi S on The Trace, then 1 mi W on Hillman Ferry Rd. 2015 rates: $12 to $40. Mar 1 to Nov 30. (270)362-8230

GRAYSON — C5 *Carter*

⬋ GRAYSON LAKE (State Pk) From Jct of I-64 & SR-7 (exit 172), S 11.2 mi on SR-7 (R). 2015 rates: $20 to $24. Apr 1 to Oct 31. (606)474-9727

⬆ VALLEY BREEZE RV CAMPGROUND **Ratings: 4/NA/5.5** (Campground) 2015 rates: $24 to $27. (606)474-6779 878 State Highway 1947, Grayson, KY 41143

GREENUP — B5 *Greenup*

⬇ GREENBO LAKE STATE RESORT PARK (State Pk) From Jct of US-23 & SR-1, S 8 mi on SR-1 to park entrance rd, W 2.9 mi (L) or From Jct of I-64 & SR-1 (exit 172), N 15 mi on SR-1 to park entrance rd, W 2.9 mi (L). 2015 rates: $12 to $35. Apr 1 to Oct 31. (606)473-7324

HARRODSBURG — D4 *Mercer*

➡ **CHIMNEY ROCK RV PARK Ratings: 9/8★/8** (RV Park) From the jct of US 127 Bypass & SR 152 (E of town), E 7.3 mi. on SR 152 to Chimney Rock Rd., E 0.2 (R). **FAC:** Paved rds. (70 spaces). Avail: 15 paved, 3 pull-thrus (25 x 50), back-ins (22 x 36), accepts self-contain units only, 15 full hkups (30/50 amps), dump, laundry, LP bottles, firewood, restaurant, controlled access. **REC:** pool, Lake Herrington: marina, playground, rec open to public. Pet restrict(B). 2015 rates: $35 to $45. Apr 1 to Oct 31. No CC.
(859)748-5252 Lat: 37.75100, Lon: -84.70789
220 Chimney Rock Road, Harrodsburg, KY 40330
www.chimneyrockrvpark.com

Refer to the Table of Contents in front of the Guide to locate everything you need.

HARTFORD — A3 *Ohio*

➡ OHIO COUNTY PARK (Public) From Jct of Western Kentucky Pkwy and William Natcher Pkwy (Exit 77B), N 6.7 mi on William Natcher Pkwy to Hwy 69 (Exit 48), NE 0.8 mi (R). 2015 rates: $6 to $22. (270)298-4466

HENDERSON — A2 *Henderson*

⬆ JOHN JAMES AUDUBON (State Pk) From Jct of US-60 & US-41, N 2 mi on US-41 (R). 2015 rates: $22 to $26. Apr 1 to Nov 30. (270)826-2247

HINDMAN — D5 *Knott*

⬇ LITTCARR CAMPGROUND (Public Corps) From town, S 10 mi on Hwy 160, follow signs (L). 2015 rates: $20 to $28. Apr 1 to Oct 11. (606)642-3052

HORSE CAVE — D3 *Hart*

⬅ HORSE CAVE KOA **Ratings: 6.5/8★/7** (Campground) 2015 rates: $32 to $40. (270)786-2819 489 Flint Ridge Rd, Horse Cave, KY 42749

HYDEN — D5 *Leslie*

⬆ TRACE BRANCH CAMPGROUND (Public Corps) From town, N 8 mi on KY-257 to Grassy Branch Rd, N 6 mi (L). 2015 rates: $22. May 1 to Sep 29. (606)672-3670

JAMESTOWN — E3 *Russell*

⬋ KENDALL REC AREA (Public Corps) From town, S 10 mi on US-127 to Powerhouse Rd, NW 1 mi (R). 2015 rates: $15 to $21. Apr 1 to Nov 1. (270)343-4660

⬇ LAKE CUMBERLAND STATE RESORT PARK (State Pk) From Jct of Cumberland Pkwy & US-127 (exit 62), S 13 mi on US-127 (L) NOTE: Campground 4.5 mi into park. CAUTION roads are hilly with sharp curves. 2015 rates: $20 to $27. Mar 14 to Nov 29. (270)343-3111

RV Park ratings you can rely on!

KY

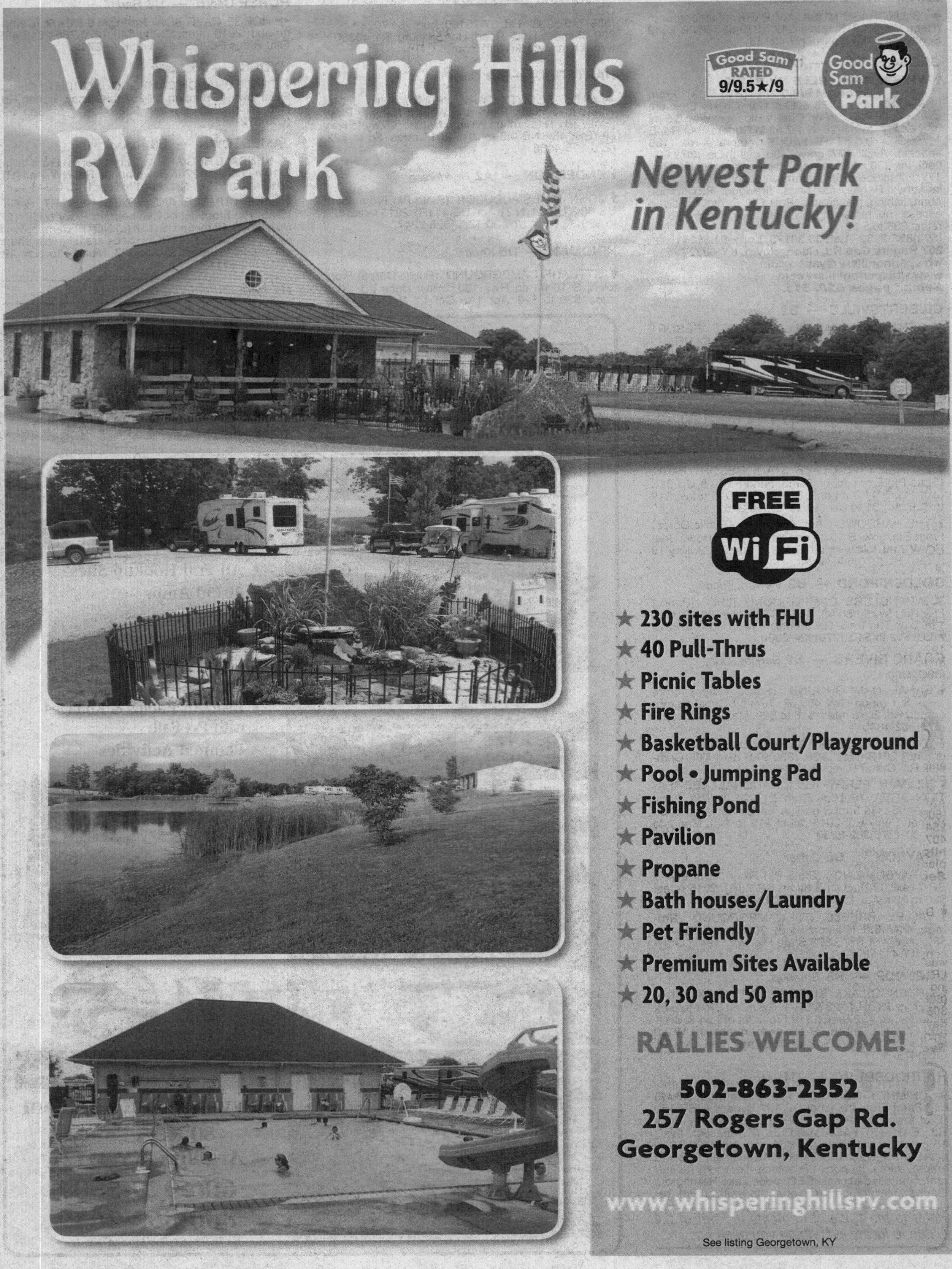
Whispering Hills
RV Park
Good Sam RATED
9/9.5★/9
Good Sam Park
Newest Park
in Kentucky!
FREE
Wi Fi
★ 230 sites with FHU
★ 40 Pull-Thrus
★ Picnic Tables
★ Fire Rings
★ Basketball Court/Playground
★ Pool • Jumping Pad
★ Fishing Pond
★ Pavilion
★ Propane
★ Bath houses/Laundry
★ Pet Friendly
★ Premium Sites Available
★ 20, 30 and 50 amp
RALLIES WELCOME!
502-863-2552
257 Rogers Gap Rd.
Georgetown, Kentucky
www.whisperinghillsrv.com
See listing Georgetown, KY

LANCASTER — D4 *Garrard*

CAMP NELSON RV PARK Ratings: 7/8.5★/7 (Campground) From Jct of US 27 & SR-52 (center of town), N 12.3 mi on US 27 to Camp Nelson Rd, E 1.5 mi (L). **FAC:** Gravel rds. 46 grass, back-ins (40 x 40), some side by side hkups, accepts self-contain units only, 36 full hkups, 10 W, 10 E (30/50 amps), WiFi $, tent sites, dump, laundry, firewood. **REC:** pool, Kentucky River: fishing, playground, rec open to public. Pet restrict(B). 2015 rates: $25.
(859)548-2113 Lat: 37.76783, Lon: -84.61656
1470 Old Lexington Rd E, Lancaster, KY 40444
willhoiterv@aol.com
campnelsonrvpark.com

LEITCHFIELD — D2 *Beckinridge, Edmonson, Madison*

DOG CREEK CAMPGROUND (Public Corps) From town, W 20 mi on Hwy 88 to SR-1015, S 1 mi, follow signs (R). 2015 rates: $15 to $22. May 15 to Sep 6. (270)524-5454

MOUTARDIER (Public Corps) From town, S 12 mi on Hwy 259 to Hwy 2067, E 1.5 mi, follow signs (R). 2015 rates: $15 to $24. May 1 to Oct 17. (270)286-4230

NOLIN LAKE (State Pk) From jct US 62 & Hwy 259: Go 17 mi S on Hwy 259, then E and follow signs. Apr 1 to Oct 31. (270)286-4240

WAX CAMPGROUND (Public Corps) From town, S 7 mi on Hwy 259 to Hwy 226, E 1 mi to KY-88, S 9 mi, follow signs (R). 2015 rates: $15 to $24. May 15 to Sep 6. (270)242-7578

LEXINGTON — C4 *Fayette, Madison*

LEXINGTON See also Frankfort, Richmond & Salvisa.

KENTUCKY HORSE PARK CAMPGROUND (Public) From Jct of I-75 & SR-1973 (exit 120), E 0.7 mi on SR-1973 (L). 2015 rates: $30 to $35. (859)259-4257

LONDON — D4 *Laurel*

DANIEL BOONE NATIONAL FOREST (WHITE OAK BOAT-IN CAMPGROUND) (Natl Pk) From town: Go 10 mi SW on Hwy 192, then 2 mi S on FR 774, then 1 mi S by private boat on the Laurel River Lake. Pit toilets. Mar 15 to Sep 15. (606)864-4163

LEVI JACKSON (State Pk) From Jct of I-75 & Hwy 192 (exit 38), E 1.8 mi on Hwy 192 to US-25, S 1.4 mi to SR-1006, E 1 mi (L). 2015 rates: $20 to $34. (606)330-2130

WESTGATE RV CAMPGROUND Ratings: 6.5/9★/6 (Campground) From Jct of I-75 & SR-80 (exit 41), W 0.3 mi on SR-80 (R). **FAC:** Gravel rds. 14 gravel, back-ins (25 x 45), accepts self-contain units only, 14 full hkups (30/50 amps), cable, WiFi, tent sites, rentals. **REC:** heated pool, playground. Pets OK. Eco-friendly. 2015 rates: $34.50. Disc: AAA.
AAA Approved
(606)878-7330 Lat: 37.14901, Lon: -84.11594
254 Russell Dyche Memorial Hwy, London, KY 40741
http://www.kentuckytourism.com/places_to_stay/westgate-rv-camping/2495/
See ad this page, 511.

Travel Services

DAY BROS AUTO & RV SALES Sale of new & pre-owned RVs. Sale of supplies & parts. Repair service. Storage of RVs. **SERVICES:** RV, RV appliance, MH mechanical, staffed RV wash, restrooms, RV Sales. RV storage. RV supplies, LP, dump, emergency parking, RV accessible. waiting room. Hours: M-Sat, 8am to 5pm.
(606)877-1530 Lat: 37.06552, Lon: -84.05779
3054 S. Laurel Rd, London, KY 40744
daybrosrvsales@hotmail.com
www.daybrosrvsales.com
See ad this page.

LOUISA — C6 *Lawrence*

THE FALLS CAMPGROUND, INC **Ratings: 5.5/NA/7** (Campground) 2015 rates: $32. May 1 to Nov 1. (606)686-3398 6072 N Hwy 3, Louisa, KY 41230

YATESVILLE LAKE CAMPGROUND (State Pk) From Jct of US-23 & SR-32, SW 4.7 mi on SR-32 to SR-3215, NW 2.7 mi (R). 2015 rates: $21 to $25. Apr 1 to Oct 31. (606)673-1490

LOUISVILLE — C3 *Fayette, Meade*

LOUISVILLE AREA MAP

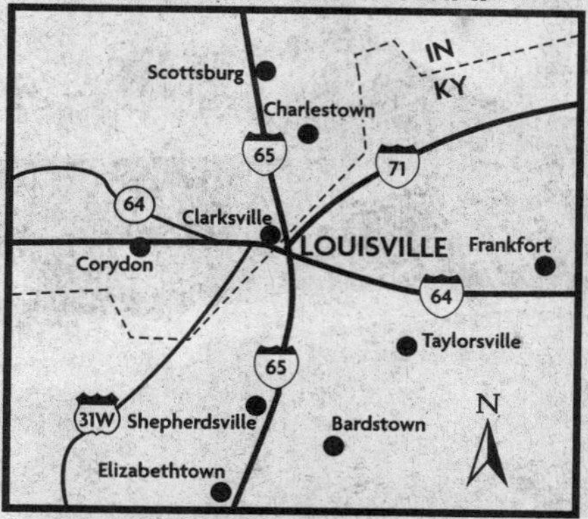

For more detail and a broader overview, please see our full-color state maps at the front of the Kentucky & Indiana state sections.

Symbols on map indicate towns within a 40 mile radius of Louisville where campgrounds are listed. Check listings for more information.

In KY, see also Bardstown, Elizabethtown, Frankfort, Shepherdsville & Taylorsville.

In IN, see also Charlestown, Clarksville, Corydon & Scottsburg.

Things to See and Do

KENTUCKY DERBY MUSEUM Exhibits and multi-media show. Interactive exhibits. Memorabilia of thoroughbred racing. Live thoroughbred horse exhibit. Partial handicap access. RV accessible. Restrooms, food. Hours: 8am to 5pm. Adult fee: $14. ATM.
(502)637-1111 Lat: 38.20604, Lon: -85.77166
704 Central Ave, Louisville, KY 40208
info@derbymuseum.org
www.derbymuseum.org
See ad page 508 (Welcome Section).

LYNCH — E5 *Harlan*

PORTAL #31 RV PARK (Public) From Jct of I-75 & US-25E (exit 27), SE 34.5 mi to US 119, E 51 mi to Hwy 160, S 3.8 mi (R). 2015 rates: $15. (606)848-1530

MCDANIELS — D2 *Breckinridge*

AXTEL (Public Corps) From town, N 4.5 mi on KY-79 (L). 2015 rates: $17 to $34. Apr 17 to Nov 1. (270)257-2584

LAUREL BRANCH (Public Corps) From town, N 2 mi on Hwy 259 to Hwy 110, W 1 mi (L). Pit toilets. 2015 rates: $10 to $19. May 2 to Oct 30. (270)257-8839

NORTH FORK (Public Corps) From Jct of KY-79 & KY-259, N 1 mi on KY-259, follow signs (R). 2015 rates: $17 to $24. May 1 to Sep 15. (270)257-8139

Say you saw it in our Guide!

MONTICELLO — E4 *Wayne*

CONLEY BOTTOM RESORT CAMPGROUND **Ratings: 6/8.5★/8** (Campground) 2015 rates: $24 to $34. (606)348-6351 270 Conley Bottom Rd, Monticello, KY 42633

FALL CREEK CAMPGROUND (CORPS OF ENGINEERS) (Public) From jct SR 90 & SR 1275: Go 5 mi N on SR 1275 (Follow signs). 2015 rates: $20 to $35. May 1 to Sep 12. (606)348-6042

MORGANFIELD — A2 *Union*

MOFFITT REC AREA (Public) From town, SE 6.4 mi on SR-56, S 2 mi on SR-141 to SH-2153, S 3 mi (R). 2015 rates: $9 to $12. Apr 1 to Oct 31. (270)333-4845

MOUNT OLIVET — C4 *Robertson*

BLUE LICKS BATTLEFIELD (State Pk) From Jct of US-68 & SR-165, S 0.5 mi on US-68 (R). 2015 rates: $12 to $26. Apr 1 to Oct 31. (859)289-5507

MOUNT VERNON — D4 *Rockcastle*

RENFRO VALLEY RV PARK Ratings: 6.5/8.5★/8 (Campground) From Jct of I-75 & US-25 (exit 62), N 0.7 mi on US-25 (R). **FAC:** Gravel rds. 149 gravel, 57 pull-thrus (28 x 58), back-ins (26 x 44), 132 full hkups, 17 W, 17 E (30/50 amps), cable, WiFi, rentals, dump, laundry, LP gas, restaurant. **REC:** rec open to public. Pets OK. No tents. 2015 rates: $35 to $37.60. Disc: AAA.
AAA Approved
(800)765-7464 Lat: 37.38835, Lon: -84.32966
2385 Richmond St, Mount Vernon, KY 40456
info@renfrovalley.com
www.renfrovalley.com

MURRAY — B2 *Callaway*

WILDCAT CREEK REC AREA (Public) From jct Hwy 94 & Hwy 280 E of town: Go 5-1/4 mi E on Hwy 280, then 2.1 mi NE on Hwy 614E. Follow signs. 2015 rates: $35 to $45. (270)436-5628

NANCY — E4 *Pulaski*

PULASKI COUNTY PARK (Public) From Jct of US-27 & SR-80, SW 7 mi on SR-80 to local rte 1248, SE 0.1 mi (E). 2015 rates: $10 to $15. Apr 1 to Oct 31. (606)636-6450

OLIVE HILL — C5 *Carter*

CARTER CAVES STATE RESORT PARK (State Pk) From Jct of I-64 & US-60 (exit 161), N 1.4 mi on US-60E to KY-182, N 3 mi (L). 2015 rates: $22 to $32. Apr 1 to Nov 15. (606)286-4411

OWENSBORO — A3 *Daviess*

OWENSBORO See also Falls of Rough, Hartford, Henderson, Leitchfield & McDaniels.

DIAMOND LAKE RESORT **Ratings: 9.5/8★/7** (RV Park) 2015 rates: $30 to $32. (270)229-4900 7301 Hobbs Rd, Owensboro, KY 42301

WINDY HOLLOW CAMPGROUND & RECREATION AREA, INC **Ratings: 6.5/8★/7** (Campground) 2015 rates: $35. (270)785-4150 5141 Windy Hollow Rd, Owensboro, KY 42301

PADUCAH — B1 *McCracken*

PADUCAH See also Benton, Eddyville, Gilbertsville & Smithland.

Take time now to plan a road trip with your pet for meaningful memories that last a lifetime. Read more in our Pampered Pet Parks feature at the front of the Guide.

PADUCAH (CONT)

DUCK CREEK RV PARK
Ratings: 9/9.5★/8 (RV Park) From Jct I 24 & SR 1954/Bus Loop 24 (exit 11), N 0.5 mi on SR 1954 (R).

BIG RIG FRIENDLY-EZ IN/OUT!
1/2 mi N of I-24; LONG pull-thru sites-30/50 amp-upgraded wifi-cable-pool & dog park wash station. Fish/boat on KY Lake & Lake Barkley; golfing nearby. Visit Historic Downtown Paducah and The Nat'l Quilt Museum!

FAC: Gravel rds. (95 spaces). Avail: 89 gravel, 30 pull-thrus (24 x 80), back-ins (24 x 40), accepts self-contain units only, 89 full hkups (30/50 amps), WiFi, dump, laundry, groc, LP gas, firewood. **REC:** pool, Bee Branch Creek: fishing, rec open to public. Pets OK. Partial handicap access, no tents. Big rig sites, eco-friendly, 2015 rates: $35 to $38. Disc: military.
(800)728-5109 Lat: 37.02137, Lon: -88.58667
2540 John L Puryear Dr, Paducah, KY 42003
info@duckcreekrvpark.com
www.duckcreekrvpark.com
See ad opposite page, 511.

FERN LAKE CAMPGROUND & RV PARK
Ratings: 7.5/9.5★/8.5 (RV Park) From Jct of I-24 & SR-305 (exit 3), SW 1/4 mi on SR-305 (R). **FAC:** Paved/gravel rds. 60 gravel, 41 pull-thrus (22 x 60), back-ins (25 x 50), accepts self-contain units only, 45 full hkups, 15 W, 15 E (30/50 amps), WiFi, tent sites, dump, laundry, firewood. **REC:** Fern Lake: fishing, playground. Pets OK. Partial handicap access. Big rig sites, eco-friendly, 2015 rates: $35. Disc: military.
(270)444-7939 Lat: 37.09643, Lon: -88.69545
5535 Cairo Rd, Paducah, KY 42001
info@fernlakecampground.net
www.fernlakecampground.net
See ad this page, 511.

VICTORY RV PARK & CAMPGROUND
Ratings: 7.5/9★/9 (Campground) From Jct of I-24 & SR-1954 (Exit 11), S 0.5 mi on SR-1954 to SR-3075 (Lyndon Rd), E 2.1 mi on SR-3075 (Lyndon Rd) to SR-450 (Oaks Rd), S 1.7 mi on SR-450 (Oaks Rd) to Shemwell Rd, S 0.2 mi on Shemwell Rd (L). **FAC:** Gravel rds. (39 spaces). Avail: 29 gravel, 18 pull-thrus (30 x 70), back-ins (30 x 50), accepts self-contain units only, 29 full hkups (30/50 amps), seasonal sites, cable, WiFi, tent sites, dump, laundry, LP gas, fire rings, firewood. **REC:** pond, fishing, playground. Pet restrict(B). Big rig sites, 2015 rates: $30.
(270)898-2099 Lat: 36.97293, Lon: -88.55957
4300 Shemwell Lane, Paducah, KY 42003
victoryrvpark@yahoo.com
victoryrvpark.com
See ad this page.

PARK CITY — E3 *Edmonson*

DIAMOND CAVERNS RV RESORT & GOLF CLUB **Ratings: 7/5.5/7.5** (Membership Pk) 2015 rates: $37. (800)405-6188 1878 Mammoth Cave Pkwy, Park City, KY 42160

MAMMOTH CAVE/ HEADQUARTERS CAMPGROUND (Natl Pk) From Jct of I-65 & Hwy 70 (Cave City exit 53), W 3.6 mi on Hwy 70, NW 5.3 mi SH-255 (L). 2015 rates: $17 to $20. May 15 to Sep 16. (800)967-2283

PIKEVILLE — D6 *Pike*

(COE-FISHTRAP LAKE) FISH TRAP LAKE SHELTERS (Public) From jct Hwy 80 & US 119: Go 9-1/2 mi E on US 119 to Meta, then 16 mi S on Hwy 194. May 24 to Sep 17. (606)437-7496

PRESTONSBURG — D6 *Floyd*

GERMAN BRIDGE CAMPGROUND (Public Corps) From town, N 6 mi on SH-321 to KY-304, SE 1 mi. 2015 rates: $8. May 25 to Sep 7. (606)874-3947

JENNY WILEY STATE RESORT PARK (State Pk) From Jct of US-23 & Hwy 3, E 2.2 mi on Hwy 3 to Hwy 3051, E 1.4 mi. Follow signs (R). 2015 rates: $21 to $30. Apr 1 to Oct 31. (606)889-1790

RENFRO VALLEY — D4 *Rockcastle*

RENFRO VALLEY See also Berea, London & Mount Vernon.

RENFRO VALLEY KOA Ratings: 9/9.5★/8.5 (RV Park) From Jct of I-75 & US-25 (exit 62), N 1.3 mi on US-25 (R). **FAC:** Paved/gravel rds. (104 spaces). 100 Avail: 48 paved, 52 gravel, 76 pull-thrus (24 x 60), back-ins (22 x 50), 72 full hkups, 28 W, 28 E (30/50 amps), seasonal sites, cable, WiFi, tent sites, rentals, dump, laundry, groc, LP gas, fire rings, firewood. **REC:** pool, playground. Pet restrict(B). Partial handicap access. Eco-friendly, 2015 rates: $42 to $57.
(800)562-2475 Lat: 37.39549, Lon: -84.33357
184 Koa Kampground Rd, Mount Vernon, KY 40456
renfrovalleykoa@hotmail.com
www.renfrovalleykoa.com

RICHMOND — D4 *Madison*

FORT BOONESBOROUGH (State Pk) From Jct of I-75 & SR-627 (exit 95), N 5.5 mi on SR-627 to SR-388, E 0.2 mi (L). Note: Fort has separate entrance. 2015 rates: $28 to $37. (859)527-3454

RUSSELL SPRINGS — E3 *Russell*

INDIAN HILLS RUSSELL SPRINGS KOA **Ratings: 9/8.5★/7** (Campground) 2015 rates: $29.60 to $42. Apr 1 to Oct 31. (270)866-5616 1440 Hwy 1383, Russell Springs, KY 42642

PINECREST RV PARK RESORT **Ratings: 6.5/8★/6.5** (Condo Pk) 2015 rates: $35. (270)866-5615 1080 Hwy 1383, Russell Springs, KY 42642

SALVISA — C4 *Mercer*

CUMMINS FERRY RESORT CAMPGROUND & MARINA Ratings: 9.5/8.5★/9 (RV Park) From Jct of Blue Grass Pkwy & US 127 (Exit 59), S 7.5 mi on US 127 to SR-1988 (Cummins Ferry Rd), E 5.5 mi (E). **FAC:** Paved rds. (90 spaces). Avail: 60 paved, 22 pull-thrus (40 x 80), back-ins (40 x 35), 52 full hkups, 8 W, 8 E (30/50 amps), seasonal sites, WiFi, tent

KY

SALVISA (CONT)

CUMMINS FERRY RESORT (CONT)
sites, dump, laundry, firewood. **REC:** pool, Kentucky River: fishing, marina, playground. Pets OK. Partial handicap access. Big rig sites, 2015 rates: $38.
(859)865-2003 Lat: 37.88818, Lon: -84.77386
2558 Cummins Ferry Rd, Salvisa, KY 40372
cfr@cumminsferry.com
cumminsferry.com

SASSAFRAS — D5 *Knott*

↓ CARR CREEK (State Pk) From Jct of Daniel Boone Pkwy/SR-80 & SR-15 (exit 59), S 18.5 mi on SR-15 (L). 2015 rates: $20 to $24. Apr 1 to Oct 31. (606)642-4050

SCOTTSVILLE — E2 *Allen*

↑ BAILEY'S POINT CAMPGROUND (Public Corps) From town, N 7 mi on 31E to Hwy 252, N 1.1 mi to Hwy 517, E 2 mi, follow signs (L). Pit toilets. 2015 rates: $17 to $23. Apr 17 to Oct 24. (270)622-6959

↑ TAILWATER CAMPING AREA (Public Corps) From Glasgow, N 4 mi on 31E to KY-252, N 4.2 mi, follow signs (L). 2015 rates: $18. May 4 to Sep 8. (270)622-7732

↓ WALNUT CREEK MARINA (Public) From town, NE 6.4 mi Hwy 31E, S 0.7 mi on Hwy 252 to CR-1855, E 2 mi (L). Pit toilets. 2015 rates: $8 to $10. Apr 15 to Oct 15. (270)622-5858

SHEPHERDSVILLE — C3 *Bullitt*

↓ GRANDMA'S RV CAMPING **Ratings: 6/9★/7.5** (RV Park) 2015 rates: $27 to $30. (502)543-7023 159 Dawson Dr, Shepherdsville, KY 40165

→ LOUISVILLE SOUTH KOA **Ratings: 8.5/8.5★/8** (RV Park) 2015 rates: $56 to $81. (800)562-1880 2433 Hwy 44E, Shepherdsville, KY 40165

The RVers' Guide to NASCAR helps RV travelers get the most out of North America's most thrilling sporting event. Turn to the front of the Guide and we'll give you the inside track on how to get high-speed thrills at major NASCAR venues.

SLADE — D5 *Powell, Wolfe*

↓ NATURAL BRIDGE STATE RESORT PARK (State Pk) From Jct of Mt Pkwy & SR-11 (exit 33), S 2.5 mi on SR-11 (L). 2015 rates: $14 to $28. Mar 16 to Nov 15. (606)663-2214

SMITHLAND — B2 *Livingston*

↑ BIRDSVILLE RV & CAMPGROUND **Ratings: 4.5/9★/7.5** (Campground) 2015 rates: $21 to $24. Mar 1 to Nov 30. (270)928-2772 972 River Rd, Smithland, KY 42081

SOMERSET — D4 *Dewayne, Pulaski*

← CUMBERLAND POINT REC AREA (Public Corps) From town, W 10 mi on Hwy 80 to Hwy 235, S 1 mi to Hwy 761, W 9 mi (E). 2015 rates: $18 to $20. May 15 to Sep 12. (606)871-7886

← FISHING CREEK REC AREA (Public Corps) From town, W 5 mi on Hwy 80 to Hwy 1248, NE 2 mi (L). 2015 rates: $20 to $25. May 1 to Sep 26. (606)679-5174

↓ WAITSBORO REC AREA & CAMPGROUND (Public Corps) From town, S 5 mi on US-27, follow signs (R). 2015 rates: $14 to $20. May 1 to Sep 29. (606)561-5513

STAFFORDSVILLE — C6 *Johnson*

↑ PAINTSVILLE LAKE (Public) From Jct of US-23 & SR 40, W 2 mi on SR 40 to Ky 2275, N 1.4 mi (N). 2015 rates: $27 to $31. (606)297-8486

STEARNS — E4 *McCreary*

↓ BIG SOUTH FORK NATIONAL RIVER & REC. AREA (BLUE HERON CAMPGROUND) (Public) From jct US 27 & Hwy 92: Go 1 mi W on Hwy 92, then 1 mi S on Hwy 1651, then 9 mi S on Hwy 741. 2015 rates: $17. Apr 1 to Oct 31. (606)376-5073

Wasn't that a beautiful campground you visited ten years ago? But can you remember where it was? Use our "Find-it-Fast" index, located in the back of the Guide. It's an alphabetical list, by state, of every private and public park and campground in the Guide.

STURGIS — D1 *Union*

→ UNION COUNTY FAIR & EXPO CENTER (Public) From jct SR-109 & US-60: Go 1 mi E on US-60. (270)333-4107

TAYLORSVILLE — C3 *Spencer*

→ TAYLORSVILLE LAKE (State Pk) E-Bnd From Jct of I-64 & KY 55 (exit 32), S 14 mi on KY 55 to KY 44, E 5.2 mi to KY 248, SE 1.9 mi (R) or W-Bnd From Jct of I 64 & KY 53 (exit 35) S 6.2 mi on KY-53 to KY-44 SW 6.2 mi to KY-248, SE 1.9 mi (R). 2015 rates: $21 to $27. Apr 1 to Dec 15. (502)477-0086

WALTON — B4 *Boone*

↙ BIG BONE LICK (State Pk) From Jct of US-42 & SR-338, NW 3 mi on SR-338 (L). 2015 rates: $22 to $26. Apr 1 to Oct 31. (859)384-3522

← **OAK CREEK CAMPGROUND**
Ratings: 9/9★/9 (Campground) From Jct of I-75 & SR-16 (Exit 171), SW 0.8 mi on SR-16 to Oak Creek Dr, NW 200 ft (L); or From Jct of I-71 & SR-14 (Exit 72), E 1.8 mi on SR-14 to SR-16, N 3.3 mi (L). Sharp left turn, swing wide. **FAC:** Paved/gravel rds. (102 spaces). Avail: 50 gravel, 5 pull-thrus (22 x 55), back-ins (25 x 50), some side by side hkups, accepts self-contain units only, 50 W, 50 E (30/50 amps), seasonal sites, WiFi, tent sites, dump, mobile sewer, laundry, groc, fire rings, firewood. **REC:** pool, McCoy's Fork Creek: playground, rec open to public. Pets OK. Eco-friendly, 2015 rates: $34. Disc: AAA, military.
(859)485-9131 Lat: 38.84937, Lon: -84.63050
13329 Oak Creek Rd, Walton, KY 41094
oakcreek@fuse.net
www.oakcreekcampground.com
See ad pages 896, 511.

Got something to tell us? We welcome your comments and suggestions regarding the ratings for a particular campground, or our rating system in general. Please email them to: travelguidecomments@goodsamfamily.com

Tim Mueller

WELCOME TO
Louisiana

DATE OF STATEHOOD	WIDTH: 130 MILES (210 KM)	PROPORTION OF UNITED STATES
APRIL 30, 1812	LENGTH: 379 MILES (610 KM)	1.38% OF 3,794,100 SQ MI

Louisiana has staked out a corner of the American imagination as the go-to place for rich food, Dixieland jazz and roaring good times. The blending of French, Spanish, African and Native American cultures in a geographically unique land has spawned such a distinct population that more reality television shows are filmed in Louisiana than in any other state.

Learn

Six nations have claimed Louisiana at one time or another, and bits and pieces of all of them can be found in New Orleans' French Quarter. This area functions as a real-life outdoor architecture and history museum. More formally, the nine museums of the Louisiana State Museum system began here in 1906 on opposite sides of Jackson Square in the Spanish-flavored former government buildings of the Cabildo and the Presbytère. The most recent additions to the network have been the Old U.S. Mint in New Orleans, built in 1835 by the Greek Revival enthusiast William Strickland; the Wedell-Williams Aviation & Cypress Sawmill Museum in Patterson; and the Louisiana Sports Hall of Fame & Northwest Louisiana History Museum in Natchitoches, the oldest city in Louisiana.

All six of those national flags flew over the Pentagon Barracks dirt fort overlooking the Mississippi River in Baton Rouge. On one side of the historic outpost stands America's tallest state capitol building, which was championed by populist governor Huey P. Long in the 1930s. Nicknamed "Kingfish," Long was assassinated on the steps of the 450-foot high limestone tower on September 8, 1935. Down the street is the castle-like Old Louisiana State Capitol from the 1840s, which is doing duty as a historical museum.

Along the Mississippi River, the Great River Road features a procession of antebellum plantation houses that stand as a testament to a way of American life gone by. The oldest, Destrehan Plantation, still features the original West Indian Creole manor house from where the indigo and sugar cane operations were orchestrated. The 28 live oaks that line the entrance drive to Oak Alley have appeared in so many movies that they should hold Screen Actors Guild cards.

Play

Louisiana has the fifth-longest shoreline of any state, with 397 miles of coast. However, sandy beaches are a novelty in the Pelican State. Grand Isle, a barrier island south of New Orleans, offers the state's most traditional "day at the beach" for vacationers. Holly Beach, south of Lake Charles, marks the western edge of the Cajun Riviera, a 30-mile run on Route 82 through

Top 3 Tourism Attractions:
1) French Quarter
2) Avery Island
3) Honey Island Swamp Tour

Nickname: Pelican State

State Flower: Magnolia

State Bird: Eastern Brown Pelican

People: Louis Armstrong, trumpet player; Truman Capote, novelist; Mahalia Jackson, gospel singer; Jerry Lee Lewis, singer and pianist

Major Cities: New Orleans, Baton Rouge (capital), Shreveport, Lafayette, Lake Charles

Topography: Flat lowlands on the coastal plain of the Gulf of Mexico and Mississippi Alluvial Plain

Climate: Semitropical and humid subtropical climate with a rainy coast

Tim Mueller

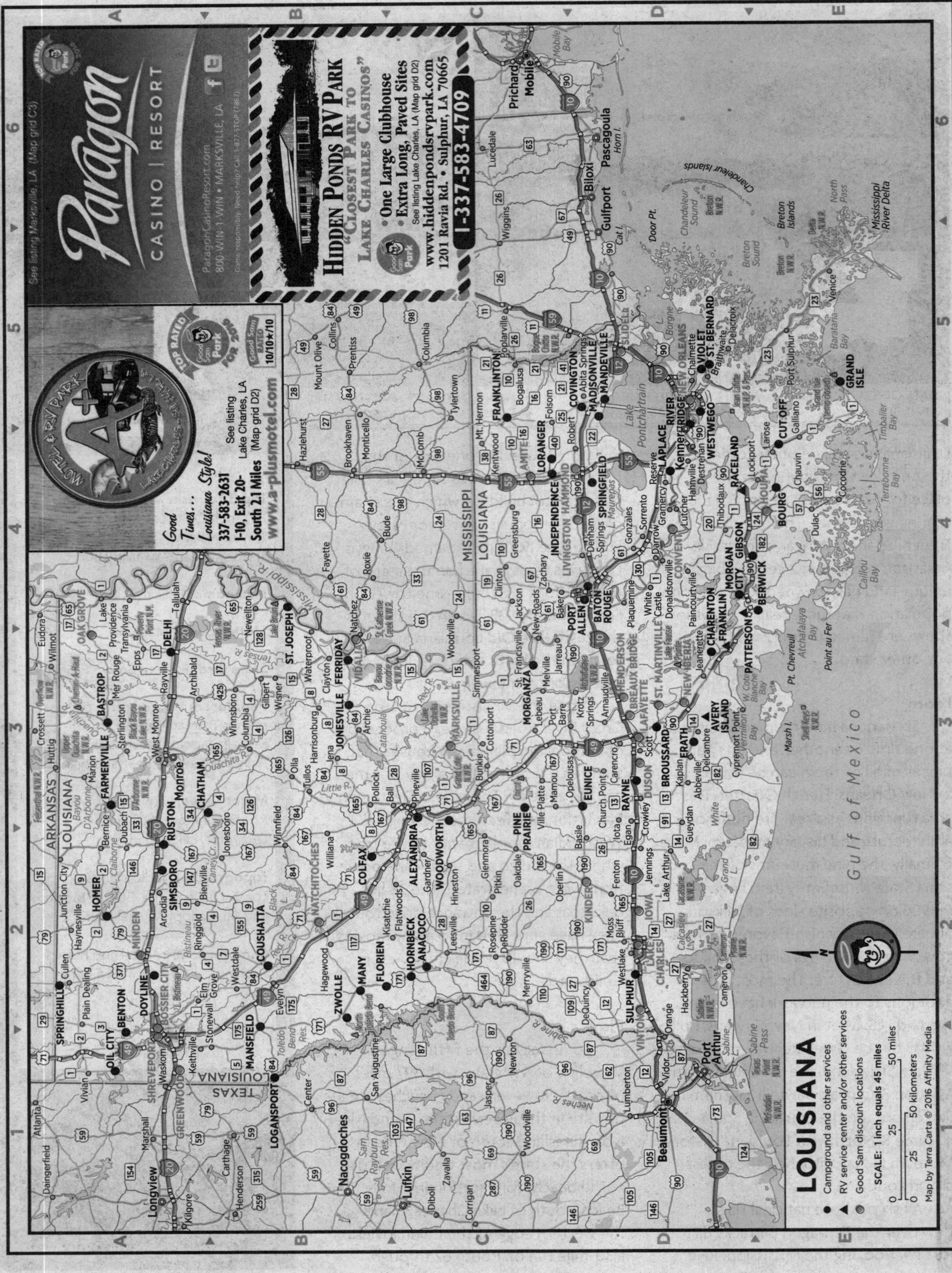
See listing Marksville, LA (Map grid C3)
Paragon
CASINO | RESORT
ParagonCasinoResort.com
800-WIN-1-WIN • MARKSVILLE, LA
HIDDEN PONDS RV PARK
"CLOSEST PARK TO LAKE CHARLES CASINOS"
• One Large Clubhouse
• Extra Long, Paved Sites
See listing Lake Charles, LA (Map grid D2)
www.hiddenpondsrvpark.com
1201 Ravia Rd. • Sulphur, LA 70665
1-337-583-4709
A+ MOTEL & RV PARK
TOP RATED Good Sam Park FOR 2016
Good Sam RATED 10/10★/10
Good Times... Louisiana Style!
337-583-2631
I-10, Exit 20-
South 2.1 Miles
See listing Lake Charles, LA (Map grid D2)
www.a-plusmotel.com
Gulf of Mexico
LOUISIANA
Campground and other services
RV service center and/or other services
Good Sam discount locations
SCALE: 1 inch equals 45 miles
Map by Terra Carta © 2016 Affinity Media

1

LAKE CHARLES
SOUTHWEST LOUISIANA
CONVENTION & VISITORS BUREAU

Taste the Cajun's favorite finger food along the Southwest Louisiana Boudin Trail! Explore natural Gulf beaches, hike through trails over the marsh for bird-watching and view alligators in their natural habitat. Experience Cajun/Creole food & culture. Start your Creole Nature Trail All-American Road adventure here.

800-456-7952 • www.visitlakecharles.org/adventure

2

It's Gumbo for Your Soul!

ST. LANDRY PARISH
SOUTH CENTRAL LOUISIANA

Shop 500+ antique vendors, experience the racetrack casino, hear live Cajun and Zydeco music, enjoy a historic walking tour, and attend festivals that celebrate our culture. Choose from eight RV/Campground locations off I-49 between Alexandria and Lafayette in Southwest Louisiana.
Come visit St. Landry Parish – It's Gumbo for Your Soul!

877-948-8004 • www.cajuntravel.com

3

Vermilion Parish
TOURIST COMMISSION
ça fait chaud!
www.MostCajun.com

Vermilion Parish, "the Most Cajun place on earth!" Sure, we're known for our food, but we're more than a great meal - authentic Cajun culture, festivals, marshlands, nature, true Southern hospitality and more. Come visit, your place at the table is ready! Located 30 minutes from Lafayette and New Iberia.

337-898-6600 • www.MostCajun.com

4

BAYOU *Lafourche*
AREA CONVENTION & VISITORS BUREAU

Come Live the Bayou Life!
Drive your RV to Bayou Lafourche and get away to a bayou kind of life with Cajun culture, food and fishing. Just 45 minutes from New Orleans, Bayou Lafourche is the gateway to Cajun Country and the Gulf of Mexico.

877-537-5800 • www.VisitLafourche.com

5

New Orleans
PLANTATION COUNTRY

Make A Date With History
In New Orleans Plantation Country, embark on a swamp tour, enjoy Louisiana cuisine, and visit history at majestic plantations, including an RV resort.

866-204-7782
VisitNOPC.com

6

TANGIPAHOA *Tourism*
TANGIPAHOA PARISH CONVENTION & VISITORS BUREAU

Conveniently located at the Crossroads of the South, Tangipahoa Parish is the place where fun meets adventure. The area features shopping districts, a wildlife refuge, historic downtowns, museums, first class campgrounds, plus much more. Stay for a day or a lifetime at the intersection of Louisiana Interstates 55 and 12!

800-542-7520 • www.tangitourism.com

7

LOUISIANA Northshore
St. Tammany Parish
LouisianaNorthshore.com

St. Tammany Parish/Louisiana's Northshore has two waterfront state parks, Fontainebleau and Fairview-Riverside. There's also family-friendly campgrounds with sandy beaches, clear rivers, cabins and campsites.

800-634-9443
www.LouisianaNorthshore.com/camp

LA

coastal marshes and bayous. This is part of the Creole Nature Trail All-American Road, which draws visitors for birding, fishing, crabbing and shell collecting.

Louisiana boasts more than two dozen state parks, and you can bet they all offer some sort of water recreation. Ancient wetlands anchored by cypress and tupelo swamps abound, and the Atchafalaya wilderness is America's largest river swamp. Airboats, kayaks and flat-bottomed boats all carry tourists into these murky, mysterious wonderlands. For touring at a faster pace, consider the ATV Swamp Tours in Prairieville, where all-terrain vehicles can negotiate more than 40 miles of often wet swampland trails.

Jackson Square is one of the must-visit spots in New Orleans. Tour Louisiana

Experience

With more than 400 festivals, Louisiana likes to bill itself as the Festival Capital of America, and when you are home to Mardi Gras, you back up that boast. New Orleans gets all the feature stories for its Fat Tuesday celebration in February, but this is a statewide party with more than a dozen colorful parades in Monroe, Shreveport, Houma and elsewhere. For more family-oriented New Orleans fun, the French Quarter Festival featuring jazz, blues and zydeco music brings more than 700,000 celebrants to the Crescent City for the free events.

The diverse Louisiana culture always seems to be bursting onto the streets somewhere. In Lafayette, the Festival International de Louisiane honors the region's French heritage with one of the country's best world music festivals. Embrace your inner pirate in Lake Charles, where local require 12 days to fit in all the celebrations to salute the high-seas buccaneer Jean Lafitte during Contraband Pirate Days.

Taste

No state is more associated with its food than Louisiana. To navigate the state's menus, you will need to know the difference between the two signature styles of cuisine: Cajun and Creole. Although they are often tossed into the same linguistic pot, Cajun and Creole cultures are distinctly different. Creole cooking is often associated with the big city and uses tomatoes; Cajun is usually shorthand for country food, and the gumbo will not contain tomatoes. And if you want that cuisine on a sandwich, you will be ordering a Po'boy.

TRAVEL & TOURISM

Louisiana Office of Tourism
800-99-GUMBO
www.louisianatravel.com
nbroussard@crt.la.gov

Visitor Centers
318-938-5613
greenwood@crt.la.gov

I-20 West—Mound
318-574-5674
mound@crt.la.gov

U.S. 84—Vidalia
318-336-7008
vidalia@crt.la.gov

I-49—Alexandria
318-767-6000
alexandria@crt.la.gov

I-10 East—Vinton
337-589-7774
vinton@crt.la.gov

I-10 Atchafalaya
337-228-1094
atchafalaya@crt.la.gov

U.S. 61—St. Francisville
225-635-6962
stfrancisville@crt.la.gov

State Capitol
225-342-7317
statecapitolwc@crt.la.gov

Capitol Park Welcome Center
225-342-8119
capitolpark@crt.la.gov

I-55—Kentwood
985-229-8338
kentwood@crt.la.gov

I-59—Pearl River
985-646-6450
pearlriverwc@crt.la.gov

I-10 West—Slidell
985-646-6451
slidell@crt.la.gov

New Orleans
504-568-5661
neworleanswc@crt.la.gov

Louisiana Office of State Parks
888-677-1400, 225-342-8111
www.lastateparks.com

River Barge Excursion Lines
888-GO-BARGE
www.riverbarge.com

OUTDOOR RECREATION

Louisiana Dept. of Wildlife and Fisheries
225-765-2800
www.wlf.state.la.us

SHOPPING

Magazine Street
866-679-4764, 504-342-4435
www.magazinestreet.com

Maskarade
504-568-1018
www.themaskstore.com

Riverwalk Marketplace
504-522-1555
www.riverwalkmarketplace.com

River Cruising
225-765-2800
www.wlf.state.la.us

The Shop at the Top
www.louisianaoldstatecapitol.org

Featured Good Sam Parks

LOUISIANA

Good Sam Park

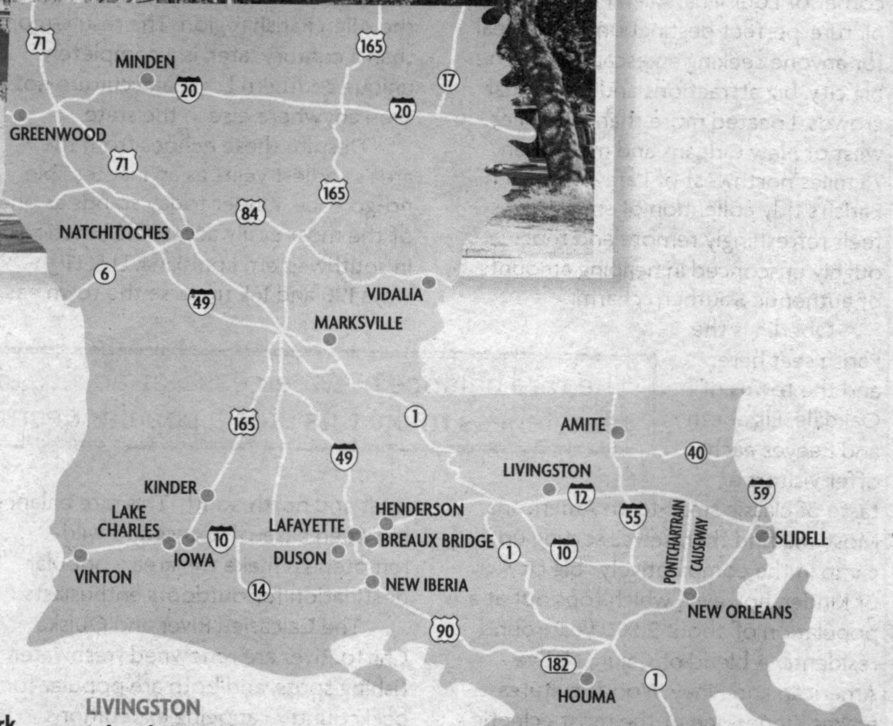

When you stay with Good Sam, you can expect the highest degree of cleanliness and friendliness, and better yet, you get 10% off campground fees.

If you're not already a Good Sam member you can purchase your membership at one of these locations:

AMITE
Natalbany Creek Campground & RV Park
(985)748-4311

BREAUX BRIDGE
Poche's RV Park
(337)332-0326

DUSON
Frog City RV Park
(337)873-9085

GREENWOOD
Travelcenters Of America RV Park
(318)938-6360

HENDERSON
Cajun Palms RV Resort
(337)667-7772

HOUMA
Capri Court Campground
(800)428-8026

IOWA
Cypress Bend RV Park
(877)409-2784

KINDER
Coushatta Luxury RV Resort at Red Shoes Park
(800)584-7263

LAFAYETTE
Bayou Wilderness RV Resort
(337)896-0598

LAKE CHARLES
A+ Motel & RV Park
(337)583-2631
Hidden Ponds RV Park
(337)583-4709
Twelve Oaks RV Park
(337)439-2916

LIVINGSTON
Lakeside RV Park
(225)686-7676

MARKSVILLE
Paragon Casino RV Resort
(800)946-1946

MINDEN
Cinnamon Creek RV Park
(318)371-5111

NATCHITOCHES
Nakatosh Campground
(318)352-0911

NEW IBERIA
KOC Kampground
(337)364-6666

NEW ORLEANS
French Quarter RV Resort (FQRV)
(504)586-3000
Jude Travel Park Of New Orleans
(800)523-2196

SLIDELL
New Orleans East Kampground
(800)562-2128
Pine Crest RV & MH Park Of New Orleans
(800)879-5936

VIDALIA
River View RV Park and Resort
(318)336-1400

VINTON
VRV Campground
(866)589-2300

For more Good Sam Parks go to listing pages

LA

Getty Images/iStockphoto

ALLEN PARISH/KINDER

Soak in authentic Louisiana charm in the heart of the bayou

Tucked into the heart of the southwest corner of Louisiana, Allen Parish is a picture-perfect destination that's ideal for anyone seeking an escape from the big city, big attractions and big tourist crowds. Located more than 200 miles west of New Orleans and more than 75 miles northwest of Lafayette, Allen Parish's tidy collection of small towns feels refreshingly remote and thoroughly ensconced in heaping amounts of authentic Southern charm.

Oberlin is the Parish seat here, and the towns of Oakdale, Elizabeth and Reeves each offer visitors a taste of classic small-town Americana. Most will find themselves setting up camp in the comparatively "big city" of Kinder, however, which tops out at a population of about 2,500 year-round residents. A blend of Cajun, Native American and Piney Woods cultures makes Kinder one of the most eclectic and diverse tiny towns one could ever hope to experience. From its handful of streets, the rest of the Parish's 766 square miles are a breeze to explore.

> The rare balance between ease-of-access and wild remoteness make this area a popular destination.

Kinder's Cajun Spirit

It wasn't until 1912 that the Parish was officially named, stringing together a handful of settlements that had been formed in the decade prior. Kinder—formed in 1903 and taking its name from the general store once operated by James Kinder—was one such location. Settlement in the region and Kinder specifically was a melting pot. Acadians (precursors to the Cajuns), Spanish, French, British and east coast Americans were all present in the early years of the Allen Parish region. The result, more than a century later, is a completely unique southern Louisiana culture not seen anywhere else in the state.

Despite these echoes from the area's earliest years as an inaccessible no-go zone, Kinder today stands as one of the most easily accessible junctions in southwestern Louisiana. U.S. Highways 190 and 165 traverse the town east-west and north-south. This rare balance between ease-of-access and wild remoteness make the area a popular destination for outdoors enthusiasts.

The Calcasieu River and Ouiska Chitto River are renowned freshwater fishing spots, and both are popular for backcountry canoeing expeditions. Anglers shouldn't expect to haul in trophy-sized catch with any regularity, but spotted bass are plentiful. Hunters, hikers, birdwatchers and backcountry campers head straight for the West Bay Wildlife Management Area. At 60,000 acres, it offers an abundance of space to zero in on a range of game, including deer, goose, duck and turkey.

Let it Ride at Coushatta

For a decidedly less wild bout of fun in the great outdoors, the Koasati Pines Golf Club is located right next door to Kinder's other main attraction, the Coushatta Casino Resort. The course features an 18-hole, par-72 championship layout dotted with pine stands, large oaks and glassy lakes. A special "gambling hole" ties the course in nicely with the casino next door, while a variety of holes feature multiple approaches, making for a fun but challenging day on the greens.

Whether you stop for a round at Koasati Pines or not, a trip to the Coushatta Casino is a must for all visitors to Kinder. Coushatta is one of the largest land-based casinos in the state and also includes an on-site RV resort, luxury hotel, six restaurants and a full schedule of live entertainment.

Even those traveling with children will find the casino to be a surprisingly family-friendly destination. In addition to its 100,000-square-foot gaming floor—featuring close to 3,000 slot machines—Coushatta is home to a massive pool and water park as well as Kids Quest play center. The pool features swim-up bars, a lazy river and a selection of water slides, while Kids Quest offers an exciting mix of arcade games, craft centers and an indoor playground.

For More Information

Allen Parish Tourist Commission
888-639-4868
www.allenparish.com

Louisiana Office of Tourism
800-994-8626
www.louisianatravel.com

LUXURY RV RESORT
COUSHATTA
KINDER, LA
AT RED SHOES PARK
Coushatta Luxury RV Resort
at Red Shoes Park
Over 100 concrete, full hook-up, pull-through RV pads
40 landscaped acres • 100 chalets • 2.6 acre lake with pier • Bathhouse
Lodge with fireplace & game room • Luxuriously heated swimming pool
Laundry facilities • Free cable TV & Wi-Fi • Lucky Paws Dog Park
Children's playground • Tennis, basketball, volleyball & shuffleboard courts
Horseshoe pits • Handicapped access available • Shuttles to & from the casino
18-hole, par 72 championship golf course - Koasati Pines • Live Bingo
Over 2800 Slots • Over 70 Table Games • Off-Track Betting
COUSHATTA
CASINO RESORT
KINDER, LOUISIANA
LOUISIANA'S BEST BET!
800.584.7263 | coushattacasinoresort.com
777 Coushatta Drive | Kinder, LA |
Management reserves the right to alter or cancel any promotion without notice. Events and dates subject to change.
Coushatta supports responsible gaming. Call 877-770-7867. Coushatta Casino Resort is owned and operated by the Coushatta Tribe of Louisiana.
Kinder
Alexandria
165
Houston
Lafayette
10
EXIT 44
Lake Charles
TOP RATED
Good Sam Park
FOR 2016
FREE NIGHT'S STAY
For every night purchased, get one FREE night-up to 5 nights FREE when you present your
2016 Good Sam RV Travel Guide & Campground Directory displaying this offer at check-in.
Valid at RV sites only • Based on availability | Expires 12/31/2016
See listing Kinder, LA

Jerrye & Roy Klotz, MD

AVOYELLES PARISH/MARKSVILLE AREA

Cool your heels at the crossroads of the Pelican State

Set up camp in Avoyelles Parish in central Louisiana and you'll quickly discover why the area has been known as the crossroads of the Pelican State since as far back as the 18th century.

The artsy riverside city of Alexandria is an easy 40 miles away to the northwest. Lafayette and Baton Rouge are less than a two-hour drive away to the south, where they each burst with great Cajun food and culture on the inland edges of the bayou. And 170 miles away to the southeast sits always-rollicking New Orleans, which makes for a boisterous and fun-filled daytrip any time of year.

In short, from Avoyelles Parish, the rest of the very best of the south is readily at hand, making it an ideal junction to either stop and peruse while passing through, or use as a quaint and quiet base camp from which to branch out and explore the entire southern half of the state.

Most visitors will find themselves drawn to the parish seat of Marksville, which by default serves as the parish's closest offering to a "big city." Home to only about 5,000 year-round residents, Marksville's roots lie with Marc Eliche, an Italian immigrant whose wagon wheel broke while he was passing through the area in 1794. Eliche looked about, noticed how gorgeous the landscape was and decided to simply stay put instead.

He quickly established a trading post to help others passing through the area and he gradually became known as Mark, instead of Marc. He later obtained grants for a vast swath of land in the area, which gradually became known to travelers as Mark's Place. The jump to Marksville was a short one from there.

Marksville's roots lie with Marc Eliche, an Italian immigrant whose wagon wheel broke while he was passing through the area in 1794.

A Wilderness Smorgasbord

Outdoorsy types and nature enthusiasts will have trouble deciding where to begin. The surrounding buffet of freshwater lakes and rivers make for fantastic fishing and hunting, while the Spring Bayou Wildlife Management Area and Grande Cote National Wildlife Refuge provide vast tracts of protected wilderness to roam and explore. You'll also discover a robust population of American Bald Eagles to observe.

The Spring Bayou WMA, located just 2 miles east of Marksville, covers more than 12,000 acres of wetland and bayou in the Red River drainage basin. It's a popular location for hunters, with game that includes deer, rabbit, bobcat, mink and a range of waterfowl. More than 40 percent of the WMA is water, making this a haven for anglers. Largemouth bass, catfish, panfish, drum and garfish are plentiful.

For a dose of history, head to the Marksville State Historic Site, home to ancient burial mounds belonging to prehistoric Native Americans.

Go Gaming

When it's time to blow off steam, the Paragon Casino Resort in Marksville is the place. Check out the gaming floor, tropical pool with a swim-up bar, full-service spa, movie theater, golf course and a nightly slate of live entertainment.

For More Information

Avoyelles Commission of Tourism
800-833-4195
www.travelavoyelles.com

Louisiana Office of Tourism
800-994-8626
www.louisianatravel.com

Bayous abound near Avoyelles Parish. Getty Images/iStockphoto

TOP RATED
Good Sam Park
FOR 2016
Paragon RV Resort
A Perfect 10/10★/10
Six Years in a Row!
ROLL IN TO RESORT LIVING
Paragon RV Resort in Marksville, Louisiana has been awarded another perfect 10/10★/10 by the Good Sam RV Travel & Savings Guide for cleanliness, environment and facilities! The resort features a world-class casino with slots and table games. Amenities include a full-service spa, shopping, an arcade, Kid's Quest, a three-screen cinema, fabulous dining choices, a championship golf course and live entertainment. Enjoy a spacious lodge, three swimming pools and free Wi-Fi. It's the perfect RV oasis!
Ask about Good Sam discounts.
Call 800-WIN-1-WIN or visit ParagonOffers.com
BEST OVERALL PROPERTY
BEST ENTERTAINMENT
BEST CASINO PERSONNEL
BEST GOLF COURSE
Paragon
CASINO | RESORT
ParagonCasinoResort.com
800-WIN-1-WIN • MARKSVILLE, LA
Restrictions may apply. Visit website for more information.
Game responsibly. Need help? Call 1-877-STOP (7867).
See listing Marksville, LA

BATON ROUGE

Louisiana's capital rivals the Big Easy in fun and food

The capital of Louisiana and the state's second-largest city after New Orleans, Baton Rouge has lots to see and do within its city limits. Situated on the banks of the Mississippi River Delta, this vibrant city ships out 61 million tons of cargo every year. It also attracts legions of visitors who seek its cultural and recreational attractions.

> Although Baton Rogue is very much a modern city, its cultural traditions are celebrated both in ecclectic museums and in daily life.

The city gets its name, French for "red stick," from early settlers who noticed a red pole that marked the border between the hunting grounds of the local Houma and Bayougoula tribes.

The first Europeans came here in 1699, and the city has been controlled by a number of nations ever since, finally secured to the United States after the American Civil War. Although there was an early French presence (a fort was built here in 1719), much of the modern character comes from the migration of French-speaking Acadians who came here during the French-Indian War. Although Baton Rogue is very much a modern city, its cultural traditions are celebrated both in museums and in daily life, and it's an excellent place to learn about the state's rich and unique heritage while sampling some of the finest Creole and Cajun cuisine that Louisiana has to offer.

One of the best places to learn about local life is the Louisiana State University Rural Life Museum, full of historic buildings (and reproductions) that give insight into what life was like in the 18th and 19th centuries. The 25-acre open-air museum is full of artifacts, informational panels and old farm equipment, giving visitors a realistic and interactive way to understand the region's agricultural past.

The Louisiana State Museum also deals with the region's history and culture, beyond rural life, and is full of displays on everything from the Civil Rights Movement to the shrimping industry. The Shaw Center for the Arts is a multi-use arts building used for both visual and performing arts. The LSU Museum of Art is housed here and features traveling exhibits and a permanent collection of painting, sculpture and photography from around the world. The Shaw Center is also home to the Manship Theatre, which plays host to a large number of theatrical and musical performances throughout the year.

Family Fun

The Baton Rouge Zoo features animals from around the world, including a Parrot Paradise full of colorful birds, a Realm of the Tiger exhibit dedicated to the striped cats and an aquarium focusing on local water life. There's also the small Cypress Bayou Railroad tourist train that takes children and adults along the zoo's perimeter.

One of the city's most popular spots for kids and grownups alike is the *USS Kidd*, a U.S. Navy destroyer that saw action in the Pacific during WWII. Today, it serves as a floating educational museum. The Blue Bayou Water Park, with wave pools and water slides—including the world's largest in-line water slide—is a great place to take kids, especially on hot summer days when the heat and humidity can make even the most patient of visitors a little cranky.

Culinary Capital

Baton Rogue is one of the world's top spots for authentic Creole and Cajun food. Food tours that make stops at numerous downtown Baton Rogue restaurants are a popular way to sample local cuisine and are great for foodies

The Baton Rouge skyline. Getty Images/iStockphoto

who want a little history and context with their meals.

Tony's Seafood is a market with both fresh and ready-to-eat food, from fried catfish to boudin to muffuletta. They also have a ton of mixes for those who want to try out their hand at cooking up local specialties back at home—just be warned that it's a popular spot with locals and can get packed.

Louisiana Lagniappe Restaurant is another great place to try fresh Cajun and Creole items, from fried catfish to crab cakes. The word *lagniappe* is Cajun for "a little something extra," and it's customary to give guests at bars and restaurants a bit of *lagniappe*, such as a plate of chips or an extra shot of whiskey. The portions are huge and come with *lagniappe*, so come with a good appetite!

Parrain's Seafood Restaurant is another hit with locals and visitors alike—along with fried fish they offer plenty of other local treats, from alligator to healthier grilled varieties of fish.

Mansurs On The Boulevard serves a more upscale take on local specialties and has a huge wine list.

And if you're in the mood for something other than Creole and Cajun fare, there are plenty of restaurants serving cuisine from around the world, from Zorba's Greek Bistro, a casual Greek restaurant, to Tsunami, which serves fresh sushi.

History buffs should take time to tour the state's two capitol buildings. The Old State Capitol and current capitol buildings are showcases in Gothic and Art Deco styles, respectively.

For More Information

Baton Rouge Area Convention and Visitors Bureau
800-LAROUGE
www.visitbatonrouge.com

Louisiana Office of Tourism
800-99-GUMBO
www.louisianatravel.com

Louisiana State Capitol Building. Getty Images/iStockphoto

LA

 See map page 526

Getty Images/iStockphoto

SPOTLIGHT LA

CAJUN COAST/ST MARY PARISH

Find bayou bliss at the arch of the Louisiana boot

Let the *lagniappe* come rolling in on a trip to Louisiana's Cajun Coast. Translated into English, that "little something extra" is evident in the history and culture of this unique, fun-loving area. Located on the arch of Louisiana's boot along the Gulf of Mexico, this region is a compelling collection of wild wetlands, beautiful coast and vibrant Cajun culture. It's a must for anyone who wants a true taste of the Pelican State.

> Get muddy alongside the locals in a crawfishing expedition and enjoy the spoils at a classic crawfish boil. Nothing beats the feeling of catching your own dinner.

St. Mary Parish was established in 1811 after the territorial government divided the Attakapas region. Abundant natural resources, including petroleum and seafood, helped cement the parish's place in the regional economy.

Franklin, the parish seat, was settled by the French, Acadian, German, Danish and Irish while Louisiana was still a foreign colony. English settlers migrated there after the Louisiana Purchase in 1803, and sugar plantations soon populated the area. The town of Patterson once claimed the largest cypress sawmill in the world, as well as the site of Wedell-Williams Air Service, which provided charter trips to New Orleans in the 1920s and 1930s.

Bayou Teche Scenic Byway traverses St. Mary Parish and divides to French Cajun culture to the Upper Tech and Anglo-Saxon culture to the Lower Teche. Moss-draped live oaks and historic properties line the Byway as it winds 125 miles through south-central Louisiana.

Cane Country

Discover sugar cane mills and plantation homes along Bayou Teche, and stop at the Chitimacha Museum in the community of Charenton to learn about the early inhabitants of modern-day Louisiana. The Chitimacha tribe is renowned for its basket weaving crafts and maintains a reservation near Charenton.

More than 420 historic buildings grace the streets of Franklin. Wander through the town's historic district to view antebellum homes, Victorian cottages and a shopping district that's straight out of the 1800s. Step inside Oaklawn Manor, a Greek Revival plantation home that's the resident of a former governor. The home features European antiques and an extensive Audubon collection.

Bayou Teche stretches for 135 miles and is part of the National Water Trails System. Tour the waterway by canoe or kayak and enjoy the natural beauty up close at your own pace. Take a swamp tour through the Atchafalaya National Heritage Area and learn about the wildlife that inhabits the diverse ecosystem as well as the region's importance in the fur trade. Break out the binoculars along your journey for a peek at any of

Cabins at Cypremort Point State Park. Cajun Coast Visitors & Tourism Bureau

several species thriving in the preserve. Egrets, eagers, Swainson's warbler and wintering geese are just a few you'll spot here.

Get to know life on an offshore oil rig at the International Petroleum Museum in Morgan City. The historic rig on the site is the museum's centerpiece, and a guided tour teaches visitors about the industry and its impact on the economy and livelihood of Louisianans. Climb aboard the *Amelia Belle,* a riverboat-turned-casino near Lake Palourde, and try your luck at table games and slot machines before dining on a Cajun buffet.

Brownell Memorial Park & Carillon Tower invites residents and visitors alike to enjoy music played twice an hour by 61 bronze bells that were cast in Holland. The 9.5-acre community park sits next to Lake Palourde and is a designated bird sanctuary.

Test your golf mettle in Patterson at the Atchafalaya at Idlewild, a course that has been in the Top 50 by *Golfweek*. The course pays tribute to the surrounding scenery with its 18 holes named for cultural features of the basin. Golfers of all skill levels find a challenging game here, along with a unique common green that hosts holes 9 and 18.

Party Down, Cajun Style

The people of the Cajun Coast love a good celebration, and they host several events throughout the year to mark historic occasions and recognize the region's unique character. Bayou Teche Black Bear Festival in Franklin honors the Louisiana black bear with educational seminars, field trips, music and fireworks. The event is held in conjunction with the Bayou Teche Wooden Boat Show, in which antique and modern wooden vessels line the waterway.

Christmas, Mardi Gras and autumn festivities each garner their own events, as well as offshore-focused fetes such as the curiously paired Shrimp & Petroleum Festival. This five-day event is Louisiana's oldest state-chartered harvest festival and features a blessing of the fleet.

Cajun Country's coastal location offers an abundance of fishing opportunities, both on and offshore. Angle for speckled trout and redfish in the marshes, or head out deep into the Gulf of Mexico for snapper or dolphin fish. Get muddy alongside the locals in a crawfishing expedition and enjoy the spoils of your efforts at a classic crawfish boil.

Set sail or take a cool dip in Vermilion Bay at Cypremort Point State Park. Cypremort Point is located between Grand Isle and Cameron and is the only location near the Gulf of Mexico that is accessible by car. The boat launch just outside the entrance to the park provides access to the Gulf or the bay, and the Louisiana marshlands surrounding the park are home to alligator, deer, black bears and red foxes as well as dozens of bird species.

For More Information

Cajun Coast Visitors & Tourism Bureau
800-256-2931
www.cajuncoast.com

Louisiana Office of Tourism
800-99-GUMBO
www.louisianatravel.com

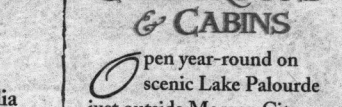

LA

HAMMOND/TANGIPAHOA PARISH

Explore a community with deep roots in Louisiana heritage

Loosely translated, "Tangipahoa" means "those who gather corn," a reference to the Acolapissa People who inhabited the region when brothers Pierre and Jean le Moyne arrived to colonize southern Louisiana at the turn of the 18th century. And while corn might have been the defining feature of the area 300 years ago, today the parish's name might as well stand for "location, location, location."

Tangipahoa Parish sits just across the waters of Lake Pontchartrain from New Orleans, and sits within easy reach of both western Alabama and southern Mississippi. The Gulf of Mexico is a stone's throw to the east and, because the parish isn't part of the swampy bayou ecosystem that defines so much of the rest of southern Louisiana, interstates 55 and 12 run directly through, rapidly connecting Tangipahoa with the rest of the state. Set up camp here and you'll be positioned at the crossroads of the south.

> A total of 95 officially designated historic buildings dating between 1880 and 1944 can be found here.

The prime location has helped make the parish (and the town of Hammond in particular) a major commercial and transportation center. In fact, the area has been a main thoroughfare for trade and inter-regional traffic since the days when Native Americans used it to travel between western Louisiana and settlements in Mobile and Pensacola further east.

Hammond History

Start your explorations in the small city of Hammond, a pioneer-era settlement turned railroad town that's blossomed into a major distribution center for the American South.

If you're a history buff, you'll be well-served by kicking things off with a walk through Hammond's Historic District, which is part of the city's downtown core. A total of 95 officially designated historic buildings dating between 1880 and 1944 can be found here, displaying a range of architectural stylings, from the Victorian era to Renaissance Revival.

An afternoon at the African American Heritage Museum is another must for those with a nose for history and art. Featuring eight galleries, more

Boats moored on a marina on Lake Pontchartrain. Getty Images/iStockphoto

A classic Conoco pump in Hammond. Infrogmation of New Orleans

than 20 original large-scale murals and a massive collection of historic artifacts, the museum profiles the stories and contributions of African Americans throughout the country's history.

Of course, you can't visit southern Louisiana without meeting an alligator or two. And at Kliebert's Alligator and Turtle Farm, located just south of downtown Hammond, you can meet a few hundred. This fully operational alligator and turtle farm offers visitors an informative behind-the-scenes tour that includes a guided Swamp People Trail walk. Throughout the tour, visitors will see 18-foot-long alligators, a 15-foot-long python and more than 40,000 different turtles.

> Throughout the tour, visitors will see 18-foot-long gators, a 15-foot-long python and more than 40,000 turtles.

A trio of family-fun attractions round out the must-visit list for Hammond. For the speedsters, there's River Road Go-Kart Track, home to a multi-use track and multiple sizes of karts fit for all ages and experience levels, including kids. For the rambunctious, there's Safari Quest, a 3,000-square-foot fun center home to laser tag, ropes courses, climbing trees, a state-of-the-art arcade and giant human hamster balls. Finally, for the education-minded, there's the Louisiana Children's Discovery Center, where more than 30 different interactive exhibits and activities are tailored exclusively to toddlers, young children and teenagers.

Louisiana Small-town Life

Outside of Hammond, the rest of Tangipahoa Parish is dotted with quaint small towns and communities that offer a quiet, relaxed pace. Amite City, Independence and Ponchatoula are particularly popular. Each one has its own designated historic district, making them a delight to stroll and explore.

Amite City is situated just west of the Tangipahoa River, making it a popular spot for kayakers, anglers and canoeists. As the parish seat, this is also the home for the Tangipahoa Parish Fair, held annually each September. In March, the town hosts the annual Oyster Festival.

Ponchatoula, for its part, calls itself the "Strawberry Capital of the World," so be sure to taste some of its prized wares while passing through. The town hosts the Strawberry Festival every April, and the event has become so popular it's now the second-largest free festival in the entire state of Louisiana. The town is also home to the Collinswood School Museum, which first opened as a one-room schoolhouse in 1876, and now serves the region as a general history museum. Items on display range from 10,000-year-old Native American artifacts to relics from the Civil War.

Finally, don't miss a visit to Camp Moore, located near the town of Kentwood. This original Confederate military training camp dates to 1861 and now serves as an interactive museum. The grounds were once used as a staging area and training facility, the largest of its kind in the state of Louisiana. Today, Camp Moore tells the story of the Civil War as seen through the eyes of the common foot soldier, from the battles they fought to the games they played to fill the hours between combat training sessions.

For More Information

Tangipahoa Parish Convention & Visitors Bureau
800-542-7520
www.tangi-cvb.org

Louisiana Office of Tourism
800-994-8626
www.louisianatravel.com

Infrogmation of New Orleans

HOUMA

Find the best of the Bayou in this slice of Louisiana heaven

Water defines the small community of Houma in southern Louisiana. Located deep in the swampy marshes and wetlands of balmy bayou country—just an hour's drive southwest of New Orleans—this charming postcard town is a popular jumping-off point for backcountry fishing trips, hunting charters, swamp tours and wildlife watching expeditions. Even in the very center of town, navigation by boat is absurdly commonplace, as a network of criss-crossing canals and shipping channels make the suburbs as accessible by shrimp boat as they are by car.

Make no mistake, this is bayou country, where the Mississippi River delta stands between the Gulf of Mexico and inland Louisiana. More than 65 percent of Terrebone Parish is classified as either wetland or open water, and if that wasn't enough to produce a distinct enough culture over the course of nearly 300 years of history, there's the colorful Cajun for good measure.

As such, you might want to brush up on your Cajun phraseology before landing in town. A mix of French, Acadian French (descendants of French settlers exiled from Nova Scotia in 1755) and English, Cajun words are as spicy and fun-loving as the foods for which the culture is so renowned. Craving some couche-couche, boudin or pain perdu? Get your tongue ready to order and your taste buds ready to savor some culinary delights.

Cajun cuisine itself is easy to make. It's a blend of classic French and Southern cooking with a pinch or two of secret influence from Germany, Spain, the Canary Islands, the Philippines and various Native American cultures. Toss the lot in a bowl, mix for 300 years and *voilà*! There may be no more richly nuanced culinary tradition in the world than real, authentic Cajun cuisine. And out-of-the-way small towns like Houma are the places to find it.

Make no mistake, this is bayou country, where the Mississippi River delta stands between the Gulf of Mexico and inland Louisiana.

Hit Houma's Downtown

Start in Houma's historic downtown core to go for a stroll. A self-guided walking tour that offers insight into the history of the town is available for history buffs. Among the sights are Terrebonne Parish Courthouse and a shrimp-packing plant that was founded in 1893. As you wander, the culinary tour will likely take care of itself, as Historic Downtown Houma is packed with mouthwatering restaurants and cafes.

Hikers, bird-watchers, anglers, hunters and boaters will want to spend some time exploring Mandalay National Wildlife Refuge, which covers 4,416 acres full of ponds, levees and man-made canals. If you're visiting between October and May you'll want to keep your eyes trained on the cypress-tree canopy for wintering bald eagles.

Greet the Gators

For a quick-and-easy day trip, nearby Gibson is home to a pair of family-friendly attractions that offer fun for all ages. The Wildlife Gardens provides visitors with the opportunity to walk through a live cypress swamp, tour a small alligator farm and see a 110-pound loggerhead turtle.

Also in Gibson is Greenwood Gator Farm, which annually houses and hatches between 5,000 and 10,000 baby alligators. Visitors enjoy a range of informative live shows, enjoy a behind-the-scenes tour and learn how to safely catch and hold baby alligators.

For More Information

Houma Area Convention & Visitors Bureau
985-868-2732
www.houmatravel.com

Louisiana's
BAYOU COUNTRY
Travel less than an hour southwest of New Orleans and you'll enter Louisiana's Bayou Country – Houma, Louisiana. Bordered by the bountiful Gulf of Mexico, surrounded by rich, coffee-colored bayous and shaded by an endless canopy of moss-draped cypress trees. Here in the Houma area, you'll find a rare blend of nature, as well as our centuries-old Cajun history that is infused in everything from our cooking and music to our architecture and lifestyle.
Houma
Louisiana's Bayou Country
HOUMATRAVEL.COM | 1-800-688-2732 | REQUEST A HOUMA VISITOR GUIDE TODAY!
See listing Houma, LA

 See map page 526

PAXTONimages.com for Peter A Mayer Advertising

LAFAYETTE

Celebrate Acadian culture in the Cajun capital

The 120,000-person city of Lafayette has plenty to offer visitors, particularly those interested in local culture and Louisiana history. Straddling the banks of the Vermilion River that runs through southwestern Louisiana, the city dates back to 1821, when it was founded by Jean Mouton, an Acadian settler. It was renamed Lafayette in 1884, in honor of the Marquis de Lafayette, who was well known for his support of the patriots during the Revolutionary War.

Cajun Capital

Lafayette is the de facto capital of Cajun Country and is celebrated for its strong musical traditions and street dances. Mardi Gras is feted here with fervor, and on Friday afternoons, the streets come to life with *fais-dodos* (street dances). There are also numerous museums in the city for history- and culture-loving travelers.

Visitors wanting to learn more about local culture should start their visit at the Acadian Cultural Center, which traces the history of the Acadian (Cajun) people of the region through exhibits, films, educational events and guided tours. The center is inside Jean Lafitte National Historical Park and Preserve, and every Tuesday through Friday, park rangers give talks on the history and culture of the region. Other on-site attractions include daily 9 am screenings of *The Cajun Way: Echoes of Acadia*, a half-hour-long film about the history of the Acadian people. The park also offers a Junior Ranger program for children, in which young visitors can earn badges and certificates by participating in educational activities and scavenger hunts. In spring and fall, rangers take visitors on guided tours aboard the Cocodrie, a traditionally built bayou boat.

Mardi Gras is feted here with fervor, and on Friday afternoons, the streets come to life with fun and spontaneous *fais-dodos* (street dances).

Another must-see destination is Acadian Village, a recreated 19th-century community with restored houses, neat walking paths and well-tended gardens. Learn how Acadians lived and worked in the age before phones, automobiles and the Internet.

In a similar vein, Vermilionville is a site that will be enjoyed by those interested in Acadian, Creole and Native American cultural traditions. This

The Acadian Cultural Center, also known as Vermilionville.
PAXTONimages.com for Peter A Mayer Advertising

Zydeco music isn't hard to find in Lafayette. Getty Images/iStockphoto

STAY HAPPY
HAPPIEST CITY IN AMERICA
Wall Street Journal's MARKETWATCH.COM
Lafayette is at the heart of Louisiana's Cajun & Creole Country, an area known for its swampland dotted with moss draped cypress trees teeming with wildlife. With plenty of outdoor adventures it's no wonder people are heading down south with a smile on their face.
STAY LAFAYETTE
LAFAYETTETRAVEL.COM/HAPPY
800 346 1958
See listing Lafayette, LA

Acadian Village is a collection of buildings that simulates an Acadian community in the 1800s. Jay Faugot Photography

23-acre living history museum focuses on life in the region between 1765 and 1890 and includes seven traditional restored homes for guests to explore. These include a reproduction chapel based on 18th-century Catholic churches, a Greek Revival house filled with traditional textiles, and a number of classical Acadian homes. There's even a reproduction schoolhouse with an old wood stove. The center also hosts cultural events throughout the year, including exhibits on indigenous traditions, Mardi Gras, Black history and Acadian culture. It's a great place for children, and along with demonstrations by local craftspeople. There's even a summer camp.

Cajun and Zydeco music are also celebrated with fervor in Lafayette, and the city has some great festivals. Along with the annual Mardi Gras celebrations, there's the Scott Boudin Festival, a family-friendly celebration of local food, culture and music that's held in the first weekend of April.

The 11-day-long Cajun Heartland State Fair is a state fair with a Cajun twist, and the Festivals Acadiens et Creoles are a collection of celebrations that fete Cajun and French Creole cultures. Every spring in March and April, the Lafayette Science Museum Foundation hosts the Bach Lunch, a lunchtime concert series held at the Parc Sans Souci as a benefit for the museum's programs. Visitors can listen to live music—including plenty of Cajun and Zydeco bands—while dining on specially prepared meals from some of the city's most loved local restaurants.

If you're visiting Lafayette in the fall of spring, be sure to catch the Downtown Alive concert series, held every Friday in the downtown district. Community and culture come together for music, food and drink in a convival atmosphere that is uniquely Lafayette.

Natural Attractions

Though Lafayette is certainly a culture capital, there's also plenty for lovers of nature and the great outdoors. Oak trees are particularly celebrated in the region, and in 1934 a local academic and botanist created the Live Oak Society, a membership organization for oak trees. A single human member acts as the honorary chairperson for registering trees, but otherwise all the members are of the arboreal persuasion. Various trees have held the presidency and vice presidency of the society, and while many have since succumbed to old age, there are plenty of younger oaks that take their place in this quirky—but certainly beneficial—local club.

Lafayette's Vermilion Bay is also a great spot for angling, and charter boats can be hired to take visitors out to fish. The waters are home to huge redfish, flounder, speckled trout and sheepshead.

Those interested in ecology won't want to miss Acadiana Park, a 110-acre natural area that's home to the Nature Station, an education and research center that's open to visitors every day. Along with over three miles of nature trails, the Nature Station offers special night hikes (held throughout the year on the last Saturday of the month) and kayak launches, as well as special programs designed to inspire a love of nature in young children.

For More Information

Lafayette Convention and Visitors Bureau
800-346-1958
www.lafayettetravel.com

Louisiana Office of Tourism
800-677-4082
www.louisianatravel.com

See map page 526

LAKE CHARLES

Party in town or cast a line in a storied body of water

In southwestern Louisiana, on the banks of Calcasieu River and about 30 miles north of the Gulf of Mexico, Lake Charles is a medium-size city best known for its strong Cajun influences and numerous festivals. Lake Charles and its surrounding regions are also home to numerous parks, casinos and museums, making it an ideal stop for those looking for a mix of activities.

Spread out over a 40-block span of downtown Lake Charles, the Charpentier Historic District is a must-see for anyone who loves old architecture. The homes here mostly date from the late Victorian era, and visitors can take a self-guided walking or driving tour by contacting the Lake Charles/Southwest Louisiana Convention & Visitors Bureau or downloading the bureau's Historic Tour app.

The Mardi Gras Museum is situated in an old school and features all kinds of colorful costumes and bedazzling masks from past Mardi Gras celebrations held in Lake Charles. It's considered the world's largest collection of Mardi Gras costumes and memorabilia, and there's even a float on display. The Imperial Calcasieu Museum is full of historical artifacts from around the region and is a good place to learn more about Southern Louisiana history. Traveling art and history exhibits are sometimes held in the Historic City Hall. There's also a Children's Museum with lots of hands-on science exhibits and play areas.

Adults might want to note that there are two casinos within city limits: L'Aubrege Casino Resort and Golden Nugget. Delta Downs Racetrack Casino and Hotel is located in nearby Vinton, and the Isle of Capri Casino & Hotel is in Westlake. Coushatta Casino Resort in nearby Kinder is also an option.

> The Creole nature trail stretches for miles through the region's wetlands and dishes out stunning views of green vistas populated by birds and alligators.

The culinary scene here ranges from quaint bistros, such as the 121 Artisan Bistro, to more casual spots, such as Hollier's Cajun Kitchen. Lake Charles is also a great spot to try out some boudin sausages, Cajun snack sausages sold in shops and restaurants throughout Southwest Louisiana—there's even a "Boudin Trail" map available through the visitors bureau that lists some of the top places to try the snack sausages.

Festivals of Lake Charles

Mardi Gras has been feted in Lake Charles since 1882, when the Mardi Gras King Momus first docked in the city. The event lost some of its fervor by the middle of the 20th century, but it was rekindled in the late '70s. Today, it attracts upwards of 150,000 people.

Another popular festivity, Contraband Days, is held over the first couple of weeks in May and attracts 200,000-plus visitors. The festival gets it name from Contraband Bayou, which was once home to lots of pirate activity. The festival launches every year with a reenactment of a pirate ship bombardment, complete with the raising of a Jolly Roger flag. The next 12 days see numerous festivities, from parades, rides, Cajun cook-offs, boat races, firework shows and special activities for children.

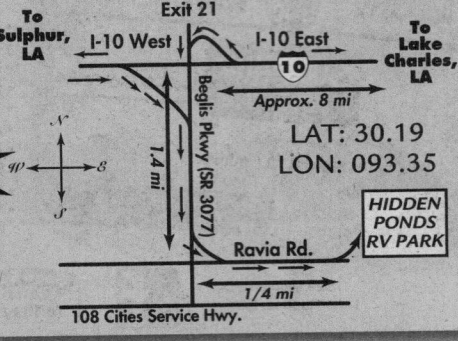

Held every year, the Arts & Crabs festival is a celebration of local cuisine, culture and art with—as the name suggests—a big focus on crabs. Guests can sample crabby specialties ranging from crabmeat beignets to crab gazpacho paired with craft brews from Louisiana's favorite breweries.

The annual Black Heritage Festival features entertainment from gospel, Zydeco and blues bands as well as numerous food booths featuring traditional African American and Creole foods. There's also a crafts fair and a kids' section, and those who want to burn off extra calories can even try out "Zydeco Aerobics."

The Downtown Crawfish Festival is another big hit and includes a parade, a carnival, a crawfish eating contest and live entertainment from Creole bands. The festival also includes a pageant, in which local girls and women of all ages compete to be crowned the Crawfish Festival Queen. The Iowa Rabbit Festival, in the nearby suburb of Iowa, also features a pageant, though in this case the contestants are of the furry, long-eared, hopping variety.

The Creole Nature Trail has earned the status of All-American Road.
PAXTONimages.com for Peter A Mayer Advertising

Lakeside Nature

There are plenty of natural sites in and around Lake Charles. The Creole nature trail stretches for miles through the region's wetlands and dishes out stunning views of green vistas populated by birds and alligators. South of Lake Charles, the Sabine Wetlands Park Nature Walkway is a boardwalk that winds through several wetlands areas. Climb an observation deck to get a panoramic view.

Like many Louisiana cities, Lake Charles has some very old oak trees, including the Sallier Oak. Located behind the Imperial Calcasieu Museum, the tree is believed to be almost 400 years old. The Bord Du Lac Park next to the lake that gives the city its name is a beautiful spot to relax, while Drew Park has play structures for children. Prien Lake Park has spots to go canoeing, while Sam Houston Jones State Park off Highway 378 features lots of trails, swamplands and campsites. Golfers can tee-off at the sprawling Contraband Bayou Golf Club at L'Auberge Du Lac, at the Mallard Cove Golf Course, or at the Gray Plantation Golf Course.

Wild in Louisiana
Ready to go birdwatching? The Sabine National Wildlife Refuge, about 10 miles south of Lake Charles on State Highway 27, protects the habitat for migratory waterfowl and other birds. The refuge consists of a basin of wetlands located between the Gulf's beach cheniers (oak ridges) and the coastal prairie, which is one of the most productive and fertile areas of North America.

The refuge encompasses 124,511 acres of fresh, intermediate and brackish marshes and is one of the largest estuarine-dependent marine species nurseries in southwest Louisiana. It has also been designated as an "Internationally Important Bird Area" because of the numerous wading, water and marsh

A 10-foot-long gator. Lake Charles/Southwest Louisiana Convention & Visitors Bureau

LA

A charming home in the Lake Charles Historic District. PAXTONimages.com for Peter A Mayer Advertising

Hoisting a beaded umbrella during Mardi Gras.
Lake Charles/Southwest Louisiana Convention & Visitors Bureau

birds that utilize it throughout the year. More than 280,000 people visit the refuge annually, and the exhibits in the refuge visitor center and the Wetland Walkway are considered two of the principal tourist attractions in southwest Louisiana. The refuge is an integral part of the Creole Nature Trail All American Road.

Cruising Lake Charles

Lake Charles can boast of having some of the most interesting sightseeing drives in the country. Set aside some time to cruise around the lake and take in the attractions.

Along the lakefront on Shell Beach Drive, visitors will find large antebellum family estates. One of these mansions was the home of famous country music star Lynn Anderson, who occupied it with her husband, Louisiana oilman Harold Stream III, while she lived in Lake Charles.

The stretch of Shell Beach that borders the lake is also lined with beautiful century-old oak trees. One estate in particular along Shell Beach is home to a famous 170-year-old oak tree known as the "Calcasieu Manor Tree." This oak tree is registered with the Live Oak Society of the Louisiana Garden Club Federation. The "Calcasieu Manor" tree also has a caretaker, and seedlings are harvested from the tree and sent to the coastline to be used in conservation preservation. There are three more old established oak trees located in the front of the property that were planted as seedings from this 170-year-old tree!

A Pirate From the Past

There are also many tales of the famous pirate Jean Lafitte, who is said to have docked in Lake Charles in the early 1800s. One story involving Lafitte has to do with the oldest house in Lake Charles: the Sallier-Barbe House located on Shell Beach Drive. Charles Sallier and his wife, Catherine, were quite good friends with the pirate, but Sallier had become jealous of his wife and Lafitte. As legend tells it, one day Charles Sallier thought that Catherine was having an affair with the buccaneer. In his rage, the husband picked up his pistol and shot Catherine.

When Catherine fell to the ground, he thought he had killed her, so he fled, never to be heard from again. However, Catherine survived the shot because of a simple piece of jewelry. When the pistol was fired, the bullet lodged in the large brooch Catherine was wearing. This brooch is a family heirloom that the Barbe family still treasures.

For More Information

Lake Charles/Southwest Louisiana Convention & Visitors Bureau
337-436-9588
www.visitlakecharles.org

Louisiana Office of Tourism
800-99-GUMBO
www.louisianatravel.com

Courtesy of McIlhenny Co.

NEW IBERIA

Spice up your travels by visiting the home of Tabasco

The small city of New Iberia on the Bayou Teche traces its history back to 1779, when Andalusian settlers moved into the area. French Acadians from Nova Scotia (later known as Cajuns) settled in the area not long after, and today the city and its surrounding region are best known for Cajun and Creole food and culture, particularly its biggest export: Tabasco Sauce, which has been produced and bottled on the nearby Avery Island for almost a century and a half.

Today, visitors can take walking tours along the city's East Main Street residential district. Main Street is home to the Bayou Teche Museum, which features cultural artifacts from the Bayou Teche region and is open Thursday through Saturday throughout the year. New Iberia also has the oldest rice mill in the U.S. that still uses a belt-driven power to this day. Other attractions include the antebellum Shadows-on-the-Teche, a National Historic Landmark mansion flanked by tall old oak trees coated in drooping Spanish moss.

Gardens and Birds

Gardens are another big attraction in the city, from the 25-acre Rip Van Winkle Gardens that wrap around the Joseph Jefferson Mansion to the gardens surrounding Antique Roseville, also known as the Renoudet Cottage, which now houses a restaurant and tea room. The grounds provide a habitat to over 100 types of antique roses as well as native plants ranging from cypress trees to Louisiana irises. The city also has a replica of the Grotto of Lourdes in France, which has beautifully landscaped grounds that include a gigantic oak tree that's more than 150 years old.

One of the most spectacular natural sites in the area is the 200-acre Jungle Gardens, featuring plants from around the world. This includes varietals developed on the island by the garden's founder, Edward Avery McIlhenny, an accomplished botonist and founder of Tabasco.

> Visitors to the Tabasco factory can learn about the aging process of Tabasco Sauce and try samples of the company's lesser-known sauces.

Tabasco Sauce

Just outside of New Iberia, Avery Island is home to Louisiana's famous Tabasco brand of pepper sauce, developed by the McIlhenny Company in 1868 and now sold around the world. Visitors to the factory can learn about the aging process of Tabasco Sauce and try samples of the company's lesser-known sauces and related products (including jelly beans made in conjunction with Jelly Belly) at the on-site Tabasco Country Store. Tours take place every day (except on major holidays), and visitors can watch pepper sauce being bottled from Monday through Thursday.

The new Avery Island experience gives visitors a chance to sample great Cajun dishes on a Tabasco Food Tour. Expanded offerings,a new visitor center and a Creole-cottage cafeteria-style restaurant will add to the experience.

Festivals

There's no shortage of festivals in New Iberia. In March, the Great Gator Race, a fundraiser for a local organization that supports rural Louisiana communities, features a race of some 5,000 plastic alligators along the Bayou Teche. In the same month, the Acadiana Dragon Boat Festival brings out teams of dedicated rowers and plenty of local spectators.

Other festivities include the World Championship Gumbo Cookoff—held in the second weekend in October—and the Cajun Hot Sauce Festival. The city's best-known event is arguably the Annual Sugar Cane Festival, now in its 74th year, which honors the sugar industry with parades and live music performances.

For More Information

LA

Iberia Travel
888-942-3742
www.iberiatravel.com

Louisiana Office of Tourism
800-99-GUMBO
www.louisianatravel.com

See listing New Iberia, LA

Getty Images/iStockphoto

NEW ORLEANS

Crescent city parties on—even after Mardi Gras

Renowned for its culinary excellence and nonstop festive atmosphere, New Orleans attracts food buffs and revelers from across the globe. And although the Big Easy is best known for its annual Mardi Gras celebrations, Louisiana's most popular destination has plenty of fantastic things to do year-round. Indeed, the eclectic city is characterized by warm weather, gorgeous old architecture, a boisterous nightlife scene and some of the finest jazz clubs on the planet.

The so-called Big Easy got its start in 1718, when French colonists settled along the Mississippi River and named their new trading post after a city in their home country. New Orleans retains its Gallic elements to this day, from local architecture to the integration of French terms into the local vernacular.

Over the years, the city has endured fires, wars and devastating natural disasters—including 2005's Hurricane Katrina. However, New Orleans has picked itself up again. Despite hardships, the local people here, known for their carefree attitudes and welcoming hospitality, have continued to help this festive city let the good times roll—or as the French-speaking population says, *laissez les bons temps rouler*!

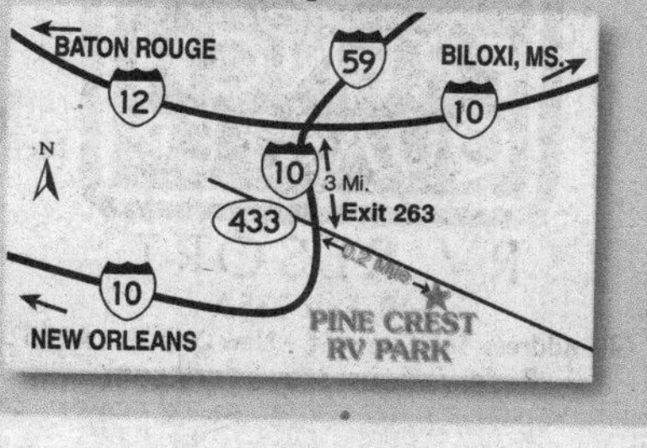

Historic Neighborhoods

New Orleans' major attraction is the historic 18th-century French Quarter, the oldest neighborhood in town, known for its gorgeous old architecture and quaint, European-style cobbled streets. At the heart of the French Quarter is Jackson Square, home to the Cathedral-Basilica of St. Louis, among the oldest continuously operating cathedrals in the country. Here guests can get a caricature drawn by a local artist, have their fortunes told, or hire a horse-drawn carriage to take them on a tour of the beautiful old city.

All visitors to New Orleans should make a point to stop by the world-famous Café du Monde, known for its fluffy beignets dusted in powdered sugar and its steaming hot cups of chicory-infused coffee, served 24 hours a day. While you're at it, stop by the French Market, an indoor-outdoor open-air market that sells handicrafts and local food items, including Tabasco sauce and Cajun spice blends. There are also a number of stalls and restaurants serving classic dishes, including jambalaya, gumbo and po'boy sandwiches.

The party scene is on Bourbon Street, and gets particularly rowdy when football fans from across the country come to town to see the New Orleans Saints play at the Mercedes-Benz Superdome. Orleans Street is much more chic and features high-end shops, antique stores, and its fair share of knickknack dealers.

Most visitors to New Orleans also make a point of heading out to the historic Garden District, known for its Italianate, Greek Revival, and Victorian homes—many of which are enormous mansions—ornately decorated with wrought-iron balconies and gates. This verdant part of town is most easily reached on the St. Charles Streetcar (aka the Streetcar Named Desire), which departs from the city's Central Business District, adjacent to the French Quarter. The Garden District has its own cemetery—Lafayette Cemetery No. 1—filled with gorgeous, eerie old tombs that make it a popular attraction for history buffs and art lovers. The city's oldest graveyard, St. Louis Cemetery No. 1, sees even more visitors.

Cutting the rug at the French Quarter Festival. Chris Granger

And if all that weren't enough, there are also regular tours that head out to many of the beautiful old plantation houses in the surrounding countryside, including Oak Alley, which has been featured in numerous films and TV shows, from "Interview With a Vampire" to "Days of Our Lives."

Mardi Gras and Jazz

Dubbed "the Greatest Free Show on Earth," Mardi Gras is the city's biggest tourist attraction, held every winter just before Lent. Although it has a reputation of being a debauchery-filled affair, it's not just for party animals; families can also find some fun amongst the crowds, especially those who want to sit and watch the elaborate parade floats from the sidelines. St. Charles Avenue in the Garden District is recommended for families with children, and glittering strings of plastic beads can be spotted in the trees that line the old avenue throughout the year.

The city's other big draw, especially for music lovers, is the New Orleans Jazz & Heritage Festival, known locally as Jazz Fest, one of the biggest music festivals in the United States. It's a weeklong celebration of local food, culture, and, of course, jazz music.

For More Information

New Orleans Convention and Visitors Bureau
800-672-6124
www.neworleanscvb.com

Louisiana Office of Tourism
800-677-4082
www.louisianatravel.com

Getty Images/iStockphoto

ST MARTIN PARISH

Experience Pelican State cool in a small cluster of towns

Slung between the comparatively big and boisterous cities of Lafayette to the west and Baton Rouge to the east, St. Martin Parish in southern Louisiana ties together a collection of classic small towns. Down-to-earth charm, zero crowds and vast tracts of gorgeous, wild landscapes make setting up camp here a richly rewarding reprieve for anyone seeking a bit of rest and relaxation.

Understanding the lay of the land in St. Martin Parish can be tricky for first-time visitors, since this is the only parish in the state to have non-contiguous regions. But this is more of a blessing than a cartographer's curse. The parish's unique layout means it sports three very distinct terrains—the Atchafalaya Basin, prairie plain and lush bayou—giving it a degree of variety not seen elsewhere in the state.

Regardless of where you decide to set up camp, take the time to explore the parish's collection of incredible small towns, especially St. Martinville ("Home of Evangeline"), Breaux Bridge ("Crawfish Capital of the World") and Henderson ("Gateway to the Atchafalaya Basin").

> The Atchafalaya Basin is the largest river basin in North America, with cypress forests and vast range of wildlife.

Evangeline's Legacy

In St. Martinville the literary legend of Evangeline (the eponymous character from Henry Wadsworth Longfellow's 1847 poem) still echoes loudly, perhaps no more so than at Evangeline Oak Park. Established near the turn of the century, the park and its famous oak tree have stood in honor of Longfellow's poem for more than a century. The legend fits in nicely with the surprising history of St. Martinville, which in the early 1800s was referred to as "Petit Paris," due to its rich performance arts scene.

Acadian ancestry is strongest here, as a quick visit to the Museum of the Acadian Memorial reveals. Dedicated to telling the story of the region's early Acadians who traveled from maritime Eastern Canada after being exiled by the British in the middle of the 18th century, the museum is a must for anyone with even a hint of southern Louisiana ancestry. While here, check out the local architecture. Attractions like the oustanding Soulier House, with its ornate railings and eye-catching round cupola, epitomize the architec-

LA

The statue of the mythic Evangeline evokes the region's bittersweet past.
Wikid77

The Soulier House is a St. Martinville architectural gem. Z28scrambler

tural style of the region.

The African-American Museum in St. Martinville is another must-visit, especially for students of history. The museum's deeply moving exhibits shed light on the rise and fall of the slave trade, as well as the hardships faced by people of color in the decades following the end of the Civil War. The museum's crown jewel is a 26-foot-high mural by Dennis Paul Williams, which depicts the historical accomplishments of some of St. Martinville's free people of color.

Over in Breaux Bridge, ready yourself for the mouthwatering smells of crawfish cook-offs and crawfish BBQs. From its roots as a simple suspension bridge crossing over the Bayou Teche to its self-anointed status as the "crawfish capital of the world," the community of Breaux Bridge is exactly as down-to-earth as it sounds. Its Historic Downtown District is dotted with heritage buildings, and guided walking tours can be arranged with a stop at the Breaux Bridge Visitors Center.

Breaux Bridge also plays host to the Crawfish Festival, which is a statewide favorite. The event spans three days every May, featuring a mix of live music, Cajun cuisine, dance contests, a carnival midway, a parade and—of course—a crawfish-eating contest.

Backcountry Travel

Those looking to journey out into the great outdoors for a day of hiking or a variety of backcountry adventure tours, fishing trips or hunting charters will want to make their way to the small town of Henderson. This humble outpost didn't even appear anywhere in official print until the 1930s and has its roots in the old village of nearby Atchafalaya. Today, the vibrant community serves as the gateway to Atchafalaya National Wildlife Refuge.

The Atchafalaya Basin is the largest river basin in North America, full of meandering rivers, cypress forests and a vast range of wildlife. Alligators are a common sight, but only if you're keeping your eyes carefully peeled. The gators here are generally shy and avoid contact with humans. The refuge is also listed on the Atchafalaya loop of the American Wetland Birding Trail, making this a popular destination for bird watchers keen on adding lots of new entries to their log books.

A handful of the species native to the refuge are endangered, and hunting restrictions apply, so be sure to consult with the Department of Wildlife and Fisheries before heading out on the trail of some of the larger game. The safest route is to sign up on a chartered hunting tour led by a local outfitter or backcountry guide.

For first-time visitors to the region, the bayou can seem like another planet, and that's just part of its charm. It doesn't take long for the down-to-earth vibe, lively Louisiana spirit and incredibly flavorful Cajun cooking to win you over for good.

For More Information

Louisiana Department of Culture, Recreation and Tourism
800-99-GUMBO
www.louisianatravel.com

St. Martin Parish Tourist Commission
337-442-1597
www.cajuncountry.org

Louisiana

CONSULTANTS

Fain & Lynda Little

ABBEVILLE — D3 *Vermilion*

ABBEVILLE RV PARK (Public) E-bnd: From jct of I-10 & exit 82: Go S 1 mi on LA-1111/LA-13 Truck Rte, then S 15 mi on LA-13, then E 10 mi on LA-14, then S 1/2 mi on Bus 14 (Port St) (R); W-bnd: From jct of I-10 & exit 100: Go S 2 mi on LA-3184, then SW 4 mi on LA-3073, then S 15-1/2 mi on US-167, then N 1/2 mi on Port St. (L). **FAC:** Gravel rds. (50 spaces). Avail: 39 gravel, back-ins (30 x 45), accepts full hkup units only, 39 full hkups (30/50 amps), WiFi, dump. **REC:** rec open to public. Pet restrict(B). No tents. 2015 rates: $25 to $30. No CC.
(337)898-4042 Lat: 29.83218, Lon: -92.29704
1501 W. Port St., Abbeville, LA 70510
info@abbevillervpark.com
www.abbevillervpark.com

PALMETTO ISLAND (State Pk) From Jct of US 167 & LA 14 BYP: Go E 0.4 mi on LA 14 BYP to LA 82 (N State St), then S 3.6 mi to Jct of LA 82 & LA 330, then W 4.6 mi on LA 82 to LA 690, then E 0.9 mi to Pleasant Rd, then S 1.8 mi (L). 2015 rates: $20 to $34. (337)893-3930

Things to See and Do

VERMILION PARISH TOURIST COMMISSION Visitors center with brochures, information & assistance on local accommodations, restaurants & attractions. Closed Sat & Sun. Brochures available on weekends. RV accessible. Restrooms. Hours: 9am to 5pm. No CC.
(337)898-6600 Lat: 29.98071, Lon: -92.11395
1907 Veteran's Memorial Dr, Abbeville, LA 70511
info@vermilion.org
www.vermilion.org
See ad page 527 (Welcome Section).

ALEXANDRIA — C3 *Rapides*

ALEXANDRIA See also Colfax & Marksville.

RAPIDES COLISEUM (PARISH PARK) (Public) From jct US 71/US 165 & Hwy 28 W: Go 1 mi W on Hwy 28. 2015 rates: $14. (318)442-9581

Things to See and Do

PARAGON CASINO RESORT Full service casino, hotel and RV park. Live entertainment, restaurants, 18 hole golf course, indoor aquatic center, and 3 screen theatre. Partial handicap access. RV accessible. Restrooms, food. Hours: 24 hrs.
(800)WIN-1-WIN Lat: 31.10674, Lon: -92.05903
711 Paragon Place, Marksville, LA 71351
mail@paragoncasinoresort.com
www.paragoncasinoresort.com
See primary listing at Marksville and ad page 533 (Spotlight Avoyelles Parish/Marksville Area), 526 (LA Map) and ad Magazine Section page 107.

AMITE — C4 *St Helena*

NATALBANY CREEK CAMPGROUND & RV PARK
Ratings: 10/8★/9 (RV Park) From jct of I-55 (exit 46) & LA-16: Go W 2-1/4 mi on LA-16. (R) Note: Behind Cash Magic Casino. **FAC:** Paved rds. (123 spaces). Avail: 100 paved, patios, 4 pull-thrus (24 x 60), back-ins (40 x 60), 100 full hkups (30/50 amps), WiFi, rentals, dump, laundry, controlled access. **REC:** pool, Natalbany Creek: fishing, playground. Pets OK. Partial handicap access, no tents. Big rig sites, 2015 rates: $35 to $45. Disc: military.
(985)748-4311 Lat: 30.714906, Lon: -90.569551
30218 La-16 West, Amite, LA 70422
natalbanycreekcampground@gmail.com
www.natalbanycreekcampground.net
See ad pages 538 (Spotlight Hammond/Tangipahoa Parish), 529.

Tell them you saw them in this Guide!

ANACOCO — C2 *Vernon*

SOUTH TOLEDO BEND (State Pk) From jct US 171 & Hwy 111/392: Go 10-1/2 mi W on Hwy 111/392, then 1 mi N on Hwy 191, then 1/2 mi W on Bald Eagle Rd. 2015 rates: $20 to $34. (337)286-9075

AVERY ISLAND — D3 *Iberia*

Things to See and Do

TABASCO The TABASCO Country Store & Restaurant —TABASCO Sauces, condiments, collectibles, gift boxes & gourmet foods. Visitor Center & Factory Tours. Partial handicap access. RV accessible. Restrooms, food. Hours: 9am to 4pm.
(800)634-9599 Lat: 29.89695, Lon: -91.90971
Hwy 329, Avery Island, LA 70513
www.tabasco.com
See ad page 550 (Spotlight New Iberia).

BASTROP — A3 *Morehouse*

CHEMIN-A-HAUT (State Pk) From jct of US-165 & US-425: Go N 9-3/4 mi on US-425, then E 1/4 mi on Loop Park Rd. (L). 2015 rates: $20 to $34. (888)677-2436

BATON ROUGE — D4 *East Baton Rouge*

A SPOTLIGHT Introducing Baton Rouge's colorful attractions appearing at the front of this state section.

BATON ROUGE See also Gonzales, Livingston, Morganza & Port Allen.

BATON ROUGE KOA Ratings: 8.5/9★/8 (RV Park) 2015 rates: $46. (800)562-5673 7628 Vincent Rd, Denham Springs, LA 70726

BREC'S FARR PARK EQUESTRIAN CENTER RV CAMPGROUND (Public) E-bnd: From Jct of I-10 & Exit 155A (right lane on bridge), exit to 2nd left on exit ramp to Nicholson Dr, S 1.7 mi to Skip Bertman Dr, W 0.5 mi to River Rd, S 1.9 mi (L) or W-bnd: From Jct of I-10 & College Dr (exit 158), S 5.3 mi (College becomes Lee Dr then Brighton Ln) to River Rd, S 0.5 mi (L). 2015 rates: $20. (225)769-7805

NATALBANY CREEK CAMPGROUND & RV PARK
Ratings: 10/8★/9 (RV Park) From jct of I-110 S & I-10 E: Go E 3-3/4 mi on I-10 E, then merge on I-12 (exit 159), then E 15-3/4 mi on I-12, then N 1-3/4 mi on LA-447/Walker Rd S, then E 1-1/2 mi on US-190, then N 17 mi on LA-449, then E 12-1/4 mi on LA-16 (L) Note: Behind Cash Magic Casino. **FAC:** Paved rds. (123 spaces). Avail: 100 paved, patios, 4 pull-thrus (24 x 60), back-ins (40 x 60), 100 full hkups (30/50 amps), WiFi, rentals, dump, laundry, controlled access. **REC:** pool, Natalbany Creek: fishing, playground. Pets OK. Partial handicap access. Big rig sites, 2015 rates: $35 to $45.
(985)748-4311 Lat: 30.714906, Lon: -90.569551
30218 La-16 West, Amite, LA 70422
natalbanycreekcampground@gmail.com
www.natalbanycreekcampground.net
See primary listing at Amite and ad page 538 (Spotlight Hammond/Tangipahoa Parish).

Travel Services

BLANCHARD TRAILER SALES RV sales of towables and fifth wheels, parts and supplies and service. **SERVICES:** RV, RV appliance, restrooms, RV Sales. RV supplies, dump, emergency parking, RV accessible. waiting room. Hours: 8:30am to 5:30pm.
(225)355-4449 Lat: 30.49212, Lon: -91.12421
6632 Airline Hwy, Baton Rouge, LA 70805
btsrv@hotmail.com
www.blanchardbr.com
See ad this page.

Visit Camping World on your RV travels to stock up on accessories and supplies while on the road. Find the nearest SuperCenter at CampingWorld.com

Things to See and Do

LOUISIANA TRAVEL PROMOTION ASSOCIATION The Louisiana Travel Promotion Association is a non-profit, private sector trade association representing the State's travel and hospitality industry. Hours: 8am to 5pm. No CC.
(225)346-1857 Lat: 30.43841, Lon: -91.13286
tschultz@ltpa.org
www.ltpa.org
See ad page 527 (Welcome Section).

BENTON — A2 *Bossier*

CYPRESS-BLACK BAYOU REC AREA (Public) From Jct of I-220 & Airline Dr (exit 12), N 5.4 mi on Airline Dr to Linton Rd, NE 4.2 mi, follow signs (R). 2015 rates: $20 to $23. (318)965-0007

BERWICK — E4 *St Mary*

CYPRESS LAKE RV RESORT Ratings: 7.5/9★/7 (Campground) 2015 rates: $35 to $40. (985)399-5981 100 Cypress Dr, Berwick, LA 70342

BOSSIER CITY — A2 *Bossier*

DIAMONDJACKS CASINO RESORT RV PARK
Ratings: 10/9.5★/7.5 (RV Park) From jct of I-20 (exit 20) & Diamond Jacks Blvd: Go S 500 ft on Diamond Jacks Blvd, then stay in left lane on Diamond Jacks Blvd (E). **FAC:** Paved rds. 32 paved, patios, 20 pull-thrus (30 x 68), back-ins (30 x 38), 32 full hkups (30/50 amps), cable, WiFi, laundry, restaurant. **REC:** heated pool, whirlpool, Red River. Pets OK. Partial handicap access, no tents. Big rig sites, 2015 rates: $28 to $34.
(318)678-7661 Lat: 32.51099, Lon: -93.72498
711 Diamond Jacks Blvd., Bossier City, LA 71111
www.diamondjacks.com
See ad this page.

RED RIVER SOUTH MARINA & RESORT Ratings: 5.5/NA/6.5 (RV Park) 2015 rates: $25 to $30. (318)747-9545 250 Red River South Marina Rd, Bossier City, LA 71112

Things to See and Do

DIAMONDJACKS CASINO RESORT Hotel, restaurants, gaming and entertainment with RV Park. Partial handicap access. RV accessible. Restrooms, food. Hours: 24 hours. ATM.
(866)552-9629 Lat: 32.51107, Lon: -93.72533
711 Diamond Jacks Blvd, Bossier City, LA 71111
www.diamondjacks.com
See ad this page.

BOURG — E4 *Terrebonne*

GRAND BOIS PARK (Public) From Jct of SR-90 & Hwy 24, E 12 mi on Hwy 24 (R). 2015 rates: $12. (985)594-7410

BREAUX BRIDGE — D3 *St Martin*

PIONEER ACADIAN VILLAGE RV PARK Ratings: 6/9★/6.5 (Campground) 2015 rates: $30 to $50. (337)332-4678 296 Degeyter Rd, Breaux Bridge, LA 70517

LA

BREAUX BRIDGE (CONT)

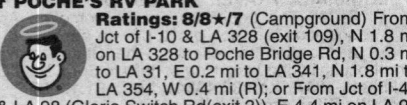

POCHE'S RV PARK
Ratings: 8/8★/7 (Campground) From Jct of I-10 & LA 328 (exit 109), N 1.8 mi on LA 328 to Poche Bridge Rd, N 0.3 mi to LA 31, E 0.2 mi to LA 341, N 1.8 mi to LA 354, W 0.4 mi (R); or From Jct of I-49 & LA 98 (Gloria Switch Rd(exit 2)), E 4.4 mi on LA 98 to LA 354, N 4.2 mi (L). **FAC:** Gravel/dirt rds. (89 spaces). 74 Avail: 49 paved, 25 gravel, 4 pull-thrus (30 x 70), back-ins (30 x 55), 74 full hkups (30/50 amps), WiFi, tent sites, rentals, dump, laundry, fire rings, firewood. **REC:** pool, pond, fishing, playground, rec open to public. Pet restrict(B). Partial handicap access. Big rig sites, eco-friendly, 2015 rates: $35.
(337)332-0326 Lat: 30.33806, Lon: -91.92475
1080 Sawmill Hwy, Breaux Bridge, LA 70517
info@pochesrvpark.com
pochesrvpark.com
See ad pages 558, 529.

Things to See and Do

ST MARTIN PARISH TOURIST COMMISSION
St. Martin Parish is in the heart of Cajun Country. Brochures and assistance on attractions, accommodations, RV Parks and restaurants. Restrooms. Hours: 9am to 5pm. No CC.
(888)565-5939 Lat: 30.27530, Lon: -91.89767
314 E Bridge St, Breaux Bridge, LA 70517
ddr@cajuncountry.org
www.cajuncountry.org
See ad page 554 (Spotlight St Martin Parish).

BROUSSARD — D3 *Lafayette, St Martin*

MAXIE'S CAMPGROUND Ratings: 5.5/6/5.5 (Campground) From jct of I-10/I-49 (exit 103A) & Evangeline Thruway: Go S 9 mi on Evangeline Thruway/US.90/ Future I-49 (R); or From jct of LA-96 & US-90: Go NW 1-1/2 mi on US-90 (L). **FAC:** Paved rds. (64 spaces). Avail: 4 gravel, back-ins (25 x 50), 4 full hkups (30/50 amps), WiFi, laundry. Pets OK. No tents. 2015 rates: $26.
(337)837-6200 Lat: 30.14923, Lon: -91.95059
4350 Hwy 90E, Broussard, LA 70518
jason@maxiescampground.com
www.maxiescampground.com

CHARENTON — D3 *St Mary*

CYPRESS BAYOU CASINO RV PARK **Ratings: 6.5/NA/8.5** (RV Park) 2015 rates: $30. (337)923-7184 832 Martin Luther King Road, Charenton, LA 70523

CHATHAM — A3 *Jackson*

JIMMIE DAVIS (State Pk) From jct of US-167 & LA-4 (in Jonesboro): Go E 12-3/4 mi on LA-4 to Lakeshore Dr, then SE 1-1/2 mi on Lakeshore Dr, then S 1-1/2 mi on State Park Rd. (E). 2015 rates: $20 to $34. (318)249-2595

Replace clogged air filters. A clogged air filter can cut a vehicle's fuel efficiency by 10 percent.

COLFAX — B2 *Grant*

COLFAX RECREATION AREA RV PARK & CAMPGROUND (Public) From Jct of I-49 & Hwy 8 (exit 99), N 11 mi on Hwy 8E to Main St, E 0.4 mi to Hwy 158, NW 0.9 mi to Lock & Dam sign, W 0.3 mi (R). 2015 rates: $32. (318)627-2640

CONVENT — D4 *St James*

POCHE PLANTATION RV RESORT
Ratings: 9/9.5★/9.5 (RV Park) E-bnd From Jct of I-10 & Exit 179, S 15.6 mi on LA44 (L) W-bnd From Jct of I-10 & Exit 194 (LA 641/3213), S 7 mi to LA 44, W 7.8 mi (R). **FAC:** Gravel rds. (85 spaces). 35 Avail: 24 paved, 11 gravel, patios, 21 pull-thrus (25 x 60), back-ins (28 x 60), 35 full hkups (30/50 amps), seasonal sites, cable, WiFi, laundry. **REC:** pool, whirlpool. Pets OK. Partial handicap access, no tents. Big rig sites, 2015 rates: $20 to $35. Disc: AAA.
(225)715-9510 Lat: 30.01306, Lon: -90.82739
6554 Louisiana Hwy 44, Convent, LA 70723
innkeeper@pocheplantation.com
pocheplantation.com
See ad this page.

SUGAR HILL RV PARK
Ratings: 5/8.5★/7.5 (RV Park) From Jct of I-10 & Exit 182 (LA-22), SW 0.4 mi on LA-22 to LA-70, SE 4.2 mi on LA-20 to LA-44, SE 2.9 mi (L). **FAC:** Paved/gravel rds. (161 spaces). Avail: 40 gravel, patios, back-ins (40 x 75), 40 full hkups (30/50 amps), seasonal sites, cable, WiFi, dump, laundry, LP gas. Pets OK. No tents. Big rig sites, 2015 rates: $21 to $34.
(225)715-9510 Lat: 30.07004, Lon: -90.89014
9450 Highway 44, Convent, LA 70723
info@sugarhillrvpark.com
www.sugarhillrvpark.com
See ad this page.

COUSHATTA — B2 *Red River*

GRAND BAYOU RESORT (Public) From Jct of I-49 & LA-177 (exit 162), NE 6 mi on LA-177 to US-84, SE 2.8 mi to US-84E, E 5.2 mi to LA-784, E 1.3 mi (R). 2015 rates: $19 to $25. (318)932-0066

COVINGTON — D5 *St Tammany*

LAND-O-PINES FAMILY CAMPGROUND **Ratings: 8.5/7/7** (Campground) 2015 rates: $38 to $65. (800)443-3697 17145 Million Dollar Rd, Covington, LA 70435

CUT OFF — E4 *Lafourche*

SOUTHERN MARSH RV PARK
(RV Park) (Planned) At Jct of LA 3162 & LA 3235 (behind Casino, Gas, Grill) (E). **FAC. REC.** No CC, no reservations.
(985)325-4445 Lat: 29.46114, Lon: -90.32099
16816 Hwy 3235, Cut Off, LA 70345
andrew@southernmarshrv.com
www.southermarshrvpark.com
See ad this page.

DELHI — A3 *Richland*

POVERTY POINT RESERVOIR (State Pk) From jct of I-20 (exit 153) & LA-17: Go N 2-1/2 mi on LA-17. (R). 2015 rates: $20 to $34. (318)878-7536

DOYLINE — A2 *Webster*

LAKE BISTINEAU (State Pk) W-bnd: From Jct of I-20 & LA-371 (exit 47), S 3.4 mi on LA-371 to LA-164, W 6.5 mi to LA-163, S 6.9 mi (L); or E-bnd: From Jct of I-20 & LA-157 (exit 33), S 600 ft on LA-157 to LA-3227, E 2 mi to LA-164, E 4.4 mi to LA-163, S 6.9 mi (L). 2015 rates: $20 to $34. (318)745-3503

The RVers' Guide to NASCAR helps RV travelers get the most out of North America's most thrilling sporting event. Turn to the front of the Guide and we'll give you the inside track on how to get high-speed thrills at major NASCAR venues.

DUSON — D3 *Acadia, Lafayette*

FROG CITY RV PARK
Ratings: 9/9.5★/8.5 (RV Park) From Jct of I-10 (exit 92) & LA-95, S 0.4 mi on LA-95 to Service Rd (Daulat Dr), W 1000 ft (E) or From Jct of US 90 & LA 95, N 0.5 mi on LA 95 to Service Rd, W 1000 ft (E). **FAC:** Paved rds. (62 spaces). Avail: 22 gravel, 22 pull-thrus (30 x 70), 22 full hkups (30/50 amps), seasonal sites, cable, WiFi, tent sites, dump, laundry, groc, LP gas, restaurant. **REC:** pool, whirlpool. Pet restrict(B/Q). Partial handicap access. Big rig sites, eco-friendly, 2015 rates: $39. Disc: military. ATM.
(337)873-9085 Lat: 30.24533, Lon: -92.19544
3003 Daulat Dr, Duson, LA 70529
manager@lafayettervpark.com
www.lafayettervpark.com
See ad pages 544 (Spotlight Lafayette), 529.

Travel Services

ROADY'S LUCKY DEUCES TRAVEL PLAZA
Truck Stop with restaurant or fast food. RV parking. Convenience store and casino. Oil Change, tire repair and propane. **SERVICES:** Tire, MH mechanical, restaurant, restrooms. RV supplies, LP, emergency parking, RV accessible. waiting room. Hours: Open 24 hrs. ATM.
(337)873-5400 Lat: 30.24582, Lon: -92.19385
3002 Daulat Dr, Duson, LA 70529
luckydeucescasino@gmail.com
See ad page 544 (Spotlight Lafayette).

ERATH — D3 *Vermilion*

QUALITY SPORTS AUTHORITY & RV PARK **Ratings: 5.5/8/8** (Campground) 2015 rates: $22 to $38. (337)937-4368 12725 North Rd, Erath, LA 70533

EUNICE — D3 *Evangeline, St Landry*

LAKEVIEW PARK & BEACH **Ratings: 7/7.5/8** (Campground) 2015 rates: $27 to $45. (337)457-2881 1717 Veteran Memorial Hwy, Eunice, LA 70535

FARMERVILLE — A3 *Union*

LAKE D'ARBONNE (State Pk) From Jct of SR-15 & SR-2 (in town), W 5 mi on SR-2 to Evergreen Rd, S 0.3 mi (L). 2015 rates: $20 to $34. (318)368-2086

FERRIDAY — B3 *Concordia*

SPORTSMAN'S LODGE **Ratings: 4.5/5/5** (Campground) 2015 rates: $30 to $50. (318)757-4381 101 Sportsmans Lane, Ferriday, LA 71334

FLORIEN — B2 *Sabine*

HODGES GARDENS (State Pk) From Jct of US 171 & SR 6 (in Many), S 14.5 mi on US 171 (L). One time entrance fee charged (office hours 8am to 5pm). 2015 rates: $20. (318)586-4020

FRANKLIN — D3 *St Mary*

Things to See and Do

CAJUN COAST VISITORS & CONVENTION BUREAU Visitors center open 6 days a week with brochures, information & assistance on accommodations & attractions. (Closed Sun). Restrooms. Hours: 8:30am to 4:30pm. No CC.
(337)828-2555 Lat: 29.80765, Lon: -91.53707
15307 Hwy 90, W Frontage Rd, Franklin, LA 70538
info@cajuncoast.com
www.cajuncoast.com
See ad page 537 (Spotlight Cajun Coast/St Mary Parish).

How can you tell whether you're traveling in the right direction? The arrow in each listing denotes the compass direction of the facility in relation to the listed town. For example, an arrow pointing straight up indicates that the facility is located due north from town. An arrow pointing down and to the right indicates that the facility is southeast of town.

FRANKLIN (CONT)

GREVEMBERG HOUSE MUSEUM This Greek Revival Home contains fine antiques, documented wallpaper & early artifacts from St Mary Parish. Partial handicap access. RV accessible. Restrooms. Hours: 10am to 4pm (closed major holidays) Adult fee: $10. No CC.
(337)828-2092 Lat: 29.80214, Lon: -91.49634
407 Sterling Rd, Franklin, LA 70538
info@grevemberghouse.com
www.grevemberghouse.com
See ad page 537 (Spotlight Cajun Coast/St Mary Parish).

FRANKLINTON — C5 *Washington*

BOGUE CHITTO (State Pk) From jct of LA-10 & LA-25/LA-16: Go S 5-1/2 mi on LA-25, then E 1-1/4 on State Park Blvd. (L). 2015 rates: $20 to $34. (886)677-7312

GIBSON — D4 *Terrebonne*

HIDEAWAY PONDS RECREATIONAL RESORT **Ratings: 8/8/8** (Membership Pk) 2015 rates: $39. (985)575-9928 6367 Bayou Black Dr, Gibson, LA 70356

GONZALES — D4 *Ascension*

LAMAR-DIXON EXPO CENTER RV PARK (Public) From Jct of I-10 & LA 30 (Exit 177), W 0.4 mi on LA 30 to St Landry Avenue, S 0.9 mi (R). **FAC:** Paved/gravel rds. (250 spaces). 200 Avail: 150 gravel, 50 grass, 100 pull-thrus (20 x 65), back-ins (20 x 65), 200 full hkups (30/50 amps), WiFi, dump. **REC:** pond, fishing, rec open to public. Pets OK. Partial handicap access, no tents. 2015 rates: $25 to $35. ATM.
(225)621-1700 Lat: 30.19744, Lon: -90.95360
9039 S. St. Landry Ave, Gonzales, LA 70737
fmagee@lamardixonexpocenter.com
www.lamardixonexpocenter.com
See ad page 534 (Spotlight Baton Rouge).

Things to See and Do

LAMAR-DIXON EXPO CENTER The purpose of the Expo Center is to provide the community with a multi-use facility, with emphasis on equestrian & 4-H activities & to attract diverse entertainment for the community. Partial handicap access. RV accessible. Restrooms. Hours: 8am to 4:30pm. ATM.
(225)621-1700 Lat: 30.19744, Lon: -90.9536
9039 S. St. Landry Ave, Gonzales, LA 70737
fmagee@apgov.us
www.ascensionparish.net
See ad page 534 (Spotlight Baton Rouge).

GRAND ISLE — E5 *Jefferson*

GRAND ISLE (State Pk) From jct of I-10 & US-90: Go S 108 mi, then go SE 68 mi on LA-308/LA-3235/LA-1, then NE 1/4 mi on Admiral Craik Dr. (R). 2015 rates: $20 to $34. (985)787-2559

GREENWOOD — A1 *Caddo*

SOUTHERN LIVING RV PARK **Ratings: 7.5/9/7.5** (RV Park) 2015 rates: $28. (318)938-1808 9010 Greenwood Rd, Greenwood, LA 71033

TRAVELCENTERS OF AMERICA RV PARK
Ratings: 7.5/9★/8 (RV Park) From Jct of I-20 (exit 5) & Greenwood Rd: Go W 1/4 mi on N service Rd (R). **FAC:** Paved rds. (49 spaces). Avail: 14 paved, patios, 10 pull-thrus (24 x 55), back-ins (24 x 60), 14 full hkups (30/50 amps), cable, WiFi $, dump, laundry, groc. **REC.** Pets OK. No tents. Big rig sites, eco-friendly, 2015 rates: $28.
(318)938-6360 Lat: 32.44591, Lon: -93.95191
8590 Greenwood Rd, Greenwood, LA 71033
www.tatravelcenters.com
See ad pages 563, 529.

HAMMOND — D4 *Tangipahoa*

A SPOTLIGHT A spotlight introducing Hammond's colorful attractions appearing at the front of this state section.

HAMMOND See also Amite, Covington, Independence, Livingston & Loranger.

CALLOWAY RV & CAMPGROUND **Ratings: 7.5/7/5.5** (Campground) 2015 rates: $30 to $33. (985)542-8094 14154 W Club Deluxe Rd, Hammond, LA 70403

NATALBANY CREEK CAMPGROUND & RV PARK
Ratings: 10/8★/9 (RV Park) From jct of I-55 & US-190 W: Go N 15-1/2 mi on I-55 (exit 46) & LA-16, then W 2-1/4 mi on LA-16. (R) Note: Behind Cash Magic Casino. **FAC:** Paved rds. (123 spaces). Avail: 100 paved, patios, 4 pull-thrus (24 x 60), back-ins (40 x 60), 100 full hkups (30/50 amps), WiFi, rentals, dump, laundry, controlled access. **REC:** pool, Natalbany Creek: fishing, playground. Pets OK. Partial handicap access. Big rig sites, 2015 rates: $35 to $45. Disc: military.
(985)748-4311 Lat: 30.714906, Lon: -90.569551
30218 La-16 West, Amite, LA 70422
natalbanycreekcampground@gmail.com
www.natalbanycreekcampground.net
See primary listing at Amite and ad page 538 (Spotlight Hammond/Tangipahoa Parish).

PUNKIN PARK CAMPGROUND **Ratings: 6/7/6** (Campground) 2015 rates: $34.35. (225)567-3418 43037 North Billville Rd, Hammond, LA 70403

REUNION LAKE RV RESORT (RV Resort) (Planned) From Jct of I-12 and LA445 (exit47), N100 yards on LA445 (R) Scheduled to open Dec 2015. **FAC. REC.** No CC, no reservations.
(985)240-2213 Lat: 30.48529, Lon: -90.33242
ne corner of Hwy 445 & I-12, Ponchatoula, LA 70454
www.reunionlakerv.com
See primary listing at Robert and ad page 539 (Spotlight Hammond/Tangipahoa Parish).

Travel Services

CAMPING WORLD OF HAMMOND As the nation's largest retailer of RV supplies, accessories, services and new and used RVs, Camping World is committed to making your total RV experience better. **SERVICES:** Tire, RV appliance, restrooms. RV supplies, emergency parking, RV accessible. waiting room. Hours: 8am to 6pm. (866)810-7323 Lat: 30.48239, Lon: -90.542378 43135 Pumpkin Center Road, Hammond, LA 70403 www.campingworld.com

Things to See and Do

TANGIPAHOA PARISH CONVENTION & VISITORS BUREAU Visitors center with brochures & information on accommodations, restaurants & attractions in the area. Open 7 days a week. Sat & Sun hrs 9am to 3pm. Class A parking with tow. Partial handicap access. RV accessible. Restrooms. Hours: 8am to 4pm. No CC.
(800)542-7520 Lat: 30.51956, Lon: -90.50766
13143 Wardline Rd, Hammond, LA 70401
info@tangitourism.com
www.tangitourism.com
See ad page 527 (Welcome Section).

HENDERSON — D3 *St Martin*

ALLEMOND POINT CAMPGROUND Ratings: 5.5/6.5/5.5 (Campground) From Jct of I-10 (exit 115/Henderson) & Hwy LA-347: Go S 220 ft on LA-347 to LA-352 (E-bnd traffic; Move to left turn lane immediately), then E 2-3/4 mi to Levee, then S 2-1/4 mi on LA-352/Henderson Levee Road. (R). **FAC:** Gravel rds. 23 gravel, 10 pull-thrus (30 x 58), back-ins (35 x 50), 23 full hkups (30/50 amps), WiFi, tent sites, dump, laundry, LP bottles, firewood. **REC:** Bayou Amy: fishing, marina. Pets OK. Partial handicap access. 2015 rates: $30 to $35. Disc: AAA.
AAA Approved
(337)228-2384 Lat: 30.30547, Lon: -91.75712
1337 Henderson Levee Rd, Henderson, LA 70517
info@mcgeeslanding.com
www.mcgeeslanding.com

CAJUN PALMS RV RESORT
Ratings: 10/10★/10 (RV Park) From Jct of I-10 (exit 115) & LA-347/Henderson: Go NE 1/2 mi on LA-347/ Grand Point Hwy, then E 1/4 mi on N Barn Rd. (L).

CAJUN PALMS RV RESORT
A full service resort located in Henderson, Louisiana (St Martin Parish), just 1/2 mile north of I-10. Visit our top rated campground & let us make your stay enjoyable!

FAC: Paved rds. (338 spaces). Avail: 300 paved, patios, 173 pull-thrus (40 x 65), back-ins (40 x 50), 300 full hkups (30/50 amps), seasonal sites, cable, WiFi, rentals, dump, laundry, groc, LP gas, firewood, restaurant, controlled access. **REC:** pool, whirlpool, pond, fishing, playground. Pet restrict(B). Partial handicap access, no tents. Big rig sites, eco-friendly, 2015 rates: $32 to $74. ATM.
(337)667-7772 Lat: 30.32344, Lon: -91.82259
1055 N Barn Rd, Breaux Bridge, LA 70517
amanda@cajunpalms.com
www.cajunpalms.com
See ad pages 559, 529, 554 (Spotlight St Martin Parish).

FRENCHMEN'S WILDERNESS CAMPGROUND
Ratings: 9/9.5★/9 (Campground) From Jct of I-10 & Butte La Rose Rd (exit 121), S 0.7 mi on Butte La Rose Rd (R). **FAC:** Paved/gravel rds. 140 Avail: 40 gravel, 100 grass, patios, 4 pull-thrus (30 x 60), back-ins (45 x 60), 140 full hkups (30/50 amps), WiFi $, rentals, laundry, LP gas, fire rings, firewood. **REC:** pool, Lake Bigeaux: fishing, playground. Pet restrict(B) $. No tents. Big rig sites, 2015 rates: $29 to $35.
(337)228-2616 Lat: 30.33561, Lon: -91.71028
2026 Atchafalaya River Hwy, Breaux Bridge, LA 70517
frenchmanswilderness@gmail.com
www.frenchmanswildernesscamp.com
See ad page 554 (Spotlight St Martin Parish).

Things to See and Do

CRAWFISH TOWN USA Boiled, fried & grilled seafood and chargrilled steaks. Lunch & Dinner 7 days a week. Large parking area for RVs at first entrance. Partial handicap access. RV accessible. Restrooms, food. Hours: 11am to 9pm. ATM.
(337)667-6148 Lat: 30.32527, Lon: -91.82628
2815 Grand Point Hwy, Henderson, LA 70517
wendy@crawfishtownusa.com
www.crawfishtownusa.com
See ad page 554 (Spotlight St Martin Parish).

PREHISTORIC PARK 12 acre park with life-sized dinosaur replicas, some animated. Buried bone sand box for young paleontologists, snack bar and gift shop. Food. Adult fee: $12.
(337)981-3466 Lat: 30.32340, Lon: -91.82232
1135 North Barn Rd., Breaux Bridge, LA 70517
www.prehistoric-park.com
See ad pages 559, 554 (Spotlight St Martin Parish).

HOMER — A2 *Claiborne*

LAKE CLAIBORNE (State Pk) E-bnd: From Jct of I-20 & SR-154 (exit 61), N 7.1 mi on SR-154 to SR-518, NE 8.5 mi to SR-146, S 1 mi (L); or W-bnd: From Jct of I-20 & SR-9 (exit 67), N 7.5 mi on SR-9 to SR-518, NE 8 mi to SR-146, S 1 mi (L). 2015 rates: $20 to $34. (877)226-7652

HORNBECK — C2 *Sabine*

PLEASURE POINT-SABINE RIVER AUTHORITY (Public) From Jct of SR-392 & SR-191, N 3.4 mi on SR-191 to park access rd, W 1.1 mi (E). 2015 rates: $15 to $25. (318)565-4810

HOUMA — E4 *Terrebonne*

A SPOTLIGHT Introducing Houma's colorful attractions appearing in the front of this state section.

HOUMA See also Charenton & Morgan City.

CAPRI COURT CAMPGROUND
Ratings: 7/7.5/7.5 (Campground) From Jct of US-90 (exit 204) & SR-316, SE 1.8 mi on SR-316 (R); or from Jct of LA-182 & SR-316, NW 3 mi on SR-316 (L). **FAC:** Paved/gravel rds. (45 spaces). 19 Avail: 9 gravel, 10 grass, 5 pull-thrus (26 x 60), back-ins (30 x 50), 19 full hkups (30/50 amps), WiFi, tent sites, dump, laundry, fire rings. **REC:** Saint Louis Canal: fishing. Pet restrict(B). Partial handicap access. Big rig sites, 2015 rates: $29.80 to $33.40. Disc: military.
AAA Approved
(800)428-8026 Lat: 29.67093, Lon: -90.72442
105 Capri Court, Houma, LA 70364
capricrt@bellsouth.net
www.capricourtrvpark.com
See ad pages 540 (Spotlight Houma), 529.

Things to See and Do

HOUMA AREA CONVENTION & VISITORS BUREAU Visitors center open 7 days a week with brochures & information on accommodations, restaurants & attractions in the area. Class A RV turn around. Free dump. Open Saturday & Sunday 9:30am to 3:30pm. Partial handicap access. RV accessible. Restrooms. Hours: 9am to 5pm. No CC.
(800)688-2732 Lat: 29.67761, Lon: -90.78638
114 Tourist Dr., Gray, LA 70359
info@houmatravel.com
www.houmatravel.com
See ad page 541 (Spotlight Houma) & RV Trips of a Lifetime in Magazine Section.

INDEPENDENCE — C4 *Tangipahoa*

INDIAN CREEK CAMPGROUND & RV PARK **Ratings: 7.5/7.5/6.5** (Campground) 2015 rates: $32 to $48. (985)878-6567 53013 West Fontana Rd., Independence, LA 70443

LA

IOWA — D2 *Calcasieu*

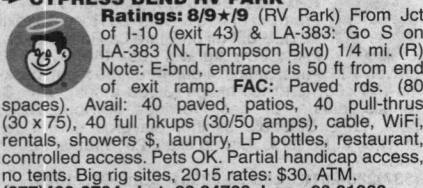

➔ CYPRESS BEND RV PARK
Ratings: 8/9★/9 (RV Park) From Jct of I-10 (exit 43) & LA-383: Go S on LA-383 (N. Thompson Blvd) 1/4 mi. (R) Note: E-bnd, entrance is 50 ft from end of exit ramp. **FAC:** Paved rds. (80 spaces). Avail: 40 paved, patios, 40 pull-thrus (30 x 75), 40 full hkups (30/50 amps), cable, WiFi, rentals, showers $, laundry, LP bottles, restaurant, controlled access. Pets OK. Partial handicap access, no tents. Big rig sites, 2015 rates: $30. ATM.
(877)409-2784 Lat: 30.24703, Lon: -93.01363
717 N Thompson, Iowa, LA 70647
cypressbendrv@aol.com
See ad pages 547 (Spotlight Lake Charles), 529.

JONESVILLE — B3 *Catahoula*

➔ LAKEVIEW PARADISE RV PARK
(RV Park) (Not Visited) From Jct of US 84 & Hwy 129, Go South 7 miles on Hwy 129 (R). **FAC:** Gravel rds. 45 paved, patios, 5 pull-thrus (20 x 65), back-ins (20 x 65), 45 full hkups (30/50 amps), WiFi, laundry, fire rings. **REC:** Cocodrie Lake: fishing, rec open to public. Pets OK. Big rig sites, 2015 rates: $30 to $50. No CC.
(318)386-0300 Lat: 31.49915, Lon: -91.70159
3873 Highway 129, Jonesville, LA 71343
office@lakeviewparadise.com
www.lakeviewparadise.com
See ad this page.

KINDER — D2 *Allen*

A SPOTLIGHT Introducing Allen Parish/Kinder's colorful attractions appearing at the front of this state section.

Looking for a new or used RV? Camping World is America's largest retailer of RVs. Click CampingWorld.com or visit SuperCenters nationwide.

↑ COUSHATTA LUXURY RV RESORT AT RED SHOES PARK
Ratings: 10/10★/10 (RV Resort) From jct of I-10 & US-165 (exit 44): Go N 22-1/2 mi on US-165 (L); or from jct of I-49 & US-165 (exit 86): Go S 55 mi on US-165 (R).

LOUISIANA'S PREMIER CASINO RESORT
Louisiana's Best Bet! Enjoy 2850 slots, 70 table games, 6 restaurants, 500+ luxurious rooms, RV resort with furnished chalets, 2 nightclubs, supervised childcare, teen arcade, award-winning championship golf course and more.

FAC: Paved rds. 107 paved, patios, 105 pull-thrus (35 x 70), back-ins (35 x 70), 107 full hkups (30/50 amps), cable, WiFi, rentals, dump, laundry, groc, restaurant. **REC:** heated pool, pond, fishing, golf, playground. Pets OK. Partial handicap access, no tents. Big rig sites, 14 day max stay, eco-friendly, 2015 rates: $20 to $65. Disc: AAA. ATM.
(800)584-7263 Lat: 30.54197, Lon: -92.81937
711 Pow Wow Parkway, Kinder, LA 70648
rmaggard@coushattacasinoresort.com
www.coushattacasinoresort.com
See ad pages 531 (Spotlight Allen Parish/Kinder), 529.

Things to See and Do

↑ COUSHATTA CASINO RESORT Casino, Hotel, RV Park with Chalets, Golf Course and Restaurants. Partial handicap access. RV accessible. Restrooms, food. Hours: Open 24 hrs. Adult fee: $79 to $299. ATM.
(800)584-7263 Lat: 30.54197, Lon: -92.81937
777 Coushatta Drive, Kinder, LA 70648
www.coushattacasinoresort.com
See ad page 531 (Spotlight Allen Parish/Kinder).

Check out the travel services section of this Guide to find services that you'll find handy in your travels.

↑ KOASATI PINES AT COUSHATTA CASINO RESORT 18 hole, par 72 championship golf course, pro shop, driving range, putting green, bar and grill. Partial handicap access. Restrooms, food. Hours: 7am to 5pm. Adult fee: $35 to $65.
(800)584-7263 Lat: 30.55450, Lon: -92.80516
300 Koasati Drive, Kinder, LA 70648
www.coushattacasinoresort.com
See ad page 531 (Spotlight Allen Parish/Kinder).

↓ PARAGON CASINO RESORT Full service casino with slots, all table games, kid's quest & marketplace buffet. Live entertainment, 7 restaurants, 18 hole golf course, 500 room hotel, indoor aquatic center, spa, 3 screen theatre & over 185 spacious RV sites. Partial handicap access. RV accessible. Restrooms, food. Hours: 24 hrs. ATM.
(800)WIN-1-WIN Lat: 31.10674, Lon: -92.05903
711 Paragon Place, Marksville, LA 71351
mail@paragoncasinoresort.com
www.paragoncasinoresort.com
See primary listing at Marksville and ad page 533 (Spotlight Avoyelles Parish/Marksville Area), 526 (LA Map) and ad Magazine Section page 107.

LAFAYETTE — D3 *Lafayette*

A SPOTLIGHT Introducing Lafayette's colorful attractions appearing at the front of this state section.

LAFAYETTE See also Abbeville, Breaux Bridge, Broussard, Carencro, Duson, Henderson, New Iberia, Opelousas, Rayne & St Martinville.

↑ ACADIANA PARK CAMPGROUND (Public) From Jct of I-10 & SR-167, S 1 mi on SR-167 to Willow St, E 0.8 mi to LA Ave, N 0.7 mi to E Alexander St, E 0.5 mi (L). 2015 rates: $13. (337)291-8388

➚ BAYOU WILDERNESS RV RESORT
Ratings: 9/9★/9.5 (RV Park) From Jct of I-10 & I-49/US 167 (Exit 103-B), N 2.5 mi on I-49/US 167 to Gloria Switch Rd (Exit 2), E 2.3 mi to N Wilderness Trail, N 0.7 mi (R) Note: Left turn 25 ft past bridge. **FAC:** Paved/gravel rds. 121 gravel, 121 pull-thrus (25 x 65), 121 full hkups (30/50 amps), cable, WiFi, tent sites, dump, laundry, groc, LP gas, controlled access. **REC:** pool, pond, fishing, playground. Pet restrict(B). Partial handicap access. Big rig sites, eco-friendly, 2015 rates: $34 to $42. Disc: military.
(337)896-0598 Lat: 30.30500, Lon: -91.98429
600 North Wilderness Trail, Carencro, LA 70520
info@bwrvr.com
www.bwrvr.com
See ad this page, 529.

➔ CAJUN PALMS RV RESORT
Ratings: 10/10★/10 (RV Park) From jct & I-10 (exit 101) and LA-182: Go 14 mi E on I-10 (exit 115/LA-347), then 1/2 mi NE on LA-347, then 1/4 mi E on N Barn Road (L). **FAC:** Paved rds. (338 spaces). Avail: 300 paved, patios, 173 pull-thrus (40 x 65), back-ins (40 x 50), 300 full hkups (30/50 amps), seasonal sites, cable, WiFi, rentals, dump, laundry, groc, LP gas, firewood, restaurant, controlled access. **REC:** pool, whirlpool, pond, fishing, playground. Pet

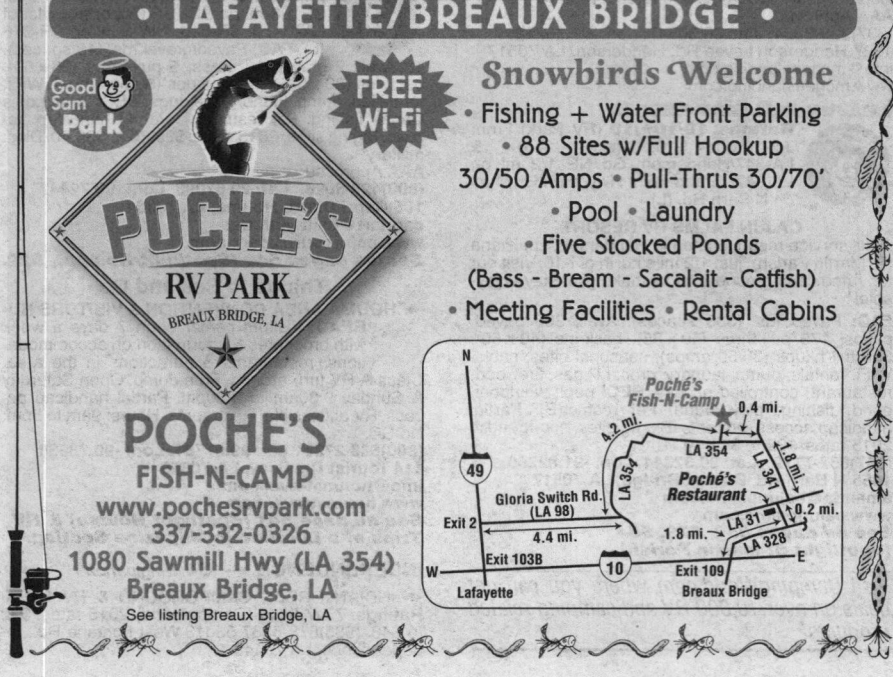

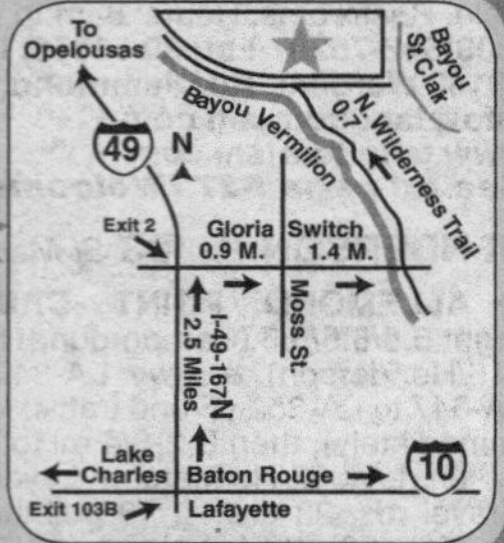

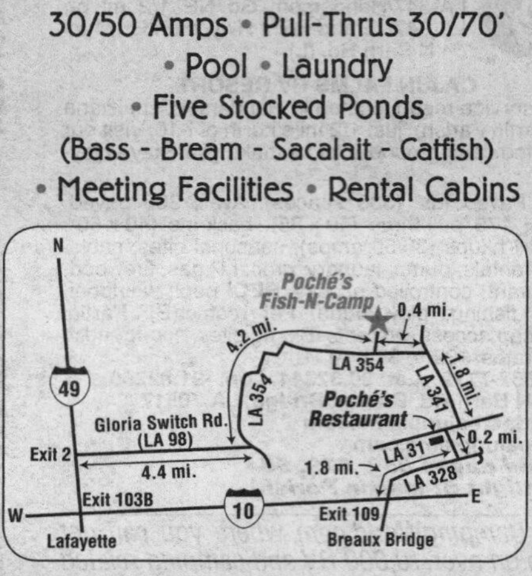

www.cajunpalms.com
Cajun Palms RV Resort
337-667-7772
1-10 Exit 115 North .6 Miles
1055 North Barn Road
Breaux Bridge, Louisiana 70517
See listing Henderson, LA
Good Sam Park
OUR MASCOT LEE ROY
FUN FOR ALL AGES
• Over 300 Deluxe RV Spots and 25 Cabins
• Twenty Waterfront Cabins • Pull-Thrus and Back-Ins
• Full hookups, 30/50 Amp • Water and Sewer
• 70+ Channels of Digital Cable • Clubhouse
• Resort Style Pool • Hot Tub • Kiddie Pool
• Video Arcade • State-of-the-Art Theatre
• Business Meeting Room • Coin Operated Laundry Facilities
• Wi-Fi Internet Throughout the Resort • Convenience Store
• Fishing In Stocked Pond
• Live Entertainment • We Rent Golf Carts
LeeRoy's Tiki Bar • Sawyer's Island
Charlie's Bar & Grill • Shirley's Snack Shack
Captain Hates' Hideaway • The Upper Deck
PREHISTORIC PARK
HENDERSON · LA
Next to RV Park
(337) 981-3466

LA

LAFAYETTE (CONT)

CAJUN PALMS RV RESORT (CONT)
restrict(B). Partial handicap access. Big rig sites, eco-friendly, 2015 rates: $32 to $74. ATM.
(337)667-7772 Lat: 30.32344, Lon: -91.82259
1055 N Barn Road, Breaux Bridge, LA 70517
amanda@cajunpalms.com
www.cajunpalms.com
See primary listing at Henderson and ad pages 559, 554 (Spotlight St Martin Parish).

KOA KAMPGROUND OF LAFAYETTE Ratings: 9.5/9★/8.5 (RV Park) From Jct of I-10 & Hwy 93 (exit 97, Scott), S 200 ft on Hwy 93 (R) or From Jct of I-10 & I-49, W 5.6 mi on I-10 to Hwy 93 (exit 97), S 1000 ft on Hwy 93 (R). **FAC:** Paved rds. (160 spaces). Avail: 105 paved, 80 pull-thrus (22 x 55), back-ins (22 x 50), some side by side hkups, 96 full hkups, 9 W, 9 E (30/50 amps), seasonal sites, cable, WiFi, tent sites, rentals, dump, laundry, groc, LP gas, fire rings, firewood. **REC:** pool, pond, fishing, playground. Pet restrict(B). Partial handicap access. 2015 rates: $42.50 to $49.50.
AAA Approved
(337)235-2739 Lat: 30.24645, Lon: -92.11150
537 Apollo Rd, Scott, LA 70583
twosonskoa@aol.com
www.koa.com

Things to See and Do

LAFAYETTE CONVENTION & VISITORS COMMISSION Visitors center open seven days a week with brochures, information & assistance on accommodations, restaurants & attractions in Cajun Country.

THE HAPPIEST CITY IN AMERICA
Lafayette, the heart of Louisiana Cajun & Creole Country, known for its swampland, moss draped cypress trees teeming with wildlife & outdoor adventures! No wonder people are heading down south with a smile on their face.

Partial handicap access. RV accessible. Restrooms. Hours: 9am to 5pm. No CC.
(800)346-1958 Lat: 30.24259, Lon: -92.01248
1400 NW Evangeline Thruway, Lafayette, LA 70501
info@lafayettetravel.com
www.lafayettetravel.com
See ad page 543 (Spotlight Lafayette) & RV Trips of a Lifetime and ad page 107 in Magazine Section.

PARAGON CASINO RESORT Full service casino, hotel and RV park. Live entertainment, restaurants, 18 hole golf course, indoor aquatic center, and 3 screen theater. Partial handicap access. RV accessible. Restrooms, food. Hours: 24 hrs.
(800)WIN-1-WIN Lat: 31.10674, Lon: -92.05903
711 Paragon Place, Marksville, LA 71351
mail@paragoncasinoresort.com
www.paragoncasinoresort.com
See primary listing at Marksville and ad page 533 (Spotlight Avoyelles Parish/Marksville Area), 526 (LA Map) and ad Magazine Section page 107.

LAKE CHARLES — D2 *Calcasieu*

A SPOTLIGHT Introducing Lake Charles' colorful attractions appearing at the front of this state section.

LAKE CHARLES See also Fenton, Iowa, Kinder, Sulphur & Vinton.

Look in the Guide to Seasonal Sites to find places you can stay for a month, a season or longer.

A+ MOTEL & RV PARK
Ratings: 10/10★/10 (RV Park) From Jct of I-10 & LA 27 (exit 20): Go S 2.1 mi on LA 27 (L). **FAC:** Paved rds. (134 spaces). Avail: 54 paved, patios, 41 pull-thrus (30 x 70), back-ins (30 x 65), 54 full hkups (30/50 amps), seasonal sites, cable, WiFi, rentals, laundry, LP gas. **REC:** pool, wading pool, whirlpool, pond, fishing, playground. Pet restrict(B). Partial handicap access, no tents. Big rig sites, eco-friendly, 2015 rates: $33 to $37. Disc: military. ATM.
(337)583-2631 Lat: 30.1813, Lon: -93.37601
4631 Hwy 27 South, Sulphur, LA 70665
mike@a-plusmotel.com
www.a-plusmotel.com
See ad pages 545 (Spotlight Lake Charles), 529, 526 (LA Map).

BAYOU MARINO RV PARK Ratings: 6/9.5★/7 (RV Park) From jct I-10 (exit 27) and LA378, go N 1.3 mi on LA378 to Shady Ln, then E 0.2 mi on Shady Ln to Carlin Dr, N 0.2 mi (R). **FAC:** Paved rds. (29 spaces). Avail: 4 paved, 4 pull-thrus (28 x 58), 4 full hkups (30/50 amps), WiFi, laundry, LP gas. **REC:** Bayou Marino: fishing. Pet restrict(B). Partial handicap access. 2015 rates: $35 to $40.
(337)274-3337 Lat: 30.259509, Lon: -93.253858
2200 Carlin Drive, Westlake, LA 70669
richard.baggett@gmail.com

HIDDEN PONDS RV PARK
Ratings: 8/8★/7.5 (RV Park) From Jct of I-10 & Beglis Pkwy (Arizona St, exit 21): Go S 1-1/2 mi on Beglis Pkwy to Ravia Rd, then E 1/4 mi. (L). **FAC:** Paved rds. (158 spaces). Avail: 10 paved, 10 pull-thrus (24 x 70), 10 full hkups (30/50 amps), cable, WiFi, rentals, laundry, LP gas. **REC:** pond, fishing. Pets OK. Partial handicap access, no tents. Big rig sites, eco-friendly, 2015 rates: $25 to $29. Disc: military.
(337)583-4709 Lat: 30.19104, Lon: -93.35461
1201 Ravia Rd, Sulphur, LA 70665
hiddenponds@camtel.net
www.hiddenpondsrvpark.com
See ad pages 546 (Spotlight Lake Charles), 529, 526 (LA Map).

LITTLE LAKE CHARLES RV RESORT **Ratings: 8.5/8/8** (Campground) 2015 rates: $30 to $70. (877)433-2400 4200 Luke Powers Rd, Lake Charles, LA 70615

SAM HOUSTON JONES (State Pk) W-bnd: From Jct of I-10 & US-171 (exit 33), N 3.7 mi on US-171 to SR-378, W 2.8 mi to SR-378 Spur, W 1 mi to Sutherland Rd, S 0.4 mi (R); or From Jct of I-10 & SR-378 (exit 27 in Westlake), N 5 mi on SR-378 to SR-378 Spur, E/N/W 2.4 mi to Sutherland Rd, S 0.4 mi (R). 2015 rates: $20 to $34. (337)855-2665

TWELVE OAKS RV PARK
Ratings: 8.5/8.5★/9 (RV Park) From jct of I-10 & US-171 (exit 33): Go N 1-1/4 mi on US-171 to Conoco St, then E 1/4 mi. (E). **FAC:** Paved rds. (70 spaces). Avail: 10 paved, patios, 10 pull-thrus (28 x 70), 10 full hkups (30/50 amps), cable, WiFi, rentals, laundry. **REC.** Pet restrict(B). Partial handicap access, no tents. Big rig sites, eco-friendly, 2015 rates: $40 to $45.
(337)439-2916 Lat: 30.26553, Lon: -93.17696
2736 Conoco St, Lake Charles, LA 70601
twelveoaksrv@yahoo.com
www.twelveoaksrv.com
See ad pages 547 (Spotlight Lake Charles), 529.

VRV CAMPGROUND
Ratings: 8.5/8.5★/8.5 (Campground) From I-10 in Lake Charles, go west to exit 8 (LA-108), N 1 blk to Goodwin St, then W 1 blk to Azema St, then S 500 ft (E). **FAC:** Paved/gravel rds. (140 spaces). 25 Avail: 11 paved, 14 gravel, 25 pull-thrus (30 x 75), 25 full hkups (30/50 amps), WiFi, tent sites, rentals, laundry, LP gas. **REC:** pool, playground. Pet restrict(B). Partial handicap access. Big rig sites, 2015 rates: $28 to $30. Disc: AAA, military.
AAA Approved
(866)589-2300 Lat: 30.18563, Lon: -93.57234
1514 Azema St, Vinton, LA 70668
See primary listing at Vinton and ad page 548 (Spotlight Lake Charles).

WHISPERING MEADOW RV PARK
Ratings: 8/9.5★/9.5 (RV Park) From Jct of I-10 & West Lake (exit 27): Go East on exit ramp to LA 378 (Sampson St), then North 3 mi on Sampson St/Westwood Rd (R) Caution: E-Bnd stay in left exit lane to make left turn under I-10. **FAC:** Paved rds. (53 spaces). Avail: 3 paved, 3 pull-thrus (30 x 68), 3 full hkups (30/50 amps), cable, WiFi, rentals, dump, laundry, LP gas, firewood. Pet restrict(B). Partial handicap access, no tents. Big rig sites, RV age restrict, 2015 rates: $38. Disc: AAA, military.
(337)433-8188 Lat: 30.28103, Lon: -93.25788
3210 Westwood Rd, Westlake, LA 70669
whisperingmeadowrvpark@yahoo.com
www.whisperingmeadowrvpark.com

Things to See and Do

LAKE CHARLES SOUTHWEST LOUISIANA CONVENTION & VISITORS BUREAU Visitor's center open 7 days a week. Brochures, information & assistance on local accommodations, restaurants & attractions. Free coffee. Gift Shop. Weekend hours 8am to 3pm. Partial handicap access. Restrooms. Hours: 8am to 5pm.
(800)456-7952 Lat: 30.23650, Lon: -93.22929
1205 N Lakeshore Dr, Lake Charles, LA 70601
touristinfo@visitlakecharles.org
www.visitlakecharles.org
See ad page 527 (Welcome Section).

LAPLACE — D4 *St John The Baptist*

R & S MH & RV PARK (MHP)
Ratings: 7/8★/7 (Campground) From Jct of I-10 & US-51 (exit 209), SW 3 mi on US-51 to US-61, SE 1.7 mi (R); or From Jct of I-55 & US-51 (exit 1), SW 3.2 mi on US-51 to US-61, SE 1.7 mi (R). **FAC:** Paved rds. (37 spaces). Avail: 15 gravel, 2 pull-thrus (30 x 65), back-ins (30 x 45), 15 full hkups (30/50 amps), cable, WiFi, laundry. Pets OK. No tents. 2015 rates: $32.
(985)652-5531 Lat: 30.04956, Lon: -90.45912
1174 E Airline Hwy, Laplace, LA 70068
sgallo@rtconline.com
See ad this page.

Things to See and Do

NEW ORLEANS PLANTATION COUNTRY Information on what to see, to do, or to stay in the River Parishes. Tour packages available. Partial handicap access. RV accessible. Restrooms. Hours: 8am to 4pm. No CC.
(866)204-7782 Lat: 30.07394, Lon: -90.47623
2900 Hwy 51, Laplace, LA 70068
info@visitnopc.com
www.neworleansplantationcountry.com
See ad page 527 (Welcome Section).

LIVINGSTON — D4 *Livingston*

LAKESIDE RV PARK
Ratings: 10/10★/9.5 (RV Park) From Jct of I-12 (exit 22) & LA 63/Frost Rd, S 1 mi on Frost Rd (L). **FAC:** Paved rds. (139 spaces). Avail: 77 paved, patios, 13 pull-thrus (28 x 85), back-ins (30 x 55), 77 full hkups (30/50 amps), WiFi, rentals, laundry, groc, LP gas, fire rings, firewood. **REC:** pool, Campground Lake: fishing, playground. Pet restrict(B). Partial handicap access, no tents. Big rig sites, eco-friendly, 2015 rates: $35 to $52. Disc: military.
(225)686-7676 Lat: 30.45488, Lon: -90.74368
28370 S Frost Rd, Livingston, LA 70754
info@lakeside-rvpark.com
www.lakeside-rvpark.com
See ad pages 535 (Spotlight Baton Rouge), 529 & Snowbird Destinations in Magazine Section.

LOGANSPORT — B1 *De Soto*

SABINE RIVER RV PARK **Ratings: 6/8.5/8** (RV Park) 2015 rates: $20 to $25. (318)564-5311 17418 Hwy 5, Logansport, LA 71049

LORANGER — C4 *Tangipahoa*

SWEETWATER CAMPGROUND & RIDING STABLES **Ratings: 7/7/7** (Campground) 2015 rates: $28 to $61. (877)890-6868 57056 North Cooper Rd, Loranger, LA 70446

MADISONVILLE — D5 *St Tammany*

FAIRVIEW RIVERSIDE (State Pk) From Jct of I-12 (exit 57) & LA-1077: Go S 7 mi on LA-1077 to Madisonville, then E 2 mi on LA-22. (L). 2015 rates: $20 to $34. (985)845-3318

MANDEVILLE — D5 *St Tammany*

FONTAINEBLEAU (State Pk) From jct of I-12 (exit 65) & LA-59: Go S 3-1/2 mi on LA-59, then SE 2-1/2 mi on US-190. (L). 2015 rates: $20 to $34. (985)624-4443

Things to See and Do

ST TAMMANY PARISH TOURIST COMMISSION Tourism & visitors information about St. Tammany Parish. Hours: 8am to 5pm. No CC.
(800)634-9443 Lat: 30.41679, Lon: -90.04126
68099 Highway 59, Mandeville, LA 70471
www.LouisianaNorthShore.com
See ad page 527 (Welcome Section).

MANSFIELD — B2 *De Soto*

➔ NEW ROCKDALE RV/MOBILE HOME PARK **Ratings: 3.5/5/4** (RV Park) 2015 rates: $22. (318)871-9918 103 Henry Circle, Mansfield, LA 71052

MANY — B2 *Sabine*

CYPRESS BEND PARK-SABINE RIVER AUTHORITY (Public) From Jct of SR-6 & SR-191, S 3 mi on SR-191 to Cypress Bend Rd, SW 3 mi (1.5 mi past golf resort entrance) (R). 2015 rates: $20 to $25. (318)256-4114

MARKSVILLE — C3 *Avoyelles*

A SPOTLIGHT Introducing Avoyelles Parish/Marksville Area's colorful attractions appearing at the front of this section.

PARAGON CASINO RV RESORT

Ratings: 10/10★/10 (RV Park) From jct of LA-1 & LA-115/107 (in Marksville): Go S 1-1/2 mi on LA-1 (L).

PARAGON RV RESORT, MARKSVILLE, LA
Amenities include a world-class casino, a spa, shops, arcade, Kids Quest, a three-screen cinema, fabulous dining choices, a beautiful golf course and live entertainment. Your Louisiana RV resort oasis awaits at Paragon!

FAC: Paved rds. 205 paved, patios, 166 pull-thrus (35 x 80), back-ins (35 x 60), 205 full hkups (30/50 amps), cable, WiFi, rentals, dump, laundry, restaurant. **REC:** pool, whirlpool, golf, shuffleboard, playground, rec open to public. Pets OK. Partial handicap access, no tents. Big rig sites, 14 day max stay, eco-friendly, 2015 rates: $17 to $32. ATM.
(800)946-1946 Lat: 31.10556, Lon: -92.05825
124 Earl J Barbry Sr Blvd., Marksville, LA 71351
paragoncasinoresort.com
See ad pages 533 (Spotlight Avoyelles Parish/Marksville Area), 529, 526 (LA Map) and ad Magazine Section page 107.

Things to See and Do

PARAGON CASINO RESORT Full service casino, hotel and RV park. Live entertainment, restaurants, 18 hole golf course, indoor aquatic center, and 3 screen theatre. Partial handicap access. RV accessible. Restrooms, food. Hours: 24 hrs. ATM.
(800)WIN-1-WIN Lat: 31.10674, Lon: -92.05903
711 Paragon Place, Marksville, LA 71351
mail@paragoncasinoresort.com
www.paragoncasinoresort.com
See ad pages 533 (Spotlight Avoyelles Parish/Marksville Area), 526 (LA Map) and ad Magazine Section page 107.

PARAGON CASINO'S TAMAHKA TRAILS GOLF CLUB Tamaka Trails is an 18-hole championship golf course associated with Paragon Casino and part of the Audubon Golf Trail. Partial handicap access. RV accessible. Restrooms, food. Hours: 7:30am to 6:45pm. Adult fee: $49 to $59.
(800)946-1946 Lat: 31.10502, Lon: -92.05721
222 Slim Lemoine Rd, Marksville, LA 71351
mail@paragoncasinoresort.com
www.paragoncasinoresort.com
See ad pages 533 (Spotlight Avoyelles Parish/Marksville Area), 526 (LA Map) and ad Magazine Section page 107.

TRIBAL MUSEUM & CULTURAL RESOURCE CENTER An Educational and Cultural complex on a Native American Reservation, including a museum, gift shop, conservation/restoration laboratory, meeting rooms and distance learning facility. Partial handicap access. Restrooms. Hours: 9am to 5pm.
(318)253-9767 Lat: 31.110888, Lon: -92.063031
151 Melacon Drive, Marksville, LA 71351
www.tunicabiloxi.org
See ad pages 533 (Spotlight Avoyelles Parish/Marksville Area), 526 (LA Map) and ad Magazine Section page 107.

MINDEN — A2 *Webster*

MINDEN See also Arcadia, Doyline, Homer, Ruston & Simsboro.

Want to see what our inspectors see? The exact reproductions of the rating guidelines our inspectors used for this edition of the Guide are printed in the front of the book. Try using them on your next trip to perform your own inspection. Since our rating system is based on objective criteria, we're confident that your ratings will be similar to ours.

CINNAMON CREEK RV PARK

Ratings: 6/9★/8 (RV Park) From jct of I-20 (exit 44) & LA-371: Go N 1/4 mi on LA-371 (L). **FAC:** Gravel rds. (83 spaces). Avail: 63 gravel, 7 pull-thrus (24 x 55), back-ins (24 x 48), some side by side hkups, 63 full hkups (30/50 amps), cable, WiFi, tent sites, laundry. **REC.** Pets OK. Partial handicap access. Big rig sites, 2015 rates: $30.
(318)371-5111 Lat: 32.59511, Lon: -93.33955
12996 Hwy 371, Minden, LA 71055
trishstanley@suddenlink.net
www.cinnamoncreekrvpark.com
See ad pages 563, 529.

MONROE — A3 *Ouachita*

MONROE See also Arcadia, Bastrop, Chatham, Farmerville, Minden, Ruston, Simsboro & West Monroe.

AZALEA GARDENS MH COMMUNITY Ratings: 3/NA/7.5 (RV Area in MHP) From jct Hwy 139 & Hwy 594: Go SE on Hwy 594, then E on Swartz School Rd/Stubbs Ritchie Rd, then S on Dolly Drive (L). **FAC:** Paved rds. (80 spaces). Avail: 2 grass, back-ins (40 x 60), accepts self-contain units only, 2 full hkups (30 amps). **REC.** Pets OK. 2015 rates: $35. No CC.
(318)345-2692 Lat: 32.56852, Lon: -91.98096
400 Dolly Dr., Monroe, LA 71203
azalea@towermgmt.com
www.azaleagardensmhc.com

➔ OUACHITA RV PARK **Ratings: 6/6.5/5** (Campground) 2015 rates: $30.40. (318)343-8672 7300 Frontage Rd, Monroe, LA 71202

MORGAN CITY — D4 *St Mary*

MORGAN CITY See also Charenton & Houma.

KEMPER WILLIAMS PARK
(Public) From Jct of US-90 & W end of Atchafalaya River Bridge, W 3.7 mi on US-90 to Cotton Rd, S 0.3 mi (R) or W-bnd: From Jct of US-90 & Berwick exit, W 4.5 mi on US-90 to Cotton Rd, S 0.3 mi (R) CAUTION: RR crossing. **FAC:** Paved/gravel rds. (209 spaces). Avail: 189 gravel, 4 pull-thrus (20 x 50), back-ins (18 x 45), some side by side hkups, 26 full hkups, 163 W, 163 E (30/50 amps), WiFi, tent sites, dump, laundry. **REC:** golf, playground, rec open to public. Pets OK. Partial handicap access. Big rig sites, 2015 rates: $25 to $30. No CC.
(985)395-2298 Lat: 29.67192, Lon: -91.29311
264 Cotten Rd, Patterson, LA 70392
kwp@stmaryparishla.gov
www.kemperwilliamspark.com
See ad page 537 (Spotlight Cajun Coast/St Mary Parish).

LAKE END PARK & CAMPGROUND
(Public) W-bnd: From Jct of US-90 & SR-70 (Brashear Ave), N 1.5 mi on SR-70 (R); or E-bnd: From Jct of US-90 & SR-182/70 (Morgan City exit), N 1.5 mi on SR-70 (R). **FAC:** Paved/gravel rds. (154 spaces). 144 Avail: 129 gravel, 15 grass, 9 pull-thrus (26 x 60), back-ins (30 x 50), 144 full hkups (30/50 amps), WiFi $, tent sites, dump, laundry, fire rings, firewood. **REC:** Lake Palourde: swim, fishing, marina, playground, rec open to public. Pet restrict(B). Partial handicap access. Big rig sites, 2015 rates: $40.
(985)380-4623 Lat: 29.70431, Lon: -91.18966
2300 La Hwy 70, Morgan City, LA 70380
lep@cityofmc.com
www.lakeendpark.net
See ad page 537 (Spotlight Cajun Coast/St Mary Parish).

Things to See and Do

➔ **CAJUN COAST VISITORS & CONVENTION BUREAU** Exhibits and swamp view. Our new visitors center is your gateway to the Cajun Coast, with brochures, information & assistance on accommodations, restaurants & attractions in the area. Partial handicap access. RV accessible. Restrooms. Hours: 9am to 5pm Mon to Fri, 10am to 3 pm Wknd. No CC.
(800)256-2931 Lat: 29.69728, Lon: -91.18237
900 Dr. Martin Luther King Blvd., Morgan City, LA 70380
info@cajuncoast.com
www.cajuncoast.com
See ad page 537 (Spotlight Cajun Coast/St Mary Parish) & RV Trips of a Lifetime in Magazine Section.

MORGANZA — C3 *Pointe Coupee*

MAXEY CARE RV PARK **Ratings: 5.5/8★/7.5** (Campground) 2015 rates: $27. (225)694-3929 641 S Hwy 1, Morganza, LA 70759

NATCHITOCHES — B2 *Natchitoches*

NATCHITOCHES See also Colfax, Gardner, Marksville & Woodworth.

NAKATOSH CAMPGROUND

Ratings: 6/7.5/7 (Campground) From Jct of I-49 & SR-6 (exit 138), W 0.2 mi on SR-6. Entrance is at west end of Chevron truck stop(R). **FAC:** Gravel rds. (41 spaces). Avail: 21 gravel, 21 pull-thrus (30 x 60), 21 full hkups (30/50 amps), WiFi, tent sites, laundry. **REC:** rec open to public. Pets OK. Partial handicap access. Big rig sites, 2015 rates: $29 to $33.
(318)352-0911 Lat: 31.72595, Lon: -93.16362
5428 Hwy 6, Natchitoches, LA 71457
k.lott@lottoil.com
www.nakatoshcampgrounds.com
See ad this page, 529.

RED RIVER MIDWAY MARINA Ratings: 5.5/NA/7 (Campground) From jct US-71 & LA-477: Go S 1 mi on LA-477 (L). **FAC:** Gravel rds. 30 Avail: 2 paved, 28 gravel, back-ins (30 x 60), 30 full hkups (30/50 amps), WiFi, tent sites, rentals, restrooms only, laundry, groc, LP gas, restaurant. **REC:** Red River: fishing, marina. Pets OK. Big rig sites, 2015 rates: $30 to $35.
(318)646-0097 Lat: 31.45192, Lon: -92.58509
175 J. E. Jones Road, Natchitoches, LA 71457
jnelson@redrivermidwaymarinastmaurice.com
www.redrivermidwaymarina.com

NEW IBERIA — D3 *Iberia*

A SPOTLIGHT Introducing New Iberia's colorful attractions appearing at the front of this state section.

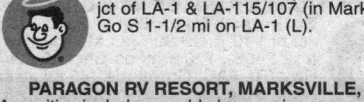

CAJUN RVERA PARK
(Public) From Jct Hwy 90 (exit 126) & Hwy 3212: Go 2.5 mi NE on Hwy 3212 (R). **FAC:** Paved rds. (185 spaces). Avail: 150 paved, 91 pull-thrus (30 x 75), back-ins (30 x 75), 150 full hkups (30/50 amps), WiFi, dump, laundry, controlled access. **REC:** heated pool, pond, fishing, rec open to public. Pets OK. Partial handicap access. Big rig sites, 2015 rates: $30 to $35.
(337)256-8681 Lat: 30.04846, Lon: -91.95061
911 Northwest Bypass (Hwy 3212), New Iberia, LA 70560
info@cajunrvera.com
www.cajunrvera.com
See ad page 550 (Spotlight New Iberia).

CHASE'S RV PARK
Ratings: 4/4.5/5 (RV Park) From Jct of US-90 & Hwy 83 (Weeks Island Rd), S 0.2 mi on Hwy 83 (R). **FAC:** Paved/gravel rds. (91 spaces). Avail: 15 grass, patios, 8 pull-thrus (25 x 45), back-ins (20 x 35), mostly side by side hkups, 15 full hkups (30 amps), cable, WiFi, laundry. **REC.** Pet restrict(B). No tents. 2015 rates: $24 to $25. No CC.
(337)365-9865 Lat: 29.95794, Lon: -91.82340
3004 Weeks Island Rd, New Iberia, LA 70560
See ad page 549 (Spotlight New Iberia).

KOC KAMPGROUND
Ratings: 8.5/10★/8 (Campground) From Jct of US-90 & Lewis St (Exit 129), S 0.1 mi on Lewis St to Frontage Rd, W 0.8 mi (L). **FAC:** Paved/gravel rds. (200 spaces). 75 Avail: 20 paved, 50 gravel, 5 grass, patios, 5 pull-thrus (30 x 50), back-ins (30 x 50), 75 full hkups (30/50 amps), cable, WiFi, tent sites, rentals, dump, laundry, fire rings. **REC:** pool, pond, fishing, playground. Pet restrict(B). Partial handicap access. Eco-friendly, 2015 rates: $25 to $27.50. Disc: military.
(337)364-6666 Lat: 29.97348, Lon: -91.84486
3104 Curtis Ln, New Iberia, LA 70560
kockampground@aol.com
www.kockampground.com
See ad pages 529, 550 (Spotlight New Iberia).

LA

NEW IBERIA (CONT)

Things to See and Do

IBERIA PARISH CONVENTION & VISITORS BUREAU Visitor center with brochures & assistance on attractions, accommodations, RV parks & restaurants. Open Monday thru Saturday. Partial handicap access. RV accessible. Restrooms. Hours: 9am to 5pm. No CC.
(888)942-3742 Lat: 29.98559, Lon: -91.85158
2513 Hwy 14, New Iberia, LA 70560
info@iberiatravel.com
www.iberiatravel.com
See ad page 550 (Spotlight New Iberia).

KONRIKO COMPANY STORE/CONRAD RICE MILL America's oldest rice mill. Gift shop. Closed Sun. RV accessible. Restrooms. Hours: 9am to 5pm. Adult fee: $4.
(800)551-3245 Lat: 29.99774, Lon: -91.81145
307 Ann St, New Iberia, LA 70560
info@conradricemill.com
www.conradricemill.com
See ad page 550 (Spotlight New Iberia).

RIP VAN WINKLE GARDENS Twenty-five acre semi-tropical landscaped garden with year-round explosion of color. Joseph Jefferson Mansion tours. Partial handicap access. RV accessible. Restrooms, food. Hours: 9am to 5pm. Adult fee: $10.
(337)359-8525 Lat: 29.97253, Lon: -91.97551
5505 Rip Van Winkle Rd, New Iberia, LA 70650
rvwgdns@yahoo.com
www.ripvanwinklegardens.com
See ad page 550 (Spotlight New Iberia).

SHADOWS-ON-THE-TECHE Home to four generations of the Weeks family. This pre-Civil War plantation home on Bayou Teche is one of the last remaining examples of Classical, English & French architecture. Restrooms. Hours: 9am to 5pm (Mon to Sat) Adult fee: $4.50 to $10. No CC.
(877)200-4924 Lat: 30.00372, Lon: -91.81543
317 E Main St, New Iberia, LA 70560
pat_kahle@nthp.org
www.shadowsontheteche.org
See ad page 550 (Spotlight New Iberia).

Our rating system isn't just tough, it's thorough. We know the kinds of things that are important to you — like clean restrooms and showers, attractive, secure, well-tended grounds, and extras like swimming pools. We give the first rating for development of facilities, the second for cleanliness and physical characteristics of restrooms and showers, and the third for visual appearance.

Like Us on Facebook.

NEW ORLEANS — D5 *Jefferson, Orleans*

NEW ORLEANS AREA MAP

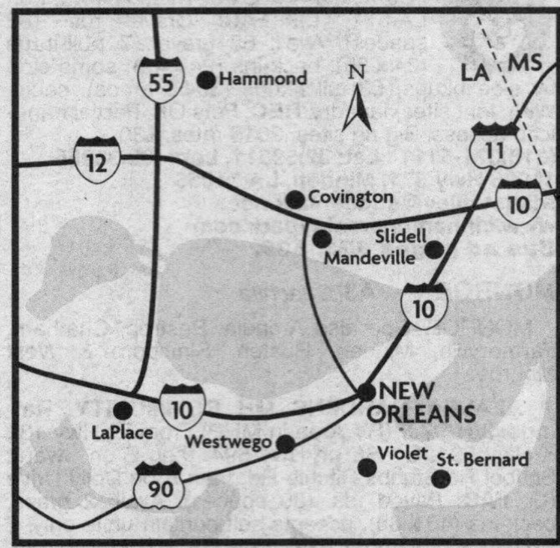

For more detail and a broader overview, please see our full-color state map at the front of the Louisiana state section.

Symbols on map indicate towns within a 50 mile radius of New Orleans where campgrounds are listed. Check listings for more information.

See also Covington, Hammond, LaPlace, Mandeville, Slidell, St. Bernard, Violet & Westwego.

A SPOTLIGHT Introducing New Orleans' colorful attractions appearing at the front of this state section.

BAY HIDE AWAY RV PARK & CAMPGROUND
Ratings: 9/9.5★/10 (Campground) From New Orleans go East to Jct of I-10 (exit 2 Welcome Center) & Hwy 607/US-90, SE 8.6 mi on Hwy 607/US-90to Lakeshore Rd, S0.5 mi (L). **FAC:** Gravel rds. 40 gravel, 23 pull-thrus (30 x 65), back-ins (30 x 65), 40 full hkups (30/50 amps), WiFi, laundry, fire rings, firewood. **REC:** pool, pond, fishing, playground. Pet restrict(B). Big rig sites, eco-friendly, 2015 rates: $25 to $50. Disc: military.
(228)466-0959 Lat: 30.29210, Lon: -089.45656
8360 Lakeshore Rd, Bay St Louis, MS 39520
bayhideawayrv@gmail.com
www.bayhideaway.com
See primary listing at Bay St Louis, MS and ad this page.

FRENCH QUARTER RV RESORT (FQRV)
Ratings: 10/9.5★/8 (RV Park) From Jct of I-10 & Basin St (exit 235 A for Orleans Ave/Vieux Carre), S 0.3 mi on Basin St to Crozat St, W 100 ft to FQRV entrance, N 550 ft (L) NOTE: Move to right lane after exiting onto Basin St. **FAC:** Paved rds. (52 spaces). Avail: 47 paved, patios, back-ins (30 x 60), 47 full hkups (30/50 amps), WiFi, rentals, laundry, controlled access. **REC:** pool, whirlpool, playground. Pets OK. Partial handicap access, no tents. Big rig sites, eco-friendly, 2015 rates: $105. Disc: military. ATM.
AAA Approved
(504)586-3000 Lat: 29.96187, Lon: -90.07276
500 N. Clairborne Ave., New Orleans, LA 70112
stay@fqrv.com
www.fqrv.com
See ad pages 552 (Spotlight New Orleans), 529.

JUDE TRAVEL PARK OF NEW ORLEANS
Ratings: 8.5/10★/8 (RV Park) From Jct of I-10 & US-90/Chef Menteur Hwy (exit 240B), E 0.8 mi on Chef Menteur Hwy (R). **FAC:** Gravel rds. (46 spaces). Avail: 31 gravel, back-ins (20 x 45), 31 full hkups (30/50 amps), seasonal sites, cable, WiFi, tent sites, laundry, controlled access. **REC:** pool, whirlpool. Pets OK. Eco-friendly, 2015 rates: $30 to $55. Disc: AAA, military.
(800)523-2196 Lat: 30.01183, Lon: -90.00045
7400 Chef Menteur Hwy, New Orleans, LA 70126
judetravelpark@judetravelpark.com
www.judetravelparkofneworleans.com
See ad pages 552 (Spotlight New Orleans), 529 & Snowbird Destinations in Magazine Section.

PARC D'ORLEANS Ratings: 4/5.5/5 (Campground) 2015 rates: $50. (504)243-3052 7676 Chef Menteur Hwy, New Orleans, LA 70126

PINE CREST RV & MH PARK OF NEW ORLEANS
Ratings: 9/9★/9.5 (RV Park) From jct I-610 & I-10: Go NE 25 mi on I-10 (exit 263), then SE 1/4 mi on LA-433. (R). **FAC:** Paved rds. (202 spaces). Avail: 36 paved, 36 pull-thrus (30 x 60), 36 full hkups (30/50 amps), WiFi, tent sites, dump, laundry, LP gas. **REC:** Campground Lake: fishing, shuffleboard, playground. Pet restrict(B). Big rig sites, eco-friendly, 2015 rates: $36.
(800)879-5936 Lat: 30.24194, Lon: -89.75796
2601 Old Spanish Trail, Slidell, LA 70461
pinecrestrvpark@gmail.com
www.pinecrestrv.com
See primary listing at Slidell and ad page 551 (Spotlight New Orleans).

PONTCHARTRAIN LANDING Ratings: 8.5/9.5★/9 (RV Park) 2015 rates: $69 to $229. (877)376-7850 6001 France Rd, New Orleans, LA 70126

REUNION LAKE RV RESORT
(RV Resort) (Planned) From Jct of I-12 and LA445 (exit 47), N 100 yards on LA 445 (R) Scheduled to open Dec 2015. **FAC. REC.** No CC, no reservations.
(985)240-2213 Lat: 30.48529, Lon: -90.33242
Ne corner of Hwy 445 & I-12, Ponchatoula, LA 70454
www.reunionlakerv.com
See primary listing at Robert and ad page 539 (Spotlight Hammond/Tangipahoa Parish).

RIVERBOAT TRAVEL PARK Ratings: 7/7/5 (Campground) E-bnd: From Jct of I-10 & Downman Rd (exit 240A), N 0.5 mi on Downman Rd to Chef Menteur Hwy (US-90), E 0.3 mi (R); or W-bnd: From Jct of I-10 & Chef Menteur Hwy/US-90 (exit 240B), W 0.1 mi on Chef Menteur Hwy/US-90 (L). **FAC:** Paved rds. (61 spaces). Avail: 46 gravel, back-ins (18 x 42), 46 full hkups (30/50 amps), cable, WiFi, tent sites,

Tell them you saw them in this Guide!

NEW ORLEANS (CONT)

RIVERBOAT TRAVEL PARK (CONT)
laundry, groc, controlled access. **REC:** pool. Pets OK. 2015 rates: $36. Disc: AAA. ATM.
AAA Approved
(800)726-0985 Lat: 30.01007, Lon: -90.01488
6232 Chef Menteur Hwy, New Orleans, LA 70126
riverboatrvpark@hotmail.com
www.riverboattravelpark.com

OAK GROVE — A3 *West Carroll*

7 OAKS RV CAMPGROUND
Ratings: 5/NA/6.5 (RV Park) From jct I-20 (exit 153) & Hwy 17: Go N on Hwy 17 (R). **FAC:** Gravel rds. (158 spaces). Avail: 142 gravel, back-ins (20 x 50), mostly side by side hkups, accepts self-contain units only, 142 full hkups (30/50 amps), seasonal sites, WiFi Hotspot. **REC.** Pets OK. Partial handicap access. 2015 rates: $25 to $30. No CC.
(318)428-5282 Lat: 32.85302, Lon: -91.40174
10284 Hwy 17 South, Oak Grove, LA 71263
lingocenterog@yahoo.com
www.lingocenterog.com
See ad opposite page.

OIL CITY — A1 *Caddo*

EARL WILLIAMSON PARK/CADDO LAKE PARK (CADDO PARISH) (Public) From jct Hwy 220 & Hwy 1 (N Market): Go 18 mi N on Hwy 1. 2015 rates: $6 to $12. (318)995-7139

OPELOUSAS — D3 *St Landry*

OPELOUSAS See also Eunice, Pine Prairie & Ville Platte.

OPELOUSAS SOUTH CITY PARK (Public) From Jct of I-49 & US-190 (exit 19B), W 1 mi on US-190 to Market St, S 0.8 mi (E). 2015 rates: $10. (337)948-2560

Things to See and Do

ST LANDRY PARISH TOURIST COMMISSION The St. Landry Parish Visitor Information Center, made with reclaimed and recycled material, is the only green visitor center in Louisiana and one of the nation's few. The center promotes sustainable practices old and new. Partial handicap access. RV accessible. Restrooms. Hours: 9am to 5pm. No CC.
(877)948-8004 Lat: 30.58419, Lon: -92.05184
978 Kennerson Rd, Opelousas, LA 70570
info@cajuntravel.net
www.cajuntravel.com
See ad page 527 (Welcome Section).

PATTERSON — D4 *St Mary*

Things to See and Do

ATCHAFALAYA AT IDLEWILD The Atchafalaya At Idlewild golf course is a championship design surrounded by wildlife and beauty found only in the heart of the Atchafalaya Basin and a member of the Audubon Golf Trail. Partial handicap access. RV accessible. Restrooms, food. Hours: 7am to 8pm. Adult fee: $40 to $68.
(985)395-4653 Lat: 29.66681, Lon: -91.29240
400 Cotten Rd., Patterson, LA 70392
news@atchafalayagolf.com
www.atchafalayagolf.com
See ad page 537 (Spotlight Cajun Coast/St Mary Parish).

PINE PRAIRIE — C3 *Evangeline*

CROOKED CREEK REC AREA (Public) From Jct of SR-13/SR-106 & SR-3187 (1 mi N of Pine Prairie), W 4.6 mi on SR-3187 to entrance rd, N 0.5 mi (E) or From Jct of US-167 & SR-106 (Bayou Chicot), W 4.5 mi on SR 106 to Jct of SR-134 3187, W 4.6 mi on SR 3187 to entrance rd, N 0.5 mi (E). 2015 rates: $20 to $27. (337)599-2661

PORT ALLEN — D4 *West Baton Rouge*

CAJUN COUNTRY CAMPGROUND **Ratings: 6.5/7/7** (Campground) 2015 rates: $35 to $40. (800)264-8554 4667 Rebelle Ln, Port Allen, LA 70767

RACELAND — D4 *Lafourche*

Things to See and Do

BAYOU LAFOURCHE AREA CVB Visitor information on things to see and do in a historic Parish. Partial handicap access. RV accessible. Restrooms. Hours: 9 am to 5 pm. No CC.
(877)537-5800 Lat: 29.70665, Lon: -90.57236
4484 Hwy 1, Raceland, LA 70394
info@visitlafourche.com
www.visitlafourche.com
See ad page 527 (Welcome Section).

RAYNE — D3 *Acadia*

CITY OF RAYNE RV PARK (Public) From jct I-10 (exit 87) & Hwy 98/35: Go 1/4 mi S on Hwy 98/35, then 200 yards W on Oak St, then NW on Gossen Memorial Dr to Frog Festival Blvd. (R) Note: Register at City Hall or Police Station after hours. 2015 rates: $20. (337)334-3121

RIVER RIDGE — D5 *Jefferson*

NEW ORLEANS WEST KOA **Ratings: 8/8.5★/7** (Campground) 2015 rates: $35.95 to $52.95. (504)467-1792 11129 Jefferson Hwy, River Ridge, LA 70123

ROBERT — D4 *Tangipahoa*

PASSPORT TO LEISURE **Ratings: 8/8★/7.5** (Membership Pk) 2015 rates: $44.40 to $72.15. (985)542-1507 46049 Hwy 445 N, Robert, LA 70455

REUNION LAKE RV RESORT
(RV Resort) (Planned) From Jct of I-12 and LA445 (exit 47), N 100 yards on LA445 (R) Scheduled to open December 2015. **FAC. REC.** No CC, no reservations.
(985)240-2213 Lat: 30.48529, Lon: -90.33242
Ne Corner of Hwy 445 & I-12, Ponchatoula, LA 70454
reunionlakerv.com
See ad page 539 (Spotlight Hammond/Tangipahoa Parish).

YOGI BEAR'S JELLYSTONE PARK **Ratings: 7/8★/7.5** (RV Park) 2015 rates: $30 to $65. (985)542-1507 46049 Hwy 445N, Robert, LA 70455

RUSTON — A2 *Lincoln*

LINCOLN PARISH PARK (Public) From Jct of I-20 & SR-33 (exit 86), N 3.5 mi on SR-33 (L). 2015 rates: $25. (318)251-5156

SHREVEPORT — A1 *Caddo*

SHREVEPORT See also Benton, Bossier City, Greenwood, Logansport, Mansfield & Minden.

GLEN LEAF MH COMMUNITY
Ratings: 5.5/NA/8 (RV Park) From jct I-20 (exit 8) & Hwy 526: Go S 0.3 mi on Hwy 526, then E 1 mi.on Hwy 511(W 70th St.), then S 0,2 mi on Glen Leaf Road (R). **FAC:** Paved rds. (215 spaces). Avail: 12 grass, back-ins (30 x 60), accepts self-contain units only, 12 full hkups (30 amps), seasonal sites. **REC:** pool, playground. Pets OK. 2015 rates: $25. No CC.
(318)687-9797 Lat: 32.44491, Lon: -93.88989
7400 Glen Leaf Dr, Shreveport, LA 71129
glenleaf@towermgmt.com
www.glenleafmhc.com

SHREVEPORT/BOSSIER KOA
Ratings: 8/9.5★/9.5 (RV Park) From jct I-20 (exit 10) & Pines Rd: Go S 0.6 mi on Pines Rd, then W 1 mi on W 70th St. (R); or From jct I-49 & LA-3132 (exit 201): Go W 6-1/4 mi on LA-3132 (exit 1D), then W 2 mi on 70th St. (R). **FAC:** Paved/gravel rds. (100 spaces). 85 Avail: 10 paved, 75 gravel, patios, 66 pull-thrus (35 x 90), back-ins (25 x 45), 85 full hkups (30/50 amps), cable, WiFi, tent sites, rentals, laundry, groc, LP gas. **REC:** pool, pond, fishing, playground. Pet restrict(B). Partial handicap access. Big rig sites, 2015 rates: $35 to $43.
(318)687-1010 Lat: 32.44376, Lon: -93.87823
6510 W 70th Street, Shreveport, LA 71129
shreveportkoa@gmail.com
http://koa.com/campgrounds/shreveport/
See ad this page.

SIMSBORO — A2 *Lincoln*

ANTIQUE VILLAGE RV PARK
Ratings: 6/9★/8.5 (RV Park) From jct of I-20 (exit 77) & LA-507: Go S 1/4 mi on LA-507/Martha St (R). **FAC:** Gravel rds. (64 spaces). Avail: 2 gravel, patios, back-ins (25 x 60), 2 full hkups (30/50 amps), WiFi, laundry, fire rings, firewood. **REC:** pond, fishing. Pets OK. Partial handicap access, no tents. Big rig sites, eco-friendly, 2015 rates: $30.
(318)247-1744 Lat: 32.54169, Lon: -92.78809
3027 Martha St., Simsboro, LA 71275
antiquervpark@att.net
See ad this page.

SLIDELL — D5 *St Tammany*

SLIDELL See also Covington, Madisonville, Mandeville & New Orleans.

NEW ORLEANS EAST KAMPGROUND
Ratings: 7/8.5★/8 (Campground) From Jct of I-10 & SR-433 (exit 263), SE 0.9 mi on SR-433. (R) Do not rely on GPS. Call for directions. **FAC:** Paved/gravel rds. (84 spaces). Avail: 30 gravel, 30 pull-thrus (24 x 65), some side by side hkups, 30 full hkups (30/50 amps), WiFi, tent sites, dump, laundry, LP gas. **REC:** pool, Salt Bayou: fishing, playground. Pets OK. Partial handicap access. Big rig sites, 2015 rates: $35 to $39. Disc: AAA.
AAA Approved
(800)562-2128 Lat: 30.23987, Lon: -89.75403
56009 Hwy 433, Slidell, LA 70461
noeast@sonic.net
www.neworleanseastkampground.com
See ad pages 552 (Spotlight New Orleans), 529.

The RVers' Guide to NASCAR - We'll give you the inside track on how to get high-speed thrills at major NASCAR venues. Turn to the front of the Guide to get the most out of North America's most thrilling sporting event.

LA

SLIDELL (CONT)

PINE CREST RV & MH PARK OF NEW ORLEANS

Ratings: 9/9★/9.5 (RV Park) From Jct of I-10 (exit 263) & LA-433, SE 0.2 mi on LA-433 (R).

PLEASANT AND FRIENDLY HOSPITALITY
Great local restaurants nearby. Swamp Tour pickup at the park. Rental car company will pick you up at the park. Only 30 minutes to downtown New Orleans or to the Gulf Coast beaches. Enjoy the city and return to relax.

FAC: Paved rds. (202 spaces). Avail: 36 paved, 36 pull-thrus (30 x 60), 36 full hkups (30/50 amps), WiFi, tent sites, dump, laundry, LP gas. **REC:** Campground Lake: fishing, shuffleboard, playground. Pet restrict(B). Big rig sites, eco-friendly, 2015 rates: $36.
(800)879-5936 Lat: 30.24194, Lon: -89.75796
2601 Old Spanish Trail, Slidell, LA 70461
pinecrestrvpark@gmail.com
www.pinecrestrv.com
See ad pages 551 (Spotlight New Orleans), 529 & Snowbird Destinations in Magazine Section.

SPRINGFIELD — D4 *Livingston*

TICKFAW (State Pk) From I-55 & LA-22 (exit 26), W 5.4 mi on LA-22 to LA-1037, SW 6.3 mi to Patterson Rd, follow signs (E); or From I-12 & LA-43 (exit 32), S 2.8 mi on LA-43 to LA-22, E 0.1 mi to LA-1037, S 6.3 mi to Patterson Rd, follow signs (E). Caution: Due to unique ecology, park rds subject to flooding, call first. 2015 rates: $18 to $28. (225)294-5020

SPRINGHILL — A2 *Webster*

FRANK ANTHONY RV PARK (Public) From jct Hwy 157 & US 371: Go 1 block S on US 371, then 2 blocks E on West Church St. (318)539-5681

ST BERNARD — D5 *St Bernard*

FANZ RV PARK

Ratings: 5.5/6/7.5 (RV Area in MHP) E-bnd: From Jct of I-10 & Exit 236B (LA39/N Claiborne), E 15 mi on LA-39 (Claiborne turns into N Robertson) to LA-46, E 2 mi (R) Note: W-bnd, exit at 236C. **FAC:** Paved rds. (140 spaces). Avail: 40 grass, back-ins (38 x 90), 40 full hkups (30/50 amps), seasonal sites, WiFi, tent sites, laundry, LP gas. **REC:** Bayou Terre: fishing. Pet restrict(B). Big rig sites, 2015 rates: $35. No CC.
(504)682-4900 Lat: 29.86985, Lon: -89.83447
2100 West Fanz Rd, St Bernard, LA 70085
cfanz@cox.net
http://www.visitstbernard.com/listings/stay/fanz-mobile-home-estates-rv-park#.VW3Xhes-Ab0
See ad this page.

ST JOSEPH — B4 *Tensas*

LAKE BRUIN (State Pk) From jct US-65 & LA-607: Go E 1 blk on LA-607, then N 1/2 mi on LA-605, then E 6-1/2 mi on LA-604, then SW 1/4 mi on Lake Bruin Rd. (L). 2015 rates: $20 to $34. (318)766-3530

ST MARTINVILLE — D3 *St Martin*

CATFISH HEAVEN AQUAFARM & RV PARK

Ratings: 9/9★/8 (Campground) From Jct of I-10 & exit 109, S 1.6 mi on LA-28 to Bridge St (LA-336-1), (R turn), S 0.2 mi to LA-31 (E Main St), SE (L turn) 4 mi to LA-314, S 2.6 mi to LA-353, E 0.1 mi (R); or From Jct of I-10 & exit 104, S 2.4 mi on Louisiana Ave to Carmel Dr, E 1.4 mi to LA-353 (Lake Martin), SE 6.4 mi (R). **FAC:** Paved/gravel rds. (45 spaces). Avail: 34 paved, 20 pull-thrus (20 x 60), back-ins (18 x 50), 34 full hkups (30/50 amps), WiFi, tent sites, dump, laundry, LP gas. **REC:** pool, wading pool, whirlpool, pond, fishing, playground, rec open to public. Pets OK. Partial handicap access. 2015 rates: $27 to $35. Disc: AAA, military.
(337)394-9087 Lat: 30.19232, Lon: -91.88134
1554 Cypress Island Hwy, Saint Martinville, LA 70582
goodtimes@catfishheaven.com
www.catfishheaven.com
See ad page 558.

LAKE FAUSSE POINTE (State Pk) From Jct of LA-31 & LA-96 (in town), NE 3.3 mi on LA-96 to LA-679, E 4 mi to LA-3083, E 4 mi (cross bridge) to Levee Rd, S 7.5 mi (R). 2015 rates: $20 to $34. (337)229-4764

SULPHUR — D2 *Calcasieu*

SWEETGUM MOBILE HOME & RV COMMUNITY Ratings: 5/NA/5.5 (RV Area in MHP) From Jct of I-10 & LA 27 S (exit 20): Go S 2 mi on LA 27 S. (R). **FAC:** Paved rds. (129 spaces). Avail: 29 grass, back-ins (40 x 100), accepts self-contain units only, 29 full hkups (30/50 amps), WiFi, laundry. **REC.** Pet restrict(B). No tents. Big rig sites, 2015 rates: $25.
(337)583-4741 Lat: 30.18534, Lon: -93.37619
4314 S. Hwy 27, Lot 73, Sulphur, LA 70665
sweetgum@towermgmt.com
sweetgummhc.com

VIDALIA — B3 *Concordia*

RIVER VIEW RV PARK AND RESORT

Ratings: 9/9★/9.5 (RV Park) From Jct of US-65/US-84 & LA-131 (on the West side of Mississippi River Bridge), S 0.8 mi on LA-131 (also Martin Luther King Ave) (L). **FAC:** Paved/gravel rds. (194 spaces). 184 Avail: 110 paved, 23 gravel, 51 grass, 141 pull-thrus (30 x 70), back-ins (30 x 50), 184 full hkups (30/50 amps), seasonal sites, WiFi, tent sites, rentals, dump, laundry, LP gas, firewood. **REC:** pool, whirlpool, Mississippi River: fishing, playground. Pet restrict(B). Partial handicap access. Big rig sites, eco-friendly, 2015 rates: $29.95 to $38.95. Disc: AAA, military.
AAA Approved
(318)336-1400 Lat: 31.55576, Lon: -91.43441
100 River View Pkwy, Vidalia, LA 71373
rvmanager@vidalialanding.com
riverviewrvpark.com
See ad pages 666 (Spotlight Mississippi River Destinations), 529.

VILLE PLATTE — C3 *Evangeline*

CHICOT (State Pk) From Jct of I-49 (exit 23) & US-167: Go NW 16-1/2 mi on US-167, then N 7 mi on LA-3042. (R). 2015 rates: $20 to $34. (337)363-2403

VINTON — D2 *Calcasieu*

VRV CAMPGROUND

Ratings: 8.5/8.5★/8.5 (Campground) From Jct of I-10 (exit 8) & LA-108: Go N 1 blk on LA-108 to Goodwin St, then W 1 blk to Azema St, then S 500 ft. (E). **FAC:** Paved/gravel rds. (140 spaces). 25 Avail: 11 paved, 14 gravel, 25 pull-thrus (30 x 75), 25 full hkups (30/50 amps), WiFi, tent sites, rentals, laundry, LP gas. **REC:** pool, playground. Pet restrict(B). Partial handicap access. Big rig sites, 2015 rates: $28 to $30. Disc: AAA, military.
AAA Approved
(866)589-2300 Lat: 30.18563, Lon: -93.57234
1514 Azema St, Vinton, LA 70668
See ad pages 548 (Spotlight Lake Charles), 529.

VIOLET — D5 *St Bernard*

ST BERNARD (State Pk) From Jct of I-10 & I-510/SR-47 (exit 246A), S 9.2 mi on I-510/SR-47 to SR-46 (St Bernard Hwy), E 7.5 mi to SR-39, SW 0.7 mi (L). 2015 rates: $20 to $34. (504)682-2101

WESTWEGO — D5 *Jefferson*

BAYOU SEGNETTE (State Pk) From jct of Westbank Expwy/Business US-90 & Lapalco Ave: Go SE 2 mi on Lapalco Ave (E). 2015 rates: $20 to $34. (888)677-2296

WOODWORTH — C3 *Rapides*

INDIAN CREEK REC AREA (State Pk) From Jct of US-165 & Robinson Bridge Rd (at sign in town), E 0.4 mi on Robinson Bridge Rd to Indian Creek Rd, follow signs SE 2.5 mi (E); or From Jct of I-49 & Parish Rd 22 (Exit 73), W 2.2 mi on Parish Rd 22 (Robinson Bridge Rd) to Indian Creek Rd, SE 2.5 mi (E). 2015 rates: $20 to $38. (318)487-5058

Replace clogged air filters. A clogged air filter can cut a vehicle's fuel efficiency by 10 percent.

ZWOLLE — B2 *Sabine*

NORTH TOLEDO BEND (State Pk) From Jct of SR-171 & SR-475 (in town), S 100 ft on SR-475 to SR-482, W 2.3 mi to SR-3229, W 4 mi to N Toledo Park Rd, follow signs 2.4 mi (E). 2015 rates: $20 to $34. (318)645-4723

SAN MIGUEL-SABINE RIVER AUTHORITY (Public) From Jct of SR-475 & SR-191, S 3 mi on SR-191 to Carters Ferry Rd, follow signs, SW 2.5 mi (R). 2015 rates: $20. (318)645-6748

Got a big rig? Look for listings indicating "big rig sites." These campgrounds are made for you, with 12'-wide roads and 14' overhead clearance. They guarantee that 25% or more of their sites measure 24' wide by 60' long or larger, and have full hookups with 50-amp electricity.

Maine Vacations and Tours

WELCOME TO Maine

DATE OF STATEHOOD	WIDTH: 210 MILES (340 KM)	PROPORTION OF UNITED STATES
MARCH 15, 1820	LENGTH: 320 MILES (515 KM)	0.93% OF 3,794,100 SQ MI

The image of Maine immediately conjures up rocky coastlines and a populace that can be as independently rugged as the nooks and crannies of its Atlantic Ocean coves. Mainers take a special pride in their autonomy, along with the relative isolation that comes with being the least densely populated state in the East.

Learn

Maine's maritime heritage goes back to 1607, when the Popham Colony settlers constructed the first English-built ship in the New World, *Virginia of Sagadahoc*, at the mouth of the Kennebec River.

The state's ocean-going heritage is explored at the Kittery Historical and Naval Museum. The Maine Maritime Museum in Bath is built near the site where warships have been launched into the Kennebec River from the Bath Iron Works since 1884.

"Up North," in Maine's interior, more than 90 percent of the area is covered by trees. The Kennebec-Chaudiere Corridor penetrates the heart of the Pine Tree State for 230 miles on its way to Quebec City in Canada, revealing the story of the North Woods as it rambles. Along the route is Augusta, the state capital on the Kennebec River.

Play

Including its many islands, Maine's famous rocky coast is more than 3,000 miles long. Sightseeing cruises explore the harbors and coastal villages aboard the fabled Maine Windjammer Fleet, which features seven vessels designated as National Historic Landmarks, including America's two oldest working

Top 3 Tourism Attractions:
1) Acadia National Park
2) Maine Lighthouses
3) Eartha, The Revolving Globe

Nickname: Pine Tree State

State Flower: White Pine Cone & Tassel

State Bird: Chickadee

People: Stephen King, writer; Henry Wadsworth Longfellow, poet; Nelson Rockefeller, vice president; Margaret Chase Smith, first woman elected to both houses of Congress and run for president

Major Cities: Portland, Lewiston, Bangor, South Portland, Auburn (Augusta, capital)

Topography: Appalachian Mountains; western borders—rugged terrain; southern coast—long sandy beaches; northern coast—rocky promontories, peninsulas, fjords

Climate: Humid continental climate with warm, humid summers and frigid winters

Maine Vacations and Tours

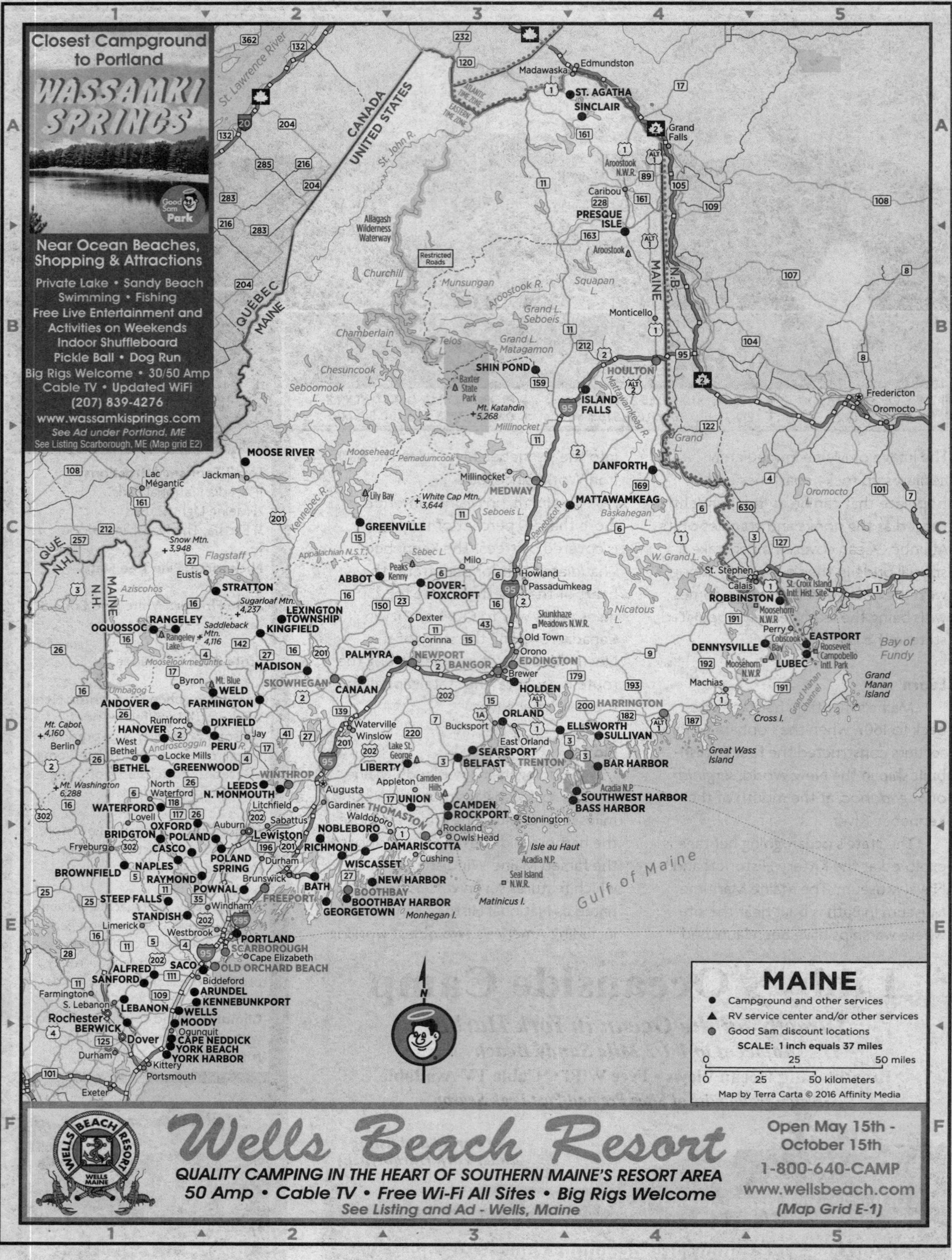
MAINE
Campground and other services
RV service center and/or other services
Good Sam discount locations
SCALE: 1 inch equals 37 miles
0 25 50 miles
0 25 50 kilometers
Map by Terra Carta © 2016 Affinity Media
CANADA
UNITED STATES
QUÉBEC
MAINE
N.B.
N.H.
Gulf of Maine
Bay of Fundy
ST. AGATHA
SINCLAIR
PRESQUE ISLE
HOULTON
SHIN POND
ISLAND FALLS
DANFORTH
MATTAWAMKEAG
MEDWAY
MOOSE RIVER
GREENVILLE
ABBOT
DOVER-FOXCROFT
STRATTON
LEXINGTON TOWNSHIP
KINGFIELD
RANGELEY
OQUOSSOC
PALMYRA
NEWPORT
BANGOR
EDDINGTON
MADISON
SKOWHEGAN
CANAAN
HOLDEN
WELD
FARMINGTON
ANDOVER
DIXFIELD
HANOVER
PERU
BETHEL
GREENWOOD
LIBERTY
SEARSPORT
BELFAST
ORLAND
ELLSWORTH
SULLIVAN
HARRINGTON
TRENTON
BAR HARBOR
SOUTHWEST HARBOR
BASS HARBOR
ROBBINSTON
DENNYSVILLE
EASTPORT
LUBEC
WINTHROP
LEEDS
N. MONMOUTH
UNION
CAMDEN
ROCKPORT
THOMASTON
WATERFORD
OXFORD
BRIDGTON
POLAND
CASCO
NAPLES
BROWNFIELD
RAYMOND
POLAND SPRING
NOBLEBORO
RICHMOND
DAMARISCOTTA
WISCASSET
NEW HARBOR
BATH
BOOTHBAY
BOOTHBAY HARBOR
GEORGETOWN
FREEPORT
POWNAL
STEEP FALLS
STANDISH
PORTLAND
SCARBOROUGH
OLD ORCHARD BEACH
SACO
ALFRED
SANFORD
ARUNDEL
KENNEBUNKPORT
LEBANON
WELLS
BERWICK
MOODY
CAPE NEDDICK
YORK BEACH
YORK HARBOR

schooners. Whale watching excursions are staples of the docks at Bar Harbor.

Maine's love of the outdoors boasts a vibrant heritage. Leon Leonwood Bean founded the company that bears his name in Freeport, and the L.L. Bean flagship store still does business. The Appalachian Trail begins in Baxter State Park on mile-high Mount Katahdin.

On the southern coast of Maine, the jagged coastline gives way to miles of white sand and picture-postcard New England beach towns. Acadia National Park on Mount Desert Island is America's finest seaside national park.

Experience

Maine produces one-quarter of all of America's blueberries, and the official state fruit is feted in August in Machias at the Wild Blueberry Festival. Farmers don't grow as many potatoes in Maine as they used to, but the Maine Potato Blossom Festival in Fort Fairfield has been packing them in since 1937. The Harvest on the Harbor fall festival in Portland is the largest food and wine event in Northern New England.

Taste

When it comes to food, Maine is synonymous with lobster. These crustaceans love Maine for the cold, clean waters found off its coast, and diners love the bounty from the state's 5,900 lobster harvesters. For five days in mid-summer, all Mainers celebrate their beloved crustacean in Rockland's Harbor Park at the Maine Lobster Festival.

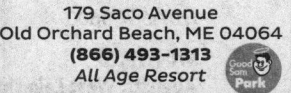

TRAVEL & TOURISM

Maine Office of Tourism
888-624-6345
www.visitmaine.com

Aroostook County Tourism
888-216-2463
www.vistaroostook.com

Greater Bangor CVB
800-916-6673
www.visitbangormaine.com

DownEast Acadia Regional Tourism
888-665-3278
www.downeastacadia.com

Kennebec & Moose River Valley Tourism
800-393-8629
www.kennebecvalley.org

Maine Beaches Association
www.mainebeachesassociation.com

Maine Highlands
800-91-MOOSE
www.themainehighlands.com

Maine Lakes & Mountains Tourism Council
888-688-0099
www.mainelakesandmountains.com

Maine's Midcoast
www.Mainesmidcoast.com

Greater Portland and Casco Bay Tourism Region
207-772-5800
www.visitportland.com

OUTDOOR RECREATION

Golf Maine
877-553-4653
www.golfme.com

Maine Association of Sea Kayak Guides
www.maineseakayakguides.com

Maine State Golf Association
207-846-3800
www.mesga.org

Ski Maine Association
207-773-7669
www.skimaine.com

Featured Good Sam Parks

MAINE

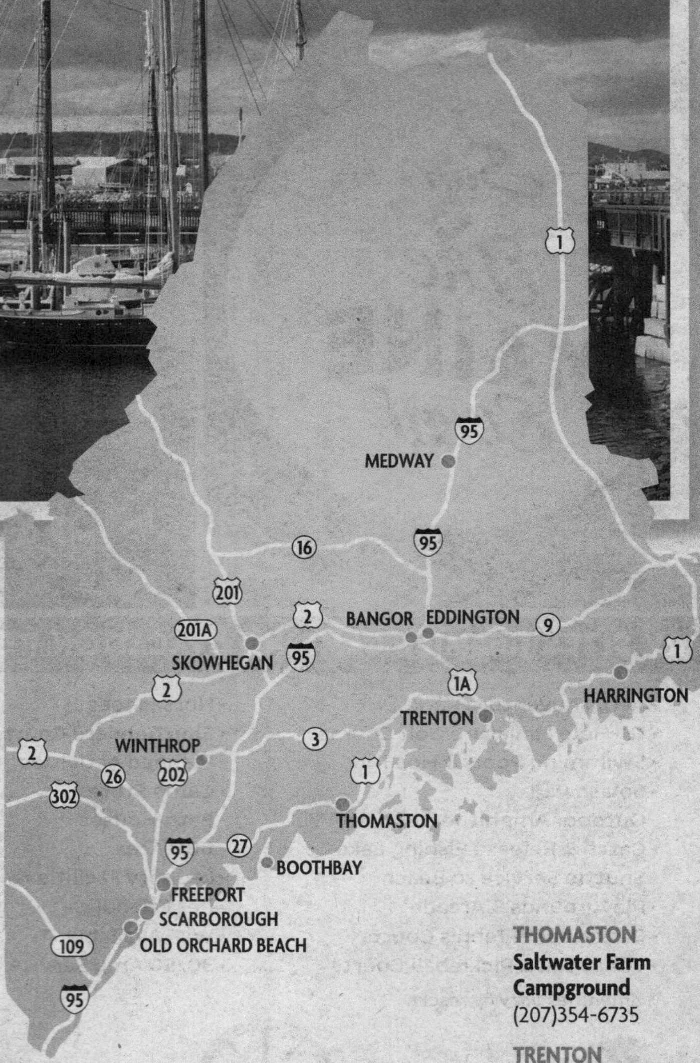

When you stay with Good Sam, you can expect the highest degree of cleanliness and friendliness, and better yet, you get 10% off campground fees.

If you're not already a Good Sam member you can purchase your membership at one of these locations:

BANGOR
Paul Bunyan Campground
(207)941-1177
Pleasant Hill Campground
(207)848-5127
Pumpkin Patch RV Resort
(207)848-2231

BOOTHBAY
Shore Hills Campground & RV Park
(207)633-4782

EDDINGTON
Cold River Campground
(207)922-2551

FREEPORT
Cedar Haven Family Campground
(207)869-5026

HARRINGTON
Sunset Point Campground At Harrington
(207)483-4412

MEDWAY
Katahdin Shadows Campground
(207)746-9349

OLD ORCHARD BEACH
Wagon Wheel RV Resort & Campground
(888)543-0516
Wild Acres RV Resort & Campground
(888)451-3586

SCARBOROUGH
Wassamki Springs Campground
(207)839-4276

SKOWHEGAN
Two Rivers Campground
(207)474-6482

THOMASTON
Saltwater Farm Campground
(207)354-6735

TRENTON
Timberland Acres RV Park
(207)667-3600

WINTHROP
Augusta-West Lakeside Resort Kampground
(207)377-9993

For more Good Sam Parks go to listing pages

Maine

CONSULTANTS

Bob & Vicki Auer

ABBOT — C2 *Piscataquis*

BALSAM WOODS CAMPGROUND **Ratings: 9/9★/9** (Campground) 2015 rates: $33 to $44. May 22 to Oct 12. (207)876-2731 112 Pond Rd, Abbot, ME 04406

ACADIA NATIONAL PARK — D4 *Hancock*

ACADIA NATIONAL PARK See also Bar Harbor, Bass Harbor, Ellsworth, Southwest Harbor & Trenton.

ALFRED — E1 *York*

WALNUT GROVE CAMPGROUND **Ratings: 8/8/8.5** (Campground) 2015 rates: $32 to $48. May 1 to Oct 12. (207)324-1207 599 Gore Rd., Alfred, ME 04002

ANDOVER — D1 *Oxford*

SOUTH ARM CAMPGROUND **Ratings: 5.5/8★/8** (Campground) 2015 rates: $28 to $36. May 15 to Sep 30. (207)364-5155 62 Kennett Dr, Andover, ME 04216

ARUNDEL — E1 *York*

BENTLEY'S SALOON, MOTEL & CAMPGROUND **Ratings: 6/9★/8.5** (Campground) 2015 rates: $30 to $50. Apr 1 to Nov 1. (207)985-8966 1601 Portland Rd., Arundel, ME 04046

AUBURN — E2 *Androscoggin*

AUBURN See also Freeport, Naples, Oxford, Poland, Poland Spring & Winthrop.

AUGUSTA — D2 *Kennebec, Waldo*

AUGUSTA See also Leeds, North Monmouth, Richmond & Winthrop.

We shine "Spotlights" on interesting cities and areas.

Explore America's Top RV Destinations!

From fishing along the Cape to boating on the Great Lakes, we've put the Spotlight on North America's most popular travel destinations. Turn to the Spotlight articles in our State and Province sections to learn more.

BANGOR — D3 *Penobscot*

PAUL BUNYAN CAMPGROUND
Ratings: 8/9★/8.5 (Campground) From Jct of I-95 & Rte 222 (Union St exit 184), NW 2.8 mi on Rte 222 (L); or From Jct of Rte 2 & Billings Rd (in Hermon), NE 3.4 mi on Billings Rd to Rte 222, SE 1.4 mi (R).

A COUNTRY OASIS WITHIN THE CITY
Experience the Sights & Sounds of Bangor from Paul Bunyan Campground - Family owned & operated for 25 years. Waterfront Concerts, Stock car & Canoe races, Discovery Museum, American Folk Festival, or relax by our heated pool!

FAC: Paved/gravel rds. (52 spaces). Avail: 42 gravel, 19 pull-thrus (30 x 72), back-ins (30 x 52), 12 full hkups, 30 W, 30 E (30/50 amps), seasonal sites, WiFi, tent sites, dump, laundry, groc, fire rings, firewood. **REC:** heated pool, pond, fishing, playground. Pet restrict(B/Q). Eco-friendly, 2015 rates: $29 to $40. Disc: AAA, military. May 1 to Oct 15.
AAA Approved
(207)941-1177 Lat: 44.82877, Lon: -68.84183
1858 Union St, Bangor, ME 04401
Radhachey@gmail.com
www.paulbunyancampground.com
See ad this page, 568.

PLEASANT HILL CAMPGROUND
Ratings: 8.5/9★/8.5 (Campground) From Jct of I-95 (exit 184) & Rte 222 (Union St), W 5 mi on Rte 222 (L). **FAC:** Paved/gravel rds. (107 spaces). 69 Avail: 19 gravel, 50 grass, 25 pull-thrus (30 x 70), back-ins (30 x 60), 17 full hkups, 52 W, 52 E (30/50 amps), seasonal sites, cable, WiFi $, tent sites, rentals, dump, mobile sewer, laundry, LP gas, fire rings, firewood. **REC:** heated pool, pond, fishing, playground. Pets OK. Partial handicap access. Big rig sites, eco-friendly, 2015 rates: $32 to $42. Disc: AAA, military. May 1 to Oct 13.
AAA Approved
(207)848-5127 Lat: 44.84800, Lon: -68.87812
45 Mansell Rd., Hermon, ME 04401
info@pleasanthillcampground.com
www.pleasanthillcampground.com
See ad this page, 568.

Things change ... last year's rates serve as a guideline only.

PUMPKIN PATCH RV RESORT
Ratings: 8.5/9.5★/9.5 (RV Park) From Jct of I-95 (Exit 180) & Cold Brook Rd: Go 2 1/2 mi W on Cold Brook Rd, then 1 1/2 mi W on Rt 2, then 1/2 mi N on Billings Rd (R).

FRIENDLIEST RV PARK IN NEW ENGLAND
Quiet, relaxing country atmosphere catering to adults, near Bangor, ME. Many interesting places nearby including museums & Stephen King's home. Sports enthusiasts will enjoy golf, stock car & harness racing, fishing & casino.

FAC: All weather rds. (75 spaces). Avail: 65 all weather, 44 pull-thrus (40 x 75), back-ins (40 x 56), 55 full hkups, 10 W, 10 E (30/50 amps), seasonal sites, cable, WiFi, dump, laundry, fire rings, firewood. **REC.** Pet restrict(B). Partial handicap access, no tents. Big rig sites, eco-friendly, 2015 rates: $35 to $40. Disc: AAA, military. May 1 to Oct 15.
(207)848-2231 Lat: 44.8164730, Lon: -68.9023388
149 Billings Rd., Hermon, ME 04401
rvoffice@pumpkinpatchrv.com
www.pumpkinpatchrv.com
See ad this page, 568.

Find it fast! To locate a town on a map, follow these easy instructions: Look for the map grid code after the town heading in the listing section and match it to the letters and numbers on the map borders. Draw a line horizontally from the letter and vertically from the number. You'll find the town near the intersection of the two lines.

ME

BAR HARBOR — D4 *Hancock*

➔ ACADIA/BLACKWOODS (Natl Pk) From Jct of SR-3 & SR-233 (in Bar Harbor), S 5 mi on SR-3 (L). Reservations required May to Oct. For reservations call (800)365-CAMP. 2015 rates: $30. May 1 to Oct 31. (207)288-3274

↖ BAR HARBOR CAMPGROUND **Ratings: 8/9★/8** (Campground) 2015 rates: $38 to $44. May 28 to Oct 13. (207)288-5185 409 State Hwy 3, Bar Harbor, ME 04609

↖ BAR HARBOR OCEANSIDE KOA **Ratings: 8/9★/8** (Campground) 2015 rates: $50 to $115. Apr 15 to Oct 30. (207)288-3520 136 County Rd, Bar Harbor, ME 04609

↖ BAR HARBOR WOODLANDS KOA **Ratings: 8.5/9★/9** (Campground) 2015 rates: $46 to $70. May 23 to Sep 21. (207)288-5139 1453 State Hwy 102, Bar Harbor, ME 04609

↖ **HADLEY'S POINT CAMPGROUND**
Ratings: 8.5/9★/8.5 (Campground) From Jct of Rtes 102 & 3, E 3 mi on Rte 3 to Hadley Point Rd, N 0.25 mi (R).

FAMILY OWNED & OPERATED FOR 40 YRS
Catering to families who want the fun of camping with proximity to Acadia Nat'l Park and Bar Harbor. Tent camping, 20-30-50 amp service sites, and NEW CABINS provide options for all types of campers.

FAC: Paved/gravel rds. 130 Avail: 10 gravel, 120 grass, 8 pull-thrus (32 x 56), back-ins (26 x 54), 15 full hkups, 115 W, 115 E (30/50 amps), WiFi, tent sites, rentals, showers $, dump, mobile sewer, laundry, LP gas, fire rings, firewood. **REC:** heated pool, shuffleboard, playground. Pets OK. Big rig sites, eco-friendly, 2015 rates: $37 to $42. May 15 to Oct 15.
AAA Approved
(207)288-4808 Lat: 44.43797, Lon: -68.31459
33 Hadley Point Rd., Bar Harbor, ME 04609
www.hadleyspoint.com
See ad this page.

↖ MT. DESERT NARROWS CAMPING RESORT **Ratings: 8/7.5/7.5** (Campground) 2015 rates: $36 to $93. May 15 to Oct 10. (207)288-4782 1219 State Hwy 3, Bar Harbor, ME 04609

↓ NARROWS TOO CAMPING RESORT **Ratings: 9/9★/8.5** (RV Park) 2015 rates: $40 to $114. May 1 to Oct 17. (207)667-4300 1150 Bar Harbor Rd., Trenton, ME 04605

BASS HARBOR — D4 *Hancock*

↓ BASS HARBOR CAMPGROUND **Ratings: 7.5/8.5★/7.5** (Campground) 2015 rates: $35 to $55. May 15 to Oct 15. (207)244-5857 342 Harbor Dr, Bass Harbor, ME 04653

BATH — E2 *Sagadahoc*

↓ MEADOWBROOK CAMPING AREA **Ratings: 8.5/7.5/7** (Campground) 2015 rates: $32 to $43. May 1 to Oct 1. (207)443-4967 33 Meadowbrook Rd., Phippsburg, ME 04562

BELFAST — D3 *Waldo*

↑ MOORINGS OCEANFRONT RV RESORT **Ratings: 6.5/8★/8.5** (Campground) 2015 rates: $51 to $72. May 1 to Oct 24. (207)338-6860 191 Searsport Ave., Belfast, ME 04915

BERWICK — E1 *York*

➔ BEAVER DAM CAMPGROUND **Ratings: 8/9★/8** (Campground) 2015 rates: $42 to $46. May 15 to Sep 30. (207)698-2267 551 School St., Berwick, ME 03901

BETHEL — D1 *Oxford*

↑ BETHEL OUTDOOR ADVENTURE AND CAMPGROUND **Ratings: 7/6.5/6.5** (Campground) 2015 rates: $35 to $40. May 15 to Oct 15. (207)824-4224 121 Mayville Rd-Us Rte 2, Bethel, ME 04217

BOOTHBAY — E2 *Lincoln*

↖ **SHORE HILLS CAMPGROUND & RV PARK**
Ratings: 8/9.5★/9 (Campground) From Jct of US-1 & SR-27, S 7.5 mi on SR-27 (R). **FAC:** Paved/gravel rds. (136 spaces). Avail: 116 gravel, 15 pull-thrus (30 x 84), back-ins (30 x 62), 82 full hkups, 34 W, 34 E (30/50 amps), seasonal sites, cable, WiFi, tent sites, rentals, showers $, dump, laundry, groc, LP gas, fire rings, firewood, controlled access. **REC:** Cross River: swim, fishing, playground. Pet restrict(B). Big rig sites, 2015 rates: $44 to $52. Disc: AAA. May 15 to Oct 14. ATM, no CC.
AAA Approved
(207)633-4782 Lat: 43.90510, Lon: -69.61994
553 Wiscasset Rd., Boothbay, ME 04537
camping@shorehills.com
www.shorehills.com
See ad this page, 568.

BOOTHBAY HARBOR — E2 *Lincoln*

↓ GRAY HOMESTEAD OCEANFRONT CAMPING **Ratings: 6.5/8★/7.5** (Campground) 2015 rates: $40 to $50. May 15 to Oct 13. (207)633-4612 21 Homestead Rd, Southport, ME 04576

BRIDGTON — E1 *Cumberland*

↑ LAKESIDE PINES CAMPGROUND **Ratings: 5/5.5/5.5** (Campground) 2015 rates: $44. May 15 to Sep 15. (207)647-3935 54 Lakeside Pines Rd (Hwy 117), Bridgton, ME 04009

BROWNFIELD — E1 *Oxford*

➔ **RIVER RUN CANOE & CAMPGROUND Ratings: 6/9/8.5** (Campground) From jct Hwy 160 and Hwy 113 (1/2 mile North of Brownfield): Go 1 mi North on Hwy 160 across Saco River Bridge. (R). **FAC:** Gravel rds. 27 Avail: 12 grass, 15 dirt, back-ins (75 x 100), WiFi Hotspot, tent sites, showers $, laun-

BROWNFIELD (CONT)

RIVER RUN CANOE (CONT)
dry, fire rings, firewood, controlled access. **REC:** Saco River: swim, fishing, rec open to public. Pets OK. Partial handicap access. Eco-friendly, 2015 rates: $15 to $75. May 26 to Sep 1.
AAA Approved
(207)452-2500 Lat: 43.95685, Lon: -70.88131
191 Denmark Rd, Brownfield, ME 04010
theparkers@fairpoint.net
www.riverruncanoe.com

➔ SHANNON'S SANCTUARY **Ratings: 7.5/6.5/8** (Campground) 2015 rates: $32 to $35. May 15 to Oct 15. (207)452-2274 379 Denmark Road, Brownfield, ME 04010

WOODLAND ACRES CAMPGROUND **Ratings: 7.5/8.5★/8** (Campground) 2015 rates: $34 to $45. May 15 to Oct 15. (207)935-2529 33 Woodland Acres Dr., Brownfield, ME 04010

BUCKSPORT — D3 *Hancock*

BUCKSPORT See also Bangor, Holden, Orland & Searsport.

CAMDEN — D3 *Knox*

CAMDEN HILLS (State Pk) From town, N 2 mi on US-1 (L). 2015 rates: $15 to $35. May 18 to Sep 13. (207)236-3109

CANAAN — D2 *Somerset*

➔ SKOWHEGAN/KENNEBEC VALLEY KOA **Ratings: 9/10★/8** (Campground) 2015 rates: $39 to $50. May 15 to Oct 12. (207)474-2858 18 Cabin Rd., Canaan, ME 04924

CAPE NEDDICK — F1 *York*

DIXON'S COASTAL MAINE CAMPGROUND **Ratings: 6/8.5★/8.5** (Campground) 2015 rates: $34 to $48. May 14 to Sep 17. (207)363-3626 1740 US Route 1, Cape Neddick, ME 03902

CASCO — E1 *Cumberland*

POINT SEBAGO RESORT
Ratings: 8/8.5★/9 (Campground) From Jct of HWY-85 & US-302: Go 5 mi N on US-302, then 1 mi W at Casco Alliance Church (Pt. Sebago Rd) (R). **FAC:** Paved/gravel rds. (223 spaces). Avail: 88 gravel, 5 pull-thrus (30 x 60), back-ins (30 x 50), 88 full hkups (30/50 amps), seasonal sites, cable, WiFi, tent sites, rentals, dump, laundry, groc, LP bottles, fire rings, firewood, restaurant, controlled access. **REC:** Sebago Lake: swim, fishing, marina, golf, shuffleboard, playground. Pet restrict(Q). Partial handicap access. Big rig sites, eco-friendly, 2015 rates: $67 to $108. Disc: AAA, military. May 1 to Oct 31. ATM.
(207)655-3821 Lat: 43.91928, Lon: -70.55020
261 Point Sebago Rd., Casco, ME 04015
information@pointsebago.com
www.pointsebago.com
See ad this page.

DAMARISCOTTA — E2 *Lincoln*

➔ **LAKE PEMAQUID CAMPING**
Ratings: 8.5/8.5★/8 (Campground) From Jct Hwy 130 & Bus US-1: Go 1 mi NE on Bus US-1, then 2 mi S on Biscay Rd, then 1/4 mi E on Egypt Rd, then E on Twin Cove Ln (E). **FAC:** Paved/gravel rds. (263 spaces). 233 Avail: 11 paved, 52 gravel, 170 dirt, 12 pull-thrus (24 x 70), back-ins (24 x 46), 167 full hkups, 66 W, 66 E (30/50 amps), seasonal sites, WiFi Hotspot, tent sites, rentals, showers $, dump, laundry, groc, LP bottles, fire rings, firewood, controlled access. **REC:** heated pool, whirlpool, Pemaquid Lake: swim, fishing, marina, playground. Pets OK. Partial handicap access. Big rig sites, eco-friendly, 2015 rates: $26 to $49. May 25 to Sep 30. ATM.
AAA Approved
(207)563-5202 Lat: 44.03130, Lon: -69.46107
100 Twin Cove Lane, Damariscotta, ME 04543
lakepem@tidewater.net
www.lakepemaquid.com
See ad page 572.

DANFORTH — C4 *Washington*

➔ GREENLAND COVE CAMPGROUND **Ratings: 8/8★/7.5** (Campground) 2015 rates: $30. May 15 to Oct 1. (207)448-2863 70 Brown Rd., Danforth, ME 04424

DENNYSVILLE — D5 *Washington*

COBSCOOK BAY (State Pk) From Jct of SR-86 & US-1, S 4 mi on US-1 to unnamed cnty rd, E 0.5 mi (L). Note: 40' RV length maximum. 2015 rates: $14 to $24. May 15 to Oct 15. (207)726-4412

We appreciate your business!

DIXFIELD — D2 *Oxford*

MOUNTAIN VIEW CAMPGROUND Ratings: 7.5/7.5/7.5 (Campground) From Jct of US-2 & Rte 142, NE 1.5 mi on Rte 142 (L). **FAC:** Paved rds. (60 spaces). Avail: 37 grass, 22 pull-thrus (24 x 63), back-ins (22 x 45), 31 full hkups, 6 W, 6 E (30 amps), seasonal sites, WiFi Hotspot, tent sites, rentals, dump, laundry, fire rings, firewood. **REC:** pool, Webb River: fishing, playground, rec open to public. Pets OK. Eco-friendly, 2015 rates: $28 to $30. Disc: AAA, military. May 1 to Oct 31. No CC.
(207)562-8285 Lat: 44.55287, Lon: -70.45269
200 Mountainview Dr., Dixfield, ME 04224
gwelch@twc.com
www.mountainviewcampground.net

PEJEPSCOOK CAMPGROUND **Ratings: 6/10★/6.5** (Campground) 2015 rates: $24. May 10 to Oct 10. (207)779-7356 569 Main St., Dixfield, ME 04224

DOVER-FOXCROFT — C3 *Piscataquis*

PEAKS-KENNY (State Pk) From Jct of SR-150 & SR-153, N 4.5 mi on SR-153 to campground rd, W 2 mi (E). Note: 35' RV length maximum. 2015 rates: $15 to $25. May 15 to Sep 1. (207)564-2003

EASTPORT — D5 *Washington*

SEAVIEW CAMPGROUND & CABINS **Ratings: 6.5/9/7** (Campground) 2015 rates: $45 to $53. May 15 to Oct 15. (207)853-4471 16 Norwood Rd., Eastport, ME 04631

Thank You to our active and retired military personnel. A dedicated section of Military Listings for places to camp can be found at the back of the Guide.

Your neighbor just told you about a great little campground in Kentucky M what was the name of it again? The "Find-it-Fast" index in the back of the Guide can help. It's an alphabetical listing, by state, of every private and public park in the Guide.

ME

EDDINGTON — D3 *Penobscot*

COLD RIVER CAMPGROUND
Ratings: 9/7.5★/8.5 (Campground) From Jct of I-95 & I-395 (exit 182A), E 1 mi on I-395 to Rte 9 (exit 4), NE 5.7 mi to N Jct of Rte 9 & Rte 178 (in Eddington), N 1 mi on Rte 178 (R). **FAC:** Gravel rds. (68 spaces). 38 Avail: 28 gravel, 10 grass, 14 pull-thrus (30 x 62), back-ins (30 x 35), 30 full hkups, 8 W, 8 E (30/50 amps), seasonal sites, cable, WiFi, tent sites, rentals, dump, laundry, groc, LP gas, fire rings, firewood. **REC:** pool, playground, rec open to public. Pet restrict(B). Eco-friendly, 2015 rates: $36.50 to $42.50. Disc: AAA, military. May 1 to Oct 15.
(207)922-2551 Lat: 44.83841, Lon: -68.69318
211 Riverside Dr., Eddington, ME 04428
info@ColdRiverCampground.com
www.coldrivercampground.com
See ad this page, 568.

A campground rating is based on ALL facilities available at the park.

ELLSWORTH — D3 *Hancock*

BRANCH LAKE CAMPING AREA **Ratings: 6/7/6.5** (Campground) 2015 rates: $37 to $43. May 15 to Oct 1. (207)667-5174 180 Hansons Landing Rd, Ellsworth, ME 04605

FOREST RIDGE CAMPGROUND AND RV PARK **Ratings: 8/8.5★/8.5** (Campground) 2015 rates: $47 to $52. May 1 to Oct 15. (207)664-7070 40 Flockamoosen Way, Ellsworth, ME 04605

LAMOINE (Public) From jct US-1 & Hwy-184: Go 10 mi SE on Hwy-184. Note: 45' RV length maximum. 2015 rates: $15 to $25. May 19 to Oct 15. (207)667-4778

PATTEN POND CAMPING RESORT **Ratings: 8.5/8/7.5** (RV Park) 2015 rates: $34 to $55. May 15 to Oct 10. (207)667-7600 1470 Bucksport Rd., Ellsworth, ME 04605

FARMINGTON — D2 *Franklin*

TROLL VALLEY CAMPGROUND **Ratings: 3.5/6/5** (Campground) 2015 rates: $28 to $35. May 16 to Oct 18. (207)778-3656 283 Red Schoolhouse Rd., Farmington, ME 04938

FREEPORT — E2 *Cumberland*

BLUEBERRY POND CAMPGROUND
Ratings: 7.5/7.5★/8 (Campground) From I-295 (Exit 22) & Hwy 125/136: Go 2-1/2 mi N on Hwy 136, then 1-1/2 mi W on Poland Rd (L). **FAC:** Gravel rds. (29 spaces). Avail: 24 gravel, 3 pull-thrus (40 x 60), back-ins (40 x 60), 9 full hkups, 15 W, 15 E (30/50 amps), seasonal sites, WiFi, tent sites, rentals, dump, laundry, fire rings, firewood. **REC:** pool, pond, playground, rec open to public. Pets OK. Partial handicap access. Big rig sites, eco-friendly, 2015 rates: $44. Disc: AAA, military. May 15 to Oct 30.
(877)290-1381 Lat: 43.90992, Lon: -70.14292
218 Poland Range Rd., Pownal, ME 04069
fun@blueberrycampground.com
www.blueberrycampground.com
See ad this page.

CEDAR HAVEN FAMILY CAMPGROUND
Ratings: 8/9★/8.5 (Campground) From Jct I-295 (exit 22) & Hwy 125: Go 1-1/2 mi N on Hwy 125, then 1/2 mi NE on Baker Rd. (L). **FAC:** Gravel rds. (41 spaces). Avail: 33 gravel, 7 pull-thrus (30 x 60), back-ins (30 x 45), 22 full hkups, 11 W, 11 E (30/50 amps), seasonal sites, WiFi, tent sites, rentals, dump, laundry, fire rings, firewood, controlled access. **REC:** pond, swim, playground. Pets OK. Partial handicap access. Big rig sites, eco-friendly, 2015 rates: $39 to $44. Disc: military. May 1 to Oct 31.
(207)869-5026 Lat: 43.88460, Lon: -70.08972
39 Baker Rd., Freeport, ME 04032
info@cedarhavenfamilycampground.com
www.cedarhavenfamilycampground.com
See ad this page, 568.

DESERT DUNES OF MAINE CAMPGROUND **Ratings: 7/7.5/7.5** (Campground) 2015 rates: $38 to $44. May 7 to Oct 16. (207)865-6962 95 Desert Rd. Freeport, ME 04032

FREEPORT DURHAM KOA **Ratings: 8.5/9.5★/9** (Campground) 2015 rates: $33 to $58. Apr 15 to Nov 1. (207)688-4288 82 Big Skye Ln., Durham, ME 04222

FREEPORT (CONT)

➔ RECOMPENCE SHORE CAMPGROUND **Ratings: 6.5/7/7.5** (Campground) 2015 rates: $26 to $48. May 1 to Oct 31. (207)865-9307 134 Burnett Rd, Freeport, ME 04032

⬇ WINSLOW MEMORIAL PARK (Public) From Jct of US-1 & S Freeport Rd, E 0.9 mi on S Freeport Rd to Staples Point Rd, SE 2 mi (R). 2015 rates: $16 to $35. May 4 to Oct 4. (207)865-4198

GEORGETOWN — E2 *Sagadahoc*

⬇ SAGADAHOC BAY CAMPGROUND **Ratings: 6/6.5/5** (Campground) 2015 rates: $45 to $58. May 1 to Nov 1. (207)371-2014 9 Molly Point Lane, Georgetown, ME 04548

GREENVILLE — C2 *Piscataquis*

⬆ LILY BAY (State Pk) From Jct of Hwy 6/15 & Kokadjo Rd, N 9 mi on Kokadjo Rd (L). Note: 45' RV length maximum. 2015 rates: $14 to $24. May 19 to Sep 7. (207)695-2700

⬇ MOOSEHEAD FAMILY CAMPGROUND **Ratings: 5/NA/7.5** (Campground) Pit toilets. 2015 rates: $30 to $45. May 1 to Oct 31. (207)695-2210 312 Moosehead Lake Rd. (Route 15), Greenville, ME 04441

GREENWOOD — D1 *Oxford*

⬇ LITTLEFIELD BEACHES CAMPGROUND **Ratings: 6.5/7/7.5** (Campground) 2015 rates: $38 to $44. May 15 to Sep 25. (207)875-3290 13 Littlefield Lane, Greenwood, ME 04255

HANOVER — D1 *Oxford*

➚ STONY BROOK RECREATION & CAMPING **Ratings: 8.5/8/8** (Campground) 2015 rates: $28 to $38. (207)824-2836 3036 Main St., Hanover, ME 04237

HARRINGTON — D4 *Washington*

➚ **SUNSET POINT CAMPGROUND AT HARRINGTON**
Ratings: 7.5/8.5★/8.5 (Campground) From Jct of US-1A & US-1 in town, NE 0.8 mi on US-1 to Marshville Rd, S 2.8 mi (R) Do Not take Cates Rd if GPS directs you there. **FAC:** Gravel rds. 21 gravel, 4 pull-thrus (46 x 76), back-ins (30 x 60), 13 full hkups, 8 W, 8 E (30/50 amps), WiFi, tent sites, rentals, dump, laundry, fire rings, firewood. **REC:** Harrington River: swim, fishing. Pets OK. Big rig sites, eco-friendly, 2015 rates: $29 to $35. May 15 to Oct 15.
(207)483-4412 Lat: 44.58952, Lon: -67.78480
24 Sunset Point Rd., Harrington, ME 04643
kurt0347@aol.com
www.sunsetpointcampground.com
See ad pages 570, 568.

HOLDEN — D3 *Penobscot*

➘ HOLDEN FAMILY CAMPGROUND **Ratings: 8/8.5★/8** (Campground) 2015 rates: $40. May 1 to Oct 15. (207)989-0529 108 Main Rd., Holden, ME 04429

HOULTON — B4 *Aroostook*

⬆ **MY BROTHER'S PLACE CAMPGROUND**
Ratings: 8.5/9★/9 (Campground) From Jct of I-95 & Rte 1 (exit 302), N 2 mi on Rte 1 (R). **FAC:** Paved rds. (77 spaces). Avail: 75 grass, 65 pull-thrus (28 x 100), back-ins (25 x 78), some side by side hkups, 50 full hkups, 25 W, 25 E (30/50 amps), seasonal sites, WiFi, tent sites, rentals, dump, laundry, groc, fire rings, firewood. **REC:** pond, swim, playground. Pets OK. Partial handicap access. Big rig sites, eco-friendly, 2015 rates: $28 to $38. May 10 to Oct 15.
(207)532-6739 Lat: 46.17073, Lon: -67.84026
659 North St., Houlton, ME 04730
mybrotherspl@aol.com
mybrothersplace.mainerec.com
See ad this page.

ISLAND FALLS — B4 *Aroostook*

➚ BIRCH POINT LODGE CAMPGROUND & COTTAGE RESORT **Ratings: 6.5/7.5★/7.5** (Campground) 2015 rates: $28 to $35. May 14 to Oct 15. (207)463-2515 33 Birch Point Ln, Island Falls, ME 04747

KENNEBUNKPORT — E1 *York*

⬆ HEMLOCK GROVE CAMPGROUND **Ratings: 8/9★/8.5** (Campground) 2015 rates: $53. May 15 to Oct 15. (207)985-0398 1299 Portland Rd, US Route 1, Kennebunkport, ME 04046

➔ **RED APPLE CAMPGROUND**
Ratings: 9/10★/10 (RV Park) From Jct of ME Tpke & Rte 35 (exit 25), SE 1.8 mi on Rte 35 to US-1, N 1.5 mi to Old Post Rd, E (right) 0.7 mi to Sinnott Rd, E (continue straight) 1.5 mi (L). **FAC:** Paved rds. (140 spaces). Avail: 58 paved, 9 pull-thrus (35 x 68), back-ins (38 x 45), 39 full hkups, 19 W, 19 E (30/50 amps), seasonal sites, cable, WiFi, tent sites, rentals, dump, laundry, fire rings, firewood. **REC:** shuffleboard, playground. Pets OK. Partial handicap access. Big rig sites, eco-friendly, 2015 rates: $55.56 to $60.19. May 6 to Oct 10. No CC.
(207)967-4927 Lat: 43.39128, Lon: -70.49303
111 Sinnott Rd., Kennebunkport, ME 04046
redapple@roadrunner.com
www.redapplecampground.com
See ad this page.

➚ SALTY ACRES CAMPGROUND **Ratings: 6/5.5/6** (Campground) 2015 rates: $30 to $57. May 11 to Oct 12. (207)967-2483 277 Mills Rd, Rt 9, Kennebunkport, ME 04046

KINGFIELD — D2 *Franklin*

⬆ DEER FARM CAMPGROUND **Ratings: 3.5/6/5.5** (Campground) 2015 rates: $24 to $30. May 15 to Oct 11. (207)265-4599 495 Tufts Pond Rd., Kingfield, ME 04947

LEBANON — E1 *York*

➘ FLAT ROCK BRIDGE FAMILY RESORT **Ratings: 7.5/7/7.5** (Campground) 2015 rates: $51 to $64. May 15 to Sep 25. (207)339-9465 21 Flat Rock Bridge Rd., Lebanon, ME 04027

ME

LEBANON (CONT)

POTTER'S PLACE ADULT CAMPING AREA **Ratings: 6.5/8/8.5** (Campground) 2015 rates: $28. May 1 to Oct 15. (207)457-1341 115 Bakers Grant Rd., Lebanon, ME 04027

SALMON FALLS RIVER CAMPING RESORT Ratings: 8/8/7.5 (Campground) From Jct of Spaulding Tpke & Exit 16, E 3 mi on US 202 (R). **FAC:** Gravel rds. (190 spaces). 60 Avail: 40 gravel, 20 grass, 50 pull-thrus (30 x 70), back-ins (25 x 55), 40 full hkups, 20 W, 20 E (30/50 amps), seasonal sites, cable, WiFi $, tent sites, dump, mobile sewer, groc, LP bottles, fire rings, firewood, controlled access. **REC:** heated pool, Salmon Falls River: swim, fishing, playground, rec open to public. Pets OK. Eco-friendly, 2015 rates: $45 to $60. Disc: AAA, military. May 15 to Oct 15.
AAA Approved
(207)339-8888 Lat: 43.33906, Lon: -70.93483
44 Natural High Rd., Lebanon, ME 04027
Cheryl@sfrcr.com
www.sfrrv.com

LEEDS — D2 *Androscoggin*

RIVERBEND CAMPGROUND **Ratings: 7.5/8★/8** (Campground) 2015 rates: $28 to $35. May 1 to Oct 13. (207)524-5711 1540 Route 106, Leeds, ME 04263

LEXINGTON TOWNSHIP — C2 *Somerset*

HAPPY HORSESHOE CAMPGROUND **Ratings: 7.5/9.5★/8.5** (Campground) 2015 rates: $35 to $40. May 25 to Sep 8. (207)628-3471 1100 Long Falls Dam Rd., Lexington Township, ME 04961

LIBERTY — D3 *Waldo*

LAKE ST GEORGE (State Pk) From town, E 25 mi on Rte 3 (R). Note: 35' RV length maximum. 2015 rates: $15 to $25. May 18 to Sep 13. (207)589-4255

LUBEC — D5 *Washington*

SUNSET POINT RV PARK **Ratings: 7/8★/7.5** (Campground) 2015 rates: $35 to $40. May 20 to Oct 15. (207)733-2272 37 Sunset Rd., Lubec, ME 04652

MADISON — D2 *Somerset*

YOGI BEAR'S JELLYSTONE PARK Ratings: 9/9★/9 (Campground) From Jct US-2 & US-201 (in Skowhegan): Go 3 1/2 mi N on US-201 (R). **FAC:** Paved/gravel rds. (98 spaces). Avail: 58 gravel, 1 pull-thrus (30 x 80), back-ins (30 x 50), 58 full hkups (30/50 amps), seasonal sites, cable, WiFi, tent sites, rentals, dump, laundry, groc, LP gas, fire rings, firewood. **REC:** pool, pond, fishing, playground, rec open to public. Pets OK. Partial handicap access. Big rig sites, eco-friendly, 2015 rates: $32 to $49. Disc: AAA, military. May 15 to Oct 12.
(207)474-7353 Lat: 44.79830, Lon: -69.74904
221 Lakewood Rd., Madison, ME 04950
camping@yonderhill.com
www.yonderhilljellystone.com

MATTAWAMKEAG — C4 *Penobscot*

MATTAWAMKEAG WILDERNESS PARK CAMPGROUND (Public) From Jct of SR-157 & US-2, S 0.1 mi on US-2 to park access rd, E 9 mi (L). 2015 rates: $22 to $35. May 25 to Sep 30. (207)290-0205

MEDWAY — C3 *Penobscot*

KATAHDIN SHADOWS CAMPGROUND Ratings: 9/9.5★/8 (Campground) From Jct of I-95 & Rte 157 (exit 244), W 1.7 mi on Rte 157 (R). **FAC:** Paved/gravel rds. (114 spaces). 74 Avail: 51 gravel, 23 grass, 14 pull-thrus (26 x 74), back-ins (30 x 40), some side by side hkups, 41 full hkups, 33 W, 33 E (30/50 amps), seasonal sites, WiFi, tent sites, rentals, dump, mobile sewer, laundry, groc, LP gas, fire rings, firewood. **REC:** heated pool, playground. Pets OK. Partial handicap access. Big rig sites, eco-friendly, 2015 rates: $34 to $36.
(207)746-9349 Lat: 45.61613, Lon: -68.55294
118 Katahdin Shadows Dr., Medway, ME 04460
katshadcamp@midmaine.com
www.katahdinshadows.com
See ad this page, 568.

PINE GROVE CAMPGROUND & COTTAGES **Ratings: 5/4.5/6** (Campground) 2015 rates: $29 to $31. May 15 to Oct 15. (207)746-5172 822 Grindstone Rd, Medway, ME 04460

MOODY — E1 *York*

MOODY BEACH RV **Ratings: 9/8.5★/8.5** (Membership Pk) 2015 rates: $41 to $61. Apr 15 to Oct 15. (888)237-3211 266 Post Rd, Wells, ME 04090

MOOSE RIVER — C2 *Somerset*

MOOSE RIVER CAMPGROUND & CABINS Ratings: 6/7.5/7 (Campground) From Jct of Rtes 201 & 15/6, N 3.5 mi on Rte 201 to Heald Stream Rd, E 1.4 mi (R). **FAC:** Gravel rds. (26 spaces). Avail: 16 gravel, 6 pull-thrus (24 x 84), back-ins (33 x 57), 4 full hkups, 12 W, 12 E (30/50 amps), seasonal sites, cable, WiFi, tent sites, rentals, dump, mobile sewer, fire rings, firewood. **REC:** Heald Stream: fishing, playground. Pets OK. Partial handicap access. Big rig sites, eco-friendly, 2015 rates: $35 to $45. Disc: AAA. May 15 to Oct 15.
AAA Approved
(207)668-4400 Lat: 45.65070, Lon: -70.24356
107 Heald Stream Rd, Moose River, ME 04945
littlebigwood@hotmail.com
www.mooserivercampground.org

NAPLES — E1 *Cumberland*

COLONIAL MAST CAMPGROUND **Ratings: 8/8.5★/7** (Campground) 2015 rates: $34 to $51. (207)693-6652 23 Colonial Mast Rd, Naples, ME 04055

FOUR SEASONS CAMPING AREA Ratings: 7/7/7 (Campground) From Jct of US-302 & Rte 11/114, NW 3 mi on US-302 (R). **FAC:** Gravel rds (115 spaces). 50 Avail: 45 gravel, 5 grass, 3 pull-thrus (32 x 80), back-ins (30 x 44), 50 W, 50 E (20/30 amps), seasonal sites, WiFi, tent sites, rentals, showers $, dump, mobile sewer, groc, fire rings, firewood, controlled access. **REC:** Long Lake: swim, fishing, playground. Pets OK. Partial handicap access. 2015 rates: $35 to $66. May 13 to Oct 13.
AAA Approved
(207)693-6797 Lat: 43.98938, Lon: -70.64899
1741 Roosevelt Trail, Naples, ME 04055
info@fourseasonscampingarea.com
www.fourseasonscampingarea.com

LOON'S HAVEN FAMILY CAMPGROUND **Ratings: 7.5/8.5★/8.5** (Campground) 2015 rates: $28 to $65. May 15 to Oct 15. (207)693-6881 41 Loon's Haven Dr., Naples, ME 04055

NAPLES KOA CAMPGROUND **Ratings: 9/10★/9** (Campground) 2015 rates: $40 to $75. May 1 to Oct 15. (207)693-5267 295 Sebago Rd. (Route 114/11), Naples, ME 04055

SEBAGO LAKE (State Pk) From Jct of Hwy 302 & Hwy 11/114, S 2 mi on Hwy 11/114 to State Park Rd, W 1 mi (L). Note: 35' RV length maximum. 2015 rates: $15 to $35. May 1 to Oct 15. (207)693-6613

NEW HARBOR — E2 *Lincoln*

SHERWOOD FOREST CAMPSITE **Ratings: 6.5/7/6** (Campground) 2015 rates: $36 to $41. May 15 to Oct 15. (207)677-3642 32 Pemaquid Trail, New Harbor, ME 04554

NEWPORT — D3 *Penobscot*

CHRISTIES CAMPGROUND & COTTAGES Ratings: 7.5/9★/8 (Campground) From Jct of I-95 & Rte 7 (exit 161), N 1 mi on Rte 7 to Rte 2/100, W 0.75 mi (R). **FAC:** Gravel/dirt rds. (71 spaces). 21 Avail: 8 gravel, 13 grass, 11 pull-thrus (24 x 57), back-ins (28 x 56), 8 full hkups, 13 W, 13 E (30 amps), seasonal sites, WiFi, rentals, showers $, dump, mobile sewer, laundry, groc, LP gas, fire rings, firewood. **REC:** Sebasticook Lake: swim, fishing, playground. Pets OK. Partial handicap access, no tents. Eco-friendly, 2015 rates: $27 to $30. Disc: AAA, military. May 15 to Nov 27.
AAA Approved
(800)688-5141 Lat: 44.82956, Lon: -69.23859
83 Christies Campground Rd, Newport, ME 04953
pnewhall@myfairpoint.net
www.christiescampground.com

MOOSEHEAD TRAIL CAMPGROUND (Campground) (Too New to Rate) 2015 rates: $45. May 15 to Oct 10. (207)974-6241 781 Moosehead Tr, Newport, ME 04953

SEBASTICOOK LAKE CAMPGROUND Ratings: 8/8.5/7 (Campground) From Jct of I-95 & Rte 7 (exit 161), N 1 mi on Rte 7 to Rte 2, W 0.5 mi on Rte 2/7 (R). **FAC:** Paved/gravel rds. (60 spaces). Avail: 30 grass, 8 pull-thrus (24 x 84), back-ins (24 x 46), some side by side hkups, 2 full hkups, 28 W, 28 E (20/30 amps), seasonal sites, WiFi $, tent sites, rentals, showers $, dump, mobile sewer, laundry, groc,

NEWPORT (CONT)

SEBASTICOOK LAKE (CONT)
LP gas, fire rings, firewood. **REC:** heated pool, Sebasticook Lake: swim, fishing, playground. Pets OK $. Partial handicap access. Eco-friendly, 2015 rates: $28 to $32. Disc: AAA. May 13 to Oct 8.
AAA Approved
(207)368-5047 Lat: 44.82629, Lon: -69.23351
52 Tent Village Rd., Newport, ME 04953
info@mainervpark.com
www.mainervpark.com

NOBLEBORO — E2 *Lincoln*

DUCK PUDDLE CAMPGROUND **Ratings: 7.5/6/6** (Campground) 2015 rates: $42 to $60. May 1 to Oct 13. (207)563-5608 60 Campground Rd., Nobleboro, ME 04555

NORTH MONMOUTH — D2 *Kennebec*

BEAVER BROOK CAMPGROUND **Ratings: 6.5/7/7.5** (Campground) 2015 rates: $37 to $51. May 13 to Oct 10. (207)933-2108 1 Wilson Pond Rd., North Monmouth, ME 04265

NORTHPORT — D3 *Waldo*

NORTHPORT CAMPGROUND **Ratings: 7/6.5/6.5** (Campground) 2015 rates: $32 to $37. May 15 to Oct 12. (207)338-2077 14 Chelsea Lane, Northport, ME 04849

OLD ORCHARD BEACH — E2 *York*

HID'N PINES FAMILY CAMPGROUND Ratings: 9/9.5★/9.5 (Campground) From Jct of ME Tpke & I-195 (exit 36), E 1.2 mi on I-195 to Rte 1, NE 3 mi to Rte 98, S 2 mi (L). **FAC:** Paved rds. (304 spaces). 256 Avail: 173 gravel, 17 grass, 66 dirt, 8 pull-thrus (38 x 60), back-ins (38 x 50), 138 full hkups, 113 W, 113 E (30/50 amps), seasonal sites, cable, WiFi, tent sites, dump, laundry, fire rings, firewood, controlled access. **REC:** heated pool, playground. Pet restrict(Q) $. Partial handicap access. Big rig sites, eco-friendly, 2015 rates: $35 to $70. May 13 to Sep 4.
AAA Approved
(207)934-2352 Lat: 43.52456, Lon: -70.38098
8 Cascade Rd., Old Orchard Beach, ME 04064
info@mainefamilycamping.com
www.mainefamilycamping.com

NE'RE BEACH FAMILY CAMPGROUND Ratings: 7/7/5.5 (Campground) From Jct of ME Tpke & I-195 (exit 36), E 2 mi on I-195 to Rte 5, NE 1.5 mi (L). **FAC:** Gravel rds. (35 spaces). Avail: 20 grass, back-ins (20 x 42), 20 full hkups (30/50 amps), seasonal sites, cable, WiFi, tent sites, dump, laundry, fire rings, firewood. **REC:** pool. Pet restrict(B). 2015 rates: $60. May 15 to Oct 13.
AAA Approved
(207)934-7614 Lat: 43.51555, Lon: -70.38113
38 Saco Ave., Old Orchard Beach, ME 04064
nerebeach@yahoo.com
www.nerebeach.com

OLD ORCHARD BEACH CAMPGROUND
Ratings: 9.5/9★/9.5 (Campground) From Jct I-95 (exit 36) & I-195: Go 2 mi E on I-195, then Rt 5 joins I-195, immediate R. **FAC:** Paved/gravel rds. 186 Avail: 186 all weather, 5 pull-thrus (40 x 80), back-ins (40 x 60), 186 full hkups (30/50 amps), cable, WiFi, tent sites, dump, laundry, groc, fire rings, firewood, controlled access. **REC:** pool, playground. Pets OK. Partial handicap access. Big rig sites, eco-friendly, 2015 rates: $50 to $60. Disc: military. May 1 to Oct 31.
(207)934-4477 Lat: 43.509397, Lon: -70.429062
27 Ocean Park Rd., Old Orchard Beach, ME 04064
relax@gocamping.com
www.gocamping.com
See ad opposite page.

PARADISE PARK RESORT CAMPGROUND **Ratings: 9.5/10★/9** (Campground) 2015 rates: $62 to $68. May 14 to Oct 13. (207)934-4633 50 Adelaide Rd., Old Orchard Beach, ME 04064

PINEHIRST RV RESORT **Ratings: 8.5/5.5/6.5** (RV Park) 2015 rates: $76. Apr 15 to Oct 18. (866)679-3819 7 Oregon Ave., Old Orchard Beach, ME 04064

POWDER HORN FAMILY CAMPING RESORT Ratings: 9/9.5★/9.5 (Campground) From Jct of ME Tpke & I-195 (exit 36), E 1.2 mi on I-195 to US-1, N 3 mi to Rte 98, S 1.8 mi (L). **FAC:** Paved rds. (482 spaces). 263 Avail: 56 gravel, 171 grass, 36 dirt, 24 pull-thrus (33 x 60), back-ins (34 x 45), 167 full hkups, 96 W, 96 E (30/50 amps), seasonal sites, cable, WiFi, tent sites, dump, laundry, groc, fire rings, firewood, controlled access. **REC:** heated pool, wading pool, whirlpool, shuffleboard, playground. Pet restrict(Q) $. Partial handicap access. Big rig sites, eco-friendly, 2015 rates: $35 to $78. May 13 to Oct 10. ATM.
AAA Approved
(207)934-4733 Lat: 43.52847, Lon: -70.38670
48 Cascade Rd., Old Orchard Beach, ME 04064
info@mainecampgrounds.com
www.mainecampgrounds.com

WAGON WHEEL RV RESORT & CAMPGROUND
Ratings: 8.5/9.5★/9 (Campground) From Jct ME Tpke & I-195 (exit 36), E 2 mi on I-195 to Rte 5, E 0.4 mi to Old Orchard Rd, S 0.1 mi (L).

ENJOY THE PINNACLE OF MAINE CAMPING
Minutes from the best attractions of Old Orchard Beach, this resort has excellent accommodations, including a great selection of vacation rentals. Enjoy planned events at the activity area or cool off at our new splash pad!

FAC: Paved rds. (281 spaces). Avail: 98 grass, 1 pull-thrus (30 x 60), back-ins (30 x 40), 98 full hkups (30/50 amps), seasonal sites, cable, WiFi, tent sites, rentals, dump, laundry, groc, LP bottles, fire rings, firewood, controlled access. **REC:** pool, whirlpool, playground. Pets OK. Partial handicap access. Big rig sites, eco-friendly, 2015 rates: $44 to $74. Disc: AAA, military. May 1 to Oct 15.
AAA Approved
(888)543-0516 Lat: 43.51007, Lon: -70.39730
3 Old Orchard Rd, Old Orchard Beach, ME 04064
wagonwheel@suncommunities.com
www.wagonwheelrvresort.com
See ad pages 567 (Welcome Section), 1463 (Welcome Section), 568 & Family Camping, RV Trips of a Lifetime in Magazine Section.

WASSAMKI SPRINGS CAMPGROUND
Ratings: 8.5/9★/9 (Campground) From Jct I-95 (Exit 46) & Hwy 22: Go 3 mi W on Hwy 22, then 1/4 mi N on Saco St (L). **FAC:** Paved/gravel rds. (256 spaces). 156 Avail: 45 grass, 111 dirt, 22 pull-thrus (30 x 60), back-ins (30 x 45), 126 full hkups, 30 W, 30 E (30/50 amps), seasonal sites, cable, WiFi, tent sites, dump, mobile sewer, laundry, groc, LP gas, fire rings, firewood, controlled access. **REC:** Wassamki Springs Lake: swim, fishing, playground, rec open to public. Pet restrict(B). Partial handicap access. Big rig sites, eco-friendly, 2015 rates: $30 to $64. Disc: AAA, military. May 1 to Oct 15.
(207)839-4276 Lat: 43.64687, Lon: -70.39875
56 Saco St., Scarborough, ME 04074
wassamkisprings@aol.com
www.wassamkisprings.com
See primary listing at Scarborough and ad page 577.

WILD ACRES RV RESORT & CAMPGROUND
Ratings: 9/9★/8.5 (Campground) From Jct of ME Tpke & I-195 (exit 36), E 2 mi on I-195 to Rte 5, E 1.5 mi (R).

UNCOVER THE WILD SIDE OF MAINE
Explore over 75 acres of picturesque grounds with a wonderful array of amenities available. As the closest campground to Old Orchard Beach, this breathtaking resort has easy beach access and features an aerial adventure park!

FAC: Paved rds. (587 spaces). 347 Avail: 227 gravel, 95 grass, 25 dirt, 61 pull-thrus (30 x 60), back-ins (30 x 40), 252 full hkups, 95 W, 95 E (30/50 amps), seasonal sites, cable, WiFi, tent sites, rentals, dump, laundry, groc, LP bottles, fire rings, firewood, controlled access. **REC:** heated pool, whirlpool, pond, fishing, shuffleboard, playground. Pet restrict(B/Q). Partial handicap access. Big rig sites, eco-friendly, 2015 rates: $46 to $87. Disc: AAA, military. May 1 to Oct 15.
AAA Approved
(888)451-3586 Lat: 43.51004, Lon: -70.39773
179 Saco Ave., Old Orchard Beach, ME 04064
wildacres@suncommunities.com
www.sunrvresorts.com
See ad pages 567 (Welcome Section), 568, 1463 (Welcome Section) & Family Camping, RV Trips of a Lifetime in Magazine Section.

OQUOSSOC — D1 *Franklin*

BLACK BROOK COVE CAMPGROUND **Ratings: 4/7/6** (Campground) 2015 rates: $30. May 1 to Oct 31. (207)486-3828 3 Balsam Rd, Lincoln Plantation, ME 04216

CUPSUPTIC LAKE PARK AND CAMPGROUND LLC Ratings: 7/8/8.5 (Campground) From Jct Hwy 4 & Hwy 16 West: Go 4-1/2 mi NW on Hwy 16 West (L). **FAC:** Gravel rds. (51 spaces). Avail: 36 gravel, back-ins (50 x 80), 17 full hkups, 19 W, 19 E (30/50 amps), seasonal sites, cable, WiFi Hotspot, tent sites, rentals, dump, mobile sewer, laundry, groc, LP bottles, fire rings, firewood. **REC:** Cupsuptic Lake: swim, fishing, playground, rec open to public. Pets OK $. Partial handicap access. Big rig sites, eco-friendly, 2015 rates: $32 to $42. May 1 to Oct 13.
(207)864-5249 Lat: 45.01266, Lon: -70.83212
route16 West (960 Wilson Mills Rd. or 7 Cupsuptic Campground Rd.), Adamstown Township, ME 04964
info@cupsupticcampground.com
www.cupsupticcampground.com

ORLAND — D3 *Hancock*

BALSAM COVE CAMPGROUND **Ratings: 8/7.5/7** (Campground) 2015 rates: $38 to $58. May 15 to Sep 28. (207)469-7771 286 Back Ridge Rd., Orland, ME 04472

SHADY OAKS CAMPGROUND & CABINS **Ratings: 9/8.5★/8.5** (Campground) 2015 rates: $40 to $43. May 1 to Oct 15. (207)469-7739 32 Leaches Point, Orland, ME 04472

OXFORD — D1 *Oxford*

TWO LAKES CAMPING AREA **Ratings: 7/6/6** (Campground) 2015 rates: $35 to $45. May 1 to Oct 13. (207)539-4851 215 Campground Lane, Oxford, ME 04270

PALMYRA — D3 *Somerset*

PALMYRA GOLF & CAMPING **Ratings: 7.5/9★/9** (Campground) 2015 rates: $31.26 to $33.76. May 15 to Oct 15. (207)938-5677 147 Lang Hill Rd., Palmyra, ME 04965

PERU — D2 *Oxford*

HONEY RUN BEACH & CAMPGROUND **Ratings: 6/7.5★/7.5** (Campground) 2015 rates: $35. May 28 to Sep 6. (207)562-4913 456 East Shore Rd., Peru, ME 04290

POLAND — E2 *Androscoggin*

RANGE POND CAMPGROUND
Ratings: 7.5/8/8 (Campground) From Jct of Hwy 26 & Hwy 122: Go 1 1/2 mi E on Hwy 122, then 1/4 mi N on Empire Rd, then 1/2 mi W on Plains Rd (R). **FAC:** Dirt rds. (110 spaces). 66 Avail: 24 gravel, 32 grass, 10 dirt, 23 pull-thrus (20 x 60), back-ins (20 x 60), 52 full hkups, 14 W, 14 E (30/50 amps), seasonal sites, cable, WiFi, tent sites, rentals,

ME

POLAND (CONT)

RANGE POND CAMPGROUND (CONT)
dump, laundry, groc, LP gas, fire rings, firewood. **REC:** heated pool, pond, fishing, playground. Pets OK. Eco-friendly, 2015 rates: $34 to $36. Disc: military. Apr 15 to Oct 15.
(207)998-2624 Lat: 44.04317, Lon: -70.34547
94 Plains Rd., Poland, ME 04274
rpcg88@aol.com
www.rangepondcamp.com
See ad this page.

POLAND SPRING — E2 *Androscoggin*

POLAND SPRING CAMPGROUND Ratings: 7.5/8/7.5 (Campground) From Jct I 95 (exit 63) & Hwy 26: Go 12 mi N on Hwy 26, then 1/2 mi E on Connor Lane (E). **FAC:** Dirt rds. (115 spaces). Avail: 68 dirt, 4 pull-thrus (38 x 78), back-ins (25 x 50), 25 full hkups, 43 W, 43 E (30/50 amps), seasonal sites, WiFi, tent sites, rentals, showers $, dump, mobile sewer, laundry, groc, LP gas, fire rings, firewood, controlled access. **REC:** heated pool, Lower Range Pond: swim, fishing, playground. Pets OK $. Partial handicap access. Big rig sites, eco-friendly, 2015 rates: $35 to $43. May 1 to Oct 13.
AAA Approved
(207)998-2151 Lat: 44.04427, Lon: -70.37509
128 Connor Lane, Poland Spring, ME 04274
info@polandspringcamp.com
www.polandspringcamp.com

PORTLAND — E2 *Cumberland*

PORTLAND See also Freeport, Old Orchard Beach, Saco & Scarborough.

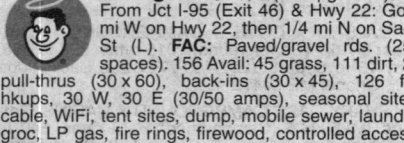

WASSAMKI SPRINGS CAMPGROUND
Ratings: 8.5/9★/9 (Campground) From Jct I-95 (Exit 46) & Hwy 22: Go 3 mi W on Hwy 22, then 1/4 mi N on Saco St (L). **FAC:** Paved/gravel rds. (256 spaces). 156 Avail: 45 grass, 111 dirt, 22 pull-thrus (30 x 60), back-ins (30 x 45), 126 full hkups, 30 W, 30 E (30/50 amps), seasonal sites, cable, WiFi, tent sites, dump, mobile sewer, laundry, groc, LP gas, fire rings, firewood, controlled access. **REC:** Wassamki Springs Lake: swim, fishing, playground, rec open to public. Pet restrict(B). Partial handicap access. Big rig sites, eco-friendly, 2015 rates: $30 to $64. Disc: AAA, military. May 1 to Oct 15.
(207)839-4276 Lat: 43.64687, Lon: -70.39875
56 Saco St, Scarborough, ME 04074
wassamkisprings@aol.com
www.wassamkisprings.com
See primary listing at Scarborough and ad page 577.

POWNAL — E2 *Cumberland*

BRADBURY MOUNTAIN (State Pk) From town center: Go 1 mi E on Hwy-9. Note: 35' RV length maximum. Pit toilets. 2015 rates: $11.77 to $20.33. (207)688-4712

Nobody said it was easy being a 10. And our rating system makes it even tougher. Check out 10/10/10 RV parks and campgrounds in the front of the guide.*

PRESQUE ISLE — B4 *Aroostook*

ARNDT'S AROOSTOOK RIVER LODGE & CAMPGROUND Ratings: 7.5/8/8 (Campground) From Jct of US-1 & Rte 163, E 3 mi on Rte 163 to Rte 205, N 0.7 mi (R). **FAC:** Gravel rds. 55 grass, 7 pull-thrus (36 x 68), back-ins (36 x 63), some side by side hkups, 26 full hkups, 29 W, 29 E (30/50 amps), WiFi Hotspot, tent sites, rentals, dump, laundry, fire rings, firewood. **REC:** pool, Aroostook River: swim, fishing, playground. Pets OK. Eco-friendly, 2015 rates: $30 to $35. May 15 to Oct 15.
(207)764-8677 Lat: 46.72257, Lon: -67.95078
95 Parkhurst Siding Rd, Presque Isle, ME 04769
clare@arndtscamp.com
www.arndtscamp.com

AROOSTOOK (State Pk) From Jct of I-95 & Rte 1, N 38 mi on Rte 1 to Spraqueville Rd, W 1 mi to State Park Rd, S 1 mi (E). 2015 rates: $10.70 to $19.26. (207)768-8341

NEIL E MICHAUD CAMPGROUND **Ratings: 3.5/4.5/6** (Campground) 2015 rates: $26 to $29. May 1 to Oct 15. (207)769-1951 164 Houlton Rd, Presque Isle, ME 04769

RANGELEY — D1 *Franklin*

RANGELEY LAKE (State Pk) From Jct of SR-16 & SR-4, S 4 mi on SR-4 to S Shore Dr, W 6 mi (R). Note: 35' RV length maximum. 2015 rates: $15 to $25. May 15 to Sep 15. (207)864-3858

RAYMOND — E1 *Cumberland*

KOKATOSI CAMPGROUND
Ratings: 7.5/7.5/7.5 (Campground) From Jct of US-302 & Rte 85, NE 6.5 mi on Rte 85 (R). **FAC:** Gravel rds. (156 spaces). Avail: 71 dirt, 4 pull-thrus (30 x 60), back-ins (25 x 40), 61 full hkups, 10 W, 10 E (30/50 amps), seasonal sites, cable, WiFi Hotspot, tent sites, rentals, dump, laundry, groc, LP gas, fire rings, firewood, controlled access. **REC:** Crescent Lake: swim, fishing, playground. Pets OK. Partial handicap access. Eco-friendly, 2015 rates: $42 to $53. May 15 to Oct 13.
(207)627-4642 Lat: 43.95949, Lon: -70.46437
635 Webbs Mills Rd, Raymond, ME 04071
kokatosi@fairpoint.net
www.kokatosicampground.com
See ad this page.

RICHMOND — E2 *Sagadahoc*

AUGUSTA-GARDINER KOA **Ratings: 8.5/9★/7.5** (Campground) 2015 rates: $48 to $56. May 8 to Oct 12. (207)582-5086 30 Mallard Dr, Richmond, ME 04357

ROBBINSTON — C5 *Washington*

HILLTOP CAMPGROUND **Ratings: 8/7/6** (Campground) 2015 rates: $36 to $38. May 15 to Oct 15. (207)454-3985 317 Ridge Rd., Robbinston, ME 04671

ROCKLAND — E3 *Knox*

ROCKLAND See also Appleton, Camden, Cushing, Damariscotta, Rockport,Thomaston & Union.

ROCKPORT — D3 *Knox*

CAMDEN HILLS RV PARK **Ratings: 8/7.5/7.5** (Campground) 2015 rates: $34 to $58. May 15 to Oct 15. (207)236-2498 30 Applewood Rd (Route 90), Rockport, ME 04856

MEGUNTICOOK RV RESORT **Ratings: 8/7.5★/7.5** (Campground) 2015 rates: $39 to $58. May 15 to Oct 13. (207)594-2428 620 Commercial St, Rockport, ME 04856

Looking for a new or used RV? Camping World is America's largest retailer of RVs. Click CampingWorld.com or visit SuperCenters nationwide.

Closest Campground to Portland
WASSAMKI SPRINGS
Cable TV, WiFi, 50 Amp Big Rigs Welcome Dog Run
Near Ocean Beaches, Portland's Old Port, Casco Bay, Shopping and Attractions
Enjoy Live Entertainment on Weekends
Private Lake
One Mile Sandy Beach
AAA APPROVED
Good Sam RATED 8.5/9★/9
Good Sam Park
Portland Headlight
Free Live Entertainment & Scheduled Activities on Weekends for All Ages
WiFi • Cable • Big Rigs Welcome • Store
Fishing • Swimming • Sports Fields & Playgrounds
Pavilion/Game Room/Arcade • Horseshoes
Snack Bar • Open, Wooded & Waterfront Sites
E,W,S 30 & 50 • Seasonal Sites Available
Wassamki Springs Campground
56 Saco Street • Scarborough, ME 04074
(207) 839-4276
www.wassamkisprings.com
Owned and Operated Since 1970
ail: wassamkisprings@aol.com
Open May 1 - October 15
Northern Groove Band
Casco Bay Sunset
See listing Scarborough, ME

SACO — E1 *York*

HOMESTEAD BY THE RIVER FAMILY CAMPGROUND
Ratings: 7/8/8 (Campground) From Jct of ME Tpke & I-195 (exit 36), E 0.3 mi on I-195 to Industrial Park Rd (exit 1), S 0.6 mi to Rte 112, NW 2.6 mi to Louden Rd, W (L) 1.5 mi to Rte 5, NW (R) 0.3 mi (R). (Do not rely on GPS) Max RV Length 38'. **FAC:** Gravel rds. (45 spaces). Avail: 22 grass, 6 pull-thrus (40 x 100), back-ins (30 x 75), 10 full hkups, 12 W, 12 E (30/50 amps), seasonal sites, WiFi, tent sites, showers $, dump, mobile sewer, laundry, groc, LP bottles, fire rings, firewood, controlled access. **REC:** Saco River: swim, fishing, playground. Pet restrict(B/Q). Eco-friendly, 2015 rates: $35 to $40. May 15 to Oct 13.
(207)282-6445 Lat: 43.54345, Lon: -70.51596
235 New County Rd. (Route 5), Biddeford, ME 04005
info@homesteadbytheriver.com
www.homesteadbytheriver.com
See ad this page.

SACO/OLD ORCHARD BEACH KOA
Ratings: 9.5/9.5/8.5 (Campground) From Jct of ME Tpke & I-195 (exit 36), E 1.2 mi on I-195 to US-1 (exit 2B), N 1.6 mi (L).

DISCOVER MAINE CAMPING AT ITS BEST
Enjoy a great family get away in Maine - just minutes from Old Orchard Beach! Resort features include room sites, vacation rentals, heated pool, snack bar, free shuttle rides to the beach and our famous blueberry pancakes!

FAC: All weather rds. 77 gravel, 52 pull-thrus (26 x 65), back-ins (26 x 46), 58 full hkups, 19 W, 19 E (30/50 amps), cable, WiFi, tent sites, rentals, dump, mobile sewer, laundry, groc, LP gas, fire rings, firewood, restaurant, controlled access. **REC:** heated pool, whirlpool, playground. Pets OK $. Partial handicap access. Big rig sites, eco-friendly, 2015 rates: $45 to $95. Disc: military. May 1 to Oct 15.
AAA Approved
(877)518-8811 Lat: 43.53452, Lon: -70.42697
814 Portland Rd., Saco, ME 04072
sacokoa@suncommunities.com
www.oldorchardbeachkoa.com
See ad pages 567 (Welcome Section), 1463 (Welcome Section) & Family Camping, RV Trips of a Lifetime in Magazine Section.

Travel Services

SEACOAST RVS Open 7 days a week. RV service, parts and accessories. RV sales new and used. Propane. **SERVICES:** RV, RV appliance, engine/chassis repair, mobile RV svc, emergency rd svc, staffed RV wash, restrooms, RV Sales. Rentals, RV storage. **TOW:** RV. RV supplies, LP, emergency parking, RV accessible. waiting room. Hours: 9am to 5pm.
(207)282-3511 Lat: 43.52230, Lon: -70.42789
729 Portland Road, Saco, ME 04072
seacoastrv@seacoastrv.com
www.seacoastrv.com
See ad page 575.

SANFORD — E1 *York*

APACHE CAMPGROUND
Ratings: 8/8★/8 (Campground) From Jct of ME Tpke & Rte 109 (exit 19), W 9 mi on Rte 109 to Rte 4, N 2 mi to New Dam Rd, E 1.4 mi to Bernier Rd, N 0.7 mi (R). **FAC:** Paved/gravel rds. (150 spaces). Avail: 20 grass, 15 pull-thrus (40 x 63), back-ins (35 x 45), 20 full hkups (30/50 amps), seasonal sites, WiFi Hotspot, tent sites, showers $, dump, laundry, groc, fire rings, firewood, controlled access. **REC:** pool, Estes Lake: fishing, shuffleboard, playground. Pets OK. Partial handicap access. Big rig sites, eco-friendly, 2015 rates: $35 to $40. May 1 to Sep 30.
(207)324-5652 Lat: 43.44076, Lon: -70.71047
165 Bernier Rd, Sanford, ME 04073
See ad this page.

YELLOWSTONE PARK **Ratings: 6.5/7/6.5** (Campground) 2015 rates: $22 to $36. May 15 to Sep 15. (207)324-7782 2245 Main St, Sanford, ME 04073

SCARBOROUGH — E2 *Cumberland*

BAYLEY'S CAMPING RESORT **Ratings: 9/9★/9** (Campground) 2015 rates: $35 to $85. May 1 to Oct 18. (207)883-6043 275 Pine Point Rd., Scarborough, ME 04074

WASSAMKI SPRINGS CAMPGROUND
Ratings: 8.5/9★/9 (Campground) From Jct I-95 (Exit 46) & Hwy 22: Go 3 mi W on Hwy 22, then 1/4 mi N on Saco St (L). **FAC:** Paved/gravel rds. (256 spaces). 156 Avail: 45 grass, 111 dirt, 22 pull-thrus (30 x 60), back-ins (30 x 45), 126 full hkups, 30 W, 30 E (30/50 amps), seasonal sites, cable, WiFi, tent sites, dump, mobile sewer, laundry, groc, LP gas, fire rings, firewood, controlled access. **REC:** Wassamki Springs Lake: swim, fishing, playground, rec open to public. Pet restrict(B). Partial handicap access. Big rig sites, eco-friendly, 2015 rates: $30 to $64. Disc: AAA, military. May 1 to Oct 15.
AAA Approved
(207)839-4276 Lat: 43.64687, Lon: -70.39875
56 Saco St., Scarborough, ME 04074
wassamkisprings@aol.com
www.wassamkisprings.com
See ad pages 577, 568, 566 (ME Map).

WILD DUCK ADULT CAMPGROUND
Ratings: 8/9.5★/9 (Campground) From Jct of ME Tpke & Exit 42 (Haigis Pkwy), E 1.5 mi on Haigis Pkwy to US-1, S 1.5 mi to Rte 9 (Pine Point Rd), E (left) 0.25 mi to Dunstan Landing Rd, SE 0.3 mi (R). **FAC:** Paved rds. (60 spaces). Avail: 45 gravel, 8 pull-thrus (20 x 80), back-ins (30 x 65), 41 full hkups, 4 W, 4 E (30/50 amps), seasonal sites, cable, WiFi $, tent sites, rentals, dump, laundry, fire rings, firewood, controlled access. **REC:** Scarborough River: fishing. Pets OK. Age restrict may apply, big rig sites, eco-friendly, 2015 rates: $33 to $65. Disc: AAA, military. Apr 24 to Oct 19.
(207)883-4432 Lat: 43.56564, Lon: -70.38078
39 Dunstan Landing Rd., Scarborough, ME 04074
info@wildduckcampground.com
www.wildduckcampground.com
See ad this page.

SEARSPORT — D3 *Waldo*

SEARSPORT SHORES OCEANFRONT CAMPING **Ratings: 7.5/8.5★/8** (Campground) From Jct of SR-3 & US-1 in Belfast, N 5 mi on US-1 (R). **FAC:** Gravel rds. 97 Avail: 50 grass, 30 grass, 17 dirt, 6 pull-thrus (30 x 75), back-ins (34 x 48), 97 W, 97 E (20/30 amps), WiFi, tent sites, rentals, dump, mobile sewer, laundry, LP gas, fire rings, firewood. **REC.** Atlantic/Penobscot Bay: swim, fishing, playground. Pet restrict(Q). Partial handicap access. Eco-friendly, 2015 rates: $49 to $84. May 7 to Oct 12.
AAA Approved
(207)548-6059 Lat: 44.44235, Lon: -68.93571
216 West Main St., Searsport, ME 04974
relax@campocean.com
www.campocean.com

SHIN POND — B3 *Penobscot*

SHIN POND VILLAGE CAMPGROUND & COTTAGES **Ratings: 6/8★/7.5** (Campground) 2015 rates: $29.99. May 1 to Oct 31. (207)528-2900 1489 Shin Pond Rd, Mount Chase, ME 04765

SINCLAIR — A4 *Aroostook*

WATERS EDGE RV RESORT & CAMPGROUND **Ratings: 6.5/9★/7** (Campground) 2015 rates: $30. May 1 to Oct 1. (207)543-6061 334 Sinclair Rd, Sinclair, ME 04779

SKOWHEGAN — D2 *Somerset*

TWO RIVERS CAMPGROUND
Ratings: 9/9★/9 (Campground) From Jct of US-201 & US-2, E 2 mi on US-2 (R).

ON THE BANKS OF THE KENNEBEC RIVER
and Wesserunsett Stream with 1,300 feet of waterfront offering spectacular wildlife observing, fishing, boating & kayaking or relax by a cozy campfire, roast marshmallows or fry up the day's big catch!

FAC: Paved/gravel rds. (65 spaces). Avail: 47 grass, 26 pull-thrus (30 x 100), back-ins (30 x 50), 30 full hkups, 17 W, 17 E (30/50 amps), seasonal sites, cable, WiFi, tent sites, rentals, dump, mobile sewer, laundry, LP gas, fire rings, firewood. **REC:** pool, Kennebec River: swim, fishing, playground. Pets OK. Partial handicap access. Big rig sites, eco-friendly,

Say you saw it in our Guide!

Like Us on Facebook.

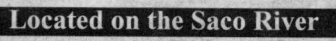

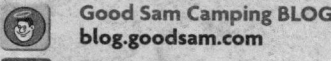

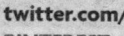

SKOWHEGAN (CONT)

TWO RIVERS CAMPGROUND (CONT)
2015 rates: $40 to $43. Disc: AAA, military. May 15 to Oct 15. No CC.
AAA Approved
(207)474-6482 Lat: 44.77072, Lon: -69.67702
327 Canaan Rd., Skowhegan, ME 04976
info@tworvrs.com
www.tworvrs.com
See ad opposite page, 568.

SOUTHWEST HARBOR — D4 *Hancock*

ACADIA/SEAWALL (Natl Pk) From Jct of SR-102 & SR-102A, S 5 mi on SR-102A (R). Entrance fee required. Note: 35' RV length maximum. 2015 rates: $30. May 20 to Sep 30. (207)244-3600

SMUGGLER'S DEN CAMPGROUND **Ratings: 8/8.5★/8.5** (Campground) 2015 rates: $30 to $60. May 22 to Oct 25. (207)244-3944 20 Main St., Southwest Harbor, ME 04679

ST AGATHA — A4 *Aroostook*

LAKEVIEW CAMPING RESORT **Ratings: 6.5/9★/8** (Campground) 2015 rates: $28 to $39. May 20 to Oct 1. (207)543-6331 9 Lakeview Dr, Saint Agatha, ME 04772

STANDISH — E1 *Cumberland*

FAMILY-N-FRIENDS CAMPGROUND **Ratings: 7.5/7.5/7.5** (Campground) 2015 rates: $29 to $48. Apr 27 to Oct 13. (207)642-2200 140 Richville Rd., Standish, ME 04084

STEEP FALLS — E1 *Cumberland*

ACRES OF WILDLIFE CAMPGROUND Ratings: 7/8/7.5 (Campground) From Jct of ME Tpke Exit 46 & Rte 22, W 0.4 mi on Connector Rd to Rte 22, W 3 mi on Rte 22 to Rte 114, NW 4 mi to Rte 25 (in Gorham), NW 9 mi to Rte 113, NE 6 mi to campground rd, NE 3 mi (E). **FAC:** Gravel rds. (270 spaces). 220 Avail: 60 gravel, 80 grass, 80 dirt, 6 pull-thrus (30 x 40), back-ins (20 x 28), 45 full hkups, 175 W, 175 E (30/50 amps), seasonal sites, WiFi, tent sites, rentals, dump, mobile sewer, laundry, groc, LP gas, fire rings, firewood, restaurant, controlled access. **REC:** Rainbow Lake: swim, fishing, shuffleboard, playground, rec open to public. Pets OK $. Partial handicap access. Eco-friendly, 2015 rates: $28 to $61. May 1 to Oct 19. ATM.
AAA Approved
(207)675-2267 Lat: 43.81731, Lon: -70.63296
60 Acres Of Wildlife Rd., Steep Falls, ME 04085
office@acresofwildlife.com
www.acresofwildlife.com

STETSON — D3 *Penobscot*

STETSON SHORES CAMPGROUND **Ratings: 6.5/7.5★/6.5** (Campground) 2015 rates: $36. May 8 to Sep 27. (207)296-2041 304 Lakins Rd., Stetson, ME 04488

STRATTON — C2 *Franklin*

CATHEDRAL PINES CAMPGROUND **Ratings: 6.5/7.5/8** (Campground) 2015 rates: $30 to $35. May 15 to Oct 1. (207)246-3491 945 Arnold Trail Hwy (Rte 27), Eustis, ME 04936

SULLIVAN — D4 *Hancock*

MOUNTAINVIEW CAMPGROUND ON THE OCEAN **Ratings: 5/7/6.5** (Campground) 2015 rates: $32 to $40. May 15 to Oct 15. (207)422-6408 2695 US Hwy 1, Sullivan, ME 04664

THOMASTON — E3 *Knox*

SALTWATER FARM CAMPGROUND
Ratings: 8/8.5★/8.5 (Campground) From Jct Hwy 97 & US-1: Go 1 3/4 mi N on US-1, then (at Prison Craft Store) go 1 1/2 mi E on Wadsworth St (L) Caution: Bridge clearance is 13'3". Do not use on GPS-Follow directions. **FAC:** Gravel rds. (40 spaces). 30 Avail: 20 gravel, 10 grass, back-ins (35 x 58), 30 full hkups (30/50 amps), seasonal sites, WiFi, rentals, dump, laundry, fire rings, firewood. **REC:** heated pool, whirlpool, St George River: fishing. Pet restrict(Q). No tents. Big rig sites, eco-friendly, 2015 rates: $35 to $54. May 15 to Oct 4.
(207)354-6735 Lat: 44.06145, Lon: -69.19724
47 Kalloch Ln, Cushing, ME 04563
sfc@midcoast.com
www.saltwaterfarmcampground.com
See ad this page, 568.

TRENTON — D3 *Hancock*

TIMBERLAND ACRES RV PARK
Ratings: 9.5/9.5★/9 (Campground) From Jct of US-1 & SR-3 (in Ellsworth), E 2 mi on SR-3 (R). **FAC:** Paved rds. (220 spaces). 120 Avail: 110 gravel, 10 grass, 66 pull-thrus (30 x 100), back-ins (30 x 50), 100 full hkups, 20 W, 20 E (30/50 amps), seasonal sites, WiFi, tent sites, dump, laundry, LP gas, fire rings, firewood. **REC:** pool, shuffleboard, playground. Pets OK. Partial handicap access. Big rig sites, eco-friendly, 2015 rates: $29 to $47. Disc: military. May 15 to Oct 15.
(207)667-3600 Lat: 44.50719, Lon: -68.38911
57 Bar Harbor Rd., Trenton, ME 04605
info@timberlandacresrvpark.com
www.timberlandacresrvpark.com
See ad pages 570, 568.

UNION — D3 *Knox*

MIC MAC COVE CAMPGROUND, INC. **Ratings: 5.5/7.5/6.5** (Campground) 2015 rates: $35 to $40. May 1 to Oct 12. (207)785-4100 210 Mic Mac Lane, Union, ME 04862

WATERFORD — D1 *Oxford*

PAPOOSE POND FAMILY CAMPGROUND AND CABINS **Ratings: 7.5/9★/8.5** (Campground) 2015 rates: $31 to $90. May 14 to Oct 13. (207)583-4470 700 Norway Rd., Waterford, ME 04088

WELD — D2 *Franklin*

MT BLUE (State Pk) From town, NW 3 mi on SR-142 to West rd, S 3.5 mi (L). Note: 35' RV length maximum. 2015 rates: $15 to $25. May 15 to Oct 1. (207)585-2347

Tell them you saw them in this Guide!

WELLS — E1 *York*

BEACH ACRES
Ratings: 7/8.5★/7.5 (RV Park) From Jct of ME Tpke, Rtes 109 & 9 (exit 19), E 1.5 mi on Rte 109/9 to US-1, S 2.25 mi to Eldridge Rd, E 0.1 mi (L). **FAC:** Paved/gravel rds. (365 spaces). Avail: 45 grass, back-ins (36 x 44), 5 full hkups, 40 W, 40 E (30/50 amps), seasonal sites, WiFi Hotspot, tent sites, showers $, dump, laundry, fire rings, firewood, controlled access. **REC:** pool, shuffleboard, playground. No pets. Eco-friendly, 2015 rates: $45 to $54. May 6 to Oct 12. No CC.
AAA Approved
(207)646-5612 Lat: 43.29098, Lon: -70.58703
76 Eldridge Rd., Wells, ME 04090
beachacres@beachacres.com
www.beachacres.com
See ad this page.

GREGOIRE'S CAMPGROUND **Ratings: 6/7/7.5** (Campground) 2015 rates: $32 to $43. May 15 to Sep 15. (207)646-3711 697 Sanford Rd., Wells, ME 04090

OCEAN VIEW COTTAGES & CAMPGROUND Ratings: 8/7.5/7 (Campground) From Jct of ME Tpke & Rtes 9/109 (exit 19 Wells-Sanford), E 1.5 mi on Rtes 9/109 to US-1, N (left) 100 ft to Harbor Rd, E 600 ft (L). **FAC:** Gravel rds. (108 spaces). Avail: 53 dirt, back-ins (24 x 44), 22 full hkups, 31 W, 31 E (30/50 amps), seasonal sites, cable, WiFi, tent sites, rentals, showers $, dump, laundry, fire rings, firewood. **REC:** pool, shuffleboard, playground. Pet restrict(Q). Eco-friendly, 2015 rates: $45 to $65. May 1 to Oct 13.
AAA Approved
(207)646-3308 Lat: 43.32281, Lon: -70.57625
84 Harbor Rd., Wells, ME 04090
www.oceanviewcampground.com

RIVERSIDE PARK CAMPGROUND Ratings: 6.5/7.5/7 (Campground) From Jct of ME Tpke, Rtes 9 & 109 (exit 19 Wells-Sanford), E 1.5 mi on Rte 9/109 to US-1, N 1.5 mi (R). **FAC:** Paved rds. (130 spaces). 40 Avail: 20 paved, 20 grass, 4 pull-thrus (25 x 52), back-ins (25 x 44), 24 full hkups, 16 W, 16 E (30/50 amps), seasonal sites, cable, WiFi $, tent sites, showers $, laundry, groc, fire rings, firewood. **REC:** pool, Merriland River: fishing, playground. Pets

Find it Fast! Use our alphabetized index of campgrounds and parks.

WELLS (CONT)

RIVERSIDE PARK CAMPGROUND (CONT)
OK. Eco-friendly, 2015 rates: $43 to $57. Disc: AAA, military. May 8 to Oct 15.
AAA Approved
(207)646-3145 Lat: 43.34330, Lon: -70.56156
2295 Post Rd. (US-1), Wells, ME 04090
info@riversidefamilycamping.com
www.riversidecampground-wells.com

SEA-VU CAMPGROUND
Ratings: 9.5/9.5★/9.5 (Campground) From Jct of ME Tpke & Rte 109 (exit 19 Wells-Sanford), E 1.5 mi on Rte 109 to US-1, N 0.4 mi (R). **FAC:** Paved rds. (229 spaces). 64 Avail: 54 gravel, 10 grass, back-ins (40 x 60), 64 full hkups (30/50 amps), seasonal sites, cable, WiFi, tent sites, dump, laundry, groc, LP gas, fire rings, firewood, controlled access. **REC:** heated pool, wading pool, playground, rec open to public. Pets OK. Partial handicap access. Big rig sites, eco-friendly, 2015 rates: $45 to $65. May 15 to Oct 15.
AAA Approved
(207)646-7732 Lat: 43.32695, Lon: -70.57598
1733 Post Rd., Wells, ME 04090
seavu@maine.rr.com
www.sea-vucampground.com
See ad this page.

SEA-VU WEST **Ratings: 9.5/10★/9** (Campground) 2015 rates: $45 to $65. May 15 to Oct 15. (207)646-0785 23 College Dr., Wells, ME 04090

STADIG CAMPGROUND **Ratings: 6.5/7.5/7.5** (Campground) 2015 rates: $30 to $38. May 25 to Oct 15. (207)646-2298 146 Bypass Rd, Wells, ME 04090

WELLS BEACH RESORT
Ratings: 10/10★/9 (RV Park) From Jct of ME Tpke (I-95) & Rte 109 (exit 19, Wells-Sanford), E 1.5 mi on Rte 109 to US-1, S 1.4 mi (R). **FAC:** Paved rds. (231 spaces). Avail: 201 all weather, 100 pull-thrus (30 x 65), back-ins (30 x 65), 201 full hkups (30/50 amps), seasonal sites, cable, WiFi, tent sites, dump, laundry, groc, fire rings, firewood, controlled access. **REC:** heated pool, swim, playground. Pet restrict(Q). Partial handicap access. Big rig sites, eco-friendly, 2015 rates: $70 to $93. May 15 to Oc 15.
AAA Approved
(207)646-7570 Lat: 43.30372, Lon: -70.58595
1000 Post Rd. - US Route 1, Wells, ME 04090
Wellsbeachresort@maine.rr.com
www.wellsbeach.com
See ad opposite page, 566 (ME Map).

Our Guide to Seasonal Sites will help you find places you can stay for extended periods of time.

WEST BETHEL — D1 *Oxford*

PLEASANT RIVER CAMPGROUND **Ratings: 7.5/8.5★/8.5** (Campground) 2015 rates: $32 t $38. May 1 to Oct 31. (207)836-2000 800 West Bethel Rd., West Bethel, ME 04286

WINTHROP — D2 *Kennebec*

AUGUSTA-WEST LAKESIDE RESORT KAMPGROUND
Ratings: 8/9★/7.5 (Campground) From Jct I-95 (Exit 109) & US-202: Go mi W on US-202, then 1/2 mi S on Highland Ave, then 3/4 mi W (R) on Homes Brook Rd (E). **FAC:** Gravel rds. (100 spaces). 4 Avail: 20 grass, 20 dirt, 20 pull-thrus (40 x 80), backins (40 x 50), 10 full hkups, 30 W, 30 E (30/50 amps) seasonal sites, WiFi, tent sites, rentals, dump, mobile sewer, laundry, groc, LP bottles, fire rings, firewood controlled access. **REC:** pool, Anna- besscook Lake swim, fishing, marina, playground. Pets OK $ Eco-friendly, 2015 rates: $30 to $38. May 15 to Se 30. ATM.
(207)377-9993 Lat: 44.27736, Lon: -69.97444
183 Holmes Brook Ln, Winthrop, ME 04364
augustawest@fairpoint.net
www.augustawestkampground.com
See ad opposite page, 568.

MORE TO LIFE CAMPGROUND **Ratings: 6/7/7** (Campground) 2015 rates: $30 to $35. May 15 to Oc 15. (207)395-4908 48 Lady Slipper Ln., Winthrop, ME 04364

WISCASSET — E2 *Lincoln*

CHEWONKI CAMPGROUND Ratings: 7/8.5★/8 (Campground) From Jct of US-1 & Rte 27, S 3.5 mi on US-1 to Rte 144, SE 0.25 mi to Chewonki Neck Rd, S 1 mi (R). **FAC:** Gravel rds. (47 spaces). Avail: 43 grass, 5 pull-thrus (20 x 60), backins (30 x 50), 14 full hkups, 29 W, 29 E (20/30 amps) seasonal sites, WiFi Hotspot, tent sites, rentals showers $, dump, fire rings, firewood. **REC:** pool wading pool, Montsweag River: fishing, playground Pet restrict(B/Q). Partial handicap access Eco-friendly, 2015 rates: $48 to $78. May 15 to Oc 15.
(207)882-7426 Lat: 43.95744, Lon: -69.71824
235 Chewonki Neck Rd, Wiscasset, ME 04578
campcontact@chewonkicampground.com
www.chewonkicampground.com

YORK BEACH — F1 *York*

FLAGGS RV RESORT **Ratings: 4.5/NA/6.5** (RV Park) 2015 rates: $42 to $60. May 1 to Oct 15 (207)363-5050 68 Garrison Ave, York Beach, ME 03909

YORK BEACH CAMPER PARK **Ratings: 6/8.5★/7** (Campground) 2015 rates: $46. May 22 to Oct 15. (207)363-1343 11 Cappy's Ln., York Beach, ME 03910

YORK HARBOR — F1 *York*

LIBBY'S OCEANSIDE CAMP
Ratings: 7.5/10★/8 (RV Park) From Jct of I-95 & The York's Exit 7, E 0.3 mi on connector rd to US-1, S 0.3 mi to Rte 1A, N 3 mi (R). **FAC:** Paved/gravel rds. (95 spaces). 55 Avail: 2 paved, 53 grass, 10 pull-thrus (20 x 65), back-ins (20 x 50), 55 full hkups (30/50 amps), seasonal sites, cable, WiFi, laundry, fire rings, firewood. **REC:** Atlantic Ocean: swim, fishing. Pet restrict(Q). Partial handicap access, no tents. Eco-friendly, 2015 rates: $55 to $97. May 15 to Oct 15.
AAA Approved
(207)363-4171 Lat: 43.14707, Lon: -70.62620
725 York St., York, ME 03909
libbyscampground@gmail.com
www.libbysoceancamping.com
See ad pages 582, 565 (Welcome Section).

Our rating system isn't just tough, it's thorough. We know the kinds of things that are important to you — like clean restrooms and showers, attractive, secure, well-tended grounds, and extras like swimming pools. We give the first rating for development of facilities, the second for cleanliness and physical characteristics of restrooms and showers, and the third for visual appearance.

Slow down. For most vehicles, fuel efficiency begins to drop rapidly at 60 mph. Driving within the speed limit can improve fuel efficiency by up to 23 percent.

The RVers' Guide to NASCAR - We'll give you the inside track on how to get high-speed thrills at major NASCAR venues. Turn to the front of the Guide to get the most out of North America's most thrilling sporting event.

ME

Clark Vandergrift

WELCOME TO
Maryland

DATE OF STATEHOOD	WIDTH: 90 MILES (145 KM)	PROPORTION OF UNITED STATES
APRIL 28, 1788	LENGTH: 250 MILES (402 KM)	0.33% OF 3,794,100 SQ MI

Often called “America in Miniature,” Maryland offers a diverse landscape. Ocean beaches and mountain ranges are a short drive from each other; north and south mingle here, and a world-class city and rural region exist side by side. The state's peaceful country lanes and scenic byways lead to destinations filled with beauty, history and culture. Activities range from fishing and boating, to hiking, biking and antiquing.

Learn

The first Marylanders were Native Americans who spoke Algonquian languages. In the 1500s, an Italian named Giovanni da Verrazano became the first European visitor, followed by English settlers in the 1600s. It was 1632 when King Charles I granted George Calvert, Lord Baltimore, the land south of the 40th parallel to the Potomac River. Calvert died before settling the new colony, so his son, Cecilius, became the Lord Proprietor of Maryland and named the colony “Terra Maria,” or Maryland” in honor of the king's wife, Queen Henrietta Maria.

During the Revolutionary War, 400 soldiers in the First Maryland Regiment fought a British force of 10,000 and helped General George Washington's army escape, earning Maryland the nickname the “Old Line State.” Washington depended on the Maryland Line throughout the war.

The War of 1812 — Chesapeake Campaign brought British warships to the port city of Baltimore and the bombardment of Fort McHenry. Witnessing the bombing while being held under guard by the British on an American truce ship, Francis Scott Key penned the words to the Star Spangled Banner. The bombings lasted for 25 hours, but the ramparts of Fort McHenry withstood the “bombs bursting in air.” The Fort McHenry National Monument and Historic Shrine is open for self-guided tours.

During the Civil War Maryland was a slave state that remained with the Union. On September 17, 1862, General Robert E. Lee made his first attempt to invade the North. His Confederate army was intercepted by the Army of the Potomac near the Maryland town of Sharpsburg and in the “Bloodiest Day of the Civil War” there were more than 22,000 casualties. The fighting interpreted at the Antietam National Battlefield was indecisive but Lee's foray into the northern states was thwarted.

The Old Line State has always been at the forefront of America's transportation craze. The Baltimore & Ohio Railroad Museum in Baltimore is a fascinating, fun place for kids, families and lovers of history. The museum is located on a 40-acre historic site and preserves the largest collection of American railroad treasures in the world. Cumberland, a town in western Mary-

Top 3 Tourism Attractions:
1) Baltimore Inner Harbor
2) Deep Creek Lake
3) Crystal Grottoes Caverns

Nickname: Free State

State Flower: Black-eyed Susan

State Bird: Baltimore Oriole

People: Matthew Henson, North Pole explorer; Johns Hopkins, founder of hospital and university; Francis Scott Key, writer of the national anthem; George Herman “Babe” Ruth, baseball player

Major Cities: Baltimore, Frederick, Rockville, Gaithersburg, Bowie, (Annapolis, capital)

Topography: Coastal plain on both sides of the Chesapeake Bay; north—Piedmont Plateau, Blue Ridge Mountains

Climate: Temperate climate with monthly average temps between 87° in July and 24° in January

Clark Vandergrift

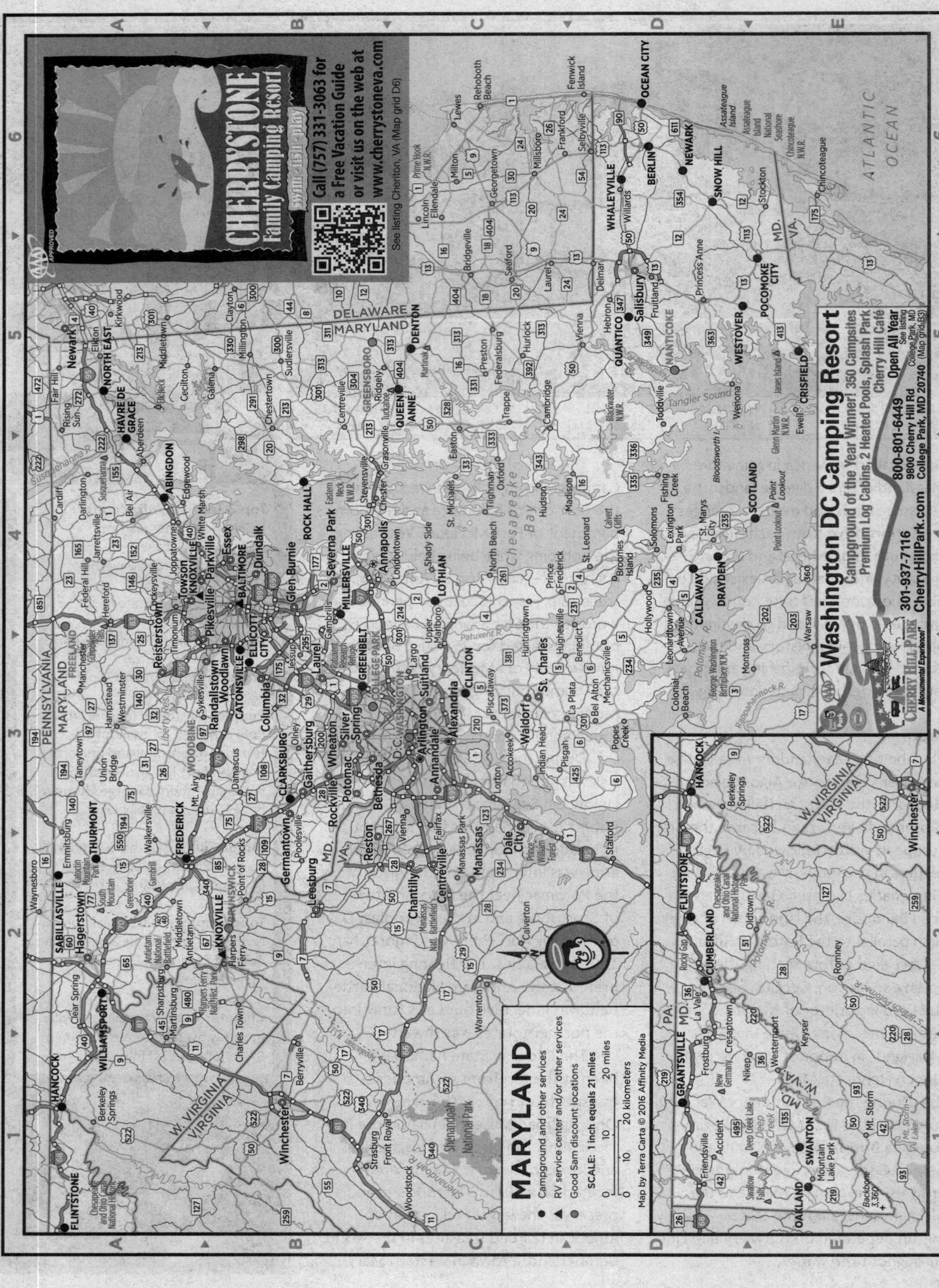
MARYLAND
Campground and other services
RV service center and/or other services
Good Sam discount locations
SCALE: 1 inch equals 21 miles
0 10 20 miles
0 10 20 kilometers
Map by Terra Carta © 2016 Affinity Media
CHERRYSTONE
Family Camping Resort
swim · fish · play
Call (757) 331-3063 for a Free Vacation Guide or visit us on the web at www.cherrystoneva.com
See listing Cheriton, VA (Map grid D6)
Washington DC Camping Resort
Campground of the Year Winner! 350 Campsites
Premium Log Cabins, 2 Heated Pools, Splash Park
Cherry Hill Café
Open All Year
CHERRY HILL PARK
A Monumental Experience!
301-937-7116
CherryHillPark.com
800-801-6449
9800 Cherry Hill Rd
College Park, MD 20740
See listing College Park, MD (Map grid B3)
PENNSYLVANIA
MARYLAND
DELAWARE
W. VIRGINIA
VIRGINIA
ATLANTIC OCEAN
Chesapeake Bay
BALTIMORE
ANNAPOLIS
OCEAN CITY
FREDERICK
HAGERSTOWN
SALISBURY
WASHINGTON D.C.

land, provides access to the Chesapeake & Ohio Canal National Historical Park. The C&O Canal, aka the "Grand Old Ditch," was the key to George Washington's plan to open the West.

Play

The beauty of the Chesapeake Bay, America's largest estuary, has a way of turning even landlubbers into weekend sailors. The bay extends almost 200 miles from Havre de Grace, Maryland, south to Virginia Beach. Smith Island, in the middle of the bay, is a popular destination accessed only by private boats and passenger-only ferries.

Maryland's Eastern Shore remains an unspoiled outdoor playground of pine forests and saltwater marshes. The resort town of Ocean City has a classic summer beach vibe with a boardwalk and miles of white-sand beaches. Directly south of Ocean City is Assateague Island, a barrier island. Assateague's northern section, which is Assateague State Park, is in Maryland and is accessed via a small connecting bridge. The island is famous for its herd of wild ponies that roam the dunes and beaches.

Experience

The Fells Point Fun Festival, held in Baltimore's waterfront neighborhood of Fells Point, began as a spotlight for historic downtown Baltimore in 1967 but has evolved into an October celebration that attracts 700,000 devotees of all things Maryland. Maryland's Flagship and Goodwill Ambassador, the tall ship Pride of Baltimore II is on hand for cruises around the Inner Harbor where you'll learn about the renaissance of Baltimore's waterfront and this interesting city's history. Nearby family-friendly attractions include Harborplace, the National Aquarium and the Maritime Museum.

The Preakness Stakes, the second jewel in thoroughbred racing's Triple Crown, is the largest single-day sporting event in the state. Even non-race fans can find something entertaining in the weeks leading up to "the Run for the Black-Eyed Susans" at Pimlico Race Course on the third Saturday in May.

Taste

Entire vacations have been planned around Maryland's rich culinary treasures, especially its seafood. Try the blue crabs sprinkled with Old Bay Seasoning (created by McCormick & Company, founded in Baltimore), succulent fresh oysters or Chesapeake Bay rockfish (striped bass) — you won't be disappointed. Quench your thirst with a local fresh-brewed beer and finish off your meal with a slice of luscious multilayered Smith Island Cake — it's the official state dessert.

TRAVEL & TOURISM

Maryland Office of Tourism
800-543-1036, 410-767-3400
www.visitmaryland.org

Alleghany County Dept. of Tourism
301-777-5134, 800-425-2067
www.mdmountainside.com

Annapolis-Anne Arundel County CVB
410-280-0445
www.visitannapolis.org

Visit Baltimore
410-659-7300
www.baltimore.org

Cambridge
410-228-4020
www.choosecambridge.com

Ocean City CVB
410-723-8600, 800-626-2326
www.ococean.com

Prince George's County CVB
301-925-8300
www.visitprincegeorges.com

Queen Anne's County Office of Tourism
410-604-2100
www.discoverqueenannes.com

Somerset County Tourism
410-651-2968, 800-521-9189
www.visitsomerset.com

Tourism Council of Frederick County
800-999-3613, 301-600-2888
www.fredericktourism.org

Worcester County Tourism
410-632-3110, 800-852-0335
www.visitworcester.org

OUTDOOR RECREATION

Department of Parks and Recreation
www.pgparks.com

Maryland Recreation and Parks Association
www.mrpanet.org

SHOPPING

AAA Antiques Mall Inc.
410-551-4101
www.aaaantiquesmallmd.com

Arts at Canal Place
301-777-8199
www.artsplaceatpuccini.com

Arundel Mills
410-540-5100
www.arundelmills.com

Featured Good Sam Parks

MARYLAND

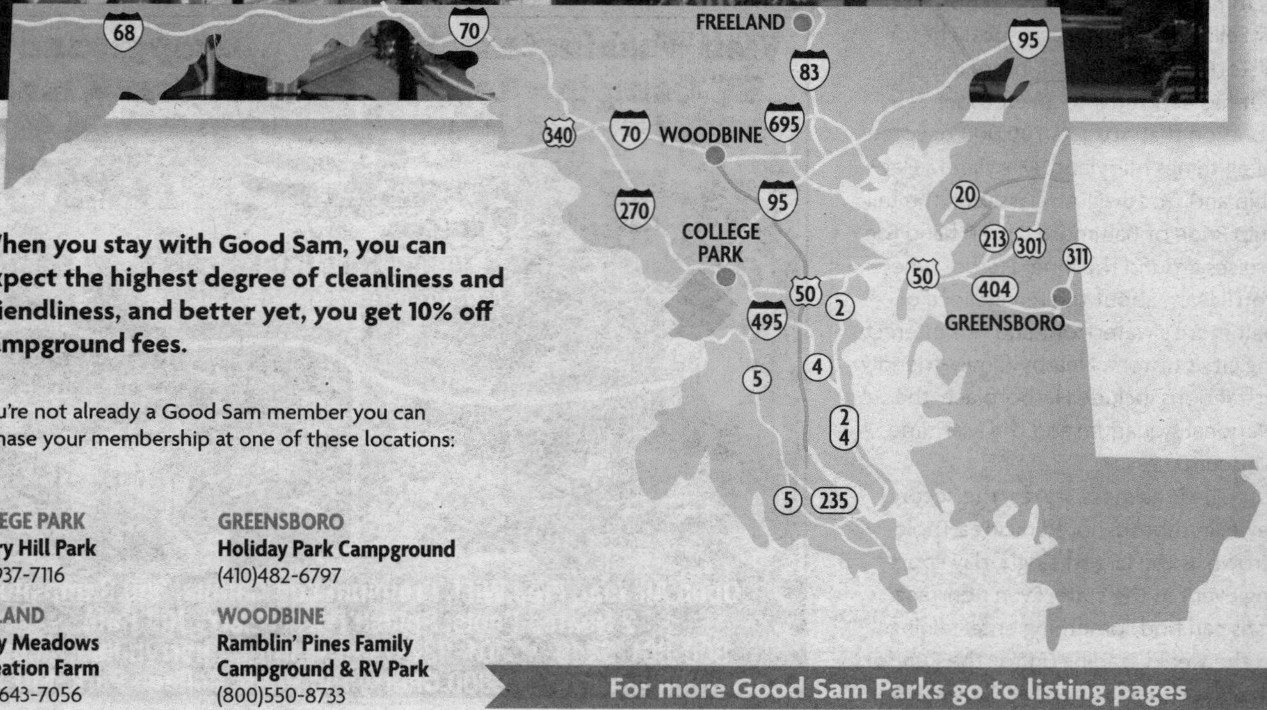

When you stay with Good Sam, you can expect the highest degree of cleanliness and friendliness, and better yet, you get 10% off campground fees.

If you're not already a Good Sam member you can purchase your membership at one of these locations:

COLLEGE PARK
Cherry Hill Park
(301)937-7116

FREELAND
Merry Meadows Recreation Farm
(800)643-7056

GREENSBORO
Holiday Park Campground
(410)482-6797

WOODBINE
Ramblin' Pines Family Campground & RV Park
(800)550-8733

For more Good Sam Parks go to listing pages

Maryland

CONSULTANTS

Ken & Kathy Wente

ABINGDON — A4 *Harford*

BAR HARBOR RV PARK & MARINA
Ratings: 9/9★/9.5 (RV Park) From Jct of I-95 & Hwy 543 (exit 80): Go 1-1/2 mi S on Hwy 543, then 1-1/2 mi W on US 40, then 3/4 mi SE on Long Bar Harbor Rd, then 1/2 mi E on Baker Ave (E).

RESERVE YOUR WATERFRONT SITE TODAY!
Enjoy the spectacular views from our waterfront sites. Fishing, crabbing, kayaking, padde boarding and swimming— All available for your relaxing stay!

FAC: Paved/gravel rds. (93 spaces). 73 Avail: 39 paved, 34 gravel, patios, back-ins (30 x 50), 73 full hkups (30/50 amps), seasonal sites, cable, WiFi, dump, laundry, groc, LP gas, fire rings, firewood, controlled access. **REC:** pool, wading pool, Bush River: fishing, playground. Pet restrict(B/Q). No tents. 2015 rates: $57 to $62.
AAA Approved
(800)351-CAMP Lat: 39.46031, Lon: -76.24424
4228 Birch Ave, Abingdon, MD 21009
info@barharborrvpark.com
www.barharborrvpark.com
See ad this page.

BALTIMORE — B4 *Baltimore*

BALTIMORE See also Abingdon, College Park, Millersville & Woodbine.

BERLIN — D6 *Worcester*

ASSATEAGUE NATL SEASHORE/BAYSIDE (Natl Pk) From Jct of US-50 & SR-611, SE 9 mi on SR-611 (R). $15 Entrance fee required in addition to camping fees. Pit toilets. 2015 rates: $20 to $25. (410)641-3030

ASSATEAGUE NATL SEASHORE/OCEANSIDE (Natl Pk) From Jct of US-50 & SR-611, SE 9 mi on SR-611 (R). $15 Entrance fee required in addition to camping fees. Pit toilets. 2015 rates: $20 to $25. May 15 to Oct 1. (410)641-3030

Read many of our brand new RV Trips of a Lifetime for 2016 in the front of the Guide. Find the rest Online!

BRUNSWICK — B2 *Frederick*

BRUNSWICK FAMILY CAMPGROUND
Ratings: 6.5/7.5★/8 (Campground) From Jct of I-70 & US 340 (Exit 52B): Go 13-1/2 mi SW on US 340, then 2-1/2 mi S on Hwy 17, then at the round-a-bout take 3rd exit, then 500 ft SE on East "A" St, then 1/2 mi S (across 2 sets of RR tracks), Then 3/4 mi SE to end of gravel Rd (R). **FAC:** Paved/gravel rds. 48 grass, 12 pull-thrus (25 x 60), back-ins (25 x 50), 48 W, 48 E (30/50 amps), WiFi, tent sites, dump, groc, fire rings, firewood. **REC:** Potomac River: swim, fishing, playground. Pets OK. Partial handicap access. 14 day max stay, eco-friendly, 2015 rates: $45. Disc: military. Mar 25 to Nov 1.
(301)834-9952 Lat: 39.31108, Lon: -77.62648
40 Canal Towpath Road, Brunswick, MD 21716
river@rivertrail.com
www.potomacrivercampground.com
See ad page 266.

CALLAWAY — D4 *St Mary's*

TAKE-IT-EASY CAMPGROUND **Ratings: 8.5/8★/7.5** (Campground) 2015 rates: $45 to $55. (301)994-0494 45285 Take-It-Easy Ranch Rd, Callaway, MD 20620

CATONSVILLE — B3 *Baltimore*

PATAPSCO VALLEY SP (HILTON AREA) (Public) From jct I-695 (exit 13) & Hwy 144 (Frederick Rd): Go 3/4 mi W on Hwy 144, then 2 mi S on Hilton Ave. 2015 rates: $20 to $25. (410)461-5005

MD

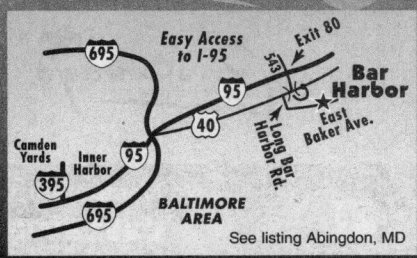

CLARKSBURG — B3 *Montgomery*

LITTLE BENNETT REGIONAL PARK (Public) From Jct of I-270 & SR-121 (exit 18) (Clarksburg), NE 0.6 mi on SR-121 (Stringtown Rd) to SR-355 (Fredrick Rd), N 0.9 mi (R). 2015 rates: $31 to $49. Mar 29 to Oct 31. (301)528-3430

CLINTON — C3 *Prince Georges*

L F COSCA REGIONAL PARK (Public) From Jct of I-95 & SR-5 (exit 7A), S 4 mi on SR-5 to SR-223, W 0.7 mi to Brandywine Rd, S 0.9 mi to Thrift Rd, W 1.1 mi (E). 2015 rates: $10 to $23. (301)868-1397

How much will it all cost? Use this as a guide: Rates shown are the minimum and maximum for two adults in one RV at the time of inspection (excluding any additional fees for items not at the site). Remember, these rates serve as guidelines only. It's always best to call ahead for the most current rate information.

COLLEGE PARK — B3 *Prince Georges*

CHERRY HILL PARK

Ratings: 9.5/10★/9.5 (RV Park) S-bnd: From Jct of I-95 & Hwy 212/Powder Mill Rd (exit 29B, Calverton): Go 1-1/4 mi W on Hwy 212/Powder Mill Rd, then (Lt turn) go 1 mi S on Cherry Hill (R); or From Beltway I-495/95 & US-1/ Baltimore Ave (exit 25): Go 1/2 mi S on US-1/Baltimore Ave, then (Rt turn) go 1 mi on Cherry Hill Rd (L).

A MONUMENTAL EXPERIENCE!
As the closest RV park and campground to Washington, D.C., Cherry Hill Park is the perfect place to stay while camping and exploring our nation's capital. Come visit and have a Monumental Experience!

FAC: Paved rds. 350 gravel, patios, 33 pull-thrus (30 x 70), back-ins (30 x 40), 350 full hkups (30/50 amps), cable, WiFi, tent sites, rentals, dump, laundry, groc, LP gas, fire rings, firewood, controlled access. **REC:** heated pool, whirlpool, pond, fishing, playground. Pets OK. Partial handicap access. Big rig sites, eco-friendly, 2015 rates: $65 to $75. Disc: AAA, military. ATM.
AAA Approved
(301)937-7116 Lat: 39.02510, Lon: -76.94028
9800 Cherry Hill Rd, College Park, MD 20740
info@cherryhillpark.com
www.cherryhillpark.com
See ad pages 266, 585 (Welcome Section), 586, 584 (MD Map), 1217 (VA Map).

We appreciate your business!

CRISFIELD — E5 *Somerset*

JANES ISLAND (State Pk) From town, NE 2 mi on SR-358 (L). 2015 rates: $21.49 to $30. Mar 27 to Nov 29. (410)968-1565

CUMBERLAND — D2 *Allegany*

GREEN RIDGE STATE FOREST (State Pk) From town, E 20 mi on I-68 to Exit 64 (R). Primitive camping only. Pit toilets. 2015 rates: $10. (301)478-3124

DENTON — C5 *Caroline*

MARTINAK (State Pk) From town, E 2 mi on SR-404 to Deep Shore Rd, S 1 mi (L). 2015 rates: $18.49 to $26.49. Mar 27 to Nov 29. (410)820-1668

DRAYDEN — D4 *St Mary's*

DENNIS POINT MARINA & CAMPGROUND **Ratings: 6.5/9★/6.5** (Campground) 2015 rates: $45 to $60. (301)994-2288 46555 Dennis Point Way Drayden, MD 20630

ELLICOTT CITY — B3 *Howard*

PATAPSCO VALLEY/HOLLOFIELD AREA (State Pk) From Jct of I-695 & Rte 40, W 3 mi on Rte 40 (R). 2015 rates: $20 to $25. (410)461-5005

FLINTSTONE — A1 *Allegany*

ROCKY GAP (State Pk) From Jct of I-68 (Exit 50) N 0.7 mi to Pleasant Valley Rd (rt turn), NE 1.7 mi to Campers Hill Rd (L). 2015 rates: $25 to $30. May 1 to Dec 13. (888)432-2267

FREDERICK — A2 *Frederick*

GAMBRILL (State Pk) From town, NW 6 mi on US-40 to Gambrill Pk Rd, N 0.5 mi to park entrance 2015 rates: $20 to $25. Apr 2 to Nov 23. (301)271-7574

FREELAND — A4 *Baltimore*

MERRY MEADOWS RECREATION FARM

Ratings: 9.5/9★/9.5 (Campground) From Jct I-83 & Hwy 439 (exit 36): Go 1/4 mi W on Hwy 439, then 1 mi N on Hwy 45, then 3 mi W on Freeland Rd (L). **FAC:** Paved rds. (260 spaces). 110 Avail: 30 paved, 80 gravel, 30 pull-thrus (25 x 75), back-ins (30 x 50), 105 full hkups, 5 W, 5 E (30/50 amps), seasonal sites, cable, WiFi, tent sites, rentals, dump, laundry, groc, LP gas, fire rings, firewood, controlled access. **REC:** pool, Merry Meadow Stream: fishing, playground. Pet restrict(B). Partial handicap access. Big rig sites, eco-friendly, 2015 rates: $24.80 to $57. Disc: AAA, military.
AAA Approved
(800)643-7056 Lat: 39.69508, Lon: -76.69828
1523 Freeland Rd, Freeland, MD 21053
mmrf@comcast.net
www.merrymeadows.com
See ad opposite page, 586.

GRANTSVILLE — D1 *Garrett*

NEW GERMANY (State Pk) From Jct of I-68 & Chestnut Ridge Rd (exit 22), S 3.5 mi on Chestnut Ridge Rd to New Germany Rd, S 2 mi, park (L). 2015 rates: $16.75 to $116.75. Apr 3 to Nov 30. (301)895-5453

GREENBELT — B3 *Prince George*

GREENBELT (Natl Pk) From I-95/495 (Capital Beltway), take exit 23 Kemilworth Ave S (Rte 201) to Greenbelt Rd E (Rte 193), E 0.25 mi (R). 2015 rates: $16. (301)344-3948

GREENSBORO — B5 *Caroline*

➔ HOLIDAY PARK CAMPGROUND
Ratings: 8/9★/8.5 (Campground) From Jct of Hwy 313 & Hwy 314, E 0.3 mi on Hwy 314 to Wothers Rd, N 0.2 mi to Boyce Mill Rd, NE 0.7 mi to Drapers Mill Rd, N 2.3 mi (L). **FAC:** Paved/gravel rds. (200 spaces). Avail: 150 dirt, 28 pull-thrus (27 x 60), back-ins (25 x 60), some side by side hkups, 150 W, 150 E (30/50 amps), seasonal sites, cable, WiFi Hotspot, tent sites, rentals, dump, mobile sewer, laundry, groc, LP gas, fire rings, firewood, controlled access. **REC:** pool, Choptank River: fishing, shuffleboard, playground. Pet restrict(B). Eco-friendly, 2015 rates: $38 to $50. Disc: AAA, military. Apr 1 to Nov 15.
AAA Approved
(410)482-6797 Lat: 39.00788, Lon: -75.76484
14620 Drapers Mill Rd, Greensboro, MD 21639
holiday@dmv.com
www.holidaypark.com
See ad this page, 586 & Family Camping in Magazine Section.

Things to See and Do

➔ HOLIDAY PARK GOSPEL CONCERTS Gospel Concerts. May 1 to Oct 15. Restrooms, food.
(410)482-6797 Lat: 39.00788, Lon: -75.76484
14620 Drapers Mill Rd, Greensboro, MD 21639
holiday@dmv.com
www.holidaypark.com
See ad this page.

HAGERSTOWN — A2 *Washington*

➔ FORT FREDERICK (State Pk) From town: Go 18 mi W on I-70 to exit 12, then 1 mi S on Hwy 56. Pit toilets. (301)842-2155

➘ GREENBRIER (State Pk) From Jct of I-70 & (US-40) Exit 42, W 3 mi on US-40 (L). Steep entrance. 2015 rates: $21.49 to $30. Apr 1 to Oct 30. (301)791-4767

HANCOCK — A1 *Washington*

➔ HAPPY HILLS CAMPGROUND **Ratings: 7/7.5/7.5** (Campground) 2015 rates: $35 to $38. (301)678-7760 12617 Seavolt Rd, Hancock, MD 21750

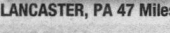

MD

HAVRE DE GRACE — A4 *Harford*

SUSQUEHANNA (State Pk) From Jct of I-95 & Rte 155 (exit 89), N 2.8 mi on Rte 155, N 1.5 mi. SH 161, E .8 mi. 2015 rates: $21.49 to $29.49. Mar 27 to Oct 30. (410)557-7994

KNOXVILLE — B2 *Frederick*

Things to See and Do

RIVER & TRAIL OUTFITTERS Rafting, Tubing, Kayaking, Canoeing, Biking & a Zip Line. They also have special trips to a Vineyard and a Micro-brewery. Near Harpers Ferry W.V. Mar 25 to Nov 1. Restrooms.
(301)695-5177 Lat: 39.33055, Lon: -77.70340
604 Valley Road, Knoxville, MD 21716
river@rivertrail.com
www.rivertrail.com
See ad page 266.

LOTHIAN — C4 *Anne Arundel*

ADVENTURE BOUND **Ratings: 8/7/7.5** (Campground) 2015 rates: $44 to $66. (410)741-9558 5381 Sands Rd, Lothian, MD 20711

MILLERSVILLE — B4 *Anne Arundel*

CAPITOL KOA KAMPGROUND **Ratings: 8.5/9.5★/8.5** (Campground) 2015 rates: $65 to $82. Mar 1 to Nov 15. (800)KOA-0248 768 Cecil Ave North, Millersville, MD 21108

NANTICOKE — D5 *Wicomico*

ROARING POINT WATERFRONT CAMPGROUND
Ratings: 6/8★/8 (Campground) From Jct of US 50 Bus & Hwy 349 (in Salisbury): Go 20 mi SW on Hwy 349, then 1/4 mi W on Nanticoke Wharf Rd (L). **FAC:** Gravel rds. (110 spaces). Avail: 30 grass, back-ins (50 x 50), 6 full hkups, 24 W, 24 E (30/50 amps), seasonal sites, tent sites, dump, mobile sewer, groc, LP gas, fire rings, firewood, controlled access. **REC:** Nanticoke River/Tangier Sound: swim, fishing, playground, rec open to public. Pets OK. Big rig sites, eco-friendly, 2015 rates: $38 to $50. Apr 1 to Nov 1.
(410)873-2553 Lat: 38.26168, Lon: -75.91141
2360 Nanticoke Wharf Rd, Nanticoke, MD 21840
www.roaringpoint.com
See ad this page.

NEWARK — D6 *Worcester*

ISLAND RESORT PARK **Ratings: 7/8/8.5** (Campground) 2015 rates: $45 to $65. Apr 18 to Jan 1. (888)641-9838 9537 Croppers Island Rd, Newark, MD 21841

NORTH EAST — A5 *Cecil*

ELK NECK (State Pk) From Jct of US-40 & SR-272, S 10.2 mi on SR-272 (E). 2015 rates: $11.75 to $38.49. (410)287-5333

OAKLAND — E1 *Garrett*

DEEP CREEK LAKE (State Pk) From Jct of US-219 & Glendale Rd, NE 2 mi on Glendale Rd to State Park Rd, NW 1 mi (L). 2015 rates: $25 to $30. Apr 15 to Dec 15. (301)387-5563

SWALLOW FALLS (State Pk) From town, NW 8 mi on Herrington Manor Rd (L). 2015 rates: $11.75 to $35. May 22 to Sep 7. (301)387-6938

OCEAN CITY — D6 *Worcester*

ASSATEAGUE (State Pk) From Jct of Rte 50 & 611, S 9 mi on Rte 611 (R). Call 888-432-2267 for reservations. 2015 rates: $20. Apr 14 to Oct 16. (410)641-2918

CASTAWAYS RV RESORT & CAMPGROUND
Ratings: 10/9★/10 (RV Park) From Jct of US 50 & Hwy 611: Go 2-1/4 mi SW on Hwy 611, then 1-1/2 mi E on Eagles Nest Rd (Stay Left at Y in Rd) (R).

CLOSEST CAMPGROUND TO OCEAN CITY!
Simply remarkable camping! Overlooking Assateague Island on the shores of beautiful Sinepuxent Bay, spend the day on our private bayfront beach or ride the free shuttle into Ocean City. Luxury camping at nature's doorstep!

FAC: Paved rds. (347 spaces). Avail: 42 paved, 300 all weather, back-ins (40 x 60), 342 full hkups (30/50 amps), seasonal sites, cable, WiFi, tent sites, rentals, laundry, groc, LP gas, fire rings, firewood, restaurant, controlled access. **REC:** pool, whirlpool, Sinepuxent Bay: swim, fishing, playground. Pet restrict(B/Q). Partial handicap access. Big rig sites, eco-friendly, 2015 rates: $61 to $170. Apr 1 to Nov 1. ATM.
(888)733-9497 Lat: 38.30493, Lon: -75.11965
12550 Eagles Nest Rd, Berlin, MD 21811
castawaysreservations@suncommunities.com
www.castawaysrvoc.com
See ad pages 588, 1463 (Welcome Section) & Family Camping, RV Trips of a Lifetime in Magazine Section.

FRONTIER TOWN RV RESORT & CAMPGROUND
Ratings: 9/9★/9.5 (Campground) From Jct US 50 & Hwy 611: Go 3-3/4 mi SW on Hwy 611 (L).

OCEAN CITY'S WILD WEST ADVENTURE
Explore this premier waterfront campground, located along the Sinepuxent Bay, and you'll discover exhilarating attractions right on-site, like a High Ropes Adventure Park, Wild West Show, Water Park, and Cowboy Mini-Golf.

FAC: Paved/gravel rds. (565 spaces). 523 Avail: 254 gravel, 269 grass, back-ins (40 x 60), 282 full hkups, 193 W, 193 E (30/50 amps), cable, WiFi, tent sites, rentals, dump, laundry, groc, LP gas, fire rings, firewood, restaurant. **REC:** pool, wading pool, Sinepuxent Bay: fishing, shuffleboard, playground, rec open to public. Pet restrict(B). Partial handicap access. Big rig sites, eco-friendly, 2015 rates: $42 to $116. Mar 11 to Nov 27. ATM.
(800)228-5590 Lat: 38.29154, Lon: -75.15011
8428 Stephen Decatur Hwy, Ocean City, MD 21843
info@frontiertown.com
www.frontiertown.com
See ad this page, 1463 (Welcome Section) & Family Camping, RV Trips of a Lifetime in Magazine Section.

Nobody said it was easy being a 10. And our rating system makes it even tougher.

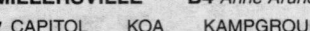

RAMBLIN' PINES CAMPGROUND

Right in the Middle of the Great American Vacation

OPEN ALL YEAR

Reduced Rates for Extended Stay!

Good Sam Park

Good Sam RATED 9.5/9★/9.5

AAA

FREE Wi-Fi

- Cable TV
- Heated Pool
- Fishing Pond
- Game Room
- Big Rig Sites
- Full Hookups
- 30-50 Amps
- Pull-Thrus
- Cabins
- Exercise Room
- Pet Exercise Area
- Mini Golf
- Jumping Pillow
- Secure, Paved RV Storage with Electric Hookups

INTERSTATE 70

INTERSTATE 70 EXIT 73

MasterCard VISA DISCOVER

NEAR
Baltimore,
Annapolis
Washington DC,
Gettysburg PA,
Lancaster PA,
Hershey PA

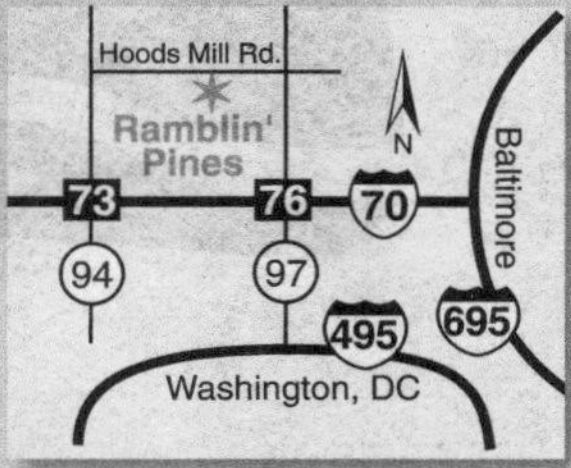

801 Hoods Mill Rd • Woodbine, MD 21797
(410) 795-5161 • (800) 550-8733

www.ramblinpinescampground.com

See listing Woodbine, MD

MD

POCOMOKE CITY — E5 *Worcester*

POCOMOKE RIVER/MILBURN LANDING AREA (State Pk) From Jct of SR-12 & SR-354, SW 7 mi on SR-354 (L). 2015 rates: $18.49 to $24.49. (410)632-2566

QUANTICO — D5 *Wicomico*

SANDY HILL FAMILY CAMP **Ratings: 5/7/5** (Campground) 2015 rates: $30 to $33. Mar 15 to Dec 15. (410)873-2471 5752 Sandy Hill Rd, Quantico, MD 21856

QUEEN ANNE — C5 *Queen Anne*

TUCKAHOE SP (State Pk) From jct Hwy 404 & Hwy 480: Go 1/10 mi N, then 5 mi N on Eveland Rd. 2015 rates: $21.49 to $30. Mar 27 to Nov 27. (410)820-1668

ROCK HALL — B4 *Kent*

BAYSHORE CAMPGROUND **Ratings: 7.5/8/9.5** (Campground) 2015 rates: $55 to $80. (410)639-7485 4228 Eastern Neck Rd, Rock Hall, MD 21661

SABILLASVILLE — A2 *Frederick*

CATOCTIN MOUNTAIN PARK/OWENS CREEK CAMPGROUND (Natl Pk) From Jct of US-15 & MD-77, W 3 mi on MD-77 to Park Central Rd, N 4 mi to park access rd, E 1 mi (E). (Max trailer length 22ft.). 2015 rates: $25. May 1 to Nov 1. (301)663-9388

SCOTLAND — E4 *St Mary's*

POINT LOOKOUT (State Pk) From Jct of SR-235 & SR-5, S 4.7 mi on SR-5 (E). 2015 rates: $25 to $35. Mar 29 to Oct 28. (301)872-5688

SNOW HILL — D6 *Worcester*

POCOMOKE RIVER/SHAD LANDING AREA (State Pk) From town, S 4 mi on US-113 (R). 2015 rates: $21.49 to $27.49. (410)632-2566

SWANTON — E1 *Garrett*

BIG RUN SP (State Pk) From I-68 (exit 22): Go S on Chestnut Ridge Rd to New Germany Rd to Big Run Rd. (No water available). Call (888)432-2267 for reservations. Pit toilets. (301)895-5453

THURMONT — A2 *Frederick*

CUNNINGHAM FALLS (State Pk) From town, W 3 mi on MD-77 to Catoctin Hollow Rd, S 0.5 mi (R). Call (888)432-2267 for reservations. 2015 rates: $21.49 to $61.75. Apr 1 to Oct 30. (301)271-7574

We give you what you want. First, we surveyed thousands of RVers just like you. Then, we developed our exclusive Triple Rating System for campgrounds based on the results. That's why our rating system is so good at explaining the quality of facilities and cleanliness of campgrounds.

CUNNINGHAM FALLS SP (MANOR AREA) (State Pk) From town: Go 3 mi S on US 15. 2015 rates: $25 to $30. (301)271-7574

WESTOVER — D5 *Somerset*

LAKE SOMERSET CAMPGROUND Ratings: 8/8.5★/8.5 (Campground) From Jct of US 113 & US 13: Go 8 mi NW on US 13, then 50 ft W to Lake Somerset Lane (between Marker 12 & 13), then immediate (L). **FAC:** Paved/gravel rds. (110 spaces). 60 Avail: 30 gravel, 30 grass, 30 pull-thrus (35 x 85), back-ins (30 x 45), 60 full hkups (30/50 amps), seasonal sites, WiFi Hotspot, tent sites, rentals, dump, laundry, LP gas, fire rings, firewood. **REC:** pool, pond, fishing, playground, rec open to public. Pets OK. Big rig sites, eco-friendly, 2015 rates: $38.
(410)957-1866 Lat: 38.11875, Lon: -75.67076
8658 Lake Somerset Ln, Westover, MD 21871
lakesomerset@yahoo.com
www.lakesomerset.com

WHALEYVILLE — D6 *Worcester*

FORT WHALEY RV RESORT & CAMPGROUND Ratings: 9/9★/9.5 (RV Park) From Jct of US 50 & Hwy 528 (S end of Ocean City): Go 13 3/4 mi W on US 50 to Hwy 610 (Whaleyville), entrance is on SE corner of intersection (L).

OLD WEST MEETS EAST COAST
Nestled among the towering pines, this peaceful Maryland campground is just minutes from Ocean City! Enjoy spacious accommodations with a great selection of amenities, plus access to many of the attractions at Frontier Town.

FAC: Paved/gravel rds. 169 Avail: 7 paved, 160 gravel, 2 grass, 14 pull-thrus (30 x 50), back-ins (30 x 50), 66 full hkups, 70 W, 70 E (30/50 amps), cable, WiFi, tent sites, rentals, dump, laundry, groc, LP gas, fire rings, firewood, controlled access. **REC:** pool, pond, fishing, shuffleboard, playground. Pet restrict(B). Eco-friendly, 2015 rates: $34 to $93. Mar 11 to Nov 27. ATM.
(888)322-7717 Lat: 38.38407, Lon: -75.31191
11224 Dale Road, Whaleyville, MD 21872
info@fortwhaley.com
www.fortwhaley.com
See ad page 590, 1463 (Welcome Section) & Family Camping, RV Trips of a Lifetime in Magazine Section.

WILLIAMSPORT — A2 *Washington*

HAGERSTOWN/ANTIETAM BATTLEFIELD KOA **Ratings: 8.5/8.5★/8.5** (Campground) 2015 rates: $38.80 to $76. Mar 25 to Nov 30. (800)562-7607 11759 Snug Harbor Lane, Williamsport, MD 21795

YOGI BEAR'S JELLYSTONE PARK CAMP-RESORT/HAGERSTOWN Ratings: 9/9★/9.5 (Campground) From Jct of I-81 & Hwy 68 (exit 1): Go 1-1/4 mi E on SR 68 (R); or From Jct of I-70 and Hwy 632 (exit 28): Go 2-3/4 mi SW on Hwy 632, then 3/4 mi W on Hwy 68W (L). **FAC:** Paved/gravel rds. 163 gravel, 109 pull-thrus (40 x 75), back-ins (25 x 50), 137 full hkups, 26 W, 26 E (30/50 amps), cable, WiFi, tent sites, rentals, dump, laundry, groc, LP gas, fire rings, firewood. **REC:** heated pool, wading pool, playground. Pets OK. Partial handicap access. Big rig sites, 14 day max stay, eco-friendly, 2015 rates: $38 to $139. Mar 25 to Nov 1. ATM.
(301)223-7117 Lat: 39.58083, Lon: -77.79605
16519 Lappans Rd, Williamsport, MD 21795
reservations@jellystonemaryland.com
www.jellystonemaryland.com

WOODBINE — A3 *Carroll*

RAMBLIN' PINES FAMILY CAMPGROUND & RV PARK Ratings: 9.5/9★/9.5 (Campground) E-bnd: From Jct of I-70 & Hwy 94 (exit 73): Go 3-1/2 mi N on Hwy 94, then 2-1/4 mi E on Hoods Mill Rd (R); W-bnd: From Jct of I-70 & Hwy 97 (exit 76): Go 2-3/4 mi N on Hwy 97, (left turn) onto Hoods Mill Rd, W 1/2 mi (L). **FAC:** Paved rds. (200 spaces). Avail: 140 gravel, 14 pull-thrus (30 x 70), back-ins (30 x 70), 140 full hkups (30/50 amps), seasonal sites, WiFi, tent sites, rentals, dump, laundry, groc, LP gas, fire rings, firewood, controlled access. **REC:** heated pool, pond, fishing, shuffleboard, playground. Pet restrict(B). Partial handicap access. Big rig sites, 2015 rates: $57.50. Disc: AAA, military.
AAA Approved
(800)550-8733 Lat: 39.36728, Lon: -77.02505
801 Hoods Mill Rd, Woodbine, MD 21797
rpines@qis.net
www.ramblinpinescampground.com
See ad pages 591, 586 & Family Camping in Magazine Section.

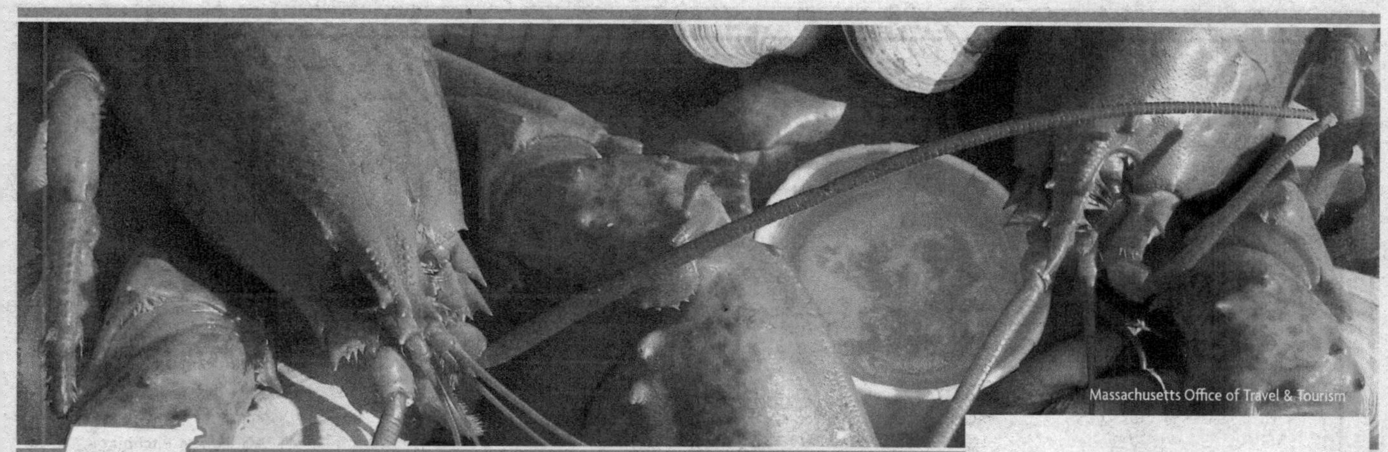

Massachusetts Office of Travel & Tourism

WELCOME TO

Massachussetts

DATE OF STATEHOOD	WIDTH: 183 MILES (295 KM)	PROPORTION OF UNITED STATES
FEB. 6, 1788	LENGTH: 113 MILES (182 KM)	0.28% OF 3,794,100 SQ MI

Few states in the nation can boast as many pivotal historic events as Massachusetts. The Pilgrims landed on Cape Cod Bay, the American Revolution erupted in Lexington and Concord, and some of the country's best colleges can be found on ivy-covered campuses in the Bay State.

For many travelers, Massachusetts is synonymous with Cape Cod. Shaped like a giant arm flexing out into the Atlantic Ocean, the Cape is fringed with 60 public beaches along its 559 miles of shoreline. The Cape Cod National Seashore features a good share of those miles. Off the southern coast are the popular vacation destinations of Nantucket Island and Martha's Vineyard.

Rural Berkshire County comprises the western third of Massachusetts. Covered by the Berkshire Hills, the region hosts classic hikes like Monument Mountain in Great Barrington, the Ice Glen in Stockbridge, Mount Washington in South Egremont and Batholomew's Cobble in Ashley Falls.

Make sure to visit during the Boston Marathon, New England's largest spectator sporting event. The road race winds 26.2 hilly miles through Greater Boston. No less celebratory is the annual St. Patrick's Day Parade, when the city celebrates its Irish heritage in Boston on the Sunday nearest to March 17. Come Independence Day, the city mounts the Boston Harborfest.

On the coast, the town of Plymouth, site of the first Thanksgiving, continues to celebrate the local bounty every November.

Top 3 Tourism Attractions:
1) Boston's Freedom Trail
2) Fenway Park
3) Old Sturbridge Village

Nickname: Bay State

State Flower: Mayflower

State Bird: Chickadee

People: Susan B. Anthony, civil rights leader; Clara Barton, American Red Cross founder; Leonard Bernstein, conductor and composer; Emily Dickinson, poet; Theodore "Dr. Seuss" Geisel, writer and cartoonist; Christa McAuliffe, teacher, astronaut; Edgar Allen Poe, writer

Major Cities: Boston (capital), Worcester, Springfield, Lowell, Cambridge

Topography: Jagged, indented coast around Cape Cod; central—flatland yielding to stony upland pastures; west—gentle hills

Climate: Humid continental climate with warm summers and cold, snowy winters

TRAVEL & TOURISM

Massachusetts Office of Travel & Tourism
800-227-MASS, 617-973-8500
www.massvacation.com

Greater Boston CVB
888-SEE-BOSTON
www.bostonusa.com

The Berkshire Visitors Bureau
413-743-4500, 800-237-5747
www.berkshires.org

Cape Cod Chamber of Commerce
888-33-CAPECOD, 888-332-2732
www.capecodchamber.org

Martha's Vineyard Chamber of Commerce
508-693-0085, 800-505-4815
www.mvy.com

Greater Merrimack Valley CVB
800-443-3332, 978-250-9704
www.merrimackvalley.org

Mohawk Trail Association
866-743-8127, 413-743-8127
www.mohawktrail.com

Nantucket Island Chamber of Commerce
508-228-1700
www.nantucketchamber.org

Southeastern Massachusetts CVB
800-288-6263, 508-997-1250
www.bristol-county.org

OUTDOOR RECREATION

Ferry Service
www.islandferry.com

Fishing & Hunting
www.mass.gov-massoutdoors
508-389-6300, 617-626-1520

SHOPPING

Cape Ann Artisans
www.capeannartisans.com

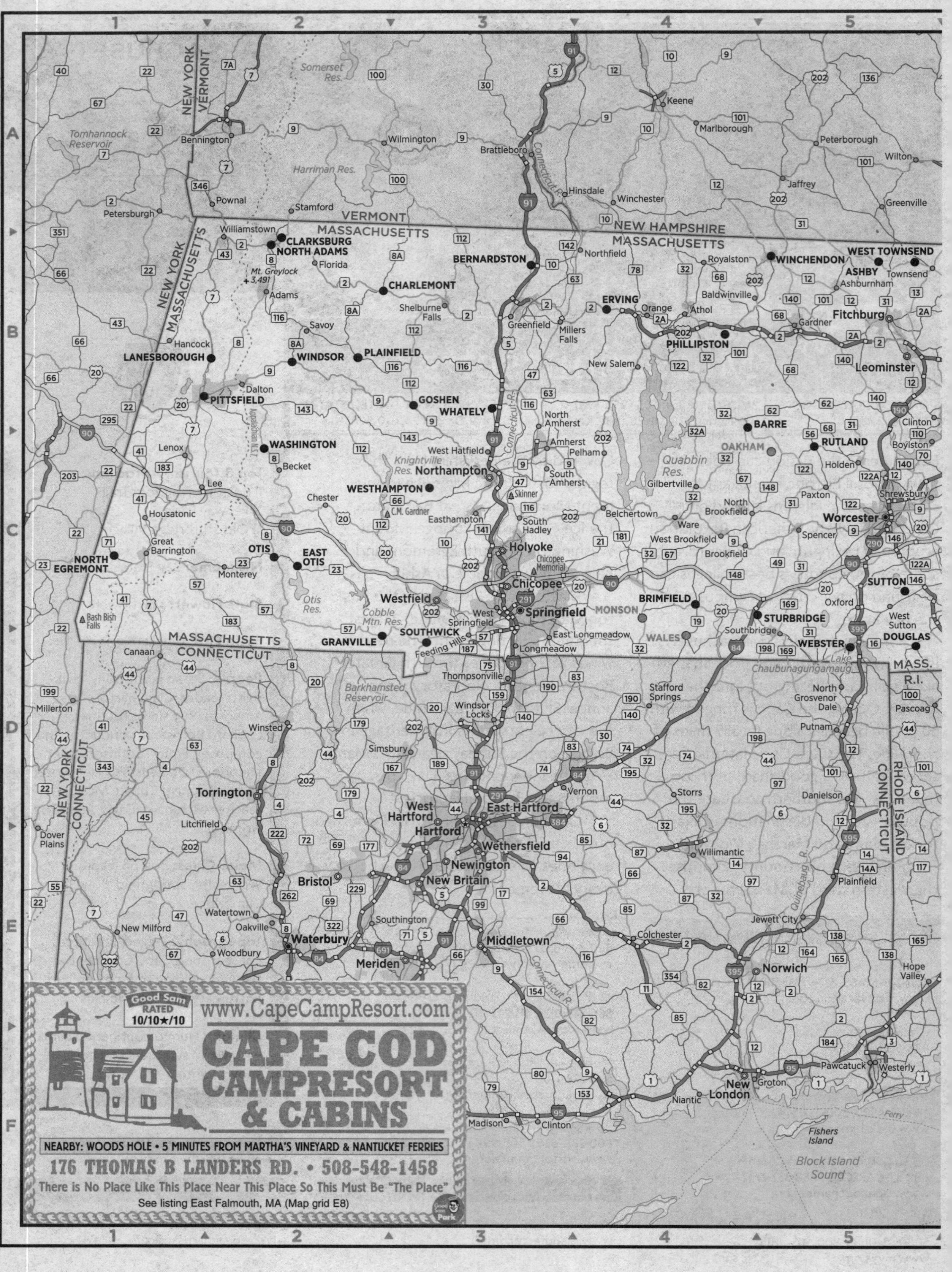
NEW YORK
VERMONT
NEW HAMPSHIRE
MASSACHUSETTS
CONNECTICUT
RHODE ISLAND
Bennington
Pownal
Petersburgh
Stamford
Wilmington
Brattleboro
Hinsdale
Winchester
Keene
Marlborough
Peterborough
Jaffrey
Wilton
Greenville
Somerset Res.
Harriman Res.
Tomhannock Reservoir
Williamstown
CLARKSBURG
NORTH ADAMS
Florida
Mt. Greylock 3,491
Adams
CHARLEMONT
Shelburne Falls
Savoy
Hancock
LANESBOROUGH
WINDSOR
PLAINFIELD
Dalton
PITTSFIELD
Lenox
Lee
WASHINGTON
Becket
GOSHEN
WHATELY
BERNARDSTON
Northfield
Greenfield
Millers Falls
ERVING
Orange
Athol
Royalston
WINCHENDON
WEST TOWNSEND
Townsend
ASHBY
Ashburnham
Baldwinville
Gardner
Fitchburg
PHILLIPSTON
Leominster
New Salem
North Amherst
Amherst
Pelham
South Amherst
BARRE
OAKHAM
RUTLAND
Holden
Clinton
Boylston
Quabbin Res.
Gilbertville
West Hatfield
Northampton
Knightville Res.
WESTHAMPTON
Chester
C.M. Gardner
Skinner
Easthampton
South Hadley
Holyoke
Belchertown
Ware
North Brookfield
West Brookfield
Brookfield
Paxton
Shrewsbury
Worcester
Spencer
Housatonic
Great Barrington
NORTH EGREMONT
OTIS
EAST OTIS
Monterey
Otis Res.
Bash Bish Falls
Westfield
Cobble Mtn. Res.
West Springfield
Chicopee
Chicopee Memorial
Springfield
MONSON
BRIMFIELD
WALES
East Longmeadow
Longmeadow
SOUTHWICK
GRANVILLE
Feeding Hills
STURBRIDGE
Southbridge
SUTTON
Oxford
West Sutton
DOUGLAS
WEBSTER
Lake Chaubunagungamaug
MASS.
R.I.
Canaan
Millerton
Barkhamsted Reservoir
Thompsonville
Windsor Locks
Stafford Springs
North Grosvenor Dale
Pascoag
Putnam
Winsted
Simsbury
Torrington
Litchfield
Dover Plains
West Hartford
Hartford
East Hartford
Vernon
Storrs
Danielson
Wethersfield
Newington
New Britain
Bristol
Willimantic
Plainfield
Watertown
Oakville
Southington
New Milford
Waterbury
Woodbury
Meriden
Middletown
Colchester
Jewett City
Norwich
Hope Valley
Pawcatuck
Westerly
New London
Groton
Niantic
Madison
Clinton
Fishers Island
Block Island Sound
Ferry
Connecticut R.
Quinebaug R.
Appalachian N.S.T.

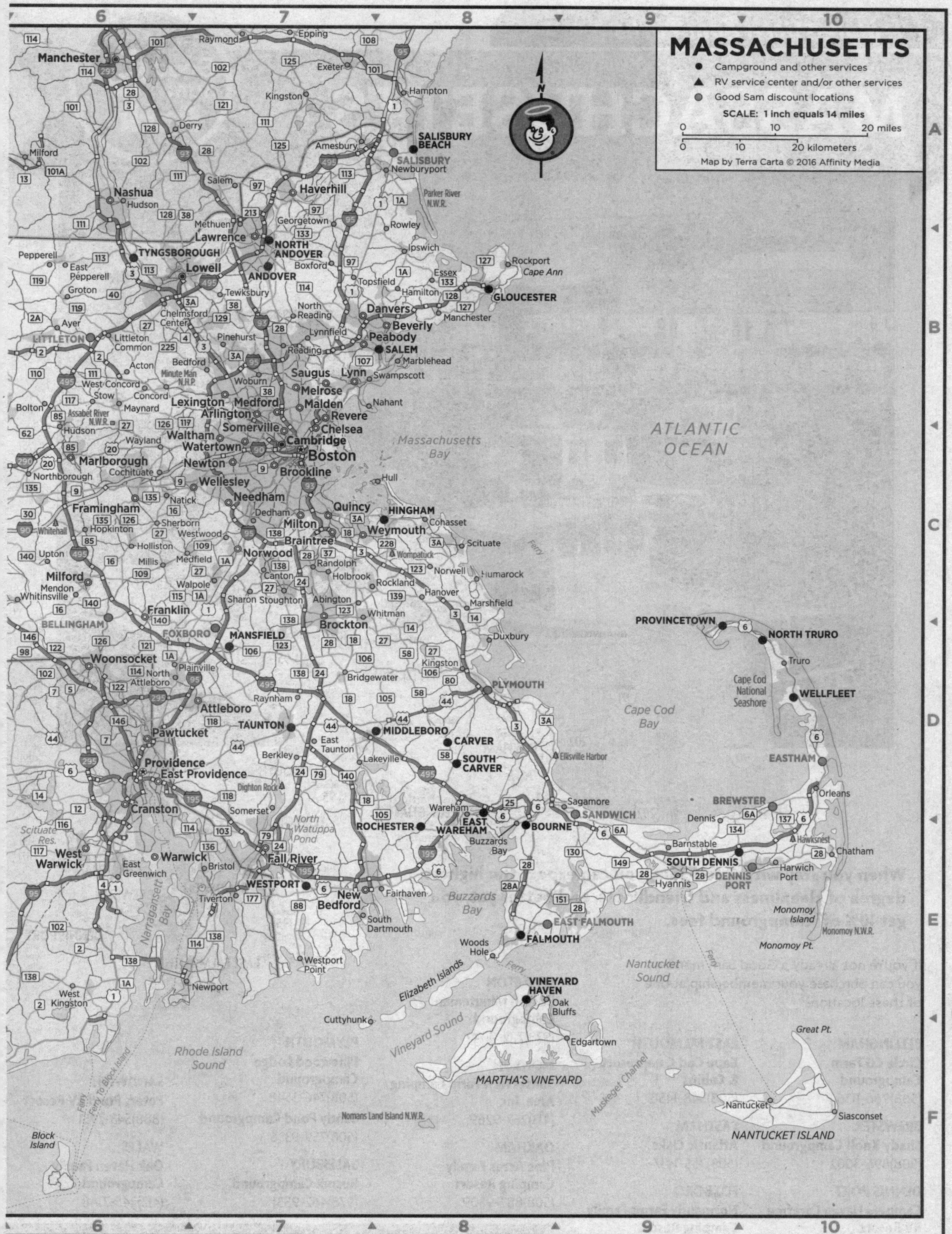
MASSACHUSETTS
Campground and other services
RV service center and/or other services
Good Sam discount locations
SCALE: 1 inch equals 14 miles
0 10 20 miles
0 10 20 kilometers
Map by Terra Carta © 2016 Affinity Media
N
ATLANTIC OCEAN
Massachusetts Bay
Cape Cod Bay
Buzzards Bay
Nantucket Sound
Vineyard Sound
Rhode Island Sound
Narragansett Bay
Muskeget Channel
Ferry
Ferry To Block Island
Manchester
Nashua
Lawrence
Haverhill
NORTH ANDOVER
ANDOVER
TYNGSBOROUGH
Lowell
SALISBURY BEACH
SALISBURY
Newburyport
GLOUCESTER
Rockport
Cape Ann
Danvers
Beverly
Peabody
SALEM
Marblehead
Lynn
Saugus
Melrose
Malden
Revere
Chelsea
Lexington
Medford
Arlington
Somerville
Waltham
Watertown
Cambridge
Boston
Newton
Brookline
Wellesley
Needham
Framingham
Marlborough
LITTLETON
Quincy
HINGHAM
Weymouth
Milton
Braintree
Norwood
Milford
Franklin
BELLINGHAM
FOXBORO
MANSFIELD
Woonsocket
Brockton
Attleboro
Pawtucket
Providence
East Providence
Cranston
West Warwick
Warwick
TAUNTON
MIDDLEBORO
CARVER
SOUTH CARVER
PLYMOUTH
Fall River
WESTPORT
New Bedford
ROCHESTER
EAST WAREHAM
Wareham
BOURNE
SANDWICH
FALMOUTH
EAST FALMOUTH
Woods Hole
Elizabeth Islands
Cuttyhunk
VINEYARD HAVEN
Oak Bluffs
Edgartown
MARTHA'S VINEYARD
Nomans Land Island N.W.R.
PROVINCETOWN
NORTH TRURO
Truro
Cape Cod National Seashore
WELLFLEET
EASTHAM
Orleans
BREWSTER
Dennis
Barnstable
SOUTH DENNIS
DENNIS PORT
Hyannis
Harwich Port
Chatham
Monomoy Island
Monomoy N.W.R.
Monomoy Pt.
Great Pt.
Nantucket
Siasconset
NANTUCKET ISLAND
Block Island
Newport
West Kingston
Westport Point
South Dartmouth
Fairhaven
Tiverton
Bristol
East Greenwich

Featured Good Sam Parks

MASSACHUSETTS

When you stay with Good Sam, you can expect the highest degree of cleanliness and friendliness, and better yet, you get 10% off campground fees.

If you're not already a Good Sam member you can purchase your membership at one of these locations:

BELLINGHAM
Circle CG Farm Campground
(508)966-1136

BREWSTER
Shady Knoll Campground
(508)896-3002

DENNIS PORT
Campers Haven Carefree RV Resort
(508)398-2811

EAST FALMOUTH
Cape Cod Campresort & Cabins
(508)548-1458

EASTHAM
Atlantic Oaks
(508)255-1437

FOXBORO
Normandy Farms Family Camping Resort
(866)673-2767

LITTLETON
Boston Minuteman Campground
(978)772-0042

MONSON
Sunsetview Farm Camping Area, Inc
(413)267-9269

OAKHAM
Pine Acres Family Camping Resort
(508)882-9509

PLYMOUTH
Pinewood Lodge Campground
(508)746-3548
Sandy Pond Campground
(508)759-9336

SALISBURY
Rusnik Campground
(978)462-9551

SANDWICH
Peters Pond RV Resort
(888)543-7951

WALES
Oak Haven Family Campground
(413)245-7148

For more Good Sam Parks go to listing pages

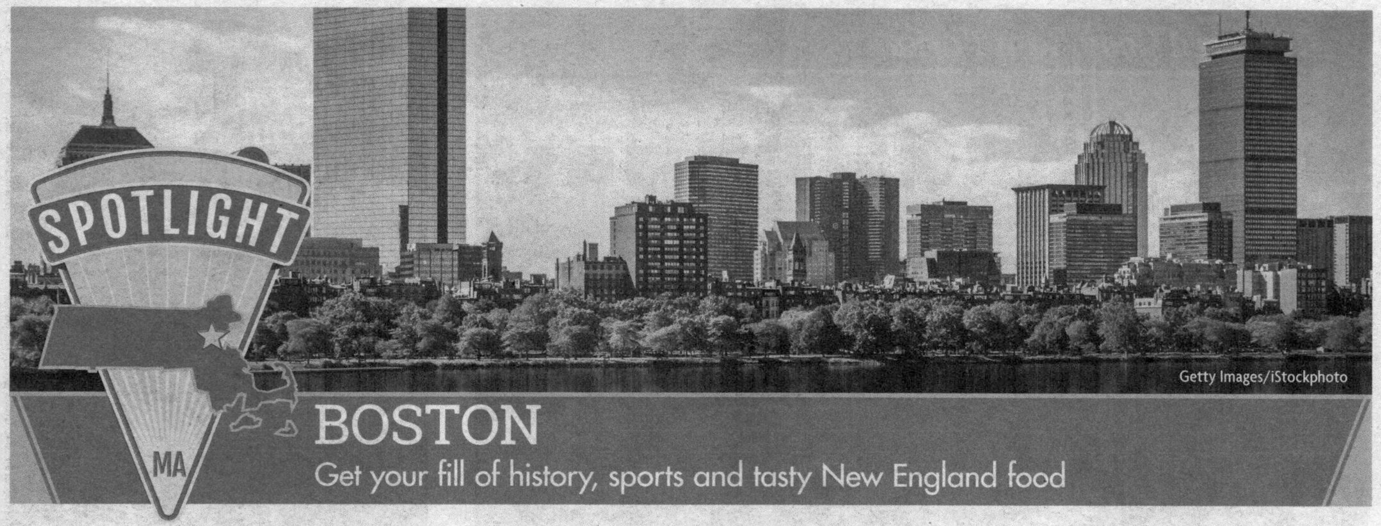

Getty Images/iStockphoto

BOSTON

Get your fill of history, sports and tasty New England food

As one of America's oldest cities, Boston is a must-visit for anyone interested in United States history. A number of significant historic events took place in Boston, including the Boston Tea Party, the Boston Massacre and the Siege of Boston, and it's a city that celebrates its rich cultural heritage in its numerous historical and cultural institutions.

> Set out on the Freedom Trail, a two-and-a half-mile pedestrian circuit that passes by 16 important historical sites across town, including the Boston Common.

English pilgrims first settled this atmospheric Massachusetts capital in the 1630s and it takes its name from the English town of Boston, in Lincolnshire. Not long after its settlement, Boston developed into the biggest city in British America. The population grew again in the early to mid-1800s, due largely to massive Irish immigration that came as a result of the potato famine. And though with just under 650,000

MA

Built in 1877, Trinity Church overlooks Copley Square. Getty Images/iStockphoto

Crews compete in the Charles Regatta.
Greater Boston CVB

residents Boston is no longer the largest city in the region, it's still quite an important hub for New England cultural and intellectual life, thanks to its many museums, historic sites and universities.

History and Culture

One of the city's most important attractions is the Freedom Trail, a two-and-a half-mile pedestrian circuit that passes by 16 important historical sites across town. These include King's Chapel and its Burying Ground, Park Street Church, the Paul Revere House and Boston Common, to name a few. Visitors to the trail will want to stop at Bunker Hill, where the famous 1775 battle of the same name—the first major battle of the Revolutionary War—took place. The Freedom Trail also passes by the *USS Constitution*, a historic warship that was launched in 1797 that saw action against the British in the War of 1812.

Boston's beautiful Public Garden, which dates back to the Victorian era, is another popular site. The 24-acre botanical site was established in 1837 on what was once a salt marsh, and has a huge variety of native and introduced trees from around the world flanking its meandering pathways.

Culture lovers will enjoy a visit to the Museum of Fine Arts, which houses a stunning collection of 18th- and 19th-century American and European paintings. Boston's award-winning Symphony Orchestra is also among the country's finest.

City of Sports

Sports lovers might want to plan their trip around a Red Sox game at Fenway Park, the oldest Major League Baseball stadium in the country. The Park opened in 1912 and 50-minute tours are available daily. This sporty city is also home to a number of other major league teams, including the Boston Celtics (basketball) and the Boston Bruins (hockey), which play at TD Garden. There's also a Sports Museum featuring memorabilia from all the city's major teams. The New England Patriots (football) and the New England Revolution (soccer) both play at the Gillette Stadium in Foxborough, 30 miles away.

Boston's best-known athletic event, however, is the Boston Marathon, the world's largest marathon with almost 40,000 runners and nearly half a million

> Visitors who love a good brew won't want to miss a visit to local breweries and beer pubs, including Boston Beer Works, the Samuel Adams Brewery and the Atlantic Beer Garden.

visitors. It's held annually on Patriots Day (the third Monday in April) and is reserved specifically for runners who have previously participated in marathons and qualified by completing the 26.2-mile distance in good time. The marathon was the site of a terrorist attack in 2013, but despite this tragic occurrence, the event has carried on, in the true spirit of Boston's perseverance and dedication to sportsmanship.

Culinary Culture

Foodies won't want to miss some of Boston's many excellent eateries. New England specialties such as prime ribs, steaks, lamb chops and lobster—as well as the city's famous baked beans—can be enjoyed at Durgin Park, or visitors can dig into fresh seafood at the Union Oyster House, which has been serving local diners since 1826, making it one of the oldest continuously operating restaurant in the country. Boston is also an excellent shopping destination and its Newbury Street has plenty of boutiques and chain stores as well as great restaurants featuring cuisine from around the world.

There's also a strong beer culture in the city, and visitors who love a good brew won't want to miss a visit to local breweries and beer pubs, including Boston Beer Works, the Samuel Adams Brewery and the Atlantic Beer Garden. You can even visit the Cheers pub shown during the opening credits of the popular 1980s sitcom. And if you visit during Saint Patrick's Day, be prepared for lots of Guinness imbibing as the large Irish-American population celebrates Ireland's national saint. South Boston's Saint Patrick's Day Parade takes place on the Sunday closest to March 17 and is considered the second-largest parade in the country, garnering a viewership of around 600,000 people per year.

For More Information

Greater Boston Convention & Visitors Bureau
888-733-2678
www.bostonusa.com

Massachusetts Office of Travel & Tourism
800-227-6277
www.massvacation.com

The Harvard campus on the Charles River. Getty Images/iStockphoto

MA

Getty Images/iStockphoto

CAPE COD

Set up camp in a perennial vacation destination

Stretching outward into the Atlantic from the easternmost end of Massachusetts, Cape Cod has been a popular summer getaway since the late 1800s. Its long coastline and favorable climate, which is less extreme than the rest of the surrounding areas, make it a perennial magnet for tourism. There are 15 towns in total, along with nearly 600 miles of coastline and around 60 public beaches.

The area known as Cape Cod is divided into multiple sections. The Upper Cape is the part closest to mainland Massachusetts and includes the towns of Bourne, Sandwich, Mashpee and Falmouth. Further east, the Mid-Cape has a warmer climate and is home to Barnstable, Yarmouth and Dennis. The beaches here are a little warmer, and there's more commercial activity in the Mid-Cape than anywhere else. The rest of the Cape is called the Outer Cape, or Lower Cape, and includes the legendary islands of Nantucket and Martha's Vineyard. Explore the region's many trails, roads or bike paths, or find a quiet beach and relax in the sand.

> Cape Cod boasts 15 towns in total, along with nearly 600 miles of coastline and around 60 public beaches.

The Upper Cape

The Upper Cape town of Mashpee was predominantly a Wampanoag Indian town until the 1960s, and visitors interested in the tribe's history won't want to miss the Wampanoag Indian Museum. The town is also home to the Cape Cod Children's Museum, which boasts a planetarium and other attractions for children of all ages. Outdoorsy folk can go hiking in the 2,000- acre Waquoit Bay National Estuarine Research Reserve or go freshwater fishing at Lowell Holly, home to the Mashpee and Wakeby ponds and huge stands of holly. Falmouth is best known for its road race held every August. Within Falmouth, the village of Woods

Provincetown Harbor's skyline is dominated by the Provincetown Library.
Getty Images/iStockphoto

See listing East Falmouth, MA

MA

Hole has great sportfishing, cute old buildings, and a marvelous aquarium with an outdoor sea pool and free admission for all.

The Mid-Cape

The Mid-Cape is the commercial hub of Cape Cod and is a starting-off point for whale-watching cruises. The West Barnstable Train Station is open on Saturdays in spring through late fall and has numerous exhibits tracing the railroad history in the area. There are also plenty of beaches in the area, especially around the town of Dennis.

The Outer Cape

Sometimes called the Lower Cape, the Outer Cape boasts ample attractions. The town of Truro is home to Highland Light Station, the oldest lighthouse on the peninsula, and its adjacent museum features old relics from the Cape's whaling industry. Eastham has many more lighthouses and is the start of many hiking and biking trails. Wellfleet contains plenty of old-time charm, from the town's old drive-in theater to the Preservation Hall, a 1910 church that's been restored and transformed into a community center.

Provincetown, at the very tip of the Cape, has long attracted artists who come here for its gorgeous views and bohemian atmosphere. Commercial Street is full of art galleries and history lovers will enjoy the Provincetown Museum, with exhibitions on Pilgrim history. Another fascinating attraction is the Provincetown Library, which houses a half-scale model of a fishing schooner. The 66-foot-long replica is based on the Rose Dorothea, a vessel built in 1905 that was known for its speed.

Martha's Vineyard

Just seven miles off of peninsular Cape Cod, Martha's Vineyard is a popular vacation spot for East Coasters during the summer months. The island was once inhabited only by the indigenous Wampanoag people, and many still live there today. In the 17th century, Europeans settled on the island, and it became a hub for the whaling industry in the 19th century. It would later become a popular spot for celebrities and well-heeled vacationers, who are drawn in by the island's gorgeous beaches and quaint towns.

A classic Cape Cod Beach House. Getty Images/iStockphoto

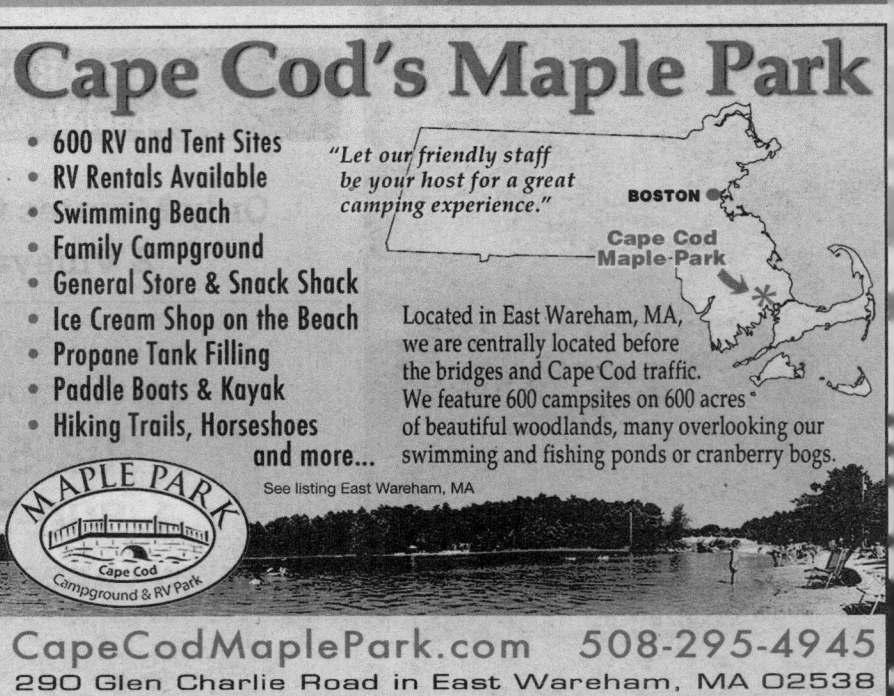

A fishing trawler at the Provincetown pier. Getty Images/iStockphoto

Nature lovers will love the colorful clay Gay Head Cliffs and the elegantly manicured Japanese-style Mytoi Garden. History buffs can learn more about the island at Martha's Vineyard Museum or simply wander through the charming lanes of the colonial town of Edgartown. The quaint dollhouselike Gingerbread Cottages in Oaks Bluff are popular with kids and adults alike, and Riverhead Field is a great spot for families to try their hand at disc golfing.

It's worth the ferry ride to get to this charming getaway.

Nantucket

Nantucket's population swells in the summer months when wealthy New Englanders descend en masse upon the quaint island 30 miles off the Massachusetts coast. Popular island activities include sunbathing, shopping, cycling and trying out the local cuisine. The island also has plenty of 19th-century buildings, many of which sprung up during Nantucket's heyday as a center for the whaling industry. Popular attractions include the Brant Point Lighthouse, which was originally built back in 1746. The history of whaling is explained in depth at the Nantucket Whaling Museum, and those interested in shipwrecks may want to stop by the Nantucket Shipwreck & Lifesaving Museum. Children and adults can take advantage of the ecology education programs offered by the Maria Mitchell Association, and early risers won't want to miss the glorious sunrises over the island's eastern shore at Siasconset Beach.

See the island on a two wheeler. The many smooth bike paths found on Nantucket are safe for cyclists of all skill levels. Hiking trails also wind throughout the region. The Barn Walk Trail, a 3 mile round trip, takes walkers to panoramic vistas that overlook Cisco Beach. During your journey, keep an eye out for nesting Ospreys.

If you're a fan of flowers, you can visit one of the local farms that cultivate colorful blooms. Check out Moors End Farm, a 28-acre property that sells flowers along with sweet corn, tomatoes and annuals.

Before you leave, don't forget to pick up a pair of Nantucket Reds, the island's famous rust-hued shorts, at Murray's Toggery Shop.

For More Information

Cape Cod Convention & Visitors Bureau
888-332-2732
www.capecodchamber.org

Massachusetts Office of Travel & Tourism
800-227-6277
www.massvacation.com

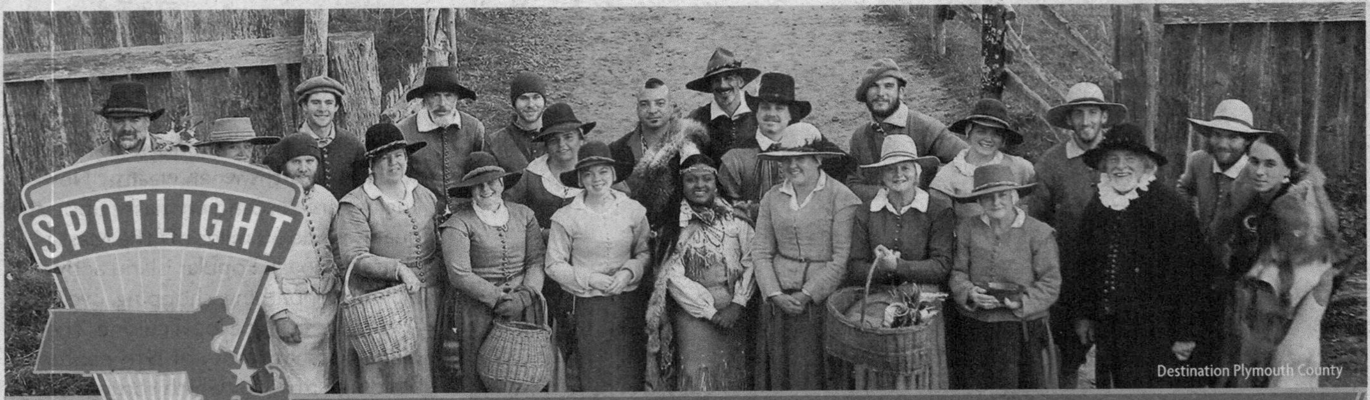

Destination Plymouth County

PLYMOUTH

Make a pilgrimage to a town that started a holiday

From the most famous stepping stone in American history to the first Thanksgiving, the town of Plymouth needs little introduction when it comes to the realm of legend and lore. It was here, in 1620, that the Pilgrims made their first colony.

Having braved the perilous journey across the Atlantic in search of a place to practice their religion in freedom, the Pilgrims came upon the modern-day coast of Massachusetts. Sailing into the calm, protected waters of Cape Cod Bay on the *Mayflower*, they set their sights upon the even calmer, even more protected waters of Plymouth Harbor. As legend tells it, they first alighted on land by stepping first on a small boulder—now known far and wide as the Plymouth Rock.

As in those early days, the modern-day city of Plymouth starts at the water's edge and moves inland. When you first arrive in town most of your attention will be directed at Pilgrim Memorial State Park, which hugs the shores of Plymouth Bay and serves as a kind of doorstep to the downtown area.

Harvesting cranberries from one of the bogs in Plymouth County.
Destination Plymouth County

More than a million people visit this small and humble park annually. The allure of walking in the footsteps of the pilgrims is a major reason why, but so is the park's main attraction: Plymouth Rock. Totaling 10 tons of granite and half buried in sand, the rock is often an underwhelming sight to first-time visitors who are expecting something grander or more visceral. The question of whether or not the rock was actually the first stepping stone to the New World for the inhabitants of the *Mayflower* is also in question. But the magnitude of the rock's symbolism is hard to deny. It not only represents the triumph of an incredible journey, undertaken in the face of discrimination, but also of the years of suffering and hardship that followed.

Mayflower Memories

To learn more about that incredible journey and struggle for survival, you'll want to pay visits to three attractions, each of them operated by the Plimoth Plantation. If you're already at the water's edge, trying to convince yourself the rock is bigger than it looks, start at the *Mayflower II*, which is docked just a short distance away. This fully re-created version of the original *Mayflower* gives curious tour-goers a chance to see what life was like aboard a 17th-century tall ship that braved the high seas of the Atlantic en route to the New World. On deck you'll encounter guides dressed in period costume who recount tales of the journey and life on board the ship.

From the *Mayflower II*, head to the Plimoth Grist Mill, located just a short walk from the waterfront, perched on the shores of Town Brook. The current mill was completed in 1970 but is an exact replica of the one first built in 1636, after the colonists approved the construction of a water-powered corn mill on the same site. The mill is open for touring daily, giving visitors a chance to learn how water from the Town Brook is diverted to mill corn on 200-year-old stones.

Rounding out the triple crown of Plimoth Plantation replicas and reproductions is a re-creation of a 17th-century English village, located at the plantation's headquarters just a few miles east of the city center. Costumed guides and actors populate the village, which is constantly abuzz with communal activity and livestock. Visitors are free to roam the village at their own pace and interact with the actors freely. You might even walk in on a family of pilgrims in the middle of dinner, discussing the colony's news of the day.

Give Thanks for Plymouth

If traveling back in time and chatting with figures of yesteryear isn't quite your cup of tea, more conventional experiences are also available for history buffs. The Pilgrim Hall Museum and the Jenney Museum are each located directly in the center of town, and each is bursting with incredible collections full of artifacts detailing the life and times of the pilgrims. The Pilgrim Hall Museum is a must-visit. Here you can view William Bradford's Bible and the cradle of Peregrine White, the first baby of European descent born in North America.

Finally, if you're visiting near the end of November you'll be in for a major treat. It should come as no surprise that the birthplace of Thanksgiving takes the holiday more than a little seriously. For more than 350 years, the community of Plymouth has celebrated this historic occasion of peace-building and cooperation.

The town's annual Thanksgiving Celebration unfolds over the course of three days each year, weaving a mix of guided walks, live concerts, parades and culminating with a massive outdoor food festival. People dress up as pilgrims and various historic organizations set up living history exhibits throughout town and along the waterfront, where the *Mayflower II* sits anchored in the background.

For More Information

Destination Plymouth County
508-747-7533
www.seeplymouth.com

Massachusetts Office of Travel & Tourism
800-227-6277
www.massvacation.com

MA

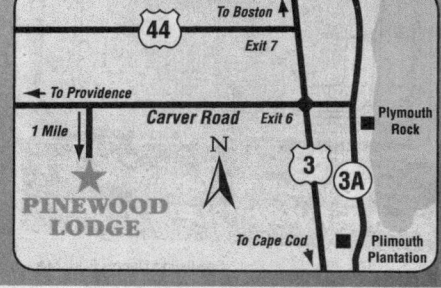

ASHBY — B5 *Middlesex*

THE PINES CAMPGROUND **Ratings: 6.5/6.5/8** (Campground) 2015 rates: $38. (978)386-7702 39 Davis Rd, Ashby, MA 01431

BARRE — B4 *Worcester*

CAMP COLDBROOK GOLF & RV RESORT **Ratings: 7.5/6.5/7** (Campground) 2015 rates: $48. Apr 15 to Oct 15. (978)355-2090 864 Old Coldbrook Rd, Barre, MA 01005

BELLINGHAM — C6 *Norfolk*

CIRCLE CG FARM CAMPGROUND
Ratings: 9.5/9★/9.5 (RV Park) From Jct of MA Pike & I-495, S 12 mi on I-495 to Hwy 126 (exit 18), S 1 mi (L); or From Jct of I-95 & I-495, N 13 mi on I-495 to Hwy 126 (exit 18), S 1 mi (L). **FAC:** Paved rds. (150 spaces). 90 Avail: 63 gravel, 27 grass, 20 pull-thrus (27 x 63), back-ins (25 x 51), some side by side hkups, 63 full hkups, 27 W, 27 E (30/50 amps), seasonal sites, cable, WiFi, tent sites, dump, mobile sewer, laundry, groc, LP gas, fire rings, firewood, controlled access. **REC:** pool, pond, swim, fishing. Pet restrict(B/Q). Big rig sites, eco-friendly, 2015 rates: $38 to $57. Disc: AAA, military. AAA Approved
(508)966-1136 Lat: 42.10128, Lon: -71.47256
131 N Main St, Bellingham, MA 02019
info@circlecgfarm.com
www.circlecgfarm.com
See ad pages 599 (Spotlight Boston), 596.

Park owners want you to be satisfied with your stay. Get to know them.

BERKLEY — D7 *Bristol*

Travel Services

CAMPING WORLD OF BERKLEY As the nation's largest retailer of RV supplies, accessories, services and new and used RVs, Camping World is committed to making your total RV experience better. RV Accessories: (855)869-1876. **SERVICES:** RV Sales. RV supplies, LP. Hours: 8:00 - 6:00.
(888)710-5457 Lat: 41.839492, Lon: -71.012277
137 Myricks Street, Berkley, MA 02779
www.campingworld.com

BERNARDSTON — B3 *Franklin*

TRAVELER'S WOODS OF NEW ENGLAND INC **Ratings: 7/8.5★/8.5** (Campground) 2015 rates: $24 to $27. May 1 to Oct 15. (413)648-9105 152 River Street, Bernardston, MA 01337

BOSTON — C7 *Suffolk*

A SPOTLIGHT Introducing Boston's colorful attractions appearing at the front of this state section.

BOSTON See also Bellingham, Foxboro, Gloucester, Littleton, Mansfield, Plymouth & Salisbury.

BOSTON MINUTEMAN CAMPGROUND
Ratings: 9/10★/10 (Campground) From Jct of I-495 & Rte 2A (exit 30), W 3 mi on Rte 2A (L). **FAC:** Paved/gravel rds. (99 spaces). Avail: 89 gravel, 19 pull-thrus (30 x 54), back-ins (30 x 50), 51 full hkups, 38 W, 38 E (30/50 amps), seasonal sites, cable, WiFi, tent sites, rentals, dump, laundry, groc, LP gas, fire rings, firewood. **REC:** heated pool, playground. Pets OK. Partial handicap access. Big rig sites, eco-friendly, 2015 rates: $46 to $57. Disc: AAA, military. May 1 to Oct 19.
(978)772-0042 Lat: 42.55035, Lon: -71.53736
264 Ayer Road, Littleton, MA 01460
info@minutemancampground.com
www.minutemancampground.com
See primary listing at Littleton and ad page 599 (Spotlight Boston).

NORMANDY FARMS FAMILY CAMPING RESORT
Ratings: 10/10★/10 (Campground) From Jct of I-95 & Rte 1 (exit 9), S 6.7 mi on Rte 1 to Thurston St, E 1.3 mi (R); or From Jct of I-495 & Rte 1 (exit 14A), N 1 mi on Rte 1 to Thurston St (2nd traffic light), E 1.3 mi (R). **FAC:** All weather rds. (393 spaces). Avail: 383 all weather, patios, 262 pull-thrus (40 x 60), back-ins (33 x 48), 229 full hkups, 110 W, 110 E (30/50 amps), seasonal sites, cable, WiFi, tent sites, rentals, dump, mobile sewer, laundry, groc, LP gas, fire rings, firewood, controlled access. **REC:** heated pool, whirlpool, pond, swim, fishing, shuffleboard, playground. Pets OK. Partial handicap access. Big rig sites, eco-friendly, 2015 rates: $51 to $84. Disc: military. Apr 1 to Nov 30. ATM.
(866)673-2767 Lat: 42.04033, Lon: -71.28069
72 West St, Foxboro, MA 02035
camp@normandyfarms.com
www.normandyfarms.com
See primary listing at Foxboro and ad page 597 (Spotlight Boston).

PINEWOOD LODGE CAMPGROUND
Ratings: 8/9★/10 (Campground) From of US 44 & SR 3 (ext 7) S1mi on SR 3 to Carver Rd (exit 6B), W 2.8 mi to Pinewood R .5 mi(R). **FAC:** Paved/gravel rds. (290 spaces). Avail: 170 gravel, 19 pull-thrus (25 x 60), back-ins (39 x 50), 68 full hkups, 102 W, 102 E (30/50 amps), seasonal sites, cable, WiFi $, tent sites, rentals, showers $, dump, mobile sewer, laundry, groc, LP gas, fire rings, firewood, controlled access. **REC:** Pinewood Lake: swim, fishing, playground. Pet restrict(B/Q) $. Partial handicap access. Big rig sites, eco-friendly, 2015 rates: $41 to $53. Disc: military. May 1 to Oct 30. ATM.
(508)746-3548 Lat: 41.92654, Lon: -70.73417
190 Pinewood Rd, Plymouth, MA 02630
camp@pinewoodlodge.com
www.pinewoodlodge.com
See primary listing at Plymouth and ad page 605 (Spotlight Plymouth).

BOURNE — E8 *Barnstable*

BAY VIEW CAMPGROUND
Ratings: 9.5/10★/9.5 (Campground) From Jct of I-195 & I-495/Rte 25, SE 9 mi on Rte 25 to Bourne bridge (over bridge to Rotary) to Rte 28S, S 1.2 mi (R). **FAC:** Paved rds. (420 spaces). 130 Avail: 80 gravel, 50 dirt, 7 pull-thrus (35 x 70), back-ins (30 x 45), 90 full hkups, 40 W, 40 E (30/50 amps), seasonal sites, cable, WiFi, tent sites, dump, laundry, groc, LP bottles, fire rings, firewood, restaurant. **REC:** pool, shuffleboard, playground. Pet restrict(Q). Partial handicap access. Big rig sites, 2015 rates: $53 to $65. May 1 to Oct 15.
(508)759-7610 Lat: 41.72547, Lon: -70.58525
260 Macarthur Blvd, Bourne, MA 02532
info@bayviewcampground.com
www.bayviewcampground.com
See ad page 600 (Spotlight Cape Cod).

BOURNE SCENIC PARK (Public) From Jct I-495 & US-6, go around Rotary, staying on US-6, N 300 ft on (R) (Beneath north end of Bourne Bridge). 2015 rates: $44 to $52. Apr 1 to Oct 30. (508)759-7873

BREWSTER — D10 *Barnstable*

NICKERSON (State Pk) From Jct of Hwy 6A & Hwy 6, W 1.5 mi on Hwy 6A (L). Note: No outside firewood permitted. 2015 rates: $15 to $17. Apr 17 to Nov 1. (508)896-3491

SHADY KNOLL CAMPGROUND
Ratings: 7.5/10★/9 (Campground) From Jct of SR-6 & Hwy 137 (exit 11), N 5 mi on Hwy 137 to Jct of Rte 6A & Hwy 137 (E) Maximum trailer length 35'. **FAC:** Gravel rds. (100 spaces). Avail: 55 gravel, 6 pull-thrus (29 x 67), back-ins (23 x 50), 20 full hkups, 35 W, 35 E (20/30 amps), seasonal sites, cable, WiFi, tent sites, dump, laundry, fire rings, firewood. **REC:** Cape Cod Bay: playground. Pet restrict(Q) $. Partial handicap access. 2015 rates: $51 to $63. May 15 to Oct 10.
(508)896-3002 Lat: 41.75742, Lon: -70.08859
1709 Main St, Brewster, MA 02631
shady_knoll@capecamping.com
www.shadyknoll.com
See ad pages 602 (Spotlight Cape Cod), 596.

SWEETWATER FOREST CAMPING RESORT **Ratings: 6/9★/9** (Campground) 2015 rates: $48 to $60. Apr 1 to Nov 1. (508)896-3773 676 Harwich Rd, Brewster, MA 02631

BRIMFIELD — C4 *Hampden*

VILLAGE GREEN FAMILY CAMPGROUND **Ratings: 7.5/9★/7.5** (Campground) 2015 rates: $32. May 1 to Nov 1. (413)245-3504 228 Sturbridge Rd, Brimfield, MA 01010

CAPE COD — D10 *Barnstable*

A SPOTLIGHT Introducing Cape Cod's colorful attractions appearing at the front of this state section.

CAPE COD (CONT)

CAPE COD See also Bourne, Brewster, Dennis Port, East Falmouth, East Wareham, Eastham, Falmouth, North Truro, Plymouth, Provincetown, Sandwich, South Dennis & Wellfleet.

BAY VIEW CAMPGROUND
Ratings: 9.5/10★/9.5 (Campground) From Jct of I-195 & I-495/Rte 25, SE 9mi on Rte 25 to Bourne bridge (over bridge to Rotary) to Rte 28S, S 1.2mi (R). **FAC:** Paved rds. (420 spaces). 130 Avail: 80 gravel, 50 dirt, 7 pull-thrus (35 x 70), back-ins (30 x 45), 90 full hkups, 40 W, 40 E (30/50 amps), seasonal sites, cable, WiFi, tent sites, dump, laundry, groc, LP bottles, fire rings, firewood, restaurant. **REC:** pool, shuffleboard, playground. Pet restrict(Q). Partial handicap access. Big rig sites, 2015 rates: $45 to $65. May 1 to Oct 15.
(508)759-7610 Lat: 41.72547, Lon: -70.58525
260 Macarthur, Bourne, MA 02532
info@bayviewcampground.com
www.bayviewcampground.com
See primary listing at Bourne and ad page 600 (Spotlight Cape Cod).

CAPE COD CAMPRESORT & CABINS
Ratings: 10/10★/10 (Campground) From Jct of Rte 28 S & Thomas B Lander Rd, E 2.5mi on Thomas B Landers Rd (R). **FAC:** Paved rds. (230 spaces). Avail: 210 paved, 2 pull-thrus (30 x 80), back-ins (30 x 55), 210 full hkups (30/50 amps), seasonal sites, WiFi, tent sites, rentals, dump, laundry, groc, fire rings, firewood, controlled access. **REC:** heated pool, wading pool, whirlpool, pond, swim, fishing, playground. Pet restrict(B) $. Partial handicap access. Big rig sites, 2015 rates: $69 to $107. May 1 to Oct 15.
(508)548-1458 Lat: 41.60614, Lon: -70.57675
176 Thomas B Landers Rd, East Falmouth, MA 02536
camp@campresort.com
wwwcapecampresort.com
See primary listing at East Falmouth and ad page 601 (Spotlight Cape Cod), 594 (MA Map).

CARVER — D8 *Plymouth*

SHADY ACRES **Ratings: 8/10★/7.5** (Campground) 2015 rates: $52 to $68. Apr 15 to Oct 15. (508)866-4040 20 Shoestring Rd, Carver, MA 02330

CHARLEMONT — B2 *Franklin*

COUNTRY AIRE CAMPGROUND
Ratings: 9/9★/9 (Campground) From Jct of I-91 & Rte 2 (exit 26), W 13 mi on Rte 2 (R). **FAC:** Paved/gravel rds. (165 spaces). Avail: 96 grass, 55 pull-thrus (30 x 75), back-ins (30 x 55), 27 full hkups, 45 W, 45 E (30/50 amps), seasonal sites, cable, WiFi, tent sites, rentals, showers $, dump, mobile sewer, laundry, groc, LP gas, fire rings, firewood, controlled access. **REC:** heated pool, Wilder Brook: fishing, playground. Pet restrict(B/Q). Big rig sites, eco-friendly, 2015 rates: $35 to $40. Disc: military. May 1 to Oct 31. ATM.
(413)625-2996 Lat: 42.6210041, Lon: -72.7906029
1753 Mohawk Trail, Shelburne Falls, MA 01370
countryairecampground@verizon.net
www.countryairecampground.com
See ad this page.

MOHAWK TRAIL STATE FOREST (State Pk) From town: Go 4 mi W on Hwy 2.Note: No outside firewood permitted. 2015 rates: $12 to $14. Apr 16 to Oct 11. (413)339-5504

CLARKSBURG — B2 *Berkshire*

CLARKSBURG (State Pk) From town: Go N on Hwy 8, then follow signs on Middle Rd. Note: No outside firewood permitted. 2015 rates: $12 to $14. May 21 to Oct 11. (413)664-8345

DENNIS PORT — E10 *Barnstable*

CAMPERS HAVEN CAREFREE RV RESORT
Ratings: 9/9/9 (RV Park) From Jct of US 6 & Hwy 134 (Exit 9A), S 2 mi on Hwy 134 (then cross Rte 28) to Swan River Rd, S 1 mi to Lower County Rd, E 0.3 mi to Old Wharf Rd, SE 0.75 mi (L). No pets June, July, August. **FAC:** Paved rds. (275 spaces). 30 Avail: 20 paved, 10 gravel, patios, 5 pull-thrus (30 x 75), back-ins (21 x 38), 30 full hkups (30/50 amps), seasonal sites, cable, WiFi, tent sites, rentals, showers $, dump, mobile sewer, laundry, groc, controlled access. **REC:** Atlantic Ocean: swim, playground. No pets. Partial handicap access. Eco-friendly, 2015 rates: $49 to $73. May 1 to Oct 14.
(508)398-2811 Lat: 41.651456, Lon: -70.14147
184 Old Wharf Rd, Dennis Port, MA 02639
campershaven@carefreervresorts.com
www.carefreervresorts.com
See ad opposite page, 596.

DOUGLAS — D5 *Worcester*

LAKE MANCHAUG CAMPING **Ratings: 7/7.5/9** (Campground) 2015 rates: $50 to $75. May 1 to Oct 1. (508)476-2471 76 Oak Street, Douglas, MA 01516

EAST FALMOUTH — E8 *Barnstable*

CAPE COD CAMPRESORT & CABINS
Ratings: 10/10★/10 (Campground) From Jct of Rte 28S & Thomas B Landers Rd, E 2.5 mi on Thomas B Landers Rd (R).

SCENIC OLDE CAPE COD
We are located in the heart of scenic Olde Cape Cod. Relax on the beach or around one of the pools. If you wish, a short drive will bring you to the ferries to the islands, or take a day trip to Provincetown or Hyannis.

FAC: Paved rds. (230 spaces). Avail: 210 paved, 2 pull-thrus (30 x 80), back-ins (30 x 55), 210 full hkups (30/50 amps), seasonal sites, WiFi, tent sites, rentals, dump, laundry, groc, fire rings, firewood, controlled access. **REC:** heated pool, wading pool, whirlpool, pond, swim, fishing, playground. Pet restrict(B) $. Partial handicap access. Big rig sites, 2015 rates: $69 to $107. May 1 to Oct 15.
(508)548-1458 Lat: 41.60614, Lon: -70.57675
176 Thomas B Landers Rd, East Falmouth, MA 02536
camp@capecampresort.com
www.capecampresort.com
See ad pages 601 (Spotlight Cape Cod), 596, 594 (MA Map).

EAST OTIS — C2 *Berkshire*

LAUREL RIDGE CAMPING AREA, INC **Ratings: 6.5/5/6.5** (Campground) 2015 rates: $36. May 4 to Oct 13. (800)538-CAMP 40 Old Blandford Rd, Otis, MA 01029

EAST WAREHAM — D8 *Plymouth*

CAPE COD'S MAPLE PARK CAMPGROUND & RV PARK
Ratings: 7.5/8★/7.5 (Campground) From Jct of Rte 25 & SR-6 (exit 2), E 0.6 mi on SR-6 to Glen Charlie Rd, N 2 mi (L). **FAC:** Paved/gravel rds. (450 spaces). Avail: 269 dirt, 3 pull-thrus (30 x 70), back-ins (23 x 40), some side by side hkups, 200 full hkups, 69 W, 69 E (30/50 amps), seasonal sites, WiFi Hotspot, tent sites, rentals, showers $, dump, laundry, groc, LP bottles, fire rings, firewood, controlled access. **REC:** pond, swim, fishing, playground. Pet restrict(B). Partial handicap access. 2015 rates: $38 to $68. May 1 to Oct 15.
(508)295-4945 Lat: 41.78107, Lon: -70.65061
290 Glen Charlie Rd, East Wareham, MA 02538
info@capecodmaplepark.com
www.capecodmaplepark.com
See ad page 602 (Spotlight Cape Cod).

EASTHAM — D10 *Barnstable*

ATLANTIC OAKS
Ratings: 8/10★/9 (Campground) From Jct of US-6 & Orleans Rotary, N 4 mi on US-6 (R). **FAC:** Gravel rds. (100 spaces). Avail: 70 gravel, 70 pull-thrus (30 x 70), 70 full hkups (30/50 amps), seasonal sites, cable, WiFi, tent sites, rentals, laundry, groc, LP gas, fire rings, firewood, controlled access. **REC:** Atlantic Ocean: playground. Pet restrict(B/Q) $. Partial handicap access. Big rig sites, eco-friendly, 2015 rates: $56 to $68. May 1 to Nov 1.
(508)255-1437 Lat: 41.84536, Lon: -69.98421
3700 State Hwy, Eastham, MA 02642
atlanticoaks3700@capecamping.com
www.atlanticoaks.com
See ad pages 602 (Spotlight Cape Cod), 596.

ERVING — B4 *Franklin*

ERVING STATE FOREST (State Pk) From town: Go E on Hwy 2, then turn at fire station & follow signs. Note: No outside firewood permitted. 2015 rates: $12 to $14. May 21 to Sep 6. (978)544-3939

FALMOUTH — E8 *Barnstable*

SIPPEWISSETT CAMPGROUND/CABINS Ratings: 6/6/7.5 (Campground) From Jct of US-6 & Rte 28 (Bourne Bridge), S 12.5 mi on Rte 28 to Sippewissett (Rte 28A) exit (Palmer Ave), SW 0.5 mi (R). NOTE: Suggested unit length under 34 ft. **FAC:** Poor paved/dirt rds. (100 spaces). 58 Avail: 29 grass, 29 dirt, back-ins (20 x 31), 58 W, 58 E (20/30 amps), seasonal sites, WiFi, tent sites, rentals, dump, mobile sewer, laundry, fire rings, firewood, controlled access. **REC:** playground. No pets. 2015 rates: $50. May 15 to Oct 15. ATM.
AAA Approved
(508)548-2542 Lat: 41.57755, Lon: -70.62939
836 Palmer Ave, Falmouth, MA 02540
information@sippewissett.com
www.sippewissett.com

Treat your pet to a fabulous camping experience by staying at one of the Pampered Pet Parks featured in the front of the Guide.

FOXBORO — D7 *Norfolk*

NORMANDY FARMS FAMILY CAMPING RESORT
Ratings: 10/10★/10 (Campground) From Jct of I-95 & Rte 1 (exit 9), S 6.7 mi on Rte 1 to Thurston St, E 1.3 mi (R); or From Jct of I-495 & Rte 1 (exit 14A), N 1 mi on Rte 1 to Thurston St (2nd traffic light), E 1.3 mi (R).

YOUR LUXURY CAMPING DESTINATION
Nestled deep in the woods between Boston & Cape Cod, Normandy Farms is a luxury camping destination that has been a family tradition since 1971 and widely recognized as one of the premier resorts in the world.

FAC: All weather rds. (393 spaces). Avail: 383 all weather, patios, 262 pull-thrus (40 x 55), back-ins (33 x 48), 229 full hkups, 110 W, 110 E (30/50 amps), seasonal sites, cable, WiFi, tent sites, rentals, dump, mobile sewer, laundry, groc, LP gas, fire rings, firewood, controlled access. **REC:** heated pool, whirlpool, pond, swim, fishing, shuffleboard, playground. Pets OK. Partial handicap access. Big rig sites, eco-friendly, 2015 rates: $60 to $84. Disc: military. Apr 1 to Nov 30. ATM.
(866)673-2767 Lat: 42.04033, Lon: -71.28069
72 West St, Foxboro, MA 02035
camp@normandyfarms.com
www.normandyfarms.com
See ad pages 597 (Spotlight Boston), 596 & Pampered Pets in Magazine Section.

GLOUCESTER — B8 *Essex*

CAPE ANN CAMP SITE
Ratings: 5.5/7.5/7.5 (Campground) From Jct of Hwy 128 & Concord St (exit 13), N 0.7 mi on Concord St to Atlantic St, E 0.6 mi (L). **FAC:** Paved/gravel rds. (230 spaces). 190 Avail: 15 paved, 95 grass, 80 dirt, back-ins (22 x 45), some side by side hkups, 45 full hkups, 145 W, 145 E (30/50 amps), seasonal sites, WiFi Hotspot, tent sites, showers $, dump, groc, fire rings, firewood. **REC.** Pets OK. Big rig sites, 2015 rates: $50 to $60. May 15 to Oct 15.
(978)283-8683 Lat: 42.63966, Lon: -70.70058
80 Atlantic St, Gloucester, MA 01930
info@capeanncampsite.com
www.capeanncampsite.com
See ad opposite page.

GOSHEN — B3 *Hampshire*

D A R SF (State Pk) From town, NW 0.25 mi on Rte 9 to Rte 112, N 0.75 mi, E 0.75 mi (L). Note: No outside firewood permitted. 2015 rates: $12 to $14. (413)268-7098

GRANVILLE — D2 *Hampden*

PROSPECT MOUNTAIN CAMPGROUND/RV PARK **Ratings: 8/7/6.5** (Campground) 2015 rates: $37 to $52. May 1 to Oct 15. (888)550-4762 1349 Main Rd (Rt 57), Granville, MA 01034

HINGHAM — C8 *Norfolk, Plymouth*

WOMPATUCK (State Pk) In town, S 1.75 mi on Central St/SR-228 to Free St, E 1 mi to Union St, S 1.5 mi (R). Note: No outside firewood permitted. 2015 rates: $12 to $14. May 1 to Oct 11. (781)749-7160

LANESBOROUGH — B2 *Berkshire*

HIDDEN VALLEY CAMPGROUND **Ratings: 7/6/7** (Campground) 2015 rates: $33 to $38. (413)447-9419 15 Scott Rd, Lanesborough, MA 01237

LENOX — C1 *Berkshire*

WOODLAND HILLS CAMPGROUND
Ratings: 7/8/9.5 (Campground) From Main St. & SR-183: Go W 4.5 mi on SR-183 to SR-102, then W 6 mi on SR-102 to SR-22, then S 1.5 mi on SR-22 to Middle Rd, then W .5 mi on Middle Rd to Fog Hill Rd, then N .75 mi on Fog Hill Rd (L). **FAC:** Gravel rds. (190 spaces). Avail: 90 grass, 3 pull-thrus (30 x 50), back-ins (30 x 45), 47 full hkups, 43 W, 43 E (30/50 amps), seasonal sites, WiFi, tent sites, rentals, showers $, dump, mobile sewer, laundry, groc, LP gas, fire rings, firewood. **REC:** pond, swim, fishing, playground. Pets OK. Eco-friendly, 2015 rates: $35 to $39. May 15 to Oct 10.
(518)392-3557 Lat: 42.34490, Lon: -73.44202
360 Fog Hill Rd, Austerlitz, NY 12017
info@whcg.net
www.whcg.net
See primary listing at Austerlitz, NY and ad page 824.

Take an RV Trip of a Lifetime! Check out trip ideas at the front of the Guide - you'll find something for the history buff, the food lover or even your wild side!

SPRINGFIELD/STURBRIDGE AREA

Good Sam Park
Good Sam RATED 9/9.5★/9
WIFI HOTSPOT

SERVING CAMPERS FOR OVER 45 YEARS

- Big Rigs • Call For Best Route
- 30/50-Amp Pull-Thru Sites
- Swimming Pool & Pond w/Beach

(413) 267-9269
www.Sunsetview.com
See listing Monson, MA

LITTLETON — B6 *Middlesex*

BOSTON MINUTEMAN CAMPGROUND
Ratings: 9/10★/10 (Campground) From Jct of I-495 & Rte 2A (exit 30), W 3 mi on Rte 2A (L). **FAC:** Paved/gravel rds. (99 spaces). Avail: 89 gravel, 19 pull-thrus (30 x 54), back-ins (30 x 50), 51 full hkups, 38 W, 38 E (30/50 amps), seasonal sites, cable, WiFi, tent sites, rentals, dump, laundry, groc, LP gas, fire rings, firewood. **REC:** heated pool, playground. Pets OK. Partial handicap access. Big rig sites, eco-friendly, 2015 rates: $53 to $57. Disc: AAA, military. May 6 to Oct 16.
AAA Approved
(978)772-0042 Lat: 42.55035, Lon: -71.53736
264 Ayer Road, Littleton, MA 01460
info@minutemancampground.com
www.minutemancampground.com
See ad pages 599 (Spotlight Boston), 596.

MANSFIELD — D7 *Norfolk, Bristol*

CANOE RIVER CAMPGROUND
Ratings: 8.5/7.5/8.5 (Campground) From Jct of I-495 & Rte 123 (exit 10), E 0.8 mi on Rte 123 to Newland St, N 2 mi (L); or From Jct of I-95 (exit 7A), Rte 140S & Hwy 106, E 3 mi on Hwy 106 to East St, S 0.4 mi onto Mill St (bear right), S 0.5 mi (R). **FAC:** Paved/gravel rds. (250 spaces). 160 Avail: 100 gravel, 60 grass, 23 pull-thrus (27 x 52), back-ins (30 x 65), 160 full hkups (30/50 amps), seasonal sites, WiFi $, tent sites, rentals, showers $, dump, laundry, groc, LP gas, fire rings, firewood, controlled access. **REC:** pool, pond, swim, fishing, playground. Pet restrict(B/Q). Partial handicap access. 2015 rates: $42 to $50. Apr 15 to Oct 15. ATM.
AAA Approved
(508)339-6462 Lat: 42.01951, Lon: -71.18079
137 Mill St, Mansfield, MA 02048
office@canoeriver.com
www.canoeriver.com
See ad page 598 (Spotlight Boston).

MIDDLEBORO — D8 *Plymouth*

BOSTON/CAPE COD KOA KAMPGROUND **Ratings: 8.5/10★/9.5** (Campground) 2015 rates: $44 to $66. Mar 1 to Nov 15. (800)562-3046 438 Plymouth Street, Middleboro, MA 02346

MONSON — C4 *Hampden*

PARTRIDGE HOLLOW CAMPING AREA **Ratings: 7.5/9★/9** (Campground) 2015 rates: $30 to $45. Apr 20 to Oct 15. (413)267-5122 72 Sutcliffe Rd, Monson, MA 01057

SUNSETVIEW FARM CAMPING AREA, INC
Ratings: 9/9.5★/9 (Campground) E-bnd: From Jct of MA Pike & Rte 32 (exit 8), S 2.5 mi on Rte 32 to Fenton Rd, E 0.5 mi to Town Farm Rd, S 1.5 mi (L); or N-bnd: From CT: From Jct of I-84 & Rte 32 (exit 70), N 17 mi on Rte 32 to Brimfield Rd (in town), E 2 mi to Town Farm Rd, N 0.5 mi (R). **FAC:** Gravel rds. (200 spaces). 80 Avail: 50 grass, 30 dirt, 26 pull-thrus (30 x 60), back-ins (33 x 43), 55 full hkups, 25 W, 25 E (30/50 amps), seasonal sites, WiFi, tent sites, showers $, dump, mobile sewer, laundry, groc, fire rings, firewood, controlled access. **REC:** pool, pond, swim, playground. Pet restrict(Q). Partial handicap access. Big rig sites, eco-friendly, 2015 rates: $38 to $56. Apr 15 to Oct 15.
AAA Approved
(413)267-9269 Lat: 42.12160, Lon: -72.29462
57 Town Farm Rd, Monson, MA 01057
camp@sunsetview.com
www.sunsetview.com
See ad this page, 596.

NORTH ADAMS — B2 *Berkshire*

HISTORIC VALLEY CAMPGROUND (Public) From Jct of SR-2 & E Main St, W 0.25 mi on E Main St to Kemp Ave, S 1 mi (E). 2015 rates: $30 to $35. May 15 to Oct 15. (413)662-3198

NORTH ANDOVER — B7 *Essex*

HAROLD PARKER SF (State Pk) From Jct of I-93 & Hwy 125, N 2.5 mi on Hwy 125 (R). Note: No outside firewood permitted. 2015 rates: $12 to $14. May 21 to Oct 11. (978)686-3391

We rate what RVers consider important.

Big Rig Friendly
Lakeside Cabins & RV Rentals
www.PineAcresResort.com
508-882-9509

NORTH EGREMONT — C1 *Berkshire*

PROSPECT LAKE PARK **Ratings: 6.5/5.5/7** (Campground) 2015 rates: $32 to $36. May 1 to Oct 15. (413)528-4158 50 Prospect Lake Rd, North Egremont, MA 01230

NORTH TRURO — D10 *Barnstable*

ADVENTURE BOUND CAMPING RESORTS-NORTH TRURO **Ratings: 7/9★/8** (Campground) 2015 rates: $74. Apr 1 to Oct 30. (508)487-1847 46 Highland Rd, North Truro, MA 02652

HORTON'S CAMPING RESORT **Ratings: 4.5/5.5/6.5** (Campground) 2015 rates: $56 to $74. May 30 to Sep 30. (508)487-1847 71 South Highland Rd, North Truro, MA 02652

NORTH OF HIGHLAND **Ratings: 5.5/8.5★/7.5** (Campground) 2015 rates: $40. May 22 to Oct 10. (508)487-1191 52 Head of Meadow Dr, North Truro, MA 02652

OAKHAM — C5 *Worcester*

PINE ACRES FAMILY CAMPING RESORT

Ratings: 10/10★/10 (Campground) From Jct of Hwy 122 & Hwy 148, SW 2 mi on Rte 148 to Spencer Rd, S 0.1 mi to Bechan Rd, E 0.4 mi (L).

DISCOVER YOUR FAMILY FUN GETAWAY
We offer a variety of campsites and rentals for everyone's pleasure. Enjoy boating and fishing on the lake or relax at the pool while the kids play in the splashpad. You don't need to travel far to experience being away!

FAC: Paved rds. (350 spaces). Avail: 260 paved, 5 pull-thrus (30 x 60), back-ins (35 x 55), 150 full hkups, 110 W, 110 E (30/50 amps), seasonal sites, cable, WiFi $, tent sites, rentals, dump, mobile sewer, laundry, groc, LP gas, fire rings, firewood, restaurant, controlled access. **REC:** heated pool, whirlpool, Lake Dean: swim, fishing, playground. Pet restrict(Q) $. Partial handicap access. Big rig sites, eco-friendly, 2015 rates: $41 to $70. Disc: military. ATM.
(508)882-9509 Lat: 42.34019, Lon: -72.02689
203 Bechan Rd, Oakham, MA 01068
camp@pineacresresort.com
www.pineacresresort.com
See ad opposite page, 596.

OTIS — C2 *Berkshire*

TOLLAND STATE FOREST (State Pk) From Jct of MA Pike (I-90) & Rte 20 (exit 2), E 8 mi on Rte 20 to Rte 8S, S 5 mi to Rte 23, E 4 mi to Reservoir Rd, S follow signs (L). Note: No outside firewood permitted. 2015 rates: $12 to $14. May 21 to Oct 25. (413)269-6002

PHILLIPSTON — B4 *Worcester*

LAMB CITY CAMPGROUND

Ratings: 9/9★/9 (Campground) E-bnd: From Jct of Rtes 2 & 2A (Exit 19), N 0.1 mi on Rte 2A to Royalston Rd, W 0.5 mi (L); or W-bnd: From Jct of Rtes 2 & 2A (Exit 19), W 300 ft on Rte 2A to Royalston Rd, W 0.5 mi (L). **FAC:** Paved/gravel rds. (230 spaces). 70 Avail: 35 gravel, 35 grass, 6 pull-thrus (30 x 67), back-ins (30 x 50), 58 full hkups, 12 W, 12 E (30/50 amps), seasonal sites, cable, WiFi, tent sites, rentals, dump, laundry, groc, LP gas, fire rings, firewood, controlled access. **REC:** pool, wading pool, pond, swim, fishing, shuffleboard, playground. Pet restrict(B). Big rig sites, eco-friendly, 2015 rates: $31 to $44. Disc: AAA. ATM.
(800)292-5262 Lat: 42.57687, Lon: -72.13142
85 Royalston Rd, Phillipston, MA 01331
lambcity@comcast.net
www.lambcity.com
See ad this page.

PITTSFIELD — B1 *Berkshire*

BONNIE BRAE CABINS & CAMPSITES **Ratings: 6/8/7.5** (Campground) 2015 rates: $39. May 1 to Oct 15. (413)442-3754 108 Broadway, Pittsfield, MA 01201

PLAINFIELD — B2 *Hampshire*

PEPPERMINT PARK CAMPING RESORT **Ratings: 8.5/7.5/8** (Campground) 2015 rates: $38 to $42. (413)634-5385 169 Grant St, Plainfield, MA 01070

PLYMOUTH — D8 *Plymouth*

ELLIS HAVEN CAMPING RESORT **Ratings: 7.5/7/7.5** (Campground) 2015 rates: $52 to $55. May 1 to Oct 13. (508)746-0803 531 Federal Furnace Rd, Plymouth, MA 02360

INDIANHEAD RESORT **Ratings: 4.5/6/7.5** (Campground) 2015 rates: $40. Apr 13 to Oct 10. (508)888-3688 1929 State Rd, Plymouth, MA 02360

PINEWOOD LODGE CAMPGROUND

Ratings: 8/9★/10 (Campground) From jct of US 44 & SR 3 (exit 7) S on SR 3 1 mi to Carver Rd (exit 6B), W 2.8 mi to Pinewood R, S 0.5 mi (ahead).

PLYMOUTH-BETWEEN BOSTON & CAPE COD
This beautiful campground is nestled in 200 acres of white pine forest & pristine Pinewood Lake. Come and join us for fishing, swimming or boating in "The Land of Pinewood," where friendships glow as warm as the campfire.

FAC: Paved/gravel rds. (290 spaces). Avail: 170 gravel, 19 pull-thrus (25 x 60), back-ins (39 x 50), 68 full hkups, 102 W, 102 E (30/50 amps), seasonal sites, cable, WiFi, tent sites, rentals, showers $, dump, mobile sewer, laundry, groc, LP gas, fire rings, firewood, controlled access. **REC:** Pinewood Lake: swim, fishing, playground. Pet restrict(B/Q) $. Partial handicap access. Big rig sites, eco-friendly, 2015 rates: $35 to $70. Disc: military. May 1 to Oct 30. ATM.
AAA Approved
(508)746-3548 Lat: 41.92654, Lon: -70.73417
190 Pinewood Rd, Plymouth, MA 02360
camp@pinewoodlodge.com
www.pinewoodlodge.com
See ad pages 605 (Spotlight Plymouth), 596.

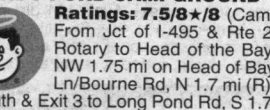

SANDY POND CAMPGROUND

Ratings: 7.5/8★/8 (Campground) From Jct of I-495 & Rte 25 (exit 3), to Rotary to Head of the Bay Rd, (1st Rt) NW 1.75 mi on Head of Bay to Plymouth Ln/Bourne Rd, N 1.7 mi (R); or Jct of Rte 3 South & Exit 3 to Long Pond Rd, S 1.75 mi on Long Pond Rd to Halfway Pond, W 0.75 mi to Bourne Rd, S 4.3 mi (L). **FAC:** Gravel rds. (225 spaces). Avail: 140 grass, 12 pull-thrus (38 x 63), back-ins (36 x 48), 65 full hkups, 75 W, 75 E (30/50 amps), seasonal sites, cable, WiFi, tent sites, rentals, showers $, dump, mobile sewer, laundry, groc, LP gas, fire rings, firewood, controlled access. **REC:** pond, swim, fishing, playground. Pet restrict(B/Q) $. Partial handicap access. Big rig sites, eco-friendly, 2015 rates: $52 to $61. Disc: AAA, military. Apr 15 to Oct 15. ATM.
AAA Approved
(508)759-9336 Lat: 41.79281, Lon: -70.60384
834 Bourne Rd, Plymouth, MA 02360
info@sandypond.com
www.sandypond.com
See ad pages 604 (Spotlight Plymouth), 596.

Travel Services

PINEWOOD LODGE RV SERVICE Mobile RV Service & Supplies. May 1 to Oct 30. **SERVICES:** RV appliance, mobile RV svc, restrooms. RV supplies, LP, dump, emergency parking, RV accessible. waiting room. Hours: 9am to 5pm. ATM.
(508)746-3548 Lat: 41.92281, Lon: -70.73928
190 Pinewood Dr, Plymouth, MA 02360
camp@pinewoodlodge.com
www.pinewoodlodge.com
See ad page 605 (Spotlight Plymouth).

PROVINCETOWN — D9 *Barnstable*

COASTAL ACRES CAMPING COURT **Ratings: 4.5/9★/7.5** (Campground) 2015 rates: $56 to $60. Apr 1 to Nov 1. (508)487-1700 76 R Bayberry Ave, Provincetown, MA 02657

ROCHESTER — E8 *Plymouth*

GATEWAY TO CAPE COD **Ratings: 8/7.5/8** (Membership Pk) 2015 rates: $47 to $60. Apr 20 to Oct 15. (800)405-6188 90 Stevens Rd, Rochester, MA 02770

RUTLAND — C5 *Worcester*

POUT & TROUT FAMILY CAMPGROUND **Ratings: 6/5/5** (Campground) 2015 rates: $29. Apr 14 to Oct 18. (508)886-6677 94 River Rd, Rutland, MA 01543

SALEM — B8 *Essex*

WINTER ISLAND PARK (Public) From jct Derby St & Fort Ave in town: Go 3/4 mi NE on Fort Ave, then 1/2 mi E on Winter Island Rd. 2015 rates: $37 to $47. May 1 to Nov 1. (978)745-9430

SALISBURY — A8 *Essex*

BLACK BEAR CAMPGROUND

Ratings: 9/9.5★/9.5 (Campground) N-bnd: From Jct of I-495 & I-95, N 0.5 mi on I-95 to Exit 60 to 1st set of lights (Main St), E 0.1 mi (L); or S-bnd: From Jct of I-95 & Exit 60, exit rd to 1st set of lights (Main St), E 0.1 mi (L). **FAC:** Gravel rds. (262 spaces). Avail: 192 gravel, 20 pull-thrus (32 x 65), back-ins (30 x 50), 192 full hkups (30/50 amps), seasonal sites, cable, WiFi, tent sites, showers $, dump, laundry, fire rings, firewood, controlled access. **REC:** pool, playground. Pet restrict Partial handicap access. Big rig sites, 2015 rates: $45 to $55. May 15 to Sep 30.
(978)462-3183 Lat: 42.87089, Lon: -70.88153
54 Main St, Salisbury, MA 01952
bbcamping@aol.com
www.blackbearcamping.com
See ad page 610.

RUSNIK CAMPGROUND

Ratings: 8/8.5★/8.5 (Campground) N-bnd: From Jct of I-495 & Rte 110 (exit 55), E 3.5 mi on Rte 110 to Rte 1, N 1 mi (L); or S-bnd: From Jct of I-95 & Rte 110/exit 58 (or I-95 N-bnd/exit 58A), E 2.4 mi on Rte 110 to Rte 1, N 1 mi (L). **FAC:** Gravel rds. (150 spaces). 60 Avail: 30 grass, 30 dirt, back-ins (30 x 38), 60 W, 60 E (30 amps), seasonal sites, WiFi Hotspot, tent sites, rentals, showers $, dump, mobile sewer, laundry, fire rings, firewood, controlled access. **REC:** pool, shuffleboard, playground. Pets OK. 2015 rates: $32 to $42. May 15 to Oct 10.
(978)462-9551 Lat: 42.85521, Lon: -70.87157
115 Lafayette Rd, Salisbury, MA 01952
rusnik2001@aol.com
www.rusnikcampground.com
See ad pages 606, 596.

SALISBURY BEACH STATE RESERVATION (State Pk) From Jct I-95 & SR-110, E 3.5 mi on SR-110 to Rte 1A, E 2 mi (R). 2015 rates: $15 to $17. Apr 16 to Nov 28. (877)422-6762

THE PINES CAMPING AREA

Ratings: 7/8/7.5 (Campground) From Jct of I-95 & Rte 110 (exit 58), E 3 mi on Rte 110 to Rte 1A, E 0.5 mi to Glenwood Ave, S 100 ft to CCC Rd, SE 0.5 mi (E). **FAC:** Poor gravel/dirt rds. (180 spaces). 40 Avail: 20 gravel, 20 dirt, 5 pull-thrus (24 x 40), back-ins (20 x 38), some side by side hkups, 4 full hkups, 36 W, 36 E (30/50 amps), seasonal sites, WiFi Hotspot, tent sites, showers $, dump, mobile sewer, laundry, groc, LP gas, fire rings, firewood, controlled access. **REC:** heated pool, playground. Pets OK. Partial handicap access. 2015 rates: $39 to $45. Apr 15 to Oct 15.
(978)465-0013 Lat: 42.83494, Lon: -70.84493
28 Ccc Rd, Salisbury, MA 01952
pinescampingarea@comcast.net
www.pinescampingarea.com
See ad this page.

Our inspectors look for the same things you do. Our unique Triple Rating System is based on years of market research, analysis and surveys from RVers like you. One thing you suggested was the need for separate ratings on facility completeness, restroom cleanliness/construction, and visual appearance/environmental quality. So we give three ratings, each based on a scale of 1 to 10, 10 being best and 5 being average. To give you an idea how tough we are, less than 1% of inspected campgrounds receive 10/10/10 ratings.*

MA

SALISBURY BEACH — A8 *Essex*

BEACH ROSE RV PARK
Ratings: 10/10★/10 (RV Park) N-Bnd: From Jct of I-495 & Rte 110/exit 55, E 3.5 mi on Rte 110 to Rte 1, N 500 ft to Rte 1A, E 1.3 mi (L); OR S-Bnd: From Jct of I-95 & Rte 110/exit 58, E 2.4 mi on Rte 110 to Rte 1, N 500 ft to Rte 1A, E 1.3 mi (L). **FAC:** Paved rds. 50 paved, 1 pull-thrus (30 x 100), back-ins (30 x 60), 50 full hkups (30/50 amps), cable, WiFi, showers $, dump, laundry, LP gas, fire rings, firewood, controlled access. **REC:** heated pool. Pet restrict(Q) $. Partial handicap access, no tents. Big rig sites, eco-friendly, 2015 rates: $40 to $63. Apr 1 to Nov 15.
(800)382-2230 Lat: 42.84009, Lon: -70.83549
147 Beach Rd, Salisbury, MA 01952
info@beachroservpark.com
www.beachroservpark.com
See ad this page.

Thank You to our active and retired military personnel. A dedicated section of Military Listings for places to camp can be found at the back of the Guide.

SANDWICH — D9 *Barnstable*

DUNROAMIN' COTTAGES & TRAILER PARK
Ratings: 7/NA/8 (RV Park) From Jct US-6 & Hwy 130, S 3 mi on Hwy 130 to Quaker Meeting House Rd, E 3/4 mi on Quaker Meeting House Rd to Cotuit Rd, S 1 mi on Cotuit to John Ewer Rd, W 500 ft on John Ewer (R). **FAC:** Gravel rds. (66 spaces). Avail: 10 gravel, 10 pull-thrus (40 x 70), 10 full hkups (30/50 amps), seasonal sites, WiFi, rentals, laundry. **REC:** pond, swim, playground. Pet restrict(B). No tents. 2015 rates: $37 to $41. Apr 17 to Oct 18.
(508)477-0541 Lat: 41.6851370, Lon: -70.4785248
5 John Ewer Rd, Sandwich, MA 02563-2668
dunroamintrailer@aol.com
www.dunroamintrailerpark.com
See ad this page.

PETERS POND RV RESORT
Ratings: 9.5/9★/9.5 (Campground) From Jct of Rte 6 & Hwy 130 (exit 2), S 3 mi on Hwy 130 to Quaker Meeting House Rd, E 0.8 mi to Cotuit Rd, S 0.7 mi (R).

NEAR THE CAPE COD NATIONAL SEASHORE
One of the finest campgrounds in the Cape Cod area! Peters Pond is situated along a spring-fed lake and offers RV sites and vacation rentals with amenities like an aqua park and beach area, arcade, pool and sand volleyball.

FAC: Paved rds. (407 spaces). Avail: 111 dirt, 3 pull-thrus (33 x 87), back-ins (30 x 60), 95 full hkups, 16 W, 16 E (30/50 amps), seasonal sites, cable, WiFi, tent sites, rentals, dump, laundry, groc, LP gas, fire rings, firewood, controlled access. **REC:** heated pool, Peters Pond: swim, fishing, shuffleboard, playground. Pets OK. Partial handicap access. Big rig sites, eco-friendly, 2015 rates: $52 to $97. Apr 15 to Oct 15.
AAA Approved
(888)543-7951 Lat: 41.69091, Lon: -70.48066
185 Cotuit Rd, Sandwich, MA 02563
peterspond@suncommunities.com
www.peterspond.com
See ad pages 603 (Spotlight Cape Cod), 596, 1463 (Welcome Section) & Family Camping, RV Trips of a Lifetime in Magazine Section.

SCUSSET BEACH STATE RESERVATION (State Pk) From Jct of US-6 & SR-3, E 1.2 mi on Scusset Beach Rd (R). Reservations Only. Note: No outside firewood permitted. 2015 rates: $15 to $17. (508)888-0859

SHAWME-CROWELL (State Pk) From Jct of US-6 & SR-6A, E 2 mi on SR-6A to SR-130, S 0.5 mi (R). Note: No outside firewood permitted. 2015 rates: $12 to $14. (508)888-0351

SOUTH CARVER — D8 *Plymouth*

MYLES STANDISH SF (State Pk) From town, E 3 mi on Cranberry Rd (L). Note: No outside firewood permitted. 2015 rates: $12 to $14. May 15 to Oct 11. (508)866-2526

SOUTH DENNIS — E10 *Yarmouth*

OLD CHATHAM ROAD RV RESORT **Ratings: 6.5/4.5/6.5** (RV Park) 2015 rates: $50 to $70. Apr 15 to Oct 31. (800)405-6188 310 Old Chatham Rd, South Dennis, MA 02660

SOUTHWICK — D3 *Hampden*

SODOM MOUNTAIN CAMPGROUNDS **Ratings: 7.5/8★/8.5** (Campground) 2015 rates: $39 to $51. May 1 to Oct 10. (413)569-3930 233 S Loomis St, Southwick, MA 01077

SPRINGFIELD — C3 *Hampden*

SPRINGFIELD See also Brimfield, Granville, Monson, Otis, Southwick, Sturbridge, Wales, Westhampton & Whately.

RV Park ratings you can rely on!

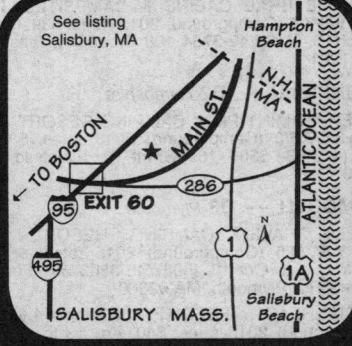

STURBRIDGE — C5 *Worcester*

STURBRIDGE RV RESORT **Ratings: 7.5/10★/8.5** (Membership Pk) 2015 rates: $38 to $56. Apr 1 to Nov 1. (800)405-6188 19 Mashapaug Rd, Sturbridge, MA 01566

WELLS (State Pk) From town, E 2 mi on Rte 20 to Rte 49, N 1 mi to park access rd (L). Note: No outside firewood permitted. 2015 rates: $12 to $14. May 8 to Oct 11. (508)347-9257

YOGI BEAR'S STURBRIDGE JELLYSTONE PARK **Ratings: 8.5/9/9** (Campground) 2015 rates: $33 to $89. (508)347-9570 30 River Rd, Sturbridge, MA 01566

SUTTON — C5 *Worcester*

OLD HOLBROOK PLACE **Ratings: 5.5/7/7.5** (Campground) 2015 rates: $34 to $50. May 30 to Sep 15. 114 Manchaug Rd, Sutton, MA 01590

SUTTON FALLS CAMPING AREA **Ratings: 6.5/5/7** (Campground) 2015 rates: $30 to $50. Apr 15 to Oct 1. (508)865-3898 90 Manchaug Road, Sutton, MA 01590

TAUNTON — D7 *Bristol*

MASSASOIT (State Pk) From Jct of US-44 & SR-18, S 2 mi on SR-18 to Taunton St., W 2.5 mi (L). Note: No outside firewood permitted. 2015 rates: $12 to $14. Apr 15 to Oct 15. (508)822-7405

TYNGSBORO — B6 *Middlesex*

BERRY'S GROVE CAMPGROUND, INC **Ratings: 4/NA/7** (Campground) 2015 rates: $40. (978)649-3141 35 Davis St, Tyngsboro, MA 01879

VINEYARD HAVEN — E8 *Dukes*

MARTHAS VINEYARD FAMILY CAMPGROUND, INC
Ratings: 8/9.5★/9 (Campground) From Vineyard Haven Ferry, S 0.25 mi on Water St to Beach St (R), SW 0.25 mi to Edgartown Rd (L), S 1 mi (R) Note: RVs under 40', campground does not allow dogs. **FAC:** Gravel rds. (128 spaces). Avail: 103 gravel, 1 pull-thru (30 x 40), back-ins (30 x 32), 25 full hkups, 78 W, 78 E (30/50 amps), seasonal sites, WiFi, tent sites, rentals, dump, laundry, groc, fire rings, firewood. **REC:** Atlantic Ocean: playground. Pets OK. Eco-friendly. 2015 rates: $62. May 22 to Oct 15.
(508)693-3772 Lat: 41.43530, Lon: -70.61029
569 Edgartown Rd, Vineyard Haven, MA 02568
info@campmv.com
www.campmv.com
See ad page 603 (Spotlight Cape Cod).

WALES — D4 *Hampden*

OAK HAVEN FAMILY CAMPGROUND
Ratings: 8.5/9.5★/9 (Campground) From Jct of I-84 & SR-32 (Exit 70 in Connecticut), N 5 mi on SR-32 to Rte 190, E 0.3 mi to SR-19, N 1 mi to MA State Line, Continue N on MA Rte 19, N 2.7 mi (R). **FAC:** Gravel rds. (140 spaces). 55 Avail: 14 gravel, 41 grass, 18 pull-thrus (36 x 60), back-ins (30 x 50), some side by side hkups, 17 full hkups, 38 W, 38 E (30 amps), seasonal sites, WiFi, tent sites, showers $, dump, laundry, groc, LP gas, fire rings, firewood, controlled access. **REC:** pool, playground. Pet restrict(Q). Partial handicap access. 2015 rates: $38 to $48. Disc: military.
(413)245-7148 Lat: 42.06793, Lon: -72.22202
22 Main St., Wales, MA 01081
camp@oakhavencampground.com
www.oakhavencampground.com
See ad this page, 596.

WASHINGTON — C2 *Berkshire*

SUMMIT HILL CAMPGROUND **Ratings: 6.5/4.5/6.5** (Campground) 2015 rates: $45. May 1 to Sep 30. (413)623-5761 34 Old Middlefield Rd, Washington, MA 01223

Our rating system isn't just tough, it's thorough. We know the kinds of things that are important to you — like clean restrooms and showers, attractive, secure, well-tended grounds, and extras like swimming pools. We give the first rating for development of facilities, the second for cleanliness and physical characteristics of restrooms and showers, and the third for visual appearance.

WEBSTER — D5 *Worcester*

INDIAN RANCH **Ratings: 9/9.5★/9** (RV Park) 2015 rates: $50 to $85. May 1 to Oct 15. (508)943-3871 200 Gore Rd, Webster, MA 01570

WEBSTER FAMILY CAMPGROUND Ratings: 6/6/5.5 (Campground) From Jct of I-395 & Rte 16 (exit 2), E 2 mi on Rte 16 (R). **FAC:** Gravel rds. (104 spaces). Avail: 92 dirt, 29 pull-thrus (20 x 52), back-ins (22 x 41), some side by side hkups, 38 full hkups, 54 W, 54 E (30/50 amps), seasonal sites, cable, WiFi, tent sites, dump, mobile sewer, laundry, groc, LP gas, fire rings, firewood. **REC:** pool, playground. Pets OK. 2015 rates: $36 to $40. Disc: AAA, military.
AAA Approved
(866)562-1895 Lat: 42.05822, Lon: -71.82288
106 Douglas Rd, Webster, MA 01570
wbcamp_1@msn.com
www.webstercamp.com

WELLFLEET — D10 *Barnstable*

MAURICE'S CAMPGROUND **Ratings: 5.5/8★/7.5** (Campground) 2015 rates: $51. May 24 to Oct 13. (508)349-2029 80 Rte 6, Wellfleet, MA 02667

WEST TOWNSEND — B5 *Middlesex*

PEARL HILL (State Pk) From Jct of SR-119 & New Fitchburg Rd, S .9 mi on New Fitchburg Rd to Bayberry Hill Rd, W 2.2 mi. Note: No outside firewood permitted. 2015 rates: $12 to $14. May 21 to Oct 11. (978)597-8802

Check out those views! From awe-inspiring redwood giants to the soaring towers of the Golden Gate Bridge, we've put the Spotlight on North America's most popular travel destinations. Turn to the Spotlight articles in our State and Province sections to learn more.

WESTHAMPTON — C3 *Hampshire*

NORTHAMPTON - SPRINGFIELD KOA **Ratings: 9/9★/9** (Campground) 2015 rates: $38 to $57. Apr 20 to Oct 31. (413)527-9862 139 South Rd, Westhampton, MA 01027

WESTPORT — E7 *Bristol*

HORSENECK BEACH STATE RESERVATION (State Pk) From Jct of I-195 & SR-88, S 13 mi on SR-88 (E). Note: No outside firewood permitted. 2015 rates: $15 to $17. May 15 to Oct 15. (508)636-8817

WHATELY — B3 *Franklin*

WHITE BIRCH CAMPGROUND **Ratings: 7/5.5/6** (Campground) 2015 rates: $39. May 1 to Oct 23. (413)665-4941 214 North St., South Deerfield, MA 01373

WINCHENDON — B5 *Worcester*

LAKE DENNISON RECREATION AREA (State Pk) From Jct of US-202 & SR-68 in Baldwinville, N 3 mi on US-202 (L). Note: No outside firewood permitted. 2015 rates: $12 to $14. May 21 to Sep 6. (978)939-8962

OTTER RIVER (State Pk) From N end of town, N 1 mi on US-202 (L). Note: No outside firewood permitted. 2015 rates: $12 to $14. May 21 to Oct 11. (978)939-8962

WINDSOR — B2 *Berkshire*

WINDSOR STATE FOREST (Public) From town: Go E on Hwy 9, then N on River Rd. Note: No outside firewood permitted. Pit toilets. (413)684-0948

According to some studies, almost 50 percent of RVers camp with pets! Find out more about the joys of traveling with your four-legged companions in our Pampered Pet Parks feature at the front of the Guide.

MA

JOHN McCORMICK

WELCOME TO Michigan

DATE OF STATEHOOD	WIDTH: 386 MILES (621 KM)	PROPORTION OF UNITED STATES
JAN. 26, 1837	LENGTH: 456 MILES (734 KM)	2.55% OF 3,794,100 SQ MI

With the second longest continuous coastline of any U.S. state (after Alaska), it's no wonder Michigan revels in its moniker, "Water Wonderland." Some 3,288 miles of rugged shoreline fringe the wilderness of Michigan's Upper Peninsula, where old-growth forests give way to sand dunes and where the timeless charms of lighthouses, bobbing sailboats and quaint harbors prevail. Along scenic byways, blueberry fields, apple orchards, cornfields and acres of vineyards reveal the state's bounties.

The "Motor City" has certainly had a bad run of it, but Detroit's phoenix is rising. In historic Brush Park, new wine bars, arty cafés, sleek restaurants and restored movie palaces are regenerating formerly abandoned neighborhoods. With its shrine to college football, Michigan Stadium in Ann Arbor is a paradigm for college town living that boasts a vibrant mix of restaurants, bars, boutiques, independent movie theaters and superb art museums. On Michigan's Upper Peninsula, Mackinac Island feels like stumbling onto the set of a BBC Victorian period drama.

History

Whatever your vantage point, you are never more than six miles away from a body of water (11,000 of them are inland lakes) and 85 miles from one of four Great Lakes: Huron, Erie, Michigan and Superior, which contain more than 80 percent of North America's fresh water supply. The five-mile suspension Mackinac Bridge connects the Upper Peninsula (U.P.) to the Lower Peninsula or "mitten." For much of the 20th century, manufacturing industries provided Michigan's main source of revenue, thanks in no small way to the auto industry. In 1897, the Olds Motor Vehicle Company opened a factory in state capital Lansing, shortly followed by the founding of the Ford Motor Company in Detroit in 1903. With the mass production of the Ford Model T, Detroit established itself as the auto industry's world capital.

Top 3 Tourism Attractions:
1) Mackinac Island
2) Henry Ford Museum
3) Traverse City

Nickname: Wolverine State

State Flower: Apple Blossom

State Bird: Robin

People: William Boeing, aircraft manufacturer; Earvin "Magic" Johnson, basketball superstar; John Harvey and William Keith Kellogg, founders of the Kellogg Company; Charles Lindbergh, pilot; Tom Selleck, actor; David Spade, comedian/actor

Major Cities: Detroit, Grand Rapids, Warren, Sterling Heights, Lansing (capital), Ann Arbor

Topography: Lower Peninsula—low rolling hills. Upper Peninsula: east—level with swamps; west—higher, more rugged

Climate: Temperate, with well-defined seasons; known for snowy, cold winters

Arace Photographic

Play

Michigan's state forest system is the largest in the eastern U.S. The Upper Peninsula is one of the nation's ultimate wilderness adventures with pristine scenery, prime wildlife viewing, undisturbed beaches, no industry and few people. Porcupine Mountains State Park, or "The Porkies," distills the essence of Michigan's beautiful Upper Peninsula.

Michigan's coastline offers something for everyone. Visitors enjoy clambering up the monumental dunes of Sleeping Bear Dunes, a 35-mile stretch of towering dunes, forests and beaches that is consistently voted as one of the most beautiful places in North America. Ludington State Park (100 miles northwest of Grand Rapids) courts families with activities galore.

Experience

Held annually in St. Joseph, the Blossomtime Festival, the oldest festival in Michigan (100 years), is a week-long riot of color and taste. Spring blooms and the arrival of the season of plenty are celebrated with one of the largest fruit markets in the U.S., the Grand Floral parade, a Miss Blossomtime Pageant and a 5k run. In Monroe, the second week in August, the annual River Raisin Jazz Festival attracts over 35,000 jazz aficionados.

Taste

A 10-minute drive outside Traverse City, Trattoria Stella (www.stellatc.com) is located in a characterful 19th-century hospital complex that used to be the Northern Michigan Asylum. Delicious and sustainable iterations of Italian classics include veal scallopini, bucatini with eggplant "meatballs," oysters, pig brain and George's Bank cod. In Ann Arbor, Zingerman's Delicatessan (www.zingermansdeli.com) has garnered a cult following. When President Obama is in town, he grazes on Zingerman's "killer" Reuben sandwich. In Detroit, the casual but cool Green Dot Stables (www.greendotstables.com) is known for its creative sliders, which range from a lean lamb patty to a quinoa burger.

TRAVEL & TOURISM

Travel Michigan
888-78-GREAT
www.michigan.org

Detroit Metro CVB
800-DETROIT
www.visitdetroit.com

Frankenmuth CVB
800-FUN-TOWN
www.frankenmuth.org

Experience Grand Rapids
800-678-9859, 616-459-8287
www.visitgrandrapids.org

Holland Area CVB
800-506-1299
www.holland.org

Indian River Area Tourist Bureau
231-238-9325
www.irtourism.com

Experience Jackson
517-764-4440
www.experiencejackson.com

Discover Kalamazoo
800-888-0509, 269-488-9000
www.discoverkalamazoo.com

Greater Lansing CVB
888-252-6746
www.lansing.org

Mackinaw Area Visitors Bureau
800-666-0160, 231-436-5664
www.mackinawcity.com

St. Ignace Visitors Bureau
800-338-6660
www.stignace.com

Southwestern Michigan Tourist Council
269-925-6301
www.swmichigan.org

Traverse City CVB
800-872-8377
www.traversecity.com

Upper Peninsula
800-562-7134
www.uptravel.com

OUTDOOR RECREATION

The Golf Association of Michigan
248-478-9242
www.gam.org

League of Michigan Bicyclists
517-334-9100
www.michigan.gov

Michigan Association of Paddle Sport Providers
www.michigancanoe.com

Michigan Charter Boat Association
800-MCBA-971
www.micharterboats.com

Michigan Department of Natural Resources
517-373-1280
www.mdnr-elicense.com

SHOPPING

Bay Antiques Center
www.bayantiquectr.com

Great Lakes Crossing
www.greatlakescrossingoutlets.com

Michigania
517-484-1137
www.greatlakescrossingoutlets.com

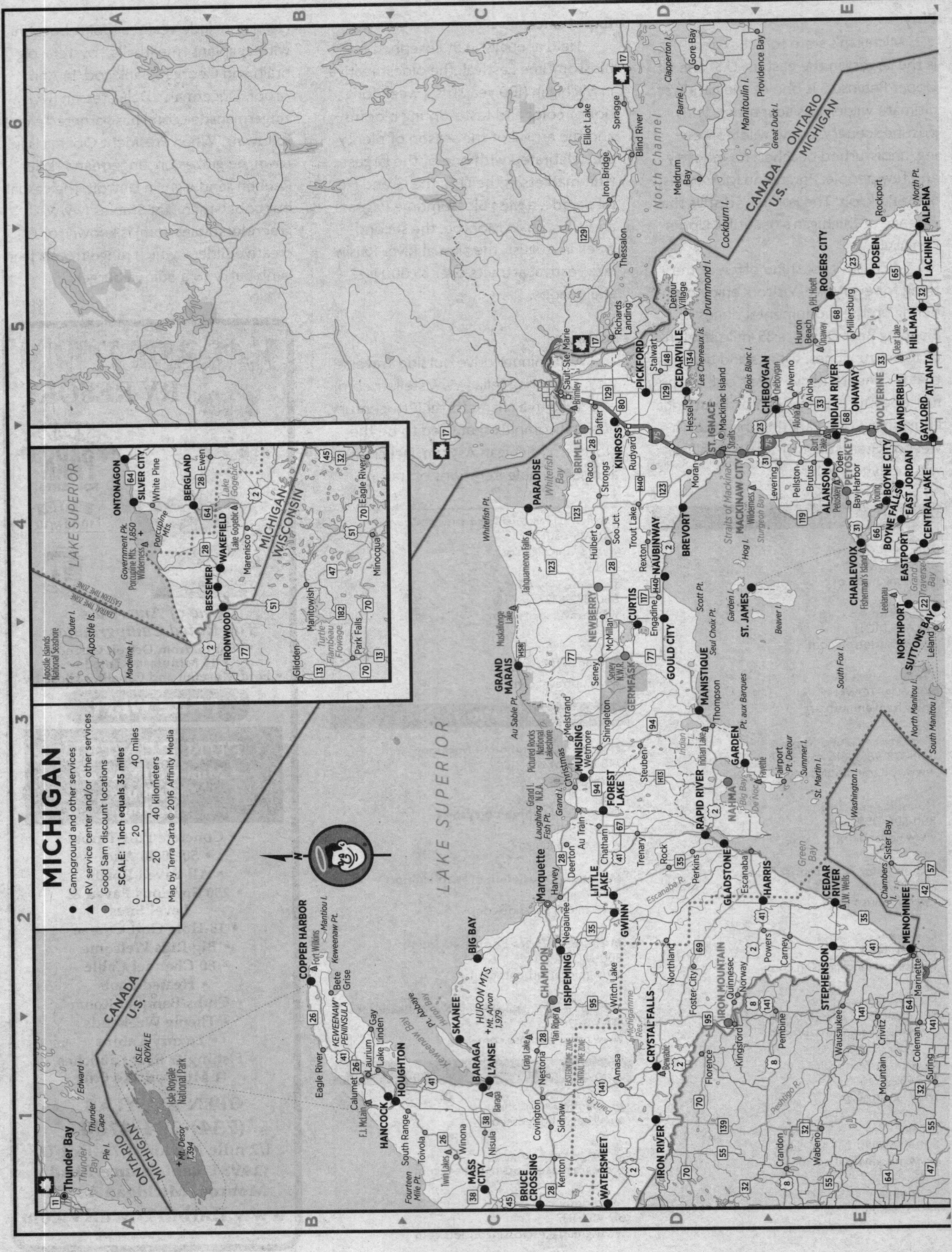
MICHIGAN
Campground and other services
RV service center and/or other services
Good Sam discount locations
SCALE: 1 inch equals 35 miles
0 20 40 miles
0 20 40 kilometers
Map by Terra Carta © 2016 Affinity Media
LAKE SUPERIOR
CANADA
U.S.
ONTARIO
MICHIGAN
WISCONSIN
Thunder Bay
Isle Royale National Park
KEWEENAW PENINSULA
COPPER HARBOR
HOUGHTON
HANCOCK
L'ANSE
BARAGA
SKANEE
BIG BAY
MASS CITY
BRUCE CROSSING
WATERSMEET
IRON RIVER
CRYSTAL FALLS
ISHPEMING
CHAMPION
Marquette
GWINN
LITTLE LAKE
FOREST LAKE
MUNISING
GRAND MARAIS
PARADISE
NEWBERRY
CURTIS
GERMFASK
GOULD CITY
MANISTIQUE
GARDEN
RAPID RIVER
GLADSTONE
HARRIS
IRON MOUNTAIN
STEPHENSON
CEDAR RIVER
MENOMINEE
NAUBINWAY
BREVORT
ST. IGNACE
MACKINAW CITY
KINROSS
BRIMLEY
PICKFORD
CEDARVILLE
Sault Ste. Marie
ST. JAMES
CHEBOYGAN
INDIAN RIVER
ONAWAY
ROGERS CITY
POSEN
ALPENA
LACHINE
HILLMAN
ATLANTA
WOLVERINE
VANDERBILT
GAYLORD
PETOSKEY
ALANSON
BOYNE CITY
BOYNE FALLS
EAST JORDAN
CENTRAL LAKE
CHARLEVOIX
EASTPORT
NORTHPORT
SUTTONS BAY
IRONWOOD
BESSEMER
WAKEFIELD
BERGLAND
ONTONAGON
SILVER CITY
North Channel
Drummond I.
Manitoulin I.
Green Bay

LAKE HURON
LAKE MICHIGAN
LAKE ERIE
CANADA
U.S.
ONT.
OHIO
MICHIGAN
INDIANA
WISCONSIN
ILLINOIS
Saginaw Bay
Green Bay
L. St. Clair
Lake Winnebago

Featured Good Sam Parks

MICHIGAN

Good Sam Park

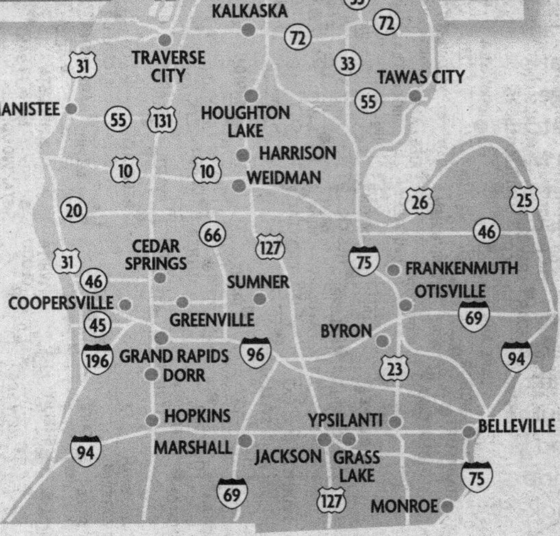

When you stay with Good Sam, you can expect the highest degree of cleanliness and friendliness, and better yet, you get 10% off campground fees.

If you're not already a Good Sam member you can purchase your membership at one of these locations:

BELLAIRE
Chain O'Lakes Campground
(231)533-8432

BELLEVILLE
Wayne County RV Park & Fairgrounds
(734)697-7002

BRIMLEY
Bay Mills Casino RV Park
(888)422-9645

BYRON
Myers Lake Campground
(810)266-4511

CEDAR SPRINGS
Lakeside Camp Park
(616)696-1735

CHAMPION
Michigamme Shores Campground Resort
(906)339-2116

COOPERSVILLE
Conestoga Grand River Campground
(616)837-6323

DORR
Hungry Horse Campground
(616)681-9843

FRANKENMUTH
Yogi Bear's Jellystone Park Camp-Resort
(989)652-6668

GRAND RAPIDS
Woodchip Campground
(616)878-9050

GRASS LAKE
Holiday RV Campground
(517)522-5846

GREENVILLE
Three Seasons Family Campground
(616)754-5717

HARRISON
Countryside Campground
(989)539-5468
Hidden Hill Family Campground
(989)539-9372

HOPKINS
Hidden Ridge RV Resort
(888)451-2180

HOUGHTON LAKE
Houghton Lake Travel Park Campground
(989)422-3931

JACKSON
Greenwood Acres Family Campground
(517)522-8600

KALKASKA
Kalkaska RV Park & Campground
(231)258-9863

MACKINAW CITY
Mackinaw Mill Creek Camping
(231)436-5584

MANISTEE
Insta Launch Campground & Marina
(866)452-8642
Little River Casino RV Park
(866)572-4386

MARSHALL
Camp Turkeyville RV Resort
(269)781-4293

MONROE
Camp Lord Willing Management RV Park & Campground
(877)210-8700

NEWBERRY
Kritter's Northcountry Campground & Cabins
(906)293-8562

OTISVILLE
Covenant Hills Camp
(810)631-4531

PETOSKEY
Petoskey Motorcoach Resort
(888)366-2666

ST IGNACE
Castle Rock Lakefront Campground
(906)643-9222
Lakeshore RV Park
(906)643-9522
Tiki RV Park & Campground
(906)643-7808

SUMNER
Leisure Lake Family Campground Inc
(989)875-4689

TAWAS CITY
Tawas River RV Park
(989)362-4988

TRAVERSE CITY
Holiday Park Campground
(231)943-4410
Traverse Bay RV Resort
(231)938-5800

WEIDMAN
Gammy Woods Campground
(989)644-2267

WOLVERINE
Elkwood Campground
(231)525-6774

YPSILANTI
Detroit/Greenfield RV Park
(734)482-7722

For more Good Sam Parks go to listing pages

FRANKENMUTH

Raise your beer stein to a town that keeps the Bavarian spirit alive

Michigan's Little Bavaria, Frankenmuth sits about 15 miles southeast of Saginaw and its culture is a lively blend of Old World German and modern America. Frankenmuth is a family-friendly destination with activities for visitors of all ages. During the summer, visitors can catch a summer concert on Sundays in Memorial Park or watch the sunset from Frankenmuth Holz Brucke, a historic covered bridge that spans the Cass River.

Give young ones a thrill at the Adventure Park, where they can traverse trails that are strung up between the treetops. Enjoy a taste of Frankenmuth's German heritage at Bavarian Inn and browse unique souvenirs at the shops on the inn's second floor. Just look for the building's castle-like architectural profile.

Beat the heat at Zehnder's Splash Village, a unique indoor water park that's 50,000 square feet and features a family raft ride, zero-entry pool and tube slides.

When the air turns chilly, the Frankenmuth Corn Maze is a lively way to spend an afternoon. Wind your way through five acres of corn stalks and hop on a hayride on Saturday afternoons. Life-size board games played outside on the lawn bring out the kid in everyone.

If you're traveling during the summer, make room on your schedule for the Bavarian Festival, which features a parade with colorful floats along with a host of celebrations. Watch the maypole dance, drink a tall brew or simply marvel at the wide variety of traditional Bavarian attire.

Celebrate Bavaria

Of course, no Bavarian town would be complete without an Oktoberfest celebration. Frankenmuth doesn't disappoint—the star of autumn celebrates German culture, food and music, and authentic Hofbrauhaus beer that's shipped directly from the famous Munich brewer. Weiner dog races add a touch of whimsy to the festivities.

Winter means Christmas in Frankenmuth, and the town hosts Bronner's Christmas Wonderland, the world's largest Christmas store. When the season is at its peak, Frankenmuth lights up with twinkling bulbs and streamers. But the holiday is celebrated year-round here, particularly at Silent Night Memorial Chapel and Christmas Town USA.

When spring arrives, the town pulls out brightly colored Easter displays and hosts a Bavarian Easter celebration that includes egg hunts, brunches and a visit from the Easter bunny.

Celebrate the simple, hardworking life of farmers at Grandpa Tiny's Farm. This historic farm and petting zoo offers guided tours and wagon rides.

The town's brewing heritage is the star of Lager Mill, a historic structure housing a museum and craft beer store featuring more than 400 varieties. More European flavors are ripe for the taking at Zehnder's Marketplace, home to European delicacies and a bakery that churns out breads, pastries and cookies.

For More Information

Frankenmuth
800-386-8696
www.frankenmuth.org

Travel Michigan
888-78-GREAT
www.michigan.org

Dancing around the maypole during the Frankenmuth Bavarian Festival. Frankenmuth.org

See listing Frankenmuth, MI

Getty Images/iStockphoto

MACKINAW CITY

This small Michigan gem packs a vacation's worth of attractions

Although it's one of Michigan's most-visited cities, Mackinaw City is a tiny place, with just over 800 full-time residents. However, during the warm summer months, the local population swells as visitors from around the Midwest descend upon the town in large numbers.

Mackinaw is a major jumping-off point for other destinations in the Mackinac Straits area, including popular Mackinac Island. The city sits at the northern tip of Michigan's Lower Peninsula and is linked to the Upper Peninsula by Mackinac Bridge, one of the city's best-known attractions. The bridge, known as the "Mighty Mac," is the world's fifth-longest suspension bridge between cable anchorages, with a span of 26,372 feet (nearly five miles).

Visitors who want to learn more about the bridge can stop by the Mackinaw Bridge Museum above MaMa Mia's restaurant. The museum was founded by one of the ironworkers who helped build the bridge. Exhibits include spinning wheels used to stretch wire across the bridge's towers and a gorgeous, handcrafted scale model of the bridge that showcases the span's intricate structure.

> Known as the "Mighty Mac," the bridge is the world's fifth-longest suspension span between cable anchorages.

Lumberjack History

Mackinaw City sits in a forested area and was once a major hub for timber production, as evidenced by some of its most popular attractions. Visitors young and old love the Jack Pine Lumberjack Shows, held May-September. These hourlong performances feature dueling lumberjacks who compete by showing off their skills with saws and axes. The shows include wood-chopping, axe-throwing and log-rolling competitions. There's even a chain-saw carving demonstration.

The Historic Mill Creek Discovery Park is another popular attraction, and here guests can learn about the area's timber industry through entertaining lumberjack demonstrations and talks by costumed interpreters. There's also an adventure program in the park that features a canopy walk, a zip line and a climbing wall, as well as three miles of nature trails and plenty of play areas for children.

Mansions on Mackinac Island. Getty Images/iStockphoto

Mackinac's Grand Hotel.
Getty Images/Hemera

MI

Lakeside Lighthouses

The area around Mackinaw City is known for its numerous lighthouses, many of which are open to visitors. The best known is the Old Mackinac Point Lighthouse, open May through early October. This lighthouse sits just east of the Mackinac Bridge and is a good place to learn more about the history of these vital lights and the lives of their keepers. The Keepers' Quarters feature three rooms of artifacts and an exhibit on the lighthouse's history. The barn is used to screen a 15-minute film about shipwrecks in the area, and visitors take guided tours up to the top of the lighthouse tower at no extra charge (although children must be 4 feet tall to participate).

About two miles west of the city, McGulpin's Point Lighthouse is open to visitors in warmer months. It first became operational in 1869 and remained in operation until 1906. Its design inspired other lighthouses, including the Eagle Harbor Light and the White River Light in Michigan, as well as Wisconsin's Sand Island Light. The new Discovery Trail at McGulpin Point transports visitors back 9,000 years, when the region was inhabited by early Native Americans. An enhanced self-guided cell phone tour, provided by TourSphere, is available throughout the grounds.

Every year, the region hosts the four-day Lighthouse Festival, which attracts lighthouse lovers from around the world. Lighthouse cruises are available both during the festival and throughout the warmer months.

Mackinac Island

Mackinaw serves as the main gateway to Mackinac Island, a car-free island accessible from the city by passenger ferry. Though you can't bring motorized vehicles onto this tiny island, bicycles are welcome, and guests who don't want to get around on foot or by using pedal power have the option of relying on elegant horse-drawn carriages instead.

The ferry ride from Mackinaw City to the island takes about 15 minutes, making it a good spot for a day trip. There are two butterfly conservatories: the Wings of Mackinac Butterfly Conservatory and the Original Mackinac Island Butterfly House & Insect World, both of which house an abundance of colorful butterflies and exotic plants. Children won't want to miss the Liberty Lego Display, an expansive exhibit made of 750,000 Lego pieces. There's also a Haunted Theatre, which features a wax museum with monster figures, and the Haunted History Tour, rich with information about local history and ghostly tales.

The island is a great setting for outdoor activities, including the 2,250-acre Mackinac Island State Park. Features include Devil's Kitchen (a limestone cavern), Point Lookout, which has sweeping views of the area, and Skull Cave, a former burial ground that English fur trader Alexander Henry used as a refuge during Pontiac's Rebellion in 1763.

For More Information

Mackinaw City
800-666-0160

Travel Michigan
888-784-7328
www.michigan.org

Michigan

CONSULTANTS

Stan & Julie Grabiec

ADRIAN — K5 *Lenawee*

CAMP SEQUOIA
Ratings: 7/8.5★/8.5 (Campground) From Jct of US 23N/Exit 17 & M-50, W 13.5 on M-50 to Rodgers Hwy S, 0.7 mi to E Russell Rd, W 0.1 mi to N Raisin Center Rd, S 2 mi to Gady Rd, W 1.7 mi (L). **FAC:** Paved/gravel rds. (120 spaces). Avail: 35 grass, back-ins (30 x 60), 35 W, 35 E (30/50 amps), seasonal sites, WiFi Hotspot, tent sites, dump, mobile sewer, fire rings, firewood. **REC:** pool, Lake Cherokee: fishing, playground. Pet restrict(B/Q). Partial handicap access. 2015 rates: $25 to $35. May 1 to Oct 1.
(517)264-5531 Lat: 41.957815, Lon: -83.974262
2675 Gady Rd, Adrian, MI 49221
Megan@campatsequoia.com
www.campatsequoia.com
See ad this page.

ALANSON — E4 *Emmet*

MACKINAW SF/MAPLE BAY (State Pk) From Jct US-31 & Brutus Rd, E 3.5 mi on Brutus Rd to Maple Bay Rd, S 0.5 mi, follow signs. Pit toilets. 2015 rates: $13. (989)732-9392

ALBION — J4 *Calhoun*

ROCKEY'S CAMPGROUND Ratings: 7/8.5★/8.5 (Campground) From Jct of I-94 & 28 Mile Rd (exit 121), N 6.9 mi on 28 Mile Rd (R). **FAC:** Gravel rds. (100 spaces). Avail: 35 grass, 1 pull-thrus (30 x 50), back-ins (40 x 40), 35 W, 35 E (30 amps), seasonal sites, cable, WiFi, tent sites, rentals, dump, mobile sewer, laundry, groc, LP gas, fire rings, firewood. **REC:** Bass Lake: swim, fishing, playground. Pet restrict(B/Q). Partial handicap access. 2015 rates: $33 to $39. Disc: military. May 15 to Oct 1.
(517)857-2200 Lat: 42.36195, Lon: -84.76437
19880 27 1/2 Mile Rd, Albion, MI 49224
rockeys@springcom.com
www.rockeyscampground.com

ALGONAC — J6 *St Clair*

ALGONAC (State Pk) From town, N 4 mi on M-29, follow signs (L). Entrance fee required. 2015 rates: $18 to $29. (810)765-5605

ALLEGAN — J3 *Allegan*

ALLEGAN STATE GAME AREA (State Pk) From town: Go 6 mi W on Monroe Road, then 1 mi S on 48th St, then 1 mi W on 116th Ave. Pit toilets. 2015 rates: $12. (269)673-2430

TRI PONDS FAMILY CAMP RESORT **Ratings: 9/9★/8** (Campground) 2015 rates: $35 to $45. May 1 to Oct 31. (269)673-4740 3687 Dumont Rd, Allegan, MI 49010

ALLENDALE — H3 *Ottawa*

ALLENDALE WEST GRAND RAPIDS KOA **Ratings: 8.5/8/8.5** (Campground) 2015 rates: $41 to $47. Apr 15 to Oct 31. (616)895-6601 8275 Warner Street, Allendale, MI 49401

ALPENA — E5 *Alpena*

CAMPERS COVE RV PARK & CANOE LIVERY Ratings: 8/8★/7.5 (Campground) From Jct of US-23 & Long Rapids Rd (N of town), W 6 mi on Long Rapids Rd (L). **FAC:** Paved/gravel rds. (86 spaces). Avail: 59 grass, 8 pull-thrus (30 x 65), back-ins (40 x 55), some side by side hkups, 18 full hkups, 41 W, 41 E (30 amps), seasonal sites, cable, WiFi, tent sites, rentals, dump, mobile sewer, laundry, groc, LP gas, fire rings, firewood. **REC:** heated pool, Lake Winyah: swim, fishing, playground. Pets OK. Partial handicap access. 2015 rates: $37. May 1 to Oct 15.
(989)356-3708 Lat: 45.11539, Lon: -83.55656
5005 Long Rapids Rd, Alpena, MI 49707
info@camperscove.org
www.camperscovecampground.com

LONG LAKE COUNTY PARK (Public) From town, N 10 mi on US-23 to Long Lake Park Rd, W 0.5 mi, follow signs (L). 2015 rates: $17 to $26. May 15 to Oct 15. (989)595-2401

THUNDER BAY CAMPGROUND **Ratings: 2/6/7** (Campground) 2015 rates: $25. Apr 1 to Nov 30. (989)354-2528 4250 US Highway 23 S, Alpena, MI 49707

ALTO — H4 *Kent*

TYLER CREEK GOLF CLUB & CAMPGROUND **Ratings: 7.5/9★/7.5** (Campground) 2015 rates: $33 to $45. Apr 15 to Oct 15. (616)868-6751 13495 92nd St, Alto, MI 49302

ANN ARBOR — J5 *Washtenaw*

ANN ARBOR See also Adrian, Belleville, Brighton, Chelsea, Dearborn, Dundee, Grass Lake, Howell, Jackson, Milford, Munith, New Hudson, Onsted, Pinckney, Tecumseh, Tipton, Wixom & Ypsilanti.

ATLANTA — E5 *Alpena, Montmorency*

CLEAR LAKE (State Pk) From Jct of M-32 & M-33, N 9.6 mi on M-33 (L). 2015 rates: $17 to $24. Apr 15 to Dec 1. (989)785-4388

MACKINAW SF (TOMAHAWK CREEK FLOODING) (State Pk) From town: Go 13 mi N on Hwy 33, then 1 mi E on Tomahawk Lake Rd. Pit toilets. 2015 rates: $13. (989)785-4388

MACKINAW SF/AVERY LAKE (State Pk) From Jct of SR-32 & CR-487, S 6 mi on CR-487 to Avery Lake Rd, W 3 mi, follow signs (R). Entrance fee required. Pit toilets. 2015 rates: $13. Apr 1 to Nov 1. (989)785-4251

MACKINAW SF/BIG OAKS (State Pk) From Jct of SR-32 & CR-487, SW 10 mi on Cr-487 to Avery Lake Rd, follow signs to entrance. Pit toilets. 2015 rates: $15. (989)785-4251

MACKINAW SF/ESS LAKE (State Pk) From town, N 8 mi on SR-33 to CR-624, E 10 mi to park access rd, N 1.5 mi, follow signs (L). Pit toilets. 2015 rates: $13. Apr 1 to Nov 1. (989)785-4388

MACKINAW SF/JACKSON LAKE (State Pk) From Jct of SR-32 & SR-33, N 6 mi to entrance (E). Pit toilets. 2015 rates: $13. (989)785-4388

AU GRES — G5 *Arenac*

AU GRES CITY PARK & CAMPGROUND (Public) From Jct of US-23 & Main St, N 0.1 mi on Main St (L). **FAC:** Paved rds. (109 spaces). Avail: 79 grass, 10 pull-thrus (30 x 70), back-ins (25 x 40), some side by side hkups, 30 full hkups, 49 W, 49 E (30 amps), WiFi, tent sites, dump, fire rings, firewood. **REC:** Au Gres River: fishing, shuffleboard, playground, rec open to public. No pets. 2015 rates: $32. Apr 15 to Oct 15.
AAA Approved
(989)876-8310 Lat: 44.049472, Lon: -83.686336
522 Park Street, Au Gres, MI 48703
cityofaugres@centurytel.net
www.cityofau-gres-mi.org

BAD AXE — G6 *Huron*

CAMPER'S HAVEN FAMILY CAMPGROUND **Ratings: 7.5/9★/8.5** (Campground) 2015 rates: $35. Apr 15 to Oct 15. (989)269-7989 2326 S Van Dyke, Bad Axe, MI 48413

HURON COUNTY PARKS (Public) From the Jct of M-142 (Pigeon Rd) & M-53 (N Van Dyke Rd) S 1.5 mi on N Van Dyke Rd to E Huron Rd E 0.2 mi to S Hanselman Rd S 0.3 mi (R). 2015 rates: $13 to $35. (989)269-6404

BALDWIN — G3 *Lake*

PERE MARQUETTE OAKS CONDOMINIUM RV PARK Ratings: 9.5/9.5★/10 (Condo Pk) From South Jct of M-37 & US-10, S 3.6 mi on M-37 to 76th St, W 3.5 mi (R) Note: Minimum length for RV is 22 feet. No tents or pop ups. **FAC:** Paved rds. (100 spaces). Avail: 20 paved, patios, back-ins (50 x 110), 20 full hkups (30/50 amps), seasonal sites, cable, WiFi, laundry, fire rings. **REC:** heated pool, whirlpool, playground. Pets OK. Partial handicap access, no tents. Big rig sites, eco-friendly. 2015 rates: $45. Apr 15 to Oct 30. No CC.
(231)898-2665 Lat: 43.85121, Lon: -85.92175
6150 W 76th St., Baldwin, MI 49304
webmaster@peremarquettervpark.com
www.peremarquettervpark.com

WHISPERING OAKS CAMPGROUND & CABINS Ratings: 5.5/9★/7.5 (Campground) From Jct of US 10 & M-37 in Baldwin, S 2.5 mi on M-37 (L). **FAC:** Gravel rds. (49 spaces). Avail: 21 grass, 3 pull-thrus (30 x 75), back-ins (30 x 45), 21 W, 21 E (30 amps), seasonal sites, WiFi, tent sites, rentals, dump, laundry, fire rings, firewood. **REC:** playground. Pet restrict(Q). Partial handicap access. 2015 rates: $30. Apr 1 to Oct 31.
(231)745-7152 Lat: 43.86325, Lon: -85.85057
8586 M-37 South, Baldwin, MI 49304
Staff@whisperingoakscampground.hypermart.net
www.michigancampground.com

BARAGA — C1 *Baraga*

BARAGA (State Pk) From Jct of M-38 & US-41, S 1 mi on US-41, follow signs (R). Entrance fee required. 2015 rates: $17 to $20. Apr 15 to Nov 15. (906)353-6558

OJIBWA RV PARK **Ratings: 8.5/NA/7.5** (Campground) 2015 rates: $20. (800)323-8045 16449 Michigan Ave, Baraga, MI 49908

BARRYTON — G4 *Missaukee*

MERRILL-GORREL CAMPGROUND (Public) From the jct of US-10 & M-66/30th Ave: S 3.0 mi on M-66 to 3 mi Rd, W 6.7 mi to Evergreen Rd S 0.1 mi (R). 2015 rates: $15 to $18. Apr 1 to Oct 27. (989)382-7158

BATTLE CREEK — J4 *Calhoun*

CREEK VALLEY
Ratings: 3.5/NA/7 (Campground) From Jct of I-94 & Hwy 37 (Exit 95): N 8.5 mi on Hwy 37 (R). **FAC:** Paved/dirt rds. 22 gravel, back-ins (25 x 40), some side by side hkups, accepts self-contain units only, 22 full hkups (30/50 amps), WiFi. **REC:** playground. Pet restrict(B). Partial handicap access, no tents. 2015 rates: $30.
(269)964-9577 Lat: 42.36041, Lon: -85.23280
70 Creek Valley Circle, Battle Creek, MI 49017
Creekvalley@att.net
www.creekvalleydevelopment.com
See ad this page.

FORT CUSTER STATE REC AREA (State Pk) From Jct of I-94 & 35th St (exit 85), N 1 mi on 35th St to M-96, E 6.2 mi, follow signs (R). Entrance Fee Required. 2015 rates: $16 to $21. (269)731-4200

HIDEAWAY HILLS FAMILY CAMPGROUND **Ratings: 5.5/4/6.5** (Campground) 2015 rates: $35. May 1 to Oct 1. (269)962-1600 21901 Collier Ave, Battle Creek, MI 49017

BAY CITY — G5 *Bay*

BAY CITY STATE REC AREA (State Pk) From Jct of I-75 & Beaver Rd (exit 168), E 5 mi on Beaver Rd, follow signs (E). Entrance fee required. 2015 rates: $18 to $25. May 1 to Oct 31. (989)684-3020

BEAR LAKE — F3 *Manistee*

HOPKINS PARK CAMPGROUND (Public) In town, off US-31, follow signs (R). 2015 rates: $20 to $22. (231)383-2402

KAMPVILLA RV PARK **Ratings: 7.5/9.5★/9** (Campground) 2015 rates: $36. Apr 15 to Oct 15. (800)968-0027 16632 US-31 (Pleasanton Highway), Bear Lake, MI 49614

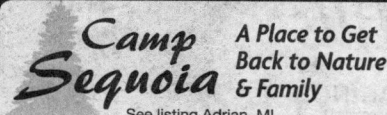

MI

BEAVERTON — G5 *Gladwin*

◄ CALHOUN CAMPGROUND (CITY PARK) (Public) From town: Go 1/2 mi S on Hwy 18, then 2 mi W on Brown, then 200 yards S on Roehrs Rd. 2015 rates: $14 to $24. May 15 to Sep 30. (989)312-4401

BELDING — H4 *Ionia*

▼ DOUBLE R RANCH **Ratings: 5.5/5/4.5** (Campground) 2015 rates: $35 to $41. May 1 to Oct 7. (877)794-0520 4424 N Whites Bridge Rd, Belding, MI 48809

BELLAIRE — F4 *Antrim*

CHAIN O'LAKES CAMPGROUND
Ratings: 8/8★/8 (Campground) From Jct. of US-131 & M-88: W. 07 mi. on M-88 (R). **FAC:** Paved/gravel rds. (53 spaces). 44 Avail: 13 paved, 15 gravel, 16 grass, 8 pull-thrus (30 x 100), back-ins (30 x 40), 44 full hkups (30/50 amps), seasonal sites, WiFi, tent sites, rentals, dump, laundry, groc, fire rings, firewood. **REC:** heated pool, playground. Pets OK. Eco-friendly, 2015 rates: $38.
(231)533-8432 Lat: 44.92464, Lon: -85.18591
7231 S M 88, Bellaire, MI 49615
reserve@chainolakescamp.com
www.chainolakescamp.com
See ad this page, 616.

BELLEVILLE — J5 *Wayne*

WAYNE COUNTY RV PARK & FAIRGROUNDS
Ratings: 6.5/8/8 (Public) From Jct of I-94 & Belleville Rd (exit 190), W 0.3 mi on North Service Rd to Quirk Rd, N 0.2 mi to fairgrounds (R). **FAC:** Gravel rds. 95 grass, 59 pull-thrus (26 x 60), back-ins (29 x 68), some side by side hkups, 34 full hkups, 61 W, 61 E (30/50 amps), WiFi, tent sites, dump, mobile sewer, laundry, LP gas, fire rings, firewood. **REC:** rec open to public. Pet restrict(Q). Partial handicap access. Big rig sites, 2015 rates: $39. Disc: military. Apr 1 to Oct 31.
(734)697-7002 Lat: 42.22324, Lon: -83.49414
10871 Quirk Rd, Belleville, MI 48111
rvfairgrounds@gmail.com
www.waynecountyfairgrounds.net
See ad pages 625, 616.

Travel Services

CAMPING WORLD OF BELLEVILLE/DETROIT
As the nation's largest retailer of RV supplies, accessories, services and new and used RVs, Camping World is committed to making your total RV experience better. **SERVICES:** RV, tire, RV appliance, MH mechanical, staffed RV wash. RV supplies, emergency parking, RV accessible. waiting room. Hours: 8am to 6pm.
(800)446-8929 Lat: 42.220417, Lon: -83.470653
43646 I-94 Service Drive North, Belleville, MI 48111
www.campingworld.com

BENTON HARBOR — J3 *Berrien*

► EDEN SPRINGS PARK **Ratings: 5.5/7.5/6.5** (Campground) 2015 rates: $35. (269)927-3302 793 M-139, Benton Harbor, MI 49022

BENZONIA — F3 *Benzie*

▼ TIMBERLINE CAMPGROUND **Ratings: 7.5/9★/8** (Campground) 2015 rates: $36. Mar 15 to Nov 1. (231)882-9548 2788 Benzie Hwy, Benzonia, MI 49616

VACATION TRAILER PARK & CANOE LIVERY
Ratings: 8.5/8★/8.5 (Campground) N-bnd: From Jct of US 31 & M-115, S 2 mi on US 31/M-115 (R); or S-bnd: From Jct of US 31 & M-115, N 1 mi on US 31/M-115 (L). **FAC:** Gravel rds. (120 spaces). Avail: 100 grass, 2 pull-thrus (25 x 50), back-ins (25 x 45), 20 full hkups, 80 W, 80 E (20/30 amps), seasonal sites, cable, WiFi, tent sites, rentals, dump, mobile sewer, laundry, fire rings, firewood. **REC:** heated pool, Betsie River: fishing, playground. Pets OK. Partial handicap access. Eco-friendly, 2015 rates: $39.50. Disc: AAA.
AAA Approved
(800)482-5101 Lat: 44.60210, Lon: -86.09931
2080 Benzie Hwy, Benzonia, MI 49616
camping@vacationtrailer.com
www.vacationtrailer.com

BERGLAND — A4 *Ontonagon*

▲ LAKE GOGEBIC (State Pk) From Jct of US-2 & M-64, W 10 mi on M-64, follow signs (R). Entrance fee required. 2015 rates: $13 to $31. Apr 15 to Nov 15. (906)842-3341

◄ ONTONAGON COUNTY PARK (Public) From Jct of Hwy 64 & M-28, W 5 mi on M-28 to M-64, S 2 mi (L). Pit toilets. 2015 rates: $7 to $9. May 1 to Sep 30. (906)575-3952

BERRIEN SPRINGS — K3 *Berrien*

▼ SHAMROCK PARK (Public) N-bnd: From Jct I 94 (Exit 30) & US 31, S 10 mi on US 31 to Exit 15 (MI 139/Old US 31), SE 3.3 mi (name changes to Old US 31, then to N Cass St) to Ferry St, NE 0.3 mi on Ferry St (Name changes to Old US 31) to Genoa Rd, N 65 yds (L). 2015 rates: $17 to $27. (269)473-5691

BESSEMER — A4 *Gogebic*

► ALPINE CAMPGROUND **Ratings: 4/7/6** (Campground) 2015 rates: $30.50. (906)667-0737 e8072 US 2, Bessemer, MI 49911

BIG BAY — C2 *Marquette*

▲ PERKINS COUNTY PARK (Public) In Marquette, from Jct of US-41 & Wright St, N 4 mi on Wright St to CR-550, N 26 mi, follow signs (R). 2015 rates: $16 to $30. May 15 to Sep 15. (906)345-9353

BIG RAPIDS — G4 *Mecosta*

◄ CRAN-HILL RANCH FAMILY CAMPGROUND **Ratings: 6.5/8.5★/8.5** (Campground) 2015 rates: $42. Apr 15 to Oct 15. (231)796-7669 14444 17 Mile Rd, Rodney, MI 49342

BIRCH RUN — H5 *Saginaw*

► PINE RIDGE RV CAMPGROUND **Ratings: 6/9★/8.5** (Campground) 2015 rates: $37. May 1 to Oct 31. (989)624-9029 11700 Gera Rd, Birch Run, MI 48415

BITELY — G3 *Oceana*

PETTIBONE LAKE PARK (Public) From Jct of US-10 & SR-37, S 10 mi on SR-37 to 15 Mile Rd, E 2 mi to Pettibone Dr. Pit toilets. 2015 rates: $16. Apr 24 to Oct 18. (231)689-1190

BOYNE CITY — E4 *Charlevoix*

YOUNG (State Pk) From Jct of SR-75 & CR-56 (Boyne City Rd), NW 2 mi on CR-56, follow signs (L). Entrance fee required. 2015 rates: $16 to $29. Apr 1 to Dec 1. (231)582-7523

BOYNE FALLS — E4 *Charlevox*

► CHANDLER HILL CAMPGROUND **Ratings: 5/8.5★/8** (Campground) 2015 rates: $28. May 1 to Nov 1. (231)549-7878 2930 Magee Rd, Boyne Falls, MI 49713

BREVORT — D4 *Mackinac*

LAKE SUPERIOR SF/LITTLE BREVORT LAKE-NORTH (State Pk) From US 2 in town: Go 2 mi NE on Carp River Rd & Worth Rd. Pit toilets. 2015 rates: $13. (906)477-6048

BRIDGMAN — K3 *Berrien*

◄ WEKO BEACH (Public) From Jct of I-94 & Red Arrow Hwy (exit 16), N 1 mi on Red Arrow Hwy to Lake St, W 1 mi, follow signs (R). 2015 rates: $25 to $30. May 1 to Oct 15. (269)465-3406

BRIGHTON — J5 *Livingston*

BRIGHTON SRA (State Pk) From Jct of I-96 & exit 147 (Spencer Rd), SW 5 mi on Spencer Rd (Main St) (Brighton Rd), to Chilson Rd, S 1.5 mi to Bishop Lake, E 0.75 mi (R). Entrance fee required. 2015 rates: $21. Apr 15 to Nov 3. (810)229-6566

BRIMLEY — D4 *Chippewa, Mackinac*

BAY MILLS CASINO RV PARK
Ratings: 7/8.5/8.5 (Campground) From Jct of M-28 & M-221 N 3 mi on M-221 to Lakeshore Dr, W 2 mi (L). **FAC:** Gravel rds. 120 gravel, 118 pull-thrus (35 x 60), back-ins (30 x 50), 73 full hkups, 47 W, 47 E (30/50 amps), cable, WiFi, tent sites, dump, laundry, LP gas, fire rings, firewood, restaurant. **REC:** Lake Superior: fishing, golf, rec open to public. Pets OK. Partial handicap access.

BRIMLEY (CONT)

BAY MILLS CASINO RV PARK (CONT)
2015 rates: $21 to $29. Disc: AAA. May 1 to Oct 30. ATM.
(888)422-9645 Lat: 46.42384, Lon: -84.60386
11386 West Lakeshore Dr, Brimley, MI 49715
kmperron@4baymills.com
www.baymillscasinos.com
See ad opposite page, 616.

➔ BRIMLEY (State Pk) From Jct I75 & MI 28, W 7.7 mi on MI 28 to MI 221, N 2.5 mi to 6 Mile Road, E 0.8 mi (L). Entrance fee required. 2015 rates: $16 to $23. Apr 15 Nov 9. (906)248-3422

Things to See and Do

BAY MILLS CASINO & RESORT Indian Casino w/resort hotel on Lake Superior. Golf Course & RV park across the road. Four restaurants & lounges. Partial handicap access. RV accessible. Restrooms, food. Hours: Open 24 hours. Adult fee: $69 to $185. ATM.
(888)422-9645 Lat: 46.42291, Lon: -84.60328
11386 West Lakeshore Dr, Brimley, MI 49715
kmperron@4baymills.com
www.4baymills.com
See ad opposite page.

WILD BLUFF GOLF COURSE Wild Bluff offers 18 holes of championship golf, a world class double teed driving range, two practice putting greens, wide fairways, and large greens. May 3 to Oct 15. Restrooms. Hours: 7am to 7pm. Adult fee: $15 to $35. ATM.
(888)422-9645 Lat: 46.42073, Lon: -84.60387
11335 W. Lakeshore Dr, Brimley, MI 49715
rlussenhop@4baymills.com
www.wildbluff.com
See ad opposite page.

BROOKLYN — J5 *Jackson, Lenawee, Washtenaw*

JUNIPER HILLS CAMPGROUND **Ratings: 6.5/6.5/7.5** (Campground) 2015 rates: $30 to $40. May 1 to Oct 31. (888)396-8300 13500 US Hwy 12, Brooklyn, MI 49230

BRUCE CROSSING — C1 *Ontonagon*

STANNARD TOWNSHIP PARK (Public) From Jct US 45 & M28 in Bruce Crossing, N 0.1 mi on US 45 (R) Pay in drop box. 2015 rates: $10 to $13. May 15 to Oct 31. (906)827-3778

BUCHANAN — K3 *Berrien*

BEAR CAVE RESORT **Ratings: 7/8★/8** (RV Resort) 2015 rates: $42 to $45. May 1 to Oct 31. (269)695-3050 4085 Bear Cave Rd, Buchanan, MI 49107

➔ **FULLER'S RESORT & CAMPGROUND ON CLEAR LAKE**
Ratings: 8/9★/9 (Campground) S-bnd: Jct of I-94 & US-12 (Exit 4A), E 17 mi on US-12 to Bakertown Rd, N 1.6 mi to Elm Valley Rd, W 0.7 mi to E Clear Lake Rd, N 1 mi (E). **FAC:** Gravel rds. (196 spaces). 136 Avail: 25 gravel, 66 grass, 45 dirt, 6 pull-thrus (30 x 60), back-ins (33 x 40), 6 full hkups, 86 W, 86 E (30/50 amps), seasonal sites, WiFi, tent sites, rentals, dump, mobile sewer, laundry, groc, LP gas, fire rings, firewood, restaurant. **REC:** Clear Lake: swim, fishing, playground, rec open to public. Pet restrict(B). 2015 rates: $39 to $44. Apr 15 to Nov 1.
(269)695-3785 Lat: 41.83436, Lon: -86.41836
1622 E Clear Lake Rd, Buchanan, MI 49107
info@fullersresort.com
www.fullersresort.com
See ad this page.

BUCKLEY — F3 *Grand Traverse*

TRAVERSE CITY KOA
Ratings: 9/9.5★/9.5 (Campground) From Jct. of US 31 & M-37, S. on M-37, 9.6 mi (R). **FAC:** Paved/gravel rds. 119 Avail: 75 gravel, 44 grass, 17 pull-thrus (30 x 65), back-ins (30 x 65), 64 full hkups, 55 W, 55 E (30/50 amps), cable, WiFi, tent sites, rentals, dump, mobile sewer, laundry, groc, LP gas, fire rings, firewood. **REC:** heated pool, playground. Pet restrict(B). Partial handicap access. Big rig sites, eco-friendly, 2015 rates: $34 to $57. May 1 to Oct 15.
(800)249-3203 Lat: 44.54561, Lon: -85.67769
9700 S M 37, Buckley, MI 49620
info@traversecitykoa.com
www.traversecitykoa.com
See ad page 640.

BYRON — H5 *Genesee*

MYERS LAKE CAMPGROUND
Ratings: 8/9.5★/9 (Campground) From Jct of US-23 & Silver Lake Rd (Exit 79), W 9.2 mi on Silver Lake Rd to Murray Rd, S 200 ft (R).

A PREMIER FAMILY CAMPGROUND!
"Come experience another great lake!" Myers Lake is a beautiful destination to experience the pristine lakeshore and bountiful Christian hospitality. Our alcohol-free setting is the perfect place for family fun for everyone.

FAC: Gravel rds. (114 spaces). 101 Avail: 1 gravel, 100 grass, back-ins (30 x 42), 62 W, 101 E (30/50 amps), seasonal sites, WiFi, tent sites, rentals, dump, mobile sewer, laundry, LP gas, fire rings, firewood, controlled access. **REC:** Myers Lake: swim, fishing, playground. Pet restrict(Q). Partial handicap access. Eco-friendly, 2015 rates: $42. May 1 to Oct 15.
(810)266-4511 Lat: 42.80721, Lon: -83.88188
10575 W Silver Lake Rd, Byron, MI 48418
info@myerslake.org
www.myerslake.org
See ad this page, 616 & Family Camping in Magazine Section.

CADILLAC — G4 *Missaukee, Wexford*

BIRCHWOOD RESORT & CAMPGROUND **Ratings: 5/7.5★/6.5** (Campground) 2015 rates: $34 to $37. (231)775-9101 6545 E M-115, Cadillac, MI 49601

➔ CAMP CADILLAC **Ratings: 8/9★/8.5** (Campground) 2015 rates: $36. Apr 15 to Oct 15. (231)775-9724 10621 E 34 Rd, Cadillac, MI 49601

MITCHELL (State Pk) From Jct of M-115 & M-55, NW 0.25 mi on M-115 (R). Entrance fee required. 2015 rates: $29 to $35. (231)775-7911

CASEVILLE — G6 *Huron*

ALBERT E SLEEPER (State Pk) From town, NE 5 mi on Hwy M 25 (R). Entrance fee required. 2015 rates: $25 to $27. Apr 17 to Oct 18. (800)447-2757

➔ CASEVILLE COUNTY PARK (Public) From the Jct of Port Austin Rd (M-25) & Oak St in Downtown Caseville: N 0.3 mi. on Port Austin Rd, cont. on Main St (L). 2015 rates: $35 to $50. Apr 15 to Oct 31. (989)856-2080

CASS CITY — G6 *Tuscola*

EVERGREEN PARK (Public) From jct Hwy 46 & Hwy 53: Go 9 mi N on Hwy 53. 2015 rates: $24 to $30. (989)872-6600

CEDAR — F3 *Leelanau*

LEELANAU PINES CAMPGROUNDS **Ratings: 8/9★/8** (Campground) 2015 rates: $63. May 1 to Oct 15. (231)228-5742 6500 E Leelanau Pines Dr, Cedar, MI 49621

CEDAR RIVER — E2 *Menominee*

J W WELLS (State Pk) From town, S 1 mi on M-35 (L). Entrance fee required. 2015 rates: $17 to $22. Apr 15 to Oct 15. (906)863-9747

KLEINKE PARK (MENOMINEE COUNTY PARK) (Public) From jct CR G-12 & Hwy 35: Go 6 mi S on Hwy 35. 2015 rates: $15 to $24. (906)753-4582

Visit Camping World on your RV travels to stock up on accessories and supplies while on the road. Find the nearest SuperCenter at CampingWorld.com

CEDAR SPRINGS — H4 *Kent*

LAKESIDE CAMP PARK
Ratings: 9/9.5★/9.5 (Campground) From Jct of US-131 & M-46 (17 Mile Rd exit 104), E 0.1 mi on 17 Mile Rd to White Creek Ave, S 0.25 mi (R). **FAC:** Paved rds. (146 spaces). Avail: 81 grass, 14 pull-thrus (30 x 50), back-ins (30 x 50), 41 full hkups, 40 W, 40 E (30/50 amps), seasonal sites, WiFi, tent sites, rentals, dump, laundry, groc, fire rings, firewood. **REC:** Waller Lake: swim, fishing, playground. Pet restrict(B). Partial handicap access. Big rig sites, eco-friendly, 2015 rates: $32 to $36. Apr 29 to Oct 9.
(616)696-1735 Lat: 43.21363, Lon: -85.57161
13677 White Creek Ave, Cedar Springs, MI 49319
www.lakesidecamppark.com
See ad pages 627, 616.

CEDARVILLE — D5 *Mackinac*

➔ **CEDARVILLE RV PARK**
Ratings: 8/9★/8 (Condo Pk) From Jct of I-75 & M-134 (exit 359), E 17.5 mi on M-134 thru Cedarville to Bay St, S 0.3 mi to Grove St, W 0.2 mi (L). **FAC:** Paved rds. (51 spaces). Avail: 27 grass, back-ins (30 x 50), 27 full hkups (30/50 amps), seasonal sites, WiFi, laundry, fire rings, firewood. **REC:** Lake Huron: swim, fishing. Pet restrict(Q). No tents. 2015 rates: $36 to $55. May 1 to Oct 1.
(906)484-3351 Lat: 45.99680, Lon: -84.34982
634 Grove St, Cedarville, MI 49719
info@cedarvillervpark.com
www.cedarvillervpark.com
See ad this page.

CENTRAL LAKE — E4 *Cheboygan*

➔ THURSTON PARK (Public) From Jct of M-88 & State St, E 2 blks on State St to Lake St, S 1 blk (E). 2015 rates: $20 to $25. Apr 25 to Oct 17. (231)544-6483

CHAMPION — C2 *Marquette*

MICHIGAMME SHORES CAMPGROUND RESORT
Ratings: 9/9★/9 (Campground) From Jct of US-41 & M-95, W 5 mi on US-41 (L). **FAC:** Paved rds. 81 Avail: 70 gravel, 11 grass, 10 pull-thrus (28 x 60), back-ins (30 x 50), 58 full hkups, 23 W, 21 E (30/50 amps), WiFi, tent sites, rentals, dump, laundry, groc, LP gas, fire rings, firewood. **REC:** Lake Michigamme: swim, fishing, playground, rec open to public. Pet restrict(Q). Partial handicap access. Big rig sites, 2015 rates: $45. May 1 to Oct 15.
AAA Approved
(906)339-2116 Lat: 46.53201, Lon: -88.00750
64 Purple Rd, Michigamme, MI 49861
ftshores@aol.com
www.michigammeshores.com
See ad pages 634, 616.

VAN RIPER (State Pk) From Jct of Hwy 95 & US-41, W 3.8 mi on US-41, follow signs (L). Entrance fee required. 2015 rates: $12 to $23. May 1 to Nov 1. (906)339-4461

CHARLEVOIX — E4 *Charlevoix*

FISHERMAN'S ISLAND (State Pk) From town: Go 5 mi S on US 31, turn right on Bell Bay Rd, then go 2-1/2 mi on Bell Bay Rd to posted entrance. Pit toilets. 2015 rates: $12. (231)547-6641

CHARLOTTE — J4 *Eaton*

EATON COUNTY FAIRGROUNDS (Public) From Jct of I-69 & M-50 (exit 60), W 0.7 mi on M-50 to Cochran Ave, S 0.3 mi on Cochran Ave (L). Call for availability. 2015 rates: $15. May 1 to Oct 1. (517)649-8580

CHEBOYGAN — E5 *Cheboygan*

ALOHA (State Pk) From Cheboygan, S 9 mi on M-33 to M-212, W 1 mi (E). Entrance fee required. 2015 rates: $18 to $30. May 1 to Oct 11. (231)625-2522

CHEBOYGAN (CONT)

CHEBOYGAN (State Pk) From Jct of SR-27 & US-23, E 5 mi on US-23, follow signs (L). Entrance fee required. 2015 rates: $16 to $22. (231)627-2811

WATERWAYS CAMPGROUND **Ratings: 7/7/8.5** (Campground) 2015 rates: $40. May 1 to Oct 15. (888)882-7066 9575 M 33 Hwy, Cheboygan, MI 49721

CHELSEA — J5 *Jackson*

WATERLOO REC AREA/PORTAGE LAKE (State Pk) From Jct of I-94 & Mt Hope Rd (exit 150), N 2.4 mi on Mt Hope Rd to Seymour Rd, W 1.7 mi, follow signs (R) Entrance fee required. 2015 rates: $18 to $26. (734)475-8307

WATERLOO SRA/SUGARLOAF (State Pk) From Jct of I-94 & Exit 153 (Clear Lake Rd), N 4 mi on Clear Lake Rd to Loveland Rd, E 1.1 mi, follow signs (L). Entrance fee required. 2015 rates: $24 to $26. May 15 to Sep 13. (734)475-8307

CLARE — G4 *Isabella*

HERRICK REC AREA (Public) From Jct of US/Bus-10 & Bus-27, E 2.25 mi on US/Bus-10 to Summerton Rd, S 0.75 mi to Herrick Rd, E 0.25 mi (R). 2015 rates: $20 to $25. (989)386-2010

CLAYTON — K5 *Lenawee*

LAKE HUDSON STATE RECREATION AREA (State Pk) From jct US 127 & Hwy 34: Go 6-1/2 mi E on Hwy 34, then 1-1/2 mi S on Hwy 156. Pit toilets. 2015 rates: $17. (517)445-2265

CLIMAX — J4 *Kalamazoo*

COLD BROOK COUNTY PARK (Public) From Jct of I 94 & Mercury Dr (Exit 92), S 0.3 mi on Mercury Dr to MN Ave E, West 1.5 mi (R). 2015 rates: $22. Apr 15 to Oct 31. (269)746-4270

COLDWATER — K4 *Branch*

ANGEL COVE PARK (Public) From Jct of I-69 & US-12, W 3.5 mi on US-12 to River Rd, N 4 mi, follow signs (L). 2015 rates: $25. Apr 15 to Oct 15. (517)278-8541

BRANCH COUNTY MEMORIAL PARK (Public) From jct I-69 & US-12: Go 3 mi W on US-12, then 1/2 mi S on Behnke Rd. 2015 rates: $20 to $25. May 1 to Oct 15. (517)279-2254

HARBOR COVE RV RESORT (RV Resort) (Under Construction) From Jct I69 & US12: Go 2 1/2 mi W on US12, then 6/10 mi S on Butters Ave, then 2/10 mi W on Race St (R). **FAC.** 200 Avail: 100 paved, 100 grass, 200 pull-thrus (34 x 80), 200 full hkups (30/50 amps), dump, laundry. **REC.** Pets OK. Big rig sites, 2015 rates: $50. Apr 1 to Oct 31.
(517)279-2683 Lat: 41.93312, Lon: -85.02795
632 Race St, Coldwater, MI 49036
Harborcovervresort@yahoo.com
www.harborcovervresort.com/
See ad this page.

WAFFLE FARM CAMPGROUNDS
Ratings: 6.5/10★/9.5 (Campground) From Jct of I-69 & Jonesville Rd (exit 16), W 2.5 mi on Jonesville Rd to Union City Rd, N 0.75 mi (L). **FAC:** Gravel rds. (355 spaces). Avail: 110 grass, 24 pull-thrus (25 x 75), back-ins (28 x 75), 17 full hkups, 93 W, 93 E (30/50 amps), seasonal sites, cable, WiFi, tent sites, rentals, dump, groc, LP gas, firewood. **REC:** Craig-Morrison Chain of 7 Lakes: swim, fishing, playground. Pet restrict(B). Partial handicap access. 2015 rates: $30 to $38. Apr 15 to Oct 15.
AAA Approved
(517)278-4315 Lat: 41.99736, Lon: -85.02510
790 N Union City Rd, Coldwater, MI 49036
info@wafflefarm.com
www.wafflefarm.com
See ad this page.

COLOMA — J3 *Van Buren*

COLOMA/ST JOSEPH KOA **Ratings: 8.5/8.5/9** (Campground) 2015 rates: $41 to $52. May 1 to Oct 15. (269)849-3333 3527 Coloma Rd, Riverside, MI 49084

DUNE LAKE CAMPGROUND **Ratings: 5.5/7.5★/8.5** (Campground) 2015 rates: $27 to $30. May 1 to Oct 1. (269)764-8941 80855 CR-376, Coloma, MI 49038

COOPERSVILLE — H3 *Ottawa*

CONESTOGA GRAND RIVER CAMPGROUND
Ratings: 8.5/8★/8 (Campground) From Jct of I-96 & 68th Ave (exit 16), S 3 mi on 68th Ave to Leonard St, W 4 mi to 96th Ave, S 0.5 mi to Oriole, W 600 ft (L); or From Jct of I-96 & 112th St (exit 16), S 2.4 mi on 112th St to Leonard St, SE 3.5 mi to 96th Ave, S 0.5 mi to Oriole, W 600 ft (L). **FAC:** Gravel rds. (90 spaces). Avail: 70 gravel, 3 pull-thrus (25 x 60), back-ins (28 x 50), 23 full hkups, 47 W, 47 E (30/50 amps), seasonal sites, WiFi, tent sites, rentals, dump, mobile sewer, laundry, fire rings, firewood. **REC:** heated pool, Grand River: fishing, marina, playground. Pet restrict(B). Partial handicap access. Big rig sites, 2015 rates: $39 to $50. May 1 to Oct 31.
(616)837-6323 Lat: 43.02983, Lon: -86.03256
9720 Oriole Dr, Coopersville, MI 49404
gasquith@mapleisland.net
www.conestogacampground.com
See ad pages 626, 616.

COPPER HARBOR — B2 *Keweenaw*

FORT WILKINS (State Pk) From Jct of US-41 & Hwy 26, E 1 mi on US-41 to park access rd, E 1.6 mi (R). Entrance fee required. 2015 rates: $18 to $26. Apr 15 to Nov 15. (906)289-4215

LAKE FANNY HOOE RESORT & CAMPGROUNDS **Ratings: 8/9★/8.5** (Campground) 2015 rates: $44. May 15 to Oct 15. (906)289-4451 505 Second St, Copper Harbor, MI 49918

COVERT — J3 *Van Buren*

COVERT PARK BEACH & CAMPGROUND (Public) From I-196 exit 13 (Covert): Go W 1 mile to park. 2015 rates: $29 to $32. May 15 to Oct 15. (269)764-1421

COVERT/SOUTH HAVEN KOA **Ratings: 9/9.5★/9.5** (Campground) 2015 rates: $41.95 to $74.95. Apr 15 to Oct 15. (269)764-0818 39397 M-140 Highway, Covert, MI 49043

CRYSTAL FALLS — D1 *Iron*

BEWABIC (State Pk) From Jct of US-141 & US-2, W 3 mi on US-2, follow signs (L). Entrance fee required. 2015 rates: $17 to $21. (906)875-3324

COPPER COUNTRY SF/GLIDDEN LAKE (State Pk) From town, E 4.5 mi on M-69 to Lake Mary Rd, S 1.5 mi to NE-side of lake (R). Pit toilets. 2015 rates: $13. (906)875-3324

Say you saw it in our Guide!

PAINT RIVER HILLS CAMPGROUND **Ratings: 2/8/7.5** (Campground) 2015 rates: $20 to $22. May 15 to Nov 30. (906)875-4977 525 Paint River Hills Road, Crystal Falls, MI 49920

PENTOGA PARK (Public) From Iron Mountain, NE 23.6 mi on US-2 to CR-424, S & W 9 mi on CR 424, follow signs (R). Entrance fee required. 2015 rates: $22 to $23. May 15 to Sep 30. (906)265-3979

RUNKLE LAKE MUNICIPAL PARK (Public) From Jct of US 2 & M69, in Crystal Falls, E 0.75 mi on M69 to Runkle Lake Rd (park sign), N 0.2 mi on Runkle Lake Rd (L). 2015 rates: $12 to $20. May 23 to Sep 7. (906)875-3051

CURRAN — F5 *Oscoda*

AU SABLE SF/MCCOLLUM LAKE (State Pk) From town, NW 8.5 mi on M-72 to Mc Collum Lake Rd, follow signs (R). Pit toilets. 2015 rates: $13. (989)848-5405

CURTIS — D3 *Mackinac*

LAKE SUPERIOR SF (SOUTH MANISTIQUE LAKE) (State Pk) From town: Go 3 mi W on S Curtis Rd, then 2 mi S on Long Point Rd, then 1/2 mi SE, on West side of lake. Pit toilets. 2015 rates: $13. (906)293-5131

LOG CABIN RESORT & CAMPGROUND **Ratings: 7.5/7/7.5** (Campground) 2015 rates: $31 to $39. May 1 to Oct 1. (906)586-9732 18024 H42, Curtis, MI 49820

DAVISON — H5 *Genesee*

WOLVERINE CAMPGROUND (Public) From Jct of I-75 & Mt Morris Rd exit, E 14.5 mi on Mt Morris Rd to Baxter Rd, S 0.25 mi (R); or From Jct of M-15 & Mt Morris Rd, E 2.6 mi to Baxter Rd, S 0.25 mi (R). 2015 rates: $14 to $24. May 20 to Sep 8. (800)648-7275

DEARBORN — J6 *Wayne*

DEARBORN CAMPGROUND (Public) From the Jct of I-96 Exit 155B (Milford Rd) N on Milford Rd 4.3 mi to General Motors Rd W 0.8 mi (R). 2015 rates: $19 to $31. May 1 to Nov 1. (248)684-6000

DECATUR — J3 *Van Buren*

OAK SHORES CAMPGROUND **Ratings: 8.5/7.5/8** (Campground) 2015 rates: $34 to $47. Apr 15 to Oct 15. (269)423-7370 86232 CR-215, Decatur, MI 49045

TIMBER TRAILS RV PARK **Ratings: 7.5/9★/9** (Campground) 2015 rates: $35. May 1 to Sep 30. (269)423-7311 84981-47 1/2 St, Decatur, MI 49045

DETROIT — J6 *Wayne*

DETROIT AREA MAP

Symbols on map indicate towns within a 45 mile radius of Detroit where campgrounds are listed. Check listings for more information.

In MI, see also Algonac, Belleville, Dundee, Holly, Howell, Monroe, New Hudson, Ortonville, Petersburg, Pinckney, Waterford & Ypsilanti.
In ON, see also Amherstburg, Belle River & Windsor

DORR — J3 *Allegan*

HUNGRY HORSE CAMPGROUND **Ratings: 9/9.5★/10** (Campground) From Jct of US-131 & 142nd Ave (exit 68), W 3.5 mi on 142nd Ave (L). **FAC:** Paved/gravel rds. (98 spaces). Avail: 71 grass, 15 pull-thrus (30 x 70), back-ins (25 x 50), 47 full hkups, 24 W, 24 E (30/50 amps), seasonal sites, WiFi, tent sites, rentals, dump, mobile sewer, laundry, groc, fire rings, firewood. **REC:** heated pool, wading pool, shuffleboard, playground. Pet restrict(B). Partial handicap access. Big rig sites, 2015 rates: $35 to $40. May 1 to Oct 15.
(616)681-9843 Lat: 42.72209, Lon: -85.74385
2016 142nd Avenue, Dorr, MI 49323
hungryhorsecampground@gmail.com
www.hungryhorsecampground.com
See ad pages 627, 616.

DUNDEE — K5 *Monroe*

WILDERNESS CAMPGROUND Ratings: 5.5/8.5★/7.5 (Campground) From Jct of US 23 & M-50, Exit 17, (in Dundee), E 4 mi on M-50 to Meanwell Rd, S 1 mi on Meanwell Rd (R). **FAC:** Gravel rds. (100 spaces). Avail: 50 grass, 10 pull-thrus (35 x 77), back-ins (35 x 55), 50 W, 50 E (30/50 amps), seasonal sites, tent sites, rentals, dump, mobile sewer, groc, fire rings, firewood. **REC:** Lake Wilderness: swim, fishing, playground. Pet restrict(B/Q). Partial handicap access. 2015 rates: $25 to $35. Apr 15 to Oct 15.
(734)529-5122 Lat: 41.93612, Lon: -83.613691
1350 Meanwell Rd, Dundee, MI 48131
wildernesscampgroundindundee@yahoo.com
www.wildernesscampgroundmichigan.com

DURAND — H5 *Shiawassee*

HOLIDAY SHORES RV PARK **Ratings: 7/NA/9.5** (RV Park) 2015 rates: $35. May 1 to Oct 31. (989)288-4444 10915 Goodall Rd, Durand, MI 48429

Tell them you saw them in this Guide!

WALNUT HILLS FAMILY CAMPGROUND LLC **Ratings: 6/9★/7.5** (Campground) From Jct I-69 & Grand River Rd (Exit 113), SE 3.3 mi on Grand River Rd to Cole Rd, SE 2.1 mi to Reed Rd, S 1 mi on Reed Rd - turns into Lehring Rd (L). **FAC:** Gravel rds. (191 spaces). Avail: 111 grass, 3 pull-thrus (35 x 75), back-ins (35 x 60), 111 W, 111 E (20/30 amps), seasonal sites, tent sites, rentals, dump, mobile sewer, groc, fire rings, firewood, controlled access. **REC:** Shiawasse River: swim, fishing, playground, rec open to public. Pets OK. Partial handicap access. Eco-friendly, 2015 rates: $37. Apr 29 to Oct 2.
(989)634-9782 Lat: 42.84018, Lon: -84.00864
7685 E. Lehring Rd, Durand, MI 48429
walnuthillscampground@gmail.com
www.walnuthillsfamilycampground.com
See ad this page.

EAST HIGHLAND — J5 *Oakland*

HIGHLAND REC AREA (State Pk) From Jct of US-23 & US-59, E 10 mi on US-59; or From Jct of I-75 & US-59, W 16 mi on US-59, follow signs (L). Entrance fee required. Pit toilets. 2015 rates: $13. (248)889-3750

EAST JORDAN — E4 *Charlevoix*

EAST JORDAN TOURIST PARK (Public) From Jct of M-32 & M-66, N 0.1 mi on M-66 (R). 2015 rates: $26 to $36. Apr 15 to Oct 15. (231)536-2561

WOODEN SHOE PARK (VILLAGE PARK) (Public) From jct Hwy-66 & East Jordan-Ellsworth Rd: Go 7 mi W on East Jordan-Ellsworth Rd, follow signs. May 15 to Sep 15. (231)588-6382

EAST TAWAS — F5 *Iosco*

EAST TAWAS CITY PARK (Public) At Jct of US-23 & Newman St. 2015 rates: $20 to $35. (989)362-5562

TAWAS POINT (State Pk) From Jct of US-23 & Tawas Beach Rd exit, SE 2.5 mi on Tawas Beach Rd, follow signs (E). Entrance fee required. 2015 rates: $29. Apr 15 to Oct 30. (989)362-5041

EASTPORT — E4 *Antrim*

BARNES PARK CAMPGROUND (Public) From Jct of US-31 & SR-88, W .25 mi on SR-88/becomes Barnes Park Rd (E). 2015 rates: $22 to $26. May 8 to Oct 21. (231)599-2712

ELK RAPIDS — F4 *Antrim*

HONCHO REST CAMPGROUND **Ratings: 7/9★/8** (Campground) 2015 rates: $40 to $45. May 1 to Oct 1. (231)264-8548 8988 Cairn Highway, Elk Rapids, MI 49629

EMMETT — H6 *St Clair*

EMMETT KOA **Ratings: 8/9.5★/9** (Campground) 2015 rates: $50.50 to $61.25. Apr 19 to Oct 20. (888)562-5612 3864 Breen Rd, Emmett, MI 48022

EMPIRE — F3 *Leelanau*

INDIGO BLUFFS RV PARK **Ratings: 8/9.5★/9** (Campground) 2015 rates: $47. May 15 to Oct 15. (231)326-5050 6760 W Empire Hwy M-72, Empire, MI 49630

INDIGO BLUFFS RV RESORT **Ratings: 9.5/NA/10** (Condo Pk) 2015 rates: $65. May 15 to Oct 15. (231)326-5050 6760 W Empire Hwy M-72, Empire, MI 49630

ESCANABA — D2 *Delta*

FULLER PARK (Public) From town, S 15 mi on M-35 (L). 2015 rates: $18 to $20. May 20 to Sep 15. (906)786-1020

PARK PLACE OF THE NORTH **Ratings: 4/6.5/7.5** (Campground) 2015 rates: $25. May 1 to Oct 15. (906)786-8453 e4575 M 35, Escanaba, MI 49829

PIONEER TRAIL PARK (Public) N-bnd: On US-2/41 at N-end of town/Escanaba River Bridge (R). 2015 rates: $32. May to Oct 15. (906)786-1020

ESSEXVILLE — G5 *Bay*

FINN ROAD CAMPGROUND & BOAT LAUNCH (HAMPTON TOWNSHIP) (Public) From jct Hwy 15 & Hwy 25: Go 5 mi E on Hwy 25, then 2 mi N on Finn Rd. 2015 rates: $19 to $23. May 1 to Oct 31. (989)894-0055

EVART — G4 *Osceola*

RIVERSIDE PARK (Public) From Jct of US-131 & US-10, E 14 mi on US-10 to Main St, S 0.1 mi to 9th St, E 0.25 mi, follow signs (L). 2015 rates: $15 to $25. May 1 to Sep 30. (231)734-5901

FENWICK — H4 *Montcalm*

SNOW LAKE KAMPGROUND Ratings: 9/8.5★/8 (Campground) From Jct of M-57 & M-66, S 3 mi on M-66 to Snows Lake Rd, E 0.75 mi (R). **FAC:** Gravel rds. (309 spaces). 129 Avail: 32 gravel, 97 grass, 69 pull-thrus (26 x 65), back-ins (30 x 50), 81 full hkups, 48 W, 48 E (30/50 amps), seasonal sites, WiFi $, tent sites, rentals, dump, mobile sewer, laundry, groc, LP gas, fire rings, firewood, restaurant, controlled access. **REC:** heated pool, wading pool, whirlpool, Snow Lake: fishing, shuffleboard, playground, rec open to public. Pet restrict(B). Partial handicap access. Big rig sites, 2015 rates: $36. May 1 to Oct 1. ATM.
(989)248-3224 Lat: 43.13369, Lon: -85.05791
644 E Snows Lake Rd, Fenwick, MI 48834
camp@snowlakekampground.com
www.snowlakekampground.com

FIFE LAKE — F4 *Grand Traverse*

PERE MARQUETTE SF/SPRING LAKE (State Pk) From Jct of US-131 & Hwy 186, SW 1.5 mi on US-131 to park access rd, S 0.5 mi, follow signs (R). Pit toilets. 2015 rates: $13. (231)775-7911

FOREST LAKE — D3 *Alger*

ESCANABA RIVER SF (FOREST LAKE) (State Pk) From town: Go 1/4 mi W on Hwy 94, then 2 mi S on Campground Rd. Pit toilets. 2015 rates: $13. (906)346-9201

FOUNTAIN — G3 *Mason*

TIMBER SURF RESORT **Ratings: 5.5/7.5/6.5** (Campground) 2015 rates: $30. Apr 1 to Nov 30. (231)462-3468 6575 Dewey Rd, Fountain, MI 49410

FRANKENMUTH — H5 *Saginaw*

YOGI BEAR'S JELLYSTONE PARK CAMP-RESORT **Ratings: 9.5/10★/9.5** (RV Park) N-bnd: From Jct of I-75 & M-83 (Exit 136), E 2 mi on M-83 (Birch Run Rd) to M-83 (Gera Rd), N 5 mi to Weiss St, NE .01 mi (R). **FAC:** Paved rds. 260 Avail: 64 paved, 167 gravel, 29 grass, 48 pull-thrus (25 x 65), back-ins (25 x 60), some side by side hkups, 160 full hkups,

MI

FRANKENMUTH (CONT)

YOGI BEAR'S JELLYSTONE (CONT)
100 W, 100 E (30/50 amps), WiFi, tent sites, rentals, dump, laundry, groc, LP gas, firewood, controlled access. **REC:** heated pool, whirlpool, playground. Pets OK. Partial handicap access. Big rig sites, 2015 rates: $44 to $66. Mar 1 to Dec 31. ATM.
AAA Approved
(989)652-6668 Lat: 43.31699, Lon: -83.73384
1339 Weiss St, Frankenmuth, MI 48734
reservations@frankenmuthjellystone.com
www.frankenmuthjellystone.com
See ad pages 618 (Spotlight Frankenmuth), 616 & RV Trips of a Lifetime in Magazine Section.

Things to See and Do

BRONNER'S CHRISTMAS WONDERLAND
The World's largest Christmas store. Open 361 days a year. This amazing store is the size of 1-1/2 football fields with over 50,000 trims, gifts & collectibles. Light refreshments available in Season's Eatings snack area. Partial handicap access. RV accessible. Restrooms, food. Hours: 9am to 9pm: Mon to Sat; 12pm to 7pm:Sun. ATM.
(989)652-9931 Lat: 43.31436, Lon: -83.73823
25 Christmas Lane, Frankenmuth, MI 48734
info@bronners.com
www.Bronners.com
See ad page 618 (Spotlight Frankenmuth) & RV Trips of a Lifetime in Magazine Section.

FRANKFORT — F3 *Benzie*

BETSIE RIVER CAMPSITE **Ratings: 4.5/8/9** (Campground) 2015 rates: $32 to $34. May 1 to Oct 1. (231)352-9535 1923 River Rd, Frankfort, MI 49635

FREDERIC — F4 *Crawford*

AU SABLE SF (UPPER MANISTEE RIVER) (State Pk) From town: Go 6-1/2 mi W on CR 612, then S on Manistee Rd. Pit toilets. 2015 rates: $13. (989)348-7068

AU SABLE SF/JONES LAKE (State Pk) From town, E 9 mi on CR-612, follow signs (R). Pit toilets. 2015 rates: $13. (989)348-7068

HAPPI DAYS CAMPGROUND **Ratings: 2.5/7.5/7.5** (Campground) 2015 rates: $26.50. May 1 to Oct 31. (989)390-5146 7486 W Batterson Rd, Frederic, MI 49733

GARDEN — D3 *Delta*

FAYETTE HISTORIC PARK (State Pk) From Jct of US-2 & M-183, SW 17 mi on M-183 (R). Entrance fee required. Pit toilets. 2015 rates: $17 to $19. Apr 15 to Nov 15. (906)644-2603

PORTAGE BAY SF CAMPGROUND (State Pk) From town, W 2.6 mi on 16th Rd., S 3.25 mi on LL Rd., SE 2 mi 100 Rd. Pit toilets. 2015 rates: $13. (906)644-2603

GAYLORD — E4 *Otsego*

GAYLORD KOA **Ratings: 9/9.5★/10** (Campground) 2015 rates: $49 to $64. May 1 to Oct 15. (800)562-4146 5101 Campfires Parkway, Gaylord, MI 49735

OTSEGO LAKE (State Pk) From Jct of I-75 & Old US-27, S 6 mi on Old US-27, follow signs (R). Entrance fee required. 2015 rates: $18 to $28. Apr 6 to Nov 1. (989)732-5485

GERMFASK — D3 *Schoolcraft*

BIG CEDAR CAMPGROUND & CANOE LIVERY
Ratings: 6.5/9★/8.5 (Campground) S-bnd: From Jct of US-28 & M-77, S 7.5 mi on M-77 (L); or N-bnd: From Jct of US-2 & M-77, N 10 mi on M-77 (R). **FAC:** Gravel rds. 50 grass, 9 pull-thrus (30 x 65), back-ins (30 x 60), 9 full hkups, 41 W, 41 E (15/30 amps), WiFi Hotspot, tent sites, dump, laundry, fire rings, firewood. **REC:** Manistique River: swim, fishing, playground. Pet restrict(B). 2015 rates: $25 to $29. May 1 to Oct 15.
(906)586-6684 Lat: 46.24265, Lon: -85.92641
7936 M77, Germfask, MI 49836
bigcedar_up@yahoo.com
www.bigcedarcampground.com

NORTHLAND OUTFITTERS **Ratings: 5/6/8.5** (Campground) 2015 rates: $30. May 1 to Oct 15. (906)586-9801 8174 Hwy M-77, Germfask, MI 49836

GLADSTONE — D2 *Delta*

GLADSTONE BAY CAMPGROUND (Public) From N jct Hwy 35 & US 2/41: Go 1/2 mi S on US 2/41, then 1 mi E on Delta Ave. 2015 rates: $25 to $30. May 7 to Oct 7. (906)428-1211

GLADWIN — G5 *Clare, Gladwin*

GLADWIN CITY PARK (Public) From Jct of SR-61 & Antler St, S 0.5 mi on Antler St (R). 2015 rates: $25. May 1 to Nov 30. (989)426-8126

RIVER VALLEY RV PARK **Ratings: 7/8/9** (Campground) 2015 rates: $33. May 1 to Oct 1. (989)386-7844 2165 S Bailey Lake Ave, Gladwin, MI 48624

GLEN ARBOR — F3 *Leelanau*

SLEEPING BEAR DUNES NATL LAKESHORE/D H DAY (Natl Pk) From town, W 1.5 mi on SR-109, follow signs (R). Pit toilets. 2015 rates: $12. Apr 4 to Nov 29. (231)326-5134

GLENNIE — F5 *Alcona*

ALCONA PARK (Public) From Jct of M-72 & M-65, S 7 mi on M-65 to Bamfield Rd, W 4.5 mi, follow signs (R). 2015 rates: $12 to $26. Apr 15 to Dec 1. (989)735-3881

We appreciate your business!

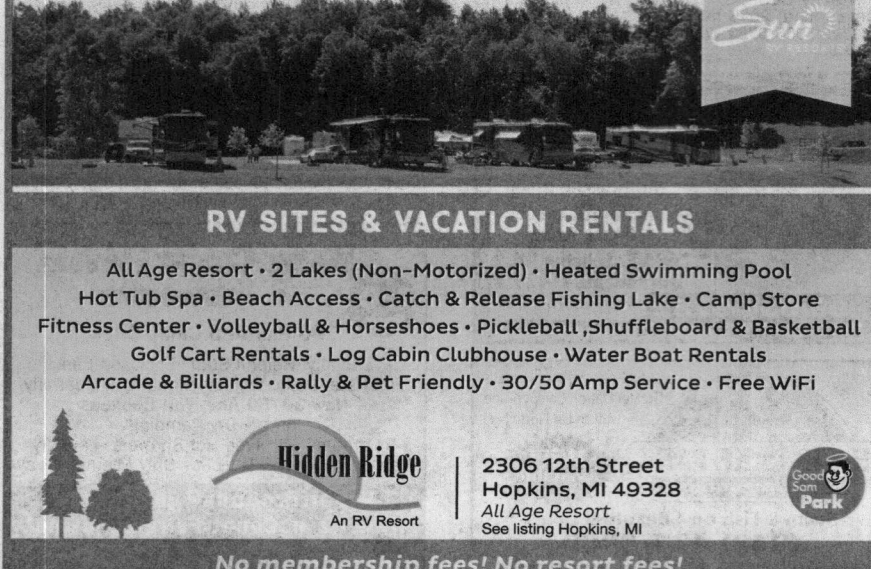

GOULD CITY — D3 *Mackinac*

MICHIHISTRIGAN BAR CAMPGROUND & CABINS **Ratings: 3.5/7/7.5** (Campground) 2015 rates: $24 to $28. (906)477-6983 w17838 Hwy US 2, Gould City, MI 49838

GOWEN — H4 *Montcalm*

LINCOLN PINES RESORT Ratings: 8/8.5★/7.5 (Campground) From the Jct of US 131 & Exit 120 (M-46) E on M-46 12 mi to Greenville Rd S 13.1 mi to Sidney Rd W. 3.0 Mi to 19 Mile Rd N 1.7 Mi to Lincoln Pines Rd (E). **FAC:** Paved rds. (339 spaces). Avail: 25 grass, patios, 4 pull-thrus (30 x 60), back-ins (30 x 50), 25 full hkups (30/50 amps), seasonal sites, WiFi Hotspot, tent sites, rentals, laundry, fire rings, firewood. **REC:** Lincoln Lake: swim, fishing, shuffleboard, playground. Pets OK. Partial handicap access. Eco-friendly, 2015 rates: $40 to $45. Apr 15 to Oct 15.
(616)984-2100 Lat: 43.24990, Lon: -85.34621
13033 19 Mile Rd, Gowen, MI 49326
info@lincolnpinesresort.com
www.lincolnpinesresort.com

GRAND HAVEN — H3 *Ottawa*

CAMPERS PARADISE, INC. **Ratings: 5/8★/5.5** (Campground) 2015 rates: $35. May 15 to Oct 15. (616)846-1460 800 Robbins Rd, Grand Haven, MI 49417

EASTPOINTE RV RESORT (RV Resort) (Too New to Rate) From Jct I-96 & M104 (Cleveland St): Go 7 mi W on M104, then 1 mi S on US 31 S, then 3/4 mi E on Fulton Ave (L). **FAC:** Paved rds. (150 spaces). Avail: 84 paved, back-ins (30 x 80), 84 full hkups (30/50 amps), seasonal sites, cable, WiFi, laundry, firewood, controlled access. **REC:** heated pool, whirlpool, Grand River: fishing. Pets OK. Big rig sites, 2015 rates: $60 to $75. May 1 to Oct 1.
(616)414-8137 Lat: 43.06311, Lon: -86.20590
200 N Beechtree St, Grand Haven, MI 49417
Info@eastpointervresort.com
www.eastpointervresort.com

GRAND HAVEN (State Pk) From Jct of US-31 & Washington Ave, N 0.75 mi on Washington Ave to Harbor Ave, W 0.75 mi (R). Entrance fee required. 2015 rates: $27 to $29. Mar 26 to Oct 30. (616)847-1309

OUTDOOR ADVENTURES GRAND HAVEN RESORT **Ratings: 8.5/8/9** (Campground) 2015 rates: $10. (989)671-1125 10990 US 31N, Grand Haven, MI 49417

GRAND JUNCTION — J3 *Van Buren*

WARNER CAMP RV PARK **Ratings: 5.5/6.5/7.5** (Campground) 2015 rates: $25. May 1 to Oct 1. (269)434-6844 60 55th St, Grand Junction, MI 49056

GRAND MARAIS — C3 *Alger*

LAKE SUPERIOR SF (BLIND SUCKER NO. 2) (State Pk) From town: Go 16 mi E on Grand Marais Truck Trail. Pit toilets. 2015 rates: $13. (906)658-3338

PICTURED ROCKS NATL LAKESHORE/HURRICANE RIVER (Natl Pk) From Grand Marais, W 12 mi on CR-H58, follow signs (R). Pit toilets. 2015 rates: $14. May 15 to Oct 31. (906)387-3700

PICTURED ROCKS NATL LAKESHORE/TWELVEMILE BEACH (Natl Pk) From Grand Marais, W 16 mi on CR-H58, follow signs (R). Pit toilets. 2015 rates: $16. May 15 to Oct 31. (906)387-3700

WOODLAND PARK (Public) From NW end of town, W 0.5 mi on M-77, follow signs (R). 2015 rates: $18 to $25. Apr 20 to Oct 15. (906)494-2613

Before you head north, know the rules and regulations for crossing the border into Canada. Read all about it in our Crossing into Canada section.

GRAND RAPIDS — H3 *Kent*

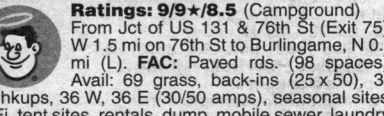

WOODCHIP CAMPGROUND
Ratings: 9/9★/8.5 (Campground) From Jct of US 131 & 76th St (Exit 75), W 1.5 mi on 76th St to Burlingame, N 0.1 mi (L). **FAC:** Paved rds. (98 spaces). Avail: 69 grass, back-ins (25 x 50), 33 full hkups, 36 W, 36 E (30/50 amps), seasonal sites, WiFi, tent sites, rentals, dump, mobile sewer, laundry, fire rings, firewood. **REC:** pool, playground. Pet restrict(B). Partial handicap access. 2015 rates: $42 to $45. May 1 to Oct 1.
AAA Approved
(616)878-9050 Lat: 42.82798, Lon: -85.70352
7501 Burlingame SW, Byron Center, MI 49315
info@woodchipcampground.com
www.woodchipcampground.com
See ad this page, 616.

Travel Services

CAMPING WORLD OF GRAND RAPIDS As the nation's largest retailer of RV supplies, accessories, services and new and used RVs, Camping World is committed to making your total RV experience better. **SERVICES:** Tire, RV appliance, staffed RV wash, restrooms. RV supplies, LP, dump, emergency parking, RV accessible. waiting room. Hours: 8am to 6pm.
(888)240-7995 Lat: 42.826239, Lon: -85.669525
201 76th Street SW, Grand Rapids, MI 49548
dselleck@campingworld.com
www.campingworld.com

GRANT — H3 *Newaygo*

CHINOOK CAMPING **Ratings: 7/6.5/7.5** (Campground) 2015 rates: $28. Apr 15 to Oct 15. (231)834-7505 5471 W 112th St, Grant, MI 49327

SALMON RUN CAMPGROUND AND VIC'S CANOES **Ratings: 5/8★/6.5** (Campground) 2015 rates: $29 to $36. May 15 to Oct 15. (231)834-5494 4845 Felch Ave, Grant, MI 49327

GRASS LAKE — J5 *Jackson*

APPLE CREEK CAMPGROUND & RV PARK
Ratings: 8.5/9★/9.5 (Campground) From Jct of I-94 & Mt Hope Rd (Exit 150), S 2.7 mi on Mt Hope Rd to Michigan Ave, W 0.8 mi to Wolf Lake Rd, S 3.5 mi to Orban Rd (L), .4 mi (R). **FAC:** Gravel rds. (180 spaces). Avail: 95 grass, 10 pull-thrus (30 x 60), back-ins (30 x 50), 95 W, 95 E (30 amps), seasonal sites, WiFi, tent sites, rentals, dump, mobile sewer, laundry, groc, LP gas, fire rings, firewood, controlled access. **REC:** heated pool, pond, fishing, playground. Pet restrict(B/Q). Age restrict may apply, 2015 rates: $30. Disc: military. Apr 15 to Nov 30.
(517)522-3467 Lat: 42.19659, Lon: -84.20709
11185 Orban Rd, Grass Lake, MI 49240
mbrennan@modempool.com
www.applecreekrv.com
See ad page 630.

Take time now to plan a road trip with your pet. Read more in our Pampered Pet Parks feature at the front of the Guide.

HOLIDAY RV CAMPGROUND
Ratings: 8.5/9★/8 (Campground) From Jct I-94 & Race Rd (Exit 147), S 0.2 mi on Race Rd to Ann Arbor Rd, E 0.4 mi to Knight Rd, E 0.8 mi. **FAC:** Gravel rds. 158 gravel, 4 pull-thrus (25 x 50), back-ins (25 x 50), 56 full hkups, 102 W, 102 E (30/50 amps), WiFi, tent sites, dump, mobile sewer, laundry, groc, LP gas, fire rings, firewood. **REC:** pool, pond, fishing, shuffleboard, playground. Pet restrict(B). Partial handicap access. Eco-friendly, 2015 rates: $35. Disc: military. Apr 15 to Oct 31.
(517)522-5846 Lat: 42.29149, Lon: -84.23745
9625 Knight Rd, Grass Lake, MI 49240
browder7288@aol.com
www.holidayrvcampground.com
See ad pages 630, 616.

GRAYLING — F4 *Crawford, Oscoda*

AU SABLE SF (CANOE HARBOR) (State Pk) From town: Go 14 mi SE on Hwy 72. Pit toilets. 2015 rates: $13. (989)275-5151

AU SABLE SF (LAKE MARGRETHE) (State Pk) From jct Hwy 93 & Hwy 72: Go 5 mi W on Hwy 72, then 1/4 mi S on McIntyres Landing Rd, then 2 mi W on gravel road. Pit toilets. 2015 rates: $13. (989)348-7068

AU SABLE SF (MANISTEE RIVER BRIDGE) (State Pk) From town: Go 8 mi W on Hwy 72. Pit toilets. 2015 rates: $13. (989)348-7068

HARTWICK PINES (State Pk) From Jct of I-75 & Harwick Pines Rd (exit 259), NE 2 mi on Harwick Pines Rd (L). Entrance fee required. 2015 rates: $18 to $35. May 1 to Oct 31. (989)348-7068

RIVER PARK CAMPGROUND **Ratings: 4/6.5/7** (Campground) 2015 rates: $30. (989)348-9092 2607 Peters Rd, Grayling, MI 49738

YOGI BEAR'S JELLYSTONE PARK CAMP-RESORT **Ratings: 7/9.5★/9** (Campground) 2015 rates: $47. May 1 to Oct 15. (989)348-2157 370 W 4 Mile Rd, Grayling, MI 49738

GREENVILLE — H4 *Montcalm*

THREE SEASONS FAMILY CAMPGROUND
Ratings: 7/8/8 (Campground) From Jct of M-91 & M-57, N 2.5 mi on M-91 to Peck Rd, E 1 mi on Peck Rd to Fitzner, N 0.8 mi on Fitzner to Fuller Rd, E 1 mi (L). **FAC:** Poor gravel/dirt rds. (161 spaces). Avail: 56 grass, 10 pull-thrus (35 x 50), back-ins (36 x 40), 2 full hkups, 29 W, 54 E (30/50 amps), seasonal sites, WiFi, tent sites, dump, mobile sewer, laundry, LP bottles, fire rings, firewood. **REC:** pool, Fish Lake: fishing, playground. Pet restrict(B). 2015 rates: $30 to $33. Apr 30 to Oct 15.
(616)754-5717 Lat: 43.22492, Lon: -85.21114
6956 W Fuller Rd, Greenville, MI 48838
threeseasonscampground@gmail.com
www.threeseasonscampground.com
See ad this page, 616.

GWINN — D2 *Marquette*

ESCANABA RIVER SF/BASS LAKE (State Pk) From town, SE 1.2 mi on Rice Lake Dr.(L). Pit toilets. 2015 rates: $15. (906)339-4461

FARQUAR-METSA TOURIST PARK (Public) From Jct of M-35 & Iron St, E 0.35 mi on Iron St (L). 2015 rates: $20. May 29 to Sep 30. (906)346-9217

HANCOCK — B1 *Houghton*

HANCOCK CAMPGROUND (Public) From Jct of US 41 & CR 203 (Quincy St-in Hancock), W 1.3 mi on CR 203 /Quincy St (changes to Jasberg St) (L). 2015 rates: $20 to $22. May 15 to Oct 15. (906)482-7413

MCLAIN (State Pk) From town, N 10 mi on M-203, follow signs (L). Entrance fee required. 2015 rates: $18 to $28. (906)482-0278

HARBOR BEACH — G6 *Huron*

HARBOR BEACH NORTH PARK CAMPGROUND (Public) From Jct of M-142 & M-25 (Huron St, in Harbor Beach), N 0.8 mi on M-25 (L). 2015 rates: $23 to $24. May 1 to Oct 31. (989)479-9554

WAGENER COUNTY PARK (Public) From the Jct of State St & S. Lakeshore Rd (M-25): S 5.3 mi on S. Lakeshore Rd. (L). 2015 rates: $18 to $35. May 1 to Oct 15. (989)479-9131

HARRIS — D2 *Delta, Menominee*

ISLAND RESORT & CASINO RV PARK **Ratings: 8.5/8.5/9.5** (Campground) 2015 rates: $20. May 1 to Nov 30. (800)682-6040 w399 US 2 & US 41, Harris, MI 49845

HARRISON — G4 *Clare, Missaukee, Osceola*

CAMP WITHII **Ratings: 4/9★/7** (Campground) 2015 rates: $30. Apr 15 to Oct 8. (989)539-3128 1820 Hampton Rd, Harrison, MI 48625

COUNTRYSIDE CAMPGROUND
Ratings: 9/10★/9 (Campground) From Jct of Bus US-127 & M-61 (in town), W 0.7 mi on M-61 to Byfield Dr, N 0.1 mi (L). **FAC:** Gravel rds. (75 spaces). Avail: 44 grass, 33 pull-thrus (35 x 70), back-ins (30 x 65), 27 full hkups, 17 W, 17 E (30/50 amps), seasonal sites, WiFi, tent sites, rentals, dump, laundry, fire rings, firewood. **REC:** heated pool, play-

We rate what RVers consider important.

HARRISON (CONT)

COUNTRYSIDE CAMPGROUND (CONT)
ground. Pets OK. Partial handicap access. Big rig sites, 2015 rates: $40. May 1 to Oct 15.
(989)539-5468 Lat: 44.02108, Lon: -84.81320
805 Byfield Dr, Harrison, MI 48625
info@countrysidecampgroundandcabins.com
www.countrysidecampgroundandcabins.com
See ad pages 627, 616.

DOWNHOUR'S SHADY ACRES CAMPGROUND **Ratings: 7/7.5★/7** (Campground) 2015 rates: $25. Apr 15 to Oct 15. (989)539-3111 7785 Jacks Road, Harrison, MI 48625

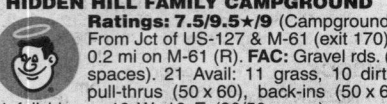

HIDDEN HILL FAMILY CAMPGROUND
Ratings: 7.5/9.5★/9 (Campground) From Jct of US-127 & M-61 (exit 170) W 0.2 mi on M-61 (R). **FAC:** Gravel rds. (45 spaces). 21 Avail: 11 grass, 10 dirt, 6 pull-thrus (50 x 60), back-ins (50 x 60), 11 full hkups, 10 W, 10 E (30/50 amps), seasonal sites, WiFi, tent sites, rentals, dump, laundry, fire rings, firewood. **REC:** shuffleboard, playground. Pet restrict(B/Q). Big rig sites, eco-friendly, 2015 rates: $34. Apr 15 to Oct 31.
AAA Approved
(989)539-9372 Lat: 43.99150, Lon: -84.77884
300 N Clare Ave, Harrison, MI 48625
manager@hiddenhillcampground.com
www.hiddenhillcampground.com
See ad pages 627, 616.

LAKE GEORGE CAMPGROUND **Ratings: 8.5/7.5/9** (Campground) 2015 rates: $36. May 1 to Oct 30. (989)588-4075 1935 S Jackson, Harrison, MI 48625

WILSON (State Pk) From Jct of SR-61 & Old US-127, N 0.6 mi on Old US-127, follow signs (R). Entrance fee required. 2015 rates: $22. Apr 1 to Dec 1. (989)539-3021

HARRISVILLE — F6 *Alcona*

HARRISVILLE (State Pk) From town, S 0.5 mi on US-23 to park access rd, E 0.1 mi, follow signs (L). Entrance fee required. 2015 rates: $25 to $27. May 9 to Oct 26. (989)724-5126

HART — G3 *Oceana*

JOHN GURNEY MUNICIPAL PARK (Public) From Jct of US-31 & Exit 149 (Polk Rd), E. 1.9 mi on Polk Rd to S Griswold St, N 0.8 mi (R). 2015 rates: $22 to $26. Apr 15 to Oct 15. (231)873-4959

HASTINGS — J4 *Barry*

CAMP MICHAWANA CHRISTIAN RV CAMP Ratings: 7.5/8★/8 (Campground) From Jct of M-37 & M-43 (W of town), S 6 mi on M-43 to Head Lake Rd, W 0.8 mi (L). **FAC:** Gravel rds. 56 gravel, patios, 5 pull-thrus (25 x 60), back-ins (30 x 60), 12 full hkups, 44 W, 44 E (30/50 amps), WiFi, tent sites, rentals, dump, mobile sewer, laundry, firewood. **REC:** Long Lake: swim, fishing, playground. Pets OK. Big rig sites, 2015 rates: $30. May 1 to Oct 3.
(269)623-3035 Lat: 42.56612, Lon: -85.36983
5800 Head Lake Rd, Hastings, MI 49058
rvcampground.michawana@gmail.com
www.michawanacamp.org

WELCOME WOODS CAMPGROUND & RV PARK **Ratings: 5/9★/6.5** (Campground) 2015 rates: $26 to $28. May 1 to Oct 15. (269)945-2803 522 Welcome Road, Hastings, MI 49058

WHISPERING WATERS CAMPGROUND **Ratings: 7.5/10★/8.5** (Campground) 2015 rates: $40. Apr 29 to Sep 25. (269)945-5166 1805 N Irving Rd, Hastings, MI 49058

HIGGINS LAKE — F4 *Roscommon*

HIGGINS LAKE KOA **Ratings: 7.5/7/8** (Campground) 2015 rates: $46 to $51. May 1 to Oct 24. (800)562-3351 3800 W Federal Hwy, Roscommon, MI 48653

HILLMAN — E5 *Montmorency*

EMERICK PARK (Public) From Jct Hwy 65 & Hwy 32: W 7.5 mi on Hwy 32 to State St, N 5 mi (R). 2015 rates: $12 to $18. May 1 to Oct 31. (989)733-0613

JACK'S LANDING RESORT **Ratings: 5.5/5.5/7.5** (Campground) 2015 rates: $33. May 1 to Oct 1. (989)742-4370 20836 Tennis Rd, Hillman, MI 49746

THUNDER BAY RESORT **Ratings: 7.5/NA/9.5** (RV Resort) 2015 rates: $39. Apr 1 to Nov 30. (989)742-4502 27800 M-32, Hillman, MI 49746

HILLSDALE — K4 *Hillsdale*

GATEWAY PARK CAMPGROUND **Ratings: 9/9★/10** (Campground) 2015 rates: $40 to $45. Apr 15 to Oct 15. (517)437-7005 4111 W Hallett Rd, Hillsdale, MI 49242

6 LAKES CAMPGROUND **Ratings: 4.5/5.5/6.5** (Campground) 2015 rates: $30. May 1 to Nov 30. (517)439-5660 2155 Hudson Rd, Hillsdale, MI 49242

HOLLAND — J3 *Ottawa*

HOLLAND (State Pk) From Jct of US-31 & Lakewood Blvd, W 1.2 mi on Lakewood Blvd to Douglas Ave, SW 5.4 mi on Douglas Ave/Ottawa Beach Rd (R) Note: Entrance fee required. 2015 rates: $27 to $33. Apr 1 to Oct 31. (616)399-9390

OAK GROVE RESORT **Ratings: 10/9.5★/10** (Campground) 2015 rates: $40 to $55. May 1 to Oct 1. (616)399-9230 2011 Ottawa Beach Rd, Holland, MI 49424

HOLLY — J5 *Oakland*

GROVELAND OAKS COUNTY PARK
(Public) From Jct of I-75 & Exit 101 (Grange Hall Rd), E 1 mi on Grange Hall Rd to Dixie Hwy, N .3 mi (L). **FAC:** Paved/gravel rds. 267 grass, back-ins (50 x 50), some side by side hkups, 267 W, 267 E (30/50 amps), WiFi Hotspot, tent sites, rentals, dump, mobile sewer, laundry, fire rings, firewood, controlled access. **REC:** Stewart Lake: swim, fishing, playground, rec open to public. Pets OK. Partial handicap access. 14 day max stay, 2015 rates $27 to $38. May 17 to Sep 22.
(248)858-1400 Lat: 42.818699, Lon: -83.551605
14555 Dixie Hwy, Holly, MI 48442
ocparks@oakgov.com
www.destinationoakland.com
See ad this page.

HOLLY KOA FUN PARK **Ratings: 7.5/8.5★/8** (Campground) 2015 rates: $52.25 to $60.50. Apr 15 to Nov 1. (248)634-0803 7072 Grange Hall Rd, Holly, MI 48442

HOLLY SRA (State Pk) From Jct of I-75 & Grange Hall Rd (exit 101), E 1.5 mi on Grange Hall Rd to Mc Ginnis Rd (R). Entrance fee required. 2015 rates: $17 to $24. Apr 1 to Nov 1. (248)634-8811

SEVEN LAKES (State Pk) From Jct of I-75 & Grange Hall Rd (exit 110), W 5 mi on Grange Rd to Fish Lake Rd, N 0.75 mi (L). 2015 rates: $22. Apr 1 to Nov 1. (248)634-7271

HOLTON — H3 *Muskegon*

BLUE LAKE COUNTY PARK (MUSKEGON COUNTY PARK) (Public) From jct Hwy 120 & US 31 (Russell Rd exit): Go 10-1/4 mi N on Russell Rd (CR B23), then 1 mi E on Owassippi Rd, then 1/4 mi N on Nichols Rd. 2015 rates: $26. May 15 to Sep 15. (231)894-5574

OAK KNOLL FAMILY CAMPGROUND **Ratings: 5/7.5/7.5** (Campground) 2015 rates: $38. May 15 to Sep 30. (231)894-6063 1522 E. Fruitvale Rd, Holton, MI 49425

HOMER — J4 *Calhoun*

LIGHTHOUSE VILLAGE RV RESORT **Ratings: 8/9★/8** (Campground) 2015 rates: $10. Apr 15 to Oct 15. (517)568-4343 1001 24 Mile Rd, Homer, MI 49245

HONOR — F3 *Benzie, Leelanau*

PERE MARQUETTE SF (VETERAN'S MEMORIAL) (State Pk) From town: Go 3-1/2 mi E on US 31. Pit toilets. 2015 rates: $13. (231)276-9511

PERE MARQUETTE SF/PLATTE RIVER (State Pk) From town, E 2.5 mi on US-31 to Goose Rd, SE 1.5 mi, follow signs (L). Pit toilets. 2015 rates: $13. Apr 1 to Nov 1. (231)276-9511

SLEEPING BEAR DUNES NATL LAKE SHORE/PLATTE RIVER (Natl Pk) From Jct of US-31 & CR-708, NW 5 mi on CR-708 to M-22, S 0.25 mi to Lake Michigan Rd, W 0.25 mi (R). 2015 rates: $16 to $24. (231)325-5881

HOPKINS — J3 *Allegan*

EAST LAKE CAMPING **Ratings: 6.5/7/7.5** (Campground) 2015 rates: $39 to $49. May 1 to Oct 1. (269)793-7177 3091 Weiks Dr, Hopkins, MI 49328

Camping World offers new and used RV sales and so much more! Over 85 SuperCenters nationwide, a state-of-the-art call center and award-winning website. Find out more at CampingWorld.com

HOPKINS (CONT)

HIDDEN RIDGE RV RESORT
Ratings: 10/9.5★/9.5 (RV Park) From Jct of US 131 & 124th Ave (exit 59), W 0.1 mi on 124th Ave to 12th St, S 0.3 mi (R). Note: Minimum RV length 22' - no pop-ups.

DISCOVER MICHIGAN'S HIDDEN GEM
Conveniently located between Kalamazoo and Grand Rapids, Hidden Ridge is nestled in the countryside of Western Michigan. Relax at the heated pool and hot tub, enjoy a lake view or try out the new basketball and tennis courts!

FAC: Paved rds. (277 spaces). Avail: 177 paved, patios, 12 pull-thrus (45 x 80), back-ins (45 x 75), 177 full hkups (30/50 amps), seasonal sites, cable, WiFi, rentals, dump, laundry, groc, LP gas, fire rings, firewood, controlled access. **REC:** heated pool, whirlpool, Grebe Lake: fishing, shuffleboard, playground. Pet restrict(B/Q). Partial handicap access, no tents. Big rig sites, RV age restrict, 2015 rates: $44 to $55. Apr 1 to Oct 30.
AAA Approved
(888)451-2180 Lat: 42.59022, Lon: -85.66425
2306 12Th St, Hopkins, MI 49328
hiddenridgerv@suncommunities.com
www.hiddenridgerv.com
See ad pages 626, 1463 (Welcome Section), 616 & Family Camping in Magazine Section.

MILLER LAKE CAMPGROUND **Ratings: 6/6/7** (Campground) 2015 rates: $30 to $45. May 1 to Oct 1. (269)672-7139 2130 Miller Lake Dr, Hopkins, MI 49328

HOUGHTON — B1 *Houghton*

CITY OF HOUGHTON RV PARK (Public) From Jct of US 41 & Lakeshore Dr (north side of Houghton), NW 1.1 mi on Lakeshore Dr. (R) Follow signs. Self-contained RVs only. 2015 rates: $30. May 1 to Oct 30. (906)482-8745

HOUGHTON LAKE — F4 *Roscommon*

AU SABLE SF/HOUGHTON LAKE (State Pk) From Jct of Old US-27 & Hwy 55, N 5 mi on Old US-27 to CR-300, E 1 mi (R). 2015 rates: $17. Apr 15 to Sep 15. (989)821-6125

AU SABLE/REEDSBURG DAM (State Pk) From Jct of Hwy 127 & CR-300, NW 2.2 mi on CR-300, follow signs (L). Pit toilets. 2015 rates: $13. (989)422-5192

HOUGHTON LAKE TRAVEL PARK CAMPGROUND
Ratings: 9/9.5★/9 (Campground) From Jct of US-127 & M-55 (Houghton Lake Dr Exit 194), E 0.1 mi on M-55 to Cloverleaf Ln, S 0.4 mi on Cloverleaf Ln (R). **FAC:** Gravel rds. (71 spaces). Avail: 38 grass, 38 pull-thrus (35 x 60), 17 full hkups, 21 W, 21 E (30/50 amps), seasonal sites, WiFi, tent sites, rentals, dump, mobile sewer, laundry, groc, LP gas, fire rings, firewood. **REC:** heated pool, playground. Pets OK. Big rig sites, 2015 rates: $43. Apr 1 to Oct 15.
(989)422-3931 Lat: 44.32914, Lon: -84.80383
370 Cloverleaf Ln, Houghton Lake, MI 48629
hltpcampground@gmail.com
www.houghtonlaketravelparkcampground.com
See ad this page, 616.

WEST HOUGHTON LAKE CAMPGROUND **Ratings: 6/6/7** (Campground) 2015 rates: $35. (989)422-5130 9371 W. Houghton Lake Dr, Houghton Lake, MI 48629

WOODED ACRES FAMILY CAMPGROUND **Ratings: 7/9★/8.5** (Campground) 2015 rates: $40. Apr 1 to Nov 30. (989)422-3413 997 Federal Ave, Houghton Lake, MI 48629

County names are provided after the city names. If you're tracking the weather, this is the information you'll need to follow the reports.

Travel Services

CAMPING WORLD OF HOUGHTON LAKE As the nation's largest retailer of RV supplies, accessories, services and new and used RVs, Camping World is committed to making your total RV experience better. RV Accessories: (888)833-4424. **SERVICES:** RV, tire, RV appliance, staffed RV wash, RV Sales. RV supplies, LP, emergency parking, RV accessible. waiting room. Hours: 8am to 5pm.
(888)514-9498 Lat: 44.299299, Lon: -84.749613
2735 W Houghton Lake Dr, Houghton Lake, MI 48629
www.campingworld.com

HOWELL — J5 *Livingston*

LAKE CHEMUNG OUTDOOR RESORT
Ratings: 9/9.5★/9.5 (RV Park) From Jct of I-96 & Exit 145 (Grand River Ave), NW on Grand River Ave, 3 mi to Hugh Rd, N .2 mi (R). **FAC:** Paved rds. (320 spaces). Avail: 20 paved, 10 pull-thrus (30 x 70), back-ins (30 x 50), 20 full hkups (50 amps), seasonal sites, WiFi Hotspot, laundry, groc, LP bottles, fire rings, firewood, controlled access. **REC:** heated pool, wading pool, whirlpool, Lake Chemung: swim, fishing, marina, golf, playground. Pet restrict(Q). Partial handicap access, no tents. Big rig sites, 2015 rates: $40. No CC.
(517)546-6361 Lat: 42.59304, Lon: -83.85342
320 S Hughes Rd, Howell, MI 48843
lcori@comcast.net
www.lcori.com
See ad this page.

TAYLOR'S BEACH CAMPGROUND **Ratings: 7/8.5★/6.5** (Campground) 2015 rates: $28 to $49. Apr 1 to Oct 31. (517)546-2679 6197 N Burkhart Rd, Howell, MI 48856

HUDSONVILLE — H3 *Ottawa*

BALDWIN OAKS CAMPGROUND, LLC **Ratings: 8/7/5.5** (Campground) 2015 rates: $30 to $31. May 1 to Sep 30. (616)669-1600 4700 Baldwin St, Hudsonville, MI 49426

INDIAN RIVER — E4 *Cheboygan*

BURT LAKE (State Pk) From Jct of I-75 & SR-68 (exit 310), W 0.3 mi on SR-68 to US-27, S 0.3 mi, follow signs (R). Entrance fee required. 2015 rates: $18 to $28. (231)238-9392

INDIAN RIVER RV RESORT & CAMPGROUND **Ratings: 9.5/10★/8.5** (Campground) 2015 rates: $41 to $44. May 1 to Oct 1. (231)238-0035 561 N Straits Hwy, Indian River, MI 49749

YOGI BEAR'S JELLYSTONE PARK CAMP-RESORT **Ratings: 7.5/8.5★/8.5** (Campground) 2015 rates: $49. May 15 to Sep 30. (231)238-8259 2201 E. M-68, Indian River, MI 49749

INTERLOCHEN — F4 *Manistee*

INTERLOCHEN (State Pk) From Jct of US-31 & M-137, S 2 mi on M-137, follow signs (L). Entrance fee required. 2015 rates: $12 to $23. Apr 15 to Nov 1. (231)276-9511

IONIA — H4 *Ionia*

ALICE SPRINGS RV PARK & CAMPGROUND **Ratings: 8.5/9★/9.5** (RV Park) 2015 rates: $39. Apr 15 to Oct 15. (616)527-1608 5087 Alice Court, Ionia, MI 48846

IONIA SRA (State Pk) From Jct of I-96 & Jordan Lake Rd (Exit 64), N 3.4 mi on Jordan Lake Rd (E). Entrance fee required. 2015 rates: $16 to $20. Mar 31 to Nov 31. (616)527-3750

IRON MOUNTAIN — D1 *Dickinson, Iron*

LAKE ANTOINE COUNTY PARK (Public) From Jct of US-2 & Lake Antoine Rd, N 1.5 mi on Lake Antoine Rd, follow signs (L). 2015 rates: $20 to $24. May 25 to Sep 7. (906)774-8875

RIVERS BEND RV PARK & CAMPGROUND **Ratings: 7/8★/7.5** (Campground) 2015 rates: $28. May 15 to Oct 15. (906)779-1171 N 3905 Pine Mountain Rd, Iron Mountain, MI 49801

SUMMER BREEZE CAMPGROUND & RV PARK
Ratings: 8/9.5★/9 (Campground) From Jct of US-2 & N M-95, N 1.25 mi on M-95 to Twin Falls Rd, W 0.2 mi (R). **FAC:** Gravel rds. (70 spaces). Avail: 64 grass, 44 pull-thrus (40 x 100), back-ins (40 x 70), 30 full hkups, 34 W, 34 E (30/50 amps), seasonal sites, WiFi, tent sites, rentals, dump, mobile sewer, laundry, groc, fire rings, firewood. **REC:** heated pool, playground, rec open to public. Pets OK. Big rig sites, eco-friendly, 2015 rates: $30. May 1 to Oct 15.
(906)774-7701 Lat: 45.88147, Lon: -88.05629
w8576 Twin Falls Rd, Iron Mountain, MI 49801
sbreeze@charter.net
www.summerbreezecampground.com

IRON RIVER — D1 *Iron*

KLINT SAFFORD MEMORIAL RV PARK (Public) From the Jct of US 2 & M-189 (center of town), E 0.2 mi on US 2 to River St, S 0.1mi to Genesee St, E 250 feet (R). **FAC:** Paved rds. (32 spaces). Avail: 22 paved, back-ins (40 x 70), 15 full hkups, 7 W, 7 E (30 amps), cable, WiFi, tent sites, dump, fire rings, firewood. **REC:** Iron River: fishing, rec open to public. Pets OK. Partial handicap access. 2015 rates: $35. May 1 to Dec 1.
(906)265-3822 Lat: 46.091459, Lon: -88.638406
50 E. Genesee Street, Iron River, MI 49935
info@iron.org
www.ironriver.org

THE IRON RIVER RV PARK (Public) From Jct of US 2 & M-189, (center of town), E 0.2 mi on US 2 to River St, S 0.1 mi to Genesse St, E 250 feet (R). 2015 rates: $26 to $35. Apr 1 to Dec 1. (906)265-3822

IRONS — G3 *Lake*

IRONS RV PARK AND CAMPGROUND **Ratings: 8.5/9.5★/8** (Campground) 2015 rates: $28 to $35. Apr 15 to Oct 15. (231)266-2070 4623 West 10 1/2 Mile Road, Irons, MI 49644

IRONWOOD — B4 *Gogebic*

CURRY PARK CAMPGROUND (Public) From Jct of US 2 & Superior St, W 0.1 mi on US 2 (R). 2015 rates: $10 to $20. May 15 to Oct 15. (906)932-5050

LITTLE GIRL'S POINT COUNTY PARK (Public) From Jct of US-2 & CR-505, NW 18 mi on CR-505, follow signs (R); or From Jct of US-2 & Saxon, E 11 mi on Saxon to CR-505 (R). 2015 rates: $15 to $20. May 8 to Sep 30. (906)667-4428

ISHPEMING — C2 *Marquette*

COUNTRY VILLAGE RV PARK **Ratings: 9/9/8** (RV Park) 2015 rates: $45. May 15 to Oct 15. (906)486-0300 1200 Country Lane, Ishpeming, MI 49849

ITHACA — H4 *Gratiot*

JUST-IN-TIME CAMPGROUND **Ratings: 6.5/5.5/6.5** (Campground) 2015 rates: $30. May 1 to Oct 15. (989)875-2865 8421 E Pierce Rd, Ithaca, MI 48847

Wasn't that a beautiful campground you visited ten years ago? But can you remember where it was? Use our "Find-it-Fast" index, located in the back of the Guide. It's an alphabetical list, by state, of every private and public park and campground in the Guide.

RV Park ratings you can rely on!

MI

JACKSON — J5 *Jackson*

GREENWOOD ACRES FAMILY CAMPGROUND
Ratings: 9.5/9.5★/9 (Campground) From Jct of I-94 & Race Rd (exit 147), S 0.2 mi on Race Rd to Ann Arbor Rd, W 0.8 mi to Portage Rd, S 1.25 mi to Greenwood Rd, E 0.4 mi to Hilton Rd (L) Note: Must be 25 to reserve site, no motorcycles in park. **FAC:** Paved rds. (1000 spaces). Avail: 200 grass, 40 pull-thrus (40 x 60), back-ins (40 x 60), 100 full hkups, 100 W, 100 E (30/50 amps), seasonal sites, WiFi, tent sites, dump, mobile sewer, laundry, groc, LP gas, fire rings, firewood, restaurant, controlled access. **REC:** pool, Goose Lake: swim, fishing, golf, shuffleboard, playground. Pets OK. Partial handicap access. Big rig sites, 2015 rates: $44. Apr 1 to Oct 31. ATM. AAA Approved
(517)522-8600 Lat: 42.26888, Lon: -84.26007
2401 Hilton Rd, Jackson, MI 49201
office@greenwoodacrescampground.com
www.greenwoodacrescampground.com
See ad pages 625, 616.

HIDEAWAY RV PARK **Ratings: 5.5/7.5★/6.5** (Campground) 2015 rates: $35. Apr 15 to Oct 15. (517)522-5858 3500 Updyke Rd, Jackson, MI 49240

JOHANNESBURG — F5 *Otsego*

MACKINAW SF/BIG BEAR LAKE (State Pk) From Jct of Hwy 32 & I-75, E 18 mi on Hwy 32 to Meridian Line Rd, S 1.2 mi to Little Bear Lake Rd, SW 0.5 mi to 2nd entrance 0.7 mi (L). Pit toilets. 2015 rates: $13. May to Oct. (989)732-5485

JONES — K3 *Cass*

CAMELOT CAMPGROUND **Ratings: 6.5/6.5/7.5** (Campground) 2015 rates: $33. Apr 15 to Oct 15. (269)476-2473 14630 M-60, Jones, MI 49061

JONESVILLE — K4 *Hillsdale*

WAY BACK IN CAMPGROUND
Ratings: 5.5/6.5/7 (Campground) From I-69 & Exit 16 (Jonesville Rd) E on Jonesville Rd 14.9 mi (L). **FAC:** Gravel rds. (43 spaces). Avail: 19 gravel, 7 pull-thrus (40 x 60), back-ins (40 x 60), 19 W, 19 E (30/50 amps), seasonal sites, WiFi, tent sites, rentals, dump, mobile sewer, groc, fire rings, firewood. **REC:** St. Joseph River: fishing, playground. Pets OK. Partial handicap access. Age restrict may apply, 2015 rates: $27 to $30. Apr 1 to Nov 1.
(517)849-0082 Lat: 41.985495, Lon: -84.684186
3590 Jonesville Rd, Jonesville, MI 49250
waybackin@ymail.com
www.waybackin.com
See ad page 628.

KALAMAZOO — J4 *Kalamazoo*

MARKIN GLEN COUNTY PARK
(Public) From Jct of I-94 & US-131 (Exit 44), N 7.5 mi on US-131 to 'D' Ave, E 3.5 mi to N Westnedge Ave, S 2.75 mi (R). **FAC:** Paved rds. 38 paved, patios, 7 pull-thrus (30 x 60), back-ins (30 x 50), 38 full hkups (30/50 amps), tent sites, dump, fire rings, firewood, controlled access. **REC:** Man Made Ponds: swim, fishing, playground, rec open to public. Pets OK. Partial handicap access. Big rig sites, 14 day max stay, 2015 rates: $26. Apr 29 to Oct 30.
(269)383-8778 Lat: 42.33703, Lon: -85.59034
5300 N. Westnedge Ave, Kalamazoo, MI 49004
parks@kalcounty.com
www.kalamazoocountyparks.com
See ad this page.

KALEVA — F3 *Wexford*

KALEVA VILLAGE PARK (Public) In town, at Jct of N. Highbridge Rd. & 9 Mile Rd. Pit toilets. 2015 rates: $10 to $15. (616)362-3366

KALKASKA — F4 *Kalkaska*

KALKASKA RV PARK & CAMPGROUND
Ratings: 8.5/9★/8.5 (Campground) From Jct. of US-131 & M-72, E 1.3 mi on M-72 (R). **FAC:** Gravel rds. (92 spaces). Avail: 82 gravel, 27 pull-thrus (30 x 60), back-ins (25 x 50), 16 full hkups, 66 W, 66 E (20/30 amps), seasonal sites, cable, WiFi, tent sites, rentals, dump, mobile sewer, laundry, groc, LP bottles, fire rings, firewood. **REC:** heated pool, playground, rec open to public. Pet restrict(Q). Eco-friendly, 2015 rates: $41. Apr 15 to Oct 30.
(231)258-9863 Lat: 44.71378, Lon: -85.16216
580 M-72 SE, Kalkaska, MI 49646
gclark53@gmail.com
www.kalkaskacampground.com
See ad pages 639, 616.

PERE MARQUETTE SF (CCC BRIDGE) (State Pk) From town: Go 10 mi SE on Hwy 72 & Sunset Trail Rd. Pit toilets. 2015 rates: $13. (231)922-5270

PERE MARQUETTE SF/GUERNSEY LAKE (State Pk) From town, W 7.7 mi on Island Lake Rd to Campground Rd, S 1 mi, follow signs (R). Pit toilets. 2015 rates: $13. (231)922-5270

KINROSS — D4 *Chippewa*

KINROSS RV PARK EAST (Public) From jct I-75 (exit 378) & Hwy 80: Go 2-3/4 mi E on Hwy 80, then 1 blk N on Riley St. 2015 rates: $12 to $20. (906)495-3023

KINROSS RV PARK WEST (TOWNSHIP PARK) (Public) From I-75 (exit 378): Go 1/2 mi E on Tone Rd, then 1/2 mi N on Fair Rd. 2015 rates: $12 to $20. (906)495-5381

L'ANSE — C1 *Houghton*

CURWOOD PARK (FORMERLY L'ANSE TOWNSHIP PARK) (Public) From Jct of US-41 & Broad St, NE 1 mi on Broad St to Skanee Rd, NE 1.5 mi (L). 2015 rates: $20. May 15 to Oct 15. (906)524-6985

L'ANSE TOWNSHIP PARK & CAMPGROUND (Public) From Jct of US 41 & Broad St (sign for downtown L'Anse), N 0.8 mi on Broad St to Main St, 2 mi NE on Main (name changes to Skanee Rd) to Crebassa Dr, L on Crebassa Dr (L). Caution: steep hill. 2015 rates: $15 to $20. May 1 to Oct 31. (906)524-6985

LACHINE — E5 *Alpena*

BEAVER LAKE CAMPGROUND (Public) From Jct of M-32 & M-65, S 10 mi on M-65 to Beaver Lake Park Rd, W 1.5 mi, follow signs (E). 2015 rates: $17 to $28. May 15 to Oct 15. (989)379-4462

LAINGSBURG — H5 *Shiawassee*

SLEEPY HOLLOW (State Pk) From Lansing, N 14 mi on US-127, follow signs (L); or From Jct of US-127 & Price Rd, E 5 mi on Price Rd (L). Entrance fee required. 2015 rates: $20. Apr 26 to Nov 4. (517)651-6217

LAKE ANN — F3 *Benzie*

PERE MARQUETTE SF/LAKE ANN (State Pk) From Jct of US-31 & Reynolds Rd, N 4 mi on Reynolds Rd, follow signs (R). Pit toilets. 2015 rates: $13. (231)276-9511

LAKE CITY — F4 *Houghton, Missaukee*

CROOKED LAKE PARK (MISSAUKEE COUNTY PARK) (Public) From jct Hwy 66 & Jennings Rd: Go 4 mi W on Jennings Rd, then 1 mi N on LaChonce Rd. 2015 rates: $20 to $30. (231)839-4945

MAPLE GROVE CITY PARK (Public) From Jct of Hwy 55 & E Union St, E 0.4 mi on Union St, follow signs (R). 2015 rates: $10. May to Nov. (231)839-4429

MISSAUKEE COUNTY PARK (Public) From Jct of M-55 & M-66, N 0.1 mi on M-66 to Fisher St, W 0.2 mi (L). 2015 rates: $25 to $30. May 15 to Oct 1. (231)839-4945

PERE MARQUETTE SF (LONG LAKE) (State Pk) From town: Go 3-1/2 mi NW on Hwy 66 & Goose Lake Rd. Pit toilets. 2015 rates: $13. (231)775-7911

PERE MARQUETTE SF/GOOSE LAKE (State Pk) From Jct of M-66 & Goose Lake Rd, NW 2.5 mi on Goose Lake Rd, follow signs (E). Pit toilets. 2015 rates: $13. (231)775-7911

LAKE LEELANAU — F3 *Leelanau*

LAKE LEELANAU RV PARK **Ratings: 8.5/10★/9.5** (Campground) 2015 rates: $59 to $79. May 1 to Oct 31. (231)256-7236 3101 Lake Shore Dr, Lake Leelanau, MI 49653

LAKEVIEW — H4 *Montcalm*

LAKEVIEW FAMILY CAMP **Ratings: 6/6.5/7** (Campground) 2015 rates: $29. May 1 to Oct 15. (855)352-6896 5300 W Cutler Rd, Lakeview, MI 48850

TOWNLINE LAKE CAMPGROUND **Ratings: 4.5/6/7.5** (Campground) 2015 rates: $28 to $35. May 1 to Oct 30. (989)352-7346 6223 Cutler Rd, Lakeview, MI 48850

LANSING — J4 *Ingham*

LANSING COTTONWOOD CAMPGROUND
Ratings: 8.5/10★/8.5 (Campground) From Jct of US 127 & Exit 11 (Jolly Rd), W 0.7 mi on Dunkell Rd to Jolly Rd, W 0.4 mi to Aurelius Rd, S 0.3 mi (L). **FAC:** Gravel rds. (120 spaces). 110 Avail: 11 gravel, 99 grass, 11 pull-thrus (30 x 60), back-ins (30 x 50), some side by side hkups, 11 full hkups, 99 W, 99 E (30/50 amps), seasonal sites, WiFi, tent sites, dump, mobile sewer, laundry, groc, fire rings, firewood. **REC:** pool, pond, fishing, playground. Pets OK. Partial handicap access. Eco-friendly, 2015 rates: $35. Apr 15 to Oct 29.
(517)393-3200 Lat: 42.67877, Lon: -84.52201
5339 Aurelius Rd, Lansing, MI 48911
cottoncamp@aol.com
www.lansingcottonwoodcampground.com
See ad this page.

LAPEER — H6 *Lapeer*

METAMORA-HADLEY SRA (State Pk) From Jct of I-75 & SR-24, N 15 mi on SR-24 to Pratt Rd, W 2.3 mi to Herd Rd, S 0.66 mi (L) or From Jct of I-69 & SR-24 (exit 155), S 4.8 mi on SR-24 to Pratt Rd, W 2.3 mi to Herd Rd, S 0.7 mi (L). Entrance fee required. 2015 rates: $17 to $24. Apr 1 to Oct 30. (810)797-4439

WATER TOWER TRAVEL TRAILER PARK (Public) From Jct of I-69 & M-24 (exit 155), N 2.8 mi on M-24 (R). 2015 rates: $25. May 1 to Oct 31. (810)664-4296

LAWRENCE — J3 *Van Buren*

YORE PLACE RESORT & CAMPGROUND **Ratings: 6.5/7/7** (Campground) 2015 rates: $20 to $25. Apr 15 to Oct 31. (269)427-7908 59381 44Th Ave, Lawrence, MI 49064

LE ROY — G4 *Osceola*

ROSE LAKE PARK (OSCEOLA COUNTY PARK) (Public) From town: Go 2 mi N on Old US 131, then 4 mi E on 18 Mile Rd. 2015 rates: $17 to $25. May 8 to Sep 27. (231)768-4923

LEONARD — H6 *Oakland*

ADDISON OAKS COUNTY PARK CAMPGROUND (Public) From the Jct of I-75 Bus & Route 59 (Huron St) Pontiac MI: W 1.3 mi on Huron St to N. Telegraph Rd, N. 1.7 mi to County Center Dr, S 0.4 mi to Pontiac Rd., W 0.2 mi to Watkins Lake Rd to Buick St NW to 0.1 mi (L). **FAC:** Gravel rds. 174 gravel, back-ins (50 x 50), some side by side hkups, 174 W, 174 E (30/50 amps), tent sites, rentals, dump, mobile sewer, laundry, fire rings, firewood, controlled access. **REC:** Adams Lake: swim, fishing, playground, rec open to public. Pets OK. Partial handicap access. 2015 rates: $27 to $34. May 1 to Oct 17.
(248)858-1400 Lat: 42.658628, Lon: -83.342725
1480 West Romeo Rd, Leonard, MI 48328
ocparks@oakgov.com
www.destinationoakland.com
See ad page 628.

Directional arrows indicate the campground's position in relation to the nearest town.

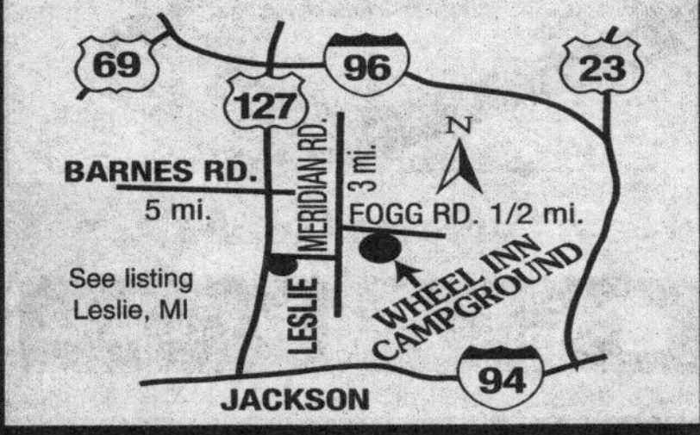

LESLIE — J5 *Ingham*

WHEEL INN CAMPGROUND & WHITE TAIL ACRES ARCHERY
Ratings: 6/4/6.5 (Campground) From Jct of US 127 & Exit 61 (Barnes Rd), E 3 mi on Barnes Rd to Meridian Rd, S 3 mi to Fogg Rd, E 0.4 mi (R). **FAC:** Gravel rds. (150 spaces). Avail: 98 grass, 60 pull-thrus (30 x 80), back-ins (30 x 60), 25 full hkups, 73 W, 73 E (20/30 amps), WiFi, tent sites, dump, mobile sewer, fire rings, firewood. **REC:** pond, fishing, playground, rec open to public. Pet restrict(B). Partial handicap access. 2015 rates: $25.
(517)589-8097 Lat: 42.47149, Lon: -84.343799
240 Fogg Rd, Leslie, MI 49251
ataylor3d@aol.com
See ad this page.

LEWISTON — F5 *Montmorency*

MACKINAW SF/LITTLE WOLF LAKE (State Pk) From town, SE 3 mi on CR-489 to W Wolf Lake Rd, E 2 mi (L). Pit toilets. 2015 rates: $13. (989)785-4251

LEXINGTON — H6 *Sanilac*

LEXINGTON PARK (Public) From jct Hwy 90 & Hwy 25: Go 3 mi N on Hwy 25. 2015 rates: $21 to $25. (810)359-7473

LINWOOD — G5 *Bay*

LINWOOD BEACH MARINA & CAMPGROUND **Ratings: 5/8★/6** (Campground) 2015 rates: $33 to $41. May 1 to Nov 1. (989)697-4415 135 S Linwood Beach Rd, Linwood, MI 48634

LITTLE LAKE — D2 *Marquette*

ESCANABA RIVER SF/LITTLE LAKE (State Pk) From Jct of US-41 & M-35, NW 36 mi on M-35 at E end of lake (R). Pit toilets. 2015 rates: $13. (906)339-4461

LOVELLS — F5 *Crawford*

AU SABLE SF/SHUPAC LAKE (State Pk) From Jct of Hwy 612 & Twin Bridge Rd, N 2 mi on Twin Bridge Rd to gravel rd, E 0.5 mi, follow signs (E). Pit toilets. 2015 rates: $13. (989)348-7068

LUDINGTON — G3 *Mason*

CARTIER PARK CAMPGROUND (Public) From W Jct of US-31 & US-10, W 3.1 mi on US-10 to M-116 (Lakeshore Dr), N 1.7 mi (R). 2015 rates: $22 to $32. May 1 to Oct 15. (231)845-1522

KIBBY CREEK TRAVEL PARK **Ratings: 8.5/8.5★/8.5** (Campground) 2015 rates: $37 to $39. Apr 15 to Oct 15. (800)574-3995 4900 W Deren Rd, Ludington, MI 49431

Say you saw it in our Guide!

LUDINGTON (State Pk) From Jct of M-116 & US-10, N 6 mi on M-116, follow signs (E). Entrance fee required. 2015 rates: $18 to $33. Apr 15 to Nov 1. (231)843-2423

MASON COUNTY CAMPGROUND & PICNIC AREA (Public) From jct US 10/31 & US 31: Go 4 mi S on US 31, then 1/2 mi S on Old US 31, then 1-1/2 mi W on Chauvez Rd. 2015 rates: $23 to $27. (231)845-7609

PONCHO'S POND
Ratings: 9.5/10★/10 (RV Park) From W Jct of US-31 & US-10, W 1.5 mi on US-10 to Pere Marquette Rd, S 0.1 mi (L). **FAC:** Paved rds. (265 spaces). 186 Avail: 118 paved, 68 gravel, patios, 88 pull-thrus (30 x 80), back-ins (30 x 60), 186 full hkups (30/50 amps), seasonal sites, cable, WiFi, tent sites, rentals, laundry, LP gas, fire rings, firewood. **REC:** heated pool, whirlpool, pond, fishing, playground. Pet restrict(Q). Partial handicap access. Big rig sites, 2015 rates: $50 to $54. Apr 1 to Oct 31.
(888)308-6602 Lat: 43.95357, Lon: -86.41292
5335 W Wallace Road, Ludington, MI 49431
poncho@poncho.com
www.poncho.com
See ad this page.

VACATION STATION RV RESORT **Ratings: 10/10★/10** (RV Park) 2015 rates: $35 to $65. Apr 15 to Oct 15. (800)499-1060 4895 W US-10, Ludington, MI 49431

LUPTON — F5 *Alcona*

RIFLE RIVER REC AREA (State Pk) From Jct of I-75 & Exit 202, N 20 mi on SR-33, E 5 mi on CR-28 (Rose City Rd) to park (R). Entrance fee required. 2015 rates: $13 to $24. (989)473-2258

LUTHER — G3 *Lake*

PERE MARQUETTE SF/SILVER CREEK (State Pk) From Jct of M-37 & Old 63, E 8 mi on Old 63 to State Rd, N 6 mi, follow signs (L) Entrance fee required. Pit toilets. 2015 rates: $13. (231)745-9465

MACKINAW CITY — D4 *Cheboygan, Emmet, Mackinaw*

MACKINAW CITY/MACKINAC ISLAND KOA **Ratings: 8/9.5★/7.5** (Campground) 2015 rates: $35 to $48. May 1 to Oct 15. (800)562-1738 566 Trail's End Rd, Mackinaw City, MI 49701

MI

MACKINAW CITY (CONT)

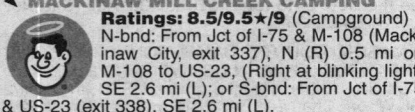

MACKINAW MILL CREEK CAMPING
Ratings: 8.5/9.5★/9 (Campground) N-bnd: From Jct of I-75 & M-108 (Mackinaw City, exit 337), N (R) 0.5 mi on M-108 to US-23, (Right at blinking light) SE 2.6 mi (L); or S-bnd: From Jct of I-75 & US-23 (exit 338), SE 2.6 mi (L).

SHORELINE CAMPSITES & CABINS
Our beautiful mile of Lake Huron shoreline and 200 acre park makes our camping experience unique. We offer a variety of campsites and cabin settings where you will be sure to find your own special site.

FAC: Paved rds. (562 spaces). 550 Avail: 250 gravel, 300 grass, 10 pull-thrus (40 x 70), back-ins (40 x 70), 350 full hkups, 200 W, 200 E (30/50 amps), seasonal sites, WiFi, tent sites, rentals, dump, groc, LP gas, fire rings, firewood. **REC:** heated pool, Lake Huron: swim, fishing, golf, playground. Pet restrict(B/Q). Partial handicap access. Big rig sites, eco-friendly, 2015 rates: $25 to $65. May 1 to Oct 25.
(231)436-5584 Lat: 45.75106, Lon: -84.68562
9730 US 23, Mackinaw City, MI 49701
office@campmackinaw.com
www.campmackinaw.com
See ad pages 631, 620 (Spotlight Mackinaw City), 616.

TEE PEE CAMPGROUND INC **Ratings: 7/9.5★/9** (Campground) 2015 rates: $33 to $40. May 5 to Oct 15. (231)436-5391 11262 W US-23, Mackinaw City, MI 49701

WILDERNESS (State Pk) From Jct of I-75 & Wilderness Park Dr, W 10 mi on Trails End Rd, follow signs (R). Entrance fee required. 2015 rates: $20 to $29. Apr to Dec. (231)436-5381

Things to See and Do

MACKINAW CLUB GOLF COURSE Within minutes of Mackinaw City Mackinaw Club Golf Course was designed by renowned golf architect Jerry Mathews. It has a lot of great scenery, is challenging and fun at an affordable price. May 1 to Oct 15. Food. Hours: 7:30am to 7:30pm. Adult fee: $15 to $38.
(231)537-4955 Lat: 45.72292, Lon: -84.73203
11891 N. Mackinaw Highway, Carp Lake, MI 49718
info@mackinawclub.com
www.mackinawclub.com
See ad page 620 (Spotlight Mackinaw City).

MANCELONA — F4 *Antrim, Kalkaska*

WHISPERING PINES RV RESORT & CAMPGROUND **Ratings: 7.5/9★/8.5** (Campground) 2015 rates: $38 to $42. May 15 to Oct 15. (231)535-0461 3060 Mancelona Rd, Mancelona, MI 49659

MANISTEE — G3 *Mason, Manistee*

INSTA LAUNCH CAMPGROUND & MARINA
Ratings: 8.5/9.5★/7.5 (Campground) From Jct. of US-31 & M-55, S. 0.4 mi on US-31 to Park Ave. E. 0.1 mi. (R). **FAC:** All weather rds. (182 spaces). Avail: 102 grass, 6 pull-thrus (30 x 80), back-ins (30 x 45), some side by side hkups, 35 full hkups, 67 W, 67 E (30/50 amps), seasonal sites, WiFi, tent sites, rentals, showers $, dump, laundry, groc, LP bottles, fire rings, firewood. **REC:** Big Manistee River: swim, fishing, marina, playground, rec open to public. Pet restrict(B/Q). Partial handicap access. Eco-friendly, 2015 rates: $24 to $36. Apr 1 to Nov 15.
(866)452-8642 Lat: 44.26497, Lon: -86.30504
20 Park Ave, Manistee, MI 49660
jim@instalaunch.com
www.instalaunch.com
See ad pages 631, 616.

We give campgrounds one rating for amenities, a second for restrooms and a third for visual appearance and environmental quality. That's the Triple Rating System.

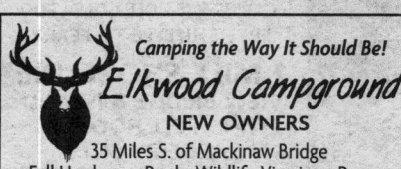

LITTLE RIVER CASINO RV PARK
Ratings: 10/10★/10 (RV Park) From Jct of US 31 & M-55, N 3.1 mi on US 31 to M-22, W 0.1 mi (L). Follow signs to RV Park.

LITTLE RIVER CASINO RESORT RV PARK
Roll in for fun! Our deluxe RV park is designed for our guests who love life on the road with all the comforts of home. 95 spaces with level concrete pads. Plus the full use of the casino and its restaurants.

FAC: Paved rds. (95 spaces). Avail: 85 paved, 39 pull-thrus (30 x 70), back-ins (35 x 50), 50 full hkups, 35 W, 35 E (30/50 amps), seasonal sites, cable, WiFi, dump, laundry, LP bottles, restaurant. **REC:** heated pool, whirlpool, playground, rec open to public. Pets OK. Partial handicap access, no tents. Big rig sites, eco-friendly, 2015 rates: $29.99 to $44.99. Disc: AAA. Apr 1 to Nov 1. ATM.
(866)572-4386 Lat: 44.28675, Lon: -86.24335
2700 Orchard Hwy, Manistee, MI 49660
frontdesksupervisors@lrcr.com
www.LRCR.com
See ad opposite page, 616.

MATSON'S BIG MANISTEE RIVER CAMPGROUND Ratings: 6.5/9★/7.5 (Campground) From the Jct of US 31 and M 55, E 8.8 mi on M 55 to Skocelas Rd, N 3 mi to Becker Rd, W 0.8 mi to Bialik Rd, N 0.7 mi (E) Caution: Steep, narrow interior roads. **FAC:** Gravel rds. (75 spaces). 50 Avail: 26 grass, 24 dirt, back-ins (25 x 38), 6 full hkups, 44 W, 44 E (30 amps), seasonal sites, WiFi Hotspot, tent sites, rentals, dump, laundry, groc, firewood. **REC:** Big Manistee River: fishing. Pets OK. Partial handicap access. 2015 rates: $28 to $32. Apr 1 to Dec 1. (888)556-2424 Lat: 44.28244, Lon: -86.15938 2680 Bialik Rd, Manistee, MI 49660 matsonscampground@gmail.com www.matsonscampground.com

ORCHARD BEACH (State Pk) From Jct of US-31 & SR-110, N 1.4 mi on SR-110, follow signs (L). Entrance fee required. 2015 rates: $28 to $35. Apr 1 to Dec 1. (231)723-7422

Things to See and Do

LITTLE RIVER CASINO RESORT A Casino Resort with 292-room luxury hotel, a 1,600 seat event center, and an expanding collection of slots and table games. Partial handicap access. RV accessible. Restrooms, food. Hours: Always Open. ATM.
(888)568-2244 Lat: 44.28675, Lon: -86.24335
2700 Orchard Highway, Manistee, MI 49660
fun@lrcr.com
www.lrcr.com
See ad opposite page.

MANISTIQUE — D3 *Schoolcraft*

HIAWATHA NATIONAL FOREST (CAMP SEVEN LAKE) (Natl Pk) From town: Go 9-1/2 mi W on CR-442, then 7-1/2 mi N on CR-437, then 4 mi W on CR-443, then 1/4 mi N on FR-2218. Pit toilets. 2015 rates: $16 to $28. May 15 to Oct 7. (906)428-5800

INDIAN LAKE (SOUTH SHORE) (State Pk) From Jct of US-2 & CR-149, N 3.5 mi on CR-149 to CR-442, E 0.6 mi (L) (Entrance Fee Required). 2015 rates: $16 to $24. Apr 15 to Nov 1. (906)341-2355

INDIAN LAKE (WEST SHORE) (State Pk) From town, SW 5.4 mi on US-2, N 3 mi on M-149 to CR-442, W 0.5 mi, follow the signs (R). Entrance fee required. Pit toilets. 2015 rates: $16. Apr 15 to Nov 1. (906)341-2355

INDIAN LAKE TRAVEL RESORT
Ratings: 7.5/9★/8 (Campground) From Jct of US-2 & CR-149 N 3.5 mi on CR-149 to Stop Sign, Turn left, Cont. on CR-149 1.0 mi. to CR-455, N 0.5 mi (R). **FAC:** Gravel rds. (60 spaces). Avail: 53 grass, 4 pull-thrus (24 x 65), back-ins (24 x 55), some side by side hkups, 40 full hkups, 13 W, 13 E (30/50 amps), seasonal sites, WiFi, tent sites, dump, laundry, LP bottles, fire rings, firewood. **REC:** Indian Lake: swim, fishing, playground. Pets OK. Big rig sites, 2015 rates: $24 to $26. May 1 to Sep 30. No CC.
(906)341-2807 Lat: 45.94759, Lon: -86.36396
202 S County Rd 455, Manistique, MI 49854
www.indianlaketravelresort.com
See ad this page.

MANTON — F4 *Wexford*

LAKE BILLINGS RV PARK (Public) From Jct of US 131 & exit 191 (SR 42-Manton), W 1 mi on SR 42 to Bus 131N (Michigan Ave), 0.4 mi to E Main St, E 0.2 mi to Park Dr, N 0.1 mi (Straight ahead). 2015 rates: $20 to $22. Apr 15 to Oct 15. (231)824-6454

PERE MARQUETTE SF (BAXTER BRIDGE) (State Pk) From town: Go 6 mi W on Hwy 42, then 6 mi N on Rd 31. Pit toilets. 2015 rates: $13. (231)775-7911

PERE MARQUETTE SF (OLD US 131) (State Pk) From town: Go 6 mi N on US 131 & Old US 131. Pit toilets. 2015 rates: $13. (231)775-7911

MARCELLUS — K3 *Cass*

CRANBERRY LAKE CAMPGROUND **Ratings: 5/5/6** (Campground) 2015 rates: $30. May 1 to Oct 1. (269)646-3336 10301 Bent Road, Marcellus, MI 49067

MARION — G4 *Osceola*

VETERANS MEMORIAL PARK (VILLAGE PARK) (Public) From jct Hwy 115 & Hwy 66: Go 5 mi N on Hwy 66. 2015 rates: $14 to $20. Apr 15 to Dec 1. (231)667-0100

Our rating system isn't just tough, it's thorough. We know the kinds of things that are important to you — like clean restrooms and showers, attractive, secure, well-tended grounds, and extras like swimming pools. We give the first rating for development of facilities, the second for cleanliness and physical characteristics of restrooms and showers, and the third for visual appearance.

MARQUETTE — C2 *Marquette*

GITCHE GUMEE RV PARK & CAMPGROUND **Ratings: 4.5/5.5/7.5** (Campground) 2015 rates: $20 to $39. (906)249-9102 2048 Sh 28 East, Marquette, MI 49855

MARQUETTE TOURIST PARK (Public) From Jct of US 41 & Front St (in Marquette, go straight when US 41 turns W), N 1.7 mi on Front St to Fair Ave, W 0.2 mi to Presque Isle Ave, N 0.5 mi to Wright St, W 0.4 mi to Sugarloaf, N 0.4 mi (L). 2015 rates: $18 to $32. May 15 to Oct 15. (906)228-0465

OJIBWA CASINO RV PARK **Ratings: 5.5/NA/8** (RV Park) 2015 rates: $1. (888)560-9905 105 Acre Trail, Marquette, MI 49855

MARSHALL — J4 *Calhoun*

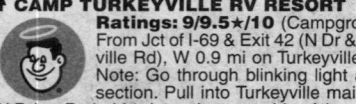

CAMP TURKEYVILLE RV RESORT
Ratings: 9/9.5★/10 (Campground) From Jct of I-69 & Exit 42 (N Dr & Turkeyville Rd), W 0.9 mi on Turkeyville Rd (L) Note: Go through blinking light at intersection. Pull into Turkeyville main lot on N Drive. Park drive is on the west side of the main lot. **FAC:** Gravel rds. 127 gravel, 23 pull-thrus (40 x 70), back-ins (40 x 60), 127 full hkups (30/50 amps), WiFi, rentals, dump, laundry, fire rings, firewood, restaurant. **REC:** heated pool, pond, fishing, playground. Pet restrict(B/Q). Partial handicap access, no tents. Big rig sites, 2015 rates: $45. Apr 1 to Oct 31.
(269)781-4293 Lat: 42.347296, Lon: -84.995507
18935 15 1/2 Mile Rd, Marshall, MI 49068
campturkeyville@turkeyville.com
www.campturkeyville.com
See ad this page, 616.

QUALITY CAMPING INC. **Ratings: 8/9★/9** (Campground) 2015 rates: $30. May 1 to Oct 31. (517)767-4161 5775 Old US 27 S, Marshall, MI 49068

TRI-LAKE TRAILS CAMPGROUND **Ratings: 6/5.5/6** (Campground) 2015 rates: $34. May 1 to Oct 1. (269)781-2297 219 Lyon Lake Rd, Marshall, MI 49068

MASS CITY — C1 *Ontonagon*

TWIN LAKES (State Pk) From Mass City, NE 15 mi on M-26; or From Houghton & Hancock, SW 26 mi on M-26, follow signs (E). Entrance fee required. 2015 rates: $18 to $24. Apr 15 to Oct 15. (906)288-3321

MEARS — G3 *Oceana*

HIDEAWAY CAMPGROUND **Ratings: 6.5/8.5★/8** (Campground) 2015 rates: $45 to $55. May 1 to Oct 1. (231)873-4428 9671 W Silver Lake Rd, Silver Lake, MI 49436

SANDY SHORES CAMPGROUND **Ratings: 7.5/10★/8.5** (Campground) 2015 rates: $45 to $53. May 1 to Sep 30. (231)873-3003 8595 W Silver Lake Rd, Silver Lake, MI 49436

SILVER CREEK RV RESORT **Ratings: 10/10★/10** (RV Park) 2015 rates: $30 to $70. Apr 1 to Oct 31. (866)832-7601 1441 N. 34th Ave, Silver Lake, MI 49436

SILVER HILLS CAMPGROUND **Ratings: 6.5/6.5/8** (Campground) 2015 rates: $34 to $50. May 6 to Sep 11. (231)873-3976 7594 W Hazel Rd, Silver Lake, MI 49436

SILVER LAKE RESORT AND CAMPGROUND **Ratings: 8/10★/9.5** (Campground) 2015 rates: $37 to $55. May 1 to Sep 30. (231)873-7199 1786 N 34th Ave, Silver Lake, MI 49436

Like Us on Facebook.

TIMBERLAKE RESORT & RV CLUB **Ratings: 7.5/7/6** (Membership Pk) 2015 rates: $5 to $30. (231)873-3285 4370 North Ridge Road, Mears, MI 49436

MECOSTA — G4 *Mecosta*

BLUEGILL LAKE FAMILY CAMPING RESORT **Ratings: 6/7.5/7** (Campground) 2015 rates: $30 to $40. Apr 15 to Nov 1. (231)972-4455 15854 Pretty Lake Drive, Mecosta, MI 49332

SCHOOL SECTION LAKE PARK (Public) From Jct of 46 & 127 (Exit 127), S 1 mi on Bus 127 to M-20 W, 22 mi to 9 mile Rd, S 2 mi to 90th Ave (R). 2015 rates: $20. May 7 to Oct 5. (231)972-7450

MENOMINEE — E2 *Menominee*

RIVER PARK CAMPGROUND (Public) From Jct of US-41 & 10th Ave, S 0.25 mi on 10th Ave, behind Kmart (R). 2015 rates: $25 to $30. May 15 to Oct 15. (906)863-5101

MEREDITH — G4 *Clare*

AU SABLE SF (HOUSE LAKE) (Public) From town: Go 2-1/2 mi NE on Meredith Grade Rd. Pit toilets. 2015 rates: $13. (989)386-4067

AU SABLE SF/TROUT LAKE (State Pk) From town: Go 3 mi N on Meredith Grade Rd. Pit toilets. 2015 rates: $13. (989)386-4067

MERRILL — H5 *Saginaw*

LAKE OF DREAMS CAMPGROUND Ratings: 6.5/9★/8.5 (Campground) From Jct of I-127 & I-46 (Exit 127), E 15 mi on I-46 to Fenmore Rd, S 0.4 mi (R). **FAC:** Gravel rds. (249 spaces). Avail: 99 grass, back-ins (50 x 80), 99 W, 99 E (30/50 amps), seasonal sites, WiFi, tent sites, rentals, dump, groc, fire rings, firewood. **REC:** pond, swim, fishing, playground. Pets OK. Partial handicap access. Eco-friendly, 2015 rates: $29. Apr 15 to Oct 15.
(989)643-0403 Lat: 43.24256, Lon: -84.21256
1000 S Fenmore, Merrill, MI 48637
Info@lakeofdreamscampground.com
www.lakeofdreamscampground.com

MESICK — F3 *Manistee, Wexford*

NORTHERN EXPOSURE CAMPGROUND (Public) From town, W 1 mi on M-115 to cnty rd (Hodenpyle Dam Rd), SW 4.4 mi to N shore of Hodenpyle Dam Impoundment of Manistee River, follow signs (E). 2015 rates: $25 to $40. May 1 to Oct 15. (800)563-7425

MIDDLEVILLE — J4 *Barry*

INDIAN VALLEY CAMPGROUND & CANOE LIVERY
Ratings: 8/8.5★/8 (Campground) From Jct of I-96 & M-50 (exit 52), S 3 mi on M-50 to 84th St, W 3.4 mi to Whitneyville Rd, S 3 mi to 108th St, W 0.3 mi (L); or From Jct of US-131 & 100th St (exit 72), E 6 mi on 100th St to Patterson Rd, S 1 mi to 108th St, E 5 mi (R). **FAC:** Paved/gravel rds. (150 spaces). Avail: 90 gravel, 15 pull-thrus (38 x 65), back-ins (35 x 30), 21 full hkups, 69 W, 69 E (30/50 amps), seasonal sites, WiFi, tent sites, rentals, dump, mobile sewer, laundry, groc, LP gas, fire rings, firewood, controlled access. **REC:** heated pool, Thornapple River: swim, fishing, playground, rec open to public. Pet restrict(Q). Partial handicap access. 2015 rates: $37. Apr 10 to Oct 20.
AAA Approved
(616)891-8579 Lat: 42.76868, Lon: -85.46311
8200 108th St SE, Middleville, MI 49333
www.indianvalleycampgroundandcanoe.com
See ad page 627.

YANKEE SPRINGS SRA/DEEP LAKE RUSTIC CAMPGROUND (State Pk) From Jct of US-131 & M-179 (exit 61), E 10 mi on M-179 to Yankee Springs Rd, S 1.5 mi (R) Entrance fee required. Pit toilets. 2015 rates: $12. Apr 1 to Dec 1. (269)795-9081

YANKEE SPRINGS SRA/GUN LAKE CAMPGROUND (State Pk) From Jct of US-131 & M-179 (exit 61), E 7 mi on M-179 to Briggs Rd, S 0.5 mi, follow signs (R). Entrance fee required. 2015 rates: $16 to $24. Apr 1 to Nov 30. (269)795-9081

MIDLAND — G5 *Bay*

RIVER RIDGE CAMPGROUND INC **Ratings: 9/9★/9** (Campground) 2015 rates: $41. May 1 to Oct 15. (989)842-5184 1989 W Pine River Rd, Breckenridge, MI 48615

VALLEY PLAZA RESORT RV PARK
Ratings: 8/8.5★/8.5 (RV Park) E-bnd: From Jct of US 10 & Waldo Rd exit, S 2.2 mi on Waldo Rd to Bay City Rd, E 1 mi (L). **FAC:** Paved rds. 77 Avail: 12 paved, 65 gravel, patios, 46 pull-thrus (30 x 65), back-ins (30 x 60), 77 full hkups (30/50 amps), cable, WiFi, tent sites, fire rings, firewood, restaurant. **REC:** heated pool, whirlpool, pond, swim, fishing, playground, rec open to public. Pets OK. Partial handicap access. Big rig sites, 2015 rates: $44. Disc: AAA.
(989)496-3151 Lat: 43.60691, Lon: -84.16515
5217 Bay City Rd, Midland, MI 48642
Jtroberts@charter.net

MILFORD — J5 *Oakland*

CAMP DEARBORN (Public) From Jct of I-96 & Milford Rd (exit 155), N 4.5 mi on Milford Rd to General Motors Rd, W 0.9 mi (R). 2015 rates: $21 to $32. May 1 to Nov 1. (248)684-6000

MIO — F5 *Oscoda*

AU SABLE SF (MIO POND) (State Pk) From town: Go 3 mi N on Hwy 72 & W on Popps Rd. Pit toilets. 2015 rates: $13. (989)826-3211

MIO PINE ACRES CAMPGROUND Ratings: 6.5/8.5★/7.5 (Campground) From Jct of M-33 & M-72, W 1 mi on M-72 (L). **FAC:** Gravel rds. (100 spaces). 83 Avail: 12 gravel, 71 grass, 12 pull-thrus (30 x 65), back-ins (30 x 40), 83 W, 83 E (30/50 amps), seasonal sites, WiFi, tent sites, rentals, dump, laundry, groc, LP gas, fire rings, firewood. **REC:** playground. Pet restrict(B). 2015 rates: $28 to $32. Apr 1 to Nov 30.
(989)826-5590 Lat: 44.65147, Lon: -84.14599
1215 W 8th St, Mio, MI 48647
info@miopineacres.com
www.miopineacres.com

OSCODA COUNTY PARK (Public) From town, N 1 mi on SR-72 to S side of Mio Dam Impoundment of Au Sable River (R). 2015 rates: $25 to $27. Apr 15 to Dec 1. (989)826-5114

MONROE — K6 *Monroe*

CAMP LORD WILLING MANAGEMENT RV PARK & CAMPGROUND
Ratings: 8/9.5★/8.5 (Campground) From Jct of I-75 & Nadeau Rd (exit 18), W 1.2 mi on Nadeau Rd to SR-125, N 0.8 mi to Stumpmier Rd, W 1 mi (R). **FAC:** Paved/gravel rds. 100 gravel, 9 pull-thrus (40 x 80), back-ins (40 x 70), 100 full hkups (30/50 amps), WiFi, tent sites, rentals, dump, laundry, LP gas, fire rings, firewood. **REC:** Lord Willing Lake: swim, fishing, playground. Pets OK. Partial handicap access. Big rig

Don't miss a thing! Check out the Table of Contents for everything the Guide has to offer.

Know The Rules Of The Road!

RV-related laws in every state and province, including: Fishing licenses, bridge and tunnel restrictions and highway information numbers for every state and province.

Find the Rules in the front of this Guide.

MONROE (CONT)

CAMP LORD WILLING (CONT)
sites, eco-friendly, 2015 rates: $35 to $42. Disc: AAA, military.
(877)210-8700 Lat: 41.97838, Lon: -83.39321
1600 Stumpmier Rd, Monroe, MI 48162
camplordwilling@yahoo.com
www.clwrvpark.com
See ad opposite page, 616.

HARBORTOWN RV RESORT
Ratings: 10/10★/10 (RV Park) From Jct of I-75 & La Plaisance Rd (exit 11), W 0.6 mi on La Plaisance Rd (L).

Come stay at a luxury resort & enjoy our go-karts, mini-golf, batting cages along with our large event weekends. Experience a vacation you deserve at a premier resort with activities for the whole family - Harbortown Resort.

FAC: Paved rds. (248 spaces). Avail: 188 paved, 105 pull-thrus (35 x 60), back-ins (35 x 50), 138 full hkups, 50 W, 50 E (30/50 amps), seasonal sites, cable, WiFi, tent sites, rentals, dump, laundry, groc, fire rings, firewood. **REC:** heated pool, playground, rec open to public. Pets OK. Partial handicap access. Big rig sites, 2015 rates: $41 to $54.
(734)384-4700 Lat: 41.88726, Lon: -83.39610
14931 Laplaisance Rd, Monroe, MI 48161
harbortown@harbortownrv.com
www.harbortownrv.com
See ad page 613 (Welcome Section).

WM. C. STERLING (State Pk) From Jct of I-75 & Dixie Hwy (Exit 15), E 0.75 mi on Dixie Hwy (R). Entrance fee required. 2015 rates: $22 to $33. (734)289-2715

MONTAGUE — H3 *Muskegon*

LUCKY LAKE CAMPGROUND & OUTDOOR CENTER, LLC Ratings: 4/NA/7 (Campground) S-bnd: From Jct of US 31 & Winston Rd (Exit 136), E 0.2 mi on Winston Rd (L). **FAC:** Poor gravel rds. 250 grass, 30 pull-thrus (35 x 100), back-ins (35 x 60), 28 W, 28 E (30/50 amps), WiFi Hotspot, tent sites, pit toilets, mobile sewer, fire rings, firewood. **REC:** Lucky Lake: swim, fishing, rec open to public. Pets OK. 2015 rates: $35. May 1 to Nov 1.
(231)894-3500 Lat: 43.50777, Lon: -86.36426
3280 Winston Road, Rothbury, MI 49437
luckylakecampground@gmail.com
www.luckylakecampground.com

MEINERT COUNTY PARK (Public) From Jct of US-31 & Fruitvale Rd, W 0.5 mi on Fruitvale Rd to Old Bus 31, N 0.9 mi to Meinert Rd, W 4.6 mi (R) Vehicle use fee required. 2015 rates: $28. May 1 to Sep 27. (231)894-4881

TRAILWAY CAMPGROUND (Public) From S Jct of Bus Hwy 31 & US-31 (Montague/Whitehall exit), W 2.3 mi on Bus Hwy 31 (R) Note: No campfires. 2015 rates: $33 to $35. May 1 to Oct 15. (231)894-4903

WHITE RIVER RV PARK & CAMPGROUND **Ratings: 7.5/9.5★/8.5** (Campground) 2015 rates: $47 to $50. May 1 to Oct 15. (231)894-4708 735 Fruitvale Rd, Montague, MI 49437

MORLEY — H4 *Mecosta*

MECOSTA PINES CAMPGROUND Ratings: 8/9★/9 (Campground) From the Jct of US 131 & Exit 125 (Jefferson Rd) E 1.5 mi on Jefferson Rd (R). **FAC:** Gravel rds. (111 spaces). Avail: 51 grass, 7 pull-thrus (45 x 60), back-ins (45 x 60), 11 full hkups, 40 W, 40 E (30/50 amps), seasonal sites, WiFi, tent sites, rentals, dump, mobile sewer, laundry, LP gas, fire rings, firewood. **REC:** heated pool, Little Muskegon: fishing, playground. Pet restrict(B). Partial handicap access. Big rig sites, 2015 rates: $38. Apr 15 to Oct 16.
(231)856-4556 Lat: 43.48958, Lon: -85.45216
550 S Talcott, Morley, MI 49336
mecostapines@gmail.com
www.mecostapinescampground.com

Tell them you saw them in this Guide!

MOSCOW — K5 *Hillsdale*

MOSCOW MAPLES RV PARK **Ratings: 6.5/5/6.5** (Campground) 2015 rates: $27 to $42. May 1 to Oct 15. (517)688-9853 8291 E. Chicago Rd, Moscow, MI 49257

MOUNT PLEASANT — G4 *Isabella*

DEERFIELD NATURE PARK (Public) From jct US 10 & US 127: Go 13 mi South on US 127 (to Lansing), then .7 mi to US 127 Bus exit toward Mt. Pleasant, then 1.4 mi on N Mission St/US 127 BR, then 6.4 mi on E High St/ M-20 to park. Pit toilets. 2015 rates: $20. (989)772-2879

SOARING EAGLE HIDEAWAY RV PARK **Ratings: 10/10★/10** (RV Park) 2015 rates: $49 to $72. Apr 1 to Oct 31. (989)817-4800 5514 E Airport Rd, Mount Pleasant, MI 48858

THE HILL CAMPGROUND **Ratings: 5/6.5/7** (Campground) 2015 rates: $22. (989)772-2285 7525 E Tomah Rd, Mount Pleasant, MI 48858

MUNISING — D3 *Alger, Delta, Schoolcraft*

MUNISING TOURIST PARK (Public) From M-28 in downtown Munising, W 3 mi on M-28 (R). 2015 rates: $23 to $37. May 15 to Oct 20. (906)387-3145

OTTER LAKE CAMPGROUND **Ratings: 5/6/7.5** (Campground) 2015 rates: $20 to $25. May 25 to Oct 1. (906)387-4648 E 7609 Otter Lake Rd, Munising, MI 49862

WANDERING WHEELS CAMPGROUND **Ratings: 6/8/7.5** (Campground) 2015 rates: $49.95. May 15 to Oct 15. (906)387-3315 e10102 Hwy M-28 East, Munising, MI 49862

MUNITH — J5 *Jackson*

THE OAKS CAMPGROUND **Ratings: 6.5/7.5/8** (Campground) 2015 rates: $30. (517)596-2747 7800 Cutler Rd, Munith, MI 49259

MUSKEGON — H3 *Muskegon*

DUCK CREEK RV RESORT **Ratings: 10/10★/10** (RV Park) 2015 rates: $45 to $63. Apr 22 to Oct 15. (231)766-3646 1155 W Riley Thompson Rd, Muskegon, MI 49445

MUSKEGON KOA **Ratings: 7/8/7** (Campground) 2015 rates: $40 to $50. May 1 to Oct 11. (800)562-3902 3500 N Strand Rd, Muskegon, MI 49445

P J HOFFMASTER (State Pk) From Jct of US-31 & Pontaluna Rd, W 3 mi on Pontaluna Rd, follow signs (L). Entrance fee required. 2015 rates: $20 to $30. Apr 9 to Oct 25. (231)798-3711

PIONEER COUNTY PARK (Public) From Jct of US-31 & SR-120, SW 1 mi on SR-120 to Giles Rd, W 6 mi to Scenic Drive, N 0.2 mi (L). Entrance fee required. 2015 rates: $26. May 1 to Sep 27. (231)744-3580

NAHMA — D3 *Delta*

UPPER PENINSULA GOLF & LAKE RESORT
Ratings: 6/7★/6 (RV Resort) From Jct of US 2 & CR 495, S 5 mi on CR 495 (L). **FAC:** Gravel rds. 50 grass, back-ins (35 x 55), 50 W, 50 E (30 amps), WiFi Hotspot, tent sites, rentals, dump, groc, LP bottles, fire rings, firewood. **REC:** Lake Michigan: swim, fishing, golf, playground. Pets OK. 2015 rates: $25. May 30 to Nov 1.
(906)644-2728 Lat: 45.83862, Lon: -86.66409
13723 Main St, Nahma, MI 49864
info@upperpeninsulagolfandlakeresort.com
www.upperpeninsulagolfandlakeresort.com

NAUBINWAY — D4 *Macinac*

LAKE SUPERIOR SF (BIG KNOB) (State Pk) From town: Go 14 mi SW on US 2 & Big Knob Rd. Pit toilets. 2015 rates: $13. (906)293-5131

LAKE SUPERIOR SF (HOG ISLAND POINT) (State Pk) From jct Hwy 117 & US 2: Go 13 mi E on US 2. Pit toilets. 2015 rates: $13. (906)477-6048

LAKE SUPERIOR SF (MILAKOKIA LAKE) (State Pk) From jct Hwy 117 & US 2: Go 11-1/2 mi W on US 2, then 1-1/2 mi S on Pike Lake Grade. Pit toilets. 2015 rates: $13. (906)293-5131

NEW ERA — G3 *Oceana*

HOLIDAY CAMPING RESORT **Ratings: 8.5/8.5/8** (Campground) 2015 rates: $40. May 1 to Oct 1. (231)861-5220 5483 W Stony Lake Rd, New Era, MI 49446

STONY HAVEN CAMPGROUND & CABINS **Ratings: 5/6/7.5** (Campground) 2015 rates: $26.25 to $35. May 1 to Oct 30. (231)861-5201 8079 W Stony Lake Rd, New Era, MI 49446

NEW HUDSON — J5 *Oakland*

HAAS LAKE PARK RV CAMPGROUND
Ratings: 8/9.5★/9.5 (Campground) From Jct of I-96 & Wixom Rd (exit 159), S 0.25 mi on Wixom Rd to Grand River, W 2.3 mi to Haas Rd, S 1.5 mi (E). **FAC:** Gravel rds. (440 spaces). Avail: 120 gravel, 15 pull-thrus (30 x 60), back-ins (30 x 60), 70 full hkups, 50 W, 50 E (30/50 amps), seasonal sites, WiFi Hotspot, dump, mobile sewer, laundry, groc, LP gas, fire rings, firewood, controlled access. **REC:** Haas Lake: swim, fishing, golf, playground. Pet restrict(B). Partial handicap access, no tents. Eco-friendly, 2015 rates: $46. Mar 29 to Nov 5.
(248)437-0900 Lat: 42.48126, Lon: -83.57915
25800 Haas Rd, New Hudson, MI 48165
service@haaslake.com
www.haaslakepark.com
See ad page 625.

NEWAYGO — H3 *Newaygo*

CROTON TOWNSHIP PARK (Public) From jct Hwy 37 & Hwy 82: Go 8 mi E on CR to the E side of Muskegon River at Croton Dam. 2015 rates: $15 to $23. (231)652-4642

ED HENNING CAMPGROUND (Public) From Jct of M 37 & Croton Rd, E 0.3 mi on Croton Rd (R). 2015 rates: $16 to $25. Apr 24 to Oct 18. (231)652-1202

NEWAYGO (State Pk) Take US-131 to exit 125, then go 5 mi W to Beech St, then N on Beech St to park entrance. Pit toilets. 2015 rates: $12. (231)856-4452

NEWBERRY — D4 *Luce*

KRITTER'S NORTHCOUNTRY CAMPGROUND & CABINS
Ratings: 6.5/8.5★/8.5 (Campground) From Jct of M-28 & M-123, N 8.2 mi on M-123 (L). **FAC:** Gravel rds. 40 grass, 40 pull-thrus (35 x 75), 8 full hkups, 32 W, 32 E (30/50 amps), cable, WiFi, tent sites, rentals, dump, laundry, fire rings, firewood. **REC:** playground. Pets OK. Partial handicap access. Big rig sites, 2015 rates: $32. May 12 to Oct 10.
(906)293-8562 Lat: 46.42406, Lon: -85.51071
13209 State Hwy M 123, Newberry, MI 49868
northcountrycampground@gmail.com
www.northcountrycampground.com
See ad this page, 616.

LAKE SUPERIOR SF (MOUTH OF TWO HEARTED RIVER) (State Pk) From jct Hwy-28 & Hwy-123: Go 7-1/2 mi N on Hwy-123, then 15 mi NW on CR-407, then 10 mi NE on CR-412, then 3 mi NW on CR-423. Pit toilets. 2015 rates: $13. (906)492-3415

LAKE SUPERIOR SF (PERCH LAKE) (State Pk) From jct Hwy-28 & Hwy-123: Go 7-1/2 mi N on Hwy-123, then 19 mi NW on CR-407. Pit toilets. 2015 rates: $13. (906)658-3338

We appreciate your business!

MI

NEWBERRY (CONT)

MUSKALLONGE LAKE (State Pk) From Jct of M-123 & M-28, N 7 mi on M-123 to H-37, NW 26 mi, follow signs (L). Entrance fee required. 2015 rates: $18 to $32. May 3 to Oct 30. (906)658-3338

NEWBERRY KOA KAMPGROUND

Ratings: 8/9.5★/8.5 (Campground) From Jct of M-123 & M-28, E 0.25 mi on M-28 (L). **FAC:** Paved/gravel rds. 75 dirt, 39 pull-thrus (30 x 58), back-ins (30 x 45), 8 full hkups, 67 W, 67 E (30/50 amps), WiFi, tent sites, rentals, dump, mobile sewer, laundry, fire rings, firewood. **REC:** heated pool, playground. Pets OK. Eco-friendly, 2015 rates: $50. May 1 to Oct 15.
(906)293-5762 Lat: 46.30377, Lon: -85.50413
13724 State Hwy M-28, Newberry, MI 49868
koanewberry@yahoo.com
www.koa.com/campgrounds/newberry/
See ad page 635.

NILES — K3 *Cass*

SPAULDING LAKE CAMPGROUND LLC

Ratings: 8/9★/9 (Campground) From Jct of I-80/90 (IN Toll Rd) & IN 933, Exit 77, (Changes to M 51 in Michigan), N 6 mi on IN 933/MI 51 to Bell Rd, E 1 mi to 17th St, S 1 block to Bell Rd, E 1 mi (L).

BEAUTIFUL FAMILY FRIENDLY RV PARK

Located in the beautiful southwest region of Michigan's Lower Peninsula between Chicago & Detroit, just 20 miles from the towering dunes of the shores of Lake Michigan. Fishing in our stocked lake 6 miles from Notre Dame.

FAC: Gravel rds. 120 grass, 44 pull-thrus (30 x 60), back-ins (30 x 40), some side by side hkups, 120 full hkups (30/50 amps), WiFi, tent sites, laundry, fire rings, firewood. **REC:** Spaulding Lake: swim, fishing, playground. Pets OK. Big rig sites, eco-friendly, 2015 rates: $32. Apr 1 to Oct 31. No CC.
AAA Approved
(269)684-1393 Lat: 41.79405, Lon: -86.21507
33524 Bell St, Niles, MI 49120
spauldingcampground@yahoo.com
www.spauldinglake.com
See ad page 481.

NORTH BRANCH — H6 *Lapeer*

SUTTER'S RECREATION AREA Ratings: 7.5/9.5★/8.5 (Campground) From Jct of I-69 & M-24 (Exit 155), N 13.4 mi on M-24 to North Branch Rd (M90), E 1.5 mi to McKibbon Rd, S 0.5 mi to Tozer Rd, W 0.4 mi (R). **FAC:** Gravel rds. (220 spaces). Avail: 20 grass, 2 pull-thrus (30 x 60), back-ins (30 x 50), 3 full hkups, 17 W, 17 E (30 amps), seasonal sites, WiFi, tent sites, dump, mobile sewer, laundry, groc, LP gas, fire rings, firewood. **REC:** pond, swim, fishing, playground. Pet restrict(B/Q). Partial handicap access. 2015 rates: $30 to $35. Apr 15 to Nov 1. No CC.
(810)688-3761 Lat: 43.21991, Lon: -83.29165
1601 Tozer Rd, North Branch, MI 48461

WASHAKIE GOLF & RV RESORT Ratings: 8/7.5/8 (Campground) From Jct of I-69 & M53 (Van Dyke Rd), N 9.1 mi to Burnside Rd, W 7.3 mi (R). **FAC:** Gravel rds. (100 spaces). Avail: 20 gravel, back-ins (32 x 50), 20 W, 20 E (30 amps), seasonal sites, WiFi, rentals, dump, laundry, LP bottles, fire rings, firewood, restaurant. **REC:** Lake Washakie: swim, fishing, golf, playground, rec open to public. Pets OK. Partial handicap access, no tents. 2015 rates: $32. May 1 to Oct 31. ATM, no CC.
(810)688-3235 Lat: 43.20697, Lon: -83.22041
3461 Burnside Rd, North Branch, MI 48461
washakiegolfrv@yahoo.com
www.washakiegolfrv.com

NORTH MUSKEGON — H3 *Muskegon*

MUSKEGON (State Pk) From Jct of US-31 & SR-120, W 2.8 mi on SR-120 to Ruddiman St, W 5 mi, follow signs (E). Entrance fee required. 2015 rates: $18 to $32. May 2 to Oct 27. (231)744-3480

We rate what RVers consider important.

NORTHPORT — E4 *Grand Traverse*

LEELANAU (State Pk) From Jct of SR-22 & SR-201, N 8 mi on SR-201(E). Entrance fee required. Pit toilets. 2015 rates: $13. May 3 to Nov 3. (231)386-5422

OMER — G5 *Arenac*

BIG BEND FAMILY CAMPGROUND **Ratings: 7/8.5★/7.5** (Campground) 2015 rates: $30 to $34. Apr 1 to Oct 30. (989)653-2267 513 Conrad Rd, Standish, MI 48658

RIVERBEND CAMPGROUND AND CANOE RENTAL **Ratings: 7/7.5/8** (Campground) 2015 rates: $32. May 1 to Dec 15. (989)653-2576 1165 N. Main St., Omer, MI 48749

ONAWAY — E5 *Presque Isle*

MACKINAW SF (SHOEPAC LAKE) (State Pk) From jct Hwy-68 & Hwy-33: Go 10-1/2 mi S on Hwy-33, then 2 mi E on Tomahawk Lake Hwy, then 1 mi N on access road. Pit toilets. 2015 rates: $13. (989)785-4388

MACKINAW SF/BLACK LAKE (State Pk) From Jct of US-23 & Black River Rd, SE 11 mi on Black River Rd. to Twin Lakes Rd, E 3mi to Doriva Beach rd., S 1.4 mi. Pit toilets. 2015 rates: $13. (989)785-2811

ONAWAY (State Pk) From town, N 6 mi on M-211 (E). Entrance fee required. 2015 rates: $17 to $21. Apr 11 to Nov 2. (989)733-8279

ONSTED — K5 *Lenawee*

HAYES (State Pk) From Jct of US-127 and US-12 in Cement City, E 12.5 mi on US-12 (L); or From Jct of US-23 & US-12 in Ypsilanti, W 25.8 mi on US-12 (R). Entrance fee required. 2015 rates: $25. Apr 9 to Oct 25. (517)467-7401

ONTONAGON — A4 *Ontonagon*

ONTONAGON TOWNSHIP PARK (Public) From Jct of US-45 & Houghton St, NE 1 mi on Houghton St (L). 2015 rates: $19 to $30. May 1 to Sep 30. (906)884-2930

RIVER ROAD RV PARK & CAMP GROUND **Ratings: 5.5/7.5/6.5** (Campground) 2015 rates: $35. (906)884-4600 600 River Rd, Ontonagon, MI 49953

ORTONVILLE — H5 *Brandon, Clarkston, Flint, Oakland*

CLEARWATER RV PARK **Ratings: 7.5/8/7.5** (Campground) 2015 rates: $40 to $55. Apr 15 to Oct 15. (248)627-3820 1140 M-15 (S Ortonville Rd), Ortonville, MI 48462

OSCODA — F6 *Alcona, Iosco*

AU SABLE SF/VAN ETTEN LAKE (State Pk) From Jct of US-23 & F-41, NW 3 mi on F-41 to park access rd, N 0.1 mi, follow signs (R). Pit toilets. 2015 rates: $13. (989)362-5041

OLD ORCHARD PARK (Public) From Jct of US-23 & River Rd, W 8 mi on River Rd, follow signs (R). 2015 rates: $16 to $35. Mar to Nov. (989)739-7814

OSCODA KOA KAMPGROUND **Ratings: 8.5/9.5★/7.5** (Campground) 2015 rates: $48.41 to $66.41. Apr 29 to Oct 16. (800)562-9667 3591 Forest Rd, Oscoda, MI 48750

OSSINEKE — F5 *Alcona*

MACKINAW SF/OSSINEKE (State Pk) From Jct of US-23 & Old Ossineke Rd, NE 2 mi on Old Ossineke Rd, follow signs (R). Entrance fee required. Pit toilets. 2015 rates: $13. (989)785-5126

OTISVILLE — H5 *Genesee*

COVENANT HILLS CAMP

Ratings: 7/9★/9 (Campground) From Jct of I-69 & M-15 (Exit 145), N 13 mi on M-15 to Farrand Rd, E 0.6 mi (L). **FAC:** Gravel rds. (321 spaces). 301 Avail: 50 gravel, 251 grass, 55 pull-thrus (30 x 70), back-ins (30 x 45), 301 full hkups (30/50 amps), seasonal sites, WiFi, tent sites, rentals, dump, fire rings, firewood. **REC:** Pleasant Lake: swim, fishing, playground, rec open to public. Pets OK. Partial handicap access. 2015 rates: $34. Apr 1 to Nov 1.
(810)631-4531 Lat: 43.195409, Lon: -83.506603
10359 E. Farrand Rd, Otisville, MI 48463
camp@CovenantHills.org
www.covenanthills.org
See ad this page, 616.

OTSEGO — J3 *Allegan*

ADVENTURE RESORTS OF AMERICA **Ratings: 6.5/8.5★/8.5** (Membership Pk) 2015 rates: $15. May 1 to Oct 7. (269)459-8308 8368 West C Ave, Kalamazoo, MI 49009

OTTAWA LAKE — K5 *Monroe*

COVERED WAGON CAMP RESORT Ratings: 8.5/6/7 (Campground) From Jct of US-23 & St Anthony Rd (exit 5), E 0.25 mi on St Anthony Rd (R). **FAC:** Paved rds. (113 spaces). 60 Avail: 12 paved, 48 grass, 20 pull-thrus (24 x 50), back-ins (22 x 55), some side by side hkups, 21 full hkups, 39 W, 39 E (30 amps), seasonal sites, WiFi, tent sites, rentals, dump, mobile sewer, laundry, groc, fire rings, firewood, controlled access. **REC:** pool, pond, fishing, playground, rec open to public. Pet restrict(B). Partial handicap access. Age restrict may apply, 2015 rates: $30 to $35. Disc: AAA, military. Apr 15 to Nov 1.
(734)856-3058 Lat: 41.79821, Lon: -83.68232
5639 St Anthony Rd (M-151), Ottawa Lake, MI 49267
wagon10@bex.net
www.coveredwagoncamp.com

OTTER LAKE — H5 *Genesee*

GENESEE OTTER LAKE CAMPGROUND **Ratings: 7.5/8.5★/8** (Campground) 2015 rates: $25 to $30. May 1 to Oct 1. (810)793-2725 12260 Ferrand Rd, Otter Lake, MI 48464

OTTER LAKE VILLAGE PARK (Public) From Jct of SR-24 & Otter Lake Rd, W 7 mi on Otter Lake Rd to 11th St, NE 0.2 mi to Genesee Rd, W 0.2 mi, follow signs (R). 2015 rates: $20 to $35. Apr 15 to Oct 15. (810)793-4258

PARADISE — C4 *Chippewa, Luce*

LAKE SUPERIOR SF (BODI LAKE) (State Pk) From town: Go 17 mi W on Hwy 123, then N on CR 500 & CR 437. Pit toilets. 2015 rates: $13. (906)492-3415

LAKE SUPERIOR SF (CULHANE LAKE) (State Pk) From town: Go 17 mi W on Hwy 123, then N on CR 500 (Northwestern Rd N). Pit toilets. 2015 rates: $13. (906)492-3415

LAKE SUPERIOR SF (PIKE LAKE) (State Pk) From town: Go 17 mi W on Hwy 123, then N on CR 500, then W on CR 414. Pit toilets. 2015 rates: $13. (906)492-3415

LAKE SUPERIOR SF/ANDRUS LAKE (State Pk) From Jct of Hwys 28 & 123, N 23 mi on Hwy 123 to Wire Rd, N 5 mi to Vermillion Rd, W 2 mi, follow signs (L). Pit toilets. 2015 rates: $13. (906)293-3293

TAHQUAMENON FALLS (State Pk) From town, SW 12 mi on M-123 (L). Entrance fee required. 2015 rates: $13 to $25. (906)492-3415

PARIS — G4 *Mecosta*

PARIS PARK (Public) From Jct of US-131 & 19 Mi Rd, E 1.5 mi on 19 Mi Rd to Northland Dr, N 4 mi (R). 2015 rates: $18 to $25. May 4 to Oct 4. (231)796-3420

PENTWATER — G3 *Mason, Oceana*

CHARLES MEARS (State Pk) From Jct of Bus US-31 & Lowell St, W 0.4 mi on Lowell St, follow signs (R). Entrance fee required. 2015 rates: $31. Apr 1 to Oct 1. (231)869-2051

HILL & HOLLOW CAMPGROUND **Ratings: 7.5/9★/8.5** (Campground) 2015 rates: $46 to $51. May 1 to Oct 15. (231)869-5811 8915 N Bus US-31, Pentwater, MI 49449

WHISPERING SURF CAMPING RESORT **Ratings: 7.5/7/7.5** (Campground) 2015 rates: $39 to $44. May 1 to Oct 31. (231)869-5050 7070 S Lakeshore Dr, Pentwater, MI 49449

PETERSBURG — K5 *Monroe*

MONROE COUNTY KOA **Ratings: 8/8/8** (Campground) 2015 rates: $54 to $69. Apr 10 to Oct 30. (734)856-4972 15600 Tunnicliffe Rd, Petersburg, MI 49270

PIROLLI PARK RV RESORT **Ratings: 8/9.5★/9** (Campground) 2015 rates: $47. (734)279-1487 6030 Sylvania-Petersburg Rd, Petersburg, MI 49270

TOTEM POLE PARK LLC Ratings: 6.5/10★/8.5 (Campground) From Jct of US-23 & Summerfield Rd (Exit 9), NW 2.6 mi on Summerfield Rd to Lulu Rd, W 0.4 mi (L). **FAC:** Gravel rds. (130 spaces). 29 Avail: 6 gravel, 23 grass, 6 pull-thrus (30 x 85), back-ins (38 x 65), 6 full hkups, 23 W, 23 E (30/50 amps), seasonal sites, WiFi, tent sites, dump, fire rings, controlled access. **REC:** pond, swim, fishing, playground. Pet restrict(Q). Partial handicap access. Age restrict may apply, big rig sites, eco-friendly, 2015 rates: $36. May 1 to Sep 30. No CC, no reservations.
(800)227-2110 Lat: 41.88034, Lon: -83.67795
16333 Lulu Rd, Petersburg, MI 49270
info@totempolepark.com
www.totempolepark.com

Had a great stay? Let us know by emailing us travelguidecomments@goodsamfamily.com

PETOSKEY — E4 *Emmet*

HEARTHSIDE GROVE MOTORCOACH RESORT **Ratings: 10/10★/9.5** (Condo Pk) 2015 rates: $89.95 to $119.95. (888)476-8388 2400 US 31 North, Petoskey, MI 49770

MAGNUS PARK
(Public) From Jct of US-31 & Lake St, W 0.7 mi on Lake St (L). **FAC:** Paved/gravel rds. 72 grass, 19 pull-thrus (25 x 60), back-ins (28 x 40), 36 full hkups, 36 W, 36 E (20/30 amps), WiFi, tent sites, dump, fire rings. **REC:** Little Traverse Bay Lake Michigan: swim, fishing, playground, rec open to public. Pet restrict(Q). Partial handicap access. 2015 rates: $25. Apr 28 to Oct 22.
(231)347-1027 Lat: 45.37388, Lon: -84.97249
901 W. Lake St, Petoskey, MI 49770
magnus@petoskey.us
www.petoskey.us
See ad this page.

PETOSKEY (State Pk) From town, N 3 mi on SR-31 to Rte 119, W 1.5 mi, follow signs (L). Entrance fee required. 2015 rates: $31 to $33. May 15 to Nov 1. (231)347-2311

PETOSKEY KOA RV & CABIN RESORT Ratings: 10/10★/10 (Campground) From Jct of US-31N & M-119 (E of town), N 1 mi on US-31N (R). **FAC:** Paved rds. (169 spaces). Avail: 120 paved, patios, 31 pull-thrus (35 x 60), back-ins (35 x 45), 92 full hkups, 28 W, 28 E (30/50 amps), seasonal sites, cable, WiFi, tent sites, rentals, dump, laundry, groc, LP gas, fire rings, firewood, controlled access. **REC:** heated pool, whirlpool, pond, playground. Pet restrict(B). Partial handicap access. Big rig sites, eco-friendly, 2015 rates: $50.95 to $71. May 1 to Oct 12.
(800)562-0253 Lat: 45.39577, Lon: -84.89305
1800 US-31 North, Petoskey, MI 49770
petkoa@msn.com
www.petoskeykoa.com

PETOSKEY MOTORCOACH RESORT
Ratings: 10/10★/10 (RV Park) From Jct of US 131 & US 31, S 5 mi on US 31 (L).

LUXURY IN NORTHERN MICHIGAN
The Petoskey RV Resort sets the standard for quality & beauty. Located in Northern Michigan along Lake Michigan's shoreline. Enjoy the grand lodge, tennis, Wifi, pool, spa and saunas. Nearby golf, fine dining and beaches.

FAC: Paved rds. 75 paved, patios, back-ins (40 x 90), 75 full hkups (50 amps), cable, WiFi, laundry, controlled access. **REC:** heated pool, whirlpool. Pet restrict(Q). Partial handicap access, no tents. Big rig sites, RV age restrict, eco-friendly, 2015 rates: $62 to $108. May 1 to Oct 1.
(888)366-2666 Lat: 45.35840, Lon: -85.05435
5505 Charlevoix Ave, Petoskey, MI 49770
Bay_front@sunlandrvresorts.com
www.petoskeymotorcoachresort.com
See ad this page, 616.

PEWAMO — H4 *Ionia*

MAPLE RIVER CAMPGROUND **Ratings: 5.5/NA/6.5** (Campground) Pit toilets. 2015 rates: $35. (989)981-6792 15420 French Rd, Pewamo, MI 48873

PICKFORD — D5 *Chippewa*

LAKE SUPERIOR SF (MUNUSCONG RIVER) (State Pk) From jct Hwy 48 & Hwy 129: Go 8 mi E & N on Sterlingville Rd. Pit toilets. 2015 rates: $13. (906)248-3422

PINCKNEY — J5 *Livingston*

HELL CREEK RANCH & CAMPGROUND Ratings: 7.5/10★/8 (Campground) From the intersection of M-36 W & Howell St in Pinckney: L on Howell St, 1.3 mi to Paterson Lake Rd (R); 1 mi to Cedar Lake Rd (L). **FAC:** Gravel rds. (100 spaces). 80 Avail: 10 paved, 70 grass, back-ins (50 x 60), 80 W, 80 E (30 amps), seasonal sites, WiFi, tent sites, dump, fire rings, firewood. **REC:** heated pool, pond, playground, rec open to public. Pets OK. Partial handicap access. 2015 rates: $30 to $35. Disc: AAA, military. Apr 1 to Oct 31.
AAA Approved
(734)878-3632 Lat: 42.44028, Lon: -83.96528
10866 Cedar Lake Rd, Pinckney, MI 48169
Hellcreekranch1@gmail.com
www.hellcreekranch.com

PINCKNEY SRA (State Pk) From US-23 & N Territorial Rd (exit 49), W 14 mi on N Territorial Rd to Hadley Rd, N (right) 4.2 mi to Kaiser Rd, E 0.8 mi, follow signs (R). Entrance fee required. 2015 rates: $18 to $28. Apr 15 to Dec 1. (734)426-4913

PINCONNING — G5 *Bay*

PINCONNING PARK (Public) From Jct of I-75 & Pinconning Rd (Exit 181), E 4.6 mi on Pinconning Rd (L). Entrance fee required. 2015 rates: $23. (989)879-5050

PORT AUSTIN — G6 *Huron*

OAK BEACH COUNTY PARK (Public) From the Jct of M-25 & M-53 in Downtown Port Austin: SW 8.6 mi on M-25 E (L). 2015 rates: $25 to $35. May 1 to Oct 15. (989)856-2344

PORT CRESCENT (State Pk) From Jct of Hwys 53 & 25, SW 5 mi on Hwy 25, follow signs (R). 2015 rates: $29 to $31. Apr 1 to Dec 1. (989)738-8663

PORT HOPE — G6 *Huron*

LIGHTHOUSE COUNTY PARK (Public) From of Jct of Sand Beach Rd (M-142) & Main St (M-25) in Downtown Harbor Beach: N 13.6 mi on Main St to Lighthouse Rd, E 1.1 mi (L). 2015 rates: $18 to $35. May 1 to Oct 15. (989)428-4749

STAFFORD COUNTY PARK (Public) From Jct of M 25 & State St in Port Hope: E 0.5 mi on State St to Huron St, N 0.2 mi (L). 2015 rates: $21 to $30. May 1 to Oct 15. (989)428-4213

PORT HURON — H6 *Garland, Huron, St Clair*

LAKEPORT (State Pk) From Jct of I-94 & M-25, N 15 mi on M-25 (R). 2015 rates: $23. Apr 11 to Nov 3. (810)327-6224

PORT HURON KOA Ratings: 9/10★/10 (Campground) From Jct of I-69 & Wadhams Rd (exit 196), N 0.5 mi on Wadhams Rd to Lapeer Rd, E 0.8 mi (R). **FAC:** Paved/gravel rds. (289 spaces). 269 Avail: 33 paved, 125 gravel, 111 grass, 60 pull-thrus (30 x 60), back-ins (30 x 60), 121 full hkups, 148 W, 148 E (30/50 amps), seasonal sites, cable, WiFi, tent sites, rentals, dump, mobile sewer, laundry, groc, LP bottles, fire rings, firewood, restaurant, controlled access. **REC:** pool, shuffleboard, playground. Pets OK. Partial handicap access. Big rig sites, 2015 rates: $55 to $87. May 1 to Oct 27. ATM.
(800)562-0833 Lat: 42.98424, Lon: -82.52879
5111 Lapeer Rd, Kimball, MI 48074
phkoa@aol.com
www.koa.com

PORT SANILAC — H6 *Lapeer, Sanilac*

FORESTER PARK (Public) From jct Hwy 46 & Hwy 25: Go 6 1/2 mi N on Hwy 25. 2015 rates: $20 to $28. (810)622-8715

LAKE HURON CAMPGROUND **Ratings: 8/9.5★/8.5** (Campground) 2015 rates: $33 to $59. Apr 15 to Oct 31. (810)622-0110 2353 N. Lakeshore Rd, Port Sanilac, MI 48419

POSEN — E5 *Alpena, Presque Isle*

SUNKEN LAKE COUNTY PARK (Public) From Jct of M-32 & M-65, N 5 mi on M-65 to Long Rapids, N 0.1 mi to Leer Rd, N 5 mi, follow signs (E). 2015 rates: $17 to $26. May 15 to Oct 1. (989)379-3055

QUINCY — K4 *Branch*

QUINCY MARBLE LAKE (BRANCH COUNTY PARK) (Public) From jct I-69 & US-12: Go 5 mi E on US-12, then 1/4 S on Lake Blvd. (517)639-4414

RAPID RIVER — D2 *Delta*

VAGABOND RESORT **Ratings: 6/4.5/6** (Campground) 2015 rates: $30. May 1 to Nov 1. (906)474-6122 8935 County 513T Rd, Rapid River, MI 49878

WHITEFISH HILL RV PARK **Ratings: 6.5/8/7.5** (RV Park) 2015 rates: $35 to $50. Apr 30 to Oct 3. (906)280-5438 8455 US 2, Rapid River, MI 49878

RAVENNA — H3 *Muskegon*

CROCKERY CREEK RV PARK **Ratings: 9/9★/9** (Campground) 2015 rates: $45. May 1 to Oct 15. (231)853-0220 13812 Apple Ave, Ravenna, MI 49451

REED CITY — G4 *Mecosta*

RAMBADT MEMORIAL PARK (Public) From Jct of US-131 & US-10, E 0.1 mi on US-10 to Patterson, S 0.5 mi to Park St, E 0.5 mi, follow signs (L). 2015 rates: $14. May 15 to Oct 31. (231)832-2245

ROCKFORD — H4 *Kent*

WABASIS LAKE PARK (Public) From Jct of US-131 & SR-57, E 10 mi on SR-57 to Wabasis Ave, S 3 mi (L). 2015 rates: $22 to $37. Apr 24 to Nov 1. (616)691-8056

ROGERS CITY — E5 *Presque Isle*

P H HOEFT (State Pk) From Jct of Hwy 68 & US-23, NW 4.3 mi on US-23, follow signs (R). Entrance fee required. 2015 rates: $17 to $34. Apr 1 to Dec1. (989)734-2543

ROSCOMMON — F4 *Crawford*

NORTH HIGGINS LAKE (State Pk) From Jct of I-75 & West Higgins (exit 244), W 5 mi on West Higgins (L). Entrance fee required. 2015 rates: $18 to $31. Apr 1 to Dec1. (989)821-6125

RV Park ratings you can rely on!

MI

ROSCOMMON (CONT)

➔ NORTHERN NIGHTS FAMILY CAMPGROUND **Ratings: 5/9★/8** (Campground) 2015 rates: $32 to $42. May 1 to Oct 4. (989)821-6891 2380 W Burdell Rd, Roscommon, MI 48653

SOUTH HIGGINS LAKE (State Pk) From Jct of I-75 & SR-18, (exit 239), S 0.1 mi on SR-18 to CR-103, W 3 mi to CR-100, S 3 mi, follow signs (R). Entrance fee required. 2015 rates: $30 to $37. Apr 15 to Nov 30. (989)821-6374

ROTHBURY — H3 *Oceana*

DOUBLE JJ RESORT **Ratings: 5/7.5/6.5** (Campground) 2015 rates: $65. Apr 1 to Oct 30. (231)894-4444 5900 Water Road, Rothbury, MI 49452

SANFORD — G5 *Midland*

AU SABLE SF (BLACK CREEK) (State Pk) From town: Go 3 mi NW on Saginaw Rd & W River Rd. Pit toilets. 2015 rates: $13. Apr 15 to Sep 15. (989)386-4067

SAULT STE MARIE — C5 *Chippewa*

➔ AUNE-OSBORN RV PARK (Public) From Jct of I-75 & Bus 75/Ashmun (Exit 392), NE 3.5 mi on Bus 75/Ashman to Portage/Riverside, E 2.0 mi (L). 2015 rates: $27 to $29. May 15 to Oct 15. (906)632-3268

KEWADIN CASINO PARK **Ratings: 5/8.5/7** (Campground) 2015 rates: $15. May 1 to Oct 31. (906)635-4926 2186 Shunk Rd, Sault Ste Marie, MI 49783

➔ SOO LOCKS CAMPGROUND **Ratings: 6/9★/7** (Campground) 2015 rates: $27 to $31. May 1 to Oct 20. (906)632-3191 1001 E Portage Ave, Sault Ste Marie, MI 49783

SAWYER — K3 *Berrien*

KAMP ACROSS FROM DUNES Ratings: 7.5/9.5★/9.5 (Campground) From Jct of I-94 & Sawyer Rd (exit 12), W 0.5 mi on Sawyer Rd to Red Arrow Hwy, N 1.5 mi (R). **FAC:** Paved/gravel rds. (62 spaces). Avail: 6 gravel, 4 pull-thrus (30 x 50), back-ins (35 x 40), 6 full hkups (30/50 amps), seasonal sites, WiFi, rentals, showers $, dump, fire rings, firewood. **REC:** pool $, pond, playground. Pets OK. No tents. Big rig sites, 2015 rates: $50. May 1 to Oct 31. (269)426-4971 Lat: 41.90169, Lon: -86.59416 12011 Red Arrow Hwy, Sawyer, MI 49125 dougryskamp@yahoo.com www.kampacrossfromthedunes.net

WARREN DUNES (State Pk) From Jct of I-94 & Bridgeman Red Arrow Hwy (exit 16), SW 3 mi on Red Arrow Hwy (R). Entrance fee required. 2015 rates: $22 to $37. Apr 1 to Oct 31. (269)426-4013

SCOTTVILLE — G3 *Mason, Oceana*

CRYSTAL LAKE FAMILY CAMPGROUND **Ratings: 7/7.5/7** (Campground) 2015 rates: $39. May 1 to Oct 15. (231)757-4510 1884 W Hansen Rd, Scottville, MI 49454

SCOTTVILLE RIVERSIDE PARK (Public) From Jct of US-31 & US-10/31, E 8 mi on US-10/31 (Ludington) to S Main St, S 0.5 mi, follow signs (L). 2015 rates: $17 to $22. May 1 to Oct 31. (231)757-2429

SEARS — G4 *Osceola*

➔ CRITTENDEN PARK (OSCEOLA COUNTY PARK) (Public) From jct US 131 & US 10: Go 13 mi E on US 10, then 5 mi SE on Big Lake. 2015 rates: $17 to $25. May 8 to Sep 27. (231)734-2588

SEBEWAING — G5 *Huron*

➔ SEBEWAING COUNTY PARK (Public) From Jct of M-25 & Pine St in Downtown Sebewaing: W 0.5 mi on Pine St to Miller St., S 0.3 mi to Union St., NW 0.1 mi (E). 2015 rates: $18 to $35. May 1 to Oct 15. (989)883-2033

SHELBY — G3 *Oceana*

SILVER LAKE (State Pk) From town, SW 4 mi on CR-B15, follow signs (R). Entrance fee required. 2015 rates: $20 to $29. Apr 20 to Oct 31. (231)873-3083

SILVER CITY — A4 *Ontonagon*

PORCUPINE MTNS. (UNION BAY CAMPGROUND) (State Pk) From town: Go 3 mi W on Hwy 107. 2015 rates: $16 to $25. (906)885-5275

SKANEE — C1 *Baraga*

➔ COPPER COUNTRY SF (BIG ERIC'S BRIDGE) (State Pk) From town: Go 6 mi E on Skanee-Big Bay Rd. Pit toilets. 2015 rates: $13. (906)353-6558

SOMERSET CENTER — K5 *Hillsdale*

SOMERSET BEACH CAMPGROUND Ratings: 7.5/8.5★/8.5 (Campground) From Jct of US-127 & US-12, W 3.7 mi on US-12 to Fairway Dr, S 0.5 mi to Brooklawn Dr, W 0.4 mi (R). **FAC:** Gravel rds. (251 spaces). Avail: 206 grass, back-ins (30 x 45), 206 E (30 amps), seasonal sites, WiFi, tent sites, rentals, dump, mobile sewer, laundry, LP gas, fire rings, firewood. **REC:** Mission Lake: swim, fishing, playground, rec open to public. Pets OK. Partial handicap access. Eco-friendly, 2015 rates: $30.
(517)688-3783 Lat: 42.04195, Lon: -84.43036 9822 Brooklawn Ct, Somerset Center, MI 49282 info@somersetbeach.org www.somersetbeach.org
See ad this page.

SOUTH HAVEN — J3 *Allegan, Van Buren*

COUSINS CAMPGROUND **Ratings: 7/8.5★/8.5** (Campground) 2015 rates: $44. May 15 to Oct 15. (269)637-1499 7317 North Shore Drive, South Haven, MI 49090

➔ **SOUTH HAVEN SUNNY BROOK RV RESORT Ratings: 10/10★/10** (Condo Pk) From Jct of I-196 & CR 388 (Phoenix Rd Exit 20), E 2.2 mi on CR 388/ Phoenix Rd (L). **FAC:** Paved rds. (181 spaces). Avail: 127 paved, patios, back-ins (45 x 90), 127 full hkups (30/50 amps), seasonal sites, WiFi, laundry, fire rings, firewood, controlled access. **REC:** heated pool, whirlpool, Butter Nut Lake: fishing, shuffleboard, playground. Pet restrict(Q). Partial handicap access, no tents. Big rig sites, RV age restrict, 2015 rates: $52 to $69. Apr 15 to Oct 31.
(888)499-5253 Lat: 42.40413, Lon: -86.21006 68300 CR 388 Phoenix Rd, South Haven, MI 49090 info@sunnybrookrvresort.com www.sunnybrookrvresort.com
See ad this page.

VAN BUREN (State Pk) From Jct of I-196 & Covert Rd exit (Blue Star Hwy), N 3 mi on Blue Star Hwy to Ruggles Rd, E 1 mi (E). Entrance fee required. 2015 rates: $18 to $27. Apr 1 to Dec 1. (269)637-2788

➔ YOGI BEAR'S JELLYSTONE PARK CAMP-RESORT **Ratings: 9/10★/10** (Campground) 2015 rates: $30 to $75. Apr 15 to Oct 30. (269)637-6153 03403 64th Street, South Haven, MI 49090

SOUTHFIELD — J6 *Oakland*

Things to See and Do

SUN COMMUNITIES Sun RV Resorts caters to everyone with a great selection of vacation destinations perfect for all ages and exclusive resorts for active adults. No CC.
(888)886-2477
www.sunrvresorts.com
See ad pages 275 (Welcome Section), 1463 (Welcome Section).

Say you saw it in our Guide!

Everyone wants to be noticed. Tell your RV Park that you found them in the this Guide.

SPRING LAKE — H3 *Ottawa*

TANGLEFOOT RV PARK (Public) From Jct of US-31 & SR-104, E 0.3 mi on SR-104 to Jackson St, S 0.1 mi to Exchange St, W 0.1 mi, follow signs (L). 2015 rates: $40. Apr 15 to Oct 15. (616)842-1393

ST CLAIR — H6 *St Clair*

SAINT CLAIR (THOUSAND TRAILS) **Ratings: 8/7/7.5** (Membership Pk) 2015 rates: $40. May 1 to Oct 31. (810)329-7129 1299 Wadhams Rd, Saint Clair, MI 48079

ST IGNACE — D4 *Mackinac*

CASTLE ROCK LAKEFRONT CAMPGROUND
Ratings: 7.5/8★/8.5 (Campground) From Jct of I-75 & Bus Loop I-75 (exit 348), SE 0.2 mi on Bus Loop I-75 to Mackinac Tr, NE 0.25 mi (R). **FAC:** Paved/gravel rds. (99 spaces). Avail: 88 grass, 8 pull-thrus (30 x 60), back-ins (28 x 39), 17 full hkups, 71 W, 71 E (20/50 amps), seasonal sites, WiFi, tent sites, dump, laundry, fire rings, firewood. **REC:** Lake Huron: swim, fishing, playground. Pets OK. 2015 rates: $36. Disc: military. May 15 to Oct 15. AAA Approved
(906)643-9222 Lat: 45.90890, Lon: -84.73885
2811 Mackinac Trail, St Ignace, MI 49781
Castlerockcampground@gmail.com
www.campmich.com
See ad pages 631, 616.

LAKESHORE RV PARK
Ratings: 8.5/9★/8 (Campground) From Jct of I-75 & US-2 (exit 344), W 1.4 mi on US-2 to Point La Barbe Rd, S 1.5 mi (R); or E-bnd: From Jct of US-2 & Point La Barbe Rd, E 1 mi on Point La Barbe Rd (L). **FAC:** Gravel rds. (55 spaces). Avail: 53 gravel, 33 pull-thrus (28 x 60), back-ins (28 x 60), 53 full hkups (30/50 amps), seasonal sites, WiFi, tent sites, dump, laundry, fire rings, firewood. **REC:** Lake Michigan: swim, fishing. Pets OK. Big rig sites, 2015 rates: $40. May 1 to Oct 15.
(906)643-9522 Lat: 45.85478, Lon: -84.78150
W 1234 Point La Barbe Rd, St Ignace, MI 49781
lakeshoreparkcampground@yahoo.com
www.lakeshoreparkcampground.com
See ad opposite page, 616.

ST IGNACE-MACKINAC ISLAND KOA
Ratings: 8/9★/9 (Campground) From Jct of I-75 & US-2, W 2.5 mi on US-2 (R). **FAC:** Gravel rds. 145 gravel, 83 pull-thrus (40 x 70), back-ins (30 x 50), 45 full hkups, 100 W, 100 E (30/50 amps), cable, WiFi, tent sites, rentals, dump, mobile sewer, laundry, groc, fire rings, firewood. **REC:** heated pool, playground, rec open to public. Pets OK. Partial handicap access. 2015 rates: $53. May 1 to Oct 31.
(906)643-9303 Lat: 45.85422, Lon: -84.77376
w1118 US 2, St Ignace, MI 49781
1simikoa@charter.net
www.simikoa.com
See ad opposite page.

STRAITS (State Pk) From Jct of I-75 & US-2 (exit 344A), E 0.3 mi on US-2 to Church St, S 0.2 mi (R). Michigan Recreation Access pass is required to enter. 2015 rates: $16 to $28. Apr 5 to Nov 30. (906)643-8620

TIKI RV PARK & CAMPGROUND
Ratings: 6.5/8.5★/7.5 (Campground) N-bnd: From Jct of I-75 & Bus I-75/US 2 (exit 344A), N 3 mi on Bus I-75 (State St) to S Airport Rd, W 0.1 mi (L). **FAC:** Gravel rds. (85 spaces). 81 Avail: 51 gravel, 30 grass, 30 pull-thrus (30 x 60), back-ins (30 x 50), 31 full hkups, 50 W, 50 E (30/50 amps), seasonal sites, WiFi, tent sites, dump, laundry, fire rings, firewood. **REC.** Pets OK. Partial handicap access. Big rig sites, 2015 rates: $36. Disc: AAA. May 1 to Oct 31.
(906)643-7808 Lat: 45.88198, Lon: -84.72785
200 S Airport Rd, St Ignace, MI 49781
tikicamp@yahoo.com
www.tikirvpark.com
See ad opposite page, 616.

ST JAMES — D4 *Charlevoix*

MACKINAW SF (BEAVER ISLAND) (State Pk) From Charlevoix: Take ferry to St. James on Beaver Island, then go 7 mi S on East Side Dr. Pit toilets. 2015 rates: $10. (989)732-3541

STANWOOD — G4 *Mecosta*

BROWER COUNTY PARK (Public) From Jct of US-131 & Eight Mile Rd, W 1 mi on Eight Mile Rd to Old State Rd, SW 2 mi to Polk Rd, W 1 mi (E). Entrance fee required. 2015 rates: $24. Apr 1 to Oct 27. (231)823-2561

RIVER RIDGE RV RESORT & MARINA **Ratings: 10/9.5★/10** (RV Park) 2015 rates: $45 to $55. Apr 15 to Oct 31. (231)823-8338 22265 8 Mile Road, Stanwood, MI 49346

STEPHENSON — E2 *Menominee*

COYOTE RV PARK & CAMPGROUND **Ratings: 4/6.5/7.5** (Campground) 2015 rates: $25. May 1 to Nov 30. (906)753-4946 w6182 Cty Rd G12, Stephenson, MI 49887

SHAKEY LAKES COUNTY PARK (Public) From Jct of US-41 & CR G-12, W 12 mi on CR-G-12 (R). Entrance fee required. 2015 rates: $15 to $24. May 23 to Sep 8. (906)753-4582

STERLING — G5 *Arenac*

OUTDOOR ADVENTURES RIFLE RIVER RESORT **Ratings: 7.5/8.5/9** (Membership Pk) 2015 rates: $30. May 15 to Oct 15. (989)671-1125 334 Melita Rd, Sterling, MI 48659

RIVER VIEW CAMPGROUND & CANOE LIVERY **Ratings: 7.5/9★/8.5** (Campground) 2015 rates: $40. May 1 to Oct 15. (989)654-2447 5755 Townline Rd, Sterling, MI 48659

STOCKBRIDGE — J5 *Ingham*

HEARTLAND WOODS FAMILY RV **Ratings: 7/9★/8** (Membership Pk) 2015 rates: $32 to $45. May 15 to Oct 15. (517)565-3500 5120 Freiermuth Rd., Stockbridge, MI 49285

STURGIS — K4 *St Joseph*

GREEN VALLEY CAMPGROUND **Ratings: 7/8.5/8** (Campground) 2015 rates: $21 to $30. May 1 to Oct 15. (269)651-8760 25499 W Fawn River Rd, Sturgis, MI 49091

SUMNER — H4 *Gratiot*

LEISURE LAKE FAMILY CAMPGROUND INC
Ratings: 7.5/9★/9.5 (Campground) From Jct of US-127 & Exit 117 (Ithaca exit), W 10 mi on Center St (changes to Washington Rd) to Warner Rd, S 0.7 mi (L). **FAC:** Gravel rds. (157 spaces). Avail: 87 grass, 8 pull-thrus (40 x 60), back-ins (40 x 50), 41 full hkups, 46 W, 46 E (30/50 amps), seasonal sites, WiFi, tent sites, rentals, dump, mobile sewer, laundry, groc, LP gas, fire rings, firewood, controlled access. **REC:** Leisure Lake: swim, fishing, playground. Pet restrict(B). Partial handicap access. Eco-friendly, 2015 rates: $32 to $45. May 1 to Oct 31.
(989)875-4689 Lat: 43.28189, Lon: -84.77698
505 S Warner Rd, Sumner, MI 48889
camp@leisurelakefamilycampground.com
www.leisurelakefamilycampground.com
See ad pages 629, 616.

SUTTONS BAY — E4 *Leelanau*

WILD CHERRY RESORT **Ratings: 7.5/NA/9.5** (RV Park) 2015 rates: $49 to $75. May 1 to Nov 1. (231)271-5550 8563 E Horn Rd, Lake Leelanau, MI 49653

TAWAS CITY — F5 *Arenac, Iosco*

NORTHERN BEAR PAW RV PARK Ratings: 7.5/10★/9.5 (RV Park) From Jct of US 23 & M-55, W 10.2 mi on M-55 (L). **FAC:** Gravel rds. (67 spaces). Avail: 46 gravel, 7 pull-thrus (40 x 70), back-ins (40 x 60), 36 full hkups, 10 W, 10 E (30/50 amps), seasonal sites, WiFi, tent sites, dump, laundry, fire rings, firewood. **REC:** East Branch Au Gres River: fishing, playground. Pets OK. Partial handicap access. Big rig sites, 2015 rates: $17 to $28. No CC. (989)362-8000 Lat: 44.27782, Lon: -83.71539 4793 M55, Tawas City, MI 48763 northernbearpaw@yahoo.com northernbearpawrvpark.com

TAWAS RIVER RV PARK
Ratings: 6/8★/6.5 (Campground) From Jct of I-75 & M-55, E. 35 mi on M-55 to Nunn Rd, N 0.2 mi (R). **FAC:** Gravel rds. (87 spaces). Avail: 25 grass, 5 pull-thrus (30 x 70), back-ins (30 x 60), some side by side hkups, 5 full hkups, 20 W, 20 E (30/50 amps), seasonal sites, cable, WiFi, tent sites, dump, mobile sewer, laundry, fire rings, firewood. **REC:** Tawas River: fishing, playground. Pets OK. Eco-friendly, 2015 rates: $35. May 1 to Oct 15.
(989)362-4988 Lat: 44.28074, Lon: -83.51463
560 E M-55, Tawas City, MI 48763
info@tawasriverrvpark.com
tawasriverrvpark.com
See ad this page, 616.

TAWAS RV PARK **Ratings: 7.5/9★/8.5** (Campground) 2015 rates: $25 to $28. May 1 to Oct 31. (989)362-0005 1453 Townline Rd, Tawas City, MI 48763

TECUMSEH — K5 *Lenauce, Lenawee*

INDIAN CREEK CAMP & CONFERENCE CENTER
Ratings: 8/9.5★/9 (Campground) From Jct of US-23 & M-50 (exit 17), W 10.4 mi on M-50 to Ford Hwy, N 2.5 mi (R). **FAC:** Gravel rds. (40 spaces). 30 Avail: 20 gravel, 10 grass, 13 pull-thrus (25 x 70), back-ins (30 x 60), 25 full hkups, 5 W, 5 E (30 amps), seasonal sites, WiFi, tent sites, rentals, dump, laundry, fire rings, firewood, controlled access. **REC:** heated pool, pond, fishing, playground, rec open to public. Pets OK. Eco-friendly, 2015 rates: $48. Disc: military. Apr 15 to Oct 15.
(517)423-5659 Lat: 42.03202, Lon: -83.86915
9415 Tangent Hwyr, Tecumseh, MI 49286
rdorman@tecumsehteamquest.com
www.indiancreekcamping.com

TIPTON — K5 *Lewanee*

JA DO CAMPGROUND **Ratings: 5.5/8/8** (Campground) 2015 rates: $30. May 1 to Oct 15. (517)431-2111 5603 Michigan Ave, Tipton, MI 49287

TRAVERSE CITY — F4 *Grand Traverse*

HOLIDAY PARK CAMPGROUND
Ratings: 9/9.5★/10 (Campground) From SW Jct of M-37 & US-31, SW 1 mi on US-31 (R). Note: No Motorcycles. **FAC:** Paved rds. (217 spaces). Avail: 137 all weather, 62 pull-thrus (40 x 65), back-ins (40 x 65), 137 full hkups (30/50 amps), seasonal sites, cable, WiFi, dump, laundry, LP gas, fire

MI

TRAVERSE CITY (CONT)

HOLIDAY PARK CAMPGROUND (CONT)
rings, firewood. **REC:** Silver Lake: swim, fishing, playground. Pets OK. Partial handicap access, no tents. Big rig sites, eco-friendly. 2015 rates: $46 to $59. Apr 25 to Oct 25.
(231)943-4410 Lat: 44.67111, Lon: -85.67390
4860 US-31S, Traverse City, MI 49685
www.holidayparktc.com
See ad this page, 616.

LITTLE RIVER CASINO RV PARK
Ratings: 10/10★/10 (RV Park) From Jct US 31 & M-55, N 3.1 mi on US 31 to M-22, W 0.1 mi (L). Follow signs to RV Park. **FAC:** Paved rds. (95 spaces). Avail: 85 paved, 39 pull-thrus (30 x 70), back-ins (35 x 50), 50 full hkups, 35 W, 35 E (30/50 amps), seasonal sites, cable, WiFi, dump, laundry, LP bottles, restaurant. **REC:** heated pool, whirlpool, playground, rec open to public. Pets OK. Partial handicap access. Big rig sites, eco-friendly. 2015 rates: $29.99 to $44.99. Disc: AAA. Apr 1 to Nov 1. ATM.
(866)572-4386 Lat: 44.28675, Lon: -86.24335
2700 Orchard Hwy, Manistee, MI 49660
frontdesksupervisors@lrcr.com
www.LRCR.com
See primary listing at Manistee and ad page 633.

NORTHWESTERN MICHIGAN FAIR ASSOCIATION CAMPGROUND **Ratings: 4/7/6.5** (Campground) 2015 rates: $20. May 1 to Oct 15. (231)943-4150 3606 Blair Townhall Rd, Traverse City, MI 49685

PERE MARQUETTE SF/ARBUTUS LAKE NO 4 (State Pk) From Jct of Hwys 37 & 113, E 6 mi on Hwy 113 into Kingsley, N 10 mi on W side of lake, follow signs (R). Pit toilets. 2015 rates: $13. May 31 to Sep 6. (231)922-5270

TIMBER RIDGE RV & RECREATION RESORT **Ratings: 8/8/8** (Campground) 2015 rates: $40 to $68. Apr 1 to Nov 15. (231)947-2770 4050 Hammond Rd, Traverse City, MI 49696

TRAVERSE BAY RV RESORT
Ratings: 10/10★/10 (Condo Pk) From N Jct of US 31N & Hwy 72, E 1.5 mi on Hwy 72 (L). Note: RVs restricted to Class "A" & "C" Motorhomes & Fifth Wheels 10 years or approval and minimum 28'. **FAC:** Paved rds. 217 paved, patios, back-ins (48 x 100), 217 full hkups (30/50 amps), cable, WiFi, laundry. **REC:** heated pool, whirlpool, pond. Pet restrict(Q). Partial handicap access, no tents. Big rig sites, RV age restrict, eco-friendly. 2015 rates: $65 to $85. May 1 to Oct 31.
(231)938-5800 Lat: 44.77329, Lon: -85.46457
5555 M-72 East, Williamsburg, MI 49690
info@traversebayrv.com
www.traversebayrv.com
See ad pages 639, 616.

TRAVERSE CITY (State Pk) From town, E 2 mi on US-31, follow signs (R). Entrance fee required. 2015 rates: $31. (231)922-5270

UNION CITY — K4 *Branch*

POTAWATOMIE RECREATION AREA, LLC **Ratings: 7/9★/8** (Campground) 2015 rates: $23 to $30. Apr 15 to Oct 15. (517)278-4289 1117 Bell Rd, Union City, MI 49094

VANDERBILT — E4 *Otsego*

MACKINAW SF/PICKEREL LAKE (State Pk) From town, E 10 mi on Sturgeon Valley Rd to Pickerel Lake Rd, N 0.5 mi, follow signs (L). Pit toilets. 2015 rates: $13. (989)983-4101

VASSAR — H5 *Tuscola*

BER WA GA NA CAMPGROUND **Ratings: 7.5/7/7** (Campground) 2015 rates: $34. May 1 to Nov 1. (989)673-7125 2601 W Sanilac Rd (M-46), Vassar, MI 48768

KRYSTAL LAKE CAMPGROUND **Ratings: 7/7/7.5** (Campground) 2015 rates: $38. Apr 15 to Oct 15. (989)843-0591 5475 Washburn Road, Vassar, MI 48768

WESLEYAN WOODS CONFERENCE CENTER & CAMPGROUND (Public) From Jct of Hwy I-75 & M-46 (Exit 149A), E 19 mi to Ringle Rd, S 1 mi to Caine Rd, E 0.5 mi (R). 2015 rates: $28 to $32. May 1 to Oct 15. (989)823-8840

WAKEFIELD — B4 *Gogebic*

PORCUPINE MOUNTAINS (State Pk) From Ontonagon, W 13 mi on M-64 to M-107, W 3 mi(R); or From town, W 3 mi on M-107, follow signs (R). Entrance fee required. 2015 rates: $15 to $27. Apr 5 to Nov 3. (906)885-5275

SUNDAY LAKE CAMPGROUND & EDDY LAKE PARK (Public) From Jct of Hwy 28 & US-2: W 1 mi on US-2 to Lakeshore Dr, N 0.5 mi. Continue on Eddy Park Rd (R). 2015 rates: $20 to $30. May 23 to Oct 1. (906)224-4481

WATERFORD — J5 *Oakland*

PONTIAC LAKE REC AREA (State Pk) From Jct of I-75 & M-59, W 12 mi on M-59 to Teggerdine Rd, N 2.5 mi (R). Entrance fee required. 2015 rates: $19. May 1 to Oct 31. (248)666-1020

WATERSMEET — D1 *Gogebic*

OTTAWA NATIONAL FOREST (MARION LAKE CAMPGROUND) (Natl Pk) From jct US 45 & US 2: Go 3-3/4 mi E on US 2, then 1-1/2 mi N on FR 3980. Pit toilets. 2015 rates: $14. (906)358-4551

WAYLAND — J4 *Allegan*

DAISY PARK CAMPGROUND **Ratings: 4.5/8/8.5** (Campground) 2015 rates: $28 to $35. May 1 to Oct 15. (269)792-2081 189 126th Ave, Wayland, MI 49348

WEIDMAN — G4 *Isabella*

COLDWATER LAKE FAMILY PARK (Public) From Jct of Bus-27 (Mission St) & M-20 (High St), W 7 mi on M-20 to Winn Rd, N 5 mi to Beal City Rd, W 2 mi to Littlefield Rd, S 0.25 mi (R). 2015 rates: $20 to $25. (989)772-0911

GAMMY WOODS CAMPGROUND
Ratings: 6/9★/9 (Campground) From Jct of US-127 & Exit 143 (Pickard Rd), W 12.2 mi on Pickard Rd to Coldwater Rd, N 4 mi on Coldwater Rd (L). **FAC:** Gravel rds. (79 spaces). Avail: 64 grass, 6 pull-thrus (35 x 70), back-ins (35 x 60), 64 W, 64 E (30 amps), seasonal sites, WiFi Hotspot, tent sites, rentals, dump, mobile sewer, LP gas, fire rings, firewood. **REC:** pond, swim, playground. Pets OK. Partial handicap access. Eco-friendly. 2015 rates: $29. May 1 to Nov 1.
(989)644-2267 Lat: 43.6665278, Lon: -84.982778
1855 N Coldwater Rd, Weidman, MI 48893
manager@gammywoodscampground.com
www.gammywoodscampground.com
See ad pages 635, 616.

WELLSTON — G3 *Manistee, Wexford*

TWIN OAKS CAMPGROUND
Ratings: 6/9.5★/8.5 (Campground) From Jct of Hwy 37 & Hwy 55, W 4.5 mi on Hwy 55 to Moss Rd, N 0.8 mi (R). **FAC:** Gravel rds. (65 spaces). 44 Avail: 36 grass, 8 dirt, 7 pull-thrus (40 x 55), back-ins (35 x 55), 18 full hkups, 26 W, 26 E (20/30 amps), seasonal sites, WiFi, tent sites, rentals, dump, laundry, groc, fire rings, firewood. **REC:** playground. Pets OK. Eco-friendly. 2015 rates: $40.
(877)442-3102 Lat: 44.23445, Lon: -85.89006
233 Moss Rd, Wellston, MI 49689
twinoaks@kaltelnet.net
www.twinoakscamping.com

WEST BRANCH — F5 *Ogemaw*

AU SABLE SF (AMBROSE LAKE) (State Pk) From town: Go 11 mi N on CR 15 & CR 20. Pit toilets. 2015 rates: $13. (989)275-4622

BEAVER TRAIL CAMPGROUND **Ratings: 5/9★/7.5** (Campground) 2015 rates: $29. (989)345-7745 4408 Grass Lake Rd, West Branch, MI 48661

LORANGER PINES RV PARK **Ratings: 6.5/9.5★/8.5** (Campground) 2015 rates: $33. May 1 to Nov 1. (989)343-0261 1700 Crawford Lane, West Branch, MI 48661

WEST BRANCH RV PARK (Public) From Jct of I-75 & Exit 212, N 1.5 mi on exit rd (L). 2015 rates: $20 to $25. Apr 1 to Oct 15. (989)345-3295

WHITE CLOUD — G3 *Oceana, Sandy Beach*

BIG BEND TOWNSHIP PARK (Public) From town, E 9 mi on Baseline Rd to S Beech Ave, S 2 mi (E). 2015 rates: $24 to $26. Apr 15 to Oct 15. (231)689-6325

OXBOW TOWNSHIP PARK (Public) From Jct of US-131 & Jefferson Rd, W 9 mi on Jefferson Rd to Chestnut, N 2.5 mi, follow signs (E). 2015 rates: $24 to $26. Apr 15 to Oct 15. (231)856-4279

SANDY BEACH COUNTY PARK (Public) From Jct of SR-37 & CR-Baseline, E 6 mi on CR-Baseline to Elm Ave, S 4 mi to 30th St, E 0.6 mi (L). 2015 rates: $16 to $36. (231)689-1229

WHITE CLOUD CITY CAMPGROUND (Public) From the Jct. of US-131 & M-20 (Exit 131): W 15.9 mi on M-20 cont. on E. Wilcox Ave 0.8 mi (L). 2015 rates: $22. Apr 15 to Sep 28. (231)689-2021

WILLIAMSBURG — F4 *Grand Traverse*

PERE MARQUETTE SF/SCHECK'S PLACE (State Pk) From town, N 1.4 mi on CR-611 to River Rd, E 4 mi, follow signs (L). Pit toilets. 2015 rates: $13. May 1 to Oct 15. (231)922-5270

WHITEWATER TOWNSHIP PARK (Public) From town, E 6 mi on Hwy 31/72 to Hwy 72, E 4 mi to Elk Lake Rd (near Turtle Creek Casino), N 3 mi to Park Rd, E 1 mi (E). 2015 rates: $23 to $28. May 8 to Sep 30. (231)267-5141

WIXOM — J5 *Oakland*

PROUD LAKE SRA (State Pk) From Jct of I-96 & Wixom Rd (exit 159), N 4.4 mi on Wixom Rd to Glengary Rd, E 0.5 mi (L). Entrance fee required. 2015 rates: $23 to $25. May 1 to Oct 30. (248)685-2433

WOLVERINE — E4 *Cheboygan*

ELKWOOD CAMPGROUND
Ratings: 6.5/8★/7.5 (Campground) From Jct. I-75 & Afton Rd. (exit 301) E. 0.9 mi on Afton Rd to Molineaux Rd, S. 4.6 mi on Molineaux Rd, changes to Lance Lake Rd, (R). **FAC:** Gravel rds. (70 spaces). Avail: 60 grass, 15 pull-thrus (36 x 65), back-ins (38 x 55), 13 full hkups, 47 W, 47 E (30/50 amps), seasonal sites, tent sites, rentals, dump, mobile sewer, laundry, groc, LP gas, fire rings, firewood. **REC:** heated pool, playground. Pets OK. 2015 rates: $30. May 1 to Dec 31.
(231)525-6774 Lat: 45.22856, Lon: -84.54328
2733 Lance Lake Rd, Wolverine, MI 49799
Reservations@elkwoodcamp.com
www.elkwoodcamp.com
See ad pages 632, 616.

STURGEON VALLEY CAMPGROUND **Ratings: 5.5/8.5★/8** (Campground) 2015 rates: $32. (231)525-8301 15247 Trowbridge Rd, Wolverine, MI 49755

YPSILANTI — J5 *Washtenaw*

DETROIT/GREENFIELD RV PARK
Ratings: 8/9.5★/9 (Campground) From Jct of I-94 & Rawsonville Rd (exit 187), S 1 mi on Rawsonville Rd to Textile Rd, W 1 mi to Bunton Rd, S 0.7 mi (R). **FAC:** Gravel rds. 184 Avail: 164 gravel, 20 grass, 111 pull-thrus (30 x 60), back-ins (30 x 40), 119 full hkups, 65 W, 65 E (30 amps), WiFi, tent sites, rentals, dump, laundry, groc, LP gas, fire rings, firewood. **REC:** Greenfield Lake: swim, fishing, playground, rec open to public. Pet restrict(B). Partial handicap access. 2015 rates: $48. Disc: AAA, military. Apr 1 to Oct 31.
(734)482-7722 Lat: 42.19270, Lon: -83.56292
6680 Bunton Rd, Ypsilanti, MI 48197
info@detroitgreenfield.com
www.detroitgreenfield.com
See ad pages 612 (Welcome Section), 616.

ZEELAND — J3 *Ottawa*

DUTCH TREAT CAMPING & RECREATION
Ratings: 9/8.5★/8 (Campground) From the Jct of I-196 & Exit 52 (Adams St) W 0.6 to 104th Ave N 1.5 mi to Gordon St. E 0.2 mi (R). **FAC:** Paved/gravel rds. (125 spaces). Avail: 100 grass, back-ins (30 x 50), some side by side hkups, 93 full hkups, 7 W, 7 E (30/50 amps), seasonal sites,

ZEELAND (CONT)

DUTCH TREAT CAMPING (CONT)
WiFi, tent sites, dump, laundry, groc, fire rings, firewood. **REC:** heated pool, pond, fishing, playground. Pets OK. Partial handicap access. 2015 rates: $36. Apr 1 to Nov 1.
(616)772-4303 Lat: 42.80482, Lon: -86.03553
10300 Gordon Ave, Zeeland, MI 49464
www.dutchtreatcamping.com
See ad page 628.

Our rating system isn't just tough, it's thorough. We know the kinds of things that are important to you — like clean restrooms and showers, attractive, secure, well-tended grounds, and extras like swimming pools. We give the first rating for development of facilities, the second for cleanliness and physical characteristics of restrooms and showers, and the third for visual appearance.

Getty Images/iStockphoto

WELCOME TO
Minnesota

DATE OF STATEHOOD	WIDTH: 200 - 350 MILES (320 - 560 KM)	PROPORTION OF UNITED STATES
MAY 11, 1858	LENGTH: 400 MILES (645 KM)	2.29% OF 3,794,100 SQ MI

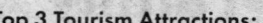

You've heard about the Land of 10,000 Lakes. Now meet real Minnesota in person to enjoy the full charms of this singular Midwestern state.

Minnesota is ideal for outdoors enthusiasts. The state boasts 267,000 acres of state park land; nowhere is a Gopher State resident more than 50 miles from a state park.

There are so many lakes in Minnesota that 150 of them are named Long Lake. The per capita rate of boat ownership is the highest in America—nearly one in every six Minnesotans owns a watercraft.

Eight of Minnesota's most spectacular state parks are huddled along the 150-mile drive of Highway 61 on the edge of Lake Superior's North Shore. The thick pine forests conceal pristine rivers heading to Lake Superior, the mightiest of the Great Lakes. Waterfalls can be found at Gooseberry Falls in Two Harbors, Tettegouche State Park, Judge C.R. Magney State Park and Grand Portage State Park.

In Minnesota, winter isn't a bad word. There are more than 20,000 miles of snowmobile trails and some of the Midwest's best downhill skiing runs.

Ready to party? The Saint Paul Winter Carnival is America's oldest winter celebration. When the ice melts, the Minneapolis Aquatennial, which began in 1940, celebrates the region's lakes, rivers and streams with 70 events. All that freshwater is used in Duluth at the Great Lakes Aquarium, one of the country's few water zoos devoted to only freshwater fish.

Top 3 Tourism Attractions:
1) Mall of America
2) Itasca State Park
3) Pipestone National Monument

Nickname: Land of 10,000 Lakes

State Flower: Lady Slipper

State Bird: Common Loon

People: Bob Dylan, singer and songwriter; Judy Garland, singer and actress; Roger Maris, baseball player; Charles Schulz, cartoonist; Richard W. Sears, founder of Sears, Roebuck and Company

Major Cities: Minneapolis, St. Paul (capital), Rochester, Duluth, Bloomington

Topography: Central—hills, lakes; northeast—rocky ridges, deep lakes; northwest—flat plains; south—rolling plains, deep river valleys

Climate: Continental climate with cold, frigid winters and hot summers

TRAVEL & TOURISM

Explore Minnesota Tourism
888-868-7476
www.exploreminnesota.com

Bloomington
800-346-4289
www.bloomington.org

Duluth Area Chamber of Commerce
800-438-5884, 218-722-4011
www.visitduluth.com

Visit Grand Rapids
800-355-9740, 218-326-9607
www.visitgrandrapids.com

Greater Grand Forks CVB
800-866-4566, 701-746-0444
www.visitgrandforks.com

Lake of thé Woods Tourism Bureau
800-382-3474
www.lakeofthewoodsmn.com

Meet Minneapolis
888-676-MPLS
www.minneapolis.org

Minnesota Historical Society
888-727-8386
www.mnhs.org

Rochester Convention & Visitors Bureau
www.visitrochestermn.com

St. Cloud Area CVB
www.granitecountry.com

St. Paul CVB
800-627-6101
www.visitsaintpaul.com

OUTDOOR RECREATION

Minnesota Dept. of Natural Resources
888-646-6367
www.mndnr.gove

Minnesota Canoe Association
www.canoe-kayak.org

Explore Minnesota Tourism
888-868-7476, 888-646-6367
www.dnr.state.mn.us

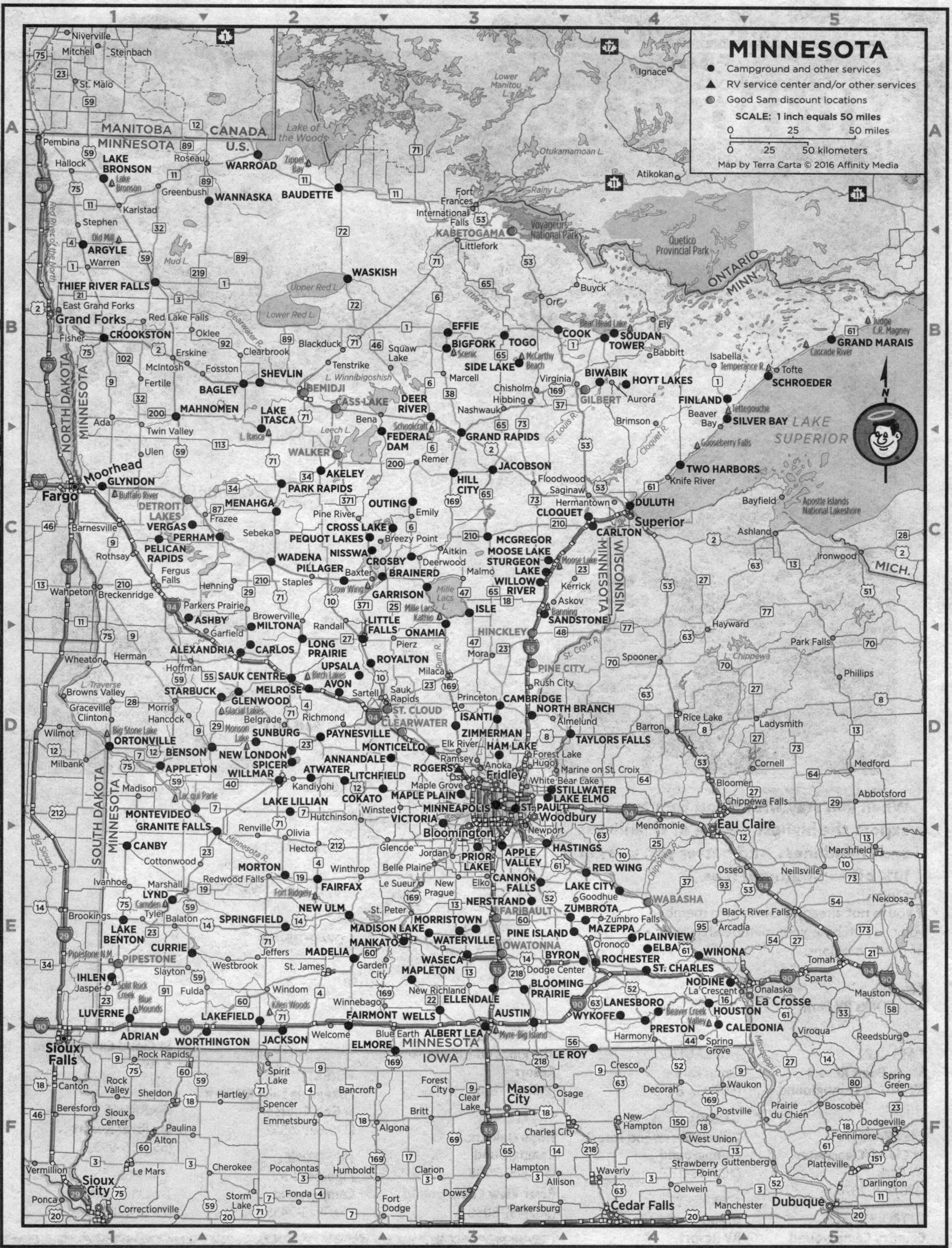
MINNESOTA
Campground and other services
RV service center and/or other services
Good Sam discount locations
SCALE: 1 inch equals 50 miles
0 25 50 miles
0 25 50 kilometers
Map by Terra Carta © 2016 Affinity Media
MANITOBA
CANADA
MINNESOTA
U.S.
ONTARIO
MINN.
NORTH DAKOTA
SOUTH DAKOTA
WISCONSIN
IOWA
MICH.
LAKE SUPERIOR
Lake of the Woods
Upper Red L.
Lower Red L.
Leech L.
Mille Lacs L.
Voyageurs National Park
Quetico Provincial Park
Apostle Islands National Lakeshore
WARROAD
LAKE BRONSON
WANNASKA
BAUDETTE
ARGYLE
THIEF RIVER FALLS
WASKISH
KABETOGAMA
Grand Forks
CROOKSTON
EFFIE
BIGFORK
TOGO
COOK
SOUDAN TOWER
GRAND MARAIS
SIDE LAKE
SHEVLIN
BAGLEY
BEMIDJI
CASS LAKE
DEER RIVER
BIWABIK
HOYT LAKES
GILBERT
SCHROEDER
FINLAND
SILVER BAY
MAHNOMEN
LAKE ITASCA
FEDERAL DAM
GRAND RAPIDS
WALKER
AKELEY
PARK RAPIDS
JACOBSON
HILL CITY
TWO HARBORS
Moorhead
GLYNDON
Fargo
DETROIT LAKES
MENAHGA
OUTING
CLOQUET
DULUTH
Superior
CARLTON
VERGAS
PERHAM
CROSS LAKE
PEQUOT LAKES
MCGREGOR
MOOSE LAKE
STURGEON LAKE
WILLOW RIVER
PELICAN RAPIDS
WADENA
NISSWA
CROSBY
PILLAGER
BRAINERD
GARRISON
ISLE
SANDSTONE
ASHBY
MILTONA
LITTLE FALLS
ONAMIA
HINCKLEY
ALEXANDRIA
CARLOS
LONG PRAIRIE
ROYALTON
SAUK CENTRE
UPSALA
AVON
PINE CITY
STARBUCK
MELROSE
GLENWOOD
ST. CLOUD
CLEARWATER
CAMBRIDGE
NORTH BRANCH
ISANTI
ZIMMERMAN
HAM LAKE
TAYLORS FALLS
ORTONVILLE
SUNBURG
PAYNESVILLE
BENSON
NEW LONDON
SPICER
MONTICELLO
ANNANDALE
APPLETON
WILLMAR
ATWATER
LITCHFIELD
ROGERS
Fridley
STILLWATER
LAKE ELMO
COKATO
MAPLE PLAIN
LAKE LILLIAN
MINNEAPOLIS
ST. PAUL
Woodbury
MONTEVIDEO
VICTORIA
Bloomington
GRANITE FALLS
CANBY
HASTINGS
PRIOR LAKE
APPLE VALLEY
RED WING
MORTON
CANNON FALLS
FAIRFAX
LAKE CITY
WABASHA
LYND
NERSTRAND
FARIBAULT
ZUMBROTA
NEW ULM
MORRISTOWN
MAZEPPA
LAKE BENTON
SPRINGFIELD
MADISON LAKE
WATERVILLE
PINE ISLAND
PLAINVIEW
MANKATO
OWATONNA
ELBA
WINONA
CURRIE
PIPESTONE
MADELIA
WASECA
BYRON
ROCHESTER
ST. CHARLES
MAPLETON
IHLEN
NODINE
La Crosse
BLOOMING PRAIRIE
ELLENDALE
LANESBORO
HOUSTON
LUVERNE
LAKEFIELD
FAIRMONT
WELLS
AUSTIN
WYKOFF
PRESTON
CALEDONIA
ADRIAN
WORTHINGTON
JACKSON
ALBERT LEA
ELMORE
LE ROY
Sioux Falls
Mason City
Eau Claire
Cedar Falls
Dubuque
Sioux City

Featured Good Sam Parks

MINNESOTA

Good Sam Park

When you stay with Good Sam, you can expect the highest degree of cleanliness and friendliness, and better yet, you get 10% off campground fees.

If you're not already a Good Sam member you can purchase your membership at one of these locations:

BEMIDJI
Royal Oaks RV Park
(218)751-8357

CASS LAKE
Stony Point Resort RV Park & Campground
(218)335-6311

CLEARWATER
St Cloud/Clearwater RV Park
(320)558-2876

DETROIT LAKES
Country Campground
(218)847-9621

FARIBAULT
Camp Faribo
(507)332-8453

GILBERT
Gilbert Sherwood Forest Campground
(218)748-2221

HINCKLEY
Grand Casino Hinckley RV Resort
(800)472-6321

KABETOGAMA
The Pines Of Kabetogama Resort
(218)875-2000

OWATONNA
Hope Oak Knoll Campground
(507)451-2998
River View Campground
(507)451-8050

PINE CITY
Pokegama Lake RV Park & Golf Course
(320)629-6552

PIPESTONE
Pipestone RV Campground
(507)825-2455

ST CLOUD
St Cloud Campground & RV Park
(320)251-4463

WABASHA
Big River Resort
(651)565-9932

WALKER
Trails RV Park
(218)547-1138

For more Good Sam Parks go to listing pages

Getty Images/iStockphoto

SPOTLIGHT

MN

HINCKLEY

Gaming, golfing and exploration greet visitors to this vibrant Minnesota town

he tiny city of Hinckley, Minnesota, is a opular stop-off point between Minne-polis-Saint Paul and Duluth. Among its nost popular attractions is the Grand Casino Hinckley, which boasts a wide rray of slots, table games and video oker. Also popular is the Hinckley Fire Auseum and an enormous antiques nall that spans over 10,000 square feet.

The area where Hinckley now tands was once a stronghold of the Djibwe Indians, who traded furs in the egion. The area was later settled by Europeans, who were enticed by the arge white-pine forests that blanketed he surroundings. In 1869, the first saw-nill was built, and the railroad reached he town in the same year, paving the vay for Hinckley's future as a major center of logging in the region. For the next two decades, Hinckley boomed s a logging town. In 1894, a tragic fire ook the lives of over 400 residents nd destroyed over 300,000 acres, but he town recovered in grand style, and oday the Hinckley Fire Museum pays nomage to the victims.

Blackjack and Buffets

Today, Hinckley is a stopping-off point for exploring attractions in the region, but the little town has a few of its own points of interest that are worth checking out. It's best known for the Grand Casino. This large casino has lots of gaming and entertainment options, and you'll find an events and conven-tion center on-site that regularly hosts concerts and events. Recent performers have included the likes of Travis Tritt and ZZ Top. Select from a variety of restaurants in the casino. The casino also offers a buffet with all kinds of meats along with salads, seafood specialties, and a great selection of desserts.

Bring your golf bag, because Hinck-ley's Grand National Golf Club provides a beautiful 18-hole course with lush fairways and challenging hazards.

Birding and Banning

Other attractions in the region include Banning State Park, near Sandstone. It's a great place for kayaking and thrill seekers can try out the rapids at Drag-on's Tooth, Mother's Delight, Blueberry Slide, and the forebodingly named Hell's Gate. There are also plenty of hiking trails along with drive-in boat launches, opportunities for fishing, and both camping and RV sites.

Birders will want to pay a visit to the Audubon Center of the North Woods, which offers lots of interest-ing programs for children and adults. Every June, the center hosts a "Birding Bonanza Weekend," a weekend-long birding festival packed with opportuni-ties to see the natural habitats of some of the park's many species of avians.

The 34,000-acre St. Croix State Park, Minnesota's largest state park, has two major rivers flowing through it: the Saint Croix River and the Kettle River, both of which are great for fishing and canoeing.

For More Information

Hinckley Convention and Visitors Bureau
800-952-4282
www.hinckleymn.com

Explore Minnesota Tourism
888-TOURISM
www.exploreminnesota.com

Golfing in Hinckley is a popular pastime. Getty Images/iStockphoto

See listing Hinckley, MN

Getty Images/iStockphoto

MINNEAPOLIS

Outdoor recreation mingles with colorful culture on the Mississippi

It served as a major fur trading center and lumber shipping hub during the 1700s and 1800s. In the 1970s, Mary Tyler Moore turned the world on with her smile as she wandered the city's landscapes in the opening credits of her primetime TV show every week. Musical acts from Hüsker Dü to Prince forged their careers in the city, and today it remains a vital industrial, cultural and business hub.

> Lake Calhoun, the city's largest lake, offers a fishing pier and a boat dock as well as sandy beaches for soaking up the sun and cooling off in the water.

Rich in history but always forward thinking, Minneapolis is one of the most fascinating cities in the Midwest. Sitting on the mighty Mississippi River, the city welcomes visitors with towering skyscrapers and cozy cafes alike. Set aside lots of time to explore both the sophisticated metropolitan districts and its rustic outlying areas.

Where to Start

Minnehaha Falls Regional Park is one of the city's treasured natural spaces. The 53-foot falls were made legendary in Henry Wadsworth Longfellow's poem, "Song of Hiawatha." Travel the paved trail around the park, and visit the Longfellow House Hospitality Center, housed in a two-thirds scale replica of the poet's home in Massachusetts. Minnehaha Falls is part of the Grand Rounds Scenic Byway, a 50-mile recreation loop that encompasses Minneapolis.

Nearby, Nicollet Island is the only inhabited island on the Mississippi River, where historic homes beckon visitors to see Victorian architecture from the seat of a horse-drawn carriage. Visit Nicollet Island Inn for a cool cocktail at the 150-year-old bar.

Mississippi isn't the region's only major waterway. To the east is the St. Croix River, and here you'll find Taylors Falls, a historic village community that can be explored through an audiovisual walking tour as well as stops at one of the town's municipal parks. Wild Mountain/Taylors Falls Recreation is a year-round destination for families seeking fun of all kinds. Wild Mountain offers scenic boat tours, kayak and canoe rentals, alpine slides and wintertime skiing and snow tubing.

For a glimpse of nature, check out the Como Park Zoo & Conservatory, one of the last free zoos in the United States. This attraction is highlighted by a variety of gardens—from sunken to tropical—under a sprawling, ornate greenhouse.

City O' Lakes

Minneapolis lakes are city treasures and popular destinations for recreation. Rent a paddleboat at Lake Harriet or drop a line to hook some muskies. The band shell on the north shore of the lake hosts numerous live music events

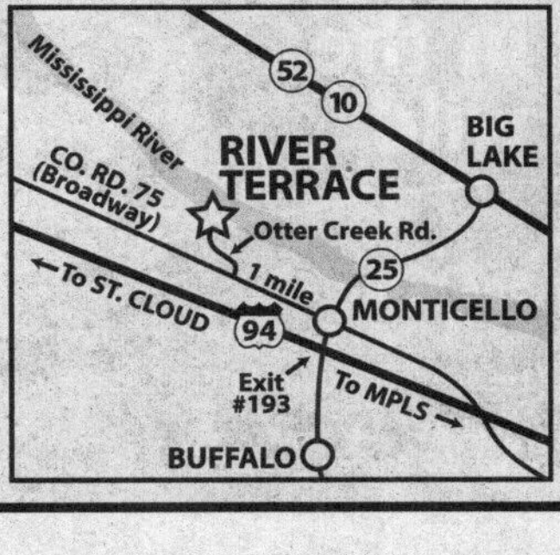

MN

The greenhouse at the Como Park Zoo & Conservatory. Getty Images/iStockphoto

during the summer. Lake Calhoun, the city's largest lake, offers a fishing pier and a boat dock as well as sandy beaches for soaking up the sun and cooling off in the water. Lake of the Isles lets small, four-legged visitors run free at an off-leash dog park.

Golfers enjoy the greens at Hiawatha Golf Club next to Lake Hiawatha. The 140-acre course features a par 73 and is dotted with mature trees, 12 ponds and 30 sand traps. A nine-hole golf course at Fort Snelling offers varied holes and a signature seventh hole—a par four that's just 228 yards, but bounded by water hazards.

Minneapolis Sculpture Garden is a premier destination for fans of bold and creative outdoor art, such as the Spoonbridge and Cherry. The adjacent Cowles Conservatory hosts seasonal displays of tropical plants and orchids.

Follow the locals to Calhoun Square for shopping and dining, Minneapolis-style. Friday afternoons welcome local vendors to showcase their wares, from artwork to jewelry to gourmet treats. Live music is played on Saturday evenings, and local eateries host trivia nights and karaoke throughout the week.

Museums and More

The Walter Library houses the University of Minnesota's science and engineering collection, but it's also an architectural treasure. The library was first built in 1923 and was renovated from 1999-2002. Be sure to check out the astrolabe chandelier that hangs in the center of the lobby, and see if you can spot all 225 owls that are perched throughout the building.

Each of the three stages at Guthrie Theater hosts world-class performances from Shakespeare to Sondheim and beckons patrons with a full-service restaurant and stunning views of St. Anthony Falls and the Stone Arch Bridge. Productions are staged year-round, ensuring visitors can catch a great show at any time.

Walk through history on a visit to Fort Snelling, built at the junction of the Mississippi and Minnesota rivers in 1825 on a bluff overlooking the confluence. More than 120 years of military service have been recorded at the site, which today hosts educational programs and celebrations honoring the men and women who fought in U.S. conflicts from the Civil War to World War II.

Mill City Museum preserves the remains of what was once the world's largest flour mill while teaching visitors about the industry and its impact on the growth and progress of Minneapolis. Explore the Baking Lab and take an eight-story elevator ride, and then watch a model mill explode as you learn how flour dust can turn a mill into rubble.

Across the river sits the Bell Museum of Natural History, which is part of the University of Minnesota. In addition to permanent installations that detail the geologic and zoologic history of the region, the museum hosts activities for kids and happy-hour forums for adults. Group tours are available to ensure guests get the most out of their visit.

Rain or shine, the treasures at the Minneapolis Institute of Arts invite visitors to explore the creative genius of world-renowned painters, sculptors and photographers. In addition to permanent collections, visiting exhibits rotate frequently, so there's always something new to see. The Institute also invites guests to take classes and enjoy concerts throughout the year.

Just outside of Minneapolis is the Pavek Museum of Broadcasting, where visitors learn about the history of sharing news and entertainment over the airwaves. Collections include antique radios, televisions and broadcasting equipment. Television viewers who remember the 1970s should make a pilgrimage to the Mary Tyler Moore House, the TV star's fictional residence. Take another trip down memory lane at the Minnesota Streetcar Museum, where guests enjoy 15-minute streetcar rides on the antique trolleys that once traversed the city.

For More Information

Meet Minneapolis
888-676-6757
www.minneapolis.org

Explore Minnesota Tourism
888-868-7476
www.exploreminnesota.com

Minnesota

CONSULTANTS

Fred & Susan Denischuk

ADRIAN — F1 *Nobles*

ADRIAN MUNICIPAL CAMPGROUND (Public) From Jct of I-90 & SR-91 (exit 26), S 0.3 mi on SR-91 o Franklin St, W 0.3 mi (E). 2015 rates: $26 to $30. Apr 15 to Oct 15. (507)483-2820

AITKIN — C3 *Aitkin*

PETE'S RETREAT FAMILY CAMPGROUND & RV PARK **Ratings: 8/9.5★/10** (Campground) 2015 rates: $48 to $65. May 1 to Oct 1. (320)684-2020 22337 State Hwy 47, Aitkin, MN 56431

AKELEY — C2 *Hubbard*

AKELEY CITY PARK & CAMPGROUND (Public) From Jct of Hwys 64 & 34, W 0.3 mi on Hwy 34, follow signs (E). 2015 rates: $29. May 15 to Sep 15. (218)652-2172

ALBERT LEA — E3 *Freeborn*

ALBERT LEA/AUSTIN KOA KAMPGROUND Ratings: 8.5/9.5★/8 (Campground) From Jct of I-90 & CR-46 (exit 166), E 0.5 mi on CR-46 (R). From I-35, take exit 11 (CR-46), E 7 mi (R). **FAC:** Gravel rds. (77 spaces). 72 Avail: 66 gravel, 6 grass, 36 pull-thrus (35 x 65), back-ins (30 x 60), some side by side hkups, 29 full hkups, 43 W, 43 E (30/50 amps), seasonal sites, WiFi, tent sites, rentals, dump, laundry, groc, LP gas, fire rings, firewood. **REC:** heated pool, wading pool, playground. Pets OK. 2015 rates: $36.50 to $44. Disc: AAA. Apr 15 to Oct 15.
(507)373-5170 Lat: 43.66155, Lon: -93.18270
84259 County Road 46, Hayward, MN 56043
hulettann@hotmail.com
www.koa.com

HICKORY HILLS CAMPGROUND **Ratings: 7/7.5/7** (Campground) 2015 rates: $32 to $45. Apr 15 to Oct 15. (507)852-4555 15694 717 Ave, Albert Lea, MN 56007

MYRE/BIG ISLAND (State Pk) From Jct of I-35 & Exit 11/CR-46, E 1 mi on CR-46 to CR-38, S 2 mi (R). Reservation fee & vehicle permit required. 2015 rates: $15 to $23. (507)379-3403

ALEXANDRIA — D2 *Douglas*

ALEXANDRIA RV PARK **Ratings: 7/NA/8** (RV Park) 2015 rates: $32. May 1 to Oct 15. (320)763-5121 910 34th Ave W, Alexandria, MN 56308

ANNANDALE — D2 *Wright*

SCHROEDER COUNTY PARK (Public) From Jct of Hwys 55 & 24, N 4.5 mi on Hwy 24 to CR-E 39, E 0.5 mi to Ireland Rd, S 0.25 mi (R). 2015 rates: $25. Apr 30 to Sep 30. (320)274-8870

APPLE VALLEY — E3 *Dakota*

LEBANON HILLS REGIONAL PARK CAMPGROUND (Public) From Jct of I-35 E & Cliff Rd (Exit 93), E 0.6 mi to Johnny Cake Ridge Rd, S 1 mi (L). **FAC:** Paved/gravel rds. 93 Avail: 58 gravel, 35 grass, 3 pull-thrus (30 x 65), back-ins (30 x 60), 58 full hkups, 24 W, 24 E (30/50 amps), WiFi Hotspot, tent sites, dump, laundry, fire rings, firewood. **REC:** pond, playground, rec open to public. No pets. Partial handicap access. Big rig sites, 14 day max stay, 2015 rates: $25 to $36. May 1 to Oct 13.
(651)688-1376 Lat: 44.77421, Lon: -93.18652
12100 Johnny Cake Ridge Road, Apple Valley, MN 55124
parks@co.dakota.mn.us
www.co.dakota.mn.us/parks/Activities/Camping/Pages/default.aspx
See ad page 648 (Spotlight Minneapolis).

APPLETON — D1 *Swift*

APPLETON MUNICIPAL CAMPGROUND (Public) From Jct of SR-7/US-59 (N of town) & SR-119, S 0.4 mi (L) on SR-7/US-59 (L). 2015 rates: $15. May 1 to Oct 30. (320)289-1363

ARGYLE — B1 *Marshall*

OLD MILL (State Pk) From Jct of US-75 & SR-4, E 11 mi on SR-4 to CR-4, N 1 mi to CR-39, N 0.5 mi (L); or From Jct of US-59 & SR-4, W 11 mi on SR-4 to CR-4, N 1 mi (L). Reservation fee. 2015 rates: $15 to $23. (218)437-8174

ASHBY — C1 *Grant*

PRAIRIE COVE CAMPGROUND AND RV PARK **Ratings: 6/6/7.5** (RV Park) 2015 rates: $30. May 1 to Oct 1. (218)747-2931 29188 State Hwy 78, Ashby, MN 56309

ATWATER — D2 *Kandiyohi*

KANDIYOHI COUNTY PARK #3 (Public) From Atwater, W 3 mi on US-12 to cnty rd, N 4 mi to Diamond Lake, follow signs (L) Entrance Fee Required $4. Reservation fee. 2015 rates: $27.25. (320)974-8520

AUSTIN — E3 *Mower*

BEAVER TRAILS JELLYSTONE PARK CAMP-RESORT **Ratings: 8.5/10★/9** (Campground) 2015 rates: $53 to $95. Apr 15 to Oct 15. (507)584-6611 21943 630th Ave, Austin, MN 55912

AVON — D2 *Stearns*

EL RANCHO MANANA CAMPGROUND & RIDING STABLE Ratings: 7.5/7.5/8 (Campground) From Jct of I-94 & CR-9 (exit 153), S 9 mi on CR-9 to Manana Rd, E 0.7 mi to Ranch Rd, N 1.3 mi (E). CAUTION: Narrow, tight, winding interior roads. **FAC:** Gravel rds. (185 spaces). Avail: 120 grass, 20 pull-thrus (28 x 40), back-ins (28 x 35), 30 full hkups, 90 W, 90 E (30/50 amps), seasonal sites, WiFi Hotspot, tent sites, dump, mobile sewer, laundry, groc, LP bottles, fire rings, firewood, controlled access. **REC:** Long Lake: swim, fishing, playground, rec open to public. Pets OK. 2015 rates: $44 to $54. May 1 to Oct 2. ATM.
(320)597-2740 Lat: 45.52213, Lon: -94.49214
27302 Ranch Road, Richmond, MN 56368
elrancho@meltel.net

BAGLEY — B2 *Clearwater*

BAGLEY CITY PARK (Public) From Jct of US-2 & SR-92, N 0.4 mi on SR-92 (L). 2015 rates: $11 to $20. May 15 to Oct 1. (218)694-2865

BAUDETTE — A2 *Lake of the Woods*

LAKE OF THE WOODS CAMPGROUND/MHP **Ratings: 6.5/6.5/6.5** (Campground) 2015 rates: $32 to $37. May 1 to Oct 10. (218)634-1694 2769 28th Street NW, Baudette, MN 56623

TIMBER MILL PARK & CAMPGROUND (Public) From Jct Hwy 72 & Hwy 11 (on East side of Baudette), W 0.8 mi on Hwy 11 to Tourist Park Ave NE, N 300 ft (R). 2015 rates: $28. May 15 to Oct 1. (218)634-1850

ZIPPEL BAY (State Pk) From jct Hwy 11 & Hwy 172: Go 12 mi N on Hwy 172, then 6 mi W on CR 8, then 1 mi N on CR 34. Pit toilets. 2015 rates: $15 to $23. (218)783-6252

BEMIDJI — B2 *Beltrami*

BEMIDJI See also Bagley, Cass Lake & Walker.

HAMILTON'S FOX LAKE CAMPGROUND Ratings: 8.5/9.5★/9 (Campground) From Jct of US-2 & US-71: Go N 10 mi on US-71 to CR-22 (2556 Island View Dr. NE), then W 4 mi (L). **FAC:** Gravel rds. (70 spaces). Avail: 28 grass, 12 pull-thrus (30 x 55), back-ins (35 x 60), 28 full hkups (30/50 amps), seasonal sites, cable, WiFi, tent sites, dump, laundry, groc, LP bottles, fire rings, firewood. **REC:** Fox Lake: swim, fishing, playground. Pet restrict(B). Partial handicap access. Eco-friendly, 2015 rates: $43. May 3 to Sep 20.
(218)586-2231 Lat: 47.61481, Lon: -94.84045
2556 Island View Dr NE, Bemidji, MN 56601
hamiltonsseo@gmail.com
www.camponfoxlake.com
See ad this page.

KOA BEMIDJI **Ratings: 8/9.5★/8.5** (Campground) 2015 rates: $38 to $50. May 1 to Oct 10. (218)444-7562 510 Brightstar Rd NW, Bemidji, MN 56601

LAKE BEMIDJI (State Pk) From Jct of Hwy 2 & US-71, N 4 mi to Glidden Rd, SE on Glidden, follow signs (L). Entrance fee & reservation fee required. Note: 50' RV length limit. 2015 rates: $15 to $23. (218)755-3843

ROYAL OAKS RV PARK Ratings: 8/9.5★/10 (RV Park) W-bnd: From Jct of US-2 & SR71S, R .02 mi to Peaceful Meadows Ln, R .01 mi to Fenske Farm Ln, R .01 mi E-bnd: Stay right on US-2 bypass (3rd exit) from Jct of US-2 & SR-71, S between mile post 116 & 117 (exit 71 S), L .02 mi on 197 to Peaceful Meadows Ln, R .01 mi to Fenske Farm Ln, R .01 mi. **FAC:** Gravel rds. (63 spaces). Avail: 49 gravel, 8 pull-thrus (30 x 80), back-ins (30 x 80), 49 full hkups (30/50 amps), seasonal sites, cable, WiFi, tent sites, laundry, groc, fire rings, firewood. **REC:** playground. Pets OK. 2015 rates: $29 to $32. May 1 to Oct 1.
(218)751-8357 Lat: 47.43380, Lon: -94.86197
2874 Fenske Farm Lane SE, Bemidji, MN 56601
royaloaksrvpark@ymail.com
www.royaloaksrvpark.com
See ad this page, 644.

BENSON — D2 *Swift*

AMBUSH PARK CAMPGROUND (Public) From Jct of Hwys 29 & 9, W 1 mi on Hwy 9, follow signs (R). 2015 rates: $21.98 to $27.47. May 1 to Oct 1. (320)843-4775

Like Us on Facebook.

MN

BIGFORK — B3 *Itasca*

GEORGE WASHINGTON SF/OWEN LAKE (Public) From town, SE 10 mi on CR-7 to CR-340, E 7 mi to CR-52, N 1.5 mi to Forestry Rd, W 1 mi, follow signs (E). Pit toilets. 2015 rates: $12. May15 to Nov 1. (218)743-3362

SCENIC (State Pk) From town, SE 7 mi on CR-7 to Scenic State Park Rd, N 1 mi (R). Reservation fee. 2015 rates: $15 to $23. (218)743-3362

BIWABIK — B4 *St Louis*

VERMILION TRAIL CAMPGROUND (Public) From Jct of SR-135 & CR 4 (East of town), E 0.3 mi on SR-135 (R). 2015 rates: $13 to $19. May to Sep. (218)865-6705

BLOOMING PRAIRIE — E3 *Mower*

BROOKSIDE CAMPGROUND **Ratings: 7.5/8.5/8** (Campground) 2015 rates: $33 to $53. May 1 to Sep 30. (507)583-2979 52482-320th St, Blooming Prairie, MN 55917

BRAINERD — C2 *Cass, Crow Wing*

CROW WING (State Pk) From Jct of SR-210 & SR-371, SW 9 mi on SR-371 to CR-27, W 1 mi (E). Entrance fee & reservation fee required. Note: 45' RV length maximum. 2015 rates: $15 to $23. (218)825-3075

CROW WING LAKE CAMPGROUND **Ratings: 8.5/8.5/10** (Campground) 2015 rates: $50 to $58. May 1 to Oct 1. (218)829-6468 2393 Crow Wing Camp Road, Brainerd, MN 56401

GULL LAKE RECREATION AREA (Public Corps) From town, NW 7 mi on Hwy 371 to CR-125 (Gull Lake Dam Rd), W 3 mi (E). 2015 rates: $26. May 1 to Oct 31. (218)829-3334

LUM PARK CAMPGROUND (Public) From Jct of SH-371 & SH-210, E 4 mi on SH-210 to Lum Park Rd, N 0.2 mi (R). 2015 rates: $30 to $35. May 1 to Oct 15. (218)828-2320

BYRON — E4 *Olmsted*

OXBOW COUNTY PARK (Public) From Jct of US-14 & CR-5, N 3 mi on CR-5 to CR-105, N 1 mi follow signs (L). 2015 rates: $15. May 1 to Oct 4. (507)775-2451

CALEDONIA — E4 *Houston*

BEAVER CREEK VALLEY (State Pk) From Jct SR-44 & SR-76, W 1 mi on SR-76 to CR-1, W 4 mi, follow signs (E). Reservation fee. 2015 rates: $16 to $20. Apr 15 to Oct 1. (507)724-2107

CAMBRIDGE — D3 *Isanti*

FAIRGROUNDS CAMPGROUND (ISANTI CO. AGRICULTURAL SOCIETY) (Public) From jct Hwy 65 & Hwy 95: Go 1/2 mi E on Hwy 95. 2015 rates: $20 to $25. May 1 to Oct 1. (763)689-2555

CANBY — E1 *Yellow Medicine*

STONE HILL REGIONAL PARK (Public) From Jct of US-75 & SR-68 (in town), W 0.1 mi on SR-68, follow signs 2 mi (L). 2015 rates: $15 to $22.50. May 1 to Oct 1. (507)223-7586

CANNON FALLS — E3 *Dakota, Goodhue*

CANNON FALLS CAMPGROUND LLC Ratings: 8/9★/9 (Campground) From Jct of US-52 & SR-19, E 2.3 mi on SR-19 to Oak Lane (E of town), S 0.1 mi (R). **FAC:** Paved rds. (200 spaces). 95 Avail: 19 gravel, 76 grass, back-ins (24 x 45), some side by side hkups, 23 full hkups, 72 W, 72 E (30/50 amps), seasonal sites, showers $, dump, mobile sewer, laundry, groc, LP bottles, fire rings, firewood. **REC:** heated pool, playground. Pets OK. Partial handicap access, no tents. 2015 rates: $41 to $53. Apr 25 to Oct 4.
(507)263-3145 Lat: 44.50891, Lon: -92.87501
30365 Oak Lane, Cannon Falls, MN 55009
www.cannonfallscampground.com

LAKE BYLLESBY REGIONAL PARK CAMPGROUND (Public) From Jct of US-52 & CR-86, W 30 ft on CR-86 to Harry Ave, S 2.2 mi (L). **FAC:** Paved rds. 35 Avail: 1 paved, 34 gravel, patios, back-ins (30 x 60), 35 W, 35 E (30/50 amps), WiFi Hotspot, tent sites, dump, groc, fire rings, firewood. **REC:** Lake Byllesby: swim, fishing, playground, rec open to public. No pets. Partial handicap access. 14 day max stay, 2015 rates: $25. Apr 29 to Oct 11.
(507)263-4447 Lat: 44.51391, Lon: -92.94715
7650 Echo Point Rd, Cannon Falls, MN 55009
parks@co.dakota.mn.us
www.dakotacounty.us
See ad page 648 (Spotlight Minneapolis).

CARLOS — D2 *Douglas*

LAKE CARLOS (State Pk) From Jct of US-29 & CR-38, W 1.5 mi on CR-38 (L). Reservation fee. Note: 50' RV length limit. 2015 rates: $15 to $23. (320)852-7200

CARLTON — C4 *Carlton*

JAY COOKE (State Pk) From town, E 2 mi on Hwy 210 (R). Entrance fee required. $4 daily, $20 annual. Reservation fee. 2015 rates: $15 to $23. (218)384-4610

CASS LAKE — B2 *Beltrami, Cass*

STONY POINT RESORT RV PARK & CAMPGROUND Ratings: 9.5/9.5★/9.5 (Campground) From Jct of US 2 & SR-371, E 1.8 mi on US 2 - between MP 131 & 132 (L). **FAC:** Paved rds. (175 spaces). Avail: 60 all weather, 28 pull-thrus (30 x 85), back-ins (30 x 50), 45 full hkups, 15 W, 15 E (30/50 amps), seasonal sites, WiFi $, tent sites, rentals, dump, mobile sewer, laundry, groc, LP gas, fire rings, firewood, restaurant. **REC:** wading pool, Cass Lake: swim, fishing, marina, playground. Pets OK $. Partial handicap access. Big rig sites, eco-friendly, 2015 rates: $33.30 to $41. May 1 to Oct 15. ATM.
AAA Approved
(218)335-6311 Lat: 47.37891, Lon: -94.57393
5510 US 2 NW, Cass Lake, MN 56633
stonypoint@arvig.net
www.stonyptresortcasslake.com
See ad pages 649, 644.

CLEARWATER — D3 *Stearns*

A-J ACRES Ratings: 7.5/6.5/7 (Campground) From Jct of I-94 & SR-24 (Exit 178), S 0.1 mi on SR-24 to CR-145, W 0.9 mi on CR-145 to 195th St, W 0.7 mi (L). **FAC:** Gravel rds. (200 spaces). Avail: 75 grass, 10 pull-thrus (35 x 70), back-ins (35 x 55), 12 full hkups, 63 W, 63 E (30/50 amps), seasonal sites, WiFi Hotspot, tent sites, dump, laundry, groc, fire rings, firewood, controlled access. **REC:** Feldges & Dallas Lakes: swim, fishing, playground. Pets OK. Big rig sites, eco-friendly, 2015 rates: $40. May 1 to Oct 1.
(320)558-2847 Lat: 45.404352, Lon: -94.089665
1300 195th Street E, Clearwater, MN 55320
ajacres@frontiernet.net
www.ajacrescampground.com

ST CLOUD/CLEARWATER RV PARK Ratings: 8.5/10★/9.5 (Campground) From Jct of I-94 & SR-24 (exit 178), N 0.5 mi on SR-24 to CR-75, W 1 mi to CR-143, SW 0.3 mi (R); From Jct of US-10 & SR 24 (Clearlake), S 3.5 mi on SR-24 to CR-75, W 1 mi to CR-143, SW 0.3 mi (R). **FAC:** Gravel rds. (100 spaces). Avail: 60 gravel, 45 pull-thrus (30 x 70), back-ins (30 x 55), 28 full hkups, 32 W, 32 E (30/50 amps), seasonal sites, WiFi Hotspot, tent sites, rentals, dump, laundry, groc, LP bottles, fire rings, firewood. **REC:** heated pool, wading pool, playground. Pets OK. Partial handicap access. Big rig sites, eco-friendly, 2015 rates: $33.60 to $50. May 1 to Oct 10.
(320)558-2876 Lat: 45.42377, Lon: -94.06521
2454 CR-143, Clearwater, MN 55320
stcloudclearwaterrvpark@msn.com
www.time2camp.com
See ad pages 656, 644.

Get the Facts! Essential tips and travel info can be found in the Welcome Section at the beginning of each State/Province.

CLOQUET — C4 *Carlton*

CLOQUET/DULUTH KOA Ratings: 8.5/10★/ (Campground) From Jct of I-35 & SR-45 (exit 239), S 2 mi on SR-45 to CR-3, W 0.8 mi (R). **FAC:** Gravel rds. (48 spaces). 45 Avail: 25 gravel, 20 grass, 28 pull-thrus (25 x 55), back-ins (22 x 45), mostly side by side hkups, 10 full hkups, 35 W, 35 E (30/50 amps), seasonal sites, WiFi, tent sites, dump, mobile sewer, laundry, groc, LP gas, fire rings, firewood. **REC:** heated pool, whirlpool, playground. Pet restrict(Q). Partial handicap access. 2015 rates: $32 to $47. May 1 to Oct 15.
(218)879-5726 Lat: 46.67933, Lon: -92.44062
1381 Kampground Road, Cloquet, MN 55720
clqkoa@gmail.com
www.cloquetkoa.com

SPAFFARD PARK (Public) From Jct of Hwys 45 & 33, W 1 blk on Hwy 45 to Broadway, N 1 mi (L). 2015 rates: $25. May 9 to Oct 10. (218)879-1675

COKATO — D2 *Wright*

COLLINWOOD COUNTY PARK (Public) From town, W 2.5 mi on US-12 to Rhodes Ave, S 2 mi (E). Reservation fee. 2015 rates: $16 to $25. Apr 30 to Sep 15. (320)286-2801

COOK — B3 *Itasca*

KABETOGAMA STATE FOREST/WAKEMUP BAY CAMPGROUND (State Pk) From town: Go 2-1/2 mi N on CR 24, then 3 mi E on CR 78, then 1 mi N. Pit toilets. 2015 rates: $14. (218)753-2245

CROOKSTON — B1 *Polk*

CENTRAL PARK CAMPGROUND (Public) From Jct US-75 & US-2 (Robert St E), E 2 blks on Robert St E to Ash St, N 1/2 blk (R). 2015 rates: $8 to $12. May 15 to Sep 30. (218)281-1232

CROSBY — C3 *Crow Wing*

CROSBY MEMORIAL PARK (Public) From Jct of SR-6 & SR-210, S 0.1 mi on SR-210 to 2nd St, SE 0.05 mi (L). 2015 rates: $25. May 10 to Oct 1. (218)546-5021

CROW WING SF/GREER LAKE CAMPGROUND (State Pk) From town, N 12 mi on SR-6 to CR-36, W 3 mi to CR-14, S 1.5 mi to access rd, W 2 mi, follow signs (R). 2015 rates: $14. May to Oct. (218)546-5926

CROSS LAKE — C3 *Crow Wing*

RONALD LOUIS COULTIER REC PARK (Public Corps) At Jct of Cnty Rds 66 & 3 (E). 2015 rates: $20 to $36. May 1 to Sep 30. (218)692-2025

CURRIE — E1 *Murray*

LAKE SHETEK (State Pk) From Jct of Hwy 30 & CR-38, N 2 mi on CR-38 to CR-37, W 2 mi (R). Reservation fee. 2015 rates: $15 to $23. (507)763-3256

SCHREIER'S ON SHETEK CAMPGROUND Ratings: 8/8★/9.5 (Campground) From Jct of SR-30 & CR-38 (in town), N 2 mi on CR-38 to CR-37, W 0.1 mi to 200th Ave, N 1 mi to 181st, W 0.5 mi (R). **FAC:** Gravel rds. (121 spaces). Avail: 22 all weather, patios, back-ins (30 x 50), 12 full hkups, 10 W, 10 E (30/50 amps), seasonal sites, WiFi, tent sites, dump, laundry, groc, LP bottles, fire rings, firewood. **REC:** Lake Shetek: swim, fishing, shuffleboard, playground, rec open to public. Pets OK. Partial handicap access. Eco-friendly, 2015 rates: $32. May 1 to Oct 15.
(507)763-3817 Lat: 44.11344, Lon: -95.67523
35 Resort Road, Currie, MN 56123
schremks@frontiernet.net
www.schreiersonshetek.com

DEER RIVER — B3 *Cass, Itasca*

SCHOOLCRAFT (State Pk) From Jct of US-2 & MN-6, S 8.5 mi on MN-6 to Itasca 28, W 2.5 mi to Cass 74, N 1.5 mi, follow signs (R). Vehicle permit & reservation fee required. Note: 40' RV length limit. Pit toilets. 2015 rates: $15 to $23. (218)247-7215

WINNIE DAM CAMPGROUND (Public Corps) From town, W 1 mi on US-2 to Hwy 46, N 11 mi to Hwy 9, W 2 mi (E). Pit toilets. 2015 rates: $18 to $20. May 1 to Sep 15. (218)326-6128

DETROIT LAKES — C1 *Becker*

DETROIT LAKES See also Perham & Vergas.

DETROIT LAKES (CONT)

COUNTRY CAMPGROUND
Ratings: 8.5/9.5★/10 (Campground) N-bnd: From Jct of I-94 (Exit 50) & US-59, N 35 mi on US-59 to CR-22 (R), .05 mi to 130th St (R), 1 mi to 260th Ave.(L), .7 mi (R). S-bnd: From Jct of US-10 & US-59, S 4.7 mi on US-59 to CR-22 (L), .05 mi to 130th St (R), 1 mi to 260th Ave.(L), .7 mi (R). **FAC:** Gravel rds. 30 Avail: 30 all weather, patios, 16 pull-thrus (40 x 60), back-ins (40 x 60), 30 full hkups (30/50 amps), cable, WiFi, tent sites, dump, laundry, groc, fire rings, firewood. **REC:** Glawe Lake: playground. Pets OK. Partial handicap access. Big rig sites, eco-friendly. 2015 rates: $35. May 1 to Oct 1.
(218)847-9621 Lat: 46.46179, Lon: -95.51412
13639 260th Ave, Detroit Lakes, MN 56501
countrycampground.mn@aol.com
www.countrycampground.org
See ad opposite page, 644.

DETROIT LAKES AMERICAN LEGION CAMPGROUND (Public) From Jct of Hwy 10 & Washington Ave, S 0.9 mi on Washington Ave to W Lake Dr, W 0.5 mi to Jct of Legion Rd (R) Note: 45' RV length maximum. 2015 rates: $31 to $37. May 15 to Oct 15. (218)847-3759

FOREST HILLS RV & GOLF RESORT **Ratings: 9.5/9.5★/10** (RV Park) 2015 rates: $60. May 1 to Sep 30. (800)482-3441 22931 185th Street, Detroit Lakes, MN 56501

LONG LAKE CAMPSITE & RV RESORT
Ratings: 6/6/7 (Campground) From Jct of US-59 & US-10, W 2.5 mi on US-10 to W Long Lake Rd, S 0.6 mi (L). **FAC:** Gravel rds. (89 spaces). 39 Avail: 20 gravel, 19 grass, 10 pull-thrus (30 x 60), back-ins (20 x 35), 15 full hkups, 24 W, 24 E (30 amps), seasonal sites, dump, mobile sewer, groc, fire rings, firewood. **REC:** Long Lake: swim, fishing, playground. Pet restrict(B). No tents. Eco-friendly. 2015 rates: $31. May 1 to Sep 20.
(218)847-8920 Lat: 46.82517, Lon: -95.90867
17421 West Long Lake Road, Detroit Lakes, MN 56501
See ad opposite page.

DULUTH — C4 *Carlton, St Louis*

DULUTH See also Cloquet, Two Harbors & Superior, WI.

BUFFALO VALLEY RV CAMPING **Ratings: 5.5/8.5/8** (Campground) 2015 rates: $39 to $45. May 1 to Nov 1. (218)628-7019 2590 Guss Road, Duluth, MN 55810

DULUTH INDIAN POINT CAMPGROUND Ratings: 5.5/7.5/7.5 (RV Park) N-bnd: I-35, Exit 251 (R) 1.2 mi on Cody St to Hwy 23 (Grand Ave) (R) 1.8 mi to 75th St (L) .3 mi on 75th St (L) S-bnd: I-35, Exit 252 (R) .6 mi on exit ramp to Hwy 23 (Grand Ave) (R) 1.2 mi to 75th St (L) .2 mi on 75th St (L). **FAC:** Gravel rds. 82 gravel, 8 pull-thrus (30 x 80), back-ins (30 x 55), 7 full hkups, 75 W, 75 E (30/50 amps), WiFi, tent sites, showers $, dump, laundry, fire rings, firewood. **REC:** Spirit Lake: fishing, marina. Pet restrict(B/Q). 2015 rates: $41 to $48. May 1 to Oct 15.
(855)777-0652 Lat: 46.72192, Lon: -92.18375
7000 Pulaski St, Duluth, MN 55807
infodipc@duluthindianpointcampground.com
www.duluthindianpointcampground.com

FOND DU LAC CAMPGROUND AND BOAT LANDING Ratings: 6/6.5/7.5 (Campground) From Jct of I-35 & SR-23 (Exit 251B), SW 9.2 mi on SR-23/Evergreen Memorial Hwy (L). **FAC:** Gravel rds. 55 gravel, 12 pull-thrus (35 x 75), back-ins (35 x 50), 5 full hkups, 35 W, 35 E (30/50 amps), WiFi, tent sites, dump, fire rings, firewood. **REC:** St. Louis: swim, fishing, playground. Pet restrict(B/Q). 2015 rates: $30 to $40. May 1 to Oct 15. No CC, no reservations.
(218)780-2319 Lat: 46.66031, Lon: -92.28057
13404 Hwy 23, Duluth, MN 55808
fmjvine@gmail.com
www.fonddulaccampground.com

LAKEHEAD BOAT BASIN & RV PARKING Ratings: 6/7.5/5 (RV Park) From Jct of I-35 & Lake Ave (exit 256B), SE 0.1 mi on Lake Ave (get in right lane) to Railroad St, SW 0.1 mi to South Lake Ave (immediate left lane), SE 0.7 mi (over aerial bridge) to 10th St, W 0.1 mi (E). **FAC:** Paved rds. 30 paved, back-ins (24 x 45), 12 full hkups, 18 W, 18 E (30/50 amps), WiFi, dump. **REC:** Lake Superior: fishing, marina. Pets OK. No tents. Big rig sites, 2015 rates: $34 to $39. May 15 to Sep 15.
(218)722-1757 Lat: 46.77487, Lon: -92.09156
1000 Minnesota Ave, Duluth, MN 55802
lbb@lakeheadboatbasin.com
www.lakeheadboatbasin.com

OGSTON'S RV PARK **Ratings: 8/9★/9** (RV Park) 2015 rates: $38 to $40. May 1 to Oct 1. (218)729-9528 5020 Ogston Dr, Saginaw, MN 55779

SPIRIT LAKE MARINA & RV PARK Ratings: 5.5/9.5★/6.5 (RV Park) N-Bnd: From Jct I-35 (Exit 251): Go R 1.2 mi on Cody St. to Hwy 23 (Grand Ave), then R 2.8 mi to Riverside Dr., then L 0.3 mi on Riverside Dr. (L). S-Bnd: From I-35 (Exit 252): Go R 0.6 mi on exit ramp to Hwy 23 (Grand Ave), then R 2.2 mi to Riverside Dr., then L 0.2 mi on Riverside Dr. (L). **FAC:** Gravel rds. (38 spaces). Avail: 25 gravel, back-ins (35 x 60), 25 W, 25 E (30/50 amps), seasonal sites, WiFi, dump, laundry, fire rings, firewood. **REC:** St. Louis River: fishing, marina, rec open to public. Pet restrict(B/Q). Partial handicap access, no tents. 2015 rates: $38 to $49. Apr 1 to Oct 30.
(218)628-3578 Lat: 46.70710, Lon: -92.20372
121 Spring Street, Duluth, MN 55807
infoslmrv@spiritlakemarinarv.com
www.spiritlakemarinarv.com

SPIRIT MOUNTAIN CAMPGROUND (CITY PARK) (Public) At I-35 (exit 249) & Spirit Mountain Place. 2015 rates: $33 to $36. (218)628-2891

EFFIE — B3 *Itasca*

BASS LAKE (Public) From Jct of SR-38 & SR-1, E 11 mi on SR-1 to Bass Lake Rd, S 2 mi, follow signs (L). Pit toilets. 2015 rates: $8. May 15 to Nov 15. (218)327-2850

ELBA — E4 *Winona*

WHITEWATER (State Pk) From Jct of Hwys 14 & 74, N 9 mi on Hwy 74 (L). Entrance fee and reservation fee required. 2015 rates: $15 to $31. (507)932-3007

ELLENDALE — E3 *Steele*

CRYSTAL SPRINGS RV RESORT Ratings: 6.5/9.5★/8.5 (RV Park) From Jct of I-35 & SR-30 (Exit 26), E 50 ft on SR-30 to SW 35th Ave (Frontage Rd), S 0.1 mi (L). **FAC:** Gravel rds. 34 Avail: 34 all weather, 2 pull-thrus (35 x 90), back-ins (40 x 80), 34 full hkups (30/50 amps), WiFi, dump, laundry, fire rings. **REC:** pond, fishing. Pet restrict(B). Partial handicap access, no tents. Big rig sites, eco-friendly. 2015 rates: $29 to $31. May 1 to Oct 31. No CC.
(507)398-3297 Lat: 43.86536, Lon: -93.27609
15649 35th Ave SW, Ellendale, MN 56026
info@crystalspringsrvresort.com
www.crystalspringsrvresort.com

ELMORE — F3 *Faribault*

FARIBAULT COUNTY/WOODS LAKE PARK (Public) From Jct of I-90 & US-169 (exit 119), S 9 mi on US-169 to CR-2, W 1.2 mi, N 0.5 mi, follow signs (L). 2015 rates: $20. May 1 to Oct 1. (507)943-3543

FAIRFAX — E2 *Nicollet*

FORT RIDGELY (State Pk) From Jct of Hwys 19 & 4, S 7 mi on Hwy 4 (R). Reservation fee. 2015 rates: $15 to $23. (507)426-7840

FAIRMONT — E2 *Martin*

FLYING GOOSE CAMPGROUND Ratings: 8/9.5★/9 (Campground) From Jct of I-90 & CR-53 (exit 107), S 1.2 mi on CR-53 to CR-26, W 0.7 mi (L). **FAC:** Paved/gravel rds. (130 spaces). 50 Avail: 20 gravel, 30 grass, 38 pull-thrus (30 x 60), back-ins (35 x 45), mostly side by side hkups, 24 full hkups, 26 W, 26 E (30/50 amps), seasonal sites, WiFi, tent sites, rentals, showers $, dump, mobile sewer, laundry, groc, LP gas, fire rings, firewood. **REC:** Lake Imogene: swim, fishing, playground. Pets OK. Big rig sites, RV age restrict, eco-friendly. 2015 rates: $40 to $45. May 1 to Oct 31.
(507)235-3458 Lat: 43.651860, Lon: -94.363595
2521 115th St, Fairmont, MN 56031
info@flyinggoosecampground.com
www.flyinggoosecampground.com

FARIBAULT — E3 *Rice*

CAMP FARIBO
Ratings: 9/8.5★/10 (Campground) From Jct of I-35 & SR-60 (exit 56), E 0.3 mi on SR-60 to Western/Bagley Ave, S 1.5 mi (L). **FAC:** Paved/gravel rds. (70 spaces). Avail: 40 gravel, 20 pull-thrus (30 x 60), back-ins (31 x 55), 40 full hkups (30/50 amps), seasonal sites, WiFi, tent sites, showers $, dump, laundry, groc, LP bottles, fire rings, firewood. **REC:** heated pool, playground. Pet restrict(B). Eco-friendly. 2015 rates: $30 to $41. Apr 15 to Oct 15.
(507)332-8453 Lat: 44.27100, Lon: -93.30194
21851 Bagley Ave, Faribault, MN 55021
campfaribo@hotmail.com
www.campfaribo.com
See ad pages 654, 644.

FEDERAL DAM — C2 *Cass*

LEECH LAKE REC AREA (Public Corps) In town, W of CR-8, adjacent to town, follow signs (L). 2015 rates: $24 to $40. May 1 to Oct 31. (218)654-3145

FINLAND — B4 *Lake*

FINLAND SF (State Pk) From town, E 0.5 mi on CR-6 (R). Pit toilets. 2015 rates: $12. May 15 to Sep 30. (218)226-6365

FINLAND SF/ECKBECK CAMPGROUND (State Pk) From town, S 3 mi on SR-1 (L). Pit toilets. 2015 rates: $12. May15 to Sep 2. (218)226-6365

GARRISON — C3 *Crow Wing*

CAMP HOLIDAY RESORT & CAMPGROUND **Ratings: 8/8/9** (Campground) 2015 rates: $29 to $50. May 1 to Sep 30. (218)678-2495 27406 Round Lake Road, Deerwood, MN 56444

GILBERT — B4 *St Louis*

GILBERT SHERWOOD FOREST CAMPGROUND
Ratings: 7/9★/9 (Public) From Jct of US 53 & SR-37E, E 2.6 mi on SR-37E to Sherwood Forest Drive, N 0.6 mi on Sherwood Forest Drive (R). **FAC:** Paved rds. (58 spaces). 50 Avail: 12 paved, 38 gravel, 9 pull-thrus (24 x 100), back-ins (30 x 60), 24 full hkups, 11 W, 12 E (20/30 amps), WiFi, tent sites, dump, fire rings, firewood, controlled access. **REC:** Lake Ore-Be-Gone: swim, fishing, playground, rec open to public. Pets OK. Partial handicap access. 2015 rates: $25 to $27. May 1 to Oct 1.
(218)748-2221 Lat: 47.48543, Lon: -92.46304
301 Ore-Be-Gone Dr, Gilbert, MN 55741
camgroundgilbertmn@org
www.gilbertmn.org
See ad this page, 644.

WEST FORTY RV PARK Ratings: 4/7/8 (RV Park) From Jct of US-53 & SR-37E, E 2.1 mi on SR-37E (L). **FAC:** Paved/gravel rds. (49 spaces). Avail: 33 gravel, 22 pull-thrus (30 x 75), back-ins (30 x 50), 28 full hkups, 5 W, 5 E (30/50 amps), seasonal sites, tent sites, dump, firewood. Pets OK. Eco-friendly. 2015 rates: $23 to $26. May 1 to Oct 31. No CC.
(218)749-2821 Lat: 47.473088, Lon: -92.482924
#245 Highway 37, Gilbert, MN 55741
west40rv@gmail.com
www.westfortyrvpark.com

GLENWOOD — D2 *Pope*

CHALET CAMPGROUNDS (Public) From town, S 0.5 mi on Franklin St (L). 2015 rates: $15 to $20. May 1 to Oct 1. (320)634-5433

GLYNDON — C1 *Clay*

BUFFALO RIVER (State Pk) From Jct of Hwys 10 & 9, E 1.5 mi on Hwy 10 (R). Vehicle permit & reservation fee required. 2015 rates: $15 to $23. (218)498-2124

Tell them you saw them in this Guide!

GRAND MARAIS — B5 *Cook*

CASCADE RIVER (State Pk) From town, SW 9 mi on US-61 (R); Or from Duluth, NE 100 mi on US-61 (Northshore Dr) to Park Entrance Rd, MP 101 N 0.7 mi (E). Reservation fee. Note: 35' length maximum. 2015 rates: $15 to $23. (218)387-3053

GRAND MARAIS RV PARK & CAMPGROUND (Public) From Jct of Hwy 61 & 8th Ave W (SW end of town), S 100 ft on 8th Ave W (R). Reservation fee required. 2015 rates: $33 to $40. (800)998-0959

JUDGE C R MAGNEY (State Pk) From town, NE 14 mi on MN-61 (L). Reservation fee. Note: 45' length maximum. 2015 rates: $15 to $23. (218)387-3039

GRAND RAPIDS — C3 *Itasca*

PRAIRIE LAKE CAMPGROUND **Ratings: 5.5/5/6.5** (Campground) 2015 rates: $31.95 to $33.95. May 1 to Oct 1. (218)326-8486 30730 Wabana Rd, Grand Rapids, MN 55744

GRANITE FALLS — E2 *Yellow Medicine*

PRAIRIE VIEW RV PARK & CAMPGROUND
Ratings: 10/10★/10 (RV Park) From Jct of Hwy 23 & Hwy 212 (in town) S. 2.2 mi on Hwy 23 to Hwy 274, S 0.4 mi on Hwy 274 to Prairies Edge Lane E 0.8 mi (L). Note: Don't use GPS coordinates. **FAC:** Paved rds. 26 paved, 16 all weather, patios, 26 pull-thrus (50 x 75), back-ins (25 x 65), 42 full hkups (30/50 amps), WiFi, tent sites, rentals, laundry, groc, LP gas, fire rings, firewood, restaurant. **REC:** heated pool, wading pool, whirlpool, playground. Pets OK. Partial handicap access. Big rig sites, eco-friendly, 2015 rates: $24. May 1 to Nov 1.
(866)293-2121 Lat: 44.76416, Lon: -95.52927
5616 Prairies Edge Lane, Granite Falls, MN 56241
rvpark@prairiesedgecasino.com
www.prairiesedgecasino.com
See ad this page.

UPPER SIOUX AGENCY (State Pk) From jct Hwy 23 & Hwy 67 south of town: Go 8 mi E on Hwy 67. 2015 rates: $15 to $31. May 1 to Oct 26. (320)564-4777

HAM LAKE — D3 *Anoka*

HAM LAKE CAMPGROUND **Ratings: 7/9.5★/9** (Campground) 2015 rates: $28 to $35. May 1 to Oct 31. (763)434-5337 2400 Constance Blvd N.e., Ham Lake, MN 55304

HASTINGS — E3 *Washington, Dakota*

SAINT CROIX BLUFFS REGIONAL PARK (Public) From town, N 1 mi on Hwy 61 to SR-95, N 2 mi to US-10, E 2.6 mi to CR-21, N 0.5 mi (R). Entrance fee required. 2015 rates: $15 to $22. (651)430-8240

HILL CITY — C3 *Aitkin*

QUADNA MT MOTEL & RV PARK **Ratings: 6/6/7** (Campground) 2015 rates: $25 to $30. May 15 to Oct 15. (218)697-2880 400 Quadna Rd, Hill City, MN 55748

HINCKLEY — D3 *Pine*

GRAND CASINO HINCKLEY RV RESORT
Ratings: 10/10★/10 (RV Park) From Jct of I-35 & SR-48 (Exit 183), E 1 mi on SR-48 (R). **FAC:** Paved rds. (271 spaces). Avail: 251 paved, patios, back-ins (35 x 65), 251 full hkups (30/50 amps), seasonal sites, cable, WiFi, rentals, laundry, groc, fire rings, firewood, restaurant, controlled access. **REC:** heated pool, whirlpool, golf, shuffleboard, playground. Pets OK. Partial handicap access, no tents. Big rig sites, 2015 rates: $27 to $35.
(800)472-6321 Lat: 46.00981, Lon: -92.91177
777 Lady Luck Drive, Hinckley, MN 55037
hinsmk@grcasinos.com
www.grandcasinomn.com
See ad this page, 646 (Spotlight Hinckley), 644.

PATHFINDER VILLAGE ST CROIX **Ratings: 8/8/8** (Membership Pk) 2015 rates: $30 to $40. Apr 15 to Sep 30. (320)384-7985 49200 State Hwy 48 #2, Hinckley, MN 55037

ST CROIX (State Pk) From Jct of I-35 & Hwy 48, E 15 mi on Hwy 48 to CR-22, S 5 mi (E). Reservation fee. 2015 rates: $15 to $23. (320)384-6591

ST CROIX RIVER RESORT Ratings: 8/9/8 (Campground) From Jct of I-35 & SR-48 (exit 183), E 23.5 mi on SR-48 to CR-173, N 1 mi (R). **FAC:** Gravel rds. (168 spaces). 108 Avail: 79 gravel, 29 grass, 2 pull-thrus (30 x 45), back-ins (30 x 50), some side by side hkups, 6 full hkups, 102 W, 102 E (30/50 amps), seasonal sites, WiFi Hotspot, tent sites, rentals, dump, mobile sewer, laundry, groc, fire rings, firewood. **REC:** heated pool, St Croix River: swim, fishing, playground. Pets OK. 2015 rates: $38 to $48. May 1 to Oct 18.
(800)231-0425 Lat: 46.02562, Lon: -92.44513
40756 Grace Lake Rd, Hinckley, MN 55037
www.midwestoutdoorresorts.com

Things to See and Do

GRAND CASINO HINCKLEY Casino. Partial handicap access. RV accessible. Restrooms, food. ATM.
(800)472-6321 Lat: 46.01073, Lon: -92.90183
777 Lady Luck Dr, Hinckley, MN 55037
www.grandcasinomn.com
See ad this page, 646 (Spotlight Hinckley).

HOUSTON — E4 *Houston*

MONEY CREEK HAVEN INC **Ratings: 6.5/6.5/8.5** (Campground) 2015 rates: $38 to $42. Apr 15 to Oct 15. (507)896-3544 18502 County Road 26, Houston, MN 55943

HOYT LAKES — B4 *St Louis*

FISHERMAN'S POINT CAMPGROUND (Public) From Jct of I-53 & Hwy 135 (Gilbert cutoff), E 22 mi on Hwy 135 to Hwy 110, E 4 mi to Hoyt Lakes Rd, S 1 mi (R). 2015 rates: $12.50. May 1 to Sep 15. (218)225-3337

IHLEN — E1 *Pipestone*

SPLIT ROCK CREEK (State Pk) From Jct of Hwys 30 & 23, S 6 mi on Hwy 23 to CR-2, E 3 blks to CR-20, S 0.75 mi (L). Entrance fee & reservation fee required. 2015 rates: $15 to $23. (507)348-7908

ISANTI — D3 *Isanti*

COUNTRY CAMPING TENT & RV PARK Ratings: 7.5/7.5/7.5 (Campground) From Jct of US-65 & CR-5, W 2.4 mi on CR-5 to CR-10, S 0.4 mi to CR-68, S 1.1 mi (L). **FAC:** Gravel rds. (100 spaces). 73 Avail: 15 gravel, 58 grass, 6 pull-thrus (28 x 100), back-ins (28 x 70), 7 full hkups, 51 W, 51 E (30/50 amps), seasonal sites, WiFi, tent sites, dump, laundry, groc, LP gas, fire rings, firewood. **REC:** heated pool, wading pool, Rum River: fishing, playground. Pets OK. Partial handicap access. 2015 rates: $36 to $45. Disc: AAA. May 1 to Oct 1. ATM.
AAA Approved
(763)444-9626 Lat: 45.46515, Lon: -93.28468
27437 Palm Street NW, Isanti, MN 55040
gocamping@country-camping.com
www.country-camping.com

Tell your RV Campground that you found them in this Guide.

ISLE — C3 *Cook*

FATHER HENNEPIN (State Pk) From Jct of Hwys 47 & 27, W 1 mi on Hwy 27 (R). Entrance fee required. Reservation fee. 2015 rates: $20 to $24. (320)676-8763

SOUTH ISLE FAMILY CAMPGROUND **Ratings: 7.5/7.5★/8.5** (Campground) 2015 rates: $38 to $50. Apr 25 to Oct 15. (320)676-8538 39002 Highway 47, Isle, MN 56342

JACKSON — F2 *Jackson*

ANDERSON-BROWN-ROBERTSON COUNTY PARKS (Public) From town, S 6 mi on Hwy 71 to CR-4, W 5 mi (R). 2015 rates: $7 to $15. May 15 to Oct 1. (507)847-2240

JACKSON KOA KAMPGROUND **Ratings: 8.5/9.5★/9** (Campground) 2015 rates: $35 to $43. Apr 15 to Oct 15. (800)KOA-5670 2035 Hwy 7 N, Jackson, MN 56143

JACOBSON — C3 *Aitkin*

SAVANNA STATE FOREST/HAY LAKE CAMPGROUND (State Pk) From town: Go 2-1/2 mi S on Hwy 65,then 3 mi E, then 1 mi S. Pit toilets. 2015 rates: $14. (218)426-3271

KABETOGAMA — B3 *St Louis*

THE PINES OF KABETOGAMA RESORT
Ratings: 9/8.5★/8.5 (RV Resort) From Hwy 53 South: Go 1.3 mi N on Gamma Rd, then 1.6 mi E on Gappa Rd, then 0.2 mi N on Burma Rd (R). **FAC:** All weather rds. (30 spaces). Avail: 24 all weather, 12 pull-thrus (35 x 65), back-ins (35 x 40), 24 full hkups (15/50 amps), seasonal sites, WiFi, rentals, laundry, fire rings, firewood. **REC:** Lake Kabetogama: fishing, playground. Pets OK. Big rig sites, 2015 rates: $60 to $100. May 1 to Oct 15.
(218)875-2000 Lat: 48.438714, Lon: -93.019634
12443 Burma Rd, Kabetogama, MN 56669
vacation@thepineskab.com
thepineskab.com
See ad this page, 644.

LAKE BENTON — E1 *Lincoln*

HOLE-IN-THE-MOUNTAIN COUNTY PARK (Public) From Jct of US-75 & Hwy 14, W 0.5 mi on Hwy 14 (L). 2015 rates: $15 to $20. May 15 to Oct 1. (507)368-9350

LAKE BRONSON — A1 *Kittson*

LAKE BRONSON (State Pk) From Jct of US-59 & CR-28, E 2 mi on CR-28 (E). Reservation fee. Note: 50' RV length limit. 2015 rates: $15 to $23. (218)754-2200

LAKE CITY — E4 *Wabasha*

FRONTENAC (State Pk) From town, NW 7 mi on US-61 to CR-2, NE 1 mi, follow signs (L). Entrance fee required. Reservation fee. Note: 53' RV length maximum. 2015 rates: $15 to $23. (651)345-3401

LAKE PEPIN CAMPGROUNDS & TRAILER COURT
Ratings: 4.5/7.5★/7 (Campground) From Jct US-63 & U-61 S, NW 1.4 mi on US-61/63 (R). **FAC:** Gravel rds. (54 spaces). Avail: 48 grass, 9 pull-thrus (30 x 45), back-ins (28 x 40), some side by side hkups, 26 full hkups, 18 W, 18 E (30/50 amps), seasonal sites, tent sites, dump, fire rings, firewood. **REC:** playground. Pets OK. 2015 rates: $28 to $30. Apr 15 to Oct 15. No CC.
(651)345-2909 Lat: 44.46281, Lon: -92.28629
1818 North High, Lake City, MN 55041
See ad this page.

LAKE ELMO — D3 *Washington*

LAKE ELMO PARK RESERVE CAMPGROUND (Public) From Jct of I-94 & Kelvin Ave. (exit 251), N 1 mi on CR-19 (E). Entrance fee required. 2015 rates: $15 to $55. (651)430-8370

LAKE ITASCA — C2 *Clearwater*

ITASCA/BEAR PAW CAMPGROUND (State Pk) From Park Rapids, N 20 mi on US-71, follow signs (L). 2015 rates: $20 to $24. (218)699-7251

ITASCA/PINE RIDGE (State Pk) From Park Rapids, N 20 mi on US-71 (L). 2015 rates: $20 to $24. (218)699-7251

LAKE LILLIAN — D2 *Kandiyohi*

KANDIYOHI COUNTY PARK # 1 (Public) From Jct of US-71 & SR-7, E 3 mi on SR-7 to SR-44/45th St., N 3 mi (R). Reservation fee. 2015 rates: $27.25. (320)995-6599

KANDIYOHI COUNTY PARK #2 (Public) From jct Hwy-7 & CR-8: Go 4 mi N on CR-8, then 1-3/4 mi NW on CR-132. (320)664-4707

LAKEFIELD — E2 *Jackson*

KILEN WOODS (State Pk) From Jct of Hwy 86 & I-90, N 6 mi on Hwy 86 to CR-24, E 5 mi, follow signs (R). Entrance fee required. $4 daily, $20 Season. Reservation fee. Pit toilets. 2015 rates: $15 to $23. (507)662-6258

LANESBORO — E4 *Fillmore*

EAGLE CLIFF CAMPGROUND & LODGING, INC Ratings: 8/8.5/9.5 (Campground) From Jct of SR-52 & SR-16, E 9 mi on SR-16 (L). **FAC:** All weather rds. (217 spaces). Avail: 126 grass, 8 pull-thrus (45 x 55), back-ins (45 x 55), 20 full hkups, 106 W, 106 E (30/50 amps), seasonal sites, WiFi $, tent sites, rentals, showers $, dump, laundry, groc, LP bottles, fire rings, firewood. **REC:** Root River: swim, fishing, playground, rec open to public. Pets OK. Partial handicap access. Big rig sites, 2015 rates: $35 to $37. Apr 15 to Oct 20.
(507)467-2598 Lat: 43.74523, Lon: -91.93793
35455 State Hwy 16, Lanesboro, MN 55949
eaglecliffcampground@gmail.com
www.eagle-cliff.com

SYLVAN PARK CAMPGROUND (Public) From Jct of US-16 & Parkway Ave (in Lanesboro), N 0.2 mi on Parkway Ave (R). 2015 rates: $30. (507)467-3722

LE ROY — F4 *Mower*

LAKE LOUISE (State Pk) From Jct of Hwy 56 & CR-14, N 1.5 mi on CR-30 (L). Reservation fee. Note: 45' RV length limit. Pit toilets. 2015 rates: $15 to $23. (507)324-5249

LITCHFIELD — D2 *Meeker*

LAKE RIPLEY CAMPGROUND (Public) From Jct of US-12 & SR-22, S 1.5 mi on SR-22 (R). 2015 rates: $20 to $25. May 2 to Oct 15. (320)693-7201

LITTLE FALLS — D2 *Harrison*

CHARLES A. LINDBERGH (State Pk) From Jct of N Hwy 10 & Hwy 27 exit, W 2 mi on Hwy 27 to Lindbergh Dr, S 1 mi (R). Reservation fee. Note: 50' RV length limit. 2015 rates: $15 to $23. (320)616-2525

LONG PRAIRIE — D2 *Todd*

CAMP S'MORE CAMPGROUND Ratings: 5/8.5★/8.5 (Campground) N-bnd: From Jct of SR-27 & US 71: Go N .07 mi on US-71 (L). **FAC:** Gravel rds. (26 spaces). Avail: 22 gravel, 8 pull-thrus (40 x 50), back-ins (40 x 50), 15 full hkups, 5 W, 5 E (30/50 amps), seasonal sites, tent sites, dump, fire rings, firewood. **REC:** playground. Pets OK. 2015 rates: $33. May 1 to Oct 15.
(320)732-2517 Lat: 45.98838, Lon: -94.86597
24797 US 71, Long Prairie, MN 56347
info@campsmoremn.com
www.campsmoremn.com

LUVERNE — E1 *Rock*

BLUE MOUNDS (State Pk) From Jct of US-75 & I-90, N 5 mi on US-75 to CR-20, E 1 mi (E). Reservation fee. Note: 50' RV length limit. 2015 rates: $18 to $22. (507)283-1307

LYND — E1 *Lyon*

CAMDEN (State Pk) From Lynd, SW 3 mi on Hwy 23 (R). Reservation fee. 2015 rates: $15 to $23. (507)865-4530

MADELIA — E2 *Watonwan*

MADELIA CAMPGROUND (Public) From Hwy 60 & Main St, W 0.2 mi on Main St to Old Hwy 60, SW 1 mi (R). 2015 rates: $17 to $22. Apr 15 to Oct 1. (507)642-3245

MADISON LAKE — E3 *Blue Earth*

BRAY PARK (BLUE EARTH COUNTY PARK) (Public) From jct US-14 & Hwy-60: Go 4 mi N on Hwy-60, then 1-1/2 mi E on Hwy-60, then 2 mi S on CR-48. 2015 rates: $10 to $15. May 1 to Oct 31. (507)304-4025

MAHNOMEN — B1 *Mahnomen*

SHOOTING STAR CASINO & RV PARK Ratings: 9.5/9.5★/8.5 (RV Park) From Jct of US-59 & SR-200 (N of town), S 1.1 mi on US-59 (R). **FAC:** Paved rds. 47 paved, 28 pull-thrus (25 x 60), back-ins (25 x 30), 47 full hkups (30/50 amps), WiFi, tent sites, rentals, dump, laundry, fire rings, firewood, restaurant. **REC:** heated pool, whirlpool, Wild Rice River: rec open to public. Pets OK. Partial handicap access. Big rig sites, 2015 rates: $20. May 1 to Oct 30. AAA Approved
(800)453-STAR Lat: 47.30598, Lon: -95.96423
777 Casino Drive, Mahnomen, MN 56557
www.starcasino.com

MANKATO — E3 *Blue Earth*

MANKATO See also Waseca & Waterville.

MINNEOPA (State Pk) From Jct of Hwys 60 & 68, W 1 mi on Hwy 68, follow signs (R). Reservation fee. 2015 rates: $15 to $23. (507)389-5464

MAPLE PLAIN — D3 *Hennepin*

BAKER PARK RESERVE (Public) From Jct of Hwy 12 & CR-19, N 1.5 mi on CR-19, located on Lake Independence, follow signs (L). 2015 rates: $17 to $25. Apr 30 to Oct 20. (763)694-7662

MAPLETON — E3 *Blue Earth*

DALY PARK (BLUE EARTH COUNTY PARK) (Public) From town: Go 3 mi S on CR-7, then 2 mi W on CR-191. 2015 rates: $15. May 1 to Oct 31. (507)524-3000

MAZEPPA — E4 *Wabasha*

PONDEROSA CAMPGROUND (Public) From Jct of US-52 & CR-12 (MP66), E 2 mi on CR-12 to CR-27, N 3.5 mi, follow signs (L). 2015 rates: $28 to $35. Apr 14 to Oct 14. (507)843-3611

MCGREGOR — C3 *Aitkin*

SANDY LAKE REC AREA (Public Corps) From town, N 13 mi on Hwy 65 (R). 2015 rates: $24 to $48. May 1 to Sep 30. (218)426-3482

SAVANNA PORTAGE (State Pk) From town, N 7 mi on Hwy 65 to CR-14, NE 10 mi (R). Reservation fee. 2015 rates: $15 to $23. (218)426-3271

MELROSE — D2 *Stearns*

BIRCH LAKES SF (Public) From Jct of CR-13 & CR-17, E 1.5 mi on CR-17 to Birch Lake Rd, N 2 mi to forest rd (E). Reservation fee. Pit toilets. 2015 rates: $14. (218)365-4966

MENAHGA — C2 *Wadena*

HUNTERSVILLE/HUNTERSVILLE LANDING (State Pk) From jct CR 17 & CR 23: Go 1 mi N on CR 23, then 3 mi E on CR 18, then 1 mi S, then 2 mi E. Pit toilets. 2015 rates: $12. (218)266-2100

MILTONA — D2 *Douglas*

LAZY DAYS CAMPGROUND **Ratings: 7/7/8** (Campground) 2015 rates: $40 to $45. May 1 to Oct 1. (218)943-3000 10247 County Rd 36 NE, Miltona, MN 56354

MINNEAPOLIS — D3 *Anoka, Hennepin*

ST. PAUL/ MINNEAPOLIS AREA MAP

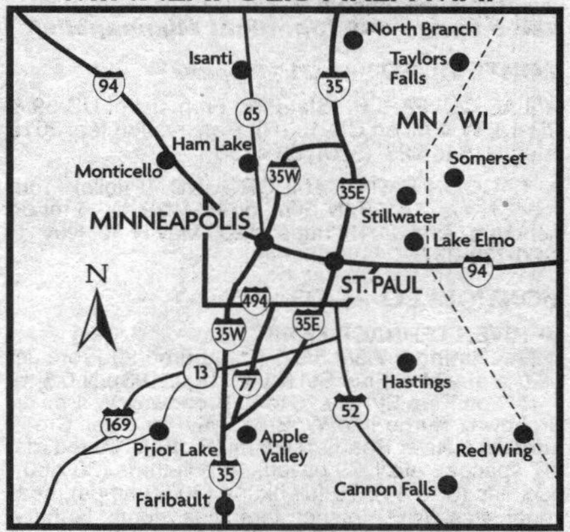

Symbols on map indicate towns within a 50 mile radius of St. Paul where campgrounds are listed. Check listings for more information.

In MN, see also Apple Valley, Cannon Falls, Faribault, Ham Lake, Hastings, Isanti, Lake Elmo, Monticello, North Branch, Prior Lake, Red Wing, Stillwater & Taylors Falls.

In WI, see Somerset.

A SPOTLIGHT Introducing Minneapolis's colorful attractions appearing at the front of this state section.

LOWRY GROVE RV PARK/MHP
Ratings: 7/7.5/6 (RV Area in MHP) From Jct of I-35W & St Anthony/Industrial Blvd (exit 22), N 1 mi on St Anthony Blvd to Kenzie Terrace, SW 0.3 mi (R). **FAC:** Paved rds. (80 spaces). 30 Avail: 12 paved, 18 gravel, 3 pull-thrus (30 x 60), back-ins (28 x 45), 30 full hkups (50 amps), seasonal

Check our family camping destinations article in the front of the Guide highlighting the best places to camp in every state and province.

MN

MINNEAPOLIS (CONT)

LOWRY GROVE RV PARK/MHP (CONT)
sites, WiFi, laundry. Pets OK. No tents. 2015 rates: $38 to $44.
AAA Approved
(612)781-3148 Lat: 45.01416, Lon: -93.22506
2501 Lowry Ave NE, St Anthony, MN 55418
adeline@pljrealty.com
www.pljrealty.com
See ad page 647 (Spotlight Minneapolis).

MINNEAPOLIS NW KOA CAMPGROUND
Ratings: 8.5/10★/9 (Campground) From Jct of I-94 & CR-30 (exit 213), left 0.2 mi on Maple Grove Pkwy (get in rt lane, CR-30 turns R at McDonalds), W 1.7 mi on CR-30 to CR-101, turn R 1 mi (R). **FAC:** Gravel rds. (150 spaces). 130 Avail: 100 gravel, 30 grass, 50 pull-thrus (30 x 65), back-ins (30 x 55), mostly side by side hkups, 41 full hkups, 89 W, 89 E (30/50 amps), seasonal sites, WiFi, tent sites, rentals, dump, laundry, groc, LP gas, fire rings, firewood. **REC:** pool, shuffleboard, playground. Pet restrict(B). Big rig sites, 2015 rates: $41 to $48. Disc: military. Apr 1 to Oct 15.
(763)420-2255 Lat: 45.14474, Lon: -93.52097
10410 Brockton Lane N, Minneapolis, MN 55311
mplsnwkoa@aol.com
www.mplsnwkoa.com
See ad page 648 (Spotlight Minneapolis).

MONTEVIDEO — D1 *Chippewa*

LAC QUI PARLE (State Pk) From Jct of US-59 & CR-13, W 4 mi on CR-13 (R). Reservation fee. 2015 rates: $15 to $23. (320)752-4736

LAGOON PARK CAMPGROUND (Public) From Jct of Hwys 7 & 29, N .3 mi on Hwy 29, W .5 mi on Ashmore Ave. 2015 rates: $20. May 1 to Nov 1. (320)269-6575

MONTICELLO — D3 *Wright*

RIVER TERRACE PARK
Ratings: 7.5/7.5/9.5 (Campground) From Jct of I-94 & Pine St/Hwy 25 (Exit 193), N 0.5 mi on Pine St/Hwy 25 to E. Broadway, W 1 mi on Broadway (turns into W. Broadway) to Otter Creek (turns into River Road), N 0.5 mi (R). **FAC:** Paved rds. (87 spaces). Avail: 79 paved, 10 pull-thrus (30 x 60), back-ins (30 x 40), 79 full hkups (30/50 amps), seasonal sites, WiFi Hotspot, tent sites, dump, laundry, fire rings, firewood. **REC:** Mississippi River: swim, fishing, playground. Pets OK. 2015 rates: $32 to $35. Apr 1 to Oct 31. No CC.
(763)295-2264 Lat: 45.31569, Lon: -93.81706
1335 River St W, Monticello, MN 55362
See ad page 647 (Spotlight Minneapolis).

Thank you for being one of our best customers!

MOOSE LAKE — C3 *Carlton*

MOOSE LAKE (State Pk) From Jct of I-35 & Hwy 43 (Willow River exit), W 0.5 mi on Hwy 43 to Hwy 61, N 0.2 mi to park access rd, E 0.75 mi, follow signs (L). Reservation fee. 2015 rates: $15 to $23. (218)485-5420

MOOSE LAKE CITY PARK & CAMPGROUND (Public) From Jct of I-35 & SR-73, W 1.5 mi on SR-73 to 2nd St, E 0.3 mi to Birch St, N 0.1 mi to 4th St, E 0.1 mi (E). 2015 rates: $24 to $29. May 8 to Sep 27. (218)485-4761

MORRISTOWN — E3 *Rice*

CAMP MAIDEN ROCK WEST **Ratings: 7/7.5/7.5** (Campground) 2015 rates: $36 to $42. May 15 to Sep 30. (507)685-2280 24505 Jackson Ave, Morristown, MN 55052

MORTON — E2 *Redwood*

JACKPOT JUNCTION CASINO CAMPGROUND **Ratings: 8.5/NA/8.5** (RV Park) Pit toilets. 2015 rates: $35. Apr 15 to Oct 15. (800)946-0077 39375 County Hwy 24, Morton, MN 56270

NERSTRAND — E3 *Rice*

NERSTRAND BIG WOODS (State Pk) From Jct of SR-246/Main St (in town) & Cherry St, W 0.5 mi on SR-246 to CR-40, W 1.2 mi (R). ($7 vehicle park entry fee). 2015 rates: $15 to $23. (507)333-4840

NEW LONDON — D2 *Kandiyohi*

KANDIYOHI COUNTY PARK #7 (Public) From jct US 71 & CR 40: Go 4 mi W on CR 40, then 2 mi N on CR 5. (320)354-4453

NEW ULM — E2 *Brown*

FLANDRAU (State Pk) From Jct US-14 & SR-15, S 1.5 mi on SR-15 to 10th South St, W 1 mi, to Summit Ave, S 0.1 mi, follow signs (R). Reservation fee. 2015 rates: $18 to $22. (507)233-9800

NISSWA — C2 *Crow Wing*

FRITZ'S RESORT & CAMPGROUND Ratings: 8.5/9/8.5 (Campground) From Jct of SR-371 & CR-77 (in Nisswa), N 3 mi on SR-371 (L). **FAC:** Paved rds. (92 spaces). Avail: 22 grass, 10 pull-thrus (28 x 50), back-ins (22 x 50), 22 full hkups (30/50 amps), seasonal sites, cable, WiFi, rentals, showers $, dump, laundry, LP bottles, fire rings, firewood. **REC:** Edna Lake: swim, fishing, playground. No pets. No tents. 2015 rates: $36 to $43. May 1 to Oct 1. (218)568-8988 Lat: 46.53592, Lon: -94.30696
26483 Hwy 371, Nisswa, MN 56468
fritzrst@uslink.net
www.fritzsresort.com

NODINE — E4 *Winona*

GREAT RIVER BLUFFS (State Pk) From jct I-90 (exit 266) & CR 12: Go N to end of CR 12, then 1 mi E on CR 3 (Scenic Apple Blossom Dr), then right 1 mi on gravel access road. 2015 rates: $15 to $23. (507)643-6849

NORTH BRANCH — D3 *Chisago*

WILD RIVER (State Pk) From Jct of I-35 & SR-95, E 10 mi on SR-95 to CR-12, NE 3.5 mi (E). Entrance fee required. Reservation fee. 2015 rates: $15 to $31. (651)583-2125

ONAMIA — C3 *Mille Lacs*

MILLE LACS KATHIO (State Pk) From town, N 8 mi on US-169 to CR-26, S 1 mi (R). Reservation fee. 2015 rates: $15 to $23. (320)532-3523

ORTONVILLE — D1 *Swift, Big Stone*

BIG STONE LAKE (State Pk) From Jct of Hwy 7 & US-12, NW 8 mi on Hwy 7, follow signs (L). Reservation fee. 2015 rates: $16 to $20. May 25 to Sep 7. (320)839-3663

LAKESHORE RV PARK INC. Ratings: 8.5/10★/9 (Campground) From Jct of US-12 & SR-7W (in town), NW 2.7 mi on SR-7W (L). **FAC:** Gravel rds. (94 spaces). Avail: 29 gravel, 13 pull-thrus (20 x 50), back-ins (20 x 40), 29 full hkups (30/50 amps), seasonal sites, cable, WiFi, tent sites, rentals, laundry, groc, LP gas, fire rings, firewood. **REC:** heated pool, whirlpool, Big Stone Lake: swim, fishing, marina, shuffleboard, playground, rec open to public. Pets OK. Partial handicap access. Big rig sites, eco-friendly, 2015 rates: $43.95 to $46.95. Disc: AAA. Apr 1 to Oct 1.
(800)9FORFUN Lat: 45.33483, Lon: -96.46350
39445 Lakeshore Rv Park Rd, Ortonville, MN 56278
lakeshorervpark@wat.midco.net
lakeshorervpark.com

OUTING — C3 *Cass*

LAND O' LAKES SF/CLINT CONVERSE CAMPGROUND (State Pk) From town, N 2 mi on Hwy 6 to CR-48 (Lake Washburn Rd), W 2 mi (R). Pit toilets. 2015 rates: $14. (218)528-4566

OWATONNA — E3 *Steele*

HOPE OAK KNOLL CAMPGROUND
Ratings: 7/8.5/8.5 (Campground) From Jct of I-35 & CR-4 (exit 32), E 0.7 mi on CR-4 to CR-3, S 0.2 mi (L). **FAC:** Paved/gravel rds. (90 spaces). 40 Avail: 20 gravel, 20 grass, 20 pull-thrus (40 x 65), back-ins (30 x 45), mostly side by side hkups, 12 full hkups, 28 W, 28 E (30/50 amps), seasonal sites, WiFi, tent sites, dump, laundry, groc, LP bottles, fire rings, firewood. **REC:** playground. Pets OK. 2015 rates: $31 to $33. Apr 15 to Oct 7.
(507)451-2998 Lat: 43.95430, Lon: -93.24379
9545 CR-3, Owatonna, MN 55060
See ad this page, 644.

RICE LAKE (State Pk) From Jct I-35 & Exit 42A/Hoffman Dr, E 0.6 mi on Hoffman Dr to East Rose (CR-19), E 7 mi to park entrance rd (R). Reservation fee. 2015 rates: $15 to $23. (507)455-5871

RIVER VIEW CAMPGROUND
Ratings: 8.5/10★/10 (Campground) From Jct of I-35 & US-14 (Exit 40B), W 0.8 mi on US-14 to CR-7, left 0.5 mi on CR-7 to CR-18, left 1.1 mi on CR-18 to park entrance (L). **FAC:** Gravel rds. (115 spaces). 40 Avail: 20 gravel, 20 grass, patios, 20 pull-thrus (25 x 60), back-ins (25 x 45), 14 full hkups, 26 W, 26 E (30/50 amps), seasonal sites, WiFi, tent sites, rentals, dump, laundry, groc, fire rings, firewood. **REC:** heated pool, wading pool, Straight River:

OWATONNA (CONT)

RIVER VIEW CAMPGROUND (CONT)
fishing, playground. Pets OK. 2015 rates: $35 to $50. Apr 15 to Oct 15.
(507)451-8050 Lat: 44.05203, Lon: -93.25350
2554 SW 28th St, Owatonna, MN 55060
rvcg.contact@gmail.com
riverviewcampgroundminnesota.com
See ad opposite page, 644.

PARK RAPIDS — C2 *Clearwater, Hubbard*

PAUL BUNYAN SF/MANTRAP LAKE (State Pk) From Jct of SR-34 & CR-4, N 12 mi on CR-4 to CR-24, E 1.5 mi to CR-104, N 0.75 mi, follow signs (R). Pit toilets. 2015 rates: $14. (218)266-2100

VAGABOND VILLAGE CAMPGROUND **Ratings: 8.5/9.5★/8.5** (Campground) 2015 rates: $32 to $47. May 15 to Oct 1. (218)732-5234 23801 Green Pines Road, Park Rapids, MN 56470

PAYNESVILLE — D2 *Meeker*

LAKE KORONIS REGIONAL PARK & CAMPGROUND (Public) From town, SE 5 mi on Hwy 55, S 0.25 mi on US-4 to CSAH-20, W 4 mi (L); or From Jct of US-23 & CSAH-20, S 1.9 mi on CSAH-20, (continue on) E 1.5 mi, follow signs (R). Reservation fee. 2015 rates: $16 to $45. May 1 to Sep 30. (320)276-8843

PELICAN RAPIDS — C1 *Otter Tail*

MAPLEWOOD (State Pk) From Jct of Hwy 108 & US-59, E 7 mi on Hwy 108 (R). Reservation fee. 2015 rates: $15 to $23. (218)863-8383

SHERIN MEMORIAL CAMPGROUND (CITY PARK) (Public) In town on Hwy-108. 2015 rates: $10 to $15. May 15 to Sep 15. (218)863-6571

PEQUOT LAKES — C2 *Crow Wing*

RV RESORT VILLAGE AT THE PRESERVE **Ratings: 10/9.5★/9.5** (Condo Pk) 2015 rates: $33 to $65. Apr 1 to Oct 31. (218)568-8009 28668 Hurtig Road, Pequot Lakes, MN 56472

WILDWEDGE GOLF & RV PARK **Ratings: 7/9.5★/8** (RV Park) 2015 rates: $37 to $44. May 1 to Oct 1. (218)568-5000 32620 Paul Bunyan Trail Park, Pequot Lakes, MN 56472

PERHAM — C2 *Otter Tail*

GOLDEN EAGLE RV VILLAGE **Ratings: 8.5/8/9** (Membership Pk) 2015 rates: $35. May 15 to Sep 15. (218)346-4386 42488 480th Ave, Perham, MN 56573

PILLAGER — C2 *Cass*

PILLSBURY SF/ROCK LAKE CAMPGROUND (State Pk) From town, W 0.5 mi on Hwy 210 to CR-1, N 6 mi, turn left. Note: 30' RV length limit. Pit toilets. 2015 rates: $14. (218)825-3075

PINE CITY — D3 *Pine*

POKEGAMA LAKE RV PARK & GOLF COURSE
Ratings: 7/8.5★/8 (Campground) From Jct of I-35 & CR-11 (Exit 171), W 4 mi on CR-11 (L). **FAC:** Paved/gravel rds. (180 spaces). Avail: 44 gravel, 26 pull-thrus (35 x 90), back-ins (30 x 60), 44 full hkups (30/50 amps), seasonal sites, WiFi Hotspot, showers $, dump, fire rings, firewood. **REC:** heated pool, Pokegama Lake: swim, fishing, marina, golf, playground. Pets OK. No tents. RV age restrict, 2015 rates: $34. May 1 to Oct 15. ATM.
(320)629-6552 Lat: 45.86949, Lon: -93.04791
19193 Island Resort Road, Pine City, MN 55063
pokegamarvpark@yahoo.com
www.woischkes.com
See ad this page, 644.

SNAKE RIVER (State Pk) From town, E 6 mi on CR-8 to CR-118, E 3 mi, follow signs (L). Reservation fee. Pit toilets. 2015 rates: $14. May 5 to Nov 5. (651)583-2125

PINE ISLAND — E4 *Goodhue*

HIDDEN MEADOWS RV PARK INC **Ratings: 7/7/7** (Campground) 2015 rates: $32 to $37. Apr 8 to Nov 1. (507)356-8594 6450 120th Street NW, Pine Island, MN 55963

PIPESTONE — E1 *Pipestone*

PIPESTONE RV CAMPGROUND
Ratings: 8.5/8/9 (Campground) From Jct of US-75 & SR-23 (N side of town), N 0.4 mi on US-75 to NE 9th St (CR-22), W 0.6 mi (R); or From Jct of I-90 & SR-23 (exit 1), N 28 mi on SR-23 to Hiawatha Ave, N 1.4 mi (R). **FAC:** Gravel rds. (77 spaces). 49 Avail: 28 gravel, 21 grass, 31 pull-thrus (35 x 60), back-ins (30 x 65), some side by side hkups, 31 full hkups, 18 W, 18 E (30/50 amps), seasonal sites, cable, WiFi, tent sites, rentals, dump, laundry, groc, fire rings, firewood. **REC:** heated pool, playground. Pets OK. Big rig sites, eco-friendly, 2015 rates: $30 to $36. Disc: AAA. May 1 to Oct 1.
AAA Approved
(507)825-2455 Lat: 44.00942, Lon: -96.31737
919 N Hiawatha Ave, Pipestone, MN 56164
pipestonervcampground@gmail.com
http://pipestonecampground.com/
See ad this page, 644.

PLAINVIEW — E4 *Wabasha*

CARLEY (State Pk) From town: Go 4 mi S on CR 10. Note: 30' RV length maximum. Pit toilets. 2015 rates: $15 to $23. (507)932-3007

PRESTON — E4 *Fillmore*

MAPLE SPRINGS CAMPGROUND INC & COUNTRY STORE Ratings: 6/NA/9 (Campground) From Jct of SR-16 & CR-5 (South of Wykoff), S 4.1 mi on CR-5 to CR-118, E 1.4 mi (L). **FAC:** Gravel rds. (67 spaces). Avail: 48 grass, back-ins (40 x 50), 11 full hkups, 23 W, 37 E (30/50 amps), seasonal sites, WiFi, tent sites, pit toilets, groc, fire rings, firewood. **REC:** Forrestville Creek: swim, fishing. Pet restrict(B). Eco-friendly, 2015 rates: $30. Apr 1 to Oct 31.
(507)352-2056 Lat: 43.63523, Lon: -92.23599
21606 Co 118, Preston, MN 55965
maplecamp@gmail.com
www.maplespringscampground.com

THE OLD BARN RESORT **Ratings: 8/7/8.5** (Campground) 2015 rates: $44. Apr 1 to Nov 1. (800)552-2512 24461 Heron Road, Preston, MN 55965

PRIOR LAKE — E3 *Scott*

DAKOTAH MEADOWS RV PARK **Ratings: 10/9.5★/9** (Campground) 2015 rates: $29 to $42. (800)653-CAMP 2341 Park Place NW, Prior Lake, MN 55372

RED WING — E4 *Goodhue*

TREASURE ISLAND RV PARK
Ratings: 9.5/9.5★/7.5 (RV Park) From Jct of US-61 & CR-18 (NW of town), N 2.5 mi on CR-18 to Sturgeon Lake Rd, E 1.3 mi (L). **FAC:** Paved rds. (95 spaces). Avail: 80 paved, 73 pull-thrus (30 x 60), back-ins (30 x 45), 80 full hkups (30/50 amps), seasonal sites, WiFi, tent sites, dump, laundry, firewood, restaurant. **REC:** heated pool, whirlpool, Sturgeon Lake: marina, rec open to public. Pets OK. Big rig sites, 2015 rates: $27 to $38. Apr 1 to Oct 31. ATM.
(800)222-7077ext2334 Lat: 44.63210, Lon: -92.64603
5630 Sturgeon Lake Road, Red Wing, MN 55089
summer.ryan@ticasino.com
www.ticasino.com
See ad this page.

Things to See and Do

TREASURE ISLAND RESORT & CASINO Casino and hotel. RV accessible. Restrooms, food. Hours: 24 hours.
(800)222-7077 Lat: 44.63205, Lon: -92.64842
5734 Sturgeon Lake Road, Red Wing, MN 55066
www.treasureislandcasino.com
See ad this page.

ROCHESTER — E4 *Olmsted*

ROCHESTER See also Lanesboro, Pine Island, Preston, St Charles & Zumbrota.

AUTUMNWOODS RV PARK Ratings: 7.5/10★/10 (RV Park) From Jct of I-90 & US-63 (Exit 209), N 2.1 mi on US-63 to CR-16, W 200 ft to 11th Ave SW, N 0.6 mi (R). **FAC:** Paved/gravel rds. (93 spaces). Avail: 87 gravel, patios, 32 pull-thrus (34 x 74), back-ins (34 x 65), 87 full hkups (30/50 amps), seasonal sites, WiFi, laundry, fire rings, firewood. **REC.** Pet restrict(B). Partial handicap access, no tents. Big rig sites, 2015 rates: $35 to $44. Mar 15 to Nov 15.
(507)990-2983 Lat: 43.92723, Lon: -92.47765
1067 Autumnwoods Circle SW, Rochester, MN 55902
autumnwoodsrv@gmail.com
www.autumnwoodsrvpark.com

We appreciate your business!

ROCHESTER (CONT)

KOA ROCHESTER/MARION **Ratings: 8.5/9.5★/8.5** (Campground) 2015 rates: $38 to $43. Mar 15 to Oct 31. (507)288-0785 5232 65th Ave SE, Rochester, MN 55904

ROGERS — D3 *Hennepin*

Travel Services

CAMPING WORLD OF ROGERS As the nation's largest retailer of RV supplies, accessories, services and new and used RVs, Camping World is committed to making your total RV experience better. **SERVICES:** Tire, RV appliance, restrooms. RV supplies, emergency parking, RV accessible. waiting room. Hours: 8am to 6pm. (800)801-8177 Lat: 45.194108, Lon: -93.54853 21200 Rogers Dr., Rogers, MN 55374 www.campingworld.com

ROYALTON — D2 *Benton, Morrison*

TWO RIVERS CAMPGROUND **Ratings: 8.5/9★/10** (Campground) 2015 rates: $35 to $59.50. May 1 to Oct 1. (320)584-5125 5116 145th St N.w., Royalton, MN 56373

SANDSTONE — C3 *Pine*

BANNING (State Pk) From Jct of I-35 & Hwy 23 (exit 195), E 1.9 mi on Hwy 23, follow signs (R). 2015 rates: $18 to $22. (320)245-2668

SAUK CENTRE — D2 *Stearns*

SINCLAIR LEWIS (Public) From Jct of I-94 & US-71, N 1 mi on US-71 to Park Lane, W 0.2 mi, follow signs (R). Reservation fee. 2015 rates: $18 to $25. May 1 to Oct 15. (320)352-2203

SCHROEDER — B5 *Cook*

TEMPERANCE RIVER (State Pk) From town, NE 1 mi on SR-61, follow signs (R). Entrance fee & reservation fee required. 2015 rates: $15 to $31. (218)663-7476

SHEVLIN — B2 *Clearwater*

LONG LAKE COUNTY CAMPGROUND (Public) From Jct of SR-2 & SR-92, S 20 mi on SR-92 to Clearwater County Campground Rd (R). 2015 rates: $29 to $35. May 8 to Sep 20. (218)657-2275

SIDE LAKE — B3 *St Louis*

MCCARTHY BEACH (State Pk) From Jct of Hwy 65 & Hwy 1, W 4 mi on Hwy 1 to CR-542, W 1 mi to fork in road, bear right (CR-542), N 3 mi (R). Note: 40' RV length limit. 2015 rates: $15 to $23. (218)254-7979

SILVER BAY — B4 *Lake*

TETTEGOUCHE (State Pk) From town: Go 4-1/2 mi NE on Hwy 61. 2015 rates: $15 to $31. (218)226-6365

SOUDAN — B4 *St Louis*

MCKINLEY PARK CAMPGROUND (Public) From Jct of US-169 & Main St exit, exit Main St, N 1.2 mi, follow signs (E). 2015 rates: $26.50 to $39.50. May 1 to Sep 30. (218)753-5921

SPICER — D2 *Kandiyohi*

KANDIYOHI COUNTY PARK #5 (Public) From town, N 2.5 mi on SR-23 to CR-30, E 4 mi, follow signs (R). Reservation fee. 2015 rates: $30.90. (320)796-5564

SPRINGFIELD — E2 *Brown*

ROTHENBURG CAMPGROUND (Public) From Jct of US-14 & Cass Ave (in Springfield), S 0.4 mi on Cass Ave (L). Past Chamber of Commerce. **FAC:** Gravel rds. 41 Avail: 16 paved, 25 gravel, back-ins (37 x 50), 17 full hkups, 24 W, 24 E (30/50 amps), WiFi, tent sites, dump, firewood. **REC:** pool, Big Cottonwood River: fishing, playground, rec open to public. Pets OK. 2015 rates: $25 to $28. May 1 to Oct 1. (507)723-3517 Lat: 44.23721, Lon: -94.97390 33 S. Cass Ave, Springfield, MN 56087 commctr@newulmtel.net www.springfieldmn.org

ST CHARLES — E4 *Winona*

LAZY D CAMPGROUND & TRAIL RIDES **Ratings: 7.5/9★/8.5** (Campground) 2015 rates: $29 to $49. Apr 15 to Nov 30. (507)932-3098 18748 County Rd 39, Altura, MN 55910

ST CLOUD — D3 *Benton, Stearns*

ST CLOUD See also Avon, Clearwater, Monticello & Royalton.

ST CLOUD CAMPGROUND & RV PARK
Ratings: 9/9.5★/9.5 (RV Park) From Jct of US-10 & SR-23, E 0.1 mi on SR-23 to CR-8 (14th Ave SE), S 0.1 mi on CR-8, E 1 mi on CR-8 (L) S-bnd: From Jct of SR-23 & CR-8, E 1 mi on CR-8 to 2nd St SE, S 1 mi on 2nd St SE (R). **FAC:** Gravel rds. (102 spaces). 84 Avail: 71 gravel, 13 grass, 45 pull-thrus (35 x 70), back-ins (35 x 55), some side by side hkups, 60 full hkups, 17 W, 17 E (30/50 amps), seasonal sites, WiFi, tent sites, rentals, dump, laundry, groc, LP gas, fire rings, firewood. **REC:** heated pool, playground. Pets OK. Partial handicap access. Big rig sites, eco-friendly, 2015 rates: $38 to $44. May 1 to Oct 12.
(320)251-4463 Lat: 45.57012, Lon: -94.11298
2491 2nd St SE, St Cloud, MN 56304
info@stcloudcampground.com
www.stcloudcampground.com
See ad this page, 644.

Laundry & dishwasher detergent liquids contain up to 80 percent water. It costs energy and packaging to bring this water to the consumer. When there is a choice - choose dry powders.

ST PAUL — D3 *Dakota, Ramsey, Washington*

ST. PAUL/ MINNEAPOLIS AREA MAP

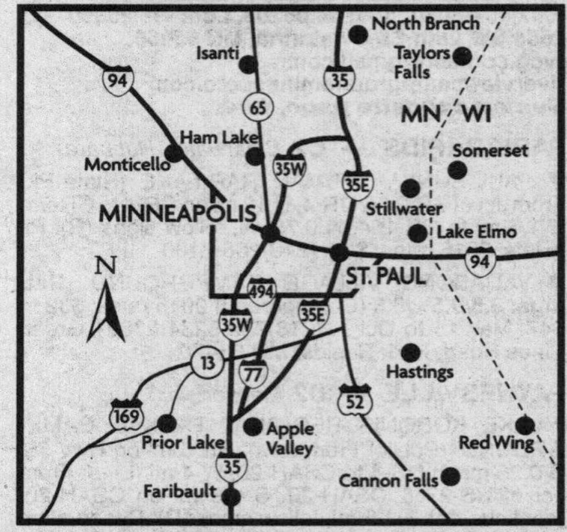

Symbols on map indicate towns within a 50 mile radius of St. Paul where campgrounds are listed. Check listings for more information.

In MN, see also Apple Valley, Cannon Falls, Faribault, Ham Lake, Hastings, Isanti, Lake Elmo, Monticello, North Branch, Prior Lake, Red Wing, Stillwater & Taylors Falls.

In WI, see Somerset.

ST PAUL EAST RV PARK
Ratings: 8.5/10★/9 (Campground) From Jct of I-94 & MN 95 (Exit 253) S 0.2 mi to Hudson Rd, W 1 mi to Settlers Ridge Parkway, S 0.3 mi (R). **FAC:** Paved/gravel rds. 70 gravel, patios, 45 pull-thrus (30 x 55), back-ins (30 x 40), 35 full hkups, 35 W, 35 E (30/50 amps), WiFi, tent sites, rentals, dump, mobile sewer, laundry, LP gas, fire rings, firewood, controlled access. **REC:** heated pool, playground. Pet restrict(B/Q). Partial handicap access. Eco-friendly, 2015 rates: $44 to $48. Apr 20 to Oct 1.
(651)436-6436 Lat: 44.94098, Lon: -92.88426
568 Settlers Ridge Parkway, Woodbury, MN 55129
stpauleastrvpark@aol.com
www.stpauleastrvpark.com
See ad page 654.

STARBUCK — D2 *Pope*

GLACIAL LAKES (State Pk) From town, S 3 mi on SR-29 to CR-41, S 2 mi (L). Reservation fee. Note: 45' RV length maximum. 2015 rates: $15 to $23. (320)239-2860

HOBO PARK CAMPGROUND (Public) From Jct of US-29 & US-28, S 0.5 mi on US-29 (L). Reservations recommended. 2015 rates: $35 to $51. May 1 to Sep 30. (320)239-2336

STILLWATER — D3 *Washington*

WILLIAM O'BRIEN (State Pk) From Jct of I-94 & Hwy 95, N 20 mi on Hwy 95 (L). Entrance fee required. Reservation fee. 2015 rates: $15 to $31. (651)433-0500

STURGEON LAKE — C3 *Pine*

TIMBERLINE RV RESORT **Ratings: 7.5/8/8** (Campground) 2015 rates: $38 to $60. May 1 to Sep 30. (218)372-3272 9152 Timberline Road, Sturgeon Lake, MN 55783

SUNBURG — D2 *Kandiyohi*

MONSON LAKE (State Pk) From town: Go 1-1/2 mi W on Hwy 9, then 2-1/2 mi S on CR 95. 2015 rates: $15 to $23. (320)366-3797

TAYLORS FALLS — D4 *Chisago*

↓ INTERSTATE (State Pk) From town, S 1 mi on Hwy 8 (L). Reservation fee. Note: 45' RV length maximum. 2015 rates: $15 to $23. (651)465-5711

← **WILDWOOD CAMPGROUND Ratings: 7.5/7.5/8** (Campground) From Jct of US-8 & SR-95, W 3 mi on US-8 (R). **FAC:** Gravel rds. (200 spaces). 135 Avail: 90 gravel, 45 grass, 27 pull-thrus (50 x 70), back-ins (45 x 50), mostly side by side hkups, 45 full hkups, 45 W, 45 E (30/50 amps), seasonal sites, WiFi, tent sites, dump, fire rings, firewood. **REC:** heated pool, playground. Pet restrict(Q) $. 2015 rates: $47. May 1 to Oct 15.
(651)465-6315 Lat: 45.38392, Lon: -92.69743
20078 Lake Blvd, Taylors Falls, MN 55084
camp@wildmountain.com
www.wildmountain.com

THIEF RIVER FALLS — B1 *Pennington*

↓ THIEF RIVER FALLS TOURIST PARK (Public) From Jct of Hwy 32 & Oakland Park Rd, S 0.25 mi on Oakland Park Rd (L). 2015 rates: $15 to $20. May 5 to Oct 15. (218)681-2519

TOGO — B3 *Itasca*

← GEORGE WASHINGTON STATE FOREST/THISTLEDEW LAKE CAMPGROUND (State Pk) From town: Go 4-1/2 mi W on Hwy 1, then 2 mi S on access road. Pit toilets. 2015 rates: $14. (218)254-7979

TOWER — B4 *St Louis*

↙ BEAR HEAD LAKE (State Pk) From town, SW 12 mi on Hwy 169 to CR-128 (Bear Head State Park Rd), S 7 mi, follow signs (R). Reservation fee. 2015 rates: $20 to $24. May 15 to Sep 1. (218)365-7229

↓ FORTUNE BAY RESORT RV PARK **Ratings: 7.5/8/8.5** (RV Park) 2015 rates: $25 to $30. (800)555-1714 1430 Bois Forte Road, Tower, MN 55790

↑ HOODOO POINT CAMPGROUNDS (Public) From Jct of US-169 & SR-135, N 100 yds on US-169 to Hoodoo Point Rd, N 1.2 mi (L). 2015 rates: $25 to $40. May 1 to Oct 1. (218)753-6868

TWO HARBORS — C4 *Lake*

↑ BURLINGTON BAY CAMPGROUND (Public) From the Jct of Hwy 61 & Park Rd (North end of town), S 100 ft (L). 2015 rates: $24 to $35. May 15 to Oct 15. (218)834-2021

↑ CLOQUET VALLEY STATE FOREST/INDIAN LAKE CAMPGROUND (State Pk) From town: Go 13 mi N on CR 2, then 12 mi W on CR 14, then 1 mi N. Pit toilets. 2015 rates: $12. Apr 29 to Oct 30. (218)226-6377

↗ GOOSEBERRY FALLS (State Pk) From town, NE 14 mi on US-61 (R). Entrance fee ($4) & reservation fee required. Note: 40' RV length maximum. 2015 rates: $20. (218)595-7100

UPSALA — D2 *Morrison*

← CEDAR LAKE MEMORIAL PARK (Public) From Jct of SR-238 & Abaca Rd. (in town), W 3 mi on CR-19 (R). 2015 rates: $32 to $44. (320)573-2983

VERGAS — C1 *Otter Tail*

↙ HEISLERS COUNTRY CAMPGROUND **Ratings: 5/8.5★/7.5** (Campground) 2015 rates: $25 to $35. May 1 to Oct 1. (218)342-2233 31870 County Hwy 130, Vergas, MN 56587

VICTORIA — D3 *Carver*

↓ LAKE AUBURN CARVER PARK (Public) From Jct of SR-7 & Carver CR-11, S 2 mi on Carver CR-11, follow signs (R). Pit toilets. 2015 rates: $15.44 to $18.71. Apr 24 to Oct 24. (763)694-1112

WABASHA — E4 *Wabasha*

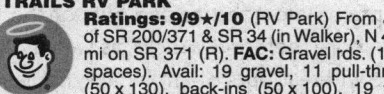

→ **BIG RIVER RESORT**
Ratings: 7/10★/9.5 (RV Park) From Jct of US-61 & SR-60, N 0.6 mi on SR-60 to Hiawatha Dr E, E 0.8 mi (R). **FAC:** Gravel rds. (28 spaces). Avail: 22 gravel, patios, 4 pull-thrus (40 x 60), back-ins (35 x 60), 22 full hkups (30/50 amps), seasonal sites, cable, WiFi, rentals, laundry, fire rings, firewood. Pets OK. No tents. Big rig sites, 2015 rates: $39.50. Apr 15 to Oct 15.
(651)565-9932 Lat: 44.37442, Lon: -92.02294
1110 Hiawatha Drive East, Wabasha, MN 55981
info@bigriverresort.com
www.bigriverresort.com
See ad this page, 644.

WADENA — C2 *Wadena*

↗ SUNNYBROOK PARK & CAMPGROUND (Public) From Jct of US-71 & US-10, E 0.9 mi on US-10 to Harry Rich Dr, N 0.1 mi (R). 2015 rates: $15 to $30. May 1 to Oct 1. (218)631-7711

WALKER — C2 *Cass*

↑ **TRAILS RV PARK**
Ratings: 9/9★/10 (RV Park) From Jct of SR 200/371 & SR 34 (in Walker), N 4.1 mi on SR 371 (R). **FAC:** Gravel rds. (106 spaces). Avail: 19 gravel, 11 pull-thrus (50 x 130), back-ins (50 x 100), 19 full hkups (30/50 amps), seasonal sites, WiFi, laundry, fire rings, firewood. **REC:** heated pool, playground. Pets OK $. Partial handicap access, no tents. Big rig sites, RV age restrict, eco-friendly, 2015 rates: $44 to $49. May 1 to Oct 15.
(218)547-1138 Lat: 47.14456, Lon: -94.63233
9424 State 371 NW, Walker, MN 56484
trailsrvpark@gmail.com
www.trailsrvpark.com
See ad this page, 644.

WANNASKA — A2 *Roseau*

↘ HAYES LAKE (State Pk) From town, S 15 mi on Hwy 89 to CR-4, E 9 mi, follow signs (E). Reservation fee. Note: 40' RV length maximum. 2015 rates: $16 to $20. (218)425-7504

WARROAD — A2 *Roseau*

→ WARROAD CITY CAMPGROUND (Public) From Jct of SR-11 & Lake St, E 1 mi on Lake St (L). 2015 rates: $25 to $35. May 3 to Oct 12. (218)386-1004

WASECA — E3 *Waseca*

→ KIESLER'S CAMPGROUND AND RV RESORT **Ratings: 8.5/10★/9** (Campground) 2015 rates: $48 to $71. Apr 24 to Oct 4. (507)835-3179 14360 Old Hwy 14, Waseca, MN 56093

WASKISH — B2 *Beltrami*

↗ BIG BOG/WASKISH CAMPGROUND (State Pk) From Jct of CR-40 & Hwy 72, S 0.1 mi on Hwy 72 (L). 2015 rates: $12. (218)647-8592

WATERVILLE — E3 *Le Sueur*

↗ KAMP DELS **Ratings: 9.5/9.5★/9.5** (Campground) 2015 rates: $35 to $70.50. Apr 20 to Oct 10. (507)362-8616 14842 Sakatah Lake Rd, Waterville, MN 56096

→ SAKATAH LAKE (State Pk) From Jct of SR-13 & SR-60, E 1 mi on SR-60, follow signs (L). Vehicle permit & reservation fee required. 2015 rates: $15 to $23. (507)362-4438

WELLS — E3 *Faribault*

↓ FARIBAULT COUNTY/PIHLS PARK (Public) From Jct of I-90 & Hwy 22 (exit 138), S 1 mi on Hwy 22 (R). 2015 rates: $20. May 1 to Oct 1. (507)553-5864

WILLMAR — D2 *Kandiyohi*

← SIBLEY (State Pk) From town, W 5 mi on Hwy 9 to US-71, S 1 mi (R). Entrance fee & reservation fee required. 2015 rates: $15 to $23. (320)354-2055

WILLOW RIVER — C3 *Pine*

→ GENERAL C.C. ANDREWS STATE FOREST (WILLOW RIVER CAMPGROUND) (State Pk) E on North St to Int-35 service road. Pit toilets. 2015 rates: $14. (320)245-2668

WINONA — E4 *Winona*

↑ PRAIRIE ISLAND CAMPGROUND (Public) From Jct of US-61 & Pelzer St, NE 1.5 mi on Pelzer St to Prairie Island Rd, E 1 mi (R). 2015 rates: $20 to $25. May 1 to Oct 1. (507)452-4501

WORTHINGTON — F2 *Nobles*

↖ OLSON PARK & CAMPGROUND (Public) From Jct of I-90 & Hwy 60, W 4.9 mi on Hwy 60 to CR-10, N 1 mi, follow signs (L). 2015 rates: $18 to $26. Apr 1 to Oct 31. (507)329-0760

WYKOFF — E4 *Fillmore*

↘ FORESTVILLE-MYSTERY CAVE (State Pk) From Jct of MN-16 & CR-5, S 4 mi on CR-5 to CR-118, E 2 mi, follow signs (R). Entrance fee & reservation fee required. Note: 50' RV length maximum. 2015 rates: $29. (507)352-5111

ZIMMERMAN — D3 *Sherburne*

← SAND DUNES SF/ANN LAKE CAMPGROUND (State Pk) From Jct of US-169 & CR-4, W 6 mi on CR-4 to 168 St, S 1.5 mi, follow signs (L). Pit toilets. 2015 rates: $14. (763)878-2325

ZUMBROTA — E4 *Goodhue*

↖ SHADES OF SHERWOOD CAMPGROUND **Ratings: 7/7.5/7.5** (Campground) 2015 rates: $29 to $53. Apr 23 to Oct 15. (507)732-5100 14334 Sherwood Trail, Zumbrota, MN 55992

↑ ZUMBROTA COVERED BRIDGE PARK (Public) From Jct of Hwys 52 & 58, N 1 mi on Hwy 58 (L). 2015 rates: $20. May 15 to Nov 1. (507)732-7318

Find it fast! To locate a town on a map, follow these easy instructions: Look for the map grid code after the town heading in the listing section and match it to the letters and numbers on the map borders. Draw a line horizontally from the letter and vertically from the number. You'll find the town near the intersection of the two lines.

How can you tell whether you're traveling in the right direction? The arrow in each listing denotes the compass direction of the facility in relation to the listed town. For example, an arrow pointing straight up indicates that the facility is located due north from town. An arrow pointing down and to the right indicates that the facility is southeast of town.

How much will it all cost? Use this as a guide: Rates shown are the minimum and maximum for two adults in one RV at the time of inspection (excluding any additional fees for items not at the site). Remember, these rates serve as guidelines only. It's always best to call ahead for the most current rate information.

MN

Getty Images/iStockphoto

WELCOME TO
Mississippi

DATE OF STATEHOOD	WIDTH: 188 MILES (303 KM)	PROPORTION OF UNITED STATES
DEC. 10, 1817	LENGTH: 352 MILES (566 KM)	1.28% OF 3,794,100 SQ MI

Mississippi is the birthplace of the blues, Elvis Presley and Oprah Winfrey. It is also where the teddy bear was born in 1902, when President Theodore Roosevelt decided to spare the life of a hapless bear during a hunting trip. The first lung transplant took place in Mississippi, and the USA International Ballet Competition attracts the world's best young dancers to the Magnolia State every four years. Mississippi just may not be what you may think it is.

Mississippi's 119 public lakes and 123,000 miles of stream support 175 species of game fish. The world-record white crappie, a 5-pound 3-ouncer, was hauled from Enid Reservoir, which hosts several tournaments. Paddlers can test the Mississippi River, which forms much of the state's western border.

On the Gulf of Mexico, charter captains know the ins and outs of the offshore reefs and wrecks, as well as the whereabouts of amberjack, cobia and red snapper. Places like Biloxi serve up some of the best seafood dishes in the United States.

In Natchez, wealthy cotton planters erected stately antebellum mansions on the bluffs above the Mississippi. The doors to these homes open for one month during the Natchez Spring Pilgrimage. In Vicksburg, Civil War history is preserved.

Check out an Ole Miss football game in the town of University, visit author William Faulkner's home in Oxford, rock with Elvis at his birthplace in Tupelo and walk the Blues Trail, which honors icons like Robert Johnson.

Top 3 Tourism Attractions:
1) Natchez Trace Parkway
2) Vicksburg National Military Park
3) Elvis Presley Birthplace

Nickname: Magnolia State

State Flower: Magnolia

State Bird: Mockingbird

People: Brett Favre, football quarterback; Jim Henson, puppeteer; James Earl Jones, actor; Elvis Presley, singer; Oprah Winfrey, talk-show host

Major Cities: Jackson (capital), Gulfport, Southaven, Hattiesburg, Biloxi

Topography: Low, fertile delta between Yazoo and Mississippi rivers. Sandy coastal terraces, piney woods, prairie; northeast—sandy hills

Climate: Mild and temperate climate, short winters and long, humid summers

TRAVEL & TOURISM

Mississippi Development Authority
866-SEE-MISS
www.visitmississippi.org

Columbus-Lowndes CVB
662-329-1191, 800-327-2686
www.columbus-ms.org

Jackson Convention and Visitors Bureau
601-960-1891, 800-354-7695
www.visitjackson.com

Mississippi Gulf Coast CVB
888-467-4853, 228-896-6699
www.gulfcoast.org

Mississippi Delta Tourism Association
800-626-3764
www.visitthedelta.com

Mississippi's West Coast-Hancock County Tourism Development Bureau
228-463-9222, 800-466-9048
www.mswestcoast.org

Natchez Convention and Visitors Bureau
601-446-6345, 800-647-6724
www.visitnatchez.org

Ocean Springs Chamber of Commerce
228-875-4424
www.oceanspringschamber.com

Tupelo Convention and Visitors Bureau
662-841-6521, 800-533-0611
www.tupelo.net

OUTDOOR RECREATION

Mississippi Outdoor Club
www.mscanoeclub.org

Fishing-Boating & Hunting
601-432-2400
www.mdwfp.com

Mississippi Golf Information
601-359-3297
www.visitmississippi.org/golftrip

Outdoor Recreation & Outfitters
866-733-6477
www.visitmississippi.org

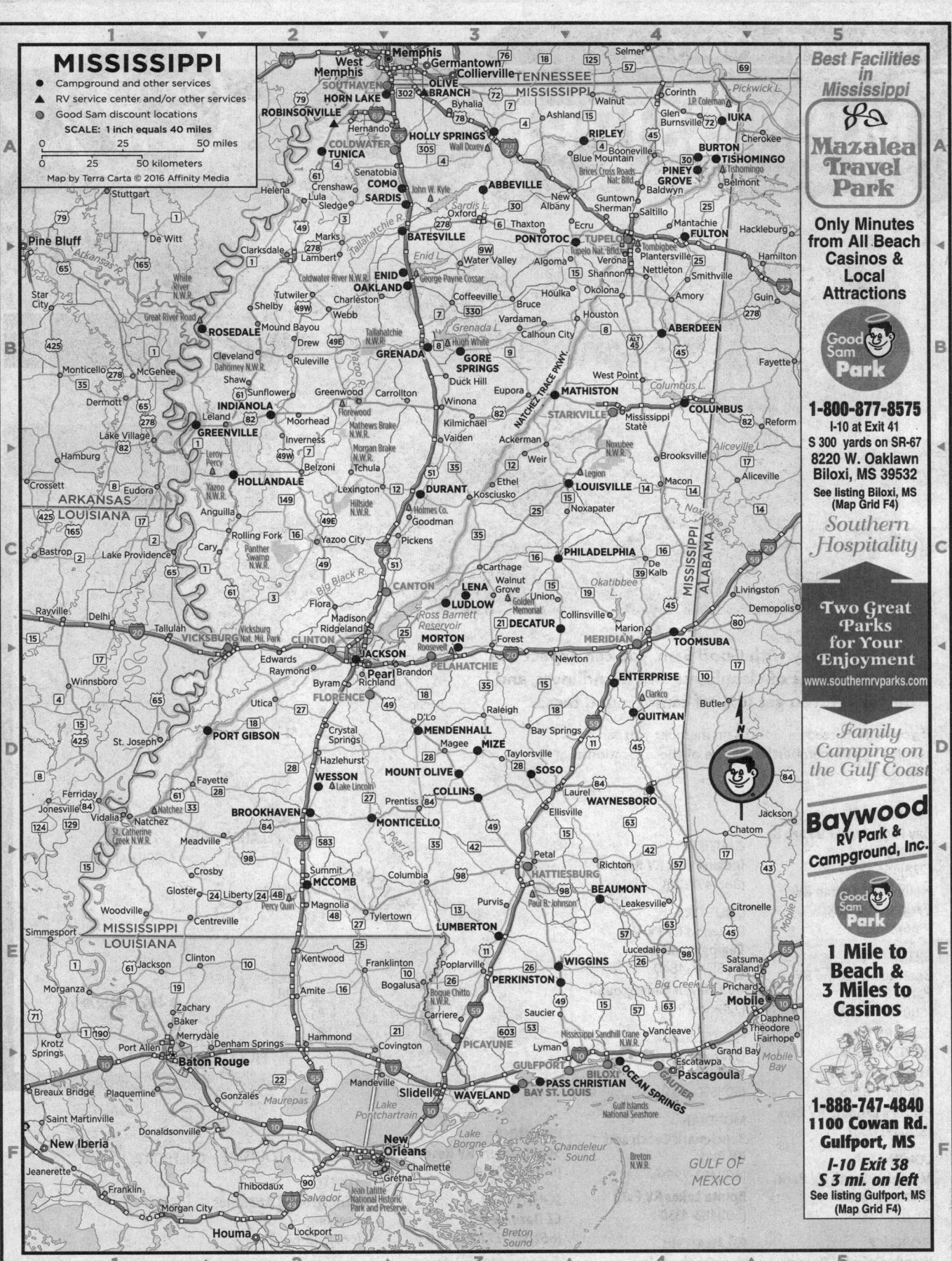

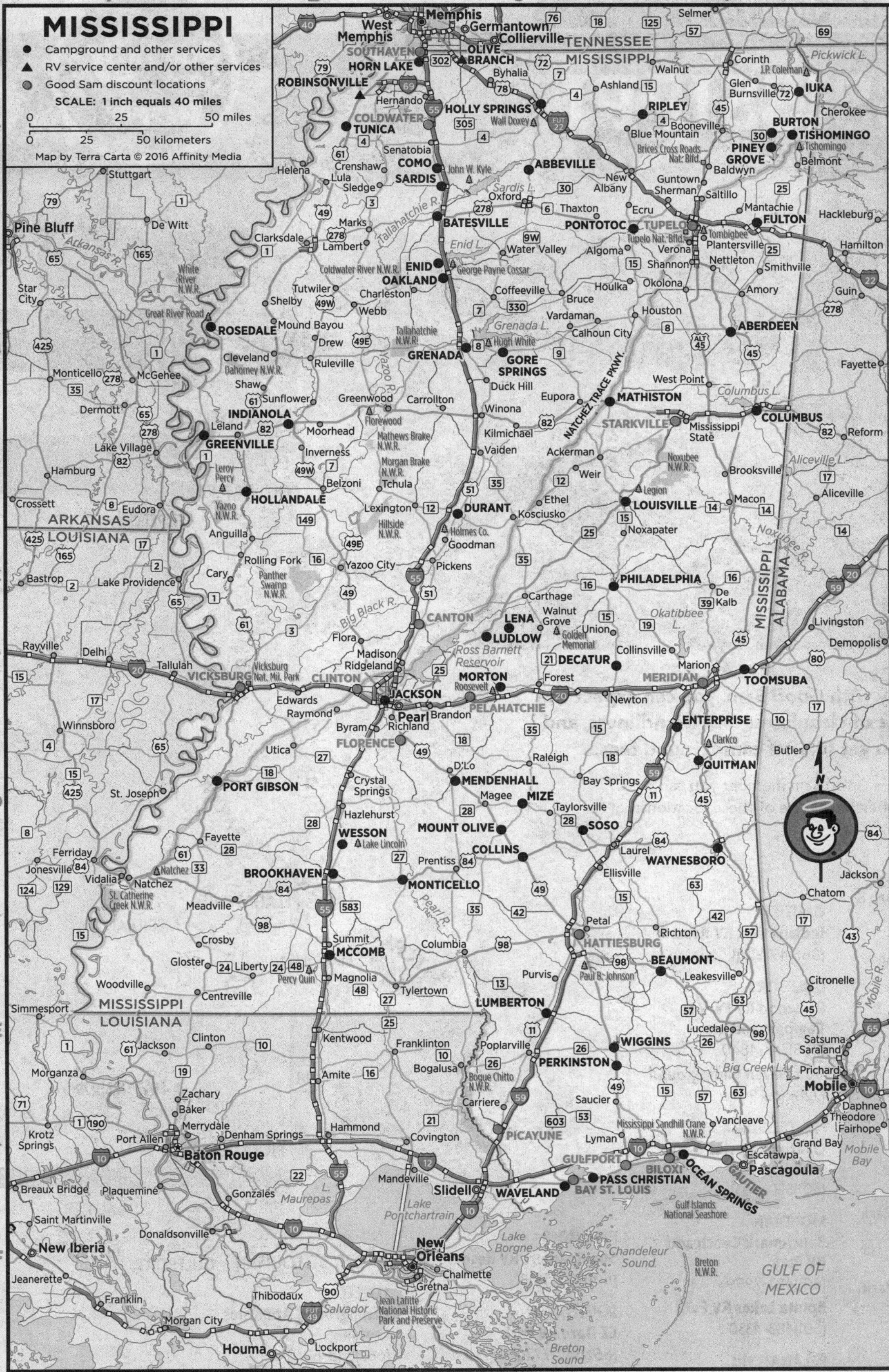
MISSISSIPPI
Campground and other services
RV service center and/or other services
Good Sam discount locations
SCALE: 1 inch equals 40 miles
0 25 50 miles
0 25 50 kilometers
Map by Terra Carta © 2016 Affinity Media
SOUTHAVEN
HORN LAKE
OLIVE BRANCH
ROBINSONVILLE
HOLLY SPRINGS
TUNICA
COLDWATER
RIPLEY
IUKA
BURTON
TISHOMINGO
PINEY GROVE
COMO
SARDIS
ABBEVILLE
BATESVILLE
PONTOTOC
TUPELO
FULTON
ENID
OAKLAND
ROSEDALE
ABERDEEN
GRENADA
GORE SPRINGS
MATHISTON
STARKVILLE
COLUMBUS
INDIANOLA
GREENVILLE
HOLLANDALE
DURANT
LOUISVILLE
PHILADELPHIA
CANTON
LENA
LUDLOW
DECATUR
VICKSBURG
CLINTON
JACKSON
MORTON
PELAHATCHIE
MERIDIAN
TOOMSUBA
ENTERPRISE
QUITMAN
FLORENCE
MENDENHALL
MIZE
SOSO
PORT GIBSON
WESSON
MOUNT OLIVE
COLLINS
WAYNESBORO
BROOKHAVEN
MONTICELLO
HATTIESBURG
BEAUMONT
MCCOMB
LUMBERTON
WIGGINS
PERKINSTON
PICAYUNE
GULFPORT
BILOXI
OCEAN SPRINGS
GAUTIER
PASS CHRISTIAN
BAY ST. LOUIS
WAVELAND
TENNESSEE
ARKANSAS
LOUISIANA
ALABAMA
GULF OF MEXICO

Featured Good Sam Parks

MISSISSIPPI

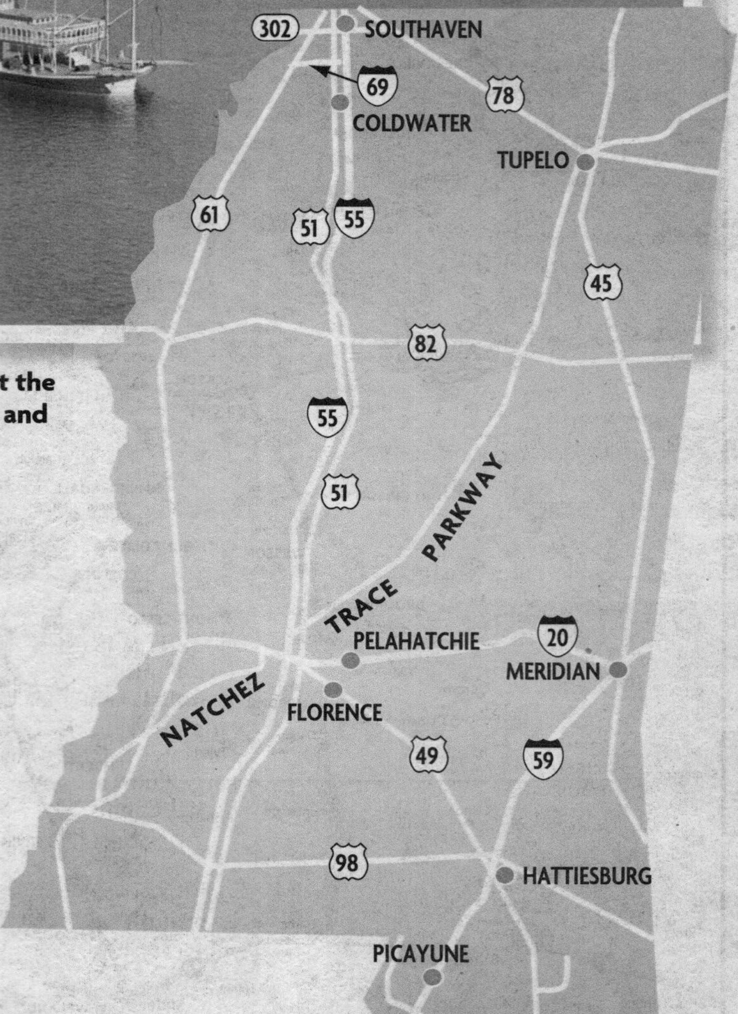

When you stay with Good Sam, you can expect the highest degree of cleanliness and friendliness, and better yet, you get 10% off campground fees.

If you're not already a Good Sam member you can purchase your membership at one of these locations:

BAY ST LOUIS
Bay Hide Away RV Park & Campground
(228)466-0959
Hollywood Casino RV Park- Gulf Coast
(866)758-2591

BILOXI
Boomtown Casino RV Park
(800)627-0777
Cajun RV Park
(877)225-8699
Mazalea Travel Park
(800)877-8575
Parker's Landing RV Park
(228)392-7717

COLDWATER
Memphis-South RV Park & Campground
(662)622-0056

FLORENCE
Wendy Oaks RV Resort
(601)845-CAMP

GAUTIER
Indian Point RV Resort
(866)497-1011

GULFPORT
Baywood RV Park & Campground Inc
(888)747-4840
Gulf Haven Campground
(228)863-9096

HATTIESBURG
Okatoma Resort & RV Park
(601)520-6631

MERIDIAN
Benchmark Coach and RV Park
(601)483-7999
Bonita Lakes RV Park
(601)483-4330

PELAHATCHIE
Yogi On the Lake
(601)854-6621

PICAYUNE
Sun Roamers RV Resort
(601)798-5818

SOUTHAVEN
EZ Daze RV Park
(662)342-7720

TUPELO
Campground At Barnes Crossing
(662)844-6063

For more Good Sam Parks go to listing pages

Visit Mississippi

GULF COAST

The Magnolia State makes the most out of its small strip of coast

Spanning 62 miles of gorgeous waterfront, Mississippi's balmy southern shoreline sits in the backyard of New Orleans and on the doorstep of the Gulf of Mexico. Sparkling views, fantastic beaches and a smorgasbord of charming seaside towns make it a popular destination for anyone looking for a place to rest, relax and have a little fun in the sun.

Moving from east to west through the counties of Jackson, Harrison and Hancock, visitors can effortlessly hop their way though the towns of Moss Point, Pascagoula, Gautier, Ocean Springs, D'Iberville, Biloxi, Gulfport, Long Beach, Pass Christian, Diamondhead, Bay St. Louis and Waveland. If you're a window-shopper or someone who likes to sit on a cafe patio, people-watching and taking in the sights, the Mississippi Gulf Coast is for you.

> The region changed national flags countless times between the establishment of the earliest French colony in 1698 and the end of the American Civil War in 1865.

The beaches are the undisputed main attractions here, tying together a region that's renowned for recreation. Dusted with soft white sand and protected by chains of barrier islands offshore, the surf is relatively gentle and perfect for families with small children. The beaches of Pass Christian and Long Beach are particularly popular for those seeking calmer waters.

Surfers on the hunt for livelier waters will want to hop on the passenger ferry in Gulfport to West Ship Island, where a 12-mile long beach offers bigger waves more suited to water sports. The beach here has been frequently cited as among the best in the country, and the scenic ferry ride often includes spontaneous dolphin sightings—free of charge.

This being the Gulf Coast, anglers will think they've gone to heaven. More

A golden eagle crowns Jackson's ornate capitol building.
Visit Mississippi

MS

Long Beach's 500-year-old Friendship Oak survived Hurricane Katrina. Visit Mississippi

than 200 different species of fish are found in abundance here, including bass, catfish, perch, drum and shark. All manner of fishing is available, from freshwater to saltwater to pier fishing to wade fishing.

> Biloxi is home to eight world-class casino resorts that combine gaming with a variety of other visitor perks, such as championship golfing, spa packages and more.

Gulf Coast's Historic Gumbo

After you've arrived and spent some time here on the Mississippi Gulf Coast, you'll begin to discover the region's rich diversity of culture, which is no doubt due to its long and eventful history. Originally inhabited by the Biloxi Indians, colonial-era expansion and exploration turned the entire coastline into a giant game of political chairs for the better part of 150 years.

The region changed national flags countless times between the establishment of the earliest French colony in 1698 and the end of the American Civil War in 1865. In fact, if you were born here in the latter half of the 18th century and lived to see the end of the Civil War, you would have found yourself living under the rule of six different national flags: British, Spanish, French, American, Confed-

MS

erate and the Republic of Florida (which lasted for all of 74 days).

Much of this incredible history can be explored at the Museum of History in downtown Ocean Springs. Known as the "City of Discovery," Ocean Springs was the site of the first permanent settlement on the Mississippi Gulf Coast, making it a natural place for a museum that curates the history of the region.

For a more hands-on glimpse into the history of the coast, the Old Spanish Fort in Pascagoula (built in 1718) and Fort Massachusetts on West Ship Island are absolute must-visits. Construction on the latter began just before the outbreak of the Civil War and changed hands several times—even while unfinished—prior to the war's end. Park Rangers lead narrated tours through the defensive fort, highlighting its sturdy craftsmanship and telling tales of its volatile military history.

Wild Waters

Today the games of political brinkmanship are long gone, and the most volatile aspect of life on the Mississippi Gulf Coast is the occasional gulf storm or hurricane—a concern that's not to be taken lightly. The devastation wrought by Hurricane Katrina in 2005 can still be felt here, especially in the town of Biloxi, where the Biloxi Bay Bridge was completely washed away.

The bridge has since been rebuilt but many places along the coast are still in recovery. The Hurricane Katrina Memorial in downtown Biloxi stands as a strong reminder of the loss of life and widespread devastation. The memorial consists of a 12-foot-tall black granite slab (symbolizing the height of the storm surge) amid personal art from Katrina victims.

Historic Biloxi Lighthouse. Visit Mississippi

When you're ready for a little fun that doesn't involve sand or surf, Biloxi is home to eight world-class casino resorts that combine gaming with a variety of other visitor perks, such as championship golfing, spa packages, live entertainment and play centers for kids.

For More Information

Mississippi Gulf Coast Regional Convention & Visitors Bureau
228-896-6699
www.gulfcoast.org

Mississippi Development Authority
866-733-6477
www.visitmississippi.org

MISSISSIPPI RIVER DESTINATIONS

Follow America's most storied waterway on this fantastic trip

The Mississippi River is as storied as it is iconic, occupying a central role in the heart, history and culture of the Magnolia State. Since the state's earliest days of discovery and settlement the river has served as an integral mode of transportation and agricultural irrigation, fueling the growth of communities up and down its twisting, winding shores.

Today, a trip along the course of the Mississippi—even if done by RV—is akin to a trip back in time. When European explorers mapped the mouth of the river in the 16th century, considering it of vital strategic importance, they had no way of knowing they were anchored on the shores of a river so vast that it stretched another 2,320 miles further inland, or that it drained water from more than half the continent.

Each of the small towns and unincorporated communities that now either hug the water's edge or find themselves within a stone's throw of it are there because of the Mississippi, and one such stretch of the river is particularly compelling.

Mississippi's Memphis

Beginning in South Memphis, on the Mississippi side of the city, a trip south via U.S. Route 61 to the sister towns of Vidalia and Natchez makes for a scenic journey full of small-town charm, major American history and family-fun attractions. Along the way, the towns of Tunica, Clarksdale, Cleveland, Greenville and Vicksburg offer lots of opportunities to get out and stretch your legs, do some window-shopping and savor some mouthwatering southern cooking.

In Tunica, make your way straight for the Visitors Center. It's not only the best place to find information on local sights and events, but it's also the home of the Gateway to the Blues Museum. The town itself is a popular stop along the Mississippi Blues Trail and the museum's offbeat collections reflect that.

> Vicksburg is best known in history as being the site of a vicious 47-day siege at the height of the Civil War.

After exploring the history of the blues, the Tunica RiverPark is the town's next best gathering point. Home to a range of nature trails and picnic areas, the RiverPark also features sunset riverboat cruises and a scenic river-viewing platform. It's also the home of the Mississippi River Museum, which gives guests the chance to follow in the footsteps of early explorers and take a peek at life on the bottom of the riverbed by way of four large freshwater aquariums.

After moving through Clarksdale, Cleveland and Greenville from Tunica, you'll arrive in the scenic town of Vicksburg. Perched high on a bluff overlooking a sharp eastward bend in the Mississippi, Vicksburg is best known in history as being the site of a vicious 47-day siege at the height of the Civil War. Visitors can explore the battle and its aftermath at Vicksburg National Military Park, a site that still bears the original fortifications of the outpost as well as the remains of an ironclad gunboat.

MS

Tunica's Visitor Center pays homage to the area's music legacy. Visit Mississippi

Illinois Monument at the Vicksburg Military Park.
Visit Mississippi

For more lighthearted fare, head to the Biedenharn Coca-Cola Museum (where the very first bottle of Coca-Cola was bottled) or to one of the town's four world-class casinos. Guided walking tours that highlight Vicksburg's dazzling collection of authentic antebellum homes are also a popular activity for first-time visitors.

If you're visiting in September you'll find yourself in the midst of the Jim Bowie Festival, an annual event held to commemorate Bowie's infamous riverside fight.

Superlative Sister Cities

At the tail end of your trip south along the winding shores of the mighty Mississippi you'll find yourself in Natchez, which sits directly across the water from Vidalia. These idyllic sister cities are the epitome of quaint southern charm. Each town is infused with hints and notes from of a variety of cultures—French, British, African, Native American—that stems from hundreds of years of settlement here by explorers and visitors from around the globe.

In Vidalia make a trip to the Riverwalk for a chance to watch an endless stream of historic riverboats steaming to and fro. Sign yourself up for an historic walking tour and learn how in 1938 the entire city lifted up and moved a mile inland as part of an unprecedented river-widening project. If you're visiting in September you'll find yourself in the midst of the Jim Bowie Festival, an annual event commemorating Bowie's infamous riverside gun-slinging fight.

According to local history, Bowie, a renowned pioneer and soldier, was involved in an alcohol-fueled brawl with several locals. Bowie was shot twice and stabbed several times, but he successfully defended himself with the long, curved knife that would later bear his name. Bowie's legend would be cemented when he died in the Battle of the Alamo in Texas. His noteriety would spread as far as England, and in 1960s London, an aspiring rock star named David Jones adopted the name to win wider appeal among the masses. Performer David Bowie went on to be a groundbreaking pop icon with hits like "Fame" and "Let's Dance."

Across the water in Natchez, history buffs will gravitate to the Natchez National Historical Park and the Grand Village of the Natchez Indians. The former tells the history of European settlement and expansion in the region, while the latter tells the history of region's original inhabitants, the Natchez Indians.

Likewise, the Natchez Trails are a hit with most visitors. Not exactly hiking trails in the traditional sense, the Natchez Trails weave through the town's historic downtown core and along a bluff overlooking the river. Interpretive signs can found along the way, shedding light on the history of the town and its significant structures. Two distinct trails—a nature trail and city trail—lead to new discoveries.

For More Information

Mississippi Development Authority
866-733-6477
www.visitmississippi.org

Mississippi

CONSULTANTS

Fain & Lynda Little

ABBEVILLE — A3 *Lafayette*

SARDIS LAKE/HURRICANE LANDING (Public Corps) 7 mi W off State Rte 7, on park access rd (E). 2015 rates: $18. (662)563-4531

ABERDEEN — B4 *Monroe*

BLUE BLUFF REC AREA (Public Corps) From Jct of Hwy 45 & Meridian St (in town), N 2 mi on Meridian St (R). 2015 rates: $16 to $18. (662)369-2832

MORGAN'S LANDING PARK (Public) From jct MS 8 & MS 25 & US 45: Go 1-1/2 mi E on US 45 then 1/2 mi S on Darracot Access Rd, then 1 mi E on Sharpley Bottom Rd. (662)369-7805

BATESVILLE — A3 *Panola*

BATESVILLE CIVIC CENTER (Public) From Jct I-55 & exit 243 (US 278/Hwy6), Go E 0.6 mi to Medical Center Dr., then S 0.2 mi (L) (continue to S end of property. Turn right between buildings). **FAC:** Paved rds. 20 paved, patios, back-ins (25 x 55), 20 full hkups (30/50 amps), WiFi. **REC.** Pets OK. 2015 rates: $30. No CC.
(662)563-1392 Lat: 34.30722, Lon: -089.90955
290 Civic Center Drive, Batesville, MS 38606
info@batesvilleciviccenter-ms.com
www.batesvilleciviccenter-ms.com
See ad this page.

BAY ST LOUIS — F3 *Hancock*

A SPOTLIGHT A spotlight introducing the Gulf Coast's colorful attractions appearing at the front of this state section.

BAY ST LOUIS See also Biloxi, Gautier, Gulfport, Lumberton, Perkinston & Picayune.

BAY HIDE AWAY RV PARK & CAMPGROUND
Ratings: 9/9.5★/10 (Campground) E-bnd: From Jct of I-10 (exit 2 Welcome Center) & Hwy 607/US-90, SE 8.6 mi on Hwy 607/US-90 to Lakeshore Rd, S 0.5 mi (L); or W-bnd: From Jct of I-10 (exit 13) & Hwys 43/603, S 5.2 mi on Hwys 43/603 to US-90, W 4.7 mi to Lakeshore Rd, S 0.5 mi (L). **FAC:** Gravel rds. 40 gravel, 23 pull-thrus (30 x 65), back-ins (30 x 65), 40 full hkups (30/50 amps), WiFi, laundry, fire rings, firewood. **REC:** pool, pond, fishing, playground. Pet restrict(B). No tents. Big rig sites, eco-friendly, 2015 rates: $25 to $50. Disc: military.
(228)466-0959 Lat: 30.29210, Lon: -089.45656
8360 Lakeshore Rd, Bay St Louis, MS 39520
bayhideawayrv@gmail.com
www.bayhideaway.com
See ad pages 562, 660 & Snowbird Destinations Magazine Section.

BAY ST LOUIS RV PARK (RV Park) (Not Visited) From Jct of I-10 & SR 603, Go South 5 miles on SR 603 to SR 90, then East 1.6 mi (R). **FAC:** Gravel rds. 70 grass, 20 pull-thrus (20 x 60), back-ins (28 x 40), 70 full hkups (30/50 amps), WiFi, tent sites, rentals, laundry, LP gas. **REC.** Pets OK. Partial handicap access. 2015 rates: $34.95 to $41.95. No CC.
(228)467-2080 Lat: 30.30881, Lon: -89.33005
814 Hwy 90, Bay St Louis, MS 39520
See ad this page.

HOLLYWOOD CASINO RV PARK- GULF COAST
Ratings: 10/10★/9.5 (RV Park) E-Bnd: From Jct of I-10 & SR-607 (exit 2), SE 7 mi on SR-607 to US-90, E 9 mi to Blue Meadow Rd, N 0.6 mi to Hollywood Blvd, E 1.3 mi (E); or W-Bnd: From Jct of I-10 & SR-603 (exit 13), SE 5.2 mi on SR-603 to US-90, E 3.5 mi to Blue Meadow Rd, N 0.6 mi to Hollywood Blvd, E 1.3 mi (E). **FAC:** Paved rds. 100 paved, patios, 6 pull-thrus (25 x 45), back-ins (30 x 60), 100 full hkups (30/50 amps), cable, WiFi, laundry, restaurant. **REC:** pool, whirlpool, Jourdan River: marina, golf, rec open to public. Pets OK. Partial handicap access, no tents. Big rig sites, eco-friendly, 2015 rates: $35 to $45. ATM.
(866)758-2591 Lat: 30.33264, Lon: -89.35424
711 Hollywood Blvd., Bay St Louis, MS 39520
www.hollywoodcasinogulfcoast.com
See ad pages 663 (Spotlight Gulf Coast), 660.

MCLEOD WATER PARK (Public) From town: Go 10 mi N on Hwy 603, then turn W on Texas Flatt Rd. (228)467-1894

Things to See and Do

HOLLYWOOD CASINO-GULF COAST Full service casino (min age 21 yrs). Lazy River, pool, hot tub, spa, 4 restaurants, hotel and meeting rooms, gaming and buffet. Partial handicap access. RV accessible. Restrooms, food. Hours: 24hrs. ATM.
(866)758-2591 Lat: 30.33311, Lon: -89.35583
711 Hollywood Blvd., Bay St Louis, MS 39520
www.hollywoodcasinobsl.com
See ad page 663 (Spotlight Gulf Coast).

THE BRIDGES GOLF COURSE AT HOLLYWOOD CASINO An Arnold Palmer course. Par 72. Hollywood Casino & Good Sam RV Park on site. RV accessible. Restrooms, food. Hours: 7am to 9pm. Adult fee: $62 to $99. ATM.
(866)758-2591 Lat: 30.33260, Lon: -89.35420
711 Hollywood Blvd., Bay St Louis, MS 39520
www.hollywoodcasinobsl.com
See ad page 663 (Spotlight Gulf Coast).

BEAUMONT — E4 *Perry*

LAKE PERRY (State Pk) From town, S 3 mi on FS-314/Lake Perry Rd, E 0.8 mi (R). 2015 rates: $15. (601)928-3720

BILOXI — F4 *Harrison, Jackson*

A SPOTLIGHT A spotlight introducing the Gulf Coast's colorful attractions appearing at the front of this state section.

BILOXI See also Bay St. Louis, Gautier, Gulfport, Lumberton, Perkinston & Picayune.

BOOMTOWN CASINO RV PARK
Ratings: 7/NA/7 (RV Park) From Jct of I-10 & I-110, Go South on I-110 to Bayview Ave, E 0.5 mi (R). **FAC:** Paved rds. 50 paved, 2 pull-thrus (24 x 70), back-ins (24 x 45), accepts full hkup units only, 50 full hkups (30/50 amps), cable, WiFi, restaurant. **REC:** rec open to public. Pets OK. Partial handicap access. Big rig sites, 2015 rates: $39 to $45. ATM, no CC.
(800)627-0777 Lat: 30.41074, Lon: -88.88664
676 Bayview Ave., Biloxi, MS 39530
www.boomtownbiloxi.com
See ad pages 663 (Spotlight Gulf Coast), 660.

Average site width and length are indicated in many campground listings to give you an idea of how much room and privacy you can expect.

CAJUN RV PARK
Ratings: 9/10★/8.5 (RV Park) From Jct of I-10 & I-110 (Exit 46A), S 5.4 mi on I-110 to Hwy 90W (Beach Blvd), W 3.3 mi on US-90 (R).

EXPLORE. PLAY. RELAX. IN BILOXI
Come enjoy our spacious sites, friendly staff and beautiful park. Across from the beach. Complimentary casino shuttle, excellent WIFI access. 1-877-225-8699 www.cajunrvpark.com

FAC: All weather rds. (130 spaces). 100 Avail: 60 gravel, 40 grass, 50 pull-thrus (24 x 60), back-ins (36 x 60), 100 full hkups (30/50 amps), seasonal sites, cable, WiFi, laundry, LP gas. **REC:** pool, playground. Pet restrict(B). Partial handicap access, no tents. Big rig sites, eco-friendly, 2015 rates: $39 to $52. Disc: AAA, military.
AAA Approved
(877)225-8699 Lat: 30.39553, Lon: -88.94861
1860 Beach Blvd., Biloxi, MS 39531
cajunrvpark@gmail.com
www.cajunrvpark.com
See ad pages 662 (Spotlight Gulf Coast), 660 & RV Trips of a Lifetime in Magazine Section.

FOX'S RV PARK & APTS **Ratings: 4.5/4.5/3** (RV Park) 2015 rates: $40. (228)388-2149 190 B Beauvoir Rd, Biloxi, MS 39531

MAJESTIC OAKS RV RESORT **Ratings: 9/9.5★/9.5** (RV Park) 2015 rates: $38.50 to $44. (228)436-4200 1750 Pass Rd, Biloxi, MS 39531

MARTIN LAKE RESORT **Ratings: 8/7.5/6** (Membership Pk) 2015 rates: $34 to $38. (228)875-9157 14605 Parker Rd, Biloxi, MS 39532

MAZALEA TRAVEL PARK
Ratings: 7.5/8/8 (RV Park) From Jct of I-10 & SR-67 (exit 41), S 0.3 mi on SR-67 (R). **FAC:** Paved rds. (144 spaces). Avail: 124 paved, patios, 40 pull-thrus (25 x 80), back-ins (25 x 45), 124 full hkups (30/50 amps), cable, WiFi $, dump, laundry, groc, LP gas. **REC:** playground. Pet restrict(B/Q). No tents. 2015 rates: $28 to $32.
(800)877-8575 Lat: 30.45786, Lon: -88.97319
8220 W Oaklawn Rd., Biloxi, MS 39532
wmsentr@aol.com
www.southernrvparks.com
See ad pages 664 (Spotlight Gulf Coast), 660, 659 (MS Map).

OAKLAWN RV PARK **Ratings: 6.5/9★/7.5** (RV Park) 2015 rates: $30 to $32. (228)392-1233 8400 W Oaklawn Rd #37, Biloxi, MS 39532

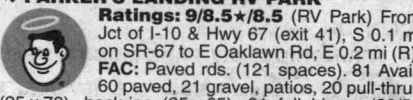

PARKER'S LANDING RV PARK
Ratings: 9/8.5★/8.5 (RV Park) From Jct of I-10 & Hwy 67 (exit 41), S 0.1 mi on SR-67 to E Oaklawn Rd, E 0.2 mi (R). **FAC:** Paved rds. (121 spaces). 81 Avail: 60 paved, 21 gravel, patios, 20 pull-thrus (25 x 70), back-ins (25 x 65), 81 full hkups (30/50 amps), seasonal sites, cable, WiFi, tent sites, rentals, dump, laundry, LP gas, firewood. **REC:** pool, Parker's Creek: fishing. Pet restrict(B). 2015 rates: $32.40 to $46.
(228)392-7717 Lat: 30.45820, Lon: -88.96755
7577 E Oaklawn Rd, Biloxi, MS 39532
parkers_landing@yahoo.com
www.parkerslandingpark.com
See ad this page, 660.

SOUTHERN COMFORT CAMPING RESORT **Ratings: 8/7.5/6** (RV Park) 2015 rates: $40 to 48. (228)432-1700 1766 Beach Blvd, Biloxi, MS 39531

We rate what RVers consider important.

BILOXI (CONT)

Things to See and Do

DOGWOOD HILLS GOLF CLUB Challenging 18 hole golf course with a full-service grill and fully equipped pro shop and practice range. Restrooms, food. Hours: Dawn to dusk. Adult fee: $27 to $32.
(228)392-9805 Lat: 30.55172, Lon: -89.01113
17476 Dogwood Hills Dr, Biloxi, MS 39532
info@dogwoodhillsgolfclub.com
www.dogwoodhillsgolfclub.com
See ad page 664 (Spotlight Gulf Coast).

BROOKHAVEN — D2 *Lincoln*

LINCOLN CIVIC CENTER RV PARK (Public) From jct I-55 (exit 42): Go 1/2 mi SE on Union St Extended NE, then 3-1/4 mi E on W Industrial Park Rd NE. **FAC:** Paved rds. 39 paved, 5 pull-thrus (25 x 60), back-ins (25 x 60), 39 full hkups (30/50 amps), WiFi, dump. **REC:** rec open to public. Pets OK. Partial handicap access, no tents. Big rig sites, 2015 rates: $25. No CC.
(601)823-9064 Lat: 31.59889, Lon: -90.40907
1096 Belt Line Dr NE, Brookhaven, MS 39601
qjordan@co.lincoln.ms.us
www.lincolnciviccenter.com
See ad this page.

BURTON — A4 *Prentiss*

PINEY GROVE (Public Corps) From Jct of Hwy 4 & Hwy 30 E (in town), E 11 mi on Hwy 30 E to CR-3501 (in Burton), S 3 mi, follow signs. 2015 rates: $18 to $20. Mar 1 to Nov 15. (662)728-1134

CANTON — C3 *Madison*

MOVIETOWN RV PARK
Ratings: 7/9★/8 (RV Park) From Jct of I-55 & SR-22 (exit 119), W 0.5 mi on SR-22 to Virlilia Rd, N 0.4 mi (R). **FAC:** Paved/gravel rds. (114 spaces). Avail: 67 gravel, 50 pull-thrus (45 x 65), back-ins (35 x 40), 67 full hkups (30/50 amps), WiFi, tent sites, rentals, laundry. **REC:** playground. Pets OK. Big rig sites, eco-friendly, 2015 rates: $26. Disc: AAA, military.
AAA Approved
(601)859-7990 Lat: 32.60736, Lon: -090.08420
109 Movietown Dr., Canton, MS 39046
info@movietownrv.com
www.movietownrv.com
See ad page 671.

RV PARK AT THE MULTIPURPOSE COMPLEX (Public) From Jct of I 55 & SR 22 (exit 119), W 0.5 mi on SR 22 to Watford Pkwy, S 0.6 mi (L). Self-contained units only. 2015 rates: $15. (601)859-4830

CLINTON — C2 *Hinds*

SPRINGRIDGE RV PARK/MOBILE HOME ESTATES
Ratings: 7.5/9.5★/7.5 (RV Area in MHP) From Jct of I-20 & Springridge Rd (exit 36), S 0.4 mi on Springridge Rd (L). **FAC:** Paved rds. (92 spaces). Avail: 42 paved, 30 pull-thrus (20 x 55), back-ins (20 x 33), mostly side by side hkups, 42 full hkups (30/50 amps), WiFi, tent sites, laundry. **REC:** pool, playground. Pets OK. 2015 rates: $33. Disc: military.
(601)924-0947 Lat: 32.32169, Lon: -90.32380
499 Springridge Rd., Clinton, MS 39056
Springridgemhp@gmail.com
www.springridgervp.com
See ad page 671.

Our travel services section will help you find services that you'll find handy in your travels.

COLDWATER — A3 *Tate*

ARKABUTLA LAKE/DUB PATTON AREA (Public Corps) From town, W 9.5 mi on Rte 304 to cnty rd, NE 4 mi, follow signs (R). 2015 rates: $16 to $20. (662)562-6261

ARKABUTLA LAKE/HERNANDO POINT (Public Corps) From Jct of I-55 & Coldwater (exit 54), W 2 mi on exit rd to US-51, N to Wheeler Rd, W 6 mi (L). Reservations required. 2015 rates: $16 to $20. (662)562-6261

MEMPHIS-SOUTH RV PARK & CAMPGROUND
Ratings: 6.5/8.5★/6 (Campground) From Jct of I-55 & Hwy 306 (Exit 271), W 0.2 mi on Hwy 306 to Campground Dr (E). **FAC:** Gravel rds. (82 spaces). Avail: 47 gravel, 47 pull-thrus (40 x 60), 47 full hkups (30/50 amps), WiFi, tent sites, laundry, firewood. **REC:** pool, pond, fishing, playground, rec open to public. Pet restrict(B). Big rig sites, eco-friendly, 2015 rates: $34. Disc: AAA, military.
(662)622-0056 Lat: 34.69600, Lon: -89.96660
256 Campground Dr, Coldwater, MS 38618
memphissouthrv@aol.com
www.memphissouthrv.com
See ad pages 1089, 660.

SOUTH ABUTMENT CAMPGROUND (COE-ARKABUTLA LAKE) (Public Corps) From town: Go 10 mi W on Arkabutla Rd. Follow signs N to the dam. 2015 rates: $18 to $20. (662)562-6261

COLLINS — D3 *Covington*

LAKE MIKE CONNER (Public) From Jct of US-49 & US-84, W 0.3 mi on US-84 to Lake Mike Conner Rd, S 6 mi, NW 0.5 mi on Blackjack New Chapel Rd. 2015 rates: $15. (601)765-4024

COLUMBUS — B4 *Clay, Lowndes*

BROWN'S RV PARK
Ratings: 3.5/NA/5.5 (Campground) From Jct of US-82 & Military Rd (E of Downtown), SW 0.3 mi on Military Rd to traffic light, N 0.1 mi (R). **FAC:** Gravel rds. 23 gravel, 3 pull-thrus (18 x 45), back-ins (25 x 45), accepts self-contain units only, 22 full hkups, 1 W, 1 E (30/50 amps), dump, laundry. **REC.** Pets OK. No tents. 2015 rates: $15 to $18. No CC.
(662)328-1976 Lat: 33.51765, Lon: -88.41633
2002 Bluecutt Rd, Columbus, MS 39705
brownsrv@cableone.net
See ad this page.

LAKE LOWNDES (State Pk) From Jct of US 82 & Stokes Rd (Stokes/New Hope exit) (East of Town), S 0.4 mi on Stokes Rd to SR 182, W 2 mi to New Hope Rd, S 3.9 mi, E 1 mi (follow signs) (E). 2015 rates: $20 to $24. (662)328-2110

PARKWOOD RV PARK
Ratings: 4.5/NA/6.5 (Campground) From Jct of US-45/US-82/SR-12 & SR-182/Main St (West of downtown Columbus), NW 0.1 mi on Main St to Plymouth Rd, E 0.2 mi (E). **FAC:** Gravel rds. 30 gravel, 5 pull-thrus (25 x 65), back-ins (25 x 60), 30 full hkups (30/50 amps), WiFi, tent sites, dump, laundry. Pets OK. Big rig sites, 2015 rates: $25. No CC.
(662)386-3047 Lat: 33.50297, Lon: -88.43562
319 E. Plymouth Rd, Columbus, MS 39705
kdsparkwood@gmail.com
www.parkwoodrvpark.com
See ad this page.

TOMBIGBEE/DEWAYNE HAYES CAMPGROUND (Public Corps) From town, W 4 mi on US-45 to Hwy 373, W 1.5 mi to Stenson Creek Rd, NW 2 mi to Barton's Ferry Rd, W 0.5 mi (L). 2015 rates: $16 to $20. (662)434-6939

TOMBIGBEE/TOWN CREEK REC AREA (Public Corps) From Jct of US-45 & US-50, W 6 mi on US-50 to Witherspoon Rd, N 0.25 mi (E). 2015 rates: $10 to $20. (662)494-4885

COMO — A3 *Lafayette*

SARDIS LAKE/TECKVILLE (Public Corps) From I-55 exit 62 (SR-310), E 16 mi on SR-310 to park access rd, SE 2.1 mi (E). Pit toilets. 2015 rates: $15. Mar to Dec. (662)563-4531

DECATUR — C3 *Newton*

TURKEY CREEK WATER PARK (Public) From Jct of I-20 & SR-15 (exit 109), N 7 mi on SR-15 to Broad St, W 0.4 mi to S 7th Ave, S 3.8 mi (follow signs) (R). 2015 rates: $22. (601)635-3314

DURANT — C3 *Holmes*

HOLMES COUNTY (State Pk) From Jct of I-55 & exit 150, E 0.8 mi on State Park Rd (E). 2015 rates: $18. (662)653-3351

ENID — B3 *Yalobusha*

ENID LAKE/CHICKASAW HILL (Public Corps) From Jct of I-55 & Exit 233, follow exit rd to Enid Dam Rd/CR-36 (Enid Lake Field Office), N 3 mi on Chapel Hill Rd to Pope Water Valley Rd, E 7 mi to Chicksaw Rd, S 1.5 mi (L). 2015 rates: $10 to $14. (662)563-4571

ENID LAKE/WALLACE CREEK (Public Corps) From Jct of I-55 & Enid Dam exit 233, E 1 mi on Enid Dam Rd to CR-36, N 3.5 mi (R). 2015 rates: $10 to $18. (662)563-4571

ENID LAKE/WATER VALLEY LANDING (Public Corps) From Jct of I-55 & SR-32 (Oakland exit), E 17 mi on SR-32 to CR-53, NW 2.7 mi (R). 2015 rates: $14. Mar 1 to Oct 31. (601)563-4571

PERSIMMON HILL (Public Corps) From Jct of I-55 & Enid Dam Rd (exit 233), E 1 mi on Enid Dam Rd, S 2 mi across dam (L). 2015 rates: $10 to $18. Mar 1 to Oct 31. (662)563-4571

ENTERPRISE — D4 *Clarke*

DUNN'S FALLS WATER PARK (PAT HARRISON WATERWAY DISTRICT) (Public) From jct I-20 & I-59: Go 6 mi S on I-59 (exit 142), then 4 mi W & S on paved road (cross back over I-59, follow signs). 2015 rates: $15. (601)655-8550

FLORENCE — D2 *Rankin*

WENDY OAKS RV RESORT
Ratings: 6.5/7.5★/8.5 (RV Park) From Florence traffic light on US 49, go 5 mi S on US Hwy 49, under railroad trestle, then make a U turn and go 1/2 mi N on US Hwy 49(R). **FAC:** Gravel rds. (32 spaces). 24 Avail: 2 paved, 22 gravel, 18 pull-thrus (33 x 120), back-ins (33 x 75), 24 full hkups (30/50 amps), WiFi Hotspot, tent sites, laundry, fire rings. **REC:** pond, fishing, rec open to public. Pet restrict(B). Eco-friendly, 2015 rates: $30 to $35. Disc: military. No CC.
(601)845-CAMP Lat: 32.10961, Lon: -90.05539
4160 Hwy 49 S, Florence, MS 39073
wendyoaksrvresort@gmail.com
See ad this page, 660.

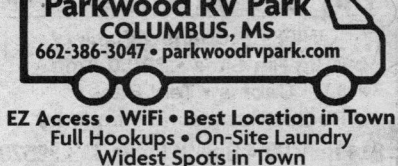

SAVE! Over $1,000 in coupons can be found at the front of the Guide!

Enjoy shopping over 10,000 RV products at great prices, at CampingWorld.com.

FULTON — A4 *Itawamba*

TOMBIGBEE/WHITTEN PARK (Public Corps) From Jct of US-78 & Hwy 25, N 200 yds on Hwy 25 to access rd, N 4.5 mi, follow signs (L). 2015 rates: $18 to $20. (662)862-7070

GAUTIER — F4 *Jackson*

A SPOTLIGHT A spotlight on the Gulf Coast's colorful attractions appearing at the front of this state section.

INDIAN POINT RV RESORT
Ratings: 9/8.5★/9.5 (Campground) From Jct of I-10 & exit 61 (Gautier Vancleave Rd), S 1.8 mi on Gautier Vancleave Rd to Indian Point Parkway, E 1.4 mi (E). **FAC:** Paved rds. (200 spaces). 100 Avail: 50 paved, 50 gravel, patios, 10 pull-thrus (20 x 65), back-ins (20 x 60), 100 full hkups (30/50 amps), seasonal sites, cable, WiFi, rentals, dump, laundry, LP gas, firewood, restaurant. **REC:** pool, Sioux Bayou: fishing, playground. Pet restrict(B/Q). No tents. Eco-friendly, 2015 rates: $25 to $32.
(866)497-1011 Lat: 30.40631, Lon: -88.63450
1600 Indian Point Parkway, Gautier, MS 39553
ip@indianpt.com
www.indianpt.com
See ad pages 661 (Spotlight Gulf Coast), 660.

SANTA MARIA RV PARK **Ratings: 8/8★/7** (Campground) 2015 rates: $28. (228)522-3009 5800 Martin Bluff Rd, Gautier, MS 39553

SHEPARD (State Pk) From Jct of US-90 & Ladnier Rd, S 1.4 mi on Ladnier Rd to Graveline Rd, E 1.3 mi (L). 2015 rates: $13 to $18. (228)497-2244

GORE SPRINGS — B3 *Grenada*

NORTH GRAYSPORT (Public Corps) From Jct of I-55 & Hwy 8, E 4 mi to 333 Scenic Drive, follow signs to Dam area (R). For reservations call 877-444-6777. 2015 rates: $14. (662)226-1679

GREENVILLE — B1 *Washington*

PECAN GROVE RV PARK
Ratings: 8/9★/9 (RV Park) S-bnd: From Jct of US 65 & US 82 (in Lake Village), S 2.7 mi on US 65 & US 82 (R); or N-bnd: Jct US 65 & US 82, 1.7 mi on US 65 & US 82 (L). **FAC:** Gravel rds. (110 spaces). Avail: 70 gravel, 70 pull-thrus (35 x 75), 70 full hkups (30/50 amps), seasonal sites, cable, WiFi, tent sites, rentals, laundry, groc, firewood. **REC:** Lake Chicot: fishing, playground. Pet restrict(B). Big rig sites, 2015 rates: $30 to $32. Disc: AAA, military. No CC.
(870)265-3005 Lat: 33.29582, Lon: -91.27629
3768 Highway 82 & 65 South, Lake Village, AR 71653
info@pecangrove.net
www.turnoninn.com
See primary listing at Lake Village, AR and ad page 114.

WARFIELD POINT PARK (Public) From Jct of US-82 & SR-1, W 6 mi on US-82 to park access rd, N 2 mi (R). 2015 rates: $13 to $15. (662)335-7275

GRENADA — B3 *Grenada*

FROG HOLLOW CAMPGROUND/RV PARK LLC **Ratings: 7/8/7.5** (Campground) 2015 rates: $28.89 to $29.96. (662)226-9042 601 Hwy 7 N, Grenada, MS 38901

HUGH WHITE (State Pk) From Jct of I-55 & SR-8 (exit 206), E 4.3 mi on SR-8 to Scenic Loop 333, N 2.5 mi, follow signs (bear left before dam) (L). 2015 rates: $18. (662)226-4934

GULFPORT — F3 *Harrison*

A SPOTLIGHT A spotlight intro ducting the Gulf Coast's colorful attractions appearing at the front of this state section.

GULFPORT See also Bay St Louis, Biloxi, Gautier, Lumberton, Perkinston & Picayune.

BAYWOOD RV PARK & CAMPGROUND INC
Ratings: 8.5/8/8 (Campground) From Jct of I-10 & Lorraine/Cowan Rd (exit 38), S 3 mi on Lorraine/Cowan Rd (L); or From Jct of US-90 & Cowan Rd, N 1.2 mi on Cowan Rd (R). **FAC:** Paved rds. (117 spaces). Avail: 49 paved, 9 pull-thrus (24 x 60), back-ins (24 x 50), 49 full hkups (30/50 amps), cable, WiFi, dump, laundry, LP gas. **REC:** pool, playground. Pet restrict(B/Q). No tents. 2015 rates: $28 to $30.
(888)747-4840 Lat: 30.40159, Lon: -89.02446
1100 Cowan Rd, Gulfport, MS 39507
www.southernrvparks.com
See ad pages 664 (Spotlight Gulf Coast), 659 (MS Map), 660.

CAMPGROUNDS OF THE SOUTH
Ratings: 7/8★/6 (RV Park) From Jct of I-10 & US-49 (Exit 34B), N 0.3 mi on US-49 to Landon Rd, E 0.8 mi to Three Rivers Rd, N 0.2 mi (R). **FAC:** Paved rds. (140 spaces). 50 Avail: 40 paved, 10 grass, 16 pull-thrus (25 x 70), back-ins (25 x 50), 50 full hkups (30/50 amps), cable, WiFi, laundry. **REC.** Pet restrict(B). Partial handicap access, no tents. 2015 rates: $25. Disc: AAA. No CC.
AAA Approved
(228)539-2922 Lat: 30.43745, Lon: -89.08292
10406 Three Rivers Rd, Gulfport, MS 39503
rvpark01@aol.com
www.campgroundsofthesouth.com
See ad this page.

COUNTRY SIDE RV PARK
Ratings: 7.5/7/8 (Campground) From Jct of I-10 & US-49N (exit 34B), N 10 mi on US-49N (R). **FAC:** Gravel rds. (32 spaces). Avail: 16 gravel, 2 pull-thrus (30 x 75), back-ins (30 x 50), 16 full hkups (30/50 amps), cable, tent sites, laundry, LP gas. **REC:** pool, pond, fishing. Pet restrict(B/Q). Big rig sites, 2015 rates: $25. Disc: AAA, military. No CC.
(228)539-0807 Lat: 30.58176, Lon: -89.12587
20278 Hwy 49, Saucier, MS 39574
csrv@bellsouth.net
countrysidervpark.com
See ad this page.

GULF HAVEN CAMPGROUND
Ratings: 8.5/10★/8.5 (Campground) From the junction of I-10 & US - 49 (exit 34A), S 4.4 mi on US - 49 to US -90 (W Beach Blvd), W 1.2 mi (R). **FAC:** All weather rds. 77 Avail: 77 all weather, 17 pull-thrus (35 x 60), back-ins (35 x 60), 77 full hkups (30/50 amps), cable, WiFi, laundry, LP gas. **REC.** Pet restrict(B). Partial handicap access, no tents. Big rig sites, 2015 rates: $39.50. Disc: military.
(228)863-9096 Lat: 30.35841, Lon: -89.11216
500 Broad Ave, Gulfport, MS 39501
gulfhaven@gulfhavencampground.net
www.gulfhavencampground.com
See ad pages 664 (Spotlight Gulf Coast), 660 & Snowbird Destinations in Magazine Section.

HARRISON COUNTY FAIRGROUNDS (Public) From jct I-10 (exit 28) & County Farm Rd: Go 7-1/2 mi N on County Farm Rd. (228)832-0080

HATTIESBURG — E3 *Covington, Forrest*

HATTIESBURG See also Lumberton.

OKATOMA RESORT & RV PARK
Ratings: 8.5/7/9 (Campground) From Jct of I-59 & US 49, N 6.8 mi on US 49 to Lux Rd, E 1 mi to Okatoma River Rd, N 1 mi (L). Call before using GPS. **FAC:** Gravel/dirt rds. 78 gravel, 16 pull-thrus (30 x 60), back-ins (30 x 50), 78 full hkups (30/50 amps), cable, WiFi, tent sites, rentals, dump, laundry, LP gas, firewood. **REC:** pool, wading pool, whirlpool, Okatoma Lakes: fishing, playground, rec open to public. Pet restrict(B). Eco-friendly, 2015 rates: $28.
(601)520-6631 Lat: 31.45664, Lon: -89.42043
221 Okatoma River Rd, Hattiesburg, MS 39401
fabaker2001@okatomaresort.com
www.okatomaresort.com
See ad this page, 660.

PAUL B JOHNSON (State Pk) From S Jct of US 98 & US 49, S 8.2 mi on US 49 (R). 2015 rates: $20 to $24. (601)582-7721

SHADY COVE RV PARK **Ratings: 5.5/4.5/4.5** (Campground) 2015 rates: $35. (601)268-1077 7836 US Hwy 49N, Hattiesburg, MS 39402

HOLLANDALE — C2 *Washington*

LEROY PERCY (State Pk) W-bnd: From Jct of US 61 & SR 12, W 5.5 mi on SR 12 (R) or; E-bnd: From Jct of Hwy 1 & SR 12, E 7.5 mi on SR 12 (L). 2015 rates: $18 to $20. (662)827-5436

HOLLY SPRINGS — A3 *Marshall*

HOLLY SPRINGS NF (CHEWALLA LAKE CAMPGROUND) (Natl Forest) From town: Go 5 mi NE on Hwy 4, then 1 mi S on CR 634, then 1 mi E on FR 611. 2015 rates: $7 to $20. Mar 8 to Dec 2. (662)236-6550

WALL DOXEY (State Pk) From Jct of US-78 & SR-7 (S. of Holly Springs), S 5.8 mi on SR-7 (R). 2015 rates: $18. (662)252-4231

HORN LAKE — A3 *DeSoto*

MEMPHIS JELLYSTONE CAMP RESORT
Ratings: 10/9.5★/9 (RV Park) From Jct of I-55 & Church Rd (exit 287), W 1.0 mi on Church Rd to US-51, N 0.8 mi to Audubon Point Dr, E 500 ft (E). **FAC:** Paved rds. (135 spaces). Avail: 60 paved, patios, 60 pull-thrus (32 x 70), 60 full hkups (30/50 amps), cable, WiFi, tent sites, rentals, laundry, LP gas, fire rings, firewood. **REC:** pool, pond, playground. Pet restrict(B/Q). Partial handicap access. Big rig sites, eco-friendly, 2015 rates: $45 to $55. Disc: AAA, military.
(662)280-8282 Lat: 34.94511, Lon: -90.01627
1400 Audubon Point Drive, Horn Lake, MS 38637
reservations@memphisjellystone.com
www.memphisjellystone.com
See ad page 1091.

INDIANOLA — B2 *Sunflower*

WILLIE'S LAST RESORT (RV Park) (Too New to Rate) From Jct of US 82 & US 49W, Go W on US 82 to Sunflower Ave, then S to 2nd St (E) (on grounds of BB King Museum). **FAC:** Paved rds. 14 paved, 6 pull-thrus (20 x 70), back-ins (15 x 35), accepts self-contain units only, 14 W, 14 E (30/50 amps), tent sites, dump. **REC:** rec open to public. Pets OK. 2015 rates: $25 to $30. No CC.
(662)887-4551 Lat: 33.449043, Lon: -90.642296
508 2nd St, Indianola, MS 38751
pittsfarms@bellsouth.net

IUKA — A4 *Tishomingo*

J P COLEMAN (State Pk) From Jct of US-72 & SR-25, N 4.5 mi on SR-25 to State Park Rd (CR-989), NE 6.2 mi to CR-321, SE 1.2 mi (E). 2015 rates: $20 to $24. (662)423-6515

JACKSON — D2 *Hinds, Madison, Rankin*

JACKSON See also Canton, Clinton, Florence & Pelahatchie.

HOMEWOOD MANOR
(RV Area in MHP) (Seasonal Stay Only) From I-55 and Briarwood exit, Go left on N. State St, then stay on N. State St past Cedars of Lebanon Rd. (L). **FAC:** Paved rds. (97 spaces). Avail: 1 grass, back-ins (18 x 40), accepts self-contain units only, 1 full hkups (30/50 amps), seasonal sites, rentals. Pet restrict no CC.
(601)366-1421 Lat: 32.37117, Lon: -90.16505
5330 N. State St, Jackson, MS 39206
homewoodmanor@statestreetgroup.com
www.homewoodcommunities.com
See ad page 671.

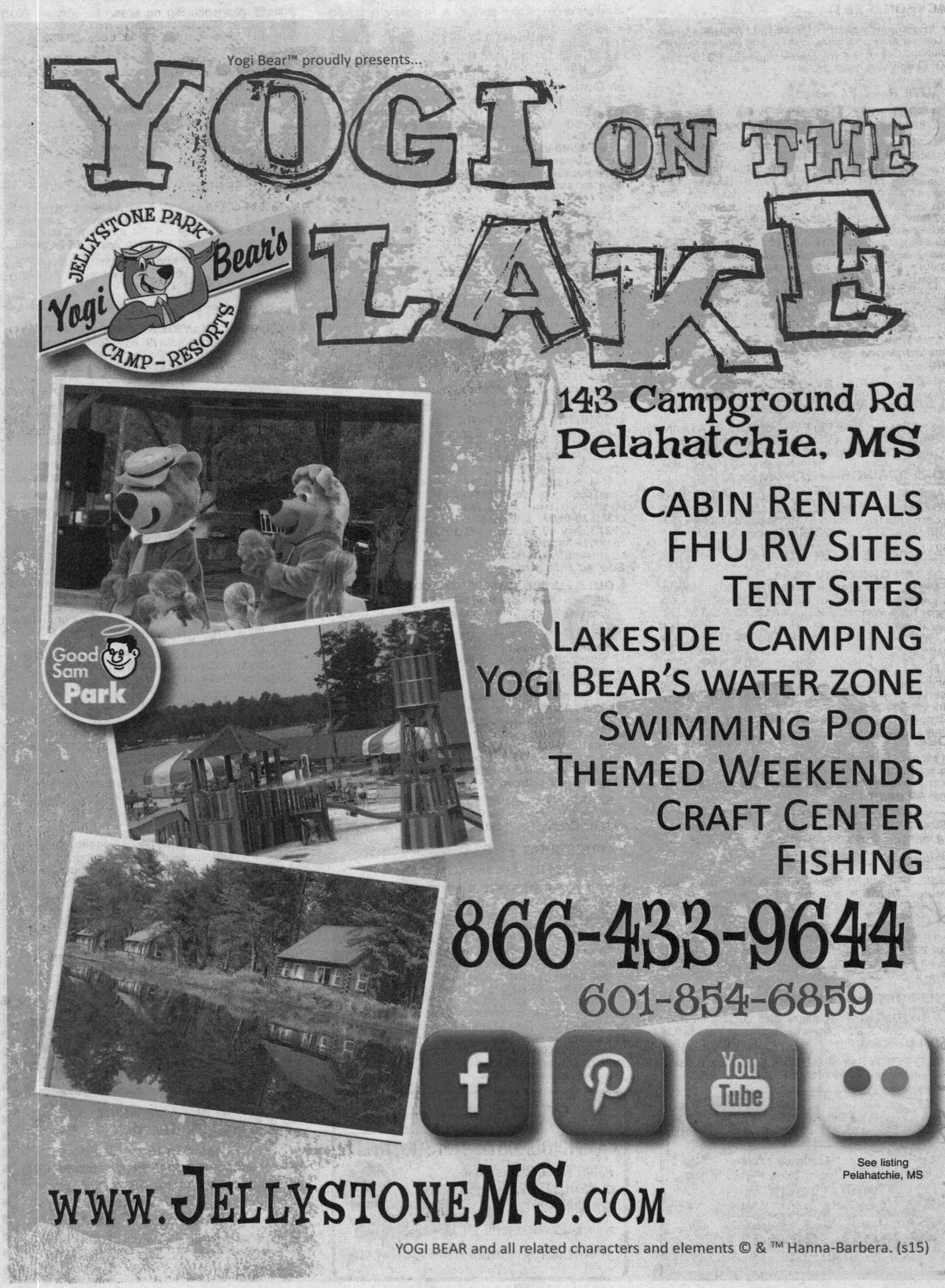
Yogi Bear™ proudly presents...
YOGI ON THE LAKE
JELLYSTONE PARK™
Yogi Bear's
CAMP-RESORTS
143 Campground Rd
Pelahatchie, MS
CABIN RENTALS
FHU RV SITES
TENT SITES
LAKESIDE CAMPING
YOGI BEAR'S WATER ZONE
SWIMMING POOL
THEMED WEEKENDS
CRAFT CENTER
FISHING
Good Sam Park
866-433-9644
601-854-6859
f
You Tube
See listing
Pelahatchie, MS
www.JellystoneMS.com
YOGI BEAR and all related characters and elements © & ™ Hanna-Barbera. (s15)

JACKSON (CONT)

LE FLEUR'S BLUFF (State Pk) From Jct of I 55 & Lakeland Dr (exit 98B), E 0.7 mi on Lakeland Dr to Lakeland Ter, S 0.2 mi (R). 2015 rates: $13 to $18. (601)987-3923

MOVIETOWN RV PARK

Ratings: 7/9★/8 (RV Park) From Jackson go north on I-55 to SR-22 (exit 119), W 0.5 mi on SR-22 to Virillia Rd, N 0.4 mi (R). **FAC:** Paved/gravel rds. (114 spaces). Avail: 67 gravel, 50 pull-thrus (45 x 65), back-ins (35 x 40), 67 full hkups (30/50 amps), WiFi, tent sites, rentals, laundry. **REC:** playground. Pets OK. Big rig sites, eco-friendly, 2015 rates: $26. Disc: AAA, military.
(601)859-7990 Lat: 32.60736, Lon: -090.08420
109 Movietown Dr., Canton, MS 39046
Info@movietownrv.com
www.movietownrv.com
See primary listing at Canton and ad page 671.

ROSS BARNETT/GOSHEN SPRINGS CAMPGROUND (Public) From Jct of I-55 & Lakeland Dr/SR-25 (exit 98B), NE 22 mi on Lakeland Dr to SR-43, W 2.9 mi (R). 2015 rates: $18 to $22. (601)829-2751

ROSS BARNETT/TIMBERLAKE CAMPGROUND (Public) From I-55 to Lakeland Dr/SR-25 (exit 98B), NE 6 mi on Lakeland Dr/SR-25 to Old Fannin Rd (becomes Northshore Parkway), N 3.7 mi (L). 2015 rates: $18 to $24. (601)992-9100

Travel Services

CAMPING WORLD OF JACKSON As the nation's largest retailer of RV supplies, accessories, services and new and used RVs, Camping World is committed to making your total RV experience better. RV Accessories: (844)760-6692. **SERVICES:** MH mechanical, RV Sales. RV supplies. Hours: 8 am to 6 pm.
(888)664-9256 Lat: 32.223876, Lon: -90.224904
4601 I-55 South Frontage Rd., Jackson, MS 39212
www.campingworld.com

LENA — C3 *Leake*

LOW HEAD DAM (ROSS BARNETT RESERVOIR) (Public) From jct Natchez Trace Parkway & Hwy 43: Go 7 mi E on Hwy 43, then 10 mi N on Hwy 25, then 3 mi NW on Utah Rd, then 5 mi W on Lowhead Dam Rd. (601)654-9359

ROSS BARNETT/LEAKE COUNTY WATER PARK (Public) From Jct of SR-43 & SR-25 (E of reservoir), N 11.5 mi on SR-25 to Utah Rd, N 2 mi to Park Rd (Left 10ft, immediate Right, follow signs), N 1.2 mi (E). 2015 rates: $18 to $22. (601)654-9359

LOUISVILLE — C4 *Winston*

LEGION (State Pk) From Northern Jct of SR-15 & SR-25, N 5.5 mi on SR-25 to N Columbus Rd, SW 3.5 mi (R). Caution: Narrow Roads. 2015 rates: $20. (662)773-8323

Use our handy Snowbird Destinations guide in the front of the Guide to find RV-friendly destinations throughout the Sunbelt.

LUDLOW — C3 *Scott*

ROSS BARNETT/COAL BLUFF PARK (Public) From Jct of SR-43 & SR-25 (E of reservoir), N 10.3 mi on SR-25 to Riverbend Rd, W 1.9 mi to Coal Bluff Rd, N 1.3 mi (E). 2015 rates: $18 to $22. (601)654-7726

LUMBERTON — E3 *Lamar*

LITTLE BLACK CREEK CAMPGROUND & PARK

Ratings: 7/7.5/9.5 (Campground) From I-59 & Hwy 13 (exit 41), Go W on Hwy 13 to US 11, then N to Little Black Creek Rd/ Myrick Ave, then W 8 mi to park (E). **FAC:** Paved rds. 125 Avail: 17 paved, 108 grass, 17 pull-thrus (25 x 60), back-ins (35 x 45), 108 full hkups, 17 W, 17 E (30/50 amps), tent sites, rentals, dump, laundry, groc, fire rings, firewood. **REC:** Little Black Creek: swim, fishing. Pets OK. Big rig sites, 2015 rates: $25 to $28.
(601)794-2957 Lat: 31.51852, Lon: -89.29393
2159 Black Creek Rd., Lumberton, MS 39455
lbc2159@gmail.com
www.lbccampground.com
See ad this page.

LITTLE BLACK CREEK WATER PARK (Public) NB:Jct I-59 & SR-13 (exit 41) N 1.9 mi on SR-13 to US-11, N 0.2 mi to Myrick Ave, NW 6.5 mi, follow signs (L) SB:Jct I-59 & SR-589 (exit 51) W 0.2 mi on US 11 S 0.2 mi to Shelby Speights Rd, NW 0.5 mi to Purvis to Batesville Rd, SW 3.5 mi to Corinth Rd, SW 1.2 mi to Little Black Creek Rd, SW 1.7 mi R. 2015 rates: $19 to $22. (601)794-2957

MATHISTON — B3 *Choctaw*

NATCHEZ TRACE PKWY/JEFF BUSBY CAMPGROUND (Natl Pk) From US-82 (in town) to milepost 204, S 9 mi on Natchez Trace Pkwy, at MP-193.1, follow signs. (800)305-7417

MCCOMB — E2 *Pike*

BOGUE CHITTO WATER PARK CAMPGROUND (PEARL RIVER BASIN DEV. DIST.) (Public) From jct I-55 & Hwy 98 east (exit 15A): Go 12 mi E on Hwy 98, then at Brown Bogue Chitto Water Park sign, go 1 mi S on Dogwood Trail. 2015 rates: $16 to $20. (601)684-9568

PERCY QUIN (State Pk) From Jct of I 55 & Fernwood Rd (exit 13), W 0.7 mi on Fernwood Rd to SR 48, N 0.1 mi (L). 2015 rates: $18 to $24. (601)684-3938

MENDENHALL — D3 *Simpson*

D'LO WATER PARK (Public) From Mendenhall, W 2 mi on SH-149 (R). 2015 rates: $20. (601)847-4310

MERIDIAN — C4 *Lauderdale*

MERIDIAN See also Toomsuba.

BENCHMARK COACH AND RV PARK

Ratings: 7.5/9★/8.5 (RV Park) From Jct of I-20/I-59 & US 45N (exit 157 B), N 1.7 mi on US 45 to Marion/Russell exit, W 1 mi to Dale Dr, N 1 mi (R). **FAC:** Gravel rds. 27 paved, 8 all weather, 27 pull-thrus (25 x 75), back-ins (25 x 60), 35 full hkups (30/50 amps), cable, WiFi, laundry, LP gas. Pet restrict(B). No tents. Big rig sites, eco-friendly, 2015 rates: $25 to $33. Disc: military.
(601)483-7999 Lat: 32.42741, Lon: -88.64233
6420 Dale Dr., Meridian, MS 39342
info@benchmarkrv.net
www.benchmarkrv.net
See ad this page, 660.

BONITA LAKES RV PARK

Ratings: 8.5/9★/7.5 (RV Park) From the Jct of I-20 and exit 156 (Jimmy Rodgers Pkwy), South 1 mile on Jimmy Rodgers Pkwy. to Hwy 19, E 0.2 mi. (L). **FAC:** Paved/gravel rds. (161 spaces). Avail: 50 paved, patios, 20 pull-thrus (24 x 65), back-ins (26 x 50), 50 full hkups (30/50 amps), seasonal sites, cable, WiFi, laundry, LP bottles, firewood. **REC:** pool, pond, fishing. Pet restrict(B). No tents. Big rig sites, 2015 rates: $30. ATM.
(601)483-4330 Lat: 32.36793, Lon: -88.64987
694 Mitchum Rd, Meridian, MS 39301
ronaldmcdevitt@aol.com
See ad this page, 660.

HILL COUNTRY RV AND MH COMMUNITY

Ratings: 5.5/NA/6.5 (RV Area in MHP) From Jct of I-20 & Hwy 39N (exit 154B), NW 7.7 mi on Hwy 39N to Briarwood Rd, E 0.8 mi (L). Reservations Required. **FAC:** Paved rds. (200 spaces). Avail: 10 gravel, patios, back-ins (24 x 80), accepts full hkup units only, 10 full hkups (30/50 amps), cable, WiFi Hotspot. **REC:** pool, playground. Pet restrict(B). No tents. Big rig sites, 2015 rates: $28.
(601)679-7300 Lat: 32.47190, Lon: -88.66029
383 Briarwood Rd, Meridian, MS 39305
hillcountry@towermgmt.com
www.towerrvparks.com

NANABE CREEK CAMPGROUND Ratings: 2/6.5/5.5 (Campground) From Jct of I-20/59 & Russell-Mt Gilead Rd (Exit 160/Russell), N 1 mi on Russell-Mt Gilead Rd (R). **FAC:** Gravel rds. (45 spaces). Avail: 5 gravel, 5 pull-thrus (24 x 60), 5 full hkups (30/50 amps), tent sites, laundry, firewood. Pets OK. Big rig sites, 2015 rates: $27. Disc: AAA. No CC.
AAA Approved
(601)485-4711 Lat: 32.40330, Lon: -88.58127
1933 Russell- Mt Gilean Rd, Meridian, MS 39301
maryjo@nanabervpark.com
www.nanabervpark.com

OKATIBBEE WATER PARK (PAT HARRISON WATERWAY DISTRICT) (Public) From jct I-20/59 (exit 150) & Hwy 19: Go 5 mi N on Hwy 19, then 8 mi N on Pine Spring Rd. Follow signs. 2015 rates: $22 to $24. (601)737-2370

TWILTLEY BRANCH (Public Corps) From Jct of I-20 & Hwy 19 exit, N 12 mi on Hwy 19 to Okatibbee Dam Rd, follow Okatibbee Lake signs (E). 2015 rates: $12 to $20. (601)626-8068

MS

MIZE — D3 *Smith*

LAKE ROSS BARNETT (Public) From Jct of Mize & SR-35, S 2.4 mi on SR-35, W 1.9 mi on cnty rd, S 0.5 mi (R). 2015 rates: $15. (601)733-2611

MONTICELLO — D2 *Lawrence*

ATWOOD WATER PARK (Public) From town: Go 1 mi E on Hwy-84. (601)587-2711

MORTON — C3 *Scott*

ROOSEVELT (State Pk) From Jct of I 20 & SR 13 (exit 77), N 0.6 mi on SR 13 (L). 2015 rates: $14 to $24. (601)732-6316

MOUNT OLIVE — D3 *Covington*

DRY CREEK WATER PARK (PAT HARRISON WATERWAY DISTRICT) (Public) From jct US 49 & park road: Go 4-1/2 mi W on park road. Follow signs. 2015 rates: $18.19. (601)797-4619

NATCHEZ — D1 *Adams*

A SPOTLIGHT A spotlight introducing Mississippi River Destinations colorful attractions appearing at the front of this state section.

NATCHEZ (State Pk) From N Jct of US-61 (NE of Natchez) & US-84, N 5.1 mi on US-61 to State Park Rd, E 0.3 mi to Wickcliff, N 0.3 mi (R). 2015 rates: $18 to $20. (601)442-2658

PLANTATION MOBILE HOME & RV PARK **Ratings: 5/6/5** (Campground) 2015 rates: $30 to $50. (601)442-5222 1 Fredrick Rd., Natchez, MS 39120

RIVER VIEW RV PARK AND RESORT
Ratings: 9/9★/9.5 (RV Park) From Jct of US 61 & US 84, NW 3.5 mi on US 84 to LA 131/Martin Luther King Ave. First left after bridge, SE 0.8 mi (L). **FAC:** Paved/gravel rds. (194 spaces). 184 Avail: 110 paved, 23 gravel, 51 grass, 141 pull-thrus (30 x 70), back-ins (30 x 50), 184 full hkups (30/50 amps), seasonal sites, WiFi, tent sites, rentals, dump, laundry, LP gas, firewood. **REC:** pool, whirlpool, Mississippi River: fishing, playground. Pet restrict(B). Partial handicap access. Big rig sites, eco-friendly, 2015 rates: $29.95 to $38.95. Disc: AAA, military.
(318)336-1400 Lat: 31.555576, Lon: -91.43441
100 River View Pkwy, Vidalia, LA 71373
rvmanager@vidalialanding.com
riverviewrvpark.com
See primary listing at Vidalia, LA and ad page 666 (Spotlight Mississippi River Destinations).

OAKLAND — B3 *Yalobusha*

GEORGE P COSSAR (State Pk) From Jct of I-55 & SR-32 (exit 227), E 2.5 mi on SR-32 to park rd, N 1.7 mi (E). 2015 rates: $20. (662)623-7356

OCEAN SPRINGS — F4 *Jackson*

GULF ISLANDS NATIONAL SEASHORE/DAVIS BAYOU CAMPGROUND (Natl Pk) From Jct of I-10 & CR-609 (exit 50), S 3 mi on CR-609 to US-90, E 2.6 mi to Park Rd, S 2 mi (R). 2015 rates: $16. (228)875-3962

OLIVE BRANCH — A3 *DeSoto*

Travel Services

CAMPING WORLD OF OLIVE BRANCH/MEMPHIS As the nation's largest retailer of RV supplies, accessories, services and new and used RVs, Camping World is committed to making your total RV experience better. RV Accessories: (855)888-6568. **SERVICES:** MH mechanical, RV Sales. RV supplies. Hours: 8am - 6pm.
(888)763-4369 Lat: 34.978836, Lon: -89.862500
8150 New Craft Road, Olive Branch, MS 38654
www.campingworld.com

PASS CHRISTIAN — F3 *Harrison*

TLC WOLF RIVER RESORT **Ratings: 7.5/8.5★/7.5** (Membership Pk) 2015 rates: $10. (228)452-9100 23098 Freddie Frank Rd, Pass Christian, MS 39571

PELAHATCHIE — D3 *Rankin*

YOGI ON THE LAKE
Ratings: 9/10★/10 (RV Park) From Jct of I 20 (exit 68) & Hwy 43, N 2.2 mi on Hwy 43 to Lake Rd, W 1.1 mi to Campground Rd, N 0.2 mi (E).

YOGI BEAR SOUTH'S BEST KEPT SECRET
Just 15 miles east of Jackson. Yogi on the Lake is the family vacation destination in the South. Friendly, clean and active atmosphere. We will greet you and make your stay your most memorable camping vacation of the year.

FAC: Paved/gravel rds. 164 Avail: 17 paved, 147 gravel, 75 pull-thrus (30 x 60), back-ins (33 x 58), 164 full hkups (30/50 amps), cable, WiFi, tent sites, rentals, dump, laundry, groc, LP gas, fire rings, firewood, restaurant, controlled access. **REC:** heated pool, Pelahatchie Lake: swim, fishing, playground, rec open to public. Pet restrict(B/Q). Big rig sites, eco-friendly, 2015 rates: $26 to $55. Disc: military. ATM.
(601)854-6621 Lat: 32.33208, Lon: -89.81064
143 Campground Rd, Pelahatchie, MS 39145
info@jellystonems.com
www.jellystonems.com
See ad pages 670, 660 & Family Camping in Magazine Section.

PERKINSTON — E3 *Stone*

DIAMOND LAKE RV PARK **Ratings: 6.5/NA/7.5** (Campground) 2015 rates: $25 to $27. (228)234-5253 997 Hwy 49, Perkinston, MS 39573

PHILADELPHIA — C3 *Neshoba*

BURNSIDE LAKE PARK (Public) From town, NE 5 mi on Hwy 15 (L). 2015 rates: $10. (601)656-4101

PICAYUNE — E3 *Hancock, Pearl River*

PICAYUNE See also Bay St Louis, Biloxi, Gulfport & Slidell, LA.

SUN ROAMERS RV RESORT
Ratings: 9.5/9.5★/9.5 (RV Park) From Jct of I-59 & SR 43 S (exit 4), E 0.8 mi on SR 43S to Stafford Rd, S 0.6 mi to Mississippi Pines Blvd, W 500 ft (E).

CLOSE TO GULF COAST ATTRACTIONS
Perfectly located between New Orleans, Gulfport casinos & all major attractions. Experience the beauty & entertainment that Southern Mississippi & North Shore Louisiana offer. Great family destination! Club rallies welcome!

FAC: All weather rds. (154 spaces). 118 Avail: 12 paved, 49 all weather, 57 gravel, 11 pull-thrus (25 x 60), back-ins (28 x 60), 118 full hkups (30/50 amps), WiFi, tent sites, rentals, dump, laundry, LP gas. **REC:** pool, Sun Roamers Lake: fishing, rec open to public. Pet restrict(B/Q). Partial handicap access. Big rig sites, eco-friendly, 2015 rates: $30 to $36. Disc: military.
(601)798-5818 Lat: 30.509977, Lon: -89.649839
41 Mississippi Pines Blvd, Picayune, MS 39466
Sunroamersrvresortpicayune@gmail.com
www.sunroamers.com
See ad this page, 660 & Snowbird Destinations in Magazine Section.

PONTOTOC — A4 *Pontotoc*

HOWARD STAFFORD PARK & LAKE (Public) From Jct of Hwys 6 & 9, W 0.5 mi on Hwy 9S to Lake Dr, S (E). Call park for more camping information. 2015 rates: $13. (662)489-5792

PORT GIBSON — D2 *Claiborne*

GRAND GULF MILITARY PARK & CAMPGROUND (Public) From Jct of US 61 & SR 462, W 7 mi on SR 462, follow signs (R); or From Jct of Natchez Trace Pkwy & US 61, N 6.5 mi on US 61 to SR 462, W 7 mi, follow signs (R). 2015 rates: $20. (601)437-5911

NATCHEZ TRACE PKWY/ROCKY SPRINGS CAMPGROUND (Natl Pk) From Jct of US-61 & SR 18, N 2 mi on SR-18, at MP-54.8, follow signs. (800)305-7417

QUITMAN — D4 *Clarke*

ARCHUSA CREEK WATER PARK (Public) From Jct of US 45 & SR 18, W 2.1 mi on SR 18 to SR 511, SE 0.3 mi to Shiloh Rd, S 0.4 mi (R). 2015 rates: $15 to $22. (601)776-6956

CLARKCO (State Pk) From Jct of US 45 & SR 145 (N of Quitman), NE 0.3 mi on SR 145 (R). 2015 rates: $20 to $24. (601)776-6651

RIPLEY — A4 *Tippah*

TIPPAH COUNTY LAKE (Public) From Jct SR-4 & SR-15, N 5 mi on SR-15 to CR-410/Tippah Lake Rd, W 2.5 mi (E). 2015 rates: $15. (662)837-9850

ROBINSONVILLE — A2 *Tunica*

ROBINSONVILLE See also Coldwater, Horn Lake, Sardis, Southaven & Tunica.

Things to See and Do

HOLLYWOOD CASINO Hollywood Casino. Slot machines, table games,restaurants, entertainment. RV accessible. Restrooms, food. Hours: 24 hrs. ATM.
(800)871-0711 Lat: 34.81365, Lon: -90.41623
1150 Casino Strip Blvd, Robinsonville, MS 38664
www.hollywoodcasinotunica.com
See ad page 665 (Spotlight Mississippi River Destinations).

RIVER BEND LINKS GOLF COURSE Designed by Clyde B. Johston, ASGCA, River Bend Links is a fresh opportunity for great golf 6,923 yds long, par 72 links-style golf course is the only true Scottish course in the mid-South. Mar 1 to Nov 31. RV accessible. Restrooms, food. Hours: 4am to 8pm.
(888)539-9990 Lat: 34.81140, Lon: -90.41670
1205 Nine Lakes Dr, Robinsonville, MS 38664
www.riverbendlinks.com
See ad page 665 (Spotlight Mississippi River Destinations).

ROSEDALE — B2 *Bolivar*

GREAT RIVER ROAD (State Pk) From Jct of SR-1 & SR-8, W 0.8 mi on park access rd (E). Due to flooding 2011, TL was unable to inspect this park's facilities. Info & rating are from previous year's Directory. 2015 rates: $20. (662)759-6762

LAKE CHARLIE CAPPS (Public) From town, E 1 mi on SR-8 (L). Pit toilets. 2015 rates: $15. (662)759-6444

SARDIS — A3 *Lafayette, Panola*

JOHN W KYLE (State Pk) S-bnd: From Jct of I-55 & SR-315 (exit 252), E 6.8 mi on SR-315 (R); or N-bnd: From Jct of I-55 & SR-35 (exit 246), N 7 mi on SR-35 to SR-315, N 2 mi (L). 2015 rates: $18 to $24. (662)487-1345

SARDIS LAKE/CLEAR CREEK (Public Corps) From Jct of I-55 & Hwy 6, E appx 20 mi on Hwy 6 to SR-314 (in Oxford), N 8 mi, follow signs (E). 2015 rates: $18. Apr 1 to Sep 30. (662)563-4531

SARDIS LAKE/OAK GROVE (Public Corps) From Jct of I-55 & SR-315 (exit 252), E 8 mi on SR-315, below dam on lower lake (R). 2015 rates: $18. Apr 1 to Sep 30. (662)563-4531

SARDIS LAKE/PATS BLUFF (Public Corps) From Batesville, E 11.3 mi on SR-315 to John W Kyle SP sign, N 2.5 mi, follow signs (E). 2015 rates: $6. Apr 1 to Sep 30. (662)563-4531

SOSO — D3 *Jones*

BIG CREEK WATER PARK 10 (Public) From Jct of I-59 & US-84W (exit 95B), W 11.9 mi on US-84W to Cooley Park Rd, S 0.6 mi (R). 2015 rates: $15 to $22. (601)763-8555

SOUTHAVEN — A3 *DeSoto*

EZ DAZE RV PARK

Ratings: 10/10★/9 (Campground) From Jct of I-55 & Church Rd (Exit 287), W 0.2 mi on Church Rd to Pepper Chase Dr, N 0.5 mi to W E Ross Pkwy, W 0.2 mi (R).

NORTH MISSISSIPPI'S PREMIER RV PARK

We go the extra mile with a reinforced storm room. Let our massage therapist relax those tired muscles. We're a first class RV park with paved sites, patios, & showcase bathrooms located near Memphis & Tunica.

FAC: Paved rds. (136 spaces). Avail: 101 paved, patios, 47 pull-thrus (25 x 75), back-ins (25 x 60), 101 full hkups (30/50 amps), cable, WiFi, laundry, LP gas. **REC:** pool, whirlpool, playground. Pet restrict(B). Partial handicap access, no tents. Big rig sites, eco-friendly, 2015 rates: $40. Disc: military.
(662)342-7720 Lat: 34.94186, Lon: -89.99883
536 W.e. Ross Pkwy, Southaven, MS 38671
ezdazervpark@yahoo.com
www.ezdazervpark.com
See ad pages 1090, 660.

SOUTHAVEN RV PARK

Ratings: 7.5/9.5★/8 (Campground) From Jct of I-55 & Stateline Rd (Exit 291), E 0.5 mi on Stateline Rd (L). **FAC:** Paved rds. (43 spaces). Avail: 10 paved, patios, 10 pull-thrus (20 x 65), 10 full hkups (30/50 amps), cable, WiFi, laundry, LP gas. Pets OK. No tents. 2015 rates: $35. Disc: military.
(662)393-8585 Lat: 34.991865, Lon: -89.994161
270 Stateline Rd, Southaven, MS 38671
Southavenrvpark270@gmail.com
www.southavenrvpark.com
See ad page 1091.

STARKVILLE — B4 *Oktibbeha*

MISSISSIPPI STATE-JOHN W STARR MEMORIAL RVP (Public) From Starkville, S 7.6 mi to St Mark Rd, E 100 yds (R). Reservations required. 2015 rates: $20. (662)325-4720

THE PINES MH AND RV COMMUNITY

Ratings: 6.5/NA/7 (RV Area in MHP) From Jct of SR-25 & SR-12 (SW of Starkville), E 2.9 mi on SR-12 to Louisville St, S 0.5 mi (R). **FAC:** Paved rds. (250 spaces). Avail: 51 gravel, 1 pull-thrus (35 x 80), back-ins (35 x 70), accepts full hkup units only, 51 full hkups (30/50 amps), WiFi Hotspot. **REC:** pool, playground. Pet restrict(B/Q). No tents. Big rig sites, 2015 rates: $30.
(662)323-6423 Lat: 33.44667, Lon: -88.82215
1000 Louisville St, Starkville, MS 39759
thepines@towermgmt.com
www.thepinesmhp.com

TISHOMINGO — A4 *Tishomingo*

TISHOMINGO (State Pk) From Jct of Natchez Trace Pkwy & park entrance road (MP 304), NE 0.5 mi on park entrance rd to CR 90 (park rd), E 0.5 mi, follow signs (E). 2015 rates: $18. (662)438-6914

TOOMSUBA — C4 *Lauderdale*

LAKE TOM BAILEY (Public) From town, W 1.25 mi on US-80, N 1.3 mi. 2015 rates: $15. (601)632-4679

MERIDIAN EAST/TOOMSUBA KOA **Ratings: 9/9★/8** (Campground) 2015 rates: $37.46 to $44.75. (601)632-1684 3953 Koa Campgroun Rd, Toomsuba, MS 39364

TUNICA — A2 *Tunica*

A SPOTLIGHT A spotlight introducing the Mississippi Gulf Coast's colorful attractions appearing at the front of this state section.

HOLLYWOOD CASINO HOTEL & RV PARK

Ratings: 9/9★/8.5 (RV Park) From Jct of US-61 & Casino Strip Blvd., W. 8 mi.(L). **FAC:** Paved rds. 123 paved, 13 pull-thrus (24 x 75), back-ins (22 x 45), 123 full hkups (30/50 amps), WiFi, dump, laundry, LP gas, restaurant. **REC:** heated pool, whirlpool, golf, rec open to public. Pets OK. No tents. 7 day max stay, 2015 rates: $19.99.
(800)871-0711 Lat: 34.81169, Lon: -90.41673
1150 Casino Strip Blvd, Robinsonville, MS 38664
www.hollywoodcasinotunica.com
See ad page 665 (Spotlight Mississippi River Destinations).

SAM'S TOWN GAMBLING HALL RV PARK **Ratings: 9/9★/8** (RV Park) 2015 rates: $18. (800)456-0711 1477 Casino Strip Resorts Blvd, Robinsonville, MS 38664

TUPELO — A4 *Lee*

CAMPGROUND AT BARNES CROSSING

Ratings: 8/9★/9.5 (Campground) E-bnd: From Jct of US 78 & Natchez Trace Pkwy, N 2.6 mi on Natchez Trace Pkwy to Bus. Hwy 145-South, S 0.5 mi (L); or W-bnd: From Jct of US 78 & US 45 (Exit 86B), N 1.3 mi on US 45 to Barnes Crossing Rd, W 0.5 mi to Hwy 145, N 0.5 mi (R). **FAC:** Paved rds. 54 gravel, 25 pull-thrus (24 x 68), back-ins (20 x 35), some side by side hkups, 54 full hkups (30/50 amps), cable, WiFi, laundry. **REC.** Pets OK. No tents. Big rig sites, 2015 rates: $35 to $39. No CC.
(662)844-6063 Lat: 34.32301, Lon: -88.70340
125 Road 1698, Tupelo, MS 38804
cgbarnescrossing@comcast.net
www.cgbarnescrossing.com
See ad pages 674, 660.

ELVIS PRESLEY LAKE CAMPGROUND (State Pk) From Jct of US 78 & N Veterans Blvd (NE of downtown Tupelo), NE 0.2 mi on Veterans Blvd to CR-1460, E 1.7 mi to CR-995, N 0.6 mi (E). Follow signs, marked well. 2015 rates: $18. (662)620-6314

NATCHEZ TRACE RV PARK

Ratings: 7.5/8.5★/8.5 (Campground) From Jct of Natchez Trace Pkwy & US-78, SW 12.5 mi on Natchez Trace Pkwy to CR-506 (between MP-251 & MP-252 Pontocola Rd), E 400 ft (R); or From Jct of US 245 & Pontocola Rd (CR-506), W 7 mi on CR-506 (L). **FAC:** Gravel rds. 27 gravel, 21 pull-thrus (25 x 65), back-ins (30 x 40), 21 full hkups, 6 W, 6 E (30/50 amps), tent sites, dump, laundry, LP gas, firewood. **REC:** pool, pond, fishing. Pets OK. Big rig sites, eco-friendly, 2015 rates: $28. No CC.
(662)767-8609 Lat: 34.14589, Lon: -88.81812
189 CR-506, Shannon, MS 38868
wez@dixieconnect.com
www.natcheztracervpark.com

TOMBIGBEE (State Pk) From Jct of US-78 & Veterans Blvd, S 2 mi on Veterans Blvd to SR-6, SE 3.3 mi to park access rd (State Park Rd), E 2.8 mi, follow signs (R). 2015 rates: $18 to $20. (662)842-7669

TRACE (State Pk) E-bnd: From Jct of SR-41 & SR-6/Pontotoc exit (W of Tupelo), E 7.2 mi on SR-6 to Faulkner Rd (CR-65), N 2.1 mi (L); or W-bnd: From Jct of Natchez Trace Pkwy & SR-6 (W of Tupelo), W 7.8 mi on SR-6 to Faulkner Rd (CR-65), N 2.1 mi (L). 2015 rates: $14 to $24. (662)489-2958

Travel Services

CAMPER CITY RV repair, parts and storage available on site. **SERVICES:** RV, tire, RV appliance, RV Sales. RV storage. **TOW:** RV, auto. RV supplies, dump, emergency parking, RV accessible. waiting room. Hours: 8am to 5pm. No CC.
(662)844-2371 Lat: 34.23999, Lon: -88.77028
4895 Cliff Gookin Blvd, Tupelo, MS 38801
See ad page 674.

Our rating system isn't just tough, it's thorough. We know the kinds of things that are important to you — like clean restrooms and showers, attractive, secure, well-tended grounds, and extras like swimming pools. We give the first rating for development of facilities, the second for cleanliness and physical characteristics of restrooms and showers, and the third for visual appearance.

Don't camp without it ... Our 2016 listings are your key to travel satisfaction.

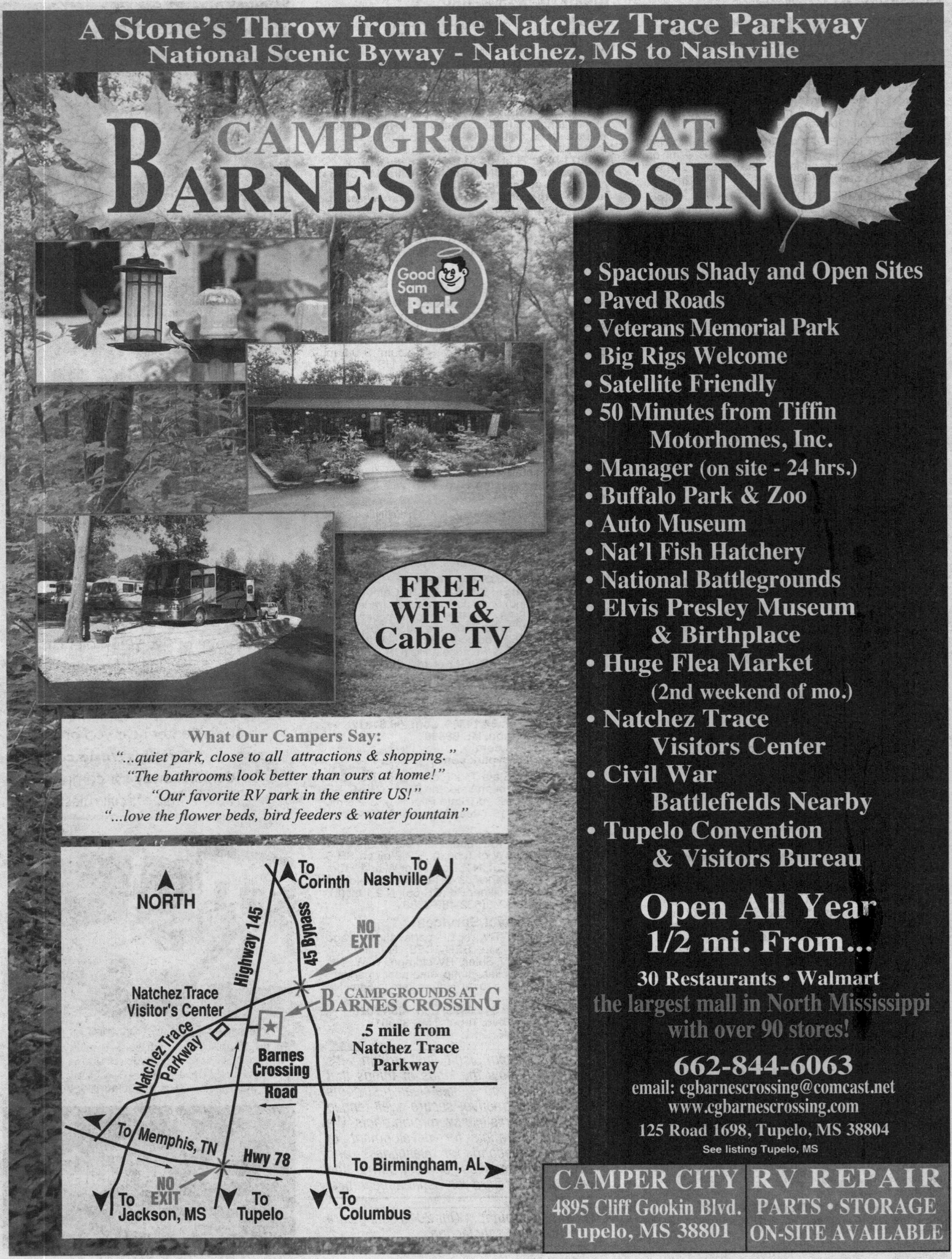
A Stone's Throw from the Natchez Trace Parkway
National Scenic Byway - Natchez, MS to Nashville
CAMPGROUNDS AT
BARNES CROSSING
Good Sam Park
• Spacious Shady and Open Sites
• Paved Roads
• Veterans Memorial Park
• Big Rigs Welcome
• Satellite Friendly
• 50 Minutes from Tiffin Motorhomes, Inc.
• Manager (on site - 24 hrs.)
• Buffalo Park & Zoo
• Auto Museum
• Nat'l Fish Hatchery
• National Battlegrounds
• Elvis Presley Museum & Birthplace
• Huge Flea Market (2nd weekend of mo.)
• Natchez Trace Visitors Center
• Civil War Battlefields Nearby
• Tupelo Convention & Visitors Bureau
FREE WiFi & Cable TV
What Our Campers Say:
"...quiet park, close to all attractions & shopping."
"The bathrooms look better than ours at home!"
"Our favorite RV park in the entire US!"
"...love the flower beds, bird feeders & water fountain"
NORTH
To Corinth
To Nashville
Highway 145
45 Bypass
NO EXIT
Natchez Trace Visitor's Center
CAMPGROUNDS AT BARNES CROSSING
.5 mile from Natchez Trace Parkway
Natchez Trace Parkway
Barnes Crossing Road
To Memphis, TN
Hwy 78
To Birmingham, AL
NO EXIT
To Jackson, MS
To Tupelo
To Columbus
Open All Year
1/2 mi. From...
30 Restaurants • Walmart
the largest mall in North Mississippi with over 90 stores!
662-844-6063
email: cgbarnescrossing@comcast.net
www.cgbarnescrossing.com
125 Road 1698, Tupelo, MS 38804
See listing Tupelo, MS
CAMPER CITY
4895 Cliff Gookin Blvd.
Tupelo, MS 38801
RV REPAIR
PARTS • STORAGE
ON-SITE AVAILABLE

VICKSBURG — C2 *Warren*

A SPOTLIGHT A spotlight introducing Mississippi River Destination's colorful attractions appearing at the front of this state section.

VICKSBURG See also Clinton.

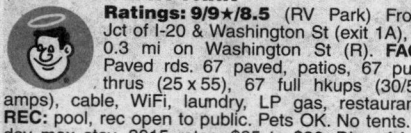

AMERISTAR RV PARK

Ratings: 9/9★/8.5 (RV Park) From Jct of I-20 & Washington St (exit 1A), N 0.3 mi on Washington St (R). **FAC:** Paved rds. 67 paved, patios, 67 pull-thrus (25 x 55), 67 full hkups (30/50 amps), cable, WiFi, laundry, LP gas, restaurant. **REC:** pool, rec open to public. Pets OK. No tents. 3 day max stay, 2015 rates: $25 to $30. Disc: AAA.
(800)700-7770 Lat: 32.31550, Lon: -90.89589
725 Lucy Bryson St, Vicksburg, MS 39180
www.ameristar.com
See ad page 665 (Spotlight Mississippi River Destinations).

MAGNOLIA RV PARK RESORT **Ratings: 8/8.5★/6.5** (RV Park) 2015 rates: $27 to $29. (601)631-0388 211 Miller St, Vicksburg, MS 39180

Visit CampingWorld.com where you can get deals on over 10,000 RV and camping related products!

RIVER TOWN CAMPGROUND

Ratings: 8/7/8 (Campground) From Jct of I 20 & US 61S (exit 1B), S 6 mi on US 61 S (L). **FAC:** Gravel rds. 108 gravel, 59 pull-thrus (45 x 62), back-ins (45 x 60), 108 full hkups (30/50 amps), WiFi, laundry, LP gas. **REC:** pool, playground. Pets OK. No tents. Big rig sites, 2015 rates: $27. Disc: military.
(601)630-9995 Lat: 32.23720, Lon: -090.92283
5900 Hwy 61 South, Vicksburg, MS 39180
rt5900a@att.net
www.rivertown-campground.com
See ad page 666 (Spotlight Mississippi River Destinations).

Things to See and Do

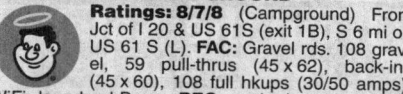

AMERISTAR CASINO Casino, Hotel and restaurants. Partial handicap access. RV accessible. Restrooms, food. Hours: Open 24 hours. ATM.
(800)700-7770 Lat: 32.31417, Lon: -90.89909
4116 Washington St, Vicksburg, MS 39180
www.ameristar.com
See ad page 665 (Spotlight Mississippi River Destinations).

Read many of our brand new RV Trips of a Lifetime for 2016 in the front of the Guide. Find the rest Online!

WAVELAND — F3 *Hancock*

BUCCANEER (State Pk) From Jct of US-90 & Nicholsan Ave/SR-603, S 1.2 mi on Nicholsan Ave to Central Ave, W 0.7 mi to Coleman, S 0.4 to Beach Blvd, W 2.7 mi, follow signs (R). Some facilities may be limited due to reconstruction from Hurricane Katrina. 2015 rates: $13 to $35. (228)467-3822

WAYNESBORO — D4 *Wayne*

MAYNOR CREEK WATER PARK (Public) From Jct of US 45 & US 84, W 4.1 mi on US 84 to Reservoir Rd, S 3 mi (L). 2015 rates: $18 to $20. (601)735-4365

WESSON — D2 *Copiah, Lincoln*

LAKE LINCOLN (State Pk) From Jct of I 55 & Sylvarena Rd (exit 51), E 3.8 mi on Sylvarena Rd to US 51, S 0.1 mi to Main St, NE 0.3 mi to E Railroad St, NE 0.7 mi to Timberlane Rd, E 2.3 mi, where road becomes Sunset Rd, SE 1.3 mi (L). 2015 rates: $20 to $24. (601)643-9044

WIGGINS — E3 *Stone*

FLINT CREEK WATER PARK (Public) From Jct SR-26 & SR-29, N 2 mi on SR-29, follow signs (L). 2015 rates: $28 to $30. (601)928-3051

Look in the Guide to Seasonal Sites to find places you can stay for a month, a season or longer.

MS

Getty Images/iStockphoto

WELCOME TO Missouri

DATE OF STATEHOOD	WIDTH: 240 MILES (385 KM)	PROPORTION OF UNITED STATES
AUG. 10, 1821	LENGTH: 300 MILES (480 KM)	1.84% OF 3,794,100 SQ MI

Top 3 Tourism Attractions:
1) Gateway Arch
2) Branson/Silver Dollar City
3) Bass Pro Shops

Nickname: Show-Me State

State Flower: Hawthorn

State Bird: Bluebird

People: Maya Angelou, poet and author; Mark Twain (Samuel Clemens), author and humorist; Yogi Berra, baseball catcher; Walter Cronkite, TV newscaster; John Goodman, actor; Rush Limbaugh, radio and TV talk-show host

Major Cities: Kansas City, Saint Louis, Springfield, Independence, Columbia, (Jefferson City, capital)

Topography: North of Missouri River—rolling hills, fertile plains, moist prairie; south—hilly, rough with deep, narrow valleys; southeast—alluvial plain

Climate: Humid continental climate with cool to cold winters and long, hot summers

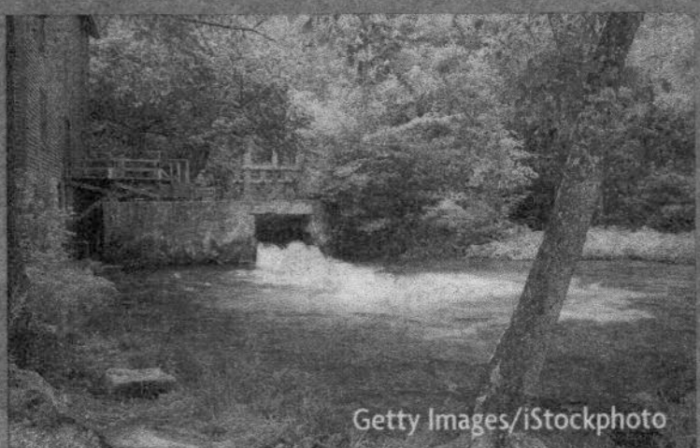
Getty Images/iStockphoto

Seasoned politicians have been known to shift adroitly between "Missour-ee" and "Missour-uh" in the same speech to mollify all their constituents. However, all Missourians stand together in their pride as the "Show-Me" state. Indeed, from Kansas City to St. Louis to Branson, Missouri locals have good reason to feel pride in their state. From scenic lakes and rivers to world-famous barbecue sauce, Missouri always shows travelers a great time.

Learn

At 630 feet tall, St. Louis' iconic Gateway Arch, America's tallest monument and the world's tallest arch, is part of a larger park officially known as the Jefferson National Expansion Memorial. The complex recognizes Missouri's westward vision: The state was the stepping-off point for Meriwether Lewis and William Clark's Corps of Discovery, the Pony Express, the Santa Fe Trail and the Oregon Trail.

In St. Joseph, the Pony Express National Museum tells the story of the 2,000-mile mail relay that began at the brick-faced Pikes Peak Stables on Penn Street. Modern-day explorers can also pick up the Lewis and Clark National Historic Trail at several Missouri sites, including the Boathouse and Nature Center in St. Charles and the National Frontier Trails Center in Independence. While in Independence, tour the home of Missouri's only president at the Harry S. Truman National Historic Site.

The scenic rolling hills of Missouri were one of the attractions to travel along Route 66 in the middle of the 20th century. Many sites remain, including Eads Bridge, the world's first steel-truss bridge. Route 66 State Park in the resort community of Times Beach on the Meramec River preserves a stretch of the historic Mother Road.

Play

The Ozark Mountains—so old and worn down that no peaks exceed 3,000 feet—are America's most extensive

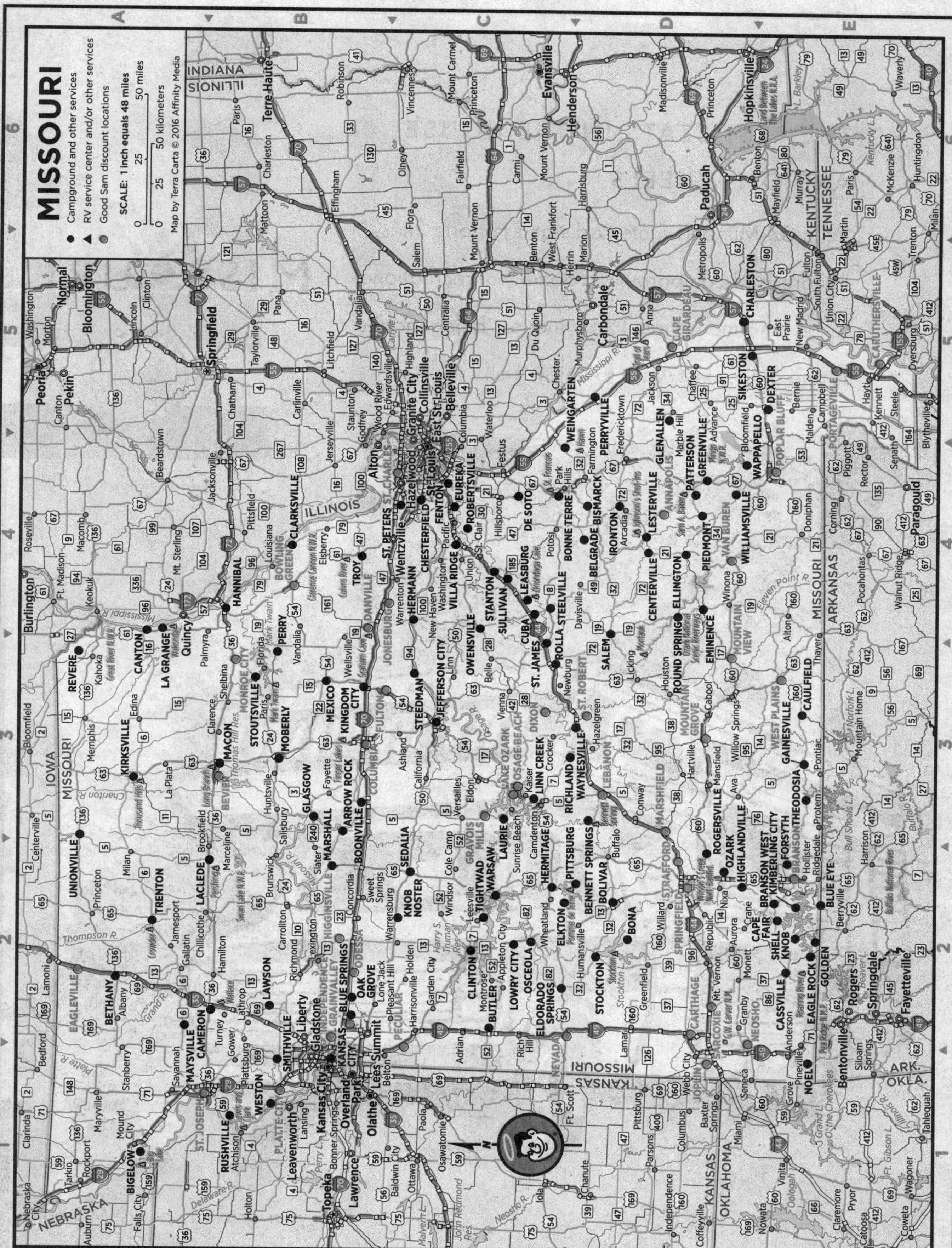
MISSOURI
Campground and other services
RV service center and/or other services
Good Sam discount locations
SCALE: 1 inch equals 48 miles
0 25 50 miles
0 25 50 kilometers
Map by Terra Carta © 2016 Affinity Media
IOWA
MISSOURI
ILLINOIS
INDIANA
KENTUCKY
TENNESSEE
ARKANSAS
OKLAHOMA
KANSAS
NEBRASKA
Kansas City
St. Louis
Springfield
Jefferson City
Columbia
Joplin
Branson
Hannibal
Cape Girardeau
Peoria
Evansville
Paducah
Topeka
Lawrence
Olathe
Fayetteville
Springdale
Bentonville
Rogers
Terre Haute

MO

 See map page 677

ST. JOSEPH

Found just an hour north of Kansas City (and throughout the pages of history), no travels through northwestern Missouri could be considered complete without a stop in St. Joseph. See the stables where the Pony Express began in 1860, explore the circa 1877 railroad depot at Patee House Museum, and tour the house where Jesse James met his end in 1882.

HERMANN

The Hermann Wine Trail is composed of seven phenomenal wineries, each with its own calendar of special events held throughout the year. One such vineyard, Adam Puchta Winery, is America's oldest continuously owned and operated family farm winery. Another can't-miss is Hermannhof Winery, which is home to 10 stone cellars and brick superstructures that are included on the National Register of Historic Places.

LAKE OF THE OZARKS

With more than 1,150 total miles of shoreline, the Lake of the Ozarks is one of the Midwest's largest lake destinations. And with that much water comes that much fun. Rent a boat from Adventure Boat Rentals, try parasailing with Paradise Parasail, visit the slides at Big Surf waterpark, take a fishing tour with Big Ed's Guide Service, or golf one of 15 top-rated courses. Better yet, adopt the Missouri mindset and make time to enjoy it all.

STE. GENEVIEVE

On the bluffs of the Mississippi River, just an hour south of St. Louis, you find the charming town of Ste. Genevieve. Founded in 1735, Ste. Gen is the oldest permanent European settlement in the state of Missouri, which immediately qualifies it as a shopping and antiquing mecca. Shops such as First Settlement Antiques, Simple to Sassy and St. Mary's Antique Mall feature collectibles and home décor that give any home a little extra personality. And don't forget to stop by Sara's Ice Cream and Antiques to literally put a "cherry on top" of your memorable trip.

BRANSON

Known as the "Live Music Show Capital of the World," Branson has dozens of live performance theaters and a variety of family-friendly shows to choose from at any given time. From musicians to magicians to actors to acrobats, this home for the performing arts is always waiting to show you a great time.

mountain range between the Appalachians and the Rockies. The Mark Twain National Forest is lubricated by turquoise-blue springs pumping millions of gallons of underground water to the surface each day.

More than 6,000 limestone caves have been identified under the Missouri soil. State parks hold the entrance key to four of the best caverns for touring: Onondaga Cave, Cathedral Cave at Onondaga Cave State Park, Fisher Cave at Meramec State Park and Ozark Caverns at Lake of the Ozarks State Park.

St. Louis Art Museum, Forest Park Missouri Division of Tourism

Experience

Reuben Branson opened a store in the Ozarks in the 1880s, and for most of the next century, the small town it served was no different than the scores of other Missouri towns. Then in 1959, the Baldknobbers Jamboree played the first live music show in Branson. Today, the "Live Entertainment Capital of the World" fills 50 theaters, and you can even see a half-scale replica of the *RMS Titanic* at the Titanic Museum.

When Samuel Clemens grew up in the town of Hannibal, the locals had no idea that he'd grow up to publish *Huck Finn, Tom Sawyer* and other iconic novels under the pen name Mark Twain. The Twain on Main Festival celebrates the life and works of America's greatest 19th-century writer from its centerpiece, Mark Twain Boyhood Home & Museum. National Tom Sawyer Days is a Hannibal tradition for wholesome family fun. Another famous Missourian, outlaw Jesse James, has a festival in his honor in his hometown of Kearney.

St. Louis is known for throwing a party—it hosted both the Olympic Games and the World's Fair in 1904. The city had been practicing since 1878 when the Veiled Prophet Fair was first staged. Today the Veiled Prophet Parade launches "America's Biggest Birthday Party"—the local version of the July 4 holiday. You can be certain plenty of hometown Anheuser-Busch products flow during the festivities.

TRAVEL & TOURISM

Missouri Division of Tourism
800-519-2100
www.visitmo.com

AgriMissouri
866-466-8283
www.AgriMissouri.com

Branson/Lakes Area Chamber of Commerce and CVB
www.explorebranson.com

Cape Girardeau Convention & Visitors Bureau
800-777-0068, 573-335-1631
www.visitcape.com

Columbia Convention & Visitors Bureau
800-652-0987, 573-875-1231
www.visitcolumbiamo.com

Greater Saint Charles Convention & Visitors Bureau
800-366-2427
www.historicstcharles.com

Hannibal Convention & Visitors Bureau
866-263-4825, 573-221-2477
www.visithannibal.com

Hermann Area Chamber of Commerce
www.visithermann.com

Independence Department of Tourism
www.visitIndependence.com

Jefferson City Convention & Visitors Bureau
www.visitjeffersoncity.com

Visit KC
800-767-7700, 816-221-5242
www.visitkc.com

Lake of the Ozarks Convention & Visitors Bureau
800-386-5253, 573-348-1599
www.funlake.com

Missouri Wine & Grape Board
800-392-9463
www.MissouriWine.org

Rolla Area Chamber of Commerce & Visitor Center
888-809-3817, 573-364-3577
www.visitrolla.com

St. Joseph Convention & Visitors Bureau
800-785-0360
www.stjomo.com

St. Louis Convention & Visitors Commission
800-325-7962, 314-421-1023
www.explorestlouis.com

Springfield Convention & Visitors Bureau Route 66 Tourist Information Center
800-678-8767, 417-881-5300
www.springfieldmo.org

OUTDOOR RECREATION

Missouri Canoe & Floaters Assn.
www.missouricanoe.org

Missouri Dept. of Conservation
573-751-4115
www.mdc.mo.gov-fish

National Caves Association
270-749-2228
www.missouricaves.com

SHOPPING

Bluestem Missouri Crafts
www.bluestemcrafts.com

Branson Landing
417-239-3002
www.BransonLanding.com

Country Club Plaza
816-753-0100
www.CountryClubPlaza.com

The District
573-442-6816
www.DiscoverTheDistrict.com

Ste. Genevieve Historic District
800-373-7007
www.VisitSteGen.com/attractions/shopping

Riverport Market
660-338-9989

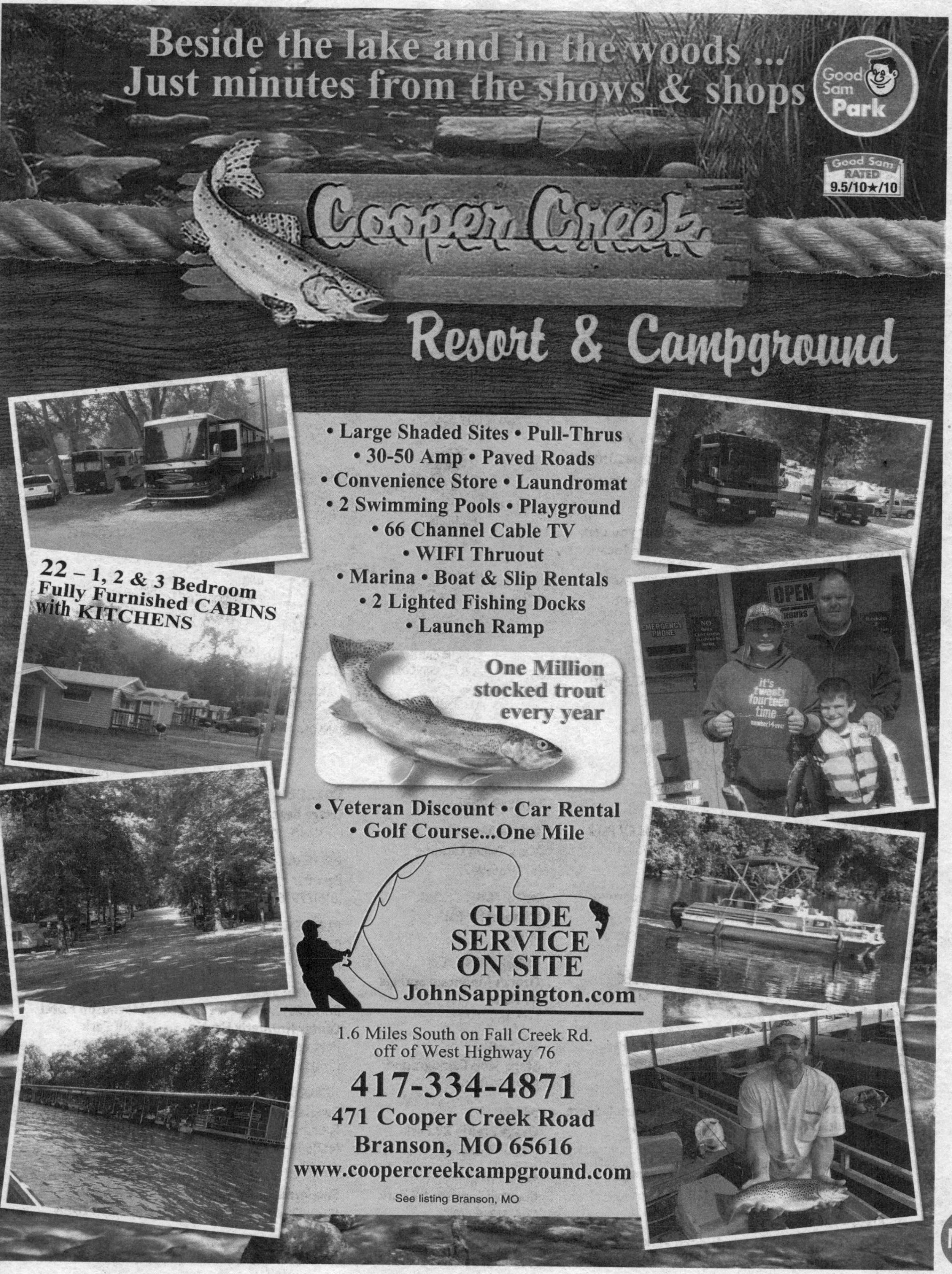
Beside the lake and in the woods ...
Just minutes from the shows & shops
Good Sam Park
Good Sam RATED 9.5/10★/10
Cooper Creek
Resort & Campground
22 – 1, 2 & 3 Bedroom Fully Furnished CABINS with KITCHENS
• Large Shaded Sites • Pull-Thrus
• 30-50 Amp • Paved Roads
• Convenience Store • Laundromat
• 2 Swimming Pools • Playground
• 66 Channel Cable TV
• WIFI Thruout
• Marina • Boat & Slip Rentals
• 2 Lighted Fishing Docks
• Launch Ramp
One Million stocked trout every year
• Veteran Discount • Car Rental
• Golf Course...One Mile
GUIDE SERVICE ON SITE
JohnSappington.com
1.6 Miles South on Fall Creek Rd. off of West Highway 76
417-334-4871
471 Cooper Creek Road
Branson, MO 65616
www.coopercreekcampground.com
See listing Branson, MO

Featured Good Sam Parks

MISSOURI

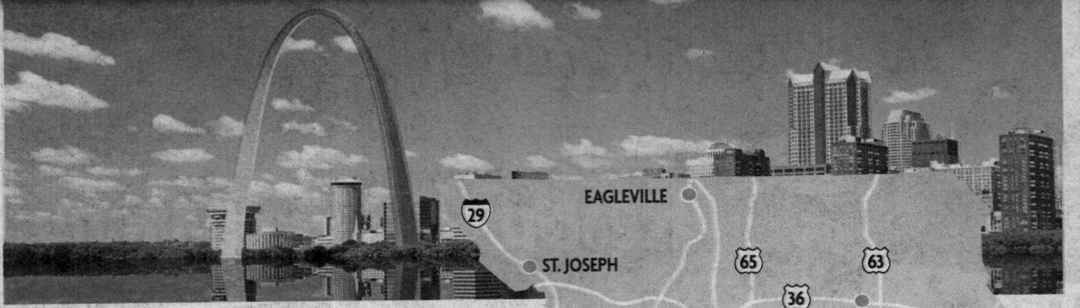

When you stay with Good Sam, you can expect the highest degree of cleanliness and friendliness, and better yet, you get 10% off campground fees.

If you're not already a Good Sam member you can purchase your membership at one of these locations:

ANNAPOLIS
Big Creek RV Park
(573)598-1064

BEVIER
Shoemaker's RV Park
(660)773-5313

BOWLING GREEN
Cozy C RV Campground, LLC
(573)324-3055

BRANSON
America's Best Campground
(800)671-4399
Blue Mountain Campground
(417)338-2114
Branson Lakeside RV Park
(417)334-2915
Branson Tree House Adventures & RV Park
(800)338-2504
Branson's Ozark Country Campground
(800)968-1300
Cooper Creek Campground & Resort
(417)334-4871
Musicland Kampground
(888)248-9080
Oak Grove RV Park
(888)334-4781
Tall Pines Campground
(800)425-2300

CAPE GIRARDEAU
The Landing Point RV Park
(573)334-7878

CARTHAGE
Big Red Barn RV Park
(417)358-2432

CARUTHERSVILLE
Lady Luck Casino & RV Park
(573)333-6000

COLUMBIA
Cottonwoods RV Park
(573)474-2747

DANVILLE
Lazy Day Campground
(573)564-2949

DIXON
Boiling Spring Campground LLC
(573)759-7294

EAGLEVILLE
Eagle Ridge RV Park
(660)867-5518

GRAIN VALLEY
Trailside RV Park & Store
(800)748-7729

LAKE OZARK
Riverview RV Park
(573)365-1122

LEBANON
Hidden Valley Outfitters
(417)533-5628

MARSHFIELD
RV Express 66
(417)859-7837

MONROE CITY
Mark Twain Landing
(573)735-9422

MOUNTAIN GROVE
Missouri RV Park
(417)926-4104

MOUNTAIN VIEW
Ozark's Mountain Springs RV Park
(417)469-3351

NEOSHO
Stage Stop Campground
(417)455-1221

NEVADA
Osage Prairie RV Park
(417)667-2267

ODESSA
Country Gardens RV Park
(816)633-8720

OSAGE BEACH
Osage Beach RV Park
(573)348-3445

PECULIAR
Peculiar Park Place
(816)779-6300

PLATTE CITY
Basswood Resort
(800)242-2775

PORTAGEVILLE
Bootheel RV Park & Event Center (formerly Hayti-Portageville RV Park)
(573)359-1580

SARCOXIE
Beagle Bay RV Haven & Campground, LLC
(417)548-0000

ST CHARLES
Sundermeier RV Park
(800)929-0832

ST JOSEPH
AOK Campground & RV Park, LLC
(816)324-4263
Beacon RV Park
(816)279-5417

ST ROBERT
Magnuson Hotel & RV Park
(573)336-3036

STRAFFORD
Paradise In the Woods RV Park & Campground
(417)859-2175

WEST PLAINS
Chipmunk Crossing RV Park
(417)256-0788

For more Good Sam Parks go to listing pages

LAKE OF THE OZARKS©
Hook Some Memories
MO 5473
MISSOURI
enjoy the show
Golf
Fishing
Outdoors
Events
Attractions
funlake.com
800-Fun-Lake
See listing Osage Beach, MO

Missouri

CONSULTANTS

Ed & Susan DeWitt

ANNAPOLIS — D4 *Iron*

➜ **BIG CREEK RV PARK** **Ratings: 10/10★/10** (RV Park) Jct of I-55S & US Rte-67: Go 34 mi S on US Rte-67, then 9 mi W on Hwy-221, then 9 mi S on Hwy-21, then 4 mi SW on Hwy-49 (L). **FAC:** All weather rds. (49 spaces). Avail: 39 all weather, 21 pull-thrus (35 x 70), back-ins (35 x 85), 39 full hkups (30/50 amps), seasonal sites, WiFi, laundry, LP gas, fire rings, firewood. **REC:** pool, Big Creek: swim, fishing, playground. Pets OK. Partial handicap access, no tents. Big rig sites, eco-friendly, 2015 rates: $36. Disc: military.
(573)598-1064 Lat: 37.41949, Lon: -90.69618
47247 Hwy 49, Annapolis, MO 63620
bigcreekrvpark@gmail.com
www.bigcreekrvpark.com
See ad pages 691, 694, 682.

➜ HIGHWAY K PARK (Public Corps) From Jct of Hwy K & RR 49, W 5 mi on Hwy K (L). 2015 rates: $14 to $20. May 15 to Sep 15. (573)751-4133

ARROW ROCK — B3 *Saline*

➜ ARROW ROCK STATE HISTORIC SITE (State Pk) From Jct of I-70 & SR-41, N 13 mi on SR-41 (R). 2015 rates: $13 to $28. (660)837-3330

BELGRADE — D4 *Washington*

MARK TWAIN NF (COUNCIL BLUFF LAKE CAMPGROUND) (Natl Forest) From town: Go 5 mi W on Hwy C, then 7 mi S on Hwy DD. 2015 rates: $10 to $20. (573)766-5765

BENNETT SPRINGS — D3 *Dallas*

➜ BENNETT SPRING (State Pk) From Jct of I-44 & SR-64, W 12 mi on SR-64 to SR-64A, S 0.8 mi (R). 2015 rates: $13 to $26. (417)532-4338

BETHANY — A2 *Harrison*

➜ **QUAIL RIDGE RV PARK Ratings: 2.5/NA/4** (Campground) From Jct of I-35 & US 136 (Exit 92), E 0.1 mi on US 136 (R) Note: turn before Taco Bell (behind Subway/Taco Bell bldg). **FAC:** Gravel rds. 10 gravel, patios, 10 pull-thrus (24 x 60), accepts self-contain units only, 10 full hkups (30/50 amps). Pets OK. No tents. 2015 rates: $25. No CC.
(660)373-0835 Lat: 40.26489, Lon: -94.01276
4132 Miller St, Bethany, MO 64424
fbennett@grm.net

Want to see what our inspectors see? The exact reproductions of the rating guidelines our inspectors used for this edition of the Guide are printed in the front of the book. Try using them on your next trip to perform your own inspection. Since our rating system is based on objective criteria, we're confident that your ratings will be similar to ours.

BEVIER — B3 *Macon*

➜ **SHOEMAKER'S RV PARK** **Ratings: 8/7.5/6** (Campground) From Jct US-63 & US-36: Go 5 mi W on US-36 to Bevier exit, then 1/4 mi E on south frontage road. **FAC:** Gravel rds. (100 spaces). Avail: 90 gravel, patios, 35 pull-thrus (25 x 65), back-ins (25 x 35), 90 full hkups (30/50 amps), seasonal sites, WiFi, tent sites, rentals, dump, laundry, firewood, restaurant. **REC:** Idle Lake: swim, fishing, playground. Pets OK. Big rig sites, 2015 rates: $25.
(660)773-5313 Lat: 39.75630, Lon: -92.56458
955 N Macon St, Bevier, MO 63532
shoemakers@cvalley.net
www.shoemakersrv.com
See ad this page, 682.

BIGELOW — A1 *Holt*

➜ BIG LAKE (State Pk) From Jct of I-29 & Hwy 159, SW 9 mi on Hwy 159 to Hwy 111, N 3 mi (L). 2015 rates: $12 to $26. (660)442-3770

BISMARCK — D4 *St Francois*

➜ SAINT JOE PARK (State Pk) From town, W 0.5 mi on Rte W to Bray Rd, N 0.1 mi to Harrington Rd, NW 4.7 mi (R). 2015 rates: $13 to $21. (573)431-1069

BLUE EYE — E2 *Taney*

➜ BAXTER CAMPGROUND (Public Corps) From town, W 5 mi on Hwy H (E). 2015 rates: $16 to $21. May 1 to Sep 15. (417)779-5370

COW CREEK PARK (COE TABLE ROCK LAKE) (Public Corps) From town: Go 2 mi S on Hwy-86, then 2 mi N on access road. (417)779-5377

➜ MILL CREEK PARK (Public Corps) From town, N 4 mi on Hwy 13 to Hwy A W 1 mi (E). 2015 rates: $21. Apr 1 to Oct 30. (417)779-5378

➜ OLD HIGHWAY 86 PARK (Public Corps) From town, E 5.5 mi on Hwy 86 to Hwy UU, N 1.5 mi (E). 2015 rates: $21. Apr 1 to Oct 31. (417)779-5376

BLUE SPRINGS — B2 *Jackson*

BLUE SPRINGS LAKE CAMPGROUND (JACKSON COUNTY PARK) (Public) From jct I-70 & I-470: Go 2 mi S on I-470 to exit 14, then 2/10 mi E on Bowlin Rd to park entrance, then N to campground entrance. (816)503-4805

BOLIVAR — D2 *Polk*

➜ RED CEDAR RV PARK **Ratings: 6.5/8.5★/8** (RV Park) 2015 rates: $25. (417)599-8504 5110 S Scenic Rd, Bolivar, MO 65613

BONA — D2 *Dade*

➜ CEDAR RIDGE PARK (Public Corps) From town, E 8 mi on Hwy 32 to Hwy 245, S 5 mi to SR-RA, N 1 mi (E). 2015 rates: $12 to $20. Apr 16 to Sep 30. (417)995-2045

BONNE TERRE — D4 *St Francois*

➜ SAINT FRANCOIS PARK (State Pk) From town, N 4 mi on Hwy 67 (R). 2015 rates: $13 to $21. (573)358-2173

BOONVILLE — B3 *Cooper*

➜ **BLACK OAKS MH AND RV COMMUNITY Ratings: 4/NA/6.5** (RV Area in MHP) From Jct of I-70 & Exit 101: Go 2 mi N (toward Boonville) on Hwy 5/Ashley Rd (R). **FAC:** Paved rds. 13 Avail: 8 gravel, 5 grass, back-ins (30 x 60), accepts full hkup units only, 13 full hkups (30/50 amps), WiFi. **REC:** playground. Pets OK. No tents. 2015 rates: $25. No CC.
(660)882-6420 Lat: 38.93555, Lon: -92.77679
1338 W Ashley Rd, Lot 2, Boonville, MO 65233
blackoaks@towermgmt.com
blackoaksmhc.com/rv.htm

BOWLING GREEN — B4 *Pike*

➜ **COZY C RV CAMPGROUND, LLC** **Ratings: 8/10★/9** (RV Park) From Jct of US-61 & US-54, E 2.5 mi on US-54 (R). **FAC:** Gravel rds. 45 gravel, 15 pull-thrus (25 x 60), back-ins (25 x 60), 45 full hkups (30/50 amps), WiFi, tent sites, dump, laundry, LP gas, firewood, restaurant. **REC:** pond, fishing, rec open to public. Pet restrict(B). Big rig sites, eco-friendly, 2015 rates: $27.50.
(573)324-3055 Lat: 39.372758, Lon: -91.164243
16733 US-54, Bowling Green, MO 63334
cozycamp@wildblue.net
www.cozyccampground.com
See ad pages 694, 682.

Things change ... last year's rates serve as a guideline only.

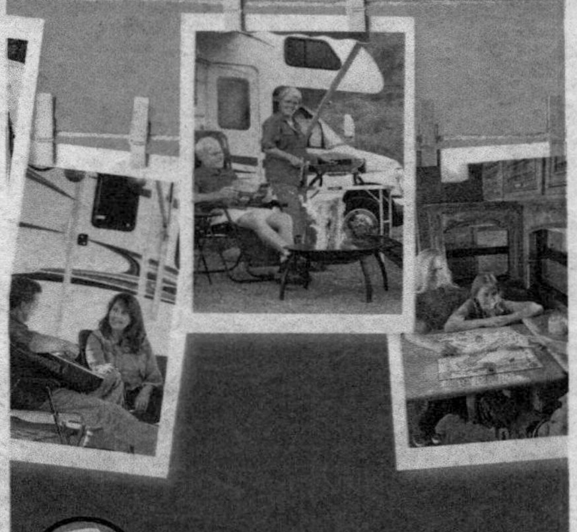

BRANSON — E2 *Stone, Taney*

BRANSON See also Blue Eye, Cape Fair, Forsyth, Kimberling City, Ozark, MO & Omaha, AR.

AMERICA'S BEST CAMPGROUND
Ratings: 9.5/9.5★/10 (RV Park) From Jct of US 65 & SR-248, W 1.7 mi on SR-248 (move to right turning lane), continue N 1.3 mi on SR-248 to Buena Vista Rd, W 0.3 mi (L) Note: Use these directions, do not use GPS.

"EXPERIENCE THE DIFFERENCE" AT ABC
America's Best Campground's convenient location is city close & country quiet. FREE WiFi, rallies & groups welcome. Come see why Good Sam Club's members voted us their exclusive Welcome Mat Award Winner 9 consecutive years!

FAC: Paved rds. (160 spaces). Avail: 158 gravel, patios, 136 pull-thrus (28 x 70), back-ins (28 x 50), 158 full hkups (30/50 amps), seasonal sites, WiFi, tent sites, rentals, dump, laundry, groc, LP gas. **REC:** pool, whirlpool, playground. Pets OK. Partial handicap access. Big rig sites, eco-friendly, 2015 rates: $39. Disc: military.
(800)671-4399 Lat: 36.68314, Lon: -93.25802
499 Buena Vista Rd, Branson, MO 65616
fun4uabc@aol.com
www.abc-branson.com
See ad pages 686, 682 & RV Trips of a Lifetime in Magazine Section.

Thank you for being one of our best customers!

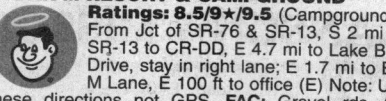

BAR M RESORT & CAMPGROUND
Ratings: 8.5/9★/9.5 (Campground) From Jct of SR-76 & SR-13, S 2 mi on SR-13 to CR-DD, E 4.7 mi to Lake Bluff Drive, stay in right lane; E 1.7 mi to Bar M Lane, E 100 ft to office (E) Note: Use these directions not GPS. **FAC:** Gravel rds. (22 spaces). Avail: 12 gravel, back-ins (24 x 60), mostly side by side hkups, 12 full hkups (30/50 amps), seasonal sites, WiFi, tent sites, rentals, dump, laundry, fire rings, firewood. **REC:** pool, whirlpool, Table Rock Lake: swim, fishing, playground. Pets OK. Eco-friendly, 2015 rates: $30 to $45. Disc: military. Apr 1 to Nov 1.
(417)338-2593 Lat: 36.59143, Lon: -93.36874
207 Bar M Lane, Branson West, MO 65737
barmresort@aol.com
www.barmresort.com
See ad this page.

BLUE MOUNTAIN CAMPGROUND
Ratings: 9/9.5/9 (Campground) From Jct of Hwy 65 & Hwy 465/Ozark Mtn Highroad, S 7.0 mi on Hwy 465 to Hwy 76, W 1.9 mi (L). **FAC:** Paved rds. (50 spaces). 40 Avail: 5 paved, 35 gravel, 19 pull-thrus (20 x 60), back-ins (18 x 55), 40 full hkups (30/50 amps), seasonal sites, cable, WiFi $, tent sites, rentals, dump, laundry. **REC:** pool, playground. Pets OK. Big rig sites, eco-friendly, 2015 rates: $25.50. Disc: military. No CC.
(417)338-2114 Lat: 36.67452, Lon: -93.33730
8766 State Hwy 76, Branson, MO 65737
amainegem@yahoo.com
See ad page 688, 682.

BRANSON KOA & CONVENTION CENTER **Ratings: 9.5/9★/8.5** (Campground) 2015 rates: $38 to $82. (800)562-4177 397 Animal Safari Rd, Branson, MO 65616

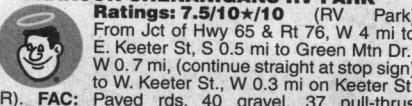

BRANSON LAKESIDE RV PARK
Ratings: 8.5/10★/9 (Public) Jct of Hwy 65 & Hwy 248 (Branson Landing Exit): Exit Branson Landing Blvd to circle, take 3rd exit, then stay in L lane (R lane ends) thru 3 traffic lights, then straight into park Note: Do not cross ridge & do not use GPS. **FAC:** Paved rds. (179 spaces). 160 Avail: 104 paved, 56 gravel, 61 pull-thrus (22 x 90), back-ins (22 x 60), mostly side by side hkups, 160 full hkups (30/50 amps), cable, WiFi, dump, laundry, LP gas. **REC:** Lake Taneycomo: fishing, marina. Pets OK. Partial handicap access, no tents. Big rig sites, 28 day max stay, 2015 rates: $22.50 to $37.
(417)334-2915 Lat: 36.635797, Lon: -93.218509
300 South Boxcar Willie Dr, Branson, MO 65616
campground@bransonmo.gov
bransonlakesidervpark.com
See ad page 688, 682.

BRANSON SHENANIGANS RV PARK
Ratings: 7.5/10★/10 (RV Park) From Jct of Hwy 65 & Rt 76, W 4 mi to E. Keeter St, S 0.5 mi to Green Mtn Dr., W 0.7 mi, (continue straight at stop sign) to W. Keeter St., W 0.3 mi on Keeter St. (R). **FAC:** Paved rds. 40 gravel, 37 pull-thrus (20 x 55), back-ins (20 x 35), 40 full hkups (30/50 amps), cable, WiFi, laundry. **REC.** Pets OK. Partial handicap access, no tents. Big rig sites, eco-friendly, 2015 rates: $37. Disc: military.
(800)338-7275 Lat: 36.63740, Lon: -93.29393
3675 Keeter St, Branson, MO 65616
bransonshenanigans@gmail.com
bransonrvparks.com

BRANSON STAGECOACH RV PARK **Ratings: 8/9★/8** (Campground) 2015 rates: $30. (800)446-7110 5751 State Hwy 165, Branson, MO 65616

BRANSON • MISSOURI

Your Hosts Jim And Sue Alkire

Beautiful Campsites

We Have Cabins!

- Free Wi-Fi
- Convenience/Gift Shop
- Concrete Patios BBQ Grills & Picnic Tables
- New FREEDOM RING Firepit and Pavilion
- 136 Pull-Thrus
- 30/50/100 Amp Service
- Cable TV • Pool & Spa
- Air Conditioned Camping Cabins/Deluxe Cabins
- 300 Seat Meeting Hall
- RV Wash
- BIG RIG PARADISE!!

Good Sam RATED 9.5/9.5★/10

Good Sam Members and Veterans 15% DISCOUNT WITH CASH OR CHECK

TOP RATED Good Sam Park FOR 2016

See listing Branson, MO

CCW WELCOME

Tent For Troops Participant

VETERANS DISCOUNT

Your pets are welcome at ABC, no breed or number restrictions

INFO: (417) 336-4399
RESERVATIONS: (800) 671-4399
E-mail: americasbestcampground@gmail.com
499 Buena Vista Road, Branson, MO 65616
Check Our Website for Current Rates & Specials
www.abc-branson.com

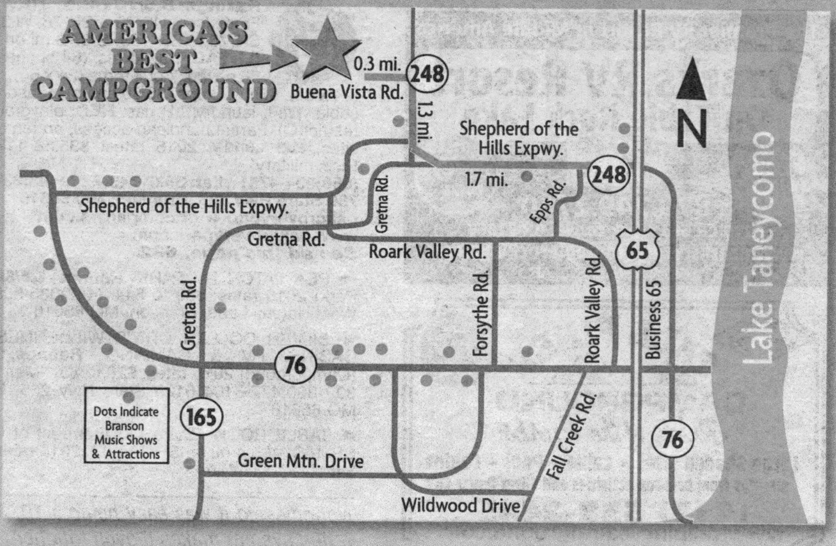

WE SELL BRANSON SHOW TICKETS!
Win Tickets to these Fabulous Shows with advance reservations.
Call for details.

The Bretts
Billy Dean and Steel Horses
Legends in Concert
Buckets N Boards
Mickey Gilley Theatre Six
Branson's IMAX Entertainment Complex
Doug Gabriel presents #1 Hits Tribute Show
A tribute to John Denver, a country music legend, starring James Garrett, of the two-time Grammy award winning group The Kendalls
The Tinoco's Magnificent Seven Variety Show
A Tribute to Marty Robbins and Classic Country Stars
Hamners' Unbelievable Variety
Smoke on the Mountain
Sunday Gospel Jubilee
Christmas on the Trail Chuckwagon Dinner Show
Grand Jubilee
Roundup on the Trail
Down Home Country
Illusionist Rick Thomas
Comedy Jamboree
Dolly Parton's Dixie Stampede Dinner Attraction
The Osmonds Music Legends
Baldknobbers Jamboree
The Lettermen
Titanic – World's Largest Museum Attraction – Branson • Missouri
Christmas Spectacular
70's Music Celebration! Barry Williams
The Haygoods
Pierce Arrow
Clay Cooper Theatre
Sons of the Pioneers

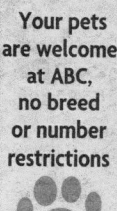

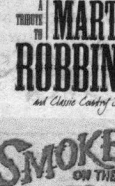

MO

BRANSON (CONT)

← BRANSON TREE HOUSE ADVENTURES & RV PARK **Ratings: 9/9/10** (Campground) From Jct of US-65 & State Hwy 465/Ozark Mountain Highroad (North of Branson), Go W 7 mi on State Hwy 465 to Hwy 76, W 2.5 mi (L). **FAC:** Gravel rds. (40 spaces). Avail: 32 gravel, patios, 15 pull-thrus (34 x 60), back-ins (32 x 70), 32 full hkups (30/50 amps), seasonal sites, WiFi, tent sites, rentals, dump, laundry, LP gas, firewood. **REC:** pool, playground. Pets OK. Partial handicap access. Big rig sites, eco-friendly, 2015 rates: $39.95 to $59.95. Disc: military.
(800)338-2504 Lat: 36.67536, Lon: -93.34683
159 Acorn Acres Lane, Branson West, MO 65737
camp@bransonrvpark.com
www.bestbransonrvpark.com
See ad pages 685, 682.

BRANSON VIEW CAMPGROUND **Ratings: 9.5/9/8.5** (Campground) From Jct of Hwy 65 & Hwy 465/Ozark Mtn Highroad, S 7 mi on Hwy 465 & Hwy 76, W 0.5 mi on Hwy 76 to Hwy 265, S 3.5 mi on Hwy 265 (L). **FAC:** Paved rds. (40 spaces). Avail: 35 paved, 30 pull-thrus (24 x 90), back-ins (24 x 65), some side by side hkups, 35 full hkups (30/50 amps), seasonal sites, cable, WiFi, rentals, laundry, groc. **REC:** pool, playground. Pets OK. Partial handicap access, no tents. Big rig sites, 2015 rates: $38. Disc: military.
(417)338-1038 Lat: 36.63439, Lon: -93.30525
2362 State Highway 265, Branson, MO 65616
bransonviewcampground@gmail.com
www.thebransonviewcampground.com

→ BRANSON VIEW ESTATES MOBILE HOME & RV PARK **Ratings: 3/NA/7** (RV Area in MHP) From Jct of Ozark Mountain Highroad (MO-465N) & MO State Hwy F: go 2 mi E on State Hwy F (L). **FAC:** Gravel rds. 10 gravel, back-ins (22 x 70), accepts self-contain units only, 10 full hkups (50 amps). Pets OK. No tents. Big rig sites, 2015 rates: $25. No CC.
(417)561-2255 Lat: 36.716218, Lon: -93.191969
2543 State Hwy F, Branson, MO 65616
See ad page 685.

BRANSON'S OZARK COUNTRY CAMPGROUND **Ratings: 8.5/9.5★/10** (Campground) From Jct of US 65 & SR-76, W 3.3 mi on SR-76 to SR-165, S 2.5 mi on SR-165 to Quebec Dr, N 0.4 mi (L). **FAC:** Gravel rds. (72 spaces). 41 Avail: 2 paved, 39 gravel, patios, 10 pull-thrus (28 x 50), back-ins (28 x 50), 41 full hkups (30/50 amps), seasonal sites, cable, WiFi, laundry, LP gas. **REC:** pool, playground. Pets OK. No tents. Big rig sites, eco-friendly, 2015 rates: $42.
(800)968-1300 Lat: 36.60095, Lon: -93.23547
679 Quebec Dr, Branson, MO 65616
occ@bransoncampground.com
www.bransoncampground.com
See ad this page, 682.

← CARSON'S COUNTRY COURT Ratings: 7/9★/5.5 (RV Area in MHP) From Hwy 65 S & Exit 248 (Shepherd of the Hills Expressway); Go W 1.6 mi on Rt 248 and stay right (R). **FAC:** Paved/gravel rds. (53 spaces). Avail: 10 gravel, patios, 5 pull-thrus (16 x 48), back-ins (18 x 34), 10 full hkups (30/50 amps), seasonal sites, WiFi, laundry. **REC.** Pets OK. Eco-friendly, 2015 rates: $25. Disc: AAA, military.
AAA Approved
(417)334-3084 Lat: 36.668452, Lon: -93.249186
2166 State Hwy 248, Branson, MO 65616
office@carsonsrvpsrk.com
www.carsonsrvpark.com

Directional arrows indicate the campground's position in relation to the nearest town.

← COMPTON RIDGE CAMPGROUND Ratings: 9.5/9.5★/8 (Campground) 2015 rates: $35 to $52.50. (800)233-8648 5040 State Hwy 265, Branson, MO 65616

← COOPER CREEK CAMPGROUND & RESORT **Ratings: 9.5/10★/10** (Campground) From Jct of US-65 & SR-76, W 1 mi on SR-76 to Fall Creek Rd, 1.6 mi on Fall Creek Rd, L on River Ln, then .1 mi to L on Cooper Creek Rd.

ON LAKE TANEYCOMO-TROUT FISHING AT its best, lies 14 wooded acres of campsites & cabins-COOPER CREEK-rated by Good Sam among top 3% parks in US. EZ access to shows/attractions & minimal traffic hassle, come 'home' to peace, woods & lakeside-ready to relax.

FAC: Paved rds. 70 gravel, 18 pull-thrus (28 x 60), back-ins (30 x 50), 70 full hkups (30/50 amps), cable, WiFi, tent sites, rentals, laundry, groc, fire rings, firewood. **REC:** pool, Lake Taneycomo: fishing, marina, playground. Pet restrict(B). Big rig sites, eco-friendly, 2015 rates: $32 to $47. Disc: military. Mar 10 to Dec 1.
(417)334-4871 Lat: 36.618319, Lon: -93.247985
471 Cooper Creek Road, Branson, MO 65616
coopercreek@suddenlink.net
www.coopercreekresort.com
See ad pages 681 (Welcome Section), 682 & RV Trips of a Lifetime in Magazine Section.

→ HOLIDAY HILLS RESORT & CAMPGROUND Ratings: 8/7/9 (Membership Pk) 2015 rates: $10 to $22. (417)334-4443 2380 E Hwy 76, Branson, MO 65616

← INDIAN POINT PARK (Public Corps) From Jct of Hwys 76 & 76/60, S 2.8 mi on Hwy 76/60 (E). 2015 rates: $16 to $21. Apr 1 to Oct 30. (417)338-2121

LONG CREEK PARK (Public Corps) From Jct of Hwys 65 & 86, W 3 mi on Hwy 86 to Lake Rd 86-50, SW 1.5 mi (E). 2015 rates: $16 to $21. Apr 1 to Sep 14. (417)334-8427

← MUSICLAND KAMPGROUND **Ratings: 9.5/10★/9.5** (Campground) From Jct of US-65 & Hwy-248, W 1.9 mi on Hwy-248 to Gretna Rd. (stay in left lane, continue straight ahead) 3.1 mi (L). **FAC:** Paved rds. 104 gravel, 11 pull-thrus (22 x 60), back-ins (22 x 50), 91 full hkups, 13 W, 13 E (30/50 amps), WiFi, tent sites, rentals, dump, laundry, LP gas, controlled access. **REC:** pool. Pet restrict(Q). Big rig sites, eco-friendly, 2015 rates: $39.95. Disc: AAA, military. Mar 1 to Nov 30.
(888)248-9080 Lat: 36.63338, Lon: -93.28418
116 Gretna Rd, Branson, MO 65616
musicland@tri-lakes.net
www.musiclandkampground.com
See ad this page, 682.

← OAK GROVE RV PARK **Ratings: 8.5/10★/8.5** (RV Park) From Jct of US-65 & SR-76, W 3.3 mi on SR-76 to SR-165, S 0.75 mi on SR-165 (L). **FAC:** Paved rds. (64 spaces). Avail: 58 paved, 7 pull-thrus (24 x 60), back-ins (24 x 60), 58 full hkups (30/50 amps), seasonal sites, cable, WiFi, laundry, LP gas. **REC:** playground. Pet restrict(Q). Partial handicap access, no tents. Big rig sites, eco-friendly, 2015 rates: $35.58 to $37.39. Disc: military.
(888)334-4781 Lat: 36.61743, Lon: -93.22723
780 Stare Hwy 165, Branson, MO 65616
oakgrovervpark@lottcompanies.com
www.oakgrovervpark.com
See ad this page, 682.

← PEA PATCH RV PARK Ratings: 8.5/8/4.5 (RV Park) 2015 rates: $39 to $44. (417)335-3958 3330 West Harvey Lane, Branson, MO 65616

← SILVER DOLLAR CITY'S WILDERNESS LOG CABINS, RV & CAMPING Ratings: 9/9.5/7.5 (Campground) 2015 rates: $28 to $32. Mar 1 to Dec 30. (800)477-5164 5125 State Hwy 265, Branson, MO 65616

TABLE ROCK (State Pk) From Jct of US-65 & SR-165, W 5.4 mi on SR-165 (L). 2015 rates: $12 to $46. (417)334-4704

Nobody said it was easy being a 10. And our rating system makes it even tougher.

City of Fountains, Kansas City
Romantic Get-A-Ways
Rallies
Weekend Fun
Family Reunions
Big Rig Pull-Thrus
FHU Sites
Lodges
CABIN RENTALS
CLUBHOUSE w/ Kitchen
EXPERIENCE THE COMFORT OF
BASSWOOD RESORT
PLATTE CITY, MO
800-242-2775
816-858-5556
Minutes from everything K.C. has to offer
Legacy RV RESORTS
Good Sam Park
OPEN YEAR ROUND
See listing Platte City, MO

See listing Monroe City, MO

BRANSON (CONT)

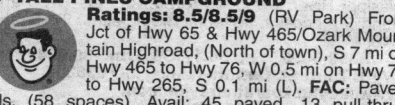

TALL PINES CAMPGROUND
Ratings: 8.5/8.5/9 (RV Park) From Jct of Hwy 65 & Hwy 465/Ozark Mountain Highroad, (North of town), S 7 mi on Hwy 465 to Hwy 76, W 0.5 mi on Hwy 76 to Hwy 265, S 0.1 mi (L). **FAC:** Paved rds. (58 spaces). Avail: 45 paved, 13 pull-thrus (24 x 65), back-ins (25 x 60), 45 full hkups (30/50 amps), seasonal sites, WiFi, tent sites, rentals, laundry, groc, LP gas, firewood. **REC:** pool, playground. Pets OK. Big rig sites, 2015 rates: $37.50. Disc: AAA. Mar 1 to Dec 1.
AAA Approved
(800)425-2300 Lat: 36.66093, Lon: -93.33172
5558 Hwy 265, Branson, MO 65616
information@tallpinescampground.com
www.tallpinescampground.com
See ad page 688, 682.

TANEYCOMO LAKEFRONT RESORT & RV PARK **Ratings: 6.5/6.5/6.5** (RV Park) 2015 rates: $25. (800)949-9975 365 Valencia Rd, Branson, MO 65616

TREASURE LAKE RESORT **Ratings: 9/8.5/8** (Membership Pk) 2015 rates: $15.20 to $20. (800)455-2961 1 Treasure Lake Dr, Branson, MO 65616

TURKEY CREEK RV VILLAGE **Ratings: 8/9.5★/8** (RV Park) 2015 rates: $29. (417)335-8004 1376 US Bus 65, Hollister, MO 65672

WILLOW TREE RV PARK **Ratings: 8.5/8/7** (RV Park) 2015 rates: $35. Apr 1 to Dec 15. (877)922-6766 3381 Shepherd of the Hills Expressway, Branson, MO 65616

BRANSON WEST — E2 *Stone*

CASTLE VIEW RV PARK **Ratings: 9.5/9.5★/9** (Membership Pk) 2015 rates: $10 to $21. (417)338-4392 1000 Castle View, Branson West, MO 65737

Travel Services

SAM'S TRAILER SERVICE Branson's authorized ONAN and Cummins dealer & service center with RV supplies, parts & propane. **SERVICES:** RV, RV appliance, MH mechanical, restrooms. RV supplies, LP, emergency parking, RV accessible. waiting room. Hours: 8:30am to 5pm M-F, 8:30am to 12pm Sat.
(417)338-2313 Lat: 36.67584, Lon: -93.34254
8810 State Hwy 76, Reeds Spring, MO 65737
1sts@centurytel.net
See ad page 685.

BUTLER — C2 *Bates*

DIEHLS CORNER RV PARK **Ratings: 3/NA/5.5** (RV Park) 2015 rates: $25. (660)679-1687 rr 2, Box 150/7045 NE Bus 49 Loop at Passaic, Butler, MO 64730

CAMERON — B2 *Clay*

WALLACE (State Pk) From Jct of I-35 & Wallace State Park exit (Hwy 69), S 0.5 mi on Hwy 69 to Hwy 121, E 2 mi (E). 2015 rates: $13 to $21. (816)632-3745

CANTON — A4 *Lewis*

CITY OF CANTON MISSISSIPPI PARK
(Public) From Jct of US 61 & SR-16, E 1.1 mi on SR-16 to 4th St, N 0.1 mi to Henderson St, E 0.2 mi (E) Call for reservations. **FAC:** Paved rds. 23 paved, back-ins (16 x 35), accepts self-contain units only, 14 full hkups, 9 W, 9 E (30/50 amps), tent sites, pit toilets, dump, fire rings. **REC:** Mississippi River: fishing, playground, rec open to public. Pets OK. Partial handicap access. Big rig sites, 2015 rates: $20.
(573)288-4413 Lat: 40.138463, Lon: -91.515728
700 N Front St, Canton, MO 63435
cpp51618@centurytel.net
www.showmecanton.com
See ad this page.

CAPE FAIR — E2 *Taney*

CAPE FAIR PARK (Public Corps) From town, S 1 mi on Hwy 76-82/Lake Rd (E). 2015 rates: $16 to $21. Apr 1 to Oct 31. (417)538-2220

CAPE GIRARDEAU — D5 *Cape Girardeau*

CAPE CAMPING & RV PARK
Ratings: 9.5/8.5★/9 (RV Park) From Jct of I-55 & Exit 99, E 1.5 mi on Hwy 61/Kings Highway (L). **FAC:** Paved/gravel rds. (90 spaces). 52 Avail: 2 paved, 50 gravel, 52 pull-thrus (25 x 75), 52 full hkups (30/50 amps), seasonal sites, WiFi, tent sites, laundry, LP gas, fire rings, firewood. **REC:** pool, pond, fishing, playground. Pets OK. Partial handicap access. Big rig sites, eco-friendly, 2015 rates: $35.
(573)332-8888 Lat: 37.335343, Lon: -89.576333
1900 N Kings Hwy, Cape Girardeau, MO 63701
crvinfo@capervpark.com
www.capervpark.com

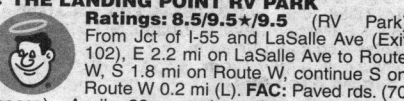

THE LANDING POINT RV PARK
Ratings: 8.5/9.5★/9.5 (RV Park) From Jct of I-55 and LaSalle Ave (Exit 102), E 2.2 mi on LaSalle Ave to Route W, S 1.8 mi on Route W, continue S on Route W 0.2 mi (L). **FAC:** Paved rds. (70 spaces). Avail: 29 paved, patios, 8 pull-thrus (24 x 60), back-ins (24 x 60), 29 full hkups (30/50 amps), WiFi, tent sites, dump, laundry, LP gas, fire rings, firewood. **REC:** playground. Pets OK. Big rig sites, eco-friendly, 2015 rates: $35. Disc: military.
(573)334-7878 Lat: 37.30957, Lon: -89.54956
3020 Boutin Dr, Cape Girardeau, MO 63701
rv@thelandingpoint.com
www.thelandingpoint.com
See ad this page, 682.

TRAIL OF TEARS (State Pk) From Jct of I-55 & US-61 (exit 105, N of town), N 1 mi on US-61 to SR-177, E 10 mi (L). 2015 rates: $13 to $26. (573)290-5268

CARTHAGE — D2 *Jasper*

BALLARD'S CAMPGROUND Ratings: 6/9★/7 (Campground) From Jct of I-44 & Exit 18 A (59S), S 0.25 mi on 59S (L). **FAC:** Gravel rds. (30 spaces). Avail: 22 gravel, 18 pull-thrus (18 x 65), back-ins (20 x 60), mostly side by side hkups, 8 full hkups, 14 W, 8 E (30/50 amps), seasonal sites, WiFi, tent sites, dump, laundry, LP gas, fire rings, firewood. **REC:** pond, fishing. Pets OK. Big rig sites, 2015 rates: $21 to $25.
(417)359-0359 Lat: 37.06194, Lon: -94.31213
13965 Ballard Loop, Carthage, MO 64836
ballardscampground@hughes.net

BIG RED BARN RV PARK
Ratings: 9/9.5★/10 (RV Park) N-bnd: From Jct of I-44 & US 71N, Exit 18-B, Go N 3.2 mi on US 71 to SR-571(Garrison Av), E 0.1 mi on Garrison to S Grand, S 1 mi on Grand to US 71 to SR-571 (Elm Rd)-(L); S-bnd: From Jct of US 71, Exit HH (Fir Rd), E 0.7 mi on Fir to Garrison (SR-571), W 0.25 mi on Garrison to S Grand to Elm (L). **FAC:** Paved rds. (63 spaces). Avail: 55 all weather, patios, 46 pull-thrus (27 x 70), back-ins (20 x 50), 55 full hkups (30/50 amps), seasonal sites, cable, WiFi, tent

CARTHAGE (CONT)

BIG RED BARN RV PARK (CONT)
sites, dump, laundry, LP gas, firewood. **REC:** playground. Pet restrict(B). Big rig sites, 2015 rates: $40. Disc: military.
(417)358-2432 Lat: 37.08160, Lon: -94.31213
13625 Elm Rd, Carthage, MO 64836
info@bigredbarnrvpark.com
www.brbrv.com
See ad pages 695, 682.

COACHLIGHT RV PARK
Ratings: 8.5/NA/9.5 (RV Park) N-bnd: From Jct of I-44 & I-49 (US-71) Exit 18-B(S of town), N 1 mi on I-49 to Exit 47 (Cedar Rd) across frwy to S Outer Rd, S 500 ft (R); or S-bnd: From Jct of I-49 (US-71), take Exit 47 (Cedar Rd), W 500 ft on Cedar Rd to S Outer Rd, S 500 ft (R). **FAC:** Paved rds. (80 spaces). Avail: 50 gravel, 50 pull-thrus (24 x 80), accepts self-contain units only, 50 full hkups (30/50 amps), seasonal sites, cable, WiFi, dump, laundry. **REC.** Pets OK. Partial handicap access, no tents. Big rig sites, 2015 rates: $32.
(417)358-3666 Lat: 37.09344, Lon: -94.31466
5305 S Garrison Ave, Carthage, MO 64836
sales@coachlightrv.com
www.coachlightrv.com
See ad page 694.

Travel Services

COACHLIGHT RV SALES & SERVICE Sales and award winning service on all types off recreational vehicles. Large parts store and indoor showroom. Open year round. **SERVICES:** RV, RV appliance, MH mechanical, restrooms, RV Sales. RV supplies, dump, emergency parking, RV accessible. waiting room. Hours: 8am to 5pm M-F, 8am to 3pm Sat.
(417)358-7444 Lat: 37.09374, Lon: -94.31337
5327 S Garrison Ave, Carthage, MO 64836
sales@coachlightrv.com
www.coachlightrv.com
See ad page 694.

Things to See and Do

CARTHAGE CONVENTION & VISITORS BUREAU Information center for Carthage historical area. Brochures & maps for area attractions, as well as information on the infamous Route 66. Partial handicap access. Restrooms. Hours: Monday - Friday 8:30 A to 5:00 P. No CC.
(866)357-8687 Lat: 37.17576, Lon: -94.31394
402 S. Garrison, Carthage, MO 64836
Wdouglas@ecarthage.com
www.visit-carthage.com
See ad this page.

CARUTHERSVILLE — E5 *Pemiscot*

LADY LUCK CASINO & RV PARK
Ratings: 8.5/10★/10 (RV Park) From Jct of I-55 & Exit 19: E 5-1/4 mi on State Hwy 84 (Hwy 84 turns into Third Street) (L) ; or From Jct of I-155 & MO-84/412 (Exit 6): N 5-1/4 mi on Hwy 84 (turns into Ward St) to Third Street, E 1/10 mi (L). **FAC:** Paved rds. 27 paved, patios, 18 pull-thrus (20 x 68), back-ins (20 x 40), 27 full hkups (30/50 amps), WiFi Hotspot, laundry, restaurant. **REC:** Mississippi River: rec open to public. Pets OK. Partial handicap access, no tents. Big rig sites, 2015 rates: $40. ATM.
(573)333-6000 Lat: 36.17798, Lon: -89.66492
777 E Third St, Caruthersville, MO 63830
www.ladyluckcaruthersville.com
See ad pages 676 (Welcome Section), 682.

Things to See and Do

LADY LUCK CASINO CARUTHERSVILLE Full service Riverboat & Casino, 600+ slots, video poker bar, 11 table games, Otis & Henry's Restaurant & Snackbar, Lone Wolf Entertainment Lounge, Amphitheater & Expo Center. Casino open 24 hr on week-ends. Partial handicap access. RV accessible. Restrooms, food. Hours: 9am to 3am. ATM.
(573)333-6000 Lat: 36.11344, Lon: -89.38942
777 E Third St, Caruthersville, MO 63830
ladyluckcaruthersville.com
See ad page 676 (Welcome Section).

CASSVILLE — E2 *Barry, Taney*

BIG M PARK (Public Corps) From town, E 8 mi on CR-M (E). 2015 rates: $16 to $23. May 1 to Sep 15. (417)271-3190

OAKHILL COURT CABINS & RV PARK **Ratings: 7/8★/7** (Campground) 2015 rates: $25. (800)291-9442 21778 State Hwy 112, Cassville, MO 65625

ROARING RIVER (State Pk) From Jct of SR-37 & SR-112, S 7 mi on SR-112 (R). 2015 rates: $13 to $23. (417)847-2539

CAULFIELD — E3 *Howell*

CLOUD 9 RANCH **Ratings: 8.5/6/7.5** (Membership Pk) 2015 rates: $10 to $30. (417)284-7321 PO Box 50, Caulfield, MO 65626

CENTERVILLE — D4 *Reynolds*

MARK TWAIN NATIONAL FOREST (SUTTON BLUFF CAMPGROUND) (Natl Pk) From town: Go 3 mi NE on Hwy-21, then 7 mi NW on FR-2233, then 3 mi S on FR-2236. 2015 rates: $10 to $20. Mar 26 to Nov 2. (573)648-9293

CHARLESTON — D5 *Mississippi*

BOOMLAND RV PARK & CAMPGROUND **Ratings: 3/4.5/3** (Campground) 2015 rates: $12. (573)683-6108 100 Beasley Park Rd, Charleston, MO 63834

CHESTERFIELD — C4 *St Louis*

DR EDMUND A BABLER MEMORIAL (State Pk) From Jct of Hwys 44 & 100, E 11 mi on Hwy 100 to Hwy 109, W 0.5 mi on Jct C, N 4 mi, follow signs (L). Two-night minimum stay on weekends. 2015 rates: $13 to $21. (636)458-3813

Say you saw it in our Guide!

CLARKSVILLE — B4 *Pike*

TIEVOLI HILLS RESORT **Ratings: 8/6/7.5** (Membership Pk) 2015 rates: $33. (573)242-3577 25795 Hwy N, Clarksville, MO 63336

CLINTON — C2 *Henry*

COZY CORNER RV PARK **Ratings: 9/9★/8** (RV Park) 2015 rates: $30. (660)885-8824 460 SE 91, Clinton, MO 64735

SPARROWFOOT PARK (Public Corps) From town, S 4 mi on Hwy 13 to park access rd, E 1 mi (E). 2015 rates: $8 to $18. (660)885-7546

COLUMBIA — B3 *Boone, Monroe*

COTTONWOODS RV PARK
Ratings: 9.5/10★/9.5 (RV Park) From Jct of I-70 & US-63 (exit 128A), N 3 mi on US-63 to Oakland Gravel Rd (paved), NE 0.25 mi (R); or S-bnd: From Jct of US-63 & Prathersville Rd, E 0.2 mi to Oakland Gravel Rd (paved), S 0.25 mi (L). **FAC:** Paved rds. 97 gravel, patios, 63 pull-thrus (24 x 60), back-ins (24 x 50), 97 full hkups (30/50 amps), WiFi, tent sites, dump, laundry, groc, LP gas, fire rings, firewood. **REC:** pool, playground. Pets OK. Partial handicap access. Big rig sites, eco-friendly, 2015 rates: $30 to $40. Disc: AAA.
(573)474-2747 Lat: 39.00736, Lon: -92.30191
5170 Oakland Gravel Rd, Columbia, MO 65202
contact@cottonwoodspark.com
www.cottonwoodspark.com
See ad this page, 682.

FINGER LAKES (State Pk) From town, N 10 mi on US-63 (E). 2015 rates: $12 to $23. (573)443-5315

PINE GROVE MH AND RV COMMUNITY
Ratings: 6.5/NA/7 (RV Area in MHP) From Jct I-70 & Hwy 63 (Exit 128A): Go 3/4 mi N on Hwy 63, then 1/2 mi E on Clark Lane (R). **FAC:** Paved rds. 50 paved, patios, 9 pull-thrus (20 x 60), back-ins (18 x 40), accepts full hkup units only, 50 full hkups (30/50 amps), WiFi. **REC:** playground. Pet restrict(B). No tents. Big rig sites, 2015 rates: $28. No CC.
(573)474-4412 Lat: 38.95477, Lon: -92.32635
3900 Clark Ln, Columbia, MO 65202
pinegrove@towermgmt.com
www.pinegrovemhc.com

Travel Services

CAMPING WORLD OF COLUMBIA As the nation's largest retailer of RV supplies, accessories, services and new and used RVs, Camping World is committed to making your total RV experience better. RV Accessories: (888)228-6167. **SERVICES:** RV, RV appliance, MH mechanical, restrooms, RV Sales. RV supplies, LP, RV accessible. waiting room. Hours: 8am - 6pm.
(888)690-9564 Lat: 38.960157, Lon: -92.202078
8877 Interstate 70 Dr NE, Columbia, MO 65202
Mike.Wolfe@campingworld.com
www.campingworld.com

CUBA — C4 *Crawford*

MERAMEC VALLEY CAMPGROUND & RV PARK **Ratings: 8/8.5★/7.5** (RV Park) 2015 rates: $45. (573)885-2541 1360 Hwy Uu, Cuba, MO 65453

DANVILLE — B4 *Montgomery*

GRAHAM CAVE (State Pk) From Jct of I-70 & CR-TT, W 2 mi on CR-TT (E). 2015 rates: $12 to $21. (573)564-3476

KAN-DO KAMPGROUND & RV PARK **Ratings: 8/8/8** (Campground) 2015 rates: $25 to $34. (573)564-7993 99 Hwy Tt, Montgomery City, MO 63361

LAZY DAY CAMPGROUND
Ratings: 10/9.5★/9.5 (Campground) From Jct of I-70 & Hwy J (Exit 170), S 1.4 mi on Hwy J (L) Note: use directions, do not use GPS. **FAC:** All weather rds. 63 Avail: 63 all weather, 61 pull-thrus (26 x 70), back-ins (27 x 57), some side by side hkups, 54 full hkups, 9 W, 9 E (30/50 amps), WiFi, tent sites, dump, laundry, groc, LP gas, fire rings, firewood. **REC:** pool, pond, fishing, rec open to public. Pets OK. Big rig sites, eco-friendly, 2015 rates: $34. Disc: military.
(573)564-2949 Lat: 38.895929, Lon: -91.559385
214 Hwy J, Danville, MO 63361
lazydaycamping@aol.com
www.lazydaycampground.com
See ad pages 699, 682.

DE SOTO — C4 *Washington*

WASHINGTON (State Pk) From Jct of SR-110 & SR-21, S 9 mi on SR-21 (R). 2015 rates: $13 to $21. (636)586-5768

DEXTER — E5 *Stoddard*

WILDWOOD RV PARK **Ratings: 5.5/NA/5.5** (RV Park) 2015 rates: $25. (573)624-6214 2106 N Outer Rd, Dexter, MO 63841

DIXON — C3 *Pulaski*

BOILING SPRING CAMPGROUND LLC
Ratings: 8.5/8.5/9 (RV Park) From Jct I-44 & Hwy 28 (Exit 163): Go N 6 mi on Hwy 28, then E 3-4/10 mi on Hwy PP (R) Note: Last 0.2 mi is gravel rd. Due to flooding in 2015, Good Sam Enterprises was unable to inspect this park's facilities. Ratings are from previous year's Guide. **FAC:** Gravel rds. (52 spaces). 46 Avail: 30 gravel, 16 grass, 3 pull-thrus (25 x 60), back-ins (22 x 55), 30 full hkups, 15 W, 16 E (30/50 amps), seasonal sites, tent sites, dump, laundry, groc, LP gas, fire rings, firewood. **REC:** Gasconade River: swim, fishing, rec open to public. Pets OK. Eco-friendly. 2015 rates: $25 to $35. Disc: military. May 15 to Oct 15.
(573)759-7294 Lat: 37.888277, Lon: -92.040779
18700 Cliff Road, Dixon, MO 65459
larryh@dixoncamping.com
www.dixoncamping.com
See ad this page, 682.

MISSOURI FESTIVAL & RV PARK
(RV Park) (Not Visited) E-Bnd: From I-44 & Hwy 28 (Exit 163): Go N 13 mi Hwy 28 to Dixon, then W 1-1/2 mi on Hwy C, then N 4 mi on Hwy 133 (R). OR W-Bnd: From I-44 & Hwy D (Exit 172): Go N 9-1/10 mi on Hwy D, then E 2-8/10 mi on Hwy 28 to Dixon, then W 1-1/2 mi on Hwy C, then N 4 mi on Hwy 133 (R). **FAC:** Gravel rds. 70 gravel, 7 pull-thrus (24 x 80), back-ins (35 x 45), 70 full hkups (30/50 amps), WiFi Hotspot, dump, fire rings, firewood, restaurant. **REC:** rec open to public. Pet restrict No tents. Big rig sites, 2015 rates: $28. May 1 to Oct 31.
(573)759-2378 Lat: 37.999204, Lon: -92.121595
19452 Hwy 133, Dixon, MO 65459
info@missourifestivalandrvpark.com
www.missourifestivalandrvpark.com
See ad this page.

EAGLE ROCK — E2 *Barry*

EAGLE ROCK PARK (Public Corps) From town, S 3 mi on Hwy 86 (R). 2015 rates: $16 to $20. May 1 to Sep 15. (417)271-3215

PARADISE COVE CAMPING RESORT
Ratings: 6.5/10★/9.5 (Campground) From Jct Hwy 86 & Hwy P: Go 1 mi S on Hwy P to Missouri/Arkansas State Line, then 2-1/2 mi W on Lake Rd P3 (Stateline Rd). **FAC:** Paved/gravel rds. 21 Avail: 5 gravel, 16 grass, 1 pull-thrus (25 x 60), back-ins (20 x 30), 5 full hkups, 16 E (30/50 amps), WiFi, tent sites, showers $, dump, laundry, fire rings, firewood, controlled access. **REC:** Table Rock Lake: fishing, playground. Pets OK. Partial handicap access. Eco-friendly, 2015 rates: $16 to $26. Disc: military. No CC.
(417)271-4888 Lat: 36.50326, Lon: -93.73661
18828 Fr 2300, Eagle Rock, MO 65641
paradisecoveresort@gmail.com
www.passport-america.com/campgrounds/campgrounddetails.aspx?campgroundID=1139
See ad page 688.

EAGLEVILLE — A2 *Harrison*

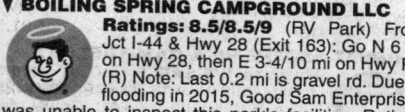

EAGLE RIDGE RV PARK
Ratings: 9.5/8.5/8.5 (Campground) S-Bnd: From Jct of I-35 & CR-N (Exit 106), W 0.5 mi on CR-N to US 69, S 1 mi (R); or N-Bnd: From Jct of I-35 & CR-A (Exit 99), W 0.2 mi on CR-A to US 69, N 5 mi (L). **FAC:** All weather rds. 31 gravel, 14 pull-thrus (24 x 70), back-ins (40 x 50), 22 full hkups, 8 W, 8 E (30/50 amps), WiFi, tent sites, dump, laundry, groc, LP gas, fire rings, firewood. **REC:** pool, pond, fishing, shuffleboard, playground. Pets OK. Big rig sites, 2015 rates: $32. Disc: AAA. No CC.
(660)867-5518 Lat: 40.44821, Lon: -93.99392
22708 W 182nd St, Eagleville, MO 64442
eagleridgervparkmo@gmail.com
www.eagleridgervpark.webs.com
See ad this page, 682.

EL DORADO SPRINGS — C2 *Cedar, St Clair*

ARROWHEAD POINT RV PARK & CAMPGROUND **Ratings: 7.5/9★/8** (Campground) 2015 rates: $22 to $27. Mar 15 to Dec 1. (417)876-3016 755 SW Hwy 54, Osceola, MO 64776

ELKTON — C2 *Hickory*

LIGHTFOOT LANDING PUBLIC USE AREA (Public Corps) From town, S 10 mi on Hwy 83 to CR-RB, E 3 mi (L). 2015 rates: $14 to $20. Apr 16 to Sep 30. (417)282-6890

ELLINGTON — D4 *Wayne*

WEBB CREEK PARK (Public Corps) From town, S 2 mi on Hwy 21 to Hwy H, E 10 mi (E). 2015 rates: $14 to $18. May 15 to Sep 15. (573)223-7777

EMINENCE — D4 *Carter*

OZARK SCENIC RIVERWAY/ALLEY SPRING (Natl Pk) From town, W 6 mi on Hwy 106 (L). 2015 rates: $17 to $33. (573)323-4236

EUREKA — C4 *Jefferson, St Louis*

ST LOUIS WEST/HISTORIC ROUTE 66 KOA **Ratings: 9/9★/8** (Campground) 2015 rates: $59. (636)257-3018 18475 US Hwy 66, Pacific, MO 63069

YOGI BEAR'S JELLYSTONE PARK RESORT AT SIX FLAGS **Ratings: 8.5/8.5★/8** (Campground) 2015 rates: $26.95 to $59.95. Apr 1 to Oct 3. (636)938-5925 5300 Fox Creek Rd, Pacific, MO 63069

Travel Services

BYERLY RV CENTER RV sales plus the areas largest parts and services facilities. Easy access at I-44 and Hwy 109. **SERVICES:** RV, RV appliance, MH mechanical, restrooms, RV Sales. Rentals. RV supplies, LP, emergency parking, RV accessible. waiting room. Hours: M-Sa 8:30am to 6pm.
(636)938-2000 Lat: 38.50573, Lon: -90.61671
295 E 5th Street, Eureka, MO 63025
sales@byerlyrv.com
byerlyrv.com
See ad page 701.

FENTON — C4 *St Louis*

BELLEVILLE RV ESTATES **Ratings: 4.5/NA/7.5** (RV Area in MHP) 2015 rates: $35. (636)343-9182 #1 Heritage Court, Fenton, MO 63026

FORSYTH — E2 *Taney*

BEAVER CREEK (Public Corps) From town, E 4 mi on Hwy 160 to Hwy O, S 2.5 mi (R). 2015 rates: $18 to $19. Apr 1 to Oct 31. (417)546-3708

JELLYSTONE CAMP RESORT **Ratings: 10/9.5★/9** (RV Park) 2015 rates: $49 to $74. (417)546-3000 11020 E State Hwy 76, Forsyth, MO 65653

RIVER RUN PARK (Public Corps) From Jct of US-160 & 76, S 0.5 mi on US-76 (R). 2015 rates: $19 to $20. May 1 to Sep 30. (417)546-3646

SHADOW ROCK PARK (Public) N-bnd on US-160 at Jct of SR-76 (R). Call park for reservations. 2015 rates: $12 to $15. Mar to Oct. (417)546-2876

FULTON — B3 *Callaway*

HIDDEN OAKS RV PARK & CAMPGROUND, LLC **Ratings: 2.5/8.5★/5** (Campground) 2015 rates: $25. Apr 1 to Oct 31. (573)592-8834 4855 Hidden Oaks, Fulton, MO 65251

RED MAPLES MH AND RV COMMUNITY
Ratings: 5/NA/8.5 (RV Area in MHP) From Jct of I-70 & US-54 (exit 148), S 9.1 mi on US-54W to Hwy H, E 0.1 mi on 54 W to NN, S 0.1 mi (L). **FAC:** Paved rds. 15 gravel, back-ins (30 x 65), 15 full hkups (30/50 amps), WiFi. **REC:** playground. Pet restrict(B). No tents. 2015 rates: $30.
(573)642-4282 Lat: 38.91389, Lon: -91.98127
5315 Red Maples Ln, Fulton, MO 65251
redmaples@towermanagement.com
www.towerrvparks.com

GAINESVILLE — E3 *Ozark*

PONTIAC PARK (Public Corps) From town, S 0.2 mi on Hwy W (E). 2015 rates: $15 to $18. (870)679-2222

GLASGOW — B3 *Howard*

STUMP ISLAND PARK & CAMPGROUND (Public) From Jct of Hwy 240 & Old Hwy 87, S 0.5 mi on Old Hwy 87 (R). 2015 rates: $7 to $10. Apr to Nov. (660)338-2377

GLENALLEN — D5 *Bollinger*

CASTOR RIVER RV PARK **Ratings: 7/6/7** (RV Park) 2015 rates: $22 to $30. Apr 15 to Oct 31. (573)495-2485 state Highway Y, Glenallen, MO 63751

GOLDEN — E2 *Stone*

VINEY CREEK (Public Corps) From town, NW 4 mi on US-J (E). 2015 rates: $16 to $21. May 1 to Sep 14. (417)271-3860

GRAIN VALLEY — B2 *Jackson*

TRAILSIDE RV PARK & STORE
Ratings: 9.5/9.5★/8.5 (Campground) From Jct of I-70 & CR-AA (Grain Valley Exit 24), S 80 ft on CR-AA to US 40 West, W 0.3 mi to OOIDA Dr, N 0.1 mi to R.D. Mize, W 0.3 mi (R) Note: Do not use GPS, call park. **FAC:** Paved rds. 69 gravel, 40 pull-thrus (23 x 65), back-ins (18 x 45), 39 full hkups, 30 W, 30 E (30/50 amps), WiFi, tent sites, dump, mobile sewer, laundry, groc, LP gas. **REC:** pool, playground. Pet restrict(B). Partial handicap access. Big rig sites, 28 day max stay, eco-friendly, 2015 rates: $34 to $36.
(800)748-7729 Lat: 39.022096, Lon: -94.210532
1000 R.D. Mize Rd, Grain Valley, MO 64029
trvpark@gmail.com
www.trailsidervpark.com
See ad this page, 682.

Travel Services

CAMPING WORLD OF GRAIN VALLEY/KANSAS CITY As the nation's largest retailer of RV supplies, accessories, services and new and used RVs, Camping World is committed to making your total RV experience better. RV Accessories: (855)809-9218. **SERVICES:** RV, RV appliance, restrooms, RV Sales. RV supplies, LP, RV accessible. waiting room. Hours: 8am - 6pm. (888)504-5167 Lat: 39.025210, Lon: -94.224800 3001 NE Jefferson, Grain Valley, MO 64029 kenny.durham@campingworld.com www.campingworldofkansascity.com

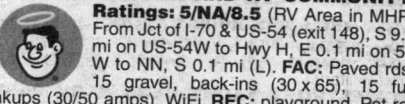

Heading South? We have lots of Snowbird Destination ideas to explore at the front of the Guide.

Like Us on Facebook.

GRAVOIS MILLS — C3 *Morgan*

HAVA SPACE RV PARK & CAMPGROUND **Ratings: 7.5/9★/8** (RV Park) 2015 rates: $30. (573)372-3466 13242 Montana Rd, Gravois Mills, MO 65037

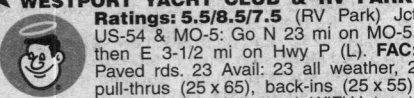

WESTPORT YACHT CLUB & RV PARK Ratings: 5.5/8.5/7.5 (RV Park) Jct US-54 & MO-5: Go N 23 mi on MO-5, then E 3-1/2 mi on Hwy P (L). **FAC:** Paved rds. 23 Avail: 23 all weather, 2 pull-thrus (25 x 65), back-ins (25 x 55), 10 full hkups, 13 W, 13 E (30/50 amps), WiFi Hotspot, tent sites, dump, fire rings, firewood. **REC:** Lake of Ozarks: swim, fishing, marina, rec open to public. Pets OK. Big rig sites, 2015 rates: $35.
(573)372-6112 Lat: 38.261021, Lon: -92.778886
16319 P Road, Gravois Mills, MO 65037
justin@westportyachtclub.com
www.westportyachtclub.com
See ad page 696.

GREENVILLE — D4 *Wayne*

GREENVILLE CAMPGROUND (Public Corps) From town, S 2 mi on US-67 (R). 2015 rates: $10 to $36. Mar 29 to Nov 18. (573)224-3884

HANNIBAL — B4 *Marion, Ralls*

HANNIBAL See also Bowling Green, Canton, La Grange & Monroe City.

MARK TWAIN CAVE & CAMPGROUND **Ratings: 8/8.5★/7.5** (Campground) 2015 rates: $28 to $32. Apr 1 to Nov 1. (800)527-0304 300 Cave Hollow Road, Hannibal, MO 63401

HERMANN — C4 *Gasconade*

HERMANN CITY PARK (Public) In town, Hwy 100 to Gasconade St, N 0.5 mi (R). 2015 rates: $15 to $30. Mar 24 to Oct 31. (573)486-5400

HERMITAGE — C2 *Hickory*

DAMSITE AREA (Public Corps) From town, S 3 mi on Hwy 254, W 0.5 mi (L). 2015 rates: $12 to $22. Apr 16 to Sep 30. (417)745-2244

NEMO LANDING AREA (Public Corps) From Jct of Hwys 254 & 64, S 4 mi on Hwy 64 (L). 2015 rates: $12 to $20. Apr 16 to Sep 30. (417)993-5529

OUTLET PARK (Public Corps) From town, S 4 mi on Hwy 254 (R). 2015 rates: $12 to $20. Apr 16 to Sep 30. (417)745-2290

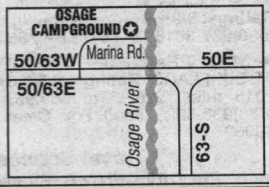

WHEATLAND PARK (Public Corps) From town, S 4 mi on Hwy 83 to Hwy 254, S 3 mi to Hwy 254/25, S 2 mi (E). 2015 rates: $12 to $20. Apr 16 to Sep 30. (417)745-6411

HIGGINSVILLE — B2 *Clay, Lafayette*

FAIRGROUND PARK (Public) From Jct of I-70 & Hwy 13, N 4 mi on Hwy 13 (R). 2015 rates: $10. (660)584-7313

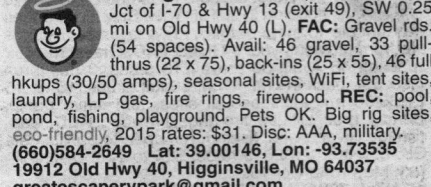

GREAT ESCAPE RV & CAMP RESORT Ratings: 9/8.5★/7.5 (RV Park) From Jct of I-70 & Hwy 13 (exit 49), SW 0.25 mi on Old Hwy 40 (L). **FAC:** Gravel rds. (54 spaces). Avail: 46 gravel, 33 pull-thrus (22 x 75), back-ins (25 x 55), 46 full hkups (30/50 amps), seasonal sites, WiFi, tent sites, laundry, LP gas, fire rings, firewood. **REC:** pool, pond, fishing, playground. Pets OK. Big rig sites, eco-friendly, 2015 rates: $31. Disc: AAA, military.
(660)584-2649 Lat: 39.00146, Lon: -93.73535
19912 Old Hwy 40, Higginsville, MO 64037
greatescapervpark@gmail.com
www.greatescape-camping.com

HIGHLANDVILLE — D2 *Christian*

HWY 160 RV PARK **Ratings: 4/NA/6.5** (RV Park) 2015 rates: $20. (417)443-5000 8180 Hwy 160 South, Highlandville, MO 65669

INDEPENDENCE — B2 *Jackson*

THE CAMPUS RV PARK Ratings: 8/8.5/8.5 (Campground) West bnd: From Jct of I-435 & Truman Rd (Exit 60): go E 3 mi on Truman, S 0.4 mi on Pleasant, W 0.1 mi on Pacific (R) East bnd: From Jct I-70 & MO-291: go N 4 mi on MO-291, W 2 mi on Truman Rd, S 0.4 mi on Pleasant, W 0.1 mi on Pacific (R) Note: Follow directions or call park, don't use GPS. **FAC:** Paved rds. 30 paved, patios, 3 pull-thrus (25 x 45), back-ins (25 x 55), 30 full hkups (30/50 amps), WiFi, laundry. **REC.** Pets OK. Partial handicap access, no tents. Big rig sites, eco-friendly, 2015 rates: $29.50.
(816)254-1815 Lat: 39.087823, Lon: -94.423977
500 W Pacific, Independence, MO 64050
www.campusrv.com

IRONTON — D4 *Iron*

TAUM SAUK (State Pk) From jct Hwy 21 and Hwy CC: Go 4 mi W on Hwy CC. Pit toilets. 2015 rates: $13. (573)546-2450

JEFFERSON CITY — C3 *Cole*

BINDER CAMPGROUND (Public) From Jct of Hwy 50 & Bus 50 (St Martins Apache Flats Exit), W 1.2 mi on Bus 50 to Binder Rd, N 0.3 mi to Rainbow Dr, W 0.1 mi (R). 2015 rates: $15. (573)634-6482

MARI OSA DELTA CAMPGROUND **Ratings: 6.5/8★/7** (Campground) 2015 rates: $24 to $27. (573)455-2452 285 Mari Osa Delta Lane, Jefferson City, MO 65101

OSAGE CAMPGROUND & MORE Ratings: 6.5/NA/5 (Campground) From Jct of US-50/US-63 & US-54 (in Jefferson City), E 10 mi on US-50/US-63 to Marina Rd (public access rd before Osage River), E 0.4 mi (L). **FAC:** Gravel rds. (36 spaces). Avail: 24 grass, 14 pull-thrus (26 x 100), back-ins (40 x 70), accepts full hkup units only, 24 full hkups (30/50 amps), seasonal sites, WiFi, dump, laundry, fire rings, firewood. **REC:** Osage River: fishing, playground. Pets OK. No tents. 2015 rates: $24.50.
(573)395-4066 Lat: 38.49335, Lon: -92.00226
10407 Marina Rd, Jefferson City, MO 65101
osagecamp1@aol.com
See ad this page.

Things to See and Do

MISSOURI DIVISION OF TOURISM Visit Welcome Centers at Major Highway entrances into State for Missouri travel information. Including free maps & brochures. Partial handicap access. RV accessible. Restrooms, food. Hours: 8am to 5pm. No CC.
(573)526-5900 Lat: 38.57873, Lon: -92.17515

JEFFERSON CITY (CONT)

MISSOURI DIVISION OF TOURISM (CONT)
301 W. High Street, Truman Bldg, Rm 290, Jefferson City, MO 65101
tourism@visitmo.com
www.visitmo.com
See ad page 678 (Welcome Section).

JONESBURG — C4 *Montgomery*

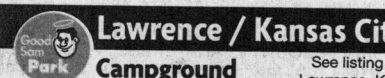

JONESBURG GARDENS CAMPGROUND
Ratings: 8/9★/7 (Campground) From Jct of I-70 & Exit 183 (Hwy E), N 0.1 mi to outer service rd, W 0.6 mi to Hwy E, N 0.2 mi (R). **FAC:** Gravel rds. 45 gravel, 36 pull-thrus (24 x 60), back-ins (15 x 20), some side by side hkups, 45 full hkups (30/50 amps), WiFi, tent sites, rentals, laundry, groc, LP gas, fire rings, firewood. **REC:** heated pool, pond, fishing, playground, rec open to public. Pets OK. Eco-friendly, 2015 rates: $30 to $34.
(636)488-5630 Lat: 38.86069, Lon: -91.31316
15 Hwy E, Jonesburg, MO 63351
jonesburggardens@aol.com
www.jonesburggardenscampground.com

JOPLIN — D1 *Newton*

JOPLIN See also Carthage, Nevada & Sarcoxie.

DOWNSTREAM Q STORE RV PARK **Ratings: 8.5/NA/8** (RV Park) 2015 rates: $30. (417)626-6750 4777 Downstream Blvd, Joplin, MO 64804

KOA JOPLIN **Ratings: 9/9.5★/7.5** (Campground) 2015 rates: $50 to $61. (417)623-2246 4359 Dakota Lane, Joplin, MO 64804

Travel Services

CUMMINS CENTRAL POWER Cummins Central Power is the exclusive distributor for Cummins and Onan products in the Midwest. 12 full-service locations in Nebraska, Kansas, Missoiri, Iowa, South Dakota and Illinois support engine and generator customers. **SERVICES:** Tire, engine/chassis repair, restrooms. RV storage. Emergency parking, RV accessible. waiting room. Hours: 7:30am - 12:30am Mon-Fri.
(417)623-1661 Lat: 37.054750, Lon: -94.452636
4915 E 32nd St, Joplin, MO 64801
centralpower@cummins.com
cumminscentralpower.com
See ad page 732.

Tell them you saw them in this Guide!

KANSAS CITY — B1 *Clay*

METROPOLITAN KANSAS CITY AREA MAP

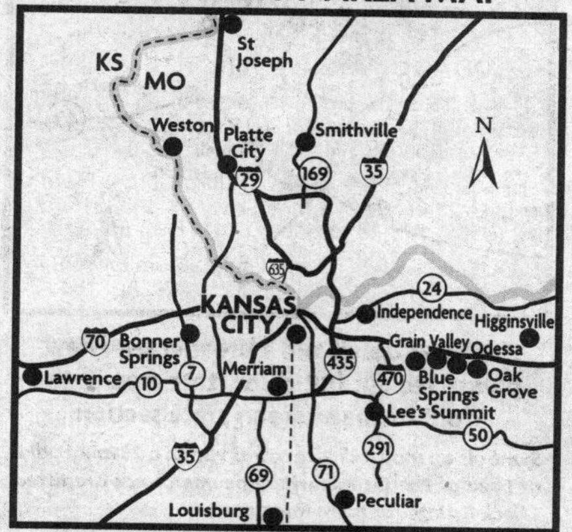

Symbols on map indicate towns within a 40 mile radius of Kansas City where campgrounds are listed. Check listings for more information.

In MO, see also Blue Springs, Grain Valley, Higginsville, Independence, Lee's Summit, Oak Grove, Odessa, Peculiar, Platte City, Smithville, St Joseph & Weston.
In KS, see also Bonner Springs, Lawrence, Louisburg & Merriam.

We appreciate your business!

COUNTRY GARDENS RV PARK
Ratings: 8/10★/9.5 (RV Park) E-Bnd: From Jct of I-70 & Hwy 131(Exit 37B), N 0.1 mi on Hwy 131 to N Outer Rd, W 0.6 mi (R). **FAC:** Paved rds. (45 spaces). 37 Avail: 19 paved, 18 gravel, patios, 9 pull-thrus (28 x 70), back-ins (28 x 60), 37 full hkups (30/50 amps), seasonal sites, WiFi, laundry, LP gas. **REC.** Pets OK. Partial handicap access. Big rig sites, eco-friendly, 2015 rates: $30 to $40.
(816)633-8720 Lat: 39.00970, Lon: -93.97156
7089 Outer Rd, Odessa, MO 64076
info@countrygardensrv.com
www.countrygardensrv.com
See primary listing at Odessa and ad page 697.

LONGVIEW LAKE CAMPGROUND (Public) From Jct of US-71 & I-470, E 4.2 mi on I-470 to View High Dr (exit 5), S 2.9 mi to Longview Dr. W 0.4 on Longview Dr (follow signs to campground on no name rd), 2 mi (E). 2015 rates: $17 to $28. Apr 1 to Sep 30. (816)503-4800

WORLDS OF FUN VILLAGE **Ratings: 9.5/9.5★/8.5** (RV Park) 2015 rates: $38 to $50. (816)454-4545 8000 Parvin Rd., Kansas City, MO 64161

Travel Services

CUMMINS CENTRAL POWER Cummins Central Power is the exclusive distributor for Cummins and Onan parts in the Midwest. 12 full-service locations in Nebraska, Missouri, Iowa, South Dakota and Illinois support engine and generator customers. **SERVICES:** RV appliance, MH mechanical, engine/chassis repair, mobile RV svc, emergency rd svc, restrooms. **TOW:** RV, auto. RV supplies, LP, emergency parking, RV accessible. waiting room. Hours: 7a-Midnt M-F,Sat 7a-3:30p,Coachcare M-F.
(816)414-8200 Lat: 39.167532, Lon: -94.483031
8201 NE Parvin Road, Kansas City, MO 64068
centralpower@cummins.com
cumminscentralpower.com
See ad page 732.

KIMBERLING CITY — E2 *Stone, Taney*

AUNTS CREEK PARK (Public Corps) From town, N 3 mi on Hwy 13 to SR-00, W 3 mi (E). 2015 rates: $16 to $20. May 1 to Sep 14. (417)739-2792

AUNTS CREEK RV PARK **Ratings: 7/6.5/6** (Campground) 2015 rates: $24 to $28. (800)587-1112 2799 State Hwy Oo, Reeds Spring, MO 65737

PORT OF KIMBERLING MARINA & RESORT **Ratings: 7.5/9.5★/6.5** (Campground) 2015 rates: $21 to $32. (800)439-3500 72 Marina Way, Kimberling City, MO 65686

We rate what RVers consider important.

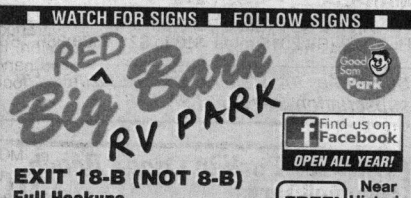

KINGDOM CITY — B3 *Osage, Callaway*

← HANSON HILLS CAMPGROUND **Ratings: 8.5/5.5/6.5** (Campground) 2015 rates: $23 to $28. (573)642-8600 3643 CR 221, Kingdom City, MO 65262

KIRKSVILLE — A3 *Adair*

← LAKEROAD VILLAGE RV PARK Ratings: 6/8.5★/6 (RV Park) From Jct of US-63 & Potter Ave, W 1.4 mi on Potter Ave (L). **FAC:** Paved rds. (46 spaces). Avail: 12 gravel, 4 pull-thrus (35 x 80), back-ins (35 x 60), 12 full hkups (30/50 amps), seasonal sites, laundry. Pets OK. No tents. Big rig sites, 2015 rates: $30.
AAA Approved
(660)665-2228 Lat: 40.21260, Lon: -92.60928
23067 Potter Trail, No 1, Kirksville, MO 63501
lakeroadrv@hughes.net

↙ THOUSAND HILLS (State Pk) From town, W 2 mi on Hwy 6 to Hwy 157, S 2 mi (L). 2015 rates: $13 to $21. (660)665-6995

KNOB NOSTER — C2 *Benton*

↙ KNOB NOSTER (State Pk) From town, W 1 mi on US-50 to Hwy 23, S 2 mi (R). 2015 rates: $13 to $36. (660)563-2463

LA GRANGE — A4 *Lewis*

↑ WAKONDA (State Pk) From town, S 3 mi on US-61 to Rte B exit, follow signs (L). 2015 rates: $13 to $21. (573)655-2280

LACLEDE — B2 *Clay*

← PERSHING (State Pk) From town, W 3 mi on US-36 to SR-130, S 2 mi (R). 2015 rates: $12 to $26. (660)963-2299

How can you tell whether you're traveling in the right direction? The arrow in each listing denotes the compass direction of the facility in relation to the listed town. For example, an arrow pointing straight up indicates that the facility is located due north from town. An arrow pointing down and to the right indicates that the facility is southeast of town.

Our inspectors look for the same things you do. Our unique Triple Rating System is based on years of market research, analysis and surveys from RVers like you. One thing you suggested was the need for separate ratings on facility completeness, restroom cleanliness/construction, and visual appearance/environmental quality. So we give three ratings, each based on a scale of 1 to 10, 10 being best and 5 being average. To give you an idea how tough we are, less than 1% of inspected campgrounds receive 10/10/10 ratings.*

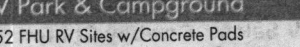

LAKE OF THE OZARKS — C3 *Miller*

LAKE OF THE OZARKS AREA MAP

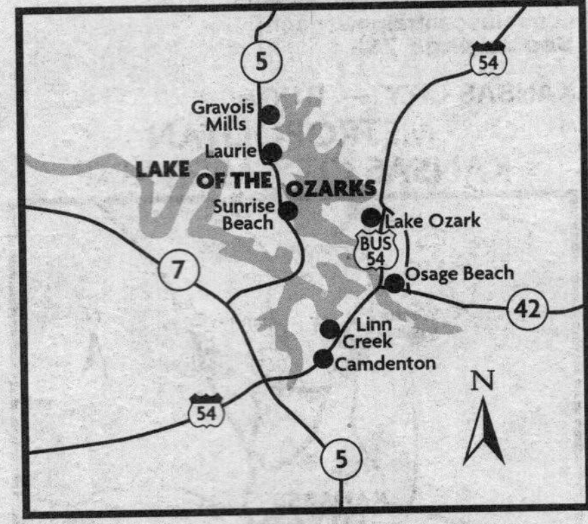

For more detail and a broader overview, please see our full-color state map at the front of the Missouri state section.

Symbols on map indicate towns within a 25 mile radius of Lake of the Ozarks where campgrounds are listed. Check listings for more information.

See also Camdenton, Gravois Mills, Lake Ozark, Laurie, Linn Creek, Osage Beach & Sunrise Beach.

LAKE OZARK — C3 *Miller*

↖ CROSS CREEK RV PARK **Ratings: 8.5/8/8** (Campground) 2015 rates: $40. Apr 11 to Nov 1. (888)250-3885 41 Old Trail Dr, Eldon, MO 65026

↖ MAJESTIC OAKS PARK **Ratings: 8.5/9★/8.5** (Campground) 2015 rates: $35. Apr 1 to Oct 31. (573)365-1890 8 Majestic Oaks Rd, Eldon, MO 65026

→ RIVERVIEW RV PARK
Ratings: 9/10★/10 (Campground) N-bnd: From Jct US-54 & Bus US-54 (S of town): Go E 1 mi on US-54, then N 100 yards on Woodriver Rd (watch carefully for small sign) (R); OR S-bnd: From North Jct Bus US-54 & US-54: Go W 2.3 mi on US-54, then S immediately after Osage River Bridge on Woodriver Rd (L). **FAC:** Gravel rds. 75 gravel, 7 pull-thrus (34 x 40), back-ins (30 x 45), 75 full hkups (30/50 amps), WiFi, tent sites, dump, laundry, groc, LP gas. **REC:** pool, Osage River: fishing, playground, rec open to public. Pets OK. Big rig sites, eco-friendly, 2015 rates: $32. Disc: AAA, military.
(573)365-1122 Lat: 38.189437, Lon: -92.606648
398 Woodriver Road, Lake Ozark, MO 65049
info@riverviewrvparkllc.com
www.riverviewrvparkllc.com
See ad this page, 682.

LAURIE — C3 *Morgan*

→ LAURIE RV PARK **Ratings: 6/7.5/8** (Campground) 2015 rates: $32. (573)374-8469 515 Hwy O, Laurie, MO 65037

LAWSON — B2 *Clay*

↙ WATKINS MILL (State Pk) From Jct of US-69 & Hwy 92, W 1.5 mi on Hwy 92. 2015 rates: $13 to $21. (816)580-3387

LEASBURG — C4 *Crawford*

→ ONONDAGA CAVE (State Pk) From Jct of I-44 & Hwy H (Leasburg exit), S 6 mi on Hwy H (R). 2015 rates: $12 to $26. (573)245-6576

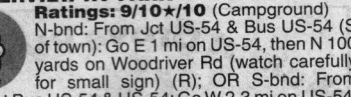

↓ OZARK OUTDOORS/RIVERFRONT RESORT **Ratings: 8/6.5/8** (Campground) 2015 rates: $25 to $50. (800)888-0023 200 Ozark Outdoors Lane, Leasburg, MO 65535

LEBANON — D3 *Laclede*

↙ HAPPY TRAILS RV PARK
Ratings: 9/9★/7 (Campground) From Jct of I-44 & cnty rd (exit 123), S 100 yds on Cnty Rd to S outer rd, E 0.2 mi (R). **FAC:** Paved/gravel rds. (36 spaces). Avail: 30 gravel, 30 pull-thrus (20 x 65), 13 full hkups, 17 W, 17 E (30/50 amps), seasonal sites, WiFi, tent sites, rentals, dump, laundry, groc, LP gas, fire rings, firewood. **REC:** pool, Mockingbird Lake: fishing, playground, rec open to public. Pets OK. Big rig sites, 2015 rates: $28 to $34. Disc: AAA.
(417)532-3422 Lat: 37.59793, Lon: -92.72136
18376 Campground Rd, Phillipsburg, MO 65722
reservations@happytrailsrvpark.com
www.happytrailrvpark.com

↗ HIDDEN VALLEY OUTFITTERS
Ratings: 7/9.5★/10 (RV Park) Jct US-44 & MO-5/MO-64: Go N 13 mi on MO-5/MO-64, then W 14 mi on MO-64W, then N 250 ft on Co Rd WW-962/Harvest Rd, then W Marigold Rd (L). **FAC:** Paved/gravel rds. (151 spaces). Avail: 52 paved, patios, 40 pull-thrus (22 x 52), back-ins (22 x 52), 52 full hkups (30/50 amps), seasonal sites, WiFi Hotspot, tent sites, dump, laundry, groc, fire rings, firewood, controlled access. **REC:** Niangua River: swim, fishing, playground, rec open to public. Pets OK. Partial handicap access. Big rig sites, eco-friendly, 2015 rates: $35. Disc: military. Mar 1 to Oct 31.
(417)533-5628 Lat: 37.738053, Lon: -92.859129
27101 Marigold Rd, Lebanon, MO 65536
info@hvoutfitters.com
www.hvoutfitters.com
See ad this page, 682.

LEES SUMMIT — B2 *Jackson*

↙ FLEMING PARK/BLUE SPRINGS CAMPGROUND (Public) From Jct of I-70 & I-470 (Exit 14), S 2.5 mi on I-470 to Bowlin Rd, E 0.4 mi on Bowlin Rd to NE Campground Rd, N 0.4 (E). 2015 rates: $21 to $28. May 16 to Sep 3. (816)503-4800

JACOMO CAMPGROUND AT FLEMING PARK (JACKSON COUNTY PARK) (Public) W'bound from I-470 (exit 10A): Go 1-3/4 mi E on Colbern Rd to park entrance, then 1/2 mi N to campground entrance. E'bound from I-470 (exit 9) & Douglas St: Go 1/4 mi N, then 2-1/2 mi E on Colbern Rd to park entrance, then 1/2 mi N to campground entrance. 2015 rates: $17 to $28. (816)795-8200

LESTERVILLE — D4 *Wayne*

↙ JOHNSON'S SHUT-INS (State Pk) From Jct of Hwy 49/72 & CR-N, N 6 mi on CR-N (R). 2015 rates: $12 to $52. (573)546-2450

LINN CREEK — C3 *Camden*

→ OZARK TRAILS RV PARK **Ratings: 7.5/8/7.5** (Campground) 2015 rates: $28 to $32. (573)346-5490 #1 Campground Dr, Linn Creek, MO 65052

LOWRY CITY — C2 *St Clair*

→ TALLEY BEND PARK (Public Corps) From Jct of Hwys 13 & C, E 6 mi on Hwy C/becomes Hwy C (R). 2015 rates: $8 to $18. (660)664-2024

MACON — B3 *Monroe*

← LONG BRANCH (State Pk) From Jct of Hwys 63 & 36, W 3 mi on Hwy 36 to park access rd, follow signs (E). 2015 rates: $12 to $23. (660)773-5229

MARSHALL — B2 *Saline*

↖ VAN METER (State Pk) From town, NW 12 mi on Hwy 122 (R). 2015 rates: $13 to $21. (660)886-7537

Subscribe to Trailer Life Magazine. For a subscription, call 800-825-6861.

MARSHFIELD — D3 *Webster*

RV EXPRESS 66
Ratings: 9/10★/8.5 (RV Park) From Jct of I-44 & Hwy 38 (Spur Rd) Exit 100: Go S 300 ft on Hwy 38/Spur Rd, take immediate L to enter park. **FAC:** Paved rds. (16 spaces). Avail: 12 paved, patios, 7 pull-thrus (22 x 70), back-ins (23 x 65), 12 full hkups (30/50 amps), seasonal sites, cable, WiFi, laundry. **REC:** pool. Pets OK. Partial handicap access. Big rig sites, eco-friendly, 2015 rates: $30. Disc: military.
(417)859-7837 Lat: 37.34329, Lon: -92.92887
1469 Spur Drive, Marshfield, MO 65706
rvexpress66@gmail.com
www.rvexpress66.com
See ad pages 699, 682.

MAYSVILLE — A2 *DeKalb*

PONY EXPRESS RV PARK & CAMPGROUND **Ratings: 7/8.5/7** (RV Park) 2015 rates: $30. Apr 1 to Oct 31. (816)449-2039 4469 S Hwy 33, Maysville, MO 64469

MEXICO — B3 *Saline*

LAKEVIEW PARK (Public) From Jct of I-70 & US-54, N 17 mi on US-54 to Lakeview St, W 0.1 mi, S on Fairground (E). Pit toilets. 2015 rates: $8 to $10. Apr 1 to Oct 31. (573)581-2100

MOBERLY — B3 *Randolph*

ROTHWELL PARK CAMPGROUND (CITY PARK) (Public) From jct US 63 & US 24: Go 3 mi W on US 24, then 1/4 mi S on Rothwell Park Rd. 2015 rates: $8 to $20. (660)263-6757

MONROE CITY — B3 *Ralls*

INDIAN CREEK REC AREA (Public Corps) From Jct of Hwy 24 & Hwy HH, S 1.5 mi on Hwy HH to park access rd, E 3 mi (E). 2015 rates: $8 to $24. (573)735-4097

MARK TWAIN LANDING
Ratings: 10/10★/10 (RV Park) From Jct of US-36 & MO-J, S 7.7 mi on MO-J (R).

From our RV & tent sites, cabins, and motel you can walk to our Playland with go carts, bumper boats, miniature golf & more. Splash around in our water park and ride the waves.

FAC: Paved rds. 36 paved, patios, back-ins (27 x 60), 36 full hkups (30/50 amps), cable, WiFi, tent sites, rentals, laundry, groc, fire rings, firewood, restaurant, controlled access. **REC:** pool, pond, fishing, playground, rec open to public. Pet restrict(B). Partial handicap access. Big rig sites, eco-friendly, 2015 rates: $42 to $59. Disc: AAA, military. ATM.
(573)735-9422 Lat: 39.55193, Lon: -91.66148
42819 Landing Ln, Monroe City, MO 63456
info@marktwainlanding.com
www.marktwainlanding.com
See ad pages 690, 682 & Family Camping in Magazine Section.

Things to See and Do

MARK TWAIN LANDING WATER PARK One of Missouri's three largest wave pools, water slides, lazy river, activity & toddler pools. 5 water slides. Tiki bar, snack bar & gift shop. May 24 to Sep 1. partial handicap access. RV accessible. Restrooms, food. Hours: 11am to 7pm daily. Adult fee: $25. ATM.
(573)735-4242 Lat: 39.56224, Lon: -91.66084
42819 Landing Ln, Monroe City, MO 63456
waterpark@marktwainlanding.com
www.marktwainlanding.com
See ad page 690.

MOUNTAIN GROVE — D3 *Wright*

MISSOURI RV PARK
Ratings: 8.5/9★/8 (Campground) From Jct of Hwy 95 & US-60, W 2 mi on US-60 to Bus 60 exit, W 1 mi on N Outer Rd (follow signs) (R). **FAC:** Paved/gravel rds. (60 spaces). Avail: 50 gravel, 35 pull-thrus (25 x 75), back-ins (24 x 70), 50 full hkups (30/50 amps), seasonal sites, WiFi, tent sites, laundry, groc. **REC:** pool, playground. Pets OK. Big rig sites, eco-friendly, 2015 rates: $28.
(417)926-4104 Lat: 37.13215, Lon: -92.32218
2325 Missouri Park Dr, Mountain Grove, MO 65711
mopark@centurytel.net
www.morvpark.net
See ad this page, 682.

MOUNTAIN VIEW — D3 *Howell*

OZARK'S MOUNTAIN SPRINGS RV PARK
Ratings: 8.5/10★/9 (RV Park) E-bnd: From Jct of Hwy 60 & Hwy 63, E 4 mi on Hwy 60 (L); or W-bnd: From Jct of Hwy 17 & Hwy 60 (in Mountain View), W 12 mi on Hwy 60 (R). **FAC:** Paved rds. 60 gravel, 53 pull-thrus (24 x 60), back-ins (20 x 40), 60 full hkups (30/50 amps), WiFi, tent sites, rentals, dump, laundry, firewood. **REC:** playground. Pet restrict(B). Partial handicap access. Big rig sites, eco-friendly, 2015 rates: $28.50 to $30.50. Disc: military.
(417)469-3351 Lat: 36.97207, Lon: -91.86797
5475 US Hwy 60, Mountain View, MO 65548
rwaldron611@gmail.com
www.ozarksrvpark.com
See ad this page, 682.

NEOSHO — D2 *Newton*

STAGE STOP CAMPGROUND
Ratings: 5/8.5★/8 (Campground) From Jct I-49 & Hwy 86 (Exit 27): Go 1/4 mi E on Hwy 86 to Hammer Rd., then 3/4 mi N on Hammer Rd (R). **FAC:** All weather rds. (14 spaces). Avail: 10 all weather, 5 pull-thrus (25 x 70), back-ins (25 x 45), 10 full hkups (30/50 amps), seasonal sites, WiFi, laundry, firewood. **REC.** Pets OK. No tents. Big rig sites, 2015 rates: $20. No CC, no reservations.
(417)455-1221 Lat: 36.83990, Lon: -94.42200
12201 Hammer Rd, Neosho, MO 64850
stagestopcampground@netadv.net
www.stagestopcampground.net
See ad pages 695, 682.

NEVADA — C2 *Vernon*

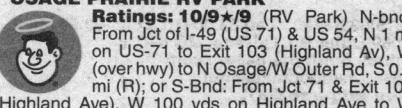

OSAGE PRAIRIE RV PARK
Ratings: 10/9★/9 (RV Park) N-bnd: From Jct of I-49 (US 71) & US 54, N 1 mi on US-71 to Exit 103 (Highland Av), W (over hwy) to N Osage/W Outer Rd, S 0.5 mi (R); or S-Bnd: From Jct 71 & Exit 103 (Highland Ave), W 100 yds on Highland Ave to W Outer Rd, S 0.5 mi (R). **FAC:** All weather rds. (46 spaces). Avail: 44 all weather, 15 pull-thrus (20 x 60), back-ins (20 x 55), 44 full hkups (30/50 amps), seasonal sites, WiFi, tent sites, dump, laundry, groc, firewood. **REC:** pool, playground. Pets OK. Big rig sites, eco-friendly, 2015 rates: $35 to $38. Disc: military.
(417)667-2267 Lat: 37.85331, Lon: -94.34613
1501 N Osage Blvd, Nevada, MO 64772
osageprairierv@yahoo.com
www.osageprairie.com
See ad this page, 682.

NOEL — E1 *McDonald*

RIVER RANCH RESORT **Ratings: 8.5/8/7.5** (Campground) 2015 rates: $30 to $60. May 15 to Sep 15. (800)951-6121 101 River Road, Noel, MO 64854

OAK GROVE — B2 *Jackson*

KOA KANSAS CITY EAST **Ratings: 8.5/9.5★/8.5** (Campground) 2015 rates: $42.90 to $70. (816)690-6660 303 NE 3rd St, Oak Grove, MO 64075

LAKE PARADISE RESORT **Ratings: 7.5/5.5/5.5** (Membership Pk) 2015 rates: $37 to $44. (816)690-4113 985 NW 1901st Rd, Lone Jack, MO 64070

ODESSA — B2 *Lafayette*

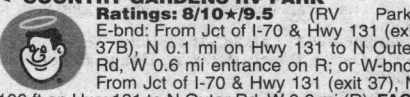

COUNTRY GARDENS RV PARK
Ratings: 8/10★/9.5 (RV Park) E-bnd: From Jct of I-70 & Hwy 131 (exit 37B), N 0.1 mi on Hwy 131 to N Outer Rd, W 0.6 mi entrance on R; or W-bnd: From Jct of I-70 & Hwy 131 (exit 37), N 100 ft on Hwy 131 to N Outer Rd, W 0.6 mi (R). **FAC:** Paved rds. (45 spaces). 37 Avail: 19 paved, 18 gravel, patios, 9 pull-thrus (28 x 70), back-ins (28 x 60), 37 full hkups (30/50 amps), seasonal sites, WiFi, laundry, LP gas. **REC.** Pets OK. Partial handicap access, no tents. Big rig sites, RV age restrict, eco-friendly, 2015 rates: $30 to $40.
(816)633-8720 Lat: 39.00970, Lon: -93.97156
7089 Outer Rd, Odessa, MO 64076
info@countrygardensrv.com
www.countrygardensrv.com
See ad this page, 682.

RV Park ratings you can rely on!

Got a different point of view? We want to know. Rate the campgrounds you visit using the rating guidelines located in front of this Guide, then compare your ratings to ours.

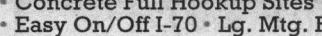

ODESSA (CONT)

Things to See and Do

ONE GOOD TASTE COUNTRY STORE Unique country store featuring cheese samples, ham & meat sticks, Amish-style bulk foods & spices, old fashioned snacks, candies, jams & pickled fruit & vegetables, greeting cards, candles & gifts and wood stoves. Partial handicap access. RV accessible. Food. Hours: Mon-Sat 8a to 6p Sun 9a to 6p.
(816)633-8720 Lat: 39.00970, Lon: -93.97156
7089 Outer Rd, Odessa, MO 64076
info@countrygardensrv.com
www.onegoodtaste.com
See ad page 697.

OSAGE BEACH — C3 *Miller*

LAKE OF THE OZARKS (State Pk) From Jct of US-54 & Hwy 42, E 4 mi on Hwy 42 to Hwy 134, S 5 mi (L). 2015 rates: $12 to $36. (573)348-2694

OSAGE BEACH RV PARK
Ratings: 9/9.5★/9.5 (Campground) From Jct US 54 Expressway & SR-42/Osage Beach Parkway North Exit: Go N 1/2 mi on SR-42,then E 1/4 mi on (watch for sign on right) to Access Road (watch for sign on R), then S 1/10 mi to office (R). **FAC:** Gravel rds. 49 gravel, 30 pull-thrus (26 x 70), back-ins (34 x 54), 49 full hkups (30/50 amps), cable, WiFi, rentals, dump, laundry, LP gas. **REC:** pool, wading pool, shuffleboard, playground. Pet restrict(B/Q). No tents. Big rig sites, eco-friendly, 2015 rates: $35. Disc: AAA. Mar 28 to Nov 3.
(573)348-3445 Lat: 38.152729, Lon: -92.602989
3949 Campground Lane, Osage Beach, MO 65065
info@osagebeachrvpark.net
www.osagebeachrvpark.net
See ad pages 696, 682.

Things to See and Do

LAKE OF THE OZARKS CONVENTION & VISITORS BUREAU Convention & Visitors Bureau. Call for free vacation guide. Partial handicap access. Restrooms. Hours: 8am to 5pm M-F. No CC.
(800)386-5253 Lat: 38.11933, Lon: -92.68165
5815 Osage Beach Parkway, Osage Beach, MO 65065
info@funlake.com
www.FunLake.com
See ad page 683.

OSCEOLA — C2 *St Clair*

OSCEOLA RV PARK (Public) S-bnd: Jct SR-13 & Bus 13/Truman Rd (N of town at Hospital H sign), W 0.5 mi on Bus 13/Truman to Parkview Dr, N 300 ft (L); or N-bnd: Jct SR-13 & Bus 13/SR-82 (S of town), W 0.1 on Bus 13/SR-82 to Bus 13, W 1 mi to Lakeshore Dr, N 0.3 mi to Parkview Dr, N 300 ft (L). 2015 rates: $15.50 to $16. (417)646-8675

OWENSVILLE — C4 *Gasconade*

LOST VALLEY LAKE RESORT **Ratings: 8.5/9.5/9.5** (Membership Pk) 2015 rates: $20 to $30. (573)764-2129 2334 Hwy Zz, Owensville, MO 65066

OZARK — D2 *Christian*

OZARK RV PARK **Ratings: 5.5/NA/6.5** (RV Park) 2015 rates: $25. (417)581-3203 320 N 20th St, Ozark, MO 65721

STAGE STOP RV PARK Ratings: 3/NA/4.5 (RV Park) From jct US 65 & exit CC & J (Fremont Hills): Go 1/2 mi E on Rte J, then 1/4 mi S on 17th St to W. Boat, turn R. **FAC:** Gravel rds. (36 spaces). Avail: 26 gravel, 26 pull-thrus (21 x 65), accepts self-contain units only, 26 full hkups (30/50 amps), seasonal sites, WiFi. **REC:** rec open to public. Pets OK. No tents. Big rig sites, 2015 rates: $25. No CC, no reservations.
AAA Approved
(417)830-1184 Lat: 37.02393, Lon: -93.22998
5251 N 17th Street, Ozark, MO 65721
stagestoprv@aol.com
www.STAGESTOPRV.com

PATTERSON — D4 *Wayne*

SAM A BAKER (State Pk) From Jct of SR-34 & SR-67, W 5 mi to SR-143, N to park entrance (R). 2015 rates: $13 to $21. (573)856-4411

PECULIAR — C2 *Cass*

PECULIAR PARK PLACE
Ratings: 9/10★/9 (RV Park) From Jct of I-70 & I-435: S 10 mi on I-435 to I-49/Hwy 71S, then S 16 mi on I-49/Hwy 71S to Peculiar Exit 167, cross over Hwy to Outer Rd, S 1.5 mi (L). **FAC:** All weather rds. 24 Avail: 24 all weather, patios, 18 pull-thrus (24 x 75), back-ins (24 x 65), accepts self-contain units only, 24 full hkups (30/50 amps), WiFi, showers $, dump, laundry, groc, LP gas. **REC:** shuffleboard. Pet restrict(B/Q). No tents. Big rig sites, RV age restrict, eco-friendly, 2015 rates: $32 to $34. Disc: military. No CC.
(816)779-6300 Lat: 38.70666, Lon: -94.43732
22901 SE Outer Rd, Peculiar, MO 64078
ppprvpark@aol.com
peculiarparkplacervpark.com
See ad pages 695, 682.

PERRY — B3 *Ralls*

FRANK RUSSELL REC AREA (Public Corps) From Jct of Hwy 36 & CR-J, S 12 mi on CR-J (R). 2015 rates: $18. May 2 to Oct 5. (573)735-4097

RAY BEHRENS REC AREA (Public Corps) From Jct of Hwys 154 & J, N 7 mi on Hwy J (L). 2015 rates: $16 to $24. Apr 3 to Nov 23. (573)735-4097

PERRYVILLE — D5 *Perry*

SOUTHEAST MISSOURI JELLYSTONE PARK CAMP - RESORT **Ratings: 9/9.5/7.5** (Campground) 2015 rates: $34 to $56. Apr 1 to Nov 2. (573)547-8303 300 Lake Drive, Perryville, MO 63775

PIEDMONT — D4 *Wayne*

BLUFF VIEW PARK (Public Corps) From town, NW 1 mi on SR-49 to Rte AA, W 6 mi (E). 2015 rates: $14 to $20. May 15 to Sep 15. (573)223-7777

PIEDMONT PARK (Public Corps) From town, SW 7 mi on Rte-HH to Lake Rd 3, N 0.5 mi (L). 2015 rates: $14 to $40. Apr 15 to Sep 30. (573)223-7777

RIVER ROAD PARK (Public Corps) From town, SW 6 mi on Hwy HH (L). 2015 rates: $16 to $40. (573)223-7777

PITTSBURG — D2 *Hickory*

PITTSBURG LANDING PUBLIC USE AREA (Public Corps) From town, S 1 mi on Hwy 64 to SR-RA, E 4 mi (E). (417)852-4291

POMME DE TERRE (State Pk) From town, N 1.7 mi on SR-64, NW 2 mi on SR-64B (E). 2015 rates: $13 to $23. (417)852-4291

PLATTE CITY — B1 *Platte*

BASSWOOD RESORT
Ratings: 9.5/9.5★/9 (RV Park) From Jct of I-29 & SR-92 (exit 18), E 3.4 mi on SR-92 to N Winan Rd, N 1.7 mi to Interurban Rd, NW 0.3 mi (L).

WELCOME TO BASSWOOD RESORT
Enjoy this KC resort and 73-acre country estate with beautifully secluded, lakeside country-modern lodging and accommodations and a national award-winning RV resort.

FAC: Paved rds. (149 spaces). 100 Avail: 45 paved, 55 gravel, 44 pull-thrus (24 x 80), back-ins (30 x 65), 100 full hkups (30/50 amps), seasonal sites, cable, WiFi, tent sites, rentals, dump, laundry, groc, LP gas, fire rings, firewood, restaurant, controlled access. **REC:** pool, Basswood Lakes: fishing, shuffleboard, playground. Pet restrict(B). Partial handicap access. Big rig sites, 2015 rates: $42 to $60.
(800)242-2775 Lat: 39.34479, Lon: -94.74609
15880 Interurban Dr, Platte City, MO 64079
info@basswoodresort.com
www.basswoodresort.com
See ad pages 689, 682 & Family Camping in Magazine Section.

New to RVing? Be sure to check out the all the great articles on getting the most out of your RV, at the front of the Guide.

Things to See and Do

BASSWOOD COUNTRY STORE Full service store. Locals shop in store all year round. Partial handicap access. RV accessible. Restrooms, food. Hours: 8 am to 7 pm.
(800)242-2775 Lat: 39.34479, Lon: -94.74609
15880 Interurban Rd., Platte City, MO 64079
info@basswoodresort.com
www.basswoodresort.com
See ad page 689.

POPLAR BLUFF — E4 *Butler*

CAMELOT RV CAMPGROUND
Ratings: 7/8/8.5 (RV Park) W-bnd: From Jct of US-60 & Springfield/St Louis Exit, go 1.5 mi on Springfield/St Louis exit (R); or E-bnd: From Jct of US-60 & Poplar Bluff Exit, go 3 mi on Poplar Bluff exit (L); or N-bnd: From Jct of Hwy 67 & Springfield/St Louis Exit, go 1.5 mi on Springfield (R). **FAC:** Gravel rds. 76 gravel, 35 pull-thrus (28 x 65), back-ins (30 x 55), 76 full hkups (30/50 amps), cable, WiFi, laundry, LP gas. **REC.** Pet restrict(B). No tents. Big rig sites, eco-friendly, 2015 rates: $35. Disc: military. No CC.
(573)785-1016 Lat: 36.80490, Lon: -90.46138
4728 Hwy 67 N, Poplar Bluff, MO 63901
camelotrv@hotmail.com
www.camelotrvcampground.com

PORTAGEVILLE — E5 *New Madrid*

BOOTHEEL RV PARK & EVENT CENTER (FORMERLY HAYTI-PORTAGEVILLE RV PARK)
Ratings: 8.5/9★/7.5 (Campground) S-bnd: From Jct I 55 & Wardell (Exit 27): Go E on Mo-A 300 feet, then S on Mo-BB/East Outer Rd 3 mi (L); or N-bnd: From Jct I 55 & Hayti (Exit 19): Go E on Hwy 84 250 feet, then N on East Outer Rd 5-1/2 mi (R) Note: Do not use GPS. **FAC:** Gravel rds. 37 grass, patios, 31 pull-thrus (28 x 65), back-ins (25 x 45), 26 full hkups, 11 W, 11 E (30/50 amps), WiFi, tent sites, rentals, dump, laundry, groc, firewood. **REC:** pool, playground, rec open to public. Pets OK. Partial handicap access. Big rig sites, eco-friendly, 2015 rates: $27.49 to $37.49. Disc: military.
(573)359-1580 Lat: 36.307078, Lon: -89.700427
2824 E Outer Rd, Portageville, MO 63873
bootheelrvpark@hotmail.com
See ad this page, 682.

REVERE — A3 *Clark*

BATTLE OF ATHENS SHS (State Pk) From Jct of US-81 & Hwy CC, E 1 mi on Hwy CC, follow signs (L). 2015 rates: $13 to $21. Apr 1 to Nov 30. (660)877-3871

RICHLAND — D3 *Pulaski*

GASCONADE HILLS RESORT **Ratings: 7.5/9.5★/8.5** (Campground) 2015 rates: $27 to $30. Mar 1 to Oct 31. (573)765-3044 28425 Spring Rd, Richland, MO 65556

ROBERTSVILLE — C4 *Franklin*

ROBERTSVILLE (State Pk) From Jct of I-44 & Hwy O, S 5 mi on Hwy O (R). 2015 rates: $12 to $44. (636)257-3788

ROGERSVILLE — D2 *Greene*

SILVER BELL RV PARK/MHP
Ratings: 6/8/7 (RV Area in MHP) W-bnd: From Jct of US-60 & SR-125, W 0.5 mi on US-60 (R) E-bnd: From Jct of US-65 & US-60 go 7 mi on US-60 to traffic light @ Farm Rd 125, make U-turn to US-60 W 1.2 mi (R). **FAC:** Paved rds. 36 paved, 18 pull-thrus (24 x 75), back-ins (20 x 60), mostly side by side hkups, 36 full hkups (30/50 amps), laundry. Pets OK. No tents. Big rig sites, 2015 rates: $25 to $22. No CC.
(417)299-5511 Lat: 37.11820, Lon: -93.13007
7711 E. Hwy 60, Rogersville, MO 65742
jackie@threestoneproperties.com
www.threestoneproperties.com
See ad opposite page.

ROLLA — C3 *Phelps*

MARK TWAIN NF (LANE SPRING CAMPGROUND) (Natl Forest) From jct Hwy-72 & US-63: Go 12 mi S on US-63, then 1 mi W on FR-1892. Pit toilets. 2015 rates: $8 to $16. Apr 1 to Oct 31. (573)364-4621

THREE SPRINGS RV PARK & CAMPGROUND **Ratings: 8/7.5/6.5** (Campground) 2015 rates: $22 to $24. (573)201-1579 24125 Phelps CR 6050, Rolla, MO 65401

To get the most out of your Guide, refer to the Table of Contents in the front of the book.

ROUND SPRING — D4 *Shannon*

OZARK SCENIC RIVERWAY/PULLTITE (Natl Pk) From town, N 17 mi on Hwy 19 to Rte EE, W 4 mi (E). 2015 rates: $14 to $17. (573)323-4236

OZARK SCENIC RIVERWAY/ROUND SPRING (Natl Pk) From Jct of US-60 & SR-19, N 25 mi on SR-19 (R). 2015 rates: $14 to $20. (573)858-3297

RUSHVILLE — B1 *Buchanan*

LEWIS & CLARK (State Pk) From town, SW 20 mi on Hwy 59 to Hwy 45, SE 1 mi (R). 2015 rates: $13 to $21. (816)579-5564

SALEM — D4 *Dent*

HAPPY PAPPY'S MONTAUK RV PARK & STORE **Ratings: 6/NA/7.5** (RV Park) 2015 rates: $30. Mar 1 to Oct 31. (573)548-7777 8787 Hwy 119, Salem, MO 65560

MONTAUK (State Pk) From town, SE 2 mi on SH 137, E 10.3 mi on SH-W. 2015 rates: $12 to $26. (573)548-2201

OZARK SCENIC RIVERWAY/TWO RIVERS (Natl Pk) From town, W 5.5 mi on SR-106, N 3 mi on SR-V (E). 2015 rates: $5 to $33. (573)323-4236

SARCOXIE — D2 *Jasper*

BEAGLE BAY RV HAVEN & CAMPGROUND, LLC
Ratings: 9/7.5/7.5 (Campground) From Jct of I-44 & CR-U (Exit 29, Sarcoxie), E 0.5 mi on CR-U (parallel to I-44) (L). **FAC:** Gravel rds. (36 spaces). Avail: 21 gravel, 21 pull-thrus (24 x 70), 21 full hkups (30/50 amps), seasonal sites, WiFi, tent sites, rentals, laundry, LP gas, firewood. **REC:** pool, pond, fishing, playground. Pets OK. Big rig sites, 2015 rates: $20 to $25. Disc: military.
(417)548-0000 Lat: 37.07829, Lon: -94.09103
2041 Cimmaron Road, Sarcoxie, MO 64862
beaglebayrv@gmail.com
beaglebayrv.com
See ad pages 695, 682.

SEDALIA — C2 *Pettis*

MISSOURI STATE FAIRGROUNDS
(Public) From Jct of US-50 & US-65, S 0.5 mi on US-65 to 16th St, W 0.5 mi to Clarendon, S 1 blk (L). **FAC:** Paved rds. 1350 grass, 500 pull-thrus (15 x 45), back-ins (15 x 45), 250 full hkups, 1100 W, 1100 E (30/50 amps), WiFi Hotspot, tent sites, dump. **REC:** playground, rec open to public. Pets OK. Partial handicap access. Big rig sites, 2015 rates: $25.
(660)530-5600 Lat: 38.698496, Lon: -93.255040
2503 W 16th St, Sedalia, MO 65301
steve.allison@mda.mo.gov
www.mostatefair.com
See ad this page.

SHELL KNOB — E2 *Stone, Taney*

CAMPBELL POINT PARK (Public Corps) From town, SE 6 mi on Rte YY (L). 2015 rates: $16 to $23. Apr 1 to Oct 31. (417)858-3903

VIOLA PARK (Public Corps) From town, SW 5 mi on Hwy 39 to Laker Rd 39-48, W 1 mi (E). 2015 rates: $16 to $21. Apr 1 to Sep 15. (417)858-3904

SIKESTON — D5 *Scott New Madrid*

HINTON RV PARK **Ratings: 6.5/8.5★/7.5** (RV Park) 2015 rates: $31. (800)327-1457 2863 E. Malone Ave, Sikeston, MO 63801

TOWN & COUNTRY RV PARK **Ratings: 6/5.5/8** (RV Park) 2015 rates: $25 to $52. (573)472-1339 1254 U.s. Hwy 62 East, Sikeston, MO 63801

SMITHVILLE — B1 *Clay*

CAMP BRANCH CAMPGROUND (Public) From town, N 4 mi on Hwy 169 to Hwy W, E 3 mi to Collins Rd, S 1 mi (R). 2015 rates: $18 to $44. (816)407-3400

CROWS CREEK (CLAY COUNTY PARK) (Public) From jct I-35 & Hwy 92: Go 4-1/2 mi W on Hwy 92, then 3-1/2 mi N on CR E. 2015 rates: $18 to $44. (816)532-0803

SMITH'S FORK RV PARK (Public) From Jct of I-435 & US 169 (Exit 41B), N 5 mi on US 169 to CR-DD, E 1.9 mi to Litton Way, N 200 ft to Smith Fork Dr, W 0.4 mi (L). 2015 rates: $20 to $23. Apr 15 to Oct 15. (816)532-1028

SPRINGFIELD — D2 *Greene*

SPRINGFIELD See also Bolivar, Carthage, Ozark, Marshfield & Rogersville.

BRANSON VIEW ESTATES MOBILE HOME & RV PARK
Ratings: 3/NA/7 Jct US-60 & US-65: Go S 29-1/2 mi on US-65S, then (Exit MO-265) S 3/10 mi on Ozark Mountain Highroad/MO-465, then E 2-3/10 mi on MO State Hwy F (L). **FAC:** Gravel rds. 10 gravel, back-ins (22 x 70), accepts full hkup units only, 10 full hkups (50 amps). Pets OK. 2015 rates: $25. No CC.
(417)561-2255 Lat: 36.72455, Lon: -93.19427
2543 State Hwy F, Branson, MO 65616
See primary listing at Branson and ad page 685.

OZARK HIGHLANDS MHC/RV PARK
Ratings: 7/8.5/5.5 (RV Area in MHP) From Jct of I-44 & Hwy 65 (Exit 82A), S 5.5 mi on Hwy 65 to Hwy 60 (Exit James River Freeway), W 1.4 mi to Glenstone Exit, N 0.3 mi to Peele St, W 100 ft (R). **FAC:** Paved rds. (89 spaces). 59 Avail: 35 paved, 24 gravel, 9 pull-thrus (15 x 60), back-ins (20 x 43), 59 full hkups (30/50 amps), seasonal sites, WiFi, laundry. **REC:** heated pool. Pet restrict(B/Q). No tents. Big rig sites, 2015 rates: $30.
(417)881-0066 Lat: 37.13654, Lon: -93.24921
3731 S Glenstone Ave, Springfield, MO 65804
ozarkhighlands@towermgmt.com
www.ozarkhighlandsmhc.com

Park policies vary. Ask about the cancellation policy when making a reservation.

SPRINGFIELD/RT 66 KOA **Ratings: 9/10★/9.5** (Campground) 2015 rates: $40 to $65. (417)831-3645 5775 W Farm Road 140, Springfield, MO 65802

TIMBERCREST PARK Ratings: 6/NA/7.5 (RV Area in MHP) East: I-44 & Hwy 360/James River Fwy; Go 12 mi SE to Glenstone Exit, then E at light, Go 2 blks, turn E at Nature Center sign. Go 2 blks, enter prk. West: I-44 & Hwy 65S to James River Fwy; Go W 0.5 mi to Glenstone exit, S @ light, across overpass, 1st turn E @ Nature Center sign, go 2 blks enter prk. **FAC:** Paved rds. 30 paved, patios, 10 pull-thrus (30 x 65), back-ins (30 x 65), 30 full hkups (30/50 amps), WiFi. Pets OK. Big rig sites, 2015 rates: $40.
(417)881-8004 Lat: 37.136492, Lon: -93.249065
4219 South Glenstone, Springfield, MO 65804
jhfowll@yahoo.com
www.passport-america.com/

Travel Services

CUMMINS CENTRAL POWER Dealer of diesel power motors & parts. **SERVICES:** Tire, RV appliance, MH mechanical, engine/chassis repair, mobile RV svc, emergency rd svc, restrooms. **TOW:** RV, auto. RV supplies, LP, emergency parking, RV accessible. waiting room. Hours: Mon-Fri 7am - 10pm.
(417)865-0505 Lat: 37.238404, Lon: -93.231993
3100 E. Kearney St, Springfield, MO 65803
See ad page 732.

ST CHARLES — C4 *St Charles*

MARQUETTE MOBILE VILLAGE, INC/MHP
Ratings: 6/NA/6.5 (RV Area in MHP) E-Bnd: From Jct I-70E & Hwy 94/First Capital Dr (Exit 228): Go W 50 yds on Hwy 94W/First Capital Drive, then E 1/2 mi on Veterans Memorial Pkwy (R) OR W-bnd: From Jct I-70W & Fifth St (Exit 229A): Go S 1/10 mi on Fifth St, then W 1 mi on Veterans Memorial Pkwy (L). **FAC:** Paved rds. (104 spaces). Avail: 10 paved, patios, back-ins (40 x 80), 10 full hkups (30/50 amps). **REC:** playground. Pet restrict

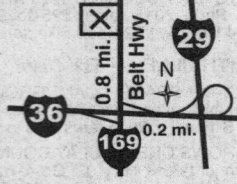

ST CHARLES (CONT)

MARQUETTE MOBILE VILLAGE, (CONT)
Partial handicap access, no tents. Big rig sites, 2015 rates: $45. No CC.
(636)724-3630 Lat: 38.774091, Lon: -90.510717
1701 Veterans Memorial Pkwy Lot #35, St Charles, MO 63303
nstiefer@att.com
www.rvmarquette.com
See ad opposite page.

↑ SUNDERMEIER RV PARK
Ratings: 8.5/10★/9 (RV Park) E-bnd: From Jct I-70 & SR-370 (exit 224): Go E 7-1/2 mi on SR-370, then W 4/10 mi on SR-94/N 3rd St (Exit 7), then E 1/10 mi on Transit St (L) OR W-bnd From Jct I-270 & SR-370 (Exit 22B): Go W 5-1/2 mi on SR-370, then W 4/10 mi on SR-94/N 3rd St (Exit 7), then E 1/10 mi on Transit St (L). **FAC:** Paved rds, 110 paved, patios, 39 pull-thrus (28 x 80), back-ins (28 x 55), 110 full hkups (30/50 amps), WiFi, laundry, LP gas. **REC.** Pet restrict(B). Partial handicap access, no tents. Big rig sites, eco-friendly, 2015 rates: $53 to $58. Disc: military.
(800)929-0832 Lat: 38.79822, Lon: -90.47381
111 Transit St, St Charles, MO 63301
reservations@sundermeierrvpark.com
www.sundermeierrvpark.com
See ad this page, 682.

County names help you follow the local weather report.

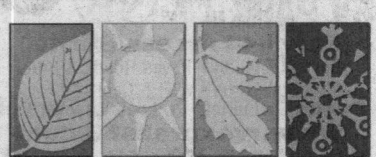

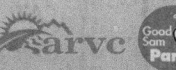

ST JAMES — C3 *Crawford*

MERAMEC SPRINGS COUNTRY STORE & RV PARK **Ratings: 7/9★/8.5** (Campground) 2015 rates: $27. Mar 1 to Oct 31. (573)265-3796 20458 Highway 8, St James, MO 65559

PHEASANT ACRES RV PARK **Ratings: 6.5/8.5/9** (RV Park) 2015 rates: $25 to $28. (573)265-5149 20279 Highway 8 East, St James, MO 65559

ST JOSEPH — B1 *Andrew, Buchanan*

AOK CAMPGROUND & RV PARK, LLC
Ratings: 8.5/9★/8.5 (RV Park) From Jct of I-29 & Bus 71 (exit 53), N 0.5 mi on Bus 71 to CR 360, W 0.5 mi (L). **FAC:** Gravel rds. (54 spaces). Avail: 36 gravel, 30 pull-thrus (24 x 75), back-ins (24 x 60), 36 full hkups (30/50 amps), seasonal sites, cable, WiFi, tent sites, laundry, fire rings, firewood. **REC:** pool, Lake AOK: fishing, playground. Pets OK. Partial handicap access. Big rig sites, eco-friendly, 2015 rates: $28 to $32.
(816)324-4263 Lat: 39.864889, Lon: -94.816186
12430 County Rd 360, St Joseph, MO 64505
aokexit53@gmail.com
aokcamping.com
See ad opposite page, 682.

BEACON RV PARK
Ratings: 8/9.5★/8 (RV Park) From Jct of I-29 (exit 46B) & US-36, W 0.2 mi on US-36 to US-169, N 0.8 mi (L). **FAC:** Paved rds. (28 spaces). Avail: 23 paved, 15 pull-thrus (30 x 60), back-ins (25 x 60), 23 full hkups (30/50 amps), seasonal sites, cable, WiFi, laundry. Pets OK. No tents. Big rig sites, 2015 rates: $36. Disc: AAA.
(816)279-5417 Lat: 39.759011, Lon: -94.804979
822 S. Belt Hwy, St Joseph, MO 64507
beaconrvparks@aol.com
www.beaconrvpark.com
See ad opposite page, 682.

SHARP RV PARK Ratings: 6.5/8.5★/5 (Campground) From Jct of I-29 & US- 59 (exit 53), S 0.25 mi on US-59 (R). **FAC:** Gravel rds. (22 spaces). Avail: 14 gravel, 5 pull-thrus (25 x 65), back-ins (22 x 50), 14 full hkups (30/50 amps), seasonal sites, WiFi, tent sites, laundry. **REC.** Pets OK. 2015 rates: $30. No CC.
(816)262-5799 Lat: 39.85276, Lon: -94.81459
18890 Hwy 59, St Joseph, MO 64505
sharprvpark@yahoo.com
www.sharprvpark.com

Enjoy the scenery as you travel North America. We exclusively rate campgrounds for their visual appearance and environmental quality, and represent their score, 1 through 10, as the third rating in our Triple Rating System.

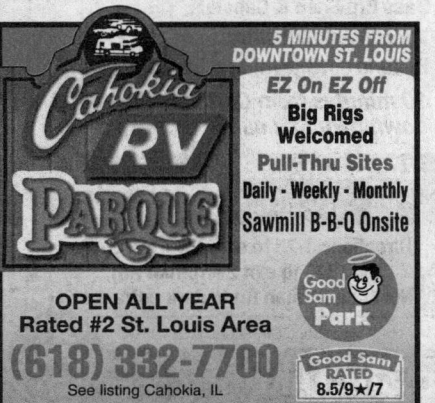

Things to See and Do

PONY EXPRESS MUSEUM The famous Overland Mail service by horseback began here on April 3, 1860. The state-of-the-art exhibits illustrate the need, creation, operation & termination of the Pony Express. Call for additional hours and rates. Partial handicap access. Hours: 9am to 5pm M-Sat. Adult fee: $6.
(816)279-5059 Lat: 39.75623, Lon: -94.84857
914 Penn, St Joseph, MO 64503
www.ponyexpress.org
See ad opposite page.

ST JOSEPH VISITORS BUREAU Information on St Joseph & all area attractions. RV accessible. Restrooms. Hours: 8am-5pm M-F. No CC.
(800)785-0360 Lat: 39.76665, Lon: -94.85537
109 S 4th St, St Joseph, MO 64501
www.stjomo.com
See ad opposite page.

ST LOUIS — C4 *St Louis*

ST LOUIS AREA MAP

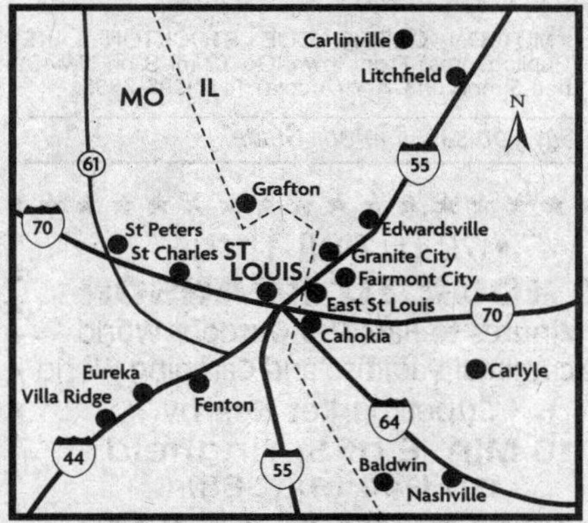

Symbols on map indicate towns within a 50 mile radius of St Louis where campgrounds are listed. Check listings for more information.

In MO, see also Eureka, Fenton, St Charles, St Peters & Villa Ridge.

In IL, see also Baldwin, Cahokia, Carlinville, Carlyle, East St Louis, Edwardsville, Fairmont City, Grafton, Granite City, Litchfield & Nashville.

ST LOUIS RV PARK **Ratings: 8.5/9.5★/6.5** (Campground) 2015 rates: $35 to $39. (314)241-3330 900 N Jefferson Ave, St Louis, MO 63106

ST PETERS — C4 *St Charles*

370 LAKESIDE PARK RV AND CAMPGROUND (Public) From Jct I-70 & Hwy 370 (Exit 224): Go E 2 mi on Hwy 370, then N 1 mi on Truman Rd/Lakeside Park Dr (Exit 2), enter on Lakeside Park Dr (L). **FAC:** Paved rds. 50 paved, patios, 20 pull-thrus (35 x 71), back-ins (35 x 61), 50 full hkups (30/50 amps), WiFi, tent sites, dump, laundry, fire rings, firewood. **REC:** Lakeside Park Lake: fishing, playground, rec open to public. Pet restrict(Q). Partial handicap access. Big rig sites, 2015 rates: $30 to $50.
(636)387-LAKE Lat: 38.821918, Lon: -90.564047
1000 Lakeside Park Dr, St Peters, MO 63376
lakesidefrontdesk@stpetersmo.net
www.stpetersmo.net/rvpark
See ad page 702.

Our inspectors look for the same things you do. Our unique Triple Rating System is based on years of market research, analysis and surveys from RVers like you. One thing you suggested was the need for separate ratings on facility completeness, restroom cleanliness/construction, and visual appearance/environmental quality. So we give three ratings, each based on a scale of 1 to 10, 10 being best and 5 being average. To give you an idea how tough we are, less than 1% of inspected campgrounds receive 10/10/10 ratings.*

Don't take any chances when it comes to cleanliness. We rate campground restrooms and showers for cleanliness and physical characteristics such as supplies and appearance.

ST ROBERT — D3 *Pulaski*

➔ **MAGNUSON HOTEL & RV PARK** **Ratings: 8.5/NA/6.5** (Campground) From Jct of I-44 & Hwy Z (Exit 163), SW 0.2 mi on Hwy Z (R). **FAC:** Paved/gravel rds. (15 spaces). Avail: 10 paved, 5 pull-thrus (20 x 65), back-ins (18 x 60), 10 full hkups (30/50 amps), seasonal sites, cable, WiFi, laundry. **REC:** pool, rec open to public. Pets OK. Partial handicap access, no tents. 2015 rates: $35. Disc: military.
(573)336-3036 Lat: 37.82998, Lon: -92.10536
14175 Hwy Z, St Robert, MO 65584
magnusonhotelstrobert@gmail.com
See ad this page, 682.

STANTON — C4 *Franklin*

➚ STANTON/MERAMEC KOA KAMPGROUND **Ratings: 8.5/9.5★/8** (Campground) 2015 rates: $40 to $48. Mar 1 to Nov 30. (573)927-5215 74 Hwy W, Sullivan, MO 63080

STEEDMAN — C3 *Callaway*

➚ WILDWOOD ASSOC. RV PARK **Ratings: 7.5/5.5/5.5** (Membership Pk) 2015 rates: $27. (573)676-5317 7233 Wildwood Estates Dr, Steedman, MO 65077

Refer to the Table of Contents in front of the Guide to locate everything you need.

STEELVILLE — C4 *Crawford*

➔ BASS RIVER RESORT **Ratings: 7/8.5★/7.5** (Campground) 2015 rates: $30.50 to $36.75. (800)392-3700 204 Butts Rd, Steelville, MO 65565

← CANDY CANE RV PARK **Ratings: 7/7.5/7** (Campground) 2015 rates: $25. (573)775-2889 11 Hwy M, Steelville, MO 65565

➔ HUZZAH VALLEY RESORT **Ratings: 7.5/8.5★/9** (Campground) 2015 rates: $13.55 to $40. (800)367-4516 970 E Hwy 8, Steelville, MO 65565

STOCKTON — D2 *Cedar, Dade*

➔ CRABTREE COVE (Public Corps) From town, E 2 mi on Hwy 32 (R). 2015 rates: $12 to $18. Apr 16 to Sep 30. (417)276-6799

↓ HAWKER POINT (Public Corps) From town, S 6 mi on Hwy 39 to Rte H, E 5.2 mi (E). 2015 rates: $12 to $18. Apr 16 to Sep 30. (417)276-7266

➘ MASTERS CAMPGROUND (Public Corps) From town, SE 10 mi on Hwy 32 to CR-RA, S 3.5 mi (E). 2015 rates: $10 to $14. May 15 to Sep 15. (417)276-3113

MUTTON CREEK (COE STOCKTON LAKE) (Public Corps) From town: Go 12 mi S on Hwy-39, then 5 mi E on CR-Y (Arcola). (417)995-3355

Say you saw it in our Guide!

↓ ORLEANS TRAIL CAMPGROUND (Public Corps) From town, S 0.75 mi on Hwy 39 to SR-RB, E 0.5 mi (E). 2015 rates: $12. May 15 to Sep 15. (417)276-6948

↓ RUARK BLUFF PARK (Public Corps) From town, S 12 mi on Hwy 39 to Rte Y, E 4.5 mi to Rte H, S 1 mi (E). 2015 rates: $12 to $18. (417)637-5279

↓ STOCKTON (State Pk) From Jct of SR-32 & SR-39, S 4 mi on SR-39 to SR-215, SE 5 m (across bridge). 2015 rates: $13 to $40. (417)276-4259

➔ STOCKTON MOBILE HOME & RV PARK **Ratings: 4/NA/7** (RV Park) 2015 rates: $14. Apr 15 to Nov 3. (417)276-8212 416 North 4th St, Stockton, MO 65785

STOUTSVILLE — B3 *Monroe*

↓ MARK TWAIN (State Pk) From Jct of US-24 & SR-107, S 6 mi on SR-107 (R). 2015 rates: $13 to $21. Apr 1 to Oct 31. (573)565-3440

STRAFFORD — D2 *Greene*

➔ **PARADISE IN THE WOODS RV PARK & CAMPGROUND** **Ratings: 9/9.5★/9.5** (Campground) W-bnd: From Jct I-44 (Exit 96) & Evergreen Rd: Go 2 1/4 mi W on N service rd, then 1 block N on Grier Branch Rd. Turn (R). E-bnd: From Jct I-84 (Exit 88), turn L, returning over Hwy-44, then R (East) 4.5 mi on Evergreen Rd, then W (L) on Grier Branch Rd. **FAC:** Gravel rds. 42 gravel, 42 pull-thrus (24 x 80), 42 full hkups (30/50 amps), WiFi, tent sites, laundry, groc, LP gas. **REC:** pool, pond, fishing, playground, rec open to public.

STRAFFORD (CONT)

PARADISE IN THE WOODS RV (CONT)
Pets OK. Big rig sites, eco-friendly, 2015 rates: $30. (417)859-2175 Lat: 37.285548, Lon: -93.039360
2481 Grier Branch Rd, Strafford, MO 65757
clark_22423@msn.com
See ad pages 697, 682.

RV PARK STRAFFORD
Ratings: 6/6.5/6 (RV Park) From Jct of I-44 & SR-125 (exit 88), S 0.1 mi on SR-125 to SR-00, E 200 ft (L). **FAC:** Gravel rds. (45 spaces). Avail: 37 gravel, 18 pull-thrus (25 x 75), back-ins (25 x 50), 37 full hkups (30/50 amps), seasonal sites, WiFi Hotspot, dump, laundry, LP gas. **REC:** playground. Pets OK. No tents. Big rig sites, 2015 rates: $25. No CC.
(417)736-3382 Lat: 37.27112, Lon: -93.10089
313 E Old Rte 66, Strafford, MO 65757
See ad opposite page.

Travel Services

CAMPING WORLD OF STRAFFORD/SPRINGFIELD As the nation's largest retailer of RV supplies, accessories, services and new and used RVs, Camping World is committed to making your total RV experience better. RV Accessories: (888)818-7828. **SERVICES:** RV, tire, RV appliance, MH mechanical, staffed RV wash, restrooms, RV Sales. RV supplies, LP, dump, RV accessible. waiting room. Hours: 8am - 6pm. (888)494-3955 Lat: 37.272125, Lon: -93.123826 373 E Evergreen Rd., Strafford, MO 65757 www.campingworld.com

SULLIVAN — C4 *Crawford, Franklin*

MERAMEC (State Pk) From Jct of I-44 & Hwy 185 (exit 226), S 4 mi on Hwy 185 (R). 2015 rates: $13 to $26. (573)468-6072

THEODOSIA — E3 *Ozark*

BUCK CREEK PARK (Public Corps) From town, S 6 mi on Hwy 125 to Buck Creek Park access rd, follow signs (R). 2015 rates: $14 to $19. (417)785-4313

THEODOSIA PARK (Public Corps) From town, E 1 mi on US-160, follow signs (R). 2015 rates: $14 to $54. May 1 to Sep 30. (417)425-2700

TIGHTWAD — C2 *Henry*

BUCKSAW CAMPGROUND (Public Corps) From Jct MO Hwy 7 to County Hwy U, S 3 mi on CR U to 803 Rd, SE 1.3 mi (R). 2015 rates: $14 to $22. (660)477-3402

WINDSOR CROSSING PARK (Public Corps) From Windsor, S 10 mi on Hwy Y to Hwy PP, S 3 mi (L). Pit toilets. 2015 rates: $6 to $10. (660)477-9275

TRENTON — A2 *Grundy*

CROWDER (State Pk) From Jct of Hwy 6 & SR-146, N 1 mi on SR-146 (R). 2015 rates: $12 to $26. Mar 1 to Nov 30. (660)359-6473

Check out those views! From awe-inspiring redwood giants to the soaring towers of the Golden Gate Bridge, we've put the Spotlight on North America's most popular travel destinations. Turn to the Spotlight articles in our State and Province sections to learn more.

TROY — B4 *Lincoln*

CUIVRE RIVER (State Pk) From Jct of US-61 & SR-47, E 3 mi on SR-47 to SR-147, N 2 mi, follow signs (E). 2015 rates: $13 to $26. (636)528-7247

UNIONVILLE — A3 *Putnam*

UNIONVILLE CITY PARK (Public) From Jct of US-136 & SR-5, N 3 blks on SR-5 (L). 2015 rates: $8 to $10. Apr to Oct. (660)947-2438

VAN BUREN — D4 *Carter*

BIG SPRING RV CAMP
Ratings: 8.5/10★/9 (Campground) From Jct of US-60 & MO Hwy-103, S 0.3 mi on MO Hwy-103, continue 1 block, turn on Chicopee Rd, E 0.3 mi (L) Note: Do not follow GPS for Pine St. **FAC:** Gravel rds. 45 Avail: 38 gravel, 7 grass, 16 pull-thrus (44 x 80), back-ins (40 x 45), 45 full hkups (30/50 amps), cable, WiFi, tent sites, rentals, dump, laundry, groc, fire rings, firewood. **REC:** Current River: swim, fishing, shuffleboard, rec open to public. Pet restrict(Q). Partial handicap access. Big rig sites, eco-friendly, 2015 rates: $29.50. Disc: military.
(573)323-8328 Lat: 36.986556, Lon: -91.005048
501 Chicopee Road, Van Buren, MO 63965
bsrvc@yahoo.com
www.currentriver.com
See ad page 701.

OZARK SCENIC RIVERWAY/BIG SPRING (Natl Pk) From town, S 4 mi on Hwy 103 (R). 2015 rates: $17 to $20. (573)323-4236

THE FAMILY CAMPGROUND ON THE CURRENT RIVER (Campground) (Rebuilding) 2015 rates: $42 to $51. Apr 15 to Oct 15. (573)323-4447 county Road M 127, Van Buren, MO 63965

VILLA RIDGE — C4 *Franklin*

PIN OAK CREEK RV PARK **Ratings: 8.5/7/7.5** (RV Park) 2015 rates: $38 to $47. (636)451-5656 1302 Highway "at", Villa Ridge, MO 63089

WAPPAPELLO — D4 *Butler, Wayne*

PEOPLES CREEK CAMPGROUND (Public Corps) From town, N 2 mi on Hwy D (L). 2015 rates: $16 to $40. Apr 19 to Sep 29. (573)222-8234

REDMAN CREEK CAMPGROUND (Public Corps) From town, S 2 mi on Hwy T (L). 2015 rates: $10 to $48. Apr 1 to Oct 31. (573)222-8233

WARSAW — C2 *Benton*

BERRY BEND PARK (Public Corps) From town, SW 5 mi on Hwy 7 to Hwy Z, S 1.8 mi (L). 2015 rates: $14 to $18. (660)438-3872

BERRY BEND PARK EQUESTRIAN CAMPGROUND (Public Corps) From town, SW 5 mi on Hwy 7 to Hwy Z, W 4 mi to SW 1231 BC, S 2 mi (L). 2015 rates: $8 to $18. (660)438-3812

The RVers' Guide to NASCAR helps RV travelers get the most out of North America's most thrilling sporting event. Turn to the front of the Guide and we'll give you the inside track on how to get high-speed thrills at major NASCAR venues.

DEERREST CAMPPARK **Ratings: 3.5/6/5.5** (Campground) 2015 rates: $17. Mar 15 to Oct 30. (660)438-6005 807 Gasoline Alley, Warsaw, MO 65355

HARRY S TRUMAN (State Pk) From Jct of US-65 & SR-7, W 8 mi on SR-7 to Hwy UU, N 2.5 mi (E). 2015 rates: $12 to $52. (660)438-7711

LONG SHOAL PARK (Public Corps) From town, W 8 mi on Hwy 7 (E). 2015 rates: $14 to $22. (660)438-2342

OSAGE BLUFF PARK (Public Corps) From town, S 2 mi on Hwy 65 to White Branch exit (Old Hwy 65), S 1 mi to Hwy 83, S 5 mi (R). 2015 rates: $8 to $18. (660)438-3873

THIBAUT POINT PARK (Public Corps) From town, N 8 mi on Hwy 65 to Hwy T, W 3 mi to Rd 218, S 1 mi (L). 2015 rates: $8 to $18. (660)438-2470

WAYNESVILLE — D3 *Pulaski*

ROUBIDOUX SPRINGS CAMPGROUND (CITY PARK) (State Pk) From jct I-44 (exit 156) & Hwy H & Business I-44: Go 1-3/4 mi NE on Business I-44. (573)774-6171

WEINGARTEN — C4 *Ste Genevieve*

HAWN (State Pk) From Jct of I-55 & Hwy 32, W 11 mi on Hwy 32 to Hwy 144, S 4 mi (E). 2015 rates: $12 to $26. (573)883-3603

WEST PLAINS — E3 *Howell*

CHIPMUNK CROSSING RV PARK
Ratings: 10/10★/10 (RV Park) From Jct of US-63 & SR-17 (S of West Plains), S 8 mi on SR-17 (L). **FAC:** All weather rds. 18 Avail: 18 all weather, 3 pull-thrus (30 x 85), back-ins (30 x 100), 18 full hkups (30/50 amps), WiFi, tent sites, dump, laundry, firewood, controlled access. **REC:** pool, pond, fishing, playground. Pets OK. Big rig sites, eco-friendly, 2015 rates: $28 to $32. Disc: military. Apr 1 to Sep 30. No CC.
(417)256-0788 Lat: 36.60530, Lon: -91.84785
11738 State Rte 17, West Plains, MO 65775
rvwestplains@yahoo.com
www.chipmunkcrossing.com
See ad this page, 682.

ROAD RUNNER RV PARK **Ratings: 4.5/8.5★/7.5** (RV Park) 2015 rates: $30. (417)255-0213 4598 County Rd 4620, West Plains, MO 65775

WESTON — B1 *Platte*

WESTON BEND (State Pk) From town, S 1 mi on Hwy 45 (L). 2015 rates: $13 to $21. (816)640-5443

WILLIAMSVILLE — D4 *Wayne*

LAKE WAPPAPELLO (State Pk) From town, S 15 mi on Hwy 67 to SR-172, E 8 mi (E). 2015 rates: $10 to $24. (573)297-3232

Don't camp without it ... Our 2016 listings are your key to travel satisfaction.

 See map page 705

National Park Service

WELCOME TO
Montana

DATE OF STATEHOOD	WIDTH: 630 MILES (1,015 KM)	PROPORTION OF UNITED STATES
NOV. 8, 1889	LENGTH: 255 MILES (410 KM)	3.88% OF 3,794,100 SQ MI

One never forgets Big Sky Country after experiencing the vistas along U.S. Route 2 near Glacier National Park in the northwest corner of the state. During summer, the clear skies seem to add new meaning to the word "blue." At night, the firmament is peppered with more stars than the eye can count. You could spend much of your time stargazing, but save room on your schedule for visiting the many fascinating communities and hiking, fishing and exploring the seemingly endless open spaces.

Learn

There is no better place to grasp what Montana is all about than the Grant-Kohrs Ranch National Historic Site. After Conrad Kohrs bought Johnny Grant's spread for $19,200 in 1866, he wound up running 50,000 head of cattle across 10 million acres of Montana prairie. Today the federal government still maintains a working ranch in the park.

While vast herds of cattle roamed the plains, most 19th-century settlers came to Montana for gold. Some strikes resulted in towns like Helena, which eventually became the state capital. So much silver and gold came out of Butte that it was called "The Richest Hill on Earth." The mining heritage of those cities is much on display today while others, like Bannack, became ghost towns. The first territorial capital, Bannack is preserved as a state park, and visitors can enter any of the 50 or so deserted wooden buildings on Main Street that are not locked.

Montana's rich Native American heritage is represented by 11 tribal nations. The Lakota Sioux and Cheyenne warriors took up arms for one of the last times to preserve their way of life on June 25 and 26 of 1876 against federal troops led by Lt. Col. George Armstrong Custer. The Little Bighorn Battlefield is a short trip outside of Billings, Montana's largest city. The site of the conflict is now a fascinating national monument.

Play

"They don't call it the Crown of the Continent for nothing," say boosters of Glacier National Park. With its 700 miles of trails and 25 active glaciers, Glacier is considered one of the nation's top parks. The only road in the park is the 53-mile Going-to-the-Sun Road. Travel it in style in 1930s-era buses, which are known as Red Jammers.

The federal government oversees 31 million acres of public land in Montana, and the state administers another 54 state parks, which makes for lots of space for backcountry adventures in America's largest landlocked state.

Nestled into a bowl of 10,000-foot peaks on the northern doorstep of Yellowstone National Park, Bozeman

MONTANA

Top 3 Tourism Attractions:
1) Glacier National Park
2) Yellowstone National Park
3) Lewis and Clark Trail

Nickname: Treasure State

State Flower: Bitterroot

State Bird: Western Meadowlark

People: Gary Cooper, actor; Phil Jackson, basketball player and coach; Evel Knievel, daredevil motorcyclist; David Lynch, director; Dave McNally, baseball player; Martha Raye, actress; Charlie Russell (artist); Jeannette Rankin (first woman elected to U.S. Congress); Dana Carvey, comedian

Major Cities: Billings, Missoula, Great Falls, Bozeman, Butte, (Helena, capital)

Topography: Rocky Mountains in western third of state; eastern two-thirds—gently rolling northern great plains

Climate: Due to Continental Divide, west has a milder climate than east, where winters can be harsh

Montana Office of Tourism

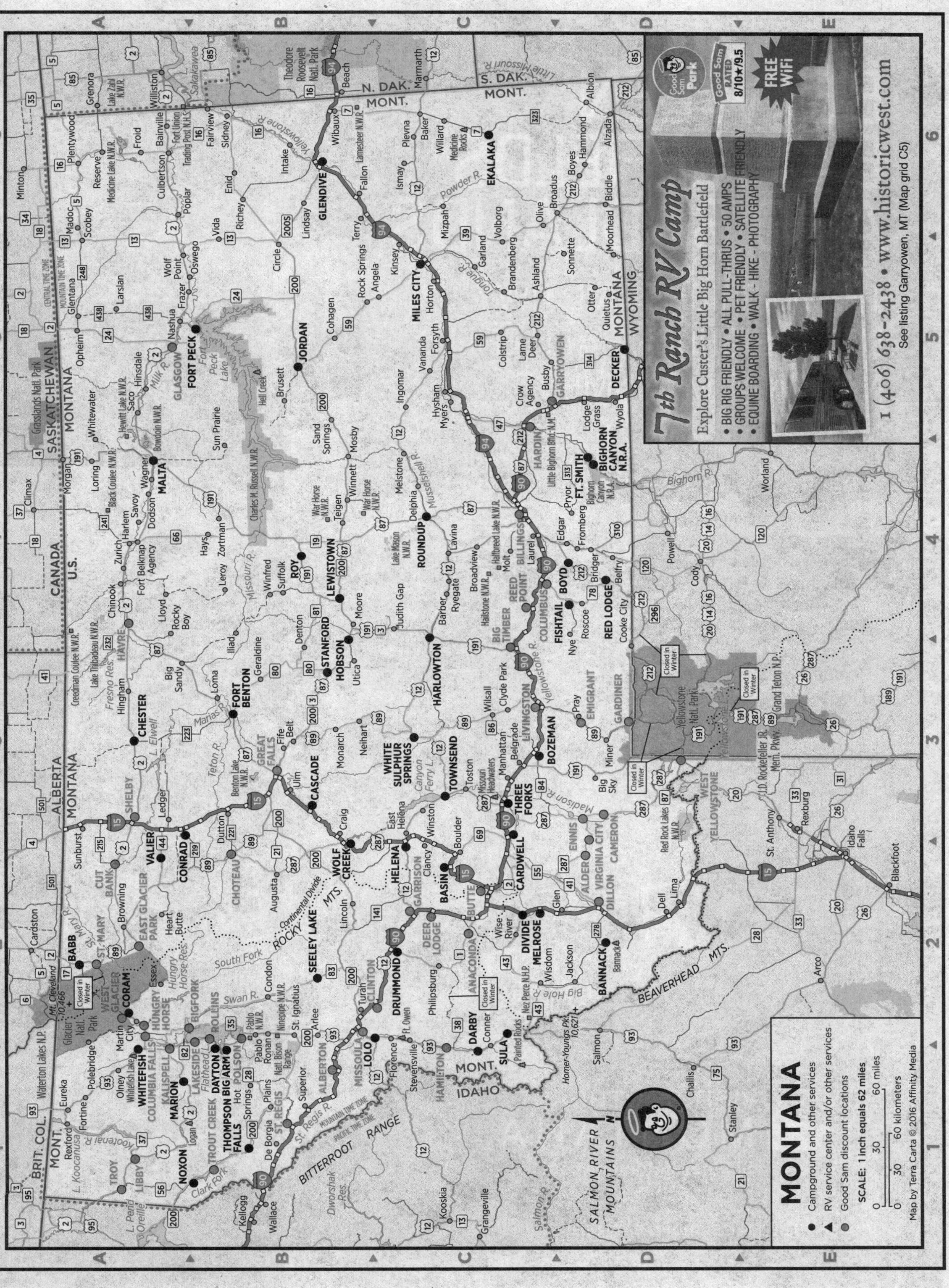
MONTANA
Campground and other services
RV service center and/or other services
Good Sam discount locations
SCALE: 1 inch equals 62 miles
0 30 60 miles
0 30 60 kilometers
Map by Terra Carta © 2016 Affinity Media
7th Ranch RV Camp
Explore Custer's Little Big Horn Battlefield
• BIG RIG FRIENDLY • ALL PULL-THRUS • 50 AMPS
• GROUPS WELCOME • PET FRIENDLY • SATELLITE FRIENDLY
• EQUINE BOARDING • WALK • HIKE • PHOTOGRAPHY
1 (406) 638-2438 • www.historicwest.com
See listing Garryowen, MT (Map grid C5)
Good Sam Park
Good Sam RATED 8/10★/9.5
FREE WiFi

has achieved cult status as an outdoor town. Lauded for its access to world-class skiing and trout fishing, the town is also known for dinosaur remains.

Think of what the Super Bowl is for football players and what Carnegie Hall is for sopranos. That's what Montana rivers are for fly fishermen. More than 450 miles have been designated "blue-ribbon" trout waters, and the names Big Hole, Yellowstone, Madison and Flathead fill every angler's bucket list.

Experience

The Flathead Valley comes alive in February to honor Ullr, the Nordic god of snow, whom locals contend has settled with his royal family in nearby Big Mountain. The Whitefish Winter Carnival features a snow queen, yetis and other colorful characters, making it one of the most intriguing winter events in the U.S. The Festival of Nations in Red Lodge brings together the cultures of the American West every summer. Native Americans dress in traditional garb and share crafts and customs. Every August, the Crow Fair Celebration features 1,500 teepees, making it "the teepee capital of the world."

Taste

They still talk about "bonanzas" and "mother lodes" in Montana, but the reference is not to gold anymore—it's to wild huckleberries. The "purple gold" berries are related to blueberries, but don't bring that up around Montanans who see no comparison of their tart, flavorful native fruit with its domesticated cousin. The purple gems make great pie ingredients.

TRAVEL & TOURISM

Travel Montana
800-VISIT-MT
www.visitmt.com

Central Montana
406-761-5036, 800-527-5348
www.centralmontana.com

Glacier Country
800-338-5072, 406-532-3234
www.glaciermt.com

Missouri River Country
800-653-1319, 406-653-1319
www.missouriver.visitmt.com

Southeast Montana
800-346-1876
www.southeastmt.com

Southwest Montana
800-879-1159, 406-846-1943
www.goldwest.visitmt.com

Yellowstone Country
800-736-5276, 406-556-8680
www.yellowstone.visitmt.com

OUTDOOR RECREATION

Montana Fish, Wildlife & Parks
406-444-2535
fwp.mt.gov

Montana Mountain Bike Alliance
800-847-4868
www.montanamountainbikealliance.com

Montana State Parks
800-847-4868
www.visitmt.com/stateparks

SHOPPING

Depot Antique Mall
www.depotantiques.com

Last Chance Gulch Pedestrian Mall
www.downtownhelena.com

Featured Good Sam Parks

MONTANA

Good Sam Park

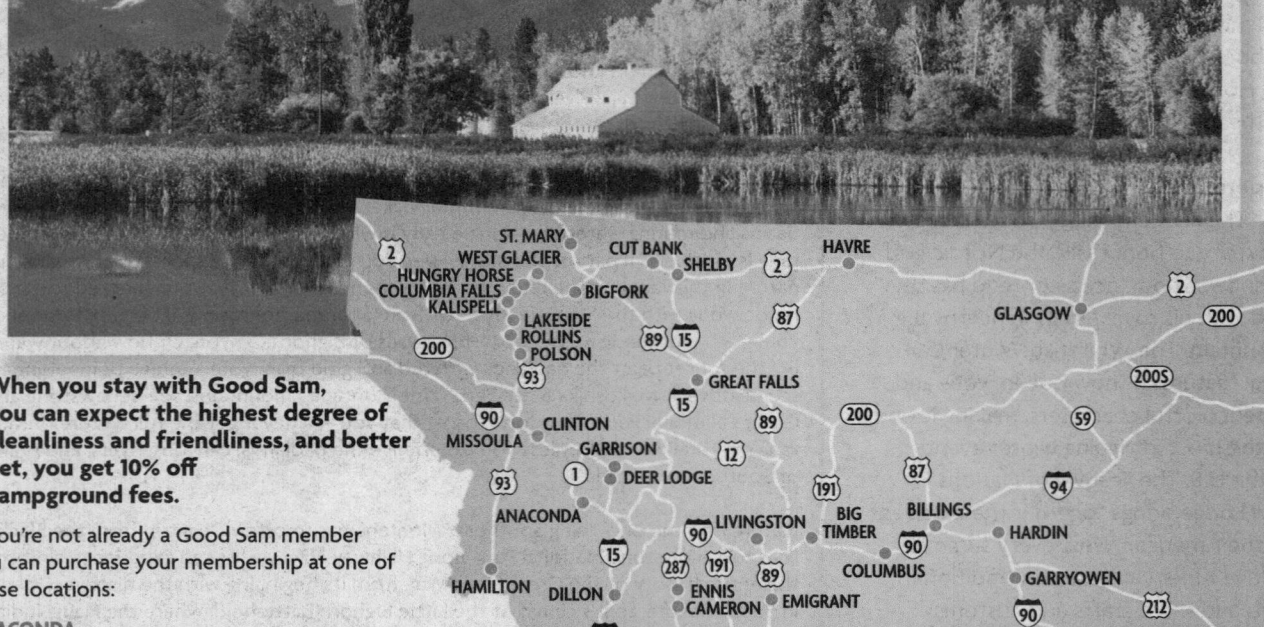

When you stay with Good Sam, you can expect the highest degree of cleanliness and friendliness, and better yet, you get 10% off campground fees.

If you're not already a Good Sam member you can purchase your membership at one of these locations:

ANACONDA
Fairmont RV Park & Campground
(406)797-3505

BIG TIMBER
Spring Creek Campground & Trout Ranch
(406)932-4387

BIGFORK
Outback Montana RV Park & Campground
(406)837-6973

BILLINGS
Billings Village RV Park
(406)248-8685
Yellowstone River RV Park & Campground
(406)259-0878

CAMERON
Driftwaters Resort
(406)682-3088

CLINTON
Bearmouth Chalet RV Park
(406)825-9950

COLUMBIA FALLS
Columbia Falls RV Park
(888)401-7268

COLUMBUS
Mountain Range RV Park
(406)322-1140

CUT BANK
Riverview RV Park
(406)873-4151

DEER LODGE
Indian Creek RV Park & Campground
(800)294-0726

DILLON
Countryside RV Park
(406)683-9860
Southside RV Park
(406)683-2244

EMIGRANT
Yellowstone's Edge RV Park
(406)333-4036

ENNIS
Ennis RV Village
(866)682-5272

GARDINER
Rocky Mountain RV Park and Lodging
(406)848-7251

GARRISON
Riverfront RV Park
(406)560-0248

GARRYOWEN
7th Ranch RV Camp
(406)638-2438

GLASGOW
Cottonwood Inn & RV Park
(800)321-8213
Shady Rest RV Park
(406)228-2769

GREAT FALLS
Dick's RV Park
(406)452-0333

HAMILTON
Black Rabbit RV Park
(866)707-5050

HARDIN
Grandview Camp & RV Park
(406)665-2489

HAVRE
Evergreen Campground
(406)265-8228
Havre RV Park
(800)278-8861

HUNGRY HORSE
Mountain Meadow RV Park & Cabins
(406)387-9125

KALISPELL
Glacier Pines RV Park
(406)752-2760
Rocky Mountain 'Hi' RV Park and Campground
(800)968-5637

LAKESIDE
Edgewater RV Resort
(406)844-3644

LIVINGSTON
Osens RV Park and Campground
(406)222-0591

MISSOULA
Jellystone RV Park
(800)318-9644
Jim & Mary's RV Park
(406)549-4416

POLSON
Eagle Nest RV Resort
(406)883-5904

ROLLINS
Rollins RV Park & Restaurant
(406)844-3501

SHELBY
Shelby RV Park and Resort
(406)434-2233
Trails West RV Park
(406)424-8436

ST MARY
Johnson's of St Mary Campground & RV Park
(406)732-4207

WEST GLACIER
Glacier Haven RV & Campground
(406)888-9987
North American RV Park & Yurt Village
(800)704-4266

WEST YELLOWSTONE
Buffalo Crossing RV Park
(406)646-4300
Yellowstone Grizzly RV Park
(406)646-4466
Yellowstone Holiday RV Campground & Marina
(406)646-4242

For more Good Sam Parks go to listing pages

ANACONDA

Find stacks of fun in this historic corner of Montana

In the southwestern corner of Montana, at the base of the Pintler Mountains, Anaconda is a charming and historic city near some of the state's finest outdoor recreational areas. This mile-high city began as a copper mining town in the 1880s. It was founded by Marcus Daly, an Irish immigrant and copper entrepreneur who wanted to call the town Copperopolis because of the sheer quantities of the valuable metal. Daly set up smelting works to process ore from the Butte mines 25 miles away.

To this day, the Smelter Stack is Anaconda's most iconic landmark, its image appearing in the most unusual of places, even in a stained-glass window in a local church. Also known as the Stack, the 585-foot-high landmark is considered the world's largest freestanding masonry structure. Although the smelter itself was closed and dismantled over 30 years ago, the stack stands to this day in the Anaconda Smoke Stack State Park, now an interpretive sight. The area around the smelter is also home to a golf course, Old Works, which was designed by golfing superstar Jack Nicklaus. Golf Week Magazine ranked it one of the top courses in Montana, and it has proven popular with golfers of all skill levels.

Anyone who grew up watching old westerns should make a point of stopping by the Grant-Kohrs Ranch, a historic site run by the National Park Service that teaches visitors what life was like for cattlemen in the Wild West.

Outdoorsy Anaconda

Along with its numerous historical attractions, Anaconda also makes a great base for outdoors enthusiasts. The area is home to a number of ranches offering horseback riding in warmer months, and there are plenty of spots to swim, kiteboard, picnic or hike in the general vicinity.

Twenty-three miles west of Anaconda, Georgetown Lake offers lots of outdoor activities and is a great place to commune with nature, no matter the season. The 3,700-acre lake sits 6,425 feet above sea level and is an average of 16 feet deep.

For More Information

The Anaconda Visitors Center & Chamber of Commerce
406-563-2400
www.anacondamt.org

Travel Montana
800-847-4868
www.visitmt.com

Shop at Camping World and SAVE with over $1,000 of coupons. Check the front of the Guide for yours!

ALBERTON — B1 *Mineral*

RIVER EDGE RESORT
Ratings: 5.5/8/7.5 (Campground) From Jct I-90 & Alberton (exit 75): Go 1/8 mi S on exit Rd, then 1/8 mi E on S Frontage Rd (R). Elev 3000 ft. **FAC:** Gravel rds. 16 gravel, 9 pull-thrus (25 x 70), back-ins (24 x 40), some side by side hkups, 9 full hkups, 7 W, 7 E (30 amps), WiFi Hotspot, tent sites, rentals, dump, laundry, fire rings, firewood, restaurant. **REC:** Clark Fork: swim, fishing, rec open to public. Pets OK. 14 day max stay, 2015 rates: $35. ATM.
(406)722-3338 Lat: 47.00389, Lon: -114.49164
168 S Frontage Rd, Alberton, MT 59820
info@riveredgemt.com
www.riveredgemt.com
See ad page 719.

ALDER — D2 *Madison*

RUBY VALLEY CAMPGROUND & RV PARK
Ratings: 6.5/8/7 (RV Park) From Jct of Hwy 357 & Hwy 287 : Go 1/2 mi E on Hwy 287 (L). Elev 5200 ft. **FAC:** Gravel rds. 32 gravel, 32 pull-thrus (20 x 85), 32 full hkups (20/30 amps), WiFi, tent sites, rentals, dump, laundry, groc, LP gas, fire rings, firewood. **REC:** pond, Koa Pond: fishing, playground. Pet restrict(B). 2015 rates: $38 to $48.
(406)842-5677 Lat: 45.32113, Lon: -112.09963
2280 Mt Hwy 287, Alder, MT 59710
jimsibert@qnet.com
Rubyvalleycampground.com

ANACONDA — C2 *Silver Bow*

A SPOTLIGHT Introducing Anaconda's colorful attractions appearing at the front of this state section.

BIG SKY RV PARK & CAMPGROUND Ratings: 6.5/8★/7.5 (Campground) 2015 rates: $35. (406)563-2967 350 Copper Sands, Anaconda, MT 59711

FAIRMONT RV PARK & CAMPGROUND
Ratings: 8/9.5★/9 (RV Park) From Jct I-90 & Hwy 441 / Fairmont Rd (Exit 211): Go 2-1/2 mi W on Fairmont Rd (L). Elev 5150 ft.

IN THE HEART OF THE ROCKY MOUNTAINS
We're among 10,000 ft. mountain peaks and spectacular woodlands, yet close to historic towns, world renowned golf & fishing & the famous Fairmont Hot Springs Resort. Come & enjoy the great outdoors with your family & friends.

FAC: Gravel rds. (113 spaces). Avail: 103 gravel, 37 pull-thrus (31 x 75), back-ins (30 x 48), 103 full hkups (30/50 amps), seasonal sites, WiFi, tent sites, rentals, dump, laundry, groc. **REC:** playground. Pets OK. Big rig sites, eco-friendly, 2015 rates: $37 to $43. Disc: AAA, military. Apr 15 to Oct 15. ATM.
(406)797-3505 Lat: 46.04197, Lon: -112.80511
1700 Fairmont Rd, Anaconda, MT 59711
fairmontrvpark@aol.com
www.fairmontrvresort.com
See ad pages 709 (Spotlight Anaconda), 708.

Travel Services

RV WIZARD Area wide Mobile RV Service and Maintenance including Electrical Systems, Water Heaters, Furnaces, Gas Generators, AC, LP Inspections and RV Appliances. RVIC and RVTC Certified. Based in Anaconda at Fairmont Campground. Elev 5150 ft. Apr 15 to Oct 15. **SERVICES:** RV appliance, mobile RV svc, restrooms. RV supplies, dump, emergency parking, RV accessible. waiting room. Hours: 8am to 5pm.
(406)209-1794 Lat: 46.04197, Lon: -112.80511
1700 Fairmont Rd, Anaconda, MT 59711
rvwizardllc@aol.com
See ad page 709 (Spotlight Anaconda).

Like Us on Facebook.

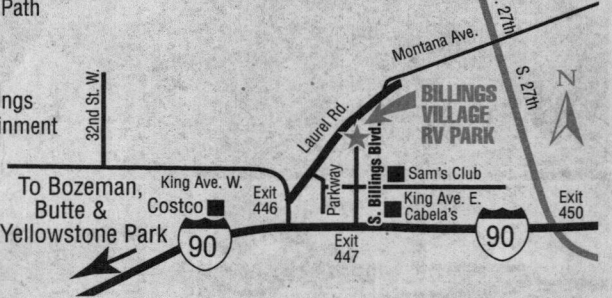

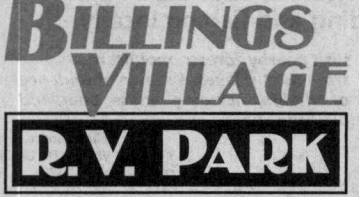

BABB — A2 *Glacier*

GLACIER/MANY GLACIER CAMPGROUND (Natl Pk) From town, W 13 mi on Many Glacier Valley Rd (L). Note: 35' RV length limit. 2015 rates: $10 to $20. May 25 to Sep 17. (406)888-7800

BANNACK — D2 *Bannack*

BANNACK (State Pk) From jct Hwy 278 & county road: Go 4 mi S on county road. 2015 rates: $15 to $23. (406)834-3413

BASIN — C2 *Jefferson*

MERRY WIDOW RV PARK & HEALTH MINE **Ratings: 5/5/5** (Campground) 2015 rates: $20.87 to $24.08. Mar 1 to Nov 15. (406)225-3220 29 Frontage Road, Basin, MT 59631

BIG ARM — B1 *Lake*

FLATHEAD LAKE/BIG ARM (State Pk) From town, N 14 mi on US-93 (R). 2015 rates: $15 to $28. Mar to Nov. (406)752-5501

BIG TIMBER — C3 *Sweet Grass*

BIG TIMBER / GREYCLIFF KOA Ratings: 8.5/8/7.5 (Campground) From Jct I-90 & Exit 377: Go 1/4 mi W on Frontage Rd (R). Elev 3900 ft. **FAC:** Gravel rds. 56 gravel, 41 pull-thrus (28 x 60), back-ins (31 x 40), 33 full hkups, 23 W, 23 E (30/50 amps), WiFi, tent sites, rentals, dump, laundry, groc, LP bottles, firewood. **REC:** heated pool, whirlpool, KOA Creek: fishing, playground. Pets OK. Big rig sites, 2015 rates: $51. Disc: AAA, military. May 15 to Sep 7. ATM.
(406)932-6569 Lat: 45.77384, Lon: -109.79918
693 Hwy 10E, Big Timber, MT 59011
bigtimberkoa@hotmail.com
www.koa.com

SPRING CREEK CAMPGROUND & TROUT RANCH
Ratings: 7/8.5★/9 (Campground) E-bnd: From US 191 & Bus 90 (exit 367): Go 1/8 mi N on 191, then 1 mi E on US 191 / Bus 90, then 2-1/2 mi S on Hwy 298 / McLeod St (L) or W-bnd: From I-90 & I-90 Bus (exit 370): Go 2-1/4 mi W on Bus Loop I-90, then 2-1/2 mi S on Hwy 298 (L). Elev 4315 ft. **FAC:** Gravel rds. 57 Avail: 9 gravel, 48 grass, 16 pull-thrus (40 x 70), back-ins (32 x 60), some side by side hkups, 12 full hkups, 45 W, 45 E (30/50 amps), WiFi, tent sites, rentals, dump, mobile sewer, laundry, groc, fire rings, firewood. **REC:** Boulder River: fishing, playground, rec open to public. Pets OK. Big rig sites, 2015 rates: $38.50 to $44. Disc: military. Apr 1 to Nov 15.
(406)932-4387 Lat: 45.80212, Lon: -109.96097
257 Main Boulder Rd. Hwy 298 S, Big Timber, MT 59011
screservations@itstriangle.com
www.springcreekcampground.com
See ad opposite page, 708.

BIGFORK — A2 *Flathead, Lake*

FLATHEAD LAKE/WAYFARERS (State Pk) From town, S 0.5 mi on Hwy 35. 2015 rates: $15 to $28. Mar 15 to Nov 15. (406)752-5501

OUTBACK MONTANA RV PARK & CAMPGROUND
Ratings: 5.5/8★/6.5 (Campground) From Jct US 93 & Hwy 82: Go 7 mi E on Hwy 82, then 7 mi S on Hwy 35 (L) From Jct US 93 & Hwy 35: Go 27 mi E on Hwy 35 (R) (MP 27). Elev 3000 ft. **FAC:** Gravel rds. (49 spaces). Avail: 44 gravel, 19 pull-thrus (20 x 80), back-ins (20 x 40), 34 full hkups, 10 W, 10 E (30/50 amps), seasonal sites, WiFi, tent sites, rentals, showers $, dump, LP gas, fire rings, firewood. **REC:** playground. Pet restrict(B). Eco-friendly, 2015 rates: $30. Disc: military.
(406)837-6973 Lat: 48.01315, Lon: -114.05511
13772 Outback Lane, Bigfork, MT 59911
camp@outbackmontana.com
www.outbackmontana.com
See ad opposite page, 708.

BIGHORN CANYON NATIONAL REC — D4 *Big Horn, Carbon*

BIGHORN CANYON NRA/BARRY'S LANDING (Natl Pk) From Lovell, W 3 mi on Hwy 14A, N 25 mi on SR-37 (through Hillsboro). Pit toilets. 2015 rates: $5. (406)666-2412

BILLINGS — C4 *Yellowstone*

BILLINGS KOA HOLIDAY **Ratings: 8.5/9.5★/9.5** (Campground) 2015 rates: $65 to $89. Apr 15 to Oct 15. (406)252-3104 547 Garden Ave, Billings, MT 59101

BILLINGS VILLAGE RV PARK
Ratings: 7.5/9.5★/8.5 (RV Park) From Jct I-90 & S Billings Blvd (exit 447): Go 1/2 mi N on S Billings Blvd (R). Elev 3100 ft.

RV PARK IN THE HEART OF BILLINGS
Stay with us and visit all the sites of Billings, MT. Museums, Moss Mansion, Pompeys Pillar, The Yellowstone River & Custer Battle Field. Award winning golf courses nearby. Enjoy free Wi-Fi for daily & weekly stays & Cable TV

FAC: Paved rds. (81 spaces). Avail: 74 paved, back-ins (30 x 60), 74 full hkups (30/50 amps), seasonal sites, cable, WiFi, laundry. **REC:** playground. Pet restrict No tents. Big rig sites, 2015 rates: $45 to $50. Disc: AAA, military.
(406)248-8685 Lat: 45.76357, Lon: -108.53542
325 S Billings Blvd, Billings, MT 59101
www.billingstrailervillagervpark.com
See ad opposite page, 708.

EASTWOOD ESTATES/MHP & RV PARK Ratings: 4/4.5/5 (RV Park) From Jct I-90 & US 87 (exit 452): Go 1/2 mi S on US 87 S, then 1/2 mi E on US 87 E (L). Elev 3200 ft. **FAC:** Paved rds. (59 spaces). Avail: 24 gravel, 3 pull-thrus (25 x 50), back-ins (23 x 38), 24 full hkups (30/50 amps), seasonal sites, laundry. Pet restrict(B). No tents. 2015 rates: $30 to $33. No reservations.
(406)245-7733 Lat: 45.79840, Lon: -108.43930
1803 Hwy 87 E, Billings, MT 59101

Tell them you saw them in this Guide!

YELLOWSTONE RIVER RV PARK & CAMPGROUND
Ratings: 9.5/9.5★/9 (Campground) W-bnd: From Jct I-90 & Hwy 3 / 27th St (exit 450): Go 1/8 mi S on 27th St, then 1/4 mi SW on Garden Ave (L) or E-bnd: From Jct I-90 & S Billings Blvd (exit 447): Go 1/4 mi S on S Billings Blvd, then 3 mi E on S Frontage Rd/Garden Ave (R). Elev 3100 ft.

CAMP CLOSE TO THE YELLOWSTONE RIVER
From shopping to dining, playing tourist to visiting National Parks, our family owned campground is close to it all. With easy access on & off I-90 you'll love our immaculate grounds, pull thru sites, swimming pool & spa.

FAC: Paved rds. (108 spaces). Avail: 88 gravel, 83 pull-thrus (18 x 65), back-ins (20 x 37), mostly side by side hkups, 63 full hkups, 25 W, 25 E (30/50 amps), seasonal sites, cable, WiFi, tent sites, rentals, dump, laundry, fire rings, firewood. **REC:** heated pool, whirlpool, Yellowstone River: fishing, playground. Pets OK. Partial handicap access. Eco-friendly, 2015 rates: $39 to $68. Disc: AAA, military.
(406)259-0878 Lat: 45.76385, Lon: -108.48350
309 Garden Ave, Billings, MT 59101
info@yellowstoneriverrvpark.com
www.yellowstoneriverrvpark.com
See ad this page, 708.

Things to See and Do

VISIT SOUTHEAST MONTANA Southeast Montana is here to promote tourism by increasing awareness of the region, and showcasing the cultural heritage. The Southeast Montana region consists of 13 counties and two Indian Reservations. Hours: M-F 9:00am to 5:00pm. No CC.
(800)346-1876 Lat: 45.77402, Lon: -108.49533
Info@southeastmontana.com
www.southeastmontana.com
See ad page 706 (Welcome Section).

BOYD — D4 *Carbon*

COONEY (State Pk) From Jct of I-90 & US-212 (Laurel exit), SW 22 mi on US-212 to Boyd, W 5 mi on cnty rd (E). Entrance fee required. 2015 rates: $15 to $28. (406)445-2326

BOZEMAN — C3 *Gallatin, Madison*

BEAR CANYON CAMPGROUND
Ratings: 9/8.5★/8.5 (Campground) From Jct I-90 & Bear Canyon Rd (exit 313): Go 1/8 mi S on Bozeman Trail Rd (L). Elev 5000 ft. **FAC:** Paved/gravel rds. (81 spaces). Avail: 68 gravel, 31 pull-thrus (25 x 68), back-ins (25 x 35), 35 full hkups, 33 W, 33 E (30/50 amps), seasonal sites, WiFi, tent sites, rentals, dump, laundry, groc. **REC:** heated pool,

BOZEMAN (CONT)

BEAR CANYON CAMPGROUND (CONT)
playground. Pets OK. Big rig sites, 2015 rates: $40. May 1 to Oct 1.
(800)438-1575 Lat: 45.65149, Lon: -110.94595
4000 Bozeman Trail Road, Bozeman, MT 59715
Office@bearcanyoncampground.com
bearcanyoncampground.com
See ad page 711.

BOZEMAN KOA **Ratings: 8.5/9★/8** (Campground) 2015 rates: $64 to $85. (406)587-3030 81123 Gallatin Rd (US-191), Bozeman, MT 59718

RED MOUNTAIN CAMPGROUND BLM (Public) From town, SW 29 mi on SR-84 (R). Pit toilets. 2015 rates: $8. Apr 1 to Dec 1. (406)683-2337

SUNRISE CAMPGROUND
Ratings: 7.5/8.5★/7.5 (Campground) From Jct of I-90 & E Main / Bus 90 (exit 309): Go 1/2 mi E on frntg rd (R). Elev 4600 ft. **FAC:** Paved/gravel rds. 50 gravel, 35 pull-thrus (21 x 64), back-ins (18 x 50), mostly side by side hkups, 50 full hkups (30/50 amps), WiFi, tent sites, dump, laundry, LP gas. **REC:** playground. Pets OK. 2015 rates: $30. Apr 1 to Oct 30.
(877)437-2095 Lat: 45.67352, Lon: -111.00343
31842 Frontage Rd, Bozeman, MT 59715
www.sunriservcampground.com
See ad this page.

BUTTE — C2 *Silver Bow, Butte*

BUTTE See also Anaconda.

BUTTE MONTANA KOA **Ratings: 7.5/8.5★/7.5** (Campground) 2015 rates: $35 to $70. Apr 15 to Oct 31. (406)782-8080 1601 Kaw Ave, Butte, MT 59701

FAIRMONT RV PARK & CAMPGROUND
Ratings: 8/9.5★/9 (RV Park) From Jct of I-90 & I-15 (Exit 121) : Go 8 mi W on I-90, then 2-1/2 mi W on Fairmont Rd (Exit 211) (L). Elev 5150 ft. **FAC:** Gravel rds. (113 spaces). Avail: 103 gravel, 37 pull-thrus (31 x 75), back-ins (30 x 48), 103 full hkups (30/50 amps), seasonal sites, WiFi, tent sites, rentals, dump, laundry, groc. **REC:** playground. Pets OK. Big rig sites, eco-friendly, 2015 rates: $37 to $43. Disc: AAA, military. Apr 15 to Oct 15. ATM.
(406)797-3505 Lat: 46.04197, Lon: -112.80511
1700 Fairmont Rd, Anaconda, MT 59711
fairmontrvpark@aol.com
www.fairmontrvresort.com
See primary listing at Acaconda and ad page 709 (Spotlight Anaconda).

2 BAR LAZY H RV PARK **Ratings: 6/7/6.5** (Campground) 2015 rates: $30 to $34. (406)782-5464 122015 W Browns Gulch Rd, Butte, MT 59701

We appreciate your business!

CAMERON — D3 *Madison*

DRIFTWATERS RESORT
Ratings: 6.5/8.5★/6.5 (RV Park) From Jct US 287 & Hwy 87: Go 2-1/2 mi W on US 287 (L) (MP 11). Elev 6100 ft. **FAC:** Gravel rds. (21 spaces). Avail: 17 gravel, 17 pull-thrus (26 x 65), 17 full hkups (30/50 amps), seasonal sites, WiFi, tent sites, rentals, laundry, firewood, restaurant. **REC:** playground. Pets OK. Partial handicap access. Big rig sites, 2015 rates: $32. May 1 to Dec 1.
(406)682-3088 Lat: 44.84769, Lon: -111.53249
31 Sagebrush Way, Cameron, MT 59720
driftwaters@live.com
www.driftwatersresort.com
See ad pages 723, 708.

CARDWELL — C3 *Jefferson*

CARDWELL STORE & RV PARK **Ratings: 4.5/5/4** (Campground) 2015 rates: $35. (406)287-5092 770 Hwy 2E, Cardwell, MT 59721

CASCADE — B3 *Cascade*

PREWETT CREEK INN RV PARK **Ratings: 5/6/6.5** (RV Park) 2015 rates: $35. Apr 1 to Oct 31. (406)468-9244 2468 Old US Hwy 91, Cascade, MT 59421

CHESTER — A3 *Liberty*

SANFORD PARK (Public) From Jct of US-2 & SR-223, S 14 mi on SR-223 to SR-366, W 8 mi. (406)759-5077

CHOTEAU — B2 *Teton*

CHOTEAU MOUNTAIN VIEW CAMPGROUND
Ratings: 5.5/9★/7 (RV Park) From Jct Hwy 89 & Hwy 221: Go 1mi E on Hwy 221 (L). Elev 3800 ft. **FAC:** Gravel rds. 44 gravel, 44 pull-thrus (28 x 45), 20 full hkups, 24 W, 24 E (30/50 amps), WiFi Hotspot, tent sites, rentals, laundry. **REC:** playground. Pets OK. 2015 rates: $32 to $45. Disc: AAA, military. May 1 to Nov 1.
(406)466-2615 Lat: 47.81617, Lon: -112.166435
85 Hwy 221, Choteau, MT 59422
campchoteau@gmail.com
campchoteaumt.com

CLINTON — C2 *Granite, Missoula*

BEARMOUTH CHALET RV PARK
Ratings: 7/8.5★/7.5 (Campground) From Jct I-90 & Exit 138: Go 1/8 mi N on Mullan Rd, then 3/4 mi E on Drummond / Frontage Rd (R). Elev 3750 ft. **FAC:** Gravel rds. 45 gravel, 30 pull-thrus (31 x 75), back-ins (30 x 60), 45 W, 45 E (30/50 amps), tent sites, rentals, dump, mobile sewer, laundry, LP gas, fire rings, firewood. **REC:** Clarks Fork: swim, fishing. Pets OK. Eco-friendly, 2015 rates: $35 to $40. May 1 to Oct 31. ATM, no CC.
(406)825-9950 Lat: 46.69785, Lon: -113.42168
1611 Drummond Frontage Rd, Clinton, MT 59825
info@bearmouthchalet.com
www.bearmouthchalet.com
See ad this page, 708.

BEAVERTAIL HILL (State Pk) From I-90 (milepost 130/Beavertail Hill exit): Go 1/4 mi S on county road. 2015 rates: $20 to $25. May 1 to Oct 31. (406)542-5500

EKSTROM'S STAGE STATION **Ratings: 5/6/8** (Campground) 2015 rates: $35 to $55. May 1 to Sep 30. (406)825-3183 81 Rock Creek Rd, Clinton, MT 59825

TURAH RV PARK LLC **Ratings: 7/9★/8** (RV Park) From Jct I-90 & Turah Rd (exit 113): Go 2 mi E on Turah Rd (R). Elev 3350 ft. **FAC:** Paved rds. 26 gravel, 14 pull-thrus (30 x 115), back-ins (30 x 70), 26 full hkups (30/50 amps), cable, WiFi, tent sites, rentals, dump, laundry, groc, LP gas, fire rings, firewood. **REC:** Clark Fork: fishing, playground. Pets OK. Partial handicap access. Big rig sites, 2015 rates: $33. Disc: military.
(406)258-9773 Lat: 46.82061, Lon: -113.80779
13555 Turah Rd, Clinton, MT 59825
turahrvpark@aol.com

COLUMBIA FALLS — A2 *Flathead*

COLUMBIA FALLS RV PARK
Ratings: 7/9.5★/9 (RV Park) E-bnd: From Jct US 93 & Hwy 40: Go 7-3/4 mi E (L) or W-bnd: From Jct US 2 & Hwy 206: Go 1-1/5 mi W on US 2 (R). Elev 3000 ft. **FAC:** Paved/gravel rds. (73 spaces). Avail: 58 gravel, 44 pull-thrus (27 x 75), back-ins (27 x 90), 58 full hkups (30/50 amps), seasonal sites, cable, WiFi, tent sites, dump, laundry, groc, LP gas. **REC.** Pets OK. Partial handicap access. Big rig sites, eco-friendly, 2015 rates: $38 to $50. Disc: AAA. Apr 1 to Oct 31.
(888)401-7268 Lat: 48.36837, Lon: -114.17921
103 Hwy 2 E, Columbia Falls, MT 59912
www.columbiafallsrvpark.com
See ad this page, 708.

GLACIER PARK WESTERN INN & CAMPGROUND **Ratings: 8/9★/8** (Campground) 2015 rates: $30 to $45. (406)892-7686 7285 US Hwy 2 East, Columbia Falls, MT 59912

GLACIER PEAKS RV PARK Ratings: 6/7.5/7.5 (Campground) From Jct US 2 & Hwy 40 : Go 1/4 mi W on Hwy 40 (R). Elev 3000 ft. **FAC:** Paved/gravel rds. (58 spaces). Avail: 38 gravel, 36 pull-thrus (25 x 70), back-ins (25 x 70), 31 full hkups, 7 W, 7 E (30/50 amps), seasonal sites, cable, WiFi, tent sites, rentals, showers $, laundry. Pets OK. Partial handicap access. Big rig sites, 2015 rates: $42.
(800)268-4849 Lat: 48.37107, Lon: -114.24574
3185 Hwy 40, Columbia Falls, MT 59912
info@glacierpeaksrvpark.com
www.glacierpeaksrvpark.com

LA SALLE RV PARK **Ratings: 5/5.5/6.5** (Campground) 2015 rates: $45. (406)892-4668 5618 Hwy 2 W, Columbia Falls, MT 59912

MOUNTAIN VIEW RV PARK **Ratings: 6.5/8.5★/7.5** (Campground) 2015 rates: $28.50. (406)892-2500 3621 Hwy 40, Columbia Falls, MT 59912

COLUMBUS — C4 *Stillwater*

ITCH-KEP-PE PARK (CITY PARK) (Public) At South edge of town on Hwy-78 at bridge. Apr 1 to Oct 31. (406)322-5313

MOUNTAIN RANGE RV PARK
Ratings: 7/9★/7 (RV Park) From Jct I-90 & Hwy 78 (exit 408): Go 1/4 mi N on Hwy 78, then 1/8 mi E on Mountain Range Rd (E). Elev 3650 ft. **FAC:** Gravel rds. (42 spaces). Avail: 37 gravel, 31 pull-thrus (27 x 74), back-ins (27 x 66), 26 full hkups, 11 E (30/50 amps), seasonal sites, WiFi, dump, laun-

COLUMBUS (CONT)

MOUNTAIN RANGE RV PARK (CONT)
dry. Pets OK. No tents. 2015 rates: $34. Apr 15 to Oct 15.
AAA Approved
(406)322-1140 Lat: 45.64758, Lon: -109.24483
19 Mountain Range Rd, Columbus, MT 59019
hionmt@montana.net
www.campingmontana.com
See ad opposite page, 708.

CONRAD — A3 *Pondera*

PONDERA RV PARK
Ratings: 5.5/7.5/5.5 (RV Park) From Jct I-15 & Conrad (exit 339): Go 1-1/4 mi S on Main St, then 1/8 mi W on 7th Ave S. Elev 3550 ft. **FAC:** Gravel rds. (45 spaces). Avail: 21 gravel, 5 pull-thrus (30 x 48), back-ins (22 x 50), 21 full hkups (30/50 amps), seasonal sites, cable, WiFi, tent sites, laundry. Pets OK. 2015 rates: $35. No CC.
(406)271-2263 Lat: 48.16582, Lon: -111.95140
713 S Maryland Street, Conrad, MT 59425
mail@conradrv.com
www.conradrvpark.com
See ad this page.

We shine "Spotlights" on interesting cities and areas.

CORAM — A2 *Flathead*

SUNDANCE RV PARK & CAMPGROUND **Ratings: 7/9★/6** (Campground) 2015 rates: $35. May 1 to Oct 15. (866)782-2677 10545 US Hwy 2E, Coram, MT 59913

CUT BANK — A2 *Glacier*

RIVERVIEW RV PARK
Ratings: 6.5/8.5★/7.5 (Campground) From Jct Hwy 2 & CR-213 (in town): Go 1/8 mi W on Hwy 2, then 1/2 mi SW on 4th (dead end) Attention: Do not use truck route. Elev 3800 ft. **FAC:** Gravel rds. (36 spaces). Avail: 28 gravel, 28 pull-thrus (22 x 80), 28 W, 28 E (30/50 amps), seasonal sites, cable, WiFi, tent sites, rentals, dump, mobile sewer, laundry. **REC:** Cut Bank River: fishing. Pets OK. Partial handicap access. Eco-friendly, 2015 rates: $32 to $35. Apr 1 to Oct 30.
(406)873-4151 Lat: 48.63374, Lon: -112.34364
401 4th Ave, S.w., Cut Bank, MT 59427
riverviewrvparkmt@gmail.com
www.riverviewrvparkmt.com
See ad this page, 708.

DARBY — C1 *Ravalli*

PAINTED ROCKS (State Pk) From Hamilton: Go S 17 mi on US 93, then SW 23 mi on Route 473. Note: 25' RV length limit. Pit toilets. (406)542-5500

DAYTON — B1 *Lake*

LAKE MARY RONAN (State Pk) From US 93 in town: Go 7 mi W on access road. Pit toilets. 2015 rates: $15 to $28. May 17 to Sep 15. (406)849-5082

DECKER — D5 *Big Horn*

TONGUE RIVER RESERVOIR (State Pk) From town: Go 6 mi N on Hwy 314, then 1 mi E on county road. Pit toilets. 2015 rates: $15 to $25. (406)234-0900

DEER LODGE — C2 *Powell*

DEER LODGE See also Anaconda, Garrison.

DEER LODGE KOA **Ratings: 5.5/6/6.5** (Campground) 2015 rates: $37 to $40. Apr 1 to Oct 30. (800)562-1629 330 Park, Deer Lodge, MT 59722

INDIAN CREEK RV PARK & CAMPGROUND
Ratings: 7/10★/7.5 (RV Park) From Jct I-90 & Bus I-90 (exit 184): Go 1/8 mi W on Bus I-90 (L). Elev 4200 ft.

CAMP, DINE, FUEL-UP AND EXPLORE!
Explore Historic Deer Lodge Valley from our Top Rated facilities. We offer friendly service & savings on gas & diesel. We're surrounded by mountain views and close to town, attractions, museums and numerous outdoor events.

FAC: Gravel rds. (72 spaces). Avail: 62 gravel, 61 pull-thrus (25 x 75), back-ins (25 x 50), 62 full hkups (30/50 amps), seasonal sites, cable, WiFi, tent sites, dump, laundry, groc, LP gas, firewood, restaurant. Pets OK. Partial handicap access. Big rig sites, eco-friendly, 2015 rates: $30 to $35. Disc: AAA, military. ATM.
(800)294-0726 Lat: 46.40931, Lon: -112.72398
745 Maverick Lane, Deer Lodge, MT 59722
indiancreekdeerlodge@gmail.com
www.indiancreekcampground.net
See ad this page, 708.

DILLON — D2 *Beaverhead*

COUNTRYSIDE RV PARK
Ratings: 8/9★/9 (RV Park) From Jct I-15 & Hwy 278 (exit 59) : Go 1/2 mi W on Hwy 278 (L). Elev 5200 ft. **FAC:** Paved/gravel rds. (44 spaces). 34 Avail: 2 paved, 32 gravel, 19 pull-thrus (32 x 70), back-ins (32 x 65), 34 full hkups (30/50 amps), seasonal sites, WiFi, tent sites, rentals, laundry, LP gas, firewood. **REC:** Ernie's Pond: fishing.

Traveling with a Fido? Many campground listings indicate pet-friendly amenities and pet restrictions.

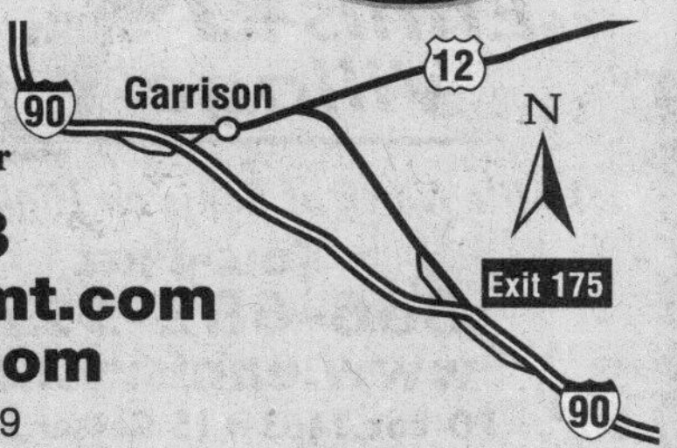

DILLON (CONT)

COUNTRYSIDE RV PARK (CONT)
Pets OK. Partial handicap access. Big rig sites, 2015 rates: $35. Disc: AAA, military.
AAA Approved
(406)683-9860 Lat: 45.18039, Lon: -112.70324
30 Sawmill Rd, Dillon, MT 59725
parkinfo@csrvmt.com
www.countrysidervparkmontana.com
See ad this page, 708.

← DILLON KOA **Ratings: 7.5/6.5/7.5** (Campground) 2015 rates: $41. (800)562-2751 735 W Park St, Dillon, MT 59725

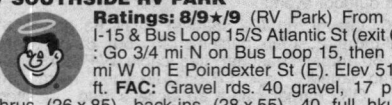

↓ **SOUTHSIDE RV PARK**
Ratings: 8/9★/9 (RV Park) From Jct I-15 & Bus Loop 15/S Atlantic St (exit 62) : Go 3/4 mi N on Bus Loop 15, then 1/4 mi W on E Poindexter St (E). Elev 5150 ft. **FAC:** Gravel rds. 40 gravel, 17 pull-thrus (26 x 85), back-ins (28 x 55), 40 full hkups (30/50 amps), WiFi, rentals, laundry. **REC:** Blacktail Creek: fishing. Pet restrict(B). No tents. Big rig sites, 2015 rates: $39. Disc: AAA, military. Mar 1 to Dec 1.
AAA Approved
(406)683-2244 Lat: 45.21014, Lon: -112.64606
104 E Poindexter, Dillon, MT 59725
www.southsidervpark.com
See ad pages 713, 708.

DIVIDE — C2 *Silver Bow*

DIVIDE BRIDGE (BLM) (Public Corps) From town: Go 2-1/2 mi W on Hwy 43. Pit toilets. 2015 rates: $6. May 15 to Sep 15. (406)533-7600

DRUMMOND — C2 *Granite*

↓ DRUMMOND CITY PARK (Public) From Jct of I-90 & Old Hwy 10 (Exit 153), S 0.5 mi on Old Hwy 10 (L). 2015 rates: $10. May 15 to Oct 1. (406)288-3231

EAST GLACIER PARK — A2 *Glacier*

← **GLACIER MEADOW RV PARK**
Ratings: 7/9★/7.5 (Campground) From Jct US 2 & Hwy 49 (East Glacier): Go W 17 mi on US 2 (L) (MP 191.5) or From Jct US 2 & Hwy To The Sun (West Glacier): Go 37 mi E on US 2 (R) (MP 191.5). Elev 4430 ft. **FAC:** All weather rds. (44 spaces). Avail: 40 gravel, 26 pull-thrus (25 x 65), back-ins (30 x 50), some side by side hkups, 25 W, 40 E (30/50 amps), seasonal sites, WiFi Hotspot, tent sites, dump, mobile sewer, laundry, LP gas, fire rings, firewood. **REC:** shuffleboard, playground. Pets OK. 2015 rates: $39.50. Disc: AAA. May 15 to Sep 30.
(877)612-2267 Lat: 48.26699, Lon: -113.44082
15735 US-2 East, Essex, MT 59916
stay@glaciermeadowrvpark.com
www.glaciermeadowrvpark.com

↑ GLACIER/TWO MEDICINE (Natl Pk) From Jct of US-2 & SR-49, NW 5 mi on SR-49 to Two Medicine CG Rd, W 7 mi (R). Note: 32' RV length limit. 2015 rates: $20. May 25 to Sep 17. (406)888-7800

EKALAKA — C6 *Carter*

MEDICINE ROCKS (State Pk) From Baker: Go S 25 mi on MT 7 to mile post 10, then W on CR 1 mi. Pit toilets. (406)234-0926

EMIGRANT — D3 *Park*

↑ **YELLOWSTONE'S EDGE RV PARK**
Ratings: 8/10★/9.5 (RV Park) From Jct I-90 & US 89 S (exit 333): Go 18 mi S on US 89 (L). Elev 4875 ft. **FAC:** Gravel rds. (81 spaces). 64 Avail: 2 paved, 62 gravel, 48 pull-thrus (30 x 60), back-ins (30 x 65), 64 full hkups (30/50 amps), seasonal sites, WiFi, rentals, laundry, groc, LP gas. **REC:** Yellowstone River: fishing. Pets OK. Partial handicap access, no tents. Big rig sites, eco-friendly, 2015 rates: $51 to $59. May 1 to Oct 10.
(406)333-4036 Lat: 45.41712, Lon: -110.68227
3502 US Hwy 89 S, Livingston, MT 59047
edge@mtrv.com
www.mtrv.com
See ad this page, 708.

How much does a fishing license cost in Idaho? Can you turn right on a red light in Rhode Island? Check the Table of Contents for the page location for annual updates of important towing laws, rules of the road, bridge and tunnel information and fishing license fees.

ENNIS — D3 *Madison*

← **CAMPER CORNER**
Ratings: 6/9★/7.5 (Campground) From Jct US 287 & MT 287: Go 1/4 mi W on MT 287 (R). Elev 4928 ft. **FAC:** Grave rds. (17 spaces). Avail: 10 gravel, back ins (30 x 30), 10 full hkups (30/50 amps) seasonal sites, WiFi, tent sites, laundry. Pets OK 2015 rates: $35.
(406)682-4430 Lat: 45.34976, Lon: -111.73354
300 W. Main Street, Ennis, MT 59729
campercornerrvpark@gmail.com
campercornerrvpark.com
See ad this page.

↑ **ENNIS RV VILLAGE**
Ratings: 7.5/10★/9.5 (RV Park From Jct US 287 & MT Hwy 287: Go 1 mi N on US 287 (R). Elev 5000 ft.

YOUR BASE TO THE YELLOWSTONE AREA!
Float or wade on the river with your fly rod. Hike up streams to fish or just enjoy the fresh air, exercise & remarkable views. Historic towns & fine dining near by. Stay for a day, a week, a month. An hour to Bozeman.

FAC: Gravel rds. (76 spaces). Avail: 66 gravel, 64 pull-thrus (32 x 78), back-ins (30 x 70), 66 full hkups (30/50 amps), seasonal sites, WiFi, tent sites, dump laundry. **REC.** Pets OK. Partial handicap access. Big rig sites, 2015 rates: $28 to $36. Apr 1 to Nov 1
AAA Approved
(866)682-5272 Lat: 45.36608, Lon: -111.72832
15 Geyser St, Ennis, MT 59729
info@ennisrv.com
www.ennisrv.com
See ad this page, 722, 708.

FISHTAIL — D4 *Stillwater*

CUSTER/PINE GROVE CAMPGROUND (Nat Forest) From town: Go 1 mi W on Hwy 419, then 7 mi SW on Hwy 425, then 8 mi S on FR 72. Pit toilets 2015 rates: $8. May 9 to Sep 23. (406)587-9054

FORT BENTON — B3 *Chouteau*

→ BENTON RV PARK & CAMPGROUND **Ratings: 6/8.5★/7** (RV Park) 2015 rates: $29. Apr 1 to Oct 31. (406)622-5015 2410 Chouteau St, Fort Benton, MT 59442

FORT PECK — B5 *Valley*

➔ DOWNSTREAM (Public Corps) From town, SE 2 mi on Yellowstone Dr (L). 2015 rates: $16 to $18. May 1 to Oct 30. (406)526-3411

➔ FORT PECK WEST (Public Corps) From town, W 1.5 mi on Hwy 117, W 0.5 mi on Hwy 24, S 0.5 mi on Duck Creek Rd (L). 2015 rates: $10. May 15 to Sep 1. (406)526-3411

FORT SMITH — D4 *Big Horn*

➔ BIGHORN CANYON NRA/AFTERBAY (Natl Pk) From Hardin, Jct of I-90 & CR-313, S 44 mi on CR-313 (R). Pit toilets. 2015 rates: $5. (406)666-2412

GARDINER — D3 *Park*

GARDINER See also Emigrant.

➔ **ROCKY MOUNTAIN RV PARK AND LODGING**
Ratings: 7.5/10★/9 (RV Park) N-bnd: From Yellowstone Park entrance : Go 1/8 mi N on US 89, then E on 4th St, immediate right on Jardine Rd (stay on paved rd) (R) S-bnd: From Jct I-90 & US 89 (exit 333): Go 53 mi S on US 89, then E on 4th St, immediate right on Jardine Rd (stay on paved rd) (R). Elev 5400 ft. **FAC:** Gravel rds. 65 gravel, 29 pull-thrus (28 x 60), back-ins (20 x 58), 65 full hkups (30/50 amps), WiFi, rentals, laundry. **REC.** Pet restrict(B/Q). Partial handicap access, no tents. Big rig sites, 2015 rates: $43 to $62. May 1 to Sep 30.
(406)848-7251 Lat: 45.03323, Lon: -110.70300
14 Jardine Rd, Gardiner, MT 59030
info@rockymountainrvpark.com
www.rockymountainrvpark.com
See ad this page, 708.

➔ YELLOWSTONE RV PARK Ratings: 5/8/8 (Campground) From Yellowstone Nat'l Park entrance in Gardine : Go 1-1/4 mi N on US 89 (L) Caution: Steep entrance. Elev 5300 ft. **FAC:** Gravel rds. (46 spaces). Avail: 8 gravel, 8 pull-thrus (26 x 55), 8 full hkups (30/50 amps), seasonal sites, WiFi, tent sites, laundry. **REC:** Yellowstone River: fishing. Pets OK. Partial handicap access. 2015 rates: $54. Disc: AAA, military. Apr 1 to Nov 1.
AAA Approved
(406)848-7496 Lat: 45.03886, Lon: -110.72432
121 Hwy 89 S, Gardiner, MT 59030
www.ventureswestinc.com

Things change ... last year's rates serve as a guideline only.

GARRISON — C2 *Powell*

➔ **RIVERFRONT RV PARK**
Ratings: 8.5/8.5★/8 (RV Park) W-Bnd: From Jct I-90 & exit 175: Go 1/2 mi N on Frontage Rd (L), E-Bnd: From Jct I-90 & exit 175: Go 1/2 mi W on Frontage Rd to stop sign, Go 1/2 mi N on Frontage Rd (L). Elev 4360 ft.

TIRED OF ORDINARY RV PARKS?
We deliver VIP service. Our park hosts personally take you to your long, wide pull-thru full hookup site. Overnight sites are 100' long and 40' wide. Enjoy our shade, lawns and river. Special monthly rates.

FAC: Paved rds. (50 spaces). Avail: 38 gravel, 31 pull-thrus (26 x 110), back-ins (32 x 70), some side by side hkups, 38 full hkups (30/50 amps), seasonal sites, WiFi, tent sites, rentals, showers $, dump, laundry, LP gas, fire rings, firewood. **REC:** Little Blackfoot River: fishing, playground. Pets OK. Partial handicap access. Big rig sites, eco-friendly, 2015 rates: $32 to $34. Disc: AAA, military.
(406)560-0248 Lat: 46.51918, Lon: -112.79559
115 Riverfront Ln, Garrison, MT 59731
hausschillo@juno.com
www.riverfrontrvparkmt.com
See ad pages 713, 708.

GARRYOWEN — C5 *Big Horn*

➔ **7TH RANCH RV CAMP**
Ratings: 8/10★/9.5 (Campground) From Jct I-90 & Garryowen (exit 514) : Go 3 mi S on Railroad frontage road, then 1/2 mi E on Reno Creek Rd (R). Elev 3200 ft.

RV PARK AT CUSTER'S LITTLE BIGHORN
Discover historic Montana. Next door to Custer's Little Bighorn Battlefield, minutes from the Crow Fair Powwow. Explore Sheridan, WY. Enjoy our serene & scenic views & 70' pull thrus. Free Wi-Fi & ice cream. Horse friendly.

FAC: Gravel rds. (66 spaces). Avail: 63 gravel, 63 pull-thrus (30 x 80), 45 full hkups, 18 W, 18 E (30/50 amps), seasonal sites, WiFi, tent sites, rentals, dump, laundry, firewood, controlled access. **REC:** playground. Pets OK. Partial handicap access. Big rig sites, eco-friendly, 2015 rates: $38 to $43. Disc: military. May 1 to Oct 1.
(406)638-2438 Lat: 45.49222, Lon: -107.38070
7th Ranch Reno Creek Rd, Garryowen, MT 59031
7thranch@historicwest.com
www.historicwest.com
See ad this page, 708, 705 (MT Map).

Enjoy shopping over 10,000 RV products at great prices, at CampingWorld.com.

GLACIER NATIONAL PARK — A2 *Glacier*

GLACIER NATIONAL PARK AREA MAP

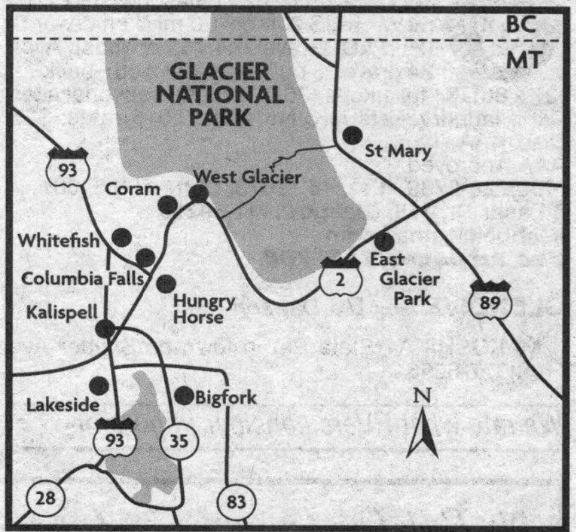

For more detail and a broader overview, please see our full-color state map at the front of the Montana state section.

Symbols on map indicate towns within a 50 mile radius of Glacier National Park where campgrounds are listed. Check listings for more information.

See also Bigfork, Columbia Falls, Coram, East Glacier Park, Hungry Horse, Kalispell, Lakeside, St Mary, West Glacier & Whitefish.

GLASGOW — A5 *Valley*

➔ **COTTONWOOD INN & RV PARK**
Ratings: 8.5/9★/8 (RV Park) From Jct US 2 & Hwy 24 (Glasgow): Go 1-3/4 mi W on US 2 (L). **FAC:** Gravel rds. 22 gravel, 5 pull-thrus (30 x 80), back-ins (35 x 65), 22 full hkups (30/50 amps), WiFi, tent sites, rentals, laundry, restaurant. **REC:** heated pool, whirlpool, rec open to public. Pets OK. Big rig sites, 2015 rates: $35 to $47. Disc: AAA. Apr 1 to Oct 31. ATM.
(800)321-8213 Lat: 48.19318, Lon: -106.62399
45 1st Ave NE, Glasgow, MT 59320
cottonwood@cwimt.net
www.cottonwoodinn.net
See ad this page, 708.

GLASGOW (CONT)

SHADY REST RV PARK
Ratings: 6/8★/7.5 (RV Park) From Jct US 2 & Hwy 24 (Glasgow): Go 1-1/2 mi W on US 2, then 1/8 mi N on Lasar Dr (E). **FAC:** Gravel rds. (40 spaces). Avail: 34 gravel, 8 pull-thrus (22 x 86), back-ins (27 x 60), 34 full hkups (30/50 amps), seasonal sites, WiFi, laundry. Pets OK. No tents. 2015 rates: $35. Disc: AAA.
AAA Approved
(406)228-2769 Lat: 48.19673, Lon: -106.62061
8 Lasar Dr, #15, Glasgow, MT 59230
jlschock@gmail.com
See ad pages 715, 708.

GLENDIVE — **B6** *Dawson*

MAKOSHIKA (State Pk) In town on Snyder Ave. (406)377-6256

We rate what RVers consider important.

GREAT FALLS — **B3** *Cascade*

DICK'S RV PARK
Ratings: 7/8★/8 (RV Park) From Jct I-15 & 10th Ave S (Exit 278): Go 1/8 mi E on 10th Ave S to Exit 0, then 1/4 mi N on 14th St SW, then 1/4 mi E on 13th Ave SW (dead end) (R) From Jct of US-87 (15th St) & 10th Ave S: Go 2 1/2 mi W on 10th Ave S to Exit 0, then (same as above from Exit 0) W-bnd: Call for directions. Elev 3300 ft. **FAC:** Gravel rds. (144 spaces). 114 Avail: 65 paved, 49 gravel, 61 pull-thrus (30 x 65), back-ins (30 x 65), 110 full hkups, 4 E (30/50 amps), seasonal sites, WiFi, tent sites, dump, laundry, LP gas. **REC.** Pets OK. Partial handicap access. Big rig sites, 2015 rates: $38. Disc: AAA. ATM.
AAA Approved
(406)452-0333 Lat: 47.49077, Lon: -111.33057
1403 11th St SW, Great Falls, MT 59404
reservations@dicksrvpark.com
www.dicksrvpark.com
See ad this page, 708.

GREAT FALLS KOA **Ratings: 6.5/7/7** (Campground) 2015 rates: $66.20. (406)727-3191 1500 51st St S, Great Falls, MT 59405

HALL — **C2** *Granite*

BOULDER CREEK LODGE AND RV PARK (RV Park) (Not Visited) W-Bnd: From Jct I-90 & exit 154: Go 500ft S on Sorenson Ln to Frontage Rd, Go .9mi W on Frontage Rd to MT Hwy 1, Go 15mi S on MT Hwy 1 (R), E-Bnd: From Jct I-90 & exit 153(MT Hwy 1): Go 15mi S on MT Hwy 1 (R). **FAC:** Gravel rds. 10 gravel, patios, 10 pull-thrus (25 x 45), 7 full hkups, 3 W, 3 E (30/50 amps), WiFi Hotspot, tent sites, rentals, dump, laundry, fire rings, firewood, restaurant. **REC:**

A campground rating is based on ALL facilities available at the park.

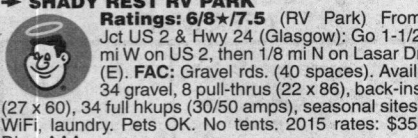

HALL (CONT)

BOULDER CREEK LODGE AND RV (CONT)
Boulder Creek: fishing, playground. Pets OK. 2015 rates: $40. May 15 to Nov 21.
(406)859-3190 Lat: 46.469507, Lon: -113.235998
4 Boulder Creek Rd, Hall, MT 59837
bouldercreeklodgemontana@gmail.com
www.bouldercreeklodgemontana.com

HAMILTON — C1 *Ravalli*

ANGLERS ROOST ON THE BITTERROOT RIVER
Ratings: 6.5/6.5/7 (Campground) From Jct US 93 & Hwy 269/531 (Hamilton): Go 3-1/2 mi S on US 93 (R) (MP 43.8). Elev 3600 ft. **FAC:** Paved/gravel rds. (59 spaces). Avail: 39 grass, 18 pull-thrus (30 x 75), back-ins (36 x 60), 20 full hkups, 19 W, 19 E (30/50 amps), seasonal sites, WiFi, tent sites, dump, laundry, groc, LP gas, fire rings, firewood. **REC:** Bitterroot River: swim, fishing, rec open to public. Pet restrict(Q). 2015 rates: $31. Disc: AAA. AAA Approved
(406)363-1268 Lat: 46.19957, Lon: -114.16685
815 Hwy 93 S, Hamilton, MT 59840
anglersroost@montana.com
www.anglersroost-montana.com
See ad opposite page.

BLACK RABBIT RV PARK
Ratings: 7.5/9.5★/7.5 (RV Park) From Jct Hwy 269/531 & US 93 (Hamilton): Go 1-3/4 mi N on US 93 (L) (Milepost 49). Elev 3540 ft. **FAC:** Gravel rds. (59 spaces). Avail: 39 gravel, 39 pull-thrus (23 x 60), 39 full hkups (30/50 amps), seasonal sites, cable, WiFi, tent sites, dump, laundry, firewood. **REC:** Bitterroot River: swim, fishing. Pet restrict(B). Partial handicap access. 2015 rates: $37.50. Disc: AAA, military.
(866)707-5050 Lat: 46.27390, Lon: -114.15956
2101 N 1st St, Hamilton, MT 59840
brabbit@bigsky.net
www.blackrabbitrv.com
See ad opposite page, 708.

HARDIN — C5 *Big Horn*

GRANDVIEW CAMP & RV PARK
Ratings: 7/8.5★/8 (Campground) From Jct I-90 & Hwy 313 (exit 495): Go 1/2 mi S on Hwy 313 / Mitchell Ave (R). Elev 3000 ft.

RV PARK IN BIG HORN & CUSTER COUNTY
Spend your Montana vacation with us & see the Historical Sites. Little Bighorn Battlefield, Custer's Last Stand Reenactment, Chief Plenty Coups Museum, Clark's Pompeys Pillar. Quick on & off access from I-90. Big Rig sites.

FAC: Gravel rds. (56 spaces). Avail: 53 gravel, 12 pull-thrus (30 x 90), back-ins (30 x 75), 47 full hkups, 6 E (30/50 amps), seasonal sites, cable, WiFi, tent sites, rentals, dump, laundry, firewood. **REC:** playground. Pets OK. Partial handicap access. Big rig sites, eco-friendly, 2015 rates: $28 to $38. Disc: AAA, military.
(406)665-2489 Lat: 45.73930, Lon: -107.61404
1002 N Mitchell, Hardin, MT 59034
reserve@grandviewcamp.com
www.grandviewcamp.com
See ad opposite page, 708.

HARDIN KOA **Ratings: 7.5/8/6.5** (Campground) 2015 rates: $40. Apr 1 to Oct 15. (406)665-1635 2205 Hwy 47 N, Hardin, MT 59034

HARLOWTON — C3 *Wheatland*

CHIEF JOSEPH PARK (Public) From Jct of US-12 & US-191, E 0.5 mi on US-12/191 (L). 2015 rates: $3 to $11. Apr 15 to Oct 1. (406)632-5523

Time and rates don't stand still. Remember that last year's rates serve as a guideline only. Call ahead for the most current rate information.

HAVRE — A4 *Blaine, Hill*

EVERGREEN CAMPGROUND
Ratings: 7.5/9★/8 (Campground) From Jct US 87 & US 2: Go 4 mi S on US-87 (L) (MP 107.5). Elev 2600 ft. **FAC:** Gravel rds. 25 grass, 5 pull-thrus (24 x 60), back-ins (20 x 60), 18 full hkups, 7 W, 7 E (30/50 amps), WiFi, tent sites, rentals, dump, laundry, fire rings, firewood. **REC:** playground. Pets OK. Eco-friendly, 2015 rates: $35. Apr 1 to Nov 15.
(406)265-8228 Lat: 48.50896, Lon: -109.78938
7350 Hwy 87 West/Gps: 4850 72nd Ave West, Havre, MT 59501
evrgreen@ttc-cmc.net
See ad this page, 708.

GREAT NORTHERN FAIR & CAMPGROUNDS (Public) From town, W 1 mi on US-2 (L). 2015 rates: $20. Apr 15 to Nov 15. (406)265-7121

HAVRE RV PARK
Ratings: 8.5/9★/8 (RV Park) From Jct US 87 & US 2: Go 4 mi E on US 2 (L) (Check in at Conoco Station). Elev 2600 ft. **FAC:** Paved rds. (54 spaces). Avail: 44 paved, 13 pull-thrus (20 x 50), back-ins (20 x 35), 44 full hkups (30/50 amps), seasonal sites, WiFi Hotspot, tent sites, rentals, laundry, groc. **REC:** heated pool, whirlpool, rec open to public. Pets OK. Partial handicap access. 2015 rates: $45. Disc: AAA. ATM.
(800)278-8861 Lat: 48.55199, Lon: -109.66289
1415 1st St, Havre, MT 59501
emporiumstationhavre@gmail.com
www.havremt.com/duckinn/emporium.htm
See ad this page, 708.

Travel Services

WESTERN TRAILER & MARINE SALES Onsite new and used fifth wheels, travel trailers & boats for sale. Parts department, accessories, and repair service. Elev 2600 ft. **SERVICES:** RV, RV appliance, MH mechanical, mobile RV svc, emergency rd svc, restrooms, RV Sales. RV supplies, emergency parking, RV accessible. waiting room. Hours: M-F 8am to 5pm, Sat 8am to 3pm.
(406)265-4572 Lat: 48.55597, Lon: -109.65546
1865 Hwy 2E, Havre, MT 59501
clyde@bresnan.net
www.westerntrailersales.com
See ad this page.

HELENA — C2 *Broadwater, Lewis & Clark*

CANYON FERRY/CHINAMANS GULCH (State Pk) From town, E 9 mi on US-287 to Hwy 284, NE 10 mi (R). 2015 rates: $8. (406)475-3310

CANYON FERRY/COURT SHERIFF (Public) From town, E 11 mi on US-12 to MP 55 (secondary 284), NE 9 mi (R). 2015 rates: $10. (406)475-3310

CANYON FERRY/HELLGATE (State Pk) From town, E 9 mi on US-287 to SR-284 (MP 55), NE 18 mi (R). 2015 rates: $8. (406)475-3310

CANYON FERRY/RIVERSIDE (State Pk) From town, E 9 mi on US-287 to Hwy 284, NE 9 mi to Eagle Bay Dr., NW 1 mi (R). 2015 rates: $8. May 26 to Sep 1. (406)475-3310

HAUSER LAKE SRA/BLACK SANDY (State Pk) From town, N 7 mi on I-15 to Lincoln Rd exit/SR-453, E 4 mi to cnty rd, N 3 mi, follow signs (R). 2015 rates: $15 to $25. May 17 to Sep 15. (406)495-3270

LINCOLN ROAD RV PARK **Ratings: 7.5/9.5★/8.5** (RV Park) 2015 rates: $40. (800)797-3725 850 West Lincoln Rd, Helena, MT 59602

HOBSON — B4 *Judith Basin*

ACKLEY LAKE (State Pk) From jct US 87 & Hwy 400: Go 5 mi S on Hwy 400, then 2 mi SW on county road. Pit toilets. 2015 rates: $15 to $23. (406)454-5840

Remember, ratings are based on ALL available facilities.

HUNGRY HORSE — A2 *Flathead*

CROOKED TREE MOTEL & RV PARK Ratings: 7.5/7/7.5 (Campground) From Jct US 93 & Hwy 4 : Go 13 mi E on Hwy 40 / US 2 (L) Note: Hwy 40 becomes US 2 in Columbia Falls. Elev 3100 ft. **FAC:** Gravel rds. (26 spaces). Avail: 20 grass, 5 pull-thrus (35 x 55), back-ins (35 x 45), 20 full hkups (30/50 amps), seasonal sites, WiFi, rentals, laundry. **REC:** heated pool, playground, rec open to public. Pets OK. No tents. 2015 rates: $32.71. Apr 15 to Nov 15.
(406)387-5531 Lat: 48.38588, Lon: -114.07220
8688 Hwy 2 E, Hungry Horse, MT 59919
crookedt@centurytel.net

MOUNTAIN MEADOW RV PARK & CABINS
Ratings: 7.5/10★/9 (Campground) From Jct US 93 & Hwy 40: Go 14-1/2 mi E on Hwy 40 / US 2 (R). Hwy 40 becomes US 2 in Columbia Falls. Elev 3200 ft. **FAC:** Gravel rds. 54 gravel, 43 pull-thrus (30 x 80), back-ins (30 x 48), 31 full hkups, 23 W, 23 E (30/50 amps), WiFi, tent sites, rentals, dump, mobile sewer, laundry, fire rings, firewood. **REC:** pond, fishing. Pets OK. Partial handicap access. Big rig sites, 2015 rates: $44 to $47. Disc: AAA, military. May 1 to Oct 1. AAA Approved
(406)387-9125 Lat: 48.38768, Lon: -114.04578
9125 US Hwy 2E, Hungry Horse, MT 59919
mmrvpark@gmail.com
www.mmrvpark.com
See ad pages 722, 708.

JORDAN — B5 *Garfield*

HELL CREEK (State Pk) From Jct of Hwy 200 & Cnty Rd (at milepost 213), N 26 mi on cnty rd (R). 2015 rates: $15 to $28. May 17 to Sep 15. (406)557-2362

KALISPELL — A1 *Flathead, Lincoln*

KALISPELL See also BigFork, Columbia Falls, Hungry Horse, Lakeside & Whitefish.

GLACIER PINES RV PARK
Ratings: 9.5/9.5★/8.5 (RV Park) From Jct US 2 & Hwy 35 : Go 1-1/2 mi E on Hwy 35 (R). Elev 2950 ft. **FAC:** Paved/gravel rds. (90 spaces). Avail: 80 gravel, 65 pull-thrus (22 x 58), back-ins (20 x 52), 62 full hkups, 18 W, 18 E (30/50 amps), seasonal sites, cable, WiFi, dump, laundry, LP gas, fire rings, firewood. **REC:** heated pool, playground. Pets OK. Partial handicap access, no tents. Eco-friendly, 2015 rates: $39. Disc: AAA, military. AAA Approved
(406)752-2760 Lat: 48.22402, Lon: -114.25481
120 Swan Mountain Drive, Kalispell, MT 59901
office@glacierpines.com
www.glacierpines.com
See ad pages 718, 708.

LIONS BITTERROOT REC YOUTH CAMP (Public) From Jct of US-93 & US-2, W 20 mi on US-2 to Pleasant Valley Rd., NW 5 mi to Bitterroot Rd., (L). Pit toilets. 2015 rates: $8. May 15 to Oct 1. (406)854-2744

Our rating system isn't just tough, it's thorough. We know the kinds of things that are important to you — like clean restrooms and showers, attractive, secure, well-tended grounds, and extras like swimming pools. We give the first rating for development of facilities, the second for cleanliness and physical characteristics of restrooms and showers, and the third for visual appearance.

KALISPELL (CONT)

➔ ROCKY MOUNTAIN 'HI' RV PARK AND CAMPGROUND

Ratings: 8.5/9★/8.5 (Campground) From Jct US-93 & US-2: Go 4 3/4 mi NE on US-2, then 1 mi E on Reserve Dr, then 3/4 mi N on Helena Flats Rd (R) Or S-Bnd : From Jct US 2 & Hwy 40: Go 8-1/4 mi S on US 2, then 1 mi E on Rose Crossing, then 1/4 mi S on Helena Flats (L). Elev 3000 ft.

RELAX & ENJOY MONTANA OUTDOORS

See what's in our backyard! Explore Glacier National Park, going to The Sun Road, Flathead Lake as well as magnificent fishing, hiking & sightseeing. Return for a quiet night's sleep, no trains or traffic noise here!

FAC: Paved/gravel rds. (98 spaces). Avail: 78 gravel, 30 pull-thrus (27 x 80), back-ins (25 x 50), 78 full hkups (30/50 amps), seasonal sites, cable, WiFi, tent sites, rentals, dump, laundry, groc, fire rings, firewood. **REC:** Spring Creek: swim, fishing, playground. Pets OK. Big rig sites, 2015 rates: $33. Disc: AAA, military. ATM.

AAA Approved

(800)968-5637 Lat: 48.25195, Lon: -114.25155
825 Helena Flats Rd, Kalispell, MT 59901
rmhc@bigsky.net
www.glaciercamping.com
See ad this page, 708.

➔ SPRUCE PARK ON THE RIVER **Ratings: 7.5/7.5/7** (Campground) 2015 rates: $35. (406)752-6321 1985 Mt Hwy 35, Kalispell, MT 59901

LAKESIDE — B2 *Powell*

⬆ EDGEWATER RV RESORT

Ratings: 8.5/9/7.5 (RV Park) S-bnd : From Jct US 93 & US 2 (Kalispell): Go 14-1/2 mi S on US 93 (R) or N-bnd : From Jct US 93 & I-90 (Missoula): Go 97 mi N on US 93 (L). Elev 3000 ft. **FAC:** Paved rds. 38 gravel, patios, 20 pull-thrus (21 x 60), back-ins (21 x 50), 38 full hkups (30/50 amps), cable, WiFi, rentals, laundry. **REC:** Flathead Lake: swim, fishing. Pet restrict(B). Partial handicap access, no tents. Big rig sites, eco-friendly, 2015 rates: $49.99. May 1 to Sep 30.

AAA Approved

(406)844-3644 Lat: 48.02254, Lon: -114.22707
7140 Hwy US 93 S, Lakeside, MT 59922
montanaedgewater@aol.com
www.edgewaterrv.com
See ad this page, 708.

LEWISTOWN — B4 *Fergus*

⬆ MOUNTAIN ACRES RV PARK

Ratings: 7/8★/7 (RV Park) From Jct US 87 & Hwy 191: Go 1/4 mi N on Hwy 191 (L). Elev 3900 ft. **FAC:** Paved rds. 36 gravel, 10 pull thrus (32 x 65), back-ins (25 x 75), 36 full hkups (30/50 amps), WiFi, tent sites, dump, laundry. **REC** playground, rec open to public. Pet restrict(B). Big rig sites, 2015 rates: $30 to $37.

(406)538-7591 Lat: 47.07223, Lon: -109.42958
103 Rocklyn Ave, Lewistown, MT 59457
mtnacresmhp@gmail.com
See ad this page.

LIBBY — A1 *Lincoln*

➔ TWO BIT OUTFIT RV PARK **Ratings: 6/8.5★/7.5** (Campground) 2015 rates: $30. Apr 1 to Nov 1. (406)293-8323 17 Two Bit Circle, Libby, MT 59923

➔ WOODLAND RV PARK

Ratings: 8/8.5★/8.5 (Campground) From Jct US 2 & Hwy 37 (Libby, MT): Go 1-1/4 mi W on US 2 (L). **FAC:** All weather rds. (50 spaces). Avail: 44 all weather, patios, 17 pull-thrus (35 x 90), back-ins (35 x 60), 44 full hkups (30/50 amps), seasonal sites, cable, WiFi, tent sites, rentals, showers $, dump, laundry, LP gas. **REC:** Parmenter Creek: fishing. Pets OK. Big rig sites, 2015 rates: $35 to $40. Apr 1 to Oct 30.

(406)293-8395 Lat: 48.39722, Lon: -115.57455
31480 US Highway 2, Libby, MT 59923
info@woodlandrvpark.com
www.woodlandrvpark.com

RV Park ratings you can rely on!

Say you saw it in our Guide!

LIVINGSTON — C3 *Park*

LIVINGSTON See also Bozeman & Emigrant.

LIVINGSTON PARADISE VALLEY KOA **Ratings: 8.5/8.5★/7.5** (Campground) 2015 rates: $38 to $53. May 1 to Oct 15. (800)562-2805 163 Pine Cr Rd, Livingston, MT 59047

OSENS RV PARK AND CAMPGROUND
Ratings: 7.5/10★/8.5 (RV Park) From Jct I-90 & US 89 (exit 333) : Go 1/2 mi S on US 89, then 1/8 mi W on Merrill Ln (R). Elev 4500 ft. **FAC:** Gravel rds. (42 spaces). Avail: 39 gravel, 17 pull-thrus (30 x 75), back-ins (25 x 65), 21 full hkups, 18 W, 18 E (30/50 amps), seasonal sites, cable, WiFi, tent sites, rentals, dump, laundry. **REC.** Pet restrict(Q). Big rig sites, 2015 rates: $34 to $46. Apr 15 to Oct 31.
(406)222-0591 Lat: 45.63677, Lon: -110.58023
20 Merrill Ln, Livingston, MT 59047
info@osensrvpark.com
www.osensrvpark.com
See ad opposite page, 708.

ROCK CANYON RV PARK **Ratings: 7/8.5★/7.5** (RV Park) 2015 rates: $40. May 1 to Oct 15. (406)222-7355 5070 Hwy 89 S #24, Livingston, MT 59047

LOLO — C2 *Missoula*

LOLO HOT SPRINGS RV PARK, CAMPGROUND & CABINS **Ratings: 5.5/4.5/5.5** (Campground) 2015 rates: $32.10. (406)273-2294 38500 West Hwy 12, Lolo, MT 59847

THE SQUARE DANCE CENTER & CAMPGROUND
Ratings: 6.5/7.5★/8 (Campground) From Jct US 93 & US 12 (Lolo): Go 2-3/4 mi W on US 12 (L). Elev 3300 ft. **FAC:** Paved/gravel rds. 61 gravel, 8 pull-thrus (35 x 75), back-ins (30 x 60), 25 full hkups, 36 W, 36 E (30/50 amps), WiFi, tent sites, dump, mobile sewer. **REC:** Lolo Creek: fishing. Pet restrict(B). Eco-friendly, 2015 rates: $25 to $30. May 1 to Sep 30.
(406)273-0141 Lat: 46.74831, Lon: -114.13528
9955 Lolo Creek Rd/Hwy 12, Lolo, MT 59847
sqrdance@bresnan.net
www.lolocampndance.com
See ad this page.

Find it Fast! Use our alphabetized index of campgrounds and parks.

MALTA — A4 *Phillips*

EDGEWATER INN & RV PARK **Ratings: 7/6.5/5** (RV Park) 2015 rates: $28 to $40. (406)654-1302 47176 US Hwy 2, Malta, MT 59538

TRAFTON (Public) From Jct of US-191 & Hwy 2 (Trafton Park Rd), N 0.1 mi on Trafton Park Rd (E). 2015 rates: $3. May 15 to Nov 1. (406)654-1251

MARION — A1 *Flathead*

LOGAN (State Pk) From town, W 60 mi on US-2 to milepost 77 (L). 2015 rates: $15 to $28. (406)752-5501

MCGREGOR LAKES RV **Ratings: 8.5/9.5★/8.5** (Campground) 2015 rates: $33. (406)858-2261 12255 Hwy #2 W, Marion, MT 59925

MELROSE — C2 *Beaverhead*

THE SPORTSMAN MOTEL, CABINS & RV **Ratings: 6/8.5★/8** (Campground) 2015 rates: $27. (406)835-2141 540 Main St, Melrose, MT 59743

MILES CITY — C5 *Custer*

BIG SKY CAMP & RV PARK Ratings: 8.5/9.5★/8 (Campground) From Jct I-94 & US 12 (Exit 141): Go 1/8 mi W on US 12 (L). **FAC:** Gravel rds. 19 gravel, 19 pull-thrus (22 x 80), 9 full hkups, 10 W, 10 E (30 amps), cable, WiFi, tent sites, dump, laundry. **REC:** pool, playground. Pets OK. 2015 rates: $22 to $27. No CC.
(406)234-1511 Lat: 46.42569, Lon: -105.79127
1294 US Hwy 12, Miles City, MT 59301
bigskyrv@midrivers.com
www.bigskycampandrvpark.com

MILES CITY KOA KAMPGROUND
Ratings: 8/7.5/7.5 (Campground) From Jct I-94 & Bus Loop 94 (exit 135): Go 2-1/2 mi NE on Bus Loop 94, then 1/8 mi N on 4th St, then 1/8 mi W on Palmer (R). **FAC:** Gravel rds. 58 gravel, 45 pull-thrus (27 x 68), back-ins (27 x 64), 47 full hkups, 11 W, 11 E (30/50 amps), cable, WiFi, tent sites, rentals, dump, laundry, groc, fire rings, firewood. **REC:** heated pool, Tongue River/Yellowstone River: fishing, playground. Pets OK. Big rig sites, 2015 rates: $41 to $48. Disc: AAA, military. Apr 15 to Oct 31.
(406)232-3991 Lat: 46.40639, Lon: -105.85884
1 Palmer, Miles City, MT 59301
milescitykoa@gmail.com
www.koa.com
See ad this page.

MISSOULA — B2 *Missoula*

MISSOULA See also Alberton & Lolo.

JELLYSTONE RV PARK
Ratings: 9.5/10★/9.5 (RV Park) From Jct of I-90 & US 93 (exit 96): Go 1/2 mi N on US 93 (L). Elev 3200 ft. **FAC:** Paved rds. 110 gravel, 81 pull-thrus (40 x 65), back-ins (24 x 48), 81 full hkups, 29 W, 29 E (30/50 amps), WiFi, tent sites, rentals, dump, laundry, groc, firewood. **REC:** heated pool, wading pool, playground, rec open to public. Pets OK. Partial handicap access. Big rig sites, eco-friendly, 2015 rates: $39.95 to $46.95. Disc: AAA, military. May 1 to Oct 15.
(800)318-9644 Lat: 46.96015, Lon: -114.13509
9900 Jellystone Dr, Missoula, MT 59808
info@campjellystonemt.com
www.jellystonemt.com
See ad this page, 708.

JIM & MARY'S RV PARK
Ratings: 8.5/10★/9 (RV Park) From Jct I 90 & US 93 (Exit 96): Go 1 mi N on US 93 (R). Elev 3200 ft. **FAC:** Paved rds. 69 gravel, 49 pull-thrus (38 x 80), back-ins (40 x 75), 69 full hkups (30/50 amps), cable, WiFi, laundry, LP bottles. **REC.** Pets OK. Partial handicap access, no tents. Big rig sites, eco-friendly, 2015 rates: $39.25. Disc: military.
(406)549-4416 Lat: 46.96463, Lon: -114.13062
9800 Hwy 93 N, Missoula, MT 59808
jimandmarys@montana.com
www.jimandmarys.com
See ad this page, 708.

MISSOULA KOA Ratings: 9.5/9★/8.5 (RV Park) From Jct I-90 & Reserve St (exit 101): Go 1-1/2 mi S on Reserve St, then 1/8 mi W on England Blvd, then 1/8 mi N on Tina (R). Elev 3200 ft. **FAC:** Paved rds. (130 spaces). Avail: 109 gravel, 103 pull-thrus

MISSOULA (CONT)

MISSOULA KOA (CONT)
(24 x 60), back-ins (24 x 50), 94 full hkups, 15 W, 15 E (30/50 amps), seasonal sites, cable, WiFi, tent sites, rentals, dump, laundry, groc, fire rings, firewood, restaurant. **REC:** heated pool, whirlpool, playground. Pet restrict(B). Partial handicap access. Big rig sites, 14 day max stay, eco-friendly, 2015 rates: $32.60 to $80. Disc: military. ATM.
AAA Approved
(800)562-5366 Lat: 46.89722, Lon: -114.04277
3450 Tina Ave, Missoula, MT 59808
reservations@missoulakoa.com
www.missoulakoa.com

NOXON — B1 *Lincoln, Sanders*

TWO RIVERS RV PARK **Ratings: 6.5/8.5★/7.5** (Campground) 2015 rates: $29. Apr 1 to Nov 15. (406)847-2291 30 Blue Jay Lane, Noxon, MT 59853

POLSON — B2 *Lake*

EAGLE NEST RV RESORT
Ratings: 9.5/10★/9.5 (RV Park) From Jct US 93 & Hwy 35: Go 1/4 mi E on Hwy 35 (L). Elev 3200 ft. **FAC:** Paved rds. (56 spaces). Avail: 44 gravel, patios, 23 pull-thrus (28 x 64), back-ins (28 x 50), 44 full hkups (30/50 amps), seasonal sites, WiFi, tent sites, laundry. **REC:** heated pool, whirlpool, playground. Pets OK $. Eco-friendly, 2015 rates: $37 to $57. Disc: AAA, military. May 1 to Oct 15.
(406)883-5904 Lat: 47.69175, Lon: -114.12009
35800 Eagle Nest Dr (Mt 35), Polson, MT 59860
info@eaglenestrv.com
www.eaglenestrv.com
See ad this page, 708.

FLATHEAD LAKE/FINLEY POINT (State Pk) From Jct of US-93 & SR-35, N 6 mi on SR-35 to Finley Point Rd, W 4 mi (R). 2015 rates: $15 to $28. May 1 to Nov 15. (406)752-5501

FLATHEAD RIVER RESORT **Ratings: 7/7.5/7** (Condo Pk) 2015 rates: $56. (406)883-6400 9 Regatta Rd, Polson, MT 59860

POLSON MOTORCOACH & RV RESORT
Ratings: 10/10★/10 (Condo Pk) From Jct US 93 & Hwy 35 : Go 3 mi N on US 93, then 1/4 mi W on Irvine Flats Rd (R) (MP-62). Elev 3000 ft. **FAC:** Paved rds. (61 spaces). Avail: 49 paved, patios, back-ins (45 x 75), 49 full hkups (50 amps), seasonal sites, WiFi, laundry, groc, LP gas. **REC:** heated pool, whirlpool, playground. Pet restrict(B/Q). Partial handicap access, no tents. Big rig sites, eco-friendly, 2015 rates: $65 to $120. Disc: military. Apr 15 to Oct 15.
(406)883-2333 Lat: 47.69986, Lon: -114.18446
200 Irvine Flats Rd, Polson, MT 59860
reservations@polsonrvresort.com
www.polsonrvresort.com
See ad this page.

POLSON/FLATHEAD LAKE KOA
Ratings: 9/10★/10 (RV Park) From Jct US 93 & Hwy 35 : Go 3 mi N on US 93, then 1/4 mi W on Irvine Flats Rd (R) (MP-62). Elev 3000 ft. **FAC:** Paved/gravel rds. (41 spaces). Avail: 35 gravel, patios, 35 pull-thrus (30 x 60), 26 full hkups, 9 W, 9 E (30/50 amps), seasonal sites, WiFi, rentals, dump, laundry, groc, LP gas, fire rings, firewood. **REC:** heated pool, whirlpool, playground. Pet restrict(B/Q). Partial handicap access, no tents. Big rig sites, eco-friendly, 2015 rates: $35 to $70. Disc: military. Apr 15 to Oct 15.
(406)883-2151 Lat: 47.69986, Lon: -114.18446
200 Irvine Flats Rd, Polson, MT 59860
info@polsonrvresort.com
www.polsonkoa.com
See ad this page.

RED LODGE — D4 *Carbon, Stillwater*

CUSTER/PARKSIDE CAMPGROUND (Natl Forest) From town: Go 12 mi SW on US 212, then 1/2 mi SW on FR 421. Pit toilets. 2015 rates: $16. May 9 to Sep 23. (406)587-9054

PERRY'S RV & CAMPGROUND Ratings: 4.5/6.5/6.5 (Campground) From Jct US 212 & Hwy 78: Go 3-1/2 mi S on US 212 (L) Caution: Narrow roads. Elev 5800 ft. **FAC:** Paved/gravel rds. (48 spaces). Avail: 43 gravel, 18 pull-thrus (26 x 55), back-ins (26 x 45), 43 W, 43 E (30/50 amps), seasonal sites, WiFi, tent sites, rentals, dump, fire rings, firewood. **REC:** Rock Creek: fishing. Pets OK. 2015 rates: $35. Disc: AAA, military. May 25 to Oct 1. No CC.
AAA Approved
(406)446-2722 Lat: 45.15140, Lon: -109.27289
6664 S. Hwy 212, Red Lodge, MT 59068
contact@perrysrv.us
www.perrysrv.com

RED LODGE KOA **Ratings: 7/6.5/7** (Campground) 2015 rates: $30 to $50. (800)562-7540 7464 Hwy 212, Red Lodge, MT 59068

REED POINT — C4 *Stillwater*

OLD WEST RV PARK & CAMPGROUND **Ratings: 5.5/7.5/5** (Campground) 2015 rates: $30. Apr 15 to Oct 1. (406)326-2394 5 South Division St., Reed Point, MT 59069

ROLLINS — B2 *Lake*

FLATHEAD LAKE/WEST SHORE UNIT (State Pk) From town: Go 5 mi N on US 93. Pit toilets. 2015 rates: $20 to $25. May 17 to Sep 15. (406)844-3066

Nobody said it was easy being a 10. And our rating system makes it even tougher.

ROLLINS RV PARK & RESTAURANT
Ratings: 8/10★/8 (RV Park) From Jct US 93 & Hwy 28: Go 9 mi N on US 93 (R); From Jct US 93 & Hwy 82: Go 17.5 mi S on US 93 (L). Elev 3000 ft. **FAC:** Paved rds. (43 spaces). Avail: 32 gravel, back-ins (30 x 40), 32 full hkups (30/50 amps), seasonal sites, WiFi, rentals, dump, laundry, firewood, restaurant. **REC:** Flathead Lake: swim, fishing, playground. Pets OK. Partial handicap access. 2015 rates: $48. Disc: AAA, military. Apr 1 to Oct 1.
(406)844-3501 Lat: 47.889298, Lon: -114.215717
23711 Hwy 93, Rollins, MT 59931
info@rollinsrvpark.com
www.rollinsrvpark.com
See ad this page, 708.

ROUNDUP — C4 *Musselshell, Yellowstone*

COWBELLES CORRAL (Public) From Jct of Main St & E Second, E 0.5 mi on E Second/at Fairground (L). (406)323-1966

ROY — B4 *Fergus*

JAMES KIPP RECREATION AREA (BLM) (Public) From town: Go 30 mi N on US 191 to the Missouri River. Pit toilets. 2015 rates: $12. Apr 1 to Dec 1. (406)538-1900

SEELEY LAKE — B2 *Missoula*

PLACID LAKE (State Pk) From town: Go 3 mi S on Hwy 83, then 3 mi W on county road. Pit toilets. 2015 rates: $20 to $28. May 17 to Sep 15. (406)677-6804

SALMON LAKE (State Pk) From town: Go 5 mi S on Hwy 83. Pit toilets. 2015 rates: $15 to $25. (406)677-6804

SHELBY — A3 *Toole*

LAKE SHEL-OOLE CAMPGROUND (Public) From town, N 0.75 mi on I-15 Bus Loop to exit 364, S 0.5 mi (L). 2015 rates: $15. May 15 to Sep 15. (406)434-5222

LEWIS & CLARK RV PARK
Ratings: 6.5/8.5★/8 (RV Park) From Jct Hwy 2 & I-15 : Go 1 mi N on I-15 to exit 364, then 1/4 mi SE on Oilfield Ave (R). Elev 3350 ft. **FAC:** Gravel rds. 60 Avail: 18 paved, 42 gravel, 60 pull-thrus (25 x 65), 42 full hkups, 18 W, 18 E (30/50 amps), WiFi, tent sites, dump, laundry, LP gas. Pet restrict(Q). Big rig sites, 2015 rates: $30 to $35. Apr 15 to Sep 30.
(406)434-2710 Lat: 48.52361, Lon: -111.85973
1535 Oilfield Ave I-15 Exit 364, Shelby, MT 59474
lewisandclarkrvpark@hotmail.com
www.lewisandclarkrvpark.com
See ad this page.

Park owners want you to be satisfied with your stay. Get to know them.

SHELBY (CONT)

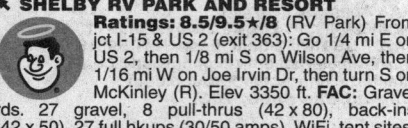

SHELBY RV PARK AND RESORT
Ratings: 8.5/9.5★/8 (RV Park) From jct I-15 & US 2 (exit 363): Go 1/4 mi E on US 2, then 1/8 mi S on Wilson Ave, then 1/16 mi W on Joe Irvin Dr, then turn S on McKinley (R). Elev 3350 ft. **FAC:** Gravel rds. 27 gravel, 8 pull-thrus (42 x 80), back-ins (42 x 50), 27 full hkups (30/50 amps), WiFi, tent sites, rentals, laundry. **REC:** heated pool, whirlpool, rec open to public. Pets OK. Partial handicap access. 2015 rates: $35 to $50. Disc: AAA. ATM.
AAA Approved
(406)434-2233 Lat: 48.51212, Lon: -111.87481
455 Mckinley, Shelby, MT 59474
st7195@townpump.com
www.shelbymtrvpark.com
See ad opposite page, 708.

TRAILS WEST RV PARK
Ratings: 6.5/9.5★/7.5 (RV Park) From Jct I-15 & US 2 (exit 363): Go 1/2 mi W on US 2, then 1/8 mi S on Adams Rd (L) Behind Best Western. Elev 3350 ft. **FAC:** Paved/gravel rds. (32 spaces). Avail: 27 gravel, 6 pull-thrus (30 x 60), back-ins (28 x 54), 27 full hkups (30/50 amps), seasonal sites, WiFi, tent sites, rentals, laundry. Pets OK. Partial handicap access. 2015 rates: $35 to $40. Disc: AAA. ATM.
AAA Approved
(406)424-8436 Lat: 48.51652, Lon: -111.88288
770 Adams Rd, Shelby, MT 59474
trailswestrv@3rivers.net
www.trailswestrvpark.com
See ad opposite page, 708.

WILLIAMSON RIVER (Public) From Jct of US-2 & I-15 frntg rd (in town), S 7 mi on I-15 frntg rd (L). 2015 rates: $8 to $15. May 15 to Sep 15. (406)434-5222

ST MARY — A2 *Glacier*

GLACIER/RISING SUN (Natl Pk) From town, W 6 mi on Going-To-The-Sun Rd (R). Note: 25' RV length limit. 2015 rates: $20. May 25 to Sep 10. (406)888-7800

GLACIER/ST MARY (Natl Pk) From Babb, S 10 mi on US-89 (R). For reservations call (800)365-CAMP. 2015 rates: $10 to $23. Jun 1 to Sep 1. (406)888-7800

JOHNSON'S OF ST MARY CAMPGROUND & RV PARK
Ratings: 6/8★/7.5 (Campground) From Jct US 89 & Going To The Sun Rd : Go 1/4 mi N on US 89, then 1/8 mi NE on access Rd (R). Elev 4550 ft. **FAC:** Paved/gravel rds. 88 Avail: 56 gravel, 32 grass, 66 pull-thrus (20 x 65), back-ins (15 x 70), some side by side hkups, 47 full hkups, 41 W, 41 E (20/30 amps), WiFi Hotspot, tent sites, rentals, dump, laundry, LP gas, fire rings, firewood, restaurant. **REC:** rec open to public. Pets OK. Partial handicap access. 2015 rates: $42 to $50. Disc: military. May 15 to Sep 15. ATM.
(406)732-4207 Lat: 48.74997, Lon: -113.42624
21 Red Eagle Road, St Mary, MT 59417
info@johnsonsofstmary.com
www.johnsonsofstmary.com
See ad this page, 708.

ST MARY-GLACIER PARK KOA **Ratings: 7.5/8.5★/8.5** (Campground) 2015 rates: $40 to $75. May 16 to Sep 30. (800)562-1504 106 West Shore, St Mary, MT 59417

Things to See and Do

JOHNSON'S CAFE OF ST MARY Homemade family style meals, homemade soup, breads, entrees and desserts. Family owned and operated for over sixty three years and three generations, decorated with family memorabilia and antiques. Elev 4550 ft. May 15 to Sep 15. Restrooms, food. Hours: 7:30 am to 9 pm. ATM.
(406)732-5565 Lat: 48.74983, Lon: -113.42602
21 Red Eagle Road, St Mary, MT 59417
info@johnsonsofstmary.com
www.johnsonsofstmary.com
See ad this page.

ST REGIS — B1 *Mineral*

CAMPGROUND ST REGIS
Ratings: 8.5/9.5★/9.5 (Campground) From Jct I-90 & Hwy 135 (St Regis exit 33): Go 0.2 mi N on Hwy 135 (to flashing red light), then 0.5 mi W on Mullan Rd, then 0.5 mi S on Little Joe Rd to Frontage Rd, then 0.5 mi W on Frontage Rd (R). Elev 2700 ft. **FAC:** Paved/gravel rds. (75 spaces). Avail: 70 gravel, 35 pull-thrus (32 x 100), back-ins (40 x 40), 14 full hkups, 56 W, 56 E (30/50 amps), seasonal sites, WiFi, tent sites, dump, laundry, groc, LP gas, fire rings, firewood. **REC:** heated pool, playground. Pets OK. Big rig sites, eco-friendly, 2015 rates: $36 to $40. Disc: AAA, military. Apr 1 to Oct 1.
AAA Approved
(406)649-2470 Lat: 47.30125, Lon: -115.13348
44 Frontage Rd West, St Regis, MT 59866
moose@campgroundstregis.com
www.campgroundstregis.com

NUGGET RV PARK
Ratings: 9/9.5★/10 (RV Park) From Jct I-90 & Hwy 135 (St Regis, exit 33): Go 1/8 mi N on Hwy 135, then 1 mi E on Mullan Rd (L). Elev 2600 ft. **FAC:** Paved/gravel rds. 64 gravel, 64 pull-thrus (30 x 75), 64 full hkups (30/50 amps), WiFi, tent sites, rentals, dump, laundry, LP gas, fire rings, firewood. **REC:** heated pool, playground. Pets OK. Partial handicap access. Big rig sites, eco-friendly, 2015 rates: $32.40 to $42.23. Disc: AAA, military. Apr 1 to Oct 31.
(888)800-0125 Lat: 47.28981, Lon: -115.08279
1037 Old Highway 10 East, St Regis, MT 59866
jim@nuggetrvpark.com
www.nuggetrvpark.com

STANFORD — B3 *Judith Basin*

LEWIS & CLARK/DRY WOLF CAMPGROUND (State Pk) From town: Go 17-1/2 mi SW on gravel CR 251, then 5-1/2 mi SW on FR 251. Pit toilets. 2015 rates: $5. May 26 to Sep 1. (406)566-2292

SULA — C2 *Ravalli*

SULA COUNTRY STORE & RESORT Ratings: 6.5/8.5/7 (Campground) From Jct US 93 & Hwy 43 (Montana / Idaho border): Go 13 mi N on US 93 (R). Elev 4450 ft. **FAC:** Gravel rds. 19 gravel, 7 pull-thrus (30 x 68), back-ins (30 x 60), some side by side hkups, 7 full hkups, 12 W, 12 E (30 amps), WiFi, tent sites, rentals, dump, laundry, groc, fire rings, firewood, restaurant. **REC:** whirlpool, Eastfork Bitterroot: fishing, playground. Pets OK $. Partial handicap access. 2015 rates: $25. Disc: AAA.
AAA Approved
(406)821-3364 Lat: 45.83684, Lon: -113.98251
7060 Hwy 93 S, Sula, MT 59871
sularesort@montana.com
www.bitterroot-montana.com

THOMPSON FALLS — B1 *Sanders*

BIRDLAND BAY RV RESORT **Ratings: 6.5/8★/7** (Campground) 2015 rates: $28.04. May 1 to Oct 1. (406)827-4757 2148 Blue Slide Rd, Thompson Falls, MT 59873

THOMPSON FALLS (State Pk) From Thompson Falls: Go NW 1 mi on MT 200. Pit toilets. 2015 rates: $15 to $20. May 17 to Sep 15. (406)752-5501

THREE FORKS — C3 *Broadwater, Gallatin*

CAMP THREE FORKS **Ratings: 6/6.5/8** (Campground) 2015 rates: $38. May 21 to Sep 15. (406)285-3611 15 Koa Rd, Three Forks, MT 59752

DAILEY LAKE (State Pk) From Jct I-90 & US-89, S 21 mi on US-89 to Murphy Lane, E 1 mi to SR-540, S 10.6 mi to Dailey Lake Rd., E 3.3. 2015 rates: $7 to $12. (406)994-4042

LEWIS AND CLARK CAVERNS (State Pk) From Jct of I-90 & US-287, SW 15 mi on US-287 to Hwy 2, W 5 mi (R). 2015 rates: $15 to $25. May 17 to Sep 15. (406)287-3541

TOWNSEND — C3 *Broadwater*

CANYON FERRY/INDIAN ROAD (State Pk) From town, N 1 mi on US-287 milepost 75 (R). 2015 rates: $8. (406)475-3310

CANYON FERRY/SILOS (State Pk) From town, N 7 mi on US-287 to Silos Rd., E 1 mi (E). 2015 rates: $10. May 9 to Sep 12. (406)266-3100

CANYON FERRY/WHITE EARTH (State Pk) From Jct of US-287 & West Shore CR, E 5 mi on West Shore CR (E). 2015 rates: $10. (406)475-3921

SILOS TOWNSEND/CANYON FERRY LAKE KOA Ratings: 8/8/8.5 (RV Park) W-Bnd: From Jct I-90 & US 287 (exit 274) : Go 38 mi N on US 287, then 3/4 mi E on Silos Rd (MP 70) (L) S-Bnd: From Jct I-15 & US 287 / US 12 (exit 192): Go 26 mi S on US 287 / US 12, then 3/4 mi E on Silos Rd (MP 70) (L). Elev 3850 ft. **FAC:** Gravel rds. 56 gravel, 56 pull-thrus (32 x 55), 41 full hkups, 15 W, 15 E (30/50 amps), WiFi, tent sites, rentals, dump, laundry, groc, LP gas, fire rings, firewood, restaurant. **REC:** Canyon Ferry Lake: swim, fishing, marina, playground, rec open to public. Pets OK. 2015 rates: $48.50.
(406)266-3100 Lat: 46.41417, Lon: -111.58062
81 Silos Rd, Townsend, MT 59644
info@canyonferrylakekoa.com
www.canyonferrylakekoa.com

TROUT CREEK — B1 *Sanders*

TROUT CREEK MOTEL & RV PARK **Ratings: 7/8.5★/9** (Campground) 2015 rates: $28. (406)827-3268 2972 Hwy 200, Trout Creek, MT 59874

TROY — A1 *Lincoln*

KOOTENAI RIVER CAMPGROUND
Ratings: 6.5/8★/6.5 (Campground) From Jct US 2 & Hwy 56 : Go W 5-1/2 mi W on US 2 (R). **FAC:** Paved/gravel rds. 25 gravel, 20 pull-thrus (30 x 65), back-ins (28 x 50), some side by side hkups, 10 full hkups, 15 W, 15 E (30 amps), WiFi, tent sites, rentals, dump, laundry, fire rings, firewood. **REC:** Kootenai River: fishing. Pets OK. Eco-friendly, 2015 rates: $28. May 1 to Oct 30.
(406)295-4090 Lat: 48.50027, Lon: -115.91982
11251 US Hwy 2, Troy, MT 59935
kootenaicamp@gmail.com
www.kootenairivercampground.com

VALIER — A2 *Pondera*

LAKE FRANCES CITY PARK CAMPGROUND (Public) From Jct of SR-44 & Teton Rd, W 0.4 mi on Teton Rd (R). 2015 rates: $10 to $15. May to Sep. (406)279-3361

VIRGINIA CITY — D3 *Madison*

VIRGINIA CITY RV PARK
Ratings: 6.5/9★/7.5 (Campground) From Jct US 287 & Hwy 287 : Go 14 mi W on Hwy 287 (L). Elev 6000 ft. **FAC:** Gravel rds. 26 gravel, 10 pull-thrus (28 x 68), back-ins (26 x 38), some side by side hkups, 12 full hkups, 13 W, 13 E (30/50 amps), WiFi, tent sites, rentals, dump, laundry, fire rings, firewood. **REC.** Pets OK. 2015 rates: $35 to $42. Disc: military. May 5 to Sep 20.
(406)843-5493 Lat: 45.29474, Lon: -111.92751
1302 E. Wallace Rd, Virginia City, MT 59755
info@virginiacityrvpark.com
www.virginiacityrvpark.com

WEST GLACIER — A2 *Glacier, Flathead*

GLACIER CAMPGROUND Ratings: 6/8/8 (Campground) From Jct US 93 & Hwy 40: Go 22-1/2 mi E on Hwy 40 / US 2 (R) MP-152 (Note: Hwy 40 becomes US 2 in Columbia Falls). Elev 3400 ft. **FAC:** Paved/gravel rds. 156 gravel, 7 pull-thrus (20 x 65), back-ins (20 x 40), some side by side hkups, 80 W,

WEST GLACIER (CONT)

GLACIER CAMPGROUND (CONT)
156 E (20/30 amps), WiFi Hotspot, tent sites, rentals, dump, mobile sewer, laundry, LP gas, fire rings, firewood, restaurant. **REC.** Pets OK. 14 day max stay, eco-friendly, 2015 rates: $35. Disc: AAA, military. May 15 to Sep 30. ATM.
AAA Approved
(888)387-5689 Lat: 48.48156, Lon: -113.99587
12070 Hwy 2, West Glacier, MT 59936
www.glaciercampground.com

➜ GLACIER HAVEN RV & CAMPGROUND
Ratings: 7.5/9★/8.5 (Campground)
E-bnd: From Jct US 2 & Going to the Sun Hwy (West Glacier): Go 20 mi E on US 2 (R) (MP 173.4) or W- bnd: From Jct US 2 & Hwy 49 (East Glacier): Go 35 mi W on US 2, (L) (MP 173.4). Elev 3850 ft. **FAC:** Gravel rds. 19 gravel, 4 pull-thrus (35 x 65), back-ins (35 x 45), 19 full hkups (30/50 amps), WiFi, tent sites, rentals, dump, laundry, fire rings, firewood, restaurant. **REC:** Middle Fork of the Flathead River: fishing. Pets OK $. Big rig sites, eco-friendly, 2015 rates: $43.30. Disc: AAA, military. Apr 15 to Nov 1.
AAA Approved
(406)888-9987 Lat: 48.36491, Lon: -113.66320
14297 US Hwy 2 East, Essex, MT 59916
info@glacierhavenrv-campground.com
glacierhavenrv-campground.com
See ad this page, 708.

⬆ GLACIER/APGAR CAMPGROUND (Natl Pk) From Jct US-2 & Going-To-The-Sun Rd, N 2 mi on Going-To-The-Sun Rd to Apgar Village (E). Note: 40' RV length limit. 2015 rates: $20. (406)888-7800

⬆ GLACIER/AVALANCHE CAMPGROUND (Natl Pk) From Jct of US-2 & Going-To-The-Sun Rd, NE 13 mi on Going-To-The-Sun Rd (R). Note: 26' RV length limit. 2015 rates: $20. Jun 10 to Sep 5. (406)888-7800

⬉ GLACIER/FISH CREEK (Natl Pk) From Jct US-2 & Going-To-The-Sun Rd, N 2 mi on Going-To-The-Sun Rd to Camas Rd, NW 4 mi to Fish Creek Rd, N 1 mi (E). For reservations call (800)365-CAMP. 2015 rates: $23. Jun 1 to Sep 5. (406)888-7800

➜ NORTH AMERICAN RV PARK & YURT VILLAGE
Ratings: 7.5/9★/8 (Campground)
From Jct US 2 & Hwy 206: Go 8-1/2 mi E on US 2 (R) (MP 147.5). Elev 3200 ft. **FAC:** Paved/gravel rds. (60 spaces). Avail: 50 gravel, 47 pull-thrus (30 x 62), back-ins (27 x 48), 50 full hkups (30/50 amps), seasonal sites, WiFi, rentals, dump, laundry, firewood. **REC:** playground. Pets OK. Partial handicap access, no tents.

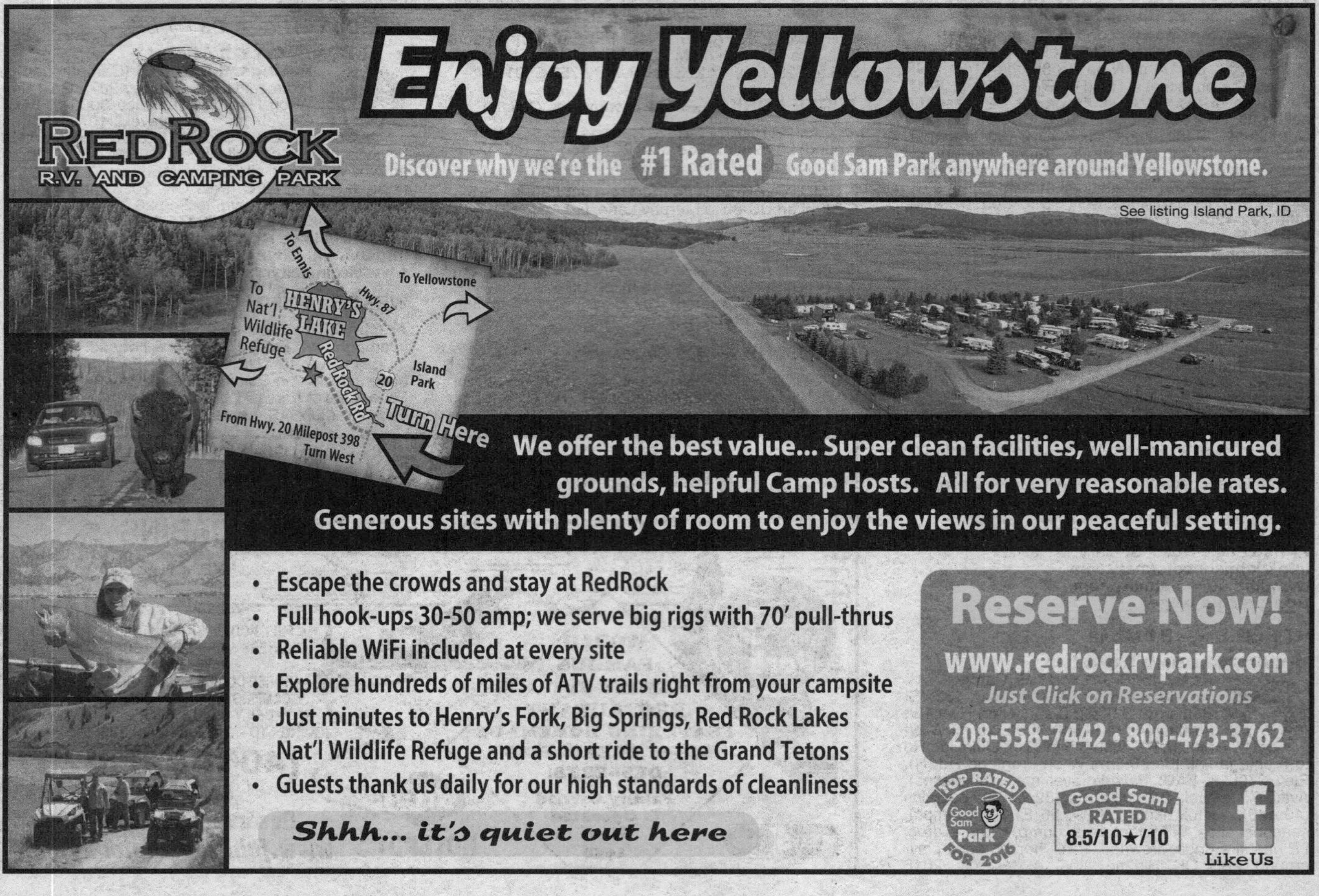

WEST GLACIER (CONT)

NORTH AMERICAN RV PARK & (CONT)
2015 rates: $38.50 to $44. Disc: military. Apr 1 to Oct 31.
(800)704-4266 Lat: 48.43769, Lon: -114.04032
10640 US Hwy 2 East, Coram, MT 59913
northamericanrv@aol.com
www.northamericanrvpark.com
See ad pages 713, 708.

SAN-SUZ-ED RV PARK & CAMPGROUND **Ratings: 6/9★/8** (Campground) 2015 rates: $44. May 1 to Oct 30. (800)630-2623 11505 Hwy 2 E, West Glacier, MT 59936

WEST GLACIER KOA **Ratings: 8.5/9.5★/9** (Campground) 2015 rates: $59.89 to $94.89. May 1 to Oct 1. (406)387-5341 355 Halfmoon Flats Rd, West Glacier, MT 59936

WEST YELLOWSTONE — D3 *Gallatin, Madison*

WEST YELLOWSTONE See also Island Park, ID.

BUFFALO CROSSING RV PARK
Ratings: 7.5/9★/9 (RV Park) From Jct US 20/Firehole Ave & US 191/Canyon St: Go 1/8 mi S on US 191/Canyon St (L). Elev 6700 ft.

EXPLORE OUR NATION'S 1ST NAT'L PARK
Stay at West Yellowstone's closest lodging to Yellowstone National Park. Enjoy our New Facility, including spacious Full service RV sites. Then shop, eat & experience Yellowstone's Imax Theatre with state-of-the-art film tech

FAC: Gravel rds. 25 gravel, patios, 15 pull-thrus (30 x 70), back-ins (25 x 45), 25 full hkups (30/50 amps), WiFi, laundry. **REC:** rec open to public. Pets OK. Partial handicap access, no tents. Big rig sites, 2015 rates: $33.99 to $54.99. Disc: AAA, military. May 11 to Oct 17.
(406)646-4300 Lat: 44.65804, Lon: -111.09965
101 B South Canyon St, West Yellowstone, MT 59758
ghales@yellowstoneimax.com
www.buffalocrossingrvpark.com
See ad this page, 708.

HIDE-A-WAY RV PARK **Ratings: 4/8★/6.5** (RV Park) 2015 rates: $34 to $45. May 1 to Oct 1. (406)646-9049 320 North Electric, West Yellowstone, MT 59758

MADISON ARM RESORT & MARINA Ratings: 6/8★/7.5 (Campground) From Jct US 20/191 & US 287: Go 3-1/2 mi N on US 191/287, then 5-1/2 mi W on Madison Arm Rd (E) (Caution: 5-1/2 mi of sand/dirt road, washboard like when not graded). Elev 6600 ft. **FAC:** Gravel rds. 57 gravel, 4 pull-thrus (20 x 36), back-ins (24 x 36), 44 full hkups, 13 W, 13 E (20/30 amps), WiFi, tent sites, rentals, laundry, groc, LP gas, fire rings, firewood. **REC:** Hebgen Lake: swim, fishing, marina, rec open to public. Pet restrict(Q). 2015 rates: $43 to $48. Disc: military. May 15 to Oct 1.
AAA Approved
(406)646-9328 Lat: 44.73560, Lon: -111.18633
5475 Madison Arm Rd, West Yellowstone, MT 59758
madisonarmresort@gmail.com
madisonarmresort.com

PONY EXPRESS RV PARK Ratings: 6/8.5★/6.5 (RV Park) From Jct US 20 / US 191 & US 287: NE corner of Jct (L) (Must check in at Brandin' Iron Inn on corner). Elev 6700 ft. **FAC:** Gravel rds. 16 gravel, 16 pull-thrus (18 x 36), 16 full hkups (30/50 amps), WiFi, rentals, laundry. Pets OK. No tents. 2015 rates: $29 to $39. Disc: AAA.
AAA Approved
(800)217-4613 Lat: 44.66235, Lon: -111.09769
201 Canyon St., West Yellowstone, MT 59758
info@brandiniron.com
www.yellowstonevacations.com

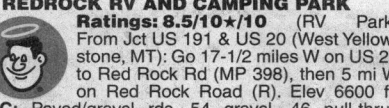

REDROCK RV AND CAMPING PARK
Ratings: 8.5/10★/10 (RV Park) From Jct US 191 & US 20 (West Yellowstone, MT): Go 17-1/2 miles W on US 20 to Red Rock Rd (MP 398), then 5 mi W on Red Rock Road (R). Elev 6600 ft. **FAC:** Paved/gravel rds. 54 gravel, 46 pull-thrus (32 x 60), back-ins (45 x 42), 54 full hkups (30/50 amps), WiFi, tent sites, dump, laundry, groc, fire rings, firewood, controlled access. **REC:** Henry's Lake: swim, fishing, playground, rec open to public. Pet restrict(B). Partial handicap access. Big rig sites, eco-friendly, 2015 rates: $50 to $54. May 1 to Sep 25.
(800)473-3762 Lat: 44.60362, Lon: -111.41644
3707 Red Rock Rd, Island Park, ID 83429
office@redrockrvpark.com
www.redrockrvpark.com
See primary listing at Island Park, ID and ad page 722.

RUSTIC WAGON RV CAMPGROUND & CABINS Ratings: 6/9★/8 (Campground) From Jct of US 191/287 & US 20: Go 1/2 mi W on US 20 (R). Elev 6700 ft. **FAC:** Paved/gravel rds. 45 Avail: 38 gravel, 7 grass, patios, 14 pull-thrus (24 x 70), back-ins (24 x 34), 40 full hkups, 5 W, 5 E (30/50 amps), cable, WiFi, tent sites, rentals, dump, laundry. **REC:** playground. Pet restrict(Q). 2015 rates: $49.95 to $52.95. Disc: AAA. Apr 15 to Oct 30. No CC.
AAA Approved
(406)646-7387 Lat: 44.66382, Lon: -111.11260
635 Hwy 20, West Yellowstone, MT 59758
welcome@rusticwagonrv.com
www.rusticwagonrv.com

WAGON WHEEL RV CAMPGROUND & CABINS Ratings: 6/9★/7.5 (RV Park) From Jct US 20 & US 191/287: Go 1/4 mi W on US 20, then 1/8 mi N on Faithful St, then 1/8 mi W on Gibbon Ave (L). Elev 6700 ft. **FAC:** Gravel rds. 36 gravel, patios, 5 pull-thrus (24 x 60), back-ins (18 x 40), some side by side hkups, 36 full hkups (20/30 amps), cable, WiFi, tent sites, rentals, laundry. **REC.** Pets OK. 2015 rates: $44.95 to $49.95. Disc: AAA. May 30 to Oct 1. No CC.
AAA Approved
(406)646-7872 Lat: 44.66384, Lon: -111.10703
408 Gibbon Ave, West Yellowstone, MT 59758
dorit@wyellowstone.com
www.wagonwheelrv.com

YELLOWSTONE GRIZZLY RV PARK
Ratings: 8.5/9.5★/10 (RV Park) From Jct Hwy 20 & US 191/Canyon St: Go 1/2 mi S on US 191/Canyon St, then 1/8 mi W on Gray Wolf Ave. Elev 6700 ft. **FAC:** Paved rds. 222 gravel, patios, 108 pull-thrus (30 x 70), back-ins (30 x 45), 222 full hkups (30/50 amps), WiFi, tent sites, rentals, dump, laundry, groc. **REC:** playground. Pets OK. Partial handicap access. Big rig sites, eco-friendly, 2015 rates: $35.50 to $67.95. Disc: AAA, military. May 1 to Oct 15.
AAA Approved
(406)646-4466 Lat: 44.65559, Lon: -111.10413
210 S Electric St., West Yellowstone, MT 59758
camp@grizzlyrv.com
www.grizzlyrv.com
See ad this page, 708.

YELLOWSTONE HOLIDAY RV CAMPGROUND & MARINA
Ratings: 8.5/9.5★/8.5 (Campground) From Jct of US 191 & US 287: Go 5-1/2 mi W on US 287 (L). Elev 6600 ft. **FAC:** Gravel rds. (36 spaces). Avail: 31 gravel, patios, 11 pull-thrus (40 x 72), back-ins (36 x 68), 31 full hkups (30/50 amps), seasonal sites, WiFi, tent sites, rentals, dump, laundry, LP gas, fire rings, firewood. **REC:** Hebgen Lake: swim, fishing, marina, rec open to public. Pets OK. Partial handicap access, no tents. Big rig sites, eco-friendly, 2015 rates: $37 to $63. May 15 to Sep 30.
(406)646-4242 Lat: 44.80320, Lon: -111.21670
16990 Hebgen Lake Rd, West Yellowstone, MT 59758
Info@yellowstoneholiday.com
www.yellowstoneholiday.com
See ad this page, 708.

YELLOWSTONE PARK / WEST GATE KOA **Ratings: 9/8.5/9** (Campground) From Jct of US 20/191 & US 287: Go W 6 mi on US 20 (R). Elev 6600 ft. **FAC:** Paved/gravel rds. 244 gravel, patios, 109 pull-thrus (30 x 75), back-ins (30 x 55), 175 full hkups, 69 W, 69 E (30/50 amps), WiFi, tent sites, rentals, dump, laundry, groc, LP gas, fire rings, firewood, restaurant. **REC:** heated pool, whirlpool, playground. Pets OK. Partial handicap access. Big rig sites, 2015 rates: $45 to $81. May 22 to Oct 1. ATM.
AAA Approved
(800)562-7591 Lat: 44.68688, Lon: -111.21663
3305 Targhee Pass/Us 20, West Yellowstone, MT 59758
ypkoa@aol.com
www.yellowstonekoa.com

YELLOWSTONE/ MOUNTAINSIDE KOA JOURNEY **Ratings: 8/10★/8** (Campground) 2015 rates: $45 to $72. May 22 to Oct 1. (877)935-5690 1545 Targhee Pass Hwy, West Yellowstone, MT 59758

WHITE SULPHUR SPRINGS — C3 *Meagher*

CONESTOGA CAMPGROUND **Ratings: 7.5/9★/8.5** (Membership Pk) 2015 rates: $39. May 1 to Oct 31. (406)547-3890 815 8th Ave SW, White Sulphur Springs, MT 59645

WHITEFISH — A1 *Flathead, Jefferson*

WHITEFISH LAKE (State Pk) From Whitefish, W 3 mi on US-93 (R). 2015 rates: $15 to $30. (406)752-5501

WHITEFISH RV PARK **Ratings: 6.5/8/7** (Campground) 2015 rates: $42 to $47. (406)862-7275 6404 Hwy 93 S, Whitefish, MT 59937

WHITEFISH/GLACIER PARK KOA **Ratings: 8.5/8.5/8** (Campground) 2015 rates: $46 to $78. (800)562-8734 5121 US-93 S, Whitefish, MT 59937

WOLF CREEK — B2 *Lewis & Clark*

HOLTER LAKE (BUREAU OF LAND MGMT.) (Public Corps) From I-15 (exit 226): Go 3 mi SE along Missouri River. Pit toilets. 2015 rates: $10 to $15. Mar 15 to Oct 15. (406)235-4314

LOG GULCH (BLM) (Public Corps) From I-25 (exit 226): Go 3 mi E on paved road, then 8 mi on gravel road. Pit toilets. (406)235-4480

Things change ... last year's rates serve as a guideline only.

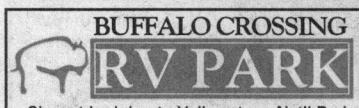

Know The Rules Of The Road!
RV-related laws in every state and province, including: Fishing licenses, bridge and tunnel restrictions and highway information numbers for every state and province.
Find the Rules in the front of this Guide.

Nebraska Tourism

WELCOME TO Nebraska

DATE OF STATEHOOD	WIDTH: 210 MILES (340 KM)	PROPORTION OF UNITED STATES
MARCH 1, 1867	LENGTH: 430 MILES (692 KM)	2.04% OF 3,794,100 SQ MI

Visiting Nebraska today, it's easy to see how the fertile farmlands, rolling hills and vibrant culture lure RVers to experience this corner of America's heartland.

Learn

Lots of Nebraska sites tell the story of pioneer life on the Plains. The Sod House Museum in Gothenburg chronicles how settlers dug up the grassy ground to build shelters. Modern attractions also merit attention: The Union Pacific Bailey Yard in North Platte is the world's largest railroad classification yard. Visitors can watch from the eight-story Golden Spike Tower.

Play

Any time the University of Nebraska hosts a home football game, the contest becomes the biggest event in the state. The Lincoln-based school has sold out every home game since 1962, and by kickoff, Memorial Stadium becomes the "Third Largest City in Nebraska."

The Omaha Summer Arts Festival sees Nebraska's biggest city come together for multicultural performances from over 100 of America's finest visual artists. While in town, visit a steakhouse for a taste of the region's most famous plate.

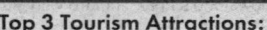

Top 3 Tourism Attractions:
1) Chimney Rock National Historic Site
2) Niobrara National Scenic River
3) Cabela's sporting goods megastore

Nickname: Cornhusker State

State Flower: Goldenrod

State Bird: Western Meadowlark

People: Fred Astaire, dancer; Marlon Brando, actor; Warren Buffett, stock investor; Dick Cheney, vice president; Henry Fonda, actor; Joyce C. Hall, founder of Hallmark cards

Major Cities: Omaha, Lincoln (capital), Bellevue, Grand Island, Kearney

Topography: Plains with rolling hills, streams and rivers, lakes and wetlands; central—sand dunes; northwest—badlands

Climate: Continental climate with highly variable temperatures from season to season

TRAVEL & TOURISM

Nebraska Dept. of Economic Development
877-NEBRASKA
www.visitnebraska.gov

Columbus-Platte County CVB
402-564-2769
www.visitcolumbusne.com

Fremont & Dodge County CVB
402-753-6414
www.fdcvb.org

Grand Island-Hall County CVB
800-658-3178
www.visitgrandisland.com

Hastings & Adams County CVB
402-461-2370
www.visithastingsnebraska.com

Norfolk-Madison County CVB
407-371-2932
www.visitnorfolkne.com

Greater Omaha CVB
402-444-4660, 866-937-6624
www.visitomaha.com

OUTDOOR RECREATION

Nebraska Game and Parks Commission
402-471-0641

Nebraska Department of Roads
www.roads.nebraska.gov

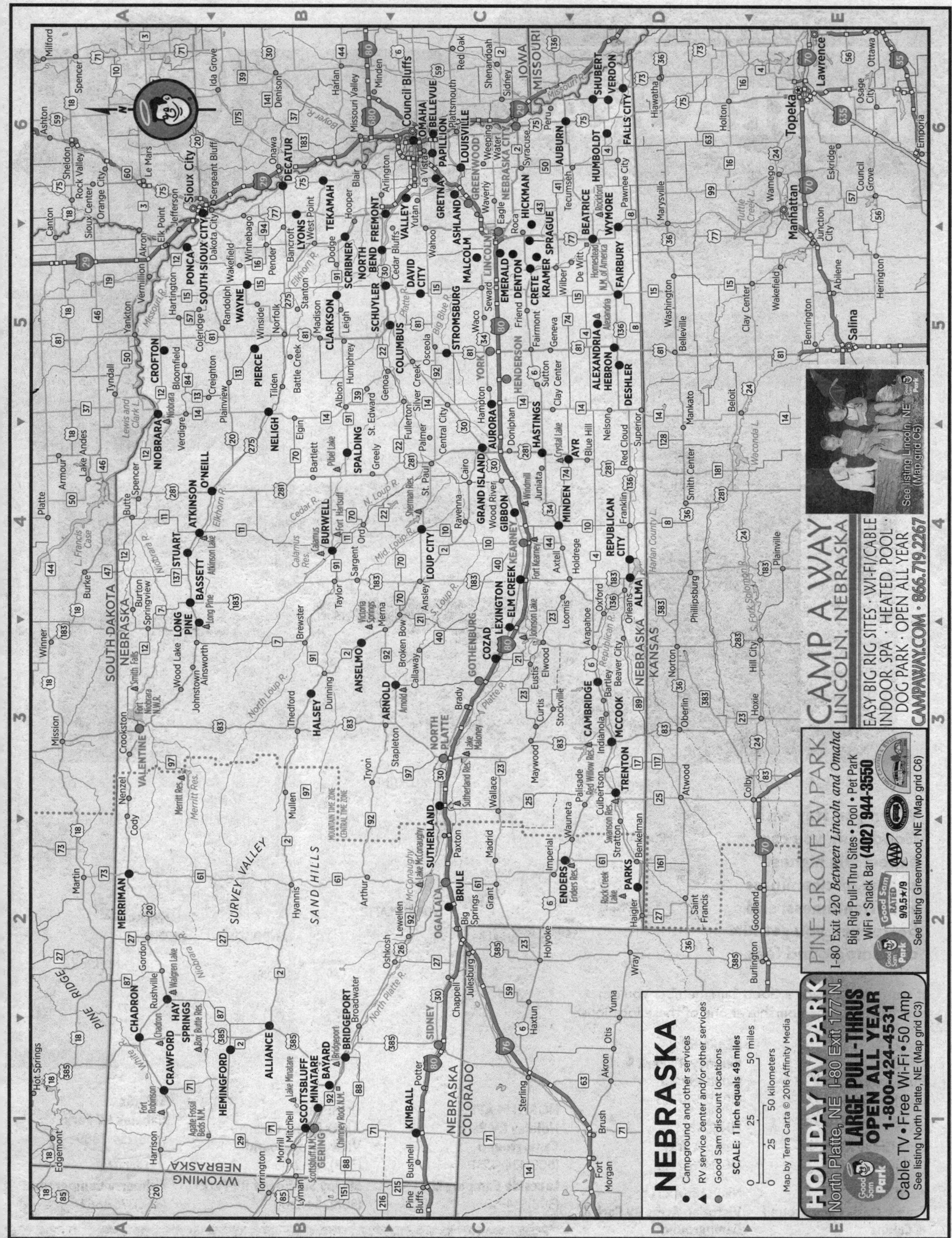
NEBRASKA
● Campground and other services
▲ RV service center and/or other services
● Good Sam discount locations
SCALE: 1 inch equals 49 miles
0 25 50 miles
0 25 50 kilometers
Map by Terra Carta © 2016 Affinity Media
HOLIDAY RV PARK
North Platte, NE I-80 Exit 177 N.
LARGE PULL-THRUS
OPEN ALL YEAR
1-800-424-4531
Cable TV • Free Wi-Fi • 50 Amp
See listing North Platte, NE (Map grid C3)
PINE GROVE RV PARK
I-80 Exit 420 Between Lincoln and Omaha
Big Rig Pull-Thru Sites • Pool • Pet Park
WiFi • Snack Bar (402) 944-3550
Good Sam RATED 9/9.5★/9
See listing Greenwood, NE (Map grid C6)
CAMP A WAY
LINCOLN, NEBRASKA
EASY BIG RIG SITES · WI-FI/CABLE
INDOOR SPA · HEATED POOL
DOG PARK · OPEN ALL YEAR
CAMPAWAY.COM • 866.719.2267
See listing Lincoln, NE (Map grid C5)
NE

Featured Good Sam Parks

NEBRASKA

When you stay with Good Sam, you can expect the highest degree of cleanliness and friendliness, and better yet, you get 10% off campground fees.

If you're not already a Good Sam member you can purchase your membership at one of these locations:

GERING
Robidoux RV Park
(308)436-2046

GREENWOOD
Pine Grove RV Park
(402)944-3550

HENDERSON
Prairie Oasis Campground & Cabins
(402)723-5227

KEARNEY
Kearney RV Park & Campground
(308)237-7275

LINCOLN
Camp A Way
(402)476-2282

NEBRASKA CITY
Victorian Acres RV Park & Campground
(402)873-6866

NORTH PLATTE
Holiday RV Park & Campground
(800)424-4531
Lakeside Camping LLC
(308)534-5077

OGALLALA
Area's Finest Country View Campground
(308)284-2415
Sleepy Sunflower RV Park
(308)284-1300

SIDNEY
Cabela's RV Park
(308)254-7889

VALENTINE
Fishberry Campground
(866)376-1662

For more Good Sam Parks go to listing pages

NE

Nebraska

CONSULTANTS

Duane & Bev Finger

AINSWORTH — A3 *Brown*

KELLER PARK SRA (State Pk) From Jct of Hwys 20 & 183, N 9 mi on Hwy 183 (L).Entrance fee required. Pit toilets. 2015 rates: $7 to $15. (402)684-2921

ALEXANDRIA — D5 *Jefferson*

ALEXANDRIA STATE REC AREA (State Pk) From Jct of US-77 & US-136 (in Beatrice), W 37 mi on US-136 to SR-53 (in town), N 6 mi to park access, E 3 mi (R). Entrance fee required. Pit toilets. 2015 rates: $7 to $13. Apr to Oct. (402)729-5777

ALLIANCE — B1 *Box Butte*

J & C RV PARK **Ratings: 4/NA/7.5** (Campground) 2015 rates: $25. (308)762-3860 2491 S Hwy 385, Alliance, NE 69301

SUNSET MOTEL & RV PARK **Ratings: 4/6.5/4.5** (Campground) 2015 rates: $25 to $30. (800)767-8660 1210 E Hwy 2, Alliance, NE 69301

ALMA — D4 *Harlan*

ALMA RV PARK (Public) From Jct of US-183 & South St, E 0.6 mi on South St (R). Extended stay discount. 2015 rates: $20. Apr 15 to Oct 15. (308)928-3102

HARLAN CNTY RES/METHODIST COVE (Public Corps) From Jct of Hwy 183 & South St (RD-B), E 2 mi on South St (R). 2015 rates: $12 to $24. May 1 to Sep 30. (308)799-2105

ANSELMO — B3 *Custer*

VICTORIA SPRINGS SRA (State Pk) From town, E 6 mi on Spur 21A (R). Entrance fee required. 2015 rates: $11 to $17. May 1 to Nov 30. (308)749-2235

ARNOLD — C3 *Custer*

ARNOLD SRA (State Pk) From Jct of US-83 & SR-92, E 16 mi on SR-92 to SR-40, S 1 mi (R). Entrance fee required. Pit toilets. 2015 rates: $7 to $13. (308)749-2235

ASHLAND — C6 *Cass, Saunders*

EUGENE T MAHONEY (State Pk) From Jct of I-80 & SR-66 (exit 426), W 0.5 mi on SR-66 (R). 2015 rates: $20 to $26. (402)944-2523

MEMPHIS STATE RECREATION AREA (State Pk) From town: Go 8 mi N on Hwy 63, then 1 mi W on CR D. Pit toilets. 2015 rates: $7. (402)471-5497

ATKINSON — A4 *Holt*

ATKINSON LAKE SRA (State Pk) From Jct of US-20 & SR-11, W 1 mi on US-20 to park access rd, SW 0.25 mi (R). Entrance fee required. Pit toilets. 2015 rates: $7 to $13. (402)925-5313

WHEEL INN RV PARK **Ratings: 3.5/7★/5** (Campground) 2015 rates: $22. (402)925-5117 702 N. Carburry, Atkinson, NE 68713

AUBURN — C6 *Nemaha*

LONGSCREEK RV PARK **Ratings: 6/7.5/6** (Campground) 2015 rates: $24. (402)274-3143 517 J St., Auburn, NE 68305

AURORA — C5 *Hamilton*

STREETER PARK (Public) From Jct of I-80 & SR-14 (exit 332), N 3 mi on SR-14 to Hwy 34, W 0.25 mi (R). Apr 1 to Oct 31. (402)694-6992

AYR — C4 *Adams*

CRYSTAL LAKE SRA (State Pk) From Jct of SR-74 & cnty rd (unnamed-gravel rd in town), N 1.5 mi on cnty rd, follow signs (E). Pit toilets. 2015 rates: $7 to $13. (308)385-6210

BASSETT — A4 *Rock*

BASSETT CITY PARK (Public) In town, W 1 blk on US-20 (L). (402)684-3338

BAYARD — B1 *Morrill*

BAYARD See also Gering & Scottsbluff.

CHIMNEY ROCK PIONEER CROSSING **Ratings: 5/9★/6.5** (Campground) 2015 rates: $25 to $30. (308)631-4478 10012 Road 75, Bayard, NE 69334

BEATRICE — D5 *Gage*

BIG INDIAN NRD REC AREA (Public) From town, S 6 mi (3 mi N of Odelle) on Hwy 8. Pit toilets. (402)228-3402

CHAUTAUQUA PARK (Public) From Jct of US-136 & US-77, S 1 mi on US-77 to Grable Ave., E 0.3 mi (L). 2015 rates: $18. (402)228-5248

RIVERSIDE PARK (Public) From Jct of US-77 & US-136, W 1 mi on US-136 to Sumner St, N 0.3 mi (E). 2015 rates: $18. Apr to Oct. (402)228-5248

ROCKFORD STATE REC AREA (State Pk) From Jct of US-136 & SR-4, E 7 mi on SR-4 to Rockford Lake Cnty Rd, S 2 mi (L). Entrance fee required. Pit toilets. 2015 rates: $7 to $15. (402)729-5777

BELLEVUE — C6 *Sarpy*

HAWORTH PARK (CITY PARK) (Public) At the east edge of town at jct Hwy 370 & Payne Dr at the Missouri River. 2015 rates: $20 to $25. (402)293-3122

BRIDGEPORT — B1 *Morrill*

BRIDGEPORT STATE RECREATION AREA (State Pk) 1/10 mi W of town off US 26. Pit toilets. 2015 rates: $7. (308)436-3777

MEADOWLARK RV PARK & MOTEL **Ratings: 4/7/4.5** (Campground) 2015 rates: $25 to $30. (308)262-0410 nw Hwy 385, Bridgeport, NE 69336

BRULE — C2 *Keith*

EAGLE CANYON HIDEAWAY **Ratings: 7/7.5/7.5** (Campground) 2015 rates: $30 to $36. Mar 15 to Dec 15. (866)866-LAKE 1086 Lakeview West Rd, Brule, NE 69127

BURWELL — B4 *Garfield*

CALAMUS RESERVOIR (State Pk) From town, N 2 mi on Windy Hill Rd., W 3.25 mi. on Pebble Creek Rd., NW 2.25 mi on Dam Rd. 2015 rates: $7 to $18. (308)346-5666

CAMBRIDGE — D3 *Frontier*

MEDICINE CREEK STATE REC AREA (TRAIL 4) (State Pk) From town, W 2 mi on US-6/34 to Medicine Creek Dam Rd, N 8.3 mi to Trail 4, W 1 mi (E). Entrance fee required. 2015 rates: $7 to $18. (308)697-4667

CHADRON — A1 *Dawes*

CHADRON (State Pk) From Jct of US-385 & US-20, S 8.4 mi on US-385 (R). Entrance fee required. 2015 rates: $7 to $18. Apr 15 to Nov 15. (308)432-6167

EAGLES REST RV PARK **Ratings: 5/8.5★/6.5** (Campground) 2015 rates: $30 to $35. (308)432-4349 #1 Stockade Rd, Chadron, NE 69337

CLARKSON — B5 *Colfax*

CLARKSON CITY PARK (Public) From Jct of Pine St & 3rd St, N 0.05 mi on Pine St to 1st St, E 0.2 mi (E). 2015 rates: $10. May 1 to Oct 1. (402)892-3100

COLUMBUS — C5 *Platte*

LOUP PARK (Public) From Jct of US-30 & 18th Ave, N 4 mi on 18th Ave to 83rd St, W 1 mi (L). May 1 to Nov 1. (402)564-3171

COZAD — C3 *Dawson*

JOHNSON LAKE SRA/INLET AREA (State Pk) From Jct of I-80 & US 283 (Exit 237), S 7.4 mi to Johnson Lake Rd, W 0.1 mi on Johnson Lake Rd (L) Entrance fee required. 2015 rates: $12 to $18. May 1 to Oct 31. (308)785-2685

CRAWFORD — A1 *Dawes*

FORT ROBINSON (State Pk) From Jct of SR-20 & 1st St (downtown), W 3 mi on SR-20 (R). Entrance fee required. 2015 rates: $18 to $24. (308)665-2900

CRETE — C5 *Saline*

TUXEDO PARK (Public) From Jct of US-33 & W 13th St, W 1.9 mi on W 13th St to CR-2100, N 2 mi (E). 2015 rates: $8. Apr 1 to Oct 15. (402)826-4315

CROFTON — A5 *Knox*

← COTTONWOOD (Public Corps) From Yankton, SD, W 4 mi on SD-52, S 1 mi on Dam Toe Rd (L). 2015 rates: $16 to $18. Apr 17 to Oct 19. (402)667-7873

↑ LEWIS AND CLARK SRA/BLOOMFIELD AREA (State Pk) From town, N 7 mi on SR-121 to CR-R54E, W 7 mi (R). Entrance fee required. 2015 rates: $7 to $18. (402)388-4169

↑ LEWIS AND CLARK SRA/MILLER CREEK (State Pk) From town, N 7 mi on SR-121 to CR-R54C, W 8 mi (R). Entrance fee required. Pit toilets. 2015 rates: $7 to $18. (402)388-4169

DAVID CITY — C5 *Butler*

↘ DAVID CITY PARK (Public) From Jct of S Hwy 15 & Kansas St exit, E 0.3 mi on Kansas St (L). 2015 rates: $10. Apr 1 to Oct 31. (402)367-3135

DECATUR — B6 *Burt*

→ BECK MEMORIAL PARK (Public) From Jct of 7th St & Broadway, S 0.4 mi on Broadway to 13th St, E 0.05 mi to 3rd Ave, N 0.05 mi to 11th St, E 0.05 mi (L). 2015 rates: $11 to $14. Apr 1 to Nov 1. (402)349-5360

DENTON — C5 *Lancaster*

↑ CONESTOGA SRA (State Pk) From Denton, N 2 mi on SR-55A to cnty rd, W 0.5 mi (L). Pit toilets. 2015 rates: $7 to $15. (402)796-2362

DESHLER — D5 *Thayer*

→ DESHLER CITY PARK (Public) From Jct of Hwy 136 & 1st St, S .3 mi on 1st St to Hebron Ave, E 0.2 mi to 4th St, S 0.6 mi (L). (402)365-4260

ELM CREEK — C4 *Johnson*

SANDY CHANNEL STATE RECREATION AREA (State Pk) From town: Go 3-1/2 mi S on US 183. Pit toilets. Sep 15 to May 1. (308)865-5305

EMERALD — C5 *Lancaster*

↖ PAWNEE STATE REC AREA (State Pk) From Jct of SR-79 & US-34, W 4.1 mi on US-34 to 112th St, S 1.4 mi (R). 2015 rates: $7 to $18. (402)796-2362

ENDERS — C2 *Chase*

↘ ENDERS RESERVOIR SRA (State Pk) From town, S 2 mi on US-6/61 (R). Entrance fee required. 2015 rates: $7 to $15. (308)394-5899

FAIRBURY — D5 *Jefferson*

→ ROCK CREEK STATION STATE HISTORICAL PARK (State Pk) From Jct of US-136 & Hwy 15, S 1 mi on Hwy 15 to PWS Rd, E 5.5 mi to 573 Ave, S 1 mi to 710 Ave, E 1.5 mi (E). Entrance fee required. 2015 rates: $12 to $18. (402)729-5777

Directional arrows indicate the campground's position in relation to the nearest town.

FALLS CITY — D6 *Richardson*

← STANTON LAKE PARK (Public) From Jct of Hwy 73 & 25th St, W 1 mi on 25th St (E). 2015 rates: $15. (402)245-2851

FREMONT — B6 *Dodge*

← FREMONT LAKES SRA (State Pk) From Jct of US-77 & US-30, W 3.5 mi on US-30 (L). 2015 rates: $12 to $18. (402)727-2922

GERING — B1 *Scotts Bluff*

← **ROBIDOUX RV PARK**
Ratings: 8.5/8.5★/9.5 (Public) N-bnd: On NE 71 take Gering exit (R): then 1-1/2 mi N on Five Rocks Rd (L); S-Bnd: From Jct of NE 71 & NE 92: keep S 4-3/4 mi on Ave I (becomes Five Rocks Rd) (R). Elev 4100 ft. **FAC:** Paved rds. 42 paved, patios, 27 pull-thrus (35 x 65), back-ins (35 x 40), 37 full hkups, 5 W, 5 E (30/50 amps), cable, WiFi, tent sites, dump, laundry. **REC:** playground. Pets OK. Partial handicap access. Big rig sites, 2015 rates: $24 to $30.
(308)436-2046 Lat: 41.81134, Lon: -103.67503
585 Five Rocks Rd, Gering, NE 69341
rvpark@gering.org
www.gering.org/rvpark.html
See ad this page, 726.

GIBBON — C4 *Buffalo*

↓ WINDMILL SRA (State Pk) From Jct of I-80 & Gibbon (exit 285), N 0.5 mi on Gibbon (R). Entrance fee required. 2015 rates: $12 to $18. (308)468-5700

GOTHENBURG — C3 *Dawson*

↓ **GOTHENBURG BLUE HERON CAMPGROUND**
Ratings: 6/8.5★/7 (Campground) From Jct of I-80 & NE 47 (exit 211): Go 1000 ft S on SR-47 (R). Elev 2505 ft. **FAC:** Paved/gravel rds. 58 paved, 51 pull-thrus (25 x 40), back-ins (25 x 30), mostly side by side hkups, 14 full hkups, 44 W, 43 E (30/50 amps), cable, tent sites, rentals, dump, laundry, groc, LP gas, fire rings, firewood. **REC:** pool, wading pool, Platte River: fishing, playground. Pets OK. Partial handicap access. Eco-friendly, 2015 rates: $28 to $35. Disc: military. Apr 1 to Oct 30.
(308)537-7387 Lat: 40.91056, Lon: -100.16778
1102 South Lake Ave, Gothenburg, NE 69138
blueheroncampgroundne@gmail.com
http://www.goodsamcamping.com.s3.amazonaws.com/gsparks/731004655/index.html
See ad this page.

↑ LAFAYETTE PARK (Public) From Jct of US-30 & US-47, N 1 mi on US-47 (L). 2015 rates: $10 to $15. Apr 15 to Nov 15. (308)537-2299

GRAND ISLAND — C4 *Hall, Hamilton*

↘ GRAND ISLAND KOA **Ratings: 9/9.5★/9** (Campground) 2015 rates: $35 to $45. Apr 1 to Oct 13. (800)562-0850 904 South B Rd, Doniphan, NE 68832

↓ MORMON ISLAND STATE REC AREA (State Pk) From Jct of I-80 & US-281 (exit 312), N 0.2 mi on US-281 (R). Entrance fee required. 2015 rates: $12 to $18. (308)385-6211

Things to See and Do

↓ **STUHR MUSEUM OF THE PRAIRIE PIONEER**
One of America's largest living history museums and greatest treasures. 200 acres & more than 100 structures (including Henry Fonda's birthplace). Antique farm machinery & auto collection, 1890's railroad town, arboretum & museum shop. Partial handicap access. RV accessible. Restrooms, food. Hours: M-Sa - 9 AM to 5 PM; Sun - 12 PM to 5 PM. Adult fee: $6 to $8.
(308)385-5316 Lat: 40.88286, Lon: -98.37450
3133 West Hwy 34, Grand Island, NE 68801
info@stuhrmuseum.org
www.stuhrmuseum.org
See ad page 724 (Welcome Section).

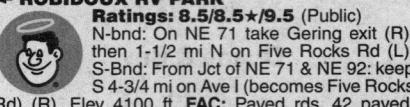

GREENWOOD — C6 *Cass, Lancaster*

PINE GROVE RV PARK
Ratings: 9/9.5★/9 (Campground) W Bnd: From Jct I-80 & NE 63 (exit 420): Go 100 ft N on NE 63; then 1/2 mi W on Mynard Rd (L) or; E Bnd: From Jct I-80 & NE 63 (exit 420): On NE 63 go N over I-80; continue past ramps another 100'; then 1/2 mi W on Mynard Rd (L). **FAC:** Paved/gravel rds. 100 gravel, 77 pull-thrus (44 x 80), back-ins (44 x 35), 100 full hkups (30/50 amps), WiFi, tent sites, dump, laundry, groc, firewood. **REC:** pool, wading pool, shuffleboard, playground. Pets OK. Big rig sites, eco-friendly, 2015 rates: $32 to $48. Disc: AAA, military.
AAA Approved
(402)944-3550 Lat: 40.97150, Lon: -96.39558
23403 Mynard Rd, Greenwood, NE 68366
pinegrovervpark@windstream.net
www.pinegrovervpark.com
See ad opposite page, 726, 725 (NE Map).

GRETNA — C6 *Sarpy*

WEST OMAHA KOA **Ratings: 8.5/7.5/7.5** (Campground) 2015 rates: $38 to $50. (800)562-1632 14601 Hwy 6, Gretna, NE 68028

HALSEY — B3 *Thomas*

NEBRASKA NF (BESSEY RECREATION COMPLEX) (Natl Forest) From town: Go 2 mi W on Hwy 2, then 1/2 mi S on Spur Hwy 86B. 2015 rates: $8 to $11. (308)533-2257

HASTINGS — C4 *Adams*

ADAMS COUNTY FAIRGROUNDS (Public) From W Jct of US-281, US-6/US-34 & S Baltimore Ave, N 0.2 mi on S Baltimore Ave (R). 2015 rates: $12.84 to $22.47. (402)462-3247

HAY SPRINGS — A2 *Sheridan*

WALGREN LAKE STATE REC AREA (State Pk) From Jct of US-20 & SR-87 (in town), E 3 mi on US-20 to park access cnty rd, S 3 mi to park entrance, E 0.6 mi (R). Pit toilets. 2015 rates: $7. (308)432-6167

HEBRON — D5 *Thayer*

RIVERSIDE PARK (Public) From Jct of Hwy 81 & Jefferson Ave., W .8 mi. to 7th st., S 1 block. 2015 rates: $3 to $5. May 1 to Nov 30. (402)768-6322

HEMINGFORD — B1 *Dawes*

BOX BUTTE RESERVOIR SRA (State Pk) From Jct of SR-87 & Mainstreet (cnty rd), N 10 mi on cnty rd to park access rd, W 1 mi (E). Pit toilets. 2015 rates: $7 to $13. (308)665-2903

HENDERSON — C5 *York*

PRAIRIE OASIS CAMPGROUND & CABINS
Ratings: 8/10★/9 (Campground) From Jct of I-80 & CR 93A/Henderson Interchange (Exit 342): Go 1500 ft N on Henderson Interchange (R) Note: Do not follow GPS. **FAC:** Gravel rds. 31 gravel, 31 pull-thrus (20 x 70), some side by side hkups, 21 full hkups, 10 W, 10 E (30/50 amps), WiFi, tent sites, rentals, dump, laundry, fire rings, firewood. **REC:** pond, fishing. Pets OK. 29 day max stay, 2015 rates: $28 to $32.50. Disc: AAA, military. Mar 1 to Nov 31.
(402)723-5227 Lat: 40.82602, Lon: -97.80544
913 Road B, Henderson, NE 68371
camp@prairieoasiscampground.com
www.prairieoasiscampground.com
See ad pages 733, 726.

HICKMAN — C6 *Lancaster*

STAGECOACH SRA (State Pk) From Jct of US-77 & SR-33, S 4 mi on US-77 to Panama rd, E 3.5 mi (L). Entrance fee required. Pit toilets. 2015 rates: $7 to $15. (402)796-2362

WAGON TRAIN STATE REC AREA (State Pk) From Jct of SR-33 & US-77, S 2 mi on US-77 to CR-S55G, E 6 mi (E). Entrance fee required. Pit toilets. 2015 rates: $7 to $15. (402)796-2362

HUMBOLDT — D6 *Richardson*

HUMBOLDT LAKE PARK (Public) From Jct of SR-105 & SR-4, S 1 mi (N side of lake) on SR-105 (R). 2015 rates: $10. Apr to Sep. (402)862-2171

KEARNEY — C4 *Buffalo*

FORT KEARNY SRA (State Pk) From Jct of I-80 & SR-10, S 3 mi on SR-10 (Minden exit #279) to L-50A, W 2 mi then N 1 mi (E). Entrance fee required. 2015 rates: $12 to $18. Mar to Oct. (308)865-5305

KEARNEY RV PARK & CAMPGROUND
Ratings: 8.5/8.5★/8.5 (RV Park) From Jct I-80 (Exit 272) & Hwy 44 (2nd Ave): Go 1/4 mi N on Hwy 44, then 1/4 mi E on Talmadge, then 1/4 mi S on Central Ave, then 3/4 mi E on 1st St (Archway Pkwy) (L). **FAC:** Gravel rds. 76 Avail: 37 paved, 39 gravel, patios, 76 pull-thrus (30 x 100), 76 full hkups (30/50 amps), WiFi, tent sites, laundry, LP gas. **REC:** Getaway Bay: swim, fishing, playground. Pets OK. Partial handicap access. Big rig sites, eco-friendly, 2015 rates: $35 to $40. Disc: AAA, military.
(308)237-7275 Lat: 40.67049, Lon: -99.06927
1140 E 1st Street, Kearney, NE 68847
info@kearneyrv.com
www.kearneyrv.com
See ad this page, 726.

Travel Services

CUMMINS CENTRAL POWER Cummins Central Power is the exclusive distributor for Cummins and Onan products in the mid-west. 12 full service locations in NE, MO, KS, IA, SD & IL support engine and generator customers. **SERVICES:** Engine/chassis repair, mobile RV svc, restaurant, restrooms. RV storage. **TOW:** RV, auto. Emergency parking, RV accessible. waiting room. Hours: Mon-Fri 7:30am to 5:30pm; Sat 7am-3:30pm.
(308)234-1994 Lat: 40.67772, Lon: -99.081703
515 Central Avenue, Kearney, NE 68847
centralpower@cummins.com
www.cumminscentralpower.com
See ad page 732.

KIMBALL — C1 *Kimball*

OLIVER RESERVOIR STATE RECREATION AREA (State Pk) From jct Hwy 71 & US 30: Go 8 mi W on US 30. Pit toilets. 2015 rates: $7. (308)436-3777

KRAMER — C5 *Saline*

OLIVE CREEK STATE RECREATION AREA (State Pk) From town: Go 2-3/4 mi SE. Pit toilets. 2015 rates: $7. (402)796-2362

LEXINGTON — C3 *Dawson*

JOHNSON LAKE SRA/MAIN AREA (State Pk) From Jct of I-80 & US-283, S 7 mi on US-283 to park access rd, N 0.6 mi (L). Entrance fee required. 2015 rates: $12 to $18. (308)785-2685

LINCOLN — C5 *Lancaster*

CAMP A WAY
Ratings: 9/9.5★/9.5 (Campground) From Jct of I-80 (Downtown Exit) (exit 401/401A) & I-80/Hwy 34 E: Go 1/4 mi S on Hwy 34 E, then 1/4 mi W on Superior St (exit 1), then 1/4 mi N on Campers Circle (E). **FAC:** Paved/gravel rds. 91 gravel, patios, 47 pull-thrus (35 x 70), back-ins (40 x 45), 91 full hkups (30/50 amps), cable, WiFi, tent sites, rentals, dump, laundry, groc, fire rings, firewood. **REC:** heated pool, whirlpool, playground. Pets OK. Big rig sites, eco-friendly, 2015 rates: $37.57 to $48.39. Disc: AAA, military.
AAA Approved
(402)476-2282 Lat: 40.85753, Lon: -96.71765
200 Campers Circle, Lincoln, NE 68521
contact@campaway.com
www.campaway.com
See ad this page, 726, 725 (NE Map).

STATE FAIR PARK CAMPGROUND (State Pk) From jct I-80 (exit 401) & I-180: Go S on I-180, follow signs to 14th St & Cornhusker Hwy. 2015 rates: $22 to $28. (402)473-4287

LONG PINE — A3 *Brown*

LONG PINE SRA (State Pk) From Jct of US-183 & US-20, E 2.5 mi on US-20 (R). Entrance fee required. Pit toilets. 2015 rates: $7 to $9. (402)684-2921

LOUISVILLE — C6 *Cass*

LOUISVILLE SRA (State Pk) W-bnd: From Jct of I-80 & SR-50, S 11 mi on SR-50 (R); or E-bnd: From Jct of I-80 & SR-66 (Exit 426), S 8.5 mi on SR-66 to SR-50, N 1.8 mi (L). 2015 rates: $11 to $18. (402)234-6855

LOUP CITY — C4 *Sherman*

BOWMAN LAKE REC AREA (State Pk) From town, W 0.5 mi on Hwy 10 (L). Entrance fee required. Pit toilets. 2015 rates: $7. (308)745-0230

SHERMAN RESERVOIR STATE REC AREA (State Pk) In town, from Jct of Hwy 92 & O St, E .8 mi on O st., N 1 blk to N St., E 2.2 mi to Trail 3, N 1 mi to Trail 5, E .25 mi. Entrance fee required. 2015 rates: $7. May to Nov. (308)745-0230

LYONS — B6 *Burt*

◄ ISLAND PARK CAMPGROUND (Public) From Jct of Hwy 77 & Main St, W 1 mi on Main St (L). 2015 rates: $12. Apr 15 to Oct 15. (402)687-2485

MALCOLM — C5 *Lancaster*

◄ BRANCHED OAK SRA (State Pk) From Jct of SR-79 & W Raymond Rd, W 3.1 mi on Raymond Rd (R). Entrance fee required. 2015 rates: $7 to $24. (402)783-3400

MCCOOK — D3 *Frontier*

▲ RED WILLOW RESERVOIR SRA (State Pk) From Jct of US-6/34 & US-83, N 10 mi on US-83 to park access Cnty Rd, W 1 mi to park entrance, N 0.25 mi (L). Entrance fee required. 2015 rates: $7 to $18. (308)345-5899

MERRIMAN — A2 *Cherry*

► COTTONWOOD LAKE REC AREA (State Pk) From Jct of SR-61 & US-20 (in town), E 0.5 mi on US-20 to park rd, S 0.25 mi (E). Pit toilets. 2015 rates: $7. (308)684-3428

MINATARE — B1 *Scotts Bluff*

▲ LAKE MINATARE STATE REC AREA (State Pk) From town, N 9 mi on US-26/Stonegate Rd (R). Entrance fee required. 2015 rates: $7 to $18. Jan 15 to Oct 15. (308)783-2911

MINDEN — C4 *Kearney*

MINDEN See also Kearney.

▲ **PIONEER VILLAGE CAMPGROUND** (Campground) (Rebuilding) From Jct of I-80 & NE 10 (exit 279): Go 12-1/4 mi S on NE 10, then 1000 ft E on US 6/34 (L). **FAC:** Poor gravel rds. 65 gravel, 27 pull-thrus (18 x 60), back-ins (18 x 55), mostly side by side hkups, 8 full hkups, 39 W, 39 E (30/50 amps), WiFi, tent sites, dump, laundry. **REC.** Pets OK. 2015 rates: $30 to $40. Disc: military.
(308)832-2750 Lat: 40.50442, Lon: -98.94964
224 East Hwy 6, Minden, NE 68959
manager@pioneervillage.com
www.pioneervillage.org
See ad this page.

Things to See and Do

▲ **HAROLD WARP PIONEER VILLAGE FOUNDATION** Pioneer Village, 50,000 historic items of Americana from 1830 to present: 350 antique autos, 26 bldgs on 20 acres, sod house, school, land office & more. Glassware, quilts, farm machinery, toys, aircraft, seven generations of period rooms. RV accessible. Restrooms, food. Hours: 9am to 4:30pm; Summer-9am to 6pm. Adult fee: $7.25 to $14.25.
(308)832-1181 Lat: 40.50442, Lon: -98.94964
138 East Hwy 6, Minden, NE 68959
manager@pioneervillage.com
www.pioneervillage.org
See ad this page.

NEBRASKA CITY — C6 *Otoe*

► RIVERVIEW MARINA SRA (State Pk) From Jct of US-75 & SR-2, E 3 mi on SR-2 to 6th St, N 2 mi to Marina (L). Entrance fee required. 2015 rates: $17. (402)873-7222

◄ **VICTORIAN ACRES RV PARK & CAMPGROUND** **Ratings: 8.5/9.5★/9.5** (Campground) E-bnd: From Jct of Hwy 75 & Hwy 2: Go 1-1/4 mi E on Hwy 2 (L); or W-bnd: From Jct of I-29 (in Iowa) & Hwy 2 (exit 10): Go 4 mi W on Hwy 2 (R). **FAC:** All weather rds. 69 gravel, 69 pull-thrus (28 x 60), some side by side hkups, 69 full hkups (30/50 amps), WiFi, tent sites, dump, laundry, LP gas, fire rings, firewood. **REC:** playground. Pets OK $. Partial handicap access. Big rig sites, eco-friendly, 2015 rates: $29 to $32. Disc: AAA, military. Mar 1 to Nov 30.
(402)873-6866 Lat: 40.65916, Lon: -95.84187
6591 Hwy 2, Nebraska City, NE 68410
info@victorianacresrvpark.com
www.victorianacresrvpark.com
See ad this page, 726.

NELIGH — B5 *Antelope*

▼ RIVERSIDE PARK (Public) In town, S-bnd on US-275 at southern Jct of L St (L). 2015 rates: $5 to $12. Apr 1 to Oct 1. (402)887-4066

NIOBRARA — A5 *Knox*

▲ NIOBRARA SRA (State Pk) From Jct of SR-12 & SR-14, W 1.2 mi on SR-12 (R). Entrance fee required. 2015 rates: $9 to $18. (402)857-3373

NORTH PLATTE — C3 *Lincoln*

↖ BUFFALO BILL STATE RECREATION AREA (State Pk) From Jct of I-80 & US-83 (Exit 177 N), N 2.3 mi on US-83 to Rodeo Dr (US-30), W 1.6 mi to Buffalo Bill Ave, N 0.9 mi to dirt road, NE 0.3 mi (E). Entrance fee required. 2015 rates: $7 to $13. (308)535-8035

▼ **HOLIDAY RV PARK & CAMPGROUND** **Ratings: 8.5/9.5★/9.5** (Campground) From Jct of I-80 & US 83 (Exit 177 North): Go 1000 ft N on US 83, then 1/2 mi E & S on E Halligan Dr (frontage rd) (L). Elev 2800 ft. **FAC:** Paved rds. 92 gravel, 72 pull-thrus (30 x 70), back-ins (30 x 55), 80 full hkups, 12 W, 12 E (30/50 amps), cable, WiFi, tent sites, dump, laundry, groc. **REC:** heated pool, playground. Pets OK. Big rig sites, eco-friendly, 2015 rates: $29 to $39. Disc: AAA, military. AAA Approved
(800)424-4531 Lat: 41.11088, Lon: -100.75699
601 E. Halligan Dr, North Platte, NE 69101
holidayparkne@hotmail.com
www.holidayparkne.com
See ad this page, 726, 725 (NE Map).

▼ LAKE MALONEY SRA (State Pk) From Jct of I-80 & SR-83, S 4 mi on SR-83 to park access rd, W 0.6 mi (E). Entrance fee required. Pit toilets. 2015 rates: $7 to $15. (308)535-8025

↘ **LAKESIDE CAMPING LLC** **Ratings: 5.5/8/6** (Campground) From Jct I-80 & Newberry Rd (56G) (Exit 179): Go 1000 ft N on Newberry Rd, then 1000 ft E on Halligan Dr (R) Note: Do not rely on GPS. Elev 2800 ft. **FAC:** Gravel rds. 66 dirt, 36 pull-thrus (26 x 70), back-ins (32 x 55), 25 full hkups, 41 W, 41 E (30/50 amps), tent sites, dump, laundry. **REC:** pond, swim, fishing, playground. Pets

Like Us on Facebook.

Don't miss the best part! Look in the front of most state sections for articles that focus on areas of special interest to RVers. These "Spotlights" tell you about interesting tourist destinations you might otherwise miss.

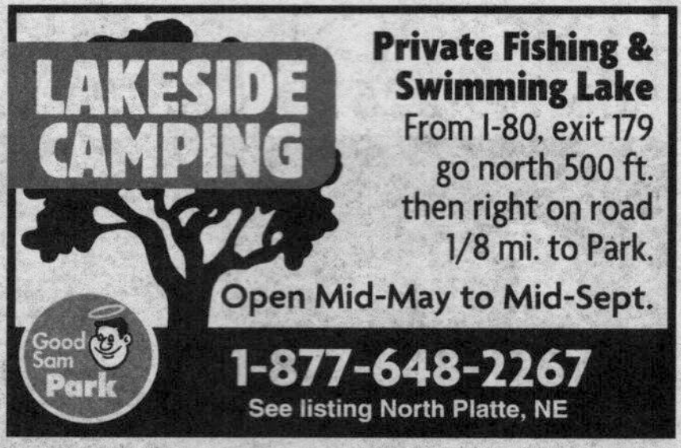

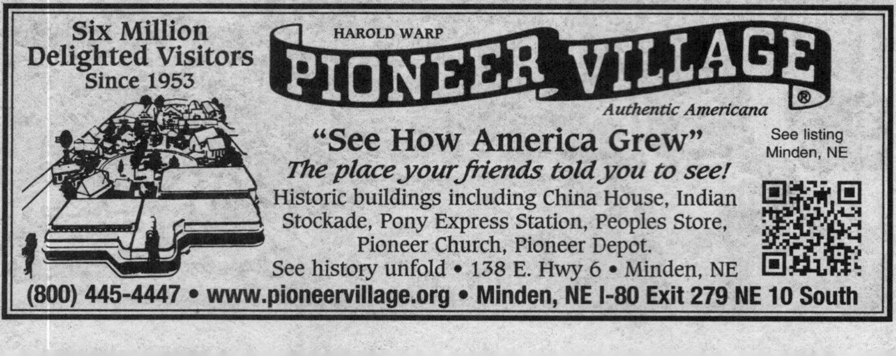

NE

NORTH PLATTE (CONT)

LAKESIDE CAMPING LLC (CONT)
OK. Big rig sites, 2015 rates: $28 to $34. Disc: AAA, military. May 1 to Sep 30. No CC.
AAA Approved
(308)534-5077 Lat: 41.10759, Lon: -100.71956
3800 Hadley Dr, North Platte, NE 69101
lakesidecamping@hotmail.com
See ad opposite page, 726.

O'NEILL — A4 *Holt*

CARNEY PARK CAMPGROUND (Public) From Jct of US-20 & US-281, S 0.4 mi on US-281 (L). 2015 rates: $10. (402)336-3640

OGALLALA — C2 *Keith*

OGALLALA See also Brule & Lewellen.

AREA'S FINEST COUNTRY VIEW CAMPGROUND
Ratings: 8.5/9★/8.5 (Campground) From Jct of I-80 & NE 61 (exit 126): Go 1/2 mi S on NE 61, Then 1/4 mi E on CR East 80 (R). Elev 2950 ft. **FAC:** Gravel rds. 49 gravel, 46 pull-thrus (24 x 100), back-ins (25 x 40), 49 full hkups (30/50 amps), cable, WiFi, tent sites, dump, laundry, fire rings, firewood. **REC:** heated pool, playground. Pets OK. Big rig sites, 2015 rates: $33.50. Disc: AAA, military.
AAA Approved
(308)284-2415 Lat: 41.10519, Lon: -101.71488
120 Road East 80, Ogallala, NE 69153
camp@cvcampground.com
www.cvcampground.com
See ad this page, 726.

LAKE MCCONAUGHY SRA (EAGLE CANYON) (Public) From town: Go 16 mi NW on US-26, then N on Eagle Canyon Rd. 2015 rates: $30 to $34. (866)866-5253

LAKE MCCONAUGHY SRA/CEDAR VUE (State Pk) From town, NE 12 mi on SR-61 to SR-92, W 12 mi to Public Rd 13 (L). Entrance fee required. 2015 rates: $7 to $24. (308)284-8800

LAKE MCCONAUGHY/LEMOYNE BAY (State Pk) From town, NE 12 mi on SR-61 to SR-92, W 6.5 mi to Public Rd 6, S .5 mi (L). Entrance fee required. 2015 rates: $7 to $24. (308)284-8800

LAKE MCCONAUGHY/MARTIN BAY/LONE EAGLE CG (State Pk) From Jct of US-30 & SR-61, NE 12 mi on SR-61 to SR-92, W 4.6 mi to Public Rd 4, S .5 mi (L). Entrance fee required. 2015 rates: $7 to $24. (308)284-8800

LAKE MCCONAUGHY/SPRING PARK (State Pk) From Jct of US-30 & SR-61, NE 12 mi on SR-61 to SR-92, W 7.2 mi to Public Rd 9, S 0.5 mi (L). Entrance fee required. Pit toilets. 2015 rates: $7 to $24. (308)284-8800

LAKE OGALLALA SRA (State Pk) From Jct of I-80 & SR-61, N 14.6 mi on Hwy 61 N (over dam) to Keystone Lake Rd, E 1.6 mi (R). Entrance fee required. 2015 rates: $7 to $18. (308)284-8800

SLEEPY SUNFLOWER RV PARK
Ratings: 8.5/10★/7.5 (Campground) From Jct of I-80 & NE 61 (exit 126): Go 500 ft S on NE 61, then 1/4 mi E on Prospector Dr (L). Elev 3300 ft. **FAC:** All weather rds. 44 Avail: 44 all weather, 30 pull-thrus (24 x 60), back-ins (25 x 30), mostly side by side hkups, 36 full hkups, 8 W, 8 E (30/50 amps), WiFi, tent sites, rentals, dump, laundry, groc. **REC:** playground. Pets OK. Big rig sites, 2015 rates: $28 to $33. Disc: AAA, military.
(308)284-1300 Lat: 41.11292, Lon: -101.70861
221 Road East 85, Ogallala, NE 69153
sleepysunflowerrvpark@yahoo.com
www.sleepysunflower.com
See ad this page, 726.

OMAHA — C6 *Douglas*

OMAHA See also Ashland, Bellevue, Greenwood & Gretna, NE and Council Bluffs, IA.

GLENN CUNNINGHAM LAKE (CITY PARK) (Public) From jct I-680 & 72nd St exit: Go 1/2 mi N on 72nd St, then 4/5 mi W on Rainwood Rd. 2015 rates: $15. Apr 12 to Oct 14. (402)444-4628

N P DODGE MEMORIAL PARK (Public) From Jct of I-680 & 30th St, S 1/2 blk on 30th St to McKinley, E 2 blks to John Pershing Dr, N 1 mi (R). Note: Only cash payments are accepted. 2015 rates: $15. May 24 to Oct 15. (402)444-5920

PINE GROVE RV PARK
Ratings: 9/9.5★/9 (Campground) From Jct I-480 & I-80 (in Omaha): Go 33 mi W on I-80; at I-80 (Exit 420) & NE 63; Go 100 ft N on NE 63; then 1/2 mi W on Mynard Rd (L). **FAC:** Paved/gravel rds. 100 gravel, 77 pull-thrus (44 x 80), back-ins (44 x 35), 100 full hkups (30/50 amps), WiFi, tent sites, dump, laundry, groc, firewood. **REC:** pool, wading pool, shuffleboard, playground. Pets OK. Big rig sites, eco-friendly, 2015 rates: $32 to $48. Disc: AAA, military.
(402)944-3550 Lat: 40.97150, Lon: -96.3958
23403 Mynard Rd, Greenwood, NE 68366
pinegrovervpark@windstream.net
www.pinegrovervpark.com
See primary listing at Greenwood and ad pages 728, 725 (NE Map).

Travel Services

CUMMINS CENTRAL POWER Cummins Central Power is the exclusive distributor for Cummins and Onan products in the Midwest. 12 full service locations in Nebraska, Missouri, Kansas, Iowa, South Dakota and Illinois support engine and generator customers. **SERVICES:** MH mechanical, engine/chassis repair, mobile RV svc, restrooms. Emergency parking, RV accessible. waiting room. Hours: 7am to Midnight.
(402)551-7678 Lat: 41.16117, Lon: -96.12729
10088 S. 136th St, Omaha, NE 68138
centralpower@cummins.com
www.centralpower.cummins.com
See ad page 732.

PAPILLION — C6 *Sarpy*

WALNUT CREEK LAKE & REC AREA (Public) From Jct of I-80 & Hwy 370 (Exit 439), E 4.8 mi on Hwy 370 to 96th St, S 0.8 mi to Schram Rd, W 0.6 mi (R). Pit toilets. 2015 rates: $16. Mar 1 to Dec 1. (402)679-9889

PARKS — D2 *Dundy*

ROCK CREEK LAKE (State Pk) From Jct of US-61 & US-34, W 12 mi on US-34 to Parks, NW 5.5 mi to Rock Creek Lake (R). Pit toilets. 2015 rates: $7. (402)471-1623

PIERCE — B5 *Pierce*

WILLOW CREEK SRA (State Pk) From town, SW 1.5 mi (L). Entrance fee required. 2015 rates: $12 to $18. (402)329-4053

PONCA — A5 *Dixon*

PONCA (State Pk) From Jct of SR-20 & SR-12, N 9 mi on SR-12 to 26 E, 3 mi (E) Entrance fee required. 2015 rates: $12 to $18. Apr 15 to Oct 31. (402)755-2284

REPUBLICAN CITY — D4 *Harlan*

HARLAN CNTY RES/GREMLIN COVE (Public Corps) From town, S 1.5 mi on Reservoir Rd (R). 2015 rates: $8 to $10. May to Sep. (308)799-2105

HARLAN CNTY RES/PATTERSON HARBOR (Public Corps) From town, S 3.3 mi on Reservoir Rd (past Dam) to RD-3, W 1 mi (E). 2015 rates: $26 to $28. Apr 1 to Sep 30. (308)799-4600

HARLAN COUNTY RES/HUNTER COVE (Public Corps) From town, S 1.5 mi on Reservoir Rd to Rd-B, W 1 mi (L). 2015 rates: $14 to $20. May 1 to Sep 30. (308)799-2105

SOUTH OUTLET (COE HARLAN COUNTY LAKE) (Public Corps) From town: Go 1-1/2 mi S on Acces Rd A, then E below dam on RD 1A. Pit toilets. 2015 rates: $6. (308)799-2105

SCHUYLER — B5 *Colfax*

SCHUYLER PARK (Public) From Jct US-30 & SR-15, S 1.5 mi on SR-15 (L). 2015 rates: $15 to $20. Apr 1 to Oct 31. (402)352-3101

SCOTTSBLUFF — B1 *Scotts Bluff*

SCOTTSBLUFF See also Bayard, Gering & Minatare.

RIVERSIDE PARK CAMPGROUND (CITY PARK) (Public) From jct US 26 & S Beltline Hwy: Go 3-3/4 mi W on S Beltline Hwy (Truck Route). 2015 rates: $10 to $20. May 1 to Sep 30. (308)632-6342

SCRIBNER — B5 *Dodge*

DEAD TIMBER SRA (State Pk) From town, N 5 mi on Hwy 275 to cnty rd, follow signs E 1.5 mi & S 0.5 mi (R). Entrance fee required. Pit toilets. 2015 rates: $7 to $15. (402)727-2922

SHUBERT — D6 *Nemaha, Richardson*

INDIAN CAVE (State Pk) From Jct of I-29 & SR-136 (exit 110), W 8 mi on SR-136 to SR-67, S 9.1 mi to Spur 64 E, E 4.9 mi (E). Entrance fee required. 2015 rates: $12 to $18. May 1 to Oct 31. (402)883-2575

SIDNEY — C1 *Cheyenne*

CABELA'S RV PARK
Ratings: 7.5/9★/8.5 (RV Park) From Jct of I-80 & NE 17J (Exit 59/Upland Parkway): Go 1/4 mi N on NE 17J, then 1/2 mi W on Old Post Rd (L). Elev 4867 ft. **FAC:** Gravel rds. 53 gravel, 35 pull-thrus (34 x 70), back-ins (25 x 40), 31 full hkups, 22 E (30/50 amps), cable, WiFi, tent sites, dump, laundry, LP gas, restaurant. **REC:** playground. Pets OK.

SIDNEY (CONT)

CABELA'S RV PARK (CONT)
Partial handicap access. Big rig sites, 2015 rates: $22 to $34.50.
(308)254-7889 Lat: 41.11584, Lon: -102.95868
115 Cabela Dr, Sidney, NE 69160
cabelas/rvpark@cabelas.com
www.cabelas.com
See ad pages 727, 726.

Things to See and Do

➜ **CABELA'S** Quality outdoor merchandise in a 85,000 sq ft showroom. A decor of museum-quality animal displays, huge aquariums & trophy animals interacting in realistic re-creations of their natural habitats. Elev 4867 ft. partial handicap access. RV accessible. Restrooms, food. Hours: 8am to 8pm M-S 10am to 6pm Sun. ATM.
(308)254-7889 Lat: 41.11584, Lon: -102.95868
115 Cabela Dr, Sidney, NE 69160
www.cabelas.com
See ad page 727.

Don't miss a thing! Check out the Table of Contents for everything the Guide has to offer.

SOUTH SIOUX CITY — A6 *Dakota*

SCENIC PARK CAMPGROUND (Public) From I-29, go to exit 148 (Wesley Parkway); Go across Veterans Memorial bridge to Riverview Dr, turn left and go 8 blocks on Riverview; or From Hwy 20, go to 77 North/Cornhusker Dr to Dakota Ave, go across Dakota Ave on to 9th St, at 9th & G St, turn left, go 3 blocks and turn right on to Riverview. 2015 rates: $15 to $25. (402)494-7531

SPALDING — B4 *Greeley*

PIBEL LAKE SRA (State Pk) From town, S 7 mi on US-281 to cnty rd, E 1 mi (L). Pit toilets. 2015 rates: $7. (308)728-3221

SPRAGUE — C5 *Lancaster*

BLUESTEM STATE RECREATION AREA (State Pk) From town: Go 3 mi W. Pit toilets. 2015 rates: $7. (402)796-2362

STROMSBURG — C5 *Polk*

BUCKLEY PARK (Public) From Jct of US-81 & SR-92, S 5 mi on US-81 (R). (402)764-2561

STUART — A4 *Holt*

STUART MUNICIPAL PARK (Public) From Jct of US-20 & Main St, N 1 mi on Main St (R). 2015 rates: $10. Mar to Nov. (402)924-3647

SUTHERLAND — C3 *Lincoln*

SUTHERLAND RESERVOIR SRA (State Pk) From Jct of I-80 & SR-25, S 2 mi on SR-25 to blacktop rd, SW 0.4 mi (L). Pit toilets. 2015 rates: $7. (308)535-8025

TEKAMAH — B6 *Burt*

PELICAN POINT SRA (State Pk) From Jct of US-75 & cnty rd, E 8 mi on cnty rd, follow signs (E). Entrance fee required. Pit toilets. 2015 rates: $9. (402)468-5611

SUMMIT LAKE SRA (State Pk) From Jct of Hwy 75 & cnty rd, W 5 mi on cnty rd, follow signs (R). Entrance fee required. Pit toilets. 2015 rates: $7 to $9. (402)468-5611

Had a great stay? Let us know by emailing us travelguidecomments@goodsamfamily.com

TRENTON — D3 *Hitchcock*

SWANSON RESERVOIR STATE REC AREA (State Pk) From town, W 5 mi on US-34 (L). 201 rates: $7 to $18. May to Sep. (308)345-5899

VALENTINE — A3 *Cherry*

BIG ALKALI LAKE STATE WILDLIFE MANAGEMENT AREA (State Pk) From town: Go 17 mi S o US-83, then 5 mi W on Hwy-483, then 2 mi S on san road. Pit toilets.

FISHBERRY CAMPGROUND
Ratings: 7.5/9★/9 (Campground) From Jct of US 20 & US 83: Go 5 mi N on US 83 (R). Elev 2728 ft. **FAC:** Grave rds. 22 gravel, 22 pull-thrus (20 x 100 mostly side by side hkups, 22 full hkup (30/50 amps), WiFi, laundry, fire rings, firewood **REC:** pond. Pets OK. Partial handicap access, n tents. Eco-friendly, 2015 rates: $30. Disc: military May 15 to Nov 1.
(866)376-1662 Lat: 42.93285, Lon: -100.57162
90440 US Hwy 83, Valentine, NE 69201
director@fishberrycampground.com
www.fishberrycampground.com
See ad this page, 726.

MERRITT RESERVOIR STATE RECREATION AREA (State Pk) From town: Go 25 mi SW o CR-166. 2015 rates: $7 to $15. (402)376-3320

WACKY WEST TRAVEL PARK Ratings: 6/8★/5.5 (Campground) 2015 rates: $29.90 (402)376-1771 702 E 'c' Street, Valentine, NE 6920

VALLEY — C6 *Douglas*

TWO RIVERS SRA (State Pk) From Jct of US-92 & 264th St, S 1 mi on 264th St to F St, W 1 mi (E) Entrance fee required. 2015 rates: $12 to $21. Ma 1 to Sep 30. (402)359-5165

VERDON — D6 *Richardson*

VERDON SRA (State Pk) From Jct of US-75 & US-73, E 6 mi on US-73 (L). Entrance fee required Pit toilets. 2015 rates: $7. (402)883-2575

WAYNE — B5 *Wayne*

LIONS CAMPER PARK (Public) From Jct o Hwys 15 & 35, E 1.5 mi on Hwy 35 (L). Apr 1 to Oc 1. (402)375-4803

WAYNE (CONT)

VICTOR PARK (Public) From Jct of Hwys 35 & 15, S 0.8 mi on Hwy 15 (R). 2015 rates: $7. (402)375-1300

WYMORE — D5 *Gage*

WYMORE ARBOR STATE PARK (Public) From Hwy 77 & 'M' St, E 0.3 mi on 'M' St (L). 2015 rates: $18. Apr 15 to Oct 15. (402)645-3377

Our rating system isn't just tough, it's thorough. We know the kinds of things that are important to you — like clean restrooms and showers, attractive, secure, well-tended grounds, and extras like swimming pools. We give the first rating for development of facilities, the second for cleanliness and physical characteristics of restrooms and showers, and the third for visual appearance.

YORK — C5 *York*

YORK See also Henderson.

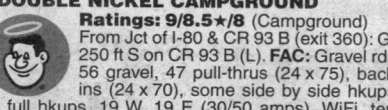

DOUBLE NICKEL CAMPGROUND

Ratings: 9/8.5★/8 (Campground) From Jct of I-80 & CR 93 B (exit 360): Go 250 ft S on CR 93 B (L). **FAC:** Gravel rds. 56 gravel, 47 pull-thrus (24 x 75), back-ins (24 x 70), some side by side hkups, 32 full hkups, 19 W, 19 E (30/50 amps), WiFi, tent sites, dump, laundry, groc, fire rings, firewood. **REC:** pool, golf, playground. Pets OK. Big rig sites, 29 day max stay, eco-friendly, 2015 rates: $26 to $42. Disc: AAA, military. Mar 15 to Oct 30.
AAA Approved
(402)728-5558 Lat: 40.81945, Lon: -97.46327
907 Road S, Waco, NE 68460
doublenickelcampground@gmail.com
www.doublenickelcampground.com

Subscribe to MotorHome Magazine! Questions? Change of address? Call 800-678-1201.

The RVers' Guide to NASCAR - We'll give you the inside track on how to get high-speed thrills at major NASCAR venues. Turn to the front of the Guide to get the most out of North America's most thrilling sporting event.

Getty Images/iStockphoto

WELCOME TO
Nevada

DATE OF STATEHOOD	WIDTH: 322 MILES (519 KM)	PROPORTION OF UNITED STATES
OCT. 31, 1864	LENGTH: 492 MILES (787 KM)	2.91% OF 3,794,100 SQ MI

Nevada is a land of vast distances punctuated by compelling stops along the way. From Vegas to Reno to Elko, visitors here quickly learn that the destination at the end of the road is worth the trip.

Las Vegas was a town of dirt streets when the first casinos opened. Today, there are scores of gaming houses to sample, and depending on who's counting, Vegas is the most visited town in America. Luckily, there are more hotel rooms here than any place on earth.

Before Las Vegas exploded, Reno was the main city in Nevada. According to boosters, it's "The Biggest Little City in the World." Yes, casinos thrive here, but so does tourism to a slew of nearby outdoorsy attractions. Carson City, meanwhile, has been the Nevada capital since territorial days, and it exudes a residential Victorian charm.

For a state that is nearly all desert, Nevada's biggest outdoor treasures are water-based. When the 726-foot high Hoover Dam—still the highest concrete dam in America—plugged the Colorado River in Black Canyon in 1935, it created the continent's largest reservoir, Lake Mead. More than one million people take the Hoover Dam tour each year and even more folks play on the lake's water and hike along the shore.

At 6,229 feet above sea level, Lake Tahoe is one of the world's largest alpine lakes. The glacial water is so clear that if you fumbled your smartphone over the edge of a boat, you could watch it drop almost all the way down.

Top 3 Tourism Attractions:
1) Las Vegas Strip
2) Hoover Dam
3) Red Rock Canyon National Conservation Area

Nickname: Silver State

State Flower: Sagebrush

State Bird: Mountain Bluebird

People: Andre Agassi, tennis player; James E. Casey, founder of UPS; Kyle and Kurt Busch, race car drivers; Julia Mancuso, Olympic skier

Major Cities: Las Vegas, Henderson, Reno, North Las Vegas, Sparks, (Carson City, capital)

Topography: Rugged north-south mountain ranges; south—part of Mojave Desert and Colorado River Canyon

Climate: Sunny, dry, with a wide variation in daily temps; south—desert climate; north—cooler mountain climate

TRAVEL & TOURISM

Nevada Commission on Tourism
800-NEVADA-8
www.travelnevada.com

Battle Mountain Chamber of Commerce and Visitor Center
775-635-8245
www.battlemountainchamber.com

Carson City CVB
800-NEVADA-1, 775-687-7410
www.visitcarsoncity.com

Lake Tahoe Visitors Authority
800-AT-TAHOE, 775-588-5900
www.bluelaketahoe.com

Las Vegas Convention & Visitors Authority
702-892-7575, 877-847-4858
www.visitlasvegas.com

Pahrump Valley Chamber of Commerce
775-727-5800
www.pahrumpchamber.com

Reno-Sparks Chamber of Commerce
775-337-3030
www.reno-sparkschamber.org

Old Crystal Bar Visitor Center
775-847-4386
www.virginiacitynv.org

Virginia City Convention & Tourism Authority
775-847-4386

White Pine County Tourism & Recreation
775-289-3720, 800-496-9350
www.elynevada.net

Winnemucca Convention & Visitors Authority
775-623-5071, 800-962-2638
www.winnemucca.com

OUTDOOR RECREATION

Golf Nevada
golf.travelnevada.com

Diamond Peak: Incline Village
775-832-1177
www.diamondpeak.com

Hiking: Bureau of Land Management
775-861-6400

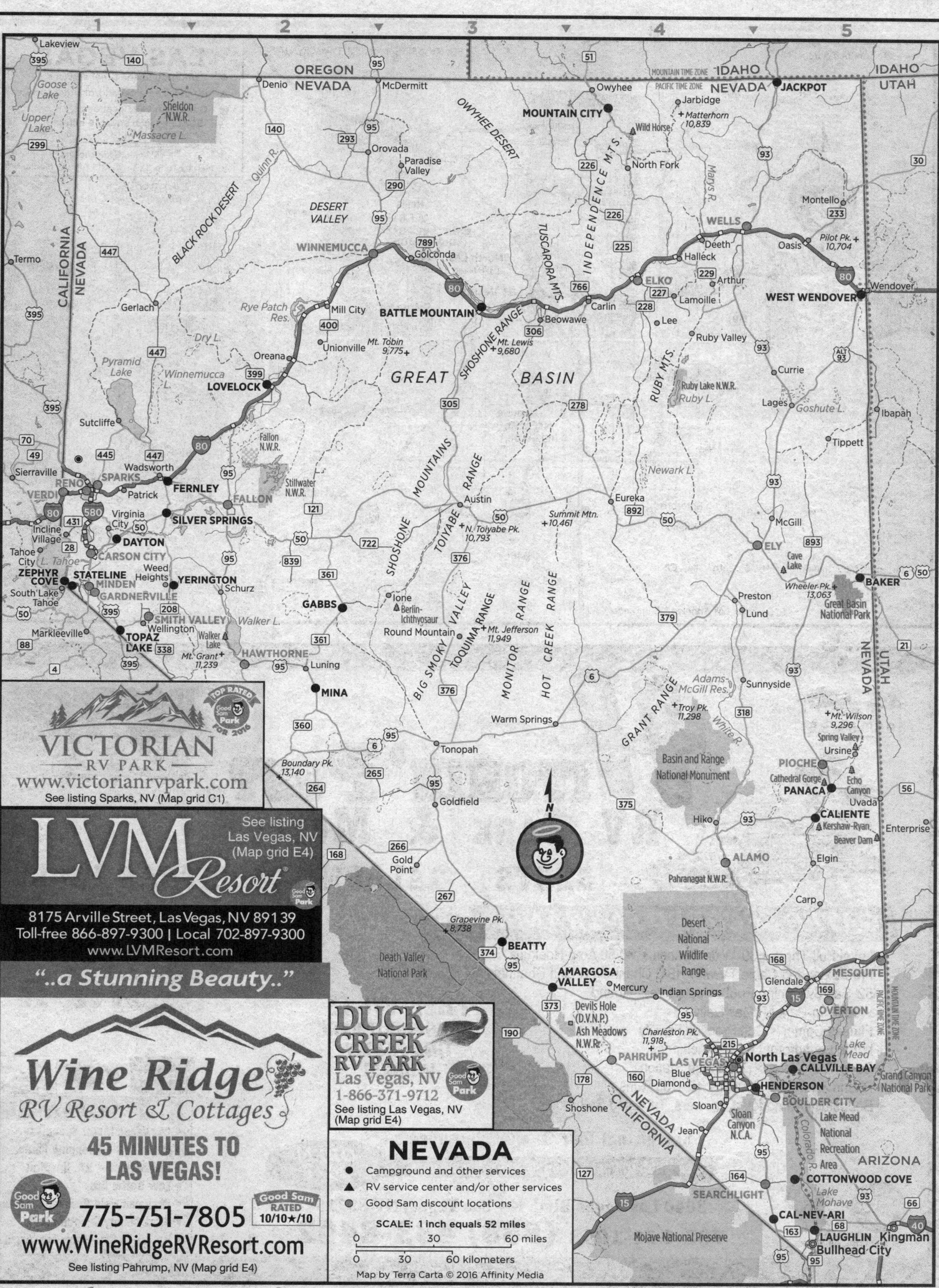
OREGON
NEVADA
IDAHO
NEVADA
IDAHO
UTAH
CALIFORNIA
NEVADA
NEVADA
UTAH
NEVADA
CALIFORNIA
ARIZONA
MOUNTAIN TIME ZONE
PACIFIC TIME ZONE
Lakeview
Goose Lake
Upper Lake
Sheldon N.W.R.
Massacre L.
Denio
McDermitt
Owyhee
JACKPOT
Jarbidge
Matterhorn 10,839
MOUNTAIN CITY
Wild Horse
North Fork
OWYHEE DESERT
Orovada
Paradise Valley
DESERT VALLEY
BLACK ROCK DESERT
Quinn R.
INDEPENDENCE MTS.
TUSCARORA MTS.
Marys R.
Montello
WELLS
Deeth
Halleck
Oasis
Pilot Pk. 10,704
Termo
WINNEMUCCA
Golconda
ELKO
Arthur
Lamoille
WEST WENDOVER
Wendover
Gerlach
Rye Patch Res.
Mill City
BATTLE MOUNTAIN
Carlin
Beowawe
Lee
Ruby Valley
Dry L.
Unionville
Mt. Tobin 9,775
SHOSHONE RANGE
Mt. Lewis 9,680
Pyramid Lake
Oreana
Winnemucca L.
LOVELOCK
GREAT BASIN
RUBY MTS.
Currie
Ruby Lake N.W.R.
Ruby L.
Lages
Goshute L.
Ibapah
Sutcliffe
Fallon N.W.R.
Tippett
Sierraville
Wadsworth
RENO
SPARKS
FERNLEY
VERDI
Patrick
Stillwater N.W.R.
FALLON
SHOSHONE MOUNTAINS
TOIYABE RANGE
Austin
Newark L.
Eureka
Incline Village
Virginia City
SILVER SPRINGS
N. Toiyabe Pk. 10,793
Summit Mtn. 10,461
McGill
DAYTON
CARSON CITY
Tahoe City
L. Tahoe
ELY
Cave Lake
ZEPHYR COVE
STATELINE
Weed Heights
YERINGTON
MINDEN
GARDNERVILLE
Schurz
South Lake Tahoe
GABBS
Ione
Berlin-Ichthyosaur
MONITOR RANGE
HOT CREEK RANGE
Preston
Lund
Wheeler Pk. 13,063
Great Basin National Park
BAKER
SMITH VALLEY
Wellington
Walker L.
Walker Lake
Markleeville
TOPAZ LAKE
Mt. Grant 11,239
HAWTHORNE
Round Mountain
TOQUIMA RANGE
Mt. Jefferson 11,949
BIG SMOKY VALLEY
Luning
MINA
Sunnyside
Adams-McGill Res.
GRANT RANGE
Troy Pk. 11,298
White R.
Mt. Wilson 9,296
Spring Valley
Ursine
Warm Springs
Tonopah
Boundary Pk. 13,140
Basin and Range National Monument
PIOCHE
Cathedral Gorge
PANACA
Echo Canyon
Uvada
Goldfield
CALIENTE
Kershaw-Ryan
Beaver Dam
Enterprise
Hiko
ALAMO
Elgin
Gold Point
Pahranagat N.W.R.
Carp
Grapevine Pk. 8,738
BEATTY
Death Valley National Park
Desert National Wildlife Range
AMARGOSA VALLEY
Mercury
Indian Springs
Glendale
MESQUITE
OVERTON
Devils Hole (D.V.N.P.)
Ash Meadows N.W.R.
Charleston Pk. 11,918
PAHRUMP
LAS VEGAS
North Las Vegas
Lake Mead
CALLVILLE BAY
Blue Diamond
HENDERSON
BOULDER CITY
Grand Canyon National Park
Shoshone
Sloan
Sloan Canyon N.C.A.
Lake Mead National Recreation Area
Jean
Colorado R.
COTTONWOOD COVE
Lake Mohave
SEARCHLIGHT
CAL-NEV-ARI
Mojave National Preserve
LAUGHLIN
Bullhead City
Kingman
NEVADA
Campground and other services
RV service center and/or other services
Good Sam discount locations
SCALE: 1 inch equals 52 miles
0 30 60 miles
0 30 60 kilometers
Map by Terra Carta © 2016 Affinity Media

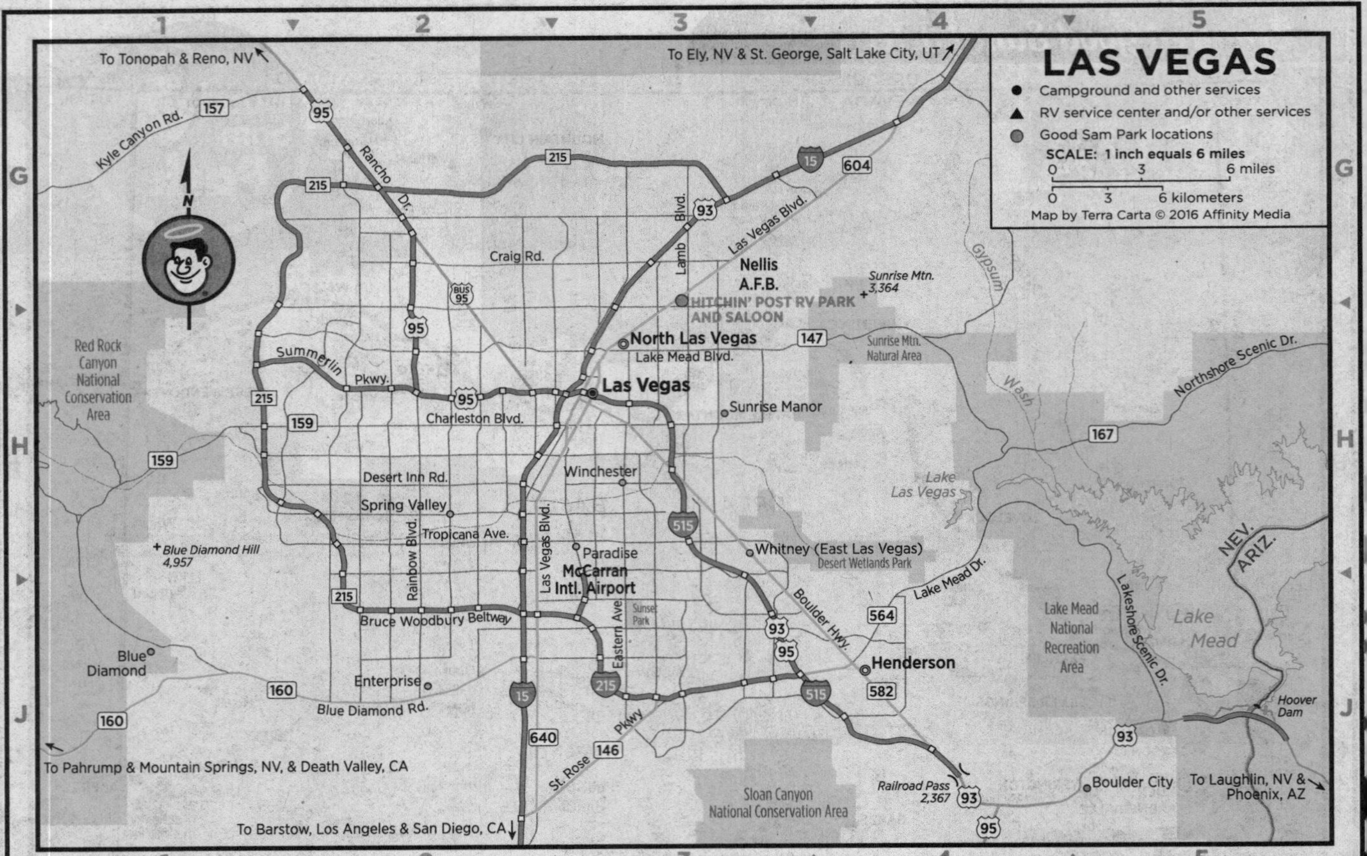
LAS VEGAS
Campground and other services
RV service center and/or other services
Good Sam Park locations
SCALE: 1 inch equals 6 miles
0 3 6 miles
0 3 6 kilometers
Map by Terra Carta © 2016 Affinity Media
To Tonopah & Reno, NV
To Ely, NV & St. George, Salt Lake City, UT
Kyle Canyon Rd.
Rancho Dr.
Craig Rd.
Lamb Blvd.
Las Vegas Blvd.
Nellis A.F.B.
HITCHIN' POST RV PARK AND SALOON
Sunrise Mtn. 3,364
Gypsum
North Las Vegas
Lake Mead Blvd.
Sunrise Mtn. Natural Area
Red Rock Canyon National Conservation Area
Summerlin Pkwy.
Las Vegas
Charleston Blvd.
Sunrise Manor
Wash
Northshore Scenic Dr.
Desert Inn Rd.
Winchester
Lake Las Vegas
Spring Valley
Tropicana Ave.
Rainbow Blvd.
Blue Diamond Hill 4,957
Paradise
Whitney (East Las Vegas)
Desert Wetlands Park
McCarran Intl. Airport
NEV. ARIZ.
Lake Mead Dr.
Boulder Hwy.
Lakeshore Scenic Dr.
Lake Mead National Recreation Area
Lake Mead
Bruce Woodbury Beltway
Eastern Ave.
Sunset Park
Blue Diamond
Henderson
Enterprise
Blue Diamond Rd.
Hoover Dam
St. Rose Pkwy
To Pahrump & Mountain Springs, NV, & Death Valley, CA
Railroad Pass 2,367
Boulder City
To Laughlin, NV & Phoenix, AZ
Sloan Canyon National Conservation Area
To Barstow, Los Angeles & San Diego, CA

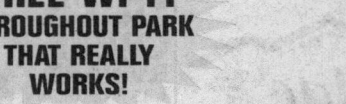

NV

Featured Good Sam Parks

NEVADA

Good Sam Park

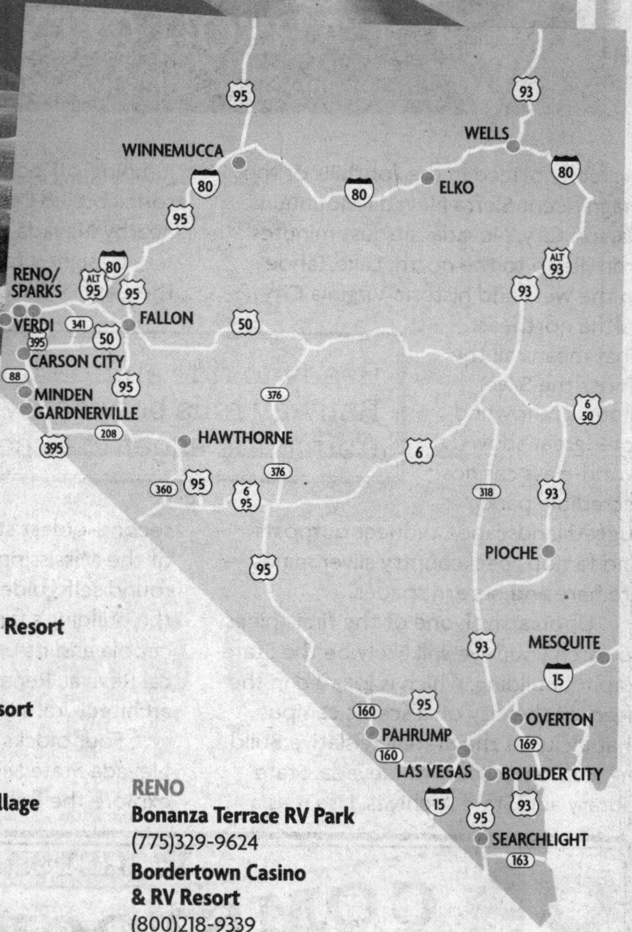

When you stay with Good Sam, you can expect the highest degree of cleanliness and friendliness, and better yet, you get 10% off campground fees.

If you're not already a Good Sam member you can purchase your membership at one of these locations:

BOULDER CITY
Canyon Trail RV Park
(702)293-1200
Lake Mead RV Village
(702)293-2540

CARSON CITY
Camp-N-Town RV Park
(800)872-1123
Comstock Country RV Resort
(775)882-2445
Gold Dust West Casino & RV Park
(775)885-9000

ELKO
Double Dice RV Park
(775)738-5642
Gold Country RV Park
(800)621-1332
Iron Horse RV Resort
(800)782-3556

FALLON
Fallon RV Park
(775)867-2332

GARDNERVILLE
Topaz Lodge, Casino & RV Park
(800)962-0732

HAWTHORNE
Scotty's RV Park & Napa Auto Supply
(775)945-3411
Whiskey Flats RV Park
(775)945-1800

LAS VEGAS
Arizona Charlie's Boulder RV Park
(800)970-7280
Duck Creek RV Park
(866)371-9712
Hitchin' Post RV Park
(888)433-8402
Las Vegas RV Resort
(702)451-8005
LVM Resort
(866)897-9300
Oasis Las Vegas RV Resort
(800)566-4707
Riviera RV Park
(702)457-8700

MESQUITE
Desert Skies RV Resort
(928)347-6000
Sun Resorts RV Park
(702)346-6666

MINDEN
Carson Valley RV Resort & Casino
(800)321-6983
Silver City RV Resort
(800)997-6393

OVERTON
Lake Mead RV Village At Echo Bay
(702)394-4000

PAHRUMP
Lakeside Casino & RV Resort
(888)558-5253
Nevada Treasure RV Resort
(800)429-6665
Pahrump Oasis RV Resort
(775)727-5100
Preferred RV Resort
(800)445-7840
Wine Ridge RV Resort & Cottages
(775)751-7805

PIOCHE
Eagle Valley Resort
(775)962-5293

RENO
Bonanza Terrace RV Park
(775)329-9624
Bordertown Casino & RV Resort
(800)218-9339
Keystone RV Park
(800)686-8559
Silver Sage RV Park
(888)823-2002

SEARCHLIGHT
Cottonwood Cove Resort
(702)297-1464

SPARKS
River's Edge RV Park
(775)358-8533
Sparks Marina RV Park
(775)851-8888
Victorian RV Park
(800)955-6405

VERDI
Gold Ranch Casino & RV Resort
(877)792-6789

WELLS
Angel Lake RV Park
(775)752-2745
Mountain Shadows RV Park
(775)752-3525

WINNEMUCCA
New Frontier RV Park
(775)621-5277
Winnemucca RV Park
(775)623-4458

For more Good Sam Parks go to listing pages

CARSON CITY

See the Silver State's true colors in its fantastic capital city

Perfectly placed in the foothills of the magnificent Sierra Nevada Mountains, Carson City, Nevada, sits just minutes from Reno to the north, Lake Tahoe to the west and historic Virginia City to the northeast. That means all the things the Silver State is renowned for—great shows, world-class casinos, incredible parks, rugged landscapes, pioneer outposts and famous backcountry silver mines—are here and here in spades.

Upon arrival, one of the first things to catch your eye will likely be the State Capitol Building, which is located in the heart of the city on a scenic campus that includes the State Legislative Building, Supreme Court of Nevada, State Library and State Archives. Use it as a jumping-off point to explore the historic core of Carson City, as well as the nearby Nevada State Museum.

Designed for a mere $250 in 1870, the Capitol Building stands as the second-oldest structure of its kind west of the Mississippi. It also offers year-round self-guided tours that highlight the building's famous silver-painted cupola and its unique blend of Classical Revival, Renaissance and Italianate architectural styles.

> Ready to ride an iron horse? The restored V&T Railway rolls between Virginia City and Carson for train buffs eager to experience 19th-century travel.

Four blocks to the north at the Nevada State Museum, visitors can explore the full sweep of Nevada history, from prehistoric times (don't miss the country's largest mammoth, reconstructed to appear caught in the throes of an agonizing action scene) to the modern day. Highlights include the building itself (from 1870 to 1893, it served as the Carson City Mint), tours of a restored underground mine and a massive working press that was used to stamp silver coins.

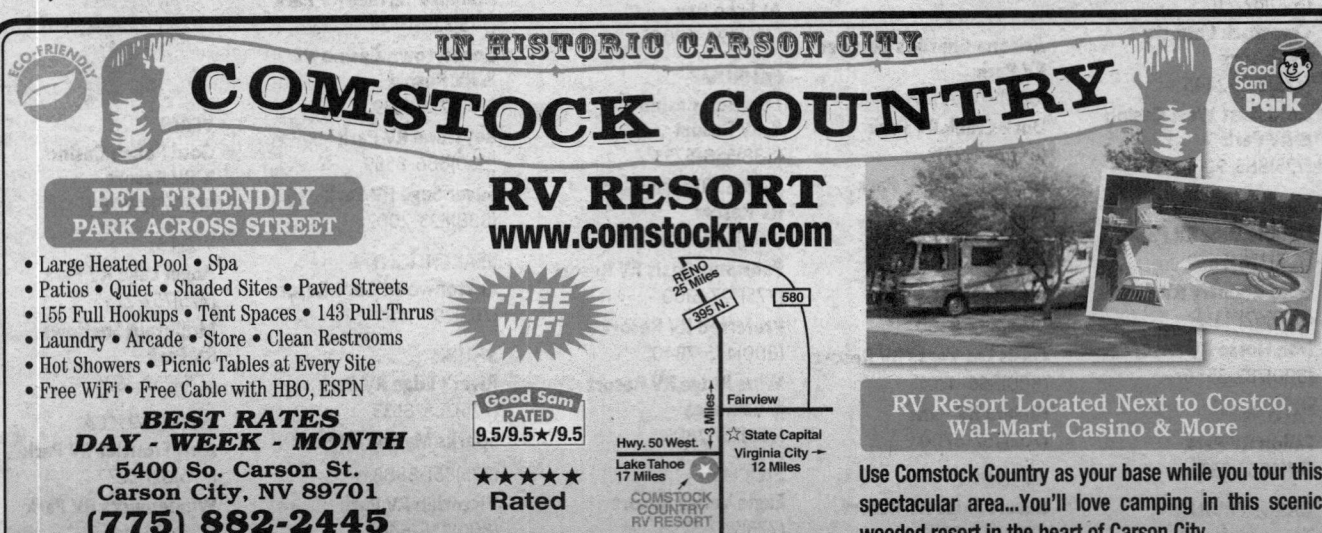

Dyed-in-the-wool history buffs will also want to pay a visit to the Nevada State Railroad Museum (2 miles south of the Capitol) and the Bowers Mansion Museum (12 miles to the north). The Railroad Museum is home to 65 locomotives and train cars (40 of which were built prior to the turn-of-the-

Skeleton of an Ice Age mammoth in the Nevada State Museum. Getty Images/iStockphoto

The Nevada Statehouse Capitol in Carson City.
Getty Images/iStockphoto

century), while the Bowers Mansion Museum features guided tours through a classic 19th-century estate populated with period furniture and artifacts. The restored V&T Railway rolls between Virginia City and Carson for rail buffs eager to experience 19th-century travel.

Wild in the West

Slightly further afield, a day trip to the Wild West town of Virginia City rounds out the must-visit playlist for history enthusiasts. It was here that Samuel Clemens first adopted his Mark Twain pen name and here that the heroes in the fictional television show "Bonanza" battled the black hats.

Virginia City visitors on the hunt for an authentic Wild West experience are greeted with a network of restored wooden sidewalks, preserved Old West buildings and eclectic museums telling the story of the town and the Comstock Lode, which produced more money than the entire California Gold Rush.

Last but certainly not least, there's the crown jewel of western Nevada and eastern California—Lake Tahoe. If you're a nature enthusiast or an outdoors lover, this is nirvana. Take your pick of recreational activity — kayaking, hiking, biking, horseback riding, boating, scuba diving, rock climbing, off-roading, sunbathing—it's all here.

Depending on where you decide to plant your beach umbrella or set up camp, the lake itself is only about 20 miles west of downtown Carson City. Lake Tahoe State Park, meanwhile, envelopes the city's western limits and stretches for more than 13,000 acres across the Carson Mountain Range. That means you'll find yourself standing on the doorstep of miles and miles of well-maintained hiking trails snaking their way through lush, protected forest teeming with wildlife. Make sure your camera's batteries are fully charged.

Beachcombing, Nevada Style

When exploring the Lake Tahoe area from Carson City, most visitors will find themselves drawn to Incline Village on the northern shore of the lake and Sand Harbor State Park on the eastern shore. The latter is home to gorgeous white sandy beaches and deep blue waters, making it the perfect spot for a picnic or day on the beach. Incline Village, meanwhile, is your classic small-town community. Founded by loggers in 1878, today it's home to secluded mountain estates, quaint waterfront cafes and a tidy smattering of easily strolled streets.

If you're visiting during the summer months, Sand Harbor will be buzzing with its annual lakeside Shakespeare Festival, while the north shore hills will be crawling with mountain bikers from around the world. Cave Rock near Zephyr Cove at the southern end of the lake is a popular spot for boating and fishing. Winter months dust the surrounding mountain peaks with blankets of snow, and throw Diamond Peak Ski Area and Mount Rose into full gear, drawing ski-bums and snowboarders from far and wide.

In short, the entire Lake Tahoe area remains a hive of activity year-round, with enough to please everyone, from hardcore adrenaline-junkies seeking aggressive downhill fun to those moving at a more casual pace.

While Reno and Las Vegas tend to steal most of the Nevada spotlight for tourists, truly savvy travelers will find everything the state is famous for within easy reach of Carson City.

For More Information

Carson City Convention and Visitors Bureau
775-687-7140
www.visitcarsoncity.com

Nevada Commission on Tourism
775-687-4322
www.travelnevada.com

Travel Nevada

SPOTLIGHT

NV

LAS VEGAS

Discover the thrills behind the bright lights

Las Vegas has come a long way in eight and a half decades. From sporting just a single paved road in 1931 to becoming the undisputed entertainment capital of the world (now home to more than 130,000 hotel rooms) the city has witnessed an almost unprecedented evolution and transformation—both on a technological and philosophical scale.

Long gone are the old Wild West-inspired days of boozy Sin City, when organized crime and dangerous racketeering outfits were in their heyday. Today, the Strip is lined with glamorous casinos, luxury hotels and family-friendly attractions that have made the city as renowned for its world-class shows and live entertainment as it is for its ocean of blackjack tables and glittering slot-machines.

Long gone are the old Wild West-inspired days of boozy Sin City. Today, the Strip is lined with glamorous casinos, luxury hotels and family-friendly attractions.

Look no farther than Fremont Street, one of the city's oldest thoroughfares and easily its most iconic.

Once the center of old Las Vegas and home to the city's classic suite of shady high-roller casino properties, Fremont is now a buzzing hotbed of world-class restaurants, high-end boutiques and miscellaneous attractions. Gluing it all together is the world's largest video screen—Viva Vision—a 1,500-foot-long (by 90-feet-wide) display sporting 12.5 million LED lights. It bursts with free light shows nightly.

Fremont is also home to newly opened SlotZilla, a combination zip line and thrill ride that runs from the mouth of the world's largest slot machine. By buckling in for a ride, brave guests can zip their way down the entire length of Fremont—just beneath the flashing lights and displays of Viva Vision—in mere minutes.

Adrenaline junkies will also want to take a trip to the top of Stratosphere Tower. Here, the world's highest thrill ride begins on the 108th floor and rockets straight up for a series of controlled free-fall descents. Of course, if floating weightlessly over the desert and then

NV

falling rapidly toward it isn't quite your kettle of fish, be sure to still pay a visit to the Stratosphere's Observation Deck. At 1,149 feet, it offers truly mesmerizing views of the surrounding cityscape and desert. If that's not enough, take a spin on the 550-tall High Roller, which is billed as the largest observation wheel in the world.

Past and Present

If you're travelling with kids, the Shark Reef Aquarium at Mandalay Bay is one of the more rewarding experiences. Spanning 14 exhibits and featuring more than 2,000 animals, plan to spend (and enjoy) a significant amount of time here. The experience includes a massive underwater jungle environment—complete with sunken shipwreck—home to not only sharks, but also crocodiles and an 8-foot long Komodo dragon.

History buffs won't be disappointed here either. The Nevada State Museum at Springs Preserve features the massive skeletal remains of an ice-age wooly mammoth, the imprints of a 225-million-year-old ichthyosaur and myriad cutting-edge displays telling the story of Las Vegas from prehistory to modern times. The Origen Museum at Springs Reserve brings the desert ecosystem to life with interactive exhibits that will thrill visitors of all ages.

Of course, since Las Vegas beats to a slightly eclectic drum, some of its very best museums follow suit. Of particular note, don't miss the National Museum

The High Roller Observation Wheel.
Getty Images/iStockphoto

of Organized Crime and Law Enforcement (also known more simply as "The Mob Museum") and the Neon Museum, home to more than 150 classic buzzing signs culled from the history of the Strip.

When it's time for a break from the bright lights and big casinos, a range of worthy day-trips are on offer.

Outside of Glitter Gulch

Red Rock Canyon, 17 miles west of the Strip, offers some of the best hiking, mountain-biking and horseback-riding trails in the Southwest. For an extended Mojave Desert experience, pair a trip to Red Rock Canyon with a longer trek to Death Valley, 142 miles west of the Strip.

And no first-time visit to Las Vegas would be complete without a hop, skip and a jump over to the mighty Hoover Dam. Just 34 miles to the southeast, a drive to the Hoover Dam and a stop for lunch at nearby Boulder City makes for an easy day-trip for families traveling with kids.

Situated on the border between Arizona and Nevada in the Black Canyon of the Colorado River, this 726-foot-high structure will take your breath away. Take a tour of the power plant and dam, which was built in 1931 and features elaborate Art Deco designs on the spillways, four towers and power plant. You can also opt to simply cross over the dam to take in the views.

There are two guided tours: the Dam Tour lasts about an hour, while the Power Plant Tour is only about 30 minutes long. Either way, you'll want to plan your visit so that you have at least two hours for your entire visit to ensure you get to see everything there is to see. The Visitor Center also offers air conditioning, which is much sought-after, especially in the scorching-hot summer months. Get to the dam early in the day, since pedestrians are not allowed on top of the dam after dark.

West of Vegas, Red Rock Canyon thrills visitors with its crimson hues. Travel Nevada

The small town of Searchlight is another day trip that's worth taking. Located less than an hour south of Vegas, Searchlight is a charming community with several eclectic attractions for lovers of Southwest culture and water recreation.

Searchlight was a rugged gold-mining town until the construction of the Davis Dam across the Colorado River in 1951. This created Lake Mohave, which immediately summoned vacationers from Southern California. Today, no beacon is needed to find the recreational opportunities around Searchlight, a tiny enclave of about 500 that services campers, boaters and outdoor explorers. Cottonwood Cove on the lake, about 14 miles to the east, is renowned for its largemouth bass.

There are no stoplights to impede traffic through town on Route 95. On this strip, you can find some small casinos and the eclectic Jack's Trading Post. Down Cottonwood Road, the small Searchlight Historic Museum has an outdoor mining exhibit and keeps the flame burning for past famous residents, including silent movie stars Rex Bell and Clara Bow. The couple founded the Walking Box Ranch, which is now in the National Register of Historic Places. Also honored in the museum is Edith Head, Hollywood costume designer who won a record eight Oscars. Head spend much of her childhood in Searchlight. Also highlighted at the museum is the region's colorful gold-mining history.

Hikers have long marked Searchlight on their bucket list maps of places to visit. Spirit Mountain south of town is 5,600 feet of craggy nooks and crannies that were sacred to the desert peoples of the Colorado River. The pygmy forests of pinyon pines and junipers give the access road its name: Christmas Tree Pass. Several routes of varying difficulty ascend the garden-like granite peak that is the high point of the surrounding Newberry Mountains.

Fremont Street is a popular nighttime hangout in Las Vegas.
Getty Images

Minutes outside of Las Vegas, the Springs Preserve educates visitors on efficient irrigation. Travel Nevada

From the top, views stretch to the Mojave National Preserve in the west to the Colorado River to the east.

The King Still Reigns

Back in Vegas, don't forget to pay homage to "the King." Graceland Presents Elvis: The Exhibition features a permanent display of Elvis Presley memorabilia that tells the story of one of music's most dynamic pioneers. Follow Elvis' life as a child in Tupelo, Mississippi, and retrace his rise to stardom.

Exhibits include Elvis Mania, which covers the 1956 recording of his first album and his groundbreaking appearance on the Ed Sullivan Show; Elvis in the Army, which examines his brief hitch as a soldier based in Germany; Graceland, following Elvis' purchase of a 17,000-square-foot property on 13 acres in Memphis, Tennessee; Elvis in Hollywood, a filmography of the star's silver screen performances; and Elvis in Las Vegas, which pays special attention to his explosive performances in America's gambling capital.

The Elvis on the Road exhibit explores the King's legendary love of cars. In his lifetime, the singer purchased more than 200 vehicles.

Vegas for All

If you don't consider yourself "a Vegas person," think again. Whatever your taste, pace or entertainment preference, Las Vegas has a custom tour itinerary waiting for you in a dozen different flavors. Two of the most rewarding activities are simply strolling the Strip after dark—taking in the bright lights and ogling at the mesmerizing architectural displays of each major casino—and hopping happily from gourmet buffet to gourmet buffet. Take a break from gambling and let your eyes take in the splendor.

For More Information

Las Vegas Convention and Visitors Authority
866-983-4279
www.vegas.com

Nevada Commission on Tourism
775-687-4322
www.travelnevada.com

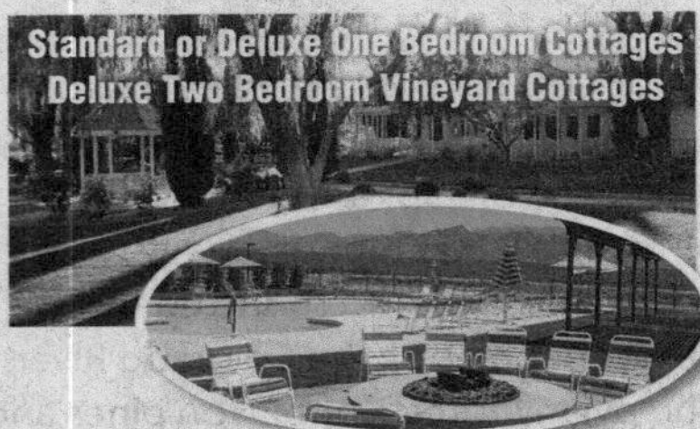

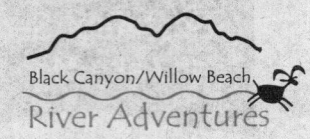

Nevada Culture

SPOTLIGHT NV

PAHRUMP

Get away from the bright lights and back to nature

Tucked away in the sun-soaked southern tip of Nevada—just 60 miles west of Las Vegas—the small Mojave Desert town of Pahrump has rapidly become a city on the rise. The first telephone lines and paved roads didn't appear here until the 1960s, yet today the community plays host to a mix of world-class wineries, preeminent national parks and even a luxury motor sports speedway. Add it all up and you have an ideal spot to set up camp, park the RV and go exploring.

Most visitors find themselves stopping in Pahrump while en route from Las Vegas to Death Valley, which lies just 60 miles (about an hour's drive) to the west across the California border. For this, the town is a popular place to stop and have lunch, stretch the legs and recharge for the final push to Death Valley.

Try going against the grain and turn this logic on its head. Rather than simply stopping in Pahrump while traveling between Vegas and Death Valley, set up shop in Pahrump and use it as a quiet small-town base-camp to branch out and explore some of southern Nevada's busiest attractions.

Set up shop in Pahrump and use it as a quiet small-town base-camp to branch out and explore some of southern Nevada's busiest attractions.

Pahrump Pathways

This is particularly savvy advice for outdoors enthusiasts and anyone on the prowl for some rugged desert recreation. Hikers, mountain bikers and off-road junkies drown in trail choices here. Carpenter Canyon, Wallace Canyon and Wheeler Wash are among the most popular, offering spectacular views of Pahrump Valley and the Spring Mountains.

The Elk Meadows Trails is another collection of renowned trails popular with mountain bikers, but keep your eyes peeled as you pick up speed—the trails are named Elk Meadows for a reason, and wild elk often find themselves wandering onto the runs.

For a more relaxed exploration of the incredible Mojave landscapes surrounding Pahrump, get in your vehicle and head 40 miles east to Red Rock Canyon National Conservation

Corvettes hit the track at the Ron Fellows Performance Driving School. Chris Moran/TravelNevada

Area. Cruise the 13-mile scenic byway that loops around the canyon, offering breathtaking views from dedicated observation points. Dozens of well-maintained hiking trails snake their way through the wilderness at Red Rock Canyon as well, so if the mood to hoof it on foot strikes there's plenty of opportunity.

Other major points of interest and attractions for recreation seekers are the Spring Mountains National Recreation Area (94 miles to the east), Ash Meadows National Wildlife Refuge (28 miles to the west) and Goldwell Open Air Museum (79 miles to the northwest).

The Spring Mountains NRA is home to massive Charleston Peak (the third highest peak in the state), and an array of historic sites, hiking trails, campsites and crisp mountain springs. During winter, the mountain is also home to the Las Vegas Ski and Snowboard Resort.

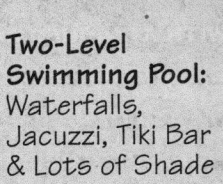

At the Ash Meadows National Wildlife Refuge, visitors can explore the largest official oasis left in the Mojave Desert. The refuge is home to prehistoric desert fish, fossil water left behind from the last ice age, the highest concentration of indigenous species in the country and 500-foot-deep Devils Hole (which local legend argues is actually a mysterious bottomless pit).

Explore Past and Present

Goldwell Open Air Museum is one of the more unusual attractions in all of Nevada—a feat by any definition. Here, in 1984, Belgian artist Albert Szukalski installed and unveiled a major public sculpture that depicted The Last Supper. Six more sculptures were eventually added to the site by other artists, leaving behind one of the world's most striking open-air art galleries.

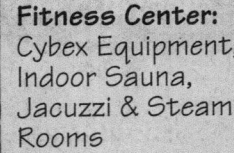

For its part, the Pahrump Valley Museum is surprisingly vast. Covering nearly 10,000 square feet indoors and paired with four acres of space out-

The Pahrump Balloon Festival adds color to the desert sky. © Photography by Horace Langford Jr.

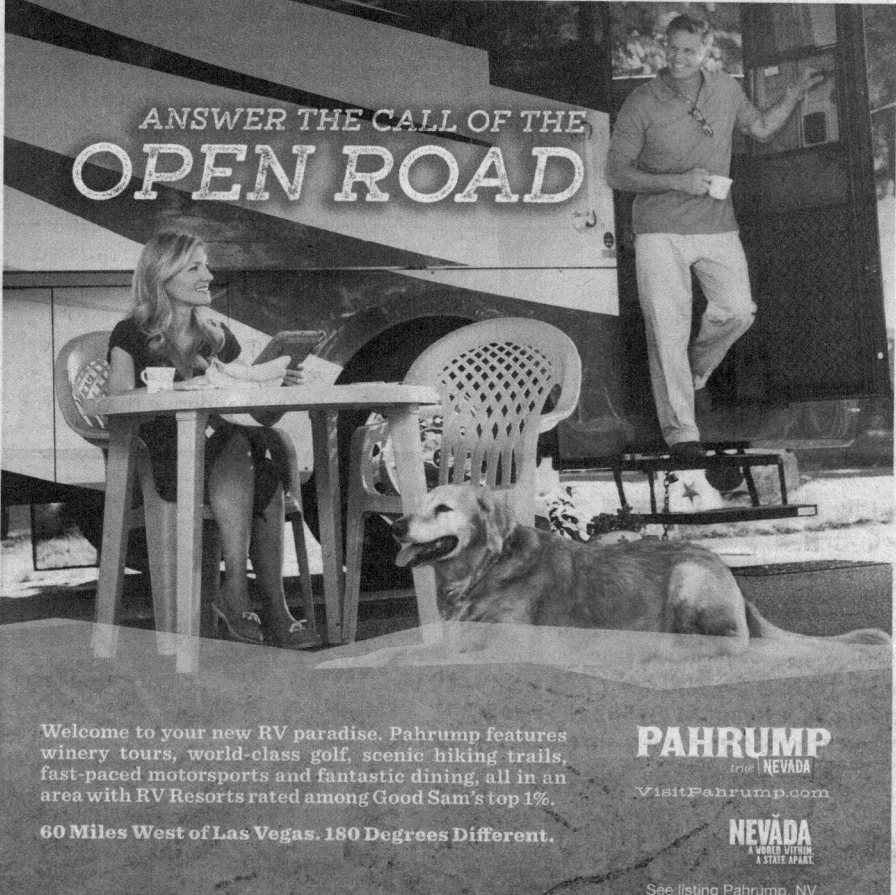

doors, the museum's highlights include original artwork and letters from Abraham Lincoln, exhibits detailing nuclear weapons testing and "Main Street Pahrump"—a life-sized recreation of bygone eras using fully restored historic buildings. If you're a history buff, plan to spend a good deal of time here, combing through the myriad informative displays and exhibits.

Wine connoisseurs can pencil in a pair of trips to the Pahrump Valley Winery (on the eastern edge of town) and the Sanders Family Winery (on the southern edge of town). Each location hosts daily wine tastings, informative tours and gorgeous grounds to explore.

Speed demons flock to the Spring Mountain Motorsports Ranch in Pahrump, which offers driving schools, racetrack rentals and space for events. With six miles of challenging track, drivers can find endless opportunities to hone their high-speed skills. Lovers of Corvettes can indulge in their passion of putting this iconic American speedster to the test when attending the Ron Fellows Performance Driving School, held at Spring Mountain.

There's no way to easily define the booming town of Pahrump. At once a laid-back small desert community and a vibrant city on the rise, the community offers visitors everything from premiere outdoor recreation to world-class entertainment options.

For More Information

Town of Pahrump
775-727-5107
www.pahrumpnv.org

Nevada Commission on Tourism
775-687-4322
www.travelnevada.com

RENO/SPARKS

Fun for the whole family in the 'Biggest Little City in the World'

Long before Las Vegas became the preeminent gambling destination in the United States, the original "Sin City" thrived. Reno's bright lights and flashy casinos pioneered an entire entertainment industry built around gambling, live shows and luxury resorts.

Originally stemming from a need to weather the volatile ups and downs of a fledgling 19th-century mining economy, gambling in Reno started underground, and illegal. But that changed swiftly when, in 1931, the state legalized casinos. What soon became known as the "Biggest Little City in the World" never looked back.

Today, visitors to Reno and its sister city of Sparks will find a surprisingly family-friendly atmosphere, packed with attractions for kids as well as adults. Like Las Vegas further south, Reno has blossomed well beyond its reliance on gambling to attract visitors from far and wide.

Once you've had your photos snapped in front of the famous Reno Arch (spanning Virginia Street at the corner of Virginia and Commercial Row), head over to the newly opened Reno Tahoe Visitors Center and pick a self-guided tour map. Use it to stroll the historic downtown core at your own pace before diving into a whistle-stop tour of the major attractions.

> During Hot August Nights, the streets of Reno and Sparks travel back in time to the golden post-war era of muscle cars, rolled-up T-shirt sleeves and the first forays of rock 'n' roll rebellion.

Kid Stuff

If you are, in fact, travelling with kids, then a trio of family fun centers will no doubt catch your eye. Atlantis, Boomtown and Wild Island each offer swaths of cutting-edge video and arcade games, as well as a litany of miscellaneous highlights, such as mini-golf at Boomtown and go-kart racing at Wild Island.

Two other popular spots for families are the Sierra Safari Zoo and the Animal Ark Wildlife Sanctuary. Both are located less than 25 miles north of downtown Reno, and each offers visitors a chance to meet, feed and interact with hundreds of exotic animals, including bears, wallabies, monkeys, lions and wolves.

When you're ready to flex some of your intellectual muscles, head to the Nevada Museum of Art, situated directly in the downtown core. Docent-led tours are offered for art history aficionados, but even the most casual of observers will enjoy spending a few carefree hours wandering through the

The Depression-era Thunderbird Yacht cruises past Edgewood Tahoe during the American Century Celebrity Golf Championship. TravelNevada

Taking off during the Great Reno Balloon Race. The Girl Jerz/TravelNevada

museum's four thematic sections. All told, the museum displays more than 2,000 works from the 19th and 20th centuries at any given time.

In a similar vein, the Wilbur D. May Center (just a few blocks to the north, near the edge of Rancho San Rafael Park) is a must-visit for history buffs and art lovers. Its massive private collections are especially eclectic. Reflecting the world travels and priceless artifacts collected by ranching tycoon Wilbur D. May, the exhibits range from Tang Dynasty pottery and ancient African artwork to Greek sculptures and Italian amulets.

Also part of the May Center is a massive botanical garden that showcases the plants and animals that live in the ecological transition zone that bridges the Sierra Nevada Mountains with the Great Basin Desert.

The National Automobile Museum is the final piece of the must-visit-museum trifecta. Easily one of the most popular attractions in all of Reno (it's been voted one of the five greatest automobile museums in the country), the Automobile Museum displays more than 200 classic and special-interest

Kayakers hone their skills in preparation for the Reno River Festival, held at Wingfield Park on the Truckee River in downtown Reno. TravelNevada

Reno's arching welcome sign aptly describes the fun-filled Western city.
Kevin Clifford/RSCVA

cars ranging from vehicles used in World War II to those used at the dawn of auto racing.

If you're visiting in September, don't miss the Great Reno Balloon race, which sees scores of colorfully designed hot air balloons ascend skyward for the win. Equally spectacular are the colorful watercraft that grace the surface of nearby Lake Tahoe. From the Tahoe Queen paddleboat to the Thunderbird Yacht, you'll be dazzled by the sights found on this grand body of water.

Spark Fun in Sparks

When it's time for a dose of fresh air, nearby Sparks is a popular spot for anyone looking for a bit of outdoor fun and relaxation—without needing to trek far into the surrounding backcountry.

Rock Park, located along the Truckee River in Sparks, features premier white-water rafting, kayaking and tubing adventures. And Sparks Marina Park, with its 80-acre lake, is the go-to spot for swimming, boating, fishing and even scuba diving.

Visit Sparks in summer for the Best in the West Nugget Rib Cook-Off. Watch top barbecue chefs cook up mouth-watering cuts of meat, then sample the results of their labor.

Travel back in time and experience railroad history at the Sparks Museum and Cultural Center. Here, you'll find a vintage steam locomotive, a cupola caboose and Pullman executive car. Also on display is a one-room Glendale Schoolhouse and a monument to the Chinese rail workers who helped build the American West.

Finally, if you're visiting the Reno-Sparks area during the summer months, aim for the infamous Hot August Nights festival in August. Every year during the first week in August, the streets of both cities travel back in time to the golden post-war era of muscle cars, rolled-up T-shirt sleeves and the first forays of rock 'n' roll.

Like Las Vegas to the south, Reno has evolved well beyond its roots as an edgy desert destination for gamblers. A downtown core packed with world-class restaurants, shops and hotels makes it a great place to visit and explore without ever throwing a pair of dice or pulling a slot lever.

For More Information

Visit Reno Tahoe
800-367-7366
www.visitrenotahoe.com

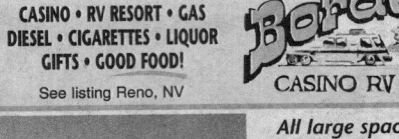

Nevada Commission on Tourism
800-638-2328
www.travelnevada.com

Nevada

CONSULTANTS

Frank & Suzy Whitmore

ALAMO — D4 *Lincoln*

PICKETTS RV PARK **Ratings: 6/8★/7** (RV Park) Sbnd: From Jct SR-318 & US-93: Go SW 12 mi on US-93 (R) Nbnd: From I-15 & Hwy 93: Go N 89 mi on Hwy 93 (L). Elev 3450 ft. **FAC:** Gravel rds. 30 gravel, 16 pull-thrus (15 x 50), back-ins (15 x 40), some side by side hkups, 30 full hkups (30/50 amps), cable, WiFi, rentals, laundry, LP gas. Pets OK. No tents. 2015 rates: $28 to $31. Disc: AAA, military.
(775)725-3300 Lat: 37.36081, Lon: -115.15804
115 Broadway St, Alamo, NV 89001
pickettsrvpark@gmail.com
www.pickettsrvpark.com
See ad this page.

AMARGOSA — E3 *Nye*

AMARGOSA VALLEY RV PARK **Ratings: 5/5.5/6** (Campground) 2015 rates: $21.40. (775)764-1932 2642 E Highway 95, Amargosa Valley, NV 89020

AMARGOSA VALLEY — E3 *Nye*

LONGSTREET INN CASINO RV PARK **Ratings: 5/6/4.5** (Campground) 2015 rates: $18. (775)372-1777 4400 S. Highway 373, Amargosa Valley, NV 89020

BAKER — C5 *White Pine*

BORDER INN & RV PARK **Ratings: 6/7/7** (Campground) 2015 rates: $25. (775)234-7300 hwy 50 & Hwy 6, Baker, NV 89311

GREAT BASIN/BAKER CREEK (Natl Pk) From town, W 5 mi on Hwy 488 to Nfd-590, S 3 mi (L). Pit toilets. 2015 rates: $12. May 1 to Oct 15. (775)234-7331

GREAT BASIN/UPPER LEHMAN CREEK (Natl Pk) From town, W 5 mi on Hwy 488 to Nfd-446, N 3 mi (L). Pit toilets. 2015 rates: $12. Apr 15 to Oct 15. (775)234-7331

GREAT BASIN/WHEELER PEAK CAMPGROUND (Natl Pk) From town, W 5 mi on Hwy 488 to Nfd 446, N 8.5mi (E). CAUTION: Steep, winding roads. RVs over 24 ft not permitted. Pit toilets. 2015 rates: $12. Jun to Oct. (775)234-7331

WHISPERING ELMS MOTEL/RV PARK & TENT CAMPING **Ratings: 6/6/5.5** (Campground) 2015 rates: $25 to $30. (775)234-9900 120 Baker Ave, Baker, NV 89311

BATTLE MOUNTAIN — B3 *Lander*

CLARK PARK **Ratings: 5.5/9.5★/7.5** (RV Park) E-bnd From I-80 (Exit 231): Go 1/8 mi L, then (immediate R, on Palmer St) to Clark Blvd (E); or W-bnd-From I-80 (Exit 231): Go 600 ft R on Bryles Ranch Rd, then L on Palmer to Clark Blvd (E). Elev 4500 ft. **FAC:** Gravel rds. (72 spaces). Avail: 32 gravel, back-ins (28 x 40), mostly side by side hkups, 32 full hkups (30/50 amps), seasonal sites, cable, WiFi, rentals, showers $, laundry. **REC:** playground. Pets OK. Partial handicap access, no tents. RV age restrict, 2015 rates: $30 to $35.
(775)635-9600 Lat: 40.6405160, Lon: -116.9417946
645 W Humboldt, Battle Mountain, NV 89820
http://www.chamberorganizer.com/battlemountain/mem_clarkpark

BEATTY — E3 *Nye*

BEATTY RV PARK **Ratings: 6/8.5★/6** (Campground) 2015 rates: $25. (775)553-2732 mile Marker 63, Hwy 95 N, Beatty, NV 89003

DEATH VALLEY INN & RV PARK **Ratings: 6/9★/7.5** (Campground) 2015 rates: $35. (775)553-9702 300 South Highway 95, Beatty, NV 89003

BOULDER CITY — F5 *Clark*

CANYON TRAIL RV PARK **Ratings: 9.5/9.5★/9.5** (RV Park) From Jct of US 93 & US 95: Go 1-1/4 mi S on US 93, then 1-1/4 mi N on Veteran's Memorial (Industrial Rd), bridge clearance-14 ft 6 in (L) From Jct of Boulder Dam & US 93: Go 7-1/2 mi W on US 93, then 600 yds W on Industrial Rd (R). **FAC:** Paved rds. 156 gravel, 86 pull-thrus (30 x 50), back-ins (30 x 50), some side by side hkups, 156 full hkups (30/50 amps), cable, WiFi, dump, laundry. **REC:** heated pool, whirlpool, shuffleboard. Pet restrict(Q). Partial handicap access, no tents. Big rig sites, eco-friendly, 2015 rates: $40. Disc: AAA, military.
AAA Approved
(702)293-1200 Lat: 35.97750, Lon: -114.85030
1200 Industrial Rd, Boulder City, NV 89005
info@canyontrailrvparknv.com
www.canyontrailrvparknv.com
See ad this page, 737.

LAKE MEAD NRA/BOULDER BEACH (Natl Pk) From Jct of US-93 & Lakeshore Rd, N 2 mi on Lakeshore Rd (R). 2015 rates: $10. (702)293-2540

LAKE MEAD RV VILLAGE **Ratings: 9/9★/10** (RV Park) From Jct of US 93 & Lakeshore Rd: Go 2 mi N on Lakeshore Rd (R) Admission to national park required.

NEAR LAS VEGAS ON LAKE MEAD
Centrally located near Hoover Dam & 30 mi from Las Vegas. The largest big rig park on Lake Mead. Quiet, scenic lake views. Lake Marinas nearby for swimming-fishing-boating-jet skiing. Great fun with family and friends.

FAC: Paved rds. (115 spaces). Avail: 30 paved, patios, 30 pull-thrus (18 x 110), 30 full hkups (30/50 amps), seasonal sites, cable, WiFi, dump, laundry, groc, LP gas, fire rings, firewood. **REC:** Lake Mead: swim, fishing, rec open to public. Pet restrict(Q). Partial handicap access, no tents. Eco-friendly, 2015 rates: $30 to $45.
(702)293-2540 Lat: 36.03496, Lon: -114.80093
268 Lakeshore Drive, Boulder City, NV 89005
lmrvfd@gmail.com
www.lakemeadrvvillage.com
See ad pages 742 (Spotlight Las Vegas), 737 & RV Trips of a Lifetime in Magazine Section.

CAL-NEV-ARI — F5 *Clark*

CAL-NEV-ARI MARKET & RV PARK **Ratings: 4.5/8/6.5** (RV Park) 2015 rates: $22. (702)297-1115 #2 Spirit Mountain Lane, Cal-Nev-Ari, NV 89039

CALIENTE — D5 *Lincoln*

BEAVER DAM (State Pk) From town, N 6 mi on US-93, E 28 mi on gravel road (L). Steep and winding access road. Vehicles over 25 ft not recommended. Entrance fee. Pit toilets. 2015 rates: $14 to $30. Apr 1 to Nov 15. (775)726-3564

YOUNG'S RV PARK **Ratings: 5.5/8★/7** (RV Park) 2015 rates: $23. (775)726-3418 1350 South Front St., Caliente, NV 89008

CALLVILLE BAY — E5 *Clark*

LAKE MEAD NRA/CALLVILLE BAY (Natl Pk) From Jct of US-93 & Northshore Rd, NE 26 mi on Northshore Rd (R). 2015 rates: $10 to $20. (702)293-8990

CARSON CITY — C1 *Carson*

A SPOTLIGHT Introducing Carson City's colorful attractions appearing at the front of this state section.

CARSON CITY See also Minden, Zephyr Cove & Virginia City.

CAMP-N-TOWN RV PARK **Ratings: 8/9★/8** (RV Park) From US-395 (Exit 43): Go 2 mi S on N Carson St (R). From Jct of US-50 W & US 395: Go 4 mi N on S Carson St (L). From Jct of US-50 E & US 395: Go 1.2 mi W on US-50E (Williams) to Carson St. N 1 mi on Carson St (L). Elev 4722 ft. **FAC:** Paved rds. (157 spaces). Avail: 100 gravel, 90 pull-thrus (28 x 75), back-ins (25 x 40), 100 full hkups (30/50 amps), seasonal sites, cable, WiFi, tent sites, dump, laundry. **REC.** Pet restrict(B). 2015 rates: $35 to $38. Disc: AAA, military.
(800)872-1123 Lat: 39.18180, Lon: -119.76804
2438 N Carson St., Carson City, NV 89706
www.campntown.com
See ad this page, 737.

COMSTOCK COUNTRY RV RESORT **Ratings: 9.5/9.5★/9.5** (RV Park) From Jct of US 395 (Carson St) & US 50 W: Go 1600 ft S on NV 395, then 750 ft W on Old Clear Creek Rd (R). Elev 4780 ft. **FAC:** Paved rds. (150 spaces). Avail: 90 gravel, patios, 75 pull-thrus (32 x 60), back-ins (32 x 45), 90 full hkups (30/50 amps), seasonal sites, cable, WiFi, tent sites, dump, laundry, groc, LP gas. **REC:** heated pool, whirlpool. Pets OK $. Partial handicap access. Eco-friendly, 2015 rates: $34 to $44. Disc: AAA.
AAA Approved
(775)882-2445 Lat: 39.1060675, Lon: -119.7716798
5400 S Carson St., Carson City, NV 89701
www.comstockrv.com
See ad pages 738 (Spotlight Carson City), 737.

DAVIS CREEK PARK (Public) From town, N 11 mi on US-395 to Old US-395, W 0.5 mi (L). 2015 rates: $20. (775)849-0684

GOLD DUST WEST CASINO & RV PARK **Ratings: 10/9★/8** (RV Park) From Jct of I-580 (US 395) & US 50: Go 400 ft SW on US 50 (L). Elev 4600 ft. **FAC:** Paved rds. 45 paved, 20 pull-thrus (21 x 46), back-ins (21 x 40), 45 full hkups (30/50 amps), WiFi, rentals, dump, laundry, restaurant. **REC:** pool, whirlpool. Pet restrict(B/Q). Partial handicap access, no tents. 2015 rates: $28 to $33. Disc: AAA.
(775)885-9000 Lat: 39.17385, Lon: -119.74263
2171 E William St., Carson City, NV 89701
hotelreservations@bhwk.com
www.gdwcasino.com
See ad pages 739 (Spotlight Carson City), 737.

WASHOE LAKE (State Pk) From Jct of US-395 & Hwy 50, N 13 mi to Lake Blvd, N 3 mi (L) Entrance fee. Max RV size 45'. 2015 rates: $14 to $30. (775)687-4319

Keep one Guide at home, and one in your RV! To purchase additional North American Edition copies, call 877-209-6655.

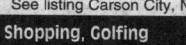

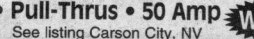

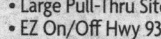

CARSON CITY (CONT)

Things to See and Do

➔ **GOLD DUST WEST** 24 hour Casino & The Grille Restaurant, 36-lane bowling center. Gold Dust Casino Carson City your one-stop shop. Also Ole Ole Restaurent. Elev 4780 ft. partial handicap access. RV accessible. Restrooms, food. Hours: 24 hours. ATM.
(775)885-9000 Lat: 39.14703, Lon: -119.74548
2171 E William St, Carson City, NV 89701
www.gdwcasino.com
See ad page 739 (Spotlight Carson City).

COTTONWOOD COVE — E5 *Clark*

➔ LAKE MEAD NRA/COTTONWOOD COVE CAMPGROUND (Natl Pk) From Jct of SR-95 & CR-164, E 14 mi on CR-164/Cottonwood Rd (E). 2015 rates: $10. (702)297-1464

Things to See and Do

➔ **COTTONWOOD COVE MARINA ON LAKE MOHAVE** A full service marina. Partial handicap access. Restrooms, food. Hours: 8 am to 5 pm. ATM.
(702)297-1464 Lat: 35.49113, Lon: -114.68621
10000 Cottonwood Cove Rd, Searchlight, NV 89046
cottonwoodadm@aol.com
www.cottonwoodcoveresort.com
See ad page 743 (Spotlight Las Vegas).

DAYTON — C1 *Lyon*

➔ **DAYTON RV PARK Ratings: 8/8/8.5** (RV Park) From Jct of NV 341 & NV 50: Go 3 mi on NV 50, then 60 Ft on W on Pike St (L). Elev 4400 ft. **FAC:** Paved rds. (50 spaces). Avail: 30 paved, 11 pull-thrus (26 x 65), back-ins (20 x 50), 30 full hkups (30/50 amps), seasonal sites, cable, WiFi, laundry. Pets OK. No tents. 2015 rates: $35 to $37.
AAA Approved
(775)246-9300 Lat: 39.23201, Lon: -119.59329
75 E Pike St, Dayton, NV 89403
info@daytonrvpark.com
www.daytonrvpark.com

ELKO — B4 *Elko*

➔ **DOUBLE DICE RV PARK**
Ratings: 8/10★/7.5 (RV Park) From Jct of I-80 & exit 303 (Jennings Way): Go 500 ft E on Jennings Way, then 3/4 mi E on Idaho St (R). Elev 5200 ft. **FAC:** Paved/gravel rds. (140 spaces). Avail: 55 gravel, 55 pull-thrus (18 x 65), 55 full hkups (30/50 amps), seasonal sites, cable, WiFi, laundry, LP gas, restaurant. **REC.** Pet restrict(Q) $. No tents. Eco-friendly, 2015 rates: $39. Disc: AAA, military. ATM.
AAA Approved
(775)738-5642 Lat: 40.8591803, Lon: -115.7371117
3730 Idaho St, Elko, NV 89801
thedice37@aol.com
www.doubledicervpark.com
See ad this page, 737.

➔ **ELKO RV PARK**
Ratings: 6.5/6/7 (RV Park) At I-80 & Exit 314 (Ryndon Devil's Gate): Go 50 ft S on Ryndon Devil's Gate (R). Elev 5170 ft. **FAC:** Gravel rds. (119 spaces). Avail: 30 gravel, 30 pull-thrus (30 x 54), 30 full hkups (30/50 amps), seasonal sites, WiFi, tent sites, dump, laundry, groc, LP gas. **REC:** Humboldt River. Pet restrict(B/Q) $. 2015 rates: $32. Disc: AAA, military. ATM.
(775)738-3448 Lat: 40.9480232, Lon: -115.5977891
507 Scott Road, Elko, NV 89801
elkorvatryndon@aol.com
www.elkorvparkatryndon.biz
See ad this page.

➚ **GOLD COUNTRY RV PARK**
Ratings: 9/8.5/8 (RV Park) From Jct of I-80 & exit 303 (Jennings Way): Go 500 ft E on Jennings Way, then .1mi S on Idaho St (L). Elev 5100 ft. **FAC:** Paved rds. (26 spaces). Avail: 13 gravel, back-ins (24 x 40), 13 full hkups (30/50 amps), seasonal sites, WiFi, rentals, dump, laundry, restaurant. **REC:** pool. Pets OK. 2015 rates: $30. Disc: AAA. ATM, no CC.
(800)621-1332 Lat: 40.8484222, Lon: -115.7460989
2050 Idaho Street, Elko, NV 89801
toni.jewell@playelko.com
www.goldcountryinnelko.com/hotel/rv-park
See ad this page, 737.

➔ **IRON HORSE RV RESORT**
Ratings: 9/10★/9.5 (RV Park) From Jct of I-80 & Exit 303 (Jennings Way): Go 500 ft S on Jennings Way (not marked), then 1/4 mi E on East Idaho St (R). Elev 5100 ft. **FAC:** Paved rds. (92 spaces). Avail: 34 gravel, patios, 20 pull-thrus (28 x 75), back-ins (28 x 58), some side by side hkups, 34 full hkups (30/50 amps), seasonal sites, cable, WiFi, rentals, dump, laundry, restaurant. **REC:** heated pool, wading pool, whirlpool, playground. Pet restrict(B). No tents. Big rig sites, eco-friendly, 2015 rates: $32 to $47. Disc: AAA.
AAA Approved
(800)782-3556 Lat: 40.8562062, Lon: -115.7400041
3400 East Idaho St, Elko, NV 89801
info@ironhorservresort.com
www.ironhorservresort.com
See ad this page, 737.

SOUTH FORK SRA (State Pk) From Jct I-80 (exit 301) & Hwy 227, SE 7 mi on Hwy 227, S 6 mi on Hwy 228 (E). Entrance fee required. 2015 rates: $14 to $30. May 1 to Oct 15. (775)744-4346

Things to See and Do

➔ **HILTON GARDEN INN ELKO & CASINO** Offers 84 rooms & 6 Suites, full service restaurant, Great American Grill, indoor pool & spa, fitness center, 24 hr business center, self laundry, banquet/conference room. Next to Iron Horse RV Resort. Elev 5150 ft. RV accessible. Restrooms, food. Hours: 24 hrs. ATM.
(877)777-7307 Lat: 40.83893, Lon: -115.76294
3650 East Idaho St, Elko, NV 89801
www.elko.gardeninn.com
See ad this page.

ELY — C5 *White Pine*

➘ CAVE LAKE (State Pk) From town, N 17.6 mi to SR-486, E 7 mi on SR-486 (R). 2015 rates: $14 to $30. May 1 to Oct 15. (775)296-1505

↓ KOA OF ELY **Ratings: 8/8.5★/8** (Campground) 2015 rates: $29.99 to $47.99. (800)562-6671 15936 Pioche Hwy, Ely, NV 89301

➔ **PROSPECTOR HOTEL & GAMBLING HALL & RV PARK Ratings: 6.5/NA/6** (RV Park) From Jct of US-50/6 & US-93: Go 1 mi N on US-93 (L). Elev 6400 ft. **FAC:** Poor gravel/dirt rds. (22 spaces). Avail: 17 gravel, 6 pull-thrus (28 x 60), back-ins (28 x 40), 17 full hkups (30/50 amps), seasonal sites, WiFi, rentals, dump, laundry, restaurant. **REC:** heated pool, whirlpool. Pets OK. No tents. Big rig sites, 2015 rates: $22.50. ATM, no reservations.
AAA Approved
(800)750-0557 Lat: 39.25415, Lon: -114.87305
1501 E Aultman St., Ely, NV 89301
prospector@mwpower.com

↑ **VALLEY VIEW RV PARK**
Ratings: 7/9★/8 (RV Park) From Jct of Hwys 50, 6 & 93: Go 2 mi NE on Hwy 93 (R). Elev 6400 ft. **FAC:** Gravel rds. (46 spaces). Avail: 26 gravel, 12 pull-thrus (22 x 60), back-ins (23 x 60), 26 full hkups (30/50 amps), seasonal sites, cable, WiFi, laundry, LP gas. Pets OK. No tents. 2015 rates: $28 to $32. Disc: AAA, military.
(775)289-3303 Lat: 39.2720024, Lon: -114.8515076
40 US-93, Ely, NV 89301
valleyviewrvelynevada.com

WARD CHARCOAL OVENS SHP (State Pk) From Jct I-93 & US-50, SW 11 mi to Cave Valley Rd (R) Entrance fee. Pit toilets. 2015 rates: $14 to $30. (775)289-1693

Tell them you saw them in this Guide!

FALLON — C2 *Churchill*

FALLON RV PARK
Ratings: 7/8.5★/7.5 (RV Park) From Jct of US-95 & US-50: Go 5 mi W on US-50 (L). Elev 4000 ft. **FAC:** Paved rds. (64 spaces). Avail: 47 paved, 28 pull-thrus (33 x 70), back-ins (30 x 60), 47 full hkups (30/50 amps), seasonal sites, cable, WiFi, tent sites, dump, laundry, groc, LP gas, firewood. **REC:** playground. Pet restrict(B). Partial handicap access. Big rig sites, eco-friendly, 2015 rates: $35 to $39. Disc: AAA, military. ATM.
(775)867-2332 Lat: 39.48666, Lon: -118.86687
5787 Reno Hwy, Fallon, NV 89406
fallonrv@gmail.com
www.fallonrv.com
See ad opposite page, 737.

Things to See and Do

FALLON RV PARK COUNTRY STORE & GIFT SHOP Country store and gift store. Sells licensed beverages, liquor, groceries and fuel. Elev 4000 ft. partial handicap access. RV accessible. Restrooms, food. Hours: 5am to 12am. ATM.
(775)867-2332 Lat: 39.48660, Lon: -118.86687
5787 Reno Hwy, Fallon, NV 89406
fallonrv@gmail.com
www.fallonrv.com
See ad opposite page.

FERNLEY — C1 *Lyon*

DESERT ROSE RV PARK
Ratings: 7.5/9★/7 (RV Park) From Jct of I-80 & exit 48 (Alt US-95 S/Alt US-50 E): Go 1 mi S on Alt US 95, then 4 mi E on US 50 (R). Elev 4200 ft. **FAC:** Gravel rds. (115 spaces). 90 Avail: 50 paved, 40 gravel, patios, 63 pull-thrus (25 x 65), back-ins (25 x 30), 90 full hkups (30/50 amps), seasonal sites, cable, WiFi, tent sites, dump, laundry, LP gas. **REC.** Pet restrict(B) $. Partial handicap access. 2015 rates: $35. Disc: AAA, military.
(877)767-3478 Lat: 39.592391, Lon: -119.156128
3285 US Highway 50 E, Fernley, NV 89408
desertroserv@aol.com
www.desertroserv.com

FERNLEY RV PARK **Ratings: 8/8.5/7.5** (RV Park) 2015 rates: $28. (775)575-5222 550 W Main, Fernley, NV 89408

GABBS — C2 *Nye*

BERLIN-ICHTHYOSAUR (State Pk) From Jct Hwy 361 & Hwy 844, E 22 mi on Hwy 844. Entrance Fee required. Pit toilets. 2015 rates: $14 to $30. (775)964-2440

Your neighbor just told you about a great little campground in Kentucky — what was the name of it again? The "Find-it-Fast" index in the back of the Guide can help. It's an alphabetical listing, by state, of every private and public park in the Guide.

GARDNERVILLE — C1 *Douglas*

TOPAZ LODGE, CASINO & RV PARK
Ratings: 8.5/8/8 (Campground) From Jct of NV 208 (Holbrook Jct) & US 395: Go 2-1/4 mi SE on US 395 (L). Elev 4900 ft. **FAC:** Paved rds. (59 spaces). Avail: 49 gravel, 6 pull-thrus (24 x 80), back-ins (23 x 45), 43 full hkups, 6 W, 6 E (30/50 amps), seasonal sites, cable, WiFi, rentals, dump, groc, LP gas, firewood, restaurant. **REC:** heated pool, Topaz Lake: fishing. Pets OK. No tents. Eco-friendly, 2015 rates: $22. ATM.
(800)962-0732 Lat: 38.6948184, Lon: -119.5478248
1979 US Hwy 395 South, Gardnerville, NV 89410
rick@topazlodge.com
www.topazlodge.com
See ad this page, 737.

HAWTHORNE — D2 *Mineral*

SCOTTY'S RV PARK & NAPA AUTO SUPPLY
Ratings: 5.5/8.5★/5.5 (Campground) From Jct of US 95 S (5th St) & J St: Go 500 ft N on J St (R). Elev 4300 ft. **FAC:** Gravel/dirt rds. (19 spaces). Avail: 16 gravel, patios, 12 pull-thrus (22 x 60), back-ins (20 x 40), 16 full hkups (30/50 amps), seasonal sites, cable, WiFi, tent sites, laundry, groc, LP bottles. **REC.** Pets OK. 2015 rates: $22. Disc: AAA, military. ATM.
(775)945-3411 Lat: 38.5247133, Lon: -118.6195033
1005 5th Street, Hawthorne, NV 89415
tina.napa@att.net
See ad this page, 737.

WHISKEY FLATS RV PARK
Ratings: 8/9.5★/8.5 (RV Park) From the Jct of NV 359 & US 95: Go 1 mi N on US 95(L). Elev 4200 ft. **FAC:** Gravel rds. (60 spaces). Avail: 40 paved, 40 pull-thrus (26 x 60), 40 full hkups (30/50 amps), seasonal sites, cable, WiFi, tent sites, dump, laundry, groc, LP gas. **REC.** Pets OK. Partial handicap access. Big rig sites, 2015 rates: $24.55 to $26.82.
(775)945-1800 Lat: 38.5374469, Lon: -118.6332281
3045 Hwy 95, Hawthorne, NV 89415
stay@whiskeyflats.net
www.whiskeyflats.net
See ad this page, 737.

HENDERSON — F5 *Clark*

LAKE MEAD NRA/LAS VEGAS BAY CAMPGROUND (Natl Pk) From Jct of US-93 & Lakeshore Rd exit, N 9 mi on Lakeshore Rd (R). 2015 rates: $10. (702)293-8990

Travel Services

CAMPING WORLD OF HENDERSON As the nation's largest retailer of RV supplies, accessories, services and new and used RVs, Camping World is committed to making your total RV experience better. **SERVICES:** Tire, RV appliance, restrooms. RV supplies, RV accessible. waiting room. Hours: 8am - 6pm.
(800)646-4093 Lat: 35.99945, Lon: -114.93896
1600 S Boulder Hwy, Henderson, NV 89015
www.campingworld.com

JACKPOT — A5 *Elko*

CACTUS PETES RV PARK Ratings: 8/8★/7.5 (RV Park) From US 93 & (NV/ID Border): Go 1-1/4 mi S on US 93 (L). Elev 5200 ft. **FAC:** Paved rds. (91 spaces). Avail: 84 paved, 50 pull-thrus (30 x 60), back-ins (26 x 50), 84 full hkups (30 amps), seasonal sites, cable, WiFi, rentals, dump, laundry, restaurant. **REC:** heated pool, whirlpool. Pets OK. Partial handicap access, no tents. 2015 rates: $18 to $24. Disc: AAA.
AAA Approved
(800)821-1103 Lat: 41.97978, Lon: -114.67201
Keno Drive, Jackpot, NV 89825
www.ameristarcasino.com

We appreciate your business!

LAKE TAHOE — C1 *Douglas*

LAKE TAHOE AREA MAP

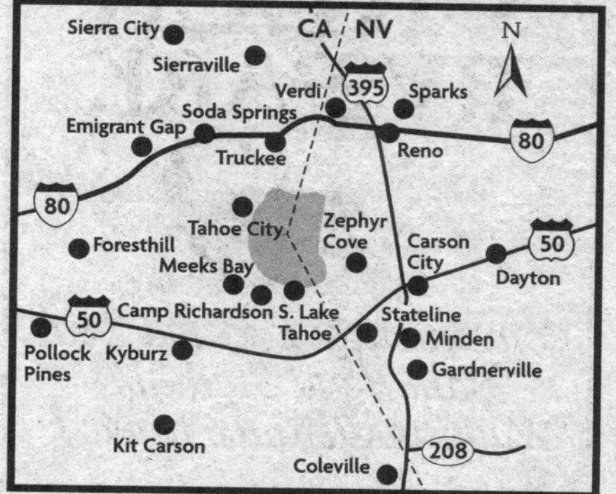

Symbols on map indicate towns within a 50 mile radius of Lake Tahoe where campgrounds are listed. Check listings for more information.

In NV, see also Carson City, Dayton, Gardnerville, Minden, Reno, Sparks, Stateline, Verdi & Zephyr Cove.

In CA, see also Camp Richardson, Coleville, Emigrant Gap, Foresthill, Kit Carson, Kyburz, Meeks Bay, Pollock Pines, Sierra City, Sierraville, Soda Springs, South Lake Tahoe, Tahoe City & Truckee.

LAS VEGAS — E4 *Clark, Las Vegas*

A SPOTLIGHT Introducing Las Vegas' colorful attractions appearing at the front of this state section.

LAS VEGAS See also Boulder City.

ARIZONA CHARLIE'S BOULDER RV PARK
Ratings: 10/9.5/9 (RV Park) From Jct of I-515 (US 93/95 Expwy) & Boulder Hwy (exit 70): Go 2 mi S on Boulder Hwy (L). **FAC:** Paved rds. (221 spaces). Avail: 201 paved, 92 pull-thrus (20 x 70), back-ins (20 x 40), 201 full hkups (30/50 amps), seasonal sites, cable, WiFi, laundry, restaurant. **REC:** heated

Heading to a privately owned park? Be sure to read how our inspection team rated it in the Guide "How to Use This Travel Guide" section.

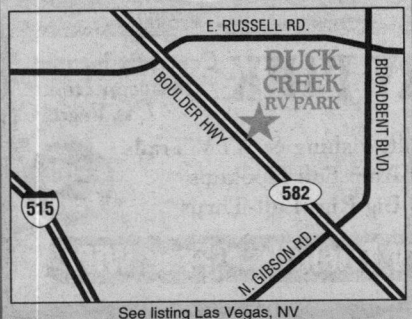

LAS VEGAS (CONT)

ARIZONA CHARLIE'S BOULDER (CONT) pool, whirlpool. Pet restrict(B/Q). Partial handicap access, no tents. 2015 rates: $32. Disc: AAA, military. **(800)970-7280 Lat: 36.12466, Lon: -115.07733 4445 Boulder Hwy, Las Vegas, NV 89121 www.arizonacharlies.com**
See ad pages 741 (Spotlight Las Vegas), 737.

CIRCUS CIRCUS RV PARK **Ratings: 9/8.5/7** (RV Park) 2015 rates: $36 to $75. (702)691-5988 500 Circus Circus Drive, Las Vegas, NV 89109

CLARK COUNTY SHOOTING COMPLEX'S RV PARK (Public) From Jct of US 95 & Hwy 215 (Bruce Woodbury Beltway): Go 3-1/4 mi E on Hwy 215, then 4-1/4 mi N on N. Decatur Blvd (E). 2015 rates: $20. (702)455-2000

What will it cost to catch a salmon in Alaska? State-by-state fishing license information is listed in the front section of the Guide.

DUCK CREEK RV PARK
Ratings: 10/9★/8.5 (RV Park) From Jct of I-515 & Sunset Rd (Exit 64): Go 1 mi E on Sunset Rd, then 1-1/4 mi N on N Boulder Hwy (R).

SPREAD YOUR WINGS AT DUCK CREEK
Come spread your wings and enjoy our friendly staff and the excitement of Las Vegas. Short drive to the Las Vegas strip. Free WIFI, heated pool & jacuzzi, showers, laundry room & recreation room, cookouts and movie nights.

FAC: Paved rds. (207 spaces). Avail: 102 paved, patios, 22 pull-thrus (24 x 78), back-ins (24 x 36), 102 full hkups (30/50 amps), seasonal sites, WiFi, laundry. **REC:** heated pool, whirlpool, playground. Pet restrict(B). Partial handicap access, no tents.

Find 'em fast. Our advertisers often include extra information or provide a detailed map in their ads to help you find their facilities quickly and easily.

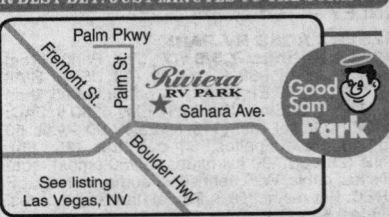

LAS VEGAS (CONT)

DUCK CREEK RV PARK (CONT)
Eco-friendly, 2015 rates: $27 to $45. Disc: AAA, military.
(866)371-9712 Lat: 36.08047, Lon: -115.02583
6635 Boulder Highway, Las Vegas, NV 89122
duckcreekrv@gmail.com
www.duckcreekrvparklv.com
See ad opposite page, 737, 735 (NV Map).

HITCHIN' POST RV PARK
Ratings: 9.5/9.5★/9.5 (RV Park) S-bnd: From Jct of I-15 & Exit 50 (Lamb): Go 2 mi S on Lamb, then 500 ft S on Las Vegas Blvd (L) or N-bnd: From Jct of I-15 & Craig Rd (exit 48): Go 1-1/4 mi E on Craig Rd, then 1 mi SE on Lamb Blvd, then 500 ft on Las Vegas Blvd (L) Note: Call for updated directions.

FRIENDLIEST RV PARK IN LAS VEGAS!
Highly rated, affordable & gated. Try your luck on our slots, relax in our heated pool, enjoy our Saloon open 24/7, dine in our restaurant & Beer Garden on property. Stop-Stay-Enjoy! Free WiFi, Cable TV & HBO. We have it all.

FAC: Paved rds. (196 spaces). Avail: 98 gravel, 98 pull-thrus (30 x 70), 98 full hkups (30/50 amps), seasonal sites, cable, WiFi, rentals, laundry, restaurant, controlled access. **REC:** heated pool. Pet restrict(Q). Partial handicap access, no tents. Big rig sites, eco-friendly, 2015 rates: $33. Disc: AAA. ATM. AAA Approved
(888)433-8402 Lat: 36.24390, Lon: -115.05432
3640 Las Vegas Blvd North, Las Vegas, NV 89115
office@hprvp.com
www.hprvp.com
See ad pages 736 (NV Featured Map), 737 & Snowbird Destinations in Magazine Section.

KINGS ROW TRAILER PARK **Ratings: 5.5/5/4.5** (RV Area in MHP) 2015 rates: $18. (702)457-3606 3660 Boulder Hwy, Las Vegas, NV 89121

LAS VEGAS KOA AT SAM'S TOWN **Ratings: 9.5/8/7** (RV Park) 2015 rates: $25 to $39. (800)562-7270 5225 Boulder Highway, Las Vegas, NV 89122

LAS VEGAS RV **Ratings: 8/6.5/7** (Membership Pk) 2015 rates: $32. (800)405-6188 4295 Boulder Highway, Las Vegas, NV 89121

LAS VEGAS RV RESORT
Ratings: 10/10★/10 (RV Park) From Jct of Boulder Hwy & Nellis Blvd: Go 1/4 mi N on Nellis Blvd (R). **FAC:** Paved rds. (385 spaces). Avail: 150 paved, 148 pull-thrus (30 x 60), back-ins (28 x 50), 150 full hkups (30/50 amps), seasonal sites, WiFi, rentals, laundry, controlled access. **REC:** heated pool, whirlpool. Pet restrict(B/Q). Partial handicap access, no tents. Age restrict may apply, big rig sites, RV age restrict, eco-friendly, 2015 rates: $29 to $45.
(702)451-8005 Lat: 36.09558, Lon: -115.04333
3890 S Nellis Blvd, Las Vegas, NV 89121
info@lasvegasrvresort.com
www.lasvegasrvresort.com
See ad opposite page, 737.

LVM RESORT
Ratings: 10/10★/10 (Condo Pk) From Jct of & I-215 & I-15: Go 3/4 mi S on I-15 (Exit 33), then 1 mi SW on Blue Diamond West (SR160), then 1/4 mi N on Arville St (L).

LVM RESORT
Award-winning, luxury Class A resort, offering the best in motorcoach accommodations. A tropical, serene setting with 24-hour security, moments away from the world-class entertainment and dining of the Las Vegas Strip.

FAC: Paved rds. (407 spaces). Avail: 200 paved, patios, back-ins (30 x 65), 200 full hkups (30/50 amps), seasonal sites, cable, WiFi, laundry, restaurant, controlled access. **REC:** heated pool, whirlpool. Pet restrict(B/Q). Partial handicap access, no tents. Big rig sites, eco-friendly, 2015 rates: $61 to $105. Disc: AAA, military.
(866)897-9300 Lat: 36.04130, Lon: -115.19949
8175 Arville St, Las Vegas, NV 89139
info@lvmresort.com
www.lvmresort.com
See ad pages 743 (Spotlight Las Vegas), 737, 735 (NV Map).

MAIN STREET STATION HOTEL-CASINO-BREWERY & RV PARK **Ratings: 6/7.5/3.5** (RV Park) 2015 rates: $14 to $19. (800)634-6255 200 North Main, Las Vegas, NV 89101

Everyone wants to be noticed. Tell your RV Park that you found them in the this Guide.

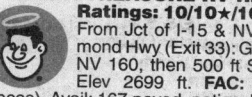

NEVADA TREASURE RV RESORT
Ratings: 10/10★/10 (RV Resort) From Jct of I-15 & NV 160/W Blue Diamond Hwy (Exit 33): Go NW 60-1/2 mi on NV 160, then 500 ft S on Leslie St (L). Elev 2699 ft. **FAC:** Paved rds. (202 spaces). Avail: 167 paved, patios, back-ins (36 x 50), 167 full hkups (30/50 amps), seasonal sites, WiFi, laundry, LP gas, restaurant, controlled access. **REC:** heated pool, whirlpool, rec open to public. Pets OK. Partial handicap access, no tents. Big rig sites, eco-friendly, 2015 rates: $40 to $60. Disc: AAA.
(800)429-6665 Lat: 36.30349, Lon: -116.01604
301 West Leslie St., Pahrump, NV 89060
frontdesk@nvtreasure.com
www.nvtreasure.com
See primary listing at Pahrump and ad page 746 (Spotlight Pahrump).

OASIS LAS VEGAS RV RESORT
Ratings: 10/10★/9 (RV Resort) From Jct of I-15 & Blue Diamond Rd (Exit 33): Go 1/4 mi E on Blue Diamond Rd (R) Note: S-bnd, move immediately to right lane from exit ramp.

LAS VEGAS PREMIER RV RESORT
Park your RV & enjoy the sights & sounds of Las Vegas. Take a day trip to Hoover Dam, Laughlin, Lake Mead, Grand Canyon, Death Valley. Enjoy our pool tournament, horseshoes, or a meal at Oasis Cafe. Monthly rates available.

FAC: Paved rds. (700 spaces). Avail: 350 paved, patios, 282 pull-thrus (24 x 60), back-ins (24 x 40), 350 full hkups (30/50 amps), seasonal sites, cable, WiFi, dump, laundry, groc, LP gas, restaurant, controlled access. **REC:** heated pool, whirlpool. Pet restrict(B/Q). Partial handicap access, no tents. Big rig sites, eco-friendly, 2015 rates: $43 to $82. Disc: AAA, military. ATM.
(800)566-4707 Lat: 36.04291, Lon: -115.17673
2711 W Windmill Lane, Las Vegas, NV 89123
customersupport@oasislasvegasrvresort.com
www.oasislasvegasrvresort.com
See ad pages 740 (Spotlight Las Vegas), 737.

RIVIERA RV PARK
Ratings: 8/8/6.5 (RV Park) From Jct of I-515 & Boulder Hwy (Fremont St): Go 2 mi N on Boulder Hwy/Fremont St, then 500 ft E on St. Louis St, then 1/4 mi S On Palm St (L). **FAC:** Paved rds. (137 spaces). Avail: 39 gravel, patios, 14 pull-thrus (25 x 60), back-ins (25 x 60), 39 full hkups (30/50 amps), seasonal sites, WiFi, laundry. **REC:** heated pool, whirlpool. Pet restrict(Q). No tents. Eco-friendly, 2015 rates: $26.61.
(702)457-8700 Lat: 36.14707, Lon: -115.10078
2200 Palm Street, Las Vegas, NV 89104
rivierarv@westcoastmhp.com
www.rivierarvpark.com
See ad opposite page, 737.

ROADRUNNER RV PARK **Ratings: 7.5/10★/8** (RV Park) 2015 rates: $16 to $20. (702)456-4711 4711 Boulder Highway, Las Vegas, NV 89121

Travel Services

CAMPING WORLD STORE OF LAS VEGAS As the nation's largest retailer of RV supplies, accessories, services and new and used RVs, Camping World is committed to making your total RV experience better. RV Accessories: (877)594-3353. **SERVICES:** RV, RV appliance, staffed RV wash, restrooms, RV Sales. RV supplies, LP, RV accessible. waiting room. Hours: 8am - 6pm.
(888)706-1299 Lat: 35.92804, Lon: -115.19440
13175 South Las Vegas Blvd., Las Vegas, NV 89044
www.campingworld.com

HITCHIN' POST TRAILER SALES Reliable Sales & Service. **SERVICES:** RV, tire, RV appliance, restrooms, RV Sales. RV supplies. Hours: 8am to 5pm. ATM.
(702)644-1819 Lat: 36.24390, Lon: -115.05432
3640 Las Vegas Blvd North, Las Vegas, NV 89115
www.hitchinpostrv.com
See ad page 736 (NV Featured Map).

Things to See and Do

ARIZONA CHARLIE'S BOULDER HOTEL, CASINO, RV PARK Casino. Partial handicap access. Restrooms, food. Hours: 24 hrs. ATM.
(877)951-0002 Lat: 36.12407, Lon: -115.07643
4575 Boulder Highway, Las Vegas, NV 89121
www.arizonacharlies.com
See ad page 741 (Spotlight Las Vegas).

Subscribe to MotorHome Magazine! Questions? Change of address? Call 800-678-1201.

HITCHIN' POST SALOON On park property, full-service bar, restaurant, poker machines, outdoor beer garden, horseshoe pits, pool tables, dart boards. Open all year, 24 hours. Partial handicap access. Restrooms, food. Hours: 24 hrs. ATM.
(888)433-8402 Lat: 36.24390, Lon: -115.05432
3650 Las Vegas Blvd N, Las Vegas, NV 89115
office@hprvp.com
www.hpsslv.com
See ad page 736 (NV Featured Map).

OASIS CAFE Serving Breakfast & Lunch. Partial handicap access. Restrooms, food. Hours: 7:30 am to 2:00 pm. ATM.
(800)566-4707 Lat: 36.04277, Lon: -115.17676
2711 W Windmill Ln, Las Vegas, NV 89123
www.oasislasvegasrvresort.com
See ad page 740 (Spotlight Las Vegas).

OASIS LAS VEGAS RV RESORT SPECIAL EVENTS CENTER A beautiful facility for: Wedding Receptions, Wedding Ceremonies, Business Meeting and all types of Parties and Banquets. Partial handicap access. Restrooms, food. Hours: As Needed. ATM.
(702)260-2050 Lat: 36.04277, Lon: -115.17676
2711 W Windmill Ln, Las Vegas, NV 89123
www.oasislasvegas.com
See ad page 740 (Spotlight Las Vegas).

THE DINER AT LVM Food and Beverages. Food. Hours: Mon-Sat 7:30am-2:30pm; Sun 8:30am-1:30pm.
(702)263-0146 Lat: 36.04144, Lon: -115.19978
8175 Arville, Las Vegas, NV 89139
info@lasvegasmotorcoachresort.com
www.lvmresort.com
See ad page 743 (Spotlight Las Vegas).

LAUGHLIN — F5 *Clark*

LAUGHLIN/AVI CASINO KOA **Ratings: 8.5/8/7.5** (RV Park) 2015 rates: $20 to $50. (800)562-4142 10000 Aha Macav Parkway, Laughlin, NV 89029

PALMS RIVER RESORT
Ratings: 9.5/9★/10 (RV Park) From Jct of Hwy 95 & Hwy 163(in AZ) S 24mi on Hwy 95 to Needles Hwy/River Rd), N 3 mi on Needles Hwy/River Rd (R) Note: No pop-up trailers. **FAC:** Paved rds. (184 spaces). Avail: 51 all weather, 23 pull-thrus (45 x 80), back-ins (45 x 80), accepts full hkup units only, 51 full hkups (30/50 amps), WiFi, rentals, laundry, groc, LP gas, firewood, controlled access. **REC:** pool, wading pool, whirlpool, Colorado River: swim, fishing, playground. Pet restrict(B). Partial handicap access. RV age restrict, eco-friendly, 2015 rates: $33 to $40. Disc: AAA, military.
(760)326-0333 Lat: 34.88409, Lon: -114.64516
4170 Needles Hwy, Needles, CA 92363
reservations@palmsriverresort.com
www.palmsriverresort.com
See primary listing at Needles, CA and ad page 200.

RIVERSIDE RESORT RV PARK **Ratings: 8.5/8/8.5** (RV Park) 2015 rates: $25 to $29. (800)227-3849 1650 S Casino Dr, Laughlin, NV 89029

LOVELOCK — B2 *Pershing*

RYE PATCH SRA (State Pk) From town, N 22 mi on I-80 to exit 129, W 1 mi (L) Entrance fee required. 2015 rates: $14 to $30. (775)538-7321

MESQUITE — E5 *Clark*

CASABLANCA RV PARK RESORT **Ratings: 6.5/8/6.5** (RV Park) 2015 rates: $20. (877)438-2929 950 West Mesquite Boulevard, Mesquite, NV 89027

Making campground reservations? Remember to ask about the cancellation policy when making your reservation.

MESQUITE (CONT)

➔ **DESERT SKIES RV RESORT** **Ratings: 10/9.5★/9.5** (RV Park) From Jct of I-15 & Sandhill Blvd (Exit 122): Go 200 ft S on Sandhill Blvd, then 1-1/2 mi E on Hillside Dr (Hwy 91) (R). **FAC:** Paved rds. (321 spaces). Avail: 161 all weather, 13 pull-thrus (32 x 65), back-ins (33 x 46), 161 full hkups (30/50 amps), seasonal sites, cable, WiFi, laundry, LP bottles. **REC:** heated pool, whirlpool. Pets OK. Partial handicap access, no tents. Big rig sites, eco-friendly, 2015 rates: $35 to $49.
(928)347-6000 Lat: 36.81907, Lon: -114.04140
350 E. Hwy 91, Mesquite, NV 89027
info@desertskiesresorts.com
www.desertskiesrv.com
See ad this page, 737.

➔ OASIS RV PARK RESORT **Ratings: 5.5/8/6** (RV Park) 2015 rates: $20. (800)896-4567 897 West Mesquite Boulevard, Mesquite, NV 89027

➘ SOLSTICE MOTORCOACH RESORT **Ratings: 8/9.5★/9.5** (RV Park) 2015 rates: $33.59 to $55.99. (702)346-8522 345 Mystic Drive, Mesquite, NV 89034

⬆ **SUN RESORTS RV PARK** **Ratings: 8.5/10★/9** (RV Park) From I-15 and Mesquite (exit 122): Go 1/4 mi S on Sandhill Blvd, then 1/4 mi E on Hillside (R). **FAC:** Paved rds. (71 spaces). Avail: 41 gravel, 24 pull-thrus (33 x 87), back-ins (30 x 54), 41 full hkups (30/50 amps), seasonal sites, cable, WiFi, laundry. **REC.** Pet restrict(Q). No tents. Big rig sites, eco-friendly, 2015 rates: $30 to $40.
(702)346-6666 Lat: 36.80971, Lon: -114.06168
401 E Old Mill Rd, Mesquite, NV 89027
sunresortsrv@yahoo.com
www.sunresortsrv.com
See ad pages 755, 737.

⬆ **VIRGIN VALLEY FOOD MART & RV PARKING** (RV Spaces) From Jct I-15 & N Sandhill Blvd (Exit 122): Go N 1 block on N Sandhill Blvd (R). **FAC:** Paved rds. 110 paved, WiFi, dump, groc, LP gas. Pets OK. No tents. 2015 rates: $.75 hr/3hr minimum. ATM, no CC, no reservations.
(702)346-8881 Lat: 36.814854, Lon: -114.064223
200 Mesa Blvd, Mesquite, NV 89027
www.247virginvalleyfoodmart.com
See ad this page.

MINA — D2 *Mineral*

⬇ SUNRISE VALLEY RV PARK **Ratings: 4/7/7** (Campground) 2015 rates: $25. Mar 2 to Nov 1. (775)573-2214 us Hwy 95, Mina, NV 89422

MINDEN — C1 *Douglas*

⬆ **CARSON VALLEY RV RESORT & CASINO** **Ratings: 10/9★/8.5** (RV Park) From Jct of NV 88 & US 395: Go 1/2 mi SE on US 395 (L). Elev 4750 ft. **FAC:** Paved rds. 59 paved, 25 pull-thrus (25 x 54), back-ins (25 x 35), 59 full hkups (30/50 amps), cable, WiFi, rentals, dump, laundry, groc, restaurant. **REC:** heated pool, whirlpool. Pets OK. Partial handicap access, no tents. Eco-friendly, 2015 rates: $25 to $42. ATM.
(800)321-6983 Lat: 38.95660, Lon: -119.76958
1627 US Hwy 395 N, Minden, NV 89423
reservations@carsonvalleyinn.com
www.carsonvalleyinn.com
See ad this page, 737.

⬆ **SILVER CITY RV RESORT** **Ratings: 10/9★/9** (RV Park) From Jct of NV 88 & US 395: Go 7-1/4 mi N on US 395 (R). Elev 4620 ft. **FAC:** Paved rds. (200 spaces). Avail: 100 paved, 90 pull-thrus (31 x 50), back-ins (31 x 40), 100 full hkups (30/50 amps), seasonal sites, cable, WiFi, tent sites, dump, laundry, groc, LP gas, firewood.

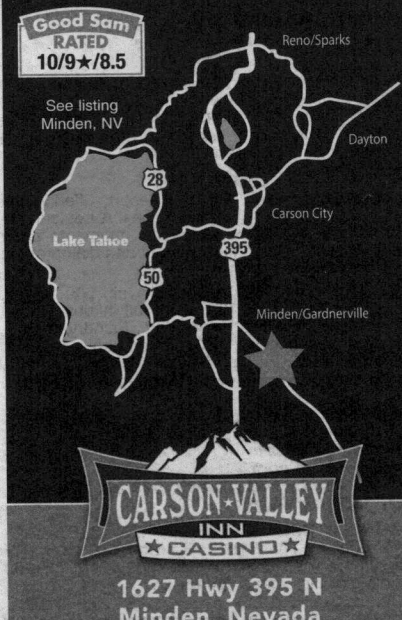

MINDEN (CONT)

SILVER CITY RV RESORT (CONT)
REC: heated pool, whirlpool, pond, fishing, playground. Pet restrict(B/Q) $. Partial handicap access. Big rig sites, eco-friendly, 2015 rates: $39.95. Disc: AAA, military. ATM.
AAA Approved
(800)997-6393 Lat: 39.06916, Lon: -119.77960
3165 Hwy 395 N, Minden, NV 89423
info@silvercityrvresort.com
www.silvercityrvresort.com
See ad opposite page, 737.

Things to See and Do

CARSON VALLEY INN HOTEL & CASINO Casino w/slots, videos, blakjack, craps, keno, race/sports bk, poker rm, 3 dining fac., 2 lounges, free nightly live cabaret entertainment. INN Club offers benefits casino play. Free to join. Indoor pool, 2 spas & fitness center. Elev 4750 ft. partial handicap access. RV accessible. Restrooms, food. Hours: 24 hours. ATM.
(775)782-9711 Lat: 38.95660, Lon: -119.76958
1627 US Hwy 395 N, Minden, NV 89423
info@carsonvalleyinn.com
www.carsonvalleyinn.com
See ad opposite page.

MOUNTAIN CITY — A4 *Elko*

WILD HORSE STATE RECREATION AREA (State Pk) From town: Go 19 mi SE on Hwy-225. Max RV size 45'. 2015 rates: $14 to $30. (775)385-5939

OVERTON — E5 *Clark*

LAKE MEAD NRA/ECHO BAY (Natl Pk) From Jct of US-93 & Lakeshore Rd, N 11 mi on Lakeshore Rd to Northshore, NE 37 mi (R). 2015 rates: $10. (702)394-4000

LAKE MEAD RV VILLAGE AT ECHO BAY
Ratings: 7.5/7.5/7 (RV Park) From Jct of SR 564 E & SR 147 W: Go 35 mi N on SR 147 W, then 4 1/2 mi W on Echo Bay Rd (R) Admission to National Park Required. **FAC:** Paved rds. (54 spaces). Avail: 34 gravel, back-ins (30 x 50), 34 full hkups (30/50 amps), seasonal sites, WiFi, laundry, groc, LP gas, firewood. **REC:** Lake Mead: swim, fishing, rec open to public. Pet restrict(Q). No tents. 2015 rates: $28 to $30.
(702)394-4000 Lat: 36.29975, Lon: -114.42146
600 Echo Bay Rd, Overton, NV 89040
lmrvecho@mvdsl.com
www.lakemeadrvvillage.com
See ad pages 742 (Spotlight Las Vegas), 737.

ROBBINS NEST MHC
Ratings: 7/9★/8.5 (RV Area in MHP) From Jct I-15 & SR 169 (Exit 93): Go E 11.7 mi on SR 169 (R). **FAC:** Gravel rds. (152 spaces). Avail: 46 gravel, 12 pull-thrus (30 x 45), back-ins (30 x 45), 46 full hkups (30/50 amps), seasonal sites, WiFi, dump, laundry. **REC.** Pet restrict(B). Partial handicap access, no tents. 2015 rates: $20. Disc: AAA, military. No CC.
(702)397-2364 Lat: 36.52692, Lon: -114.44160
479 S Moapa Valley Blvd., Overton, NV 89040
stan.wiebe@ascentia.us
ascentia.us/nevada/robbins-nest
See ad this page.

VALLEY OF FIRE (State Pk) From Jct of I-15 & SR-169, SW 18 mi on SR-169 (L). Entrance fee required. 2015 rates: $14 to $30. (702)397-2088

PAHRUMP — E4 *Nye*

A SPOTLIGHT Introducing Pahrump's colorful attractions appearing at the front of this state section.

PAHRUMP See also Shoshone, CA.

Do you know how to read each part of a listing? Check the How to Use This Campground Guide in the front.

LAKESIDE CASINO & RV RESORT
Ratings: 10/10★/10 (RV Resort) From Jct of Hwy 160 & Homestead Rd (S end of town): Go S 3-3/4 mi on Homestead Rd, then W 100 ft on Thousandaire Rd (R). Elev 2700 ft.

ESCAPE TO THE OASIS IN THE DESERT
Relax at Lakeside- enjoy our hot tub, swimming pool, sandy beach, cabanas, fire pits, pedal boats & fish in our 7 acre lake. A short walk to the casino for 24 hour action, cafe, buffet and bar. Come relax at Lakeside!

FAC: Paved rds. (159 spaces). Avail: 129 paved, patios, 15 pull-thrus (30 x 70), back-ins (30 x 58), 129 full hkups (30/50 amps), seasonal sites, WiFi, laundry, groc, LP gas, firewood, restaurant. **REC:** pool, whirlpool, Lakeside Lake: fishing, playground. Pet restrict(Q). Partial handicap access, no tents. Big rig sites, eco-friendly, 2015 rates: $29.99 to $49.99. Disc: AAA, military. ATM.
(888)558-5253 Lat: 36.12054, Lon: -115.96387
5870 S Homestead Road, Pahrump, NV 89048
infogcg@goldencasinogroup.com
www.lakesidecasinopahrump.com
See ad pages 745 (Spotlight Pahrump), 737 & Snowbird Destinations in Magazine Section.

NEVADA TREASURE RV RESORT
Ratings: 10/10★/10 (RV Resort) From Jct of SR-372 & SR-160: Go N 7-1/2 mi on SR-160, then go 500 ft on Leslie St (L). Elev 2699 ft.

A JEWEL IN THE DESERT
World Class amenities at affordable rates! Experience total relaxation within our perfectly manicured grounds. Paved & landscaped Big Rig sites, Pool w/Waterfall, Fitness Center/Spa & much more!

FAC: Paved rds. (202 spaces). Avail: 167 paved, patios, back-ins (36 x 50), 167 full hkups (30/50 amps), seasonal sites, WiFi, laundry, LP gas, restaurant, controlled access. **REC:** heated pool, whirlpool, rec open to public. Pets OK. Partial handicap access, no tents. Big rig sites, eco-friendly, 2015 rates: $40 to $60. Disc: AAA.
AAA Approved
(800)429-6665 Lat: 36.30349, Lon: -116.01604
301 West Leslie St., Pahrump, NV 89060
frontdesk@nvtreasure.com
www.nvtreasure.com
See ad pages 746 (Spotlight Pahrump), 737 & Snowbird Destinations in Magazine Section.

PAHRUMP OASIS RV RESORT
Ratings: 8.5/9★/8.5 (RV Park) S bnd: From Jct of Hwys 160 & 372: Go 1/2 mi S on Hwy 160 (L). Elev 2700 ft. **FAC:** Paved rds. (140 spaces). 65 Avail: 55 paved, 10 gravel, patios, 45 pull-thrus (35 x 70), back-ins (30 x 55), mostly side by side hkups, 65 full hkups (30/50 amps), seasonal sites, cable, WiFi, laundry, restaurant. **REC:** pool, whirlpool. Pets OK. Partial handicap access, no tents. Age restrict may apply, big rig sites, 2015 rates: $43.15. Disc: AAA.
(775)727-5100 Lat: 36.20409, Lon: -115.97794
1101 S Hwy 160, Pahrump, NV 89048
29078@hotel.bestwestern.com
www.bwpahrump.com/rvpark.php
See ad pages 747 (Spotlight Pahrump), 737.

PREFERRED RV RESORT
Ratings: 9/9★/9 (Membership Pk) From Jct of SR-160 & Crawford Way: Go NE 1/4 mi on Crawford Way (R). Elev 2700 ft. **FAC:** Gravel rds. (270 spaces). Avail: 50 gravel, patios, 25 pull-thrus (20 x 60), back-ins (35 x 45), mostly side by side hkups, 50 full hkups (30/50 amps), seasonal sites, WiFi, rentals, dump, laundry, LP gas, controlled access. **REC:** heated pool, whirlpool, shuffleboard, playground. Pets OK. Partial handicap access, no tents. Eco-friendly, 2015 rates: $33.
(800)445-7840 Lat: 36.21096, Lon: -115.98184
1801 E Crawford Way, Pahrump, NV 89048
reservations@preferredrv.com
www.preferredrv.com
See ad this page, 737.

SADDLE WEST HOTEL CASINO & RV PARK **Ratings: 8.5/9★/7** (RV Park) 2015 rates: $25. (800)433-3987 1220 S Hwy 160, Pahrump, NV 89048

WINE RIDGE RV RESORT & COTTAGES
Ratings: 10/10★/10 (RV Park) From Jct of SR-160 & Winery Rd: Go 3/4 mi on Winery Rd (L). Elev 2850 ft.

MODERN AMENITIES, MOUNTAIN VIEWS
Top Resort: 10/10/10. HWY 160 & Winery Rd. 42 Cottages; new 2-bed Casitas; large, 42 one bed cottages, 129 perfect FHU 50-amp level RV sites. Private bath suites, 2 pools w/spa, free LD phone, free waffle breakfast M-F.

FAC: Paved rds. (139 spaces). Avail: 94 all weather, patios, 19 pull-thrus (33 x 60), back-ins (33 x 60), 94 full hkups (30/50 amps), seasonal sites, WiFi, rentals, laundry, restaurant. **REC:** pool, whirlpool. Pets OK. No tents. Big rig sites, eco-friendly, 2015 rates: $28. Disc: AAA, military.
(775)751-7805 Lat: 36.19531, Lon: -115.94223
3800 Winery Road, Pahrump, NV 89048
wineridgerv@gmail.com
www.wineridgervresort.com
See ad pages 744 (Spotlight Las Vegas), 737, 735 (NV Map) See ad inside back cover & Snowbird Destinations in Magazine Section.

Things to See and Do

LAKESIDE CASINO Casino with games, entertainment, 24-hr restaurant & buffet. Elev 2700 ft. partial handicap access. Restrooms, food. Hours: 24 Hrs. ATM.
(775)751-7770 Lat: 36.13294, Lon: -115.95801
5870 S Homestead Rd, Pahrump, NV 89048
www.lakesidecasinopahrump.com
See ad page 745 (Spotlight Pahrump).

PAHRUMP NEVADA Tourist Information for the town of Pahrump, located between Las Vegas and Death Valley. Enjoy the peaceful surroundings of picturesque mountain ranges, wide open spaces and the lush rolling hills of one of Southern Nevada's treasures. Elev 2600 ft.

PAHRUMP-TRUE NEVADA
Located between Las Vegas & Death Valley, Pahrump is a destination unlike any other. Beautiful scenery, top notch golf courses, two wineries & perfectly-rated parks. Visit Pahrump to experience True Nevada.

Hours: 9 am to 5 pm. No CC.
(775)751-6853 Lat: 36.21058, Lon: -115.99591
400 N Hwy 160, Pahrump, NV 89060
aledbetter@pahrumpnv.org
www.visitpahrump.com
See ad page 747 (Spotlight Pahrump).

PANACA — D5 *Lincoln*

CATHEDRAL GORGE (State Pk) From Jct of US-93 & SR-319, N 1 mi on US-93 to park access rd (W side of US-93), W 1.5 mi (L). Entrance fee required. 2015 rates: $14 to $30. (775)728-4460

PIOCHE — D5 *Lincoln*

EAGLE VALLEY RESORT
Ratings: 5.5/7.5★/5.5 (Campground) From Jct Hwy 93 & 322: Go E 16 miles (R). Elev 5400 ft. **FAC:** Poor gravel/dirt rds. (55 spaces). Avail: 43 gravel, 4 pull-thrus (25 x 60), back-ins (25 x 45), 43 full hkups (30/50 amps), WiFi Hotspot, rentals, laundry, groc, LP bottles, fire rings, firewood. **REC.**

PIOCHE (CONT)

EAGLE VALLEY RESORT (CONT)
Pets OK. Partial handicap access. 2015 rates: $21. ATM.
(775)962-5293 Lat: 37.97930, Lon: -114.21068
12555 Sr 322, Pioche, NV 89043
eaglevalleyresort@gmail.com
eaglevalleynv.com
See ad this page, 737.

➔ ECHO CANYON (State Pk) From Jct of US-93 & SR-322, E 4 mi on SR-322 to SH-86, S 8 mi (L). 2015 rates: $14 to $30. (775)962-5103

➔ SPRING VALLEY (State Pk) From Jct of Hwy 93 & SR-322, E 18 mi on SR-322 (E). 2015 rates: $14 to $30. (775)962-5102

RENO — C1 *Washoe*

A SPOTLIGHT Introducing Reno/Sparks' colorful attractions appearing at the front of this state section.

RENO/SPARKS See also Verdi.

↑ BONANZA TERRACE RV PARK
Ratings: 6.5/8.5★/8 (RV Park) From Jct of I-80 & US-395 (Exit 15): Go 4 mi N on US 395 (Exit 72), then 1-1/4 mi SW on Bus 395, then 500 ft W on Hoge Rd, then 1/4 mi S on Stoltz Rd (L). Elev 4900 ft. **FAC:** Paved rds. (79 spaces). 39 Avail: 19 paved, 20 gravel, 3 pull-thrus (24 x 40), back-ins (24 x 45), 39 full hkups (30/50 amps), seasonal sites, cable, WiFi, laundry. Pet restrict(B/Q) $. Partial handicap access, no tents. Eco-friendly, 2015 rates: $34 to $38. Disc: AAA, military.
(775)329-9624 Lat: 39.57092, Lon: -119.83090
4800 Stoltz Rd, Reno, NV 89506
See ad this page, 737.

↑ BORDERTOWN CASINO & RV RESORT
Ratings: 9/8.5★/9.5 (RV Park) From Jct of US-395 & Exit 83: Go 1/4 mi NW on Frontage Rd (L). Elev 5000 ft. **FAC:** Paved rds. 50 paved, patios, 48 pull-thrus (24 x 70), back-ins (23 x 50), 50 full hkups (30/50 amps), cable, WiFi, dump, laundry, groc, LP gas, restaurant. **REC.** Pets OK. Partial handicap access, no tents. Big rig sites, 28 day max stay, eco-friendly, 2015 rates: $30.11 to $37.87. Disc: AAA, military.
(800)218-9339 Lat: 39.66960, Lon: -119.99990
19575 US-395, Reno, NV 89508
info@bordertowncasinorv.com
www.bordertowncasinorv.com
See ad pages 750 (Spotlight Reno/Sparks), 737.

← KEYSTONE RV PARK
Ratings: 7.5/8.5/8 (RV Park) From Jct of I-80 & Keystone Ave (Exit 12): Go 1/4 mi S on Keystone Ave, then 500 ft W on to 4th St (R). Elev 4500 ft. **FAC:** Paved rds. (102 spaces). Avail: 70 paved, back-ins (23 x 40), 70 full hkups (30/50 amps), seasonal sites, cable, WiFi, rentals, dump, laundry. Pets OK. No tents. RV age restrict, eco-friendly, 2015 rates: $35 to $39. Disc: AAA.
(800)686-8559 Lat: 39.5265724, Lon: -119.8309026
1455 W 4th St., Reno, NV 89503
info@keystonervpark.com
www.keystonervpark.com
See ad pages 750 (Spotlight Reno/Sparks), 737.

➔ RV PARK AT GRAND SIERRA RESORT Ratings: 8.5/7.5/5.5 (RV Park) 2015 rates: $35 to $50. (775)789-2147 2500 E 2nd St., Reno, NV 89595

↑ SHAMROCK RV PARK
Ratings: 9.5/10★/9.5 (RV Park) From Jct of I-80 & US-395 (Exit 15): Go 3 mi N on US-395 (Exit 71), then 1 mi W on Parr Blvd (L). Elev 4900 ft. **FAC:** Paved rds. (121 spaces). Avail: 60 paved, patios, 50 pull-thrus (28 x 56), back-ins (28 x 40), 60 full hkups (30/50 amps), seasonal sites, cable, WiFi, dump, laundry, LP gas. **REC:** heated pool. Pets OK. Partial handicap access, no tents. Eco-friendly, 2015 rates: $33 to $37. Disc: AAA.
(775)329-5222 Lat: 39.53842, Lon: -119.82376
260 Parr Blvd, Reno, NV 89512
shamrockrvreno@yahoo.com
www.shamrockrv.com
See ad this page.

↓ SILVER SAGE RV PARK
Ratings: 7.5/9★/7 (RV Park) From Jct of US-395, I-80(Exit 64) Moana Lane: Go W on Moana Lane 1/2 mi to S Virginia St, then N 1/4 mi on S Virginia St (R). Elev 4458 ft.

RENO'S MOST CONVENIENT RV PARK
Reno's most deluxe and convenient RV Park with full hookups. Located within minutes of shopping, malls, restaurants, and casinos. Security gates and video cameras, cable, and Free Wi-Fi.

FAC: Paved rds. (43 spaces). Avail: 30 paved, patios, back-ins (23 x 50), 30 full hkups (30/50 amps), seasonal sites, cable, WiFi, laundry, controlled access. **REC.** Pets OK. Partial handicap access, no tents. Eco-friendly, 2015 rates: $36.75 to $41.15. Disc: AAA, military.
AAA Approved
(888)823-2002 Lat: 39.47937, Lon: -119.78943
2760 S. Virginia St., Reno, NV 89502
info@silversagervpark.com
www.silversagervpark.com
See ad pages 748 (Spotlight Reno/Sparks), 737.

Things to See and Do

↑ BORDERTOWN CASINO Live sports book, and gaming. Restaurant with food and drink specials. Open 24 hrs. Elev 5000 ft. partial handicap access. RV accessible. Restrooms, food. Hours: 24 hrs. ATM.
(800)443-4383 Lat: 39.66960, Lon: -119.99990
19575 US-395, Reno, NV 89508
bordertowncasinorv.com
See ad page 750 (Spotlight Reno/Sparks).

SEARCHLIGHT — F5 *Clark*

← COTTONWOOD COVE RESORT
Ratings: 6.5/8.5★/7 (RV Park) From Jct of US-95 & SR 164 (Cottonwood Cove Rd) in Searchlight: Go E 14 mi on Cottonwood Cove Rd (E).

FUN AT THE LAKE
Located on the shores of Lake Mohave, enjoy swimming, fishing & boating. Amenities include cable TV, laundry, restroom shower facility, community center, restaurant & store. Located halfway between Laughlin and Las Vegas.

FAC: Dirt rds. 72 dirt, patios, 29 pull-thrus (18 x 80), back-ins (20 x 32), some side by side hkups, 72 full hkups (30/50 amps), rentals, dump, laundry, groc, LP gas, firewood, restaurant. **REC:** Lake Mohave: swim, fishing, marina, shuffleboard, rec open to public. Pet restrict(Q). Partial handicap access, no tents. Eco-friendly, 2015 rates: $32 to $36. ATM.
(702)297-1464 Lat: 35.49122, Lon: -114.68630
10000 Cottonwood Cove Rd, Searchlight, NV 89046
ccarter@foreverresorts.com
www.cottonwoodcoveresort.com
See ad pages 743 (Spotlight Las Vegas), 737.

Nobody takes to the road like we do. In many listings we tell you the surface type and condition of interior campground roads.

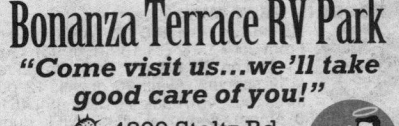

SILVER SPRINGS — C1 *Lyon*

FORT CHURCHILL STATE HISTORIC PARK (State Pk) From town, S 8 mi on Hwy 95A to Fort Churchill Rd, W 1 mi (L). Pit toilets. 2015 rates: $14 to $30. (775)577-2345

LAHONTAN SRA (State Pk) From town, W 18 mi on US-50 (L). Entrance fee required. 2015 rates: $14 to $30. (775)867-3500

SMITH VALLEY — C1 *Lyon*

WALKER RIVER RESORT RV PARK
Ratings: 8.5/9★/9 (Campground) From Jct of Hwy 395 & Hwy 208: Go 22-1/2 E on Hwy 208, then 2-1/2 mi N on Hudson Way (R). Elev 4734 ft. **FAC:** Dirt rds. (128 spaces). Avail: 118 dirt, 108 pull-thrus (24 x 42), back-ins (26 x 50), mostly side by side hkups, 82 full hkups, 36 W, 36 E (30/50 amps), seasonal sites, WiFi, tent sites, rentals, dump, laundry, groc, LP gas, firewood. **REC:** heated pool, whirlpool, Walker River: swim, fishing, golf. Pets OK. Eco-friendly, 2015 rates: $36 to $46. Disc: AAA. Apr 1 to Oct 31. ATM, no CC.
AAA Approved
(800)446-2573 Lat: 38.82501, Lon: -119.27477
700 Hudson Way, Smith Valley, NV 89430
resortservices@aol.com
www.wrresort.com

SPARKS — C1 *Washoe*

A SPOTLIGHT Introducing Reno/Spark's colorful attractions appearing at the front of this state section.

RIVER'S EDGE RV PARK
Ratings: 9/8.5/7 (RV Park) From Jct I-80 & Rock Blvd (Exit 17): Go S 3/4 on Rock Blvd (R). Elev 4400 ft. **FAC:** Paved rds. (164 spaces). Avail: 53 paved, 37 pull-thrus (23 x 50), back-ins (23 x 30), 53 full hkups (30/50 amps), seasonal sites, cable, WiFi, rentals, dump, laundry. **REC:** heated pool, Truckee River: swim, fishing, rec open to public. Pet restrict(B/Q). 2015 rates: $33.71 to $35.75. Disc: AAA, military.
(775)358-8533 Lat: 39.52128, Lon: -119.76516
1405 S Rock Blvd, Sparks, NV 89431
riversedge775@yahoo.com
www.riversedgervparksparks.com
See ad this page, 737.

SPARKS MARINA RV PARK
Ratings: 10/10★/10 (RV Park) From Jct of I-80 & Exit 20 (Sparks Blvd): Go 1/4 min N on Sparks Blvd, then 1/2 mi W on E Lincoln Way (R). Elev 4500 ft. **FAC:** Paved rds. 204 paved, 121 pull-thrus (30 x 65), back-ins (30 x 39), 204 full hkups (30/50 amps), cable, WiFi, laundry, groc, LP gas. **REC:** heated pool, whirlpool. Pet restrict(B/Q). Partial handicap access, no tents. Big rig sites, 28 day max stay, eco-friendly, 2015 rates: $23 to $49. Disc: AAA.
AAA Approved
(775)851-8888 Lat: 39.5375145, Lon: -119.7243844
1200 E Lincoln Way, Sparks, NV 89434
inquirysmrvp@sbcglobal.net
www.sparksmarinarvpark.com
See ad opposite page, 737.

VICTORIAN RV PARK
Ratings: 10/10★/9 (RV Park) From Jct of Hwy 395 & I-80 (Exit 19): Go 1/4 mi N on McCarren Blvd, then 1/4 mi W on Nichols Blvd (L). Elev 4600 ft.

VISIT TOP RATED VICTORIAN RV PARK
The Victorian RV Park offers our guests the finest RV experience when visiting Northern Nevada. We are centrally located near gaming and all of the great events in Reno/Sparks. Book your next stay with us online today!

FAC: Paved rds. (85 spaces). Avail: 45 paved, patios, 21 pull-thrus (24 x 60), back-ins (25 x 30), 45 full hkups (30/50 amps), seasonal sites, cable, WiFi, dump, laundry, groc. **REC:** heated pool, whirlpool. Pets OK. Partial handicap access, no tents. Eco-friendly, 2015 rates: $34 to $42. Disc: AAA, military.
(800)955-6405 Lat: 39.5354284, Lon: -119.7407624
205 Nichols Blvd, Sparks, NV 89431
info@victorianrvpark.com
www.victorianrvpark.com
See ad pages 749 (Spotlight Reno/Sparks), 737, 735 (NV Map).

STATELINE — C1 *Douglas*

LAKE TAHOE BASIN MGMT. UNIT USFS (NEVADA BEACH CAMPGROUND) (Natl Pk) From town: Go 2 mi N on US-50, then 1/2 mi W on Elks Point Rd. 2015 rates: $28 to $32. May 17 to Oct 13. (775)588-5562

TOPAZ LAKE — C1 *Douglas*

Things to See and Do

TOPAZ LODGE CASINO Gaming and Restaurant Dining. Elev 4900 ft. partial handicap access. RV accessible. Restrooms, food. Hours: 24 hrs. ATM.
(775)266-3338 Lat: 38.6948184, Lon: -119.5478248
1979 US Hwy 395 South, Gardnerville, NV 89410
www.topazlodge.com
See ad page 753.

VERDI — C1 *Washoe*

GOLD RANCH CASINO & RV RESORT
Ratings: 10/9.5★/9.5 (RV Park) From Jct of I-80 & NV 40 (Gold Ranch Rd): Go 500 ft S on Gold Ranch Rd (R). Elev 5000 ft. **FAC:** Paved rds. (105 spaces). Avail: 70 paved, 64 pull-thrus (30 x 75), back-ins (30 x 60), 70 full hkups (30/50 amps), seasonal sites, cable, WiFi, laundry, groc, LP gas, restaurant. **REC:** heated pool, whirlpool. Pet restrict(Q). Partial handicap access, no tents. Big rig sites, 2015 rates: $29 to $38. Disc: AAA, military. ATM.
AAA Approved
(877)792-6789 Lat: 39.50182, Lon: -120.00085
320 Gold Ranch Road, Verdi, NV 89439
goldranch@goldranchrvcasino.com
www.goldranchrvcasino.com
See ad opposite page, 737.

RENO/BOOMTOWN KOA **Ratings: 9/8/8** (RV Park) 2015 rates: $35 to $65. (888)562-5698 i-80 W At Garson Rd, Verdi, NV 89439

Things to See and Do

GOLD RANCH CASINO/RV RESORT Casino, Restaurants and Gaming. Elev 5000 ft. partial handicap access. RV accessible. Restrooms, food. Hours: 24 hrs. ATM.
(775)345-6789 Lat: 39.50192, Lon: -120.00108
P. O. Box 160, Verdi, NV 89439
goldranch@goldranchrvcasino.com
www.goldranchrvcasino.com
See ad opposite page.

WELLS — A4 *Elko*

ANGEL LAKE RV PARK
Ratings: 7/10★/7.5 (Campground) From Jct I-80 & Exit 351 (South Humboldt Ave): Go 50 ft S on South Humboldt Ave (L) ; From Jct I-80 & US Hwy 93: I-80 W to exit 351 (South Humbolt Ave): Go 50 ft S on South Humbolt Ave (L). Elev 5600 ft. **FAC:** Gravel rds. (48 spaces). Avail: 18 gravel, 18 pull-thrus (24 x 70), 18 full hkups (30/50 amps), seasonal sites, WiFi, tent sites, dump, laundry. Pets OK. Partial handicap access. Big rig sites, 28 day max stay, eco-friendly, 2015 rates: $25 to $38. Disc: AAA, military.
(775)752-2745 Lat: 41.1029657, Lon: -114.9722416
124 South Humbodlt, Wells, NV 89835
angellakervwellsnv@gmail.com
www.angellakerv.com
See ad this page, 737.

CROSSROADS RV PARK **Ratings: 2.5/7.5★/4** (Membership Pk) 2015 rates: $27.75. (702)379-8388 734 6th St., Wells, NV 89835

MOUNTAIN SHADOWS RV PARK
Ratings: 6/9★/8 (Campground) From Jct of I-80 & Humboldt Ave (exit 351): Go 1/4 mi N on Humboldt Ave (L). Elev 5600 ft. **FAC:** Gravel rds. (38 spaces). Avail: 31 gravel, 26 pull-thrus (25 x 53), back-ins (25 x 34), 31 full hkups (30/50 amps), seasonal sites, cable, WiFi, tent sites, dump, laundry. Pets OK. Partial handicap access. 2015 rates: $30. Disc: military.
AAA Approved
(775)752-3525 Lat: 41.1078066, Lon: -114.9743594
807 Humboldt Ave, Wells, NV 89835
mtnshadowsrvpark@frontier.com
mtnshadowsrvpark.com
See ad this page, 737.

WEST WENDOVER — B5 *Elko*

WENDOVER NEVADA/KOA **Ratings: 7.5/8/7** (Campground) 2015 rates: $38 to $48. (775)664-3221 651 North Camper Dr., West Wendover, NV 89883

WINNEMUCCA — B2 *Humboldt*

I-80 WINNEMUCCA KOA Ratings: 9.5/9.5★/9.5 (RV Park) From Jct of I-80 & Exit 180 (East Winnemucca Blvd): Go 3/4 mi E on East Winnemucca Blvd (R). Elev 4295 ft. **FAC:** Paved rds. (149 spaces). Avail: 96 gravel, 82 pull-thrus (27 x 63), back-ins (25 x 40), 96 full hkups (30/50 amps), seasonal sites, cable, WiFi, tent sites, rentals, dump, laundry, groc, LP gas. **REC:** heated pool, shuffleboard, playground. Pets OK $. Partial handicap access. Big rig sites, eco-friendly, 2015 rates: $19 to $37.50. ATM.
(800)562-7554 Lat: 40.9808482, Lon: -117.7069327
5575 E Winnemucca Blvd, Winnemucca, NV 89445
winnemucca@koa.com
www.koa.com

WINNEMUCCA (CONT)

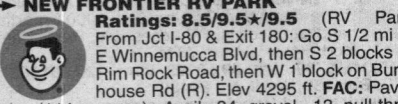

➔ NEW FRONTIER RV PARK
Ratings: 8.5/9.5★/9.5 (RV Park) From Jct I-80 & Exit 180: Go S 1/2 mi on E Winnemucca Blvd, then S 2 blocks on Rim Rock Road, then W 1 block on Bunkhouse Rd (R). Elev 4295 ft. **FAC:** Paved rds. (114 spaces). Avail: 84 gravel, 13 pull-thrus (30 x 100), back-ins (33 x 70), 84 full hkups (30/50 amps), seasonal sites, cable, WiFi, rentals, dump, laundry, groc, restaurant. **REC.** Pets OK. Partial handicap access. Big rig sites, eco-friendly, 2015 rates: $32 to $34. Disc: AAA, military.
(775)621-5277 Lat: 40.982068, Lon: -117.699536
4360 Rim Rock Rd, Winnemucca, NV 89445
contact@newfrontierrvpark.com
www.newfrontierrvpark.com
See ad pages 759, 737.

➔ WINNEMUCCA RV PARK
Ratings: 9/8★/8.5 (RV Park) E-Bnd: From Jct I-80 & Exit 178: Go S 500 ft to E Winnemucca Blvd, then go 1 mi on E Winnemucca Blvd (L).W-Bnd: From Jct I-80 & Exit 178: Go S on E Second St to E Winnemucca Blvd, then go 1 mi on E Winnemucca Blvd (L). Elev 4200 ft. **FAC:** Gravel rds. (100 spaces). Avail: 50 gravel, 50 pull-thrus (22 x 70), mostly side by side hkups, 50 full hkups (30/50 amps), seasonal sites, cable, WiFi, dump, laundry, groc, LP gas. **REC:** heated pool, playground. Pets OK. No tents. Eco-friendly, 2015 rates: $36. Disc: AAA, military.
(775)623-4458 Lat: 40.978864, Lon: -117.711829
5255 E Winnemucca Blvd, Winnemucca, NV 89445
winnemuccarvpark@gmail.com
www.winnemuccarvpark.biz
See ad pages 759, 737.

Our travel services section will help you find services that you'll find handy in your travels.

YERINGTON — C1 *Lyon*

➘ GREENFIELD RV PARK & MHP **Ratings: 5/4.5/4.5** (RV Area in MHP) 2015 rates: $30 to $35. (775)463-4912 500 W Goldfield Ave, Yerington, NV 89447

➘ WEED HEIGHTS RV PARK Ratings: 6.5/8.5★/6 (Campground) From Jct of NV 339 & SR-95A: Go 1/4 mi N on US-95A, then SW 2 mi on Birch Dr (unmarked, note sign promoting Weed Heights), then 150 ft NW on Austin St (R). Elev 4600 ft. **FAC:** Paved/gravel rds. (96 spaces). Avail: 64 gravel, 44 pull-thrus (20 x 65), back-ins (20 x 40), 54 full hkups, 10 W, 10 E (30 amps), seasonal sites, WiFi $, tent sites, dump, laundry. **REC:** shuffleboard. Pets OK. 2015 rates: $25 to $30. Disc: AAA, military. No CC.
AAA Approved
(775)463-4634 Lat: 38.98722, Lon: -119.20806
2 Austin St., Yerington, NV 89447
weedheights.rvpark@live.com
www.weedheights.com

Tell your RV Campground that you found them in this Guide.

ZEPHYR COVE — C1 *Douglas*

➔ ZEPHYR COVE RESORT RV PARK & CAMPGROUND **Ratings: 8.5/6/7.5** (Campground) 2015 rates: $62 to $83. (775)589-4907 760 Hwy 50, Zephyr Cove, NV 89448

Take an RV Trip of a Lifetime!

Check out our itineraries for the Food Lover, Living History, Picture Perfect and On the Wild Side! These once-in-a-lifetime journeys are required fun for RVers of all ages.

Browse the RV Trips of a Lifetime, with routes and handy maps, in the front of this Guide.

Getty Images/iStockphoto

WELCOME TO
New Hampshire

DATE OF STATEHOOD	WIDTH: 68 MILES (110 KM)	PROPORTION OF UNITED STATES
JUNE 21, 1788	LENGTH: 190 MILES (305 KM)	0.25% OF 3,794,100 SQ MI

No state takes its motto more seriously than New Hampshire. John Stark, the hero of the Battle of Bennington in the American Revolution, uttered the famous words, "Live free or die," which became the state motto. The state even went to the Supreme Court to win the right to prosecute anyone who tried to cover up the motto on license plates (the state lost).

Learn

New Hampshire established an independent government six months before the Continental Congress got around to issuing the Declaration of Independence. The state has preserved the homesteads of many of its prominent natives, including the two-room log cabin in Franklin of statesman Daniel Webster. You can see the farm of poet Robert Frost in Derry; the home, studios and gardens of sculptor Augustus Saint-Gaudens in Cornish; and the boyhood home of Franklin Pierce in Hillsborough. Pierce rose to become 14th president of the United States and is still the only chief executive from one of the country's "small" states.

You can find New Hampshire history in unexpected places. In the tiny village of Warren, visitors will discover a Redstone intermediate range ballistic missile, a type of rocket that's in the same class as the vehicle that hurtled Granite Stater Alan Shepard into space in 1961. On Market Street in Portsmouth, the USS Albacore, the first of America's modern submarines when it was built at the Portsmouth Naval Yard and commissioned in 1953, sits ready for boarding as a National Historic Landmark.

Play

People have been hankering to get to the top of Mount Washington, New England's tallest peak, for as long as there has been a New Hampshire. The nation's first hiking trail was hacked to the peak's 6,288-foot summit in 1819. Later came a coach road in 1861, and then the world's first mountain railroad, the Mount Washington Cog Railway, in 1869. All are used today. Despite its beautiful appearance, Mount Washington isn't always nice—wind gusts of 231 miles per hour have been recorded.

The Presidential Range in the White Mountains, of which Mount Washington is the star, is one of the premier hiking destinations in the country. New Hampshire hosts 48 peaks higher than 4,000 feet, which makes it a mecca for climbers. The mountains attract so many winter enthusiasts to the snowboarding parks, cross-country trails and 20 resorts that skiing is the official state sport.

New Hampshire possesses just a sliver of Atlantic Ocean frontage, only 13 miles and most of it rocky. There is enough sand to support five oceanside

Top 3 Tourism Attractions:
1) Mount Washington Auto Road
2) Robert Frost Farm
3) Hampton Beach

Nickname: Granite State

State Flower: Purple Lilac

State Bird: Purple Finch

People: Alan B. Shepard Jr., first American in space; Earl Silas Tupper, founder of Tupperware

Major Cities: Manchester, Nashua, Concord (capital), Derry, Rochester

Topography: Low rolling coast with countless hills and mountains rising out of a central plateau

Climate: Humid continental climate with warm humid summers and cold, wet winters

Karen Bobotas

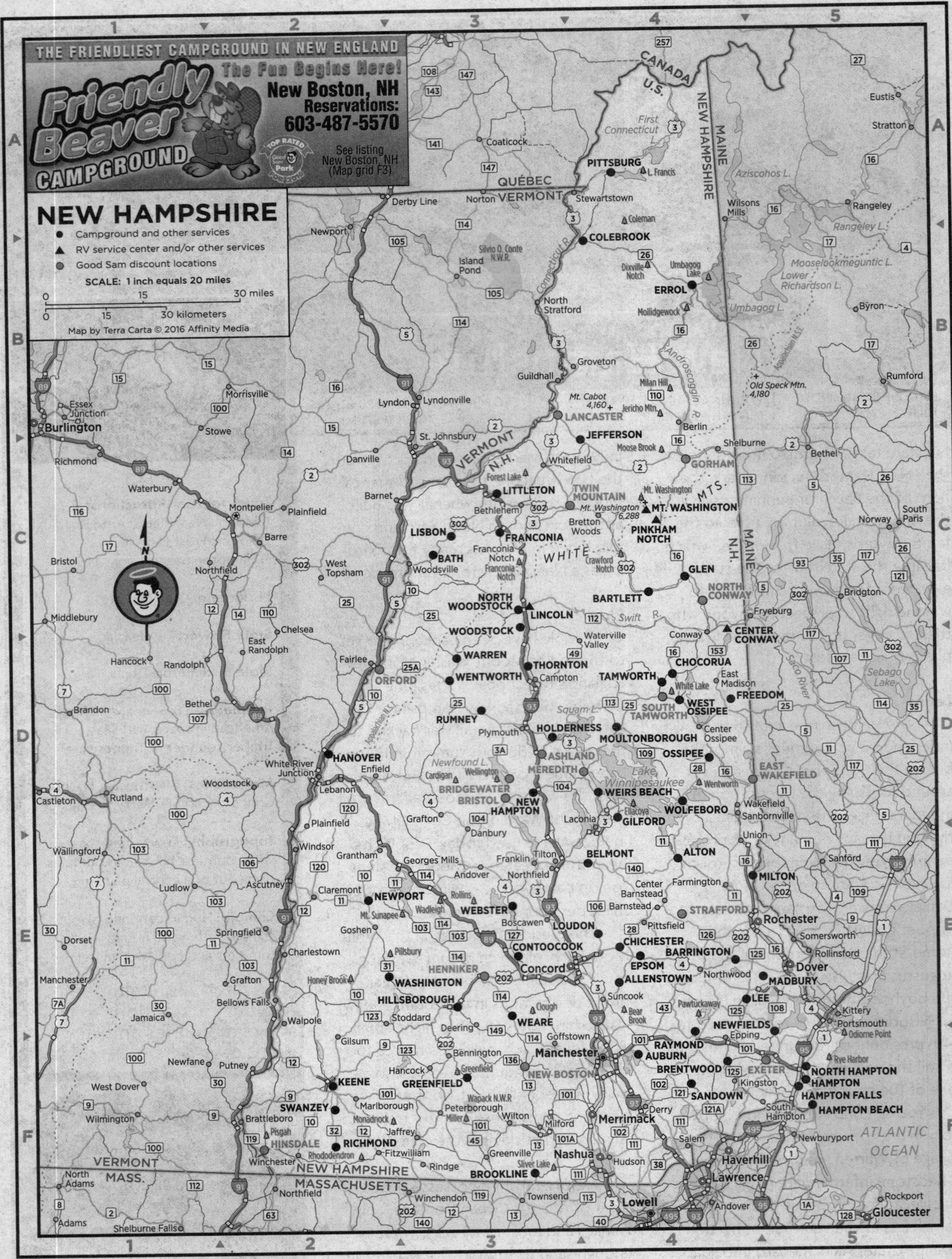
THE FRIENDLIEST CAMPGROUND IN NEW ENGLAND
Friendly Beaver CAMPGROUND
The Fun Begins Here!
New Boston, NH
Reservations:
603-487-5570
See listing New Boston, NH (Map grid F3)
NEW HAMPSHIRE
Campground and other services
RV service center and/or other services
Good Sam discount locations
SCALE: 1 inch equals 20 miles
0 15 30 miles
0 15 30 kilometers
Map by Terra Carta © 2016 Affinity Media
CANADA
U.S.
QUÉBEC
VERMONT
NEW HAMPSHIRE
MAINE
MASSACHUSETTS
ATLANTIC OCEAN
WHITE MTS.
PITTSBURG
COLEBROOK
ERROL
LANCASTER
JEFFERSON
GORHAM
LITTLETON
TWIN MOUNTAIN
MT. WASHINGTON
PINKHAM NOTCH
LISBON
FRANCONIA
BATH
GLEN
NORTH CONWAY
BARTLETT
NORTH WOODSTOCK
LINCOLN
WOODSTOCK
CENTER CONWAY
WARREN
THORNTON
ORFORD
WENTWORTH
CHOCORUA
TAMWORTH
FREEDOM
SOUTH TAMWORTH
WEST OSSIPEE
RUMNEY
HOLDERNESS
MOULTONBOROUGH
HANOVER
ASHLAND
OSSIPEE
MEREDITH
EAST WAKEFIELD
BRIDGEWATER
BRISTOL
NEW HAMPTON
WEIRS BEACH
WOLFEBORO
GILFORD
BELMONT
ALTON
MILTON
NEWPORT
WEBSTER
STRAFFORD
LOUDON
CHICHESTER
CONTOOCOOK
BARRINGTON
HENNIKER
EPSOM
ALLENSTOWN
MADBURY
WASHINGTON
HILLSBOROUGH
LEE
WEARE
NEWFIELDS
RAYMOND
AUBURN
NORTH HAMPTON
BRENTWOOD
EXETER
HAMPTON
KEENE
GREENFIELD
NEW BOSTON
HAMPTON FALLS
SANDOWN
SWANZEY
HAMPTON BEACH
RICHMOND
HINSDALE
BROOKLINE
Concord
Manchester
Nashua
Merrimack
Rochester
Dover
Portsmouth
Haverhill
Lawrence
Lowell
Burlington
Montpelier

NH

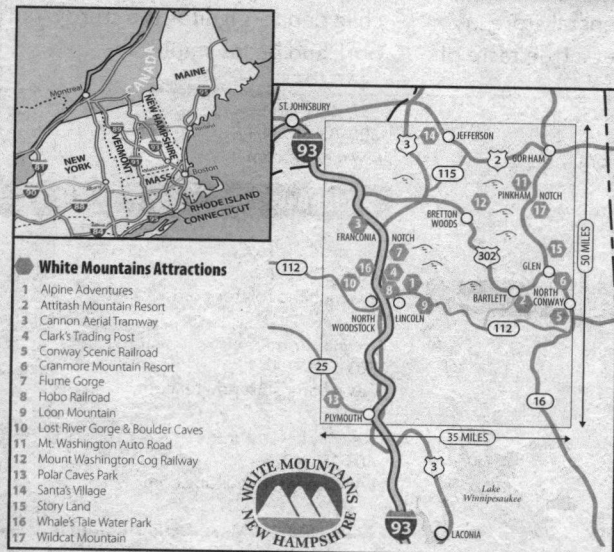

 See map page 762

Mount Major is a scenic, rocky summit that is a popular hiking destination.
NH Division of Travel and Tourism

state parks, however, with Hampton Beach offering a mile-long boardwalk. Note to dog owners—dogs are not permitted in any of the Seacoast state parks.

Glaciers were busy in New Hampshire in the last ice age, carving the 800-foot Flume Gorge in Franconia Notch State Park and gouging more than 1,300 lakes in the state. The largest, Lake Winnipesaukee, covers 69 square miles and boasts more than 250 islands waiting for exploration by canoe or kayak. On its shores, the town of Wolfeboro calls itself the oldest summer resort in America because the colonial governor built a mansion house in town in the mid-1700s. Today, it lives up to that tradition, making visitors feel at home amid stunning New England scenery.

Experience

There is no surer sign of spring than New Hampshire Maple Weekend in March, when 60 sugar houses open their doors to demonstrate the ancient craft of maple sugaring. You will find horse-drawn carriage tours of the orchards and sap-collecting operations with plenty of syrupy samples waiting for visitors at the end.

There is no crazier time to visit New Hampshire than on the eve of the presidential primary every fourth year.

There is no crazier time to visit New Hampshire than on the eve of the presidential primary every fourth year. Aspiring candidates blanket the state in anticipation of the election, and you just might run into a future president in any barbershop or general store in the Granite State. To get a true taste of the political blitzkrieg, visit the Balsams Grand Resort Hotel in Dixville Notch, where midnight voting yields the first returns of the election.

In summer, towns across the state revive the tradition of Old Home Week, a celebration of home and hearth started in 1899 by New Hampshire Governor Frank W. Rollins. By 1907, the concept of honoring one's hometown with reunions and public gatherings had spread to all of the New England states and as far away as Australia. Today, the concept of "homecoming" is part of our vocabulary.

New Hampshire is the second most forested state in America. October is given over to the leaf-peepers, as the birches and maples and oaks show off their finest autumn wear. Fall foliage tours duck in and out of quaint New England villages with whitewashed frame buildings, quiet farms, covered bridges and beautiful mountain byways.

Taste

Any cuisine tour of New Hampshire will yield plenty of apple- and maple-based dishes. You'll find lots of fresh seafood as well, but for a classic taste of yore, you'll need to track down New Hampshire Yankee bean pot chili. The dish is based on a hunk of salt pork cooked with a batch of yellow-eye beans. Tossing in dried whole ancho chile peppers ignites the sturdy Yankee pork and beans staple.

TRAVEL & TOURISM

New Hampshire Dept. of Resources and Economic Development
603-271-2665
www.visitnh.gov

Androscoggin Valley Chamber of Commerce
800-992-7480, 603-752-6060
www.androscogginvalleychamber.com

Hampton Beach
603-643-3115
www.hamptonbeach.org

Hanover Area Chamber of Commerce
603-926-8717
www.hanoverchamber.org

North Country Chamber of Commerce
603-237-8939, 800-698-8939
www.northcountrychamber.org

White Mountains Attractions
800-FIND MTS, 603-745-8720
www.visitwhitemountains.com

OUTDOOR RECREATION

New Hampshire Fish & Game
603-271-3511
www.wildlife.state.nh.us

New Hampshire Snowmobile Assn.
603-273-0220
www.nhsa.com

New Hampshire State Parks
603-271-3556
www.nhstateparks.org

Ski New Hampshire
800-88-SKI-NH
www.skinh.com

SHOPPING

Granite State Candies
888-225-2591
www.nhchocolates.com

Hampshire Pewter
603-569-4944
www.hampshirepewter.com

Keepsake Quilting
603-253-4026
www.keepsakequilting.com

New Hampshire Antique Dealers Assn.
www.nhada.org

NH

Featured Good Sam Parks

NEW HAMPSHIRE

Good Sam Park

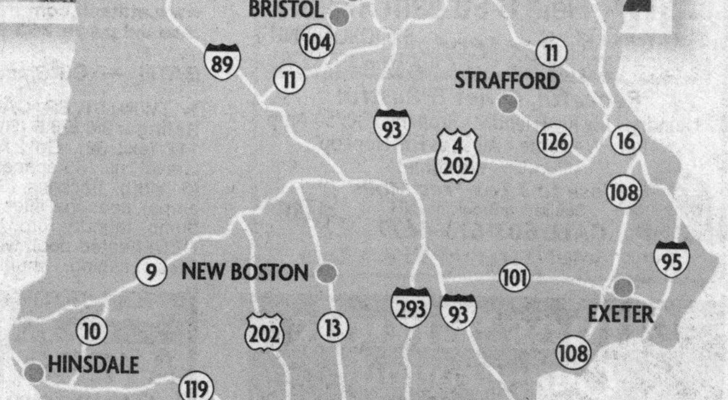

When you stay with Good Sam, you can expect the highest degree of cleanliness and friendliness, and better yet, you get 10% off campground fees.

If you're not already a Good Sam member you can purchase your membership at one of these locations:

ASHLAND
Ames Brook Campground
(603)968-7998

BRIDGEWATER
Newfound RV Park
(603)744-3344

BRISTOL
Davidson's Countryside Campground
(603)744-2403

EXETER
Exeter Elms Family Campground
(603)778-7631

GORHAM
Timberland Campground
(603)466-3872

HINSDALE
Hinsdale Campground At Thicket Hill Village
(603)336-8906

LANCASTER
Mountain Lake Camping Resort
(603)788-4509

MEREDITH
Twin Tamarack Family Camping & RV Resort
(603)279-4387

NEW BOSTON
Friendly Beaver Campground
(603)487-5570

SOUTH TAMWORTH
Riverbend Campground
(603)323-9133

STRAFFORD
Crown Point Campground
(603)332-0405

For more Good Sam Parks go to listing pages

New Hampshire

CONSULTANTS

Jeff & Peggy Harmann

ALLENSTOWN — E4 *Merrimack*

BEAR BROOK SP (State Pk) From jct US 3 & Hwy 28: Go 3 mi NE on Hwy 28, then follow signs. 2015 rates: $25. May 24 to Oct 21. (603)485-9665

ALTON — E4 *Belknap*

TURTLE KRAAL RV PARK **Ratings: 8/9★/8.5** (RV Park) 2015 rates: $43. May 1 to Nov 1. (603)855-2377 14 Fox Trot Loop, Alton, NH 03809

ASHLAND — D3 *Belknap, Grafton*

AMES BROOK CAMPGROUND
Ratings: 9/10★/9.5 (Campground) From Jct of I-93 & Exit 24 (Rtes 3 & 25), Go 0.75 mi S on Rte 3 & 25 to Rte 132, then 0.25 mi S to Winona Rd, then 0.5 mi S (R) (Avoid S end of Winona Rd, low bridge). **FAC:** Gravel rds. (85 spaces). Avail: 47 gravel, 10 pull-thrus (37 x 62), back-ins (50 x 64), 44 full hkups, 3 W, 3 E (30/50 amps), seasonal sites, cable, WiFi, tent sites, dump, laundry, groc, LP gas, fire rings, firewood. **REC:** pool, Ames Brook: fishing, playground. Pet restrict(Q). Big rig sites, eco-friendly, 2015 rates: $37 to $43. Disc: AAA, military. May 13 to Oct 15.
AAA Approved
(603)968-7998 Lat: 43.68811, Lon: -71.62290
104 Winona Rd, Ashland, NH 03217
info@amesbrook.com
www.amesbrook.com
See ad this page, 765.

AUBURN — F4 *Rockingham*

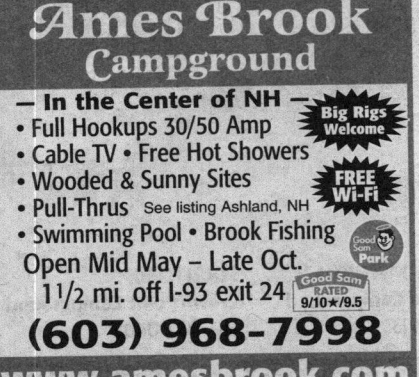

CALEF LAKE CAMPING AREA Ratings: 5/8★/8 (Campground) From jct Hwy 101 & Hwy 121, Go 4 mi SE on Hwy 121. **FAC:** Gravel rds. (153 spaces). Avail: 53 gravel, no slide-outs, back-ins (28 x 40), 20 full hkups, 33 W, 33 E (30 amps), seasonal sites, WiFi Hotspot, tent sites, dump, laundry, LP gas. **REC:** Calef Lake: swim, playground. Pets OK. 2015 rates: $32 to $37.
AAA Approved
(603)483-8282 Lat: 42.97333, Lon: -71.31726
593 Chester Rd (Hwy 121), Auburn, NH 03032
info@caleflakecampingarea.com
www.caleflakecampingarea.com

BARRINGTON — E4 *Strafford*

AYERS LAKE FARM CAMPGROUND & COTTAGES
Ratings: 6.5/8.5★/9 (Campground) From Jct Hwy 16 (Spaulding Tpk) (Exit 13) & US 202, Go 5 mi SW on US 202 (Washington St.) (R). **FAC:** Gravel rds. (50 spaces). Avail: 20 dirt, 5 pull-thrus (22 x 40), back-ins (22 x 40), some side by side hkups, 15 full hkups, 5 W, 5 E (30/50 amps), seasonal sites, cable, WiFi Hotspot, tent sites, rentals, dump, laundry, fire rings, firewood, controlled access. **REC:** Ayers Lake: swim, fishing. Pet restrict(B/Q). Eco-friendly, 2015 rates: $50 to $60. Disc: AAA. May 20 to Oct 12. No CC.
AAA Approved
(603)335-1110 Lat: 43.24852, Lon: -71.04981
497 Washington St (US 202), Barrington, NH 03825-6116
http://www.ayerslakecampground.com/
See ad this page.

BARRINGTON SHORES CAMPGROUND Ratings: 8.5/8.5★/8 (Campground) From Jct of Rtes 4 & 125 (Lee traffic circle), Go 3 mi N on Rte 125 to Beauty Hill Rd, then 1 mi W to Hall Rd, then 1 mi S (R). GPS address use: 70 Hall Rd, Barrington, NH. **FAC:** Gravel rds. (142 spaces). 62 Avail: 30 gravel, 32 dirt, 3 pull-thrus (30 x 60), back-ins (32 x 50), 43 full hkups, 19 W, 19 E (30/50 amps), seasonal sites, WiFi, tent sites, rentals, dump, mobile sewer, laundry, groc, LP gas, fire rings, firewood, controlled access. **REC:** Swains Lake: swim, fishing, playground. Pets OK. Partial handicap access. Eco-friendly, 2015 rates: $44 to $54. May 11 to Sep 16.
AAA Approved
(603)664-9333 Lat: 43.18462, Lon: -71.02653
7 Barrington Shores Drive, Barrington, NH 03825
bashores@metrocast.net
www.barringtonshores.com

BARTLETT — C4 *Carroll*

CRAWFORD NOTCH SP (DRY RIVER CAMPGROUND) (State Pk) From town: Go 12 mi NW on US 302. 2015 rates: $25. Apr 27 to Dec 1. (603)374-2272

Things to See and Do

ATTITASH MOUNTAIN RESORT Nor'Easter Mtn Coaster, Alpine Slides, Horseback Riding, Mtn Biking, Aquaboggan Water Slides, Play Pool, Scenic Chair Ride, Climbing wall, Bungy Trampoline, Zip Tour. RV accessible. Restrooms, food. Hours: 10am to 6pm. Adult fee: $49. ATM.
(800)223-7669 Lat: 44.0781180, Lon: -71.283881
775 Rt 302, Bartlett, NH 03812
info@attitash.com
www.attitash.com
See ad page 763 (Welcome Section).

BATH — C3 *Grafton*

TWIN RIVER CAMPGROUND & COTTAGES Ratings: 8/6.5/8.5 (RV Park) From Jct of I 93 & Rte 112 (exit 32), Go 21 mi W on Rte 112. (L). **FAC:** Gravel rds. (55 spaces). Avail: 20 grass, 1 pull-thrus (31 x 60), back-ins (31 x 60), 20 full hkups (30/50 amps), seasonal sites, cable, WiFi, tent sites, rentals, dump, laundry, groc, LP gas, fire rings, firewood. **REC:** heated pool, wading pool, Wild Ammonoosuc River: fishing, shuffleboard, playground. Pet restrict(B/Q). Eco-friendly, 2015 rates: $34 to $42. Disc: AAA. May 15 to Oct 15. ATM.
AAA Approved
(603)747-3640 Lat: 44.15157, Lon: -71.97594
4 Twin River Lane, Bath, NH 03740
info@twinrivernh.com
www.twinrivernh.com

BELMONT — E4 *Belknap*

SILVER LAKE PARK CAMPGROUND & CABINS **Ratings: 6.5/8.5★/8.5** (Campground) 2015 rates: $35 to $45. May 15 to Oct 12. (603)524-6289 389 Jamestown Rd, Belmont, NH 03220

BRENTWOOD — F4 *Rockingham*

3 PONDS CAMPGROUND INC Ratings: 7/7.5/7.5 (Campground) From Jct of Rtes 101 & 125 (in Epping), Go 1.2 mi S on Rte 125 to North Rd, then 1 mi E (L). **FAC:** Gravel rds. (141 spaces). Avail: 29 grass, 7 pull-thrus (24 x 54), back-ins (24 x 54), 29 W, 29 E (30/50 amps), seasonal sites, WiFi Hotspot, tent sites, showers $, dump, laundry, firewood. **REC:** pond, swim, fishing, playground. Pet restrict(B/Q). 2015 rates: $38 to $40. Disc: AAA, military. May 15 to Oct 1.
AAA Approved
(603)679-5350 Lat: 43.01120, Lon: -71.05801
146 North Rd, Brentwood, NH 03833
info@3pondscampground.net
www.3pondscampground.net

BRIDGEWATER — D3 *Grafton*

NEWFOUND RV PARK
Ratings: 7.5/9.5★/10 (RV Park) From Jct of I-93 Exit 23 & Rte 104, Go 6 mi W on Rte 104 to Rte 3A, then 5 mi N (R). **FAC:** Paved/gravel rds. (45 spaces). Avail: 37 gravel, 32 pull-thrus (33 x 90), back-ins (33 x 62), 37 full hkups (30/50 amps), seasonal sites, cable, WiFi, tent sites, laundry, fire rings, firewood. **REC:** Newfound Brook: fishing, playground. Pet restrict(Q). Big rig sites, 2015 rates: $40 to $48. Disc: military. May 1 to Oct 31.
(603)744-3344 Lat: 43.65494, Lon: -71.73593
792 Mayhew Turnpike (Rte 3A), Bridgewater, NH 03222
newfoundrv@gmail.com
www.newfoundrvpark.com
See ad this page, 765.

BRISTOL — D3 *Grafton*

DAVIDSON'S COUNTRYSIDE CAMPGROUND
Ratings: 7.5/9★/9 (Campground) From Jct of I-93 & Rte 104 (exit 23), Go 2 mi W on Rte 104 to River Rd, then 1/2 mi N (R). **FAC:** Gravel rds. (110 spaces). 30 Avail: 14 gravel, 16 grass, 9 pull-thrus (24 x 50), back-ins (28 x 50), 6 full hkups, 24 W, 24 E (30/50 amps), seasonal sites, WiFi, tent sites, rentals, showers $, dump, groc, fire rings, firewood, controlled access. **REC:** pool, Pemigewasset River: swim, fishing, playground. Pets OK. Partial handicap access. Eco-friendly, 2015 rates: $34 to $38. Disc: military. May 22 to Oct 12.
(603)744-2403 Lat: 43.609857, Lon: -71.669594
100 Schofield Rd, Bristol, NH 03222
davidsons@metrocast.net
www.davidsonscamp.com
See ad pages 770, 765.

BROOKLINE — F3 *Hillsborough*

FIELD & STREAM RV PARK LLC
Ratings: 7.5/10★/9 (Campground) From Jct of US-3 (Everett Tpke) & Rte 130 (exit 6), Go 12 mi W on Rte 130 to SR-13, then 1 mi S to Mason Rd (at caution light), then 0.8 mi W to Dupaw-Gould Rd, then 0.2 mi N (R). **FAC:** Gravel rds. (54

BROOKLINE (CONT)

FIELD & STREAM RV PARK LLC (CONT)
spaces). Avail: 21 paved, patios, 5 pull-thrus (29 x 64), back-ins (29 x 53), 21 full hkups (30/50 amps), seasonal sites, cable, WiFi, dump, laundry, LP gas, fire rings, firewood, controlled access. **REC:** The Pond: fishing, playground. Pet restrict(B). Partial handicap access, no tents. Big rig sites, eco-friendly, 2015 rates: $42. Disc: AAA, military.
AAA Approved
(603)673-4677 Lat: 42.74161, Lon: -71.68649
7 Dupaw-Gould Rd, Brookline, NH 03033
info@fieldnstreamrvpark.com
www.fieldnstreamrvpark.com
See ad opposite page.

CENTER CONWAY — D4 *Carroll*

Travel Services

CAMPING WORLD OF CONWAY As the nation's largest retailer of RV supplies, accessories, services and new and used RVs, Camping World is committed to making your total RV experience better. RV Accessories: (855)530-1773. **SERVICES:** RV, tire, RV appliance, MH mechanical, staffed RV wash, restrooms, RV Sales. RV supplies, LP, RV accessible. waiting room. Hours: 8am to 5pm.
(888)654-6730 Lat: 43.99544, Lon: -71.063472
1571 E. Main Street, Center Conway, NH 03813
rgriffin@campingworld.com
www.campingworld.com

CHICHESTER — E4 *Merrimack*

GREAT MEADOW CAMPGROUND **Ratings: 8.5/8.5★/6.5** (Campground) 2015 rates: $33 to $38. May 1 to Oct 15. (603)798-5124 78 Dover Rd, Chichester, NH 03258

Travel Services

CAMPING WORLD OF CHICHESTER As the nation's largest retailer of RV supplies, accessories, services and new and used RVs, Camping World is committed to making your total RV experience better. RV Accessories: (866)393-6437. **SERVICES:** RV, RV appliance, MH mechanical, engine/chassis repair, staffed RV wash, restrooms, RV Sales. RV supplies, LP, emergency parking, RV accessible. waiting room. Hours: 8am - 6pm.
(888)603-6076 Lat: 43.244849, Lon: -71.406518
165 Dover Road, Chichester, NH 03258
jastewart@campingworld.com
www.campingworld.com

CHOCORUA — D4 *Carroll*

CHOCORUA CAMPING VILLAGE KOA
Ratings: 9/10★/10 (Campground) From Northern Jct of Hwy 16 & Rte 25W, Go 3 mi N on Hwy 16 (R). Do not use GPS. Call for directions. **FAC:** Paved/gravel rds. (135 spaces). Avail: 85 dirt, 20 pull-thrus (30 x 60), back-ins (22 x 50), 65 full hkups, 20 W, 20 E (30/50 amps), seasonal sites, cable, WiFi, tent sites, rentals, dump, laundry, groc, LP gas, fire rings, firewood, controlled access. **REC:** pool, Moore's Pond: swim, fishing, playground. Pet restrict(B/Q) $. Big rig sites, eco-friendly, 2015 rates: $40 to $86. May 1 to Oct 18.
AAA Approved
(888)237-8642 Lat: 43.85611, Lon: -71.20572
893 White Mountain Hwy (Nh Rt 16), Tamworth, NH 03886
info@chocoruacamping.com
www.chocoruacamping.com
See ad this page.

COLEBROOK — B4 *Coos*

COLEMAN SP (State Pk) From jct US 3 & Hwy 26: Go 6-3/4 mi E on Hwy 26, then 5-1/2 mi N on Diamond Pond Rd. 2015 rates: $25 to $29. May 10 to Oct 13. (603)237-5382

CONCORD — E3 *Merrimack*

CONCORD See also Auburn, Barrington, Belmont, Chichester, Contoocook, Epsom, Henniker, Hillsboro, New Boston, Weare, Webster.

CHERRYSTONE FAMILY CAMPING RESORT
Ratings: 9/9.5★/9.5 (Campground) From I 93 in Concord: Go S on I 93 to I 95, S on I 95 to Hwy 1 (in Delaware), S on Hwy 1 to Hwy 13, S on Hwy 13 to SR-680, W 1.5 mi (E). **FAC:** Paved/gravel rds. (539 spaces). 503 Avail: 5 gravel, 498 grass, 100 pull-thrus (30 x 70), back-ins (30 x 45), 358 full hkups, 145 W, 145 E (30/50 amps), seasonal sites, WiFi, tent sites, rentals, dump, mobile sewer, laundry, groc, LP gas, firewood, restaurant. **REC:** pool, Chesapeake Bay: swim, fishing, shuffleboard, playground. Pet restrict(B/Q). Partial handicap access. Big rig sites, eco-friendly, 2015 rates: $17 to $68. ATM.
(757)331-3063 Lat: 37.28557, Lon: -76.01077
1511 Townfield Dr, Cape Charles, VA 23310
info@cherrystoneva.com
www.cherrystoneva.com
See primary listing at Cheriton, VA and ad pages 1233, 587, 584 (MD Map), 1217 (VA Map) & ad Magazine Section page 103.

CONTOOCOOK — E3 *Merrimack*

SANDY BEACH RV RESORT **Ratings: 8/7/7.5** (RV Park) 2015 rates: $36 to $47. May 8 to Oct 13. (603)746-3591 677 Clement Hill Rd, Contoocook, NH 03229

EAST WAKEFIELD — D4 *Carroll*

LAKE IVANHOE CAMPGROUND & INN
Ratings: 7.5/9★/8 (Campground) From Jct of Rte 16 & Wakefield Rd, Go 0.5 mi E on Wakefield Rd to Rte 153, then 2.5 mi N to Acton Ridge Rd, then 1.2 mi E (L). **FAC:** Gravel rds. (68 spaces). 38 Avail: 18 grass, 20 dirt, 5 pull-thrus (26 x 46), back-ins (28 x 46), 25 full hkups, 13 W, 13 E (30/50 amps), seasonal sites, cable, WiFi, tent sites, rentals, dump, laundry, LP gas, fire rings, firewood, controlled access. **REC:** Lake Ivanhoe: swim, fishing, shuffleboard, playground. Pet restrict(B/Q). Eco-friendly, 2015 rates: $37 to $48. May 15 to Oct 15.
(603)522-8824 Lat: 43.60455, Lon: -70.99014
631 Acton Ridge Rd, East Wakefield, NH 03830
office@lakeivanhoe.com
www.lakeivanhoe.com

EPSOM — E4 *Merrimack*

BLAKE'S BROOK FAMILY CAMPGROUND **Ratings: 5.5/6.5/8** (Campground) 2015 rates: $36 to $39. May 1 to Oct 15. (603)736-4793 76 Mountain Rd, Epsom, NH 03234

CIRCLE 9 RANCH CAMPGROUND **Ratings: 7/7/6.5** (Campground) 2015 rates: $30 to $38. (603)736-3111 39 Windymere Dr, Epsom, NH 03234

EPSOM VALLEY CAMPGROUND **Ratings: 5/7.5★/6.5** (Campground) 2015 rates: $30 to $35. May 18 to Oct 15. (603)736-9758 990 Suncook Valley Hwy, Epsom, NH 03234

LAZY RIVER FAMILY CAMPGROUND **Ratings: 6/5/6** (Campground) 2015 rates: $30. May 15 to Oct 15. (603)798-5900 427 Goboro Rd, Epsom, NH 03234

ERROL — B4 *Coos*

UMBAGOG LAKE CAMPGROUND SP (State Pk) From jct Hwy 16 & Hwy 26: Go 7-3/4 mi E on Hwy 26. 2015 rates: $35. May 3 to Nov 11. (603)482-7795

EXETER — F5 *Rockingham*

EXETER ELMS FAMILY CAMPGROUND
Ratings: 8/8.5★/8 (Campground) From Jct of I-95 & Rte 107 (Exit 1), Go 2.6 mi NW on Rte 107 to Rte 150, then 4.1 mi NW to Rte 108, then 0.2 mi N (R). **FAC:** Gravel rds. (144 spaces). 74 Avail: 10 gravel, 64 dirt, 2 pull-thrus (25 x 50), back-ins (28 x 50), 14 full hkups, 60 W, 60 E (30/50 amps), seasonal sites, WiFi, tent sites, rentals, showers $, dump, mobile sewer, laundry, groc, LP bottles, fire rings, firewood, controlled access. **REC:** pool, Exeter River: fishing, playground. Pets OK $. Eco-friendly, 2015 rates: $40 to $55. May 1 to Oct 15.
(603)778-7631 Lat: 42.95880, Lon: -70.95536
190 Court Street, Exeter, NH 03833
info@exeterelms.com
www.exeterelms.com
See ad this page, 765.

GREEN GATE CAMPGROUND **Ratings: 7/8★/6.5** (Campground) 2015 rates: $40 to $44. May 15 to Sep 15. (603)772-2100 185 Court St, Exeter, NH 03833

FRANCONIA — C3 *Grafton*

FRANCONIA NOTCH SP (LAFAYETTE CAMPGROUND) (State Pk) No N'bound access. N'bound on I-93: turn around at Tramway exit 2, then go back 2-1/2 mi S on I-93. S'bound: At I-93 (Lafayette Place/Campground exit). 2015 rates: $25. (603)745-8391

FRANSTED FAMILY CAMPGROUND Ratings: 8/8★/9.5 (Campground) From Jct of I-93 & Exit 38, Go 0.1 mi W on exit rd to Rte 18, then 1.2 mi SE (left) (R). **FAC:** Paved/gravel rds. (47 spaces). Avail: 23 gravel, 7 pull-thrus (30 x 60), back-ins (40 x 45), 9 full hkups, 14 W, 14 E (30/50 amps), seasonal sites, cable, WiFi, tent sites, rentals, dump, mobile sewer, laundry, groc, LP gas, fire rings, firewood. **REC:** Meadow Brook: swim, fishing, playground. Pet restrict(B/Q). Big rig sites, eco-friendly, 2015 rates: $46 to $49. May 15 to Oct 12.
AAA Approved
(603)823-5675 Lat: 44.21709, Lon: -71.73225
974 Profile Rd Rte 18, Franconia, NH 03580
info@franstedcampground.com
www.franstedcampground.com

Things to See and Do

CANNON AERIAL TRAMWAY/FRANCONIA NOTCH STATE PARK Ride an 80-passenger cable car to the summit of a 4200' mountain. Elev 4200 ft. RV accessible. Restrooms, food. Hours: 9am to 5pm. Adult fee: $17. ATM.
(603)823-8800 Lat: 44.10219, Lon: -71.68284
9 Franconia Notch State Park, Franconia, NH 03580
nhparks@dred.state.nh.us
www.cannonmt.com
See ad page 763 (Welcome Section).

THE FLUME/FRANCONIA NOTCH STATE PARK Visitors Center for the Flume, towering moss-covered granite walls, past cascading waterfalls, historic covered bridges. Self-guided 2 mile loop walk. May 15 to Oct 31. RV accessible. Restrooms, food. Hours: 9am to 5pm. Adult fee: $16. ATM.
(603)745-8391 Lat: 44.0989, Lon: -71.6706
852 Daniel Webster Hwy, Lincoln, NH 03251
www.nhstateparks.org
See ad page 763 (Welcome Section).

FREEDOM — D4 *Carroll*

DANFORTH BAY CAMPING & RV RESORT
Ratings: 9/10★/9 (Campground) From Jct of Rte 16 & Rte 41 (in West Ossipee), Go 0.5 mi E on Rte 41 to Ossipee Lake Rd, then 4.8 mi SE to Shawtown Rd, then 1 mi NE (R). **FAC:** Paved/gravel rds. (308 spaces). 193 Avail: 4 paved, 178 gravel, 11 grass, 24 pull-thrus (30 x 60), back-ins (30 x 40), 128 full hkups, 65 W, 65 E (30/50 amps), seasonal sites, cable, WiFi, tent sites, rentals, showers $, dump, laundry, groc, LP gas, fire rings, firewood, controlled access. **REC:** heated pool, wading pool, Danforth Bay: swim, fishing, playground. Pet restrict(Q). Partial handicap access. Big rig sites, eco-friendly, 2015 rates: $35 to $80.
(603)539-2069 Lat: 43.81906, Lon: -71.11747
196 Shawtown Rd, Freedom, NH 03836
reservations@danforthbay.com
www.danforthbay.com
See ad page 774.

THE BLUFFS RV RESORT
Ratings: 9/10★/9 (RV Park) From Jct of Rte 16 & Rte 41 (in West Ossipee), Go 0.5 mi E on Rte 41 to Ossipee Lake Rd, then 4.8 mi SE to Shawtown Rd, then 1 mi NE (R). One week minimum stay, age 50 and older. **FAC:** Paved/gravel rds. (297 spaces). Avail: 12 gravel, back-ins (30 x 65), accepts full hkup units only, 12 full hkups (30/50 amps), seasonal sites, cable, WiFi, rentals, laundry,

FREEDOM (CONT)

THE BLUFFS RV RESORT (CONT)
groc, LP gas, fire rings, firewood, controlled access. **REC:** heated pool, pond, fishing. Pet restrict(Q). Partial handicap access, no tents. Age restrict may apply, big rig sites, eco-friendly, 2015 rates: $46 to $54. Apr 18 to Nov 2.
(603)539-2069 Lat: 43.83240, Lon: -71.11064
196 Shawton Rd, Freedom, NH 03836
seasonal@danforthbay.com
www.nhrvresort.com
See ad page 774.

GILFORD — D4 *Belknap*

➜ ELLACOYA STATE BEACH/RV CAMPGROUND (State Pk) From Jct of I-93 & I-393/Rtes 4 & 202 (exit 15E), E 3 mi on I-393/4/202 to Rte 106, N 17.5 mi to Rte 3/11 Bypass, NE 5 mi to Rte 11, SE 3.5 mi (L). 2015 rates: $47. May 24 to Oct 13. (603)293-7821

➜ GUNSTOCK (BELKNAP COUNTY PARK) (Public) From Jct of I-93 & Rte 3 (exit 20), NE 7 mi on Rte 3 to Rte 3/11 Bypass, NE 3 mi to Rte 11A, E 5.5 mi (R). 2015 rates: $30 to $58. (603)293-4341

GLEN — C4 *Carroll*

← GLEN ELLIS FAMILY CAMPGROUND **Ratings: 8.5/9.5★/9.5** (Campground) 2015 rates: $40 to $50. May 26 to Oct 13. (603)383-4567 83 Glen Ellis Campground Rd, Glen, NH 03838

↑ GREEN MEADOW CAMPING AREA **Ratings: 7/8★/7.5** (Campground) 2015 rates: $36 to $46. May 24 to Oct 14. (603)383-6801 37 Green Meadow Campground Rd, Glen, NH 03838

Things to See and Do

↑ **STORY LAND** Children's theme park, 22 themed rides including new wooden roller coaster, live shows, interactive play areas, storybook characters and all your favorite nursery rhyme animals set on 35 acres. May 23 to Oct 12. partial handicap access. RV accessible. Restrooms, food. Hours: 9:30am to 6pm. Adult fee: $31.99. ATM.
(603)383-4186 Lat: 44.11585, Lon: -71.18362
850 Nh Rte 16, Glen, NH 03838
www.storylandnh.com
See ad page 763 (Welcome Section).

GORHAM — C4 *Coos*

MOOSE BROOK SP (State Pk) From west jct Hwy 16 & US 2: Go 1-1/4 mi W on US 2, then 1/2 mi N on Jimtown Rd. 2015 rates: $25. May 24 to Oct 14. (603)466-3860

We've listened to thousands of RVers like you, so we know exactly how to rate campgrounds. Got feedback? Call us!877-209-6655

➜ **TIMBERLAND CAMPGROUND**
Ratings: 8.5/9★/9 (Campground) From Jct of US-2 & Rte 16, Go 4.5 mi E on US-2 (L). **FAC:** Gravel rds. 50 Avail: 34 gravel, 8 grass, 8 dirt, 22 pull-thrus (32 x 60), back-ins (32 x 35), 26 full hkups, 24 W, 24 E (30/50 amps), WiFi Hotspot, tent sites, rentals, showers $, dump, laundry, groc, fire rings, firewood, controlled access. **REC:** heated pool, Androscoggin River: fishing, playground. Pet restrict(B/Q). Big rig sites, eco-friendly, 2015 rates: $35 to $40. Disc: military. May 10 to Oct 20.
(603)466-3872 Lat: 44.40877, Lon: -71.08881
809 State Route 2, Shelburne, NH 03581
info@timberlandcampgroundnh.com
www.timberlandcampgroundnh.com
See ad this page, 765.

➜ **WHITE BIRCHES CAMPING PARK Ratings: 8/7/7.5** (Campground) From Jct of US 2 & Hwy 16S, Go 1.8 mi E on US 2 (R). GPS use Mt Moriah Dr (Do not drive up Mt. Moriah Dr). **FAC:** Gravel rds. (59 spaces). 27 Avail: 14 grass, 13 dirt, 15 pull-thrus (32 x 65), back-ins (32 x 56), 20 full hkups, 7 W, 7 E (30/50 amps), seasonal sites, WiFi, tent sites, rentals, showers $, dump, laundry, groc, LP gas, fire rings, firewood, controlled access. **REC:** pool, Androscoggin River: fishing, playground. Pets OK. Big rig sites, 2015 rates: $30 to $39. May 1 to Oct 25.
AAA Approved
(603)466-2022 Lat: 44.3870, Lon: -71.13950
218 State Rte 2, Shelburne, NH 03581
whbirch@ncia.net
www.whitebirchescamping.com

GREENFIELD — F3 *Hillsborough*

← GREENFIELD (State Pk) From Jct of SR-31 & SR-136, W 1 mi on SR-136, follow signs (R). 2015 rates: $25. May 24 to Oct 13. (603)547-3497

HAMPTON — F5 *Rockingham*

↓ **TIDEWATER CAMPGROUND LP**
Ratings: 8/10★/8.5 (Campground) From Jct of I-95 & Rte 101 (Exit 2), Go 2.5 mi E on Rte 101 to US 1, then 0.2 mi S (R). Do not rely on GPS, No dogs allowed. **FAC:** Paved/gravel rds. (188 spaces). 68 Avail: 62 gravel, 6 grass, 4 pull-thrus (25 x 60), back-ins (28 x 60), 68 full hkups (30/50 amps), seasonal sites, WiFi, tent sites, showers $, groc, fire rings, firewood, controlled access. **REC:** pool, playground. No pets. Big rig sites, eco-friendly, 2015 rates: $39 to $47. May 15 to Oct 15.
(603)926-5474 Lat: 42.93121, Lon: -70.84587
160 Lafayette Rd, Hampton, NH 03842
tidewatercampground@gmail.com
tidewatercampgroundnh.com
See ad this page.

Say you saw it in our Guide!

HAMPTON BEACH — F5 *Rockingham*

↓ HAMPTON STATE BEACH/RV CAMPGROUND (State Pk) From Jct of I-95 & Rte 101 (exit 2), E 3 mi on Rte 101 to Rte 1A, S 2 mi (L). 3 day min stay. Note: No Pets April 1st-Sept. 15th. 2015 rates: $50. May 22 to Oct 12. (603)926-3784

HAMPTON FALLS — F5 *Rockingham*

← **WAKEDA CAMPGROUND LLC**
Ratings: 7.5/8.5★/10 (Campground) From Jct of I-95 & Rte 107 (exit 1), Go 0.5 mi E on Rte 107 to US-1, then 1.7 mi N to Rte 88, then 3.7 mi W (L). **FAC:** Paved rds. (338 spaces). 135 Avail: 5 paved, 90 gravel, 40 grass, 9 pull-thrus (22 x 86), back-ins (30 x 60), 68 full hkups, 28 W, 28 E (30/50 amps), seasonal sites, WiFi Hotspot, tent sites, rentals, showers $, dump, laundry, groc, LP bottles, fire rings, firewood. **REC:** playground. Pets OK. Partial handicap access. Big rig sites, eco-friendly, 2015 rates: $45 to $51. Disc: military. May 15 to Oct 1.
(603)772-5274 Lat: 42.95631, Lon: -70.90453
294 Exeter Rd, Rt 88, Hampton Falls, NH 03844
www.wakedacampground.com
See ad this page.

HANCOCK — F3 *Hillsborough*

↓ SEVEN MAPLES CAMPGROUND **Ratings: 7/8.5★/8** (Campground) 2015 rates: $36 to $39. May 1 to Oct 13. (603)525-3321 24 Longview Rd, Hancock, NH 03449

HANOVER — D2 *Grafton*

STORRS POND RECREATION AREA (State Pk) From jct I-89 & I-91 in VT: Go 5 mi N on I-91 (exit 13-Hanover, NH-Dartmouth College), then turn E and cross the Connecticut River into Hanover, NH (street becomes Wheelock St), 1 mi E on Wheelock St, 1 mi N on Hwy 10, then 1 mi E on Reservoir. 2015 rates: $38. (603)643-2134

HENNIKER — E3 *Merrimack*

➜ KEYSER POND CAMPGROUND **Ratings: 6.5/7.5/7** (Campground) 2015 rates: $32 to $40. May 15 to Oct 15. (603)428-7741 1739 Old Concord Rd, Henniker, NH 03242

➜ **MILE-AWAY CAMPGROUND**
Ratings: 7.5/8.5★/7.5 (Campground) From Jct of I-89 & Rtes 202/9 (exit 5), Go 5 mi W on Rtes 202/9 to Old W Hopkinton Rd, then 1 mi NE (L). **FAC:** Gravel rds. (145 spaces). 45 Avail: 20 gravel, 25 dirt, 3 pull-thrus (24 x 60), back-ins (24 x 48), 45 full hkups (30/50 amps), seasonal sites, cable, WiFi, tent sites, rentals, showers $, dump, laundry, LP gas, fire rings, firewood. **REC:** heated pool, pond, French Pond: swim, fishing, playground.

Like Us on Facebook.

HENNIKER (CONT)

MILE-AWAY CAMPGROUND (CONT)
Pets OK. Partial handicap access. Big rig sites, eco-friendly, 2015 rates: $36. Disc: AAA.
(603)428-7616 Lat: 43.18948, Lon: -71.77221
479 Old W Hopkinton Rd, Henniker, NH 03242
camping@mileaway.com
www.mileaway.com

HILLSBORO — E3 *Hillsborough*

OXBOW CAMPGROUND **Ratings: 7.5/7.5/8** (Campground) 2015 rates: $36. May 1 to Oct 31. (603)464-5952 8 Oxbow Rd, Deering, NH 03244

HINSDALE — F2 *Cheshire*

HINSDALE CAMPGROUND AT THICKET HILL VILLAGE
Ratings: 7.5/9.5★/9 (Campground) From Jct of I-91 & Rte 5, (Exit 1 in Brattleboro, VT), Go 1.1 mi NE on Rte 5 to Rte 119, then (in VT) 4.5 mi S, (L). **FAC:** Gravel rds. (89 spaces). Avail: 33 gravel, 8 pull-thrus (35 x 60), back-ins (35 x 60), 17 full hkups, 16 W, 16 E (30/50 amps), seasonal sites, cable, WiFi, tent sites, dump, laundry, LP gas, fire rings, firewood. **REC:** pool, wading pool, playground. Pet restrict(B/Q). Partial handicap access. Big rig sites, 2015 rates: $39 to $43. Apr 17 to Oct 31.
(603)336-8906 Lat: 42.79731, Lon: -72.51586
29 Pine St, Hinsdale, NH 03451
hinsdale@campingnow.com
www.campingnow.com
See ad this page, 765.

HOLDERNESS — D3 *Belknap*

OWLS LANDING CAMPROUND Ratings: 8/6.5/7 (Campground) From Jct of I-93 & US Rte 3 (Exit 24), Go 7.5 mi E on US Rte 3 (R). **FAC:** Gravel rds. (70 spaces). 23 Avail: 8 gravel, 15 dirt, 2 pull-thrus (25 x 50), back-ins (27 x 50), mostly side by side hkups, 12 full hkups, 11 W, 11 E (30 amps), seasonal sites, cable, WiFi, tent sites, dump, laundry, groc, LP gas, fire rings, firewood. **REC:** heated pool, playground. Pets OK. Eco-friendly, 2015 rates: $35 to $40. Disc: AAA, military. May 22 to Oct 15.
AAA Approved
(603)279-6266 Lat: 43.72519, Lon: -71.56382
245 US Rte 3, Holderness, NH 03245
camp@owlslanding.com
www.owlslanding.com

JEFFERSON — C4 *Coos*

FORT JEFFERSON CAMPGROUND **Ratings: 6.5/5.5/6** (Campground) 2015 rates: $28 to $33. May 15 to Oct 15. (603)586-4510 1468 Presidential Hwy, Jefferson, NH 03583

LANTERN RESORT MOTEL & CAMPGROUND **Ratings: 8.5/10★/10** (Campground) 2015 rates: $40 to $48. May 15 to Oct 14. (603)586-7151 571 Presidential Hwy (Rt 2), Jefferson, NH 03583

Things to See and Do

SANTA'S VILLAGE Visit with Santa, feed his reindeer, Christmas themed amusement park. May 1 to Dec 31. partial handicap access. Restrooms, food. Hours: 9:30am to 5pm. Adult fee: $30. ATM.
(603)586-4445 Lat: 44.42635, Lon: -71.49405
528 Presidential Hwy (Rt 2), Jefferson, NH 03583
santa@santasvillage.com
www.santasvillage.com
See ad page 763 (Welcome Section).

"Full hookups" in a campground listing means there are water, electric and sewer hookups at the sites.

KEENE — F2 *Cheshire*

WHEELOCK PARK CAMPGROUND (Public) From Jct of SR-9 & SR-12, N 0.5 mi on SR-12 to West St, W .7 mi on West St/Park Ave (R). For reservations after May 20, call (603)357-9832. 2015 rates: $20 to $35. May 28 to Sep 10. (603)357-9832

LANCASTER — B3 *Coos*

MOUNTAIN LAKE CAMPING RESORT
Ratings: 9/10★/10 (Campground) From Jct of US-3 & US-2 (in town), Go 4.5 mi S on US-3 (R).

WE INVITE YOU TO CREATE MEMORIES
We've created a warm, comfortable place for your family to enjoy; kayaking, fishing, swimming in our lake or heated pool with new waterslides, hiking, golfing or enjoying the many attractions in the White Mountains of NH.

FAC: Paved/gravel rds. (63 spaces). Avail: 51 gravel, 7 pull-thrus (32 x 60), back-ins (35 x 55), 45 full hkups, 6 W, 6 E (30/50 amps), seasonal sites, cable, WiFi, tent sites, rentals, dump, laundry, groc, LP gas, fire rings, firewood. **REC:** heated pool, Mountain Lake: swim, fishing, playground, rec open to public. Pet restrict(B). Big rig sites, eco-friendly, 2015 rates: $57 to $67.50. May 15 to Oct 15.
(603)788-4509 Lat: 44.43043, Lon: -71.58969
485 Prospect St (Rt 3), Lancaster, NH 03584
mtnlake@ne.rr.com
www.mtnlakecampground.com
See ad this page, 765.

LEE — E4 *Strafford*

FERNDALE ACRES CAMPGROUND Ratings: 7.5/7.5★/8 (Campground) From Jct of Rtes 4 & 125 (Lee Traffic Circle), Go 1.5 mi S on Rte 125 to Bennett Rd, then 0.5 mi E to Rte 155, then 0.1 mi N to Wednesday Hill Rd, then 1.4 mi to entrance rd, then 1 mi S (E). **FAC:** Paved/gravel rds. (120 spaces). 45 Avail: 15 grass, 30 dirt, 3 pull-thrus (40 x 40), back-ins (24 x 42), 20 full hkups, 25 W, 25 E (30 amps), seasonal sites, WiFi Hotspot, tent sites, showers $, dump, laundry, groc, fire rings, firewood. **REC:** pool, Lamprey River: swim, fishing, playground. Pet restrict(B/Q). Age restrict may apply, RV age restrict, eco-friendly, 2015 rates: $38. May 15 to Sep 15.
AAA Approved
(603)659-5082 Lat: 43.11750, Lon: -70.99706
130 Wednesday Hill Rd, Lee, NH 03861
ferndaleacres@gmail.com
www.ferndaleacrescampground.com

LINCOLN — C3 *Grafton*

Things to See and Do

ALPINE ADVENTURES Alpine Adventures ziplining, off-roading in a Swiss army vehicle, misty flip into Big Airbag, Stunt Zone, Aerial Adventure Park and the Bird House. RV accessible. Restrooms.
(603)745-9911 Lat: 44.038942, Lon: -71.674929
41 Main Street, Lincoln, NH 03251
info@alpinezipline.com
http://www.alpinezipline.com/
See ad page 763 (Welcome Section).

CLARK'S TRADING POST Trained Bear Shows, Stream Train Rides, Museums, Haunted House, Antique Photos, Gift Shops, Candle Shop, Avery's Garage, The Peppermint Saloon, Blaster Boats, Climbing Tower, Segway Rides. May 16 to Oct 12. RV accessible. Restrooms, food. Hours: 9:30am to 6pm. Adult fee: $20. ATM.
(603)745-8913 Lat: 44.04781, Lon: -71.68594
110 US-Rt 3, Lincoln, NH 03251
info@clarkstradingpost.com
www.clarkstradingpost.com
See ad page 763 (Welcome Section).

Tell them you saw them in this Guide!

HOBO RAILROAD Dinner, Sightseeing Train, Santa Train, Santa Express Train. May 15 to Dec 23. partial handicap access. RV accessible. Restrooms, food. Hours: 10am to 3pm. Adult fee: $16.
(603)745-2135 Lat: 44.039216, Lon: -71.679097
64 Railroad St, Lincoln, NH 03251
ride@hoborr.com
www.hoborr.com
See ad page 763 (Welcome Section).

LOON MOUNTAIN NH longest aerial ride on 7000 ft long gondola tramway, mountain biking, Sunday mountaintop brunch, bungee jumping, zipline, adventure packages. May 28 to Oct 16. partial handicap access. Restrooms, food. Hours: 9:30am to 6pm. Adult fee: $15. ATM.
(603)745-8111 Lat: 44.05765, Lon: -71.63430
60 Loon Mountain Rd, Lincoln, NH 03251
info@loonmtn.com
www.loonmtn.com
See ad page 763 (Welcome Section).

THE WHALE'S TALE WATERPARK Waterpark. Jun 1 to Sep 7. partial handicap access. RV accessible. Restrooms, food. Hours: 10am to 6pm. Adult fee: $35. ATM.
(603)745-8810 Lat: 44.07237, Lon: -71.68571
481 Daniel Webster Hwy, Lincoln, NH 03251
info@whalestalewaterpark.net
www.whalestalewaterpark.net
See ad page 763 (Welcome Section).

LISBON — C3 *Grafton*

LITTLETON/LISBON KOA **Ratings: 8.5/8.5★/9** (Campground) 2015 rates: $42 to $58. May 1 to Oct 19. (603)838-5525 2154 Rte 302, Lisbon, NH 03585

LITTLETON — C3 *Grafton*

CRAZY HORSE CAMPGROUND
Ratings: 9/9.5★/9 (Campground) From Jct of I-93 & Rte 135 (Exit 43), Go 0.1 mi SW on Rte 135 to Rte 135/18, then 1 mi W to Hilltop Rd, then 1.5 mi NW (R). **FAC:** Gravel rds. (175 spaces). 93 Avail: 63 gravel, 30 dirt, 15 pull-thrus (32 x 64), back-ins (32 x 50), 55 full hkups, 38 W, 38 E (30/50 amps), seasonal sites, cable, WiFi $, tent sites, rentals, showers $, dump, laundry, groc, LP gas, fire rings, firewood. **REC:** pool, pond, fishing, playground. Pets OK. Big rig sites, eco-friendly, 2015 rates: $36 to $42. Disc: AAA, military.
(603)444-2204 Lat: 44.32219, Lon: -71.84888
788 Hilltop Rd, Littleton, NH 03561
mail@crazyhorsenh.com
www.crazyhorsenh.com
See ad this page.

LOUDON — E3 *Merrimack*

CASCADE CAMPGROUND **Ratings: 8/7/7.5** (Campground) 2015 rates: $38. May 1 to Oct 15. (603)224-3212 379 Route 106 South, Loudon, NH 03307

MADBURY — E5 *Strafford*

OLD STAGE CAMPGROUND **Ratings: 8/9.5★/8.5** (Campground) 2015 rates: $42. May 1 to Oct 3. (603)742-4050 46 Old Stage Rd, Madbury, NH 03823

MEREDITH — D4 *Belknap*

← **CLEARWATER CAMPGROUND Ratings: 8.5/8.5★/8** (Campground) From Jct of I-93 & Rte 104 (exit 23), Go 3 mi E on Rte 104 (R). **FAC:** Gravel rds. (141 spaces). Avail: 43 gravel, 4 pull-thrus (25 x 60), back-ins (24 x 58), 23 full hkups, 20 W, 20 E (30/50 amps), seasonal sites, cable, WiFi $, tent sites, rentals, dump, laundry, groc, fire rings, firewood, controlled access. **REC:** Pemigewasset Lake: swim, fishing, playground. Pets OK. Eco-friendly. 2015 rates: $25 to $51. Disc: military. May 15 to Oct 12.
(603)279-7761 Lat: 43.61927, Lon: -71.58715
26 Campground Rd, Meredith, NH 03253
info@clearwatercampground.com
www.clearwatercampground.com

→ HARBOR HILL CAMPING AREA **Ratings: 9/9★/9** (Campground) 2015 rates: $42 to $45. May 22 to Oct 12. (603)279-6910 189 Nh Rte 25, Meredith, NH 03253

← **MEREDITH WOODS 4 SEASON CAMPING AREA**
Ratings: 9.5/9.5★/9 (Campground) From Jct of I-93 & Rte 104 (exit 23), Go 3 mi E on Rte 104 (L). **FAC:** Paved rds. (100 spaces). Avail: 25 gravel, back-ins (28 x 66), 25 full hkups (30/50 amps), seasonal sites, cable, WiFi $, tent sites, rentals, laundry, groc, fire rings, firewood, controlled access. **REC:** heated pool, whirlpool, playground. Pets OK. Big rig sites, 2015 rates: $32 to $50. Disc: military.
(603)279-5449 Lat: 43.62006, Lon: -71.58573
551 Nh Rte 104, Meredith, NH 03253
info@meredithwoods.com
www.meredithwoods.com
See ad this page.

← **TWIN TAMARACK FAMILY CAMPING & RV RESORT**
Ratings: 8.5/9.5★/9 (Campground) From Jct of I-93 & Rte 104 (exit 23), Go 2.5 mi E on Rte 104 (L) Do not use GPS, call park. **FAC:** Gravel rds. (236 spaces). 122 Avail: 86 gravel, 36 dirt, 13 pull-thrus (30 x 60), back-ins (24 x 60), 51 full hkups, 71 W, 71 E (30/50 amps), seasonal sites, cable, WiFi, tent sites, rentals, dump, mobile sewer, laundry, groc, fire rings, firewood, controlled access. **REC:** pool, whirlpool, Pemigewasset Lake: swim, fishing, playground. Pets OK. Big rig sites, eco-friendly. 2015 rates: $40 to $48. May 17 to Oct 14.
(603)279-4387 Lat: 43.62182, Lon: -71.58923
41 Twin Tamarack Rd, New Hampton, NH 03256
twintamarack@metrocast.net
www.twintamarackcampground.com
See ad this page, 765 & RV Trips of a Lifetime in Magazine Section.

MILTON — E4 *Strafford*

↑ **MI-TE-JO CAMPGROUND**
Ratings: 8.5/9.5★/9.5 (Campground) From Jct of Rte 16 (Spaulding Tpke) & Rte 75 (exit 17), Go 1 mi SE on Rte 75 to Rte 125, then 3.2 mi NE to Townhouse Rd, then 1 mi E to campground, then 0.5 mi NE (E). **FAC:** Gravel rds. (202 spaces). Avail: 89 gravel, 13 pull-thrus (35 x 80), back-ins (30 x 48), 89 full hkups (30/50 amps), seasonal sites, cable, WiFi, tent sites, rentals, dump, laundry, groc, LP gas, fire rings, firewood, controlled access. **REC:** Northeast Pond (Lake): swim, fishing, shuffleboard, playground. Pets OK. Partial handicap access. Big rig sites, eco-friendly, 2015 rates: $50 to $55. May 15 to Oct 10.
(603)652-9022 Lat: 43.44353, Lon: -70.96904
111 Mi-Te-Jo Rd, Milton, NH 03851
info@mi-te-jo.com
www.mi-te-jo.com
See ad this page.

MOULTONBOROUGH — D4 *Carroll*

↗ **LONG ISLAND BRIDGE CAMPGROUND LLC**
Ratings: 7/8.5★/9 (Campground) From Jct of Rtes 3 & 25 (in Meredith), NE 7 mi on Rte 25 to Moultonboro Neck Rd, S 7 mi (L) Do not use GPS. **FAC:** Paved/gravel rds. (96 spaces). Avail: 37 gravel, 5 pull-thrus (24 x 45), back-ins (24 x 45), 17 full hkups, 20 W, 20 E (30/50 amps), seasonal sites, cable, WiFi Hotspot, tent sites, rentals, showers $, dump, laundry, fire rings, firewood, controlled access. **REC:** Lake Winnipesaukee: swim, fishing, playground. Pet restrict(B/Q). 21 day max stay, eco-friendly, 2015 rates: $38 to $48. May 15 to Oct 15. No CC.
(603)253-6053 Lat: 43.66676, Lon: -71.34689
29 Long Island Rd, Moultonborough, NH 03254
libcg1@juno.com
www.longislandbridgecampgroundnh.com
See ad this page.

MOUNT WASHINGTON — C4 *Coos*

Things to See and Do

↑ **MT WASHINGTON COG RAILWAY** Railway has unique speciality-built coal-fired steam or bio-diesel locomotives that climb to the top of Mt. Washington, the Northeast's highest peak. Museum, restaurant, gift shop & RV parking. Open rain, snow or shine. May 1 to Oct 31. partial handicap access. RV accessible. Restrooms, food. Hours: 9am to 4pm. Adult fee: $68. ATM.
(800)922-8825 Lat: 44.26967, Lon: -71.35088
Base Rd 6 mi off Rte 302, Bretton Woods, NH 03589
info@thecog.com
www.thecog.com
See ad page 763 (Welcome Section).

Tell your RV Campground that you found them in this Guide.

NEW BOSTON — F3 *Hillsborough*

↓ **FRIENDLY BEAVER CAMPGROUND**
Ratings: 9/10★/9 (Campground) From Jct of Rtes 77 & 136 & 13 (in town), Go 100 ft S on Rte 13 to Old Coach Rd, then 2 mi W (R).

NEW ENGLAND'S #1 FUN DESTINATION!
The Super Vacation Spot in So. NH, Friendly Beaver has LOTS of Activities for All Ages! From our Indoor & 3 Outdoor Pools, GAZEBOS, New Cabins to Theme Weekends & Activities for Children Young & Old, there'll be NO BOREDOM!!

FAC: Gravel rds. (278 spaces). Avail: 71 gravel, 5 pull-thrus (30 x 70), back-ins (30 x 60), 36 full hkups, 35 W, 35 E (30/50 amps), seasonal sites, WiFi $, tent sites, rentals, dump, mobile sewer, laundry, groc, fire rings, firewood. **REC:** heated pool, wading pool, playground. Pet restrict(B). Partial handicap access. Big rig sites, eco-friendly, 2015 rates: $46 to $48. ATM.
(603)487-5570 Lat: 42.98180, Lon: -71.71950
98 Cochran Hill Rd, New Boston, NH 03070
Reservations@friendlybeaver.com
www.friendlybeaver.com
See ad pages 772, 765, 762 (NH Map) & Family Camping in Magazine Section.

How can you tell whether you're traveling in the right direction? The arrow in each listing denotes the compass direction of the facility in relation to the listed town. For example, an arrow pointing straight up indicates that the facility is located due north from town. An arrow pointing down and to the right indicates that the facility is southeast of town.

CELEBRATING 36+ YEARS ESTABLISHED 1979!
Friendly Beaver CAMPGROUND
Reader's Choice Winner 2014/15
WINNER UNION LEADER Readers' Choice 2015
WINNER UNION LEADER Readers' Choice 2014
MasterCard
VISA
TOP RATED Good Sam Park FOR 2016
9:00 am - 5:00 pm (Eastern Time)
Visit our web pages at:
www.friendlybeaver.com
Old Coach Road,
New Boston, NH 03070
Background picture is our new Blueberry walking trail
(603) 487-5570
Tent & Trailer Sites
Water, Electric and Sewer Hookups
Cabins • Tables
Fireplaces
General Store
Wood • Ice
Lounging Patio
Dumping Station
Two Large Rec Halls: 1 For Adults And 1 For Children & Teens
Christmas in July
Theme Weekends
Free Wagon Rides
Movies
Saturday Night Entertainment
Country & Western Dances
Arts & Crafts
Children's Activities
Free WiFi at Adult and Children's Rec Hall
Why not try our Weekday Getaway SPECIAL?
SUNDAY thru THURSDAY
Camp TWO Nights and Receive a THIRD Night FREE!
Must request discount at time of making your reservation

FRIENDLIEST CAMPGROUND IN NEW ENGLAND
CONCORD
N
89
13
114
77
Chase
93
Weare
13
149
MANCHESTER
FRIENDLY BEAVER
114
93
77
Goffstown
136
New Boston
114
Old Coach Rd.
Bedford
13
Stop Sign
77
13
100 Ft.
Old Coach Rd.
Milford
101
13
FOUR AWESOME POOLS:
• 20x40 Swim Pool
• 20x40 Sport Pool (Water Basketball & Water Volleyball)
• 16x32 Wading Pool
• Indoor Heated Pool Open Year Round
SUPER PLAYGROUND:
• Beautifully Crafted Wood Replicas of a Pirate Ship, Airplane, Space Ship, Fire Truck, & a 40 Foot Train
Good Sam RATED 9/10★/9
FRIENDLY BEAVER CAMPGROUND GOES GREEN PLEASE RECYCLE!
NEW HAMPSHIRE Pledged To Quality Camping CAMPGROUND OWNERS' ASS'N.
APPROVED CAMPGROUND

NEW HAMPTON — D3 *Belknap, Grafton*

↓ YOGI BEAR'S JELLYSTONE PARK CAMP-RESORT **Ratings: 7.5/7/8** (Campground) 2015 rates: $49 to $74. May 22 to Oct 10. (603)968-9000 35 Jellystone Park, New Hampton, NH 03256

NEWFIELDS — F5 *Rockingham*

↗ **GREAT BAY CAMPING LLC**
Ratings: 8/8★/8.5 (Campground) From Jct of I-95 & SR-101-W (Exit 2), Go 3.8 mi W on SR-101 to SR-108 (Exit 11), then 4 mi N (R) turn into Shell gas station, driveway is on the side. **FAC:** Gravel rds. (68 spaces). Avail: 33 grass, 2 pull-thrus (45 x 72), back-ins (45 x 50), some side by side hkups, 27 full hkups, 6 W, 6 E (30/50 amps), seasonal sites, WiFi, tent sites, dump, laundry, fire rings, firewood. **REC:** pool, Squamscott River: fishing, playground. Pet restrict(B/Q). Big rig sites, 2015 rates: $35 to $45. May 15 to Oct 1.
(603)778-0226 Lat: 43.04475, Lon: -70.92528
56-60 Route 108, Newfields, NH 03856
info@greatbaycamping.com
www.greatbaycamping.com
See ad page 768.

NEWPORT — E2 *Sullivan*

↓ CROW'S NEST CAMPGROUND **Ratings: 8/8.5★/7** (Campground) From Jct of I-89 and Rte 11 (exit 12), Go 11 mi W on Rte 11, then 2 mi S on Rte 10 (R). **FAC:** Gravel rds. (103 spaces). 77 Avail: 30 grass, 47 dirt, 4 pull-thrus (27 x 75), back-ins (28 x 39), some side by side hkups, 30 full hkups, 47 W, 47 E (30/50 amps), seasonal sites, WiFi $, tent sites, rentals, showers $, dump, laundry, groc, LP gas, fire rings, firewood. **REC:** pool, wading pool, Sugar River: swim, fishing, playground. Pet restrict(B/Q). Partial handicap access. Big rig sites, eco-friendly, 2015 rates: $34 to $42. Disc: AAA. May 15 to Oct 15.
(603)863-6170 Lat: 43.33227, Lon: -72.16999
529 S Main St, Newport, NH 03773
camping@crowsnestcampground.com
www.crowsnestcampground.com

NORTH CONWAY — C4 *Carroll*

↑ EASTERN SLOPE CAMPING AREA **Ratings: 8.5/7.5/7** (RV Park) 2015 rates: $38.99 to $48.99. May 15 to Oct 17. (603)447-5092 584 White Mountain Hwy/Nh Rt 16, Conway, NH 03818

↓ **SACO RIVER CAMPING AREA**
Ratings: 9/10★/9 (Campground) From S Jct of US-302 & Rte 16, Go 500 yds N on Rte 16/302 (L). **FAC:** Paved/gravel rds. 174 Avail: 104 gravel, 55 grass, 15 dirt, 41 pull-thrus (40 x 75), back-ins (44 x 50), 133 full hkups, 41 W, 41 E (30/50 amps), cable, WiFi, tent sites, rentals, showers $, dump, mobile sewer, laundry, LP gas, fire rings, firewood, controlled access. **REC:** heated pool, Saco River: swim, fishing, shuffleboard, playground, rec open to public. Pet restrict(B/Q) $. Big rig sites, 29 day max stay, eco-friendly, 2015 rates: $43 to $64. May 7 to Oct 11.
(603)356-3360 Lat: 44.01897, Lon: -71.11526
1550 White Mountain Hwy, North Conway, NH 03860
reservations@sacorivercampingarea.com
www.sacorivercampingarea.com
See ad opposite page.

↓ **THE BEACH CAMPING AREA**
Ratings: 7.5/8.5★/7 (Campground) From N Jct of Rts 113 & 16 (in town), Go 1.5 mi N on Rt 16 (L). **FAC:** Paved/dirt rds. (110 spaces). Avail: 92 dirt, 9 pull-thrus (30 x 60), back-ins (30 x 45), 92 full hkups (20/30 amps), seasonal sites, cable, WiFi, tent sites, dump, laundry, groc, LP gas, fire rings, firewood. **REC:** Saco River: swim, fishing, shuffleboard, playground. Pet restrict(B/Q) $. 2015 rates: $45 to $49. May 15 to Oct 15.
(603)447-2723 Lat: 43.99945, Lon: -71.11143
776 White Mountain Hwy/Rte 16, North Conway, NH 03818
www.thebeachcampingarea.com

Things to See and Do

↑ **CONWAY SCENIC RAILROAD** Old time train rides of varying duration (1 hr to 5 1/2 hrs) from restored Victorian depot. Partial handicap access. RV accessible. Restrooms, food. Hours: 9:30am to 5:30pm. Adult fee: $16 to $35.
(800)232-5251 Lat: 44.05239, Lon: -71.12876
38 Norcross Circle, North Conway, NH 03860
info@conwayscenic.com
www.conwayscenic.com
See ad page 763 (Welcome Section).

↑ **CRANMORE MOUNTAIN ADVENTURE PARK** Summer and winter activities; aerial adventure park, mountain adventure park, 5 aerial adventure courses, scenic chairlift, fitness center, 57 skiing trails, ski lessons, hiking, tubing park, giant swing, daycare, equip rentals. Partial

NORTH CONWAY (CONT)

CRANMORE MOUNTAIN (CONT)
handicap access. RV accessible. Restrooms, food. Hours: 10am to 6pm. ATM.
(603)356-5543 Lat: 44.055888, Lon: -71.109591
1 Skimobile Rd, North Conway, NH 03860
info@cranmore.com
www.cranmore.com
See ad page 763 (Welcome Section).

NORTH HAMPTON — F5 *Rockingham*

SHEL-AL CAMPGROUND
Ratings: 6.5/10★/9.5 (Campground) From Jct of I-95 & Rte 107 (exit 1), Go 0.1 mi E on Rte 107 to US-1, then 7 mi N (R). **FAC:** Paved/gravel rds. (64 spaces). Avail: 33 gravel, back-ins (26 x 40), 33 full hkups (30/50 amps), seasonal sites, WiFi Hotspot, tent sites, showers $, fire rings, firewood. **REC:** playground. Pets OK. Eco-friendly, 2015 rates: $44 to $46. Disc: military. May 15 to Oct 1.
AAA Approved
(603)964-5730 Lat: 42.98238, Lon: -70.83180
115 Lafayette Rd, North Hampton, NH 03862
camp@shel-al.com
www.shel-al.com
See ad page 768.

NORTH WOODSTOCK — C3 *Grafton*

LOST RIVER VALLEY CAMPGROUND **Ratings: 7/7.5/7.5** (Campground) 2015 rates: $35 to $41. May 15 to Oct 12. (603)745-8321 951 Lost River Road, North Woodstock, NH 03262

Things to See and Do

LOST RIVER GORGE AND BOULDER CAVES Ice age formation, boulder formed caves & waterfalls, gift shop & snack bar. Open weather permitting. Call. Last ticket sold 1 hr before closing. May 15 to Oct 18. RV accessible. Restrooms, food. Hours: 9am to 5pm. Adult fee: $18.
(603)745-8031 Lat: 44.03715, Lon: -71.78500
1712 Lost River Rd, North Woodstock, NH 03262
lostriver@visitwhitemountains.com
www.lostrivergorge.com
See ad page 763 (Welcome Section).

WHITE MOUNTAINS ATTRACTIONS ASSOC Visitors center for the White Mountains attractions, offering information, discount passes and gift shop. Partial handicap access. RV accessible. Restrooms. Hours: 8:30am to 5pm.
(603)745-8720 Lat: 44.03569, Lon: -71.67701
200 Kancamagus Hwy, North Woodstock, NH 03262
info@visitwhitemountains.com
www.visitwhitemountains.com
See ad page 763 (Welcome Section).

ORFORD — D2 *Grafton*

JACOBS BROOK CAMPGROUND
Ratings: 7/8.5★/8.5 (Campground) From Jct of I-91 & Fairlee/Orford exit (exit 15, VT), Go 300 yds E on connector rd to Rte 5, then 0.5 mi NE to Rte 25A, then 0.3 mi E to Rte 10, then 0.5 mi N to Archer Town Rd (at cemetery), then 1 mi NE to High Bridge Rd, then 0.3 mi NE (R) Reservations only. **FAC:** Gravel rds. (43 spaces). 25 Avail: 10 gravel, 15 grass, 3 pull-thrus (27 x 66), back-ins (26 x 52), 10 full hkups, 15 W, 15 E (30 amps), seasonal sites, WiFi, tent sites, showers $, dump, fire rings, firewood. **REC:** pool, Jacobs Brook: fishing, playground. Pets OK. Eco-friendly, 2015 rates: $35 to $38. May 28 to Oct 14.
(603)353-9210 Lat: 43.89788, Lon: -72.11966
46 High Bridge Rd, Orford, NH 03777
talk_to_us@jacobsbrookcampground.com
www.jacobsbrookcampground.com

OSSIPEE — D4 *Carroll*

BEAVER HOLLOW CAMPGROUND
Ratings: 9/9★/9 (Campground) From jct Hwy 28 & Hwy 16, Go 1.5 mi S on Hwy 16 (L). **FAC:** Gravel rds. (135 spaces). 50 Avail: 25 gravel, 20 grass, 5 dirt, 35 pull-thrus (35 x 60), back-ins (30 x 45), 46 full hkups, 4 W, 4 E (30/50 amps), seasonal sites, WiFi, tent sites, rentals, dump, laundry, LP gas, fire rings, firewood, controlled access. **REC:** heated pool, playground. Pet restrict(B/Q). Big rig sites, eco-friendly, 2015 rates: $40. Disc: AAA, military.
AAA Approved
(603)539-4800 Lat: 43.68835, Lon: -71.09339
700 Rte 16, Ossipee, NH 03864
inquiry@beaverhollowcampground.com
www.beaverhollowcampground.com
See ad this page.

PINKHAM NOTCH — C4 *Coos*

Things to See and Do

MOUNT WASHINGTON AUTO ROAD Trip to summit of the highest peak in Northeastern US. RV accessible. Restrooms, food. Hours: 8am to 5pm. Adult fee: $35. ATM.
(603)466-3988 Lat: 44.28901, Lon: -71.22525
1 Mount Washington Auto Road, Gorham, NH 03581
info@mtwashingtonautoroad.com
www.mtwashingtonautoroad.com
See ad page 763 (Welcome Section).

WILDCAT MOUNTAIN Gondola Skyride, Zip Rider Cable, Disc Golf, guided tours, stocked trout pond, Lunch N' Ride packages. (Summer and Fall). Skiing, snowboarding, ski school (Winter & Spring). RV accessible. Restrooms, food. Hours: 10am to 4pm. Adult fee: $15. ATM.
(888)754-9453 Lat: 44.26436, Lon: -71.23948
542 Rt 16, Pinkham Notch, NH 03581
info@skiwildcat.com
www.skiwildcat.com
See ad page 763 (Welcome Section).

PITTSBURG — A4 *Coos*

LAKE FRANCIS SP (State Pk) From town: Go 7 mi N on US-3. 2015 rates: $25 to $35. May 17 to Nov 11. (603)538-6965

RAYMOND — F4 *Rockingham*

PAWTUCKAWAY SP (State Pk) From jct Hwy 101 (exit 5) & Hwy 156: Go 2 mi N on Hwy 156, then 2 mi NW on Mountain Rd. 2015 rates: $25 to $30. May 3 to Oct 26. (603)895-3031

PINE ACRES RESORT **Ratings: 8/8/8** (Campground) 2015 rates: $44 to $64. Apr 15 to Oct 15. (603)895-2519 74 Freetown Rd, Raymond, NH 03077

RICHMOND — F2 *Cheshire*

SHIR-ROY CAMPING AREA Ratings: 7.5/8★/7 (Campground) From Jct of Rtes 10 & 119 (in Winchester), E 6 mi on Rte 119 to Rte 32, S 0.4 mi (L). **FAC:** Gravel rds. (120 spaces). 90 Avail: 46 gravel, 44 grass, 18 pull-thrus (36 x 56), back-ins (36 x 56), some side by side hkups, 88 full hkups, 2 W, 2 E (30/50 amps), seasonal sites, WiFi Hotspot, tent sites, rentals, dump, laundry, groc, fire rings, firewood. **REC:** Cass Pond: swim, fishing, playground. Pet restrict(Q). 2015 rates: $32 to $43. May 25 to Oct 14. No CC.
AAA Approved
(603)239-4768 Lat: 42.74457, Lon: -72.26905
136 Athol Rd, Richmond, NH 03470
Camp@Shir-Roy.com
www.shir-roy.com

RUMNEY — D3 *Grafton*

RIVERBROOK RV RESORT **Ratings: 8.5/8.5★/7.5** (Campground) 2015 rates: $24 to $48. (888)786-2333 1120 Mt Moosilauke Hwy, Rumney, NH 03266

Things to See and Do

POLAR CAVES PARK Self-guided tours, 9 glacial caves, nature trails, Maple Sugar Museum, snack bar, deer exhibit, two distinctive gift shops, glacial gardens, mining sluice, Klondike mine. Group rates available. Last ticket sold 1 hr before closing. May 10 to Oct 12. RV accessible. Restrooms, food. Hours: 9am to 5pm. Adult fee: $16.50.
(603)536-1888 Lat: 43.78248, Lon: -71.78145
705 Rumney Rte 25, Rumney, NH 03264
info@polarcaves.com
www.polarcaves.com
See ad page 763 (Welcome Section).

SANDOWN — F4 *Rockingham*

ANGLE POND GROVE CAMPING AREA Ratings: 7.5/8★/6 (Campground) From Jct of I-93 & SR-111 (exit 3), Go 11 mi E on Rte 111 to SR-121A, then 0.5 mi N (L). **FAC:** Gravel rds. (136 spaces). Avail: 18 grass, back-ins (24 x 40), 18 full hkups (30/50 amps), seasonal sites, WiFi, tent sites, rentals, showers $, laundry, LP bottles, fire rings, firewood, controlled access. **REC:** pond, Angle Pond: swim, fishing, shuffleboard, playground, rec open to public. No pets. Eco-friendly, 2015 rates: $35 to $40. May 15 to Oct 15.
AAA Approved
(603)887-4434 Lat: 42.89960, Lon: -71.14914
9 Pillsbury Rd, Sandown, NH 03873
camp@anglepondgrove.com
www.anglepondgrove.com

SOUTH TAMWORTH — D4 *Carroll*

RIVERBEND CAMPGROUND
Ratings: 7/8.5★/7.5 (RV Park) From jct Hwy 16 & Hwy 25, Go 7 mi W on Hwy 25, then 100 ft W on Hwy 113 (Bearcamp Hwy) (L). **FAC:** Gravel rds. (30 spaces). Avail: 25 gravel, 9 pull-thrus (30 x 60), back-ins (30 x 40), some side by side hkups, 25 full hkups (30/50 amps), seasonal sites, WiFi, tent sites, dump, laundry, fire rings, firewood. **REC:** pool, Bearcamp River: fishing, playground. Pets OK. Big rig sites, 2015 rates: $35 to $50. May 15 to Oct 15.
(603)323-9133 Lat: 43.82838, Lon: -71.32797
11 Jackman Pond Rd (Jct of Rt-25 & 113W), South Tamworth, NH 03883
info@riverbend-nh.com
www.riverbend-nh.com
See ad this page, 765.

STRAFFORD — E4 *Strafford*

CROWN POINT CAMPGROUND
Ratings: 9.5/9.5★/10 (Campground) From Jct of Spaulding Tpke exit 14 & Ten Rod Road, Go 0.2 mi S to Rte 11/Main St, then E 0.1 mi E to Twombly St, then 0.3 mi SW to Rte 202A, then 4 mi W to First Crown Point Rd, then 0.3 mi N (L). **FAC:** Gravel rds. (135 spaces). Avail: 50 all weather, 1 pull-thru (24 x 60), back-ins (34 x 44), 50 full hkups (30/50 amps), seasonal sites, cable, WiFi, tent sites, rentals, dump, mobile sewer, laundry, groc, LP gas, fire rings, firewood, controlled access. **REC:** heated pool, pond, swim, fishing, playground. Pet re-

We appreciate your business!

We rate what RVers consider important.

STRAFFORD (CONT)

CROWN POINT CAMPGROUND (CONT)
strict(B/Q). Big rig sites, eco-friendly, 2015 rates: $49 to $68. Disc: AAA. May 15 to Oct 15.
(603)332-0405 Lat: 43.28605, Lon: -71.06756
79 First Crown Point Rd, Strafford, NH 03884
camp@crownpointcampground.com
www.crownpointcampground.com
See ad this page, 765.

SWANZEY — F2 *Cheshire*

ASHUELOT RIVER CAMPGROUND **Ratings: 7/8.5/7** (Campground) 2015 rates: $35 to $42. May 1 to Oct 31. (603)357-5777 152 Pine St, Swanzey, NH 03446

SWANZEY LAKE CAMPING AREA **Ratings: 6.5/8★/6.5** (Campground) 2015 rates: $34 to $36. Apr 15 to Nov 1. (603)352-9880 88 E Shore Rd, Swanzey, NH 03446

TAMWORTH — D4 *Carroll*

TAMWORTH CAMPING AREA
Ratings: 7/8.5★/8 (Campground) From Jct of Hwys 25W & 16, Go 0.5 mi N on Hwy 16 to Depot Rd, W 3 mi (L). **FAC:** Gravel rds. (100 spaces). Avail: 75 gravel, 5 pull-thrus (35 x 60), back-ins (30 x 46), 14 full hkups, 61 W, 56 E (30/50 amps), seasonal sites, cable, WiFi Hotspot, tent sites, rentals, showers $, dump, laundry, LP bottles, fire rings, firewood, controlled access. **REC:** Swift River: swim, fishing, shuffleboard, playground. Pets OK. Big rig sites, eco-friendly, 2015 rates: $34 to $49. May 15 to Oct 15.
AAA Approved
(603)323-8031 Lat: 43.84639, Lon: -71.25764
194 Depot Rd, Tamworth, NH 03886
info@tamworthcamping.com
www.tamworthcamping.com
See ad this page.

THORNTON — D3 *Grafton*

GOOSE HOLLOW CAMPGROUND **Ratings: 7/6.5/8** (RV Park) 2015 rates: $43. (603)726-2000 35 Burbank Hill Rd, Thornton, NH 03285

PEMI RIVER CAMPGROUND **Ratings: 6/6.5/7.5** (Campground) 2015 rates: $40 to $45. May 1 to Oct 15. (603)726-7015 2458 US Rte 3, Thornton, NH 03285

TWIN MOUNTAIN — C3 *Coos*

BEECH HILL CAMPGROUND & CABINS
Ratings: 8/9★/8.5 (Campground) From Jct of US-3 & US-302, W 1.8 mi on US-302 (R). **FAC:** Gravel rds. (107 spaces). 74 Avail: 50 grass, 24 dirt, back-ins (30 x 60), 24 full hkups, 50 W, 50 E (30/50 amps), seasonal sites, cable, WiFi, tent sites, rentals, dump, laundry, groc, LP gas, fire rings, firewood, controlled access. **REC:** heated pool, Ammonoosuc River: swim, fishing, shuffleboard, playground. Pets OK. Big rig sites, eco-friendly, 2015 rates: $37.50 to $47.50. May 15 to Oct 15. ATM.
(603)846-5521 Lat: 44.27367, Lon: -71.57516
970 Rte 302W, Twin Mountain, NH 03595
beechhill@ncia.net
www.beechhill.com
See ad this page.

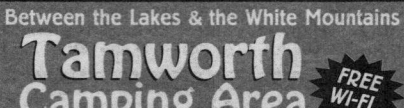

TARRY HO CAMPGROUND & CABINS
Ratings: 7/9.5★/8.5 (Campground) From Jct of I-93 & US 302 (Exit 40), E 9 mi on US 302 (R); or From Jct of I-93 & US 3 (Exit 35), N 9 mi on US 3 to US 302, W 0.5 mi (L). **FAC:** Gravel rds. (50 spaces). Avail: 44 grass, back-ins (30 x 45), 29 full hkups, 15 W, 15 E (30/50 amps), seasonal sites, WiFi, tent sites, rentals, dump, fire rings, firewood. **REC:** pool, Ammonoosuc River: fishing, playground, rec open to public. Pets OK $. Eco-friendly, 2015 rates: $39 to $49. Disc: AAA, military. May 15 to Nov 12.
(603)846-1026 Lat: 44.27195, Lon: -71.55331
373 Rte 302 West, Twin Mountain, NH 03595
Stay@tarryho.com
www.tarryho.com

TWIN MOUNTAIN MOTOR COURT & RV PARK
Ratings: 7.5/NA/8 (RV Park) N-bnd: From Jct of I-93 & Rte 3 (exit 35), N 9 mi on Rte 3 (L); or S-bnd: From Jct of I-93 & Rte 302 (exit 40), E 10.8 mi on Rte 302 to Rte 3, S 1 mi (R). **FAC:** Gravel rds. 18 gravel, 18 pull-thrus (32 x 85), accepts full hkup units only, 18 full hkups (30 amps), cable, WiFi, rentals, laundry, fire rings, firewood. **REC:** pool, Ammonoosuc River: fishing, playground. Pet restrict(B). No tents. 2015 rates: $40. Disc: AAA, military. May 1 to Oct 15.
AAA Approved
(603)846-5574 Lat: 44.26808, Lon: -71.55940
554 Rte 3 S, Twin Mountain, NH 03595
Tmmcrv@gmail.com
www.tmmcrv.com

TWIN MOUNTAIN/MT.WASHINGTON KOA Ratings: 8.5/9.5★/8.5 (Campground) From Jct of US-3 & US-302, Go 2 mi N on US-3 to SR-115, then 0.8 mi N (R). **FAC:** Gravel rds. 60 gravel, 21 pull-thrus (25 x 65), back-ins (25 x 45), some side by side hkups, 36 full hkups, 24 W, 24 E (30/50 amps), cable, WiFi, tent sites, rentals, dump, laundry, groc, LP gas, fire rings, firewood. **REC:** heated pool, playground. Pet restrict(B). Big rig sites, eco-friendly, 2015 rates: $40 to $65. May 14 to Oct 11.
AAA Approved
(603)846-5559 Lat: 44.30476, Lon: -71.53220
372 Rte 115, Twin Mountain, NH 03595
campkoa@roadrunner.com
www.twinmountainkoa.com

WARREN — D3 *Grafton*

MOOSE HILLOCK CAMPGROUND **Ratings: 7.5/8.5★/8** (Campground) 2015 rates: $52 to $79. May 16 to Oct 14. (603)764-5294 96 Batchelder Brook Rd - Rte 118 N, Warren, NH 03279

SCENIC VIEW CAMPGROUND **Ratings: 8/8.5★/8** (Campground) 2015 rates: $39 to $49. May 16 to Oct 12. (603)764-9380 18 Gingerbread Lane, Warren, NH 03279

WASHINGTON — E2 *Sullivan*

PILLSBURY SP (State Pk) From town: Go 4 mi N on Hwy 31. Pit toilets. 2015 rates: $23. May 24 to Oct 20. (603)863-2860

WEARE — E3 *Hillsborough*

AUTUMN HILLS CAMPGROUND **Ratings: 7.5/7.5★/7.5** (Campground) 2015 rates: $37 to $42. May 1 to Oct 15. (603)529-2425 285 S Stark Hwy, Weare, NH 03281

COLD SPRINGS CAMP RESORT Ratings: 9.5/10★/10 (RV Resort) From S Jct of I-93 & I-293, Go 3 mi W on I-293 to Rte 101, then 1.5 mi W to Rte 114, then 12 mi NW to Barnard Hill Rd, then 0.2 mi N (R). **FAC:** Paved rds. (380 spaces). Avail: 100 gravel, 11 pull-thrus (33 x 64), back-ins (24 x 60), 96 full hkups, 4 W, 4 E (30/50 amps), seasonal sites, cable, WiFi, tent sites, rentals, showers $, dump, laundry, groc, LP gas, fire rings, firewood, restaurant, controlled access. **REC:** heated pool, wading pool, whirlpool, pond, swim, shuffleboard, playground. Pet restrict(B) $. Partial handicap access. Big rig sites, eco-friendly, 2015 rates: $60 to $64. May 1 to Oct 12. ATM.
(603)529-2528 Lat: 43.05372, Lon: -71.68923
62 Barnard Hill Rd, Weare, NH 03281
info@coldspringscampresort.com
www.coldspringscampresort.com

WEBSTER — E3 *Merrimack*

COZY POND CAMPING RESORT **Ratings: 6.5/7/8** (Campground) 2015 rates: $39 to $47. May 8 to Oct 12. (603)428-7701 541 Battle St, Webster, NH 03303

WEIRS BEACH — D4 *Belknap*

HACK-MA-TACK FAMILY CAMPGROUND **Ratings: 6/6.5/6** (Campground) 2015 rates: $35 to $45. May 22 to Oct 12. (603)366-5977 rt 3, Weirs Beach, NH 03246

PAUGUS BAY CAMPGROUND **Ratings: 7/8.5★/8** (Campground) 2015 rates: $44 to $48. May 15 to Oct 15. (603)366-4757 96 Hilliard Rd, Weirs Beach, NH 03246

PINE HOLLOW CAMPGROUND
Ratings: 8.5/8.5★/8.5 (Campground) From Jct Hwy 104 & US 3, Go 0.75mi S on US 3 (R). **FAC:** Paved/gravel rds. (40 spaces). 25 Avail: 20 paved, 5 gravel, back-ins (35 x 40), 13 full hkups, 12 W, 12 E (30 amps), seasonal sites, cable, WiFi, tent sites, dump, laundry, fire rings, firewood, controlled access. **REC:** pool. Pet restrict(B). 2015 rates: $38 to $45. May 1 to Oct 12.
(603)366-2222 Lat: 43.61581, Lon: -71.48027
656 Endicott N, Weirs Beach, NH 03247-5024
camp@pinehollowcampground.com
www.pinehollowcampground.com
See ad this page.

Follow the arrow. The arrow in each listing indicates where the facility is located in relation to the listed town.

WENTWORTH — D3 *Grafton*

PINE HAVEN CAMPGROUND **Ratings: 7/8★/7.5** (Campground) 2015 rates: $36.95 to $42.95. May 15 to Oct 15. (603)786-2900 29 Pine Haven Campground Rd, Wentworth, NH 03282

WEST OSSIPEE — D4 *Carroll*

WHITE LAKE SP (State Pk) From jct Hwy 16 & Hwy 25: Go 1-1/2 mi N on Hwy 16. 2015 rates: $25 to $30. May 24 to Oct 13. (603)323-7350

Find it fast! To locate a town on a map, follow these easy instructions: Look for the map grid code after the town heading in the listing section and match it to the letters and numbers on the map borders. Draw a line horizontally from the letter and vertically from the number. You'll find the town near the intersection of the two lines.

WOLFEBORO — D4 *Carroll*

WOLFEBORO CAMPGROUND **Ratings: 5.5/8★/7.5** (Campground) From S Jct of Hwy 28 & Rte 109 (in town), Go 4.5 mi N on Hwy 28 to Haines Hill Rd, then 1000 ft NE, up hill (R). **FAC:** Gravel rds. 25 dirt, back-ins (28 x 40), 25 full hkups (30/50 amps), WiFi, tent sites, showers $, groc, LP gas, fire rings, firewood. Pet restrict(Q). 2015 rates: $32. May 15 to Oct 15.
AAA Approved
(603)569-9881 Lat: 43.63483, Lon: -71.15269
61 Haines Hill Rd, Wolfeboro, NH 03894
www.wolfeborocampground.com

WOODSTOCK — C3 *Grafton*

LINCOLN/WOODSTOCK KOA **Ratings: 8/9.5★/8.5** (Campground) 2015 rates: $39 to $78. May 1 to Oct 18. (800)562-9736 1000 Eastside Rd, Woodstock, NH 03293

How much does a fishing license cost in Idaho? Can you turn right on a red light in Rhode Island? Check the Table of Contents for the page location for annual updates of important towing laws, rules of the road, bridge and tunnel information and fishing license fees.

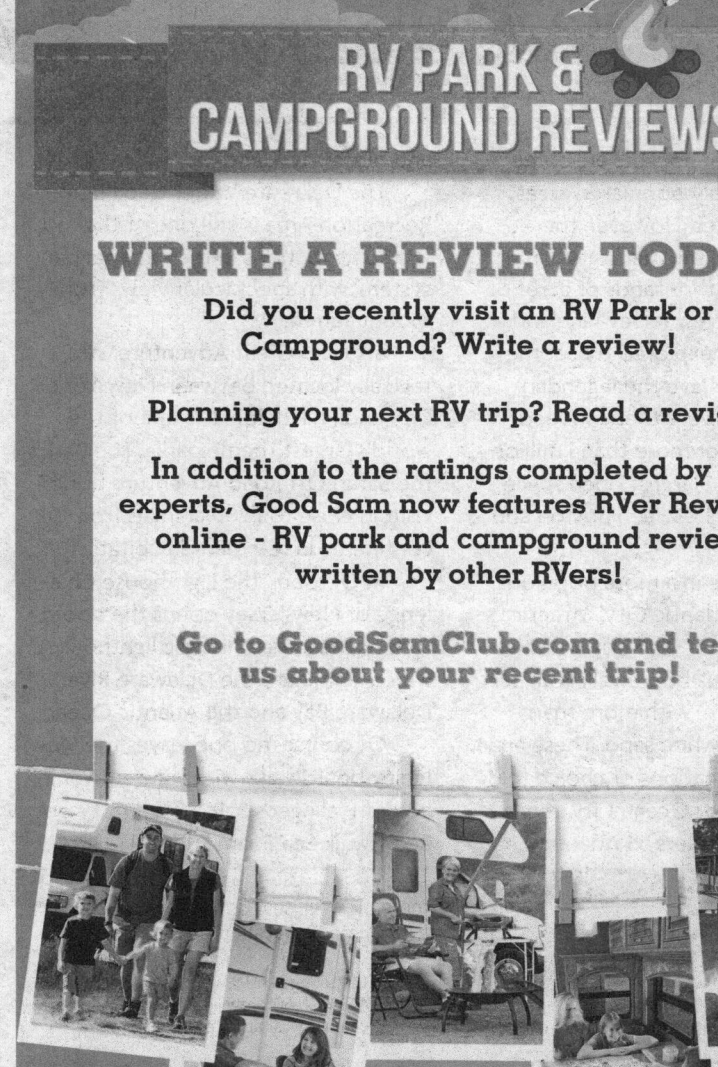

NH

Getty Images/iStockphoto

WELCOME TO New Jersey

DATE OF STATEHOOD	WIDTH: 70 MILES (113 KM)	PROPORTION OF UNITED STATES
DEC. 18, 1787	LENGTH: 170 MILES (273 KM)	0.23% OF 3,794,100 SQ MI

New Jersey's urban pockets are some of the most densely populated areas in the United States. However, the so-called Garden State earns its name with hundreds of thousands of acres of open space. The New Jersey Pinelands are so vast and unexplored that some New Jerseyites believe the legendary Jersey Devil still dwells there. Indeed, the Pinelands cover more than 1 million acres of land—the largest open space on the East Coast between Boston and Richmond, Virginia.

For adventure in a more populous area, check out Atlantic City, "America's Favorite Playground." The city with the casinos and famous boardwalk is all part of the Jersey Shore, with more than 100 miles of soft, white sand. These are the summer destinations of choice for families heading for Ocean City, teens to Wildwood, gamblers to Atlantic City and birders to Cape May.

The Delaware Water Gap National Recreation Area is still one of the most visited attractions in the national park system, with spectacular views from Mount Tammany.

Six Flags Great Adventure, strategically located between New York City and Philadelphia, is one of the world's largest theme parks. The park's the Safari Off Road Adventure brings visitors close to 1,200 animals from six continents in re-created habitats.

In October, the Lighthouse Challenge of New Jersey opens the doors to 11 of the state's historic lighthouses, which illuminate the Delaware River, Delaware Bay and the Atlantic Ocean.

Of course, no one leaves the New Jersey boardwalks without a souvenir box of Fralinger's Salt Water Taffy or Boardwalk Sea Foam Fudge.

TRAVEL & TOURISM

New Jersey Department of Tourism
800-VISIT NJ, 609-777-0885
www.visitnj.org

Atlantic City Convention & Visitors Authority
888-228-4748
www.atlanticcitynj.com

Garden State Wine Growers Association
www.newjerseywines.com

Meadowlands Liberty CVB
877-MLCVB-US
www.meadowlandslibertcvb.com

New Jersey Lighthouse Society
www.njlhs.org

Ocean City Boardwalk
800-BEACH-NJ, 609-399-1412
www.OceanCityVacation.com

Ocean City Welcome Center
800-BEACH-NJ, 609-399-1412
www.OceanCityVacation.com

Ocean County Public Affairs and Tourism
732-929-2000
www.oceancountytourism.com

South Jersey Tourism Corp.
856-757-9400
www.visitsouthjersey.com

Southern Shore Tourism Council
609-463-6415, 800-227-2297
www.njsouthernshore.com

Top 3 Tourism Attractions:
1) Atlantic City Boardwalk
2) Ocean City Boardwalk
3) Six Flags Great Adventure Theme Park/Six Flags Wild Safari

Nickname: Garden State

State Flower: Purple Violet

State Bird: Eastern Goldfinch

People: Bud Abbott and Lou Costello, comedy team; Buzz Aldrin, astronaut; Charles Addams, creator of Addams Family cartoons; Jon Bon Jovi, musician; Joseph Campbell, founder of the Campbell Soup Company

Major Cities: Newark, Jersey City, Paterson, Elizabeth, Edison, (Trenton, capital)

Topography: Northwest—Appalachian Valley; northeast-southwest—mountain ranges, Piedmont Plateau, low plains, high ridges; southeast—coastal plain

Climate: Moderate climate with cold winters and warm, humid summers

OUTDOOR RECREATION

New Jersey Division of Fish & Wildlife
609-292-2965
www.nj.gov-dep

New Jersey State Golf Association
908-241-GOLF
www.njsga.org

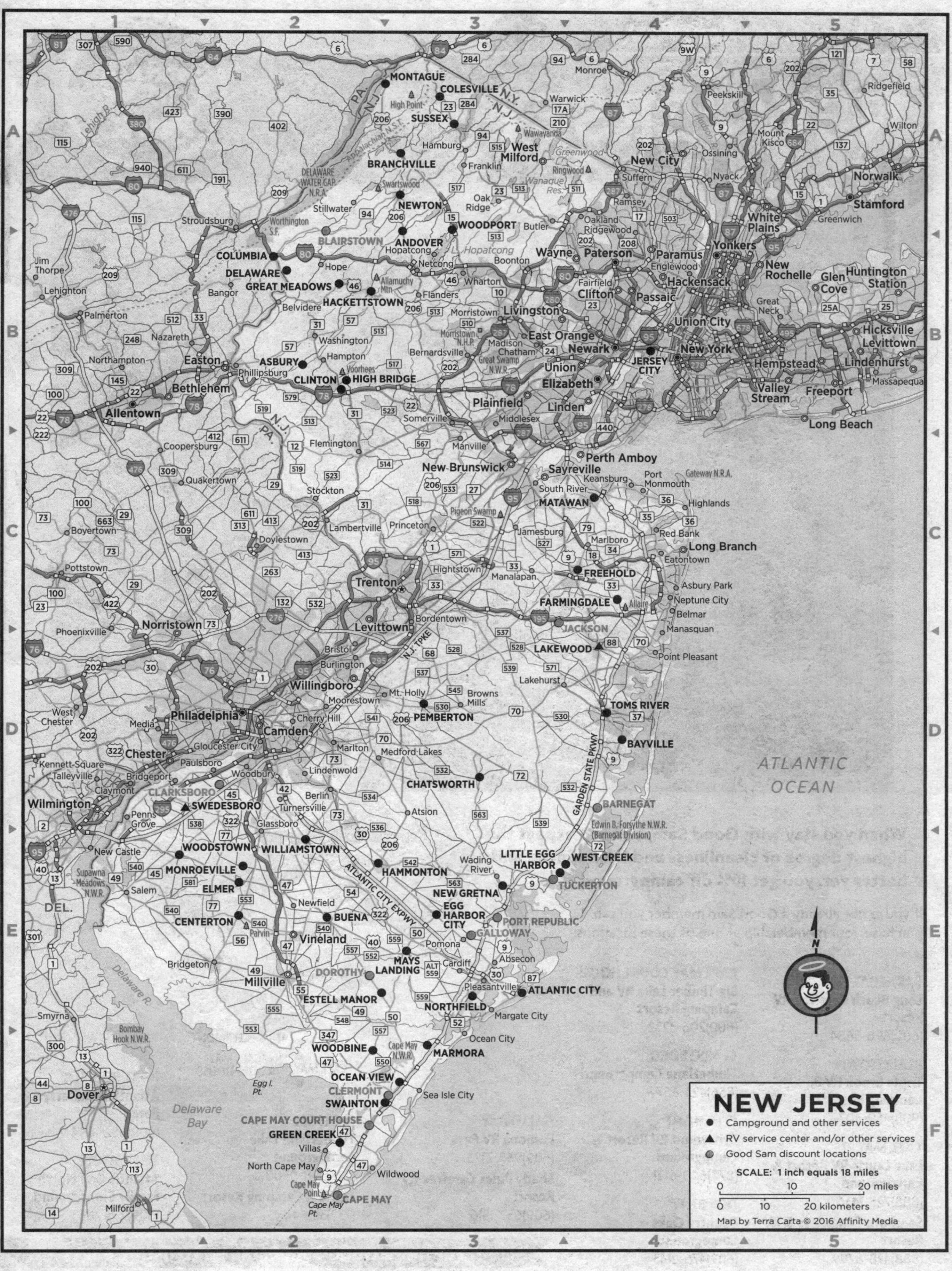
NEW JERSEY
Campground and other services
RV service center and/or other services
Good Sam discount locations
SCALE: 1 inch equals 18 miles
0 10 20 miles
0 10 20 kilometers
Map by Terra Carta © 2016 Affinity Media
ATLANTIC OCEAN
Delaware Bay
MONTAGUE
COLESVILLE
SUSSEX
BRANCHVILLE
NEWTON
WOODPORT
ANDOVER
BLAIRSTOWN
COLUMBIA
DELAWARE
GREAT MEADOWS
HACKETTSTOWN
ASBURY
CLINTON
HIGH BRIDGE
MATAWAN
FREEHOLD
FARMINGDALE
JACKSON
LAKEWOOD
TOMS RIVER
BAYVILLE
PEMBERTON
CHATSWORTH
BARNEGAT
LITTLE EGG HARBOR
WEST CREEK
TUCKERTON
NEW GRETNA
EGG HARBOR CITY
PORT REPUBLIC
GALLOWAY
HAMMONTON
WILLIAMSTOWN
WOODSTOWN
MONROEVILLE
ELMER
CENTERTON
BUENA
CLARKSBORO
SWEDESBORO
MAYS LANDING
DOROTHY
ESTELL MANOR
NORTHFIELD
ATLANTIC CITY
WOODBINE
MARMORA
OCEAN VIEW
CLERMONT
SWAINTON
CAPE MAY COURT HOUSE
GREEN CREEK
CAPE MAY
JERSEY CITY
New York
Newark
Trenton
Philadelphia
Camden
Wilmington
Allentown
Bethlehem
Easton
Paterson
Yonkers
Stamford
Long Beach
GARDEN STATE PKWY
ATLANTIC CITY EXPWY
N.J. TPKE

Featured Good Sam Parks

NEW JERSEY

Good Sam Park

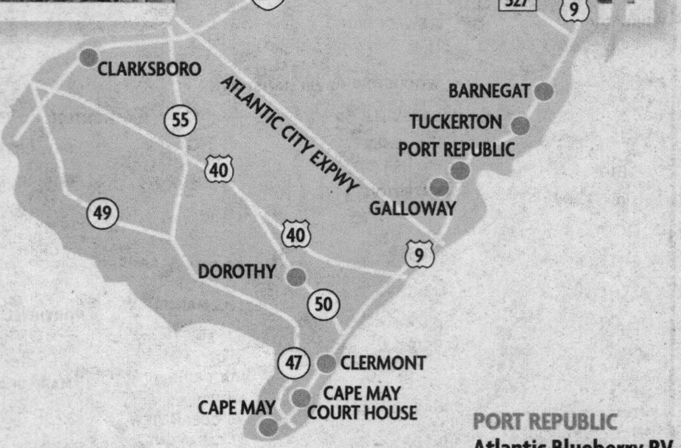

When you stay with Good Sam, you can expect the highest degree of cleanliness and friendliness, and better yet, you get 10% off campground fees.

If you're not already a Good Sam member you can purchase your membership at one of these locations:

BARNEGAT
Long Beach Carefree RV Resort
(609)698-5684

BLAIRSTOWN
Triple Brook RV & Camping Resort
(908)459-4079

CAPE MAY
Lake Laurie RV Resort & Campground
(888)725-1436
Seashore Campsites & RV Resort
(888)478-8799

CAPE MAY COURT HOUSE
Big Timber Lake RV and Camping Resort
(800)206-3232

CLARKSBORO
Timberlane Campground
(856)423-6677

CLERMONT
Driftwood RV Resort & Campground
(877)600-6121

DOROTHY
Country Oaks Campground
(609)476-2143

GALLOWAY
Pomona RV Park
(609)965-2123
Shady Pines Carefree RV Resort
(609)652-1516

JACKSON
Timberland Lake Campground
(732)928-0500
Tip Tam Camping Resort
(732)363-4036

PORT REPUBLIC
Atlantic Blueberry RV Park
(609)652-1644

TUCKERTON
Atlantic City North Family Campground
(609)296-9163

For more Good Sam Parks go to listing pages

ATLANTIC CITY

Wander the world's most famous boardwalk

Welcome to the glittering Atlantic City boardwalk, a six-mile-long open-air playground bridging white sandy beaches and rolling Atlantic surf with a buffet of world-class restaurants, shops, casinos and luxury hotels. It's almost hard to believe it all started as a way of simply keeping sand from being tracked into hotel lobbies and train cars.

It was 1870, and an exacerbated hotel owner and railroad conductor had just successfully petitioned the city to build a wooden boardwalk, all in the pursuit of saving their carpets and floors. The finished walk cost $5,000, was only one mile in length and had to be picked back up again at the end of each summer season and stored for the winter. A bizarre city ordinance also barred commerce from within 100 feet of the walk.

But like sand tracked from beach to heel to hotel lobby, the early inertia of the boardwalk was hard to contain or altogether control. Less than 20 years after the walk's first plank was laid, the ordinance barring commerce was "tossed to sea," as some put at the time. Stores, stalls and stands flooded the increasingly popular beachfront. Business boomed and the boardwalk was continuously expanded, reinvented and transformed over the course of the next century into the powerhouse of entertainment we know today.

Business boomed and the boardwalk was continuously expanded, reinvented and transformed over the course of the next century into the powerhouse of entertainment we know today.

Boardwalk Empire

The history and growth of the boardwalk is a fascinating tale, and can be explored in-depth at the Atlantic City Historical Museum. Located on Garden Pier, it showcases the rise of the boardwalk into a world-class entertainment destination with a slate of state-of-the-art interactive digital exhibits. The collections also include artifacts and paraphernalia from some of the earliest Miss America pageants.

Looks can be deceiving here, however. Even as the uncontested gambling capital of the entire eastern seaboard—home to the likes of the Trump Taj Mahal, Golden Nugget and the Tropicana—the city has managed to somehow still retain a measure of its humble and practical roots. The beaches are free, the boardwalk is an attraction in itself, and one of the best things a visitor can do is simply snag a bite or two of some authentic Atlantic City salt water taffy (invented when a storm surge flooded a candy store).

If you're a recreation hound or outdoorsy type, you can safely skip the glitzy casinos entirely and spend all of your time on the beach or in the water.

Casinos along the waterfront in Atlantic City, New Jersey. Getty Images/iStockphoto

Absecon Lighthouse in Atlantic City. Getty Images/iStockphoto

Downtown Beach, Crystal Beach and Delaware Avenue Beach are popular surfing spots. A variety of on-site vendors provide board rentals and surfing lessons. Kayakers and windsurfers can find similar options at Jackson Avenue Beach. For anglers, Maine Avenue is a busy spot, but all beaches are open to shallow-water surf fishing in the early mornings and late evenings, so avoid the crowds by watching the sun rise or set while casting for some trophy-class Striped Bass.

> Ripley's Believe It or Not! Odditorium is filled to the brim with some of the strangest artifacts and artistic exhibits you'll ever see. See shrunken heads and a laser maze.

Family-Friendly Fun

If you're traveling with kids, a quartet of family-friendly attractions will arouse your attention. The Steel Pier amusement park, the Ripley's Believe It or Not! Odditorium, the Atlantic City Aquarium and the Monopoly Monument at the corner of Boardwalk and Park Place are all must-visits.

Steel Pier first opened in 1898, and throughout its colorful history has played host to entertainers like Frank Sinatra and The Beatles. Today it's home to more than 25 thrill rides, a classic Ferris wheel, a row of challenging carnival games and a range of eclectic exhibits.

The Ripley's Believe It or Not! Odditorium, for its part, is for the curious and the strong-willed. It's filled to the brim with some of the strangest artifacts and artistic exhibits you'll ever see, from shrunken heads and roulette tables made of jellybeans, to a giant Laser Maze and a spider web made of scissors.

For a more educational experience, head to the Atlantic City Aquarium, located at Historic Gardiner's Basin. It's home to the likes of loggerhead sea turtles, moray eels, tropical sharks and a range of exotic reptiles.

Finally there's the Monopoly Monument. As you walk the boardwalk you'll notice a central theme surrounding the streets and avenues that spill onto the waterfront. Properties and place-names in the legendary board game were named after existing streets and places in Atlantic City. Today, a life-sized version of the game sits at the corner of the real Boardwalk and real Park Place, making it one of the absolute must-visit photo-op stops of any visit to Atlantic City.

It's been more than a century now, and there's just no stopping Atlantic City. From sand to anti-commerce laws to the competition from Las Vegas to surging tropical storms—the boardwalk has stared down them all and continues to thrive.

For More Information

Atlantic City Convention and Visitors Authority
609-348-7100
www.atlanticcitynj.com

New Jersey Department of Tourism
609-599-6540
www.visitnj.org

CAPE MAY COUNTY

Victorian charm reigns in this historic coastal region

The spirit of small-town America and the charming aesthetic found in classic Normal Rockwell paintings are defining characteristics of Cape May County, New Jersey. Tree-lined streets and Victorian-inspired homes with tidy porches and crisp American flags are buffered by friendly mom-and-pop shops and a distinct lack of big-box outlets.

Nowhere is that more apparent than in the city of Cape May itself, where in 1878 a small fire nearly burned the entire community to the ground. When all was said and done, more than 40 acres had been razed, leaving behind a massive swath of charred rubble. The ensuing reconstruction resulted in an explosion of ornate Victorian-era homes and resorts, most or all of which still stand to this day—and in tip-top shape, no less.

While many think of Atlantic City when it comes to beachside vacationing on the eastern seaboard, Cape May County's 30-mile ribbon of white sandy beachfront has been attracting visitors and resorters for more than a century. Popular landing spots are Ocean City, Sea Isle City, Avalon, Stone Harbor the Wildwoods (North Wildwood, West Wildwood and Wildwood Crest) and, of course, Cape May at the peninsulas extreme southern tip.

An Ocean of Fun

Ocean City is a popular and slightly quieter alternative to the thronging crowds found in Atlantic City a short distance to the north. The city has cultivated its family-friendly image since 1879, when it outlawed the sale of alcohol. Ever since it's been a dry town, more geared toward activities like mini golf and music festivals than gambling. Gillian's Wonderland Pier is the premier must-visit attraction, offering more than 38 rides and midway activities for visitors of all ages.

As you move south down the eastern side of the Cape the crowds grow thinner and the communities quieter. Sea Isle City and Avalon are popular laid-back vacation spots for water sports, shopping and sunbathing. Stone Harbor, just north of the Wildwoods, is a great place to window-shop, and wildlife enthusiasts will want to check out the eco-conservationist programs, tours and exhibits at the Wetlands Institute near the center of town.

In the Wildwoods—comprised of North Wildwood, West Wildwood and Wildwood Crest—a 3-mile boardwalk buzzes with an assortment of amusement rides, roller coasters, waterparks and a world-class selection of beachfront restaurants. It's classic Americana on full display. Morey's Piers is the star of the show, offering the usual beachfront amusement park selection of coasters, thrill rides, carnival games and bumper cars. It's also the home of a shipwreck-inspired water park, tropical island beach club and cliff dive themed water slide. Splash Zone Water, home to man-made whitewater rapids, is another popular attraction in the Wildwoods.

 See map page 779

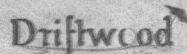

Visit Victorian Times

Cape May, at the extreme southern tip of the peninsula, is one of the oldest resorting communities in the country. Its slate of Victorian-inspired homes and tree-lined streets make it a treat to simply stroll and explore on foot. A trip to the top of the Cape May Lighthouse is a must-do, and a tour of the Emlen Physick Estate offers insight into life on the Cape May coast, circa 1879.

If you're a history buff visiting the Cape, you'll want to set aside a significant portion of your time to scour the entire peninsula from top to bottom. You can slowly hop your way from north to south and east to west exploring a range of eclectic museums that cover everything from rock-and-roll to Naval aviation.

The Stone Harbor Museum, Sea Isle City Historical Museum and Avalon Museum provide insight into the history of each community and the Cape at large. Other popular museums include the American Lifesaving Station (dating back to 1895), the Doo Wop Museum (celebrating America's rock-and-roll history) and the Hereford Inlet Lighthouse (dating to 1874).

A heron soars over Cape May County. Getty Images/iStockphoto

At the northern end of the Cape, the Cape May County Zoo features free admission and guided tours. More than 100 species of animals are on display, including lions, tigers, giraffes and zebras. The Zoo is part of the Cape May County Park, which is full of picnic areas and open-pit barbecues, making the area a nice day-trip alternative from the beaches and amusement park rides of eastern Cape May County.

From its quiet historic communities dotted with Victorian homes and eclectic shops, to its buzzing beachfronts loaded with roller coasters and thrill rides, Cape May County offers something for everyone.

For More Information

Cape May Chamber of Commerce
609-884-5508
www.capemaychamber.com

New Jersey Department of Tourism
609-599-6540
www.visitnj.org

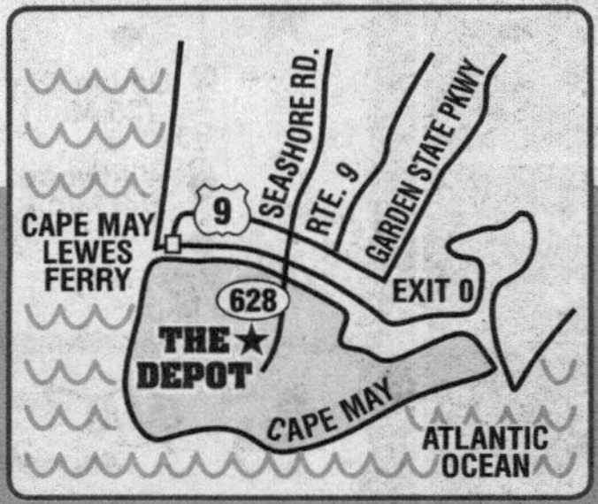

New Jersey

CONSULTANTS

Greg & Maureen Baron

ANDOVER — B3 *Sussex*

PANTHER LAKE CAMPING RESORT **Ratings: 7.5/7.5/7.5** (Campground) 2015 rates: $49 to $59. Apr 1 to Oct 31. (973)347-4440 6 Panther Lake Rd, Andover, NJ 07821

Want to know how we rate? Our campground inspection guidelines are detailed in the front pages of the Guide.

Our rating system isn't just tough, it's thorough. We know the kinds of things that are important to you — like clean restrooms and showers, attractive, secure, well-tended grounds, and extras like swimming pools. We give the first rating for development of facilities, the second for cleanliness and physical characteristics of restrooms and showers, and the third for visual appearance.

RV Park ratings you can rely on!

ASBURY — B2 *Warren*

JUGTOWN MOUNTAIN CAMPSITES **Ratings: 5.5/7.5/5** (Campground) 2015 rates: $35 to $38. (908)735-5995 1074 Hwy 173, Asbury, NJ 08802

ATLANTIC CITY — E3 *Atlantic*

A SPOTLIGHT Introducing Atlantic City's colorful attractions appearing at the front of this state section.

BARNEGAT — D4 *Ocean*

BROOKVILLE CAMPGROUND

Ratings: 6/8.5★/8 (Campground) From North: Jct of Garden State Pkwy & Exit 69 (CR 532), W 3.5 mi on CR 532 to Brookville Rd (CR 611), S 1.1 mi to Jones Rd, E 0.4 mi (E); or From South: Jct of Garden State Pkwy & Exit 67 (SR-72), NW 5.3 mi on SR-72 to CR-554, E 0.9 mi to Brookville Rd (CR 611), N 0.8 mi to Jones Rd, E 0.4 mi(E). **FAC:** Gravel rds. (82 spaces). Avail: 45 gravel, back-ins (30 x 50), some side by side hkups, 45 full hkups (30 amps), seasonal sites, tent sites, rentals, dump, fire rings, firewood. **REC:** pool, Brookville Lake: fishing,

Say you saw it in our Guide!

See listing Barnegat, NJ

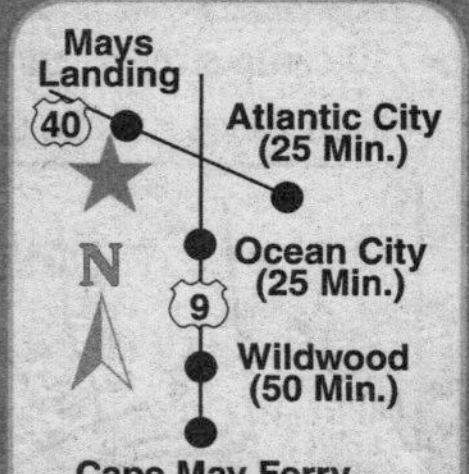

BARNEGAT (CONT)

BROOKVILLE CAMPGROUND (CONT)
playground. Pets OK. 2015 rates: $37.50. Apr 15 to Oct 1. No CC.
(609)698-3134 Lat: 39.78153, Lon: -74.30737
224 Jones Road - 120, Barnegat, NJ 08005
www.brookvillecampground.com
See ad opposite page.

← LONG BEACH CAREFREE RV RESORT
Ratings: 8/9★/9 (RV Park) From Jct of Garden State Parkway & Rte 72 (Exit 63), W 4.1 mi on Rte. 72 (R). **FAC:** Gravel rds. (225 spaces). Avail: 10 gravel, 3 pull-thrus (22 x 45), back-ins (22 x 46), 10 W, 10 E (30/50 amps), seasonal sites, cable, WiFi $, tent sites, rentals, dump, mobile sewer, laundry, groc, LP bottles, fire rings, firewood, controlled access. **REC:** pool, playground. Pets OK. Partial handicap access. 2015 rates: $39 to $57. Disc: military. Apr 1 to Nov 1.
(609)698-5684 Lat: 39.76128, Lon: -74.31589
30 Route 72, Barnegat, NJ 08005
longbeach@carefreervresorts.com
www.carefreervresorts.com
See ad pages 789, 780.

BAYVILLE — D4 *Ocean*

← CEDAR CREEK CAMPGROUND **Ratings: 8/8/7.5** (Campground) 2015 rates: $49.50 to $62.95. (732)269-1413 1052 Atlantic City Blvd, Bayville, NJ 08721

BLAIRSTOWN — B3 *Warren*

← TRIPLE BROOK RV & CAMPING RESORT
Ratings: 8/8★/9 (Campground) From Jct of I-80 & CR-521 (exit 12/Hope), S 1.2 mi on CR-521 to CR-609, W 3.2 mi to Nightingale Rd, N 1.2 mi to Honey Run Rd, E 0.5 mi, follow signs (L). **FAC:** Paved/gravel rds. (220 spaces). 125 Avail: 65 gravel, 60 grass, 3 pull-thrus (40 x 50), back-ins (40 x 50), 25 full hkups, 100 W, 100 E (30 amps), seasonal sites, WiFi, tent sites, rentals, dump, mobile sewer, laundry, groc, LP gas, fire rings, firewood, controlled access. **REC:** pool, whirlpool, pond, fishing, shuffleboard, playground. Pet restrict(B/Q). Partial handicap access. Eco-friendly, 2015 rates: $45 to $50. Apr 19 to Oct 25. ATM.
AAA Approved
(908)459-4079 Lat: 40.91205, Lon: -75.01910
58 Honey Run Rd, Blairstown, NJ 07825
info@triplebrook.com
www.triplebrook.com
See ad opposite page, 780.

BRANCHVILLE — A3 *Sussex*

↑ HARMONY RIDGE CAMPGROUND **Ratings: 7/6/7** (Campground) 2015 rates: $30 to $40. (973)948-4941 23 Risdon Dr, Branchville, NJ 07826

↑ KYMER'S CAMPING RESORT **Ratings: 7/7.5/8** (Campground) 2015 rates: $48 to $53. Apr 1 to Oct 31. (973)875-3167 69 Kymer Rd, Branchville, NJ 07826

Like Us on Facebook.

STOKES STATE FOREST (State Pk) From jct CR-519 & US-206: Go 3 mi NW on US-206. Pit toilets. 2015 rates: $20 to $25. Apr 1 to Oct 31. (973)948-3820

BUENA — E2 *Atlantic*

→ BUENA VISTA CAMPGROUND
Ratings: 6.5/5.5/6 (Campground) From Jct of US-40 & Hwy 54, E 0.02 mi on US-40 (L). **FAC:** Poor paved/gravel rds. (675 spaces). 385 Avail: 185 grass, 200 dirt, 4 pull-thrus (40 x 60), back-ins (25 x 48), 385 W, 385 E (20/30 amps), seasonal sites, WiFi Hotspot, tent sites, rentals, dump, laundry, LP gas, fire rings, firewood, controlled access. **REC:** pool, Buena Vista Lake: fishing, shuffleboard, playground. Pets OK. Partial handicap access. Eco-friendly, 2015 rates: $30 to $38. Apr 1 to Oct 31.
(856)697-5555 Lat: 39.5127631, Lon: -74.9219376
775 Harding Hwy, Box A-2, Buena, NJ 08310
info@buenavistacampground.com
www.BuenaVistaCampground.com
See ad this page.

CAPE MAY — F2 *Cape May*

↑ BEACHCOMBER CAMPING RESORT **Ratings: 8.5/8.5/10** (Campground) From Jct of Garden State Pkwy & SR-47 (exit 4A), N 0.4 mi on SR-47 to US-9, S to Seashore Rd, N 0.1 mi (L). **FAC:** Paved/gravel rds. (700 spaces). 200 Avail: 50 grass, 150 dirt, patios, back-ins (35 x 55), 140 full hkups, 60 W, 60 E (30/50 amps), seasonal sites, cable, WiFi $, tent sites, rentals, showers $, dump, laundry, groc, LP gas, fire rings, firewood, controlled access. **REC:** pool, wading pool, Beachcomber Lake: swim, fishing, shuffleboard, playground. Pet restrict(Q). Partial handicap access. Eco-friendly, 2015 rates: $36 to $80. Apr 15 to Oct 31. ATM.
AAA Approved
(609)886-6035 Lat: 39.00466, Lon: -74.89120
462 Seashore Rd, Cape May, NJ 08204
beachcomberoffice@yahoo.com
www.beachcombercamp.com

↑ HOLLY SHORES CAMPING RESORT **Ratings: 9.5/10★/10** (Campground) From Jct of Garden State Pkwy & SR-47 (exit 4A), W 0.5 mi on SR-47 to US-9, S 1 mi (L). **FAC:** Paved/gravel rds. (300 spaces). Avail: 160 all weather, patios, back-ins (30 x 55), 150 full hkups, 10 W, 10 E (30/50 amps), seasonal sites, cable, WiFi $, tent sites, rentals, showers $, dump, mobile sewer, laundry, groc, LP gas, fire rings, firewood, controlled access. **REC:** heated pool, wading pool, whirlpool, shuffleboard, playground. Pets OK. Partial handicap access. Big rig sites, eco-friendly, 2015 rates: $38 to $76. Apr 12 to Oct 31. ATM.
AAA Approved
(877)494-6559 Lat: 39.00121, Lon: -74.89027
491 Rte 9, Cape May, NJ 08204
info@hollyshores.com
www.hollyshores.com

Keeping pets quiet and on a leash is common courtesy. "Pet Restrictions" which you'll find in some listings refers to limits on size, breed or quantity of pets allowed.

↑ LAKE LAURIE RV RESORT & CAMPGROUND
Ratings: 7.5/9★/8 (Campground) From Jct of Garden State Pkwy & SR-109 (exit 0), N 0.6 mi on SR-109 to US-9, N 1.2 mi (R).

FINEST CAMPING IN CAPE MAY
Stay in the heart of the Jersey Cape with ocean beaches just minutes away. Enjoy updated amenities like newly renovated pickleball, tennis and basketball courts, fish or swim at the private lake or explore the nature trails!

FAC: Paved/gravel rds. (660 spaces). Avail: 350 dirt, back-ins (24 x 36), some side by side hkups, 30 full hkups, 320 W, 320 E (20/30 amps), seasonal sites, cable, WiFi, tent sites, rentals, dump, mobile sewer, laundry, groc, LP gas, fire rings, firewood, controlled access. **REC:** pool, wading pool, Lake Laurie: swim, fishing, playground. Pet restrict(B/Q). Partial handicap access. Eco-friendly, 2015 rates: $44 to $73. Apr 1 to Oct 31.
AAA Approved
(888)725-1436 Lat: 38.98317, Lon: -74.90297
669 Rte 9, Cape May, NJ 08204
lakelaurie@suncommunities.com
www.lakelaurie.com
See ad pages 1463 (Welcome Section), 784 (Spotlight Cape May County), 780 & Family Camping, RV Trips of a Lifetime in Magazine Section.

↑ SEASHORE CAMPSITES & RV RESORT
Ratings: 9.5/10★/9.5 (Campground) From Jct of Garden State Pkwy & SR-47 (exit 4A), N 0.9 mi on SR-47 to SR-626 (Railroad Ave), S 2.7 mi (R); or From Cape May-Lewes Ferry, E 1.9 mi on US-9N to SR-626 N (Seashore Rd), N 1.2 mi (L).

THE ULTIMATE JERSEY SHORE ADVENTURE
Explore an abundance of beaches, boardwalks and nature preserves in the Cape May area. Stay on 90 acres of wooded grounds with features like a filtered lake and beach, lighted tennis and basketball courts, and miniature golf.

FAC: Paved rds. (675 spaces). 237 Avail: 66 paved, 61 gravel, 110 dirt, patios, 19 pull-thrus (25 x 61), back-ins (30 x 45), 95 full hkups, 142 W, 142 E (30/50 amps), seasonal sites, cable, WiFi, tent sites, rentals, showers $, dump, mobile sewer, laundry, groc, LP gas, fire rings, firewood, controlled access. **REC:** heated pool, wading pool, Seashore Lake: swim, fishing, shuffleboard, playground. Pets OK. Partial handicap access. Big rig sites, eco-friendly, 2015 rates: $32 to $71. Disc: AAA, military. Apr 15 to Oct 31. ATM.
AAA Approved
(888)478-8799 Lat: 38.982564, Lon: -74.906687
720 Seashore Rd, Cape May, NJ 08204
seashore@suncommunities.com
www.seashorecampsites.com
See ad pages 1463 (Welcome Section), 780, 784 (Spotlight Cape May County) & Family Camping, RV Trips of a Lifetime in Magazine Section.

Tell them you saw them in this Guide!

CAPE MAY (CONT)

THE DEPOT TRAVEL PARK
Ratings: 7.5/10★/10 (Campground) From Jct of Garden State Pkwy & SR-109 (Exit 0), NW 0.6 mi on SR-109 to US-9, W 0.4 mi to Seashore Rd, changes to Broadway (Rte 626), S 1.8 mi (R).

A SHORT WALK TO CAPE MAY BEACHES!
Closest campground to Cape May beaches and all the attractions that make Cape May one of the most popular places to vacation in southern New Jersey! We have the facilities to provide you with a relaxing and affordable stay.

FAC: Paved rds. (150 spaces). Avail: 100 grass, 2 pull-thrus (30 x 60), back-ins (30 x 45), 53 full hkups, 47 W, 47 E (30/50 amps), seasonal sites, cable, WiFi, tent sites, rentals, dump, laundry, LP gas, firewood, controlled access. **REC:** playground. Pets OK. Partial handicap access. Big rig sites, eco-friendly, 2015 rates: $42.50 to $54.50. May 1 to Oct 12. No CC.
(609)884-2533 Lat: 38.94340, Lon: -74.92953
800 Broadway, West Cape May, NJ 08204
depottravelpark@comcast.net
www.thedepottravelpark.com
See ad page 785 (Spotlight Cape May County).

CAPE MAY COUNTY — F2 *Cape May*

A SPOTLIGHT Introducing Cape May's wonderful attractions appearing at the front of this state section.

CAPE MAY COURT HOUSE — F2 *Cape May*

ADVENTURE BOUND CAMPING RESORTS-CAPE MAY **Ratings: 7.5/6.5/7** (Campground) 2015 rates: $46 to $67. Apr 1 to Oct 31. (609)465-4440 240 W Shellbay Ave, Cape May Court House, NJ 08210

AVALON CAMPGROUND
Ratings: 8.5/8.5/9 (Campground) From Jct of Garden State Pkwy & Rte 601 (exit 13), W 0.4 mi on Rte 601 to US-9, N 1.5 mi (L). **FAC:** Paved rds. (320 spaces). Avail: 120 gravel, back-ins (25 x 40), some side by side hkups, 25 full hkups, 95 W, 95 E (20/30 amps), seasonal sites, cable, WiFi Hotspot, tent sites, rentals, showers $, dump, laundry, groc, LP gas, fire rings, firewood, controlled access. **REC:** pool, shuffleboard, playground. Pet restrict(B). Partial handicap access. Eco-friendly, 2015 rates: $57 to $69. Apr 11 to Oct 12.
AAA Approved
(609)624-0075 Lat: 39.14686, Lon: -74.76510
1917 Rte 9 N, Cape May Court House, NJ 08210
avaloncmpg@aol.com
www.avaloncampground.com
See ad this page.

BIG TIMBER LAKE RV AND CAMPING RESORT
Ratings: 9/9.5★/9.5 (Campground) From Jct of Garden State Pkwy & Rte 601 (exit 13), W 0.5 mi on Rte 601 to US-9, S 0.8 mi to CR-646, W 1 mi (R); or From Dennisville, S 1.7 mi on SR-47 to Rte 657, S 3 mi to Rte 646, E 0.8 mi (L).

ENJOY HISTORIC CAPE MAY
Big Timber Lake is your ticket to a fabulous location and vacation destination! Take in all the charm of downtown Cape May or entertain yourself with resort amenities like a heated pool, basketball, arcade and miniature golf.

FAC: Paved/gravel rds. (498 spaces). Avail: 234 dirt, 8 pull-thrus (25 x 50), back-ins (30 x 50), 161 full hkups, 73 W, 73 E (30/50 amps), seasonal sites, cable, WiFi, tent sites, rentals, showers $, dump, laundry, groc, LP gas, fire rings, firewood, restaurant, controlled access. **REC:** heated pool, wading pool, Big Timber Lake: swim, fishing, shuffleboard, playground. Pets OK. Partial handicap access. Eco-friendly, 2015 rates: $50 to $84. Apr 15 to Oct 18. ATM.
AAA Approved
(800)206-3232 Lat: 39.12596, Lon: -74.81107
116 Swainton-Goshen Rd, Cape May Court House, NJ 08210
bigtimber@suncommunities.com
www.bigtimberlake.com
See ad pages 1463 (Welcome Section), 780, 784 (Spotlight Cape May County) & Family Camping, RV Trips of a Lifetime in Magazine Section.

KING NUMMY TRAIL CAMPGROUND **Ratings: 8/9.5★/8** (Campground) 2015 rates: $34 to $46. Apr 24 to Oct 1. (609)465-4242 205 S Delsea Dr, Cape May Court House, NJ 08210

SHELLBAY FAMILY CAMPING RESORT **Ratings: 8.5/9/8.5** (Campground) 2015 rates: $50. May 15 to Oct 1. (609)465-4770 227 W Shellbay Ave, Cape May Court House, NJ 08210

CENTERTON — E2 *Salem*

PARVIN (State Pk) From Jct of SR-47 & CR-540, W 5 mi on Almond Rd. (L). 2015 rates: $20 to $25. Apr 1 to Oct 31. (856)358-8616

CHATSWORTH — D3 *Burlington*

WADING PINES CAMPING RESORT
Ratings: 7.5/8/8.5 (Campground) S-bnd: From Jct of Garden State Pkwy & Rte 72 (exit 63), W 15 mi on Rte 72 to Rte 532, W 4 mi to Rte 563, S 9.1 mi to Godfrey Bridge Rd, W 1 mi (L); or E-bnd: From Jct of Atlantic City Expwy (exit 17) & SR-50 (becomes CR-563), NE 16 mi on CR-563 to Godfrey Bridge Rd, W 1 mi (L). **FAC:** Gravel rds. (284 spaces). Avail: 184 dirt, 18 pull-thrus (25 x 50), back-ins (30 x 60), 40 full hkups, 144 W, 144 E (30/50 amps), seasonal sites, cable, tent sites, rentals, dump, mobile sewer, laundry, groc, LP gas, fire rings, firewood, controlled access. **REC:** pool, Wading River: fishing, shuffleboard, playground. Pets OK. Eco-friendly, 2015 rates: $35 to $65. Apr 15 to Nov 15. ATM.
(888)726-1313 Lat: 39.68933, Lon: -74.54359
85 Godfrey Bridge Rd, Chatsworth, NJ 08019
info@wadingpines.com
www.wadingpines.com
See ad page 782 (Spotlight Atlantic City).

CLARKSBORO — D2 *Gloucester*

TIMBERLANE CAMPGROUND
Ratings: 9.5/10★/10 (Campground) S-bnd: From Jct of I-295 & Rte 667 (Exit 18), SE 1 mi on Rte 667 to Friendship Rd, W 0.3 mi to Timberlane Rd, N 200 ft (L); or N-bnd: From Jct of I-295 & Timberlane Rd (Exit 18), E 0.8 (R).

CITY CLOSE, COUNTRY QUIET PARK
Timberlane is located in the hub of the tri-state area. Closest park to Philadelphia, PA. Big rigs welcome, WiFi available, Free cable, game room, beautiful pool and much more. 60 mi to Atlantic City, 90 mi to NY City.

FAC: Paved rds. (96 spaces). Avail: 71 gravel, patios, 60 pull-thrus (30 x 60), back-ins (30 x 50), 71 full hkups (30/50 amps), seasonal sites, cable, WiFi, tent sites, rentals, dump, laundry, LP gas, fire rings, firewood. **REC:** pool, wading pool, pond, fishing, playground. Pets OK. Partial handicap access. Big rig sites, eco-friendly, 2015 rates: $46 to $49. Disc: AAA, military.
AAA Approved
(856)423-6677 Lat: 39.80741, Lon: -75.23718
117 Timberlane Road, Clarksboro, NJ 08020
info@timberlanecampground.com
www.timberlanecampground.com
See ad pages 1008, 780.

CLERMONT — F3 *Cape May*

DRIFTWOOD RV RESORT & CAMPGROUND
Ratings: 9/9.5★/9.5 (Campground) From Jct of US 9 & SR-83, S 0.1 mi on US 9 (R).

BEACHES AND BOARDWALKS
Adventure awaits you at the beaches and boardwalks of Avalon and Wildwoods with attractions like amusement rides, arcades and shopping! Resort amenities include a private lake, two pools and new tennis and basketball courts.

FAC: Paved rds. (700 spaces). 61 Avail: 21 paved, 40 dirt, 11 pull-thrus (30 x 60), back-ins (30 x 45), 36 full hkups, 25 W, 25 E (30/50 amps), seasonal sites, cable, WiFi, tent sites, rentals, showers $, dump, laundry, groc, LP gas, fire rings, firewood, controlled access. **REC:** pool, Campground Lake: swim, fishing, playground. Pets OK. Partial handicap access. Big rig sites, 2015 rates: $42 to $71. Apr 15 to Oct 15. ATM
AAA Approved
(877)600-6121 Lat: 39.15004, Lon: -74.76440
1955 Rte 9 North, Clermont, NJ 08210
driftwood@suncommunities.com
www.driftwoodcampingresorts.com
See ad pages 1463 (Welcome Section), 784 (Spotlight Cape May County), 780 & Family Camping, RV Trips of a Lifetime in Magazine Section.

DRIFTWOOD TOO CAMPING RESORT **Ratings: 9/9★/8** (Campground) 2015 rates: $40 to $68. Mar 5 to Nov 30. (609)624-9015 1142 Rte 83, Cape May Court House, NJ 08210

CLINTON — B2 *Hunterdon*

SPRUCE RUN REC AREA (State Pk) From Jct of I-78 & Hwy 31 (Clinton exit), N 3.2 mi on Hwy 31 to Van Syckels Rd, W 1 mi (L). 2015 rates: $20 to $25. Apr 1 to Oct 31. (908)638-8572

COLESVILLE — A3 *Sussex*

HIGH POINT (State Pk) From town: Go 3 mi N on Hwy-23. 2015 rates: $20 to $25. May 15 to Oct 15. (973)875-4800

COLUMBIA — B2 *Warren*

CAMP TAYLOR CAMPGROUND **Ratings: 7/9/8** (Campground) 2015 rates: $39. Apr 15 to Oct 31. (908)496-4333 85 Mt. Pleasant Rd, Columbia, NJ 07832

WORTHINGTON SF (State Pk) From town, W on Hwy 80 to Millbrooke exit, N 3 mi on Millbrooke to Old Mine Rd (L) Campground is temporarily closed due to flooding. 2015 rates: $20 to $25. Apr 1 to Dec 31. (908)841-9575

DELAWARE — B2 *Warren*

DELAWARE RIVER FAMILY CAMPING RESORT **Ratings: 8/7.5/8.5** (Campground) 2015 rates: $49. Apr 1 to Oct 31. (908)475-4517 100 Rte 46, Delaware, NJ 07833

DOROTHY — E2 *Atlantic*

COUNTRY OAKS CAMPGROUND
Ratings: 9/9★/10 (Campground) From Jct of Rte 50 & Rte 40 (in May's Landing), S 1.1 mi on Rte 50 to Rte 669 (11th Ave), SW 5.5 mi to S Jersey (turn before RR tracks), NW 1.2 mi (R). **FAC:** Gravel rds. (140 spaces). Avail: 40 gravel, patios, 10 pull-thrus (30 x 65), back-ins (32 x 40), 38 full hkups, 2 W, 2 E (30/50 amps), seasonal sites, cable, WiFi, tent sites, rentals, dump, laundry, groc, LP gas, fire rings, firewood, controlled access. **REC:** pool, wading pool, playground. Pet restrict(Q). Big rig sites, eco-friendly, 2015 rates: $52 to $56. Apr 15 to Oct 15.
(609)476-2143 Lat: 39.41626, Lon: -74.83604
13 S Jersey Avenue, Dorothy, NJ 08317
countryoakscamp@verizon.net
www.countryoakscampground.com
See ad pages 786, 780.

EGG HARBOR CITY — E3 *Atlantic*

BEST HOLIDAY TRAV-L-PARK HOLLY ACRES **Ratings: 6/6.5/7** (Campground) 2015 rates: $38 to $47. Apr 15 to Oct 31. (609)965-2287 218 S Frankfurt Avenue, Egg Harbor City, NJ 08215

EGG HARBOR LAKE CAMPGROUND **Ratings: 6/7.5/7** (Campground) 2015 rates: $47. May 27 to Oct 1. (609)965-0330 2400 Philadelphia Ave, Egg Harbor City, NJ 08215

TURTLE RUN CAMPGROUND **Ratings: 8/6.5/6.5** (Campground) 2015 rates: $38 to $50. Apr 1 to Oct 31. (609)965-5343 3 Cedar Lane, Egg Harbor City, NJ 08215

ELMER — E2 *Salem*

YOGI BEAR'S JELLYSTONE PARK-ELMER **Ratings: 8/7.5/8.5** (Campground) 2015 rates: $55 to $99. Apr 1 to Oct 31. (800)252-2890 49 Beal Rd, Elmer, NJ 08318

ESTELL MANOR — E3 *Cumberland*

PLEASANT VALLEY FAMILY CAMPGROUND
Ratings: 8/9.5★/9 (Campground) From Jct of US 40 & SR-50, S 1.3 mi on SR-50 to S. River Rd, W 0.3 mi (L). **FAC:** Gravel rds. (250 spaces). Avail: 45 dirt, back-ins (50 x 60), 45 full hkups (30/50 amps), seasonal sites, cable, WiFi Hotspot, tent sites, rentals, dump, laundry, groc, LP gas, fire rings, firewood, controlled access. **REC:** pool, wading pool, whirlpool, shuffleboard, playground. Pet

We salute you! Our Military Listings indicate campgrounds for use exclusively by active and retired military personnel.

Canada — know the rules, regulations and tips before crossing the border. This is listed at the beginning of the country.

ESTELL MANOR (CONT)

PLEASANT VALLEY FAMILY (CONT)
restrict(B). Big rig sites, 2015 rates: $45 to $55. Apr 15 to Oct 15.
(609)625-1238 Lat: 39.43053, Lon: -74.739173
60 South River Rd, Mays Landing, NJ 08319
info@pleasantvalleycamping.com
www.pleasantvalleycamping.com
See ad page 790.

FARMINGDALE — C4 *Monmouth*

ALLAIRE (State Pk) From town, S 3 mi on CR-524 (L); or I-195 exit 31A. 2015 rates: $20 to $25. (732)938-2371

FREEHOLD — C4 *Monmouth*

PINE CONE RESORT **Ratings: 8/7.5/8** (Campground) 2015 rates: $43 to $58. (732)462-2230 340 Georgia Rd., Freehold, NJ 07728

TURKEY SWAMP PARK (Public) From Jct of I-195 & Jackson Mills Rd (exit 22), N 2.5 mi on Jackson Mills Rd to Georgia Rd, W 0.9 mi to park entrance. 2015 rates: $35 to $39. Apr 1 to Nov 15. (732)462-7286

GALLOWAY — E3 *Atlantic*

POMONA RV PARK
Ratings: 9/9.5★/9.5 (Campground) S-bnd: From Jct of Garden State Pkwy & CR-575 (exit 44), S 5 mi on CR-575 (L) E-bnd: From Jct of Atlantic City Expressway & CR-575 (exit 12), N 3 mi on CR 575 (R). **FAC:** Gravel rds. (100 spaces). Avail: 65 gravel, patios, 10 pull-thrus (35 x 60), back-ins (30 x 32), 65 full hkups (30/50 amps), seasonal sites, cable, WiFi, tent sites, rentals, laundry, groc, LP gas, fire rings, firewood. **REC:** pool, whirlpool, playground. Pets OK. Big rig sites, eco-friendly, 2015 rates: $51 to $56. Disc: military.
(609)965-2123 Lat: 39.474524, Lon: -74.583979
536 S. Pomona Rd, Galloway, NJ 08240
info@pomonarvpark.com
www.pomonarvpark.com
See ad pages 782 (Spotlight Atlantic City), 780.

SHADY PINES CAREFREE RV RESORT
Ratings: 9/9.5★/9.5 (RV Park) From Jct of US-9 & US-30, W 1.2 mi on US-30 to 6th Ave, N 1.5 mi (L). **FAC:** Paved rds. (140 spaces). Avail: 60 all weather, 4 pull-thrus (30 x 60), back-ins (30 x 43), 60 full hkups (30/50 amps), seasonal sites, WiFi, rentals, dump, LP gas, fire rings. **REC:** pool. Pet restrict(B). Partial handicap access, no tents. Eco-friendly, 2015 rates: $52. Disc: military.
(609)652-1516 Lat: 39.46121, Lon: -74.50665
443 S 6th Ave, Galloway, NJ 08205
shadypines@carefreervresorts.com
http://www.carefreervresorts.com/shadypines
See ad this page, 780.

GREAT MEADOWS — B2 *Warren*

JENNY JUMP STATE FOREST (State Pk) From jct US 46 & Hwy 611: Go 5 mi NW on Hwy 611 to Far View Rd. 2015 rates: $20 to $25. Apr 1 to Oct 31. (908)459-4366

GREEN CREEK — F2 *Cape May*

ACORN CAMPGROUND **Ratings: 7.5/7/7** (Campground) 2015 rates: $53 to $59. May 2 to Sep 28. (609)886-7119 419 Delsea Dr S, Green Creek, NJ 08210

HACKETTSTOWN — B2 *Warren*

STEPHENS (State Pk) From town: Go 2 mi N on Willow Grove Rd. 2015 rates: $20 to $25. Apr 1 to Oct 31. (908)852-3790

HAMMONTON — E2 *Atlantic, Burlington*

INDIAN BRANCH PARK CAMPGROUND **Ratings: 7.5/6/7** (Campground) 2015 rates: $37 to $47. May 1 to Sep 30. (609)561-4719 2021 Skip Morgan Dr, Hammonton, NJ 08037

WHARTON SF/ATSION FAMILY SITES (State Pk) From Jct of Rtes 30 & 206, N 7 mi on Rte 206 to Atsion Rd (R). 2015 rates: $20 to $25. Apr 1 to Oct 31. (609)268-0444

We appreciate your business!

WHARTON STATE FOREST (GODFREY BRIDGE CAMP) (State Pk) From jct US 30 & CR 542: Go 15 mi NE on CR 542 & CR 563. (Trailers 21 ft or less). Pit toilets. 2015 rates: $3 to $5. (609)561-0024

HIGH BRIDGE — B2 *Hunterdon*

VOORHEES (State Pk) From town, N 2 mi on Hwy 513 (L). 2015 rates: $20 to $25. Apr 1 to Oct 31. (908)638-8572

JACKSON — C3 *Monmouth, Ocean*

BUTTERFLY CAMPING RESORT **Ratings: 7.5/9★/8.5** (Campground) 2015 rates: $55 to $62. Apr 1 to Oct 31. (732)928-2107 360 Butterfly Rd, Jackson, NJ 08527

INDIAN ROCK RV PARK
Ratings: 8/7/8.5 (Campground) From Jct of I-195 & Exit 16 (CR-537), E 0.5 mi on CR-537 to CR-571, S 4.5 mi to CR-528, W 1.5 mi (R). **FAC:** Gravel rds. (150 spaces). Avail: 110 dirt, 1 pull-thrus (30 x 65), back-ins (30 x 50), 60 full hkups, 50 W, 50 E (30/50 amps), seasonal sites, WiFi, tent

JACKSON (CONT)

INDIAN ROCK RV PARK (CONT)
sites, dump, laundry, groc, LP gas, fire rings, firewood, controlled access. **REC:** pool, pond, fishing, playground. Pet restrict(B). Partial handicap access. Eco-friendly, 2015 rates: $49 to $59. Disc: military.
(732)928-0034 Lat: 40.10042, Lon: -74.41549
920 West Veterans Hwy, Jackson, NJ 08527
info@indianrockrvpark.com
www.indianrockrvpark.com
See ad page 789 & Pampered Pets in Magazine Section.

TIMBERLAND LAKE CAMPGROUND
Ratings: 7/8.5★/8.5 (Campground) From Jct of I-195 & CR-537 (exit 16), SW 3.3 mi on CR-537 to Hawkin Rd, SE 0.2 mi to Reed Rd, E 0.6 mi (R). **FAC:** Gravel rds. (220 spaces). Avail: 140 dirt, 59 pull-thrus (35 x 60), back-ins (39 x 60), 65 full hkups, 75 W, 75 E (30/50 amps), seasonal sites, cable, WiFi Hotspot, tent sites, rentals, dump, mobile sewer, groc, LP gas, fire rings, firewood, controlled access. **REC:** pool, Timberland Lake: fishing, playground. Pets OK. Partial handicap access. Eco-friendly, 2015 rates: $46 to $56. Disc: AAA, military. ATM.
(732)928-0500 Lat: 40.11889, Lon: -74.45748
1335 Reed Rd, Jackson, NJ 08527
info@timberlandlakecampground.com
www.timberlandlakecampground.com
See ad pages 789, 780.

TIP TAM CAMPING RESORT
Ratings: 9/9★/8.5 (Campground) From Jct of NJ Tpke & I-195 (exit 7A), E 14.25 mi on I-195 to CR-527 (exit 21), S 0.2 mi to CR-526, E 5.7 mi to Brewer's Bridge Rd, S 1.8 mi (L); or From Jct of Garden State Pkwy & CR-549 (exit 91), S 1.5 mi on CR-549 to CR-526, W 6.1 mi to Brewers Bridge Rd, S 1.8 mi (L). **FAC:** Paved/gravel rds. (200 spaces). Avail: 100 dirt, back-ins (30 x 40), some side by side hkups, 60 full hkups, 40 W, 40 E (30/50 amps), seasonal sites, cable, WiFi, tent sites, rentals, showers $, dump, laundry, groc, LP gas, fire rings, firewood, controlled access. **REC:** pool, playground. Pet restrict(Q). Eco-friendly, 2015 rates: $47 to $57. Disc: AAA, military. Apr 15 to Sep 30.
AAA Approved
(732)363-4036 Lat: 40.10068, Lon: -74.27188
301 Brewers Bridge Rd, Jackson, NJ 08527
tiptam@aol.com
www.tiptam.com
See ad pages 789, 780.

JERSEY CITY — B4 *Hudson*

LIBERTY HARBOR MARINA & RV PARK
Ratings: 7/8.5★/6.5 (RV Park) From Jct of NJ Tpk I-95, (North or South), to Exit 14C (Holland Tunnel exit) I-78 E, 8.7 mi on I-78 E to Marin Blvd, (Last Signal/Exit before Holland Tunnel), S 1.3 mi (R).

Liberty Harbor is the closest RV Park to New York City. View the Statue of Liberty from your site. N.Y. waterway ferry leaves from park. Short walk to subway, restaurant on site. Enjoy the beauty of Manhattan's skyline.

FAC: Paved rds. 70 Avail: 16 paved, 54 gravel, back-ins (18 x 40), 70 W, 70 E (30/50 amps), WiFi, tent sites, dump, mobile sewer, laundry, restaurant, controlled access. **REC:** Hudson River: fishing, marina. Pets OK. Partial handicap access. Eco-friendly, 2015 rates: $80.
(201)516-7500 Lat: 40.71222, Lon: -74.04333
11 Marin Blvd, Jersey City, NJ 07302
info@libertyharborrv.com
www.libertyharborrv.com
See ad page 836.

JERSEY SHORE — C6 *Lycoming*

JERSEY SHORE AREA See also Atlantic City, Barnegat & Galloway.

Thank you for being one of our best customers!

LAKEWOOD — D4 *Ocean*

Travel Services

CAMPING WORLD OF LAKEWOOD As the nation's largest retailer of RV supplies, accessories, services and new and used RVs, Camping World is committed to making your total RV experience better. RV Accessories: (800)746-7787. **SERVICES:** RV, tire, RV appliance, staffed RV wash, RV Sales. RV supplies, waiting room. Hours: 8am to 6pm.
(888)719-1631 Lat: 40.04927, Lon: -74.22071
1359 River Avenue, Lakewood, NJ 08701
Bcarp@campingworld.com
www.campingworld.com

LITTLE EGG HARBOR — E3 *Ocean*

BAKER'S ACRES
Ratings: 8/8.5★/9 (Campground) From jct Garden State Pkwy (exit 58) & Hwy 539: Go 1/4 mi SE on Hwy 539, then 1-3/4 mi E on Thomas Ave, then 1/4 mi SE on Railroad Dr. **FAC:** Gravel rds. (220 spaces). Avail: 70 dirt, 6 pull-thrus (25 x 35), back-ins (30 x 35), 19 full hkups, 51 W, 51 E (30 amps), seasonal sites, cable, WiFi $, tent sites, rentals, dump, mobile sewer, laundry, groc, LP bottles, fire rings, firewood. **REC:** pool, playground. Pet restrict(Q). Partial handicap access. 2015 rates: $42.30 to $51. Disc: military. May 1 to Oct 31.
(609)296-2664 Lat: 39.63484, Lon: -74.31412
230 Willets Ave, Little Egg Harbor, NJ 08087
mrsacres@bakersacres.com
www.bakersacres.com
See ad this page.

MARMORA — F3 *Cape May*

WHIPPOORWILL CAMPGROUND **Ratings: 9/9★/9** (Campground) 2015 rates: $61.50. Apr 1 to Oct 31. (609)390-3458 810 S Shore Rd, Marmora, NJ 08223

MATAWAN — C4 *Middlesex*

CHEESEQUAKE (State Pk) From Jct of Garden State Pkwy & Matawan Rd (exit 120), follow signs (E) 11 ft height restriction for vehicles entering camping area. 2015 rates: $20 to $25. Apr 1 to Oct 31. (732)566-2161

MAYS LANDING — E3 *Atlantic*

MAYS LANDING RV RESORT **Ratings: 7/NA/7** (Campground) 2015 rates: $28 to $80. Apr 1 to Oct 31. (609)476-2811 1079 12th Ave, Mays Landing, NJ 08330

WINDING RIVER CAMPGROUND
Ratings: 8/9★/9 (Campground) From Jct of US-322 & SR-50, NW 4.5 mi on US-322 to CR-559, S 2 mi (L).

WINDING RIVER CAMPGROUND
Welcome to Winding River Campground. Atlantic City area's finest in camping, located on the pristine Egg Harbor River. We rent canoes, kayaks and tubes. Make great family memories at Winding River Campground.

FAC: Gravel rds. (103 spaces). 33 Avail: 15 gravel, 18 dirt, back-ins (40 x 68), 33 full hkups (30 amps), seasonal sites, WiFi Hotspot, tent sites, rentals, showers $, dump, laundry, groc, LP bottles, fire rings, firewood, controlled access. **REC:** heated pool, Great Egg Harbor River: fishing, playground. Pets OK. Eco-friendly, 2015 rates: $48. May 1 to Oct 15. ATM.
AAA Approved
(609)625-3191 Lat: 39.49235, Lon: -74.77119
6752 Weymouth Rd, Mays Landing, NJ 08330
windingrivercampgroundnj@msn.com
www.windingrivercamping.com
See ad page 786.

Take your Guide with you wherever you go! The front section is chock-full of vital reference information and all new 2016 travel editorial you'll want to keep handy all the time.

Things to See and Do

WINDING RIVER CANOEING & KAYAKING Canoes, kayaks and tube rentals for the Egg Harbor River. May 1 to Oct 15. RV accessible. Restrooms. Hours: 9am to 5pm. ATM.
(609)625-3191 Lat: 39.48858, Lon: -74.76993
6752 Weymouth Rd, Mays Landing, NJ 08330
windingrivercampgroundnj@msn.com
www.windingrivercamping.com
See ad page 786.

MONROEVILLE — E2 *Salem*

OLD CEDAR CAMP Ratings: 7.5/6/7.5 (Campground) Rtes 55 & 553 (exit 45), S .05 mi on RT 553 to CR-538, NW 2.8 mi to CR-609, SW 1.3 mi to Foote Ln, SE .05 mi (L). **FAC:** Gravel rds. (170 spaces). 100 Avail: 60 grass, 40 dirt, 20 pull-thrus (21 x 50), back-ins (20 x 32), 50 full hkups, 50 W, 50 E (30/50 amps), seasonal sites, WiFi, tent sites, rentals, dump, laundry, groc, LP gas, fire rings, firewood. **REC:** pool, Old Cedar Lake: fishing, shuffleboard, playground. Pets OK. Partial handicap access. 2015 rates: $33 to $39. Apr 15 to Oct 15.
AAA Approved
(800)582-3327 Lat: 39.64167, Lon: -75.16506
274 Richwood Rd, Monroeville, NJ 08343
camp@oldcedarcampground.com
www.oldcedarcampground.com

OLDMAN'S CREEK CAMPGROUND **Ratings: 5.5/5.5/4.5** (Campground) 2015 rates: $40. (856)478-4502 174 Laux Rd, Monroeville, NJ 08343

MONTAGUE — A3 *Sussex*

ROCKVIEW VALLEY CAMPGROUND AND RESORT **Ratings: 6/6/7** (Campground) 2015 rates: $35. May 1 to Oct 15. (973)293-3383 59 River Rd, Montague, NJ 07827

NEW GRETNA — E3 *Burlington, Ocean, Wrightstown*

BASS RIVER SF (State Pk) N-bnd: From Jct Garden State Pkwy & SR-9 (exit 50), N 2.5 mi on SR-9 to Greenbush Rd (in town), N 1.5 mi to Stage Rd (R); or S-bnd: From Jct Garden State Pkwy & Greenbush Rd (exit 52), S 1.5 mi on Greenbush to Stage Rd, N 0.5 mi (L). 2015 rates: $20 to $25. (609)296-1114

CHIPS FOLLY FAMILY CAMPGROUND **Ratings: 7/7.5/6.5** (Campground) 2015 rates: $40.50 to $45. (609)296-4434 100 Chips Folly Rd, New Gretna, NJ 08224

PILGRIM LAKE CAMPGROUNDS **Ratings: 3.5/7/5.5** (Campground) 2015 rates: $36 to $39. May 1 to Oct 31. (609)296-4725 940 Stage Road, New Gretna, NJ 08224

TIMBERLINE LAKE CAMPING RESORT Ratings: 7.5/7/8 (Campground) From Jct of US 9 & CR-679 in New Gretna, N 3.7 mi on CR-679 (L). **FAC:** Gravel/dirt rds. (170 spaces). 30 Avail: 10 gravel, 10 grass, 10 dirt, 8 pull-thrus (30 x 50), back-ins (30 x 50), some side by side hkups, 30 W, 30 E (30/50 amps), seasonal sites, cable, WiFi, tent sites, rentals, dump, mobile sewer, laundry, groc, fire rings, firewood, controlled access. **REC:** pool, Timberline Lake: swim, fishing, playground. Pets OK. Eco-friendly, 2015 rates: $45 to $55. Disc: AAA, military. May 1 to Oct 16.
AAA Approved
(609)296-7900 Lat: 39.63322, Lon: -74.47987
365 Rte. 679, New Gretna, NJ 08224
camp@timberlinelake.com
www.timberlinelake.com

NEWTON — A3 *Sussex*

SWARTSWOOD (State Pk) From Jct of CH-519 & CH-622, W 4.2 mi. Turn left onto Rt 619 1/2 mi S. 2015 rates: $20 to $25. (973)383-5230

THE GREAT DIVIDE CAMPGROUND Ratings: 8/8.5/9 (Campground) From Jct of US-206 & CR-611 (in Springdale), W 0.6 mi on CR-611 to Huntsville Rd, S 1 mi (L). **FAC:** Paved/gravel rds. (148 spaces). 75 Avail: 45 gravel, 30 grass, 1 pull-thru (20 x 40), back-ins (20 x 34), 50 full hkups, 25 W, 25 E (20/30 amps), seasonal sites, cable, WiFi Hotspot, tent sites, rentals, dump, mobile sewer, laundry, groc, LP bottles, fire rings, firewood, controlled access. **REC:** heated pool, Campground Lake: swim, fishing, playground, rec open to public. Pets OK. Partial handicap access. Eco-friendly, 2015 rates: $42 to $59. Disc: military. May 15 to Oct 15. ATM.
AAA Approved
(973)383-4026 Lat: 40.99587, Lon: -74.77868
68 Phillips Rd, Newton, NJ 07860
info@campthegreatdivide.com
www.campthegreatdivide.com

Our travel services section will help you find services that you'll find handy in your travels.

NORTHFIELD — E3 *Atlantic*

BIRCH GROVE PARK (CITY PARK) (Public) From jct US-322 & US-9: Go 2 mi S on US-9, then 1/4 mi W on Hwy 662 (Mill Rd), then 1/8 mi N on Burton Rd. 2015 rates: $25 to $35. Apr 1 to Sep 30. (609)641-3778

OCEAN VIEW — F3 *Cape May*

FRONTIER CAMPGROUND Ratings: 6/9.5★/8.5 (Campground) S-bnd: From Jct of Garden State Pkwy & Rte 623 (exit 25), W 0.5 mi on Rte 623 to Rte 9, S 5 mi to Rte 50, W 2.5 mi (R); or N-bnd: From Jct of Garden State Pkwy & Rte 50 (exit 20), W 2.5 mi on Rte 50 (R). **FAC:** Gravel rds. (192 spaces). Avail: 76 dirt, back-ins (25 x 45), 22 full hkups, 54 W, 54 E (20/30 amps), seasonal sites, cable, WiFi $, tent sites, rentals, laundry, LP gas, fire rings, firewood. **REC:** playground. Pet restrict(B). Eco-friendly, 2015 rates: $38 to $70. Apr 15 to Oct 13. AAA Approved
(800)277-4109 Lat: 39.24260, Lon: -74.71278
84 Tyler Rd, Ocean View, NJ 08230
frontiercampground@gmail.com
www.frontiercampground.com

OCEAN VIEW RESORT CAMPGROUND
Ratings: 9.5/10★/9.5 (Campground) From Jct of Garden State Pkwy & CR-625 (exit 17), W 0.4 mi on CR-625 to US-9, N 0.3 mi (L).

JERSEY SHORE AT ITS BEST
We invite you to visit our top rated, family operated camping resort. Our perfect location is within 3 miles of the ocean beaches & midway between Ocean City & Wildwood. You'll be glad you came - and hate to leave!

FAC: Paved rds. (1175 spaces). Avail: 450 dirt, 40 pull-thrus (30 x 62), back-ins (30 x 45), 450 full hkups (30/50 amps), seasonal sites, cable, WiFi, tent sites, rentals, showers $, laundry, groc, LP gas, fire rings, firewood, restaurant, controlled access. **REC:** pool, wading pool, Trails End Lake: swim, fishing, golf, shuffleboard, playground. Pets OK. Partial handicap access. Big rig sites, eco-friendly, 2015 rates: $39 to $74. Apr 11 to Oct 13. ATM.
AAA Approved
(609)624-1675 Lat: 39.18104, Lon: -74.73096
2555 Rte 9, Ocean View, NJ 08230
camp@ovresort.com
www.ovresort.com
See ad page 783 (Spotlight Cape May County).

SEA GROVE CAMPING RESORT Ratings: 7.5/6.5/8 (Campground) From Jct of Garden State Pkwy & CR-625 (exit 17), W 0.25 mi on CR-625 to US-9, N 0.5 mi (L). **FAC:** Paved/gravel rds. (170 spaces). Avail: 80 dirt, back-ins (30 x 47), 20 full hkups, 60 W, 60 E (20/30 amps), seasonal sites, cable, WiFi Hotspot, tent sites, rentals, dump, laundry, groc, LP gas, fire rings, firewood, controlled access. **REC:** pool, shuffleboard, playground. Pets OK. Partial handicap access. Eco-friendly, 2015 rates: $30 to $58. Apr 1 to Nov 1.
(609)624-3529 Lat: 39.18626, Lon: -74.72454
2665 Route 9, Ocean View, NJ 08230
sgresort@aol.com
www.seagroveresort.com

TAMERLANE CAMPGROUND Ratings: 8.5/6.5/6.5 (Campground) From Jct of Garden State Pkwy & CR-625 (exit 17), W 0.25 mi on CR-625 to US-9, S 1 mi (R). **FAC:** Paved/gravel rds. (300 spaces). Avail: 12 dirt, back-ins (25 x 36), 12 full hkups (30/50 amps), seasonal sites, cable, WiFi, tent sites, dump, laundry, groc, fire rings, firewood, controlled access. **REC:** heated pool, playground. Pets OK. Partial handicap access. 2015 rates: $45. Disc: AAA. Apr 1 to Oct 1.
AAA Approved
(609)624-0767 Lat: 39.16370, Lon: -74.74802
2241 US-9, Ocean View, NJ 08230
tcg4me@aol.com

Travel Services

OCEAN VIEW TRAILER SALES RV Sales, Supplies and RV body repair. **SERVICES:** RV, RV appliance, restrooms, RV Sales. RV storage. RV supplies, LP, RV accessible. Hours: 8:30am to 5pm. Closed Tues.
(609)624-0370 Lat: 39.18016, Lon: -74.72936
2555 Shore Rd (Rte 9), Ocean View, NJ 08230
www.oceanviewtrailersales.com
See ad page 783 (Spotlight Cape May County).

PEMBERTON — D3 *Burlington*

BRENDAN T BYRNE STATE FOREST (State Pk) From town, SW 17 mi on Rte 70, follow signs (L). 2015 rates: $20 to $25. (609)726-1191

SAVE! Over $1,000 in coupons can be found at the front of the Guide!

PORT REPUBLIC — E3 *Atlantic*

ATLANTIC BLUEBERRY RV PARK
Ratings: 7.5/8/7 (Campground) From Jct of Atlantic City Expressway & Rte 50 & 563 (exit 17), N 6.7 mi on Rte 50 & 563 to Rte 624 E 6.5 mi (R). **FAC:** Gravel/dirt rds. (178 spaces). Avail: 88 dirt, 31 pull-thrus (25 x 45), back-ins (25 x 40), 47 full hkups, 41 W, 41 E (30/50 amps), seasonal sites, WiFi, tent sites, dump, mobile sewer, laundry, LP gas, fire rings, firewood, controlled access. **REC:** pool, wading pool, playground. Pet restrict(B). Partial handicap access. 2015 rates: $40 to $50. Apr 1 to Oct 31.
(609)652-1644 Lat: 39.53006, Lon: -74.50526
283 Clarks Landing Rd, Port Republic, NJ 08241
info@atlanticblueberryrvp.com
www.atlanticblueberryrvp.com
See ad this page, 780.

CHESTNUT LAKE RV CAMPGROUND **Ratings: 8/8.5/7** (Membership Pk) 2015 rates: $46. Apr 22 to Oct 11. (609)652-1005 631 Chestnut Neck Rd, Port Republic, NJ 08241

SUSSEX — A3 *Sussex*

PLEASANT ACRES FARM CAMPGROUND **Ratings: 8.5/8.5★/8.5** (Campground) 2015 rates: $58. (800)722-4166 61 Dewitt Rd, Sussex, NJ 07461

TALL TIMBERS CAMPGROUND Ratings: 8.5/7/6 (Campground) From Jct CR-284 (Main St) & Rt-23 (Hamburg Ave), SE 1.5 mi on Rt-23 to CR-565 (Glenwood Rd), E 3.5 mi on CR-565 to Tall Timbers Rd, N .6 mi on Tall Timbers to Gatehouse. **FAC:** Paved rds. (973 spaces). Avail: 25 gravel, back-ins (35 x 60), 25 full hkups (30/50 amps), seasonal sites, WiFi Hotspot, laundry, groc, LP gas, controlled access. **REC:** heated pool, Campground Lake: swim, fishing, playground. Pets OK. No tents. Eco-friendly, 2015 rates: $35. May 1 to Oct 31.
(973)875-1991 Lat: 41.21582, Lon: -74.53568
100 Tall Timbers Rd, Sussex, NJ 07461
rentals@talltimbers.net
www.talltimbers.net

SWAINTON — F2 *Cape May*

SEA PINES RV RESORT & CAMPGROUND **Ratings: 8.5/7/8** (Membership Pk) 2015 rates: $45. May 9 to Oct 13. (866)319-2700 1535 Rte 9, Swainton, NJ 08210

SWEDESBORO — E2 *Gloucester*

Travel Services

CAMPING WORLD OF SWEDESBORO/BRIDGEPORT As the nation's largest retailer of RV supplies, accessories, services and new and used RVs, Camping World is committed to making your total RV experience better. **SERVICES:** Tire, RV appliance, staffed RV wash, restrooms, RV supplies, RV accessible. waiting room. Hours: 8am - 6pm.
(800)889-8923 Lat: 39.768010, Lon: -75.354239
602 Heron Dr (Pureland), Swedesboro, NJ 08085
Cw29@campingworld.com
www.campingworld.com

TOMS RIVER — D4 *Ocean*

SURF N STREAM Ratings: 7/6.5/7 (Campground) N-bnd: From Jct of Garden State Pkwy & US-9 (exit 83), N 0.3 mi on US-9 to CR-571, W 1.5 mi (L); or S-bnd: From Jct of Garden State Pkwy & SR-70 (exit 88), W 4 mi on SR-70 to CR-527S, S 2 mi (R). **FAC:** Gravel rds. (202 spaces). Avail: 75 dirt, 29 pull-thrus (22 x 52), back-ins (25 x 34), mostly side by side hkups, 60 full hkups, 15 W, 15 E (30 amps), seasonal sites, cable, WiFi, tent sites, dump, laundry, groc, LP gas, fire rings, firewood, controlled access. **REC:** pool, wading pool, Tom's River: fishing, playground. Pets OK. 2015 rates: $46 to $66. Disc: AAA, military.
AAA Approved
(732)349-8919 Lat: 40.00256, Lon: -74.23588
1801 Ridgeway Rd, Toms River, NJ 08757
campinfo@surfnstream.com
www.surfnstream.com

TUCKERTON — E3 *Ocean*

ATLANTIC CITY NORTH FAMILY CAMPGROUND
Ratings: 9/10★/9 (Campground) From Jct of Garden State Pkwy & CR-539 (exit 58), E 0.1 mi on CR-539 to Poormans Pkwy(frontage rd), S 4.2 mi to Stage Rd, E 0.7 mi to access rd, SW 0.5 mi (E).

BEACHES AND BOARDWALK!
Explore Atlantic City & Long Beach Island - beaches, boardwalk, casinos & pristine shorelines. Nestled in the New Jersey Pine Barrens ACN has fun for the entire family and is the perfect spot to relax & explore the NJ coast!

FAC: Gravel rds. (176 spaces). Avail: 86 dirt, 12 pull-thrus (30 x 60), back-ins (30 x 42), 45 full hkups, 41 W, 41 E (30/50 amps), seasonal sites, WiFi $, tent sites, rentals, dump, mobile sewer, laundry, groc, LP gas, fire rings, firewood. **REC:** pool, playground. Pets OK. Partial handicap access. Eco-friendly, 2015 rates: $53 to $60. Disc: AAA, military. ATM.
AAA Approved
(609)296-9163 Lat: 39.61115, Lon: -74.40824
450 Ishmael Rd, Tuckerton, NJ 08087
campacn@aol.com
www.campacn.com
See ad pages 781 (Spotlight Atlantic City), 780.

WEST CREEK — E4 *Ocean*

SEA PIRATE CAMPGROUND Ratings: 9/9/9.5 (Campground) From Jct of Garden State Pkwy & SR-72 (exit 63), SE 1 mi on SR-72 to US-9, S 4.9 mi (L). **FAC:** Gravel rds. (232 spaces). 69 Avail: 39 gravel, 30 dirt, 34 pull-thrus (40 x 70), back-ins (30 x 40), 50 full hkups, 19 W, 19 E (30/50 amps), seasonal sites, cable, WiFi, tent sites, rentals, dump, mobile sewer, laundry, groc, LP gas, fire rings, firewood, controlled access. **REC:** pool, pond, Weir Creek: fishing, playground, rec open to public. Pets OK $. Partial handicap access. Big rig sites, eco-friendly, 2015 rates: $52 to $67. Apr 24 to Oct 12. ATM.
AAA Approved
(609)296-7400 Lat: 39.63040, Lon: -74.31009
148 Main Street, West Creek, NJ 08092
info@sea-pirate.com
www.sea-pirate.com

WILLIAMSTOWN — E2 *Glouster*

HOSPITALITY CREEK CAMPGROUND **Ratings: 9.5/9.5★/9** (Campground) 2015 rates: $70 to $105. Apr 17 to Oct 4. (856)629-5140 117 Coles Mill Rd, Williamstown, NJ 08094

WOODBINE — F2 *Cape May*

BELLEPLAIN SF (State Pk) From Jct of Cnty Rtes 550/557, NW 1.4 mi on CR-550 (L). 2015 rates: $20 to $25. (609)861-2404

WOODPORT — A3 *Morris*

MAHLON DICKERSON RESERVATION (MORRIS COUNTY PARK) (Public) From jct I-80 (exit 34) & Hwy 15: Go 5 mi N on Hwy 15, then 4 mi E on Weldon Rd. 2015 rates: $20. Mar 1 to Nov 30. (973)697-3140

WOODSTOWN — E1 *Salem*

FOUR SEASONS CAMPGROUND
Ratings: 7.5/7/7.5 (Campground) From Jct of US-40 & CR-581, S 1.3 mi on CR-581 to CR-615 (Woodstown-Daretown Rd), W 200 ft (R). **FAC:** Gravel rds. (427 spaces). 90 Avail: 25 grass, 65 dirt, 37 pull-thrus (25 x 50), back-ins (18 x 36), some side by side hkups, 34 full hkups, 56

NJ

WOODSTOWN (CONT)

FOUR SEASONS CAMPGROUND (CONT)
W, 56 E (30/50 amps), seasonal sites, WiFi $, tent sites, rentals, dump, laundry, groc, LP gas, fire rings, firewood, restaurant. **REC:** pond, swim, fishing, playground. Pets OK. Partial handicap access. Eco-friendly, 2015 rates: $35 to $40. Feb 1 to Dec 31.
(856)769-3635 Lat: 39.61949, Lon: -75.27445
158 Woodstown-Daretown Rd, Pilesgrove, NJ 08098
info@fourseasonscamping.com
www.fourseasonscamping.com
See ad page 1008.

Join the flock and head south during the winter. Use our handy Snowbird guide in the front of the Guide to find RV-friendly destinations throughout the Sunbelt. Snowbird Destinations features the top Snowbird roosts and lists great Campgrounds in compelling areas.

Getty Images/iStockphoto

NM

WELCOME TO

New Mexico

DATE OF STATEHOOD	WIDTH: 342 MILES (550 KM)	PROPORTION OF UNITED STATES
JAN. 6, 1912	LENGTH: 370 MILES (595 KM)	3.20% OF 3,794,100 SQ MI

OK, New Mexico wins the tourism motto contest. But does the Land of Enchantment live up to the boast? Certainly few states have a richer culture to draw upon to beguile visitors.

There is less surface water by percentage in New Mexico than any other state, but fishing and boating enthusiasts can get their fix of the wet stuff at Elephant Butte, an irrigation lake on the Rio Grande River that's the state's largest body of water. Catch the big one there, dock your boat at one of the nearby marinas or go strolling on one of its beautiful sand beaches.

Thanks to the drug-dealing chronicled on television's "Breaking Bad," New Mexico's deserts have received plenty of screen time, but there are enough trees here to support five national forests and a national grassland covering several million acres. Back in 1950, the Lincoln National Forest was as famous as Walter White when an orphaned five-pound bear cub was discovered clinging to a tree in a forest fire. The two-month old survivor was enlisted as the living symbol for Smokey the Bear.

More than 119 fantastic limestone caves are preserved in the Carlsbad Caverns National Park. Go above ground and see the stunning dunes of the White Sands National.

The population of New Mexico's largest city, Albuquerque, surges for nine days in early October during the Albuquerque International Balloon Fiesta, the world's largest hot air balloon festival.

The state's rich past is honored in cities like Santa Fe, which annually hosts the centuries-old Traditional Spanish Market. The event is bathed in the creations of 350 local artists competing in one of the largest juried art shows in the United States.

Top 3 Tourism Attractions:
1) White Sands National Monument
2) Carlsbad Caverns National Park
3) Georgia O'Keeffe Museum

Nickname: Land of Enchantment

State Flower: Yucca

State Bird: Roadrunner

People: John Denver, singer and songwriter; William Hanna, "Yogi Bear" and "Flintstones" creator

Major Cities: Albuquerque, Las Cruces, Rio Rancho, Santa Fe (capital), Roswell

Topography: Eastern third—Great Plains; central third—Rocky Mountains; western third—high plateau

Climate: Mild, arid or semi-arid continental climate with light precipitation, abundant sunshine, low relative humidity

TRAVEL & TOURISM

New Mexico Tourism Dept.
505-827-7400
www.newmexico.org

Albuquerque CVB
800-284-2282
www.visitalbuquerque

Visit Gallup
505-863-1220
www.gallupnm.com

Las Cruces CVB
575-541-2444
www.lascrucescvb.org

Tourism Santa Fe
800-777-2489
www.santafe.org

OUTDOOR RECREATION

Continental Divide Trail Alliance
303-838-3760
www.cdtrail.org

Golf New Mexico
www.nmgolf.net

New Mexico Dept. of Game & Fish
505-476-8000
www.wildlife.state.nm.us

SHOPPING

Albuquerque Old Town
www.albuquerqueoldtown.com

Ford Smith Gallery
505-988-3732
www.fordsmithfineart.com

Santa Fe Premium Outlets
www.fashionoutletssantafe.com

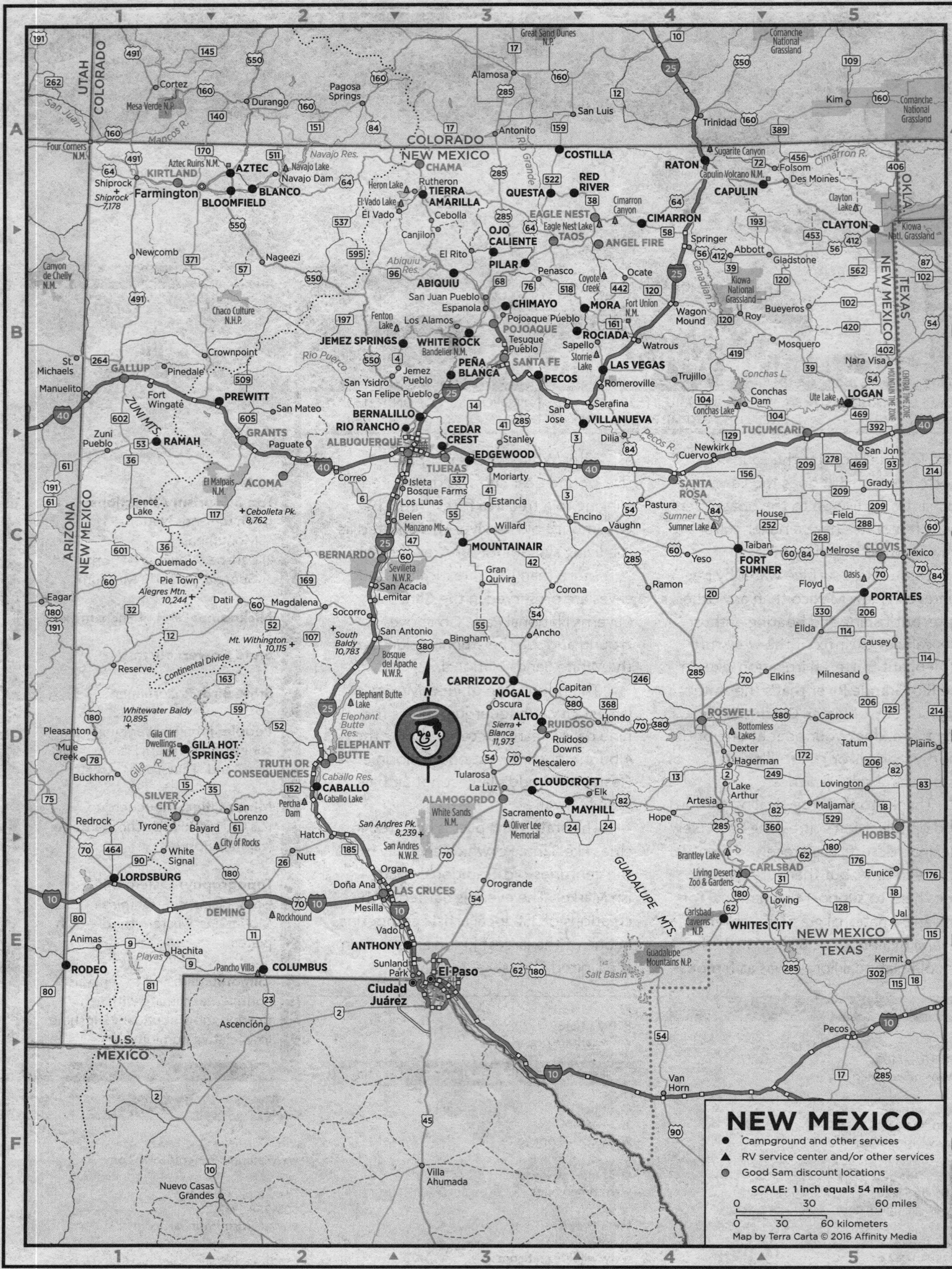
NEW MEXICO
Campground and other services
RV service center and/or other services
Good Sam discount locations
SCALE: 1 inch equals 54 miles
0 30 60 miles
0 30 60 kilometers
Map by Terra Carta © 2016 Affinity Media
UTAH
COLORADO
ARIZONA
NEW MEXICO
TEXAS
OKLA.
U.S.
MEXICO
Great Sand Dunes N.P.
Comanche National Grassland
Mesa Verde N.P.
Four Corners N.M.
Cortez
Durango
Pagosa Springs
Alamosa
San Luis
Antonito
Trinidad
Kim
Aztec Ruins N.M.
Navajo Res.
Navajo Lake
Navajo Dam
KIRTLAND
AZTEC
BLANCO
BLOOMFIELD
Farmington
Shiprock
Shiprock 7,178
CHAMA
Heron Lake
Rutheron
TIERRA AMARILLA
El Vado Lake
El Vado
Cebolla
Canjilon
COSTILLA
RED RIVER
QUESTA
EAGLE NEST
Eagle Nest Lake
Cimarron Canyon
CIMARRON
RATON
Sugarite Canyon
Capulin Volcano N.M.
CAPULIN
Folsom
Des Moines
Cimarron R.
Clayton Lake
CLAYTON
Kiowa Natl. Grassland
OJO CALIENTE
TAOS
ANGEL FIRE
Springer
Abbott
Gladstone
El Rito
Abiquiu Res.
ABIQUIU
PILAR
Penasco
Coyote Creek
Ocate
Newcomb
Nageezi
Canyon de Chelly N.M.
Chaco Culture N.H.P.
San Juan Pueblo
Espanola
CHIMAYO
MORA
Fort Union N.M.
Wagon Mound
Kiowa National Grassland
Roy
Bueyeros
Fenton Lake
Los Alamos
Pojoaque Pueblo
POJOAQUE
ROCIADA
JEMEZ SPRINGS
WHITE ROCK
Bandelier N.M.
Tesuque Pueblo
Sapello
Storrie Lake
Watrous
Mosquero
Crownpoint
St. Michaels
GALLUP
Pinedale
Manuelito
Rio Puerco
Jemez Pueblo
PEÑA BLANCA
SANTA FE
PECOS
LAS VEGAS
Romeroville
Trujillo
Conchas L.
Nara Visa
Fort Wingate
PREWITT
ZUNI MTS.
San Ysidro
San Felipe Pueblo
San Mateo
Serafina
San Jose
VILLANUEVA
Conchas Dam
Conchas Lake
Ute Lake
LOGAN
CENTRAL TIME ZONE
MOUNTAIN TIME ZONE
BERNALILLO
RIO RANCHO
GRANTS
CEDAR CREST
Stanley
Dilia
Pecos R.
Newkirk
TUCUMCARI
Zuni Pueblo
RAMAH
Paguate
ALBUQUERQUE
EDGEWOOD
TIJERAS
Moriarty
Cuervo
San Jon
El Malpais N.M.
ACOMA
Correo
Isleta
Bosque Farms
Los Lunas
Estancia
SANTA ROSA
Grady
Fence Lake
Cebolleta Pk. 8,762
Belen
Manzano Mts.
Willard
Encino
Pastura
Vaughn
Sumner L.
Sumner Lake
House
Field
Quemado
BERNARDO
MOUNTAINAIR
Taiban
FORT SUMNER
Yeso
Melrose
CLOVIS
Texico
Pie Town
Alegres Mtn. 10,244
Sevilleta N.W.R.
San Acacia
Lemitar
Gran Quivira
Corona
Ramon
Floyd
Oasis
PORTALES
Eagar
Datil
Magdalena
Socorro
Elida
Causey
Mt. Withington 10,115
South Baldy 10,783
San Antonio
Bingham
Ancho
Reserve
Continental Divide
Bosque del Apache N.W.R.
CARRIZOZO
Capitan
NOGAL
Oscura
Elkins
Milnesand
Whitewater Baldy 10,895
Elephant Butte Lake
Elephant Butte Res.
ALTO
Sierra Blanca 11,973
RUIDOSO
Ruidoso Downs
Hondo
ROSWELL
Caprock
Pleasanton
Gila Cliff Dwellings N.M.
GILA HOT SPRINGS
Mule Creek
ELEPHANT BUTTE
TRUTH OR CONSEQUENCES
Caballo Res.
CABALLO
Caballo Lake
Mescalero
Bottomless Lakes
Dexter
Hagerman
Tatum
Plains
Buckhorn
Gila R.
Tularosa
La Luz
CLOUDCROFT
Elk
MAYHILL
Lake Arthur
Lovington
SILVER CITY
San Lorenzo
Percha Dam
ALAMOGORDO
White Sands N.M.
Sacramento
Oliver Lee Memorial
Artesia
Maljamar
Redrock
Tyrone
Bayard
San Andres Pk. 8,239
Hope
HOBBS
City of Rocks
Hatch
San Andres N.W.R.
White Signal
Nutt
Brantley Lake
LORDSBURG
Organ
Living Desert Zoo & Gardens
CARLSBAD
Eunice
Doña Ana
LAS CRUCES
Orogrande
GUADALUPE MTS.
Loving
DEMING
Rockhound
Mesilla
Jal
Vado
Carlsbad Caverns N.P.
WHITES CITY
Animas
ANTHONY
Hachita
Playas L.
Guadalupe Mountains N.P.
Kermit
RODEO
Pancho Villa
COLUMBUS
Sunland Park
El Paso
Ciudad Juárez
Salt Basin
Ascención
Pecos
Van Horn
Villa Ahumada
Nuevo Casas Grandes

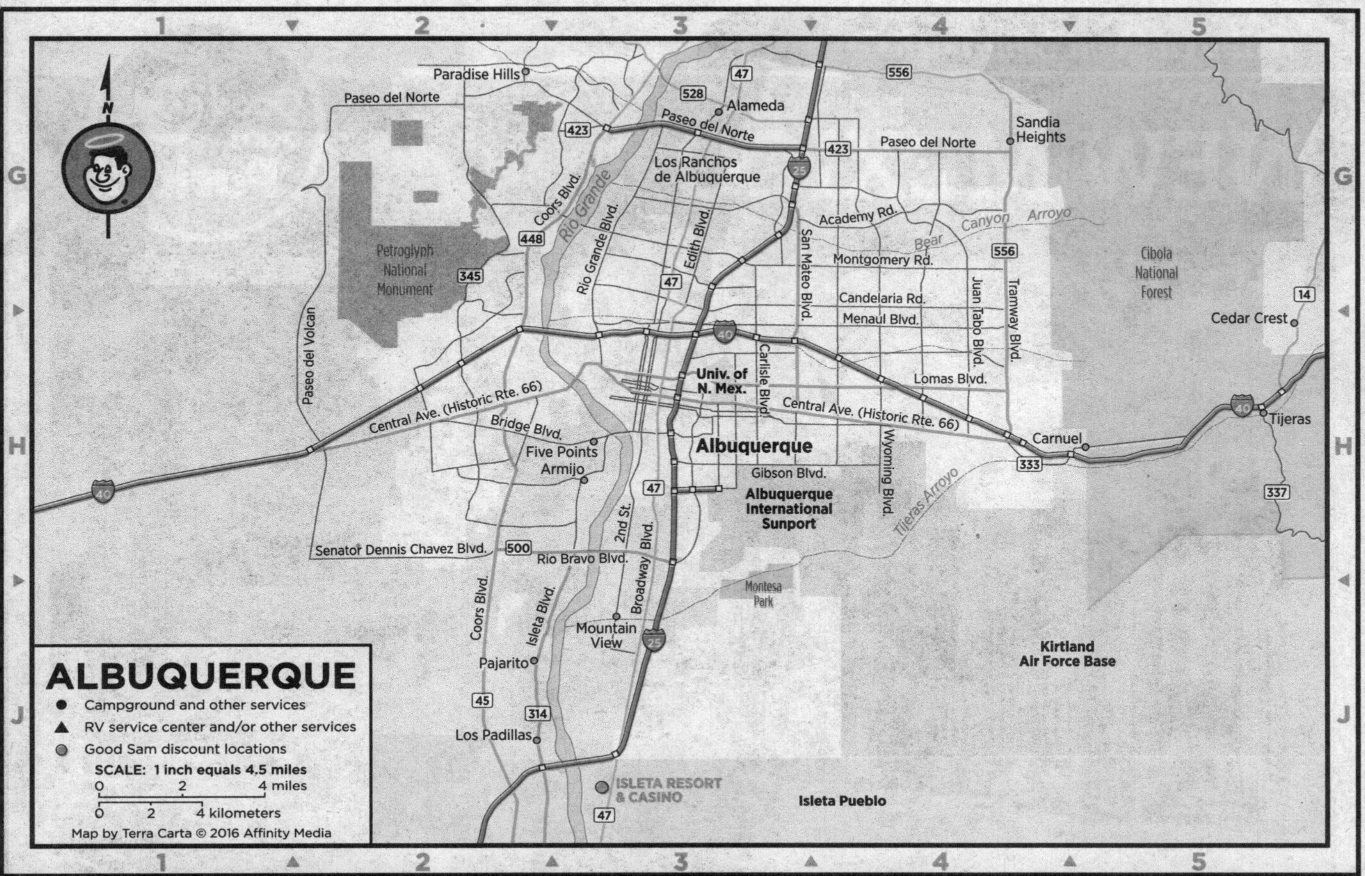

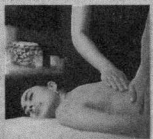

ALBUQUERQUE
Campground and other services
RV service center and/or other services
Good Sam discount locations
SCALE: 1 inch equals 4.5 miles
0 2 4 miles
0 2 4 kilometers
Map by Terra Carta © 2016 Affinity Media
Paradise Hills
Paseo del Norte
Alameda
Sandia Heights
Los Ranchos de Albuquerque
Coors Blvd.
Rio Grande
Rio Grande Blvd.
Edith Blvd.
Academy Rd.
Canyon Arroyo
Bear
Montgomery Rd.
San Mateo Blvd.
Juan Tabo Blvd.
Tramway Blvd.
Cibola National Forest
Petroglyph National Monument
Candelaria Rd.
Menaul Blvd.
Cedar Crest
Paseo del Volcan
Univ. of N. Mex.
Carlisle Blvd.
Lomas Blvd.
Central Ave. (Historic Rte. 66)
Bridge Blvd.
Tijeras
Carnuel
Five Points
Armijo
Albuquerque
Gibson Blvd.
Wyoming Blvd.
Tijeras Arroyo
Albuquerque International Sunport
Senator Dennis Chavez Blvd.
Rio Bravo Blvd.
2nd St.
Broadway Blvd.
Montesa Park
Coors Blvd.
Isleta Blvd.
Mountain View
Kirtland Air Force Base
Pajarito
Los Padillas
ISLETA RESORT & CASINO
Isleta Pueblo
NM

Featured Good Sam Parks

NEW MEXICO

Good Sam Park

When you stay with Good Sam, you can expect the highest degree of cleanliness and friendliness, and better yet, you get 10% off campground fees.

If you're not already a Good Sam member you can purchase your membership at one of these locations:

ALAMOGORDO
Boot Hill RV Resort, LLC
(575)439-6224

ALBUQUERQUE
American RV Park
(505)831-3545

Coronado Village Mobile Home & RV Resort
(505)823-2515

Enchanted Trails RV Park & Trading Post
(505)831-6317

Isleta Lakes & RV Park
(505)244-8102

ANGEL FIRE
Angel Fire Resort
(800)633-7463

CHAMA
Sky Mountain Resort RV Park
(575)756-1100

CLOVIS
Clovis RV Park
(575)742-5035

DEMING
A Deming Roadrunner RV Park
(575)546-6960

Little Vineyard RV Park
(800)413-0312

EAGLE NEST
Golden Eagle RV Park & Store LLC
(800)388-6188

ELEPHANT BUTTE
Cedar Cove RV Park
(575)744-4472

Elephant Butte Lake RV Resort
(575)744-5996

GALLUP
USA RV Park
(505)863-5021

LAS CRUCES
Hacienda RV & Rally Resort
(888)686-9090

Siesta RV Park
(800)414-6816

Sunny Acres RV Park
(877)800-1716

POJOAQUE
Roadrunner RV Park
(505)455-2626

ROSWELL
Town & Country RV Park
(575)624-1833

RUIDOSO
Circle B RV Park
(575)378-4990

SANTA FE
Los Suenos de Santa Fe RV Resort & Campground
(505) 473-1949

Rancheros de Santa Fe Campground
(505)466-3482

Santa Fe Skies RV Park
(877)565-0451

The Trailer Ranch RV Resort & 55+ Community
(505)471-9970

SANTA ROSA
Santa Rosa Campground
(575)472-3126

TAOS
Taos Valley RV Park & Campground
(575)758-4469

For more Good Sam Parks go to listing pages

Getty Images/iStockphoto

ANGEL FIRE

Discover high-altitude adventure in this recreation hot spot

The rugged beauty of New Mexico is the center of attention in Angel Fire. This resort community welcomes skiers, golfers and many more adventurous travelers. But you don't have to be a daredevil to enjoy Angel Fire—relaxation and rejuvenation come in ample supply as well.

Angel Fire sits nearly 9,000 feet above sea level in the Southern Rocky Mountains. From here, Wheeler Peak—the highest point in New Mexico—can easily be seen. Hiking is a popular warm-weather activity, and Angel Fire's trail systems provide varying levels of difficulty for visitors of all skill levels. Trails pass through grassy meadows and thickly forested areas, and all offer spectacular views of the surrounding landscape.

The trails around Angel Fire are inviting to mountain bikers, ranging in difficulty from family-friendly to adrenaline-boosting. The extensive South Boundary Trail begins south of the town and winds through Carson National Forest. If young adventurers want to ride above the earth, send them down a 1,600-foot tandem zip line over the forest floor. More relaxing aerial transportation is available on Angel Fire chairlifts, which run year-round and offer stunning views from Agua Fria Peak.

Colorful Skies

Brightly colored hot air balloons waft through the sky over Angel Fire during its summer festival. Watch the balloons glide by from the ground or arrange for a ride in a basket.

Seeking more terrestrial pursuits? Carson National Forest sits adjacent to Angel Fire and is a prime spot for fishing and hunting. Trout are the prize catch in the streams that run through the forest, including native Rio Grande cutthroat trout. Small game in the forest includes grouse, mourning dove, gray squirrel and banned-tailed pigeon. Elk, turkey, Rocky Mountain bighorn sheep and mule deer make up the large-game set for avid hunters.

Just north of Angel Fire, on the Enchanted Circle Scenic Byway, the mountains of the Moreno Valley surround Eagle Nest Lake. Trout and salmon thrive in the lake, where boat fishing and ice fishing are popular activities. Take a boat ride, go kayaking and canoeing, or simply relax on the banks. Eagle Nest Lake is a prime bird-watching spot, so pack your binoculars.

New Mexico's Past

The Enchanted Circle Byway is an 84-mile loop that takes day-trippers around Wheeler Peak. Head north from Angel Fire and stop to visit the memorial chapel in Vietnam Veterans Memorial State Park. Further north, in the town of Eagle Nest, lies Laguna Vista Lodge and Saloon, which once served as one of the state's earliest bordellos. The nearby Gateway Museum features exhibits on gold panning and early railroad travel in the region.

A hot air balloon floats over Angel Fire's rugged landscape. Getty Images/iStockphoto

For More Information

Angel Fire Convention & Visitors Bureau
866-668 7787
www.angelfirefun.com

New Mexico Tourism Department
800-827-7400
www.newmexico.org

ANGEL FIRE
RV RESORT
NEW MEXICO
Good Sam Park
INTRODUCING THE
Next Generation of RV Resorts
Located in the heart of the Enchanted Circle Scenic Byway
GOOD SAM RATED:
10/10★/10 • #1 in New Mexico • Top 100 in the U.S.
angelfirervresort.com • (888) 976-1541 • rvresort@angelfireresort.com
Latitude, Longitude: 36.4237, -105.30983
YEAR ROUND RESORT
See listing Angel Fire, NM

New Mexico Tourism

ELEPHANT BUTTE

Rugged New Mexico desert meets crystal, refreshing water

Elephant Butte Lake State Park is an outdoor destination with postcard-worthy scenery and an abundance of recreational opportunities. Whether you want to kayak across the calm water or launch a sailboat into the sunset, Elephant Butte satisfies outdoors enthusiasts of all types.

Motorized and nonmotorized boating is permitted on the lake, as are personal watercraft, canoes and kayaks. Fish from a boat on the lake or from the pier, and take advantage of a knowledgeable guide to help you find the best spots for catching walleye, crappie, white and black bass, and stripers.

Elephant Butte Lake has a handful of accessible sandy beaches for relaxing under the New Mexico sun and cooling off in the water. Camping on the beach is permitted and is a great way to watch the sun set over the rocky horizon after a full day on the water.

Enchanting Landscapes

The terrain at Elephant Butte looks daunting, but it is an excellent host to four hiking trails that range from primitive paths to paved surfaces. For an easy, scenic loop to traverse, head to the Paseo del Rio campground at the lake's southern tip. A more adventurous trek awaits visitors on the 10.5-mile West Lakeshore Trail, which runs the length of the lake's western edge. Look out for jackrabbits and lizards, and enjoy the scenery from points such as Black Bluff Overlook and Fray Cristobal Mountain Overlook.

Elephant Butte is a popular birding destination thanks to the riparian habitat that beckons egrets, herons, pelicans and some unusual gulls. In the scrubby cliffs near Rock Canyon, keen-eyed watchers can spot sparrows and horned larks.

Hunting with a state-issued license is a permitted and popular pastime in the area around Elephant Butte Lake. Big game pursuits focus on antelope, desert bighorn, deer and elk. Bird-hunting adventures are built around healthy populations of mallards, canvasbacks, wigeons and teals. Also around Elephant Butte, hunters will find opportunities to hunt turkey, quail and dove—check out guided opportunities to ensure a successful hunt.

Away from the lake, golfers are welcome at Turtleback Mountain Resort for a game or two on the Sierra del Rio course. The 18-hole championship course winds over various elevation changes with a scenic backdrop featuring the Turtleback Mountain Range and the Rio Grande, as well as 89 bunkers and four lakes.

The resort community of Elephant Butte hosts events year-round including a hot air balloon regatta, Elephant Days Festival, Oktoberfest, a luminaria beach walk and a floating lights parade on the lake.

Face the Truth or Consequences

Visit a town with one of the quirkiest names around—Truth or Consequences—and soak in the hot springs that have made this a prime resort community. Out of a rift along the Rio Grande, thermal hot water flows freely to the surface at temperatures between 98 to 115 degrees. Trace elements of 38 different minerals have been detected in the water, and these minerals are believed to hold many health benefits for visitors to the Hot Springs Bathhouse Historic and Commercial District.

Geronimo Springs Museum tells the story of the region's Native American history.
New Mexico Tourism

Downtown Truth or Consequences is home to Geronimo Springs Museum. This gem is home to Old West artifacts including pottery and arrowheads, as well as a re-created miner's cabin and a room devoted to the famous Apache shaman, Geronimo.

Pay respects to the men and women who served on behalf of their nation at the Hamilton Military Museum, where exhibits memorialize the lives and work of soldiers, sailors and marines in major conflicts. The museum is adjacent to a Vietnam War Memorial replica on the grounds of Veterans Memorial Park in Truth or Consequences.

West of Elephant Butte, the living ghost town of Cuchillo draws visitors to explore the San Jose Catholic Church, built in 1907, and the supposedly haunted Cuchillo Bar. If a daytrip with stunning scenery suits you, head out to the town of Chloride, at the western edge of Sierra County. Just 11 residents call this former mining town home, and visitors can wander through the old Pioneer Store that serves as a museum before visiting the Monte Cristo Saloon and Dance Hall, which today operates as a gallery featuring works by local artists.

Further to the south, a trip to Las Palomas reveals another living ghost town. With fewer than 200 residents today, Las Palomas still has an active Catholic church and is a gateway to Indian pueblo ruins that date to around A.D. 500. Kingston tells yet another tale of mining boom-and-bust; here, hotels put up Mark Twain, Butch Cassidy and the Sundance Kid, and other characters, both famous and infamous, during the town's heyday.

Today the Percha Bank Museum opens on weekdays to share artifacts and local artists' creations.

For More Information

Elephant Butte Chamber of Commerce
575-744-4708
www.ebcocnm.com

New Mexico Tourism Department
505-827-7400
www.newmexico.org

Getty Images/iStockphoto

SANTA FE

Explore the compelling past of a centuries-old city

Some 13 years before the Mayflower nudged up against the shores of Plymouth Rock in 1620, the small township of Santa Fe was established in what is now New Mexico. More than 400 years later, this one-time seat of power for the 17th century Spanish Empire stands as the oldest capital city in North America, and the oldest city of European ancestry west of the Mississippi.

In fact, over the course of that 400-year history, the city has served as the capital for no less than four distinct political sovereigns: the Spanish Kingdom of New Mexico, the Mexican province of Nuevo Mejico, the American territory of New Mexico and (since 1912) for the state of New Mexico.

If this is your first time in Santa Fe, the first thing you'll notice is how picturesque and replete with ornate architecture the city is. Since the early days of New Mexico's statehood, the city has fought hard to preserve and promote its cultural heritage, resulting in a rich assortment of protected buildings and landmarks.

Santa Fe Aesthetics

But architecture and artifacts aren't the only ways to explore Santa Fe's rich culture heritage and history. Arts enthusiasts will be in their element, as the city is home to more than 250 galleries showcasing everything from traditional pottery and sculptures to contemporary photography and paintings.

If you don't know where to start, aim for Canyon Road in the city's historic district. This easy-to-stroll half-mile stretch in the foothills of the Sangre de Cristo Mountains has been attracting artists for centuries.

Closer to the center of town, don't miss the Georgia O'Keefe Museum, where the single largest repository of the late artist's works is displayed.

Sunny Hikes

When it's time to stretch your legs and get some fresh air, the surrounding foothills, forests and rocky mountain peaks provide a rich assortment of options. The Santa Fe National Forest lies just to the east, and the Rio Grande lies just to the west.

For More Information

Tourism Santa Fe
800-777-2489
www.santafe.org

New Mexico Tourism Department
800-827-7400
www.newmexico.org

New Mexico

CONSULTANTS

Fain & Lynda Little

ABIQUIU — B3 *Rio Arriba*

RIANA CAMPGROUND (COE - ABIQUIU RESERVOIR) (Public Corps) From town: Go 7 mi N on US 84, then 1-1/2 mi W on Hwy 96. 2015 rates: $12 to $16. Apr 15 to Oct 14. (505)685-4371

ACOMA — C2 *Cibola*

SKY CITY RV PARK, CASINO & CULTURAL CENTER
Ratings: 7.5/9.5★/7.5 (RV Park) From jct of I-40 & exit 102: Go 1/4 mi N on exit rd (L). Elev 6154 ft. **FAC:** Paved rds. 42 paved, 42 pull-thrus (30 x 85), 42 full hkups (30/50 amps), cable, WiFi, dump, laundry. **REC:** heated pool, whirlpool, rec open to public. Pets OK. Partial handicap access, no tents. Big rig sites, 2015 rates: $22.40. ATM.
(505)552-7913 Lat: 35.07888, Lon: -107.55772
I-40, Exit 102, Acoma, NM 87034
www.skycity.com

ALAMOGORDO — D3 *Otero*

ALAMOGORDO WHITE SANDS KOA **Ratings: 8/8.5★/7** (Campground) 2015 rates: $33 to $37. (575)437-3003 412 24th St, Alamogordo, NM 88310

BOOT HILL RV RESORT, LLC
Ratings: 7.5/9★/8.5 (RV Park) S-bnd: From Jct of NM State Hwy 54/70 in Tularosa, South 5.8 mi on Hwy 54/70 (L); or N-bnd: From N Jct of 54/70 & Hwy 82 in Alamogordo, N 3.7 mi (R). Note: Turn right between two big yellow boots. **FAC:** Gravel rds. 41 gravel, 19 pull-thrus (32 x 83), back-ins (30 x 70), 41 full hkups (30/50 amps), WiFi, rentals, laundry. **REC.** Pet restrict(B). No tents. Big rig sites, eco-friendly. 2015 rates: $27. Disc: military.
(575)439-6224 Lat: 32.99759, Lon: -105.98949
1 Dog Ranch Rd, Alamogordo, NM 88310
Newmexico@boothillrv.net
www.boothillrv.com
See ad this page, 796.

DESERT PARADISE MH & RV VILLAGE **Ratings: 5.5/8.5★/7** (RV Park) 2015 rates: $25 to $30. (575)434-2266 1090 US Highway 70 West, Alamogordo, NM 88310

OLIVER LEE MEMORIAL (State Pk) From S Jct of US-70 & US-54, S 8.8 mi on US-54 to CR-16, E 4 mi (E). 2015 rates: $8 to $18. (575)437-8284

WHITE SANDS MANUFACTURED HOMES AND RV COMMUNITY
Ratings: 9/9.5★/7.5 (RV Area in MHP) N-bnd: From S Jct of US-54 & US-70/82, NE 1.2 mi on US-54/70/82 - White Sands Blvd (R); or S-bnd: From N Jct of US-54/70 & US-82, S 3.8 mi on US-54/70/82 - White Sands Blvd (L). Elev 4200 ft. **FAC:** Paved rds. (86 spaces). 59 Avail: 29 paved, 30 gravel, patios, 29 pull-thrus (23 x 50), back-ins (26 x 50), 59 full hkups (30/50 amps), cable, WiFi, laundry. **REC:** pool, playground. Pets OK. Partial handicap access, no tents. 2015 rates: $33.75.
AAA Approved
(575)437-8388 Lat: 32.88579, Lon: -105.95703
607 S White Sands, Alamogordo, NM 88310
info@westernm.com
www.westernm.com/whitesands/
See ad this page.

ALBUQUERQUE — C3 *Bernalillo, Santa Fe*

ALBUQUERQUE See also Bernalillo, Cedar Crest, Edgewood, Rio Rancho & Tijeras.

ALBUQUERQUE CENTRAL KOA **Ratings: 9.5/9★/7.5** (Campground) 2015 rates: $45 to $69. (505)296-2729 12400 Skyline Rd NE, Albuquerque, NM 87123

We rate what RVers consider important.

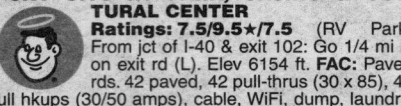

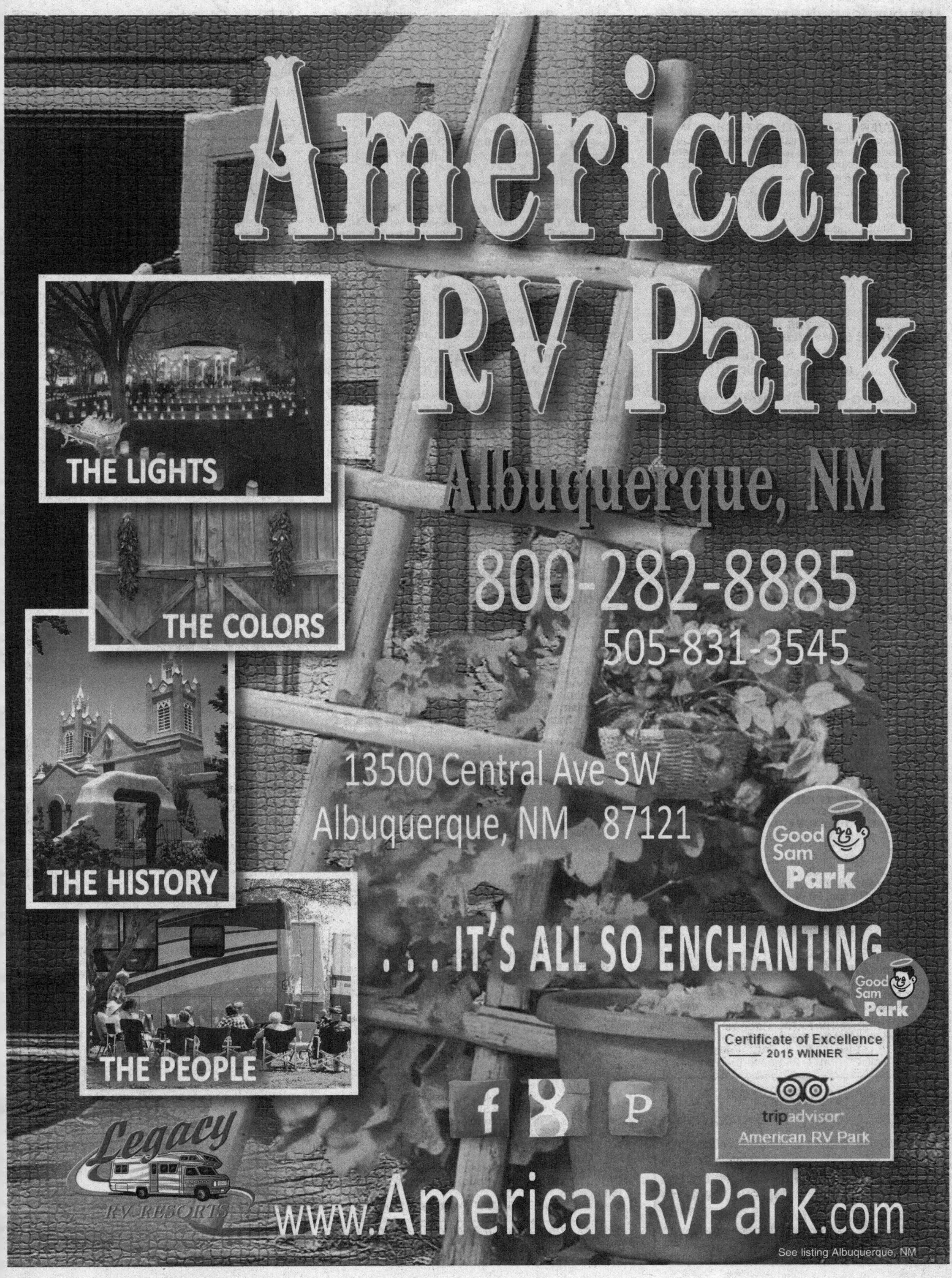
American
RV Park
Albuquerque, NM
800-282-8885
505-831-3545
THE LIGHTS
THE COLORS
THE HISTORY
THE PEOPLE
13500 Central Ave SW
Albuquerque, NM 87121
Good Sam Park
. . . IT'S ALL SO ENCHANTING
Good Sam Park
Certificate of Excellence
2015 WINNER
tripadvisor
American RV Park
Legacy
RV RESORTS
www.AmericanRvPark.com
See listing Albuquerque, NM

ALBUQUERQUE (CONT)

← **AMERICAN RV PARK**
Ratings: 10/10★/9 (RV Park) E-bnd: From jct of I-40 & exit 149: Go 1/2 mi W on S frntg rd (L); or W-bnd: From jct of I-40 & exit 149: Go 1/4 mi S on overpass to S frntg rd, then 1/2 mi W (L). Elev 5672 ft.

ALBUQUERQUE-IT'S ALL SO ENCHANTING!
The lights, the colors, the history, the people. Our RV Park includes everthing to make your stay a relaxed and pleasant experience with daily, weekly and monthly rates available.

FAC: Paved rds. (218 spaces). Avail: 148 paved, patios, 133 pull-thrus (25 x 60), back-ins (27 x 50), 148 full hkups (30/50 amps), cable, WiFi, tent sites, rentals, dump, laundry, LP gas. **REC:** heated pool, whirlpool, playground, rec open to public. Pets OK. Partial handicap access. Big rig sites, eco-friendly, 2015 rates: $35 to $41. Disc: AAA. ATM.
(505)831-3545 Lat: 35.06019, Lon: -106.79693
13500 Central Ave S.w., Albuquerque, NM 87121
info@americanrvpark.com
www.americanrvpark.com
See ad pages 803, 796 & Snowbird Destinations in Magazine Section.

→ BALLOON VIEW RV PARK **Ratings: 8/8★/6.5** (RV Park) 2015 rates: $35. (505)345-3716 500 Tyler Rd NE, Albuquerque, NM 87113

↑ **CORONADO VILLAGE MOBILE HOME & RV RESORT**
Ratings: 9/8★/7.5 (RV Area in MHP) From Jct of I-25 & Exit 233: Go 3/4 mi S on West Service Rd (R). Gates close at 8pm. **FAC:** Paved rds. (321 spaces). Avail: 15 dirt, 2 pull-thrus (20 x 65), back-ins (25 x 60), 15 full hkups (30/50 amps), seasonal sites, WiFi, laundry, controlled access. **REC:** pool, whirlpool, playground. Pet restrict(B). No tents. Big rig sites, 2015 rates: $34.
(505)823-2515 Lat: 35.178269, Lon: -106.585647
8401 Pan American Freeway N.e., Albuquerque, NM 87113
coronadovillage@thesman.com
thesman.com/coronado
See ad pages 802, 796.

↘ **EL RANCHO RV PARK**
Ratings: 5.5/NA/6.5 (RV Park) From jct of I-40 & Wyoming Blvd (exit 164): Go 1 mi S on Wyoming to Central, then 150 feet W to Wisconsin, then 150 feet S to entrance (L). Elev 5447 ft. **FAC:** Paved rds. (86 spaces). Avail: 66 gravel, patios, back-ins (25 x 45), accepts full hkup units only, 66 full hkups (30/50 amps), WiFi. Pet restrict(B). No tents. 2015 rates: $25 to $40. Disc: AAA, military.
(505)266-1455 Lat: 35.07223, Lon: -106.55160
201 Wyoming SE Space 90, Albuquerque, NM 87123
manager@elranchorvpark.com
www.elranchorvpark.com
See ad page 802.

← **ENCHANTED TRAILS RV PARK & TRADING POST**
Ratings: 9/9★/8.5 (RV Park) From jct of I-40 & Atrisco Vista Blvd/Exit 149 (W side of town), exit to N frntg rd, then go 1-1/2 mi (R). Elev 5672 ft. **FAC:** Paved/gravel rds. 135 gravel, 127 pull-thrus (20 x 80), back-ins (20 x 50), some side by side hkups, 115 full hkups, 20 W, 20 E (30/50 amps), WiFi, rentals, dump, laundry, LP gas. **REC:** heated pool, whirlpool. Pets OK. Partial handicap access, no tents. 2015 rates: $34 to $37. Disc: AAA.
AAA Approved
(505)831-6317 Lat: 35.05987, Lon: -106.81025
14305 Central NW, Albuquerque, NM 87121
info@enchantedtrails.com
enchantedtrails.com
See ad pages 802, 796.

← **HIGH DESERT RV PARK Ratings: 8/9★/7** (RV Park) From jct of I-40 & Exit 149: Go 1/4 mi W on S Frntg Rd (L). Elev 5670 ft. **FAC:** Paved rds. (75 spaces). Avail: 25 gravel, 25 pull-thrus (25 x 64), 25 full hkups (30/50 amps), WiFi, dump, laundry, LP gas. **REC.** Pet restrict(B). Partial handicap access, no tents. Big rig sites, 2015 rates: $28.95 to $30.95. Disc: AAA, military.
AAA Approved
(505)839-9035 Lat: 35.06088, Lon: -106.78813
13000 Frontage Rd. SW, Albuquerque, NM 87121
highdesertrvpark@gmail.com
www.highdesertrvpark.net

↓ **ISLETA LAKES & RV PARK**
Ratings: 8/9.5★/8.5 (RV Park) From jct of I-25 & exit 215 (Hwy 47): Go 1/4 mi S to Isleta Lakes Rd (TR-15), then 1/2 mi W (E). Elev 5200 ft.

ISLETA LAKES CASINO & RV PARK
Enjoy the natural beauty of the Southwest. Our 50 full-service RV sites are equipped with all the necessities +WIFI, convenience store, lakes & fishing. Golf, Casino, bowling, family fun nearby. Come spread your wings.

FAC: Paved/gravel rds. 50 gravel, patios, 42 pull-thrus (30 x 45), back-ins (30 x 45), 50 full hkups (30/50 amps), cable, WiFi, dump, laundry, groc, controlled access. **REC:** Isleta Lake: fishing, golf, playground, rec open to public. Pet restrict(B). Partial handicap access, no tents. 2015 rates: $35. ATM.
(505)244-8102 Lat: 34.94548, Lon: -106.67424
4051 Hwy 47, Albuquerque, NM 87105
Isleta.com/camping
See ad pages 795 (NM Featured Map), 796 & RV Trips of a Lifetime in Magazine Section.

← **ROUTE 66 RV RESORT**
(RV Resort) (Planned) Elev 5200 ft. **FAC. REC.** No CC, no reservations.
(505)352-7866 Lat: 35.02693, Lon: -106.95236
interstate 40 exit 140, Albuquerque, NM 87121
route66rvresort@poldc.com
www.rt66Casino.com
See ad page 802.

→ **TURQUOISE TRAIL CAMPGROUND & RV PARK**
Ratings: 7.5/8.5★/7.5 (Campground) From Jct I-40 & Exit 175 (Cedar Crest/Hwy 14): Go 4 mi N on Hwy 14 (L). Elev 7200 ft. **FAC:** Gravel rds. 57 gravel, 37 pull-thrus (26 x 70), back-ins (28 x 60), some side by side hkups, 47 full hkups, 10 W, 10 E (30/50 amps), WiFi, tent sites, dump, laundry. **REC:** playground. Pets OK. Big rig sites, 2015 rates: $29.95 to $32.95.
(505)281-2005 Lat: 35.14287, Lon: -106.36741
22 Calvary Rd, Cedar Crest, NM 87008
turquoisetrailrv@gmail.com
turquoisetrailcampground.com
See primary listing at Cedar Crest and ad page 802.

Travel Services

← **CAMPING WORLD OF ALBUQUERQUE** As the nation's largest retailer of RV supplies, accessories, services and new and used RVs, Camping World is committed to making your total RV experience better. RV Accessories: (866)393-6446. **SERVICES:** RV, tire, RV appliance, MH mechanical, staffed RV wash, restrooms, RV Sales. RV supplies, LP, RV accessible. waiting room. Hours: 8am to 6pm.
(888)870-4392 Lat: 35.059254, Lon: -106.810134
14303 Central Ave N.W. Suite B, Albuquerque, NM 87121
kcoughran@cwrvsales.com
www.campingworld.com

Things to See and Do

↓ **ISLETA EAGLE GOLF COURSE** 18 hole championship golf course. Elev 5200 ft. RV accessible. Restrooms, food. Hours: 8am to 4pm. ATM.
(505)848-1900 Lat: 34.93822, Lon: -106.67068
11001 Broadway SE, Albuquerque, NM 87105
www.isleta.com
See ad page 795 (NM Featured Map).

↓ **ISLETA RESORT & CASINO** 201 Guest rooms; 100,000 sq ft casino; relaxing indoor/outdoorpool; restaurants/cocktail lounges and a 2,500 seat theatre for concerts and events. 18 hole championship golf course & pro shop. Elev 5200 ft. partial handicap access. RV accessible. Restrooms, food. Hours: 12am to 11:59pm. No CC.
(505)724-3800 Lat: 34.94553, Lon: -106.67432
11000 Broadway SE, Albuquerque, NM 87105
Isleta.com
See ad page 795 (NM Featured Map).

Don't camp without it ... Our 2016 listings are your key to travel satisfaction.

ALTO — D3 *Lincoln*

↑ BONITO HOLLOW RV PARK & CAMPGROUND **Ratings: 6/9★/9** (Campground) 2015 rates: $29 to $39. Apr 1 to Oct 15. (575)336-4325 221 Hwy 37, Alto, NM 88312

ANGEL FIRE — B4 *Colfax*

A SPOTLIGHT A Spotlight on Angel Fire's colorful attractions appearing at the front of this state section.

↖ **ANGEL FIRE RESORT**
Ratings: 10/10★/10 (RV Resort) From Jct of US 64 & SR 434, Go W 0.8 mi on US 64(L). Elev 8300 ft.

NEW MEXICO'S NEW PREMIER RV RESORT
Our family friendly destination in the Southern Rockies is open year-round! Enjoy zipline adventures, mountain biking, fishing, great golf & many other activities. In winter, ski & enjoy all of our snow related fun! Welcome!

FAC: Paved rds. 102 paved, patios, 85 pull-thrus (40 x 90), back-ins (40 x 90), accepts self-contain units only, 102 full hkups (30/50 amps), cable, WiFi, laundry, fire rings, controlled access. **REC:** heated pool $, whirlpool. Pets OK. Partial handicap access. Big rig sites, eco-friendly, 2015 rates: $59 to $65. Disc: military.
(800)633-7463 Lat: 36.42370, Lon: -105.30983
27500 Hwy 64, Angel Fire, NM 87710
reservations@angelfireresort.com
www.angelfireresort.com
See ad pages 798 (Spotlight Angel Fire), 796.

↑ **MONTE VERDE RV PARK & CAMPGROUND**
Ratings: 6/9★/8 (RV Park) From Jct of US-64 & SR-434: Go 1-1/3 mi S on SR-434 (R). Elev 8300 ft. **FAC:** Gravel rds. 28 gravel, 8 pull-thrus (25 x 60), back-ins (25 x 55), 19 full hkups, 9 W, 9 E (30 amps), WiFi, tent sites, showers $, dump, LP gas, firewood. **REC.** Pets OK. 2015 rates: $35 to $40. May 15 to Oct 15. No CC.
(575)377-3404 Lat: 36.41142, Lon: -105.29463
3521 Hwy 434, Angel Fire, NM 87710
monteverderv@yahoo.com
www.monteverderv.com
See ad this page.

ANTHONY — E3 *Dona Ana*

↑ EL PASO WEST RV PARK **Ratings: 6.5/9.5★/6** (RV Park) 2015 rates: $31. (575)882-7172 1415 Anthony Dr, Anthony, NM 88021

AZTEC — A2 *San Juan*

↗ NAVAJO LAKE/COTTONWOOD (State Pk) From town, E 10 mi on Hwy 64 to Hwy 511, NE 8 mi to Hwy 173, W 1.1 mi to CR-4280, NW 2.7 mi (R). 2015 rates: $8 to $18. (505)632-2278

BERNALILLO — B3 *Bernalillo, Sandoval*

→ ALBUQUERQUE NORTH KOA **Ratings: 8.5/10★/8** (Campground) 2015 rates: $36.75 to $41.75. (800)562-3616 555 south Hill Rd, Bernalillo, NM 87004

← CORONADO CAMPGROUND (Public) From Jct of I-25 & Exit 242B, W on Hwy 550 1.6 mi (Old Hwy 44-over Rio Grande River), N 0.5 mi on Kuaua, follow signs (E). Call for maximum stay limit. 2015 rates: $14 to $22. (505)980-8256

BERNARDO — C2 *Socorro*

← **KIVA RV PARK & HORSE MOTEL**
Ratings: 6/7.5★/8 (Campground) From jct of I-25 & Hwy 60 (exit 175), (watch for cell phone tower): Go 1/4 mi S on W frntg rd (L). Elev 4800 ft. **FAC:** Gravel/dirt rds. (34 spaces). Avail: 16 gravel, 16 pull-thrus (30 x 60), 16 full hkups (30/50 amps), WiFi, tent sites, laundry. **REC.** Pets OK. Partial handicap access. Big rig sites, eco-friendly, 2015 rates: $28. Disc: AAA. No CC.
(505)861-0693 Lat: 34.41623, Lon: -106.84294
21 Old Highway 60 west, Bernardo, NM 87006
admin@kivarvparkandhorsemotel.com
www.kivarvparkandhorsemotel.com

BLANCO — A2 *San Juan*

↗ NAVAJO LAKE/SIMS MESA (State Pk) From Jct of US-64 & Hwy 527, NW 9.2 mi to CR-636, W 4.9 mi to CR-490, NW 2.9 mi, W 1.8 mi. 2015 rates: $8 to $18. (505)632-2278

BLOOMFIELD — A2 *San Juan*

↗ DESERT ROSE AT FOUR CORNERS **Ratings: 8.5/9.5★/8** (Campground) 2015 rates: $36.50 to $39.50. (505)632-8339 1900 E Blanco Blvd, Bloomfield, NM 87413

BLOOMFIELD (CONT)

NAVAJO LAKE/PINE RIVER (State Pk) From Jct of US-64 & SR-511, N 15 mi on SR-511 (R). 2015 rates: $8 to $18. May 15 to Sep 15. (505)632-2278

CABALLO — D2 *Sierra*

CABALLO LAKE (State Pk) S-bnd: From Jct of I-25 & Hwy 152 (exit 63), E 0.1 mi on Hwy 152 to Hwy 187, S 3 mi (L); or N-bnd: From Jct of I-25 & Hwy 187 (exit 59), N 0.8 mi on Hwy 187 (R) (Reservations available). 2015 rates: $8 to $18. (575)743-3942

CABALLO LAKE RV PARK Ratings: 5/NA/7.5 (RV Park) From Jct of I-25 & Exit 59 (Hwy 187), N 1.8 mi on Hwy 187 (Mile Marker 22) (R). Elev 4300 ft. **FAC:** Gravel rds. 19 gravel, 19 pull-thrus (35 x 55), 19 full hkups (30/50 amps), WiFi. **REC.** Pets OK. No tents. Eco-friendly, 2015 rates: $15. No CC.
(575)743-0502 Lat: 32.90865, Lon: -107.31178
14279 Hwy 187 Mile Marker 22, Caballo, NM 87931
cjatcaballo@yahoo.com
caballolakervpark.net

PERCHA DAM (State Pk) From town, S 6.2 mi on I-25, follow signs (R). 2015 rates: $8 to $18. (575)743-3942

CAPULIN — B2 *Union*

CAPULIN RV PARK **Ratings: 4.5/8★/6** (Campground) 2015 rates: $27. (575)278-2921 7 S. Santa Fe Ave, Capulin, NM 88414

CARLSBAD — E4 *Eddy*

BRANTLEY LAKE (State Pk) From Jct of US-285 & US-62/180, N 12.3 mi on US-285 to Capitan Reef Rd/CR-30, E 4 mi on Captain Reef Rd/CR-30 (L). 2015 rates: $8 to $18. (575)457-2384

CARLSBAD KOA **Ratings: 9/9.5★/9** (RV Park) 2015 rates: $48 to $68. (575)457-2000 # 2 Manthei Rd, Carlsbad, NM 88220

CARLSBAD RV PARK & CAMPGROUND
Ratings: 8.5/7/6 (Campground) From S Jct of US-285 & US-62/180: Go 1-3/4 mi SW on US-62/180 (R). Elev 3110 ft. **FAC:** Gravel rds. (110 spaces). Avail: 25 gravel, 21 pull-thrus (22 x 55), back-ins (24 x 45), some side by side hkups, 21 full hkups, 4 W, 4 E (30/50 amps), cable, WiFi, tent sites, rentals, dump, laundry, groc. **REC:** heated pool, playground. Pet restrict(B). 2015 rates: $34 to $42. Disc: AAA, military.
(575)885-6333 Lat: 32.36790, Lon: -104.23533
4301 National Parks Hwy, Carlsbad, NM 88220
sales@carlsbadrvpark.com
www.carlsbadrvpark.com
See ad this page.

CARRIZOZO — D3 *Lincoln*

VALLEY OF FIRES RECREATION AREA (BLM) (Public) From jct US 54 & US 380: Go 3 mi NW on US 380. 2015 rates: $12 to $18. (575)648-2241

CEDAR CREST — C3 *Bernalillo*

TURQUOISE TRAIL CAMPGROUND & RV PARK
Ratings: 7.5/8.5★/7.5 (Campground) From Jct of I-40 & Exit 175 (Cedar Crest/Hwy 14): Go 4 mi N on Hwy 14 (L). Elev 7200 ft. **FAC:** Gravel rds. 57 gravel, 37 pull-thrus (26 x 70), back-ins (28 x 60), some side by side hkups, 47 full hkups, 10 W, 10 E (30/50 amps), WiFi, tent sites, dump, laundry. **REC:** playground. Pets OK. Big rig sites, 2015 rates: $29.95 to $32.95.
(505)281-2005 Lat: 35.14287, Lon: -106.36741
22 Calvary Rd, Cedar Crest, NM 87008
turquoisetrailrv@gmail.com
www.turquoisetrailcampground.com
See ad page 802.

CHAMA — A3 *Rio Arriba*

LITTLE CREEL RESORT
Ratings: 7/7.5/7 (RV Park) From Jct of US-84/64 & Hwy 17: Go 3/4 mi S on US-84/64 (R). Elev 7852 ft. **FAC:** Paved/gravel rds. (63 spaces). Avail: 53 gravel, 36 pull-thrus (25 x 68), back-ins (25 x 45), 53 full hkups (30/50 amps), seasonal sites, WiFi, tent sites, laundry. **REC:** Chama River: fishing, playground. Pets OK. Big rig sites, 2015 rates: $25 to $45.
(575)756-2382 Lat: 36.87194, Lon: -106.58287
2631 State Hwy 84/64, Chama, NM 87520
lcresort@windstream.net
www.littlecreelresort.com
See ad this page.

RIO CHAMA RV PARK
Ratings: 6.5/8.5★/9 (RV Park) From Jct of US-84 & Hwy 17: Go 2 mi N on Hwy 17 (R). Elev 7860 ft. **FAC:** Gravel rds. 73 grass, 56 pull-thrus (24 x 70), back-ins (21 x 40), 53 full hkups, 20 W, 20 E (30/50 amps), WiFi, tent sites, dump, fire rings, firewood, controlled access. **REC:** Rio Chama River: fishing. Pet restrict(B/Q). Big rig sites, 2015 rates: $30 to $43. May 1 to Oct 1.
(575)756-2303 Lat: 36.90905, Lon: -106.57687
182 N Hwy 17, Chama, NM 87520
riochamarv@verizon.net
www.riochamarv.com
See ad this page.

Looking for places the "locals" frequent? Make friends with park owners and staff to get the inside scoop!

SKY MOUNTAIN RESORT RV PARK
Ratings: 7.5/9.5★/9 (RV Park) From Jct of US Hwy 84/64 & Hwy 17: Go 1 mi S on Hwy 64/84 (R). Elev 7860 ft. **FAC:** Gravel rds. 46 gravel, 11 pull-thrus (30 x 60), back-ins (35 x 45), 46 full hkups (30/50 amps), WiFi, laundry, firewood. **REC:** Rio Chama: fishing. Pet restrict(B/Q). No tents. Big rig sites, 2015 rates: $29 to $39. Disc: AAA, military. May 15 to Oct 15.
AAA Approved
(575)756-1100 Lat: 36.86493, Lon: -106.58147
2743 S US Hwy 84/64, Chama, NM 87520
reservations@skymountainresort.com
www.skymountainresort.com
See ad this page, 796.

CHIMAYO — B3 *Rio Arriba*

SANTA CRUZ LAKE RECREATION AREA (BLM) (Public) From jct Hwy 76 & Hwy 596: Go S on Hwy 596. Pit toilets. 2015 rates: $7 to $9. (575)758-8851

CIMARRON — A4 *Colfax*

PONIL CAMPGROUND **Ratings: 3.5/6/4.5** (Campground) 2015 rates: $30. (575)376-2343 31130 Hwy 64, Cimarron, NM 87714

CLAYTON — A5 *Union*

CLAYTON LAKE (State Pk) From town, N 10 mi on Hwy 370 (L). 2015 rates: $8 to $18. (575)374-8808

CLAYTON RV PARK **Ratings: 7.5/8★/6.5** (Campground) 2015 rates: $30 to $34. (575)374-9508 903 S 5th St & Aspen, Clayton, NM 88415

CLOUDCROFT — D3 *Otero*

LINCOLN NATIONAL FOREST (SILVER CAMPGROUND) (Natl Pk) From jct US 82 & Hwy 244: Go 1-1/2 mi NW on Hwy 244, then 3/10 mi S on FR 24. 2015 rates: $18. Apr 18 to Oct 15. (575)682-2551

LINCOLN NF (PINES CAMPGROUND) (Natl Pk) From jct US 82 & Hwy 244: Go 1/2 mi NW on Hwy 244. 2015 rates: $18 to $36. May 16 to Sep 3. (575)682-2551

LINCOLN NF (SLEEPY GRASS CAMPGROUND) (Natl Forest) From town: Go 1 mi S on Hwy 130, then 1 mi E on FR 24B. Pit toilets. 2015 rates: $15 to $29. May 16 to Sep 3. (575)682-2551

CLOVIS — C5 *Curry*

AKER'S RV PARK **Ratings: 3.5/NA/7** (RV Park) 2015 rates: $30. (575)763-3240 1800 E Grand Ave, Clovis, NM 88101

CLOVIS RV PARK
Ratings: 7.5/9.5★/7 (RV Park) From Jct US 60/84 & US 70 (Prince St.): Go 2.3 mi N on Prince St. (R). Elev 4200 ft. **FAC:** Paved/gravel rds. (68 spaces). Avail: 10 gravel, 5 pull-thrus (25 x 75), back-ins (25 x 45), 10 full hkups (30/50 amps), seasonal sites, cable, WiFi, laundry, LP gas. **REC.** Pets

RV Park ratings you can rely on!

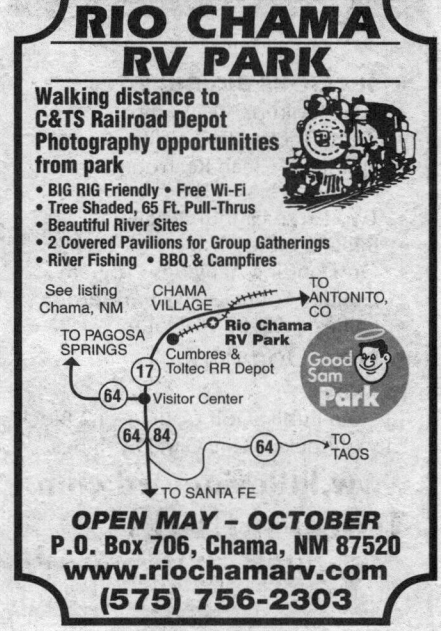

CLOVIS (CONT)

CLOVIS RV PARK (CONT)
OK. Partial handicap access, no tents. Big rig sites, 2015 rates: $38.50.
(575)742-5035 Lat: 34.42928, Lon: -103.19644
3009 N. Prince St, Clovis, NM 88101
Clovisrvpark@gmail.com
clovisrvpark.com
See ad pages 805, 796.

← TRAVELER'S WORLD CAMPGROUND
Ratings: 7/9★/7.5 (Campground) On W side of Clovis: From Jct of Hwys 70 (Prince St) & 60/84 (1st St): Go 4 mi W on Hwy 60/84 (2 mi. Past the 4 way stop) (L). Elev 4300 ft. **FAC:** Gravel rds. (50 spaces). Avail: 20 gravel, 20 pull-thrus (27 x 70), 20 full hkups (30/50 amps), seasonal sites, cable, WiFi, dump, laundry, LP gas. **REC:** playground. Pet restrict(B). No tents. Big rig sites, 2015 rates: $28 to $30. Disc: AAA, military.
(575)763-8153 Lat: 34.40425, Lon: -103.25998
1361 US Hwy 60/84, Clovis, NM 88101
twc_clovis@yahoo.com
www.travelersworldcampground.com
See ad this page.

← WEST GRAND RV PARK **Ratings: 4/7/5** (RV Park) 2015 rates: $27.50. (575)762-9240 2309 West Grand Ave, Clovis, NM 88101

COLUMBUS — E2 *Luna*

← PANCHO VILLA (State Pk) From Jct of SR-11 & SR-9, W 0.1 mi on SR-9 (L). 2015 rates: $8 to $18. May 1 to Aug 31. (575)531-2711

COSTILLA — A3 *Taos*

CARSON NATIONAL FOREST (CIMARRON CAMPGROUND) (Natl Pk) From jct Hwy 522 & Hwy 196: Go 29 mi SE on Hwy 196/FR 1950 (primitive access). Pit toilets. 2015 rates: $16. May 23 to Oct 27. (575)586-0520

We make finding the perfect campground easier. Just use the "Find-it-Fast" index in the back of the Guide. It's a complete, state-by-state, alphabetical listing of our private and public park listings.

DEMING — E2 *Grant, Hidalgo, Luna*

→ A DEMING ROADRUNNER RV PARK
Ratings: 7.5/8★/7 (RV Park) From Jct of I-10 & Pine St (E Deming, exit 85): Go W 1.5 mi on Pine St (R). Elev 4300 ft. **FAC:** Gravel rds. (83 spaces). Avail: 43 gravel, 43 pull-thrus (25 x 60), mostly side by side hkups, 43 full hkups (30/50 amps), cable, WiFi, tent sites, laundry, LP gas. **REC:** whirlpool. Pets OK. Big rig sites, 2015 rates: $28.90.
(575)546-6960 Lat: 32.26903, Lon: -107.72798
2849 E Pine St, Deming, NM 88030
ademingroadrunnerrvpark@gmail.com
www.roadrunner-rv.com
See ad this page, 796 & Snowbird Destinations in Magazine Section.

↖ CITY OF ROCKS (State Pk) From town, NW 24 mi on US-180 to SH-61, NE 3.3 mi, N 1.4 mi (L). 2015 rates: $8 to $18. (575)536-2800

→ DREAM CATCHER RV PARK **Ratings: 4.5/8★/6.5** (Membership Pk) 2015 rates: $21. (575)544-4004 4400 E Pine St, Deming, NM 88030

↑ HIDDEN VALLEY RANCH RV RESORT **Ratings: 5/7.5/5.5** (Membership Pk) 2015 rates: $25.62. (575)546-3071 12100 Hidden Valley Rd. NW, Deming, NM 88030

→ LITTLE VINEYARD RV PARK
Ratings: 9/9★/8 (RV Park) From Jct of I-10 & Pine St (exit 85), SW 1.4 mi on Pine St (R). Elev 4300 ft. **FAC:** Gravel rds. (144 spaces). Avail: 100 gravel, 100 pull-thrus (32 x 70), 100 full hkups (30/50 amps), cable, WiFi, laundry, LP gas. **REC:** heated pool, whirlpool. Pet restrict(B). No tents. Big rig sites, 2015 rates: $26. Disc: AAA.
AAA Approved
(800)413-0312 Lat: 32.26908, Lon: -107.72642
2901 E Pine St, Deming, NM 88030
littlevineyard.com
See ad this page, 796 & Snowbird Destinations in Magazine Section.

↘ ROCKHOUND (State Pk) From town, S 4 mi on Hwy 11 to SR-141, E 7 mi, follow signs (E). 2015 rates: $8 to $18. (575)546-6182

← 81 PALMS SENIOR RV RESORT **Ratings: 8.5/8.5★/7.5** (RV Park) 2015 rates: $28 to $30. (575)546-7434 2800 W Pine St, Deming, NM 88030

EAGLE NEST — A4 *Colfax*

↗ ANGEL NEST RV RETREAT **Ratings: 6/8★/6.5** (RV Park) From jct of US-64 & Hwy 38: Go 1 mi SW on Hwy 64 to Marina Way, then 1/4 mi SE (L). Elev 8283 ft. **FAC:** Gravel rds. 68 gravel, back-ins (33 x 50), 61 full hkups, 7 W, 7 E (30/50 amps), WiFi, tent sites, dump, laundry. **REC.** Pets OK. 2015 rates: $42 to $45. May 1 to Oct 1.
AAA Approved
(575)377-0533 Lat: 36.54067, Lon: -105.27508
Hcr 71 Box 3, Eagle Nest, NM 87718
Angelnest.rvretreat@gmail.com

↓ GOLDEN EAGLE RV PARK & STORE LLC
Ratings: 7.5/9.5★/8.5 (RV Park) From Jct of Hwy 38 & US-64: Go 1/4 mi SW on US-64 (R). Elev 8300 ft. **FAC:** Gravel rds. 65 gravel, 20 pull-thrus (20 x 64), back-ins (20 x 50), accepts full hkup units only, 65 full hkups (30/50 amps), WiFi, rentals, dump, laundry, groc, LP gas, firewood. **REC.** Pets OK. Partial handicap access, no tents. Eco-friendly, 2015 rates: $39.95 to $41.95. Disc: military.
(800)388-6188 Lat: 36.55264, Lon: -105.27055
540 W Therma (Hwy 64), Eagle Nest, NM 87718
goldeneaglerv@msn.com
goldeneaglerv.com
See ad this page, 796.

EDGEWOOD — C3 *Santa Fe*

→ ROUTE 66 RV PARK **Ratings: 3.5/NA/4.5** (RV Park) 2015 rates: $35 to $40. (505)281-0893 1981 Rte 66, Edgewood, NM 87015

Are you using a friend's Guide? Want one of your own? Call 877-209-6655.

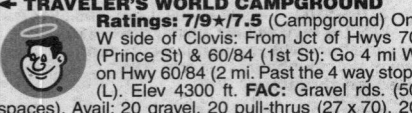

ELEPHANT BUTTE — D2 *Sierra*

A SPOTLIGHT Introducing Elephant Butte's colorful attractions appearing at the front of this state section.

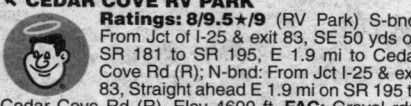

CEDAR COVE RV PARK
Ratings: 8/9.5★/9 (RV Park) S-bnd: From Jct of I-25 & exit 83, SE 50 yds on SR 181 to SR 195, E 1.9 mi to Cedar Cove Rd (R); N-bnd: From Jct I-25 & exit 83, Straight ahead E 1.9 mi on SR 195 to Cedar Cove Rd (R). Elev 4600 ft. **FAC:** Gravel rds. (140 spaces). Avail: 40 gravel, patios, 39 pull-thrus (32 x 80), back-ins (40 x 60), 40 full hkups (30/50 amps), seasonal sites, WiFi, rentals, laundry, groc. **REC.** Pets OK. Partial handicap access, no tents. Big rig sites, eco-friendly, 2015 rates: $40 to $45. Disc: AAA, military.
(575)744-4472 Lat: 33.19827, Lon: -107.23897
Hwy 195, 48 Cedar Cove Dr., Elephant Butte, NM 87935
Info@cedarcovervpark.com
www.cedarcovervpark.com
See ad this page, 796.

ELEPHANT BUTTE LAKE RV RESORT
Ratings: 9/10★/9.5 (RV Resort) From Jct of I-25 & Hwy 181 (exit 83), SE 0.1 mi on Hwy 181 to Hwy 195 (follow signs for Elephant Butte State Park), SE 3.25 mi (R). Elev 4674 ft. **FAC:** Paved/gravel rds. (144 spaces). Avail: 37 all weather, 63 gravel, 28 pull-thrus (22 x 70), back-ins (35 x 60), 100 full hkups (30/50 amps), seasonal sites, cable, WiFi, dump, laundry. **REC:** heated pool, whirlpool. Pets OK. Partial handicap access, no tents. Big rig sites, eco-friendly, 2015 rates: $38 to $56. Disc: AAA. ATM.
(575)744-5996 Lat: 33.18578, Lon: -107.21793
402 Hwy 195, Elephant Butte, NM 87935
rv@ebresort.com
ebresort.com
See ad pages 800 (Spotlight Elephant Butte), 796 & Snowbird Destinations in Magazine Section.

Things to See and Do

ELEPHANT BUTTE INN & SPA A retreat offering lake view rooms, conference rooms, heated swimming pool, The Ivory Tusk Tavern & Restaurant and The Ivory Spa & Salon; all on Elephant Butte Lake. Elev 4674 ft. Restrooms, food. No CC.
Lat: 33.18606, Lon: -107.21697
401 Hwy 195, Elephant Butte, NM 87935
www.ebresort.com
See ad page 800 (Spotlight Elephant Butte).

FARMINGTON — A1 *San Juan*

MOM & POP RV PARK
Ratings: 5.5/8/6 (RV Park) E-bnd: From Jct of Main St & W Murray St (truck route in town): Go 3 mi E on W Murray St to Illinois Ave, then 500 ft N (L); or W-bnd: From Jct of US-64 & E Murray St (truck route): Go 500 ft W on E Murray St to Illinois Ave, then 500 ft N (L). Elev 5345 ft. **FAC:** Paved rds. 33 paved, 6 pull-thrus (25 x 65), back-ins (24 x 40), 31 full hkups, 2 W, 2 E (30 amps), WiFi, tent sites, dump. Pet restrict(B). Partial handicap access. 2015 rates: $22. No CC.
(505)327-3200 Lat: 36.72071, Lon: -108.18717
901 Illinois Ave, Farmington, NM 87401
See ad this page.

FORT SUMNER — C4 *De Baca*

SUMNER LAKE (State Pk) From town: Go 10 mi N on US 84, then 6 mi W on Hwy 203. 2015 rates: $8 to $18. Apr 1 to Sep 30. (575)355-2541

Got something to tell us? We welcome your comments and suggestions regarding the ratings for a particular campground, or our rating system in general. Please email them to: travelguidecomments@goodsamfamily.com

VALLEY VIEW RV PARK
Ratings: 4/NA/5 (RV Park) From Jct of Hwys 60 & 84 (in town): Go 3/4 mi E on Hwy 60/84 (R). Elev 4000 ft. **FAC:** Gravel rds. 20 gravel, 11 pull-thrus (45 x 90), back-ins (45 x 90), 20 full hkups (30/50 amps), WiFi. Pets OK. No tents. Big rig sites, 2015 rates: $20.
(575)355-2380 Lat: 34.46712, Lon: -104.23190
1435 E Sumner Ave, Fort Sumner, NM 88119
btkmuseum@plateautel.net
billythekidmuseumfortsumner.com
See ad this page.

Things to See and Do

BILLY THE KID MUSEUM Best privately owned museum in the SW. Collection of Billy the Kid & early Western memorabilia. RV accessible. Restrooms. Hours: 8:30am to 5pm. Adult fee: $5 per person.
(575)355-2380 Lat: 34.46608, Lon: -104.22885
1435 E Sumner, Fort Sumner, NM 88119
btkmuseum@plateautel.net
billythekidmuseumfortsumner.com
See ad this page.

GALLUP — B1 *McKinley*

RED ROCK PARK (Public) E-bnd: From Jct of I-40 & Hwy 118 (exit 26), E 3.5 mi on Hwy 118 to SR-566, N 0.5 mi (L); or W-bnd: From Jct of I-40 & Hwy 118 (exit 33), W 4.2 mi on Hwy 118 to SR-566, N 0.5 mi (L). 2015 rates: $20. (505)722-3839

USA RV PARK
Ratings: 9.5/10★/9.5 (RV Park) From jct of I-40 & exit 16 (Historic Route 66/W US Hwy 66/Hwy 118/Bus Loop 40): Go 1 mi E on W US Hwy 66/Hwy 118/Bus Loop 40 (R) (don't rely solely on gps). Elev 6469 ft.

NEW MEXICO'S PREMIER RV PARK
Family owned & operated. Our park is beautifully landscaped with paved roads. All the finest amenities including free Wi-Fi, sparkling restrooms & showers & a BBQ dinner. Pet friendly. Active duty military stay for free.

FAC: Paved rds. (105 spaces). Avail: 81 gravel, 81 pull-thrus (24 x 80), mostly side by side hkups, 48 full hkups, 33 W, 33 E (30/50 amps), cable, WiFi, tent sites, rentals, dump, laundry, groc, LP gas, restaurant. **REC:** heated pool, playground. Pet restrict(B/Q). Big rig sites, 2015 rates: $29.95 to $35.95. Disc: AAA, military.
(505)863-5021 Lat: 35.50738, Lon: -108.81196
2925 W Hwy 66, Gallup, NM 87301
manager@usarvpark.com
www.usarvpark.com
See ad pages 808, 796.

Things to See and Do

USA RV BBQ BBQ restaurant serving dinner, desserts & fountain drinks. Elev 6469 ft. May 10 to Oct 10. Food. Hours: 5:30pm to 8:30pm.
(505)863-5021 Lat: 35.50738, Lon: -108.81196
2925 W Hwy 66, Gallup, NM 87301
manager@usarvpark.com
usarvpark.com
See ad page 808.

Don't miss the best part! Look in the front of most state sections for articles that focus on areas of special interest to RVers. These "Spotlights" tell you about interesting tourist destinations you might otherwise miss.

NM

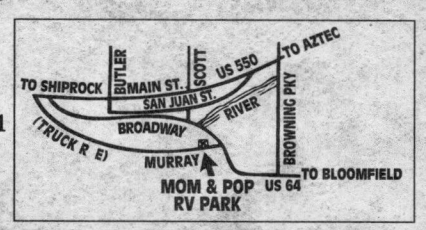

Good Sam
RATED
9.5/10★/9.5
USA RV PARK
ROUTE
US
66
GALLUP, NM
www.usarvpark.com
contact@usarvpark.com
USA RV PARK
NEW MEXICO'S PREMIER RV & CAMPING FACILITY
USA RV Park is a short distance from spectacular national and tribal parks including Mesa Verde, El Morro, Chaco Canyon, Canyon de Chelly, Hubbell's Trading Post, Window Rock, Zuni, Four Corners, Monument Valley, and the Painted Desert.
▪ Sparkling Restrooms
▪ Convenience Store & Gift Shop
▪ Active Duty Military Stay Free
▪ 30/50 Amp Sites
▪ Long Pull-Thrus
▪ Family Owned & Operated
▪ Free Wi-Fi Internet
▪ Camping Cabins
▪ Propane Tank
▪ Heated Outdoor Pool
▪ Pet Friendly
▪ Laundry Facility
▪ Putting Green
▪ Playground
▪ Entertainment Room with Television
▪ BBQ Dinner
▪ Open Year Round
▪ Beautifully Landscaped with Paved Roads
Good Sam Park
ESCAPEES RV CLUB
FAMILY MOTOR COACH ASSOC.
AARP
505.863.5021
2925 West Historic Highway 66 • Gallup, New Mexico 87301 • I-40 Exit 16 • 1 Mile East on Highway 66 • USA RV Park on right
See listing Gallup, NM

GILA HOT SPRINGS — D1 *Grant*

CAMPBELL'S GILA HOT SPRINGS RV PARK
Ratings: 4/7/5.5 (Campground) From Jct of US-180 & Hwy 152 (E of Silver City): Go E 14 mi on Hwy 152 to Hwy 35, N 27 mi to Hwy 15, N 14 mi (L). Note: Trailers over 22' avoid Hwy 15 from Silver City. Elev 5600 ft. **FAC:** Gravel/dirt rds. 17 gravel, 17 pull-thrus (18 x 60), some side by side hkups, 17 full hkups (30 amps), tent sites, laundry. **REC:** whirlpool, Gila River: fishing, playground, rec open to public. Pets OK. 2015 rates: $20. No CC.
AAA Approved
(575)536-9551 Lat: 33.19447, Lon: -108.21037
Hc 68 Box 80, Silver City, NM 88061
gilahotspringsranch@gilanet.com
www.gilahotspringsranch.com

GRANTS — C2 *Cibola*

BAR S RV PARK
Ratings: 7/9.5★/7.5 (RV Park) From jct of I-40 & Exit 79: Go 500 feet NE on Exit 79 to Pinon Dr (between Chevron & Love Truck Stop), then 1/4 mi NW (R). Elev 6575 ft. **FAC:** Gravel rds. (50 spaces). Avail: 30 gravel, 30 pull-thrus (27 x 70), 30 full hkups (30/50 amps), cable, WiFi, laundry. **REC.** Pet restrict(B). Partial handicap access, no tents. Big rig sites, 2015 rates: $20 to $23.
(505)876-6002 Lat: 35.18674, Lon: -107.90083
1860 Pinon Ave, Grants, NM 87021
darinsimpson2003@yahoo.com
See ad this page.

BLUE SPRUCE RV PARK
Ratings: 6/9★/6.5 (RV Park) From jct of I-40 & Hwy 53 (Exit 81 or 81A): Go 500 feet S on Hwy 53 (R). Elev 6460 ft. **FAC:** Gravel rds. (25 spaces). Avail: 15 gravel, 12 pull-thrus (18 x 65), back-ins (22 x 30), 9 full hkups, 6 W, 6 E (30/50 amps), cable, WiFi, tent sites, dump, laundry. **REC.** Pet restrict(B). Partial handicap access. 2015 rates: $17 to $19.
(505)287-2560 Lat: 35.15159, Lon: -107.87491
1708 Zuni Canyon Rd, Grants, NM 87020
darinsimpson2003@yahoo.com

GRANTS/CIBOLA SANDS KOA Ratings: 8/8.5★/7.5 (RV Park) 2015 rates: $42 to $47. Feb 1 to Dec 31. (888)562-5608 26 Cibola Sands Loop, Grants, NM 87020

LAVALAND RV PARK
Ratings: 6.5/9★/7 (RV Park) From I-40 (exit 85): Go 100 yards S on Santa Fe Ave (R). Elev 6400 ft. **FAC:** Gravel rds. 51 gravel, 40 pull-thrus (30 x 60), back-ins (30 x 50), 39 full hkups, 12 W, 12 E (30/50 amps), WiFi, tent sites, dump, laundry. **REC.** Pets OK. 2015 rates: $28.
(505)287-8665 Lat: 35.12231, Lon: -107.83311
1901E Santa Fe Ave, Grants, NM 87020
kade@lavalandrvpark.com
lavalandrvpark.com
See ad this page.

HOBBS — D5 *Lea*

HARRY MCADAMS CAMPGROUND (Public) From town, NW 6 mi on NM-18 to Jack Gomez, W 0.6 mi (R). 2015 rates: $18. (575)392-5845

HOBBS RV PARK **Ratings: 6/NA/7.5** (RV Park) 2015 rates: $28. (575)393-3226 100 S Marland Blvd, Hobbs, NM 88240

ZIA RVILLAS RV RESORT & RALLY PARK
Ratings: 8/8.5/6.5 (Campground) From West Country Rd/Joe Harvey Blvd & Hwy 18 (Lovington Hwy), 4 mi NW on HWy 18 to N. World Dr (R). Elev 3622 ft. **FAC:** Paved/gravel rds. (166 spaces). Avail: 10 gravel, 9 pull-thrus (33 x 70), back-ins (35 x 60), 10 full hkups (30/50 amps), seasonal sites, cable, WiFi, laundry, LP gas. **REC:** pool. Pet restrict(B). Partial handicap access, no tents. Big rig sites, 2015 rates: $35. Disc: AAA, military.
(575)392-7887 Lat: 32.77707, Lon: -103.19558
6720 North World Dr, Hobbs, NM 88242
www.ziarvillas.com
See ad this page.

JEMEZ SPRINGS — B3 *Sandoval*

FENTON LAKE (State Pk) From town: Go 9 mi N on Hwy 4, then 5 mi W on Hwy 126. Pit toilets. 2015 rates: $8 to $18. May 1 to Oct 15. (575)829-3630

KIRTLAND — A1 *San Juan*

HOMESTEAD RV PARK
Ratings: 6/9.5★/7 (RV Park) From the jct of Hwy 64 & Rd 6500: Go 1 block N on Rd 6500, then 1 block E on Rd 6432. (R). **FAC:** Gravel rds. (65 spaces). Avail: 35 gravel, 30 pull-thrus (30 x 65), back-ins (30 x 38), accepts full hkup units only, 35 full hkups (30/50 amps), cable, WiFi, tent sites, rentals, dump, LP bottles. Pet restrict(B). Partial handicap access. Big rig sites, 2015 rates: $30.
(505)598-9181 Lat: 36.744870, Lon: -108.35794
11 Rd 6432, Kirtland, NM 87417
info@homesteadrvparknm.com
homesteadrvparknm.com
See ad this page.

LAS CRUCES — E2 *Dona Ana*

HACIENDA RV & RALLY RESORT
Ratings: 8.5/9.5★/8.5 (RV Park) From Jct of I-10 & Ave de Mesilla (exit 140), S 0.1 mi on Ave de Mesilla to Stern Dr (first immediate left), E 0.2 mi (R). Elev 4000 ft. **FAC:** Paved rds. 113 gravel, 85 pull-thrus (25 x 60), back-ins (27 x 36), some side by side hkups, 113 full hkups (30/50 amps), cable, WiFi, laundry. **REC:** whirlpool. Pets OK. Partial handicap access, no tents. Big rig sites, 2015 rates: $28 to $53. Disc: military.
(888)686-9090 Lat: 32.28677, Lon: -106.78869
740 Stern Dr., Las Cruces, NM 88005
info@haciendarv.com
www.haciendarv.com
See ad pages 810, 796.

LAS CRUCES KOA **Ratings: 7.5/8.5★/7.5** (Campground) 2015 rates: $36 to $54. (575)526-6555 814 Weinrich Rd, Las Cruces, NM 88007

LEASBURG DAM (State Pk) From Jct of US-70 & I-25, N 15 mi on I-25 to exit 19 (park access rd), W 1 mi (E). Open at 7 am, closed at sunset. 2015 rates: $8 to $18. (575)524-4068

SIESTA RV PARK
Ratings: 6.5/8★/6.5 (RV Park) From Jct of I-10 & I-25, W 5 mi on I-10 to Exit 140 (Avenida De Mesilla), S 0.4 mi (L). Elev 3900 ft. **FAC:** Gravel rds. (53 spaces). Avail: 43 gravel, 42 pull-thrus (20 x 50), back-ins (25 x 36), 32 full hkups, 11 W, 11 E (30 amps), cable, WiFi, tent sites, dump, laundry.

NM

LAS CRUCES (CONT)

SIESTA RV PARK (CONT)
REC. Pets OK. 2015 rates: $31 to $37. Disc: AAA, military.
AAA Approved
(800)414-6816 Lat: 32.28383, Lon: -106.79447
1551 Ave de Mesilla, Las Cruces, NM 88005
siesta@zianet.com
www.siestarvpark.com
See ad pages 809, 796.

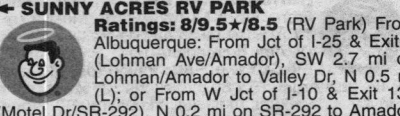

SUNNY ACRES RV PARK
Ratings: 8/9.5★/8.5 (RV Park) From Albuquerque: From Jct of I-25 & Exit 3 (Lohman Ave/Amador), SW 2.7 mi on Lohman/Amador to Valley Dr, N 0.5 mi (L); or From W Jct of I-10 & Exit 139 (Motel Dr/SR-292), N 0.2 mi on SR-292 to Amador, E 1.2 mi to Valley Dr, N 0.5 mi (L). Elev 4000 ft. **FAC:** Gravel rds. (100 spaces). Avail: 65 gravel, 16 pull-thrus (33 x 85), back-ins (39 x 60), 65 full hkups (30/50 amps), cable, WiFi, laundry. **REC.** Pet restrict(Q). Partial handicap access, no tents. Big rig sites, 2015 rates: $30.82 to $40. Disc: AAA.
AAA Approved
(877)800-1716 Lat: 32.31033, Lon: -106.79692
595 N Valley Dr, Space #75, Las Cruces, NM 88005
admin@sunnyacresrv.com
www.sunnyacresrv.com
See ad pages 809, 796 & Snowbird Destinations in Magazine Section.

Travel Services

BOGART'S AUTO & RV SERVICE Full service Auto & RV. Elev 3900 ft. **SERVICES:** tire, RV appliance, MH mechanical, engine/chassis repair. **TOW:** RV, auto. RV supplies, LP, emergency parking, waiting room. Hours: 8AM to 5PM.
(575)524-0881 Lat: 32.28441, Lon: -106.77419
2210 S Valley Dr, Las Cruces, NM 88005

LAS VEGAS — B4 *San Miguel*

LAS VEGAS KOA
Ratings: 9/9★/8.5 (Campground) From Jct of I-25 (exit 339) & US-84: Go 100 ft S on US-84 to frntg rd, then 1/2 mi SW (R). Elev 6595 ft. **FAC:** Gravel rds. 53 gravel, 36 pull-thrus (25 x 70), back-ins (25 x 35), 33 full hkups, 20 W, 20 E (30/50 amps), cable, WiFi, tent sites, rentals, dump, laundry, LP gas, fire rings, firewood. **REC:** heated pool, playground. Pet restrict(B). Eco-friendly, 2015 rates: $36 to $42. Disc: AAA.
(505)454-0180 Lat: 35.51124, Lon: -105.25275
76 County Rd A 25 A, Las Vegas, NM 87701
koalvnm@desertgate.com
www.koa.com
See ad this page.

STORRIE LAKE (State Pk) From Jct of I-25 & exit 347 (Grand Ave) SW 0.8 mi on Grand Ave to Mountain View Dr, W 0.8 mi to 7th St (Hwy 518), N 3 mi (L). 2015 rates: $8 to $18. (505)425-7278

LOGAN — B5 *Quay*

UTE LAKE (State Pk) From Jct of US-54 & Hwy 540, SW 2.4 mi on Hwy 540 (L). 2015 rates: $8 to $18. Nov 1 to Mar 31. (575)487-2284

LORDSBURG — E1 *Hidalgo*

LORDSBURG KOA
Ratings: 9/8.5★/7.5 (Campground) From Jct of I-10 & Main St (exit 22), S 0.1 mi on Main St to Maple St, W 0.1 to Lead, S 0.2 to Park (E). Follow signs. Elev 4230 ft. **FAC:** Gravel rds. 63 gravel, 63 pull-thrus (24 x 60), some side by side hkups, 45 full hkups, 18 W, 18 E (30/50 amps), cable, WiFi, tent sites, rentals, dump, laundry, groc, LP gas. **REC:** pool, playground. Pet restrict(B). Partial handicap access. Big rig sites, 2015 rates: $35 to $37.
(575)542-8003 Lat: 32.34105, Lon: -108.71713
1501 Lead St, Lordsburg, NM 88045
lordskoa@aznex.net
koa.com
See ad this page.

MAYHILL — D3 *Otero*

DEER SPRING RV PARK **Ratings: 6.5/8.5★/8.5** (RV Park) 2015 rates: $25. Apr 1 to Oct 31. (575)687-3464 2089 Rio Penasco Rd, Mayhill, NM 88339

RIO PENASCO RV CAMP **Ratings: 6/7.5/7.5** (RV Park) 2015 rates: $23. (575)687-3715 2180 Rio Penasco Rd, Mayhill, NM 88339

MORA — B4 *Mora*

COYOTE CREEK (State Pk) From Jct of Hwys 518 & 434, N 17 mi on Hwy 434; or From Jct of Hwys 121 & 434, S 18 mi on Hwy 434 (L). 2015 rates: $8 to $18. (575)387-2328

MORPHY LAKE (State Pk) From town: Go 4 mi S on Hwy 94, then W on dirt road. Check local conditions, 4-wheel drive might be required. Pit toilets. 2015 rates: $8 to $18. Mar 13 to Oct 15. (575)387-2328

MOUNTAINAIR — C3 *Torrance*

MANZANO MOUNTAINS SP (State Pk) From town: Go 13 mi N on Hwy 55, then 3 mi W on Hwy 253. Call ahead for park status. 2015 rates: $8 to $18. Apr 24 to Nov 1. (505)847-2820

NOGAL — D3 *Lincoln*

STONE MOUNTAIN RV RESORT **Ratings: 5/7.5★/5.5** (RV Park) 2015 rates: $35. (575)354-0698 510 Hwy 37, Nogal, NM 88341

OJO CALIENTE — C1 *Taos*

OJO CALIENTE MINERAL SPRINGS RESORT & SPA RV PARK Ratings: 5.5/7.5/7 (RV Park) From jct US 285 & Hwy 414: Go 1/4 mi W on Hwy 414. Elev 6200 ft. **FAC:** Gravel/dirt rds. 29 gravel, back-ins (18 x 50), some side by side hkups, 29 W, 29 E (20/30 amps), WiFi, tent sites, rentals, dump, controlled access. **REC:** whirlpool, swim, rec open to public. Pets OK. 2015 rates: $40.
AAA Approved
(800)222-9162 Lat: 36.30518, Lon: -106.05111
50 Los Banos Drive, Hwy 414, Ojo Caliente, NM 87549
guestrelations@ojospa.com
www.ojospa.com

PECOS — B3 *San Miguel*

SANTA FE NATIONAL FOREST (HOLY GHOST CAMPGROUND) (Natl Pk) From town: Go 14 mi N on Hwy 63, then 1-1/2 mi NW on FR 122. Pit toilets. 2015 rates: $8. May 1 to Oct 30. (505)757-6121

SANTA FE NATIONAL FOREST (JACK'S CREEK CAMPGROUND) (Natl Pk) 21 miles N of Pecos on Hwy 63 & Forest Rd 555. Pit toilets. 2015 rates: $10. (505)757-6121

PENA BLANCA — B3 *Sandoval*

COCHITI LAKE REC AREA (Public Corps) From town, S 17 mi on I-25 to NM-16, NW 8.4 mi to NM-22, N 4 mi (R). 2015 rates: $12 to $20. (505)465-0307

TETILLA PEAK REC AREA (Public Corps) From town, SW on I-25 13 mi, W 3.8 mi on NM-16 to La Bajada Rd, N 10 mi (E). 2015 rates: $12 to $20. Apr 15 to Oct 15. (505)465-0307

PILAR — B3 *Taos*

ORILLA VERDE REC AREA (Public) From town, SW 5.6 mi on US-68, W 6.5 mi on Hwy 570. 2015 rates: $15. (575)758-8851

POJOAQUE — B3 *Santa Fe*

ROADRUNNER RV PARK
Ratings: 5.5/NA/7 (RV Park) From jct of 84/285 & W Gutierrez St (in Pojoaque): Go 100 feet W to O'GO Wii St, then 500 feet S on O'GO Wii St to entrance (R). Elev 6000 ft. **FAC:** Gravel rds. (60 spaces). Avail: 50 gravel, 50 pull-thrus (35 x 60), accepts full hkup units only, 50 full hkups (30/50 amps), seasonal sites, WiFi, groc. **REC:** rec open to public. Pet restrict(B). No tents. Big rig sites, 2015 rates: $29.70. Disc: AAA.
(505)455-2626 Lat: 35.88034, Lon: -106.01300
55 O'go Wii, Pojoaque, NM 87506
roadrunnerrvpark07@gmail.com
buffalothunderresort.com
See ad pages 801 (Spotlight Santa Fe), 796.

Things to See and Do

CITIES OF GOLD CASINO & HOTEL Slots, luxury hotel, tasty buffet & sports bar. Elev 6000 ft. partial handicap access. RV accessible. Restrooms, food. Hours: 12am to 11:59pm. ATM.
(800)455-3313 Lat: 35.89003, Lon: -106.02017
10-B Cities of Gold Road, Santa Fe, NM 87506
morewinners@citiesofgold.com
citiesofgold.com
See ad page 801 (Spotlight Santa Fe).

WELLNESS & HEALING ARTS CULTURAL CENTER Pueblo of Pojoaque Wellness & Healing Arts Center available to guests of Roadrunner RV Park. Healing Arts, Massage, Acupuncture, Classes, Aquatic Programs & Physical Therapy. Elev 7000 ft. Restrooms. Hours: 6am to 8pm. No CC.
(505)455-9355 Lat: 35.89006, Lon: -106.01349
www.pojoaquewellness.com
See ad page 801 (Spotlight Santa Fe).

PORTALES — C5 *Roosevelt*

OASIS (State Pk) From Jct of US-70 & SR-467, N 5 mi on SR-467 to Oasis Rd, W 2 mi (E). 2015 rates: $8 to $18. (575)356-5331

PREWITT — B2 *Cibola*

BLUEWATER LAKE (State Pk) From Jct of I-40 & Hwy 412 (exit 63), S 7 mi on Hwy 412, follow signs (L). 2015 rates: $8 to $18. (505)876-2391

QUESTA — A3 *Taos*

CARSON NATIONAL FOREST (COLUMBINE CAMPGROUND) (Natl Pk) From town: Go 5 mi E on Hwy-38. Pit toilets. 2015 rates: $17. May 23 to Sep 29. (303)567-3000

RAMAH — C1 *Cibola, McKinley*

EL MORRO RV PARK & ANCIENT WAY CAFE **Ratings: 2.5/6/6.5** (Campground) 2015 rates: $25. (505)783-4612 Hc 61 Box 44, Ramah, NM 87321

RATON — A4 *Colfax*

KICKBACK RV PARK **Ratings: 5/6.5/6** (RV Park) 2015 rates: $30 to $32. (575)445-1200 1025 Frontage Rd, Raton, NM 87740

RATON (CONT)

NRA WHITTINGTON CENTER CAMPGROUNDS Ratings: 4.5/6.5/7 (Campground) From jct I-25 (exit 446) & US 64: Go 4 mi SW on US 64. **FAC:** Gravel/dirt rds. 124 dirt, 124 pull-thrus (25 x 50), some side by side hkups, 124 full hkups (30/50 amps), tent sites, laundry, LP gas, controlled access. **REC.** Pets OK. Partial handicap access. 2015 rates: $27 to $30.
AAA Approved
(575)445-3615 Lat: 36.77122, Lon: -104.48255
34025 Hwy 64 West, Raton, NM 87740
reservations@nrawc.org
www.nrawc.org

RATON KOA **Ratings: 6.5/7.5/6.5** (Campground) 2015 rates: $31.88 to $34.88. (575)445-3488 1330 S 2nd St, Raton, NM 87740

RATON PASS CAMP & CAFE **Ratings: 6.5/9★/7.5** (Campground) 2015 rates: $33.84. Mar 1 to Nov 1. (575)445-8500 46020 I-25, Raton, NM 87740

SUGARITE CANYON (State Pk) From jct I-25 & Hwy 72: Go 6 mi E on Hwy 72, then 2 mi N on Hwy 526. 2015 rates: $8 to $18. (575)445-5607

SUMMERLAN RV PARK **Ratings: 6/8.5★/6** (RV Park) 2015 rates: $29.50 to $34.50. (575)445-9536 1900 S Cedar St, Raton, NM 87740

RED RIVER — A3 *Taos*

RED RIVER RV PARK **Ratings: 5.5/7.5★/7** (RV Park) 2015 rates: $32 to $38. May 1 to Oct 30. (575)754-6187 100 High Cost Trail, Red River, NM 87558

ROAD RUNNER RV RESORT **Ratings: 8/9.5★/9** (RV Resort) 2015 rates: $51.05 to $56.02. (575)754-2286 1371 E Main St, Red River, NM 87558

RIO RANCHO — B3 *Sandoval, Bernalillo*

STAGECOACH STOP RV PARK **Ratings: 10/9.5★/8.5** (RV Park) 2015 rates: $39 to $44. (505)867-1000 3650 State Hwy 528 NE, Rio Rancho, NM 87144

ROCIADA — B3 *San Miguel*

PENDARIES RV RESORT **Ratings: 6.5/8/7.5** (RV Park) 2015 rates: $32 to $41. May 15 to Oct 15. (800)820-8304 rt #105 Park Place #103, Rociada, NM 87742

RODEO — E1 *Hidalgo*

RUSTY'S RV RANCH **Ratings: 7/8.5★/9** (Campground) 2015 rates: $24 to $26.40. (575)557-2526 854 The Rv Way, Rodeo, NM 88056

ROSWELL — D4 *Chaves*

BOTTOMLESS LAKES (State Pk) From Jct of US-380 & US-285, E 10.2 mi on US-380 to SR-409, S 3.1 mi (R). For Reservations Call (877)644-7787. 2015 rates: $8 to $18. (575)624-6058

EXCLUSIVE! Every listing includes a special "arrow" symbol. This valuable tool shows you where the facility is located (N, S, E, W, NE, NW, SE, SW) in relation to the town.

TOWN & COUNTRY RV PARK
Ratings: 9/10★/8 (RV Park) From Jct of US-70/380 (2nd St) & US-285 (Main St) in the center of Roswell: Go 3-1/2 mi S on Main St to Brasher Rd, then 1/10 mi W (R). Elev 3586 ft. **FAC:** Paved rds. (119 spaces). Avail: 50 all weather, 29 gravel, 70 pull-thrus (24 x 85), back-ins (25 x 50), some side by side hkups, accepts full hkup units only, 79 full hkups (30/50 amps), cable, WiFi, laundry. **REC:** pool. Pets OK. Partial handicap access, no tents. Big rig sites, eco-friendly, 2015 rates: $35. Disc: AAA, military.
(575)624-1833 Lat: 33.35122, Lon: -104.52476
331 W Brasher Rd., Roswell, NM 88203
managertownandcountry@yahoo.com
www.townandcountryrvpark.com
See ad this page, 796 & Snowbird Destinations in Magazine Section.

TRAILER VILLAGE RV PARK
Ratings: 7.5/9★/8 (RV Park) From Jct of Bus US-285 (Main St) & Bus US-380 (2nd St): Go 1-1/2 mi E on US-380 (2nd St) (R). Elev 3932 ft. **FAC:** Gravel rds. 73 gravel, patios, 21 pull-thrus (30 x 65), back-ins (35 x 45), 73 full hkups (30/50 amps), cable, WiFi, rentals, laundry, groc, LP gas. **REC.** Pets OK. No tents. Big rig sites, eco-friendly, 2015 rates: $32.50 to $38.50. Disc: military.
(575)623-6040 Lat: 33.39368, Lon: -104.49871
1706 E Second St., Roswell, NM 88201
trailervillage2003@gmail.com
trailervillagervpark.com
See ad this page.

Subscribe to Trailer Life Magazine. For a subscription, call 800-825-6861.

RUIDOSO — D3 *Lincoln*

CIRCLE B RV PARK
Ratings: 8.5/9.5★/9 (RV Park) From Jct of US-70 & Hwy 48, E 4 mi on US-70 at Mile Marker 265 (south side of road), 3.5 mi E of racetrack (R). Elev 6121 ft. **FAC:** Paved rds. (135 spaces). Avail: 100 gravel, 63 pull-thrus (35 x 65), back-ins (30 x 50), 100 full hkups (30/50 amps), seasonal sites, cable, WiFi, rentals, dump, laundry. **REC.** Pets OK. No tents. Big rig sites, eco-friendly, 2015 rates: $38 to $43.
(575)378-4990 Lat: 33.34706, Lon: -105.56913
26514 E Hwy 70, Ruidoso Downs, NM 88346
www.circlebrv.com
See ad this page, 796.

Exclusive! According to our research, restroom cleanliness is of the utmost concern to RVers. Of course, you knew that already. The cleanest campgrounds have a star in their restroom rating!

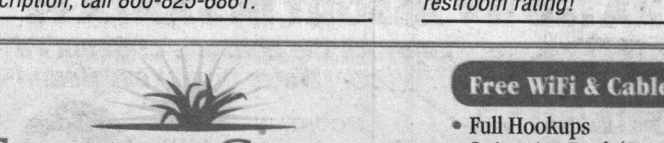

NM

Lend a hand. During the busy season park services are stretched to the max! Please do your best to keep your area "ship-shape".

So you're the one with "pooch" duty? Please make a clean sweep of it! Your fellow RVers will appreciate it!

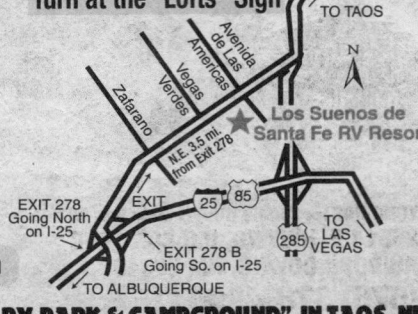

RUIDOSO (CONT)

EAGLE CREEK RV RESORT
Ratings: 8/NA/9.5 (RV Park) From Jct of Hwy 48 & Hwy 532, W 0.5 mi (L). **FAC:** Gravel rds. 48 gravel, 22 pull-thrus (30 x 60), back-ins (25 x 50), 48 full hkups (30/50 amps), WiFi, laundry, firewood, controlled access. **REC:** Eagle Creek. Pets OK. No tents. Big rig sites, eco-friendly, 2015 rates: $35 to $40. Apr 1 to Nov 1.
(575)336-1131 Lat: 33.39780, Lon: -105.68465
159 Ski Run Rd, Alto, NM 88312
eaglecreek@bajabb.com
eaglecreekrvresort.com

RAINBOW LAKE CABIN & RV RESORT **Ratings: 5.5/7.5/6** (RV Park) 2015 rates: $26.99 to $38.99. (575)630-2267 806 Carrizzo Canyon Rd, Ruidoso, NM 88345

RIVERSIDE RV PARK
Ratings: 6.5/NA/8 (RV Park) From Jct of Sudderth & Gavilian Canyon Rd, NW 0.5 mi on Gavilan Canyon Rd (R). Elev 6800 ft. **FAC:** Gravel rds. 30 gravel, back-ins (25 x 47), accepts self-contain units only, 30 full hkups (30/50 amps), cable, WiFi, rentals, dump, laundry, firewood. **REC:** Rio Ruidoso: fishing. Pets OK. No tents. Eco-friendly, 2015 rates: $36 to $45.
(575)257-3428 Lat: 33.32673, Lon: -105.63415
298 Gavilan Canyon Rd., Ruidoso, NM 88345
riversiderv@gmail.com
www.riversidervparkruidoso.com
See ad page 811.

TWIN SPRUCE RV PARK
Ratings: 9/9★/8.5 (Campground) W-Bnd: From Jct of US-70 & Sudderth Dr: Go 1-14 mi W on US 70 (L); or E-Bnd: US-70 W of town between MM 259 & MM 260 (R). Elev 6700 ft. **FAC:** Paved/gravel rds. 111 gravel, patios, 36 pull-thrus (27 x 60), back-ins (25 x 40), 111 full hkups (30/50 amps), cable, WiFi, tent sites, rentals, dump, laundry, LP gas. **REC:** heated pool. Pets OK. 2015 rates: $31.95 to $41.95. Disc: AAA, military.
(575)257-4310 Lat: 33.31091, Lon: -105.64015
25996 US Hwy70, Ruidoso, NM 88345
twinspruce2000@yahoo.com
twinsprucervpark.com
See ad this page.

Travel Services

CIRCLE B RV PARTS RV parts and accessories. Elev 6100 ft. RV supplies, dump, emergency parking, waiting room. Hours: 9 AM to 6 PM.
(575)378-4990 Lat: 33.349747, Lon: -105.569964
26514 Hwy 70, Ruidoso Downs, NM 88346
www.circlebrv.com
See ad page 811.

Things to See and Do

RUIDOSO VISITOR CENTER AND TOURISM OFFICE Ruidoso is located in the southern Rocky Mountains of south-central New Mexico. Ruidoso & Billy the Kid Country features spectacular mountain vistas, outdoor adventure activities, theatre, casinos,

RUIDOSO (CONT)

RUIDOSO VISITOR CENTER AND (CONT) year-round golf. RV accessible. Restrooms. Hours: 8am to 5pm. No CC.
(877)784-3676 Lat: 33.19796, Lon: -105.40642
720 Sudderth Rd, Ruidoso, NM 88345
director@discoverruidoso.com
discoverruidoso.com

SANTA FE — B3 *Sandoval, Santa Fe*

SANTA FE See also Espanola, Pojoaque.

HYDE MEMORIAL (State Pk) From Jct of Washington Ave & Hwy 475 (Artist Rd.), NE 7.5 mi on Hwy 475 (E). Entrance fee required. Pit toilets. 2015 rates: $8 to $18. (505)983-7175

LOS SUENOS DE SANTA FE RV RESORT & CAMPGROUND
Ratings: 8/8.5/8 (RV Park) From Jct of I-25 & Cerrillos Rd (exit 278 or 278B): Go 3-3/4 mi NE on Cerrillos Rd (R). Elev 6567 ft. **FAC:** Paved rds. (95 spaces). Avail: 60 gravel, patios, 25 pull-thrus (25 x 68), back-ins (25 x 47), 60 full hkups (30/50 amps), seasonal sites, WiFi, tent sites, rentals, dump, laundry, LP gas. **REC:** heated pool, playground. Pet restrict(B). Big rig sites, 2015 rates: $41 to $51. Disc: AAA.
AAA Approved
(505)473-1949 Lat: 35.64505, Lon: -106.00641
3574 Cerrillos Rd, Santa Fe, NM 87507
Santaferv@gmail.com
www.lossuenosrv.com
See ad opposite page, 817, 796.

RANCHEROS DE SANTA FE CAMPGROUND
Ratings: 8.5/9★/9 (Campground) From Jct of I-25 & Exit 290 (NM 300/Old Las Vegas Hwy): Go 1/3 mi N on US 285 to N Frntg Rd, SE (turn right) then 1 mi (L). Elev 7200 ft. **FAC:** Paved/gravel rds. (125 spaces). Avail: 100 dirt, 72 pull-thrus (24 x 55), back-ins (22 x 50), 53 full hkups, 47 W, 47 E (30/50 amps), seasonal sites, cable, WiFi, tent sites, rentals, dump, laundry, groc, LP gas, fire rings, firewood. **REC:** heated pool, playground. Pets OK. Eco-friendly, 2015 rates: $31 to $44. Disc: AAA. Mar 15 to Oct 31.
(505)466-3482 Lat: 35.54580, Lon: -105.86404
736 Old Las Vegas Hwy, Santa Fe, NM 87505
camp@rancheros.com
www.rancheros.com
See ad pages 814, 796.

ROADRUNNER RV PARK
Ratings: 5.5/NA/7 (RV Park) From Santa Fe, Go N on US 84/285 to O'GO Wii St, then 500 ft S on O'GO Wii St to entrance (R). Elev 6000 ft. **FAC:** Gravel rds. (60 spaces). Avail: 50 gravel, 50 pull-thrus (35 x 60), accepts full hkup units only, 50 full hkups (30/50 amps), seasonal sites, WiFi, groc. **REC:** rec open to public. Pet restrict(B). Big rig sites, 2015 rates: $29.70. Disc: AAA.
(505)455-2626 Lat: 35.88034, Lon: -106.01300
55 O'go Wii, Pojoaque, NM 87506
roadrunnerrvpark07@gmail.com
buffalothunderresort.com
See primary listing at Pojoaque and ad page 801 (Spotlight Santa Fe).

SANTA FE KOA **Ratings: 7.5/9★/8.5** (Campground) 2015 rates: $39.50 to $48.50. Mar 1 to Nov 1. (505)466-1419 934 Old Las Vegas Hwy, Santa Fe, NM 87505

SANTA FE SKIES RV PARK
Ratings: 8/10★/10 (RV Park) N-bnd: From Jct of I-25 & Exit 276 (SR-599) Go 1/2 mi SE on SR-599 to NM 14, continue straight across NM 14 to park on Ridge (L); or S-bnd: From Jct of I-25 & Exit 276, SE (stay left) under I-25 to NM 14, continue straight across NM 14 to park on Ridge (L). Elev 6633 ft. **FAC:** Paved/gravel rds. (98 spaces). Avail: 88 gravel, patios, 53 pull-thrus (27 x 75), back-ins (40 x 45), 86 full hkups, 2 W, 2 E (30/50 amps), seasonal sites, WiFi, dump, laundry, LP gas. **REC.** Pets OK. Partial handicap access, no tents. Big rig sites, eco-friendly, 2015 rates: $37 to $46. Disc: AAA, military.
(877)565-0451 Lat: 35.58863, Lon: -106.04477
14 Browncastle Ranch, Santa Fe, NM 87508
www.santafeskiesrvpark.com
See ad pages 815, 796 & RV Trips of a Lifetime in Magazine Section.

THE TRAILER RANCH RV RESORT & 55+ COMMUNITY
Ratings: 9/9.5★/9 (RV Park) From Jct of I-25 & Cerrillos Rd (exit 278 or 278B): Go 3-1/2 mi NE on Cerrillos Rd (L) or (S bnd) From (North of Santa Fe) US-285/St Francis Dr to Cerrillos Rd, then 3-1/2 mi SW (R). Elev 7000 ft. **FAC:** Paved rds. (120 spaces). 52 Avail: 24 paved, 28 gravel, patios, 9 pull-thrus (22 x 50), back-ins (24 x 60), 52 full hkups (30/50 amps), cable, WiFi, laundry, LP gas. **REC:** heated pool. Pets OK. No tents. Age restrict may apply, big rig sites, eco-friendly, 2015 rates: $37 to $45. Disc: AAA.
(505)471-9970 Lat: 35.64796, Lon: -106.00501
3471 Cerrillos Rd, Santa Fe, NM 87507
rv@trailerranch.com
www.trailerranch.com
See ad opposite page, 796.

Things to See and Do

BUFFALO THUNDER CASINO & RESORT Buffalo Thunder Casino, the beauty of Santa Fe, the action and excitement of Las Vegas. Elev 6000 ft. partial handicap access. RV accessible. Restrooms, food. Hours: 12am to 11:59pm. ATM.
(505)455-5555 Lat: 35.86096, Lon: -105.99789
20 Buffalo Thunder Trail, Santa Fe, NM 87506
buffalothunderresort.com
See ad page 801 (Spotlight Santa Fe).

Don't camp without it ... Our 2016 listings are your key to travel satisfaction.

NM

Rancheros de Santa Fe Campground
Santa Fe's most scenic RV resort and campground
Quiet, wooded camping only minutes from Old Town Santa Fe. Rancheros de Santa Fe is known to visitors from all over the world for its scenic, natural setting. Located on historic Route 66, adjacent to the Santa Fe Trail, Rancheros de Santa Fe offers a beautiful destination for your visit.
Good Sam Park
To Taos
285
NORTH
St. Francis Drive
OLD TOWN SANTA FE
N
Old Las Vegas Hwy (NM 300)
Exit 282
25
Exit 284 Old Pecos Trail
To Albuquerque
RANCHEROS DE SANTA FE CAMPGROUND
25
To Las Vegas, NM
Exit 290
285
SOUTH
See listing Santa Fe, NM
To I-40
•Big Rig Friendly •Cable TV •Free Wi-Fi•Pool
•Propane •Laundromat •Clean Rest Rooms
•Camping Cabins •Early Season Rates
•Southwest Gift Shop •Dog Run •Hiking Trail
505-466-3482
rancheros.com
736 Old Las Vegas Highway
Santa Fe, NM 87505

NM

See listing Santa Fe, NM

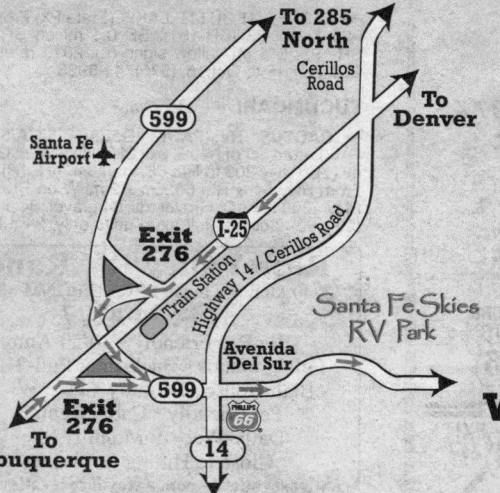

SANTA ROSA — C4 *Guadalupe*

➜ SANTA ROSA CAMPGROUND
Ratings: 8/8.5★/8.5 (RV Park) W-bnd: From Jct of I-40 & Bus I-40 (exit 277): Go 1 mi W on Bus I-40 (R); or E-bnd: From Jct of I-40 & Bus I-40 (exit 275): Go 1mi E on Bus I-40 (L). Elev 4803 ft. **FAC:** Paved/gravel rds. 73 gravel, 70 pull-thrus (25 x 75), back-ins (21 x 38), some side by side hkups, 28 full hkups, 45 W, 45 E (30/50 amps), cable, WiFi, tent sites, rentals, dump, laundry, LP gas, fire rings, firewood, restaurant. **REC:** heated pool, playground. Pets OK. Big rig sites, eco-friendly, 2015 rates: $30 to $40. Disc: AAA.
AAA Approved
(575)472-3126 Lat: 34.94622, Lon: -104.66194
2136 Historic Route 66, Santa Rosa, NM 88435
santarosacampground@gmail.com
santarosacampground.com
See ad this page, 796.

SANTA ROSA LAKE (State Pk) From Jct of I-40 & 2nd St, N 1 blk on 2nd St to Eddy St, E 7 blks to 8th St, N 7.5 mi (E). 2015 rates: $8 to $18. (575)472-3110

SILVER CITY — D1 *Grant*

➜ MANZANO'S RV PARK **Ratings: 7/8.5★/9** (RV Park) 2015 rates: $28. (575)538-0918 103 Flury Lane, Silver City, NM 88061

ROSE VALLEY RV RANCH
Ratings: 7.5/8.5★/9 (RV Park) From Jct of Hwy 180 & Hwy 90, E 1.1 mi on Hwy 180 to Memory Lane, S 0.2 mi on Memory Ln (L). From Deming: Continue W on Hwy 180 to Memory Lane, S 0.2 mi on Memory Lane (L). Elev 5938 ft. **FAC:** Gravel rds. (68 spaces). Avail: 30 gravel, 14 pull-thrus (35 x 70), back-ins (25 x 58), 30 full hkups (30/50 amps), WiFi, rentals, dump, laundry. **REC.** Pets OK. Partial handicap access, no tents. Big rig sites, 2015 rates: $34 to $38. Disc: AAA.
AAA Approved
(575)534-4277 Lat: 32.78563, Lon: -108.25633
2040 Memory Ln, Silver City, NM 88061
stay@rosevalleyrv.com
rosevalleyrv.com
See ad this page.

➜ SILVER CITY KOA **Ratings: 9/9.5★/7.5** (Campground) 2015 rates: $35 to $45. (575)388-3351 11824 Hwy 180E, Silver City, NM 88022

SILVER CITY RV PARK **Ratings: 7/8.5/7** (RV Park) 2015 rates: $32. (866)538-2239 1304 N Bennett St., Silver City, NM 88061

TAOS — B3 *Taos*

TAOS VALLEY RV PARK & CAMPGROUND
Ratings: 7.5/9★/8.5 (Campground) From N Jct of US-64 & SR-68 (Downtown Taos Plaza): Go 2-1/2 mi S on SR-68 to Este Es Rd, then 500 ft E (R). Elev 7151 ft. **FAC:** Gravel rds. 64 Avail: 15 paved, 49 gravel, 42 pull-thrus (25 x 65), back-ins (24 x 35), 39 full hkups, 25 W, 25 E (30/50 amps), WiFi, tent sites, dump, laundry, LP gas. **REC:** playground. Pet restrict(B). Big rig sites, 2015 rates: $35 to $46. Disc: AAA.
AAA Approved
(575)758-4469 Lat: 36.37000, Lon: -105.59292
120 Estes Es Rd, Taos, NM 87571
TaosValleyRV@gmail.com
www.taosrv.com
See ad opposite page, 812, 796.

TIERRA AMARILLA — A3 *Rio Arriba*

EL VADO LAKE (State Pk) From Jct of US-84 & SR-112, W 13.5 mi on SR-112 (R). 2015 rates: $8 to $18. Apr 1 to Nov 30. (575)588-7247

HERON LAKE (State Pk) From town, W 6 mi on SR-95 (R). Entrance fee required. 2015 rates: $8 to $18. May 15 to Sep 15. (575)588-7470

TIJERAS — C3 *Bernalillo*

➜ HIDDEN VALLEY RV MOUNTAIN RESORT Ratings: 7/8.5★/7 (Membership Pk) From jct I-40 & SR 14/333/337: Go 2-1/4 mi E on I-40 (exit 178-Zuzax Rd), then 1 block E on S Frontage Rd (East 333) (Turn right at gas station up the hill to park). Elev 6607 ft. **FAC:** Poor gravel/dirt rds. 101 gravel, 64 pull-thrus (17 x 68), back-ins (22 x 50), 98 full hkups, 3 W, 3 E (30/50 amps), WiFi Hotspot, tent sites, dump, laundry. **REC:** heated pool, playground. Pet restrict(B). 2015 rates: $37.50.
AAA Approved
(505)281-3363 Lat: 35.10495, Lon: -106.33939
844-B State Hwy 333, Tijeras, NM 87059
info@hiddenvalley-rvpark.com
hiddenvalley-rvpark.com

TRUTH OR CONSEQUENCES — D2 *Sierra*

CIELO VISTA RV PARK
Ratings: 6.5/7/7.5 (RV Park) S-Bnd: From Jct of I-25 & Exit 79 (Date St/Broadway/Bus 25), S 2.7 mi on Date St/Broadway/Bus 25 (R) or N-Bnd: From Jct of I-25 & Exit 75 (Broadway), N 2.8 mi on Broadway/Bus 25 (L). Elev 4260 ft. **FAC:** Paved/gravel rds. (70 spaces). Avail: 20 gravel, patios, 19 pull-thrus (27 x 58), back-ins (27 x 40), 20 full hkups (30/50 amps), cable, tent sites, laundry. **REC.** Pet restrict(B). 2015 rates: $36. Disc: AAA. No CC.
(575)894-3738 Lat: 33.12759, Lon: -107.26112
501 S Broadway, Truth or Consequences, NM 87901
pattyv48@windstream.net
www.cielovistarvpark.com

➜ ELEPHANT BUTTE LAKE (State Pk) From Jct of I-25 & exit 83 (SR-181), SE 0.1 mi on SR-181 to SR-195, E 4 mi, follow signs (L). 2015 rates: $8 to $18. Mar 15 to Oct 15. (575)744-5923

TUCUMCARI — B5 *Quay*

➜ CACTUS RV PARK Ratings: 5/NA/5.5 (RV Park) From Jct of I-40 & exit 332 (Hwy 209): Go 1-1/2 mi N on Hwy 209 to Rte 66, then 3/4 mi E (R). S bnd: From Hwy 54 & Rte 66: Go 1/2 mi W on Rte 66. (L). Elev 4000 ft. **FAC:** Gravel rds. 34 gravel, 34 pull-thrus (25 x 90), accepts full hkup units only, 34 full hkups

TUCUMCARI (CONT)

CACTUS RV PARK (CONT)
(30/50 amps), cable, WiFi. Pets OK. No tents. Big rig sites, 2015 rates: $24.50 to $26.50. Disc: AAA. (575)461-2501 Lat: 35.17137, Lon: -103.71044 1316 E Route 66 Blvd, Tucumcari, NM 88401 cactusrvpark@qwestoffice.net www.cactusrvpark.com

↖ CONCHAS LAKE (State Pk) From Tucumcari, NW 32 mi on SR-104 (R). 2015 rates: $8 to $18. (575)868-2270

How can you tell whether you're traveling in the right direction? The arrow in each listing denotes the compass direction of the facility in relation to the listed town. For example, an arrow pointing straight up indicates that the facility is located due north from town. An arrow pointing down and to the right indicates that the facility is southeast of town.

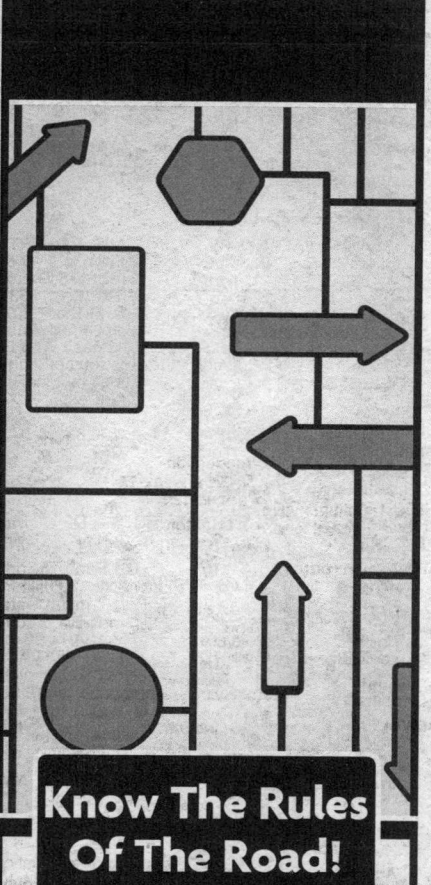

↘ **MOUNTAIN ROAD RV PARK**
Ratings: 6.5/9★/7.5 (RV Park) From Jct of I-40 & US-54/Mountain Rd (exit 333): Go 1/2 mi N on US-54 (L). Elev 4085 ft. **FAC:** Gravel rds. 60 gravel, 60 pull-thrus (24 x 60), 60 full hkups (30/50 amps), cable, WiFi, tent sites, laundry. **REC:** playground. Pets OK. Big rig sites, 2015 rates: $22.50 to $25. Disc: AAA, military.
(575)461-9628 Lat: 35.16258, Lon: -103.70305
1700 Mountain Rd., Tucumcari, NM 88401
See ad this page.

→ TUCUMCARI KOA **Ratings: 8/8★/7** (Campground) 2015 rates: $31.50 to $42. (575)461-1841 6299 Quay Rd Al, Tucumcari, NM 88401

Wasn't that a beautiful campground you visited ten years ago? But can you remember where it was? Use our "Find-it-Fast" index, located in the back of the Guide. It's an alphabetical list, by state, of every private and public park and campground in the Guide.

VILLANUEVA — B4 *San Miguel*

↑ VILLANUEVA (State Pk) From Jct of I-25 & SR-3 (Villanueva State Park exit), S 13 mi on SR-3; or From Jct of I-40 & SR-3 (exit 230), N 21 mi on SR-3 (R). 2015 rates: $8 to $18. (575)421-2957

WHITE ROCK — B3 *Los Alamos*

↙ BANDELIER NATL MON/JUNIPER CAMPGROUND (Natl Pk) From town, SW 7 mi on SR-4 (L). Entrance fee required. 2015 rates: $12. (505)672-3861

WHITES CITY — E4 *Eddy*

↑ WHITE'S CITY CARLSBAD CAVERNS RV PARK **Ratings: 5/6/5** (Campground) 2015 rates: $36 to $40. (575)785-2291 17 Carlsbad Caverns Hwy, Whites City, NM 88268

We salute you! Our Military Listings indicate campgrounds for use exclusively by active and retired military personnel.

NM

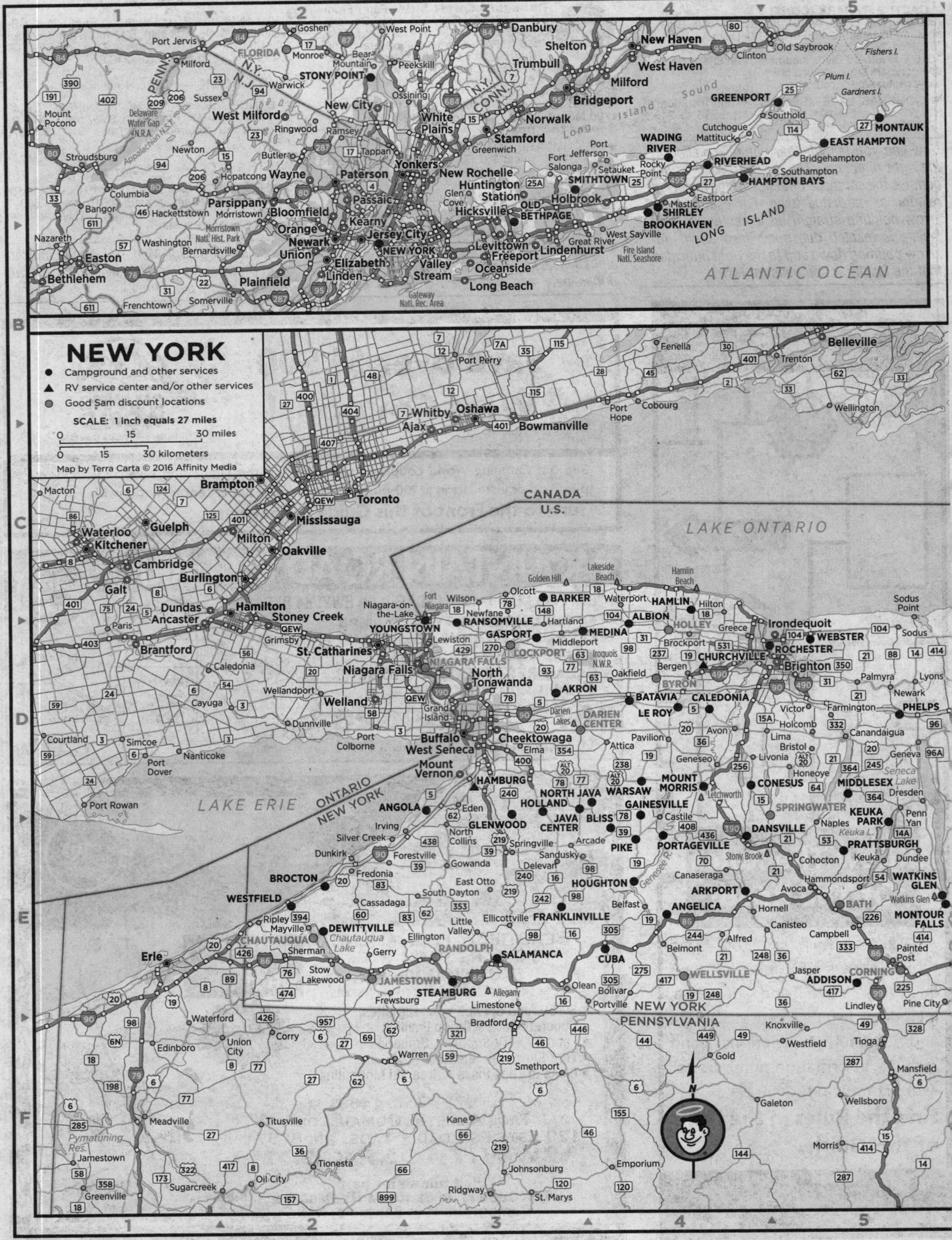
NEW YORK
Campground and other services
RV service center and/or other services
Good Sam discount locations
SCALE: 1 inch equals 27 miles
0 15 30 miles
0 15 30 kilometers
Map by Terra Carta © 2016 Affinity Media
CANADA
U.S.
LAKE ONTARIO
LAKE ERIE
ONTARIO
NEW YORK
PENNSYLVANIA
ATLANTIC OCEAN
LONG ISLAND
Long Island Sound
STONY POINT
West Milford
Port Jervis
Goshen
West Point
Danbury
Shelton
New Haven
West Haven
Trumbull
Milford
Bridgeport
Norwalk
Stamford
White Plains
Yonkers
New Rochelle
Paterson
Wayne
Passaic
Parsippany
Bloomfield
Kearny
Jersey City
Orange
Newark
NEW YORK
Union
Elizabeth
Linden
Plainfield
Easton
Bethlehem
Huntington Station
Hicksville
OLD BETHPAGE
Holbrook
SMITHTOWN
Levittown
Freeport
Lindenhurst
Valley Stream
Oceanside
Long Beach
WADING RIVER
RIVERHEAD
GREENPORT
MONTAUK
EAST HAMPTON
HAMPTON BAYS
SHIRLEY
BROOKHAVEN
Toronto
Brampton
Mississauga
Oakville
Milton
Waterloo
Kitchener
Guelph
Cambridge
Burlington
Hamilton
Stoney Creek
Brantford
St. Catharines
Niagara Falls
Welland
Oshawa
Whitby
Ajax
Bowmanville
Belleville
YOUNGSTOWN
RANSOMVILLE
BARKER
GASPORT
LOCKPORT
NIAGARA FALLS
North Tonawanda
MEDINA
ALBION
HOLLEY
HAMLIN
CHURCHVILLE
ROCHESTER
WEBSTER
Irondequoit
Brighton
AKRON
BATAVIA
CALEDONIA
LE ROY
BYRON
DARIEN CENTER
PHELPS
Buffalo
West Seneca
Cheektowaga
Mount Vernon
HAMBURG
ANGOLA
NORTH JAVA
HOLLAND
JAVA CENTER
BLISS
WARSAW
MOUNT MORRIS
GAINESVILLE
CONESUS
SPRINGWATER
MIDDLESEX
KEUKA PARK
DANSVILLE
PRATTSBURGH
GLENWOOD
PIKE
PORTAGEVILLE
BROCTON
WESTFIELD
HOUGHTON
ARKPORT
WATKINS GLEN
FRANKLINVILLE
ANGELICA
BATH
MONTOUR FALLS
DEWITTVILLE
CHAUTAUQUA
RANDOLPH
SALAMANCA
CUBA
WELLSVILLE
ADDISON
CORNING
JAMESTOWN
STEAMBURG
Erie
Olean
Bradford
Warren
Meadville
Titusville
Jamestown
Emporium
St. Marys
Wellsboro
Mansfield

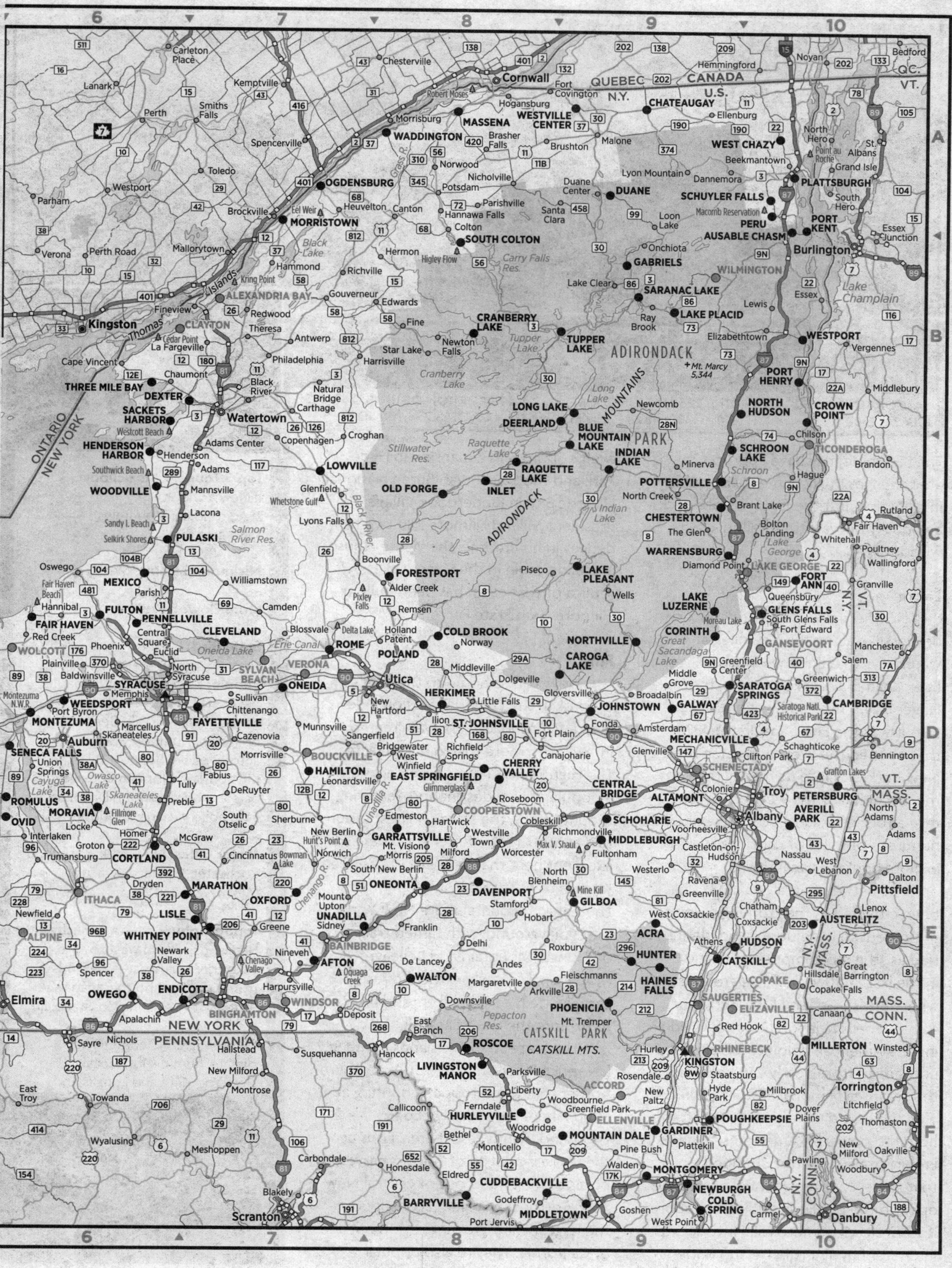
6
7
8
9
10
A
B
C
D
E
F
Carleton Place
Chesterville
Cornwall
QUEBEC
CANADA
QC.
VT.
N.Y.
U.S.
Noyan
Bedford
Hemmingford
Lanark
Kemptville
Robert Moses
Fort Covington
Hogansburg
CHATEAUGAY
Ellenburg
Perth
Smiths Falls
Morrisburg
MASSENA
WESTVILLE CENTER
WADDINGTON
Brasher Falls
Brushton
Malone
WEST CHAZY
North Hero
Point au Roche
St. Albans
Grand Isle
Spencerville
Norwood
Beekmantown
Toledo
OGDENSBURG
Potsdam
Nicholville
Duane Center
DUANE
Lyon Mountain
Dannemora
PLATTSBURGH
Westport
Parham
Eel Weir
Heuvelton
Canton
Parishville
Hannawa Falls
Santa Clara
SCHUYLER FALLS
South Hero
Brockville
MORRISTOWN
Colton
Macomb Reservation
PERU
PORT KENT
Loon Lake
Essex Junction
SOUTH COLTON
AUSABLE CHASM
Burlington
Mallorytown
Black Lake
Hermon
Higley Flow
Carry Falls Res.
Onchiota
Verona
Perth Road
Hammond
Richville
GABRIELS
WILMINGTON
Kring Point
Thousand Islands
Lake Clear
SARANAC LAKE
Lewis
Essex
Lake Champlain
Gouverneur
Edwards
ALEXANDRIA BAY
Fineview
Redwood
Kingston
CLAYTON
Theresa
Fine
CRANBERRY LAKE
Ray Brook
LAKE PLACID
Cedar Point
La Fargeville
Antwerp
Newton Falls
Tupper Lake
TUPPER LAKE
Elizabethtown
WESTPORT
Vergennes
Cape Vincent
Philadelphia
Star Lake
Harrisville
ADIRONDACK
Mt. Marcy 5,344
PORT HENRY
Chaumont
Natural Bridge
Cranberry Lake
Middlebury
THREE MILE BAY
Black River
DEXTER
Carthage
LONG LAKE
Long Lake
Newcomb
NORTH HUDSON
CROWN POINT
ONTARIO
NEW YORK
SACKETS HARBOR
Watertown
DEERLAND
MOUNTAINS
Westcott Beach
Croghan
Copenhagen
BLUE MOUNTAIN LAKE
PARK
Chilson
Adams Center
Raquette Lake
Stillwater Res.
TICONDEROGA
HENDERSON HARBOR
Henderson
SCHROON LAKE
Adams
LOWVILLE
INDIAN LAKE
Minerva
Brandon
Southwick Beach
RAQUETTE LAKE
Schroon L.
Hague
WOODVILLE
Mannsville
Glenfield
OLD FORGE
INLET
POTTERSVILLE
North Creek
Whetstone Gulf
Black River
Lacona
Lyons Falls
Indian Lake
Brant Lake
Rutland
Fair Haven
Sandy I. Beach
ADIRONDACK
CHESTERTOWN
Bolton Landing
Selkirk Shores
PULASKI
Salmon River Res.
The Glen
Whitehall
Lake George
Poultney
WARRENSBURG
Oswego
Boonville
Diamond Point
LAKE GEORGE
Wallingford
Fair Haven Beach
MEXICO
Williamstown
FORESTPORT
Piseco
LAKE PLEASANT
FORT ANN
Granville
Hannibal
Parish
Alder Creek
Pixley Falls
Wells
Queensbury
FULTON
Camden
Remsen
LAKE LUZERNE
GLENS FALLS
FAIR HAVEN
PENNELLVILLE
Holland Patent
Moreau Lake
South Glens Falls
Red Creek
Central Square
CLEVELAND
Blossvale
Delta Lake
COLD BROOK
CORINTH
Fort Edward
Norway
NORTHVILLE
WOLCOTT
Phoenix
Euclid
Oneida Lake
Erie Canal
ROME
Great Sacandaga Lake
GANSEVOORT
Manchester
POLAND
Plainville
North Syracuse
SYLVAN BEACH
VERONA
CAROGA LAKE
Greenfield Center
Salem
Baldwinsville
Middleville
Middle Grove
Montezuma N.W.R.
SYRACUSE
ONEIDA
Utica
Dolgeville
Greenwich
SARATOGA SPRINGS
Memphis
Sullivan
HERKIMER
Gloversville
Broadalbin
Saratoga Natl. Historical Park
WEEDSPORT
Chittenango
New Hartford
Little Falls
JOHNSTOWN
GALWAY
CAMBRIDGE
Port Byron
MONTEZUMA
Marcellus
FAYETTEVILLE
Ilion
ST. JOHNSVILLE
Fonda
Amsterdam
Auburn
Skaneateles
Cazenovia
Munnsville
Sangerfield
Fort Plain
MECHANICVILLE
Schaghticoke
SENECA FALLS
Morrisville
BOUCKVILLE
Bridgewater
Richfield Springs
Canajoharie
Glenville
Clifton Park
Bennington
Union Springs
Fabius
West Winfield
CHERRY VALLEY
SCHENECTADY
Grafton Lakes
Cayuga Lake
Owasco Lake
HAMILTON
EAST SPRINGFIELD
Tully
Leonardsville
Glimmerglass
CENTRAL BRIDGE
Colonie
Troy
PETERSBURG
Skaneateles Lake
DeRuyter
Unadilla R.
ALTAMONT
VT.
MASS.
ROMULUS
Preble
Roseboom
AVERILL PARK
North Adams
MORAVIA
Fillmore Glen
South Otselic
Sherburne
Edmeston
COOPERSTOWN
SCHOHARIE
Albany
OVID
Locke
New Berlin
Hartwick
Cobleskill
Richmondville
Voorheesville
Adams
Interlaken
Homer
McGraw
Hunt's Point
GARRATTSVILLE
Westville
MIDDLEBURGH
Groton
Mt. Vision
Town
Max V. Shaul
Castleton-on-Hudson
Nassau
Trumansburg
CORTLAND
Cincinnatus
Bowman Lake
Norwich
Morris
Milford
Worcester
Fultonham
West Lebanon
South New Berlin
North Blenheim
Westerlo
Dalton
Chenango R.
Dryden
ONEONTA
Ravena
Pittsfield
MARATHON
DAVENPORT
Mine Kill
ITHACA
OXFORD
Mount Upton
Stamford
GILBOA
Greenville
Chatham
Lenox
Newfield
LISLE
UNADILLA
Hobart
West Coxsackie
Coxsackie
AUSTERLITZ
Greene
Sidney
Franklin
ACRA
WHITNEY POINT
BAINBRIDGE
Delhi
Roxbury
Athens
HUDSON
ALPINE
Newark Valley
Nineveh
AFTON
De Lancey
Andes
HUNTER
CATSKILL
N.Y.
MASS.
Spencer
Chenango Valley
Oquaga Creek
WALTON
Great Barrington
Fleischmanns
HAINES FALLS
COPAKE
Hillsdale
Elmira
OWEGO
ENDICOTT
Harpursville
Margaretville
Arkville
Copake Falls
MASS.
Apalachin
BINGHAMTON
WINDSOR
Downsville
PHOENICIA
SAUGERTIES
ELIZAVILLE
Canaan
CONN.
NEW YORK
Deposit
Pepacton Res.
Mt. Tremper
CATSKILL PARK
Red Hook
PENNSYLVANIA
Sayre
Nichols
Hallstead
East Branch
ROSCOE
CATSKILL MTS.
RHINEBECK
MILLERTON
Winsted
Susquehanna
Hancock
LIVINGSTON MANOR
Hurley
KINGSTON
New Milford
Parksville
Staatsburg
Rosendale
ACCORD
East Troy
Towanda
Montrose
Liberty
New Paltz
Hyde Park
Millbrook
Torrington
Ferndale
Woodbourne
Greenfield Park
Litchfield
Callicoon
HURLEYVILLE
ELLENVILLE
POUGHKEEPSIE
Dover Plains
Thomaston
Woodridge
GARDINER
Bethel
MOUNTAIN DALE
Wyalusing
New Milford
Oakville
Meshoppen
Monticello
Pine Bush
Plattekill
Pawling
Carbondale
Walden
MONTGOMERY
Woodbury
Honesdale
Eldred
CUDDEBACKVILLE
N.Y.
CONN.
Blakely
NEWBURGH
Godeffroy
COLD SPRING
Scranton
BARRYVILLE
MIDDLETOWN
Goshen
Carmel
Danbury
Port Jervis
West Point

NY

 See map pages 818 and 819

Getty Images/iStockphoto

WELCOME TO
New York

DATE OF STATEHOOD	WIDTH: 285 MILES (455 KM)	PROPORTION OF UNITED STATES
JULY 26, 1788	LENGTH: 330 MILES (531 KM)	1.44% OF 3,794,100 SQ MI

The Big Apple may have appropriated the New York name in the public imagination, but the Empire State packs an equally big vacation wallop, even without NYC.

Learn

Nowhere does New York history unwind like along the 524 miles of waterways that link the Hudson River, Lake Champlain, Lake Ontario, the Finger Lakes, Niagara River and Lake Erie. It was the Erie Canal in the 1820s that opened the West and catapulted New York City into its role as the commerce capital of the world. You can take a tour on a canal boat, hike or bike hundreds of miles of canal trailways or explore heritage canal towns.

The Battle of Saratoga in 1777 has been crowned as the "turning point of the American Revolution" and identified as "the most important battle in the last 1,000 years." The grounds where British General John Burgoyne surrendered England's hopes at dividing the American colonies are almost unchanged from nearly 240 years ago at the Saratoga National History Park.

You would expect New York to be home to powerful Americans, and the Empire State does not disappoint on that score. Four presidential homes are open to the public, including Theodore Roosevelt's Sagamore Hill Historic Site in Oyster Bay, Franklin Delano Roosevelt's Springwood mansion in Hyde Park and the Martin Van Buren National Historic Site in Kinderhook Village. President Millard Fillmore had two residences in his lifetime: the White House and a log cabin in the Finger Lakes. A replica of that cabin has been built in Fillmore Glen State Park.

Play

New York is home to the largest park in the United States outside Alaska. Adirondack Park was created in 1892 with more than 6 million acres. The High Peaks in the Adirondacks are a popular hiking destination, featuring Mount Marcy, the state's highest mountain at 5,343 feet. Winter sports are so excellent here that Lake Placid has been tabbed to host two Winter Olympics. The Catskill Mountains are New York City's playground, with famed trails on Hunter Mountain and Belleayre Mountain. Meanwhile, the old resort carriage trails enable bikers and hikers to explore the Gunks as well.

There are so many islands in the St. Lawrence River on New York's northern border that they stopped counting at 1,000. There are actually 1,864 in the Thousand Islands resort area. Eons ago, the restless activity of glaciers carved 11 pools of meltwater out of central New York. Today, the Finger Lakes support the largest wine-growing region outside of California. They're also popular

Top 3 Tourism Attractions:
1) New York City
2) Adirondack Mountains
3) Niagara Falls

Nickname: Empire State

State Flower: Rose

State Bird: Bluebird

People: Kareem Abdul-Jabbar, basketball player; Lucille Ball, actress; William "Bill" Bennett, politician; Humphrey Bogart, actor; William Bonney "Billy the Kid", outlaw; Norman Rockwell, painter and illustrator; Dr. Jonas Salk, polio vaccine developer

Major Cities: New York, Buffalo, Rochester, Yonkers, Syracuse, (Albany, capital)

Topography: East—Appalachian Highlands extend west toward Lake Erie; northeast—lowlands from Lake Ontario to Canada; southeast— Atlantic Coastal plain

Climate: Humid continental climate; humid subtropical in New York City and Long Island

NYSDED-Photo by Darren McGee

NY

among tourists.

New York created the country's first state park at Niagara Falls in 1885; the iconic waterfall is not even the highest cascade in the state's system of 180 parks. That would be the 215-foot Taughannock Falls near Ithaca. The parks include beaches on two Great Lakes and the Atlantic Ocean; Lake Champlain, which is so murky that it hosts its own monster, affectionately known as Champ"; and the chasms and spectacular gorges of Central New York.

Experience

The last weekend in July brings the induction of new members to the Baseball Hall of Fame in Cooperstown. The ceremonies at the nation's most hallowed sports museum are an occasion to not only celebrate the national pastime but to honor a way of life in small-town America. An even older American sporting tradition takes place in August at Saratoga Race Course, where horse racing's premier meet has drawn the nation's elite since 1863.

New York brims with entertainment outside the Big Apple. The Lucille Ball Comedy Festival takes place each summer in Jamestown. The event was started by television's greatest comedienne in her hometown in the 1980s. Ready for the Twilight Zone? The Rod Serling Film Festival takes place in his hometown of Binghamton. And for those who missed the touchstone of a generation, a plaque has been placed at the site of Max Yasgur's farm commemorating 1969's Woodstock Festival. Concerts are still held at the nearby Bethel Woods Center for the Arts.

Taste

While it may be nearly impossible to come up with a definitive New York dish, it likely springs from a New York City delicatessen. Arnold Reuben was the first to pile corned beef, Swiss cheese and sauerkraut on rye bread and slather it with Russian dressing, and the sandwich has been named for him since its invention in 1914. Katz's Deli teamed pastrami and corned beef into one of America's most popular sandwiches.

TRAVEL & TOURISM

New York Department of Economic Development
800-CALL-NYS, 518-474-4116
www.iloveny.com

The Adirondacks
800-487-6867
www.visitadirondacks.com

Buffalo Niagara CVB
716-852-0511, 800-BUFFALO
www.wrightnowinbuffalo.com

Catskill Association for Tourism Services
800-NYS-CATS
www.visitthecatskills.com

Central-New York
800-233-8778
www.roundthebend.com/central

Finger Lakes
800-530-7488
www.fingerlakes.org

Long Island
www.discoverlongisland.com

New York City
212-484-1200
www.nycgo.com

Thousand Islands
800-847-5263, 315-482-2520
www.visit1000islands.com

OUTDOOR RECREATION

New York State Boater's Guide and/or Launch Site Book
518-474-0456
www.nysparks.com

New York State Dept. of Environmental Conservation, Resources Bureau of Fisheries
www.dec.ny.gov

Off-Road Vehicles
www.nysorva.org

Outfitters/guides
www.nysoga.com

Riding Trails
www.ptny.org

Wineries
www.newyorkwines.org

SHOPPING

Hickory Dickory Dock
888-646-7474
www.hickorydock.com

NBC Experience Store
877-841-2128
www.nbcexperiencestore.com

Where It All Began Bat Company
607-547-7101
www.wiabbatco.com

Featured Good Sam Parks

NEW YORK

Good Sam Park

When you stay with Good Sam, you can expect the highest degree of cleanliness and friendliness, and better yet, you get 10% off campground fees.

If you're not already a Good Sam member you can purchase your membership at one of these locations:

ALEXANDRIA BAY
Swan Bay Resort
(315)482-7926

ALPINE
Cool Lea Camp
(607)594-3500

BAINBRIDGE
Tall Pines Campground & Canoeing
(607)563-8271

BATH
Hickory Hill Family Camping Resort
(607)776-4345

BINGHAMTON
Belden Hill Campground LLC
(607)693-1645

BYRON
Southwoods RV Resort
(585)548-9002

CHAUTAUQUA
Camp Chautauqua Camping Resort
(716)789-3435

CLAYTON
Merry Knoll 1000 Islands Campground
(315)686-3055

COOPERSTOWN
Cooperstown-Shadow Brook Campground
(607)264-8431
Meadow-Vale Campsites
(607)293-8802

COPAKE
Camp Waubeeka
(518)329-4681

CORNING
Camp Bell Campground
(800)587-3301

DARIEN CENTER
Skyline RV Resort Inc
(585)591-2021

ELIZAVILLE
Brook N Wood Family Campground
(888)625-3186

ELLENVILLE
Jellystone Park (TM) at Birchwood Acres
(888)726-4073
Skyway Camping Resort Inc
(800)447-5992

FLORIDA
Black Bear Campground Inc
(845)651-7717

GANSEVOORT
Adirondack Gateway Campground
(518)792-0485
Coldbrook Campsites
(518)584-8038

HOLLEY
Hickory Ridge Golf & RV Resort
(585)638-0220

ITHACA
Pinecreek Campground
(607)273-1974
Spruce Row Campground & RV Park
(607)387-9225

JAMESTOWN
Hidden Valley Camping Area
(716)569-5433

LAKE GEORGE
King Phillips Campground
(518)668-5763
Ledgeview Village RV Park
(518)798-6621

LOCKPORT
Niagara County Camping Resort
(716)434-3991

NIAGARA FALLS
AA Royal Motel & Campground
(716)693-5695
Niagara Falls Campground & Lodging
(716)731-3434

RHINEBECK
Interlake RV Park & Sales
(845)266-5387

SAUGERTIES
Rip Van Winkle Campgrounds Inc
(800)246-3357

SCHENECTADY
Arrowhead Marina & RV Park
(518)382-8966

SYLVAN BEACH
Oneida Pines Campground
(315)245-1377

VERONA
The Villages At Turning Stone
(315)361-7275

WELLSVILLE
Trout Run Camp Resort
(585)596-0500

WILMINGTON
North Pole Resorts
(518)946-7733

WINDSOR
Lakeside Campground
(607)655-2694

WOLCOTT
Cherry Grove Campground
(315)594-8320

For more Good Sam Parks go to listing pages

New York

CONSULTANTS

Jim & Julie Golden

ACCORD — F9 *Ulster*

RONDOUT VALLEY RESORT **Ratings: 8.5/7.5/9** (Membership Pk) 2015 rates: $45 to $61. (845)626-5521 105 Mettacahonts Rd, Accord, NY 12404

SOHI CAMPGROUND
Ratings: 8.5/9.5★/9 (Campground) From jct of I 87 & US 209: go south 14 mi, then west on CR 2 for 4 mi, then north on Woodland Rd (R). **FAC:** Paved/gravel rds. (75 spaces). Avail: 55 grass, patios, 6 pull-thrus (30 x 55), back-ins (30 x 55), 55 full hkups (30/50 amps), seasonal sites, cable, WiFi, tent sites, dump, laundry, fire rings, firewood. **REC:** pool, pond, fishing, playground. Pets OK. Big rig sites, 2015 rates: $38 to $45. May 15 to Oct 15.
(845)687-7377 Lat: 41.8798, Lon: -74.21870
425 Woodland Rd, Accord, NY 12404
sohicampground@hotmail.com
www.sohicampground.com

ACRA — E9 *Greene*

WHIP-O-WILL CAMPSITE **Ratings: 7.5/7/7.5** (Campground) 2015 rates: $35 to $40. Apr 10 to Oct 12. (518)622-3277 644 County Rd 31, Purling, NY 12470

ADDISON — E5 *Steuben*

SUNFLOWER ACRES FAMILY CAMPGROUND **Ratings: 7.5/9.5★/8** (Campground) From Jct of US-15 & CR-5 (Presho exit), W 0.5 mi on CR-5 to N Glendenning Rd (becomes Stead School Rd), N 2.8 mi to Tinkertown Rd, E 0.1 mi (R). **FAC:** Poor gravel/dirt rds. (100 spaces). Avail: 50 grass, 30 pull-thrus (40 x 50), back-ins (40 x 50), 17 full hkups, 33 W, 33 E (30 amps), seasonal sites, WiFi, tent sites, dump, laundry, groc, LP gas, fire rings, firewood. **REC:** pool, pond, fishing, playground. Pets OK. 2015 rates: $28 to $30. May 1 to Oct 15.
(607)523-7756 Lat: 42.06382, Lon: -77.20958
1488 Sunflower Blvd, Addison, NY 14801
sunfloweracres@hughes.net
www.sunfloweracresfamilycampground.com

AFTON — E7 *Chenango*

KELLYSTONE PARK
Ratings: 7.5/6.5/7.5 (Campground) From Jct of I-88 & SR-41 (exit 7), S 5.2 mi on SR-41 to Hawkins Rd, E 0.2 mi (L); or From Jct of SR-17 (Quickway) & SR-41 (exit 82), N 9 mi on SR-41 to Hawkins Rd, E 0.2 mi (L). **FAC:** All weather rds. (180 spaces). Avail: 20 grass, 20 pull-thrus (50 x 70), mostly side by side hkups, 20 full hkups (30/50 amps), seasonal sites, tent sites, showers $, dump, laundry, fire rings. **REC:** pool, pond, fishing, golf, playground. Pet restrict(B). Partial handicap access. Big rig sites, 2015 rates: $39. Disc: AAA, military. Apr 15 to Oct 1.
AAA Approved
(607)639-1090 Lat: 42.17018, Lon: -75.52540
51 Hawkins Rd, Nineveh, NY 13813
kellystone_park@yahoo.com
www.kellystonepark.net
See ad opposite page.

AKRON — D3 *Erie*

SLEEPY HOLLOW LAKE Ratings: 7/9★/8.5 (Campground) From Jct of I-90 (Thruway) & SR-77 (exit 48A), S 1 mi on SR-77 to SR 5, W 3 mi to Crittenden Rd, S 3 mi to Siehl Rd, E 0.5 mi (L). **FAC:** Gravel rds. (245 spaces). 65 Avail: 25 gravel, 40 grass, 15 pull-thrus (28 x 65), back-ins (35 x 55), some side by side hkups, 65 W, 65 E (30/50 amps), seasonal sites, WiFi, tent sites, rentals, showers $, dump, mobile sewer, groc, LP gas, fire rings, firewood, restaurant, controlled access. **REC:** Sleepy Hollow Lake: swim, fishing, playground. Pets OK. Partial handicap access. 2015 rates: $36 to $39. Disc: AAA, military. May 1 to Oct 12. ATM.
AAA Approved
(716)542-4336 Lat: 42.95591, Lon: -78.47083
13800 Siehl Rd, Akron, NY 14001
sleepyhollowlake@yahoo.com
sleepyhollowlakeresort.com

ALBION — D4 *Orleans*

LAKESIDE BEACH (State Pk) From town, N 8 mi on SR-98 to W end Lake Ontario State Pkwy, W 2.2 mi (R). 2015 rates: $21 to $27. May 13 to Oct 10. (585)682-4888

ALEXANDRIA BAY — B7 *Jefferson*

GRASS POINT (State Pk) From Jct of I-81 & SR-12, SW 1 mi on SR-12 (R). 2015 rates: $15 to $21. May 17 to Sep 1. (315)686-4472

KEEWAYDIN (State Pk) From Jct SR-26 & SR-12, W 1 mi on SR-12 (R). 2015 rates: $15. May 24 to Sep 1. (315)482-3331

KRING POINT (State Pk) From Jct of I-81 & Rte 12, NE 14 mi on Rte 12 to Kring Point Rd, W 2 mi (L). 2015 rates: $15 to $21. May 3 to Oct 13. (315)482-2444

SWAN BAY RESORT
Ratings: 10/9.5★/10 (RV Park) From jct I-81 N & Rte 411: Go 8.6 mi N on I-81 to exit 50N, then go right to Rte 12 East, then go .9 mi (L). **FAC:** Paved rds. 71 paved, patios, 9 pull-thrus (40 x 80), back-ins (40 x 80), 71 full hkups (30/50 amps), WiFi, rentals, dump, laundry, groc, LP bottles, fire rings, firewood, controlled access. **REC:** heated pool, St Lawrence River: swim, fishing, marina, playground. Pets OK. Partial handicap access. Big rig sites, eco-friendly, 2015 rates: $55 to $115. May 1 to Oct 31.
(315)482-7926 Lat: 44.298963, Lon: -75.963537
43615 State Route 12, Alexandria Bay, NY 13607
manager@swanbayresort.com
www.swanbayresort.com
See ad this page, 823.

WELLESLEY ISLAND (State Pk) From business center: Go 6 mi S on Hwy 12, then cross 1000 Island Bridge (Toll). 2015 rates: $15. May 10 to Oct 13. (315)482-2722

ALPINE — E6 *Schuyler*

COOL LEA CAMP
Ratings: 6.5/9.5★/9 (Campground) From Jct of Rts 224 & 228 (in Odessa) 2.5 N on Rt 228. (R). **FAC:** Gravel rds. (73 spaces). 48 Avail: 43 gravel, 5 grass, 4 pull-thrus (30 x 60), back-ins (30 x 40), some side by side hkups, 19 full hkups, 29 W, 29 E (30/50 amps), seasonal sites, WiFi Hotspot, tent sites, rentals, showers $, dump, mobile sewer, fire rings, firewood. **REC:** Cayuta Lake: swim, fishing, playground. Pet restrict(Q) $. Partial handicap access. Big rig sites, 2015 rates: $40 to $58. Disc: military. May 15 to Oct 15.
(607)594-3500 Lat: 42.3616, Lon: -76.7440
2620 Cool-Lea Camp Dr, Alpine, NY 14805
coollea2@aol.com
www.coolleacamp.com
See ad pages 844, 823.

ALTAMONT — D9 *Albany*

THOMPSON'S LAKE (State Pk) From town, W 4 mi on Hwy 156, SE 2 mi on Hwy 157 (L). Reservations recommended. 2015 rates: $15 to $19. May 3 to Sep 1. (518)872-1674

ANGELICA — E4 *Allegany*

EVERGREEN TRAILS CAMPGROUND **Ratings: 6.5/9.5★/9** (Campground) 2015 rates: $30 to $35. May 1 to Oct 31. (585)466-7993 8403 CR 15, Angelica, NY 14709

ANGOLA — D3 *Erie*

EVANGOLA (State Pk) From town, SW 1 mi on NY-5, follow signs (R). 2015 rates: $15 to $32. Apr 12 to Oct 30. (716)549-1802

ARKPORT — E4 *Allegany*

SUN VALLEY CAMPSITES **Ratings: 8/8.5★/9** (Campground) 2015 rates: $31 to $41. May 1 to Oct 18. (607)545-8388 10740 Poags Hole Rd, Arkport, NY 14807

AUSABLE CHASM — A10 *Clinton*

AUSABLE CHASM CAMPGROUND **Ratings: 7/8.5/8** (Campground) 2015 rates: $35 to $40. May 27 to Oct 14. (518)834-9990 634 Rt 373, Ausable Chasm, NY 12911

AUSTERLITZ — E10 *Columbia*

WOODLAND HILLS CAMPGROUND
Ratings: 7/8/9.5 (Campground) From Jct of I-90 & SR-22 (Exit 3B), S 2 mi on SR-22 to Middle Rd, W 0.75 mi on Middle Rd to Fog Hill Rd, W 0.75 mi (L). **FAC:** Gravel rds. (190 spaces). Avail: 90 grass, 3 pull-thrus (30 x 50), back-ins (30 x 45), 47 full hkups, 43 W, 43 E (30/50 amps), seasonal sites, WiFi, tent sites, rentals, showers $, dump, mobile sewer, laundry, groc, LP gas, fire rings, firewood. **REC:** pond, swim, fishing, playground. Pets OK. Eco-friendly, 2015 rates: $35 to $39. May 15 to Oct 10.
(518)392-3557 Lat: 42.34490, Lon: -73.44202
386 Fog Hill Rd, Austerlitz, NY 12017
info@whcg.net
www.whcg.net
See ad this page.

AVERILL PARK — D10 *Rensselaer*

ALPS FAMILY CAMPGROUND **Ratings: 8.5/6/8** (Campground) 2015 rates: $30 to $32. May 1 to Oct 15. (518)674-5565 1928 State Route 43, Averill Park, NY 12018

BAINBRIDGE — E7 *Broome, Chenango, Delaware*

GENERAL CLINTON PARK (Public) From I-88 (exit 8) & SR-206: Go .5mi NW on SR-206, then 1.5mi NE on SR-7 (R). 2015 rates: $25. May 1 to Oct 31. (607)967-3781

OQUAGA CREEK (State Pk) From Jct of Hwy 17 & Rte 8 exit 84 (at Deposit), N 3 mi on Rte 8 to CR-20, N 9 mi (L). 2015 rates: $15 to $19. May 9 to Oct 12. (607)467-4160

RIVERSIDE RV CAMPING
Ratings: 2.5/8/6.5 (Campground) From Jct of I-88 & SR-206 (exit 8), W 0.2 mi on SR-206 to Roundabout 3rd Exit onto CR-39, S 0.1 mi (R). Behind Susquehanna Motor Lodge. **FAC:** Gravel rds. (14 spaces). Avail: 7 grass, 7 pull-thrus (35 x 70), 7 full hkups (30 amps), seasonal sites, cable, tent sites, rentals, dump, fire rings, firewood. **REC:** Susquehanna River: fishing. Pets OK. Partial handicap access.

Say you saw it in our Guide!

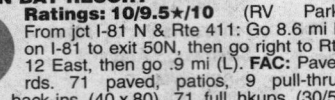

Like Us on Facebook.

BAINBRIDGE (CONT)

RIVERSIDE RV CAMPING (CONT)
2015 rates: $25. Disc: military. Apr 15 to Oct 15.
(607)967-2102 Lat: 42.29019, Lon: -75.47633
1303 CR 39, Bainbridge, NY 13733
flyingtigers@frontiernet.net
See ad opposite page.

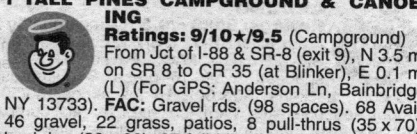

TALL PINES CAMPGROUND & CANOEING
Ratings: 9/10★/9.5 (Campground) From Jct of I-88 & SR-8 (exit 9), N 3.5 mi on SR 8 to CR 35 (at Blinker), E 0.1 mi (L) (For GPS: Anderson Ln, Bainbridge NY 13733). **FAC:** Gravel rds. (98 spaces). 68 Avail: 46 gravel, 22 grass, patios, 8 pull-thrus (35 x 70), back-ins (30 x 60), 37 full hkups, 31 W, 31 E (30/50 amps), seasonal sites, cable, WiFi, tent sites, rentals, dump, mobile sewer, laundry, groc, LP gas, fire rings, firewood, restaurant. **REC:** pool, Unadilla River: fishing, playground. Pets OK. Partial handicap access. Big rig sites, eco-friendly, 2015 rates: $32 to $52. May 1 to Oct 10.
(607)563-8271 Lat: 42.34134, Lon: -75.39986
anderson Lane, Bainbridge, NY 13733
tallpinescampground@yahoo.com
www.tallpinescampground-ny.com
See ad pages 826, 823.

BARKER — C3 *Niagara*

GOLDEN HILL (State Pk) From Jct of Rtes 18 & 269 (County Line Rd), N 1 mi on County Line Rd to Lower Lake Rd, W 1 mi (R). One time entrance fee $2.75. 2015 rates: $15 to $21. Apr 9 to Oct 11. (716)795-3885

BARRYVILLE — F8 *Sullivan*

KITTATINNY CAMPGROUNDS **Ratings: 7/7/7** (Campground) 2015 rates: $11 to $18. Apr 15 to Oct 31. (845)557-8611 3854 SR-97, Barryville, NY 12719

BATAVIA — D4 *Genesee*

LEI-TI RECREATION RESORT Ratings: 9/8.5/9 (Campground) From Jct of I-90 & SR-98 (exit 48), S 1 mi on SR-98 to SR-63, S 2.8 mi to Shepard Rd, S 0.5 mi to Putnam Rd, SW 1 mi to Francis Rd, S 2 mi (L); or From Jct of SR-98 & SR-20, E 4.1 mi on SR-20 to Francis Rd, N 3.1 mi (R). **FAC:** Gravel rds. (260 spaces). 20 Avail: 8 gravel, 12 grass, 7 pull-thrus (40 x 80), back-ins (40 x 60), 20 full hkups (30/50 amps), seasonal sites, WiFi, rentals, dump, mobile sewer, laundry, groc, LP gas, fire rings, firewood, controlled access. **REC:** pool, Lei Ti Lake: swim, fishing, shuffleboard, playground. Pet restrict(B/Q). Partial handicap access, no tents. Big rig sites, 2015 rates: $45. May 1 to Oct 19. ATM.
AAA Approved
(585)343-8600 Lat: 42.93060, Lon: -78.16242
9979 Francis Rd, Batavia, NY 14020
leiti@leiti.com
www.leiti.com

BATH — E5 *Steuben*

BABCOCK HOLLOW FAMILY CAMPGROUND **Ratings: 7/9.5★/7** (Campground) 2015 rates: $35. May 1 to Oct 15. (607)776-7185 5932 County Route 11, Bath, NY 14810

CAMPERS HAVEN **Ratings: 8.5/8.5★/7.5** (Campground) 2015 rates: $35 to $45. Apr 15 to Oct 15. (607)776-0328 6832 CR-15 Knight Settlement Rd, Bath, NY 14810

HICKORY HILL FAMILY CAMPING RESORT
Ratings: 9/10★/9.5 (Campground) From Jct of I-86 & SR-54 (Exit 38), N 1.4 mi on SR-54 to the Y intersection, left at Y, on to Haverling St. (CR-13), N 2.0 mi (L). Note: Minimum 3 day stay on holiday weekends. **FAC:** All weather rds. (216 spaces). 136 Avail: 104 gravel, 32 grass, patios, 60 pull-thrus (30 x 65), back-ins (35 x 65), 104 full hkups, 32 W, 32 E (30/50 amps), seasonal sites, cable, WiFi, tent sites, rentals, dump, laundry, groc, LP gas, fire rings, firewood. **REC:** heated pool, pond, shuffleboard, playground. Pets OK. Partial handicap access. Big rig sites, eco-friendly, 2015 rates: $40 to $75. Disc: military. May 1 to Oct 31. ATM.
(607)776-4345 Lat: 42.36459, Lon: -77.30989
7531 County Route 13, Bath, NY 14810
camp@hickoryhillcampresort.com
www.hickoryhillcampresort.com
See ad pages 828, 823.

Travel Services

CAMPING WORLD OF BATH As the nation's largest retailer of RV supplies, accessories, services and new and used RVs, Camping World is committed to making your total RV experience better. RV Accessories: (866)851-7700. **SERVICES:** RV appliance, MH mechanical, staffed RV wash, restrooms, RV Sales. RV supplies, LP, emergency parking, RV accessible, waiting room. Hours: 8am to 6pm.
(888)672-0357 Lat: 42.342706, Lon: -77.337673
500 W. Morris Street, Bath, NY 14810
ted.thompson@campingworld.com
www.campingworld.com

BINGHAMTON — E7 *Broome*

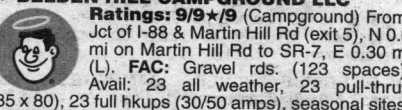

BELDEN HILL CAMPGROUND LLC
Ratings: 9/9★/9 (Campground) From Jct of I-88 & Martin Hill Rd (exit 5), N 0.6 mi on Martin Hill Rd to SR-7, E 0.30 mi (L). **FAC:** Gravel rds. (123 spaces). Avail: 23 all weather, 23 pull-thrus (35 x 80), 23 full hkups (30/50 amps), seasonal sites, WiFi, tent sites, rentals, dump, laundry, LP gas, fire rings, firewood. **REC:** pond, swim, fishing, golf, playground. Pets OK. Big rig sites, 2015 rates: $33 to $38. Apr 1 to Oct 30.
(607)693-1645 Lat: 42.20245, Lon: -75.69941
1843 State Route 7, Harpursville, NY 13787
beldenhillcamp@aol.com
www.beldenrvpk.com
See ad this page, 823.

CHENANGO VALLEY (State Pk) From Jct of I-88 & SR-369, NE 5 mi on SR-369 (L). 2015 rates: $15 to $23. May 10 to Oct 13. (607)648-5251

BLISS — E4 *Wyoming*

FAUN LAKE **Ratings: 7/7.5/8** (Membership Pk) 2015 rates: $28. May 1 to Oct 15. (585)322-7300 5124 Pleasant Valley Rd, Bliss, NY 14024

BLUE MOUNTAIN LAKE — C9 *Hamilton*

LAKE DURANT (ADIRONDACK SF) (State Pk) From jct Hwy 30 & Hwy 28: Go 3 mi E on Hwy 28. 2015 rates: $20. (518)352-7797

BOUCKVILLE — D7 *Madison*

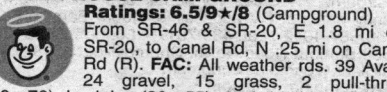

CIDER HOUSE CAMPGROUND
Ratings: 6.5/9★/8 (Campground) From SR-46 & SR-20, E 1.8 mi on SR-20, to Canal Rd, N .25 mi on Canal Rd (R). **FAC:** All weather rds. 39 Avail: 24 gravel, 15 grass, 2 pull-thrus (30 x 70), back-ins (30 x 55), 24 full hkups, 6 W, 15 E (30 amps), WiFi, tent sites, rentals, dump, fire rings, firewood. **REC:** playground, rec open to public. Pets OK. 2015 rates: $25 to $30. May 27 to Oct 1.
AAA Approved
(315)825-8477 Lat: 42.89322, Lon: -75.54935
3570 Canal Rd, Bouckville, NY 13310
campground@ciderhouseantiques.com
www.ciderhouseantiques.com

BROCTON — E2 *Chautauqua*

LAKE ERIE (State Pk) From Jct of I-90 & SR-380 (exit 60), N 0.75 mi on SR-380 to SR-5, E 9 mi (R). 2015 rates: $15 to $21. May 16 to Oct 12. (716)792-9214

BROOKHAVEN — A4 *Suffolk*

SOUTHHAVEN COUNTY PARK (Public) From Long Island Expwy (I-495, exit 68S): Go S on William Floyd Pkwy to 4th traffic light, then W on Victory Ave, then 1/2 mi N on River Rd. (631)854-1414

BUFFALO — D3 *Erie*

CHAUTAUQUA LAKE KOA
Ratings: 10/10★/10 (Campground) From Buffalo I-90 S to Exit 60, go SE on US-394 for 6 mi, at Jct with SR-430, go 4 mi NE to Thumb Rd. Go E 0.5 mi (L). **FAC:** All weather rds. (246 spaces). Avail: 10 paved, 101 all weather, patios, 106 pull-thrus (50 x 80), back-ins (40 x 60), 84 full hkups, 27 W, 27 E (30/50 amps), seasonal sites, cable, WiFi, tent sites, rentals, dump, laundry, groc, LP gas, fire rings, firewood, controlled access. **REC:** heated pool, playground. Pet restrict(B). Partial handicap access. Big rig sites, 2015 rates: $39 to $64. Disc: military. May 1 to Oct 15.
(716)386-3804 Lat: 42.22885, Lon: -79.42983
5652 Thum Road, Dewittville, NY 14728
camping@chautauqualakekoa.com
www.chautauqualakekoa.com
See primary listing at Dewittville and ad page 826.

You have high expectations, so we point out campgrounds, service centers and tourist attractions with elevations over 2,500 feet.

BYRON — D4 *Genesee*

SOUTHWOODS RV RESORT
Ratings: 9.5/9★/10 (Campground) W-bnd: From Jct of I-90 & SR-19 (exit 47), N 3.2 mi on SR-19 to SR-262, W 4.6 mi (L); or E bnd: From Jct of I-90 & SR-98 (exit 48), N 3.5 mi on SR-98 to SR-262, E 7.8 mi (R) Note: Min 3 day stay on holiday weekends. **FAC:** All weather rds. (233 spaces). 126 Avail: 72 gravel, 54 grass, 65 pull-thrus (30 x 70), back-ins (40 x 70), 63 full hkups, 63 W, 63 E (30/50 amps), seasonal sites, cable, WiFi, tent sites, rentals, dump, mobile sewer, laundry, groc, LP gas, fire rings, firewood, controlled access. **REC:** heated pool, playground. Pet restrict(Q). Partial handicap access. Big rig sites, eco-friendly, 2015 rates: $32 to $40. May 1 to Oct 31.
(585)548-9002 Lat: 43.07756, Lon: -78.03600
6749 Townline Rd, Byron, NY 14422
scu74@aol.com
www.southwoodsrvresort.com
See ad pages 822 (Welcome Section), 823.

NY

CALEDONIA — D4 *Livingston*

GENESEE COUNTRY CAMPGROUND **Ratings: 7/9/8.5** (Campground) 2015 rates: $29. May 1 to Oct 31. (585)538-4200 40 Flint Rd, Caledonia, NY 14423

CAMBRIDGE — D10 *Washington*

LAKE LAUDERDALE CAMPGROUND **Ratings: 6.5/8/8.5** (Campground) 2015 rates: $32 to $35. May 1 to Oct 15. (518)677-8855 744 CR-61, Cambridge, NY 12816

CANANDAIGUA — D5 *Ontario*

BRISTOL WOODLANDS CAMPGROUND **Ratings: 6/5.5/7.5** (Campground) 2015 rates: $40 to $42. May 1 to Oct 20. (585)229-2290 4835 South Hill Rd, Canandaigua, NY 14424

KOA CANANDAIGUA/ROCHESTER KAMPGROUND **Ratings: 10/9.5★/9.5** (Campground) 2015 rates: $34 to $51. Apr 1 to Nov 1. (585)398-3582 5374 Canandaigua Farmington Town Line Rd, Canandaigua, NY 14425

CAROGA LAKE — D9 *Fulton*

ADIRONDACK/CAROGA LAKE (State Pk) From town, S 1 mi on Hwy 29A (R). Campground is on E-side of Caroga Lake. Entrance fee required. 2015 rates: $20. May 16 to Aug 31. (518)835-4241

CATSKILL — E9 *Greene*

INDIAN RIDGE CAMPGROUND **Ratings: 7/8/7.5** (Campground) 2015 rates: $40 to $50. May 15 to Oct 15. (518)943-4513 1446 Leeds Athens Rd, Catskill, NY 12414

CENTRAL BRIDGE — D9 *Schoharie*

HIDE-A-WAY CAMPSITES **Ratings: 6/8.5★/7.5** (Campground) 2015 rates: $30 to $32. May 15 to Oct 15. (518)868-9975 107 Janice Ln, Central Bridge, NY 12035

CHATEAUGAY — A9 *Franklin*

HIGH FALLS PARK **Ratings: 6.5/5.5/8** (Campground) 2015 rates: $30 to $35. May 1 to Oct 15. (518)497-3156 34 Cemetery Rd (Jerdon Rd), Chateaugay, NY 12920

Replace clogged air filters. A clogged air filter can cut a vehicle's fuel efficiency by 10 percent.

CHAUTAUQUA — E2 *Chautauqua*

CAMP CHAUTAUQUA CAMPING RESORT
Ratings: 9.5/9.5★/10 (Campground) From Jct of I-86/SR-17 & SR-394 (exit 8), N 2 mi on SR-394 (R).

BEST CAMPING IN WESTERN NEW YORK
On the shores of Chautauqua Lake. Camp Chautauqua, a family resort has all amenities in the heart of Western New York's natural playground. 2000 ft of lakeside w/ docks. Near Chautauqua Institution. Open all year.

FAC: All weather rds. (250 spaces). Avail: 100 all weather, 69 pull-thrus (35 x 70), back-ins (35 x 70), 75 full hkups, 25 W, 25 E (30/50 amps), seasonal sites, cable, WiFi Hotspot, tent sites, dump, mobile sewer, laundry, groc, LP gas, fire rings, firewood, controlled access. **REC:** heated pool, wading pool, Lake Chautauqua: swim, fishing, marina, playground. Pet restrict(Q). Partial handicap access. Big rig sites, eco-friendly, 2015 rates: $27.50 to $65. Disc: military. ATM.
(716)789-3435 Lat: 42.16918, Lon: -79.43985
3900 W Lake Rd, Stow, NY 14785
camp@campchautauqua.com
www.campchautauqua.com
See ad this page, 823.

Visit CampingWorld.com where you can get deals on over 10,000 RV and camping related products!

CHERRY VALLEY — D8 *Otsego*

BELVEDERE LAKE RESORT **Ratings: 7.5/7.5/9** (Campground) 2015 rates: $40 to $45. May 1 to Oct 4. (607)264-8182 270 Gage Rd, Cherry Valley, NY 13320

CHESTERTOWN — C9 *Warren*

RANCHO PINES CAMPGROUND **Ratings: 8/8.5★/9** (Campground) 2015 rates: $35. May 20 to Oct 10. (518)494-3645 2854 Schroon River Rd, Chestertown, NY 12817

RIVERSIDE PINES CAMPSITES Ratings: 7.5/9★/9 (Campground) From Jct of I-87 & SR-8 (exit 25), E 0.1 mi on SR-8 to Schroon River Rd, N 0.5 mi (L) Note: 37' max RV length. **FAC:** Gravel rds. (64 spaces). Avail: 14 gravel, 10 pull-thrus (35 x 60), back-ins (35 x 50), 14 full hkups (30 amps), seasonal sites, cable, WiFi, tent sites, rentals, laundry, groc, LP gas, fire rings, firewood, restaurant. **REC:** Schroon River: swim, fishing, playground. Pets OK. Partial handicap access. 2015 rates: $35. May 15 to Oct 13. No CC.
AAA Approved
(518)494-2280 Lat: 43.67559, Lon: -73.78074
1 Carl Turner Rd, Chestertown, NY 12817
info@riversidepines.com
www.riversidepines.com

CHURCHVILLE — D4 *Monroe*

Travel Services

CAMPING WORLD OF CHURCHVILLE As the nation's largest retailer of RV supplies, accessories, services and new and used RVs, Camping World is committed to making your total RV experience better. RV Accessories: (866)393-6438. **SERVICES:** Tire, RV appliance, MH mechanical, engine/chassis repair, staffed RV wash, restrooms, RV Sales. RV supplies, LP, dump, emergency parking, RV accessible. Hours: 8am to 6pm. (888)687-4042 Lat: 43.078175, Lon: -77.850348
1000 Sanford Road North, Churchville, NY 14428
tmicikiuk@campingworld.com
www.campingworld.com

To get the most out of your Guide, refer to the Table of Contents in the front of the book.

CLAYTON — B6 *Jefferson*

CEDAR POINT (State Pk) From Jct of SR-12 & SR-12E, SW 6 mi on SR-12E (R) Note: A $2.75 walk-up fee is also charged. 2015 rates: $15 to $27. May 3 to Oct 13. (315)654-2522

MERRY KNOLL 1000 ISLANDS CAMPGROUND
Ratings: 9/9.5★/9.5 (Campground) From Jct of SR-12 & SR-12E, S 2.5 mi on SR-12E (R). **FAC:** Paved rds. (75 spaces). Avail: 16 grass, 8 pull-thrus (30 x 50), back-ins (30 x 60), 16 full hkups (30/50 amps), seasonal sites, WiFi, tent sites, rentals, dump, mobile sewer, laundry, groc, fire rings, firewood. **REC:** pool, St Lawrence River: fishing, playground. Pet restrict(B). Big rig sites, eco-friendly, 2015 rates: $38 to $42. Disc: military. May 1 to Oct 15. No CC.
(315)686-3055 Lat: 44.22028, Lon: -76.12776
38115 Rt 12E, Clayton, NY 13624
mryknoll@gisco.net
www.merryknollcampground.com
See ad this page, 823.

CLEVELAND — D7 *Oneida*

WHISPERING WOODS CAMPGROUND **Ratings: 6.5/6.5/7** (Campground) 2015 rates: $36 to $44. May 1 to Oct 13. (315)675-8100 965 Stone Barn Rd, Cleveland, NY 13042

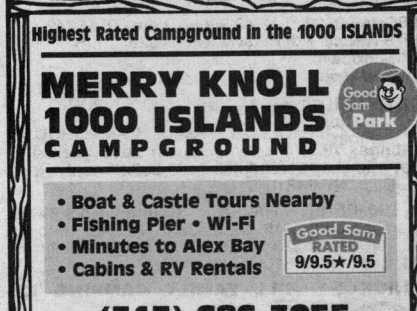

COLD BROOK — D8 *Herkimer*

TRAILS END CAMPGROUND **Ratings: 7/7/8** (Campground) 2015 rates: $33 to $56. May 1 to Oct 1. (315)826-7220 438 Macarthur Rd, Cold Brook, NY 13324

COLD SPRING — F9 *Putnam*

CLARENCE FAHNESTOCK MEMORIAL (State Pk) From jct Hwy-9 & Hwy-301: Go 8 mi E on Hwy-301. 2015 rates: $15 to $19. (845)225-7207

CONESUS — D4 *Livingston*

CONESUS LAKE CAMPGROUND **Ratings: 9/9★/8.5** (Campground) 2015 rates: $39 to $43. May 15 to Oct 15. (585)346-CAMP 5609 E Lake Rd, Conesus, NY 14435

COOPERSTOWN — D8 *Otsego*

COOPERSTOWN BEAVER VALLEY CABINS & CAMPSITES Ratings: 8/8.5/9 (Campground) From Jct of SR-28 & SR-80 (in Cooperstown), S 4 mi on SR-28 to Seminary Rd, NW 1.5 mi to Towers Rd, SW 1 mi (L). **FAC:** Gravel rds. (54 spaces). 46 Avail: 30 gravel, 16 grass, 9 pull-thrus (25 x 60), back-ins (25 x 40), 13 full hkups, 23 W, 23 E (30 amps), seasonal sites, WiFi, tent sites, rentals, showers $, dump, mobile sewer, laundry, groc, LP gas, fire rings, firewood. **REC:** heated pool, pond, Beaver Pond: fishing, playground, rec open to public. Pets OK. 2015 rates: $39 to $46. Disc: military. May 20 to Oct 14.
AAA Approved
(607)293-7324 Lat: 42.65370, Lon: -74.99923
138 Towers Rd, Milford, NY 13807
info@beavervalleycampground.com
www.beavervalleycampground.com

COOPERSTOWN KOA **Ratings: 8/9★/8.5** (Campground) 2015 rates: $49 to $60. May 1 to Oct 14. (315)858-0236 565 Ostrander Rd, Richfield Springs, NY 13439

COOPERSTOWN-SHADOW BROOK CAMPGROUND
Ratings: 9/10★/10 (Campground) From Jct of SR-80E & Main St, SE 0.75 mi on Main St (becomes CR-31), N 10 mi on CR-31 (L); or From Jct of US-20 & CR-31 (in E Springfield), S 1 mi on CR-31 (R). **FAC:** All weather rds. (97 spaces). 69 Avail: 32 gravel, 37 grass, 22 pull-thrus (30 x 50), back-ins (40 x 50), 19 full hkups, 50 W, 50 E (30/50 amps), seasonal sites, WiFi, tent sites, rentals, dump, mobile sewer, laundry, groc, LP gas, fire rings, firewood. **REC:** heated pool, pond, fishing, playground. Pet restrict(B). Partial handicap access. Big rig sites, 2015 rates: $36 to $54. Disc: military. May 6 to Oct 15.
(607)264-8431 Lat: 42.81622, Lon: -74.82526
2149 County Hwy 31, Cooperstown, NY 13326
reservations@cooperstowncamping.com
www.cooperstowncamping.com
See ad opposite page, 823.

HARTWICK HIGHLANDS CAMPGROUND
Ratings: 9.5/10★/9.5 (Campground) S-bnd: From Jct of SR-28 & SR-80 (in Cooperstown), S 4 mi on SR-28 to Seminary Rd, NW 1.5 mi (R); or N-bnd: From Jct of I-88 & SR-28 (Exit 17), N 12.5 mi on SR-28 to Seminary Rd, NW 1.5 mi (R). Do not use GPS. **FAC:** All weather rds. (57 spaces). Avail: 47 all weather, 15 pull-thrus (40 x 80), back-ins (40 x 70), 45 full hkups, 2 W, 2 E (30/50 amps), seasonal sites, WiFi, tent sites, rentals, dump, laundry, LP gas, fire rings, firewood, controlled access. **REC:** heated pool, playground. Pets OK. Partial handicap access. Big rig sites, 2015 rates: $47. May 15 to Oct 12. ATM.
(607)547-1996 Lat: 42.66006, Lon: -74.98296
131 Burke Hill Rd, Milford, NY 13807
camping@hartwickhighlandscg.com
www.hartwickhighlandscg.com
See ad this page.

MEADOW-VALE CAMPSITES
Ratings: 8.5/9★/9 (Campground) From Jct of I 88 & SR 205 (exit 13), N 11 mi on SR 205 to CR 11B in Mt Vision, W 0.25 mi on CR 11B and then follow campground signs for 6 mi (R). **FAC:** Gravel rds. (89 spaces). Avail: 32 gravel, 7 pull-thrus (35 x 70), back-ins (40 x 50), 32 W, 32 E (30/50 amps), seasonal sites, WiFi, tent sites, rentals, showers $, dump, mobile sewer, laundry, groc, LP gas, fire rings, firewood, controlled access. **REC:** pool, Meadow-Vale Lake: fishing, playground. Pets OK. 2015 rates: $38 to $42. Disc: military. May 13 to Oct 10.
(607)293-8802 Lat: 42.60516, Lon: -75.12328
505 Gilbert Lake Rd, Mount Vision, NY 13810
meadowvale@oecblue.com
www.meadow-vale.com
See ad this page, 823.

COPAKE — E10 *Columbia*

CAMP WAUBEEKA
Ratings: 7.5/8.5/8.5 (Campground) From Jct of SR-22 & SR-23, S 2.9 mi on SR-22 to Farm Rd (CR-7/7A), SW 1.7 mi (R). **FAC:** Paved/gravel rds. (324 spaces). Avail: 120 grass, 14 pull-thrus (35 x 60), back-ins (30 x 50), 120 full hkups (30/50 amps), seasonal sites, cable, WiFi $, tent sites, rentals, LP gas, fire rings, firewood, controlled access. **REC:** pond, swim, fishing, playground, rec open to public. Pet restrict(Q). Partial handicap access. Big rig sites, 2015 rates: $28 to $50. Disc: military. May 1 to Oct 15.
(518)329-4681 Lat: 42.11651, Lon: -73.54502
133 Farm Rd, Copake, NY 12516
info@campwaubeeka.com
www.campwaubeeka.com
See ad this page, 823.

COPAKE KOA Ratings: 9.5/10★/9.5 (Campground) From Jct of SR-22 & SR-23, S 2.9 mi on SR-22 to Farm Rd (CR-7/7A), SW 3 mi (L). **FAC:** All weather rds. (225 spaces). 120 Avail: 50 gravel, 70 grass, patios, 29 pull-thrus (40 x 125), back-ins (30 x 45), 120 full hkups (30/50 amps), seasonal sites, cable, WiFi, tent sites, rentals, laundry, groc, LP gas, fire rings, firewood, controlled access. **REC:** heated pool, playground. Pet restrict(B). Partial handicap access. Big rig sites, eco-friendly, 2015 rates: $55 to $78. Disc: military. May 9 to Oct 12. ATM.
(518)329-2811 Lat: 42.0931, Lon: -73.5806
2236 County Route 7, Copake, NY 12516
copake@hotmail.com
www.copakekoa.com

CORINTH — D9 *Saratoga*

ALPINE LAKE RV RESORT **Ratings: 8/7/8.5** (Campground) 2015 rates: $57 to $69. May 1 to Oct 12. (518)654-6260 78 Heath Rd, Corinth, NY 12822

RIVER ROAD CAMPGROUND **Ratings: 6.5/5.5/8** (Campground) 2015 rates: $45. May 25 to Oct 15. (518)654-6630 5254 Rte 9N, Corinth, NY 12822

NY

CORNING — E5 *Steuben*

CAMP BELL CAMPGROUND
Ratings: 8.5/9.5★/9 (Campground) From Jct of I-86 & SR-333 (exit 41), E 0.5 mi on SR-333 to SR-415, N 0.75 mi (L). **FAC:** Gravel rds. (89 spaces). Avail: 57 grass, 16 pull-thrus (25 x 55), back-ins (35 x 50), some side by side hkups, 57 W, 57 E (20/30 amps), seasonal sites, cable, WiFi, tent sites, rentals, dump, mobile sewer, laundry, groc, LP gas, fire rings, firewood. **REC:** heated pool, playground, rec open to public. Pets OK. Partial handicap access. 2015 rates: $32 to $39. Disc: AAA, military. May 1 to Oct 20.
(800)587-3301 Lat: 42.23565, Lon: -77.18454
8700 Sr 415, Campbell, NY 14821
info@campbellcampground.com
www.campbellcampground.com
See ad pages 828, 823.

FERENBAUGH CAMPGROUND
Ratings: 7.5/8★/9 (Campground) From Jct of I-86 (SR-17) & SR-414 (exit 46), N 5.2 mi on SR-414 (R). **FAC:** Gravel rds. (149 spaces). 119 Avail: 100 gravel, 19 grass, 40 pull-thrus (50 x 75), back-ins (50 x 60), 33 full hkups, 86 W, 86 E (30/50 amps), seasonal sites, cable, WiFi, tent sites, rentals, dump, mobile sewer, laundry, groc, LP

CORNING (CONT)

FERENBAUGH CAMPGROUND (CONT) gas, fire rings, firewood. **REC:** pool, pond, fishing, playground. Pets OK. Big rig sites, 2015 rates: $34 to $69. Disc: AAA, military. Apr 15 to Nov 1.
AAA Approved
(607)962-6193 Lat: 42.20272, Lon: -76.99130
4248 Sr 414, Corning, NY 14830
ferenbaugh@ferenbaugh.com
http://www.ferenbaugh.com
See ad this page.

CORTLAND — E6 *Cortland*

COUNTRY MUSIC PARK **Ratings: 5.5/9★/7.5** (Campground) 2015 rates: $28. Apr 15 to Oct 15. (607)753-0377 1824 State Route 13 N, Cortland, NY 13045

YELLOW LANTERN KAMPGROUND **Ratings: 7.5/7/7** (Campground) 2015 rates: $32 to $36. Apr 1 to Oct 30. (607)756-2959 1770 State Route 13 N, Cortland, NY 13045

CRANBERRY LAKE — B8 *St Lawrence*

CRANBERRY LAKE CAMPGROUND (ADIRONDACK SF) (State Pk) From town: Go 1-1/2 mi off Hwy 3. 2015 rates: $20. May 17 to Oct 26. (315)848-2315

CROWN POINT — B10 *Essex*

CROWN POINT CAMPGROUND (Public) From town, N 4 mi on Rtes 9 & 22N, E 4 mi on Bridge Rd, follow signs (R). 2015 rates: $18. May 17 to Oct 13. (518)597-3603

CUBA — E4 *Allegany*

MAPLE LANE CAMPGROUND Ratings: 5.5/8★/6 (Campground) From Jct of I-86 (SR-17) & SR-305 (exit 28), N 600 ft on SR-305 to Maple Lane (L). **FAC:** All weather rds. (46 spaces). Avail: 36 gravel, 24 pull-thrus (22 x 97), back-ins (30 x 35), some side by side hkups, 20 full hkups, 16 W, 16 E (30/50 amps), seasonal sites, WiFi, tent sites, rentals, dump, laundry, fire rings. Pets OK. Partial handicap access. Big rig sites, 2015 rates: $30 to $35. Disc: military. Apr 15 to Oct 30. No CC.
(585)968-1677 Lat: 42.22790, Lon: -78.27831
5233 Maple Lane, Cuba, NY 14727

CUDDEBACKVILLE — F8 *Orange*

DEERPARK/NEW YORK CITY NW KOA **Ratings: 8/10★/8** (Campground) 2015 rates: $49 to $77. (845)754-8388 108 Guymard Turnpike, Cuddebackville, NY 12729

DANSVILLE — E4 *Livingston, Steuben*

SKYBROOK CAMPGOUND INC **Ratings: 5.5/8.5★/7.5** (Campground) 2015 rates: $28 to $33. May 1 to Oct 1. (585)335-6880 10816 Mccurdy Rd, Dansville, NY 14437

STONY BROOK (State Pk) From town, S 3 mi on Hwy 36 (L) or Exit 4 on I-390, S 1.2 mi. 2015 rates: $15 to $19. May 3 to Oct 13. (585)335-8111

DARIEN CENTER — D3 *Genesee*

DARIEN LAKE THEME PARK RESORT **Ratings: 7.5/8/8.5** (Campground) 2015 rates: $89 to $244. May 10 to Oct 12. (585)599-2211 9993 Allegheny Rd, Darien Center, NY 14040

DARIEN LAKES (State Pk) From Jct of US-20 and Harlow Rd, N 0.25 mi on Harlow Rd (R). 2015 rates: $12 to $27. May 10 to Oct 20. (585)547-9242

SKYLINE RV RESORT INC
Ratings: 7.5/8.5★/7.5 (Campground) From Jct of US-20 & SR-238, SE 3 mi on SR-238 to Town Line Rd, N 0.5 mi (R). **FAC:** Paved/gravel rds. (325 spaces). Avail: 75 grass, 3 pull-thrus (35 x 60), back-ins (35 x 50), some side by side hkups, 12 full hkups, 63 W, 63 E (30/50 amps), seasonal sites, WiFi, showers $, dump, mobile sewer, groc, LP bottles, fire rings, firewood. **REC:** heated pool, pond, fishing, shuffleboard, playground. Pet restrict(B/Q). No tents. 2015 rates: $39 to $44. May 2 to Oct 13.
(585)591-2021 Lat: 42.88498, Lon: -78.30741
10933 Town Line Rd, Darien Center, NY 14040
Adele@skylinervresort.com
www.skylinervresort.com
See ad pages 839, 823.

DAVENPORT — E8 *Delaware*

BEAVER SPRING LAKE CAMPGROUND Ratings: 8/8.5★/8 (Campground) From Jct of I-88 (exit 15) & SR-23, E 12 mi on SR-23 to Beaver Spring Lake Rd. .25 mi (L) (Note: 3 night minimum on holiday weekends.). **FAC:** Gravel rds. (100 spaces). Avail: 70 grass, 16 pull-thrus (35 x 100), back-ins (35 x 100), 70 full hkups (30/50 amps), seasonal sites, WiFi, tent sites, rentals, dump, laundry, groc, LP gas, fire rings, firewood. **REC:** pool, Beaver Spring Lake: fishing, playground. Pets OK. Big rig sites, 2015 rates: $40 to $45. Disc: AAA, military. Apr 15 to Oct 31.
AAA Approved
(607)278-5293 Lat: 42.47681, Lon: -74.83337
263 Beaver Spring Rd, Davenport, NY 13750
bslcg@stny.rr.com
www.beaverspringlake.com

DEERLAND — B8 *Hamilton*

FORKED LAKE CAMPGROUND (ADIRONDACK SF) (State Pk) From business center: Go 3 mi W off Hwy-30 (access by foot or boat only). Pit toilets. 2015 rates: $18. May 17 to Sep 1. (518)624-6646

DEWITTVILLE — E2 *Chautauqua*

CHAUTAUQUA LAKE KOA
Ratings: 10/10★/10 (Campground) From Jct of I-86/SR-17 & SR-430 (exit 10), W 6 mi on SR-430 to Thum Rd, E 0.5 mi (L) Note: Min 3 day stay on holiday weekends. **FAC:** All weather rds. (246 spaces). Avail: 10 paved, 101 all weather, patios, 106 pull-thrus (50 x 80), back-ins (40 x 60), 84 full hkups, 27 W, 27 E (30/50 amps), seasonal sites, cable, WiFi, tent sites, rentals, dump, laundry, groc, LP gas, fire rings, firewood, controlled access. **REC:** heated pool, playground. Pet restrict(B). Partial handicap access. Big rig sites, 2015 rates: $39 to $64. Disc: military. May 1 to Oct 15.
(716)386-3804 Lat: 42.22885, Lon: -79.42983
5652 Thum Rd, Dewittville, NY 14728
camping@chautauqualakekoa.com
www.chautauqualakekoa.com
See ad page 826.

DEXTER — B7 *Jefferson*

BLACK RIVER BAY CAMPGROUND **Ratings: 6.5/6.5/8.5** (Campground) 2015 rates: $36 to $38. May 1 to Oct 15. (315)639-3735 16129 Foster Park Rd, Dexter, NY 13634

DUANE — A9 *Franklin*

ADIRONDACK/MEACHAM LAKE (State Pk) From town, S 21 mi on Hwy 30 (L). 2015 rates: $20. May 18 to Oct 7. (518)483-5116

EAST HAMPTON — A5 *Suffolk*

CEDAR POINT (SUFFOLK COUNTY PARK) (Public) From town: Go E on Hwy 27 (Montauk Hwy), then N on Stephens Hands Path to Old Northwest Rd, then follow signs to Alewive Brook Rd. (631)852-7620

EAST SPRINGFIELD — D8 *Otsego*

GLIMMERGLASS (State Pk) From town, E 3 mi on Mainstreet to CR-31, N 7 mi (L). 2015 rates: $15. May 10 to Oct 13. (607)547-8662

ELIZAVILLE — E9 *Columbia*

BROOK N WOOD FAMILY CAMPGROUND
Ratings: 8/8/9.5 (Campground) From Jct US 9 and Rte 23: Go 10 mi S to CR 8, then left on CR 8, then E 1 mi (R). From Jct US 9 and SR 199: Go 9 mi N on US 9 to CR 8, E 1 mi (R). **FAC:** Gravel rds. (150 spaces). 105 Avail: 7 gravel, 98 grass, 5 pull-thrus (30 x 80), back-ins (30 x 50), 96 full hkups, 9 W, 9 E (30/50 amps), seasonal sites, cable, WiFi, tent sites, rentals, dump, laundry, groc, LP gas, fire rings, firewood. **REC:** heated pool, Doove Kill Creek: fishing, playground. Pet restrict(B). Age restrict may apply, big rig sites, eco-friendly, 2015 rates: $46 to $55. Disc: military. Apr 25 to Oct 31.
(888)625-3186 Lat: 42.09116, Lon: -73.78814
1947 County Rt 8, Elizaville, NY 12523
camp@brooknwood.com
www.brooknwood.com
See ad pages 841, 823.

Treat your pet to a fabulous camping experience by staying at one of the Pampered Pet Parks featured in the front of the Guide. Many of the parks on this list offer perks like dog runs, dog washing stations and dog walking services. Some of the parks even conduct pet parades during special holidays.

ELLENVILLE — F9 *Ulster*

JELLYSTONE PARK (TM) AT BIRCHWOOD ACRES
Ratings: 10/9.5★/9.5 (Campground) From Jct of SR-209 & SR-52 (in Ellenville), W 8.5 mi on SR-52 to Martinfeld Rd, S 1 mi (L).

THE FINEST CAMPING IN THE CATSKILLS
Nestled in the foothills of the New York Catskill Mountains, this family-friendly resort is sure to create memories that last a lifetime! Amenities include a 5-acre fishing lake, swimming and splash pool, and jumping pillow!

FAC: All weather rds. (273 spaces). Avail: 215 all weather, back-ins (40 x 60), 112 full hkups, 103 W, 103 E (30/50 amps), seasonal sites, cable, WiFi, tent sites, rentals, dump, laundry, groc, LP gas, fire rings, firewood. **REC:** heated pool, whirlpool, Birchwood Lake: fishing, shuffleboard, playground. Pet restrict(Q). Partial handicap access. Big rig sites, 2015 rates: $75 to $77. May 1 to Oct 12.
AAA Approved
(888)726-4073 Lat: 41.739768, Lon: -74.54472
85 Martinfeld Road, Greenfield Park, NY 12345
jellystonebirchwood@suncommunities.com
www.nyjellystone.com
See ad pages 1463 (Welcome Section), 823, 821 (Welcome Section) & Family Camping in Magazine Section.

SKYWAY CAMPING RESORT INC
Ratings: 10/10★/10 (Campground) From Jct of SR-52 & US-209 (in Ellenville), W 5 mi on SR-52 to Mountaindale Rd., SW 1.2 mi (L). **FAC:** All weather rds. (147 spaces). Avail: 67 all weather, back-ins (35 x 65), 67 full hkups (30/50 amps), seasonal sites, cable, WiFi, tent sites, rentals, laundry, groc, LP gas, fire rings, firewood. **REC:** heated pool, whirlpool, Skyway Lake: fishing, shuffleboard, playground. Pets OK. Partial handicap access. Big rig sites, eco-friendly, 2015 rates: $59 to $69. Disc: military. May 1 to Oct 14.
(800)447-5992 Lat: 41.72902, Lon: -74.50907
99 Mountaindale Rd, Greenfield Park, NY 12435
skywaycamping@gmail.com
www.skywaycamping.com
See ad this page, 823.

ENDICOTT — E7 *Broome*

PINE VALLEY RV PARK & CAMPGROUND Ratings: 7.5/8/8 (Campground) From Jct of SR-17 & SR-17C (Exit 66), E 3.5 mi on SR-17C to Glendale Dr, N 1.75 mi on (Glendale Dr becomes Leona), to Day Hollow Rd, W 0.5 mi on Day Hollow Rd to Boswell Hill Rd, N 2.5 mi (R). Note: GPS users call to verify. **FAC:** Gravel rds. (115 spaces). 60 Avail: 47 grass, 13 dirt, 2 pull-thrus (45 x 80), back-ins (45 x 60), 32 full hkups, 28 W, 28 E (30/50 amps), seasonal sites, WiFi $, tent sites, dump, mobile sewer, laundry, groc, LP gas, fire rings, firewood, controlled access. **REC:** pond, swim, fishing, playground. Pets OK. Partial handicap access. Big rig sites, 2015 rates: $30 to $39. May 1 to Sep 30.
(607)785-6868 Lat: 42.14686, Lon: -76.09034
600 Boswell Hill Rd, Endicott, NY 13760
pinevalley@baka.com
www.pinevalleycampground.com

FAIR HAVEN — C6 *Cayuga, Wayne*

FAIR HAVEN BEACH (State Pk) From city, N 2 mi on park rd (E). 2015 rates: $15 to $25. Apr 11 to Oct 19. (315)947-5205

HOLIDAY HARBOR CAMPGROUND & MARINA Ratings: 6/8/7.5 (Campground) From Jct of SR-104 & SR-104A, E 3.5 mi on SR-104 to Blind Sodus Bay Rd, N 3 mi to park entrance (L). **FAC:** Gravel rds. (105 spaces). 24 Avail: 4 gravel, 20 grass, back-ins (40 x 70), some side by side hkups, 1 full hkups, 23 W, 23 E (30/50 amps), seasonal sites, WiFi, tent sites, showers $, dump, laundry, fire rings, firewood. **REC:** Lake Ontario: fishing, marina, playground. Pets OK. Partial handicap access. 2015 rates: $26 to $33. Disc: AAA. Apr 15 to Oct 15. No CC.
AAA Approved
(315)947-5244 Lat: 43.33636, Lon: -76.73473
9415 Blind Sodus Bay Rd, Red Creek, NY 13143
holidayharborrvpark@ymail.com
www.holidayharborrv.com

FAYETTEVILLE — D7 *Onondaga*

GREEN LAKES (State Pk) From I-481 Exit 5E, W 2.9 mi on CH-53, S 2.4 mi on CH-55, w 2.3 mi on SH-290. 2015 rates: $15 to $21. May 10 to Oct 13. (315)637-6111

FLORIDA — A2 *Orange*

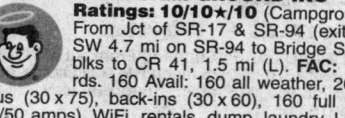

BLACK BEAR CAMPGROUND INC
Ratings: 10/10★/10 (Campground) From Jct of SR-17 & SR-94 (exit 126), SW 4.7 mi on SR-94 to Bridge St, W 2 blks to CR 41, 1.5 mi (L). **FAC:** Paved rds. 160 Avail: 160 all weather, 20 pull-thrus (30 x 75), back-ins (30 x 60), 160 full hkups (30/50 amps), WiFi, rentals, dump, laundry, LP bottles, fire rings, firewood. **REC:** pool, pond, fishing, shuffleboard, playground. Pet restrict(B). Partial handicap access, no tents. Big rig sites, 2015 rates: $60 to $80. Disc: military.
(845)651-7717 Lat: 41.32242, Lon: -74.37340
197 Wheeler Rd, Florida, NY 10921
info@blackbearcampground.com
www.blackbearcampground.com
See ad pages 837, 823.

FORESTPORT — C8 *Oneida*

KAYUTA LAKE CAMPGROUND **Ratings: 8.5/7/8.5** (Campground) 2015 rates: $37 to $47. May 1 to Oct 15. (315)831-5077 10892 Campground Rd, Forestport, NY 13338

FORT ANN — C10 *Washington*

MOOSE HILLOCK CAMPING RESORT-NY **Ratings: 9.5/9.5★/8.5** (Campground) 2015 rates: $49 to $80. May 16 to Oct 12. (518)792-4500 10366 St Rt - 149, Fort Ann, NY 12827

FRANKLINVILLE — E3 *Cattaraugus*

TRIPLE R CAMPING RESORT & TRAILER SALES Ratings: 10/10★/10 (Campground) S-bnd: From Jct of SR-98 & SR-16, S 1.9 mi on SR-16 to Elm St (traffic light), W 1.5 mi to Bryant Hill Rd, W 0.3 mi (L); or N-bnd: From Jct of I-86 (SR-17) & SR-16 (Exit 27), N 12 mi on SR-16 to Elm St (traffic light), W 1.5 mi to Bryant Hill Rd, W 0.3 mi (L). **FAC:** All weather rds. (218 spaces). Avail: 54 all weather, patios, 24 pull-thrus (45 x 70), back-ins (45 x 65), 54 full hkups (30/50 amps), seasonal sites, cable, WiFi, tent sites, rentals, dump, mobile sewer, laundry, groc, LP gas, fire rings, firewood, restaurant, controlled access. **REC:** heated pool, wading pool, pond, fishing, playground. Pets OK. Partial handicap access. Big rig sites, eco-friendly, 2015 rates: $44. Disc: AAA, military. Apr 15 to Oct 15.
(716)676-3856 Lat: 42.33503, Lon: -78.49229
3491 Bryant Hill Rd, Franklinville, NY 14737
info@triplercamp.com
www.triplercamp.com

FULTON — C6 *Oswego*

NORTH BAY CAMPGROUNDS (Public) From Jct of SR-3 & SR-481, W 1.3 mi on SR-3 to Phillips St, S 0.1 mi (E). 2015 rates: $17 to $20. May 15 to Sep 15. (315)592-2256

GABRIELS — B9 *Franklin*

BUCK POND CAMPGROUND (State Pk) From town, NE 0.5 mi on CR-30 (L). 2015 rates: $20. May 19 to Sep 7. (518)891-3449

GAINESVILLE — D4 *Wyoming*

WOODSTREAM CAMPSITE
Ratings: 7.5/8.5/9 (Campground) From Jct of SR-19 & SR-78 (N of town), S 1.5 mi on SR-19 to School Rd, E 0.5 mi (R). **FAC:** Gravel rds. (220 spaces). 110 Avail: 14 gravel, 96 grass, 14 pull-thrus (50 x 70), back-ins (50 x 50), some side by side hkups, 15 full hkups, 95 W, 94 E (30/50 amps), seasonal sites, WiFi Hotspot, tent sites, rentals, showers $, dump, mobile sewer, laundry, groc, LP gas, fire rings, firewood. **REC:** pond, swim, fishing, playground. Pets OK. Big rig sites, 2015 rates: $27 to $40. May 1 to Oct 15.
(877)226-7669 Lat: 42.63011, Lon: -78.12268
5440 School Rd, Gainesville, NY 14066
www.woodstreamcampsite.com
See ad this page.

GALWAY — D9 *Saratoga*

MCCONCHIE'S HERITAGE ACRES **Ratings: 7/6.5/6.5** (Campground) 2015 rates: $27 to $32. May 1 to Oct 1. (518)882-6605 2501 Northline Rd, Galway, NY 12074

GANSEVOORT — D10 *Saratoga*

ADIRONDACK GATEWAY CAMPGROUND
Ratings: 7.5/7.5/8 (RV Park) From Jct of I-87 & US-9 (exit 17N), N 0.25 mi on US-9 to Fawn Rd, E 0.25 mi to Fortsville Rd, S 0.25 mi (R). **FAC:** Gravel rds. (339 spaces). 119 Avail: 50 gravel, 32 grass, 37 dirt, 40 pull-thrus (35 x 50), back-ins (20 x 45), some side by side hkups, 15 full hkups, 104 W, 104 E (30/50 amps), seasonal sites, cable, WiFi Hotspot $, tent sites, rentals, dump, mobile sewer, laundry, LP gas, fire rings, firewood, controlled access. **REC:** pool, pond, fishing, playground. Pet restrict(Q). Partial handicap access. 2015 rates: $33 to $53. Disc: AAA, military. May 1 to Oct 15.
(518)792-0485 Lat: 43.23417, Lon: -73.68325
427 Fortsville Rd, Gansevoort, NY 12831
info@adirondackgatewaycampgrounds.com
www.AdirondackGatewayCampgrounds.com
See ad pages 840, 823.

COLDBROOK CAMPSITES
Ratings: 8/8.5/8 (Campground) From Jct of I 87 & Ballard Rd (Exit 16), E 100 yds on Ballard Rd to Gurn Springs Rd, N 0.6 mi (R). **FAC:** Gravel rds. (269 spaces). 119 Avail: 110 gravel, 9 grass, 7 pull-thrus (40 x 60), back-ins (50 x 50), 119 full hkups (30/50 amps), seasonal sites, cable, WiFi $, tent sites, dump, laundry, LP gas, fire rings, firewood. **REC:** pool, pond, fishing, playground. Pet restrict(Q). Partial handicap access. Big rig sites, 2015 rates: $38 to $46. Disc: AAA, military. May 1 to Oct 15.
(518)584-8038 Lat: 43.17547, Lon: -73.70387
385 Gurnsprings Rd, Gansevoort, NY 12831
coldbrookcampgrounds@gmail.com
www.ColdbrookResortCampgrounds.com
See ad this page, 823.

SARATOGA RV PARK **Ratings: 6.5/6/8** (Campground) 2015 rates: $35 to $45. May 15 to Oct 15. (518)798-1913 4894 Rte 50, Gansevoort, NY 12831

GARDINER — F9 *Ulster*

YOGI BEAR'S JELLYSTONE PARK AT LAZY RIVER Ratings: 9/9.5★/9.5 (Campground) From Jct of US-44/55 & SR-32, W 4 mi on US-44/55 to Albany Post Rd, S 0.2 mi (across bridge) to Bevier Rd, E 0.5 mi (L). **FAC:** Paved rds. (144 spaces). 94 Avail: 90 gravel, 4 grass, 30 pull-thrus (30 x 80), back-ins (30 x 80), 78 full hkups, 16 W, 16 E (30/50 amps), seasonal sites, cable, WiFi Hotspot, tent sites, rentals, dump, mobile sewer, laundry, groc, LP gas, fire rings, firewood, controlled access. **REC:** heated pool, Wallkill River: fishing, shuffleboard, playground. Pets OK. Partial handicap access. Big rig sites, 2015 rates: $45 to $93. Disc: military. Apr 16 to Nov 1.
(845)255-5193 Lat: 41.68324, Lon: -74.16542
50 Bevier Rd, Gardiner, NY 12525
rangersmith@lazyriverny.com
www.lazyriverny.com

GARRATTSVILLE — E8 *Otsego*

YOGI BEAR'S JELLYSTONE PARK AT CRYSTAL LAKE **Ratings: 9/8★/8** (Campground) 2015 rates: $43 to $53. May 9 to Oct 13. (607)965-8265 111 E Turtle Lake Rd, Garrattsville, NY 13342

GASPORT — D3 *Niagara*

NIAGARA HARTLAND RV RESORT Ratings: 6.5/6/7.5 (Campground) E-bnd: From Jct of I-90 & SR-78 (exit 49), N 19 mi on SR-78 to SR-104, E 6.3 mi to Hartland Rd, N 3.9 mi (R); or W-bnd: From Jct of I-90 & SR-77 (exit 48A), NE 21 mi on SR-77 to Gasport Rd, N 10 mi (R). **FAC:** Gravel rds. (115 spaces). Avail: 50 gravel, 15 pull-thrus (28 x 70), back-ins (40 x 50), 50 full hkups (30/50 amps), seasonal sites, tent sites, dump, laundry, groc, fire rings, firewood. **REC:** Lake Charles: swim, fishing, playground. Pet restrict(B). Big rig sites, 2015 rates: $32. Disc: AAA, military. May 15 to Oct 15.
AAA Approved
(800)571-4829 Lat: 43.29232, Lon: -78.57070
2383 Hartland Rd, Gasport, NY 14067
www.niagarahartlandrv.com

GILBOA — E9 *Schoharie*

COUNTRY ROADS CAMPGROUND
Ratings: 8.5/7/7.5 (Campground) From Jct of SR-23 & SR-30 (Grand Gorge), N 3 mi on SR-30 to SR-990V (Gilboa), N on Wycoff Rd (changes to Kingsley Rd), N 1.7 mi to Peaceful Rd, W 0.3 (E). Call for alternate directions. **FAC:** Gravel rds. (104 spaces). 66 Avail: 43 gravel, 23 grass, 2 pull-thrus (30 x 60), back-ins (45 x 60), 62 full hkups, 4 W, 4 E (20/30 amps), seasonal sites, WiFi, tent sites, rentals, showers $, dump, laundry, groc, fire rings, firewood. **REC:** pool, whirlpool, playground. Pets OK. 2015 rates: $41 to $43. Disc: AAA. May 15 to Oct 12.
AAA Approved
(518)827-6397 Lat: 42.43206, Lon: -74.42739
144 Peaceful Rd, Gilboa, NY 12076
camp@countryroadscampground.com
www.countryroadscampground.com
See ad this page.

NICKERSON PARK CAMPGROUND
Ratings: 9/10★/8.5 (Campground) From jct Hwy 23 & Hwy 30: Go 5-1/2 mi N on Hwy 30, then 1 mi E on Stryker Rd (CR 13). **FAC:** Gravel rds. (282 spaces). Avail: 169 grass, back-ins (50 x 50), 95 full hkups, 74 W, 74 E (30/50 amps), seasonal sites, cable, WiFi, tent sites, dump, mobile sewer, laundry, groc, LP gas, fire rings, firewood. **REC:** pool, Schoharie Creek: swim, fishing, playground. Pets OK. Big rig sites, 2015 rates: $42 to $44. May 1 to Oct 15.
(607)588-7327 Lat: 42.41364, Lon: -74.46341
378 Stryker Rd, Gilboa, NY 12076
info@nickersonparkcampground.com
www.nickersonparkcampground.com
See ad this page.

GLENS FALLS — C10 *Warren*

MOREAU LAKE (State Pk) From Jct of US-87 & Rte 9 (exit 17S), S 0.25 mi on Rte 9 to Old Saratoga Rd, 0.5 mi (R). 2015 rates: $15 to $19. May 3 to Sep 1. (518)793-0511

GLENWOOD — E3 *Erie*

SPRAGUE BROOK PARK (Public) From Jct of SR 39 & SR 240, N 6 mi on SR 240 to Foute Rd, E 0.3 mi on Foute Rd to second entrance (L) Checks or money orders only. 2015 rates: $15 to $22. (716)592-2804

GREENPORT — A5 *Suffolk*

EASTERN LONG ISLAND KAMPGROUND INC **Ratings: 8/9/8.5** (Campground) 2015 rates: $70 to $80. May 1 to Nov 1. (631)477-0022 690 Queen St, Greenport, NY 11944

MCCANN'S TRAILER PARK & CAMPGROUND (Public) From Jct of CR-48 & Moores Ln, S 0.5 mi on Moores Ln (L). 2015 rates: $35. May 1 to Oct 31. (631)477-0043

HAINES FALLS — E9 *Greene*

NORTH/SOUTH LAKE (State Pk) From Jct of Rte 23A & CR-18, NE 3 mi on CR-18 (E). 2015 rates: $22. May 4 to Oct 12. (518)589-5058

HAMBURG — D3 *Erie*

Travel Services

CAMPING WORLD OF HAMBURG/BUFFALO
As the nation's largest retailer of RV supplies, accessories, services and new and used RVs, Camping World is committed to making your total RV experience better. RV Accessories: (855)660-3857. **SERVICES:** RV appliance, MH mechanical, staffed RV wash, restrooms, RV Sales. RV supplies, LP, RV accessible. Hours: 8am - 6pm. (888)668-8973 Lat: 42.735545, Lon: -78.840574
5533 Camp Road, Hamburg, NY 14075
www.campingworld.com

Tell them you saw them in this Guide!

HAMILTON — D7 *Madison*

LEBANON RESERVOIR CAMPGROUND **Ratings: 7/8.5/9** (Campground) 2015 rates: $35 to $45. May 15 to Oct 15. (315)824-2278 6277 Reservoir Rd, Hamilton, NY 13346

HAMLIN — C4 *Monroe*

HAMLIN BEACH (State Pk) From business center: Go 4 mi N on Hwy 19, then 2 mi W on Lake Ontario Pkwy. 2015 rates: $21 to $25. May 10 to Oct 20. (585)964-2462

HAMPTON BAYS — A4 *Suffolk*

SEARS BELLOWS (SUFFOLK COUNTY PARK) (Public) From Sunrise Hwy (Hwy 27, exit 65N): Go N on Bellows Pond Rd. (631)852-8290

HENDERSON HARBOR — C6 *Jefferson*

KOA 1000 ISLANDS AT ASSOCIATION ISLAND
Ratings: 10/10★/9 (Campground) From Jct of I-81 & Rt 178 (Exit 41), W 9 mi on Rt 178 to Snowshoe Rd, NW 2.5 mi to end, cross causeway to island (E) CAUTION: Registration and security gate closed at 8:00pm. Note: Min 3 day stay on holiday weekends.

ONE-OF-A-KIND-ISLAND GETAWAY!
Watch world class sunsets or sunrises from our unique island resort located a mile into Lake Ontario, accessed by Causeway. Enjoy activities on-site or in the local Thousand Islands Region. All RVers are welcome to have fun!

FAC: Paved rds. (305 spaces). Avail: 260 all weather, 26 pull-thrus (40 x 85), back-ins (35 x 60), 260 full hkups (30/50 amps), seasonal sites, WiFi, tent sites, rentals, dump, laundry, groc, fire rings, firewood, controlled access. **REC:** pool, Lake Ontario: fishing, shuffleboard, playground. Pet restrict(B/Q). Partial handicap access. Big rig sites, 2015 rates: $35 to $80. Disc: military. May 15 to Oct 12. ATM.
(800)393-4189 Lat: 43.88678, Lon: -76.23120
15530 Snowshoe Rd, Henderson, NY 13650
info@associationislandkoa.com
www.associationislandkoa.com
See ad this page.

THE "WILLOWS" ON THE LAKE RV PARK & RESORT **Ratings: 7.5/7/9** (Campground) 2015 rates: $38 to $45. Apr 15 to Oct 15. (315)938-5977 11609 Sr 3, Adams, NY 13605

HERKIMER — D8 *Herkimer*

HERKIMER DIAMOND CAMPGROUND KOA **Ratings: 8/9/9** (Campground) 2015 rates: $35 to $69. Apr 15 to Oct 31. (315)891-7355 4626 Sr 28N, Herkimer, NY 13350

Park policies vary. Ask about the cancellation policy when making a reservation.

HOLLAND — D3 *Erie*

THREE VALLEY RESORT **Ratings: 6.5/3/4.5** (Membership Pk) 2015 rates: $40. Apr 15 to Sep 15. (716)537-2372 9766 Olean Rd/Rt 16, Holland, NY 14080

HOLLEY — D4 *Orleans*

HICKORY RIDGE GOLF & RV RESORT
Ratings: 9.5/9.5★/8.5 (RV Park) From Jct of SR 104 & SR 387 (Fancher Rd), S 3.3 mi on SR 387 (Fancher Rd) to Padelford Rd, continue S 0.2 mi on Padelford Rd to Lynch Rd, W 500 ft (L) Note: 3 day minimum on holidays. **FAC:** All weather rds. (71 spaces). Avail: 43 all weather, 32 pull-thrus (40 x 80), back-ins (40 x 75), 40 full hkups, 3 W, 3 E (30/50 amps), seasonal sites, cable, WiFi, tent sites, rentals, dump, laundry, groc, LP gas, fire rings, firewood, restaurant. **REC:** pool, Lake McCargo: fishing, golf, playground. Pets OK. Partial handicap access. Big rig sites, 2015 rates: $44 to $56. May 1 to Oct 31.
(585)638-0220 Lat: 43.14041, Lon: -78.5569
15870 Lynch Rd, Holley, NY 14470
rvinfo@hickoryridgegolfresort.com
www.hickoryridgegolfresort.com
See ad opposite page, 823.

RED ROCK PONDS RV RESORT **Ratings: 9/9★/10** (Campground) 2015 rates: $40 to $52. May 1 to Oct 18. (585)638-2445 16097 Canal Rd, Holley, NY 14470

Things to See and Do

HICKORY RIDGE GOLF COURSE An 18-hole championship golf course, snack shop, golf packages & on-site golf cart rentals. May 1 to Oct 31. RV accessible. Restrooms. Hours: 7:00 to 6:00. Adult fee: $21 to $28.
(585)638-4653 Lat: 43.23479, Lon: -78.09894
15870 Lynch Rd, Holley, NY 14470
info@hickoryridgegolfresort.com
www.hickoryridgegolfresort.com
See ad opposite page.

HOUGHTON — E4 *Allegany*

HOUGHTON/LETCHWORTH KOA **Ratings: 8.5/7.5/8** (Campground) 2015 rates: $40 to $47. May 1 to Oct 15. (585)567-4211 7632 Centerville Rd, Houghton, NY 14744

HUDSON — E10 *Columbia*

LAKE TAGHKANIC (State Pk) From business center: Go 11 mi S on Hwy-82. 2015 rates: $15 to $19. May 10 to Oct 19. (518)851-3631

HUNTER — E9 *Greene*

DEVIL'S TOMBSTONE (State Pk) From Jct of Hwy 214 & SR-23A, S 4 mi on Hwy 214 (E). Pit toilets. 2015 rates: $16. May 19 to Sep 7. (845)688-7160

HURLEYVILLE — F8 *Sullivan*

MORNINGSIDE PARK (Public) From Jct of Rte 17 & Exit 107, N 5 mi on CR-161 to Rte 42, N 2 mi to Brickman Rd, W 2 mi (R). 2015 rates: $20 to $35. May 22 to Oct 12. (845)434-5877

INDIAN LAKE — C9 *Hamilton*

ADIRONDACK/LEWEY LAKE (State Pk) From town, S 12 mi on Hwy 30 (R). 2015 rates: $20. May 18 to Oct 7. (518)648-5266

INLET — C8 *Hamilton*

ADIRONDACK/LIMEKILN LAKE (State Pk) From town, E 1 mi on Hwy 28, S 2 mi (R). Entrance fee required. 2015 rates: $20. May 18 to Sep 2. (315)357-4401

ITHACA — E6 *Tompkins*

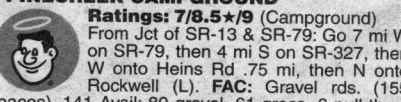

PINECREEK CAMPGROUND
Ratings: 7/8.5★/9 (Campground) From Jct of SR-13 & SR-79: Go 7 mi W on SR-79, then 4 mi S on SR-327, then W onto Heins Rd .75 mi, then N onto Rockwell (L). **FAC:** Gravel rds. (155 spaces). 141 Avail: 80 gravel, 61 grass, 6 pull-thrus (40 x 60), back-ins (30 x 55), some side by side hkups, 56 full hkups, 85 W, 85 E (30/50 amps), seasonal sites, WiFi Hotspot, tent sites, rentals, dump, laundry, groc, LP gas, fire rings, firewood. **REC:** pool, pond, fishing, playground. Pet restrict(B). 2015 rates: $32 to $48. Disc: military. May 1 to Oct 15.
(607)273-1974 Lat: 42.407555, Lon: -76.611647
28 Rockwell Rd, Newfield, NY 14867
info@pinecreekcampground.com
www.pinecreekcampground.com
See ad this page, 823.

ROBERT H TREMAN (State Pk) From Jct of SR-13 & Rte 327, W 0.25 mi on Rte 327 (L). 2015 rates: $15 to $21. Apr 19 to Nov 16. (607)273-3440

SPRUCE ROW CAMPGROUND & RV PARK
Ratings: 7.5/8.5/9 (Campground) From Jct of SR-13 & SR-96, N 7 mi on SR-96 to Jacksonville Rd, N 0.4 mi on Jacksonville Rd to Kraft Rd, E 1 mi (R). Note: 3 day min stay on holiday weekend. **FAC:** Gravel rds. (180 spaces). Avail: 90 grass, 5 pull-thrus (50 x 65), back-ins (50 x 65), some side by side hkups, 23 full hkups, 67 W, 67 E (20/30 amps), seasonal sites, WiFi, tent sites, rentals, dump, mobile sewer, groc, LP gas, fire rings, firewood. **REC:** pool, pond, fishing, playground. Pet restrict(B). Partial handicap access. 2015 rates: $32 to $39. May 1 to Oct 12.
(607)387-9225 Lat: 42.51597, Lon: -76.58714
2271 Kraft Rd, Ithaca, NY 14850
sprucerowcampground@yahoo.com
www.sprucerow.com
See ad this page, 823.

TAUGHANNOCK FALLS (State Pk) From business center: Go 8 mi N on Hwy-89. 2015 rates: $15 to $19. (607)387-6739

JAMESTOWN — E2 *Chautauqua*

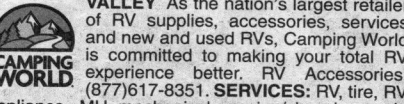

HIDDEN VALLEY CAMPING AREA
Ratings: 8.5/10★/9.5 (Campground) From the jct of Exit I-86 at Exit 11 (Strunk Rd), S 0.4 mi on Strunk Rd to State 430 (Fluvanna Ave), E 1.5 mi on Fluvanna to Washington St, S 4.2 mi on Washington St (US-60 Truck Route) to Kiantone Rd(CR-49), S 4.4 mi on Kiantone Rd (R). CAUTION: AVOID EXIT 12 ON I-86 LOW CLEARANCE. **FAC:** Gravel rds. (225 spaces). Avail: 50 grass, 14 pull-thrus (28 x 60), back-ins (40 x 40), 50 W, 50 E (30/50 amps), seasonal sites, cable, WiFi, tent sites, rentals, dump, mobile sewer, laundry, groc, LP gas, fire rings, firewood. **REC:** pool, Kiantone Creek: fishing, playground. Pets OK. Eco-friendly, 2015 rates: $35 to $44. Disc: military. Apr 15 to Oct 15.
(716)569-5433 Lat: 42.006430, Lon: -79.182245
299 Kiantone Rd, Jamestown, NY 14701
hiddenvalley@hiddenvalleycampingarea.com
www.hiddenvalleycampingarea.com
See ad this page, 823.

County names help you follow the local weather report.

JAVA CENTER — D3 *Wyoming*

BEAVER MEADOW FAMILY CAMPGROUND **Ratings: 7.5/7/8** (Campground) 2015 rates: $30 to $45. May 1 to Oct 13. (585)457-3101 1455 Beaver Meadow Rd, Java Center, NY 14082

JOHNSTOWN — D9 *Fulton*

ROYAL MOUNTAIN CAMPSITES **Ratings: 6.5/7/8.5** (Campground) 2015 rates: $30. Apr 15 to Oct 15. (877)725-9838 4948 Hwy 29, Johnstown, NY 12095

KEUKA PARK — E5 *Yates*

KEUKA LAKE (State Pk) From Jct of Hwy 54A & Hwy 14A, SW 6 mi on Hwy 54A to Pepper Rd, S 0.25 mi (R). Pets need rabies certification. 2015 rates: $15 to $21. May 3 to Oct 20. (315)536-3666

KINGSTON — F9 *Ulster*

Travel Services

CAMPING WORLD OF KINGSTON/HUDSON VALLEY As the nation's largest retailer of RV supplies, accessories, services and new and used RVs, Camping World is committed to making your total RV experience better. RV Accessories: (877)617-8351. **SERVICES:** RV, tire, RV appliance, MH mechanical, engine/chassis repair, mobile RV svc, staffed RV wash, restrooms, RV Sales. **TOW:** RV. RV supplies, LP, emergency parking, RV accessible. Hours: 8am to 6pm.
(888)872-8949 Lat: 41.945873, Lon: -74.03013
124 New York 28/Onteora Trail, Kingston, NY 12401
www.campingworld.com

LAKE GEORGE — C10 *Warren*

ADIRONDACK CAMPING VILLAGE
Ratings: 8.5/10★/9 (Campground) N-bnd: From Jct of I-87 & US-9 (exit 22), N 1.5 mi on US-9 (R); or S-bnd: From Jct of I-87 & US-9 (exit 23), S 2.5 mi on US-9 (L). **FAC:** All weather rds. (175 spaces). Avail: 150 dirt, 12 pull-thrus (30 x 60), back-ins (30 x 42), 87 full hkups, 63 W, 63 E (30/50 amps), seasonal sites, cable, WiFi Hotspot, tent sites, rentals, dump, laundry, groc, fire rings, firewood, controlled access. **REC:** heated pool, wading pool, shuffleboard, playground. Pets OK. Big rig sites, 2015 rates: $31 to $59. Disc: AAA, military. May 15 to Sep 15.
AAA Approved
(518)668-5226 Lat: 43.45428, Lon: -73.73279
43 Finkle Farm Rd, Lake George, NY 12845
info@adirondackcampingvillage.com
www.adirondackcampingvillage.com
See ad this page.

We appreciate your business!

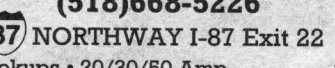

LAKE GEORGE RV PARK
1966 CELEBRATING 50 YEARS! 2016
50 Years of Fun!
JOIN THE CELEBRATION AT LAKE GEORGE RV PARK!
Enjoy thrilling camping enhanced by amazing amenities at our beautiful Adirondack resort. Make treasured memories with us as we celebrate our 50th year!
GuestRated
Rated in Top 1% of all US parks since 1966.
TOP RATED PARK FOR 2016
RATED 10/10★/10
888-572-6490 • WWW.LAKEGEORGERVPARK.COM
74 State Route 149, Lake George, NY 12845-3501
Just off Exit 20 of Interstate 87, near the area's most popular attractions, restaurants and shops.
See listing Lake George, NY

Lake George NY... Quiet & Peaceful
"Ledgeview is our Adirondack Paradise...
We initially visited over ten summers ago and basically never left. Our travels have taken us across the country and we are always happy to return to our RV park home at Ledgeview. This superbly maintained and managed park provides a restful, friendly escape, while being conveniently located to seemingly endless summertime and fall activities."
—Lin and Jack S., Ponce Inlet, FL
Good Sam Park
www.LedgeView.com
RV Park Lake George, NY
Ledgeview RV Park has been specifically designed to cater to the requirements of even the largest RVs.
Enjoy
Free Wi-Fi
• Large Wooded Sites
• Easy Pull-thrus
• Full Hookups 30 & 50 Amps
• Cable TV / Wi-Fi
• Laundry Facilities
• Pool / Rec Hall
• Playground
• Fun Cycles
• Horseshoes / Bocce
• Shuffle Board and More
Conveniently located off I-87 and close to all local attractions.
321 State Route 149
Lake George, NY 12845 (518) 798-6621
1-888-353-5936
See listing Lake George, NY

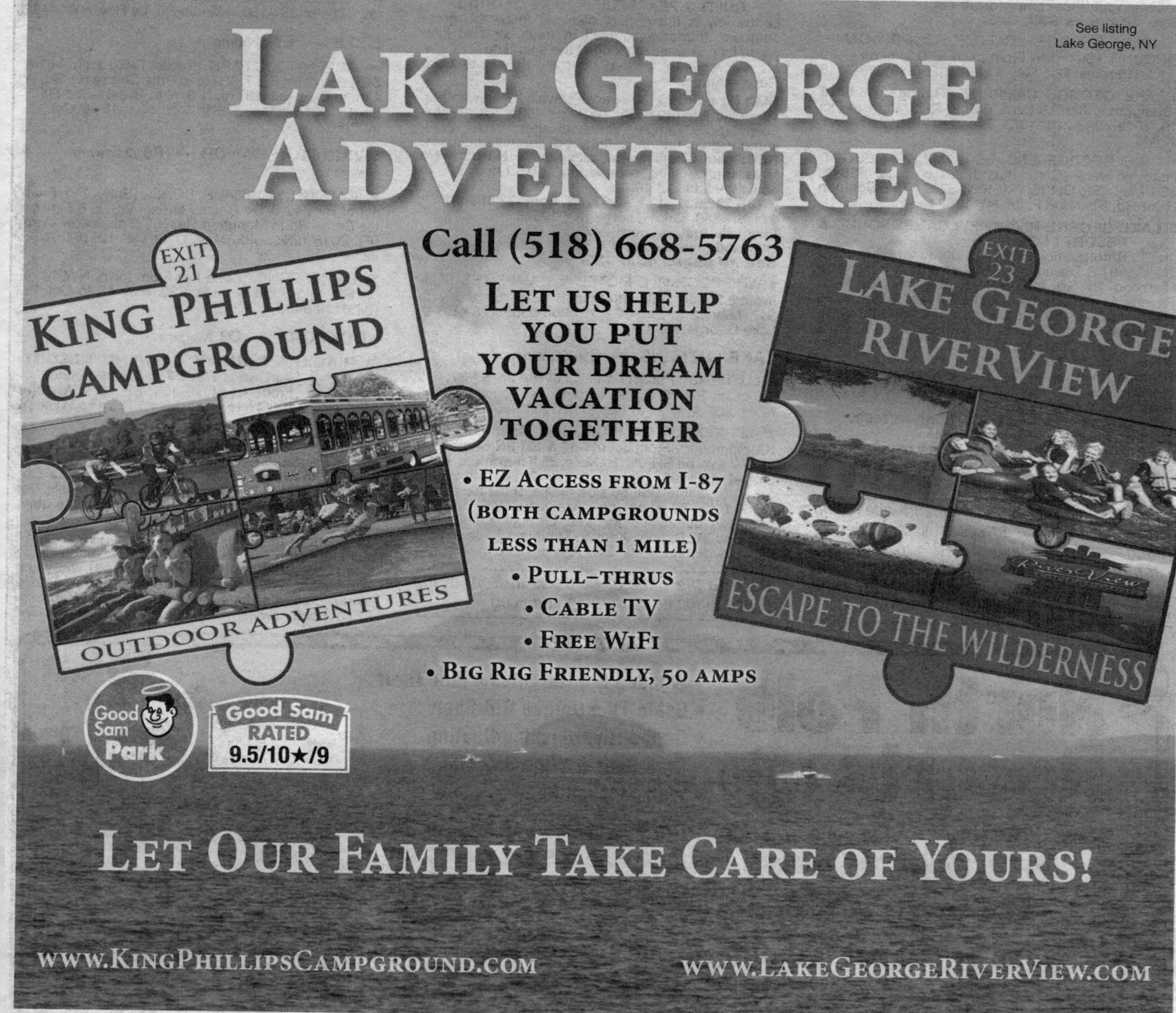
See listing
Lake George, NY
LAKE GEORGE ADVENTURES
Call (518) 668-5763
EXIT 21
KING PHILLIPS CAMPGROUND
OUTDOOR ADVENTURES
LET US HELP YOU PUT YOUR DREAM VACATION TOGETHER
• EZ ACCESS FROM I-87 (BOTH CAMPGROUNDS LESS THAN 1 MILE)
• PULL-THRUS
• CABLE TV
• FREE WIFI
• BIG RIG FRIENDLY, 50 AMPS
EXIT 23
LAKE GEORGE RIVERVIEW
ESCAPE TO THE WILDERNESS
Good Sam Park
Good Sam RATED 9.5/10★/9
LET OUR FAMILY TAKE CARE OF YOURS!
WWW.KINGPHILLIPSCAMPGROUND.COM
WWW.LAKEGEORGERIVERVIEW.COM

LAKE GEORGE (CONT)

ADVENTURE RESORTS OF AMERICA **Ratings: 6/6.5/8** (Membership Pk) 2015 rates: $45 to $49. May 1 to Oct 13. (800)340-2267 969 E Schroon River Rd, Diamond Point, NY 12824

HEARTHSTONE POINT (State Pk) From town, N 2 mi on SR-9N (R). 2015 rates: $22. May 19 to Sep 16. (518)668-5193

KING PHILLIPS CAMPGROUND
Ratings: 9.5/10★/9 (RV Park) From Jct of I-87 & US-9N (exit 21), N 0.2 mi on US-9N to US-9, S 0.8 mi to Bloody Pond Rd, E 0.1 mi (R).

CONVENIENTLY LOCATED TO ATTRACTIONS
Your outdoor adventure begins here-in the middle of all the fun the Lake George area has to offer: Trolley Stop & Bike Trails take you to Village & Beaches, Great Escape, Outlet Shopping and all premier area attractions.

FAC: All weather rds. (222 spaces). 97 Avail: 83 all weather, 4 grass, 10 dirt, patios, 16 pull-thrus (35 x 60), back-ins (35 x 44), 80 full hkups, 17 W, 17 E (30/50 amps), seasonal sites, cable, WiFi, tent sites, dump, laundry, groc, LP gas, fire rings, firewood, controlled access. **REC:** pool, shuffleboard, playground. Pets OK. Big rig sites, eco-friendly, 2015 rates: $39.50 to $56.50. Disc: military. May 1 to Oct 31.
(518)668-5763 Lat: 43.39415, Lon: -73.69948
14 Bloody Pond Rd, Lake George, NY 12845
reservations@kingphillipscampground.com
www.kingphillipscampground.com
See ad pages 833, 823.

LAKE GEORGE BATTLEGROUND CAMPGROUND (State Pk) From town, S 0.3 mi on US-9 (L). 2015 rates: $22. May 5 to Oct 12. (518)668-3348

LAKE GEORGE CAMPSITE **Ratings: 8/6.5/6.5** (Campground) 2015 rates: $49 to $57. May 1 to Oct 15. (518)798-6218 1053 Rte 9, Queensbury, NY 12804

LAKE GEORGE ESCAPE CAMPING RESORT **Ratings: 8/9/9** (Campground) 2015 rates: $55 to $80. May 15 to Oct 15. (518)623-3207 175 E Schroon River Rd, Diamond Point, NY 12824

LAKE GEORGE RIVERVIEW CAMPGROUND & RESORT LLC
Ratings: 8/9.5★/9 (Campground) From Jct of I-87 & Diamond Pt Rd (exit 23), W 0.25 mi on Diamond Pt Rd to US-9, N 0.2 mi (R). **FAC:** Paved/gravel rds. (94 spaces). 65 Avail: 40 gravel, 25 grass, 10 pull-thrus (30 x 50), back-ins (26 x 45), some side by side hkups, 44 full hkups, 21 W, 21 E (30/50 amps), seasonal sites, cable, WiFi, tent sites, dump, groc, LP gas, fire rings, firewood. **REC:** pool, Schroon River: swim, fishing, playground. Pets OK. Big rig sites, eco-friendly, 2015 rates: $30 to $59. Disc: military. May 15 to Oct 15.
(518)623-9444 Lat: 43.48995, Lon: -73.76002
3652 Sr 9, Lake George, NY 12845
reservations@lakegeorgeriverview.com
www.lakegeorgeriverview.com
See ad page 833.

Did you know we sent 35 husband-wife RVing teams out this year to scour North America, rating and inspecting RV parks and campgrounds? You can rest easy when you read our listings, knowing we've already been there.

LAKE GEORGE RV PARK
Ratings: 10/10★/10 (RV Park) From Jct of I-87 & US-9 (exit 20), N 0.5 mi on US-9 to SR-149, E 0.5 mi (R) Note: 3 night minimum on holiday weekends.

AWARD WINNING FAMILY CAMPING RESORT
Rated in top 1% of all US campgrounds since 1966. Experience the best amenities, service and location in the Adirondack region. Indoor heated pool, trolley shuttle, spacious landscaped sites, BIG RIG and dog friendly.

FAC: Paved rds. (368 spaces). Avail: 356 all weather, 280 pull-thrus (30 x 60), back-ins (30 x 56), 356 full hkups (50 amps), seasonal sites, cable, WiFi, rentals, dump, laundry, groc, LP gas, fire rings, firewood, controlled access. **REC:** heated pool, wading pool, pond, fishing, shuffleboard, playground. Pets OK. Partial handicap access, no tents. Big rig sites, eco-friendly, 2015 rates: $62 to $95. May 6 to Oct 10. ATM.
AAA Approved
(518)792-3775 Lat: 43.36922, Lon: -73.69109
74 SR-149, Lake George, NY 12845
info@lakegeorgervpark.com
www.lakegeorgervpark.com
See ad page 832 & Pampered Pets, RV Trips of a Lifetime in Magazine Section.

LEDGEVIEW VILLAGE RV PARK
Ratings: 10/10★/9.5 (RV Park) From Jct of I-87 & US-9 (exit 20), N 0.5 mi on US-9 to SR-149, E 1.5 mi (L).

QUIET & PEACEFUL IN LAKE GEORGE
Ledgeview is the perfect place to enjoy the great outdoors. Immerse yourself in fresh air and lush green foliage while relaxing at the sparkling pool. We are conveniently located near all of favorite Lake George attractions.

FAC: Paved rds. (130 spaces). Avail: 77 all weather, 17 pull-thrus (50 x 75), back-ins (50 x 70), 77 full hkups (30/50 amps), seasonal sites, cable, WiFi, laundry, groc, fire rings, firewood, controlled access. **REC:** pool, shuffleboard, playground. No pets. No tents. Big rig sites, eco-friendly, 2015 rates: $48 to $55. May 5 to Oct 10.
(518)798-6621 Lat: 43.37792, Lon: -73.66963
321 SR-149, Lake George, NY 12845
info1@ledgeview.com
www.ledgeview.com
See ad pages 833, 823.

WHIPPOORWILL MOTEL & CAMPSITES **Ratings: 6.5/8.5/8.5** (Campground) 2015 rates: $42 to $47. May 15 to Sep 20. (518)668-5565 1784 SR-9, Lake George, NY 12845

LAKE LUZERNE — C9 *Warren*

LUZERNE (Public) From Jct of Rte 9N & I-87, SW 6.5 mi on Rte 9N (L). $5 entrance fee required. 2015 rates: $22. May 17 to Sep 7. (518)696-2031

MT KENYON CAMPGROUND Ratings: 7/8/7.5 (Campground) From Jct of I-87 & SR-9N South (exit 21), W 4 mi on SR-9N (R) Note: 35 ft maximum. **FAC:** Gravel rds. (95 spaces). Avail: 75 dirt, back-ins (25 x 40), some side by side hkups, 9 full hkups, 66 W, 66 E (20/30 amps), seasonal sites, WiFi Hotspot, tent sites, dump, laundry, groc, LP bottles, fire rings, firewood. **REC:** pool, Kenyon Mountain Stream: fishing, playground. Pets OK. Age restrict may apply, 2015 rates: $35 to $38. Disc: military. May 15 to Sep 30.
AAA Approved
(518)696-2905 Lat: 43.2245, Lon: -73.4638
1571 Lake Ave, Lake Luzerne, NY 12846
www.mtkenyon.com

Refer to the Table of Contents in front of the Guide to locate everything you need.

LAKE PLACID — B9 *Essex*

LAKE PLACID See also Wilmington.

LAKE PLEASANT — C9 *Hamilton*

ADIRONDACK/MOFFITT BEACH (State Pk) From town, E 2.5 mi on Hwy 8 (L). 2015 rates: $22. May 18 to Oct 7. (518)548-7102

LITTLE SAND POINT (Public) E-bnd: From Jct of Hwy 8 & Old Piseco Rd (at S end of lake), E 5 mi on Old Piseco Rd (R); or W-bnd: From Jct of Hwy 8 & Old Piseco Rd, W 3 mi on Old Piseco Rd (L). Entrance fee required. 2015 rates: $20. May 17 to Sep 1. (518)548-7585

POINT COMFORT CAMPGROUND (ADIRONDACK SF) (State Pk) From business center: Go 10 mi SW on Hwy 8, then 3/4 mi N on CR 24. Pit toilets. 2015 rates: $20. (518)548-7586

LE ROY — D4 *Genesee*

THE RIDGE NY (FORMERLY FROST RIDGE) **Ratings: 8/7/7.5** (Campground) 2015 rates: $36 to $54. (585)768-4883 8101 Conlon Rd, Le Roy, NY 14482

TIMBERLINE LAKE PARK **Ratings: 6.5/5/6** (Campground) 2015 rates: $38. May 1 to Oct 15. (585)768-6635 8150 Vallance Rd, Le Roy, NY 14482

LISLE — E7 *Broome*

GREENWOOD PARK (Public) From Jct of I-81 & SR-26 (exit 8), S 3.7 SR-26 to Cnty Cherry Hill Rd, W 4 mi to Caldwell Hill Rd, N 3 mi to Greenwood Rd, 1 mi (L). 2015 rates: $18 to $22. May 15 to Oct 15. (607)862-9933

LIVINGSTON MANOR — F8 *Delaware, Sullivan*

CATSKILL/MONGAUP POND (State Pk) From Jct of Hwy 17 & De Bruce Rd (exit 96), E 6.5 mi on De Bruce Rd to Mongaup Rd, N 3.5 mi, follow signs (E). 2015 rates: $22. May 17 to Oct 13. (845)439-4233

LITTLE POND (State Pk) From town, NW 14 mi on Rte 17 (L). 2015 rates: $22. May 17 to Oct 13. (845)439-5480

LOCKPORT — D3 *Niagara*

NIAGARA COUNTY CAMPING RESORT
Ratings: 7/7.5/7.5 (Campground) From Jct of SR-104, SR-78 & Wheeler Rd (4 mi N of Lockport), E 3 mi on Wheeler Rd (L).

QUIET COUNTRY CAMPING
Minutes to Niagara Falls, Erie Canal and Lake Ontario. Cable TV & WiFi, cottage and cabin rentals. Pet and family friendly! Come relax & enjoy some quiet time & all that the nearby area has to offer!

FAC: Gravel rds. (240 spaces). Avail: 100 grass, 47 pull-thrus (30 x 55), back-ins (30 x 46), some side by side hkups, 100 W, 100 E (30/50 amps), seasonal sites, cable, WiFi, tent sites, rentals, dump, mobile sewer, groc, fire rings, firewood, controlled access. **REC:** pond, swim, fishing, playground. Pets OK.

LOCKPORT (CONT)

NIAGARA COUNTY CAMPING (CONT)
Eco-friendly, 2015 rates: $43 to $45. Disc: AAA, military. May 8 to Oct 15.
AAA Approved
(716)434-3991 Lat: 43.23201, Lon: -78.62844
7369 Wheeler Rd, Lockport, NY 14094
camp@niagaracamping.com
www.niagaracamping.com
See ad pages 838, 823.

LONG ISLAND — B4 *Nassau, Soffolk*

Travel Services

W E S TRAILER SALES, INC Trailer sales & service. **SERVICES:** RV, RV appliance, restrooms, RV Sales. RV storage. RV supplies, LP, dump, emergency parking, RV accessible. waiting room. Hours: 8 AM to 5 PM.
(631)727-5852 Lat: 40.91477, Lon: -72.83493
6166 Route 25, Wading River, NY 11792
Westrailersales.com
See primary listing at Wading River and ad page 835.

LONG LAKE — B9 *Hamilton*

ADIRONDACK/LAKE EATON (State Pk) From town, NW 2 mi on Hwy 30 (L). 2015 rates: $20. May 18 to Oct 7. (518)624-2641

LAKE HARRIS (State Pk) From town, W 3 mi on Rte 28N (L). 2015 rates: $18. May 19 to Sep 9. (518)582-2503

LOWVILLE — C7 *Lewis*

WHETSTONE GULF (State Pk) From town, S 6 mi on SR-26 (R) $2.75 one time walk-up fee. 2015 rates: $15 to $21. May 24 to Sep 7. (315)376-6630

MARATHON — E7 *Cortland*

COUNTRY HILLS CAMPGROUND **Ratings: 7/8/8.5** (Campground) 2015 rates: $30 to $35. Apr 26 to Oct 15. (607)849-3300 1165 Muckey Rd, Marathon, NY 13803

MASSENA — A8 *St Lawrence*

MASSENA INTERNATIONAL KAMPGROUND **Ratings: 8/8.5★/8** (Campground) 2015 rates: $29 to $39. May 1 to Oct 25. (315)769-9483 84 CR 42A, Massena, NY 13662

MECHANICVILLE — D10 *Rensselaer*

ADVENTURE BOUND CAMPING AT DEER RUN **Ratings: 8/7.5/8.5** (Campground) 2015 rates: $58 to $68. Apr 18 to Oct 18. (518)664-2804 200 Deer Run Dr (SR-67), Schaghticoke, NY 12154

MEDINA — D3 *Orleans*

MEDINA/WILDWOOD LAKE KOA **Ratings: 8/9/9** (Campground) 2015 rates: $44 to $80. May 1 to Oct 12. (585)735-3310 2711 County Line Rd, Medina, NY 14103

MEXICO — C6 *Oswego*

J & J CAMPGROUND **Ratings: 7/9★/7** (Campground) 2015 rates: $30 to $32. (315)963-1108 291 Tubbs Rd, Mexico, NY 13114

YOGI BEAR'S JELLYSTONE PARK CAMP-RESORT AT MEXICO **Ratings: 8/9.5★/9.5** (Campground) 2015 rates: $39 to $61. May 1 to Oct 25. (315)963-7096 601 CR-16, Mexico, NY 13114

MIDDLEBURGH — E9 *Schoharie*

MAX V SHAUL (State Pk) From town, S 5 mi on Hwy 30 (R). 2015 rates: $15. May 23 to Sep 1. (518)827-4711

MIDDLESEX — D5 *Yates*

FLINT CREEK CAMPGROUND **Ratings: 6.5/7.5/7** (Campground) 2015 rates: $37 to $39. May 1 to Oct 31. (585)554-3567 1455 Phelps Rd, Middlesex, NY 14507

MIDDLETOWN — F9 *Orange*

KORN'S CAMPGROUNDS **Ratings: 7/7/7.5** (Campground) 2015 rates: $50. May 1 to Oct 15. (845)386-3433 60 Meyer Rd, Middletown, NY 10940

MILLERTON — F10 *Dutchess*

TACONIC/COPAKE FALLS AREA (State Pk) From Jct of SR-22 & Rte 344, E 1 mi on Rte 344 (L). 2015 rates: $15 to $19. May 3 to Nov 30. (518)329-3993

MONTAUK — A5 *Suffolk*

HITHER HILLS (State Pk) From town, W 3 mi on Old Montauk Hwy (L). RESERVATIONS REQUIRED. 2015 rates: $28 to $64. Jun to Sep. (631)668-2554

MONTEZUMA — D6 *Seneca*

HEJAMADA CAMPGROUND & RV PARK Ratings: 8/8.5/7.5 (Campground) From Jct of I-90 & SR-414 (Exit 41), S 0.01 mi to SR-414 to SR-318, E 4 mi to US 5/US 20, E 1.5 mi to SR-90, N 3.5 mi to Fuller Rd, S 0.02 mi to Mc Donald Rd, SE 0.08 mi (R). **FAC:** Gravel rds. (196 spaces). 109 Avail: 19 gravel, 90 grass, back-ins (50 x 70), 20 full hkups, 89 W, 89 E (30/50 amps), seasonal sites, WiFi, tent sites, rentals, dump, mobile sewer, laundry, groc, LP gas, fire rings, firewood. **REC:** pool, pond, fishing, playground. Pets OK. Partial handicap access. Big rig sites, 2015 rates: $32 to $55. Disc: AAA. May 1 to Oct 15.
AAA Approved
(315)776-5887 Lat: 42.99593, Lon: -76.68989
748 Mcdonald Rd, Port Byron, NY 13140
larso692000@yahoo.com
www.hejamadacampground.com

MONTGOMERY — F9 *Orange*

WINDING HILLS PARK (Public) From Jct of I 87 & 17K, W 12 mi to Old Rt 17K (follows signs), N 0.3 mi (R) Caution: Maximum length 35'. Note: Three day minimum stay holiday weekends. 2015 rates: $20 to $35. (845)457-4918

MONTOUR FALLS — E5 *Schuyler*

MONTOUR MARINA & CAMPSITE (Public) From Jct of SR-14 & Marina Dr (in town), N 0.5 mi on Marina Dr (L). 2015 rates: $35 to $50. May 1 to Oct 15. (607)210-4124

MORAVIA — D6 *Cayuga*

FILLMORE GLEN (State Pk) From Jct of Hwy 90 & SR-38, N 3 mi on SR-38 (R). 2015 rates: $15 to $23. May 3 to Oct 13. (315)497-0130

MORRISTOWN — A7 *St Lawrence*

JACQUES CARTIER (State Pk) From Jct of Rtes 37 & 12, S 2 mi on Rte 12 to unnamed rd, W 100 ft, follow signs (L). 2015 rates: $15 to $21. May 17 to Sep 14. (315)375-6371

MOUNT MORRIS — D4 *Livingston*

LETCHWORTH (State Pk) From Jct of Hwys 36 & 39, S 2 mi on Hwy 36 to park rd (park entrance), S 5.5 mi (L). 2015 rates: $21 to $27. (585)493-3600

MOUNTAIN DALE — F9 *Sullivan*

MOUNTAIN DALE PARK (Public) From Jct of Rte 17 & Rockhill (exit 109), N 8 mi on Cr-58 to Mountain Dale, E 2 mi to Park Hill Rd., E 1 mi. 2015 rates: $33.90. May 1 to Sep 24. (845)434-7337

NEW YORK CITY — B2 *New York*

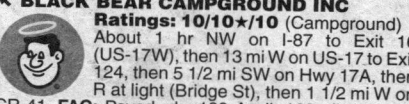

BLACK BEAR CAMPGROUND INC Ratings: 10/10★/10 (Campground) About 1 hr NW on I-87 to Exit 16 (US-17W), then 13 mi W on US-17 to Exit 124, then 5 1/2 mi SW on Hwy 17A, then R at light (Bridge St), then 1 1/2 mi W on CR-41. **FAC:** Paved rds. 160 Avail: 160 all weather, 20 pull-thrus (30 x 75), back-ins (30 x 60), 160 full hkups (30/50 amps), WiFi, rentals, dump, laundry, LP bottles, fire rings, firewood. **REC:** pool, pond, fishing, shuffleboard, playground. Pet restrict(B). Partial handicap access, no tents. Big rig sites, 2015 rates: $60 to $80. Disc: military.
(845)651-7717 Lat: 41.32242, Lon: -74.3734
197 Wheeler Rd, Florida, NY 10921
info@blackbearcampground.com
www.blackbearcampground.com
See primary listing at Florida and ad page 837.

E2. C5. F1. It's not a cipher; it's our easy-to-use map grid. Draw a line horizontally from the letter, vertically from the number, in the map border. "X" will mark a spot near your destination.

Park owners want you to be satisfied with your stay. Get to know them.

NY

Call Toll Free: (800) 646-2066 for Reservations Or Book Online Today
Liberty Harbor Rv
The Closest Rv Park to New York City
15 Minutes
From New York City
What You Will Find At Our Park:
70 sites (water and electric)
Dump station / Honeywagon Service
Full restrooms with hot showers
Laundry room
Subway & Ferry to NYC
Bus tours daily to New York City
Restaurant/Bar on premises
FREE Wi-Fi
12 Tent sites Available
24 hour security and on-site manager
View of New York Skyline, Statue of Liberty, Ellis Island, Liberty Science Center and Liberty State Park from your campsite
RESERVE ONLINE
11 Luis Munoz Marin Blvd. Jersey City, NJ 07302
Phone: 201.516.7500
Email: info@libertyharborrv.com
www.libertyharborrv.com
*Open Year Round
See listing Jersey City, NJ

www.blackbearcampground.com
OPEN ALL YEAR
• Extended Stays
• Large RVs Welcome
• Full Hookups
• 50-Amp Service
845-651-7717
197 Wheeler Road
P.O. Box 82
Florida, NY 10921
info@blackbearcampground.com
VISA
MasterCard
DISCOVER
Guided New York City Tours Direct from Campground
Mid-May to End of October. Highlights Include: Times Square, Ground Zero Memorial, 911 Memorial, Statue of Liberty, Ellis Island
Nearest Full-Service Campground to New York City!
Black Bear
CAMPGROUND
Good Sam RATED 10/10★/10
See listing Florida, NY
Good Sam Park

NY

NEWBURGH — F9 *Orange*

NEW YORK CITY NORTH/NEWBURGH KOA **Ratings: 10/9.5★/9.5** (Campground) 2015 rates: $50 to $70. Mar 28 to Nov 1. (845)564-2836 119 Freetown Highway, Plattekill, NY 12568

Check out those views! From awe-inspiring redwood giants to the soaring towers of the Golden Gate Bridge, we've put the Spotlight on North America's most popular travel destinations. Turn to the Spotlight articles in our State and Province sections to learn more.

NIAGARA FALLS — D3 *Niagara*

AA ROYAL MOTEL & CAMPGROUND Ratings: 7.5/8/8 (Campground) From Jct of I-90 (exit 50) & I-290, W 0.1 mi on US-62 N (Exit 3), N 5.7 mi on US-62 (R); or From Jct of I-190 N & US-62 S (exit 22), S 7.7 mi on US-62 (R). **FAC:** Paved rds. 30 paved, 6 pull-thrus (30 x 80), back-ins (30 x 50), 30 full hkups (30/50 amps), WiFi, tent sites, rentals, laundry, fire rings, firewood. **REC.** Pets OK. Partial handicap access. Big rig sites, 2015 rates: $60 to $70. Disc: AAA, military. **(716)693-5695 Lat: 43.07530, Lon: -78.86127** 3333 Niagara Falls Blvd, North Tonawanda, NY 14120 **mike@royalmotelandcampground.com www.royalmotelandcampground.com** ***See ad opposite page, 823.***

BRANCHES OF NIAGARA CAMPGROUND & RESORT Ratings: 10/10★/10 (Campground) From Jct of I-190 & Whitehaven Rd (Exit 19), E 0.75 mi on Whitehaven Rd (R). **FAC:** All weather rds. 61 Avail:

NIAGARA FALLS (CONT)

BRANCHES OF NIAGARA (CONT)

61 all weather, 5 pull-thrus (40 x 60), back-ins (40 x 50), 32 full hkups, 29 W, 29 E (30/50 amps), WiFi, tent sites, rentals, dump, laundry, groc, LP gas, fire rings, firewood. **REC:** heated pool, Whitehaven Lake: fishing, playground. Pets OK. Partial handicap access. Big rig sites, 2015 rates: $44 to $81. Disc: military. Apr 11 to Oct 31.
(877)321-2267 Lat: 43.02412, Lon: -78.99089
2659 Whitehaven Rd, Grand Island, NY 14072
info@branchesofniagara.com
www.branchesofniagara.com

← CINDERELLA MOTEL & CAMPSITE **Ratings: 4.5/8/7** (Campground) 2015 rates: $40 to $45. Apr 1 to Oct 31. (716)773-2872 2797 Grand Island Blvd, Grand Island, NY 14072

↓ **NIAGARA FALLS CAMPGROUND & LODGING**

Ratings: 9/10★/8.5 (Campground) From Jct of I-290W & US-62N (exit 3), N 10 mi on US-62N (R); or From Jct of I-190N & US-62S (exit 22), S 4.5 mi on US-62S (L) Note: Min 2 night stay on holiday weekend. **FAC:** All weather rds. 55 Avail: 55 all weather, 30 pull-thrus (25 x 75), back-ins (20 x 50), 49 full hkups, 6 W, 6 E (30/50 amps), WiFi, tent sites, rentals, dump, laundry, fire rings, firewood. **REC:** pool, playground. Pets OK. Partial handicap access. Big rig sites, 2015 rates: $49 to $66. Disc: military. Apr 1 to Nov 1.
(716)731-3434 Lat: 43.09658, Lon: -78.91627
2405 Niagara Falls Blvd, Niagara Falls, NY 14304
nfcampground@yahoo.com
www.niagarafallscampground.com
See ad opposite page, 823.

← NIAGARA FALLS KOA **Ratings: 9/9.5★/8** (Campground) 2015 rates: $31 to $105. Apr 1 to Oct 31. (716)773-7583 2570 Grand Island Blvd, Grand Island, NY 14072

↑ NIAGARA FALLS NORTH/LEWISTON KOA **Ratings: 8/9.5/9** (Campground) 2015 rates: $49 to $64. Apr 15 to Oct 15. (800)562-8715 1250 Pletcher Rd, Youngstown, NY 14174

We rate what RVers consider important.

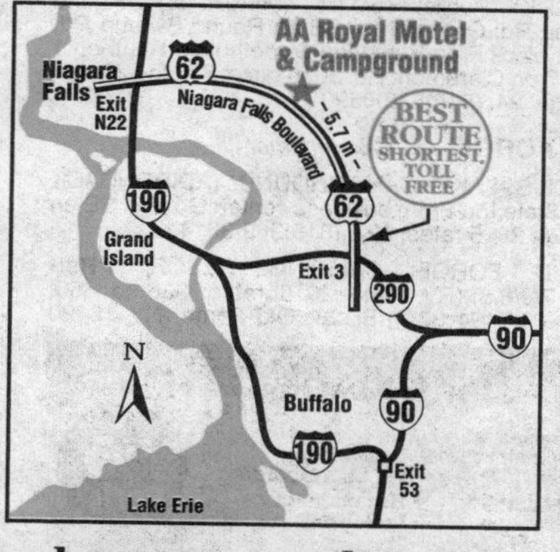

NORTH HUDSON — B10 *Essex*

YOGI BEAR'S JELLYSTONE PARK AT PARADISE PINES CAMPING RESORT Ratings: 9.5/10★/9.5 (Campground) From Jct of I-87 & Blue Ridge Rd (exit 29), E 0.1 mi on Blue Ridge Rd (L). **FAC:** All weather rds. (142 spaces). 130 Avail: 81 gravel, 49 grass, 22 pull-thrus (35 x 75), back-ins (35 x 42), 95 full hkups, 35 W, 35 E (30/50 amps), seasonal sites, WiFi, tent sites, rentals, dump, mobile sewer, laundry, groc, LP gas, fire rings, firewood, controlled access. **REC:** heated pool, wading pool, Schroon River: fishing, shuffleboard, playground. Pet restrict(B). Big rig sites, 2015 rates: $52 to $63. Disc: military. May 1 to Oct 15. ATM.
(518)532-7493 Lat: 43.95274, Lon: -73.73006
4035 Blue Ridge Rd, North Hudson, NY 12855
office@adirondacksjellystone.com
www.adirondacksjellystone.com

NORTH JAVA — D4 *Wyoming*

JELLYSTONE PARK (TM) OF WESTERN NEW YORK
Ratings: 8.5/9.5★/9.5 (Campground) From Jct of SR-78/SR-98 & Peedee Rd, E 1.6 mi on Peedee Rd to Youngers Rd, S 0.7 mi (R) Note: Min 3 day min. stay on holiday weekends.

THE ULTIMATE CAMPING EXPERIENCE
Situated in the heart of New York, this is the perfect location for your next vacation. Enjoy spacious sites with a great selection of vacation rentals and a phenomenal amenity package, which includes Yogi Bear's Water Zone!

FAC: Gravel rds. (302 spaces). 210 Avail: 25 paved, 111 gravel, 74 grass, 68 pull-thrus (40 x 75), back-ins (25 x 30), some side by side hkups, 128 full hkups, 82 W, 82 E (30/50 amps), seasonal sites, WiFi, tent sites, rentals, dump, mobile sewer, laundry, groc, LP gas, fire rings, firewood, controlled access. **REC:** heated pool, wading pool, pond, fishing, playground. Pet restrict(Q) $. Partial handicap access. Big rig sites, 2015 rates: $64 to $93. Disc: AAA. May 1 to Oct 12. ATM.
AAA Approved
(877)469-7590 Lat: 42.64137, Lon: -78.30985
5204 Youngers Road, North Java, NY 14113
Infojwn@suncommunities.com
www.wnyjellystone.com
See ad pages 1463 (Welcome Section), 821 (Welcome Section) & Family Camping in Magazine Section.

NORTHVILLE — D9 *Fulton*

ADIRONDACK/SACANDAGA CAMPGROUND (State Pk) From Amsterdam, N 35 mi on Rte 30 (L). Entrance fee required. 2015 rates: $20. May 19 to Oct 8. (518)924-4121

NORTHAMPTON BEACH CAMPGROUND (ADIRONDACK SF) (State Pk) From business center: Go 1-1/2 mi S on Hwy 30, then SE. 2015 rates: $22. (518)863-6000

OGDENSBURG — A7 *St Lawrence*

LISBON BEACH AND CAMPGROUND (Public) From jct Hwy 812 & Hwy 37: Go 5 mi E on Hwy 37. 2015 rates: $24 to $32. May 1 to Oct 1. (315)393-5374

OLD BETHPAGE — B3 *Nassau*

BATTLE ROW CAMPGROUND (NASSAU COUNTY PARK) (Public) From jct I-495 (exit 48) & Round Swamp Rd: Go 1-3/4 mi SE on Round Swamp Rd, then 1 block E on Bethpage-Sweethollow Rd, then 1 block S on Claremont Rd. 2015 rates: $10 to $20. Apr 5 to Nov 24. (516)572-8690

OLD FORGE — C8 *Herkimer*

NICK'S LAKE CAMPGROUND (ADIRONDACK SF) (State Pk) From business center: Go 2 mi SE on Hwy-28. 2015 rates: $22. (315)369-3314

OLD FORGE CAMPING RESORT **Ratings: 7/8/8.5** (RV Park) 2015 rates: $36 to $50. (800)226-7464 3347 Sr 28, Old Forge, NY 13420

SINGING WATERS CAMPGROUND **Ratings: 6.5/8/7.5** (Campground) 2015 rates: $45 to $50. (315)369-6618 1334 Sr 28, Old Forge, NY 13420

ONEIDA — D7 *Madison*

VERONA BEACH (State Pk) From jct I-90 & Hwy-13: Go 7 mi NW on Hwy-13. 2015 rates: $15 to $20. May 9 to Oct 12. (315)762-4463

ONEONTA — E8 *Otsego*

DEER HAVEN CAMPGROUND & CABINS **Ratings: 7.5/9★/9** (Campground) 2015 rates: $35 to $45. May 25 to Oct 12. (607)433-9654 180 Deer Haven Lane, Oneonta, NY 13820

GILBERT LAKE (State Pk) From Jct of I-88 & SR-205, N 10 mi on SR-205 to CR-11A, W to CR-12, NW 4 mi (R). 2015 rates: $15 to $21. May 10 to Oct 13. (607)432-2114

SUSQUEHANNA TRAIL CAMPGROUND **Ratings: 6.5/6/8.5** (Campground) 2015 rates: $35 to $65. Apr 1 to Nov 1. (607)432-1122 4292 State Hwy 7, Oneonta, NY 13820

OVID — D6 *Seneca*

SNED-ACRES FAMILY CAMPGROUND **Ratings: 7.5/7.5/7** (Campground) 2015 rates: $29.25 to $35.50. Apr 15 to Nov 1. (607)869-9787 6590 S Cayuga Lake Rd, Ovid, NY 14521

OWEGO — E6 *Tioga*

HICKORIES PARK (Public) From Jct of SR-17C & Hickories Park Rd (exit 65), S 0.5 mi on Hickories Park Rd (E). 2015 rates: $25 to $30. (607)687-1199

OXFORD — E7 *Chenango*

BOWMAN LAKE (State Pk) From town, W 6.3 mi on SR-220, N 1.3 mi Bowman Rd. (R). 2015 rates: $15. May 10 to Oct 13. (607)334-2718

PARISH — C6 *Oswego*

BASS LAKE RESORT- TRAVEL RESORTS OF AMERICA **Ratings: 8.5/9★/9.5** (Campground) 2015 rates: $50. May 1 to Nov 1. (315)625-4101 132 Crim Rd, Parish, NY 13131

PENNELLVILLE — C6 *Oswego*

PLEASANT LAKE RV PARK **Ratings: 6/5.5/8** (Campground) 2015 rates: $35 to $38. May 1 to Oct 13. (315)668-2074 65 Wigwam Dr, Pennellville, NY 13132

PERU — A10 *Clinton*

AUSABLE POINT (Public) From Plattsburgh, S 12 mi on US-9 (L). 2015 rates: $22. May 17 to Oct 13. (518)561-7080

IROQUOIS RV PARK & CAMPGROUND **Ratings: 7.5/8/8.5** (Campground) 2015 rates: $36 to $38. May 1 to Oct 1. (518)643-9057 270 Bear Swamp Rd, Peru, NY 12972

PETERSBURGH — D10 *Rensselaer*

AQUA VISTA CAMPGROUND **Ratings: 7.5/7/6.5** (Campground) 2015 rates: $35 to $39.50. May 1 to Sep 30. (518)658-3659 72 Armsby Rd, Petersburgh, NY 12138

BROKEN WHEEL CAMPGROUND **Ratings: 6.5/6.5/9** (Campground) 2015 rates: $31. May 1 to Oct 15. (518)658-2925 61 Broken Wheel Rd, Petersburgh, NY 12138

PHELPS — D5 *Ontario, Seneca*

CHEERFUL VALLEY CAMPGROUND
Ratings: 8.5/9.5★/9 (Campground) From Jct of I-90 & SR-14 (exit 42), N 0.5 mi on SR-14 (L). **FAC:** Paved rds. (125 spaces). 75 Avail: 1 gravel, 74 grass, 12 pull-thrus (50 x 70), back-ins (40 x 70), 19 full hkups, 56 W, 56 E (30/50 amps), seasonal sites, WiFi, tent sites, rentals, dump, mobile sewer, laundry, groc, LP gas, fire rings, firewood. **REC:** pool, Canandaigua Outlet River: fishing, shuffleboard, playground. Pet restrict(Q). 2015 rates: $30 to $50. May 1 to Oct 15.
(315)781-1222 Lat: 42.96652, Lon: -76.98105
1412 Route 14, Phelps, NY 14532
cheerfulvalley@gmail.com
www.cheerfulvalleycampground.com
See ad opposite page.

JUNIUS PONDS CABINS & CAMPGROUND LLC
Ratings: 9.5/9★/9 (Campground) From Jct of I-90 & SR-318 (Exit 42), E 0.7 mi on SR-318 to Townline Rd, N 0.3 mi (E).Caution: Follow these directions, GPS not always reliable. **FAC:** Paved rds. (227 spaces). Avail: 51 all weather, 41 pull-thrus (45 x 80), back-ins (40 x 70), 41 full hkups, 10 W, 10 E (30/50 amps), seasonal sites, WiFi, tent sites, rentals, dump, laundry, groc, LP gas, fire rings, firewood. **REC:** pool, pond, fishing, playground. Pets OK. Partial handicap access. Big rig sites, 2015 rates: $35 to $37.50. Apr 15 to Oct 15.
(315)781-5120 Lat: 42.95481, Lon: -76.96121
1475 W Townline Rd, Phelps, NY 14532
campjpcc@gmail.com
www.juniuspondscabinsandcampground.com
See ad opposite page.

PHOENICIA — E9 *Ulster*

CATSKILL/KENNETH L WILSON (State Pk) Nbound: From Jct of Hwy 87 & exit 19/Kingston exit (in Kingston), W 20 ft at traffic circle to Rte 28, NW 21 mi to Rte 212 (in Mt Tremper), E 0.5 mi to Rte 40/Wittenberg, E 5 mi (R). 2015 rates: $22. May 12 to Oct 12. (845)679-7020

CATSKILL/WOODLAND VALLEY (State Pk) From town, W 0.5 mi on Rte 28 to Woodland Valley Rd, S 5 mi (L). 2015 rates: $20. May 12 to Oct 12. (845)688-7647

PIKE — E4 *Wyoming*

ROLLING ACRES GOLF COURSE & CAMPGROUND **Ratings: 4.5/7.5/6.5** (Campground) 2015 rates: $30. May 1 to Oct 15. (585)567-8557 7795 Dewitt Rd, Pike, NY 14130

PLATTSBURGH — A10 *Clinton*

CUMBERLAND BAY (State Pk) From Jct. US Hwy 9 & Rte 314, E .5 Mi on Rte 314. 2015 rates: $15 to $21. May 10 to Oct 13. (518)563-5240

PLATTSBURGH RV PARK **Ratings: 7/6.5/8** (RV Park) 2015 rates: $35 to $42. May 5 to Oct 15. (518)563-3915 7182 Rt 9, Plattsburgh, NY 12901

SHADY OAKS RV PARK **Ratings: 7.5/8/8.5** (Campground) 2015 rates: $35 to $42. May 1 to Sep 30. (518)562-0561 70 Moffitt Rd, Plattsburgh, NY 12901

POLAND — D8 *Oneida*

ADIRONDACK GATEWAY CAMPGROUND & LODGE
Ratings: 8/7/8 (Campground) From Jct of I-90 & SR-8 (exit 31), NE 17.4 mi on SR-8 to Hall Rd, E 0.4 mi to Burt Rd, N 0.3 mi (E). **FAC:** Gravel rds. (50 spaces). Avail: 38 grass, 10 pull-thrus (40 x 70), back-ins (50 x 70), some side by side hkups, 30 full hkups, 8 W, 8 E (30/50 amps), seasonal sites, WiFi Hotspot, tent sites, rentals, dump, laundry, fire rings, firewood. **REC:** heated pool, pond, fishing, playground. Pets OK. 2015 rates: $28 to $35. Disc: military. May 15 to Oct 13.
(315)826-5335 Lat: 43.26618, Lon: -74.98141
244 Burt Rd, Cold Brook, NY 13324
agccoldbrook@yahoo.com
www.adirondackgatewaycampground.net
See ad page 843.

WEST CANADA CREEK CAMPSITES Ratings: 9/8.5★/9.5 (Campground) From Jct of I-90 & SR-8 (exit 31), N 11 mi on SR-8 (L). **FAC:** Gravel rds. (68 spaces). Avail: 48 grass, 10 pull-thrus (45 x 60), back-ins (45 x 50), 38 full hkups, 10 W, 10 E (30/50 amps), seasonal sites, cable, WiFi, tent sites, rentals, dump, laundry, LP gas, fire rings, firewood. **REC:** pool, West Canada Creek: fishing, playground. Pets OK. Partial handicap access. 2015 rates: $31 to $60. Disc: military. May 1 to Oct 15.
(315)826-7390 Lat: 43.23104, Lon: -75.07569
12275 SR-28, Poland, NY 13431
camp@westcanadacreekcampsites.com
www.westcanadacreekcampsites.com

PORT HENRY — B10 *Essex*

BULWAGGA BAY CAMPGROUND & RV PARK (Public) From center of town: Go 1/4 mi S on Hwy 9N/22, then 500 feet E on Bulwagga Rd (follow signs). 2015 rates: $28 to $40. May 1 to Sep 30. (518)546-7500

PORT HENRY CHAMP BEACH CAMPGROUND & RV PARK (Public) From center of town (Hwy 9N/22): Go 100 yards E on Dock St, then 1/4 mi N on Hwy 9N/22, then 1/8 mi E on Beach Rd (curve to the right). 2015 rates: $30 to $40. May 9 to Oct 5. (518)546-7123

PORT KENT — A10 *Essex*

PORT KENT CAMPSITE **Ratings: 5/7/8** (Campground) 2015 rates: $25 to $30. May 15 to Oct 15. (518)834-9011 93 Rte 373, Port Kent, NY 12975

PORTAGEVILLE — E4 *Wyoming*

ADVENTURE BOUND CAMPING RESORT **Ratings: 6/6.5/8** (Campground) 2015 rates: $39 to $49. May 1 to Oct 15. (585)493-2794 7350 Tenefly Rd, Portageville, NY 14536

We shine "Spotlights" on interesting cities and areas.

POTTERSVILLE — C9 *Warren*

EAGLE POINT (State Pk) From town, N 2 mi on SR-9 (R). 2015 rates: $22. May 17 to Sep 7. (518)494-2220

POUGHKEEPSIE — F9 *Dutchess*

MILLS-NORRIE (State Pk) From Jct of CR-41 & US-9, N 3.4 mi on US-9 to Old Post Rd, W 0.1 mi (L). 2015 rates: $15 to $19. May 10 to Oct 27. (845)889-4646

PRATTSBURGH — E5 *Steuben*

BUD VALLEY CAMPGROUND **Ratings: 6/9.5★/7** (Campground) 2015 rates: $30 to $35. May 1 to Oct 15. (607)522-3270 10378 Presler Rd, Prattsburgh, NY 14873

PULASKI — C6 *Oswego*

BEAR'S SLEEPY HOLLOW PARK **Ratings: 6/7.5/7.5** (Campground) 2015 rates: $40. Mar 1 to Nov 1. (315)298-5560 7065 SR-3, Pulaski, NY 13142

BRENNAN BEACH RV RESORT **Ratings: 8.5/7.5/9** (Campground) 2015 rates: $46 to $68. May 1 to Oct 15. (315)298-2242 80 Brennan Beach, Pulaski, NY 13142

SELKIRK SHORES (State Pk) From Jct of SR-13 & SR-3, S 1.5 mi on SR-3 (R). 2015 rates: $15 to $21. May 10 to Oct 19. (315)298-5737

STREAMSIDE RV PARK & GOLF COURSE **Ratings: 7/NA/7.5** (Campground) 2015 rates: $25. Apr 15 to Oct 15. (315)298-6887 800 Tinker Tavern, Pulaski, NY 13142

RANDOLPH — E3 *Cattaraugus*

POPE HAVEN CAMPGROUND
Ratings: 9/9★/9.5 (Campground) From Jct of I-86 & SR 394 (Main St) (exit 16), E 1.4 mi (thru town) on SR-394 (Main St.) to SR-241, N 3.5 mi to Pope Rd, E 100 ft (L). **FAC:** All weather rds. (175 spaces). 70 Avail: 45 gravel, 25 grass, 15 pull-thrus (36 x 70), back-ins (35 x 70), 11 full hkups, 59 W, 59 E (30/50 amps), seasonal sites, WiFi, tent sites, rentals, showers $, dump, mobile sewer, laundry, groc, LP gas, fire rings, firewood, controlled access. **REC:** pool, pond, fishing, playground. Pets OK. Partial handicap access. Big rig sites, 2015 rates: $28 to $42. Disc: AAA, military. May 1 to Oct 15.
(716)358-4900 Lat: 42.20759, Lon: -78.99732
11948 Pope Rd, Randolph, NY 14772
rangermike@popehaven.com
www.popehaven.com

RANSOMVILLE — D3 *Niagara*

NIAGARA WOODLAND CAMPGROUND **Ratings: 7/5.5/6.5** (Campground) 2015 rates: $36 to $40. May 8 to Oct 18. (716)791-3101 3435 New Rd, Ransomville, NY 14131

RAQUETTE LAKE — C8 *Hamilton*

BROWN TRACT POND CAMPGROUND (ADIRONDACK SF) (Natl Forest) From business center: Go 2 mi NW on Town Rd. 2015 rates: $18. (315)354-4412

EIGHTH LAKE (ADIRONDACK SF) (State Pk) From town: Go 5 mi W on Hwy-28. 2015 rates: $22. May 17 to Oct 13. (315)354-4120

GOLDEN BEACH CAMPGROUND (State Pk) From town, E 2 mi on SR-28 (L). 2015 rates: $20. May 17 to Sep 1. (315)354-4230

RHINEBECK — F9 *Dutchess*

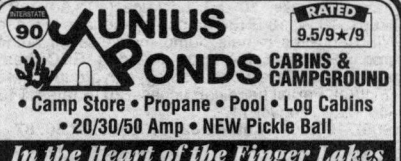

INTERLAKE RV PARK & SALES
Ratings: 9.5/9.5★/9.5 (Campground) From Jct of US 9 & SR-9G (N of town), S 3.5 mi on SR-9G to Slate Quarry Rd (CR-19), E 3.5 mi on CR-19 to Lake Dr, S 0.3 mi (L). **FAC:** Paved rds. (159 spaces). Avail: 79 grass, back-ins (35 x 60), 46 full hkups, 33 W, 33 E (30/50 amps), seasonal sites, cable, WiFi, tent sites, rentals, dump, mobile sewer, laundry, groc, fire rings, firewood, controlled access. **REC:** heated pool, wading pool, Interlake: fishing, playground. Pet restrict(B). Big rig sites, eco-friendly, 2015 rates: $48 to $57. Disc: military. Apr 15 to Oct 19.
(845)266-5387 Lat: 41.90408, Lon: -73.81268
428 Lake Dr, Rhinebeck, NY 12572
interlakervpark@aol.com
www.interlakervpark.com
See ad this page, 823.

RIVERHEAD — A4 *Suffolk*

INDIAN ISLAND PARK (SUFFOLK COUNTY PARK) (Public) From jct Hwy 24 & CR 105: Go E on CR 105 past golf course. 2015 rates: $25. (631)852-3232

ROCHESTER — D5 *Monroe*

ROCHESTER See also Byron, Caledonia, Conesus, Phelps & Webster.

RV Park ratings you can rely on!

ROME — D7 *Oneida*

DELTA LAKE (State Pk) From town, N 6 mi on Hwy 46 (L). 2015 rates: $15. May 9 to Sep 1. (315)337-4670

ROMULUS — D6 *Seneca*

SAMPSON (State Pk) From Jct of Hwy 5/20 & Rte 96A, S 11 mi on Rte 96A (R); or From town, S 4 mi on Rte 14 to Rte 5/20, E 1 mi to Rte 96A, S 11 mi (R). Note: All sites closed Sept. 22-30, 2013. 2015 rates: $15 to $21. Apr 25 to Oct 15. (315)585-6392

ROSCOE — F8 *Delaware, Sullivan*

RUSSELL BROOK CAMPSITE **Ratings: 7/8/8.5** (Campground) 2015 rates: $35. May 1 to Oct 31. (607)498-5416 731 Russell Brook Rd, Roscoe, NY 12776

SACKETS HARBOR — B6 *Jefferson*

WESTCOTT BEACH (State Pk) From town, W 8 mi on Arsenal St/NY SR-3 (R). 2015 rates: $15 to $21. May 17 to Sep 1. (315)646-2239

SALAMANCA — E3 *Cattaraugus*

ALLEGANY (QUAKER AREA) (State Pk) From Hwy-17 (Exit 18): Go S on Hwy-280, then E on Park Rd 3. 2015 rates: $15 to $25. Mar 27 to Nov 25. (716)354-2182

ALLEGANY (RED HOUSE AREA) (State Pk) From Hwy 17 (exit 19): Go E on Allegany State Park Rd 2, then S on Allegany State Park Rd 1. 2015 rates: $15 to $25. (716)354-9121

SARANAC LAKE — B9 *Franklin*

ADIRONDACK/MEADOWBROOK (State Pk) From town, N 4 mi on Rte 86 (L). 2015 rates: $18. May 18 to Sep 2. (518)891-4351

SARATOGA SPRINGS — D9 *Saratoga*

SARATOGA ESCAPE LODGES & RV RESORT **Ratings: 7.5/8/9.5** (Campground) 2015 rates: $49 to $54. May 1 to Oct 1. (518)893-0537 265 Brigham Rd, Greenfield Center, NY 12833

WHISPERING PINES CAMPSITES **Ratings: 7/6.5/7.5** (Campground) 2015 rates: $38 to $44. May 1 to Oct 31. (855)687-2267 550 Sand Hill Rd, Greenfield Center, NY 12833

SAUGERTIES — E9 *Ulster*

BLUE MOUNTAIN CAMPGROUND **Ratings: 7.5/9.5★/7.5** (Campground) From jct I-87 (exit 20) & Hwy 212: Go 1/8 mi W on Hwy 212, then 4-1/2 mi N on Hwy 32. **FAC:** All weather rds. (25 spaces). Avail: 20 gravel, 2 pull-thrus (18 x 40), back-ins (14 x 52), mostly side by side hkups, 20 full hkups (30 amps), seasonal sites, WiFi, tent sites, rentals, dump, laundry, groc, fire rings, firewood. **REC:** pool, play-

NY

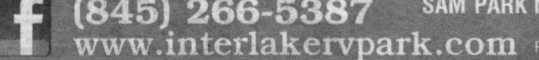

SAUGERTIES (CONT)

BLUE MOUNTAIN CAMPGROUND (CONT)
ground. Pet restrict(B). 2015 rates: $52.99. Disc: AAA, military. Apr 15 to Oct 15.
(845)246-7564 Lat: 42.14174, Lon: -74.00209
3783 Rte 32, Saugerties, NY 12477
bluemtncampground@yahoo.com
www.bluemountaincampground.com

RIP VAN WINKLE CAMPGROUNDS INC
Ratings: 10/9★/9 (Campground) From Jct of I-87 & SR-212 (exit 20), W 2.4 mi on SR-212 to CR-35, N 0.5 mi (L). **FAC:** All weather rds. (176 spaces). Avail: 106 all weather, 34 pull-thrus (40 x 75), back-ins (40 x 60), 100 full hkups, 6 W, 6 E (30/50 amps), seasonal sites, cable, WiFi, tent sites, rentals, showers $, dump, laundry, groc, LP gas, fire rings, firewood, controlled access. **REC:** heated pool, Plattekill River: swim, fishing, playground. Pets OK. Partial handicap access. Big rig sites, 2015 rates: $40 to $54. Disc: AAA, military. Apr 1 to Oct 15.
AAA Approved
(800)246-3357 Lat: 42.09249, Lon: -74.01863
149 Blue Mountain Rd (Cr-35), Saugerties, NY 12477
camping@ripvanwinklecampground.com
www.ripvanwinklecampground.com
See ad this page, 823.

SAUGERTIES/WOODSTOCK JOURNEY KOA
Ratings: 9/9.5★/9.5 (Campground) N-bnd: From Jct of I-87 & SR 212 (exit 20), W 2.5 mi on SR-212 (R); or S-bnd: From Jct of I-87 & SR 32 (exit 20), S 0.1 mi on SR 32 to SR-212, W 2.5 mi (R). **FAC:** Gravel rds. 70 Avail: 70 all weather, 29 pull-thrus (30 x 85), back-ins (30 x 60), 34 full hkups, 36 W, 36 E (30/50 amps), cable, WiFi, tent sites, rentals, dump, laundry, groc, LP gas, fire rings, firewood, controlled access. **REC:** heated pool, pond, fishing, playground. Pets OK. Partial handicap access. Big rig sites, eco-friendly, 2015 rates: $37 to $63. Disc: AAA, military. Apr 1 to Oct 30.
AAA Approved
(845)246-4089 Lat: 42.08341, Lon: -74.01849
882 Rte 212, Saugerties, NY 12477
saugertieskoa@hotmail.com
saugertieskoa.com

SCHENECTADY — D9 *Schenectady*

ARROWHEAD MARINA & RV PARK
Ratings: 7/9★/9 (Campground) From I-90 (exit 26), W 1 mi on I-890 to SR-5, W 300 ft to Van Buren Ln, S 0.1 mi to Pump House Rd, W (right) 0.2 mi (L). **FAC:** Paved/gravel rds. (60 spaces). Avail: 48 all weather, patios, 9 pull-thrus (40 x 100), back-ins (35 x 60), 34 full hkups, 14 W, 14 E (30/50 amps), seasonal sites, cable, WiFi, tent sites, dump, mobile sewer, laundry, fire rings, firewood. **REC:** Mohawk River: fishing, marina. Pets OK. Big rig sites, 2015 rates: $34 to $37. May 15 to Oct 15. No CC.
(518)382-8966 Lat: 42.84938, Lon: -74.01415
2 Van Buren Ln, Glenville, NY 12302
arrowheadmrvp@gmail.com
www.arrowheadmrvp.com
See ad this page, 823.

FROSTY ACRES RV & CAMPING RESORT
Ratings: 7/9.5★/8.5 (Membership Pk) 2015 rates: $40 to $45. May 15 to Oct 12. (518)864-5352 1560 Skyline Dr, Schenectady, NY 12306

SCHOHARIE — D9 *Schoharie*

TWIN OAKS CAMPGROUND Ratings: 7.5/8.5★/7.5 (Campground) From Jct of I-88 & SR-145 (Exit 22), S 1 mi on SR-145 to Ecker Hollow Rd (CR-41), W 3.6 mi to Twin Oaks Ln (private rd), N 0.2 mi (E). Note: Call for more info. **FAC:** Gravel rds. (108 spaces). 35 Avail: 11 gravel, 24 grass, 10 pull-thrus (25 x 50), back-ins (30 x 38), some side by side hkups, 11 full hkups, 24 W, 24 E (30 amps), seasonal sites, WiFi, tent sites, rentals, showers $, dump, mobile sewer, laundry, LP gas, fire rings, firewood. **REC:** Big Bass Lake: fishing, playground. Pets OK. 2015 rates: $35 to $39. May 15 to Oct 12.
(518)827-5641 Lat: 42.64401, Lon: -74.37369
142 Twin Oaks Ln, Schoharie, NY 12157
camp@twinoaks.com
www.twinoaksny.com

SCHROON LAKE — C9 *Essex*

ADIRONDACK/SHARP BRIDGE (State Pk) From town, N 15 mi on Hwy 9 (R). $3 entrance fee required. 2015 rates: $18. May 19 to Sep 7. (518)532-7538

SCHUYLER FALLS — A10 *Clinton*

MACOMB RESERVATION (State Pk) From town, S 0.25 mi on Hwy 22B to Norrisville Rd, W 3 mi to Campsite Rd, S 0.5 mi (R). 2015 rates: $15 to $21. May 24 to Sep 1. (518)643-9952

SENECA FALLS — D6 *Seneca*

CAYUGA LAKE/EAST CAMP (State Pk) From Jct of I-90 & SR-414 (Exit 41),S 0.25 mi on SR-414 to Rte 318, E 4.2 mi to Jct of Rtes 5 & 20, E 5 mi on Rte 5 to Rte 90, S 4 mi (L). 2015 rates: $15 to $21. May 2 to Oct 14. (315)568-5163

OAK ORCHARD MARINA & CAMPGROUND **Ratings: 6/6/7.5** (Campground) 2015 rates: $32 to $36. May 1 to Oct 12. (315)365-3000 508 Rt 89, Savannah, NY 13146

SHIRLEY — A4 *Suffolk*

SMITH POINT PARK (SUFFOLK COUNTY PARK) (Public) From Long Island Expwy (I-495, exit 68): Go S on William Floyd Pkwy to the end on Fire Island. 2015 rates: $25. (631)852-1313

SMITHTOWN — A3 *Suffolk*

BLYDENBURGH (Public) From Jct of Hwys 347 & 454, W 1.5 mi on Hwy 454 (R). 2015 rates: $25. Apr 3 to Oct 13. (631)854-3712

SOUTH COLTON — B8 *St Lawrence*

HIGLEY FLOW (State Pk) From Potsdam, S 14 mi on Rte 56 to Cold Brook Dr, W 2.5 mi (R). 2015 rates: $15 to $21. May 17 to Sep 1. (315)262-2880

SPRINGWATER — E5 *Livingston*

HOLIDAY HILL CAMPGROUND
Ratings: 9/9.5★/9.5 (Campground) From Jct of I-390 & Rte 15 (exit 3) N 3.9 mi to Walker Rd, E 0.6 mi to Strutt St, N 3.6 mi, follow signs (L) Caution: if towing do not use Marvin Hill Rd. Enter on (L). **FAC:** All weather rds. (167 spaces). 36 Avail: 18 gravel, 8 grass, 10 dirt, back-ins (40 x 50), 18 full hkups, 18 W, 18 E (30 amps), seasonal sites, cable, WiFi, tent sites, rentals, dump, mobile sewer, laundry, groc, LP bottles, fire rings, firewood. **REC:** heated pool, pond, Bass Pond: fishing, playground. Pet restrict(Q). Partial handicap access. 2015 rates: $40 to $45. May 1 to Oct 11.
(800)719-2267 Lat: 42.62631, Lon: -77.56787
7818 Marvin Hill Rd, Springwater, NY 14560
info@holidayhillcampground.com
www.holidayhillcampground.com

ST JOHNSVILLE — D8 *Fulton, Montgomery*

CRYSTAL GROVE DIAMOND MINE & CAMPGROUND **Ratings: 4.5/6.5/8** (Campground) 2015 rates: $35. Apr 15 to Oct 15. (518)568-2914 161 CR-114, St Johnsville, NY 13452

ST JOHNSVILLE CAMPSITE & MARINA (CITY PARK) (Public) From I-90 (Canajoharie exit): Cross Mohawk River and go 10 mi W on Hwy 5, then 1/4 mi S on Bridge St to Marina Dr. (518)568-7406

STEAMBURG — E3 *Cattaraugus*

ONOVILLE MARINA AND CAMPGROUND (Public) From I-86 (exit 17): Go 9-1/4 mi S on West Perimeter Rd. 2015 rates: $25. (716)354-2615

STONY POINT — A2 *Suffolk*

BEAVER POND CAMPGROUND (State Pk) From Jct of Hwy 6 & SR-202, S to Rte 9W, S 12 mi to Stony Point, S 7 mi to CR-106 (exit 15), W 2 mi (R) 2015 rates: $15. Apr 25 to Oct 12. (845)947-2792

SYLVAN BEACH — D7 *Oneida*

MAYFAIR CAMPGROUND **Ratings: 7/6.5/9** (RV Park) 2015 rates: $41. May 1 to Oct 15 (315)245-3870 3250 Old Rt 49, Blossvale, NY 13308

ONEIDA PINES CAMPGROUND
Ratings: 7/8.5★/8 (Campground) From I-90: Take exit 34 at Canustuta then take Rte 13N through Sylvan Beach, then turn left at the Y Hill onto Rte 49 West, then take second left onto Mulholland Rd, then 1/4 mile (R). **FAC:** All weather rds (109 spaces). Avail: 84 grass, 7 pull-thrus (35 x 75) back-ins (40 x 50), 84 full hkups (30/50 amps), seasonal sites, WiFi Hotspot, tent sites, dump, laundry groc, fire rings, firewood. **REC:** pond, fishing, playground. Pet restrict(Q). Partial handicap access. Big rig sites, eco-friendly, 2015 rates: $35 to $45. May 1 to Oct 15.
(315)245-1377 Lat: 43.135949, Lon: -75.45531
2045 Mulholland Rd, North Bay, NY 13123
Oneidapines@outlook.com
www.3pinesoneidalake.com
See ad this page, 823.

TA-GA-SOKE CAMPGROUNDS Ratings: 7.5/5.5/8 (Campground) 2015 rates: $41 to $45. Apr 26 to Oct 14. (800)831-1744 7820 Higginsvilee Rd, Blossvale, NY 13308

THE LANDING CAMPGROUND Ratings: 6.5/7/7 (Campground) 2015 rates: $37 to $45 Apr 30 to Oct 1. (315)245-9951 2796 Kellogg Road Blossvale, NY 13308

TREASURE ISLE RV PARK Ratings: 7.5/8.5★/9 (Campground) From Jct of I-90 & SR-13 (exit 34), N 8.7 mi on SR-13 to Vienna Rd (stoplight), E 4 mi on Vienna Rd/Haskins Rd (R). Do not use GPS. **FAC:** Poor gravel/dirt rds. (75 spaces) Avail: 10 grass, 5 pull-thrus (45 x 70), back-ins (45 x 60), 10 W, 10 E (30/50 amps), seasonal sites WiFi, dump, mobile sewer, laundry, LP gas, fire rings firewood. **REC:** Fish Creek River: swim, fishing, playground. Pet restrict(Q). Partial handicap access, no tents. 2015 rates: $36 to $39. Disc: AAA, military. Apr 22 to Oct 10.
AAA Approved
(315)245-5228 Lat: 43.23065, Lon: -75.67639
3132 Haskins Rd, Blossvale, NY 13308
leannesilber@gmail.com
www.treasureislervpark.com

SYRACUSE — D6 *Onondaga*

Travel Services

CAMPING WORLD OF SYRACUSE As the nation's largest retailer of RV supplies, accessories, services and new and used RVs, Camping World is committed to making your total RV experience better. RV Accessories: (866)393-6439. **SERVICES:** RV, tire, RV appliance, MH mechanical, staffed RV wash, RV Sales. RV supplies LP, emergency parking. Hours: 8am to 6pm.
(888)627-9431 Lat: 43.109200, Lon: -76.283231
7030 Interstate Island Road, Syracuse, NY 13209
www.campingworld.com

Things change ... last year's rates serve as a guideline only.

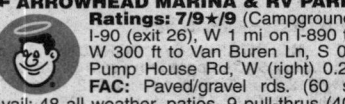

THREE MILE BAY — B6 *Jefferson*

LONG POINT (State Pk) From Jct of SR-12E & SR-57, S 12 mi on SR-57, becomes State Park Rd (L). Pets need rabies certification. 2015 rates: $15 to $21. May 24 to Sep 1. (315)649-5258

TICONDEROGA — C10 *Essex*

BROOKWOOD RV RESORT
Ratings: 6/9.5★/8.5 (Campground) From Jct of I-87 (exit 28) & Rte 74: Go 16 mi E on Rte 74, then go right on NY 9N, then at traffic circle go right, then go 4 mi S (R). **FAC:** Gravel rds. (75 spaces). Avail: 16 gravel, 6 pull-thrus (30 x 60), back-ins (25 x 42), 16 full hkups (30/50 amps), seasonal sites, WiFi Hotspot, tent sites, rentals, showers $, dump, laundry, groc, LP bottles, fire rings, firewood. **REC:** Trout Brook: playground. Pets OK. Partial handicap access. Big rig sites, eco-friendly, 2015 rates: $39. May 15 to Oct 15.
(518)585-4462 Lat: 43.4832, Lon: -73.2919
133 State Route 9N, Ticonderoga, NY 12883
camping@brookwoodrvresort.com
www.brookwoodrvresort.com

PARADOX LAKE (State Pk) From Exit 28 on Rte 87, E 4 mi on Rte 74 (L). 2015 rates: $18. May 19 to Oct 12. (518)532-7451

PUTNAM POND (State Pk) From Jct of SR-9N/22 & SR-74, W 6 mi on SR-74 (L). Entrance fee required. 2015 rates: $18. May 19 to Sep 7. (518)585-7280

ROGERS ROCK CAMPGROUND (ADIRONDACK SF) (State Pk) From town: Go 7 mi SW on Hwy-9N. 2015 rates: $22. (518)585-6746

TUPPER LAKE — B9 *Franklin*

FISH CREEK POND (State Pk) From town, E 12 mi on Rte 30 (L). Entrance fee required. 2015 rates: $22. Apr 14 to Nov 11. (518)891-4560

ROLLINS POND (Public) From Jct of SR-3 & SR-30 (in town), E 12 mi on SR-30 (L). 2015 rates: $20. May 19 to Sep 3. (518)891-3239

UNADILLA — E7 *Delaware*

DELAWARE VALLEY/UNADILLA KOA **Ratings: 8.5/9/8.5** (Campground) 2015 rates: $41 to $46. May 1 to Oct 15. (607)369-9030 242 Union Church Road, Franklin, NY 13775

UTICA — D8 *Oneida*

UTICA See also Poland, Rome, Oneida, Herkimer.

VERONA — D7 *Oneida*

THE VILLAGES AT TURNING STONE
Ratings: 10/10★/10 (RV Park) From Jct of I-90 (exit 33) & SR-365, W 1 mi on SR-365 (R).

ADVENTURE ABOUNDS IN VERONA, NY
Enjoy nature's playground at this top-rated New York park. Hike and bike acres of terrain, swim, and enjoy themed weekends the whole season through. Entire world-class resort experience is just 5 minute shuttle ride away!

FAC: Paved rds. (175 spaces). Avail: 155 paved, 50 pull-thrus (50 x 60), back-ins (50 x 50), 155 full hkups (30/50 amps), seasonal sites, cable, WiFi, dump, laundry, groc, LP gas, fire rings, firewood. **REC:** heated pool, wading pool, whirlpool, pond, fishing, golf, playground. Pets OK. Partial handicap access, no tents. Big rig sites, 2015 rates: $40 to $55. Disc: AAA. Apr 15 to Oct 15.
(315)361-7275 Lat: 43.10667, Lon: -75.60643
5065 Sr 365, Verona, NY 13478
info@turningstone.com
www.turningstone.com
See ad this page, 823.

Things to See and Do

TURNING STONE RESORT CASINO Casino type games, restaurants, golf course. Partial handicap access. RV accessible. Restrooms, food. Hours: 24 hours. ATM.
(800)771-7711 Lat: 43.11591, Lon: -75.59235
5218 Patrick Rd, Verona, NY 13478
www.turningstone.com
See ad this page.

WADDINGTON — A8 *St Lawrence*

COLES CREEK (State Pk) From Jct of SR-345 & SR-37, NE 4 mi on SR-37 (L). 2015 rates: $15 to $21. May 10 to Sep 7. (315)388-5636

Say you saw it in our Guide!

WADING RIVER — A4 *Suffolk*

WILDWOOD (State Pk) From Jct of I-495 & SR-46 (exit 68N), N 8 mi on SR-46 to SR-25A, E 3 mi to Sound Rd, E 0.5 mi to Hulse Landing Rd, N 0.3 mi (R) (One time entrance fee $2.75). 2015 rates: $15 to $31. Apr 5 to Oct 14. (631)929-4314

Travel Services

W E S TRAILER SALES, INC Trailer sales & service. **SERVICES:** RV, RV appliance, restrooms, RV Sales. RV storage. RV supplies, LP, dump, emergency parking, RV accessible. waiting room. Hours: 8am to 5pm.
(631)727-5852 Lat: 40.91477, Lon: -72.83493
6166 Route 25, Wading River, NY 11792
www.westrailersales.com
See ad page 835.

WALTON — E8 *Delaware*

BEAR SPRING MOUNTAIN (Public) From town, SE 4.5 mi on Rte 206, S 1 mi on E Trout Brook Rd (R). 2015 rates: $18. May 17 to Sep 1. (607)865-6989

WARRENSBURG — C9 *Warren*

LAKE GEORGE SCHROON VALLEY RESORT **Ratings: 8/7.5/9** (Campground) 2015 rates: $23 to $52. May 10 to Oct 15. (800)405-6188 1730 Schroon River Rd, Warrensburg, NY 12885

SCHROON RIVER CAMPSITES LLC **Ratings: 6.5/6.5/7.5** (Campground) 2015 rates: $38 to $47. May 15 to Oct 4. (518)623-2171 686 Schroon River Rd, Warrensburg, NY 12885

WARSAW — D4 *Wyoming*

DREAM LAKE CAMPGROUND **Ratings: 8/8/8.5** (Campground) 2015 rates: $30 to $58. May 1 to Oct 25. (585)786-5172 4391 Old Buffalo Rd, Warsaw, NY 14569

WATKINS GLEN — E5 *Schuyler*

WARREN W CLUTE MEMORIAL PARK
(Public) From Jct of Hwys 14 & 414 (in town), N 0.5 mi on Hwy 414 (R). For GPS aided location use "Boat Launch Road.". **FAC:** Paved/gravel rds. (130 spaces). Avail: 60 grass, 17 pull-thrus (25 x 50), back-ins (25 x 50), 60 full hkups (30/50 amps), cable, WiFi, tent sites, dump, LP bottles, fire rings, firewood. **REC:** Seneca Lake: swim,

NY

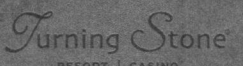

WATKINS GLEN (CONT)

WARREN W CLUTE MEMORIAL (CONT)
fishing, playground. Pets OK. Partial handicap access. Big rig sites, 2015 rates: $55. May 9 to Oct 14.
(607)535-4438 Lat: 42.38424, Lon: -76.86022
155 S Clute Park Drive, Watkins Glen, NY 14891
parksdept@watkinsglen.us
www.watkinsglen.us/clute-park-campground
See ad page 843.

WATKINS GLEN (State Pk) From Jct of Rtes 14 & CR-409, W 2.6 mi to Whites Hollow Rd, S .2 mi. 2015 rates: $15 to $27. May 5 to Oct 21. (607)535-4511

WATKINS GLEN/CORNING KOA CAMPING RESORT **Ratings: 10/10★/10** (Campground) 2015 rates: $53 to $94. Apr 18 to Oct 26. (800)562-7430 1710 Route 414 S, Watkins Glen, NY 14891

WEBSTER — D5 *Monroe*

WEBSTER PARK (Public) From town, N 3 mi on Webster Rd. to Lake Rd, W 1.5 mi (L). 2015 rates: $25. Apr 1 to Oct 31. (585)872-5326

WEEDSPORT — D6 *Cayuga*

RIVERFOREST PARK **Ratings: 8/7.5/8.5** (Campground) 2015 rates: $34 to $38. May 1 to Oct 12. (315)834-9458 9439 Riverforest Rd, Weedsport, NY 13166

WELLSVILLE — E4 *Allegany*

TROUT RUN CAMP RESORT
Ratings: 7.5/8.5/8 (Campground) From jct 19 & 417: Go 2 mi S on Route 19 (R). **FAC:** Paved rds. (156 spaces). Avail: 131 grass, patios, 12 pull-thrus (50 x 100), back-ins (50 x 100), 131 full hkups (30/50 amps), seasonal sites, WiFi, tent sites, rentals, dump, laundry, groc, LP gas, fire rings, firewood. **REC:** Genesee River: swim, fishing, playground. Pets OK. Partial handicap access. Big rig sites, 2015 rates: $35. Apr 15 to Nov 30. ATM.
(585)596-0500 Lat: 42.52914, Lon: -77.552201
2137 Stannards Rd, Wellsville, NY 14895
info@troutruncamping.com
www.troutruncamping.com
See ad this page, 823.

WEST CHAZY — A10 *Clinton*

TWIN ELLS CAMPSITE **Ratings: 8/8.5★/8** (Campground) 2015 rates: $27. May 1 to Oct 12. (518)493-6151 255 Laplante Rd, Beekmantown, NY 12992

WESTFIELD — E2 *Chautauqua*

WESTFIELD-LAKE ERIE KOA **Ratings: 8.5/9★/7.5** (Campground) 2015 rates: $41 to $51. Apr 18 to Nov 1. (800)562-3973 8001 Rte 5 (East Lake Road), Westfield, NY 14787

WESTPORT — B10 *Essex*

BARBER HOMESTEAD PARK **Ratings: 8/9/8.5** (Campground) 2015 rates: $33 to $38. May 25 to Oct 12. (518)962-8989 68 Barber Ln, Westport, NY 12993

You can be the king of the road, but you still have to be safe. Be sure to use the valuable information provided in the Road and Highway Safety Information pages, and check out the Road and Highway Information Telephone Numbers. You can locate both by referring to the Table of Contents at the front of the Guide.

WESTVILLE CENTER — A9 *Franklin*

BABBLING BROOK RV PARK **Ratings: 6.5/8/7.5** (Campground) 2015 rates: $35. May 4 to Sep 30. (518)358-4245 1623 County Route 4, Westville Center, NY 12953

WHITNEY POINT — E7 *Broome*

UPPER LISLE CAMPGROUND (Public) From Jct of I-81 & Rte 26E (exit 8), E 0.25 mi on Rte 26E to Rte 11, N 0.25 mi to SR-26N, N 5 mi (L). Pit toilets. 2015 rates: $10. May 1 to Sep 30. (607)692-4612

WILMINGTON — B9 *Essex*

ADIRONDACK/WILMINGTON NOTCH (State Pk) From town, W 3.5 mi on Rte 86 (R). Entrance fee required. 2015 rates: $18. May 5 to Oct 8. (518)946-7172

LAKE PLACID/WHITEFACE MT KOA **Ratings: 8.5/8.5/8** (Campground) 2015 rates: $46 to $58. (518)946-7878 77 Fox Farm Rd, Wilmington, NY 12997

NORTH POLE RESORTS
Ratings: 9/10★/10 (Campground) N-bnd: From Jct of I-87 & SR-73 (Exit 30), NW 16 mi on SR-73 to SR-9N, 10 mi N on SR-9N to SR-86, W 5 mi on SR-86 to Jct 431, continue on SR-86 W 0.2 mi (L); or S-bnd: From Jct of I-87 & SR-9N (Exit 34), S 16 mi on SR-9N to SR-86, W 5 mi on SR-86 to Jct 431, continue on SR-86 W 0.2 mi (L). **FAC:** Paved/gravel rds. 113 Avail: 95 gravel, 18 grass, 40 pull-thrus (30 x 80), back-ins (26 x 56), 78 full hkups, 35 W, 35 E (30/50 amps), cable, WiFi, tent sites, rentals, dump, laundry, groc, LP gas, fire rings, firewood. **REC:** heated pool, Ausable River: fishing, playground. Pet restrict(B/Q). Big rig sites, eco-friendly, 2015 rates: $48 to $50. Apr 10 to Oct 25. ATM.
(518)946-7733 Lat: 44.38745, Lon: -73.82469
5644 Rte 86, Wilmington, NY 12997
info@northpoleresorts.com
www.northpoleresorts.com
See ad pages 834, 823.

WINDSOR — E7 *Broome*

FOREST LAKE CAMPGROUND Ratings: 7/8/8.5 (Campground) From Jct of SR-17 & Old SR-17 (Exit 80), E 1.3 mi on Old SR-17 to Ostrander Rd, NW 2.5 mi (R). Note: 3 days minimum stay on holiday weekends. **FAC:** All weather rds. (93 spaces). Avail: 17 all weather, back-ins (30 x 60), 17 full hkups (30/50 amps), seasonal sites, WiFi, tent sites, dump, mobile sewer, laundry, fire rings, firewood, controlled access. **REC:** Forest Lake: swim, fishing, playground. Pet restrict(B). Big rig sites, 2015 rates: $35. May 1 to Oct 15. No CC.
AAA Approved
(607)655-1444 Lat: 42.09387, Lon: -75.59882
574 Ostrander Rd, Windsor, NY 13865
barbmirch@yahoo.com
www.forestlakewindsorny.com

Traveling with a Fido? Many campground listings indicate pet-friendly amenities and pet restrictions.

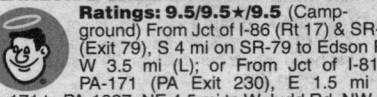

LAKESIDE CAMPGROUND
Ratings: 9.5/9.5★/9.5 (Campground) From Jct of I-86 (Rt 17) & SR-79 (Exit 79), S 4 mi on SR-79 to Edson Rd, W 3.5 mi (L); or From Jct of I-81 & PA-171 (PA Exit 230), E 1.5 mi on PA-171 to PA-1027, NE 4.5 mi to W Judd Rd, NW 0.6 mi to Hargrave Rd, NE 0.8 mi (R). Note: Re GPS; call ahead. **FAC:** All weather rds. (110 spaces). Avail: 50 all weather, 11 pull-thrus (30 x 75), back-ins (30 x 50), 39 full hkups, 11 W, 11 E (30/50 amps), seasonal sites, WiFi, tent sites, rentals, showers $, dump, laundry, groc, LP gas, fire rings, firewood, controlled access. **REC:** Lakeside Lake: swim, fishing, playground. Pet restrict(Q). Big rig sites, 2015 rates: $40 to $43. May 1 to Oct 1.
AAA Approved
(607)655-2694 Lat: 42.01727, Lon: -75.68268
336 Hargrave Rd, Windsor, NY 13865
theresa@ilovecamping.com
www.ilovecamping.com
See ad page 823.

PINE CREST CAMPGROUND **Ratings: 6.5/8/7.5** (Campground) 2015 rates: $40 to $48. May 15 to Sep 30. (607)655-1515 280 State Rte 79, Windsor, NY 13865

WOLCOTT — D6 *Wayne*

CHERRY GROVE CAMPGROUND
Ratings: 9.5/9★/8 (Campground) From Jct of SR-104 & Ridge Rd (E of town), W 300 ft on Ridge Rd (R). **FAC:** All weather rds. (105 spaces). Avail: 25 all weather, 20 pull-thrus (30 x 75), back-ins (30 x 50), 25 full hkups (30/50 amps), seasonal sites, WiFi $, tent sites, rentals, dump, laundry, LP gas, fire rings, firewood. **REC:** pool, shuffleboard, playground. Pet restrict(B/Q). Big rig sites, eco-friendly, 2015 rates: $34 to $39. Apr 15 to Oct 15.
(315)594-8320 Lat: 43.22414, Lon: -76.78472
12669 Ridge Rd, Wolcott, NY 14590
cherrygrove03@gmail.com
www.cherrygrovecampground.com
See ad this page, 823.

LAKE BLUFF CAMPGROUND **Ratings: 7/8/9.5** (Campground) 2015 rates: $34 to $39. Apr 15 to Oct 18. (315)587-4517 7150 Garner Rd, Wolcott, NY 14590

WOODVILLE — C6 *Jefferson*

SOUTHWICK BEACH (State Pk) From I-81 & CR-193 Jct (exit 40), W 4 mi. (E). Entrance Fee Required. 2015 rates: $15 to $21. May 10 to Oct 13. (315)846-5338

YOUNGSTOWN — D3 *Niagara*

FORT NIAGARA SP (FOUR MILE CAMPSITE) (State Pk) From town: Go 4 mi E on Hwy-18. 2015 rates: $15 to $23. (716)745-7273

Say you saw it in our Guide!

Stephen Beaudet

WELCOME TO
North Carolina

DATE OF STATEHOOD	WIDTH: 150 MILES (241 KM)	PROPORTION OF UNITED STATES
NOV. 21, 1789	LENGTH: 560 MILES (901 KM)	1.42% OF 3,794,100 SQ MI

For most of its existence, North Carolina was known as a place of tobacco farms, textile mills and antebellum mansions on stately country lanes. The farms and mills are mostly gone, replaced by high-tech research complexes and modern banks. In its colorful cities you'll find craft breweries, but the stock cars are still big. Only five states attract more tourists than modern-day North Carolina.

Learn

Explorations of North Carolina history begin on Roanoke Island in the Outer Banks. Unfortunately, the Lost Colony of English settlers disappeared without a trace, and their fate is left to speculation by visitors to the preserved historic site.

Pivotal Revolutionary War battlefields are preserved in the Guilford Courthouse National Military Park in Greensboro and Moores Creek National Battlefield in Currie. Civil War history is relived on the North Carolina coast at Fort Macon State Park and Fort Fisher State Recreation Area. And the *USS North Carolina* battleship moored in downtown Wilmington delivers a slice of World War II Marine life.

The Wright Brothers National Memorial in Kitty Hawk looks much the same as it did when bicycle mechanics Orville and Wilbur Wright came in the winter of 1903. The area's soft sand provided safe landings for the early aviators, who often crashed their planes before perfecting their designs.

Play

Those sand piles are part of the Outer Banks, 200 miles of Atlantic Ocean barrier islands. Today, America's first protected national seashore is a vacationer's delight. In past centuries, not so much—mariners called the treacherous shoals off Cape Hatteras the "Graveyard of the Atlantic." Even the country's tallest brick lighthouse, the famous black-and-white stripe Cape Hatteras Light, didn't always help.

Top 3 Tourism Attractions:
1) Great Smoky Mountains National Park
2) Biltmore Estate
3) Wright Brothers National Memorial

Nickname: Tar Heel State

State Flower: Dogwood

State Bird: Cardinal

People: Howard Cosell, sports journalist; Billy Graham, evangelist; Andy Griffith, actor; Sugar Ray Leonard, boxer; Richard Petty, race car driver; Soupy Sales, actor and comedian; Randy Travis, singer

Major Cities: Charlotte, Raleigh (capital), Greensboro, Winston-Salem, Durham

Topography: East—coastal plains, tidewater; central—Piedmont Plateau; west—Appalachian Mountains contain Blue Ridge and Great Smoky mountains

Climate: Humid, subtropical climate with short, mild winters, sultry summers and distinct, refreshing spring and fall seasons

Brad Styron

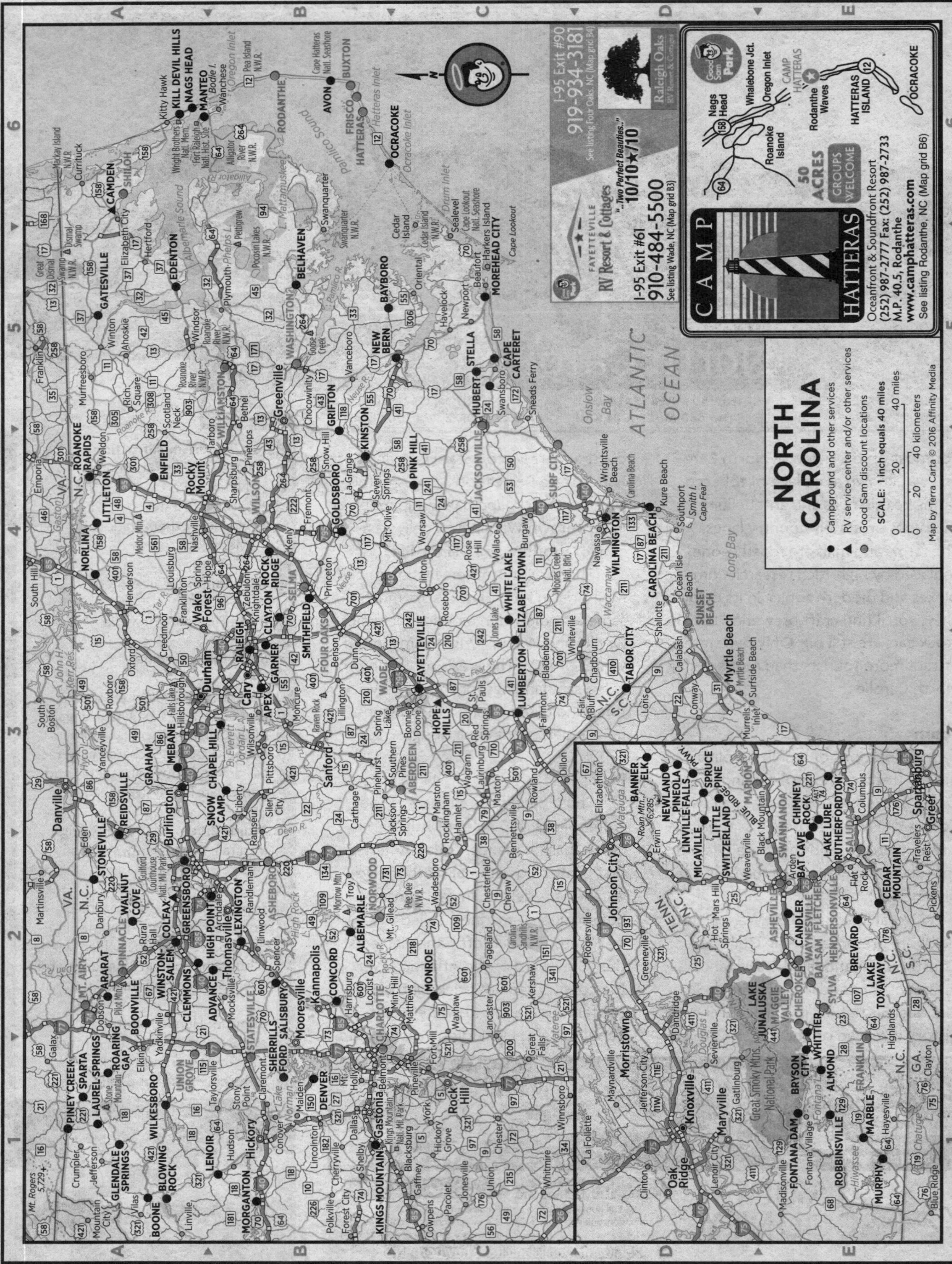
NORTH CAROLINA
Campground and other services
RV service center and/or other services
Good Sam discount locations
SCALE: 1 inch equals 40 miles
0 20 40 miles
0 20 40 kilometers
Map by Terra Carta © 2016 Affinity Media
ATLANTIC OCEAN
I-95 Exit #90
919-934-3181
See listing Four Oaks, NC (Map grid B4)
Raleigh Oaks RV Resort & Cottages
FAYETTEVILLE RV Resort & Cottages
"Two Perfect Beauties"
10/10★/10
I-95 Exit #61
910-484-5500
See listing Wade, NC (Map grid B3)
CAMP HATTERAS
50 ACRES
GROUPS WELCOME
Oceanfront & Soundfront Resort
(252) 987-2777 Fax: (252) 987-2733
M.P. 40.5, Rodanthe
www.camphatteras.com
See listing Rodanthe, NC (Map grid B6)

See listing Manteo, NC
Stir the Soul
We're drawn to open spaces. Natural settings that stir the soul and inspire us. The Outer Banks of North Carolina, a chain of barrier islands shaped by wind and water. Connected by the elements. Just open spaces and endless possibilities. Get in touch with us.
The Outer Banks®
OF NORTH CAROLINA
877-629-4386 | OuterBanksSoul.com

NC

The Blue Ridge Parkway is one of America's most visited units of the National Park Service, and 250 of its 469 miles connect Virginia to the Great Smoky Mountains National Park across western North Carolina. Along the way, the two-lane roadway visits Mount Mitchell, the highest point east of the Mississippi River; Biltmore, America's largest private house; and enough waterfalls in Pisgah National Forest to enable Transylvania County to tout itself as "the Land of Waterfalls."

Hollywood has discovered North Carolina scenery and staked out several movie studios. The DuPont State Forest starred in "The Hunger Games," Lake Lure stood in for the Catskills of the 1950s in "Dirty Dancing" and Chimney Rock State Park provided the dramatic backdrop for "The Last of the Mohicans."

Experience

North Carolina barbecue has earned a place in culinary legend, and for good reason. Over the decades, two types of barbecue have evolved. In Eastern style, "every part of the hog except the squeal" is slow-cooked; in Western style (also known as Lexington style) only the pork shoulder of the pig is used. Eastern style barbecue sauce is vinegar and red pepper-based; Western style barbecue includes ketchup or tomato products as a third main ingredient. It all gets sorted out at the Lexington Barbecue Festival.

At the Grandfather Mountain Highland Games, descendants of Scottish settlers and fans of all things Scottish celebrate their heritage with contests of strength. The mountain itself is an International Biosphere Reserve.

Even though it has been nearly 50 years since "The Andy Griffith Show" aired, its portrayal of small-town life continues to resonate in America. Nowhere is that more apparent than during Mayberry Days in Mount Airy in September.

Taste

Pepsi-Cola was born in Caleb Davis Bradham's drug store in New Bern in 1893, but that is not North Carolina's most beloved soda pop. That would be Cheerwine, a wild cherry-flavored potion concocted in 1917 by L.D. Peeler in his store in Salisbury. Today, the Carolina Beverage Corporation is the oldest soft drink company in America and is run by the same family.

- STAY A WHILE -

The Outer Banks

The Outer Banks is a 200-mile-long string of narrow barrier islands off the coast of North Carolina and a small portion of Virginia, beginning in the southeastern corner of Virginia Beach on the east coast of the United States. The islands cover most of the North Carolina coastline, separating the Currituck Sound, Albemarle Sound and Pamlico Sound from the Atlantic Ocean.

The Outer Banks is a major tourist destination and is known around the world for its temperate climate and wide expanse of open beachfront.

The Wright brothers' first flight in a controlled, powered, heavier-than-air vehicle took place on the Outer Banks on December 17, 1903, at Kill Devil Hills near the seafront town of Kitty Hawk. The Wright Brothers National Monument commemorates the historic flights, and First Flight Airport is a small, general-aviation airfield located there.

The English Roanoke Colony—where the first person of English descent, Virginia Dare, was born on American soil—vanished from Roanoke Island in 1587. "The Lost Colony," written and performed to commemorate the original colonists, is the second longest running outdoor drama in the United States and its theater acts as a cultural focal point for much of the Outer Banks.

The treacherous seas off the Outer Banks and a large number of shipwrecks that have occurred there have given these seas the nickname Graveyard of the Atlantic. The Graveyard of the Atlantic Museum is located in Hatteras Village near the United States Coast Guard facility and Hatteras ferry.

www.outerbanks.org/Travel-Guide

TRAVEL & TOURISM

North Carolina Dept of Tourism
800-VISIT-NC, 919-733-4171
www.visitnc.com

Visit Charlotte
800-722-1994, 704-334-2282
www.visitcharlotte.com

Durham Convention & Visitors Bureau
800-446-8604, 919-687-0288
www.durham-nc.com

Greensboro Area Convention & Visitors Bureau
800-344-2282, 336-274-2282
www.visitgreensboro.com

North Carolina Brunswick Islands
800-795-7263, 910-755-5517
www.ncbrunswick.com

Wilmington Beaches CVB
910-341-4030
www.wilmingtonandbeaches.com

Visit Raleigh
800-849-8499
www.visitraleigh.com

OUTDOOR RECREATION

North Carolina Fishing
www.ncwildlife.org/fishing

North Carolina State Parks
www.ncparks.gov

SHOPPING

Appalachian Craft Center
www.appalachiancraftcenter.com

Carolina Premium Outlets
www.premiumoutlets.com/carolina

Ninth Street Shopping District
www.ninthst.com

North Carolina Remembered
919-782-5808
www.ncremembered.citysearch.com

Wilcox Emporium Warehouse
828-262-1221

Featured Good Sam Parks

NORTH CAROLINA

Good Sam Park

NC

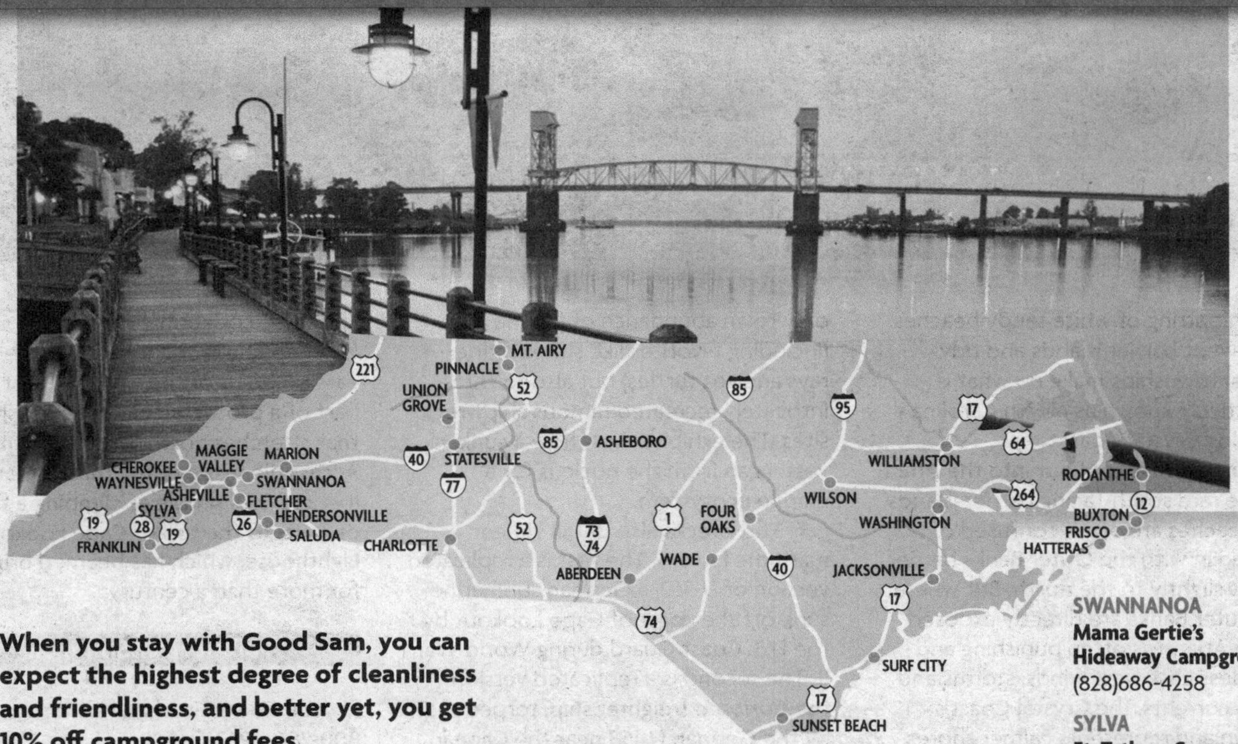

When you stay with Good Sam, you can expect the highest degree of cleanliness and friendliness, and better yet, you get 10% off campground fees.

If you're not already a Good Sam member you can purchase your membership at one of these locations:

ABERDEEN
Oasis Of North Carolina
(910)266-8372

ASHEBORO
Zooland Family Campground, LLC
(336)381-3422

ASHEVILLE
Asheville Bear Creek RV Park
(800)833-0798
Asheville Taps RV Park
(828)299-8277

BUXTON
Cape Woods Campground
(252)995-5850

CHARLOTTE
Camping at Charlotte Motor Speedway
(704)455-4445
Carowinds Camp Wilderness Resort
(704)587-9116

CHEROKEE
Fort Wilderness Campground and RV Park
(828)497-9331
Happy Holiday Campground
(828)497-9204
Yogi In the Smokies
(828)497-9151

FLETCHER
Rutledge Lake RV Resort
(828)654-7873

FOUR OAKS
Four Oaks Lodging & RV Resort
(919)963-3596
Raleigh Oaks RV Resort & Cottages
(919)934-3181

FRANKLIN
The Great Outdoors RV Resort
(828)349-0412

FRISCO
Frisco Woods Campground
(252)995-5208

HATTERAS
Hatteras Sands Campground
(252)986-2422

HENDERSONVILLE
Jaymar Travel Park
(828)685-3771
Lakewood RV Resort
(888)819-4200
Town Mountain Travel Park
(828)697-6692

JACKSONVILLE
Cabin Creek Campground
(910)346-4808

MAGGIE VALLEY
Stonebridge Campgrounds
(828)926-1904

MARION
Buck Creek RV Park
(828)724-4888

MOUNT AIRY
Mayberry Campground
(336)789-6199

PINNACLE
Greystone RV Park
(336)368-5588

RODANTHE
Camp Hatteras
(252)987-2777

SALUDA
Orchard Lake Campground
(828)749-3901

STATESVILLE
Midway Campground Resort
(855)882-7999

SUNSET BEACH
Brunswick Beaches Camping Resort
(855)579-2267

SURF CITY
Lanier's Campground
(910)328-9431

SWANNANOA
Mama Gertie's Hideaway Campground
(828)686-4258

SYLVA
Ft. Tatham Campground Carefree RV Resort
(828)586-6662

UNION GROVE
Van Hoy Farms Family Campground
(704)539-5493

WADE
Fayetteville RV Resort & Cottages
(910)484-5500

WASHINGTON
Tranter's Creek Resort & Campground
(252)948-0850

WAYNESVILLE
Creekwood Farm RV Park
(828)926-7977

WILLIAMSTON
Pierce RV Park
(252)799-0111

WILSON
Kamper's Lodge Of America
(252)237-0905

For more Good Sam Parks go to listing pages

Crystal Coast Tourism Authority

CRYSTAL COAST

Climb the stairs of an iconic lighthouse and hit the surf

A scenic string of white sandy beaches, windswept barrier islands and tidy coastal townships make up what is collectively known as North Carolina's sparkling Crystal Coast.

Jutting eastward out into the Atlantic, the rare south-facing barrier islands and beaches are often confused or lumped in with the Outer Banks barrier islands slightly to the north. But where the Outer Banks are directly exposed to the Atlantic's often punishing and relentless east-west winds, storms and ocean currents, the Crystal Coast's bend inland represents calmer shores.

Bank on the Banks

Unlike shipwrecked pirates of centuries past, folks who visit the Crystal Coast today will find themselves drawn happily to Bogue Banks, a 21-mile-long island that constitutes the bulk of the Crystal Coast, and which separates the Atlantic Ocean from Bogue Sound. The Banks are home to the communities of Emerald Isle, Indian Beach, Salter Path, Pine Knoll Shores and Atlantic Beach.

Emerald Isle and Indian Beach are popular water-sports destinations for summer-rental cottagers. Salter Path, located further east at Bogue Banks' narrowest juncture, is a tiny fishing village that's home to some of the Banks' original descendants. The communities of Pine Knoll Shores and Atlantic Beach tend to attract the bulk of the crowds visiting Bogue Banks.

Fascinating Fish and Fighting Ships

At Pine Knoll Shores, those traveling with kids won't want to miss the North Carolina Aquarium, which is home not only to an abundance of marine life (including favorites like sharks, stingrays and sea turtles) but also to three intricately recreated famous shipwreck sites. The exhibits show how a sunken vessel can form the nucleus for a marine ecosystem.

The wrecks also detail violent maritime history. The first is a replicated version of *U-352*, a German submarine sunk off the coast of Cape Lookout by the U.S. Coast Guard during World War II. The second is a replicated version the *Caribsea* freighter ship, torpedoed by the German *U-158* near the Cape in 1942. And the third replication is the crown jewel of the collection: *Queen Anne's Revenge*, Blackbeard's infamous pirate ship. For all the terror it inspired on the high seas, its end was pedestrian. It ran aground in Beaufort Inlet in 1718.

One of the Best Beaches

Just east of Pine Knoll Shores at Atlantic Beach, sunbathers, surfers and sandcastle aficionados can enjoy free access to what's been routinely selected as one of the best beaches in the country. It's also the jumping-off point to Fort Macon State Park, home to the Civil War fort of the same name.

From Bogue Banks, your next stop should be a hop across the water to Beaufort and Harkers Island.

Nearby Harkers Island is mostly full of private homes and communities, but from here you can catch daily ferries that offer easy day trips to nearby Shackleford Banks (an undeveloped island that's home to more than 100 wild horses—most likely descendants from abandoned shipwrecked horses) and Cape Lookout.

Cape Lookout, located at the far eastern point of the Crystal Coast, is part of a protected National Seashore that stretches northward for 56 miles. Accessible by boat, the must-do activity here is as simple as climbing a flight of stairs to the top of Cape Lookout Lighthouse, which has beamed brightly for more than a century.

For More Information

Crystal Coast Tourism Authority
800-786-6962
www.crystalcoastnc.org

North Carolina Department of Tourism
800-VISIT-NC
www.visitnc.com

Pathway to Cape Lookout Lighthouse.
Getty Images/iStockphoto

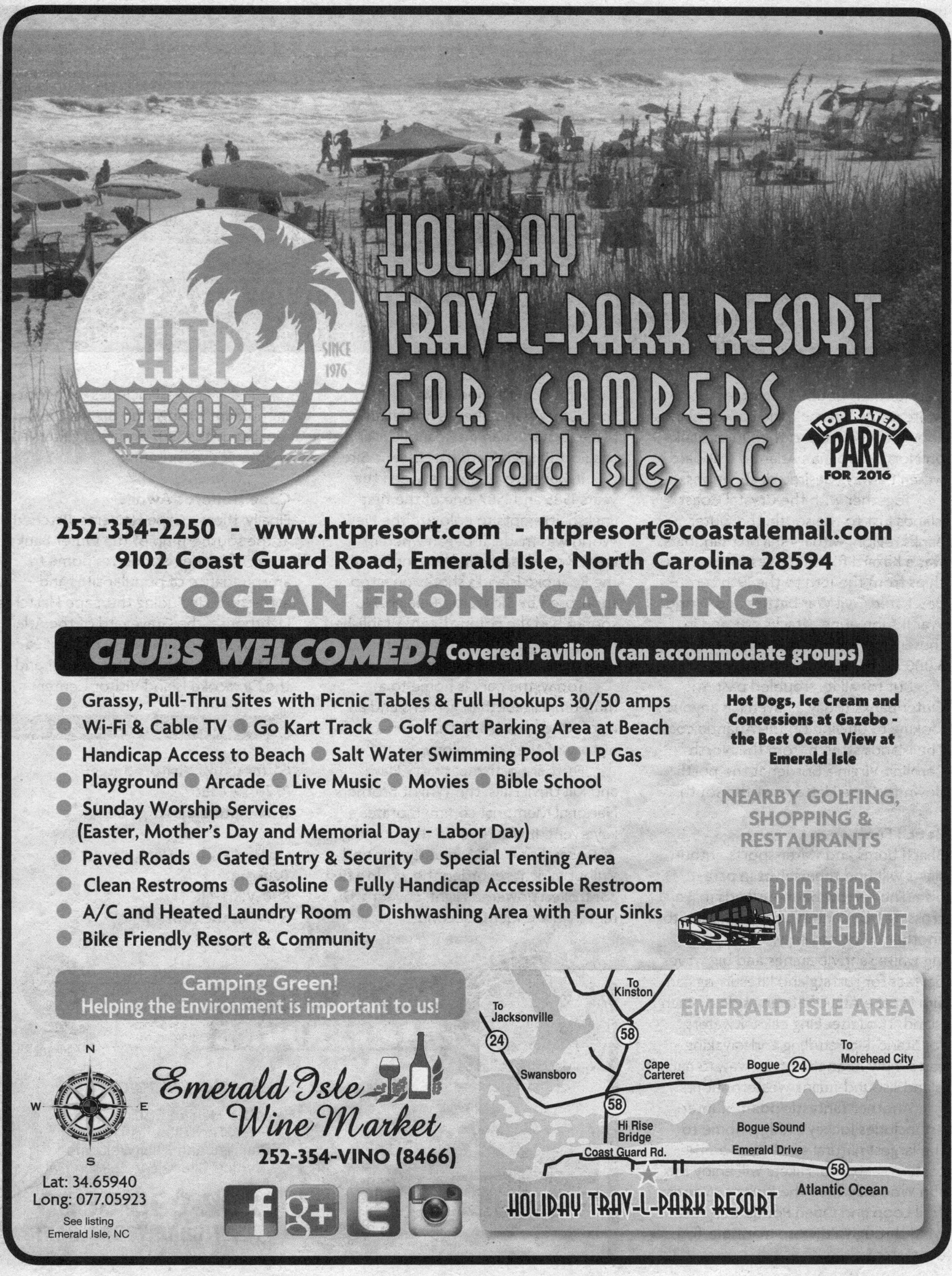
HTP RESORT
SINCE 1976
HOLIDAY TRAV-L-PARK RESORT FOR CAMPERS
Emerald Isle, N.C.
TOP RATED PARK FOR 2016
252-354-2250 - www.htpresort.com - htpresort@coastalemail.com
9102 Coast Guard Road, Emerald Isle, North Carolina 28594
OCEAN FRONT CAMPING
CLUBS WELCOMED! Covered Pavilion (can accommodate groups)
Grassy, Pull-Thru Sites with Picnic Tables & Full Hookups 30/50 amps
Wi-Fi & Cable TV • Go Kart Track • Golf Cart Parking Area at Beach
Handicap Access to Beach • Salt Water Swimming Pool • LP Gas
Playground • Arcade • Live Music • Movies • Bible School
Sunday Worship Services (Easter, Mother's Day and Memorial Day - Labor Day)
Paved Roads • Gated Entry & Security • Special Tenting Area
Clean Restrooms • Gasoline • Fully Handicap Accessible Restroom
A/C and Heated Laundry Room • Dishwashing Area with Four Sinks
Bike Friendly Resort & Community
Hot Dogs, Ice Cream and Concessions at Gazebo - the Best Ocean View at Emerald Isle
NEARBY GOLFING, SHOPPING & RESTAURANTS
BIG RIGS WELCOME
Camping Green! Helping the Environment is important to us!
N
W
E
S
Lat: 34.65940
Long: 077.05923
See listing Emerald Isle, NC
Emerald Isle Wine Market
252-354-VINO (8466)
EMERALD ISLE AREA
To Kinston
To Jacksonville
24
58
Swansboro
Cape Carteret
Bogue
To Morehead City
Hi Rise Bridge
Bogue Sound
Coast Guard Rd.
Emerald Drive
Atlantic Ocean
HOLIDAY TRAV-L-PARK RESORT

 See map page 846

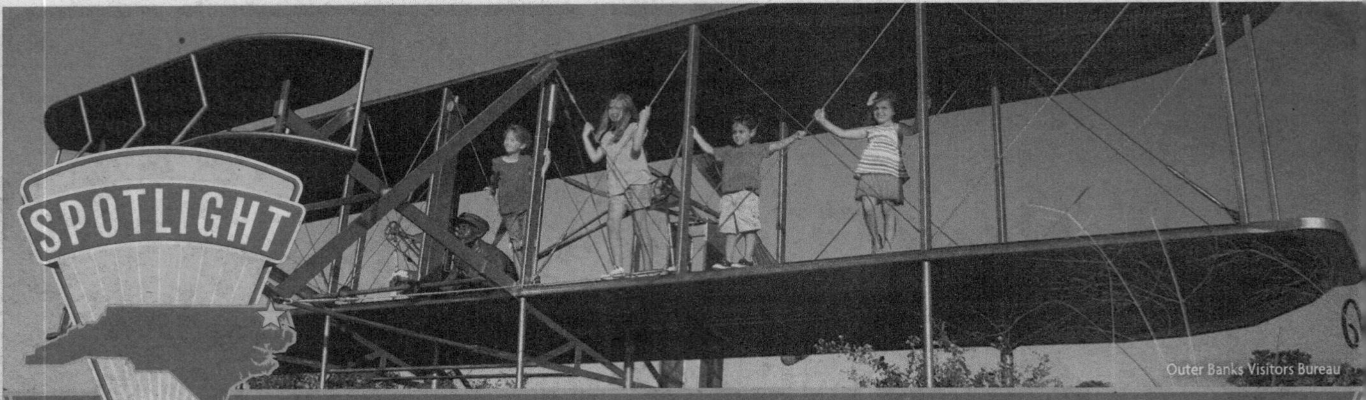

Outer Banks Visitors Bureau

OUTER BANKS/CAPE HATTERAS

A swashbuckling history gives way to easygoing charm on the Atlantic shore

Despite their ribbons of gorgeous white sandy beaches, the barrier islands known collectively as the Outer Banks on North Carolina's Atlantic seaboard weren't always desired destinations.

Together with the Crystal Coast islands just to the south, the Outer Banks region, with its shifting sandbars, was a hazard for pirate vessels and tall ships from the 16th to the 19th centuries. Later, Civil War battles and World War II submarine attacks erupted in these waters. All told, there are roughly 3,000 shipwrecks off the shores.

But for all its troubled past, the Outer Banks today a haven for anyone looking to unwind on the Atlantic coast. The islands stretch from the North Carolina-Virginia border at the north down to Cape Hatteras at the south.

Beach Fun

Beach bums and water-sports enthusiasts will find themselves in paradise. The narrow barrier islands make crossing from one type of shoreline to another quick and easy. Those seeking white sandy beaches and big waves perfect for surfing and kitesurfing can aim for the Atlantic-facing side of each island. Those seeking calmer waters for Stand-Up Paddling and kayaking can simply head the other way, to each island's sound-facing western shores.

Another fantastic point of interest includes Jockey's Ridge, home to the largest natural sand dune on the eastern seaboard. Hikers will enjoy Buxton Woods, where the Buxton Woods Trail Loop and Open Ponds Trail each wind through a diverse maritime-forest ecosystem.

Colorful Past Comes Alive

For history buffs, there's no better place to start than on Roanoke Island at the Fort Raleigh National Historic Site.

It was here where, between the years 1585 and 1587, one of the first English attempts to colonize the New World was made. It began when 117 men, women and children landed on the Roanoke Island's shores on a trip sponsored by Sir Walter Raleigh. No sooner had the colony been established than it disappeared without a trace, a nagging mystery that lingers to this day.

Today, the park is home to a museum, Elizabethan gardens and an outdoor drama troop that reenacts the history of the Lost Colony.

Further north, near Kitty Hawk and Kill Devil Hills, the Wright Brothers National Memorial commemorates a key event. It was here on the morning of December 17, 1903, that Orville and Wilbur Wright recorded the world's first controlled powered flight, covering 120 feet in just under 12 seconds.

The Memorial includes a 60-foot monument sitting atop Big Kill Devil Hill replicas of the 1902 and 1903 gliders and an interactive museum.

Cape Hatteras Awaits

Finally, there's Cape Hatteras. Perched at the southern tip of the Outer Banks' string of barrier islands, it's home to an abundance of popular sites and attractions, including the Cape Hatteras Lighthouse, the Graveyard of the Atlantic Museum, the Museum of the Sea, the Hatteras Island Visitor Center and the Ocracoke Island Visitor Center.

For More Information

Outer Banks Visitors Bureau
877-629-4386
www.outerbanks.org

North Carolina Department of Tourism
800-VISIT-NC
www.visitnc.com

NC

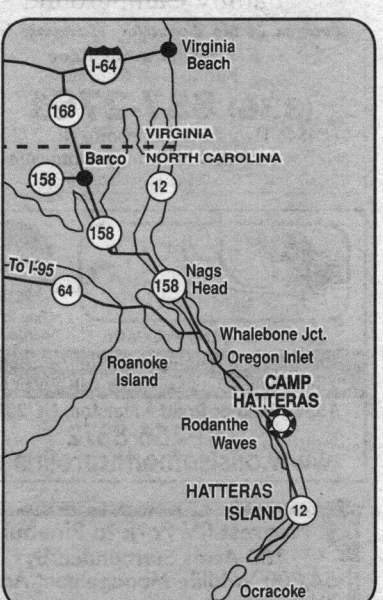

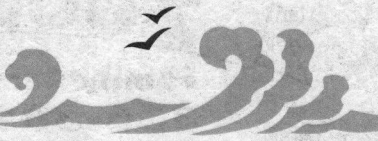

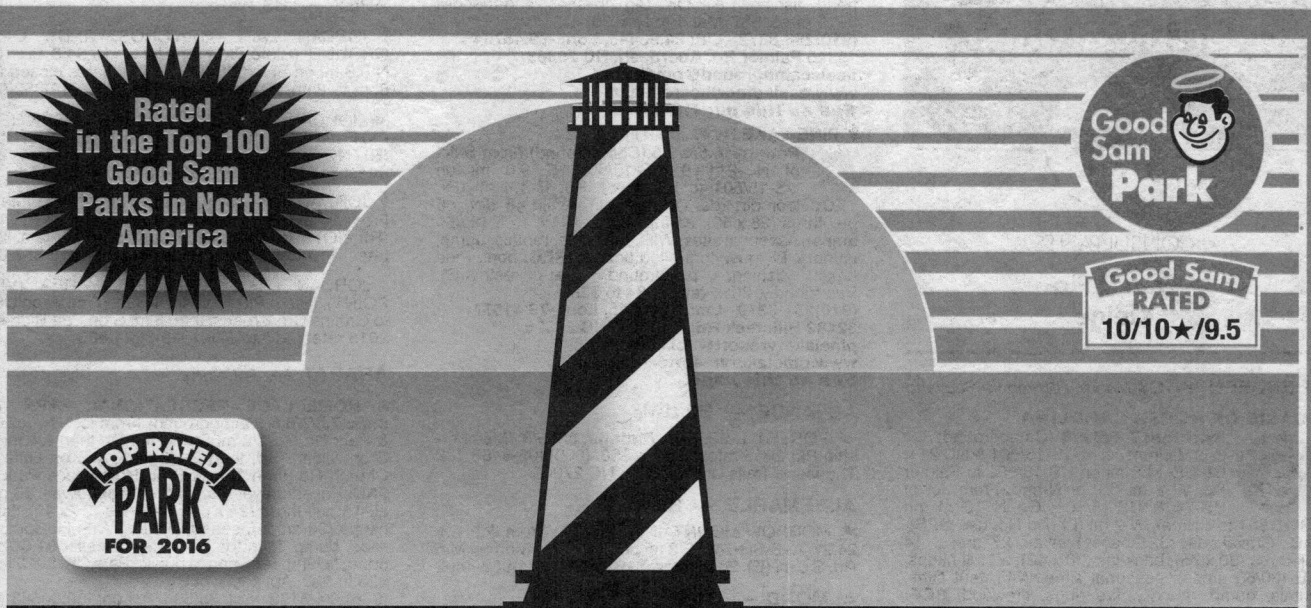

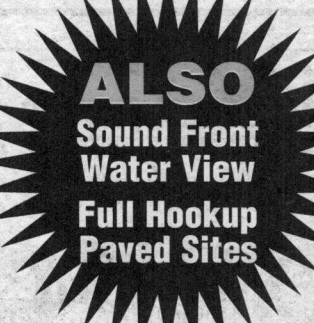

ABERDEEN — C3 *Moore, Richmond, Scotland*

OASIS OF NORTH CAROLINA
Ratings: 7.5/9★/9 (Campground) S-bnd: From Jct of US-15/501 & NC 211: Go SE 14.5 mi on US-15/501 to Palmer Rd, W 2 mi (L); or N-bnd: From Jct of US-74 & US-15/501: Go N 12 mi on US-15/501 to Palmer, W 2 mi (L) (Do Not use GPS). **FAC:** Gravel rds. (32 spaces). Avail: 27 grass, 14 pull-thrus (30 x 75), back-ins (30 x 40), 22 full hkups, 5 E (30/50 amps), seasonal sites, WiFi, tent sites, rentals, dump, laundry, fire rings, firewood. **REC:** pond, fishing. Pets OK. Big rig sites, eco-friendly, 2015 rates: $37. Mar 1 to Nov 30.
(910)266-8372 Lat: 34.90445, Lon: -79.46764
15340 Palmer Rd, Aberdeen, NC 28363
oasiscampground@gmail.com
www.oasisofnorthcarolina.us
See ad this page, 849.

A campground rating is based on ALL facilities available at the park.

PINE LAKE RV RESORT
Ratings: 6.5/6/5.5 (Campground) From S Jct of NC-211 & US-15/501, S 9.6 mi on US-15/501 to Hill Creek Rd, E 1.9 mi (R). **FAC:** Poor dirt rds. (75 spaces). Avail: 45 dirt, 45 pull-thrus (28 x 50), 35 full hkups, 10 W, 10 E (30/50 amps), seasonal sites, WiFi, tent sites, rentals, dump, laundry, LP gas, controlled access. **REC:** pool, Pine Lake: fishing, playground. Pet restrict(B). Eco-friendly, 2015 rates: $34 to $38.
(910)281-3319 Lat: 34.98546, Lon: -79.41577
32482 Hillcreek Rd, Wagram, NC 28396
pinelakervresort@aol.com
www.pinelakervresortcamp.com
See ad this page.

ADVANCE — B2 *Davie*

FOREST LAKE RV **Ratings: 8/7.5/8** (Membership Pk) 2015 rates: $38 to $58. (800)405-6188 192 Thousand Trails Dr, Advance, NC 27006

ALBEMARLE — B2 *Stanly*

MORROW MOUNTAIN (State Pk) From Jct Hwy 24/27/73 & SR-740, E 3 mi on SR-740 to Morrow Mtn Rd, S 5 mi (E). 2015 rates: $15 to $25. (704)982-4402

ALMOND — E1 *Swain*

TUMBLING WATERS CAMPGROUND **Ratings: 3.5/7/6** (Campground) 2015 rates: $28. Mar 1 to Dec 1. (828)479-3814 1612 Panther Creek Rd, Almond, NC 28702

APEX — B3 *Wake*

JORDAN LAKE SRA/CROSSWINDS CAMPGROUND (State Pk) From Jct of US 64 & SR-1008, N 0.3 mi on SR-1008 (R). NOTE: Gates closed from 8pm to 8am. 2015 rates: $15 to $25. (919)362-0586

JORDAN LAKE SRA/PARKERS CREEK (State Pk) From Jct of US-64 & SR-1008, W 2.2 mi on US-64 (R). NOTE: Gates closed from 8pm to 8am. 2015 rates: $15 to $25. (919)362-0586

JORDAN LAKE SRA/POPLAR POINT (State Pk) From Jct of US-64 & SR-1008, S 0.5 mi on SR-1008 (R). NOTE: Gates closed from 8pm to 8am. 2015 rates: $15 to $25. Mar 15 to Nov 30. (919)362-0586

JORDAN LAKE STATE REC. AREA (VISTA POINT) (State Pk) From town: Go 12 mi W on US 64 to Griffins Crossroads, then 3 mi S on Pea Ridge Rd. 2015 rates: $15 to $25. (919)362-0586

ARARAT — A2 *Surry*

HOMEPLACE RECREATIONAL PARK Ratings: 7.5/7/6.5 (Campground) From jct I-74 (exit 13) & Park Dr: Go 1/2 mi S on Park Dr, then 3/4 mi E & S on Siloam Rd, then 2-1/2 mi E & S on Little Mtn Church Rd, then 1/4 mi S on Homeplace Park Rd. **FAC:** Paved/gravel rds. (155 spaces). Avail: 30 gravel, 15 pull-thrus (24 x 60), back-ins (24 x 45), 30 full hkups (30 amps), seasonal sites, WiFi Hotspot, tent sites, dump, laundry, controlled access. **REC:** pool, pond, fishing, rec open to public. Pets OK. 2015 rates: $28 to $30. Apr 1 to Oct 31.
(336)374-5173 Lat: 36.39578, Lon: -80.58683
119 Waterloo Lane, Ararat, NC 27007
www.homeplacepark.com

ASHEBORO — B2 *Randolph*

DEEP RIVER CAMPGROUND & RV PARK, INC. Ratings: 7.5/7.5/5.5 (Campground) From Jct of US-220 & US-64: Go E 5.8 mi on US-64 to Loflin Pond Rd, N 1.5 mi to Mc Dowell Country Tr, E 0.1 mi (L). **FAC:** Gravel rds. (56 spaces). Avail: 10 gravel, 10 pull-thrus (20 x 60), some side by side hkups, 10 W, 10 E (30/50 amps), seasonal sites, cable, WiFi Hotspot, tent sites, dump, laundry, LP gas, fire rings, firewood. **REC:** pool, Deep River: fishing, playground, rec open to public. Pet restrict(B). 2015 rates: $35.
(336)629-4069 Lat: 35.74667, Lon: -79.72965
814 Mcdowell Country Trail, Asheboro, NC 27203
Info@deeprivercampground.com
www.deeprivercampground.com

ASHEBORO (CONT)

HOLLY BLUFF FAMILY CAMPGROUND
Ratings: 7/4.5/6.5 (Campground) From Jct of US-64 & NC-49 (W of town), SW 7.5 mi on NC-49 (R). **FAC:** Gravel rds. (90 spaces). Avail: 50 gravel, 21 pull-thrus (25 x 45), back-ins (20 x 45), 48 full hkups, 2 W, 2 E (30/50 amps), seasonal sites, WiFi, tent sites, dump, fire rings, firewood. **REC:** pool, playground. Pets OK. 2015 rates: $30 to $32. Apr 1 to Oct 31. No CC.
(336)857-2761 Lat: 35.64439, Lon: -79.95941
4846 NC Hwy 49 S, Asheboro, NC 27205
www.hollybluffcampground.com
See ad opposite page.

ZOOLAND FAMILY CAMPGROUND, LLC
Ratings: 8.5/9★/9 (Membership Pk) From Jct of US 64 & US 220 (Bypass), S 4.7 mi on US 220 (Bypass) to exit 68 (Ulah-Troy), W 1.2 mi on Dawson-Miller Rd to Pisgah Covered Bridge Rd, SW 1.4 mi (L). **FAC:** Gravel rds. (167 spaces). 147 Avail: 88 gravel, 59 grass, 88 pull-thrus (30 x 65), back-ins (30 x 50), 88 full hkups, 59 W, 59 E (30/50 amps), seasonal sites, WiFi, tent sites, dump, laundry, LP gas, fire rings, firewood. **REC:** pool, Little River: fishing, playground. Pets OK. Partial handicap access. Big rig sites, 2015 rates: $31.50 to $34.50.
(336)381-3422 Lat: 35.60306, Lon: -79.85032
3671 Pisgah Covered Bridge Rd, Asheboro, NC 27205
reservations.zfc@rtmc.net
www.zoolandfc.com
See ad opposite page, 849.

ASHEVILLE — E2 *Buncombe, Haywood, Yancey*

ASHEVILLE See also Candler, Fletcher, Hendersonville, Swannanoa, Lake Lure, Bat Cave, Chimney Rock.

ASHEVILLE BEAR CREEK RV PARK
Ratings: 10/10★/9.5 (RV Park) W-bnd: From Jct of I-40 & NC-191 (exit 47), cross NC-191 to S Bear Creek Rd, W 0.6 mi (L); or E-bnd: From Jct of I-40 & NC-191 (exit 47), N 0.1 mi on NC-191 to S Bear Creek Rd, W 0.6 mi (L); or From Jct of I-26 & NC-191 (exit 31), N 1.1 mi on NC-191 to S Bear Creek Rd, W 0.6 mi (L).

BILTMORE HOUSE VIEWS AND MORE
We're so close to the Biltmore House you can see it from our park. Stay on our BIG, level concrete sites (Free WI-FI) and buy your tickets from us. You'll enjoy the sightseeing and the peace and quiet at the end of the day.

FAC: Paved rds. 114 paved, patios, 26 pull-thrus (30 x 60), back-ins (30 x 60), 114 full hkups (30/50 amps), cable, WiFi, dump, laundry, LP gas. **REC:** heated pool, playground. Pets OK. No tents. Big rig sites, eco-friendly, 2015 rates: $40 to $45.
AAA Approved
(800)833-0798 Lat: 35.55749, Lon: -82.60465
81 S Bear Creek Rd, Asheville, NC 28806
camping@ashevillebearcreek.com
www.ashevillebearcreek.com
See ad pages 856, 849.

ASHEVILLE TAPS RV PARK
Ratings: 6/9/9 (RV Park) From Jct of I-40 & Exit 55, N 0.1 mi on Porter Cove Rd to US-70/Tunnel Rd, W (left) 0.3 mi (L); or From Jct of Blue Ridge Pkwy (MP-383) & US-70, E 0.2 mi on US-70 (R). **FAC:** Gravel rds. (47 spaces). 32 Avail: 17 paved, 15 gravel, 23 pull-thrus (28 x 50), back-ins (28 x 45), 18 full hkups, 14 W, 14 E (30/50 amps), seasonal sites, cable, WiFi, dump, LP gas, fire rings. Pets OK. No tents. 2015 rates: $37.50 to $41.50.
(828)299-8277 Lat: 35.58342, Lon: -82.46906
1325 Tunnel Rd, Asheville, NC 28805
www.ashevilletapsrvpark.com
See ad opposite page, 849.

Like Us on Facebook.

BLUE RIDGE PKWY/MOUNT PISGAH (Natl Pk) From Jct of I-26 & Hwy 191, S 2 mi on Hwy 191 to Blue Ridge Pkwy, S 14 mi at MP-408.6 (R). 2015 rates: $16 to $19. May 8 to Oct 24. (828)648-2644

CAMPFIRE LODGINGS
Ratings: 7.5/10★/10 (Campground) From Jct of I-240 (Exit 4A) & US-19/23/70, N 5.8 mi on US-19/23/70 to New Stock Rd (Exit 21), E 0.1 mi to US-19 Bus, S 0.6 mi to Old Marshall Hwy, W 0.4 mi to Appalachian Village Rd, SW 0.4 mi (E). Elev 2500 ft. **FAC:** Gravel rds. 19 Avail: 6 paved, 13 gravel, patios, back-ins (30 x 65), 19 full hkups (30/50 amps), cable, WiFi, tent sites, rentals, laundry, LP gas, fire rings, firewood. **REC:** pond, fishing. Pets OK. Partial handicap access. Big rig sites, 2015 rates: $45 to $65.
(828)658-8012 Lat: 35.66001, Lon: -82.59213
116 Appalachian Village Rd, Asheville, NC 28804
info@campfirelodgings.com
www.campfirelodgings.com
See ad this page.

FRENCH BROAD RIVER CAMPGROUND **Ratings: 3.5/4.5/4.5** (Campground) 2015 rates: $37. (828)658-0772 1030 Old Marshall Hwy, Asheville, NC 28804

WILSON'S RIVERFRONT RV PARK **Ratings: 7/7.5/6.5** (Campground) 2015 rates: $36. (828)254-4676 225 Amboy Rd, Asheville, NC 28806

Check out the travel services section of this Guide to find services that you'll find handy in your travels.

Did you know we sent 35 husband-wife RVing teams out this year to scour North America, rating and inspecting RV parks and campgrounds? You can rest easy when you read our listings, knowing we've already been there.

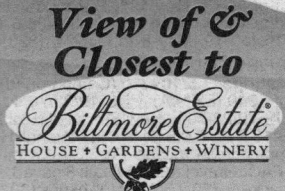

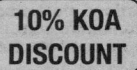

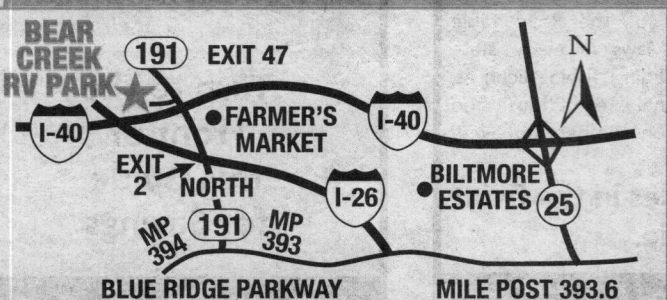

AVON — B6 *Dare*

SANDS OF TIME CAMPGROUND & RV PARK **Ratings: 5.5/UI/8** (Campground) 2015 rates: $45 to $48. (252)995-5596 40523 North End Rd, Avon, NC 27915

BALSAM — E2 *Jackson*

MOONSHINE CREEK CAMPGROUND
Ratings: 7.5/10★/9.5 (Campground) From Waynesville Jct of I-40 & US-23/74 (Exit 27), S 12 mi on US-23/74 to CR-1471, just past Mile Marker 93.7 (Candlestick Ln), SE 200 ft to CR-1701, SW 0.5 mi onOld Balsam Depot Rd, (straight past Post Office, hairpin turn back over RR tracks, past Balsam Mtn Inn), 1.5 mi on Dark Ridge Rd (L). Elev 3200 ft. **FAC:** Gravel rds. (79 spaces). Avail: 66 gravel, back-ins (30 x 50), 46 full hkups, 20 W, 20 E (30/50 amps), seasonal sites, WiFi Hotspot, tent sites, rentals, dump, laundry, groc, LP gas, fire rings, firewood. **REC:** Moonshine Creek: fishing, playground. Pet restrict(B). 2015 rates: $37 to $42. Apr 1 to Nov 1.
(828)586-6666 Lat: 35.51720, Lon: -83.05807
2486 Dark Ridge Rd, Sylva, NC 28779
moonshinecreek@hotmail.com
www.moonshinecreek.com
See ad page 858.

BANNER ELK — D3 *Watauga*

GRANDFATHER CAMPGROUND **Ratings: 6/6/7.5** (Campground) 2015 rates: $25 to $35. (800)788-2582 125 Profile View Dr, Banner Elk, NC 28604

BAT CAVE — E2 *Henderson*

CREEKSIDE MOUNTAIN CAMPING Ratings: 7.5/7.5/7 (Campground) Jct I-26 & US64 (Ext 49A), E 12 mi to US74, N 3.5 mi to Grant Mtn Rd (R). **FAC:** Paved/gravel rds. (36 spaces). 23 Avail: 8 gravel, 15 grass, 2 pull-thrus (30 x 60), back-ins (30 x 60), 8 full hkups, 15 W, 15 E (30 amps), seasonal sites, WiFi Hotspot, tent sites, rentals, dump, laundry, groc, fire rings, firewood. **REC:** pool, Hickory Nut Creek: fishing, rec open to public. Pets OK. Partial handicap access. 2015 rates: $29.95 to $36.95.
(800)248-8118 Lat: 35.46585, Lon: -82.32703
us Hwy 74-A at Grant Mountain Road, Bat Cave, NC 28710
Info@creeksidecamping.com
www.creeksidecamping.com

BAYBORO — B5 *Pamlico*

RIVERS EDGE FAMILY CAMPGROUND **Ratings: 5.5/8/8** (Campground) 2015 rates: $38 to $40. (252)559-3603 149 Tempe Gut Rd, Bayboro, NC 28515

BELHAVEN — B5 *Beaufort, Hyde*

RIVERSIDE CAMPGROUND
Ratings: 5/9★/6.5 (Campground) From Jct of US-264 & NC-45, N 2 mi on NC-45 to Riverside Campground Rd, SW 0.3 mi (R). **FAC:** Gravel/dirt rds. 50 grass, 40 pull-thrus (30 x 100), back-ins (25 x 45), some side by side hkups, 35 full hkups, 15 W, 15 E (30/50 amps), WiFi Hotspot, tent sites, rentals, dump, laundry, LP gas, firewood. **REC:** Pungo River: fishing, playground. Pets OK. Partial handicap access. Big rig sites, eco-friendly, 2015 rates: $25 to $35.
(252)945-9012 Lat: 35.58481, Lon: -76.51648
272 Riverside Campground Rd, Belhaven, NC 27810
brooke.riverside@yahoo.com
See ad this page.

BLOWING ROCK — A1 *Watauga*

BLUE RIDGE PKWY/JULIAN PRICE MEMORIAL PARK (Natl Pk) From town, S 4 mi on Blue Ridge Pkwy at MP-297 (R). 2015 rates: $16 to $19. May 8 to Oct 24. (828)963-5911

Find it Fast! Use our alphabetized index of campgrounds and parks.

BOONE — A1 *Watauga*

BOONE KOA
Ratings: 8.5/10★/9 (Campground) From Jct of US-421/221 & NC-194, N 2.8 mi on NC-194 to Ray Brown Rd, W 1.1 mi (R). Elev 3700 ft. **FAC:** Gravel rds. (135 spaces). Avail: 67 gravel, 63 pull-thrus (24 x 60), back-ins (24 x 60), 56 full hkups, 11 W, 11 E (30/50 amps), seasonal sites, WiFi Hotspot, tent sites, rentals, dump, laundry, groc, fire rings, firewood. **REC:** heated pool, playground. Pets OK. Big rig sites, eco-friendly, 2015 rates: $37 to $45. May 1 to Oct 31.
(828)264-7250 Lat: 36.25924, Lon: -81.66096
123 Harmony Mtn Ln, Boone, NC 28607
boonekoa@bellsouth.net
www.boonekoa.com
See ad this page.

FLINTLOCK CAMPGROUND
Ratings: 7/10★/8 (Campground) N-bnd: From Jct of US 221 & NC-105, N 13.6 mi on NC-105 (L); or S-bnd: From Jct of US-321/US-321 truck rte & NC-105, SW 3.5 mi on NC-105 (R). Elev 3200 ft. **FAC:** Paved/gravel rds. (84 spaces). 67 Avail: 25 paved, 42 gravel, patios, 7 pull-thrus (24 x 70), back-ins (24 x 50), 67 full hkups (30 amps), seasonal sites, cable, WiFi, tent sites, rentals, dump, laundry, firewood. **REC:** Laurel Creek: fishing, playground. Pets OK. Partial handicap access. 2015 rates: $34. Apr 1 to Nov 9.
(888)850-9997 Lat: 36.20540, Lon: -81.72825
171 Flintlock Campground Dr, Boone, NC 28607
flintlockcg@gmail.com
www.flintlockcampground.com
See ad this page.

HONEY BEAR CAMPGROUND & NATURE CENTER **Ratings: 7/6.5/6** (Campground) 2015 rates: $37. Apr 1 to Oct 31. (828)963-4586 229 Honey Bear Campground Rd, Boone, NC 28607

BOONVILLE — A2 *Yadkin*

HOLLY RIDGE FAMILY CAMPGROUND INC. **Ratings: 8.5/7.5/7** (Campground) 2015 rates: $37 to $45. (336)367-7756 5140 River Rd, Boonville, NC 27011

BREVARD — E2 *Transylvania*

ADVENTURE VILLAGE AND LODGINGS **Ratings: 6/8/7.5** (Campground) 2015 rates: $30. (828)862-5411 15 Adventure Ridge Rd, Brevard, NC 28712

BRYSON CITY — E1 *Swain*

DEEP CREEK TUBE CENTER & CAMPGROUND **Ratings: 6.5/6.5/7** (Campground) 2015 rates: $29 to $45. Apr 1 to Oct 31. (828)488-6055 1090 W Deep Wood Rd, Bryson City, NC 28713

GREAT SMOKY MTN/DEEP CREEK CAMPGROUND (Natl Pk) From town, N 3 mi on Deep Creek Rd (R). 2015 rates: $17. Apr 11 to Oct 31. (865)436-1200

SMOKY MOUNTAIN MEADOWS CAMPGROUND
Ratings: 6/8★/8 (Campground) From Jct of US-74 & Exit 64/Alarka Rd: Go S 1.5 mi on Alarka Rd to E Alarka Rd, E 0.7 mi (L). Elev 2700 ft. **FAC:** Gravel rds. 28 grass, 16 pull-thrus (26 x 68), back-ins (28 x 43), 21 full hkups, 7 W, 7 E (30 amps), WiFi, tent sites, rentals, dump, laundry, firewood. **REC:** East Alarka Creek: playground. Pets OK. 2015 rates: $28 to $35. Apr 1 to Oct 30.
(828)488-3672 Lat: 35.37600, Lon: -83.45620
755 E Alarka Rd, Bryson City, NC 28713
info@smokymtnmeadows.com
www.smokymtnmeadows.com
See ad this page.

BUXTON — B6 *Dare*

CAPE HATTERAS NATL SEASHORE/CAPE POINT (Natl Pk) From town, SW 3 mi on SR-12 (R). 2015 rates: $20. May to Sep. (252)473-2111

CAPE WOODS CAMPGROUND
Ratings: 7.5/9★/9.5 (Campground) S-bnd: From Jct of US-158/64/164 & NC-12, S 47.4 mi on NC-12 to Buxton Back Rd (at PNC Bank), SE 0.7 mi (L); or N-bnd: From Okracoke/Hatteras Ferry, N 10.5 mi on NC-12 to Buxton Back Rd (across from school), E 0.6 mi (R). **FAC:** Gravel rds. (113 spaces). Avail: 29 grass, patios, 14 pull-thrus (25 x 65), back-ins (27 x 50), 23 full hkups, 6 W, 6 E (30/50 amps), seasonal sites, cable, WiFi, tent sites, rentals, dump, laundry, LP bottles, fire rings, firewood, controlled access. **REC:** pool, pond, fishing, playground. Pets OK. Partial handicap access. Big rig sites, 2015 rates: $42 to $62. Mar 15 to Dec 1.
(252)995-5850 Lat: 35.26500, Lon: -75.54049
47649 Buxton Back Rd, Buxton, NC 27920
Capewoodscampground@yahoo.com
www.capewoods.com
See ad pages 852 (Spotlight Outer Banks/Cape Hatteras), 849.

NC

CAMDEN — A6 *Camden*

Things to See and Do

CAMDEN COUNTY TOURISM DEVELOPMENT AUTHORITY Tourism information for area campgrounds, parks & community events. Hours: 9am to 5pm. No CC.
(252)771-8333 Lat: 36.32970, Lon: -76.17478
www.camdencountync.gov
See ad page 845 (Welcome Section).

CANDLER — E2 *Buncombe*

ASHEVILLE-WEST KOA
Ratings: 9/9★/9 (Campground) From Jct of I-40 & US-19/23 (exit 37), S 200 ft on unmarked rd to US-19/23, W 0.4 mi to Wiggins Rd, N 0.2 mi (R). **FAC:** Paved/gravel rds. 74 gravel, 27 pull-thrus (35 x 60), back-ins (32 x 42), 46 full hkups, 28 W, 28 E (30/50 amps), cable, WiFi, tent sites, rentals, dump, laundry, groc, LP gas, fire rings, firewood. **REC:** pool, pond, playground. Pet restrict(B). Partial handicap access. Big rig sites, eco-friendly, 2015 rates: $34.31 to $42.41.
(800)562-9015 Lat: 35.54281, Lon: -82.75952
309 Wiggins Rd, Candler, NC 28715
kamperservices@ashevillekoa.com
www.ashevillekoa.com
See ad page 855.

CAPE CARTERET — C5 *Onslow*

GOOSE CREEK RESORT **Ratings: 8/7.5/8.5** (RV Park) 2015 rates: $58 to $71. (800)405-6188 350 Red Barn Rd, Newport, NC 28570

Tell them you saw them in this Guide!

CAPE CARTERET (CONT)

WATERWAY RV RESORT **Ratings: 7.5/6.5/8** (RV Park) 2015 rates: $73. (800)405-6188 850 Cedar Point Blvd, Swansboro, NC 28584

CAROLINA BEACH — D4 *New Hanover*

CAROLINA BEACH (State Pk) From Jct of US-421 & Dow Rd, W 0.8 mi on Dow Rd (R). 2015 rates: $15 to $20. (910)458-8206

CEDAR MOUNTAIN — E2 *Transylvania*

BLACK FOREST FAMILY CAMPING RESORT
Ratings: 9/10★/9.5 (Campground) N-bnd: From Jct of I-85 & Exit 48/Hwy 276, NW 36.3 mi on Hwy 276 to Caesars Head St Pk, con't 3 mi to Summer Rd, E 0.4 mi (R); or S-bnd: From Jct of US-64 & US-276 (in downtown Brevard), SE 12.6 mi on US-276 to Summer Rd, E 0.4 mi (R). Elev 3000 ft. **FAC:** Gravel rds. 64 gravel, back-ins (30 x 60), 32 full hkups, 32 W, 32 E (30/50 amps), cable, WiFi, tent sites, rentals, dump, laundry, groc, fire rings, firewood, controlled access. **REC:** heated pool, playground. Pets OK. Partial handicap access. Big rig sites, eco-friendly, 2015 rates: $34 to $43. Mar 15 to Nov 1.
(828)884-2267 Lat: 35.13372, Lon: -82.63499
280 Summer Rd, Cedar Mountain, NC 28718
www.blackforestcampground.com
See ad page 857.

CHAPEL HILL — B3 *Orange*

SPRING HILL PARK Ratings: 5.5/NA/7.5 (RV Park) From Jct of I-40 & NC-54 (Exit 273A), W 3 mi on NC-54 (go under bridge and exit right) continue 3.8 mi to Jones Ferry Rd exit, SW 0.9 mi to Old Greensboro Rd, W 4 mi to Spring Hill Rd, N 0.2 mi on gravel rd along W side of church (E). **FAC:** Gravel rds. 66 gravel, 7 pull-thrus (30 x 100), back-ins (40 x 75), accepts full hkup units only, 66 full hkups (30/50 amps), cable, WiFi, LP gas. **REC:** playground. Pets OK. No tents. Big rig sites, 2015 rates: $32.
(919)967-4268 Lat: 35.90015, Lon: -79.16986
3500-1A Old Greensboro Rd, Chapel Hill, NC 27516
www.springhillpark.com

CHARLOTTE — B1 *Mecklenburg*

CHARLOTTE See also Concord, Denver; Fort Mill, SC.

CAMPING AT CHARLOTTE MOTOR SPEEDWAY
Ratings: 7/8.5/8 (Campground) From Jct of I-77 & I-85, N 11 mi on I-85 to Bruton Smith Blvd (Exit 49), E 1.4 mi (L). Entrance at zMax Dragway sign at Charlotte Motor Speedway.

WALK TO CHARLOTTE MOTOR SPEEDWAY
This full service RV camping area is available for each event held at Charlotte Motor Speedway, zMax Dragway & The Dirt Track & are also available for daily camping on non-event days.

FAC: Paved rds. 441 gravel, 56 pull-thrus (30 x 100), back-ins (30 x 50), some side by side hkups, 441 full hkups (30/50 amps), WiFi, tent sites, dump, laundry, firewood. **REC:** pond, playground, rec open to public. Pet restrict Big rig sites, 2015 rates: $25 to $30.
(704)455-4445 Lat: 35.35896, Lon: -80.69059
6600 Bruton Smith Blvd, Concord, NC 28027
camping1@charlottemotorspeedway.com
www.charlottemotorspeedway.com
See ad this page, 849.

Look in the Guide to Seasonal Sites to find places you can stay for a month, a season or longer.

CAROWINDS CAMP WILDERNESS RESORT
Ratings: 9/8.5★/8 (Campground) From Jct of I-77 & Exit 90 (NC/SC Border), W 1 mi to Catawba Trace, N 0.1 mi (L). **FAC:** Paved rds. 142 paved, 39 pull-thrus (31 x 78), back-ins (31 x 60), 142 full hkups (30/50 amps), WiFi, tent sites, rentals, dump, laundry, groc. **REC:** pool, shuffleboard. Pets OK. Partial handicap access. Big rig sites, 2015 rates: $41.99 to $75.99. Disc: AAA, military. ATM.
(704)587-9116 Lat: 35.10394, Lon: -80.94766
14523 Carowinds Blvd, Charlotte, NC 28273
www.carowinds.com
See ad this page, 849.

ELMORE RV PARK (RV Spaces) From Jct I-85 & Sugar Creek Rd (Exit 41), E 1.5 mi on Sugar Creek Rd to Left on Tryon St. Go 0.5 mi on Tryon St (US 29) (R) Note: RV Park is located next to Phil Jackson's Auto Sales. **FAC:** Paved/gravel rds. 44 Avail: 31 paved, 13 gravel, back-ins (24 x 48), accepts full hkup units only, 44 full hkups (30/50 amps), WiFi. Pets OK. No tents. 2015 rates: $32. Disc: military.
(704)597-1323 Lat: 35.25742, Lon: -80.78529
4824 N Tryon St, Charlotte, NC 28213
rvpark@carolina.rr.com
www.elmorervpark.com

MCDOWELL NATURE PRESERVE (Public) From Jct of I-77 & Carowinds Blvd, NW 2 mi on Carowinds Blvd to Hwy 49, S 4 mi (R). 2015 rates: $15 to $33. (704)583-1284

YATES FAMILY CAMPING Ratings: 4.5/NA/5.5 (Campground) From Jct I-85 & Bruton Smith Blvd. (exit 49) SE 1.9 mi on Bruton Smith Blvd to Concord Pkwy (Hwy 29), SE .2 mi on Hwy 29 to Morehead Rd., SE .9 mi to Hudspeth Rd, SW .2 mi (L) "Race Week Rates" $30-$50/night. **FAC:** Gravel rds. 48 gravel, 11 pull-thrus (24 x 90), back-ins (23 x 45), mostly side by side hkups, 21 full hkups, 27 W, 27 E (30/50

CHARLOTTE (CONT)

YATES FAMILY CAMPING (CONT)
amps), WiFi, tent sites, pit toilets, firewood. **REC.** Pets OK. Big rig sites, 2015 rates: $20. No CC.
(704)773-9349 Lat: 35.33917, Lon: -80.68106
6285 Hudspeth Rd, Harrisburg, NC 28075
roaul@msn.com
www.yatesfamilycamping.com

Things to See and Do

CAROWINDS Theme park with 14 different attractions at one location. Partial handicap access. Restrooms, food. Hours: 10am to 10pm. Adult fee: $42 to $58. ATM.
(800)888-4FUN Lat: 35.10158, Lon: -80.93516
14523 Carowinds Blvd, Charlotte, NC 28241
carowinds.com
See ad opposite page.

CHEROKEE — E2 *Jackson, Swain*

ADVENTURE TRAIL CAMPGROUND **Ratings: 7/6/6.5** (Campground) 2015 rates: $30 to $35. May 1 to Oct 31. (828)497-3651 276 Adventure Trail Rd, Whittier, NC 28789

CHEROKEE CAMPGROUND & CRAIG'S LOG CABINS **Ratings: 5/6.5/7** (Campground) 2015 rates: $35 to $45. Apr 1 to Oct 31. (828)497-9838 91 Hwy 19N, Cherokee, NC 28719

CHEROKEE/GREAT SMOKIES KOA **Ratings: 8.5/7/8.5** (Campground) 2015 rates: $33 to $75. (828)497-9711 92 Koa Kampground Rd, Cherokee, NC 28719

FORT WILDERNESS CAMPGROUND AND RV PARK
Ratings: 8.5/7.5★/7 (Campground) From Jct of US-74 & US-441 (exit 74): Go N 1.6 mi on US-441 to Shoal Creek Rd, W 0.5 mi (R). **FAC:** Paved rds. (107 spaces). 57 Avail: 16 paved, 41 gravel, 28 pull-thrus (20 x 55), back-ins (25 x 35), 57 full hkups (30/50 amps), seasonal sites, cable, WiFi, tent sites, rentals, dump, laundry, groc, fire rings, firewood. **REC:** pool, playground. Pets OK. 2015 rates: $35 to $40. Disc: AAA.
(828)497-9331 Lat: 35.44239, Lon: -83.33170
284 Fort Wilderness Rd, Whittier, NC 28789
c.roestenberg@yahoo.com
www.fortwilderness.net
See ad this page, 849.

GREAT SMOKEY MOUNTAIN RV CAMPING RESORT
Ratings: 7.5/6/6 (RV Park) From West Jct US-19 & US-441: Go 1-1/2 mi S on US-441 (L). **FAC:** Paved/gravel rds. (240 spaces). 30 Avail: 15 gravel, 15 grass, 10 pull-thrus (25 x 55), back-ins (25 x 55), 30 full hkups (30 amps), seasonal sites, cable, WiFi, laundry, groc, LP gas, fire rings, firewood. **REC:** pool, Soco Creek: playground. Pet restrict No tents. 2015 rates: $35. May 1 to Oct 31.
(828)497-2470 Lat: 35.45993, Lon: -83.31349
17 Old Soco Rd, Whittier, NC 28789
gsmrvcr@yahoo.com
www.gsmrvcr.com
See ad this page.

GREAT SMOKY MOUNTAINS NATIONAL PARK (BALSAM MOUNTAIN CAMPGROUND) (Natl Pk) From town: Go 4 mi N on US 441, 12 mi E on Blue Ridge Pkwy to MP 458, then 8 mi N on Balsam Mtn. Rd. 2015 rates: $14. May 23 to Oct 13. (423)436-1200

GREAT SMOKY MTN/SMOKEMONT (Natl Pk) From Jct of US-19 & US-441 (Newfound Gap Rd), N 9 mi on US-441 (R). 2015 rates: $17 to $20. (828)497-9270

HAPPY HOLIDAY CAMPGROUND
Ratings: 9/9★/9.5 (Campground) From W Jct of US 74 & US 441N, N 3.8 mi on US 441N to Bus-441N, NE 0.8 mi to US 19N, N 3.3 mi (L); or From Jct of Blue Ridge Pkwy (MP-455.5) & US 19, SW 7.6 mi on US 19S (R). **FAC:** Paved/gravel rds. 322 Avail: 20 gravel, 302 grass, 149 pull-thrus (35 x 75), back-ins (35 x 50), 257 full hkups, 65 W, 65 E (30/50 amps), cable, WiFi, tent sites, rentals, dump, laundry, groc, LP gas, fire rings, firewood, controlled access. **REC:** pool, Soco Creek: fishing, playground. Pet restrict(B). Partial handicap access. Big rig sites, 2015 rates: $37 to $49. Mar 15 to Oct 31.
(828)497-9204 Lat: 35.47145, Lon: -83.24694
1553 Wolfetown Rd (US-19), Cherokee, NC 28719
info@happyholidayrv.com
www.happyholidayrv.com
See ad this page, 849.

RIVER VALLEY CAMPGROUND **Ratings: 7/7.5/7.5** (Campground) 2015 rates: $34 to $39. Apr 1 to Nov 1. (828)497-3540 2978 Big Cove Rd, Cherokee, NC 28719

TIMBERLAKE CAMPGROUND **Ratings: 5/7.5★/6.5** (Campground) 2015 rates: $30 to $34. May 1 to Nov 1. (828)497-7320 3270 Conley's Creek Rd, Whittier, NC 28789

YOGI IN THE SMOKIES
Ratings: 8.5/10★/9 (Campground) From W Jct of US-19 & US-441, N 2.2 mi on US-441 to Big Cove Rd, NE 7.7 mi (R). Elev 2500 ft.

GOOD TIME AND FUN SHINE EVERYDAY!
A great campground featuring comfortable cabins and beautiful campsites, nestled deep in the Smoky Mountains. We have everything to make your stay a relaxed and pleasant experience. Daily, weekly and monthly rates available.
FAC: Gravel rds. (135 spaces). Avail: 133 gravel, 23 pull-thrus (18 x 58), back-ins (25 x 45), some side by side hkups, 82 full hkups, 51 W, 51 E (30/50 amps), seasonal sites, cable, WiFi Hotspot, tent sites, rentals, dump, laundry, groc, LP gas, fire rings, firewood. **REC:** heated pool, Raven Fork River: fishing, playground. Pet restrict(B). Eco-friendly, 2015 rates: $40 to $68. Disc: AAA.
(828)497-9151 Lat: 35.55402, Lon: -83.25894
317 Galamore Bridge Rd, Cherokee, NC 28719
yogibear@jellystone-cherokee.com
www.JellystoneCherokee.com
See ad pages 860, 849 & Family Camping in Magazine Section.

Pamper Your Pet on the Road - turn to our Pampered Pet Parks feature at the front of the Guide for great tips and advice when traveling with pets.

NC

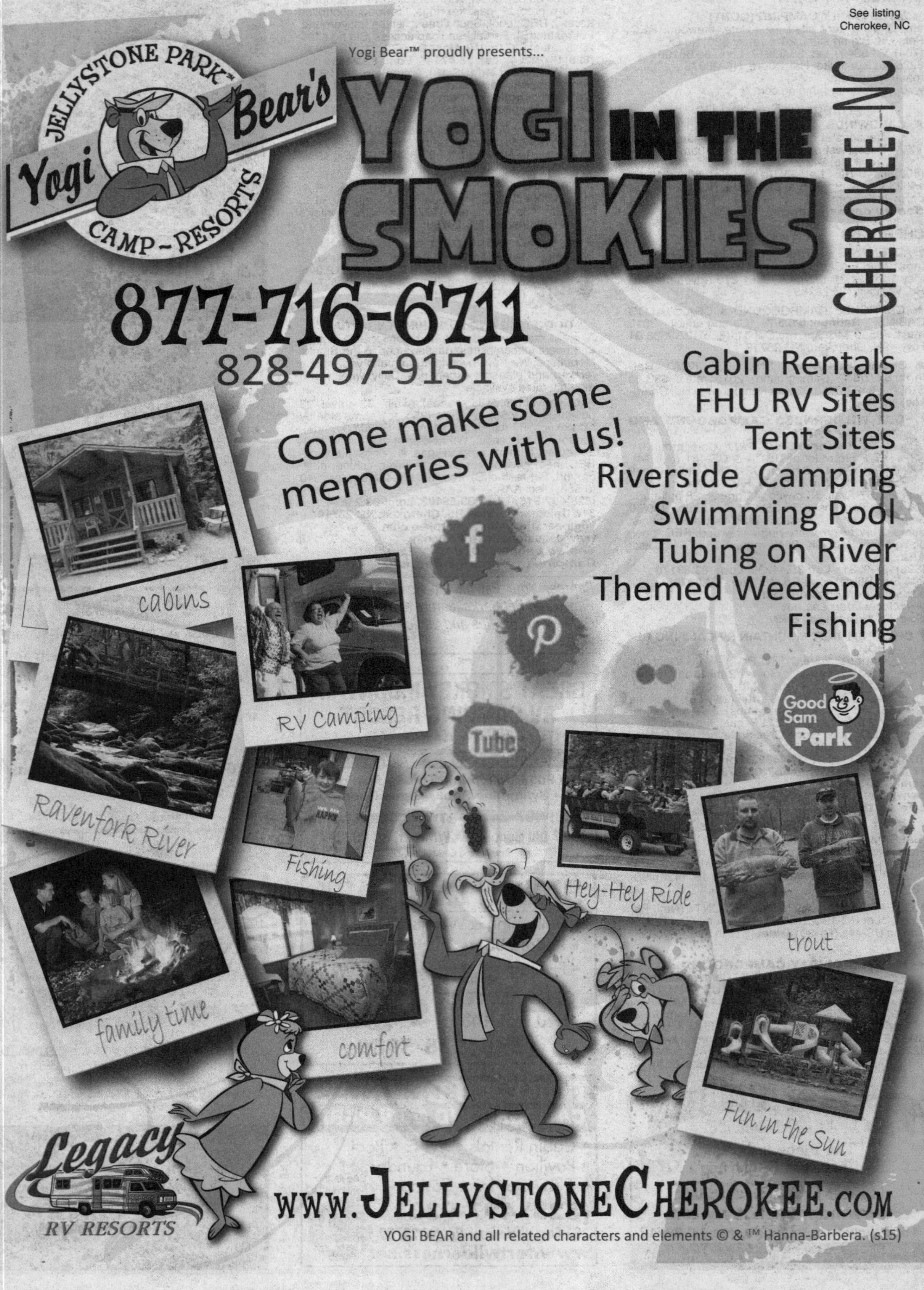
See listing
Cherokee, NC
Yogi Bear™ proudly presents...
JELLYSTONE PARK™
Yogi Bear's
CAMP-RESORTS
YOGI IN THE SMOKIES
CHEROKEE, NC
877-716-6711
828-497-9151
Come make some
memories with us!
Cabin Rentals
FHU RV Sites
Tent Sites
Riverside Camping
Swimming Pool
Tubing on River
Themed Weekends
Fishing
Good Sam Park
cabins
RV Camping
Ravenfork River
Fishing
Hey-Hey Ride
trout
family time
comfort
Fun in the Sun
Legacy
RV RESORTS
www.JELLYSTONECHEROKEE.COM
YOGI BEAR and all related characters and elements © & ™ Hanna-Barbera. (s15)

CHIMNEY ROCK — E3 *Rutherford*

HICKORY NUT FALLS FAMILY CAMPGROUND Ratings: 6.5/7.5/6.5 (Campground) From Jct of I-26 & US 64 (Exit 49A), E 12.5 mi on US 64 to NC-9, SE 2.1 mi on US 64/NC 74A/NC9 (R). **FAC:** Paved/gravel rds. (63 spaces). Avail: 13 gravel, back-ins (20 x 35), 13 full hkups (30 amps), seasonal sites, WiFi Hotspot, tent sites, rentals, dump, laundry, LP gas, firewood. **REC:** Rocky Broad River: swim, fishing, playground. Pet restrict(B). 2015 rates: $32 to $42. Apr 1 to Oct 31.
(828)625-4014 Lat: 35.44049, Lon: -82.25679
639 Main St., Chimney Rock, NC 28720
www.hickorynutfallsfamilycampground.com

CLAYTON — B4 *Johnston*

COOPERS RV PARK **Ratings: 5.5/NA/8** (RV Area in MHP) 2015 rates: $35. (919)359-8060 13528 Hwy 70 W, Clayton, NC 27520

CLEMMONS — A2 *Forsyth*

TANGLEWOOD PARK (Public) From Jct of I-40 & Harper Rd (Exit 182), S 0.3 mi on Harper Rd to Hwy 158 (Clemmons Rd), W 0.3 mi (L). 2015 rates: $31. Mar 1 to Dec 1. (336)703-6400

COLFAX — A2 *Forsyth*

Travel Services

CAMPING WORLD OF COLFAX As the nation's largest retailer of RV supplies, accessories, services and new and used RVs, Camping World is committed to making your total RV experience better. RV Accessories: (888)240-8007. **SERVICES:** RV, RV appliance, MH mechanical, staffed RV wash, restrooms, RV Sales. RV supplies, LP, dump, emergency parking, RV accessible. waiting room. Hours: 8am to 6pm.
(888)495-9166 Lat: 36.094589, Lon: -79.997827
8615 Triad Drive, Colfax, NC 27235
www.campingworld.com

CONCORD — B2 *Cabarrus*

GLENWOOD ACRES RV PARK
Ratings: 5.5/NA/7 (RV Park) From Jct of I-85 & Bruton Smith Blvd (Exit 49), E 1.9 mi on Bruton Smith Blvd to Concord Parkway (Hwy 29), S 0.1 mi to Moorehead Rd, W 200 yds to Delrae Circle (R). **FAC:** Paved rds. (100 spaces). 50 Avail: 10 gravel, 40 grass, 10 pull-thrus (25 x 100), back-ins (25 x 50), accepts self-contain units only, 50 full hkups (30/50 amps), seasonal sites, WiFi Hotspot, dump, groc. **REC.** Pets OK. No tents. Big rig sites, 2015 rates: $30.
(704)455-9282 Lat: 35.35078, Lon: -80.69362
4632 Delrae Circle, Concord, NC 28027
phillipalittle@gmail.com
www.glenwoodacresrvpark.com
See ad page 858.

Travel Services

CAMPING WORLD OF CONCORD/TOM JOHNSON As the nation's largest retailer of RV supplies, accessories, services and new and used RVs, Camping World is committed to making your total RV experience better. **SERVICES:** RV, RV appliance, MH mechanical, staffed RV wash, restrooms, RV Sales. RV supplies, LP, emergency parking, RV accessible. waiting room. Hours: 8am to 6pm.
(704)837-1934 Lat: 35.36043, Lon: -80.69294
6700 Bruton Smith Blvd, Concord, NC 28027
mark@tomjohnsoncamping.com
www.campingworld.com

Things to See and Do

CHARLOTTE MOTOR SPEEDWAY NASCAR, Sprint Cup, Nationwide & Camping World Truck Series Racing. Also Host: Three of the Nation's Largest Car Shows, Stock Car Racing & Driving Schools. Call for available Tours & rates. Partial handicap access. RV accessible. Restrooms, food. Hours: 9am to 5pm. ATM.
(800)455-3267 Lat: 35.35246, Lon: -80.68806
5555 Concord Parkway South, Concord, NC 28027
tickets@charlottemotorspeedway.com
www.charlottemotorspeedway.com
See ad page 858.

DENVER — B1 *Catawba*

CROSS COUNTRY CAMPGROUND **Ratings: 8.5/8.5★/6.5** (Campground) 2015 rates: $35. (704)483-5897 6254 Hwy 150 East, Denver, NC 28037

EDENTON — A5 *Chowan*

ROCKY HOCK CAMPGROUND Ratings: 6/8★/7.5 (Campground) From Jct of US 17 & NC 32 (Exit 227): N 5.4 mi on NC 32 to Rocky Hock Rd, W 1.2 mi to Rocky Hock Creek Rd, SW 0.2 mi to Harris Landing Rd, NW 1.7 mi to Tynch Town Rd, W 0.8 mi to David's Red Barn Lane (L) NOTE: Follow Blue Camp Signs At Each Turn. **FAC:** Gravel rds. 32 gravel, 12 pull-thrus (25 x 70), back-ins (40 x 70), 32 full hkups (30/50 amps), WiFi $, tent sites, laundry, firewood. **REC:** pond, fishing, golf, rec open to public. Pets OK. Big rig sites, 2015 rates: $35.
(252)221-4695 Lat: 36.15547, Lon: -76.71048
1008 David's Red Barn Ln, Edenton, NC 27932
rhcampground@net-change.com
www.rockyhockcampground.com

ELIZABETHTOWN — C3 *Bladen*

JONES LAKE (State Pk) From town, N 4 mi on Hwy 242 (L). 2015 rates: $15 to $25. (910)588-4550

EMERALD ISLE — C5 *Carteret*

HOLIDAY TRAV-L-PARK RESORT FOR CAMPERS
Ratings: 9.5/10★/10 (Campground) From Jct of NC-24 & NC-58, S 2 mi on NC-58 to Coast Guard Rd (traffic light), S 200 ft (L). **FAC:** Paved rds. (300 spaces). Avail: 181 grass, 124 pull-thrus (30 x 60), back-ins (28 x 65), 161 full hkups, 20 W, 20 E (30/50 amps), seasonal sites, cable, WiFi $, tent sites, rentals, dump, laundry, groc, LP gas, firewood, controlled access. **REC:** pool, wading pool, Atlantic Ocean: swim, fishing, playground, rec open to public. Pet restrict(B) $. Partial handicap access. Big rig sites, eco-friendly, 2015 rates: $50 to $115. Mar 15 to Dec 10. ATM.
(252)354-2250 Lat: 34.65940, Lon: -77.05923
9102 Coast Guard Rd, Emerald Isle, NC 28594
htpresort@coastalemail.com
www.htpresort.com
See ad page 851 (Spotlight Crystal Coast).

Things to See and Do

EMERALD ISLE WINE MARKET Extensive selection of wines from North Carolina and around the world, as well as gifts and accessories for wine lovers. Partial handicap access. Restrooms, food. Hours: 7am to 10pm. ATM.
(252)354-8466 Lat: 34.66007, Lon: -77.05972
9102 Coast Guard Rd, Emerald Isle, NC 28594
See ad page 851 (Spotlight Crystal Coast).

ENFIELD — A4 *Halifax*

ENFIELD/ROCKY MOUNT KOA **Ratings: 8/8★/8** (Campground) 2015 rates: $35 to $40. (252)445-5925 101 Bell Acres, Enfield, NC 27823

FAYETTEVILLE — C3 *Cumberland*

LAZY ACRES CAMPGROUND
Ratings: 7.5/10★/7.5 (RV Park) From Jct of I-95 & Claude Lee Rd (exit 44), W 1 mi on Claude Lee Rd to Lazy Acres Rd, E 0.3 mi, follow campground signs (E). **FAC:** Gravel/dirt rds. 48 dirt, patios, 23 pull-thrus (30 x 70), back-ins (30 x 50), 48 full hkups (30/50 amps), cable, WiFi, dump, laundry, LP gas, fire rings, firewood. **REC:** pool, pond,

We appreciate your business!

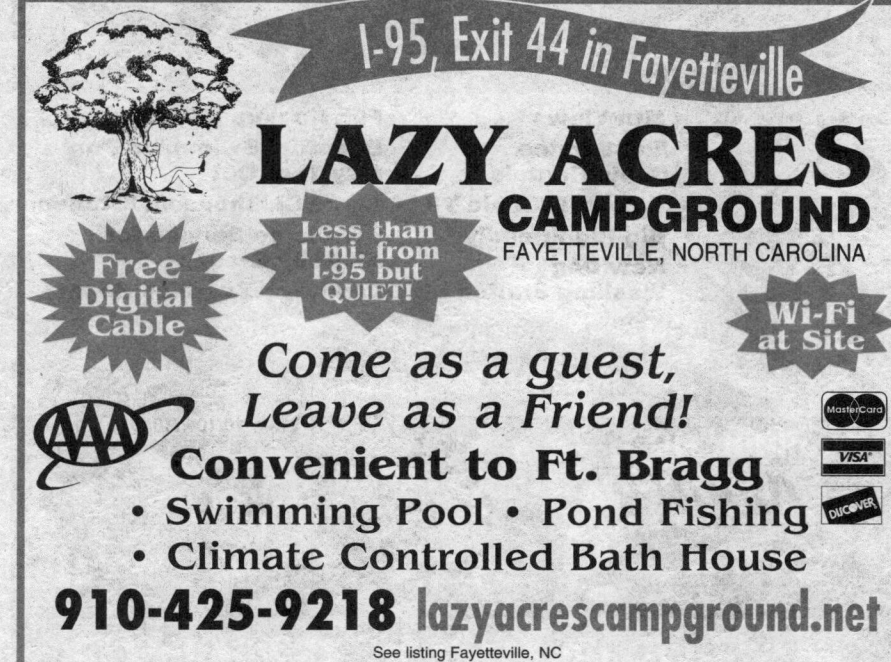

FAYETTEVILLE (CONT)

LAZY ACRES CAMPGROUND (CONT)
fishing, playground. Pet restrict(B). No tents. Big rig sites, eco-friendly, 2015 rates: $37.
AAA Approved
(910)425-9218 Lat: 34.97455, Lon: -78.88683
821 Lazy Acres St, Fayetteville, NC 28306
lazyacresoffice@yahoo.com
www.lazyacrescampground.net
See ad page 861.

FLETCHER — E2 *Henderson*

RUTLEDGE LAKE RV RESORT
Ratings: 9/9.5★/10 (Campground) From Jct of I-26 & NC-280 (exit 40), E 1 mi on NC-280 (Airport Rd) to Rutledge Rd, S 1 mi (L). **FAC:** Paved/gravel rds. (96 spaces). 86 Avail: 1 paved, 85 gravel, 6 pull-thrus (33 x 50), back-ins (33 x 50), 86 full hkups (30/50 amps), seasonal sites, cable, WiFi, rentals, laundry, LP gas, fire rings, firewood, controlled access. **REC:** heated pool, Rutledge Lake: fishing, playground. Pet restrict(B/Q). Partial handicap access, no tents. Eco-friendly, 2015 rates: $48 to $76. Disc: AAA.
AAA Approved
(828)654-7873 Lat: 35.44103, Lon: -82.52161
170 Rutledge Rd, Fletcher, NC 28732
info@campingnorthcarolina.com
www.rutledgelake.com
See ad pages 855, 849.

Our Guide to Seasonal Sites will help you find places you can stay for extended periods of time.

FONTANA DAM — E1 *Graham*

FONTANA VILLAGE CAMPGROUND (Public) From N end of town, N 1 mi on SR-28 to park access rd, E 0.2 mi (E). 2015 rates: $20 to $40. Apr to Oct. (828)498-2211

FOUR OAKS — B4 *Johnston*

FOUR OAKS LODGING & RV RESORT
Ratings: 7/8★/8 (Campground) S-bnd: From Jct of I-95 & US 301/701/NC 96 (Exit 90), on exit ramp turn left in break in island on US-301S, S 0.2 mi (R); or N-bnd: From Jct of I-95 & US-301/701/NC96 (Exit 90), W 0.2 mi on US-701 to US-301, S 0.3 mi (L).

CONVENIENT TO I-95 (ON HWY 301)
We have a place for everyone. Long RV sites, tent sites & deluxe motel rooms. Six golf courses within 15-20 min. Lots of historical sites. Several performing theaters & shopping for everyone less than 5 miles away!

FAC: Gravel rds. 24 grass, 4 pull-thrus (25 x 80), back-ins (22 x 70), 24 full hkups (30/50 amps), cable, WiFi, tent sites, rentals, dump, groc, LP gas, fire rings. **REC.** Pet restrict(B). Eco-friendly, 2015 rates: $20 to $40. Disc: AAA, military.
AAA Approved
(919)963-3596 Lat: 35.45765, Lon: -78.39428
4606 US Hwy 301 South, Four Oaks, NC 27524
Rich@fouroakslodging.com
www.fouroaksrvresort.com
See ad this page, 849.

We rate what RVers consider important.

RALEIGH OAKS RV RESORT & COTTAGES
Ratings: 10/10★/10 (RV Resort) From Jct of I-95 & US-701 (exit 90), S 0.4 mi on US-701 (L).

TOTALLY RENOVATED RALEIGH LOCATION
Easy I-95 access: NC #90. Near Carolina Premium Outlets. Free waffle breakfast daily, free WiFi & Cable. Playground, Mini-golf, 150 HUGE, level RV sites, 21+ cottages, 2 pools, spa, fitness center & 18 private bath suites.

FAC: All weather rds. 150 Avail: 150 all weather, 110 pull-thrus (35 x 80), back-ins (35 x 65), 150 full hkups (30/50 amps), cable, WiFi, rentals, laundry, LP gas, fire rings, firewood. **REC:** pool, whirlpool, playground. Pets OK. Partial handicap access, no tents. Big rig sites, 2015 rates: $30 to $40.
(919)934-3181 Lat: 35.45131, Lon: -78.38793
497 US 701S, Four Oaks, NC 27524
raleighoaksrv@gmail.com
www.raleighoaksrvresort.com
See ad pages 871, 846 (NC Map), 849 See ad inside back cover & Snowbird Destinations in Magazine Section.

FRANKLIN — E1 *Macon*

FRANKLIN See also Dillard, GA.

CARTOOGECHAYE CREEK CAMPGROUND **Ratings: 5/6/5** (RV Park) 2015 rates: $24. Apr 1 to Nov 1. (828)524-8553 91 No Name Rd, Franklin, NC 28734

COUNTRY WOODS RV PARK Ratings: 7.5/8★/8 (RV Park) S-bnd: From W Jct of US-441/23/64 Bypass & US-441, S 2.2 mi on US-441 (R); or N-bnd: On US-23/441, 1.5 mi N of Smoky Mountain Visitors Center (L). **FAC:** Paved/gravel rds. (72 spaces). Avail: 10 gravel, patios, 7 pull-thrus (18 x 65), back-ins (20 x 40), 10 full hkups (30/50 amps), seasonal sites, cable, WiFi, laundry, fire rings, firewood. **REC.** Pet restrict(Q). No tents. Eco-friendly, 2015 rates: $35. Apr 1 to Oct 31.
(828)524-4339 Lat: 35.13504, Lon: -83.39897
60 Countrywoods Dr, Franklin, NC 28734
cwoodsrv@dnet.net
www.countrywoodsrvpark.com

CULLASAJA RIVER RV PARK Ratings: 8/8/6.5 (Campground) From E Jct of US-441/23/64 bypass & US-64/NC-28, E 5 mi on US-64/NC-28 (R). **FAC:** Gravel rds. (90 spaces). Avail: 20 gravel, patios, 14 pull-thrus (25 x 65), back-ins (25 x 60), 20 full hkups (30/50 amps), seasonal sites, WiFi, tent sites, dump, laundry, LP gas, fire rings, firewood. **REC:** Cullasaja River: swim, fishing. Pets OK. 2015 rates: $28 to $33.
AAA Approved
(800)843-2795 Lat: 35.14158, Lon: -83.29814
6269 Highlands Rd, Franklin, NC 28734
info@campnc.com
www.campnc.com

FRANKLIN RV PARK & CAMPGROUND
Ratings: 6/9.5★/9.5 (RV Park) From Jct of US 441 & US 64, S 3.2 mi on US 441 to Addington Bridge Rd, W 0.1 mi to Old Addington Bridge Rd, N 0.1 mi (L). **FAC:** Gravel rds. 23 gravel, 3 pull-thrus (25 x 70), back-ins (24 x 50), some side by side hkups, 23 full hkups (30/50 amps), cable, WiFi, fire rings, firewood. **REC:** Dowdle Branch Stream. Pet restrict(B). No tents. Big rig sites, 2015 rates: $38 to $48. Apr 1 to Nov 15.
(828)349-6200 Lat: 35.12317, Lon: -83.39516

RV Park ratings you can rely on!

FRANKLIN (CONT)

FRANKLIN RV PARK & (CONT)
230 Old Addington Bridge Rd, Franklin, NC 28734
info@franklinrvpark.com
www.franklinrvpark.com
See ad opposite page.

↘ **OLD CORUNDUM MILLSITE CAMPGROUND Ratings: 6/8★/6** (Campground) From E Jct of US-441/23/64 Bypass & US-64/NC-28, E 4.2 mi on US-64/NC-28 to SR-1697 (Old Highlands Rd), SE 0.1 mi to Nickajack Rd, W 200 yds (L). **FAC:** Gravel rds. (81 spaces). Avail: 36 gravel, patios, 5 pull-thrus (18 x 45), back-ins (20 x 45), 36 full hkups (30 amps), seasonal sites, WiFi Hotspot, tent sites, dump, laundry, fire rings, firewood. **REC:** Cullasaja River: swim, fishing, playground. Pet restrict(Q). 2015 rates: $32 to $35. Disc: AAA, military. Apr 1 to Oct 31.
AAA Approved
(828)524-4663 Lat: 35.14416, Lon: -83.30931
80 Nickajack Rd, Franklin, NC 28734
ocmc@frontier.co
www.ocmcampground.com

↖ OUTSIDE INN CAMPGROUND **Ratings: 4.5/8.5★/7** (Campground) 2015 rates: $22. Apr 1 to Nov 1. (828)349-1846 7374 Lower Burningtown Rd, Franklin, NC 28734

↗ PINES RV PARK **Ratings: 7.5/8.5★/8** (Campground) 2015 rates: $30 to $34. (828)524-4490 4724 Murphy Rd, Franklin, NC 28734

↑ **THE GREAT OUTDOORS RV RESORT**
Ratings: 10/10★/10 (RV Park) N-bnd: From Jct of US 64 & US 441/23: Go N 6.2 mi on US 441 to Echo Valley Rd, W 200 ft (R); or S-bnd: From Jct of US 74 & US 23/441 (Exit 81A): Go S 13.8 mi on US 23/441 to Echo Valley Rd, W 200 ft (R). **FAC:** Paved rds. 63 Avail: 63 all weather, back-ins (35 x 60), accepts full hkup units only, 63 full hkups (30/50 amps), cable, WiFi, rentals, laundry, groc, LP gas, fire rings. **REC:** pool. Pet restrict(B). Partial handicap access, no tents. Big rig sites, 2015 rates: $43.95.
(828)349-0412 Lat: 35.23335, Lon: -83.34779
321 Thumpers Trail, Franklin, NC 28734
info@gorvresort.com
www.gorvresort.com
See ad opposite page, 849.

FRISCO — B6 *Dare*

CAPE HATTERAS NATIONAL SEASHORE (FRISCO CAMPGROUND) (Natl Pk) From center of town on Hwy 12: Go 2 mi E following signs. 2015 rates: $20. Apr to Oct. (252)473-2111

↑ **FRISCO WOODS CAMPGROUND**
Ratings: 8.5/10★/9 (Campground) S-bnd: From Jct of US-158 & NC-12, S 53.4 mi on NC-12 (R); or N-bnd: From Ocracoke/Hatteras Ferry, N 5.9 mi on NC-12, in town (L).

PAMLICO SOUND WATERFRONT CAMPING
Located on the Pamlico Sound within Cape Hatteras National Seashore, Frisco Woods is a family oriented waterfront campground. Enjoy our outdoor pool, windsurfing, kitesurfing or launching your kayak near your campsite.

FAC: Paved rds. 200 Avail: 120 grass, 80 dirt, back-ins (25 x 45), 93 full hkups, 107 W, 107 E (30/50 amps), cable, WiFi, tent sites, rentals, dump, laundry, groc, LP gas, firewood. **REC:** pool, Pamlico Sound: fishing, playground. Pet restrict(Q). Partial handicap access. 2015 rates: $40 to $71. Disc: military. Mar 1 to Dec 1.
(252)995-5208 Lat: 35.23956, Lon: -75.62009
53124 Hwy 12, Frisco, NC 27936
fwcstaff@thefriscowoodscampground.com
www.thefriscowoodscampground.com
See ad pages 864, 849 & Family Camping in Magazine Section.

Follow the arrow. The arrow in each listing indicates where the facility is located in relation to the listed town.

Take an RV Trip of a Lifetime!

Check out our itineraries for the Food Lover, Living History, Picture Perfect and On the Wild Side! These once-in-a-lifetime journeys are required fun for RVers of all ages.

Browse the RV Trips of a Lifetime, with routes and handy maps, in the front of this Guide.

The RV That's Right For You

Which recreational vehicle is right for you? Our handy overview in the front of this Guide helps prospective buyers decide which RV type fits their lifestyle, travel needs and budget, from folding camping trailers to motorhomes.

NC

FRISCO WOODS CAMPGROUND
EST. 1975
HATTERAS ISLAND N.C.
Cape Hatteras' Only Wooded Waterfront Campground
"We've put the camp back in camping"
• Full Hookups • Laundry • WiFi • LP Gas • 30/50 Amps • Cable TV • Convenience Store
• Tent Sites • Game Room • 4 Bathhouses • 32 Camping Cabins • Outdoor Pavilion
• One Mile to 4WD Accessible Beaches • Large Pool Overlooking Pamlaico Bay
Kite Surfing
Wind Surfing
Fishing
Crabbing
Oystering
Birdwatching
Kayaking
Beach Equipment
(800) 948-3942 • (252) 995-5208
Visit Our Web Site At:
www.thefriscowoodscampground.com
See listing Frisco, NC
Good Sam Park
Your Family Campground
53124 NC-12, Frisco, NC 27936
Good Sam RATED 8.5/10★/9

GARNER — B3 *Wake*

70 EAST MOBILE ACRES & RV PARK (RV Spaces) From Jct of I-40 and US Hwy 70 (Exit 306) (East 70 towards Clayton), E 1 mi on US Hwy 70 (L). Entrance: Keep left past mini storage. Call upon arrival for escort. **FAC:** Paved/gravel rds. (80 spaces). Avail: 60 gravel, 30 pull-thrus (40 x 90), back-ins (40 x 80), accepts full hkup units only, 60 full hkups (30/50 amps), seasonal sites, WiFi. Pet restrict(B/Q). No tents. Big rig sites, 2015 rates: $35 to $40.
(919)772-6568 Lat: 35.68525, Lon: -78.54195
134 Walnut Dr, Garner, NC 27529
www.rvinraleigh.com
See ad page 871.

Travel Services

CAMPING WORLD OF GARNER/RALEIGH As the nation's largest retailer of RV supplies, accessories, services and new and used RVs, Camping World is committed to making your total RV experience better. RV Accessories: (855)872-5504. **SERVICES:** Tire, RV appliance, MH mechanical, staffed RV wash, restrooms, RV Sales. RV supplies, LP, dump, waiting room. Hours: 8am to 6pm.
(888)857-0451 Lat: 35.681296, Lon: -78.532253
2300 US 70 Business, Garner, NC 27529
www.campingworld.com

GATESVILLE — A5 *Gates*

MERCHANTS MILLPOND (State Pk) From town: Go 6 mi NE on Hwy 1403. 2015 rates: $15 to $20. (252)357-1191

GLENDALE SPRINGS — A1 *Ashe*

RACCOON HOLLER CAMPGROUND Ratings: 7.5/7.5★/8 (Campground) N-bnd: From Jct of Blue Ridge Pkwy & NC-16, N 3.5 mi on Blue Ridge Pkwy (between MP-257 & 258) to Raccoon Holler Rd, W 0.1 mi (R); or N-bnd: From Jct of US-421 & NC-16, N 18 mi on NC-16 to Old Wilkesboro Rd, N 0.3 mi to Raccoon Holler Rd, E 0.4 mi (L). Elev 3200 ft. **FAC:** Paved/gravel rds. (210 spaces). Avail: 100 gravel, 6 pull-thrus (20 x 50), back-ins (20 x 50), 50 full hkups, 50 W, 50 E (30/50 amps), seasonal sites, cable, WiFi, tent sites, dump, laundry, groc, LP gas, fire rings, firewood. **REC:** pond, fishing, shuffleboard, playground. Pet restrict(B/Q). Partial handicap access. 2015 rates: $35. Apr 20 to Oct 31.
AAA Approved
(336)982-2706 Lat: 36.35695, Lon: -81.37570
493 Raccoon Holler Rd, Glendale Springs, NC 28629
janmill@skybest.com
www.raccoonholler.com

GOLDSBORO — B4 *Wayne*

CLIFFS OF THE NEUSE (State Pk) From Jct of US-70 & SR-111, S 8 mi on US-70 to CR-1743 (E). 2015 rates: $15 to $20. Mar 15 to Nov 30. (919)778-6234

Travel Services

DALY RV Family owned & operated since 1997 - One Stop shop for all your RV needs. **SERVICES:** RV, RV appliance, restrooms, RV Sales. RV supplies, LP. Hours: 8:30am to 5:00pm (closed Mon)
(800)972-8995 Lat: 35.43785, Lon: -78.08336
3369 Hwy 70 W, Goldsboro, NC 27530
info@dalyrv.com
www.dalyrv.com

Find it fast! To locate a town on a map, follow these easy instructions: Look for the map grid code after the town heading in the listing section and match it to the letters and numbers on the map borders. Draw a line horizontally from the letter and vertically from the number. You'll find the town near the intersection of the two lines.

GRAHAM — A3 *Alamance*

HIDDEN LAKE PARK Ratings: 5.5/4.5/6 (Campground) From Jct of I-40/I-85 & NC 54 (Exit 148), E 6.5 mi on N 54 (L). **FAC:** Fair paved/gravel rds. Avail: 60 gravel, 7 pull-thrus (25 x 50), back-ins (20 x 50), 30 full hkups, 30 W, 30 E (30/50 amps), tent sites, dump, firewood. **REC:** Hidden Lake, fishing, playground, rec open to public. Pet restrict(S). 2015 rates: $25.
(336)578-5980 Lat: 36.00077, Lon: -79.29863
4460 S NC 54 E, Graham, NC 27253
jmajors59@bellsouth.net
See ad page 859.

GREENSBORO — A2 *Guilford*

GREENSBORO CAMPGROUND **Ratings: 9/9★/8.5** (RV Park) 2015 rates: $40. (877)274-4143 1896 Trox St, Greensboro, NC 27406

HAGAN STONE CITY PARK (Public) From Jct of I-85 & US-421, S 6 mi on US-421 to Hagan-Stone Park Rd, W 2 mi (R). 2015 rates: $15 to $20. (336)674-0472

GRIFTON — B4 *Lenoir, Pitt*

CONTENTNEA CREEKSIDE RV & TRAIL PARK (Public) From Jct of US 264 (E) & NC Hwy 11, S 20 mi on Hwy 11 to S Highland Dr, S 3 mi on Highland Dr (across bridge) to Contentnea Dr, E 0.5 mi (L). 2015 rates: $10 to $15. (252)524-5168

HATTERAS — B6 *Dare*

HATTERAS SANDS CAMPGROUND Ratings: 7.5/10★/7 (Campground) S-bnd: From Jct of US 158 & NC-12, S 58.9 mi to Eagle Pass Rd, E 0.5 mi (R); or N-bnd: From Ocracoke/Hatteras Ferry, N 0.5 mi on NC-12 to Eagle Pass Rd, E 0.2 mi (L). **FAC:** Paved rds. 89 paved, 20 pull-thrus (24 x 48), back-ins (30 x 45), 52 full hkups, 20 W, 20 E (30/50 amps), cable, WiFi, tent sites, rentals, dump, laundry. **REC:** pool, Hatteras Inlet: fishing, playground. Pets OK. 2015 rates: $42 to $57. Disc: AAA, military. Mar 1 to Dec 1.
AAA Approved
(252)986-2422 Lat: 35.21357, Lon: -75.69552
57316 Eagle Pass Rd, Hatteras, NC 27943
hatterassandscg@gmail.com
www.hatterassandsrvpark.com
See ad this page, 849.

Things to See and Do

HATTERAS ISLAND WELCOME CENTER Information for local attractions & camping. Partial handicap access. RV accessible. Restrooms. Hours: 9am to 5pm.
(877)629-4386 Lat: 35.21947, Lon: -75.69072
57190 Kohler Rd, Hatteras, NC 27943
information@outerbanks.org
www.outerbanks.org
See ad page 847 (Welcome Section) and ad Magazine Section page 118.

HENDERSON — A4 *Vance, Warren*

KERR LAKE SRA/BULLOCKSVILLE PARK (Public) From Jct of I-85 & SR-1244 (Manson Exit), NW 2.5 mi on SR-1244 to SR-1366, NW 4 mi (R). 2015 rates: $15 to $25. Apr 1 to Sep 30. (252)438-7791

KERR LAKE SRA/HENDERSON POINT (Public) From Jct of I-85 & SR-39, N 20 mi on SR-39 to CR-1356, NE 2 mi to CR-1359 (R). 2015 rates: $15 to $25. Apr 1 to Sep 30. (252)438-7791

HENDERSONVILLE — E2 *Henderson*

APPLE VALLEY TRAVEL PARK **Ratings: 5.5/7/6.5** (RV Area in MHP) 2015 rates: $27 to $29. Apr 1 to Nov 1. (828)685-8000 1 Apple Orchard Rd, Hendersonville, NC 28792

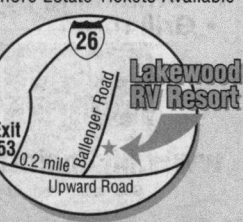

JAYMAR TRAVEL PARK Ratings: 9/10★/9 (RV Area in MHP) From Jct of I-26 & US-64 (exit 49A), E 2.7 mi on US-64 (L). **FAC:** Paved rds. 30 paved, patios, 12 pull-thrus (24 x 100), back-ins (25 x 48), some side by side hkups, 30 full hkups (30/50 amps), cable, WiFi, laundry. **REC:** shuffleboard. Pet restrict(Q). No tents. Big

HENDERSONVILLE (CONT)

JAYMAR TRAVEL PARK (CONT)
rig sites, 2015 rates: $28 to $33. Apr 20 to Nov 5. No CC.
(828)685-3771 Lat: 35.36902, Lon: -82.40796
140 Jaymar Park Dr, Hendersonville, NC 28792
jaymarnc@yahoo.com
www.jaymarnc.com
See ad pages 865, 849.

LAKEWOOD RV RESORT
Ratings: 9.5/10★/10 (RV Park) From Jct of I-26 & Upward Rd (exit 53), E 0.2 mi on Upward Rd (unmarked) to Ballenger Rd (Left), NE 0.2 mi (Right) to main entrance (R). **FAC:** Paved rds. (100 spaces). Avail: 69 gravel, patios, 26 pull-thrus (30 x 75), back-ins (30 x 60), 69 full hkups (30/50 amps), seasonal sites, cable, WiFi, rentals, laundry, LP gas. **REC:** heated pool, pond, fishing, shuffleboard. Pet restrict(B/Q). No tents. Age restrict may apply, eco-friendly, 2015 rates: $45. Disc: AAA.
(888)819-4200 Lat: 35.30124, Lon: -82.40148
15 Timmie Ln, Flat Rock, NC 28731
info@lakewoodrvresort.com
www.lakewoodrvresort.com
See ad pages 865, 849.

RED GATES RV PARK **Ratings: 5/8★/6** (Campground) 2015 rates: $32. Apr 1 to Nov 1. (828)685-8787 314 Red Gates Ln, Hendersonville, NC 28792

TOWN MOUNTAIN TRAVEL PARK
Ratings: 7/10★/9 (Campground) From Jct of I-26 & Exit 53/Upward Rd, W 0.8 mi on Upward Rd to Old Upward Rd, NW 0.3 mi (R). **FAC:** Paved rds. 21 gravel, patios, back-ins (36 x 75), 21 full hkups (30/50 amps), cable, WiFi, tent sites, rentals, firewood. **REC.** Pet restrict(B/Q). Big rig sites, eco-friendly, 2015 rates: $38 to $40.
(828)697-6692 Lat: 35.29497, Lon: -82.42639
48 Town Mountain Rd, Hendersonville, NC 28792
info@townmountaintravelpark.com
www.townmountaintravelpark.com
See ad this page, 849.

Treat your pet to a fabulous camping experience by staying at one of the Pampered Pet Parks featured in the front of the Guide.

Travel Services

CAMPING WORLD OF HENDERSONVILLE/ASHEVILLE As the nation's largest retailer of RV supplies, accessories, services and new and used RVs, Camping World is committed to making your total RV experience better. RV Accessories: (855)530-1772. **SERVICES:** RV, tire, RV appliance, MH mechanical, engine/chassis repair, staffed RV wash, restrooms, RV Sales. RV storage. RV supplies, LP, dump, emergency parking, RV accessible. waiting room. Hours: 8am to 6pm.
(888)865-1310 Lat: 35.40494, Lon: -82.51602
2918 North Rugby Rd., Hendersonville, NC 28791
www.campingworld.com

HIGH POINT — B2 *Guilford*

OAK HOLLOW FAMILY CAMPGROUND
(Public) From Jct of I-85 Bus & US 311 Bypass (Exit 66) to Johnson St, S 0.3 mi to Oakview Rd, E 0.4 mi to Centennial St, N 0.1 mi (L). **FAC:** Paved/gravel rds. 84 Avail: 60 paved, 24 gravel, back-ins (22 x 45), mostly side by side hkups, 84 full hkups (30/50 amps), cable, WiFi, tent sites, laundry, controlled access. **REC:** pool, Oak Hollow: fishing, marina, golf, playground, rec open to public. Pet restrict(B). Partial handicap access. 21 day max stay, 2015 rates: $35. No reservations.
(336)883-3492 Lat: 36.00881, Lon: -80.00196
3415 N Centennial St, High Point, NC 27265
Lamar.lee@highpointnc.gov
www.highpointnc.gov/pr
See ad this page.

HOPE MILLS — C3 *Cumberland*

Travel Services

CAMPING WORLD OF HOPE MILLS/FAYETTEVILLE As the nation's largest retailer of RV supplies, accessories, services and new and used RVs, Camping World is committed to making your total RV experience better. RV Accessories: (855)872-5503. **SERVICES:** RV appliance, staffed RV wash, restrooms, RV Sales. RV supplies, LP, dump, emergency parking. Hours: 8am - 6pm.
(888)741-0295 Lat: 34.947729, Lon: -78.928682
5117 U.s. Hwy 301 S., Hope Mills, NC 28348
www.campingworld.com

HUBERT — C5 *Onslow*

HAWKINS CREEK CAMPGROUND
Ratings: 6/7.5★/8 (Campground) From center of town: Go 1-3/4 mi NW on Hwy 24, then 1/4 mi S on Hwy 172, then 1/4 mi E on Starling Rd (E). **FAC:** Paved/gravel rds. (88 spaces). Avail: 12 gravel, 12 pull-thrus (30 x 50), 12 full hkups (30/50 amps), seasonal sites, cable, WiFi, tent sites, dump,

Take time now to plan a road trip with your pet. Read more in our Pampered Pet Parks feature at the front of the Guide.

LP gas, fire rings. **REC:** pond, fishing. Pets OK. 2015 rates: $35. No CC.
AAA Approved
(910)340-4131 Lat: 34.70933, Lon: -77.22890
252 Reid Acres Ln, Hubert, NC 28539
reid@hawkinscreekcampground.com
www.hawkinscreekcampground.com
See ad this page.

JACKSONVILLE — C5 *Onslow*

CABIN CREEK CAMPGROUND
Ratings: 8/9★/9 (Campground) From W Jct of US-17 & NC-24/US-258, S 4.8 mi on US-17 (R). **FAC:** Paved/gravel rds (100 spaces). Avail: 40 grass, 30 pull-thrus (24 x 85), back-ins (30 x 65), 40 full hkups (30/50 amps), seasonal sites, cable, WiFi, tent sites, rentals, dump, laundry, LP gas, firewood. **REC:** pond, fishing, playground, rec open to public. Pet restrict(B/Q). Partial handicap access. Big rig sites eco-friendly, 2015 rates: $32.50 to $39. Disc: AAA military.
(910)346-4808 Lat: 34.69166, Lon: -77.47868
3200 Wilmington Hwy, Jacksonville, NC 28540
cabincreekcampground@yahoo.com
www.cabincreekcampground.com
See ad this page, 849.

KILL DEVIL HILLS — A6 *Dare*

OBX CAMPGROUND Ratings: 5.5/8.5/9 (RV Park) From Hwy 158 & Colington Rd, W 2.2 mi to Marshy Rd, S 600 ft on Marshy Rd (R). **FAC:** Gravel rds. (48 spaces). Avail: 28 gravel, back-ins (30 x 60), 28 full hkups (30/50 amps), cable, WiFi, dump, laundry. Pets OK. 2015 rates: $60.
(252)564-4741 Lat: 36.01023, Lon: -75.69008
126 Marshy Ridge Rd., Kill Devil Hills, NC 27948
Beasley@obxcampground.com
www.obxcampground.com

KINGS MOUNTAIN — B1 *Cleveland*

HOUNDS GATEWAY CAMPGROUND AND FUN PARK Ratings: 8/9.5★/5.5 (Campground) From Jct I-85 & Dixon School Rd (exit 5), W 1 mi to Hwy 216, N 1.5 mi (R) Note: Park open with continued expansion. **FAC:** Gravel rds. 43 gravel, back-ins (35 x 50), 43 full hkups (30/50 amps), WiFi, tent sites rentals, dump, laundry, restaurant. **REC:** pool Hounds Lake: fishing, playground, rec open to public Pets OK. Partial handicap access. 2015 rates: $25
(704)739-4474 Lat: 35.16430, Lon: -81.20863
114 Raven Circle, Kings Mountain, NC 28086
mebrown@carolina.rr.com
www.houndsgatewaycampground.com

KINSTON — B4 *Lenoir*

NEUSEWAY NATURE PARK & CAMPGROUND (Public) From Jct of US 70 & NC 11, NE 1 mi on NC 11, 0.1 mi on River Bank Rd (L). 2015 rates: $12. (252)939-3367

LAKE JUNALUSKA — E2 *Haywood*

LAKE JUNALUSKA CAMPGROUND **Ratings: 7.5/5.5/7** (Campground) 2015 rates: $30 to $32. Apr 1 to Oct 31. (800)222-4930 50 Camp Adventure Rd, Waynesville, NC 28785

LAKE LURE — E3 *Rutherford*

RIVER CREEK CAMPGROUND **Ratings: 7.5/7/7** (Campground) 2015 rates: $35. (828)287-3915 217 River Creek Dr, Rutherfordton, NC 28139

RUTHERFORD MOUNTAIN CAMPGROUND **Ratings: 5/9★/7** (Campground) 2015 rates: $40. Apr 15 to Oct 1. (828)286-9006 234 Otter Creek Rd, Union Mills, NC 28167

LAKE TOXAWAY — E2 *Transylvania*

MOUNTAIN FALLS LUXURY MOTORCOACH RESORT Ratings: 10/10★/10 (Condo Pk) E-bnd: From Jct of US-64 & NC-281 (S), E 1.9 mi on US-64 (R); or W-bnd: From Jct of US-64 & NC-281, W 0.8 mi on US-64 (L) Class A Motorhomes only. Elev 3000 ft. **FAC:** Paved rds. 74 paved, patios, back-ins (40 x 90), 74 full hkups (30/50 amps), cable, WiFi, laundry, controlled access. **REC:** heated pool, whirlpool, pond, fishing, golf. Pet restrict(Q). Partial handicap access, no tents. Big rig sites, 2015 rates: $75 to $105.
(828)966-9350 Lat: 35.11997, Lon: -82.93661
20 Resorts Blvd, Lake Toxaway, NC 28747
info@mountain-falls.com
www.mtn-falls.com

RIVERBEND RV PARK **Ratings: 5.5/8.5★/8** (RV Park) 2015 rates: $30 to $35. May 1 to Oct 31. (828)966-4214 hwy 281 N, 1400 Blue Ridge Rd, Lake Toxaway, NC 28747

LAUREL SPRINGS — A1 *Alleghany*

MILLER'S CAMPING Ratings: 6/8★/8 (Campground) From Jct of Blue Ridge Pkwy & NC-18, N 0.8 mi on Blue Ridge Pkwy, between MP-247 & 248 (L). Elev 3000 ft. **FAC:** Paved/gravel rds. (64 spaces). 11 Avail: 8 gravel, 3 grass, patios, 2 pull-thrus (40 x 50), back-ins (40 x 50), 11 full hkups (30 amps), seasonal sites, WiFi, tent sites, rentals, laundry, firewood. **REC:** Laurel Creek: fishing. Pets OK. 2015 rates: $29. Apr 1 to Oct 31. No CC.
(336)359-2828 Lat: 36.39530, Lon: -81.23260
33 Campground Rd, Laurel Springs, NC 28644
info@millerscamping.com
www.millerscamping.com

LENOIR — B1 *Caldwell*

GREEN MOUNTAIN PARK RESORT **Ratings: 7.5/8★/7** (Membership Pk) 2015 rates: $55. Apr 1 to Nov 1. (800)405-6188 2495 Dimmette Rd, Lenoir, NC 28645

Like Us on Facebook.

LEXINGTON — B2 *Davidson*

CROSS WINDS FAMILY CAMPGROUND
Ratings: 8.5/9.5★/9 (Campground) N-bnd: Jct I-85 & Hwy 150 (exit 84), W .5 mi on Hwy 150 to Old Salisbury Rd, SW .25 mi to Sowers Rd W 500 ft (immed R) on Campground Dr(R) S-bnd: Jct I-85 & NC150 (exit 84), W 300 ft to Sowers Rd W 500 ft (immed R) on Campground Dr (R). **FAC:** Paved/gravel rds. (72 spaces). Avail: 62 gravel, 27 pull-thrus (40 x 90), back-ins (30 x 70), 62 full hkups (30/50 amps), seasonal sites, cable, WiFi, tent sites, laundry, LP gas, fire rings, firewood. **REC:** pool, pond, fishing, playground. Pets OK. Partial handicap access. Big rig sites, eco-friendly, 2015 rates: $38 to $41.
(336)853-4567 Lat: 35.73109, Lon: -80.38230
160 Campground Ln, Linwood, NC 27299
camping@crosswindsfamilycampground.com
www.crosswindsfamilycampground.com
See ad this page.

HIGH ROCK LAKE/MARINA & CAMPGROUND Ratings: 8/8★/8 (RV Park) From Jct of I-85 & NC-8 (exit 91), S 6.6 mi on NC-8 to Wafford Rd (flashing yellow light), E 1.25 mi on Wafford Rd (becomes Wafford Circle), proceed to sign on right (R). **FAC:** Paved/gravel rds. (95 spaces). Avail: 35 gravel, 17 pull-thrus (22 x 55), back-ins (25 x 45), 35 full hkups (30/50 amps), seasonal sites, cable, WiFi, rentals, dump, laundry, LP gas, fire rings, firewood. **REC:** pool, High Rock Lake: fishing, marina, playground. Pet restrict(B). No tents. 2015 rates: $40. Disc: AAA.
(336)798-1196 Lat: 35.68364, Lon: -80.25145
1013 Wafford Circle, Lexington, NC 27292
Highrock@triad.twcbc.com
www.highrocklakecampground.com

LINVILLE FALLS — D3 *Burke*

BLUE RIDGE PKWY/LINVILLE FALLS (Natl Pk) From Jct of US-40 & US-221, N 20 mi on US-221 to Blue Ridge Pkwy, N 1 mi at MP-316.3 (R). 2015 rates: $16 to $19. May 8 to Oct 24. (828)765-7818

LINVILLE FALLS TRAILER LODGE & CAMPGROUND **Ratings: 5/8.5★/8.5** (Campground) 2015 rates: $35 to $40. May 1 to Nov 1. (828)765-2681 717 Gurney Franklin Rd, Newland, NC 28647

Explore America's Top RV Destinations! Turn to the Spotlight articles in our State and Province sections to learn more.

LITTLE SWITZERLAND — D3 *McDowell*

BLUE RIDGE PKWY/CRABTREE MEADOWS (Natl Pk) From Jct of I-40 & SR-221, N 11 mi on SR-221 to SR-226, NW 7 mi to Parkway Rd, S 8 mi at MP-339.5 (R). 2015 rates: $16. May 1 to Oct 31. (828)271-4779

LITTLETON — A4 *Warren*

LAKE GASTON RV RESORT / OUTDOOR WORLD **Ratings: 6.5/8/8.5** (Membership Pk) 2015 rates: $45 to $49. Apr 1 to Oct 23. (800)405-6188 561 Fleming Dairy Rd, Littleton, NC 27850

LUMBERTON — C3 *Robeson*

LUMBERTON/I-95 KOA **Ratings: 7.5/7.5/6.5** (Campground) 2015 rates: $36 to $41. (910)739-4372 465 Kenric Rd, Lumberton, NC 28360

MAGGIE VALLEY — E2 *Haywood*

STONEBRIDGE CAMPGROUNDS
Ratings: 9/7.5/7 (Campground) From W Jct of I-40 & US-276 (Exit 20), S 5.5 mi on US-276 (Jonathan Creek Rd) to US-19, W 1.7 mi (R). Elev 3200 ft.

STONEBRIDGE & THE SMOKEY MOUNTAINS
Located in the beautiful Maggie Valley, North Carolina. The Great Smokey Mountains, Blue Ridge Parkway and Asheville with the Biltmore Estate await you. Stay and view our spectacular fall colors.

FAC: Paved/gravel rds. (230 spaces). 150 Avail: 100 gravel, 50 grass, 100 pull-thrus (25 x 60), back-ins (20 x 50), mostly side by side hkups, 150 full hkups (30/50 amps), seasonal sites, cable, WiFi, tent sites, rentals, dump, laundry, fire rings, firewood. **REC:** pool, Johnathan Creek: fishing, playground. Pet restrict(B). Partial handicap access. Big rig sites, 2015 rates: $30 to $40.
(828)926-1904 Lat: 35.51754, Lon: -83.05923
1786 Soco Rd, Maggie Valley, NC 28751
info@stonebridgecampgrounds.com
www.stonebridgecampgrounds.com
See ad this page, 849.

EXCLUSIVE! Military Listings in the back of the Guide indicate campgrounds for use exclusively by active and retired military personnel.

NC

Good Sam Park
CREEKWOOD FARM
RV PARK
At the Gateway to the Maggie Valley and the Great Smoky Mountains National Park
4696 Jonathan Creek Rd.
Waynesville, NC 28785
Haywood County
828-926-7977 • 800-862-8110
See listing Waynesville, NC
125 LARGE SITES ON 11 ACRES
• 20/30/50 Amps All Sites
• Creekside Sites
• Private Individual Bathrooms
• TV/Card Room
• Laundry Room
• Historic Barn for Meetings
• Modem Hookup
• Ice/Propane Available
• Cable TV
• Open All Year
• Free Wifi
creekwoodfarmrv@main.nc.us • www.creekwoodfarmrv.com
I-40, Exit 20, 1 Mile South On US 276
VISA
MasterCard
AAA

MANTEO — A6 *Dare*

THE REFUGE ON ROANOKE ISLAND
Ratings: 7/9.5★/8.5 (RV Park) From Jct of US 64/264 & NC 345, S 3 mi on NC 345 (L). **FAC:** Gravel rds. (63 spaces). Avail: 14 gravel, back-ins (30 x 50), 14 full hkups (30/50 amps), seasonal sites, cable, WiFi, laundry. **REC:** pool, pond, fishing. Pets OK. Partial handicap access, no tents. Big rig sites, eco-friendly, 2015 rates: $42 to $62.
(252)473-1096 Lat: 35.85332, Lon: -75.64425
2881 NC Hwy 345, Wanchese, NC 27981
info@refuge-roanokeisland.com
www.refuge-roanokeisland.com
See ad this page.

Things to See and Do

OUTER BANKS VISITORS BUREAU Obtain information on the distinct communities of the Outer Banks with over 20 national, state & historic sites & over 100 miles of dynamic barrier islands, beaches & unique coastal restaurants with fresh local seafood.

THE OUTER BANKS OF NORTH CAROLINA
OBX marks the spot for what you seek. Relaxation? We've got it. Adventure? We've got it. Freshest seafood? You'll find it here. Visit outerbanks.org or call 877-629-4386 to get your free guide and start planning your trip.

Partial handicap access. RV accessible. Restrooms. Hours: 9am to 5pm.
(877)629-4386 Lat: 35.88594, Lon: -75.66800
One Visitor Center Circle, Manteo, NC 27954
information@outerbanks.org
www.outerbanks.org
See ad page 847 (Welcome Section) & RV Trips of a Lifetime and ad page 118 in Magazine Section.

MARBLE — E1 *Cherokee*

CREEKSIDE RV PARK **Ratings: 6/8★/7** (RV Park) 2015 rates: $30. Apr 1 to Nov 1. (828)837-4123 68 Old Peach Tree Rd, Marble, NC 28905

MARION — D3 *McDowell*

BUCK CREEK RV PARK
Ratings: 8.5/9★/10 (RV Park) From Jct of I-40 & NC-226 (exit 86), NW 6 mi on NC 226/US 221 to US-70, W 1.8 mi to NC-80, N 1.9 mi to Tom's Creek Rd, E .01 mi (L). **FAC:** Gravel rds. (74 spaces). Avail: 30 gravel, 5 pull-thrus (30 x 62), back-ins (30 x 50), 30 full hkups (30/50 amps), seasonal sites, cable, WiFi, laundry, fire rings, firewood. **REC:** Buck Creek: swim, fishing. Pet restrict(B). No tents. Big rig sites, eco-friendly, 2015 rates: $36 to $48. Apr 1 to Nov 1. No CC.
(828)724-4888 Lat: 35.71869, Lon: -82.07405
2576 Tom's Creek Rd, Marion, NC 28752
www.buckcreekcampground.com
See ad this page, 849.

LAKE JAMES (State Pk) From town: Go 5 mi NE on Hwy 126. 2015 rates: $15 to $20. Mar 1 to Nov 30. (828)584-7728

MOUNTAIN STREAM RV PARK Ratings: 6/10★/10 (RV Park) From Jct of I-40 (exit 86) & NC-226, NW 7 mi on NC 226/US 221 to US-70, W 1.8 mi to NC-80, N 7 mi (R). **FAC:** Gravel rds. 35 gravel, back-ins (30 x 50), 35 full hkups (30/50 amps), cable, WiFi, fire rings, firewood. **REC:** Buck Creek: fishing. Pets OK. No tents. 2015 rates: $38 to $53. Apr 1 to Nov 30.
(877)724-9013 Lat: 35.73877, Lon: -82.13332
6954 Buck Creek Rd, Marion, NC 28752
camp@mountainstreamrvpark.com
www.mountainstreamrvpark.com

TOM JOHNSON CAMPING WORLD CAMPGROUND **Ratings: 8/9.5★/9** (RV Park) 2015 rates: $30. (800)225-7802 348 Resistoflex Rd, Marion, NC 28752

YOGI BEARS JELLYSTONE PARK MARION NC **Ratings: 8/8/7.5** (Campground) 2015 rates: $42 to $64. Mar 15 to Nov 15. (828)652-7208 1210 Deacon Dr, Marion, NC 28752

Travel Services

CAMPING WORLD OF MARION/TOM JOHNSON As the nation's largest retailer of RV supplies, accessories, services and new and used RVs, Camping World is committed to making your total RV experience better. RV Accessories: (828)634-4412. **SERVICES:** RV, tire, RV appliance, MH mechanical, restaurant, staffed RV wash, restrooms, RV Sales. RV storage. RV supplies, LP, dump, emergency parking, RV accessible. waiting room. Hours: 8am to 6pm.
(800)225-7802 Lat: 35.69128, Lon: -82.05900
1885 US Hwy 70 W, Marion, NC 28752
www.campingworld.com

MEBANE — A3 *Alamance*

JONES STATION RV PARK Ratings: 6.5/9.5★/9 (Campground) From Jct of I-40 & Mebane Oaks Rd (exit 154), S 2.1 mi on Mebane Oaks Rd to Cook St, W 1.3 mi to Jones Dr, S 0.3 mi (L). **FAC:** Gravel rds. 36 gravel, 17 pull-thrus (30 x 80), back-ins (30 x 30), 36 full hkups (30/50 amps), WiFi, fire rings, firewood. **REC:** playground. Pet restrict(B). Partial handicap access, no tents. 2015 rates: $38. Disc: AAA, military. No CC.
(919)568-0153 Lat: 36.03161, Lon: -79.27805
2710 Jones Dr, Mebane, NC 27302
jonesstationrvpark@gmail.com
www.JonesStationRVPark.com

MICAVILLE — D3 *Yancey*

PATIENCE PARK/TOE RIVER CAMPGROUND (Public) From Jct of Hwys 19E & 80S, S 4 mi on Hwy 80 to Blue Rock Rd, E 2 mi (L). 2015 rates: $16 to $20. Apr to Oct. (828)675-5104

MONROE — C2 *Union*

CANE CREEK PARK/UNION COUNTY (Public) From Jct of US-74 & Hwy 200 (Skyway Dr in Monroe), S 12.8 mi on Hwy 200 to Potter Rd, E 3.2 mi to Cane Creek Rd, S 1.6 mi (E). 2015 rates: $18.75 to $30. (704)843-3919

MOREHEAD CITY — C5 *Carteret*

WATERS EDGE RV PARK **Ratings: 5.5/9/8.5** (Campground) 2015 rates: $35 to $49. (252)247-0494 1463 Hwy 24, Newport, NC 28570

WHISPERING PINES RV PARK **Ratings: 9/10★/9** (RV Park) 2015 rates: $64. (800)405-6188 25 Whispering Pines, Newport, NC 28570

MORGANTON — B1 *Burke*

RIVERSIDE GOLF & RV PARK
Ratings: 5.5/NA/5 (Campground) From Jct of I-40 & Jamestown Rd (Exit 100), N 2.1 mi on Jamestown Rd (becomes Independence Blvd North of US 70) (R). **FAC:** Gravel rds. 30 gravel, 18 pull-thrus (26 x 67), back-ins (26 x 60), 30 full hkups (30/50 amps), cable, WiFi, dump. **REC:** Catawba River: fishing, rec open to public. Pets OK. No tents. Big rig sites, 2015 rates: $30.
(828)433-6464 Lat: 35.73854, Lon: -81.72483
611 Independence Blvd, Morganton, NC 28655
riversidegolfrv@gmail.com
www.riversidegolfrvpark.com
See ad this page.

STEELE CREEK PARK **Ratings: 7.5/6.5/7** (Campground) 2015 rates: $25 to $32. Apr 1 to Nov 1. (828)433-5660 7081 Nc-181 N, Morganton, NC 28655

MOUNT AIRY — A2 *Surry*

BEECHNUT FAMILY CAMPGROUND **Ratings: 6/5/7** (Campground) 2015 rates: $40 to $45. (336)320-3802 315 Beechnut Lane, Mount Airy, NC 27030

MAYBERRY CAMPGROUND
Ratings: 8/8★/8 (Campground) From Jct of I 74 & Hwy 601 (Exit 11) SW 0.3 mi on Hwy 601 to South McKinney Road, SE 0.3 mi to Rustic Village Trail, NE 0.2 mi (E). **FAC:** Gravel rds. 106 gravel, 38 pull-thrus (32 x 73), back-ins (30 x 60), 106 full hkups (30/50 amps), cable, WiFi, tent sites, laundry, firewood. **REC:** pond, fishing, playground. Pets OK. Par-

Get the Facts! Essential tips and travel info for can be found in the Welcome Section at the beginning of each State/Province.

NC

MOUNT AIRY (CONT)

MAYBERRY CAMPGROUND (CONT)
tial handicap access. Big rig sites, eco-friendly, 2015 rates: $33.50.
AAA Approved
(336)789-6199 Lat: 36.45433, Lon: -80.63666
114 Bunker Rd, Mount Airy, NC 27030
mayberrycamp@embarqmail.com
www.mayberrycampground.com
See ad this page, 849.

VETERAN'S MEMORIAL PARK, INC
(RV Spaces) From Jct of I-74 & NC-601 (ext 11), E 3 mi on NC-601 to NC-52 By Pass, 3.5 mi N to Starlite Rd, E 0.5 mi to Lebanon St, S 0.75 mi (R). **FAC:** Gravel rds. 54 grass, back-ins (30 x 60), some side by side hkups, 42 full hkups, 12 W, 12 E (30/50 amps), tent sites. Pets OK. 2015 rates: $30. No CC.
(336)786-2236 Lat: 36.51492, Lon: -80.61877
691 W Lebanon St, Mount Airy, NC 27030
vpark1946@gmail.com
www.veteransparkmtairy.org
See ad this page.

MURPHY — E1 *Cherokee*

MURPHY/PEACE VALLEY KOA **Ratings: 8/8.5★/8.5** (Campground) 2015 rates: $32 to $39. (828)837-6223 117 Happy Valley Rd, Marble, NC 28905

RIVERS EDGE MOUNTAIN RV RESORT **Ratings: 7/6.5/7.5** (Condo Pk) 2015 rates: $39 to $59. (828)361-4517 1750 Hilltop Rd, Murphy, NC 28906

VALLEY RIVER RESORT
(RV Park) (Under Construction) Jct US-64 & US-19/US-74, N 3.2 on US-19/US-74 to Regal Rd (L). **FAC:** Paved rds. 10 paved, back-ins (30 x 60), 10 full hkups (30/50 amps). Pets OK. 2015 rates: $40 to $45. No CC, no reservations.
(828)349-3390 Lat: 35.12161, Lon: -84.00114
975 Regal Rd, Murphy, NC 28906
lcjones6456@yahoo.com
www.valleyriverresort.com
See ad this page.

NAGS HEAD — A6 *Dare*

CAPE HATTERAS NATL SEASHORE/OREGON INLET (Natl Pk) From town, S 10 mi on Hwy 12 (L). 2015 rates: $20. Apr 5 to Oct 14. (252)473-2111

Things to See and Do

WHALEBONE WELCOME CENTER Information for towns tourist info for Outer Banks. Partial handicap access. RV accessible. Restrooms. Hours: 9am to 5pm.
(252)441-6644 Lat: 35.90427, Lon: -75.59780
2 NC Hwy 12, Nags Head, NC 27959
information@outerbanks.org
www.outerbanks.org
See ad page 847 (Welcome Section) and ad Magazine Section page 118.

NEW BERN — C5 *Craven*

MOONLIGHT LAKE RV PARK & COTTAGES **Ratings: 6/9/5** (Campground) 2015 rates: $32. (252)745-9800 180 Moonlight Lake Dr, New Bern, NC 28560

NEW BERN KOA **Ratings: 9/9★/9** (Campground) 2015 rates: $41 to $78. (800)562-3341 1565 B St, New Bern, NC 28560

NEWLAND — D3 *Avery*

SECLUDED VALLEY CAMPGROUND **Ratings: 6.5/6/8** (Campground) 2015 rates: $30 to $35. May 1 to Oct 15. (828)765-4810 8555 US Hwy 19E, Newland, NC 28657

NORLINA — A4 *Warren*

KERR LAKE SRA/COUNTY LINE PARK (Public) From Jct of I-85 & SR-1244 (Manson exit), NW 6 mi on SR-1244 to SR-1200, N 3 mi to SR-1203, NW 3 mi (E). 2015 rates: $15 to $25. Apr 1 to Sep 30. (252)438-7791

KERR LAKE SRA/KIMBALL POINT PARK (Public) From Jct of I-85 & SR-1244, (Manson Exit), NW 6 mi on SR-1244 to SR-1200, N 5 mi to SR-1204, NW 2 mi (E). 2015 rates: $15 to $25. Apr 1 to Oct 31. (252)438-7791

NORTH TOPSAIL BEACH — C4 *Onslow, Pender*

NORTH TOPSAIL BEACH See also Surf City.

NORWOOD — B2 *Stanly*

NORWOOD CAMPGROUND
Ratings: 8/8.5★/6.5 (Campground) US-52: Turn (N) on Bowers Rd, go 1.5 mi, turn (E) on Lake Shore Dr, go 1.2 mi, turn (N) on Berry Hill Dr, go 3 mi, campground on right (follow directions not GPS). **FAC:** Gravel rds. (88 spaces). Avail: 18 gravel, 4 pull-thrus (24 x 60), back-ins (24 x 40), 18 full hkups (30/50 amps), seasonal sites, cable, WiFi, tent sites, rentals, dump, laundry, LP gas, fire rings, firewood. **REC:** pool, pond, fishing, playground. Pets OK. Partial handicap access. 2015 rates: $30 to $38. Disc: military.
(704)474-3800 Lat: 35.24907, Lon: -80.10399
1216 Berry Hill Dr, Norwood, NC 28128
norwoodcamping@windstream.net
norwoodcamping.com

Check our family camping destinations article in the front of the Guide highlighting the best places to camp in every state and province.

OCRACOKE — B6 *Hyde*

➨ CAPE HATTERAS NATL SEASHORE/OCRACOKE (Natl Pk) From town, E 3 mi on Hwy 12 (R). For reservations call (877)444-6777. Reservations period Memorial Day through Labor Day. 2015 rates: $23. Apr to Oct. (252)473-2111

OUTER BANKS — B6 *Dare*

OUTER BANKS AREA MAP

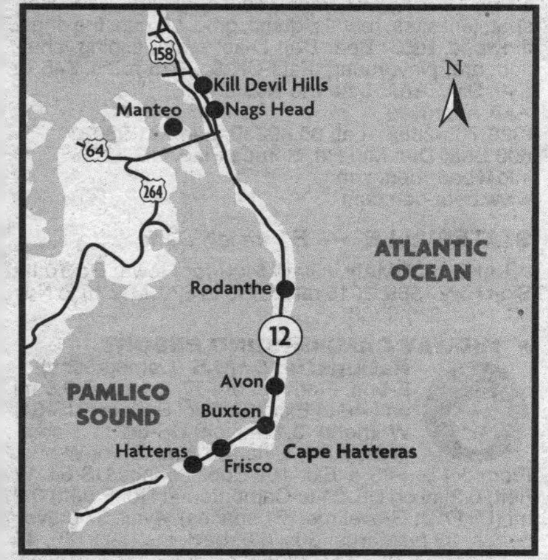

For more detail and a broader overview, please see our full-color state map at the front of the North Carolina state section.

Symbols on map indicate towns within a 50 mile radius of Outer Banks where campgrounds are listed. Check listings for more information.

See also Avon, Buxton, Frisco, Hatteras, Kill Devil Hills, Manteo, Nags Head & Rodanthe.

A SPOTLIGHT Introducing Outer Banks colorful attractions appearing at the front of this state section.

PINEOLA — D3 *Avery*

⬇ **DOWN BY THE RIVER CAMPGROUND Ratings: 8/9.5★/10** (Campground) From Jct of US-221 & NC-181, S 0.2 mi on NC-181S (R); or From Jct of Blue Ridge Parkway & NC 181 (between mile posts 312 & 313), N 1.4 mi on NC 181 (L). Elev 3500 ft. **FAC:** Paved/gravel rds. (114 spaces). 29 Avail: 18 paved, 11 gravel, patios, 20 pull-thrus (50 x 48), back-ins (50 x 48), 29 full hkups (30/50 amps), seasonal sites, WiFi, tent sites, dump, laundry, firewood. **REC:** Linville River: fishing. Pet restrict(Q). Big rig sites, 2015 rates: $32 to $58. May 1 to Oct 31. No CC. (828)733-5057 Lat: 36.02685, Lon: -81.89603
292 River Campground Rd, Pineola, NC 28662
info@downbytherivercampground.com
www.downbytherivercampground.com

Tell them you saw them in this Guide!

PINEY CREEK — A1 *Alleghany*

➚ RIVERCAMP USA **Ratings: 6.5/7.5★/7.5** (Campground) 2015 rates: $30 to $35. Apr 15 to Nov 1. (336)359-2267 2221 Kings Creek Rd, Piney Creek, NC 28663

PINK HILL — C4 *Duplin, Lenoir*

⬆ CABIN LAKE COUNTY PARK (Public) From the Jct of NC 41 and NC 111 (Beulaville), N 4.5 mi on NC 111 to Cabin Lake Rd, E 0.7 mi on Cabin Lake Rd (R). Please call for reservations. 2015 rates: $30. (910)298-3648

PINNACLE — A2 *Surry*

⬇ **GREYSTONE RV PARK**

Ratings: 6.5/9.5★/9 (RV Park) From Jct Hwy 52 & Pilot Knob Park Rd (exit 131), go east .5 mi (L). **FAC:** Gravel rds. 10 paved, 10 pull-thrus (38 x 50), 10 full hkups (30/50 amps), WiFi, LP bottles, fire rings, firewood. **REC:** pond, fishing. Pets OK. Partial handicap access. Eco-friendly, 2015 rates: $40 to $48. Disc: military.
(336)368-5588 Lat: 36.34180, Lon: -80.44803
1164 Pilot Knob Park Rd, Pinnacle, NC 27043
info@greystonervpark.com
www.greystonervpark.com
See ad this page, 849.

⬆ PILOT MOUNTAIN (State Pk) From Winston-Salem, N 24 mi on US-52 (R). 2015 rates: $15 to $20. Mar 15 to Nov 30. (336)325-2355

RALEIGH — B3 *Durham, Wake*

RALEIGH See also Chapel Hill, Clayton, Durham, Four Oaks, Garner, Selma.

⬆ FALLS LAKE SRA/ROLLINGVIEW (Public) From Jct of Hwy 50 & Hwy 98, W 7 mi on Hwy 98 to Baptist Rd, N 3 mi (E). 2015 rates: $15 to $25. (919)676-1027

FALLS LAKE STATE REC. AREA (HOLLY POINT CAMPGROUND) (State Pk) From jct Hwy 50 & Hwy 98: Go 1/2 mi E on Hwy 98, then N on Ghoston Rd, then N on New Light Rd. 2015 rates: $15 to $25. (919)676-1027

⬅ **NORTH CAROLINA STATE FAIRGROUNDS Ratings: 6.5/UI/8** (Campground) From Jct of I-40 & Wade Ave (Exit 289), E 2 mi on Wade Ave to Blue Ridge Rd, S 0.5 mi to Trinity Rd, W 0.5 mi to Youth Center Dr, S 0.1 mi (R). **FAC:** Paved/gravel rds. 52 gravel, back-ins (30 x 50), 52 full hkups (30/50 amps), WiFi, tent sites, dump. **REC:** pond, fishing. Pets OK. Partial handicap access. 14 day max stay, 2015 rates: $25 to $30. No CC, no reservations. (919)612-6767 Lat: 35.79676, Lon: -78.71752
1025 Blue Ridge Rd, Raleigh, NC 27607
fairgrounds.camping@lists.ncmail.net
www.ncstatefair.org

⬅ WILLIAM B UMSTEAD (State Pk) From town, NW 6 mi on US-70 (R). OPEN THURS to SUN ONLY. 2015 rates: $15 to $20. Mar 15 to Dec 1. (919)571-4170

REIDSVILLE — A2 *Rockingham*

⬆ LAKE REIDSVILLE RECREATION PARK (Public) From Jct of US 29N & US 29 Business, N 3 mi on US 29 Business to Waterworks Rd, W 1 mi (L). 2015 rates: $15 to $17. (336)349-4738

ROANOKE RAPIDS — A4 *Halifax*

➨ THE RV RESORT AT CAROLINA CROSSROADS **Ratings: 9/10★/10** (RV Park) 2015 rates: $37.50 to $42.50. (252)538-9776 415 Wallace Forks Rd, Roanoke Rapids, NC 27870

We appreciate your business!

ROARING GAP — A1 *Alleghany*

STONE MOUNTAIN (State Pk) From jct US 21 & Hwy 1002: Go 7 mi SW on Hwy 1002 to John P. Frank Pkwy. 2015 rates: $15 to $25. (336)957-8185

ROBBINSVILLE — E1 *Graham*

⬉ **STECOAH RV RESORT** (RV Spaces) Jct of Hwy 19 & NC-28, NW 9 mi on NC-28 to Hyde Town Rd, SW 0.4 mi (R). Elev 2700 ft. **FAC:** Gravel rds. (20 spaces). Avail: 18 gravel, back-ins (60 x 70), 18 full hkups (30/50 amps), seasonal sites. Pets OK. 2015 rates: $30.
(239)707-3469 Lat: 35.36834, Lon: -83.68462
415 Hyde Town Rd, Robbinsville, NC 28771
tom@stecoahvalleyrv.com
www.stecoahvalleyrv.com

ROCK RIDGE — B4 *Wilson*

➚ **ROCK RIDGE CAMPGROUND Ratings: 4.5/3.5/4.5** (Campground) From Jct of I-95 & NC-42 (exit 116), W 0.9 mi on NC-42 to Rock Ridge School Rd, NW 1 mi (R). **FAC:** Dirt rds. (110 spaces). Avail: 70 gravel, 40 pull-thrus (18 x 55), back-ins (18 x 55), mostly side by side hkups, 50 full hkups, 20 W, 20 E (20/30 amps), seasonal sites, WiFi, dump, laundry, LP bottles. **REC:** pool, pond, fishing, playground. Pets OK. No tents. 2015 rates: $25 to $28. Disc: AAA.
AAA Approved
(252)291-4477 Lat: 35.70847, Lon: -78.07615
7030-B Rock Ridge School Rd, Sims, NC 27880
www.rockridgecampgroundnc.com

RODANTHE — B6 *Dare*

⬇ **CAMP HATTERAS**

Ratings: 10/10★/9.5 (Membership Pk) S-bnd: From Jct of US-158/64/264 & NC-12, S 24.7 mi on NC-12 (L); or N-bnd: From Jct of Ocracoke/Hatteras Ferry & NC-12, N 34.3 mi on NC-12 (R) (Mile Post 40.5). **FAC:** Paved rds. 409 paved, patios, 12 pull-thrus (30 x 60), back-ins (32 x 60), 409 full hkups (30/50 amps), cable, WiFi, tent sites, rentals, laundry, LP gas, firewood, controlled access. **REC:** heated pool, wading pool, whirlpool, Atlantic Ocean: swim, fishing, shuffleboard, playground. Pets OK $. Partial handicap access. Big rig sites, eco-friendly, 2015 rates: $49 to $107. Disc: military.
(252)987-2777 Lat: 35.57815, Lon: -75.46606
24798 Hwy 12, Mile Post 40.5, Waves, NC 27968
camping@camphatteras.com
www.camphatteras.com
See ad pages 853 (Spotlight Outer Banks/Cape Hatteras), 849, 846 (NC Map).

⬇ CAPE HATTERAS KOA **Ratings: 8/10★/8** (Campground) 2015 rates: $38 to $132. (800)562-5268 25099 NC Hwy 12, Rodanthe, NC 27968

⬇ **OCEAN WAVES CAMPGROUND**

Ratings: 9/9★/8.5 (Campground) S-bnd: From Jct of US-158/164/264 & NC-12, S 25.3 mi on NC-12, in Waves (L); or N-bnd: From Okracoke/Hatteras Ferry, N 33.8 mi on NC-12 (R). **FAC:** Paved rds. (70 spaces). Avail: 64 paved, back-ins (30 x 60), 64 full hkups (30/50 amps), seasonal

RODANTHE (CONT)

OCEAN WAVES CAMPGROUND (CONT)
sites, cable, WiFi, tent sites, laundry, groc. **REC:** pool, Atlantic Ocean: fishing, playground. Pets OK. Partial handicap access. Big rig sites, 2015 rates: $44 to $48. Mar 15 to Nov 15.
(252)987-2556 Lat: 35.57164, Lon: -75.46723
25313 Hwy 12, Rodanthe, NC 27982
oceanwaves@oceanwavescampground.com
www.oceanwavescampground.com
See ad page 871.

ST CLAIR LANDING CAMPGROUND **Ratings: 5.5/8★/8.5** (Campground) 2015 rates: $45 to $50. Mar 1 to Dec 1. (252)987-2850 25028 Hwy NC 12, Rodanthe, NC 27968

RUTHERFORDTON — E3 *Rutherford*

FOUR PAWS KINGDOM CAMPGROUND
Ratings: 8/10★/10 (RV Park) From Jct of Hwy 221 & US 64/74A, W 1.9 mi on US64/74A to Coopers Gap Rd, W 3.3 mi to Lazy Creek Dr (R). **FAC:** Paved/gravel rds. 38 Avail: 2 paved, 36 gravel, 25 pull-thrus (35 x 70), back-ins (35 x 65), 38 full hkups (30/50 amps), WiFi, rentals, laundry, fire rings, firewood. **REC:** pond, swim, fishing. Pets OK. Partial handicap access, no tents. Big rig sites, eco-friendly, 2015 rates: $38 to $44. Apr 1 to Nov 27.
(828)287-7324 Lat: 35.37524, Lon: -82.03004
335 Lazy Creek Dr, Rutherfordton, NC 28139
camping@4pawskingdom.com
www.4pawskingdom.com
See ad page 867.

SALISBURY — B2 *Rowan*

DAN NICHOLAS PARK (Public) From I-85 (exit 79), follow signs (L) ; or From I-85 (exit 75), follow signs (L). 2015 rates: $17 to $24. (704)216-7803

SALUDA — E2 *Henderson, Polk*

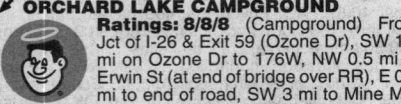

ORCHARD LAKE CAMPGROUND
Ratings: 8/8/8 (Campground) From Jct of I-26 & Exit 59 (Ozone Dr), SW 1.2 mi on Ozone Dr to 176W, NW 0.5 mi to Erwin St (at end of bridge over RR), E 0.1 mi to end of road, SW 3 mi to Mine Mtn Rd, SW 1.5 mi to Orchard Lake Rd (L). **FAC:** Paved/gravel rds. (137 spaces). Avail: 82 gravel, 16 pull-thrus (40 x 75), back-ins (35 x 40), 82 full hkups (30/50 amps), seasonal sites, WiFi, tent sites, rentals, dump, laundry, groc, fire rings, firewood. **REC:** Orchard Lake: swim, fishing, golf, playground, rec open to public. Pets OK. Big rig sites, eco-friendly, 2015 rates: $45. Apr 1 to Nov 1.
AAA Approved
(828)749-3901 Lat: 35.20119, Lon: -82.35665
460 Orchard Lake Rd, Saluda, NC 28773
mgr@orchardlakecampground.com
www.orchardlakecampground.com
See ad pages 866, 849.

Nobody said it was easy being a 10. And our rating system makes it even tougher. Check out 10/10/10 RV parks and campgrounds in the front of the guide.*

SELMA — B4 *Johnston*

RVACATION RV PARK
Ratings: 8/10★/9.5 (RV Park) From Jct of I-95 & Exit 98 (Selma exit), SE 100 ft on CR-1927 (Selma-Pine Level Rd) to Campground Rd, NE 0.4 mi (R). **FAC:** Gravel rds. 80 Avail: 2 paved, 78 gravel, 65 pull-thrus (50 x 75), back-ins (50 x 90), 75 full hkups, 5 W, 5 E (30/50 amps), WiFi, dump, laundry, LP gas, firewood. **REC:** pool, RVacation Lake: fishing, playground. Pets OK. No tents. Big rig sites, eco-friendly, 2015 rates: $20 to $39. Disc: AAA.
(919)965-5923 Lat: 35.53176, Lon: -78.26275
428 Campground Rd, Selma, NC 27576
camping@rvacation.us
www.rvacation.us
See ad this page.

SHALLOTTE — D4 *Brunswick*

SHALLOTTE See also Sunset Beach.

S & W CAMPGROUND (RV Spaces) From NE Jct of Bus US-17 & SR-130/Holden Beach Rd, SE 1.2 mi on SR-130/Holden Beach Rd (R). **FAC:** Gravel rds. (30 spaces). Avail: 10 grass, back-ins (30 x 60), accepts full hkup units only, 10 full hkups (30/50 amps), seasonal sites, cable, WiFi. Pet restrict(Q). No tents. Big rig sites, 2015 rates: $40.
(910)754-8576 Lat: 33.97662, Lon: -78.35340
532 Holden Beach Rd SW, Shallotte, NC 28470
Lindastephens1948@atmc.net
www.holdenbeachandshallottenccampground.com

SHAWBORO — A6 *Currituck*

SHAWBORO See also Shiloh.

SHERRILLS FORD — B1 *Catawba*

LAKE NORMAN RV RESORT **Ratings: 9/9.5★/10** (RV Park) 2015 rates: $48 to $78. (877)489-6033 6738 East NC Hwy 150, Sherrills Ford, NC 28673

SHILOH — A6 *Camden, Currituck*

NORTH RIVER CAMPGROUND & RV PARK
Ratings: 10/10★/9 (Campground) From Jct of NC 168 & NC 34: Go SW 3.5 mi on NC 34 to Indian Town Rd, S 8.2 to Garrington Island Rd, E 1.5 mi (R). **FAC:** Paved rds. (107 spaces). Avail: 92 all weather, patios, 4 pull-thrus (27 x 80), back-ins (27 x 65), 92 full hkups (30/50 amps), seasonal sites, cable, WiFi, tent sites, rentals, dump, laundry, groc, LP gas, fire rings, firewood, controlled access. **REC:** pool, pond, swim, fishing, playground. Pet restrict(Q). Partial handicap access. Big rig sites, eco-friendly, 2015 rates: $42.
(252)336-4414 Lat: 36.30453, Lon: -76.02126
256 Garrington Island Rd, Shawboro, NC 27973
www.northrivercampground.com
See ad page 845 (Welcome Section).

SMITHFIELD — B4 *Johnston*

SMITHFIELD See also Calyton, Four Oaks, Garner, Selma.

SNOW CAMP — B3 *Alamance*

CANE CREEK CAMPGROUND & RV PARK **Ratings: 4/NA/7** (Campground) Pit toilets. 2015 rates: $25. (336)376-8324 1256 Longest Acre Rd, Snow Camp, NC 27349

SPARTA — A1 *Alleghany*

BLUE RIDGE PKWY/DOUGHTON PARK (Natl Pk) From Jct of SR-18 & Blue Ridge Pkwy, N 8 mi on Blue Ridge Pkwy at MP-239 (E). 2015 rates: $16. May 1 to Oct 31. (336)372-8877

Use our handy Snowbird Destinations guide in the front of the Guide to find RV-friendly destinations throughout the Sunbelt.

SPRUCE PINE — D3 *Avery, McDowell, Mitchell*

BEAR DEN FAMILY CAMPGROUND Ratings: 6.5/4.5/7 (Campground) From Jct of Blue Ridge Pkwy & US-221 (Linville Falls), SW 7.3 mi on Blue Ridge Pkwy S to Bear Den Mountain Rd (at MP-324.8), SE 0.6 mi (E). Elev 3000 ft. **FAC:** Poor paved/gravel rds. (58 spaces). Avail: 43 gravel, 12 pull-thrus (20 x 50), back-ins (20 x 45), 30 full hkups, 13 W, 13 E (30/50 amps), seasonal sites, WiFi Hotspot, tent sites, rentals, dump, groc, LP gas, fire rings, firewood. **REC:** Bear Den Lake: swim, fishing, shuffleboard, playground. Pets OK $. 2015 rates: $45 to $49. Disc: AAA. Mar 1 to Nov 30.
AAA Approved
(828)765-2888 Lat: 35.89230, Lon: -81.98021
600 Bear Den Mtn Rd, Spruce Pine, NC 28777
info@bear-den.com
www.bear-den.com

STATESVILLE — B1 *Iredell, Davie*

LAKE NORMAN (State Pk) From town: Go 10 mi S on Hwy 1569. 2015 rates: $15 to $20. Mar 15 to Nov 30. (704)528-6350

MIDWAY CAMPGROUND RESORT
Ratings: 9/10★/9.5 (Campground) E-bnd: From Jct of I-77 & I-40, E 9.6 mi on I-40 to Exit 162/Cool Springs/ US-64, W (right) 0.1 mi on US-64 to Campground Rd, E (left) 0.2 mi (L); or W-bnd: From Jct of I-40 & Exit 162/Cool Springs/US-64, W (left) 0.2 mi on US-64 to Campground Rd, E (left) 0.2 mi (L). **FAC:** Gravel rds. (61 spaces). Avail: 57 gravel, patios, 28 pull-thrus (30 x 60), back-ins (30 x 50), 45 full hkups, 12 W, 12 E (30/50 amps), seasonal sites, cable, WiFi, tent sites, rentals, dump, laundry, groc, LP gas, fire rings, firewood. **REC:** pool, pond, fishing, playground. Pet restrict(B). Big rig sites, 2015 rates: $39.91 to $48.91. Disc: AAA, military. ATM.
(855)882-7999 Lat: 35.86609, Lon: -80.70650
114 Midway Dr, Statesville, NC 28625
camp@midwaycampground.com
www.midwaycampground.com
See ad this page, 874, 849.

Travel Services

CAMPING WORLD OF STATESVILLE As the nation's largest retailer of RV supplies, accessories, services and new and used RVs, Camping World is committed to making your total RV experience better. RV Accessories: (888)224-3059. **SERVICES:** RV, tire, RV appliance, MH mechanical, staffed RV wash, restrooms, RV Sales. RV supplies, LP, dump, emergency parking, RV accessible. waiting room. Hours: 8am to 6pm.
(888)699-4002 Lat: 35.766688, Lon: -80.860638
1220 Morland Drive, Statesville, NC 28677
agood@campingworldrvsales.com
www.campingworld.com

STELLA — C5 *Cataret*

WHITE OAK SHORES CAMPING & RV RESORT **Ratings: 9.5/9★/10** (Campground) 2015 rates: $55 to $85. (252)393-3244 400 Wetherington Landing Rd, Stella, NC 28582

STONEVILLE — A2 *Rockingham*

DAN RIVER CAMPGROUND **Ratings: 6.5/7.5★/7** (Campground) 2015 rates: $27 to $33. Mar 15 to Oct 31. (336)427-8530 724 Webster Rd, Stoneville, NC 27048

Don't miss out on great savings - find over $1,000 in Camping World coupons at the front of the Guide!

SUNSET BEACH — D4 *Brunswick*

BRUNSWICK BEACHES CAMPING RESORT
Ratings: 9/9.5★/9.5 (Campground) From Jct of NC 17 & NC 904, E 0.7 mi on NC 904 (R). **FAC:** Paved/gravel rds. (94 spaces). Avail: 84 gravel, 66 pull-thrus (30 x 68), back-ins (26 x 60), 69 full hkups, 15 W, 15 E (30/50 amps), seasonal sites, cable, WiFi, tent sites, rentals, dump, laundry, groc, LP gas, fire rings, firewood, controlled access. **REC:** pool, pond, fishing, playground. Pets OK. Partial handicap access. Big rig sites, 2015 rates: $40 to $65. Disc: military.
(855)579-2267 Lat: 33.93691, Lon: -78.50161
7200 Koa Dr, Sunset Beach, NC 28468
brunswickbeachescamping@gmail.com
www.brunswickbeachescamping.com
See ad opposite page, 849.

SURF CITY — C4 *Pender*

SURF CITY See also Jacksonville.

LANIER'S CAMPGROUND
Ratings: 8/8.5★/7.5 (Campground) From Jct of Hwy 17 & 50, S 4.3 mi on Hwy 50 (E Ocean Rd) to Little Kinston Rd, S 0.6 mi to Spot Lane, W 0.4 mi (E). **FAC:** Gravel rds. (465 spaces). Avail: 60 grass, back-ins (25 x 60), 31 full hkups, 29 W, 29 E (30/50 amps), seasonal sites, WiFi Hotspot, tent sites, dump, laundry, groc, LP gas, firewood, controlled access. **REC:** pool, Intercoastal Waterway: fishing, playground, rec open to public. Pet restrict(B). Partial handicap access. Big rig sites, eco-friendly, 2015 rates: $29 to $48. Disc: military.
(910)328-9431 Lat: 34.43169, Lon: -77.56998
1161 Spot Lane, Holly Ridge, NC 28445
linda@lanierscampgroundnc.com
www.lanierscampgroundnc.com
See ad this page, 849 & Family Camping in Magazine Section.

SWANNANOA — E2 *Buncombe*

ASHEVILLE EAST KOA Ratings: 9/8.5★/8.5 (Campground) From Jct of I-40 & Patton Cove Rd (exit 59): Go N 0.3 mi on Patton Cove Rd to US-70, E 1.6 mi (L). **FAC:** Paved rds. 200 gravel, 11 pull-thrus (24 x 63), back-ins (24 x 47), 112 full hkups, 88 W, 88 E (30/50 amps), cable, WiFi, tent sites, rentals, dump, laundry, groc, LP gas, fire rings, firewood. **REC:** pool, pond, fishing, playground. Pet restrict(B). 2015 rates: $43.50 to $47.50.
(828)686-3121 Lat: 35.60144, Lon: -82.37441
2708 Hwy 70 East, Swannanoa, NC 28778
akoaeast@bellsouth.net
www.ashevilleeastkoa.com

The RVers' Guide to NASCAR helps RV travelers get the most out of North America's most thrilling sporting event. Turn to the front of the Guide and we'll give you the inside track on how to get high-speed thrills at major NASCAR venues.

MAMA GERTIE'S HIDEAWAY CAMPGROUND
Ratings: 8.5/10★/10 (Campground) From Jct of I-40 & Patton Cove Rd (exit 59), S 0.5 mi on Patton Cove Rd (L).

A SMALL PIECE OF PARADISE
Keeping with the splendor of our beautiful state, we have preserved a natural setting for our guests in combination with modern amenities and convenience.

FAC: Paved rds. 45 Avail: 2 paved, 43 gravel, patios, 23 pull-thrus (30 x 60), back-ins (30 x 60), 38 full hkups, 7 W, 7 E (30/50 amps), cable, WiFi, tent sites, rentals, dump, laundry, LP gas, fire rings, firewood, controlled access. **REC.** Pets OK. Partial handicap access. Big rig sites, eco-friendly, 2015 rates: $37 to $70.
(828)686-4258 Lat: 35.58622, Lon: -82.40493
15 Uphill Rd, Swannanoa, NC 28778
info@mamagerties.com
www.mamagerties.com
See ad pages 854, 849.

SYLVA — E2 *Jackson*

FT. TATHAM CAMPGROUND CAREFREE RV RESORT
Ratings: 8.5/8.5★/8 (Campground) From Jct of US-23/74 & US-441 (exit 81), S 6.7 mi on US-441 to Garland Buchanan Rd, E 100 ft to Tatham Creek Rd, N 0.1 mi (L). Elev 2700 ft. **FAC:** Paved/gravel rds. (93 spaces). Avail: 36 gravel, 6 pull-thrus (22 x 64), back-ins (20 x 50), 36 full hkups (30/50 amps), seasonal sites, WiFi, tent sites, rentals, dump, laundry. **REC:** pool, Savannah Creek, Tatham's Creek: fishing, shuffleboard, playground. Pet restrict(B). 2015 rates: $37. Apr 1 to Nov 1.
(828)586-6662 Lat: 35.29310, Lon: -83.26910
175 Tatham's Creek Rd, Sylva, NC 28779
forttatham@carefreervresorts.com
www.carefreervresorts.com
See ad this page, 849.

TABOR CITY — D3 *Columbus*

CARROLL WOODS RV PARK AT GRAPEFULL SISTERS VINEYARD **Ratings: 9/9.5★/9.5** (Membership Pk) 2015 rates: $37 to $45. (910)653-5538 95 Dots Drive, Tabor City, NC 28463

YOGI BEARS JELLYSTONE PARK AT DADDY JOE'S **Ratings: 9.5/9.5★/9.5** (Campground) 2015 rates: $35 to $77. (877)668-8586 626 Richard Wright Rd, Tabor City, NC 28463

UNION GROVE — A1 *Iredell*

VAN HOY FARMS FAMILY CAMPGROUND
Ratings: 8.5/8★/9 (RV Park) From Jct of I-77 & NC-901S (exit 65), E 0.1 mi on NC-901S to Jericho Rd, S 0.3 mi (L). **FAC:** Gravel rds. (94 spaces). 54 Avail: 42 gravel, 12 grass, 22 pull-thrus (30 x 65), back-ins (30 x 60), 54 full hkups (30/50 amps), seasonal sites, WiFi, rentals, dump, laundry, LP gas, firewood. **REC:** pool, Razor Back Stream: rec open to public. Pets OK. No tents. Big rig sites, eco-friendly, 2015 rates: $45 to $50. Disc: AAA.
(704)539-5493 Lat: 36.00120, Lon: -80.83113
742 Jericho Rd, Harmony, NC 28634
casey@vanhoyfarms.com
www.vanhoyfarms.com
See ad this page, 849.

WADE — B3 *Cumberland*

FAYETTEVILLE RV RESORT & COTTAGES
Ratings: 10/10★/10 (RV Resort) From Jct of I-95 & Exit 61 (Wade-Stedman Rd), E 0.3 mi on Wade-Stedman Rd (L).

PERFECT HALF WAY NORTH SOUTH I-95
Top Resort: 10/10/10. Easy I-95 access: NC #61. Near For Bragg; special military & LONG TERM rates. Huge FHU 50-amp sites, Charming cottages. Fitness center, 2 pools, playground, free WiFi & Cable. Free waffle breakfast.

FAC: All weather rds. (188 spaces). Avail: 120 all weather, 101 pull-thrus (35 x 90), back-ins (30 x 55), 120 full hkups (30/50 amps), seasonal sites, cable, WiFi, rentals, dump, laundry, groc, LP gas, fire rings, firewood. **REC:** pool, whirlpool, pond, fishing, playground. Pets OK. Partial handicap access, no tents. Big rig sites, eco-friendly, 2015 rates: $51. Disc: AAA, military.
(910)484-5500 Lat: 35.15698, Lon: -78.70762
6250 Wade-Stedman Rd, Wade, NC 28395
info@fayettevillervresort.com
www.fayettevillervresort.com
See ad pages 861, 849, 846 (NC Map) See ad inside back cover & Snowbird Destinations in Magazine Section.

WALNUT COVE — A2 *Stokes*

HANGING ROCK (State Pk) From town, W 5 mi on SR-1001 (Moore's Spring Rd), follow signs (R). 2015 rates: $15 to $20. (336)593-8480

WASHINGTON — B5 *Pitt*

TRANTER'S CREEK RESORT & CAMPGROUND
Ratings: 9/10★/9.5 (Campground) From Jct of US-17 & US-264, W 1.5 mi on 264 to Clarks Neck Rd, SW 1.6 mi (R). **FAC:** Paved/gravel rds. (218 spaces). Avail: 40 grass, 12 pull-thrus (36 x 100), back-ins (32 x 70), 40 full hkups (30/50 amps), seasonal sites, WiFi, tent sites, rentals, laundry, LP gas, fire rings, firewood, controlled access. **REC:** pool, Tranter's Creek: fishing, playground. Pets OK. Partial handicap access. Big rig sites, eco-friendly, 2015 rates: $35 to $47.50. Disc: military.
(252)948-0850 Lat: 35.56544, Lon: -77.10311
6573 Clarksville Neck Rd, Washington, NC 27889
camp@tranterscreekresort.com
www.tranterscreekresort.com
See ad pages 874, 849.

TWIN LAKES RV RESORT **Ratings: 7.5/7.5/8.5** (Campground) 2015 rates: $41 to $54. (800)405-6188 1618 Memory Lane, Chocowinity, NC 27817

NC

WAYNESVILLE — E2 *Haywood*

WAYNESVILLE See also: Balsam, Candler, Maggie Valley, Sylva.

CREEKWOOD FARM RV PARK **Ratings: 8.5/9.5★/8.5** (Campground) From Jct of I-40 & US-276 (exit 20), S 1 mi on US-276 (L); or From W Jct of US-19 & US-276, N 4.7 mi on US-276 (R) Note: (Please follow these directions not GPS). Elev 3000 ft.

IN THE MOUNTAINS OF NORTH CAROLINA
Find spacious sites with full hook ups, WiFi and cable TV. 2 red cedar rental cabins. Clean restrooms & laundry. Also a 100 year barn & silo. Enjoy Jonathan Creek. We are the gateway to the Smoky Mountains and Maggie Valley.

FAC: Gravel rds. (125 spaces). Avail: 60 all weather, 7 pull-thrus (30 x 90), back-ins (30 x 50), 60 full hkups (30/50 amps), seasonal sites, cable, WiFi, tent sites, rentals, dump, laundry, LP gas, fire rings, firewood. **REC:** Jonathan Creek: swim, fishing. Pets OK. Partial handicap access. Big rig sites, 2015 rates: $41 to $85. Disc: AAA, military.
AAA Approved
(828)926-7977 Lat: 35.58744, Lon: -83.00944
4696 Jonathan Creek Rd, Waynesville, NC 28785
creekwoodfarmrv@main.nc.us
www.creekwoodfarmrv.com
See ad pages 868, 849.

GREAT SMOKY MTN/CATALOOCHEE (Natl Pk) From Jct of I-40 & US-276, SW 0.5 mi on US-276 to Cove Creek Rd, follow signs (R). 2015 rates: $20. Mar 14 to Oct 31. (865)436-1200

PRIDE RV RESORT **Ratings: 9/9★/8** (Membership Pk) 2015 rates: $41 to $51. (800)926-8191 4394 Jonathan Creek Rd, Waynesville, NC 28785

TRAILS END RV PARK Ratings: 7/NA/8.5 (RV Park) From Jct of I 40 & US 276 (Exit 20): Go S 3.5 mi on US 276 to Hemp Hill Rd, W 1 mi to Shelton Cove Rd, SW 0.2 mi (L). **FAC:** Gravel rds. (46 spaces). Avail: 26 gravel, back-ins (30 x 60), 26 full hkups (30/50 amps), seasonal sites, cable, WiFi, laundry, firewood. **REC:** Shelton Cove Branch: fishing. Pets OK. No tents. Big rig sites, 2015 rates: $35 to $42.
(828)421-5295 Lat: 35.55802, Lon: -83.03720
219 Shelton Cove Rd, Waynesville, NC 28785
info@trailsendrvparknc.com
trailsendrvparknc.com

WINNGRAY FAMILY CAMPGROUND **Ratings: 7.5/6/7.5** (Campground) From Jct of I-40 & US-276 (exit 20): Go S 3 mi on US-276 (R) or From W Jct of US-19 & US-276: Go N 2.5 mi on US-276 (L). Elev 3000 ft. **FAC:** Paved rds. (150 spaces). 120 Avail: 60 gravel, 60 grass, 50 pull-thrus (30 x 50), back-ins (30 x 55), some side by side hkups, accepts self-contain units only, 100 full hkups, 20 W, 20 E (30/50 amps), seasonal sites, WiFi, tent sites, dump, laundry, LP gas. **REC:** Jonathan Creek: fishing. Pet restrict 2015 rates: $36 to $39.
(828)926-3170 Lat: 35.55782, Lon: -83.02270
26 Winngray Ln, Waynesville, NC 28785
billwinngray@aol.com
www.winngraycampground.com
See ad page 869.

WHITE LAKE — C4 *Bladen*

CAMP CLEARWATER FAMILY CAMPGROUND **Ratings: 8.5/9.5★/8.5** (Campground) From Jct Hwy 41 & Hwy 53: Go 2-1/2 mi SE on Hwy 53, then 1/4 mi NE on White Lake Dr (L) Note: For GPS, use White Lake for city, do not use zip code. **FAC:** Paved/gravel rds. (1012 spaces). 100 Avail: 5 paved, 95 grass, 100 pull-thrus (30 x 70), 100 full hkups (30/50 amps), seasonal sites, cable, WiFi, tent sites, laundry, groc, controlled access. **REC:** White Lake: swim, fishing, playground. Pets OK. Partial handicap access. Big rig sites, 2015 rates: $50 to $55. ATM, no CC.
(910)862-3365 Lat: 34.632323, Lon: -78.489428
2038 White Lake Dr, White Lake, NC 28337
kristy@campclearwater.com
www.campclearwater.com
See ad page 861.

WHITTIER — E2 *Jackson, Swain*

FLAMING ARROW CAMPGROUND, INC **Ratings: 8/8.5★/8** (Campground) 2015 rates: $45. (877)497-6161 283 Flaming Arrow Dr, Whittier, NC 28789

HOLLY COVE RV RESORT Ratings: 8.5/10★/8.5 (RV Park) From Cherokee Jct US-74 & US-441 : Go 2.5 mi SE on US-441/US-74 (mm 76.5), then 500 feet E on West Piney Mountain Rd, then 1/4 mi N on Holly Cove Rd (E). **FAC:** Paved rds. (50 spaces). Avail: 7 gravel, 4 pull-thrus (25 x 60), back-ins (24 x 50), 7 full hkups (30/50 amps), seasonal sites, cable, WiFi, laundry, fire rings. **REC:** heated pool, pond, fishing. Pets OK. Partial handicap access, no tents. Eco-friendly, 2015 rates: $32. May 1 to Nov 1. No CC.
(828)631-0692 Lat: 35.39770, Lon: -83.28909
341 Holly Cove Rd, Whittier, NC 28789
hollycove1@aol.com
hollycovervresort.com

TUCKASEEGEE RV RESORT **Ratings: 8/10★/9** (RV Park) 2015 rates: $40. (828)497-3598 78 Wilmont Rd, Whittier, NC 28789

WILKESBORO — A1 *Wilkes*

BANDIT'S ROOST PARK (Public Corps) From Jct of US-421 & SR-268, W 6 mi on SR-268 to Jess Walsh Rd, N 0.5 mi (E). 2015 rates: $24. Apr 1 to Oct 30. (336)921-3190

WARRIOR CREEK PARK (Public Corps) From town, W 7.5 mi on SR-268 (R). 2015 rates: $22. Apr 15 to Oct 14. (336)921-2177

WILLIAMSTON — B5 *Martin*

FARM COUNTRY CAMPGROUND Ratings: 8/9.5★/6.5 (Campground) From Jct of Hwy 64 & Prison Camp Rd (exit 512), S 2 mi on Prison Camp Rd to Eds Grocery Rd, S 2 mi on Ed's Grocery Rd (R). **FAC:** Gravel rds. 35 grass, 35 pull-thrus (40 x 100), 35 full hkups (30/50 amps), WiFi, tent sites, dump, laundry, LP gas, fire rings, firewood. **REC:** pool, pond, rec open to public. Pets OK. Partial handicap access. Big rig sites, 2015 rates: $30 to $35.
(252)789-8482 Lat: 35.778510, Lon: -77.141275
2301 Eds Grocery Rd, Williamston, NC 27892
farmcountrycampground@centurylink.net
www.farmcountrycampground.com

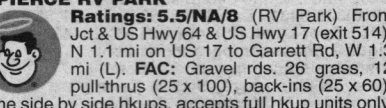

GREEN ACRES FAMILY CAMPGROUND **Ratings: 6.5/6.5/6.5** (Campground) From Jct of US-64 & US-17, S 3 mi on US-17 to Rodgers School Rd, W 1.3 mi (R) or From Jct of US-264 & US-17, N 15 mi on US-17 to Rodgers School Rd, W 1.3 (R). **FAC:** Dirt rds. (175 spaces). 110 Avail: 60 grass, 50 dirt, 50 pull-thrus (25 x 56), back-ins (25 x 45), 30 full hkups, 80 W, 74 E (20/30 amps), seasonal sites, WiFi, tent sites, rentals, dump, laundry, groc, LP gas, fire rings, firewood. **REC:** pool, pond, fishing, golf, playground. Pets OK. Eco-friendly, 2015 rates: $27 to $35. Disc: AAA, military.
AAA Approved
(888)792-3939 Lat: 35.78261, Lon: -77.08698
1679 Green Acres Rd, Williamston, NC 27892
bgreene@embarqmail.com
www.greenacresnc.com
See ad this page.

PIERCE RV PARK **Ratings: 5.5/NA/8** (RV Park) From Jct & US Hwy 64 & US Hwy 17 (exit 514), N 1.1 mi on US 17 to Garrett Rd, W 1.3 mi (L). **FAC:** Gravel rds. 26 grass, 12 pull-thrus (25 x 100), back-ins (25 x 60), some side by side hkups, accepts full hkup units only, 26 full hkups (30/50 amps), WiFi, firewood. Pets OK. No tents. 2015 rates: $28. No CC.
(252)799-0111 Lat: 35.82889, Lon: -77.08832
2295 Garrett Rd, Williamston, NC 27892
jpierce02@live.com
www.pierce-rv-park-williamston-nc.com
See ad this page, 849.

WILMINGTON — D4 *New Hanover*

WILMINGTON KOA **Ratings: 9/9.5★/9** (Campground) 2015 rates: $49 to $125. (888)562-5699 7415 Market Street, Wilmington, NC 28411

WILSON — B4 *Wilson*

KAMPER'S LODGE OF AMERICA **Ratings: 8/8★/8.5** (Campground) N-bnd: Jct I-95 & US 301 (Exit 107), N 18 mi on US 301 (L); or S-bnd: I-95 & US 64 (Exit 138), E 3 mi on US 64 to US 301 S, S 17 mi (R). **FAC:** Gravel rds. 53 Avail: 23 gravel, 30 grass, patios, 35 pull-thrus (30 x 70), back-ins (30 x 60), 53 full hkups (30/50 amps), WiFi, tent sites, rentals, dump, laundry, groc, LP gas, firewood. **REC:** pool, playground, rec open to public.

Park owners want you to be satisfied with your stay. Get to know them.

Directional arrows indicate the campground's position in relation to the nearest town.

WILSON (CONT)

KAMPER'S LODGE OF AMERICA (CONT)
Pets OK. Big rig sites, eco-friendly, 2015 rates: $30 to $35.
(252)237-0905 Lat: 35.74475, Lon: -77.87302
3465 US Hwy 301N, Wilson, NC 27893
kamperslodge3465@aol.com
www.kamperslodge.com
See ad opposite page, 849.

WINSTON-SALEM — A2 *Forsyth*

WINSTON-SALEM See also Advance, Greensboro, Pinnacle, Walnut Grove.

Treat your pet to a fabulous camping experience by staying at one of the Pampered Pet Parks featured in the front of the Guide. Many of the parks on this list offer perks like dog runs, dog washing stations and dog walking services. Some of the parks even conduct pet parades during special holidays.

NC

North Dakota Tourism Division

WELCOME TO North Dakota

DATE OF STATEHOOD	WIDTH: 211 MILES (340 KM)	PROPORTION OF UNITED STATES
NOV. 2, 1889	LENGTH: 340 MILES (545 KM)	1.86% OF 3,794,100 SQ MI

The Corps of Discovery led by Meriwether Lewis and William Clark blazed the trail to North Dakota in 1803, but travelers seldom follow their lead—the state attracts fewer tourists than any other. It's a shame, because North Dakota boasts an abundance of treasures that should be cherished by all.

Learn

Theodore Roosevelt came to the Dakota Territory in 1883 to hunt buffalo, and returned five months later to rebuild his life after the deaths of his wife and mother on the same day. The lessons he learned in the "perfect freedom" of the West were to shape America after he became president nearly two decades later.

Before the dreamers and doers arrived in Dakota Territory, there were endless herds of bison grazing in the wide-open grasslands. With wild bison all but gone in 1959, the World's Largest Buffalo Monument was erected at the entrance to Frontier Village in Jamestown, an outdoor museum where original pioneer buildings were collected from around the Great Plains. The 60-ton cement bovid now also marks the entrance to the National Buffalo Museum, which interprets the role of this great land mammal.

The North Dakota Heritage Center & State Museum at the state capitol ties North Dakota history together, from the Corridor of History, with its great-tusked mastodon skeleton, to the exploits of the *USS North Dakota* battleship. The art deco capitol tower is the tallest building in the state. In Fargo, Bonanzaville brings together 43 historic buildings to re-create a plains village. The Pioneer Days festival in August is city's the biggest party.

Play

The Dakota Badlands are made for trail-riding and exploring. Theodore Roosevelt National Park alone spreads 100 miles of trails across the western edge of the state. Little Missouri State

Top 3 Tourism Attractions:
1) Theodore Roosevelt National Park
2) Lawrence Welk Homestead
3) International Peace Garden

Nickname: Sioux State

State Flower: Wild Prairie Rose

State Bird: Western Meadowlark

People: Angie Dickinson, actress; Carl Ben Eielson, pioneering pilot; Louis L'Amour, author; Peggy Lee, singer; Lawrence Welk, band leader

Major Cities: Fargo, Bismarck (capital), Grand Forks, Minot, West Fargo

Topography: East—flat Red River Valley; central—rolling drift prairie; west—Missouri Plateau of the Great Plains

Climate: Continental climate with cold winters and hot summers

North Dakota Tourism Division

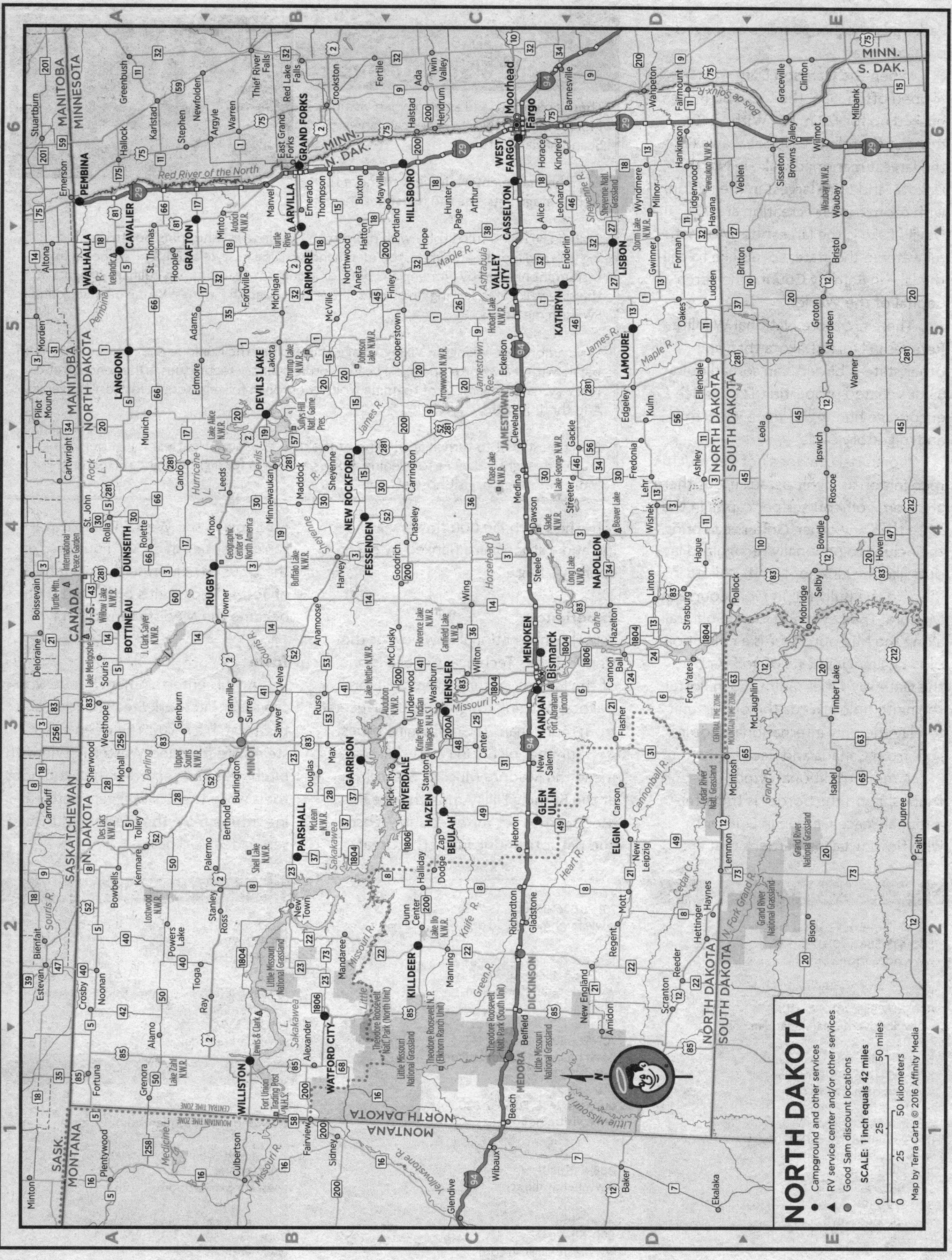
NORTH DAKOTA
Campground and other services
RV service center and/or other services
Good Sam discount locations
SCALE: 1 inch equals 42 miles
0 25 50 miles
0 25 50 kilometers
Map by Terra Carta © 2016 Affinity Media
MANITOBA
MINNESOTA
SASKATCHEWAN
MONTANA
SOUTH DAKOTA
CANADA
U.S.
N. DAKOTA
MINN.
S. DAK.
CENTRAL TIME ZONE
MOUNTAIN TIME ZONE
ND
PEMBINA
WALHALLA
CAVALIER
LANGDON
GRAFTON
GRAND FORKS
ARVILLA
LARIMORE
DEVILS LAKE
HILLSBORO
WEST FARGO
Fargo
Moorhead
CASSELTON
VALLEY CITY
KATHRYN
LISBON
LAMOURE
JAMESTOWN
NEW ROCKFORD
FESSENDEN
DUNSEITH
BOTTINEAU
RUGBY
MINOT
NAPOLEON
MENOKEN
Bismarck
MANDAN
HENSLER
GARRISON
RIVERDALE
HAZEN
BEULAH
GLEN ULLIN
PARSHALL
ELGIN
KILLDEER
WATFORD CITY
WILLISTON
MEDORA
DICKINSON
Red River of the North
Missouri R.
James R.
Sheyenne R.
Souris R.
Little Missouri R.
Yellowstone R.
Lake Sakakawea
Lake Oahe
Devils L.
Theodore Roosevelt Natl. Park (North Unit)
Theodore Roosevelt Natl. Park (South Unit)
International Peace Garden
Geographic Center of North America
Little Missouri National Grassland
Sheyenne Natl. Grassland
Cedar River Natl. Grassland
Grand River National Grassland

Park adds another 30 miles of rugged passages nearby.

When the Garrison Dam was topped off in 1956, the Missouri River backed up for 178 miles. With 1,340 miles of shoreline, Lake Sakakawea is the largest man-made lake in North Dakota, and third largest in the nation, with room for 35 recreation areas. Devil's Lake is the largest body of natural water in the state. Locals like to call the lake in Ramsey County the Perch Capital of the World.

There are more National Wildlife Refuges in North Dakota than any other state—birders can spread out at 63 designated properties, 12 of which encourage hunting of deer, waterfowl and migratory birds.

North Dakota does not get much recognition as a golf paradise, but there are more golf courses per capita in the state than any other. Golfers can bring their clubs to nationally recognized layouts like the Links of North Dakota in Ray and the Bully Pulpit Golf Course in Medora. The Lewis and Clark Golf Trail along the Missouri River is a collection of 19 challenging tests of golf. And at the Gateway Cities Golf Club in Portal, the ninth hole affords the opportunity to play the only international shot in golf, from Canada and back.

A more traditional symbol of friendship on the border is the International Peace Garden in Dunseith with flowing lawns, gardens that are refreshed with 150,000 flowers, a carillon and a stone cairn flanked by each country's flag.

Experience

The International Powwow at the United Tribes Technical College is one of the leading cultural events in North Dakota, bringing together 1,500 dancers from more than 70 Great Plains tribes.

Summer nights in North Dakota mean the Medora Musical. Staged at the Burning Hills Amphitheatre in Medora, this act mixes country, gospel and patriotic music into "The Greatest Show in the West." The extravaganza first began as "Ol' Four Eyes" in the 1950s to celebrate the centennial of Teddy Roosevelt's birth, and then became the Medora Musical in 1965.

Taste

At this entertainment venue, you can savor Pitchfork Steak Fondue and then watch a show. The deep-fried steaks are fondued Western-style with pitchforks and served with baked potatoes, while the Coal Diggers performing troupe from the Medora Musical serenade the diners.

- STAY A WHILE -

North Dakota's Norsk Hostfest

There's plenty to see and do when visiting Norsk Høstfest, North America's largest Scandinavian festival!

From big-name entertainment to more than 30 free stage acts, the fun is just gearing up.

Scandinavia is on full display with more than 100 Høstfest shopping booths, including genuine Nordic and imported merchandise. Dine in style at En To Tre fine dining restaurant headed by Norwegian chefs, or indulge in Scandinavian culinary delights at the sidewalk cafes serving favorites such as Royal Danish Pastries, Viking on a Stick and Swedish meatballs.

Walk among the Vikings in Viking Village and explore their unique crafts and watch them battle with real swords and axes! Learn Nordic culinary techniques, experience Arctic Norway, catch a glimpse of roaming trolls or enroll in folk classes at Høstfest University. And this is just the start!

Don't be so fast to turn in at the end of the day—because Høstfest is just beginning! From free nightly dances to evening movies, you're in for a great night at Høstfest! For more information, visit hostfest.com.

TRAVEL & TOURISM

North Dakota Tourism Division
800-435-5663, 701-328-2525
www.ndtourism.com

Bismarck-Mandan CVB
800-767-3555, 701-222-4308
www.discoverbismarckmandan.com

Buffalo City Tourism Foundation
800-222-4766, 701-251-9145
www.tourjamestown.com

Devils Lake Chamber-Tourism Office
800-233-8048, 701-662-4903
www.devilslakend.com

Dickinson CVB
800-279-7391
www.dickinsoncvb.com

Fargo-Moorhead CVB
701-282-3653, 800-235-7654
www.fargomoorhead.org

Greater Grand Forks CVB
800-866-4566, 701-746-0444
www.visitgrandforks.com

Medora Chamber of Commerce
701-623-4910
www.medorandchamber.com

Minot CVB
800-264-2626, 701-857-8206
www.visitminot.org

Valley City
888-845-1891
www.hellovalley.com

Willison CVC
800-615-9041
www.visitwilliston.com

OUTDOOR RECREATION

North Dakota Game & Fish Department
701-328-6300
www.gf.nd.gov

North Dakota Parks and Recreation Department
701-328-5357
www.parkrec.nd.gov

SHOPPING

Dakota Square
www.shopdakotasquare.com

Kirkwood Mall
701-223-3500
www.shopkirkwoodmall.com

West Acres Shopping Centre
800-783-6450
www.westacres.com

Featured Good Sam Parks

NORTH DAKOTA

Good Sam Park

ND

When you stay with Good Sam, you can expect the highest degree of cleanliness and friendliness, and better yet, you get 10% off campground fees.

If you're not already a Good Sam member you can purchase your membership at one of these locations:

DICKINSON
North Park RV Campground
(701)227-8498

JAMESTOWN
Jamestown Campground
(701)252-6262

MEDORA
Red Trail Campground
(800)621-4317

MINOT
Roughrider Campground
(701)852-8442

For more Good Sam Parks go to listing pages

 See map page 877

Getty Images/iStockphoto

MEDORA

Follow the trail of adventure blazed by Theodore Roosevelt

The sprawling and still sparsely populated badlands of eastern North Dakota are forever intertwined with two equally intertwined themes: the romance of a rough-and-tumble American frontier and the legacy of President Theodore Roosevelt, an avid conservationist. Nowhere are those two themes more readily on display than in the tiny town of Medora.

Tucked away in the middle of two massive national parks, and sitting on the shores of the Little Missouri River, Medora (population 129) serves as the home base for anyone looking to branch out and explore eastern North Dakota at large. Bismarck, the closest major population center, lies 133 miles to the east. Interstate 94 skirts the northern city limits of Medora, making arrival and departure fairly painless, but this is still much the same countryside that an adventurous Teddy Roosevelt came to know and love so well in his youth.

The same largely undeveloped landscape full of corrugated cliffs, steep gullies and richly colored stratified-rock hills are here in abundance. So is the thriving wildlife population—bison, elk, pronghorn, mule deer, wild horses and bighorn sheep all fill the badlands. The only noticeable change the late president would be likely to notice today is that his name graces an area he once roamed as a burgeoning cattle rancher and amateur big-game hunter.

Thus, for the very same reasons that a brash 25-year-old Teddy Roosevelt fell in love with the picturesque landscapes surrounding what is now Medora, visitors today looking for wild countryside full of great hunting, hiking, fishing and exploring are in for a treat.

Roosevelt's Rugged Playground

Theodore Roosevelt National Park will consume most of your time here, and justifiably so. Spanning more than 70,000 acres, its relative isolation and massive size means crowds are almost nonexistent year-round.

The park is divided into two sections, the South Unit and the North Unit. If you're short on time or simply wish to orient yourself before diving in a little bit deeper, take a self-guided tour on the South Unit's 36-mile-long Scenic Loop Drive. Marked overlooks along the way provide context on the park's natural history. Don't miss the panoramic views from Scoria Point Overlook, Skyline Vista and Buck Hill.

For a slightly deeper exploration into the park, head 70 miles north to the North Unit's scenic drive. This one only covers 14 miles, but features stunning canyon views and a greater chance of viewing some big wildlife like bison or bighorn sheep.

As you're snaking your way around the badlands, don't miss Elkhorn Ranch (where Theodore Roosevelt grazed his cattle), Maltese Cross Cabin (Roosevelt's first ranch-style home) and Peaceful Valley Ranch (where visitors can saddle up for guided horseback trail rides).

Where the Grass Grows

Little Missouri National Grasslands is another popular spot for outdoors enthusiasts, though it's significantly more remote. It spans more than a million acres, just north of Theodore Roosevelt National Park. Nature photographers will revel in the grasslands' rich concentration of antelope, eagles and bighorn sheep.

Little Missouri River from Theodore Roosevelt National Park. Getty Images/iStockphoto

To round out the nature theme, take a trip to nearby Dickinson (36 miles to the east) and spend the day at the Dakota Dinosaur Museum. It's only open from May 1 to Labor Day each year, but if you're lucky enough to be in the area during that time of the year, make sure to give it a visit. The museum showcases a mix of sculptures and life-size skeletal displays, including a 37-foot-long replica of an Allosaurus from the late Jurassic period.

When you're ready for a break from natural history and natural attractions, head to the Billings County Museum or the Chateau de Mores State Historic Site. The former is a quaint small-town museum, housed in what was once the Billings County Courthouse, built circa 1880. It displays an eclectic mix of artifacts that help piece together the story of Medora, eastern North Dakota and the county in general.

The Chateau de Mores, for its part, is an absolute must-visit for history buffs. Once the home of the town's founder, a French nobleman who was known as the Marquis de Mores, the 1880s-style 26-room estate is for all intents and purposes a time machine. The chateau's rooms are fully restored and its original furnishings are arranged to resemble how the estate would have appeared in 1885. Guided tours of the chateau are available, and interpretive exhibits can be perused at your own pace in the on-site museum.

To put it simply, if you're an outdoors lover you'll be right at home in Medora. Likewise, if you harbor any romance for the allure of a rugged wilderness frontier that's attracted adventurers from far and wide for more than a century, then Medora is where you want to set up camp and go exploring yourself.

For More Information

Medora Area Convention and Visitors Bureau
701-623-4830
www.medorand.com

North Dakota Tourism Division
800-435-5663
www.ndtourism.com

North Dakota

CONSULTANTS

Duane & Bev Finger

ARVILLA — B6 *Grand Forks*

TURTLE RIVER (State Pk) From town, W 22 mi on Hwy 2, follow signs (R). Entrance fee required. 2015 rates: $10 to $30. (701)594-4445

BEULAH — C3 *Mercer*

BEULAH BAY REC AREA - LAKE SAKAKAWEA (MUNICIPAL PARK) (Public) From jct Hwy-49 & Hwy-200: Go 15 mi N on Hwy-49, follow signs. 2015 rates: $10 to $25. May 15 to Sep 15. (701)873-5852

BEULAH BAY RECREATION AREA (Public Corps) From town N, 15 mi on Hwy 49 to Beulah Bay Rd., E 2 mi on Beulah Bay Rd. (L). 2015 rates: $10 to $21. May 1 to Sep 30. (701)873-5916

BISMARCK — C3 *Burleigh*

BISMARCK KOA KAMPGROUND
Ratings: 9/10★/9 (Campground) From Jct of I-94 & Bismarck Expressway (exit 161): Go 1 mi N on Centennial Rd (L). **FAC:** Gravel rds. 94 Avail: 82 gravel, 12 grass, 56 pull-thrus (30 x 60), back-ins (30 x 55), 65 full hkups, 29 W, 29 E (30/50 amps), WiFi, tent sites, rentals, dump, mobile sewer, laundry, groc, LP gas, fire rings, firewood. **REC:** heated pool, playground. Pets OK. Big rig sites, 2015 rates: $39 to $49. Disc: military.
(701)222-2662 Lat: 46.84657, Lon: -100.73248
3720 Centennial Rd, Bismarck, ND 58503
bismarckkoa@midconetwork.com
www.koa.com
See ad this page.

GENERAL SIBLEY PARK (Public) From Jct of I-94 & SH-810, SW 5.2 mi, S 4 mi on Washington St. 2015 rates: $22. May 9 to Oct 1. (701)222-1844

BOTTINEAU — A3 *Bottineau*

LAKE METIGOSHE (State Pk) From town: Go 14 mi NE on County Rd, then E on Hwy-43. 2015 rates: $10 to $25. (701)263-4651

TOMMY TURTLE PARK (Public) From ND Hwy 5 & Jay St: Go 1 blk N on Jay St (L). 2015 rates: $15. May 1 to Oct 15. (701)228-3030

CASSELTON — C6 *Cass*

GOVERNORS' RV PARK
Ratings: 8/8/6 (Campground) From Jct of I-94 (Exit 331) & Hwy 18: Go 500 ft N on Hwy 18 (Governors Dr), then 200 ft W on service rd (R). **FAC:** Paved/gravel rds. 45 gravel, 20 pull-thrus (25 x 70), back-ins (30 x 50), 45 full hkups (30/50 amps), WiFi, tent sites, rentals, dump, laundry, fire rings, restaurant. **REC:** heated pool $, wading pool, whirlpool, rec open to public. Pets OK. Partial handicap access. Big rig sites, 2015 rates: $39. Disc: AAA, military. Apr 1 to Nov 1.
AAA Approved
(888)847-4524 Lat: 46.87633, Lon: -97.21260
2050 Governors Dr, Casselton, ND 58012
daysinn@cassinn.com
See ad this page.

CAVALIER — A5 *Pembina*

ICELANDIC (State Pk) From jct Hwy-5 & Hwy-18: Go 5 mi W on Hwy-5. 2015 rates: $10 to $25. (701)265-4561

DEVILS LAKE — B5 *Ramsey*

GRAHAMS ISLAND (State Pk) From town, W 10 mi on Hwy 19 to 72nd Ave./CR 0322, S 5 mi (across bridge). 2015 rates: $10 to $30. (701)766-4015

DICKINSON — C2 *Stark*

NORTH PARK RV CAMPGROUND
Ratings: 7/9.5★/8.5 (Campground) From Jct I-94 (exit 61) & 3rd Ave/Hwy 22: Go 1/2 mi N on 3rd Ave/Hwy 22, then 1/2 mi E on 21st St, then 500 ft N on 5th Ave (R). Elev 2536 ft. **FAC:** Gravel rds. (100 spaces). Avail: 30 gravel, 27 pull-thrus (24 x 90), back-ins (30 x 95), mostly side by side hkups, 30 full hkups (30/50 amps), seasonal sites, WiFi, tent sites, dump, laundry. **REC.** Pet restrict(B/Q). Partial handicap access. Big rig sites, eco-friendly, 2015 rates: $33. No CC.
AAA Approved
(701)227-8498 Lat: 46.90662, Lon: -102.77717
2320 Buckskin Dr, Dickinson, ND 58601
campnorthpark@yahoo.com
www.campnorthpark.com
See ad this page, 879.

PATTERSON LAKE RECREATION AREA (CITY PARK) (Public) From I-94 (exit 59): Go 3 mi W on Old Hwy 10, then 1 mi S. 2015 rates: $12 to $24. (701)456-2056

DUNSEITH — A4 *Rolette*

INTERNATIONAL PEACE GARDEN CAMPGROUND (Public) From town, N 13 mi on US-281 (L). $10 entrance fee. 2015 rates: $14 to $22. Jun 1 to Sep 30. (701)263-4390

ELGIN — D3 *Grant*

SHEEP CREEK DAM (Public) From Jct of SR-49 & SR-21, S 1 mi on SR-49 (becomes gravel, 68th St.), S 4.3 mi (R). Pit toilets. May 1 to Oct 31. (701)584-2354

FARGO — C6 *Cass*

LINDENWOOD PARK (Public) From Jct of I-94 & US-81 (exit 351), N 0.25 mi on US-81 to 17th Ave, E 8 blks (R). 2015 rates: $28. May 1 to Oct 15. (701)232-3987

FESSENDEN — B4 *Wells*

FESSENDEN CITY PARK (Public) From Jct of Hwys 52 & 15, E 0.5 mi on Hwy 15 (L). 2015 rates: $10 to $15. May 1 to Oct 1. (701)547-3291

GARRISON — B3 *McLean*

DOUGLAS CREEK BAY RECREATION AREA (Public Corps) 17-1/2 mi W on Hwy 37 (Emmett), then 5 mi S, 4 mi E on CR. Pit toilets. (701)654-7411

EAST TOTTEN TRAIL (COE-LAKE SAKAKAWEA) (Public Corps) From jct Hwy 37 & US 83: Go 5 mi S on US 83. Pit toilets. May 1 to Sep 30. (701)654-7411

FORT STEVENSON (State Pk) From Jct of SR-37 & CR-15, S 3 mi on CR-15 (E). Entrance fee required. 2015 rates: $10 to $30. (701)337-5576

GLEN ULLIN — C3 *Morton*

GLEN ULLIN MEMORIAL PARK (Public) From town, W 0.5 mi on CR-139/Hwy 10 (L). Pit toilets. 2015 rates: $15 to $18. (701)348-3683

GRAFTON — A6 *Walsh*

LEISTIKOW PARK CAMPGROUND (CITY PARK) (Public) From jct I-29 (exit 176) & Hwy 17: Go 10 mi W on Hwy 17, then 6 blocks N on Cooper Ave, then 1 mi W on Fifth St. 2015 rates: $20. (701)352-1842

GRAND FORKS — B6 *Grand Forks*

GRAND FORKS CAMPGROUND
Ratings: 7/9.5★/8.5 (Campground) From Jct I-29 (Exit 138) & Bus US-81/32nd Ave: Go 500 ft W on 32nd Ave, then 1 mi S on S 42nd St (gravel rd) (R). **FAC:** Gravel rds. 128 Avail: 63 gravel, 65 grass, 65 pull-thrus (30 x 60), back-ins (30 x 55), 106 full hkups, 22 W, 22 E (30/50 amps), WiFi, tent sites, dump, laundry, fire rings, firewood. **REC:** playground. Pets OK. Partial handicap access. Big rig sites, eco-friendly, 2015 rates: $35. Apr 1 to Nov 1.
(701)772-6108 Lat: 47.87374, Lon: -97.09012
4796 S. 42nd St, Grand Forks, ND 58201
www.grandforkscampground.com
See ad this page.

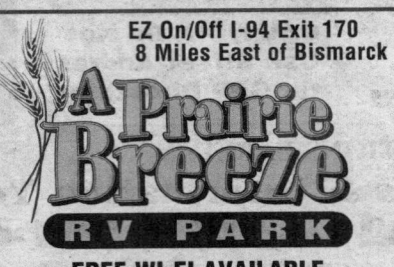

HAZEN — C3 *Mercer*

HAZEN BAY RECREATION AREA (Public) From jct Hwy 200 & CR 27: Go 15 mi N on CR 27. 2015 rates: $10 to $21. May 15 to Sep 15. (701)748-6948

LEWIS & CLARK RV PARK (Public) From Jct of Hwy 200 & Main St (unmarked street), follow signs, S 0.2 mi on Main St (L). 2015 rates: $10 to $20. May 1 to Sep 15. (701)748-2267

HENSLER — C3 *Oliver*

CROSS RANCH (State Pk) From Jct of I-94 & Hwy 25 (exit 147), N 18.5 mi on Hwy 25 (road curves west), N 5 mi on County Rd, E 3 mi on County Rd, N 2 mi (R). Entrance fee required to access this campground. 2015 rates: $10 to $25. (701)794-3731

HILLSBORO — C6 *Traill*

HILLSBORO CAMPGROUND & RV PARK **Ratings: 5/9★/6** (Campground) 2015 rates: $25. (701)636-5205 203-6th St SW, Hillsboro, ND 58045

JAMESTOWN — C5 *Stutsman*

FRONTIER FORT CAMPGROUND Ratings: 6/6/4.5 (Campground) From Jct of I-94 (Exit 258) & US-281: Go 1/2 mi N on US-281, then 1/2 mi E on 17th St. SW (R) Don't rely on GPS. Call for directions. **FAC:** Paved/gravel rds. 61 Avail: 61 all weather, 28 pull-thrus (25 x 60), back-ins (26 x 50), mostly side by side hkups, 52 full hkups, 9 W, 9 E (30/50 amps), WiFi, tent sites, dump, laundry, firewood, restaurant. **REC:** playground, rec open to public. Pets OK. Partial handicap access. 2015 rates: $25 to $50. Disc: AAA, military. Apr 1 to Nov 15. No CC. AAA Approved
(701)252-7492 Lat: 46.89038, Lon: -98.70508
1838 3rd Ave SE, Jamestown, ND 58401
frontierfort@live.com

JAMESTOWN CAMPGROUND
Ratings: 7.5/9★/8.5 (Campground) W-bnd: From exit 256 off I-94: Go S (L) over interstate, then 1 mi W (R) on south frontage road (R) (Gravel) E-bnd: From exit 256 off I-94: Go S (R) 100 ft, then 1 mi W (R) on south frontage road (R) Don't rely on GPS-Call for directions. **FAC:** Gravel rds. 48 gravel, 42 pull-thrus (22 x 75), back-ins (22 x 52), mostly side by side hkups, 30 full hkups, 18 W, 18 E (30/50 amps), WiFi, tent sites, rentals, dump, mobile sewer, laundry, fire rings, firewood. **REC:** playground. Pet restrict(B). Eco-friendly, 2015 rates: $28 to $38. May 1 to Oct 1.
(701)252-6262 Lat: 46.89122, Lon: -98.77707
3605 80th Ave SE, Jamestown, ND 58401
jamestown.campground@yahoo.com
See ad this page, 879.

JAMESTOWN DAM/LAKESIDE MARINA CAMPGROUND (Public) From town, N 3.5 mi on SR-20 to 30th St., W 0.5 mi (L). 2015 rates: $9 to $14. May to Sep. (701)252-1183

SMOKEY'S CAMPGROUND & LANDING (STUTSMAN COUNTY PARK) (Public) From jct I-94 & US 281: Go 10-1/2 mi N on US 281, then 1-3/4 mi E on paved road. 2015 rates: $10 to $15. May 1 to Sep 15. (701)252-0659

KATHRYN — C5 *Barnes*

LITTLE YELLOWSTONE PARK (BARNES COUNTY PARK) (Public) From jct Hwy 1 & Hwy 46: Go 6 mi E on Hwy 46. Pit toilets. May 1 to Oct 31. (701)762-4450

KILLDEER — C2 *Dunn*

LITTLE MISSOURI (State Pk) From town: Go 17 mi N on Hwy-22. (701)764-5256

LAMOURE — D5 *LaMoure*

LAMOURE COUNTY MEMORIAL PARK (Public) From Jct of CR-34 & CR-63, N 1 mi on CR-63 (R). 2015 rates: $7. May to Oct. (701)883-5856

LANGDON — A5 *Cavalier*

LANGDON CITY PARK CAMPGROUND (Public) From Jct of SR-1 & SR-5, W 0.4 mi on SR-5, N 2 blks 7th St. (E). 2015 rates: $6 to $20. May 1 to Oct 30. (701)256-2155

LARIMORE — B5 *Grand Forks*

LARIMORE DAM RECREATION AREA CAMPGROUND (Public) Westbound from Jct I-29 (Exit 141) & US-2: Go 23 mi W on US-2, then 2 mi S & W on CR-4A/18th Ave NE (R). Eastbound from Jct Hwy 18 & US 2: Go 2 mi E o n US 2, then 2 mi S & W on CR-4A//18th Ave NE (R). 2015 rates: $25. May 1 to Oct 1. (701)343-2078

Don't miss a thing! Check out the Table of Contents for everything the Guide has to offer.

LISBON — D5 *Ransom*

SANDAGER CAMPGROUND (Public) From jct Hwy 32 & Hwy 27 (in Lisbon); go 3 blks N on Hwy 32 (Main St); then 4 blks W on 2nd Ave West; then 1 blk NE on Ash St; then 1 blk NW on 1st Ave; then L on Parkway Dr & follow signs. 2015 rates: $18. Apr 15 to Oct 31. (701)683-3010

MANDAN — C3 *Morton*

FORT ABRAHAM LINCOLN (State Pk) From town, S 7 mi on Hwy 1806 (E). Entrance fee required. 2015 rates: $10 to $30. (701)667-6340

MEDORA — C1 *Billings*

A SPOTLIGHT Introducing Medora's colorful attractions appearing at the front of this state section.

MEDORA CAMPGROUND **Ratings: 7/4.5/7.5** (Campground) 2015 rates: $25 to $40. May 21 to Sep 15. (800)633-6721 3370 Pool Dr, Medora, ND 58645

RED TRAIL CAMPGROUND
Ratings: 6.5/9★/7 (Campground) E-bnd only: From I-94 (Exit 24): Go 2 mi SE on Bus I-94/Pacific Ave, then 1/4 mi SW (R) on E River Rd, S to Red Trail St (L). W-bnd: From I-94 (Exit 27): Go 1 1/2 mi W on Bus I-94/Pacific Ave, then 1/4 mi SW (L) on E River Rd S to Red Trail St (L) Do not rely on GPS. **FAC:** Paved/gravel rds. 120 Avail: 3 paved, 117 gravel, 21 pull-thrus (28 x 60), back-ins (28 x 60), 56 full hkups, 46 W, 64 E (30/50 amps), cable, WiFi, tent sites, dump, mobile sewer, laundry, groc. **REC:** playground. Pets OK. Partial handicap access. Big rig sites, eco-friendly, 2015 rates: $29 to $47. May 15 to Sep 30.
(800)621-4317 Lat: 46.90896, Lon: -103.52471
Red Trail Street, Medora, ND 58645
www.redtrailcampground.com
See ad pages 881 (Spotlight Medora), 879.

THEODORE ROOSEVELT/COTTONWOOD CAMPGROUND (Natl Pk) E-bnd: From Jct I-94 & exit 24, SE 1.4 mi on service rd to park access rd, N 5.5 mi(L); or W-bnd: From Jct I-94 & exit 27, SW 1 mi on service rd to park access rd, N 5.5 mi (R). Entrance fee required. 2015 rates: $5 to $10. (701)623-4730

MENOKEN — C3 *Burleigh*

A PRAIRIE BREEZE RV PARK
Ratings: 5/8★/8 (Campground) From Jct of I-94 & Exit 170 (Menoken exit): Go 1000 ft S on Rd to Menoken (R). **FAC:** Gravel rds. 42 gravel, 42 pull-thrus (30 x 80), mostly side by side hkups, 42 full hkups (30/50 amps), WiFi, tent sites, dump, laundry. **REC.** Pets OK. Partial handicap access. Big rig sites, 2015 rates: $25 to $30. Apr 1 to Nov 1. No CC.
(701)224-8215 Lat: 46.83446, Lon: -100.54261
2810 158th St NE, Menoken, ND 58558
prairiebreeze@outlook.com
See ad opposite page.

MINOT — B3 *Ward*

ROUGHRIDER CAMPGROUND
Ratings: 7/9.5★/8.5 (Campground) From Jct of US-83 & US 2/US-52: Go 4 mi W on US-2/52, then 1/2 mi N on paved CR-18 (54th St) (R). **FAC:** Gravel rds. 90 gravel, 58 pull-thrus (21 x 55), back-ins (22 x 55), 63 full hkups, 25 W, 27 E (30/50 amps), WiFi, tent sites, dump, laundry, LP bottles, fire rings, firewood. **REC:** Souris River: fishing, playground. Pet restrict(B). Eco-friendly, 2015 rates: $45. Disc: military.
(701)852-8442 Lat: 48.24165, Lon: -101.37107
500 54th St NW, Minot, ND 58703
roughriderrvpark@gmail.com
www.roughridercampground.com
See ad this page, 78, 879.

Things to See and Do

NORSK HOSTFEST 5 night/4 day Scandinavian festival celebrates the heritage & culture of 5 Nordic countries. Scandinavian cuisine, shopping, entertainment & RV camping during the festival. Sep 29 to Oct 3. partial handicap access. RV accessible. Restrooms, food. Hours: 7:30am to 12 am.
(701)852-2368 Lat: 48.33561, Lon: -101.26148
2005 Burdick Expy East, Minot, ND 58701
leannmellum@hostfest.com
www.hostfest.com
See ad page 876 (Welcome Section).

ND

NAPOLEON — D4 *Logan*

BEAVER LAKE (State Pk) From town, S 17 mi on Hwy 3 to CR-Burnstad (R). 2015 rates: $12 to $25. (701)452-2752

NEW ROCKFORD — B4 *Eddy*

NORTH RIVERSIDE PARK (Public) At Jct of Hwys 15 & 281 (L). 2015 rates: $5. (701)947-2461

PARSHALL — B2 *Mountrail*

PARSHALL BAY REC AREA (Public) From Jct of SR-23 & SR-37, S 2 mi on SR-37 to 37th St., W & S 4 mi, W 5.7 mi 36th St. 2015 rates: $7.50 to $12. May 15 to Sep 15. (701)862-3362

Had a great stay? Let us know by emailing us travelguidecomments@goodsamfamily.com

PEMBINA — A6 *Pembina*

FORT DAER CAMPGROUND (Public) From Canadian border, S 2 mi on I-29 (E). 2015 rates: $15. May 31 to Sep 15. (701)825-6819

RIVERDALE — C3 *McLean*

DOWNSTREAM CAMPGROUND-GARRISON DAM (Public Corps) From town, W 1 mi on Hwy 200 to rd next to dam, follow signs (E). 2015 rates: $12 to $18. May 16 to Sep 29. (701)654-7411

LAKE SAKAKAWEA (State Pk) From Jct of Hwys 83 & 200, W 9 mi on Hwy 200 to W-side of Garrison Dam & park grounds (R). Entrance fee required. 2015 rates: $10 to $30. (701)487-3315

WOLF CREEK REC AREA (Public Corps) From Jct of Tourist Rte/Missouri Dr & Hwy 200, E 1 mi on Hwy 200, follow sign (E). Pit toilets. 2015 rates: $10. (701)654-7411

RUGBY — B4 *Pierce*

OAKWOOD INN & RV PARK **Ratings: 4.5/6.5/5.5** (Campground) 2015 rates: $20 to $32. Apr 1 to Nov 1. (701)776-5272 601 Hwy 2 SW, Rugby, ND 58368

Take an RV Trip of a Lifetime! Check out trip ideas at the front of the Guide - you'll find something for the history buff, the food lover or even your wild side!

VALLEY CITY — C5 *Barnes*

EAST ASHTABULA CROSSING CAMPGROUND (Public Corps) From town, N 14 mi on CR-21 (R). 2015 rates: $26 to $52. May 1 to Sep 30. (701)845-2970

EGGERTS LANDING (Public Corps) From town, N 12 mi on CR-21 (L). 2015 rates: $26. May 1 to Sep 30. (701)845-2970

MEL RIEMAN REC AREA (Public Corps) From town, N 1 mi on CR-21 to Valley Rd (CR-19), NW 9 mi (L). 2015 rates: $25 to $26. May 1 to Sep 30. (701)845-2970

WALHALLA — A5 *Pembina*

WALHALLA RIVERSIDE PARK (Public) From Jct of SR-32 & Mountain Ave, S 0.2 mi on Mountain Ave (E). 2015 rates: $25. May 15 to Sep 15. (701)549-3289

WATFORD CITY — B2 *McKenzie*

THEODORE ROOSEVELT/JUNIPER (Natl Pk) From town, S 15 mi on US-85 to park access rd, W 5 mi (L). 2015 rates: $5 to $10. (701)842-2333

Thank You to our active and retired military personnel. A dedicated section of Military Listings for places to camp can be found at the back of the Guide.

WATFORD CITY TOURIST PARK (Public) From Jct of US-85 & SR-23, E 1 mi on SR-23 (R). 2015 rates: $25. May 1 to Oct. (701)570-3677

WEST FARGO — C6 *Cass*

RED RIVER VALLEY FAIR CAMPGROUND (CASS COUNTY) (Public) From jct I-94 (exit 343) & Hwy 10: Go 1/4 mi E on Hwy 10, then 1/4 mi S on CR 28. 2015 rates: $20 to $25. May 1 to Nov 1. (701)282-2200

WILLISTON — B1 *Williams*

LEWIS & CLARK (State Pk) From town, E 18 mi on Hwy 1804 to park access road, S 3 mi (L) $5 entrance fee required. 2015 rates: $10 to $30. (701)859-3071

CLEAN RESTROOMS GET A STAR

Campgrounds that receive the maximum 5 points for restroom cleanliness (toilets, showers, floors, walls and sinks/counters/mirrors) are honored with a star beside their total restroom rating. RATED 10/10★/10

Getty Images/iStockphoto

WELCOME TO Ohio

DATE OF STATEHOOD	WIDTH: 220 MILES (355 KM)	PROPORTION OF UNITED STATES
MARCH 1, 1803	LENGTH: 220 MILES (355 KM)	1.18% OF 3,794,100 SQ MI

Ohio has it all. Hit the beach on the shores of Lake Erie or the banks of the Ohio River, or hike the Appalachian foothills to the southeast. Feel the beat of the Rock and Roll Hall of Fame in Cleveland and savor the big-city charm of Cincinnati.

Record-breaking amusement parks and the world's largest Amish enclave invite visitors who seek something different. If you're a foodie, check out the KitchenAid Experience in Greenville and see the original Model H mixer. Set sail on Lake Erie from the quaint town of Port Clinton, or walk along the banks of the historic Erie Canal.

Learn

Professional baseball, professional football, airplanes, and rock and roll all have deep roots in Ohio, and visitors can trace the origins of each one at fabulous museums. Visit the Cincinnati Reds Hall of Fame to learn about the 1869 Red Stockings, baseball's first professional team, which finished the season 57-0. Check out the Professional Football Hall of Fame in Canton, where the National Football League formed in 1920 at the Hupmobile automotive dealership. Many of those early teams—the Bears, Packers and Eagles, for starters—still play to this day.

At the Rock and Roll Hall of Fame in Cleveland, visitors can learn about local disk jockey Alan Freed, who popularized the term, "rock 'n' roll." Take wing in Dayton, home to the National Museum of the United States Air Force. Local sons Orville and Wilbur Wright built their first flying machine here. The Inventors Hall of Fame is at home in Akron, and Ohioans boast lots of contribution to this tribute to innovation.

Ohio was admitted to the Union in 1803 and went on to and send eight native sons to the White House—tying Virginia as the birthplace of U.S. presidents. The Hayes Presidential Center at Spiegel Grove in Fremont, dedicated to Ohio-born Rutherford B. Hayes, is considered the prototype to the modern presidential library.

OH

Top 3 Tourism Attractions:
1) Cedar Point Amusement Park/ Resort
2) Rock and Roll Hall of Fame and Museum
3) Pro Football Hall of Fame

Nickname: Buckeye State

State Flower: Scarlet Carnation

State Bird: Cardinal

People: Neil Armstrong, astronaut; Thomas Edison, inventor; Paul Newman, actor; Jack Nicklaus, golfer; Jesse Owens, Olympic track star

Major Cities: Columbus (capital), Cleveland, Cincinnati, Toledo, Akron

Topography: East—generally rolling plains, Allegheny Plateau; north—Lake Erie plains extending southward; west—plains

Climate: Mostly a humid continental zone with a generally temperate climate

Randall L. Schieber

OHIO
Campground and other services
RV service center and/or other services
Good Sam discount locations
SCALE: 1 inch equals 35 miles
0 25 50 miles
0 25 50 kilometers
Map by Terra Carta © 2016 Affinity Media
LAKE ERIE
CANADA
U.S.
ONTARIO
OHIO
MICHIGAN
INDIANA
KY.
W. VA.
PA.
Toledo
CLEVELAND
Youngstown
Mansfield
Marion
Columbus
Dayton
Cincinnati
Springfield
Lima
Findlay
Zanesville
Cambridge
Marietta
Parkersburg
Portsmouth
Huntington
Charleston
Wheeling
Ann Arbor
Windsor
Jackson
Frankfort

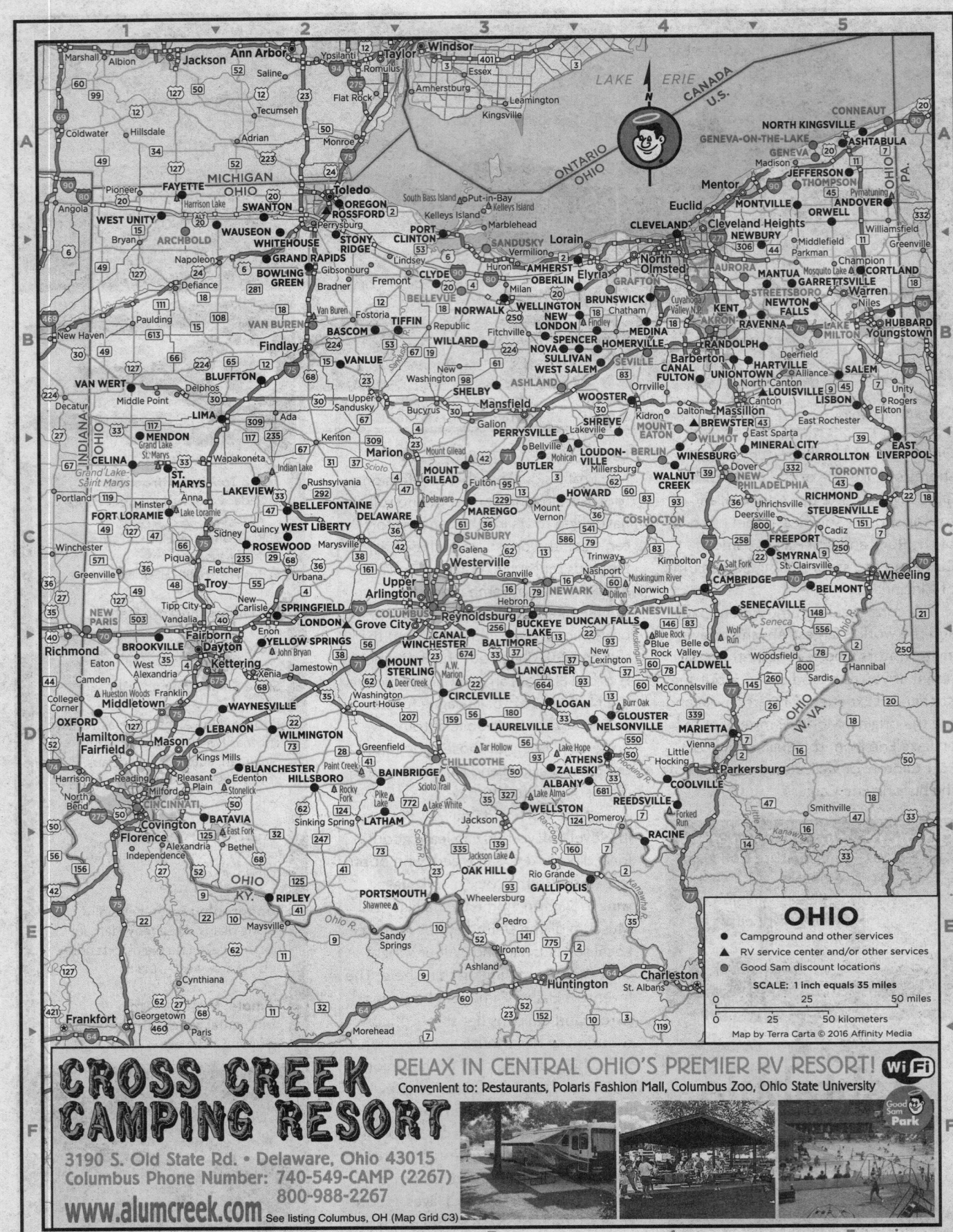

Experience

Started in 1849, the Ohio State Fair in Columbus is one of America's largest get-togethers. The fair celebrates Buckeye State products and its people over the course of 11 days in mid-summer. During the cold months, Winterfest in Bowling Green features three days of chilly weather competitions.

On the 76-mile Amish Country Scenic Byway, RVs must share the road with horse-drawn buggies as they traverse the largest community of the "plain people" in the United States. The indoctrination point for Ohio Amish Country is the Amish & Mennonite Heritage Center in Berlin. From here, browse quaint villages, where 21st-century life has been slow to intrude.

About two hours to the west is Columbus, the Ohio state capital and the 15th largest city in America. World-class museums, cultural attractions and architecture thrive in this metropolis.

Play

On the shore of Lake Erie, Cedar Point Amusement Park dishes out thrills. The park hosts 3 million visitors each summer, and more people ride roller-coasters here than in any amusement park in America. Before careening down the track, get a great view of the lake from 200 feet above the ground—if you can keep your eyes open.

The Wayne National Forest in southeastern Ohio is the state's only national forest, an amalgam of old farming tracts that provide 300 miles of trails for all-terrain vehicles, mountain bikers and equestrians. Nearby is the star of the Ohio's outdoors, the Hocking Hills. The thick woodlands reveal their caves, waterfalls and rugged cliffs grudgingly to willing explorers.

Did you know that America's first national park of the 21st Century was created in Cleveland? Cuyahoga National Park preserves the "crooked river" that was settled by Native Americans 12,000 years ago. The main trail through Cuyahoga National Park is the nearly 20 miles of the Towpath Trail along the route of the historic Ohio & Erie Canal. Ten trailheads make it easy to hike the crushed limestone path. The park is one of many in northeast Ohio that lead through massive jumbles of cracked limestone known as "ledges."

The Holden Arboretum in Kirtland is one of the nation's finest tree museums, with more than 6,000 varieties of plants and trees spread over 3,446 acres. It also allows dogs.

Taste

Thomas Kiradjieff first started serving Cincinnati chili in his Empress Chili diner in 1922, when customers asked for chili on top of their spaghetti. Now there are hundreds of chili parlors in the Ohio Valley dishing out some 2 million pounds of chili to adoring Cincinnatians who order short-hand as three-way (chili, spaghetti, cheese), four-way (add onions) and five-way (add kidney beans). Enjoy it with Oyster crackers on the side. The cinnamon-spiced favorite gets its own day in Cincinnati in September at Chilifest on Yeatman's Cove.

OH

TRAVEL & TOURISM

Ohio Tourism Division
800-BUCKEYE
www.DiscoverOhio.com

Ashland Area CVB
877-581-2345, Ext. 1003
www.visitashlandohio.com

Belmont County TC
800-356-5082
www.belmontcountytourism.org

Cincinnati USA Regional Tourism Network
859-581-2260
www.cincinnatiusa.com

Visit Cleveland
800-362-0727
www.cleveland.com/visit

Delaware County CVB
888-335-6446
www.visitdelohio.com

Dublin CVB
800-245-8387
www.irishisanattitude.com

Experience Columbus
866-397-2657
www.experiencecolumbus.com

Fairfield Co. Visitors & Convention Bureau
800-626-1296
www.visitfairfieldcounty.org

Fremont-Sandusky Co. CVB
800-255-8070
www.lakeeriesfavoriteneighbor.com

Gahanna CVB
614-418-9122
www.visitgahanna.org

Greater Springfield CVB
800-803-1553
www.visitspringfieldohio.com

Greater Toledo CVB
800-243-4667
www.dotoledo.org/gtcvb

Grove City Area
800-539-0405, 614-539-8747
www.visitgrovecityoh.com

Licking County CVB and Welcome Center
800-589-8224
www.lccvb.com

Loudonville-Mohican CVB
877-266-4422
www.loudonville-mohican.com

Mansfield-Richland County CVB
800-642-8282
www.mansfieldtourism.com

Marion Area
800-371-6688
www.visitmarionohio.com

Ohio DNR, Wildlife Division
614-265-6300, 800-945-3543
www.ohiodnr.com/wildlife

Ohio Wine Producers Assn.
800-227-6972, 440-466-4417
www.ohiowines.org

Scioto County Visitors Bureau
740-343-1116
www.ohiorivvertourism.org

OUTDOOR RECREATION

Ohio State parks
866-OHIOPARKS
Parks.ohiodnr.gov

SHOPPING

Aurora Premium Outlets
www.premiumoutlets.com/aurora

Chapel Hill Mall
330-633-7100
www.chapelhillmall.com

Easton Town Center
614-337-2200
www.eastontowncenter.com

The Holmes County Flea Market
330-893-0900
www.holmesfleamarket.com

Libbey Glass Factory Outlet
419-727-2374, 888-794-8469
www.libbey.com

Lodi Station Outlets
www.lodistation.com

Featured Good Sam Parks

OHIO

Good Sam Park

When you stay with Good Sam, you can expect the highest degree of cleanliness and friendliness, and better yet, you get 10% off campground fees.

If you're not already a Good Sam member you can purchase your membership at one of these locations:

AKRON
Countryside Campground
(330)628-1212

ARCHBOLD
Sauder Village RV Park
(800)590-9755

AURORA
Roundup Lake Campground
(330)562-9100

BELLEVUE
Gotta Getaway RV Park
(800)305-9644

BERLIN
Berlin RV Park & Campground
(330)674-4774
Scenic Hills RV Park
(330)893-3607

CHILLICOTHE
Sun Valley Campground
(740)775-3490

CINCINNATI
Indian Springs Campground, LLC
(888)550-9244

COLUMBUS
Cross Creek Camping Resort
(740)549-2267

CONNEAUT
Evergreen Lake Park
(440)599-8802

COSHOCTON
Colonial Campground & RV Park
(740)502-9245

GENEVA
Kenisee's Grand River Campground
(440)466-2320

GENEVA-ON-THE-LAKE
Indian Creek RV & Camping Resort
(888)420-0893

GRAFTON
American Wilderness Campground
(440)926-3700

MOUNT EATON
Evergreen Park RV Resort
(888)359-6429

NEW PARIS
Arrowhead Campground
(937)996-6203

NEW PHILADELPHIA
Wood's Tall Timber Resort
(330)602-4000

NEWARK
Lazy River At Granville
(740)366-4385

SANDUSKY
Camp Sandusky
(419)626-1133
Huron River Valley Resort & Campground
(419)433-4118
Milan Travel Park
(800)433-4627

SEVILLE
Maple Lakes Recreational Park
(330)336-2251

STREETSBORO
Woodside Lake Park
(866)241-0492

SUNBURY
Autumn Lakes
(740)625-6600

THOMPSON
Heritage Hills RV Park
(440)298-1311

TORONTO
Austin Lake RV Park & Cabins
(740)544-5253

VAN BUREN
Pleasant View Recreation
(419)299-3897

WILMOT
Baylor Beach Park
(888)9BAYLOR

ZANESVILLE
Wolfies Campground
(740)454-0925

For more Good Sam Parks go to listing pages

Tourism Ohio

AMISH COUNTRY

America's largest community of "plain people" opens its doors to visitors

Take a journey back in time and enjoy life at a slower pace in Amish Country, Ohio. This collection of thriving communities offers entertainment, outdoor adventure, shopping and unique historical sites for visitors.

Here, the Amish life can be experienced in the crafts and delicacies of the simple-living locals. You can also learn about their history, which saw the first families of Swiss Anabaptists come to America in the 1700s. Staying true to their beliefs of modest, uncomplicated living, the Amish have continued to eschew electricity, automobiles and other modern developments, clinging to virtues grounded in the Bible. Ohio's Amish country is home to the largest population of "plain people" in the United States.

Amish life is serene yet somewhat hidden from the outside world, but some residents open their doors to visitors. Yoder's Amish Home invites guests to observe the daily life and work of Amish families who call Ohio home. Tour the barn and see baby animals, then hop in an iconic buggy for a jaunt through Ohio's scenic countryside. In the fall, family members make treats like apple butter and pumpkin butter, and farm visitors can chip in.

Yoder's Amish Home invites guests to observe the daily life and work of Amish families who call Ohio home.

In nearby Berlin, the Amish & Mennonite Heritage Center displays the history of the Amish faith in the Behalt Cyclorama. You'll also find a pioneer barn and a restored Conestoga wagon. Amish education and devotional coverings—headwear for Amish and Mennonite women and men—are also part of the heritage center experience. Stay immersed in Amish life at Schrock's Amish Farm and Village, with shopping and education opportunities, as well as buggy rides and tours of an Amish home and farm.

Charming Trips

Explore the natural beauty of Amish Country on a trail ride through communities such as Charm, where stables open to guests who seek a relaxing equestrian experience. At the end of the day, sip wine and enjoy finely crafted cheese from a local winery and cheesehouse.

The Millersburg Victorian House Museum showcases 28 rooms outfitted in the Queen Anne style. On display are a host of Victorian artifacts and pieces along with examples of the history of Holmes County. Visit the Millersburg Glass Museum at the Holmes County Cultural Center, where guests learn about the history of the local glass plant and see the evolution of the plant's craftsmanship and works of art.

Animal Attractions

Go "wild" at the Farm at Walnut Creek, where more than 500 animals from six different continents are on exhibit. Visitors can get up close and personal with giraffes, camels, zebras and kangaroos alongside horses, llamas and deer at this educational farm in the community of Sugarcreek.

Get in touch with nature at The Wilderness Center, a nonprofit nature preserve with 10 miles of hiking trails that wind through old-growth forests and prairies. Enjoy the Wildlife Observation Room or the Planetarium.

For More Information

Visit Amish Country
877-643-8824
www.visitamishcountry.com

Ohio Tourism Division
800-282-5393
www.discoverohio.com

Evergreen PARK
RV RESORT
In the Heart of Amish Country
Good Sam Park
Good Sam RATED 10/10★/10
See listing Mount Eaton, OH
87 Full Hookup Sites • Paved Roadways • Big Rigs • Pull-Thrus • 20/30/50 Amp • Cable TV • Wi-Fi
Evergreen PARK
RV RESORT
LAUNDROMAT
Miller Ave.
16359 Dover Rd. • Dundee, OH 44624 • 888-359-6429
www.evergreenparkrvresort.com • evergreenpark@wifi7.com

Ohio

CONSULTANTS

John & Shirley Bujnovsky

AKRON — B4 *Summit*

AKRON See also Aurora, Brunswick, Hartville, Medina, Randolph, Ravenna, Seville, Streetsboro & Uniontown.

CHEROKEE PARK CAMPGROUND
Ratings: 6.5/8.5★/6.5 (Campground) From Jct of I-76 & SR-43 (exit 33), S 2.4 mi on SR-43 to unmarked rd (watch for park sign on L), E 0.2 mi (E); or From Jct of US-224 & SR 43, N 3.1 mi on SR 43, E on unmarked rd (watch for park sign) (E). **FAC:** Gravel rds. (120 spaces). 30 Avail: 15 gravel, 15 grass, 4 pull-thrus (25 x 50), back-ins (30 x 45), mostly side by side hkups, 30 W, 30 E (30/50 amps), seasonal sites, WiFi Hotspot, tent sites, dump, mobile sewer, laundry, LP gas, fire rings, firewood. **REC:** pond, swim, fishing, shuffleboard, playground. Pet restrict(B). Partial handicap access. Eco-friendly, 2015 rates: $30 to $36. Apr 20 to Oct 20.
(330)673-1964 Lat: 41.09056, Lon: -81.38881
3064 State Route 43, Mogadore, OH 44260
cherokeeparkcampground@gmail.com
www.cherokeeparkcampground.com
See ad this page.

COUNTRYSIDE CAMPGROUND
Ratings: 9/8★/9 (Campground) From Jct of US-224 & SR-43, N 2.4 mi on Sr-43 (L). **FAC:** Paved/gravel rds. (86 spaces). Avail: 25 gravel, 8 pull-thrus (28 x 74), back-ins (25 x 50), 25 full hkups (30 amps), seasonal sites, WiFi $, tent sites, rentals, dump, laundry, groc, LP gas, fire rings, firewood, controlled access. **REC:** heated pool, Mogadore Reservoir: fishing, playground. Pet restrict(B). Eco-friendly, 2015 rates: $35 to $41. May 1 to Oct 15.
(330)628-1212 Lat: 41.06194, Lon: -81.34738
2687 State Route 43, Mogadore, OH 44260
gtbrain@aol.com
www.countrysidecampgrounds.com
See ad this page, 889.

MAPLE LAKES RECREATIONAL PARK
Ratings: 8/8.5★/8.5 (RV Park) From Jct of I-76 & I-277 go W 15.5 mi on I-76 to OH-3 (Exit 2) go N 0.9 mi to Blake Rd, go 1 mi E(L). **FAC:** Poor paved/dirt rds. (198 spaces). 68 Avail: 64 gravel, 4 grass, patios, 20 pull-thrus (30 x 60), back-ins (30 x 50), 62 full hkups, 6 W, 6 E (30/50 amps), seasonal sites, WiFi $, tent sites, rentals, dump, mobile sewer, laundry, groc, LP bottles, fire rings, firewood, controlled access. **REC:** heated pool, pond, fishing, playground, rec open to public. Pet restrict(Q). Partial handicap access. Eco-friendly, 2015 rates: $44. Apr 15 to Oct 1.
(330)336-2251 Lat: 41.03119, Lon: -81.80145
4275 Blake Rd, Seville, OH 44273
maplelakes@maplelakes.com
www.mapleslakes.com
See primary listing at Seville and ad page 904.

PORTAGE LAKES (State Pk) From Jct of I-76 and I-277, E 2 miles on I-277, to OH-93, S 8 miles on OH-93 enter on the (L). Pit toilets. 2015 rates: $27. (330)644-2220

Travel Services

CAMPING WORLD OF AKRON As the nation's largest retailer of RV supplies, accessories, services and new and used RVs, Camping World is committed to making your total RV experience better. RV Accessories: (800)875-0600. **SERVICES:** RV, tire, RV appliance, MH mechanical, mobile RV svc, staffed RV wash, restrooms, RV Sales. RV supplies, LP, emergency parking, RV accessible. waiting room. Hours: 8am to 6pm.
(888)721-5964 Lat: 40.978922, Lon: -81.486322
1005 Interstate Parkway, Akron, OH 44312
www.campingworld.com

ALBANY — D4 *Athens*

LAKE SNOWDEN EDUCATIONAL AND RECREATION PARK (Public) From jct US 50/32 & CR 681: Go 1 mi N on US 50/32. 2015 rates: $24 to $33. (740)698-6373

AMHERST — A4 *Lorain*

SERVICE PLAZA-VERMILLION VALLEY (Public) From town, E 2 mi on Ohio Tpke at MP-139.5 (R). Overnight rest area (Between Exits 135 & 142). 2015 rates: $20. (440)234-2081

ANDOVER — A5 *Ashtabula*

BAY SHORE FAMILY CAMPING **Ratings: 8.5/9★/9** (Campground) 2015 rates: $39 to $41. Apr 15 to Oct 16. (440)293-7202 7124 Pymatuning Lake Rd, Andover, OH 44003

HOLIDAY CAMPLANDS **Ratings: 7.5/8★/7.5** (Membership Pk) Apr 20 to Oct 15. (440)293-7116 4273 Pymatuning Lake Rd, Andover, OH 44003

JEFFCO LAKES RESORTS **Ratings: 6/5.5/5** (Campground) 2015 rates: $35. May 1 to Oct 15. (440)293-7485 6758 Hayes Rd, Andover, OH 44003

ANDOVER (CONT)

PYMATUNING (State Pk) From town, E 1.5 mi on SR-85 to Lake Rd, S 4 mi (L). 2015 rates: $21 to $34. (440)293-6030

WILDWOOD ACRES FAMILY CAMPGROUND **Ratings: 6/NA/6** (Campground) Pit toilets. 2015 rates: $27 to $29. Apr 17 to Oct 18. (440)293-6838 6091 Marvin Rd, Andover, OH 44003

ARCHBOLD — A1 *Fulton*

SAUDER VILLAGE RV PARK
Ratings: 8/9★/8.5 (Campground) From Jct of I-80 (OH Tpke) & Exit 25/SR-66: Go S 3.9 mi on SR-66 to SR-2, E 0.25 mi (R) Register at Sauder Heritage Inn. **FAC:** Paved rds. 77 gravel, 11 pull-thrus (34 x 75), back-ins (40 x 60), 37 full hkups, 40 W, 40 E (50 amps), WiFi Hotspot, tent sites, dump, laundry, fire rings, firewood, restaurant. **REC:** pool, pond, fishing, shuffleboard, playground, rec open to public. Pets OK. Partial handicap access. Big rig sites, 14 day max stay, eco-friendly, 2015 rates: $26 to $47. Disc: AAA, military. Apr 15 to Oct 31. ATM.
AAA Approved
(800)590-9755 Lat: 41.54320, Lon: -84.30272
22611 Sr 2, Archbold, OH 43502
sauderheritageinn@saudervillage.org
www.saudervillage.org
See ad this page, 889.

Things to See and Do

HISTORIC SAUDER VILLAGE Historic rural village. May 1 to Oct 28. partial handicap access. RV accessible. Restrooms, food. Hours: 10am to 5pm Tues - Sun. Adult fee: $10 to $15. ATM.
(800)590-9755 Lat: 41.54320, Lon: -84.30272
22611 Sr 2, Archbold, OH 43502
sauderheritageinn@saudervillage.org
www.saudervillage.org
See ad this page.

MUSEUM AT SAUDER VILLAGE Pioneer machinery, kitchen tools and quilts. History of development of Black Swamp from native Americans thru 1920s. May 1 to Oct 28. partial handicap access. RV accessible. Restrooms, food. Hours: 10am to 5pm. Adult fee: $0. ATM.
(800)590-9755 Lat: 41.54320, Lon: -84.30272
22611Sr 2, Archbold, OH 43502
sauderheritageinn@saudervillage.org
www.saudervillage.org
See ad this page.

Check the air pressure on your tires and inflate any that are lower than the pressure recommended in the owner's manual. Properly inflated tires can increase fuel efficiency by 3.3 percent.

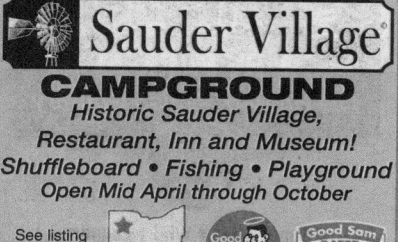

OLD BARN RESTAURANT AT SAUDER VILLAGE Pioneer themed restaurant, buffet and menu service. Partial handicap access. RV accessible. Restrooms, food. Hours: 11 am to 8pm. ATM.
(800)590-9755 Lat: 41.54320, Lon: -84.30272
22611 Sr 2, Archbold, OH 43502
Sauderheritageinn@saudervillage.org
www.saudervillage.org
See ad this page.

ASHLAND — B3 *Ashland*

HICKORY LAKES CAMPGROUND
Ratings: 7/8★/7.5 (Campground) From Jct of I-71 (exit 186) & SR-250, E 6.3 mi on SR-250 to TWP Rd-63, N 0.9 mi to TWP Rd-1300, E 0.6 mi (R). **FAC:** Gravel rds. (170 spaces). 60 Avail: 28 gravel, 32 grass, 7 pull-thrus (36 x 60), back-ins (30 x 40), 60 W, 60 E (30/50 amps), seasonal sites, WiFi, tent sites, rentals, dump, mobile sewer, groc, LP gas, fire rings, firewood, controlled access. **REC:** pond, swim, fishing, playground. Pets OK. Age restrict may apply, eco-friendly, 2015 rates: $40 to $45. Apr 15 to Sep 30.
(419)869-7587 Lat: 40.85699, Lon: -82.13276
23 Township Rd 1300, West Salem, OH 44287
hickorylakescampground@gmail.com
www.hickorylakescampground.com
See ad this page.

ASHTABULA — A5 *Ashtabula*

HIDE-A-WAY LAKES CAMPGROUND **Ratings: 7.5/5/7.5** (Campground) 2015 rates: $33 to $38. Apr 15 to Oct 15. (440)992-4431 2034 South Ridge Rd W, Ashtabula, OH 44004

Things to See and Do

ASHTABULA CO. CONVENTION & VISITORS BUREAU Tourist information for Ashtabula County & Lake Erie area,including 18 covered bridges, the longest covered bridge in the U.S., 20 wineries, 2 wild & scenic rivers, plus 30 mi of Lake Erie coastline. Restrooms. Hours: 10am to 4pm. No CC.
(800)337-6746 Lat: 41.78965, Lon: -80.85386
1850 Ashtabula-Austinburg Rd, Austinburg, OH 44010
jkrysa@visitashtabulacounty.com
www.visitashtabulacounty.com
See ad page 885 (Welcome Section).

ATHENS — D4 *Athens*

STROUDS RUN (State Pk) From jct US 33 (Columbus Rd exit) & N Lancaster Rd: Go E on N Lancaster Rd, which becomes Columbia Ave then Strouds Run Rd (CR 20). Pit toilets. 2015 rates: $19. (740)767-3570

AURORA — B4 *Portage*

ROUNDUP LAKE CAMPGROUND
Ratings: 8/8★/7.5 (Campground) From Jct of I-80 & SR-44 (exit 193), N 6 mi on SR-44 to Hwy 82, W 2 mi (L). **FAC:** Paved/gravel rds. (295 spaces). 151 Avail: 76 gravel, 75 grass, patios, 41 pull-thrus (32 x 75), back-ins (36 x 70), 56 full hkups, 95 W, 95 E (30/50 amps), seasonal sites, WiFi $, tent sites, rentals, dump, mobile sewer, laundry, LP gas, fire rings, firewood, controlled access. **REC:** heated pool, wading pool, 50 Acre Lake: swim, fishing, playground. Pets OK. Partial handicap access. Big rig sites, eco-friendly, 2015 rates: $32 to $58. Disc: AAA, military. May 1 to Oct 31.
(330)562-9100 Lat: 41.29983, Lon: -81.22289
3392 SR-82, Mantua, OH 44255
info@rounduplakecampground.com
www.rounduplakecampground.com
See ad pages 901, 889.

We rate what RVers consider important.

BAINBRIDGE — D2 *Pike, Ross*

PAINT CREEK (State Pk) From Jct of SR-41 & US-50, W 5 mi on US-50 (R). 2015 rates: $24 to $28. (937)393-4284

PIKE LAKE (State Pk) From Jct of US-50 & Potts Hill Rd, SE 4 mi on Potts Hill Rd to Pike Lake Rd, S 3 mi (L). Pit toilets. 2015 rates: $18 to $22. (740)493-2212

BALTIMORE — D3 *Fairfield*

RIPPLING STREAM CAMPGROUND **Ratings: 4.5/8★/6.5** (RV Area in MHP) 2015 rates: $28. Apr 1 to Oct 31. (740)862-6065 3640 Reynoldsburg-Baltimore Rd, Baltimore, OH 43105

BASCOM — B2 *Seneca*

MEADOWBROOK PARK (Public) From Jct of SR-635 & SR-18, E 1 mi on SR-18 (R). 2015 rates: $30. Apr 1 to Nov 1. (419)937-2242

BATAVIA — D1 *Hamilton*

EAST FORK (State Pk) From Jct of I-275E & SR-32E, E 10 mi on SR-32E to Half Acre Rd, S 1.5 mi to Old SR-32E, E 0.1 mi (R). 2015 rates: $28. (513)734-4323

BELLEFONTAINE — C2 *Logan*

A & E CAMPING RESORT **Ratings: 6/6.5/7** (Campground) 2015 rates: $30. (937)593-0220 3299 St Rte 540, Bellefontaine, OH 43311

BACK 40 LTD **Ratings: 7/5/7.5** (Campground) 2015 rates: $35. May 1 to Oct 28. (937)468-7492 959 CR-111E, Rushsylvania, OH 43347

OHIO STATE EAGLES RECREATION PARK **Ratings: 6/5/7** (Campground) 2015 rates: $25. Apr 1 to Nov 1. (937)593-1565 5118 US 68N, Bellefontaine, OH 43311

BELLEVUE — B3 *Huron*

GOTTA GETAWAY RV PARK
Ratings: 8/8.5★/8 (RV Park) From Jct of I-80/90 (OH-Tpke) Exit 110/SR-4: S 5.3 mi on SR-4 to US 20, E 1.2 mi (L). **FAC:** Paved/gravel rds. (87 spaces). Avail: 54 grass, 32 pull-thrus (20 x 60), back-ins (20 x 33), 54 W, 54 E (30/50 amps), seasonal sites, WiFi Hotspot, tent sites, rentals, dump, mobile sewer, laundry, LP bottles, fire rings, firewood. **REC:** heated pool, pond, fishing, playground. Pet restrict(Q). Partial handicap access. Eco-friendly, 2015 rates: $35 to $38. May 1 to Oct 31.
(800)305-9644 Lat: 41.26128, Lon: -82.76744
4888 US Hwy 20E, Bellevue, OH 44811
info@GottaGetawayRVPark.com
www.gottagetawayrvpark.com
See ad pages 903, 889.

BELMONT — C5 *Belmont*

BARKCAMP (State Pk) From Jct of I-70 & SR-149 (exit 208), S 1 mi on SR-149, E 1 mi Fox Trail Rd. 2015 rates: $21 to $23. (740)484-4064

BERLIN — C4 *Holmes*

BERLIN See also Mount Eaton, New Philadelphia, Shreve, Walnut Creek, Wilmot & Winesburg.

BERLIN (CONT)

← BERLIN RV PARK & CAMPGROUND
Ratings: 6.5/9.5★/9 (Campground) W-bnd: From Jct of I-77 & SR-39 (Exit 83), W 18 mi on SR-39 (L); or E-bnd: From Jct of US 62 (SR-39), E 4.5 mi on US 62 (SR-39) (R). **FAC:** Gravel rds. 40 gravel, 25 pull-thrus (30 x 65), back-ins (30 x 50), 31 full hkups, 9 W, 9 E (30/50 amps), WiFi, tent sites, dump, fire rings, firewood. **REC:** playground. Pets OK. Partial handicap access. Big rig sites, eco-friendly, 2015 rates: $29 to $41. Disc: military. Apr 1 to Dec 1.
(330)674-4774 Lat: 40.55285, Lon: -81.83573
5898 State Route 39, Millersburg, OH 44654
info@berlinrvpark.com
berlinrvpark.com
See ad pages 893, 889.

→ SCENIC HILLS RV PARK
Ratings: 7.5/NA/9 (RV Park) W-bnd: From Jct of I-77 & SR-39 (Exit 83), W 15 mi on SR-39, to Township Hwy 367 (blinking light), S 0.1 mi on Twp-367 (R); or E-bnd: From Jct of US 62 & SR-39 (at Berlin), E 1 mi on SR-39 to Township Rd 367 (at blinking light), S 0.1 mi on Twp Rd 367 (R). **FAC:** Paved/gravel rds. 112 gravel, 40 pull-thrus (30 x 86), back-ins (30 x 75), accepts self-contain units only, 112 full hkups (30/50 amps), WiFi, dump, laundry, fire rings, firewood. Pet restrict(B). No tents. Big rig sites, eco-friendly, 2015 rates: $35. Apr 1 to Nov 1. No CC. AAA Approved
(330)893-3607 Lat: 40.56152, Lon: -81.79321
4483 Township Hwy 367, Millersburg, OH 44654
shrvp@wifi7.com
www.scenichillsrvpark.com
See ad this page, 889.

BLANCHESTER — D2 *Clinton*

← STONELICK (State Pk) From Jct of SR-133 & SR-727, S 3 mi on SR-727, follow signs (L). 2015 rates: $26. Apr 1 to Oct 31. (513)734-4323

RV Park ratings you can rely on!

BLUFFTON — B2 *Hancock*

BLUFFTON/FINDLAY SW KOA **Ratings: 8/7/7.5** (Campground) 2015 rates: $42 to $58. (800)562-3460 3506 Tr-34, Bluffton, OH 45817

BOWLING GREEN — B2 *Wood*

FIRE LAKE CAMPER PARK **Ratings: 6.5/7.5/6.5** (Campground) 2015 rates: $27 to $34. May 1 to Oct 15. (888)879-2267 13630 West Kramer Rd, Bowling Green, OH 43402

BREWSTER — B4 *Stark*

Things to See and Do

BAYLOR BEACH WATERPARK 2 acre man-made lake, sand bottom, grassy beaches. 90 ft. Slide & 4 kid slides, diving boards, log rolls, picnicking, grills, concessions, mini-golf, paddle boats, sand volleyball, playground. Shelters available for rent. May 26 to Sep 1. partial handicap access. RV accessible. Restrooms, food. Hours: 11am to 7pm. Adult fee: $3 to $7.
(330)767-3031 Lat: 40.68686, Lon: -81.59955
8777 Manchester Ave. SW, Navarre, OH 44662
www.baylorbeachpark.com
See ad page 890 (Spotlight Amish Country).

BROOKVILLE — D1 *Montgomery*

DAYTON TALL TIMBERS RESORT KOA **Ratings: 8.5/10★/10** (Campground) 2015 rates: $37 to $55. Apr 1 to Nov 1. (800)562-3317 7796 Wellbaum Rd, Brookville, OH 45309

BRUNSWICK — B4 *Medina*

WILLOW LAKE PARK INC
Ratings: 7/5.5/6.5 (Campground) From Jct of I-71 & SR-303 (exit 226), W 3.2 mi on SR-303 to Substation Rd, S 1.8 mi (R). **FAC:** Gravel rds. (250 spaces). 40 Avail: 20 gravel, 20 grass, 30 pull-thrus (35 x 50), back-ins (18 x 32), 40 W, 40 E (30/50 amps), seasonal sites, WiFi, tent sites, showers $, dump, mobile sewer, groc, fire rings, firewood. **REC:** Willow Lake: swim, fishing, playground, rec open to public. Pets OK. 2015 rates: $30 to $40. May 1 to Oct 18. No CC.
(330)225-6580 Lat: 41.21796, Lon: -81.84265
2400 Substation Rd, Brunswick, OH 44256
ajkwlp@aol.com
www.willowlakepark.net
See ad opposite page.

BUCKEYE LAKE — C3 *Licking*

BUCKEYE LAKE COLUMBUS EAST KOA **Ratings: 8.5/10★/9** (Campground) 2015 rates: $48.39 to $83.52. Apr 1 to Oct 31. (740)928-0706 4460 Walnut Rd, Buckeye Lake, OH 43008

BUTLER — C3 *Richland*

RIVER TRAIL CROSSING RV PARK **Ratings: 6/6/8.5** (Campground) 2015 rates: $29 to $32. May 1 to Oct 15. (419)883-3888 1597 SR-97, Butler, OH 44822

CALDWELL — D4 *Noble*

WOLF RUN (State Pk) From Jct of I-77 & Belle Valley exit (Rte 821), S 0.5 mi on Rte 821 to Rte 215, NE 0.9 mi to Wolf Run Rd, N 0.3 mi (R). Pit toilets. 2015 rates: $25. Apr 1 to Nov 1. (740)732-5035

CAMBRIDGE — C4 *Guernsey*

SALT FORK (State Pk) From Jct of I-77 & US-22, E 7 mi on US-22, N 2 mi on SH-285. 2015 rates: $24 to $37. (740)432-1508

SPRING VALLEY CAMPGROUND Ratings: 8/9.5★/9.5 (Campground) From Jct of I-77 & I-70, W 1 mi on I-70 to SR-209 (exit 178), S 0.1 mi to Dozer Rd, W 1 mi (L). **FAC:** Paved/gravel rds. (199 spaces). 139 Avail: 95 gravel, 44 grass, patios, 22 pull-thrus (30 x 100), back-ins (30 x 36), 103 full hkups, 36 W, 36 E (50 amps), seasonal sites, cable, WiFi, tent sites, dump, laundry, groc, LP gas, fire rings, firewood. **REC:** pool, Spring Valley Lake: swim, fishing, playground, rec open to public. Pet restrict(B). Big rig sites, 2015 rates: $30 to $36.
(740)439-9291 Lat: 40.02594, Lon: -81.58722
8000 Dozer Rd, Cambridge, OH 43725
mail@campspringvalley.com
www.campspringvalley.com

CANAL FULTON — B4 *Stark*

CLAY'S PARK RESORT
Ratings: 8/9/8.5 (Campground) N of Town, From Jct of Hwy 21 & Hwy 93, S 1.3 mi on Hwy 93 to Patterson Rd, E 0.5 mi (L) Rates include 2 day park passes, 1 night stay. **FAC:** Paved/gravel rds. (550 spaces). 150 Avail: 50 gravel, 100 grass, 20 pull-thrus (50 x 90), back-ins (50 x 50), some side by side hkups, 50 full hkups, 100 W, 100 E (50 amps), seasonal sites, WiFi $, tent sites, rentals, dump, mobile sewer, laundry, groc, LP gas, fire rings, firewood, restaurant, controlled access. **REC:** heated pool, Clay's Park Lake: fishing, playground, rec open to public. Pet restrict(Q). Partial handicap access. Big rig sites, 2015 rates: $35 to $46. May 1 to Nov 1. ATM.
(330)854-6691 Lat: 40.86121, Lon: -81.58204
13190 Patterson Rd, North Lawrence, OH 44666
info@clayspark.com
www.clayspark.com
See ad page 892.

CANAL WINCHESTER — D3 *Franklin*

JACKSON LAKE CAMPGROUND PARK LLC **Ratings: 7.5/4.5/6** (RV Park) 2015 rates: $43. (614)837-2656 3715 Cedar Hill Rd. NW, Canal Winchester, OH 43110

CANTON — B4 *Stark*

CUTTY'S SUNSET CAMPING RESORT
Ratings: 9/9★/9 (RV Park) From Jct of I-77 & US-62 (exit 107B), E 7.4 mi on US -62 to SR-44, N 6.4 mi to SR-619, E 0.3 mi (R). **FAC:** Paved rds. (480 spaces). Avail: 80 gravel, 15 pull-thrus (30 x 70), back-ins (30 x 50), 60 full hkups, 20 W, 20 E (50 amps), seasonal sites, WiFi $, tent sites, dump, laundry, groc, LP gas, fire rings, firewood, restaurant, controlled access. **REC:** heated pool, shuffleboard, playground. Pet restrict(Q). Partial handicap access. Big rig sites, eco-friendly, 2015 rates: $38 to $54. Disc: military. May 1 to Oct 15.
(330)533-7965 Lat: 40.95177, Lon: -80.24632
8050 Edison St NE, Louisville, OH 44641
info@cuttyssunset.com
www.cuttyssunset.com
See primary listing at Hartville and ad page 892.

CARROLLTON — C5 *Carroll*

ABC COUNTRY CAMPING & CABINS **Ratings: 6.5/7.5/6** (Campground) 2015 rates: $25. May 1 to Oct 15. (330)735-3220 4105 Fresno Rd NW, Carrollton, OH 44615

COZY RIDGE CAMPGROUND **Ratings: 5.5/5.5/7** (Campground) 2015 rates: $28. Apr 15 to Oct 15. (330)735-2553 4145 Fresno Rd NW, Carrollton, OH 44615

PETERSBURG MARINA (MUSKINGUM CONSERVANCY DISTRICT) (Public) From town: Go 4 mi S on Hwy-332, then W on CR-22. (330)627-4270

CELINA — C1 *Mercer*

KOZY KAMP GROUND **Ratings: 7/6.5/8.5** (Campground) 2015 rates: $35. Apr 1 to Oct 15. (419)268-2275 5134 Its It Rd, Celina, OH 45822

CHILLICOTHE — D3 *Ross*

GREAT SEAL (State Pk) From town, N 3 mi on US-23 to Delano Rd, E 3.5 mi to Marietta Rd, S 0.5 mi (L). Pit toilets. 2015 rates: $16 to $20. Mar 1 to Dec 31. (740)887-4818

SCIOTO TRAIL SP (State Pk) From Jct of US-35 & US-23, S 10 mi on US-23 to SR-372, E 0.5 mi to Stoney Creek Rd, E 2 mi to Lake Rd, N 0.5 mi (E); or from town, SE 10 mi on US-35 to Higby Rd, W 1.5 mi to Three Locks Rd, N 3 mi to Stoney Creek Rd, W 3 mi to Lake Rd, N 0.5 mi (E). Pit toilets. 2015 rates: $16 to $24. (740)887-4818

SUN VALLEY CAMPGROUND
Ratings: 6.5/9★/8.5 (Campground) From Jct of US 35 & CR-550, take CR-550 exit, go W 2 mi on CR-550 (R).

HISTORIC MOUNDS COUNTRY
Nestled in historic Ross County. 4 mi W of Chillicothe, between Great Seal, Hocking Hills, Scioto Trail and Rocky Fork State Parks. Quiet country setting with RV Park amenities, including FREE Wi-Fi.

FAC: Paved/gravel rds. (50 spaces). 27 Avail: 14 gravel, 13 grass, patios, 3 pull-thrus (24 x 100), back-ins (20 x 78), 10 full hkups, 17 W, 17 E (30/50 amps), seasonal sites, WiFi, tent sites, dump, fire rings, firewood. **REC:** pond, fishing, playground. Pets OK. Big rig sites, 2015 rates: $38. Disc: military. No CC.
(740)775-3490 Lat: 39.38718, Lon: -83.08459
10105 CR-550, Chillicothe, OH 45601
sunvalley550@roadrunner.com
www.sunvalleycampground.freeservers.com
See ad opposite page, 889.

OH

CINCINNATI — D1 *Hamilton*

CINCINNATI AREA MAP

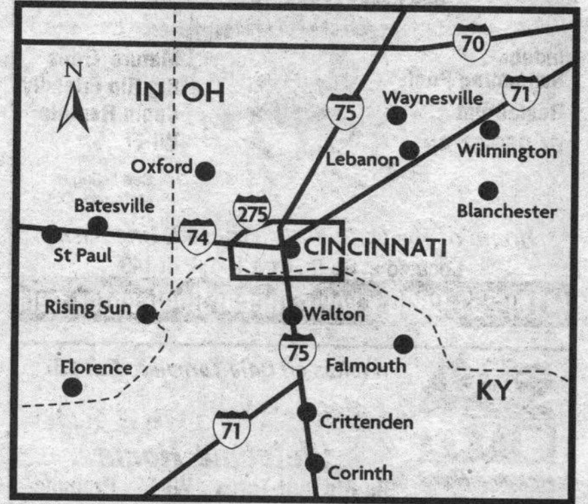

Symbols on map indicate towns within a 50 mile radius of Cincinnati where campgrounds are listed. Check listings for more information.

In OH, see also Blanchester, Lebanon, Oxford, Waynesville & Wilmington.

In IN, see also Batesville, Florence, Rising Sun & St Paul.

In KY, see also Corinth, Crittenden, Falmouth & Walton.

CINCINNATI (CONT)

INDIAN SPRINGS CAMPGROUND, LLC
Ratings: 8.5/9.5★/9 (Campground) From Jct of I-275 & US 50 (Exit 16): Go E 2.2 mi on US 50 to State Line Rd, N 0.4 mi (R).

VISIT OHIO, INDIANA & KENTUCKY
Easy access to all 3 states. Only 20 minutes to Cincinnati. Creation Museum to the South. Riverboat Gambling to the West. 16 acre fishing lake & lakeside sites. Easy on, off with Big Rigs. Pull Thrus, paddle boats & more.

FAC: All weather rds. (73 spaces). Avail: 71 gravel, 13 pull-thrus (33 x 80), back-ins (33 x 60), 71 full hkups (30/50 amps), WiFi, laundry, LP gas, fire rings, firewood. **REC:** Indian Springs Lake: fishing, playground. Pet restrict(B/Q). Partial handicap access, no tents. Big rig sites, eco-friendly, 2015 rates: $40 to $45. Disc: AAA.
AAA Approved
(888)550-9244 Lat: 39.15564, Lon: -84.82011
3306 State Line Rd, North Bend, OH 45052
iscg@fuse.net
www.indianspringscampground.com
See ad pages 895, 889.

MIAMI WHITEWATER FOREST CAMPGROUND (GREAT PARKS OF HAMILTON COUNTY)
(Public) From Jct of I-74 & Dry Fork Rd, E 0.5 mi on Dry Fork Rd to West Rd, S 0.5 mi (L). **FAC:** Paved rds. 46 gravel, back-ins (30 x 40), 46 E (30 amps), WiFi Hotspot, tent sites, dump, groc, fire rings, firewood. **REC:** Miami Whitewater Forest Lake: fishing, golf, playground, rec open to public. Pets OK. Partial handicap access. 14 day max stay, 2015 rates: $28. Disc: military. Mar 6 to Dec 14.
(513)367-9632 Lat: 39.254208, Lon: -84.762176
9001 Mt Hope Rd, Harrison, OH 45030
camping@greatparks.org
www.greatparks.org
See ad page 895.

WINTON WOODS CAMPGROUND (GREAT PARKS OF HAMILTON COUNTY)
(Public) From Jct of I-275 & Winton Rd (Exit 39), S 3.5 mi on Winton Rd, L on Lakeview Drive, follow signs (R). **FAC:** Paved rds. 105 Avail: 12 paved, 93 gravel, 12 pull-thrus (25 x 65), back-ins (30 x 45), 37 full hkups, 68 E (30/50 amps), WiFi, tent sites, rentals, dump, mobile sewer, laundry, groc, fire rings, firewood, controlled access. **REC:** Winton Lake: fishing, marina, golf, playground, rec open to public. No pets. Partial handicap access. Age restrict may apply, big rig sites, 14 day max stay, 2015 rates: $28 to $48. Disc: military. Mar 1 to Dec 1.
(513)851-2267 Lat: 39.28711, Lon: -84.52606
10245 Winton Rd., Cincinnati, OH 45231
camping@greatparks.org
www.greatparks.org
See ad page 895.

Things to See and Do

GREAT PARKS OF HAMILTON COUNTY Central management and info center. Call for reservations: (513)851-CAMP to visit Miami Whitewater Forest (West), Winton Woods (North), Steamboat Bend (East). Partial handicap access. RV accessible. Restrooms. Hours: 9am to 5pm. No CC.
(513)521-7275 Lat: 39.25697, Lon: -84.51997
10245 Winton Rd, Cincinnati, OH 45231
camping@greatparks.org
www.greatparks.org
See ad page 895.

HICKEY'S BARBER SHOP Barber Shop. Restrooms. Hours: 10:00 am to 6:00 pm. No CC.
(513)353-9555 Lat: 39.15570, Lon: -84.82003
3306 State Line Rd, North Bend, OH 45052
iscg@fuse.com
See ad page 895.

STEAMBOAT BEND CAMPGROUND (GREAT PARKS OF HAMILTON COUNTY) Day use park. Apr 1 to Oct 31. No CC.
(513)851-2267 Lat: 39.029011, Lon: -84.32922
8401 Steamboat Dr, Cincinnati, OH 45255
camping@greatparks.org
www.greatparks.org
See ad page 895.

CIRCLEVILLE — D3 *Pickaway*

A W MARION (State Pk) From Jct of Hwy 188 & SR-22, E 4 mi on SR-22 to East Ringold Southern Rd, N 1 mi to Warner Huffer Rd, E 0.5 mi (L). Pit toilets. 2015 rates: $20 to $24. Apr 1 to Oct 31. (740)869-3124

Say you saw it in our Guide!

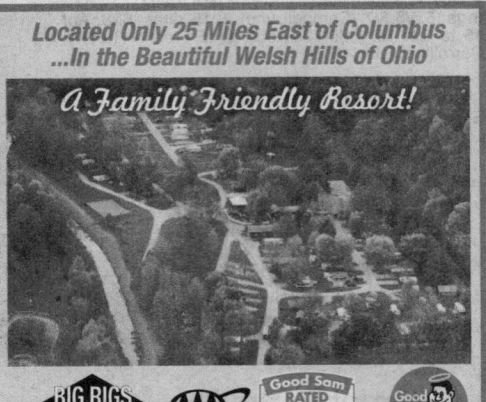

CLEVELAND — A4 *Cuyahoga*

CLEVELAND See also Aurora, Grafton & Streetsboro.

AMERICAN WILDERNESS CAMPGROUND
Ratings: 8/8.5★/9.5 (Campground) From Jct of I-80 & I-480 & SR 10, SW 2.2 mi on SR 10 to SR 83, S 7.3 on SR 83 (L). **FAC:** Gravel rds. (166 spaces). Avail: 56 gravel, 23 pull-thrus (38 x 95), back-ins (30 x 78), 56 W, 56 E (30/50 amps), seasonal sites, WiFi, tent sites, rentals, dump, mobile sewer, laundry, groc, fire rings, firewood, controlled access. **REC:** American Wilderness Lakes: swim, fishing, playground. Pets OK. Partial handicap access. Eco-friendly, 2015 rates: $38 to $42. Disc: military. May 1 to Oct 15.
(440)926-3700 Lat: 41.222443, Lon: -82.01795
17273 Avon Belden Rd Sr 83, Grafton, OH 44044
staff@americanwildernesscampground.com
www.americanwildernesscampground.com
See primary listing at Grafton and ad page 896.

CLYDE — B3 *Sandusky*

LEAFY OAKS CAMPGROUND Ratings: 7.5/5.5/8 (Campground) W-bnd: From Jct US-20 & SR-101 (at Clyde): Go 8 mi S on SR-101 (L) E-bnd: From Jct US-20 & OH-19, go 8 mi S on OH-19, then 1/4 mi SE on OH-19, then 1 1/2 mi NE on SR-101 N (R) (GPS maybe incorrect). **FAC:** Gravel rds. (235 spaces). 65 Avail: 9 gravel, 56 grass, 9 pull-thrus (34 x 40), back-ins (34 x 40), some side by side hkups, 15 full hkups, 50 W, 50 E (30/50 amps), seasonal sites, WiFi $, tent sites, rentals, dump, mobile sewer, laundry, groc, LP gas, fire rings, firewood, controlled access. **REC:** pond, swim, fishing, shuffleboard, playground, rec open to public. Pets OK. Age restrict may apply, 2015 rates: $28 to $47. Disc: military. Apr 15 to Oct 15.
(419)639-2887 Lat: 41.22493, Lon: -83.02395
6955 State Route 101, Clyde, OH 43410
leafyoakscamp@aol.com
leafyoaks.com

COLUMBUS — C3 *Franklin*

COLUMBUS See also Marengo & Sunbury.

ALTON RV PARK
Ratings: 6/7.5★/7.5 (RV Park) E-Bnd: From Jct of I-70 & SR-142 (Exit 85), S 2.2 mi on SR-142 to US 40, E 4.1 mi (L) N-Bnd: Fr Jct of I-270 & US 40 (Exit 7), W 3 mi on US 40, W of town (R). Reservations required 11/15-4/15. (GPS City GALLOWAY). **FAC:** Gravel rds. (35 spaces). Avail: 20 gravel, 18 pull-thrus (24 x 60), back-ins (20 x 50), 20 full hkups (30/50 amps), seasonal sites, WiFi, tent sites, dump. Pet restrict(B). Big rig sites, eco-friendly, 2015 rates: $40.
(614)878-9127 Lat: 39.95030, Lon: -83.17577
6552 W Broad St, Galloway, OH 43119
info@altonrvpark.com
www.altonrvpark.com
See ad opposite page.

AUTUMN LAKES
Ratings: 10/10★/10 (Campground) From Jct I-270 & I-71: Go N 15 mi to Exit 131 (SR -36/37), then E 0.2 mi to SR 656, then N 8.5 mi to Porter Central, then S 0.2 mi (L). **FAC:** Paved rds. (140 spaces). Avail: 36 all weather, patios, 14 pull-thrus (30 x 63), back-ins (30 x 50), 36 full hkups (50 amps), seasonal sites, WiFi $, tent sites, rentals, dump, laundry, groc, LP gas, fire rings, firewood, controlled access. **REC:** pool, pond, fishing, playground. Pets OK. Partial handicap access. Big rig sites, eco-friendly, 2015 rates: $42 to $62. Apr 15 to Oct 15. ATM.
(740)625-6600 Lat: 40.32518, Lon: -82.78952
8644 Porter Central Rd, Sunbury, OH 43074
autumnlakescampground@gmail.com
www.autumnlakescampground.com
See primary listing at Sunbury and ad page 905.

CROSS CREEK CAMPING RESORT
Ratings: 10/10★/10 (Campground) From Jct of I-71 (Exit 131) & SR-36/37: Go 3 mi W on SR-36/37, then 3 mi S on Lackey (Old State Rd).

TWO TIME NATIONAL AWARD WINNER
Twenty minutes North of Columbus. I-71 Exit 131. Close to world-famous Columbus Zoo, Ohio State University, Muirfield & next to Alum Creek Marina. 120 restaurants & Polaris Fashion Place 10 minutes away. Meet me at the Creek!

FAC: Paved rds. (200 spaces). Avail: 158 all weather, patios, 46 pull-thrus (40 x 65), back-ins (35 x 65), 136 full hkups, 22 W, 22 E (30/50 amps), seasonal sites, WiFi, tent sites, rentals, dump, laundry, groc, LP gas, fire rings, firewood. **REC:** pool, Alum Creek Lake: fishing, playground. Pet restrict(B). Partial handicap access. Big rig sites, eco-friendly, 2015 rates: $34 to $66. Disc: AAA. ATM.
AAA Approved
(740)549-2267 Lat: 40.22369, Lon: -82.93030
3190 S Old State Rd, Delaware, OH 43015
crosscreek@alumcreek.com
www.alumcreek.com/cccr/
See ad pages 898, 889, 886 (OH Map).

LAZY RIVER AT GRANVILLE
Ratings: 9.5/10★/9.5 (RV Park) From Jct of I-270 & State Rte 161 E go E on SR 161 17 mi/ continue on OH-16/37E 4 mi to OH-661, Go N 3.2 mi on OH-661 to Dry Creek Rd NE, then E 1.3 mi on Dry Creek Rd NE (R). **FAC:** Paved rds. (195 spaces). Avail: 141 gravel, patios, 45 pull-thrus (37 x 80), back-ins (30 x 60), 86 full hkups, 55 W, 55 E (30/50 amps), seasonal sites, cable, WiFi $, tent sites, rentals, dump, laundry, groc, LP gas, fire rings, firewood. **REC:** heated pool, Dry Creek: shuffleboard, playground, rec open to public. Pets OK. Partial handicap access. Big rig sites, eco-friendly, 2015 rates: $35 to $60. Disc: AAA. ATM.
(740)366-4385 Lat: 40.11492, Lon: -82.49932
2340 Dry Creek Rd NE, Granville, OH 43023
camp@lazyriveratgranville.com
www.lazyriveratgranville.com
See primary listing at Newark and ad page 896.

Our rating system isn't just tough, it's thorough. We know the kinds of things that are important to you — like clean restrooms and showers, attractive, secure, well-tended grounds, and extras like swimming pools. We give the first rating for development of facilities, the second for cleanliness and physical characteristics of restrooms and showers, and the third for visual appearance.

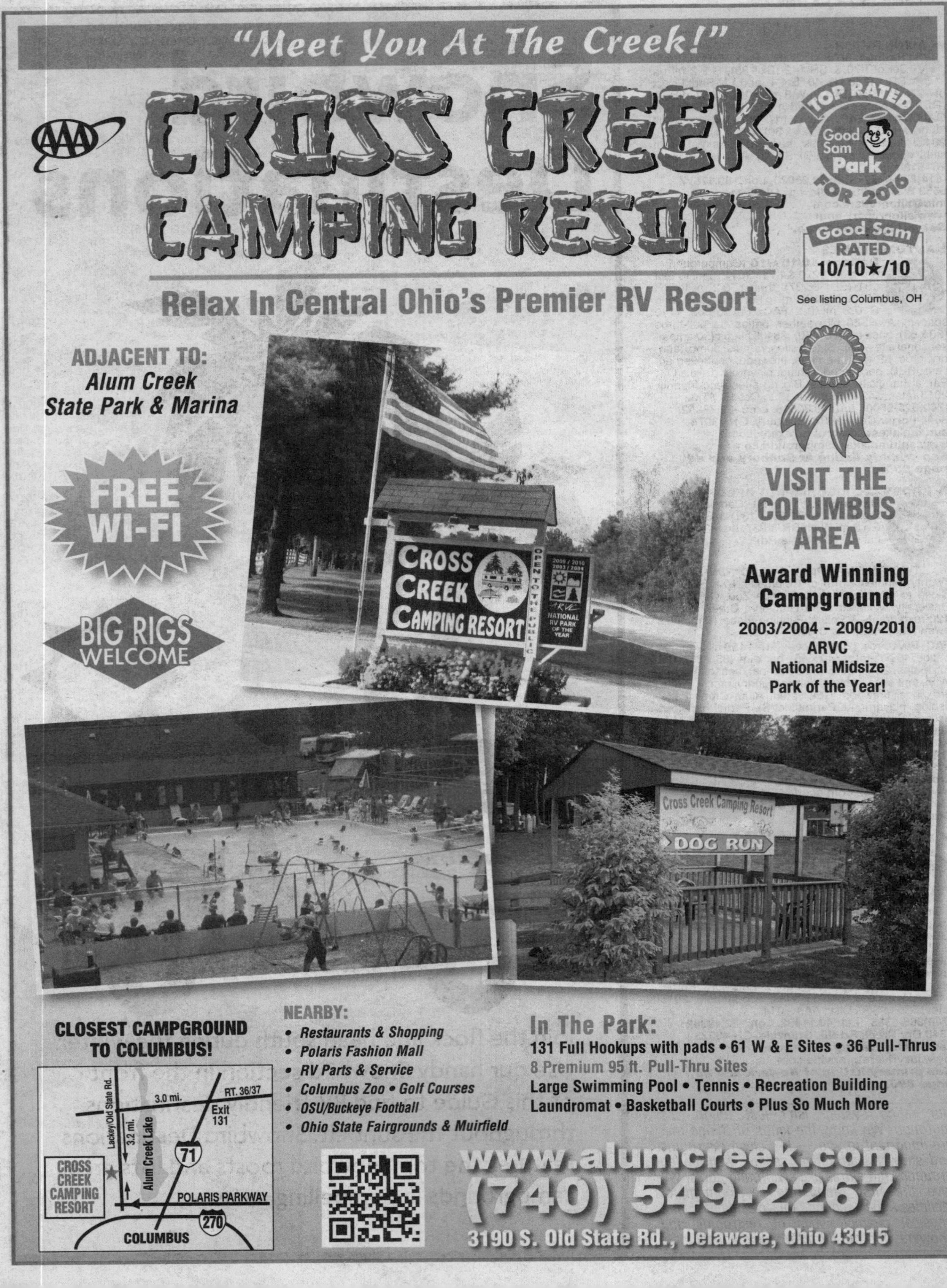
"Meet You At The Creek!"
AAA
CROSS CREEK
CAMPING RESORT
TOP RATED
Good Sam Park
FOR 2016
Good Sam
RATED
10/10★/10
See listing Columbus, OH
Relax In Central Ohio's Premier RV Resort
ADJACENT TO:
Alum Creek
State Park & Marina
FREE
WI-FI
BIG RIGS
WELCOME
CROSS
CREEK
CAMPING RESORT
OPEN TO THE PUBLIC
2009 / 2010
2003 / 2004
ARVC
NATIONAL
RV PARK
OF THE
YEAR
VISIT THE
COLUMBUS
AREA
Award Winning
Campground
2003/2004 - 2009/2010
ARVC
National Midsize
Park of the Year!
Cross Creek Camping Resort
DOG RUN
CLOSEST CAMPGROUND
TO COLUMBUS!
Lackey/Old State Rd.
3.0 mi.
RT. 36/37
Exit
131
3.2 mi.
Alum Creek Lake
71
CROSS
CREEK
CAMPING
RESORT
POLARIS PARKWAY
270
COLUMBUS
NEARBY:
• Restaurants & Shopping
• Polaris Fashion Mall
• RV Parts & Service
• Columbus Zoo • Golf Courses
• OSU/Buckeye Football
• Ohio State Fairgrounds & Muirfield
In The Park:
131 Full Hookups with pads • 61 W & E Sites • 36 Pull-Thrus
8 Premium 95 ft. Pull-Thru Sites
Large Swimming Pool • Tennis • Recreation Building
Laundromat • Basketball Courts • Plus So Much More
www.alumcreek.com
(740) 549-2267
3190 S. Old State Rd., Delaware, Ohio 43015

CONNEAUT — A5 *Ashtabula*

EVERGREEN LAKE PARK
Ratings: 7/8.5★/9 (Campground) From Jct of I-90 & SR-7 (exit 241), N 0.5 mi on SR-7 to Gateway Ave, W 0.1 mi to Center Rd, S 0.4 mi (R). **FAC:** Paved/gravel rds. (280 spaces). 60 Avail: 52 gravel, 8 grass, patios, 30 pull-thrus (35 x 63), back-ins (35 x 52), 12 full hkups, 48 W, 48 E (50 amps), seasonal sites, WiFi, tent sites, rentals, dump, mobile sewer, groc, LP gas, fire rings, firewood, controlled access. **REC:** pond, swim, fishing, shuffleboard, playground. Pets OK. Partial handicap access. Big rig sites, eco-friendly, 2015 rates: $33 to $35. Disc: AAA, military. May 1 to Oct 15. ATM. AAA Approved
(440)599-8802 Lat: 41.92657, Lon: -80.57098
703 Center Rd, Conneaut, OH 44030
camper@suite224.net
www.evergreenlake.com
See ad pages 1000, 889.

WINDY HILL GOLF COURSE & CAMPGROUND **Ratings: 4/7/6.5** (Campground) 2015 rates: $29. May 1 to Oct 1. (440)594-5251 6231 Weaver Rd, Conneaut, OH 44030

Travel Services

EVERGREEN LAKE RV SALES & SERVICE On site RV service, Mobile RV service, Licensed tech. May 1 to Oct 15. **SERVICES:** RV appliance, mobile RV svc, restrooms, RV Sales. RV supplies, LP, dump, emergency parking, RV accessible. waiting room. Hours: 9am to 6pm. ATM.
(440)599-8802 Lat: 41.91731, Lon: -80.57166
703 Center Rd, Conneaut, OH 44030
camper@suite224.net
www.evergreenlake.com
See ad page 1000.

COOLVILLE — D4 *Athens*

CARTHAGE GAP CAMPGROUND **Ratings: 7/9★/8** (Campground) 2015 rates: $30. Apr 15 to Oct 31. (740)667-3072 22575 Brimstone Rd, Coolville, OH 45723

CORTLAND — B5 *Trumbull*

MOSQUITO LAKE (State Pk) From Jct of SR-46 & SR-305, W 2 mi on SR-305 (R). 2015 rates: $20 to $26. (330)638-5700

COSHOCTON — C4 *Coshocton*

COLONIAL CAMPGROUND & RV PARK
Ratings: 7.5/9★/8.5 (Campground) From intersection of I-77 & US 36 (exit 65) go West 10 miles on US 36 to County Road 10, go 1 mile North on CR 10 (R). **FAC:** All weather rds. (48 spaces). 38 Avail: 14 gravel, 24 grass, 1 pull-thrus (30 x 60), back-ins (30 x 60), 27 full hkups, 11 W, 11 E (50 amps), seasonal sites, WiFi, tent sites, dump, laundry, LP gas, fire rings, firewood. **REC:** playground. Pets OK. Eco-friendly, 2015 rates: $30. Disc: military.
(740)502-9245 Lat: 40.31068, Lon: -81.82422
24688 County Road 10, Coshocton, OH 43812
info@colonialcampground.com
colonialcampground.com
See ad this page, 889.

LAKE PARK CAMPGROUNDS (Public) From Jct of US-36 & SR-83, N 0.5 mi on SR-83 (L). 2015 rates: $20 to $27. Apr to Nov. (740)622-7528

DAYTON — D1 *Greene*

DAYTON See also Brookville, Enon, Lebanon, Springfield & Waynesville.

ENON BEACH CAMPGROUND
Ratings: 6.5/5/5.5 (Campground) From Jct of I-70 & I-675 take I-70, E 3 mi to Exit 47 (Enon exit), NE 1.3 mi, on exit rd to Donnellsville/Enon, S 0.2 mi on Enon Rd. (R). **FAC:** Paved rds. (117 spaces). 69 Avail: 13 paved, 47 gravel, 9 grass, 15 pull-thrus (40 x 54), back-ins (40 x 36), some side by side hkups, 15 full hkups, 54 W, 54 E (30/50 amps), seasonal sites, WiFi Hotspot, tent sites, dump, laundry, LP bottles, fire rings, firewood. **REC:** wading pool, Enon Lake: swim, fishing, playground. Pet restrict(B). Eco-friendly, 2015 rates: $37.50. No CC.
(937)882-6431 Lat: 39.89004, Lon: -83.93584
2401 Enon Rd, Springfield, OH 45502
djj84161h@yahoo.com
www.enonbeach.com
See primary listing at Springfield and ad page 899.

Travel Services

STOOPS Freightliner service center. **SERVICES:** MH mechanical, engine/chassis repair, emergency rd svc, guest serv, restrooms. Emergency parking, RV accessible. waiting room. Hours: 7am to 12am.
(800)950-8782 Lat: 39.866718, Lon: -84.068192
7800 Center Point 70 Blvd., Dayton, OH 45424
www.stoops.com
See ad page 892.

DEERSVILLE — C5 *Harrison*

TAPPAN LAKE PARK
(Public) From Jct of US-36 & US-250, E 15 mi on US-250 to CR-55, W 3.5 mi (R). **FAC:** Paved rds. (567 spaces). 227 Avail: 100 gravel, 127 dirt, no slide-outs, 5 pull-thrus (14 x 45), back-ins (14 x 50), 25 full hkups (30 amps), WiFi Hotspot, tent sites, rentals, dump, mobile sewer, laundry, LP bottles, fire rings, firewood, restaurant, controlled access. **REC:** Tappan Lake: swim, fishing, marina, playground, rec open to public. Pets OK. Partial handicap access. 2015 rates: $27 to $35. Disc: military. ATM, no reservations.
(740)922-3649 Lat: 40.31751, Lon: -81.186521
8400 Mallarnee Rd, Deersville, OH 44693
tappanpark@mwcd.com
www.tappanparkohio.org
See ad page 888 (Welcome Section).

DELAWARE — C3 *Delaware*

ALUM CREEK (State Pk) From Jct of I-71 & Hwy 37, W 3 mi on Hwy 37 to CR-10, S 3 mi (L). 2015 rates: $26 to $38. (740)548-4631

CROSS CREEK CAMPING RESORT
Ratings: 10/10★/10 (RV Resort) From Jct of US Hwy 23 & State Rte 36/37, go E 4.5 mi on SR 36 to Lackey Old State Rd, go S 3.2 mi (R). **FAC:** Paved rds. (200 spaces). Avail: 158 all weather, patios, 46 pull-thrus (40 x 65), back-ins (35 x 65), 136 full hkups, 22 W, 22 E (30/50 amps), seasonal sites, WiFi, tent sites, rentals, dump, laundry, groc, LP gas, fire rings, firewood. **REC:** pool, Alum Creek Lake: fishing, playground. Pet restrict(B). Partial handicap access. Big rig sites, eco-friendly, 2015 rates: $34 to $66. Disc: AAA. ATM.
(740)549-2267 Lat: 40.22369, Lon: -82.93030
3190 S Old State Rd, Delaware, OH 43015
crosscreek@alumcreek.com
www.alumcreek.com/cccr/
See primary listing at Columbus and ad page 898.

DELAWARE (State Pk) From town, N 5 mi on US-23 (R). 2015 rates: $24 to $28. Apr to Dec. (740)548-4631

DUNCAN FALLS — C4 *Muskingum*

BLUE ROCK (State Pk) From Jct of SR-60 & CR-45 (Cutler Lake Rd, S of Duncan Falls), E 6 mi on CR-45 (R). Pit toilets. 2015 rates: $18. May 1 to Oct 31. (866)644-6727

EAST LIVERPOOL — C5 *Columbiana*

BEAVER CREEK (State Pk) FromJct SR 7 & US 30, N 7.9 mi on SR 7, to Bell School Rd, E 1.2 mi on Bell School Rd, enter at the second left on Echo Dell RD. 2015 rates: $24. May 1 to Oct 31. (330)385-3091

It's the law! Rules of the Road and Towing Laws are updated each year. Be sure to consult this chart to find the laws for every state on your traveling route.

FAIRFIELD — D1 *Butler, Hamilton*

Travel Services

CAMPING WORLD OF FAIRFIELD As the nation's largest retailer of RV supplies, accessories, services and new and used RVs, Camping World is committed to making your total RV experience better. **SERVICES:** RV appliance, MH mechanical, RV Sales. RV supplies. Hours: 8am - 7pm.
(513)285-6978 Lat: 39.337590, Lon: -84.528799
5300 Dixie Hwy, Fairfield, OH 45014
www.campingworld.com

FAYETTE — A1 *Fulton*

HARRISON LAKE (State Pk) From Jct of Hwy 66 & US-20, SW 2 mi on Hwy 66 to CR-M, W 1.5 mi (R). 2015 rates: $16 to $26. (419)237-2593

FINDLAY — B2 *Hancock*

FINDLAY See also Bluffton, Van Buren, Vanlue & Tiffin.

FORT LORAMIE — C1 *Shelby*

LAKE LORAMIE (State Pk) From Jct of SR-119 & SR-66, S 1 mi on SR-66 (L). 2015 rates: $27. Apr 1 to Oct 31. (937)295-2011

FREEPORT — C5 *Belmont, Harrison*

CLENDENING LAKE CAMPGROUND
(Public) From town, N 3 mi on SR-800 to SR-799, E 2 mi (L). **FAC:** Paved rds. (90 spaces). 55 Avail: 4 gravel, 51 dirt, no slide-outs, back-ins (25 x 35), 4 full hkups, 51 E (30 amps), tent sites, rentals, dump, LP bottles, fire rings, firewood. **REC:** Clendening Lake: swim, fishing, marina, playground, rec open to public. Pets OK. Partial handicap access. 14 day max stay, 2015 rates: $20 to $23. Disc: military. Apr 1 to Sep 30.
(740)658-3691 Lat: 40.242409, Lon: -81.222433
79100 Bose Rd, Freeport, OH 43973
clendeningmarina@mwcd.com
www.clendeningmarinaohio.org
See ad page 888 (Welcome Section).

GALLIPOLIS — E4 *Gallia*

GALLIA COUNTY JUNIOR FAIRGROUNDS (Public) From town, W 4 mi on US-35 (L). 2015 rates: $20. (740)446-4120

GARRETTSVILLE — B5 *Portage*

KOOL LAKES FAMILY RV PARK **Ratings: 6.5/5.5/5.5** (Campground) 2015 rates: $45 to $65. May 1 to Oct 15. (440)548-8436 12990 Nelson Ledge Road (SR282), Garrettsville, OH 44231

GENEVA — A5 *Ashtabula*

GENEVA (State Pk) From Jct of I-90 & SR-534 (exit 218), N 7 mi on SR-534 (L). 2015 rates: $26 to $35. Apr to Nov. (440)466-8400

Like Us on Facebook.

OH

GENEVA (CONT)

↓ **KENISEE'S GRAND RIVER CAMPGROUND** **Ratings: 7.5/10★/9.5** (Campground) From Jct of I-90 & SR-534 (exit 218), S 0.7 mi on SR-534 to SR-307/S River Rd E 1 mi (R). **FAC:** Gravel rds. (300 spaces). Avail: 12 gravel, 12 pull-thrus (30 x 70), 12 full hkups (30/50 amps), seasonal sites, WiFi $, tent sites, dump, mobile sewer, groc, LP gas, fire rings, firewood, restaurant, controlled access. **REC:** Grand Lake at Kenisee's: swim, fishing, shuffleboard, playground. Pets OK. Partial handicap access. Big rig sites, eco-friendly, 2015 rates: $35. May 1 to Oct 15. ATM.
(440)466-2320 Lat: 41.76295, Lon: -80.92174
4680 State Route 307E, Geneva, OH 44041
pkeniseegrc@windstream.net
www.keniseegrc.com
See ad this page, 889.

↑ WILLOW LAKE CAMPGROUND **Ratings: 7.5/9.5★/8.5** (Campground) 2015 rates: $38. May 15 to Oct 15. (440)466-0150 3935 N Broadway, Geneva, OH 44041

Travel Services

↓ **KENISEE'S GRAND RIVER RV SALES & SERVICE** RV sales, supplies, towing, emergency parking and dump station. **SERVICES:** RV, RV Sales. **TOW:** RV. RV supplies, dump, emergency parking, RV accessible. waiting room. Hours: 10am to 6pm. ATM.
(440)466-6520 Lat: 41.76295, Lon: -80.92174
4680 Rt 307 E, Geneva, OH 44041
keniseerv@hotmail.com
www.keniseegrc.com
See ad this page.

GENEVA-ON-THE-LAKE — A5 *Ashtabula*

➔ **INDIAN CREEK RV & CAMPING RESORT** **Ratings: 8.5/10★/9** (Campground) E-bnd: From Jct of I-90 & SR-534 (exit 218), N 6.4 mi on SR-534 to SR-531, E 2 mi (R); or W-bnd: From Jct of I-90 & SR-45 (exit 223), N 6 mi on SR-45 to SR-531, W 4 mi (L).

EXPERIENCE THE SHORES OF LAKE ERIE
Stay at a one-stop campground with on-site conveniences like a grocery store, gas station and full restaurant and lounge. Our 110 acres include easy access to Lake Erie, heated pools, miniature golf and planned activities.

FAC: Paved/gravel rds. (632 spaces). 250 Avail: 55 gravel, 195 grass, patios, 120 pull-thrus (40 x 75), back-ins (35 x 50), 54 full hkups, 196 W, 196 E (30/50 amps), seasonal sites, cable, WiFi, tent sites, rentals, dump, laundry, groc, LP gas, fire rings, firewood, restaurant, controlled access. **REC:** heated pool, pond, fishing, playground. Pets OK. Partial handicap access. Big rig sites, 2015 rates: $40 to $75. ATM. AAA Approved
(888)420-0893 Lat: 41.81439, Lon: -80.91064
4710 Lake Rd East, Geneva-On-The-Lake, OH 44041
indiancreekoh@suncommunities.com
www.indiancreekresort.com
See ad pages 1463 (Welcome Section), 887 (Welcome Section), 889 & Family Camping in Magazine Section.

Things to See and Do

➔ **THE LOFT RESTAURANT** Gas service station, restaurant, bar and lounge. RV accessible. Restrooms, food. Hours: Tues-Sun 11 am to 2:30 am. ATM.
(440)466-8512 Lat: 41.81438, Lon: -80.91064
4720 Lake Road East, Geneva-on-the-Lake, OH 44041
See ad page 887 (Welcome Section).

GLOUSTER — D4 *Morgan*

↑ BURR OAK (State Pk) From Jct of SR-78 & SR-13, N 4 mi on SR-13 to CR-107, E 2 mi (E). 2015 rates: $19 to $23. (740)767-3570

GRAFTON — B4 *Lorain*

➘ **AMERICAN WILDERNESS CAMPGROUND** **Ratings: 8/8.5★/9.5** (Campground) From Jct of SR 10 & SR 83, S 7.3 mi on SR-83 (L). **FAC:** Gravel rds. (166 spaces). Avail: 56 gravel, 23 pull-thrus (38 x 95), back-ins (30 x 78), 56 W, 56 E (30/50 amps), seasonal sites, WiFi, tent sites, rentals, dump, mobile sewer, laundry, groc, fire rings, firewood, controlled access. **REC:** American Wilderness Lakes: swim, fishing, playground. Pets OK. Partial handicap access. Eco-friendly, 2015 rates: $38 to $42. Disc: military. May 1 to Oct 15.
AAA Approved
(440)926-3700 Lat: 41.22443, Lon: -82.01795
17273 Avon Belden Rd, Sr 83, Grafton, OH 44044
staff@americanwildernesscampground.com
www.americanwildernesscampground.com
See ad pages 896, 889.

GRAND RAPIDS — B2 *Wood*

↑ MARY JANE THURSTON (State Pk) From Jct US 6 & SR 65, N 3.5 mi on SR 65 enter on (L). 2015 rates: $24. (419)832-7662

HARTVILLE — B4 *Stark*

↑ **CUTTY'S SUNSET CAMPING RESORT** **Ratings: 9/9★/9** (RV Park) From Jct of State Route, OH 43 & State Route OH 619, go E 5 mi on OH 619 (Maple St/Edison St) (R). **FAC:** Paved rds. (480 spaces). Avail: 80 gravel, 15 pull-thrus (30 x 70), back-ins (30 x 50), 60 full hkups, 20 W, 20 E (50 amps), seasonal sites, WiFi $, tent sites, dump, laundry, groc, fire rings, firewood, restaurant, controlled access. **REC:** heated pool, shuffleboard, playground. Pet restrict(Q). Partial handicap access. Big rig sites, eco-friendly, 2015 rates: $38 to $54. Disc: military. May 1 to Oct 15.
(800)533-7695 Lat: 40.95177, Lon: -81.24632
8050 Edison St NE, Louisville, OH 44641
info@cuttyssunset.com
www.cuttyssunset.com
See ad page 892.

HILLSBORO — D2 *Highland*

➘ ROCKY FORK (State Pk) From town, E 3.5 mi on SR-124 to N Shore Dr, NE 1 mi (R). 2015 rates: $19 to $35. (937)393-4284

↓ SHADY TRAILS FAMILY CAMPGROUND **Ratings: 6/5.5/7.5** (Campground) 2015 rates: $25 to $27. Apr 1 to Oct 31. (937)393-5618 11145 Sunset Lane, Hillsboro, OH 45133

HOMERVILLE — B4 *Medina*

↓ HOMERVILLE KOA **Ratings: 8/9★/7.5** (Campground) 2015 rates: $42. Apr 15 to Oct 16. (330)625-2817 11450 Crawford Rd, Homerville, OH 44253

HOWARD — C3 *Knox*

➔ KOKOSING VALLEY CAMP & CANOE **Ratings: 5/6.5/6** (Campground) 2015 rates: $30. May 1 to Oct 15. (740)599-7056 25860 Coshocton Rd., Howard, OH 43028

HUBBARD — B5 *Trumbull*

↖ CHESTNUT RIDGE PARK & CAMPGROUND **Ratings: 5.5/5/7** (Campground) 2015 rates: $30. May 1 to Oct 1. (330)534-2352 6486 Chestnut Ridge Rd, Hubbard, OH 44425

JEFFERSON — A5 *Ashtabula*

← KENISEE LAKE **Ratings: 7.5/8★/8** (Membership Pk) 2015 rates: $38. Apr 22 to Oct 19. (800)405-6188 2021 Mill Creek Road, Jefferson, OH 44047

↓ MILLBROOK OUTDOOR RESORT **Ratings: 6/6.5/8** (Membership Pk) 2015 rates: $49. Apr 15 to Oct 31. (440)294-3991 4051 State Route 46 S, Jefferson, OH 44047

Everyone wants to be noticed. Tell your RV Park that you found them in the this Guide.

LAKE MILTON — B5 *Mahoning*

➔ **GREEN ACRES LAKE PARK RESORT** **Ratings: 7/9★/7** (Campground) From Jct of I-76 & SR-534 (Exit 54), N 0.25 mi on SR-534 to Creed, E 0.25 mi (R). **FAC:** Gravel rds. (175 spaces). Avail: 27 gravel, 7 pull-thrus (25 x 125), back-ins (30 x 55), some side by side hkups, 27 W, 27 E (30/50 amps), seasonal sites, tent sites, rentals, dump, mobile sewer, laundry, groc, LP gas, fire rings, firewood. **REC:** Green Acres Lake: swim, fishing, playground, rec open to public. Pets OK. Partial handicap access. Eco-friendly, 2015 rates: $27 to $39. Apr 17 to Oct 1.
(330)538-2194 Lat: 41.10963, Lon: -80.94333
15487 Creed Rd, Lake Milton, OH 44429
theoffice@greenacreslakepark.com
www.greenacreslakepark.com

LAKEVIEW — C2 *Logan*

↑ INDIAN LAKE (State Pk) From Jct of US-33 & SR-235, N 2 mi on SR-235 (R). 2015 rates: $25 to $37. Apr to Oct. (937)843-3553

LANCASTER — D3 *Fairfield*

↓ LAKEVIEW PARK **Ratings: 7/8.5★/7.5** (Campground) 2015 rates: $37 to $38. (740)653-4519 2715 Sugar Grove Rd, Lancaster, OH 43130

LATHAM — D2 *Pike*

↙ LONG'S RETREAT FAMILY RESORT **Ratings: 7.5/8/8** (RV Resort) 2015 rates: $27 to $42. Apr 1 to Oct 31. (937)588-3725 50 Bell Hollow Rd, Latham, OH 45646

LAURELVILLE — D3 *Ross*

↓ TAR HOLLOW (State Pk) From Jct of SR-180 & SR-327, S 8 mi on SR-327 to Tar Hollow Rd, W 0.25 mi (R). Pit toilets. 2015 rates: $19 to $26. (740)887-4818

LEBANON — D1 *Warren*

↖ CEDARBROOK CAMPGROUND **Ratings: 7.5/8/7.5** (Campground) 2015 rates: $30 to $48. (866)999-6433 760 Franklin Rd., Lebanon, OH 45036

➔ **OLIVE BRANCH CAMPGROUND** **Ratings: 9/9.5★/9** (Campground) From Jct of I-71 & Wilmington Rd (exit 36), E 0.3 mi on Wilmington Rd (R). **FAC:** Gravel rds. (137 spaces). Avail: 92 gravel, 16 pull-thrus (50 x 60), back-ins (35 x 60), some side by side hkups, 92 full hkups (30/50 amps), seasonal sites, WiFi, tent sites, rentals, dump, laundry, groc, LP gas, fire rings, firewood. **REC:** heated pool, pond, fishing, playground. Pet restrict(B/Q). Big rig sites, 2015 rates: $35 to $40.
(513)932-CAMP Lat: 39.42967, Lon: -84.07210
6985 Wilmington Rd, Oregonia, OH 45054
olivebranchcampgroundllc@yahoo.com
www.olivebranchcampgroundllc.com
See ad this page.

LIMA — B2 *Allen*

➘ **SUN VALLEY FAMILY CAMPGROUND** **Ratings: 6/7.5/5.5** (Campground) From jct US 33 & Hwy 196: Go 8 mi N on Hwy 196, then 3 mi E on Amherst Rd, then 2 mi N on Hay Rd, then 1 blk W on Faulkner Rd. **FAC:** Poor gravel/dirt rds. (242 spaces). Avail: 75 gravel, back-ins (30 x 55), 75 full hkups (30/50 amps), seasonal sites, tent sites, laundry, groc, LP gas, fire rings, firewood. **REC:** Sun Valley Lake: swim, fishing, shuffleboard, playground, rec open to public. Pet restrict(B). Partial handicap access. 2015 rates: $28 to $30. Apr 1 to Oct 31.
(419)648-2235 Lat: 40.67252, Lon: -83.92823
9779 Faulkner Rd, Harrod, OH 45850
info@sunvalley.com
www.sunvalleycampground.com

Travel Services

↓ **STOOPS** Freightliner service center. **SERVICES:** Engine/chassis repair, emergency rd svc, restrooms. Emergency parking, RV accessible. waiting room. Hours: 7:30am to 12am.
(800)444-1589 Lat: 40.702179, Lon: -84.097137
598 E Hanthorn Rd., Lima, OH 45804
www.stoops.com
See ad page 892.

LISBON — B5 *Columbiana*

↖ GUILFORD LAKE (State Pk) From jct of SR 45 & US 30, W 1.9 mi on US 30 to SR 172, 5.6mi N on SR 172 to Teagarden RD, 0.5 mi to Camp Blvd slight right onto Lakeside Dr (R). 2015 rates: $35. (330)222-1712

LOGAN — D3 *Hocking*

← HOCKING HILLS KOA **Ratings: 8.5/10★/10** (RV Park) 2015 rates: $49 to $79. Apr 1 to Oct 31. (800)562-0251 29150 Pattor Rd, Logan, OH 43138

LOGAN (CONT)

HOCKING HILLS SP/OLD MAN'S CAVE (State Pk) From town, S 12 mi on SR-664 (L). 2015 rates: $22 to $30. (740)385-6842

LONDON — C2 *Madison*

Travel Services

CAMPING WORLD OF LONDON As the nation's largest retailer of RV supplies, accessories, services and new and used RVs, Camping World is committed to making your total RV experience better. **SERVICES:** RV appliance, MH mechanical, RV Sales. RV supplies. Hours: 8am - 7pm.
(888)603-5204 Lat: 39.958814, Lon: -83.371896
1305 N London Delaware Rd, London, OH 43140
www.campingworld.com

LOUDONVILLE — C4 *Ashland, Knox*

CAMP TOODIK FAMILY CAMPGROUND, CABINS & CANOE LIVERY **Ratings: 8/7/8** (Campground) 2015 rates: $40 to $44. Apr 15 to Oct 31. (877)886-7866 7700 Township Road 462, Loudonville, OH 44842

MOHICAN (State Pk) From town, S 3 mi on SR-3 (R). Entrance fee required in the summertime. 2015 rates: $23 to $40. (419)994-5125

MOHICAN ADVENTURES CAMPGROUND & CABINS **Ratings: 8.5/8.5/9** (Campground) 2015 rates: $35. Apr 1 to Dec 7. (419)994-2267 3058 SR-3, Loudonville, OH 44842

MOHICAN RESERVATION CAMPGROUNDS & CANOEING Ratings: 6.5/9.5★/7.5 (Campground) From Jct of CR-3 & Twp Rd 3175 (Walley Rd), S 6.4 mi on Twp Rd 3175 (Walley Rd) (L). **FAC:** Gravel rds. (201 spaces). Avail: 126 grass, back-ins (35 x 50), some side by side hkups, 126 W, 126 E (30/50 amps), seasonal sites, WiFi, tent sites, rentals, dump, mobile sewer, laundry, groc, LP bottles, fire rings, firewood. **REC:** Mohican River: swim, fishing, playground, rec open to public. Pet restrict(Q). Partial handicap access. 2015 rates: $25 to $35. Disc: military. Apr 1 to Nov 1.
AAA Approved
(800)766-2267 Lat: 40.56079, Lon: -82.19013
23270 CR-3175, Loudonville, OH 44842
mohicamp@bright.net
www.mohicanreservation.com

Heading South? We have lots of Snowbird Destination ideas to explore at the front of the Guide.

MOHICAN WILDERNESS **Ratings: 5.5/6/7.5** (Campground) 2015 rates: $24 to $45. May 1 to Oct 31. (740)599-6741 22462 Wally Rd, Glenmont, OH 44628

RIVER RUN FAMILY CAMPGROUND **Ratings: 6.5/6.5/6.5** (Campground) 2015 rates: $40 to $44. May 1 to Oct 31. (419)994-5257 3070 CR-3175, Loudonville, OH 44842

SMITH'S PLEASANT VALLEY CAMPGROUND & CABINS **Ratings: 5.5/5/8.5** (Campground) 2015 rates: $30 to $40. Apr 15 to Oct 31. (800)376-4847 16325 CR-23, Loudonville, OH 44842

WALLY WORLD CAMPING RESORT **Ratings: 8/10★/8.5** (Membership Pk) 2015 rates: $40 to $50. (419)994-4828 16121 CR 23, Loudonville, OH 44842

LOUISVILLE — B5 *Stark*

Travel Services

CUTTY'S SUNSET RV SERVICE RV sales, supplies,body repair, RV towing, LP Gas, emergency parking and RV appliance repair. Restaurant on site. **SERVICES:** RV, RV appliance, MH mechanical, restrooms, RV Sales. **TOW:** RV. RV supplies, LP, dump, emergency parking, RV accessible. Hours: 9am to 5pm.
(330)935-2431 Lat: 40.95177, Lon: -81.24632
8050 Edison St NE, Louisville, OH 44641
info@cuttyssunset.com
www.cuttyssunset.com
See ad page 892.

MANSFIELD — B3 *Ashland, Richland*

CHARLES MILL LAKE PARK (Public) From Jct of I-71 & US-30, E 3 mi on US-30 to SR-603, S 0.5 mi to SR-430 (L). **FAC:** Paved rds. (475 spaces). 225 Avail: 49 gravel, 176 dirt, back-ins (20 x 40), 225 E (30/50 amps), WiFi Hotspot, tent sites, dump, mobile sewer, LP bottles, fire rings, firewood, controlled access. **REC:** pool, Charles Mill Lake: swim, fishing, marina, playground. Pets OK. Partial handicap access. 2015 rates: $29 to $31. Disc: military.
(419)368-6885 Lat: 40.765763, Lon: -82.372873
1277A SR-430, Mansfield, OH 44903
charlesmillpark@mwcd.org
www.charlesmillparkohio.org
See ad page 888 (Welcome Section).

MALABAR FARM (State Pk) At jct of SR 39 and SR 703, S 4 mi, then W 0. 9 mi on Pleasant Valley RD, then SW 0.9mi on Bromfield Rd. 2015 rates: $19. (419)892-2784

MANTUA — B5 *Portage*

SERVICE PLAZA-BRADY'S LEAP (Public) From town, E 6 mi on OH Tpke at MP-197.0 (R). Overnight rest area (Between Exits 193 & 209). 2015 rates: $20. (440)234-2081

MARENGO — C3 *Morrow*

CARDINAL CENTER CAMPGROUND Ratings: 9/9.5★/8 (RV Park) From Jct of I-71 & SR 61 (Exit 140), N 0.3 mi on Hwy 61, go W onto Cardinal Lane Continue NW for 0.5 mi (R). **FAC:** Paved/gravel rds. 400 gravel, 52 pull-thrus (105 x 55), back-ins (55 x 35), 200 full hkups, 200 W, 200 E (30/50 amps), WiFi, tent sites, rentals, dump, laundry, LP gas, fire rings, firewood, restaurant. **REC:** heated pool, pond, fishing, playground, rec open to public. Pets OK. Partial handicap access. Big rig sites, 2015 rates: $30 to $42. Disc: military.
(419)253-0800 Lat: 40.36950, Lon: -82.83569
616 Sr 61, Marengo, OH 43334
ccoffice@yahoo.com
www.thecardinalcenter.com
See ad page 896.

MARIETTA — D4 *Washington*

WASHINGTON COUNTY FAIR PARK (Public) From jct I-77 & Hwy 821: Go 2-1/2 mi S on Hwy 821, then 6 blocks S on Hwy 60 to Washington County Fairgrounds.(No water Nov 1 - Apr 30). 2015 rates: $35. (740)373-1347

MEDINA — B4 *Medina*

PIER-LON PARK **Ratings: 7.5/6/7.5** (Campground) 2015 rates: $35 to $39. Apr 15 to Oct 15. (330)667-2311 5960 Vandemark Rd, Medina, OH 44256

MENDON — B1 *Mercer*

➔ RIVER TRAIL CAMPGROUND **Ratings: 7/8/7.5** (RV Park) 2015 rates: $31 to $33. Apr 15 to Oct 15. (419)795-1400 7712 Deep Cut Rd, Mendon, OH 45862

MINERAL CITY — C4 *Tuscarawas*

➔ **ATWOOD LAKE PARK**
(Public) From Jct of I-77 & SR-212 (exit 93), E 11 mi on SR-212 to CR-93, E 1.5 mi (E). **FAC:** Paved rds. (600 spaces). 280 Avail: 175 gravel, 105 dirt, back-ins (26 x 50), 15 full hkups, 47 W, 218 E (30 amps), WiFi Hotspot, tent sites, dump, mobile sewer, laundry, LP bottles, fire rings, firewood, restaurant. **REC:** Atwood Lake: swim, fishing, marina, playground, rec open to public. Pets OK. Partial handicap access. 2015 rates: $27 to $35. Disc: military. No CC, no reservations.
(330)343-6780 Lat: 40.541922, Lon: -81.267936
9500 Lakeview Rd NE, Mineral City, OH 44656
atwoodpark@mwcd.org
www.atwoodparkohio.org
See ad page 888 (Welcome Section).

MONTVILLE — A5 *Geauga*

➔ COUNTRY LAKES FAMILY CAMPGROUND **Ratings: 7/7.5/5.5** (Campground) 2015 rates: $30. May 1 to Oct 3. (440)968-3400 17147 Gar Hwy 6 (SR-6), Montville, OH 44064

MOUNT EATON — B4 *Wayne*

➘ **EVERGREEN PARK RV RESORT**
Ratings: 10/10★/10 (RV Park) E-bnd: From Jct of US-250 & SR 241, S 0.4 mi on US-250 (R); or From Jct of I-77 & US-250, NW 12.6 mi on US-250 (L).

OHIO'S TOP-RATED RV RESORT
A modern, premier resort in the heart of Amish Country. Enjoy our heated, indoor pool & spa with retractable roof. Our extra large pull thru sites can accommodate the largest of rigs. Cabins & deluxe suites now available too!

FAC: Paved rds. 87 paved, 48 pull-thrus (30 x 65), back-ins (30 x 55), 87 full hkups (50 amps), cable, WiFi, rentals, dump, laundry, LP gas, fire rings, firewood. **REC:** heated pool, whirlpool, shuffleboard, playground. Pet restrict(B). Partial handicap access, no tents. Big rig sites, eco-friendly, 2015 rates: $55 to $60. ATM.
(888)359-6429 Lat: 40.69114, Lon: -81.69488
16359 Dover Rd, Dundee, OH 44624
evergreenpark@wifi7.com
www.evergreenparkrvresort.com
See ad pages 891 (Spotlight Amish Country), 889.

MOUNT GILEAD — C3 *Morrow*

➔ MOUNT GILEAD (State Pk) From Jct of I-71 (exit 151) & SR-95, W 6 mi on Hwy 95 (R). Pit toilets. 2015 rates: $19 to $23. (419)946-1961

↑ YOGI BEAR'S JELLYSTONE PARK AT DOGWOOD VALLEY **Ratings: 8/10★/9** (Campground) 2015 rates: $58 to $82. May 1 to Oct 15. (419)946-5230 4185 Township Rd 99 (Mckibben), Mount Gilead, OH 43338

MOUNT STERLING — D2 *Pickaway*

↓ DEER CREEK (State Pk) From town, S 5 mi on SR-207 to Yankeetown Rd, E 2 mi (E). 2015 rates: $25 to $29. (740)869-3124

NELSONVILLE — D4 *Hocking*

↓ HAPPY HILLS CAMPGROUND & CABINS **Ratings: 8/7.5★/7.5** (Campground) 2015 rates: $43 to $70. Apr 1 to Dec 5. (740)385-6720 22245 SR-278 S.w., Nelsonville, OH 45764

NEW LONDON — B3 *Huron*

↓ NEW LONDON RESERVOIR PARK (Public) From Jct of Hwys 162 & 60, W. 8 mi on Hwy 162, S 1 mi on Euclid Rd. 2015 rates: $20 to $35. Apr 25 to Oct 25. (419)929-8609

NEW PARIS — C1 *Darke, Preble*

↑ **ARROWHEAD CAMPGROUND**
Ratings: 9/10★/10 (RV Park) From Jct of I-70 West & US 127 (exit 10): Go N 6.8 mi to OH 722,W 6.4 mi to OH 121, N 2 mi to Thomas Rd, W on Thomas 1mi (L) or From Jct of I-70 East & US 40(exit 156B INDIANA): Go E 1.1 mi on US 40 to OH 320 N 1.5 mi to OH 121, N 8 mi to Thomas Rd W 1 mi (L). **FAC:** All weather rds. (131 spaces). Avail: 26 gravel, patios, 10 pull-thrus (35 x 70), back-ins (30 x 40), 26 full hkups (30/50 amps), seasonal sites, WiFi Hotspot, tent sites, rentals, dump, laundry, LP gas, fire rings, firewood. **REC:** pool, pond, fishing, playground. Pet restrict(B). Big rig sites, eco-friendly, 2015 rates: $39 to $49. Disc: military. Apr 15 to Nov 1.
(937)996-6203 Lat: 39.94380, Lon: -84.74400
1361 Thomas Rd, New Paris, OH 45347
patmcc@arrowhead-campground.com
www.arrowhead-campground.com
See ad pages 899, 889.

↓ NATURAL SPRINGS RESORT **Ratings: 8.5/7/7.5** (Campground) 2015 rates: $45 to $50. (888)330-5771 500 S. Washington Street, New Paris, OH 45347

Our rating system isn't just tough, it's thorough. We know the kinds of things that are important to you — like clean restrooms and showers, attractive, secure, well-tended grounds, and extras like swimming pools. We give the first rating for development of facilities, the second for cleanliness and physical characteristics of restrooms and showers, and the third for visual appearance.

NEW PHILADELPHIA — C4 *Tuscarawas*

➔ **WOOD'S TALL TIMBER RESORT**
Ratings: 9.5/9.5★/10 (RV Park) From Jct of I-77 & US 250, SR 39 (Exit 81), E 5.8 mi on SR 39 (Exit 81) to Tall Timber Rd, N 1 mi (R).

ONE OF OHIO'S FINEST RESORTS
New Zipline! Lake swimming & fishing. Rental houses, cabins & cottages. Gift shop & concession stand. Delux RV sites. Minutes off I-77. Near restaurants and the world's largest Amish Community.

FAC: Paved rds. (125 spaces). Avail: 60 all weather, patios, 20 pull-thrus (30 x 90), back-ins (30 x 45), 50 full hkups, 10 W, 10 E (30/50 amps), seasonal sites, WiFi $, tent sites, rentals, dump, laundry, LP bottles, fire rings, firewood, restaurant, controlled access. **REC:** Tall Timber Lake: swim, fishing, golf, playground, rec open to public. Pets OK. Partial handicap access. Big rig sites, eco-friendly, 2015 rates: $38 to $46. Disc: AAA. May 1 to Nov 1.
AAA Approved
(330)602-4000 Lat: 40.50385, Lon: -81.37049
1921 Tall Timber Rd. NE, New Philadelphia, OH 44663
info@woodstalltimberlake.com
www.woodstalltimberlake.com
See ad this page, 889.

Things to See and Do

↑ **MUSKINGUM WATERSHED CONSERVANCY DISTRICT** Information center for the Muskingum Watershed Conservancy District covering 5 parks, 10 lakes & 3000 campsites. Restrooms. Hours: 7am to 5pm. No CC.
(330)343-6647 Lat: 40.50720, Lon: -81.45062
1319 Third St NW, New Philadelphia, OH 44663
mwcd@raex.com
www.mwcdlakes.com
See ad page 888 (Welcome Section).

NEWARK — C3 *Licking*

NEWARK See also Buckeye Lake & Zanesville.

➔ HIDDEN HILL CAMPGROUND **Ratings: 4.5/8★/6** (Campground) 2015 rates: $30. Apr 15 to Oct 15. (740)763-2750 3246 Lopers Rd NE, Newark, OH 43055

➚ **LAZY RIVER AT GRANVILLE**
Ratings: 9.5/10★/9.5 (RV Park) From Jct of I-70 & SR-37 (exit 126), N 8 mi on SR-37 to SR-661 (Granville), N 4.5 mi to Dry Creek Rd, E 1.2 mi (R).

FAMILY FUN AT ITS BEST!
Challenge course zipline, laser tag, sprayground, sand volleyball. Mini golf and a snack bar. Weekend entertainment. Gem mining and a critter catching creek. The place where kids of all ages have fun.

FAC: Paved rds. (195 spaces). Avail: 141 gravel, patios, 45 pull-thrus (37 x 80), back-ins (30 x 60), 86 full hkups, 55 W, 55 E (30/50 amps), seasonal sites, cable, WiFi $, tent sites, rentals, dump, laundry, groc, LP gas, fire rings, firewood. **REC:** heated pool, Dry Creek: shuffleboard, playground, rec open to public. Pets OK. Partial handicap access. Big rig sites, eco-friendly, 2015 rates: $35 to $60. Disc: AAA. ATM.
AAA Approved
(740)366-4385 Lat: 40.11492, Lon: -82.49932
2340 Dry Creek Rd NE, Granville, OH 43023
camp@lazyriveratgranville.com
www.lazyriveratgranville.com
See ad pages 896, 889.

NEWBURY — B5 *Geauga*

➔ PUNDERSON (State Pk) From Jct of SR-44 & SR-87, W 2 mi on SR-87 (L). 2015 rates: $25. Apr 1 to Oct 1. (440)564-1195

NEWTON FALLS — B5 *Trumbull*

↑ RIDGE RANCH FAMILY CAMPGROUND **Ratings: 6/5/7** (Campground) 2015 rates: $35. May 1 to Oct 15. (330)898-8080 5219 Sr 303 NW, Newton Falls, OH 44444

NORTH KINGSVILLE — A5 *Ashtabula*

↑ VILLAGE GREEN CAMPGROUND (Public) From Jct of I-90 & exit 235 (Rte-193), N 3 mi on Rte-193 (R). 2015 rates: $18 to $20. Apr 15 to Oct 15. (440)224-0310

NORWALK — B3 *Huron*

↓ **INDIAN TRAIL CAMPGROUND Ratings: 7.5/7/8** (Campground) From Jct of I-80 (OH Tpke) & Exit 118/US 250, S 18 mi on US 250 (L). Park is 0.5 mi N of Fitchville, 0.1 mi S of SR-162 on US 250. **FAC:** Paved rds. (169 spaces). Avail: 77 gravel, 1 pull-thrus (25 x 85), back-ins (38 x 60), 40 full hkups, 37 W, 37 E (30/50 amps), seasonal sites, WiFi Hotspot, tent sites, rentals, dump, mobile sewer, laundry, groc, fire

NORWALK (CONT)

INDIAN TRAIL CAMPGROUND (CONT)
rings, firewood. **REC:** pool, Indian Trail Lake: fishing, playground, rec open to public. Pet restrict(B). Partial handicap access. 2015 rates: $33 to $38. Disc: military. Apr 25 to Oct 4.
(419)929-1135 Lat: 41.09436, Lon: -82.48810
1400 US-250S, New London, OH 44851
eve@campindiantrail.com
www.campindiantrail.com

NOVA — B3 *Ashland*

COUNTRY STAGE CAMPGROUND **Ratings: 6.5/6/8** (Campground) 2015 rates: $45. May 1 to Oct 18. (419)652-2267 40 C Twp Rd 1031, Nova, OH 44859

OAK HILL — E3 *Jackson*

JACKSON LAKE (State Pk) In Jackson County Jct of SR 279/SR 93,W 1.3 mi to CR 8/Tommy Been Rd, N 0.7 mi on Tommy Been Rd (R). Pit toilets. 2015 rates: $35. (740)682-6197

OBERLIN — B4 *Lorain*

SCHAUN ACRES CAMPGROUND **Ratings: 6/4.5/5.5** (Campground) 2015 rates: $30 to $35. May 1 to Oct 1. (440)775-7122 51390 Rt 303, Oberlin, OH 44074

OREGON — A2 *Lucas*

MAUMEE BAY (State Pk) From Jct of I-280 & SR-2, E 6.5 mi on SR-2 to N Curtice Rd, N 2.5 mi to Cedar Point Rd, W 1 mi (R). 2015 rates: $25 to $29. Mar 31 to Sep 30. (419)836-7758

ORWELL — A5 *Ashtabula*

PINE LAKES CAMPGROUND **Ratings: 6.5/5.5/8** (Campground) 2015 rates: $32 to $35. May 10 to Oct 15. (440)437-6218 3001 Hague Rd., Orwell, OH 44076

OXFORD — D1 *Butler*

HUESTON WOODS (State Pk) From town go S 2 mi on Hwy 27 to Todd Road, (R) on Butler Israel. Follow signs. 2015 rates: $26. (513)523-6347

PERRYSVILLE — C3 *Ashland, Richland*

PLEASANT HILL LAKE PARK
(Public) From Jct of I-71 & SR-39, E on SR-39 to SR-95, W 10 mi (L). **FAC:** Paved rds. (440 spaces). 220 Avail: 4 gravel, 216 dirt, back-ins (40 x 50), 20 full hkups, 20 S, 200 E (15/30 amps), WiFi Hotspot, tent sites, rentals, dump, mobile sewer, LP bottles, fire rings, firewood, controlled access. **REC:** Pleasant Hill Lake: swim, fishing, marina, playground, rec open to public. Pets OK. Partial handicap access. 2015 rates: $31 to $37. Disc: military.
(419)938-7884 Lat: 40.645794, Lon: -82.344135
3431 Sr 95, Perrysville, OH 44864
pleasanthillpark@mwcd.org
See ad page 888 (Welcome Section).

East or west? North or south? The directional arrow in the service center and tourist attractions' listings can point you in the right direction from the town it is listed in.

PORT CLINTON — A3 *Ottawa*

CEDARLANE RV PARK
Ratings: 8.5/8.5/9 (Campground) W-bnd: From W Jct of SR-53 & SR-2, E 6.3 mi on SR-53N/SR-2 to E Jct of SR-53N/SR-2 (Catawba Island exit), N 4.5 mi on SR-53N (L); or E-bnd: From E Jct of SR-2 & SR-53N (Catawba Island exit), N 4.5 mi on SR-53N (L). **FAC:** Paved/gravel rds. (285 spaces). 67 Avail: 65 gravel, 2 grass, 39 pull-thrus (30 x 60), back-ins (25 x 60), 23 full hkups, 44 W, 44 E (30/50 amps), seasonal sites, WiFi, tent sites, rentals, dump, mobile sewer, laundry, groc, LP gas, fire rings, firewood, controlled access. **REC:** heated pool, wading pool, playground. Pets OK. Partial handicap access. Big rig sites, eco-friendly, 2015 rates: $43 to $68. Disc: military. May 1 to Oct 15.
(419)797-9907 Lat: 41.55335, Lon: -82.83780
2926 NE Catawaba Rd (Rte 53N), Port Clinton, OH 43452
cedarlanereservations@yahoo.com
www.cedarlanervpark.com
See ad this page.

EAST HARBOR (State Pk) From Jct of SR-2 & SR-269N, N 6 mi on SR-269N (R). 2015 rates: $29. (419)734-5857

ERIE ISLANDS RESORT & MARINA **Ratings: 7/7.5/8.5** (RV Resort) 2015 rates: $35.95 to $49.95. Apr 1 to Nov 1. (419)734-9117 4495 W Darr-Hopfinger Rd, Port Clinton, OH 43452

KELLEYS ISLAND (State Pk) From Newman's dock on Kelley's Island, E 0.5 mi on Water St to Division St, N 2 mi (R). 2015 rates: $33. May 1 to Oct 30. (419)746-2546

MIDDLE BASS ISLAND (State Pk) Take ferry from Port Clinton to MIDDLE BASS ISLAND. Pit toilets. 2015 rates: $20. Mar 19 to Sep 15. (419)797-4530

SOUTH BASS ISLAND (State Pk) Take ferry from Catawba Island to S Bass Island, N 0.5 mi on Langram Rd to Meechan Rd, E 0.25 mi to Catawba Ave, N 0.1 mi (R). 2015 rates: $34. Apr 1 to Oct 1. (419)734-4424

TALL TIMBERS CAMPGROUND **Ratings: 7/7/7.5** (Campground) 2015 rates: $35 to $42. May 1 to Oct 31. (419)732-3938 340 Christy Chapel Rd, Port Clinton, OH 43452

PORTSMOUTH — E3 *Scioto*

LAZY VILLAGE CAMPGROUND & RV PARK **Ratings: 7/5.5/7** (Campground) 2015 rates: $35 to $40. (740)858-2409 13610 US-52, West Portsmouth, OH 45663

SHAWNEE (State Pk) From town, W 10.2 mi on SR-52, N 6 mi on SR-125. 2015 rates: $16 to $25. (740)858-4561

RACINE — E4 *Meigs*

KOUNTRY RESORT CAMPGROUND **Ratings: 8/6/8** (Membership Pk) 2015 rates: $34. Apr 1 to Oct 31. (740)992-6488 44705 Resort Rd, Racine, OH 45771

New to RVing? Be sure to check out the all the great articles on getting the most out of your RV, at the front of the Guide.

RANDOLPH — B5 *Portage*

FRIENDSHIP ACRES PARK Ratings: 7.5/7/5 (Campground) From jct I-76 & Hwy 44: Go 3-1/2 mi S on Hwy 44. **FAC:** Gravel rds. (250 spaces). Avail: 75 grass, 10 pull-thrus (40 x 70), back-ins (40 x 60), some side by side hkups, 35 full hkups, 40 W, 40 E (50 amps), seasonal sites, WiFi $, tent sites, dump, mobile sewer, laundry, groc, LP gas, fire rings, firewood, restaurant, controlled access. **REC:** heated pool, Randolph Lake: fishing, playground, rec open to public. Pets OK. Partial handicap access. 2015 rates: $32. May 1 to Oct 15. ATM, no CC.
AAA Approved
(330)325-9527 Lat: 41.03119, Lon: -81.24939
2210 Oh 44, Randolph, OH 44265
FAParkInc@aol.com
www.friendshipacrespark.com

RAVENNA — B5 *Portage*

COUNTRY ACRES CAMPGROUND **Ratings: 8/8.5★/8.5** (Campground) 2015 rates: $47. Apr 15 to Oct 15. (330)358-2774 9850 Minyoung Rd, Ravenna, OH 44266

WEST BRANCH (State Pk) From Jct of SR-14 & SR-5, E 3.7 mi on SR-5 to Rock Springs Rd, S 0.2 mi to Park Entrance Rd, E 2 mi (E). 2015 rates: $20 to $34. (330)296-3239

REEDSVILLE — D4 *Meigs*

FORKED RUN SP (State Pk) From Jct of Hwys 681 & 124, S 3 mi on Hwy 124 (R). 2015 rates: $16 to $24. (740)378-6206

RICHMOND — C5 *Jefferson*

JEFFERSON LAKE (State Pk) From Jct of Hwy 152 & SR-43, NW 2.5 mi on SR-43 to CR-54, N 5 mi (L). Pit toilets. 2015 rates: $17. May to Sep. (740)765-4459

OH

RIPLEY — E2 *Brown*

EAGLE CREEK MARINA (COE) (Public Corps) From jct US-52 & US-62/68: Go 1-1/2 mi E on US-52/62/68. Pit toilets. May 1 to Nov 1. (937)392-4989

ROSEWOOD — C2 *Champaign*

KISER LAKE (State Pk) At jct of SR 29/SR 235, S 0. 75 mi on SR 235 to Possom Hollow Rd,E 1.5 mi on Possom Hollow Rd, to Kiser Lake Rd, N 1.3 mi (End). Pit toilets. 2015 rates: $24. (937)362-3822

ROSSFORD — A2 *Wood*

Travel Services

CAMPING WORLD OF ROSSFORD/TOLEDO
As the nation's largest retailer of RV supplies, accessories, services and new and used RVs, Camping World is committed to making your total RV experience better. RV Accessories: (855)594-4482. **SERVICES:** RV, RV appliance, MH mechanical, engine/chassis repair, restrooms, RV Sales. RV supplies, RV accessible. waiting room. Hours: 8am to 6pm.
(888)710-4692 Lat: 41.560285, Lon: -83.585963
28000 Sportsman's Drive, Rossford, OH 43460
www.campingworld.com

SALEM — B5 *Columbiana*

TIMASHAMIE FAMILY CAMPGROUND **Ratings: 7/6.5/6** (RV Park) 2015 rates: $35. Apr 1 to Oct 31. (330)525-7054 28251 Georgetown Rd, Salem, OH 44460

SANDUSKY — B3 *Erie*

SANDUSKY See also Bellevue, Clyde, Huron, New London & Port Clinton.

SANDUSKY (CONT)

CAMP SANDUSKY
Ratings: 7.5/7.5/5.5 (Campground) From Jct of SR-2 & SR-101, N 0.1 mi on SR-101 (R) No pets in tents. **FAC:** Paved/gravel rds. 115 Avail: 15 gravel, 100 grass, 22 pull-thrus (25 x 60), back-ins (24 x 50), 100 full hkups, 15 W, 15 E (30/50 amps), cable, WiFi, tent sites, rentals, dump, laundry, groc, fire rings, firewood. **REC:** heated pool, playground. Pets OK. Partial handicap access. Big rig sites, eco-friendly, 2015 rates: $30 to $69. Disc: AAA, military. May 6 to Oct 10.
(419)626-1133 Lat: 41.40472, Lon: -82.72980
3518 Tiffin Ave, Sandusky, OH 44870
info@campsandusky.com
www.campsandusky.com
See ad pages 903, 889.

CAMPER VILLAGE CEDAR POINT **Ratings: 9.5/9★/9** (Campground) 2015 rates: $80 to $125. May 6 to Oct 30. (419)627-2106 1 Cedar Point Rd., Sandusky, OH 44870

CRYSTAL ROCK CAMPGROUND **Ratings: 7.5/8.5★/8** (Campground) 2015 rates: $35 to $45. Apr 15 to Nov 1. (419)684-7177 710 Crystal Rock Ave, Sandusky, OH 44870

HURON RIVER VALLEY RESORT & CAMPGROUND
Ratings: 8/8.5★/8.5 (Campground) From Jct of I-80 (Ohio Turnpike) & US-250 (Exit 118-Norwalk), Go SE 0.8 mi on US-250 to SR-13, Go N 2.1 mi on SR-13 to E Mason Rd,Go E 0.8 mi on E Mason Rd. to River Rd, Go N 2.1 mi on River Rd (L). **FAC:** Paved/gravel rds. (200 spaces). 64 Avail: 22 gravel, 42 grass, 5 pull-thrus (24 x 100), back-ins (31 x 55), 64 W, 64 E (30/50 amps), seasonal sites, WiFi $, tent sites, rentals, dump, mobile sewer, laundry, groc, LP bottles, fire rings, firewood, controlled access. **REC:** Huron Swim Lake: swim, fishing, marina, playground. Pet restrict(B/Q). Age restrict may apply, eco-friendly, 2015 rates: $38 to $44. May 1 to Oct 10.
(419)433-4118 Lat: 41.35667, Lon: -82.54938
9019 River Rd, Huron, OH 44839
letscamp@huronrivervalley.com
www.huronrivervalley.com
See ad pages 903, 889.

MILAN TRAVEL PARK
Ratings: 9/9★/7.5 (RV Park) From Jct of I-80/I-90 & US-250 N (exit 118), N 0.25 mi on US-250N (R). **FAC:** Paved rds. (85 spaces). Avail: 68 gravel, 49 pull-thrus (27 x 64), back-ins (27 x 60), 28 full hkups, 40 W, 40 E (30/50 amps), seasonal sites, WiFi, tent sites, rentals, dump, laundry, LP gas, fire rings, firewood. **REC:** heated pool, shuffleboard, playground. Pet restrict(B). Partial handicap access. Big rig sites, eco-friendly, 2015 rates: $37 to $39. Disc: military. May 1 to Nov 1.
(800)433-4627 Lat: 41.32945, Lon: -82.62167
11404 US-250N, Milan, OH 44846
milantravelpark@gmail.com
www.staycolonial.com
See ad this page, 889.

SANDUSKY/BAYSHORE ESTATES KOA
Ratings: 10/8/8 (Campground) From Jct of I-80/I-90 & US-250 (exit 118), N 10 mi on US-250 to US-6, E 1.8 mi to Shoreway Rd, N 0.1 mi (R). **FAC:** Paved rds. (206 spaces). Avail: 84 paved, 44 all weather, 61 pull-thrus (30 x 70), back-ins (40 x 50), 82 full hkups, 46 W, 46 E (30/50 amps), seasonal sites, cable, WiFi $, tent sites, rentals, dump, laundry, groc, fire rings, firewood. **REC:** heated pool, Sandusky Bay: fishing, shuffleboard, playground. Pet restrict(Q). Big rig sites, 2015 rates: $35 to $79. Disc: military. ATM.
(800)962-3786 Lat: 41.41571, Lon: -82.68585
2311 Cleveland Rd E, Sandusky, OH 44870
reservations@koasandusky.com
www.koasandusky.com
See ad page 903.

SENECAVILLE — C4 *Guernsey, Knoble*

SENECA LAKE PARK
(Public) From Jct of I-77 & SR-313 (exit 37), E 6 mi on SR-313 to SR-574, S 1.8 mi (L). **FAC:** Paved rds. (524 spaces). Avail: 167 gravel, 10 pull-thrus (20 x 45), back-ins (20 x 50), 41 full hkups, 126 W, 126 E (30/50 amps), WiFi Hotspot, tent sites, rentals, dump, laundry, LP bottles, fire rings, firewood, restaurant, controlled access. **REC:** Seneca Lake: swim, fishing, marina, playground. Pets OK. Partial handicap access. 2015 rates: $27 to $35. Disc: military. Apr 1 to Oct 31. ATM.
(740)685-6013 Lat: 39.906047, Lon: -81.421663
22172 Park Rd, Senecaville, OH 43780
senecapark@mwcd.org
www.senecaparkohio.org
See ad page 888 (Welcome Section).

SEVILLE — B4 *Medina*

MAPLE LAKES RECREATIONAL PARK
Ratings: 8/8.5★/8.5 (Campground) From Jct of I-76 & SR-3 (exit 2), N 0.9 mi on SR-3 to Blake Rd, E 1 mi (L). **FAC:** Poor paved/dirt rds. (198 spaces). 68 Avail: 64 gravel, 4 grass, patios, 20 pull-thrus (30 x 60), back-ins (30 x 50), 62 full hkups, 6 W, 6 E (30/50 amps), seasonal sites, WiFi $, tent sites, rentals, dump, mobile sewer, laundry, groc, LP bottles, fire rings, firewood, controlled access. **REC:** heated pool, pond, fishing, playground, rec open to public. Pet restrict(Q). Partial handicap access. Eco-friendly, 2015 rates: $44. Disc: military. Apr 15 to Oct 1.
(330)336-2251 Lat: 41.03119, Lon: -81.80145
4275 Blake Rd, Seville, OH 44273
maplelakes@maplelakes.com
www.maplelakes.com
See ad this page, 889.

SHELBY — B3 *Crawford*

SHELBY-MANSFIELD KOA RESORT **Ratings: 8.5/10★/9** (RV Resort) 2015 rates: $35 to $77. May 1 to Oct 15. (888)562-5607 6787 Baker 47, Shelby, OH 44875-9103

SHREVE — B4 *Holmes*

WHISPERING HILLS JELLYSTONE RV PARK **Ratings: 8.5/9★/9.5** (Campground) 2015 rates: $39 to $49. Apr 20 to Nov 30. (800)992-2435 8248 State Route 514, Big Prairie, OH 44611

SMYRNA — C5 *Harrison*

PIEDMONT MARINA MILL LAKE & CAMPGROUND
(Public) From Jct of I-70 & SR-800, N 10 mi on SR-800 (R). **FAC:** Paved rds. (88 spaces). 44 Avail: 31 gravel, 13 dirt, no slide-outs, back-ins (14 x 40), 26 full hkups, 18 W, 18 E (30 amps), WiFi Hotspot, tent sites, rentals, dump, LP bottles, fire rings, firewood, restaurant. **REC:** Piedmont Lake: swim, fishing, marina, playground, rec open to public. Pets OK. Partial handicap access. 14 day max stay, 2015 rates: $20 to $29.50. Disc: military.
(740)658-1029 Lat: 40.166746, Lon: -81.225665
32281 Marina Rd, Freeport, OH 43973
piedmontmarina@mwcd.org
See ad page 888 (Welcome Section).

SPENCER — B4 *Medina*

SUNSET LAKE CAMPGROUND Ratings: 5.5/4.5/5 (Campground) From jct Hwy-301 & Hwy-162: Go 2-1/2 mi E on Hwy-162, then 1-1/2 mi N on CR-58 (Root Rd). **FAC:** Poor gravel rds. (204 spaces). Avail: 109 grass, back-ins (35 x 50), mostly side by side hkups, 25 full hkups, 84 W, 84 E (30/50 amps), seasonal sites, tent sites, dump, laundry, groc, LP gas, fire rings, firewood, controlled access. **REC:** Sunset Lake: swim, fishing, playground. Pets OK. 2015 rates: $29. Disc: AAA. May 1 to Oct 15. No CC.
AAA Approved
(330)667-2686 Lat: 41.11676, Lon: -82.07675
5566 Root Rd, Spencer, OH 44275
www.sunsetlakecampground.com

SPRINGFIELD — C2 *Clark*

BUCK CREEK (State Pk) From Jct of I-70 & exit 62 (Rte 40), W 3 mi on Rte 40 to North Bird, N 1 mi, follow signs (E). 2015 rates: $22 to $28. (937)322-5284

ENON BEACH CAMPGROUND
Ratings: 6.5/5/5.5 (Campground) W-bnd: From Jct of I-70 & Exit 48: Go NW 0.1 mi on Enon Rd (L) or E-bnd: From Jct of I-70 & Exit 47 (Enon exit): Go NE 1.3 mi on exit rd to Donnelsville/Enon exit, S 0.2 mi on Enon Rd (R). **FAC:** Paved rds. (117 spaces). 69 Avail: 13 paved, 47 gravel, 9 grass, 15 pull-thrus (40 x 54), back-ins (40 x 36), some side by side hkups, 15 full hkups, 54 W, 54 E (30/50 amps), seasonal sites, WiFi Hotspot, tent sites, dump, laundry, LP bottles, fire rings, firewood. **REC:** wading pool, Enon Lake: swim, fishing, playground. Pet restrict(B). Eco-friendly, 2015 rates: $37.50.
(937)882-6431 Lat: 39.89004, Lon: -83.93584
2401 Enon Rd, Springfield, OH 45502
djj84161h@yahoo.com
www.enonbeach.com
See ad page 899.

TOMORROW'S STARS RV RESORT Ratings: 7.5/6.5/7 (RV Park) From Jct of I-70 & US 40 (exit 62), E 0.3 mi on US 40 (L). **FAC:** Poor paved/gravel rds. (210 spaces). 130 Avail: 100 gravel, 30 grass, patios, 15 pull-thrus (40 x 80), back-ins (40 x 70), 130 full hkups (30/50 amps), seasonal sites, WiFi Hotspot, tent sites, rentals, laundry, LP gas, fire rings, firewood. **REC:** pool, pond, fishing, shuffleboard, playground, rec open to public. Pets OK. Partial handicap access. Big rig sites, 2015 rates: $37.
AAA Approved
(937)324-2267 Lat: 39.92432, Lon: -83.68835
6716 East National Road, South Charleston, OH 45368
tomorrowsstars@aarvparks.com
www.allamericanrvparks.com

ST MARYS — C1 *Auglaize*

GRAND LAKE ST MARYS (State Pk) From town, W 1 mi on SR-703 (L). 2015 rates: $19 to $27. (419)394-3611

STEUBENVILLE — C5 *Jefferson*

STEUBENVILLE See also Toronto, OH.

STONY RIDGE — A2 *Wood*

TOLEDO EAST/STONY RIDGE KOA **Ratings: 7.5/6/5.5** (Campground) 2015 rates: $41 to $57. Mar 15 to Oct 31. (800)562-6831 24787 Luckey Rd, Perrysburg, OH 43551

STREETSBORO — B4 *Portage*

WOODSIDE LAKE PARK
Ratings: 8/9★/9 (Campground) From Jct Ohio I-80 (exit 187 Streetsboro) & I-480, W .3 mi on I-480, right exit at Frost Rd, 3 mi E on Frost Rd to Elliman, 200 yards S on Elliman (R).

WELCOME HOME-IT'S ALL ABOUT CHOICES
Peaceful, safe, clean, cozy, classic family-oriented! Minutes from: Aurora Premium Outlet Mall, Rock 'N Roll Hall of Fame and Cuyahoga Valley National Park. Neat cabins that sleep up to eight persons.

FAC: Gravel rds. (233 spaces). 47 Avail: 14 gravel, 33 grass, 14 pull-thrus (25 x 70), back-ins (30 x 45), 4 full hkups, 43 W, 43 E (30/50 amps), seasonal sites, WiFi $, tent sites, rentals, dump, mobile sewer, laundry, groc, LP gas, fire rings, firewood. **REC:** Woodside Lake: swim, fishing, playground, rec open to public. Pet restrict(Q). Partial handicap access. Age restrict may apply, big rig sites, eco-friendly, 2015

STREETSBORO (CONT)

WOODSIDE LAKE PARK (CONT)
rates: $35 to $45. Disc: AAA, military. Apr 15 to Oct 15.
AAA Approved
(866)241-0492 Lat: 41.25914, Lon: -81.30288
2486 Frost Rd, Streetsboro, OH 44241
woodside@woodsidelake.com
www.woodsidelake.com
See ad pages 896, 889.

SULLIVAN — B4 *Ashland, Lorain*

↑ RUSTIC LAKES **Ratings: 7.5/5.5/7** (Campground) 2015 rates: $34. May 1 to Oct 15. (440)647-3804 44901 New London Eastern Rd, Sullivan, OH 44880

SUNBURY — C3 *Columbus, Delaware*

↑ **AUTUMN LAKES**
Ratings: 10/10★/10 (Campground) From Jct of I-71 & SR-36/37 (Exit 131 towards Sunbury), N 0.2 mi on Wilson Rd/SR-656, N 8.5 mi to Porter Central, S 0.2 mi (L). **FAC:** Paved rds. (140 spaces). Avail: 36 all weather, patios, 14 pull-thrus (30 x 63), back-ins (30 x 50), 36 full hkups (50 amps), seasonal sites, WiFi $, tent sites, rentals, dump, laundry, groc, LP gas, fire rings, firewood, controlled access. **REC:** pool, pond, fishing, playground. Pets OK. Partial handicap access. Big rig sites, eco-friendly, 2015 rates: $42 to $62. Apr 15 to Oct 15. ATM.
(740)625-6600 Lat: 40.32518, Lon: -82.78952
8644 Porter Central Rd, Sunbury, OH 43074
autumnlakescampground@gmail.com
www.autumnlakescampground.com
See ad this page, 889.

SWANTON — A2 *Lucas*

↘ BIG SANDY CAMPGROUND **Ratings: 5/8★/4.5** (Campground) 2015 rates: $25. Apr 26 to Oct 1. (419)826-8784 4035 S Berkey Southern, Swanton, OH 43558

↓ **BLUEGRASS CAMPGROUND Ratings: 8/7/6.5** (Campground) From Jct of I-80 (OH Tpke) & Exit 52/SR-2, W 3.5 mi on SR-2 to SR-64, S 3.2 mi (L). **FAC:** Gravel rds. (96 spaces). 10 Avail: 5 gravel, 5 grass, 4 pull-thrus (30 x 50), back-ins (35 x 40), 3 full hkups, 7 W, 7 E (30/50 amps), seasonal sites, WiFi $, tent sites, dump, mobile sewer, laundry, LP gas, fire rings, firewood, controlled access. **REC:** Pine Tree Lake: swim, fishing, playground. Pet restrict(B/Q). 2015 rates: $28 to $30. Apr 1 to Oct 30.
(419)875-5110 Lat: 41.59973, Lon: -83.87512
5751 Waterville-Swanton Rd, Swanton, OH 43558
bluegrasscamp@aol.com
bluegrasscampground.com

THOMPSON — A5 *Geauga*

↗ **HERITAGE HILLS RV PARK**
Ratings: 9/8.5★/9.5 (Campground) From Jct of I-90 & Rte 528 (exit 212), S 1.9 mi on Rte 528 to Ledge Rd, S 2.5 mi (L). **FAC:** Gravel rds. (160 spaces). Avail: 30 gravel, 25 pull-thrus (50 x 75), back-ins (40 x 55), 27 full hkups, 3 W, 3 E (50 amps), seasonal sites, WiFi $, tent sites, rentals, dump, mobile sewer, laundry, groc, LP bottles, fire rings, firewood, controlled access. **REC:** heated pool, Heritage Lake: fishing, playground. Pets OK. Partial handicap access. Big rig sites, eco-friendly, 2015 rates: $37 to $40. May 1 to Oct 31.
(440)298-1311 Lat: 41.68852, Lon: -81.03385
6445 Ledge Rd, Thompson, OH 44086
info@heritagehillsrvpark.com
www.heritagehillsrvpark.com
See ad pages 896, 889.

TIFFIN — B3 *Seneca*

↖ **CLINTON LAKE CAMPING**
Ratings: 6.5/5.5/7.5 (Campground) From Jct US-224 & SR-67: Go 1/4 mi E on SR-67, then 5 mi N on CR-43, then 1-1/10 mi W on Twp Rd 122 (Center Rd) (L). **FAC:** Gravel rds. (160 spaces). Avail: 35 grass, 10 pull-thrus (30 x 40), back-ins (30 x 40), 35 W, 35 E (30 amps), seasonal sites, WiFi $, tent sites, dump, mobile sewer, groc, fire rings, firewood. **REC:** Clinton Lake: swim, fishing, playground. Pets OK. Partial handicap access. 2015 rates: $29. May 1 to Oct 15.
(419)585-3331 Lat: 41.12664, Lon: -83.06924
4990 E Twp Rd-122, Republic, OH 44867
clinton_lake20@yahoo.com
See ad this page.

↓ WALNUT GROVE CAMPGROUND **Ratings: 5/5.5/6** (Campground) 2015 rates: $30 to $39. May 1 to Oct 31. (419)448-0914 7325 S Twp Rd 131, Tiffin, OH 44883

TOLEDO — A2 *Lucas*

TOLEDO See also Bowling Green, Stony Ridge, Swanton, Van Buren & Whitehouse; Monroe, MI, Ottawa Lake, MI & Petersburg, MI.

TORONTO — C5 *Jefferson*

↗ **AUSTIN LAKE RV PARK & CABINS**
Ratings: 8.5/10★/9.5 (Campground) From Jct of Hwy 22 & SR-43 (Carrollton-Wintersville exit), N 4 mi on SR-43 to SR-152, NE 4 mi to Twp Hwy 285A, SW 1.5, follow signs (L). Do not use GPS the last 20 miles. **FAC:** Paved/gravel rds. (250 spaces). Avail: 13 all weather, 77 grass, patios, 1 pull-thrus (34 x 70), back-ins (50 x 75), 17 full hkups, 73 W, 73 E (50 amps), seasonal sites, WiFi, tent sites, rentals, showers $, dump, mobile sewer, laundry, groc, LP bottles, fire rings, firewood, controlled access. **REC:** Austin Lake: swim, fishing, playground. Pets OK. Partial handicap access. Big rig sites, eco-friendly, 2015 rates: $50.
(740)544-5253 Lat: 40.48642, Lon: -80.73744
1002 Twp Road 285A, Toronto, OH 43964
austinlakepark@gmail.com
www.austinlakepark.com
See ad opposite page, 889.

UNIONTOWN — B4 *Stark*

→ CLEARWATER JELLYSTONE **Ratings: 8.5/8.5★/8** (RV Park) 2015 rates: $44 to $61. (330)877-9800 12712 Hoover Ave NW, Uniontown, OH 44685

VAN BUREN — B2 *Hancock*

→ **PLEASANT VIEW RECREATION**
Ratings: 9/10★/10 (Campground) From Jct of I-75 & SR-613 (exit 164): Go E 0.7 mi on SR-613 to Twp Rt-218, S 0.5 mi (R). **FAC:** Paved/gravel rds. (320 spaces). Avail: 160 gravel, patios, 38 pull-thrus (28 x 75), back-ins (24 x 45), 28 full hkups, 132 W, 132 E (30/50 amps), seasonal sites, WiFi, tent sites, rentals, dump, mobile sewer, laundry, groc, LP gas, fire rings, firewood, controlled access. **REC:** pool, pond, fishing, shuffleboard, playground. Pets OK. Big rig sites, eco-friendly, 2015 rates: $26.95 to $42.95. Disc: military. Apr 1 to Nov 1.
(419)299-3897 Lat: 41.10260, Lon: -83.66089
12611 Allen Township Rd 218, Van Buren, OH 45889
campfire7@frontier.com
www.pleasantviewcampgroundandcabins.com/
See ad this page, 889.

→ VAN BUREN (State Pk) From Jct of I-75 & Hwy 613, E 1 mi on Hwy 613 to State Park Rd, S 1 mi (R). Pit toilets. 2015 rates: $16 to $24. (419)832-7662

VAN WERT — B1 *Van Wert*

← HUGGY BEAR CAMPGROUND **Ratings: 7/6.5/6.5** (Campground) 2015 rates: $32 to $38. Apr 15 to Oct 15. (419)968-2211 9065 Ringwald Rd, Middle Point, OH 45863

↙ TIMBERWOODS CAMPING RESORT **Ratings: 7/6/7** (Campground) 2015 rates: $30 to $33. Apr 1 to Nov 1. (419)238-1124 10856 A Liberty Union Rd, Van Wert, OH 45891

VANLUE — B2 *Hancock*

→ HERITAGE SPRINGS CAMPGROUND **Ratings: 8/8.5★/9.5** (Campground) 2015 rates: $33 to $38. Apr 17 to Oct 25. (419)387-7738 13891 Twp Rd 199, Vanlue, OH 45890

WALNUT CREEK — C4 *Holmes*

↑ **KANDELS' CAMPING & RV PARK Ratings: 6.5/9★/7.5** (Campground) From Jct of US-62 & SR 515, S 3.9 mi on SR 515 (L); or From Jct of SR-39 & SR-515, E 1.4 mi on SR-515 (R). **FAC:** Gravel rds. 66 gravel, 32 pull-thrus (25 x 72), back-ins (35 x 50), 32 full hkups, 34 W, 34 E (30/50 amps), WiFi, tent sites, dump, laundry, fire rings, firewood. **REC:** playground. Pet restrict(B). Partial handicap access. Big rig sites, 2015 rates: $33. Apr 1 to Oct 31.
(330)893-2720 Lat: 40.55931, Lon: -81.72054
5552 State Route 515, Millersburg, OH 44687
tdkandel@kandels-RV-camping.com
www.kandels-rv-camping.com

WAPAKONETA — C1 *Auglaize*

→ WAPAKONETA KOA **Ratings: 9/10★/9** (Campground) 2015 rates: $44 to $70. Mar 15 to Nov 15. (419)738-6016 14719 Cemetary Rd, Wapakoneta, OH 45895

WAUSEON — A2 *Fulton*

↗ SUNNY'S CAMPGROUND SHADY RECREATION AREA **Ratings: 6/7.5/6.5** (Campground) 2015 rates: $30. Apr 30 to Oct 10. (419)337-3101 12399 C.r. 13, Wauseon, OH 43567

OH

WAYNESVILLE — D2 *Clinton, Warren*

→ CAESAR CREEK (State Pk) From town, E 8 mi on SR-73 to SR-380, N 3 mi to Center Rd, W 1 mi (E). 2015 rates: $25 to $29. (937)488-4595

↗ FRONTIER CAMPGROUND **Ratings: 9/10★/9** (Campground) 2015 rates: $31.50 to $47.50. (937)488-1127 9580 Collette Rd, Waynesville, OH 45068

WELLINGTON — B4 *Lorain*

↓ FINDLEY SP (State Pk) From Jct of Hwys 18 & 58, S 2.5 mi on Hwy 58 (L). 2015 rates: $22 to $28. (440)647-4490

WELLSTON — D3 *Vinton*

↗ LAKE ALMA (State Pk) From town, N 1 mi on Hwy 93 to Hwy 349, NE 1 mi (R). Pit toilets. 2015 rates: $16 to $24. Mar 31 to Sep 30. (740)384-4474

WEST LIBERTY — C2 *Logan*

↖ OAK CREST CAMPGROUND **Ratings: 6/6.5/6** (Campground) 2015 rates: $30 to $40. Apr 15 to Oct 31. (937)593-7211 4226 Twp Rd 187, West Liberty, OH 43357

WEST SALEM — B4 *Wayne*

← HIDDEN ACRES CAMPGROUND (RV Area in MHP) (Rebuilding) 2015 rates: $36. Apr 15 to Oct 15. (419)853-4687 107 Township Road 810 #40, West Salem, OH 44287

→ TOWN & COUNTRY CAMP RESORT **Ratings: 8/6.5/6.5** (RV Park) 2015 rates: $31 to $40. Apr 1 to Nov 1. (419)853-4550 7555 Shilling Rd, West Salem, OH 44287

Tell them you saw them in this Guide!

WEST UNITY — A1 *Williams*

➔ SERVICE PLAZA-INDIAN MEADOW (Public) From town, W on OH Tpke, at MP-20.8 (R). Overnight rest area (Between Exits 13 & 15). 2015 rates: $20. (440)234-2081

WHITEHOUSE — A2 *Lucas*

➔ TWIN ACRES CAMPGROUND **Ratings: 6.5/7/7.5** (Campground) 2015 rates: $29 to $45. May 1 to Oct 15. (419)877-2684 12029 Waterville-Swanton Rd (Rte 64), Whitehouse, OH 43571

WILLARD — B3 *Huron*

➔ AUBURN LAKE PARK **Ratings: 6.5/7.5/7** (Campground) 2015 rates: $15. Apr 15 to Oct 15. (419)492-2110 6881 S.r. 103 East, New Washington, OH 44854

WILMINGTON — D2 *Clinton*

BEECHWOOD ACRES CAMPING RESORT **Ratings: 8.5/9.5★/10** (RV Park) 2015 rates: $35 to $65. Apr 1 to Oct 31. (937)289-2202 855 Yankee Rd, Wilmington, OH 45177

COWAN LAKE (State Pk) From town, S 3 mi on US-68 to Dalton Rd, W 1.5 mi (L). 2015 rates: $20 to $29. (937)383-3751

➔ WILMINGTON RV RESORT **Ratings: 7/7.5/7.5** (Membership Pk) 2015 rates: $47. Apr 18 to Oct 19. (800)405-6188 1786 State Route 380, Wilmington, OH 45177

WILMOT — C4 *Stark*

BAYLOR BEACH PARK

Ratings: 7.5/9.5★/10 (Campground) From Jct of US 250 & US 62: Go 2 mi E on US 62 (at jct US 62 & Hwy 93). (L). **FAC:** Paved rds. 60 Avail: 60 all weather, 33 pull-thrus (30 x 60), back-ins (30 x 90), 20 full hkups, 40 W, 40 E (50 amps), WiFi, tent sites, dump, mobile sewer, fire rings, firewood, controlled access. **REC:** Baylor Beach Park: swim, playground, rec open to public. Pet restrict(B/Q). Partial handicap access. Big rig sites, 14 day max stay, eco-friendly, 2015 rates: $35. Disc: AAA, military. May 1 to Oct 15.
AAA Approved
(888)9BAYLOR Lat: 40.68690, Lon: -81.59941
8777 Manchester SW, Navarre, OH 44662
www.baylorbeachpark.com
See ad pages 890 (Spotlight Amish Country), 889.

WINESBURG — C4 *Holmes*

AMISH COUNTRY CAMPSITES

Ratings: 5.5/7/8 (Campground) E-bnd: From Jct of SR-39 & US-62 (Berlin), NE 7 mi on US-62 (R); or W-bnd: From W Jct of US-250 & US-62 (Wilmot), SW 4 mi on US-62 (L). **FAC:** Gravel rds. 60 gravel, 8 pull-thrus (25 x 40), back-ins (25 x 40), 60 W, 60 E (30 amps), WiFi, tent sites, rentals, dump, fire rings, firewood. **REC.** Pets OK. 2015 rates: $29. Apr 1 to Nov 15.
AAA Approved
(330)359-5226 Lat: 40.61979, Lon: -81.69418
1930 US 62 NE, Winesburg, OH 44690
www.amishcountrycampsites.com
See ad page 894.

WOOSTER — B4 *Wayne*

MEADOW LAKE PARK **Ratings: 5/NA/6.5** (Campground) Pit toilets. 2015 rates: $30. May 1 to Nov 1. (330)435-6652 8970 Canaan Center Rd, Wooster, OH 44691

YELLOW SPRINGS — D2 *Greene*

➔ JOHN BRYAN (State Pk) From Jct of SR-343 & SR-370, S 1 mi on SR-370 (L). Pit toilets. 2015 rates: $18 to $22. (937)767-1274

Don't camp without it ... Our 2016 listings are your key to travel satisfaction.

ZALESKI — D3 *Vinton*

LAKE HOPE (State Pk) From Jct of SR-50 & Hwy 278, N 4 mi on Hwy 278, follow signs (L). 2015 rates: $16 to $24. (740)596-4938

ZANESVILLE — C4 *Muskingum*

➔ DILLON (State Pk) From Jct of SR-16 & SR-146, E 7 mi on SR-146 to Clay Littick Dr, S 1 mi to park entrance (R). 2015 rates: $26. (740)453-4377

MUSKINGUM RIVER (State Pk) From town, N 6 mi on Hwy 60 to Powellson Rd, E 11 mi to Lock & Dam #11, follow signs (L). Pit toilets. 2015 rates: $18. (740)453-4377

According to some studies, almost 50 percent of RVers camp with pets! Find out more about the joys of traveling with your four-legged companions in our Pampered Pet Parks feature at the front of the Guide.

WOLFIES CAMPGROUND

Ratings: 9/9.5★/10 (Campground) From Jct of I-70 & SR-146 W (Exit 155, Eastbound must turn left at bottom of the ramp onto Elberon), W 0.25 mi on SR-146, N 0.75 mi on OH-666, N 0.75 mi on Lewis Dr (OH-666), first right past Riverside Park, (Buckeye Dr), E 0.2 mi on Buckeye Dr (L). **FAC:** Gravel rds. 54 gravel, patios, 21 pull-thrus (30 x 65), back-ins (30 x 62), 46 full hkups, 8 W, 8 E (30/50 amps), WiFi, tent sites, rentals, dump, laundry, groc, fire rings, firewood. **REC:** heated pool, playground. Pets OK. Big rig sites, eco-friendly, 2015 rates: $34 to $36. Disc: military. ATM.
(740)454-0925 Lat: 39.96466, Lon: -81.98933
101 Buckeye Dr, Zanesville, OH 43701
wolfieskamping1@yahoo.com
www.wolfiescampground.com
See ad this page, 889.

Lend a hand. During the busy season park services are stretched to the max! Please do your best to keep your area "ship-shape".

WELCOME TO Oklahoma

DATE OF STATEHOOD	WIDTH: 230 MILES (370 KM)	PROPORTION OF UNITED STATES
NOV. 16, 1907	LENGTH: 298 MILES (480 KM)	1.84% OF 3,794,100 SQ MI

Oklahoma is full of surprises. The Sooner State has the most diverse terrain of any state in the Union. You'll also find the headquarters of 39 Native American nations and a pioneer spirit that thrives well into the 21st century.

To see real-life cowboys and cowgirls, check out the Oklahoma City Stockyards' twice-weekly auctions. Tour the National Cowboy and Western Heritage Museum in Oklahoma City to see traditional cowboy artists, photos of the American West and Oklahoma History. Oklahoma was the home of the Dust Bowl in the 1930s, but today has more artificial lakes than any state.

Fans of Route 66 will love the fact that the Sooner State retains more drivable miles of Route 66 than any other state, rolling past relics like Totem Pole Park and museums such as the Route 66 Interpretive Center in Chandler.

The rounded hills of Eastern Oklahoma boast elevations high enough to produce 77-foot Turner Falls in the Arbuckle Mountains. Big game is so abundant in the Ouachita Mountains that one of the towns is named Antlers.

For big city thrills, check out Oklahoma City's refurbished midtown district, which is lined with trendy restaurants and shops. Tulsa, meanwhile, is a haven for lovers of Art Deco architecture.

TRAVEL & TOURISM

Oklahoma Tourism & Recreation Dept.
800-652-6552, 405-230-8400
www.travelok.com

Bartlesville Area Chamber-CVB
866-364-8708, 918-336-8708
www.visitbartlesville.org

Broken Arrow CVB
918-259-2400
www.brokenarrowok.gov

Claremore CVB
877-341-8688, 918-341-8688
www.visitclaremore.org

Duncan CVB
800-782-7167
www.duncanok.org

Edmond CVB-Chamber
405-341-4344
www.visitedmondok.com

Norman CVB
www.visitnorman.com

Oklahoma City CVB
800-225-5652, 405-297-8912
www.okccvb.org

Shawnee CVB
www.visitshawnee.com

Tulsa CVB
www.tulsachamber.com

Top 3 Tourism Attractions:
1) Wichita Mountains Wildlife Refuge
2) Chisholm Trail Heritage Museum
3) Oklahoma City Zoological Park

Nickname: Sooner State

State Flower: Mistletoe

State Bird: Scissor-Tailed Flycatcher

People: Garth Brooks, singer; Ron Howard, actor, director and producer; Mickey Mantle, baseball player; Chuck Norris, martial artist and actor; Will Rogers, humorist; Sam Walton, Wal-Mart founder

Major Cities: Oklahoma City (capital), Tulsa, Norman, Broken Arrow, Lawton

Topography: West—high plains; east—hills, small mountains; east central—Arkansas River Basin; south—Red River Plains

Climate: Continental climate; cold winters, hot summers; east—humid subtropical; west—semi-arid

OK

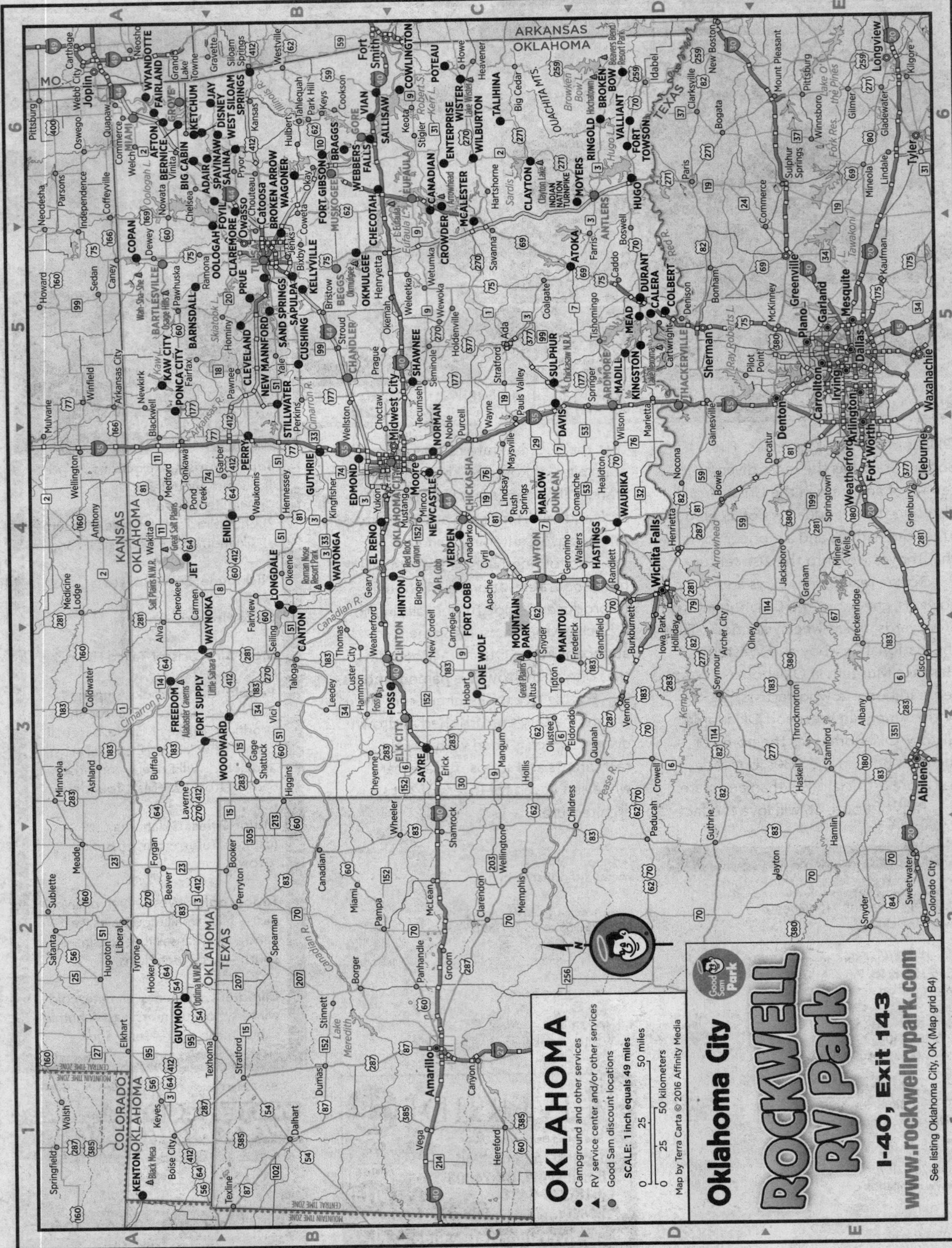
OKLAHOMA
Campground and other services
RV service center and/or other services
Good Sam discount locations
SCALE: 1 inch equals 49 miles
0 25 50 miles
0 25 50 kilometers
Map by Terra Carta © 2016 Affinity Media
Good Sam Park
Oklahoma City
ROCKWELL RV Park
I-40, Exit 143
www.rockwellrvpark.com
See listing Oklahoma City, OK (Map grid B4)
KANSAS
OKLAHOMA
TEXAS
COLORADO
ARKANSAS
MO.
OKLAHOMA CITY
TULSA
Amarillo
Wichita Falls
Dallas
Fort Worth

Featured Good Sam Parks

OKLAHOMA

When you stay with Good Sam, you can expect the highest degree of cleanliness and friendliness, and better yet, you get 10% off campground fees.

If you're not already a Good Sam member you can purchase your membership at one of these locations:

ANTLERS
Antlers RV Park
(580)298-9008

ARDMORE
Hidden Lake RV Park
(580)220-2900
Oswalt RV Resort
(580)276-2800

BARTLESVILLE
Riverside RV Resort & Campground
(918)336-6431

BEGGS
Tulsa RV Ranch
(918)267-9000

CHANDLER
Oak Glen RV Park
(405)258-2994

CHICKASHA
Pecan Grove RV Resort
(405)224-0500

ELK CITY
Elk Creek RV Park
(580)225-7865

EUFAULA
Little Turtle RV & Storage
(918)618-2140

GORE
Marval Resort
(800)340-4280

GROVE
Cedar Oaks RV Resort
(800)880-8884

LAWTON
Buffalo Bobs RV Park
(580)699-3534

MUSKOGEE
Hidden Valley RV Park
(918)681-4457

OKLAHOMA CITY
Council Road RV Park
(405)789-2103
Mustang Run RV Park
(405)577-6040
Roadrunner RV Park
(405)677-2373
Rockwell RV Park
(405)787-5992

THACKERVILLE
Winstar RV Park
(580)276-8900

TULSA
Mingo RV Park
(918)832-8824

For more Good Sam Parks go to listing pages

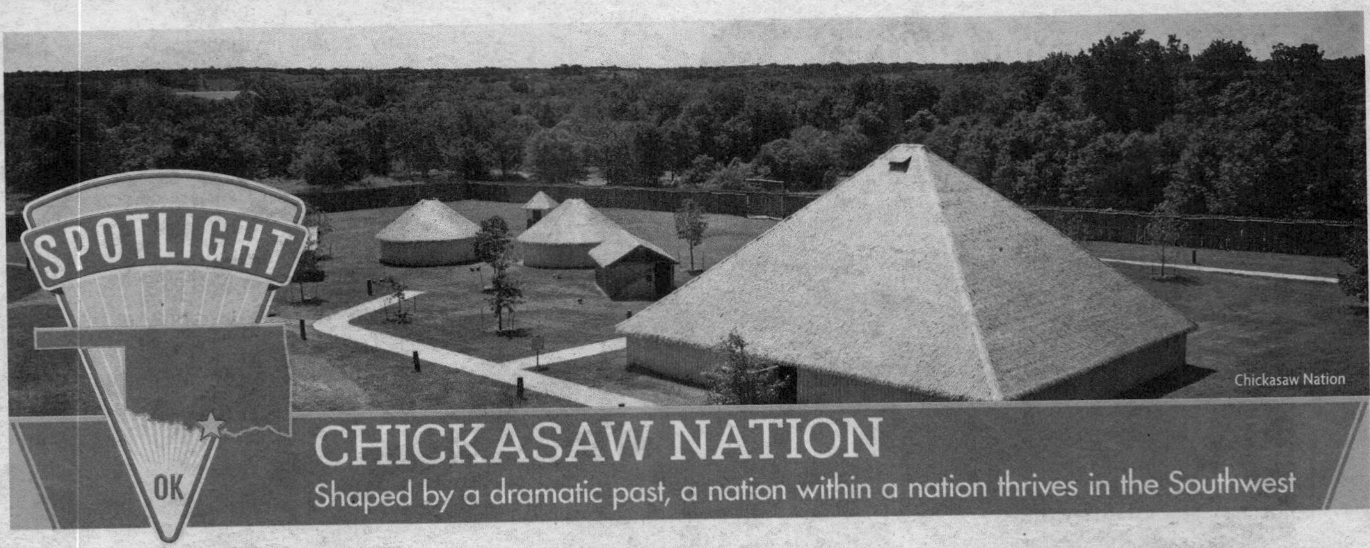

CHICKASAW NATION

Shaped by a dramatic past, a nation within a nation thrives in the Southwest

Despite being born out of turmoil, the people of Chickasaw Nation have survived to create a vital, vibrant community of great cultural import. Now a federally recognized Native American nation, Chickasaw Nation was established when the Chickasaw tribes were relocated to Indian Territory as part of the federal initiative that became known as the Trail of Tears. However, rather than let this incident define them, the citizens of Chickasaw Nation have instead gone on to create one of the most truly unique locales in the United States, a nation among states.

As you would expect, one of the great calling cards of the Chickasaw Nation is its storied culture. The first visit for the history buff inside you should be the Chickasaw Cultural Center. The vast complex includes a sprawling campus grounds consisting of a beautiful stone garden that honors many of the great citizens of Chickasaw Nation.

Also on display is a series of bronze statues commemorating the Chickasaw arrival to Indian Territory upon completing the Trail of Tears and a breathtaking amphitheater that plays host to cultural presentations and living history performances. The Chickasaw Cultural Center also boasts a bustling exhibit center, two beautifully ornate fine art galleries, a traditional village to showcase the historic lives of the original Chickasaw people and many more compelling exhibits.

Culture on Display

The Chickasaw Council House Museum in nearby Tishomingo features one of the nation's largest collections of Chickasaw art, artifacts and archive materials.

> The Chickasaw Cultural Center boasts an exhibit center, two beautifully ornate fine art galleries and replica of a traditional village.

Stop by the gift shop on your way out and browse pottery, jewelry, beadwork and paintings by Chickasaw artists. For a glimpse into the authentic past of the native citizens, make sure to visit the Kullihoma Grounds, a tribal reserve that was once used as a school and stomping grounds. Today, it continues to thrive as not only a gathering ground for the Chickasaw people, but as a looking glass into recent history. If your feet are up to it, check out all the 1,500-acres grounds, including eye-opening replicas of traditional dwellings.

Supporters of more modern art can feast their eyes on creations by Chickasaw artists and get in on the act. ARTesian Gallery & Studios, in downtown Sulphur, features an art gallery where artists can display their work for sale. Also offered are art classes for visitors in the mood to test their creative vision.

Cards and Clubs

As is the case for many Native American communities, the casino industry is one of the bedrocks of the Chickasaw Nation economy. This means that for visitors seeking to press their luck on games of chance, there are several viable options. Two deserve special

A panorama of Chickasaw people on display in the Cultural Center.—Chickasaw Nation

WinStar Golf Course Clubhouse. Chickasaw Nation

mention here, one for being the first gaming facility established by the Chickasaw Nation and the second for simply being the largest. Established in 1983 as a bingo hall, Ada Gaming Center has moved into the modern age with over 22,000 feet of electronic games and four table games to test your gambling skill.

The immense WinStar Casino & Resort, on the other hand, prides itself in being the "largest casino in the entire world." Indeed, if you are going here, bring the walking shoes, because the casino is home to 500,000 square feet of gaming, including 7,400 electronic games, 96 game tables, a bingo hall, fully functioning poker hall and off-track betting areas.

By the way, if you do happen to be in the area of the WinStar and you are the type of person who packs the clubs in the RV when going on trips, you owe it to yourself to check out the WinStar Golf Course. The beautiful course is challenging enough to be worth your time, but so not difficult that you'll want to throw your clubs in one of the many visually inviting bodies of water.

If you have kids in tow, Lazer Zone Family Fun Center needs to be on your list. The facility offers an arcade with more than 100 games, bowling lanes that glow during evening hours, miniature golf and a laser tag arena.

Dining options are copious in Chickasaw Nation, and you certainly can't go wrong with Springs at the Artesian. Located inside the Artesian Hotel in Sulphur, the restaurant features menu items starting as low as $7 and features burgers, pastas, steaks and salads. Want to go straight to dessert? Then check out Bedré Fine Chocolate. Located in Davis, this shop includes a wide selection of gourmet chocolates.

For More Information

Chickasaw Nation
580-436-2603
www.chickasaw.net

Oklahoma Tourism and Recreation Department
800-652-6552
www.travelok.com

Oklahoma

CONSULTANTS

Chuck & Alyce Grover

ADAIR — B6 *Mayes*

HORSESHOE INN & CAMPGROUND **Ratings: 6/8/6.5** (Campground) 2015 rates: $30 to $35. (918)809-3341 3296 E. 4675 Road, Adair, OK 74330

Shop at Camping World and SAVE with over $1,000 of coupons. Check the front of the Guide for yours!

AFTON — A6 *Ottawa*

MONKEY ISLAND RV RESORT

(RV Resort) (Too New to Rate) From jct of I-44 & US 59/60 (Exit 302), go S 5.5 mi on US 59 to jct of US 59 & OK 125, then S 3.0 mi. on OK 125, to jct of OK 125 & E 280, then E .1 mi on E 280 (L). **FAC:** Paved rds. 71 paved, patios, 29 pull-thrus (34 x 75), back-ins (34 x 60), 71 full hkups (30/50 amps), WiFi, rentals, dump, laundry, groc. **REC:** pool, playground. Pets OK. Partial handicap access. Big rig sites, 2015 rates: $40 to $50. Disc: military.
(918)257-6400 Lat: 36.613228, Lon: -94.869668
56140 E. 280 Road, Afton, OK 74331
info@monkeyislandrv.com
www.monkeyislandrv.com
See ad this page.

ANTLERS — D6 *Pushmataha*

ANTLERS RV PARK

Ratings: 6.5/7.5★/7 (RV Park) From Jct of Indian Nation Turnpike & SR 3 (exit Antlers/Atoka): Go E on SR 3 1-1/4 mi to N.W. J St., then N 1/4 mi on N.W. J St (R). **FAC:** Gravel rds. (29 spaces). Avail: 21 gravel, 5 pull-thrus (26 x 60), back-ins (26 x 49), 21 full hkups (30/50 amps), seasonal sites, WiFi, laundry. **REC:** pond. Pets OK. No tents. Big rig sites, 2015 rates: $22 to $24. No CC.
(580)298-9008 Lat: 34.234215, Lon: -95.634048
220 N.W. J Street, Antlers, OK 74523
bobncheryl@antlersrvparkok.com
www.antlersrvparkok.com
See ad this page, 909.

LITTLE RIVER PARK (COE PINE CREEK LAKE) (Public Corps) From town: Go 29 mi E on Hwys-7 & 3, then 3/4 mi SE on paved county road. Pit toilets. 2015 rates: $10 to $23. Apr 1 to Sep 29. (580)876-3720

Traveling with a Fido? Many campground listings indicate pet-friendly amenities and pet restrictions.

Keep one Guide at home, and one in your RV! To purchase additional North American Edition copies, call 877-209-6655.

ARDMORE — D5 *Carter*

BY THE LAKE RV PARK RESORT
(RV Park) (Too New to Rate) From jct of I-35 (exit 24) & OK-77 S: Go E 1/2 mi (L). **FAC:** Paved rds. (128 spaces). Avail: 90 paved, no slide-outs, patios, 90 pull-thrus (30 x 75), 90 full hkups (30/50 amps), seasonal sites, cable, WiFi, laundry, LP gas. **REC:** pond, fishing, playground. Pets OK. Partial handicap access. 2015 rates: $35 to $40. Disc: AAA.
(580)798-4721 Lat: 34.071006, Lon: -97.121483
1031 Lodge Road, Ardmore, OK 73401
info@bythelakerv.com
www.bythelakerv.com
See ad this page & Pampered Pets in Magazine Section.

CEDARS EDGE RV PARK **Ratings: 5.5/5.5/6.5** (Campground) 2015 rates: $25. (580)226-2266 3433 Highway 70 E, Ardmore, OK 73401

HIDDEN LAKE RV PARK
Ratings: 8/10★/9 (RV Park) From jct. of I-35 (exit 29) & US-70: Go W 1/4 mi on US-70 to Hedges Rd, then S 1-1/4 mi. (L). **FAC:** Gravel rds. (84 spaces). 30 Avail: 20 paved, 10 gravel, 30 pull-thrus (33 x 70), 30 full hkups (30/50 amps), seasonal sites, cable, WiFi, rentals, laundry, LP gas, fire rings, firewood. **REC:** pool, Hidden Lake: fishing, playground. Pet restrict(B/Q). Partial handicap access, no tents. Big rig sites, 2015 rates: $32.
(580)220-2900 Lat: 34.118151, Lon: -97.158101
4661 Hedges Rd, Ardmore, OK 73401
desk@hiddenlakerv.com
www.hiddenlakerv.com
See ad opposite page, 909.

LAKE MURRAY (State Pk) From Jct of I-35 & Exit 24 (Scenic 77), E 2.7 mi on Scenic 77 (E). 2015 rates: $20 to $30. (580)223-4044

OSWALT RV RESORT
Ratings: 6.5/10★/7 (Campground) From Jct of I-35 & Oswalt Rd (exit 21): Go W 1 block on Oswalt Rd. (L). **FAC:** Gravel rds. 26 all weather, 16 gravel, 26 pull-thrus (25 x 75), back-ins (24 x 60), 42 full hkups (30/50 amps), WiFi, dump, laundry, groc, LP gas, fire rings, firewood. **REC:** playground. Pets OK. No tents. Big rig sites, 2015 rates: $24 to $35. Disc: military.
(580)276-2800 Lat: 34.024586, Lon: -97.148551
12467 Oswalt Road, Marietta, OK 73448
lazymanlodge@yahoo.com
See ad opposite page, 909.

Travel Services

HIDDEN LAKE REPAIRS & SUPPLIES Full line of RV parts and accessories. On-site repair and service of RVs and trailers. Mobile RV Services. **SERVICES:** RV appliance, MH mechanical, mobile RV svc, emergency rd svc, restrooms. RV supplies, LP, emergency parking, RV accessible. waiting room. Hours: 8:30am to 7pm.
(580)220-2900 Lat: 34.118151, Lon: -97.158102
4661 Hedges Rd, Ardmore, OK 73401
joe@hiddenlakerv.com
www.hiddenlakerv.com
See ad opposite page.

ATOKA — C5 *Atoka*

BOGGY DEPOT (State Pk) From Jct of US-75 & SR-7 (Not Boggy Depot Rd), W 11 mi on SR-7 to park access/cnty rd, S 4 mi (L). 2015 rates: $20 to $30. (580)889-5625

MCGEE CREEK (State Pk) From Jct of US-69 & SR-3 (in town), E 17 mi on SR-3 to McGee Creek Lake Rd, N 3 mi (R). 2015 rates: $20 to $30. (580)889-5822

BARNSDALL — A5 *Osage*

BIRCH COVE (Public Corps) From town, S 1.5 mi on 8th St., follow signs (R). 2015 rates: $16 to $18. Apr 1 to Oct 30. (918)396-3170

BARTLESVILLE — A5 *Washington*

OSAGE HILLS (State Pk) E-bnd: From S Jct of US-60 & Hwy 99, N 6 mi on Hwy 99 to US-60, E 8 mi to park access rd, S 2 mi (L); or W-bnd: From Jct of US-75 & US-60, W 16 mi on US-60 to park access rd, S 2 mi (L). 2015 rates: $20 to $30. (918)336-4141

RIVERSIDE RV RESORT & CAMPGROUND
Ratings: 8/9★/8 (RV Park) From jct of US-75 & W US-60 (Pawhuska exit): Go W 1-1/2 mi on US-60, then S 1 blk on Quapaw Ave. (L). **FAC:** Paved/gravel rds. 70 gravel, 18 pull-thrus (24 x 60), back-ins (25 x 50), 53 full hkups, 17 W, 17 E (30/50 amps), cable, WiFi, dump, mobile sewer, laundry, LP gas, firewood. **REC:** pool, Caney River: fishing. Pet restrict(Q). No tents. Big rig sites, eco-friendly, 2015 rates: $30. Disc: AAA, military.
AAA Approved
(918)336-6431 Lat: 36.746178, Lon: -95.963858
1211 SE Adams Blvd., Bartlesville, OK 74003
riversidervrst@yahoo.com
www.resortrv.com
See ad pages 907 (Welcome Section), 909.

BEGGS — B5 *Okmulgee*

TULSA RV RANCH
Ratings: 7.5/10★/8 (RV Park) From jct of I-44 & Hwy 75: Go S 27 mi on Hwy 75. (L). **FAC:** Gravel rds. 118 gravel, 90 pull-thrus (30 x 80), back-ins (30 x 50), 98 full hkups, 20 W, 20 E (30/50 amps), WiFi, tent sites, rentals, dump, laundry, groc, LP gas, fire rings, firewood, restaurant. **REC:** pond, fishing, rec open to public. Pets OK. Partial handicap access. Big rig sites, RV age restrict, eco-friendly, 2015 rates: $35. Disc: military. ATM.
(918)267-9000 Lat: 35.82593, Lon: -96.05582
2538 US-75, Beggs, OK 74421
rvranchllc@gmail.com
www.tulsarvranch.com
See ad pages 924, 909.

BERNICE — A6 *Delaware*

BERNICE (State Pk) From Jct of I-44 & Afton exit (US-59), SE 6.4 mi on US-59 to SR-125, S 4.1 mi to State Park Rd, W 1.8 mi (R). 2015 rates: $20 to $30. (918)786-9447

BIG CABIN — A6 *Craig*

CABIN RV PARK
(RV Spaces) From jct I-44 & Hwy 69 (exit 283): Go S 1/2 mi on Hwy 69 (L). **FAC:** Gravel rds. 10 gravel, 10 pull-thrus (35 x 80), 10 full hkups (30/50 amps), WiFi, dump, LP gas. Pets OK. No tents. Big rig sites, 2015 rates: $30.
(918)783-5159 Lat: 36.553421, Lon: -95.220087
32046 S Hwy 69, Big Cabin, OK 74332
cabindiesel@junct.com
www.cabindieselservices.com
See ad page 914.

We appreciate your business!

We rate what RVers consider important.

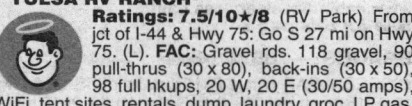

OK

BIG CABIN (CONT)

Travel Services

CABIN DIESEL SERVICE Freightliner, Western Star, Sterling, Spartan Chassis, Caterpillar, Cummins & Detroit Deisel service and repair center. **SERVICES:** MH mechanical, engine/chassis repair, restrooms. RV storage. RV supplies, LP, dump, emergency parking, RV accessible. waiting room. Hours: 8am-5pm M-F, 8am-12pm Sa.
(918)783-5159 Lat: 36.553421, Lon: -95.220087
32046 S Hwy 69, Big Cabin, OK 74332
cabindiesel@junct.com
www.cabindieselservices.com
See ad this page.

BRAGGS — B6 *Muskogee*

GREENLEAF (State Pk) From Jct of US-62 & Hwy 10, S 15 mi on Hwy 10, 3 mi S of town (L). 2015 rates: $20 to $30. (918)487-5196

BROKEN ARROW — B5 *Wagoner*

BLUFF LANDING (Public Corps) From town, E 12.7 mi on 71 St (L). 2015 rates: $15. May 1 to Sep 30. (918)489-5541

BROKEN BOW — D6 *McCurtain*

BEAVERS BEND (State Pk) From Jct of US-70 & US-259, N 6 mi on US-259 to Hwy 259-A, E 5 mi (R). 2015 rates: $20 to $30. (580)494-6538

HOCHATOWN/CARSON CREEK & STEVENS GAP AREAS (State Pk) From Jct of US-70 & US-259, N 12 mi on US-259 to State Park sign, E 3 mi on E 1965 Rd.(R). 2015 rates: $20 to $30. (580)494-6300

CALERA — D5 *Bryan*

PLATTER FLATS (Public Corps) From town, W 7.5 mi on Smiser Rd, follow signs (L). 2015 rates: $12 to $22. Apr 1 to Sep 30. (580)434-5864

CANADIAN — C6 *Pittsburg*

ARROWHEAD (State Pk) From Jct of US-69 & SR 113 (at Canadian), E 0.1 mi on SR 113 (L). 2015 rates: $20 to $30. (918)339-2204

CANTON — B4 *Blaine*

BIG BEND AREA (Public Corps) From town, W 2 mi on Hwy 51 to paved cnty rd, N 4 mi (R). 2015 rates: $15 to $22. Apr 13 to Sep 30. (580)886-2989

CANADIAN CAMPGROUND AREA (Public Corps) From town, W 1 mi on Hwy 51 to Hwy 58A, NW 1.7 mi (stay left at fork in rd) (L). 2015 rates: $18 to $22. Apr 1 to Oct 30. (580)886-3454

SANDY COVE CAMPGROUND (Public Corps) From town, W 0.5 mi on SR-51 to Rte 58A, N 5.2 mi (stay rt at Y in rd) (L). 2015 rates: $18. Apr 1 to Sep 30. (580)274-3576

CARTWRIGHT — D5 *Bryan*

BURNS RUN EAST CAMPGROUND (Public Corps) From town, W 4.5 mi on SR-91, follow signs (L). 2015 rates: $15 to $24. (580)965-4660

CHANDLER — B5 *Lincoln*

OAK GLEN RV PARK
Ratings: 6.5/9.5★/8 (Campground) Eastbound: From the jct of I-44 & OK-18 (exit 166): Go S 1 mi on OK-18, then E 3-1/2 mi on OK-66 (R) Westbound: From the jct of I-44 & OK-99 (exit 179): Go S 1/4 mi on OK-99, then W 10 mi on OK-66 (L). **FAC:** Gravel rds. (51 spaces). 14 Avail: 1 paved, 13 gravel, 14 pull-thrus (24 x 68), 14 full hkups (30/50 amps), seasonal sites, WiFi, tent sites, laundry, groc. **REC:** pond, fishing, playground. Pets OK. Big rig sites, 2015 rates: $28.
(405)258-2994 Lat: 35.706501, Lon: -96.816844
347203 East Highway 66, Chandler, OK 74834
oakglenrvpark@gmail.com
www.oakglenrvpark.com
See ad this page, 909.

CHECOTAH — B6 *McIntosh*

CHECOTAH/LAKE EUFAULA WEST KOA **Ratings: 8.5/10★/8** (Campground) 2015 rates: $36.50 to $43. (918)473-6511 i-40 & Pierce Road (exit 255), Checotah, OK 74426

GENTRY CREEK CAMPGROUND (Public Corps) From town, W 9 mi on US-266, follow signs (L). 2015 rates: $13 to $18. Apr 1 to Sep 29. (918)799-5843

LAKE EUFAULA (State Pk) S-bnd: From Jct of I-40 & Hwy 150 (exit 259), S 6 mi on Hwy 150 (L); or N-bnd: From Jct of US-69 & Hwy 150 (S of town), NW 3 mi on Hwy 150 (R). 2015 rates: $20 to $30. (918)689-5311

TERRA STARR RV PARK **Ratings: 8/8.5/6** (Campground) 2015 rates: $24 to $25. (918)689-2164 420589 E 1147 Rd, Checotah, OK 74426

CHICKASHA — C4 *Grady*

PECAN GROVE RV RESORT
Ratings: 7.5/10★/7.5 (RV Park) From jct of I-44 (H.E. Bailey Turnpike) & US-81/US-277: Go S 1/4 mi on US-81/US-277, then W 1/4 mi on W Almar Dr. (R). **FAC:** Paved rds. (71 spaces). Avail: 30 gravel, patios, 9 pull-thrus (45 x 107), back-ins (45 x 72), 30 full hkups (30/50 amps), seasonal sites, WiFi, laundry. **REC.** Pet restrict(B/Q). Partial handicap access, no tents. Big rig sites, eco-friendly, 2015 rates: $35 to $40.
(405)224-0500 Lat: 35.0205, Lon: -97.939519
600 W. Almar Drive, Chickasha, OK 73018
info@pecangrovervresort.com
www.pecangrovervresort.com
See ad this page, 909.

CLAREMORE — B6 *Rogers*

CLAREMORE EXPO RV PARK (Public) From Jct of I-44 (Will Rogers Tpke) & SR-20 (Exit 255), W 2.8 mi on SR-20 (L). 2015 rates: $27 to $32. (918)342-5357

TULSA NE WILL ROGERS DOWNS KOA **Ratings: 7/10★/7.5** (RV Park) 2015 rates: $32 to $40. (800)562-7635 20900 S 4200 Rd, Claremore, OK 74019

CLAYTON — C6 *Pushmataha*

CLAYTON LAKE (State Pk) From town, S 6 mi on US-271 (R). 2015 rates: $20 to $30. (918)569-7981

CLEVELAND — B5 *Pawnee*

COWSKIN BAY SOUTH (Public Corps) From town, S 14 mi on US-64 to cnty rd (Westport exit), W 1.5 mi (E). Note: 30' RV length limit. Pit toilets. 2015 rates: $5. May 15 to Sep 1. (918)865-2621

Tell your RV Campground that you found them in this Guide.

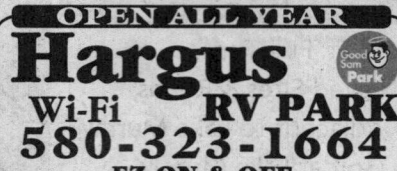

CLINTON — B3 *Custer*

HARGUS RV PARK
Ratings: 6/8/7 (RV Park) From jct o I-40 & Exit 65A (Neptune Dr): Go S 1/ mi on Neptune Dr. (R). **FAC:** All weathe rds. (64 spaces). Avail: 34 gravel, 6 pul thrus (38 x 57), back-ins (25 x 55), 34 fu hkups (30/50 amps), seasonal sites, cable, WiFi, ter sites, laundry. **REC:** playground. Pets OK. Partia handicap access. Big rig sites, eco-friendly, 201 rates: $33. Disc: military.
(580)323-1664 Lat: 35.498589, Lon: -98.977019
1410 Neptune Dr, Clinton, OK 73601
rvhargus@omega1w.net
www.rvhargus.com
See ad this page.

WATER-ZOO CAMPGROUND
Ratings: 8.5/8.5/8.5 (Campground) I-40W & Neptune Dr (exit 65A): Go N 1/4 mi on Nep tune Dr then E on Blvd of Champions, then le at traffic circle on Blvd of Champions. (L). **FAC** Paved rds. 35 paved, patios, 35 pull-thrus (35 x 80 35 full hkups (30/50 amps), WiFi $. **REC:** heated poo rec open to public. Pet restrict(B). Big rig sites, 201 rates: $49.99.
(580)323-9966 Lat: 35.496806, Lon: -98.984673
1900 Boulevard of Champions, Clinton, OK 7360
Water-Zoo@clintonamerica.com
www.water-zoo.com
See ad page 907 (Welcome Section).

COLBERT — D5 *Bryan*

BURNS RUN WEST (Public Corps) From town W 5.5 mi on Hwy 91, follow signs (R). 2015 rates: $2 to $24. Apr 1 to Sep 30. (903)965-4922

RIVER VIEW RV & RECREATIONAL PARK **Ratings: 8/9.5★/8.5** (RV Park) 2015 rates: $25 to $4 (580)296-8439 300 S Dickson Drive, Colbert, O 74733

RV STATION & RESORT **Ratings: 9/8.5/7.** (Campground) 2015 rates: $30. (580)296-2373 41 Sherrard St, Colbert, OK 74733

COOKSON — B6 *Cherokee*

SNAKE CREEK CAMPGROUND (Public Corps From town, S 6 mi on Hwy 82-100 to access rd, W mi on Snake Creek Cove Rd (R). 2015 rates: $15 t $20. (918)487-5252

COPAN — A5 *Osage, Washington*

POST OAK PARK AREA (Public Corps) From Jc Hwy 75 & 10, W 3.5 mi on Hwy 10 (R). 2015 rates $16 to $18. Apr 1 to Oct 30. (918)532-4334

WAH-SHA-SHE (State Pk) From Jct of Hwy 75 & SR-10, W 12 mi on SR-10 (L). 2015 rates: $20 to $30 (918)532-4334

WASHINGTON COVE CAMPGROUND (Publi Corps) From Jct Hwy 75 & 10, W 2 mi on Hwy 10 follow signs, N 1.5 mi (L). 2015 rates: $16. Apr 1 t Oct 30. (918)532-4334

COWLINGTON — C6 *Le Flore*

COWLINGTON POINT (Public Corps) From town S 10.5 mi on US-59, W 4 mi on CR D1172/CR E1170 follow signs (R). 2015 rates: $10 to $15. Apr 26 to Se 25. (918)775-4475

SHORT MOUNTAIN COVE (Public Corps) From town, S 12 mi on US-59 to cnty rd, W 1.5 mi, follow signs (L). 2015 rates: $11 to $15. Apr 26 to Sep 25 (918)775-4475

CROWDER — C6 *Pittsburg*

CROWDER POINT EAST (Public Corps) From town, S 2 mi on US-69, follow signs (L). 2015 rates $7. Mar 1 to Oct 31. (918)484-5135

CUSHING — B5 *Payne*

GRANDSTAFF RV PARK Ratings: 3.5/NA/ (RV Park) From jct of Hwy 33 (W Main St) & Hwy 1 (N Little Ave): Go N 1 mi on N Little Ave, then E 3/ mi on Grandstaff Rd. (R). **FAC:** Gravel rds. 22 Avail 9 paved, 13 gravel, back-ins (30 x 50), 22 full hkup

CUSHING (CONT)

GRANDSTAFF RV PARK (CONT)
(30/50 amps), WiFi. Pets OK. No tents. 2015 rates: $32. No CC.
(918)223-5207 Lat: 35.998735, Lon: -96.755009
1107 E Grandstaff, Cushing, OK 74023
jcqmrtn52@yahoo.com
www.grandstaffrvpark.com

DAVIS — C5 *Murray*

TURNER FALLS PARK (Public) From Jct of I-35 & SR-77 (exit 51), S 1.2 mi on SR-77 (R). Entrance fee required. Caution: Steep grade to camping area. 2015 rates: $25 to $37. (580)369-2988

DISNEY — A6 *Mayes*

CHEROKEE (State Pk) From Jct of SR-28 & SR-82, E 2 mi on SR-28 (L). 2015 rates: $20 to $30. (918)435-8066

DUNCAN — C4 *Stephens*

CHISHOLM TRAIL RV PARK
Ratings: 5.5/9.5★/5.5 (RV Park) From jct of OK-7 Bypass & US-81: Go S 1.5 mi on US-81. (L). **FAC:** Gravel rds. (80 spaces). Avail: 78 gravel, patios, 37 pull-thrus (24 x 60), back-ins (22 x 45), some side by side hkups, 78 full hkups (30/50 amps), WiFi, dump, laundry. **REC.** Pets OK. Partial handicap access, no tents. 2015 rates: $27.
(580)252-7300 Lat: 34.541074, Lon: -97.96679
3000 S. Hwy 81, Duncan, OK 73533
chisholmtrailrvpark@gmail.com
www.chisholmtrailrvpark.com

DUNCAN MOBILE VILLAGE
Ratings: 4.5/5.5/6.5 (Campground) From jct US-81 & OK-7 (Duncan Bypass): Go S. 1/2 mi on US-81, then W 2 blks on Green Meadow Drive (L). **FAC:** Paved rds. (176 spaces). Avail: 106 grass, back-ins (40 x 100), 106 full hkups (30/50 amps), seasonal sites, WiFi Hotspot, laundry. **REC.** Pets OK. No tents. 2015 rates: $30. No CC.
(580)255-1348 Lat: 34.484816, Lon: -97.970285
1702 Green Meadow Drive, Duncan, OK 73533
Duncan@shermanandhemstreet.com
www.duncanmobilevillage.com
See ad this page.

DURANT — D5 *Bryan*

CHOCTAW CASINO RESORT KOA
Ratings: 10/10★/10 (RV Park) From Jct of US-70 & US-69: Go S 3-1/2 mi on US-69 to Choctaw Road, then E 1/4 mi to Enterprise Dr, then N 1 block. (R). **FAC:** Paved rds. 77 paved, patios, 77 pull-thrus (30 x 80), 77 full hkups (30/50 amps), cable, WiFi, dump, laundry, groc, LP gas, firewood, restaurant. **REC:** heated pool, playground. Pet restrict(B). Partial handicap access, no tents. Big rig sites, eco-friendly, 2015 rates: $40 to $50. ATM.
(800)562-6073 Lat: 33.959965, Lon: -96.412093
3650 Enterprise Blvd., Durant, OK 74701
charlie.tyree@choctawcasinos.com
www.choctawcasinos.com
See ad this page.

RV Park ratings you can rely on!

JOHNSON CREEK (Public Corps) From town, W 10 mi on US-70, follow signs (R). 2015 rates: $20 to $40. (580)924-7316

LAKESIDE (Public Corps) From town, W 10 mi on US-70 to Streetman Rd, S 4 mi (E). 2015 rates: $20 to $22. Mar 31 to Sep 30. (580)920-0176

Things to See and Do

CHOCTAW CASINO RESORT 4600 slot machines, table games, poker, bingo, off-track betting, 330 room Tower Hotel, 10 restaurants, lounges, tropical pools, event center, RV park. Hotel room rates vary. Partial handicap access. RV accessible. Restrooms, food. Hours: 24 Hours. ATM.
(888)652-4628 Lat: 33.954184, Lon: -96.412111
3735 Choctaw Road, Durant, OK 74701
info@choctawcasinos.com
choctawcasinos.com
See ad this page.

EDMOND — B4 *Oklahoma*

ARCADIA LAKE (Public) From jct I-35 & Hwy 66: Go 2-1/2 mi E on Hwy 66. 2015 rates: $10 to $29. (405)216-7470

EL RENO — B4 *Canadian*

EL RENO WEST KOA **Ratings: 9.5/9/6.5** (RV Park) 2015 rates: $35 to $37. (405)884-2595 301 S Walbaum Rd, Calumet, OK 73014

HENSLEY'S RV PARK **Ratings: 7.5/7.5/5** (RV Park) 2015 rates: $25. (405)262-6490 2701 S Country Club Rd, El Reno, OK 73036

ELK CITY — C3 *Beckham, Washita*

ELK CITY See also Clinton.

ELK CREEK RV PARK
Ratings: 8.5/9.5★/7.5 (RV Park) From jct of I-40 (exit 38) & S. Main: Go N 500 ft on S. Main to 20th St, then E 500 ft on 20th St. (L). **FAC:** Paved/gravel rds. (89 spaces). Avail: 35 gravel, 35 pull-thrus (21 x 65), 35 full hkups (30/50 amps), seasonal sites, cable, WiFi, laundry. **REC.** Pet restrict(B). Partial handicap access, no tents. Big rig sites, eco-friendly, 2015 rates: $30 to $32. Disc: AAA, military.
AAA Approved
(580)225-7865 Lat: 35.3929, Lon: -99.401552
317 E 20th St, Elk City, OK 73644
elkcreekrv1900@cableone.net
www.elkcreekrvpark.com
See ad this page, 909.

Heading to a privately owned park? Be sure to read how our inspection team rated it in the Guide "How to Use This Travel Guide" section.

KOA ELK CITY/CLINTON **Ratings: 9/8.5★/8** (Campground) 2015 rates: $35.95 to $43.50. (800)562-4149 21167 Route 66 North, Foss, OK 73647

ENID — B4 *Garfield*

HIGH POINT MOBILE HOME & RV PARK **Ratings: 6.5/10★/6.5** (RV Area in MHP) 2015 rates: $28 to $32. (580)234-1726 2700 N. Van Buren #93, Enid, OK 73703

ENTERPRISE — C6 *Haskell*

BROOKEN COVE CAMPGROUND (Public Corps) From town, N 4 mi on SR-71, follow signs (L). 2015 rates: $18 to $20. Apr 1 to Sep 29. (877)444-6777

DAM SITE SOUTH (COE-EUFAULA LAKE) (Public Corps) From town: Go 16 mi E on Hwy 9, then 4 mi N on Hwy 71. 2015 rates: $12 to $20. Apr 1 to Sep 29. (918)799-5843

PORUM LANDING (Public Corps) From town, N 6 mi on US-69 to Texanna Rd (exit 150), follow signs (R). 2015 rates: $13 to $20. Apr 1 to Sep 29. (918)799-5843

EUFAULA — C6 *McIntosh, Pittsburgh*

BELLE STARR (Public Corps) From town, N 5 mi on US-69 to Texanna Rd, E 2 mi, follow signs (R). 2015 rates: $18 to $20. Apr 1 to Sep 29. (918)799-5843

HIGHWAY 9 LANDING (Public Corps) From town, E 8 mi on Hwy 9, follow signs (L). 2015 rates: $8 to $20. Mar 31 to Sep 28. (918)799-5843

OK

EUFAULA (CONT)

LITTLE TURTLE RV & STORAGE
Ratings: 9/10★/9 (RV Park) From jct of I-40 (exit 264) & US-69: Go S 6-1/2 mi on US-69, then E 300 yds OK-150/Texanna Rd, then S 300 yds Old US-69. (L).

OKLAHOMA'S NEWEST, FINEST I40/US69
A luxury experience awaits you. Paved 80 ft pull thru FHU sites. Pool, playground, Duck Isle for the kids. Adjacent to Lake Eufaula. Separate equestrian section each site with its own pen. Circle pen, dog park, 100 amp sites.

FAC: Gravel rds. 70 paved, 36 pull-thrus (35 x 80), back-ins (35 x 60), 70 full hkups (30/50 amps), WiFi, tent sites, laundry, LP gas. **REC:** pool, pond, fishing, playground. Pets OK. Partial handicap access. Big rig sites, eco-friendly, 2015 rates: $39.
(918)618-2140 Lat: 35.360912, Lon: -95.573372
114161 Highway 69, Eufaula, OK 74432
littleturtlervandstorage@gmail.com
www.LittleTurtleRV.com
See ad this page, 909.

YOGI BEAR'S JELLYSTONE PARK EUFAULA **Ratings: 7/7.5/4** (RV Resort) 2015 rates: $89. May 24 to Sep 2. (918)689-9644 610 Lakeshore Drive, Eufaula, OK 74432

FAIRLAND — A6 *Ottawa*

TWIN BRIDGES (State Pk) E-bnd: From Jct of I-44 & Afton exit (US-60), E 11.9 mi on US-60 (L); or W-bnd: From Wyandotte, W 3 mi on US-60 (R). 2015 rates: $20 to $30. (918)542-6969

FORT COBB — C4 *Caddo*

FORT COBB (State Pk) From Jct of Hwys 9 & 146, N 1 mi on Hwy 146 to local rd, N 4.3 mi, past golf course (R). 2015 rates: $20 to $30. (405)643-2249

FORT GIBSON — B6 *Muskogee*

HARBOR RV PARK **Ratings: 6/9★/6.5** (RV Park) 2015 rates: $25 to $30. (918)478-3300 1217 S. Scott St, Fort Gibson, OK 74434

WILDWOOD (Public Corps) From town, S 1 mi on Hwy 80-A to Hwy 80, W 4 mi (R). 2015 rates: $16 to $20. (918)682-4314

FORT SUPPLY — A3 *Woodward*

SUPPLY PARK CAMPGROUND (Public Corps) From town, S 1.5 mi on access rd (E). 2015 rates: $16 to $23. Mar 1 to Sep 30. (580)766-2001

FORT TOWSON — D6 *Choctaw*

RAYMOND GARY (State Pk) From town, E 0.5 mi on US-70 to SR-209, S 2 mi (E). 2015 rates: $20 to $30. (580)873-2307

FOSS — B3 *Custer*

FOSS (State Pk) From Jct of I-40 & SR-44 (exit 53), N 6.3 mi on SR-44 to SR-73W, W 0.2 mi (R). 2015 rates: $20 to $30. May 1 to Oct 30. (580)592-4433

FOYIL — B6 *Rogers*

BLUE CREEK (Public Corps) From town, N 10 mi on US-66 to 1st cnty rd, W 2.3 mi to EW-40, N 1.2 mi to EW-39, W 1.5 mi, follow signs (E). 2015 rates: $14 to $18. Apr 1 to Sep 30. (918)341-4244

SPENCER CREEK CAMPGROUND (Public Corps) From town, S 4 mi on Hwy 66 to Cnty Rd, W 5 mi, N 2 mi (E). 2015 rates: $14 to $18. Apr 1 to Sep 30. (918)341-3690

FREEDOM — A3 *Woodward*

ALABASTER CAVERNS (State Pk) From Jct of US-64 & Hwy 50, S 9 mi on Hwy 50 to Hwy 50A, E 0.5 mi (L). 2015 rates: $20 to $30. (580)621-3381

GORE — B6 *Cherokee, Haskell, Sequoia*

CHICKEN CREEK CAMPGROUND (Public Corps) From town, S 3 mi on SR 100-82 to cnty rd, NW 2 mi (E). 2015 rates: $13 to $18. Apr 1 to Sep 30. (918)487-5252

Want to see what our inspectors see? The exact reproductions of the rating guidelines our inspectors used for this edition of the Guide are printed in the front of the book. Try using them on your next trip to perform your own inspection. Since our rating system is based on objective criteria, we're confident that your ratings will be similar to ours.

MARVAL RESORT
Ratings: 8.5/10★/9 (Campground) From jct of I-40 & Hwy 100 (Exit 287): Go N 6 mi on Hwy 100 to 4450 Rd, then E 1/4 mi to 1011 Rd, then N 1/2 mi. (E).

MARVAL FAMILY CAMPING RESORT
Where families create memories! Fish, play, & enjoy the great outdoors along the Lower Illinois River. Log cabins, RV & tent sites, pool, splash pad, mini & disc golf, 1/2 mile of riverfront fishing, floating & swimming.

FAC: Paved/gravel rds. (162 spaces). 72 Avail: 26 paved, 46 gravel, 43 pull-thrus (38 x 70), back-ins (40 x 50), 33 full hkups, 39 W, 39 E (30/50 amps), seasonal sites, cable, WiFi, tent sites, rentals, dump, laundry, groc, LP gas, fire rings, firewood, controlled access. **REC:** heated pool, wading pool, Lower Illinois River: fishing, playground, rec open to public. Pet restrict(Q). Partial handicap access. Big rig sites, 2015 rates: $37 to $59. Disc: AAA, military. ATM.
(800)340-4280 Lat: 35.55049, Lon: -95.09678
445104 E 1011 Rd, Gore, OK 74435
Camp@marvalresort.com
www.marvalresort.com
See ad opposite page, 909 & Family Camping in Magazine Section.

STRAYHORN LANDING (Public Corps) From town, N 8 mi on Hwy 100 to Hwy 10A, N 1.5 mi to paved access rd, E 0.25 mi (R). 2015 rates: $13 to $20. Apr 1 to Sep 30. (918)487-5252

GROVE — A6 *Delaware*

CEDAR OAKS RV RESORT
Ratings: 8/9.5★/9.5 (RV Park) From jct of I-44 & Hwy 59 (exit 302): Go S 10-3/4 mi on Hwy 59 (over Sailboat Bridge), continue 1-1/4 mi. (R). **FAC:** Paved/gravel rds. 123 Avail: 123 all weather, patios, 40 pull-thrus (28 x 60), back-ins (30 x 55), 123 full hkups (30/50 amps), WiFi, dump, laundry, LP gas, firewood. **REC:** Grand Lake o' the Cherokee: fishing, shuffleboard. Pets OK. No tents.

What will it cost to catch a salmon in Alaska? State-by-state fishing license information is listed in the front section of the Guide.

MARVAL RESORT
800-340-4280
918-489-2295
You Tube
CABINS
RV SITES
TENT SITES
LODGES
Reunion Hall &
Clubhouse
GORE, OK
Trout
Capital of
Oklahoma
FAMILY
MARVAL
RESORT
FISHING & CAMPING
POOL
SPLASH PAD
MINI-GOLF
ACTIVITIES
GAME ROOM
ACTIVITIES
Welcome To
GORE
EXPERIENCE THE AREA
Good Sam Park
www.MarvalResort.com
See listing
Gore, OK

Cedar Oaks RV Resort

On Grand Lake O' The Cherokees

5 Club Rooms with Kitchen Facilities

Atlas Safe Room

WELCOME SNOWBIRDS

- BIG RIGS
- 30/50 Amp
- Full Hookups
- Long, Level Pull-Thrus with Patios
- Big, Clean Laundromat
- Great Fishing
- Boat Ramp
- Boat Slips
- 4 Rental Units
- Close to Restaurants & Shopping

See listing Grove, OK

www.cedaroaksrv.com
1550 83rd Street • Grove, OK 74344
800-880-8884 • (918) 786-4303

Good Sam Park

MasterCard VISA DISCOVER

Park GPS Settings:

North 36° 37' 05" West 94° 48' 53"

Exit 302 from Hwy I-44,
take Hwy 59 South toward Grove.
Located one mile south of Sail Boat Bridge
and 2.5 Miles North of downtown Grove.

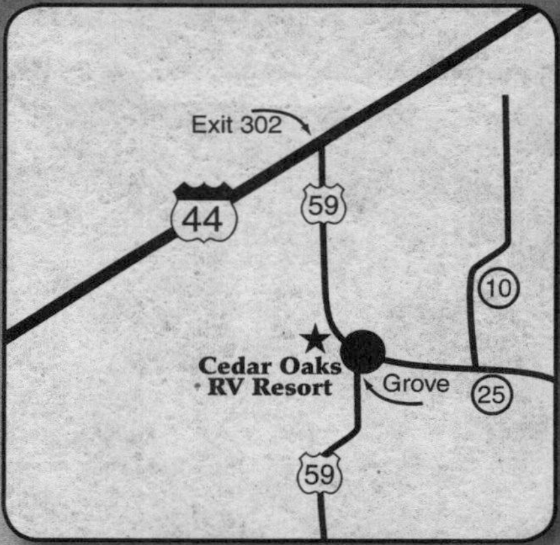

GROVE (CONT)

CEDAR OAKS RV RESORT (CONT)
Big rig sites, eco-friendly, 2015 rates: $30 to $35. Disc: military.
(800)880-8884 Lat: 36.599791, Lon: -94.786821
1550 83rd St NW, Grove, OK 74344
cedaroaksrvresort@yahoo.com
www.cedaroaksrv.com
See ad opposite page, 909.

EAGLES' LANDING RESORT & RECREATION **Ratings: 6/6.5/8** (Membership Pk) 2015 rates: $35. (918)786-6196 25301 US Hwy 59 N, Grove, OK 74344

HONEY CREEK (State Pk) From Jct of I-44 & US-59, S 15 mi on US-59 to State Park Rd, W 0.8 mi (E). 2015 rates: $20 to $30. (918)786-9447

GUTHRIE — B4 *Logan*

CEDAR VALLEY RV PARK **Ratings: 6/7.5/7** (RV Park) 2015 rates: $35. (405)282-4478 725 Masters Dr, Guthrie, OK 73044

PIONEER RV PARK **Ratings: 6/6.5/5.5** (RV Park) 2015 rates: $30 to $32. (405)282-3557 1601 E Seward Rd, Guthrie, OK 73044

GUYMON — A2 *Texas*

CORRAL DRIVE IN RV PARK **Ratings: 8/10★/8** (RV Park) 2015 rates: $30 to $37. (580)338-3748 825 W Hwy 54, Guymon, OK 73942

HASTINGS — D4 *Jefferson*

KIOWA PARK I (Public Corps) From town, NW 8 mi on Hwy 5 to cnty rd, N 3 mi, follow signs (R). 2015 rates: $14 to $18. May 1 to Sep 30. (580)963-9031

WICHITA RIDGE NORTH (COE-WAURIKA LAKE) (Public Corps) From town: Go 4 mi N on county road. Pit toilets. (580)963-2111

HINTON — C4 *Caddo*

RED ROCK CANYON (State Pk) From Jct of I-40 & US-281 (exit 101), S 5 mi on US-281 (L) Caution: Steep decline and winding road to campground area. 2015 rates: $20 to $30. (405)542-6344

HUGO — D6 *Choctaw*

HUGO LAKE (State Pk) From Indian Nations Tnpk & Hwy 70: Go 5 mi E on Hwy 70, (Hugo Lk State Park Sign), then 2 mi N on N 4285. 2015 rates: $20 to $30. (580)326-0303

KIAMICHI PARK (Public Corps) From town, E 5 mi on US-70 to N4285, N 1 mi (E). 2015 rates: $12 to $22. Mar 31 to Sep 29. (580)326-3345

VIRGIL POINT CAMPGROUND (Public Corps) From town, E 10 mi on US-70 to SR-147, N 2.6 mi to SH 147, W 1 mi, follow signs (E). 2015 rates: $15 to $22. Apr 1 to Sep 30. (580)326-3345

JAY — B6 *Delaware*

PINE ISLAND RV RESORT **Ratings: 8/6/7.5** (Membership Pk) 2015 rates: $10. (918)786-9071 32501 S 571, Jay, OK 74346

JET — A4 *Alfalfa*

GREAT SALT PLAINS (State Pk) From Jct of US-64 & Hwy 38 (in town), N 9 mi on Hwy 38 (L). 2015 rates: $20 to $30. (580)626-4731

KAW CITY — A5 *Kay*

COON CREEK COVE (Public Corps) From Jct of US-77 & Hwy 11, E 5.7 mi on Hwy 11 to N Enterpise Rd., N 2 mi to Furguson Rd., E 2 mi (R). 2015 rates: $16 to $18. Mar 1 to Nov 30. (580)762-5611

SARGE CREEK CAMPGROUND (Public Corps) From town, N 4 mi on US-77 to Hwy 11, E 13.8 mi (R). 2015 rates: $18. Mar 30 to Sep 28. (580)762-5611

WASHUNGA BAY CAMPGROUND (Public Corps) From town, N 4 mi on US-177 to Hwy 11, E 17 mi to park access rd, N 4.5 mi (R). 2015 rates: $16 to $18. May 1 to Sep 15. (580)762-5611

KELLYVILLE — B5 *Creek*

HEYBURN PARK (Public Corps) From town, W 9.4 mi on US-66 to S 337W Ave., N 4 mi to W 141st St., E 2.6 mi. 2015 rates: $14 to $16. Apr 1 to Oct 31. (918)247-6601

KENTON — A1 *Cimarron*

BLACK MESA (State Pk) N-bnd: From Kenton, E 4.5 mi on SR-325 to D0073 Rd, S 3.2 mi (E); or S-bnd: From Jct of SR-325 & US-56 (in Boise City), NW 19.5 mi on SR-325 to N0080 Rd., W 6 mi (E). 2015 rates: $20 to $30. (580)426-2222

Thank you for being one of our best customers!

KETCHUM — A6 *Mayes*

PELICAN LANDING RESORT & CAMPGROUND **Ratings: 7/6/7.5** (Membership Pk) 2015 rates: $40. (918)782-3295 32100 Hwy 85, Ketchum, OK 74349

KINGSTON — D5 *Bryan, Marshall*

BUNCOMBE CREEK CAMPGROUND (Public Corps) From town, W 2 mi on SR-32 to Enos Rd, S 4 mi to Shay Rd, W 3 mi, follow signs (E). 2015 rates: $16 to $20. (580)564-2901

CANEY CREEK (Public Corps) From town, S 5 mi on Muncrief Rd, follow signs. 2015 rates: $18 to $22. Apr 1 to Sep 30. (580)564-2632

LAKE TEXOMA (State Pk) In town, from Jct of US-70 & SR-32, E 5 mi on US-70 (R). 2015 rates: $20 to $30. (580)564-2566

LAWTON — C4 *Comanche*

BUFFALO BOBS RV PARK
Ratings: 7.5/9.5★/8.5 (RV Park) From jct of I-44 (Eastbound: exit 36; Westbound: exit 36A) & Hwy 7: Go E on 1 mi on Hwy 7, then S 500 ft on Tower Rd (L).

SOUTHWEST OK'S PREMIER RV PARK
We have the perfect place to make your stay with us a great experience. Enjoy our huge rally room and free wi-fi/cable. Easy off from I-44 with the best amenities for both you and your pet. Come enjoy the free laundry & ice!

FAC: Paved rds. (38 spaces). Avail: 10 paved, patios, 10 pull-thrus (24 x 65), 10 full hkups (30/50 amps), seasonal sites, cable, WiFi, dump, laundry. **REC.** Pets OK. Partial handicap access, no tents. Big rig sites, 2015 rates: $35. Disc: military.
(580)699-3534 Lat: 34.593778, Lon: -98.361103
1508 S.E. Tower Rd., Lawton, OK 73501
info@buffalobobsrvpark.net
www.buffalobobsrvpark.net
See ad this page, 909.

CAMP DORIS (WICHITA MTNS. WILDLIFE REFUGE) (Natl Pk) From jct US 62 & Hwy 115: Go 4 mi N on Hwy 115. 2015 rates: $10 to $20. (580)429-3222

LAKE ELLSWORTH (Public) From Jct of I-44 & US-277, W 4 mi on US-277 to Bonafield Rd, N 1 mi (R). 2015 rates: $7 to $12. (580)529-2663

LAKE LAWTONKA CITY PARK (Public) From Jct of I-44 & Hwy 49, W 3.7 mi on Hwy 49 to Hwy 58, N 2 mi (L). 2015 rates: $7 to $12. (580)529-2663

LONE WOLF — C3 *Kiowa*

QUARTZ MOUNTAIN (State Pk) From Jct of Hwys 9 & 44 (in town), S 9 mi on Hwy 44 to access rd Hwy 44A (at sign), W 1 mi (R). 2015 rates: $20 to $30. (580)563-2238

Our travel services section will help you find services that you'll find handy in your travels.

LONGDALE — B4 *Blaine*

LONGDALE CAMPGROUND (Public Corps) From town, W 2 mi on cnty rd (E). Pit toilets. 2015 rates: $10 to $11. May 1 to Sep 10. (580)274-3454

MADILL — D5 *Marshall*

BRIDGEVIEW RESORT (Public Corps) From town, E 9 mi on SR-199 to Bridgeview Rd, S 4 mi (R). 2015 rates: $20 to $25. (580)795-3979

LITTLE GLASSES RESORT & MARINA (Public) From town, E 3.4 mi on US-70 to Hwy 106, E 5 mi (E). 2015 rates: $15 to $24. (580)795-2068

MANITOU — C3 *Tillman*

LAKE FREDERICK (Public) From Jct of US-183 & Hwy 5-C, E 5 mi on Hwy 5-C to N2290, N 0.5 mi (E). 2015 rates: $6 to $9. (580)397-7551

MARLOW — C4 *Stephens*

TOWN & COUNTRY RV PARK **Ratings: 6/9.5★/7.5** (RV Park) 2015 rates: $30. (580)641-2836 2727 S. Hwy 81, Marlow, OK 73055

MCALESTER — C5 *Pittsburg*

ELM POINT (Public Corps) From town, NE 13 mi on Hwy 31 (L). Pit toilets. 2015 rates: $7 to $11. Mar 1 to Oct 31. (918)484-5135

MEAD — D5 *Bryan*

LAKE TEXOMA RV RESORT **Ratings: 7/9.5★/7** (RV Park) 2015 rates: $39. (580)931-8963 6414 Hwy 70 West, Mead, OK 73449

NEWBERRY CREEK RESORT & MARINA (Public) From town, W 8 mi on US-70 to N3630, N 2 mi (R). Pit toilets. 2015 rates: $20. Apr 15 to Nov 1. (580)924-0787

OK

MIAMI — A6 *Ottawa*

MIAMI MH & RV PARK
Ratings: 6/9★/7.5 (RV Area in MHP) From Jct of I-44 & Steve Owens Blvd/Hwy 10 (Miami exit 313): Go W 1 blk on Steve Owens Blvd/Hwy 10 (R). **FAC:** Paved/gravel rds. (112 spaces). Avail: 48 all weather, 21 pull-thrus (24 x 60), back-ins (30 x 60), 48 full hkups (30/50 amps), seasonal sites, WiFi, laundry. **REC.** Pet restrict(B). Partial handicap access, no tents. Big rig sites, 2015 rates: $30.
(918)542-2287 Lat: 36.871112, Lon: -94.855186
2001 E Steve Owens Blvd #18, Miami, OK 74354
miami@towermgt.com
www.towerrvparks.com

MOUNTAIN PARK — C3 *Jackson*

GREAT PLAINS (State Pk) From Jct of US-62 & US-183, N 7 mi on US-183 to E1570, (at sign), W 1 mi (R). 2015 rates: $20 to $30. (580)569-2032

Say you saw it in our Guide!

MOYERS — D6 *Pushmataha*

K RIVER CAMPGROUND **Ratings: 4/6.5/5** (Campground) 2015 rates: $20 to $25. (580)298-2442 415209 E 1842 Road, Moyers, OK 74557

MUSKOGEE — B6 *Muskogee, Wagoner*

CROSSROADS RV PARK **Ratings: 5.5/10★/6.5** (RV Park) 2015 rates: $20. (918)686-9104 6476 N 55th Street N, Porter, OK 74454

DAM SITE WEST (Public Corps) From town, E 6 mi on Hwy 251-A (R). 2015 rates: $15 to $20. (918)683-6618

HIDDEN VALLEY RV PARK
Ratings: 6.5/8/7 (RV Park) S-bnd: From jct of US-69 & Muskogee Turnpike (exit 26): Go S 3/4 mi on US-69. (L) N-bnd: From jct of US-69 & US-62 (Shawnee Bypass): Go N 4-1/2 mi on US-69. (R). **FAC:** Gravel rds. 60 gravel, 60 pull-thrus (30 x 75), 60 full hkups (30/50 amps), WiFi, tent sites, laundry, LP bottles. **REC:** playground. Pets OK. Big rig sites, 2015 rates: $25.
(918)681-4457 Lat: 35.833775, Lon: -95.401520
6388 Hwy 69, Porter, OK 74454
hiddenvalleyrvpark@yahoo.com
www.hiddenvalleyrvparkok.com
See ad this page, 909.

SAVE! Over $1,000 in coupons can be found at the front of the Guide!

MEADOWBROOK RV PARK
Ratings: 4/NA/6.5 (RV Park) From jct US-62/Hwy 16 & US-69: Go S 1 mi on US-69. **FAC:** Paved/gravel rds. (84 spaces). Avail: 44 paved, patios, 23 pull-thrus (34 x 70), back-ins (25 x 45), accepts full hkup units only, 44 full hkups (30/50 amps), seasonal sites. Pet restrict(B). No tents. Big rig sites, 2015 rates: $20. No CC.
(918)681-4574 Lat: 35.740215, Lon: -95.402389
1300 S 32nd Street (US-69), Muskogee, OK 74401
meadowbrook123@yahoo.com
See ad this page.

SPANIARD CREEK PARK (Public Corps) From town, S 8 mi on US-64 to Elm Grove Rd, E 5 mi (L). 2015 rates: $14 to $15. (918)487-5252

NEW MANNFORD — B5 *Creek*

NEW MANNFORD RAMP CAMPGROUND (Public Corps) From town, N 1 mi on cnty rd, follow signs (R). 2015 rates: $8 to $21. Apr 1 to Oct 31. (918)865-2096

SALT CREEK NORTH (Public Corps) From town, E 1 mi on US-51, follow signs (L). 2015 rates: $10 to $17. May 1 to Sep 10. (918)865-2845

NEWCASTLE — C4 *McClain*

A' AAA ADULT RV PARK **Ratings: 5.5/NA/8.5** (RV Park) 2015 rates: $20 to $40. (405)387-3334 3300 SW 24th Street, Newcastle, OK 73065

Like Us on Facebook.

NORMAN — C4 *Cleveland*

LAKE THUNDERBIRD (State Pk) From Jct of I-35 & Hwy 9E (exit 108A), E 15 mi on Hwy 9E (L) or From Jct of I-40 & Choctaw Rd (exit 166), S 10.8 mi on Choctaw Rd to Alameda Dr, E 1 mi (E). 2015 rates: $20 to $30. (405)360-3572

OKLAHOMA CITY — B4 *Oklahoma*

OKLAHOMA CITY See also Chandler, El Reno, Guthrie, Midwest City & Newcastle.

COUNCIL ROAD RV PARK
Ratings: 6.5/10★/7 (RV Park) From jct of I-40 & Council Rd (Exit 142): Go S 1/4 mi on Council Rd, then W 1 block on SW 8th St (L). **FAC:** Paved/gravel rds. (102 spaces). Avail: 66 gravel, patios, 66 pull-thrus (25 x 60), 66 full hkups (30/50 amps), seasonal sites, cable, WiFi, dump, laundry, LP gas. **REC.** Pet restrict(B). Partial handicap access, no tents. Big rig sites, eco-friendly, 2015 rates: $35. Disc: AAA, military.
(405)789-2103 Lat: 35.45394, Lon: -97.655151
8108 SW 8th St, Oklahoma City, OK 73128
councilrdrvpark_okc@yahoo.com
www.councilroadrvpark.com
See ad pages 922, 909.

MUSTANG RUN RV PARK
Ratings: 9.5/10★/7.5 (RV Park) From jct of I-40 & I-44: Go W 7-1/2 mi on I-40 (exit 138), then S 1/8mi on Mustang Road, then W 1/8 mi on West Service Road (entrance at Braum's Ice Cream Store) (E). **FAC:** Paved rds. 61 paved, 36 pull-thrus (30 x 75), back-ins (30 x 60), 61 full hkups (30/50 amps), cable, WiFi, laundry. **REC:** pool, playground. Pets OK. Partial handicap access. Big rig sites, 2015 rates: $45. Disc: military.
(405)577-6040 Lat: 35.467255, Lon: -97.726074
11528 W I-40 Service Road, Yukon, OK 73099
mustangrunrvpark@coxinet.net
www.mustangrunrvpark.com
See ad this page, 909.

OKLAHOMA CITY EAST KOA **Ratings: 9/10★/9.5** (Campground) 2015 rates: $44 to $69. (800)562-5076 6200 S Choctaw Rd., Choctaw, OK 73020

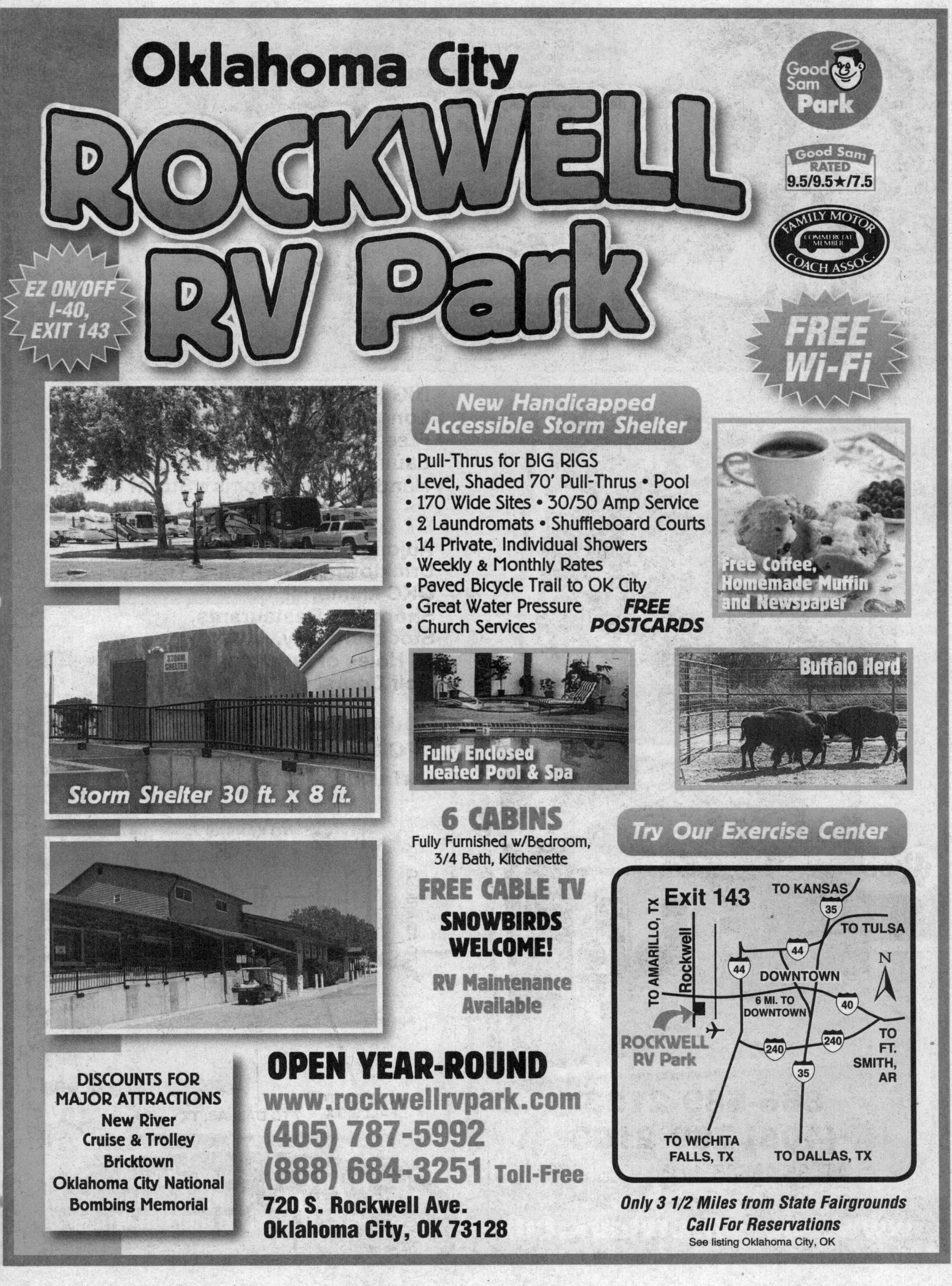
Oklahoma City
ROCKWELL
RV Park
Good Sam Park
Good Sam RATED 9.5/9.5★/7.5
FAMILY MOTOR COACH ASSOC. COMMERCIAL MEMBER
EZ ON/OFF I-40, EXIT 143
FREE Wi-Fi
New Handicapped Accessible Storm Shelter
• Pull-Thrus for BIG RIGS
• Level, Shaded 70' Pull-Thrus • Pool
• 170 Wide Sites • 30/50 Amp Service
• 2 Laundromats • Shuffleboard Courts
• 14 Private, Individual Showers
• Weekly & Monthly Rates
• Paved Bicycle Trail to OK City
• Great Water Pressure
• Church Services
FREE POSTCARDS
Free Coffee, Homemade Muffin and Newspaper
STORM SHELTER
Storm Shelter 30 ft. x 8 ft.
Fully Enclosed Heated Pool & Spa
Buffalo Herd
6 CABINS
Fully Furnished w/Bedroom, 3/4 Bath, Kitchenette
FREE CABLE TV
SNOWBIRDS WELCOME!
RV Maintenance Available
Try Our Exercise Center
Exit 143
TO KANSAS
35
TO TULSA
TO AMARILLO, TX
Rockwell
44
44
DOWNTOWN
N
6 MI. TO DOWNTOWN
40
ROCKWELL RV Park
240
240
TO FT. SMITH, AR
35
TO WICHITA FALLS, TX
TO DALLAS, TX
DISCOUNTS FOR MAJOR ATTRACTIONS
New River Cruise & Trolley
Bricktown
Oklahoma City National Bombing Memorial
OPEN YEAR-ROUND
www.rockwellrvpark.com
(405) 787-5992
(888) 684-3251 Toll-Free
720 S. Rockwell Ave.
Oklahoma City, OK 73128
Only 3 1/2 Miles from State Fairgrounds
Call For Reservations
See listing Oklahoma City, OK

Council road RV PARK

Good Sam Park

EZ On/Off
Free WiFi

See listing Oklahoma City, OK

- BIG RIG SITES • 30/50 Amps
- Long, Shaded Pull-Thrus
- Free Wi-Fi • Cable TV
- Laundry • LP • Open Year Round
- Handicap Restrooms • Storm Shelter

CLOSE TO:
Adjoining Nature/Hiking Trail, Bricktown, Riverboat & Trolley, OKC Memorial, Shopping, Restaurants, Stockyard City, 36 Holes of Public Golf Courses, OKC Airport

I-40 at Exit 142
8108 S.W. 8th St.
Oklahoma City, OK 73128

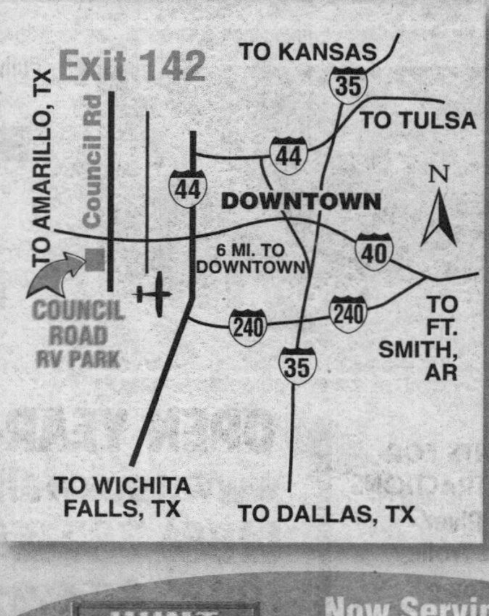

PETS WELCOME

866-589-2103
(405) 789-2103
LAT: 35.45685 LON: 97.65566

HUNT BROTHERS PIZZA
Now Serving Hunts Brothers Pizza and Hot Wings

www.councilrdrvpark.com

OKLAHOMA CITY (CONT)

ROADRUNNER RV PARK (RV Park) (Rebuilding) From jct of I-35 (exit 123A) & SE 51st St: Go N 1/4 mi on E Service Road. (R). **FAC:** Paved rds. (132 spaces). Avail: 82 paved, 42 pull-thrus (25 x 60), back-ins (25 x 45), 82 full hkups (30/50 amps), seasonal sites, cable, WiFi, laundry. **REC:** playground. Pet restrict(B). Partial handicap access, no tents. Big rig sites, 2015 rates: $31 to $35.
(405)677-2373 Lat: 35.418202, Lon: -97.488971
4740 S I-35 Service Rd, Oklahoma City, OK 73129
www.roadrunnerrvparkokc.com
See ad pages 920, 909.

ROCKWELL RV PARK **Ratings: 9.5/9.5★/7.5** (RV Park) From Jct of I-40 & Rockwell Ave (exit 143), S 0.03 mi on Rockwell Ave (L)on SE corner of Rockwell & I-40.

EZ ON/OFF I40 EXIT 143 BIG RIG FHUS
Minutes from downtown OKC with a new jogging path to the city, state fairgrounds, National Cowboy Hall of Fame, firefighters mueum, exercise center, new handicapped accessible storm shelter, private showers & cabin rentals.

FAC: Paved rds. (170 spaces). Avail: 95 gravel, 95 pull-thrus (28 x 70), 95 full hkups (30/50 amps), seasonal sites, cable, WiFi, tent sites, rentals, laundry, LP bottles. **REC:** heated pool, whirlpool, Crystal Lake: fishing, shuffleboard. Pets OK. Partial handicap access. Big rig sites, eco-friendly, 2015 rates: $35 to $40. Disc: AAA, military.
AAA Approved
(405)787-5992 Lat: 35.458429, Lon: -97.634299
720 S Rockwell Ave, Oklahoma City, OK 73128
dmlrokrv@aol.com
www.rockwellrvpark.com
See ad pages 921, 909, 908 (OK Map).

TWIN FOUNTAINS RV RESORT **Ratings: 8.5/10★/9.5** (RV Resort) 2015 rates: $44.50. (405)475-5514 2727 NE 63rd St, Oklahoma City, OK 73111

Travel Services

CAMPING WORLD OF OKLAHOMA As the nation's largest retailer of RV supplies, accessories, services and new and used RVs, Camping World is committed to making your total RV experience better. RV Accessories: (888)224-3022. **SERVICES:** RV appliance, MH mechanical, engine/chassis repair, RV Sales. RV supplies, LP, dump, emergency parking, waiting room. Hours: 8am - 6pm.
(888)596-7274 Lat: 35.605682, Lon: -97.49993
13111 N Broadway Ext, Oklahoma City, OK 73114
Greg.Justice@CampingWorld.com
www.campingworld.com

MOTLEY RV REPAIR Repair of all types of RVs and towables. Large inventory of repair parts. **SERVICES:** RV, RV appliance, MH mechanical, mobile RV svc, emergency rd svc, restrooms. RV storage. RV supplies, dump, emergency parking, RV accessible. waiting room. Hours: 8am to 6pm Tu-Fr, 8am to 5 pm M.
(405)789-4848 Lat: 35.463607, Lon: -97.660261
8300 W Reno Ave, Oklahoma City, OK 73127
motleyrvrepair@coxinet.net
www.motleyrvrepair.com
See ad page 920.

OKMULGEE — B5 *Okfuskee, Okmulgee*

DRIPPING SPRINGS (State Pk) From Jct of US-75 & SR-56, W 6.5 mi on SR-56 (L). 2015 rates: $20 to $30. Apr 15 to Oct 15. (918)756-5971

OKMULGEE (State Pk) From jct US 75 & Hwy 56: Go 5 mi W on Hwy 56. 2015 rates: $20 to $30. (918)756-5971

OOLOGAH — B5 *Rogers*

HAWTHORN BLUFF (Public Corps) From town, E 2 mi on SR-88 (L). 2015 rates: $16 to $20. Apr 1 to Sep 30. (918)443-2319

REDBUD BAY (Public Corps) From town, S 4 mi on SR-88 (L). Pit toilets. 2015 rates: $16. Apr 1 to Oct 31. (918)443-2250

PARK HILL — B6 *Cherokee*

CHEROKEE LANDING (State Pk) From Jct of Hwy 62 & Hwy 82 (S of Tahlequah), S 11 mi on Hwy 82 (R). Note: 40' RV length limit. 2015 rates: $20 to $30. (918)457-5716

Enjoy shopping over 10,000 RV products at great prices, at CampingWorld.com.

PERRY — B4 *Noble*

PERRY LAKE RV PARK (CITY PARK) (Public) From jct of I-35 & OK-77 (exit 185): Go W 1/2 mi on OK-77, then S 1 mi on CR-80. (R). **FAC:** Paved rds. 10 paved, patios, 10 pull-thrus (35 x 60), 10 full hkups (30/50 amps), tent sites, restrooms only, fire rings. **REC:** Perry Lake: swim, fishing, rec open to public. Pets OK. Big rig sites, 2015 rates: $25. Apr 1 to Nov 1. No CC.
(580)336-4684 Lat: 36.258792, Lon: -97.336521
24050 CR 80, Perry, OK 73077
information@perrychamber.net
www.perryokchamber.com
See ad this page.

PONCA CITY — A5 *Kay, Osage*

BEAR CREEK COVE (Public Corps) From Jct of Hwy 77 & Main St, E 8.3 mi on Lake Rd., S 3.7 mi N Bear Creek Rd. (E). 2015 rates: $15. May 1 to Sep 15. (580)762-5611

LAKE PONCA CAMPGROUNDS (Public) From Jct of US 60 & US 77, N 0.4 mi on US 77 to Lake Rd, E 3 mi on Lake Rd to Prentice, N 0.4 mi on Prentice (L). 2015 rates: $12. (580)767-0400

OSAGE COVE (Public Corps) From town, E 11 mi on Lake Rd to park access rd, S 0.1 mi (E). 2015 rates: $18. Mar 1 to Sep 28. (580)762-5611

SANDY PARK (Public Corps) From town, E 11 mi on Lake Rd to park access rd, N .5 mi (E). Pit toilets. 2015 rates: $12. Apr 1 to Oct 31. (580)762-5611

POTEAU — C6 *Le Flore*

LONG LAKE RESORT & RV PARK **Ratings: 6/UI/9.5** (RV Park) 2015 rates: $20 to $25. (918)647-8140 35740 US Hwy 59 S, Poteau, OK 74953

PRUE — B5 *Osage*

WALNUT CREEK (State Pk) E-bnd: From Jct of SR-99 & Osage Prue Rd, SE 10 mi on Osage Prue Rd to area #2 (R); or W-bnd: From Jct of US-64/412 & 209 W Ave/Prue Rd (6 mi W of Sand Springs), W 13 mi on Prue Rd to area #2 (L). 2015 rates: $20 to $30. Apr 1 to Nov 30. (918)865-4991

RINGOLD — D6 *McCurtain*

LOST RAPIDS PINE CREEK RESERVE (Public Corps) From Jct of Indian Nation Tpke & Hwy 3 (Antler exit), E 30 mi on Hwy 3, follow signs (R). 2015 rates: $10 to $15. Apr 1 to Sep 29. (580)876-3720

SALINA — B6 *Mayes*

SNOWDALE (State Pk) From Jct of I-44 & US-69, SW 12 mi on US-69 to SR-20, E 8 mi to park access rd, N 0.25 mi (L). 2015 rates: $20 to $30. (918)434-2651

SALLISAW — B6 *Haskell, Sequoyah*

BRUSHY LAKE (Public) From Jct of I-40 & US-59, (Exit 308), N 1.3 mi on US-59 to Maple St, N 6.5 mi on Maple St to Park Rd, S 0.8 mi (E). 2015 rates: $15. (918)775-6507

SALLISAW/FORT SMITH WEST KOA **Ratings: 8/9★/8.5** (Campground) 2015 rates: $39.89. (800)562-2797 1900 Koa Power Drive, Sallisaw, OK 74955

SAND SPRINGS — B5 *Osage*

APPALACHIA BAY (Public Corps) From town, W 12 mi on US-64 to frontage rd, W 0.25 mi to 3760 Rd, S 1 mi (E). Pit toilets. 2015 rates: $8. Apr 1 to Oct 31. (918)243-7822

LAKE KEYSTONE (State Pk) From Jct of US-64 & Hwy 151, S 1 mi on Hwy 151 (R); or From Jct of Hwys 51 & 48, E 8 mi on Hwy 51 to Hwy 151, N 0.5 mi (R). 2015 rates: $20 to $30. (918)865-4991

WASHINGTON IRVING SOUTH (Public Corps) From town, W 12 mi on US-64 to Bear Glen Rd, left, cross over expwy to frntg rd, left 0.25 mi to cnty rd, W 1 mi (E). 2015 rates: $10 to $17. (918)865-2621

SAPULPA — B5 *Creek*

SHEPPARD POINT (Public Corps) From Jct of I-44 & SR-33 (exit 211), W 7 mi on SR-33 to park access rd, S 2.4 mi, E 1.7 mi on W 141st St. (R). 2015 rates: $14 to $16. (918)247-4551

SAYRE — C3 *Beckham*

SAYRE RV PARK (Public) From jct US 40 & US 283: Go 1/2 mi N on US 283. (580)928-2260

The Guide gives you one less thing to worry about. Our directional arrows in service center and tourist attraction listings make them much easier to find.

SHAWNEE — C5 *Pottawatomi*

HEART OF OKLAHOMA EXPO CENTER (Public) From jct of I-40 & US-177 (exit 181): Go SE 3-1/2 mi on US-177 (L). **FAC:** Paved/gravel rds. 705 gravel, 100 pull-thrus (30 x 50), back-ins (25 x 35), some side by side hkups, 361 full hkups, 344 W, 344 E (30/50 amps), WiFi $, dump, laundry. Pets OK. Partial handicap access, no tents. 2015 rates: $20.
(405)275-7020 Lat: 35.347229, Lon: -96.938669
1700 W Independence St, Shawnee, OK 74804
mjackson@shawneeexpo.org
www.shawneeexpo.org
See ad page 920.

Things to See and Do

SHAWNEE CONVENTION & VISITORS BUREAU Source of information for meetings, groups and tourists in Shawnee, OK. Partial handicap access. Restrooms. Hours: 9am to 5pm. No CC.
(405)275-9780 Lat: 35.328416, Lon: -96.921846
131 North Bell, Shawnee, OK 74801
info@visitshawnee.com
www.visitshawnee.com
See ad page 920.

SPAVINAW — B6 *Mayes*

SPAVINAW (State Pk) From Jct of SR-20 & SR-82 (N of town), S 3 mi on SR-82 (L). 2015 rates: $20 to $30. (918)589-2651

STILLWATER — B5 *Payne*

LAKE CARL BLACKWELL (Public) From town, W 7 mi on Hwy 51 to Hwy 51C, N 2 mi (E). 2015 rates: $10 to $20. (405)372-5157

SULPHUR — C5 *Murray*

ARBUCKLE RV RESORT **Ratings: 8/8.5★/9** (Campground) 2015 rates: $30. (580)622-6338 774 Charles Cooper Memorial Dr, Sulphur, OK 73086

CHICKASAW/BUCKHORN (Natl Pk) From town: Go 5 mi S on US 177, then 3 mi W. 2015 rates: $16 to $24. (580)622-3161

CHICKASAW/ROCK CREEK (Natl Pk) 1 mi W of North entrance. 2015 rates: $14 to $22. (580)622-3161

CHICKASAW/THE POINT (Natl Pk) From Hwy 7 west of town: Go 5 mi S on access road. 2015 rates: $16 to $22. Mar 22 to Oct 31. (580)622-3161

TAHLEQUAH — B6 *Cherokee*

CARTER'S LANDING (Public Corps) From town, E 7 mi on Hwy 82, E 5 mi to Carters Landing Rd, E 1.3 mi (E). 2015 rates: $7 to $11. (918)487-5252

COOKSON BEND (Public Corps) From town, N 15 mi on Hwy 100 to Cookson Rd, W 2 mi (E). 2015 rates: $7 to $18. Apr 1 to Sep 30. (918)487-5252

ELK CREEK LANDING (Public Corps) From town, N 5 mi on SR 82 (L). 2015 rates: $7 to $16. Apr 1 to Sep 30. (918)487-5252

PETTIT BAY (Public Corps) From Jct of US-62 & OK-82, S 4 mi on OK-82 to Indian Rd, S 2 mi to paved rd, E 1 mi (E). 2015 rates: $10 to $20. (918)487-5252

SIZEMORE LANDING (Public Corps) From town, N 6 mi on Hwy 100 to 10A, W 2 mi to Indian Rd, N 11 mi to Sizemore, E 1 mi (E). Pit toilets. 2015 rates: $5. (918)487-5252

TALIHINA — C6 *Le Flore*

TALIMENA (Natl Pk) From Jct of US-271 & SR-63, N 7 mi on US-271 (R). 2015 rates: $20. (918)567-2052

THACKERVILLE — D5 *Love*

RED RIVER RANCH RV RESORT **Ratings: 7.5/3.5/7** (RV Park) 2015 rates: $24. (800)568-7837 19691 U. S. Hwy 77, Thackerville, OK 73459

Don't camp without it ... Our 2016 listings are your key to travel satisfaction.

OK

THACKERVILLE (CONT)

→ WINSTAR RV PARK
Ratings: 10/10★/10 (RV Park) From Jct of I-35 (exit 1) & US-77 N: Go NE 1-1/2 mi on Casino Ave, then E 1/2 mi on Vegas Rd, then N 1 blk on Merle Wolfe Rd. (L).

RELAX GOLF WIN AT WINSTAR RV PARK
Nestled in the Southern Foothills, the Winstar RV Park offers lodging next to the Winstar World Casino. Take a shuttle, enjoy our 27 hole golf course in a resort setting. Refine your skills at the golf academy.
FAC: Paved rds. 153 paved, patios, 41 pull-thrus (30 x 80), back-ins (30 x 50), 153 full hkups (30/50 amps), WiFi, tent sites, dump, laundry, restaurant. **REC:** pool, whirlpool, golf, playground, rec open to public. Pet restrict(Q). Partial handicap access. Big rig sites, 2015 rates: $30 to $50. ATM.
(580)276-8900 Lat: 33.752316, Lon: -97.126142
21902 Merle Wolfe Rd, Thackerville, OK 73459
winstar.rvpark@chickasaw.net
www.winstarworldcasino.com/rv-park
See ad pages 911 (Spotlight Chickasaw Nation), 909.

Things to See and Do

→ WINSTAR WORLD CASINO AND RESORT
Largest casino in the world with eight themed gaming plazas, 500,000 sq ft of gaming, restaurants. Partial handicap access. RV accessible. Restrooms, food. Hours: 24 Hours. ATM.
(800)622-6317 Lat: 33.757785, Lon: -97.132039
777 Casino Avenue, Thackerville, OK 73459
www.WinStarWorldCasino.com
See ad page 911 (Spotlight Chickasaw Nation).

TULSA — B5 *Tulsa*

TULSA See also Bartlesville, Beggs & Big Cabin.

↙ CHERRY HILL MH & RV COMMUNITY
Ratings: 8.5/9.5★/7.5 (RV Area in MHP) From jct of I-44 & Elwood Ave (exit 224): Go E 1-1/4 mi on S service rd (follow Elwood Ave signs), then N 1/4 mi on Elwood Ave. (L). **FAC:** Paved rds. (269 spaces). Avail: 76 gravel, patios, 3 pull-thrus (24 x 60), back-ins (30 x 50), 76 full hkups (30/50 amps), seasonal sites, WiFi, laundry. **REC:** pool, playground. Pet restrict(B). Partial handicap access, no tents. 2015 rates: $30 to $33. Disc: military.
(918)446-9342 Lat: 36.097036, Lon: -95.994642
4808 S Elwood Ave, Tulsa, OK 74107
cherryhill@towermgmt.com
www.cherryhillmhc.com

↘ EXPO-SQUARE RV PARK (Public) From Jct of I-44 & exit 229 (Yale Ave), N 3 mi on Yale Ave to 15th St, W 0.5 mi, Gate 5 Entrance (L). 2015 rates: $25 to $35. (918)744-1113

→ MINGO RV PARK
Ratings: 8/10★/8 (RV Park) E-bnd: From jct of I-244 & Mingo (exit 13A): Go N 1/4 mi on Mingo. (R); or W-bnd: From jct of I-44 & I-244: Go W 2 mi on I-244 to Garnett (exit 14), then S 1/4 mi on Garnet, then W 1 mi on Admiral, then N 1/4 mi on Mingo. (R). **FAC:** Paved rds. (250 spaces). Avail: 75 gravel, 30 pull-thrus (30 x 80), back-ins (20 x 60), 75 full hkups (30/50 amps), seasonal sites, cable, WiFi, laundry, LP gas. **REC:** playground. Pets OK. Partial handicap access, no tents. Big rig sites, 2015 rates: $31 to $35. Disc: AAA, military.
(918)832-8824 Lat: 36.167409, Lon: -95.866347
801 N Mingo Rd, Tulsa, OK 74116
mingorv@sbcglobal.net
www.mingorvpark.com
See ad page 909.

Want to know how we rate? Our campground inspection guidelines are detailed in the front pages of the Guide.

VALLIANT — D6 *McCurtain*

PINE CREEK COVE (COE-PINE CREEK LAKE) (Public Corps) From town: Go 8 mi N on county road. 2015 rates: $15 to $23. Apr 1 to Sep 29. (580)933-4215

VERDEN — C4 *Caddo*

↑ LAKE CHICKASHA (Public) From Main St, N 2 mi on cnty rd to sign, W 2 mi on cnty rd to sign, N 1 mi on cnty rd (L). 2015 rates: $10 to $15. (405)453-7915

VIAN — B6 *Sequoyah*

↑ TENKILLER (State Pk) From Jct of I-40 & Hwy 100 (exit 287), NE 11 mi on Hwy 100 (L). 2015 rates: $20 to $30. (918)489-5641

WAGONER — B6 *Wagoner*

← AFTON LANDING (Public Corps) From town, W 4.5 mi on Hwy 51 to access rd, follow signs (L). 2015 rates: $15. (918)489-5541

↑ BLUE BILL POINT (Public Corps) From town, N 4 mi on US-69 to park access rd, NE 3 mi (E). 2015 rates: $11 to $20. (918)476-6638

↗ FLAT ROCK CREEK (Public Corps) From town, N 8 mi on US-69 to Flat Rock Rd, SE 6.5 mi, follow signs (E). 2015 rates: $10 to $18. Apr 1 to Sep 30. (918)474-6766

↗ ROCKY POINT (Public Corps) From town, N 3 mi on US-69 to White Horn Cove Rd, follow signs (E). 2015 rates: $14 to $20. Apr 1 to Sep 30. (918)462-2042

← SEQUOYAH (State Pk) From Jct of US-69 & Hwy 51 (in Wagoner), E 11 mi on Hwy 51 (R). 2015 rates: $20 to $30. (918)772-2545

↗ SEQUOYAH BAY (State Pk) From town, S 5 mi on Hwy 16 to Grey Oaks Rd, E 5 mi (E). 2015 rates: $20 to $30. (918)683-0878

→ TAYLOR FERRY SOUTH (Public Corps) From town, E 4 mi on SR-51 to cnty rd, S 0.5 mi to park access rd, E 1 mi (E). 2015 rates: $16 to $20. (918)485-4792

WATONGA — B4 *Blaine*

↑ ROMAN NOSE (State Pk) From Jct of Hwy 33 & US-281/Hwy 8, N 5 mi on Hwy 8 to Hwy 8A, NW 2 mi (L). 2015 rates: $20 to $30. (580)623-4218

WAURIKA — D4 *Jefferson*

↑ CHISHOLM TRAIL RIDGE PARK (Public Corps) From town, NW 5 mi on Hwy 5, N 3 mi on CR (Advent Rd), W 1 mi to park entrance (L). 2015 rates: $14 to $18. May 1 to Sep 30. (580)439-8040

MONEKA PARK (COE-WAURIKA LAKE) (Public Corps) From town: Go 4 mi W on Hwy-5, then 1 mi N on blacktop road. Pit toilets. 2015 rates: $8. Mar 1 to Oct 31. (580)963-2111

WAYNOKA — A3 *Woods*

↓ LITTLE SAHARA (State Pk) From town, S 4 mi on US-281 (R). 2015 rates: $20 to $30. (580)824-1471

WEBBERS FALLS — B6 *Muskogee*

↑ BREWERS BEND (Public Corps) From town, W 2 mi on US-64 to cnty rd, N 5 mi (R). 2015 rates: $15. May 1 to Sep 30. (918)489-5541

WEST SILOAM SPRINGS — B6 *Delaware*

← NATURAL FALLS (State Pk) From Siloam Springs, W 6 mi on US-412 (L). 2015 rates: $20 to $30. (918)422-5802

WILBURTON — C6 *Latimer*

↑ ROBBERS CAVE (State Pk) From Jct of US-270 & Hwy 2, N 5 mi on Hwy 2 (R). 2015 rates: $20 to $30. (918)465-2565

WISTER — C6 *Le Flore*

↓ LAKE WISTER (State Pk) From Jct of US-270 E & 271, S 2 mi on US-270 to Quarry Island (off of dam), follow signs (R). 2015 rates: $20 to $30. (918)655-7212

WOODWARD — B3 *Woodward*

↗ BOILING SPRINGS (State Pk) E-bnd: From Jct of Hwys 15 & 34 (in town), N 1.4 mi on Hwy 34 to Hwy 34C, E 5 mi (E); or W-bnd: From Jct of Hwys 15 & 50 (Mooreland), N 1 mi on Hwy 50 to Hwy 50B, W 5 mi (E). 2015 rates: $20 to $30. (580)256-7664

WYANDOTTE — A6 *Ottawa*

↗ WHISPERING WOODS RV PARK **Ratings: 8/9.5/8.5** (RV Park) 2015 rates: $10. (918)666-9200 70220 East Highway 60, Wyandotte, OK 74370

It's the law! Rules of the Road and Towing Laws are updated each year. Be sure to consult this chart to find the laws for every state on your traveling route.

Getty Images/iStockphoto

WELCOME TO
Oregon

DATE OF STATEHOOD	WIDTH: 400 MILES (640 KM)	PROPORTION OF UNITED STATES
FEB. 14, 1859	LENGTH: 360 MILES (580 KM)	2.59% OF 3,794,100 SQ MI

Progressive, crunchy, inventive and fashionably hip, Oregon's cliché's are only the beginning. Green in spirit and matter, Oregon is draped with evergreen forests, expansive farmlands and more than 300 vineyards. The Oregon Coast Trail, which traces the state's rugged 360-mile shoreline, is a dramatic juxtaposition of rocky headlands, monumental dunes, seal rookeries, a forested promontory and stunning panoramas. Eastern Oregon is a world apart, an austere desert land strewn with fossils that plunges into the mighty chasm of Hells Canyon.

Considered one of the top lifestyle cities in the nation, Portland's reputation precedes itself, yet it remains a city true to itself. Populated with independent, spirited and fiercely loyal denizens, Portland's embrace of all things fresh and local, from farmer's markets to a grass roots arts scene, transcends caricature. Within easy reach of the city, Mount Hood and the Columbia River Gorge—-with the 600-foot drop of Multnomah Falls waterfall—deliver dramatic landscapes where recreational opportunities abound.

History

In 1805, Lewis and Clark mapped Oregon during their quest to find the Northwest Passage. In Astoria, at the mouth of the Columbia River, the Lewis and Clark National Historical Park is dotted with historic sites utilized by the Corps of Discovery during 1805-06. The 6.5-mile Fort to Sea Trail, from Fort Clatsop to Sunset, runs through the same forest, coastal rivers, fields and windswept dunes that the Corps traveled, covering land that was home to the Clatsop Indians who assisted the expedition.

During the summer, costumed interpreters bring the history of the fort to life. In the 1830s, pioneers embarked upon the arduous journey west on the 2,200-mile Oregon Trail, the historic east-west wagon route that linked the Missouri River to Oregon.

Top 3 Tourism Attractions:
1) Mount Hood
2) Crater Lake National Park
3) Oregon Coast Aquarium

Nickname: Beaver State

State Flower: Oregon Grape

State Bird: Western Meadowlark

People: Beverly Cleary, children's novelist; Edwin Markham, poet; Ahmad Rashad, football player and sportscaster; Doc Severinsen, trumpeter

Major Cities: Portland, Eugene, Salem (capital), Gresham, Hillsboro

Topography: West—rugged coast range, fertile Willamette River Valley; central—Cascade Mountain range of volcanic peaks; east—plateau

Climate: West—oceanic climate; east—drier east of the Cascades

Getty Images/iStockphoto

OR

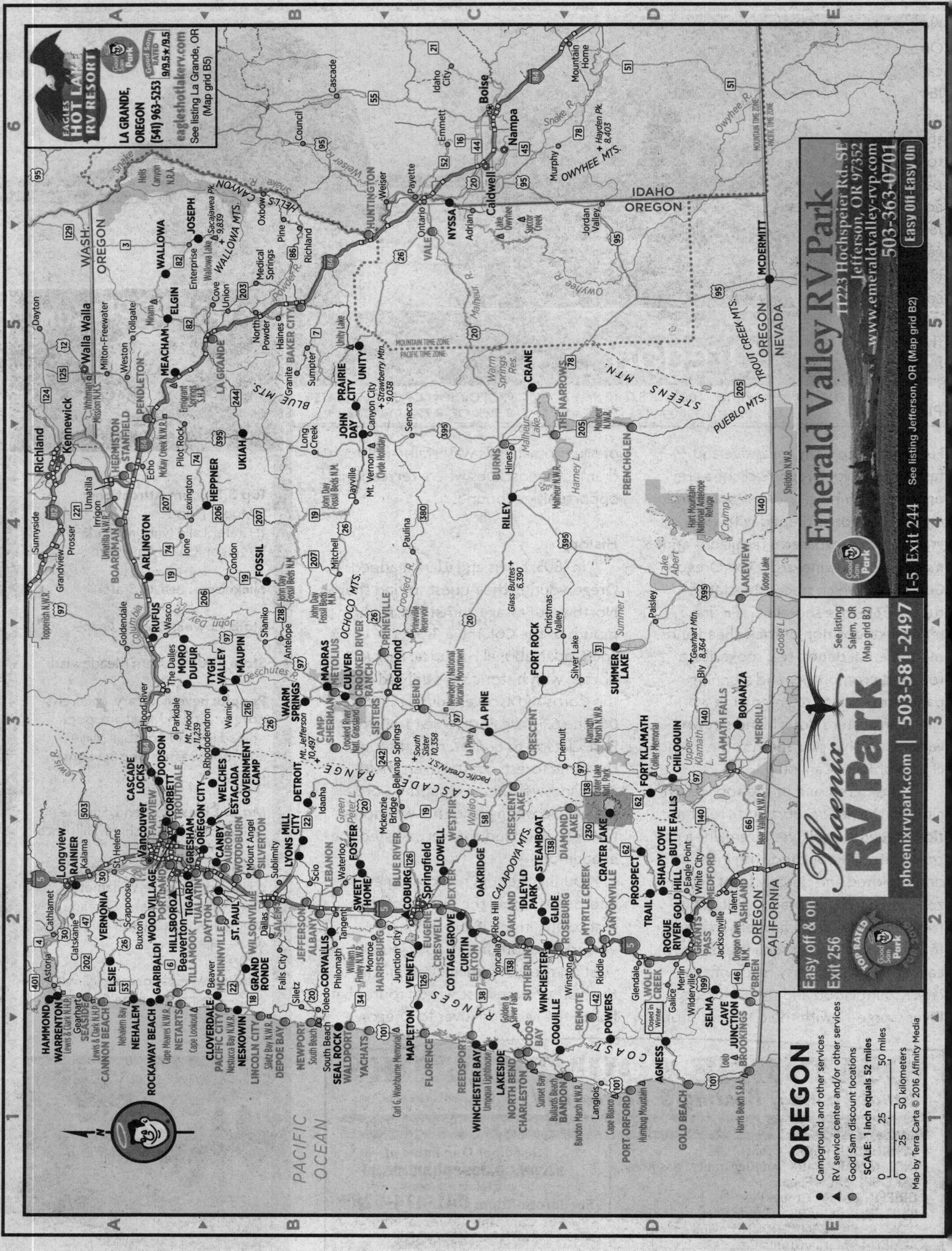
OREGON
Campground and other services
RV service center and/or other services
Good Sam discount locations
SCALE: 1 inch equals 52 miles
Map by Terra Carta © 2016 Affinity Media
PACIFIC OCEAN
EAGLES HOT LAKE RV RESORT
LA GRANDE, OREGON
(541) 963-5253
eagleshotlakerv.com
See listing La Grande, OR (Map grid B5)
Phoenix RV Park
Easy off & on Exit 256
phoenixrvpark.com | 503-581-2497
See listing Salem, OR (Map grid B2)
Emerald Valley RV Park
11223 Hochspeier Rd. SE
Jefferson, OR 97352
www.emeraldvalley-rvp.com
503-363-0701
Easy Off-Easy On
I-5 Exit 244
See listing Jefferson, OR (Map grid B2)

Near Baker City's National Historic Oregon Trail Interpretive Center, you can still see 150-year-old wagon ruts. In 1846, the border between U.S. and British territory was formally established at the 49th parallel; the territory assigned to Britain would ultimately become part of Canada. Oregon was officially admitted to the union on February 14th, 1859. The discovery of gold in the 1860s gave birth to new towns and cities. The 19th-century gold-mining town of Jacksonville is the best-preserved historic community in Oregon and boasts more than 80 buildings listed on the National Register of Historic Places.

Play

There may only be one national park in Oregon, but it's a showstopper indeed. In western Oregon, Crater Lake National Park possesses the deepest lake in the U.S. and the ninth deepest lake in the world. The eruption of the Mount Mazama volcano some 7,700 years ago (which created Crater Lake) was one of the greatest geologic catastrophes witnessed by mankind. Within the park, the Oregon Cascades (a line of volcanoes) is legendary for its excellent skiing and backcountry recreation opportunities.

There's excellent hiking, whale-watching and horse riding at Oregon Dunes National Recreation Area, a 40-mile section of beach that boasts the largest expanse of coastal sand dunes in North America. Near Terrebonne, Oregon's beautiful eastern desert unfurls from the kaleidoscopic rocks of Smith Rock State Park, the birthplace of modern sport climbing. The awe-inspiring Hells Canyon, the deepest river canyon in the U.S. (deeper even than Arizona's Grand Canyon; a mile and a half from river bed to mountain top), delivers white-knuckle whitewater rafting as well as boating, fishing, swimming and more than 900 miles of unforgettable hiking trails.

Experience

Portland's Jazz Festival is one of the nation's seminal musical events, drawing world-renowned jazz artists for 10 days every February. Between February and July, 400,000 visitors converge on Ashland to celebrate the great "British Bard" with a seasonal showcase of 11 plays, Shakespearean-themed activities and a terrific education program, produced by the Tony Award-winning Oregon Shakespeare Festival (OSF).

In late May/early June, more than 2 million people pay homage to the cultural and environmental riches of the Pacific Northwest at the legendary Portland Rose Festival. In July, the Oregon Brewers Fest in Portland offers beer lovers the chance to savor more than 20 styles of handcrafted brews, including rare and specialty beers. In venues all over Portland, Labor Day is crowned with MusicFestNW, a musical extravaganza.

Taste

One of the nation's most fertile states, where co-op groceries co-exist with organic food trucks, microbreweries, low-key bistros, gourmet restaurants and farmer's markets, it's not hard to see why Portland is frequently hailed as one of the nation's premier foodie destinations. The lauded vineyards of the Willamette Valley produce Amer-

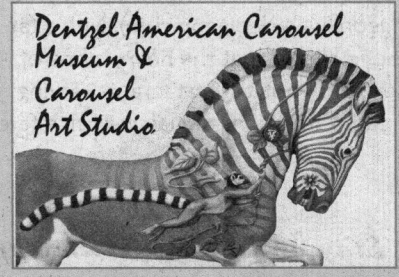

- STAY A WHILE -

Albany and Linn County

Nestled in the fertile Willamette Valley, Albany, Oregon, is a treasure chest of family-friendly events and attractions. Everyone will find something to like in Albany and Linn County—the mid-valley offers everything from hiking and fishing to museums, historic homes and concerts.

In August, watch hot air balloons launch into the summer sky each morning at the ATI Northwest Art & Air Festival. The Lebanon Strawberry Festival each June boasts the world's largest strawberry shortcake, which is served to thousands after the grand parade. Each July and December, you can board a trolley or a horse-drawn wagon and tour the historic homes, churches, and museums in Albany, dating back to the Pioneer Era. The charming small town of Brownsville was the filming location for the movie "Stand By Me"—stop by and visit sites from this classic '80s movie.

Nearly every town in the county hosts its own farmers market, with the freshest fruits, vegetables, flowers and baked goods. Music-lovers can find a show nearly any night of the week during the summer, as concerts in local parks fill the nights with music in towns throughout Linn County.

In Albany, stop to see the exquisite artwork created by hundreds of volunteers who are hand-carving and painting animals for a historic carousel. A visit to the carousel carving studio and museum while you are exploring Albany and Linn County is a memory-making experience for visitors both young and old.

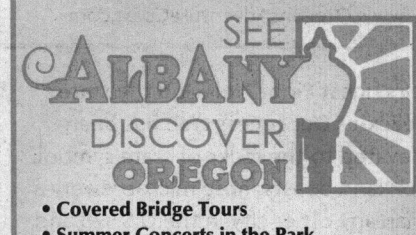

OR

- STAY A WHILE -

Oregon's Adventure Coast

When you visit the Coos Bay, North Bend and the Charleston area, you'll find many opportunities for adventure. The region is called Oregon's Adventure Coast, and it includes free access to some of the world's most beautiful scenic coastline and wide open beaches. The Pacific keeps our weather temperate year-round, rarely reaching extremes in heat or cold.

In addition to 18 RV parks to choose from, we have world-class sporting opportunities, from fishing to tackling the Oregon Sand Dunes. For tranquility, explore our bay beaches, hiking trails, bird watching and beauty of the gardens at Shore Acres State Park.

Both Coos Bay and North Bend feature bay-front boardwalks and shopping districts where you'll find restaurants, antique shops and unique gifts. The Coos Art Museum features a permanent collection of memorabilia honoring runner Steve Prefontaine, in addition to five galleries of contemporary exhibits. The new Coos History Museum is located facing Coos Bay and features exhibits that represent the original local tribes along with the history of development in this waterfront community.

If you are looking for sizzling casino action, you might strike it rich at one of our two casinos. There is also an active community of music and theater available throughout the year. You might catch a festival, from March through October, and see Holiday Lights in December.

We are an all season destination, with surprises and memories around every turn. We have a variety of fun itineraries and offer oodles of other great ideas for your next adventure!

www.OregonsAdventureCoast.com

ica's finest Pinot Noir, and the state's delicious Dungeness crab has been elevated to the ranks of state symbol. Portland boasts more microbreweries than any other city in the U.S. (28 and rising) and at Rogue (www.rogue.com), brews find their way into sauces and any bread-based culinary offerings. In Portland's Lower Burnside, the tiny Le Pigeon (www.lepigeon.com), with a tattooed rock star at the helm, is one of Portland's hottest restaurants serving creative iterations of classic French fare.

The Double Mountain Brewery & Taproom (www.doublemountainbrewery.com) in Hood River is renowned for its beer list, and its perfectly executed wood-fired pizza has achieved nothing less than cult status. In Depoe Bay, Restaurant Beck (www.restaurantbeck.com) is the epitome of fine Oregon dining. Chef-owner Justin Wills conjures a dazzling menu of modern, Pacific Northwest cuisine in an elegant dining room at the Whale Cove Inn (www.whalecoveinn.com).

TRAVEL & TOURISM

Travel Oregon
800-547-7842, 503-373-1270
www.traveloregon.com

Albany Visitors Association
541-928-0911
www.albanyvisitors.com

Ashland Chamber
541-482-3486
www.ashlandchamber.com

Astoria & Warrenton Chamber of Commerce
800-875-6807, 503-325-6311
www.oldoregon.com

Baker County Chamber of Commerce
541-523-5855
www.visitbaker.com

Visit Bend
877-245-8484, 541-382-8048
www.visitbend.com

Cannon Beach Chamber of Commerce
503-436-0434
www.cannonbeach.org

Grants Pass Visitors & Conv. Bureau
541-476-5510
www.visitgrantspass.org

Josephine County Parks
541-474-5260
www.co.josephine.or.us

Travel Klamath
541-882-1501, 800-445-6728
www.travelklamath.com

Travel Portland
877-678-5263
www.travelportland.com

Salem Convention Visitors Bureau
503-581-4325, 800-874-7012
www.travelsalem.com

Silverton Area Chamber of Commerce
503-873-5615
www.silvertonchamber.org

Tillamook Chamber of Commerce
503-842-7525
www.tillamookchamber.org

Willamette Valley Visitors Assn.
866-548-5018
www.oregonwinecountry.org

OUTDOOR RECREATION

Oregon Dept. of Fish and Wildlife
503-947-6000, 800-720-6339
www.dfw.state.or.us

Oregon Skiing
www.oregon.com/snow/downhill.cfm

SHOPPING

Columbia Gorge Premium Outlets
503-669-8060
www.premiumoutlets.com

Featured Good Sam Parks

OREGON

When you stay with Good Sam, you can expect the highest degree of cleanliness and friendliness, and better yet, you get 10% off campground fees.

If you're not already a Good Sam member you can purchase your membership at one of these locations:

ALBANY
Blue Ox RV Park
(541)926-2886

ASHLAND
Glenyan RV Park & Campground
(541)488-1785

AURORA
Aurora Acres RV Resort
(503)678-2646

BAKER CITY
Mt View RV
(541)523-4824
Oregon Trails West RV Park, Inc
(541)523-3236

BANDON
Bandon By the Sea RV Park
(541)347-5155
Bandon RV Park
(541)347-4122

BEND
Scandia RV Park
(541)382-6206

BLUE RIVER
Patio RV Park
(541)822-3596

BOARDMAN
Boardman Marina & RV Park
(541)481-7217

BROOKINGS
AtRivers Edge RV Resort
(541)469-3356
Brookings RV Park
(541)469-6849
Driftwood RV Park
(541)469-9089
Portside RV Park
(877)787-2752

BURNS
Burns RV Park
(800)573-7640

CAMP SHERMAN
Camp Sherman RV Park & Motel
(541)595-6514

CANNON BEACH
RV Resort At Cannon Beach
(800)847-2231

CANYONVILLE
Seven Feathers RV Resort
(877)839-3599

COOS BAY
AAA Midway RV Park
(541)888-9300
Alder Acres RV Park
(888)400-7275

CRESCENT
Big Pines RV Park
(541)433-2785

CRESWELL
Meadowlark RV Park
(541)525-3348

CROOKED RIVER RANCH
Crooked River Ranch RV Park
(800)841-0563

DAYTON
Willamette Wine Country RV Park
(503)864-2233

DEPOE BAY
Fogarty Creek RV Park
(541)764-2228
Sea & Sand RV Park
(541)764-2313

DEXTER
Dexter Shores RV Park
(866)558-9777

DIAMOND LAKE
Diamond Lake RV Park
(541)793-3318

ELKTON
Elkton RV Park
(541)584-2832

EUGENE
Eugene Kamping World
(800)343-3008
Premier RV Resorts - Eugene
(541)686-3152
Shamrock RV & MHP Village
(541)747-7473

FAIRVIEW
Portland Fairview RV Park
(877)777-1047

FLORENCE
B & E Wayside RV Park
(541)997-6451
Heceta Beach RV Park
(541)997-7664
Pacific Pines RV Park & Storage, Inc
(541)997-1434
Woahink Lake RV Resort
(541)997-6454

FRENCHGLEN
Steens Mountain Wilderness Resort
(541)493-2415

GOLD BEACH
Beach Resort At Turtle Rock
(800)353-9754
Four Seasons RV Resort
(541)247-4503
Honey Bear RV & Campground
(800)822-4444
Indian Creek RV Park
(541)247-7704
Ireland's Oceanview RV Park & Motel/Cabins
(541)247-0148

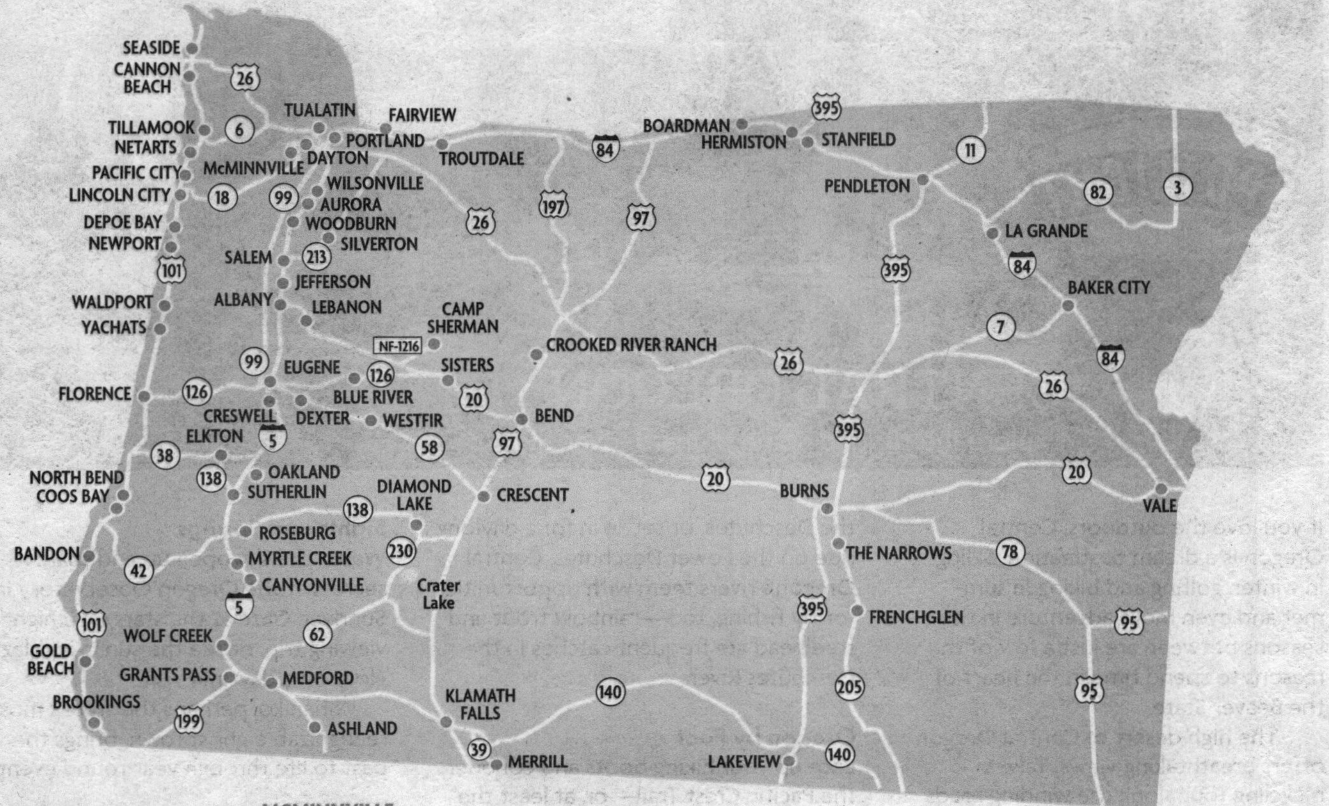

GRANTS PASS
Moon Mountain RV Resort
(877)479-1145
Rogue Valley Overniters
(541)479-2208

HERMISTON
Hat Rock Campground
(541)567-4188

JEFFERSON
Emerald Valley RV Park
(503)363-0701

KLAMATH FALLS
Oregon Motel 8 & RV Park
(541)883-3431

LA GRANDE
Eagles Hot Lake RV Park
(541)963-5253

LAKEVIEW
Junipers Reservoir RV Resort
(541)947-2050

LEBANON
Mallard Creek Golf & RV Resort
(866)632-9133

LINCOLN CITY
Logan Road RV Park
(877)564-2678
Premier RV Resorts - Lincoln City
(877)871-0663

MCMINNVILLE
Olde Stone Village RV Park
(877)472-4315

MEDFORD
Holiday RV Park
(800)452-7970
Lakewood RV Park
(541)830-1957

MERRILL
Merrill RV Park
(541)798-1654

MYRTLE CREEK
Tri City RV Park
(541)860-5000

NETARTS
Netarts Bay Garden RV Resort
(503)842-7774

NEWPORT
Pacific Shores Motorcoach Resort
(541)265-3750
Port Of Newport Marina & RV Park
(541)867-3321

NORTH BEND
The Mill Casino Hotel & RV Park
(800)953-4800

OAKLAND
Rice Hill RV Park
(866)236-0121

PACIFIC CITY
Cape Kiwanda RV Resort & Market Place
(503)965-6230

PENDLETON
Wildhorse RV Resort
(800)654-9453

PORTLAND
Columbia River RV Park
(503)285-1515
Jantzen Beach RV Park
(800)443-7248

ROSEBURG
Rising River RV Park
(541)679-7256
Twin Rivers Vacation Park
(541)673-3811

SALEM
Hee Hee Illahee RV Resort
(877)564-7295
Phoenix RV Park
(503)581-2497
Premier RV Resorts - Salem
(877)364-9990

SEASIDE
Bud's RV Park & Campground
(800)730-6855
Circle Creek RV Resort
(503)738-6070

SILVERTON
Silver Spur RV Park
(503)873-2020

SISTERS
Bend/Sisters Garden RV Resort
(541)516-3036

STANFIELD
Pilot RV Park
(541)449-1189
Stage Gulch RV Park
(541)449-1176

SUTHERLIN
Hi-Way Haven RV Park & Drive In Movie
(541)459-4557

THE NARROWS
The Narrows RV Park
(541)495-2006

TILLAMOOK
Tillamook Bay City RV Park
(503)377-2124
Tillamook RV Park
(503)354-4627

TROUTDALE
Sandy Riverfront RV Resort
(503)665-6722

TUALATIN
Roamer's Rest RV Park LLC
(503)692-6350

VALE
Vale Trails RV Park
(541)473-3879

WALDPORT
Chinook RV Park
(541)563-3485

WESTFIR
Casey's Riverside RV Park
(541)782-1906

WILSONVILLE
Pheasant Ridge RV Resort
(503)682-7829

WOLF CREEK
Sunny Valley RV Park
(541)479-0209

WOODBURN
Portland/Woodburn RV Park
(888)988-0002

YACHATS
Sea Perch RV Resort
(541)547-3505

For more Good Sam Parks go to listing pages

Getty Images/iStockphoto

CENTRAL OREGON

Explore the rugged spine of the Beaver State

If you love the outdoors, Central Oregon is a dream destination. Skiing in winter, golfing and biking in summer and even more adventure in the seasons between are just a few of the reasons to spend time in the heart of the Beaver State.

The high desert of Central Oregon offers breathtaking views. Take a bicycling tour along the winding roads of the Sisters to Smith Rock Scenic Bikeway. From the Old West town of Sisters to Smith Rock State Park, riders see the curving Deschutes River, the rugged Cascade Mountains and the iconic Smith Rock. The craggy face of this formation entices climbers from all over the world to test their skills.

Closer to the water, the Deschutes River Trail is an 18-mile trek through pine forests and ancient lava flows that dishes out views of the river as it wanders from calm waters to churning froth. The Madras Mountain Views Scenic Bikeway is a 30-mile loop that shows off the best of Oregon's volcanic peaks: Mount Jefferson, the Three Sisters Mountains (Faith, Hope and Chastity), Broken Top and Three-Fingered Jack.

Hit the Water

While there's no ocean in sight, Central Oregon knows how to keep summer visitors cool. Grab a kayak and a paddle for a trip along the Deschutes Paddle Trail, which includes 26 miles of the Little Deschutes River and 95 miles of the Deschutes River.

Gear up for more thrills on a whitewater rafting tour, with launches available from Bend and Sunriver. Choose a heat-pounding, three-mile journey on the Deschutes, or settle in for a daylong ride on the Lower Deschutes. Central Oregon's rivers teem with opportunities for fly fishing, too—rainbow trout and steelhead are frequent catches in the Deschutes River.

Oregon by Foot

Lace up your hiking boots and conquer the Pacific Crest Trail—or, at least the part that runs through Central Oregon. This portion takes hikers through the Cascade Range and perhaps is the most scenic in the state. The trail runs 40 miles through Three Sisters Wilderness, a collection of glacial lakes and lava fields, stands of fir trees and pine and Collier Glacier—one of Oregon's largest glaciers.

Sights and Springs

Watch the sky open up and share its secrets at the Oregon Observatory in Sunriver. Gaze at the stars on a night viewing trip, or see the sun in its blazing glory on a daytime visit.

Shaniko, perhaps the state's most recognizable ghost town, brings the past to life through year-round events.

For More Information

Central Oregon
800-800-8334
www.visitcentraloregon.com

Travel Oregon
800-547-7842
www.traveloregon.com

Oregon

CONSULTANTS

Chip & Karen May

AGNESS — D1 *Curry*

AGNESS RV PARK Ratings: 6.5/7.5/8 (Campground) From Jct of Hwy 101 & So Bank Rogue Rd/Agness Rd: Go E 28.3 mi on So Bank Rogue/Agness Rd (L). **FAC:** Gravel/dirt rds. 86 grass, 30 pull-thrus (28 x 60), back-ins (30 x 40), 86 full hkups (30/50 amps), WiFi, tent sites, rentals, laundry, firewood. **REC:** Rogue River: swim, fishing, rec open to public. Pet restrict(B). 2015 rates: $22 to $26. Disc: AAA.
AAA Approved
(541)247-2813 Lat: 42.55181, Lon: -124.06349
4215 Agness Rd, Agness, OR 97406
stay@rogueriverrvpark.com
www.agnessrvpark.com

ALBANY — B2 *Linn*

ALBANY See also Corvallis, Harrisburg, Lebanon & Salem.

ALBANY-CORVALLIS KOA **Ratings: 8/6.5/8** (Campground) 2015 rates: $36.33 to $41.28. (800)562-8526 33775 Oakville Rd. SW, Albany, OR 97321

BLUE OX RV PARK
Ratings: 10/9★/9.5 (RV Park) From Jct of I-5 & Hwy 20 (exit 233): Go E 0.2 mi on Hwy 20 to Price Rd, then N 0.1 mi (R) Note: Use GPS coord. or call park for precise directions. **FAC:** Paved rds. (150 spaces). Avail: 75 paved, 33 pull-thrus (32 x 66), back-ins (25 x 70), 75 full hkups (30/50 amps), seasonal sites, cable, WiFi, laundry, LP gas. **REC:** heated pool. Pets OK. Partial handicap access, no tents. Big rig sites. 2015 rates: $37.40 to $40.70. Disc: military.
(541)926-2886 Lat: 44.63279, Lon: -123.05064
4000 Blue Ox Drive SE, Albany, OR 97322
info@theblueoxrvpark.com
www.theblueoxrvpark.com
See ad this page, 930.

KNOX BUTTE RV PARK
Ratings: 8/9★/9 (RV Park) N-Bnd: From Jct of I-5 & Exit 234: Go E 0.3 mi on Knox Butte Rd (L) NOTE: S-Bnd use exit 234A. **FAC:** Paved rds. (78 spaces). 20 Avail: 10 paved, 10 gravel, 10 pull-thrus (30 x 55), back-ins (30 x 55), accepts full hkup units only, 20 full hkups (30/50 amps), seasonal sites, cable, WiFi, laundry, groc, LP gas. **REC:** Burkhart Creek. Pets OK $. Partial handicap access, no tents. 2015 rates: $37. Disc: AAA.
(541)928-9033 Lat: 44.644483, Lon: -123.055066
125 Expo Parkway NE, Albany, OR 97322
knxpark@hotmail.com
www.knoxbuttervpark.com
See ad this page.

Things to See and Do

ALBANY VISITORS ASSOCIATION Enjoy the covered bridge tour, 700 historic homes, festivals, concerts, museums, five-star restaurants. Call for visitor guide, events schedules & group meeting facilities. Come help carve animals on the carousel project. Partial handicap access. Restrooms. Hours: 9am to 5pm.
(541)928-0911 Lat: 44.63569, Lon: -123.10814
110 SE 3rd Ave, Albany, OR 97321
info@albanyvisitors.com
www.albanyvisitors.com
See ad page 927 (Welcome Section).

ARLINGTON — A4 *Gilliam*

PORT OF ARLINGTON RV & MARINA PARK (Public) From Jct of I-84 & Arlington Exit (137), N 1.1 mi on Arlington Port Rd (L). 2015 rates: $19. (541)454-2868

ASHLAND — D2 *Jackson*

ASHLAND See also Butte Falls, Medford & White City.

EMIGRANT LAKE RECREATION AREA (Public) From Jct of I-5 & SR-66, SE 5 mi on SR-66 (L). 2015 rates: $20 to $30. (541)774-8183

GLENYAN RV PARK & CAMPGROUND
Ratings: 8.5/9★/8 (Campground) From Jct of I-5 & Hwy 66 (exit 14): Go SE 3.5 mi on Hwy 66/Green Springs Hwy (R). **FAC:** Paved/gravel rds. (45 spaces). Avail: 39 gravel, 7 pull-thrus (24 x 60), back-ins (24 x 40), 11 full hkups, 28 W, 28 E (30 amps), seasonal sites, cable, WiFi, tent sites, dump, laundry, groc, LP gas, fire rings, firewood. **REC:** heated pool, pond, playground. Pets OK. Partial handicap access. Eco-friendly. 2015 rates: $35 to $38. Disc: AAA.
AAA Approved
(541)488-1785 Lat: 42.15516, Lon: -122.62914
5310 Hwy 66, Ashland, OR 97520
info@glenyanrvpark.com
www.glenyanrvpark.com
See ad this page, 930.

GRIZZLY (Public) From town, E 28 mi on Dead Indian Memorial Rd to Hyatt Prairie Rd, S 2 mi (R). Pit toilets. 2015 rates: $18. (541)774-8183

HYATT LAKE CAMPGROUND (Public) From Jct of I-5 & SR-66, E 16 mi on SR-66, Green Springs Hwy to East Hyatt Lake Rd, N 4 mi (L). 2015 rates: $12 to $15. Apr 15 to Oct 31. (541)618-2200

KLUM LANDING (Public) From town, E 19 mi on Dead Indian Memorial Rd. to Hyatt Prairie Rd, S 2 mi (R). 2015 rates: $20. Apr to Sep. (541)774-8183

THE POINT RV CAMPGROUND (JACKSON COUNTY PARKS) (Public) From jct I-5 (exit 14) and Hwy 66: Go 4 mi SE on Hwy 66, 3.5 mi to Emigrant Lake turnoff (L). 2015 rates: $20 to $30. (541)774-8183

WILLOW POINT (Public) From town, E 28 mi on Dead Indian Memorial Lake to Hyatt Prairie Rd, S 2 mi (R). Pit toilets. 2015 rates: $18. Apr 22 to Oct 30. (541)774-8183

ASTORIA — A2 *Clatsup*

ASTORIA See also Cannon Beach, Seaside, Warrenton; Ocean Park, WA.

ASTORIA/WARRENTON SEASIDE KOA **Ratings: 7/6/9** (Campground) 2015 rates: $25 to $53. (800)KOA-8506 1100 NW Ridge Rd., Hammond, OR 97121

LEWIS & CLARK GOLF & RV PARK **Ratings: 8.5/9★/9** (RV Park) 2015 rates: $28 to $44. (503)338-3386 92294 Youngs Rivers Rd, Astoria, OR 97103

AURORA — B2 *Marion*

AURORA ACRES RV RESORT
Ratings: 9.5/8.5/8 (RV Park) From Jct of I-5 & Ehlen Rd (exit 278): Go E 200 ft on Ehlen Rd (R). **FAC:** Paved rds. (130 spaces). Avail: 30 paved, 22 pull-thrus (28 x 61), back-ins (40 x 38), accepts full hkup units only, 30 full hkups (30/50 amps), seasonal sites, cable, WiFi Hotspot, laundry, groc, LP gas, firewood. **REC:** heated pool. Pet restrict(B/Q). Partial

Are you using a friend's Guide? Want one of your own? Call 877-209-6655.

How can we make a great Travel Guide even better? We ask YOU! Please share your thoughts with us. Drop us a note and let us know if there's anything we haven't thought of.

AURORA (CONT)

AURORA ACRES RV RESORT (CONT)
handicap access, no tents. Eco-friendly, 2015 rates: $37 to $42. Disc: AAA.
AAA Approved
(503)678-2646 Lat: 45.23206, Lon: -122.80788
21599 Dolores Way NE, Aurora, OR 97002
auroraacresrvparkoregon@gmail.com
www.auroraacresrv.com
See ad pages 933, 930.

BAKER CITY — B5 *Baker*

MT VIEW RV
Ratings: 10/10★/9 (RV Park) From Jct of I-84 & Campbell St (exit 304), W 1.5 mi on Campbell St to 10th St, N 1 mi to Hughes Ln, E 1000 ft (R). Elev 3405 ft. **FAC:** Paved rds. (97 spaces). Avail: 77 paved, 45 pull-thrus (25 x 70), back-ins (25 x 65), 73 full hkups, 4 W, 4 E (30/50 amps), seasonal sites, cable, WiFi $, tent sites, dump, laundry, groc, LP gas. **REC:** heated pool, whirlpool, playground, rec open to public. Pets OK. Partial handicap access. Big rig sites, 2015 rates: $33 to $35. Disc: AAA, military.
AAA Approved
(541)523-4824 Lat: 44.79564, Lon: -117.84140
2845 Hughes Ln, Baker City, OR 97814
camp@mtviewrv.com
www.mtviewrv.com
See ad this page, 930.

OREGON TRAILS WEST RV PARK, INC
Ratings: 8/9.5★/9.5 (RV Park) From Jct of I-84 & N Cedar St (exit 302), W 0.1 mi on N Cedar St (R). Elev 3425 ft. **FAC:** Paved rds. (50 spaces). 35 Avail: 6 paved, 29 gravel, 29 pull-thrus (30 x 60), back-ins (24 x 40), 35 full hkups (30/50 amps), WiFi, tent sites, laundry, groc, LP gas. **REC.** Pet restrict(B/Q). Big rig sites, 2015 rates: $28. Disc: AAA, military.
(541)523-3236 Lat: 44.80307, Lon: -117.81721
42534 N Cedar Rd., Baker City, OR 97814
otwrv1@msn.com
www.goodsamclub.com/travel/campgroundsandrvparks/generalinfo.aspx?cgid=840000628
See ad opposite page, 930.

BANDON — D1 *Coos*

BANDON BY THE SEA RV PARK
Ratings: 7.5/9★/9.5 (RV Park) On Hwy 101 at MP 276.5 (S of Bandon). **FAC:** Paved/gravel rds. (90 spaces). 57 Avail: 5 paved, 52 gravel, 45 pull-thrus (30 x 70), back-ins (30 x 60), 57 full hkups (30/50 amps), seasonal sites, cable, WiFi, tent sites, laundry. **REC.** Pets OK. Big rig sites, eco-friendly, 2015 rates: $43.50. Disc: AAA, military.
(541)347-5155 Lat: 43.08582, Lon: -124.41593
49612 Hwy 101 S, Bandon, OR 97411
reservations@bandonbythesearvpark.com
www.bandonbythesearvpark.com
See ad opposite page, 930.

BANDON RV PARK
Ratings: 8/9.5★/8 (RV Park) From Jct of US-101 & Hwy 42S (N end of town): Go S 500 ft on US-101 (R) Note: If using a GPS unit lat & lon will be more reliable than address. **FAC:** Paved rds. (45 spaces). Avail: 40 all weather, patios, 9 pull-thrus (21 x 50), back-ins (21 x 65), 40 full hkups (30/50 amps), seasonal sites, WiFi, laundry. **REC.** Pets OK. Partial handicap access, no tents. 2015 rates: $36.
(541)347-4122 Lat: 43.11916, Lon: -124.40217
935 2nd St. SE (Hwy 101), Bandon, OR 97411
bandonrvpark@bandonrvpark.com
www.bandonrvpark.com
See ad opposite page, 930.

BANDON/PORT ORFORD KOA **Ratings: 8/9/8.5** (Campground) 2015 rates: $33 to $53. Mar 1 to Nov 1. (800)562-3298 46612 Hwy 101, Langlois, OR 97450

BEACH LOOP RV PARK **Ratings: 6.5/5.5/7.5** (Campground) 2015 rates: $32. (541)347-2100 53877 Beach Loop Rd. W, Bandon, OR 97411

BULLARDS BEACH (State Pk) From Jct of US-101 & Hwy 42S (N end of town), N 2.3 mi on US-101, at MP-259 1/4 (L). 2015 rates: $20 to $24. (800)452-5687

ROBBINS NEST RV PARK **Ratings: 5.5/8★/6** (Campground) 2015 rates: $30. (541)347-2175 49034 US Hwy 101, Bandon, OR 97411

BAY CITY — B2 *Tillamook*

BAY CITY See also Cannon Beach, Garibaldi, Netarts, Pacific City & Tillamook.

BEND — C3 *Deschutes*

BEND See also Redmond & Sisters.

BEND SUNRIVER RV **Ratings: 7/6/8.5** (Membership Pk) 2015 rates: $37 to $55. (800)405-6188 17480 S. Century Dr., Bend, OR 97707

BEND/SISTERS GARDEN RV RESORT
Ratings: 10/10★/10 (RV Resort) From Jct of US Hwy 97 & US Hwy 20 (Exit 135A): Go W 14 3/4 mi on US Hwy 20 (L). Elev 3200 ft. **FAC:** Paved rds. (105 spaces). Avail: 99 paved, patios, 66 pull-thrus (30 x 70), back-ins (30 x 45), 99 full hkups (30/50 amps), WiFi, rentals, laundry, groc, LP gas, fire rings, firewood. **REC:** heated pool, whirlpool, pond, fishing, playground. Pet restrict(Q) $. No tents. Big rig sites, eco-friendly, 2015 rates: $43.20 to $64.80.
(541)516-3036 Lat: 44.25039, Lon: -121.48825
67667 Hwy 20, Bend, OR 97701
bendsistersgardenrv@gmail.com
www.bendsistersgardenrv.com
See primary listing at Sisters and ad page 936.

CROWN VILLA RV RESORT
Ratings: 9/10★/10 (RV Park) N-bnd & S-bnd: From Jct of Business-97/3rd St & Murphy Rd (S of town), E 1.2 mi on Murphy Rd to Brosterhous Rd, S 0.1 mi (R) NOTE: Do not rely on GPS or Mapquest, if unsure call the park or ck parks website. Elev 3623 ft. **FAC:** Paved rds. 104 paved, patios, 5 pull-thrus (55 x 130), back-ins (55 x 100), accepts self-contain units only, 104 full hkups (30/50 amps), cable, WiFi, rentals, laundry, LP gas. **REC:** whirlpool, shuffleboard, rec open to public. Pet restrict(B). Partial handicap access, no tents. Big rig sites, eco-friendly, 2015 rates: $36 to $84. Disc: military.
(541)388-1131 Lat: 44.01720, Lon: -121.29413
60801 Brosterhous Rd, Bend, OR 97702
info@crownvillarvresort.com
www.crownvillarvresort.com
See ad opposite page.

SCANDIA RV PARK
Ratings: 8/9★/9 (RV Park) N-bnd: From Jct of Hwy 97 & Bus 97 (S of town), N 1 mi on Bus 97 (L); or W-bnd: From Jct of Hwy 20 (From Burns) & Bus 97, S 2.2 mi on Bus 97 (R). Elev 3400 ft. **FAC:** Paved rds. (113 spaces). Avail: 48 paved, 14 pull-thrus (25 x 60), back-ins (24 x 60), 48 full hkups

BEND (CONT)

SCANDIA RV PARK (CONT)
30/50 amps), seasonal sites, cable, WiFi, laundry. REC: rec open to public. Pets OK. Partial handicap access, no tents. Big rig sites, 2015 rates: $42 to $50. Disc: military.
541)382-6206 Lat: 44.03025, Lon: -121.31153
61415 S. 3 rd. St (US Bus 97), Bend, OR 97702
deanna@scandiarv.com
www.scandiarv.com
See ad this page, 930.

SUNDANCE MEADOWS **Ratings: 7/7.5/8** Membership Pk) 2015 rates: $13. (541)389-7003 60335 Arnold Market Rd, Bend, OR 97702

TUMALO (State Pk) From Jct of US-20 & US-97 N of town), NW 3.7 mi on US-20 to Cook Ave (MP 14 3/4), SW 1.1 mi (L). 2015 rates: $22 to $30. 800)452-5687

Travel Services

JERRY'S RV SERVICE CENTER RV service, supplies, parts and accessories and a complete service department. Elev 3600 ft. **SERVICES:** RV appliance, restrooms. RV supplies, emergency parking, RV accessible. waiting room. Hours: 8am to 5:30pm.
541)382-2372 Lat: 44.03749, Lon: -121.30476
1165 SE 3rd. St (US Bus 97), Bend, OR 97702
im@jerrys-rv.com
www.jerrysrvservice.com
See ad this page.

Driving a big rig? Average site width and length measurements tell you which campgrounds can accommodate your wide load.

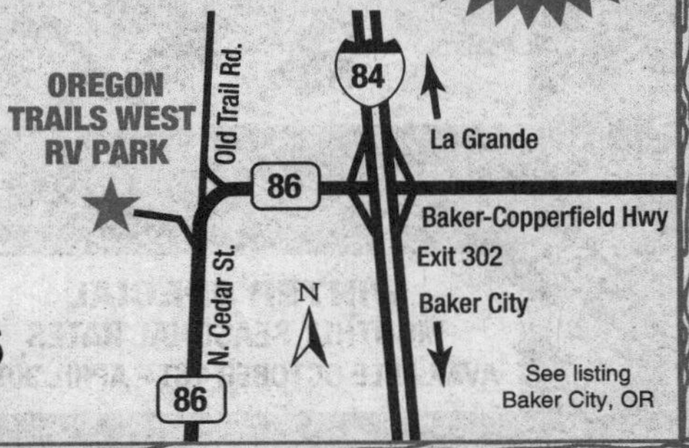

OR

Bend/Sisters Garden RV Resort
67667 Hwy. 20 | Bend, Oregon 97701 | 541-516-3036
888-503-3588 | Fax 541-516-3032
bendsistersgardenrv@gmail.com
www.bendsistersgardenrv.com
Bend/Sisters Garden
RV RESORT
See listing Sisters, OR
WINTER SPECIAL
MONTHLY SEASONAL RATES
AVAILABLE OCTOBER 1ST - APRIL 30TH
TOP RATED
Good Sam Park
FOR 2016
Good Sam
RATED
10/10★/10

BLUE RIVER — C2 *Lane*

➔ HOLIDAY FARM RV RESORT **Ratings: 7.5/8.5★/7.5** (Condo Pk) 2015 rates: $40. (541)822-3726 54432 Mckenzie Hwy, Blue River, OR 97413

PATIO RV PARK
Ratings: 7/8.5/8 (RV Park) From Jct of Hwy 126 & McKenzie River Dr (MP-49.25): Go SW 0.3 mi on McKenzie River Dr (L). **FAC:** Paved/gravel rds. (60 spaces). Avail: 40 gravel, patios, 1 pull-thrus (30 x 60), back-ins (30 x 45), 40 full hkups (30/50 amps), seasonal sites, cable, WiFi, tent sites, dump, laundry. **REC:** Mc Kenzie River: fishing. Pet restrict(B). Big rig sites, 2015 rates: $28 to $33. Disc: AAA.
(541)822-3596 Lat: 44.17464, Lon: -122.19166
55636 Mckenzie River Dr., Blue River, OR 97413
patiorvpark@gmail.com
www.patiorv.com
See ad this page, 930.

WILLAMETTE NF (DELTA CAMPGROUND) (Natl Forest) From town: Go 3-1/2 mi E on Hwy 126, then 1/3 mi S on Aufderheide Dr (FR 19). Pit toilets. 2015 rates: $16. Apr 20 to Oct 21. (801)226-3564

BOARDMAN — A4 *Morrow*

BOARDMAN MARINA & RV PARK
Ratings: 9/8.5★/9.5 (Public) From Jct of I-84 & Exit 164 (Main St), N 0.8 mi on Main St over RR tracks Bridge, stay left at fork (R). Note: Use lat-lon for GPS. **FAC:** Paved rds. 63 paved, patios, 15 pull-thrus (31 x 80), back-ins (30 x 50), 63 full hkups (30/50 amps), WiFi, tent sites, dump, laundry, firewood. **REC:** Columbia River: swim, fishing, marina, playground, rec open to public. Pets OK. Partial handicap access. Big rig sites, 14 day max stay, 2015 rates: $26.50 & $31.80.
(541)481-7217 Lat: 45.84338, Lon: -119.70760
#1 W Marine Dr., Boardman, OR 97818
info@boardmanmarinapark.com
www.boardmanmarinapark.com
See ad this page, 930.

DRIFTWOOD RV PARK & RESORT Ratings: 7.5/7.5/7.5 (RV Park) From Jct of I-84 & exit 164 (Boardman), S 1.2 mi on S Main St to Kunze Rd (2nd stop sign), W 0.8 mi (R). **FAC:** Paved/gravel rds. (108 spaces). 10 Avail: 5 paved, 5 gravel, 10 pull-thrus (28 x 50), 10 full hkups (30/50 amps), seasonal sites, WiFi, laundry. **REC:** heated pool, whirlpool, playground. Pets OK $. Partial handicap access, no tents. 2015 rates: $30.45 to $33.50. Disc: AAA, military.
(541)481-2262 Lat: 45.64862, Lon: -119.67454
800 W Kunze Ln, Boardman, OR 97818
customerservice@drifwood-rv.com
www.driftwood-rv.com

BONANZA — D3 *Klamath*

➔ GERBER RESERVOIR (Public) From town, E 10 mi on Gerber Rd (R). Pit toilets. 2015 rates: $7. (541)947-2177

BROOKINGS — E1 *Curry*

ATRIVERS EDGE RV RESORT
Ratings: 8.5/9.5★/10 (RV Park) From Jct of US-101 & S Bank Chetco River Rd (S end of Chetco River Bridge): Go E 1.5 mi on S Bank Chetco River Rd (L). Caution: S-bnd, enter S Bank Chetco Rd from R turn. **FAC:** Paved rds. (120 spaces). 90 Avail: 30 paved, 60 gravel, patios, 18 pull-thrus (30 x 60), back-ins (33 x 50), 90 full hkups (30/50 amps), seasonal sites, cable, WiFi, rentals, showers $, dump, laundry, LP gas, firewood. **REC:** Chetco River: fishing. Pet restrict(Q). Partial handicap access, no tents. Big rig sites, eco-friendly, 2015 rates: $40 to $45.
(541)469-3356 Lat: 42.07092, Lon: -124.25274

Subscribe to Trailer Life Magazine. For a subscription, call 800-825-6861.

98203 S. Bank Chetco River Rd., Brookings, OR 97415
stay@atriversedge.com
www.atriversedge.com
See ad pages 938, 930.

Do you know how to read each part of a listing? Check the How to Use This Campground Guide in the front.

OR

BROOKINGS (CONT)

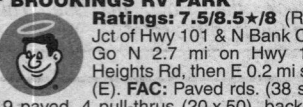

BROOKINGS RV PARK
Ratings: 7.5/8.5★/8 (RV Park) From Jct of Hwy 101 & N Bank Chetco Bridge: Go N 2.7 mi on Hwy 101 to Harris Heights Rd, then E 0.2 mi stay left at fork (E). **FAC:** Paved rds. (38 spaces). Avail: 19 paved, 4 pull-thrus (20 x 50), back-ins (18 x 45), 19 full hkups (30/50 amps), seasonal sites, cable, WiFi, tent sites, rentals, laundry. **REC.** Pets OK. 2015 rates: $32.
(541)469-6849 Lat: 42.07224, Lon: -124.30721
96707 E Harris Heights Rd., Brookings, OR 97415
brookingsrv@charter.net
www.brookingsrv.com
See ad pages 937, 930.

DRIFTWOOD RV PARK
Ratings: 8.5/9.5★/9 (RV Park) N-bnd: Jct of US-101 & W Benham Ln: Go W 0.6 mi on W Benham Ln/Lower Harbor Rd (R) S-Bnd: Jct of US-101 & CH 816/Lower Harbor Rd: Go W 0.6 mi on CH 816/Lower Harbor Rd (R). **FAC:** Paved rds. (110 spaces). 80 Avail: 10 paved, 70 gravel, patios, 24 pull-thrus (30 x 60), back-ins (30 x 40), 80 full hkups (30/50 amps), seasonal sites, cable, WiFi, laundry. **REC.** Pet restrict(B/Q). No tents. Big rig sites, eco-friendly, 2015 rates: $35.
AAA Approved
(541)469-9089 Lat: 42.04272, Lon: -124.26277
16011 Lower Harbor Rd, Brookings, OR 97415
info@driftwoodrvpark.com
www.driftwoodrvpark.com
See ad pages 937, 930.

HARRIS BEACH (State Pk) From Jct of US-101 & N Bank Chetco Bridge, N 2.2 mi on US-101 to Harris Beach State Park Rd (L). 2015 rates: $21 to $26. (800)452-5687

LOEB (State Pk) From Jct of US-101 & N Bank Chetco River Rd, NE 8 mi on N Bank Chetco River Rd (R). 2015 rates: $18 to $22. (541)469-2021

Tell them you saw them in this Guide!

PORT OF BROOKINGS HARBOR BEACHFRONT RV PARK
(Public) N-bnd: From OR border: Go N 3.8 mi on US-101 to Benham Ln, then W 0.6 mi to Boat Basin Rd, then N 0.2 mi (L); or S-bnd: From S end of Chetco River Bridge on US-101: Go W 1 mi on Lower Harbor Rd to Boat Basin Rd, N 0.2 mi (R). **FAC:** Paved rds. (107 spaces). Avail: 104 gravel, patios, 44 pull-thrus (20 x 60), back-ins (20 x 40), 78 full hkups, 9 W, 9 E (30/50 amps), cable, WiFi, tent sites, showers $, dump, laundry, firewood. **REC:** Pacific Ocean: swim, fishing, rec open to public. Pets OK. Partial handicap access. 14 day max stay, 2015 rates: $23 to $51.
(541)469-5867 Lat: 42.04272, Lon: -124.26538
16035 Boat Basin Rd., Brookings, OR 97415
beachfrontrv@port-brookings-harbor.org
www.beachfrontrvpark.com
See ad this page.

PORTSIDE RV PARK
Ratings: 9/10★/8.5 (RV Park) S-bnd: From Jct of US-101 & Lower Harbor Rd (S end of Chetco River bridge): Go W 0.6 mi on Lower Harbor Rd (L); or N-bnd: From Jct of US-101 & W Benham Ln/Lower Harbor Rd: Go NW 1 mi on W Benham Ln/Lower Harbor Rd (R). **FAC:** Paved rds. (95 spaces). Avail: 45 paved, patios, 10 pull-thrus (30 x 65), back-ins (24 x 50), 45 full hkups (30/50 amps), seasonal sites, cable, WiFi, showers $, laundry, restaurant. **REC.** Pet restrict(B). Partial handicap access, no tents. RV age restrict, 2015 rates: $34 to $48.
(877)787-2752 Lat: 42.04839, Lon: -124.26410
16219 Lower Harbor Rd., Brookings, OR 97415
rvpark@destinationbrookings.com
www.portside-rvpark.com
See ad this page, 930.

RIVERSIDE RV RESORT Ratings: 8/7.5/8 (RV Park) From Jct of US-101 & N Bank Chetco River Rd: Go E 0.4mi on North Bank Chetco River Rd (R). **FAC:** Paved rds. (25 spaces). Avail: 13 gravel, patios, 1 pull-thrus (25 x 65), back-ins (25 x 55), some side by side hkups, 13 full hkups (30/50 amps), seasonal sites, cable, WiFi, tent sites, rentals, laundry, firewood. **REC:** Chetco River: fishing. Pets OK. Partial handicap access. 2015 rates: $31 to $44. Disc: AAA, military.
AAA Approved
(541)469-4799 Lat: 42.05949, Lon: -124.26868
97666 N. Bank Chetco River Rd, Brookings, OR 97415
chetcocharlie@riverside-rv.com
www.riverside-rv.com

SEA BIRD RV PARK **Ratings: 5.5/8/6** (Campground) 2015 rates: $30. (541)469-3512 16429 Hwy 101S, Brookings, OR 97415

WHALESHEAD BEACH RESORT **Ratings: 5.5/6.5/8** (RV Park) 2015 rates: $25. (541)469-7446 19921 Whaleshead Rd., Brookings, OR 97415

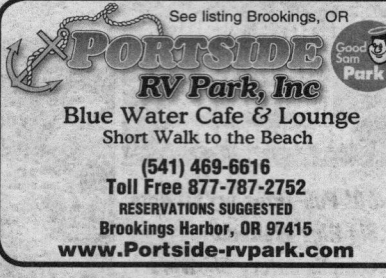

BURNS — C4 *Harney*

BURNS See also Crane.

BURNS RV PARK
Ratings: 6.5/9★/8.5 (RV Park) From Jct of US-20/395 & Hwy 78 (in town), NE 1 mi on US-20/395, NE city limits (R) Elev 4150 ft. **FAC:** Gravel rds. (49 spaces). Avail: 45 gravel, patios, 20 pull-thrus (30 x 75), back-ins (40 x 60), 45 full hkups (30/50 amps), cable, WiFi, tent sites, laundry. Pets OK. Big rig sites, eco-friendly, 2015 rates: $33 to $40. Disc: AAA.
(800)573-7640 Lat: 43.59789, Lon: -119.04924
1273 Seneca Dr., Burns, OR 97720
burnsrvpark@centurytel.net
www.burnsrvpark.com
See ad this page, 930.

BUTTE FALLS — D2 *Jackson*

ROGUE RIVER NF (WHISKEY SPRINGS CAMPGROUND) (Natl Forest) From town: Go 9-1/3 mi SE on CR 821, then 1/3 mi E on FR 3065. Pit toilets. 2015 rates: $14. (541)865-2700

WILLOW LAKE RESORT (Public) From Butte Falls, SE 8 mi on Fish Lake Road (R). 2015 rates: $20 to $30. Apr 15 to Oct 31. (541)774-8183

CAMP SHERMAN — B3 *Jefferson*

CAMP SHERMAN RV PARK & MOTEL
Ratings: 6/9★/8.5 (RV Park) From Jct of Hwy 126 & US-20 (in Sisters), Go W 10 mi on US-20 to SW Camp Sherman Rd, Then N 4 3/4 mi (Follow Camp Sherman Resort Signs) (R). Caution: On SW Camp Sherman Rd, at approx. 2 1/2 mi bear left at the Y. Elev 3022 ft. **FAC:** Gravel rds. (34 spaces). Avail: 24 gravel, back-ins (25 x 55), some side by side hkups, 10 full hkups, 14 W, 14 E (30/50 amps), WiFi, rentals, dump, laundry. **REC:** rec open to public. Pet restrict(B/Q). No tents. 2015 rates: $32 to $34. Disc: AAA.
(541)595-6514 Lat: 44.46016, Lon: -121.64706
25635 SW Forest Service Rd. #1419, Camp Sherman, OR 97730
campshermanrv@gmail.com
www.campshermanrv.com
See ad pages 965, 930.

CANBY — B2 *Clackamas*

RIVERSIDE RV PARK **Ratings: 8.5/7/6.5** (RV Park) 2015 rates: $37. (503)263-3000 24310 Hwy 99E, Canby, OR 97013

CANNON BEACH — A2 *Clatsop*

CANNON BEACH See also Nehalem & Seaside.

Nobody takes to the road like we do. In many listings we tell you the surface type and condition of interior campground roads.

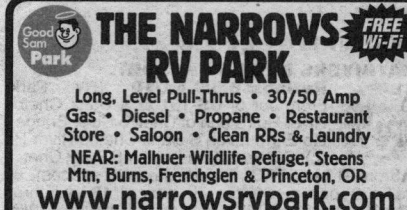

CANNON BEACH (CONT)

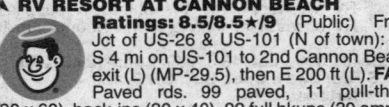

RV RESORT AT CANNON BEACH **Ratings: 8.5/8.5★/9** (Public) From Jct of US-26 & US-101 (N of town): Go S 4 mi on US-101 to 2nd Cannon Beach exit (L) (MP-29.5), then E 200 ft (L). **FAC:** Paved rds. 99 paved, 11 pull-thrus 30 x 60), back-ins (30 x 40), 99 full hkups (30 amps), able, WiFi, laundry, groc, LP gas, firewood. **REC:** eated pool, whirlpool, Ecola Creek: playground. ets OK. Partial handicap access, no tents. 2015 ates: $38 to $50. Disc: military.
800)847-2231 Lat: 45.88918, Lon: -123.95570
40 Elk Creek Road, Cannon Beach, OR 97110
nfo@cbrvresort.com
www.cbrvresort.com
See ad opposite page, 930.

CANYONVILLE — D2 *Douglas*

SEVEN FEATHERS RV RESORT **Ratings: 10/10★/10** (RV Resort) S-Bnd: From Jct of I-5 (exit 99) to Quintioosa Blvd (R); N-Bnd: From Jct of I-5 & exit 99, Go N on Frontage Rd, then under freeway 0.2 mi to Quintioosa Blvd (L).

FIRST CLASS RV RESORT WITH CASINO

n the 'Land of Umpqua' we are nestled in a canyon f douglas fir and pines where their fragrance lingers ong after quiet hours. We are located directly off I-5 t exit 99 in Canyonville.

FAC: Paved rds. 191 paved, patios, 104 pull-thrus 30 x 60), back-ins (30 x 55), accepts full hkup units nly, 191 full hkups (30/50 amps), WiFi, dump, laundry, LP gas. **REC:** heated pool, whirlpool, Jordan Creek: playground, rec open to public. Pet restrict(Q). Partial handicap access, no tents. Big rig sites, 28 day max stay, eco-friendly, 2015 rates: $42 to $50. Disc: AAA, military.
AAA Approved
877)839-3599 Lat: 42.94131, Lon: -123.29004
325 Quintioosa Blvd., Canyonville, OR 97417
v@sevenfeathersrvresort.com
www.sevenfeathersrvresort.com
See ad opposite page, 930.

STANTON PARK (DOUGLAS COUNTY PARK) Public) From town: Go 1 mi N on Hwy 99. From I-5 northbound take exit 99. From I-5 southbound take exit 101. 2015 rates: $15 to $23. (541)839-4483

Things to See and Do

SEVEN FEATHERS CASINO RESORT 24 hour casino with slots, table games, Bingo, Keno, Poker, non-smoking casino area, 5 restaurants, 298 guest room hotel, pool, hot tubs, itness center, River Rock Spa & Salon, live entertainment, and RV Resort. Partial handicap access. RV accessible. Restrooms, food. Hours: 24 hours. ATM.
800)548-8461 Lat: 42.94082, Lon: -123.28526
146 Chief Miwaleta Ln, Canyonville, OR 97417
nfo@sevenfeathers.com
www.sevenfeathers.com
See ad opposite page.

SEVEN FEATHERS TRUCK & TRAVEL CENTER Oregon's most exciting truck stop off I-5 at Exit 99. Partial handicap access. RV accessible. Restrooms, food. Hours: 24 hrs. ATM.
(541)839-3100 Lat: 42.94120, Lon: -123.29009
130 Creekside, Canyonville, OR 97417
www.sevenfeathers.com
See ad opposite page.

CASCADE LOCKS — A3 *Hood River*

CASCADE LOCKS KOA **Ratings: 8.5/8.5★/7** (Campground) 2015 rates: $32.89 to $42.89. Feb 20 to Oct 15. (800)562-8698 841 NE Forest Lane, Cascade Locks, OR 97014

CASCADE LOCKS MARINE PARK (Public) From Jct of I-84 & Wanapa St (Cascade Locks exit), E 0.5 mi on Wanapa St (L) Caution: 12' vertical clearance at entrance to park. 2015 rates: $15 to $25. (541)374-8619

CAVE JUNCTION — D2 *Josephine*

COUNTRY HILLS RESORT Ratings: 3.5/5/7.5 (Campground) From jct US 199 & Hwy 46: Go 8 mi E on Hwy-46. (R). **FAC:** Gravel rds. (34 spaces). Avail: 29 dirt, back-ins (30 x 45), 20 W, 20 E (20/30 amps), seasonal sites, WiFi Hotspot, tent sites, rentals, showers $, dump, laundry, fire rings, firewood. **REC:** Sucker Creek. Pets OK. Partial handicap access. 2015 rates: $28 to $30. Disc: AAA.
AAA Approved
(541)592-3406 Lat: 42.16417, Lon: -123.51049
7901 Caves Highway, Cave Junction, OR 97523
proprietor@countryhillsresort.com
www.countryhillsresort.com

MOUNTAIN MAN RV PARK **Ratings: 5/8/7** (Campground) 2015 rates: $26. (541)592-2656 28288 Redwood Hwy, Cave Junction, OR 97523

OL JO'S RV PARK & CAMPGROUND **Ratings: 5.5/5/7** (Campground) 2015 rates: $25 to $30. (541)592-4207 156 Ollis Rd, Cave Junction, OR 97523

CHARLESTON — C1 *Coos*

BASTENDORFF BEACH PARK (Public) From town, SW 10 mi on Cape Arago Rd, follow signs (R). 2015 rates: $15 to $24. (541)396-7759

CHARLESTON MARINA RV PARK (Public) From Jct of US-101 & Commercial Ave (in Coos Bay), follow Ocean Beaches/Charleston signs: Go W 9 mi to Boat Basin Rd, then N 0.2 mi to Kingfisher Rd, then NE 0.1 mi on Kingfisher Rd (L) NOTE: GPS user's - use coordinates or Coos Bay as the city. **FAC:** Paved rds. 100 paved, 10 pull-thrus (21 x 55), back-ins (21 x 40), some side by side hkups, 100 full hkups (30/50 amps), cable, WiFi $, rentals, dump, laundry, LP gas. **REC:** Coos Bay: fishing, marina, rec open to public. Pets OK. Partial handicap access, no tents. 2015 rates: $28.50 to $32.
(541)888-9512 Lat: 43.34360, Lon: -124.32581
63402 Kingfisher Rd, Charleston, OR 97420
rvpark@charlestonmarina.com
www.charlestonmarina.com
See ad page 940.

OCEANSIDE BEACHFRONT RV RESORT **Ratings: 7.5/8.5★/9** (Campground) From Jct of US-101 & Charleston/State Park (in Coos Bay or North Bend), W 8.5 mi on Charleston (following Charleston signs) to W-end Charleston Bridge/Cape Arago Hwy, W (continue straight) 1.8 mi (R). **FAC:** Gravel rds. 64 gravel, 20 pull-thrus (30 x 60), back-ins (31 x 35), 64 full hkups (30/50 amps), WiFi, tent sites, rentals, showers $, laundry, LP gas, fire rings, firewood. **REC:** Pacific Ocean: swim, fishing. Pets OK. Partial handicap access. Big rig sites, 2015 rates: $42 to $65. Disc: AAA, military.
(541)888-2598 Lat: 43.33957, Lon: -124.35436
90281 Cape Arago Hwy, Coos Bay, OR 97420
stay@oceansidervresort.com
www.oceansidervresort.com

SUNSET BAY (State Pk) From Jct of US-101 & Charleston Harbor (beaches) exit (in Coos Bay or North Bend), W 11.7 mi on Cape Arago Hwy/Charleston Harbor Hwy to W-end Charleston Bridge MP-12 (L). 2015 rates: $20 to $28. (800)452-5687

Things to See and Do

CHARLESTON MARINA & LAUNCH RAMP Full service marina on the Oregon Coast. Partial handicap access. RV accessible. Restrooms, food. Hours: 6 am to 10 pm. Adult fee: $5 Launch Fee.
(541)888-2548 Lat: 43.34615, Lon: -124.32403
63534 Kingfisher Rd, Charleston, OR 97420
info@charlestonmarina.com
www.charlestonmarina.com
See ad page 940.

CHILOQUIN — D3 *Klamath*

COLLIER MEMORIAL (State Pk) From Jct of US-97 & SR-62, N 8 mi on US-97 at MP 243 3/4 (R). (Watch for 2nd camping entrance). 2015 rates: $17 to $22. Apr 15 to Oct 30. (541)783-2471

SPORTSMAN'S RIVER RETREAT RV PARK & CAMPGROUND **Ratings: 4.5/6.5/6** (Campground) 2015 rates: $25. (541)783-3857 32323 Modoc Point Rd, Chiloquin, OR 97624

WALT'S RV PARK Ratings: 3.5/6/7 (Campground) From Jct of Hwy 62 & US-97: Go N 3 mi on US 97 (MP 248 3/4) (L). Elev 4200 ft. **FAC:** Gravel rds. (14 spaces). Avail: 10 gravel, 3 pull-thrus (26 x 50), back-ins (25 x 40), 8 full hkups, 2 W, 2 E (20 amps), seasonal sites, WiFi Hotspot, tent sites, firewood. **REC.** Pet restrict(B/Q). 2015 rates: $22 to $30. Disc: AAA. No CC, no reservations.
AAA Approved
(541)783-2537 Lat: 42.57328, Lon: -121.88394
38400 Hwy 97 N, Chiloquin, OR 97624
gailg14@live.com
www.waltsrvpark.com

WATERWHEEL CAMPGROUND **Ratings: 4/5/5.5** (Campground) 2015 rates: $30 to $40. (541)783-2738 200 Williamson River Dr, Chiloquin, OR 97624

CLOVERDALE — B2 *Tillamook*

CAMPER COVE RV PARK & CAMPGROUND **Ratings: 5/7★/8** (RV Park) S-bnd: From Jct of US-101 & Hwy 6 (in Tillamook), S 12 mi on US-101 (R); or N-bnd: From town, N 2 mi on US-101, at MP 77.5 (L). **FAC:** Gravel rds. (24 spaces). Avail: 20 gravel, 2 pull-thrus (22 x 60), back-ins (24 x 50), 5 full hkups, 15 W, 15 E (30 amps), tent sites, rentals, showers $, dump, laundry, fire rings, firewood. **REC:** Beaver Creek: fishing. Pet restrict(B). Partial handicap access. 2015 rates: $30.
(503)398-5334 Lat: 45.31139, Lon: -123.83773
19620 Hwy 101 South, Cloverdale, OR 97112
celiahung@aol.com
www.campercovecampground.com
See ad page 966.

COBURG — C2 *Lane*

Travel Services

CAMPING WORLD OF COBURG As the nation's largest retailer of RV supplies, accessories, services and new and used RVs, Camping World is committed to making your total RV experience better. RV Accessories: (855)811-3401. **SERVICES:** RV, RV Sales. RV supplies, LP. Hours: 8am - 6pm.
(888)629-6098 Lat: 44.131750, Lon: -123.052515
90855 Roberts Road, Coburg, OR 97408
www.campingworld.com

COOS BAY — C1 *Coos*

COOS BAY See also Bandon, Charleston, Lakeside & North Bend.

OR

COOS BAY (CONT)

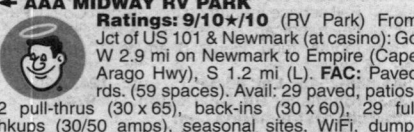

← **AAA MIDWAY RV PARK**
Ratings: 9/10★/10 (RV Park) From Jct of US 101 & Newmark (at casino): Go W 2.9 mi on Newmark to Empire (Cape Arago Hwy), S 1.2 mi (L). **FAC:** Paved rds. (59 spaces). Avail: 29 paved, patios, 2 pull-thrus (30 x 65), back-ins (30 x 60), 29 full hkups (30/50 amps), seasonal sites, WiFi, dump, laundry, LP gas. **REC:** whirlpool. Pet restrict(B). Partial handicap access, no tents. Big rig sites, eco-friendly, 2015 rates: $39.39 to $78.78. Disc: AAA, military.
(541)888-9300 Lat: 43.37425, Lon: -124.28957
92478 Cape Arago Hwy, Coos Bay, OR 97420
midwayrvpark@yahoo.com
www.midwayrvparkcoosbay.com
See ad pages 939, 930.

← **ALDER ACRES RV PARK**
Ratings: 8.5/10★/9 (RV Park) N-bnd: From Jct of US-101 & Charleston/State Pk (Coos Bay): Go W 2.3 mi on Commercial/Central/Ocean Blvd (L) S-bnd: From Jct of US-101 & Virginia Ave (Charleston/State Pk): Go W 0.7 mi on Virginia Ave, then S 2.1 mi on Broadway St/ Woodland Dr. (STAY in LEFT LN)to Ocean Blvd, then W 0.5 mi (L). **FAC:** Paved rds. (88 spaces). Avail: 26 paved, 26 pull-thrus (24 x 60), 26 full hkups (30/50 amps), seasonal sites, WiFi, laundry. **REC.** Pet restrict(Q). Partial handicap access, no tents. Big rig sites, 2015 rates: $38.50.
(888)400-7275 Lat: 43.38081, Lon: -124.24672
1800 28th Ct, Coos Bay, OR 97420
alderacresrv@me.com
www.alderacres.com
See ad this page, 930.

↘ LUCKY LOGGERS RV PARK **Ratings: 7/7/7.5** (RV Park) 2015 rates: $37.90. (541)267-6003 250 E Johnson Ave., Coos Bay, OR 97420

Travel Services

← **ALDER ACRES RV PARK STORAGE** Secure RV, car and boat storage. Large pull-thrus with electricity. RV storage. RV supplies, dump, emergency parking. Hours: 10 am to 5 pm.
(888)400-7275 Lat: 43.38081, Lon: -124.24672
1800 28th Ct., Coos Bay, OR 97420
alderacresrv@me.com
www.alderacres.com
See ad this page.

Wasn't that a beautiful campground you visited ten years ago? But can you remember where it was? Use our "Find-it-Fast" index, located in the back of the Guide. It's an alphabetical list, by state, of every private and public park and campground in the Guide.

↓ **PORTER'S RVS** RV sales, parts, service, bod repair. **SERVICES:** RV, RV appliance, mobil RV svc, restrooms, RV Sales. RV supplies RV accessible. waiting room. Hours: 8am t 5pm.
(800)746-2366 Lat: 43.35870, Lon: -124.21375
971 S Broadway, Coos Bay, OR 97420
pns@portersrv.com
www.portersrv.com
See ad this page.

Things to See and Do

→ **COOS BAY-NORTH BEND VISITOR & CON VENTION BUREAU** Coos Bay area informa tion. Partial handicap access. RV accessible Restrooms. Hours: 9am to 5pm.
(541)269-0215 Lat: 43.36822, Lon: -124.21263
50 Central Ave, Coos Bay, OR 97420
info@oregonsadventurecoast.com
www.oregonsadventurecoast.com
See ad page 928 (Welcome Section).

COQUILLE — C1 *Coos*

↑ LAVERNE COUNTY PARK (Public) From town, N 1 mi on SR-42 to Fairview Rd, N 13 mi (R). 2015 rates: $11 to $18. (541)396-7755

CORBETT — A2 *Multnomah*

↑ **CROWN POINT RV PARK Ratings: 4/5.5/7** (RV Park) From jct I-84 & NE Corbett Hill Rd (exit 22) Follow signs to park. NOTE: To avoid steep grade & sharp turns use Exit 18, then Go 6 mi SE on E Historic Columbia Hwy (R). **FAC:** Gravel rds. (22 spaces) Avail: 10 gravel, 2 pull-thrus (25 x 70), back-ins (25 x 50), 8 full hkups, 2 W, 2 E (30/50 amps), seasonal sites, WiFi, showers $, laundry. **REC.** Pet restrict(B/Q). Partial handicap access, no tents. 2015 rates: $30 to $35. Disc: AAA. No CC.
AAA Approved
(503)695-5207 Lat: 45.53127, Lon: -122.28326
3700 E Historic Columbia River Hwy., Corbett, OR 97019
http://crownpointrvpark.com/

CORVALLIS — B2 *Benton, Linn*

← BENTON OAKS RV CAMPGROUND (Public) From Jct of Hwy 34 & Hwy 20 W (in town): Go SW 3.3 mi on Hwy 20 to 53rd St, then N 1.3 mi (L). 2015 rates: $32. (541)766-6259

← SALMONBERRY COUNTY PARK CAMPGROUND (Public) From town, W 26 mi on Alsea Hwy/Hwy 34 (L). 2015 rates: $20 to $25. May 15 to Oct 15. (541)766-6871

COTTAGE GROVE — C2 *Lane*

↖ ARMITAGE PARK CAMPGROUND (Public) From Jct of Belt Line Rd & Coburg Rd, N 1.6 mi on Coburg Rd to entrance of Lane County Parks (L) 2015 rates: $30 to $33. (541)682-2000

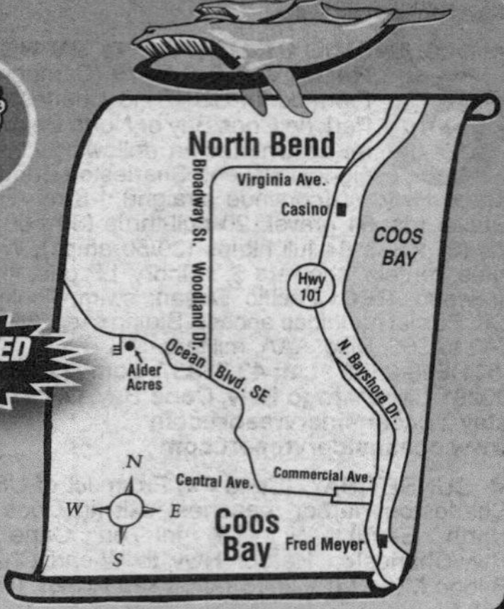

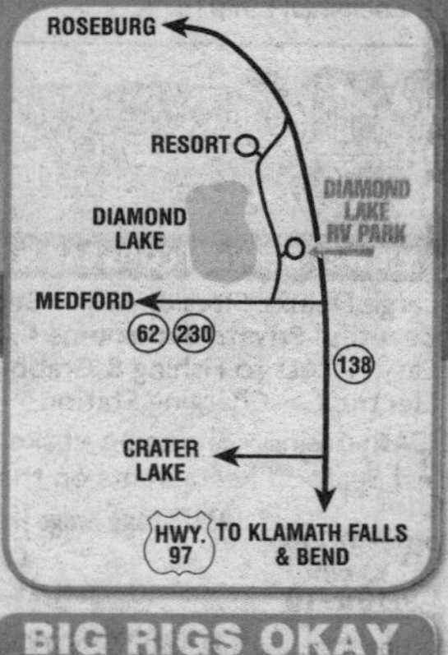

COTTAGE GROVE (CONT)

PINE MEADOWS (Public Corps) From Jct of I-5 & London Rd (Cottage Grove-exit 172), S 3.5 mi on London Rd to Reservoir Rd, SE 3 mi (R). 2015 rates: $12 to $18. May 16 to Sep 7. (541)942-8657

SCHWARZ PARK (COE - DORENA RESERVOIR) (Public Corps) From jct I-5 (exit 174): Go 4 mi SE on Row River Rd. 2015 rates: $16 to $32. Apr 25 to Sep 21. (541)942-1418

CRANE — C5 *Harney*

CRYSTAL CRANE HOT SPRINGS **Ratings: 5.5/7/7.5** (RV Park) 2015 rates: $23 to $25. (541)493-2312 59315 Hwy 78 (Mp 25), Burns, OR 97720

CRATER LAKE — D3 *Klamath*

CRATER LAKE AREA MAP

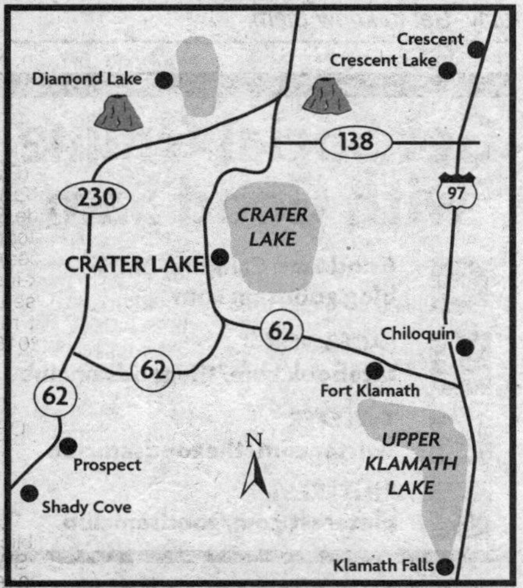

Symbols on map indicate towns within a 50 mile radius of Crater Lake where campgrounds are listed. Check listings for more information.

See also Chiloquin, Crescent, Crescent Lake, Diamond Lake, Fort Klamath, Klamath Falls, Prospect & Shady Cove.

DIAMOND LAKE RV PARK
Ratings: 7/9.5★/9 (RV Park) From Crater Lake: Go N 5.9 Miles on SR-232 to SR-138/E Diamond Lake Hwy (North Entrance to Crater Lake): then N 3 mi to SR-230/W Diamond Lake Hwy, then W 1/4 mi to NF-6592/NF-4795 (Diamond Lake Recreation Area Junction), then N 1 mi (R). Elev 5230 ft. **FAC:** Paved/gravel rds. 100 gravel, patios, 40 pull-thrus (28 x 60), back-ins (30 x 45), 100 full hkups (30/50 amps), WiFi, laundry, LP gas, fire rings, firewood. **REC:** Diamond Lake: fishing, marina. Pet restrict(Q). No tents. Big rig sites, eco-friendly, 2015 rates: $41 to $43. Disc: AAA. May 15 to Oct 1.
(541)793-3318 Lat: 43.13868, Lon: -122.13650
3500 Diamond Lake Loop, Diamond Lake, OR 97731
dlrvp@budget.net
www.diamondlakervpark.com
See primary listing at Diamond Lake and ad page 940.

MAZAMA VILLAGE CAMPGROUND (Natl Pk) From Jct of SR-62 & SR-230, NE 25 mi on SR-62 to park access rd, N 0.1 mi to Ranger pay station (R). 2015 rates: $29 to $35. Jun to Oct. (541)594-2255

CRATER LAKE NATIONAL PARK — D3 *Klamath*

CRATER LAKE See also Chiloquin, Diamond Lake & Prospect.

CRESCENT — C3 *Klamath*

BIG PINES RV PARK
Ratings: 7/9.5★/9 (RV Park) S-bnd: From Crescent: Go S 1 mi on US-97 at MP-186 1/2 (L); or N-bnd: From Jct of 58 & 97: Go N 8.8 mi on Hwy 97 at MP-186 1/2 (R). Elev 4600 ft. **FAC:** Gravel rds. (29 spaces). Avail: 24 gravel, 20 pull-thrus (45 x 100), back-ins (20 x 50), 24 full hkups (30/50 amps), cable, WiFi, tent sites, laundry, fire rings, firewood. **REC.** Pets OK. Big rig sites, eco-friendly, 2015 rates: $34.
(541)433-2785 Lat: 43.44863, Lon: -121.70522
135151 Hwy 97N, Crescent, OR 97733
camp@bigpinesrvpark.com
www.bigpinesrvpark.com
See ad this page, 930.

CRESCENT RV PARK **Ratings: 3/5.5/5.5** (Campground) 2015 rates: $28. (541)433-2950 109 Potters St. (Hwy 97), Crescent, OR 97733

CRESCENT LAKE — C3 *Klamath*

HOODOO'S CRESCENT JUNCTION RV PARK **Ratings: 5/9★/7** (RV Park) 2015 rates: $25 to $30. Apr 15 to Nov 1. (541)433-5300 20030 Crescent Lake Hwy, Crescent, OR 97733

CRESWELL — C2 *Lane*

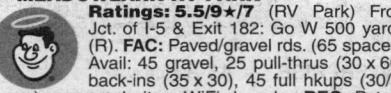

MEADOWLARK RV PARK
Ratings: 5.5/9★/7 (RV Park) From Jct. of I-5 & Exit 182: Go W 500 yards. (R). **FAC:** Paved/gravel rds. (65 spaces). Avail: 45 gravel, 25 pull-thrus (30 x 60), back-ins (35 x 30), 45 full hkups (30/50 amps), seasonal sites, WiFi, laundry. **REC.** Pet restrict(B). 2015 rates: $35.
(541)525-3348 Lat: 43.91806, Lon: -123.015825
PO Box 1024, Creswell, OR 97426
creswellrvpark@gmail.com
www.creswellrvpark.com
See ad pages 942, 930.

CROOKED RIVER RANCH — B3 *Jefferson*

CROOKED RIVER RANCH RV PARK
Ratings: 8/9★/8 (RV Park) From Jct of US 97 & Hwy 126 (in Redmond), N 7.5 mi on US 97 to Lower Bridge Way (Milepost 115 1/4), W 2.2 mi to NW 43 RD St, N 1.8 mi to Chinook Dr, NW 3.5 mi (R) Note: Call for directions. Elev 2569 ft. **FAC:** Paved/gravel rds. 83 Avail: 50 gravel, 33 grass, patios, 7 pull-thrus (24 x 60), back-ins (24 x 60), some side by side hkups, 36 full hkups, 47 W, 47 E (30/50 amps), WiFi, tent sites, showers $, dump, laundry. **REC:** heated pool, golf, playground, rec open to public. Pet restrict(B). Big rig sites, 2015 rates: $37.45 to $39.59. Disc: military.
(800)841-0563 Lat: 44.42833, Lon: -121.24252
14875 SW Hayes Rd., Crooked River Ranch, OR 97760
rvpark@crookedriverranch.com
www.crookedriverranch.com
See ad pages 959, 930.

CULVER — B3 *Jefferson*

CENTRAL OREGON KOA **Ratings: 8.5/8.5/9** (Campground) 2015 rates: $36.26 to $46.96. (800)562-1992 2435 SW Jericho Ln, Culver, OR 97734

THE COVE PALISADES (State Pk) From Jct of US-26 & US-97 (S-end of Jordan Rd), S 6.6 mi on US-97 to Iris Ln (MP-103 1/2), W 2.4 mi to SW Feather Dr, NW 1.1 mi to Fisch/Frazier Rd, N 1.5 mi to Jordan Rd (State Park sign), W 6 mi (L). 2015 rates: $21 to $30. (800)452-5687

CURTIN — C2 *Douglas*

PASS CREEK (DOUGLAS COUNTY PARK) (Public) From I-5 (exit 163): Go 1/4 mi N on W Marginal Rd. 2015 rates: $15 to $23. (541)942-3281

DAYTON — B2 *Yamhill*

WILLAMETTE WINE COUNTRY RV PARK
Ratings: 10/10★/9.5 (RV Park) From Jct of US-99W & Hwy 18/SE Dayton Bypass: Go SW 0.9 mi on Hwy 18 (L). **FAC:** Paved rds. (173 spaces). Avail: 43 paved, patios, 43 pull-thrus (26 x 65), 43 full hkups (30/50 amps), seasonal sites, cable, WiFi, rentals, laundry, LP gas. **REC:** heated pool, whirlpool, swim. Pet restrict(B/Q). Partial handicap access, no tents. Big rig sites, 2015 rates: $40 to $45. Disc: military.
(503)864-2233 Lat: 45.22731, Lon: -123.07424
16205 SE Kreder Rd, Dayton, OR 97114
reservations@wwcrvpark.com
www.wwcrvpark.com
See ad pages 955, 930.

DEPOE BAY — B1 *Lincoln*

FOGARTY CREEK RV PARK
Ratings: 8/8.5★/8 (RV Park) From town, N 2 mi on US-101 (100 ft N of Fogarty Creek State Park) (R). **FAC:** Paved rds. (53 spaces). 30 Avail: 16 all weather, 4 gravel, 10 grass, 18 pull-thrus (25 x 42), back-ins (23 x 40), 30 full hkups (30 amps), seasonal sites, cable, WiFi, laundry. **REC.** Pets OK. No tents. 2015 rates: $39.60.
(541)764-2228 Lat: 44.84371, Lon: -124.04702
3340 N Hay 101, Depoe Bay, OR 97341
info@fogartycreekrv.com
www.fogartycreekrv.com
See ad this page, 930.

SEA & SAND RV PARK
Ratings: 8/9★/9 (RV Park) S-bnd: From Jct of US 101 & Hwy 18 (N of Lincoln City), S 13.5 mi on US 101 (R); or N-bnd: From town, N 3.6 mi on US-101 (make U turn, turn about, at Lancer St), S 0.1 mi (R). Note: Up to 40 ft max allowed. **FAC:** Paved/gravel rds. 109 gravel, 16 pull-thrus (26 x 44), back-ins (28 x 40), 109 full hkups (30 amps), cable, WiFi, showers $, dump, laundry, fire rings, firewood. **REC:** Pacific Ocean: swim. Pet restrict(B/Q). Partial handicap access, no tents. 14 day max stay, 2015 rates: $35 to $59. Disc: military.
(541)764-2313 Lat: 44.861083, Lon: -124.03831
4985 N Hwy 101, Depoe Bay, OR 97341
seaandsandmngr@aol.com
www.seaandsandrvpark.com
See ad this page, 930.

DETROIT — B3 *Marion*

DETROIT LAKE (State Pk) From Jct of Hwy 22 & Forest Ave (in town), W 1.8 mi on Hwy 22 to MP-48 1/2 (L). 2015 rates: $20 to $24. Mar 15 to Oct 31. (800)452-5687

MT. HOOD NF (PENINSULA CAMPGROUND) (Natl Forest) From town: Go 27 mi SE on Hwy-224, then 21-3/4 S on FR-46, then 8-1/4 mi SE on FR-4690, then 6-1/2 mi S on FR-4220. Pit toilets. 2015 rates: $15 to $25. (503)668-1700

DETROIT (CONT)

WILLAMETTE NF (SOUTHSHORE CAMPGROUND) (Natl Forest) From town: Go 2.5 mi E on Hwy 22 to Blowout Rd. #10, then 3.5 mi on Blowout to entrance. Pit toilets. 2015 rates: $18. (541)338-7869

DEXTER — C2 *Lane*

DEXTER SHORES RV PARK
Ratings: 6.5/8★/8 (RV Park) From Jct of I-5 & Hwy 58 (Exit 188A): Go E 11.5 mi on Hwy 58 to Lost Creek Rd, then S 200 ft to Dexter Rd, E 200 ft (E). **FAC:** Gravel/dirt rds. (53 spaces). 28 Avail: 7 paved, 21 gravel, patios, 12 pull-thrus (24 x 60), back-ins (30 x 50), 28 full hkups (30/50 amps), seasonal sites, cable, WiFi, tent sites, laundry. **REC.** Pet restrict(B/Q) $. Partial handicap access. 2015 rates: $32 to $34. Disc: military.
(866)558-9777 Lat: 43.91398, Lon: -122.81008
39140 Dexter Rd, Dexter, OR 97431
dextershoresrv@gmail.com
www.dextershoresrv.com
See ad this page, 930.

DIAMOND LAKE — D3 *Douglas*

DIAMOND LAKE RV PARK
Ratings: 7/9.5★/9 (RV Park) From Jct of US-97 & SR- 138: Go W 19 mi on Hwy 138 to SR-230 (MP-83), then W 1/4 mi to NF-6592/NF-4795 (Diamond Lake Recreation Area Junction), then N 1 mi (R). Elev 5230 ft. **FAC:** Paved/gravel rds. 100 gravel, patios, 40 pull-thrus (28 x 60), back-ins (30 x 45), 100 full hkups (30/50 amps), WiFi, laundry, LP gas, fire rings, firewood. **REC:** Diamond Lake: fishing, marina. Pet restrict(Q). Partial handicap access, no tents. Big rig sites, eco-friendly. 2015 rates: $41 to $43. Disc: AAA. May 15 to Oct 1.
(541)793-3318 Lat: 43.13868, Lon: -122.13650
3500 Diamond Lake Loop, Diamond Lake, OR 97731
dlrvp@budget.net
www.diamondlakervpark.com
See ad pages 940, 930.

We appreciate your business!

DODSON — A3 *Hood River*

AINSWORTH (State Pk) From Jct of I-84 & Historic Hwy (exit 35), S 0.6 mi on Historic Hwy (L). 2015 rates: $16 to $20. Mar 14 to Oct 31. (503)695-2301

DUFUR — A3 *Wasco*

DUFUR RV PARK
Ratings: 3.5/NA/7 (RV Park) From Jct of I-84 & US-197 (at the Dalles), S 13 mi on US-197 to First St (2nd Dufur exit), W 0.4 mi (L). **FAC:** Paved/gravel rds. (26 spaces). 20 Avail: 10 gravel, 10 grass, 7 pull-thrus (20 x 45), back-ins (16 x 45), 20 full hkups (30 amps), WiFi, dump. **REC:** Fifteen Mile Creek. Pets OK. No tents. 2015 rates: $20. No CC.
(541)467-2449 Lat: 45.45156, Lon: -121.12928
#10 Aiken St, Dufur, OR 97021
See ad page 966.

ELGIN — A5 *Umatilla, Union*

HU-NA-HA RV PARK (Public) From Jct of Hwy 82 & Cedar St (in town), E 0.4 mi on Cedar St (L). 2015 rates: $25. (541)786-1662

ELKTON — C2 *Douglas*

ELKTON RV PARK
Ratings: 8/NA/9 (RV Park) From Jct of Hwy 138 & Hwy 38 (E edge of town): Go W 0.2 mi on Hwy 38 to 1st St, then S 200 yds to River Rd, then W 700 ft (L). **FAC:** Gravel rds. (45 spaces). Avail: 40 gravel, 6 pull-thrus (25 x 45), back-ins (25 x 45), 34 full hkups, 6 W, 6 E (30/50 amps), seasonal sites, WiFi, tent sites, rentals, restrooms only, dump, laundry, firewood. **REC:** Umpqua River: swim, fishing. Pets OK. 2015 rates: $34. Disc: military.
(541)584-2832 Lat: 43.63673, Lon: -123.56954
450 River Rd, Elkton, OR 97436
www.elktonrvpark.com
See ad pages 961, 930.

ELSIE — A2 *Clatsop*

SPRUCE RUN (State Pk) From Jct of US-26 & Spruce Run Rd, S 5 mi on Lower Nehalem Rd (E). Pit toilets. 2015 rates: $10. May 15 to Sep 15. (503)325-9306

ENTERPRISE — A5 *Wallowa*

ENTERPRISE See also Joseph & Wallowa.

To get the most out of your Guide, refer to the Table of Contents in the front of the book.

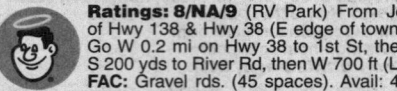

ESTACADA — B3 *Clackamas*

CLACKAMAS RIVER RV PARK **Ratings: 7.5/8★/7.5** (RV Park) 2015 rates: $32. (503)630-7000 40505 E Hwy 224, Estacada, OR 97023

MILO MCIVER (State Pk) From Jct of Hwys 224 & 211 (in town), SW 1 mi on Hwy 211 to S Hayden Rd, W 1.3 mi to S Springwater Rd, NW 1.2 mi (R). 2015 rates: $17 to $24. Mar 15 to Oct 31. (800)452-5687

MT. HOOD NF (LAZY BEND CAMPGROUND) (Natl Forest) From town: Go 10-3/4 SE on Hwy-224. 2015 rates: $21. Apr 19 to Oct 13. (503)630-4156

PROMONTORY (Public) From town, SE 7 mi on SR-224 (R). 2015 rates: $18. May 23 to Sep 14. (503)630-7229

Park owners want you to be satisfied with your stay. Get to know them.

EUGENE — C2 *Lane*

EUGENE AREA MAP

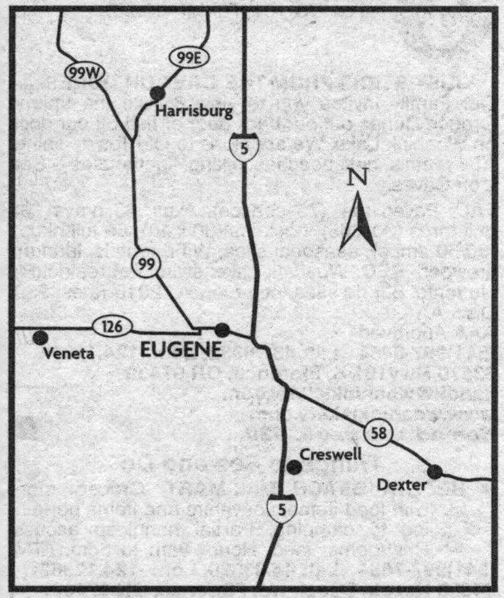

Symbols on map indicate towns within a 35 mile radius of Eugene where campgrounds are listed. Check listings for more information.

See also Creswell, Dexter, Harrisburg & Veneta.

DEERWOOD RV PARK **Ratings: 7.5/8★/8** (RV Park) 2015 rates: $42.94 to $47.70. (541)988-1139 35059 Seavy Loop Rd, Eugene, OR 97405

EUGENE KAMPING WORLD
Ratings: 8/8.5/8.5 (Campground) From Jct of I-5 & Van Duyn Rd (exit 199): Go W 0.3 mi on Van Duyn Rd/E Pearl St to S Stuart Way, then S 0.2 mi (E) Note: first turn after stop light. **FAC:** Paved rds. (110 spaces). 60 Avail: 37 paved, 23 gravel, 55 pull-thrus (22 x 65), back-ins (22 x 40), 47 full hkups, 13 W, 13 E (30/50 amps), seasonal sites, WiFi, tent sites, dump, laundry, LP gas. **REC:** playground. Pet restrict(B). Eco-friendly, 2015 rates: $35 to $39. Disc: AAA.
AAA Approved
(800)343-3008 Lat: 44.13420, Lon: -123.05683
90932 S Stuart Way, Coburg, OR 97408
eugenekampingworld2@yahoo.com
www.eugenekampingworld.com
See ad opposite page, 930.

EUGENE MOBILE VILLAGE & RV PARK
Ratings: 5.5/8.5★/7.5 (RV Area in MHP) From Jct of I-5 & 30th Ave (exit 189): Go N 0.3 mi on off ramp to Franklin Blvd, then N 1.7 mi on Franklin Blvd (L). **FAC:** Paved rds. (75 spaces). Avail: 24 paved, 9 pull-thrus (25 x 50), back-ins (20 x 45), 24 full hkups (30/50 amps), seasonal sites, WiFi, laundry. **REC.** Pet restrict(Q). No tents. 2015 rates: $28.
(541)747-2257 Lat: 44.037918, Lon: -123.028039
4750 Franklin Blvd., Eugene, OR 97403
info@eugenervpark.com
www.eugenervpark.com
See ad opposite page.

PREMIER RV RESORTS - EUGENE
Ratings: 10/10★/9.5 (RV Resort) From Jct of I-5 & Van Duyn Rd (exit 199): Go E 300 ft on Van Duyn Rd (R). **FAC:** Paved rds. (151 spaces). Avail: 87 paved, patios, 54 pull-thrus (33 x 64), back-ins (25 x 52), 87 full hkups (30/50 amps), seasonal sites, cable, WiFi, dump, laundry, LP gas. **REC:** heated pool, whirlpool, pond, fishing. Pets OK. Partial handicap access, no tents. Big rig sites, eco-friendly, 2015 rates: $42 to $49. Disc: AAA, military.
(541)686-3152 Lat: 44.13462, Lon: -123.04842
33022 Van Duyn Rd, Coburg, OR 97408
premiereugene@msn.com
www.premierrvresorts.com
See ad opposite page, 930.

RICHARDSON PARK (Public) From Jct of Beltline Rd & Hwy 99, N 0.6 mi on Hwy 99 to Clearlake Rd, W 8.5 mi (L). 2015 rates: $25. Apr 15 to Oct 15. (541)682-2000

SHAMROCK RV & MHP VILLAGE
Ratings: 8/8.5★/7 (RV Park) N-bnd: From Jct of I-5 & Franklin Blvd (Exit 189): Go N 2 mi on Franklin Blvd (R); or S-bnd: From Jct of I-5 & 30th St (Exit 189): Go E 0.1 mi on 30th St. (over the freeway) to Franklin Blvd, then N 2 mi (R). Note: RV length restriction. **FAC:** Paved rds. (113 spaces). Avail: 37 paved, 28 pull-thrus (20 x 50), back-ins (22 x 35), 30 full hkups, 7 W, 7 E (30/50 amps), seasonal sites, cable, WiFi, dump, laundry. **REC:** Willamette River: fishing. Pet restrict(B). Partial handicap access, no tents. 2015 rates: $31.
(541)747-7473 Lat: 44.04113, Lon: -123.02826
4531 Franklin Blvd, Eugene, OR 97403
manager@shamrockvillagepark.com
www.shamrockvillagepark.com
See ad opposite page, 930.

We rate what RVers consider important.

FAIRVIEW — A2 *Multnomah*

PORTLAND FAIRVIEW RV PARK
Ratings: 10/10★/9 (RV Park) From Jct of I-84 & 207th Ave N (exit 14): Go N 0.1 mi on 207th Ave to NE Sandy Blvd, then E 0.3 mi (L).

A PRIME PORTLAND LOCATION
Only minutes from Portland, rose gardens, zoo and all local attractions, just off I-84. We invite you to our clean, green and friendly park. We are big rig friendly with club room, pool and Wi-Fi for your convenience.

FAC: Paved rds. (407 spaces). Avail: 257 paved, patios, 105 pull-thrus (25 x 60), back-ins (25 x 35), accepts full hkup units only, 257 full hkups (30/50 amps), seasonal sites, cable, WiFi, laundry. **REC:** heated pool, whirlpool, pond. Pet restrict(B). No tents. Big rig sites, eco-friendly, 2015 rates: $42 to $45.
(877)777-1047 Lat: 45.54333, Lon: -122.44438
21401 NE Sandy Blvd, Fairview, OR 97024
customerservice@portlandfairviewrv.com
www.portlandfairviewrv.com
See ad pages 957, 930.

ROLLING HILLS MOBILE TERRACE RV PARK **Ratings: 7.5/7.5/7.5** (RV Park) 2015 rates: $35. (503)666-7282 20145 NE Sandy Blvd #31, Fairview, OR 97024

FLORENCE — C1 *Lane*

B & E WAYSIDE RV PARK
Ratings: 8/9.5★/8 (RV Park) From Jct of US-101 & Hwy 126 (in town): Go N 1.7 mi on US-101 (R). **FAC:** Paved rds. 25 paved, patios, back-ins (27 x 50), 25 full hkups (30 amps), cable, WiFi, laundry. **REC.** Pet restrict(B/Q). Partial handicap access, no tents. Eco-friendly, 2015 rates: $39.
(541)997-6451 Lat: 43.99962, Lon: -124.10060
3760 Hwy 101, Florence, OR 97439
info@bandewaysidervpark.com
www.bandewaysidervpark.com
See ad pages 944, 930.

CARL G WASHBURNE (State Pk) From Jct of US-101 & Hwy 126 (in town), N 15 mi on US-101 to MP-176 (R). 2015 rates: $22 to $26. (541)547-3416

OR

FLORENCE (CONT)

HARBOR VISTA CAMPGROUND (Public) From Jct of US-101 & Hwy 126 (in town), N 1.6 mi on US-101 to 35th St, W 1 mi to Rhododenron Dr, N 0.5 mi to N Jetty Rd, W 0.1 mi to Harbor Vista (L). 2015 rates: $25 to $27.50. (541)682-2000

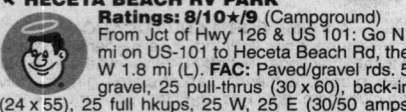

HECETA BEACH RV PARK
Ratings: 8/10★/9 (Campground) From Jct of Hwy 126 & US 101: Go N 3 mi on US-101 to Heceta Beach Rd, then W 1.8 mi (L). **FAC:** Paved/gravel rds. 50 gravel, 25 pull-thrus (30 x 60), back-ins (24 x 55), 25 full hkups, 25 W, 25 E (30/50 amps), cable, WiFi, tent sites, dump, laundry, groc, LP gas, fire rings, firewood. **REC.** Pets OK. Partial handicap access. Big rig sites, 2015 rates: $36 to $42. Disc: military.
(541)997-7664 Lat: 44.03293, Lon: -124.12868
04636 Heceta Beach Rd, Florence, OR 97439
hecetabeachrvpark@yahoo.com
www.hecetabeachrvpark.com
See ad pages 943, 930.

JESSIE M HONEYMAN (State Pk) From Jct of US-101 & Hwy 126 (in town), S 3 mi on Hwy 101 (R). 2015 rates: $22 to $31. (800)452-5687

PACIFIC PINES RV PARK & STORAGE, INC
Ratings: 9/10★/9 (RV Park) From Jct of US-101 & Hwy 126 (in town): Go N 2 mi on US-101 to 42nd St, then E 0.1 mi (R). **FAC:** Paved rds. (64 spaces). Avail: 44 paved, 40 pull-thrus (24 x 50), back-ins (22 x 40), 44 full hkups (30/50 amps), seasonal sites, cable, WiFi, dump, laundry, controlled access. **REC.** Pets OK. Partial handicap access, no tents. 2015 rates: $36.66 to $38.88.
(541)997-1434 Lat: 44.00226, Lon: -124.09975
4044 Hwy 101, Florence, OR 97439
info@pacificpinesrv.com
www.pacificpinesrv.com
See ad pages 943, 930.

RV Park ratings you can rely on!

PORT OF SIUSLAW CAMPGROUND & MARINA
(Public) From Jct of 101 & Hwy 126: Go S 0.3 mi on Hwy 101 to Nopal (follow brown port signs), then SE 0.2 mi to Harbor St, then E 0.2 mi (E). **FAC:** Paved/dirt rds. 101 gravel, back-ins (23 x 55), mostly side by side hkups, 63 full hkups, 25 W, 25 E (30/50 amps), cable, WiFi, tent sites, dump, laundry. **REC:** Siuslaw River: fishing, marina. Pets OK $. Partial handicap access. 2015 rates: $22 to $32.
(541)997-3040 Lat: 43.96901, Lon: -124.10187
100 Harbor St, Florence, OR 97439
campground@portofsiuslaw.com
www.portofsiuslaw.com
See ad page 943.

SOUTH JETTY **Ratings: 6/5.5/7** (Membership Pk) 2015 rates: $32 to $46. (800)288-7245 05010 South Jetty Rd, Florence, OR 97439

Our rating system isn't just tough, it's thorough. We know the kinds of things that are important to you — like clean restrooms and showers, attractive, secure, well-tended grounds, and extras like swimming pools. We give the first rating for development of facilities, the second for cleanliness and physical characteristics of restrooms and showers, and the third for visual appearance.

WOAHINK LAKE RV RESORT
Ratings: 9/9★/10 (RV Park) From Jct of Hwy 126 & US-101 (in town): Go S 5.1 mi on US-101 (R) (MP-195.5).

JUST STEPS FROM THE OREGON DUNES!
Our Family invites you to view & hike the unique Oregon Dunes out our back door or fish off our dock on Woahink Lake. We are close to Old Town, dining, ATV rentals, golf, beaches, hiking, lighthouses & Sea Lion Caves.

FAC: Paved rds. (75 spaces). Avail: 65 gravel, 35 pull-thrus (30 x 65), back-ins (30 x 40), 65 full hkups (30/50 amps), seasonal sites, WiFi, rentals, laundry, firewood. **REC:** Woahink Lake: swim. Pet restrict(B). No tents. Big rig sites, eco-friendly, 2015 rates: $39. Disc: AAA.
AAA Approved
(541)997-6454 Lat: 43.90332, Lon: -124.11614
83570 Hwy101 S, Florence, OR 97439
kandk@woahinklakerv.com
www.woahinklakerv.com
See ad this page, 930.

Things to See and Do

HECETA BEACH MINI-MART Grocery store with food items, souvenirs and items pertaining to camping. Partial handicap access. Restrooms, food. Hours: 8am to 6pm. ATM.
(541)997-7664 Lat: 44.03320, Lon: -124.12862
04636 Heceta Beach Rd, Florence, OR 97439
hecetabeachrvpark@yahoo.com
www.hecetabeachrvpark.com
See ad page 943.

FORT KLAMATH — D3 *Klamath*

CRATER LAKE RESORT **Ratings: 6/7/8.5** (RV Park) 2015 rates: $30. (541)381-2349 50711 Hwy 62, Fort Klamath, OR 97626

FORT ROCK — C3 *Lake*

ROCKHORSE PARK **Ratings: 4/7/5** (Campground) 2015 rates: $20 to $40. (541)576-2488 74543 Hwy 31, Fort Rock, OR 97735

FOSSIL — B4 *Wheeler*

BEAR HOLLOW PARK (Public) From Town, SE 10 mi on Hwy 19 (R). Pit toilets. 2015 rates: $5 to $10. (541)763-2010

SHELTON WAYSIDE PARK (Public) From Town, SE 13 mi on Hwy 19 (R). Pit toilets. 2015 rates: $5. Apr 15 to Nov 15. (541)763-2010

FOSTER — B2 *Linn*

RIVER BEND PARK (Public) From Jct of US-228 & Hwy 20 (Sweet Home), 6.3 mi on Hwy 20 to MP 36.4 (L) Online resv. 2015 rates: $24 to $28. (541)967-3917

FRENCHGLEN — D4 *Harney*

PAGE SPRINGS (BLM-DIAMOND CRATERS) (Public) From town: Go 4 mi E on N Steens Mountain Loop Rd. 2015 rates: $8. (541)573-4400

Park policies vary. Ask about the cancellation policy when making a reservation.

FRENCHGLEN (CONT)

➔ **STEENS MOUNTAIN WILDERNESS RESORT**
Ratings: 7.5/10★/8 (RV Park) From Jct of Hwy 205 & Steens Mountain North Loop Rd (S end of Frenchglen), SE 3 mi on Steens Mountain North Loop Rd to Resort Ln, W 0.1 mi (L). 60 mi S of Burns. Elev 4200 ft. **FAC:** Gravel rds. 38 gravel, 38 pull-thrus (45 x 90), 38 full hkups (30/50 amps), WiFi, tent sites, rentals, dump, laundry, fire rings, firewood. **REC:** Donner und Blitzen River: fishing, playground. Pets OK. Big rig sites, 2015 rates: $20 to $30.
(541)493-2415 Lat: 42.809542, Lon: -118.876643
35678 Resort Ln, Frenchglen, OR 97736
info@steensresort.com
www.steensresort.com
See ad opposite page, 930.

GARIBALDI — A2 *Tillamook*

↑ BARVIEW JETTY COUNTY PARK (Public) From Jct of SR-6 & US-101, N 14 mi on US-101 to Cedar St, W 0.25 mi (R). 2015 rates: $10 to $30. (503)322-3522

↓ **HARBORVIEW INN & RV PARK**
Ratings: 7.5/9★/8.5 (RV Park) From Jct of US 101 & So. 7th St: Go S .02 mi on So. 7th St. (R). **FAC:** Gravel rds. (30 spaces). Avail: 26 gravel, 8 pull-thrus (25 x 60), back-ins (25 x 60), 26 full hkups (30/50 amps), seasonal sites, cable, WiFi, rentals, laundry, fire rings. **REC:** Pacific Ocean: fishing. Pets OK. Partial handicap access. Big rig sites, 2015 rates: $35 to $46.
(503)322-3251 Lat: 45.556131, Lon: -123.915208
302 South 7th Streeet, Garibaldi, OR 97118
info@harborviewfun.com
www.harborviewfun.com
See ad opposite page.

← THE OLD MILL RV PARK **Ratings: 5.5/6.5/5** (RV Park) 2015 rates: $26.50 to $30.50. (503)322-0322 210 S 3rd St, Garibaldi, OR 97118

GLIDE — C2 *Douglas*

SUSAN CREEK (BLM) (Natl Pk) From east of town limits: Go 12-1/2 mi E on Hwy 138 (North Umpqua Hwy). 2015 rates: $14. Apr 18 to Oct 27. (541)440-4930

GOLD BEACH — D1 *Curry*

GOLD BEACH See also Agness, Brookings & Port Orford.

↗ ANGLER'S TRAILER VILLAGE **Ratings: 7/8.5★/6.5** (RV Park) 2015 rates: $25. (541)247-7922 95706 Jerry's Flat Rd., Gold Beach, OR 97444

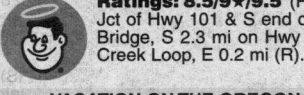

➔ **BEACH RESORT AT TURTLE ROCK**
Ratings: 8.5/9★/9.5 (RV Park) From Jct of Hwy 101 & S end of Rogue River Bridge, S 2.3 mi on Hwy 101 to Hunter Creek Loop, E 0.2 mi (R).

VACATION ON THE OREGON COAST
Cottages, RV sites, 6 RV spa sites with decks, BBQs on the banks of Hunter Creek. Walking distance to the ocean, bar & grill, local brewery. Group facility. Hear sounds of the surf, watch for whales on your next adventure.

FAC: Gravel rds. (115 spaces). Avail: 109 gravel, 22 pull-thrus (35 x 60), back-ins (40 x 45), 109 full hkups (30/50 amps), seasonal sites, cable, WiFi, tent sites, rentals, dump, laundry, LP gas, fire rings, firewood. **REC:** Hunter Creek: swim, fishing. Pets OK. Partial handicap access. Big rig sites, eco-friendly, 2015 rates: $36.89 to $72.66. Disc: AAA.
AAA Approved
(800)353-9754 Lat: 42.39079, Lon: -124.41684
28788 Hunter Creek Loop, Gold Beach, OR 97444
trr.reservation@icloud.com
www.turtlerockresorts.com
See ad pages 946, 930.

Say you saw it in our Guide!

↗ **FOUR SEASONS RV RESORT**
Ratings: 8.5/9★/9.5 (RV Park) From Jct of US-101 & N Rogue River Rd (at N end of Rogue River bridge): Go E 3.5 mi on N Rogue River Rd to N Bank Rogue, then SE 3 mi (R). **FAC:** Paved/gravel rds. (42 spaces). Avail: 28 gravel, patios, back-ins (25 x 50), 28 full hkups (30/50 amps), seasonal sites, cable, WiFi, tent sites, laundry, groc, LP gas. **REC:** Rogue River: swim, fishing. Pets OK. Eco-friendly, 2015 rates: $28 to $42.
(541)247-4503 Lat: 42.47498, Lon: -124.33765
96526 N Bank Rogue, Gold Beach, OR 97444
fourseasons@harborside.com
www.fourseasonsrv.com
See ad opposite page, 930.

↑ **HONEY BEAR RV & CAMPGROUND**
Ratings: 8/8.5★/8.5 (Campground) From town (at N end of Rogue River Bridge), N 6.5 mi on US-101 to Honey Bear Logo & Ophir Rd (MP-321), NE 2 mi (R); or From S end of Port Orford, S 19 mi on US-101 to Logo & Ophir Rd, SE 0.6 mi (L). **FAC:** Paved/gravel rds. (65 spaces). 45 Avail: 20 paved, 25 gravel, patios, 40 pull-thrus (28 x 60), back-ins (30 x 50), some side by side hkups, 33 full hkups, 12 W, 12 E (30/50 amps), seasonal sites, WiFi, tent sites, dump, laundry, fire rings, firewood, restaurant. **REC:** pond, fishing, playground. Pet restrict(Q). 2015 rates: $33 to $39. Disc: AAA, military.
AAA Approved
(800)822-4444 Lat: 42.53581, Lon: -124.39567
34161 Ophir Rd, Gold Beach, OR 97444
info@honeybearrv.com
www.honeybearrv.com
See ad this page, 930.

↗ **INDIAN CREEK RV PARK**
Ratings: 8/9★/9.5 (RV Park) From Jct of US-101 & Jerry's Flat Rd (S end of Rogue River bridge): Go E 0.5 mi on Jerry's Flat Rd (R). **FAC:** Paved rds. (95 spaces). 62 Avail: 8 paved, 44 gravel, 10 grass, patios, 7 pull-thrus (20 x 60), back-ins (21 x 40), 62 full hkups (30 amps), seasonal sites, WiFi, tent sites, laundry, groc, fire rings, firewood, restaurant. **REC:** Indian Creek: fishing. Pets OK. Partial handicap access. 2015 rates: $25 to $35.
(541)247-7704 Lat: 42.42787, Lon: -124.40374
94680 Jerry's Flat Rd, Gold Beach, OR 97444
indiancreekrv@gmail.com
www.indiancreekrv.com
See ad this page, 930.

↓ **IRELAND'S OCEANVIEW RV PARK & MOTEL/CABINS**
Ratings: 5.5/7.5/7.5 (RV Park) From jct US 101 & Jerry's Flat Rd (south end of Rogue River bridge): Go 1-1/2 mi S on US 101 (R) (Choose site, then register 100 yards N at Gold Beach Inn) NOTE: RV Park is on West side of Hwy 101. **FAC:** Paved rds. 32 paved, patios, 9 pull-thrus (25 x 50), back-ins (25 x 50), 32 full hkups (30 amps), cable, WiFi, rentals, laundry. **REC:** Pacific Ocean: swim, fishing. Pet restrict(B). No tents. 2015 rates: $29 to $39. Disc: AAA, military.
(541)247-0148 Lat: 42.40237, Lon: -124.4243
29272 Ellensburg Ave (Hwy 101), Gold Beach, OR 97444
www.irelandsrvpark.com
See ad this page, 930.

↗ KIMBALL CREEK BEND RV RESORT **Ratings: 7/8/8** (RV Park) 2015 rates: $28.50 to $41.50. (888)814-0633 97136 North Bank Rogue, Gold Beach, OR 97444

↗ LUCKY LODGE RV PARK **Ratings: 8/7.5/8** (RV Park) 2015 rates: $30 to $35. (541)247-7618 32040 Watson Ln, Gold Beach, OR 97444

↑ NESIKA BEACH RV PARK & CAMPGROUND **Ratings: 5/5.5/6** (Campground) 2015 rates: $25 to $30. (541)247-6077 32887 Nesika Rd, Gold Beach, OR 97444

↖ **OCEANSIDE RV PARK** **Ratings: 6.5/8/6.5** (RV Park) From Jct of US-101 & Moore St (light at N end of town): Go W 0.2 mi on Moore St to Airport Way, then NW 0.2 mi to S Jetty, then W 0.2 mi (L) Note: Do not use GPS coordinates to get to the park. **FAC:** Gravel rds. 87 gravel, 10 pull-thrus (21 x 55), back-ins (21 x 40), 32 full hkups, 55 W, 55 E (20/30 amps), WiFi, rentals, dump, laundry. **REC:** Pacific Ocean: fishing. Pets OK. No tents. 2015 rates: $25 to $35. (541)247-2301 Lat: 42.42067, Lon: -124.42653 94040 S. Jetty Rd, Gold Beach, OR 97444 www.oceansiderv1.com

↗ SECRET CAMP RV PARK **Ratings: 5/5/7.5** (Campground) 2015 rates: $38. (541)247-2665 95614 Jerry's Flat Rd, Gold Beach, OR 97444

Things to See and Do

➔ **INDIAN CREEK CAFE** Cafe serves breakfast and lunch. Located on Indian Creek Resort premises. Partial handicap access. RV accessible. Restrooms, food. Hours: 5:30am to 2 pm.
(541)247-0680 Lat: 42.42773, Lon: -124.40419
94680 Jerry's Flat Rd, Gold Beach, OR 97444
indiancreekrv@gmail.com
www.indiancreekrv.com
See ad this page.

RV Park ratings you can rely on!

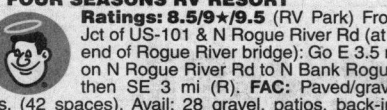

OR

Beach Resort at Turtle Rock
TOP PARKS 2015
TOP WATERFRONT RV PARKS
Premium RV Hot Tub Sites w/Your Own Deck & BBQ
Good Sam Park
TURTLE ROCK RV RESORT
WATER & FORESTED VIEWS JUST STEPS FROM THE BEACH
RV RESORT
• 115 RV Sites • Full Hookups
• Pull-Thrus • Cable TV
• Premium Hot Tub Sites
COTTAGES
• Nightly Rentals • Sleeps 4–6
• TV• Full Kitchen • Gas BBQ
• Deck with Private Spa
VACATION RENTAL HOME
Sleeps 8, Gourmet Kitchen, Hot Tub
COTTAGE SALES
VACATION HOME
Store • Kayak Rentals
Group Facilities • Exercise Room
Yoga • Holiday Potlucks
• FREE WIFI
Beach Path from RV Resort
Close to Jet Boat Rides,
Fishing, Fine & Family Restaurants,
Golf, Coastal Activities,
Concerts, Festivals
See listing Gold Beach, OR
www.turtlerockresorts.com
800-353-9754 • 541-247-9203
28788 Hunter Creek Loop
Gold Beach, OR 97444

GOLD HILL — D2 *Jackson*

CYPRESS GROVE RV PARK **Ratings: 7.5/9★/8.5** (RV Park) 2015 rates: $32. (800)758-0719 1679 Rogue River Hwy, Gold Hill, OR 97525

MEDFORD/GOLD HILL KOA Ratings: 7/9/6.5 (Campground) From Jct of I-5 & Gold Hill (Exit 40): Go E 0.3 mi on Gold Hill to Blackwell Rd, Then S 0.5 mi (R); or From town, at Jct of Hwys 234 & 99, E 0.5 mi on Hwy 99 (R). **FAC:** Paved/gravel rds. (84 spaces). Avail: 40 gravel, 27 pull-thrus (25 x 65), back-ins (22 x 38), 20 full hkups, 20 W, 20 E (30/50 amps), seasonal sites, cable, WiFi, tent sites, rentals, dump, laundry, groc, LP gas, firewood. **REC:** pool, playground. Pet restrict(B). Partial handicap access. Big rig sites, 2015 rates: $37 to $40. Disc: AAA.
AAA Approved
(800)562-7608 Lat: 42.42678, Lon: -123.03715
12297 Blackwell Rd., Central Point, OR 97502
medfordkoa@charter.net
www.koa.com

GOVERNMENT CAMP — B3 *Clackamas*

MT. HOOD NF (FROG LAKE CAMPGROUND) (Natl Forest) From town: Go 7-1/2 mi SE on US-26, then 1 mi SE on FR-2610. Pit toilets. 2015 rates: $20. Jun 7 to Oct 6. (541)328-0909

MT. HOOD NF (STILL CREEK CAMPGROUND) (Natl Forest) From town: Go 1 mi E on US-26,then 1/2 mi S on FR-2650. Pit toilets. 2015 rates: $20. May 22 to Oct 1. (503)668-1700

GRAND RONDE — B2 *Polk*

WANDERING SPIRIT RV PARK & PARK MODEL SALES Ratings: 7/8.5/8 (RV Park) From Jct of US-22 & US-18 (Valley Jct): Go SW 2.2 mi on US-18 (L). **FAC:** Paved rds. (129 spaces). Avail: 72 paved, 16 pull-thrus (20 x 50), back-ins (28 x 50), 72 full hkups (30/50 amps), seasonal sites, cable, WiFi Hotspot, tent sites, rentals, dump, laundry, groc, LP gas. **REC:** Rock Creek: swim, fishing. Pets OK. Partial handicap access. 2015 rates: $35. Disc: AAA.
AAA Approved
(503)879-5700 Lat: 45.05805, Lon: -123.61788
28800 Salmon River Hwy, Grand Ronde, OR 97347
wanderrvpark@gmail.com
www.wanderingspiritrv.com

GRANTS PASS — D2 *Josephine*

GRANTS PASS See also Meford & Wolf Creek.

GRANTS PASS OREGON KOA
Ratings: 7.5/7/9 (RV Park) From Jct of I-5 & Hugo (Exit 66): Go NE 400 ft on Monument to Jumpoff Joe Creek Rd, then E 1/3 mi (R). **FAC:** Gravel/dirt rds. (39 spaces). Avail: 19 gravel, patios, 19 pull-thrus (22 x 60), 19 full hkups (30/50 amps), seasonal sites, WiFi, tent sites, rentals, showers $, dump, laundry, groc. **REC:** Jump off Joe Creek & Waterfalls: swim, rec open to public. Pets OK. Partial handicap access. 2015 rates: $45.
(541)479-7974 Lat: 42.57027, Lon: -123.36467
699 Jumpoff Joe Creek Rd, Grants Pass, OR 97526
joecreekrvresort@msn.com
www.joecreekrv.com
See ad this page.

GRANTS PASS/REDWOOD HIGHWAY CAMPGROUND & RV PARK **Ratings: 3.5/7/6** (Campground) 2015 rates: $350 to $36. (541)476-6508 13370 Redwood Hwy., Wilderville, OR 97543

GRIFFIN PARK
(Public) From Jct of US-199 & Riverbanks Rd, N 6 mi on Riverbanks Rd to Griffin Rd, E 0.1 mi (L) Note: Cash only w/out reservation. **FAC:** Paved rds. 15 paved, 3 pull-thrus (20 x 50), back-ins (20 x 45), 15 full hkups (30/50 amps), tent sites, rentals, dump, firewood. **REC:** Rogue River: fishing, playground, rec open to public. Pets OK. Partial handicap access. 14 day max stay, 2015 rates: $30. No CC.
(800)452-5687 Lat: 42.46263, Lon: -123.48789
500 Griffin Rd., Grants Pass, OR 97527
ahoward@co.josephine.or.us
http://www.co.josephine.or.us/Page.asp?NavID=490
See ad page 925 (Welcome Section).

JACK'S LANDING RV RESORT **Ratings: 7.5/7.5/8.5** (RV Park) 2015 rates: $28 to $35. (866)785-2257 247 NE Morgan Ln, Grants Pass, OR 97526

JOSEPHINE COUNTY FAIRGROUNDS RV PARK
(Public) From: Jct of I-5 & US-199/Redwood Hwy (Exit 55), Go 4.5 mi W on US-199/Redwood Hwy (R) NOTE: Office is on the right just inside the gate of the Fairgrounds. **FAC:** Gravel rds. 30 gravel, back-ins (15 x 55), mostly side by side hkups, 30 full hkups (30/50 amps), WiFi Hotspot. Pets OK. 14 day max stay, 2015 rates: $35. Disc: AAA, military.
(541)476-3215 Lat: 42.42331, Lon: -123.342967
1451 Fairgrounds Rd., Grants Pass, OR 97527
fairgrounds@co.josephine.or.us
http://www.josephinecountyfairgrounds.com/facilities/overnight-rv-camping.html
See ad this page.

LAKE SELMAC PARK (Public) From jct Hwy 199 & Lake Shore Dr: Go 2.3 mi left on Lake Shore Dr to park. 2015 rates: $20 to $22. (541)474-5285

MOON MOUNTAIN RV RESORT
Ratings: 8/9★/9 (RV Park) From Jct of I-5 & Hwy 199 (exit 55): Go SW .02 mi on Hwy 199 to Agness Ave, then S .02 mi to Foothill Blvd (Veer R to Pearce Park Rd), then E 1.4 mi (L). **FAC:** Paved rds. (50 spaces). Avail: 23 paved, 20 pull-thrus (20 x 60), back-ins (20 x 45), 23 full hkups (30/50 amps), seasonal sites, cable, WiFi, dump, laundry, LP gas. Pets OK. Partial handicap access, no tents. Eco-friendly, 2015 rates: $38.90.
(877)479-1145 Lat: 42.43609, Lon: -123.27328
3298 Pearce Park Rd., Grants Pass, OR 97526
info@moonmountainrv.com
www.moonmountainrv.com
See ad this page, 930.

RIVERPARK RV RESORT Ratings: 8/7.5/9 (Campground) From Jct of I-5 & US-199 (Exit 55): Go W 1.8 mi on US-199 to Parkdale Dr, then S 0.3 mi on Rogue River Hwy/OR SH-99, the E 1.9 mi (L); OR - E-bnd: From Jct of Hwy US-199 & Rogue River Hwy/OR SH-99: Go E 2.5 mi on Rogue River Hwy/OR SH-99 (L). **FAC:** Paved rds. 47 paved, patios, back-ins (20 x 55), 47 full hkups (30/50 amps), cable, WiFi, tent sites, dump, laundry. **REC:** Rogue River: swim, fishing. Pets OK. 2015 rates: $33 to $40. Disc: AAA.
AAA Approved
(541)479-0046 Lat: 42.42584, Lon: -123.28212
2956 Rogue River Hwy, Grants Pass, OR 97527
donna@riverparkrvresort.com
www.riverparkrvresort.com

ROGUE VALLEY OVERNITERS
Ratings: 7.5/9★/9 (RV Park) From Jct of I-5 & 6th St (exit 58), Go S 0.2 mi on 6th St (R); or From Jct of US-199 & Hwy 99 (S end of town), Go N 2.3 mi on US-199/Hwy 99 (7th St) to Morgan Ln, then W 400 ft to 6th St, then S 500 ft (R). **FAC:** Paved rds. (93 spaces). 43 Avail: 23 paved, 20 gravel, 13 pull-thrus (24 x 70), back-ins (23 x 28), 43 full hkups (30/50 amps), seasonal sites, cable, WiFi, dump, laundry. **REC.** Pet restrict(Q). No tents. Big rig sites, 2015 rates: $28 to $35.
(541)479-2208 Lat: 42.45912, Lon: -123.32296
1806 NW 6th St, Grants Pass, OR 97526
roguevalleyoverniters@hotmail.com
www.roguevalleyoverniters.com
See ad this page, 930.

We've listened to thousands of RVers like you, so we know exactly how to rate campgrounds. Got feedback? Call us!877-209-6655

OR

GRANTS PASS (CONT)

SCHROEDER PARK (Public) From Jct of I-5 & US-199, W 2 mi on US-199 to Willow Ln, N 2.3 mi (E). **FAC:** Paved rds. 29 paved, 14 pull-thrus (19 x 65), back-ins (18 x 30), 29 full hkups (30/50 amps), tent sites, rentals, firewood. **REC:** Rogue River: fishing, rec open to public. Pets OK. Partial handicap access. 14 day max stay, 2015 rates: $30. No CC.
(800)452-5687 Lat: 42.29981, Lon: -123.28472
605 Schroeder Ln, Grants Pass, OR 97527
ahoward@co.josephine.or.us
http://www.co.josephine.or.us/Page.asp?NavID=493
See ad page 925 (Welcome Section).

SISKIYOU NF (SAM BROWN CAMPGROUND) (Natl Forest) From I-5 (exit 61): Go 12 mi W on Merlin Rd, then 15 mi W on FR 25 to FR 2512 (R) (Max length 24' due to narrow winding steep road). Pit toilets. 2015 rates: $5. (541)496-3830

WHITEHORSE PARK (Public) From Jct of I-5 & Exit 58: Go SE 0.3 mi to 6th St, then S 1.7 mi to SW G St, then W 8 mi (SW G St. turns into Upper/Lower River Rd.) (L). **FAC:** Paved rds. 8 paved, back-ins (30 x 50), 8 full hkups (20 amps), tent sites, rentals, dump, fire rings, firewood. **REC:** Rogue River: playground, rec open to public. Pets OK. 14 day max stay, 2015 rates: $30. No CC.
(800)452-5687 Lat: 42.43687, Lon: -123.45879
7613 Lower River Rd., Grants Pass, OR 97527
ahoward@co.josephine.or.us
http://www.co.josephine.or.us/Page.asp?NavID=497
See ad page 925 (Welcome Section).

Things to See and Do

JOSEPHINE COUNTY PARKS Seven Camping parks with boat ramps on the Rogue River in Grants Pass area. Reservations can be made 9 mo to 2 days in advance. On-line resv. available. www.reserveamerica.com. 800-452-5687. Partial handicap access. RV accessible. Hours: 8am to 4:30pm.
(541)474-5285 Lat: 42.42476, Lon: -123.34066
125 Ringuette St, Grants Pass, OR 97527
ahoward@co.josephine.or.us
http://www.co.josephine.or.us/
See ad page 925 (Welcome Section).

GRESHAM — A2 *Multnomah*

OXBOW (Public) From Jct of I-205 & Division St, E 13 mi on Division St, follow signs (L). Entrance fee required. GATE LOCKED AT SUNSET; OPENS AT 6:30AM. 2015 rates: $22. (800)452-5687

HAMMOND — A2 *Clatsop*

FORT STEVENS (State Pk) S-bnd: From Jct of US-101 & A1T US-101, SW 1 mi on A1T US-101 to Ridge Rd, W 3.5 mi (R); or N-bnd: From Jct of US-101 & Fort Stevens State Park Rd, NW 4.6 mi on Fort Stevens State Park Rd (L). 2015 rates: $23 to $27. (800)452-5687

HARRISBURG — B2 *Linn*

DIAMOND HILL RV PARK **Ratings: 5/6.5/5** (RV Park) 2015 rates: $30. (541)995-9279 32917 Diamond Hill Dr., Harrisburg, OR 97446

HEPPNER — B4 *Morrow*

ANSON WRIGHT COUNTY PARK (Public) From Jct of I-84 & SR-207, SW 26 mi on SR-207/ Jct 74, S 36.5 mi (R). 2015 rates: $12 to $21. May 10 to Oct 30. (541)989-9500

BULL PRAIRIE LAKE (Natl Forest) From Heppner, S 36 mi on Hwy 207 to FR-2039 (L). Pit toilets. 2015 rates: $14. May 15 to Oct 15. (541)676-9187

CUTSFORTH COUNTY PARK (Public) From town, S 1 mi on SR-207 to Willow Creek Rd, SE 22 mi (R). 2015 rates: $12 to $21. May 10 to Nov 13. (541)989-9500

HERMISTON — A4 *Umatilla*

HERMISTON See also Boardman, Irrigon, Pendleton, Stanfield & Umatilla.

HAT ROCK CAMPGROUND **Ratings: 8/8.5★/8** (Campground) N-bnd: From Jct of US-395 & Hwy 207 (in town), NE 7 mi on Hwy 207 to US-730, E 1 mi to state pk access rd, N 0.5 mi (L); or S-bnd: From Jct of I-82 & US-730 (N of town), E 8 mi on US-730 to state pk access rd, N 0.5 mi (L). **FAC:** Gravel rds. (60 spaces). Avail: 27 grass, patios, 24 pull-thrus (24 x 60), back-ins (24 x 50), some side by side hkups, 10 full hkups, 17 W, 17 E (30/50 amps), seasonal sites, WiFi, tent sites, dump, laundry, groc, fire rings, firewood, restaurant. **REC:** heated pool. Pets OK. 2015 rates: $28 to $32.
(541)567-4188 Lat: 45.91105, Lon: -119.17138
82284 Hat Rock Rd., Hermiston, OR 97838
www.hatrockcampground.com
See ad this page, 930.

PIONEER RV PARK Ratings: 8.5/9.5★/8.5 (RV Park) S-bnd: From Jct of I-82 & Powerline Rd (exit 5), S 2.2 mi on Powerline Rd to Bridge Rd, NE 0.3 mi (thru stop) to Highland, E 0.7 mi (L); or E & W-bnd: From Jct of I-84 & Hwy 207 (Exit 182), N 3.7 mi on Hwy 207 to Highland (1st stoplight), W 0.3 mi (R). **FAC:** Paved rds. (102 spaces). Avail: 47 paved, 45 pull-thrus (25 x 55), back-ins (25 x 38), 47 full hkups (30/50 amps), seasonal sites, cable, WiFi, dump, laundry. **REC.** Pet restrict(B/Q). Partial handicap access, no tents. 2015 rates: $37.03. Disc: AAA, military.
(541)564-9286 Lat: 45.83548, Lon: -119.31858
1590 W Highland Ave., Hermiston, OR 97838
pioneerrv@pioneerrv.net
www.pioneer-rv.com

HILLSBORO — A2 *Washington*

Travel Services

CAMPING WORLD OF HILLSBORO As the nation's largest retailer of RV supplies, accessories, services and new and used RVs, Camping World is committed to making your total RV experience better. RV Accessories: (800)732-2141. **SERVICES:** RV, RV appliance, staffed RV wash, restrooms, RV Sales. RV supplies, LP, emergency parking, RV accessible. waiting room. Hours: 8am to 6pm.
(888)698-4232 Lat: 45.496731, Lon: -122.914244
6503 SE Alexander St, Hillsboro, OR 97123
www.campingworld.com

HOOD RIVER — A3 *Hood River*

HOOD RIVER See also Cascade Locks, Dufur, The Dalles; White Salmon, WA.

BRIDGE RV PARK & CAMPGROUND **Ratings: 8/10★/9** (RV Park) From Jct of I-84 & Exit 64 (Hood River Bridge, in OR): Go 1 mi N across toll bridge to SR-14, then 1/8 mi E on SR-14 (R). Warning: Bridge is narrow. See park website for alternate big rig directions. **FAC:** Paved rds. (35 spaces). Avail: 29 paved, 16 pull-thrus (26 x 55), back-ins (24 x 48), 29 full hkups (30/50 amps), seasonal sites, cable, WiFi, tent sites, rentals, showers $, laundry, LP gas. **REC.** Pets OK $. Partial handicap access. Eco-friendly, 2015 rates: $45.48 Disc: AAA, military.
(509)493-1111 Lat: 45.72324, Lon: -121.48745
65271 Hwy 14, White Salmon, WA 98672
bridgerv@bridgerv.com
www.bridgerv.com
See primary listing at White Salmon, WA and ad page 1257 (Spotlight Gateway to Washington).

TOLLBRIDGE (Public) From Jct of Hwy 35 & I-84, S 17 mi on Hwy 35, to Toll Bridge Rd, W 0.4 mi (R). 2015 rates: $22 to $25. Apr 1 to Oct 31. (541)352-5522

TUCKER PARK (Public) From Jct of I-84 & US-30 (exit 62, W of town), E 1 mi on US-30 (Cascade St) to 13th/Tucker Rd, S .6 mi (left, then right), S .5 mi to 12th St., W 1 mi to Brookside Dr., S 2.9 mi to Dee Hwy, SW .4 mi. 2015 rates: $25. Apr 1 to Oct 31. (541)386-4477

VIENTO PARK (State Pk) From town, W 8 mi on I-84 (exit 56) (R). 2015 rates: $16 to $22. Apr 12 to Oct 31. (541)374-8811

HUNTINGTON — B5 *Baker, Malheur*

CATFISH JUNCTION RV PARK & CAMPGROUND **Ratings: 5.5/8.5★/8** (RV Park) From Jct of I-84 & Hwy 201 (exit 356), E 2.5 mi on Hwy 201 (L). **FAC:** Gravel rds. 44 gravel, 16 pull-thrus (26 x 65), back-ins (30 x 60), 33 full hkups, 11 W, 11 E (30/50 amps), tent sites, rentals, dump, laundry, LP gas, firewood. **REC:** Snake: fishing, playground, rec open to public. Pets OK. Partial handicap access. Big rig sites, 2015 rates: $28 to $30.
(541)262-3833 Lat: 44.26406, Lon: -117.12006
6170 Hwy 201 N, Huntington, OR 97907
catfishjunctionrv@gmail.com
www.catfishjunctionrvpark.com

FAREWELL BEND (State Pk) From Jct of I-84 & Bus US-30 (exit 353), N 1 mi on Bus US-30 (R). 2015 rates: $17 to $22. (800)551-6949

IDLEYLD PARK — C2 *Douglas*

ELK HAVEN RV RESORT Ratings: 5/8/8 (RV Park) From jct I-5 & Hwy 138 (exit 124): Go 19 1/2 mi E on Hwy 138 (L). **FAC:** Gravel/dirt rds. (43 spaces). Avail: 23 gravel, 20 pull-thrus (44 x 70), back-ins (44 x 70), 23 full hkups (30/50 amps), seasonal sites, WiFi Hotspot, tent sites, rentals, dump, laundry, fire rings, firewood. **REC:** pool, pond. Pets OK. Big rig sites, 2015 rates: $25. Disc: AAA, military.
(888)552-0166 Lat: 43.32362, Lon: -123.05078
22020 N Umpqua Hwy, Idleyld Park, OR 97447
vacation@elkhavenrv.com
www.elkhavenrv.com

UMPQUA'S LAST RESORT WILDERNESS RV PARK & CAMPGROUND **Ratings: 6.5/6.5/7** (Campground) 2015 rates: $33. (541)498-2500 115 Elk Ridge Lane, Idleyld Park, OR 97447

JEFFERSON — B2 *Manon*

EMERALD VALLEY RV PARK **Ratings: 8.5/9★/9.5** (Campground) From Jct of I-5 & Hochspeier Rd (Exit 244): Go NE 0.5 mi on Hochspeier Rd (R). **FAC:** Paved rds. (51 spaces). Avail: 13 gravel, 10 pull-thrus (30 x 62), back-ins (30 x 45), 13 full hkups (30/50 amps), seasonal sites, cable, WiFi, tent sites, laundry, LP gas. **REC.** Pets OK. Partial handicap access. Big rig sites, 2015 rates: $35. Disc: AAA.
(503)363-0701 Lat: 44.79211, Lon: -123.03292
11223 Hochspeir Rd SE, Jefferson, OR 97352
evrvp.manager@gmail.com
www.emeraldvalley-rvp.com
See ad pages 963, 930, 926 (OR Map).

JOHN DAY — B4 *Grant*

CLYDE HOLLIDAY (State Pk) From Jct of US-26 & US-395 (in town), W 7 mi on US-26, MP 155 1/4 (L). 2015 rates: $17 to $22. Mar 1 to Nov 30. (541)932-4453

GRANT COUNTY RV PARK (Public) From Jct of 395 & 26 (center of town), E 0.1 mi on Hwy 26 to Bridge St, N 0.3 mi (R). 2015 rates: $15 to $27. (541)575-1900

JOSEPH — A5 *Wallowa*

HELLS CANYON REC AREA/COPPERFIELD PARK (Public) From town, S 0.1 mi on SR-82 to Imnaha Hwy, E 8.1 mi to Wallowa Mountain Loop NFD 39, SE 55.4 mi to SH-86, NE 7.3 mi. 2015 rates: $16. (541)785-7209

Like Us on Facebook.

Refer to the Table of Contents in front of the Guide to locate everything you need.

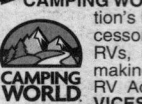

JOSEPH (CONT)

HELLS CANYON REC AREA/MCCORMICK PARK (Public) From town, S 0.1 mi on SR-82 to Imnaha Hwy, E 8.1 mi to NF-39, Wallowa Mountain Loop, SE 55.4 mi to SH-86, NE 7.3 mi to SH-71, S 7.5 mi (across river). 2015 rates: $16. (541)785-7209

WALLOWA LAKE (State Pk) From Jct of Hwy 82 (Main St) & Joseph St (in town), S 6 mi on Hwy 82 (R). 2015 rates: $21 to $30. (800)452-4185

KLAMATH FALLS — D3 *Klamath*

KLAMATH FALLS See also Chiloquin & Merrill.

KLAMATH FALLS KOA **Ratings: 9/8.5/8** (Campground) 2015 rates: $38.70 to $41.97. (541)884-4644 3435 Shasta Way, Klamath Falls, OR 97603

LAKE OF THE WOODS RESORT **Ratings: 6.5/5/6** (Campground) 2015 rates: $40 to $50. (541)949-8300 hwy 140 Mile Post 36, Medford, OR 97504

OREGON MOTEL 8 & RV PARK
Ratings: 7.5/8.5★/7 (RV Park) From Jct of Bus US-97 & US-97 (N end of town): Go N 2 mi on US-97 (MP-271) (R). Elev 4200 ft. **FAC:** Gravel rds. (32 spaces). Avail: 22 gravel, 22 pull-thrus (18 x 60), 22 full hkups (30/50 amps), seasonal sites, cable, WiFi, tent sites, rentals, dump, laundry. **REC:** heated pool. Pets OK. 2015 rates: $35 to $40. Disc: AAA.
(541)883-3431 Lat: 42.27535, Lon: -121.81142
5225 Hwy 97 North, Klamath Falls, OR 97601
oregonmotel8rvpark@yahoo.com
http://www.oregonmotel8rvpark.com
See ad this page, 930.

ROCKY POINT RESORT **Ratings: 5/7/6** (Campground) 2015 rates: $28 to $30. Apr 1 to Nov 1. (541)356-2287 28121 Rocky Point Rd., Klamath Falls, OR 97601

LA GRANDE — B5 *Union*

EAGLES HOT LAKE RV PARK
Ratings: 9/9.5★/9.5 (RV Park) From Jct of I-84 & Hwy 203 (exit 265): Go SE 4.5 mi on Hwy 203 to Hot Lake Ln, then W 0.3 mi (L). Elev 2714 ft. **FAC:** Gravel rds. (100 spaces). Avail: 96 gravel, 96 pull-thrus (30 x 90), 96 full hkups (30/50 amps), seasonal sites, WiFi, tent sites, dump, laundry, groc, firewood. **REC:** heated pool, whirlpool, playground. Pets OK. Partial handicap access. Big rig sites, eco-friendly, 2015 rates: $34. Disc: AAA, military. AAA Approved
(541)963-5253 Lat: 45.24567, Lon: -117.97006
65182 Hot Lake Ln., La Grande, OR 97850
info@eagleshotlakerv.com
www.eagleshotlakerv.com
See ad this page, 930, 926 (OR Map).

LA GRANDE RENDEZVOUS RV RESORT **Ratings: 6.5/7/7.5** (RV Park) 2015 rates: $32 to $38. (800)276-6873 2632 Bearco Loop Rd., La Grande, OR 97850

LA PINE — C3 *Deschutes*

CASCADE MEADOWS RV RESORT **Ratings: 6.5/5.5/7.5** (RV Resort) 2015 rates: $38 to $40. Apr 15 to Oct 15. (541)536-2244 53750 US Highway 97, La Pine, OR 97739

CRANE PRAIRIE RESORT **Ratings: 5.5/7/7.5** (Campground) 2015 rates: $33. (541)383-3939 crane Prairie Rd., La Pine, OR 97739

DESCHUTES/HOT SPRINGS CAMPGROUND (Natl Forest) From town: Go 5 mi N on US 97, then 17 mi E on CR 21. Pit toilets. 2015 rates: $10. (541)536-8344

LA PINE (State Pk) From Jct of US-97 & La Pine State Recreational Area Rd (MP-160 1/2, N of town), W 5.2 mi on La Pine SRA Rd (E). 2015 rates: $17 to $26. (800)452-5687

NEWBERRY RV PARK **Ratings: 4.5/6/5** (RV Park) 2015 rates: $33. (541)536-7596 52660 S. Hwy 97, La Pine, OR 97739

RIVERVIEW TRAILER PARK **Ratings: 4.5/7/6.5** (RV Park) 2015 rates: $26. (541)536-2382 52731 Huntington Rd., La Pine, OR 97739

LAKESIDE — C1 *Coos*

NORTH LAKE RV RESORT & MARINA **Ratings: 7.5/8.5★/9** (Campground) 2015 rates: $30 to $38. Apr 1 to Nov 1. (541)759-3515 2090 N Lake Rd., Lakeside, OR 97449

OSPREY POINT RV RESORT **Ratings: 7.5/6.5/8** (RV Park) 2015 rates: $33 to $49. (541)759-2801 1505 N Lake Rd., Lakeside, OR 97449

LAKEVIEW — D4 *Lake*

BASE CAMP RV PARK, INC Ratings: 6/7.5★/7 (Campground) From Jct of Hwy 140 & Hwy 395 (in town), go N 2 mi on Hwy 395 (L). Elev 4735 ft. **FAC:** Gravel/dirt rds. (30 spaces). Avail: 29 gravel, 29 pull-thrus (20 x 60), 25 full hkups, 4 W, 4 E (30/50 amps), WiFi, tent sites, dump, laundry, firewood. **REC:** playground. Pets OK. 2015 rates: $25 to $30. (541)947-4968 Lat: 42.21756, Lon: -120.36502 18020 Hwy 395 North, Lakeview, OR 97630 basecamprv@gmail.com

GOOSE LAKE (State Pk) From town, S 15 mi on US-395 to New Pine Creek, W 1 mi (R). 2015 rates: $16 to $22. May 1 to Sep 30. (541)783-2471

JUNIPERS RESERVOIR RV RESORT
Ratings: 8.5/9.5★/9 (RV Park) From Jct of US-395 & Hwy 140 (in town), W 10 mi on Hwy 140 to MP 86.5 (R). Elev 4899 ft. **FAC:** Gravel rds. (40 spaces). Avail: 36 gravel, 36 pull-thrus (30 x 80), 19 full hkups, 17 W, 17 E (30/50 amps), WiFi, tent sites, rentals, dump, laundry, firewood. **REC:** Junipers Reservoir: swim, fishing. Pets OK. Partial handicap access. Big rig sites, eco-friendly, 2015 rates: $32 to $39. Disc: AAA. May 1 to Oct 15.
(541)947-2050 Lat: 42.18312, Lon: -120.53283
PO Box 590, Lakeview, OR 97630
junipersrvresort@gmail.com
www.junipersrv.com
See ad this page, 930.

LAKE COUNTY FAIRGROUNDS & RV (Public) From Jct of Hwy 395 & Hwy 140 (in town), W .8 mi on Hwy 140 (R). 2015 rates: $12 to $18. Apr 15 to Nov 1. (541)947-2925

LEBANON — B2 *Linn*

GILL'S LANDING RV PARK (Public) Hwy 20 & Grant St (in town) E 0.6 mi on Grant St (R). 2015 rates: $30. (541)258-4917

MALLARD CREEK GOLF & RV RESORT
Ratings: 9/10★/10 (RV Park) From the Jct of Hwy 20 & Waterloo Rd 4.5 mi E (SW of Lebanon): Go NE 2.3 mi on Waterloo Rd to Berlin Rd, then E 0.3 mi to Bellinger Scale Rd, then N 0.4 mi (L). **FAC:** Paved rds. 43 paved, patios, 23 pull-thrus (32 x 60), back-ins (30 x 50), 43 full hkups (30/50 amps), WiFi, laundry, restaurant. **REC:** pond, fishing, golf, rec open to public. Pets OK. Partial handicap access, no tents. Big rig sites, 2015 rates: $42.50.
(866)632-9133 Lat: 44.51985, Lon: -122.80080
31958 Bellinger Scale Rd., Lebanon, OR 97355
rv@mallardcreekgc.com
www.mallardcreekgc.com
See ad pages 958, 930.

Reducing your speed to 55 mph from 65 mph may increase your fuel efficiency by as much as 15 percent; cut it to 55 from 70, and you could get a 23 percent improvement.

Tell them you saw them in this Guide!

OR

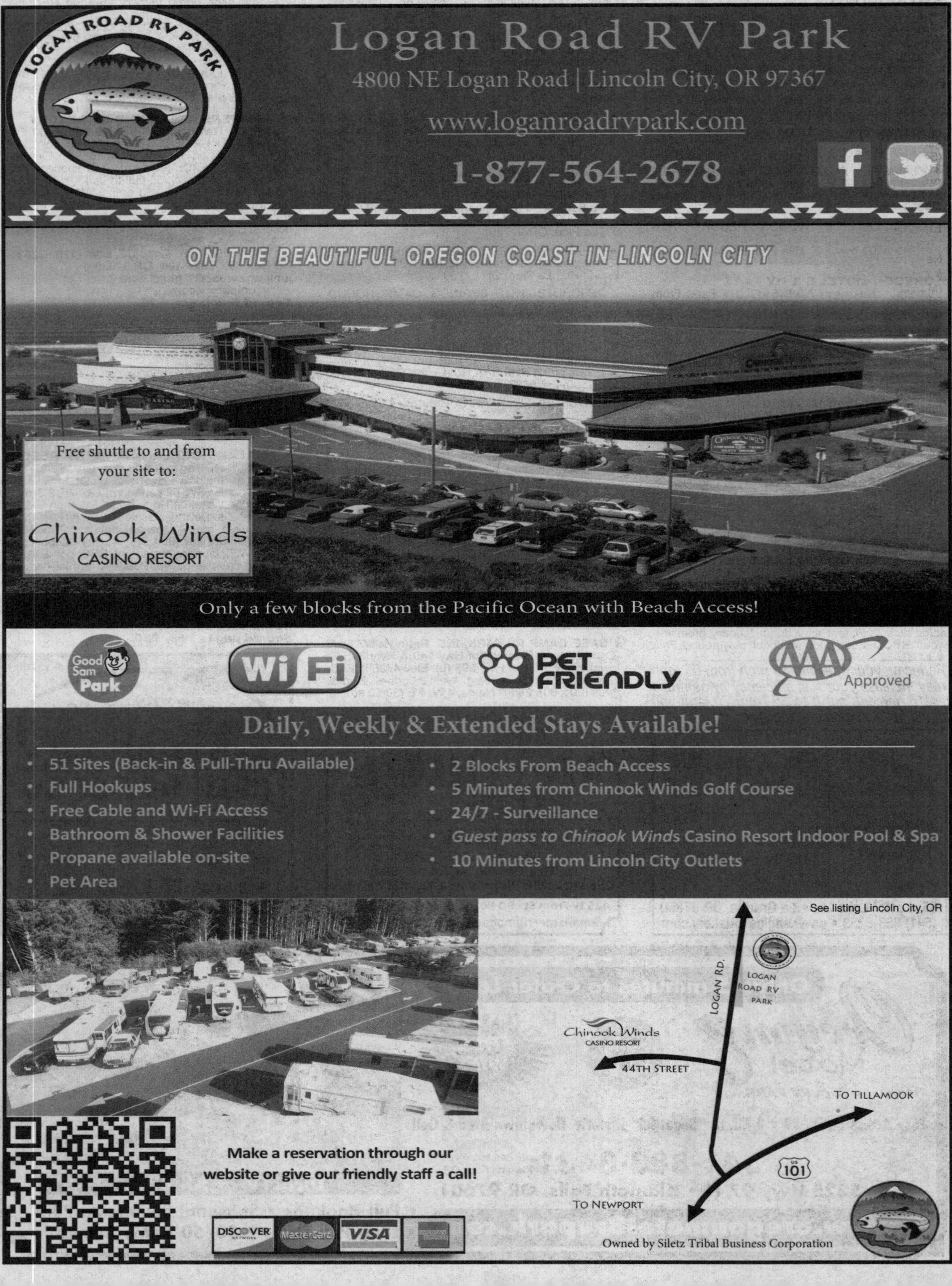
LOGAN ROAD RV PARK
Logan Road RV Park
4800 NE Logan Road | Lincoln City, OR 97367
www.loganroadrvpark.com
1-877-564-2678
ON THE BEAUTIFUL OREGON COAST IN LINCOLN CITY
Free shuttle to and from your site to:
Chinook Winds CASINO RESORT
Only a few blocks from the Pacific Ocean with Beach Access!
Good Sam Park
Wi Fi
PET FRIENDLY
AAA Approved
Daily, Weekly & Extended Stays Available!
• 51 Sites (Back-in & Pull-Thru Available)
• Full Hookups
• Free Cable and Wi-Fi Access
• Bathroom & Shower Facilities
• Propane available on-site
• Pet Area
• 2 Blocks From Beach Access
• 5 Minutes from Chinook Winds Golf Course
• 24/7 - Surveillance
• Guest pass to Chinook Winds Casino Resort Indoor Pool & Spa
• 10 Minutes from Lincoln City Outlets
See listing Lincoln City, OR
LOGAN RD.
LOGAN ROAD RV PARK
Chinook Winds CASINO RESORT
44TH STREET
TO TILLAMOOK
101
TO NEWPORT
Make a reservation through our website or give our friendly staff a call!
DISCOVER
MasterCard
VISA
Owned by Siletz Tribal Business Corporation

LEBANON (CONT)

➔ WATERLOO CAMPGROUND (Public) From Jct of Hwys 20 & 34 (in town), E 5.78 mi on Hwy 20 to Waterloo turnoff, N 1 mi on Gross (R). 2015 rates: $24 to $28. (541)967-3917

Things to See and Do

MALLARD CREEK GOLF & RV RESORT Championship course, covered driving range, PGA pros, fine & casual dining and RV Resort. Partial handicap access. RV accessible. Restrooms, food. Hours: 6:30am to 8pm. Adult fee: $35 to $40.
(541)259-4653 Lat: 44.51985, Lon: -122.80080
31966 Bellinger Scale Rd., Lebanon, OR 97355
rv@mallardcreekgc.com
www.mallardcreekgc.com
See ad page 958.

LINCOLN CITY — B2 *Lincoln*

LINCOLN CITY See also Cloverdale, Depoe Bay, Neskowin, Newport & Pacific City.

CHINOOK BEND RV RESORT **Ratings: 7/7/7.5** (Membership Pk) 2015 rates: $40 to $45. (800)203-6364 2920 Siletz Hwy, Lincoln City, OR 97367

COYOTE ROCK RV RESORT & MARINA **Ratings: 6/6/7.5** (Campground) 2015 rates: $27 to $38. (541)996-6824 1676 Siletz River Hwy, Lincoln City, OR 97367

DEVILS LAKE (State Pk) From Jct of US-101 & N 6th St/Vinyard Church exit (in town), E 0.2 mi on N 6th St/Vinyard Church (R). 2015 rates: $23 to $28. (800)452-5687

DEVILS LAKE RV PARK Ratings: 8.5/9/9.5 (RV Park) From Jct of Hwy 101 & W Devils Lake Rd (N of town): Go E 0.2 mi on W Devils Lake Rd (R). **FAC:** Paved rds. (80 spaces). Avail: 38 paved, 35 pull-thrus (24 x 65), back-ins (22 x 60), 38 full hkups (30/50 amps), seasonal sites, cable, WiFi, tent sites, rentals, laundry, LP gas. **REC:** playground. Pets OK. Partial handicap access. Big rig sites, 2015 rates: $40.50 to $45. Disc: AAA, military.
AAA Approved
(541)994-3400 Lat: 44.99580, Lon: -123.99845
4041 NE West Devils Lake Rd., Lincoln City, OR 97367
info@devilslakerv.com
www.devilslakerv.com

LINCOLN CITY KOA **Ratings: 7/9★/7.5** (Campground) 2015 rates: $35.19 to $45.09. (800)562-3316 5298 NE Park Lane, Otis, OR 97368

LOGAN ROAD RV PARK
Ratings: 8.5/10★/7.5 (RV Park) From Jct of Hwy 101 & Logan Rd (North of town): Go W & N on Logan Rd 1 mi (R). **FAC:** Paved rds. (51 spaces). Avail: 43 paved, patios, 17 pull-thrus (28 x 50), back-ins (21 x 45), 43 full hkups (30/50 amps), seasonal sites, cable, WiFi, laundry, LP gas. **REC:** heated pool. Pets OK. Partial handicap access, no tents. 2015 rates: $37 to $43. Disc: AAA, military.
AAA Approved
(877)564-2678 Lat: 45.00083, Lon: -124.00428
4800 NE Logan Rd., Lincoln City, OR 97367
manager@loganroadrvpark.com
www.loganroadrvpark.com
See ad opposite page, 930.

PREMIER RV RESORTS - LINCOLN CITY
Ratings: 9/10★/9 (RV Resort) N-Bnd: From Jct of Hwy 101 & 51st St (S of town): Go N 0.2 mi on Hwy 101 (R); or S-Bnd: From Jct of Hwy 101 & E Devils Lake Rd (outlet mall): Go S 2.5 mi on Hwy 101 (L). **FAC:** Paved rds. 92 paved, patios, 7 pull-thrus (23 x 50), back-ins (23 x 45), 92 full hkups (30/50 amps), cable, WiFi, laundry. **REC:** whirlpool. Pets OK. Partial handicap access, no tents. Big rig sites, eco-friendly, 2015 rates: $50 to $57. Disc: AAA, military.
(877)871-0663 Lat: 44.93457, Lon: -124.02222
4100 SE Hwy 101, Lincoln City, OR 97367
premierlincoln@msn.com
www.premierrvresorts.com
See ad this page, 930.

LOWELL — C2 *Lane*

CASCARA (State Pk) From I-5 (exit 189A): Go 13 mi E on Hwy 58 to Lowell exit, then N across bridge, then follow signs, then 8 mi on Big Fall Creek Rd, then right 1 mi on Peninsula Rd. Pit toilets. 2015 rates: $19. May 1 to Sep 30. (541)937-1173

LYONS — B2 *Linn*

JOHN NEAL MEMORIAL PARK (Public) From Jct of Hwy 22 & Mehama-Lyons exit, S 1 mi on Mehama-Lyons to Hwy 226, E 1.5 mi to 13th St, follow signs (R). 2015 rates: $22. Apr 26 to Sep 24. (541)967-3917

MADRAS — B3 *Jefferson*

MADRAS See also Crooked River Ranch, Culver, Metolius, Prineville & Warm Springs.

JEFFERSON COUNTY FAIRGROUNDS (Public) From the jct of Hwy 97 and Fairgrounds Rd (south end of Madras): Go 1/2 blk W on Fairgrounds Rd. 2015 rates: $18. (541)325-5050

LAKE SIMTUSTUS RV PARK **Ratings: 7/8.5★/7.5** (RV Park) 2015 rates: $30 to $40. (541)475-1085 2750 NW Pelton Dam Rd., Madras, OR 97741

PELTON PARK (Public) From North jct. US 97 & US 26: Go 9-1/2 mi NW on US 26, then 3-3/4 mi S on Pelton Dam Rd. Apr 25 to Sep 28. (541)325-5292

MAPLETON — C2 *Lane*

WHITTAKER CREEK RECREATION SITE (Public) From town, W 12.5 mi on Hwy 126 to Siuslaw River Rd, S 2 mi (R). Pit toilets. 2015 rates: $10. May 23 to Sep 21. (541)683-6600

MAUPIN — B3 *Wasco*

MAUPIN CITY PARK (Public) From Jct of Hwy 197 & Bakeoven Rd exit, SE 0.1 mi on Bakeoven Rd (L). 2015 rates: $26 to $32. (541)395-2252

MCDERMITT — E5 *Malhuer*

MITCHELLS STATELINE RV PARK **Ratings: 3/6/5.5** (RV Park) 2015 rates: $30. (541)522-8133 4112 Stateline Dr, Mcdermitt, OR 89421-0391

MCMINNVILLE — B2 *Yamhill*

MULKEY RV PARK Ratings: 7/7.5/8 (RV Park) From Jct of Hwys 99W & 18 (SW of town): Go SW 3.5 mi on Hwy 18 (L). **FAC:** Paved rds. (77 spaces). Avail: 20 gravel, 10 pull-thrus (19 x 80), back-ins (24 x 70), accepts full hkup units only, 20 full hkups (30/50 amps), seasonal sites, WiFi $, laundry, LP gas. **REC.** Pet restrict(B). Partial handicap access, no tents. 2015 rates: $30 to $32. Disc: AAA.
(877)472-2475 Lat: 45.15673, Lon: -123.26342
14325 SW Hwy18, Mcminnville, OR 97128
mulkeyrvp@onlinemac.com
www.mulkeyrvp.com

OLDE STONE VILLAGE RV PARK
Ratings: 10/10★/10 (RV Park) From Jct of Hwy 99W & E Hwy 18 bypass (S of McMinnville): Go NE 4.2 mi on Hwy 18 bypass to MP-48.25 (L). **FAC:** Paved rds. 71 paved, patios, 33 pull-thrus (28 x 65), back-ins (28 x 65), 71 full hkups (30/50 amps), cable, WiFi, laundry. **REC:** heated pool, playground. Pet restrict(B). Partial handicap access, no tents. Big rig sites, RV age restrict, eco-friendly, 2015 rates: $38.
(877)472-4315 Lat: 45.20390, Lon: -123.13534
4155 NE Three Mile Ln., Mcminnville, OR 97128
oldestonevillage@comcast.net
www.oldestonevillage.com
See ad pages 956, 930.

Things to See and Do

EVERGREEN IMAX THEATER 3D & 2D IMAX films. Partial handicap access. RV accessible. Restrooms. Hours: 9am to 5pm. Adult fee: $5 to $11.
(503)434-4180 Lat: 45.20218, Lon: -123.15159
3685 NE Three Mile Ln, Mcminnville, OR 97128
publicity@sb.org
www.evergreenmuseum.org
See ad this page.

EVERGREEN MUSEUM CAMPUS Historical aircraft & space museum, educational programs, stores, cafe, wine tasting & special Imax digital theatre. Partial handicap access. RV accessible. Restrooms, food. Hours: 9am to 5pm. Adult fee: $23 to $25.
(503)434-4180 Lat: 45.20192, Lon: -123.14547
500 NE Captain Smith King Way, Mcminnville, OR 97128
publicity@sg.org
www.evergreenmuseum.org
See ad this page.

MEACHAM — A5 *Umatilla*

EMIGRANT SPRINGS (State Pk) N-bnd: From Jct of I-84 & Exit 234, NW 0.5 mi on exit rd (L); or S-bnd: From Jct of I-84 & Exit 233, S 0.5 mi on exit rd (R). 2015 rates: $16 to $20. (541)983-2277

MEDFORD — D2 *Jackson, Klamath*

MEDFORD See also Ashland, Gold Hill, Grants Pass & Rogue River.

CANTRALL-BUCKLEY PARK (Public) From town, SW 8 mi on SR-238 to Hamilton Rd, S 1 mi (R). 2015 rates: $16. May 4 to Sep 15. (541)774-8183

We shine "Spotlights" on interesting cities and areas.

OR

MEDFORD (CONT)

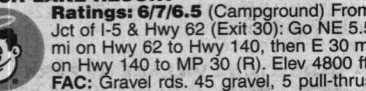

FISH LAKE RESORT
Ratings: 6/7/6.5 (Campground) From Jct of I-5 & Hwy 62 (Exit 30): Go NE 5.5 mi on Hwy 62 to Hwy 140, then E 30 mi on Hwy 140 to MP 30 (R). Elev 4800 ft. **FAC:** Gravel rds. 45 gravel, 5 pull-thrus (20 x 50), back-ins (18 x 35), some side by side hkups, 45 full hkups (20/30 amps), tent sites, rentals, showers $, laundry, groc, LP gas, fire rings, firewood, restaurant. **REC:** Fish Lake: swim, fishing, marina. Pet restrict(B/Q). Eco-friendly. 2015 rates: $40.
(541)949-8500 Lat: 42.39428, Lon: -122.31596
hwy 140 Mile Post 30, Medford, OR 97501
fishlakeresort@aol.com
www.fishlakeresort.net

HOLIDAY RV PARK
Ratings: 9.5/9.5★/8.5 (RV Park) From Jct of I-5 & Fern Valley Rd (exit 24): Go W 1000 ft on Fern Valley Rd (R). **FAC:** Paved rds. (110 spaces). Avail: 65 paved, 64 pull-thrus (22 x 70), back-ins (22 x 38), 65 full hkups (30/50 amps), seasonal sites, cable, WiFi, showers $, laundry, LP gas. **REC:** heated pool, Bear Creek. Pets OK. Partial handicap access, no tents. Eco-friendly. 2015 rates: $44.50. Disc: AAA.
(800)452-7970 Lat: 42.28236, Lon: -122.81876
201 Fern Valley Rd., Phoenix, OR 97535
kprv@aol.com
www.holidayrvpark.net
See ad this page, 930.

LAKEWOOD RV PARK
Ratings: 6/9★/8.5 (RV Park) From Jct of I-5 & Hwy 62 (Exit 30): Go N 5.2 mi on Hwy 62 to Merry Ln, then E 1/4 mi (R). **FAC:** Paved rds. (45 spaces). Avail: 15 gravel, 15 pull-thrus (24 x 60), 15 full hkups (30/50 amps), seasonal sites, cable, laundry. **REC.** Pets OK. Partial handicap access, no tents. 2015 rates: $40.40. No CC.
(541)830-1957 Lat: 42.42087, Lon: -122.84534
2564 Merry Lane, White City, OR 97503
lakewood@ccountry.net
www.lakewoodrvpark.com
See ad this page, 930.

MEDFORD OAKS RV PARK & CABINS Ratings: 7.5/8.5/8.5 (Campground) From Jct of I-5 & Hwy 62 (Exit 30/Crater Lake Hwy): Go NE 6.7 mi on Hwy 62 to Hwy 140, then E 6.8 mi on Hwy 140 (L). **FAC:** Paved/gravel rds. (51 spaces). 41 Avail: 40 gravel, 1 grass, 40 pull-thrus (50 x 55), back-ins (25 x 35), 18 full hkups, 23 W, 23 E (30/50 amps), seasonal sites, WiFi, tent sites, rentals, showers $, dump, mobile sewer, laundry, LP gas, firewood. **REC:** pool, pond, fishing, playground, rec open to public. Pet restrict(B). Eco-friendly. 2015 rates: $30 to $35.
(541)826-5103 Lat: 42.45452, Lon: -122.73381
7049 Hwy140, Eagle Point, OR 97524
stay@medfordoaks.com
www.medfordoaks.com

PEAR TREE RV PARK RESORT Ratings: 7.5/7.5★/6.5 (RV Park) From Jct of I-5 & Fern Valley Rd (exit 24): Go E 0.25 mi on Fern Valley Rd to S Phoenix Rd, then S 0.3 mi to Pear Tree Ln, then N 0.2 mi (R) Warning: Ask for directions to EXIT the park. **FAC:** Paved rds. (31 spaces). Avail: 23 paved, patios, 16 pull-thrus (24 x 75), back-ins (24 x 42), 23 full hkups (30/50 amps), seasonal sites, cable, WiFi, laundry. **REC:** pool, whirlpool. Pet restrict(Q). Partial handicap access, no tents. Big rig sites, 2015 rates: $40.
(541)535-4445 Lat: 42.27835, Lon: -122.81003
300 Pear Tree Ln., Phoenix, OR 97535
phoenixoregonamericasbest@gmail.com
www.americasbestinnphoenix.com

MERLIN — D2 *Josephine*

ALMEDA
(Public) From jct I-5 & Merlin/Galice Rd, exit 61: Go 19 mi W on Merlin/Galice Rd. (R). **FAC:** Paved/dirt rds. 5 dirt, back-ins (20 x 40), tent sites, rentals, pit toilets, dump, firewood. **REC:** Rogue River: swim, fishing, rec open to public. Pets OK. Partial handicap access. 14 day max stay, 2015 rates: $20. No CC.
(541)474-5285 Lat: 42.60548, Lon: -123.58122
14800 Merlin Galice Rd, Merlin, OR 97532
ahoward@co.josephine.or.us
www.co.josephine.or.us/Page.asp?NavID=488
See ad page 925 (Welcome Section).

INDIAN MARY PARK
(Public) From Jct of I-5 & Merlin-Galice Rd (Merlin exit 61), W 10.9 mi on Merlin-Galice Rd (R). Reservations recommended. Note: Cash only w/out resv. **FAC:** Paved rds. 58 paved, 5 pull-thrus (30 x 60), back-ins (30 x 40), 44 full hkups, 14 W, 14 E (30/50 amps), tent sites, rentals, dump, firewood. **REC:** Rogue River: swim, fishing, playground, rec open to public. Pets OK. Partial handicap access. 14 day max stay, 2015 rates: $30. No CC.
(800)452-5687 Lat: 42.55173, Lon: -123.54063
7100 Merlin/Galice Rd., Merlin, OR 97532
ahoward@co.josephine.or.us
http://www.co.josephine.or.us/Page.asp?NavID=491
See ad page 925 (Welcome Section).

MERRILL — E3 *Klamath*

MERRILL RV PARK
Ratings: 7.5/9★/7.5 (RV Park) From Jct of St Route 39 & Main: Go W on Rt 39/ W Front St (L) CAUTION: When using GPS confirm arrival at 'Merrill RV Park'. Elev 4063 ft. **FAC:** Gravel rds. (30 spaces). Avail: 10 gravel, patios, 6 pull-thrus (20 x 40), back-ins (24 x 50), some side by side hkups, 10 full hkups (30/50 amps), seasonal sites, WiFi, showers $, laundry. **REC.** Pet restrict(B). No tents. 2015 rates: $32. No CC, no reservations.
(541)798-1654 Lat: 42.023917, Lon: -121.604844
425 W Front St., Merrill, OR 97633
merrillmobilmanor@hotmail.com
See ad pages 949, 930.

METOLIUS — B3 *Jefferson*

MT VIEW RV PARK **Ratings: 7.5/8/8** (RV Park) 2015 rates: $35. (541)546-3049 500 N Jefferson Ave., Metolius, OR 97741

MILL CITY — B2 *Marion*

FISHERMEN'S BEND RECREATION SITE (Public) From town, W 1.5 mi on Hwy 22 (L). 2015 rates: $16 to $28. Apr 1 to Oct 31. (503)897-2406

MORO — A3 *Sherman*

SHERMAN COUNTY RV PARK
(Public) From Jct of US-97 & 1st St, SE 0.2 mi on 1st St (1st St becomes Lone Rock Rd) (L). **FAC:** Gravel rds. (33 spaces). Avail: 18 gravel, 16 pull-thrus (25 x 65), back-ins (25 x 50), 18 full hkups (30/50 amps), cable, WiFi, tent sites, laundry. Pets OK. 2015 rates: $20 to $25. No CC.
(541)565-3127 Lat: 45.48231, Lon: -120.72579
66067 Lone Rock Rd., Moro, OR 97039
www.sherman-county.com/govt_parks.asp
See ad page 966.

MYRTLE CREEK — D2 *Douglas*

RIVERS WEST RV PARK **Ratings: 6.5/8.5/8** (Campground) 2015 rates: $21 to $30. (541)863-7601 333 Ruckles Road, Myrtle Creek, OR 97457

TRI CITY RV PARK
Ratings: 8/9.5★/8 (Campground) From Jct of I-5 & Riddle/Hwy 99 (exit 103): Go N 1.4 mi on Riddle Rd/Hwy 99 (L). **FAC:** Paved rds. (70 spaces). Avail: 10 paved, 10 pull-thrus (24 x 50), 10 full hkups (30/50 amps), seasonal sites, cable, WiFi, showers $, dump, laundry, LP gas. Pet restrict(Q). Partial handicap access, no tents. 2015 rates: $28.28. Disc: AAA.
(541)860-5000 Lat: 42.98790, Lon: -123.32019
187 N. Old Pacific Hwy, Myrtle Creek, OR 97457
info@tricityrvpark.com
www.tricityrvpark.com
See ad this page, 930.

NEHALEM — A2 *Tillamook*

NEHALEM BAY (State Pk) From Jct of US-101 & Hwy 53 (S of town), N 2.6 mi on US-101 to state park sign (Mc Carney Rd MP-43 3/4), W 1.3 mi (E). $7 for extra vehicle. 2015 rates: $22 to $29. (503)368-5154

NEHALEM FALLS CAMPGROUND (State Pk) From jct US 101 & Hwy 53: Go 1-1/4 mi E on Hwy 53, then 1 mi S on Miami Foley Rd, then E on Foss Rd to milepost 7. Pit toilets. 2015 rates: $10. May 15 to Sep 15. (503)842-2545

NESKOWIN — B2 *Tillamook*

NESKOWIN CREEK RV RESORT **Ratings: 8/7.5/8** (Membership Pk) 2015 rates: $44. (503)392-3355 50500 Hwy 101 S, Neskowin, OR 97149

According to the Wall Street Journal, 100 billion plastic shopping bags are consumed in the United States annually. Consider toting your own reusable shopping bags instead of using plastic.

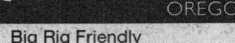

NETARTS — A2 *Tillamook*

NETARTS BAY GARDEN RV RESORT
Ratings: 7/8.5★/8.5 (RV Park) From Jct of US-101 & 3rd St/Netarts Hwy (in Tillamook): Go W 5.8 mi on 3rd St (Netarts Hwy) to Bilyeu Ave, then SW 0.2 mi (R) NOTE: Do not use GPS until you reach Tillamook. **FAC:** Paved rds. (83 spaces). 62 Avail: 4 paved, 58 gravel, patios, 11 pull-thrus (24 x 55), back-ins (24 x 40), 62 full hkups (30/50 amps), seasonal sites, WiFi, laundry. **REC:** Netarts Bay: fishing, rec open to public. Pets OK. No tents. 2015 rates: $29 to $40.
(503)842-7774 Lat: 45.42655, Lon: -123.93851
2260 Bilyeu Ave., W, Tillamook, OR 97141
info@netartsbay.com
www.netartsbay.com
See ad pages 966, 930.

NEWPORT — B1 *Lincoln*

NEWPORT See also Depoe Bay, Lincoln City, Waldport & Yachats.

BEVERLY BEACH (State Pk) From Jct of US-20 & US-101 (in town), N 6.3 mi on US-101 to MP-134 (R). 2015 rates: $22 to $26. (800)452-5687

HARBOR VILLAGE RV PARK & MHP **Ratings: 5.5/7/7** (RV Park) 2015 rates: $35. (541)265-5088 923 SE Bay Blvd., Newport, OR 97365

PACIFIC SHORES MOTORCOACH RESORT
Ratings: 10/10★/10 (Condo Pk) From Jct of US 20 & N Hwy 101: Go N 3.5 mi (L) NOTE: A & C Class Motorhomes ONLY. **FAC:** Paved rds. (210 spaces). Avail: 119 paved, patios, back-ins (35 x 70), 119 full hkups (30/50 amps), seasonal sites, cable, WiFi, laundry, controlled access. **REC:** heated pool, whirlpool, Pacific Ocean: fishing. Pet restrict(Q). Big rig sites, eco-friendly, 2015 rates: $40 to $120.
(541)265-3750 Lat: 44.682039, Lon: -124.063574
6225 N Coast Hwy 101, Newport, OR 97365
info@pacificshoresmotorcoachresort.com
www.PacificShoresMotorcoachResort.com
See ad this page, 930.

PORT OF NEWPORT ANNEX RV PARK
(Public) S-bnd: From Jct of US-101 & US-20, S 1.7 mi on US-101 to Marine Science Center exit (at S end of bridge), NE 0.5 mi on S OSU Dr (L); or N-bnd: From Jct of US-101 & 32nd (1st light), E 0.1 mi on 32nd to Ferry Slip, N 0.4 mi to Marine Science Rd, E 0.1 mi (L). **FAC:** Paved/gravel rds. 50 Avail: 10 gravel, 40 grass, back-ins (20 x 40), 50 full hkups (30/50 amps), cable, WiFi, dump, groc, restaurant. **REC:** Yoquina River: fishing, marina. Pet restrict(Q). 2015 rates: $32.
(541)867-3321 Lat: 44.62093, Lon: -124.04963
2120 SE Marine Science Dr, Newport, OR 97365
anex@portofnewport.com
www.portofnewport.com
See ad this page.

PORT OF NEWPORT MARINA & RV PARK
Ratings: 8.5/9.5★/8 (Public) S-bnd: From Jct of US-101 & US-20, S 1.7 mi on US-101 to Marine Science Center exit (at S end of bridge), NE 0.5 mi on S OSU Dr (L); or N-bnd: From Jct of US-101 & 32nd (1st light), E 0.1 mi on 32nd to Ferry Slip, N 0.4 mi to Marine Science Rd, E 0.1 mi (L). **FAC:** Paved rds. 92 paved, 45 pull-thrus (27 x 60), back-ins (27 x 32), 92 full hkups (30/50 amps), cable, WiFi, dump, laundry, groc, restaurant. **REC:** Yaquina River: fishing, marina. Pet restrict(Q). Partial handicap access, no tents. Big rig sites, 2015 rates: $18 to $43.
(541)867-3321 Lat: 44.62093, Lon: -124.04963
2120 SE Marine Science Dr., Newport, OR 97365
rv@portofnewport.com
www.portofnewport.com
See ad this page, 930.

SOUTH BEACH (State Pk) From Jct of US-20 & US-101 (in town), S 3 mi on US-101 to MP-143.5 (R). 2015 rates: $22 to $29. (800)452-5687

WHALER'S REST RESORT **Ratings: 8/7/8** (Membership Pk) 2015 rates: $40 to $49.25. (800)405-6188 50 SE 123rd, South Beach, OR 97366

NORTH BEND — C1 *Coos*

OREGON DUNES KOA **Ratings: 7/9/6.5** (Campground) 2015 rates: $45 to $70. (541)756-4851 68632 Hwy 101, North Bend, OR 97459

THE MILL CASINO HOTEL & RV PARK
Ratings: 9.5/9.5★/8.5 (RV Park) From Jct of Newmark St & US-101: Go N 0.3 mi on Hwy 101 (R). **FAC:** Paved rds. 102 paved, patios, 70 pull-thrus (28 x 62), back-ins (27 x 40), 102 full hkups (30/50 amps), cable, WiFi, laundry, LP gas, restaurant. **REC:** heated pool, whirlpool, Coos Bay. Pets OK. Partial handicap access, no tents. Big rig sites, eco-friendly, 2015 rates: $30 to $62.
AAA Approved
(800)953-4800 Lat: 43.39483, Lon: -124.21910
2665 Tremont Ave., North Bend, OR 97459
themill@themillcasino.com
www.themillcasino.com
See ad pages 939, 930.

Things to See and Do

THE MILL CASINO-HOTEL Casino with hotel, gaming, entertainment, restaurant, lounge & new RV park. Partial handicap access. RV accessible. Restrooms, food. Hours: 24 hrs. ATM.
(800)953-4800 Lat: 43.39483, Lon: -124.21910
3201 Tremont Ave., North Bend, OR 97459
themill@themillcasino.com
www.themillcasino.com
See ad page 939.

NYSSA — C6 *Malheur*

LAKE OWYHEE (State Pk) From town, SW 12 mi on SR-201 to Owyhee Ave, S 25 mi (E). 2015 rates: $16 to $22. Apr 15 to Oct 31. (800)452-5687

O'BRIEN — E2 *JOSEPHINE*

LONE MOUNTAIN RV RESORT
Ratings: 7.5/8.5★/9.5 (Campground) From Jct Hwy 199/Redwood Hwy & SR 46 (in Cave Junction): Go S 7.08 mi on Hwy 199 to Lone Mountain Rd, then W 500 ft (L). **FAC:** Paved rds. (38 spaces). Avail: 33 gravel, 7 pull-thrus (24 x 75), back-ins (28 x 50), 33 full hkups (30/50 amps), seasonal sites, WiFi, tent sites, rentals, showers $, laundry. **REC:** O'Brien Creek: swim. Pet restrict(B/Q). Partial handicap access. Big rig sites, 2015 rates: $34 to $35. Disc: AAA.
(541)596-2878 Lat: 42.06699, Lon: -123.70828
169 Lone Mountain Rd., O'brien, OR 97534
reservations@lonemountainrv.com
www.lonemountainrv.com

"Full hookups" in a campground listing means there are water, electric and sewer hookups at the sites.

OAKLAND — C2 *Douglas*

RICE HILL RV PARK
Ratings: 8.5/9★/8.5 (RV Park) N-bnd: From Jct of I-5 & Exit 148 (stay on exit rd), E 0.7 mi (L); or S-bnd: From Jct of I-5 & Exit 148, S 0.3 mi on John Long Rd (cross under freeway), N 0.8 mi on John Long Rd (L). **FAC:** Paved rds. (43 spaces). Avail: 26 paved, patios, 25 pull-thrus (30 x 75), back-ins (38 x 45), 26 full hkups (30/50 amps), seasonal sites, WiFi, tent sites, laundry, LP gas. **REC.** Pet restrict(B). Partial handicap access. Big rig sites, 2015 rates: $34. Disc: AAA. No reservations.
(866)236-0121 Lat: 43.54121, Lon: -123.28591
1120 John Long Rd., Oakland, OR 97462
ricehillrvp@yahoo.com
www.ricehill-rvpark.com
See ad pages 961, 930.

OAKRIDGE — C2 *Lane*

WILLAMETTE NF (BLACK CANYON CAMPGROUND) (Natl Forest) From town: Go 6 mi NW on Hwy-58. 2015 rates: $18. May 17 to Oct 1. (541)225-6300

WILLAMETTE NF (PACKARD CREEK CAMPGROUND) (Natl Forest) From town: Go 2 mi SE on Hwy-58, then 5 mi S on FR-21. Pit toilets. 2015 rates: $16. Apr 26 to Sep 30. (541)225-6300

ONTARIO — C6 *Malheur*

ONTARIO See also Huntington & Vale; Fruitland & Weiser, ID.

OREGON CITY — A2 *Clackamas*

CLACKAMETTE RV PARK (Public) From Jct of I 205 & 99E (Exit 9), N 0.1 mi on McLoughlin/99E (L). 2015 rates: $20 to $25. (503)496-1201

PACIFIC CITY — B2 *Tillamook*

CAPE KIWANDA RV RESORT & MARKET PLACE
Ratings: 9/9.5★/9 (RV Park) From Jct of US-101 & Brooten Rd/Pacific City Jct (MP-90.3 N of Lincoln City): Go NW 3 mi on Brooten Rd to Pacific Ave (blinking light in town), then W 0.2 mi to Kiwanda Dr, then N 1 mi (R). Note: Some GPS require Cloverdale, OR as city. **FAC:** Paved rds. (170 spaces). 125 Avail: 100 paved, 25 gravel, 22 pull-thrus (25 x 60), back-ins (28 x 40), 116 full hkups, 9 W, 9 E (30/50 amps), seasonal sites, cable, WiFi, tent sites, rentals, dump, laundry, groc, LP gas, fire rings, firewood, restaurant. **REC:** heated pool, whirlpool, playground. Pets OK. Partial handicap access. Big rig sites, eco-friendly, 2015 rates: $34.95 to $49.95. ATM.
(503)965-6230 Lat: 45.21462, Lon: -123.96878
33305 Cape Kiwanda Dr., Pacific City, OR 97135
info@capekiwandarvresort.com
www.capekiwandarvresort.com
See ad pages 954, 930.

WEBB PARK (TILLAMOOK COUNTY PARK) (Public) From town: Go 1 mi N on 3 Capes to Cape Kiwanda. 2015 rates: $19 to $29. (503)965-5001

OR

PACIFIC CITY (CONT)

↑ WHALEN ISLAND PARK (State Pk) From town, NW 5 mi on Resort Dr (L). 2015 rates: $19 to $24. (503)965-6085

Things to See and Do

↖ **CAPE KIWANDA MARKET & GIFT SHOP** The marketplace offers a deli, unique gifts and beach toys. Partial handicap access. Restrooms, food. Hours: 7am to 10pm. ATM.
(503)965-6230 Lat: 45.21511, Lon: -123.96927
33305 Kiwanda Dr, Pacific City, OR 97135
info@capekiwandarvresort.com
www.capekiwandarvresort.com
See ad this page.

↖ **DORYLAND PIZZA PARLOR** Pizza, salad bar, sandwiches, pasta,wine and beer & big screen TV. Partial handicap access. Restrooms, food. Hours: 11:30 to 9. ATM.
(503)965-6230 Lat: 45.21511, Lon: -123.96927
33305 Cape Kiwanda Dr, Pacific City, OR 97135
info@capekiwandarvresort.com
www.capekiwandarvresort.com
See ad this page.

PENDLETON — A5 *Umatilla*

PENDLETON See also Hermiston & Stanfield.

↖ PENDLETON/MOUNTAIN VIEW KOA **Ratings: 8/8.5/8.5** (RV Park) 2015 rates: $38.65 to $43.01. (541)276-1041 1375 SE 3rd St., Pendleton, OR 97801

← THE LOOKOUT RV PARK **Ratings: 7/7/6.5** (RV Park) 2015 rates: $38.87. (541)276-6014 601 Airport Rd., Pendleton, OR 97801

→ **WILDHORSE RV RESORT**
Ratings: 9/10★/9.5 (RV Park) From Jct of I-84 & Hwy 331 (exit 216), N 0.8 mi on Hwy 331 (R).

WILDHORSE RV PARK & TIPI VILLAGE
Conveniently off I-84, next to Wildhorse Resort & Casino, the Park offers full RV amenities including heated pool and spa, showers, laundry room, free Wifi and shuttle. Walking distance to Casino, golf and museum.

FAC: Paved rds. (106 spaces). 100 Avail: 52 paved, 48 gravel, 56 pull-thrus (30 x 60), back-ins (30 x 50), 100 full hkups (30/50 amps), seasonal sites, WiFi, tent sites, rentals, dump, laundry, restaurant. **REC:** heated pool, whirlpool, golf. Pets OK. Partial handicap access. Big rig sites, 2015 rates: $28.95 to $39.95.
(800)654-9453 Lat: 45.64816, Lon: -118.67534
46510 Wildhorse Blvd., Pendleton, OR 97801
info@wildhorseresort.com
www.wildhorseresort.com
See ad this page, 930.

Things to See and Do

→ **WILDHORSE GOLF COURSE** 18 holes nestled in the foothills of Oregon's Blue Mountains. RV accessible. Restrooms, food. Hours: 7am to 7 pm. Adult fee: $34 to $40. ATM.
(800)654-9453 Lat: 45.91103, Lon: -119.17135
46510 Wildhorse Blvd., Pendleton, OR 97801
info@wildhorseresort.com
www.wildhorseresort.com
See ad this page.

Follow the arrow. The arrow in each listing indicates where the facility is located in relation to the listed town.

PENDLETON (CONT)

➔ **WILDHORSE RESORT & CASINO** Over 1,200 slot machines, plus your favorite table games and bingo. Tower hotel with convention space, fine dining, buffet & lounge. Partial handicap access. RV accessible. Restrooms, food. Hours: open 24 Hrs. ATM.
(800)654-9453 Lat: 45.64816, Lon: -118.67534
46510 Wildhorse Blvd., Pendleton, OR 97801
info@wildhorseresort.com
www.wildhorseresort.com
See ad opposite page.

PORT ORFORD — D1 *Curry*

CAMP BLANCO RV PARK
Ratings: 6.5/9★/8 (RV Park) From Jct of US-101 & 20th St (N end of town): Go N 50 ft on US-101 (L). **FAC:** Paved rds. (25 spaces). Avail: 15 gravel, 13 pull-thrus (20 x 60), back-ins (20 x 50), 15 full hkups (30 amps), seasonal sites, WiFi, rentals, showers $, LP gas. **REC.** Pets OK. No tents. Eco-friendly, 2015 rates: $31. Disc: AAA, military.
(541)332-6175 Lat: 42.75430, Lon: -124.49747
2011 Oregon St. (US-101), Port Orford, OR 97465
campblanco@yahoo.com
www.campblanco.com
See ad this page.

CAPE BLANCO (State Pk) From Jct of US-101 & Madrona Ave (N end of town), N 3.7 on US-101 to Cape Blanco Rd, W 5 mi (L). 2015 rates: $16 to $20. (541)332-6774

ELK RIVER CAMPGROUND **Ratings: 5.5/5.5/6** (Campground) 2015 rates: $25. (541)332-2255 93363 Elk River Rd., Port Orford, OR 97465

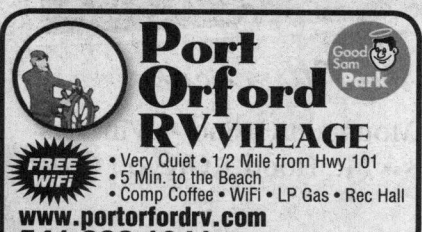

HUMBUG MOUNTAIN (State Pk) From Jct of US-101 & Jackson St (S end of town), S 6 mi on US-101, at MP-307 (L) Note: Dump station under construction at time of inspection. 2015 rates: $16 to $22. (541)332-6774

PORT ORFORD RV VILLAGE
Ratings: 8/9.5★/9.5 (RV Park) From Jct of US-101 & Madrona Ave (N end of town at MP-300): Go E 500 ft on Madrona Ave to Port Orford Loop, then N 0.5 mi (L). **FAC:** Paved rds. (42 spaces). 39 Avail: 29 gravel, 10 grass, patios, 2 pull-thrus (29 x 60), back-ins (28 x 40), 34 full hkups, 5 W, 5 E (30 amps), seasonal sites, cable, WiFi, tent sites, rentals, dump, laundry, LP gas. **REC.** Pets OK. Eco-friendly, 2015 rates: $31. No CC.
(541)332-1041 Lat: 42.76158, Lon: -124.49422
2855 Port Orford Loop Rd., Port Orford, OR 97465
portorfordrv@gmail.com
www.portorfordrv.com
See ad this page.

Park policies vary. Ask about the cancellation policy when making a reservation.

Get the Facts!

Essential tips and travel info can be found in the Welcome Section at the beginning of each State/Province.

PORTLAND — A2 *Multnomah*

PORTLAND AREA MAP

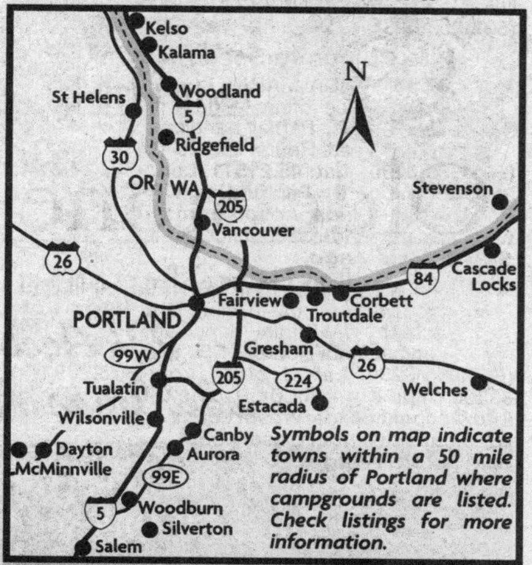

In OR, see also Aurora, Canby, Cascade Locks, Corbett, Dayton, Estacada, Fairview, Gresham, McMinnville, Salem, Silverton, St Helens, Troutdale, Tualatin, Welches, Wilsonville & Woodburn.

In WA, see also Kalama, Kelso, Ridgefield, Stevenson, Vancouver & Woodland.

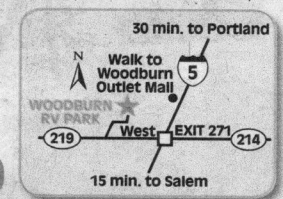

TOP RATED Good Sam Park FOR 2016

Good Sam RATED 10/10★/10

Olde Stone Village

A Village Northwest Community

Luxurious RV Accommodations Await Your Arrival

Big-Rig Friendly Pull-Thrus • DirecTV (Including HBO/Cinemax) • FREE WiFi • Pitch 'n Putt
20-30-50 Amp Service • Sports Court • Heated Seasonal Pool • Laundry Facilities
• Village Clubhouse • Beautiful Landscaping • Free Showers & Restrooms

Located in the Heart of Oregon's Wine Country

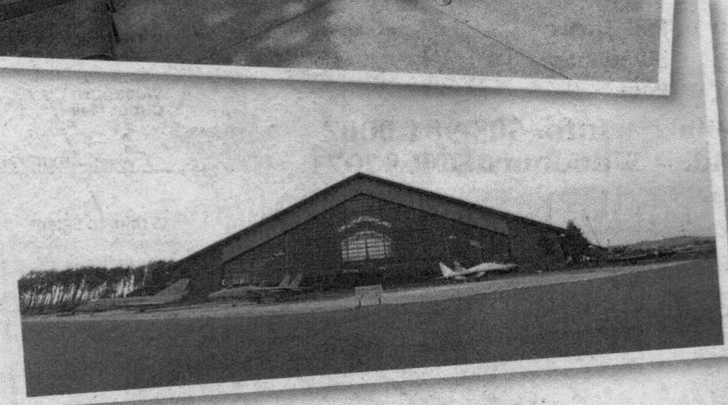

Walk or Shuttle to "Spruce Goose" at the Evergreen Aviation & Space Museum
• Digital Theatre • Wings & Waves Water Park

Nearby Attractions

Golf • Spirit Mountain Casino • Wineries
Antique Shops • Mt. Hood • Oregon Coast

Winter Monthly Special
$325 Mo. + Electricity
November Thru April

BIG RIGS WELCOME

Reservations Suggested

4155 NE Three Mile Lane • McMinnville, Oregon 97128

See listing McMinnville, OR

www.oldestonevillage.com • (877) 472-4315

OR

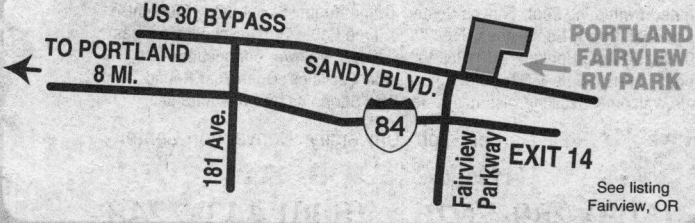

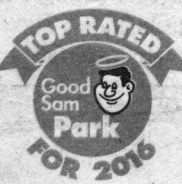

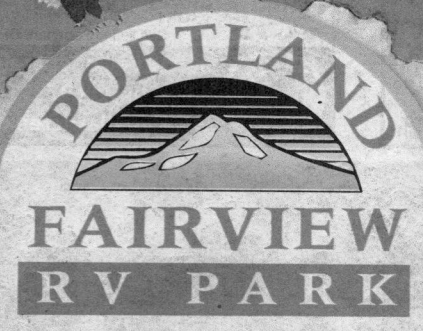

Columbia River RV Park

Experience the difference
...just off I-5 at the Columbia River!

www.columbiariverrv.com

- Spacious Sites with Landscaping • Laundry
- Free Wi-Fi • Cable TV/HBO • Showers
- Weight Room • Rec Room

10649 NE 13th Ave.
Portland, OR 97211

AAA · Good Sam Park

503-285-1515 See listing Portland, OR

ROAMERS REST RV PARK LLC

Good Sam RATED 9/9.5★/9

503-692-6350 FREE WI-FI

www.roamersrestrvpark.com

- City Bus to Portland

17585 SW Pacific Hwy.
Tualatin, OR 97062

Good Sam Park

I-5 Exit 289 West

See listing Tualatin, OR

Mallard Creek GOLF & RV RESORT

(541) 259-4653

Minutes from I-5

Stay & Play!

Good Sam RATED 9/10★/10

See listing Lebanon, OR

TOP RATED Good Sam Park FOR 2016

31958 Bellinger Scale Rd.
Lebanon, OR 97355
www.mallardcreekgc.com

Sandy Riverfront RV Resort

RIVER VIEW SITES AVAILABLE • BIG RIGS WELCOME

FREE CABLE TV & HBO
FREE WiFi

- Portland – 17 Miles
- Columbia Gorge – Boating/Fishing
- 13 Waterfalls including 620 ft. Multnomah Waterfall

1097 E. Historic Columbia River Hwy
Troutdale, Oregon
1 MILE TO I-84

503-665-6722
info@sandyrv.com
www.sandyrv.com
See listing Troutdale, OR

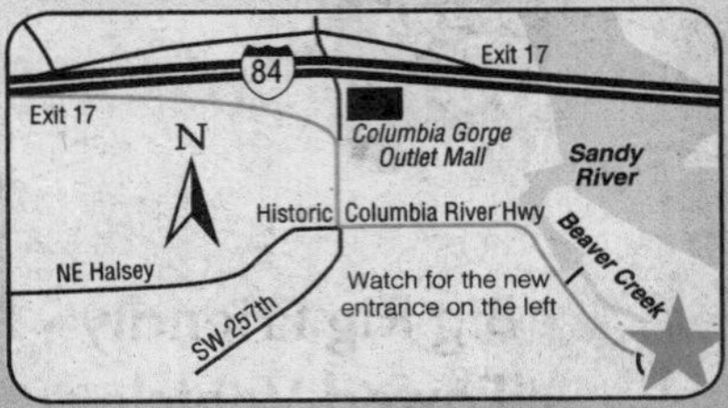

JANTZEN BEACH RV PARK

FREE WIFI

DISCOVER PORTLAND'S ISLAND TREASURE!

Located on the mighty Columbia River in the beautiful Portland area. The park has the quiet open, fresh-air feel of the country, with all the conveniences and attractions of nearby Portland. There is so much to see and do you'll never want to leave.

· Heated Swimming Pool · Fitness Center · Game Room · Playground · Clubhouse
· Basketball Court · Horseshoes · Free Wi-Fi · Free Cable TV · Grassy Picnic Areas
· 20/30/50 Amp Hookups · 60' Pull-thrus · Water & Sewer Connections
· Spotless Restrooms & Showers · Full Laundry Facilities · Open Year Round
· Pets Welcome · Walking Distance to Tax Free Shopping and Restaurants

NEAR Rose Garden · Zoo · University · Convention Center

www.jantzenbeachrv.com

(503) 289-7626 • (800) 443-7248

1503 N. Hayden Is. Dr., Portland, OR 97217
One half mile west of I-5 (exit 308)

AAA

TOP RATED Good Sam Park FOR 2016

Good Sam RATED 9.5/10★/9.5

See listing Portland, OR

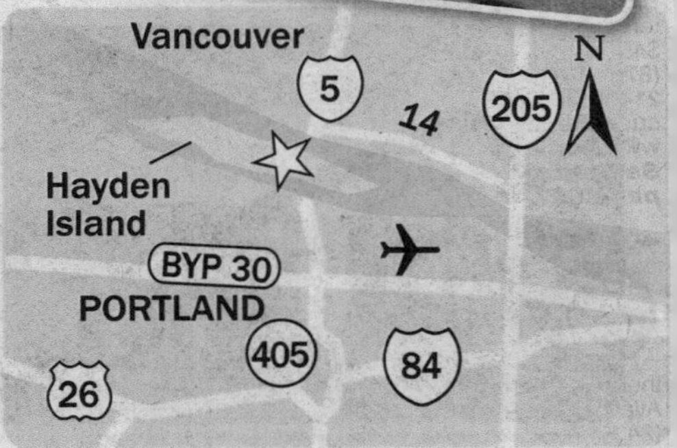

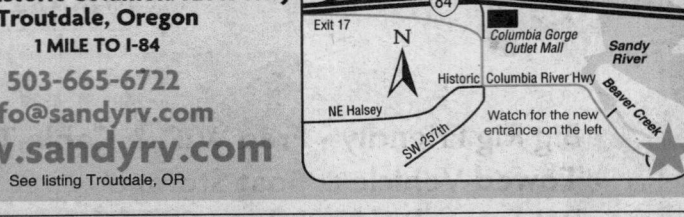

PORTLAND (CONT)

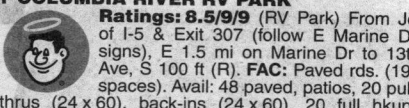

COLUMBIA RIVER RV PARK
Ratings: 8.5/9/9 (RV Park) From Jct of I-5 & Exit 307 (follow E Marine Dr. signs), E 1.5 mi on Marine Dr to 13th Ave, S 100 ft (R). **FAC:** Paved rds. (198 spaces). Avail: 48 paved, patios, 20 pull-thrus (24 x 60), back-ins (24 x 60), 20 full hkups (30/50 amps), seasonal sites, cable, WiFi, dump, laundry. **REC.** Pet restrict(B/Q). Partial handicap access, no tents. Big rig sites, 2015 rates: $32. Disc: AAA.
AAA Approved
(503)285-1515 Lat: 45.59972, Lon: -122.65307
10649 NE 13th Ave., Portland, OR 97211
manager@columbiariverrv.com
www.columbiariverrv.com
See ad opposite page, 930.

JANTZEN BEACH RV PARK
Ratings: 9.5/10★/9.5 (RV Park) From Jct of I-5 & Jantzen Beach (exit 308/N of Portland), take exit rd to N Hayden Island Dr, W 0.3 mi (R). **FAC:** Paved rds. (169 spaces). Avail: 69 paved, 9 pull-thrus (27 x 68), back-ins (30 x 50), 69 full hkups (30/50 amps), seasonal sites, cable, WiFi, laundry. **REC:** heated pool, wading pool, Columbia River: playground. Pet restrict(B). No tents. Big rig sites, eco-friendly, 2015 rates: $35. Disc: AAA.
AAA Approved
(800)443-7248 Lat: 45.61613, Lon: -122.68609
1503 N Hayden Island Dr., Portland, OR 97217
mail@jbrv.com
www.jantzenbeachrv.com
See ad opposite page, 930.

OLDE STONE VILLAGE RV PARK
Ratings: 10/10★/10 (RV Park) From Jct of Hwy 99W & E Hwy 18 bypass (S of McMinnville): Go NE 4.2 mi on Hwy 18 bypass to MP-48.25 (L). **FAC:** Paved rds. 71 paved, patios, 33 pull-thrus (28 x 65), back-ins (28 x 65), 71 full hkups (30/50 amps), cable, WiFi, laundry. **REC:** heated pool, playground. Pet restrict(B). Partial handicap access, no tents. Big rig sites, RV age restrict, eco-friendly, 2015 rates: $38.
(877)472-4315 Lat: 45.2039, Lon: -123.13534
4155 NE Three Mile Ln, Mcminnville, OR 97128
oldestonevillage@comcast.net
www.oldestonevillage.com
See primary listing at McMinnville and ad page 956.

PHEASANT RIDGE RV RESORT
Ratings: 10/10★/10 (RV Park) From Jct of I-405 & I-5 (S of Portland): Go S 12 3/4 mi on I-5 to SW Elligsen Rd/N Wilsonville (Exit 286), then E 1/2 mi on SW Elligsen Rd (L). **FAC:** Paved rds. (130 spaces). Avail: 92 paved, patios, 90 pull-thrus (30 x 60), back-ins (34 x 60), 92 full hkups (30/50 amps), seasonal sites, cable, WiFi, laundry, groc, LP gas. **REC:** heated pool, whirlpool. Pet restrict(B). Partial handicap access. Big rig sites, eco-friendly, 2015 rates: $48 to $55. Disc: AAA, military.
(503)682-7829 Lat: 45.33548, Lon: -122.76192
8275 SW Elligsen Rd, Wilsonville, OR 97070
service@pheasantridge.com
www.pheasantridge.com
See primary listing at Wilsonville and ad this page.

PORTLAND FAIRVIEW RV PARK
Ratings: 10/10★/9 (RV Park) From jct I-5 & I-84: Go 14 mi E on I-84 to 207th Ave (exit 14), then 1/4 mi N on 207th Ave, then 1/4 mi E on Sandy Blvd. **FAC:** Paved rds. (407 spaces). Avail: 257 paved, patios, 105 pull-thrus (25 x 60), back-ins (25 x 35), accepts full hkup units only, 257 full hkups (30/50 amps), seasonal sites, cable, WiFi, laundry. **REC:** heated pool, whirlpool, pond. Pet restrict(B). No tents. Big rig sites, eco-friendly, 2015 rates: $42 to $45.
(877)777-1047 Lat: 45.54333, Lon: -122.44438
21401 NE Sandy Blvd, Fairview, OR 97024
customerservice@portlandfairviewrv.com
www.portlandfairviewrv.com
See primary listing at Fairview and ad page 957.

PORTLAND/WOODBURN RV PARK
Ratings: 9.5/9.5★/8.5 (RV Park) From Jct of I-405 & I-5 (Portland): Go S 28 mi on I-5 to Hwy 214/Hwy 219 (Exit 271), then W 0.1 mi on Hwy 214/Hwy 219 to Arney Rd, then N 100 ft to stop sign, then E 0.1 mi (L). **FAC:** Paved rds. (148 spaces). Avail: 60 paved, 55 pull-thrus (25 x 60), back-ins (24 x 40), 60 full hkups (30/50 amps), seasonal sites, cable, WiFi, laundry. **REC:** heated pool, playground. Pet restrict(B). Partial handicap access. Big rig sites, eco-friendly, 2015 rates: $40. Disc: AAA, military.
(888)988-0002 Lat: 45.15336, Lon: -122.88222
115 N Arney Rd., Woodburn, OR 97071
info@woodburnrv.com
www.woodburnrv.com
See primary listing at Woodburn and ad page 955.

SANDY RIVERFRONT RV RESORT
Ratings: 9.5/9★/9.5 (RV Park) From Jct of I-5 & I-84 : Go E 15.3 mi to Exit 17, the E 0.3 mi on Frontage Rd to Graham (past Loves), then S 0.3 mi to Historic Columbia River Hwy, then E & S 0.6 mi (L). **FAC:** Paved rds. (113 spaces). Avail: 63 paved, 51 pull-thrus (24 x 60), back-ins (24 x 60), accepts full hkup units only, 63 full hkups (30/50 amps), seasonal sites, cable, WiFi, laundry. **REC:** Sandy River: swim, fishing. Pet restrict(B/Q). Partial handicap access. Big rig sites, eco-friendly, 2015 rates: $39 to $43. Disc: AAA.
(503)665-6722 Lat: 45.53779, Lon: -122.37879
1097 E Historic Columbia River Hwy, Troutdale, OR 97060
info@sandrv.com
www.sandyrv.com
See primary listing at Troutdale and ad page 958.

POWERS — D1 *Coos*

POWERS COUNTY PARK (Public) From Jct of Hwy 42 & Powers Hwy exit, W 17 mi on Powers Hwy (R). 2015 rates: $11 to $18. (541)439-2791

PRAIRIE CITY — B5 *Grant*

DEPOT PARK (Public) From Jct of State Hwy 26 & Main St, S 0.5 mi on Main St (L). 2015 rates: $16. May 1 to Oct 31. (541)820-3605

PRINEVILLE — B3 *Crook*

CROOK COUNTY RV PARK (Public) From Jct of US-26 & Main St (in town), Go S 0.8 mi on Main St (L). 2015 rates: $32.85 & $35.04. (800)609-2599

OCHOCO LAKE CAMPGROUND (Public) From Jct of US-26 & Main St (in town), NE 7 mi on US-26 (R). Dry camping only. Water is available. 2015 rates: $16. Apr 1 to Oct 15. (541)447-1209

OCHOCO LAKE CAMPGROUND (Public) From jct Main St & US 26: go 7 mi E on US 26. 2015 rates: $16. Apr 1 to Oct 31. (541)447-2599

PRINEVILLE RESERVOIR (State Pk) From Jct of US-26 & Hwy 126 (in town), E 1 mi on US-26 to Combs Flat Rd, S 1.3 mi to Prineville Reservoir Rec Area Rd, SE 14.4 mi (E). 2015 rates: $22 to $31. (541)447-4363

PRINEVILLE RESERVOIR RESORT **Ratings: 4.5/7.5★/6** (Campground) 2015 rates: $24 to $26. May 1 to Sep 15. (541)447-7468 19600 SE Juniper Canyon Rd, Prineville, OR 97754

SUN ROCKS RV RESORT **Ratings: 8/8★/5.5** (RV Park) 2015 rates: $26 to $30. (541)447-6540 14900 SE Juniper Canyon Rd., Prineville, OR 97754

PROSPECT — D2 *Jackson*

CRATER LAKE RV PARK **Ratings: 6.5/6.5/7.5** (RV Park) 2015 rates: $32.50. (541)560-3399 46611 Hwy 62, Prospect, OR 97536

JOSEPH H STEWART RECREATION AREA (State Pk) From town, SW 6 mi on Hwy 62 (R). 2015 rates: $16 to $22. Mar 1 to Oct 31. (541)560-3334

RAINIER — A2 *Columbia*

HUDSON-PARCHER PARK (Public) From town, W 2 mi on Hwy 30 to Larson Rd, S 0.3 mi, follow signs (R). 2015 rates: $20 to $25. (503)366-3984

Slow down. For most vehicles, fuel efficiency begins to drop rapidly at 60 mph. Driving within the speed limit can improve fuel efficiency by up to 23 percent.

REDMOND — C3 *Deschutes*

EXPO CENTER RV PARK
(Public) From Jct of Hwy 97 & SW Airport Way (south end of town) Exit 124/Yew, E on Airport Way 0.2 mi to SW 19th St, S 0.4 mi (L) NOTE: For GPS use 4690 SW 19th St. Redmond OR 97756. Elev 3096 ft. **FAC:** Paved rds. 106 paved, 50 pull-thrus (24 x 70), back-ins (20 x 55), 106 full hkups (30/50 amps), WiFi, tent sites, laundry. Pets OK. Partial handicap access. Big rig sites, 2015 rates: $33.
(541)585-1569 Lat: 44.23328, Lon: -121.18745
4690 SW 19th St., Redmond, OR 97756
kathyg@deschutes.org
http://expo.deschutes.org/rv
See ad page 960.

Things to See and Do

EXPO CENTER Rodeos, Horse Shows and many other events happen year round in the Expo Center. Partial handicap access. RV accessible. Restrooms, food. ATM.
(541)548-2711 Lat: 44.24025, Lon: -121.18413
3800 SW Airport Rd, Redmond, OR 97756
kathyg@deschutes.org
www.expo.deschutes.org
See ad page 960.

OR

EXPO CENTER
RV PARK
With the majestic
Cascade
Mountains
right out your door...
Open year round
We are a short distance
from the NW's finest golfing,
dining, fishing & boating. Even skiing!
Rodeos, horse shows, dog shows and
many other events happen year round
in the Expo Center.
541-548-2711 ext. 1569
FREE WiFi
www.expo.deschutes.org
Yew Ave.
Airport Way
97
19th St.
Deschutes County Fair and Expo Center
See listing
Redmond, OR

REEDSPORT — C1 *Douglas*

COHO RV PARK & MARINA **Ratings: 6/6/6.5** (RV Park) 2015 rates: $30. (541)271-5411 1580 Winchester Ave, Reedsport, OR 97467

LOON LAKE CAMPGROUND (BLM) (Public) From town: Go 12 mi E on Hwy 38, then 3 mi S on Mill Creek Rd. 2015 rates: $18 to $36. May 22 to Sep 30. (541)599-2254

LOON LAKE LODGE & RV RESORT
Ratings: 6/8.5/8 (RV Park) From Jct of Hwy 38 & Loon Lake Rd (13 mi E of Hwy 101): Go S 9 mi on Loon Lake Rd (R). **FAC:** Gravel/dirt rds. 38 gravel, 24 pull-thrus (24 x 65), back-ins (24 x 50), 38 full hkups (30/50 amps), WiFi, tent sites, rentals, laundry, groc, LP gas, fire rings, firewood, restaurant. **REC:** Loon Lake: swim, fishing, marina. Pet restrict(B). 21 day max stay, 2015 rates: $30 to $52. Disc: AAA. Apr 1 to Oct 31.
AAA Approved
(541)599-2244 Lat: 43.58447, Lon: -123.83559
9011 Loon Lake Rd, Reedsport, OR 97467
loonlakerv@loonlakerv.com
www.loonlakerv.com

SURFWOOD RV CAMPGROUND **Ratings: 5/5.5/5.5** (Campground) 2015 rates: $25. (541)271-4020 75381 US Hwy 101, Reedsport, OR 97467

WILLIAM M TUGMAN SP (State Pk) 8 mi S on US 101 on Eel Lake. 2015 rates: $17 to $24. (541)271-4118

REMOTE — D2 *Coos*

REMOTE OUTPOST RV PARK & CABINS
Ratings: 8.5/8★/8.5 (Campground) From Jct of I-5 & Hwy 42 (Exit 119): Go SW 35 mi (L) or From Jct of US Hwy 101 & Hwy 42S: Go SE 17 mi on Hwy 42S to Hwy 42, then E 27 mi on Hwy 42 (R). **FAC:** Gravel rds. (26 spaces). Avail: 20 gravel, back-ins (30 x 55), 20 full hkups (30/50 amps), seasonal sites, WiFi, rentals, showers $, laundry, LP gas, firewood. **REC:** Qoquille River: swim, fishing. Pet restrict(B) $. Big rig sites, 2015 rates: $33 to $36. Disc: military.
(541)572-5105 Lat: 42.99279, Lon: -123.87589
23146 Hwy 42, Remote, OR 97458
remoteoutpost@wildblue.net
www.remoteoutpostrv.com

RILEY — C4 *Harney*

CHICKAHOMINY CAMPGROUND (Public) From town, W 8 mi on Hwy 20 to park access rd (green sign on right),N 0.25 mi (R). Pit toilets. 2015 rates: $8. (541)573-4400

ROCKAWAY BEACH — A2 *Tillamook*

PARADISE COVE RESORT & MARINA **Ratings: 7.5/8/7.5** (Membership Pk) 2015 rates: $41. (800)445-9519 32455 Hwy 101, Rockaway Beach, OR 97136

ROGUE RIVER — D2 *Jackson*

BRIDGEVIEW RV RESORT Ratings: 9/8.5/8 (RV Park) From Jct of I-5 & Depot St (Exit 48): Go SW 0.2 mi on Depot St. (across river) to Hwy 99, then NW 500 ft (R). **FAC:** Paved rds. 40 paved, patios, 11 pull-thrus (21 x 45), back-ins (21 x 34), 40 full hkups (30/50 amps), cable, WiFi, tent sites, laundry. **REC:** Rogue River: fishing, rec open to public. Pets OK. Partial handicap access. Big rig sites, 2015 rates: $30 to $35. Disc: AAA, military.
AAA Approved
(541)582-5980 Lat: 42.43168, Lon: -123.17299
8880 Rogue River Hwy, Grants Pass, OR 97527
info@bridgeviewrvresort.com
www.bridgeviewrvresort.com

VALLEY OF THE ROGUE (State Pk) From Jct of I-5 & State Park Rd (exit-45B), W 0.2 mi on State Park Rd. 2015 rates: $20 to $28. (800)452-5687

ROSEBURG — C2 *Douglas*

ROSEBURG See also Canyonville, Elkton, Idleyld Park, Myrtle Creek, Oakland, Remote, Rice Hill, Sutherlin, Tillamook & Winchester.

AMACHER PARK/DOUGLAS COUNTY PARK (Public) From jct I-5 (exit 129) & Hwy 99: Go 3/10 mi S on Old Hwy 99. 2015 rates: $15 to $23. (541)672-4901

DOUGLAS COUNTY PARKS-PASS CREEK (Public) From Cottage Grove: S on I-5 to Curtin (Exit 163) (R). 2015 rates: $15 to $23. (541)942-3281

ON THE RIVER GOLF & RV RESORT
Ratings: 8/8.5★/9 (RV Park) S-Bnd From Jct of I-5 & Exit 113: Go W 0.7 mi on exit rd to Hwy 99, then NW (right) 1.3 mi to S Umpqua River Bridge (L); or N-Bnd: From Jct I-5 & Exit 113: Go N & W (left under freeway) on exit rd to Hwy 99, then NW (right) 1.3 mi to S Umpqua River Bridge (L). **FAC:** Paved rds. (58 spaces). Avail: 18 gravel, 13 pull-thrus (25 x 60), back-ins (29 x 45), 12 full hkups, 6 W, 6 E

Things change ... last year's rates serve as a guideline only.

OR

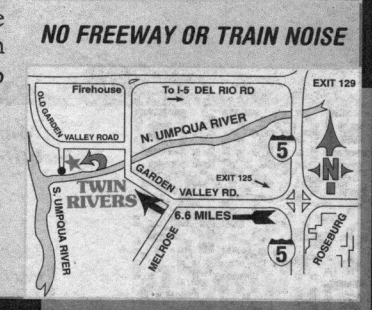

ROSEBURG (CONT)

ON THE RIVER GOLF & RV (CONT)
(30/50 amps), seasonal sites, WiFi, showers $, dump, laundry, firewood. **REC:** South Umpqua River: swim, fishing, golf, rec open to public. Pets OK. Partial handicap access, no tents. Big rig sites, 2015 rates: $28 to $35. Disc: AAA. No CC.
AAA Approved
(800)521-5556 Lat: 43.07907, Lon: -123.38622
111 Whitson Ln, Myrtle Creek, OR 97457
rps1937@gmail.com
www.ontherivergolf-rv.com

← RISING RIVER RV PARK
Ratings: 9/9★/9 (RV Park) From Jct of I-5 & US-99 (exit 119): Go S 2 mi on US-99 to Grange Rd, then SE 0.2 mi (E). **FAC:** Paved rds. (68 spaces). Avail: 11 gravel, patios, 7 pull-thrus (25 x 60), back-ins (32 x 60), 11 full hkups (30/50 amps), seasonal sites, cable, WiFi, laundry, LP gas, firewood. **REC:** South Umpqua River: swim, fishing. Pet restrict(B). Partial handicap access, no tents. Big rig sites, eco-friendly, 2015 rates: $34.
(541)679-7256 Lat: 43.13387, Lon: -123.39677
5579 Grange Rd., Roseburg, OR 97471
risingrv@charter.net
www.risingriverrv.com
See ad pages 961, 930.

← TWIN RIVERS VACATION PARK
Ratings: 8.5/9★/10 (RV Park) From Jct of I-5 & Garden Valley Rd (Exit 125): Go W 4.7 mi on Garden Valley Rd to Hwy 6 (Old Garden Valley Rd), just past bridge, then S 1.5 mi to River Forks Rd, then S.E. 0.2 mi (L).

BEAUTIFUL PRISTINE SETTING
Vickie Bryant & Family welcome you to their beautifully manicured, safe and secure oasis on the N Umpqua River where fishing is spectacular and swimming is refreshing. Come stay a night, you may never want to leave!!!

FAC: Paved rds. (69 spaces). Avail: 60 gravel, patios, 34 pull-thrus (41 x 75), back-ins (40 x 40), 60 full hkups (30/50 amps), seasonal sites, cable, WiFi, tent sites, laundry, groc, LP gas, fire rings, firewood, controlled access. **REC:** N Umpqua River: fishing, playground. Pets OK. Big rig sites, eco-friendly, 2015 rates: $25 to $34.
(541)673-3811 Lat: 43.27046, Lon: -123.43782
433 River Forks Park Rd., Roseburg, OR 97471
twinrv@earthlink.net
www.twinriversrvpark.com
See ad pages 961, 930.

We appreciate your business!

→ WHISTLER'S BEND (Public) From town, NE 12 mi on Hwy 138 to Whistler's Park Rd, NW 3 mi (E). 2015 rates: $15 to $23. (541)673-4863

RUFUS — A3 *Sherman*

→ LEPAGE PARK (Public Corps) From Jct of I-84 & exit 114, S 200 ft on exit 114 (E). 2015 rates: $22 to $25. Mar 31 to Oct 30. (541)506-4807

↑ RUFUS RV PARK **Ratings: 4/5.5/5** (RV Park) 2015 rates: $30. (541)739-2272 311 Wallace St, Rufus, OR 97050

SALEM — B2 *Marion, Polk*

SALEM See also Albany, Aurora, Dayton, Jefferson, McMinnville, Silverton, Wilsonville, Woodburn.

We rate what RVers consider important.

→ HEE HEE ILLAHEE RV RESORT
Ratings: 10/10★/10 (RV Park) From Jct of I-5 & Hwy 99E/Portland Rd (Exit 258): Go N 1/4 mi on Hwy 99E/Portland Rd to Astoria St, then NW 1/4 mi (L). **FAC:** Paved rds. (139 spaces). Avail: 36 paved, patios, 33 pull-thrus (30 x 75), back-ins (30 x 45), accepts self-contain units only, 36 full hkups (30/50 amps), seasonal sites, cable, WiFi, laundry, LP gas. **REC:** pool, whirlpool, playground. Pets OK. No tents. Big rig sites, eco-friendly, 2015 rates: $40. Disc: AAA.
AAA Approved
(877)564-7295 Lat: 44.99105, Lon: -122.99185
4751 Astoria Street, N.e., Salem, OR 97305
manager@heeheeillahee.com
www.heeheeillahee.com
See ad opposite page, 930.

According to some studies, almost 50 percent of RVers camp with pets! Find out more about the joys of traveling with your four-legged companions in our Pampered Pet Parks feature at the front of the Guide.

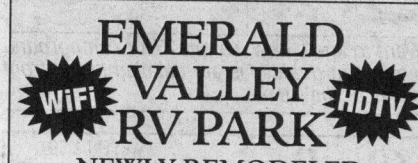

OR

SALEM (CONT)

PHOENIX RV PARK

Ratings: 9/10★/10 (RV Park) S-bnd: From Jct of I-5 & Market St (Exit 256): Go E 0.3 mi on Market to Lancaster Dr, then N 1.5 mi to Silverton Rd, then E 0.1 mi (R); or N-bnd: From Jct of I-5 & Market St (exit 256): Go E 0.3 mi on Market to Lancaster Dr, then N 1.5 mi to Silverton Rd, then E 0.1 mi (R).

BEST KEPT SECRET IN SALEM

Good Sam guests: "We will be stopping often - A well kept and clean Park - One of the most attractive parks we have ever seen! We will stay again and recommend it to other RVers. Phoenix RV is truly a first class operation."

FAC: Paved rds. (107 spaces). Avail: 47 paved, patios, 45 pull-thrus (35 x 65), back-ins (30 x 50), 47 full hkups (30/50 amps), seasonal sites, cable, WiFi, laundry, LP gas. **REC:** playground. Pet restrict(B). Partial handicap access, no tents. Big rig sites, eco-friendly, 2015 rates: $45.50. Disc: AAA, military. AAA Approved
(503)581-2497 Lat: 44.96956, Lon: -122.98185
4130 Silverton Rd NE, Salem, OR 97305
info@phoenixrvpark.com
www.phoenixrvpark.com
See ad this page, 930, 926 (OR Map).

Want to know how we rate? Our campground inspection guidelines are detailed in the front pages of the Guide.

PREMIER RV RESORTS - SALEM

Ratings: 10/10★/9.5 (RV Resort) N bnd: From Jct of I-5 & SR-22/99E Bus/Mission St (exit 253): Go W 3.8 mi on SR-22/99E Bus, then 4.3 mi on SR-22 (L) NOTE: Stay on SR-22 at Marion St. OR S bnd: From Jct of I-5 Salem Parkway/99E (exit260A): Go SW 4.5 mi on Salem Pkwy/Commercial St/99E to Marion St/22W, then W 4.3 mi (L). **FAC:** Paved rds. (164 spaces). Avail: 100 paved, 100 pull-thrus (25 x 60), 100 full hkups (30/50 amps), seasonal sites, cable, WiFi, tent sites, dump, laundry, LP gas. **REC:** heated pool, whirlpool, Rickreall Creek: fishing; playground. Pets OK. Partial handicap access. Big rig sites, eco-friendly, 2015 rates: $49 to $55. Disc: AAA, military.
(877)364-9990 Lat: 44.93074, Lon: -123.12385
4700 Salem-Dallas Hwy 22, Salem, OR 97304
premiersalem@msn.com
www.premierrvresorts.com
See ad pages 963, 930.

SALEM CAMPGROUND & RV'S Ratings: 6.5/7.5/6.5 (Campground) From Jct of I-5 & Hwy 22 (exit 253): Go E 1/4 mi on Hwy 22 to Lancaster Dr., then S 0.1 mi to Carson Dr. SE, then W 200 ft to Hagers Grove Rd, then NW 0.3 mi (E) Note: behind Home Depot. **FAC:** Paved rds. (180 spaces). Avail: 100 paved, 64 pull-thrus (20 x 60), back-ins (21 x 50), 92 full hkups, 8 W, 8 E (30/50 amps), seasonal sites, cable, WiFi, tent sites, dump, laundry, groc, LP gas. **REC:** Millcreek: playground. Pet restrict(B/Q). 2015 rates: $26 to $46. Disc: AAA. AAA Approved
(800)826-9605 Lat: 44.91227, Lon: -122.93540
3700 Hagers Grove Rd., SE, Salem, OR 97317
info@salemrv.com
www.salemrv.com

A campground rating is based on ALL facilities available at the park.

SILVER FALLS (State Pk) From Jct of SR-22 & SR-214 (MP-6 1/2, E of Salem), E 16.4 mi on SR-214, MP-25 (R). 2015 rates: $20 to $26. (800)452-5687

SEAL ROCK — B1 *Lincoln*

SEAL ROCKS RV COVE **Ratings: 5.5/6/7.5** (Campground) 2015 rates: $37 to $46. (541)563-3955 1276 NW Cross St., Seal Rock, OR 97376

SEASIDE — A2 *Clatsop*

BUD'S RV PARK & CAMPGROUND

Ratings: 7/9.5★/8.5 (Campground) From Jct of US-101 & US-26: Go N 7.25 mi on US-101(L) (Note: GPS may require Gearhart for city). **FAC:** Paved/gravel rds. (26 spaces). Avail: 16 gravel, patios, back-ins (30 x 40), 16 full hkups (30/50 amps), seasonal sites, WiFi, tent sites, dump, laundry, groc, LP gas, fire rings, firewood. **REC.** Pet restrict(B/Q). Big rig sites, 2015 rates: $44.99.
(800)730-6855 Lat: 46.03819, Lon: -123.91372
4412 Hwy 101N, Seaside, OR 97138
budsrvandgrocery@gmail.com
www.budsrv.com
See ad this page, 930.

CIRCLE CREEK RV RESORT

Ratings: 8/9★/9 (RV Park) From Jct of US-26 & US-101: Go N 1.8 mi on US-101 (MP-23 1/4) (L); or From town: Go S 0.5 mi on US-101 (MP-23 1/4) (R). **FAC:** Paved rds. 44 paved, 9 pull-thrus (40 x 55), back-ins (40 x 60), 44 full hkups (30 amps), WiFi, dump, laundry, groc, fire rings, firewood. **REC:** Necanicum River. Pets OK. No tents. Eco-friendly, 2015 rates: $46 to $54. Disc: military. Apr 1 to Nov 1.
(503)738-6070 Lat: 45.96539, Lon: -123.92495
85658 Hwy 101, Seaside, OR 97138
info@circlecreekrv.com
www.circlecreekrv.com
See ad this page, 930.

SEASIDE (CONT)

SEASIDE RESORT/THOUSAND TRAILS/ENCORE **Ratings: 8/6.5/8** (Membership Pk) 2015 rates: $42 to $65. (800)405-6188 1703 12th Ave., Seaside, OR 97138

SELMA — D2 *Josephine*

LAKE SELMAC JOSEPHINE COUNTY PARK (Public) From Jct of US-199/Redwood Hwy & Deer Creek Rd (in town): Go S 0.6 mi on US-199 to Lakeshore Dr, then E 2 mi to Reeve's Creek Rd (R). **FAC:** Paved rds. 21 dirt, back-ins (30 x 50), 18 full hkups, 3 W, 3 E (30/50 amps), tent sites, rentals, showers $, dump, fire rings, firewood. **REC:** Lake Selmac: fishing, playground, rec open to public. Pets OK. Partial handicap access. 14 day max stay, 2015 rates: $30. No CC.
(800)452-5687 Lat: 42.26800, Lon: -123.58204
500 Reeves Creek Rd, Selma, OR 97538
ahoward@co.josephine.or.us
http://www.co.josephine.or.us/Page.asp?NavID=492
See ad page 925 (Welcome Section).

LAKE SELMAC RESORT Ratings: 6/4.5/6.5 (Campground) From Jct of Redwood Hwy/199 & Lakeshore Dr: Go E 2.6 mi on Lakeshore Dr (L). **FAC:** Gravel/dirt rds. (29 spaces). Avail: 26 gravel, 13 pull-thrus (25 x 60), back-ins (25 x 45), 5 full hkups, 21 W, 21 E (30/50 amps), seasonal sites, WiFi, tent sites, rentals, dump, laundry, groc, firewood. **REC:** Lake Selmac: rec open to public. Pet restrict(B/Q). Partial handicap access. Big rig sites, 2015 rates: $40 to $45. Disc: AAA, military.
AAA Approved
(541)597-2277 Lat: 42.26298, Lon: -123.57347
2700 Lakeshore Dr., Selma, OR 97538
info@lakeselmacresort.com
www.lakeselmac.com

SHADY COVE — D2 *Jackson*

ROGUE RIVER RV PARK **Ratings: 6.5/7.5/6.5** (RV Park) 2015 rates: $37.45 to $58.85. (800)775-0367 21800 Hwy 62, Shady Cove, OR 97539

SILVERTON — B2 *Marion*

SILVER SPUR RV PARK
Ratings: 8/9.5★/9.5 (RV Park) N-Bnd: From Jct of I-5 & Chemawa Rd (Exit 260) or S-Bnd (Exit 260B): Go E 5.6 mi on Chemawa/Hazel Green Rd to Howell Prairie Rd, then S 1.3 mi to Silverton Rd, the E 3.6 mi (R) (NOTE: Follow Oregon Gardens signs). **FAC:** Gravel rds. (134 spaces). Avail: 71 gravel, 65 pull-thrus (27 x 75), back-ins (30 x 40), 71 full hkups (30/50 amps), seasonal sites, WiFi, dump, laundry, LP gas. **REC:** pond, fishing, playground, rec open to public. Pet restrict(B/Q). Partial handicap access, no tents. Big rig sites, eco-friendly, 2015 rates: $40. Disc: AAA, military.
AAA Approved
(503)873-2020 Lat: 45.00263, Lon: -122.80305
12622 Silverton Rd NE, Silverton, OR 97381
info@silverspurrvpark.com
www.silverspurrvpark.com
See ad pages 963, 930.

SISTERS — C3 *Deschutes, Jefferson, Linn*

SISTERS See also Bend, Camp Sherman & Redmond.

BEND/SISTERS GARDEN RV RESORT
Ratings: 10/10★/10 (RV Resort) From Jct of US-20 & Hwy 126 (E edge of Sisters), SE 4 mi on US-20 (R). Elev 3200 ft. **FAC:** Paved rds. (105 spaces). Avail: 99 paved, patios, 66 pull-thrus (30 x 70), back-ins (30 x 45), 99 full hkups (30/50 amps), WiFi, rentals, laundry, groc, LP gas, fire rings, firewood. **REC:** heated pool, whirlpool, pond, fishing, playground. Pet restrict(Q) $. Partial handicap access, no tents. Big rig sites, eco-friendly, 2015 rates: $43.20 to $64.80.
(541)516-3036 Lat: 44.25039, Lon: -121.48825
67667 Hwy 20, Bend, OR 97701
bendsistersgardenrv@gmail.com
www.bendsistersgardenrv.com
See ad pages 936, 965, 930, 932 (Spotlight Central Oregon).

SISTERS CREEKSIDE CAMPGROUND (Public) From town: Go E 0.25 mi on US-20 to South Locust St, then S 500 ft (L) NOTE: Cross over the bridge take 2nd Left. Elev 3200 ft. **FAC:** Paved/gravel rds. 67 gravel, 6 pull-thrus (18 x 45), back-ins (18 x 35), 25 full hkups (30/50 amps), tent sites, dump, fire rings, firewood. **REC:** Wychus Creek: fishing. Pets OK. 14 day max stay, 2015 rates: $15 to $40. Apr 15 to Oct 15.
(541)323-5218 Lat: 44.28738, Lon: -121.54275
657 E Hwy 20, Sisters, OR 97759
http://www.ci.sisters.or.us/living/city-parks-campground.html
See ad this page.

WILLAMETTE NF (BIG LAKE CAMPGROUND) (Natl Forest) From town: Go 35 mi W on Hwy 126, then 3 mi S on FR 2690. 2015 rates: $20. (801)226-3564

ST HELENS — A2 *Columbia*

BAYPORT RV PARK & CAMPGROUND (Public) From Jct of Hwy 30 & Bennett RD: Go SE 200 ft on Bennett Rd to Old Portland Rd, then NE 1/2 mi (R). 2015 rates: $28. (503)397-2888

ST PAUL — B2 *Marion*

CHAMPOEG (State Pk) From Jct of I-5 & Donald/Aurora (exit 278), W 3.6 mi on Ehlen Rd to Newberg Rd, NW 2.3 mi (R). 2015 rates: $20 to $24. (800)452-5687

OR

STANFIELD — A4 *Umatilla*

PILOT RV PARK
Ratings: 8/8.5★/9 (RV Park) From Jct of I-84 & Hwy 395 (Exit 188): Go N 0.1 mi on Hwy 395 (L). Call for best direction to enter. **FAC:** Paved rds. (48 spaces). Avail: 36 paved, patios, 15 pull-thrus (30 x 75), back-ins (30 x 55), 36 full hkups (30/50 amps), seasonal sites, cable, WiFi, dump, laundry. **REC.** Pets OK. Partial handicap access, no tents. Big rig sites, 2015 rates: $35.
(541)449-1189 Lat: 45.76518, Lon: -119.20718
2125 Hwy 395, Stanfield, OR 97875
manager@pilotrvpark.com
www.pilotrvpark.com
See ad pages 948, 930.

STAGE GULCH RV PARK
Ratings: 6.5/8.5/6.5 (RV Park) From the Jct of I-84 & 395 (Exit 188), N 1.7 mi on Hwy 395 (R). **FAC:** Paved rds. (41 spaces). Avail: 20 paved, 7 pull-thrus (22 x 60), back-ins (22 x 50), accepts full hkup units only, 20 full hkups (30/50 amps), cable, WiFi, tent sites, showers $, dump, laundry. Pets OK. Partial handicap access. 2015 rates: $27 to $29.
(541)449-1176 Lat: 45.78459, Lon: -119.21739
120 E Harding Ave., Stanfield, OR 97875
See ad pages 954, 930.

STEAMBOAT — C2 *Douglas*

UMPQUA NF (EAGLE ROCK CAMPGROUND) (Natl Forest) From town: Go 14 mi SE on Hwy-138. Pit toilets. 2015 rates: $10. May 20 to Sep 30. (541)957-3200

RV Park ratings you can rely on!

SUMMER LAKE — D3 *Lake*

ANA RESERVOIR RV PARK LLC **Ratings: 4.5/8.5★/8** (Campground) 2015 rates: $23 to $27. (541)943-3240 84594 Carlon Lane, Summer Lake, OR 97640

SUTHERLIN — C2 *Douglas*

HI-WAY HAVEN RV PARK & DRIVE IN MOVIE
Ratings: 8.5/9★/9.5 (RV Park) From Jct of I-5 & Hwy 138 (exit 136): Go W 0.2 mi on Hwy 138 to Fort McKay Rd, then SW 1/2 mi (R). **FAC:** Paved rds. (100 spaces). Avail: 37 gravel, patios, 36 pull-thrus (24 x 60), back-ins (24 x 50), 37 full hkups (30/50 amps), seasonal sites, cable, WiFi, dump, laundry, groc, LP gas. **REC:** playground. Pet restrict(B). Partial handicap access, no tents. Big rig sites, 2015 rates: $29 to $31. Disc: AAA, military.
AAA Approved
(541)459-4557 Lat: 43.38744, Lon: -123.35288
609 Fort Mckay Rd., Sutherlin, OR 97479
manager@hiwayhaven.com
www.hiwayhaven.com
See ad pages 961, 930.

SWEET HOME — B2 *Linn*

SUNNYSIDE PARK (Public) From Jct of Hwy 20 & 18th Ave (in town), E 5.2 mi on Hwy 20 to Quartzville Rd, NE 1.4 mi (R). 2015 rates: $22 to $28. Mar 21 to Nov 1. (541)967-3917

WHITCOMB CREEK PARK (Public) From town, E 3 mi on US-20 to Quartzville Rd, N 9 mi (R). Group Camping (res on-line) Note: Small rig & tent camping only. Pit toilets. 2015 rates: $22. Apr 25 to Nov 1. (541)967-3917

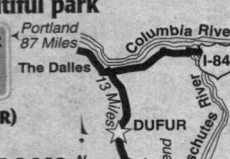

THE DALLES — A3 *Wasco*

DESCHUTES RIVER STATE REC AREA (State Pk) From town, E 12 mi on I-84 to Columbia River Hwy (exit 97), E 5 mi (R). 2015 rates: $16 to $20. (541)739-2322

MEMALOOSE (State Pk) Access from W-bnd only: From Jct of I-84 & State Park Rest Area off Ramp (milepost 73 1/4), proceed thru rest area to park (E); or E-Bnd: From Jct of I-84 & Exit 76, proceed under freeway and return, continue W 3 mi on I-84 (R). 2015 rates: $20 to $28. Mar 15 to Oct 30. (800)452-5687

THE NARROWS — C4 *Harney*

THE NARROWS RV PARK
Ratings: 7/10★/9.5 (RV Park) From Jct of Hwy 20 & Hwy 205, Go S 26 miles on Hwy 205, Then E 25ft on Sodhouse Ln (R) 26 miles South of Burns on Hwy 205. Elev 4160 ft. **FAC:** Gravel rds. (49 spaces). Avail: 41 gravel, patios, 24 pull-thrus (30 x 50), back-ins (30 x 40), 41 full hkups (30/50 amps), seasonal sites, WiFi, tent sites, rentals, showers $, dump, laundry, groc, LP gas, fire rings, firewood, restaurant. **REC.** Pets OK. Partial handicap access. Big rig sites, 2015 rates: $26 to $28.
(541)495-2006 Lat: 43.25723, Lon: -118.95840
33468 Sodhouse Lane, Princeton, OR 97721
thenarrows@highdesertair.com
www.narrowsrvpark.com
See ad pages 938, 930.

Things to See and Do

THE NARROWS RESTAURANT Full service restaurant and saloon serving American traditional meals, beer & wine. Catering meals for clubs, gift Shop, market & gas station with gasoline, diesel & propane. Elev 4160 ft. partial handicap access. RV accessible. Restrooms, food. Hours: 9am - 7pm.
(541)495-2006 Lat: 43.25460, Lon: -118.95830
33468 Sodhouse Lane, Princeton, OR 97721
thenarrows@highdesertair.com
www.narrowsrvpark.com
See ad page 938.

TILLAMOOK — A2 *Tillamook*

TILLAMOOK See also Bay City, Cloverdale, Garibaldi, Nehalem, Netarts, Pacific City, Seaside & Tillamook.

ASHLEY INN - TILLAMOOK **Ratings: 6/NA/7** (RV Park) 2015 rates: $19.95 to $34.95. (503)842-7599 1722 Mankister Rd., Tillamook, OR 97141

TILLAMOOK (CONT)

CAPE LOOKOUT (State Pk) S-bnd: From Jct of US-101 & 3rd St (in town), SW 12 mi on Whiskey Creek Rd (R); or N-bnd: From Jct of US-101 & Sand Lake/Cape Lookout Rd (N of Beaver), NW 10.5 mi on Sand Lake/Cape Lookout Rd (L). 2015 rates: $20 to $24. (800)452-5687

KILCHIS (Public) From city, N 0.5 mi on US-101 to cnty rd (Alderbrook Rd), NE 7 mi (E). 2015 rates: $19 to $24. May 1 to Sep 31. (503)842-6694

NETARTS BAY GARDEN RV RESORT
Ratings: 7/8.5★/8.5 (RV Park) From Jct of US-101 & 3rd St/Netarts Hwy (in Tillamook): Go W 5 3/4 mi on 3rd St/Netarts Hwy to Bilyeu Ave W., then SW 1/4 mi (E) : NOTE: Do not use GPS until your reach Tillamook. **FAC:** Paved rds. (83 spaces). 62 Avail: 4 paved, 58 gravel, patios, 11 pull-thrus (24 x 55), back-ins (24 x 40), 62 full hkups (30/50 amps), seasonal sites, WiFi, laundry, fire rings. **REC:** Netarts Bay: fishing, rec open to public. Pets OK. 2015 rates: $29 to $40.
(503)842-7774 Lat: 45.42655, Lon: -123.93851
2260 Bilyeu Ave W, Tillamook, OR 97141
info@netartsbay.com
www.netartsbay.com
See primary listing at Netarts and ad page 966.

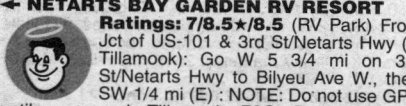

PLEASANT VALLEY RV PARK **Ratings: 6.5/8/9** (Campground) 2015 rates: $29 to $34. (503)842-4779 11880 Hwy 101, S, Tillamook, OR 97141

PORT OF TILLAMOOK CAMPGROUND (Public) From jct Hwy 6 & US 101: Go 2 mi S on US 101. 2015 rates: $19 to $29. (503)842-7152

TILLAMOOK BAY CITY RV PARK
Ratings: 7/8★/8 (RV Park) From Jct of US-101 & Hwy 6 (in town): Go N 4.5 mi on US-101 to Alderbrook Rd (MP-61 1/2), then E 0.2 mi (R). **FAC:** Gravel rds. (45 spaces). Avail: 39 gravel, 18 pull-thrus (25 x 60), back-ins (25 x 60), 26 full hkups, 13 W, 13 E (30/50 amps), seasonal sites, WiFi, tent sites, showers $, dump, laundry, firewood. **REC.** Pets OK. Partial handicap access. Big rig sites, eco-friendly, 2015 rates: $34.
(503)377-2124 Lat: 45.51115, Lon: -123.87536
7805 Alderbrook Rd., Tillamook, OR 97141
francesh@centurylink.net
www.tillamookbaycityrvpark.com
See ad opposite page, 930.

TILLAMOOK RV PARK
Ratings: 8/8★/8 (Campground) From Jct of US-101 & Hwy 6 (in town):Go N 2 mi on US-101 (L). **FAC:** Gravel rds. (31 spaces). Avail: 27 gravel, 27 pull-thrus (24 x 40), 27 full hkups (30/50 amps), seasonal sites, WiFi, tent sites, rentals, showers $, dump, laundry, fire rings, firewood. **REC.** Pet restrict(B). 2015 rates: $45.
(503)354-4627 Lat: 45.48683, Lon: -123.84614
1950 Suppress Rd N, Tillamook, OR 97141
tillamookrvpark@gmail.com
www.tillamookrvpark.com
See ad opposite page, 930.

TILLAMOOK STATE FOREST (GALES CREEK CAMPGROUND) (State Pk) From the town of Tillamook: Go 23 mi E on Hwy 6, then N on North Fork Rd. Pit toilets. 2015 rates: $10. May 15 to Oct 1. (503)357-2191

TILLAMOOK STATE FOREST (JONES CREEK CAMPGROUND) (State Pk) From the town of Tillamook: Go 23 mi E on Hwy 6, then N on North Fork Rd. Pit toilets. 2015 rates: $10. (503)842-2545

TRASK RIVER (Public) From town, E 11.8 mi on Trask River Cnty Rd (R). Pit toilets. 2015 rates: $19 to $24. (503)842-4559

WILSON RIVER RV PARK **Ratings: 5.5/6/6.5** (RV Park) 2015 rates: $30 to $38. (503)842-2750 11300 Wilson River Hwy, Tillamook, OR 97141

TRAIL — D2 *Jackson*

JOSEPH H STEWART (State Pk) From Jct of I-5 & SR-62 (exit 30 Crater Lake Hwy), NE 34 mi on SR-62 (L). 2015 rates: $16 to $22. Mar 1 to Oct 31. (541)560-3334

ROGUE ELK (Public) From Jct of I-5 & Crater Lake Hwy 62, NE 27 mi on Crater Lake Hwy 62 (L). 2015 rates: $20 to $24. Mar 15 to Oct 31. (541)774-8183

TROUTDALE — A2 *Multnomah*

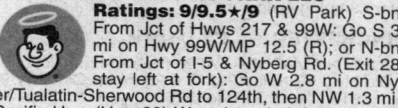

SANDY RIVERFRONT RV RESORT
Ratings: 9.5/9★/9.5 (RV Park) From Jct of I-84 & Exit 17: Go E 0.3 mi on Frontage Rd to Graham (Loves), then S 0.3 mi to Historic Columbia River Hwy, then E & S 0.6 mi (L). **FAC:** Paved rds. (113 spaces). Avail: 63 paved, 60 pull-thrus (24 x 60), back-ins (24 x 60), accepts full hkup units only, 63 full hkups (30/50 amps), seasonal sites, cable, WiFi, laundry. **REC:** Sandy River: swim, fishing. Pet restrict(B/Q). Partial handicap access, no tents. Big rig sites, eco-friendly, 2015 rates: $39 to $43. Disc: AAA.
(503)665-6722 Lat: 45.53779, Lon: -122.37879
1097 E Historic Columbia River Hwy, Troutdale, OR 97060
info@sandyrv.com
www.sandyrv.com
See ad pages 958, 930.

TUALATIN — A2 *Washington*

ROAMER'S REST RV PARK LLC
Ratings: 9/9.5★/9 (RV Park) S-bnd: From Jct of Hwys 217 & 99W: Go S 3.5 mi on Hwy 99W/MP 12.5 (R); or N-bnd: From Jct of I-5 & Nyberg Rd. (Exit 289, stay left at fork): Go W 2.8 mi on Nyber/Tualatin-Sherwood Rd to 124th, then NW 1.3 mi to Pacific Hwy (Hwy 99) West (stay in left lane), N 0.3 mi (L). **FAC:** Paved rds. (93 spaces). Avail: 53 paved, 20 pull-thrus (22 x 58), back-ins (25 x 42), 53 full hkups (30/50 amps), seasonal sites, WiFi, laundry. **REC:** Tualatin River: fishing. Pet restrict(B). Partial handicap access, no tents. Big rig sites, eco-friendly, 2015 rates: $44. Disc: AAA, military.
(503)692-6350 Lat: 45.39263, Lon: -122.80054
17585 SW Pacific Hwy, Tualatin, OR 97062
info@roamersrestrvpark.com
www.roamersrestrvpark.com
See ad pages 958, 930.

TYGH VALLEY — B3 *Wasco*

HUNT PARK-WASCO COUNTY FAIRGROUNDS (Public) From Jct of US-197 & SR-216, W 0.25 mi on SR-216 to Fairgrounds Rd, SW 2 mi, follow signs (L). 2015 rates: $20. (541)483-2288

UKIAH — B4 *Umatilla*

UKIAH-DALE/FOREST WAYSIDE (State Pk) From Jct of US-395 & CR-244, S 1.5 mi on US-395 (L). 2015 rates: $5 to $10. May 1 to Oct 18. (800)551-6949

UMATILLA — A4 *Umatilla*

UMATILLA MARINA & RV PARK
(Public) From Jct of I-82 & Brownell Ave (Exit 1), N 0.4 mi on Brownell to Third, W 0.3 mi to Quincy St, N 100 ft (R). **FAC:** Gravel rds. 26 gravel, 12 pull-thrus (37 x 60), back-ins (37 x 60), 26 full hkups (30/50 amps), WiFi, tent sites, dump, fire rings, firewood. **REC:** Columbia River: swim, fishing, marina. Pets OK. Big rig sites, 14 day max stay, 2015 rates: $31.
(541)922-3939 Lat: 45.92352, Lon: -119.32990
1710 Quincy St., Umatilla, OR 97882
www.umatillarvpark.com
See ad this page.

UNITY — B5 *Baker*

UNITY LAKE (State Pk) From town: Go 5 mi N on Hwy-7. 2015 rates: $17 to $24. Apr 1 to Oct 31. (541)932-4453

VALE — C5 *Malheur*

BULLY CREEK RESERVOIR PARK (Public) From town, NW 7 mi on Graham Blvd to Bully Creek Rd, NW 3 mi (L). 2015 rates: $15. Apr 15 to Nov 15. (541)473-2969

VALE TRAILS RV PARK
Ratings: 6.5/9★/9 (RV Park) From Jct of US-20 & US-26 (in town), N 0.2 mi on US-26/Glenn St to Hope St, E 100 yds (L). **FAC:** Gravel rds. 35 gravel, patios, 28 pull-thrus (31 x 60), back-ins (31 x 60), 35 full hkups (30/50 amps), WiFi, dump, laundry, LP gas. **REC.** Pets OK. Partial handicap access, no tents. Big rig sites, eco-friendly, 2015 rates: $33 to $35. Disc: AAA, military.
AAA Approved
(541)473-3879 Lat: 43.98602, Lon: -117.23643
511 11th Street, Vale, OR 97918
valetrailsrvpark@hotmail.com
www.valetrailsrvpark.com
See ad this page, 930.

VENETA — C2 *Lane*

FERN RIDGE SHORES RV PARK & MARINA **Ratings: 6/6.5/8.5** (RV Park) 2015 rates: $30. (541)935-2335 29652 Jeans Rd., Veneta, OR 97487

VERNONIA — A2 *Columbia*

ANDERSON PARK (Public) From Jct of SR-47 & Jefferson St, S 2 blks on Jefferson St (E). 2015 rates: $14 to $22. (503)429-5291

BIG EDDY PARK (Public) From town, N 7 mi on SR-47 (L). 2015 rates: $15 to $22. (503)397-2353

L.L. "STUB" STEWART (State Pk) From Jct of Hwy 26 & Hwy 47 (30 mi NW of Portland), N 3.55 mi on Hwy 47 (R). 2015 rates: $22 to $31. (503)324-0606

WALDPORT — B1 *Lincoln*

BEACHSIDE (State Pk) From Jct of US-101 & Hwy 34 (N of town), S 3.5 mi on US-101 (R). 2015 rates: $20 to $26. (800)452-5687

CHINOOK RV PARK
Ratings: 7/8.5★/8.5 (Campground) From Jct of Hwy 101 & Hwy 34: Go E 3.2 mi on Hwy 34 (L). **FAC:** Gravel/dirt rds. (34 spaces). 25 Avail: 14 gravel, 11 grass, patios, back-ins (30 x 50), 14 full hkups, 11 W, 11 E (30/50 amps), seasonal sites, cable, WiFi, dump, laundry, firewood. **REC:** Alsea

Like Us on Facebook.

Say you saw it in our Guide!

OR

WALDPORT (CONT)

CHINOOK RV PARK (CONT)
River: fishing. Pets OK. No tents. Eco-friendly, 2015 rates: $27 to $35.
(541)563-3485 Lat: 44.41351, Lon: -124.01540
3299 E Alsea Hwy, Waldport, OR 97394
camp@chinookrvpark.com
www.chinookrvpark.com
See ad pages 953, 930.

MCKINLEY'S MARINA & RV PARK
Ratings: 8/8.5/8.5 (RV Park) From Jct of Hwy 101 & Hwy 34: Go E 1.5 mi on Hwy 34 (L). **FAC:** Paved/gravel rds. (68 spaces). Avail: 58 paved, patios, 37 pull-thrus (24 x 60), back-ins (24 x 60), mostly side by side hkups, 58 full hkups (30/50 amps), seasonal sites, cable, WiFi, tent sites, showers $, laundry, LP gas. **REC:** Alsea River: fishing, playground, rec open to public. Pets OK. Big rig sites, 2015 rates: $34.50.
(541)563-4656 Lat: 44.43183, Lon: -124.05307
850 Hwy 34, Waldport, OR 97394
mckinleysmarina@hotmail.com
www.mckinleysrvparkandmarina.com
See ad page 967.

SIUSLAW NF (BLACKBERRY CAMPGROUND) (Natl Forest) From jct US 101 & Hwy 34: Go 18 mi E on Hwy 34 to Milepost 17-1/2. Pit toilets. 2015 rates: $22. May 17 to Sep 2. (541)547-3679

WALDPORT/NEWPORT KOA **Ratings: 7/8.5★/8.5** (Campground) 2015 rates: $29.50 to $60.50. (541)563-2250 1330 N.W. Pacific Coast Hwy., Waldport, OR 97394

WALLOWA — A5 *Wallowa*

WALLOWA RIVER RV PARK **Ratings: 7/8.5★/8.5** (RV Park) 2015 rates: $30. Apr 1 to Nov 30. (541)886-7002 503 Whiskey Creek Rd., Wallowa, OR 97885

WARM SPRINGS — B3 *Wasco*

KAH-NEE-TA RV PARK **Ratings: 9/8.5/8.5** (Campground) 2015 rates: $25 to $49. (541)553-1112 6823 Hwy 8, Warm Springs, OR 97761

WARRENTON — A2 *Clatsop*

KAMPERS WEST RV PARK **Ratings: 6.5/6/8.5** (Campground) 2015 rates: $30 to $38. (503)861-1814 1140 NW Warrenton Dr., Warrenton, OR 97146

WELCHES — B3 *Clackamas*

MT HOOD VILLAGE RESORT Ratings: 7.5/7.5/8.5 (Campground) From Jct of US-26 & Hwy 211 (in Sandy), E 13 mi on US-26 to MP-38.5 (R). **FAC:** Paved/dirt rds. (377 spaces). Avail: 274 gravel, 20 pull-thrus (35 x 60), back-ins (35 x 50), 185 full hkups, 89 W, 89 E (30/50 amps), seasonal sites, cable, WiFi Hotspot, tent sites, rentals, dump, laundry, groc, LP gas, fire rings, firewood, restaurant, controlled access. **REC:** heated pool, whirlpool, Salmon River: fishing, playground. Pet restrict(B). Partial handicap access. 2015 rates: $57 to $64. Disc: AAA.
AAA Approved
(800)405-6188 Lat: 45.35584, Lon: -121.98636
65000 E Hwy 26, Welches, OR 97067
mt_hood_village@equitylifestyle.com
www.RVontheGo.com

WESTFIR — C2 *Lane*

CASEY'S RIVERSIDE RV PARK
Ratings: 10/10★/10 (RV Park) E-bnd: From Jct of I-5 & Hwy 58 (exit 188A): Go E 31.3 mi on Hwy 58 to Westfir Rd (Old Willamette Hwy), then SE 0.4 mi (L); or W-bnd: From Jct of Hwy 97 & Hwy 58: Go W 55 mi on Hwy 58 to Westfir Rd (MP-31 1/4), then NE 0.4 mi (L). **FAC:** Paved rds. (56 spaces). Avail: 55 paved, patios, 21 pull-thrus (31 x 75), back-ins (31 x 50), 55 full hkups (30/50 amps), seasonal sites, WiFi, laundry, LP gas. **REC:** heated pool, Middle Fork Willamette River: swim, fishing, rec open to public. Pet restrict(B/Q). Partial handicap access, no tents. Big rig sites, 2015 rates: $38 to $42. Disc: AAA.
(541)782-1906 Lat: 43.75718, Lon: -122.52742
46443 Westfir Rd., Westfir, OR 97492
stay@caseysrvpark.com
www.caseysrvpark.com
See ad pages 942, 930.

WILSONVILLE — B2 *Washington*

PHEASANT RIDGE RV RESORT
Ratings: 10/10★/10 (RV Park) From Jct of I-5 & SW Elligsen Rd/N Wilsonville (exit 286): Go E 0.5 mi on SW Elligsen Rd (L). **FAC:** Paved rds. (130 spaces). Avail: 92 paved, patios, 90 pull-thrus (30 x 60), back-ins (34 x 60), 92 full hkups (30/50 amps), seasonal sites, cable, WiFi, laundry, groc, LP gas. **REC:** heated pool, whirlpool. Pet restrict(B). Partial handicap access, no tents. Big rig sites, eco-friendly, 2015 rates: $48 to $55. Disc: AAA, military.
AAA Approved
(503)682-7829 Lat: 45.33548, Lon: -122.76192
8275 SW Elligsen Rd., Wilsonville, OR 97070
service@pheasantridge.com
www.pheasantridge.com
See ad pages 959, 930.

Travel Services

CAMPING WORLD OF WILSONVILLE/PORTLAND As the nation's largest retailer of RV supplies, accessories, services and new and used RVs, Camping World is committed to making your total RV experience better. **SERVICES:** RV, tire, RV appliance, staffed RV wash, restrooms. RV supplies, LP, emergency parking, RV accessible. waiting room. Hours: 8am to 6pm.
(800)446-9039 Lat: 45.325091, Lon: -122.769802
26875 SW Boones Ferry Rd., Wilsonville, OR 97070
www.campingworld.com

WINCHESTER — C2 *Douglas*

JOHN P AMACHER PARK (Public) From Jct of I-5 & Old Hwy 99 (Exit 129), S 0.25 mi on Old Hwy 99 (R). 2015 rates: $15 to $23. May 1 to Sep 30. (541)957-7001

WINCHESTER BAY — C1 *Douglas*

SALMON HARBOR RV PARK, LLC **Ratings: 6/7/6** (RV Park) 2015 rates: $35.35. (541)271-2791 75325 Hwy 101, Winchester Bay, OR 97467

UMPQUA LIGHTHOUSE (State Pk) From Jct of US-101 & Winchester Bay/Salmon Harbor exit, S 0.8 mi on US-101 to Old Hwy 101/Lighthouse Rd, W 0.5 mi (L). 2015 rates: $20 to $28. (541)271-4118

WINCHESTER BAY RV RESORT (Public) From Jct of US-101 & Salmon Harbor Dr (Winchester Bay exit), SW 0.3 mi on Salmon Harbor Dr (R). 2015 rates: $22 to $42. (541)271-0287

WINDY COVE CAMPGROUND 'A' (Public) From Jct of Hwy 101 & Salmon Harbor Dr, SW 0.2 mi on Salmon Harbor Dr (L). 2015 rates: $15 to $23. (541)271-4138

WINDY COVE CAMPGROUND 'B' (Public) From Jct of Hwy 101 & Salmon Harbor Dr, SW 0.4 mi on Salmon Harbor Dr (L). 2015 rates: $15 to $23. (541)271-5634

WOLF CREEK — D2 *Josephine*

SUNNY VALLEY RV PARK
Ratings: 8.5/9★/8 (RV Park) N-bnd: From Jct of I-5 & Exit 71 (Sunny Valley), Go W 0.1 mi on Sunny Valley Loop Rd/Lariat Rd. to Old Stage Rd, then S 200 ft (R); or S-bnd: From Jct of I-5 & Exit 71 (Sunny Valley), S 500 ft on Old Stage Rd (R). **FAC:** Paved/gravel rds. (37 spaces). Avail: 24 gravel, 16 pull-thrus (30 x 55), back-ins (30 x 40), 4 full hkups, 20 W, 20 E (30/50 amps), seasonal sites, WiFi, tent sites, rentals, dump, laundry, groc, fire rings, firewood. **REC:** pool. Pets OK. 2015 rates: $25 to $30. Mar 1 to Oct 30.
(541)479-0209 Lat: 42.630949, Lon: -123.383355
140 Old Stage Rd., Wolf Creek, OR 97497
info@sunnyvalleycampground.com
www.sunnyvalleycampground.com
See ad pages 947, 930.

WOLF CREEK PARK
(Public) From Jct of I-5 & Wolf Creek (Exit 76): Go SW onto Old State Hwy 99S, then SW 0.3 mi to Front St., then W 0.2 mi to Main St, then S 0.3 mi (L). **FAC:** Paved rds. 12 gravel, back-ins (25 x 45), 12 W, 12 E (30 amps), tent sites, pit toilets, dump, fire rings. **REC:** playground, rec open to public. Pets OK. 14 day max stay, 2015 rates: $15. May 26 to Oct 3. No CC.
(800)452-5687 Lat: 42.69214, Lon: -123.40405
370 Main St., Wolf Creek, OR 97497
ahoward@co.josephine.or.us
http://www.co.josephine.or.us/Page.asp?NavID=496
See ad page 925 (Welcome Section).

WOOD VILLAGE — A2 *Multnomah*

Travel Services

CAMPING WORLD OF WOOD VILLAGE As the nation's largest retailer of RV supplies, accessories, services and new and used RVs, Camping World is committed to making your total RV experience better. RV Accessories: (888)240-7979. **SERVICES:** RV appliance, staffed RV wash, restrooms, RV Sales. RV supplies, dump, emergency parking, RV accessible. waiting room. Hours: 8am to 6pm.
(888)796-3028 Lat: 45.542589, Lon: -122.416176
24000 NE Sandy Blvd, Wood Village, OR 97060
www.campingworld.com

WOODBURN — B2 *Marion*

PORTLAND/WOODBURN RV PARK
Ratings: 9.5/9.5★/8.5 (RV Park) From Jct of I-5 & Hwy 214/ Hwy 219 (exit 271): Go W 0.1 mi on Hwy 214/ Hwy 219 to Arney Rd, then N 100 ft to stop sign, then E 0.1 mi (L). **FAC:** Paved rds. (148 spaces). Avail: 60 paved, 55 pull-thrus (25 x 60), back-ins (24 x 40), 60 full hkups (30/50 amps), seasonal sites, cable, WiFi, laundry. **REC:** heated pool, playground. Pet restrict(B). Partial handicap access, no tents. Big rig sites, eco-friendly, 2015 rates: $40. Disc: AAA, military.
AAA Approved
(888)988-0002 Lat: 45.15336, Lon: -122.88222
115 N Arney Rd., Woodburn, OR 97071
info@woodburnrv.com
www.woodburnrv.com
See ad pages 955, 930.

YACHATS — B1 *Lane*

SEA PERCH RV RESORT
Ratings: 9.5/10★/9.5 (RV Resort) From Jct of Hwy 126 & US 101 (in Florence): Go N 17 mi on US 101 to MP-171 (L). **FAC:** Paved rds. 24 Avail: 24 all weather, patios, back-ins (28 x 60), accepts full hkup units only, 24 full hkups (30/50 amps), WiFi, rentals, laundry. **REC:** Pacific Ocean: swim, fishing. Pets OK. Partial handicap access, no tents. Big rig sites, eco-friendly, 2015 rates: $55 to $85.
(541)547-3505 Lat: 44.23045, Lon: -124.10976
95480 Hwy 101 S - Mp 171, Yachats, OR 97498
seaperchrvresort@gmail.com
www.seaperchrvresort.com
See ad pages 943, 930.

Pamper Your Pet on the Road - turn to our Pampered Pet Parks feature at the front of the Guide for great tips and advice when traveling with pets.

We appreciate your business!

Pennsylvania Tourism

WELCOME TO
Pennsylvania

DATE OF STATEHOOD	WIDTH: 280 MILES (455 KM)	PROPORTION OF UNITED STATES
DEC. 12, 1787	LENGTH: 160 MILES (260 KM)	1.21% OF 3,794,100 SQ MI

There are few better places than the Keystone State to immerse oneself in American history. In the iconic buildings of Independence Park, "America's most historic square mile," the seeds of Revolutionary War were planted and the U.S. government came into bloom. After decades of degradation, the future is bright in the university cities of Philadelphia and Pittsburgh. The much-storied "City of Brotherly Love," where the Liberty Bell hangs in all its cracked glory, Philadelphia marries industrial prowess with a creative verve that finds expression in hip bistros, cafés, galleries and funky independent stores.

A city synonymous with steel factories, Pittsburgh defies cliché with its first-rate cultural attractions. The four museums of the Carnegie Institute triumph art, science and natural history, and pay homage to its Pop Art native son at the stellar Andy Warhol Museum. U.S. history lesson 101 continues at Gettysburg and Valley Forge, while at Laurel Highlands a number of Frank Lloyd Wright's prairie-style masterworks can be found, most notably his magnum opus, Fallingwater.

Play

Following intensive urban renewal and regeneration programs, Philadelphia flaunts more outdoor sculptures and artworks—notably murals—than any of its big-city peers. Fairmount Park is the largest landscaped urban park in the world; horseback riding, cycling, hiking and fishing are just some of the pursuits on offer amidst 9,000 acres of rolling hills, trails, woodlands and waterfront. Pennsylvania boasts an award-winning state park system. The Poconos and Allegheny National

Top 3 Tourism Attractions:
1) Hersheypark
2) Fallingwater
3) Longwood Gardens

Nickname: Keystone State

State Flower: Mountain Laurel

State Bird: Ruffed Grouse

People: Jimmy and Tommy Dorsey, band leaders; Billie Holiday, jazz-blues singer; Lee Iacocca, auto executive; Arnold Palmer, golfer; James "Jimmy" Stewart, actor

Major Cities: Philadelphia, Pittsburgh, Allentown, Erie, Reading, (Harrisburg, capital)

Topography: Central—Allegheny Mountains run southwest to northeast; southeast—piedmont, coastal plain; northwest—rugged plateau to Lake Erie

Climate: Humid continental zone with various climates according to region and elevation

Pennsylvania Tourism

PA

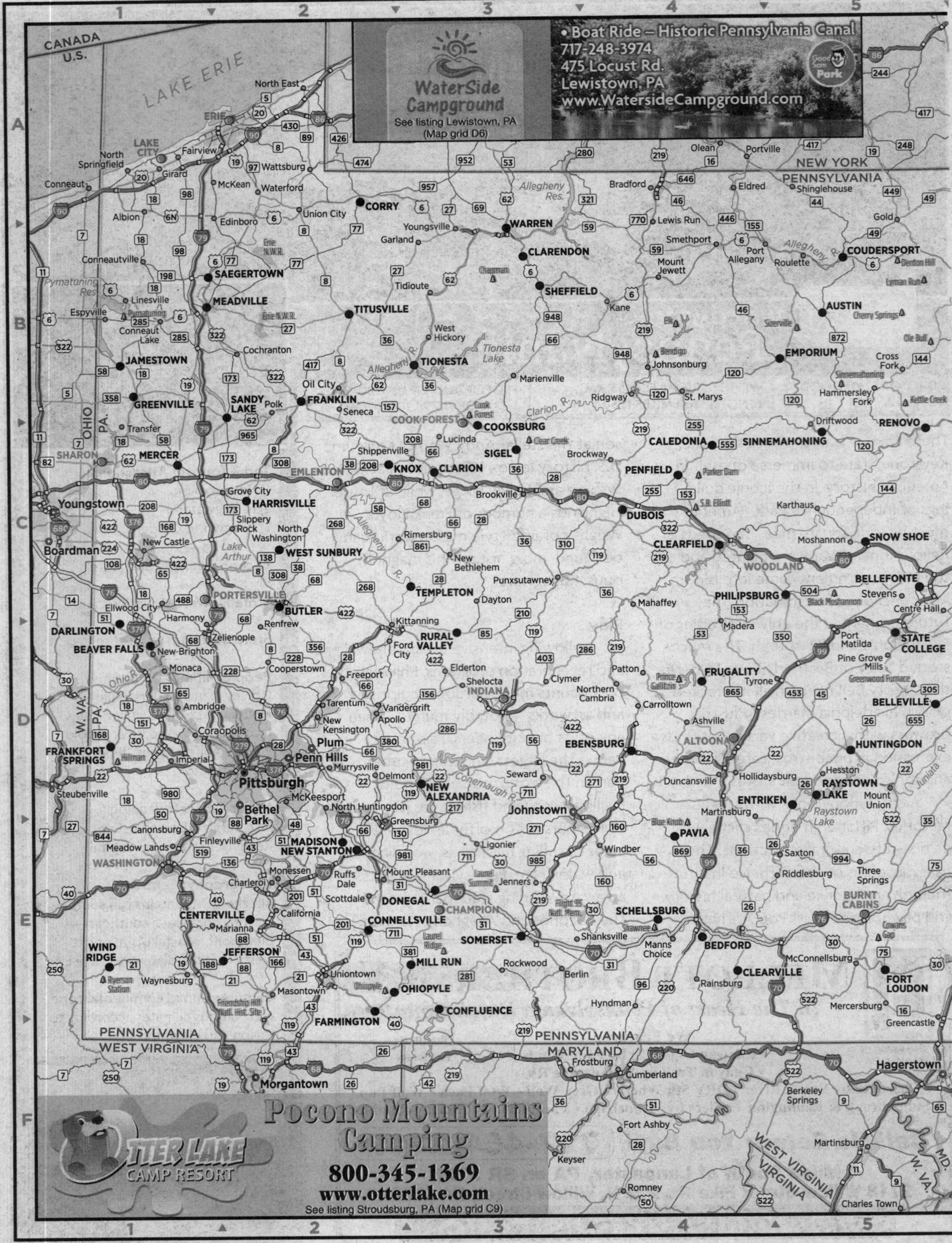
WaterSide Campground
See listing Lewistown, PA (Map grid D6)
• Boat Ride – Historic Pennsylvania Canal
717-248-3974
475 Locust Rd.
Lewistown, PA
www.WatersideCampground.com
Good Sam Park
Pocono Mountains Camping
OTTER LAKE CAMP RESORT
800-345-1369
www.otterlake.com
See listing Stroudsburg, PA (Map grid C9)
CANADA
U.S.
LAKE ERIE
NEW YORK
PENNSYLVANIA
OHIO
PA.
W. VA.
WEST VIRGINIA
MARYLAND
VIRGINIA
MD.
ERIE
CORRY
WARREN
CLARENDON
SHEFFIELD
COUDERSPORT
SAEGERTOWN
MEADVILLE
TITUSVILLE
AUSTIN
JAMESTOWN
TIONESTA
EMPORIUM
GREENVILLE
SANDY LAKE
FRANKLIN
COOKSBURG
RENOVO
MERCER
SIGEL
CALEDONIA
SINNEMAHONING
KNOX
CLARION
PENFIELD
HARRISVILLE
DUBOIS
SNOW SHOE
CLEARFIELD
WEST SUNBURY
BELLEFONTE
TEMPLETON
PHILIPSBURG
BUTLER
DARLINGTON
BEAVER FALLS
RURAL VALLEY
STATE COLLEGE
FRUGALITY
BELLEVILLE
FRANKFORT SPRINGS
EBENSBURG
HUNTINGDON
Pittsburgh
NEW ALEXANDRIA
RAYSTOWN LAKE
ENTRIKEN
Johnstown
PAVIA
MADISON
NEW STANTON
DONEGAL
CENTERVILLE
CONNELLSVILLE
SCHELLSBURG
SOMERSET
BEDFORD
WIND RIDGE
JEFFERSON
MILL RUN
CLEARVILLE
FORT LOUDON
OHIOPYLE
CONFLUENCE
FARMINGTON
Youngstown
Boardman
Morgantown
Cumberland
Hagerstown

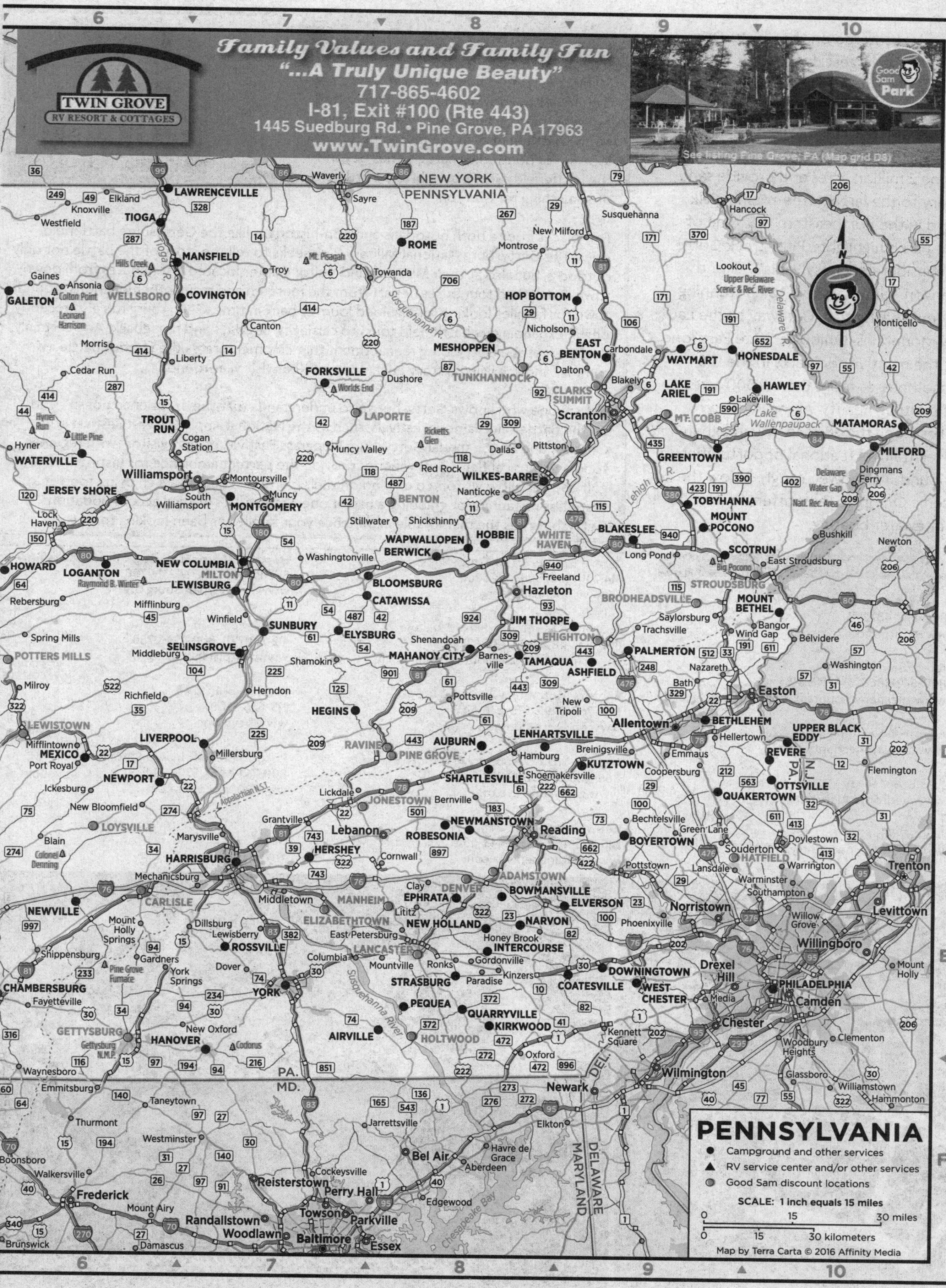
Family Values and Family Fun
"...A Truly Unique Beauty"
717-865-4602
I-81, Exit #100 (Rte 443)
1445 Suedburg Rd. • Pine Grove, PA 17963
www.TwinGrove.com
TWIN GROVE
RV RESORT & COTTAGES
Good Sam Park
See listing Pine Grove, PA (Map grid D8)
NEW YORK
PENNSYLVANIA
PA.
MD.
DEL.
MARYLAND
DELAWARE
N.J.
LAWRENCEVILLE
TIOGA
MANSFIELD
COVINGTON
GALETON
ROME
HOP BOTTOM
MESHOPPEN
FORKSVILLE
TUNKHANNOCK
EAST BENTON
WAYMART
HONESDALE
LAKE ARIEL
HAWLEY
MATAMORAS
MILFORD
TROUT RUN
WATERVILLE
JERSEY SHORE
MONTGOMERY
Williamsport
CLARKS SUMMIT
Scranton
MT. COBB
GREENTOWN
WILKES-BARRE
TOBYHANNA
MOUNT POCONO
BLAKESLEE
SCOTRUN
HOBBIE
WAPWALLOPEN
BERWICK
HOWARD
LOGANTON
NEW COLUMBIA
LEWISBURG
BLOOMSBURG
CATAWISSA
Hazleton
STROUDSBURG
BRODHEADSVILLE
MOUNT BETHEL
SUNBURY
ELYSBURG
JIM THORPE
LEHIGHTON
SELINSGROVE
MAHANOY CITY
TAMAQUA
ASHFIELD
PALMERTON
POTTERS MILLS
HEGINS
Easton
LEWISTOWN
Allentown
BETHLEHEM
LIVERPOOL
AUBURN
LENHARTSVILLE
UPPER BLACK EDDY
MEXICO
RAVINE
PINE GROVE
KUTZTOWN
REVERE
NEWPORT
SHARTLESVILLE
OTTSVILLE
JONESTOWN
QUAKERTOWN
LOYSVILLE
Lebanon
NEWMANSTOWN
ROBESONIA
Reading
BOYERTOWN
HERSHEY
HARRISBURG
HATFIELD
Trenton
ADAMSTOWN
BOWMANSVILLE
CARLISLE
DENVER
MANHEIM
EPHRATA
ELVERSON
Norristown
NEWVILLE
ELIZABETHTOWN
NEW HOLLAND
NARVON
Levittown
ROSSVILLE
LANCASTER
INTERCOURSE
Willingboro
CHAMBERSBURG
YORK
STRASBURG
COATESVILLE
DOWNINGTOWN
WEST CHESTER
Drexel Hill
PHILADELPHIA
Camden
PEQUEA
QUARRYVILLE
KIRKWOOD
Chester
GETTYSBURG
HANOVER
AIRVILLE
HOLTWOOD
Wilmington
Newark
Frederick
Bel Air
Reisterstown
Perry Hall
Towson
Parkville
Randallstown
Woodlawn
Baltimore
Essex
PENNSYLVANIA
Campground and other services
RV service center and/or other services
Good Sam discount locations
SCALE: 1 inch equals 15 miles
0 15 30 miles
0 15 30 kilometers
Map by Terra Carta © 2016 Affinity Media
PA

Forests, centered on the Kinzua Dam (one of the largest dams in the U.S.), boasts mile after mile of wilderness hiking trails.

In northern Pennsylvania, the forests of the Pennsylvania Wilds span some 2 million acres and provide sanctuary to the largest free-roaming elk herd in the northeastern U.S. One of the park's highlights, Pine Creek Gorge is considered Pennsylvania's "Grand Canyon," draws visitors to its stunning 40-mile hiking trail. Gateway to the Laurel Mountains, Ohiopyle State Park (one of the most visited parks in the U.S.) encompasses more than 19,000 acres of startling beauty. Along with scenic hikes along the 28-mile Youghiogheny River Trail, recreational opportunities abound. The Lower Yough, below the scenic Ohiopyle Falls, offers fantastic whitewater boating.

- STAY A WHILE -

Gettysburg

Many families find that it takes at least a few days to get to know Gettysburg, Pennsylvania. Whether you are searching for history on the battlefield or in the museums, or looking for nontraditional activities beyond the battlefield, Gettysburg offers a little bit of something for everyone.

Few places inspire both historians and non-historians like the Gettysburg battlefield does. The Gettysburg National Military Park seeks to tell the story of the battle not only outdoors, but also at their Museum and Visitor Center located just minutes from downtown. Battlefield tour buses depart from the museum and many other locations around town for families looking for a guided journey back in time. Gettysburg has also recently begun expanding its battlefield tours to carriages, Segways and horseback. And certainly don't forget the Gettysburg reenactment that commemorates the famous battle every summer and the living history encampments that visit year-round.

But anyone who knows Gettysburg also understands that the experience doesn't end on the battlefield. Famous festivals, such as the National Apple Harvest Festival in October and the bi-annual Gettysburg Bluegrass Festival, delight visitors with regional food and musical flair. Local wineries provide the perfect ambiance for tastings, while golf courses allow visitors to unwind on their journey. Whether it's enjoying food at a first-class restaurant or grabbing a nap at one of the area's leading accommodations, Gettysburg has the memorable experience your family has been looking for.

TRAVEL & TOURISM

Pennsylvania Tourism Office
800-847-4872
www.visitpa.com

Allegheny Mountains CVB
800-842-5866, 814-943-4183
www.alleghenymountains.com

Armstrong County Tourist Bureau
www.armstrongcounty.com

Bedford County Visitors Bureau
www.bedfordcounty.net

Brandywine Visitors Bureau
www.brandywinecountry.org

Centre County-Penn State
814-231-1400, 800-358-5466
www.visitpennstate.org

Columbia Montour Visitors Bureau
800-847-4810, 570-784-8279
www.iTourColumbiaMontour.com

Endless Mountains Visitors Bureau
800-769-8999, 570-836-5431
www.endlessmountains.org

Gettysburg Convention & Visitors Bureau
866-486-5735, 800-337-5015
www.gettysburgcvb.org

Greater Reading CVB
610-375-4085, 800-443-6610
www.readingberkspa.com

Hershey Harrisburg Regional Visitors Bureau
877-PA-PULSE, 717-231-7788
www.hersheyharrisburg.org

Visit Pittsburgh
412-281-7711, 800-359-0758
www.visitpittsburgh.com

Philadelphia CVB
215-636-3300
www.pcvb.org

Pocono Mountains Vacation Bureau, Inc.
800-762-6667, 570-421-5791
www.800poconos.com

Scranton/Lackawanna County
800-22-WELCOME
www.visitnepa.org

Featured Good Sam Parks

PENNSYLVANIA

When you stay with Good Sam, you can expect the highest degree of cleanliness and friendliness, and better yet, you get 10% off campground fees.

If you're not already a Good Sam member you can purchase your membership at one of these locations:

ADAMSTOWN
Shady Grove Campground
(717)484-4225

BENTON
Whispering Pines Camping Estates
(570)925-6810

BRODHEADSVILLE
Silver Valley Campsites
(570)992-4824

BURNT CABINS
Ye Olde Mill Campground
(717)987-3244

CARLISLE
Deer Run Camping Resort
(717)486-8168
Mountain Creek Campground
(717)486-7681

CHAMPION
Mountain Pines Campground
(724)455-3300

CLARKS SUMMIT
Highland Campground
(570)586-0145

DENVER
Hickory Run Family Camping Resort
(800)458-0612

ELIZABETHTOWN
Hershey Conewago Campground
(717)367-1179

EMLENTON
Gaslight Campground
(724)867-6981

ERIE
Presque Isle Passage RV Park & Cabin Rentals
(814)833-3272
Sparrow Pond Family Campground & Recreation
(814)796-6777
West Haven RV Park & Family Campground
(814)403-3243

GETTYSBURG
Artillery Ridge Camping Resort & Gettysburg Horse Park
(717)334-1288
Gettysburg Campground
(717)334-3304
Granite Hill Camping Resort
(717)642-8749

HATFIELD
Village Scene RV Park
(215)362-6030

HOLTWOOD
Tucquan Park Family Campground
(717)284-2156

INDIANA
Wheel-In Campground
(724)354-3693

JONESTOWN
Jonestown AOK Campground
(717)865-2526

LAKE CITY
Camp Eriez
(814)774-8381

LANCASTER
Country Acres Campground
(866)675-4745
Flory's Cottages & Camping
(717)687-6670
Mill Bridge Village and Campresort
(717)687-8181

LAPORTE
Pioneer Campground
(570)946-9971

LEHIGHTON
Stoneybrook Campground
(570)386-4088

LEWISTOWN
Waterside Campground & RV Park
(717)248-3974

LOYSVILLE
Paradise Stream Family Campground
(717)789-2117

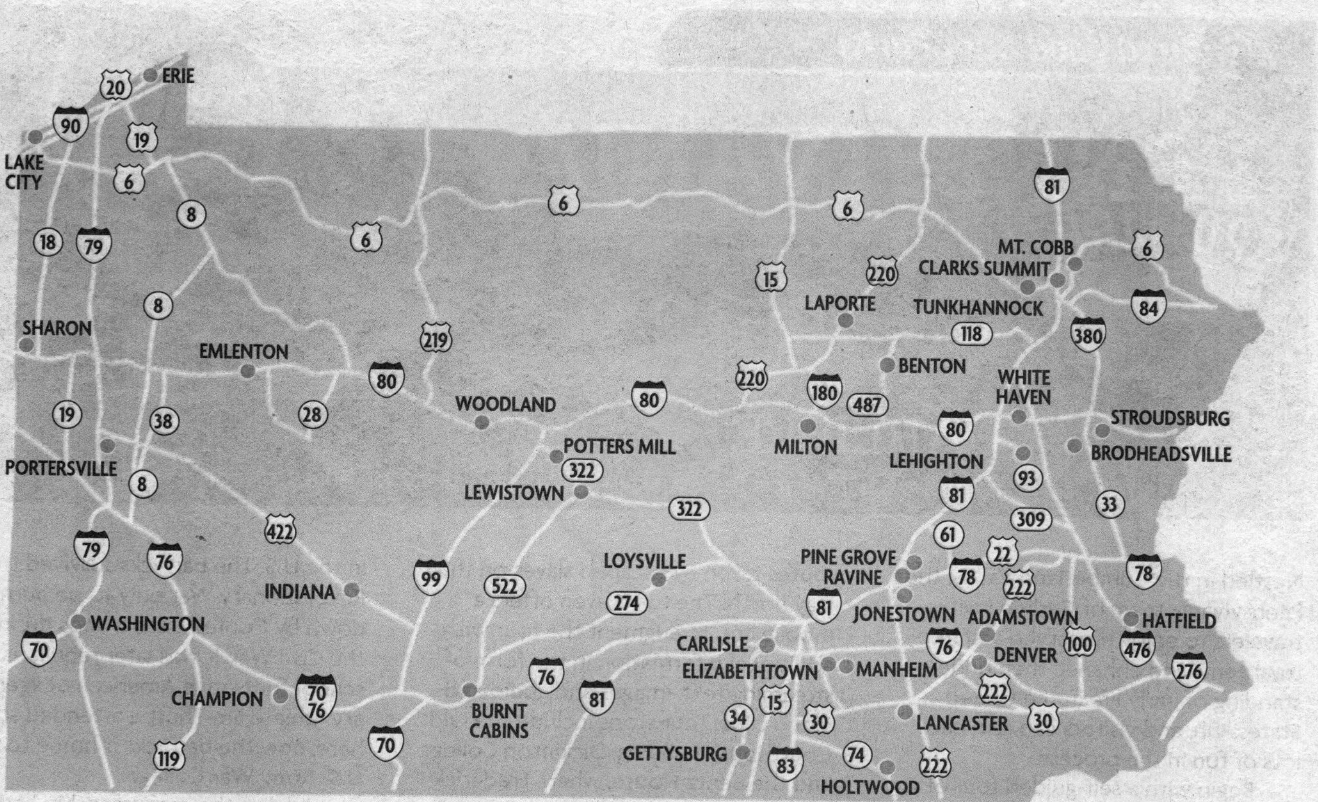

PA

MANHEIM
Pinch Pond Family Campground
(800)659-7640

MILTON
Yogi At Shangri-La
(570)524-4561

MOUNT COBB
Clayton Park Recreational Area
(570)698-6080

PINE GROVE
Twin Grove RV Resort & Cottages
(717)865-4602

PORTERSVILLE
Bear Run Campground
(888)737-2605
Rose Point Park Cabins & Campground
(724)924-2415

POTTERS MILLS
Seven Mountains Campground
(814)364-1910

RAVINE
Echo Valley Campground
(570)695-3659

SHARON
Shenango Valley RV Park
(724)962-9800

STROUDSBURG
Mountain Vista Campground
(570)223-0111
Pocono Vacation Park
(570)424-2587

TUNKHANNOCK
Cozy Creek Family Campground
(570)836-4122

WASHINGTON
Pine Cove Beach Club & RV Resort
(724)239-2900

WHITE HAVEN
Lehigh Gorge Campground
(570)443-9191

WOODLAND
Woodland Campground
(814)857-5388

For more Good Sam Parks go to listing pages

CARLISLE

Explore Civil War sites, bask in colonial history or hike untamed wilderness

Nestled in the Cumberland Valley, the Pennsylvania town of Carlisle invites travelers to enjoy preserved architectural gems and enhance their understanding of early life in the United States. Oh, and visitors can also have lots of fun in the process.

Begin with a self-guided tour of the town to learn about its role in the Civil War and in the Underground Railroad, the system of safe houses and secret routes taken by escaped slaves on their way north. The town even offers a mobile app to augment the tour with additional information in the form of streaming text, images and audio and video clips. Tour stops include the Old Courthouse building, Dickinson College and the Bentz House, where Frederick Douglass spoke in 1872.

Also worth a visit is the Carlisle Barracks, the second-oldest Army post in the U.S. The barracks survived the Revolutionary War only to be burned down by Confederate troops during the Civil War. It was later rebuilt as a school for Native Americans. Legendary athlete Jim Thorpe attended school here; now the barracks is home to the U.S. Army War College.

Admire the craftsmanship and staying power of 18th-century architecture that graces the streets of Carlisle. Stops include the Steven Duncan House, a stone structure built in the 1750s, and First Presbyterian Church, the oldest public building in Carlisle, where citizens met in 1774 to condemn the closing of the port of Boston by the British.

Cars and Carlisle

Fast-forward a few hundred years and see the best of American and foreign automakers on display at any of nine annual car shows, held at the Carlisle Fairgrounds. Visit the U.S. Army Heritage and Education Center and peruse military might on display along the one-mile Army Heritage Trail, an interactive loop dotted with equipment and vehicles such as the M-46 Patton tank and a Huey helicopter. Ready for speed? The Williams Grove speedway thrills spectators with some of the most exciting 410 sprint car racing in North America.

Take the ice-cream challenge at Pine Grove General Store, where winners are awarded with a special prize.

The Carlisle Theatre entertains patrons with a lively schedule of plays, musicals, choral events and movie screenings. The American Artisan Gallery showcases the talents of local makers, who create unique works in several media, including glass, ceramics, metal and fine art.

Enjoy the outdoors on a hike along the Appalachian Trail; the Cumberland Valley stretch is the midpoint of this legendary trail, and where you can stop in at the Appalachian Trail Museum—the nation's only museum dedicated to hiking. Along the trail, you'll often see herons and water birds resting and feeding at Conodoguinet Creek.

Take the ice-cream challenge at Pine Grove General Store, where consuming a half-gallon of the sweet treat earns victors a celebratory ice cream scoop for their trophy room. If you prefer a faster touring pace, hop on two wheels for a scenic bike ride from

PA

Military hardware through the decades is on display at the U.S. Army Heritage and Education Center.
USAHEC

Williams Grove Speedway hosts 410 sprint car racing.
Jason Walls

Carlisle to several nearby scenic stops including Boiling Springs, where the Carlisle Iron Works Furnace still stands. One of the earliest blast furnaces, this structure was built in 1761.

Pastoral Pennsylvania

Get to know the ins and outs of Pennsylvania's natural wonders at Kings Gap Environmental Education Center, where children's activities and interpretive programs for the public teach visitors about the 2,500-acre forest on Pennsylvania's South Mountain. Also on site is the Cameron/Masland Mansion; built around 1900 from local stone, it's now open for self-guided tours on Sundays through the summer, as well as during weekends in December, when the mansion gets "dressed up" in festive decorations for the holidays.

Toast to a great vacation at Molly Pitcher Brewing Company, named for a famed Revolutionary War heroine.

Cast a line into one of several great spots for fly-fishing in the Cumberland Valley. Big Spring Creek, Children's Lake and Opossum Lake are great for trout, and you can fish year-round at Laurel Lake and Mountain Creek. Take the boat out on a sunny day at North Middleton Park, where Conodoguinet Creek is easily accessible. On shore, cast a few horseshoes or just take a leisurely walk around this 15-acre retreat.

If the temperature drops, keep young family members entertained for a day at Carlisle Sports Emporium. This indoor arcade cures bad-weather blues with a variety of games and activities for guests of all ages and skill levels. Enjoy a more laid-back time hitting a few balls on the course at Cumberland Golf Club or Mayapple Golf Club.

Toast to a great vacation at Molly Pitcher Brewing Company, named for a famed Revolutionary War heroine who loaded and swabbed an artillery piece during the battle of monmouth despite incoming British fire. Even the locally crafted beers and brews carry out the colonial theme. Sip on Patriot Pale Ale or Minuteman Mild while you're here.

If a good wine is more to your liking, visit Castlerigg Wine Shop for Pennsylvania vintages to sample along with small bites to complement each varietal.

For More Information

Cumberland Valley Visitors Bureau
888-513-5130
www.visitcumberlandvalley.com

Pennsylvania Tourism
800-847-4872
www.visitpa.com

ERIE

History washes ashore in this charming port city

Erie Pennsylvania shares a vibrant mix of history and modernity with visitors, and there's plenty to explore in this lakeside community. With roots that stretch back to the Colonial era and a culture that's fed by the steady traffic of the lake that shares its name, there's no end to the discoveries that visitors can make in this charming waterfront town.

> Asbury Woods provides an expansive nature experience, with multiuse trails and a nature center with live animal habitats and a live honeybee-hive exhibit.

Museums Galore

The Erie County Historical Society is a great place to start your tour of the city. The Hagen History Center, housed in historic buildings, displays regional history and Victorian-era furnishings as well as archival resources.

From American artists to ancient tribes of other lands, the artifacts and art on display at Erie Art Museum fascinate and educate guests year-round. Every year, as many as 20 traveling exhibitions make their way to the museum, ensuring a new experience on every trip. Five historic buildings make up the museum, including the Old Customs House and the Old Pumper House, which is the oldest surviving firehouse in Erie, originally established as a marble works in 1850.

Young family members will welcome the more hands-on approach found at ExpERIEnce Children's Museum. Imaginations are inspired by opportunities to play and learn about the world around us through interactive displays for children of all ages.

Wartime Triumphs

Once controlled by the French, Erie was seized by the British prior to the Revolutionary War. It fell into American hands after that conflict, but during the War of 1812 with Britain, the area was hotly contested during the 1813 Battle of Lake Erie. The struggle ended in America's favor and ensured that the U.S., commanded by Oliver H. Perry, had control over the region. The Perry Monument is found on Presque Isle State Park and is open to the public during the summer months.

Point Betsie Lighthouse overlooks Lake Erie. Getty Images/iStockphoto

A countryside stroll outside of Erie.
Getty Images/iStockphoto

But don't just visit Presque Isle State Park for Perry. This is a sandy, sunny getaway for summer-loving visitors to Erie. The 3,200-acre peninsula is an ideal destination for bike tours on the Karl Boyes Recreation Trail.

At the base of the peninsula, the Tom Ridge Environmental Center is a resource for explorers of all ages. The center teaches visitors about the life inhabiting the peninsula and its importance to the region. Guests are invited to climb the center's 75-foot observation tower.

More tales of American naval might are collected into interactive displays at the Erie Maritime Museum. Erie's native daughter, the *U.S. Brig Niagara*, is ported here. Other exhibits include a steam generator, lighthouse memorabilia and several ship models.

Fishing is grand in Erie, with walleye in the lake during summer months, and steelhead trout in streams both east and west of the city, from spring to fall. Presque Isle Bay is a hot spot for bass, perch, northern pike and muskellunge. Sheltered lagoons around Presque Isle Bay provide calm waters for leisurely boating, and there's enough room for sailboats, jet-skis and speedboats as well.

Erie's Wild Side

Just blocks from Lake Erie lies the serene Lake Erie Arboretum at Frontier Park. More than 225 varieties of trees grow here, and a stone labyrinth invites visitors to wander around its intricately curved paths. At the Erie Zoo, the animals are the star attraction, and rightly so. See primates, wild cats, tropical birds and more in habitats designed to closely mirror their homes in the wild.

Satisfy your sporting side with a game courtesy of Erie's minor professional teams. The Erie Seawolves are the AA affiliate for baseball's Detroit Tigers; the Erie Otters are a major junior hockey team under the Ontario Hockey League; the Erie Bayhawks keep the ball moving as part of the NBA Developmental League, the professional association's official minor-league organization; and the Erie Explosion and Illusion are both a touchdown for football fans—the Illusion shine as a professional women's team in the Independent Women's Football League, while the Explosion dominate the professional indoor football circuit.

Get a little wild—and wet—on hot summer days at Erie's Waldameer & WaterWorld. This dual-attraction amusement park first came to life as a picnic spot overlooking Lake Erie, then evolved into a turn-of-the-century amusement destination, complete with wooden roller coasters, a carousel and even a pre-Prohibition beer garden. Today the park offers a combination of thrilling rides and aquatic refreshment.

Asbury Woods provides another expansive nature experience, with multiuse trails and a nature center with live animal habitats and a live honeybee-hive exhibit. Younger visitors are encouraged to visit the Little Woods play area for some back-to-nature fun. Brown's Farm Barn shows guests what a working farm in the 1800s and 1900s might have looked like, with a focus on agriculture and the responsible use of natural resources.

Enjoy the arts and culture scene at a production of the Lake Erie Ballet or a show at the Erie Playhouse. All Act Theatre Production is one of Erie's gems, promising a rousing good time for everyone. Warner Theater is a visual stunner of a movie house, reminiscent of Hollywood's Golden Age of cinema. The theater opened in 1931 and today hosts the Erie Philharmonic and Broadway productions.

For More Information

Visit Erie
800-524-ERIE
www.visiteriepa.com

Pennsylvania Tourism
800-847-4872
www.visitpa.com

GETTYSBURG

Walk the hallowed ground of soldiers who fought for freedom in Pennsylvania

The defeat of confederate General Robert E. Lee at the hands of a Union army in Gettysburg, Pennsylvania, in 1863 turned the tide of the Civil War in favor of the northern states. It makes sense, then, that Gettysburg, Pennsylvania, is the most celebrated Civil War battlefield in the United States.

Gettysburg National Military Park certainly lives up to this status. Indeed, the park is more than the battlefield; it is the site where hundreds of soldiers are now laid to rest, and where the park's museum displays relics from the battle, interactive exhibits and multimedia presentations in 22,000 square feet of space. The home of Gettysburg attorney David Wills is the place where President Abraham Lincoln fine-tuned his famous Gettysburg Address, and today the residence is a museum with five galleries and two re-created rooms open to public viewing.

> Relive the days of the Civil War on a historic walking tour through Gettysburg with knowledgeable guides.

In Soldiers' Footsteps

Touring Gettysburg on horseback is a popular way to explore the countryside and historic battlefields, but you can also learn about the battle by traveling the Civil War Trails, which feature roadside markers to guide visitors through the journey that soldiers took in the days leading up to the battle, and beyond into the duration of the Civil War.

The men and women living in Gettysburg during the war had their own stories to tell, and those stories are brought to life at the Shriver House Museum. Here, guides in period dress take guests through a restored 1860s home telling the story of the home's residents. Continue to relive the days of the Civil War on a historic walking tour through Gettysburg, with knowledgeable guides in 1860s dress helping you see life as it was during that era.

As the epicenter of the epic battle at Gettysburg, the town itself hosted wounded soldiers and frightened residents, and the Jennie Wade House is a standing piece of history worth visiting. The home has changed very little in the 150-plus years since it was built and is open to visitors to learn Jennie's story. In downtown Gettysburg, the Rupp House History Center is the site of living history displays and demonstrations. Outside town, walk around Daniel Lady Farm,

PA

Gettysburg
CAMPGROUND
Camp in Historic Gettysburg
Family Camping with a Personal Touch, where Recreation and History Meet.
Tent & RV Campsites, Cabin & Cottage Rentals, Free Wi-Fi Access, and an On-Site RV Repair Facility
Only 3 miles west of Gettysburg and convenient to Gettysburg Battlefields, Baltimore, Hershey, Lancaster and Washington, DC
History comes alive in Gettysburg … and at the Gettysburg Campground.
Good Sam Park
Choose wisely, and you will choose to camp with us!
2030 Fairfield Road (Route 116 West)
Gettysburg, Pennsylvania 17325
(717) 334-3304 • For Reservations: 1 888 879-2241
www.GettysburgCampground.com
VISA
MasterCard
DISCOVER
See listing Gettysburg, PA

where buildings once used as cover by Union and Confederate troops still bear the scars of battle, and where the barn served as a field hospital.

The drama of Gettysburg and its aftermath stirs intrigue among believers in the supernatural, and so of course there's a ghost tour for every type of paranormal enthusiast. Roam the streets of the city by candlelight and stop at locations famous for spirits and hauntings, guided by experienced and entertaining tour guides. Visit former Confederate Army hospitals, cemeteries and haunted inns for a spooky experience.

Gettysburg Bounty

Pennsylvania's rich agriculture has blossomed into agritourism, and visitors to Gettysburg are encouraged to taste the fruits of the region on the Gettysburg Wine and Fruit Trail. Year-round events celebrate apple harvests, craft beers, local wines and more. At Reid's Orchard and Winery, guests can taste local vintages and sample cider while enjoying live music in a lively atmosphere.

The First Minnesota Regiment Monument at Gettysburg.
Getty Images/iStockphoto

The natural bounty of Gettysburg makes it a popular spot for leisure and sport fishing. Drop a line in Zinkand Pond or Stevens Run for a chance to snag catfish and crappie, and visit Marsh Creek to cast for trout.

Animals are the star of the show at Land of Little Horses, a farm park where the furry, four-legged residents entertain guests with arena performances and teach them about equestrian care through hands-on activities. Explore & More Hands-On Children's Museum in town gives kids the chance to burn some energy and learn new skills inside an 1860s-era home. Themed rooms let kids explore the world through nature, architecture, art and more.

Entertainment and Views

Take in a show at the Gettysburg Community Theatre. Here, theater students and local actors come together to produce and perform beloved classic stage shows as well as modern-day musical and comedic hits. Gettysburg's revered Majestic Theater harkens back to the golden days of Hollywood, hosting movie screenings and performing arts showcases.

For More Information

Gettysburg Travel
717-334-6274
www.destinationgettysburg.com

Pennsylvania Tourism
800-847-4872
www.visitpa.com

PA

HERSHEY

Explore the many flavors of America's chocolate capital

Hershey, Pennsylvania, is associated with candy bars, Kisses and all things chocolate. But look inside the wrapper of this delightful town and you'll discover a lot more than confections.

Indeed, although Milton Hershey built much of the town—and the company that bears his name—with sweets and profits in mind, he also envisioned a community that supported the arts and contributed to American culture.

> Hersheypark is a confectionery-themed amusement destination that pays homage to the town's biggest business success—Hershey Chocolate.

Sweet Diversions

A great place to start is Hersheypark. This confectionery-themed amusement destination pays homage to the town's biggest business success—Hershey Chocolate. Rollercoasters and exhibits will awaken the candy-loving kid inside.

For more on the history of Milton Hershey's candy empire, tour Hershey's Chocolate World and Founders Hall at the Milton Hershey School. Adventure Sports in Hershey keeps the good times going for families with extra energy to burn. Go-kart tracks, miniature golf and an arcade keep everyone busy.

Get wild with the residents of ZooAmerica, Hershey's wildlife park that's home to more than 200 animals from five regions of North America. Well-known and well-loved residents include the mountain lion, black bear and American alligator—but other lesser-known creatures that are just as fascinating live here too. Meet a coati—a relative of the raccoon—an American marten or a long-eared owl. The zoo offers regular programs and behind-the-scenes tours for guests, as well.

Milton Hershey supported the arts and helped ensure his community would be able to enjoy great performances for years. Take in a show at the Hershey Area Playhouse, or enjoy a night of classical and pop performances courtesy of Hershey Symphony Orchestra. The home of the orchestra, Hershey Theatre, was built during the Great Depression for Hershey as part of his Great Building Campaign.

The Hershey Theatre features a 78-rank Aeolian-Skinner concert organ.
Hershey Entertainment and Resorts

History Beyond Hershey

Hershey isn't only about the sweets. Stop in at Hershey Derry Township Historical Society to view exhibits dedicated to the state police, early town life and architectural styles distinctive to the area. Native son and World War II hero Major Dick Winters is celebrated with a collection of wartime memorabilia and a scale reproduction of his den.

Indian Echo Caverns takes visitors underground to see ancient geological wonders. The limestone cave is a cool 52 degrees year-round, and its walls encompass water-worn formations and crystal pools. Tours through the caverns teach guests about the cave's importance to native inhabitants of the region. Nearby is Gem Mill Junction, where young explorers can pan for gemstones and dig for fossils. Additional outdoor attractions include a petting zoo and playground.

Quench an adult-size thirst at Tröegs Brewing Company, where guided tasting tours provide insights into the production of the company's tastiest creations. Samples are available for lovers of craft beers. At Cullari Vineyards and Winery, sip some of Hershey's distinctive varietals, including chocolate wines. Cassel Vineyards in nearby Hummelstown tempts taste buds with its own locally crafted wines made from six varieties of grapes.

Take your bicycles out for a spin on the fabulous trails that run through Hershey; the Jonathan Eshenour Memorial Trail winds more than 13 miles through the township. Float down Swatara Creek, a tributary of the Susquehanna River, and see if you can spot a limestone cave or two along the banks. According to local legends, horse thieves established hideouts here. If fishing is your preferred pastime, dip a line in the creek and snag some bass, catfish, sunfish or muskie.

Hershey's Sporting Life

Get out your best clubs and play a round of golf at Spring Creek Golf Course, a public course with a par of 33. If you've got a sharp eye and a penchant for patience, the Milton Hershey School manages game lands for recreational hunting, and white-tail deer culling is a popular draw for hunters from all over the region.

Roll the dice on a day trip to Hollywood Casino in Grantville and if you're lucky you'll come up a winner. Located at Penn National Race Course, the casino offers slot play, table games and a museum filled with memorabilia and props from popular Hollywood films. Live music has a starring role, too, as do the horses. If racing revs you up, stick around for a race or two and see if you can pick a winner.

Chrome fenders, whitewall tires and peppy little scooters bring visitors from far and wide to the Antique Automobile Club of America Museum. The AACA Museum is more than a mere collection; the curators strive for a fresh experience with each visit. Each permanent and featured exhibit focuses on a detailed, nostalgic aspect of automotive history. From individual automakers to famous owners and their beloved rides, the museum has something for every kind of car, motorcycle and truck lover imaginable.

PA

For More Information

Hershey Entertainment & Resorts
800-437-7439
www.hersheypa.com

Pennsylvania Tourism
800-847-4872
www.visitpa.com

Getty Images/iStockphoto

LANCASTER COUNTY

Go Dutch in this Old World corner of Pennsylvania

Lancaster County owes much of its fame to the Amish, the so-called "plain people" who have forsaken modern technology for simple lives without electricity or automobiles. And while this delightful corner of Pennsylvania offers lots of insights into this fascinating culture, it's also chock-full of attractions from its non-Amish residents.

A great place to start is the Historic Lancaster Walking Tour, which will introduce you to the stories of the county seat's earliest days. Helpful guides dressed in period clothing share the city's past (it was once the capital of the United States) and explain the area's contributions to American life through stops at more than 50 locations around Lancaster.

Stop in at Saint James Episcopal Church, a beacon of hospitality and an icon of the region. The church has stood at its present location since 1744 and is adorned with stained-glass works of art, intricate paintings and colorful tiles.

> Broadway shows are under the spotlight at Fulton Theatre, a county treasure and National Historic Landmark.

Pennsylvania German culture is rich and lively, and Historic Schaefferstown welcomes you to explore and learn about the traditions and lives of its founding residents. Visit Alexander Schaeffer House and Farm, a mid-18th-century dwelling in which residents distilled whiskey. The Thomas R. Brendle Museum displays cultural artifacts from Pennsylvania German families and the Gemberling-Re House, once a tavern, invites visitors in to see where thirsty travelers once whet their whistles.

Plain Folk and Food

Ok, so you made the trip to the region primarily for the Amish. No problem. Travel around in Amish style on a buggy ride from Kitchen Kettle Village. Whether you trot four miles or

Shoofly pie is a sweet confection made famous by Lancaster County.
Getty Images/iStockphoto

The Pool Forge Covered Bridge in Lancaster County. Getty Images/iStockphoto

meander five, be sure to pass over a covered bridge and take in the scenic countryside. Then, trek through historic Intercourse for more Amish-style fun. As you travel, you'll glean some great insights into the customs, agricultural methods and ingenuity of this community, who migrated from Europe in the 17th century to escape religious persecution. But be respectful of the Amish. Don't take photographs of them without permission, and always be polite and courteous.

If you've ever wanted to get insights into the day-to-day Amish lifestyle, head to the whimsically named community of Bird-in-Hand. The Amish Experience offers a VIP tour that allows you to visit an Amish home and watch while family members milk the cows and prepare food. Abe's Buggy Rides has been giving visitors a taste of Amish travel for nearly 50 years, and if you're lucky, the driver will let you in on the best places to try the traditional molasses treat known as Shoofly pie, the region's most famous desert.

The town of Paradise lives up to its name if you're a lover of farming. Here, Verdant View Farm celebrates the bounty of Lancaster County. Try your hand as a farmers' apprentice and help tend to the goats, milk the cows, collect eggs for breakfast and make homemade ice cream.

Toast to a great vacation at Rumspringa Brewing Company, where craft-brewed beers accompany lively conversation and tasty bar-style treats, and where wine lovers can sample vintages from the region. If you're a fan of salty snacks, you can't miss the chance to see famed Lancaster County pretzels being made by hand. Some establishments encourage guests to try and twist their own. Homemade jam is a sweet attraction here, too, and the Cannin' and Jammin' Tour is a fun way to find out how jam comes together.

Tucquan Glen Nature Preserve includes a two-mile loop that leads hikers and bikers along a tributary that feeds into the Susquehanna River.

Save room for dinner, which becomes an entertaining event at one of Lancaster's famed dinner theaters. Broadway shows are under the spotlight at Fulton Theatre, a county treasure and National Historic Landmark. Taste the fresh produce of the county at Lancaster Central Market, where goods have been sold since before the American Revolution.

Trips to the Past

Hop aboard a vintage train at Strasburg Rail Road. The coal-burning steam locomotive pulls passenger cars along America's oldest short-line railroad for 45 minutes, then drops guests back at the station to try their hand at a pump car or ride on a miniature steam train. Wander across the street to the Railroad Museum of Pennsylvania for even more great rail history, including full-size railroad equipment.

Fine country living is preserved for visitors to see and experience at Rock Ford Plantation, the home of Revolutionary War General Edward Hand. These 33 acres include a house built in Georgian domestic style and preserved in the style of the day, down to the paint colors. While the barn is not original to the property, it stands on the original location and dates to the 1780s.

See where the movement to free slaves before the Civil War played a central role in the state's history at Christiana Underground Railroad Center. The site of a skirmish over escaped slaves has become a museum honoring the Pennsylvania citizens who spurred the resistance against slavery.

Expanding Horizons

Tucquan Glen Nature Preserve includes a two-mile loop that leads hikers and bikers along a tributary that feeds into the Susquehanna River, with views of short waterfalls and a variety of trees with seasonal foliage. Also in the preserve, Fishing Creek North is a prime spot for—you guessed it—fishing. As a cold-water fishery, Fishing Creek is home to a spawning trout population that's supplemented by trout stocking. The preserve permits bow hunting and is home to white-tailed deer and turkey.

Kids can become inventors, creators and engineers at Lancaster Science Factory, where exhibits are designed to encourage children to learn more about the world around them. For more good times, Lost Treasure Golf and Maze is a delightful destination for families. Take your choice of two 18-hole miniature courses, then make your way through the open-air maze.

Savor the beautiful sunset from up high on a hot-air ballon ride over Lancaster County. The U.S. Hot Air Balloon Team hosts trips that provide views of farmland and town life, and even extend into three- and five-day tours through the Brandywine Valley.

Amish boys go fishing in a local pond. Getty Images/Hemera

For More Information

Discover Lancaster
800-723-8824
www.padutchcountry.com

Pennsylvania Tourism
800-847-4872
www.visitpa.com

PA

PITTSBURGH AND COUNTRYSIDE

Take a peek behind the steel city's hard façade

The steel town of Pittsburgh plays just as hard as it works, and the opportunities for fun and exploration are numerous. The city began as a frontier fort and the Gateway to the West, and since then has grown to a bustling metropolis built on the industries that run the nation: steel, coal, timber and limestone.

Take a downtown walking tour with the assistance of a free downloadable audio guide, and learn stories behind Pittsburgh's towering skyscrapers in just an hour. Hop in a car and ride up McArdle Roadway to the top of Mt. Washington and enjoy one of the nation's most stunning views. For a vintage ride, scale the slopes of Mount Washington on the cable cars of the Duquesne Incline, which has been running for nearly 140 years. While you're up here, visit the 280-acre Emerald View Park.

Looking Back

Discover Pittsburgh's colonial past. Fort Ligonier is a full-scale site reconstructed and restored to its 1758 glory. It defended British subjects during the French and Indian War and served as a supply station during the siege of Fort Duquesne. Tour the officers' mess, barracks, guardroom and underground magazine, and be sure to visit the sawmill, hospital and forge on-site.

Old Economy Village shares details of 19th-century life through hands-on activities like baking bread and churning butter, carding wool and making a songbook. The village was established in 1824 as a home for the Harmony Society, a religious communal group that originated in Germany. Preserved structures include the Feast Hall and Museum Building, mechanics building and wine cellar, water pump and bake oven.

The legacy of Pittsburgh's steel and coal empires is preserved at Clayton, the family home of Henry Clay Frick. Frick partnered with Andrew Carnegie to form U.S. Steel. Go back further in the city's industrial history and see an exhibit on Pittsburgh's glass industry at the Senator John Heinz History Center.

Take advantage of Carnegie's philanthropic legacy by visiting the Carnegie Museums of Pittsburgh, four distinctive museums including the Carnegie Museum of Natural History, where kids find hands-on opportunities to explore the natural world by "digging" for fossils and indulge their artistic side through crafts and art projects.

Take Wing

Bird lovers can't miss out on a trip to National Aviary, a birdcentric zoo with more than 500 residents representing

150-plus species from around the world. African penguins, canaries and more are part of the experience, which includes free-flight bird shows during the summer months.

See how residents of Pittsburgh and neighboring towns helped support the Underground Railroad, the secret network of routes and safe houses for runaway slaves that operated in the 1800s. The Blairsville Area Underground Railroad Project offers tours to the Underground Railroad Museum at Belmont Mansion, Bigham House in the Mt. Washington neighborhood and St. Matthew's AME Zion Church in Sewickley.

In Armstrong County, ride the Kiski Junction Railroad to experience railway history on a working freight train. Casino Theatre is a vaudevillian delight, welcoming theater buffs to explore its national museum dedicated to the popular entertainment form from the early 20th century. Hop aboard a carriage for a casual ride through the surrounding countryside, and come back in winter to Dragon Run Forge & Livery for a snowy sleigh ride.

Explore the Far East without leaving American soil at the Maridon Museum in Butler County. The Maridon's exhibits explore Japanese and Chinese art and culture, showcasing paintings, tapestries, ornate sculpture and pottery, as well as a unique collection of German Meissen porcelain.

Moraine State Park beckons boaters to cruise along Lake Arthur, the centerpiece of the 16,725-acre park that's a warm-water fishery open to anglers who seek northern pike, largemouth bass, crappie and bluegill. A large portion of the parkland is open to hunting and trapping during appropriate seasons, and game include waterfowl, deer, turkey, rabbit and grouse.

A wooden cable car takes tourists up the Duquesne Incline on Mount Washington.
Getty Images/iStockphoto

Go Greene

Get your fill of fall's changing foliage on a trek through Greene County. Be sure to travel over at least a couple of its seven covered bridges, all of which have been declared historical landmarks, and stop in at the Jacktown Fair, which runs in July and is the nation's oldest continuous fair. Founded in 1866, the fair features tractor pulls, a home and garden show, and parade.

Thrill seekers flock to Laurel Highlands and Ohiopyle State Park, where whitewater rafting and mountain biking are popular activities. Get a low-key rush by hiking or fishing, or take the family out to Idlewild Park and SoakZone for a day of amusement park rides, lifesize storybook tales and relaxation in an aquatic oasis. Architecture buffs should make time to see three of Frank Lloyd Wright's creations in Laurel Highlands: Fallingwater, Duncan House and Kentuck Knob are all here.

Stretch your legs and roll two wheels down Park Harbor Bike Trail in Lawrence County. This two-mile trail wanders through wildlife sanctuary. Living Treasures Wild Animal Park brings visitors face to face with petting-zoo residents and their wilder neighbors, including a Barbary lion, Canadian lynx, grey kangaroo and more. Experience history in Washington County at Meadowcroft Rockshelter, where prehistoric tribes made camp under a massive stone outcropping.

PA

For More Information

Pittsburgh Convention and Visitors Bureau
800-359-0758
www.visitpittsburgh.com

Pennsylvania Tourism
800-847-4872
www.visitpa.com

POCONO MOUNTAINS

Head for the hills to Pennsylvania's perennial playground

Spread across more than 2,400 square miles that are packed with tumbling waterfalls, crisp alpine lakes and lush forest landscapes, the entire Pocono Mountains region has served as a natural point of retreat and countryside escape for suburb-weary Pennsylvanians and big-city East Coasters for nearly two centuries.

The first hotel was established here in 1829, and in 1926 the damming of Wallenpaupack Creek (and subsequent creation of scenic Lake Wallenpaupack) spurred on a booming "mountain resort" industry which, by the time the 1970s rolled around, helped the Poconos gain a reputation as the "Honeymoon Capital of the World."

Today, visitors find themselves exploring the same inviting landscapes dotted with incredible public parks and picturesque historic sites, but a slew of additions have been made in the decades since the region was a popular honeymoon hotspot. More than 35 golf courses now call the Poconos home, as well as three massive state-of-the-art water parks, a variety of annual NASCAR events and nearly a dozen world-class ski resorts.

Fantastic Fun

The region is mostly broken down into distinct regions, each offering its own unique basket of recreational activities and local attractions.

> The Lehigh River Gorge Region is home to a variety of historic sites and museums, including the alpine town of Jim Thorpe, often referred to as the "Switzerland of America."

The Upper Delaware River Region, straddling the New York and Pennsylvania border, is home to vast tracts of pristine wilderness and river rapids that are perfect for white-water rafting adventures. The Lake Region, home to 5,700-acre Lake Wallenpaupack, serves as the heart of the Poconos. The Delaware River Region, lying along the Poconos' southeastern edge, is home to the Delaware Water Gap National Recreation Area and the historic town of Milford. The Mountain Region is where skiers and snowboarders will find the region's highest concentration of ski resorts and ski areas. And the Lehigh River Gorge Region is home to a variety of historic sites and museums, including the alpine town of Jim Thorpe, often referred to as the "Switzerland of America."

With 261 miles of dedicated hiking trails, more than 100 freshwater lakes and an abundance of pristine rivers and creeks ripe for fishing, kayaking and canoeing, the Poconos is a boon for nature lovers and outdoor recreation hounds. If you're on the prowl for the quintessential Poconos experience, kick things off at the Delaware Water Gap National Recreation Area.

Home to 27 miles of the Appalachian Trail and 100 miles of scenic roadway, the Delaware Water Gap NRA also provides access to Dingman Falls and Bushkill Falls—two of the Poconos' most renowned natural attractions. At Dingman Falls visitors can explore a network of trail systems and take in up-close misty views of an idyllic waterfall that plunges 130 feet over smooth sandstone rocks. Bushkill Falls, a short distance south from Dingman, tumbles 100 feet and is often referred to as "the Niagara of Pennsylvania."

Hickory Run State Park is another popular location for hikers and anglers. Located in the southwestern quadrant of the Poconos, it offers more than 15,000 acres of mountain foothills.

Poconos Past

History buffs will want to stop at a quartet of must-visit museums and sites. Start in the historic town of Jim Thorpe, named after the legendary football hero and Olympic athlete who went to school in Carlisle, Pennsylvania. Here, the Asa Packer Mansion Museum offers a chance to tour a Victorian-style house that was built in 1861 and still contains all of its original furniture.

Those travelling with kids will find themselves drawn to a trio of water parks when it's time for a break from biking trails, museums and waterfall hikes. Great Wolf Lodge, quirkily named H20ooohh! and Camelbeach Mountain Waterpark each offer a variety of slides, pools and activities for visitors of all ages. Camelbeach, for its part, is the largest water park in the state, and also home to a crisscrossing zip line course.

Finally, if you're a motorsports fan, the Pocono Raceway in Blakeslee hosts annual NASCAR Sprint Cup Series races, NASCAR Camping World Truck Series races and IndyCar Series races through July and August each year.

For More Information

Pocono Mountains Visitors Bureau
800-762-6667
www.800poconos.com

Pennsylvania Tourism
800-847-4872
www.visitpa.com

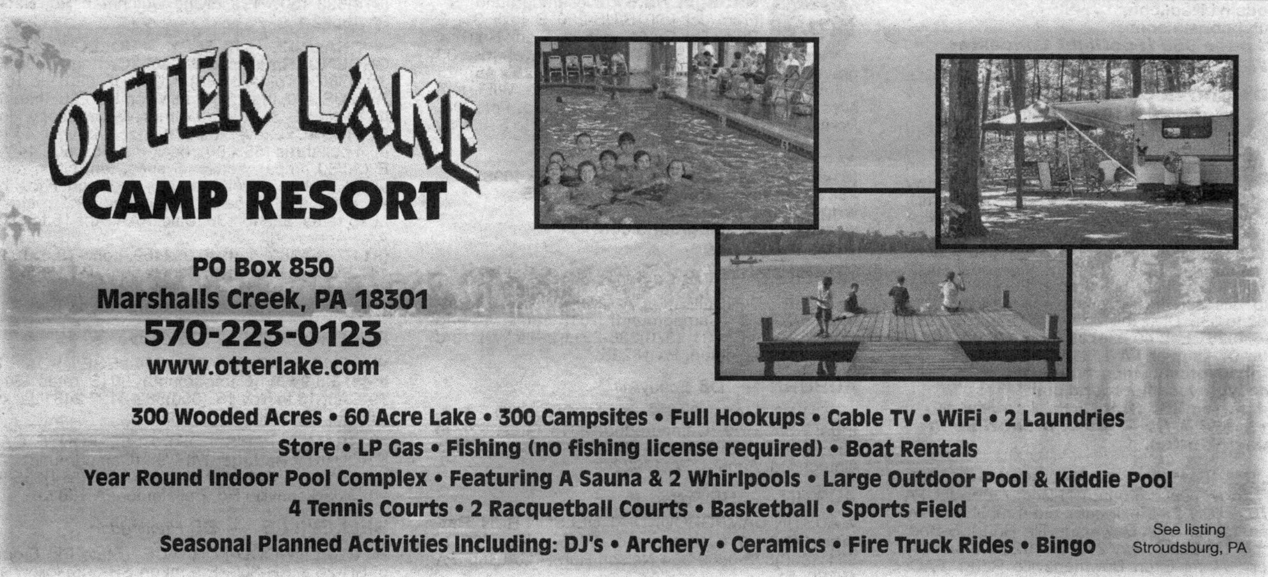

Pennsylvania

CONSULTANTS

Dan & Annette Bramos

ADAMSTOWN — E8 *Lancaster*

DUTCH COUSIN CAMPGROUND **Ratings: 6.5/8.5★/8** (Campground) From Jct of I-76 & Hwy 272 (exit 286): Go 1/4 mi N on Hwy 272, then W 1 mi W on Hill Rd(L). **FAC:** Gravel rds. (95 spaces). Avail: 40 gravel, 4 pull-thrus (18 x 75), back-ins (18 x 35), 40 full hkups (30/50 amps), seasonal sites, cable, WiFi, tent sites, rentals, dump, mobile sewer, laundry, groc, LP gas, fire rings, firewood. **REC:** playground. Pets OK. Partial handicap access. 2015 rates: $40. Disc: military.
(717)336-6911 Lat: 40.239067, Lon: -76.105951
446 Hill Rd, Denver, PA 17517
dutchcousin1@aol.com
www.dutchcousin.com
See ad page 988 (Spotlight Lancaster County).

SHADY GROVE CAMPGROUND **Ratings: 9/10★/9** (Campground) From Jct of I-76 & Colonel Howard Blvd/Hwy 1040 (exit 286): Go 1/2 mi N on Colonel Howard Blvd, then 1 mi E on Hwy 272, then 1/2 mi N on Hwy 897/West Swartzville, then 2 blks W on Poplar Dr(L). **FAC:** Gravel rds. (125 spaces). Avail: 65 gravel, 4 pull-thrus (25 x 60), back-ins (30 x 42), 65 full hkups (30/50 amps), seasonal sites, cable, WiFi, tent sites, rentals, laundry, LP gas, fire rings, firewood. **REC:** pool, Spirit Lake: fishing, playground. Pets OK. Partial handicap access. Big rig sites, eco-friendly, 2015 rates: $53 to $58. Disc: military.
(717)484-4225 Lat: 40.238733, Lon: -76.084167
65 Poplar Dr, Denver, PA 17517
office@shadygrovecampground.com
www.shadygrovecampground.com
See ad pages 988 (Spotlight Lancaster County), 974 & RV Trips of a Lifetime in Magazine Section.

SILL'S FAMILY CAMPGROUND Ratings: 8/7.5★/7 (Campground) N-Bnd: From Jct PA Tpke I-76 & Hwy 272 (exit 286): Go 4 mi N on Hwy 272, then 1/2 mi E on Bowmansville Rd(L); S-Bnd: From Jct of US-222 & Hwy 272: Go 1/2 mi S on Hwy 272, then 1/4 mi E on Bowmansville Rd(L). **FAC:** Paved/gravel rds. (120 spaces). Avail: 35 gravel, 17 pull-thrus (25 x 60), back-ins (22 x 40), some side by side hkups, 35 full hkups (30/50 amps), seasonal sites, cable, WiFi, tent sites, rentals, dump, laundry, groc, LP gas, fire rings, firewood. **REC:** heated pool, playground. Pets OK. Partial handicap access. Big rig sites, eco-friendly, 2015 rates: $42 to $51.
(717)484-4806 Lat: 40.239424, Lon: -76.037809
1906 Bowmansville Rd, Mohnton, PA 19540
sillscamp@windstream.net
www.sillscampgrounds.com

AIRVILLE — E8 *York*

OTTER CREEK CAMPGROUND Ratings: 5/6.5/7 (Campground) 2015 rates: $28 to $35. Apr 1 to Oct 31. (717)862-3628 1101 Furnace Rd, Airville, PA 17302

ALLENTOWN — D9 *Lehigh*

ALLENTOWN See also Ashfield, Bethlehem, Boyertown, Kutztown, Lenhartsville, Ottsville, Palmerton, Revere, Quakertown, Stroudsburg & Upper Black Eddy.

ALLENTOWN-LEHIGH VALLEY KOA **Ratings: 9/9★/9** (Campground) From Jct I-476(PA Tpk) & I-78/US22: Go 3 mi W on I-78/US-22(exit 49B), then 6-1/2 mi N on Hwy 100, then 1/4 mi W on Narris Rd(L) GPS Incorrect. **FAC:** Gravel rds. (89 spaces). 66 Avail: 60 gravel, 6 grass, 27 pull-thrus (28 x 70), back-ins (26 x 32), some side by side hkups, 33 full hkups, 33 W, 33 E (30/50 amps), seasonal sites, cable, WiFi, tent sites, rentals, dump, mobile sewer, laundry, groc, LP gas, fire rings, firewood. **REC:** heated pool, wading pool, Switzer Creek: fishing, playground. Pets OK. Partial handicap access. Big rig sites, eco-friendly, 2015 rates: $41 to $60. Disc: military. Apr 1 to Nov 1. ATM.
(610)298-2160 Lat: 40.65937, Lon: -75.692003
6750 Koa Dr, New Tripoli, PA 18066
info@fununlimitedllc.com
www.koa.com/campgrounds/allentown/
See ad this page.

ALTOONA — D4 *Blair*

WRIGHT'S ORCHARD STATION CAMPGROUND **Ratings: 7/8.5★/8** (Campground) From Jct I-99 S/US-220 S (exit 31) & Plank Rd: Go 3/4 mi S on Plank Rd (Bus US-220 S) (R). **FAC:** Gravel rds. 33 gravel, 8 pull-thrus (25 x 50), back-ins (25 x 45), 25 full hkups, 8 W, 8 E (30/50 amps), cable, WiFi, tent sites, dump, laundry, fire rings, firewood. Pets OK. Partial handicap access. 2015 rates: $32 to $38. May 1 to Oct 31.
AAA Approved
(814)695-2628 Lat: 40.45227, Lon: -78.40965
2381 Plank Rd, Duncansville, PA 16635
wrightscamp@verizon.net
www.wrightscampground.com
See ad this page.

ASHFIELD — D9 *Carbon*

BLUE RIDGE CAMPGROUND Ratings: 6/7.5/6.5 (Campground) 2015 rates: $35 to $60. Apr 1 to Oct 31. (570)386-2911 2489 W. Lizard Creek Rd, Lehighton, PA 18235

AUBURN — D8 *Schuylkill*

CHRISTMAS PINES CAMPGROUND Ratings: 7.5/8.5★/9 (Campground) 2015 rates: $25 to $34. Apr 11 to Oct 19. (570)366-8866 450 Red Church Rd, Auburn, PA 17922

AUSTIN — B5 *Potter*

AUSTIN CAMPGROUND AT NELSON RUN Ratings: 5/8.5★/9 (Campground) 2015 rates: $28 to $34. (800)878-0889 364 Nelson Run Rd, Austin, PA 16720

BEAVER FALLS — D1 *Beaver*

HARTS CONTENT CAMPGROUND **Ratings: 7.5/7/7** (Campground) From Jct I-79(exit 83) & Hwy 528: Go 3/4 mi NW on Hwy 528, then 3 mi N on US 19N, then 3/4 mi NW on Hwy 288, then 6 mi W on Hwy 588, the 1/2 mi SW on Glendale Rd(L). **FAC:** Gravel rds. (105 spaces). Avail: 25 gravel, 1 pull-thrus (35 x 80), back-ins (30 x 45), 10 full hkups, 15 W, 15 E (30/50 amps), seasonal sites, rentals, dump, mobile sewer, laundr LP gas, fire rings, firewood, controlled access. **REC** pool, playground. Pet restrict(Q). No tents. Big ri sites, 2015 rates: $30. Apr 15 to Oct 15.
(724)846-0005 Lat: 40.784912, Lon: -80.247724
496 Glendale Rd, Beaver Falls, PA 15010
hartscontent@gmail.com
www.hartscontentcampground.com
See ad page 993 (Spotlight Pittsburgh & Countryside).

BEDFORD — E4 *Bedford*

FRIENDSHIP VILLAGE CAMPGROUND & RV PARK **Ratings: 9/10★/10** (Campground) From Jc I-76(exit 146) & US 220: Go 300 yds N on Bus US 220, then 1-1/2 mi S on US 220, then 1-1/2 mi NW on US 30, then 1/2 mi NE on Friendship Villag Rd(E). **FAC:** Paved/gravel rds. (285 spaces). Avail 220 gravel, 86 pull-thrus (32 x 70), back-ins (30 x 60), 193 full hkups, 27 W, 27 E (30/50 amps) seasonal sites, cable, WiFi, tent sites, rentals, dump laundry, groc, LP gas, fire rings, firewood. **REC:** poo Friendship Village Lake: fishing, shuffleboard, play ground. Pet restrict(Q). Partial handicap access. Bi rig sites, eco-friendly, 2015 rates: $37 to $47. Disc AAA, military.
AAA Approved
(814)623-1677 Lat: 40.04475, Lon: -78.519008
348 Friendship Village Rd, Bedford, PA 15522
friendshipvillage@comcast.net
www.friendshipvillagecampground.com
See ad this page.

MERRITT POND CAMPGROUND Rat ings: 4/NA/7 (Campground) 2015 rates: $30 to $35 (814)623-1507 193 Flying Dutchman Rd, Bedford PA 15522

SHAWNEE SLEEPY HOLLOW CAMP GROUND Ratings: 5.5/5.5/7 (Campground) From Jct I-76/PA Tpk(exit 146) & Bus US 220: Go 1000 S on US 220, then 2-1/2 mi W on US 220, then 6-1/2 mi W on US 30, then 3/4 mi NW on Sleepy Hollow Rd(R). **FAC:** Gravel rds. (76 spaces). Avail: 44 grav el, 4 pull-thrus (55 x 80), back-ins (45 x 50), 44 W, 4 E (30/50 amps), seasonal sites, tent sites, rentals dump, mobile sewer, fire rings, firewood. **REC:** heat ed pool, shuffleboard, playground. Pet restrict(B) 2015 rates: $29 to $36. Disc: AAA. Apr 15 to Oct 31
AAA Approved
(814)733-4380 Lat: 40.052469, Lon: -78.611349
147 Sleepy Hollow Rd, Schellsburg, PA 15559
sleepyhollow147@centurylink.net
www.bedfordcounty.net/camping/sleepy

BELLEFONTE — C5 *Centre*

BELLEFONTE/STATE COLLEGE KOA Rat ings: 8.5/9★/9 (Campground) 2015 rates: $44 t $90. Apr 10 to Nov 15. (800)562-8127 2481 Jackson ville Rd, Bellefonte, PA 16823

GRAM & PAP'S FORT BELLEFONTE CAMP GROUND Ratings: 7/8★/8 (Campground) 201 rates: $40 to $48. Apr 1 to Nov 30. (814)355-982 2023 Jacksonville Rd, Bellefonte, PA 16823

BELLEVILLE — D5 *Huntingdon*

GREENWOOD FURNACE (State Pk) From Jc of SR-26 & SR-305, E 5 mi on SR-305, follow sign (R). 2015 rates: $15 to $28. Apr 10 to Oct 31 (814)667-1800

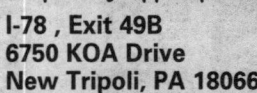

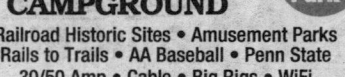

BENTON — C8 *Columbia*

RICKETTS GLEN (State Pk) From Jct SR-487 & SR-118, N 4 mi on SR-487 (R). Heavy trailer units access the park from SR-487 N from Dushore. 2015 rates: $15 to $28. (570)477-5675

WHISPERING PINES CAMPING ESTATES Ratings: 8/9.5★/9.5 (Campground) From Jct Hwy 487 & Hwy 239 (in Benton): Go 4 mi E on Hwy 239, then 1 mi S on N Bendertown Rd (R). **FAC:** Gravel rds. (58 spaces). Avail: 32 gravel, 1 pull-thrus (25 x 60), back-ins (25 x 60), 32 full hkups (30/50 amps), seasonal sites, WiFi, tent sites, rentals, showers $, groc, fire rings, firewood. **REC:** heated pool, pond, fishing, playground. Pet restrict(B/Q). Partial handicap access. Big rig sites, eco-friendly, 2015 rates: $40 to $45. Disc: military.
(570)925-6810 Lat: 41.179447, Lon: -76.318985
1557 North Bendertown Rd, Stillwater, PA 17878
info@wpce.com
www.wpce.com
See ad this page, 974.

BERWICK — C8 *Columbia*

BODNAROSA MOTEL & CAMPGROUND **Ratings: 6/10★/8** (Campground) 2015 rates: $38. (570)520-4070 1175 Salem Boulevard (U.s. 11), Berwick, PA 18603

BETHLEHEM — D9 *Northampton*

EVERGREEN LAKE Ratings: 7/9★/8.5 (Campground) From Jct US-22 & Hwy 512: Go 8-1/2 mi N on Hwy 512, then 1/2 mi W on Hwy 946, then 2-1/2 mi N on Copella Rd, then 1/4 mi E on Benders Dr (L). **FAC:** Paved/gravel rds. (256 spaces). Avail: 96 gravel, 25 pull-thrus (30 x 65), back-ins (35 x 55), some side by side hkups, 25 full hkups, 71 W, 71 E (20/30 amps), seasonal sites, cable, WiFi Hotspot, tent sites, dump, mobile sewer, laundry, LP gas, fire rings, firewood. **REC:** Evergreen Lake: swim, fishing, playground, rec open to public. Pet restrict(B). 2015 rates: $32 to $39. Apr 15 to Oct 15. ATM, no CC.
(610)837-6401 Lat: 40.812932, Lon: -75.40168
2375 Benders Dr, Bath, PA 18014
www.evergreenlake.net

BLAKESLEE — C9 *Monroe*

PEACEFUL WOODLANDS FAMILY CAMPGROUND Ratings: 7/9★/7 (Campground) From Jct of I-80 & Hwy 115(exit 284): Go 5-1/2 mi S on Hwy 115(R). **FAC:** Gravel rds. (140 spaces). Avail: 110 gravel, 8 pull-thrus (40 x 65), back-ins (45 x 50), 50 full hkups, 60 W, 60 E (20/30 amps), seasonal sites, WiFi $, tent sites, rentals, dump, groc, LP gas, fire rings, firewood, controlled access. **REC:** heated pool, wading pool, playground. Pets OK. Partial handicap access. Eco-friendly, 2015 rates: $40 to $57. Disc: AAA, military. Apr 1 to Oct 31.
AAA Approved
(570)646-9255 Lat: 41.028885, Lon: -75.498176
114 W T Family Blvd, Blakeslee, PA 18610
camping@peacefulwoodlands.com
www.peacefulwoodlands.com

BLOOMSBURG — C7 *Columbia*

INDIAN HEAD RECREATIONAL CAMPGROUND Ratings: 5.5/7.5/6.5 (Campground) From Jct I-80(exit 232) & Hwy 42: Go 3-1/4 mi S on Hwy 42, then 1/4 mi E on Train St(L). **FAC:** Gravel rds. (220 spaces). 135 Avail: 105 gravel, 30 grass, 62 pull-thrus (30 x 70), back-ins (30 x 60), mostly side by side hkups, 26 full hkups, 109 W, 100 E (30/50 amps), seasonal sites, WiFi $, tent sites, dump, mobile sewer, groc, fire rings, firewood. **REC:** Susquehanna River: fishing, playground. Pet restrict(B). Partial handicap access. 2015 rates: $36 to $40. Disc: AAA, military. May 1 to Oct 31.
(570)784-6150 Lat: 40.977359, Lon: -76.471935
340 Reading St, Bloomsburg, PA 17815
tal@sunlink.net
www.indianheadcampground.com
See ad this page.

BOWMANSVILLE — E8 *Lancaster*

OAK CREEK CAMPGROUND **Ratings: 8/8★/8** (Campground) 2015 rates: $45 to $55. Apr 1 to Nov 1. (717)445-6161 400 E Maple Grove Rd, Narvon, PA 17555

BOYERTOWN — D9 *Bucks*

LAZY K CAMPGROUND **Ratings: 7/9★/9** (Campground) 2015 rates: $38 to $46. (610)367-8576 109 Washington Rd, #106, Bechtelsville, PA 19505

BRODHEADSVILLE — C9 *Monroe*

CHESTNUT LAKE CAMPGROUND Ratings: 7/9★/8 (Campground) From Jct I-80 & US 209/33 (exit 302A): Go 5 mi S on US 209, then 4-1/4 mi W on US 209(Brodheadsville exit), then 1/4 mi S on Frable Rd, then 1/4 mi S on Frantz Rd(R). **FAC:** Gravel rds. (104 spaces). Avail: 75 gravel, back-ins (35 x 75), 57 full hkups, 18 W, 18 E (30/50 amps), seasonal sites, cable, WiFi, tent sites, dump, laundry, LP gas, fire rings, firewood. **REC:** Chestnut Lake: swim, fishing, playground. Pet restrict(B/Q). Partial handicap access. 2015 rates: $45 to $50. Disc: AAA.
AAA Approved
(570)992-6179 Lat: 40.91804, Lon: -75.378612
117 Chestnut Lake Rd, Brodheadsville, PA 18322
chestnutlakecpgd@aol.com
www.chestnutlakecampgroundpa.com

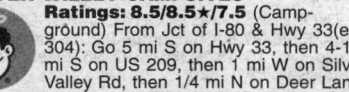

SILVER VALLEY CAMPSITES Ratings: 8.5/8.5★/7.5 (Campground) From Jct of I-80 & Hwy 33(exit 304): Go 5 mi S on Hwy 33, then 4-1/2 mi S on US 209, then 1 mi W on Silver Valley Rd, then 1/4 mi N on Deer Lane, then 1 blk W on Kennel Rd(R). **FAC:** Gravel rds. (140 spaces). Avail: 83 gravel, 16 pull-thrus (28 x 60), back-ins (23 x 50), some side by side hkups, 83 full hkups (30/50 amps), seasonal sites, cable, WiFi, tent sites, rentals, dump, laundry, groc, LP gas, fire rings, firewood, restaurant. **REC:** heated pool, pond, fishing, playground. Pet restrict(B). Partial handicap access. Big rig sites, eco-friendly, 2015 rates: $44.50 to $49.50. Disc: military.
(570)992-4824 Lat: 40.94354, Lon: -75.82684
101 Silver Valley Circle, Saylorsburg, PA 18353
svc1@ptd.net
www.silvervalleycamp.com
See ad this page, 974.

BURNT CABINS — E5 *Fulton*

YE OLDE MILL CAMPGROUND Ratings: 7/8.5★/7 (Campground) From Jct I-76/PA Tpk (exit 180) & US 522: Go 4.5 mi N on US 522, then 1/2 mi NE on Grist Mill Rd (R). **FAC:** Gravel rds. (44 spaces). Avail: 34 gravel, 12 pull-thrus (26 x 100), back-ins (30 x 40), 34 full hkups (30/50 amps), seasonal sites, cable, WiFi, tent sites, rentals, dump, mobile sewer, laundry, groc, LP gas, fire rings, firewood. **REC:** Little Aughwick Creek: fishing, playground, rec open to public. Pets OK. Big rig sites, eco-friendly, 2015 rates: $32 to $38. Disc: military.
(717)987-3244 Lat: 40.077705, Lon: -77.888009
582 Grist Mill Rd, Burnt Cabins, PA 17215
info@historicmillandcamping.com
www.historicmillandcamping.com
See ad this page, 974.

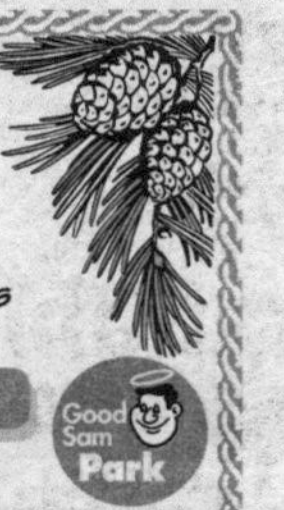

Things to See and Do

BURNT CABINS GRIST MILL A 200 year tradition from Burnt Cabins Grist Mill. Fresh, all natural flours and mixes produced daily. May 25 to Oct 31. RV accessible. Restrooms, food. Hours: 11 am Sunday or by appt. Adult fee: $2.
(717)987-3244 Lat: 40.07705, Lon: -77.888009
info@historicmillandcamping.com
www.historicmillandcamping.com
See ad this page.

BUTLER — C2 *Butler*

BUTTERCUP WOODLANDS CAMPGROUND Ratings: 8.5/10★/8.5 (Campground) From Jct I-79 (exit 88) & US 19: Go 1-1/2 mi S on US 19, then 12 mi E on Hwy 68 (L). **FAC:** Paved rds. (330 spaces). Avail: 26 grass, 7 pull-thrus (40 x 70), back-ins (35 x 60), 26 full hkups (30/50 amps), seasonal sites, cable, WiFi, tent sites, rentals, laundry, groc, LP gas, fire rings, firewood, controlled access. **REC:** pool, shuffleboard, playground. Pets OK. Partial handicap access. Big rig sites, eco-friendly, 2015 rates: $30 to $36. Apr 15 to Oct 15.
(724)789-9340 Lat: 40.850177, Lon: -79.985361
854 Evans City Rd, Renfrew, PA 16053
buttcup@zbzoom.net
www.buttercup.org

SMITH GROVE CAMPGROUND Ratings: 7.5/6/6.5 (Campground) From Jct Hwy 228/Hwy 8 & Hwy 356: Go 1-1/2 mi S on Hwy 356, then 2 mi E on Herman Rd (L). **FAC:** Paved/gravel rds. (155 spaces). Avail: 15 gravel, back-ins (30 x 45), 15 W, 15 E (30 amps), seasonal sites, WiFi Hotspot, tent sites, dump, laundry, groc, LP gas, fire rings, firewood, controlled access. **REC:** pool, pond, fishing, playground. Pet restrict(Q). Partial handicap access. 2015 rates: $33 to $35. Apr 15 to Oct 15. ATM, no CC.
AAA Approved
(724)285-3600 Lat: 40.831249, Lon: -79.780998
1085 Herman Rd, Butler, PA 16002
www.smithgrovecampground.com

CALEDONIA — C4 *Franklin*

CALEDONIA (State Pk) From town, E 4 mi on US-30 to SR-233, N 0.1 mi (L). 2015 rates: $15 to $28. Mar 1 to Dec 15. (717)352-2161

CARLISLE — E6 *Cumberland*

A SPOTLIGHT Introducing Carlisle's colorful attractions appearing at the front of this state section.

DEER RUN CAMPING RESORT Ratings: 8.5/9★/9 (Campground) From Jct of I-81 & Hwy 34 (exit 47A): Go 7 mi S on Hwy 34, then 1-1/4 mi S on Hwy 94, then 1/2 mi E on Sheet Iron Roof Rd. (R). **FAC:** Gravel rds. (170 spaces). Avail: 110 gravel, 40 pull-thrus (25 x 70), back-ins (25 x 50), 96 full hkups, 14 W, 14 E (30/50 amps), seasonal sites, cable, WiFi $, tent sites, rentals, dump, mobile sewer, laundry, groc, LP gas, fire rings, firewood. **REC:** heated pool, wading pool, pond, fishing, playground. Pets OK. Partial handicap access.

PA

CARLISLE (CONT)

DEER RUN CAMPING RESORT (CONT)
Big rig sites, eco-friendly, 2015 rates: $36 to $53. Disc: military. Apr 1 to Oct 31. ATM.
(717)486-8168 Lat: 40.095427, Lon: -77.158081
111 Sheet Iron Roof Rd, Gardners, PA 17324
deb@deerruncampingresort.com
www.deerruncampingresort.com
See ad pages 978 (Spotlight Carlisle), 974.

DOGWOOD ACRES CAMPGROUND
Ratings: 8/9.5★/9.5 (Campground) From Jct I-81 (exit 37) & Hwy 233: Go 9 mi N on Hwy 233, then 2-1/4 E on SR 944 (L) Note: Turn (L) at big green campground sign, not street sign, for other directions call park. **FAC:** Gravel rds. (93 spaces). Avail: 36 gravel, 4 pull-thrus (40 x 60), back-ins (30 x 50), 23 full hkups, 13 W, 13 E (30/50 amps), seasonal sites, cable, WiFi $, tent sites, rentals, dump, mobile sewer, groc, LP gas, fire rings, firewood. **REC:** pool, pond, fishing, playground. Pet restrict(B/Q). Partial handicap access. Big rig sites, eco-friendly, 2015 rates: $49 to $55. Disc: military. Apr 15 to Oct 30.
(717)776-5203 Lat: 40.234411, Lon: -77.399712
4500 Enola Rd, Newville, PA 17241
info@dogwoodcamping.com
www.dogwoodcamping.com
See ad page 978 (Spotlight Carlisle).

MOUNTAIN CREEK CAMPGROUND
Ratings: 8.5/8.5★/9 (Campground) From Jct of Hwy 94 & Hwy 34: Go 2 mi S on Hwy 34, then 3/4 mi W on Green Mountain Rd, then 1 mi W on Pine Grove Rd. (R).

CONVENIENT TO GETTYSBURG, CARLISLE
In PA's beautiful South Mtns, family-oriented & family-owned. Make happy memories at national car shows in Carlisle or historic Gettysburg. Surrounded by Amish & Civil War history. Activities for all ages. Open all year!

FAC: Gravel rds. (228 spaces). Avail: 123 grass, 7 pull-thrus (30 x 65), back-ins (40 x 55), some side by side hkups, 24 full hkups, 99 W, 99 E (30/50 amps), seasonal sites, WiFi, tent sites, rentals, dump, mobile sewer, laundry, groc, LP gas, fire rings, firewood, controlled access. **REC:** pool, wading pool, Mountain Creek: fishing, playground. Pets OK. Partial handicap access. Big rig sites, eco-friendly, 2015 rates: $34 to $53. Disc: AAA, military. Mar 15 to Nov 20.
(717)486-7681 Lat: 40.06383, Lon: -77.22668
349 Pine Grove Rd, Gardners, PA 17324
camp@mtncreekcg.com
www.mtncreekcg.com
See ad pages 977 (Spotlight Carlisle), 974.

WESTERN VILLAGE RV PARK
Ratings: 8.5/9.5★/9 (Campground) From Jct of I-76/Penn Tpk & US 11(exit 226): follow signs to I-81: Go 7 mi SW on I-81 (exit 45/Walnut Bottom Rd), then 1-1/4 mi SW on Walnut Bottom Rd, then 1/4 mi SE on Greenview Dr. (E). **FAC:** Gravel rds. (188 spaces). Avail: 100 gravel, 22 pull-thrus (30 x 70), back-ins (24 x 50), 100 full hkups (30/50 amps), seasonal sites, WiFi, tent sites, rentals, dump, laundry, groc, LP gas, fire rings, firewood. **REC:** pool, shuffleboard, playground. Pets OK. Partial handicap access. Big rig sites, eco-friendly, 2015 rates: $36 to $48.
(717)243-1179 Lat: 40.235989, Lon: -77.397188
200 Greenview Dr, Carlisle, PA 17015
camp@westernvillagervpark.com
www.westernvillagervpark.com
See ad page 976 (Spotlight Carlisle).

CATAWISSA — C7 *Columbia*

J & D CAMPGROUND **Ratings: 7.5/8★/7.5** (Campground) 2015 rates: $49. May 1 to Oct 15. (570)356-7700 973 Southern Dr, Catawissa, PA 17820

KNOEBELS LAKE GLORY CAMPGROUND **Ratings: 5.5/5.5/7.5** (Campground) 2015 rates: $49. Apr 15 to Oct 15. (570)356-7392 96 Eisenhower Rd, Catawissa, PA 17820

CENTERVILLE — E2 *Cumberland*

PINE GROVE FURNACE (State Pk) From Jct of I-81 & SR-233, S 8 mi on SR-233 (E). 2015 rates: $15 to $28. Mar 25 to Dec 15. (717)486-7174

CHAMBERSBURG — E6 *Franklin*

TWIN BRIDGE MEADOW FAMILY CAMPGROUND
Ratings: 5.5/9★/7.5 (Campground) From Jct I-81 (exit 16/6) & US 30: Go 6 mi W on US 30, then 1-1/4 mi N on Twin Bridge Rd. (L). **FAC:** Gravel rds. (180 spaces). Avail: 138 grass, 40 pull-thrus (40 x 60), back-ins (40 x 50), mostly side by side hkups, 138 W, 138 E (30/50 amps), seasonal sites, WiFi, tent sites, dump, mobile sewer, groc, fire rings, firewood. **REC:** Back Creek: fishing, playground. Pets OK. Partial handicap access. 2015 rates: $28 to $40. Apr 15 to Oct 15.
AAA Approved
(717)369-2216 Lat: 39.951242, Lon: -77.738942
1345 Twin Bridge Rd, Chambersburg, PA 17202
info@twinbridgecampground.com
www.twinbridgecampground.com
See ad this page.

CHAMPION — E3 *Fayette, Westmoreland*

MOUNTAIN PINES CAMPGROUND
Ratings: 8.5/8/7.5 (Campground) From Jct I-76/70/PA Tpk(exit 91) & Hwy 31: Go 2 mi E on Hwy 31, then 2 mi S on Hwy 711/Indian Creek Valley Rd(L). **FAC:** Paved/gravel rds. (716 spaces). Avail: 203 grass, back-ins (30 x 60), 203 full hkups (30/50 amps), seasonal sites, cable, WiFi $, tent sites, rentals, dump, laundry, groc, LP gas, fire rings, firewood. **REC:** heated pool, wading pool, Indian Creek: fishing, shuffleboard, playground, rec open to public. Pets OK. Partial handicap access. 2015 rates: $37 to $45. Disc: military. Apr 15 to Oct 15. ATM.
(724)455-3300 Lat: 40.066791, Lon: -79.362724
1662 Indian Creek Valley Rd, Champion, PA 1562
info@mountainpinescamping.com
www.MountainPinesCamping.com
See ad this page, 974.

CLARENDON — B3 *Warren*

CHAPMAN (State Pk) From Jct of US-6 & Chapman Dam Rd, SW 5 mi on Chapman Dam Rd/Railroad (E). 2015 rates: $15 to $28. Apr 15 to Dec 15. (814)723-0250

CLARION — C3 *Clarion*

RUSTIC ACRES RV RESORT & CAMPGROUND
Ratings: 6/8.5★/8.5 (Campground) From Jct I-80 (exit 60) & Hwy 66N: Go 3-1/4 mi N on Hwy 66N, then 1/2 mi W on Pine Terrace Rd (L). **FAC:** Paved/gravel rds. (95 spaces). Avail: 43 gravel, 20 pull-thrus (25 x 55), back-ins (25 x 40), 43 full hkups (30 amps), seasonal sites, WiFi Hotspot, tent sites, rentals, dump, laundry, groc, LP gas, fire rings, firewood. **REC:** Deer Creek: shuffleboard, play

Remember, ratings are based on ALL available facilities.

CLARION (CONT)

RUSTIC ACRES RV RESORT (CONT)
ground. Pet restrict(B). 2015 rates: $30 to $35. Disc: AAA, military.
(814)226-9850 Lat: 41.23672, Lon: -79.437763
634 Pine Terrace Rd, Shippenville, PA 16254
contact@rusticacrescampground.com
www.rusticacrescampground.com
See ad opposite page.

CLARKS SUMMIT — B9 *Lackawanna*

HIGHLAND CAMPGROUND
Ratings: 6.5/8★/7.5 (Campground) From Jct US 6 & US 11 (North): Go 1-1/2 mi W on US 6, then 1 mi N on PA-3077 (Winola Rd), then 5 mi N on Hwy 307 (Winola Rd), then 1 mi E on Highland Dr to stop sign. Go straight on dirt rd (thru stop sign) (L) Do not use GPS. **FAC:** Gravel rds. (70 spaces). Avail: 46 gravel, 4 pull-thrus (30 x 55), back-ins (30 x 50), 21 full hkups, 25 W, 25 E (30/50 amps), seasonal sites, WiFi Hotspot, tent sites, rentals, dump, laundry, fire rings, firewood. **REC:** pool, playground. Pet restrict(B). 2015 rates: $25 to $50. Disc: military. Apr 15 to Oct 31.
(570)586-0145 Lat: 41.534244, Lon: -75.736025
105 Whispering Winds Lane, Dalton, PA 18414
camphighland@epix.net
highlandcampgrounds.com
See ad opposite page, 974.

CLEARFIELD — C4 *Clearfield*

S B ELLIOTT (State Pk) At Jct of I-80 & SR-153/Exit 18 (R). 2015 rates: $15 to $28. May 10 to Sep 10. (814)765-0630

CLEARVILLE — E4 *Bedford*

HIDDEN SPRINGS CAMPGROUND
Ratings: 7.5/7.5/7.5 (Campground) From Jct US 220 & I-68/US 40 in MD: Go 4-1/2 mi E on I-68(exit 50), then 2-1/2 mi N on Pleasant Valley Rd (at PA/MD state line Pleasant Valley Rd becomes SR 3005/Beans Cove Rd), then 1-1/2 mi NE on Beans Cove Rd(L). **FAC:** Paved/gravel rds. (100 spaces). Avail: 44 gravel, 8 pull-thrus (22 x 50), back-ins (22 x 40), 27 full hkups, 17 W, 17 E (30/50 amps), seasonal sites, tent sites, rentals, dump, laundry, groc, LP gas, fire rings, firewood, controlled access. **REC:** heated pool $, pond, fishing, playground, rec open to public. Pets OK. 2015 rates: $39. May 1 to Oct 31.
(814)767-9676 Lat: 39.741439, Lon: -78.622888
815 Beans Cove Road, Clearville, PA 15535
www.hiddenspringscampground.com
See ad page 588.

COATESVILLE — E9 *Chester*

HIDDEN ACRES CAMPGROUND
Ratings: 7/7.5/7.5 (Campground) From Jct US 30 & Hwy 82: Go 1/4 mi N on Hwy 82, then 4-1/2 mi W on Hwy 340, then 1/2 mi N on Cambridge Rd, then 1/4 mi E on Baldwin Rd(L). **FAC:** Paved/gravel rds. (200 spaces). 120 Avail: 100 gravel, 20 grass, 6 pull-thrus (30 x 65), back-ins (25 x 40), 20 full hkups, 100 W, 100 E (30/50 amps), seasonal sites, WiFi Hotspot, tent sites, dump, mobile sewer, laundry, groc, fire rings, firewood. **REC:** pool, pond, fishing, playground. Pets OK. Partial handicap access. Big rig sites, 2015 rates: $31 to $48. Apr 15 to Oct 15.
(610)857-3990 Lat: 40.030453, Lon: -75.903783
103 Hidden Acres Rd, Coatesville, PA 19320
hiddenacres103@hotmail.com
www.hiddenacrespa.com
See ad this page.

CONFLUENCE — E3 *Fayette*

TUB RUN CAMPGROUND (Public Corps) From town, S 4.5 mi on Hwy 281 to Tub Run Rd, E 1 mi, follow signs (L). Off-season, call (814)395-3242. 2015 rates: $18 to $22. May 16 to Aug 30. (814)395-3242

Tell them you saw them in this Guide!

CONNELLSVILLE — E2 *Fayette*

UNIONTOWN KOA AT RIVER'S EDGE **Ratings: 9/9★/9.5** (Campground) 2015 rates: $38 to $75. (724)628-4880 1101 Riveredge Rd, Connellsville, PA 15425

COOK FOREST — C3 *Clarion*

DEER MEADOW CAMPGROUND **Ratings: 8.5/8★/9.5** (Campground) 2015 rates: $38 to $53. May 23 to Sep 7. (814)927-8125 2761 Forest Rd, Cooksburg, PA 16217

KALYUMET CAMPGROUND **Ratings: 8.5/10★/10** (Campground) 2015 rates: $43 to $53. May 1 to Oct 31. (814)744-9622 8630 Miola Rd, Lucinda, PA 16235

WHITE'S HAVEN CAMPGROUND
Ratings: 6/8.5★/8 (Campground) From Jct I-80 & SR 36, (Exit 78), N 12.7 mi on SR36 to Cathers Run Rd, S 0.1 mi (L). **FAC:** Gravel rds. (140 spaces). 15 Avail: 8 gravel, 7 grass, 2 pull-thrus (45 x 45), back-ins (45 x 60), 15 W, 15 E (30 amps), seasonal sites, WiFi Hotspot, tent sites, rentals, dump, mobile sewer, laundry, groc, LP gas, fire rings, firewood. **REC:** playground. Pets OK. Partial handicap access. Eco-friendly, 2015 rates: $35. No CC.
(814)752-2205 Lat: 41.31329, Lon: -79.16915
3058 Cathers Run, Clarington, PA 15828
outsider629@yahoo.com
www.whiteshavencampground.com
See ad this page.

COOKSBURG — C3 *Clarion*

COOK FOREST (State Pk) From Jct of SR-66 & SR-36, S 7 mi on SR-36 (L). 2015 rates: $15 to $28. May 25 to Oct 10. (814)744-8407

CORRY — A2 *Erie*

HARECREEK CAMPGROUND **Ratings: 8.5/8.5★/8.5** (Campground) 2015 rates: $37. (814)664-9684 375 Sciota St., Corry, PA 16407

COUDERSPORT — B5 *Potter*

ALLEGHENY RIVER CAMPGROUND Ratings: 8/8.5★/8.5 (Campground) From Jct US 6 & Hwy 155: Go 9 mi E on US 6 (mile marker 170) (R). **FAC:** Gravel rds. (110 spaces). 78 Avail: 22 gravel, 56 grass, back-ins (40 x 40), 16 full hkups, 62 W, 62 E (30/50 amps), seasonal sites, WiFi, tent sites, rentals, dump, mobile sewer, laundry, groc, LP gas, fire rings, firewood, controlled access. **REC:** heated pool, Allegheny River: fishing, playground. Pets OK. Eco-friendly, 2015 rates: $34 to $40. Apr 15 to Dec 5.
(814)544-8844 Lat: 41.780065, Lon: -78.153898
1737 US Rte. 6 W, Roulette, PA 16746
info@alleghenyrivercampground.com
www.alleghenyrivercampground.com

CHERRY SPRINGS (State Pk) From Jct of US-6 & W Branch Rd, SW 14 mi on W Branch Rd to Jct of SR-44 at park, follow signs (R). Pit toilets. 2015 rates: $15 to $17. Apr 10 to Nov 1. (814)435-5010

POTTER COUNTY FAMILY CAMPGROUND **Ratings: 5.5/6.5/7.5** (Campground) 2015 rates: $25 to $28. (814)274-5010 3075 E Second St (Rt 6), Coudersport, PA 16915

COVINGTON — B6 *Tioga*

TANGLEWOOD CAMPING **Ratings: 8/8.5★/9** (Campground) 2015 rates: $39 to $49. May 1 to Oct 31. (570)549-8299 787 Tanglewood Rd, Covington, PA 16917

DARLINGTON — D1 *Beaver*

CRAWFORD'S CAMPING PARK **Ratings: 6/8★/7** (Campground) 2015 rates: $25 to $30. Apr 15 to Oct 15. (724)846-5964 251 Hogson Rd, Darlington, PA 16115

Find it Fast! Use our alphabetized index of campgrounds and parks.

DENVER — E8 *Lancaster*

HICKORY RUN FAMILY CAMPING RESORT
Ratings: 8/8★/9 (Campground) From Jct PA Tpke I-76 & Hwy 272 (exit 21/286): Go 2 mi S on Hwy 272, then 2 mi W on Main/Church Rd, then 2-1/4 mi N on Leisey/Greenville Rd(L). **FAC:** Paved/gravel rds. (255 spaces). Avail: 160 gravel, 24 pull-thrus (30 x 65), back-ins (33 x 40), 100 full hkups, 60 W, 60 E (30/50 amps), seasonal sites, WiFi $, tent sites, rentals, showers $, dump, laundry, groc, LP gas, fire rings, firewood. **REC:** pool, pond, fishing, shuffleboard, playground, rec open to public. Pets OK. Partial handicap access. Big rig sites, eco-friendly, 2015 rates: $34 to $44. Disc: AAA, military. Apr 1 to Nov 1.
AAA Approved
(800)458-0612 Lat: 40.26267, Lon: -76.161371
285 Greenville Rd, Denver, PA 17517
stanst@ptd.net
www.pacampgrounds.com
See ad pages 988 (Spotlight Lancaster County), 974.

DONEGAL — E3 *Westmoreland*

DONEGAL CAMPGROUND Ratings: 7/7/7 (Campground) From Jct PA Tpk/I-70/76(exit 91) & Hwy 31: Go 1/2 mi W on Hwy 31(L). **FAC:** Paved rds. (45 spaces). Avail: 30 gravel, 18 pull-thrus (30 x 85), back-ins (30 x 50), 25 full hkups, 5 W, 5 E (30/50 amps), seasonal sites, cable, WiFi, tent sites, dump, fire rings, firewood. **REC:** pool, playground. Pets OK. Big rig sites, 2015 rates: $34 to $36. Mar 15 to Dec 15.
AAA Approved
(724)593-7717 Lat: 40.112083, Lon: -79.389074
106 Yeckel Dr, Rt 31, Donegal, PA 15628
dansheryeckel@lhtot.com
www.donegalcampground.com

KOOSER (State Pk) From town, NW 11 mi on Hwy 31W (L). 2015 rates: $15 to $28. Apr 15 to Oct 15. (814)445-8673

LAUREL HIGHLANDS CAMPLAND INC **Ratings: 6.5/6.5/6** (RV Park) 2015 rates: $41.20. (724)593-6325 1001 Clubhouse Rd, Donegal, PA 15628

DOWNINGTOWN — E9 *Chester*

BRANDYWINE CREEK CAMPGROUND **Ratings: 7/8.5★/8.5** (Campground) 2015 rates: $45. Apr 1 to Nov 1. (610)942-9950 1091 Creek Rd, Downingtown, PA 19335

DU BOIS — C4 *Clearfield*

CAYMAN LANDING AT TREASURE LAKE **Ratings: 6.5/6.5/4** (Campground) 2015 rates: $25 to $39. (814)913-1437 13 Treasure Lake, Dubois, PA 15801

EAST BENTON — B9 *Lackawanna*

LACKAWANNA (State Pk) From I-81 (exit 199): Go 3 mi W on Hwy 524, then N on Hwy 407. 2015 rates: $15 to $28. Apr 15 to Oct 21. (570)945-3239

EBENSBURG — D4 *Cambria*

WOODLAND PARK INC
Ratings: 5/5/6 (Campground) From Jct US 219 & US 22: Go 1-1/4 mi W on US 22, then 1/4 mi S on Campground Rd(E). **FAC:** Gravel rds. (200 spaces). Avail: 100 grass, 8 pull-thrus (30 x 50), back-ins (30 x 40), 90 full hkups, 10 W, 10 E (30/50 amps), seasonal sites, tent sites, showers $, laundry, groc, LP gas, fire rings, firewood. **REC:** pond, fishing, playground. Pets OK. 2015 rates: $20 to $26. Apr 15 to Oct 15.
AAA Approved
(814)472-9857 Lat: 40.447168, Lon: -78.785871
220 Campground Rd, Ebensburg, PA 15931
woodlandpark@atlanticbb.com
www.woodlandparkinc.com
See ad this page.

We appreciate your business!

PA

ELIZABETHTOWN — E7 *Lancaster*

← ELIZABETHTOWN/HERSHEY KOA **Ratings: 9/9★/9.5** (Campground) From Jct Hwy 283 & Hwy 743 (Elizabethtown/Hershey exit): Go 1-1/2 mi S on Hwy 743, then 1/2 mi E on Hwy 230 (Market St), then 1/2 mi W on W High St, then 2-1/4 mi N on Turnpike Rd(L). **FAC:** Paved/gravel rds. 158 Avail: 154 gravel, 4 grass, 21 pull-thrus (30 x 70), back-ins (35 x 45), 147 full hkups, 11 W, 11 E (30/50 amps), WiFi, tent sites, rentals, dump, laundry, groc, LP gas, fire rings, firewood. **REC:** pool, wading pool, pond, fishing, playground. Pet restrict(B). Partial handicap access. Big rig sites, eco-friendly, 2015 rates: $46.50 to $86.95. Apr 11 to Nov 2.
AAA Approved
(800)562-4774 Lat: 40.1391, Lon: -76.657239
1980 Turnpike Rd, Elizabethtown, PA 17022
hersheykoa@live.com
www.hersheykoa.com

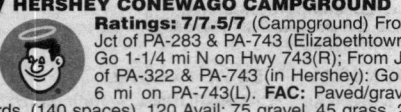

↓ **HERSHEY CONEWAGO CAMPGROUND**
Ratings: 7/7.5/7 (Campground) From Jct of PA-283 & PA-743 (Elizabethtown): Go 1-1/4 mi N on Hwy 743(R); From Jct of PA-322 & PA-743 (in Hershey): Go S 6 mi on PA-743(L). **FAC:** Paved/gravel rds. (140 spaces). 120 Avail: 75 gravel, 45 grass, 20 pull-thrus (30 x 60), back-ins (30 x 60), mostly side by side hkups, 59 full hkups, 61 W, 61 E (30 amps), seasonal sites, WiFi Hotspot, tent sites, rentals, dump, laundry, groc, LP gas, fire rings, firewood. **REC:** pool, pond, playground. Pets OK. Eco-friendly, 2015 rates: $25 to $70. Disc: AAA, military. Apr 15 to Nov 1.
AAA Approved
(717)367-1179 Lat: 40.19809, Lon: -76.60892
1590 Hershey Rd, Elizabethtown, PA 17022
camp@hersheyconewago.com
www.hersheyconewago.com
See ad pages 988 (Spotlight Lancaster County), 974.

ELVERSON — E9 *Berks*

↗ FRENCH CREEK (State Pk) From Jct of I-76 & & SH 345, N 4.5 mi on SH 345. 2015 rates: $15 to $28. (610)582-9680

ELYSBURG — C7 *Northumberland, Columbia*

↗ KNOEBELS AMUSEMENT PARK AND CAMPGROUND **Ratings: 6/5.5/5.5** (Campground) 2015 rates: $49. Apr 15 to Oct 31. (800)487-4386 391 Knoebels Blvd, Rt 487, Elysburg, PA 17824

EMLENTON — C2 *Venango*

← **GASLIGHT CAMPGROUND**
Ratings: 9/9★/9 (Campground) From Jct I-80(exit 42) & Hwy 38: Go 500 ft N on Hwy 38, then 1/4 mi W on Hwy 208/Emlenton Clintonville Rd(R). **FAC:** Gravel rds. (128 spaces). 48 Avail: 24 gravel, 24 grass, 42 pull-thrus (25 x 60), back-ins (40 x 60), 48 full hkups (30/50 amps), seasonal sites, WiFi $, tent sites, rentals, dump, laundry, groc, LP gas, fire rings, firewood. **REC:** heated pool, pond, fishing, playground. Pets OK. Big rig sites, eco-friendly, 2015 rates: $37 to $40. Disc: military. Apr 1 to Oct 31.
(724)867-6981 Lat: 41.180075, Lon: -79.745667
6297 Emlenton Clitonville Rd, Emlenton, PA 16373
peetub@aol.com
www.gaslightcampground.com
See ad pages 1005, 974.

EMPORIUM — B5 *Cameron*

↑ SIZERVILLE (State Pk) From Jct of US-120 & Rte 155, N 7 mi on Rte 155 (R). 2015 rates: $15 to $28. Apr 15 to Dec 15. (814)486-5605

ENTRIKEN — D5 *Huntingdon*

↓ TROUGH CREEK (State Pk) From Jct of Hwys 26 & 994, E 6 mi on Hwy 994 to entrance (E). Pit toilets. 2015 rates: $15 to $28. Apr 15 to Dec 15. (814)658-3847

EPHRATA — E8 *Lancaster*

↑ STARLITE CAMPING RESORT **Ratings: 7.5/8★/8.5** (Campground) 2015 rates: $42 to $48. May 1 to Oct 31. (717)733-9655 1500 Furance Hill Rd, Stevens, PA 17578

ERIE — A2 *Erie*

A SPOTLIGHT Introducing Erie's colorful attractions appearing at the front of this state section.

ERIE See also Corry, Jamestown, Lake City, Meadville, North Springfield, Titusville & Waterford.

→ LAMPE MARINA CAMPGROUND (Public) From Jct I-79(exit 183A) & Hwy 5/Hwy 290/W 12th St: Go 3-1/4 mi E on 12th St, then 1-1/2 mi N on E Bayfront Pkwy/Port Access Road(E). 2015 rates: $30 to $35. May 1 to Oct 31. (814)454-5830

→ **PRESQUE ISLE PASSAGE RV PARK & CABIN RENTALS**
Ratings: 8.5/9★/8 (Campground) From Jct I-90(exit 18) & Hwy 832: Go 0.3 mi N on Hwy 832/Sterrettania Rd, W 500 ft. on Sterrettania Rd(L). **FAC:** Gravel rds. (144 spaces). 93 Avail: 89 gravel, 4 grass, 60 pull-thrus (25 x 65), back-ins (35 x 55), mostly side by side hkups, 89 full hkups, 4 W, 4 E (30/50 amps), seasonal sites, cable, WiFi, tent sites, rentals, dump, laundry, groc, LP gas, fire rings, firewood. **REC:** heated pool, pond, fishing, playground. Pets OK. Partial handicap access. Big rig sites, eco-friendly, 2015 rates: $30 to $50. Disc: AAA, military.
(814)833-3272 Lat: 42.021447, Lon: -80.186015
6300 Sterrettania Rd (Hwy 832), Erie, PA 16415
info@presqueislepassage.com
www.PresqueIslePassage.com
See ad pages 980 (Spotlight Erie), 974.

← SARA'S CAMPGROUND **Ratings: 6.5/8.5★/6.5** (Campground) E Bnd: From jct of I-90(exit 18) & Hwy 832: Go 7-1/2 mi N on PA-832(R); N Bnd: From Jct I-79(exit 183B) & Hwy 5: Go 1-3/4 mi W on Hwy 5, then 3/4 mi N on Hwy 832(R). **FAC:** Paved/gravel rds. (381 spaces). 58 Avail: 26 gravel, 32 grass, back-ins (20 x 35), some side by side hkups, 32 full hkups, 26 W, 26 E (30/50 amps), seasonal sites, cable, WiFi, tent sites, showers $, dump, laundry, groc, fire rings, firewood, restaurant. **REC:** Lake Erie: swim, fishing, playground. Pets OK. 2015 rates: $34 to $38. Apr 1 to Oct 31. no reservations.
AAA Approved
(814)833-4560 Lat: 42.111574, Lon: -80.15548
50 Peninsula Dr, Erie, PA 16505
camp@sarascampground.com
www.sarascampground.com

↓ **SPARROW POND FAMILY CAMPGROUND & RECREATION**
Ratings: 8.5/9★/9 (Campground) From Jct I-90(exit 24) & US 19: Go 5-1/2 mi S on US 19(L). **FAC:** Gravel rds. (145 spaces). Avail: 62 gravel, 11 pull-thrus (35 x 60), back-ins (40 x 65), 57 full hkups, 5 W, 5 E (30/50 amps), seasonal sites, WiFi $, tent sites, rentals, dump, laundry, groc, LP gas, fire rings, firewood, controlled access. **REC:** heated pool, wading pool, pond, fishing, playground. Pets OK. Partial handicap access. Big rig sites, eco-friendly, 2015 rates: $38 to $64. Disc: AAA. Apr 15 to Oct 15.
AAA Approved
(814)796-6777 Lat: 41.979289, Lon: -80.014029
11103 Rt. 19 N, Waterford, PA 16441
camp@sparrowpond.com
www.sparrowpond.com
See ad this page, 974.

↗ **WEST HAVEN RV PARK & FAMILY CAMPGROUND**
Ratings: 7.5/9★/8.5 (Campground) From Jct I-90 (exit 18/Sterrettania/Presque Isle) & Hwy 832: Go 1/2 mi S on Sterrettania Rd (L); From Jct I-79 (exit 174/McKean) & West Rd: Go 2 mi W on West Rd, then 1 mi N on Sterrettania Rd (R). **FAC:** Paved/gravel rds. (158 spaces). Avail: 15 gravel, 10 pull-thrus (25 x 70), back-ins (21 x 55), 15 full hkups (30/50 amps), seasonal sites, WiFi, tent sites, rentals, showers $, dump, laundry, fire rings, firewood. **REC:** pool, pond, fishing, playground. Pets OK. Partial handicap access. Big rig sites, 2015 rates: $36 to $48. Disc: military. May 1 to Oct 23.
(814)403-3243 Lat: 42.011321, Lon: -80.19846
6601 Sterrettania Rd, Fairview, PA 16415
jodie@westhavenrvpark.com
www.westhavenrvpark.com
See ad this page, 974.

FARMINGTON — E2 *Fayette*

↗ BENNER'S MEADOW RUN CAMPING AND CABINS **Ratings: 8/7.5/8** (Campground) 2015 rates: $43 to $49. Apr 25 to Oct 20. (724)329-4097 315 Nelson Rd, Farmington, PA 15437

FORKSVILLE — B7 *Sullivan*

↓ WORLDS END (State Pk) From town, S 2 mi SR-154 (E). 2015 rates: $15 to $22.50. (570)924-3287

FORT LOUDON — E5 *Franklin*

↖ COWANS GAP (State Pk) From Jct of US-30 & SR-75 (in town), N 4 mi on SR-75 to Richmond Furnace Rd, W 3 mi (L). 2015 rates: $15 to $28. Apr 10 to Dec 15. (717)485-3948

FRANKFORT SPRINGS — D1 *Beaver*

↑ RACCOON CREEK (State Pk) From Pittsburgh, W 33 mi on Hwy 22 to SR-18 (last PA exit), N 6 mi (R). 2015 rates: $15 to $28. (724)899-2200

FRANKLIN — B2 *Venango*

↗ TWO MILE RUN COUNTY PARK (Public) From jct of SR 8 & US 322: Go 1/2 mi W on US 322, then 6 mi N on SR 417, then 1/2 mi E on Cherrytree Rd, then 3/4 mi S on Beach Rd. 2015 rates: $15 to $25. (814)676-6116

FRUGALITY — D5 *Cambria*

← PRINCE GALLITZIN (State Pk) From Jct of SR-53 & SR-253, S 1.75 mi on SR-53 to SR-1026, W 6 mi, follow signs (L). 2015 rates: $15 to $28. Apr 15 to Oct 25. (814)674-1000

GALETON — B6 *Potter*

↖ LYMAN RUN (State Pk) From Jct of US-6 & W Branch Rd, W 5 mi on W Branch Rd to Lyman Run Rd, NW 2 mi (R). 2015 rates: $15 to $28. Apr 15 to Dec 15. (814)435-5010

↓ OLE BULL (State Pk) From Jct of US-6 & Hwy 144, S 18 mi on Hwy 144 (L). 2015 rates: $15 to $28. (814)435-5000

GETTYSBURG — E6 *Adams*

A SPOTLIGHT Introducing Gettysburg's colorful attractions appearing at the front of this state section.

↓ **ARTILLERY RIDGE CAMPING RESORT & GETTYSBURG HORSE PARK**
Ratings: 8.5/9.5★/8.5 (Campground) From Jct US 15 & Hwy 134 (Taneytown Rd) (S of town): Go 2-1/4 mi N on Taneytown Rd. (R).

FREE BATTLEFIELD DIORAMA
One mile from town, full HUs & pull thru sites. Camp with & ride your own horse. Our campers admitted free to Battlefield Diorama. See the 3-day battle unfold.

FAC: Gravel rds. (177 spaces). Avail: 144 gravel, 87 pull-thrus (40 x 60), back-ins (30 x 50), 133 full hkups, 11 W, 11 E (30/50 amps), seasonal sites, WiFi, tent sites, rentals, dump, mobile sewer, laundry, groc, fire rings, firewood. **REC:** pool, pond, fishing, playground. Pets OK. Partial handicap access. Big rig sites, eco-friendly, 2015 rates: $53 to $58. Disc: military.
(717)334-1288 Lat: 39.802008, Lon: -77.22944
610 Taneytown Rd (Rte 134), Gettysburg, PA 17325
artilleryridge@comcast.net
www.artilleryridge.com
See ad pages 983 (Spotlight Gettysburg), 974.

GETTYSBURG (CONT)

➔ DRUMMER BOY CAMPING RESORT **Ratings: 8.5/8.5/8** (Campground) 2015 rates: $44 to $69. (800)293-2808 1300 Hanover Rd, Gettysburg, PA 17325

➔ GETTYSBURG BATTLEFIELD KOA KAMPGROUND **Ratings: 8.5/9★/9.5** (Campground) 2015 rates: $31 to $81. Apr 1 to Nov 1. (800)562-1869 20 Knox Rd, Gettysburg, PA 17325

➔ GETTYSBURG BATTLEFIELD RESORT AT TRAVEL RESORTS OF AMERICA PROPERTY **Ratings: 8.5/10★/9** (Membership Pk) 2015 rates: $30. (717)337-3363x1703 1960 Emmitsburg Rd, Gettysburg, PA 17325

➔ **GETTYSBURG CAMPGROUND**
Ratings: 9.5/9.5★/9.5 (Campground) From Jct of US 30 & Bus US 15 S (Lincoln Square in Gettysburg): Go 1 blk S on Bus US 15, then 3 mi W on Hwy 116/Middle St. (L).

LOCATED IN HISTORIC GETTYSBURG, PA
Gettysburg Campground is a full-facility, family campground along beautiful Marsh Creek. Convenient to Gettysburg Battlefields, Lancaster, Hershey, Baltimore, and Washington, DC.

FAC: All weather rds. 240 Avail: 240 all weather, 44 pull-thrus (25 x 70), back-ins (30 x 40), some side by side hkups, 112 full hkups, 126 W, 128 E (30/50 amps), cable, WiFi, tent sites, rentals, dump, mobile sewer, laundry, groc, LP gas, fire rings, firewood. **REC:** pool, Marsh Creek: fishing, shuffleboard, playground. Pets OK. Eco-friendly, 2015 rates: $38 to $66. Disc: AAA, military. Apr 1 to Nov 22. ATM.
AAA Approved
(717)334-3304 Lat: 39.817585, Lon: -77.2856
2030 Fairfield Rd, Gettysburg, PA 17325
camp@gettysburgcampground.com
www.gettysburgcampground.com
See ad pages 982 (Spotlight Gettysburg), 974 & Family Camping, RV Trips of a Lifetime in Magazine Section.

➔ **GRANITE HILL CAMPING RESORT**
Ratings: 7.5/8.5★/8 (Campground) From Jct of US 30 & Bus US 15: Go 528 ft S on Bus US 15, then 6 mi W on Hwy 116 (L). **FAC:** Paved/gravel rds. (330 spaces). 302 Avail: 192 gravel, 110 grass, 100 pull-thrus (40 x 55), back-ins (30 x 50), some side by side hkups, 112 full hkups, 190 W, 190 E (30/50 amps), seasonal sites, cable, WiFi Hotspot, tent sites, rentals, dump, mobile sewer, laundry, groc, LP gas, fire rings, firewood, restaurant. **REC:** pool, pond, fishing, shuffleboard, playground, rec open to public. Pets OK. Partial handicap access. Eco-friendly, 2015 rates: $44 to $66. Disc: AAA, military. ATM.
AAA Approved
(717)642-8749 Lat: 39.803872, Lon: -77.33254
3340 Fairfield Rd, Gettysburg, PA 17325
camp@granitehillcampingresort.com
www.granitehillcampingresort.com
See ad pages 981 (Spotlight Gettysburg), 974 & RV Trips of a Lifetime in Magazine Section.

↑ **MOUNTAIN CREEK CAMPGROUND**
Ratings: 8.5/8.5★/9 (Campground) From the Roundabout in Downtown Gettysburg: Go 1-1/2 mi N on Carlisle St, then 19 mi N on Hwy 34 (Carlisle St becomes Hwy 34), then 1-3/4 mi W on Pine Grove Rd(R). **FAC:** Gravel rds. (228 spaces). Avail: 123 grass, 7 pull-thrus (30 x 65), back-ins (40 x 55), some side by side hkups, 24 full hkups, 99 W, 99 E (30/50 amps), seasonal sites, WiFi, tent sites, rentals, dump, mobile sewer, laundry, groc, LP gas, fire rings, firewood, controlled access. **REC:** pool, wading pool, Mountain Creek: fishing, playground. Pet restrict(Q). Partial handicap access. Big rig sites, eco-friendly, 2015 rates: $34 to $53. Disc: AAA, military. Mar 15 to Nov 20.
(717)486-7681 Lat: 40.06383, Lon: -77.22668
349 Pine Grove Rd, Gardners, PA 17324
camp@mtncreekcg.com
www.mtncreekcg.com
See primary listing at Carlisle and ad page 977 (Spotlight Carlisle).

↓ ROUND TOP CAMPGROUND **Ratings: 9/8.5★/8.5** (Campground) 2015 rates: $39 to $79. (717)334-9565 180 Knight Rd, Gettysburg, PA 17325

Your neighbor just told you about a great little campground in Kentucky — what was the name of it again? The "Find-it-Fast" index in the back of the Guide can help. It's an alphabetical listing, by state, of every private and public park in the Guide.

Things to See and Do

➔ **ADVENTURE GOLF AT GRANITE HILL** Unique mini-golf course. Apr 1 to Oct 31. partial handicap access. Restrooms, food. Hours: 10am to 10pm. Adult fee: $4 to $5. ATM.
(717)642-8749 Lat: 39.803872, Lon: -77.33254
3340 Fairfield Rd, Gettysburg, PA 17325
camp@granitehillcampingresort.com
www.granitehillcampingresort.com
See ad page 981 (Spotlight Gettysburg).

➔ **DESTINATION GETTYSBURG** Official tourism bureau for Gettysburg, PA. Information available on housing, restaurants and places of interest in the area. Restrooms. Hours: Mon to Fri 8:30am to 5pm. No CC.
Lat: 39.829483, Lon: -77.242126
571 W Middle St., Gettysburg, PA 17325
info@destinationgettysburg.com
www.destinationgettysburg.com
See ad page 972 (Welcome Section).

➔ **GETTYSBURG BLUEGRASS FESTIVAL** Bluegrass Festival held semi-annually. May 15 to May 18. partial handicap access. Restrooms, food. Hours: 12pm to 10pm. Adult fee: $25 to $125. ATM.
(717)642-8749 Lat: 39.803872, Lon: -77.33254
3340 Fairfield Rd, Gettysburg, PA 17325
camp@granitehillcampingresort.com
www.gettysburgbluegrass.com
See ad page 981 (Spotlight Gettysburg).

➔ **STERLING PAVILION AT GRANITE HILL** Summer concert series and two Bluegrass Festivals held in Sterling Pavilion at campground. Partial handicap access. RV accessible. Restrooms, food. Hours: 10am to 10pm. Adult fee: $25 to $125. ATM.
(717)642-8749 Lat: 39.803872, Lon: -77.33254
3340 Fairfield Rd, Gettysburg, PA 17325
camp@granitehillcampingresort.com
www.granitehillcampingresort.com
See ad page 981 (Spotlight Gettysburg).

GREENTOWN — C9 *Pike*

➚ IRONWOOD POINT RECREATION AREA **Ratings: 6.5/NA/7** (Campground) 2015 rates: $32 to $38. Apr 30 to Oct 15. (570)857-0880 155 Burns Hill Rd, Greentown, PA 18426

↑ LEDGEDALE REC AREA **Ratings: 4.5/NA/6** (Campground) 2015 rates: $32 to $38. Apr 25 to Oct 17. (570)689-2181 153 Ledgedale Rd, Greentown, PA 18426

↓ PROMISED LAND (State Pk) From Jct of I-84 & SR-390 (old exit 7/new exit 26), S 5 mi on SR-390 (R) Call ahead for reservations. 2015 rates: $15 to $28. Apr 1 to Dec 15. (570)676-3428

GREENVILLE — B1 *Mercer*

➔ FARMA FAMILY CAMPGROUND **Ratings: 8/8/8** (Campground) 2015 rates: $30 to $45. May 1 to Sep 30. (724)253-4535 87 Hughey Rd, Greenville, PA 16125

HANOVER — E7 *York*

➘ CODORUS (State Pk) From Jct of SR-116 & SR-216, E 2.5 mi on SR-216 to Dubs Church Rd, S 1 mi (R). 2015 rates: $15 to $28. Apr 10 to Nov 1. (717)637-2816

Travel Services

↓ **CAMPING WORLD OF HANOVER** As the nation's largest retailer of RV supplies, accessories, services and new and used RVs, Camping World is committed to making your total RV experience better. RV Accessories: (877)786-0643. **SERVICES:** RV appliance, MH mechanical, engine/chassis repair, staffed RV wash, restrooms, RV Sales. RV supplies, LP, emergency parking, RV accessible. Hours: 8am - 6pm.
(888)776-1519 Lat: 39.755834, Lon: -76.953714
2100 Baltimore Pike, Hanover, PA 17331
www.campingworld.com

HARMONY — D1 *Butler*

↑ INDIAN BRAVE CAMPGROUND **Ratings: 6.5/6.5/6** (Campground) 2015 rates: $35 to $38. Apr 15 to Oct 15. (724)452-9204 159 Perry Hwy (US 19), Harmony, PA 16037

HARRISBURG — E7 *Dauphin*

HARRISBURG See also Carlisle, Dover, Elizabethtown, Hershey, Jonestown, Lebanon, Lewistown, Liverpool, Manheim & York.

➘ HARRISBURG EAST CAMPGROUND **Ratings: 9/10★/8** (Campground) 2015 rates: $38 to $55. (717)939-4331 1134 Highspire Rd, Harrisburg, PA 17111

Travel Services

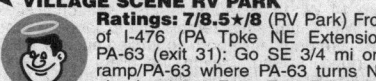

➔ **CAMPING WORLD OF HARRISBURG** As the nation's largest retailer of RV supplies, accessories, services and new and used RVs, Camping World is committed to making your total RV experience better. RV Accessories: (855)869-2365. **SERVICES:** RV, tire, RV appliance, MH mechanical, engine/chassis repair, restrooms, RV Sales. RV supplies, RV accessible. waiting room. Hours: 8am - 6pm.
(888)591-5811 Lat: 40.334081, Lon: -76.732335
7501 Allentown Blvd., Harrisburg, PA 17112
www.campingworld.com

HARRISVILLE — C2 *Butler*

➔ **YOGI BEAR'S JELLYSTONE PARK AT KOZY REST**
Ratings: 9.5/10★/10 (Campground) From Jct I-80 (exit 29) & Hwy 8: Go 5 mi S on Hwy 8, then 1/2 mi E on Hwy 58, then 2 mi N on Campground Rd (L); or From Jct of I-79 (exit 113) & Hwy 208: Go 4 mi E on Hwy 208, then 4-3/4 mi SE on Hwy 58, then 2 mi N on Campground Rd (L). **FAC:** Paved rds. (164 spaces). Avail: 83 gravel, 23 pull-thrus (35 x 75), back-ins (40 x 60), 57 full hkups, 26 W, 26 E (30/50 amps), seasonal sites, WiFi, tent sites, rentals, dump, laundry, groc, LP gas, fire rings, firewood, controlled access. **REC:** pool, playground. Pets OK. Partial handicap access. Big rig sites, eco-friendly, 2015 rates: $44 to $72. Disc: AAA, military. Apr 15 to Oct 31. ATM.
(724)735-2417 Lat: 41.15137, Lon: -79.966947
449 Campground Rd, Harrisville, PA 16038
camp@pittsburghjellystone.com
www.pittsburghjellystone.com
See ad page 993 (Spotlight Pittsburgh & Countryside).

HATFIELD — E9 *Montgomery*

➘ **VILLAGE SCENE RV PARK**
Ratings: 7/8.5★/8 (RV Park) From jct of I-476 (PA Tpke NE Extension) & PA-63 (exit 31): Go SE 3/4 mi on exit ramp/PA-63 where PA-63 turns NE (& also becomes Forty Foot Rd), then NE 2-1/4 mi on PA-63/Forty Foot Rd, then SE 1/2 mi on Koffel Rd. (L). **FAC:** Paved rds. 32 paved, patios, 3 pull-thrus (25 x 60), back-ins (30 x 45), accepts full hkup units only, 30 full hkups (30/50 amps), WiFi, dump, laundry. **REC:** playground. Pet restrict(B). Partial handicap access, no tents. Big rig sites, eco-friendly, 2015 rates: $42. Apr 1 to Nov 30. No CC.
(215)362-6030 Lat: 40.26848, Lon: -75.303431
2151 Koffel Rd, Hatfield, PA 19440
villagesceneinfo@gmail.com
www.villagesceneinfo.com
See ad pages 1008, 974.

PA

HAWLEY — B10 *Pike*

➔ WILSONVILLE REC AREA **Ratings: 6/7/7** (Campground) 2015 rates: $28 to $32. Apr 29 to Oct 16. (570)226-4382 113 Ammon Dr, Hawley, PA 18428

HEGINS — D7 *Schuylkill*

➔ **CAMP-A-WHILE**
Ratings: 8/8.5★/9 (Campground) From jct of I-81 & PA-25 (exit 112): Go W 1 mi on PA-25 (L). **FAC:** Gravel rds. 96 gravel, 4 pull-thrus (40 x 70), back-ins (23 x 40), 96 full hkups (30 amps), WiFi Hotspot, tent sites, laundry, groc, LP gas, fire rings, firewood. **REC:** pool, Pine Creek: fishing, playground. Pet restrict(Q). Eco-friendly, 2015 rates: $34 to $40. Apr 15 to Oct 25.
AAA Approved
(570)682-8696 Lat: 40.664531, Lon: -76.402201
1921 E Main St, Hegins, PA 17938
camping@epix.net
www.campawhilepa.com
See ad this page.

HERSHEY — E7 *Dauphin, Lebanon*

A SPOTLIGHT Introducing Hershey's colorful attractions appearing at the front of this state section.

HERSHEY (CONT)

HERSHEY See also Carlisle, Elizabethtown, Ephrata, Harrisburg, Jonestown, Lebanon, Manheim, Pine Grove, Ravine, York.

HERSHEYPARK CAMPING RESORT
Ratings: 9.5/10★/9 (Campground) E-bnd: From Jct of US 322/422 & Hwy 39W (Hershey Park Dr): Go 1/2 mi N on Hwy 39W (Hershey Park Dr) (L) W-bnd: From Jct of I-81 & Hwy 39E (exit 77): Go 6 mi W on Hwy 39E, then 1 mi W on Hershey Park Dr (R).

YEAR ROUND CAMPING IN HERSHEY
Hersheypark Camping Resort offers year-round family camping just minutes from your favorite Hershey attractions, including Hersheypark! For reservations, call 717-534-8999 or visit HersheyparkCampingResort.com.

FAC: All weather rds. 262 Avail: 262 all weather, 87 pull-thrus (24 x 50), back-ins (24 x 40), 250 full hkups, 12 W, 12 E (30/50 amps), cable, WiFi, tent sites, rentals, dump, laundry, groc, LP gas, fire rings, firewood. **REC:** pool, wading pool, Swatara Creek: shuffleboard, playground. Pets OK. Partial handicap access. 14 day max stay, eco-friendly, 2015 rates: $41 to $75. Disc: military. ATM.
(717)534-8999 Lat: 40.27266, Lon: -76.68993
1200 Sweet Street, Hummelstown, PA 17036
HersheyparkCampingResort@hersheypa.com
www.HersheyparkCampingResort.com
See ad page 984 (Spotlight Hershey).

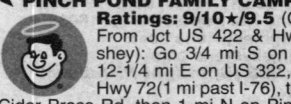

PINCH POND FAMILY CAMPGROUND
Ratings: 9/10★/9.5 (Campground) From Jct US 422 & Hwy 743 (in Hershey): Go 3/4 mi S on Hwy 743, then 12-1/4 mi E on US 322, then 3 mi S on Hwy 72(1 mi past I-76), then 1/2 mi W on Cider Press Rd, then 1 mi N on Pinch Rd(R). **FAC:** Paved/gravel rds. (186 spaces). Avail: 121 gravel, 53 pull-thrus (35 x 60), back-ins (30 x 55), 107 full hkups, 14 W, 14 E (30/50 amps), seasonal sites, cable, WiFi $, tent sites, rentals, dump, laundry, groc, LP gas, fire rings, firewood, controlled access. **REC:** pool, pond, fishing, playground. Pets OK. Partial handicap access. Big rig sites, eco-friendly, 2015 rates: $42 to $47. Disc: AAA.
(800)659-7640 Lat: 40.229546, Lon: -76.45227
3075 Pinch Rd, Manheim, PA 17545
jmspond@aol.com
www.pinchpond.com
See primary listing at Manheim and ad page 988 (Spotlight Lancaster County).

HESSTON — D5 *Huntingdon*

PLEASANT HILLS CAMPGROUND **Ratings: 8.5/8.5★/8.5** (Campground) 2015 rates: $37 to $49. Apr 15 to Oct 15. (814)658-3986 12733 Pleasant Hills Dr, Hesston, PA 16647

HOBBIE — C8 *Luzerne*

MOYER'S GROVE CAMPGROUND **Ratings: 7/6/6.5** (Campground) 2015 rates: $33 to $41. (800)722-1912 309 Moyers Grove Rd, Wapwallopen, PA 18660

HOLTWOOD — E8 *Lancaster*

MUDDY RUN RECREATION PARK (EXELON ENERGY) **Ratings: 6/8.5★/7** (Campground) 2015 rates: $30. Mar 30 to Oct 31. (717)284-5850 172 Bethesda Church Rd, Holtwood, PA 17532

TUCQUAN PARK FAMILY CAMPGROUND
Ratings: 8.5/8.5★/8.5 (Campground) From Jct Hwy 272 & Hwy 372: Go 5 mi W on Hwy 372, then 2 mi N on River Rd(R). **FAC:** Gravel rds. (155 spaces). Avail: 75 gravel, 41 pull-thrus (30 x 60), back-ins (25 x 40), 68 full hkups, 7 W, 7 E (30/50 amps), seasonal sites, WiFi, tent sites, rentals, dump, laundry, groc, LP gas, fire rings, firewood. **REC:** pool, pond, fishing, playground. Pets OK. Partial handicap access. Big rig sites, eco-friendly, 2015 rates: $43 to $47. Disc: military. ATM.
(717)284-2156 Lat: 39.857869, Lon: -76.330519
917 River Rd, Holtwood, PA 17532
tucquanpark@aol.com
www.camptucquanpark.com
See ad pages 988 (Spotlight Lancaster County), 974 & RV Trips of a Lifetime in Magazine Section.

HONESDALE — B9 *Wayne*

HONESDALE/POCONOS KOA **Ratings: 8/8★/7.5** (Campground) 2015 rates: $45 to $59.50. Mar 1 to Dec 15. (570)253-0424 50 Countryside Lane, Honesdale, PA 18431

PONDEROSA PINES CAMPGROUND Ratings: 7.5/8.5★/7.5 (Campground) From Jct US 6 & Hwy 170: Go 3-1/2 mi N on Hwy 170, then 1-1/4 mi E on Beech Grove Dr, then 1 mi N on Alden Rd(R). **FAC:** Gravel rds. (103 spaces). 53 Avail: 11 gravel, 42 grass, 4 pull-thrus (30 x 65), back-ins (30 x 60), 9 full hkups, 44 W, 44 E (30 amps), seasonal sites, WiFi Hotspot, tent sites, rentals, showers $, dump, mobile sewer, laundry, groc, LP gas, fire rings, firewood. **REC:** heated pool, Lake Ponderosa: fishing, playground, rec open to public. Pet restrict(B/Q). Eco-friendly, 2015 rates: $40 to $45. Apr 18 to Oct 19.
(570)253-2080 Lat: 41.655866, Lon: -75.335094
31 Ponderosa Dr, Honesdale, PA 18431
ponderosapines@verizon.net
www.ponderosapinescampground.com

HOP BOTTOM — B9 *Susquehanna*

SHORE FOREST CAMPGROUND Ratings: 8/8.5★/7 (Campground) From Jct I-81(exit 211) & HWY 106/HWY 92: Go 1-1/2 mi W on Hwy 106, then 3-1/2 mi W on Hop Bottom Rd, then 1/2 mi W on Forest St(R). **FAC:** Gravel rds. (160 spaces). Avail: 40 gravel, 7 pull-thrus (25 x 60), back-ins (30 x 50), 23 full hkups, 17 W, 17 E (30/50 amps), seasonal sites, cable, WiFi Hotspot, tent sites, rentals, dump, laundry, groc, LP bottles, fire rings, firewood. **REC:** heated pool, whirlpool, pond, fishing, playground. Pets OK. 2015 rates: $30 to $48. Apr 15 to Nov 1.
(570)289-4666 Lat: 41.70980, Lon: -75.75677
121 The Driveway, Hop Bottom, PA 18824
shoreforest@gmail.com
www.shoreforestcampground.com

HOWARD — C6 *Centre*

BALD EAGLE (RUSSEL P. LETTERMAN CAMPGROUND) (State Pk) From jct I-80 (exit 158) & Hwy 150: Go 9 mi N on Hwy 150. 2015 rates: $15 to $28. Apr 15 to Dec 15. (814)625-2775

PRIMITIVE CAMPGROUND AT BALD EAGLE (State Pk) I-80 (exit 158) & Hwy 150: Go 8 mi N on Rt 150 to Rt 26 S and turn right, go another 1.5 mi and left at the sign (Primitive Campground). Pit toilets. 2015 rates: $15 to $28. Apr 15 to Dec 15. (814)625-2775

HUNTINGDON — D5 *Huntingdon*

HUNTINGDON FAIRGROUNDS CAMPGROUND (Public) From jct US 22 & SR-3035: Go 1 mi SW on SR-3035. 2015 rates: $20. (814)643-2274

INDIANA — D3 *Armstrong*

WHEEL-IN CAMPGROUND
Ratings: 6.5/9.5★/9.5 (Campground) From Jct US 422 & Hwy 210: G 1/2 mi E on US 422, then 1/2 mi E o Dutch Run Rd, then 1/4 mi N on Plum creek Rd(L). **FAC:** Paved rds. (9 spaces). Avail: 40 grass, 12 pull-thrus (50 x 50 back-ins (50 x 50), 2 full hkups, 38 W, 38 E (30/5 amps), seasonal sites, WiFi, tent sites, rentals, dump mobile sewer, fire rings, firewood, controlled access **REC:** Plum Creek: fishing, shuffleboard, playground Pets OK. Eco-friendly, 2015 rates: $32 to $39. Disc military. Apr 15 to Oct 15.
(724)354-3693 Lat: 40.692597, Lon: -79.32719
113 Wheel In Campground Rd, Shelocta, P 15774
wheelin@windstream.net
wheelincampground.net
See ad this page, 974.

INTERCOURSE — E8 *Lancaster*

BEACON HILL CAMPING Ratings: 7/9.5★ (RV Park) From Jct of Hwy 340 & Hwy 772 W (i Intercourse): Go 1/2 mi N on Hwy 772 W(R). **FAC** Gravel rds. (38 spaces). Avail: 34 gravel, 12 pull-thru (27 x 48), back-ins (27 x 40), 34 full hkups (30/5 amps), seasonal sites, WiFi, tent sites, rentals, laun dry, LP gas, fire rings, firewood. **REC.** Pets OK. Pa tial handicap access. Eco-friendly, 2015 rates: $42 Apr 11 to Nov 1.
AAA Approved
(717)768-8775 Lat: 40.046281, Lon: -76.114554
128 Beacon Hill Dr., Ronks, PA 17572
beaconhillcamping@gmail.com
www.beaconhillcamping.com

JAMESTOWN — B1 *Crawford, Mercer*

PYMATUNING (State Pk) From Jct of US-322 SR-58, W 5 mi on US-322 (R). 2015 rates: $15 to $28 Apr 15 to Oct 15. (724)932-3142

JEFFERSON — E2 *Greene*

FIREHOUSE RV CAMPGROUND
Ratings: 5.5/8/7 (RV Park) From Jct I-79 (ex 19) & Hwy 19: Go 1/4 mi S on Hwy 19, the 4 mi E on Hwy 221, then 4 mi E on Hwy 18 (L). **FAC:** Gravel rds. (55 spaces). Avail: 10 gravel, pull-thrus (40 x 60), back-ins (25 x 60), accepts fu hkup units only, 10 full hkups (30/50 amps), seasona sites, WiFi, laundry. **REC.** Pets OK. No tents. Big ri sites, 2015 rates: $30. ATM, no CC.
(724)833-1955 Lat: 39.93414, Lon: -80.05331
1483 Jefferson Rd, Jefferson, PA 15344
JVFC20@windstream.net
See ad this page.

JERSEY SHORE — C6 *Clinton*

RAVENSBURG (State Pk) From town: Go 12 mi on Hwy 44 & Hwy 880. 2015 rates: $15 to $28. Ma 21 to Sep 21. (570)966-1455

JIM THORPE — C9 *Carbon*

JIM THORPE CAMPING RESORT Rat ings: 7.5/7/7 (Campground) From Jct I-476 & US 2 (exit 74): Go 6 mi S on US 209, then 2-1/4 mi W o W Broadway(L). **FAC:** Paved/gravel rds. (14 spaces). Avail: 92 gravel, 30 pull-thrus (25 x 50 back-ins (22 x 45), 51 full hkups, 41 W, 41 E (30/5 amps), seasonal sites, cable, WiFi Hotspot, tent sites rentals, dump, laundry, groc, LP gas, fire rings, fire wood, controlled access. **REC:** pool, wading poo Mauch Chunk Creek: fishing, playground. Pets OK Partial handicap access. 2015 rates: $36 to $49 Disc: AAA, military. Apr 1 to Oct 31.
AAA Approved
(570)325-2644 Lat: 40.854045, Lon: -75.776571
129 Lentz Trail, Jim Thorpe, PA 18229
camper1@ptd.net
www.jimthorpecamping.com

JONESTOWN — D7 *Lebanon*

JONESTOWN AOK CAMPGROUND
Ratings: 7.5/9★/7.5 (Campground) From Jct Hwy 72 & US 22: Go E 2.5 mile E on US 22 to Old Rte 22, SW 0.5 mi o Old Rte 22 (R). **FAC:** Paved/gravel rds (97 spaces). Avail: 89 gravel, 60 pull thrus (24 x 60), back-ins (25 x 40), some side by side hkups, 89 full hkups (30/50 amps), seasonal sites WiFi Hotspot, tent sites, rentals, dump, laundry, groc LP gas, fire rings, firewood. **REC:** pool, playground Pets OK. Partial handicap access. Eco-friendly, 201 rates: $45.
(717)865-2526 Lat: 40.42286, Lon: -76.46684
145 Old Route 22, Jonestown, PA 17038
camping@jonestownAOKcampground1.com
JonestownAOKCampground.com
See ad pages 985 (Spotlight Hershey), 974.

JONESTOWN (CONT)

JONESTOWN/HERSHEY KOA **Ratings: 8.5/9.5★/8.5** (Campground) 2015 rates: $36 to $52. (800)562-2609 11 Lickdale Rd, Jonestown, PA 17038

KIRKWOOD — E8 *Lancaster*

D & J SHADY REST
Ratings: 5/7/7.5 (Campground) From Jct of Hwy 372 & Hwy 472: Go 7 1/4 mi SE on Hwy 472(L). **FAC:** Paved/gravel rds. (89 spaces). Avail: 24 gravel, back-ins (40 x 40), 24 full hkups (30 amps), seasonal sites, WiFi, rentals, dump, fire rings, firewood. **REC:** playground. Pet restrict(Q). Partial handicap access, no tents. 2015 rates: $45.
(717)529-2020 Lat: 39.83814, Lon: -76.05786
2085 Kirkwood Pike, Kirkwood, PA 17536
djshadyrest@yahoo.com
www.djshadyrest.com
See ad this page.

KNOX — C2 *Clarion*

WOLFS CAMPING RESORT Ratings: 7.5/8★/7 (Campground) From Jct I-80(exit 53) & SR 3007: Go 1 Bk N on SR 3007(R). **FAC:** Paved/gravel rds. (500 spaces). 100 Avail: 50 gravel, 50 grass, 40 pull-thrus (30 x 65), back-ins (30 x 50), some side by side hkups, 100 full hkups (30/50 amps), seasonal sites, cable, WiFi Hotspot, tent sites, rentals, dump, laundry, groc, LP gas, fire rings, firewood, restaurant, controlled access. **REC:** heated pool, whirlpool, pond, fishing, golf, shuffleboard, playground, rec open to public. Pets OK. Partial handicap access. Big rig sites, 2015 rates: $35 to $50. Disc: AAA, military. Apr 15 to Oct 31. ATM.
AAA Approved
(800)850-9252 Lat: 41.187649, Lon: -79.542174
308 Timberwolf Run, Knox, PA 16232
info@wolfscampingresort.com
www.wolfscampingresort.com

KUTZTOWN — D9 *Berks*

PINE HILL RV PARK **Ratings: 6.5/9★/8.5** (RV Park) 2015 rates: $46 to $48. Apr 1 to Nov 1. (610)285-6776 268 Old Rte 22, Kutztown, PA 19530

LAKE ARIEL — B9 *Wayne*

SECLUDED ACRES CAMPGROUND **Ratings: 7/7.5/7** (Campground) 2015 rates: $35 to $40. Apr 15 to Oct 15. (570)226-9959 150 Marty's Main St, Lake Ariel, PA 18436

LAKE CITY — A1 *Erie*

CAMP ERIEZ
Ratings: 7/9★/8.5 (Campground) From Jct I-90(exit 16) & Hwy 98: Go 3-1/4 mi N on Hwy 98, then 2-3/4 mi W on Hwy 5(R). **FAC:** Paved rds. (177 spaces). Avail: 15 gravel, 15 pull-thrus (35 x 66), 15 W, 15 E (30/50 amps), seasonal sites, dump, fire rings, firewood, controlled access. **REC:** heated pool, Lake Erie: fishing, playground. Pets OK. No tents. 2015 rates: $35. May 1 to Oct 31. No CC.
(814)774-8381 Lat: 42.032942, Lon: -80.321238
9356 W Lake Rd, Lake City, PA 16423
bart4262@yahoo.com
See ad pages 980 (Spotlight Erie), 974.

Exclusive! According to our research, restroom cleanliness is of the utmost concern to RVers. Of course, you knew that already. The cleanest campgrounds have a star in their restroom rating!

Want to Know How We Rate Campgrounds?

RATED
10/10★/10

Turn to the "Understand the Campground Rating System" to find out how we rate and inspect parks.

LANCASTER — E8 *Lancaster*

LANCASTER AREA MAP

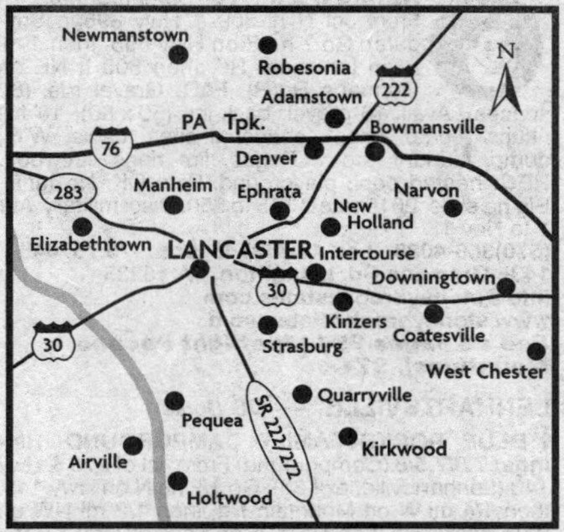

Symbols on map indicate towns within a 30 mile radius of Lancaster where campgrounds are listed. Check listings for more information.

See also Adamstown, Airville, Bowmansville, Coatesville, Denver, Downingtown, Elizabethtown, Ephrata, Holtwood, Intercourse, Kinzers, Kirkwood, Manheim, Narvon, New Holland, Newmanstown, Pequea, Quarryville, Robesonia, Strasburg & West Chester.

A SPOTLIGHT Introducing Lancaster County's colorful attractions appearing at the front of this state section.

COUNTRY ACRES CAMPGROUND
Ratings: 9/9.5★/9.5 (Campground) From Jct US 30 & Hwy 896: Go 2-1/2 mi E on US 30, then 300 ft N on Leven Rd(L). **FAC:** Gravel rds. 92 gravel, 28 pull-thrus (36 x 60), back-ins (30 x 40), 74 full hkups, 18 W, 18 E (30/50 amps), cable, WiFi, tent sites, rentals, dump, laundry, groc, fire rings, firewood, controlled access. **REC:** pool, shuffleboard, playground. Pets OK. Partial handicap access. Big rig sites, 14 day max stay, eco-friendly, 2015 rates: $46 to $62. Disc: AAA. Mar 17 to Nov 26.
AAA Approved
(866)675-4745 Lat: 40.015154, Lon: -76.146276
20 Leven Rd, Gordonville, PA 17529
countryacres@bird-in-hand.com
www.countryacrescampground.com
See ad pages 988 (Spotlight Lancaster County), 974.

FLORY'S COTTAGES & CAMPING
Ratings: 8/9.5★/8.5 (Campground) From Jct US 30 & Hwy 896: Go 1-1/2 mi E on US 30, then 1/2 mi N on Ronks Rd(R). **FAC:** Gravel rds. (71 spaces). Avail: 62 gravel, 1 pull-thrus (30 x 100), back-ins (30 x 50), 62 full hkups (30/50 amps), seasonal sites, cable, WiFi, tent sites, rentals, dump, laundry, groc. **REC:** playground. Pets OK. Big rig sites, eco-friendly, 2015 rates: $39 to $56.
(717)687-6670 Lat: 40.025031, Lon: -76.167475
99 North Ronks Rd, Ronks, PA 17572
info@floryscamping.com
www.floryscamping.com
See ad pages 988 (Spotlight Lancaster County), 974.

MILL BRIDGE VILLAGE AND CAMPRESORT
Ratings: 8.5/8.5★/8.5 (Campground) From Jct of US 30 & Hwy 896: Go 1-1/2 mi E on US 30, then 1/2 mi S on Ronks Rd(L). **FAC:** Paved/gravel rds. (104 spaces). 92 Avail: 52 gravel, 40 grass, 11 pull-thrus (25 x 50), back-ins (25 x 45), some side by side hkups, 60 full hkups, 32 W, 32 E (30/50 amps), seasonal sites, WiFi, tent sites, rentals, dump, laundry, groc, fire rings, firewood. **REC:** heated pool, Pequea Creek: fishing, shuffleboard, playground, rec open to public. Pet restrict(B/Q). 2015 rates: $42 to $67. Disc: AAA, military.
AAA Approved
(717)687-8181 Lat: 40.007094, Lon: -76.158775
101 S. Ronks Rd, Ronks, PA 17572
info@millbridge.com
www.millbridge.com
See ad pages 988 (Spotlight Lancaster County), 974.

OLD MILL STREAM CAMPGROUND
Ratings: 8/10★/8.5 (Campground) W-bnd: From Jct of US 30 & Hwy 896: Go 1-1/4 mi W on US 30 (R); E-bnd: From Jct of US 30 & US 222: Go 4-1/2 mi E on US 30 (L). **FAC:** Paved/gravel rds. 142 gravel, 5 pull-thrus (25 x 60), back-ins (25 x 50), 137 full hkups, 5 W, 5 E (30/50 amps), cable, WiFi, tent sites, rentals, dump, laundry, groc, LP gas, fire rings, firewood. **REC:** Old Mill Stream: fishing, playground. Pet restrict(Q). Partial handicap access. Big rig sites, 14 day max stay, eco-friendly, 2015 rates: $50 to $65. ATM.
(717)299-2314 Lat: 40.026926, Lon: -76.218411
2249 Lincoln Hwy (US 30E), Lancaster, PA 17602
info@oldmillstreamcampground.com
www.oldmillstreamcampground.com
See ad page 988 (Spotlight Lancaster County).

PINCH POND FAMILY CAMPGROUND
Ratings: 9/10★/9.5 (Campground) From the Jct of SR 741 & SR 283, N. 2 mi. On SR 741 to SR 722, E. 9.9 mi on SR 722 to Pinch Rd., W 1.5 mi (R). **FAC:** Paved/gravel rds. (186 spaces). Avail: 121 gravel, 53 pull-thrus (35 x 60), back-ins (30 x 55), 107 full hkups, 14 W, 14 E (30/50 amps), seasonal sites, cable, WiFi $, tent sites, rentals, dump, laundry, groc, LP gas, fire rings, firewood, controlled access. **REC:** pool, pond, fishing, playground. Pets OK. Partial handicap access. Big rig sites, eco-friendly, 2015 rates: $42 to $47. Disc: AAA. No CC.
(800)659-7640 Lat: 40.229546, Lon: -76.45227
3075 Pinch Rd., Manheim, PA 17545
jmspond@aol.com
www.pinchpond.com
See primary listing at Manheim and ad page 988 (Spotlight Lancaster County).

SHADY GROVE CAMPGROUND
Ratings: 9/10★/9 (Campground) From US 30 E/US 222 N: Go 16-1/4 mi E on US 222 N, then 1-3/4 mi NE on Hwy 272/N Reading Rd, then 1/2 mi N on W Swartzville Rd/Hwy 897, then 1/2 mi W on Poplar Dr(R). **FAC:** Gravel rds. (125 spaces). Avail: 65 gravel, 4 pull-thrus (25 x 60), back-ins (30 x 42), 65 full hkups (30/50 amps), seasonal sites, cable, WiFi, tent sites, rentals, laundry, LP gas, fire rings, firewood. **REC:** pool, Spirit Lake: playground. Pet restrict(B). Partial handicap access. Big rig sites, eco-friendly, 2015 rates: $53 to $58.
(717)484-4225 Lat: 40.238733, Lon: -76.084167
65 Poplar Dr, Denver, PA 17517
office@shadygrovecampground.com
www.shadygrovecampground.com
See primary listing at Adamstown and ad page 988 (Spotlight Lancaster County).

TUCQUAN PARK FAMILY CAMPGROUND
Ratings: 8.5/8.5★/8.5 (Campground) From jct US-222 (Hwy 272 N) and Hwy 462 W: Go 13 mi S on Hwy 272 N, then 5 mi SW on Holtwood Rd/Hwy 372, then 2 mi NW on River Rd(R). **FAC:** Gravel rds. (155 spaces). Avail: 75 gravel, 41 pull-thrus (30 x 60), back-ins (25 x 40), 68 full hkups, 7 W, 7 E (30/50 amps), seasonal sites, WiFi, tent sites, rentals, dump, laundry, groc, fire rings, firewood. **REC:** pool, pond, fishing, playground. Pets OK. Partial handicap access. Big rig sites, eco-friendly, 2015 rates: $43 to $47. Disc: military. ATM.
(717)284-2156 Lat: 39.857869, Lon: -76.330519
917 River Rd, Holtwood, PA 17532
tucquanpark@aol.com
www.camptucquanpark.com
See primary listing at Holtwood and ad page 988 (Spotlight Lancaster County).

Travel Services

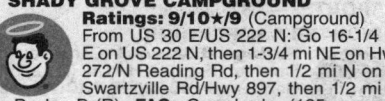

MELLOTT BROTHERS TRAILER SALES Sales of new and used motorhomes, fifth wheels and towables. Service and repair. Extensive inventory of parts and supplies. (Extended Spring, Summer & Fall Hrs.). **SERVICES:** RV, RV appliance, MH mechanical, engine/chassis repair, restrooms, RV Sales. RV supplies, LP, dump, emer-

PA

LANCASTER (CONT)

MELLOTT BROTHERS TRAILER (CONT)
gency parking, RV accessible. waiting room. Hours: 8am to 5pm, Mon-Fri.
(717)464-2311 Lat: 39.985806, Lon: -76.283627
2718 Willow Street Pike, Rte 272 North, Willow Street, PA 17584
sales@mellottbrothers.com
www.mellottbrothers.com
See ad page 969 (Welcome Section).

Things to See and Do

DISCOVER LANCASTER CONVENTION & VISITORS BUREAU Tourism Information. (Hours: Memorial weekend to Oct 31, 9am to 5pm, Mon-Sat; 10am to 4pm Sun. Nov 1 to Memorial weekend, 10am to 4pm Mon-Sun). Partial handicap access. RV accessible. Restrooms. Hours: 9am to 5pm Mon-Sat, 10am to 4pm Sun.
(800)723-8824 Lat: 40.051825, Lon: -76.255621
501 Greenfield Rd, Lancaster, PA 17601
info@padutchcountry.com
www.padutchcountry.com
See ad pages 988 (Spotlight Lancaster County), 990 (Spotlight Lancaster County).

DUTCH WONDERLAND FAMILY AMUSEMENT PARK Family fun attraction including 31 family rides, shows, mini-golf, exhibits and new water play area. May 1 to Oct 15. partial handicap access. RV accessible. Restrooms, food. Hours: 10am to 8:30pm. Adult fee: $39.99. ATM.
(866)386-2839 Lat: 40.026926, Lon: -76.218411
2249 Lincoln Hwy (US-30E), Lancaster, PA 17602
infodw@dutchwonderland.com
www.dutchwonderland.com
See ad page 988 (Spotlight Lancaster County).

LAPORTE — B7 *Sullivan*

PIONEER CAMPGROUND
Ratings: 8.5/9★/9.5 (Campground) From Jct US 220 & Hwy 42 (in Laporte): Go S 2 mi on US 220(R). **FAC:** All weather rds. (71 spaces). Avail: 41 gravel, back-ins (45 x 60), 41 W, 41 E (30/50 amps), seasonal sites, cable, WiFi, tent sites, rentals, dump, mobile sewer, laundry, groc, LP gas, fire rings, firewood. **REC:** heated pool, playground. Pet restrict(Q). Eco-friendly, 2015 rates: $40 to $50. Disc: AAA, military. Apr 1 to Dec 7.
AAA Approved
(570)946-9971 Lat: 41.399686, Lon: -76.505367
307 Pioneer Trail, Muncy Valley, PA 17758
pioneercg@epix.net
www.pioneercampground.com
See ad this page, 974.

LAWRENCEVILLE — A6 *Tioga*

TOMPKINS REC AREA (COE - COWANESQUE LAKE) (Public Corps) From jct Hwy 49 & US 15: Go 1/4 mi N on US 15, then 3 mi W on Bliss Rd. 2015 rates: $20 to $34. May 15 to Sep 29. (570)835-5281

LEHIGHTON — C9 *Carbon*

STONEYBROOK CAMPGROUND
Ratings: 9/9★/10 (Campground) From Jct Hwy 309 & Hwy 895(in Snyders): Go 7 mi E on Hwy 895, then 1 mi S on Lauchnor Rd, then 500 ft NE on Germans Rd(R). **FAC:** Gravel rds. (82 spaces). Avail: 16 gravel, back-ins (50 x 60), 16 full hkups (30/50 amps), seasonal sites, cable, WiFi, dump, laundry, groc, LP gas, fire rings, firewood. **REC:** heated pool, playground. Pets OK. No tents. Big rig sites, 2015 rates: $45 to $50. Disc: military. Apr 1 to Nov 1.
(570)386-4088 Lat: 40.758746, Lon: -75.757046
1435 Gremans Rd, Lehighton, PA 18235
info@stoneybrookestates.com
www.stoneybrookestates.com
See ad pages 994 (Spotlight Pocono Mountains), 974.

LENHARTSVILLE — D8 *Berks*

BLUE ROCKS FAMILY CAMPGROUND Ratings: 7.5/7.5/8 (Campground) From Jct of I-78 & Hwy 143 (Lenhartsville, exit 35): Go 1/2 mi N on Hwy 143, then 1/4 mi W on Mountain Rd, then 1/2 mi NW on Blue Rocks Rd, then 1/4 mi N on Sousley Rd(L). **FAC:** Gravel rds. (115 spaces). Avail: 40 gravel, 2 pull-thrus (30 x 40), back-ins (30 x 40), 11 full hkups, 29 W, 29 E (20/30 amps), seasonal sites, WiFi Hotspot, tent sites, rentals, dump, mobile sewer, laundry, groc, LP gas, fire rings, firewood, controlled access. **REC:** heated pool, wading pool, pond, fishing, playground, rec open to public. Pets OK. 2015 rates: $46 to $53. Apr 1 to Nov 1.
AAA Approved
(866)478-5276 Lat: 40.570012, Lon: -75.908951
341 Sousley Rd, Lenhartsville, PA 19534
camp@bluerockscampground.com
www.bluerockscampground.com

LEWISBURG — C7 *Union*

LEWISBURG See also Bloomsburg, Catawissa, Elysburg, Milton, Montgomery, New Columbia, Potters Mills, Selinsgrove, Sunbury.

LITTLE MEXICO CAMPGROUND **Ratings: 7.5/7.5/9** (Campground) 2015 rates: $39 to $45. Apr 15 to Oct 28. (570)374-9742 1640 Little Mexico Rd, Winfield, PA 17889

R B WINTER (State Pk) From Jct of Hwy 192 & Rte 15, W 18 mi on Hwy 192 (R). 2015 rates: $15 to $28. Apr 15 to Dec 15. (570)966-1455

LEWISTOWN — D6 *Mifflin*

WATERSIDE CAMPGROUND & RV PARK
Ratings: 9/9★/9 (Campground) From Jct Hwy 103 (in Lewistown) & US 22: Go 2-1/2 mi SW on US 22(W 4th St), then 2 mi SE on Loop Rd, then 1/2 mi S on Locust Rd (E). **FAC:** Paved/gravel rds. (236 spaces). Avail: 91 gravel, back-ins (30 x 60), 91 full hkups (30/50 amps), seasonal sites, WiFi, tent sites, rentals, showers $, dump, laundry, groc, LP gas, fire rings, firewood, controlled access. **REC:** heated pool, Juniata River: fishing, playground. Pet restrict(Q). Partial handicap access. Big rig sites 2015 rates: $47 to $54. Disc: AAA, military.
(717)248-3974 Lat: 40.558808, Lon: -77.598925
475 Locust Rd, Lewistown, PA 17044
staff@watersidecampground.com
www.watersidecampground.com
See ad this page, 974, 970 (PA Map).

Things to See and Do

BOAT RIDE - HISTORIC PENNSYLVANIA CANAL A narrated boat ride on the Pennsylvania Canal. May 25 to Oct 31. Restrooms Hours: 10am to 12pm. Adult fee: $5.
(717)248-3974 Lat: 40.558808, Lon: -77.598925
475 Locust Rd, Lewistown, PA 17044
staff@watersidecampground.com
www.watersidecampground.com
See ad this page, 970 (PA Map).

LIVERPOOL — D7 *Perry*

FERRYBOAT CAMPSITES Ratings: 7/8★/6. (Campground) From jct US 22/322 & US 11/1 (Northeast of Duncannon): Go 10-1/2 mi N on U 11/15, then 1 block E on Ferry Ln (E). **FAC** Paved/gravel rds. (278 spaces). 58 Avail: 20 grave 30 grass, 8 dirt, 10 pull-thrus (35 x 60), back-in (30 x 45), mostly side by side hkups, 55 full hkups, W, 3 E (30/50 amps), seasonal sites, cable, WiFi, te sites, rentals, dump, laundry, groc, LP gas, fire ring firewood. **REC:** Susquehanna River: fishing, shuffle board, playground. Pets OK. 2015 rates: $41 to $6 Disc: AAA, military. Apr 15 to Oct 31.
AAA Approved
(800)759-8707 Lat: 40.543513, Lon: -76.98287
32 Ferry Ln, Liverpool, PA 17045
ferryboat@tricountyi.net
www.ferryboatcampsites.com

LOGANTON — C6 *Clinton*

HOLIDAY PINES CAMPGROUND **Ratings: 8/8.5★/8** (Campground) 2015 rates: $38 t $43. Apr 1 to Dec 15. (570)725-2267 16 Pine Tre Lane, Loganton, PA 17747

LOYSVILLE — D6 *Perry*

PARADISE STREAM FAMILY CAMPGROUND
Ratings: 9/9.5★/10 (Campground) From Jct of Hwy 850 & Hwy 274 (in Loysville): Go 4-1/2 mi W on Hwy 274, the 1/4 mi S on Rt 3008 (Couchtown Rd then 1/2 mi SW on Paradise Stream Rd (R) Note: N GPS after Loysville. **FAC:** Gravel rds. (196 spaces 126 Avail: 95 gravel, 31 grass, 21 pull-thrus (40 x 75 back-ins (40 x 50), 95 full hkups, 31 W, 31 E (30/5 amps), seasonal sites, WiFi, tent sites, rentals, dum laundry, groc, LP gas, fire rings, firewood, controlle access. **REC:** heated pool, Sherman's Creek: fishin shuffleboard, playground. Pet restrict(Q). Big ri sites, eco-friendly, 2015 rates: $52 to $61. Apr 8 t Oct 30.
(717)789-2117 Lat: 40.35091, Lon: -77.424438
693 Paradise Stream Rd, Loysville, PA 17047
campparadise@embarqmail.com
www.campparadisestream.com
See ad pages 978 (Spotlight Carlisle), 974

MADISON — E2 *Westmoreland*

MADISON/PITTSBURGH SE KOA
Ratings: 8.5/8.5★/8.5 (Campground) Fro Jct I-70 & Hwy 66: Go 6 mi W on I-70(exit 54 then 1/2 mi S on Waltz Mill Road(R). **FAC** Gravel rds. (128 spaces). Avail: 60 gravel, 60 pul thrus (30 x 60), 60 full hkups (30/50 amps), season sites, cable, WiFi, tent sites, rentals, dump, laundr groc, LP gas, fire rings, firewood, controlled acces **REC:** heated pool, Tanglewood Lake: fishing, pla ground. Pet restrict(B). Partial handicap access. Bi rig sites, eco-friendly, 2015 rates: $44 to $59.
(800)562-4034 Lat: 40.207493, Lon: -79.6678431
764 Waltz Mill Rd, Ruffs Dale, PA 15679
kamping@pittsburghkoa.com
www.pittsburghkoa.com
See ad page 1009.

IAHANOY CITY — D8 *Schuylkill*

LOCUST LAKE (State Pk) From Jct of US-209 & rockton, N 3 mi to Locust Lake Rd, W 500 yds (E). 015 rates: $15 to $28. Apr 15 to Oct 20. (570)467-404

IANHEIM — E8 *Lancaster*

GRETNA OAKS CAMPING **Ratings: 3/7.5★/6.5** Campground) 2015 rates: $35 to $38. Apr 15 to Oct 1. (717)665-7120 2649 Camp Rd, Manheim, PA 7545

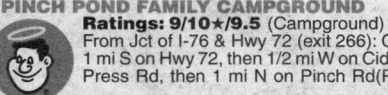

PINCH POND FAMILY CAMPGROUND
Ratings: 9/10★/9.5 (Campground)
From Jct of I-76 & Hwy 72 (exit 266): Go 1 mi S on Hwy 72, then 1/2 mi W on Cider Press Rd, then 1 mi N on Pinch Rd(R).

THE CAMPING EXPERIENCE OF YOUR LIFE
ocated in the foothills of northern Lancaster County, ve offer the perfect combination of camping fun & ouring experience. Our goal: To give you the most nemorable & enjoyable camping experience of your fe!

AC: Paved/gravel rds. (186 spaces). Avail: 121 ravel, 53 pull-thrus (35 x 60), back-ins (30 x 55), 07 full hkups, 14 W, 14 E (30/50 amps), seasonal ites, cable, WiFi $, tent sites, rentals, dump, laundry, roc, LP gas, fire rings, firewood, controlled access. **REC:** pool, pond, fishing, playground. Pets OK. Paral handicap access. Big rig sites, eco-friendly, 2015 ates: $42 to $47. Disc: AAA.
AA Approved
800)659-7640 Lat: 40.229546, Lon: -76.45227
075 Pinch Rd, Manheim, PA 17545
nspond@aol.com
www.pinchpond.com
See ad pages 988 (Spotlight Lancaster County), 974.

IANSFIELD — B6 *Tioga*

BUCKTAIL CAMPING RESORT **Ratings: 8/8★/7.5** (Campground) 2015 rates: $41.75 to 68.75. Apr 15 to Oct 31. (570)662-2923 130 Bucktail Rd, Mansfield, PA 16933

IATAMORAS — B10 *Pike*

TRI-STATE RV PARK **Ratings: 3.5/5/4.5** (RV Park) 2015 rates: $38 to $40. (800)562-2663 400 Shay Ln, Matamoras, PA 18336A

IEADVILLE — B2 *Crawford*

MEADVILLE KOA Ratings: 9/10★/9 (Campground) From Jct I-79(exit 147A) & US 6/19: Go 1-1/5 mi NE on US 6/19, the 1/2 mi N on Park Ave, then 6 mi E on SR 27/North St(L). **FAC:** Gravel rds. (147 spaces). 70 Avail: 47 gravel, 23 grass, 34 pull-thrus 40 x 60), back-ins (40 x 55), 47 full hkups, 23 W, 23 (30/50 amps), seasonal sites, cable, WiFi, tent ites, rentals, dump, laundry, groc, LP gas, fire rings, rewood, controlled access. **REC:** pool, pond, fishing, playground. Pets OK. Partial handicap access. Big rig sites, eco-friendly, 2015 rates: $38 to $61. Apr 2 to Oct 16. ATM.
814)789-3251 Lat: 41.622653, Lon: -80.038787
5164 Hwy 27, Meadville, PA 16335
amp@meadvillekoa.com
www.meadvillekoa.com

IERCER — C1 *Mercer*

MERCER/GROVE CITY KOA **Ratings: 8.5/9★/8.5** (Campground) 2015 rates: $44 to 69. Apr 1 to Oct 31. (724)748-3160 1337 Butler Pike, Mercer, PA 16137

ROCKY SPRINGS CAMPGROUND **Ratings: 9/9★/9.5** (Campground) 2015 rates: $38 to 42. May 1 to Oct 20. (724)662-1568 84 Rocky Springs Rd, Mercer, PA 16137

RV VILLAGE CAMPING RESORT **Ratings: 8/8/8.5** (Campground) From Jct I-80(exit 15) & US 19: Go 2-1/2 mi N on Hwy 19, then 3 mi N on Hwy 58, then 1/2 mi W on Skyline Rd(R). **FAC:** Gravel ds. (324 spaces). Avail: 131 grass, back-ins 40 x 60), some side by side hkups, 11 full hkups, 120 W, 120 E (30/50 amps), seasonal sites, WiFi Hotspot , tent sites, dump, laundry, groc, fire rings, firewood. **REC:** pool, pond, fishing, shuffleboard, playground. Pet restrict(B). Partial handicap access. Big rig sites, 2015 rates: $30 to $35. Apr 1 to Oct 31.
AA Approved
724)662-4560 Lat: 41.247096, Lon: -80.281885
35 Skyline Dr, Mercer, PA 16137
vvillagecampground@gmail.com
www.rvvillages.com

IESHOPPEN — B8 *Susquehanna, Wyoming*

SLUMBER VALLEY CAMPGROUND **Ratings: 7.5/8.5★/7.5** (Campground) 2015 rates: $36 to 45. Apr 15 to Oct 15. (570)833-5208 248 Meshoppen Creek Rd, Meshoppen, PA 18630

MEXICO — D6 *Juniata*

BUTTONWOOD CAMPGROUND **Ratings: 8.5/8★/9** (Campground) 2015 rates: $50 to $65. Apr 1 to Oct 31. (717)436-8334 1515 E River Road, Mifflintown, PA 17059

MIFFLINBURG — C7 *Union*

HIDDEN VALLEY CAMPING RESORT **Ratings: 7.5/7.5/8.5** (Campground) 2015 rates: $38 to $43. Apr 14 to Oct 26. (570)966-1330 162 Hidden Valley Lane, Mifflinburg, PA 17844

MILFORD — C10 *Pike*

RIVER BEACH CAMPSITES **Ratings: 6/7/7.5** (Campground) 2015 rates: $41 to $48. Mar 15 to Nov 15. (800)FLOATKC 378 US 209, Milford, PA 18337

MILL RUN — E3 *Fayette*

MILL RUN YOGI BEAR'S JELLYSTONE CAMP RESORT **Ratings: 9/10★/9.5** (Campground) 2015 rates: $62 to $95. (800)439-9644 839 Mill Run Rd, Mill Run, PA 15464

MILTON — C7 *Northumberland*

YOGI AT SHANGRI-LA
Ratings: 8.5/9.5★/9 (Campground)
From Jct I-80 (exit 212A) & Hwy 147: Go 8 mi S on Hwy 147, then 1/4 mi NW on Hwy 405N, then 3/4 mi E on Hidden Paradise Rd (E).

Our Pennsylvania RV Campground facilities include everything to make your stay a relaxed and pleasant experience with daily, weekly and monthly rates and rentals available.

FAC: Gravel rds. (155 spaces). Avail: 97 gravel, 28 pull-thrus (30 x 60), back-ins (30 x 50), 41 full hkups, 56 W, 56 E (30/50 amps), seasonal sites, cable, WiFi, tent sites, rentals, dump, mobile sewer, laundry, groc, LP gas, fire rings, firewood. **REC:** heated pool, wading pool, Chillisquaque Creek: fishing, playground. Pet restrict(Q). Partial handicap access. Big rig sites, eco-friendly, 2015 rates: $44 to $51. Disc: AAA, military. ATM.
(570)524-4561 Lat: 40.942143, Lon: -76.852069
670 Hidden Paradise Rd, Milton, PA 17847
info@slcreek.com
www.JellystoneShangri-La.com
See ad pages 1006, 974 & Family Camping in Magazine Section.

Check out those views! From awe-inspiring redwood giants to the soaring towers of the Golden Gate Bridge, we've put the Spotlight on North America's most popular travel destinations. Turn to the Spotlight articles in our State and Province sections to learn more.

Set a Destination for Family Fun!

Check out our camping destinations highlighting the best places for camping with the family in every state and province. Find a great destination, then select one of the family-friendly campgrounds listed by region throughout the article in the front of this Guide.

PA

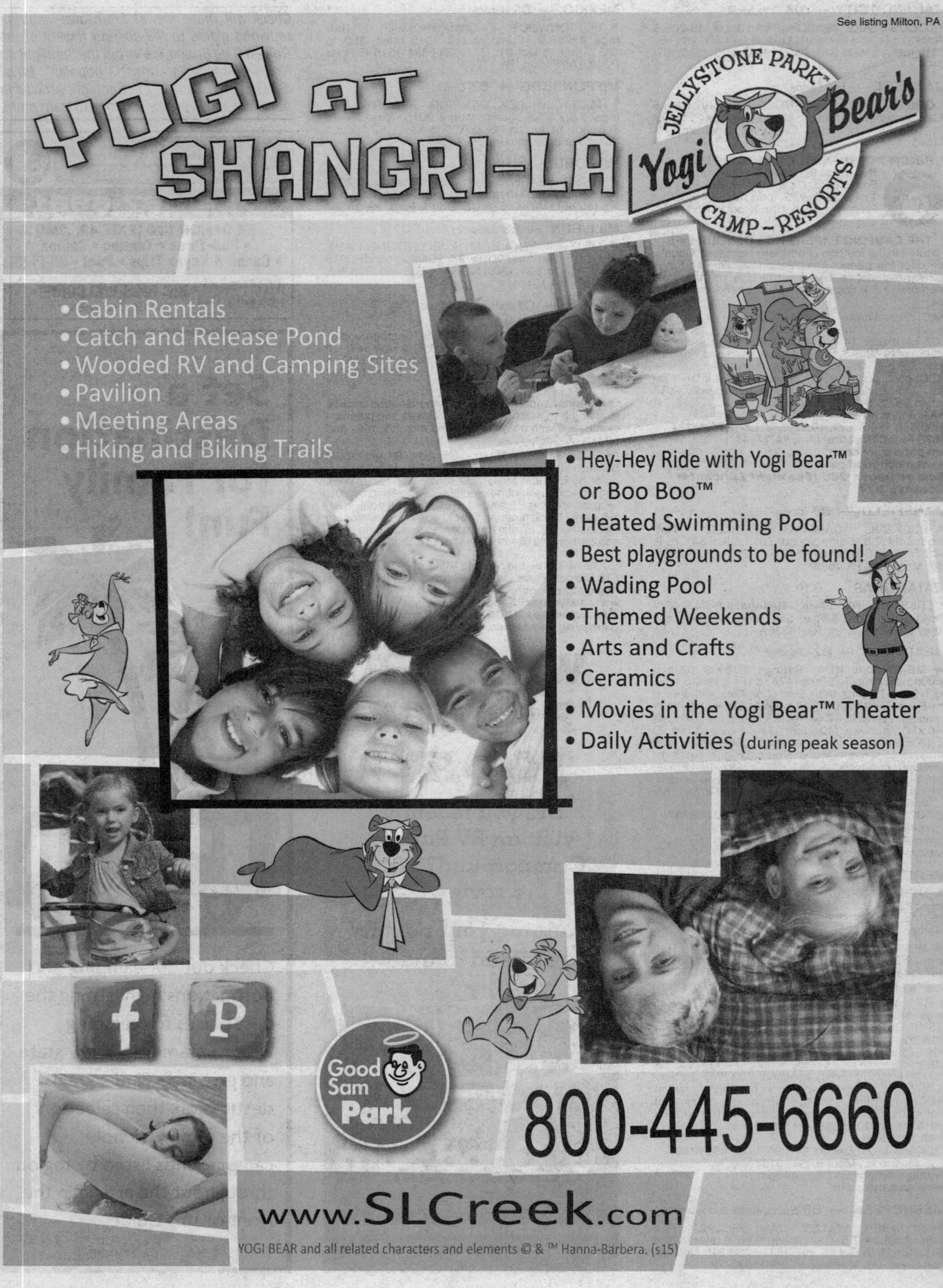
See listing Milton, PA
YOGI AT SHANGRI-LA
JELLYSTONE PARK™ Yogi Bear's CAMP-RESORTS
• Cabin Rentals
• Catch and Release Pond
• Wooded RV and Camping Sites
• Pavilion
• Meeting Areas
• Hiking and Biking Trails
• Hey-Hey Ride with Yogi Bear™ or Boo Boo™
• Heated Swimming Pool
• Best playgrounds to be found!
• Wading Pool
• Themed Weekends
• Arts and Crafts
• Ceramics
• Movies in the Yogi Bear™ Theater
• Daily Activities (during peak season)
Good Sam Park
800-445-6660
www.SLCreek.com
YOGI BEAR and all related characters and elements © & ™ Hanna-Barbera. (s15)

MONTGOMERY — C7 *Lycoming*

RIVERSIDE CAMPGROUND **Ratings: 7/5.5/6.5** (Campground) 2015 rates: $38 to $45. (570)547-6289 125 S Main St, Montgomery, PA 17752

MORRIS — B6 *Tioga*

TWIN STREAMS CAMPGROUND **Ratings: 7/9★/9** (Campground) 2015 rates: $35 to $38. Apr 15 to Dec 15. (570)353-7251 2143 Rte 287, Morris, PA 16938

MOUNT BETHEL — C10 *Northampton*

DRIFTSTONE ON THE DELAWARE Ratings: 8/9★/9 (Campground) From Jct I-80 & Hwy 94(exit 4B in NJ): Go 3/4 mi SW on Hwy 94(thru toll bridge enter PA), then follow exit ramp NE for Portland, then 3 mi S on River Rd then 1-1/4 mi S on River Rd(L) *Route has tolls. **FAC:** Paved/gravel rds. (186 spaces). Avail: 124 grass, 7 pull-thrus (50 x 80), back-ins (50 x 80), 124 W, 121 E (30/50 amps), seasonal sites, cable, WiFi, tent sites, dump, mobile sewer, laundry, groc, LP gas, fire rings, firewood. **REC:** pool, wading pool, Delaware River: fishing, playground. Pet restrict(Q). Partial handicap access. Eco-friendly, 2015 rates: $51 to $57. May 16 to Sep 18.
AAA Approved
(888)355-6859 Lat: 40.871738, Lon: -75.057629
2731 River Rd, Mount Bethel, PA 18343
office@driftstone.com
www.driftstone.com

MOUNT COBB — B9 *Lackawanna*

CLAYTON PARK RECREATIONAL AREA Ratings: 7/8.5★/8.5 (Campground) From Jct I-84(exit 8) & Hwy 247: Go 600 ft N on Hwy 247, then 3/4 mi E on Hwy 348(Mt. Cobb Hwy), then 4-1/2 mi N on Cortez Rd(SR2003), then 1/2 mi SE on Maplewood Rd, then 1/4 mi NE on Swoyer Rd(R). **FAC:** Gravel rds. (77 spaces). Avail: 17 gravel, 9 pull-thrus (35 x 65), back-ins (35 x 50), 12 full hkups, 5 W, 5 E (30/50 amps), seasonal sites, WiFi Hotspot, tent sites, rentals, showers $, dump, mobile sewer, laundry, groc, fire rings, firewood. **REC:** Lake Henry: fishing, playground. Pet restrict(B/Q). Partial handicap access. Big rig sites, eco-friendly, 2015 rates: $41 to $53. Disc: AAA, military. May 1 to Oct 15.
AAA Approved
(570)698-6080 Lat: 41.454378, Lon: -75.451048
26 Eagle Eye Dr, Lake Ariel, PA 18436
camp@claytonpark.net
www.claytonpark.net
See ad this page, 974.

MOUNT POCONO — C9 *Monroe*

MOUNT POCONO See also Blakeslee, Brodheadsville, Lake Ariel, Mount Bethel, Scotrun Stroudsburg, Tobyhanna & White Haven.

MOUNT POCONO CAMPGROUND Ratings: 9/9.5★/10 (Campground) From Jct I-380 & Hwy 940 (exit 3): Go 2-1/2 mi NE on Hwy 940, then 1/2 mi N on Hwy 196, then 1/2 mi E mi on Edgewood (R). **FAC:** Gravel rds. (127 spaces). Avail: 17 gravel, 15 pull-thrus (40 x 50), back-ins (40 x 50), 17 full hkups (30/50 amps), seasonal sites, cable, WiFi, tent sites, rentals, laundry, groc, LP gas, fire rings, firewood. **REC:** heated pool, wading pool, playground. Pets OK. Eco-friendly, 2015 rates: $45 to $55. Disc: AAA, military. May 1 to Oct 31.
AAA Approved
(570)839-8950 Lat: 41.139364, Lon: -75.350775
30 Edgewood Rd, Mount Pocono, PA 18344
mtpocono@mtpoconocampground.com
www.mtpoconocampground.com

NARVON — E8 *Lancaster*

LAKE IN WOOD RESORT Ratings: 10/10★/10 (RV Resort) From Jct of Hwy 23 & Hwy 625: Go 4-1/2 mi N on Hwy 625, then 1 mi E on Oaklyn Dr, then 1-1/2 mi NE on Yellow Hill Rd(R).

COVERED BRIDGES AND AMISH COUNTRY
With an atmosphere straight out of a fairy tale, the whole family will love our scenic grounds and unique rentals. Cool down at the pool, get creative with planned activities or have a meal at the Gnome Cafe.

FAC: Paved rds. (400 spaces). Avail: 65 paved, 60 all weather, 49 pull-thrus (45 x 60), back-ins (30 x 65), 125 full hkups (30/50 amps), seasonal sites, cable, WiFi, tent sites, rentals, dump, laundry, groc, LP bottles, fire rings, firewood, restaurant, controlled access. **REC:** heated pool, wading pool, whirlpool, Lake-In-Wood: fishing, shuffleboard, playground. Pet restrict(Q). Partial handicap access. Big rig sites, eco-friendly, 2015 rates: $56 to $64. Mar 24 to Nov 1. ATM.
AAA Approved
(717)445-5525 Lat: 40.19441, Lon: -75.97210
576 Yellow Hill Rd, Narvon, PA 17555
lakeinwood@suncommunities.com
www.lakeinwoodcampground.com
See ad pages 1463 (Welcome Section), 986 (Spotlight Lancaster County) & Family Camping, RV Trips of a Lifetime in Magazine Section.

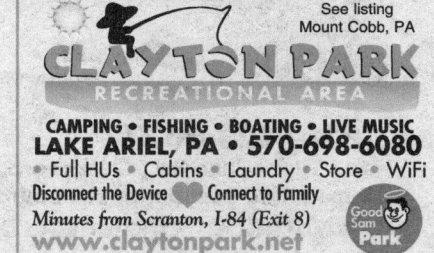

Park owners want you to be satisfied with your stay. Get to know them.

NEW ALEXANDRIA — D3 *Westmoreland*

KEYSTONE (State Pk) From town, W 4 mi on Derry Rd., N 3.8 mi on SH-981. Call for reservations. 2015 rates: $15 to $28. Apr 7 to Oct 21. (724)668-2939

NEW COLUMBIA — C7 *Union*

WILLIAMSPORT SOUTH/NITTANY MOUNTAIN KOA **Ratings: 8.5/9★/9** (Campground) 2015 rates: $43 to $90. Apr 1 to Nov 1. (570)568-5541 2751 Millers Bottom Rd, New Columbia, PA 17856

NEW HOLLAND — E8 *Lancaster*

COUNTRY HAVEN LANCASTER KOA **Ratings: 8.5/10★/10** (Campground) 2015 rates: $44 to $63. Apr 15 to Oct 30. (717)354-7926 354 Springville Rd, New Holland, PA 17557

RED RUN CAMPGROUND **Ratings: 7.5/8★/7.5** (Campground) 2015 rates: $36 to $40. Apr 1 to Nov 1. (717)445-4526 877 Martin Church Rd, New Holland, PA 17557

NEW STANTON — E2 *Westmoreland*

FOX DEN ACRES CAMPGROUND Ratings: 8/8★/8.5 (Campground) From Jct I-76/PA Tpk(exit 75) & I-70 W: Go 1/2 mi W on 1-70(exit 57), then 2 mi N on N Center Ave, then 1 Bk W on Wilson Fox Rd(L). **FAC:** Gravel rds. (160 spaces). Avail: 90 gravel, 30 pull-thrus (36 x 75), back-ins (30 x 60), 90 full hkups (30/50 amps), seasonal sites, cable, WiFi, tent sites, showers $, dump, groc, LP gas, fire rings, firewood. **REC:** pool, wading pool, Fox Lake: fishing, playground. Pets OK. Partial handicap access. Big rig sites, eco-friendly, 2015 rates: $33. May 1 to Oct 31.
(724)925-7054 Lat: 40.238588, Lon: -79.594703
390 Wilson Fox Rd, New Stanton, PA 15672
steve@foxdenacres.com
www.foxdenacres.com
See ad page 993 (Spotlight Pittsburgh & Countryside).

NEWMANSTOWN — D8 *Lebanon*

SHADY OAKS FAMILY CAMPGROUND **Ratings: 8/8.5★/6.5** (Campground) 2015 rates: $39 to $48. (717)949-3177 40 Round Barn Road, Newmanstown, PA 17073

NEWPORT — D6 *Perry*

LITTLE BUFFALO (Public) From jct US 22 & SR 34: Go 3 mi S on SR 34, then 3 mi W on Little Buffalo Rd, then 1/2 m N on Blackhill Rd. 2015 rates: $15 to $28. Apr 1 to Oct 21. (717)567-7370

NEWVILLE — E6 *Cumberland*

COLONEL DENNING (State Pk) From town, N 8 mi on Hwy 233 (R). Pit toilets. 2015 rates: $15 to $28. Apr 17 to Dec 12. (717)776-5272

OHIOPYLE — E2 *Somerset*

OHIOPYLE (State Pk) From Jct of PA Tpke (old exit 9/new exit 91) & SR-381, S 25 mi on SR-381, follow signs (E). 2015 rates: $15 to $28. Apr 1 to Dec 15. (724)329-8591

OTTSVILLE — D10 *Bucks*

BEAVER VALLEY FAMILY CAMPGROUND Ratings: 7/8★/7.5 (Campground) From Jct of Hwy 611 & Hwy 412: Go 1-1/2 mi SE on Hwy 611, then 1 mi NE on Geigel Hill Rd, stay straight 1 mi on Clay Ridge Rd (L) Office open weekends. **FAC:** Gravel rds. (85 spaces). Avail: 25 gravel, 2 pull-thrus (30 x 40), back-ins (30 x 35), 25 W, 25 E (30 amps), seasonal sites, cable, WiFi Hotspot, tent sites, rentals, dump, mobile sewer, laundry, groc, LP gas, fire rings, firewood, controlled access. **REC:** pool, wading pool, .Beaver Creek: shuffleboard, playground. Pet restrict(B/Q). Eco-friendly, 2015 rates: $39. Disc: military. Apr 1 to Oct 31.
(610)847-5643 Lat: 40.492642, Lon: -75.135781
80 Clay Ridge Rd, Ottsville, PA 18942
info@campbeavervalley.com
www.campbeavervalley.com

We salute you! Our Military Listings indicate campgrounds for use exclusively by active and retired military personnel.

PALMERTON — D9 *Carbon*

DON LAINE CAMPGROUND Ratings: 8/7.5/8 (Campground) From Jct (I-476) & US 209(exit 74): Go 8-1/4 mi E on US 209, then 500 ft S on Spruce Hollow Rd, then 8 mi SE on Church Dr, then 8 mi E on 57 Rd(R). **FAC:** Paved/gravel rds. (167 spaces). Avail: 65 gravel, 39 pull-thrus (35 x 65), back-ins (25 x 40), some side by side hkups, 59 full hkups, 6 W, 6 E (30/50 amps), seasonal sites, cable, WiFi $, dump, laundry, groc, LP gas, fire rings, firewood, controlled access. **REC:** pool, playground. Pets OK. Partial handicap access, no tents. Big rig sites, 2015 rates: $32 to $38. May 1 to Nov 1.
AAA Approved
(610)381-3381 Lat: 40.870719, Lon: -75.521168
790 57 Dr, Palmerton, PA 18071
dlaine@ptd.net
www.donlaine.com

PAVIA — E4 *Bedford*

BLUE KNOB (State Pk) From town, W 1 mi on SR-869 to Monument Rd., N 3 mi (L). 2015 rates: $15 to $28. Apr 10 to Oct 18. (814)276-3576

PENFIELD — C4 *Clearfield*

PARKER DAM (State Pk) From Jct of I-80 & SR-153 (exit 18), N 5.5 mi on SR-153, E 2.2 mi on Mud Run Rd. 2015 rates: $15 to $28. Apr 15 to Dec 15. (814)765-0630

PEQUEA — E8 *Lancaster*

PEQUEA CREEK CAMPGROUND **Ratings: 5.5/7/7.5** (Campground) 2015 rates: $32 to $35. Apr 15 to Oct 15. (717)284-4587 86 Fox Hollow Rd, Pequea, PA 17565

PHILADELPHIA — E10 *Allegheny*

PHILADELPHIA AREA MAP

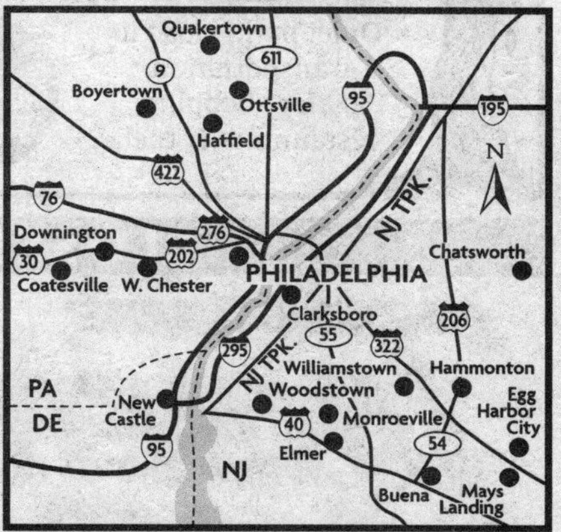

Symbols on map indicate towns within a 50 mile radius of Philadelphia where campgrounds are listed. Check listings for more information.

In PA, see also Boyertown, Coatesville, Downington, Hatfield, Ottsville, Quakertown & West Chester.
In DE, see also New Castle.
In NJ, see also Buena, Chatsworth, Clarksboro, Egg Harbor City, Elmer, Hammonton, Mays Landing, Monroeville, Williamstown & Woodstown.

CAMPUS PARK & RIDE (RV Spaces) From Jct US 30 & I-76: Go 1-1/4 mi S on I-76 to I-76(exit 346B), then 100 ft W on Wharton St, then 1/4 mi S on Warfield St(E). **FAC:** Paved rds. 50 paved, no slide-outs, back-ins (21 x 45), 12 full hkups, 12 W, 12 E (30/50

PA

PHILADELPHIA (CONT)

CAMPUS PARK & RIDE (CONT)
amps), WiFi, dump, controlled access. Pets OK. 2015 rates: $30.
(267)324-9691 Lat: 39.934114, Lon: -75.201877
1600 Warfield Street, Philadelphia, PA 19145
info@campusparkandride.com
www.campusparkandride.com/rv/
See ad this page.

TIMBERLANE CAMPGROUND
Ratings: 9.5/10★/10 (Campground)
From jct I 95 & I 676: Go S on I 676 to I 295, then S on I 295 (exit 18) to Rte 667, SE 1 mi on Rte 667 to Friendship Rd, W 0.3 mi to Timberlane Rd, N 200 ft (L).
FAC: Paved rds. (96 spaces). Avail: 71 gravel, patios, 60 pull-thrus (30 x 60), back-ins (30 x 50), 71 full hkups (30/50 amps), seasonal sites, cable, WiFi, tent sites, rentals, dump, laundry, LP gas, fire rings, firewood. **REC:** pool, wading pool, pond, fishing, playground. Pets OK. Partial handicap access. Big rig sites, eco-friendly, 2015 rates: $46 to $49. Disc: AAA, military.
(856)423-6677 Lat: 39.80741, Lon: -75.23718
117 Timberlane Rd, Clarksboro, NJ 08020
Info@timberlanecampground.com
www.timberlanecampground.com
See primary listing at Clarksboro, NJ and ad page 1008.

PHILIPSBURG — C5 *Centre*

BLACK MOSHANNON (State Pk) From business center: Go 9 mi E on Hwy 504, then 1/4 mi after park entrance, go 1/2 mi N on Cassanova-Munson Rd. 2015 rates: $15 to $28. (814)342-5960

Did you know we sent 35 husband-wife RVing teams out this year to scour North America, rating and inspecting RV parks and campgrounds? You can rest easy when you read our listings, knowing we've already been there.

PINE GROVE — D8 *Lebanon*

TWIN GROVE RV RESORT & COTTAGES
Ratings: 9/9★/9.5 (Campground)
From Jct I-81 & Hwy 443 (exit 100): Go 5 mi W on Hwy 443(R).

FAMILY FUN IN THE AMISH COUNTRYSIDE
Best Family Resort in Central PA/I-80, PA exit #100. 250 RV sites & 62 cottages on 104 wooded acres. Free WiFi & Cable. Game arcade, Ferris Wheel, Large Carousel, 2 pools w/slides, pets OK. 4 pavilions for group activities.
FAC: Paved/gravel rds. (239 spaces). Avail: 158 gravel, 70 pull-thrus (30 x 80), back-ins (25 x 50), 158 full hkups (30/50 amps), seasonal sites, cable, WiFi, tent sites, rentals, dump, laundry, groc, LP gas,

PINE GROVE (CONT)

TWIN GROVE RV RESORT (CONT)
fire rings, firewood, restaurant, controlled access. **REC:** pool, Swatara Creek: playground, rec open to public. Pet restrict(B/Q). Partial handicap access. Big rig sites, 2015 rates: $44 to $70. Disc: AAA, military. ATM.
(717)865-4602 Lat: 40.51303, Lon: -76.51501
1445 Suedburg Rd, Pine Grove, PA 17963
twingrovecamp@gmail.com
www.twingrove.com
See ad pages 970 (PA Map), 985 (Spotlight Hershey), 974 & ad inside back cover.

PITTSBURGH — D2 *Allegheny*

PITTSBURGH AREA MAP

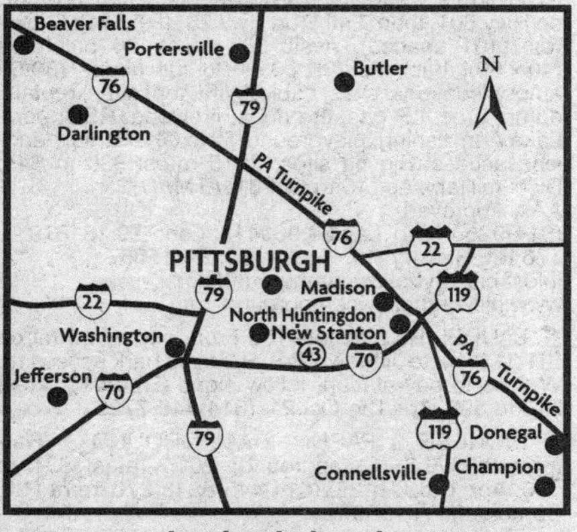

For more detail and a broader overview, please see our full-color state map at the front of the Pennsylvania state section.

Symbols on map indicate towns within a 50 mile radius of Pittsburgh where campgrounds are listed. Check listings for more information.

See also Beaver Falls, Butler, Champion, Connellsville, Darlington, Donegal, Jefferson, Madison, New Stanton, North Huntingdon, Portersville & Washington.

A SPOTLIGHT Introducing Pittsburgh's colorful attractions appearing at the front of this state section.

FOX DEN ACRES CAMPGROUND
Ratings: 8/8★/8.5 (Campground) From Grant St & I-376 E/US-22 E: Go E 14 mi on I-376E/US-22 E, then Merge onto I-76 E (PA Tpke) via Exit 85, then SE 19 mi on I-76, then S 1/2 mi on I-70 (exit 75), then NE 2 mi on US-110/PA-66 Tpke N, then W 1/4 mi on Northeast Dr/Racetrack Rd, then NW 1/4 mi on Wilson Fox Rd. (L). **FAC:** Gravel rds. (160 spaces). Avail: 90 gravel, 30 pull-thrus (36 x 75), back-ins (30 x 60), 90 full hkups (30/50 amps), seasonal sites, cable, WiFi, tent sites, showers $, dump, groc, LP gas, fire rings, firewood. **REC:** pool, wading pool, Fox Lake: fishing, playground. Pets OK. Partial handicap access. Big rig sites, eco-friendly, 2015 rates: $33. May 1 to Oct 31.
(724)925-7054 Lat: 40.238588, Lon: -79.594703
390 Wilson Fox Rd, New Stanton, PA 15672
steve@foxdenacres.com
www.foxdenacres.com
See primary listing at New Stanton and ad page 993 (Spotlight Pittsburgh & Countryside).

POCONO MOUNTAINS — C9 *Monroe*

A SPOTLIGHT Introducing Pocono Mountain's colorful attractions appearing at the front of this state section.

DELAWARE WATER GAP/POCONO MOUNTAIN KOA
Ratings: 8.5/9★/9 (Campground) From jct of I-80 & US-209 (exit 309): Go NE 6-1/4 mi on US-209 to Hollow Rd, then E 1 mi (L). **FAC:** Paved/gravel rds. (152 spaces). Avail: 127 gravel, 49 pull-thrus (25 x 65), back-ins (23 x 40), 34 full hkups, 93 W, 93 E (30/50 amps), seasonal sites, cable, WiFi, tent sites, rentals, dump, mobile sewer, laundry, groc, LP gas, fire rings, firewood. **REC:** heated pool, playground. Pets OK. Eco-friendly, 2015 rates: $49 to $69. Disc: military.
(570)223-8000 Lat: 41.050803, Lon: -75.080614
227 Hollow Road, East Stroudsburg, PA 18302
information@poconokoa.com
www.poconokoa.com
See primary listing at Stroudsburg and ad page 994 (Spotlight Pocono Mountains).

PORTERSVILLE — C1 *Butler*

BEAR RUN CAMPGROUND
Ratings: 9.5/9.5★/9 (Campground) From Jct I-79(exit 96) & Hwy 488: Go 50 yds E on Hwy 488, then 1/2 mi N on Badger Hill Rd(R). **FAC:** Paved rds. (225 spaces). 60 Avail: 19 paved, 41 gravel, 19 pull-thrus (35 x 60), back-ins (25 x 40), 31 full hkups, 29 W, 29 E (30/50 amps), seasonal sites, WiFi, tent sites, rentals, showers $, dump, laundry, groc, LP gas, fire rings, firewood, controlled access. **REC:** heated pool, Lake Arthur: swim, fishing, playground. Pet restrict(B). Partial handicap access. Big rig sites, eco-friendly, 2015 rates: $35 to $57. Disc: AAA, military. Apr 15 to Oct 30. ATM.
AAA Approved
(888)737-2605 Lat: 40.92984, Lon: -80.126231
184 Badger Hill Rd, Portersville, PA 16051
brcinc@earthlink.net
www.bearruncampground.com
See ad pages 992 (Spotlight Pittsburgh & Countryside), 974 & Family Camping in Magazine Section.

ROSE POINT PARK CABINS & CAMPGROUND
Ratings: 8.5/8.5★/9 (Campground) From Jct I-79(exit 99) & US 422: Go 3 mi W on US 422, then 1/2 mi N on Old US 422(L). **FAC:** Paved rds. (130 spaces). 32 Avail: 25 gravel, 7 grass, 7 pull-thrus (25 x 65), back-ins (20 x 35), 25 full hkups, 7 W, 7 E (30/50 amps), seasonal sites, WiFi, tent sites, rentals, dump, laundry, groc, LP gas, fire rings, firewood, controlled access. **REC:** heated pool, wading pool, pond, fishing, playground. Pet restrict(B/Q). Big rig sites, eco-friendly, 2015 rates: $35 to $45.
(724)924-2415 Lat: 40.97187, Lon: -80.18381
8775 Old US 422, New Castle, PA 16101
info@rosepointpark.com
www.rosepointpark.com
See ad this page, 974.

Things to See and Do

BEAR RUN CAMPGROUND CANOE & KAYAK RENTAL Canoe & Kayak rentals at Bear Run Campground to enjoy Lake Arthur in Moraine State Park. Apr 15 to Oct 30. partial handicap access. Restrooms. Hours: 9am to 7pm. Adult fee: $25 to $30 (1/2 half day) ATM.
(888)737-2605 Lat: 40.92984, Lon: -80.126231
184 Badger Hill Rd, Portersville, PA 16051
brcinc@earthlink.net
www.bearruncampground.com
See ad page 992 (Spotlight Pittsburgh & Countryside).

POTTERS MILLS — D6 *Centre*

POE PADDY (State Pk) From town, NW 6 mi on US-322 to Sand Mt Rd, NE 14 mi, follow signs (R). Pit toilets. 2015 rates: $15 to $28. Apr 15 to Dec 1. (814)349-2460

POE VALLEY (State Pk) From town, NW 6 mi on Hwy 322 to Sand Mt Rd, N 11 mi, follow signs (R). 2015 rates: $15 to $28. Apr 15 to Dec 1. (814)349-2460

SEVEN MOUNTAINS CAMPGROUND
Ratings: 6/8.5★/7.5 (Campground) From Jct US 322 & Hwy 144 (East of State College): Go 2-1/2 mi E on US 322(R). **FAC:** Gravel rds. (52 spaces). Avail: 36 gravel, 7 pull-thrus (30 x 85), back-ins (30 x 50), 16 full hkups, 20 W, 20 E (30/50 amps), seasonal sites, WiFi, tent sites, rentals, dump, mobile sewer, laundry, groc, fire rings, firewood. **REC:** playground. Pets OK. Partial handicap access. Big rig sites, 2015 rates: $40 to $45. Disc: AAA, military.
AAA Approved
(814)364-1910 Lat: 40.762617, Lon: -77.616241
101 Seven Mountains Campground Rd, Spring Mills, PA 16875
info@sevenmountainscampground.com
www.sevenmountainscampground.com
See ad pages 1010, 974.

QUAKERTOWN — D9 *Bucks*

QUAKERTOWN See also Allentown, Bethlehem, Boyertown, Hatfield, Revere & Ottsville.

HOMESTEAD CAMPGROUND **Ratings: 7.5/7/7** (Campground) 2015 rates: $30 to $40. (215)257-3445 1150 Allentown Rd, Green Lane, PA 18054

LITTLE RED BARN CAMPGROUND **Ratings: 8.5/8★/8.5** (Campground) 2015 rates: $40 to $47. Apr 1 to Nov 1. (866)434-1711 367 Old Bethlehem Rd, Quakertown, PA 18951

QUAKERWOODS CAMPGROUND
Ratings: 8/8★/7 (Campground) From jct of PA Tpk (Rt 476) & PA-663 (exit 32): Go E 1 mi on PA-663, then N 2 mi on Allentown Rd, then E 1/2 mi on Rosedale Rd. (R); or From jct of PA-309 & PA-663: Go W 1/4 mi on PA-663, then N 2-1/2 mi on Old Bethlehem Pike, then W 1/2 mi on Rosedale Rd. (R). **FAC:** Gravel rds. (170 spaces). Avail: 90 gravel, 4 pull-thrus (25 x 50), back-ins (25 x 35), some side by side hkups, 50 full hkups, 40 W, 40 E (30/50 amps), seasonal sites, cable, WiFi, tent sites, rentals, dump, mobile sewer, laundry, groc, LP gas, fire rings, firewood. **REC:** pool, wading pool, pond, fishing, shuffleboard, playground. Pets OK. 2015 rates: $37 to $46. Apr 1 to Oct 31.
(800)235-2350 Lat: 40.4687, Lon: -75.400287
2225 Rosedale Rd, Quakertown, PA 18951
quakerwoods@verizon.net
www.quakerwoods.com
See ad page 996.

TOHICKON FAMILY CAMPGROUND **Ratings: 7/5.5/6.5** (Campground) 2015 rates: $46 to $48. Apr 1 to Oct 31. (215)536-7951 8308 Covered Bridge Rd, Quakertown, PA 18951

PA

QUARRYVILLE — E8 *Lancaster*

YOGI BEAR'S JELLYSTONE PARK/LANCASTER SOUTH/QUARRYVILLE **Ratings: 8.5/9.5★/9.5** (Campground) From Jct US 222 & Hwy 372: Go 2-1/2 mi S on US 222, then 1-1/2 mi E on Blackburn Rd(L). **FAC:** Paved/gravel rds. 175 gravel, 16 pull-thrus (40 x 60), back-ins (40 x 60), 148 full hkups, 27 W, 27 E (30/50 amps), cable, WiFi Hotspot, tent sites, rentals, dump, laundry, groc, LP gas, fire rings, firewood. **REC:** heated pool, wading pool, pond, fishing, shuffleboard, playground. Pet restrict(Q). Partial handicap access. Big rig sites, eco-friendly, 2015 rates: $40 to $122. Apr 18 to Nov 2. ATM.
(717)786-3458 Lat: 39.853488, Lon: -76.12729
340 Blackburn Rd, Quarryville, PA 17566
Rangersmith@jellystonepa.com
www.jellystonepa.com

RAVINE — D8 *Schuylkill*

ECHO VALLEY CAMPGROUND
Ratings: 8/8.5★/8.5 (Campground) From Jct I-81 & Mollystown Rd/T634(residential rd), (exit 104): Go R off ramp & follow signs. **FAC:** Gravel rds. (112 spaces). Avail: 97 gravel, 15 pull-thrus (25 x 60), back-ins (25 x 40), 97 full hkups (30/50 amps), seasonal sites, WiFi $, tent sites, rentals, dump, laundry, groc, LP bottles, fire rings, fire-

RAVINE (CONT)

ECHO VALLEY CAMPGROUND (CONT)
wood. **REC:** pool, Black Creek: playground. Pet restrict(B). Partial handicap access. Big rig sites, eco-friendly, 2015 rates: $40 to $42.
(570)695-3659 Lat: 40.598182, Lon: -76.391087
52 Camp Rd, Tremont, PA 17981
echovalley@comcast.net
www.echovalleycamp.com
See ad pages 1009, 974.

RAYSTOWN LAKE — D5 *Huntingdon*

HERITAGE COVE RESORT **Ratings: 9/9★/8.5** (Campground) 2015 rates: $47 to $58. May 1 to Oct 31. (814)635-3386 1172 River Rd, Saxton, PA 16678

LAKE RAYSTOWN RESORT & LODGE RVC OUTDOOR DESTINATION **Ratings: 8.5/8.5★/8.5** (Campground) 2015 rates: $20 to $75. Apr 10 to Nov 1. (814)658-3500 3101 Chipmunk Crossing, Entriken, PA 16638

RENOVO — C5 *Clinton*

HYNER RUN (State Pk) From town, E 9 mi on unnamed park access rd, follow signs (L). 2015 rates: $15 to $28. Apr 10 to Dec 15. (570)923-6000

KETTLE CREEK (State Pk) From town, W 6 mi on Rte 120 to Rte 4001, N 7 mi(L). 2015 rates: $15 to $28. Apr 1 to Dec 15. (570)923-6004

REVERE — D10 *Bucks*

COLONIAL WOODS FAMILY CAMPING RESORT **Ratings: 8/8.5★/9.5** (Campground) 2015 rates: $40 to $55. Apr 4 to Nov 1. (800)887-2267 545 Lonely Cottage Dr, Upper Black Eddy, PA 18972

ROBESONIA — D8 *Lebanon*

ADVENTURE BOUND CAMPING RESORT AT EAGLES PEAK **Ratings: 8/8★/8.5** (Campground) 2015 rates: $50 to $70. Apr 1 to Oct 31. (800)336-0889 397 Eagles Peak Rd., Robesonia, PA 19551

ROME — B8 *Bradford*

PINE CRADLE LAKE FAMILY CAMPGROUND **Ratings: 8/8★/8.5** (Campground) 2015 rates: $50 to $65. May 1 to Oct 15. (570)247-2424 220 Shoemaker Rd, Rome, PA 18837

ROSSVILLE — E7 *York*

GIFFORD PINCHOT (State Pk) From town, S 3.8 mi on SH 177. 2015 rates: $15 to $28. Apr 10 to Oct 30. (717)292-4112

RURAL VALLEY — D3 *Armstrong*

SILVER CANOE CAMPGROUND **Ratings: 8.5/9.5★/7.5** (Campground) 2015 rates: $35 to $38. (724)783-6000 140 Silver Canoe Campground Ln, Rural Valley, PA 16249

SAEGERTOWN — B1 *Crawford*

COLONEL CRAWFORD PARK (Public) From Jct of I-79 & Rte 198 (Conneautville/Saegertown exit), E 8.4 mi on Rte 198 to Schultz Rd, S 1 mi, follow Woodcock Creek Lake signs in town (R). 2015 rates: $12 to $14. May 15 to Sep 15. (814)333-7372

SANDY LAKE — B2 *Mercer*

GODDARD PARK VACATIONLAND **Ratings: 8/8★/8.5** (Campground) 2015 rates: $32.50 to $41.75. Apr 15 to Oct 15. (724)253-4645 867 Georgetown Rd, Sandy Lake, PA 16145

SCHELLSBURG — E4 *Bedford*

SHAWNEE (State Pk) From Jct of US-30 & SR-96, S 1 mi on SR-96 (L). 2015 rates: $15 to $28. Apr 14 to Dec 25. (814)733-4218

Get a tune-up. Routine maintenance can up fuel efficiency by 4 percent, while fixing more serious problems can improve efficiency up to 40 percent.

SCOTRUN — C9 *Monroe*

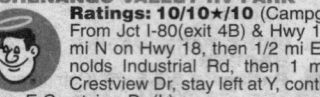

FOUR SEASONS CAMPGROUNDS
Ratings: 8.5/10★/9.5 (Campground) From Jct I-80 & Hwy 715(exit 299): Go 500 ft N on Hwy 715, then 1-3/4 mi N on Hwy 611, then 1/4 mi NW(bear left) on Scotrun Ave, then 1/2 mi W on Babbling Brook(L). **FAC:** Paved/gravel rds. (116 spaces). Avail: 58 gravel, 25 pull-thrus (30 x 65), back-ins (30 x 55), 58 full hkups (30/50 amps), seasonal sites, cable, WiFi, tent sites, laundry, groc, LP gas, fire rings, firewood, controlled access. **REC:** pool, wading pool, shuffleboard, playground. Pets OK. Eco-friendly, 2015 rates: $49 to $57. Apr 15 to Oct 10.
(570)629-2504 Lat: 41.06411, Lon: -75.33314
249 Babbling Brook Rd, Scotrun, PA 18355
fsc1@ptd.net
www.fourseasonscampgrounds.com
See ad page 994 (Spotlight Pocono Mountains).

SCRANTON — B9 *Lackawanna*

SCRANTON See also Clarks Summit, Greentown, Halwy, Honesdale, Hop Bottom, Meshoppen, Mount Cobb, Rome, Tobyhanna, Tunkhannock, Lake Ariel & Waymart.

SELINSGROVE — D7 *Snyder*

PENN AVON CAMPGROUND **Ratings: 3.5/8.5★/7.5** (Campground) 2015 rates: $43. Apr 1 to Oct 31. (570)374-9468 22 Penn Avon Trail, Rte 204, Selinsgrove, PA 17870

SHARON — C1 *Mercer*

SHENANGO PUBLIC USE AREA (COE-SHENANGO LAKE) (Public Corps) From jct I-80 & Hwy 18: Go 6-1/2 mi N on Hwy 18. 2015 rates: $19 to $34. May 16 to Aug 31. (724)646-1124

SHENANGO VALLEY RV PARK
Ratings: 10/10★/10 (Campground) From Jct I-80(exit 4B) & Hwy 18: Go 13 mi N on Hwy 18, then 1/2 mi E on Reynolds Industrial Rd, then 1 mi SE on Crestview Dr, stay left at Y, continue 1 mi SE on E Crestview Dr (L).

ONE OF A KIND EXPERIENCE!
Truly big-rig friendly. Spotlessly clean, huge heated pool. Beautiful grounds, large sites, 5-hole professional putting green. Unique shopping experience in the Serendipity Shoppe. Memory-making.

FAC: All weather rds. (193 spaces). Avail: 33 all weather, patios, 7 pull-thrus (45 x 100), back-ins (40 x 70), 33 full hkups (30/50 amps), seasonal sites, cable, WiFi, rentals, showers $, dump, laundry, groc, LP gas, fire rings, firewood, controlled access. **REC:** heated pool, Shenango River: fishing, playground. Pet restrict(Q). Partial handicap access, no tents. Big rig sites, eco-friendly, 2015 rates: $55 to $62. May 1 to Oct 15.
(724)962-9800 Lat: 41.333379, Lon: -80.377944
559 E Crestview Dr, Transfer, PA 16154
info@shenangovalleyrvpark.com
www.shenangovalleyrvpark.com
See ad pages 979 (Spotlight Erie), 974.

Things to See and Do

SERENDIPITY SHOPPE Unique gift shop featuring apparel, handbags by Baggallini, Lego toys, Melissa & Doug toys, jewelry, home decor, camping supplies, snacks and gift items. May 1 to Oct 15. partial handicap access. RV accessible. Restrooms, food. Hours: Mon to Sun 9am - 7pm.
(724)962-9800 Lat: 41.333379, Lon: -80.377944
559 E. Crestview Drive, Transfer, PA 16154
info@shenangovalleyrvpark.com
www.shenangovalleyrvpark.com
See ad page 979 (Spotlight Erie).

SHARTLESVILLE — D8 *Berks*

MOUNTAIN SPRINGS CAMPING RESORT **Ratings: 8/8.5★/8** (Campground) 2015 rates: $31 to $42. Apr 1 to Oct 31. (610)488-6859 3450 Mountain Rd, Hamburg, PA 19526

PENNSYLVANIA DUTCH CAMPGROUND **Ratings: 6.5/8.5★/6.5** (Campground) 2015 rates: $46. Apr 10 to Oct 31. (610)488-6268 136 Campsite Rd, Bernville, PA 19506

SHEFFIELD — B3 *Warren*

WHISPERING WINDS CAMPGROUND **Ratings: 8/7.5★/7.5** (Campground) 2015 rates: $32 to $36. (814)968-4377 277 Tollgate Rd, Sheffield, PA 16347

SIGEL — C3 *Jefferson*

CAMPERS PARADISE CAMPGROUND **Ratings: 7.5/9★/9.5** (Campground) 2015 rates: $42 to $47. (814)752-2393 37 Steele Dr, Sigel, PA 15860

CLEAR CREEK (State Pk) From Jct I-80 & SR-949 (old exit 12/new exit 73), N 12 mi (L). 2015 rates: $15 to $28. (814)752-2368

SINNEMAHONING — C5 *Cameron*

SINNEMAHONING (State Pk) From Jct of Rtes 120 & 872, N 8 mi on Rte 872 (R). 2015 rates: $15 to $28. Apr 14 to Dec 15. (814)647-8401

SNOW SHOE — C5 *Centre*

SNOW SHOE PARK (CITY PARK) (Public) From jct I-80 (exit 147) & SR-144: Go 1/2 mi N on SR-144. 2015 rates: $15. Apr 15 to Oct 15. (814)387-6299

SOMERSET — E3 *Somerset*

HICKORY HOLLOW CAMPGROUND Ratings: 7.5/9.5★/7.5 (Campground) From Jct I-70/I-76/Pa Tpk(exit 110) & Hwy 601S: Go 1/4 mi E on Hwy 601, then 7 mi S on Hwy 281(R). **FAC:** Gravel rds. (101 spaces). Avail: 36 gravel, 26 pull-thrus (40 x 60), back-ins (35 x 60), 36 full hkups (30/50 amps), seasonal sites, cable, WiFi, tent sites, rentals, dump, groc, LP gas, fire rings, firewood. **REC:** pool, Lake Ann: fishing, playground. Pets OK. Partial handicap access. Big rig sites, 2015 rates: $30 to $45. Disc: military. Apr 15 to Oct 31. ATM.
AAA Approved
(814)926-4636 Lat: 39.960412, Lon: -79.181879
176 Big Hickory Rd, Rockwood, PA 15557
info@hickoryhollowcampground.com
www.hickoryhollowcampground.com

LAUREL HILL (State Pk) From city, W 10 mi on SR-31 to state Jimtown Rd., S 2 mi to park access rd, W 3 mi to pay station, follow signs (R). 2015 rates: $15 to $28. Apr 1 to Oct 21. (814)445-7725

PIONEER PARK CAMPGROUND **Ratings: 9/9★/9.5** (Campground) 2015 rates: $34 to $56. Apr 1 to Oct 25. (814)445-6348 273 Trent Rd., Somerset, PA 15501

STATE COLLEGE — D5 *Centre*

STATE COLLEGE See also Bellefonte, Potters Mills & Woodland.

STRASBURG — E8 *Lancaster*

WHITE OAK CAMPGROUND Ratings: 7.5/8.5★/9 (Campground) From Jct of US 30 & Hwy 896: Go 3 mi S on Hwy 896 (continue straight through traffic light), then 3-1/2 mi S on Decatur St/May Post Office Rd, then 1/4 mi E on White Oak Rd(L). **FAC:** Paved rds. (200 spaces). Avail: 120 gravel, 12 pull-thrus (30 x 65), back-ins (30 x 40), 78 full hkups, 42 W, 42 E (30 amps), seasonal sites, WiFi, tent sites, dump, groc, fire rings, firewood. **REC:** pool, playground. Pet restrict(B). 2015 rates: $35 to $47.
AAA Approved
(717)687-6207 Lat: 39.94245, Lon: -76.14349
3156 White Oak Road, Quarryville, PA 17566
info@whiteoakcampground.com
www.whiteoakcampground.com

Like Us on Facebook.

STROUDSBURG — C10 *Monroe*

STROUDSBURG AREA MAP

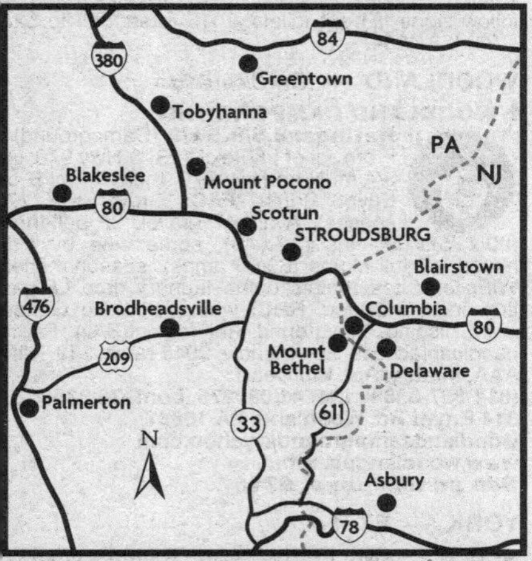

Symbols on map indicate towns within a 30 mile radius of Stroudsburg where campgrounds are listed. Check listings for more information.

In PA, see also Blakeslee, Brodheadsville, Greentown, Mount Bethel, Mount Pocono, Palmerton, Scotrun & Tobyhanna.

In NJ, see also Asbury, Blairstown, Columbia & Delaware.

DELAWARE WATER GAP/POCONO MOUNTAIN KOA
Ratings: 8.5/9★/9 (Campground) From Jct I-80(exit 309) & US-209: Go 6-1/4 mi NE on US 209, then 1 mi E on Hollow Rd (L). **FAC:** Paved/gravel rds. (152 spaces). Avail: 127 gravel, 49 pull-thrus (25 x 65), back-ins (23 x 40), 34 full hkups, 93 W, 93 E (30/50 amps), seasonal sites, cable, WiFi, tent sites, rentals, dump, mobile sewer, laundry, groc, LP gas, fire rings, firewood. **REC:** heated pool, playground. Pets OK. Eco-friendly, 2015 rates: $49 to $69. Disc: military.
(570)223-8000 Lat: 41.050803, Lon: -75.080614
227 Hollow Rd, East Stroudsburg, PA 18302
information@poconokoa.com
www.poconokoa.com
See ad page 994 (Spotlight Pocono Mountains).

MOUNTAIN VISTA CAMPGROUND
Ratings: 9/10★/10 (Campground) From Jct I-80 & US 209(exit 309): Go 3 mi N on US 209/Seven Bridges Rd, then enter roundabout, take 2nd exit follow signs for Bus US 209 to Marshalls Creek, then 1/2 mi N on Seven Bridges Rd, then 1/2 mi W on Bus US 209, then 1 mi N on Craigs Meadow Rd, then 1/2 block W on Taylor Dr(R). **FAC:** Paved/gravel rds. (185 spaces). Avail: 95 gravel, 21 pull-thrus (40 x 75), back-ins (40 x 60), 85 full hkups, 10 W, 10 E (30/50 amps), seasonal sites, cable, WiFi, tent sites, rentals, dump, mobile sewer, laundry, groc, fire rings, firewood. **REC:** pool, pond, fishing, playground. Pets OK. Big rig sites, eco-friendly, 2015 rates: $40 to $61. Apr 22 to Oct 23. ATM, no CC.
(570)223-0111 Lat: 41.045795, Lon: -75.15274
415 Taylor Drive, East Stroudsburg, PA 18301
info@mtnvistacampground.com
www.mountainvistacampground.com
See ad pages 995 (Spotlight Pocono Mountains), 974.

OTTER LAKE CAMP-RESORT
Ratings: 9/10★/10 (Campground) From Jct I-80 & US-209(exit 309): Go 3 mi N on US 209/Seven Bridges Rd, then enter roundabout, (take 2nd exit, follow signs for Bus US-209), then 1/2 mi N on Hwy 1019/Seven Bridges Rd, then 1 blk E on Bus US 209, then 7-1/2 mi NW on Marshalls Creek Rd (L).

BEAUTIFUL PRIVATE LAKE
Family camping at top-rated camp resort in Poconos. 300 wooded acres. 60-acre private lake. No-license fishing. From tent sites to Wi-Fi, something for all. Indoor pool, Softball, Archery, Ceramics and Splash pad.

FAC: Paved rds. (300 spaces). Avail: 150 gravel, 27 pull-thrus (30 x 60), back-ins (30 x 50), 120 full hkups, 30 W, 30 E (30 amps), seasonal sites, cable, WiFi, tent sites, dump, laundry, groc, LP gas, fire rings, firewood, controlled access. **REC:** heated pool, wading pool, whirlpool, Otter Lake: swim, fishing, shuffleboard, playground. Pets OK. Partial handicap access. Eco-friendly, 2015 rates: $42 to $75. ATM. AAA Approved
(570)223-0123 Lat: 41.14028, Lon: -75.15222
1639 Marshallas Creek Rd, East Stroudsburg, PA 18302
camp@otterlake.com
www.otterlake.com
See ad pages 995 (Spotlight Pocono Mountains), 970 (PA Map) & Family Camping in Magazine Section.

POCONO VACATION PARK
Ratings: 7.5/8.5★/7.5 (Campground) From Jct I-80 & Bus US 209(exit 305): Go 1-1/2 mi S on Bus US 209, then 1/3 mi W on Shafer's Schoolhouse Rd, then 1 blk S on Arnie Way (E) GPS: Use Shafer's Schoolhouse Rd. **FAC:** Gravel rds. (200 spaces). Avail: 107 gravel, 83 pull-thrus (25 x 50), back-ins (25 x 50), mostly side by side hkups, 93 full hkups, 14 W, 14 E (30/50 amps), seasonal sites, cable, WiFi, tent sites, rentals, dump, mobile sewer, groc, LP gas, fire rings, firewood. **REC:** pool, wading pool, shuffleboard, playground. Pet restrict(Q). Partial handicap access. Eco-friendly, 2015 rates: $31 to $39. Disc: AAA, military.
(570)424-2587 Lat: 40.97916, Lon: -75.25060
110 Arnie Way, Stroudsburg, PA 18360
carlet_2001@yahoo.com
www.poconovacationpark.com
See ad pages 994 (Spotlight Pocono Mountains), 974.

SUNBURY — C7 *Northumberland*

FANTASY ISLAND CAMPGROUND Ratings: 8/8.5★/7 (Campground) From Jct Hwy 61 & Hwy 147: Go 1-3/4 mi N on Hwy 147, then 500 ft E on Park Rd (L). **FAC:** Paved rds. (97 spaces). 32 Avail: 22 paved, 10 gravel, patios, back-ins (30 x 55), 32 full hkups (30/50 amps), seasonal sites, WiFi, rentals, showers $, dump, laundry, LP gas, fire rings, firewood. **REC:** heated pool, Susquehanna River: fishing, playground. Pet restrict(B/Q). Partial handicap access, no tents. 2015 rates: $40 to $45. Apr 15 to Oct 15.
(866)882-1307 Lat: 40.886721, Lon: -76.786592
401 Park Dr, Sunbury, PA 17801
fantasyislandcampground@yahoo.com
www.fantasyislandcampground.com

TAMAQUA — D8 *Schuylkill*

ROSEMOUNT CAMPING RESORT **Ratings: 8/10★/9.5** (Campground) 2015 rates: $34 to $40. Apr 15 to Oct 15. (570)668-2580 285 Valley Rd, Tamaqua, PA 18252

TEMPLETON — C3 *Armstrong*

BEAR RIDGE CAMPGROUND & RV RESORT **Ratings: 7/8★/7** (Campground) 2015 rates: $25 to $45. Apr 1 to Oct 31. (724)822-6521 345 Mt. Trails Road, Templeton, PA 16259

TIOGA — A6 *Tioga*

IVES RUN RECREATION AREA (COE-HAMMOND LAKE) (Public Corps) From jct US 15 & Hwy 287: Go 2 mi S to Tioga, turn W on continue 4 mi S on Hwy 287. 2015 rates: $20 to $34. Apr 20 to Oct 30. (570)835-5281

SCENIC VIEW CAMPGROUND **Ratings: 4/7.5★/5.5** (Campground) 2015 rates: $28. Apr 30 to Oct 31. (570)835-5700 283 Scenic View Dr, Tioga, PA 16946

TIONESTA — B3 *Forest*

KELLETTVILLE REC AREA (Public Corps) From town, N 7 mi on 62N to SR-666, E 10 mi to campground (R). 2015 rates: $10. Apr 15 to Dec 15. (814)755-3512

TIONESTA LAKE/TIONESTA REC AREA CAMPGROUND (Public Corps) From Jct of SR-36 & Elm St (in town), S 1 mi on Elm St (E). 2015 rates: $30. May 19 to Sep 1. (814)755-3512

YOUGHIOGHENY RIVER/OUTFLOW CAMPING AREA (Public Corps) From Jct of SR-36 & Elm St (in town), S 1 mi on Elm St (E). 2015 rates: $18 to $38. May 18 to Sep 9. (814)395-3242

TITUSVILLE — B2 *Venango*

OIL CREEK FAMILY CAMPGROUND **Ratings: 7/7.5★/7** (Campground) 2015 rates: $29 to $31. Apr 15 to Nov 1. (814)827-1023 340 Shreve Rd, Titusville, PA 16354

TOBYHANNA — C9 *Monroe*

HEMLOCK CAMPGROUND & COTTAGES **Ratings: 8.5/9★/9.5** (Campground) 2015 rates: $44 to $49. May 1 to Oct 31. (570)894-4388 559 Hemlock Rd, Tobyhanna, PA 18466

TOBYHANNA (State Pk) From Jct of I-380 & old exit 7/new exit 8 (SR-423, in town), N 3 mi on SR-423, follow signs (L). 2015 rates: $15 to $28. Apr 15 to Oct 21. (570)894-8336

TROUT RUN — B7 *Lewis, Lycoming*

SHESHEQUIN CAMPGROUND **Ratings: 5/9★/8.5** (Campground) 2015 rates: $35. Apr 1 to Oct 31. (888)995-9230 389 Marsh Hill Rd, Trout Run, PA 17771

TUNKHANNOCK — B8 *Wyoming*

COZY CREEK FAMILY CAMPGROUND
Ratings: 8.5/8.5★/8 (Campground) From Jct I-81 (exit 194) & US 6/11: Go NW 9 mi on US-6/11, then W 7 mi on US 6 (past SR-92) (L). **FAC:** Gravel rds. (110 spaces). Avail: 87 grass, 34 pull-thrus (40 x 50), back-ins (35 x 50), 57 full hkups, 30 W, 30 E (30/50 amps), seasonal sites, cable, WiFi $, tent sites, rentals, dump, mobile sewer, laundry, groc, LP bottles, fire rings, firewood, restaurant, controlled access. **REC:** pool, Tunkhannock Creek: swim, fishing, playground, rec open to public. Pet restrict(Q). Partial handicap access. Eco-friendly, 2015 rates: $39.95 to $59.95. Disc: military. ATM.
(570)836-4122 Lat: 41.538688, Lon: -75.946588
30 Vacation Lane, Tunkhannock, PA 18657
Info@northeastpacamping.com
www.northeastpacamping.com
See ad this page, 974.

UPPER BLACK EDDY — D10 *Bucks*

RINGING ROCKS FAMILY CAMPGROUND **Ratings: 7.5/8★/7.5** (Campground) 2015 rates: $40 to $44. Apr 1 to Oct 31. (610)982-5552 75 Woodland Dr, Upper Black Eddy, PA 18972

WAPWALLOPEN — C8 *Luzerne*

COUNCIL CUP CAMPGROUND Ratings: 5.5/5.5/6 (Campground) From I-80(exit 256) & Hwy 93: Go 2-1/2 mi N on Hwy 93, then 7 mi NW on Hwy 239, then 1 mi N on Ruckle Hill Rd(R). **FAC:** Gravel rds. (140 spaces). Avail: 58 gravel, 4 pull-thrus (22 x 90), back-ins (25 x 45), 30 full hkups, 28 W, 28 E (30/50 amps), seasonal sites, WiFi $, tent sites, rentals, dump, mobile sewer, laundry, groc, fire rings, firewood, controlled access. **REC:** Pond Creek: swim, fishing, playground. Pets OK. 2015 rates: $30. Disc: AAA, military.
AAA Approved
(570)379-2566 Lat: 41.103504, Lon: -76.097764
212 Ruckle Hill Rd, Wapwallopen, PA 18660
tik@epix.net
www.councilcupcampground.com

WARREN — B3 *McKean, Warren*

HIDDEN VALLEY CAMPING AREA
Ratings: 8.5/10★/9.5 (Campground) From the Jct of US 62 and BR 6, go N on US 62 1 mi past NY state line & turn (W) onto SR-49/Kiantone Rd (L). **FAC:** Gravel rds. (225 spaces). Avail: 50 grass, 14 pull-thrus (28 x 60), back-ins (40 x 40), 50 W, 50 E (30/50 amps), seasonal sites, cable, WiFi, tent sites, rentals, dump, mobile sewer, laundry, groc, LP gas, fire rings, firewood. **REC:** pool, Kiantone Creek: fishing, playground. Pets OK. Eco-friendly, 2015 rates: $34 to $42. Disc: military. Apr 15 to Oct 15.
(716)569-5433 Lat: 42.0832, Lon: -79.17981
299 Kiantone Rd., Jamestown, NY 14701
hiddenvalley@hiddenvalleyarea.com
www.hiddenvalleycampingarea.com
See primary listing at Jamestown, NY and ad page 831.

RED OAK CAMPGROUND Ratings: 7/6.5/7 (Campground) N-Bnd: From Jct US 6 & US 62N: Go 5-1/2 mi N on US 62N, then 4-3/4 mi E on Hatch Run Rd, then 8 mi N on Scandia Rd, then 1/4 mi E on Norman Rd(L); S-Bnd: From I-86(exit 17 in NY) & Hwy 394: Go 17 mi S on Hwy 394(becomes Scandia Rd), then 1/4 E on Norman Rd(L). **FAC:** Paved/gravel rds. (206 spaces). 75 Avail: 50 gravel, 25 grass, 5 pull-thrus (30 x 60), back-ins (30 x 45), some side by

PA

WARREN (CONT)

RED OAK CAMPGROUND (CONT)
side hkups, 16 full hkups, 59 W, 59 E (30/50 amps), seasonal sites, WiFi Hotspot, tent sites, rentals, dump, laundry, groc, LP gas, fire rings, firewood. **REC:** heated pool, playground, rec open to public. Pets OK. Big rig sites, eco-friendly, 2015 rates: $38 to $53. Disc: military.
AAA Approved
(814)757-8507 Lat: 41.964277, Lon: -78.97979
225 Norman Rd, Russell, PA 16345
redoakcampground@verizon.net
www.redoakcamping.com

WASHINGTON — E1 *Washington*

PINE COVE BEACH CLUB & RV RESORT
Ratings: 9/9★/9.5 (RV Park) From Jct of I-70 & Rte 481 (exit 35): Go 1/4 mi N on Rte 481 (L). **FAC:** Paved/gravel rds. (57 spaces). Avail: 38 gravel, back-ins (38 x 60), 38 full hkups (30/50 amps), seasonal sites, WiFi, laundry, fire rings, firewood, controlled access. **REC:** pool, wading pool, Pine Cove Lake: fishing, playground, rec open to public. Pets OK. Partial handicap access, no tents. Big rig sites, 2015 rates: $55 to $65.
(724)239-2900 Lat: 40.128104, Lon: -79.955795
1495 Rte 481, Charleroi, PA 15022
pinecovebeachclub@gmail.com
www.pinecovebeachclub.com
See ad pages 993 (Spotlight Pittsburgh & Countryside), 974.

WASHINGTON/PITTSBURGH SW KOA KAMPGROUND **Ratings: 8.5/8/7.5** (Campground) 2015 rates: $42. Mar 1 to Dec 1. (800)562-0254 7 Koa Rd, Washington, PA 15301

WATERVILLE — C6 *Lycoming*

HAPPY ACRES RESORT Ratings: 7.5/8★/8 (RV Park) From Jct US 220/Bypass & Hwy 44 N: Go 10-3/4 mi N on Hwy 44, then 3-1/4 mi N on Little Pine Creek Rd (L). **FAC:** Poor paved/gravel rds. (88 spaces). Avail: 53 gravel, 4 pull-thrus (25 x 65), back-ins (25 x 40), some side by side hkups, 20 full hkups, 33 W, 33 E (30/50 amps), seasonal sites, WiFi, tent sites, rentals, showers $, dump, mobile sewer, laundry, groc, LP gas, fire rings, firewood, restaurant. **REC:** pool, playground. Pets OK $. Big rig sites, 2015 rates: $30 to $40. ATM.
(570)753-8000 Lat: 41.048742, Lon: -76.954187
3332 Little Pine Creek Rd, Waterville, PA 17776
info@happyacresresort.net
www.happyacresresort.net

LITTLE PINE (State Pk) From Jct of US-220 Bypass & SR-44 (in Jersey Shore), N 10 mi on SR-44 to cnty rd, N 3 mi on cnty rd, follow signs (R). 2015 rates: $15 to $28. Apr 7 to Dec 15. (570)753-6000

WAYMART — B9 *Wayne*

KEEN LAKE CAMPING & COTTAGE RESORT Ratings: 9/10★/10 (Campground) From Jct of US 6 & Hwy 296: Go 1-1/2 mi E on US 6(R). **FAC:** Paved/gravel rds. (304 spaces). 139 Avail: 125 gravel, 14 grass, 4 pull-thrus (30 x 60), back-ins (30 x 50), 71 full hkups, 68 W, 68 E (30/50 amps), seasonal sites, cable, WiFi, tent sites, rentals, showers $, dump, laundry, groc, fire rings, firewood. **REC:** heated pool, Keen Lake: swim, fishing, shuffleboard, playground. Pet restrict(Q). Eco-friendly, 2015 rates: $42 to $61. Disc: military. May 1 to Oct 12. ATM.
(570)488-6161 Lat: 41.590754, Lon: -75.379873
155 Keen Lake Rd, Waymart, PA 18472
camping@keenlake.com
www.keenlake.com

WELLSBORO — B6 *Tioga*

COLTON POINT (State Pk) From Jct of US-6 & SR-287, W 8 mi on US-6 to Colton Rd, S 6 mi, follow signs (E). Pit toilets. 2015 rates: $15 to $28. May 10 to Oct 20. (570)724-3061

HILLS CREEK (State Pk) From town, W 6 mi on US-6 to Jct of US-6 & SR-660, N 5 mi on cnty rd, follow signs (R). 2015 rates: $15 to $28. Apr 10 to Oct 25. (570)724-4246

LEONARD HARRISON (State Pk) From Jct of US-6 & SR-660, W 3 mi on SR-660 to Jct of SR-362/660, W 9 mi on SR-660, follow signs (E). 2015 rates: $12 to $28. Apr 15 to Oct 25. (570)724-3061

STONY FORK CREEK CAMPGROUND **Ratings: 7.5/7.5/8** (Campground) 2015 rates: $35 to $40. (570)724-3096 658 Stony Fork Creek Rd, Wellsboro, PA 16901

WEST CHESTER — E9 *Chester*

PHILADELPHIA/WEST CHESTER KOA **Ratings: 9/8★/8** (Campground) 2015 rates: $53 to $88. Apr 1 to Oct 31. (610)486-0447 1659 Embreeville Rd, Coatesville, PA 19320

WEST SUNBURY — C2 *Butler*

BUTLER NORTH KOA AT PEACEFUL VALLEY CAMPGROUND **Ratings: 7/9.5★/6** (Campground) 2015 rates: $40 to $50. Apr 18 to Oct 23. (724)894-2421 231 Peaceful Valley Rd, West Sunbury, PA 16061

WHITE HAVEN — C9 *Carbon, Luzerne*

HICKORY RUN (State Pk) From Jct of I-80 & Rte 534 (old exit 41/new exit 274), E 6 mi on Rte 534 (R). Call for reservations. 2015 rates: $15 to $28. Apr 10 to Oct 25. (570)443-0400

LEHIGH GORGE CAMPGROUND
Ratings: 8/8.5★/8 (Campground) From jct of I-80 & PA-534 (exit 274): Go W 1/4 mi on PA-534, then W 1/4 mi on PA-940 (R); or From jct of I-476/PA Tpke (exit 95) & PA-940: Go W 2-1/2 mi on PA-940. (R). **FAC:** Paved/gravel rds. (200 spaces). Avail: 25 gravel, 25 pull-thrus (45 x 75), 25 full hkups (30 amps), seasonal sites, cable, WiFi, tent sites, laundry, groc, LP gas, fire rings, firewood, controlled access. **REC:** heated pool, pond, fishing, playground. Pets OK. Partial handicap access. Eco-friendly, 2015 rates: $43. Disc: AAA.
AAA Approved
(570)443-9191 Lat: 41.06525, Lon: -75.756282
4585 State St, White Haven, PA 18661
liz@lehighgorgecampground.com
www.lehighgorgecampground.com
See ad this page, 974.

Travel Services

LEHIGH GORGE RV CENTER Sale of new and used Motorhomes, Fifth Wheels and Travel Trailers. Largest service center in North East Pennsylvania. Huge parts inventory. **SERVICES:** RV, tire, RV appliance, MH mechanical, engine/chassis repair, restrooms, RV Sales. **TOW:** RV, auto. RV supplies, LP, emergency parking, RV accessible. waiting room. Hours: 8am to 5pm M-SA, Closed Sunday.
(570)443-9876 Lat: 41.06525, Lon: -75.756282
4585 State St, White Haven, PA 18661
jay@lehighgorgerv.com
www.lehighgorgerv.com
See ad this page.

WILKES-BARRE — C8 *Luzerne*

FRANCES SLOCUM (State Pk) From jct I-81 (exit 170B) & Hwy 309: Go 7 mi N on Hwy 309, then 4 mi E on Carverton Rd, then 1 mi N on Eighth St, then 1 mi W on Mt. Olivet Rd. 2015 rates: $15 to $28. Apr 10 to Oct 25. (570)696-3525

WIND RIDGE — E1 *Greene*

RYERSON STATION (State Pk) From town, S 2 mi on SR-3022 (Bristoria Rd) to Rte 3022, E 1.3 mi follow signs (E). Pit toilets. 2015 rates: $15 to $2 (724)428-4254

WOODLAND — C4 *Clearfield*

WOODLAND CAMPGROUND
Ratings: 8.5/9.5★/9 (Campground) From Jct of I-80(exit 123) & Hwy 970: G 3/4 mi N on Hwy 970, then 1/4 mi E Egypt Rd(R). **FAC:** Gravel rds. (7 spaces). Avail: 47 gravel, 36 pull-thr (20 x 75), back-ins (20 x 45), some side by si hkups, 47 full hkups (30/50 amps), seasonal site WiFi, tent sites, rentals, dump, laundry, groc, LP ga fire rings, firewood. **REC:** whirlpool, Lake Gene swim, fishing, playground. Pet restrict(B/Q). Part handicap access. Eco-friendly, 2015 rates: $42. Dis AAA, military. Apr 1 to Dec 1.
(814)857-5388 Lat: 41.030275, Lon: -78.335352
314 Egypt Rd, Woodland, PA 16881
woodlandcampground@yahoo.com
www.woodlandpa.com
See ad this page, 974.

YORK — E7 *York*

BEN .FRANKLIN RV PARK **Ratings: 6/9.5★** (Campground) 2015 rates: $30. (717)744-8237 13 Woodberry Rd, York, PA 17408

Park owners want you to be satisfied with you stay. Get to know them.

Getty Images/iStockphoto

WELCOME TO
Rhode Island

DATE OF STATEHOOD	WIDTH: 37 MILES (60 KM)	PROPORTION OF UNITED STATES
MAY 29, 1790	LENGTH: 48 MILES (77 KM)	0.04% OF 3,794,100 SQ MI

Used to living in America's smallest state, Rhode Islanders good-naturedly grumble that anything beyond a half-hour drive is too far. But for visitors, the appeal of the Ocean State is worth a long drive, indeed. From the opulent estates in Newport, inspiration for "The Great Gatsby," to Providence's big city thrills, Rhode Island packs a ton of fun.

RVers expecting to explore the state in a day are in for a big surprise. The Ocean State is certainly not lacking for sailing charters and guides waiting to lead deep-sea fishing expeditions. South County offers a procession of shielded pocket beaches from Watch Hill in Westerly to Scarborough Beach in Narragansett.

Rhode Island has alluring islands as well. Block Island features 17 miles of bluff-backed beaches and 25 miles of walking trails in the tradition of English countryside tramping; ferry service operates year-round. Prudence Island, reached by ferry from Bristol, offers another 475 acres of walkable terrain.

On the mainland, the Ocean State could easily pass for the Forest State. Away from the shore are management areas teeming with trails and outdoor adventures.

In Newport, the Cliff Walk extends 3.5 ocean-hugging miles in the backyards of the Newport Mansions—no amount of money can buy the ocean-front property thanks to centuries-old "fishermen's rights."

Newport became the symbol of the Gilded Age of the late 19th century, as America's rich and famous tried to top one another in building the country's most opulent "summer cottage." The world's oldest international competition, the America's Cup yacht race, began in Newport. Ten of the town's landmark mansions are open for tours.

Top 3 Tourism Attractions:
1) Newport Mansions
2) Slater Mill
3) International Tennis Hall of Fame

Nickname: The Ocean State

State Flower: Violet

State Bird: Rhode Island Red Hen

People: Jon B, musician; Nelson Eddy, singer and actor; David Hartman, TV newscaster; Gilbert Stuart, painted the George Washington that appears on the dollar bill; Meredith Vieira, TV personality

Major Cities: Providence (capital), Warwick, Cranston, Pawtucket, East Providence

Topography: East—lowlands of Narragansett Basin; west—uplands of flat rolling hills

Climate: Humid with short summers and cold winters. Weather is highly changeable

RI

TRAVEL & TOURISM

Rhode Island Tourism Division
800-556-2484
www.VisitRhodeIsland.com

Blackstone Valley Tourism Council
800-454-2882
www.blackstonevalleytourismcouncil.com

Block Island Tourism Council
800-383-BIRI, 401-466-5200

Newport & Bristol County CVB
800-326-6030
www.discovernewport.org

Providence Warwick Convention & Visitors Bureau
401-456-0200
www.goprovidence.com

South County Tourism Council
800-548-4662
www.southcountryri.com

OUTDOOR RECREATION

Rhode Island Department of Environmental Management
401-789-3094, 401-222-3575
www.dem.ri.gov

SHOPPING

Bowen's Wharf
www.bowenswharf.com

The Shops at Long Wharf
866-4-Only-RI
www.onlyinrhodeisland.com

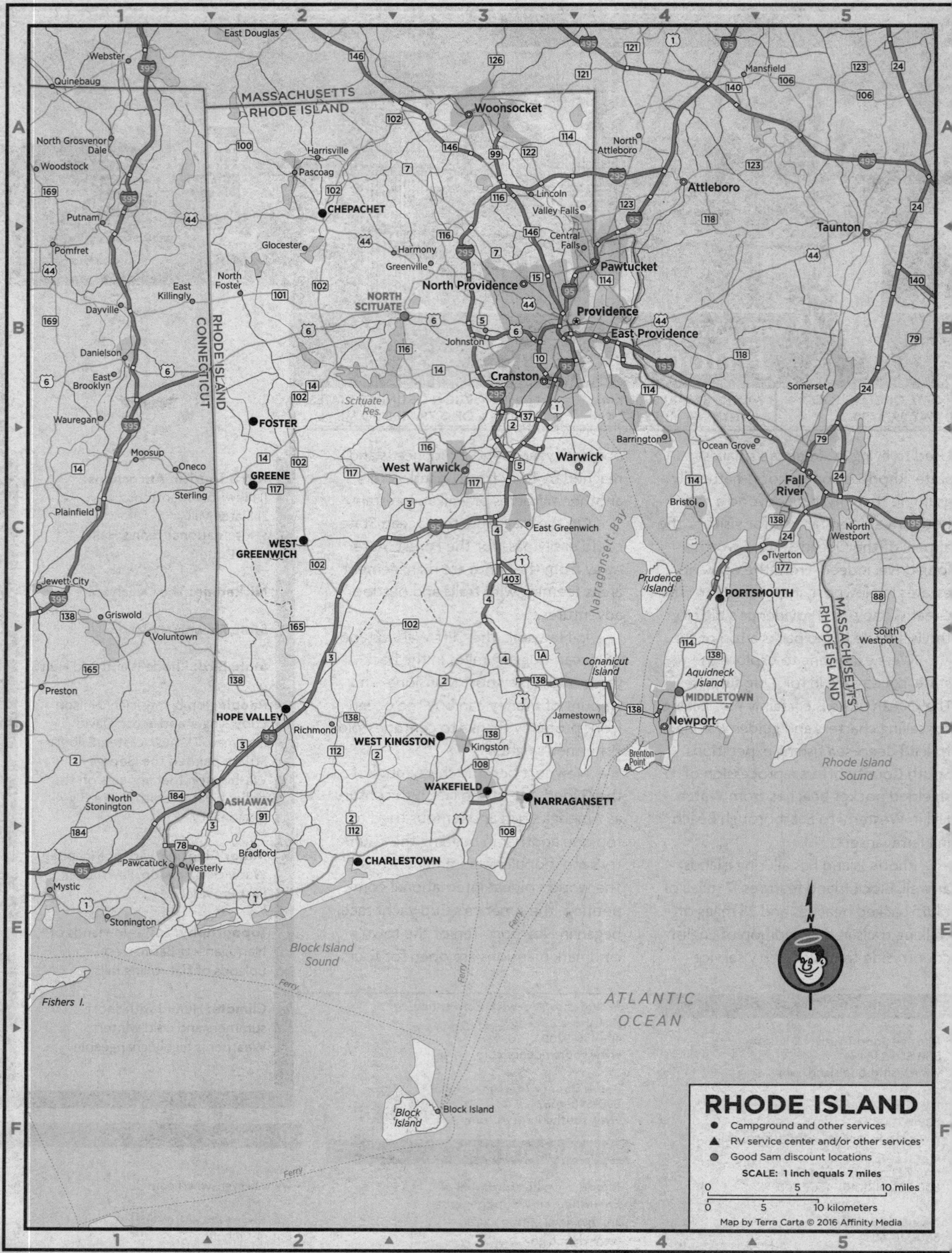
RHODE ISLAND
Campground and other services
RV service center and/or other services
Good Sam discount locations
SCALE: 1 inch equals 7 miles
0 5 10 miles
0 5 10 kilometers
Map by Terra Carta © 2016 Affinity Media
MASSACHUSETTS
RHODE ISLAND
CONNECTICUT
Woonsocket
Pawtucket
North Providence
Providence
East Providence
Cranston
Warwick
West Warwick
Johnston
Attleboro
Taunton
Fall River
North Attleboro
Mansfield
Somerset
Barrington
Ocean Grove
Bristol
Tiverton
North Westport
South Westport
Lincoln
Valley Falls
Central Falls
East Greenwich
Narragansett Bay
Prudence Island
Conanicut Island
Aquidneck Island
Jamestown
Newport
Brenton Point
PORTSMOUTH
MIDDLETOWN
CHEPACHET
NORTH SCITUATE
FOSTER
GREENE
WEST GREENWICH
HOPE VALLEY
WEST KINGSTON
WAKEFIELD
NARRAGANSETT
ASHAWAY
CHARLESTOWN
Kingston
Richmond
Bradford
Westerly
Pawcatuck
Mystic
Stonington
North Stonington
Preston
Voluntown
Griswold
Jewett City
Plainfield
Sterling
Oneco
Moosup
Wauregan
Danielson
East Brooklyn
Dayville
East Killingly
Pomfret
Putnam
Woodstock
North Grosvenor Dale
Quinebaug
Webster
East Douglas
Harrisville
Pascoag
Glocester
Harmony
Greenville
North Foster
Scituate Res.
Block Island Sound
Rhode Island Sound
ATLANTIC OCEAN
Fishers I.
Block Island
Ferry
N

Featured Good Sam Parks

RHODE ISLAND

Good Sam Park

RI

When you stay with Good Sam, you can expect the highest degree of cleanliness and friendliness, and better yet, you get 10% off campground fees.

If you're not already a Good Sam member you can purchase your membership at one of these locations:

ASHAWAY
Ashaway RV Resort
(401)377-8100

MIDDLETOWN
Meadowlark, Inc
(401)846-9455

NORTH SCITUATE
Holiday Acres Camping Resort
(401)934-0780

For more Good Sam Parks go to listing pages

Rhode Island

CONSULTANTS

Mark & Wendy Pitts

ASHAWAY — D2 *Washington*

ASHAWAY RV RESORT
Ratings: 9/9.5★/8 (RV Park) From Jct of I-95 (Exit 1) & Rte 3, S 1.8 mi to Rte 216 E (Ashaway Rd), 2.1 mi (L). **FAC:** Gravel rds. (260 spaces). Avail: 220 gravel, 20 pull-thrus (30 x 60), back-ins (30 x 60), 220 full hkups (30/50 amps), seasonal sites, cable, WiFi, rentals, laundry, LP gas, fire rings, firewood. **REC:** pool, whirlpool, shuffleboard, playground. Pet restrict(B). Partial handicap access. Big rig sites, 2015 rates: $54 to $65. Disc: military. Apr 15 to Oct 15. ATM.
(401)377-8100 Lat: 41.4120023, Lon: -71.7505510
235 Ashaway Road, Ashaway, RI 02808
info@ashawayrvresort.com
www.ashawayrvresort.com
See ad this page, 1015.

CHARLESTOWN — E2 *Washington*

BURLINGAME (State Pk) From town, S 4 mi on US-1 (R). 2015 rates: $14 to $20. Apr 12 to Oct 14. (401)322-7337

CHARLESTOWN BREACHWAY CAMPGROUND (State Pk) From Jct of Rte 1A & Charlestown Beach Rd, S 4.5 mi on Charlestown Beach Rd (E). Self-contained units only. 2015 rates: $14 to $20. Apr 15 to Oct 31. (401)364-7000

CHEPACHET — A2 *Providence*

BOWDISH LAKE CAMPING AREA **Ratings: 6/6.5/7.5** (Campground) 2015 rates: $40 to $100. May 15 to Oct 13. (401)568-8890 40 Safari Rd, Chepachet, RI 02814

GEORGE WASHINGTON MEMORIAL CAMPING AREA (State Pk) From Jct of US-44 & Rte 102, W 5.2 mi on US-44 (R). Pit toilets. 2015 rates: $14 to $20. Apr 12 to Oct 31. (401)568-2085

RV Park ratings you can rely on!

FOSTER — B2 *Providence*

GINNY-B FAMILY CAMPGROUND
Ratings: 7.5/7/8.5 (Campground) From Jct of US-6 & Cucumber Hill Rd (at CT state line), 3.5 mi on Cucumber Hill Rd to Harrington Rd, E 0.5 mi (L). **FAC:** Paved rds. (225 spaces). Avail: 7 grass, 20 pull-thrus (30 x 60), back-ins (27 x 54), some side by side hkups, 15 full hkups, 60 W, 60 (20/30 amps), seasonal sites, WiFi Hotspot, tent sites, dump, mobile sewer, laundry, groc, fire rings, firewood. **REC:** pond, swim, fishing, playground. Pets OK. Partial handicap access. 2015 rates: $36 to $3 May 1 to Sep 30.
(401)397-9477 Lat: 41.75541, Lon: -71.75465
7 Harrington Rd, Foster, RI 02825
gnnyb@aol.com
ginny-bcampground.com
See ad this page.

GREENE — C2 *Kent*

HICKORY RIDGE FAMILY CAMPGROUND **Ratings: 6/6/6.5** (Campground) 2015 rates: $4 May 1 to Oct 10. (401)397-7474 584 Victory Hwy Greene, RI 02827

HOPE VALLEY — D2 *Washington*

WHISPERING PINES **Ratings: 9/7.5/8.** (Campground) 2015 rates: $33 to $55. Apr 15 to O 15. (401)539-7011 41 Saw Mill Rd, Hope Valley, R 02832

MIDDLETOWN — D4 *Newport*

MEADOWLARK, INC
Ratings: 6/NA/7.5 (Campground) From Jct of I-95 & SR-138 (exit 3A), E 2 mi on SR-138 to SR-138A, S 1.5 mi to Prospect Ave, E 0.4 mi (R). **FAC:** Paved rds. (74 spaces). Avail: 41 grass, back-ins (24 x 45), accepts self-contain units only, 41 full hkups (30 amps), WiFi, dump, laundry. **REC:** playground. Pets OK. No tents. 2015 rates: $45 to $6 Apr 1 to Dec 1. No CC.
(401)846-9455 Lat: 41.50074, Lon: -71.27263
132 Prospect Ave, Middletown, RI 02842
http://www.trailerlifedirectory.com/travel/campgroundsandrvparks/generalinfo.aspx?cgid=720005637
See ad this page, 1015.

NARRAGANSETT — D3 *Washington*

FISHERMENS MEMORIAL (State Pk) From Jct of US-1 & SR-108, S 3.6 mi on SR-108 (R). 2015 rates $18 to $35. Apr 12 to Oct 31. (401)789-8374

NEWPORT — D4 *Newport*

PARADISE RV PARK **Ratings: 5.5/NA/7.5** (RV Park) 2015 rates: $67 to $87. May 27 to Sep 30 (401)847-1500 459 Aquidneck Ave (Rt. 138A), Middletown, RI 02842

NORTH SCITUATE — B3 *Providence*

HOLIDAY ACRES CAMPING RESORT
Ratings: 7.5/8/8 (Campground) From Jct of I-295 & Rte 44 (Exit 7B), W 2 mi on Rte 44 to Rte 116 (Smith Ave), S 1.4 mi to 4-way stop to Snake Hill Rd, W 2.8 mi (R); or From Jct of Rtes 6 & 102, N 3 mi on Rte 102 to Snake Hill Rd, E 3 mi (L). **FAC:** Poor gravel/dirt rds. (225 spaces). 45 Avail: 20 grass, 2 dirt, 8 pull-thrus (34 x 50), back-ins (30 x 50), 22 full hkups, 23 W, 23 E (30/50 amps), seasonal sites, WiFi, tent sites, rentals, showers $, dump, mobile sewer, laundry, groc, LP gas, fire rings, firewood. **REC:** Coomer's Lake: swim, fishing, shuffleboard, playground. Pet restrict(Q). Partial handicap access. 2015 rates: $40 to $50. Disc: AAA, military.
(401)934-0780 Lat: 41.87890, Lon: -71.62198
593 Snake Hill Rd, North Scituate, RI 02857
info@holidayacrescampground.com
www.holidayacrescampground.com
See ad opposite page, 1015.

Say you saw it in our Guide!

PORTSMOUTH — C4 *Newport*

MELVILLE PONDS CAMPGROUND (Campground) (Rebuilding) 2015 rates: $32 to $65. Apr 1 to Nov 1. (401)682-2424 181 Bradford Ave, Portsmouth, RI 02871

WAKEFIELD — D3 *Washington*

WORDEN POND FAMILY CAMPGROUND **Ratings: 6/8.5★/7.5** (Campground) 2015 rates: $45. May 1 to Oct 15. (888)858-9113 416 A Worden Pond Rd, Wakefield, RI 02879

WEST GREENWICH — C2 *West Greenwich*

OAK EMBERS **Ratings: 8/5.5/7** (Campground) 2015 rates: $35 to $40. May 1 to Oct 31. (401)397-4042 219 Escoheag Rd, West Greenwich, RI 02817

WEST KINGSTON — D3 *Washington*

WAWALOAM CAMPGROUND **Ratings: 9/8.5/10** (Campground) 2015 rates: $46 to $58. May 1 to Oct 31. (401)294-3039 510 Gardiner Rd, West Kingston, RI 02892

Each privately owned campground has been rated three times. The first rating is for development of facilities. The second one is for cleanliness and physical characteristics of restrooms and showers. The third is for campground visual appearance and environmental quality.

We give you what you want. First, we surveyed thousands of RVers just like you. Then, we developed our exclusive Triple Rating System for campgrounds based on the results. That's why our rating system is so good at explaining the quality of facilities and cleanliness of campgrounds.

RI

Get the Facts!

Essential tips and travel info can be found in the Welcome Section at the beginning of each State/Province.

Joe Carr Photography, Inc.

WELCOME TO
South Carolina

DATE OF STATEHOOD	WIDTH: 200 MILES (322 KM)	PROPORTION OF UNITED STATES
MAY 23, 1788	LENGTH: 260 MILES (418 KM)	0.84% OF 3,794,100 SQ MI

With its alluring coastline, plunging waterfalls and outsized role in American history, it's hard to imagine that South Carolina is the second-smallest state outside of the Northeast. But once you've experienced all that the state has to offer, you'll realize that good things come in small packages.

Myrtle Beach's 120 golf courses have made it synonymous with golf vacations. With 60 miles of white sand beaches, Myrtle Beach and the Grand Strand are also the ocean playgrounds of choice for millions of sun worshipers. Hilton Head Island, the Isle of Palms and Kiawah Island are all world-class beach and golf destinations. Hunting Island and Edisto Beach offer long, non-commercialized walks on the beach.

Head inland to explore Congaree National Park's 2,000 acres of virgin pine, tupelo and bald cypress; 20 state or national champion trees live here. The black-water rivers are ideal for canoeing, and boardwalk trails keep hikers dry from the Congaree River.

As the hub of the Upcountry, Greenville has emerged as the most vibrant mid-size city in the South. The former textile town owes much its popularity to its role as gateway to the boundless recreation opportunities in the foothills of the Appalachian Mountains. The alpine splendor includes Whitewater Falls, Table Rock, Jones Gap, Paris Mountain and Caesars Head state parks. These sit along the Blue Ridge Escarpment's dramatic break.

Top 3 Tourism Attractions:
1) Historic Charleston
2) Myrtle Beach
3) Boone Hall

Nickname: Palmetto State

State Flower: Carolina Yellow Jessamine

State Bird: Carolina Wren

People: James Brown, "godfather of soul"; Chubby Checker, singer and songwriter; Joe Frazier, Olympic heavyweight champion; Dizzy Gillespie, jazz trumpeter, bandleader, singer and composer; Vanna White, TV personality

Major Cities: Columbia (capital), Charleston, North Charleston, Mount Pleasant, Rock Hill

Topography: Northwest—Blue Ridge Mountains; central—piedmont lies between mountains and fall line; east—coastal plain

Climate: Humid subtropical climate with hot summers and winters that are not extremely cold

TRAVEL & TOURISM

South Carolina Dept. of Parks & Tourism
866-224-9339, 803-734-1700
www.discoversouthcarolina.com

Capital City-Lake Murray Country Tourism Region & Visitor Center
866-725-3935, 803-781-5940
www.lakemurraycountry.com

Charleston Area CVB
843-853-8000
www.charlestoncvb.com

Discover Upcountry Carolina Assn.
800-849-4766, 864-233-2690
www.TheUpcountry.com

Myrtle Beach Area Chamber of Commerce & Visitor Center
843-626-7444, 800-356-3016
www.VisitMyrtleBeach.com

North Myrtle Beach Area Chamber of Commerce & CVB
877-332-2662, 843-281-2662
www.northmyrtlebeachchamber.com

Old 96 District Tourism Commission
800-429-9633
www.sctravelold96.com

Olde English District Tourism Commission
800-968-5909 or 803-385-6800
www.sctravel.net

Pee Dee Tourism Commission
800-325-9005 or 843-669-0950
www.peedeetourism.com

Santee Cooper Counties Promotion Commission and Visitor Center
800-227-8510 or 803-854-2131
www.santeecoopercountry.org

SC Lowcountry & Resort Islands Tourism Commission
800-528-6870
www.SouthCarolinaLowcountry.com

Thoroughbred Country
888-834-1654, 803-649-7981
www.tbredcountry.org

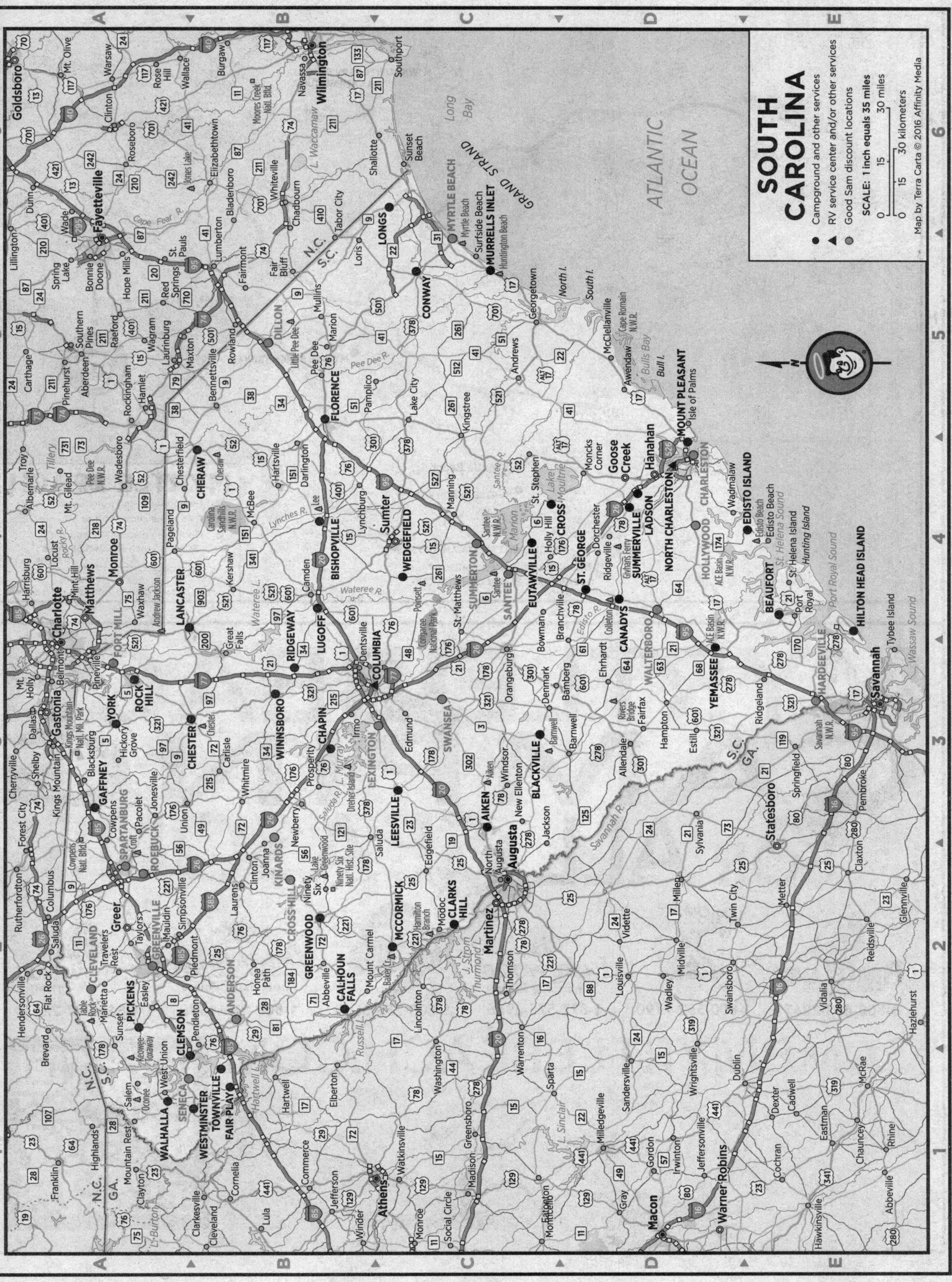
SOUTH CAROLINA
Campground and other services
RV service center and/or other services
Good Sam discount locations
SCALE: 1 inch equals 35 miles
0 15 30 miles
0 15 30 kilometers
Map by Terra Carta © 2016 Affinity Media
ATLANTIC OCEAN
GRAND STRAND
Long Bay
COLUMBIA
CHARLESTON
NORTH CHARLESTON
MYRTLE BEACH
FLORENCE
SUMTER
GREENVILLE
SPARTANBURG
ROCK HILL
AIKEN
BEAUFORT
HILTON HEAD ISLAND
Charlotte
Augusta
Savannah
Wilmington
Fayetteville
Athens
Macon

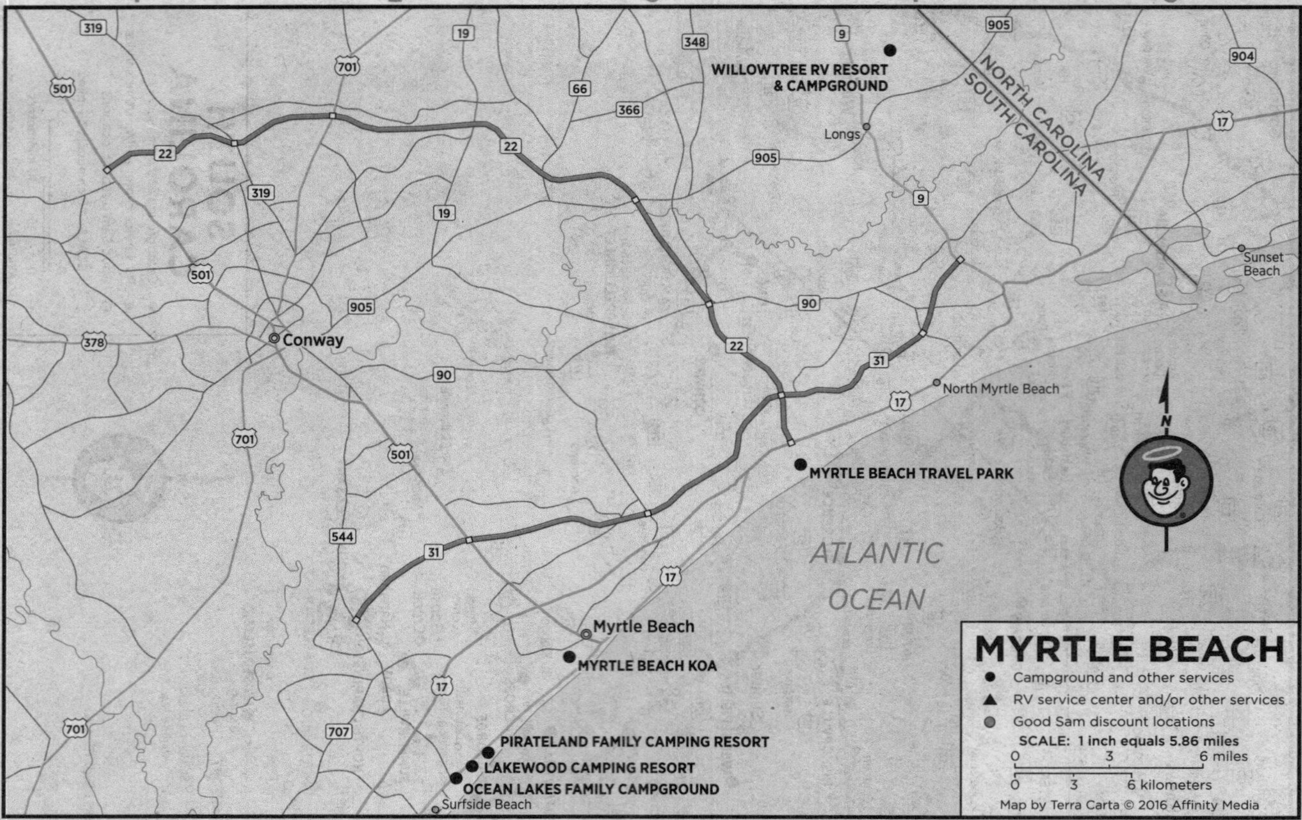
WILLOWTREE RV RESORT & CAMPGROUND
Longs
NORTH CAROLINA
SOUTH CAROLINA
Sunset Beach
Conway
North Myrtle Beach
MYRTLE BEACH TRAVEL PARK
ATLANTIC OCEAN
Myrtle Beach
MYRTLE BEACH KOA
PIRATELAND FAMILY CAMPING RESORT
LAKEWOOD CAMPING RESORT
OCEAN LAKES FAMILY CAMPGROUND
Surfside Beach
MYRTLE BEACH
Campground and other services
RV service center and/or other services
Good Sam discount locations
SCALE: 1 inch equals 5.86 miles
0 3 6 miles
0 3 6 kilometers
Map by Terra Carta © 2016 Affinity Media

Featured Good Sam Parks

SOUTH CAROLINA

Good Sam Park

When you stay with Good Sam, you can expect the highest degree of cleanliness and friendliness, and better yet, you get 10% off campground fees.

If you're not already a Good Sam member you can purchase your membership at one of these locations:

ANDERSON
Lake Hartwell Camping & Cabins
(864)287-3223

CHARLESTON
Oak Plantation Campground, LP
(843)766-5936

CLEVELAND
Solitude Pointe RV Park & Cabins
(864)836-4128

DILLON
Camp Pedro
(843)774-2411

GREENVILLE
Springwood RV Park
(864)277-9789

HARDEEVILLE
Camp Lake Jasper RV Resort
(843)784-5200

HOLLYWOOD
Lake Aire RV Park & Campground
(843)571-1271

KINARDS
Magnolia RV Park & Campground
(864)697-1214

LEXINGTON
Barnyard RV Park
(800)633-6351

MYRTLE BEACH
Briarcliffe RV Resort
(843)272-2730
Cypress Camping Resort
(843)293-0300

ROEBUCK
Pine Ridge Campground
(864)576-0302

SANTEE
Palmetto Shores RV Resort
(803)478-6336
Santee Lakes Campground
(803)478-2262

SENECA
Crooked Creek RV Park
(864)882-5040

SPARTANBURG
Spartanburg/ Cunningham RV Park
(864)576-1973

SUMMERTON
Taw Caw Campground & Marina
(803)478-2171

SWANSEA
Yogi Bear's Jellystone Park At River Bottom Farms
(803)568-4182

WALTERBORO
New Green Acres RV Park
(800)474-3450

For more Good Sam Parks go to listing pages

Getty Images/iStockphoto

CHARLESTON

Soak in the history of this quintessentially Southern town

The phrase "Southern charm" is a well-worn idiom in travelogues of the United States, but any attempt to distill the essence of Charleston, South Carolina, down to a single tidy phrase or sentence without it will be missing the mark entirely.

> The French Quarter is where the echoes of old Charleston ring loudest. Here, the cobblestone streets remain.

Like drawing water from a well, this historic coastal community is one of the few places in the American South where one can easily trace the source of such nostalgia. Horse-drawn carriages still navigate the downtown core's network of antique cobblestone streets. Antebellum architecture is everywhere, as if in too vast a supply to be considered of any special significance. And extravagant church steeples predating the American Revolution by nearly a century casually rise over the cityscape, gifting Charleston the straightforward moniker of "Holy City."

The modesty and ease with which Charleston wears its profound history and romantic glamour can only be attributed to heaping amounts of the aforementioned Southern charm.

The city itself sits on a peninsula jutting out into an inlet created by the convergence of the Ashley, Cooper and Wando rivers. Together, the waters flow into scenic Charleston Harbor, where a daily and nightly mix of narrated boat tours and gourmet dinner cruises zips back and forth across the water in a tireless maritime dance.

Walking Through History

As such, first-time visitors to Charleston are best advised to begin their explorations at Waterfront Park. Rimming the edges of the downtown peninsula, the park offers a mix of everything the city is renowned for: history, incredible ocean views and a chance to stroll about on foot. Old-fashioned park benches, water fountains and picnic areas are set against a constantly shifting backdrop of sailboats and small cruise liners.

From there, continue your exploration of the city on foot (you'll soon quickly discover that Charleston is a city best experienced by walking). Must-visit city hotspots and districts include the Charleston City Market, French Quarter and King Street.

SC

The Charleston City Market is open 364 days a year (it's closed on Christmas Day) and dates to the 1790s. It spans four city blocks and the entire open-air bazaar is now an official National Historic Landmark listed on the National Register of Historic Places. Vendors hawk all manner of products and wares, ranging from fresh produce to rare used books to artistic crafts.

The French Quarter is where the echoes of old Charleston ring loudest. Here, the main cluster of cobblestone streets and old colonial-era city walls remain, as well as a slew of art studios and art galleries. Guided walking tours are a popular activity, with docents highlighting the history of the quarter.

Take a trip into the city's agrarian past at Magnolia Plantation. Founded in 1676 by the Drayton family, Magnolia Plantation has witnessed history unfold before it from the American Revolution through the Civil War and beyond. It is the oldest public tourist site in the Lowcountry, and the oldest public gardens in America. Its sprawling grounds host thousands of plants, trees and gardens, making it a photographer's delight.

When you're ready for a break from shopping, sightseeing and navigating historic cobblestone streets, head to King Street. Here a good selection of the city's best bars, cafes and restaurants make for a perfect pit stop.

Confederates and Buccaneers

Ready for more? At the top of the list sits Fort Sumter, a crumbling stronghold located on an island in the middle of Charleston Harbor. It was here that the opening salvo of the Civil War was launched. Boat tours to the island depart daily from Patriot's Point. Once at the island, tours are continued by a National Park Service Ranger, who leads a walk through the Fort's battered remains and on-site museum.

For a touch of real brick-and-mortar history, the Old Slave Mart Museum, Old Exchange and Provost Dungeon are three of the more humbling points of interest in the city.

The Old Slave Mart Museum is exactly what it sounds like. Once a place where the buying and selling of slaves was undertaken, the building is now home to an emotionally powerful museum and educational center that sheds light on the practice (and individual experience) of slavery.

The Old Exchange and Provost Dungeon, meanwhile, is perhaps the most historic building in the entire state. Built in 1771, it served as a dungeon cellar for pirates in the 17th century, as a prison used by the British prior to the American Revolution, as a customs house and as an elegant entertaining hall. The Declaration of Independence was read from its steps, and pirates have been imprisoned in its basement. It's a building with an eclectic history, and guided tours through its historic halls are among the most popular activities in all of Charleston.

For More Information

Charleston Area Convention and Visitors Bureau
800-774-0006
www.explorecharleston.com

South Carolina Department of Parks, Recreation and Tourism
803-734-1700
www.discoversouthcarolina.com

Ruth Rackley

LAKE KEOWEE

Bring a fishing rod and a thirst for adventure to this South Carolina gem

When viewed on a map or from the air, Lake Keowee in northwestern South Carolina is often said to resemble a Christmas tree. Long, narrow and fringed with shoreline that's frayed with thousands of branching inland coves, the lake is actually a long and deep valley, one that was flooded after the construction of three massive hydroelectric dams over the course of the 1960s and 70s.

Standing on the shores of this marvelous man-made gem, it's easy to see why Lake Keowee is such a popular vacation spot for Palmetto State residents and visitors alike.

Spread across more than 18,000 acres and sporting more than 300 miles of shoreline, the lake is a popular destination for anglers, boaters, kayakers, bird watchers and backcountry hikers. To the north rise the rocky summits of Sassafras Mountain and Pinnacle Mountain—the nearest of the Blue Ridge peaks—creating a stunning alpine backdrop. And the comparatively big city of Greenville is less than an hour's drive away to the east, meaning the luxury and amenity of world-class dining, shopping and entertainment options remains close at hand.

Lakeside Living

Most will find themselves setting up camp in the towns of Seneca, Walhalla, Clemson or Salem. Each offers their own unique vibe wrapped in heaping dollops of the kind of laid-back charm one would expect from a series of small lakeside communities.

Seneca and Walhalla are particularly worthwhile, and serve as either the homes-of or stepping-stones-to a handful of the most worthwhile attractions in the entire Keowee region.

Anyone with an ear for history won't want to miss the Oconee Heritage Center or the Museum of the Cherokee, both located in Walhalla. Both places tell the stories of Native Americans through artifacts, art work and superb exhibits.

For More Information

Discover Lake Keowee
888-348-7388
www.discoverkeowee.com

South Carolina Department of Parks, Recreation and Tourism
803-734-1700
www.discoversouthcarolina.com

SC

Perry Baker/SCPRT

LAKE MARION

Make your way to this recreation mecca

Teeming with largemouth bass, ringed with well-maintained hiking trails and bursting with wildlife, Lake Marion in central South Carolina is a popular spot for anglers, campers, boaters and anyone with a love of the great outdoors.

At more than 110,000 square acres in size, the lake is far and away the largest in the state. It's even among the top 50 largest lakes in the entire country. Together with nearby Lake Moultrie on its southern flank (connected via short a man-made canal and lock system) it sprawls across five separate counties in the heart of South Carolina's Coastal Plain region, a low and flat stretch of land where the Atlantic Ocean is believed to have once reached far inland.

Most visitors will find themselves arriving at Lake Marion by way of Columbia (53 miles to the northwest) or Charleston (71 miles to the southeast). Upon arrival, visitors can set up camp in a range of towns and communities that dot the lake's shoreline, though Santee is perhaps the most conveniently located. Santee sits directly on Interstate 95, just a stone's throw from Santee State Park and just west of the single bridge that quickly connects one side of the lake with the other.

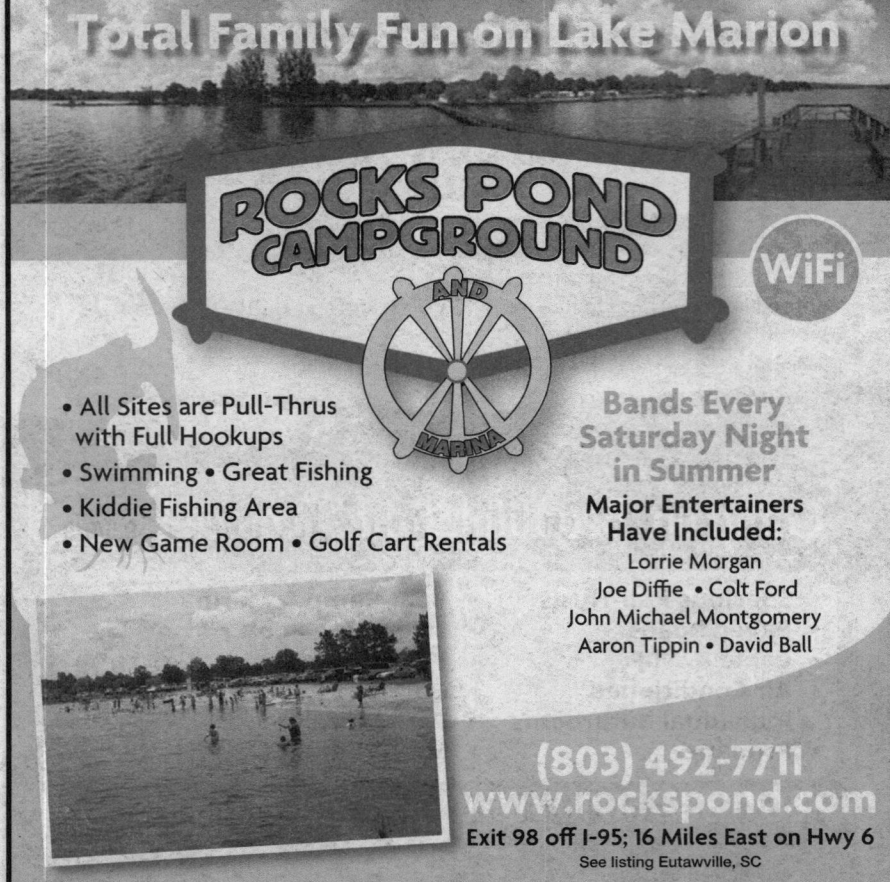

Swing in Santee

Golfers in particular will cherish their time in the small town of Santee. Home to less than 900 year-round residents, it annually attracts hundreds of thousands of visitors, many of whom are looking to hit the links at one of nearly 20 courses located within a 50-mile radius of the town's center. Lake Marion Golf Course and Santee Cooper

Great egret at Santee State Park.
April Rembert/SCPRT

Baiting a hook at Santee State Park. Deborah Holtzscheiter/SCPRT

Fishing in Santee State Park. Perry Baker/SCPRT

Country Club are both located within the town's limits and each features scenic lakeside holes, making them among the most popular courses in the area.

But fairways and putting greens aren't the only ways to savor to the great outdoors here. The lake itself remains the main attraction, and there's no shortage of recreational activities to keep busy bodies active and outdoors all year long. The typical gamut of lakeside recreational options is available in spades. Canoeing, kayaking, boating, swimming and fishing are all popular Lake Marion pastimes for visitors and locals alike. Striped bass, largemouth bass, crappie, bream and catfish call the lake home, and an abundance of bait shops dotted around the lake's shores make picking up a South Carolina fishing license quick and easy.

Most visitors will find themselves content enough to simply lace up their hiking boots and hit portions of the Palmetto Trail, six branches of which loop around the Lake Marion area. But more adventurous trail hoppers looking for a chance to go completely off-the-beaten-path will need more than a pair of hiking boots to do so. In order to trek the Cooper River Underwater Heritage Trail system, you'll need a scuba diving certification or professional scuba trainer to help you navigate this historic pathway, which features underwater shipwrecks and structures dating all the way back to the American Revolution. While it's certainly not the most accessible attraction in the area, it's easily one of the most rewarding.

Beyond Lake Marion itself, Santee State Park manages to attract most of the recreational attention in the area—and for good reason. The park is home to Nature Adventure Outfitters, which rent canoes, kayaks or stand up paddle boards for fun on the lake. If you're towing a vessel, you're in luck: Two separate boat ramps in the park make launching in the lake a quick and easy breeze, even during peak season. Hikers and bikers can explore more than ten miles of marked trails that wind through the park, including the Limestone Nature Trail, Oak Pinolly Trail and Sinkhole Pond Trail.

> Lake Marion Golf Course and Santee Cooper Country Club are both located within the town's limits and each features scenic lakeside holes.

Marion's Wild Side

Twenty miles to the east and across the lake, Santee National Wildlife Refuge is big draw for hunters and nature photographers looking to snag the perfect shot of an alligator, grey fox or bobcat.

Finally, when it's time for a break from campfires, trail heads and queuing-up at boat launches, head just south of Lake Moultrie to the Berkeley County Museum. Tucked into the corner of Old Santee Canal State Park near the small town of Moncks Corner, this 5,600-square-foot heritage museum features exhibits that tell the story of Berkeley County, with artifacts dating as far back as 12,000 years ago. The highlight is the Santee Cooper exhibit, which chronicles the New Deal-era creation of Lake Marion and Lake Moultrie as part of the Santee Cooper Hydroelectric and Navigation Project.

Make no mistake: Man-made or not, the Lake Marion region is a boon for nature lovers and outdoors enthusiasts. Park the RV, grab your fishing rod or lace up your hiking boots and explore this surprising gem in the heart of central South Carolina.

SC

For More Information

Clarendon County Chamber of Commerce
803-435-4405
www.clarendoncounty.com

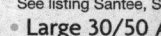

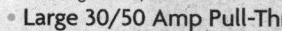

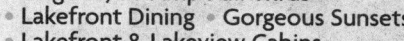

South Carolina Department of Parks, Recreation and Tourism
866-224-9339
www.discoversouthcarolina.com

SOUTH OF THE BORDER

Get a taste of Old Mexico in the heart of Dixie

If you're not paying close attention, crossing from North Carolina into South Carolina near the tiny town of Dillon can make your head spin. Here, a good 1,400 miles or so from the Mexican border, sits a vibrant, trinket-rich, taco-fueled swath of Old Mexico.

Welcome to South of the Border. No, you didn't make a wrong turn or blank out for 20 hours of driving—you've arrived at one of the quirkiest roadside stops in the country, one you won't soon forget.

The first clue that something is amiss will be when you spot a massive water tower wearing a giant Mexican sombrero, aptly known as Sombrero Tower. If your radar isn't already going off then it surely will be once you're greeted by Pedro, the 97-foot-tall mustachioed cartoon character who stands proudly over the entrance, straddling the driveway in what appears to be a pair of brightly colored mariachi pants. Your surprise Mexican adventure has begun.

> Pedro is a 97-foot-tall, mustachioed cartoon character who stands proudly over the entrance.

Bringing Mexico to the South

It all started in 1949, when a pioneering entrepreneur named Alan Schafer built a beer stand on the highway, catering to thirsty folks living in alcohol-free counties just over the border in North Carolina. At this point, it was called the South of the Border Beer Depot. The idea took root, and so Mr. Shafer added a grill to the mix, changing the name to the South of the Border Drive-In. When he added a motel, the name changed once again, to Schafer Project South of the (North Carolina) Border. Eventually, he embraced a dash of brevity, shortening the name to its current appellation, South of the Border.

Today, the 300-acre roadside complex is stuffed with family fun. Visitors can pull over for a quick pit stop and spin through the on-site theme park or hunker down in the on-site campground for a more in-depth dive into this quirky roadside playground of fun.

If you're travelling with kids, then Pedroland Park will likely attract most of your attention. The Mexican-styled theme park features a range of rides, including a Ferris wheel, bumper cars, carousel, two mini-golf courses and a

South of the Border mascot Pedro greets visitors.
South of the Border

RV camping near South of the Border. South of the Border

full-size arcade. The park is also home to Reptile Lagoon, the largest indoor exhibit of its kind in the United States. Home to a variety of snakes, alligators, crocodiles and large turtles, the exhibit gives an up-close and educational look at some of the most exotic animals in the world.

You also won't want to miss a ride to the top of Sombrero Tower. The observation deck is at an elevation of 200 feet, offering a 360-degree view of the surrounding South Carolina and North Carolina countryside. The ride to the top is done in a glass elevator to boot, so the topsy-turvy sightseeing begins as soon as you start ascending smoothly to the top.

> You won't want to miss a ride to the top of Sombrero Tower. The observation deck is 200 feet high.

Dillon's Delights

When you're ready for a break from the bright lights and spicy food of South of the Border, head a few miles south to nearby Dillon or Latta. Trains have been passing through Dillon since 1904, and the tiny town still has a turn-of-the-century look and feel. Take some time to wander Historic Downtown Dillon, which is listed on the National Register of Historic Places.

In Latta, slightly south of Dillon, history buffs will want to check out the Dillon County Museum. Housed in a restored doctor's office, the artifacts on display showcase the local and personal history of the area. Near the museum is the Betha Post Office and General Store (built in 1888) and Vidalia Academy (a turn-of-the-century schoolhouse).

If you're hankering for some exercise in the great outdoors, head for Little Pee Dee State Park, located about 12 miles southeast of South of the Border. At 835 acres, the park is large enough for a day trip escape but small enough to explore thoroughly over the course of a long weekend. Hop on the Beaver Pond Nature Trail for an easy 1.3-mile hike, or cycle along paved park biking paths.

Little Pee Dee is also home to Lake Norton, which features a fishing pier, boat ramp and a canoe or kayak rental shop. The 45-acre lake is teeming with bream, bass and catfish, making it a popular destination for anglers.

Regardless of how long you stop, South of the Border and the surrounding area has something for every type of RV traveler. As one of the quirkiest (and largest) roadside attractions in the country, it's well worth a thorough visit and makes for a great pit stop to break up a long road trip. Bring your camera to prove that you visited Old Mexico in South Carolina.

For More Information

South of the Border
843-774-2417
www.thesouthoftheborder.com

South Carolina Tourism
866-224-9339
www.discoversouthcarolina.com

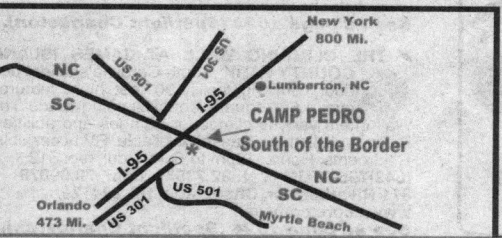

SC

CONSULTANTS
Chip & Pat Dennis

AIKEN — C3 *Aiken*

AIKEN (State Pk) From Jct of US 78 & State Park Rd (NW side of town), N 5 mi on State Park Rd, NW 300 feet on Old Tory Trail (R). Call park directly if making group reservations. 2015 rates: $14. (803)649-2857

ANDERSON — B2 *Anderson*

ANDERSON/LAKE HARTWELL KOA **Ratings: 8.5/9★/8** (Campground) 2015 rates: $35 to $60. (800)562-5804 200 Wham Rd, Anderson, SC 29625

LAKE HARTWELL CAMPING & CABINS
Ratings: 8.5/9★/8 (Campground) From Jct of I-85 (exit 11) & SC-24, NW 2.6 mi on SC-24 to O'Neal Ferry Rd, NE 0.3 mi to Ponderosa Point Rd, E 0.5 mi (E). **FAC:** Paved/gravel rds. (120 spaces). Avail: 60 gravel, 20 pull-thrus (25 x 55), back-ins (25 x 50), 20 full hkups, 40 W, 40 E (30/50 amps), seasonal sites, cable, WiFi, tent sites, rentals, dump, laundry, LP gas, fire rings, firewood. **REC:** pool, wading pool, Lake Hartwell: fishing, playground, rec open to public. Pet restrict(B). 2015 rates: $35. Disc: military.
(864)287-3223 Lat: 34.56356, Lon: -82.85714
400 Ponderosa Point, Townville, SC 29689
info@camplakehartwell.com
www.camplakehartwell.com
See ad this page, 1021.

SADLERS CREEK STATE RECREATION AREA (State Pk) From Jct of I-85 & SC-24 (Exit 11), E 5.1 mi on SC-24 to SC-187, S 7 mi to Sadlers Creek Rd, W 1.2 mi(E). Call park directly if making group reservations. Note: 40' RV length limit. 2015 rates: $15 to $19. (864)226-8950

SPRINGFIELD (Public Corps) From Jct of SC Hwy 28 By-Pass & SC Hwy 24 (in Anderson), W 4.5 mi on SC Hwy 24 to SC Hwy 187, S 4 mi to CR, W 2 mi (L). 2015 rates: $26. Apr 1 to Oct 31. (888)893-0678

BEAUFORT — E4 *Beaufort*

HUNTING ISLAND (State Pk) From E Jct of US 21 & SC-802 (SE of Beaufort), SE 17 mi on US 21 (L). Call park directly if making group reservations. Note: 40' RV length limit. 2015 rates: $17 to $38. (843)838-2011

Laundry & dishwasher detergent liquids contain up to 80 percent water. It costs energy and packaging to bring this water to the consumer. When there is a choice - choose dry powders.

TUCK IN THE WOOD CAMPGROUND
Ratings: 8/9★/8.5 (Campground) From the Jct of Hwy 170 & US-21 Bus in Beaufort: Go E 9.1 mi E on US-21 Bus, then S 2.2 mi on Martin Luther King/Lands End Rd (L). **FAC:** Gravel rds. (74 spaces). Avail: 73 dirt, 28 pull-thrus (30 x 65), back-ins (30 x 60), 73 full hkups (30/50 amps), seasonal sites, cable, WiFi, tent sites, dump, laundry, firewood. **REC:** pond, fishing, playground. Pet restrict(B). Partial handicap access. Big rig sites, eco-friendly, 2015 rates: $37.
(843)838-2267 Lat: 32.366667, Lon: -80.585833
22 Tuck In De Wood Ln, St Helena Island, SC 29920
tuckinthewood@islc.net
www.tuckinthewood.com
See ad this page.

BISHOPVILLE — B4 *Lee*

LEE STATE NATURAL AREA (State Pk) From Jct of I-20 & Road 22 (Exit 123), N 1 mi on Road 22 (L). Call park directly if making group reservations. Note: 36' RV length limit. 2015 rates: $15 to $18. (803)482-5307

BLACKVILLE — C3 *Barnwell*

BARNWELL (State Pk) From Jct of US 78 & SC-3, SW 2.5 mi on SC-3 (R). Call park directly if making group reservations. Note: 36' RV length limit. 2015 rates: $14 to $16. (803)284-2212

CALHOUN FALLS — B2 *Abbeville*

CALHOUN FALLS (State Pk) From Jct of SC-72 & SC-81, N 1.1 mi on SC-81 (L). Call park directly if making group reservations. 2015 rates: $19 to $21. (864)447-8267

CANADYS — D4 *Colleton*

COLLETON (State Pk) From Jct of I-95 & SC-61 (Exit 68), SE 2.9 mi on SC-61 to US 15, N 0.4 mi (L). Call park directly if making group reservations. 2015 rates: $15. (843)538-8206

CHAPIN — B3 *Lexington*

DREHER ISLAND (State Pk) From Jct of I-26 & RD 48/Columbia Ave (Exit 91), SW 2 mi on RD 48/Columbia Ave to US 76, NW (right) 0.3 mi to St Peters Church Rd, SW 3.4 mi to Dreher Island Rd, W 3 mi to State Park Rd, SE 2.6 mi (E). Call park directly if making group reservations. Note: 45' RV length limit. 2015 rates: $23 to $26. (803)364-4152

CHARLESTON — D4 *Charleston*

CHARLESTON See also Hollywood, Ladson & Mount Pleasant.

DOLPHIN COVE MARINA & RV PARK
(RV Park) (Under Construction) From the jct of I-26 (exit 216B) & Hwy 7/Cosgrove Ave: Go N 0.3 mi on Cosgrove Ave, then E 0.9 mi on Azalea Dr, then SE 0.7 mi on King St Extension, then SW on Summerville Ave and immediately W onto Austin Ave (R).

CHARLESTON'S BEST KEPT SECRET
NEW RV PARK OPENING EARLY 2016. Just 2 1/2 miles to the heart of Charleston, bus shuttle is avail. View the incredible sunsets over the beautiful Ashley River from our dock or Cafe's patio. Call for more info 843/744-2562.

FAC: Paved rds. 60 paved, back-ins (28 x 75), 60 full hkups (30/50 amps). **REC:** Ashley River: marina, rec open to public. Pets OK. Big rig sites, 2015 rates: $50 to $60.
(843)744-2562 Lat: 32.83199, Lon: -79.95836
2079 Austin Ave, Charleston, SC 29405
sales@dolphincovemarina.net
www.dolphincovemarina.net
See ad page 1022 (Spotlight Charleston).

Clean Green! Vinegar and baking soda can be used to clean almost anything. Mix in a little warm water with either of these and you've got yourself an all-purpose cleaner.

OAK PLANTATION CAMPGROUND, LP
Ratings: 9/9.5★/9.5 (Campground) From W Jct of I-526 & US-17, S 4.4 mi on US-17 (R).

15 MINUTES FROM HISTORIC CHARLESTON
Guests appreciate the friendly staff and picturesque setting as well as convenient location to the many attractions in the Charleston area. For sightseeing or just relaxing, let us host your next camping experience.

FAC: Paved rds. 246 Avail: 40 paved, 45 gravel, 161 grass, 134 pull-thrus (35 x 65), back-ins (35 x 65), 146 full hkups, 95 W, 95 E (30/50 amps), cable, WiFi, dump, laundry, LP gas, firewood. **REC:** pool, pond, fishing, playground. Pets OK. Partial handicap access, no tents. Big rig sites, 2015 rates: $42 to $50. Disc: military.
(843)766-5936 Lat: 32.80308, Lon: -80.10704
3540 Savannah Hwy, Charleston, SC 29455
info@oakplantationcampground.com
www.oakplantationcampground.com
See ad pages 1023 (Spotlight Charleston), 1021 & RV Trips of a Lifetime, Snowbird Destinations in Magazine Section.

RIVER'S END CAMPGROUND & RV PARK
Ratings: 9/9.5★/9 (Public) From Jct I-26 (exit 220B) & US 17: Go 61 mi SW on US 17, then 51 mi S on I-95 to I-95 (exit 94), then 10 mi E on Hwy 204, then 8 mi N on Harry Truman Parkway, then 15-1/2 mi E on US 80E, then 1/4 mi N on Polk St, then 500 ft E on Fort Ave (L). **FAC:** Gravel rds. (87 spaces). Avail: 82 gravel, 30 pull-thrus (20 x 45), back-ins (20 x 40), 75 full hkups, 7 W, 7 E (30/50 amps), cable, WiFi, tent sites, rentals, dump, laundry, LP gas, fire rings, firewood. **REC:** pool. Pet restrict(Q). Partial handicap access. 2015 rates: $44 to $99. Disc: AAA, military. ATM.
(800)786-1016 Lat: 32.02274, Lon: -80.85020
5 Fort Ave, Tybee Island, GA 31328
riversend@cityoftybee.org
www.riversendcampground.com
See primary listing at Tybee Island, GA and ad page 436.

THE CAMPGROUND AT JAMES ISLAND COUNTY PARK
(Public) From Jct of I-26 & US-17 (exit 221A S-bnd) W 2 mi on US-17 to SC-171, S 1.4 mi to SC-700/Maybank Hwy, W 1.4 mi to Riverland Dr S (left) 1.7 mi (R).

DISCOVER THE CHARMS OF CHARLESTON
Explore Historic Downtown Charleston. Indulge in fine dining and shopping. Experience the waterparks walking trails, beaches, fishing and fun festivals. All minutes away. Charleston County Parks - Everything under the sun.

FAC: Paved rds. 124 gravel, 15 pull-thrus (35 x 90), back-ins (25 x 65), 118 full hkups, 6 W, 6 E (30/50 amps), WiFi, tent sites, rentals, dump, laundry, groc, LP gas, fire rings, firewood, controlled access. **REC:** pond, fishing, playground. Pets OK. Partial handicap access. Big rig sites, 28 day max stay, 2015 rates $43 to $49.
(843)795-4386 Lat: 32.73549, Lon: -79.99193
871 Riverland Dr, Charleston, SC 29412
campground@ccprc.com
www.charlestoncampgrounds.com
See ad page 1024 (Spotlight Charleston) & Family Camping, Snowbird Destinations in Magazine Section.

Things to See and Do

SPLASH ZONE WATERPARK Water playground offering two 200 ft tube slides, a 500 ft lazy river, adventure channel featuring sprays & a waterfall, a leisure pool & a Caribbean play structure with interactive elements. May 30 to Sep 5. partial handicap access. RV accessible Restrooms, food. Hours: 10am to 6pm. Adult fee: $11.99.
(843)795-7275 Lat: 32.73557, Lon: -79.99078
871 Riverland Dr, Charleston, SC 29412
customerservice@ccprc.com
www.splashparks.com
See ad page 1024 (Spotlight Charleston).

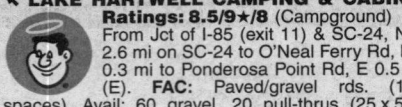

THE CLIMBING WALL AT JAMES ISLAND COUNTY PARK South Carolina's tallest outdoor climbing facility-50 feet high, features over 4,500 square feet of climbing space. The Wall offers various climbs for all ages and abilities Belay and climbing classes available. RV accessible Restrooms. Hours: 12pm to 5pm. Adult fee: $12.
(843)795-4FUN Lat: 32.73557, Lon: -79.99078
871 Riverland Dr, Charleston, SC 29412
www.ccprc.com/wall
See ad page 1024 (Spotlight Charleston).

CHERAW — B4 *Chesterfield*

CHERAW (State Pk) From SW Jct of SC-9 & US 52, S 3.7 mi on US 52 (R). Contact park directly if making group and boat-in reservations. 2015 rates: $17. (866)345-7275

CHESTER — B3 *Chester*

CHESTER (State Pk) From SW Jct of US 321 & SC-72, SW 1.5 mi on SC-72 (L). Call park directly if making group reservations. 2015 rates: $14. (803)385-2680

CLARKS HILL — C2 *McCormick*

MODOC (Public Corps) From town, S 13 mi on SR-28 to Clarks Hill, SC. Continue NW on Hwy 22 for 4 mil to entrance (L). For reservations call 1-877-444-6777. 2015 rates: $18 to $52. Mar 28 to Sep 28. (864)333-2272

CLEMSON — A1 *Pickens*

TWIN LAKES (Public Corps) From Jct of SC Hwy 123 & US-76, SE 3.5 mi on US-76 to CR-56, SW 3 mi (R). 2015 rates: $24 to $26. (888)893-0678

CLEVELAND — A2 *Greenville*

PALMETTO COVE RV PARK **Ratings: 7.5/NA/7.5** (RV Park) 2015 rates: $25. Apr 1 to Nov 15. (864)836-6221 521 Table Rock Rd, Cleveland, SC 29635

SOLITUDE POINTE RV PARK & CABINS
Ratings: 8.5/9.5★/9.5 (RV Park) From Jct I-26 & Hwy 11 (Exit 5): Go 29 mi S on Hwy 11, then 1 mi N on Hwy 8 (Caesars Head Hwy), then 1/4 mi W on Table Rock Rd (R). **FAC:** Paved rds. 13 Avail: 7 paved, 6 gravel, patios, 3 pull-thrus (30 x 58), back-ins (30 x 50), 13 full hkups (30/50 amps), WiFi, tent sites, rentals, laundry, LP gas, firewood. **REC:** Saluda River: fishing, playground. Pet restrict(B/Q). Big rig sites, 2015 rates: $35 to $38. Disc: AAA, military.
(864)836-4128 Lat: 35.06717, Lon: -82.62231
102 Table Rock Road, Cleveland, SC 29635
info@solitudepointe.com
www.solitudepointe.com
See ad pages 1032, 1021.

COLUMBIA — B3 *Lexington, Richland*

COLUMBIA See also Kinards, Lexington & Swansea.

BARNYARD RV PARK
Ratings: 8.5/10★/9.5 (RV Park) From Jct of I-26 (exit111A) & US-1, W 3 mi on US-1S (R); or From Jct of I-20 (exit 58) & US-1, E (N-bnd) 2 mi on US-1 (L). **FAC:** Paved rds. (129 spaces). Avail: 49 gravel, patios, 49 pull-thrus (30 x 85), 49 full hkups (30/50 amps), seasonal sites, WiFi, dump, laundry, LP gas. **REC.** Pets OK. Partial handicap access. Big rig sites, eco-friendly, 2015 rates: $35. Disc: AAA, military.
(800)633-6351 Lat: 33.97712, Lon: -81.15610
201 Oak Dr, Lexington, SC 29073
barnyardrvpark@sc.rr.com
www.barnyardrvpark.com
See primary listing at Lexington and ad page 1031.

SESQUICENTENNIAL (State Pk) From Jct of I-20 & US 1 (Exit 74), NE 3 mi on US 1 (R); or From Jct of I-77 & US 1 (Exit 17), NE 2.2 mi on US 1 (R). Call park directly if making group reservations. Note: 35' RV length limit. 2015 rates: $18. (803)788-2706

Travel Services

CAMPING WORLD OF COLUMBIA As the nation's largest retailer of RV supplies, accessories, services and new and used RVs, Camping World is committed to making your total RV experience better. RV Accessories: (888)818-7834. **SERVICES:** RV, tire, RV appliance, staffed RV wash, restrooms, RV Sales. RV supplies, LP, dump, RV accessible. waiting room. Hours: 8am to 6pm.
(888)686-5194 Lat: 34.053732, Lon: -81.127153
3634 Fernandina Rd, Columbia, SC 29210
www.campingworld.com

CONWAY — C5 *Horry*

BIG CYPRESS LAKE RV PARK/FISHING RETREAT
Ratings: 4/7★/7.5 (Campground) From Jct of US-378 & US-501 & US-701, S 1.4 mi on US-701 to Janette St (Janette St becomes Kates Bay Hwy), W 5.7 mi to Browns Way Shortcut Rd, S 0.6 mi (L) (Call for Reservation). **FAC:** Gravel rds. (30 spaces). Avail: 25 gravel, 10 pull-thrus (22 x 60), back-ins (24 x 46), 25 full hkups (30/50 amps), seasonal sites, WiFi $, tent sites, fire rings, firewood. **REC:** Big Cypress Lake: fishing. Pet restrict(B). Eco-friendly, 2015 rates: $35 to $55. Disc: military.
(843)902-3418 Lat: 33.78955, Lon: -79.16617
6531 Browns Way Shortcut Rd, Conway, SC 29527
rvpark@sccoast.net
www.bigcypresslake.com
See ad page 1034.

BUCKSPORT PLANTATION MARINA & RV RESORT **Ratings: 5/8/8** (RV Park) 2015 rates: $37 to $57. (843)397-5566 135 Bucksport Rd, Conway, SC 29527

CROSS — C4 *Berkeley*

CROSS/SANTEE COOPER LAKES KOA **Ratings: 7/9/8** (Campground) 2015 rates: $32 to $38. (843)753-2818 2060 Ranger Dr, Cross, SC 29436

CROSS HILL — B2 *Laurens*

ALL SEASONS FAMILY CAMPGROUND **Ratings: 4.5/NA/8** (RV Park) 2015 rates: $25. (864)998-5181 2075 Watts Bridge Rd, Cross Hill, SC 29332

LAKE GREENWOOD MOTORCOACH RESORT **Ratings: 8.5/9★/9.5** (Condo Pk) 2015 rates: $49 to $69. (864)992-4700 463 Cane Creek Rd, Cross Hill, SC 29332

MOON LANDING RV PARK & MARINA
Ratings: 7/9★/6.5 (Campground) From Jct SC 72 & SC 39, S 1.9 mi to Watts Bridge Rd, SW 4 mi (L). **FAC:** Gravel rds. (75 spaces). Avail: 10 grass, patios, 10 pull-thrus (30 x 40), 10 full hkups (30/50 amps), seasonal sites, cable, WiFi, dump, laundry, groc, LP gas, fire rings, firewood. **REC:** Lake Greenwood: fishing, marina. Pets OK. No tents. Eco-friendly, 2015 rates: $35 to $45.
(864)998-4292 Lat: 34.24670, Lon: -81.98939
4105 Watts Bridge Rd, Cross Hill, SC 29332
info@moonlandingrvpark.com
www.moonlandingrvpark.com

DILLON — B5 *Dillon*

BASS LAKE RV CAMPGROUND **Ratings: 7.5/8.5★/7.5** (Campground) 2015 rates: $36. (843)774-9100 1149 Bass Lake Place, Dillon, SC 29536

Tell them you saw them in this Guide!

DILLON (CONT)

CAMP PEDRO
Ratings: 9/8.5★/8.5 (RV Park) From Jct of I-95 (Exit 1A in NC) & US-301, 0.1 mi on US 301 (L). **FAC:** Paved rds. 100 paved, 65 pull-thrus (40 x 100), back-ins (40 x 40), 100 full hkups (30/50 amps), WiFi, tent sites, laundry, LP gas, controlled access. **REC:** heated pool, playground, rec open to public. Pets OK. Big rig sites, 2015 rates: $35. Disc: military. AAA Approved
(843)774-2411 Lat: 34.49757, Lon: -79.30655
3346 Hwy 301N, Hamer, SC 29547
info@thesouthoftheborder.com
www.thesouthoftheborder.com
See ad pages 1029 (Spotlight South of the Border), 1021.

LITTLE PEE DEE (State Pk) From Jct of I-95 & SC-34 (Exit 190), E 3.2 mi on SC-34 to SC-57, S 8.2 mi to State Park Rd, N 1.9 mi (R). Call park directly if making group reservations. 2015 rates: $16. (843)774-8872

Things to See and Do

SOUTH OF THE BORDER Tourist complex with variety of restaurants, shops, arcades & hotel/motel convention center. Also features children's amusement park, mini-golf & observation tower. Partial handicap access. RV accessible. Restrooms, food. Hours: 9AM to 9Pm. ATM.
(843)774-2411 Lat: 34.49757, Lon: -79.30655
3346 Highway 301 North, Hamer, SC 29547
www.thesouthoftheborder.com
See ad page 1029 (Spotlight South of the Border).

EDISTO ISLAND — E4 *Colleton*

EDISTO BEACH (State Pk) From Jct of Hwy 17 & SC-174, S 21.8 mi on SR-174 (L). Call park directly if making group reservations. Note: 40' RV length limit. 2015 rates: $21 to $38. (843)869-2156

EUTAWVILLE — C4 *Orangeburg*

ROCKS POND CAMPGROUND & MARINA
Ratings: 7.5/7.5/7.5 (Campground) From Jct of I-95 & SC-6 (Exit 98), SE 16 mi on Old Number Six Hwy (SC 6) to Rocks Pond Rd, NE 1.4 mi to Campground Rd E 0.6 mi (R). **FAC:** Gravel rds. (407 spaces). Avail: 200 grass, 172 pull-thrus (35 x 64), back-ins (35 x 60), 200 full hkups (30/50 amps), seasonal sites, WiFi $, tent sites, rentals, laundry, groc, LP gas, firewood, controlled access. **REC:** Lake Marion: swim, fishing, marina, playground, rec open to public. Pet restrict(B). Partial handicap access. Big rig sites, 2015 rates: $30 to $40. Disc: military.
(803)492-7711 Lat: 33.40369, Lon: -80.23383
108 Campground Rd, Eutawville, SC 29048
feedback@rockspond.com
www.rockspond.com
See ad page 1026 (Spotlight Lake Marion).

FAIR PLAY — B1 *Oconee*

CAROLINA LANDING **Ratings: 7/8/8** (Membership Pk) 2015 rates: $35. (800)405-6188 120 Carolina Landing Drive, Fair Play, SC 29643

LAKE HARTWELL STATE RECREATION AREA (State Pk) From Jct of I-85 & SC-11 (exit 1), N 0.7 mi on SC-11 (L). 2015 rates: $16 to $21. (864)972-3352

FLORENCE — B5 *Florence*

FLORENCE RV PARK **Ratings: 7.5/6.5/6.5** (Campground) 2015 rates: $30 to $40. (843)665-7007 1115 E Campground Rd, Florence, SC 29506

SWAMP FOX CAMPGROUND **Ratings: 5.5/8/7** (Campground) 2015 rates: $29 to $35. (877)251-2251 1600 Gateway Road, Florence, SC 29501

FORT MILL — A3 *York*

CHARLOTTE/FORT MILL KOA **Ratings: 8/9★/8** (Campground) 2015 rates: $35 to $65. (888)562-4430 940 Gold Hill Rd, Fort Mill, SC 29708

CROWN COVE RV PARK
Ratings: 6/8/7.5 (RV Park) From Jct of I-77 (Exit 90) & Hwy 21 (Carowinds Blvd): Go S 1.2 mi on Hwy 21, then E 2.1 mi on Regent Pkwy (R). **FAC:** Paved rds. 126 Avail: 59 paved, 67 gravel, 72 pull-thrus (30 x 65), back-ins (50 x 70), 126 full hkups (30/50 amps), cable, WiFi, dump, laundry. **REC:** pond, fishing. Pets OK. Partial handicap access, no tents. 2015 rates: $38. Disc: AAA.
(803)547-3500 Lat: 35.06010, Lon: -80.90410
8332 Regent Pkwy, Fort Mill, SC 29715
office@crowncovecamprvpark.com
www.crowncovervpark.com
See ad page 858.

GAFFNEY — A3 *Cherokee*

SPARTANBURG NORTHEAST/GAFFNEY KOA **Ratings: 9/10★/9.5** (Campground) 2015 rates: $29 to $44. (800)562-0362 160 Sarratt School Rd, Gaffney, SC 29341

GREENVILLE — A2 *Greenville*

GREENVILLE See also Anderson, Cleveland, Kinards, Roebuck, Seneca & Spartanburg.

PARIS MOUNTAIN (State Pk) From the Jct of US 276 & SC 253/SC 291 (State Park Rd), E 0.1 mi on SC 291 to SC 253, NE 2.5 mi on SC 253 to S23-334, N 0.7 mi (L). Call park directly if making tent only reservations. Note: 40' RV length limit. 2015 rates: $18 to $19. (864)244-5565

SPRINGWOOD RV PARK
Ratings: 6.5/8.5★/7 (RV Park) From the Jct of I-85 (Exit 44) & US-25/White Horse Rd: Go 2 3/4 mi S on White Horse Rd, then 1/2 mi S on Donaldson Rd (R). **FAC:** Paved rds. (72 spaces). Avail: 22 grass, patios, 4 pull-thrus (30 x 65), back-ins (30 x 45), 22 full hkups (30/50 amps), seasonal sites, WiFi. Pets OK. No tents. Big rig sites, 2015 rates: $35. No CC.
(864)277-9789 Lat: 34.76017, Lon: -82.38466
810 Donaldson Rd, Greenville, SC 29605
wyattpark@aol.com
www.springwoodrvpark.com
See ad this page, 1021.

GREENWOOD — B2 *Abbeville, Greenwood*

LAKE GREENWOOD (State Pk) From Jct of SC-246 & SC-34, E 3.5 mi on SC-34 to Island Ford Rd, N 1.4 mi (E); or From Jct of SC-246 & SC-702, S 5.2 mi on SC-702 (L). Call park directly if making group reservations. 2015 rates: $18 to $23. (864)543-3535

Dispose of old paint, chemicals, and oil properly. Don't put batteries, antifreeze, paint, motor oil, or chemicals in the trash. Use proper toxics disposal sites.

HARDEEVILLE — E3 *Jasper*

CAMP LAKE JASPER RV RESORT
Ratings: 9/9.5★/9.5 (RV Park) From Jct. of I-95 (exit 8) and Hwy 278: Go E .01 mi on Hwy 278 then 1.1 mi N on Medical Center Drive then E 1.1 mi. on Red Dam Rd (R). **FAC:** Paved rds. 30 all weather, 40 gravel, 23 pull-thrus (38 x 85), back-ins (38 x 90), 70 full hkups (30/50 amps), cable, WiFi, laundry, firewood. **REC:** pool, Lake Jasper: fishing. Pet restrict(Q) $. No tents. Big rig sites, eco-friendly, 2015 rates: $38 to $48. Disc: AAA, military.
(843)784-5200 Lat: 32.322997, Lon: -81.038788
44 Camp Lake Drive, Hardeeville, SC 29927
info@camplakejasper.com
www.camplakejasper.com
See ad opposite page, 1021.

HARDEEVILLE RV-THOMAS PARKS **Ratings: 5.5/NA/7.5** (RV Park) 2015 rates: $39 to $50. (843)784-6210 3090 South Okatie Hwy (Hwy 315), Hardeeville, SC 29927

HILTON HEAD ISLAND — E4 *Beaufort*

HILTON HEAD ISLAND See also listings in Beaufort & Hardeeville.

HILTON HEAD HARBOR RV RESORT & MARINA
Ratings: 10/10★/10 (Condo Pk) From Jct of I-95 & US-278 (exit 8), E 19 mi on US-278 to Jenkins Rd, N 0.4 mi (L).

STAY ON THE INTRACOASTAL WATERWAY
Beautiful Waterside Resort with landscaped sites & concrete pads. Enjoy excellent dining at the Sunset Grille. Charter a boat or jet-skis at our marina. Beautiful beaches & premier golf are minutes away. Ask about lot sales.

FAC: Paved rds. (200 spaces). Avail: 150 paved, patios, back-ins (30 x 65), 150 full hkups (30/50 amps), seasonal sites, cable, WiFi, dump, laundry, groc, firewood, restaurant. **REC:** pool, whirlpool, Intercostal waterway: fishing, marina, playground. Pets OK. Partial handicap access, no tents. Big rig sites, eco-friendly, 2015 rates: $54 to $69.
(843)681-3256 Lat: 32.22328, Lon: -80.77140
43-A Jenkins Rd, Hilton Head Island, SC 29926
info@hiltonheadharbor.com
www.hiltonheadharbor.com
See ad opposite page & Snowbird Destinations in Magazine Section.

HILTON HEAD ISLAND MOTORCOACH RESORT **Ratings: 10/10★/10** (Condo Pk) 2015 rates: $60 to $80. (800)722-2365 133 Arrow Rd, Hilton Head Island, SC 29928

HOLLYWOOD — E5 *Charleston*

LAKE AIRE RV PARK & CAMPGROUND
Ratings: 8/8.5★/8.5 (Campground) From W Jct of I-526 & US-17, W 7.5 mi on US-17 S to SC-162, SW 0.2 mi (L). **FAC:** Gravel rds. 87 grass, 66 pull-thrus (30 x 60), back-ins (30 x 60), 66 full hkups, 21 W, 21 E (30/50 amps), WiFi, tent sites, dump, laundry, LP gas, fire rings. **REC:** pool, Lake Rantowles: fishing, playground. Pets OK. Partial handicap access. Big rig sites, 2015 rates: $34.20. Disc: AAA, military.
AAA Approved
(843)571-1271 Lat: 32.77822, Lon: -80.14984
4375 Hwy 162, Hollywood, SC 29449
lakeairerv@juno.com
www.lakeairerv.com
See ad pages 1022 (Spotlight Charleston), 1021.

KINARDS — B3 *Newberry*

MAGNOLIA RV PARK & CAMPGROUND
Ratings: 9/9.5★/8.5 (Campground) From Jct of I-26 & SC-66 (exit 60), SW 0.1 mi on SC-66 to Fairview Church Rd, SE 0.6 mi (L). **FAC:** Gravel rds. 41 gravel, 28 pull-thrus (25 x 60), back-ins (20 x 30), 30 full hkups, 11 W, 11 E (30/50 amps), WiFi, tent sites, rentals, dump, laundry, LP gas, fire rings, firewood. **REC:** pool, playground. Pet restrict(Q). Big rig sites, eco-friendly, 2015 rates: $26 to $32. Disc: military.
(864)697-1214 Lat: 34.43320, Lon: -81.75555
567 Fairview Church Rd, Kinards, SC 29355
info@magnoliarvparksc.com
www.magnoliarvparksc.com
See ad pages 1031, 1021.

LADSON — E5 *Charleston*

CHARLESTON KOA **Ratings: 8.5/9★/8** (Campground) 2015 rates: $39. (800)562-5812 9494 Hwy 78, Ladson, SC 29456

LANCASTER — A4 *Lancaster*

ANDREW JACKSON (State Pk) From Jct of SC-9 & US 521 N, N 8 mi on US 521 (R). Call park directly if making group reservations. 2015 rates: $18. (803)285-3344

LEESVILLE — C3 *Lexington*

CEDAR POND CAMPGROUND **Ratings: 3/5/6.5** (Campground) 2015 rates: $25. (803)657-5993 4721 Fairview Rd, Leesville, SC 29070

LEXINGTON — C3 *Lexington*

BARNYARD RV PARK
Ratings: 8.5/10★/9.5 (RV Park) From Jct of I-26 & US-1 (Exit 111A), W 3 mi on US-1S (R); or From Jct of I-20 & US-1 (exit 58), E (N-bnd) 2 mi on US-1 (L).

TALK ABOUT CONVENIENCE!
Located off Hwy 1, just minutes from I-20, I-26 and many area attractions. Come stay with us, kick back, relax and we will make you feel right at home. On weekends, experience Southern hospitality at our huge flea market.

FAC: Paved rds. (129 spaces). Avail: 49 gravel, patios, 49 pull-thrus (30 x 85), 49 full hkups (30/50 amps), seasonal sites, cable, WiFi $, dump, laundry, LP gas. **REC.** Pets OK. Partial handicap access, no tents. Big rig sites, 2015 rates: $35. Disc: AAA, military.
(800)633-6351 Lat: 33.97712, Lon: -81.15610
201 Oak Dr, Lexington, SC 29073
barnyardrvpark@sc.rr.com
www.barnyardrvpark.com
See ad pages 1031, 1021.

EDMUND RV PARK
Ratings: 6/7.5/7 (RV Park) From Jct I-20 & SC-6 (Exit 55), S 7.3 mi on SC-6 to SC-302, SW 0.2 mi (R). **FAC:** Paved/dirt rds. (125 spaces). Avail: 65 grass, 65 pull-thrus (30 x 60), some side by side hkups, 65 full hkups (30/50 amps), seasonal sites, WiFi, dump, laundry. Pet restrict(B). No tents. Big rig sites, 2015 rates: $30. Disc: military. No CC.
(803)955-4010 Lat: 33.85839, Lon: -81.20519
5920 Edmund Hwy, Lexington, SC 29073
www.edmundrvpark.com
See ad this page.

Things to See and Do

THE BARNYARD FLEA MARKETS Flea Market. RV accessible. Restrooms, food. Hours: Sat 7am to 4:30pm; Sun 8am to 4:30pm. ATM, no CC.
(803)957-6570 Lat: 33.97712, Lon: -81.15610
4414 Augusta Rd, Lexington, SC 29073
www.barnyardfleamarkets.com
See ad page 1031.

Directional arrows indicate the campground's position in relation to the nearest town.

LONGS — C6 *Horry*

WILLOWTREE RV RESORT & CAMPGROUND
Ratings: 10/10★/10 (RV Park) From Jct of SC-9 & SC-905, N 1.8 mi on SC-905 to Old Buck Creek Rd, N 1.5 mi (R).

LOCATED MINUTES FROM MYRTLE BEACH
Our Top Rated Park Features Huge Paved FHU Sites, Cozy Cottages, Meeting Facilities and Affordable Storage. Snowbirds Packages Available. Come Experience Our 10/10/10 Park And See What Southern Hospitality Is All About.

FAC: Paved rds. 106 paved, patios, 85 pull-thrus (50 x 100), back-ins (50 x 80), 106 full hkups (30/50 amps), WiFi, dump, laundry, LP gas, fire rings, firewood, controlled access. **REC:** pool, wading pool, whirlpool, Lake Willowtree: swim, fishing, shuffleboard, playground. Pet restrict(B). Partial handicap access, no tents. Big rig sites, eco-friendly, 2015 rates: $45 to $69.
(866)207-2267 Lat: 33.97509, Lon: -78.71985
520 Southern Sights Drive, Longs, SC 29568
reservations@willowtreervr.com
www.willowtreervr.com
See ad page 1020 (SC Featured Map) & Family Camping, Snowbird Destinations in Magazine Section.

LUGOFF — B4 *Kershaw*

COLUMBIA CAMDEN RV PARK **Ratings: 4.5/6/6.5** (RV Park) 2015 rates: $30. (803)206-9954 1354 Ft Jackson Rd, Lugoff, SC 29078

MCCORMICK — C2 *McCormick*

BAKER CREEK (State Pk) From Jct of SC-28 & US 378, SW 3.7 mi on US 378 to park access rd, N 1.1 mi (L). Call park directly if making group reservations. 2015 rates: $18. Mar 1 to Sep 30. (864)443-2457

HAMILTON BRANCH (State Pk) From Jct of US 221/SC-28 & SC-23, N 1.6 mi on US 221/SC-28 (L). Call park directly if making group reservations. Note: 40' RV length limit. 2015 rates: $15 to $20. (864)333-2223

HAWE CREEK (Public Corps) From Jct of US-221 & US-378, SW 6 mi on US-378 to Park Rd, S 4 mi (E). For reservations call 1-877-444-6777. 2015 rates: $24 to $26. Apr 1 to Sep 28. (864)333-1100

HICKORY KNOB STATE RESORT PARK (State Pk) From Jct of SC-28 & US 378, SW 5.8 mi on US 378 to Hwy 7, N 1.5 mi (L). Call park directly if making group reservations. Note: 30' RV length limit. 2015 rates: $18. (800)491-1764

MOUNT PLEASANT — D4 *Charleston*

MT PLEASANT/CHARLESTON KOA **Ratings: 8.5/9★/9** (Campground) 2015 rates: $52 to $70. (843)849-5177 3157 Hwy 17, Mount Pleasant, SC 29466

MURRELLS INLET — C5 *Georgetown*

HUNTINGTON BEACH (State Pk) From Jct of SC-707 & US 17, SW 4.1 mi on US 17 (L). Call park directly if making group reservations. Note: 40' RV length limit. 2015 rates: $21 to $47. (843)237-4440

MYRTLE BEACH — C5 *Horry*

APACHE FAMILY CAMPGROUND & PIER
Ratings: 8.5/8★/8.5 (Campground) From Jct of US-501 & SC 22, E 28 mi on SC 22 to Kings Rd Exit, E 1.7 mi (L). **FAC:** Paved/gravel rds. (695 spaces). Avail: 287 grass, 31 pull-thrus (25 x 60), back-ins (28 x 40), 284 full hkups, 3 W, 3 E (30/50 amps), cable, WiFi $, tent sites, rentals, dump, laundry, groc, LP gas, firewood, restaurant,

SC

MYRTLE BEACH (CONT)

APACHE FAMILY CAMPGROUND & (CONT)
controlled access. **REC:** pool, wading pool, Atlantic Ocean: swim, fishing, playground, rec open to public. Pet restrict(B/Q). Partial handicap access. Big rig sites, eco-friendly, 2015 rates: $38 to $72.
AAA Approved
(800)553-1749 Lat: 33.76870, Lon: -78.78796
9700 Kings Rd, Myrtle Beach, SC 29572
info.camping@apachefamilycampground.com
www.apachefamilycampground.com
See ad page 1033 & Snowbird Destinations in Magazine Section.

BRIARCLIFFE RV RESORT
Ratings: 10/9★/8.5 (RV Resort) From Jct of US 501 & SC 22, E 28 mi on SC 22 to North Myrtle Beach Exit (US 17/N. Kings Hwy) N 1.2 mi (L). **FAC:** Paved rds. (281 spaces). Avail: 174 paved, patios, back-ins (30 x 55), 174 full hkups (30/50 amps), seasonal sites, cable, WiFi $, rentals, laundry, LP gas, controlled access. **REC:** pool, Intracoastal Waterway: shuffleboard, playground. Pets OK. Partial handicap access, no tents. Big rig sites, eco-friendly, 2015 rates: $40 to $61.
(843)272-2730 Lat: 33.79579, Lon: -78.75025
10495 N Kings Hwy, Myrtle Beach, SC 29572
briarcliffervresort@sc.rr.com
www.briarcliffervresort.com
See ad pages 1033, 1021.

CYPRESS CAMPING RESORT
Ratings: 10/9.5★/9.5 (RV Resort) From the Jct of US-31 & US-544: Go 1 mi E on US-544, then 1/4 mi N on Hwy 707, then 1/4 mi W on River Rd (L). **FAC:** All weather rds. 109 paved, 101 pull-thrus (35 x 60), back-ins (35 x 60), 109 full hkups (30/50 amps), cable, WiFi, tent sites, rentals, dump, laundry, groc, LP gas, firewood, restaurant. **REC:** pool, wading pool, Intercoastal Waterway: swim, fishing, playground. Pet restrict(B). Partial handicap access. Big rig sites, eco-friendly, 2015 rates: $35 to $65. Disc: AAA, military.
(843)293-0300 Lat: 33.68664, Lon: -78.99855
101 Cypress Rv Way, Myrtle Beach, SC 29588
info@cypresscampingresort.com
cypresscampingresort.com
See ad this page, 1021.

LAKEWOOD CAMPING RESORT
Ratings: 9.5/9.5★/9.5 (Campground) From Jct of US-501 & SC 544, SE 14.5 mi to Bus US-17, NE 0.4 mi (R).

AWARD-WINNING OCEANFRONT CAMPING
Selected as the Official Best Campground in South Carolina by Bestof.com. Spread over 200 oceanfront acres with 2000 campsites, 112 rental villas and many guest-pleasing amenities. Lakewood has it all!

FAC: Paved rds. (2000 spaces). 1103 Avail: 800 grass, 303 dirt, 43 pull-thrus (30 x 60), back-ins (25 x 50), 1083 full hkups, 20 W, 20 E (30/50 amps), seasonal sites, cable, WiFi, tent sites, rentals, dump, laundry, groc, LP gas, firewood, restaurant, controlled access. **REC:** heated pool, wading pool, whirlpool, Atlantic Ocean: swim, fishing, shuffleboard, playground. Pet restrict(B/Q). Partial handicap access. Big rig sites, eco-friendly, 2015 rates: $31 to $88. Disc: military. ATM.
AAA Approved
(877)525-3966 Lat: 33.63380, Lon: -78.95564
5901 S Kings Hwy, Myrtle Beach, SC 29575
info@lakewoodcampground.com
www.lakewoodcampground.com
See ad page 1020 (SC Featured Map) & Family Camping, Snowbird Destinations in Magazine Section.

MYRTLE BEACH (State Pk) From Jct of US 501 & Bus US 17S, S 4.2 mi on Bus US 17S (L). Call park directly if making group reservations. Note: 40' RV length limit. 2015 rates: $21 to $52. (843)238-5325

Don't miss a thing! Check out the Table of Contents for everything the Guide has to offer.

MYRTLE BEACH KOA
Ratings: 9/9★/8.5 (Campground) From Jct of US-501 & US-17, E 1 mi on US-501 to 3rd Ave S, SE 1 mi to Bus US-17 (Kings Hwy), S 0.2 mi to 5th Ave S, NW 0.2 mi (L).

THE BEST LOCATION IN MYRTLE BEACH!
Discover beautiful and friendly Myrtle Beach KOA! Our family campground features 500 large sites nestled in a spacious 60-acre naturally wooded area - in the city and only a few blocks from Atlantic Ocean beaches.

FAC: Paved rds. (420 spaces). 230 Avail: 73 gravel, 67 grass, 90 dirt, 47 pull-thrus (24 x 60), back-ins (24 x 56), some side by side hkups, 149 full hkups, 65 W, 65 E (30/50 amps), seasonal sites, cable, WiFi, tent sites, rentals, dump, laundry, groc, LP gas, fire rings, firewood, controlled access. **REC:** heated pool, wading pool, pond, fishing, playground. Pets OK $. Partial handicap access. Eco-friendly, 2015 rates: $31 to $79. ATM.
(800)562-7790 Lat: 33.68416, Lon: -78.89663
613 5th Ave S, Myrtle Beach, SC 29577
myrtlebeach@koa.net
www.myrtlebeachkoa.com
See ad page 1020 (SC Featured Map) & Family Camping, Snowbird Destinatins in Magazine Section.

MYRTLE BEACH TRAVEL PARK
Ratings: 9/10★/10 (Campground) From Jct of US-501 & SC 22, E 28 mi on SC 22 to Kings Rd Exit, E 0.6 mi (L).

ENJOY OCEANFRONT CAMPING
at Myrtle Beach Travel Park! Choose from beach sites or shaded sites all with easy access to the beautiful Atlantic Ocean. We offer modern facilities and a variety of activities for ALL ages.

FAC: Paved/gravel rds. (1150 spaces). 700 Avail: 410 grass, 290 dirt, 535 pull-thrus (30 x 55), back-ins (30 x 45), 695 full hkups, 5 W, 5 E (30/50 amps), cable, WiFi, tent sites, rentals, dump, laundry, groc, restaurant, controlled access. **REC:** heated pool, wading pool, Atlantic Ocean: swim, fishing, playground. Pets OK. Partial handicap access. Big rig sites, eco-friendly, 2015 rates: $41 to $75. ATM.
AAA Approved
(800)255-3568 Lat: 33.77719, Lon: -78.77321
10108 Kings Rd, Myrtle Beach, SC 29572
reservations@mbtravelpark.com
www.myrtlebeachtravelpark.com
See ad page 1020 (SC Featured Map) & Family Camping, Snowbird Destinations in Magazine Section.

OCEAN LAKES FAMILY CAMPGROUND
Ratings: 10/10★/10 (Campground) From Jct of US-501 & SC 544, SE 14.5 mi to Kings Hwy US 17 Bus (E).

RANKED IN THE TOP 1% OF 8,000 PARKS
Our oceanfront camping resort features outstanding amenities, activities and customer service. Enjoy all pull-thru sites, concrete pads & inclusive rates (people, pets, full hook-ups w/wi-fi). ARVC's 5 Time Park of the Year.

FAC: Paved rds. (3419 spaces). Avail: 640 paved, 219 all weather, 859 pull-thrus (35 x 53), 859 full hkups (30/50 amps), cable, WiFi, tent sites, rentals, laundry, groc, LP gas, controlled access. **REC:** heated pool, wading pool, Atlantic Ocean: swim, fishing, shuffleboard, playground. Pet restrict(B). Partial handicap access. Big rig sites, eco-friendly, 2015 rates: $31 to $79. ATM.
AAA Approved
(800)341-6659 Lat: 33.62819, Lon: -78.96142
6001 S Kings Hwy, Myrtle Beach, SC 29575
camping@oceanlakes.com
www.oceanlakes.com
See ad page 1020 (SC Featured Map) & Family Camping, Snowbird Destinations in Magazine Section.

Canada — know the rules, regulations and tips before crossing the border. This is listed at the beginning of the country.

PIRATELAND FAMILY CAMPING RESORT
Ratings: 9.5/9.5★/9.5 (Campground) From Jct of US-501 & SC 544, SE 13.5 mi to Bus US-17, NE 1.2 mi (R).

OCEANFRONT, PLUS 510' LAZY RIVER
Looking for the absolute best in oceanfront camping? Look no further. We have redefined the standards of family outdoor fun to bring you an unbeatable camping experience. Check out our specials at www.pirateland.com

FAC: Paved rds. (1495 spaces). 705 Avail: 64 paved, 541 grass, 100 dirt, 40 pull-thrus (24 x 60), back-ins (30 x 45), 705 full hkups (30/50 amps), seasonal sites, cable, WiFi, tent sites, rentals, laundry, groc, LP gas, controlled access. **REC:** heated pool, wading pool, whirlpool, Atlantic Ocean: swim, playground. Pet restrict(B). Partial handicap access. Big rig sites, eco-friendly, 2015 rates: $32 to $82. Disc: military. ATM.
(800)443-2267 Lat: 33.64136, Lon: -78.94659
5401 S Kings Hwy, Myrtle Beach, SC 29575
camppirate@aol.com
www.pirateland.com
See ad page 1020 (SC Featured Map) & Family Camping, Snowbird Destinations in Magazine Section.

Travel Services

CAMPING WORLD OF MYRTLE BEACH As the nation's largest retailer of RV supplies, accessories, services and new and used RVs, Camping World is committed to making your total RV experience better. RV Accessories: (843)215-1565. **SERVICES:** RV, RV appliance, MH mechanical, staffed RV wash, restrooms, RV Sales. RV supplies, LP, emergency parking, RV accessible. waiting room. Hours: 8am to 6pm.
(888)590-0837 Lat: 33.643865, Lon: -78.972576
2295 Dick Pond Road (Hwy 544), Myrtle Beach, SC 29575
www.campingworld.com

CAMPING WORLD OF MYRTLE BEACH As the nation's largest retailer of RV supplies, accessories, services and new and used RVs, Camping World is committed to making your total RV experience better. **SERVICES:** RV, tire, RV appliance, staffed RV wash, restrooms. RV supplies, LP, emergency parking, RV accessible. waiting room. Hours: 8am to 6pm.
(800)845-3571 Lat: 33.729448, Lon: -78.940773
3632 Waccamaw Blvd (Hwy 501), Myrtle Beach, SC 29579
www.campingworld.com

Things to See and Do

MYRTLE BEACH CAMPGROUNDS Association of six Myrtle Beach Campgrounds which promotes tourism in the area.

6 STUNNING MYRTLE BEACH CAMPGROUNDS
All offering visitors an unforgettable camping experience for all seasons. Beautiful weather and reduced rates make fall and spring favorites. Easy access - just one hour off I-95. Plan your visit today.

no CC.
(843)916-2013 Lat: 33.72413, Lon: -78.87719
ashepherd@thebrandonagency.com
www.campmyrtlebeach.com
See ad page 1020 (SC Featured Map).

NORTH CHARLESTON — D4 *Charleston*

Travel Services

CAMPING WORLD OF CHARLESTON As the nation's largest retailer of RV supplies, accessories, services and new and used RVs, Camping World is committed to making your total RV experience better. RV Accessories: (843)553-6633. **SERVICES:** RV, RV appliance, MH mechanical, staffed RV wash, restrooms, RV Sales. RV supplies, LP, dump, emergency parking, RV accessible. waiting room. Hours: 8am to 6pm.
(888)698-2069 Lat: 32.95618, Lon: -80.042877
8155 Rivers Ave, North Charleston, SC 29406
www.campingworld.com

PICKENS — A2 *Pickens*

KEOWEE-TOXAWAY (State Pk) From Jct of SC-183 & US 178, N 9 mi on US 178 to SC-11, SW 8.5 mi (R). Call park directly if making group reservations. Note: 40' RV length limit. 2015 rates: $16. (864)868-2605

TABLE ROCK (State Pk) From Jct of SC-183 & US 178, N 9 mi on US 178 to SC-11, E 4 mi to park entrance rd, N 1 mi (R). Call park directly if making group reservations. Note: 40' RV length limit. 2015 rates: $16 to $21. (864)878-9813

RIDGEWAY — B3 *Fairfield*

LITTLE CEDAR CREEK CAMPGROUND Ratings: 5.5/8★/9 (Campground) From Jct of I-77 & Peach Rd (Exit 32), E 1.6 mi on Peach Rd (R). **FAC:** Gravel rds. (24 spaces). Avail: 4 gravel, patios, 2 pull-thrus (20 x 80), back-ins (30 x 45), 4 full hkups (30/50 amps), seasonal sites, tent sites, dump, laundry, firewood. **REC:** pond, fishing, playground. Pet restrict(Q). Partial handicap access. 2015 rates: $40. No CC.
(803)234-1784 Lat: 34.17860, Lon: -80.58380
6140 E. Peach Rd, Ridgeway, SC 29130
littlecedarcreek@yahoo.com
www.littlecedarcreekcampground.com

ROCK HILL — A3 *York*

EBENEZER PARK
(Public) From Jct of I-77 (exit 82C) & SR-161: Go W (towards York) 0.8 mi on SC-161 to Mt Gallant Rd, NE 6 mi to Boatshore Rd, N 0.4 mi (E). **FAC:** Paved/gravel rds. 69 gravel, 4 pull-thrus (25 x 63), back-ins (30 x 50), 69 full hkups (30/50 amps), WiFi, tent sites, fire rings, firewood, controlled access. **REC:** Lake Wylie: swim, fishing, playground, rec open to public. Pets OK. Partial handicap access. 14 day max stay, 2015 rates: $28.
(803)366-6620 Lat: 35.02205, Lon: -81.04297
4490 Boatshore Rd, Rock Hill, SC 29732
ebenezer.park@yorkcountygov.com
http://www.yorkcountygov.com/departments/ebenezer/default.aspx
See ad page 858.

ROEBUCK — A2 *Spartanburg*

PINE RIDGE CAMPGROUND
Ratings: 9/10★/9 (Campground) From Jct of I-26 (exit 28) & US 221, NE 0.2 mi to Stillhouse Rd., SE 1 mi to Otts Shoals Rd, N 1.5 mi on Otts Shoals Rd to Pine Ridge Campground Rd. (R). **FAC:** Paved/gravel rds. (48 spaces). 18 Avail: 14 paved, 4 gravel, patios, 14 pull-thrus (30 x 65), back-ins (30 x 50), 18 full hkups (30/50 amps), seasonal sites, WiFi, tent sites, rentals, dump, laundry, LP gas, fire rings, firewood. **REC:** pool, pond, fishing, playground. Pet restrict(B). Big rig sites, 2015 rates: $35. Disc: AAA, military.
(864)576-0302 Lat: 34.84784, Lon: -81.94350
199 Pineridge Campground Rd, Roebuck, SC 29376
Pineridgecampground@gmail.com
www.pineridgecampground.com
See ad this page, 1021.

SANTEE — C4 *Clarendon, Orangeburg*

SANTEE See also Eutawville & Summerton.

PALMETTO SHORES RV RESORT
Ratings: 9/8.5★/8.5 (RV Park) From I-95 (exit 102): Go 200 yds E on Road 400. (R). **FAC:** All weather rds. (115 spaces). Avail: 85 gravel, 44 pull-thrus (40 x 75), back-ins (38 x 50), 85 full hkups (30/50 amps), WiFi, rentals, dump, laundry, groc, fire rings, firewood, restaurant, controlled access. **REC:** pool, wading pool, Lake Marion: fishing. Pet restrict(Q). Partial handicap access. Big rig sites, 2015 rates: $40 to $45. No CC.
(803)478-6336 Lat: 33.52076, Lon: -80.42763
5215 Dingle Pond Rd, Summerton, SC 29148
reservations@palmettoshoresrvresort.com
www.palmettoshoresrvresort.com
See ad pages 1027 (Spotlight Lake Marion), 1021.

SANTEE (State Pk) From Jct of I-95 & SC-6 (Exit 98), NW 1.2 mi on SC-6 to State Park Rd, N 4.6 mi (R). Call park directly if making group reservations. Note: 40' RV length limit. 2015 rates: $15 to $18. (803)854-2408

SANTEE LAKES CAMPGROUND
Ratings: 7.5/8.5/7.5 (Campground) From Jct of I-95 (exit 102) & Rd 400: Go E 0.2 mi on Rd 400 to Gordon Rd (S-14-400), S 0.2 mi on Gordon Rd (R). **FAC:** Gravel rds. (170 spaces). Avail: 150 dirt, 115 pull-thrus (30 x 60), back-ins (30 x 65), 60 full hkups, 90 W, 90 E (20/30 amps), seasonal sites, WiFi, tent sites, dump, laundry, groc, firewood. **REC:** pool, wading pool, Lake Marion: swim, fishing, playground. Pet restrict(B). 2015 rates: $35 to $38. Disc: AAA, military.
(803)478-2262 Lat: 33.51778, Lon: -80.42957
1268 Gordon Rd, Summerton, SC 29148
www.santeelakes-campground.com
See ad this page, 1021.

SENECA — A1 *Oconee*

CROOKED CREEK RV PARK
Ratings: 9.5/9/9 (RV Park) From Jct of I-85 (exit 19) & US 76/US 28, W 21.4 mi on SC 28 to SC 188, NE 3.3 mi to Ebenezer Rd, NW 1.6 mi to Arvee Ln (R) Call for directions.

LAKE KEOWEE IS OUR HOME
Our family has owned this little piece of heaven for over 100 years. We built a first-class RV park & marina to share it with those who value beautiful mountains, pristine lakes and spectacular waterfalls. Come relax with us.

FAC: Paved rds. 97 gravel, 97 pull-thrus (30 x 67), 97 full hkups (30/50 amps), WiFi, tent sites, laundry, groc, LP gas, fire rings, firewood. **REC:** pool, wading pool, Lake Keowee: swim, fishing, marina, playground. Pet restrict(B). Partial handicap access. Big rig sites, eco-friendly, 2015 rates: $30 to $40. Disc: military.
(864)882-5040 Lat: 34.76406, Lon: -82.97171
777 Arvee Ln, West Union, SC 29696
www.crookedcreekrvpark.org
See ad pages 1025 (Spotlight Lake Keowee), 1021.

HIGH FALLS PARK (Public) From town, W 9.7 mi on US-76, N 5 mi on SR-183, follow signs (L). 2015 rates: $15 to $25. Mar 1 to Nov 1. (864)882-8234

SOUTH COVE (Public) From Jct of Hwy 123/76 & Hwy 28, N 1.5 mi on Hwy 28, follow signs (R). 2015 rates: $15 to $25. (864)882-5250

Things to See and Do

CROOKED CREEK MARINA & SNACK BAR Pizza shoppe featuring fresh cooked pizza, hot dogs, chicken wings, sandwiches, hand dipped ice cream, and homemade fudge with a shaded patio for lake side dining. Marina & marine gas available. May 30 to Sep 5. ATM.
(864)784-7704 Lat: 34.76172, Lon: -82.97798
777 Arvee Ln, Seneca, SC 29696
CCRVP@trivergent.net
See ad page 1025 (Spotlight Lake Keowee).

SPARTANBURG — A2 *Spartanburg*

SPARTANBURG See also Roebuck.

CROFT STATE NATURAL AREA (State Pk) From Jct of SC-295 & SC-56, S 2.4 mi on SC-56 to Dairy Ridge Rd, E 0.2 mi (R). Call park directly if making group reservations. Note: 40' RV length limit. 2015 rates: $14 to $18. (864)585-1283

SPARTANBURG/CUNNINGHAM RV PARK
Ratings: 8/9★/8 (RV Park) From Jct of I-85 (exit 70) & I-26: Go NW 0.5 mi on I-26 (exit 17) to New Cut Rd, then W 1 mi on New Cut Rd, then SW 0.3 mi on Blackstock Rd, then W 0.5 mi on Campground Rd (R). **FAC:** Gravel rds. (96 spaces). Avail: 83 grass, 83 pull-thrus (31 x 60), 83 full hkups (30/50 amps), seasonal sites, WiFi, tent sites, dump, laundry, LP gas, firewood. **REC:** pool, playground, rec open to public. Pets OK. Big rig sites, eco-friendly, 2015 rates: $35.
(864)576-1973 Lat: 34.98549, Lon: -82.04153
600 Campground Rd, Spartanburg, SC 29303
info@cunninghamrvpark.com
www.cunninghamrvpark.com
See ad this page, 1021.

Travel Services

CAMPING WORLD OF SPARTANBURG As the nation's largest retailer of RV supplies, accessories, services and new and used RVs, Camping World is committed to making your total RV experience better. RV Accessories: (866)999-3164. **SERVICES:** RV, tire, RV appliance, MH mechanical, staffed RV wash, restrooms, RV Sales. RV supplies, LP, dump, emergency parking, RV accessible. waiting room. Hours: 8am to 6pm.
(888)515-9424 Lat: 35.100786, Lon: -82.026699
114 Best Drive, Spartanburg, SC 29303
tflourney@campingworld.com
www.campingworld.com

ST GEORGE — D4 *Dorchester*

JOLLY ACRES RV PARK & STORAGE
Ratings: 8/9★/9 (RV Park) From Jct I-95 & Hwy 78 (exit 77), E 5 mi on Hwy 78 (toward Charleston, SC) to Horne Taylor Rd, N 0.5 mi (L). **FAC:** Gravel rds. 35 Avail: 9 paved, 26 gravel, patios, 30 pull-thrus (35 x 78), back-ins (30 x 60), 23 full hkups, 12 W, 12 E (30/50 amps), WiFi, dump, laundry, LP gas. **REC:** pond, fishing, playground. Pet restrict(B). Partial handicap access, no tents. Big rig sites, 2015 rates: $32 to $35.
(843)563-8303 Lat: 33.17987, Lon: -80.51405
289 Horne Taylor Rd, St George, SC 29477
jollyacres@hughes.net
www.syrrrun.com
See ad page 1036.

We appreciate your business!

Our inspectors look for the same things you do. Our unique Triple Rating System is based on years of market research, analysis and surveys from RVers like you. One thing you suggested was the need for separate ratings on facility completeness, restroom cleanliness/construction, and visual appearance/environmental quality. So we give three ratings, each based on a scale of 1 to 10, 10 being best and 5 being average. To give you an idea how tough we are, less than 1% of inspected campgrounds receive 10/10/10 ratings.*

SC

SUMMERTON — C4 *Clarendon*

➔ TAW CAW CAMPGROUND & MARINA
Ratings: 6/7/6.5 (Campground) From Jct of I-95 (exit 108) & Hwy 102: Go S 1.7 mi on Hwy 102 to Bill Davis Rd, E 1.4 mi to Wash Davis Rd, S 1.9 mi to Rowe Dr, SE 1.2 mi to Joyner Dr, E 0.1 mi (E). **FAC:** Paved/gravel rds. (98 spaces). 14 Avail: 7 grass, 7 dirt, 1 pull-thrus (30 x 80), back-ins (21 x 58), 1 full hkups, 13 W, 13 E (30/50 amps), seasonal sites, cable, WiFi, tent sites, rentals, dump, groc, firewood. **REC:** Lake Marion: swim, fishing, marina. Pet restrict(B). Partial handicap access. 2015 rates: $42.
(803)478-2171 Lat: 33.61332, Lon: -80.34931
1328 Joyner Drive, Summerton, SC 29148
tawcaw@gmail.com
www.tawcawcampground.com
See ad this page, 1021.

SUMMERVILLE — D4 *Dorchester*

GIVHANS FERRY (State Pk) From Jct of I-26 & SC-27 (Exit 187), S 9.5 mi on SR-27 to SR-61, W 3.1 mi to Givhans Ferry Rd, N 0.25 mi (L). Call park directly for group reservations. Note: 40' RV length limit. 2015 rates: $14. (843)873-0692

SWANSEA — C3 *Lexington*

YOGI BEAR'S JELLYSTONE PARK AT RIVER BOTTOM FARMS
Ratings: 9/9.5★/9.5 (Campground) S-bnd: From Jct of I-77 & US 321 S (Exit 71), S 15 mi on US 321 to SC3, SW 6.5 mi on SC-3 to SC-178, NW 0.5 mi on 178 to Cedar Creek Rd, W 0.7 mi (L); N-bnd: From Jct of US-321 & SC 178 (S of Swansea), W 6.3 mi on SC 178 to Cedar Creek Rd, W 0.7 mi (L). **FAC:** Gravel rds. 62 grass, 29 pull-thrus (33 x 63), back-ins (35 x 61), 62 full hkups (30/50 amps), WiFi, tent sites, rentals, dump, laundry, LP gas, fire rings, firewood. **REC:** pool, pond, fishing, playground. Pet restrict(B/Q). Partial handicap access. Big rig sites, eco-friendly, 2015 rates: $36. Disc: military.
(803)568-4182 Lat: 33.66797, Lon: -81.19844
357 Cedar Creek Rd, Swansea, SC 29160
swanseajellystone@live.com
www.swanseajellystone.com
See ad pages 1031, 1021.

TOWNVILLE — B1 *Anderson*

CONEROSS PARK (Public Corps) From town, NE 2 mi on Hwy 24 to Hwy 184, N 1 mi to Coneross Creek Rd, NE 1 mi (E). 2015 rates: $18 to $26. May 1 to Sep 30. (888)893-0678

OCONEE POINT (Public Corps) From town, W 2 mi on SR-24 to CR-184, N 3.5 mi to CR-21, SE 2.5 mi (L). 2015 rates: $26. May 1 to Sep 29. (888)893-0678

WALHALLA — A1 *Oconee*

DEVILS FORK (State Pk) From Jct of SC-130 & SC-11, E 1.6 mi on SC-11 to Jocassee Lake Rd, N 3.7 mi (E). Call park directly if making group reservations. 2015 rates: $20 to $22. (866)345-7275

OCONEE (State Pk) From Jct of SC-11 & SR-28, NW 9.8 mi on SC-28 to SC-107, NE 2.5 mi (R). Call park directly if making group reservations. 2015 rates: $16 to $20. (864)638-5353

WALTERBORO — D4 *Colleton*

EAGLE RV CAMPGROUND (RV Park) (Rebuilding) 2015 rates: $30. (843)538-8731 11592 Jefferies Hwy, Walterboro, SC 29488

NEW GREEN ACRES RV PARK
Ratings: 7.5/7.5/7.5 (Campground) From Jct of I-95 & SC-63 (exit 53), W 500 ft. on SC-63 to Campground Rd, N 0.3 mi (R). **FAC:** Gravel rds. (126 spaces). 101 Avail: 26 gravel, 75 grass, 101 pull-thrus (40 x 90), 67 full hkups, 34 W, 34 E (30/50 amps), seasonal sites, cable, WiFi, dump, laundry, LP gas. **REC:** pool, playground. Pets OK. No tents. Big rig sites, 2015 rates: $30 to $32. Disc: AAA, military.
(800)474-3450 Lat: 32.88375, Lon: -80.71646
396 Campground Rd, Walterboro, SC 29488
greenacres53@lowcountry.com
www.newgreenacres.com
See ad this page, 1021.

WEDGEFIELD — C4 *Sumter*

POINSETT (State Pk) From Jct of US 76/US 378 & SC-261, S 10.3 mi on SC-261 to S-43-63, W 1.7 mi (R). Call park directly if making group reservations. Note: 40' RV length limit. 2015 rates: $18.10. (803)494-8177

WESTMINSTER — B1 *Oconee*

CHAU RAM PARK (Public) From town, W 2.5 mi on US-76 to Chau Ram Park Rd, S 1 mi, follow signs (L). 2015 rates: $12 to $25. Mar 1 to Nov 1. (877)685-2537

WINNSBORO — B3 *Fairfield*

LAKE WATEREE (State Pk) From Jct of I-77 & Rd 41 (exit 41), E 2.6 mi on Rd 41 to US-21, N 2.1 mi to River Rd 101, E 5.1 mi (L). Note: 40' RV length limit. 2015 rates: $16 to $22. (803)482-6401

YEMASSEE — D3 *Hampton*

POINT SOUTH/YEMASSEE KOA Ratings: 8.5/9★/7.5 (Campground) From Jct of I-95 (exit 33) & US-17: Go NE 0.2 mi on US-17 to Yemassee Rd (Waffle House), SE 0.2 mi to Campground Rd, SW (right) 0.5 mi (L). **FAC:** Gravel rds. 58 gravel, 31 pull-thrus (25 x 60), back-ins (25 x 40), 28 full hkups, 30 W, 30 E (30/50 amps), cable, WiFi, tent sites, rentals, dump, laundry, groc, LP gas, firewood. **REC:** pool, pond, fishing, playground. Pet restrict(B). Big rig sites, 2015 rates: $28 to $50.
AAA Approved
(800)726-5733 Lat: 32.62488, Lon: -80.88216
14 Campground Rd, Yemassee, SC 29945
pskoa@hargray.com
www.pointsouthkoa.com

THE OAKS AT POINT SOUTH **Ratings: 7/6.5/7** (Campground) 2015 rates: $49. (800)405-6188 1292 Campground Rd, Yemassee, SC 29945

YORK — A3 *York*

KINGS MOUNTAIN (State Pk) From Jct of I-85 & Hwy 216 (Exit 2 in NC), SE 7 mi on NC/SC 216 (L). Call park directly if making group reservations. Note: 40' RV length limit. 2015 rates: $16 to $18. (803)222-3209

South Dakota Department of Tourism

WELCOME TO

South Dakota

DATE OF STATEHOOD	WIDTH: 210 MILES (340 KM)	PROPORTION OF UNITED STATES
NOV. 2, 1889	LENGTH: 380 MILES (612 KM)	2.03% OF 3,794,100 SQ MI

Think of South Dakota and the vision of Sioux warriors, roaming buffalo, gold prospectors and the gunslingers of historic Deadwood spring to mind. Beyond the dramatic touchstones, South Dakota's gentle Midwest landscape of undulating prairies, windswept plains and lush valleys, dotted with Native American sites, speaks to the state's rich history and intrepid spirit.

Along South Dakota's western flanks, Rapid City forms the launch pad for the state's awe-inspiring national parks, while Sioux Falls, the largest city in the state, provides heart-warming Little House on the Prairie" nostalgia at the Laura Ingalls Wilder Memorial. The lofty Black Hills and South Dakota's iconic Mount Rushmore, with its 60-foot-tall sculptures of Presidents Washington, Jefferson, Roosevelt and Lincoln, features on every traveler's bucket list—and justifiably so.

History

South Dakota became a U.S. territory in 1803 as part of the Louisiana Purchase. In 1804, Lewis and Clark established the first permanent American settlement at Fort Pierre. The Lewis & Clark Family Center in state capital Pierre houses child-friendly artifacts related to westward expansion, such as dugout canoes, animal hides and early 19th-century journals. South Dakota's turbulent past is entwined with the history of the native Sioux, a confederacy of several tribes that speak three different dialects: Lakota, Dakota and Nakota. The 1868 Treaty of Laramie gave ownership of the Black Hills to the Lakota people. However, in 1874, when Colonel George Armstrong Custer announced the discovery of gold near Custer in the Black Hills, the Lakota people were forced from their land.

The South Dakota Cultural Heritage Center in Pierre provides a fascinating insight into Sioux life and culture, including a large tipi, traditional dress, tools and a replica of the Jefferson Peace Medal. South Dakota was incorporated

Top 3 Tourism Attractions:
1) Mount Rushmore National Park
2) Badlands National Park
3) Crazy Horse Memorial

Nickname: Mount Rushmore State

State Flower: American Pasqueflower

State Bird: Ring-necked Pheasant

People: Tom Brokaw, TV news anchor; Crazy Horse, Oglala Indian chief; Al Neuharth, founder of USA Today; Billy Mills, Olympic athlete and humanitarian; Harvey Dunn, prairie artist

Major Cities: Sioux Falls, Rapid City, Aberdeen, Brookings, Watertown, (Pierre, capital)

Topography: East—prairie plains; west—rolling hills of the Great Plains; southwest corner—Black Hills

Climate: Interior continental climate with hot summers and extremely cold winters; high winds and periodic droughts

South Dakota Department of Tourism

SD

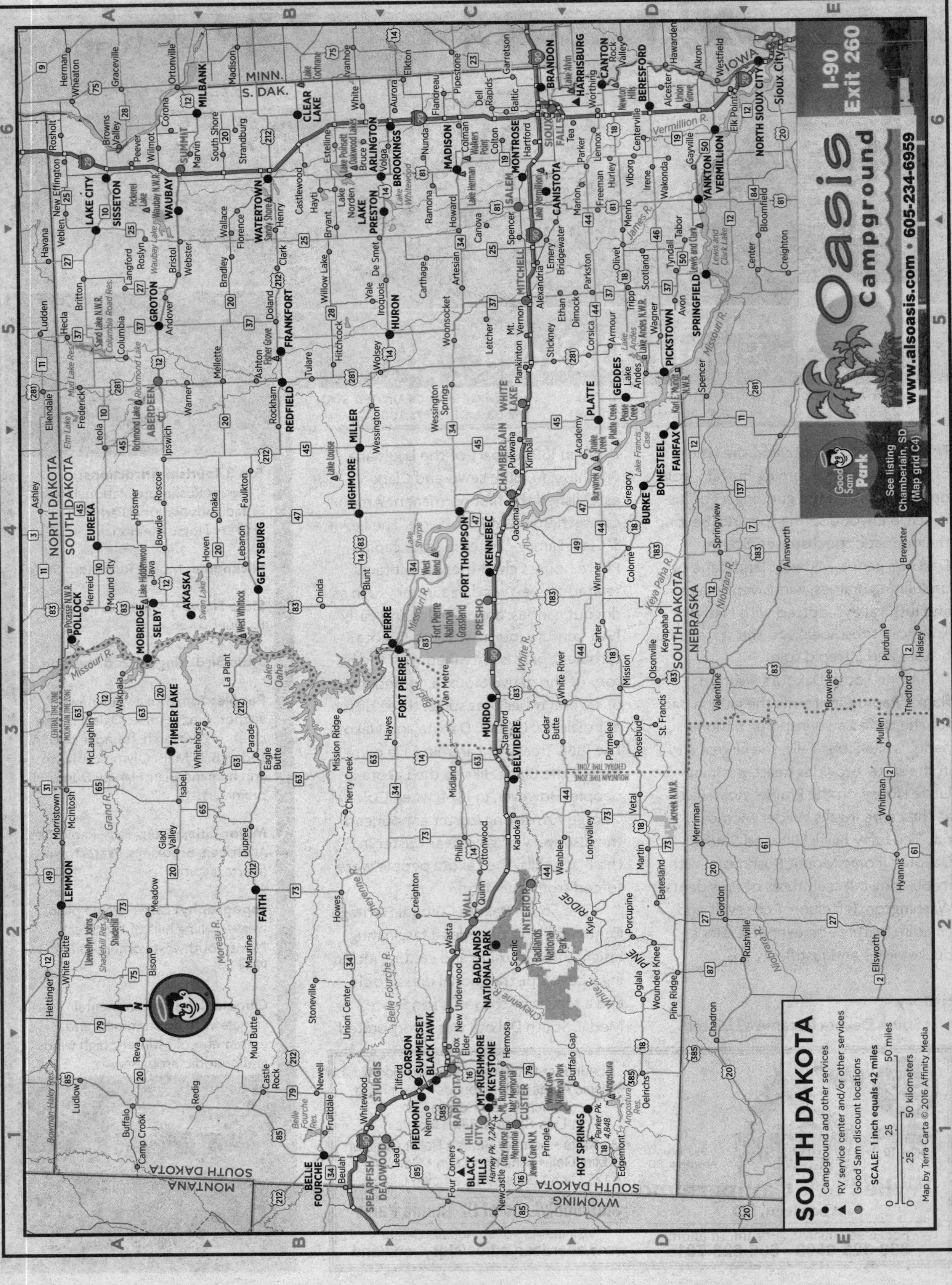
SOUTH DAKOTA
Campground and other services
RV service center and/or other services
Good Sam discount locations
SCALE: 1 inch equals 42 miles
Map by Terra Carta © 2016 Affinity Media
Oasis Campground
I-90 Exit 260
www.alsoasis.com • 605-234-6959
Good Sam Park
See listing Chamberlain, SD (Map grid C4)

South Dakota STATE PARKS

Department of Game, Fish and Parks

From rolling hills and plains to mighty mountains and thick forests, South Dakota State Parks offer great variety for nature lovers.

Lewis & Clark Recreation Area

Big Sioux Recreation Area

Custer State Park

Good Earth State Park

Photos courtesy of South Dakota Tourism

INFORMATION:
www.gfp.sd.gov
605.773.3391

RESERVATIONS:
www.CampSD.com
1.800.710.2267

SD

STAY AWHILE!

Join a family of over 200 volunteers who live and work in SD State Parks during the summer months!

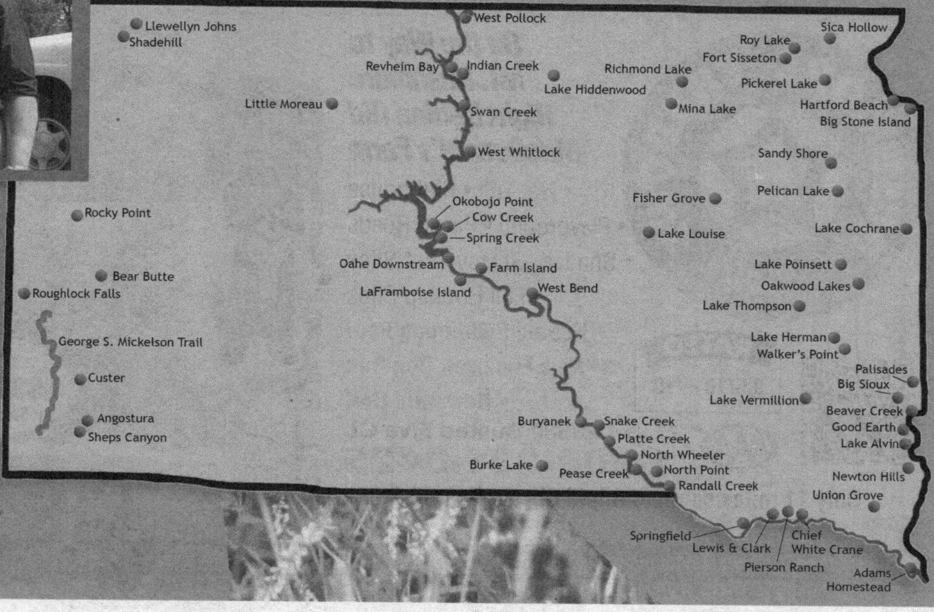

into the union on November 2, 1889, along with North Dakota. During the late 19th century, Deadwood achieved infamy as the region's lawless epicenter, a place of opium dens, saloons, brothels and gambling halls. Nowadays (with an acclaimed HBO series to its name), Deadwood is a National Historic Landmark complete with restored gaming halls, Victorian homes and Mount Moriah Cemetery, where Old West gunslinger Wild Bill Hickok is buried (he came to a grizzly end in Deadwood during a game of poker) along with that fabled frontierswomen with a heart of gold, Calamity Jane.

Play

The threshold to the West, South Dakota's wild, open lands have always summoned adventure. Furrowed with the wagon trails of homesteaders and riddled with the bullet holes of gunslingers, South Dakota's 56 state parks help unravel the history and psyche of the Old American West. With its sizzling air, surreal rock formations, vertiginous walls and pink-splashed mesas, Badlands National Park forms South Dakota's most storied wilderness. Mount Rushmore, one of the nation's most iconic images, draws around 3 million visitors each year. Carved between 1927 and 1941, from the granite of a Black Hills outcrop, the 60-foot-tall faces of presidents George Washington, Thomas Jefferson, Abraham Lincoln and Theodore Roosevelt were conceived, according to creator Gutzon Borglum, as a physical embodiment of the ideals of American government.

Less than an hour from Mount Rushmore, the longest, most intricate and brilliantly hued cave systems in the world can be explored at Wind Cave National Park and Jewel Cave National Monument. At Custer State Park, there's a star-studded cast of wildlife (bison herds, white-tailed deer, pronghorn antelope and big-horn sheep), along with scenic drives, historic sites and fishing lakes. In 1948, Korczak Ziolkowski, (who honed his skills at nearby Mount Rushmore), immortalized

- STAY A WHILE -

South Dakota State Parks

For a peek at the real South Dakota, you need only to visit a South Dakota state park. These lands will introduce you to some of the most scenic views, abundant recreational opportunities and friendliest people in the state. There is a reason they were saved for this elite group called state parks.

You really can't go wrong with any of the 60-plus parks across the state. Nearly every park offers electrical camping, swimming, water recreation, hiking and wildlife viewing. From there, parks add on activities that best fit their natural resources, from historical interpretation to rock climbing to canoeing to equestrian trails. Each park offers a unique mixture of recreational opportunities for their visitors, whether you're camping overnight or just stopping in along the way.

Some parks offer a glimpse into pure nature. They remain nearly untouched, with simple enhancements to provide access and interpretation. Visit Good Earth State Park near Sioux Falls and surround yourself with abundant wildlife, fertile flood plains, flowing river and quiet forest. Or follow the footsteps of Lewis and Clark as you hike to the top of Spirit Mound near Vermillion.

Other parks encourage you to get out and be active in nature, making use of natural and constructed features to maximize outdoor recreational opportunities. Visitors to Lewis and Clark Recreation Area near Yankton enjoy boating, hiking, biking, swimming, disc golf, volleyball, archery and much more. Or stop by Oahe Downstream Recreation Area near Pierre for a little walleye fishing on the great Missouri River.

And then there's unique. Stroll the grounds of Fort Sisseton Historic State Park near Lake City, a frontier army post with 14 refurbished buildings. Or explore all 71,000 acres of Custer State Park in the Black Hills, known for its scenic beauty, abundant recreational activities and herd of 1,300 bison.

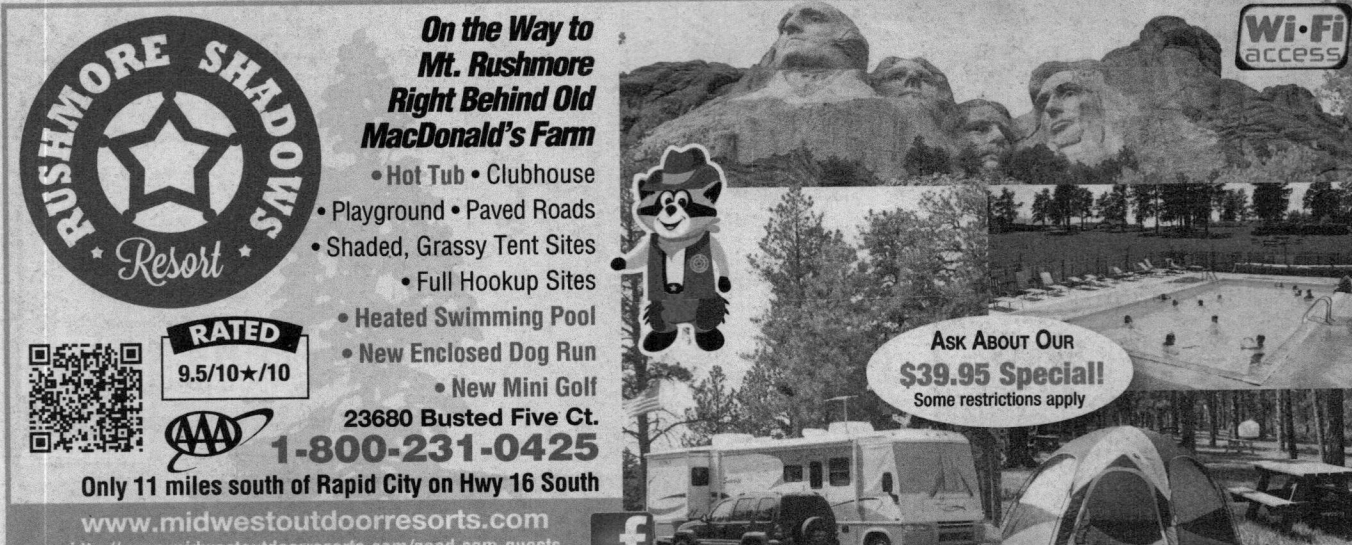

Sioux idol Crazy Horse with a breath-taking mountainside sculpture carved by hand into Thunderhead Mountains. Ziolkowski died before the sculpture was completed, but work continues under the unforgiving eye of his wife and children.

Experience

Since 1926, the Days of 76 Festival has commemorated the first pioneers of Deadwood with historic parades, live music and impressive rodeos every July. In Mitchell, at the end of August, "The World's Only Corn Palace" (a Moorish revival building complete with glorious onion domes) celebrates itself (with not a whiff of irony) with the city-wide Corn Palace Festival. The Corn Palace is redecorated every year with fresh murals fashioned from 12 different colors of corn (grown by a lucky chosen local farmer) and framed with native grasses. Mid-July, the deceptively named Jazz Fest, one of the largest free events in the Midwest, showcases performers of every genre: jazz; blues; Latin; reggae; zydeco; rock; soul; and funk. In August, the weeklong Sturgis Motorcycle Rally is a 10-day homage to the motorcycle. Along five "bike-only" blocks of Main Street, you can demo virtually every kind of bike on the market, compete in bike races, watch live music and cheer on participants of the Annual Mayor's Ride, a fundraising event.

- STAY A WHILE -

1880 Town

While traveling across South Dakota on Interstate 90 (Exit 170), take time to explore 1880 Town. You'll see over 30 original, historically correct and authentically furnished buildings from 1880 to 1920. 1880 Town displays thousands of relics, including antique buggies and wagons; toys; saloon pianos; a collection of Buffalo Bill items; and a special tribute to the late Casey Tibbs, 19-time World Champion Rodeo Cowboy. Props from the movie, Dances with Wolves, reside inside a 14-sided round barn built in 1919. As you exit the barn, the whole town lies ahead in a beautiful panoramic view. A self-guided tour of the town begins here. The Vanishing Prairie Museum houses collections from the General Custer period, Indian artifacts and cowboy memorabilia. Stop at the old bank, whet your whistle with a sarsaparilla served in a family-friendly "saloon." The Dakota Hotel still carries the scars made by cowboys' spurs on the staircase. There's a completely restored bank, a one-room schoolhouse furnished with all the "trappings" of a country school—sure to bring back many memories to those who may have attended one. There's a quaint little church at the end of Main Street, and Santa Fe Steam Liner dining cars provide an old fashioned ambiance for a snack or lunch. For history buffs or antique collectors, 1880 Town is a good place to stretch your legs and your imagination. www.1880town.com, 605-344-2236

Taste

A state made for carnivorous palates, South Dakota's restaurant menus tend toward grilled steaks, pheasant, lean buffalo burgers and elk, served in a rustic setting with a country music soundtrack. The Firehouse Brewing company (www.firehousebrewing.com), one of the most popular restaurants in Rapid City, serves palette-searing fare in the form of "Hyperventilation Wings and Rings" and firehouse-themed dishes to the tune of the "hook and ladder" (bowl of soup and a half Reuben sandwich) or Fire Caps (mushrooms topped with crab and cream cheese). For upscale dining, the elegant Landing (www.thelandingyankton.com) restaurant in Yankton offers Modern American dishes (sesame-encrusted tuna steak or mac 'n' cheese with truffles), serene river views and a well-conceived wine list. In Sioux Falls, locals wax poetic about Bob's Café (www.bobscarryout.com), which is renowned for its succulent "broasted" chicken, burger baskets, ribs and convivial atmosphere.

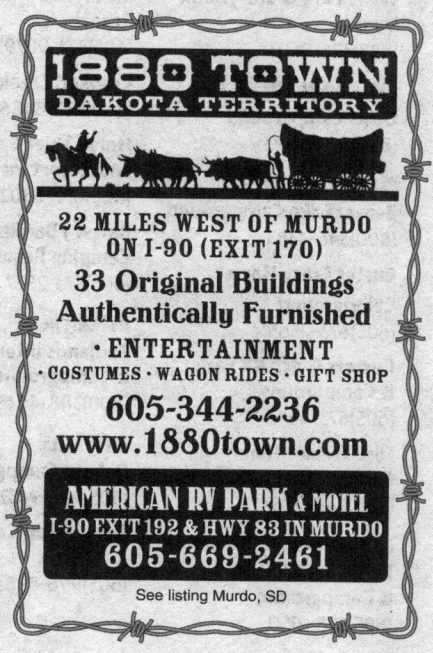

SD

TRAVEL & TOURISM

South Dakota Department of Tourism
800-732-5682, 605-773-3301
www.travelsd.com

1880 Town
605-344-2236
www.1880town.com

Black Hills and Badlands Tourism Assn.
605-355-3600
www.blackhillsbadlands.com

Glacial Lakes & Prairies Tourism CVB
800-244-8860, 605-886-7305
www.sdglaciallakes.com

South Dakota Missouri River Tourism Association
888-386-4617
www.sdmissouririver.com

Southeast South Dakota Tourism Association
888-353-7382
www.southeastsouthdakota.com

Wylie Park/Storybook Land
888-326-9693
www.aberdeen.sd.us/storybookland

OUTDOOR RECREATION

South Dakota Dept. of Game, Fish & Parks
www.gfp.sd.gov

SHOPPING

Akta Lakota Museum Gift Shop
800-798-3452
www.aktalakota.org

Cabela's
605-388-5600
www.cabelas.com

Empire Mall-Empire East
605-361-0586
www.theempiremall.com

Wall Drug
605-279-2175
www.walldrug.com

 See map page 1038

Featured Good Sam Parks

SOUTH DAKOTA

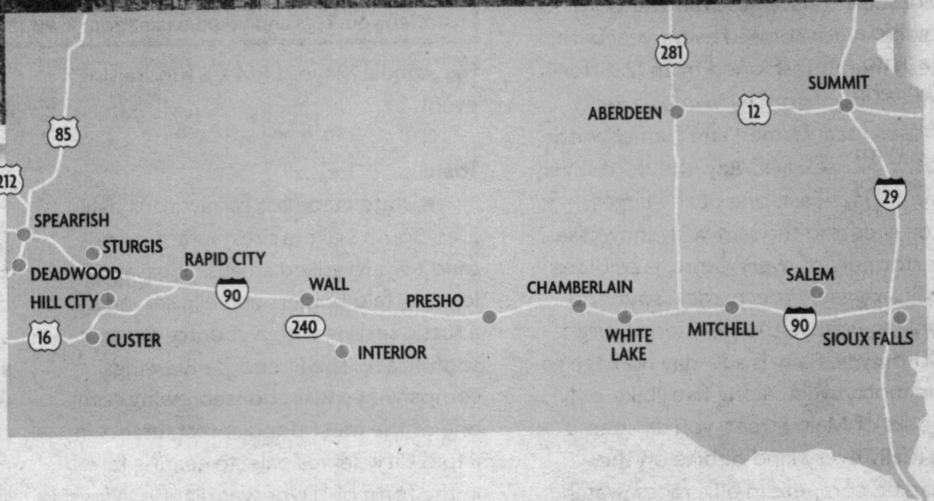

When you stay with Good Sam, you can expect the highest degree of cleanliness and friendliness, and better yet, you get 10% off campground fees.

If you're not already a Good Sam member you can purchase your membership at one of these locations:

ABERDEEN
Wylie Park & Storybook Land
(888)326-9693

CHAMBERLAIN
Oasis Campground
(800)675-6959

CUSTER
Beaver Lake Campground
(800)346-4383

Custer Crazy Horse Campground
(605)673-2565

Custers Gulch RV Park & Campground
(605)673-4647

Fort Welikit Family Campground
(888)946-2267

DEADWOOD
Fish'N Fry RV Park & Campground
(605)578-2150

HILL CITY
Black Hills Trailside Park Resort
(605)574-9079

Crooked Creek Resort Inc
(800)252-8486

Horse Thief Campground and Resort Inc
(800)657-5802

Rafter J Bar Ranch Camping Resort
(605)574-2527

INTERIOR
Badlands Interior Motel & Campground
(800)388-4643

MITCHELL
Dakota Campground
(605)996-9432

Famil-E-Fun Campground & RV Park
(605)996-8983

R & R Campground & RV Park
(605)996-8895

Rondee's RV Park
(605)996-0769

PRESHO
New Frontier RV Park
(605)895-2604

RAPID CITY
Happy Holiday Resort
(605)342-7365

Mystery Mountain Resort
(605)342-5368

Rapid City RV Park and Campground
(605)342-2751

Tee Pee Campground & RV Park
(605)343-6319

SALEM
Camp America Campground
(605)425-9085

SIOUX FALLS
Red Barn RV Park
(605)368-2268

Sioux Falls Yogi Bear
(605)332-2233

Tower Campground
(605)332-1173

SPEARFISH
Chris' Camp & RV Park
(800)350-2239

Elkhorn Ridge RV Resort & Golf Club
(877)722-1800

STURGIS
Rush No More RV Resort & Campground
(605)347-2916

SUMMIT
County Line RV Park & Campground
(605)398-6355

WALL
Arrow Campground
(800)888-1361

Sleepy Hollow Campground, LLC
(605)279-2100

WHITE LAKE
Siding 36 Motel & RV Park
(605)249-2295

For more Good Sam Parks go to listing pages

Getty Images/iStockphoto

CHAMBERLAIN/OACOMA

Go exploring in this pioneering pair of towns

On either side of a gentle bend in the Missouri River, the South Dakota townships of Chamberlain and Oacoma provide a front-row seat into America's pioneering, frontier past.

With a combined population of less than 3,000 people, these two tight-knit sister communities still manage to echo the attraction and allure of a bygone era, when fur-traders and mountain men spearheaded brave expeditions into wild, uncharted backcountry.

Both communities trace their roots back to the 1822 establishment of the Fort Kiowa fur-trading post. The Fort is most renowned for its role in the defining moment of Hugh Glass's life. A scrappy hard-nosed frontiersman, Glass set off from the Fort in 1823 as part of a 100-man trading expedition to far-away Fort Henry. Partway into the weeks-long trek, Glass was mauled by a grizzly bear and—true to the hard-nosed spirit of the time—left for dead by his fellow expedition members. Battling infection in his leg and fainting spells brought on by dehydration and starvation, Glass is reported to have crawled 200 miles back to Fort Kiowa, where he made a miraculous and full recovery.

> If hunting or fishing is your game then you'll find yourself casting in walleye-filled waters and zeroing in on an abundance of wild pheasant.

Today, the one-time site of Fort Kiowa sits underwater, the result of the damming of the Missouri River, but the scrappy frontier spirit it once represented still remains. Visitors will find themselves drawn to a mix of historic sites, interactive museums and myriad outdoor activities in vast, untamed tracts of pristine South Dakota wilderness.

Learn Lakota Lore

Make your first stop the Akta Lakota Museum and Cultural Center. Long before legendary fur trappers and rugged pioneer outposts appeared on the scene here, the Lakota people called this area home. The museum's exhibits showcase art and artifacts from the history of the Sioux nation (of which the Lakota people and language are a part), including an intricate 36-foot-long diorama depicting the stretch of prairie plain between the Missouri River and the Black Hills to the west. In addition to its cultural and historical displays, the

Al's oasis beckons travelers with food and shopping. Runner1928

American explorer Meriwether Lewis
Getty Images

museum also features the Collector's Gallery, where contemporary local artists can display and sell their artwork.

Once you've explored the museum, continue your chronological journey through the history of Chamberlain and Oacoma with a stop at the Lewis and Clark Interpretive Center, located just a few miles south of downtown Chamberlain. Admission is free and the Center is just off of Interstate 90, making it an easy must-visit even for those just passing through. Highlights include a life-sized replica of the 55-foot-long keelboat used on the legendary expedition (visitors are able to climb aboard for pictures) and an array of artifacts from Lewis and Clark's cross-continent travels.

Get a five cent cup of coffee at Al's Oasis, a stop along I-90 that offers food, souvenirs and touring for travelers. Stock up on supplies, sip a beer at the Last Chance Saloon or pull up a chair at Al's Restaurant/Lounge.

Follow Lewis and Clark

When you're ready for a nature tour of your own, hit the Native American Scenic Byway—part of which follows the Lewis and Clark motor route. The byway begins in Chamberlain and winds its way north through Crow Creek Reservation and Brule Sioux Indian Reservation, and past Lake Sharpe and Lake Francis Case. It's an easy way to explore central South Dakota's landscape of rolling foothills and bluffs.

Hikers, bird-watchers and wildlife photographers will want to head 90 miles south to the Fort Randall Dam area. Just below the dam, the area is home to one of the world's highest concentrations of wintering bald eagles, hundreds of which dot the tops of the refuge's forests of scenic cottonwood trees. During the summer months, tours of the Fort Randall Dam and Powerhouse are available. If hunting or fishing is your game, then you'll find yourself casting in walleye-filled waters and zeroing in on an abundance of wild pheasant, grouse and deer.

Set up camp or park the RV in one of several nearby campsites and go exploring. Pristine creeks, streams and lakes buzz through spring, summer and autumn with anglers. Hikers hit the region's absurd abundance of trailheads year-round, unknowingly on the historic trail of legendary fur trappers who were among the first explorers to map the area.

Rich in big-time history and small-town charm, the Chamberlain-Oacoma region still seems to buzz with the same pioneering frontier spirit that attracted fur trappers like Hugh Glass and explorers like Lewis and Clark more than 150 years ago. Vast tracts of still-untamed wilderness expand in every direction from the shores of the Missouri River, both sides of which are bracketed by small communal townships where you can still buy a cup of coffee for a nickel.

For More Information

Chamberlain Convention and Visitors Bureau
605-234-4416
www.chamberlainsd.org

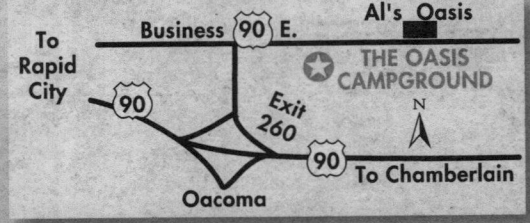

South Dakota Department of Tourism
800-732-5682
www.travelsd.com

Getty Images/iStockphoto

CUSTER

The Gold Rush spirit lives on in this corner of the west

Whispers of the Black Hills Gold Rush still echo through the tiny creek-side town of Custer in sun-soaked South Dakota. With a population of fewer than 2,000 residents and surrounded by more than a million acres of undeveloped wilderness, Custer isn't too far removed from its days as an rough-and-tumble outpost on the edge of the Wild, Wild West.

Even today, Custer's single long main street appears just as if it's been ripped from the reels of any classic western cowboy film. Part of the reason for that may be that the town dates directly back to the Wild West itself, when in 1874 gold was discovered in French Creek, which winds through the center of town. The discovery set off an otherwise illegal gold rush, as the Black Hills area was at that point still closed to white settlement. But with the promise of striking it rich, the restriction made no difference at all. Excited miners rushed in, led by Thomas Hooper. They drew a one-square-mile plot of land near the creek and just like that the town of Custer was born. Within one year, the population had swelled to more than 10,000 residents—five times the population of the town today.

The gold rush boom times ended when gold was discovered in the hills and backcountry near the town of Deadwood. That discovery dragged the bulk of panners and prospectors away, but the Wild West spirit (and aesthetic) seems to have lived on in earnest.

In the Center of It All

Today, visitors here will find themselves at the heart of a particularly attraction-filled portion of South Dakota. Rapid City, Mount Rushmore, Badlands National Park and Buffalo Gap National Grassland all lie within easy reach and make for excellent day trips. Closer to Custer itself is Custer State Park, Wind Cave National Park, Jewel Cave National Monument and the Mammoth Site of Hot Springs. Set aside plenty of time to explore abroad, but if you're camped out in Custer, be sure to pay special attention to its own nearby slate of parks, attractions and museums.

Start at Custer State Park, located just three miles east of town. A herd of more than 1,300 wild bison roam the park's rolling lowlands and fields, as well as mountain goats, bighorn sheep, elk and even a friendly family of burros.

SD

"Begging burros" at Custer State Park. www.travelsd.com

Make sure you drive along the Needles Highway, which runs through the park and is so named because of the fantastic rock spires that soar into the sky in defiance of gravity.

Exploring the park is easy. The 18-mile-long Wildlife Loop Road offers a great orientation to the park and its wild denizens, while a robust network of hiking trails is available for more in-depth exploration. Most of the trails are leftover pathways from early pioneers, ranchers and loggers, but which are now frequented by hikers, mountain bikers, horse riders and rock climbers slinking between rock walls.

To the west, Jewel Cave National Monument is another must-visit. This is officially designated as the world's second longest cave, with active explorers discovering new passageways each year. Park Rangers lead guided tours year-round. In the summer months, themed tours are offered, including the Historic Lantern Tour.

In a similar vein, 18 miles south of Custer is Wind Cave National Park, home of the fourth-longest cave in the world. As with Jewel Cave, guided tours below the surface to the cave's honeycomb-like features are led by Park Rangers year-round.

Further south still, about 39 miles from the center of town, the Mammoth Site of Hot Springs is one of the most riveting attractions in the region. To date, the remains of 61 different woolly mammoths have been discovered here, and the area is still an active paleontological dig site. Visitors to the region can enjoy a 30-minute guided tour, access to an Ice Age museum exhibit and a stroll around the dig area at their leisure.

Ancient history and geological history aren't the only highlights in the area for history buffs, however. A slew of family-friendly attractions beckon.

Standing Tall

The Crazy Horse Memorial, located just five miles north of Custer, is also home to the Indian Museum of North America and the Native American Cultural Center. Here, just a short distance from the Presidential faces etched into the side of Mount Rushmore, guests can view the world's largest in-progress mountain carving, topping out at a height of 563 feet.

Finally, for those travelling with small children, two wildly different attractions lies just a few miles southwest of Custer. The first, Four Mile Old West Town, is an open-air Wild West town featuring live re-enactments of gunslinging and gold-prospecting life on the edge of the western frontier. The other, Flintstones Bedrock City, is a combination theme park and campground that features all of the colorful characters, locations and aesthetics of the popular television cartoon series.

From its history as a town built in the wild pursuit of gold to its location in the heart of the Black Hills and Badlands region of South Dakota, Custer is a unique western-style township that begs to be visited and explored.

For More Information

Visit Custer
800-992-9818
www.visitcuster.com

South Dakota Department of Tourism
800-SDAKOTA
www.travelsd.com

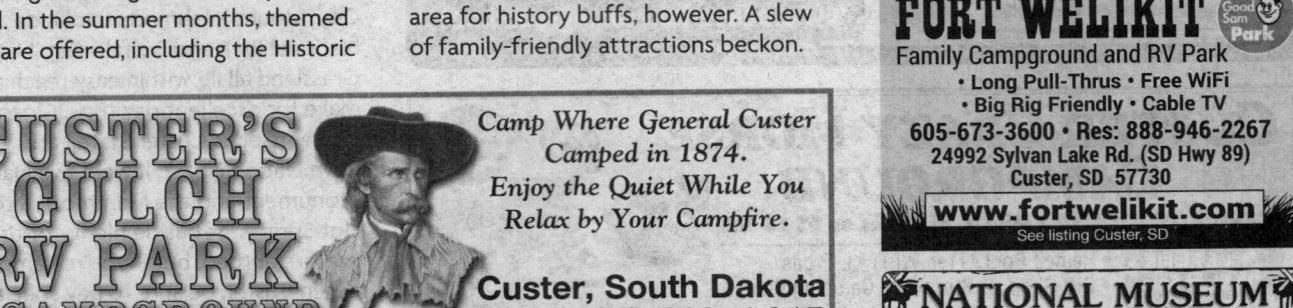

Getty Images/iStockphoto

HILL CITY

Explore the heart of the Black Hills

The Black Hills and Badlands region of South Dakota is bursting with incredible natural attractions, surreal geological formations, historic Wild West-flavored townships and major All-American attractions. Sitting at the center of it all is humble Hill City, a tiny gold rush-era community that's home to fewer than 1,000 year-round residents.

At first glance, Hill City may not seem the most likely of places to set up camp and go exploring abroad, but this charming small town is perfectly placed for those with fully loaded sightseeing itineraries. From here, visitors can range out and plan easy day trips to Badlands National Park, Buffalo Gap National Grassland, Custer State Park, Wind Cave National Park, Jewel Cave National Park, the Mammoth Site of Hot Springs and Rapid City.

Closer to town, Hill City is a major gateway to a pair of major attractions—Mount Rushmore and Black Hills National Forest.

Face-to-Face with Rushmore

Start with Mount Rushmore, located 16 miles west of Hill City near the even smaller town of Keystone. This is the undisputed main attraction in southwestern South Dakota, so expect big crowds year-round. An average of three million people flock to the Mount Rushmore National Memorial annually, making it one of the most popular attractions in the entire country.

An average of three million people flock to the Mount Rushmore National Memorial annually, making it one of the most popular attractions in the entire country.

Beyond jaw-dropping views of the mountain's famous carved faces of George Washington, Thomas Jefferson, Theodore Roosevelt and Abraham Lincoln, the site is home to an informative Visitor Center, the Presidential Trail (for up-close views of the faces) and a trio of Native American Heritage Villages.

Pair your stop at Mount Rushmore with a visit to nearby Rushmore Cave. This unique adventure park is full of zip lines, spelunking expeditions and even an interactive gunslinger adventure ride.

The other major attraction here in Hill City is one with an abundance of choice. Black Hills National Forest sprawls across 1.25 million acres of wilderness that's loaded with meandering creeks, rolling plains, lush forests and rugged foothills. Hiking, fishing, hunting, kayaking and canoeing are all popular activities among visitors.

Black Hills by Rail

For a change of pace from exploring the area by hiking boot, canoe or steering wheel, the 1880 Train is another great way to see a vast swath of the Black Hills. Departing from Hill City, this sightseeing train tour is pulled by a vintage steam engine and covers a scenic 20-mile roundtrip route.

The 1880 Train departs from each town at various points throughout the day, so this can be a great way to pencil in a trip to the National Presidential Wax Museum, located just outside of downtown Keystone. The museum features life-sized wax figures of every President in American history

For More Information

Hill City Area Chamber of Commerce
800-888-1798
www.hillcitysd.com

South Dakota Department of Tourism
800-S-DAKOTA
www.travelsd.com

George S. Mickelson Trail Hiking & Biking

HEATED SWIMMING POOL AND HOT TUB COMPLEX

The ranch is comprised of five camping areas separated by large meadows and shaded by Ponderosa pines. Choose level, shady sites in remote camping areas, or sites close to the resort activity center.

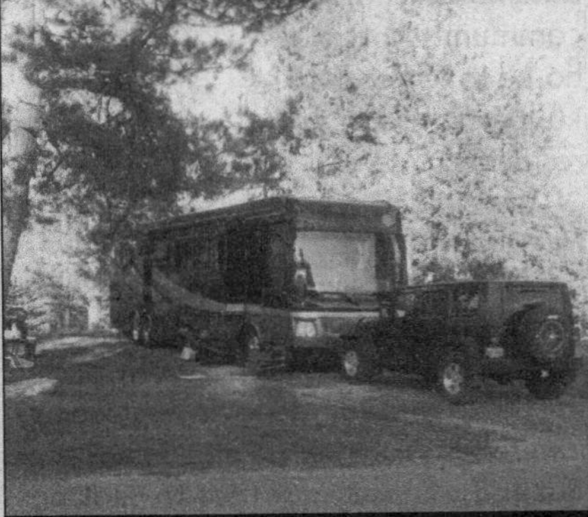

Open and Tree Shaded Sites

• Satellite Cable TV (limited sites) • Four Lakes Within Minutes

Within 8 Miles of:

• Mt. Rushmore • Crazy Horse Mountain • Custer State Park

• Playground • Large Heated Pool & Hot Tub • Snack Bar • Ice • Firewood • LP Gas Detachable Tanks Only • 50 Amp • Game Room • Rec Hall • Rafter J Bar Gift Shop & Store • Trout Stream • 24-Hour Security • NEW Basketball Court • NEW Volleyball Court

Three Styles of Camping Cabins to Choose From

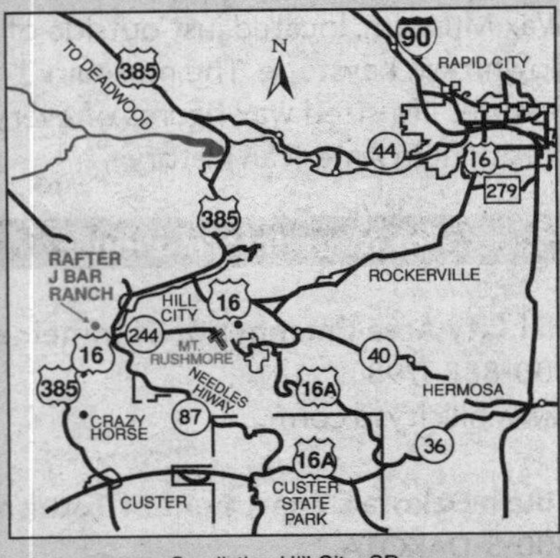

See listing Hill City, SD

web site: www.rafterj.com

Reservations Toll Free:

(888)-Rafter J
(723-8375)

Info. - (605) 574-2527

UPS & Fed Ex delivers to 12325 Rafter J Rd. Hill City, SD 57745

Add us to your GPS Lat: 43.89461 Lon: -103.59104

Good Sam Park

Good Sam RATED 9/10★/9.5

Getty Images/iStockphoto

RAPID CITY

See dinosaurs, Badlands and buffalo in this fun-filled spot in the Black Hills

Set against the eastern edges of the scenic Black Hills and sitting within easy reach of the legendary Badlands of South Dakota, historic Rapid City is an ideal place to set up camp in the southwestern corner of the state and go exploring abroad.

As the second-largest city in the state, this Gold Rush-era boomtown is home to a full selection of world-class dining, shopping and entertainment options. It also sits on the doorstep to incredible outdoor attractions like Mount Rushmore National Memorial, Black Hills National Forest, Badlands National Park, Buffalo Gap National Grassland, Custer State Park, Wind Cave National Park, Jewel Cave National Park and the Mammoth Site of Hot Springs. So find a campground, park the RV and prepare to pencil in a full slate of jam-packed day-trips that mix surreal geology with an incredible history.

Before you go exploring far and wide, though, be sure to see all that the immediate Rapid City area has to offer.

> Set atop a scenic ridge, Dinosaur Park is home to sweeping vistas that stretch for upwards of 100 miles.

Hail to the Chiefs

Start with its historic downtown district, known affectionately as the City of Presidents. At its heart is Main Street Square, a picturesque public space that plays host to a full calendar of live concerts and cultural events. The surrounding streets are dotted with life-sized bronze statues depicting America's past presidents, giving the historic district its presidential moniker.

The City of Presidents pairs nicely with a trip to the Founding Fathers Black Hills art gallery and museum, which is located a few miles south of the city center. Here, art and history intertwine to tell the story of the men who drafted and signed the Declaration of Independence. The exhibit features a life-size recreation of events inside Philadelphia's Independence Hall during the Second Continental Congress.

Black Hills Background

Continue the history theme with stops at the Journey Museum and the South Dakota Air and Space Museum. The for-

SD

Deer on the roadside of Badlands National Park. Getty Images/iStockphoto

Horseback riding outside of Rapid City. Rapid City CVB

mer is located in downtown Rapid City, while the latter sits just 14 miles east of town off of Interstate 90.

At the Journey Museum campus, guests can explore the full sweep of Black Hills history and geography by way of four different sub-museums: The Museum of Geology, the State of South Dakota Archeological Research Center, the Sioux Indian Museum and the Minnilusa Pioneer Museum. Exhibits, collections and interactive displays cover everything from the final gun-slinging days of Wild Bill Hickok in Deadwood to ancient Native American artifacts from nearby dig sites.

Statues of presidents, tales of gunslingers and archeological dig sites aren't for everyone, though, and those traveling with small children will want to spice up the sightseeing schedule with a bit of family fun. For this, a great place to start is Bear Country USA.

Located a few miles south of the city, this unique open-air safari sprawls across 200 acres of forests and meadows. Visitors enjoy a self-paced, 3-mile drive through a variety of enclosures that house black bears, reindeer, mountain goats, bighorn sheep, cougars, bobcats, pronghorns and buffalos.

Creepy Crawlies

On your way back to Rapid City, you might also want to pay a visit to Reptile Gardens, which nicely rounds out the trio of animal attractions in the immediate area. The star of the show here is the resident Komodo dragon, followed closely by a rare saltwater crocodile, but the enclosures feature a large selection of other snakes, birds and, of course, lizards in an exotic setting.

Finally, if you're looking for a taste of South Dakota's incredible geological history head to Dinosaur Park or Sitting Bull Crystal Caverns.

Dinosaur Park has been free and open to the public since 1936. Set atop a scenic ridge, the park is home to sweeping vistas that stretch for upwards of 100 miles as well as a rich history of archeological discovery. Dinosaurs from the Late Jurassic and Early Cretaceous periods have been discovered here along with prehistoric dinosaur footprints.

Sitting Bull Crystal Caverns, for its part, features anything but sweeping panoramic vistas. Here, visitors descend deep underground for guided tours of the world's largest natural displays of dogtooth spar crystal. Other highlights of the tour include a subterranean lake and underground domes known as the French Chandelier Room, Crystal Palace and Rainbow Arch.

For More Information

Rapid City CVB
800-487-3223
www.visitrapidcity.com

South Dakota Department of Tourism
800-S-DAKOTA
www.travelsd.com

Getty Images/iStockphoto

SPOTLIGHT

SD

SPEARFISH

Explore some of the most photogenic spots in the Black Hills

As visitors arrive in Spearfish, South Dakota, they're treated to much the same views the town's first settlers would have enjoyed in 1876. Nestled against the shores of a gentle creek in a scenic valley, the town is ringed by a crown of three distinct alpine peaks: Lookout Mountain, Spearfish Mountain and Crow Peak. Encircled by these majestic gems, it's no wonder the town adopted the nickname, "Queen City."

Located just 50 miles from Rapid City at the northern edges of Black Hills National Forest, Spearfish is ideally situated for those looking to explore the greater southwestern quadrant of South Dakota. Sitting directly on Interstate 90, day trips to Mount Rushmore, Crazy Horse Memorial, Custer State Park, Badlands National Park and Buffalo Gap National Grassland are made with a fair degree of ease. RV travelers who are short on time can branch out and visit the hotspots in rapid succession, while those with the luxury of more time on their hands can set up camp and spend an entire summer exploring this historic and attraction-packed slice of South Dakota. However, the local attractions merit just as much attention.

> Like so many other towns, Spearfish owes its foundation to the discovery of gold in the Black Hills area in 1876.

Golf Rush Survivor

Like so many other towns and communities in the Black Hills region, Spearfish owes its foundation to the discovery of gold in the region in 1876. Native Americans occupied the region long before the arrival of gold panners and prospectors, using spears to fish in the creek that would ultimately give the town its name. But the population exploded in the years following 1890. Unlike so many other towns and communities, Spearfish successfully weathered the boom-bust cycle of gold prospecting to survive—and thrive—to the present day.

Whether its picturesque setting had anything to do with that early survival and perseverance is up for debate, but there's no denying Spearfish's beauty. So striking is the area that, when scouting film locations for "Dances With Wolves," Kevin Costner chose Spearfish Canyon for the movie's final, climactic scenes.

As such, the canyon itself is among the most popular (and rewarding)

A rocky ridge in Spearfish Canyon.
Getty Images/iStockphoto

Spearfish Falls. Visit South Dakota

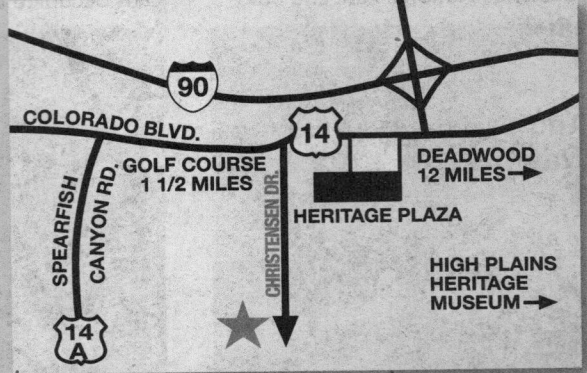

Clear water tumbles over limestone cliffs in Roughlock Falls.
Getty Images/iStockphoto

A bronze sculpture honoring fishery workers. U.S. Department of Fish and Wildlife Service

attractions for visitors making their first stops in Spearfish. Hiking is a popular activity here, with a robust system of well-maintained scenic trails snaking their way through the wilderness bracketing each side of the canyon walls. Trailheads wind their way to secluded waterfalls—including Spearfish Canyon Falls and Roughlock Falls—as well as the Rod and Gun Campground (also accessible by road).

Prefer wading to walking? Fly fishing for trout in Spearfish Creek draws anglers from far and wide to find fish in the current and wait for that big bite.

Spearfish Canyon is also home to some fantastic biking trails, with *Bicycling* magazine naming it as one of the top-50 most scenic biking paths in the country.

For an easier-on-the-knees-and-back exploration of the canyon, simply buckle up and hit the Spearfish Canyon Scenic Byway. The entire route covers 22 miles in total, with the journey beginning in downtown Spearfish. The drive features incredible views of massive limestone cliffs, gentle Spearfish Creek and tumbling Bridal Veil Falls. The speed limit is a slow-and-steady 35 miles per hour, with the byway offering plenty of spots to pull over and soak in the mesmerizing views.

Along the way, the byway is home to the Spearfish Canyon Lodge, Latchstring Restaurant and the cafe at Cheyenne Crossing Store, each providing a nice spot to stop for a bit of lunch and a chance to recharge.

Elsewhere, the Spirit of the Hills Wildlife Sanctuary and D.C. Booth Historic National Fish Hatchery are two other highly popular Spearfish area attractions. The former provides sanctuary and care for more than 300 animals which, for various reasons, can never again be released to the wild. Tours of the facilities are highly educational and provide an opportunity to get up-close views of a variety of exotic animals, including African lions.

See What's Hatching

At the D.C. Booth Historic National Fish Hatchery, guests can tour a conservationist facility that was first opened in 1896, making it one of the oldest of its kind in the country. Access is free year-round, and visitors are encouraged to stroll the grounds freely. From May to September, the Hatchery is also home to exhibits and collections displayed at the on-site Von Bayer Museum, Booth House and Railcar.

Finally, don't miss paying a visit to the High Plains Western Heritage Center. The five states of North Dakota, South Dakota, Nebraska, Wyoming and Montana all collaborate to showcase the history of Wild West pioneers and Native Americans here, where preserved artifacts, Western art and live displays are showcased.

Perched on the northern edges of Black Hills National Forest, the town of Spearfish can often find itself overshadowed by the likes of Rapid City to the southeast. But the comparatively smaller crowds, gorgeous natural settings and striking canyon vistas found in Spearfish are reward enough for savvy travelers and explorers who decide to set up camp here and explore abroad.

For More Information

Visit Spearfish
800-344-6181
www.visitspearfish.com

South Dakota Department of Tourism
800-732-5682
www.travelsd.com

SD

South Dakota

CONSULTANTS

Duane & Bev Finger

ABERDEEN — A5 *Brown*

MELGAARD PARK CAMPGROUND (CITY PARK) (Public) From Jct of Hwy 12 & State St, S 1 mi on State St, follow signs (E). 2015 rates: $26. Apr 1 to Oct 31. (605)626-7015

MINA LAKE REC AREA
(State Pk) From Aberdeen: Go 11 mi W on Hwy 12, follow signs (R). Entrance fee required. **FAC:** Paved rds. 37 gravel, back-ins (16 x 55), 37 E (20/30 amps), tent sites, rentals, dump. **REC:** Mina Lake: swim, fishing, playground, rec open to public. Pets OK. Partial handicap access. 14 day max stay, 2015 rates: $19.
(800)710-2267 Lat: 45.446704, Lon: -98.74082
402 Park Ave, Mina, SD 57451
parkinfo@state.sd.us
www.gfp.sd.gov/state-parks
See ad page 1039 (Welcome Section).

RICHMOND LAKE STATE RECREATION
(State Pk) From Jct of US-12 & US-281, W 5 mi on US-12 to park access rd, NW 6 mi (L). Entrance fee required. **FAC:** Paved rds. 24 gravel, 1 pull-thrus (20 x 50), back-ins (20 x 50), 22 E (20/30 amps), tent sites, rentals, dump. **REC:** Richmond Lake: swim, fishing, playground, rec open to public. Pets OK. Partial handicap access. 14 day max stay, 2015 rates: $15 to $19.
(800)710-2267 Lat: 45.532958, Lon: -98.619032
37908 Youth Camp Rd, Aberdeen, SD 57401
parkinfo@state.sd.us
www.gfp.sd.gov/state-parks
See ad page 1039 (Welcome Section).

WYLIE PARK & STORYBOOK LAND
Ratings: 9/9★/10 (Campground) From Jct US-12 & US-281: Go 2 1/4 mi N on US-281, then 1/4 mi W on Seratoma Pkwy (L) Don't rely on GPS - Call for directions. **FAC:** Paved rds. 115 paved, patios, 29 pull-thrus (34 x 60), back-ins (35 x 60), 77 full hkups, 38 W, 38 E (30/50 amps), WiFi, tent sites, rentals, dump, laundry, groc, fire rings, firewood. **REC:** Wylie Lake: swim, fishing, playground, rec open to public. Pets OK. Partial handicap access. Big rig sites, 2015 rates: $30 to $31. Disc: AAA. Apr 1 to Nov 1.
AAA Approved
(888)326-9693 Lat: 45.48910, Lon: -98.52437
2300 24th Ave NW, Aberdeen, SD 57401
prf@aberdeen.sd.us
www.aberdeen.sd.us/storybookland
See ad pages 1037 (Welcome Section), 1042.

Set a destination for family fun! Check our family camping destinations article highlighting the best places to camp in every state and province. Find a great destination, then select one of the family-friendly campgrounds listed by region.

Things to See and Do

ABERDEEN AQUATIC CENTER 50 meter/5-lane lap pool with 1 & 3-meter diving boards, a drop slide & variety of floatable play features. The 9000 sq. ft. leisure pool includes a mutli-level structure with waterslides & interactive features. May 30 to Aug 21. Restrooms. Hours: 1pm to 9pm. Adult fee: $5.25 to $7.25. No CC.
(605)626-7015 Lat: 45.45362, Lon: -98.47296
1029 S Dakota St, Aberdeen, SD 57401
prf@aberdeen.sd.us
www.aberdeen.sd.us/aquatics
See ad page 1037 (Welcome Section).

STORY BOOK/LAND OF OZ THEME PARKS
210-acre park featuring picnic facilities, lake & swimming beach, recreational trails, wildlife exhibits, Story Book Land, Land of Oz, train, carousel, balloon rides, paddle boat & canoe rentals. Admission free to Theme Park. Apr 15 to Oct 15. RV accessible. Restrooms, food. Hours: 10am to 9pm.
(605)626-7015 Lat: 45.49118, Lon: -98.52192
2202 24th Ave NW, Aberdeen, SD 57401
prf.@aberdeen.sd.us
www.aberdeen.sd.us/storybookland
See ad page 1037 (Welcome Section).

AKASKA — A4 *Walworth*

D & S CAMPGROUND & LODGE
Ratings: 3.5/8★/6 (Campground) From Jct US 83 & Hwy 144: Go 3 mi W on Hwy 144. (L). **FAC:** Gravel rds. 43 gravel, 20 pull-thrus (25 x 75), back-ins (25 x 75), some side by side hkups, 34 full hkups, 9 E (30/50 amps), tent sites, rentals, dump, laundry, fire rings, firewood. **REC.** Pets OK. Big rig sites, 2015 rates: $35. May 1 to Dec 1. No CC.
(605)229-1739 Lat: 45.33316, Lon: -100.12143
103 Swan Creek Rd, Akaska, SD 57420
lgillies@abe.midco.net
www.sdhuntfishguide.com
See ad this page.

SWAN CREEK REC AREA
(State Pk) From Gettysburg: W 9 mi on 142nd St. (E). Entrance fee required. **FAC:** Paved rds. 23 paved, back-ins (14 x 60), 23 E (20/30 amps), tent sites, dump. **REC:** Missouri River: fishing, rec open to public. Pets OK. Partial handicap access. 14 day max stay, 2015 rates: $13 to $17.
(800)710-2267 Lat: 45.319177, Lon: -100.3
16157A West Whitlock Rd c/o West Whitlock, Gettysburg, SD 57442
parkinfo@state.sd.us
www.gfp.sd.gov/state-parks
See ad page 1039 (Welcome Section).

ARLINGTON — B6 *Brookings*

LAKE POINSETT REC AREA
(State Pk) From town, N 12 mi on Hwy 81 to CR-2, E 2 mi (E) Entrance fee required. **FAC:** Paved rds. 108 gravel, 22 pull-thrus (14 x 50), back-ins (14 x 60), 108 E (30 amps), tent sites, rentals, dump. **REC:** Lake Poinsett: swim, fishing, playground, rec open to public. Pets OK. Partial handicap access. 14 day max stay, 2015 rates: $21 to $25.
(800)710-2267 Lat: 44.534183, Lon: -97.083956
45617 S Poinsett Dr, Arlington, SD 57212
parkinfo@state.sd.us
www.gfp.sd.gov/state-parks
See ad page 1039 (Welcome Section).

BADLANDS NATIONAL PARK — C2 *Jackson*

BADLANDS NATIONAL PARK See also Interior.

BELLE FOURCHE — B1 *Butte*

ROCKY POINT RA
(State Pk) From Belle Fourche: Go 8 mi E on SD-212. **FAC:** Gravel rds. 66 gravel, back-ins (15 x 65), 57 E (20/30 amps), tent sites, rentals, dump. **REC:** Belle Fourche Reservoir: swim, fishing, playground, rec open to public. Pets OK. Partial handicap access. 14 day max stay, 2015 rates: $15 to $21.
(800)710-2267 Lat: 44.709733, Lon: -103.710709
18513 Fisherman's Rd, Belle Fourche, SD 57717
parkinfo@state.sd.us
www.gfp.sd.gov/state-parks
See ad page 1039 (Welcome Section).

ROCKY POINT RECREATION AREA (State Pk) From Jct of US 85 & US 212 (North of Bell Fourche), E 6.4 mi on US 212 to Fishermans Rd, N 2.2 mi (E). Park entrance fee required. 2015 rates: $15 to $19. (605)584-3896

BELVIDERE — C3 *Jackson*

BELVIDERE EAST/EXIT 170 KOA **Ratings: 8.5/9.5★/9.5** (Campground) 2015 rates: $31.94 to $42.23. May 1 to Sep 30. (800)562-2134 24201 Sd Hwy 63, Midland, SD 57552

BERESFORD — D6 *Union*

UNION GROVE C/O NEWTON HILLS
(State Pk) From Jct of SR-46 & I-29, S 11 mi on I-29 to exit 38, S 2 mi (L) Note: Entrance fee required. **FAC:** Paved rds. 22 gravel, 9 pull-thrus (20 x 40), back-ins (20 x 40), 22 E (20/30 amps), tent sites, dump. **REC:** Brule Creek: playground, rec open to public. Pets OK. 14 day max stay, 2015 rates: $13 to $19.
(800)710-2267 Lat: 42.920242, Lon: -96.785322
30828-471st Ave, Beresford, SD 57004
parkinfo@state.sd.us
www.gfp.sd.gov/state-parks
See ad page 1039 (Welcome Section).

BLACK HAWK — C1 *Meade*

THREE FLAGS RV PARK **Ratings: 6/9★/7** (Campground) 2015 rates: $30 to $47.50. Apr 1 to Oct 30. (605)787-7898 9484 Three Flags Ln, Black Hawk, SD 57718

BLACK HILLS — C1 *Lawrence*

Things to See and Do

MICKELSON TRAIL (SRA) The trail is 109 miles long and contains more than 100 converted railroad bridges and 4 rock tunnels. Its gentle slopes and easy access allow people of all ages and abilities to enjoy the beauty of the Black Hills. No CC.
(800)710-2267 Lat: 44.365915, Lon: -100.345825
523 E Capitol, Pierre, SD 57501
parkinfo@state.sd.us
www.sdparks.info
See ad page 1039 (Welcome Section).

BONESTEEL — D4 *Gregory*

WHETSTONE BAY REC AREA (Public Corps) From town, W 0.25 mi on US-18 to CR-1806, N 8.75 mi (R). Pit toilets. 2015 rates: $11 to $15. (605)487-7046

BRANDON — C6 *Minnehaha*

BIG SIOUX RECREATION AREA
(State Pk) From Jct of I-90 & SR-11 (Exit 406), S 3 mi on SR-11/Splitrock Blvd to S. Sioux Blvd, NW 0.2 mi to Park St, W 0.3 mi to Park Entrance (R) Note: Entrance fee required. **FAC:** Gravel rds. 44 gravel, back-ins (18 x 75), 44 E (20/30 amps), tent sites, rentals, dump. **REC:** Big Sioux River: fishing, playground, rec open to public. Pets OK. Partial handicap access. 14 day max stay, 2015 rates: $15 to $19.
(800)710-2267 Lat: 43.57267, Lon: -96.59472
410 W Park Ave, Brandon, SD 57005
parkinfo@state.sd.us
www.gfp.sd.gov/state-parks
See ad page 1039 (Welcome Section).

BROOKINGS — C6 *Brookings*

OAKWOOD LAKES
(State Pk) From Jct of I-29 & SR-30, W 10 mi on SR-30, follow signs (R). Entrance fee required. **FAC:** Paved rds. 136 gravel, 3 pull-thrus (15 x 35), back-ins (15 x 35), 130 E (20/30 amps), tent sites, rentals, dump. **REC:** Oakwood Lakes: swim, fishing, playground, rec open to public. Pets OK. Partial handicap access. 14 day max stay, 2015 rates: $15 to $19. No CC.
(605)627-5441 Lat: 44.449753, Lon: -96.981982
20247 Oakwood Dr, Bruce, SD 57220
oakwoodlakes@state.sd.us
gfp.sd.gov/state-parks
See ad page 1039 (Welcome Section).

SEXAUER CITY PARK (Public) From Jct of I-29 & Hwy 14 (6th St), W 2 mi on Hwy 14 to Western Ave, N 0.5 mi (R). 2015 rates: $20. May 15 to Oct 15. (605)692-2708

BURKE — D4 *Gregory*

BURKE LAKE (SRA)
(State Pk) From Burke: Go 2 mi E on US-18. **FAC:** Gravel rds. 15 gravel, back-ins (18 x 46), tent sites, pit toilets. **REC:** Burke Lake: fishing, rec open to public. Pets OK. 14 day max stay, 2015 rates: $11.
(800)710-2267 Lat: 43.183192, Lon: -99.260023
29145 Burke Lake Rd, Burke, SD 57523
parkinfo@state.sd.us
www.gfp.sd.gov/state-parks
See ad page 1039 (Welcome Section).

CANISTOTA — C6 *McCook*

LAKE VERMILLION REC AREA
(State Pk) From Jct of I-90 & CR-E30 (exit 374), S 5 mi on CR-E30 to Lake Vermillion Rd (L) Note: Entrance fee required. **FAC:** Paved rds. 90 gravel, 18 pull-thrus (14 x 70), back-ins (14 x 70), some side by side hkups, 90 E (20/30 amps), tent sites, rentals, dump. **REC:** Lake Vermillion: swim, fishing, playground, rec open to public. Pets OK. Partial handicap access. 14 day max stay, 2015 rates: $15 to $19.
(800)710-2267 Lat: 43.5947, Lon: -97.185173
26140 451st Ave, Canistota, SD 57012
parkinfo@state.sd.us
gfp.sd.gov/state-parks
See ad page 1039 (Welcome Section).

CANTON — D6 *Lincoln*

NEWTON HILLS
(State Pk) 6 mi S of Canton, off CR-135: From Jct of I-29 & CR-140 (exit 56), E 12 mi on CR-140 to CR-135, N 0.25 mi (L). Entrance fee required. **FAC:** Gravel rds. 112 gravel, back-ins (14 x 60), 112 E (20/30 amps), tent sites, rentals, dump. **REC:** Lake Lakota: swim, fishing, playground, rec open to public. Pets OK. Partial handicap access. 14 day max stay, 2015 rates: $15 to $19.
(800)710-2267 Lat: 43.219041, Lon: -96.570193
28767 482nd Ave, Canton, SD 57013
parkinfo@state.sd.us
www.gfp.sd.gov/state-parks
See ad page 1039 (Welcome Section).

CHAMBERLAIN — C4 *Brule, Lyman*

A SPOTLIGHT Introducing Chamberlain/Oacoma's colorful attractions appearing at the front of this state section.

OASIS CAMPGROUND
Ratings: 8.5/9.5★/8 (Campground) From Jct of I-90 & Exit 260: Go 100 ft N on Douglas Ave, then 1/4 mi E on Bus-90/Hwy 16 (R).

OASIS CAMPGROUND
We invite you to stay & relax at the Oasis Campground, one of South Dakota's greatest locations. Complete with scenic views of Missouri River and history, art & culture to explore! Across from Al's Oasis, still $.05 coffee.

FAC: Gravel rds. 72 Avail: 58 gravel, 14 grass, 34 pull-thrus (30 x 65), back-ins (30 x 65), 72 full hkups (30/50 amps), cable, WiFi, tent sites, dump, laundry, fire rings, firewood. **REC:** heated pool, playground. Pets OK. Partial handicap access. Big rig sites, 2015 rates: $35.95. Disc: AAA, military. Apr 15 to Nov 1.
AAA Approved
(800)675-6959 Lat: 43.80205, Lon: -99.38755
605 East Sd Hwy16, Oacoma, SD 57365
mark@wildwoodsd.com
www.alsoasis.com
See ad pages 1044 (Spotlight Chamberlain/Oacoma), 1042, 1038 (SD Map).

Had a great stay? Let us know by emailing us travelguidecomments@goodsamfamily.com

Things to See and Do

OASIS PUMP N PAK Service station, convenience store, casino across from Oasis Campground. RV accessible. Restrooms, food. Hours: 6am to 5:59am. ATM.
(605)234-5325 Lat: 43.80281, Lon: -99.38435
1000 E Hwy 16, Oacoma, SD 57365
info@alsoasis.com
www.alsoasis.com
See ad page 1044 (Spotlight Chamberlain/Oacoma).

CLEAR LAKE — B6 *Deuel*

CLEAR LAKE CITY PARK (Public) From Jct of SR-22 & SR-15, N 1 mi on SR-15 (L). 2015 rates: $15. (605)874-2121

LAKE COCHRANE REC AREA
(State Pk) From Clear Lake, E 10 mi on Hwy 22, follow signs (R). Entrance fee required. **FAC:** Paved rds. 30 gravel, back-ins (17 x 60), 30 E (20/30 amps), tent sites, dump. **REC:** Lake Cochrane: swim, fishing, playground, rec open to public. Pets OK. Partial handicap access. 14 day max stay, 2015 rates: $19.
(800)710-2267 Lat: 44.714191, Lon: -96.478932
3454 Edgewater Dr, Gary, SD 57237
parkinfo@state.sd.us
www.gfp.sd.gov/state-parks
See ad page 1039 (Welcome Section).

ULVEN PARK (Public) From town, E 0.25 mi on SR-22 (R). 2015 rates: $15. (605)874-2121

CORSON — C1 *Minnehaha*

PALISADES
(State Pk) From Jct I-90 & Brandon (Exit 406): Go 10 mi N on Cnty Rd 11. Follow signs(R). Entrance fee required. **FAC:** Paved rds. 22 gravel, back-ins (20 x 60), 22 E (20/30 amps), tent sites, rentals. **REC:** Split Rock Creek: fishing, playground, rec open to public. Pets OK. Partial handicap access. 14 day max stay, 2015 rates: $15 to $19.
(800)710-2267 Lat: 43.687645, Lon: -96.517166
25495-485th Ave, Garretson, SD 57030
parkinfo@state.sd.us
www.gfp.sd.gov/state-parks
See ad page 1039 (Welcome Section).

CUSTER — C1 *Custer*

A SPOTLIGHT Introducing Custer's colorful attractions appearing at the front of this state section.

CUSTER See also Hill City & Keystone.

BEAVER LAKE CAMPGROUND
Ratings: 9/10★/9.5 (Campground) From Jct US 385 & US 16 (in town): Go 3.5 mi W on US 16 (L) Note: can also call for directions. Elev 5600 ft.

BEAVER LAKE CAMPGROUND
Relaxation. Tranquility. The way it should be. Beaver Lake Campground is centrally located to all the tourist attractions in the Black Hills. Amenities include: water slide, heated pool and playground for your family fun.

FAC: Gravel rds. 86 gravel, 25 pull-thrus (40 x 60), back-ins (35 x 60), 63 full hkups, 23 W, 23 E (30/50 amps), cable, WiFi, tent sites, rentals, dump, mobile sewer, laundry, groc, LP gas, fire rings, firewood. **REC:** heated pool, wading pool, playground, rec open to public. Pets OK. Partial handicap access. Big rig sites, eco-friendly, 2015 rates: $38 to $50. Disc: military. Mar 15 to Nov 10. ATM.
AAA Approved
(800)346-4383 Lat: 43.73967, Lon: -103.65685
12005 US Hwy 16, Custer, SD 57730
beaverlake@gwtc.net
www.beaverlakecampground.net
See ad pages 1045 (Spotlight Custer), 1042.

BIG PINE CAMPGROUND Ratings: 8/10★/9.5 (Campground) From Jct US-385 & US-16 (in town): Go 2 mi W on US-16 (R). Elev 5500 ft. **FAC:** Gravel rds. 63 gravel, 10 pull-thrus (20 x 60), back-ins (25 x 55), 35 full hkups, 27 W, 27 E (30/50 amps), WiFi, tent sites, rentals, dump, laundry, fire rings, firewood. **REC:** playground. Pets OK. Big rig sites, eco-friendly, 2015 rates: $34 to $37. Disc: military. May 20 to Oct 1.
(800)235-3981 Lat: 43.74962, Lon: -103.64046
12084 Big Pine Road, Custer, SD 57730
bigpine@gwtc.net
www.bigpinecampground.com

BLACK HILLS NF (BISMARCK LAKE CAMPGROUND) (Natl Forest) From town: Go 4 mi E on US-16A. 2015 rates: $24. May 17 to Sep 7. (605)574-4402

Looking for places the "locals" frequent? Make friends with park owners and staff to get the inside scoop!

CUSTER CRAZY HORSE CAMPGROUND
Ratings: 7/7.5/7 (Campground) From Jct US-16 & US-385 (in town): Go 1 mi N on US-16/385 (R) or Southbound from Crazy Horse Memorial: go 3 mi S on US 16/US 385. (L). Elev 5300 ft. **FAC:** Poor gravel/dirt rds. 106 gravel, 51 pull-thrus (22 x 55), back-ins (25 x 40), 69 full hkups, 37 W, 37 E (30/50 amps), WiFi, tent sites, rentals, dump, laundry, groc, LP gas, fire rings, firewood. **REC:** heated pool, playground. Pets OK. Partial handicap access. 2015 rates: $27 to $33. Disc: AAA, military. May 1 to Oct 5.
AAA Approved
(605)673-2565 Lat: 43.77704, Lon: -103.61270
1116 N 5th St, Custer, SD 57730
reservation@rushmorecabins.com
www.rushmorecabins.com
See ad pages 1045 (Spotlight Custer), 1042.

CUSTER MOUNTAIN CABINS & CAMPGROUND **Ratings: 5.5/6.5/8.5** (Campground) 2015 rates: $31.50 to $36.75. Apr 1 to Nov 30. (605)673-5440 12503 Hwy 16A, Custer, SD 57730

CUSTER/BLUE BELL
(State Pk) From Custer: Go 8 mi E on US-16A (to Visitor's Ctr), then continue 7 mi E on US-16A, then 3 mi S on SD-87 (L). Entrance fee required. Elev 5000 ft. **FAC:** Paved rds. 30 paved, back-ins (20 x 45), 30 E (30/50 amps), tent sites, rentals. **REC:** rec open to public. Pets OK. Partial handicap access. 14 day max stay, 2015 rates: $21 to $25. May 1 to Oct 31.
(800)710-2267 Lat: 43.705415, Lon: -103.5
13329 US Hwy 16A, Custer, SD 57730
parkinfo@state.sd.us
www.gfp.sd.gov/state-parks
See ad page 1039 (Welcome Section).

CUSTER/CENTER LAKE
(State Pk) From Custer: Go 10 mi E on US-16A, then 4 mi N on SD-87. (R). Elev 4686 ft. **FAC:** Paved rds. 71 gravel, back-ins (20 x 50), tent sites, pit toilets. **REC:** Center Lake: swim, fishing, playground, rec open to public. Pets OK. Partial handicap access. 14 day max stay, 2015 rates: $19. May 1 to Sep 30.
(800)710-2267 Lat: 43.807161, Lon: -103.4
13329 US Hwy 16A, Custer, SD 57730
parkinfo@state.sd.us
www.gfp.sd.gov/state-parks
See ad page 1039 (Welcome Section).

CUSTER/GAME LODGE
(State Pk) From Custer: Go 15 mi E on US-16A to Visitor Center, then continue 1 mi E on US-16A (R). Elev 4250 ft. **FAC:** Paved rds. 57 paved, back-ins (20 x 60), 57 E (20/30 amps), tent sites, rentals, dump, laundry. **REC:** pond, swim, fishing, playground, rec open to public. Pets OK. Partial handicap access. 14 day max stay, 2015 rates: $21 to $25.
(800)710-2267 Lat: 43.760274, Lon: -103.4
hc 83 Box 70, Custer, SD 57730
parkinfo@state.sd.us
www.gfp.sd.gov/state-parks
See ad page 1039 (Welcome Section).

SD

CUSTER/GRACE COOLIDGE
(State Pk) From Custer: E 14.5 mi on US-16A (R). Elev 4250 ft. **FAC:** Paved rds. 18 paved, back-ins (20 x 35), 18 E (30 amps), tent sites. **REC:** Grace Coolidge Creek: fishing, rec open to public. Pets OK. Partial handicap access. 14 day max stay, 2015 rates: $21 to $25. May 17 to Sep 30.
(800)710-2267 Lat: 43.778816, Lon: -103.402240
13329 US Hwy 16A, Custer, SD 57730
parkinfo@state.sd.us
www.gfp.sd.gov/state-parks
See ad page 1039 (Welcome Section).

CUSTER/LEGION LAKE
(State Pk) From Custer: Go 9 mi E on US-16A (L). Elev 5000 ft. **FAC:** Paved rds. 21 gravel, back-ins (20 x 50), 21 E (20/30 amps), tent sites. **REC:** Legion Lake: swim, fishing, rec open to public. Pets OK. Partial handicap access. 14 day max stay, 2015 rates: $21 to $25. May 17 to Sep 30.
(800)710-2267 Lat: 43.762262, Lon: -103.50000
13329 US Hwy 16A, Custer, SD 57730
parkinfo@state.sd.us
www.gfp.sd.gov/state-parks
See ad page 1039 (Welcome Section).

CUSTER/STOCKADE LAKE
(State Pk) From Custer: E 3 mi on US-16A (R). Elev 5280 ft. **FAC:** Gravel rds. 67 gravel, back-ins (20 x 50), 56 E (20/30 amps), tent sites, rentals. **REC:** Stockade Lake: swim, playground, rec open to public. Pets OK. Partial handicap

Park owners and staff are rightly proud of their business. Let them know how much you enjoyed your stay.

CUSTER (CONT)

CUSTER/STOCKADE LAKE (CONT)
access. 14 day max stay, 2015 rates: $21 to $25. May 17 to Sep 30.
(800)710-2267 Lat: 43.769500, Lon: -103.532556
13329 US Hwy16A, Custer, SD 57730
parkinfo@state.sd.us
www.gfp.sd.gov/state-parks
See ad page 1039 (Welcome Section).

CUSTER/SYLVAN LAKE
(State Pk) From Custer: Go 6 mi N on Hwy 89 (R). Elev 6200 ft. **FAC:** Paved rds. 25 gravel, back-ins (20 x 30), 25 E (20/30 amps), tent sites. **REC:** Sylvan Lake: fishing, rec open to public. Pets OK. Partial handicap access. 14 day max stay, 2015 rates: $21 to $25. May 17 to Sep 2.
(800)710-2267 Lat: 43.843695, Lon: -103.60000
13329 US Hwy 16A, Custer, SD 57730
parkinfo@state.sd.us
www.gfp.sd.gov/state-parks
See ad page 1039 (Welcome Section).

CUSTERS GULCH RV PARK & CAMPGROUND
Ratings: 8.5/9.5★/9.5 (Campground) From Jct of Hwy 385/Hwy 16/5th St and Hwy 16A/Hwy 89/Mt Rushmore Rd (in downtown Custer), E 3 mi on Hwy 16A (towards Custer State Park) (R). Elev 5298 ft. **FAC:** All weather rds. 70 gravel, 8 pull-thrus (45 x 75), back-ins (45 x 70), 62 full hkups, 8 E (30/50 amps), WiFi, tent sites, rentals, dump, laundry, LP gas, fire rings, firewood. **REC.** Pet restrict(B). Big rig sites, eco-friendly, 2015 rates: $34 to $45. May 4 to Sep 30.
AAA Approved
(605)673-4647 Lat: 43.76552, Lon: -103.54505
25112 Golden Valley Rd, Custer, SD 57730
custersgulch@gwtc.net
www.custersgulch.com
See ad pages 1046 (Spotlight Custer), 1042.

FORT WELIKIT FAMILY CAMPGROUND
Ratings: 7.5/10★/8 (Campground) From Jct Hwy 385 & 16A (in downtown Custer): Go .5 mi E on 16A to Hwy 89/Sylvan Lake Rd, then N 1 mi (R). Elev 5500 ft. **FAC:** Gravel rds. (65 spaces). Avail: 55 gravel, 15 pull-thrus (30 x 75), back-ins (30 x 60), 42 full hkups, 13 W, 13 E (30/50 amps), seasonal sites, cable, WiFi, tent sites, rentals, dump, laundry, LP gas, fire rings, firewood. **REC:** playground. Pets OK. Partial handicap access. Big rig sites, eco-friendly, 2015 rates: $33 to $41. Disc: AAA, military. May 1 to Oct 15.
AAA Approved
(888)946-2267 Lat: 43.78290, Lon: -103.58583
24992 Sylvan Lake Rd, Custer, SD 57730
sanctusv@gmail.com
www.fortwelikit.com
See ad pages 1046 (Spotlight Custer), 1042.

Everyone wants to be noticed. Tell your RV Park that you found them in the this Guide.

HERITAGE VILLAGE CAMPGROUND Ratings: 6/9★/7.5 (Campground) From Jct US-16/385 & US-16A (in downtown Custer) : Go 3 1/2 mi N on US-16/385 (R). Elev 5841 ft. **FAC:** Gravel rds. (35 spaces). Avail: 27 gravel, 27 pull-thrus (25 x 65), 27 full hkups (30/50 amps), seasonal sites, tent sites, rentals, dump, laundry, firewood. **REC.** Pets OK. Partial handicap access. Big rig sites, 2015 rates: $22 to $26. May 1 to Oct 15.
AAA Approved
(605)673-5005 Lat: 43.80318, Lon: -103.63796
24827 Village Ave, Crazy Horse, SD 57730
camping@heritage-village.com
www.heritage-village.com

Things to See and Do

BEAVER LAKE CAMPGROUND GIFT SHOP A convenience store that includes: limited groceries, gifts & souvenirs, video rentals, jewelry & cards, beverages and an extensive selection of RV supplies. Elev 5600 ft. Mar 15 to Nov 10. partial handicap access. RV accessible. Restrooms. Hours: 8am to 7pm. ATM.
(800)346-4383 Lat: 43.73967, Lon: -103.65685
12005 W US Hwy 16, Custer, SD 57730
beaverlake@gwtc.net
www.beaverlakecampground.net
See ad page 1045 (Spotlight Custer).

CUSTER CAR, ATV/UTV RENTAL Rent ATVs/UTVs, Cars & SUVs. All rentals include entrance pass to Custer State Park & Mount Rushmore. ATVs include Custer Forest Service permit & license plate. Located at Custers Gulch Campground. RV accessible. Hours: 8am to 7pm.
(605)673-6600 Lat: 43.76552, Lon: -103.54505
25112 Golden Valley Rd, Custer, SD 57730
custersgulch@gwtc.net
www.blackhillsrv.net
See ad page 1046 (Spotlight Custer).

The RVers' Guide to NASCAR helps RV travelers get the most out of North America's most thrilling sporting event. Turn to the front of the Guide and we'll give you the inside track on how to get high-speed thrills at major NASCAR venues.

NATIONAL MUSEUM OF WOODCARVING Museum of Woodcarving, the life work of an original animator from Disneyland, a residential woodcarving studio, gallery and gift/snack shop. May 1 to Oct 22. partial handicap access. RV accessible. Restrooms. Hours: 9am to 5pm. Adult fee: $9.99.
(605)673-4404 Lat: 43.75058, Lon: -103.63593
12111 Hwy 16W, Custer, SD 57730
woodcarv@gwtc.net
www.blackhills.com/woodcarving
See ad page 1046 (Spotlight Custer).

DEADWOOD — B1 *Lawrence*

DEADWOOD See also Belle Fourche, Nemo, Spearfish & Sturgis.

BLACK HILLS NF (ROUBAIX LAKE CAMPGROUND) (Natl Forest) From jct US-85 & US-385: Go 14 mi S on US-385, then 1 mi W on FR-255. Pit toilets. 2015 rates: $19. (605)574-4402

FISH'N FRY RV PARK & CAMPGROUND
Ratings: 8.5/8.5★/8.5 (Campground) From Jct US-385 & US-85 (SE edge of Deadwood): Go 6 mi S on US-385 (L) Use exact GPS coordinates: Lat 44.30219, Lon -103.67776. Elev 5500 ft. **FAC:** Gravel rds. 59 Avail: 35 gravel, 24 grass, 10 pull-thrus (16 x 55), back-ins (26 x 60), some side by side hkups, 31 full hkups, 21 W, 21 E (30/50 amps), WiFi, tent sites, rentals, dump, laundry, groc, fire rings, firewood, restaurant. **REC:** heated pool, Bear Butte Creek: fishing, playground. Pets OK. Big rig sites, eco-friendly, 2015 rates: $32 to $38. Disc: AAA, military. May 13 to Sep 18.
(605)578-2150 Lat: 44.30219, Lon: -103.67776
21390 Hwy 385, Deadwood, SD 57732
stay@fishnfry.com
www.fishnfry.com
See ad this page, 1042.

HIDDEN VALLEY CAMPGROUND
Ratings: 7/10★/9 (Campground) From Jct US-85 & US-385 (in Deadwood): Go 6 mi S on US-385. (R). Elev 5300 ft. **FAC:** Gravel rds. 34 gravel, patios, 5 pull-thrus (25 x 60), back-ins (25 x 45), 5 full hkups, 29 W, 29 E (30 amps), WiFi, tent sites, rentals, dump, laundry, groc, fire rings, firewood. **REC:** Paradise Creek: fishing, playground. Pets OK. Partial handicap access. 2015 rates: $30 to $35. Disc: military. May 15 to Sep 15.
(866)578-1342 Lat: 44.29731, Lon: -103.68035
21423 US Hwy 385, Deadwood, SD 57732
hiddenvalley@orbitcom.biz
www.hiddenvalleydeadwood.com
See ad this page.

STEEL WHEEL CAMPGROUND & TRADING POST
Ratings: 7/10★/7.5 (Campground) From Jct US-85 & US-385 (in Deadwood): Go 6 mi S on US-385 (R) Call for directions. Elev 5285 ft. **FAC:** Paved/gravel rds. 31 gravel, patios, 7 pull-thrus (25 x 70), back-ins (30 x 48), 28 full hkups, 3 E (30/50 amps), WiFi, tent sites, rentals, dump, laundry, groc, LP gas, fire rings, firewood, restaurant. **REC.** Pets OK. Partial handicap access. Big rig sites, 2015 rates: $30 to $38. Disc: military. ATM.
(877)596-9767 Lat: 44.29970, Lon: -103.67863
21399 US Hwy 385, Deadwood, SD 57732
steelwheel@orbitcom.biz
www.steelwheelcampground.com
See ad this page.

WHISTLER GULCH RV PARK & CAMPGROUND
Ratings: 9.5/9.5★/9 (Campground) From Jct US 85 & US 14A: Go 3 mi S on US 85 (L); or From Jct US 385 & US 85: Go .5 mi E on US 85 (R). Note: Don't use GPS - Call for directions. Elev 4800 ft. **FAC:** Paved rds. 121 Avail: 105 gravel, 16 grass, 35 pull-thrus (20 x 60), back-ins (20 x 40), 121 full hkups (30/50 amps), WiFi, tent sites, rentals, dump, laundry, groc, fire rings, firewood. **REC:** heated pool, Whitewood Creek: fishing. Pets OK. Partial handicap access.

)EADWOOD (CONT)

WHISTLER GULCH RV PARK & (CONT)
:co-friendly, 2015 rates: $35 to $48. Disc: military. ɫay 1 to Sep 30.
800)704-7139 Lat: 44.36383, Lon: -103.73485
35 Cliff St, Deadwood, SD 57732
vhistlergulch@gmail.com
www.whistlergulch.com

WILD BILL'S CAMPGROUND, SALOON & GRILL
Ratings: 6.5/8.5★/8 (Campground) From Jct US-85 & US-385 (S of Deadwood): Go 5-1/4 ni S on US-385 (L) Don't rely on GPS, call for direcions. Elev 5248 ft. **FAC:** Gravel rds. 49 gravel, backıs (20 x 45), 25 full hkups, 10 W, 24 E (30/50 amps), ViFi, tent sites, rentals, dump, laundry, fire rings, rewood, restaurant. **REC:** Bear Butte Creek: fishing, layground. Pets OK. 2015 rates: $24 to $34. Disc: AA, military. May 15 to Sep 5.
605)578-2800 Lat: 44.30967, Lon: -103.67486
1372 US Hwy 385, Deadwood, SD 57732
vildbillscamp@gmail.com
vww.wildbillscamp.com
See ad opposite page.

:UREKA — A4 *McPherson*

EUREKA CITY PARK (Public) From Jct of 47 & D-10, N on 18th, follow signs. 2015 rates: $10. 605)284-2441

:AIRFAX — D4 *Gregory*

SOUTH SCALP CREEK REC AREA (Public Corps) From town, E 4.3 mi on US-18 to CH-2, N 7 ni follow signs (E). Pit toilets. 2015 rates: $11. 605)668-2985

:AITH — B2 *Meade*

FAITH CITY PARK (Public) From Jct of US-212 & ɫain St, S 4 blks on Main St (L). (605)967-2261

:ORT PIERRE — C3 *Stanley*

COW CREEK RECREATION AREA
(State Pk) From Fort Pierre: Go 15 mi NW on Hwy 1804. Entrance fee required. **FAC:** Gravel rds. 40 gravel, back-ins (18 x 60), 31 E 20/30 amps), tent sites, rentals, dump. **REC:** Oahe Reservoir: swim, fishing, rec open to public. Pets OK. 4 day max stay, 2015 rates: $13 to $17.
800)710-2267 Lat: 44.555685, Lon: -100.5
8229 Cow Creek Rd, Fort Pierre, SD 57532
arkinfo@state.sd.us
vww.gfp.sd.gov/state-parks
See ad page 1039 (Welcome Section).

OAHE DOWNSTREAM RECREATION AREA
(State Pk) From Fort Pierre: Go 5 mi N on Hwy 1806. **FAC:** Paved rds. 204 Avail: 160 paved, 44 gravel, 1 pull-thrus (20 x 60), back-ins 20 x 50), 204 E (20/30 amps), WiFi, tent sites, rentls, dump. **REC:** Missouri River: swim, fishing, mari-a, playground, rec open to public. Pets OK. Partial andicap access. 14 day max stay, 2015 rates: $19.
800)710-2267 Lat: 44.436944, Lon: -100.4
0439 Marina Loop Rd, Fort Pierre, SD 57532
arkinfo@state.sd.us
vww.gfp.sd.gov/state-parks
See ad page 1039 (Welcome Section).

:ORT THOMPSON — C4 *Buffalo*

LEFT TAILRACE REC AREA (Public Corps) From own, S 2 mi on Hwy 47W (L). Pit toilets. 2015 rates: 8 to $14. May 15 to Sep 12. (605)245-2255

:RANKFORT — B5 *Spink*

FISHER GROVE
(State Pk) From Redfield: Go 7 mi E on US-212, N .5 mi. Entrance fee required. **FAC:** Paved rds. 22 gravel, 4 pull-thrus (14 x 75), ack-ins (14 x 65), 22 E (30 amps), tent sites, dump. **EC:** James River: fishing, golf, playground, rec pen to public. Pets OK. 14 day max stay, 2015 rates: 13 to $17.
800)710-2267 Lat: 44.883461, Lon: -98.356702
7290 Fishers Lane, Frankfort, SD 57440
arkinfo@state.sd.us
vww.gfp.sd.gov/state-parks
See ad page 1039 (Welcome Section).

:EDDES — D5 *Charles Mix*

PEASE CREEK RECREATION AREA
(State Pk) From Jct of Hwy 50 & Main St (in Lake Andes), W 8.5 mi on Hwy 50 to SD-1804, S 1.1 mi to 292nd St, W 1 mi to 373rd Ave, S mi to park entrance (R). Note: Park Entrance fee equired. **FAC:** Gravel rds. 28 gravel, back-ins 35 x 60), 23 E (20/30 amps), tent sites, dump. **REC:** ake Francis Case: fishing, playground, rec open to public. Pets OK. Partial handicap access. 14 day max stay, 2015 rates: $15 to $17.
(800)710-2267 Lat: 43.140208, Lon: -98.731855
37270-293rd St, Geddes, SD 57342
parkinfo@state.sd.us
www.gfp.sd.gov/state-parks
See ad page 1039 (Welcome Section).

Ve rate what RVers consider important.

GETTYSBURG — B4 *Potter*

WEST WHITLOCK RECREATION AREA
(State Pk) From Gettysburg: Go 13 mi W on US-212. **FAC:** Gravel rds. 101 gravel, back-ins (22 x 75), 101 E (20/30 amps), WiFi, tent sites, rentals, dump. **REC:** Lake Oahe: swim, fishing, playground, rec open to public. Pets OK. Partial handicap access. 14 day max stay, 2015 rates: $17.
(800)710-2267 Lat: 45.048094, Lon: -100.3
16157A West Whitlock Rd., Gettysburg, SD 57442
parkinfo@state.sd.us
www.gfp.sd.gov/state-parks
See ad page 1039 (Welcome Section).

GROTON — A5 *Brown*

GROTON CITY PARK (Public) From Jct of US-12 & SR-37, E 3 blks on US-12 to Main St, S 4 blks (L). 2015 rates: $20. May to Nov. (605)397-8422

HARRISBURG — D6 *Lincoln*

Things to See and Do

LAKE ALVIN (SRA) This 59 acre park is best known for its beach facilities and excellent fishing. Anglers can expect to snag walleye, northern pike, crappie, sunfish, perch, catfish and bullheads. No CC.
(800)710-2267 Lat: 43.442555, Lon: -96.609
27225 480th Ave, Harrisburg, SD 57032
parkinfo@state.sd.us
www.gfp.sd.gov/state-parks
See ad page 1039 (Welcome Section).

HIGHMORE — B4 *Hyde*

CITY PARK EAST (Public) From Jct of US-14 & SD-47, S 0.5 mi on SD-47 to 2nd St, E 2 blks (L). 2015 rates: $8. (605)852-2716

HILL CITY — C1 *Pennington*

A SPOTLIGHT Introducing Hill City's colorful attraction appearing at the front of this state section.

BLACK HILLS TRAILSIDE PARK RESORT
Ratings: 6.5/9.5★/7.5 (Campground) At South city limit of Hill City on US-16/385. (East side). Elev 5000 ft. **FAC:** Gravel rds. 33 gravel, back-ins (24 x 45), 33 full hkups (30/50 amps), cable, WiFi, tent sites, rentals, dump, fire rings, firewood. **REC:** Spring Creek: playground. Pets OK. Partial handicap access. Big rig sites, eco-friendly, 2015 rates: $39 to $55. Disc: AAA, military. May 1 to Oct 30.
AAA Approved
(605)574-9079 Lat: 43.92564, Lon: -103.57831
24024 Hwy 16/385, Hill City, SD 57745
reserve@trailsideparkresort.com
www.blackhillstrailsideparkresort.com
See ad this page, 1042.

CROOKED CREEK RESORT INC
Ratings: 9/10★/9.5 (Campground) From south city limit of Hill City: Go 2 mi S on US-16/385 (L). Elev 5000 ft. **FAC:** Paved/gravel rds. 82 Avail: 62 gravel, 20 grass, 25 pull-thrus (20 x 60), back-ins (24 x 65), 55 full hkups, 26 W, 26 E (30/50 amps), WiFi, tent sites, rentals, dump, mobile sewer, laundry, groc, LP gas, fire rings, firewood. **REC:** heated pool, Spring Creek: fishing, playground. Pet restrict(B). Big rig sites, eco-friendly, 2015 rates: $27 to $57. Disc: AAA, military. May 15 to Oct 15. ATM.
(800)252-8486 Lat: 43.89956, Lon: -103.59240
24184 Hwy 16, Hill City, SD 57745
ccrresort@gmail.com
www.crookedcreeksd.com
See ad pages 1047 (Spotlight Hill City), 1042.

HORSE THIEF CAMPGROUND AND RESORT INC
Ratings: 9/10★/9 (Campground) From south city limits of Hill City: Go 3 1/2 mi S on US-16/385, then 2 mi S & E on Hwy 87 (R). Elev 5500 ft. **FAC:** Gravel rds. 66 gravel, 40 pull-thrus (32 x 60), back-ins (32 x 60), 52 full hkups, 14 W, 14 E (30/50 amps), WiFi, tent sites, rentals, dump, laundry, groc, fire rings, firewood. **REC:** heated pool, playground. Pet restrict(B). Partial handicap access. Big rig sites, eco-friendly, 2015 rates: $35 to $45. Disc: AAA, military. May 15 to Oct 1.
(800)657-5802 Lat: 43.87023, Lon: -103.58547
24391 Sd Hwy 87, Hill City, SD 57745
camp@horsethief.com
www.horsethief.com
See ad pages 1047 (Spotlight Hill City), 1042.

MT RUSHMORE KOA **Ratings: 9/9.5★/9.5** (Campground) 2015 rates: $43.80 to $66.91. May 1 to Oct 1. (800)562-8503 12620 Hwy 244, Hill City, SD 57745

RAFTER J BAR RANCH CAMPING RESORT
Ratings: 9/10★/9.5 (Campground) From south city limits of Hill City: Go 3.0 mi S on US-16/385 (R). Elev 5280 ft.

RAFTER J BAR RANCH CAMPING RESORT
A Black Hills premier camping resort near Mt. Rushmore & other attractions. Enjoy our VERIZON 4G coverage across entire park! 5 Pristine & picturesque camping areas! Only a few minutes to Needles Hwy & Custer State Park!

FAC: Paved/gravel rds. 166 Avail: 145 gravel, 21 grass, 60 pull-thrus (40 x 60), back-ins (40 x 60), 136 full hkups, 30 W, 30 E (30/50 amps), WiFi, tent sites, rentals, dump, laundry, groc, LP gas, fire rings, firewood. **REC:** heated pool, whirlpool, Spring Creek: fishing, playground. Pet restrict(B). Partial handicap access. Big rig sites, eco-friendly, 2015 rates: $43.95 to $60.95. May 1 to Oct 1. ATM.
(605)574-2527 Lat: 43.89461, Lon: -103.59104
12325 Rafter J Rd, Hill City, SD 57745
www.rafterj.com
See ad this page, 1048 (Spotlight Hill City), 1042 & RV Trips of a Lifetime in Magazine Section.

Things to See and Do

RAFTER J BAR RANCH GIFT SHOP Large store carries: Black Hills Gold Jewelry, T-shirts, Sioux Indian Pottery, Souvenirs, Clothing, Camping Supplies, Toys, Gifts, Ice Cream & Snack Bar. Also, limited Groceries. May 1 to Oct 1. RV accessible. Restrooms, food. Hours: 8am to 7pm. ATM.
(888)RAFTERJ Lat: 43.89461, Lon: -103.59104
12325 Rafter J Rd, Hill City, SD 57745
www.rafterj.com
See ad this page, 1048 (Spotlight Hill City).

SD

HOT SPRINGS — D1 *Fall River*

ANGOSTURA REC AREA
(State Pk) From Hot Springs: SE 10 mi on US-18/385 (R). Entrance fee required. Elev 3200 ft. **FAC:** Paved rds. 166 gravel, back-ins (15 x 55), 160 E (30/50 amps), tent sites, rentals, dump, restaurant. **REC:** Angostura Reservoir: swim, fishing, marina, playground, rec open to public. Pets

Lend a hand. During the busy season park services are stretched to the max! Please do your best to keep your area "ship-shape".

HOT SPRINGS (CONT)

ANGOSTURA REC AREA (CONT)
OK. Partial handicap access. 14 day max stay, 2015 rates: $15 to $19.
(800)710-2267 Lat: 43.345873, Lon: -103.4
13157 N. Angostura Rd, Hot Springs, SD 57747
parkinfo@state.sd.us
www.gfp.sd.gov/state-parks
See ad page 1039 (Welcome Section).

COLD BROOK LAKE (Public Corps) From Jct of Hwy 385 & Evans St (in town), follow signs. Pit toilets. 2015 rates: $5. (605)745-5476

COTTONWOOD SPRINGS (Public Corps) From town, W 5 mi on US-18 to CR-17, N 2 mi (R). 2015 rates: $10. (605)745-5476

HOT SPRINGS KOA
Ratings: 9/10★/8 (Campground) From Jct US-385/US-18 & SR-79: Go .5 mi N on SR-79 (L). Elev 3300 ft. **FAC:** Gravel rds. 48 gravel, 38 pull-thrus (25 x 60), back-ins (25 x 50), 31 full hkups, 17 W, 17 E (30/50 amps), cable, WiFi, tent sites, rentals, dump, laundry, groc, LP gas, fire rings, firewood. **REC:** heated pool, playground. Pets OK. Big rig sites, eco-friendly, 2015 rates: $35 to $45. Disc: AAA, military.
AAA Approved
(800)562-0803 Lat: 43.40818, Lon: -103.39488
27585 Hwy 79, Hot Springs, SD 57747
hotsprings@koa.com
www.hskoa.com
See ad this page.

SHEPS CANYON
(Public) From jct US-385 & Hwy 71 (at Hot Springs): Go 6 mi S on Hwy 71; then 5 mi E on Sheps Canyon Rd. **FAC:** Gravel rds. 22 gravel, back-ins (15 x 80), WiFi, tent sites, dump. **REC:** Angostura Reservoir: swim, fishing, rec open to public. Pets OK. Partial handicap access. 2015 rates: $15 to $19.
(800)710-2267 Lat: 43.32550, Lon: -103.44579
28150 S Boat Ramp Rd, Hot Springs, SD 57747
parkinfo@state.sd.us
www.gfp.sd.gov/state-parks
See ad page 1039 (Welcome Section).

WIND CAVE/ELK MOUNTAIN (Natl Pk) From town, N 7 mi on US-385 (L). 2015 rates: $10. Apr 1 to Oct 1. (605)745-4600

HURON — C5 *Beadle*

MEMORIAL PARK CAMPGROUND (CITY PARK) (Public) From Jct of Hwy 37 & Hwy 14, E 0.7 mi on Hwy 14 to Jersey Ave, N 0.3 mi (L). 2015 rates: $15 to $20. Apr to Nov. (605)353-8533

SOUTH DAKOTA STATE FAIRGROUNDS & PARK (Public) From Jcts of Hwy 37 & Hwy 14, W on Hwy 14 to Lincoln, to Gate 6. 2015 rates: $20. (800)529-0900

INTERIOR — C2 *Jackson*

BADLANDS CIRCLE 10 CAMPGROUND **Ratings: 4/7/7.5** (Campground) 2015 rates: $29 to $31. Apr 15 to Oct 15. (800)231-3617 21296 Sd Hwy 240, Philip, SD 57567

BADLANDS INTERIOR MOTEL & CAMPGROUND
Ratings: 7/8★/7.5 (Campground) From Jct I-90 (Exit 131) & Hwy 240: Go 9 mi S on Hwy 240, then 2 mi S on Hwy 377. (R). Don't rely on GPS, call. **FAC:** Gravel rds. 45 Avail: 35 gravel, 10 grass, 45 pull-thrus (28 x 75), mostly side by side hkups, 20 full hkups, 12 W, 12 E (30/50 amps), WiFi, tent sites, rentals, dump, laundry, groc, fire rings, firewood. **REC:** pool, playground. Pets OK. Partial handicap access. Eco-friendly, 2015 rates: $26 to $28. Disc: AAA, military. Apr 1 to Oct 1.
AAA Approved
(800)388-4643 Lat: 43.72909, Lon: -101.97857
900 Sd Hwy 377, Interior, SD 57750
badlandsmotelcampground@gmail.com
www.badlandsinteriorcampground.com
See ad pages 1054, 1042.

BADLANDS/CEDAR PASS (Natl Pk) From Jct I-90 (exit 131) & Hwy 240: Go 8-1/2 S on Hwy 240, then 1/2 mi S on SR 377. (L). 2015 rates: $30. (605)433-5460

BADLANDS/WHITE RIVER KOA **Ratings: 9/10★/10** (Campground) 2015 rates: $38 to $68. Apr 17 to Sep 30. (800)KOA-3897 20720 Sd Hwy 44, Interior, SD 57750

KENNEBEC — C4 *Lyman*

KENNEBEC KOA **Ratings: 9/9.5★/8.5** (Campground) 2015 rates: $35 to $47. May 1 to Oct 31. (800)562-6361 307 S Hwy 273, Kennebec, SD 57544

KEYSTONE — C1 *Custer, Pennington*

KEMP'S KAMP Ratings: 6/8/9 (Campground) From Jct US-16 Alt & CR-323/Old Hill City Rd (N edge of town): Go 1.5 mi W on CR-323/Old Hill City Rd (R). Elev 4500 ft. **FAC:** Gravel rds. 37 Avail: 34 gravel, 3 grass, 8 pull-thrus (25 x 40), back-ins (25 x 55), 14 full hkups, 23 W, 23 E (30/50 amps), WiFi, tent sites, rentals, dump, firewood. **REC:** heated pool, Battle Creek: fishing. Pets OK. 2015 rates: $40 to $47. May 10 to Sep 28.
(888)466-6282 Lat: 43.90149, Lon: -103.4458
1022 Old City Road, Keystone, SD 57751
www.kempskamp.com

SPOKANE CREEK CABINS & CAMPGROUND **Ratings: 7/7.5/8** (Campground) 2015 rates: $35 to $45. May 15 to Sep 15. (800)261-9331 24631 Iron Mountain Rd, Keystone, SD 57751

LAKE CITY — A6 *Marshall*

FORT SISSETON
(State Pk) 10 mi SW of Lake City off US Hwy 10. **FAC:** Paved rds. 14 gravel, back-ins (12 x 70), 10 E (20/30 amps), WiFi, tent sites, rentals. **REC:** Kettle Lake: fishing, rec open to public. Pets OK. Partial handicap access. 14 day max stay, 2015 rates: $13 to $17.
(800)710-2267 Lat: 45.659398, Lon: -97.528266
11907 434th Ave, Lake City, SD 57247
parkinfo@state.sd.us
www.gfp.sd.gov/state-parks
See ad page 1039 (Welcome Section).

ROY LAKE
(State Pk) From Lake City: Go 3 mi SW on SD-10. **FAC:** Paved rds. 88 gravel, 6 pull-thrus (20 x 75), back-ins (20 x 60), 88 E (20/30 amps), tent sites, rentals, dump, groc, restaurant. **REC:** Roy Lake: swim, fishing, playground, rec open to public. Pets OK. Partial handicap access. 14 day max stay, 2015 rates: $15 to $19.
(800)710-2267 Lat: 45.709611, Lon: -97.448000
11545 Northside Dr, Lake City, SD 57247
parkinfo@state.sd.us
www.gfp.sd.gov/state-parks
See ad page 1039 (Welcome Section).

LAKE PRESTON — B6 *Kingsbury*

LAKE THOMPSON RECREATION AREA
(State Pk) From Jct of Hwy 14 & Main St (in Lake Preston), W 3.8 mi on Hwy 14 to 438 Ave, S 4 mi to park entrance. Entrance fee required. **FAC:** Gravel rds. 103 gravel, 21 pull-thrus (16 x 72), back-ins (16 x 72), 103 E (20/30 amps), tent sites, rentals, dump. **REC:** Lake Thompson: swim, fishing, playground, rec open to public. Pets OK. Partial handicap access. 14 day max stay, 2015 rates: $19.
(800)710-2267 Lat: 44.32346, Lon: -97.43463
21176 Flood Club Rd, Lake Preston, SD 57249
parkinfo@state.sd.us
www.gfp.sd.gov/state-parks
See ad page 1039 (Welcome Section).

LEAD — C1 *Lawrence*

RECREATIONAL SPRINGS RESORT **Ratings: 6.5/NA/7.5** (Campground) 2015 rates: $25 to $40. (605)584-1228 11201 US Highway 14A, Lead, SD 57754

LEMMON — A2 *Perkins*

LLEWELLYN JOHNS (SRA)
(State Pk) From Lemmon: Go 12 mi S on Hwy 73. **FAC:** Gravel rds. 10 gravel, back-ins (12 x 50), 10 E (20/30 amps), tent sites, pit toilets. Pets OK. 14 day max stay, 2015 rates: $15
(800)710-2267 Lat: 45.804725, Lon: -102.292348
19150 Summerville Rd, Shadehill, SD 57653
parkinfo@state.sd.us
www.gfp.sd.gov/state-parks
See ad page 1039 (Welcome Section).

SHADEHILL REC AREA
(State Pk) FromLemmon: Go 12 mi S on Hwy 73 (R). Entrance fee required. **FAC:** Gravel rds. 56 gravel, 3 pull-thrus (20 x 100), back-ins (20 x 70), 56 E (20/30 amps), tent sites, rentals, dump. **REC:** Shadehill Reservoir: swim, fishing, playground, rec open to public. Pets OK. Partial handicap access. 14 day max stay, 2015 rates: $19 to $2
(800)710-2267 Lat: 45.761144, Lon: -102.2
19150 Summerville Rd, Shadehill, SD 57638
parkinfo@state.sd.us
www.gfp.sd.gov/state-parks
See ad page 1039 (Welcome Section).

MADISON — C6 *Lake*

LAKE HERMAN
(State Pk) From Madison: Go W 2 mi on Hwy 34 to Lake Rd, S 2 mi (E). **FAC:** Paved rds. 6 gravel, 6 pull-thrus (15 x 50), back-ins (15 x 50), 69 E (20/30 amps), tent sites, rentals, dump. **REC:** Lake Herman: swim, fishing, playground, rec open to public. Pets OK. Partial handicap access. 14 day max stay, 2015 rates: $15 to $1
(800)710-2267 Lat: 43.992878, Lon: -97.160427
23409 State Park Dr, Madison, SD 57042
parkinfo@state.sd.us
www.gfp.sd.gov/state-parks
See ad page 1039 (Welcome Section).

WALKER'S POINT REC AREA
(State Pk) From Madison: Go 9 mi SE on Hwy 19 to Walker's Point Rd, E 2 mi, N 1.5 mi on township road (R). **FAC:** Paved rds. 42 gravel, 8 pull-thrus (20 x 60), back-ins (26 x 60), 42 E (20/30 amps), tent sites, rentals, dump. **REC:** Madison Lake: fishing, playground, rec open to public. Pets OK. Partial handicap access. 14 day max stay, 2015 rates: $15 to $19.
(800)710-2267 Lat: 43.956806, Lon: -97.028615
6431 Walker's Point Dr, Madison, SD 57042
parkinfo@state.sd.us
www.gfp.sd.gov/state-parks
See ad page 1039 (Welcome Section).

MILBANK — A6 *Grant*

HARTFORD BEACH
(State Pk) From Milbank: Go 15 mi N on Hwy 15. Entrance fee required. **FAC:** Paved rds. 87 gravel, back-ins (15 x 70), 87 E (20/30 amps), tent sites, rentals, dump. **REC:** Big Stone Lake: swim, fishing, playground, rec open to public. Pets OK. Partial handicap access. 2015 rates: $19
(605)432-6374 Lat: 45.402196, Lon: -96.673074
13672 Hartford Beach Rd, Corona, SD 57227
hartford@state.sd.us
gfp.sd.gov/state-parks
See ad page 1039 (Welcome Section).

MILLER — B4 *Hand*

CRYSTAL PARK (Public) From Jct of Hwy 14 7th St exit, W 3 blks on 7th St (R). (605)853-270

So you're the one with "pooch" duty? Please make a clean sweep of it! Your fellow RVers will appreciate it!

ILLER (CONT)

LAKE LOUISE REC AREA
(State Pk) From Miller, go 14 mi NW on US-14. Entrance fee required. **FAC:** Paved rds. 35 Avail: 29 paved, 6 gravel, back-ins 4 x 50), 30 E (20/30 amps), tent sites, rentals, ump. **REC:** Lake Louise: swim, fishing, playground, ec open to public. Pets OK. Partial handicap access. 4 day max stay, 2015 rates: $15 to $19.
00)710-2267 Lat: 44.620547, Lon: -99.140554
5250 191st St, Miller, SD 57362
arkinfo@state.sd.us
fp.sd.gov/state-parks
ee ad page 1039 (Welcome Section).

ITCHELL — C5 *Davison, Hanson*

DAKOTA CAMPGROUND
Ratings: 9/9.5★/9 (Campground)
From Jct of I-90 & Exit 330, S 0.2 mi on 408th Ave/Ohlman St to Spruce St, W 0.1 mi on Spruce St (R) Don't rely on GPS. Call. **FAC:** Gravel rds. 52 gravel, 2 pull-thrus (30 x 70), back-ins (30 x 70), 42 full kups, 10 W, 10 E (30/50 amps), WiFi, tent sites, entals, dump, laundry, fire rings, firewood. **REC:** ool, playground. Pets OK. Partial handicap access. ig rig sites, eco-friendly, 2015 rates: $23 to $25. isc: military. Apr 1 to Nov 30.
05)996-9432 Lat: 43.68765, Lon: -98.04991
800 W Spruce, Mitchell, SD 57301
ww.dakotacampgrounds.com
ee ad this page, 1042.

FAMIL-E-FUN CAMPGROUND & RV PARK
Ratings: 9/9.5★/9.5 (Campground)
From Jct of I-90 & Exit 325 (Betts Rd), S 0.2 mi on Betts Rd (R). Don't use GPS. **FAC:** Gravel rds. 55 gravel, 39 pull-thrus 25 x 65), back-ins (35 x 65), 55 full hkups (30/50 mps), WiFi, tent sites, rentals, dump, laundry, groc, re rings, firewood. **REC:** heated pool, playground. ets OK. Partial handicap access. Big rig sites, co-friendly, 2015 rates: $28.50 to $30. Apr 15 to Nov
05)996-8983 Lat: 43.69179, Lon: -98.14728
5473 403rd Ave, Mitchell, SD 57301
amilefun@santel.net
ww.familefuncampground.com
ee ad this page, 1042.

LAKE MITCHELL CAMPGROUND (Public) From ct of I-90 & SR-37 (Exit 330), N 3.1 mi on SR-37 to ain St, N 0.5 mi (L). 2015 rates: $28.50 to $32. Apr 5 to Oct 31. (605)995-8457

MITCHELL KOA **Ratings: 7.5/9/8.5** (Campround) 2015 rates: $26 to $48. May 1 to Nov 1. 00)562-1236 41255 Sd Hwy 38, Mitchell, SD 57301

R & R CAMPGROUND & RV PARK
Ratings: 8/8.5/8 (Campground) From Jct I-90 (exit 332) & Burr St.: Go 1000 ft N on Burr St, then 1000 ft E & S to campground entrance (behind Super 8 motel). **FAC:** Paved/gravel rds. 40 Avail: 5 aved, 35 gravel, 35 pull-thrus (30 x 70), back-ins 30 x 70), 40 full hkups (30/50 amps), cable, WiFi, ent sites, rentals, dump, laundry, groc. **REC:** heated ool, wading pool, playground. Pets OK. Partial handicap access. Big rig sites, 2015 rates: $34 to $38. Disc: AAA, military. May 15 to Oct 10.
AAA Approved
(605)996-8895 Lat: 43.69431, Lon: -98.01131
1700 S Burr St., Mitchell, SD 57301
campmitchellsd@gmail.com
www.mitchellsuper8.com
See ad this page, 1042.

RONDEE'S RV PARK
Ratings: 8.5/9.5★/8 (Campground)
From jct Hwy 37 & I-90: Go 2 mi E on I-90 (exit 332), then 1/4 mi N on Burr St. (R). **FAC:** Gravel rds. 35 gravel, 35 pull-thrus (30 x 70), 35 full hkups (30/50 amps), cable, WiFi, tent sites, rentals, dump, laundry, fire rings, firewood. **REC:** heated pool $, wading pool, whirlpool, playground. Pets OK. Partial handicap access. Big rig sites, 2015 rates: $30 to $35. Disc: AAA, military.
(605)996-0769 Lat: 43.69606, Lon: -98.01268
911 E Kay Ave, Mitchell, SD 57301
dusty@mitchelltelecom.net
www.rondeescampground.com
See ad opposite page, 1042.

MOBRIDGE — A3 *Corson, Walworth*

INDIAN CREEK REC AREA (Public Corps) From Mobridge: Go 2 mi SE on US-12. 2015 rates: $14. (605)845-7112

INDIAN CREEK REC AREA
(State Pk) From Mobridge: Go 2 mi SE on US-12. **FAC:** Gravel rds. 123 gravel, 2 pull-thrus (15 x 70), back-ins (15 x 70), 123 E (20/30 amps), tent sites, rentals, dump. **REC:** Lake Oahe: fishing, marina, playground, rec open to public. Pets OK. Partial handicap access. 14 day max stay, 2015 rates: $13 to $17.
(800)710-2267 Lat: 45.522137, Lon: -100.4
12905 - 288th Ave, Mobridge, SD 57601
parkinfo@state.sd.us
www.gfp.sd.gov/state-parks
See ad page 1039 (Welcome Section).

MONTROSE — C6 *McCook*

PIONEER CAMPGROUND (Public) From Jct of I-90 & 451st Ave., N 2 mi on 451st Ave, follow signs (L). 2015 rates: $15. May 1 to Nov 1. (605)363-5065

MOUNT RUSHMORE — C1 *Pennington*

BEAVER LAKE CAMPGROUND
Ratings: 9/10★/9.5 (Campground)
From Mount Rushmore: Go 8 mi W on Hwy 244, then 11 mi S on US 16/385, then 3-1/4 mi W on US 16 (L). Elev 5600 ft. **FAC:** Gravel rds. 86 gravel, 25 pull-thrus (40 x 60), back-ins (35 x 60), 63 full hkups, 23 W, 23 E (30/50 amps), cable, WiFi, tent sites, rentals, dump, mobile sewer, laundry, groc, LP gas, fire rings, firewood. **REC:** heated pool, wading pool, playground, rec open to public. Pets OK. Partial handicap access. Big rig sites, eco-friendly, 2015 rates: $36 to $45. Disc: military. Mar 15 to Nov 10. ATM.
(800)346-4383 Lat: 43.73967, Lon: -103.65685
12005 W Hwy 16, Custer, SD 57730
beaverlake@gwtc.net
www.beaverlakecampground.net
See primary listing at Custer and ad page 1045 (Spotlight Custer).

HEARTLAND RV PARK & CABINS
Ratings: 8/10★/8 (Campground)
From Mount Rushmore: Go 2-3/4 mi NE on US-16A/Hwy 244, then 19-1/2 mi E on Hwy 40, then 1/4 mi S on Hwy 79 (R). Elev 3300 ft. **FAC:** Gravel rds. 135 gravel, 135 pull-thrus (30 x 60), 130 full hkups, 5 W, 5 E (30/50 amps), WiFi, tent sites, rentals, dump, laundry, LP gas, fire rings, firewood. **REC:** heated pool, whirlpool, playground. Pets OK. Partial handicap access. Big rig sites, 2015 rates: $20 to $49. Disc: AAA.
(605)255-5460 Lat: 43.81876, Lon: -103.20265
24743 Hwy 79, Hermosa, SD 57744
rving@rapidnet.com
www.heartlandcampground.com
See primary listing at Rapid City and ad pages 1059, 1060.

You have high expectations, so we point out campgrounds, service centers and tourist attractions with elevations over 2,500 feet.

RAFTER J BAR RANCH CAMPING RESORT
Ratings: 9/10★/9.5 (Campground)
From Mount Rushmore: Go 8 mi W on Hwy 244, then 200 feet N on US 16/385. (L). Elev 5280 ft. **FAC:** Paved/gravel rds. 166 Avail: 145 gravel, 21 grass, 60 pull-thrus (40 x 60), back-ins (40 x 60), 136 full hkups, 30 W, 30 E (30/50 amps), WiFi, tent sites, rentals, dump, laundry, groc, LP gas, fire rings, firewood. **REC:** heated pool, whirlpool, Spring Creek: fishing, playground. Pet restrict(B). Partial handicap access. Big rig sites, eco-friendly, 2015 rates: $43.95 to $60.95. May 1 to Oct 1. ATM.
(605)574-2527 Lat: 43.89461, Lon: -103.59104
12325 Rafter J Rd, Hill City, SD 57745
www.rafterj.com
See primary listing at Hill City and ad pages 1057, 1048 (Spotlight Hill City).

RUSHMORE SHADOWS RESORT
Ratings: 9.5/10★/10 (Membership Pk) From Mount Rushmore: Go 1-1/2 mi NE on Hwy 244, then 4-1/2 mi NE on US-16A (through Keystone), then 7 mi NE on US-16. (L). Elev 4425 ft. **FAC:** Paved rds. 160 gravel, 23 pull-thrus (30 x 60), back-ins (28 x 60), 160 full hkups (30/50 amps), WiFi, tent sites, dump, laundry, groc, fire rings, firewood, controlled access. **REC:** heated pool, whirlpool, playground. Pets OK. Partial handicap access. Big rig sites, eco-friendly, 2015 rates: $35 to $62. Disc: AAA, military. May 1 to Oct 15.
(800)231-0425 Lat: 43.97309, Lon: -103.32716
23680 Busted Five Ct, Rapid City, SD 57702
stay@midwestoutdoorresorts.com
www.midwestoutdoorresorts.com
See primary listing at Rapid City and ad page 1040 (Welcome Section).

MURDO — C3 *Jones*

AMERICAN RV PARK & MOTEL
Ratings: 4.5/8.5★/6.5 (Campground) From Jct I-90 (Exit 192) & Hwy 83: Go 2 blks N on US-83, then 2 blks W on 5th St (L). **FAC:** Paved/gravel rds. 51 Avail: 9 paved, 42 gravel, 46 pull-thrus (24 x 65), back-ins (25 x 60), 20 full hkups, 31 W, 31 E (30/50 amps), WiFi, tent sites, rentals, dump, laundry, restaurant. Pets OK. Partial handicap access. Big rig sites, 2015 rates: $23.50 to $29.50. Disc: AAA. May 1 to Nov 1.
(605)669-2461 Lat: 43.88562, Lon: -100.70991
303 5th St, Murdo, SD 57559
Postmaster@AmericanRVPark.net
See ad page 1041 (Welcome Section).

Replace clogged air filters. A clogged air filter can cut a vehicle's fuel efficiency by 10 percent.

SD

MURDO (CONT)

Things to See and Do

1880 TOWN 35 original town bldgs. authentically furnished with thousands of unique relics. 1880 Town includes Dances with Wolves movie props, Gen. Custer artifacts, Santa Fe Steam Liner dining cars. Mule-drawn wagon rides & entertainment daily. May 1 to Oct 31. RV accessible. Restrooms, food. Hours: 8am to 9pm. Adult fee: $10 to $12.
(605)344-2236 Lat: 43.88241, Lon: -101.14159
Interstate 90 Exit 170, Murdo, SD 57559
info@1880town.com
www.1880town.com
See ad page 1041 (Welcome Section).

NORTH SIOUX CITY — E6 *Union*

SIOUX CITY NORTH KOA
Ratings: 9/10★/8.5 (Campground) From Jct I-29 (Exit 2) & River Dr: Go 500 ft W on River Dr, then 3/4 mi N on Streeter Dr/W Service Rd (L). **FAC:** Gravel rds. 84 gravel, patios, 76 pull-thrus (30 x 60), back-ins (28 x 45), 77 full hkups, 7 W, 7 E (30/50 amps), cable, WiFi, tent sites, rentals, dump, laundry, groc, LP gas, fire rings, firewood. **REC:** heated pool, playground. Pets OK. Partial handicap access. Big rig sites, eco-friendly, 2015 rates: $39.95 to $47.95.
(605)232-4519 Lat: 42.53638, Lon: -96.50092
675 Streeter Dr, North Sioux City, SD 57049
contact@siouxcitykoa.com
www.siouxcitykoa.com
See ad page 494.

PICKSTOWN — D5 *Charles Mix, Gregory*

NORTH POINT REC AREA
(State Pk) From Pickstown: Go 1 mi NW on US-281, follow signs (L) Entrance fee required. **FAC:** Paved rds. 115 gravel, back-ins (15 x 70), 115 E (20/30 amps), tent sites, rentals, dump. **REC:** Lake Francis Case: swim, fishing, marina, playground, rec open to public. Pets OK. Partial handicap access. 14 day max stay, 2015 rates: $19.
(800)710-2267 Lat: 43.083064, Lon: -98.550327
38180-297th St, Lake Andes, SD 57356
parkinfo@state.sd.us
www.gfp.sd.gov/state-parks
See ad page 1039 (Welcome Section).

RANDALL CREEK CAMPGROUND (COE-FORT RANDALL DAM, LAKE FRANCIS CASE)
(Public Corps) From Pickstown: Go 1 mi W on US-281. **FAC:** Paved rds. 132 gravel, back-ins (12 x 55), 132 E (20/30 amps), tent sites, rentals, dump. **REC:** Missouri River: fishing, golf, playground, rec open to public. Pets OK. 14 day max stay, 2015 rates: $19.
(800)710-2267 Lat: 43.051021, Lon: -98.555139
136 Randall Creek Rd, Pickstown, SD 57367
parkinfo@state.sd.us
www.gfp.sd.gov/state-parks
See ad page 1039 (Welcome Section).

RANDALL CREEK REC AREA (State Pk) From Jct of Hwy 50 & 281, W 1 mi (Across the dam) on US Hwy -281/18, Follow signs (L) Entrance fee required. 2015 rates: $16. Apr 30 to Oct 1. (800)710-2267

PIEDMONT — C1 *Meade*

ELK CREEK RESORT RV PARK Ratings: 8/7.5/7 (Campground) From Jct I-90 & Exit 46 (Elk Creek Rd): Go 1 mi E on Elk Creek Rd (L). Elev 3280 ft. **FAC:** Gravel rds. 30 gravel, 30 pull-thrus (25 x 60), 29 full hkups, 1 W, 1 E (30/50 amps), WiFi Hotspot, tent sites, rentals, dump, mobile sewer, laundry, fire rings, firewood. **REC:** heated pool, whirlpool, Elk Creek: fishing, playground. Pets OK. Partial handicap access. Big rig sites, 2015 rates: $25 to $40. Disc: AAA, military.
AAA Approved
(800)846-2267 Lat: 44.22752, Lon: -103.35334
8220 Elk Creek Rd, Piedmont, SD 57769
info@elkcreekresort.net
www.elkcreekresort.net

PIERRE — C3 *Hughes, Stanley*

FARM ISLAND REC AREA
(State Pk) From Pierre: Go 4 mi E on Hwy 34 (R). Entrance fee required. **FAC:** Paved rds. 90 gravel, back-ins (16 x 70), 90 E (20/30 amps), WiFi, tent sites, rentals, dump. **REC:** Missouri River: swim, fishing, playground, rec open to public. Pets OK. Partial handicap access. 14 day max stay, 2015 rates: $15 to $19.
(800)710-2267 Lat: 44.345921, Lon: -100.3
1301 Farm Island Rd, Pierre, SD 57501
parkinfo@state.sd.us
www.gfp.sd.gov/state-parks
See ad page 1039 (Welcome Section).

GRIFFIN PARK (Public) From Jct of US-83 & Sioux St, E 5 blks on Sioux St to Washington, S 2 blks (E). 2015 rates: $10 to $16. (605)773-2527

OKOBOJO POINT RECREATION AREA
(State Pk) From Pierre: Go 17 mi NW on Hwy 1804. **FAC:** Gravel rds. 17 gravel, back-ins (15 x 60), tent sites. **REC:** Lake Oahe: swim, fishing, rec open to public. Pets OK. 14 day max stay, 2015 rates: $13. No CC.
(800)710-2267 Lat: 44.57596, Lon: -100.5
19425 Okobojo Point Dr, Fort Pierre, SD 57532
parkinfo@state.sd.us
www.gfp.sd.gov/state-parks
See ad page 1039 (Welcome Section).

WEST BEND REC AREA
(State Pk) From Pierce: Go 26 mi E on Hwy 34 then 9 mi S on unnamed CR. Follow signs. (L) Entrance fee required. **FAC:** Paved rds. 121 gravel, back-ins (16 x 65), 108 E (20/30 amps), WiFi, tent sites, rentals, dump. **REC:** Lake Sharpe Reservoir: fishing, playground, rec open to public. Pets OK. Partial handicap access. 14 day max stay, 2015 rates: $15 to $19.
(800)710-2267 Lat: 44.170744, Lon: -99.721022
22154 West Bend Rd, Harrold, SD 57536
parkinfo@state.sd.us
www.gfp.sd.gov/state-parks
See ad page 1039 (Welcome Section).

Things to See and Do

SOUTH DAKOTA DEPT OF GAME, FISH & PARKS Home to breathtaking scenery, abundant wildlife, and exciting geological wonders, South Dakota offers visitors a range of things to do and see. Partial handicap access. Hours: 8am to 5pm. No CC.
(800)710-2267 Lat: 44.365360, Lon: -100.344990
523 East Capitol, Joe Foss Bldg, Pierre, SD 57501
parkinfo@state.sd.us
www.gfp.sd.gov
See ad page 1039 (Welcome Section).

Visit CampingWorld.com where you can get deals on over 10,000 RV and camping related products!

PLATTE — D5 *Charles Mix*

BURYANEK RECREATION AREA
(State Pk) From Platte: Go 20 mi NW on Hw 44. **FAC:** Gravel rds. 44 gravel, back-ir (14 x 67), 44 E (20/30 amps), tent sites, ren als, dump. **REC:** Lake Francis Case: swim, fishin playground, rec open to public. Pets OK. Parti handicap access. 14 day max stay, 2015 rates: $1 to $17.
(800)710-2267 Lat: 43.415231, Lon: -99.173167
27450 Buryanek Rd, Burke, SD 57523
parkinfo@state.sd.us
www.gfp.sd.gov/state-parks
See ad page 1039 (Welcome Section).

NORTH WHEELER
(State Pk) From Platte: Go 16 mi S on Hv 1804. **FAC:** Gravel rds. 25 gravel, back-ir (12 x 65), 25 E (20/30 amps), tent sites, p toilets. **REC:** Lake Francis Case: fishing, rec open t public. Pets OK. 14 day max stay, 2015 rates: $1 No CC.
(800)710-2267 Lat: 43.171927, Lon: -98.825553
29084 N Wheeler Rd, Geddes, SD 57342
parkinfo@state.sd.us
www.gfp.sd.gov/state-parks
See ad page 1039 (Welcome Section).

PLATTE CREEK REC AREA
(State Pk) From Jct of Hwy 45 & Hwy 44: G 8 mi W on Hwy 44, then 10 mi S on Hwy 180 (R). Entrance fee required. **FAC:** Paved rd 36 gravel, back-ins (18 x 60), 36 E (20/30 amps), te sites, dump. **REC:** Lake Francis Case: swim, fishin playground, rec open to public. Pets OK. Parti handicap access. 14 day max stay, 2015 rates: $1 to $17.
(800)710-2267 Lat: 43.298531, Lon: -98.997652
35910-282nd St, Platte, SD 57369
parkinfo@state.sd.us
www.gfp.sd.gov/state-parks
See ad page 1039 (Welcome Section).

SNAKE CREEK REC AREA
(State Pk) From Platte: Go 14 mi W on Hwy 4 (L). Entrance fee required. **FAC:** Paved rd 115 gravel, 7 pull-thrus (18 x 51), back-ir (18 x 40), 111 E (20/30 amps), tent sites, rental dump, groc, restaurant. **REC:** Lake Francis Cas swim, fishing, marina, playground, rec open to publi Pets OK. Partial handicap access. 14 day max sta 2015 rates: $14 to $18.
(800)710-2267 Lat: 43.389979, Lon: -99.119491
35316 Sd Hwy 44, Platte, SD 57369
parkinfo@state.sd.us
www.gfp.sd.gov/state-parks
See ad page 1039 (Welcome Section).

POLLOCK — A3 *Campbell*

WEST POLLOCK (SRA)
(State Pk) From Pollock: Go 3 mi SW on Hw 1804. **FAC:** Gravel rds. 29 gravel, back-ir (16 x 75), 29 E (20/30 amps), tent sites, dum **REC:** Lake Oahe: fishing, playground, rec open t public. Pets OK. 14 day max stay, 2015 rates: $1
(800)710-2267 Lat: 45.88431, Lon: -100.386798
12905-288th Ave, Mobridge, SD 57601
parkinfo@state.sd.us
www.gfp.sd.gov/state-parks
See ad page 1039 (Welcome Section).

PRESHO — C4 *Lyman*

NEW FRONTIER RV PARK
Ratings: 7.5/9.5★/8.5 (Campground) From Jct I-90 (Exit 226) US-183: Go 1/4 mi W on I-90 Bus Loo (R) Note: do not use GPS. **FAC:** Grav rds. 64 gravel, 48 pull-thrus (22 x 60 back-ins (40 x 60), some side by side hkups, 36 fu hkups, 4 W, 28 E (30/50 amps), WiFi, tent site rentals, dump, laundry, fire rings, firewood. **RE** playground. Pets OK. Partial handicap access. Big r

Tell your RV Campground that you found the in this Guide.

PRESHO (CONT)

NEW FRONTIER RV PARK (CONT)
sites, eco-friendly, 2015 rates: $25 to $40. Disc: military. Apr 1 to Nov 1.
(605)895-2604 Lat: 43.90314, Lon: -100.05262
504 E Hwy 16, Presho, SD 57568
neal@newfrontiercampground.com
www.newfrontiercampground.com
See ad opposite page, 1042.

RAPID CITY — C1 *Meade, Pennington*

RAPID CITY See also Black Hawk, Hill City, Keystone, Piedmont & Sturgis.

HAPPY HOLIDAY RESORT
Ratings: 8.5/8★/7.5 (Campground) From Jct I-90 & Exit 61 (Elkvale Rd): Go 8.8 mi S on Elkvale Rd (turns into Catron Blvd/US-16 Truck BYP) to US 16, then 2.2 mi S on US-16. (L). Elev 3200 ft. **FAC:** Paved/gravel rds. 190 gravel, patios, 146 pull-thrus (22 x 54), back-ins (23 x 50), 148 full hkups, 42 W, 32 E (30/50 amps), WiFi, tent sites, rentals, dump, laundry, groc, LP gas, fire rings, firewood. **REC:** heated pool, wading pool, whirlpool, playground. Pets OK $. Partial handicap access. 2015 rates: $40.25 to $43.50. Disc: AAA, military.
(605)342-7365 Lat: 43.99030, Lon: -103.26870
8990 S Hwy 16, Rapid City, SD 57702
camp@happyholidayrvresort.com
happyholidayrvresort.com
See ad pages 1049 (Spotlight Rapid City), 1042.

HART RANCH CAMPING RESORT CLUB (Membership Pk) From Jct I-90 (Exit 61) & US-16 Truck Rte/Hwy 79: Go 5-1/4 mi S on US-16 Truck Rte/Hwy 79 (N Elk Vale Rd), then 6 mi S on Hwy 79, then 2 mi W on Spring Creek Rd (L). Elev 3500 ft. **FAC:** Paved rds. 418 paved, patios, back-ins (35 x 60), 418 full hkups (30/50 amps), cable, WiFi, tent sites, dump, laundry, groc, LP gas, restaurant, controlled access. **REC:** heated pool, wading pool, whirlpool, shuffleboard, playground. Pets OK. Partial handicap access. Big rig sites, eco-friendly, 2015 rates: $14.50 to $49.95. Disc: AAA, military. ATM. AAA Approved
(800)605-4278 Lat: 43.96718, Lon: -103.21763
23756 Arena Drive, Rapid City, SD 57702
sales@hartranchresort.com
www.hartranchresort.com

HEARTLAND RV PARK & CABINS
Ratings: 8/10★/8 (Campground) From Jct I-90 (Exit 61) & US-16 truck rte/Hwy 79: Go 5 1/4 mi S & W on US-16 truck rte/Hwy 79 (N Elk Vale Rd), then 12.5 mi S on Hwy 79 (R). Elev 3300 ft. **FAC:** Gravel rds. 135 gravel, 135 pull-thrus (30 x 60), 130 full hkups, 5 W, 5 E (30/50 amps), WiFi, tent sites, rentals, dump, laundry, LP gas, fire rings, firewood. **REC:** heated pool, whirlpool, playground. Pets OK. Partial handicap access. Big rig sites, 2015 rates: $20 to $49. Disc: military.
AAA Approved
(605)255-5460 Lat: 43.81876, Lon: -103.20265
24743 Hwy 79, Hermosa, SD 57744
rving@rapidnet.com
www.heartlandcampground.com
See ad pages 1059, 1060.

LAKE PARK CAMPGROUND & COTTAGES
Ratings: 8/9.5★/9 (Campground) From Jct US-16 Truck Rte/Hwy 79 & I-90 (Exit 61): Go 4 mi W on I-90 (Exit 57), then 1 1/2 mi S on US-16, then 4 1/4 mi W on Hwy 44 (Omaha, Mountain View & Jackson Blvds), then 1/4 mi S on Chapel Ln (L). Elev 3240 ft. **FAC:** Paved rds. 29 gravel, 9 pull-thrus (20 x 70), back-ins (20 x 50), some side by side hkups, 23 full hkups, 6 W, 6 E (30/50 amps), cable, WiFi, tent sites, dump, laundry. **REC:** Canyon Lake: swim, fishing, playground. Pets OK. 2015 rates: $38 to $51.
(800)644-2267 Lat: 44.05876, Lon: -103.29556
2850 Chapel Ln, Rapid City, SD 57702
campnelson@lakeparkcampground.com
www.lakeparkcampground.com
See ad opposite page.

LAZY JD RV PARK **Ratings: 3.5/9.5★/6.5** (Campground) 2015 rates: $30. May 1 to Oct 1. (605)787-7036 12336 Erickson Ranch Rd, Piedmont, SD 57769

MYSTERY MOUNTAIN RESORT
Ratings: 9/9.5★/9 (Campground) From Jct I-90 & US-16W (Exit 61): Go 13.5 mi S on US-16W (R). Elev 4200 ft. **FAC:** Paved/gravel rds. 82 Avail: 14 paved, 68 gravel, 25 pull-thrus (20 x 60), back-ins (16 x 55), 42 full hkups, 40 W, 40 E (30/50 amps), WiFi, tent sites, rentals, dump, laundry, groc, fire rings, firewood. **REC:** heated pool, whirlpool, playground. Pet restrict(Q). Eco-friendly, 2015 rates: $32 to $44. Disc: AAA, military. May 15 to Sep 30. AAA Approved
(605)342-5368 Lat: 43.97365, Lon: -103.30728
13752 S Hwy 16 West, Rapid City, SD 57702
mmresortrez@aol.com
www.mysterymountain.us
See ad pages 1050 (Spotlight Rapid City), 1042.

RAPID CITY KOA **Ratings: 8.5/10★/9** (Campground) 2015 rates: $35.95 to $68.95. Apr 15 to Oct 15. (800)562-8504 3010 E Hwy 44, Rapid City, SD 57703

RAPID CITY RV PARK AND CAMPGROUND
Ratings: 9/8.5/8 (Campground) From Jct I-90 (Exit 61) & Elk Vale Rd/Hwy 16 Truck Bypass: Go 7.7 mi S on Elk Vale Rd/Hwy 16 Truck Bypass, then 1.6 mi N on East US-16. (R). GPS can be misleading. Call for directions. Elev 4200 ft. **FAC:** Paved rds. (126 spaces). Avail: 108 gravel, 47 pull-thrus (26 x 60), back-ins (26 x 60), 43 full hkups, 65 W, 65 E (30/50 amps), seasonal sites, WiFi, tent sites, rentals, dump, laundry, groc, LP bottles, fire rings, firewood. **REC:** heated pool, shuffleboard, playground. Pet restrict(B). Partial handicap access. Big rig sites, 2015 rates: $39 to $45. Disc: AAA, military.
(605)342-2751 Lat: 44.04317, Lon: -103.24416
4110 S Hwy 16, Rapid City, SD 57701
rcrvpark@gmail.com
www.rcrvpark.com
See ad pages 1050 (Spotlight Rapid City), 1042 & RV Trips of a Lifetime in Magazine Section.

RUSHMORE SHADOWS RESORT
Ratings: 9.5/10★/10 (Membership Pk) From Jct I-90 (Exit 61) & US-16 Truck/Hwy 79: Go 9 mi S & W on US-16 Truck, then 6-1/2 mi W on US-16 W (R). Elev 4425 ft. **FAC:** Paved rds. 160 gravel, 23 pull-thrus (30 x 60), back-ins (28 x 60), 160 full hkups (30/50 amps), WiFi, tent sites, dump, laundry, groc, fire rings, firewood, controlled access. **REC:** heated pool, whirlpool, playground. Pets OK. Partial handicap access. Big rig sites, eco-friendly, 2015 rates: $35 to $62. Disc: AAA, military. May 1 to Oct 15.
AAA Approved
(800)231-0425 Lat: 43.97309, Lon: -103.32716
23680 Busted Five Court, Rapid City, SD 57702
stay@midwestoutdoorresorts.com
www.midwestoutdoorresorts.com
See ad page 1040 (Welcome Section) & RV Trips of a Lifetime in Magazine Section.

TEE PEE CAMPGROUND & RV PARK
Ratings: 6/9★/6.5 (Campground) From Jct I-90 (Exit 61) & US-16 Truck Rte/Hwy 79: Go 9 mi S & W on US-16 Truck Rte/Hwy 79, then 1-1/2 mi W on US-16 (R). Elev 3900 ft. **FAC:** Gravel rds. 70 grass, 47 pull-thrus (21 x 55), back-ins (22 x 60), mostly side by side hkups, 20 full hkups, 50 W, 50 E (30/50 amps), WiFi, tent sites, rentals, dump, laundry, fire rings, firewood. **REC:** playground. Pets OK. Partial handicap access. Eco-friendly, 2015 rates: $28 to $40. Disc: AAA, military. May 1 to Sep 30.
(605)343-6319 Lat: 44.00286, Lon: -103.25418
2200 Ft Hayes Dr, Rapid City, SD 57702
peg@teepeeblackhills.com
www.teepeeblackhills.com
See ad opposite page, 1042.

WHISPERING PINES CAMPGROUND & LODGING **Ratings: 7/7/8** (Campground) From Jct I-90 & Exit 57 (Rapid City): Go 1.4 mi S on I-190, then 18 mi W on US 44 (Omaha St), then 1.3 mi NW on US-385, then 500 ft W on Silver City Rd (L). Or from Jct US-85 & US-385 (in Deadwood): Go 23 mi SW on US-385, then 500 ft W on Silver City Rd (L). Elev 4900 ft. **FAC:** Gravel rds. 44 grass, 44 pull-thrus (30 x 60), 24 full hkups, 20 W, 20 E (30/50 amps), WiFi, tent sites, rentals, dump, laundry, groc, fire rings, firewood. **REC:** heated pool, playground. Pets OK. 2015 rates: $32 to $36. Disc: military. May 15 to Sep 15.
(877)341-3667 Lat: 44.10908, Lon: -103.53337
22700 Silver City Rd, Rapid City, SD 57702
reservations@blackhillswhisperingpines.com
www.blackhillswhisperingpines.com

Things to See and Do

RUSHMORE SHADOWS RESORT GIFTS & CONVENIENCE STORE Convenience store carries limited groceries, snacks & variety of beverages: milk shakes, coffee & soft drinks. Also includes RV supplies; clothing apparel; books; Black Hills gold jewelry; toys, souvenirs plus more. Elev 4425 ft. May 1 to Oct 15. partial handicap access. RV accessible. Restrooms, food. Hours: 7am to 7pm.
(800)231-0425 Lat: 43.97309, Lon: -103.32716
23680 Busted Five Ct, Rapid City, SD 57702
stay@midwestoutdoorresorts.com
www.midwestoutdoorresorts.com
See ad page 1040 (Welcome Section).

REDFIELD — B5 *Spink*

HAV-A-REST CAMPGROUND (Public) From W Jct US-212 & US-281: Go 1/2 mi NW on US-212; then 1/2 mi E on W 4th Ave. (L). 2015 rates: $15. Apr 1 to Nov 1. (605)472-4550

SALEM — C6 *McCook*

CAMP AMERICA CAMPGROUND
Ratings: 9/9.5★/10 (Campground) From Jct of I-90 (Exit 364) & US-81: Go 1.25 mi N on US-81 (L). Do not rely on GPS. **FAC:** Paved/gravel rds. 45 gravel, 24 pull-thrus (28 x 78), back-ins (30 x 50), 39 full hkups, 6 W, 6 E (30/50 amps), WiFi, tent sites, showers $, dump, laundry, groc, fire rings, firewood. **REC:** pool, playground. Pets OK. Big rig sites, eco-friendly, 2015 rates: $30 to $37. Disc: AAA. May 1 to Oct 31.
(605)425-9085 Lat: 43.68873, Lon: -97.38890
25495 US-81, Salem, SD 57058
cmpsalem@triotel.net
www.campsalemsd.com
See ad this page, 1042.

SELBY — A4 *Walworth*

LAKE HIDDENWOOD RECREATION AREA (State Pk) From Selby: Go 5 mi NE on US 12/83. **FAC:** Gravel rds. 13 gravel, 1 pull-thrus (17 x 50), back-ins (17 x 50), 7 E (20/30 amps), tent sites, pit toilets. **REC:** Lake Hiddenwood: swim, fishing, playground, rec open to public. Pets OK. 14 day max stay, 2015 rates: $11 to $15.
(800)710-2267 Lat: 45.549856, Lon: -99.985001
hidden Wood Rd, Selby, SD 57472
parkino@state.sd.us
www.gfp.sd.gov/state-parks
See ad page 1039 (Welcome Section).

SIOUX FALLS — C6 *Minnehaha*

SIOUX FALLS See also Brandon & Canton.

Check out the travel services section of this Guide to find services that you'll find handy in your travels.

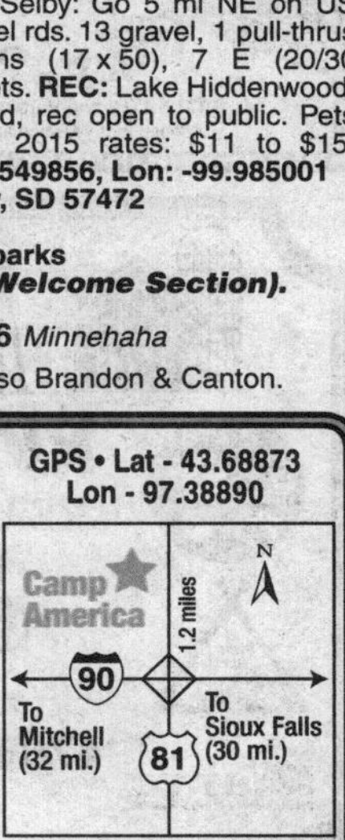

SIOUX FALLS (CONT)

BURMA CAMP & STAY (Campground) (Seasonal Stay Only) From Jct I-29 (Exit 81) & W Maple St/W Russell St: Go 1/2 mi E on W Maple St/W Russell St, then 1/4 mi S & W on N Louise Ave, then 3/4 mi N on N Louise Dr (L) (Road ends/Cul-de-sac 100 ft past entrance). **FAC:** Paved rds. (16 spaces). Avail: 1 gravel, patios, back-ins (30 x 65), accepts full hkup units only, 1 full hkups (30/50 amps), seasonal sites, controlled access. Pets OK. No tents. Big rig sites, 2015 rates: $425/mo. Apr 1 to Nov 1. No CC.
AAA Approved
(605)338-6537 Lat: 43.57030, Lon: -96.77156
2111 N Louise Dr, Sioux Falls, SD 57107
matt@burmabev.com
www.campandstay.com

RED BARN RV PARK
Ratings: 8/7.5★/8.5 (Campground) From Jct of I-90 & I-29: Go 11 mi S on I-29 (Exit 73), then 1/2 mi W on 271st St, then 1 mi S on 470th Ave, then 50 ft E on 272nd St. (R) Note: Don't rely on GPS. **FAC:** Gravel rds. (74 spaces). Avail: 25 gravel, 25 pull-thrus (25 x 60), some side by side hkups, 25 full hkups (30/50 amps), seasonal sites, WiFi Hotspot, dump, laundry, fire rings, firewood. **REC:** heated pool, shuffleboard, playground. Pets OK. Partial handicap access, no tents. Eco-friendly, 2015 rates: $34. Apr 1 to Nov 1.
(605)368-2268 Lat: 43.44520, Lon: -96.80534
47003 272nd St, Tea, SD 57064
bftea@aol.com
www.accesscamping.com
See ad this page, 1042.

SIOUX EMPIRE FAIR CAMPGROUND (Public) From Jct of I-29 & Exit 80 (Madison St), E 0.2 mi on Madison St to Fairground Rd, S 0.3 mi (R) or From Jct of I-29 & Exit 79 (W 12th St), E 0.2 mi on W 12th St to Lyons Blvd, N 0.2 mi to fairground entrance (R). 2015 rates: $25. Apr 15 to Oct 31. (605)367-7178

SIOUX FALLS KOA
Ratings: 9/9.5★/8 (Campground) From Exit 399 off I-90 (Cliff Ave): Go 1 blk N on Cliff Ave, then 1 blk E on Robur Dr. (R). **FAC:** Gravel rds. 79 Avail: 1 paved, 78 gravel, 46 pull-thrus (33 x 75), back-ins (33 x 45), 63 full hkups, 16 W, 16 E (30/50 amps), cable, WiFi, tent sites, rentals, dump, laundry, groc, firewood. **REC:** heated pool, playground. Pets OK $. Partial handicap access. Big rig sites, eco-friendly, 2015 rates: $34 to $57. May 1 to Oct 15.
(605)332-9987 Lat: 43.60676, Lon: -096.70530
1401 E Robur Dr, Sioux Falls, SD 57104
siouxfallskoa@yahoo.com
www.siouxfallskoa.com
See ad this page.

SIOUX FALLS YOGI BEAR
Ratings: 9/10★/9.5 (Campground) From Jct of I-29 & I-90: Go 6 mi E on I-90 (Exit 402), then 1 block N on CR-121. (R). **FAC:** Gravel rds. 112 gravel, 98 pull-thrus (35 x 70), back-ins (25 x 30), 98 full hkups, 14 W, 14 E (30/50 amps), cable, WiFi, tent sites, rentals, dump, laundry, groc, LP gas, fire rings, firewood. **REC:** heated pool, whirlpool, playground. Pets OK. Partial handicap access. Big rig sites, eco-friendly, 2015 rates: $25 to $45. Disc: AAA, military. ATM.
(605)332-2233 Lat: 43.61046, Lon: -96.65149
26014 478th Ave, Brandon, SD 57005
reservation@jellystonesiouxfalls.com
www.jellystonesiouxfalls.com
See ad this page, 1042.

TOWER CAMPGROUND
Ratings: 7.5/9/7.5 (Campground) N Bnd: From Jct I-29 (exit 78) & 26th St: Go .6 mi W on 26th St, then 1 mi N on Marion Rd, then .3 mi E on W 12th St/SD-42 (R). S Bnd: From Jct I-29 (exit 80) & W Madison St: Go .5 mi W on Madison St, then 1 mi S on S Ebenezer, then .3 mi E on W 12th St/SD-42 (R). **FAC:** Paved/gravel rds. (118 spaces). 72 Avail: 46 paved, 26 gravel, 7 pull-thrus (50 x 60), back-ins (50 x 50), 72 full hkups (30/50 amps), seasonal sites, cable, WiFi, tent sites, dump, laundry, firewood. **REC:** playground. Pets OK. Partial handicap access. Big rig sites, eco-friendly, 2015 rates: $36 to $40. Disc: military.
(605)332-1173 Lat: 43.54361, Lon: -96.78177
4609 W. 12th St, Sioux Falls, SD 57106
towercampground@gmail.com
www.towercampground.com
See ad pages 1061, 1042.

Travel Services

CUMMINS CENTRAL POWER Cummins Central Power is the exclusive distributor for Cummins and Onan products in the mid-west. 12 full service locations in NE, MO, KS, IA, SD & IL support engine and generator customers. **SERVICES:** Engine/chassis repair, restrooms. Emergency parking, RV accessible. waiting room. Hours: Mon-Fri 7am to 12am; Sat 7am-3:30pm.
(605)336-1715 Lat: 43.59471, Lon: -96.71970
701 East 54th St North, Sioux Falls, SD 57104
centralpower@cummins.com
www.cumminscentralpower.com
See ad page 732.

Look in the Guide to Seasonal Sites to find places you can stay for a month, a season or longer.

Things to See and Do

GOOD EARTH STATE PARK An important cultural and historical site as well as a unique nature retreat. The site itself is one of the oldest sites of long-term human habitation in the U.S. Hours: 8 to 5. No CC.
(800)710-2267 Lat: 43.475595, Lon: -96.5942
48072 270th St., Sioux Falls, SD 57108
parkinfo@state.sd.us
www.gfp.sd.gov/state-parks
See ad page 1039 (Welcome Section).

SISSETON — A6 *Roberts*

CAMP DAKOTAH **Ratings: 6.5/8.5★/7.5** (Campground) 2015 rates: $23. (605)698-7388 11885 460th Ave, Sisseton, SD 57262

SICA HOLLOW
(State Pk) From Sisseton: Go 15 mi NW on Hwy 10. **FAC:** Gravel rds. 8 grass, 8 pull-thrus (50 x 100), pit toilets. **REC:** rec open to public. Pets OK. No tents. 14 day max stay, 2015 rates: $13.
(800)710-2267 Lat: 45.7421, Lon: -97.242668
44950 Park Rd, Sisseton, SD 57262
parkinfo@state.sd.us
www.gfp.sd.gov/state-parks
See ad page 1039 (Welcome Section).

SPEARFISH — B1 *Lawrence*

A SPOTLIGHT Introducing Spearfish's colorful attractions appearing at the front of this state section.

CHRIS' CAMP & RV PARK
Ratings: 9/9.5★/9 (Campground) From Jct US-85 N & I-90: Go 4 mi E on I-90 (Exit 14), then 1/2 mi W on Bus I-90, then 3/4 mi S on Christensen Dr (R). Elev 3600 ft.

A START TO A GREAT VACATION
We welcome big rigs to sleeping bags. We are a full service campground with all amenities including 3 bath houses, 2 laundry rooms, 3 heated pools, a pet farm and tour planning. See you soon!

FAC: Paved/gravel rds. 135 Avail: 95 gravel, 40 grass, 68 pull-thrus (20 x 50), back-ins (24 x 75), 101 full hkups, 34 W, 34 E (30/50 amps), cable, WiFi, tent sites, rentals, showers $, dump, laundry, groc, fire rings, firewood. **REC:** heated pool, wading pool, playground. Pets OK. Partial handicap access. Big rig sites, eco-friendly, 2015 rates: $37 to 42. Disc: AAA. Apr 15 to Oct 15. No CC.
AAA Approved
(800)350-2239 Lat: 44.47092, Lon: -103.82711
701 Christensen Dr, Spearfish, SD 57783
chriscamp@blackhills.com
www.chriscampground.com
See ad pages 1052 (Spotlight Spearfish), 1042.

ELKHORN RIDGE RV RESORT & GOLF CLUB
Ratings: 10/9.5★/10 (RV Park) From Jct I-90 & US 85 (Exit 17): Go .6 mi SE on US 85 (R). Elev 3846 ft. **FAC:** Paved rds. 186 paved, patios, 111 pull-thrus (38 x 90), back-ins (30 x 66), 186 full hkups (50 amps), cable, WiFi, tent sites, rentals, dump, laundry, groc, LP gas, fire rings, firewood, restaurant. **REC:** heated pool, wading pool, whirlpool, golf, playground. Pets OK. Partial handicap access. Big rig sites, 2015 rates: $40 to $60. Disc: AAA, military. ATM.
AAA Approved
(877)722-1800 Lat: 44.47056, Lon: -103.73356
20189 US Hwy 85, Spearfish, SD 57783
gm@elkhornridgervresort.com
www.elkhornridgervresort.com
See ad pages 1053 (Spotlight Spearfish), 1042.

SPEARFISH CITY CAMPGROUND (Public) From Jct of I-90 & Jackson Blvd (exit 12), SW 0.6 mi on Jackson Blvd to Canyon St, S 0.7 mi on Canyon St, cross bridge (L). 2015 rates: $30 to $34. May 15 to Oct 1. (605)642-1340

SPEARFISH (CONT)

SPEARFISH KOA **Ratings: 8/9★/7.5** (Campground) 2015 rates: $29 to $55. Apr 22 to Oct 2. 800)562-0805 41 W Hwy 14, Spearfish, SD 57783

SPRINGFIELD — D5 *Bon Homme*

SPRINGFIELD RECREATION AREA

(State Pk) From Springfield: Go 1 mi E on Hwy 37 (R) Entrance fee required. **FAC:** Gravel rds. 20 gravel, 2 pull-thrus (15 x 52), back-ins 15 x 48), 19 E (20/30 amps), tent sites, rentals, dump. **REC:** Missouri River: fishing, playground, rec open to public. Pets OK. 14 day max stay, 2015 rates: $15 to $19.
800)710-2267 Lat: 42.855881, Lon: -97.884587
1412 Boat Basin Dr, Springfield, SD 57062
parkinfo@state.sd.us
www.gfp.sd.gov/state-parks
See ad page 1039 (Welcome Section).

STURGIS — B1 *Meade*

STURGIS See also Black Hawk, Deadwood, Piedmont & Spearfish.

BEAR BUTTE

(State Pk) From Jct of Hwy 79 & Junction Ave (in Sturgis): Go 3 3/4 mi E on Hwy 79/34, then continue 3 1/4 mi N on Hwy 79 (L). Entrance fee required. Elev 3181 ft. **FAC:** Gravel rds. 23 gravel, back-ins (30 x 49), 1 E (20/30 amps), tent sites, pit toilets. **REC:** Bear Butte Lake: fishing, rec open to public. Pets OK. 14 day max stay, 2015 rates: $10 to $12.
800)710-2267 Lat: 44.46128, Lon: -103.43513
20250 Hwy 79, Sturgis, SD 57785
parkinfo@state.sd.us
www.gfp.sd.gov/state-parks
See ad page 1039 (Welcome Section).

NO NAME CITY LUXURY CABINS & RV, LLC

Ratings: 9.5/9★/8 (Campground) From Jct US-14A & I-90: Go 4 mi SE on I-90 (Exit 34), then 3/4 mi E on Pleasant Valley Dr/Service Rd (R). **FAC:** All weather rds. 42 Avail: 16 gravel, 26 grass, patios, 16 pull-thrus (24 x 100), back-ins (24 x 50), 16 full hkups, 26 W, 26 E (30/50 amps), cable, WiFi, tent sites, rentals, dump, mobile sewer, laundry, LP gas, fire rings, firewood. **REC:** heated pool, whirlpool, playground. Pets OK. Partial handicap access. Big rig sites, 2015 rates: $35 to $45. Disc: AAA, military.
(605)347-8891 Lat: 44.36337, Lon: -103.46594
20899 Pleasant Valley Dr, Sturgis, SD 57785
camping@nonamecity.com
www.nonamecity.com
See ad this page.

RUSH NO MORE RV RESORT & CAMPGROUND

Ratings: 9/9.5★/10 (Campground) From Jct US-14A & I-90: Go 5 mi SE on I-90 (Exit 37), then 3/4 mi W on Pleasant Valley Rd, then 1/4 mi S on Brimstone Pl (R). Elev 3200 ft. **FAC:** Paved/gravel rds. 125 Avail: 68 gravel, 57 grass, patios, 58 pull-thrus (25 x 75), back-ins (30 x 65), 113 full hkups, 12 W, 12 E (30/50 amps), WiFi, tent sites, rentals, dump, laundry, LP gas. **REC:** heated pool, whirlpool, playground. Pets OK. Partial handicap access. Big rig sites, eco-friendly, 2015 rates: $41.99 to $54.99. Disc: AAA, military. ATM.
(605)347-2916 Lat: 44.34079, Lon: -103.46252
21137 Brimstone Pl, Sturgis, SD 57785
info@rushnomore.com
www.rushnomore.com
See ad this page, 1042.

STURGIS RV PARK

(Campground) (Not Visited) From Jct I-90 (exit 32) and Jct Ave: Go 1-1/2 mi N on Jct Ave; then 1/4 mi W on Woodland Dr (R). **FAC:** Paved/gravel rds. 152 gravel, 80 pull-thrus (30 x 80), back-ins (27 x 50), 152 full hkups (30/50 amps), WiFi, tent sites, rentals, dump, laundry. **REC.** Pets OK. Partial handicap access. Big rig sites, 2015 rates: $40. Disc: AAA, military. May 15 to Sep 15. ATM.
(605)720-1501 Lat: 44.41814, Lon: -103.51245
1175 W Woodland Dr, Sturgis, SD 57785
customerservice@sturgisdowntownrvpark.com
www.sturgisdowntownrvpark.com
See ad this page.

SUMMERSET — C1 *Meade*

Travel Services

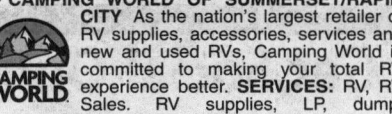

CAMPING WORLD OF SUMMERSET/RAPID CITY As the nation's largest retailer of RV supplies, accessories, services and new and used RVs, Camping World is committed to making your total RV experience better. **SERVICES:** RV, RV Sales. RV supplies, LP, dump. Hours: 8am to 5pm; closed Sun.
(844)654-6172 Lat: 44.181962, Lon: -103.328575
10400 Recreational Drive, Summerset, SD 57718
www.campingworld.com

SUMMIT — A6 *Roberts*

COUNTY LINE RV PARK & CAMPGROUND

Ratings: 8/9.5★/8.5 (Campground) From Jct of I-29 & Hwy 12 (Exit 207): Go E 1 mi on Hwy 12, then S 0.5 mi on Summit Rd (Maple St) (R). **FAC:** All weather rds. 24 Avail: 24 all weather, 24 pull-thrus (33 x 90), 24 full hkups (30/50 amps), WiFi, tent sites, rentals, dump, laundry, fire rings, firewood. Pets OK. Partial handicap access. Big rig sites, eco-friendly, 2015 rates: $28 to $38. Disc: AAA, military. Apr 1 to Oct 1.
(605)398-6355 Lat: 45.29924, Lon: -97.03634
907 Maple St, Summit, SD 57266
county_campground@hotmail.com
www.countylinecampground.com
See ad this page, 1042.

Thank you for using our 2016 Guide. Now you have all the latest information about RV parks, campgrounds and RV resorts across North America!

TIMBER LAKE — A3 *Dewey*

LITTLE MOREAU RECREATION AREA

(State Pk) From Timber Lake: Go 6 mi S on Hwy 20. **FAC:** Gravel rds. 5 gravel, back-ins (16 x 50), tent sites, pit toilets. **REC:** Moreau & Little Moreau Rivers: fishing, rec open to public. Pets OK. 14 day max stay. No CC, no reservations.
(800)710-2267 Lat: 45.349193, Lon: -101.1
6 miles South of Timberlake off Sd 20, Timber Lake, SD 57656
parkinfo@state.sd.us
www.gfp.sd.gov/state-parks
See ad page 1039 (Welcome Section).

VERMILLION — D6 *Clay*

LION'S PARK (Public) In town, 0.5 mi on Hwy 50 (L). (605)677-7064

WALL — C2 *Pennington*

ARROW CAMPGROUND

Ratings: 7.5/9★/7 (Campground) From Jct I-90 & Bus-90 (Exit 109): Go .5 mi E on Bus-90. (L). OR From Jct I-90 & Bus-90 (Exit 110): Go 3/4 mi W on Bus-90 (South Blvd). (R). Elev 2800 ft. **FAC:** Paved/gravel rds. 72 gravel, 72 pull-thrus (21 x 60), 36 full hkups, 36 W, 36 E (30/50 amps), cable, WiFi, tent sites, rentals, dump, laundry, groc. **REC:** pool, playground. Pets OK. Eco-friendly, 2015 rates: $26 to $31. May 1 to Oct 15.
AAA Approved
(800)888-1361 Lat: 43.99244, Lon: -102.24600
515 Crown St., Wall, SD 57790
arrowcg127@gmail.com
www.arrowcampground.com
See ad this page, 1042.

SLEEPY HOLLOW CAMPGROUND, LLC

Ratings: 9/10★/8 (Campground) From Jct I-90 (Exit 110): Go 1/2 mi N on Glenn, then 1/4 mi W on 4th Ave (R). **FAC:** Gravel rds. 59 gravel, 59 pull-thrus (24 x 65), 38 full hkups, 21 W, 21 E (30/50 amps), cable, WiFi, tent sites, dump, laundry, groc, fire rings, firewood. **REC:** heated pool, playground. Pets OK. Big rig sites, eco-friendly, 2015 rates: $29.75 to $34.75. Disc: AAA, military. Apr 15 to Sep 30.
AAA Approved
(605)279-2100 Lat: 43.99471, Lon: -102.24374
118 4th Ave. West, Wall, SD 57790
sleepyhollow@goldenwest.net
www.sleepyhollowsd.com
See ad this page, 1042.

WATERTOWN — B6 *Codington*

CODINGTON COUNTY MEMORIAL CAMPGROUND (Public) From Jct of Hwys 212 & 81, W 7 mi on Hwy 212 to Hwy 139, N 2.5 mi (R). 2015 rates: $19 to $22. May 1 to Oct 1. (605)882-6290

SD

WATERTOWN (CONT)

← PELICAN LAKE REC AREA
(State Pk) From Watertown: Go 4 mi W on US-212, then 1 1/2 mi S on 450th Ave. Entrance fee required. **FAC:** Paved rds. 76 gravel, back-ins (15 x 75), 76 E (20/30 amps), tent sites, rentals, dump. **REC:** Pelican Lake: swim, fishing, playground, rec open to public. Pets OK. Partial handicap access. 14 day max stay, 2015 rates: $19.
(800)710-2267 Lat: 44.852222, Lon: -97.208449
17450 450th Ave, Watertown, SD 57201
parkinfo@state.sd.us
www.gfp.sd.gov/state-parks
See ad page 1039 (Welcome Section).

← SANDY SHORE REC AREA
(State Pk) From Jct of US-212 & US-20: Go 5 mi W on US-212, follow signs (R). Entrance fee required. **FAC:** Paved rds. 20 Avail: 3 gravel, 17 grass, back-ins (15 x 40), 15 E (20/30 amps), tent sites. **REC:** Lake Kampeska: swim, fishing, playground, rec open to public. Pets OK. 14 day max stay, 2015 rates: $15 to $19.
(800)710-2267 Lat: 44.893844, Lon: -97.240953
1100 South Lake Dr, Watertown, SD 57201
parkinfo@state.sd.us
www.gfp.sd.gov/state-parks
See ad page 1039 (Welcome Section).

STOKES-THOMAS LAKE (CITY PARK) (Public) From jct US-81 & Hwy-20: Go 3 mi NW on Hwy-20 to S Lake Dr. 2015 rates: $18. May 1 to Oct 1. (605)882-6264

WAUBAY — A6 *Day*

↑ PICKEREL LAKE
(State Pk) From Waubay: Go 14 mi N on DAY CR-1 (R). Entrance fee required. **FAC:** Paved rds. 72 gravel, 5 pull-thrus (25 x 60), back-ins (25 x 60), 69 E (20/30 amps), tent sites, rentals, dump. **REC:** Pickerel Lake: swim, fishing, playground, rec open to public. Pets OK. Partial handicap access. 14 day max stay, 2015 rates: $15 to $19.
(800)710-2267 Lat: 45.485552, Lon: -97.248139
12980-446th Ave, Grenville, SD 57239
parkinfo@state.sd.us
www.gfp.sd.gov/state-parks
See ad page 1039 (Welcome Section).

WHITE LAKE — C5 *Aurora*

↓ SIDING 36 MOTEL & RV PARK
Ratings: 7/9.5★/7 (Campground)
From Jct of I-90 (Exit 296) and S Main St: Go 500 ft S on S. Main St (R) Note: On south side of Interstate-90. **FAC:** Gravel rds. 35 gravel, 35 pull-thrus (20 x 52), 35 full hkups (30/50 amps), WiFi, tent sites, rentals, dump, laundry, groc, fire rings, firewood. **REC:** playground. Pets OK. Partial handicap access. 2015 rates: $33. Disc: AAA, military.
AAA Approved
(605)249-2295 Lat: 43.7169, Lon: -98.7170
1500 S. Main Street, White Lake, SD 57383
siding36@hotmail.com
www.siding36.com
See ad this page, 1042.

YANKTON — D6 *Yankton*

← CHIEF WHITE CRANE REC AREA
(State Pk) From Yankton: Go 4 mi W on Hwy 52, then 4 mi S on Toe Rd (E). **FAC:** Paved rds. 145 paved, back-ins (15 x 75), 145 E (30/50 amps), tent sites, rentals, dump. **REC:** Lake Yankton: fishing, playground, rec open to public. Pets OK. Partial handicap access. 14 day max stay, 2015 rates: $15 to $21.
(800)710-2267 Lat: 42.851249, Lon: -97.460067
31323 Toe Rd, Yankton, SD 57078
parkinfo@state.sd.us
www.gfp.sd.gov/state-parks
See ad page 1039 (Welcome Section).

Directional arrows indicate the campground's position in relation to the nearest town.

COTTONWOOD (COE-LEWIS & CLARK LAKE) (State Pk) From town: Go 5 mi W on Hwy 52, then 1 mi S on Toe Rd. 2015 rates: $19 to $21. (800)710-CAMP

← LEWIS & CLARK RECREATION AREA
(State Pk) From Yankton: Go 4 mi W on Hwy 52. (L) Entrance fee required. **FAC:** Paved rds. 409 paved, back-ins (15 x 60), 409 E (30/50 amps), WiFi, tent sites, rentals, dump, restaurant. **REC:** Lewis & Clark Lake: swim, fishing, marina, golf, playground, rec open to public. Pets OK. Partial handicap access. 14 day max stay, 2015 rates: $19 to $21.
(800)710-2267 Lat: 42.867723, Lon: -97.521526
43349 Sd Hwy 52, Yankton, SD 57078
parkinfo@state.sd.us
www.gfp.sd.gov/state-parks
See ad page 1039 (Welcome Section).

Clean Green! Vinegar and baking soda can be used to clean almost anything. Mix in a little warm water with either of these and you've got yourself an all-purpose cleaner.

← PIERSON RANCH REC AREA
(State Pk) From Yankton: Go 4 mi W on Hw 52. (L) Entrance fee required. **FAC:** Pave rds. 67 paved, back-ins (15 x 75), 67 E (30/5 amps), tent sites, rentals, dump. **REC:** Lewis & Clar Lake: playground, rec open to public. Pets OK. Partia handicap access. 14 day max stay, 2015 rates: $1 to $21.
(800)710-2267 Lat: 42.871111, Lon: -97.485556
31144 Toe Rd, Yankton, SD 57442
parkinfo@state.sd.us
www.gfp.sd.gov/state-parks
See ad page 1039 (Welcome Section).

→ YANKTON/MISSOURI RIVER KOA **Ratings: 9/9.5★/9** (Campground) 2015 rates: $36 t $44. (605)260-1010 807 Bill Bags Rd, Yankton, SD 57078

E2. C5. F1. It's not a cipher; it's ou easy-to-use map grid. Draw a line horizontall from the letter, vertically from the number, i the map border. "X" will mark a spot near you destination.

Tennessee Tourism

WELCOME TO
Tennessee

DATE OF STATEHOOD JUNE 1, 1796	WIDTH: 120 MILES (195 KM) LENGTH: 440 MILES (710 KM)	PROPORTION OF UNITED STATES 1.11% OF 3,794,100 SQ MI

Perhaps there's something in the water in Tennessee—it seems that everyone just wants to dance. Tennessee has always been a magnet for artists and musicians: Nashville's moniker of "Music City" speaks to its status as the cradle of country music; Memphis was the capital of blues for much of the 19th century; and then there's the rock 'n' roll theme park, Graceland. From the peaks of the Great Smoky Mountains—the most-visited national park in the nation—to the undulating green valleys around Nashville and the humid lowlands that unfurl from Memphis, Tennessee's three distinct geographic regions flaunt distinct beauty and charm. And, there's more to Memphis than barbecue and Elvis.

Sure enough, in Nashville you'll witness families decked out in cowboy boots and line dancing in the streets, but, as one of Google's "Entrepreneurs Tech Hub Network" cities, Nashville has fashioned some new riffs. Along with stylish hotels, there's a hip dining scene, fashionable boutiques and world-class sights, including the storied Ryman Auditorium and the Country Music Hall of Fame. In eastern Tennessee, historic Franklin flaunts its artistic verve at every opportunity, while the laid-back riverside college towns of Knoxville and Chattanooga provide a launch pad for the state's outdoor adventures.

Play

In Memphis, within Overton Park, the 1,000-year-old Old Forest State Natural Area is listed in the National

Top 3 Tourism Attractions:
1) Grand Ole Opry
2) Graceland
3) Lookout Mountain

Nickname: Volunteer State

State Flower: Iris

State Bird: Mockingbird

People: Eddy Arnold, singer; Davy Crockett, frontiersman; Aretha Franklin, singer; Morgan Freeman, actor; Dolly Parton, singer-songwriter

Major Cities: Memphis, Nashville (capital), Knoxville, Chattanooga, Clarksville

Topography: East—Great Smoky Mountains; central—low ridges, slightly rolling terrain; west—Eastern Gulf coastal plain with streams

Climate: Temperate climate with mostly warm summers and mild winters

Tennessee Tourism

TN

- STAY A WHILE -
Tennessee State Parks

Tennessee's 56 state parks offer diverse natural, recreational and cultural experiences for individuals, families, or business and professional groups. State park features range from pristine natural areas to 18-hole championship golf courses. If you like being around water, there are great places to camp in parks that have waterfalls, rivers, lakes and streams. If you like activities, you can fish, boat, watch wildlife, bike, canoe, golf, watch an outdoor play, enjoy a festival, hike or just stroll over to the restaurant. We offer museums, nature centers and interpretative programs for both young and old. Many of our parks are built around historical events such as Civil War battles, British forts and birthplaces of famous legends. For a free brochure about Tennessee State Parks, call 888-867-2757. For additional information, visit our Web site at www.tnstateparks.com.

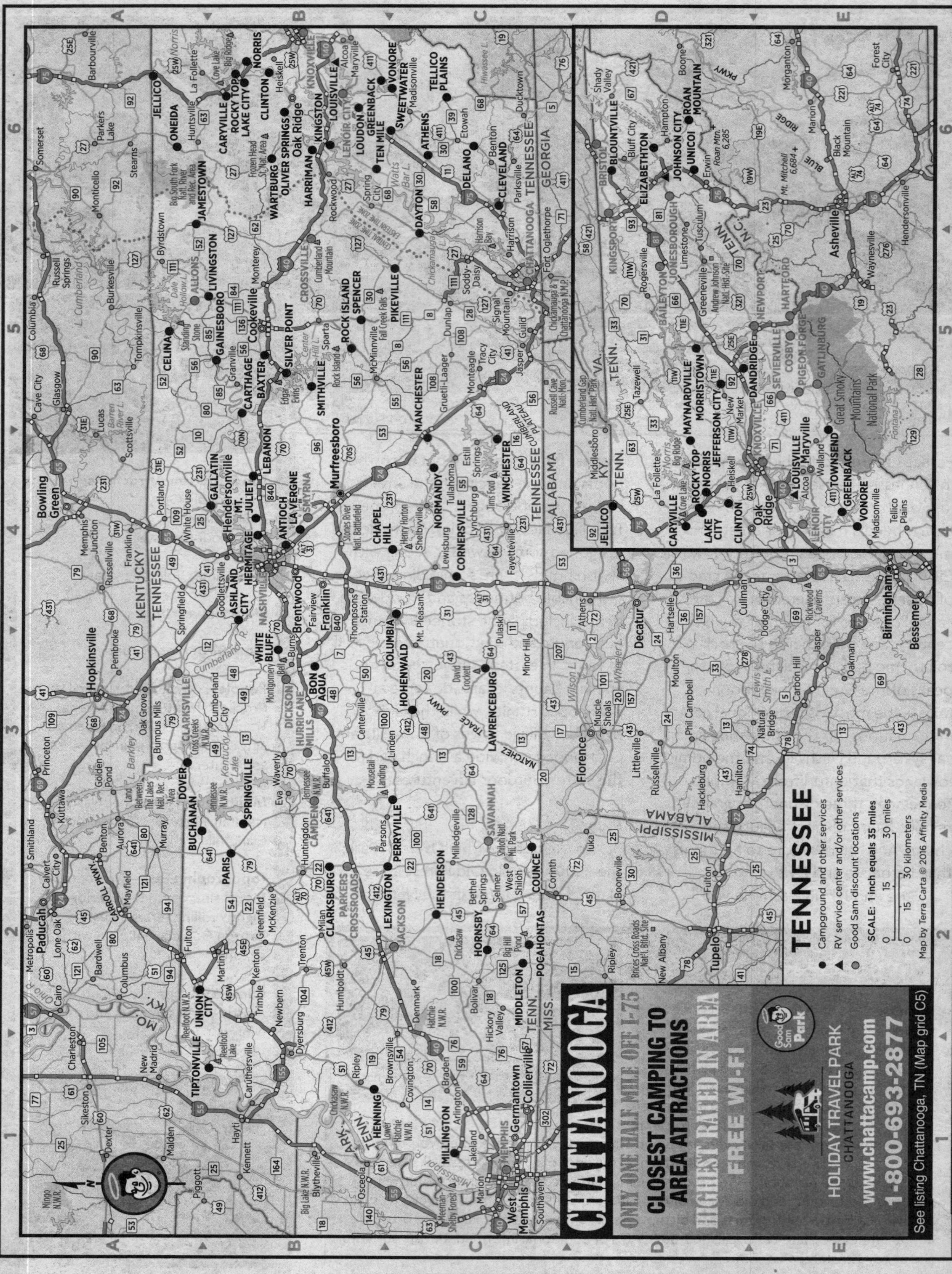
TENNESSEE
Campground and other services
RV service center and/or other services
Good Sam discount locations
SCALE: 1 inch equals 35 miles
0 15 30 miles
0 15 30 kilometers
Map by Terra Carta © 2016 Affinity Media
CHATTANOOGA
ONLY ONE HALF MILE OFF I-75
CLOSEST CAMPING TO AREA ATTRACTIONS
HIGHEST RATED IN AREA
FREE WI-FI
Good Sam Park
HOLIDAY TRAVEL PARK
CHATTANOOGA
www.chattacamp.com
1-800-693-2877
See listing Chattanooga, TN (Map grid C5)

Register of Historic Places for its unique status of never having been farmed or even tilled. Just outside Nashville, in the serene forests of the Natchez Trace, you can hike the same trails traveled by pioneers, the Pony Express and Cherokee Indians. Highlights of Great Smoky Mountains National Park ("Salamander Capital of the World") include the evocative settlement of Cades Cove, the lofty peaks of Mount Le Conte, spectacular waterfalls and more than 2,000 black bears.

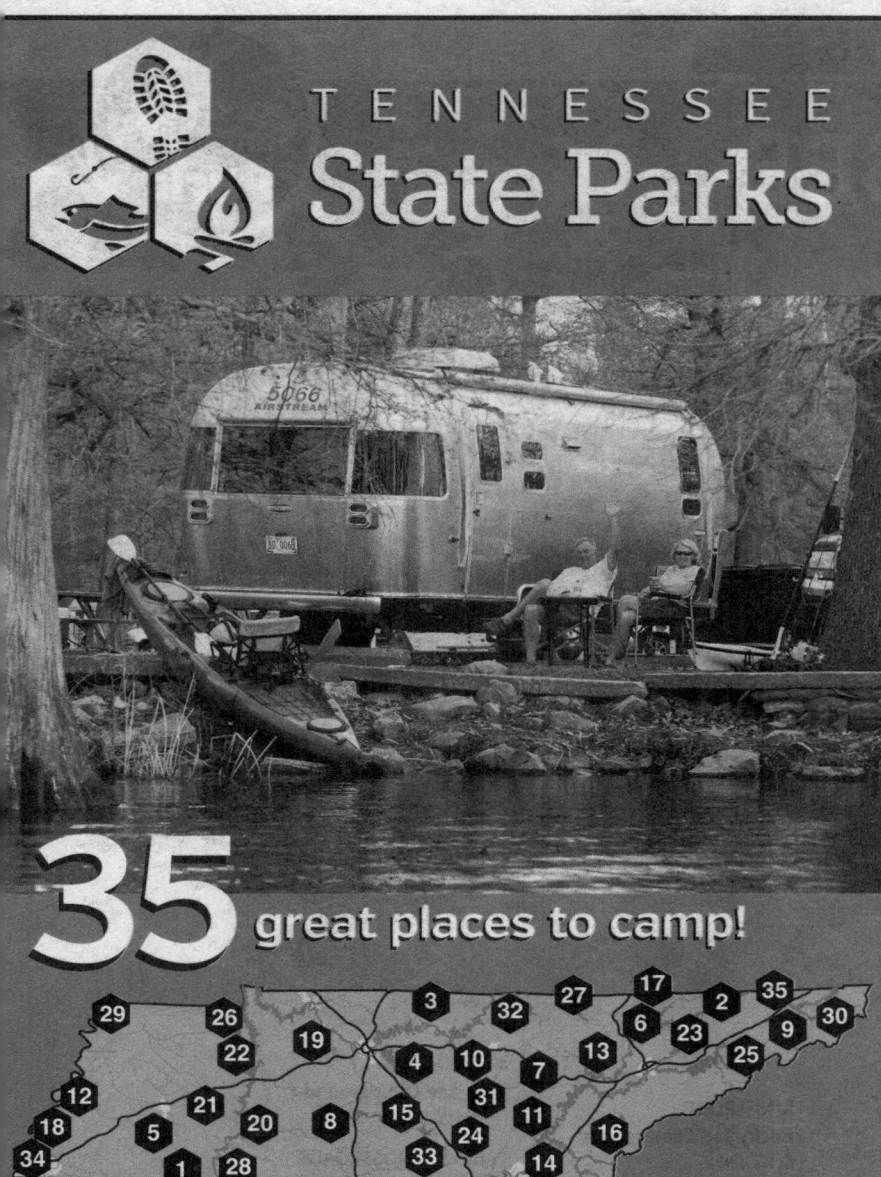

In East Tennessee, Big South Fork of the Cumberland National Recreation Area near Oneida is one of the area's best-kept secrets, affording all manner of recreational opportunities. Encompassing some 26,000 acres and more than 34 miles of trails, Fall Creek Falls is Tennessee's largest and most-visited state park, named for its awe-inspiring 256-foot waterfall, one of the highest in the eastern U.S.

TRAVEL & TOURISM

Tennessee Dept. of Tourist Development
615-741-2159
www.tnvacation.com

Memphis CVB
901-543-5300
www.memphistravel.com

Nashville CVB
800-657-6910
www.musiccityusa.com

Middle Tennessee Tourism Council
615-862-8828
www.middletennesseetourism.com

Northeast Tennessee Tourism Assn.
800-468-6882, 423-913-5550
www.netta.com

Northwest Tennessee Tourism Council
866-698-6386, 731-593-0171
www.kentuckylaketourism.com

Southeast Tennessee Tourism Association
423-424-4267
www.southeasttennessee.com

Tourism Association of Southwest Tennessee
800-462-8366, 731-616-7474
www.tast.tn.org

OUTDOOR RECREATION

Tennessee Department of Environment and Conservation
888-891-TDEC
www.tate.tn.us/environment

TN

Featured Good Sam Parks

TENNESSEE

Good Sam Park

When you stay with Good Sam, you can expect the highest degree of cleanliness and friendliness, and better yet, you get 10% off campground fees.

If you're not already a Good Sam member you can purchase your membership at one of these locations:

ALLONS
Deep Valley Campground
(931)823-2222

BAILEYTON
Baileyton RV Park & Willow View Cabins
(423)234-4992

BRISTOL
Lakeview RV Park
(423)538-5600

CHATTANOOGA
Best Holiday Trav-L-Park
(800)693-2877

CLARKSVILLE
Clarksville RV Park LLC
(931)648-8638

COSBY
Smoky Mountain Premier RV Resort
(855)557-6778

CROSSVILLE
Bean Pot Campground
(931)484-7671
Deer Run RV Resort
(931)484-3333
Spring Lake RV Resort
(877)707-1414

GATLINBURG
Camp Leconte Luxury Outdoor Resort
(865)436-8831
Smoky Bear Campground
(865)436-8372
Twin Creek RV Resort
(865)436-7081

HARTFORD
Pigeon River Campground
(888)820-8771

HURRICANE MILLS
Loretta Lynn's Ranch
(931)296-7700

JONESBOROUGH
Riverpark Campground
(423)753-5359

KINGSPORT
Rocky Top Campground & RV Park
(423)323-2535

KNOXVILLE
Volunteer Park Family Campground
(865)938-6600

LENOIR CITY
Soaring Eagle Campground & RV Park Inc
(865)376-9017

MEMPHIS
Memphis Graceland RV Park & Campground
(866)571-9236

NASHVILLE
Nashville Shores Lakeside Resort
(615)889-7050
Two Rivers Campground
(615)883-8559

NEWPORT
Tana-See Campground
(423)415-5000

PARKERS CROSSROADS
Parkers Crossroads RV Park and Campground
(731)968-9939

PIGEON FORGE
Bear Cove Village
(865)453-8117
Camp Rivers Landing RV Park
(800)848-9097
Creekside RV Park
(865)428-4801
King's Holly Haven RV Park
(888)204-0247
Mill Creek Resort
(865)428-3498
Pine Mountain RV Park
(877)753-9994
River Plantation RV Park Inc
(800)758-5267

SAVANNAH
Green Acres RV Resort
(731)926-1928

SEVIERVILLE
Ripplin' Waters Campground & Cabin Rental
(865)453-4169
Riverside RV Park & Resort
(865)453-7299
Two Rivers Landing RV Resort
(866)727-5781

SMYRNA
Nashville I-24 Campground
(615)459-5818

For more Good Sam Parks go to listing pages

Tennessee Tourism

SPOTLIGHT

CHATTANOOGA

Tennessee's rising star shines for visitors

Much has changed in a little less than five decades in Chattanooga, Tennessee. Once named the "Dirtiest City in America" in the 1960s, the *New York Times* recently called this charming riverside community one of the Top 45 places to visit—in the world.

Hyper-industrialization throughout the course of the nineteenth century was surely the cause of the first moniker, and within minutes of arrival today it's easy to see how the city has since garnered the praise of professional globetrotters. Decades of aggressive revitalization and industrial cleanup took care of the pollution; Mother Nature seems to have taken care of the rest. To put it in simple terms, there's a reason Chattanooga's new moniker is "The Scenic City."

Tucked in the picturesque southwest corner of Tennessee on either side of the Tennessee River, the city lies draped across a series of slopping ridges and gentle valleys that are slung between the Appalachian Mountains and the Cumberland Plateau.

Rambling in RiverPark

Start in Downtown Chattanooga, where uncrowded streets mix seamlessly with waterfront walking trails. Part of the Tennessee RiverPark stretches into the Downtown area, making the transition from lively city center to quiet riverside stroll quick and easy. In fact, most of the city's main attractions are clustered in the city center and a free electric shuttle covers the entire Downtown area.

The best way to explore the city, however, is by bike, and even this is a breeze. Chattanooga is home to the South's first citywide bike share system. More than 300 bikes are available at any given time from 30 different locations.

In your travels be sure to take a spin through the Bluff View Art District. As its name suggests, this hip and trendy district sits on top of a bluff overlooking the Tennessee River. Locals and visitors alike head here for some of the best restaurants, cafes and bakeries in the city.

For some family-friendly fun, head to the Tennessee Aquarium and Chattanooga Zoo. Surprisingly, the Tennessee Aquarium is the world's largest freshwater aquarium. The facility is divided into two parts—River Journey and Ocean Journey—and visitors should expect to spend one very worthwhile full day here. The Aquarium also operates the River Gorge Explorer, a 70-passenger high-speed boat that takes guests on an in-depth, two-hour tour of the Tennessee River ecosystem.

Stay on the Lookout

When it's time to get out of the city limits and explore the landscapes of southwest Tennessee head for Lookout Mountain, once a Civil War battleground. A plateau perched on a mountain and surrounded by treacherous sheer-faced cliffs, Lookout Mountain is an absolute must-visit. To take in views that claim to stretch as far as seven states, hop on the Incline Railway—the world's steepest passenger train—for a trip to the summit.

For More Information

Chattanooga CVB
800-322-3344
www.chatanoogafun.com

Tennessee Tourism
615-741-2159
www.tnvacation.com

A Civil War cannon at Point Park on Lookout Mountain. Getty Images/iStockphoto

CHATTANOOGA'S HIGHEST RATED

- Top 50 RV Parks in North America
- Convenient to all area attractions
- Free Wi-Fi
- 40 x 60 Swimming Pool
- Cabins & Cottages
- Pull-Thrus with 30/50 Amp & Sewer
- New Playground & Dog Park
- Lookout Mtn. Packages for Guests

GOOD SAM RATINGS
9/10★/10

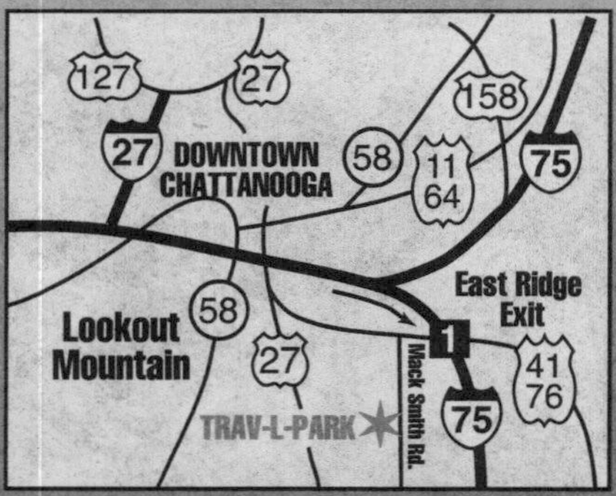

1/2 mile off I-75 exit 1
DIRECTIONS:
If Northbound on I-75, take exit 1B.
If Southbound on I-75, take exit 1.
In either case, go right at top of ramp, then left at light at Mack Smith Rd.
Follow Signs.

HOLIDAY TRAVEL PARK
CHATTANOOGA

Mack Smith Road
At I-75 East Ridge Exit
Local Phone: 1-706-891-9766
Reservations suggested: 1-800-693-2877

www.travelparkchattanooga.com

See listing Chattanooga, TN

Getty Images/iStockphoto

SPOTLIGHT TN

PIGEON FORGE

Stay a spell in Tennessee's favorite stomping ground for fun and adventure

Set against the west-facing slopes of the Great Smoky Mountains in eastern Tennessee, the town of Pigeon Forge is small in both footprint and population. But looks can be deceiving. Big music and big attractions give this otherwise quiet countryside community a bursting-at-the-seams look and feel that seems a far cry from the town's far more humble roots.

> At the Elvis Museum, visitors can view a range of authentic Elvis artifacts including his limousine and famous $250,000 ring.

The earliest settlers arrived here in 1788 when the area was still governed by North Carolina. In 1820, a man by the name of Isaac Love built an iron forge on the banks of Pigeon River and *voilà*, the future town's namesake of Pigeon Forge was born through a simple act of one-plus-one. Ten years later, Love's son built a flour and grain mill, further propelling the settlement and growth of Pigeon Forge. The mill still stands (and works) to this day under the charmingly hyper-logical name of "Old Mill."

Fast-forward to the present day, and you'll quickly discover that Pigeon Forge has built steadily on its historic foundation of straightforward, no-nonsense place-name poetry. Today, the town is synonymous with country music, gospel music and the effervescent spirit of Dolly Parton, who grew up in the Smoky Mountains region.

Entertainment Abounds

Look no further than the basket of country twang-infused attractions that bring visitors from far and wide to Pigeon Forge and the surrounding area: Dollywood, Dolly Parton's Dixie Stampede, the Southern Gospel Museum and Hall of Fame, the Elvis Presley Museum and the Chasing Rainbows Museum. But like any good country song, Pigeon Forge holds an unexpected surprise or two up its sleeve. For instance, who would expect this to be the home of a Titanic Museum or Hollywood Wax Museum? The Bottom line: Once you set up camp in Pigeon Forge, prepare to be entertained.

Start at Dollywood, the town's undisputed premiere attraction. Country music superstar Dolly Parton is part owner and the namesake of this unusual theme park, which is jam-packed with eclectic thrill rides and an endless array of live shows set across 10 uniquely

TN

The Pigeon Forge Parkway. Pigeon Forge

Pigeon Forge's Titanic replica features artifacts from the ill-fated voyage. Pigeon Forge

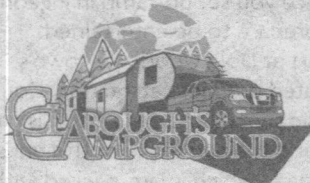

WELCOME to
THE LAND of MORE
Nothing beats camping in Pigeon Forge at the foothills of the Great Smoky Mountains. From traditional tent camping to deluxe RV camping, there is a spot for everyone, and the fun of the Parkway is just around the corner. Pigeon Forge is the place with more to see and do and more ways to enjoy the great outdoors.
ACTION ★ PACKED
PIGEON FORGE
TENNESSEE
MyPigeonForge.com

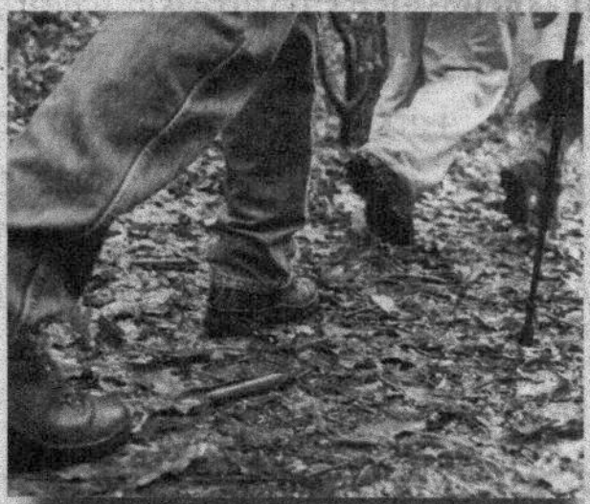

TN

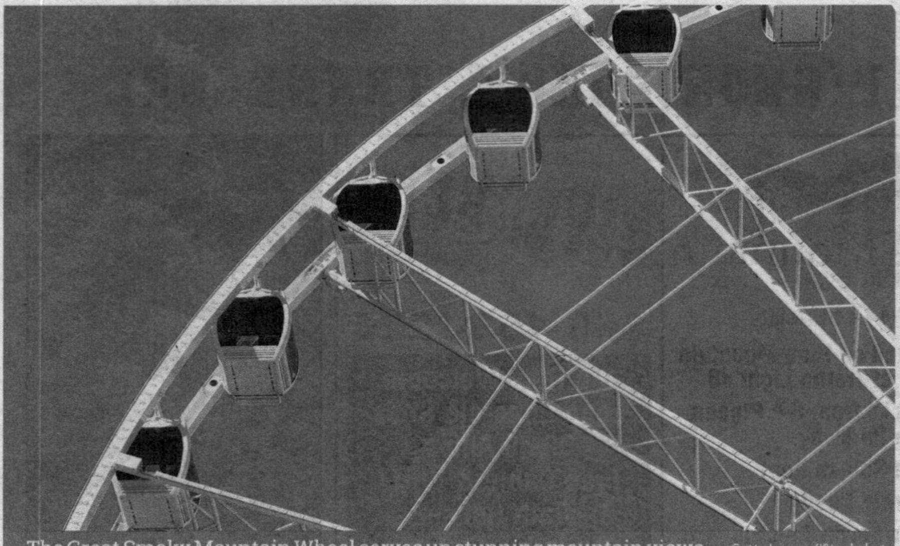
The Great Smoky Mountain Wheel serves up stunning mountain views. Getty Images/iStockphoto

Old Mill in Pigeon Forge. Getty Images/iStockphoto

themed areas. The park covers more than 150 acres and annually attracts nearly 2.5 million guests.

Dollywood is also home to Splash Country, an adjacent waterpark open during the summer months each year. A variety of wave pools and thrill-ride waterslides are available for all ages (and bravery levels).

The Elvis Museum, Southern Gospel Museum (home to the Southern Gospel Hall of Fame) and Chasing Rainbows Museum (located at Dollywood) are all must-visits for music lovers and pop culture enthusiasts. At the Elvis Museum, visitors can view a range of authentic Elvis artifacts (including his limousine and famous $250,000 ring), as well as take in a nightly mix of live shows and concerts.

Top a day of country music-inspired sightseeing off with dinner at Dolly Parton's Dixie Stampede. This lively dinner theater experience includes four-course meals served during a show featuring acrobats, show riding and live music.

Titanic Attractions
When you're ready for a complete change of pace, the Titanic Museum and Hollywood Wax Museum are the places to go. Interactive walk-through galleries and exhibits bring little-known tales and stories from the famous iceberg-doomed ship to life at the Titanic Museum, while the country's largest collection of celebrity wax figures is on guard at the Hollywood Wax Museum. Top another day of family-fun off at the Island, a sparkling new shopping and entertainment district in the center of town, and also the home to the Great Smoky Mountain Wheel, a 200-foot-tall Ferris wheel that gives riders imcomparable mountain vistas.

Finally, when it's time for some healthy outdoor fun and recreation, the Great Smoky Mountains National Park is at your fingertips. More than 10 million visitors flock to the Great Smoky Mountains each year, making it far and away the most visited national park in the country—and for good reason. More than 800 miles of maintained hiking trails weave through the park, as well as five different scenic byways.

Ninety historic buildings and structures are spread throughout the forest, along with a buffet of sparkling waterfalls. And as if that wasn't enough, this is among the best places in the country to see wild bears, as the Smokies are home to more than 1,500 black bears—approximately two per square mile.

From waterslides and Ferris wheels to black bears and wax celebrities, Pigeon Forge is among the most eclectic small towns in the country. Families traveling with small children will find more than enough to keep them occupied (and all family members smiling) while the Great Smoky Mountains National Forest offers a world of incredible outdoor recreation.

For More Information

Pigeon Forge Department of Tourism
800-251-9100
www.mypigeonforge.com

Tennessee Tourism
615-741-2159
www.tnvacation.com

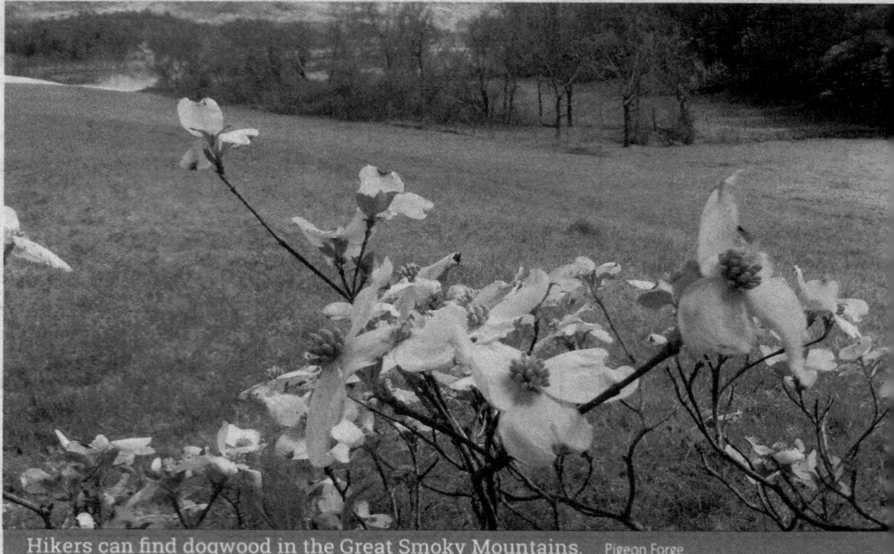
Hikers can find dogwood in the Great Smoky Mountains. Pigeon Forge

Getty Images/iStockphoto

SEVIERVILLE

Enjoy a bright gem in the Shadow of the Great Smoky Mountains

Sevierville, a city of nearly 15,000 nes-
:led in the midst of the Great Smoky Mountains, is a town rich with history, rom its first Native American settlers :o its integral role as a Revolutionary Nar battleground. That heritage is still on display today, but visitors to "Your Hometown in the Smokies" should expect more than a lesson in our past, s the town is also a major draw for adventurers, fami-ies, and, well, fans of Dolly Parton.

Dolly Parton calls Sevierville her home town. A statue of Dolly stands on the Sevier County Courthouse lawn.

Seeing the Smokies

When planning your trip, put Great Smoky Mountains National Park on he top of your list. No visit to the city would be complete without a visit to his nearby treasure, which lies just outh of town and occupies a vast wath of mountainous land on the bor-der of Tennessee and North Carolina. nterested in fishing? Grab your license and feel free to dip the line into one of he park's trout filled streams from sun-ise to sunset. Is hiking your thing? Pack up the gear and prepare to feast your eyes on bursting wildflowers, vibrant nountain streams and powerful, roar-ng waterfalls. Would you rather just ee historic buildings and landmarks? Smoky Mountain has those too, with one of the largest conglomerations of og buildings in the country. The list of istoric structures includes all manner of buildings, including barns, churches, chools and grist mills.

Make sure to give a gander what's aking place beneath the towering rocks of the Smokies. Tennessee is known as the state with the most caves, with over 8,000 vast subterranean chambers. Perhaps the most breathtakingly beautiful is Forbidden Caverns. Visitors will be treated to the site of twinkling crystal formations, overwhelming natural chimneys and grottos with intimidating names like Grotto of the Dead and Grotto of Evil Spirits.

For a good time that is even more family-friendly, Smoky Mountain Deer Farm Exotic Petting Zoo is worth your attention. Get friendly with any number of animals at this unique attraction, including camels, zebra and kangaroos.

Delve Into the Past

Those with an interest in learning about the history of Sevierville would be wise to make the Sevier County Heritage Museum an early stop on their agenda. The museum, established in 1995, features a copious amount of artifacts, memorabilia and documents to give you a window into what life was like for some of our nation's earliest citizens.

Some of the featured collections include the Library of the Smoky Mountain Historical Society.

If you're a fan of things that take wing, the Tennessee Museum of Aviation is located on over 50,000 square feet of ground near the Gatlinburg-Pigeon Forge Airport. Tours are available for individuals interested in delving into the museum's vast collection of lovingly restored "warbirds."

Do you cringe at just the mention of the word "museum"? You might enjoy Floyd Garrett's Muscle Car Museum, which features more than 90 American-made muscle cars from the 1950s, 1960s and 1970s. Also on exhibit are more than 5,000 other car-related museum pieces and a 6,000-square-foot gift shop jam-packed with items such as T-shirts, die casts, posters and more.

Dolly's Stomping Ground

Simply put, Dolly Parton is not only a world-famous actress, musician, and entertainer; she is also just a person who is proud to call Sevierville her hometown. So make sure to check out Dollywood, the spectacular theme park in nearby Pigeon Forge. With festivals, concerts, and rides galore, you'll be sure to find something for both kids and parents alike. And, by the way, if you would like to pay homage to the great lady but don't have the money for park admission, you could always just stop by the statue of Dolly Parton that is located on the Sevier County Courthouse lawn.

TN

For More Information

Sevierville, Tennessee Visitors Page
888-738-4378
www.visitsevierville.com

Tennessee Tourism
615-741-2159
www.tnvacation.com

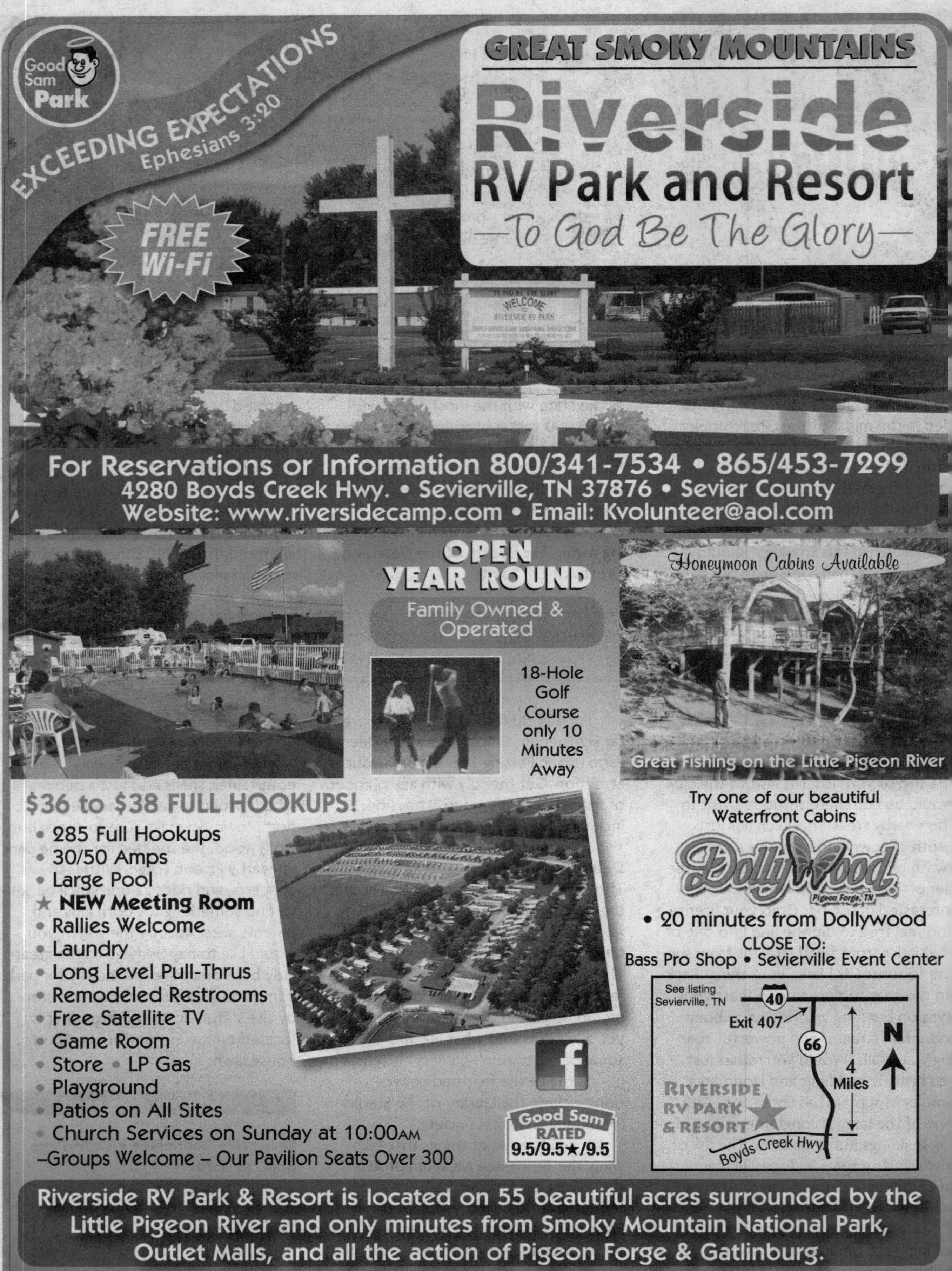
Good Sam Park
EXCEEDING EXPECTATIONS
Ephesians 3:20
FREE Wi-Fi
GREAT SMOKY MOUNTAINS
Riverside
RV Park and Resort
—To God Be The Glory—
For Reservations or Information 800/341-7534 • 865/453-7299
4280 Boyds Creek Hwy. • Sevierville, TN 37876 • Sevier County
Website: www.riversidecamp.com • Email: Kvolunteer@aol.com
OPEN YEAR ROUND
Family Owned & Operated
18-Hole Golf Course only 10 Minutes Away
Honeymoon Cabins Available
Great Fishing on the Little Pigeon River
$36 to $38 FULL HOOKUPS!
• 285 Full Hookups
• 30/50 Amps
• Large Pool
★ NEW Meeting Room
• Rallies Welcome
• Laundry
• Long Level Pull-Thrus
• Remodeled Restrooms
• Free Satellite TV
• Game Room
• Store • LP Gas
• Playground
• Patios on All Sites
• Church Services on Sunday at 10:00AM
–Groups Welcome – Our Pavilion Seats Over 300
Try one of our beautiful Waterfront Cabins
Dollywood
Pigeon Forge, TN
• 20 minutes from Dollywood
CLOSE TO:
Bass Pro Shop • Sevierville Event Center
See listing Sevierville, TN
40
Exit 407
66
4 Miles
N
RIVERSIDE RV PARK & RESORT
Boyds Creek Hwy.
Good Sam RATED 9.5/9.5★/9.5
Riverside RV Park & Resort is located on 55 beautiful acres surrounded by the Little Pigeon River and only minutes from Smoky Mountain National Park, Outlet Malls, and all the action of Pigeon Forge & Gatlinburg.

Tennessee

CONSULTANTS

Henry & Anne Goldman

ALLONS — A5 *Clay*

DEEP VALLEY CAMPGROUND
Ratings: 7.5/8.5★/9 (Campground) From Jct of I 40 & Hwy 111 (Exit 288) N 21.1 mi on Hwy 111 to Jct of Hwy 111 & Hwy 52 N 5.2 mi on Hwy 52 to Palestine Rd E 0.3 mi on Palestine RD to Hunters Cove Rd E 2.5 mi on Hunters Cove Rd (L). **FAC:** Gravel rds. 28 gravel, back-ins (25 x 44), 13 full hkups, 15 W, 15 E (30 amps), cable, WiFi, tent sites, rentals, dump, laundry, groc, fire rings, firewood. **REC:** pool, wading pool, Mitchell Creek: playground, rec open to public. Pets OK. Eco-friendly, 2015 rates: $25 to $30. Apr 1 to Nov 1.
(931)823-2222 Lat: 36.28334, Lon: -85.19325
755 Hunter Cove Road, Allons, TN 38541
deepvalleytn@outlook.com
www.deepvalleycampground.com
See ad this page, 1068.

ANTIOCH — B4 *Davidson*

ANDERSON ROAD CAMPGROUND (Public Corps) From Jct of US-41 & Bell Rd, N 1.5 mi on Bell Rd to Smith Springs Rd, E 1.1 mi to Anderson Rd, N .5 mi (L). 2015 rates: $14 to $24. Mar 1 to Oct 31. (615)361-1980

ASHLAND CITY — B4 *Cheatham*

LOCK A CAMPGROUND (COE - CHEATHAM LAKE) (Public Corps) From jct Ashland City: Go W mi on US 12 to Cheap Hill, then W 4 mi on Cheatham Dam Rd. 2015 rates: $19 to $23. Apr 1 to Oct 4. (615)792-3715

ATHENS — C6 *McMinn*

OVER-NITER RV PARK **Ratings: 7/8.5★/7.5** (RV Park) From Jct of I-75 & SR-305 (exit 52), E 0.6 mi on SR-305 (L). **FAC:** Gravel rds. (16 spaces). Avail: 10 gravel, patios, 10 pull-thrus (30 x 50), 10 full hkups (30/50 amps), seasonal sites, WiFi, laundry, LP bottles. **REC.** Pet restrict(B). Partial handicap access, no tents. Big rig sites, eco-friendly, 2015 rates: $24 to $26.
(423)507-0069 Lat: 35.49410, Lon: -84.60037
816 Hwy 305, Athens, TN 37303
janejustice@overniterrvpark.com
www.overniterrvpark.com

BAILEYTON — D5 *Greene*

BAILEYTON RV PARK & WILLOW VIEW CABINS
Ratings: 8/9★/9 (Campground) From Jct of I-81 & Hwy 172 (exit 36), N 0.7 mi on Van Hill Rd/Hwy 172 to Horton Hwy, Right turn onto Horton Hwy E 1 mi (L). **FAC:** Gravel rds. (72 spaces). Avail: 55 gravel, 30 pull-thrus (25 x 70), back-ins (28 x 55), 55 full hkups (30/50 amps), seasonal sites, cable, WiFi, tent sites, rentals, dump, laundry, groc, LP gas, firewood. **REC:** pond, fishing, playground, rec open to public. Pets OK. Big rig sites, eco-friendly, 2015 rates: $34 to $36. Disc: military.
(423)234-4992 Lat: 36.33912, Lon: -82.82330
7485 Horton Hwy, Baileyton, TN 37745
baileytonrvpark@gmail.com
www.baileytonrvpark.com
See ad this page, 1068.

BAXTER — B5 *Putnam*

TWIN LAKES CATFISH FARM & CAMPGROUND **Ratings: 4.5/NA/6.5** (Campground) 2015 rates: $27. (931)858-2333 580 Gainesboro Hwy (Hwy 56), Baxter, TN 38544

BLOUNTVILLE — D6 *Sullivan*

BRISTOL-KINGSPORT KOA **Ratings: 8.5/8.5/9** (Campground) 2015 rates: $35 to $64. (800)562-7640 425 Rocky Branch Rd, Blountville, TN 37617

BON AQUA — B3 *Hickman*

PINEY RIVER ESCAPE **Ratings: 5.5/8★/7.5** (Campground) 2015 rates: $35 to $40. (931)996-3431 6832 Piney River Road North, Bon Aqua, TN 37025

BRISTOL — D6 *Sullivan*

LAKEVIEW RV PARK
Ratings: 8.5/9.5★/9 (RV Park) From Jct of I-81 & SR 394/SR37 (exit 69) SE 5.3 mi on SR 394/37 to Hwy US 11E/US 19, S 3 mi (R). **FAC:** Gravel rds. 151 gravel, 4 pull-thrus (30 x 45), back-ins (30 x 45), 151 full hkups (30/50 amps), cable, WiFi, laundry, LP gas, fire rings, firewood. **REC:** pool, Boone Lake: fishing, playground, rec open to public. Pets OK. Partial handicap access, no tents. Eco-friendly, 2015 rates: $36 to $39. Disc: AAA, military.
(423)538-5600 Lat: 36.46511, Lon: -82.28517
4550 Hwy 11E, Bristol, TN 37618
camping@lakeviewrvpark.com
www.lakeviewrvpark.com
See ad this page, 1068.

SHADRACK CAMPGROUND
Ratings: 6.5/9.5★/7 (Campground) From the Jct of I-81 & SR-394 (exit 69), S 5.5 mi on SR-394 to US-19 (US-11E), E 2.0 mi (R). **FAC:** Gravel rds. 105 Avail: 55 gravel, 50 grass, back-ins (40 x 40), 75 full hkups, 30 W, 30 E (30/50 amps), WiFi, tent sites, rentals, dump, fire rings, firewood. **REC:** Beaver Creek: fishing. Pets OK. Big rig sites, 2015 rates: $29 to $32. Disc: military.
(423)217-1181 Lat: 36.52906, Lon: -82.24979
2537 Volunteer Pkwy, Bristol, TN 37620
Albert@shadrack.com
www.shadrackcampground.com
See ad this page.

THUNDER MOUNTAIN CAMPGROUND **Ratings: 4.5/7/6.5** (Campground) 2015 rates: $28 to $35. (423)946-2380 250 North Raceway Villa Drive, Bristol, TN 37620

Our Guide to Seasonal Sites will help you find places you can stay for extended periods of time.

BUCHANAN — A3 *Benton, Henry, Stewart*

PARIS LANDING
(State Pk) From Jct of US-641 & US-79, E 16.9 mi on US-79 (L). **FAC:** Paved rds. (50 spaces). Avail: 30 gravel, 3 pull-thrus (30 x 80), back-ins (20 x 30), 30 W, 30 E (30 amps), WiFi Hotspot, dump, laundry, restaurant. **REC:** pool $, Kentucky Lake: fishing, marina, golf, playground. Pets OK. Partial handicap access, no tents. 14 day max stay, 2015 rates: $27. No CC.
(731)641-4465 Lat: 36.43934, Lon: -88.08320
16055 Hwy 79N, Buchanan, TN 38222
tnstateparks.itinio.com
See ad page 1067 (Welcome Section).

CAMDEN — B3 *Benton*

BIRDSONG RESORT & MARINA LAKESIDE RV & TENT CAMPGROUND
Ratings: 8.5/7.5/6.5 (Campground) From Jct of I-40 & SR 191/Birdsong Rd (Exit 133), N 9.1 mi on SR 191 to Marina Rd, E 0.4 mi (L). **FAC:** Paved rds. (74 spaces). Avail: 38 paved, 7 pull-thrus (22 x 65), back-ins (22 x 45), 38 full hkups (30/50 amps), seasonal sites, WiFi, tent sites, dump, mobile sewer, laundry, LP gas, firewood. **REC:** pool, Kentucky Lake: fishing, marina, playground, rec open to public. Pets OK. Partial handicap access. 2015 rates: $40 to $46. Disc: military.
(731)584-7880 Lat: 35.96973, Lon: -88.04623
255 Marina Rd, Camden, TN 38320
bob@birdsong.com
www.birdsongresort.com

NATHAN BEDFORD FOREST
(State Pk) From Jct of US-70 & SR-191, N 10.3 mi on SR-191 (E). **FAC:** Paved/gravel rds. 37 paved, no slide-outs, back-ins (25 x 45), 37 W, 37 E (30/50 amps), tent sites, dump. **REC:** Kentucky Lake: swim, fishing, playground, rec open to public. Pets OK. 14 day max stay, 2015 rates: $16.
(731)584-6356 Lat: 36.09122, Lon: -87.98595
1825 Pilot Knob Rd, Eva, TN 38333
tnstateparks.itinio.com
See ad page 1067 (Welcome Section).

CARTHAGE — B5 *Jackson, Smith*

DEFEATED CREEK (Public Corps) From town, W 4 mi on Hwy 25 to Hwy 80, N 2 mi to Hwy 85, E 3.8 mi to Marina Ln., S 1.5 mi. Call 877-444-6777 for reservations. 2015 rates: $15 to $26. Mar 13 to Nov 3. (615)774-3141

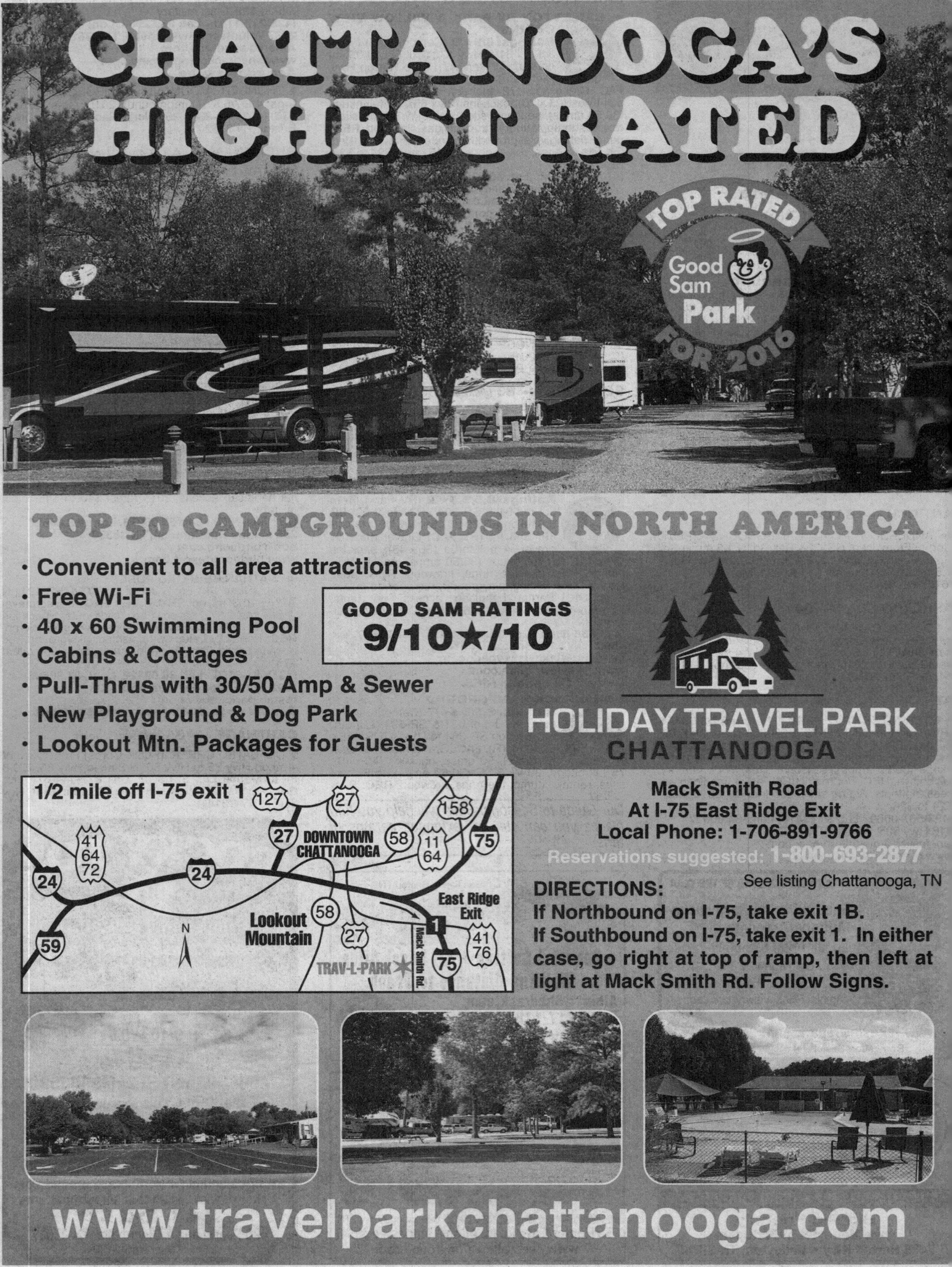
CHATTANOOGA'S HIGHEST RATED
TOP RATED
Good Sam Park
FOR 2016
TOP 50 CAMPGROUNDS IN NORTH AMERICA
• Convenient to all area attractions
• Free Wi-Fi
• 40 x 60 Swimming Pool
• Cabins & Cottages
• Pull-Thrus with 30/50 Amp & Sewer
• New Playground & Dog Park
• Lookout Mtn. Packages for Guests
GOOD SAM RATINGS
9/10★/10
HOLIDAY TRAVEL PARK
CHATTANOOGA
1/2 mile off I-75 exit 1
127
27
158
41
64
72
DOWNTOWN CHATTANOOGA
58
11
64
75
24
East Ridge Exit
Lookout Mountain
Mack Smith Rd.
41
76
59
N
TRAV-L-PARK
Mack Smith Road
At I-75 East Ridge Exit
Local Phone: 1-706-891-9766
Reservations suggested: 1-800-693-2877
See listing Chattanooga, TN
DIRECTIONS:
If Northbound on I-75, take exit 1B.
If Southbound on I-75, take exit 1. In either case, go right at top of ramp, then left at light at Mack Smith Rd. Follow Signs.
www.travelparkchattanooga.com

CARYVILLE — B6 *Campbell*

COVE LAKE
(State Pk) From Jct of I-75 & Hwy 25W (exit 134), N 0.8 mi on Hwy 25W (L). **FAC:** Paved rds. 100 gravel, 2 pull-thrus (30 x 50), back-ins (30 x 50), 100 W, 100 E (30 amps), tent sites, dump, restaurant. **REC:** pool $, Cove Lake: fishing, shuffleboard, playground. Pets OK. Partial handicap access. 14 day max stay, 2015 rates: $20. No CC.
(423)566-9701 Lat: 36.30879, Lon: -84.21110
110 Cove Lake Ln, Caryville, TN 37714
tnstateparks.itinio.com
See ad page 1067 (Welcome Section).

CELINA — A5 *Clay*

DALE HOLLOW DAM (Public Corps) From town, E 3 mi on SR-53, follow signs (R). Call 877-444-6777 for reservations. 2015 rates: $18 to $24. Apr 4 to Oct 27. (877)444-6777

CHAPEL HILL — C4 *Marshall*

HENRY HORTON STATE RESORT PARK
(State Pk) From Jct of I-65 & SR-99 (exit 46), E 12 mi on SR-99 to Jct with US-31A, S 0.4 mi (R). **FAC:** Paved rds. 56 paved, 6 pull-thrus (25 x 65), back-ins (25 x 50), 56 E (30/50 amps), tent sites, dump, restaurant. **REC:** pool $, Duck River: fishing, golf, playground. Pets OK. Partial handicap access. 14 day max stay, 2015 rates: $25. No CC.
(931)364-2222 Lat: 35.58975, Lon: -86.69477
4209 Nashville Hwy, Chapel Hill, TN 37034
tnstateparks.itinio.com
See ad page 1067 (Welcome Section).

CHATTANOOGA — C5 *Hamilton*

CHATTANOOGA AREA MAP

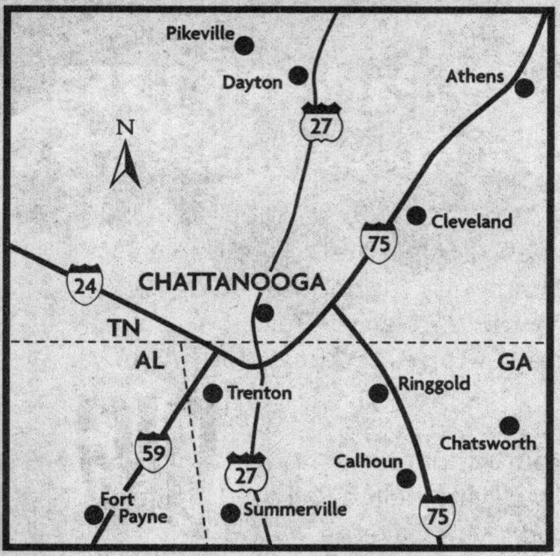

Symbols on map indicate towns within a 50 mile radius of Chattanooga where campgrounds are listed. Check listings for more information.

In TN, see also Athens, Cleveland, Dayton & Pikeville.

In GA, see also Calhoun, Chatsworth, Ringgold, Summerville & Trenton.

In AL, see also Fort Payne.

A SPOTLIGHT Introducing Chattanooga's colorful attractions appearing at the front of this state section.

BATTLEFIELD CAMPGROUND & RV PARK
Ratings: 8/9.5★/7.5 (RV Park) From Jct I-24 (exit 185a) & I-75: Go 6-1/4 mi S on 1-75 to (exit 350), then 1/4 mi W on Hwy 2/Battlefield Pkwy, then 500 ft N on Koa Blvd (E). **FAC:** Paved/gravel rds. (109 spaces). Avail: 79 gravel, 50 pull-thrus (25 x 60), back-ins (24 x 45), 39 full hkups, 40 W, 40 E (30/50 amps), seasonal sites, cable, WiFi, tent sites, rentals, dump, laundry, LP gas, fire rings, firewood. **REC:** playground. Pet restrict(B). Partial handicap access. Big rig sites, 2015 rates: $39 to $43. Disc: AAA, military.
(706)937-4166
199 Koa Blvd, Ringgold, GA 30736
Info@battlefieldrvpark.com
www.battlefieldrvpark.com
See primary listing at Ringgold, GA and ad page 1080.

Read many of our brand new RV Trips of a Lifetime for 2016 in the front of the Guide. Find the rest Online!

BEST HOLIDAY TRAV-L-PARK
Ratings: 9/10★/10 (Campground) N-bnd: From Jct of I-75 & US-41N (exit 1B, North US-41), W 0.5 mi on US-41N to Mack Smith Rd, S 0.7 mi (R); or S-bnd: From Jct of I-75 & US-41N (exit 1), W 0.25 mi on US-41N to Mack Smith Rd, S 0.7 mi (R).

CHATTANOOGA KEEPS GETTING BETTER!
And so do we! Make our park your home while you re-live Civil War history, visit the world's largest fresh-water aquarium or ride the Incline Railroad. We offer groomed, shaded sites with every amenity-just 1/2 mi off I-75.

FAC: All weather rds. (221 spaces). Avail: 161 all weather, patios, 138 pull-thrus (30 x 70), back-ins (35 x 60), 143 full hkups, 18 W, 18 E (30/50 amps), seasonal sites, cable, WiFi, tent sites, rentals, dump, laundry, LP gas, fire rings, firewood. **REC:** pool, shuffleboard, playground. Pet restrict(B). Partial handicap access. Big rig sites, eco-friendly, 2015 rates: $37 to $41. Disc: military.
(800)693-2877 Lat: 34.98624, Lon: -85.211008
1709 Mack Smith Road, Chattanooga, TN 37412
campmail@chattacamp.com
www.chattacamp.com
See ad opposite page, 1070 (Spotlight Chattanooga), 1066 (TN Map), 1068 & Snowbird Destinations in Magazine Section.

CAMPING WORLD CHATTANOOGA CAMPGROUND **Ratings: 6.5/7.5/7.5** (Campground) 2015 rates: $23 to $25. (423)892-0144 6728 Ringgold Rd, Chattanooga, TN 37412

CHATTANOOGA'S RACCOON MOUNTAIN RV PARK & CAMPGROUND
Ratings: 8.5/9★/9 (Campground) From Jct of I-24 & US-41 (exit 174), N 1.3 mi on US-41 to W Hills Dr, W 0.5 mi (E). **FAC:** Gravel rds. 100 gravel, patios, 65 pull-thrus (35 x 70), back-ins (20 x 45), 75 full hkups, 25 W, 25 E (30/50 amps), cable, WiFi, tent sites, rentals, dump, laundry, LP gas, fire rings, firewood. **REC:** pool, swim, playground, rec open to public. Pet restrict(B). Big rig sites, eco-friendly, 2015 rates: $31 to $40. Disc: military.
(423)821-9403 Lat: 35.02141, Lon: -85.40730
319 W Hills Dr, Chattanooga, TN 37419
Raccoon1@racoonmountain.com
www.raccoonmountain.com
See ad this page.

CHESTER FROST PARK (Public) From Jct of I-75 & Hwy 153, W 8 mi on Hwy 153 to Hixson Pike, N 10 mi to Gold Point Cir (there are 2 Gold Point Cirs, use 2nd one), NE 0.5 mi (L). 2015 rates: $18.5 to $25. Apr 1 to Oct 30. (423)842-3306

HARRISON BAY
(State Pk) From Jct of SR-153 & SR-58, N 8.2 mi on SR-58 to Harrison Bay Rd, NW 1.5 mi to park entrance, NW 1.5 mi (E). **FAC:** Paved rds. 128 gravel, 54 pull-thrus (30 x 50), back-ins (35 x 40), 128 W, 128 E (30/50 amps), tent sites, dump. **REC:** pool $, Chickamauga Lake: fishing, marina, shuffleboard, playground. Pets OK. No tents. 14 day max stay, 2015 rates: $16 to $25.
(423)344-6214 Lat: 35.17416, Lon: -85.11676
8411 Harrison Bay Road, Harrison, TN 37341
tnstateparks.itinio.com
See ad page 1067 (Welcome Section).

Travel Services

CAMPING WORLD OF CHATTANOOGA As the nation's largest retailer of RV supplies, accessories, services and new and used RVs, Camping World is committed to making your total RV experience better. RV Accessories: (866)999-1286. **SERVICES:** RV, tire, RV appliance, MH mechanical, engine/chassis repair, staffed RV wash, restrooms, RV Sales. RV supplies, LP, RV accessible. waiting room. Hours: 8am to 6pm.
(888)793-4139 Lat: 34.989034, Lon: -85.194508
6734 Ringgold Road, Chattanooga, TN 37412
www.campingworld.com

Things to See and Do

RACCOON MOUNTAIN CAVERNS Natural cave very close to the top of the ground therefore shows many rare formations. Ground level entrance, suitable for all ages. RV accessible. Restrooms, food. Hours: 9:00 a.m. to call. Adult fee: $7.00 to $16.00.
(423)821-9403 Lat: 35.02141, Lon: -85.40730
319 W Hills Drive, Chattanooga, TN 37419
Racoon1@racoonmountain.com
www.raccoonmountain.com
See ad this page.

Treat your pet to a fabulous camping experience by staying at one of the Pampered Pet Parks featured in the front of the Guide.

According to the Wall Street Journal, 100 billion plastic shopping bags are consumed in the United States annually. Consider toting your own reusable shopping bags instead of using plastic.

TN

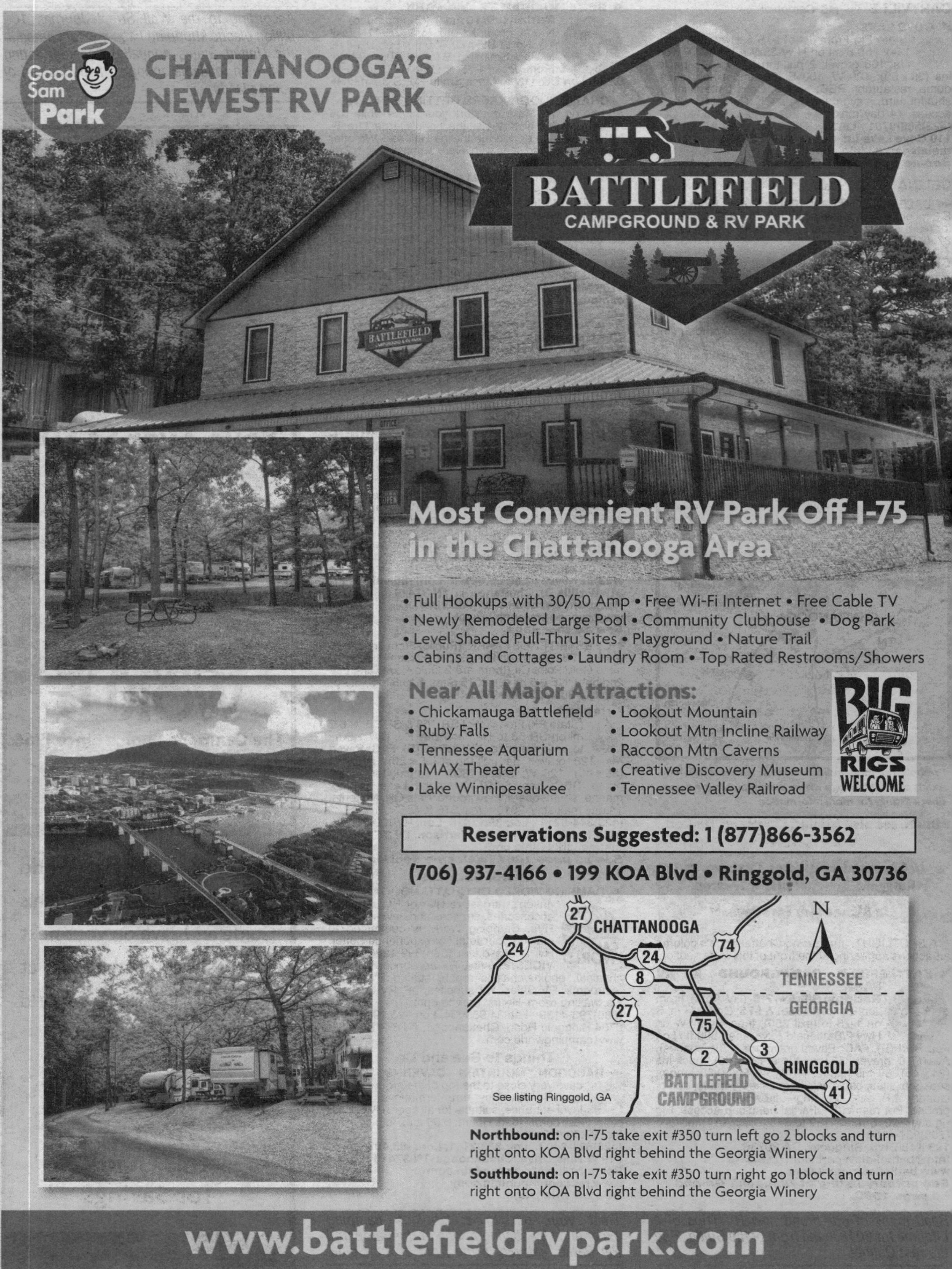
Good Sam Park
CHATTANOOGA'S NEWEST RV PARK
BATTLEFIELD
CAMPGROUND & RV PARK
Most Convenient RV Park Off I-75 in the Chattanooga Area
• Full Hookups with 30/50 Amp • Free Wi-Fi Internet • Free Cable TV
• Newly Remodeled Large Pool • Community Clubhouse • Dog Park
• Level Shaded Pull-Thru Sites • Playground • Nature Trail
• Cabins and Cottages • Laundry Room • Top Rated Restrooms/Showers
Near All Major Attractions:
• Chickamauga Battlefield
• Ruby Falls
• Tennessee Aquarium
• IMAX Theater
• Lake Winnipesaukee
• Lookout Mountain
• Lookout Mtn Incline Railway
• Raccoon Mtn Caverns
• Creative Discovery Museum
• Tennessee Valley Railroad
BIG RIGS WELCOME
Reservations Suggested: 1 (877)866-3562
(706) 937-4166 • 199 KOA Blvd • Ringgold, GA 30736
N
27
CHATTANOOGA
24
24
74
8
TENNESSEE
GEORGIA
27
75
3
2
RINGGOLD
BATTLEFIELD CAMPGROUND
41
See listing Ringgold, GA
Northbound: on I-75 take exit #350 turn left go 2 blocks and turn right onto KOA Blvd right behind the Georgia Winery
Southbound: on I-75 take exit #350 turn right go 1 block and turn right onto KOA Blvd right behind the Georgia Winery
www.battlefieldrvpark.com

CLARKSBURG — B2 *Carroll*

NATCHEZ TRACE/PIN OAK RV CAMPGROUND (State Pk) From Jct of I-40 & SR-114 (exit 116), S 11.4 mi on SR-114 (R) (Follow Signs For RV Camping). **FAC:** Paved rds. 77 gravel, 18 pull-thrus (30 x 60), back-ins (25 x 60), 77 full hkups (20/30 amps), WiFi Hotspot, tent sites, dump, laundry, groc. **REC:** Pin Oak Lake: swim, fishing, playground, rec open to public. Pets OK. Partial handicap access. 14 day max stay, 2015 rates: $25.
(800)250-8616 Lat: 35.703457, Lon: -88.297137
567 Pin Oak Lane, Lexington, TN 38351
ask.tnstateparks@tn.gov
tnstateparks.itinio.com
See ad page 1067 (Welcome Section).

CLARKSVILLE — A3 *Montgomery*

CLARKSVILLE RV PARK LLC
Ratings: 10/10★/9.5 (Campground) From Jct of I-24 & Hwy-48 (exit 1), N 0.1 mi on Hwy-48 to Tylertown Rd, W 0.3 mi (L). **FAC:** Paved/gravel rds. (67 spaces). Avail: 47 all weather, 47 pull-thrus (25 x 65), 35 full hkups, 12 W, 12 E (30/50 amps), seasonal sites, WiFi, tent sites, rentals, dump, laundry, groc, LP gas, firewood. **REC:** pool, playground. Pets OK. Partial handicap access. Big rig sites, eco-friendly, 2015 rates: $35 to $38. Disc: military.
(931)648-8638 Lat: 36.63485, Lon: -87.32224
1270 Tylertown Rd, Clarksville, TN 37040
info@clarksvillervpark.com
www.clarksvillervpark.com
See ad this page, 1068.

CLEVELAND — C6 *Bradley, Polk*

CHATTANOOGA NORTH KOA/CLEVELAND **Ratings: 8/8.5/8** (Campground) 2015 rates: $38 to $45. (800)562-9039 648 Pleasant Grove Road, Cleveland, TN 37353

CLINTON — B6 *Anderson*

CLINTON/KNOXVILLE NORTH KOA Ratings: 9/9★/7.5 (Campground) From Jct of I-75 & SR-61 (exit 122), E 0.2 mi on SR-61 (L). **FAC:** Gravel rds. (75 spaces). Avail: 33 gravel, 32 pull-thrus (25 x 55), back-ins (30 x 60), 28 full hkups, 5 W, 5 E (30/50 amps), seasonal sites, cable, WiFi, tent sites, rentals, dump, laundry, groc, LP gas, fire rings, firewood. **REC:** pool, wading pool, playground, rec open to public. Pets OK. Partial handicap access. Big rig sites, eco-friendly, 2015 rates: $38 to $45. Disc: AAA, military.
AAA Approved
(865)494-9386 Lat: 36.16998, Lon: -84.07951
2423 N. Charles G Seivers Blvd, Clinton, TN 37716
clintonkoa@gmail.com
www.koa.com/campgrounds/knoxville

COLUMBIA — C4 *Maury*

CAMPERS RV PARK **Ratings: 7/7/5.5** (Campground) 2015 rates: $30. (931)381-4112 1792 Bear Creek Pike, Columbia, TN 38401

CORNERSVILLE — C4 *Marshall*

TEXAS T CAMPGROUND **Ratings: 5/8.5★/8.5** (Campground) 2015 rates: $29.75 to $34.25. (931)293-2500 2499 Lynnville Hwy, Cornersville, TN 37047

COSBY — E5 *Cocke*

GREAT SMOKY MTN/COSBY (Natl Pk) From Jct of I-40 & Foothills Pkwy, W 7 mi on Foothills Pkwy to US-321, S 2 mi, follow signs (R). NOTE: Tunnel construction may restrict RVs-call (888)355-1849 for information. 2015 rates: $14. Apr 11 to Oct 31. (865)487-2683

SMOKY MOUNTAIN PREMIER RV RESORT
Ratings: 9/9.5★/8.5 (RV Park) (In Gatlinburg) From Jct of US 441 & US 321, E 16. mi on US 321 (R).

TENNESSEE'S 2015 PARK OF THE YEAR!
A new resort catering to Big Rigs with full hookups while keeping you in the shade, bordering the Smoky Mtn Nat'l Park. 15 Min from I-40 in Newport, close attractions include Gatlinburg and Pigeon Forge. Enjoy UTV tours here.
FAC: Gravel rds. 76 gravel, 21 pull-thrus (30 x 100), back-ins (25 x 50), 76 full hkups (30/50 amps), cable, WiFi, rentals, laundry, groc, LP bottles, fire rings, firewood, controlled access. **REC:** heated pool, playground. Pet restrict(Q). Partial handicap access. Big rig sites, eco-friendly, 2015 rates: $52 to $75. Disc: AAA, military.
(855)557-6778 Lat: 35.774628, Lon: -83.258998
4874 Hooper Hwy, Cosby, TN 37722
smprvresort@gmail.com
smokymountainpremierrvresort.com
See ad pages 1082, 1097, 1068.

COUNCE — C2 *Hardin*

TVA/PICKWICK DAM-PICKWICK RESERVOIR (Public) From Jct of Hwys 57 & 128, N 1.5 mi on Hwy 128 across dam, park is below dam (L). 2015 rates: $17 to $26. Mar 14 to Nov 17. (800)882-5263

CROSSVILLE — B5 *Cumberland*

BEAN POT CAMPGROUND
Ratings: 9/8.5★/8.5 (Campground) From Jct of I-40 & Peavine Rd (exit 322), N 1.5 mi on Peavine Rd to Bean Pot Campground Road, E 0.3 mi (E). **FAC:** Paved/gravel rds. (54 spaces). Avail: 49 gravel, 49 pull-thrus (25 x 65), 36 full hkups, 13 W, 13 E (30/50 amps), seasonal sites, cable, WiFi, tent sites, rentals, dump, laundry, groc, LP gas, fire rings, firewood. **REC:** pool, wading pool, playground. Pets OK. Partial handicap access. Big rig sites, eco-friendly, 2015 rates: $26 to $29. Disc: AAA, military.
AAA Approved
(931)484-7671 Lat: 35.97839, Lon: -84.96323
23 Bean Pot Campground Loop, Crossville, TN 38571
beanpotcampground@yahoo.com
www.beanpotcampground.com
See ad this page, 1068.

BRECKENRIDGE LAKE RESORT **Ratings: 6/8★/7** (Membership Pk) 2015 rates: $20. Mar 1 to Dec 1. (931)788-1873 395 Oak Park Circle, Crossville, TN 38572

CROSSVILLE KOA **Ratings: 8/8★/8.5** (Campground) 2015 rates: $38 to $40. (931)707-5349 6575 Hwy 70E, Crossville, TN 38555

CUMBERLAND MOUNTAIN (State Pk) From Jct of I-40 & US-127 (exit 317), S 7 mi on US-127 (R). **FAC:** Paved rds. 145 paved, back-ins (30 x 50), some side by side hkups, 145 W, 145 E (20/50 amps), tent sites, dump, restaurant. **REC:** pool $, wading pool, Byrd

Take time now to plan a road trip with your pet. Read more in our Pampered Pet Parks feature at the front of the Guide.

TN

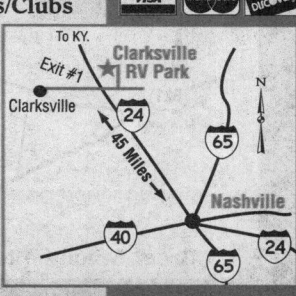

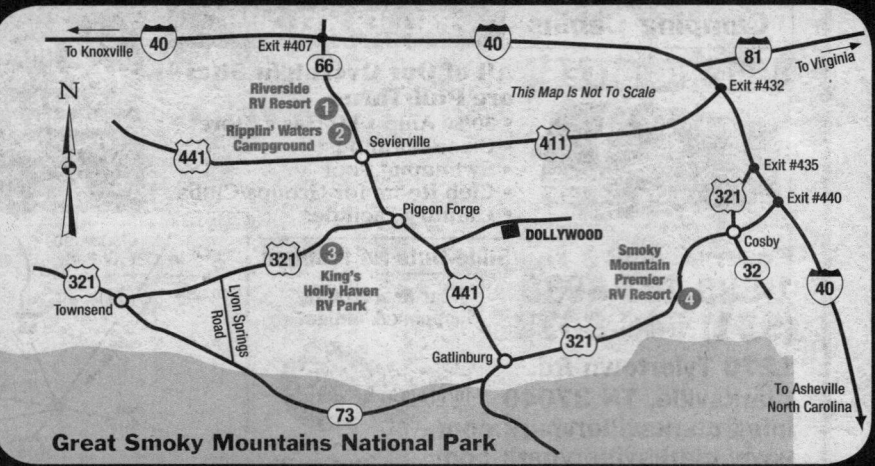

CROSSVILLE (CONT)

CUMBERLAND MOUNTAIN (CONT)
Lake: fishing, golf, playground. Pets OK. 14 day max stay, 2015 rates: $22.50 to $27.50.
(931)484-6138 Lat: 35.89747, Lon: -84.99365
24 Office Dr, Crossville, TN 38555
tnstateparks.itinio.com
See ad page 1067 (Welcome Section).

DEER RUN RV RESORT
Ratings: 9/10★/9 (RV Park) From Jct of I 40 & Hwy 101 (Exit 322), NE 1.9 mi on Hwy 101 to Peavine Fire Tower Rd, N 3.6 mi (L). **FAC:** Gravel rds. (337 spaces). Avail: 75 gravel, 12 pull-thrus (30 x 70), back-ins (30 x 50), 75 full hkups (30/50 amps), seasonal sites, cable, WiFi, tent sites, rentals, laundry, groc, LP gas, fire rings, firewood, controlled access. **REC:** pool, wading pool, Good Neighbor Lake: swim, fishing, playground. Pets OK. Partial handicap access. Big rig sites, eco-friendly, 2015 rates: $39. Disc: military. ATM.
(931)484-3333 Lat: 36.02131, Lon: -84.92984
3609 Peavine Firetower Rd, Crossville, TN 38571
info@deerrunrvresort.com
www.deerrunrvresort.com
See ad pages 1081, 1068.

SPRING LAKE RV RESORT
Ratings: 9/9★/9.5 (Campground) From Jct of I-40 & Hwy 101 (exit 322): Go N 3.6 mi on Hwy 101 (Peavine Rd) to Fairview Dr, SE 0.3 mi (L). **FAC:** All weather rds. 63 Avail: 63 all weather, patios, 5 pull-thrus (45 x 75), back-ins (45 x 75), 60 full hkups, 3 W, 3 E (30/50 amps), cable, WiFi, dump, laundry, fire rings, firewood. **REC:** Spring Lake: fishing. Pet restrict(B). No tents. Big rig sites, eco-friendly, 2015 rates: $32 to $35. Disc: AAA, military.
(877)707-1414 Lat: 35.99176, Lon: -84.92863
255 Fairview Drive, Crossville, TN 38571
slcampingrv@gmail.com
www.springlakervtn.com
See ad pages 1081, 1068.

DANDRIDGE — D5 *Cocke*

ANCHOR DOWN RV RESORT **Ratings: 10/10★/10** (RV Resort) 2015 rates: $49 to $69. Mar 9 to Dec 21. (877)784-4446 1703 Highway 139, Dandridge, TN 37725

DAYTON — C6 *Rhea*

BLUE WATER RV RESORT & MARINA **Ratings: 6.5/8/9** (RV Park) 2015 rates: $39 to $49. (423)775-3265 220 Bluewater Campground Rd, Dayton, TN 37321

DELANO — C6 *Polk*

HIAWASSEE STATE SCENIC RIVER & OCOEE RIVER (GEE CREEK CAMPGROUND)
(State Pk) From north jct Hwy 30 & US 411: Go 6 mi S on US 411 to Hwy 163, then 1 mi SE on Spring Creek Rd. **FAC.** 1 grass, no slide-outs, accepts self-contain units only, tent sites, showers $, fire rings, controlled access. **REC.** Pets OK. Partial handicap access. 14 day max stay. No CC.
(423)263-0050 Lat: 35.24105, Lon: -84.55336
404 Spring Creek Rd, Delano, TN 37325
tnstateparks.itinio.com
See ad page 1067 (Welcome Section).

Explore America's Top RV Destinations! Turn to the Spotlight articles in our State and Province sections to learn more.

DICKSON — B3 *Dickson, Hickman*

TANBARK CAMPGROUND
Ratings: 6/8/6.5 (Campground) From Jct of I-40 & SR-48 (Exit 163), S 0.3 mi on SR-48 to S Spradlin Rd, E 0.1 mi (L). **FAC:** Gravel rds. (38 spaces). 10 Avail: 4 paved, 6 gravel, 10 pull-thrus (22 x 50), 10 full hkups (30/50 amps), seasonal sites, WiFi, tent sites, dump, laundry, firewood. Pet restrict(B). 2015 rates: $28. Disc: military. No CC.
AAA Approved
(615)441-1613 Lat: 35.98405, Lon: -87.48929
125 S. Spradlin Rd., Dickson, TN 37055
tanbarkcmp@aol.com
tanbarkcampground.tripod.com
See ad this page.

DOVER — A3 *Henry, Houston, Paris, Paris Landing, Stewart*

BUMPUS MILLS (Public Corps) From town, W 4 mi on Hwy 120, follow signs (L). Call 877-444-6777 to make reservations. 2015 rates: $17 to $20. May 2 to Sep 1. (931)232-8831

DYERSBURG — B1 *Dyer*

DYERSBURG See also Caruthersville, MO.

ELIZABETHTON — D6 *Carter*

STONEY CREEK RV PARK (RV Spaces) From Jct of US-19E/321 & Hwy 91: Go N 2.8 mi on Hwy 91 to Blue Springs Rd, then S 0.2 mi to Willowsprings Rd, then N 1.2 mi (stay left at Y) to Price Rd, then NW 200 ft (R). **FAC:** Paved/gravel rds. (12 spaces). Avail: 7 gravel, back-ins (20 x 50), 7 full hkups (30/50 amps), seasonal sites, dump. Pets OK. No tents. 2015 rates: $17 to $20. No CC.
(423)474-3505 Lat: 36.37754, Lon: -82.13777
108 Price Rd., Elizabethton, TN 37643

GAINESBORO — B5 *Jackson*

SALT LICK CREEK (Public Corps) From town, W 4 mi on Hwy 25 to Hwy 80, N 2 mi to Hwy 85, E 8 mi to Smith Bend Rd, S 1 mi to park access rd, follow signs (E). Call 877-444-6777 for reservations. 2015 rates: $15 to $26. Apr 16 to Sep 1. (931)678-4718

GALLATIN — B4 *Sumner*

BLEDSOE CREEK
(State Pk) From Jct of US-31 & SR-25, E 6 mi on SR-25 to Ziegler Fort Rd, S 1.3 mi (L). **FAC:** Paved rds. 57 gravel, 19 pull-thrus (35 x 55), back-ins (35 x 55), some side by side hkups, 57 W, 57 E (30/50 amps), tent sites, dump, laundry, fire rings, controlled access. **REC:** Old Hickory Lake: fishing, playground. Pets OK. Partial handicap access. 14 day max stay, 2015 rates: $20 TO $25. No CC.
(615)452-3706 Lat: 36.37837, Lon: -86.36346
400 Ziegler Fort Rd, Gallatin, TN 37066
tnstateparks.itinio.com
See ad page 1067 (Welcome Section).

CAGES BEND (Public Corps) From Jct of US-31E & Cages Bend Rd, S 3.5 mi on Cages Bend Rd, follow signs (L). Call 877-444-6777 for reservations. 2015 rates: $20 to $24. Apr 1 to Oct 15. (615)824-4989

GATLINBURG — B4 *Cocke, Sevier*

ADVENTURE BOUND CAMPING RESORT-GATLINBURG **Ratings: 7/7.5/6** (Campground) 2015 rates: $36 to $62. Apr 1 to Nov 4. (865)436-4434 4609 E Pkwy (Hwy 321 S), Gatlinburg, TN 37738

Get the Facts! Essential tips and travel info for can be found in the Welcome Section at the beginning of each State/Province.

CAMP LECONTE LUXURY OUTDOOR RESORT
Ratings: 9/9.5★/10 (Campground) From Jct of US-441 & US-321N (traffic light #3 in downtown Gatlinburg), E 4 mi on US-321N/East Parkway (L). **FAC:** Paved rds. 18 gravel, patios, 11 pull-thrus (28 x 60), back-ins (28 x 35), 18 full hkups (30/50 amps), WiFi, tent sites, rentals, laundry, fire rings, firewood. **REC:** heated pool, playground. Pet restrict(B). Partial handicap access. Eco-friendly, 2015 rates: $39 to $59. Disc: AAA, military. Mar 1 to Nov 30.
AAA Approved
(865)436-8831 Lat: 35.73146, Lon: -83.44695
1739 East Parkway, Gatlinburg, TN 37738
stay@campleconte.com
www.campleconte.com
See ad this page, 1068.

CAMPING IN THE SMOKIES **Ratings: 5.5/7/6.5** (Campground) 2015 rates: $40 to $55. Apr 1 to Oct 31. (865)430-0350 1640 E. Parkway, Gatlinburg, TN 37738

GREAT SMOKY JELLYSTONE CAMP-RESORT **Ratings: 9.5/9.5★/9.5** (Campground) 2015 rates: $33 to $63. Mar 18 to Dec 1. (423)487-5534 4946 Hooper Hwy, Gatlinburg, TN 37722

GREAT SMOKY MTN/ELKMONT (Natl Pk) From Jct of US-441 S & Little River Rd, W 8 mi on Little River Rd (L). NOTE: Tunnel construction may restrict RVs-call (888)355-1849 for information. 2015 rates: $17 to $23. (865)436-1271

GREENBRIER ISLAND CAMPGROUND **Ratings: 5.5/6.5/7.5** (Campground) 2015 rates: $28 to $30. Apr 1 to Oct 31. (865)436-4243 2353 E Pkwy, Gatlinburg, TN 37738

OUTDOOR RESORTS/GATLINBURG **Ratings: 10/8.5★/9.5** (Condo Pk) 2015 rates: $35 to $45. (865)436-5861 4229 E Pkwy (Hwy 321N), Gatlinburg, TN 37738

SMOKY BEAR CAMPGROUND
Ratings: 10/10★/10 (RV Park) E-bnd: From Jct of I-40 & US 321S (exit 435), S 17.2 mi on US 321S (R); or W-bnd: From Jct of I-40 & US 73S (Exit 440), S 2.3 mi on US 73S to US 321S, S 11.6 mi (R). **FAC:** Paved rds. 8 paved, 36 all weather, 9 pull-thrus (30 x 80), back-ins (30 x 70), 44 full hkups (30/50 amps), WiFi, tent sites, rentals, laundry, fire rings, firewood. **REC:** heated pool, whirlpool, playground. Pets OK. Partial handicap access. Big rig sites, eco-friendly, 2015 rates: $39 to $48. Disc: military. Mar 15 to Nov 30.
(865)436-8372 Lat: 35.76258, Lon: -83.30222
4857 East Pkwy, Gatlinburg, TN 37738
smokybearcamp@comcast.net
www.smokybearcampground.com
See ad this page, 1068.

TWIN CREEK RV RESORT
Ratings: 10/10★/10 (RV Park) From Jct of US-441 & US-321N (traffic light #3 in downtown Gatlinburg), E 2 mi on US-321N/East Parkway (R). **FAC:** Paved rds. 85 paved, patios, 17 pull-thrus (30 x 55), back-ins (30 x 60), 85 full hkups (30/50 amps), cable, WiFi, rentals, laundry, groc, fire rings, firewood. **REC:** heated pool, wading pool, whirlpool, Dudley Creek: fishing, playground. Pet restrict(B/Q). No tents. Big rig sites, eco-friendly, 2015 rates: $54 to $62. Disc: AAA, military. Mar 29 to Dec 1.
(865)436-7081 Lat: 35.72597, Lon: -83.48291
1202 E Parkway, Gatlinburg, TN 37738
Sns@twincreekrvresort.com
www.twincreekrvresort.com
See ad this page, 1068.

GREAT SMOKY MOUNTAIN NATIONAL PARK — E5 *Blount, Cocke, Sevier*

GREAT SMOKY MTN NATL PK See also Gatlinburg, Newport, Pigeon Forge, Sevierville, Townsend; Cherokee, NC & Whittier, NC.

TN

"Friendliest Campground in the Smokies"

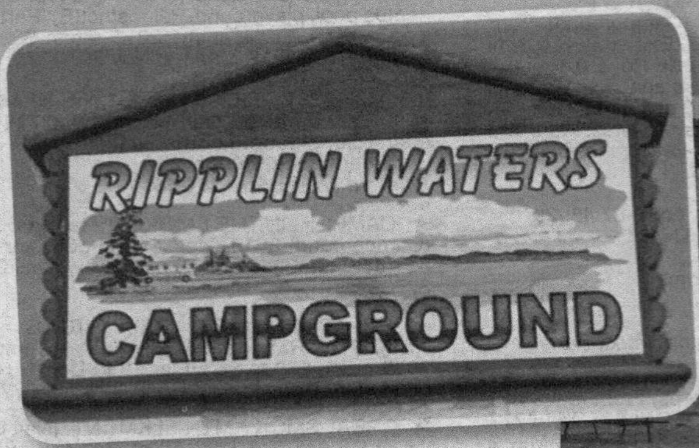

See listing Sevierville, TN

BIG RIGS WELCOME

Over 156 Sites For Your Total Comfort

- Beautiful Riverfront Sites!
- Rental Cabins
- Full Hookups • 30/50 Amps
- Great Fishing!

Great Entertainment Nearby

- The Great Smoky Mountains
- Cades Cove
- 18-Hole Golf Course Across River
- Flea Market Across Street
- Live Entertainment Close By - Dollywood
- **Foothills of the Smoky Mountains**

Kids 6 & Under FREE IN CAMPGROUND

For Information or Reservations
(865) 453-4169
Toll Free (888) 747-7546
www.ripplinwatersrv.com

1930 Winfield Dunn Pkwy. (Hwy 66)
Sevierville, TN 37876

VISA MasterCard American Express Discover

Good Sam Park

Good Sam RATED 8/8.5★/8.5

GREENBACK — B6 *Loudon*

LOTTERDALE COVE (Public) From jct Hwy 95 & US 411: Go 3-1/4 mi SW on US 411, then follow signs 4-1/4 mi N. (865)856-7284

GREENEVILLE — D5 *Greene*

DAVY CROCKETT BIRTH PLACE HISTORICAL PARK (State Pk) From Jct of US 11E & S Heritage, SE 0.7 mi on S. Heritage to Old SR-34, E 0.6 mi to Davy Crockett Rd, SW and follow signs for next 2 mi. **FAC:** Paved rds. 71 gravel, 39 pull-thrus (28 x 50), back-ins (28 x 50), 40 full hkups, 31 W, 31 E (30/50 amps), tent sites, dump, firewood, controlled access. **REC:** pool $, wading pool, Nolichuckey River: fishing, playground. Pets OK. Partial handicap access. 14 day max stay, 2015 rates: $16 to $27.50. No CC.
(423)257-2167 Lat: 36.20928, Lon: -82.65831
1245 Davy Crockett Park Rd, Limestone, TN 37681
tnstateparks.itinio.com
See ad page 1067 (Welcome Section).

KINSER PARK (Public) From jct US 321 & Hwy 70: Go 5 mi S on Hwy 70, then 5 mi E on Allens Bridge Rd. 2015 rates: $25. Mar 29 to Oct 1. (423)639-5912

HARRIMAN — B6 *Roane*

CANEY CREEK RV RESORT & MARINA **Ratings: 9.5/9★/9** (RV Park) 2015 rates: $49 to $65. (865)882-4042 3615 Roane State Hwy, Harriman, TN 37748

HARTFORD — E5 *Cocke*

PIGEON RIVER CAMPGROUND
Ratings: 7.5/9.5★/7.5 (Campground) From Jct of I-40 & Hartford Rd (Exit 447), N 0.9 mi on Hartford Rd (L).

CAMP RIGHT ON THE PIGEON RIVER
Easy on-off access from I-40. One hr from Asheville or Gatlinburg. Bordering the Great Smoky Mtns National Park. Pool, Wi-Fi, store, private bathrooms. Close to rafting, hiking, fishing & biking. Adventure packages available.

FAC: Gravel rds. 12 gravel, back-ins (30 x 50), 12 full hkups (30/50 amps), WiFi Hotspot, tent sites, rentals, laundry. **REC:** pool, Pigeon River: fishing, rec open to public. Pets OK. Eco-friendly, 2015 rates: $35 to $60. Feb 1 to Nov 30.
(888)820-8771 Lat: 35.48575, Lon: -83.09431
3375 Hartford Rd, Hartford, TN 37753
trips@smokymountainrafting.com
Campinginthesmokymountains.com
See ad this page, 1068.

HENDERSON — C2 *Chester*

CHICKASAW (State Pk) From Jct of US-45 & SR-100, W 7.6 mi on SR-100 (L). **FAC:** Paved rds. 52 paved, 8 pull-thrus (20 x 60), back-ins (25 x 40), 52 W, 52 E (20/30 amps), tent sites, dump, restaurant. **REC:** Lake Placid: swim, fishing, golf, playground. Pets OK. Partial handicap access. 14 day max stay, 2015 rates: $20.
(731)989-5141 Lat: 35.39421, Lon: -88.77162
20 Cabin Lane, Henderson, TN 38340
tnstateparks.itinio.com
See ad page 1067 (Welcome Section).

HENNING — B1 *Lauderdale*

FORT PILLOW STATE HISTORIC AREA (State Pk) From jct US 51 & Hwy 87: Go 17 mi W on 87, then 1 mi N on Hwy 207. **FAC.** 32 grass, tent sites. **REC:** playground. Pets OK. Partial handicap access. No CC.
(731)738-5581 Lat: 35.6382, Lon: -89.8383
3122 Park Rd., Henning, TN 38041
tnstateparks.itinio.com
See ad page 1067 (Welcome Section).

HERMITAGE — B4 *Wilson*

SEVEN POINTS REC AREA (Public Corps) From town, E 10 mi on I-40 to exit 221B (Old Hickory Blvd), S 0.7 mi to Bell Rd, E 1 mi to New Hope Rd, S 1.5 mi to Stewart Ferry Pike, E 1.5 mi (R). 2015 rates: $20 to $24. Mar 1 to Oct 31. (615)889-1975

HOHENWALD — C3 *Lewis*

NATCHEZ TRACE **Ratings: 7/8.5★/8.5** (Membership Pk) 2015 rates: $24. (800)405-6188 1363 Napier Rd, Hohenwald, TN 38462

NATCHEZ TRACE PKWY/MERIWETHER LEWIS CAMPGROUND (Natl Pk) From Hohenwald, E 8 mi on Hwy 20 at MP-385.9 (E). (800)305-7417

Our travel services section will help you find services that you'll find handy in your travels.

HORNSBY — C2 *Hardeman*

BIG BUCK CAMPING RESORT **Ratings: 7.5/6/7** (Membership Pk) 2015 rates: $30 to $39. (731)658-2246 205 Sparks Rd, Hornsby, TN 38044

HURRICANE MILLS — B3 *Humphreys*

BUFFALO I-40 KOA Ratings: 8.5/9★/8 (Campground) From Jct of I-40 & Hwy 13 (exit 143), N 500 ft on Hwy 13 to Barren Hollow Rd (local rd), E 0.6 mi (R). **FAC:** Gravel rds. (47 spaces). Avail: 42 gravel, patios, 27 pull-thrus (22 x 50), back-ins (25 x 40), 23 full hkups, 19 W, 19 E (30/50 amps), seasonal sites, WiFi, tent sites, rentals, dump, laundry, groc, LP gas, firewood. **REC:** pool, playground, rec open to public. Pet restrict(B). Partial handicap access. Big rig sites, 2015 rates: $34 to $45. Disc: AAA, military.
AAA Approved
(931)296-1306 Lat: 35.88104, Lon: -87.79208
473 Barren Hollow Rd, Hurricane Mills, TN 37078
buffaloriverkoa@yahoo.com
www.koa.com

LORETTA LYNN'S RANCH
Ratings: 8.5/9★/9 (Campground) From Jct of I-40 & SR-13 (Exit 143), N 8 mi on SR-13 (L). Caution: Follow directions, not GPS.

CAMPGROUND WITH CONCERT VENUE
Loretta Lynn's Ranch offers: Concerts, RV Park/Cabins, Tours, Museums, Gift Shops, Pool, Fishing, Canoes, Trail Rides, and more. Just an hour outside of Nashville in the beautiful countryside. A GREAT Family Destination!

FAC: Paved/gravel rds. 282 Avail: 36 paved, 42 gravel, 204 grass, 76 pull-thrus (20 x 60), back-ins (20 x 60), 78 full hkups, 204 W, 204 E (30/50 amps), WiFi, tent sites, rentals, dump, laundry, groc, fire rings, firewood. **REC:** pool, pond, fishing, playground,

Check out a campground's ad. In it you might find a locator map, photos, and a lot more information about the park to help you find just the right place to stay.

TN

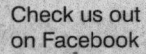

See listing Hurricane Mills, TN

HURRICANE MILLS (CONT)

LORETTA LYNN'S RANCH (CONT)
rec open to public. Pets OK. Partial handicap access. 2015 rates: $29.50 to $36.50. Disc: AAA, military. AAA Approved
(931)296-7700 Lat: 35.97752, Lon: -87.76380
8000 Highway 13S, Hurricane Mills, TN 37078
res@lorettalynn.com
www.lorettalynnranch.net
See ad opposite page, 1068.

Things to See and Do

→ LORETTA LYNN'S RANCH Tour this western town & museum and see the Old Grist Mill, coal mine, Loretta Lynn's plantation home and her childhood home in Butcher Holler. Complex also includes snack & gift shops. Hours: 9am to 5pm. Adult fee: $25.
(931)296-7700 Lat: 35.97746, Lon: -87.76308
8000 Highway 13S, Hurricane Mills, TN 37078
www.lorettalynnranch.net
See ad opposite page.

JACKSON — C2 *Madison*

↓ JACKSON RV PARK (MHP)
Ratings: 4/NA/6 (RV Area in MHP) From Jct of I 40 & US 412 (Exit 79), S 0.1 mi on US 412 (L). **FAC:** Paved rds. (41 spaces). 36 Avail: 15 paved, 21 gravel, 15 pull-thrus (15 x 50), back-ins (25 x 80), mostly side by side hkups, 36 full hkups (30/50 amps), seasonal sites, WiFi, laundry. Pets OK. No tents. 2015 rates: $30. No CC.
(731)234-2009 Lat: 35.65448, Lon: -88.87169
2223 Hollywood Dr, Jackson, TN 38305
www.jacksonrvpark.com
See ad this page.

↗ PARKWAY VILLAGE MH AND RV COMMUNITY
Ratings: 7.5/NA/8 (RV Area in MHP) From Jct of I-40 & US 70 (Exit 87), SW 3.5 mi on US 70/W Whitehall St (R). **FAC:** Paved rds. (126 spaces). Avail: 28 paved, patios, 2 pull-thrus (30 x 160), back-ins (32 x 80), some side by side hkups, 28 full hkups (30/50 amps), seasonal sites, WiFi Hotspot, laundry. **REC:** pool. Pet restrict(B/Q). No tents. Big rig sites, 2015 rates: $30.
(731)423-3331 Lat: 35.63940, Lon: -88.78071
1243 Whitehall St, Jackson, TN 38301
parkwayvillage@towermgmt.com
www.parkwayvillagemhc.com

JAMESTOWN — A6 *Fentress, Pickett*

↖ CHEROKEE RIDGE CAMP N CABINS **Ratings: 7/7.5/6.5** (Campground) 2015 rates: $25 to $30. (931)879-7696 150 Laurel Creek Campground Rd, Jamestown, TN 38556

↓ EAST FORK RESORT & STABLES **Ratings: 6/8.5/7** (Campground) 2015 rates: $18 to $30. Apr 1 to Nov 1. (931)879-1176 3598 S York Hwy, Jamestown, TN 38556

↗ MAPLE HILL RV PARK & CABINS **Ratings: 6.5/8.5/7** (Campground) 2015 rates: $27 to $30. (931)879-3025 1386 North York Hwy (US 127), Jamestown, TN 38556

↖ PICKETT
(State Pk) From Jct of US-127/Jamestown Bypass & SR-154, NE 12 mi on SR-154 to park access rd, NW 1 mi (L). CAUTION: Maximum length 25 ft. **FAC:** Paved rds. 32 Avail: 16 gravel, 16 dirt, no slide-outs, patios, 8 pull-thrus (12 x 35), back-ins (15 x 35), some side by side hkups, 32 W, 32 E (30 amps), tent sites, dump, laundry, firewood, controlled access. **REC:** Arch Lake: swim, fishing, playground. Pets OK. 14 day max stay, 2015 rates: $16.
(931)879-5821 Lat: 36.53945, Lon: -84.80085
4605 Pickett Park Hwy, Jamestown, TN 38556
tnstateparks.itinio.com
See ad page 1067 (Welcome Section).

JEFFERSON CITY — D5 *Grainger*

↑ GREENLEE OF MAY SPRINGS (Public) From Jct of US 11E & SR-92, N 5 mi on SR-92 to SR-375 (Lake Shore Rd), NE 4.5 mi to Maysprings Rd, S 0.5 mi (E). For reservations call (866)828-4802. 2015 rates: $25. (866)828-4802

↑ TVA/CHEROKEE DAM-CHEROKEE LAKE (Public) From town, W 1.5 mi on US-11E to Hwy 92, N 4.5 mi, follow signs (R). 2015 rates: $17 to $26. Mar 14 to Nov 17. (800)882-5263

JELLICO — A6 *Campbell*

↖ INDIAN MOUNTAIN
(State Pk) From jct I-75 (exit #160 & US 25 NW: Follow signs 3 mi N to park. **FAC.** 49 grass, 49 W, 49 E (30 amps), tent sites, dump. **REC:** pool, playground. Pets OK. No CC.
(423)784-7958 Lat: 36.58349, Lon: -84.13750
143 State Park Circle, Jellico, TN 37762
tnstateparks.itinio.com
See ad page 1067 (Welcome Section).

JOHNSON CITY — D6 *Washington*

JOHNSON CITY See also Bristol, Elizabethton, Jonesborough, Kingsport & Unicoi.

JONESBOROUGH — D6 *Washington*

↓ RIVERPARK CAMPGROUND
Ratings: 9/10★/9 (Campground) From Jct of I 26/Hwy 19/23 & Hwy 81 (Exit 37), N 5.0 mi on Hwy 81 (R). **FAC:** All weather rds. 32 Avail: 32 all weather, 3 pull-thrus (30 x 60), back-ins (30 x 50), 32 full hkups (30/50 amps), cable, WiFi, tent sites, rentals, dump, laundry, LP gas, fire rings, firewood. **REC:** Nolichucky River: fishing, rec open to public. Pet restrict(Q). Partial handicap access. Eco-friendly, 2015 rates: $31 to $41. Disc: military.
(423)753-5359 Lat: 36.18840, Lon: -82.45311
3937 Hwy 81 South, Jonesborough, TN 37659
bngant@rparkcamp.comcastbiz.net
www.riverparkcampground.net
See ad this page, 1068.

↘ RIVERVIEW CAMPGROUND **Ratings: 2/5.5/6** (Campground) 2015 rates: $27. (423)753-2577 408 Hwy 107, Jonesborough, TN 37659

From fishing along the Cape to boating on the Great Lakes, we've put the Spotlight on North America's most popular travel destinations. Turn to the Spotlight articles in our State and Province sections to learn more.

KINGSPORT — D5 *Sullivan*

→ ROCKY TOP CAMPGROUND & RV PARK
Ratings: 9/10★/9.5 (Campground) From Jct of I-81 & Exit 63 (Airport Pkwy), NW 0.4 mi on Airport Pkwy/Browder Rd to Pearl Ln, W 0.6 mi (R). **FAC:** Paved rds. 35 Avail: 35 all weather, patios, 8 pull-thrus (30 x 65), back-ins (30 x 60), 35 full hkups (30/50 amps), cable, WiFi, tent sites, rentals, dump, laundry, groc, LP gas, fire rings, firewood. **REC.** Pets OK. Big rig sites, eco-friendly, 2015 rates: $41.50. Disc: AAA, military.
(423)323-2535 Lat: 36.51101, Lon: -82.43996
496 Pearl Lane, Blountville, TN 37617
camping@rockytopcampground.com
rockytopcampground.com
See ad pages 1077, 1068.

→ WARRIORS PATH
(State Pk) From Jct of I-81 & SR-36 (exit 59), N 1.3 mi on SR-36 to Hemlock Rd, E 1.8 mi (L). **FAC:** Paved rds. 94 paved, back-ins (30 x 40), 94 W, 94 E (30/50 amps), tent sites, dump. **REC:** pool $, Patrick Henry Lake: fishing, marina, golf, shuffleboard, playground. Pets OK. Partial handicap access. 14 day max stay, 2015 rates: $20.
(423)239-8531 Lat: 36.49891, Lon: -82.48718
490 Hemlock Rd, Kingsport, TN 37663
tnstateparks.itinio.com
See ad page 1067 (Welcome Section).

KINGSTON — B6 *Roane*

↓ RILEY CREEK CAMPGROUND (Public) From Jct. I-40 & Hwy 58, S 5.6 mi to Old Hood Rd., E .5 mi (R). 2015 rates: $30. Apr 1 to Oct 31. (865)717-4198

KNOXVILLE — B6 *Knox*

KNOXVILLE AREA MAP

Symbols on map indicate towns within a 50 mile radius of Knoxville where campgrounds are listed. Check listings for more information.

See also Caryville, Clinton, Cosby, Dandridge, Gatlinburg, Greenback, Harriman, Jefferson City, Kingston, Lenoir City, Loudon, Maynardville, Morristown, Newport, Norris, Oliver Springs, Pigeon Forge, Sevierville, Sweetwater, Townsend & Vonore.

TN

KNOXVILLE (CONT)

➔ RACCOON VALLEY RV PARK **Ratings: 6.5/8/8** (Campground) 2015 rates: $24 to $25. (865)947-9776 908 E Raccoon Valley Rd, Heiskell, TN 37754

↓ SOUTHLAKE RV PARK **Ratings: 6.5/8/6** (Campground) 2015 rates: $35 to $38. (865)573-1837 3730 Maryville Pike, Knoxville, TN 37920

↑ **VOLUNTEER PARK FAMILY CAMPGROUND**
Ratings: 9/8.5★/7.5 (Campground) From Jct of I-75 & Raccoon Valley Rd (exit 117), W 0.2 mi on Raccoon Valley Rd (L). **FAC:** Paved/gravel rds. (140 spaces). 100 Avail: 30 paved, 70 gravel, patios, 42 pull-thrus (24 x 50), back-ins (24 x 50), 82 full hkups, 18 W, 18 E (30/50 amps), seasonal sites, cable, WiFi, tent sites, rentals, dump, laundry, groc, LP gas, fire rings, firewood. **REC:** heated pool, wading pool, playground. Pet restrict(Q). Partial handicap access. 2015 rates: $25 to $38. Disc: AAA, military.
(865)938-6600 Lat: 36.10271, Lon: -84.02594
9514 Diggs Gap Rd, Heiskell, TN 37754
volunteer.park@yahoo.com
www.volparktn.com
See ad this page, 1068.

LA VERGNE — B4 *Robertson*

↖ POOLE KNOBS REC AREA (Public Corps) From Smyrna, N 3 mi on US 41 to Fergus Rd, N 1.5 mi to Jones Mill Rd, NE 4 mi (E). Call 877-444-6777 for reservations. 2015 rates: $14 to $24. May 1 to Oct 31. (615)459-6948

LAWRENCEBURG — C3 *Lawrence*

← **DAVID CROCKETT**
(State Pk) From Jct of US-43 & US-64, W 1.4 mi on US-64 (R). **FAC:** Paved rds. 107 paved, back-ins (24 x 40), 107 W, 107 E (30 amps), tent sites, dump, restaurant, controlled access. **REC:** pool $, Lindsey Lake: fishing, playground, rec open to public. Pets OK. Partial handicap access. 14 day max stay, 2015 rates: $20.
(931)762-9408 Lat: 35.24293, Lon: -87.35422
1400 W. Gaines, Lawrenceburg, TN 38464
tnstateparks.itinio.com
See ad page 1067 (Welcome Section).

LEBANON — B4 *Wilson*

↓ **CEDARS OF LEBANON**
(State Pk) From Jct of I-40 & US-231 (exit 238), S 6.4 mi on US-231 (L). **FAC:** Paved rds. 117 gravel, 45 pull-thrus (20 x 55), back-ins (30 x 50), 117 W, 117 E (30/50 amps), tent sites, dump, laundry, fire rings, firewood. **REC:** pool $, playground. Pets OK. Partial handicap access. 14 day max stay, 2015 rates: $20.
(615)443-2769 Lat: 36.09378, Lon: -86.33527
328 Cedar Forrest Rd, Lebanon, TN 37090
tnstateparks.itinio.com
See ad page 1067 (Welcome Section).

↙ **NASHVILLE EAST/LEBANON KOA Ratings: 8.5/9★/9** (RV Park) From Jct of I-40 & SR-109 (Eastbound Exit 232A) (Westbound Exit 232), S 400 yds on SR-109 to 2nd left turn, E 2 mi on Safari Camp Rd (R); or From Jct of I-840 & Exit 72-B, NW 3.6 mi on SR-109 to Safari Camp Rd, E 2 mi (R). **FAC:** Paved/gravel rds. (88 spaces). Avail: 54 gravel, 31 pull-thrus (30 x 75), back-ins (25 x 50), 28 full hkups, 26 W, 26 E (30/50 amps), seasonal sites, WiFi, tent sites, rentals, dump, laundry, groc, LP gas, fire rings, firewood. **REC:** pool, playground. Pets OK. Big rig sites, eco-friendly, 2015 rates: $32.10 to $40.80. Disc: military.
AAA Approved
(615)449-5527 Lat: 36.18356, Lon: -86.36952
2100 Safari Camp Rd, Lebanon, TN 37090
nashvilleeast@koa.com
www.nashvilleeastkoa.com

LENOIR CITY — B6 *Loudon, Roane*

↑ LAZY ACRES RV PARK **Ratings: 6/7.5/6** (Campground) 2015 rates: $24 to $30. (865)986-3539 7502 Jackson Bend Rd, Lenoir City, TN 37772

➔ **SOARING EAGLE CAMPGROUND & RV PARK INC**
Ratings: 8/9.5★/9 (Campground) From Jct of I-40 & Buttermilk Rd West/Exit 360: Go N 50 ft on Buttermilk Rd West (R). **FAC:** Paved/gravel rds. (110 spaces). 85 Avail: 1 paved, 84 gravel, patios, 85 pull-thrus (20 x 70), 85 full hkups (30/50 amps), seasonal sites, WiFi, tent sites, dump, laundry, groc, LP gas, fire rings, firewood. **REC:** pool, Watts Bar Lake: fishing. Pet restrict(B). Big rig sites, eco-friendly, 2015 rates: $31 to $37. Disc: AAA, military.
(865)376-9017 Lat: 35.87217, Lon: -84.37732
3152 Buttermilk Rd West, Lenoir City, TN 37771
reservations@campatsoaringeagle.com
www.soaringeaglecampgroundrvpark.com
See ad this page, 1068.

↑ TVA/MELTON HILL RESERVOIR (Public) From Jct of I-40 & Hwy 95, N 1 mi on Hwy 95 (R). 2015 rates: $17 to $26. Mar 14 to Nov 17. (800)882-5263

↓ YARBERRY PENINSULA-FORT LOUDOUN LAKE (Public) From Jct I-75 & US-321, SE 3 mi on US-321 to paved rd, follow signs E 0.5 mi (E). 2015 rates: $27 to $29. Mar 15 to Nov 1. (865)755-3471

LEXINGTON — C2 *Henderson*

↑ BEECH LAKE FAMILY CAMPING RESORT **Ratings: 5/5.5/6.5** (Campground) 2015 rates: $24. (731)968-9542 495 Beech Lake Campground Road, Lexington, TN 38351

LIVINGSTON — B5 *Overton*

↖ LILLYDALE REC AREA (Public Corps) From town, NW 2 mi on SR-52 to Hwy 1209, NE 1.5 mi to Hwy 294, NW 6 mi, follow signs (E). Call 877-444-6777 for reservations. 2015 rates: $10 to $24. Apr 25 to Sep 8. (931)823-4155

↓ OBEY RIVER PARK (Public Corps) From town, SW 3 mi on SR-111 (R). 2015 rates: $15 to $24. Apr 11 to Oct 14. (931)864-6388

↖ **STANDING STONE STATE RUSTIC PARK**
(State Pk) From Jct of Hwys 111 & 52 (in Livingston), W 8.7 mi on Hwy 52 to SR-136, S 0.5 mi (L). Note: 45' RV length limit. **FAC:** Paved rds. 36 Avail: 1 paved, 35 gravel, 1 pull-thrus (32 x 50), back-ins (32 x 50), 36 W, 36 E (30/50 amps), tent sites, dump. **REC:** pool $, wading pool, Standing Stone Lake: fishing, playground. Pets OK. 14 day max stay, 2015 rates: $20.
(931)823-6347 Lat: 36.48431, Lon: -85.40669
1674 Standing Stone Park Hwy, Hilham, TN 38568
tnstateparks.itinio.com
See ad page 1067 (Welcome Section).

↑ WILLOW GROVE (Public Corps) From town, NW 2 mi on SR-52 to Hwy 1209, NE 1.5 mi to Hwy 294, NW 6 mi, follow signs (E). 2015 rates: $18 to $24. May 15 to Sep 1. (931)823-4285

LOUDON — B6 *Loudon*

↓ **EXPRESS RV PARK**
Ratings: 7/8★/4.5 (Campground) From Jct I-75 (Exit 72) & Hwy 72: Go 1/4 mi W on Hwy 72 (R). **FAC:** Paved rds. 15 paved, 15 pull-thrus (20 x 55), mostly side by side hkups, 15 W, 15 E (30/50 amps), WiFi, tent sites, rentals, dump, laundry. **REC:** pool. Pets OK. 2015 rates: $25. Disc: AAA.
(865)458-5855 Lat: 35.73436, Lon: -84.39820
15100 Hwy 72, Loudon, TN 37774
Abviloudon@gmail.com
See ad this page.

LOUISVILLE — E4 *Blount*

Travel Services

↗ **CAMPING WORLD OF LOUISVILLE/KNOXVILLE** As the nation's largest retailer of RV supplies, accessories, services and new and used RVs, Camping World is committed to making your total RV experience better. RV Accessories: (855)244-8918. **SERVICES:** RV appliance, staffed RV wash, restrooms, RV Sales.

RV Park ratings you can rely on!

LOUISVILLE (CONT)

CAMPING WORLD (CONT)
RV supplies, LP, RV accessible. waiting room. Hours: 8am to 6pm.
(888)495-3315 Lat: 35.854903, Lon: -83.962671
4223 Airport Highway, Louisville, TN 37777
www.campingworld.com

MANCHESTER — C5 *Coffee*

MANCHESTER KOA
Ratings: 10/9.5★/9.5 (Campground) From Jct of I-24 & US-41 (exit 114), SE 300 ft on US-41 to Campground Rd, N 0.5 mi (R).

Easy on/off hwy, between Nashville & Chattanooga, shopping & dining close, Big, long, wide pull-thrus, 50 amps, cable, pool, spa. Free fishing in stocked pond, nice, new looking, shady country atmosphere. Highest Awards.

FAC: All weather rds. 4 paved, 33 all weather, 37 pull-thrus (37 x 65), 37 full hkups (30/50 amps), cable, WiFi, tent sites, rentals, dump, laundry, groc, LP gas, fire rings, firewood. **REC:** pool, whirlpool, pond, fishing, playground. Pets OK. Big rig sites, 2015 rates: $46 to $65. Disc: military.
(800)562-7785 Lat: 35.46326, Lon: -86.05391
586 Campground Rd, Manchester, TN 37355
manchesterkoa@gmail.com
www.koa.com
See ad this page.

OLD STONE FORT STATE ARCHAEOLOGICAL PARK
(State Pk) From Jct of I-24 & Hwy 53 (exit 110), W 0.8 mi on Hwy 53 to US-41, N 0.7 mi (L). CAUTION: Must drive over narrow bridge (11 ft wide) to get to campground. 10 ton wt limit for 2 axles, 18 ton for 3 axles. **FAC:** Paved rds. 51 paved, back-ins (20 x 60), 51 W, 51 E (30 amps), tent sites, dump, controlled access. **REC:** Duck River: fishing, playground. Pets OK. Partial handicap access. 14 day max stay, 2015 rates: $20.
(931)723-5073 Lat: 35.49496, Lon: -86.10269
732 Stone Fort Dr, Manchester, TN 37355
tnstateparks.itinio.com
See ad page 1067 (Welcome Section).

MAYNARDVILLE — D4 *Union*

BIG RIDGE
(State Pk) From Jct of I-75 & Hwy 61 (Exit 122), E 11.6 mi on Hwy 61 (L). Note: 35' RV length limit. **FAC:** Paved rds. 50 paved, 1 pull-thrus (24 x 70), back-ins (25 x 50), 50 W, 50 E (30 amps), tent sites, dump, laundry, fire rings. **REC:** Norris Lake: swim, fishing, playground. Pets OK. Partial handicap access, no tents. 14 day max stay, 2015 rates: $20.
(865)992-5523 Lat: 36.24000, Lon: -83.93212
1015 Big Ridge Park Rd, Maynardville, TN 37807
tnstateparks.itinio.com
See ad page 1067 (Welcome Section).

MEMPHIS — C1 *Shelby*

MEMPHIS See also Millington; Marion, AR; West Memphis, AR; Horn Lake, MS; Robinsonville, MS.

SAVE! Over $1,000 in coupons can be found at the front of the Guide!

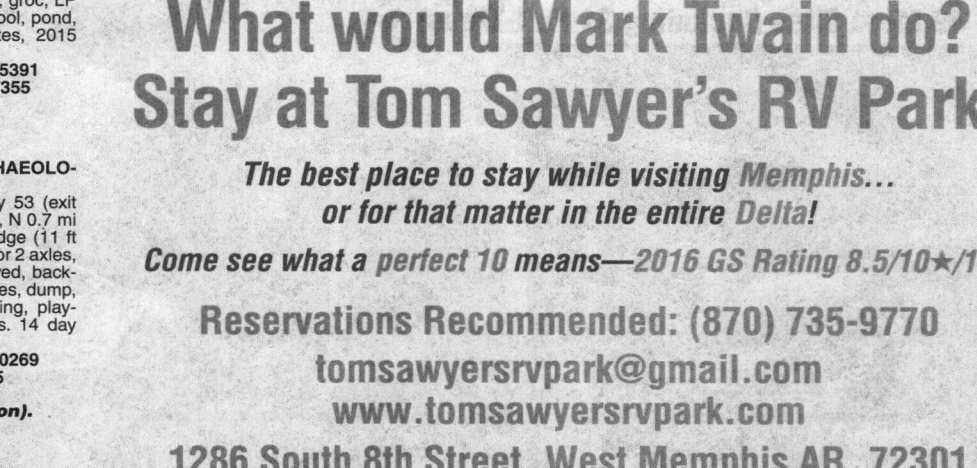

TN

NORTH MISSISSIPPI'S TOP PREMIER PARK • MINUTES FROM MEMPHIS

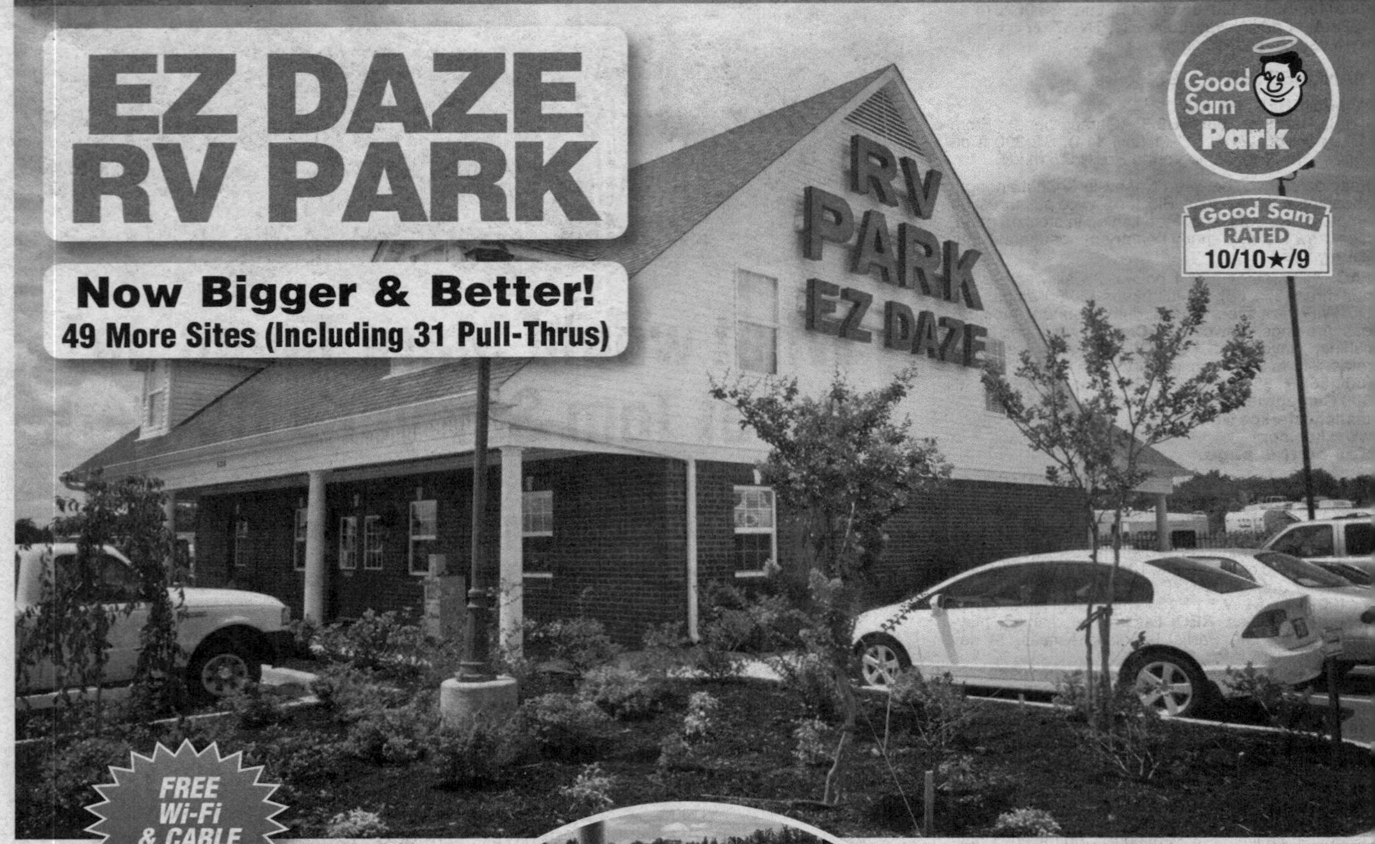

BIG RIG FRIENDLY

- Concrete Pads with Patios
- Full Hook Ups
- Superior A/C Bath and Laundry
- Pool and Hot Tub
- Massage Therapist
- Beauti Control Sold Here
- Free Facials
- Veranda • Pet Friendly
- Seasonal Sites Available

PLUS

- Private Meeting Facilities with Kitchen
- 3 Large Family Restrooms

RESERVATIONS
662-342-7720
www.ezdazervpark.com
ezdazervpark@yahoo.com

We go the extra mile for safety with a reinforced storm room/group meeting room

NEARBY ATTRACTIONS

• Graceland • Casinos • Memphis Zoo
• Fedex Forum • Landers Center
• Beale Street Blues District
• Snowden Grove Ballfield & Park

CAMPING CLUBS & RALLIES WELCOME

Behind Southaven RV Sales and Repairs

EZ On/Off I-55 Exit 287 (Church Road)
536 We Ross Parkway
Southaven, MS 38671

MEMPHIS (CONT)

AGRICENTER RV PARK
(Public) From Jct of I-40 & Germantown Rd (W-bnd-exit 16A, E-bnd-exit 16B), S 4.7 mi on Germantown Pkwy to Timbercreek Rd, W 0.1 mi (follow signs to RV park in complex) (L). **FAC:** Gravel rds. 300 Avail: 175 gravel, 125 grass, 300 pull-thrus (20 x 70), 144 full hkups, 156 W, 156 E (30/50 amps), WiFi, dump, laundry. **REC:** pond, fishing. Pets OK. Partial handicap access, no tents. 2015 rates: $27 to $30. ATM.
(901)355-1977 Lat: 35.12758, Lon: -89.80566
7777 Walnut Grove Rd, Memphis, TN 38120
mhoggard@agricenter.org
www.agricenter.org
See ad this page.

ELVIS PRESLEY BLVD RV PARK Ratings: 4.5/6/4.5 (Campground) 2015 rates: $35 to $40. (901)332-3633 3971 Elvis Presley Blvd, Memphis, TN 38116

EZ DAZE RV PARK
Ratings: 10/10★/9 (RV Park) From Memphis go south on I-55 to Church Rd (exit 287 Southaven) Go W 0.2 mi on Church Rd to Pepper Chase Dr. N 0.5 mi to W E Ross Pkwy W 0.2 mi (R). **FAC:** Paved rds. (136 spaces). Avail: 101 paved, patios, 47 pull-thrus (25 x 75), back-ins (25 x 60), 101 full hkups (30/50 amps), cable, WiFi, laundry, LP gas. **REC:** pool, whirlpool, playground. Pet restrict(B). Partial handicap access. Big rig sites, eco-friendly, 2015 rates: $40. Disc: military.
(662)342-7720 Lat: 34.94186, Lon: -89.99883
536 W.e. Ross Pkwy, Southaven, MS 38671
ezdazervpark@yahoo.com
www.ezdazervpark.com
See primary listing at Southaven, MS and ad page 1090.

MEMPHIS EAST CAMPGROUND Ratings: 7/5.5/6.5 (Campground) From Jct of I-40 & Canada Rd (exit 20), S 0.8 mi on Canada Rd to Monroe Rd, E 0.4 mi (L). **FAC:** Paved/gravel rds. (66 spaces). Avail: 35 gravel, 22 pull-thrus (21 x 80), back-ins (25 x 60), some side by side hkups, 29 full hkups, 6 W, 6 E (30/50 amps), seasonal sites, WiFi, dump, laundry, LP gas. **REC:** pool, pond, Memphis East Lake: fishing, playground, rec open to public. Pets OK. Partial handicap access, no tents. 2015 rates: $32 to $33.50. Disc: AAA.
AAA Approved
(901)388-3053 Lat: 35.21489, Lon: -89.72878
3291 Shoehorn Dr., Lakeland, TN 38002
Judy@tklcommunities.com
www.memphistravel.com

MEMPHIS GRACELAND RV PARK & CAMPGROUND
Ratings: 9/9★/8.5 (Campground) S-Bnd: From Jct of I-55 & US-51/Elvis Presley Blvd (Exit 5B), S 0.8 mi on US-51/Elvis Presley Blvd (R); or N-bnd: From Jct of I-55 & E Brooks Rd (exit 5), W 0.4 mi on E Brooks Rd to US-51/Elvis Presley Blvd, S 0.8 mi (R). **FAC:** All weather rds. 80 gravel, 36 pull-thrus (25 x 50), back-ins (20 x 40), 65 full hkups, 15 W, 15 E (30/50 amps), WiFi, tent sites, rentals, dump, laundry, LP gas. **REC:** pool, playground. Pets OK. Partial handicap access. Eco-friendly, 2015 rates: $36 to $41. Disc: military.
(866)571-9236 Lat: 35.02951, Lon: -90.01519
3691 Elvis Presley Blvd, Memphis, TN 38116
gracelandrvpark@graceland.com
www.memphisgracelandrvpark.com
See ad this page, 1068.

MEMPHIS JELLYSTONE CAMP RESORT
Ratings: 10/9.5★/9 (RV Park) From Memphis, Go south on I-55 to Church Rd (exit 287), W 1.0 mi on Church Rd to US-51, N 0.8 mi to Sudubon Point Dr, E 500 ft (E). **FAC:** Paved rds. (135 spaces). Avail: 60 paved, patios, 60 pull-thrus (32 x 70), 60 full hkups (30/50 amps), cable, WiFi, tent sites, rentals, laundry, LP gas, fire rings, fire-

Say you saw it in our Guide!

TN

See listing Nashville, TN

MEMPHIS (CONT)

MEMPHIS JELLYSTONE CAMP (CONT)
wood. **REC:** pool, pond, playground. Pet restrict(B/Q). Partial handicap access. Big rig sites, eco-friendly, 2015 rates: $45 to $55. Disc: AAA, military.
(662)280-8282 Lat: 34.94511, Lon: -90.01627
1400 Audubon Point Drive, Horn Lake, MS 38637
reservations@memphisjellystone.com
www.memphisjellystone.com
See primary listing at Horn Lake, MS and ad page 1091.

MEMPHIS-SOUTH RV PARK & CAMPGROUND
Ratings: 6.5/8.5★/6 (Campground) From Memphis, Go South on I-55 to Hwy 306 (exit 271), W 0.2 mi on Hwy 306 to Campground Dr (E). **FAC:** Gravel rds. (82 spaces). Avail: 47 gravel, 47 pull-thrus (40 x 60), 47 full hkups (30/50 amps), WiFi, tent sites, laundry, firewood. **REC:** pool, pond, fishing, playground, rec open to public. Pet restrict(B). Big rig sites, eco-friendly, 2015 rates: $34. Disc: AAA, military.
(662)622-0056 Lat: 34.69600, Lon: -89.96660
256 Campground Dr, Coldwater, MS 38618
memphissouthrv@aol.com
www.memphissouthrv.com
See primary listing at Coldwater, MS and ad page 1089.

T. O. FULLER
(State Pk) From Jct of I 55 & Mallory Ave (Exit 9), E 450 ft on Mallory Ave to Riverport Rd, S 5 mi to Plant Rd (L). **FAC:** Paved rds. 45 Avail: 14 paved, 31 gravel, 12 pull-thrus (30 x 60), back-ins (30 x 60), 45 W, 45 E (30/50 amps), tent sites, dump, laundry, fire rings, firewood. **REC:** pool $, playground. Pets OK. Partial handicap access, no tents. 14 day max stay, 2015 rates: $20.
(901)543-7581 Lat: 35.05763, Lon: -90.11354
1500 W. Mitchell Road, Memphis, TN 38109
tnstateparks.itinio.com
See ad page 1067 (Welcome Section).

MIDDLETON — C2 *Hardeman*

CHEROKEE LANDING RV **Ratings: 7/7/6.5** (Membership Pk) 2015 rates: $26. Apr 1 to Oct 29. (800)405-6188 1385 Old Stateline Rd, Saulsbury, TN 38067

MILLINGTON — C1 *Shelby*

MEEMAN-SHELBY FOREST
(State Pk) From Jct of US-51 & Hwy 388, N 6.9 mi on Hwy 388 (N Watkins Rd) to Locke Cuba Rd, W 0.7 to Bluff Rd, N 0.8 mi (L). **FAC:** Paved rds. 49 paved, back-ins (18 x 40), 49 W, 49 E (20/30 amps), dump, fire rings. **REC:** Mississippi River: fishing, playground. Pets OK. No tents. 14 day max stay, 2015 rates: $20.
(800)471-5293 Lat: 35.34371, Lon: -90.03175
910 Riddick Rd, Millington, TN 38053
tnstateparks.itinio.com
See ad page 1067 (Welcome Section).

MORRISTOWN — D5 *Hamblen*

CHEROKEE COUNTY PARK (Public) From town, N 3 mi on Hwy 25E to Cherokee Park Rd, NE .9 mi (L). 2015 rates: $15 to $20. (423)586-0325

PANTHER CREEK
(State Pk) W-bnd: From Jct of I-81 & Hwy 160 (exit 12), NW 10 mi on Hwy 160 to US-11E, NE 1.2 mi to Hwy 342, NW 2.4 mi (R); or E-bnd: From Jct of I-40 & US-11E (exit 394), NE 29.5 mi on US-11E thru Talbott to Hwy 342, NW 2.2 mi (R) Max RV length 35 ft. **FAC:** Paved rds. 50 paved, back-ins (25 x 35), 50 W, 50 E (20/50 amps), tent sites, dump, laundry, fire rings, controlled access. **REC:** pool $, wading pool, Cherokee Lake: fishing, playground. Pets OK. Partial handicap access, no tents. 14 day max stay, 2015 rates: $20 to $25. No CC.
(423)587-7046 Lat: 36.20556, Lon: -83.40733
2010 Panther Creek Rd, Morristown, TN 37814
tnstateparks.itinio.com
See ad page 1067 (Welcome Section).

MOUNT JULIET — B4 *Wilson*

CEDAR CREEK (Public Corps) From Jct of US-70 & Nonaville Rd, N 5 mi on Nonaville Rd, follow signs (R). Call 877-444-6777 for reservations. 2015 rates: $20 to $24. Apr 1 to Oct 15. (615)754-4947

Wasn't that a beautiful campground you visited ten years ago? But can you remember where it was? Use our "Find-it-Fast" index, located in the back of the Guide. It's an alphabetical list, by state, of every private and public park and campground in the Guide.

NASHVILLE — B4 *Davidson*

NASHVILLE AREA MAP

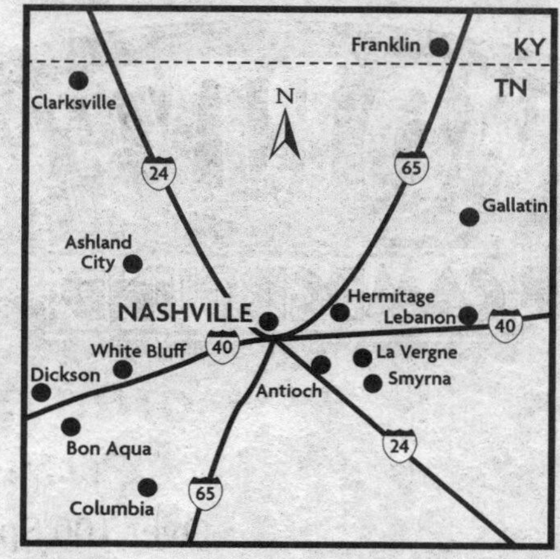

Symbols on map indicate towns within a 50 mile radius of Nashville where campgrounds are listed. Check listings for more information.

In TN, see also Antioch, Ashland City, Bon Aqua, Clarksville, Columbia, Dickson, Gallatin, Hermitage, La Vergne, Lebanon, Smyrna & White Bluff.

In KY, see also Franklin.

NASHVILLE KOA **Ratings: 9.5/10★/9** (Campground) 2015 rates: $63.02 to $72.40. (800)562-7789 2626 Music Valley Koa, Nashville, TN 37214

NASHVILLE NORTH KOA **Ratings: 9.5/9.5★/8.5** (RV Park) 2015 rates: $35 to $45. (615)859-0348 1200 Louisville Highway (31 W), Goodlettsville, TN 37072

NASHVILLE SHORES LAKESIDE RESORT
Ratings: 9.5/9.5★/9.5 (RV Park) From Jct of I-40 & Old Hickory Blvd (Exit 221 & 221B), S 0.5 mi on Old Hickory Blvd to Bell Rd, W 0.5 mi (L).

CAMPING W/FULL WATERPARK!
A family-friendly campers' paradise on Percy Priest Lake just 10 miles from downtown Nashville! Marina-boat and jet-ski rentals & downtown shuttle. A FULL waterpark with wavepool, lazy river & slides. Zip Line & Ropes Course.

FAC: Paved rds. 84 paved, patios, 25 pull-thrus (35 x 65), back-ins (30 x 60), 84 full hkups (30/50 amps), cable, WiFi, rentals, laundry, groc, fire rings, firewood, restaurant. **REC:** pool $, Percy Priest Lake: swim, fishing, marina, shuffleboard, playground, rec open to public. Pets OK. No tents. Big rig sites, 14 day max stay, eco-friendly, 2015 rates: $45 to $65. Disc: AAA. Mar 1 to Dec 1.
AAA Approved
(615)889-7050 Lat: 36.15874, Lon: -86.60826
4001 Bell Road, Nashville, TN 37076
Lodging@nashvilleshores.com
nashvilleshores.com
See ad opposite page, 1068.

NASHVILLE YOGI BEAR'S JELLYSTONE PARK **Ratings: 9/9★/8** (Campground) 2015 rates: $62 to $75. (615)889-4225 2572 Music Valley Drive, Nashville, TN 37214

TWO RIVERS CAMPGROUND
Ratings: 8.5/10★/9 (RV Park) E-bnd: From Jct of I-40 & Briley Pkwy (Exit 204), N 16.4 mi on Briley Pkwy to McGavock Pike (exit 12), W 0.2 mi to Music Valley Dr, N 1.2 mi (L); or W-bnd: From Jct of I-40 & Briley Pkway (Exit 215), N 5.3 mi on Briley Pkwy to McGavock Pike (exit 12), W 0.2 mi to Music Valley Dr, N 1.2 mi (L).

MUSIC CITY U S A
Known for country music & Grand Ole Opry. Home to historic landmarks, civil war battlefields, great golf & water fun, fine dining, world famous broadway "Honky Tonks" & fabulous Opryland Hotel! Join us for fun packed vacation

FAC: Paved/gravel rds. (104 spaces). Avail: 100 gravel, patios, 12 pull-thrus (24 x 54), back-ins (28 x 54), 74 full hkups, 26 W, 26 E (30/50 amps), seasonal sites, cable, WiFi, dump, laundry, groc. **REC:** pool, playground. Pets OK. No tents. Big rig sites, eco-friendly, 2015 rates: $37 to $48. Disc: AAA, military.
(615)883-8559 Lat: 36.23431, Lon: -86.70369
2616 Music Valley Drive, Nashville, TN 37214
tworiverscamp@bellsouth.net
www.tworiverscampground.com
See ad pages 1094, 1068.

Travel Services

CAMPING WORLD OF NASHVILLE As the nation's largest retailer of RV supplies, accessories, services and new and used RVs, Camping World is committed to making your total RV experience better. RV Accessories: (800)831-0111. **SERVICES:** RV, tire, RV appliance, MH mechanical, engine/chassis repair, staffed RV wash, restrooms, RV Sales. RV supplies, LP, RV accessible. waiting room. Hours: 8am to 6pm.
(888)869-5506 Lat: 36.160974, Lon: -86.664267
2618 Music Valley Dr., Nashville, TN 37214
www.campingworld.com

Things to See and Do

TENNESSEE STATE PARKS Call for brochures about any of Tennessee's State Parks or to make reservations 1-888-867-2757. Hours: 8am to 4:30pm. No CC.
(615)532-0001 Lat: 36.16363, Lon: -86.77901
312 Rosa L. Parks Ave. 2nd Floor, Nashville, TN 37243
kevin.easton@tn.gov
www.tnstateparks.com
See ad page 1067 (Welcome Section).

TN

Good Sam Park

See listing Nashville, TN

NEXT DOOR TO CAMPING WORLD

TWO RIVERS CAMPGROUND

Good Sam RATED 8.5/10★/9

OPEN ALL YEAR

Only Two Miles From Grand Ole Opry®

Come as a Customer, Leave as Friends!

- Over 100 Spacious RV Sites
- Full Hookups • 30/50 Amp Service
- Privately Owned & Operated
- Concrete Patios, Picnic Tables
- Clean Laundry • Clean Bath Houses
- Playground • Game Room
- Store & Gift Shop • Propane Available
- Friendly Service • Free WiFi/Cable TV
- **EVENING ENTERTAINMENT (SEASONAL) May Thru Sept**
- TOURS OF ALL AREA ATTRACTIONS
- TRANSPORTATION TO GRAND OLE OPRY® AND OPRY MILLS

Commercial Shuttle to Downtown Attractions, "Honky Tonks" & Restaurants

BEST RATES ON MUSIC VALLEY DRIVE

Enjoy a "Music City Vacation." Let our friendly and experienced staff help you plan a "customized" vacation in Nashville. They will help you see Nashville like you've never seen it before. From tickets to the Grand Ole Opry to tours that suit your special interests our staff is here to make sure you enjoy yourself while visiting Music City U.S.A.

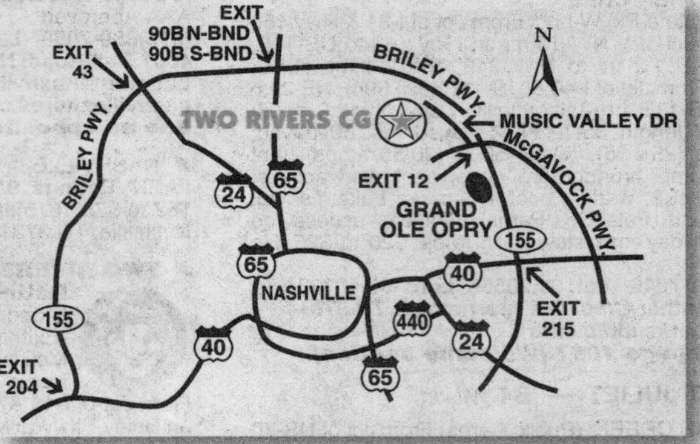

Campground Reservations & Information

(615) 883-8559 • (615) 883-8070 • FAX (615) 889-5453

2616 Music Valley Dr., Nashville, TN 37214 • www.tworiverscampground.com

1 NIGHT DEPOSIT REQUIRED

NEWPORT — E5 *Cocke*

KOA NEWPORT **Ratings: 8.5/8/9** (Campground) 2015 rates: $32 to $47. (800)562-9016 240 Koa Lane, Newport, TN 37821

TANA-SEE CAMPGROUND
Ratings: 9/9★/8.5 (Campground) From Jct of I40 & Hwy 25W (Exit 432B): Go E 0.2 mi on Hwy 25W, then S 0.1 mi on Carson Springs Rd (E). **FAC:** Gravel rds. (105 spaces). Avail: 101 gravel, 6 pull-thrus (25 x 75), back-ins (20 x 50), 101 full hkups (30/50 amps), seasonal sites, cable, WiFi, tent sites, rentals, dump, laundry, groc, fire rings, firewood. **REC:** pool, pond, playground. Pet restrict(B). Partial handicap access. Big rig sites, RV age restrict, eco-friendly, 2015 rates: $35 to $45. Disc: military.
(423)415-5000 Lat: 35.58247, Lon: -83.14733
112 Carson Springs Rd, Newport, TN 37821
tanaseecampground@yahoo.com
www.tana-seecampground.com
See ad this page, 1068.

TRIPLE CREEK CAMPGROUND **Ratings: 5/6/7** (Campground) 2015 rates: $35 to $45. Mar 1 to Nov 30. (423)465-3065 141 Lower Bogard Rd, Newport, TN 37821

NORMANDY — C4 *Coffee*

TVA/BARTON SPRINGS-NORMANDY RESERVOIR (Public) From town, E 3 mi on Huffman Rd (L). 2015 rates: $17 to $26. Mar 15 to Oct 1. (931)857-9222

NORRIS — B6 *Anderson*

TVA/LOYSTON POINT-NORRIS RESERVOIR (Public) From Jct US-441 & SR-61, E 2 mi on SR-61 to Park Rd, N 3.8 mi to Boy Scout Rd, E 0.5 mi, follow signs NE 2.5 mi to park (E). 2015 rates: $22.85 to $33.13. Apr 15 to Oct 15. (865)494-9369

OLIVER SPRINGS — B6 *Morgan*

WINDROCK PARK CAMPGROUND **Ratings: 5.5/7.5/8.5** (Campground) 2015 rates: $38. (865)435-1251 555 Windrock Park Lane, Oliver Springs, TN 37840

ONEIDA — A6 *Scott*

BIG SOUTH FORK NAT'L RIVER & REC. AREA (BANDY CREEK CAMPGROUND) (Natl Pk) From jct US 27 & Hwy 297: Go 15 mi W on Hwy 297. 2015 rates: $19 to $22. (423)569-9778

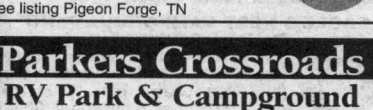

PARIS — B2 *Henry*

LITTLE EAGLE RV PARK **Ratings: 6.5/9.5★/7** (RV Park) 2015 rates: $32. (731)642-4669 14652 Hwy 79 N, Buchanan, TN 38222

PARIS LANDING/KENTUCKY LAKE KOA
Ratings: 9/9★/9.5 (Campground) From Jct of US-641 & US-79 (in Paris), NE 12 mi on US-79 E to Antioch Rd, SE 0.2 mi (L). **FAC:** Paved rds. 42 gravel, 38 pull-thrus (30 x 60), back-ins (30 x 60), 24 full hkups, 18 W, 18 E (30/50 amps), WiFi, tent sites, rentals, dump, laundry, LP bottles, fire rings, firewood. **REC:** pool, playground, rec open to public. Pet restrict(B). Partial handicap access. Big rig sites, RV age restrict, eco-friendly, 2015 rates: $39 to $45. Disc: military. Mar 15 to Oct 1.
(731)642-6895 Lat: 36.41309, Lon: -88.13212
6290 East Antioch Road, Buchanan, TN 38222
parislandingkoa@gmail.com
koa.com
See ad this page.

PARKERS CROSSROADS — B2 *Henderson*

PARKERS CROSSROADS RV PARK AND CAMPGROUND
Ratings: 8.5/NA/7.5 (Campground) From Jct of I-40 & SR-22 (Exit 108), N 1.5 mi on SR-22 (R). **FAC:** Paved/gravel rds. 36 Avail: 7 paved, 27 gravel, 2 grass, patios, 26 pull-thrus (24 x 50), back-ins (24 x 40), 34 full hkups, 2 W, 2 E (30/50 amps), cable, WiFi, tent sites, rentals, dump, laundry, LP gas, fire rings, firewood. **REC:** pool, pond, fishing, playground. Pets OK. Eco-friendly, 2015 rates: $31.50. Disc: military.
(731)968-9939 Lat: 35.809182, Lon: -88.389067
22580 Highway 22N, Yuma, TN 38390
pcrvpark@gmail.com
pcrvpark.com
See ad this page, 1068.

Check our family camping destinations article in the front of the Guide highlighting the best places to camp in every state and province.

Travel Services

PARKERS CROSSROADS RV Repair RVs, all sizes & types, including Electrical Systems, Roofs, Awnings & Steps, Generators, Water Heaters, Refrigerators, Air Conditioners & just about anything else wrong with your RV. Located halfway between Memphis & Nashville. **SERVICES:** RV, RV appliance, MH mechanical, mobile RV svc, restrooms. RV supplies, LP, dump, emergency parking, RV accessible. waiting room. Hours: 8am - 7pm.
(731)968-9939 Lat: 35.809162, Lon: -88.389067
22580 Hwy 22 North, Yuma, TN 38390
Pcrvrepair@gmail.com
www.pcrvrepair.com
See ad this page.

PERRYVILLE — C3 *Decatur*

BEECH BEND (DECATUR COUNTY PK) (Public) From jct US 412/Hwy 20 & Hwy 100: Go 1-1/2 mi S on Hwy 100. 2015 rates: $19. (731)847-4252

MOUSETAIL LANDING
(State Pk) From Jct of US-412 & SR 438, NE 2.7 mi on SR-438 (L) Caution: Steep grade in park. **FAC:** Paved/gravel rds. 24 gravel, 1 pull-thrus (30 x 90), back-ins (30 x 30), 19 W, 19 E (30/50 amps), tent sites, dump, laundry, fire rings. **REC:** Tennessee River: swim, fishing, playground. Pets OK. Partial handicap access, no tents. 14 day max stay, 2015 rates: $20. No CC.
(731)847-0841 Lat: 35.65201, Lon: -88.00294
3 Campground Road, Linden, TN 37096
tnstateparks.itinio.com
See ad page 1067 (Welcome Section).

PIGEON FORGE — E5 *Sevier*

A SPOTLIGHT Introducing Pigeon Forge's colorful attractions appearing at the front of this state section.

A WALDENS CREEK CAMPGROUND **Ratings: 6.5/8.5/7** (Campground) 2015 rates: $28 to $34. (877)908-2727 2485 Henderson Springs Rd, Pigeon Forge, TN 37863

Use our handy Snowbird Destinations guide in the front of the Guide to find RV-friendly destinations throughout the Sunbelt.

TN

PIGEON FORGE (CONT)

BEAR COVE VILLAGE

Ratings: 8.5/8.5/9 (RV Park) From Jct of Hwy 66 & Hwy 441, NE 1.4 mi on Hwy 441 to Veterans Blvd, E 5.3 mi to Whaley Dr, NE 100 ft (L). **FAC:** Paved rds. 101 paved, back-ins (24 x 50), 101 full hkups (30/50 amps), cable, WiFi, tent sites, rentals, laundry, LP gas, fire rings, firewood. **REC:** pool, pond, fishing, playground. Pet restrict(B). Partial handicap access. Eco-friendly, 2015 rates: $50 to $60. Disc: military.
(865)453-8117 Lat: 35.79168, Lon: -83.54420
3404 Whaley Dr, Pigeon Forge, TN 37863
heather@bearcovevillage.com
www.bearcovevillage.com
See ad pages 1095, 1068.

CAMP RIVERS LANDING RV PARK

Ratings: 8.5/8.5/8 (Campground) From Jct of US-441 & US-321, S 2.1 mi on US-441, (thru traffic light #8), SE 0.4 mi to Golf Drive/Day Springs Rd NE 0.2 mi (R). **FAC:** Paved rds. 116 gravel, patios, back-ins (28 x 50), 116 full hkups (30/50 amps), cable, WiFi, tent sites, laundry, fire rings, firewood. **REC:** pool, Little Pigeon River: fishing, playground. Pets OK. Partial handicap access. Big rig sites, eco-friendly, 2015 rates: $36 to $45. Disc: military.
(800)848-9097 Lat: 35.77625, Lon: -83.53915
304 Day Springs Road, Pigeon Forge, TN 37863
Info@campriverslanding.com
www.campriverslanding.com
See ad pages 1095, 1068.

CLABOUGH'S CAMPGROUND & CABINS

Ratings: 8.5/9.5★/8 (Campground) From Jct of US-441 & Wears Valley Rd (US 321): Go W 0.5 mi on Wears Valley Rd (US-321) to Sequoia Rd S 0.1 mi (E). **FAC:** Paved rds. (320 spaces). Avail: 260 gravel, patios, 70 pull-thrus (30 x 70), back-ins (25 x 50), 260 full hkups (30/50 amps), cable, WiFi, tent sites, rentals, laundry, groc, firewood, restaurant. **REC:** heated pool, wading pool, Walden's Creek: fishing, playground. Pet restrict(Q). Big rig sites, 2015 rates: $28 to $39.
(800)965-8524 Lat: 35.79956, Lon: -83.58604
405 Wears Valley Rd, Pigeon Forge, TN 37863
info@claboughcampground.com
www.claboughcampground.com
See ad page 1072 (Spotlight Pigeon Forge).

CREEKSIDE RV PARK

Ratings: 9/9★/9.5 (Campground) From Jct of US-441 & US-321, SW 0.7 mi on US-321 to Henderson Springs Rd, NW 0.2 mi (R) (2nd campground on right). **FAC:** Paved rds. (145 spaces). Avail: 115 gravel, patios, 5 pull-thrus (27 x 60), back-ins (27 x 55), 115 full hkups (30/50 amps), seasonal sites, cable, WiFi, laundry, firewood. **REC:** pool, Waldens Creek: fishing. Pets OK. Partial handicap access, no tents. Eco-friendly, 2015 rates: $28 to $42. Disc: military. Mar 1 to Jan 1.
(865)428-4801 Lat: 35.80174, Lon: -83.58911
2475 Henderson Springs Rd, Pigeon Forge, TN 37863
creeksidervpark@yahoo.com
www.creeksidervpark.com
See ad pages 1095, 1068.

EAGLE'S NEST CAMPGROUND INC

Ratings: 7/8/7.5 (Campground) From Jct of US-441 & Wears Valley Rd (US-321), S 1.5 mi on Wears Valley Rd (L). **FAC:** Gravel rds. (200 spaces). Avail: 150 gravel, 6 pull-thrus (30 x 100), back-ins (25 x 40), 108 full hkups, 42 W, 42 E (30/50 amps), seasonal sites, cable, WiFi, tent sites, dump, laundry, fire rings, firewood. **REC:** pool, Waldens Creek: fishing, playground. Pets OK. Partial handicap access. Big rig sites, 2015 rates: $35 to $ 37. Disc: military.
(800)892-2714 Lat: 35.79283, Lon: -83.60206
1111 Wears Valley Rd, Pigeon Forge, TN 37863
encamp2@aol.com
www.eaglesnestcampground.com
See ad page 1072 (Spotlight Pigeon Forge).

PIGEON FORGE (CONT)

FOOTHILLS RV PARK & CABINS

Ratings: 9/9.5★/8.5 (RV Park) From Jct. of US 441 & Wears Valley Road (US 321), S 3 mi on US 441 to Cates Lane, (200 ft before reaching traffic light #10), E 0.1 mi to Huskey St, S 750 ft (L). **FAC:** Paved rds. 32 paved, patios, back-ins (25 x 42), 32 full hkups (30/50 amps), cable, WiFi, rentals, laundry, fire rings, firewood. **REC:** pool. Pets OK. Partial handicap access, no tents. Eco-friendly, 2015 rates: $36 to $42. Apr 1 to Nov 1.
(865)428-3818 Lat: 35.77356, Lon: -83.53658
4235 Huskey St, Pigeon Forge, TN 37863
camp@foothillsrvpark.info
www.foothillsrvparkandcabins.com
See ad page 1072 (Spotlight Pigeon Forge).

KING'S HOLLY HAVEN RV PARK

Ratings: 9/9.5★/9 (Campground) From Jct of US-441 & US-321, SW 1 mi on US-321 (L). **FAC:** Paved rds. (207 spaces). Avail: 162 all weather, patios, 12 pull-thrus (25 x 60), back-ins (28 x 55), 162 full hkups (30/50 amps), seasonal sites, cable, WiFi, laundry, fire rings, firewood. **REC:** pool, Waldens Creek: fishing, playground. Pets OK. Partial handicap access, no tents. Big rig sites, eco-friendly, 2015 rates: $24 to $37.
(888)204-0247 Lat: 35.79576, Lon: -83.59064
647 Wears Valley Rd, Pigeon Forge, TN 37863
hollyhavenrvpark@aol.com
www.hollyhavenrvpark.com
See ad pages 1095, 1082, 1068, 1072 (Spotlight Pigeon Forge).

MILL CREEK RESORT

Ratings: 9.5/10★/9 (RV Resort) From South city limits at Jct US-441 & Conner Hgts Rd: Go 1/2 mi W on Conner Hgts Rd, then 100 yards N on Mill Creek Rd. **FAC:** Paved rds. 70 gravel, 16 pull-thrus (28 x 50), back-ins (25 x 35), 70 full hkups (30/50 amps), cable, WiFi $, rentals, laundry. **REC:** pool, wading pool, shuffleboard, playground. Pets OK. Partial handicap access, no tents. Eco-friendly, 2015 rates: $33 to $35. Disc: AAA, military. AAA Approved
(865)428-3498 Lat: 35.77205, Lon: -83.54616
449 W Mill Creek Rd, Pigeon Forge, TN 37863
Reservations@mcresort.com
www.mcresort.com
See ad pages 1095, 1068.

PIGEON FORGE/GATLINBURG KOA

Ratings: 9.5/9/8.5 (Campground) From Jct of US-441 & Wears Valley Rd (US-321S), S 2.1 mi on US-441 to Dollywood Ln (stop light #8), E 0.3 mi to Veterans Blvd, N 1000 ft (L). **FAC:** Paved rds. 174 Avail: 68 paved, 86 gravel, 20 grass, patios, 78 pull-thrus (32 x 70), back-ins (36 x 50), 125 full hkups, 49 W, 49 E (30/50 amps), cable, WiFi, tent sites, rentals, dump, laundry, groc, fire rings, firewood. **REC:** heated pool, whirlpool, Little Pigeon River: fishing, playground. Pets OK. Big rig sites, eco-friendly, 2015 rates: $42 to $81. Disc: military. ATM.
(865)453-7903 Lat: 35.78718, Lon: -83.54814
3122 Veterans Blvd, Pigeon Forge, TN 37863
campingkoa@aol.com
www.pigeonforgekoa.com
See ad page 1072 (Spotlight Pigeon Forge).

PINE MOUNTAIN RV PARK

Ratings: 9/10★/9.5 (RV Park) From Jct of US-441 & Pine Mountain Rd (traffic light #6 in Pigeon Forge), SE 0.4 mi on Pine Mountain Rd (L).

TOP RATED CAMPGROUND IN SMOKY MTS

The beauty of Smoky Mts is just a part of what makes our area special. Enjoy the many activities - fishing, rafting, horse riding, hiking, biking, Dollywood, or a beautiful drive through the Great Smoky Mts. Enjoy!

FAC: Paved rds. 61 paved, patios, 25 pull-thrus (35 x 45), back-ins (35 x 60), 61 full hkups (30/50 amps), cable, WiFi, rentals, laundry, fire rings, firewood. **REC:** heated pool. Pet restrict(B). Partial handicap access, no tents. Big rig sites, eco-friendly, 2015 rates: $35 to $58. Disc: military.
(877)753-9994 Lat: 35.789986, Lon: -83.566389
411 Pine Mountain Rd, Pigeon Forge, TN 37863
stay@pinemountainrvpark.com
www.pinemountainrvpark.com
See ad opposite page, 1072 (Spotlight Pigeon Forge), 1068.

Your neighbor just told you about a great little campground in Kentucky — what was the name of it again? The "Find-it-Fast" index in the back of the Guide can help. It's an alphabetical listing, by state, of every private and public park in the Guide.

RIVER PLANTATION RV PARK INC

Ratings: 9/10★/9.5 (RV Resort) From Jct of I-40 & SR-66 (exit 407), S 10 mi on SR-66/US-441 (L); or From Jct of US-441 & Hwy 66, S 1 mi on US-441 (L) Note: Merge to left lane after junction entrance S of traffic light #14.5.

RIVER PLANTATION RV RESORT is located in a peaceful valley bordered by the Little Pigeon River. Only minutes from the Smoky Mountains, Pigeon Forge & Gatlinburg. Near Dollywood, 300 factory outlet stores, and all the shows.

FAC: Gravel rds. (299 spaces). 231 Avail: 17 paved, 214 gravel, patios, 59 pull-thrus (40 x 75), back-ins (35 x 60), 231 full hkups (30/50 amps), seasonal sites, cable, WiFi, rentals, laundry, LP gas, fire rings, firewood, restaurant. **REC:** pool, wading pool, whirlpool, Little Pigeon River: fishing, playground. Pets OK. Partial handicap access, no tents. Big rig sites, eco-friendly, 2015 rates: $22.50 to $54.50. Disc: military.
(800)758-5267 Lat: 35.85151, Lon: -83.56942
1004 Parkway, Sevierville, TN 37862
riverplantation@rvcoutdoors.com
www.rvcoutdoors.com/river-plantation/
See ad opposite page, 1068 & Family Camping, RV Trips of a Lifetime in Magazine Section.

RIVERBEND CAMPGROUND

Ratings: 6/8★/7.5 (Campground) From Jct of US-441 & US-321, N 0.3 mi on US-441 to Henderson Chapel Rd (Stoplight No. 1), W 0.3 mi on Henderson Chapel Rd to Riverbend Loop SW 0.4 mi (L). **FAC:** Paved/gravel rds. (130 spaces). 120 Avail: 100 paved, 20 gravel, patios, 42 pull-thrus (24 x 60), back-ins (25 x 60), 120 full hkups (30/50 amps), seasonal sites, cable, WiFi, tent sites, laundry, firewood. **REC:** Little Pigeon River: fishing. Pets OK. Big rig sites, 2015 rates: $35 to $36. Disc: military. Mar 15 to Nov 30.
(865)453-1224 Lat: 35.80957, Lon: -83.58787
2479 Riverbend Loop 1, Pigeon Forge, TN 37863
riverbend@earthlink.net
www.riverbendcampground.com
See ad page 1072 (Spotlight Pigeon Forge).

Things to See and Do

PIGEON FORGE DEPARTMENT OF TOURISM

Promotion & Marketing agency of Pigeon Forge. Hours: 8:30 am to 5 pm. No CC.
(800)251-9100 Lat: 35.81012, Lon: -83.57903
135 Jake Thomas Road, Pigeon Forge, TN 37863
inquire@mypigeonforge.com
www.mypigeonforge.com
See ad page 1072 (Spotlight Pigeon Forge).

PIKEVILLE — C5 *Bledsoe, Van Buren*

MOUNTAIN GLEN RV PARK & CAMPGROUND **Ratings: 6.5/9.5★/8** (Campground) 2015 rates: $31. (877)716-4493 6182 Brockdell Rd, Pikeville, TN 37367

POCAHONTAS — C2 *Hardeman*

BIG HILL POND

(State Pk) From town: Go 5 mi E on Hwy 57. **FAC.** 28 gravel, tent sites, controlled access. **REC:** playground. Pets OK. Partial handicap access. 2015 rates: $13. No CC.
(731)645-7967 Lat: 35.07731, Lon: -88.72196
984 John Howell Rd, Pocahontas, TN 38061
tnstateparks.itinio.com
See ad page 1067 (Welcome Section).

ROAN MOUNTAIN — D6 *Carter*

ROAN MOUNTAIN

(State Pk) From Jct of US-19E & SR-143, S 4.5 mi on SR-143 (R). Elev 2900 ft. **FAC:** Paved rds. 87 Avail: 50 paved, 37 gravel, 1 pull-thrus (25 x 50), back-ins (25 x 40), 87 W, 87 E (30/50 amps), tent sites, dump, laundry, fire rings, firewood, controlled access. **REC:** pool $, Doe River: fishing, playground. Pets OK. 14 day max stay, 2015 rates: $20 to $27.50.
(423)772-0190 Lat: 36.16047, Lon: -82.09749
1015 Hwy 143, Roan Mountain, TN 37687
tnstateparks.itinio.com
See ad page 1067 (Welcome Section).

Like Us on Facebook.

ROCK ISLAND — B5 *Warren*

ROCK ISLAND

(State Pk) From Jct of US-70S & SR 136 (in town), N 1.2 mi on SR 136 to SR-287, NW 2.2 mi (R). **FAC:** Paved rds. 50 gravel, back-ins (30 x 45), 50 W, 50 E (30/50 amps), tent sites, dump, controlled access. **REC:** Center Hill Lake: swim, fishing, playground, rec open to public. Pets OK. Partial handicap access. 14 day max stay, 2015 rates: $20 to $27.50.
(931)686-2471 Lat: 35.80871, Lon: -85.64205
82 Beach Rd, Rock Island, TN 38581
tnstateparks.itinio.com
See ad page 1067 (Welcome Section).

ROCKY TOP — D4 *Anderson, Campbell*

NORRIS DAM

(State Pk) From Jct of I-75 & US-441 (exit 128), S 3 mi on US-441 (L) Caution: Steep, winding curves to campground (Self contained units only in winter). **FAC:** Paved rds. 75 paved, back-ins (30 x 40), 75 W, 75 E (30/50 amps), tent sites, dump, laundry. **REC:** Norris Lake: fishing, marina, playground. Pets OK. Partial handicap access. 14 day max stay, 2015 rates: $18 to $20. No CC.
(865)426-7461 Lat: 36.23251, Lon: -84.10838
125 Village Green Circle, Rocky Top, TN 37769
tnstateparks.itinio.com
See ad page 1067 (Welcome Section).

SAVANNAH — C2 *Hardin*

GREEN ACRES RV RESORT

Ratings: 9/9.5★/9.5 (Campground) From Jct of US-64 & SR-128 in Savannah, S 6.1 mi on SR-128 to Sylvan Dr, E 0.1 mi (R). **FAC:** Paved/gravel rds. 36 gravel, 10 pull-thrus (30 x 120), back-ins (30 x 65), 36 full hkups (30/50 amps), cable, WiFi, tent sites, laundry, groc, fire rings, firewood. **REC:** pool, playground, rec open to public. Pets OK. Big rig sites, eco-friendly, 2015 rates: $33. Disc: military.
(731)926-1928 Lat: 35.13920, Lon: -88.25019
215 Ziffel Circle, Savannah, TN 38372
Greenacresrvresorttn@gmail.com
www.greenacresrvparktn.com
See ad this page, 1068.

PICKWICK LANDING

(State Pk) From Jct of SR-128 & SR-57, E 0.5 mi on SR-57 to Hardin Dock Rd, N 0.9 mi (L). **FAC:** Paved rds. 48 paved, patios, 2 pull-thrus (30 x 40), back-ins (30 x 40), 48 W, 48 E (30/50 amps), tent sites, dump. **REC:** Pickwick Lake: fishing, marina, golf, playground. Pets OK. Partial handicap access. 14 day max stay, 2015 rates: $20.
(731)689-3129 Lat: 35.05224, Lon: -88.24230
box 15, Pickwick Dam, TN 38365
tnstateparks.itinio.com
See ad page 1067 (Welcome Section).

THE HISTORIC BOTEL **Ratings: 5/NA/4** (Campground) 2015 rates: $30. (731)925-8500 1010 Botel Road, Savannah, TN 38372

SEVIERVILLE — E5 *Sevier*

A SPOTLIGHT Introducing Sevierville's colorful attractions appearing at the front of this state section.

COVE CREEK RESORT & RV PARK **Ratings: 8.5/9.5★/8.5** (Campground) From Jct of Hwy 441 & Hwy 321, W 8.6 mi on Hwy 321 (L). **FAC:** Paved/gravel rds. 113 Avail: 25 paved, 88 gravel, 24

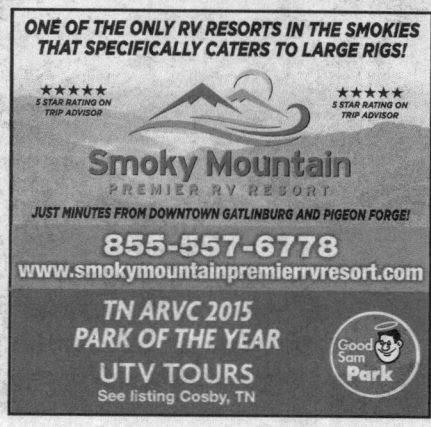

TN

SEVIERVILLE (CONT)

COVE CREEK RESORT & RV PARK (CONT)
pull-thrus (30 x 60), back-ins (30 x 60), 113 full hkups (30/50 amps), cable, WiFi, tent sites, rentals, dump, laundry, firewood. **REC:** pool, Cove Creek: fishing. Pets OK. Partial handicap access. Big rig sites, 2015 rates: $40 to $65. Disc: AAA, military.
AAA Approved
(877)570-2683 Lat: 35.72363, Lon: -83.64008
3293 Wears Valley Rd, Sevierville, TN 37862
covecreekrvresort@gmail.com
www.covecreekresort.com

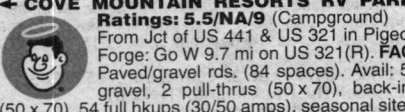

COVE MOUNTAIN RESORTS RV PARK
Ratings: 5.5/NA/9 (Campground)
From Jct of US 441 & US 321 in Pigeon Forge: Go W 9.7 mi on US 321(R). **FAC:** Paved/gravel rds. (84 spaces). Avail: 54 gravel, 2 pull-thrus (50 x 70), back-ins (50 x 70), 54 full hkups (30/50 amps), seasonal sites, cable, WiFi, firewood. **REC:** pool, Fishin' Lake: fishing, rec open to public. Pet restrict(B). No tents. Big rig sites, 2015 rates: $30.50 to $37.
(865)453-1041 Lat: 35.70979, Lon: -83.66601
3958 Wears Valley Rd, Sevierville, TN 37862
karenjerrymiller@aol.com
www.covemountainrvresort.com

RIPPLIN' WATERS CAMPGROUND & CABIN RENTAL
Ratings: 8/8.5★/8.5 (Campground)
From Jct of I-40 & Hwy 66 (exit #407), S 5 mi on Hwy 66 (R). **FAC:** Paved/gravel rds. (156 spaces). Avail: 130 gravel, 36 pull-thrus (24 x 55), back-ins (24 x 50), 130 full hkups (30/50 amps), seasonal sites, WiFi, rentals, laundry, LP gas, firewood. **REC:** pool, Little Pigeon River: fishing, playground. Pet restrict(B). Partial handicap access, no tents. Eco-friendly, 2015 rates: $32 to $38. ATM.
(865)453-4169 Lat: 35.92085, Lon: -83.58119
1930 Winfield Dunn Parkway, Sevierville, TN 37876
ripplinwatersrv@ripplinwatersrv.com
www.ripplinwatersrv.com
See ad pages 1084, 1082, 1068.

Don't miss out on great savings - find over $1,000 in Camping World coupons at the front of the Guide!

RIVERSIDE RV PARK & RESORT
Ratings: 9.5/9.5★/9.5 (Campground) From Jct of I-40 & Hwy 66 (exit 407): Go S 4 mi on Hwy 66 to Boyds Creek Rd, W 500 ft (R).

LARGEST RV RESORT IN THE SMOKIES
At Riverside RV Park & Resort you have everything under the sun. Large full service sites with extra long pull thru's or deluxe riverfront sites with easy full hookups. A friendly staff.

FAC: All weather rds. (330 spaces). 285 Avail: 2 paved, 283 gravel, patios, 123 pull-thrus (25 x 80), back-ins (25 x 45), 285 full hkups (30/50 amps), seasonal sites, WiFi, rentals, dump, laundry, LP gas, fire rings, firewood. **REC:** pool, Little Pigeon River: fishing, playground. Pet restrict(B). Partial handicap access, no tents. Big rig sites, eco-friendly, 2015 rates: $36 to $38. Disc: military.
(865)453-7299 Lat: 35.92821, Lon: -83.58670
4280 Boyds Creek Highway, Sevierville, TN 37876
kvolunteer@aol.com
www.riversidecamp.com
See ad pages 1082, 1076 (Spotlight Sevierville), 1068.

TVA/DOUGLAS DAM HEADWATER-DOUGLAS RESERVOIR (Public) From Jct I-40 & Hwy 66, S 3 mi on Hwy 66 to Hwy 139, E 3.5 mi to Hwy 338, S 2.5 mi (L). 2015 rates: $17 to $26. Mar 14 to Nov 17. (800)882-5263

TVA/DOUGLAS DAM TAILWATER-DOUGLAS RESERVOIR (Public) From Jct I-40 & Hwy 66, S 3 mi on Hwy 66 to Hwy 139, E 5 mi to Hwy 338, S 0.5 mi (L). 2015 rates: $17 to $26. Mar 14 to Nov 17. (800)882-5263

TWO RIVERS LANDING RV RESORT
Ratings: 10/10★/10 (RV Resort) From Jct of I 40 & Hwy 66 (Exit 407), S 3 mi on Hwy 66 to Knife Works Ln, W 0.1 mi to Business Center Circle (R). **FAC:** Paved rds. 55 paved, patios, back-ins (30 x 65), 55 full hkups (30/50 amps), cable, WiFi, laundry. **REC:** pool, French Broad River: fishing, playground. Pet restrict(B). Partial handicap access, no tents. Big rig sites, RV age restrict, eco-friendly, 2015 rates: $55 to $65.
(866)727-5781 Lat: 35.93486, Lon: -83.58674
2328 Business Center Circle, Sevierville, TN 37876
info@tworiversrvresort.com
www.tworiversrvresort.com
See ad this page, 1068.

SILVER POINT — B5 *Putnam*

FLOATING MILL PARK (Public Corps) From Jct of I-40 & Hwy 56 (exit 273), S 5 mi on Hwy 56 to Hurricane Dock Rd, W into campground (E). 2015 rates: $16 to $24. Apr 20 to Oct 11. (931)858-4845

LONG BRANCH PUBLIC USE AREA (Public Corps) From Jct of I-40 & exit 268, S 4.5 mi on exit rd, follow signs (R). 2015 rates: $20 to $24. Apr 14 to Oct 18. (615)548-8002

SMITHVILLE — B5 *DeKalb*

EDGAR EVINS STATE RUSTIC PARK
(State Pk) From Jct of I-40 & SR-96 (Center Hill Dam exit 268), S 7.2 mi on SR-96 (L). Caution: Interior roads have steep inclines throughout park. **FAC:** Paved rds. 60 paved, patios, back-ins (22 x 32), 60 W, 60 E (30/50 amps), tent sites, dump, laundry, fire rings. **REC:** Center Hill Lake: fishing, playground. Pets OK. Partial handicap access. 14 day max stay, 2015 rates: $20. No CC.
(931)858-2446 Lat: 36.10367, Lon: -85.81996
1630 Edgar Evins Park Rd., Silver Point, TN 38582
tnstateparks.itinio.com
See ad page 1067 (Welcome Section).

RAGLAND BOTTOM (Public Corps) From town, E 8 mi on US-70 (L). Call 877-444-6777 for reservations. 2015 rates: $20 to $24. Mar 1 to Oct 31. (931)761-3616

SMYRNA — B4 *Rutherford*

NASHVILLE I-24 CAMPGROUND
Ratings: 9/10★/8 (Campground)
E-bnd: From Jct of I-24 & Hwy 266 (E-bnd: exit 66B; or W-bnd: exit 66), NE 1.6 mi on Hwy 266 to Old Nashville Hwy, SE 1.7 mi to Rocky Fork Rd, W 0.1 mi (R). **FAC:** Paved/gravel rds. (140 spaces). Avail: 50 gravel, 35 pull-thrus (25 x 50), back-ins (25 x 50), mostly side by side hkups, 30 full hkups, 20 W, 20 E (30/50 amps), seasonal sites, WiFi, tent sites, rentals, dump, laundry, groc, LP gas. **REC:** pool, playground.

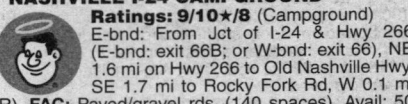

SMYRNA (CONT)

NASHVILLE I-24 CAMPGROUND (CONT)
Pet restrict(B/Q). 2015 rates: $25 to $35. Disc: military.
(615)459-5818 Lat: 35.96631, Lon: -86.53040
1130 Rocky Fork Rd, Smyrna, TN 37167
info@nashvillel24kampground.com
www.nashvillel24kampground.com
See ad pages 1093, 1068.

SPENCER — B4 *Van Buren*

FALL CREEK FALLS
(State Pk) From Pikeville, W 12 mi on SR-30 to Hwy 284, SW 4 mi (R). **FAC:** Paved rds. 66 grass, 7 pull-thrus (30 x 50), back-ins (30 x 40), some side by side hkups (30/50 amps), WiFi Hotspot, tent sites, dump, laundry, fire rings, firewood, restaurant. **REC:** pool $, wading pool, Fall Creek Lake: fishing, golf, playground. Pets OK. 14 day max stay, 2015 rates: $20 to $25.
(423)881-5298 Lat: 35.67793, Lon: -85.33936
2009 Village Camp Road, Spencer, TN 37367
tnstateparks.itinio.com
See ad page 1067 (Welcome Section).

SPRINGVILLE — B3 *Benton, Henry, Stewart*

ALMOST HOME RV PARK **Ratings: 6.5/NA/8** (RV Park) 2015 rates: $32 to $45. (731)642-3090 329 Rice Lane, Springville, TN 38256

MANSARD ISLAND RESORT & MARINA **Ratings: 4/4.5/6.5** (Campground) 2015 rates: $31.50. (731)642-5590 60 Mansard Island Dr, Springville, TN 38256

SWEETWATER — C6 *Loudon, Monroe*

SWEETWATER VALLEY KOA
Ratings: 9/9.5/10 (Campground) From Jct of I-75 & Hwy 322 (exit 62), W 0.8 mi on Hwy 322 to Murray's Chapel Rd, S 0.4 mi (L). **FAC:** Paved rds. (77 spaces). 61 Avail: 43 paved, 18 gravel, patios, 61 pull-thrus (30 x 60), 55 full hkups, 6 W, 6 E (30/50 amps), seasonal sites, cable, WiFi, tent sites, dump, laundry, groc, LP gas, fire rings, firewood. **REC:** pool, pond, fishing, playground. Pet restrict(B). Partial handicap access. Big rig sites, eco-friendly, 2015 rates: $35 to $61. Disc: military.
(800)562-9224 Lat: 35.62253, Lon: -84.50581
269 Murrays Chapel Rd, Sweetwater, TN 37874
sweetwaterkoa@hotmail.com
See ad this page.

TEN MILE — B6 *Meigs*

FOOSHEE PASS (Public) From Chattanooga, S 70 mi to exit 60 (Hwy 68), W 19 mi. 2015 rates: $14 to $17. Apr 15 to Sep 1. (423)334-4842

HORNSBY HOLLOW-WATTS BAR LAKE (Public) From Jct of Hwys 68 & I-75 (Exit 60), N 13 mi on Hwy 68 to Hwy 304N, N 6 mi (L). Cash & check only. No credit cards accepted. 2015 rates: $28.07. (423)334-1709

TIPTONVILLE — B1 *Obion*

REELFOOT LAKE
(State Pk) E-bnd: From Jct of Hwys 78 & 21 (in Tiptonville), E 5.2 mi on Hwy 21 (L); or W-bnd: From Jct of US-51 & Hwy 21 (Troy exit), W 15.5 mi on Hwy 21 (R). **FAC:** Paved/gravel rds. 100 Avail: 68 paved, 32 gravel, patios, 5 pull-thrus (25 x 50), back-ins (30 x 40), some side by side hkups, 86 W, 86 E (30 amps), tent sites, dump, laundry, controlled access. **REC:** Reelfoot Lake: fishing, playground. Pets OK. Partial handicap access. 14 day max stay, 2015 rates: $20 to $25.
(731)253-8003 Lat: 36.35212, Lon: -89.40221
3120 State Route 213, Tiptonville, TN 38079
tnstateparks.itinio.com
See ad page 1067 (Welcome Section).

TOWNSEND — E5 *Blount, Sevier*

BIG MEADOW FAMILY CAMPGROUND
Ratings: 9.5/10★/10 (RV Park) From Jct of US-321 & Hwy 73, NE 0.2 mi on US-321 to Cedar Creek Rd, W 300 ft (R). **FAC:** All weather rds. 53 paved, 25 all weather, patios, 58 pull-thrus (30 x 75), back-ins (29 x 55), 78 full hkups (30/50 amps), cable, WiFi, laundry, LP gas, firewood, controlled access. **REC:** Little River: swim, fishing, playground. Pets OK. Partial handicap access, no tents. Big rig sites, eco-friendly, 2015 rates: $45 to $55.
(888)497-0625 Lat: 35.68179, Lon: -83.73348
8215 Cedar Creek Road, Townsend, TN 37882
information@bigmeadowcampground.com
www.bigmeadowcampground.com
See ad this page.

GREAT SMOKY MTN/CADES COVE (Natl Pk) From Jct of US-411 & Little River Rd, W 26 mi on Little River Rd (L); or From Jct of US-411 & US-441, S 13 mi on US-441 to Little River Rd (R). NOTE: Tunnel construction may restrict RVs-call (888)355-1849 for information. 2015 rates: $20. May 15 to Oct 31. (865)436-2472

LAZY DAZE CAMPGROUND **Ratings: 6/7/7** (Campground) 2015 rates: $40 to $50. (865)448-6061 8429 State Hwy 73, Townsend, TN 37882

MISTY RIVER CABINS & RV RESORT (RV Park) (Rebuilding) 2015 rates: $45 to $47. (877)981-4300 5050 Old Walland Hwy, Walland, TN 37886

MOUNTAINEER CAMPGROUND **Ratings: 6.5/7.5/8** (Campground) 2015 rates: $41 to $47. (865)448-6421 8451 State Hwy 73, Townsend, TN 37882

TOWNSEND/GREAT SMOKIES KOA **Ratings: 8/9/9** (Campground) 2015 rates: $34 to $79. (800)562-3428 8533 State Hwy 73, Townsend, TN 37882

TREMONT OUTDOOR RESORT **Ratings: 8.5/9★/9** (Campground) 2015 rates: $40 to $65. (800)448-6373 118 Stables Dr, Townsend, TN 37882

Enjoy shopping over 10,000 RV products at great prices, at CampingWorld.com.

Pamper Your Pet on the Road - turn to our Pampered Pet Parks feature at the front of the Guide for great tips and advice when traveling with pets.

TN

UNICOI — D6 *Unicoi*

WOODSMOKE CAMPGROUND
Ratings: 6/8.5★/9 (Campground) W-bnd: From Jct of I-26 & SR-173 (Exit 32) left at the Jct. (under I-26) 0.1 mi to Greenoak Dr, SW 0.1 mi (R) E-bnd: From Jct of I-26 & SR-173 (Exit 32) right at the Jct. 300 ft to Greenoak Dr, SW 0.1 mi (R) Note: RV maximum length 40 ft. **FAC:** Gravel rds. (34 spaces). Avail: 29 gravel, back-ins (24 x 60), 29 full hkups (30/50 amps), seasonal sites, WiFi, tent sites, fire rings, firewood. Pet restrict(Q). Partial handicap access. RV age restrict, eco-friendly, 2015 rates: $30.
(423)743-2116 Lat: 36.20775, Lon: -82.35573
215 Woodsmoke Drive, Unicoi, TN 37692
woodsmoke@embarqmail.com
www.woodsmokecampground.com
See ad page 1087.

UNION CITY — A2 *Obion*

AAA RV PARK **Ratings: 5.5/8★/5.5** (RV Park) 2015 rates: $30. (731)446-4514 2029 Phebus Ln, Union City, TN 38261

VONORE — C6 *Monroe*

NOTCHY CREEK (Public Corps) From jct US 411 & CR 400: Go 3 mi S on CR 400, then 1-3/4 mi E (follow signs). (423)884-6280

TOQUA BEACH CAMPGROUND (Public) From jct US 411 & Hwy 360: Go 3 mi E on Hwy 360. (423)884-3317

Directional arrows indicate the campground's position in relation to the nearest town.

WARTBURG — B6 *Morgan*

FROZEN HEAD
(State Pk) From Hwy 27 in Harriman: Go N on Hwy 27, then 2 mi E on Hwy 62, then 4 mi N on Flat Fork Rd to park entrance. **FAC.** 20 grass, tent sites, fire rings. **REC:** playground. Pets OK. Partial handicap access. No CC.
(423)346-3318 Lat: 36.09931, Lon: -84.44539
964 Flat Fork Road, Wartburg, TN 37887
tnstateparks.itinio.com
See ad page 1067 (Welcome Section).

WHITE BLUFF — B3 *Dickson*

MONTGOMERY BELL STATE RESORT PARK
(State Pk) W-bnd: From Jct of I-40 & Hwy 96 (exit 182), NW 10.6 mi on Hwy 96 to US-70, E 3.7 mi (R); or E-bnd: From Jct of I-40 & Hwy 46 (exit 172), N 5.2 mi on Hwy 46 to Bus US-70, E 6 mi (R). **FAC:** Paved rds. 116 Avail: 35 paved, 81 gravel, 2 pull-thrus (25 x 50), back-ins (25 x 50), 116 W, 116 E (30/50 amps), tent sites, dump, fire rings, restaurant. **REC:** Acorn Lake, Woodhaven, Creech Hollow: swim, fishing, golf, playground. Pets OK. Partial handicap access. 14 day max stay, 2015 rates: $25.
(615)797-9052 Lat: 36.10278, Lon: -87.28303
1020 Jackson Hill Rd, Burns, TN 37029
tnstateparks.itinio.com
See ad page 1067 (Welcome Section).

Don't miss a thing! Check out the Table of Contents for everything the Guide has to offer.

WINCHESTER — F5 *Franklin*

FAIRVIEW DEVIL'S STEP CAMPGROUND (State Pk) From Town, W 3.1 mi on Hwy 50 to Fairview Rd, N 1 mi (R). 2015 rates: $20 to $25. Apr 1 to Oct 31. (800)471-5295

TIMS FORD STATE RUSTIC PARK
(State Pk) From town, W 5 mi on Hwy 50 to Mansford Rd, NW 5 mi (L). **FAC:** Paved rds. 52 paved, back-ins (38 x 25), 4 full hkups, 48 W, 48 E (20/30 amps), tent sites, dump, fire rings. **REC:** pool $, wading pool, Tim's Ford Lake: fishing, marina, golf, playground. Pets OK. Partial handicap access. 14 day max stay, 2015 rates: $20 to $25.
(931)962-1183 Lat: 35.22815, Lon: -86.25533
570 Tims Ford Drive, Winchester, TN 37398
tnstateparks.itinio.com
See ad page 1067 (Welcome Section).

Check out those views! From awe-inspiring redwood giants to the soaring towers of the Golden Gate Bridge, we've put the Spotlight on North America's most popular travel destinations. Turn to the Spotlight articles in our State and Province sections to learn more.

WELCOME TO Texas

DATE OF STATEHOOD	WIDTH: 773 MILES (1,244 KM)	PROPORTION OF UNITED STATES
DEC. 29, 1845	LENGTH: 790 MILES (1,270 KM)	7.08% OF 3,794,100 SQ MI

Texas is big. The second largest state in the nation (behind only Alaska), spanning some 261,000 miles, the Lone Star state is bigger than Britain, Germany, Belgium and Holland, combined. From the soaring monoliths of Dallas to gargantuan slabs of barbecued beef, everything in Texas overwhelms with its scale and brawn. But, aside from the state's clichéd images of cowboys and tumbling tumbleweed framed by an austere desert landscape, Texas is a cultural juggernaut. Dallas boasts world-class galleries in its sublime Arts District (the largest in the country), as well as the JFK Memorial, Dallas County Historical Plaza and an acclaimed symphony. Houston draws crowds to its iconic Space Center, superb Museum of Fine Arts and steamy Buffalo Bayou. Offbeat and folksy, Austin beats to a different drum with its dynamic music scene and come-as-you-are vibe, while San Antonio its blend of Native American and Mexican culture and takes pride in its symbol of resistance: the Alamo.

History

As the first European settlers in Texas, Spanish missionaries founded San Antonio in 1718. Following the War of Mexican Independence (1810-1821), the Mexican government allowed U.S. settlers to claim land within the territory. The population explosion that ensued caused friction and unrest between Texans and Mexico's ruling government, culminating with the battle of the Alamo on February 23, 1836. Immortalized in movies and songs, the doomed 13-day siege transformed a derelict Spanish mission in the heart of downtown San Antonio into a rallying cry for Texas's independent spirit. Texas eventually won its independence in subsequent fighting.

In 1845, after negotiations with the U.S. government, Texas joined the union. During the 20th century, Texas played a key role in space exploration. The Johnson Space Center in Houston, established in 1961, still provides Mission Control for all space flights.

Top 3 Tourism Attractions:
1) The Alamo
2) The San Antonio River Walk
3) Houston Space Center

Nickname: Lone Star State

State Flower: Bluebonnet

State Bird: Mockingbird

People: Mary Kay Ash, cosmetics entrepreneur; Carol Burnett, comedian and actress; Buddy Holly, musician; Howard Hughes, industrialist and film producer; Willie Nelson, singer and songwriter

Major Cities: Houston, San Antonio, Dallas, Austin (capital), Fort Worth

Topography: South-southeast—Gulf Coast Plain; north central—plains, hills extending over Panhandle; central—Hill Country; west-desert-like

Climate: Varies widely: west—arid; east—humid; southeast—subtropical

Texas State Travel Guide

TX

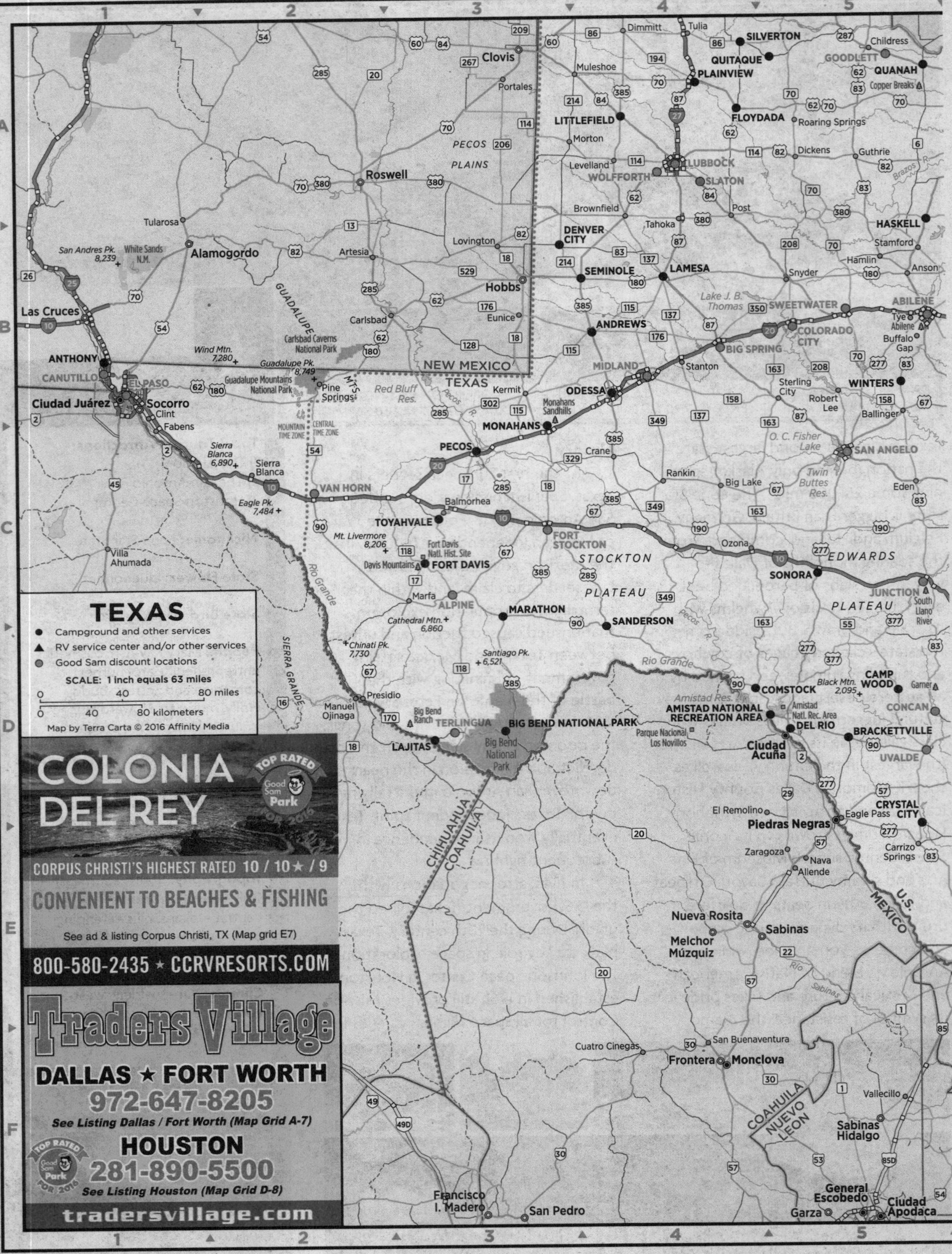

TEXAS

- ● Campground and other services
- ▲ RV service center and/or other services
- ● Good Sam discount locations

SCALE: 1 inch equals 63 miles

0 40 80 miles
0 40 80 kilometers

Map by Terra Carta © 2016 Affinity Media

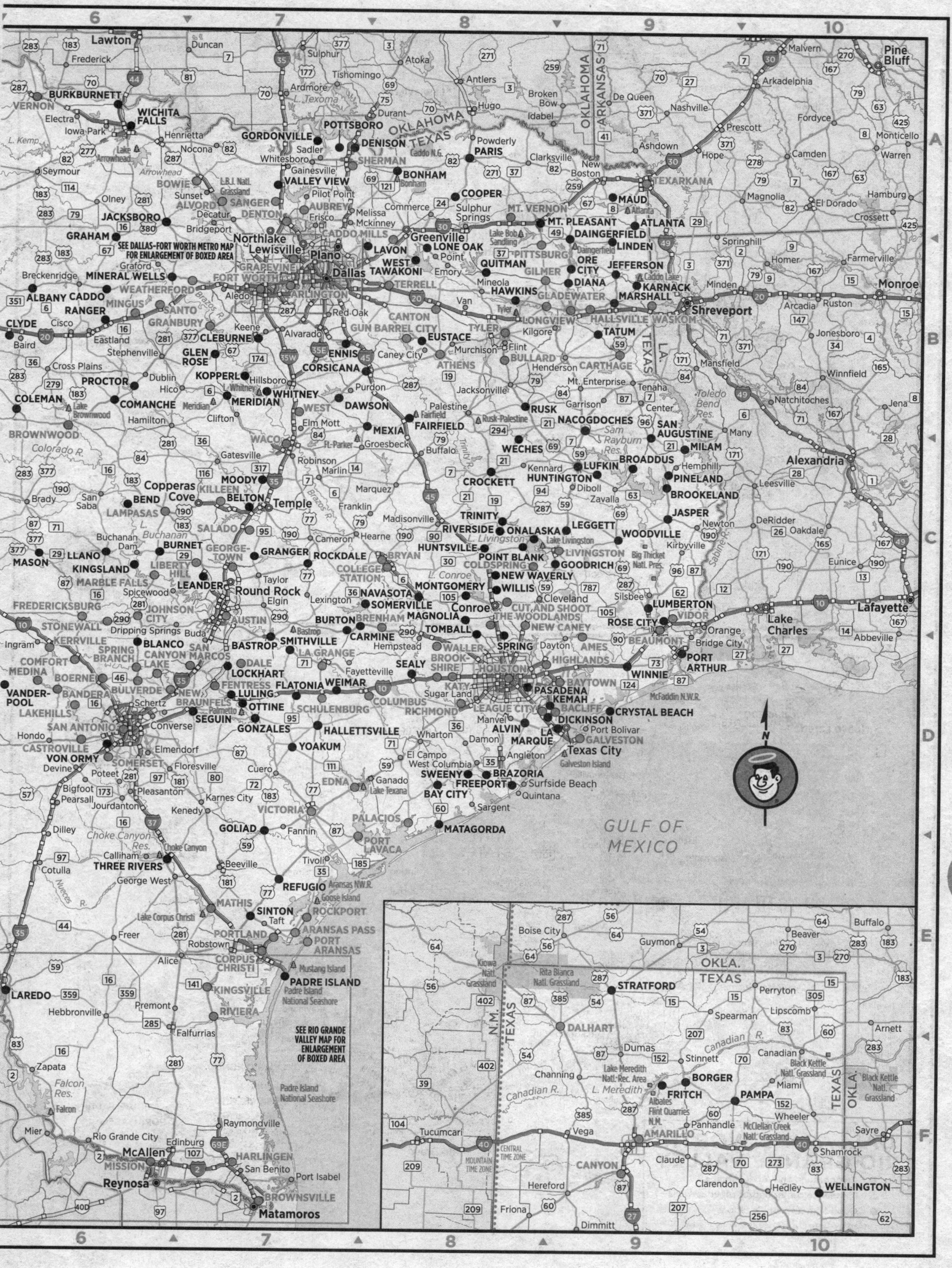
6
7
8
9
10
A
B
C
D
E
F
Lawton
Duncan
Frederick
Sulphur
Atoka
Tishomingo
Antlers
Broken Bow
Idabel
Hugo
Ardmore
Durant
L. Texoma
OKLAHOMA
TEXAS
ARKANSAS
Malvern
Pine Bluff
Arkadelphia
De Queen
Nashville
Prescott
Fordyce
Monticello
Warren
Hope
Camden
Ashdown
Texarkana
Magnolia
El Dorado
Hamburg
Crossett
Springhill
Homer
Farmerville
Minden
Monroe
Shreveport
Arcadia
Ruston
Jonesboro
Mansfield
Winnfield
Natchitoches
Jena
Toledo Bend Res.
Many
Alexandria
Leesville
DeRidder
Oakdale
Newton
Kirbyville
Eunice
Lake Charles
Lafayette
Orange
Bridge City
Abbeville
BURKBURNETT
VERNON
WICHITA FALLS
Electra
Iowa Park
Henrietta
Nocona
GORDONVILLE
POTTSBORO
DENISON
SHERMAN
Sadler
Whitesboro
Gainesville
VALLEY VIEW
BONHAM
PARIS
Powderly
Clarksville
New Boston
MAUD
ATLANTA
Seymour
BOWIE
Sunset
ALVORD
SANGER
DENTON
Olney
JACKSBORO
Decatur
Bridgeport
GRAHAM
Northlake
Lewisville
Plano
Dallas
Pilot Point
AUBREY
Melissa
Mckinney
Frisco
Commerce
COOPER
Sulphur Springs
MT. VERNON
MT. PLEASANT
DAINGERFIELD
LINDEN
CADDO MILLS
Greenville
LAVON
LONE OAK
Point
WEST TAWAKONI
Emory
QUITMAN
PITTSBURG
ORE CITY
JEFFERSON
GILMER
DIANA
KARNACK
MARSHALL
GLADEWATER
HAWKINS
Mineola
TERRELL
Van
Tyler
LONGVIEW
HALLSVILLE
WASKOM
SEE DALLAS-FORT WORTH METRO MAP FOR ENLARGEMENT OF BOXED AREA
Graford
Breckenridge
MINERAL WELLS
FORT WORTH
GRAPEVINE
ARLINGTON
WEATHERFORD
ALBANY
CADDO
RANGER
MINGUS
SANTO
Aledo
Red Oak
CANTON
GUN BARREL CITY
TYLER
Kilgore
TATUM
CLYDE
Cisco
Eastland
GRANBURY
Keene
CLEBURNE
Alvarado
EUSTACE
Flint
Baird
Stephenville
GLEN ROSE
ENNIS
Caney City
Murchison
BULLARD
CARTHAGE
Cross Plains
Dublin
CORSICANA
ATHENS
Henderson
PROCTOR
Hico
KOPPERL
Hillsboro
Mt. Enterprise
Tenaha
COLEMAN
COMANCHE
Meridian
WHITNEY
MERIDIAN
Purdon
Jacksonville
Garrison
Center
Hamilton
Clifton
WEST
DAWSON
Palestine
RUSK
NACOGDOCHES
SAN AUGUSTINE
BROWNWOOD
Elm Mott
MEXIA
FAIRFIELD
Sam Rayburn Res.
Colorado R.
WACO
Groesbeck
WECHES
MILAM
Buffalo
Robinson
Gatesville
Marlin
Kennard
LUFKIN
BROADDUS
Hemphill
Copperas Cove
KILLEEN
MOODY
CROCKETT
HUNTINGTON
PINELAND
Brady
San Saba
BEND
BELTON
Temple
Marquez
Diboll
BROOKELAND
LAMPASAS
Franklin
Zavalla
JASPER
SALADO
Madisonville
TRINITY
Buchanan Dam
BURNET
Cameron
Hearne
RIVERSIDE
ONALASKA
LEGGETT
WOODVILLE
MASON
LLANO
GEORGETOWN
GRANGER
ROCKDALE
BRYAN
HUNTSVILLE
L. Livingston
POINT BLANK
LIVINGSTON
Big Thicket Natl. Pres.
KINGSLAND
LIBERTY HILL
COLLEGE STATION
COLDSPRING
GOODRICH
MARBLE FALLS
LEANDER
Round Rock
Taylor
L. Conroe
NEW WAVERLY
Spicewood
Elgin
NAVASOTA
MONTGOMERY
WILLIS
Silsbee
LUMBERTON
FREDERICKSBURG
JOHNSON CITY
Lexington
SOMERVILLE
Conroe
Cleveland
STONEWALL
AUSTIN
Dripping Springs
Buda
BURTON
BRENHAM
MAGNOLIA
CUT AND SHOOT
THE WOODLANDS
ROSE CITY
VIDOR
Ingram
KERRVILLE
BLANCO
BASTROP
SMITHVILLE
CARMINE
TOMBALL
NEW CANEY
BEAUMONT
SPRING BRANCH
CANYON LAKE
SAN MARCOS
LA GRANGE
Hempstead
WALLER
SPRING
Dayton
AMES
PORT ARTHUR
COMFORT
MEDINA
BOERNE
BANDERA
BULVERDE
DALE
LOCKHART
FENTRESS
Fayetteville
SEALY
BROOKSHIRE
HOUSTON
HIGHLANDS
BAYTOWN
WINNIE
VANDERPOOL
LAKEHILLS
NEW BRAUNFELS
Schertz
LULING
FLATONIA
WEIMAR
COLUMBUS
KATY
Sugar Land
PASADENA
KEMAH
BACLIFF
CRYSTAL BEACH
McFaddin N.W.R.
Palmetto
OTTINE
SCHULENBURG
RICHMOND
LEAGUE CITY
DICKINSON
SAN ANTONIO
Converse
SEGUIN
GONZALES
HALLETTSVILLE
Manvel
ALVIN
Port Bolivar
Hondo
CASTROVILLE
Elmendorf
YOAKUM
Wharton
Damon
LA MARQUE
GALVESTON
Texas City
VON ORMY
SOMERSET
Floresville
El Campo
West Columbia
Angleton
Galveston Island
Devine
Poteet
Cuero
SWEENY
BRAZORIA
Bigfoot
Pearsall
Pleasanton
Ganado
Lake Texana
EDNA
FREEPORT
Surfside Beach
Quintana
Jourdanton
Karnes City
VICTORIA
BAY CITY
Sargent
Kenedy
Dilley
Choke Canyon Res.
Fannin
GOLIAD
PALACIOS
MATAGORDA
GULF OF MEXICO
Calliham
Choke Canyon
THREE RIVERS
Cotulla
George West
Beeville
PORT LAVACA
Tivoli
REFUGIO
Aransas N.W.R.
Goose Island
ROCKPORT
MATHIS
Lake Corpus Christi
SINTON
Taft
ARANSAS PASS
PORTLAND
PORT ARANSAS
Freer
Robstown
CORPUS CHRISTI
Mustang Island
Alice
PADRE ISLAND
Padre Island National Seashore
LAREDO
KINGSVILLE
Hebbronville
Premont
RIVIERA
Falfurrias
SEE RIO GRANDE VALLEY MAP FOR ENLARGEMENT OF BOXED AREA
Zapata
Falcon Res.
Falcon
Mier
Rio Grande City
Raymondville
Edinburg
McAllen
MISSION
HARLINGEN
San Benito
Port Isabel
Reynosa
BROWNSVILLE
Matamoros
Boise City
Kiowa Natl. Grassland
Rita Blanca Natl. Grassland
Guymon
Beaver
Buffalo
OKLA.
STRATFORD
Perryton
Spearman
Lipscomb
N.M.
DALHART
Arnett
Dumas
Canadian R.
Canadian
Stinnett
Black Kettle Natl. Grassland
Channing
Lake Meredith Natl. Rec. Area
BORGER
Miami
L. Meredith
FRITCH
PAMPA
Alibates Flint Quarries N.M.
Panhandle
Wheeler
McClellan Creek Natl. Grassland
Tucumcari
Vega
AMARILLO
Sayre
MOUNTAIN TIME ZONE
CENTRAL TIME ZONE
CANYON
Claude
Shamrock
Hereford
Clarendon
Hedley
WELLINGTON
Friona
Dimmitt

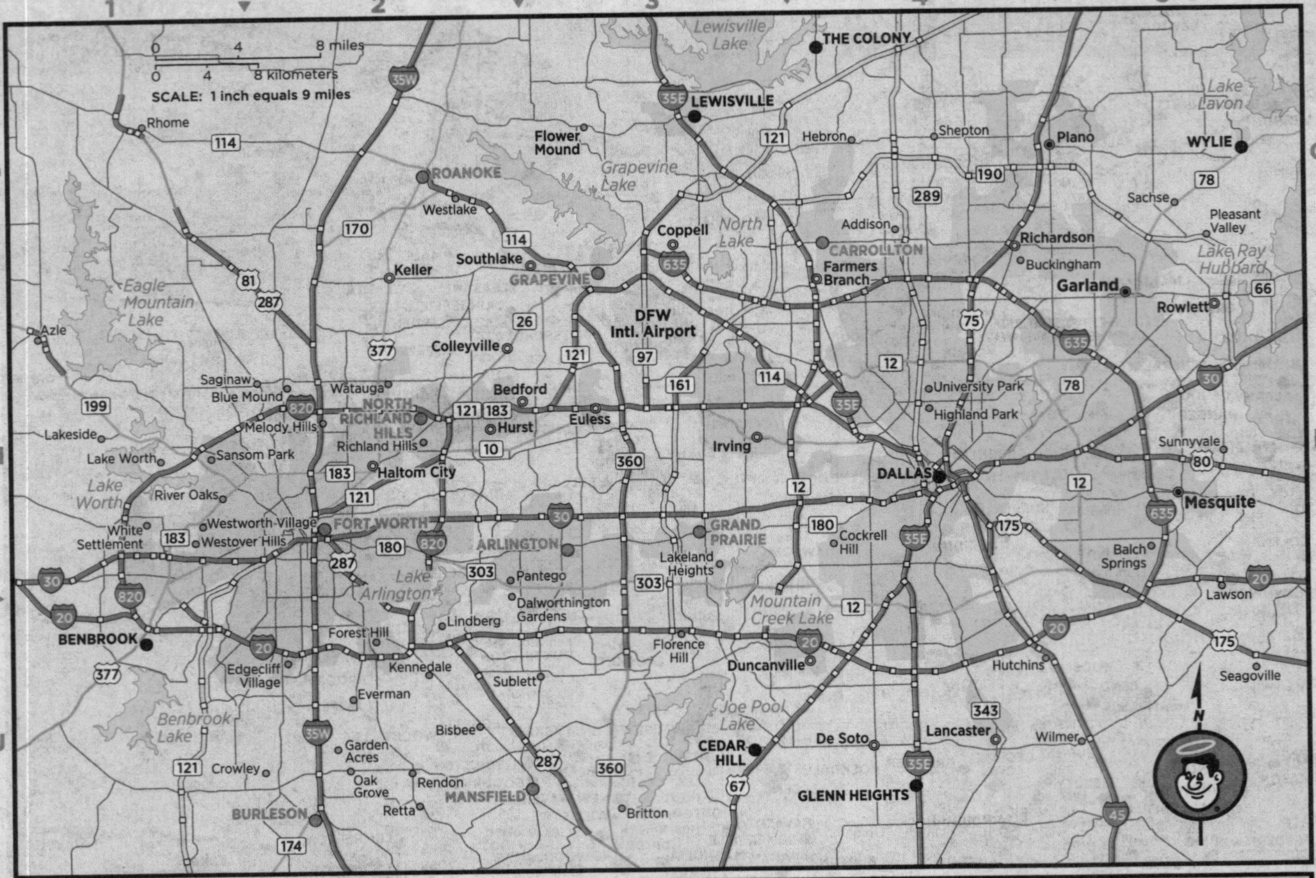

0 4 8 miles
0 4 8 kilometers
SCALE: 1 inch equals 9 miles
Lewisville Lake
THE COLONY
LEWISVILLE
Lake Lavon
Rhome
Flower Mound
Hebron
Shepton
Plano
WYLIE
ROANOKE
Grapevine Lake
Westlake
Coppell
North Lake
Addison
CARROLLTON
Richardson
Sachse
Pleasant Valley
Keller
Southlake
GRAPEVINE
Farmers Branch
Buckingham
Garland
Lake Ray Hubbard
Rowlett
Eagle Mountain Lake
Azle
DFW Intl. Airport
Colleyville
Saginaw
Blue Mound
Watauga
NORTH RICHLAND HILLS
Bedford
Euless
University Park
Highland Park
Lakeside
Melody Hills
Hurst
Richland Hills
Irving
Sunnyvale
Lake Worth
Sansom Park
Haltom City
DALLAS
Mesquite
Lake Worth
River Oaks
White Settlement
Westworth Village
Westover Hills
FORT WORTH
ARLINGTON
GRAND PRAIRIE
Cockrell Hill
Balch Springs
Lake Arlington
Pantego
Lakeland Heights
Lawson
Dalworthington Gardens
Mountain Creek Lake
BENBROOK
Forest Hill
Lindberg
Florence Hill
Duncanville
Hutchins
Edgecliff Village
Kennedale
Sublett
Seagoville
Everman
Joe Pool Lake
Benbrook Lake
Bisbee
Lancaster
De Soto
Wilmer
Garden Acres
CEDAR HILL
Crowley
Oak Grove
Rendon
GLENN HEIGHTS
MANSFIELD
Retta
Britton
BURLESON

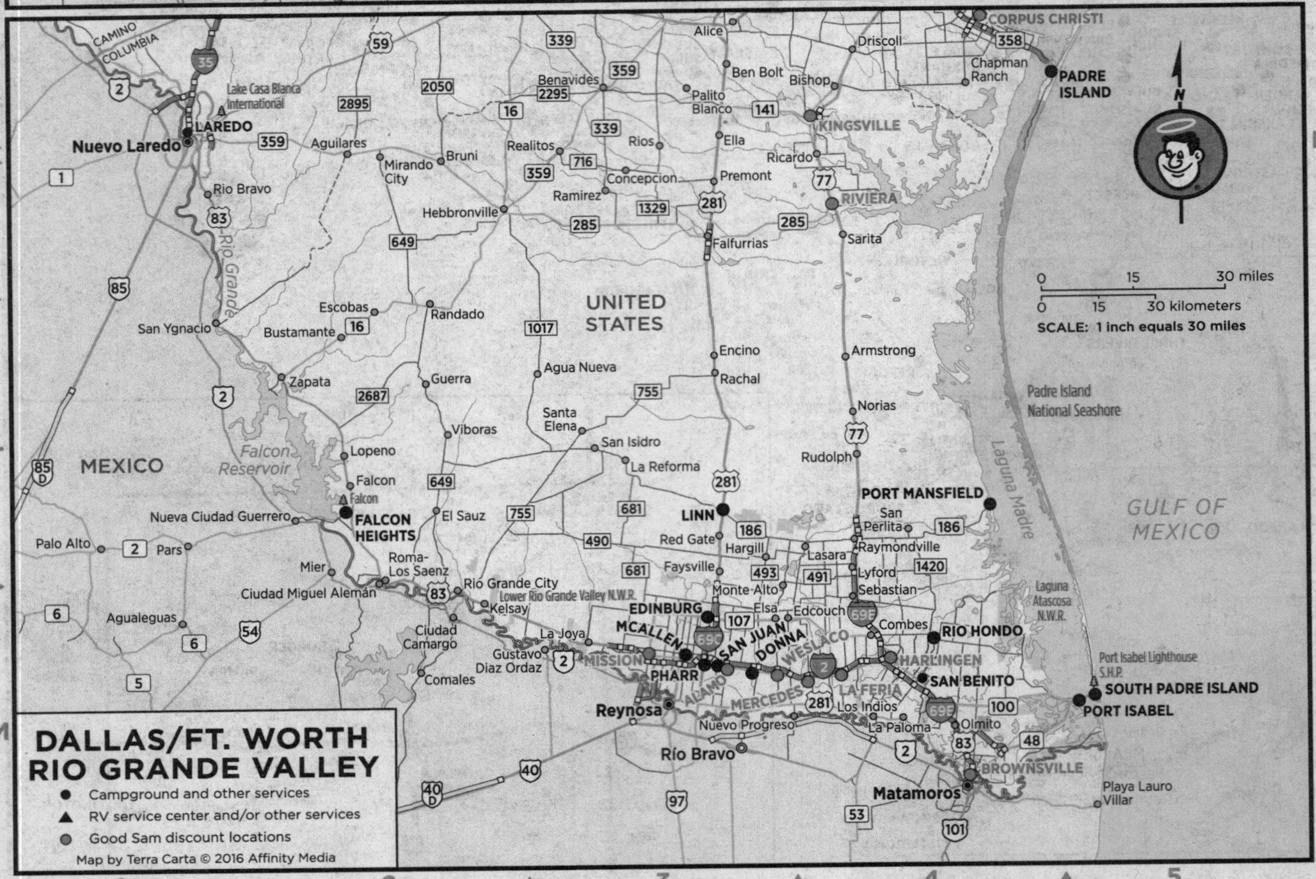

CAMINO COLUMBIA
CORPUS CHRISTI
Alice
Driscoll
Lake Casa Blanca International
Benavides
Ben Bolt
Bishop
Chapman Ranch
PADRE ISLAND
Palito Blanco
LAREDO
KINGSVILLE
Nuevo Laredo
Aguilares
Bruni
Mirando City
Realitos
Rios
Ella
Ricardo
Concepcion
Premont
Rio Bravo
Ramirez
RIVIERA
Hebbronville
Rio Grande
Falfurrias
Sarita
0 15 30 miles
0 15 30 kilometers
SCALE: 1 inch equals 30 miles
UNITED STATES
Escobas
Randado
San Ygnacio
Bustamante
Encino
Armstrong
Agua Nueva
Rachal
Zapata
Guerra
Padre Island National Seashore
Norias
Santa Elena
Viboras
San Isidro
Rudolph
MEXICO
Falcon Reservoir
Lopeno
La Reforma
Laguna Madre
Falcon
Falcon
FALCON HEIGHTS
El Sauz
LINN
PORT MANSFIELD
GULF OF MEXICO
Nueva Ciudad Guerrero
San Perlita
Red Gate
Hargill
Raymondville
Palo Alto
Pars
Lasara
Mier
Roma-Los Saenz
Faysville
Lyford
Sebastian
Ciudad Miguel Alemán
Rio Grande City
Lower Rio Grande Valley N.W.R.
Monte Alto
Laguna Atascosa N.W.R.
Agualeguas
Kelsay
EDINBURG
Elsa
Edcouch
Combes
RIO HONDO
Ciudad Camargo
La Joya
MCALLEN
SAN JUAN
DONNA
WESLACO
HARLINGEN
Gustavo Diaz Ordaz
MISSION
PHARR
ALAMO
MERCEDES
LA FERIA
SAN BENITO
Port Isabel Lighthouse S.H.P.
SOUTH PADRE ISLAND
Comales
Los Indios
PORT ISABEL
Reynosa
Nuevo Progreso
La Paloma
Olmito
Río Bravo
BROWNSVILLE
Matamoros
Playa Lauro Villar
DALLAS/FT. WORTH
RIO GRANDE VALLEY
Campground and other services
RV service center and/or other services
Good Sam discount locations
Map by Terra Carta © 2016 Affinity Media

- STAY A WHILE -

Kerrville

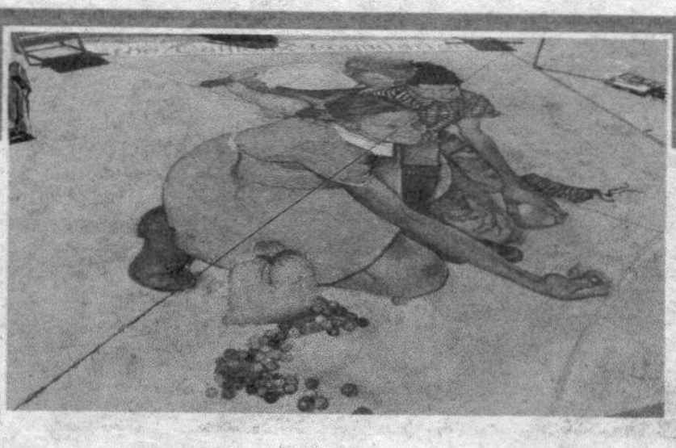

Kerrville, Texas, is a must-see, must-stay destination for RVers. This Texas-friendly community is known for its mild climate and exceptional performing and fine arts programs, all nestled in the heart of the Texas Hill Country.

RV parks with year-round events and activities are designed with the RVer in mind. You'll find year-round campground facilities for those RVers that want to experience nature at its finest! Your first visit will make it easy to understand why many Texans want to retire in the Texas Hill Country!

Enjoy the beauty of the Hill Country combined with the tranquility of the Guadalupe River. Play golf or tennis every day, photograph birds and exotic animals at area ranches or visit Texas wineries. Kerrville is the perfect location for hub and spoke activities, with some of the most scenic drives in the country.

Visit neighboring communities without relocating your RV—you're only minutes from the arts communities of Hunt and Ingram. Shop in Fredericksburg, find out what intrigued Willie and Waylon about Luckenbach, put on your hat and boots and head to Bandera, and Austin and San Antonio are short drives away.

Kerrville: An exceptional RV destination!

Play

With two national parks and 50 state parks, Texas offers a great deal more than barren desert. There are three colossal mountain ranges with peaks that exceed 7,000 feet, lush pine forests, cypress-lined bayous, rugged islands with windswept dunes and more than 350 miles of coastline. Encompassing an area of the Chihuahua desert, Big Bend National Park and its state park sibling are a hiking mecca, with more than 200 challenging trails. Tucked into the Rio Grand River, along the Mexican border, Big Bend provides refuge to a tremendous array of wildlife, including Mexican black bears and mountain lions. It is also a major migration pathway for hundreds of species of birds, including the rare Colima warbler. Just east of El Paso, Hueco Tanks State Park draws die-hard rock climbers to its low, chal-

- STAY A WHILE -

Galveston Island

At its Golden Era in the late 1800s, Galveston Island was known as the "Playground of the South"—a booming tourist destination built on its attractive beaches, convenient location, high-traffic port and numerous attractions. Galveston has reclaimed that title in recent years with an influx of new attractions and cruise ships that keep drawing visitors to this charming historic beach town on the Texas Gulf Coast.

Galveston is described as a romantic island tucked deep within the heart of south Texas. It possesses all the charm of a small southern town, yet it is only 50 miles south of Houston, the fourth-largest city in the United States.

Galveston Island is a popular year-round destination, blending temperate weather and rich history—including one of the largest and well-preserved concentrations of Victorian architecture in the country. But that's only the beginning. The island is also home to 32 miles of beaches, a wide variety of family attractions, museums, restaurants, downtown shopping, top resort hotels, and outdoor adventure activities by land or sea, including kayaking, diving, deep-sea fishing, birding, golfing, beach volleyball and more.

Much of Galveston's appeal is tied to its history, an aspect the island's tight-knit tourism community works to preserve. Popular historical attractions on the island include the 1892 Victorian mansion Bishop's Palace, 1895 Moody Mansion, the Grand 1895 Opera House and 1877 Tall Ship ELISSA. The Downtown Historic Strand Seaport District is lined with Victorian buildings that house quaint boutiques, art galleries, shops, restaurants and attractions.

www.galveston.com
888-GAL-ISLE (425-4753)

- STAY A WHILE -

Port Aransas

Port Aransas is located on the northern tip of Mustang Island along the Central Texas Gulf Coast. Eighteen miles of beautiful beach, dolphins frolicking in the channel, gentle gulf breezes and welcoming weather make the perfect backdrop for your next weekend getaway or an escape from the seasons. Our warm waters offer some of the finest fishing found anywhere, and tournaments fill almost every weekend during the summer. Take a deep-sea excursion, fish the bays and channels or cast a line in the surf or off a pier.

Hundreds of bird species visit us annually, making Port Aransas one of the most popular birding destinations in the country. With numerous vantage points to view wildlife, regardless of the time of year, you'll find Port Aransas as relaxing a rest stop as the birds do. Beachcombing for shells and driftwood along our waters and surrounding islands brings endless finds and treasures.

Adventure seekers can take part in kite boarding, jet skiing, parasailing, surfing, kayaking and much more. Our trolley will take you around town to boutiques and art galleries filled with unique coastal treasures, home décor and island style clothing. Enjoy waterside dining at our many fine restaurants and at the end of the day, experience a breathtaking sunset before returning to one of our many RV parks or campgrounds to sleep under the stars.

Come experience Port Aransas, Texas, Island Style!
Call 800-45-COAST or visit portaransas.org.

lenging routes and distinctive hand holds formed by Hueco's "tanks" (small water-carved depressions). Hueco Tanks also boasts the largest number of mask paintings in North America, with more than 200 identified throughout the park. One of the best stretches of Texas's wild coastline, Padre National Seashore forms the longest undeveloped stretch of barrier islands in the world. The narrow, 70-mile long spit of dunes and tidal flats abound with sea life, including Padre Island's most famous residents: Kemp's Ridley sea turtles.

Experience

From mid January, the Fort Worth Stock Show and Rodeo is a 23-day rodeo extravaganza that attracts more than 1 million visitors to its livestock shows, live music performances, child-friendly activities and hearty cowboy fare. In Waxahachie, from early April through May, the Scarborough Renaissance Festival features live music, sword contests and comedy performances. There's more than one Rattlesnake Roundup in Texas, but the "World's Largest" has been held in Sweetwater every March since 1958. In addition to the namesake snake hunt, when bounty hunters seize one percent of the state's rattlesnake population from their lethal dens, there's a Rattlesnake Parade, Miss Snake Charmer Pageant, Rattlesnake Dance and a barbecue cook off. Appropriately for Texas, the Dallas-based State Fair is a prodigious, three-week extravaganza that reaches a raucous crescendo with the annual "Red River Shoot-out" between the University of Texas and the University of Oklahoma. From June to mid August, the Outdoor Musical Drama in Palo Duro Canyon State Park is often cited (with a typical Texan lack of modesty) as the most spectacular outdoor musical drama in the world.

TRAVEL & TOURISM

Office of the Governor, Economic Development and Tourism
800-8888-TEX
www.TravelTex.com

Brewster County Tourism
www.visitbigbend.com

Dallas-Fort Worth Area Tourism Council
800-766-3349, 817-329-2438
www.dfwandbeyond.com

East Texas Tourism Assn.
903-757-4444
www.easttexasguide.com

Visit Houston
800-4-HOUSTON
www.visithoustontexas.com

Kerrville CVB
800-221-7958
www.kerrvilletexascvb.com

Rio Grande Valley Chamber of Commerce
956-968-3141
www.valleychamber.com

San Antonio Tourism Council
210-886-9991
www.sanantoniotourism.com

OUTDOOR RECREATION

Texas Parks & Wildlife Dept.
800-792-1112, 512-389-4800
www.tpwd.state.tx.us

SHOPPING

Jackson Street District
956-216-4910
www.traveltex.com/attractions

Prime Outlets and Tanger Outlet Center
www.primeoutlets.com

RV PARK &
CAMPGROUND REVIEWS
WRITE A REVIEW TODAY!
Did you recently visit an RV Park or Campground? Write a review!
Planning your next RV trip? Read a review!
In addition to the ratings completed by our experts, Good Sam now features RVer Reviews, online - RV park and campground reviews written by other RVers!
Go to GoodSamClub.com and tell us about your recent trip!
Good Sam
Visit GoodSamClub.com/travel
to read or write reviews

Featured Good Sam Parks

TEXAS

Good Sam Park

When you stay with Good Sam, you can expect the highest degree of cleanliness and friendliness, and better yet, you get 10% off campground fees.

If you're not already a Good Sam member you can. purchase your membership at one of these locations:

ALAMO
Casa Del Valle RV Resort
(877)828-9945

ALPINE
Lost Alaskan RV Resort
(432)837-1136

AMARILLO
Amarillo Best Wonderland RV Resort
(806)383-1700
Amarillo Ranch RV Park
(806)373-4962
Fort Amarillo RV Resort
(806)331-1700
Oasis RV Resort
(888)789-9697
Overnite RV Park
(800)554-5305

ARLINGTON
Treetops Carefree RV Resort
(800)747-0787

ATHENS
Texan RV Park
(903)677-3326

AUBREY
Shady Creek RV Park and Storage
(972)347-5384

AUSTIN
Austin Lone Star Carefree RV Resort
(512)444-6322
Crestview RV Park
(512)282-3516
La Hacienda RV Resort
(512)266-8001
Oak Forest RV Park
(512)813-2913

BANDERA
Skyline Ranch RV Park
(830)796-4958

BAYTOWN
Houston East RV Resort
(281)383-3618
Mont Belvieu RV Resort
(832)902-2200

BOERNE
Alamo Fiesta RV Resort
(800)321-2267
Top Of the Hill RV Resort
(830)537-3666

BROOKSHIRE
Houston West RV Park
(281)375-5678

BROWNSVILLE
Breeze Lake RV Campground MHP
(956)831-4427
Paul's RV Park
(956)831-4852

BULLARD
K.E. Bushman's Camp
(903)894-8221

BULVERDE
Texas 281 RV Park Ltd
(830)980-2282

BURLESON
Mockingbird Hill Mobile Home & RV Park
(817)295-3011

CANTON
Canton I-20 RV Park
(903)873-8561
Mill Creek Ranch Resort
(866)599-7275

CANYON
Palo Duro RV Park
(800)540-0567

CANYON LAKE
Summit Vacation & RV Resort
(830)964-2531

CARROLLTON
Sandy Lake MH & RV Park Carefree RV Resort
(972)242-6808

CARTHAGE
Carthage RV Campground
(903)693-6640

CASTROVILLE
Alsatian RV Resort & Golf Club
(830)931-9190

COLLEGE STATION
Karstens RV Resort
(979)774-7799

COLORADO CITY
Lone Wolf Creek RV Village
(325)728-9310

COMFORT
RV Park USA
(830)995-2900

CONCAN
Parkview Riverside RV Park
(877)374-6748

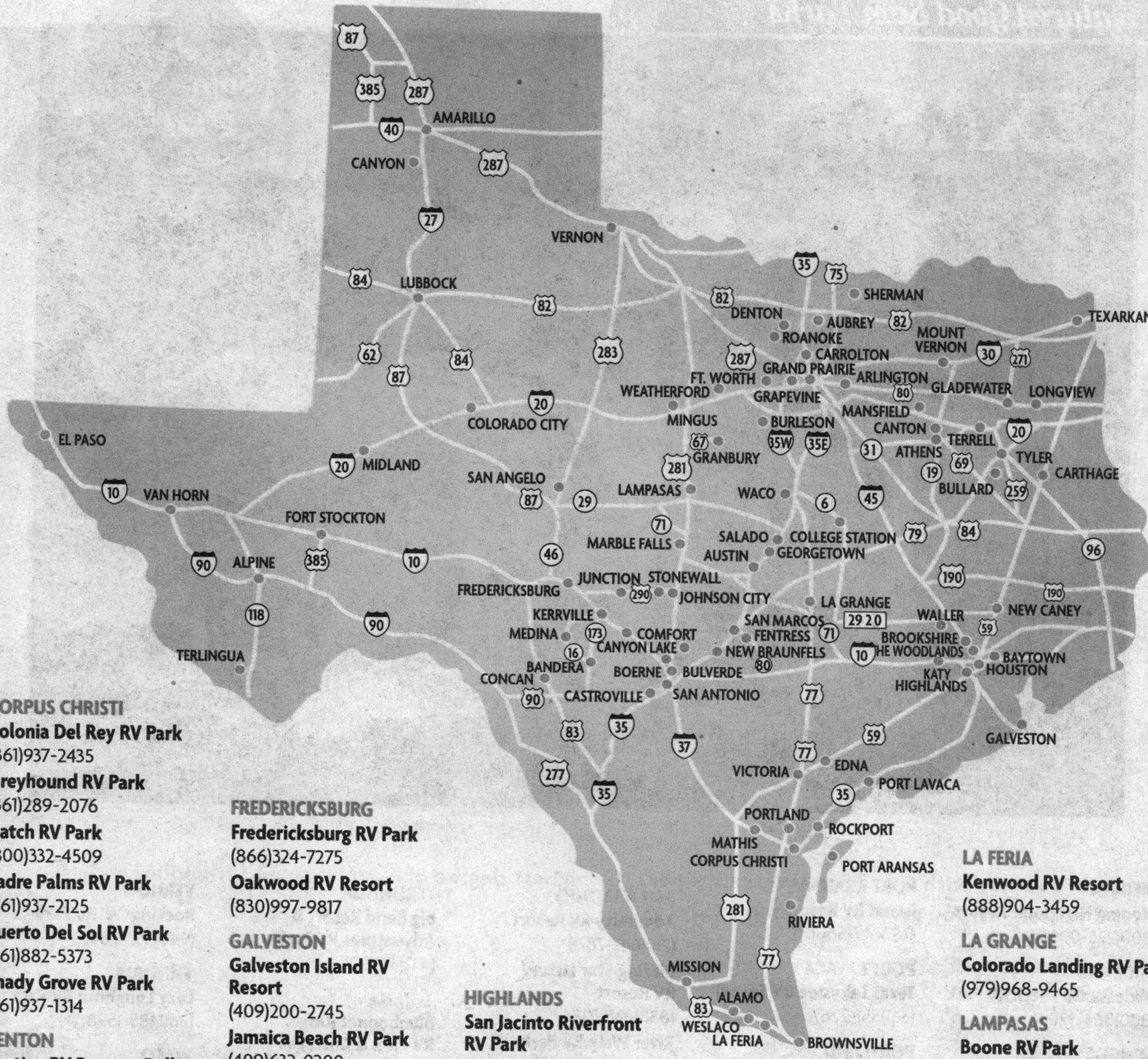

CORPUS CHRISTI
Colonia Del Rey RV Park
(361)937-2435
Greyhound RV Park
(361)289-2076
Hatch RV Park
(800)332-4509
Padre Palms RV Park
(361)937-2125
Puerto Del Sol RV Park
(361)882-5373
Shady Grove RV Park
(361)937-1314

DENTON
Destiny RV Resorts-Dallas
(888)238-1532

EDNA
Brackenridge Recreation Complex - Brackenridge Park & Campground
(361)782-5456

EL PASO
Mission RV Park
(915)859-1133

FENTRESS
Leisure Resort RV Park
(800)248-4103

FORT STOCKTON
Fort Stockton RV Park
(432)395-2494

FORT WORTH
Cowtown RV Park
(817)441-7878

FREDERICKSBURG
Fredericksburg RV Park
(866)324-7275
Oakwood RV Resort
(830)997-9817

GALVESTON
Galveston Island RV Resort
(409)200-2745
Jamaica Beach RV Park
(409)632-0200

GEORGETOWN
East View RV Ranch
(512)931-2251

GLADEWATER
Shallow Creek RV Resort
(888)984-4513

GRANBURY
Bennett's RV Ranch
(817)279-7500

GRAND PRAIRIE
Loyd Park/Joe Pool Lake
(817)467-2104
Traders Village RV Park
(972)647-8205

GRAPEVINE
The Vineyards Campground & Cabins
(888)329-8993

HIGHLANDS
San Jacinto Riverfront RV Park
(281)426-6919

HOUSTON
Advanced RV Resort
(713)433-6950
Allstar RV Resort
(713)981-6814
Eastlake RV Resort
(832)243-6919
Fallbrook RV Resort
(866)923-4988
Lakeview RV Resort
(800)385-9122
Northlake RV Resort
(281)209-1770
Southlake RV Resort
(832)804-8088
Traders Village RV Park
(281)890-5500
Westlake RV Resort
(281)463-8566

JOHNSON CITY
Roadrunner RV Park, LLC
(830)868-7449

JUNCTION
Junction North Llano River RV Park
(325)446-3138

KATY
Katy Lake RV Resort
(281)492-0044

KERRVILLE
Buckhorn Lake Resort
(830)895-0007
Johnson Creek RV Resort & Park
(830)367-3300
Take-It-Easy RV Resort
(800)828-6984

LA FERIA
Kenwood RV Resort
(888)904-3459

LA GRANGE
Colorado Landing RV Park
(979)968-9465

LAMPASAS
Boone RV Park
(888)577-5171

LONGVIEW
Fernbrook Park
(903)643-8888

LUBBOCK
Camelot Village RV Park
(806)792-6477
Lubbock RV Park, Inc
(806)747-2366

MANSFIELD
Texan RV Ranch
(817)473-1666

MARBLE FALLS
Sunset Point On Lake LBJ
(830)798-8199

MATHIS
Mustang Hollow Campground
(361)547-5201

MEDINA
Medina Highpoint Resort
(800)225-0991

MIDLAND
Midessa Oil Patch RV Park
(800)864-3204

MINGUS
Cactus Rose RV Park
(254)693-5976

MISSION
Bentsen Grove Resort MHP
(956)585-7011
Bentsen Palm Village RV Resort
(877)247-3727

MOUNT VERNON
Still Meadow RV Park
(903)588-2230

NEW BRAUNFELS
Hill Country Cottage and RV Resort
(830)625-1919

NEW CANEY
Forest Retreat RV Park
(281)354-9888

PORT ARANSAS
Island RV Resort
(361)749-5600

PORT LAVACA
Texas Lakeside RV Resort
(361)551-2267

PORTLAND
Sea Breeze RV Park
(361)643-0744

RIVIERA
Seawind RV Resort On the Bay
(361)297-5738

ROANOKE
Northlake Village RV Park
(817)430-3303

ROCKPORT
Ancient Oaks RV Park
(361)729-5051

SALADO
Tranquil Gardens RV Park
(254)947-5192

SAN ANGELO
Spring Creek Marina & RV Park, Inc
(325)944-3850

SAN ANTONIO
Admiralty RV Resort
(210)647-7878
Blazing Star Luxury RV Resort
(888)838-7186
River Walk RV Park
(210)337-6501
Stone Creek RV Park
(830)609-7759
Travelers World Carefree RV Resort
(210)532-8310

SAN MARCOS
Pecan Park Riverside RV & Cabins
(512)396-0070

SHERMAN
Lazy L RV Park
(903)870-7772

STONEWALL
Peach Country RV Park
(830)644-2233

TERLINGUA
Big Bend Resort & Adventures RV Park
(432)371-2218

TERRELL
Bluebonnet Ridge RV Park & Cottages
(972)524-9600

TEXARKANA
Shady Pines RV Park
(903)832-1268

THE WOODLANDS
Rayford Crossing RV Resort
(281)298-8008
Woodland Lakes RV Park
(936)273-6666

TYLER
#1 RV Park Of Tyler
(903)593-9101

VAN HORN
Van Horn RV Park
(432)283-2728

VERNON
Rocking "A" RV Park
(940)552-2821

VICTORIA
Lazy Longhorn RV Park
(361)485-1598

WACO
I 35 RV Park & Resort
(254)829-0698

WALLER
Lonestar Yogi
(979)826-4111

WEATHERFORD
Oak Creek RV Park
(817)594-0200

WESLACO
Snow To Sun RV Resort
(888)799-5895

For more Good Sam Parks go to listing pages

Getty Images/iStockphoto

BIG BEND NATIONAL PARK

Walk on the wild side in a west Texas wonderland

As the Rio Grande snakes its way south and eastward between Texas and Mexico—forming a natural international border between the two—it bends sharply to the north before continuing on with its Gulf of Mexico-bound trajectory. This sharp bend, known matter-of-factly as the Big Bend, is home to Big Bend National Park, a more than 800,000-acre tract of protected Chihuahuan Desert wilderness.

If you're looking for one of the most geologically diverse and historically fascinating places in the American Southwest, Big Bend National Park is it. Home to three different ecosystems (desert, mountain and river), a massive selection of wildlife and set upon a history of political conquest, Big Bend National Park is anything but generic.

Native Americans have occupied, hunted in and moved through the Big Bend area for thousands of years. As a result, the park is home to a rich array of ancient pictographs and archeological sites. Over the course of the last 500 years, the area has been claimed by six different nations and has witnessed the movements of various armies and raiding parties crossing the Rio Grande.

> Rio Grande Village boasts incredible scenery and wildlife, making it popular for nature photographers.

Geological Marvels

Today, that game of political chairs has finally settled, and the park is known more for its striking physical geography and its rich fossil beds. Once under a massive inland sea, the park has been a paleontological oasis full of sea fossils and dinosaur bones. More than 100 miles of scenic paved roadways make exploring the park's main attractions quick and easy, while more than 150 miles of backcountry road make going off-road one of the area's secret recreational treasures. Hundreds of miles of well-marked trails are available for hikers, bikers and horseback riders, while rafting, kayaking and canoeing excursions can launch on the legendary Rio Grande.

Start with a stop at any of the park's main visitor centers—Panther Junction, Chisos Basin, Castolon, Persimmon Gap or Rio Grande Village. Each provides information on nearby campgrounds, trailheads and recreational options. Three National Park Service-operated campgrounds are available in the park, including one with full RV hookups—Rio Grande Village RV Campground.

Each visitor center offers a unique selection of perks. Castolon, for instance, doubles as an attraction and historic district all in its own. It features a range of on-site exhibits and historic buildings for guests to stroll about and explore.

Chisos Basin, surrounded by sheer-faced cliffs and a smorgasbord of trail-

A fawn along Basin Road. NPS Photo/Cookie Ballou

TX

heads, is a focal point for hikers. It's also home to an outdoor amphitheater that often features educational programs during the summer.

Persimmon Gap is the main northern gateway to Big Bend National Park. Those who stop on their way in can explore to the Fossil Bone Exhibit Area or hit trailheads that weave their way to Dog Canyon or Devil's Den.

Rio Grande Village attracts tourist activity year-round, boasting warm temperatures, incredible scenery and an abundance of wildlife, making this a popular spot for nature photographers. The village is also home to a general store, laundromat, showers and full-service RV campground.

Trails and Roads

When it's time to explore the park in earnest, there may be no better way of doing so than by lacing up the hiking boots and simply hitting the old dusty trail. Big Bend National Park is a hiker's dream come true. The choices are essentially endless, with clusters of nearby trailheads offering desert hikes, mountain hikes and riverside hikes in vast supply. As always, exercise caution and if necessary consult with rangers at one of the visitor centers before venturing into the backcountry of the park.

Visitors with a soft spot for fishing will find themselves just as at home in Big Bend as folks with a penchant for hiking. To fish the legendary Rio Grande or either of its two Big Bend-area tributaries (Tornillo Creek or Terlingua Creek), simply head to a visitor center and snag a free daily fishing permit—no Texas State fishing license is required here. Then find yourself a nice quiet spot to call your own for the day.

Finally, when you're tired of exploring the park by foot or by fishing reel, hop in the car or truck and go for an auto tour. Some scenic routes require more robust off-road vehicles, but most of the park's unpaved roads can be tackled with relative ease. Two of the more popular routes are the Dagger Flat Auto Trail and Old Maverick Road. The National Park Service recommends that you check your vehicle's fluids and tires before using backcountry roads.

It's no wonder why Big Bend National Park annually attracts an average of 300,000 visitors. The real wonder is why that number isn't so much higher. At close to a million acres and featuring such a varied landscape, the park is packed with recreational hotspots and stunning natural landscapes. Take advantage of comparatively small crowds and experience this oft-overlooked natural gem in the Lone Star State.

Chisos Basin, surrounded by sheer-faced cliffs and a smorgasbord of trailheads, is a focal point for hikers.

For More Information

Big Bend National Park
432-477-2251
www.nps.gov/bibe

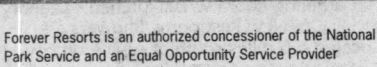

Texas State Travel Guide
800-452-9292
www.traveltex.com

Getty Images/iStockphoto

DALLAS/FORT WORTH

Everything is bigger in Texas—including this pair of larger-than-life cities

The Dallas-Fort Worth Metroplex is a multi-city mashup of historic Old West adventure and metropolitan excitement. Popular landmarks such as the Dallas World Aquarium and the Fort Worth Stockyards are worth a visit, but be sure to check out some lesser-known destinations that are just as entertaining and enlightening. You'll see the Lone Star State in a whole new light after visiting these towns.

Fort Worth

Natural beauty is treasured in Fort Worth, and the city's Botanic Gardens provide a great way to get a sense of the region's diverse flora. Wander the 115 acres of curated plants in 23 uniquely styled garden settings. From the Japanese countryside to English rose collections, the garden's sights and smells will make you want to spend a whole day there.

Let the warm summer breeze carry a cool mist your way from the Fort Worth Water Gardens, next to the Fort Worth Convention Center. While it's not for swimming—the center of the pool is a strong swirl of rushing water—the sight and sound alone will grant you a temporary oasis in the heat of the urban environment.

See a collection of diverse animals at the Fort Worth Zoo. This state-of-

The Dealy Plaza and its surrounding buildings in Dallas Getty Images/iStockphoto

the-art zoo boasts hundreds of species in natural settings and a Wild West-style town that offers kid-friendly activities such as a carousel and petting zoo. A new waterpark feature invites the little ones to cool off in the summer months.

Fort Worth's biggest outdoor show can be found at the Fort Worth Stockyards, a 98-acre historic district that once served as a vital cattle center. Immerse yourself in the city's Western history by touring the preserved buildings or taking in a rodeo. Watch an authentic cattle drive or go shopping at one of the many stores selling western gear and memorabilia.

Museums

The collection of stainless-steel and glass structures that comprise the Modern Art Museum of Fort Worth are eye-catching and inviting, and visitors who venture inside find works by Jackson Pollock and Andy Warhol.

Rough and rugged men weren't the only ones to roam the Texas plains in the days of cattle driving. The women who made history are remembered at the National Cowgirl Hall of Fame and Museum, located near the Fort Worth Museum of Science and History. The hall of fame honors pioneers such as Annie Oakley and Sacagawea, and houses more than 4,000 artifacts attributed to these great ladies of the frontier era.

The neighboring science and history museum houses a permanent children's collection of hands-on exhibits that keep kids busy for hours. Visitors also learn about the Wild West days of the region and the geology that makes up this part of the state.

Dallas

Dallas dominates the skyline of the east side of the Metroplex, and its streets are filled with eclectic shops, world-class museums and shops and dining spots soaked in true Texas character. City founder John Neely Bryan is honored in the display of a replica of his log-cabin home, which sits on Founder's Plaza, only a quarter-mile from the original homestead. Pioneer Plaza, near the Dallas Convention Center, features a life-size bronze sculpture depicting a cattle drive, along with native trees and a flowing stream on a four-acre site.

Trinity River Audubon Center is a popular destination for locals and visitors alike, and with good reason: It's home to the largest urban hardwood forest in the U.S. and boasts stunning architecture, day hikes, birding classes and guided river tours.

Dallas has its fair share of ghost tales, and if supernatural stories are your thing, pay a visit to Sons of Hermann Hall in Deep Ellum. Here, ghosts of revelers past have been known to dance in the upstairs ballroom, knock paintings off the wall and even launch a bowling ball or two down the lanes of the shuttered bowling alley in the basement.

Texas-size Fun for Kids

Kids get a kick out of trying some of the nearly 200 sodas on tap at the Soda Gallery in Bishop Arts District. This sugar-laden store features soft drinks from dozens of countries. Fair Park is another great family-friendly spot, with the Children's Aquarium and an extension of the Perot Museum of Nature and Science, whose main campus is located downtown.

While you're there, tour the Texas Discovery Gardens and the African-American Museum. If you visit in the fall, you can't pass up the chance to visit the Texas State Fair, which is held every year at Fair Park. Wave back to Big Tex, an animatronic statue that towers over the fair, and ride the gigantic Ferris Wheel to get a bird's-eye view of the festivities below.

For More Information

Dallas/Fort Worth Area Tourism Council
817-329-2438
www.dfwandbeyond.com

Texas State Travel Guide
800-452-9292
www.traveltex.com

The Dallas Texas skyline. Getty Images/iStockphoto

TX

Galveston Island CVB

SPOTLIGHT

TX

GALVESTON ISLAND

Voyage into the Lone Star State's past on this fun-filled island

Forget the Texas stereotypes of tumbleweeds, longhorn cattle and cowpokes. Galveston Island, a barrier island on the Gulf Coast just 50 miles southeast of Houston, offers boating, fishing, surfing and swimming. The eclectic communities on the island will make all visitors feel welcome, and the extensive menu of recreational activities will keep visitors of all ages busy.

Dropping a Line

Gather your fishing gear and grab some bait for a morning or evening on the 61st Street Pier. This popular destination features great fishing for a fee, and photo-worthy views of the water and the shore.

If you prefer shooting photos to dropping a line, take a break from the summer sun and visit Moody Gardens, a multi-attraction destination that includes a living rainforest, 1.5-million-gallon aquarium, and a 1800s-era paddlewheel boat that offers one-hour cruises. Get your adrenaline pumping on the ropes course and zip line, and cool off in the Gardens' water park.

Pier Into Fun

Nothing beats a seaside carnival experience, and Galveston's Historic Pleasure Pier offers just that. The family-friendly combination of midway rides, quick-dining and souvenir shopping makes for a classic summer experience.

Get a feel for historic Galveston on a walk around the Strand Historic District. This collection of shops, restaurants, galleries and museums provides a full day of exploration and discovery. Stop in at the Galveston Island Railroad Museum, and grab a bowl of gumbo to refuel for more walking through this popular destination.

See the history of flight embodied in historic aircraft on display at the Lone Star Flight Museum, which houses more than 40 aircraft. The Texas Aviation Hall of Fame celebrates the aerial accomplishments of the state's native sons and daughters. Guests can even go for rides in some of the restored planes.

For More Information

Galveston Island Convention and Visitors Bureau
888-GAL-ISLE
www.galveston.com

Texas Travel Guide
800-452-9292
www.traveltex.com

JUNCTION

This charming Texas town is more than a country crossroads

How the town of Junction in central Texas got its name is no great mystery, considering two navigable rivers and four major highways converge and intersect here. Since its founding in 1876, the town has been a crossroads and gateway to east, west and south Texas. More surprisingly, perhaps, is the official nickname of this Lone Star State town: "Land of Living Waters."

Despite its scorching central Texas setting, Junction is, in fact, home to more flowing waterways than any other town or county in the entire state. Kayaking, canoeing, river-tubing and fishing are among the most popular activities in and around this community of fewer than 3,000 residents. By spring of each year, the flow of surrounding rivers, creeks and streams picks up considerably, attracting visitors from far and wide for the remainder of summer.

The community itself is small and rural, home to less than 3,000 residents. The nearest big city, San Antonio, sits 115 miles away to the southeast. Mastering the art of supreme relaxation is the principal pastime in this township, followed closely by exploring the great outdoors.

Riding the River

The North and South forks of the Llano River attract most of the attention. Guide and equipment outfitters make it easy to kayak, canoe, raft, fish, hunt and hike the immediate area and surrounding backcountry. On river-float trips, most guides offer launch and pick-up services, allowing you to float the length of the river with transportation waiting for you downstream.

South Llano River State Park is probably the best place to start your outdoor adventures. The main park entrance is located roughly 4 miles south of downtown Junction, hugging the eastern shores of the South Llano River. At 507 acres, the park is just big enough to lose yourself in, but small enough to explore in full over the course of a lengthy visit.

The park is also home to one of the largest natural turkey roosts in the state. Hunting is prohibited, but observation blinds are littered throughout the "Turkey Roost" section of the park down along the South Llano River frontage. Aside from wild turkey, however, you're just as likely to spot white-tailed deer, bobcats and armadillos.

If you're an angler, the "Land of Living Waters" will seem like a dream come true. Both branches of the river burst with an abundance of largemouth bass, Guadalupe bass, perch, channel catfish and yellow catfish.

The Deer Horn Tree is a landmark in Junction. Billy Hathorn

History on Display

A popular hotspot for history enthusiasts is the National Museum of the Pacific War, located in the nearby German-themed town of Fredericksburg. Dedicated to showcasing the history and events in World War II's Pacific Theater, the museum's collections include a range of original artifacts and educational exhibits.

For More Information

Junction Texas
800-KIMBLE-4
www.junctiontexas.net

Texas Travel Guide
800-452-9292
www.traveltex.com

Getty Images/iStockphoto

PORT ARANSAS

Make a splash in a Texas island paradise

Bring your fishing rod, beach chair and thirst for adventure to Port Aransas, nestled on Mustang Island off the coast of Corpus Christi. This town is the ultimate Gulf Coast destination, bustling with quaint shops and fantastic restaurants along with lots of opportunities for adventure on the inviting Gulf waters and inlets.

> End the day by taking in a sunset around the island on a chartered boat ride.

Hit the Water

Fishing at Port A—as the locals call it—is one of the biggest draws to the barrier island. Charter a boat or launch your own into the surf and head out into the Gulf to chase redfish, pompano and amberjack. From the safety of the wharf, you can enjoy a sunrise catch while taking in the oceanside scenery.

Prefer riding to reeling? The waves that break off the shores of Mustang Island are big enough to ride, and if you're a seasoned surfer you'll be more than satisfied at Horace Caldwell Pier. Sandbars are the secret to the great waves, swift enough to give veterans a workout and safe enough to entice beginners. Catch a private lesson from a local, or dive in and hang ten on your own.

If surfing or angling doesn't satisfy your need for an adrenaline rush, check out the parasailing and paragliding opportunities available around Port A. Further down the island, you can paddle through 20 miles of shallow spots to enjoy fishing and bird-watching along the Mustang Island State Park Paddling Trail.

Slow things down a bit with a ferry ride out to San Jose Island. This 21-mile stretch of sandy, undeveloped paradise is a shell-hunter's dream. Dig your toes in and build a sandcastle or two; the ferry only runs a few times each day, so pack enough snacks, water and sunscreen for a few hours.

Land-based Recreation

While most small towns might offer a sandwich shop or fast-food chain spot, Port Aransas caters to guests who travel from all around the world. Take the opportunity to enjoy fine dining at any one of several great spots, many of which take advantage of the island location to create unforgettable seafood

A nature observation deck on the wetlands outside of Port Aransas. Getty Images/iStockphoto

Amphibious turtles can be found near the shores of Port Aransas.
John Fowler

TX

dishes. Save room for dessert, which you'll find at Winton's Candies. The handmade caramel and taffy treats are a delight for just about anyone.

Bicycling the beach is a great way to spend an afternoon in Port Aransas. Wheel yourself down to Port Aransas Nature Preserve at Charlie's Pasture. The preserve houses just over three miles of trails for biking and hiking, and its proximity to the birding center means you're likely to see some of the preserve's feathered residents.

Paradise Pond is a wheelchair-accessible park with boardwalks and viewing areas, as well as a sitting area near the entrance of the 2-acre habitat that lets guests enjoy butterflies and dragonflies among the flowers that draw in the beautiful insects.

Bird-lovers are in luck because Mustang Island is home to the Leonabelle Turnbull Birding Center. Visitors can stroll the boardwalk and climb the 25-foot observation tower to sneak a peek at dozens of migratory species, including roseate spoonbills, black crowned night herons and more. Free guided tours are available.

Floating Past History

Get to know the story behind Port Aransas during a visit to the Port Aransas Museum. Rotating exhibits shed light on the region's involvement in the Civil War, the maritime industry and fishing industry. Nearby, Farley Boat Works introduces visitors to the skill and craft of boat building.

The story and science of the sea are the focus of a museum at the University of Texas Marine Science Institute. Explore the institute's Visitor Center, Estuary Explorium, Wetlands Education Center and Bay Education Center to learn about marine life and its varied habitats, many of which are found and studied around Mustang Island and Port Aransas.

Discover history via kayak on the Lighthouse Lakes Trail close to nearby Aransas Pass. Amidst the redfish, mullet and birds, you'll catch a glimpse of the 68-foot tall Lydia Ann Lighthouse, activated in 1862.

Aransas Entertainment

Spend a night out and catch a performance or two at Third Coast Theater, where singer-songwriters entertain guests in this cozy, 150-seat theater situated on the property of a resort community. On a quiet morning, take in a round of golf at the only seaside golf course designed by Arnold Palmer, the Palmilla Beach Golf Club.

Despite its small size, Port Aransas offers a wealth of shopping opportunities. Spend a little cash and come home with treasures from local shops featuring gifts, apparel and artwork from local craftsmen. Port Aransas Community Theater entertains audiences with performances throughout the year.

End the day by taking in a sunset around the island on a chartered boat ride. You may even catch a glimpse of playful dolphins.

For More Information

Port Aransas Chamber of Commerce
800-45-COAST
www.portaransas.org

Texas State Travel Guide
800-452-9292
www.traveltex.com

Getty Images/iStockphoto

SAN MARCOS

Go deeper into the heart of Texas in this fun town

The quiet city of San Marcos sits halfway between the buzzing central Texas hot spots of Austin and San Antonio on Interstate 35. The trendy streets of the former are just 30 miles away to the northeast, while the rustic and historic relics of the latter are just 50 miles away to the southwest. So it's really no surprise that the tourism spotlight so rarely shines here, given its nearest neighbors.

That's a pity. This small city of less than 60,000 residents offers a perfect balance for out-of-town visitors seeking some small-town atmosphere, great public parks and easy access to world-class attractions in nearby major cities. In short, this is the ideal spot to set up camp and enjoy the best of all possible worlds while still savoring some rest, relaxation and solitude.

That formula appears to have deep roots as well. The San Marcos area is littered with archaeological dig sites, with new finds occurring all the time. One recent groundbreaking discovery unearthed artifacts dating to 12,000 years ago and the prehistoric Clovis Indians, the oldest known inhabitants of the western hemisphere. To some experts, this puts San Marcos in the running for longest continuously inhabited community on the continent.

Down by the River

If the Clovis Indians did, in fact, call this Texas Hill Country spot home, it was likely because of the San Marcos River, which winds its way straight through the layout of the town.

Today, the river still serves as one of the community's best attractions and most accessible sources of recreation. Lazy, aimless tubing is a popular pastime, especially for a place that boasts an annual average of 300 days of sunshine each year.

The headwaters of the river start at nearby San Marcos Springs. Glass-bottomed boat tours that depart from the heart of downtown San Marcos make the 4-mile journey upstream, offering incredible below-surface views.

For More Information

San Marcos Convention and Visitor Bureau
888-200-5620
www.toursanmarcos.com

Texas State Travel Guide
800-452-9292
www.traveltex.com

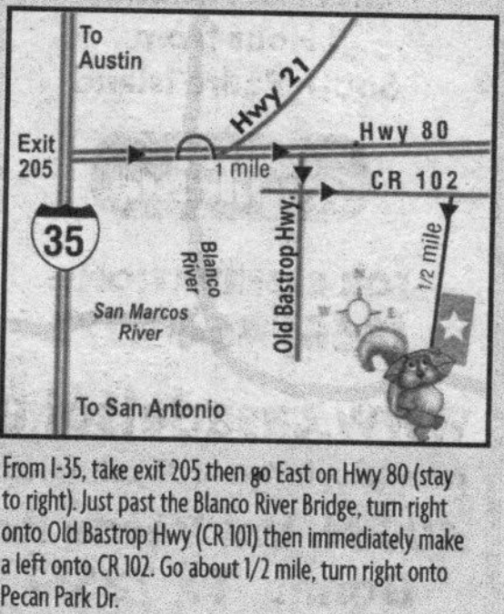

TX

Kenny Braun

SPOTLIGHT

TX

SOUTH TEXAS TROPICS

Butterflies and birds mingle with naval history and country music in this slice of the Lone Star State

The Texas Tropics is a sprawling region known for its vibrant Mexican influences and abundant natural attractions. The fertile Rio Grande Valley is a major part of this landscape, as birds, butterflies and other species gather here during long migrations. The communities of South Texas comprise a rich cultural mix of Mexican, European and early American pioneer ancestry, all offering singular appeal.

Start your trip in Laredo, where historic charm is plentiful. This colorful border town (its Mexican neighbor across the river to the west is the town of Nuevo Laredo) can be explored through a walking tour that starts at the Republic of the Rio Grande Museum. Once the residence of a rancher and former mayor of Laredo, the museum houses displays that simulate the interior of an authentic 1830s home.

> Padre Island National Seashore invites nature enthusiasts to explore 70 miles of sand, surf and grassy dunes.

The museum is located on San Agustin Plaza, where you can also explore the Villa Antigua Border Heritage Museum, San Agustin Cathedral, San Agustin Plaza, the Washington's Birthday Celebration Museum and Casa Ortiz on your walking tour. True to its community, Laredo conducts its tours in English and Spanish.

Birding on the River

Continue your travels down the southwest edge of the region to McAllen. This rapidly growing city maintains its small-town feel and puts the focus on the rugged natural beauty of the Rio Grande Valley at Quinta Mazatlan World Birding Center and the McAllen Nature Center. Quinta Mazatlan is a 1930s adobe estate that educates visitors about the region's bird populations, plant life and environmental stewardship. It is the McAllen wing of the World Birding Center under the stewardship of the City of McAllen Parks & Recreation Department. McAllen Nature Center offers a variety of nature walks for families, bird enthusiasts and photographers on a half-mile of trails.

Port Isabel Lighthouse in the Holidays.
Getty Images/iStockphoto

A movie set in the Rio Grande River Kenny Braun

Giraffes in the Brownsville Zoo.
Kenny Braun

Expand your mind at the International Museum of Art and Science. This eclectic but inspired combination of disciplines features the RioScape, an interactive science playground. Guests can also see works of talented artists.

Brownsville, at the southernmost tip of the state, is a gateway to coastal recreation. Visit the city's Historic Battlefield Trail, where the first battle of the Mexican-American War took place at Palo Alto on the trail's northern end. The 9-mile hike-and-bike trail is a former rail line and is bookended to the south by the Gladys Porter Zoo. To the east, the Port Isabel Lighthouse is a historic treasure.

Island Time

Head east toward the Gulf and enjoy one of the state's most popular oceanside destinations, South Padre Island. While it's a crowded scene during college spring break weeks, South Padre can be also a quiet family escape the rest of the year.

Take a chartered boat out into the Gulf and watch dolphins dance in the waves, or venture out onto the sand under a full moon during nesting season to see baby sea turtles (from a safe distance). Make sure you don't use your camera flash: Turtles can mistake the bright lights for the moon and become disoriented.

Learn more about the wildlife that call the Valley home at the Boca Chica unit of Las Palomas Wildlife Management Area. As part of the Las Palomas Loop, a Texas wildlife trail, Boca Chica provides a safe habitat for several species, including white-wing doves and the endangered ocelot.

Further up the coast, Padre Island National Seashore invites nature enthusiasts to explore 70 miles of sand, surf and grassy dunes. As the world's longest stretch of undeveloped barrier island, it separates the Gulf from the Laguna Madre, a rare hypersaline lagoon. Here, Kemp's ridley sea turtles return from the ocean to dig nests for their eggs, and more than 380 species of birds find cover in the native grasses. Historically, this was home to an indigenous tribe, the Malaquites. The South Padre Island Birding and Nature Center is a premier destination for bird watching. Divers can explore the several Spanish shipwrecks found off the coast.

Continue up the coast and dive into the adventure at Corpus Christi. Sport fishing, surfing or just hunting for shells along North Beach are just a few of the ways to spend your stay. Take the family to the Texas State Aquarium to watch otters play, then climb aboard the *USS Lexington* to learn about the aircraft carrier's role in military action. See how sailors live while at sea.

Art exhibits, classes and lectures are plentiful at the Art Museum of South Texas. Here, visiting collections from modern masters like Andy Warhol mingle with traditional arts and crafts from Latin America.

Stroll past the yachts and schooners docked at Corpus Christi Marina as the sun sets, then stop to dine at one of several restaurants along the bayfront. When the stars come out, so does the live music. Head to Water Street Market to take in a performance, but don't miss a stroll on the South Texas Music Walk of Fame. Fan favorites who have earned a place on the walk include Freddy Fender, Stoney LaRue, Michael Nesmith and George Strait.

For More Information

South Padre Island
800-767-2373
www.sopadre.com

Texas State Travel Guide
800-452-9292
www.traveltex.com

TX

TEXAS HILL COUNTRY

Ride a horse, drift on a river or go nuts in this pretty Lone Star landscape

One of Texas' most popular destinations is the region known as Hill Country. This collection of charming and historic cities, including the capital city of Austin, embodies the character and spirit of what the world has come to think of when they hear the name "Texas."

From Austin to Kerrville and from San Saba to Uvalde, the Hill Country is awash with Texas traditions in the form of pit-smoked barbecue joints, inner tubes drifting down rivers and late-night two-stepping in old dance halls.

Recreation and Rock 'n' Roll

The scrubby wilderness of the Hill Country is a natural habitat for deer and game birds, which means great hunting for sportsmen. Leases and private hunting trips are offered throughout the region, along with ancillary services such as processing and taxidermy. Barksdale, Bend, Harper and Ingram are just a few towns where hunters can venture into the woods in pursuit of their next trophy.

If you find yourself in Austin in the heat of the summer, take the plunge into chilly Barton Springs. This legendary watering hole is fed by underground springs and stays between 68 and 70 degrees year-round. Take a spin on the dance floor at the Broken Spoke, which has hosted the likes of Willie Nelson and Bob Wills and his Texas Playboys. For a quieter destination, the Bullock Texas State History Museum is worth spending a few hours in. Exhibits here tell the stories of people and events that shaped Texas, from a Native American tomahawk to a Kenny Rogers single.

Head west to Fredericksburg, where peach crops helped the town grow into its present-day tourist hot spot. The town's German heritage is preserved and celebrated in the Sauer-Beckmann Living History Farm. Here, visitors learn how the sausage is made, along with the mechanics of sheep-shearing and canning.

Enjoy the natural beauty of Hill Country geology at Enchanted Rock State Natural Area, where you can hike, camp and climb the massive granite dome that dominates the area's landscape. Sip on a local brew crafted at Fredericksburg Brewing Company, where ales and lagers are made on-site in the German tradition.

A short drive south, you'll find yourself in Kerrville, which sits on the edge of the spring-fed Guadalupe River and is surrounded by opportunities to enjoy live entertainment, Western art and rich scenery. Riverside Nature Center is a home to native plants and animals and provides education and access to the Kerrville River Trail, which is suitable for walking and biking.

Small Town Charms

The Museum of Western Art celebrates works of living artists who create in the style of Remington and Russell, and the Kerrville Arts & Cultural Center showcases the craft and creativity of more than 600 member artists.

With a small-town feel and a visitor's log that spans the globe, Boerne (pronounced Bernie) has something to please just about any guest. Adventurers should explore Cascade Caverns and Cave Without A Name, two natural living caves, or tube down the cool waters of the Guadalupe River. No matter when you're in Boerne, you're bound to be entertained by one of the many music festivals and art shows held throughout the year.

Take a trip over to nearby Luckenbach for live music and dancing at Luckenbach Dance Hall. This quirky little town, with an official population of three, was founded as a trading post in 1849 and more than 100 years later was a ghost town up for sale, which the aforementioned three people purchased and made into the live-entertainment destination that it is today.

Bandera, which touts itself as "the Cowboy Capital of the World," beckons travelers to revisit the Old West. Once a staging ground for cattle drives, the town celebrates its heritage with rodeos and roping demonstrations, ranch tours and frontier history lessons. Several locations offer horseback-riding

A trail ride at Hill Country State Natural Area. Kenny Braun

lessons, and the nearby Medina River is ideal for paddle-boating, kayaking and tubing. Medina Lake also plays host to boating and fishing.

Uvalde sits at the intersection of the country's two longest highways, U.S. 90 and U.S. 83, but driving will be the last thing on your mind when you see the charm that brings visitors here. Horseback riding, hunting and wildflower viewing are popular outdoor activities here.

Giant oak trees dot the cityscape thanks to careful civic planning in Uvalde's early days, and Cooks Slough Sanctuary provides a safe habitat for several bird species. Hit the links at Uvalde Memorial Golf Course, then visit Rexall Soda Fountain for retro refreshment. A driving tour of the city's heritage homes along its tree-lined streets is a great way to while away the afternoon.

Nuts, Barbecue and History

San Saba is a town many go nuts over; after all, it is the pecan capital of the world. But this northernmost Hill Country destination is more than just pies and pralines. It's chock-full of history and family fun. Visit the San Saba Historical County Museum at Mill Pond Park on a weekend afternoon to learn about life in the town's early days. Cattle, cotton and sawmills helped grow San Saba from a rugged frontier town into a bustling commercial destination in the 19th century.

Colorado Bend State Park offers spectacular views of Gorman Falls, and it's a prime destination for primitive camping, mountain biking, swimming and caving. The city hosts celebrations year-round, including rodeos, July Fourth fireworks, Christmas shows and more.

Curb your craving for authentic pit-smoked barbecue in Llano, where Cooper's draws a crowd every day. Visit the Red Top Jail, a 19th-century jail with the hanging gallows still inside, and tour the Dabbs Hotel—it was once a rest stop for infamous criminal couple Bonnie and Clyde.

For More Information

Hill Country of Texas
512-763-0051
www.texashillcountry.com

Texas State Travel Guide
800-452-9292
www.traveltex.com

TX

TYLER

Savor the scent of fresh flowers in Texas's rose capital

If you're ready to stop and smell the roses, make sure you're in Tyler, the rose capital of Texas. Spring in East Texas means bountiful blooms around every corner of this charming community. In March and April, the Azalea and Spring Flower Trail extends for eight miles through residential gardens and historic homes.

When the smell of roses isn't wafting in the air, there are perennial flowers in bloom, and more than 250 days of sunshine to be enjoyed by residents and their guests.

The best time to see the Tyler roses is in October, when the bright-red flowers are at the peak of their bloom. Horticulture enthusiasts will love learning about the care of the 32,000 bushes in town, and the surprising amount of work needed when caring for 600 rose varieties. It's during this month every year that Tyler hosts the Texas Rose Festival, highlighted by the crowning of the Rose Queen.

The Tyler Rose Museum keeps a record of every Rose Queen crowned, along with some of their hand-made gowns, going back to 1935. In the "Attic of Memories" exhibit, visitors are allowed a glimpse into life in Smith County from the past 100 years.

Trip Through Tyler History

Fly high at the Historic Aviation Memorial Museum, which is housed in a former passenger terminal at the city's airport. Walk among restored historic aircraft, including the F-4D Pantom II, a T-33 Shooting Star and an F-104A Starfighter. The world-class museum spans the history of flight from the Wright Brothers to the Space Shuttle. Compelling exhibits document the role that Tyler played in Aviation history.

See the creatures of the world's wild places at Tyler's Caldwell Zoo. The 85-acre park is home to more than 2,000 animals representing 250 species from Africa, and North and South America. Explore the mysteries of nature and the universe at the Center for Earth & Space Science Education.

For More Information

Tyler Convention and Visitors Bureau
800-235-5712
www.visittyler.com

Office of the Governor, Economic Development and Tourism
512-463-2000
www.traveltex.com

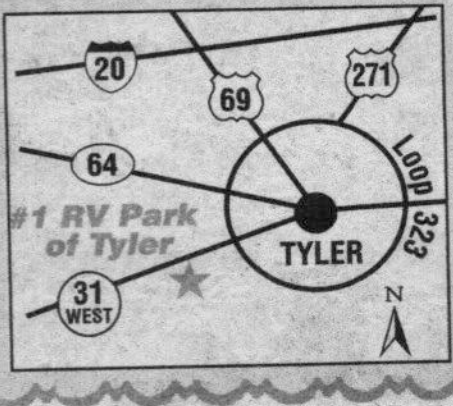

Texas

CONSULTANTS

Northern Texas

Randy & Debbie Block

Southern Texas

Gary & Sherry Wilcox

ABILENE — B5 *Taylor*

ABILENE See also Clyde.

ABILENE (State Pk) From Jct of Hwy 83/84 & FM-89 S side of Abilene (Buffalo Gap Rd), SW 13.9 mi on FM-89, follow signs (L) (Entrance fee). 2015 rates: $15 to $20. (325)572-3204

ABILENE KOA **Ratings: 9/9/7.5** (Campground) 2015 rates: $28.95 to $41.99. (325)672-3681 4851 W Stamford St, Abilene, TX 79603

ABILENE RV PARK
Ratings: 9/9.5★/8 (RV Park) E-bnd: From Jct of I-20 & Exit 292B, E 1.1 mi on S service rd (R); or W-bnd: From Jct of I-20 & Exit 294, Exit 294 & cross over frwy to S service rd, W 1 mi (L). **FAC:** All weather rds. (66 spaces). Avail: 54 gravel, 54 pull-thrus (20 x 56), 54 full hkups (30/50 amps), seasonal sites, WiFi, rentals, laundry. **REC:** pool. Pet restrict(B/Q). No tents. Big rig sites, 2015 rates: $39. Disc: AAA, military.
(325)672-2212 Lat: 32.43475, Lon: -99.62259
6195 E Ih-20, Abilene, TX 79601
abrvpark@wtconnect.com
www.abilenetexasrvpark.com
See ad this page.

BIG COUNTRY RV PARK
Ratings: 5.5/8.5/7.5 (RV Park) From jct I-20 and exit 294: Go 1/4 mi W on N access rd (R). **FAC:** Gravel rds. 77 gravel, 44 pull-thrus (30 x 100), back-ins (30 x 60), 77 full hkups (30/50 amps), WiFi, laundry, LP gas. Pets OK. No tents. Big rig sites, 2015 rates: $30.
(325)677-1401 Lat: 32.43490, Lon: -99.61012
6662 Ih20 East, Abilene, TX 79601
Sales@bigcountryrv.com
www.bigcountryrv.com
See ad this page.

Don't camp without it ... Our 2016 listings are your key to travel satisfaction.

BUCK CREEK RV PARK
Ratings: 6.5/9/8 (RV Park) From Jct of I-20 (exit 294) & Buck Creek Rd: Go 1/4 mi N on Buck Creek Rd. (L). **FAC:** Gravel rds. (50 spaces). Avail: 16 gravel, 16 pull-thrus (36 x 120), 16 full hkups (30/50 amps), seasonal sites, WiFi, laundry. Pet restrict(Q). No tents. Big rig sites, 2015 rates: $30 to $33. Disc: AAA, military.
(325)672-2825 Lat: 32.43669, Lon: -99.60571
12445 Cty Rd 108 N, Abilene, TX 79601
buckcreekrvpark@hotmail.com
www.buckcreekrvpark.com
See ad this page.

TYE RV PARK **Ratings: 4/7.5/7** (RV Park) 2015 rates: $28. (325)691-0398 441 N Access Rd, Tye, TX 79563

ALAMO — M3 *Hidalgo*

ALAMO PALMS RV RESORT **Ratings: 9/9★/8.5** (RV Area in MHP) 2015 rates: $35 to $40. (800)405-6188 1341 W Bus Hwy 83, Alamo, TX 78516

ALAMO REC-VEH PARK/MHP **Ratings: 9.5/9★/7** (RV Park) 2015 rates: $40. (956)787-8221 1320 W Frontage Road, Alamo, TX 78516

ALAMO ROSE MOBILE HOME & RV RESORT **Ratings: 9.5/9★/8.5** (RV Resort) 2015 rates: $39. (956)783-2600 938 S Alamo Rd, Alamo, TX 78516

CASA DEL VALLE RV RESORT
Ratings: 8.5/8.5★/8 (RV Park) From Jct of US-83 (Expwy) & FM-907 (N Rudy Villarreal Rd)), N 1.1 mi on FM-907 (R).

BEST RESORT IN THE RIO GRANDE VALLE
Enjoy the amenities and activities of this gated RV resort. Guests can enjoy the heated pool, fitness center, pickleball, billiards, recreation center, tennis, shuffleboard, social events and activities.
FAC: Paved rds. (387 spaces). Avail: 124 paved, patios, back-ins (30 x 57), 124 full hkups (30/50 amps), seasonal sites, WiFi Hotspot, rentals, laundry, controlled access. **REC:** heated pool, whirlpool, shuffleboard. Pet restrict(B/Q). Partial handicap access, no tents. Age restrict may apply, eco-friendly, 2015 rates: $35. Disc: AAA, military.
AAA Approved
(877)828-9945 Lat: 26.20633, Lon: -98.11859
1048 N Alamo Road, Alamo, TX 78516
casadelvalle@suncommunities.com
www.casarv.com
See ad pages 1463 (Welcome Section), 1108 & RV Trips of a Lifetime, Snowbird Destinations in Magazine Section.

TROPHY GARDENS MH & RV RESORT **Ratings: 8.5/8.5★/8** (RV Resort) 2015 rates: $39. (956)787-7717 800 State Hwy 495, Alamo, TX 78516

WINTER RANCH MHP & RV RESORT **Ratings: 8.5/8.5★/8** (RV Resort) 2015 rates: $39. (956)781-1358 600 Sh-495, Alamo, TX 78516

ALBANY — B6 *Shackelford*

FORT GRIFFIN STATE HIST PARK (State Pk) From Jct of US-180 & US-283, N 13.5 mi on US-283 (L). $2 Entrance fee per day. 2015 rates: $15 to $22. (325)762-3592

ALPINE — C3 *Brewster*

B C RANCH RV PARK Ratings: 4.5/7★/6.5 (RV Park) From Jct US 90 & Hwy 118: Go 3 mi N on Hwy 118 (L). Elev 4585 ft. **FAC:** Gravel/dirt rds. 28 dirt, 20 pull-thrus (25 x 70), back-ins (25 x 70), 20 full hkups, 4 W, 8 E (30/50 amps), WiFi, dump, laundry. **REC.** Pets OK. No tents. Big rig sites, 2015 rates: $28.50. Disc: AAA. No CC.
AAA Approved
(432)837-5883 Lat: 30.39786, Lon: -103.68104
45560 N Hwy 118, Alpine, TX 79831
www.bcranchrvpark.com

Tell them you saw them in this Guide!

TX

Join the flock and head south during the winter. Use our handy Snowbird guide in the front of the Guide to find RV-friendly destinations throughout the Sunbelt. Snowbird Destinations features the top Snowbird roosts and lists great Campgrounds in compelling areas.

Got a big rig? Look for listings indicating "big rig sites." These campgrounds are made for you, with 12'-wide roads and 14' overhead clearance. They guarantee that 25% or more of their sites measure 24' wide by 60' long or larger, and have full hookups with 50-amp electricity.

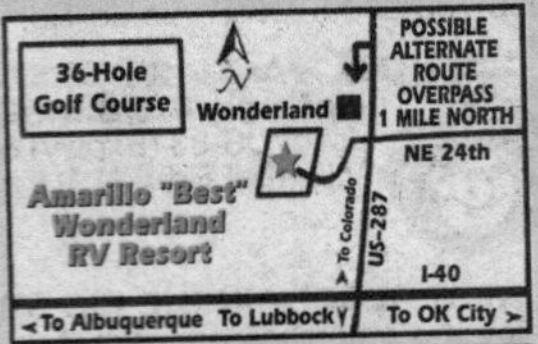

ALPINE (CONT)

LA VISTA RV PARK
Ratings: 3.5/8★/8 (RV Park) From Jct of US-67 & Hwy 118: Go 6 1/2 mi S on Hwy 118 (L). Elev 4600 ft. **FAC:** Gravel rds. 14 gravel, 14 pull-thrus (30 x 85), 14 full hkups (30/50 amps), WiFi, laundry. **REC.** Pets OK. No tents. 2015 rates: $27 to $29.
(432)364-2293 Lat: 30.28961, Lon: -103.59400
46501 State Hwy 118 S, Alpine, TX 79830
lavistarvpark.net
See ad page 1111 (Spotlight Big Bend National Park).

LOST ALASKAN RV RESORT
Ratings: 9.5/10★/10 (RV Park) From Jct of US-90 & Hwy 118: Go 1-1/2 mi N on Hwy 118 (L). Elev 4435 ft. **FAC:** Paved rds. (91 spaces). Avail: 54 gravel, 54 pull-thrus (32 x 95), 54 full hkups (30/50 amps), seasonal sites, WiFi, tent sites, rentals, laundry, LP bottles. **REC:** pool, playground. Pets OK. Partial handicap access. Big rig sites, eco-friendly, 2015 rates: $33.95 to $44.95. Disc: AAA, military.
(432)837-1136 Lat: 30.394985, Lon: -103.678981
2401 N Hwy 118, Alpine, TX 79830
lostalaskanrv@gmail.com
www.lostalaskan.com
See ad pages 1127, 1108.

ALVIN — D8 *Brazoria*

MEADOWLARK RV PARK
Ratings: 6.5/NA/9 (RV Park) From jct Hwy 6 & Hwy 35: Go 1 mi S on Hwy 35, then 2-1/4 mi W on South St.(L). **FAC:** Paved rds. (47 spaces). Avail: 12 paved, back-ins (40 x 80), 12 full hkups (30/50 amps), seasonal sites, cable, WiFi. Pet restrict No tents. Big rig sites, 2015 rates: $45. No CC.
(281)331-5992 Lat: 29.40272, Lon: -95.27377
2607 W South St, Alvin, TX 77511
mjour77542@aol.com
See ad this page.

Find it fast! To locate a town on a map, follow these easy instructions: Look for the map grid code after the town heading in the listing section and match it to the letters and numbers on the map borders. Draw a line horizontally from the letter and vertically from the number. You'll find the town near the intersection of the two lines.

\LVORD — A7 *Wise*

A +RV PARK

Ratings: 7.5/10★/9 (RV Park) From Jct of US 287 (Alvord exit) & Bus 287 (Franklin St): Go 1/4 mi N on Bus 287 N. (R). **FAC:** Gravel rds. 47 gravel, 47 pull-thrus (30 x 70), 47 full hkups (30/50 mps), WiFi, tent sites, dump, laundry, LP gas. **REC:** ond, fishing. Pet restrict(B). Partial handicap ac-ess. 2015 rates: $35. Disc: military.
940)427-9621 Lat: 33.34791, Lon: -97.68293
67 E Franklin St, Alvord, TX 76225
plusrvpark@embarqmail.com
plusrvpark.com
ee ad opposite page.

\MARILLO — F9 *Potter, Randall*

AMARILLO See also Canyon.

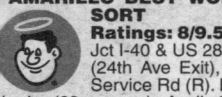

AMARILLO BEST WONDERLAND RV RE-SORT

Ratings: 8/9.5★/7.5 (RV Park) From Jct I-40 & US 287: Go 3 mi N on US 287 (24th Ave Exit), then 400 feet S on W Service Rd (R). Elev 3670 ft. **FAC:** Grav-l rds. (93 spaces). Avail: 63 gravel, 60 pull-thrus 28 x 66), back-ins (28 x 60), 63 full hkups (30/50 mps), seasonal sites, WiFi, laundry, LP gas, fire ngs. **REC:** playground. Pets OK. No tents. Big rig ites, 2015 rates: $26. Disc: military.
806)383-1700 Lat: 35.23431, Lon: -101.83167
001 Dumas Dr, Amarillo, TX 79107
nonied@msn.com
/ww.sisemoretraveland.com
ee ad opposite page, 1108.

➛ AMARILLO KOA **Ratings: 9/9.5★/8.5** (Camp-round) 2015 rates: $41.67 to $45.67. (806)335-1792 100 Folsom Rd, Amarillo, TX 79108

➛ **AMARILLO RANCH RV PARK**

Ratings: 9.5/9.5★/9 (RV Park) From Jct of I-40 (exit 74) & Whitaker Rd: Go 1/2 mi W on N Service Rd (R). Elev 3670 ft. **FAC:** Paved rds. (156 spaces). Avail: 81 gravel, 80 pull-thrus (30 x 90), back-ns (30 x 80), 81 full hkups (30/50 amps), seasonal ites, cable, WiFi, tent sites, dump, laundry. **REC:** eated pool, whirlpool, playground. Pet restrict(B). ig rig sites, 2015 rates: $37 to $39. Disc: AAA, mili-ary.
AA Approved
806)373-4962 Lat: 35.19449, Lon: -101.77150
414 Sunrise Dr, Amarillo, TX 79104
eservation@amarilloranch.com
/ww.amarilloranch.com
ee ad pages 1130-1131, 1108.

➛ **FORT AMARILLO RV RESORT**

Ratings: 9/10★/10 (RV Park) From jct I-40 (exit 64) & Loop 335: Go 1/4 mi N on W Loop 335, then 1-1/4 W on Rt 66/Amarillo Blvd W (L). Elev 3670 ft.

FORT AMARILLO EVERY TIME!
'ou'll enjoy our western setting, indoor heated pool, ot tub, fitness room, stream-fed fishing pond, il-uminated walking paths & breathtaking sunsets! luge pull thrus, free WiFi & be sure to shop at Lizzie lae's Mercantile.

'AC: Paved/gravel rds. (105 spaces). Avail: 70 grav-l, patios, 70 pull-thrus (30 x 75), 70 full hkups (30/50 mps), seasonal sites, WiFi, laundry, LP gas. **REC:** eated pool, whirlpool, pond, fishing, playground. Pet estrict(B/Q). Partial handicap access, no tents. Big ig sites, eco-friendly, 2015 rates: $43. Disc: AAA, nilitary.
806)331-1700 Lat: 35.19109, Lon: -101.95605
0101 Amarillo Blvd W, Amarillo, TX 79124
eservations@fortrvparks.com
/ww.fortrvparks.com
ee ad pages 1132, 1108.

➛ **OASIS RV RESORT**

Ratings: 10/9★/9.5 (RV Park) From Jct I-40 (Exit 60) & Arnot Rd: Go 1/2 mi S on Arnot Rd. (L).

RATED TOP 5 RV DESTINATION IN TEXAS
Velcome to Oasis RV Resort. Amarillo's NEWEST, INEST & LARGEST RV Resort. We are located in riendly Amarillo, Texas just off Interstate 40 at exit 0. A very quiet & secure location with easy on/off ccess to I-40.

'AC: Paved rds. 188 paved, patios, 105 pull-thrus 39 x 75), back-ins (39 x 50), 188 full hkups (30/50 mps), cable, WiFi, dump, laundry, LP gas. **REC:** ool, whirlpool, shuffleboard, playground. Pets OK. Partial handicap access, no tents. Big rig sites, 2015 rates: $25 to $36.50. Disc: military.
(888)789-9697 Lat: 35.18388, Lon: -102.00949
2715 Arnot Rd, Amarillo, TX 79124
info@myrvoasis.com
www.myrvoasis.com
See ad opposite page, 1108.

Are you using a friend's Guide? Want one of your own? Call 877-209-6655.

➛ **OVERNITE RV PARK**

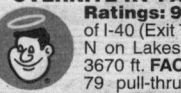

Ratings: 9/9★/9 (RV Park) From Jct of I-40 (Exit 75) & Lakeside Dr: Go 1/4 mi N on Lakeside Dr (Loop 335) (L). Elev 3670 ft. **FAC:** All weather rds. 79 gravel, 79 pull-thrus (32 x 65), 79 full hkups (30/50 amps), WiFi, laundry, LP gas. **REC:** heated pool, shuffleboard, playground. Pets OK. No tents. Big rig sites, 2015 rates: $33.
(800)554-5305 Lat: 35.19636, Lon: -101.74266
900 S Lakeside Dr, Amarillo, TX 79118
elens@juno.com
www.overnitervpark.com
See ad opposite page, 1108.

Travel Services

➛ **JACK SISEMORE TRAVELAND** Full line of parts. New & pre-owned RV sales. Full service dept with certified RV techs. Elev 3670 ft. **SERVICES:** RV, RV appliance, restrooms, RV Sales. RV storage. RV supplies, emergency parking, RV accessible. waiting room. Hours: 8:30am to 6pm.
(806)358-4891 Lat: 35.16752, Lon: -101.86811
4341 Canyon Expressway, Amarillo, TX 79110
tsisemore@clearwire.net
www.sisemoretraveland.com
See ad opposite page.

Things to See and Do

➛ **LIZZIE MAE'S MERCANTILE** Located inside Fort Amarillo RV Resort, 3,000 sq ft gifts and home decor. RV accessible. Restrooms. Hours: 8am to 6pm.
(806)331-1700 Lat: 35.19109, Lon: -101.95605
10101 Amarillo Blvd W, Amarillo, TX 79124
lizziemaes@gmail.com
www.lizziemaes.com
See ad page 1132.

Park policies vary. Ask about the cancellation policy when making a reservation.

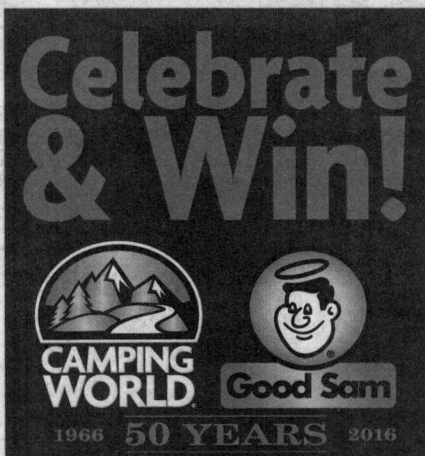

TX

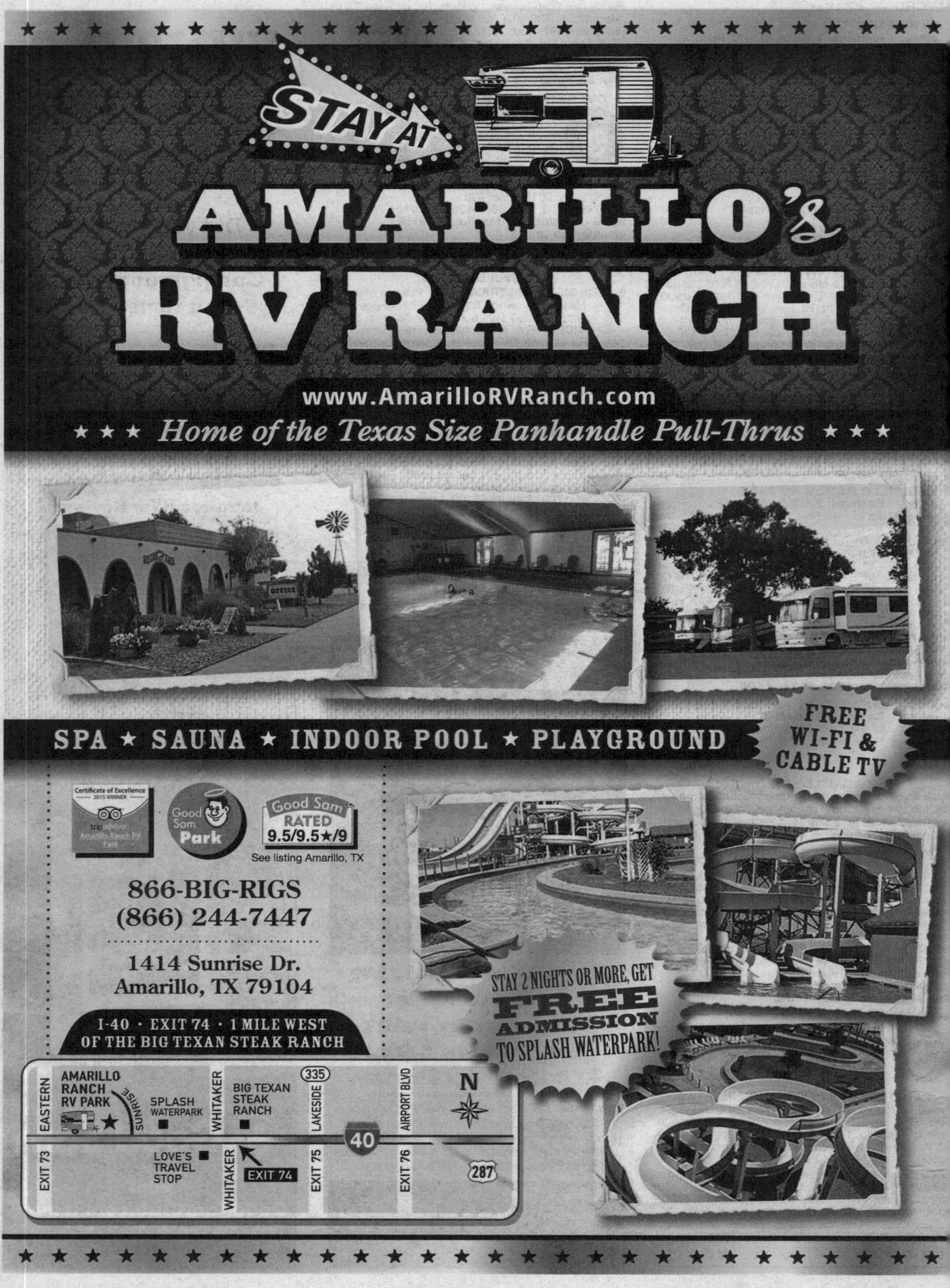
STAY AT
AMARILLO'S
RV RANCH
www.AmarilloRVRanch.com
★ ★ ★ Home of the Texas Size Panhandle Pull-Thrus ★ ★ ★
OFFICE
SPA ★ SAUNA ★ INDOOR POOL ★ PLAYGROUND
FREE WI-FI & CABLE TV
Certificate of Excellence 2015 WINNER
Good Sam Park
Good Sam RATED 9.5/9.5★/9
See listing Amarillo, TX
866-BIG-RIGS
(866) 244-7447
1414 Sunrise Dr.
Amarillo, TX 79104
I-40 · EXIT 74 · 1 MILE WEST OF THE BIG TEXAN STEAK RANCH
STAY 2 NIGHTS OR MORE, GET FREE ADMISSION TO SPLASH WATERPARK!
AMARILLO RANCH RV PARK
EASTERN
SUNRISE
SPLASH WATERPARK
WHITAKER
BIG TEXAN STEAK RANCH
335
LAKESIDE
AIRPORT BLVD
N
40
EXIT 73
LOVE'S TRAVEL STOP
WHITAKER
EXIT 74
EXIT 75
EXIT 76
287

HOME OF THE WORLD FAMOUS
FREE 72 oz STEAK DINNER™
IF EATEN IN 1 HOUR
the BIG TEXAN STEAK RANCH
™
AMARILLO, TEXAS
HISTORIC ROUTE 66
LANDMARK LEGEND
7701 I-40 EAST
AMARILLO, TX 79118
806-372-6000 TELEPHONE
800-657-7177 TOLL FREE
BIGTEXAN.COM
THE BIG TEXAN
© Safoma, LLC. All rights reserved.
© Safoma, LLC. All rights reserved.
Printed with permission of AGN Media
THE BIG TEXAN™
BREWERY™
BIG TEXAN MOTEL
BIG TEXAN GIFT SHOP
FREE LIMO SERVICE
LIVE MUSIC NIGHTLY
HANDCRAFTED BEER
BREWED ON-SITE
FEATURED IN
DRAFT MAGAZINE
Selected as one of the
"Top 10 Places to Have a Beer"

AMES — D9 *Liberty*

CEDAR GROVE RV PARK
Ratings: 7/7.5/7 (RV Park) From Jct of US-90 & FM-160 (in Ames), E 0.5 mi on US-90 (R). **FAC:** Gravel rds. 93 gravel, 25 pull-thrus (25 x 70), back-ins (25 x 50), 93 full hkups (30/50 amps), WiFi, tent sites, rentals, dump, laundry, groc, LP gas. **REC:** pond, fishing. Pet restrict(B). Big rig sites, 2015 rates: $40. ATM.
(936)334-0711 Lat: 30.05120, Lon: -94.73407
710 E Main, Ames, TX 77575
johwrigjr@aol.com
www.cedargrovervpark.com
See ad page 1135.

AMISTAD NATIONAL REC AREA — D5
Val Verde

AMISTAD NRA/SAN PEDRO FLATS (Natl Pk) From Jct of US-90 & Hwy 277, W 3 mi on US-90 to Spur Rd 454, N 0.5 mi, follow signs (R). Pit toilets. 2015 rates: $4. (830)775-7491

AMISTAD NRA/277 NORTH (Natl Pk) From Del Rio, N 11 mi on US-277, follow signs 0.5 mi (E). Pit toilets. 2015 rates: $4. (830)775-7491

ANDREWS — B4 *Andrews*

FLOREY PARK (Public) From town, N 8 mi on US-385 to County Park Rd, E 1 mi, follow sign (R). 2015 rates: $5 to $10. (432)524-1401

ANTHONY — B1 *El Paso*

ANTHONY EL PASO WEST KOA
Ratings: 6.5/8.5★/6 (RV Park) From Jct I-10 & Exit 2: Go 1-1/2 mi on N Desert Blvd (Behind Camping World) (R). Elev 3950 ft. **FAC:** Dirt rds. 92 dirt, 92 pull-thrus (35 x 60), 92 full hkups (30/50 amps), WiFi, tent sites, dump, laundry. Pet restrict(B). Big rig sites, eco-friendly, 2015 rates: $30.
(915)603-3105 Lat: 31.983311, Lon: -106.585358
8805 N. Desert Blvd., Anthony, TX 79821
http://koa.com/campgrounds/el-paso/
See ad page 1146.

Travel Services

CAMPING WORLD OF ANTHONY As the nation's largest retailer of RV supplies, accessories, services and new and used RVs, Camping World is committed to making your total RV experience better. RV Accessories: (866)650-9145. **SERVICES:** RV, tire, RV appliance, staffed RV wash, restrooms, RV Sales. RV storage. RV supplies, LP, emergency parking, RV accessible. waiting room. Hours: 8am - 6pm.
(888)691-2071 Lat: 31.973965, Lon: -106.599314
8805B N. Desert Blvd., Anthony, TX 79821
www.campingworld.com

ARANSAS PASS — E7 *San Patricio*

ARANSAS BAY RV RESORT **Ratings: 9.5/9.5★/9** (RV Park) 2015 rates: $35 to $45. (830)423-4322 501 N Avenue A, Aransas Pass, TX 78336

RANSOM ROAD RV PARK
Ratings: 9/9.5★/9 (RV Park) From Jct of Bus 35 & Commercial St (S Loop 90), SW 1.6 mi on Commercial St to Ransom Rd, E 0.1 mi (L). **FAC:** Paved rds. 128 paved, patios, 24 pull-thrus (25 x 60), back-ins (24 x 60), 128 full hkups (30/50 amps), cable, WiFi, laundry. **REC.** Pet restrict(B/Q). Partial handicap access, no tents. Big rig sites, eco-friendly, 2015 rates: $37 to $42.
(361)758-2715 Lat: 27.89045, Lon: -97.15179
240 Ransom Road, Aransas Pass, TX 78336
ransomroadrvpark@cableone.net
www.ransomroadrvparkinc.com
See ad this page.

SOUTHERN OAKS LUXURY RV RESORT
Ratings: 9/8.5/8.5 (RV Park) From Jct Hwy 181 (Portland) & Hwy 35, NE 9 mi on Hwy 35 (L) From Jct Hwy 188 (Rockport) & Hwy 35 Bypass, SW 3.3 mi on Hwy 35 Bypass (R). **FAC:** Paved rds. (195 spaces). Avail: 75 paved, patios, 15 pull-thrus (30 x 75), back-ins (30 x 80), 75 full hkups (30/50 amps), WiFi Hotspot, laundry. **REC:** heated pool. Pet restrict(B/Q). Partial handicap access, no tents. Big rig sites, RV age restrict, eco-friendly, 2015 rates: $45 to $55.
(361)758-1249 Lat: 27.92728, Lon: -97.15629
1850 Hwy 35 Bypass, Aransas Pass, TX 78336
peggy.southernoaks@yahoo.com
www.sorvresort.com
See ad this page.

ARLINGTON — H3 *Tarrant*

ARLINGTON See also Fort Worth, Glenn Heights, Grand Prairie, Lewisville, Mansfield.

DALLAS/ARLINGTON KOA **Ratings: 8.5/9/7.5** (RV Park) 2015 rates: $47.98 to $62.98. (817)277-6600 2715 S Cooper, Arlington, TX 76015

TREETOPS CAREFREE RV RESORT
Ratings: 8.5/9.5★/9.5 (RV Park) From Jct I-20 (Exit 449) & Hwy 157: Go 1/2 mi N on Hwy 157, then 1/4 mi W on Arbrook (R).

WELCOME TO TREETOPS CAREFREE RESORT
The most beautiful park in the Metroplex, neighboring the new Cowboys Stadium, Texas Rangers Ballpark, 6 Flags and more. Large pull-thrus and extra wide sites in a quiet, friendly place shaded by oak trees.

FAC: Paved rds. (166 spaces). Avail: 51 gravel, patios, 51 pull-thrus (25 x 70), 51 full hkups (30/50 amps), seasonal sites, cable, WiFi, dump, laundry, LP gas. **REC:** pool. Pet restrict(B/Q). Partial handicap access, no tents. Big rig sites, 2015 rates: $47 to $55. Disc: AAA, military.
(800)747-0787 Lat: 32.68560, Lon: -97.13859
1901 W Arbrook Blvd, Arlington, TX 76015
treetops@carefreervresorts.com
www.treetopsrv.com
See ad pages 1134, 1108.

ATHENS — B8 *Henderson*

TEXAN RV PARK
Ratings: 9.5/10★/9.5 (RV Park) From Jct of Loop 7 & US 175: Go 4 mi N on US 175. (R). **FAC:** All weather rds. (75 spaces). Avail: 45 grass, patios, 24 pull-thrus (34 x 100), back-ins (30 x 60), 35 full hkups (30/50 amps), seasonal sites, WiFi, tent sites, rentals, dump, laundry. **REC:** pool, pond, fishing. Pet restrict(B/Q). Big rig sites, 2015 rates: $30. Disc: military.
(903)677-3326 Lat: 32.26057, Lon: -95.92806
9024 US Hwy 175 W, Athens, TX 75751
texanrvpark@yahoo.com
www.texanrvpark.com
See ad this page, 1108.

ATLANTA — A9 *Cass*

ATLANTA (State Pk) From Jct of US-59 & FM-96, W 7.1 mi on FM-96 to FM-1154, N 1.7 mi to Park Rd 42 (E) (Entrance free). 2015 rates: $14 to $16. (903)796-6476

AUBREY — A7 *Denton*

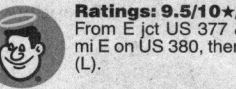

SHADY CREEK RV PARK AND STORAGE
Ratings: 9.5/10★/10 (RV Park) From E jct US 377 & US 380: Go 6-1/4 mi E on US 380, then 1 mi N on FM 1385 (L).

LOCATION *DALLAS* LOCATION
With all the amenities you've come to expect, you'll love the paved streets, pool, dog park, wifi & more. Convenient to restaurant, shopping and all that Dallas and Fort Worth have to offer, you will stay awhile! Call today.

FAC: Paved rds. (206 spaces). Avail: 80 gravel, back-ins (35 x 55), 80 full hkups (30/50 amps), seasonal sites, WiFi, laundry, LP gas. **REC:** pool, playground. Pet restrict(B). Partial handicap access. Big rig sites, 2015 rates: $30. No CC.
(972)347-5384 Lat: 33.23544, Lon: -96.89525
1893 Fm 1385, Aubrey, TX 76227
Shadycreekrvpark@gmail.com
www.shadycreekrvpark.com
See ad pages 1113 (Spotlight Dallas/Fort Worth), 1108.

AUSTIN — C7 *Travis*

AUSTIN See also Bastrop & Marble Falls.

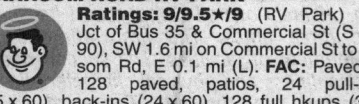

Subscribe to Trailer Life Magazine. For a subscription, call 800-825-6861.

TX

We give you what you want. First, we surveyed thousands of RVers just like you. Then, we developed our exclusive Triple Rating System for campgrounds based on the results. That's why our rating system is so good at explaining the quality of facilities and cleanliness of campgrounds.

Each privately owned campground has been rated three times. The first rating is for development of facilities. The second one is for cleanliness and physical characteristics of restrooms and showers. The third is for campground visual appearance and environmental quality.

AUSTIN (CONT)

↓ AUSTIN LONE STAR CAREFREE RV RE-SORT

Ratings: 9/8.5★/8.5 (RV Park) From Jct I-35 & Exit 227: Go 1-1/4 mi N on E Frontage Rd (R).

AUSTIN LONE STAR CAREFREE RV RESORT
Enjoy the famous music, attractions and entertainment of downtown Austin. It's just minutes from ou front door. This resort is an active RVer's paradise with state-of-the-art facilities and Texas-wide smiles

FAC: Paved/gravel rds. (156 spaces). Avail: 50 gravel, patios, 50 pull-thrus (33 x 65), 50 full hkups (30/50 amps), seasonal sites, cable, WiFi, rentals, dump laundry, groc, LP gas, controlled access. **REC:** heated pool, wading pool, playground. Pet restrict(B). Partial handicap access, no tents. Big rig sites, 2015 rates: $44 to $50. Disc: AAA, military.
(512)444-6322 Lat: 30.18552, Lon: -97.77316
7009 S I-35, Austin, TX 78744
austinlonestar@carefreervresorts.com
www.carefreervresorts.com
See ad this page, 1108.

↗ CRESTVIEW RV PARK

Ratings: 7.5/10★/7.5 (RV Park) From Jct I-35 & exit 220: Go 1/2 block W on Cabela's Dr (L). **FAC:** Paved rds. (91 spaces). Avail: 69 paved, 69 pull-thrus (21 x 75), 69 full hkups (30/50 amps), seasonal sites, cable, WiFi, laundry, LP gas. Pets OK. Partial handicap access, no tents. Big rig sites, 2015 rates: $33. Disc: AAA.
AAA Approved
(512)282-3516 Lat: 30.08011, Lon: -97.82564
PO Box 1028, 15700 S. Ih 35, Buda, TX 78610
sales@crestviewrv.com
www.crestviewrv.com
See ad pages 1133, 1108.

← EMMA LONG METROPOLITAN PARK (Public) From town, W 6.5 mi on RR-2222 to City Park Rd, S 6 mi (E). M-Th entry fee $5 per vehicle. $10 Fri-Sun per vehicle. 2015 rates: $10 to $25. (512)346-1831

Heading South? We have lots of Snowbird Destination ideas to explore at the front of the Guide.

AUSTIN (CONT)

LA HACIENDA RV RESORT
Ratings: 9.5/10★/10 (RV Park) S-Bnd: From Jct of I-35 & FM-620, S 18.7 mi on FM-620 to Hudson Bend Rd, W 1.5 mi (L); N-Bnd: From Jct of I-35 & (Exit 230) Hwy 290/71, W 7.7 mi on US 290 to TX 71, NW 7.1 mi to Ranch Road 620, N 7.9 mi to Hudson Bend Rd, NW 1.4 mi (L).

EXPLORE HISTORIC TEXAS HILL COUNTRY
This all-age luxury RV resort is located near the vibrant metropolis of Austin, the "live music capitol of the world!" Amenities include swimming pools, hot tub, putting green, and pavilion for planned activities and events.

FAC: Paved rds. (346 spaces). Avail: 176 gravel, 88 pull-thrus (40 x 90), back-ins (30 x 60), 176 full hkups (30/50 amps), seasonal sites, cable, WiFi, rentals, laundry, LP gas. **REC:** heated pool, whirlpool. Pets OK. Partial handicap access, no tents. Big rig sites, 2015 rates: $48 to $57. Disc: military.
(512)266-8001 Lat: 30.41563, Lon: -97.92986
5220 Hudson Bend Rd, Austin, TX 78734
lahaciendarvpark@yahoo.com
www.lahaciendarvpark.com
See ad opposite page, 1463 (Welcome Section), 1125 (Spotlight Texas Hill Country), 1108 & Family Camping, RV Trips of a Lifetime, Snowbird Destinations in Magazine Section.

MCKINNEY FALLS (State Pk) From Jct of I-35 & Wm Cannon Dr (exit 228), E 3.3 mi on Wm Cannon Dr to McKinney Falls Pkwy, N 1.1 mi (L) (Entrance fee). 2015 rates: $20 to $24. (512)243-1643

OAK FOREST RV PARK
Ratings: 9.5/9.5★/9 (RV Park) From Jct of I-35 (Exit 238B) & Hwy 290: Go E 6.5 mi E on Hwy 290, then 4 mi S on Decker Ln (FM 3177), then 500 ft W on Canoga (L).

AUSTIN'S BEST-OAK FOREST RV PARK
Welcome to Oak Forest RV Park. Peace and Quiet yet close enough to Austin for convenience and access to all things Austin. Whether you are looking for an RV vacation, living destination or retirement location, it's all here.

FAC: Paved rds. (162 spaces). Avail: 26 paved, 26 pull-thrus (28 x 75), 26 full hkups (30/50 amps), seasonal sites, cable, WiFi, laundry. **REC:** pool, whirlpool, shuffleboard. Pet restrict(B). Partial handicap access, no tents. Big rig sites, 2015 rates: $45. Disc: AAA, military.
(512)813-2913 Lat: 30.28498, Lon: -97.63622
8207 Canoga Ave, Austin, TX 78724
manager@oakforest-rvpark.com
www.oakforest-rvpark.com
See ad pages 1101 (Welcome Section), 1108 & Snowbird Destinations in Magazine Section.

Relax on white sandy beaches under palm fronds or get dancing at Mardi Gras; we've put the Spotlight on North America's most popular destinations. Turn to the Spotlight articles in our State and Province sections to learn more.

BACLIFF — D9 *Galveston*

KEMAH RV RESORT
Ratings: 9.5/8.5★/9 (RV Park) From Jct of I-45 & FM 518 (exit 23), E 6.5 mi on FM-518 to Hwy 146, SE 1.8 mi to Miles Rd, NE 0.3 mi (R). **FAC:** Paved rds. (107 spaces). Avail: 70 paved, 8 pull-thrus (30 x 65), back-ins (21 x 45), 70 full hkups (30/50 amps), seasonal sites, cable, WiFi, rentals, laundry. **REC:** pool, pond, playground. Pet restrict(B). No tents. Eco-friendly, 2015 rates: $35 to $39. Disc: AAA, military.
(281)559-2362 Lat: 29.51565, Lon: -95.00021
675 Miles Rd, Bacliff, TX 77518
manager@kemahrvresort.com
www.kemahrvresort.com

BANDERA — D6 *Bandera*

ANTLER OAKS LODGE AND RV RESORT **Ratings: 9/9★/8** (RV Park) 2015 rates: $40 to $59. (830)796-8111 3862 Hwy 16 North, Bandera, TX 78003

HOLIDAY VILLAGES OF MEDINA- TEXAS RESORT COMPANY **Ratings: 8.5/8/8** (Membership Pk) 2015 rates: $10. (830)796-8141 234 Private Road, Bandera, TX 78003

MANSFIELD PARK (Public) From Jct of Hwys 173 & 16, N 1.5 mi on Hwy 16 (R). 2015 rates: $15. (830)796-8448

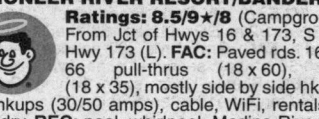

PIONEER RIVER RESORT/BANDERA
Ratings: 8.5/9★/8 (Campground) From Jct of Hwys 16 & 173, S 1 blk on Hwy 173 (L). **FAC:** Paved rds. 167 grass, 66 pull-thrus (18 x 60), back-ins (18 x 35), mostly side by side hkups, 167 full hkups (30/50 amps), cable, WiFi, rentals, dump, laundry. **REC:** pool, whirlpool, Medina River: fishing, shuffleboard, playground. Pet restrict(B/Q). No tents. RV age restrict, eco-friendly, 2015 rates: $26 to $28. Disc: AAA.
(866)371-3751 Lat: 29.72375, Lon: -99.06957
1202 Maple St, Bandera, TX 78003
pioneerrr@sbcglobal.net
www.pioneerriverresort.com
See ad page 1106 (Welcome Section).

RIVERSIDE RV PARK **Ratings: 7.5/5.5/7** (RV Park) 2015 rates: $20. (830)796-3636 760 Hwy 16 S, Bandera, TX 78003

SKYLINE RANCH RV PARK
Ratings: 8.5/9.5★/8.5 (RV Park) From N Jct of Hwys 173 & 16N (in town), W 1.1 mi on Hwy 16N (L). **FAC:** Gravel rds. 140 gravel, 119 pull-thrus (32 x 70), back-ins (32 x 60), 115 full hkups, 25 W, 25 E (30/50 amps), cable, WiFi, rentals, dump, laundry. **REC:** Medina River & Catfish Pond: swim, fishing. Pets OK. Partial handicap access, no tents. Big rig sites, eco-friendly, 2015 rates: $27 to $30. Disc: AAA, military.
(830)796-4958 Lat: 29.73007, Lon: -99.09620
2231 North Hwy 16, Bandera, TX 78003
skyline@indian-creek.net
www.skylineranchrvpark.com
See ad this page, 1108.

2 E RV GUEST RANCH RESORT **Ratings: 8.5/10★/8.5** (RV Park) 2015 rates: $35. (830)796-3628 810 Fm 470, Bandera, TX 78003

BASTROP — D7 *Bastrop*

BASTROP (State Pk) From Jct of SR-71, 95, & 21, NE 0.6 mi on SR-21 (R); or From Hwy-71 Loop 150, NW 0.7 mi on Hwy 71 (R) (Entrance fee). 2015 rates: $17 to $20. (512)321-2101

BASTROP/COLORADO RIVER/KOA **Ratings: 9.5/9.5★/9** (RV Park) 2015 rates: $45 to $55. (512)321-7500 98 Hwy 71 W, Bastrop, TX 78602

HWY 71 RV PARK **Ratings: 9/9.5★/8.5** (RV Park) 2015 rates: $30 to $45. (877)321-7275 931 Union Chapel Rd, Cedar Creek, TX 78612-3440

BAY CITY — D8 *Matagorda*

RIVERSIDE RV PARK (Public) From Jct of Hwys 35 & 60, S 3 mi on Hwy 60 to FM-2668, SW 2 mi (R). 2015 rates: $15 to $18. (979)245-0340

BAYTOWN — D9 *Chambers, Harris*

HOUSTON EAST RV RESORT
Ratings: 9.5/10★/10 (RV Park) W-bnd: From Jct of I-10 & Hwy 146 (Exit 798): Go E 1.4 mi on S Frntg Rd (R) or E-bnd: From Jct of I-10 & Exit 797, E 1.5 mi on S. Frntg Rd (L). **FAC:** Paved rds. (146 spaces). Avail: 116 paved, 50 pull-thrus (30 x 61), back-ins (30 x 70), 116 full hkups (30/50 amps), seasonal sites, cable, WiFi, rentals, laundry, LP gas, firewood, controlled access. **REC:** pool. Pet restrict(B/Q). Partial handicap access, no tents. Big rig sites, eco-friendly, 2015 rates: $44. Disc: military.
(281)383-3618 Lat: 29.82250, Lon: -94.87500
11810 I-10 E, Baytown, TX 77523
info@houstoneastrvresort.com
www.houstoneastrvresort.com
See ad pages 1157, 1108.

MONT BELVIEU RV RESORT
Ratings: 10/9.5★/10 (RV Resort) From jct I-10 and Exit 803, go S 1.2 mi on S FM 565 Rd (R). **FAC:** Paved rds. 240 paved, patios, 40 pull-thrus (30 x 65), back-ins (30 x 47), 240 full hkups (30/50 amps), cable, WiFi, rentals, laundry, fire rings, controlled access. **REC:** heated pool, whirlpool, Mont Belvieu Lake: fishing, shuffleboard. Pets OK. Partial handicap access. 2015 rates: $41.11 to $66.66. ATM.
AAA Approved
(832)902-2200 Lat: 29.83395, Lon: -094.80440
6103 S Fm 565, Baytown, TX 77523
Montbelvieu@qualityrvresorts.com
www.montbelvieurvresort.com
See ad pages 1154-1155, 1108.

BEAUMONT — D9 *Jefferson*

EAST LUCAS RV PARK **Ratings: 5.5/8★/8** (RV Park) 2015 rates: $30. (409)899-9209 2590 E Lucas Dr, Beaumont, TX 77703

GULF COAST RV RESORT
Ratings: 9.5/10★/9 (RV Park) W-bnd: From Jct of I-10 & Exit 847 (Brooks Rd/Major Dr), S 0.1 mi on Brooks Rd (R); or E-bnd: From Jct of I-10 & Exit 845 (Major Dr/Brooks Rd), E 1.6 mi on frontg rd to Brooks Rd, S 0.1 mi (R). **FAC:** Paved rds. 125 paved, patios, 125 pull-thrus (30 x 60), 125 full hkups (30/50 amps), WiFi, laundry, groc. **REC:** pool, playground. Pet restrict(B). Partial handicap access, no tents. Big rig sites, RV age re-

TX

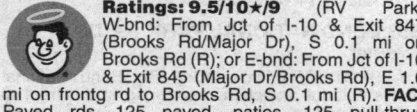

BEAUMONT (CONT)

GULF COAST RV RESORT (CONT)

strict, eco-friendly, 2015 rates: $40. Disc: AAA, military.
(866)410-7801 Lat: 30.01720, Lon: -94.17232
5175 Brooks Rd., Beaumont, TX 77705
hospitality@gulfcoastrvresort.com
www.gulfcoastrvresort.com
See ad page 1135.

HIDDEN LAKE RV RESORT
Ratings: 8.5/10★/9.5 (RV Park) E-bnd: From Jct of I-10 & Exit 845 (Major Dr), S 0.3 mi on Major Dr (FM 364) (R). W-bnd: From Jct of I-10 & Exit 847 (Brooks/Major Dr), W 1.3 mi on frntg rd to Major Dr (FM 364), S 0.3 mi (R). **FAC:** Paved rds. 70 paved, patios, 25 pull-thrus (35 x 85), back-ins (36 x 65), 70 full hkups (30/50 amps), cable, WiFi, laundry. **REC:** Lake Taylor: fishing. Pet restrict(B/Q). Partial handicap access, no tents. Big rig sites, eco-friendly, 2015 rates: $38.
(409)840-9691 Lat: 30.00291, Lon: -94.18551
6860 S. Major Dr. (Fm 364), Beaumont, TX 77705
info@hiddenlakervresort.com
www.hiddenlakervresort.com
See ad page 1135.

BELTON — C7 *Bell*

DANA PEAK (Public Corps) From town, W 5 mi on US-190 to FM-2410, SW 6 mi to Comanche Gap Rd, S 5 mi (E). 2015 rates: $20 to $36. (254)698-4282

LIVE OAK RIDGE PARK/BELTON LAKE (Public Corps) 2 mi N on Hwy-317, then 2 mi W & N on FM-439, then N on FM-2271 to N side of Belton Dam. 2015 rates: $18 to $22. (254)780-1738

UNION GROVE (Public Corps) From town, W 4 mi on US-190 to FM-1670, S 3 mi to FM-2484, W 5 mi (R). 2015 rates: $22 to $26. (254)947-0072

WESTCLIFF PARK/BELTON LAKE (Public Corps) From jct Hwy 317 & FM 439: Go 4-1/2 mi W on FM 439, then 1 mi N on Sparta Rd, then 1 mi NE on Westcliff Rd. 2015 rates: $20. (254)939-9828

BENBROOK — J1 *Tarrant*

BEAR CREEK CAMPGROUND (Public Corps) From town, S 6.2 mi on US-377 to FM-1187, E 1.4 mi to CR-1125 (Ben Day Murrin Rd), N 1.7 mi (L). Pit toilets. 2015 rates: $28. Apr 1 to Sep 30. (817)292-2400

HOLIDAY PARK (Public Corps) From town, S 6 mi on US-377 to Pearl Ranch Dr/S Lakeview Dr, E 2 mi (E). 2015 rates: $28. (817)292-2400

BEND — C6 *San Saba*

COLORADO BEND (State Pk) From town: Go 4 mi S on gravel road (unmarked CR 442). Note: Maximum length 30'. Entrance fee required. Pit toilets. 2015 rates: $14. (512)628-3240

BIG BEND NATIONAL PARK — D3 *Brewster*

A SPOTLIGHT Introducing Big Bend National Park's colorful attractions appearing at the front of this state section.

BIG BEND/COTTONWOOD CAMPGROUND (Natl Pk) From park headquarters (Panther Junction): Go 35 mi SW of park hdqtrs. Pit toilets. 2015 rates: $14. (432)477-1121

BIG BEND/RIO GRANDE VILLAGE CAMPGROUND (Natl Pk) From Jct of US-90 & US-385 (in Marathon), S 40 mi on US-385 to park entrance, S 29 mi to park hdqtrs at Panther Jct, SE 20 mi (E). Entrance fee required. 2015 rates: $14. (432)477-1121

RIO GRANDE RV PARK & CAMPGROUND
(Natl Pk) From Jct of US-90 & US-385 (in Marathon), S 40 mi to park entrance, S 29 mi to park hdqtrs at Panther Junction, SE 20 mi (E). Entrance fee required. Register at Rio Grande Village Store/Service Station. **FAC:** Paved rds. 25 paved, back-ins (15 x 50), 25 full hkups (30 amps), WiFi Hotspot, showers $, laundry, groc, LP gas, firewood. **REC:** Rio Grande River: fishing. Pets OK. Partial handicap access, no tents. 14 day max stay, 2015 rates: $33.
(432)477-2293 Lat: 29.18250, Lon: -102.96083
big Bend National Park-Basin Rural Station, Big Bend National Park, TX 79834
www.nps.gov
See ad page 1112 (Spotlight Big Bend National Park).

BIG SPRING — B4 *Howard*

WHIP IN RV PARK
Ratings: 6.5/9★/7.5 (RV Park) From Jct I-20: Go 200 ft S on Moss Lake Rd (L). **FAC:** Gravel rds. (60 spaces). Avail: 10 gravel, 10 pull-thrus (22 x 70), 10 full hkups (30/50 amps), seasonal sites, cable, WiFi, laundry. Pet restrict(B/Q). Partial handicap access, no tents. Big rig sites, 2015 rates: $30 to $33.35. Disc: AAA, military.
(432)393-5242 Lat: 32.27412, Lon: -101.36983
7000 S Service Rd, Big Spring, TX 79720
whipinrvpark@yahoo.com
www.whipinrvpark.com

BLANCO — D6 *Blanco*

BLANCO (State Pk) From Jct of US-281 & RR-165 (Loop 163, in town), S 0.3 mi on US-281 (R). CAUTION: 24,000 lb weight limit bridge at campground entrance (Entrance fee). 2015 rates: $17 to $23. (830)833-4333

BLANCO SETTLEMENT CABINS & RV PARK
Ratings: 5/7.5★/8 (RV Park) From Jct of US-281 & Loop 163: Go 1/2 mi SE on Loop 163, then 1 mi E on RR 165 (R). **FAC:** Gravel rds. (27 spaces). Avail: 6 gravel (30/50 amps), seasonal sites, WiFi, rentals, laundry. **REC:** Blanco River: swim, fishing. Pet restrict(B). No tents. 2015 rates: $30 to $35.
AAA Approved
(830)833-5115 Lat: 30.09090, Lon: -98.39875
1705 Ranch Rd 165, Blanco, TX 78606
mailblancosettlement@gmail.com
www.blancosettlement.com

BOERNE — D6 *Bexar*

ALAMO FIESTA RV RESORT
Ratings: 8.5/8.5/7.5 (RV Park) W-bnd: From Jct of I-10 & Exit 543: Go NW 1.1 mi on N Frontage Rd (R); or E-bnd: From Jct of I-10 & Exit 543: Go S Frontage Rd to U-turn under Fwy, then NW 1.1 mi on N Frontage Rd (R). **FAC:** All weather rds. (222 spaces). 130 Avail: 65 paved, 65 gravel, 130 pull-thrus (25 x 60), 130 full hkups (30/50 amps), seasonal sites, WiFi, rentals, dump, laundry, groc, LP gas. **REC:** pool, playground. Pet restrict(B). Partial handicap access, no tents. Big rig sites, 2015 rates: $40 to $55. Disc: AAA, military.
(800)321-2267 Lat: 29.76755, Lon: -98.71715
33000 Ih-10 W, Boerne, TX 78006
alamofiesta@alamofiestarv.com
www.alamofiestarv.com
See ad pages 1175, 1108.

CASCADE CAVERNS
Ratings: 7.5/9/8 (Campground) From Jct of I-10 & Exit 543 (Cascade Caverns Rd), then follow signs on Cascade Caverns Rd 2.6 mi (R). **FAC:** Paved/gravel rds. 104 gravel, 25 pull-thrus (18 x 60), back-ins (18 x 60), 45 full hkups, 11 W, 59 E (30/50 amps), WiFi, tent sites, dump, laundry, firewood, controlled access. **REC.** Pet restrict(B). 2015 rates: $35. Disc: AAA.
AAA Approved
(830)755-8080 Lat: 29.76339, Lon: -98.68066
226 Cascade Caverns Rd, Boerne, TX 78015
downunder@cascadecaverns.com
www.cascadecaverns.com
See ad page 1175.

According to some studies, almost 50 percent of RVers camp with pets! Find out more in our Pampered Pet Parks feature at the front of the Guide.

TOP OF THE HILL RV RESORT
Ratings: 9.5/10★/9 (RV Park) Fro[m] Jct I-10 & Exit 533, (FM-289/Welfare) (... of Boerne): Go NW 0.8 mi on FM-289 ... Green Cedar Rd (L). **FAC:** All weathe[r] rds. 103 Avail: 6 paved, 97 gravel, 3... pull-thrus (30 x 65), back-ins (30 x 50), 103 full hkup[s] (30/50 amps), WiFi, tent sites, rentals, laundry, gro[c] **REC:** pool, whirlpool. Pets OK. Big rig sites, 201[5] rates: $37.50 to $50.
(830)537-3666 Lat: 29.88190, Lon: -98.79990
12 Green Cedar Rd, Boerne, TX 78006
info@topofthehillrvresort.com
www.topofthehillrvresort.com
See ad pages 1174, 1108.

BONHAM — A8 *Fannin*

BONHAM (State Pk) From Jct of SR-56 & SR-7[8] S 1.4 mi on SR-78 to FM-271, E 1.9 mi (L). 201[5] rates: $20. (903)583-5022

BORGER — F9 *Hutchinson*

HUBER PARK (Public) At Jct of SR-207 (S Ma[in] St) & Cedar St (E). Pit toilets. (806)273-2883

BOWIE — A7 *Montague*

CAMPER'S PARADISE RV PARK
Ratings: 9/8.5/8.5 (RV Park) Fro[m] Jct of US 287 & Fruitland Rd: Go 1/2 ... S on E Service Rd. (L). **FAC:** Gravel rd[s] (90 spaces). Avail: 60 gravel, 48 pu[ll-] thrus (20 x 55), back-ins (20 x 55), 60 fu[ll] hkups (30/50 amps), seasonal sites, WiFi, tent site[s] dump, laundry, groc, LP gas. **REC:** pool, playgroun[d] Pet restrict(B/Q). Big rig sites, 2015 rates: $35. Dis[c:] military.
(940)872-2429 Lat: 33.48738, Lon: -97.79774
4242 US Hwy 287, Bowie, TX 76270
campparadiserv@aol.com
See ad this page.

BRACKETTVILLE — D5 *Kinney*

FORT CLARK SPRINGS RV PARK Rat[-] ings: 8.5/8.5★/7.5 (RV Park) 2015 rates: $23.5[0] (830)563-9340 80 Scales Road, Brackettville, T[X] 78832

BRAZORIA — D8 *Brazoria*

BRAZORIA LAKES RV RESORT
(RV Resort) (Under Construction) FAC[:] Paved rds. 262 paved, 262 full hkups (30/5[0] amps). **REC.** Pet restrict(B). Disc: AAA.
AAA Approved
(866)682-4632 Lat: 29.036316, Lon: -095.56839
109 Stephen F Austin Trail, Brazoria, TX 77422
Info@qualityrvresorts.com
www.qualityrvresorts.com
See ad page 1154-1155.

BRENHAM — C8 *Washington*

ARTESIAN PARK RV CAMPGROUND
Ratings: 7.5/8/7 (RV Park) From J[ct] of US-290W & Hwy 36N: Go W 7.2 mi o[n] US-290W (L). **FAC:** Gravel rds. (5... spaces). Avail: 10 gravel, 10 pull-thru[s] (22 x 55), 10 full hkups (30/50 amps) seasonal sites, WiFi, tent sites, dump, laundry. **REC** playground. Pets OK. Big rig sites, 2015 rates: $40 t[o] $42. Disc: military.
(979)836-0680 Lat: 30.19059, Lon: -96.52816
8601 Hwy 290 W, Brenham, TX 77833
info@artesianrvpark.com
www.artesianrvpark.com

BROADDUS — C9 *San Augustine*

JACKSON HILL PARK (Public Corps) Fro[m] town, SW 4 mi on Hwy 147 to FR-2851, W 1 mi (E) Pit toilets. 2015 rates: $30. Jan to Sep. (936)872[-] 9266

BROOKELAND — C9 *Jasper, Sabine*

BROOKELAND/LAKE SAM RAYBURN KOA Rat[-] ings: 7/9★/8 (RV Park) 2015 rates: $34 to $45 (800)562-1612 505 CR 212, Brookeland, TX 7593...

MILL CREEK PARK (Public Corps) From town W 1 mi on Spur 165 (E). 2015 rates: $26 to $28 (409)384-5716

TWIN DIKES PARK (Public Corps) From town, N 15 mi on US-96 to RR-255, W 5 mi (R). 2015 rates $14 to $28. Mar 1 to Sep 3. (409)384-5716

BROOKSHIRE — D8 *Waller*

HOUSTON WEST RV PARK
Ratings: 9.5/9.5★/9 (Campground) From Jct of I-10 & FM-1489 (exit 731), N 0.2 mi on FM-1489 to Cooper Rd, W 0.2 mi (L). **FAC:** All weather rds. (14... spaces). Avail: 100 gravel, 80 pull-thru[s] (30 x 70), back-ins (30 x 50), 100 full hkups (30/5[0] amps), seasonal sites, WiFi, dump, laundry, groc

BROOKSHIRE (CONT)

HOUSTON WEST RV PARK (CONT)
REC: pool, whirlpool, pond, fishing, playground. Pet restrict(B/Q). Partial handicap access, no tents. Big rig sites, eco-friendly, 2015 rates: $37 to $39. Disc: AAA, military.
AAA Approved
(281)375-5678 Lat: 29.78153, Lon: -95.97143
35303 Cooper Rd., Brookshire, TX 77423
info@hwrvpark.com
www.hwrvpark.com
See ad pages 1159, 1108 & Snowbird Destinations in Magazine Section.

BROWNSVILLE — M4 *Cameron*

BREEZE LAKE RV CAMPGROUND MHP
Ratings: 9.5/9★/8 (RV Area in MHP) S-bnd: From Jct of US-77/83 & FM-511, SE (left) 10.5 mi on FM-511 to FM-802, W 0.7 mi to Vermillion Ave, S 0.3 mi (L). **FAC:** Paved rds. (180 spaces). 90 Avail: 41 paved, 30 gravel, 19 grass, patios, 14 pull-thrus (20 x 60), back-ins (25 x 60), 90 full hkups (30/50 amps), seasonal sites, cable, WiFi $, rentals, showers $, laundry, controlled access. **REC:** heated pool, pond, fishing, shuffleboard. Pet restrict(B/Q). Partial handicap access, no tents. Age restrict may apply, big rig sites, eco-friendly, 2015 rates: $36 to $39. Disc: AAA, military.
(956)831-4427 Lat: 25.93416, Lon: -97.41729
1710 N Vermillion Ave, Brownsville, TX 78521
breezelake@att.net
www.breezelakervcampground.com/
See ad this page, 1108.

HONEYDALE MOBILE HOME & RV PARK **Ratings: 7.5/9★/6.5** (RV Area in MHP) 2015 rates: $36. (956)982-2230 505 Honeydale Rd, # 22, Brownsville, TX 78520

PAUL'S RV PARK
Ratings: 9/9.5★/8 (RV Area in MHP) From Jct of US 77/83 & Boca Chica Blvd exit, E 4 mi on Boca Chica Blvd to Minnesota Ave (FM 313), N 0.9 mi (L); or From Jct of US 77/83 & FM 802, E 4.8 mi on FM 802 to Hwy 48, SW 0.2 mi to Minnesota Ave (FM 313), S 0.8 mi (R). **FAC:** Paved rds. (150 spaces). Avail: 113 grass, patios, back-ins (27 x 35), 113 full hkups (30/50 amps), cable, WiFi $, rentals, laundry, controlled access. **REC:** heated pool, whirlpool, shuffleboard. Pet restrict(B/Q). Partial handicap access, no tents. Age restrict may apply, eco-friendly, 2015 rates: $38. Disc: AAA, military.
(956)831-4852 Lat: 25.92928, Lon: -97.43204
1129 N Minnesota, Brownsville, TX 78521
paulsrvpark@aol.com
www.paulsrvpark.com
See ad this page, 1108.

RIO RV PARK MHP **Ratings: 7.5/8.5/7.5** (RV Area in MHP) 2015 rates: $36. (956)831-4653 8801 E Boca Chica Blvd, Brownsville, TX 78521

RIVER BEND COUNTRY CLUB **Ratings: 7.5/9★/8.5** (Condo Pk) 2015 rates: $28. (956)548-0194 4541 US Military Hwy 281, Brownsville, TX 78520

WINTER HAVEN RESORT **Ratings: 9.5/9★/8.5** (RV Area in MHP) 2015 rates: $35. (956)831-7755 3501 Old Port Isabel Rd, Brownsville, TX 78526

4 SEASONS MHP & RV RESORT
Ratings: 8.5/8/8 (RV Area in MHP) From Jct of US-77/83 & FM-802, E 5 mi on FM-802 to Coffee Port Rd, W 0.3 mi (L). **FAC:** Paved rds. (205 spaces). Avail: 81 grass, patios, 10 pull-thrus (21 x 60), back-ins (25 x 40), accepts full hkup units only, 81 full hkups (30/50 amps), seasonal sites, cable, WiFi $, laundry, controlled access. **REC:** heated pool, whirlpool, Resaca River: fishing, shuffleboard. No pets. No tents. Age restrict may apply, eco-friendly, 2015 rates: $38. No CC.
(956)831-4918 Lat: 25.93772, Lon: -97.42824
6900 Coffee Port Rd, Brownsville, TX 78521
info@4seasonsmhrvresort.com
www.4seasonsmhrvresort.com
See ad page 1122 (Spotlight South Texas Tropics).

BROWNWOOD — B6 *Brown*

LAKE BROWNWOOD (State Pk) From Jct of US 67/84 & SR 279 N (in town), N 14.4 mi on SR 279 N to PR-15, E 4.8 mi (E) (Entrance fee). 2015 rates: $15 to $25. (325)784-5223

RIVERSIDE PARK RV
Ratings: 7/9★/7.5 (RV Park) From jct of Hwy 377 & Riverside Park Dr: Go 1/4 mi N on Riverside Park Dr (R). **FAC:** Paved rds. 26 paved, 26 pull-thrus (40 x 100), 26 full hkups (30/50 amps), cable, WiFi, laundry. **REC:** Pecan Bayou: playground. Pet restrict(B). 2015 rates: $48. Disc: military.
(325)642-1869 Lat: 31.730272, Lon: -98.975627
320 Riverside Park Dr, Brownwood, TX 76801
Ross@riversideparkrv.com
www.riversideparkrv.com
See ad this page.

BRYAN — C8 *Brazos*

AGGIELAND RV PARK
Ratings: 9.5/10★/7.5 (RV Park) From Jct of TX-21/US-190 & N Earl Rudder Fwy/N TX-6, NW 0.3 mi on N Earl Rudder Fwy to Colson Rd (R). **FAC:** Paved rds. (94 spaces). Avail: 74 paved, patios, 12 pull-thrus (25 x 70), back-ins (25 x 60), 74 full hkups (30/50 amps), seasonal sites, cable, WiFi, laundry, LP gas. **REC:** pool. Pet restrict(B). Partial handicap access, no tents. 2015 rates: $38. Disc: military.
(979)703-7937 Lat: 30.70001, Lon: -96.36201
3203 Colson Rd, Bryan, TX 77808
aggielandrvpark@gmail.com
www.aggielandrvpark.com
See ad page 1140.

BULLARD — B8 *Smith*

K.E. BUSHMAN'S CAMP
Ratings: 10/10★/10 (RV Park) From Jct of FM 344 & US 69: Go 1-1/2 mi S on US 69. (L). **FAC:** Paved rds. 97 paved, 25 pull-thrus (40 x 70), back-ins (30 x 65), 97 full hkups (30/50 amps), WiFi, tent sites, laundry, groc, LP bottles, firewood, controlled access. **REC:** heated pool, whirlpool, pond, fishing, playground. Pets OK. Partial handicap access. Big rig sites, eco-friendly, 2015 rates: $30. Disc: military.
(903)894-8221 Lat: 32.11974, Lon: -95.30060
51152 S. US Hwy 69N, Bullard, TX 75757
camping@kiepersol.com
www.kiepersol.com
See ad pages 1178, 1108.

Things to See and Do

K.E. BUSHMAN'S WINERY & CELEBRATION CENTER Event center and digital recording facility. Closed Sunday. Partial handicap access. RV accessible. Restrooms. Hours: 11am to 9pm.
(903)894-7505 Lat: 32.11841, Lon: -95.29756
5165 Fm 2493 E, Tyler, TX 75757
www.kiepersol.com
See ad page 1178.

BULVERDE — D6 *Comal*

GUADALUPE MOUNTAINS/PINE SPRINGS (Natl Pk) From El Paso, E 110 mi on Hwy 62/180 (L) Or From Carlsbad NM, SW 60 mi on Hwy 62/180 (R). 2015 rates: $8. (915)828-3251

TEXAS 281 RV PARK LTD
Ratings: 8.5/9★/9 (RV Park) From Jct of SR-46 & US-281: Go 3/4 mi S on US-281, then crossover & back N 1/4 mi (R). **FAC:** Paved rds. (160 spaces). Avail: 53 paved, patios, 47 pull-thrus (28 x 65), back-ins (28 x 40), 53 full hkups (30/50 amps), seasonal sites, cable, WiFi, laundry. **REC:** shuffleboard, playground. Pet restrict(B). No tents. Big rig sites, 2015 rates: $34.
(830)980-2282 Lat: 29.78960, Lon: -98.42121
33300 Hwy 281 N, Bulverde, TX 78163
reservations@texas281rvpark.com
www.texas281rvpark.com
See ad this page, 1108.

BURKBURNETT — A6 *Wichita*

BURKBURNETT/WICHITA FALLS KOA **Ratings: 8.5/9★/8** (RV Park) 2015 rates: $30 to $40. (940)569-3081 1202 East 3rd St., Burkburnett, TX 76354

BURLESON — J2 *Johnson*

JELLYSTONE PARK AT THE RUSTIC CREEK RANCH **Ratings: 9/9★/8** (Campground) 2015 rates: $25 to $81. (817)426-5037 2301 S I-35 West, Burleson, TX 76028

MOCKINGBIRD HILL MOBILE HOME & RV PARK
Ratings: 8/9.5★/9 (RV Area in MHP) S-Bound I-35W (Exit 35): Go 2-1/2 mi S on W Frontage Rd (R). N-Bound I-35W (Exit 32): Go 1-1/4 mi N on W Frontage Rd (L). **FAC:** All weather rds. (89 spaces). Avail: 20 paved, patios, 20 pull-thrus (25 x 70), 20 full hkups

TX

BURLESON (CONT)

MOCKINGBIRD HILL MOBILE (CONT)
(30/50 amps), seasonal sites, WiFi, rentals, laundry. Pet restrict(B). Partial handicap access, no tents. Big rig sites, 2015 rates: $35. Disc: AAA, military.
(817)295-3011 Lat: 32.50145, Lon: -97.29320
1990 S Burleson Blvd #20, Burleson, TX 76028
mockingbirdrv@aol.com
www.mockingbirdrvpark.com
See ad pages 1137, 1108.

BURNET — C6 *Burnet*

BIG CHIEF RV & CABIN RESORT **Ratings: 8.5/8.5/8.5** (RV Park) 2015 rates: $30 to $50. (512)793-4746 1420 Fm 690, Burnet, TX 78611

INKS LAKE (State Pk) From Jct of US-281 & Hwy 29, W 9 mi on Hwy 29 to Park Rd 4, S 3 mi (R) (Entrance fee). 2015 rates: $15 to $22. (512)793-2223

BURTON — C7 *Washington*

LAKE SOMERVILLE & TRAILWAY (NAILS CREEK UNIT) (State Pk) From jct US 290 & FM 1697: Go 11 mi W on FM 1697, then 4 mi NE on FM 180. Entrance fee required. 2015 rates: $16. (979)289-2392

CADDO — B6 *Palo Pinto*

POSSUM KINGDOM (State Pk) From Jct of US-180 & PR-33, N 14.3 mi on PR-33, on Possum Kingdom Lake (E) (Entrance fee). 2015 rates: $12 to $20. (940)549-1803

CADDO MILLS — B8 *Hunt*

DALLAS NE CAMPGROUND
Ratings: 9/9★/9 (Campground) From Jct I-30 (Exit 85) & FM-36: Go 1/4 mi N on FM-36 (L). **FAC:** Gravel rds. (87 spaces). 67 Avail: 37 gravel, 30 grass, 67 pull-thrus (30 x 85), some side by side hkups, 67 full hkups (30/50 amps), seasonal sites, WiFi, tent sites, rentals, laundry, groc, LP gas, firewood. **REC:** pool, pond, fishing, playground. Pet restrict(B). Partial handicap access. Big rig sites, 2015 rates: $38.05 to $41.67. Disc: military.
(903)527-3615 Lat: 33.02352, Lon: -96.20692
4268 Fm 36 S, Caddo Mills, TX 75135

CAMP WOOD — D5 *Uvalde*

COOKSEY PARK (Public) From town, S 3 mi on Hwy 55 (R). 2015 rates: $16. (830)597-3223

CANTON — B8 *Van Zandt*

CANTON See also Athens, Canton & Terrell.

CANTON I-20 RV PARK
Ratings: 9.5/9★/10 (RV Park) From Jct of I-20 & Exit 519, E 0.25 mi on South access rd (R). **FAC:** All weather rds. (46 spaces). Avail: 28 gravel, 24 pull-thrus (40 x 80), back-ins (35 x 50), 28 full hkups (30/50 amps), seasonal sites, WiFi, tent sites, laundry, firewood. **REC:** pool. Pets OK. Big rig sites, 2015 rates: $35. Disc: military.
(903)873-8561 Lat: 32.61606, Lon: -95.97761
24481 Ih-20, Wills Point, TX 75169
cantonl20rvpark@yahoo.com
www.cantonl20rvpark.com
See ad this page, 1108.

FIRST MONDAY TRADE DAYS RV PARK (Public) From Jct of I-20 & Exit 527/TX 19, S 1.1 mi to Hwy 64, W 1.5 mi to Edgewood Rd, E 0.7 mi (R). 2015 rates: $25 to $30. (903)567-6556

MILL CREEK RANCH RESORT
Ratings: 10/10★/10 (RV Park) From Jct I-20 (Exit 527) & Hwy 19 (Trade Days Blvd): Go 1/4 mi S on Hwy 19 (L). **FAC:** Paved rds. 100 paved, 65 pull-thrus (32 x 100), back-ins (33 x 50), 100 full hkups (30/50 amps), cable, WiFi $, rentals, laundry, groc, LP bottles, fire rings, firewood, controlled access. **REC:** pool, whirlpool, pond, fishing, playground. Pet restrict(B). Partial handicap access, no tents. Big rig sites, 28 day max stay, 2015 rates: $37 to $66. Disc: military.
(866)599-7275 Lat: 32.57360, Lon: -95.85264
2102 N. Trade Days Blvd, Canton, TX 75103
reservations@millcreekranchresort.com
www.millcreekranchresort.com
See ad this page, 1108.

WAGON TRAIN RV PARK
Ratings: 6.5/9★/8.5 (RV Park) From jct I-20 & Exit 533 (E-Bound): Go 2 mi E on S Service Rd (R). W-Bound I-20, Exit 536: Go 1/2 mi W on S Service Rd (L). **FAC:** Gravel rds. 15 gravel, 11 pull-thrus (40 x 75), back-ins (40 x 75), 15 full hkups (30/50 amps), WiFi, laundry. Pet restrict(B). 2015 rates: $30. Disc: AAA, military.
(903)963-1333 Lat: 32.5269432, Lon: -95.7248619
7869 Interstate 20, Canton, TX 75103
wagontrainrvpark@gmail.com
www.wagontrainrvpark.com

CANUTILLO — B1 *El Paso*

GASLIGHT SQUARE MOBILE ESTATES
Ratings: 9/9.5★/7 (Campground) From Jct I-10 (Exit 6) & Transmountain Rd: Go 1/2 mi W on Transmountain/Talbot Rd (L). Elev 3850 ft. **FAC:** Paved rds. (223 spaces). Avail: 2 paved, patios, 16 pull-thrus (24 x 62), back-ins (21 x 45), 23 full hkups (30/50 amps), cable, WiFi, dump, laundry. **REC:** pool, playground. Pet restrict(B/Q). Partial handicap access, no tents. 2015 rates: $25.
(915)877-2238 Lat: 31.90775, Lon: -106.59375
500 Talbot Ave, Canutillo, TX 79835
gaslightsquare@towermgmt.com
www.towerrvparks.com

CANYON — F9 *Randall*

PALO DURO CANYON (State Pk) From Jct of US-87 & SR-217, E 12.2 mi on SR-217 (E); or From Jct of I-27 & SR-217, E 10 mi on SR-217 (E) (2 mi 10% Grade Down to sites) (Entrance fee). 2015 rates: $24. (806)488-2227

PALO DURO RV PARK
Ratings: 7/8/7 (RV Park) From Jct of I-27 (Exit 106) & Hwy 217: Go 200 ft E on Hwy 217 (L). Elev 3670 ft. **FAC:** Paved/gravel rds. (82 spaces). Avail: 52 gravel, 52 pull-thrus (18 x 80), mostly side by side hkups, 52 full hkups (30/50 amps), seasonal sites, WiFi, laundry. **REC.** Pet restrict(B). No tents. Big rig sites, 2015 rates: $28. Disc: AAA, military.
AAA Approved
(800)540-0567 Lat: 34.97984, Lon: -101.87799
5707 4th Ave, Canyon, TX 79015
pdrv@msn.com
palodurorv.tripod.com
See ad this page, 1108.

CANYON LAKE — D6 *Comal*

RIO GUADALUPE RESORT **Ratings: 8/7/8** (RV Park) 2015 rates: $25 to $40. (830)964-3613 14130 River Rd, New Braunfels, TX 78132

SUMMIT VACATION & RV RESORT
Ratings: 9/9.5★/9.5 (RV Resort) From Jct FM-306 & FM-2673: Go 1-1/2 mi S on FM-2673, then 1-1/2 mi E on River Rd (R).

5-STAR RESORT NOW OPEN TO PUBLIC
Located on the beautiful Guadalupe River, just minutes to San Antonio and Austin and 5 miles to Canyon Lake. A paradise for RVers, Winter Texans and a great vacation for families. Enjoy our Tree Top Villas and Cabins too!

FAC: Paved rds. (106 spaces). Avail: 94 gravel, 18 pull-thrus (45 x 80), back-ins (45 x 60), 94 full hkups (30/50 amps), seasonal sites, WiFi, rentals, dump, laundry, fire rings, restaurant, controlled access

;ANYON LAKE (CONT)

SUMMIT VACATION & RV RESORT (CONT)
:EC: heated pool, wading pool, whirlpool, Guada-ıpe River: fishing, shuffleboard, playground. Pet re-trict(B). No tents. Big rig sites, 2015 rates: $34 to 50. Disc: military.
830)964-2531 Lat: 29.83273, Lon: -98.16363
3105 River Road, New Braunfels, TX 78132
eservations@summitresorttexas.com
ʌww.summitresorttexas.com
See ad opposite page, 1108 & Family Camping in Magazine Section.

YOGI BEAR'S JELLYSTONE PARK HILL ;OUNTRY **Ratings: 9/9★/8.5** (Campground) From ct FM 2673 & FM 306: Go 3/4 mi NW on FM 306 (L). **'AC:** Paved/gravel rds. 85 gravel, patios, 53 pull-ırus (15 x 50), back-ins (25 x 40), some side by side kups, 85 full hkups (30/50 amps), cable, WiFi, tent ites, rentals, laundry, groc, LP gas, firewood. **REC:** eated pool, whirlpool, shuffleboard, playground. Pet estrict(B). Partial handicap access. Big rig sites, 015 rates: $48 to $62. Disc: military. 830)256-0088 Lat: 29.86605, Lon: -98.17278 2915 Fm 306, Canyon Lake, TX 78133 ıfo@jellystonehillcountry.com ʌww.jellystonehillcountry.com

;ARMINE — C7 *Fayette*

DIXIELAND/TEXAS RETREAT RV PARK **Rat-ıgs: 6/8.5★/8** (Campground) 2015 rates: $30 to 35. (979)278-3805 249 Dixieland Rv Park Lane, ;armine, TX 78932

;ARROLLTON — G4 *Dallas*

SANDY LAKE MH & RV PARK CAREFREE RV RESORT
Ratings: 8.5/8.5★/7 (RV Park) From jct I-35E & Loop I-635: Go 4 mi N on I-35E (exit 444), then 1/2 mi W on Sandy Lake Rd. (L).

SANDY LAKE CAREFREE RV RESORT!
'isit all that Dallas has to offer at the Sandy Lake! his property boasts large sites, heated swimming ool, large clubhouse and exercise facilities. All within ıinutes of downtown Dallas and the Fort Worth area.

'AC: Paved rds. (217 spaces). Avail: 10 paved, 10 ull-thrus (20 x 60), 10 full hkups (30/50 amps), sea-onal sites, WiFi $, laundry. **REC:** pool. Pet re-trict(B). No tents. Big rig sites, 2015 rates: $47. Disc: ,AA, military.
972)242-6808 Lat: 32.96835, Lon: -96.93053
915 Sandy Lake Rd, Carrollton, TX 75006
andylake@carefreervresorts.com
ʌww.carefreervresorts.com/sandylake
See ad pages 1134, 1108.

;ARTHAGE — B9 *Panola*

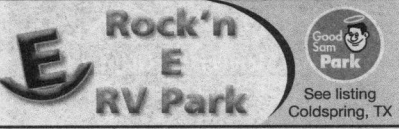

CARTHAGE RV CAMPGROUND
Ratings: 9.5/10★/8.5 (RV Park) From Jct of North US 59/US 79 & Lasalle Pkwy (Loop 59), SE 2 mi (R). **FAC:** Paved/gravel rds. 64 paved, 59 pull-thrus (35 x 65), back-ins (27 x 60), 64 full ıkups (30/50 amps), cable, WiFi, tent sites, rentals, ıump, laundry, LP gas. **REC:** pool, pond, fishing. Pets OK. Big rig sites, 2015 rates: $32.50 to $40. Disc: military.
(903)693-6640 Lat: 32.17940, Lon: -94.32709
1294 NE Loop 59, Carthage, TX 75633
u2best@sbcglobal.net
See ad this page, 1108.

CASTROVILLE — D6 *Medina*

ALSATIAN RV RESORT & GOLF CLUB
Ratings: 10/10★/10 (RV Resort) From Jct Hwy 90 & CR 4516: Go 2.5 mi on CR 4516 (R). **FAC:** Paved rds. 69 paved, patios, 23 pull-thrus (41 x 110), back-ins (41 x 80), 69 full hkups (30/50 amps), cable, WiFi, rentals, laundry, groc, LP gas, restaurant, controlled access. **REC:** heated pool, whirlpool, pond, fishing, golf. Pet restrict(B). Partial handicap access. Big rig sites, RV age restrict, eco-friendly, 2015 rates: $35 to $85. Disc: AAA, military. ATM.
(830)931-9190 Lat: 29.36310, Lon: -098.94100
1581 CR 4516, Castroville, TX 78009
info@alsatianresort.com
www.alsatianresort.com
See ad pages 1175, 1108 & Snowbird Destinations in Magazine Section.

CASTROVILLE REGIONAL PARK (Public) From Jct of US-90 & Athens St, S 0.4 mi on Athens St to Lisbon St, W 0.2 mi (E). For reservations call (830)931-0033. 2015 rates: $25. (830)931-0033

Things to See and Do

ALSATIAN RV RESORT AND GOLF COURSE
Par 71, 18 hole golf course. Full driving range & practice facility. Club house with pro shop & restaurant. Food. Hours: 6:00 AM to 7:00 PM. Adult fee: $25 to $55. ATM.
(830)931-3100 Lat: 29.36050, Lon: -098.93370
1339 County Road 4516, Castroville, TX 78009
thealsatiangolfclub@yahoo.com
www.alsatiangolfclub.com
See ad page 1175.

CEDAR HILL — J3 *Dallas*

CEDAR HILL (State Pk) From Jct of I-20 & FM-1382 (exit 457), S 3.7 mi on FM-1382 (R) (Entrance fee). 2015 rates: $10 to $30. (972)291-3900

CLEBURNE — B7 *Johnson*

CLEBURNE (State Pk) From Jct of US-67 & SR-171/174, SW 6 mi on US-67 to PR-21, S 6 mi (R). CAUTION: Bridge weight limit 15000 lbs single or tandem axle (Entrance fee). 2015 rates: $16 to $30. (817)645-4215

CLYDE — B6 *Callahan*

WHITE'S RV PARK
Ratings: 5/8.5/7 (RV Park) From W-bnd I-20 & Exit 300: Go 1 block W on S. Service Rd (L) From E-bnd I-20 & Exit 300: Go 1 block E on S. Service Rd (R). **FAC:** Gravel rds. 30 gravel, 30 pull-thrus (18 x 60), 30 full hkups (30/50 amps), WiFi Hotspot, laundry. Pet restrict Partial handicap access, no tents. 2015 rates: $25 to $28. Disc: AAA, military.
(325)893-3320 Lat: 32.41506, Lon: -99.50947
1113 S I-20 Access Road W, Clyde, TX 79510
See ad page 1127.

COLDSPRING — C8 *San Jacinto*

ROCK'N E RV PARK
Ratings: 7.5/9★/9 (Campground) From Jct of SH 150 & FM 1514 (Byrd Ave) in town, SE 1.9 mi on SH 150 to FM 222, NE 5.1 mi (L). **FAC:** Gravel rds. 43 gravel, 31 pull-thrus (30 x 100), back-ins (30 x 100), 43 full hkups (30/50 amps), WiFi, tent sites, rentals, laundry, groc, firewood. **REC:** playground. Pet restrict(B). Big rig sites, RV age restrict, 2015 rates: $32 to $35.
(936)653-8024 Lat: 30.58086, Lon: -95.05036
5221 Fm 222, Coldspring, TX 77331
rocknervpark@yahoo.com
www.rocknervpark.com
See ad this page.

WOLF CREEK PARK (Public) From Coldspring, turn left on Hwy 156, go 1 mi. to Hwy 224, turn right. Park is 5 mi. on the right. (R). 2015 rates: $21 to $24. Mar 1 to Nov 30. (936)653-4312

COLEMAN — B6 *Coleman*

HORDS CREEK LAKE/FLATROCK PARK (Public Corps) From town, W 8 mi on FM 53 to Dam Rd, S 2 mi (R). Pit toilets. 2015 rates: $16 to $44. Apr 2 to Oct 1. (325)625-2322

HORDS CREEK LAKE/LAKESIDE PARK (Public Corps) From town, W 8 mi on Hwy 153 to Hords Creek Lake, follow signs (E). 2015 rates: $16 to $26. (325)625-2322

PRESS MORRIS (Public) From town, N 14 mi on US-283 to FM-1274, W 2 mi (R). 2015 rates: $15 to $20. (915)382-4635

COLLEGE STATION — C8 *Brazos*

KARSTENS RV RESORT
Ratings: 9.5/10★/8.5 (RV Resort) From jct Hwy 6 & FM 158: Go 4 mi E on FM 158, then 2-1/2 mi N on Elmo Weedon Rd (L). **FAC:** Paved rds. 115 paved, 15 pull-thrus (40 x 75), back-ins (36 x 60), 115 full hkups (30/50 amps), WiFi, laundry, LP gas. **REC:** pool, playground. Pet restrict(B). Partial handicap access. Big rig sites, 2015 rates: $40 to $70. No CC.
(979)774-7799 Lat: 30.6816827, Lon: -96.2474069
6685 Elmo Weedon, College Station, TX 77845
karstensstorage@yahoo.com
karstensrvresort.com
See ad this page, 1108.

We appreciate your business!

New to RVing? Be sure to check out the all the great articles on getting the most out of your RV, at the front of the Guide.

TX

COLORADO CITY — B5 *Mitchell*

LAKE COLORADO CITY (State Pk) From Jct of I-20 & FM-2836 (exit 210), S 5.3 mi on FM-2836 (L) 15,000 # per axle or Tandem Bridge on FM 2836S (Entrance fee). 2015 rates: $15 to $22. (325)728-3931

How much will it all cost? Use this as a guide: Rates shown are the minimum and maximum for two adults in one RV at the time of inspection (excluding any additional fees for items not at the site). Remember, these rates serve as guidelines only. It's always best to call ahead for the most current rate information.

LONE WOLF CREEK RV VILLAGE
Ratings: 7/9★/7.5 (RV Park) From jct I-20 & Exit 217 (Hwy 208 S): Go 1/4 mi S on Hwy 208 S (L).

COME JOIN THE PACK
It can get awfully lonely out in West Texas, but you'll always find a warm Texas welcome here at the Lone Wolf. Plenty of room to kick back & relax or cool off in the beautiful swimming pool. Ya'll come see us.

FAC: Gravel/dirt rds. (58 spaces). Avail: 24 gravel, 14 pull-thrus (35 x 90), back-ins (35 x 50), 24 full hkups (30/50 amps), seasonal sites, cable, WiFi Hotspot, dump, laundry, LP gas. **REC:** pool. Pets OK. Partial handicap access. 2015 rates: $35.
(325)728-9310 Lat: 32.40348, Lon: -100.84185
1591 S Highway 208, Colorado City, TX 79512
info@lonewolfrv.com
lonewolfcreekrvvillage.com
See ad this page, 1108.

COLUMBUS — D8 *Colorado*

COLORADO RIVER RV RESORT **Ratings: 7/7/7.5** (Membership Pk) 2015 rates: $42. (800)405-6188 1062 Thousand Trails Lane, Columbus, TX 78934

Find out more about the joys of traveling with your four-legged companions in our Pampered Pet Parks feature at the front of the Guide.

COLUMBUS RV PARK
Ratings: 8.5/9.5★/8.5 (Campground) From Jct of I-10 & SR-71 (Columbus Exit # 696), S 0.3 mi on SR-71 (R). **FAC:** Gravel rds. (86 spaces). Avail: 12 gravel, 12 pull-thrus (18 x 75), mostly side by side hkups, 12 full hkups (30/50 amps), seasonal sites, WiFi, tent sites, dump laundry, firewood. **REC:** pool. Pets OK. Partial handicap access. Big rig sites, eco-friendly, 2015 rates $33 to $305. Disc: AAA, military.
(979)732-6455 Lat: 29.6871, Lon: -96.5387
1011 New World Dr., Columbus, TX 78934
columbusrv@sbcgobal.net
www.campingfriend.com/columbusrvpark/
See ad this page.

COMANCHE — B6 *Comanche*

COPPERAS CREEK (Public Corps) From town NE 5 mi on US-377 to FM-2861, N 2.5 mi (R). 2015 rates: $16 to $42. Apr 1 to Sep 30. (254)879-2498

PROMONTORY (Public Corps) From town, N 12 mi on Hwy 16 to FM-2318, E 5 mi (E). 2015 rates: $8 to $16. Apr 1 to Sep 30. (254)893-7545

Did you know we sent 35 husband-wife RVing teams out this year to scour North America rating and inspecting RV parks and campgrounds? You can rest easy when you read our listings, knowing we've already been there.

COMFORT — D6 *Kendall*

RV PARK USA
Ratings: 7.5/9★/8 (RV Park) From Jct of I-10 & Hwy 87 (exit 523), exit to SW side (R). **FAC:** All weather rds. 52 gravel, 12 pull-thrus (25 x 70), back-ins (25 x 45), 52 full hkups (30/50 amps), cable, WiFi, tent sites, rentals, laundry, LP gas. **REC.** Pet restrict(B). Partial handicap access. Big rig sites, eco-friendly, 2015 rates: $35. Disc: AAA, military.
(830)995-2900 Lat: 29.97996, Lon: -98.90713
108 Blueridge, Comfort, TX 78013
rvparkusa@hctc.net
www.rvparkusa.net
See ad pages 1163, 1108.

COMSTOCK — D4 *Val Verde*

SEMINOLE CANYON STATE HISTORICAL PARK (State Pk) From Jct of US-90 & Hwy 163 (in town), W 8.6 mi on US-90 (L) (Tours are cancelled when temp. over 100 degrees) (Entrance fee). 2015 rates: $20. (432)292-4464

CONCAN — D5 *Uvalde*

BECS STORE & RV PARK
Ratings: 7.5/9.5★/8.5 (RV Park) From Jct of Hwy 127 & US-83, N 5.7 mi on US-83 (L). **FAC:** Gravel rds. (28 spaces). Avail: 23 gravel, patios, 9 pull-thrus (50 x 80), back-ins (50 x 50), 23 full hkups (30/50 amps), seasonal sites, WiFi, tent sites, rentals, laundry, fire rings, firewood. **REC:** playground. Pet restrict(B/Q). Partial handicap access. Big rig sites, eco-friendly, 2015 rates: $32 to $60.
(830)232-5477 Lat: 29.57132, Lon: -99.74905
29015 N US Hwy 83, Concan, TX 78838
becsrv@aol.com
www.becsrv.com
See ad opposite page.

GARNER (State Pk) From Jct of Hwy 127 & US-83, N 8.3 mi on US-83 to FM-1050, E 0.2 mi (R) (Entrance fee). 2015 rates: $15 to $26. (830)232-6132

PARKVIEW RIVERSIDE RV PARK
Ratings: 8.5/9.5★/9 (RV Park) From Jct of Hwy 83 & Hwy 1050 (North of Concan), E 1.1mi on Hwy 1050 to CR-350, S 1.5 mi (R). **FAC:** Paved/gravel rds. 99 gravel, 17 pull-thrus (28 x 65), back-ins (35 x 55), 99 full hkups (30/50 amps), WiFi $, dump, laundry, groc, LP gas, fire rings, firewood. **REC:** Frio River: swim, fishing. Pets OK. Partial handicap access, no tents. Big rig sites, eco-friendly, 2015 rates: $42 to $60.
(877)374-6748 Lat: 29.58256, Lon: -99.72801
2561 County Road 350, Concan, TX 78838
parkviewrv@gmail.com
parkviewriversiderv.com
See ad opposite page, 1108 & Snowbird Destinations in Magazine Section.

COOPER — A8 *Delta*

COOPER LAKE-DOCTORS CREEK UNIT (State Pk) From Jct of Hwy 19/154 & 154, W 2.3 mi on Hwy 154 to FM 1529, S 1.6 mi (R); or From Jct of Hwy 19 & FM 1529, W 5.3 mi on FM 1529 (R) NOTE: Park only open on weekends as of April 10, 2006. (Entrance fee). 2015 rates: $16. (903)395-3100

COOPER LAKE-SOUTH SULPHUR UNIT (State Pk) From Jct of SR-19/SR-154 & FM-71, W 4.2 mi on FM-71 to FM-3505, N 1.4 mi on FM-3505 (E) (Entrance fee). 2015 rates: $16. (903)945-5256

CORPUS CHRISTI — E7 *Nueces*

CORPUS CHRISTI See also Aransas Pass, Kingsville, Mathis, Port Aransas, Portland, Riviera, Rockport & Sinton.

COLONIA DEL REY RV PARK
Ratings: 10/10★/9 (RV Park) From Jct of I-37 & Hwy 358 (Padre Island Dr), SE 15.7 mi on Hwy 358 to Waldron Rd exit, S 0.8 mi (L).

CORPUS CHRISTI'S HIGHEST RATED PARK
Located at the entrance to Padre Island. The best vacation spot on the TX Gulf Coast. Beaches, fine dining, shopping, golf courses, and many more activities.

FAC: Paved rds. (209 spaces). Avail: 25 paved, 9 all weather, patios, 34 pull-thrus (25 x 70), 34 full hkups (30/50 amps), seasonal sites, cable, WiFi, rentals, dump, laundry. **REC:** pool, whirlpool, playground. Pet restrict(B). No tents. Big rig sites, eco-friendly, 2015 rates: $38 to $45.
(361)937-2435 Lat: 27.65783, Lon: -97.28857
1717 Waldron Road, Corpus Christi, TX 78418
coloniadelrey@ccrvresorts.com
www.ccrvresorts.com
See ad pages 1142, 1108, 1102 (TX Map) & Snowbird Destinations in Magazine Section.

GREYHOUND RV PARK
Ratings: 7.5/9★/7 (RV Park) S-bnd: From Jct of I-37 & Hwy 358, SE 0.5 mi on I-37 to Navigation Blvd (exit 3A), S 0.4 mi to Leopard St, W 0.4 mi (R); or N-bnd: From Jct of, I-37, Hwy 44 & Hwy 358, N 1 mi on Hwy 358 to Leopard St, E 0.4 mi (L). **FAC:** Paved rds. (90 spaces). 40 Avail: 25 paved, 15 gravel, patios, 40 pull-thrus (25 x 64), some side by side hkups, 40 full hkups (30/50 amps), seasonal sites, cable, WiFi, dump, laundry. **REC.** Pet restrict(B). No tents. Big rig sites, eco-friendly, 2015 rates: $35 to $40.
(361)289-2076 Lat: 27.79788, Lon: -97.46089
5402 Leopard St, Corpus Christi, TX 78408
greyhound@ccrvresorts.com
www.ccrvresorts.com
See ad pages 1142, 1108.

HATCH RV PARK
Ratings: 9.5/8.5★/7.5 (RV Park) From Jct of I-37 & Nueces Bay Blvd (exit 1B in town), Go S 0.6 mi to Up River Rd then E on Up River Rd 2 blocks (R). **FAC:** Paved rds. (127 spaces). 32 Avail: 10 paved, 22 grass, patios, 32 pull-thrus (22 x 80), 32 full hkups (30/50 amps), seasonal sites, cable, WiFi, rentals, laundry, LP gas, firewood. **REC:** pool, whirlpool. Pet restrict(B/Q). No tents. Big rig sites, RV age restrict, eco-friendly, 2015 rates: $44. Disc: AAA, military.
(800)332-4509 Lat: 27.79367, Lon: -97.42455
3101 Up River Rd., Corpus Christi, TX 78408
stay@hatchrv.com
www.hatchrv.com
See ad this page, 1108 & Snowbird Destinations in Magazine Section.

MARINA VILLAGE PARK **Ratings: 4.5/4.5/5.5** (RV Area in MHP) 2015 rates: $35. (361)937-2560 229 N.a.s. Drive, Corpus Christi, TX 78418

PADRE BALLI PARK (Public) From Jct of JFK Bridge & P-22, SW 3.5 mi on P-22 (L). 2015 rates: $25. (361)949-8121

PADRE PALMS RV PARK
Ratings: 9/9★/8.5 (RV Park) From Jct of I-37 & Hwy 358 (Padre Island Dr), SE 15.5 mi on Hwy 358 to NAS Dr/CCAD exit, NE 0.4 mi to Skipper Ln, E 0.3 mi (R). **FAC:** Paved rds. (84 spaces). 59 Avail: 34 paved, 25 grass, 59 pull-thrus (17 x 70), mostly side by side hkups, 59 full hkups (30/50 amps), seasonal sites, cable, WiFi, dump, laundry. **REC:** heated pool, Laguna Madre: fishing, shuffleboard. Pet restrict(B). No tents. Eco-friendly, 2015 rates: $35 to $40.
(361)937-2125 Lat: 27.67281, Lon: -97.27090
131 Skipper Lane, Corpus Christi, TX 78418
padrepalms@ccrvresorts.com
www.ccrvresorts.com
See ad pages 1142, 1108.

PUERTO DEL SOL RV PARK
Ratings: 7/7/6.5 (RV Park) From Jct of I-37 & US-181, N 2 mi on US-181 to Beach Ave exit, continue NE 0.3 mi on E frntg rd to Beach Ave, SE 0.1 mi to Timon Blvd, NE 0.4 mi (R). **FAC:** Poor paved/dirt rds. 53 gravel, 53 pull-thrus (22 x 48), 53 full hkups (30/50 amps), WiFi $, laundry. **REC:** Corpus Christi Bay: swim, fishing. Pet restrict(B). No tents. Eco-friendly, 2015 rates: $35 to $40. Disc: AAA, military.
(361)882-5373 Lat: 27.83531, Lon: -97.37984
5100 Timon Blvd, Corpus Christi, TX 78402
info@puertodelsolrvpark.com
www.puertodelsolrvpark.com
See ad this page, 1108.

SEA BREEZE RV PARK
Ratings: 9/9★/9 (RV Park) From jct of US-181 & FM-893/Moore Ave exit, NW 1 mi on FM-893/Moore Ave to Marriott St, SW .5 mi to Doyle, S 0.2 mi (R). **FAC:** Gravel rds. (160 spaces). Avail: 100 gravel, patios, 42 pull-thrus (22 x 60), back-ins (22 x 49), some side by side hkups, 99 full hkups, 1 W, 1 E (30/50 amps), seasonal sites, WiFi, dump, laundry. **REC:** heated pool, wading pool, whirlpool, Corpus Christi Bay: fishing. Pet restrict(B/Q). Partial

We rate what RVers consider important.

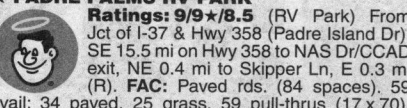

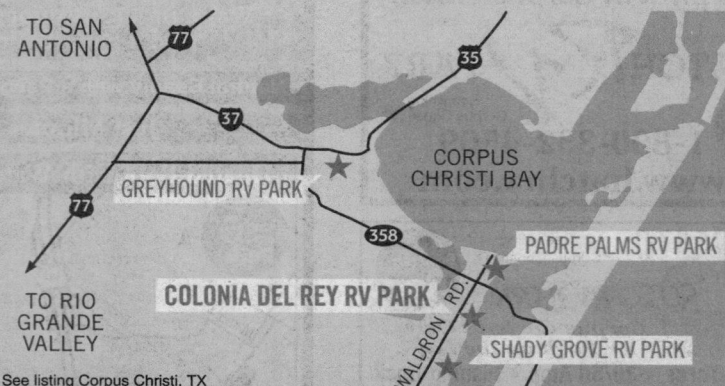

CORPUS CHRISTI (CONT)

SEA BREEZE RV PARK (CONT)
handicap access, no tents. Eco-friendly, 2015 rates: $34 to $39. Disc: AAA.
(361)643-0744 Lat: 27.88515, Lon: -097.34420
1026 Seabreeze Lane, Portland, TX 78374
seabreezerv@aol.com
wwww.seabreezerv.com
See primary listing at Portland and ad page 1141.

SHADY GROVE RV PARK
Ratings: 7/8.5★/7.5 (RV Park) From Jct of I-37 & Hwy 358 (Padre Island Dr), SE 15.7 mi on Hwy 358 to Waldron Rd exit, S 1 mi (L). **FAC:** Paved rds. (180 spaces). Avail: 18 paved, 17 all weather, 10 pull-thrus (27 x 75), back-ins (30 x 50), 35 full hkups (30/50 amps), seasonal sites, laundry. **REC.** Pet restrict(B). No tents. Big rig sites, eco-friendly, 2015 rates: $30.
(361)937-1314 Lat: 27.63951, Lon: -97.30026
2919 Waldron Rd, Corpus Christi, TX 78418
shadygrove@ccrvresorts.com
www.ccrvresorts.com
See ad opposite page, 1108.

CORSICANA — B7 *Navarro*

AMERICAN RV PARK Ratings: 6/7.5/6.5 (RV Park) From jct I-45 & Hwy 31: Go 5 mi W on Hwy 31. (L). **FAC:** Paved/gravel rds. (156 spaces). 100 Avail: 21 paved, 79 gravel, 64 pull-thrus (29 x 60), back-ins (29 x 60), some side by side hkups, 100 full hkups (30/50 amps), seasonal sites, WiFi, tent sites, laundry, LP gas. **REC:** playground. Pets OK. Partial handicap access. Big rig sites, 2015 rates: $32.25.
AAA Approved
(903)872-0233 Lat: 32.06356, Lon: -96.51471
4345 W Hwy 31, Corsicana, TX 75110

CROCKETT — C8 *Houston*

CROCKETT FAMILY RESORT Ratings: 7.5/6.5/7 (Campground) From Jct of Loop 304 & FM 229 (NW of town), W 6.8 mi on FM 229 to CR 2140, N 2 mi (E). **FAC:** Dirt rds. (161 spaces). Avail: 136 gravel, 10 pull-thrus (20 x 50), back-ins (22 x 40), mostly side by side hkups, 136 full hkups (30/50 amps), seasonal sites, cable, WiFi, tent sites, rentals, dump, laundry, firewood, restaurant. **REC:** pool, Houston County Lake: fishing, shuffleboard, playground. Pet restrict(B/Q). Big rig sites, 2015 rates: $27 to $35. Disc: AAA, military. ATM.
AAA Approved
(936)544-8466 Lat: 31.41133, Lon: -95.57894
75 Dogwood Lane West, Crockett, TX 75835
marina@crockettresort.com
www.crockettresort.com

CRYSTAL BEACH — D9 *Galveston*

BOLIVAR PENINSULA RV PARK Ratings: 5.5/7.5★/7 (RV Park) From jct Crystal Beach Drive & Hwy 87: Go 1/4 mi SW on Hwy 87 (R); or 10-1/2 mi E on Hwy 87 from Ferry Landing (L). **FAC:** Dirt rds. 90 gravel, patios, 20 pull-thrus (30 x 65), back-ins (32 x 65), 90 full hkups (30/50 amps), WiFi, tent sites, showers $, laundry. **REC:** pond, fishing. Pet restrict(B/Q). Big rig sites, 2015 rates: $28 to $34. Disc: AAA, military.
AAA Approved
(409)684-0939 Lat: 29.45576, Lon: -94.64504
1685 Hwy 87, Crystal Beach, TX 77650
bolivarrv@att.net
www.bolivarpeninsularvpark.com

PAULAS VINEYARD RV RESORT Ratings: 8.5/8.5★/8.5 (RV Park) 2015 rates: $35. (409)684-9970 1250 N Crystal Beach Rd, Crystal Beach, TX 77650

CRYSTAL CITY — E5 *Zavala*

TRIPLE R RESORT RV PARK Ratings: 8.5/8★/8 (RV Park) 2015 rates: $28. (830)374-0400 3766 Hwy 65, Crystal City, TX 78839

CUT AND SHOOT — C8 *Montgomery*

COUNTRY PLACE RV PARK
Ratings: 9/9★/9 (RV Park) From Jct of E Loop 336 & SR-105, E 3.7 mi on SR-105 to Waukegan Rd, S 0.6 mi (L). **FAC:** Gravel rds. (73 spaces). 32 Avail: 20 paved, 12 gravel, patios, 17 pull-thrus (30 x 80), back-ins (23 x 65), 32 full hkups (30/50 amps), seasonal sites, WiFi, tent sites, rentals, laundry, LP gas, firewood. **REC:** pool, pond, fishing. Pet restrict(B). Big rig sites, 2015 rates: $30. Disc: military.
(936)264-2854 Lat: 30.32497, Lon: -95.34041
3043 Waukegan Rd, Cut and Shoot, TX 77306
countryplacerv@gmail.com
www.countryplacervpark.com
See ad this page.

DAINGERFIELD — B9 *Morris*

DAINGERFIELD (State Pk) From Jct of US-259 & SR-11/49, E 2.3 mi on SR-49 (R) (Entrance fee). 2015 rates: $20 to $25. (903)645-2921

DALE — D7 *Caldwell*

LAKE FALLING STAR RV RESORT
Ratings: 9.5/10★/10 (RV Resort) From Jct of FM 713 & TX 86 (in McMahan), NE 1 mi on FM 713 (L). **FAC:** All weather rds. 50 gravel, patios, 20 pull-thrus (42 x 70), back-ins (40 x 50), 50 full hkups (30/50 amps), WiFi, rentals, laundry. **REC:** pool, Tinney Lake: fishing. Pet restrict(B/Q). No tents. Big rig sites, 2015 rates: $37 to $47. Disc: military. No CC.
(512)398-7827 Lat: 29.85479, Lon: -97.50535
7355 Fm 713, Dale, TX 78616
camp@lakefallingstarrvresort.com
www.lakefallingstarrvresort.com
See ad this page.

DALHART — E9 *Dallum, Hartley*

CORRAL RV PARK
Ratings: 8/9.5★/9 (RV Park) From Jct of US 385 & US 54: Go 1 mi E on US 54. (R). Elev 3980 ft. **FAC:** Paved rds. (85 spaces). Avail: 65 gravel, 65 pull-thrus (24 x 80), some side by side hkups, 65 full hkups (30/50 amps), seasonal sites, cable, WiFi, tent sites, laundry. **REC:** playground. Pets OK. Big rig sites, 2015 rates: $25 to $26. Disc: military.
(806)249-2798 Lat: 36.07423, Lon: -102.50671
1202 Liberal, Dalhart, TX 79022
reservations@corralrvpark.net
www.corralrvpark.net
See ad this page.

DALLAS — H4 *Dallas*

DALLAS/FORT WORTH AREA MAP

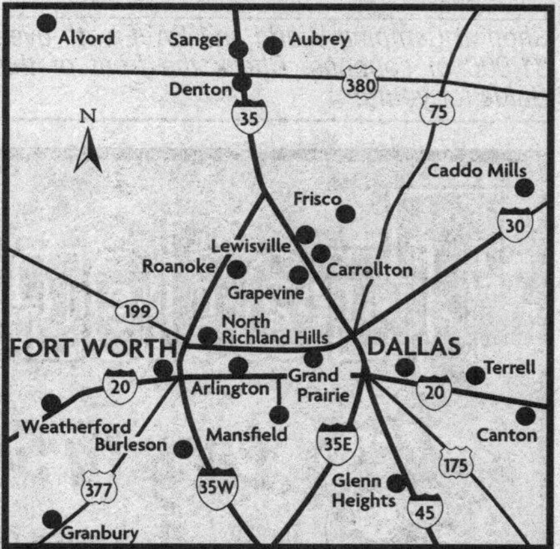

Symbols on map indicate towns within a 50 mile radius of Dallas & Fort Worth where campgrounds are listed. Check listings for more information.

See also Alvord, Arlington, Aubrey, Burleson, Caddo Mills, Canton, Carrollton, Denton, Fort Worth, Frisco, Glenn Heights, Granbury, Grand Prairie, Grapevine, Lewisville, Mansfield, North Richland Hills, Roanoke, Sanger, Terrell & Weatherford.

A SPOTLIGHT Introducing Dallas' colorful attractions appearing at the front of this state section.

TX

DALLAS (CONT)

TRADERS VILLAGE RV PARK
Ratings: 10/10★/8.5 (RV Park) From Dallas go W on I-20, exit 454 then 1mi N on Great Southwest Parkway, then 1/4 mi W on Mayfield Rd. (R). **FAC:** Paved rds. (126 spaces). Avail: 51 paved, patios, 48 pull-thrus (21 x 60), back-ins (25 x 40), 51 full hkups (30/50 amps), seasonal sites, WiFi $, tent sites, laundry, groc, LP gas. **REC:** pool, shuffleboard, playground. Pet restrict(B/Q). Partial handicap access. 2015 rates: $29.95 to $36.95. Disc: military. ATM.
(972)647-2331 Lat: 32.69274, Lon: -97.04868
2602 Mayfield Rd, Grand Prairie, TX 75052
dfwinfo@tradersvillage.com
www.tradersvillage.com
See primary listing at Grand Prairie and ad page 1144.

Shop at Camping World and SAVE with over $1,000 of coupons. Check the front of the Guide for yours!

WINSTAR RV PARK
Ratings: 10/10★/10 (RV Park) From jct of I-35 & T-114 W: Go N 68 mi on I-35, then exit 1 (TX/OK state line), then go NE 1/2 mi on frontage road, then E 1/4 mi on Merle Wolfe Road. (L). **FAC:** Paved rds. 153 paved, patios, 41 pull-thrus (30 x 80), back-ins (30 x 50), accepts self-contain units only, 153 full hkups (30/50 amps), WiFi, tent sites, rentals, dump, laundry, restaurant. **REC:** pool, whirlpool, golf, playground, rec open to public. Pet restrict(Q). Partial handicap access. Big rig sites, 2015 rates: $30 to $50. ATM.
(580)276-8900 Lat: 33.751559, Lon: -97.134619
21902 Merle Wolfe Rd, Thackerville, OK 73459
winstar.rvpark@chickasaw.net
www.winstarworldcasino.com/accommodations/view/rv-park
See primary listing at Thackerville, OK and ad page 911 (Spotlight Chickasaw Nation).

To get the most out of your Guide, refer to the Table of Contents in the front of the book.

DAWSON — B7 *Bosque, Navarro*

LIBERTY HILL PARK (Public Corps) From town NW 4 mi on FM-709 (R). 2015 rates: $18 to $36. (254)578-1431

OAK PARK (Public Corps) From town, NE 3.5 mi on SR-31 to FM-667, NW 1.5 mi (L). 2015 rates: $14 to $22. (254)578-1431

PECAN POINT PARK (COE-NAVARRO MILLS RESERVOIR) (Public Corps) From jct Hwy 31 & FM 667: Go 4 mi NW on FM 667, then 2-1/2 mi SW on FM 744, then 2 mi S on 1578, then at dead end 1/4 mi W. Pit toilets. 2015 rates: $10 to $12. Apr 1 to Sep 30. (254)578-1431

WOLF CREEK PARK (Public Corps) From town NE 3.5 mi on SR-31 to FM-667, NW 3 mi to FM-639 SW 2 mi (E). 2015 rates: $14 to $28. Apr 1 to Sep 30 (254)578-1431

DEL RIO — D5 *Val Verde*

BROKE MILL RV PARK **Ratings: 8.5/9★/7.5** (RV Park) 2015 rates: $34. (830)422-2961 6069 W US Hwy 90, Del Rio, TX 78840

LONESOME DOVE RV RANCH **Ratings: 6.5/8.5★/7.5** (RV Park) 2015 rates: $25 (830)774-1823 4832 Hwy 90 W, Del Rio, TX 78840

DENISON — A7 *Grayson*

DAM SITE (Public Corps) From Jct of Hwy 75 & Hwy 91, N 1.8 mi on Hwy 91 to Denison Dam, follow signs (R). 2015 rates: $20. Apr 1 to Oct 31. (903)465-4990

EISENHOWER (State Pk) From Jct of US-75 & SR-91 (exit 72), NW 1.7 mi on SR-91 to FM-1310, W 1.8 mi (E) (Entrance fees). 2015 rates: $15 to $25 (903)465-1956

DENTON — A7 *Denton*

DESTINY RV RESORTS-DALLAS
Ratings: 9.5/10★/9 (RV Park) From Jct of I-35E & Exit 460: Go 1 mi S on W Service Rd. (R).

COUNTRY LIVING IN THE DALLAS AREA
With great amenities and easy I 35 E (exit 460) access, your stay will be the best. Super size pull thru sites, mature trees, 2 laundries, fitness center, car & RV wash on site, swimming pool and more are here for you.

FAC: Paved rds. (165 spaces). Avail: 35 gravel, 35 pull-thrus (28 x 70), some side by side hkups, 35 full hkups (30/50 amps), seasonal sites, WiFi, dump, laundry, groc, LP gas. **REC:** pool, whirlpool, playground. Pet restrict(B/Q). Partial handicap access, no tents. Big rig sites, 2015 rates: $34 to $43. Disc: AAA.
(888)238-1532 Lat: 33.14087, Lon: -97.05124
7100 S I-35E, Denton, TX 76210
dallas@destinyrv.com
www.destinyrv.com
See ad this page, 1108.

POST OAK PLACE
Ratings: 8.5/NA/8 (RV Park) From Jct of I-35E (exit 465 B) & US 377: Go 1/2 mi S on US 377, then 250 feet W on Massey (L). **FAC:** Paved/gravel rds. (100 spaces). Avail: 20 gravel, patios, back-ins (23 x 50), 20 full hkups (30/50 amps), WiFi, laundry. **REC:** pool. Pet restrict(B/Q). No tents. 2015 rates: $28. Disc: AAA, military.
(940)387-8584 Lat: 33.18691, Lon: -97.14074
109 Massey, Denton, TX 76205
info@postoakplace.com
www.postoakplace.com
See ad page 1143.

DENTON (CONT)

Travel Services

CAMPING WORLD STORE OF DENTON/DALLAS As the nation's largest retailer of RV supplies, accessories, services and new and used RVs, Camping World is committed to making your total RV experience better. **SERVICES:** RV, tire, RV appliance, MH mechanical, staffed RV wash. RV supplies, emergency parking, RV accessible. waiting room. Hours: 8am to 6pm. (800)527-4812 Lat: 33.246169, Lon: -97.177463 5209 I-35 North, Denton, TX 76207 www.campingworld.com

DENVER CITY — B3 *Yoakum*

YOAKUM COUNTY PARK (Public) From town, N 7 mi on SR-214 (R). 2015 rates: $14. (806)592-3166

DIANA — B9 *Upshur*

BRUSHY CREEK (Public Corps) From town, NW 4 mi on HWY-49 to HWY-729, W 3.5 mi to HWY-726, S 4.9 mi (R). 2015 rates: $24 to $40. Mar 1 to Nov 30. (903)777-3491

DICKINSON — D9 *Galveston*

MARQUEE ON THE BAY
(RV Park) (Under Construction) From Hwy 146 and 29th St go 1/10 mi S on 29th st, to Ave U, then go 1/10 mi NW on Ave U, to San Leon, then go SW 1 mi on San Leon (E). **FAC:** Paved rds. 65 paved, patios, 32 pull-thrus (72 x 45), back-ins (55 x 45), 65 full hkups (30/50 amps), cable, laundry. **REC:** pool, Galveston Bay / Dickenson Bayou: fishing. Pet restrict(B/Q). Big rig sites, 2015 rates: $40 to $45. Disc: AAA, military.
(281)339-1260 Lat: 29.456286, Lon: -094.983007
9900 San Leon Drive, Dickinson, TX 77539
valerieannweber@yahoo.com
www.marqueeonthebay.com
See ad page 1150.

DONNA — M3 *Hidalgo*

BIT-O-HEAVEN RV & MOBILE HOME PARK
Ratings: 9.5/8.5★/7.5 (RV Area in MHP) From Jct of US-83 (Expwy) & FM 493: Go W 2 3/4 mi on US 83 to FM 1423, then S 1/2 mi to Bus US-83, then W 1/2 mi (L). **FAC:** Paved rds. (824 spaces). Avail: 315 grass, back-ins (30 x 50), 315 full hkups (30/50 amps), seasonal sites, WiFi, rentals, laundry, controlled access. **REC:** heated pool, whirlpool, shuffleboard. Pet restrict(Q). Partial handicap access, no tents. Age restrict may apply, eco-friendly, 2015 rates: $40. No CC.
(956)464-5191 Lat: 26.17736, Lon: -98.08983
1051 W Bus US 83, Donna, TX 78537
office@bitoheaven.net
www.bit-o-heaven.net
See ad this page.

CASA DEL SOL MH & RV RESORT
Ratings: 9/8.5/8 (RV Park) From Jct of US-83 (Expwy) & FM-1423 (Val Verde Rd), S 0.4 mi on FM-1423/Val Verde Rd (L). **FAC:** Paved rds. (350 spaces). Avail: 180 grass, patios, back-ins (24 x 56), some side by side hkups, 180 full hkups (30/50 amps), seasonal sites, WiFi Hotspot, laundry, controlled access. **REC:** heated pool, whirlpool, shuffleboard. Pet restrict(B/Q). Partial handicap access, no tents. Age restrict may apply, big rig sites, eco-friendly, 2015 rates: $50 to $60. No CC.
(956)464-2272 Lat: 26.18169, Lon: -98.08092
400 N Val Verde Rd, Donna, TX 78537
casadelsolrvresort@yahoo.com
www.casadelsol.us
See ad page 1122 (Spotlight South Texas Tropics).

MAGNOLIA PARK **Ratings: 8.5/8/6.5** (RV Area in MHP) 2015 rates: $42. (956)464-2421 3707 E. Hwy 83, Donna, TX 78537

SHADY ACRES MH & RV PARK **Ratings: 8/7.5/7.5** (RV Area in MHP) 2015 rates: $44. (956)464-2241 310 Hester Ave, Donna, TX 78537

VICTORIA PALMS RESORT **Ratings: 10/9.5★/8.5** (RV Park) 2015 rates: $38 to $54. (800)405-6188 602 N Victoria Rd, Donna, TX 78537

EDINBURG — M3 *Hidalgo*

ORANGE GROVE RV PARK
Ratings: 8.5/8/7.5 (RV Park) From Jct of US-281 & Hwy 107, E 2.4 mi on Hwy 107 (L). **FAC:** Paved rds. (350 spaces). Avail: 125 dirt, back-ins (30 x 36), 125 full hkups (30 amps), WiFi, laundry, controlled access. **REC:** heated pool, whirlpool, shuffleboard. Pets OK. Partial handicap access, no tents. Age restrict may apply, eco-friendly, 2015 rates: $42. No CC.
(956)383-7931 Lat: 26.29455, Lon: -98.10801
4901 E State Hwy 107, Edinburg, TX 78542
parkinfo@ogrvp.com
www.ogrvp.com
See ad this page.

EDNA — D7 *Jackson*

BRACKENRIDGE RECREATION COMPLEX - BRACKENRIDGE PARK & CAMPGROUND
Ratings: 8.5/9★/9 (Public) From Jct of US-59 & Hwy 111, E 7.5 mi on Hwy 111 (R). **FAC:** Paved rds. 134 Avail: 102 paved, 32 gravel, 16 pull-thrus (35 x 50), back-ins (30 x 40), 98 full hkups, 36 W, 36 E (30/50 amps), WiFi, tent sites, rentals, dump, laundry, groc, fire rings, firewood, controlled access. **REC:** Lake Texana: swim, fishing, playground, rec open to public. Pet restrict(B). Partial handicap access. Big rig sites, 2015 rates: $25 to $30.
(361)782-5456 Lat: 28.94217, Lon: -96.53882
891 Brackenridge Pkwy, Edna, TX 77957
brc@lnra.org
www.brackenridgepark.com
See ad pages 1146, 1108.

BRACKENRIDGE RECREATION COMPLEX-TEXANA PARK & CAMPGROUND
Ratings: 7/8.5/9 (Public) From Jct 111 & 59: Go 7 mi E on Hwy 111 to Brackenridge Pkwy (L). **FAC:** Paved rds. 141 paved, back-ins (30 x 50), 63 full hkups, 78 W, 78 E (30/50 amps), WiFi Hotspot, tent sites, rentals, dump, groc, fire rings, firewood, controlled access. **REC:** Lake Texana: swim, fishing, playground, rec open to public. Pet restrict(B). Partial handicap access. 2015 rates: $25 to $30.
(361)782-5718 Lat: 28.95706, Lon: -096.543812
46 Park Road 1, Edna, TX 77957
brc@lnra.org
www.brackenridgepark.com
See ad page 1146.

FIVE COATS RV PARK **Ratings: 6.5/8.5★/7** (Campground) 2015 rates: $30. (361)782-5109 87 Fm 234 South, Edna, TX 77957

TEXANA PARK & CAMPGROUND (State Pk) From Jct of US-59 & Hwy 111, E 7.2 mi on Hwy 111 (L) (Entrance fee). 2015 rates: $25 to $30. (361)782-5718

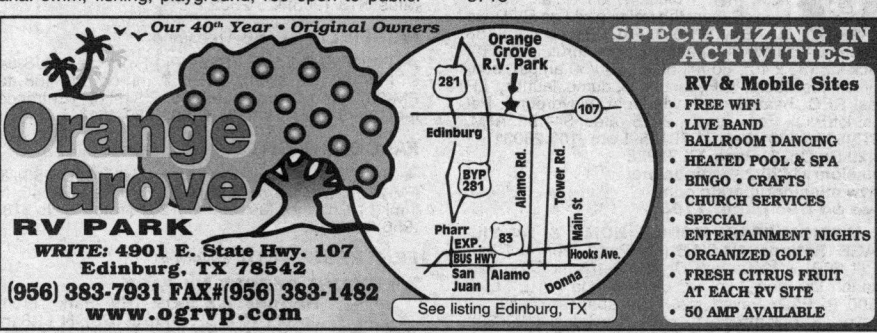

TX

EDNA (CONT)

Things to See and Do

BRACKENRIDGE MAIN EVENT CENTER The Brackenridge main event center is a multi-purpose facility that hosts a wide variety of events, situated on 188 acres adjacent to Brackenridge Park & Campground. Partial handicap access. Restrooms, food. ATM.
(361)782-7272 Lat: 28.95313, Lon: -96.54257
284 Brackenridge Pkwy, Edna, TX 77957
mec@lnra.org
www.brackenridgepark.com
See ad this page.

EL PASO — B1 *El Paso*

EL PASO See also Anthony & Canutillo.

EL PASO ROADRUNNER RV PARK **Ratings: 5.5/6.5/6** (RV Park) 2015 rates: $30. (915)598-4469 1212 Lafayette Ave, El Paso, TX 79907

HUECO TANKS STATE HISTORICAL PARK (State Pk) From Jct of US-62/180 (Montana St) & FM-659/Zargoza (E edge of town), E 8.5 mi on US-62/180 to RR-2775, N 8 mi (E) (Advance reservations required thru this park office at (915)849-6684) (Entrance fee). 2015 rates: $12 to $16. (800)792-1112

MISSION RV PARK
Ratings: 9/8.5★/7 (RV Park) From Jct I-10 & Exit 35: Go 1/4 mi N on Eastlake, then 1 block W on Rojas, then 1 block S (past the trailer park) on RV Drive (L). Elev 3770 ft. **FAC:** Paved rds. (188 spaces). Avail: 80 dirt, patios, 72 pull-thrus (20 x 70), back-ins (33 x 40), 80 full hkups (30/50 amps), seasonal sites, cable, WiFi, tent sites, dump, laundry, LP gas. **REC:** heated pool, whirlpool, playground. Pet restrict(B/Q). Eco-friendly, 2015 rates: $41.95. ATM.
(915)859-1133 Lat: 31.70105, Lon: -106.28031
1420 Rv Dr., El Paso, TX 79928
missionrv1420@sbcglobal.net
www.missionrvparklp.com
See ad this page, 1108.

MISSION TRAIL MOBILE HOME & RV VILLAGE Ratings: 4/4.5/4.5 (RV Park) From Jct I-10 (Exit 28B) & Yarbrough Dr: Go 2-1/2 mi S on Yarbrough Dr, then 1 mi SE on Alameda Av (L). Elev 3500 ft. **FAC:** Paved rds. (100 spaces). Avail: 15 gravel, 3 pull-thrus (12 x 70), back-ins (12 x 30), some side by side hkups, 15 full hkups (30/50 amps), laundry. **REC:** playground. Pet restrict(B/Q). No tents. 2015 rates: $25.
(915)859-0202 Lat: 31.70689, Lon: -106.34283
8479 Alameda Ave, El Paso, TX 79907
missiontrail@towermgmt.com
www.towerrvparks.com

Travel Services

MISSION RV PARTS & SERVICE CENTER Services RV, RV appliance, RV supplies, LP, Dump, emergency parking, waiting room. Elev 3500 ft. **SERVICES:** RV, RV appliance. RV storage. RV supplies, LP, dump, emergency parking, waiting room. Hours: 9am to 5pm. ATM.
(915)859-3344 Lat: 31.70105, Lon: -106.28031
1420 Rv Drive, El Paso, TX 79928
www.missionrvparklp.com
See ad this page.

ENNIS — B7 *Ellis*

HIGH VIEW (Public Corps) From Jct of I-45 & US-287 Bypass/Exit 247, W 4.5 mi on US-287 to Bardwell Lake exit/Hwy 34, SW 2.5 mi on Hwy 34 to High View Park Rd, SE 0.2 mi to park entrance. 2015 rates: $14 to $16. (972)875-5711

MOTT PARK (Public Corps) From town, SW 5.5 mi on SH-34 (over bridge), SE 1.7 mi on FM-985. 2015 rates: $16. Apr 1 to Sep 30. (972)875-5711

WAXAHACHIE CREEK PARK (Public Corps) From Jct of I-45 & US-287 Bypass (exit 247), W 4.5 mi on US-287 to Bardwell Lake exit/Hwy 34, SW 3 mi on Hwy 34 to Bozek Rd, NW 1.5 mi (E). 2015 rates: $14 to $18. (972)875-5711

EUSTACE — B8 *Henderson, Van Zandt*

PURTIS CREEK (State Pk) From Jct US-175 & FM-316, N 3.4 mi on FM-316 (L) (Entrance fee). 2015 rates: $18. (903)425-2332

FAIRFIELD — B8 *Freestone*

FAIRFIELD LAKE (State Pk) From Jct of US-84 & FM-488 (in town), NE 1.7 mi on FM-488 to FM-2570, N 1.2 mi to FM-3285, E 3 mi (E) (Entrance fee). 2015 rates: $9 to $18. (903)389-4514

FALCON HEIGHTS — L2 *Zapata*

FALCON (State Pk) From Jct of US-83 & FM-2098, SW 2.6 mi on FM-2098 to Park Rd 46, N 1 mi (L). Entrance fee required. 2015 rates: $8 to $18. (956)848-5327

FENTRESS — D7 *Caldwell*

LEISURE RESORT RV PARK
Ratings: 8/8.5★/9 (RV Park) From Jct of I-10 & SR-80 (exit 628), N 11.8 mi on SR-80 to FM-20, S 0.3 mi to CR-125, E 0.4 mi, follow signs (E); or From Jct of I-35 & Exit 205, SE 13.3 mi on SR-80 to FM-20, S 0.3 mi to CR-125, E 0.4 mi, follow signs (E). **FAC:** Paved/gravel rds. (117 spaces). 93 Avail: 66 paved, 27 gravel, 46 pull-thrus (22 x 90), back-ins (27 x 65), 48 full hkups, 45 W, 45 E (30/50 amps), seasonal sites, WiFi, tent sites, rentals, showers $, dump, laundry, groc, firewood, controlled access. **REC:** pool, San Marcos River: swim, fishing, playground, rec open to public. Pets OK. Partial handicap access. Big rig sites, 2015 rates: $39 to $44. Disc: military.
(800)248-4103 Lat: 29.74770, Lon: -97.77580
1 River Lane, Fentress, TX 78622
stay@leisureresort.net
www.leisureresort.net
See ad pages 1176, 1108.

FLATONIA — D7 *Fayette*

FLATONIA RV RANCH **Ratings: 5/7.5/6.5** (RV Park) 2015 rates: $30. (361)865-9290 2055 Fm 609 Flatonia, TX 78941

FLOYDADA — A4 *Floyd*

FLOYDADA OVERNIGHT RV PARK (Public) From jct Hwy 207/62 & US 70: Go 1 mi NW on US 70 to park entrance. Pit toilets. (806)983-2834

FORT DAVIS — C3 *Jeff Davis*

DAVIS MOUNTAINS (State Pk) From N Jct of Hwys 17 & 118, W 2.8 mi on Hwy 118 (L) (Entrance fee). 2015 rates: $15 to $25. (432)426-3337

MACMILLEN RV PARK **Ratings: 5/9★/6.5** (Campground) 2015 rates: $30. (432)426-2056 43424 S. Hwy 17, Fort Davis, TX 79734

FORT STOCKTON — C3 *Pecos*

FORT STOCKTON RV PARK
Ratings: 8.5/8.5★/8.5 (Campground) From Jct I-10 & Warnock Rd (exit 264), 400 yards Ni on Warnock Rd (R). Elev 3240 ft. **FAC:** Paved rds. 130 Avail: 90 paved, 40 gravel, 116 pull-thrus (32 x 70), back-ins (32 x 45), 130 full hkups (30/50 amps), cable, WiFi, tent sites, dump, laundry, groc, LP gas, restaurant. **REC:** pool, playground. Pet restrict(B). Partial handicap access. Big rig sites, eco-friendly, 2015 rates: $33 to $35. Disc: AAA, military.
(432)395-2494 Lat: 30.89432, Lon: -102.79520
3604 Koa Rd, Fort Stockton, TX 79735
manager@fortstocktonrvpark.com
www.ftstocktonrvpark.com
See ad opposite page, 1108.

Like Us on Facebook.

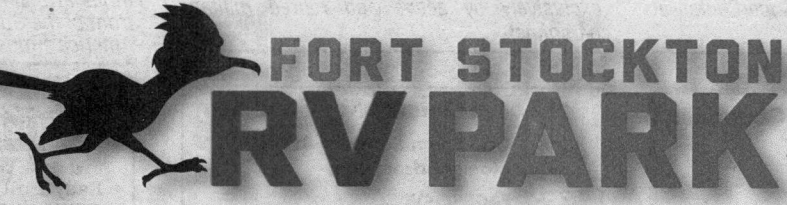

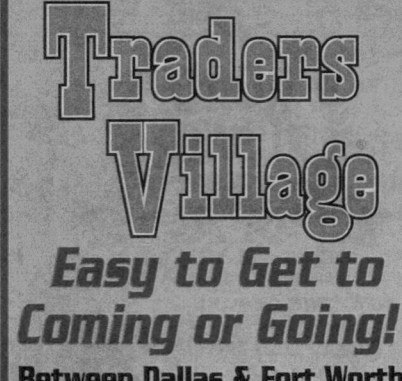

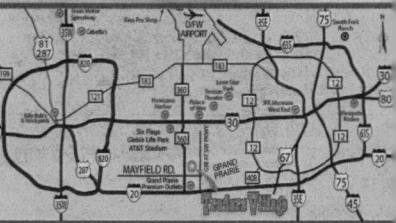

FORT WORTH — H2 *Tarrant*

DALLAS/FORT WORTH AREA MAP

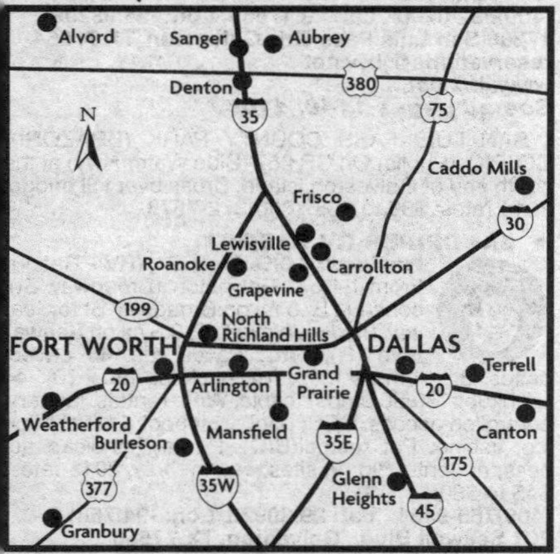

Symbols on map indicate towns within a 50 mile radius of Dallas & Fort Worth where campgrounds are listed. Check listings for more information.

See also Alvord, Arlington, Aubrey, Burleson, Caddo Mills, Canton, Carrollton, Dallas, Denton, Frisco, Glenn Heights, Granbury, Grand Prairie, Grapevine, Lewisville, Mansfield, North Richland Hills, Roanoke, Sanger, Terrell & Weatherford.

A SPOTLIGHT Introducing Fort Worth's colorful attractions appearing at the front of this state section.

COWTOWN RV PARK
Ratings: 9/9.5★/9 (RV Park) From Jct I-20 (exit 418) & Ranch House Rd: Go 1 mi E on S Frontage Rd. (R). **FAC:** Paved/gravel rds. (167 spaces). 40 Avail: 30 paved, 10 gravel, 40 pull-thrus (27 x 65), 40 full hkups (30/50 amps), seasonal sites, cable, WiFi, dump, laundry, LP gas. **REC:** pool, playground. Pet restrict(B/Q). Partial handicap access, no tents. Big rig sites, 2015 rates: $32.50. Disc: military.
(817)441-7878 Lat: 32.72986, Lon: -97.61420
7000 I-20 East, Aledo, TX 76008
cowtownrv@yahoo.com
www.cowtownrvpark.com
See ad opposite page, 1108.

LAKEVIEW RV & MH COMMUNITY
Ratings: 6.5/NA/8 (RV Park) From Jct I-20 (Exit 442B) & E Loop 820 N: Go 1 mi N on E Loop 820 N (Exit 33B), then 1/4 mi N on E Frontage Rd (R). **FAC:** Paved rds. (105 spaces). Avail: 20 gravel, patios, 2 pull-thrus (35 x 60), back-ins (35 x 60), 20 full hkups (30/50 amps), seasonal sites, WiFi, laundry. Pet restrict(Q). No tents. Big rig sites, 2015 rates: $34.
(800)767-7756 Lat: 32.69351, Lon: -97.23846
4793 E Loop 820 South, Fort Worth, TX 76119
lakeview@towermgmt.com
www.lakeviewmhc.com

We rate what RVers consider important.

TRADERS VILLAGE RV PARK
Ratings: 10/10★/8.5 (RV Park) From Ft Worth go E on I-20 exit 454 then 1 mi N on Great Southwest Parkway then 1/4 mi W on Mayfield Rd. (R). **FAC:** Paved rds. (126 spaces). Avail: 51 paved, patios, 48 pull-thrus (21 x 60), back-ins (25 x 40), 51 full hkups (30/50 amps), seasonal sites, WiFi $, tent sites, laundry, groc, LP gas. **REC:** pool, shuffleboard, playground. Pet restrict(B/Q). Partial handicap access. 2015 rates: $29.95 to $36.95. Disc: AAA, military. ATM.
(972)647-2331 Lat: 32.69274, Lon: -97.04868
2602 Mayfield Rd, Grand Prairie, TX 75052
dfwinfo@tradersvillage.com
www.tradersvillage.com
See primary listing at Grand Prairie and ad page 1144.

Travel Services

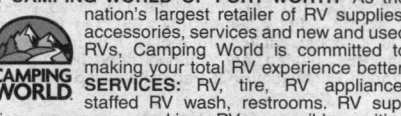

CAMPING WORLD OF FORT WORTH As the nation's largest retailer of RV supplies, accessories, services and new and used RVs, Camping World is committed to making your total RV experience better. **SERVICES:** RV, tire, RV appliance, staffed RV wash, restrooms. RV supplies, emergency parking, RV accessible. waiting room. Hours: 8am - 6pm.
(866)393-6441 Lat: 32.608872, Lon: -97.322628
10100 S. Freeway, Fort Worth, TX 76140
www.campingworld.com

FREDERICKSBURG — C6 *Gillespie*

FREDERICKSBURG KOA **Ratings: 8.5/8/8** (Campground) 2015 rates: $35 to $45. (830)997-4796 5681 US Hwy 290 East, Fredericksburg, TX 78624

FREDERICKSBURG RV PARK
Ratings: 9/10★/10 (RV Park) From Jct of US 290 & S US 87 (Washington St): Go 3/4 mi SE on Hwy 87, then 1/2 block W on Highway St (L). **FAC:** Paved rds. (105 spaces). Avail: 80 all weather, patios, 74 pull-thrus (30 x 70), back-ins (25 x 60), 80 full hkups (30/50 amps), seasonal sites, cable, WiFi, laundry. **REC:** pond, shuffleboard. Pet restrict(B). Partial handicap access, no tents. Big rig sites, 2015 rates: $45 to $50. Disc: military.
(866)324-7275 Lat: 30.26143, Lon: -98.87439
305 E Highway St, Fredericksburg, TX 78624
info@fbgrvpark.com
fbgrvpark.com
See ad this page, 1108.

RV Park ratings you can rely on!

HILL COUNTRY RV PARK Ratings: 5.5/6/6 (RV Park) From Jct of Hwy 16 & US 290: Go 2 mi E on US 290 (R). **FAC:** Gravel/dirt rds. (66 spaces). Avail: 36 dirt, 36 pull-thrus (25 x 60), 36 full hkups (30/50 amps), seasonal sites, cable, WiFi, laundry. **REC.** Pet restrict(B). No tents. Big rig sites, 2015 rates: $30.
(830)997-5365 Lat: 30.25151, Lon: -98.84858
1589 E Main St, Fredericksburg, TX 78624
reservations@hillcountryrvpark.com
www.hillcountryrvpark.com

LADY BIRD JOHNSON MUNICIPAL PARK (Public) From Jct of US-290 & SR-16S: Go 3-1/2 mi S on SR 16S, then 1/4 mi W on Lady Bird Dr (E). 2015 rates: $30. (830)997-4202

OAKWOOD RV RESORT
Ratings: 9/9★/8.5 (RV Park) From Jct US-290 & Hwy 16: Go 2-1/4 mi S on Hwy 16S, then 200 feet W on FM 2093 (R). **FAC:** Paved/gravel rds. (132 spaces). Avail: 102 gravel, patios, 38 pull-thrus (21 x 50), back-ins (25 x 55), 102 full hkups (30/50 amps), seasonal sites, cable, WiFi, dump, laundry. **REC:** pool, whirlpool, playground. Pet restrict(Q). No tents. 2015 rates: $40 to $47. Disc: AAA, military.
(830)997-9817 Lat: 30.25184, Lon: -98.89580
78 Fm 2093, Fredericksburg, TX 78624
oakwoodrv@yahoo.com
www.oakwoodrvresort.com
See ad opposite page, 1108.

TEXAS WINE COUNTRY JELLYSTONE PARK CAMP-RESORT **Ratings: 9/10★/8** (Campground) 2015 rates: $52 to $68. (830)997-6100 10618 E US Hwy 290, Fredericksburg, TX 78624

FREEPORT — D8 *Brazoria*

QUINTANA BEACH COUNTY PARK (Public) From Jct of Hwy 36/288 & FM-1495, SW 1.7 mi on FM-1495 to FM-723, NE 3 mi to 5th St, S 0.1 mi (E). 2015 rates: $20 to $32. (800)872-7578

FRITCH — F9 *Hutchinson, Moore*

LAKE MEREDITH NRA/BLUE WEST (Natl Pk) From Amarillo, N 35 mi on Hwy 287, E 15.5 mi on Ranch Rd. 1913, E 3.1 mi on Blue West Rd. Pit toilets. (806)857-3151

GALVESTON — D9 *Galveston*

A SPOTLIGHT Introducing Galveston Island's colorful attractions appearing at the front of the state section.

Say you saw it in our Guide!

TX

GALVESTON (CONT)

DELLANERA RV PARK
(Public) From Jct of I-45 & 61st St Exit (Spur Rd 342), S 1.7 mi on 61st to Seawall Blvd, W 3.2 mi (becomes San Luis Pass Rd) (L). **FAC:** Paved rds. 65 paved, patios, 21 pull-thrus (20 x 55), back-ins (18 x 40), 65 full hkups (30/50 amps), WiFi, laundry, groc. **REC:** Gulf of Mexico: swim, fishing. Pets OK. Partial handicap access, no tents. 2015 rates: $34 to $42.
(409)797-5102 Lat: 29.24207, Lon: -94.87220
10901 San Luis Pass Rd, Galveston, TX 77554
info@galvestoncvb.com
www.galvestonparkboard.org
See ad page 1116 (Spotlight Galveston Island) & Snowbird Destinations in Magazine Section.

GALVESTON ISLAND (State Pk) From Jct of I-45 & 61st St exit, S 1.7 mi on 61st St to Seawall Blvd (FM-3005), W 9.2 mi (becomes San Luis Pass Rd), (L) (Entrance fee). 2015 rates: $20 to $25. (409)737-1222

Like Us on Facebook.

GALVESTON ISLAND RV RESORT
Ratings: 10/10★/10 (RV Park) From Jct I-45 & 61st St (exit 1A), S 1.7 mi to Seawall Blvd. (FM-3005), W 17.5 mi (R). **FAC:** Paved rds. 116 paved, patios, 20 pull-thrus (35 x 70), back-ins (35 x 60), 116 full hkups (30/50 amps), cable, WiFi, laundry, groc, LP gas. **REC:** pool, whirlpool, Gulf of Mexico: fishing, shuffleboard, playground. Pets OK. Partial handicap access. Big rig sites, 2015 rates: $43 to $50. Disc: AAA, military. No CC.
(409)200-2745 Lat: 29.12071, Lon: -95.07153
23700 San Luis Pass Rd, Galveston, TX 77554
chris@outdoorresorts.com
www.galvestonrv.com
See ad this page, 1108.

JAMAICA BEACH RV PARK
Ratings: 10/10★/10 (RV Resort) From Jct of I-45 & 61st St. exit (1A), S 1.7 mi to Seawall Blvd (FM-3005), W 11 mi (R). **FAC:** Paved rds. 111 paved, patios, 111 pull-thrus (31 x 65), 111 full hkups (30/50 amps), cable, WiFi, rentals, laundry, groc, LP gas. **REC:** heated pool, whirlpool, pond, fishing, playground. Pet restrict(B/Q). Partial handicap access, no tents. Big rig sites, eco-friendly, 2015 rates: $43 to $56. Disc: AAA, military.
AAA Approved
(409)632-0200 Lat: 29.17860, Lon: -94.98208
17200 San Luis Pass Rd., Galveston, TX 77554
reservations@jbrv.net
www.jbrv.net
See ad pages 1149, 1108.

SAN LUIS PASS COUNTY PARK (BRAZORIA CO. PK) (Public) On CR 257 (Blue Water Hwy) at the south end of Galveston Island. Cross over toll bridge. 2015 rates: $30 to $35. (800)372-7578

SANDPIPER RV RESORT
Ratings: 10/9.5★/9.5 (RV Resort) From I-45 in Galveston (Broadway St) continue S .5 mi on Broadway St to Seawall Blvd (curve left), E 0.3 mi on Seawall Blvd (R). **FAC:** Paved rds. 44 paved, patios, 8 pull-thrus (30 x 70), back-ins (30 x 70), 44 full hkups (30/50 amps), cable, WiFi, rentals, laundry, controlled access. **REC:** pool, whirlpool, Gulf of Mexico: fishing. Pet restrict(B/Q). Partial handicap access, no tents. Big rig sites, eco-friendly, 2015 rates: $45 to $80.
(409)765-9431 Lat: 29.30926, Lon: -94.76811
201 Seawall Blvd., Galveston, TX 77550
sndpipr325@aol.com
www.sandpiperrvresort.com
See ad this page.

Things to See and Do

GALVESTON ISLAND CONVENTION & VISITORS BUREAU Tourism information at Galveston Island Visitors Center; 2328 Broadway, Galveston, TX 77550; (888)425-4753. Restrooms. No CC.
(409)757-5145 Lat: 29.303674, Lon: -94.793201
601 Tremont St., Galveston, TX 77550
info@galvestoncvb.com
www.galveston.com
See ad page 1105 (Welcome Section).

GEORGETOWN — C7 *Travis, Williamson*

BERRY SPRINGS RV PARK
Ratings: 7.5/9/8.5 (RV Park) N-bnd: From Jct of I-35 & Exit 265, N 1.2 mi on E Fntg Rd to Market St, E 0.3 mi (L); or S-bnd: From Jct of I-35 & Exit 266, to W Fntg Rd, (pass thru Hwy 195 intersection, stay in center ln), S 1.5 mi on W Fntg Rd, cross I-35 at double bridge, N 0.7 mi on E Fntg Rd to Market St, E 0.3 mi (L). **FAC:** Paved rds. (115 spaces). Avail: 35 gravel, patios, 35 pull-thrus (36 x 100), 35 full hkups (30/50 amps), seasonal sites, WiFi, laundry. **REC.** Pet restrict(Q). No tents. Big rig sites, 2015 rates: $30. Disc: AAA, military.
(512)864-2724 Lat: 30.69271, Lon: -97.64938
131 Market St, Georgetown, TX 78626
info@berryspringsrv.com
www.berryspringsrv.com
See ad page 1133.

EAST VIEW RV RANCH
Ratings: 8.5/8★/8.5 (RV Park) From Jct I-35 (exit 261) and Hwy 29 (University Ave): go 4mi E on Hwy 29, then 1/2mi N on Eastview Rd (R). **FAC:** All weather rds. 50 gravel, 29 pull-thrus (28 x 45), back-ins (28 x 45), 50 full hkups (30/50 amps), WiFi, laundry. **REC:** playground. Pet restrict(B). No tents. Big rig sites, 2015 rates: $28. Disc: military.
(512)931-2251 Lat: 30.65170, Lon: -97.62500
552 Eastview Dr, Georgetown, TX 78626
info@eastviewrvranch.com
www.eastviewrvranch.com
See ad pages 1133, 1108.

NEW LIFE RV PARK **Ratings: 9.5/10★/10** (RV Park) 2015 rates: $29 to $32.50. (512)931-2073 1200 County Rd 152, Georgetown, TX 78626

GILMER — B8 *Upshur*

WATTS RV PARK

Ratings: 9.5/9.5★/8.5 (RV Park) From S Jct of US 271 & SH 155: Go 3-1/4 mi SW on SH 155, then 1 mi S on Chinaberry Rd. (R). **FAC:** Gravel rds. (44 spaces). Avail: 23 paved, patios, 23 pull-thrus (25 x 60), 23 full hkups (30/50 amps), seasonal sites, WiFi, tent sites, laundry, groc, firewood. **REC:** pool, pond, fishing. Pets OK. Big rig sites, 2015 rates: $25 to $32.
(903)734-3380 Lat: 32.66553, Lon: -94.98311
2212 Chinaberry Rd, Gilmer, TX 75645
manager@wattsrvpark.com
www.wattsrvpark.com

YAMBOREE GROUNDS (Public) From Jct of Hwys 154 & 271, N 1.6 mi on Hwy 271 (R). 2015 rates: $5. (903)843-2413

GLADEWATER — B8 *Gregg*

ANTIQUE CAPITAL RV PARK

Ratings: 8.5/10★/9.5 (RV Park) From Jct US 80 & US 271: Go 3/4 mi SW on US 271, then 3/4 mi S on Loop 485. (L). **FAC:** Gravel rds. (114 spaces). Avail: 62 paved, patios, 62 pull-thrus (35 x 80), 62 full hkups (30/50 amps), seasonal sites, WiFi, laundry, LP gas. **REC:** pond, fishing, playground. Pet restrict(B/Q). Partial handicap access, no tents. Big rig sites, 2015 rates: $29. Disc: military.
(903)845-7378 Lat: 32.52381, Lon: -94.94247
500 S Loop 485, Gladewater, TX 75647
antiquecapitalrvpark@antiquecapitalrvpark.com
www.antiquecapitalrvpark.com
See ad this page.

SHALLOW CREEK RV RESORT

Ratings: 10/10★/10 (RV Park) From Jct of I-20 (exit 583) & SR 135: Go 1-1/2 mi N on SR 135 (R).

EAST TEXAS PINEY WOODS BEST
In the Longview area and Gladewater's Antique District, enjoy the golf course next door or our pool and splashpad. Nearby activities & Lonestar Speedway will round out your stay. Reserve now for this top rated destination.

FAC: Paved rds. (63 spaces). Avail: 43 paved, patios, 16 pull-thrus (31 x 90), back-ins (35 x 70), 43 full hkups (30/50 amps), seasonal sites, cable, WiFi, dump, laundry, groc, LP gas, fire rings. **REC:** pool, whirlpool, pond, fishing, golf, playground. Pet restrict(B/Q). Partial handicap access, no tents. Big rig sites, 2015 rates: $33.
(888)984-4513 Lat: 32.45467, Lon: -94.93566
5261 Hwy 135 N, Gladewater, TX 75647
rv@shallowcreek.com
www.shallowcreek.com
See ad opposite page, 1108.

GLEN ROSE — B7 *Somervell*

DINOSAUR VALLEY (State Pk) From Jct of US-67 & FM-205 (Park Rd 59), W 2.8 mi on FM-205 (Park Rd 59), NW 0.4 mi on Park Rd 59 (E) (Entrance fee). 2015 rates: $25. (254)897-4588

Tell them you saw them in this Guide!

GLENN HEIGHTS — J4 *Dallas*

DALLAS HI-HO RV PARK

Ratings: 6/8.5/7.5 (RV Park) From Jct of I-20 & I-35 E: Go 5 mi S on I-35 E (exit 412), then 2-1/2 mi W on Bear Creek Rd (L). **FAC:** Paved/gravel rds. (125 spaces). Avail: 25 gravel, 25 pull-thrus (19 x 55), 25 full hkups (30/50 amps), seasonal sites, WiFi, tent sites, dump, laundry. **REC:** playground. Pets OK. Partial handicap access. 2015 rates: $29. Disc: AAA.
AAA Approved
(972)223-4834 Lat: 32.56060, Lon: -96.85996
200 W. Bear Creek Rd, Glenn Heights, TX 75154
hihorvpark@yahoo.com
www.hihorvpark.com
See ad page 1143.

GOLIAD — E7 *Goliad*

COLETO CREEK PARK & RESERVOIR (Public) From Fannin, NE 4 mi on US-59 to Coleto Park Rd, N 0.3 mi (R). 2015 rates: $29 to $35. (361)575-6366

GOLIAD STATE HISTORICAL PARK (State Pk) From Jct of US-59 & US-183/77A, S 0.8 mi on US-183/77A (R) (Entrance fee). 2015 rates: $15 to $25. (361)645-3405

GONZALES — D7 *Gonzales*

GONZALES INDEPENDENCE PARK (Public) From town, S 1 mi on US-183 (R). 2015 rates: $25. (830)672-1324

LAKE WOOD REC AREA (Public) From town, W 4 mi on US-90A to FM-2091, S 3 mi (E). 2015 rates: $26 to $31. (830)672-2779

GOODLETT — A5 *Hardeman*

OLE TOWNE COTTON GIN RV PARK

Ratings: 9/9★/8.5 (RV Park) From jct US 287 & FM 2363/Goodlett Rd: Go 1 block N on Goodlett Rd. (L). **FAC:** All weather rds. (50 spaces). Avail: 42 gravel, patios, 23 pull-thrus (28 x 85), back-ins (27 x 60), 42 full hkups (30/50 amps), seasonal sites, WiFi, tent sites, laundry, groc. **REC:** pool. Pet restrict(B). Partial handicap access. Big rig sites, 2015 rates: $30 to $35. Disc: AAA, military.
(940)674-2477 Lat: 34.33514, Lon: -99.88112
230 Market St, Goodlett, TX 79252
oletowne2@gmail.com
http://www.campingfriend.com/OleTowne/
See ad this page.

Traveling with a Fido? Many campground listings indicate pet-friendly amenities and pet restrictions.

GOODRICH — C9 *Polk*

MAGNOLIA RV PARK & CAMPGROUND **Ratings: 6/5/8** (RV Park) 2015 rates: $30. (936)365-4910 791 Fm Road 2665, Goodrich, TX 77335

GORDONVILLE — A7 *Grayson*

BIG MINERAL RESORT, MARINA AND CAMPGROUND (Public) From town, W 14 mi on US-82, N 10 mi on SR-901, follow signs (R). 2015 rates: $17 to $25. (903)523-4287

JUNIPER POINT (Public Corps) From town, N 5 mi on US-377, follow signs (R). 2015 rates: $20 to $22. Apr 1 to Oct 1. (903)523-4022

GRAHAM — B6 *Young*

FIREMAN'S PARK (Public) From Jct of US-380, SR-16 & SR-67, S .25 mi on SH-16, E .2 mi on 5th St. 2015 rates: $12. (940)549-3324

KINDLEY PARK (Public) From town, W 6.8 mi on US-380 (L). 2015 rates: $10. (940)549-3324

GRANBURY — B7 *Hood*

BENNETT'S RV RANCH

Ratings: 8.5/10★/9 (RV Park) From Jct Hwy 144 & US 377: Go 3 1/2 mi NE on US 377(L). Register at Bennett's Camping Center. If arriving after 6 pm, call for instructions.

GREAT RV PARK GREAT DEALERSHIP
Relax under a shady oak tree while our full service RV dealership makes your needed repairs without interrupting your camping fun. Our clubhouse is great for rallies and family reunions. Visit historic Granbury and enjoy.

FAC: Paved rds. (44 spaces). Avail: 24 paved, 11 pull-thrus (30 x 57), back-ins (30 x 68), 24 full hkups (50 amps), seasonal sites, cable, WiFi, tent sites,

We appreciate your business!

GRANBURY (CONT)

BENNETT'S RV RANCH (CONT)
laundry. **REC:** playground. Pet restrict(B/Q). Partial handicap access. Big rig sites, 2015 rates: $35.
(817)279-7500 Lat: 32.45020, Lon: -97.73984
3101 Old Granbury Rd, Granbury, TX 76049
resranch@bennettsrvranch.com
www.bennettsrvranch.com
See ad pages 1151, 1108.

Travel Services

BENNETT'S CAMPING CENTER RV Sales and service since 1972, legendary service, rental RVs, large store with RV supplies, warranty service, maintenance items for your RV, extended service warranties, Service M-Sat. **SERVICES:** RV, RV appliance, restrooms, RV Sales. Rentals, RV storage. RV supplies, dump, emergency parking, RV accessible. waiting room. Hours: 9am to 5pm.
(817)279-7500 Lat: 32.45020, Lon: -97.73984
2708 E Hwy 377, Granbury, TX 76049
stacy@bennettsrv.com
www.bennettsrv.com
See ad page 1151.

GRAND PRAIRIE — H3 *Dallas, Tarrant*

LOYD PARK/JOE POOL LAKE
Ratings: 8/9.5★/9 (Public) From Jct of I-20 (exit 453 B) & SR 360: Go 4 3/4 mi S on SR 360, then 1/2 mi E on Ragland Rd. (R). **FAC:** Paved rds. 213 paved, patios, back-ins (50 x 65), 17 full hkups, 196 W, 196 E (30 amps), WiFi, tent sites, rentals, dump, groc, fire rings, firewood, controlled access. **REC:** Joe Pool Lake: swim, fishing, playground. Pets OK. Partial handicap access. 2015 rates: $20 to $28.
(817)467-2104 Lat: 32.61313, Lon: -97.06939
city of Grand Prairie, 3401 Ragland Rd, Grand Prairie, TX 75052
bhicks@gptx.org
www.loydpark.com
See ad pages 1115 (Spotlight Dallas/Fort Worth), 1108.

TRADERS VILLAGE RV PARK
Ratings: 10/10★/8.5 (RV Park) From Jct of I-20 & Great Southwest Parkway (exit 454), N 1 mi on Great Southwest Parkway to Mayfield Rd, W 0.2 mi (R).

STROLL THROUGH 1000'S OF SHOPS
Located in west side of Columbus, only minutes off I-270-Exit 7 on US 40 W. Near Metro Parks, dog park, Hollywood Casino. We feature 50 amp full hookups with level sites. Many pull thrus and clean bathhouse. Free Wi-Fi too.

FAC: Paved rds. (126 spaces). Avail: 51 paved, patios, 48 pull-thrus (21 x 60), back-ins (25 x 40), 51 full hkups (30/50 amps), seasonal sites, WiFi, tent sites, dump, laundry, groc, LP gas. **REC:** pool, shuffleboard, playground. Pet restrict(B/Q). Partial handicap access. 2015 rates: $29.95 to $36.95. Disc: AAA, military. ATM.
(972)647-8205 Lat: 32.69274, Lon: -97.04868
2602 Mayfield Rd, Grand Prairie, TX 75052
dfwrv@tradersvillage.com
www.tradersvillagervpark.com
See ad pages 1144, 1148, 1108, 1102 (TX Map).

Things to See and Do

TRADERS VILLAGE 154 acre flea market with special events. $3 per car parking fee. Partial handicap access. RV accessible. Restrooms, food. Hours: 8am to 9pm. ATM, no CC.
(972)647-2331 Lat: 32.69274, Lon: -97.04868
2602 Mayfield Rd, Grand Prairie, TX 75052
dfwinfo@tradersvillage.com
www.tradersvillage.com
See ad page 1144.

GRANGER — C7 *Williamson*

TAYLOR PARK (Public Corps) From town, S 6.1 mi on Hwy 95, E 5 mi on FM-1331 (L). 2015 rates: $18 to $22. Apr 1 to Sep 28. (512)859-2668

WILLIS CREEK (Public Corps) From Jct of SR-95 & CR-346, E 4 mi on CR-346 (E). 2015 rates: $18 to $22. (512)859-2668

WILSON H FOX PARK (Public Corps) From I-35: E on Hwy 79 to Hwy 95, N 5.9 mi on Hwy 95, E 6.5 mi on FM-1331 to entrance of Granger Dam, N to park (L). 2015 rates: $18 to $36. (512)859-2668

GRAPEVINE — G3 *Tarrant*

THE VINEYARDS CAMPGROUND & CABINS
Ratings: 9.5/8.5★/10 (Public) From E Jct Hwy 121 & Hwy 26 (Northwest Hwy): Go 2-1/2 mi SW on Hwy 26, then 1 mi N on Dooley Rd (L).

RELAX ON SHORES OF GRAPEVINE LAKE
Our nationally acclaimed campground is well-known for its peaceful setting, lovely grounds, lakefront views and accommodating staff. Spacious pull-thrus & cozy furnished cabins offer something for everyone.

FAC: Paved rds. 93 paved, patios, 30 pull-thrus (40 x 85), back-ins (40 x 70), 93 full hkups (30/50 amps), WiFi, rentals, laundry, groc, fire rings, firewood, controlled access. **REC:** Lake Grapevine: swim, fishing, marina, playground. Pets OK. Partial handicap access, no tents. Big rig sites, 2015 rates: $48 to $68. Disc: military.
(888)329-8993 Lat: 32.95549, Lon: -97.07394
1501 N Dooley, Grapevine, TX 76051
thevineyards@grapevinetexas.gov
www.vineyardscampground.com
See ad this page, 1108 & Snowbird Destinations in Magazine Section.

GREENVILLE — B8 *Hunt*

EAST TEXAS RV PARK
(Campground) (Not Visited) From jct I-30 and US Hwy 69: go 3 mi South on US 69 (L). **FAC.** (44 spaces). Avail: 42 gravel, 42 full hkups (30/50 amps), seasonal sites. **REC.** No CC, no reservations.
(903)454-8900 Lat: 33.08498, Lon: -96.04399
2935 Sh 69S, Greenville, TX 75402
Jan@easttexasrvpark.com
www.easttexasrvpark.com
See ad page 1167.

GUN BARREL CITY — B8 *Henderson*

LAKERIDGE RV PARK
Ratings: 6.5/8.5/7.5 (RV Park) From jct Hwy 198 & Hwy 334: Go 1/4 mi W on Hwy 334 (L). **FAC:** Paved/gravel rds. (64 spaces). Avail: 10 paved, 1 pull-thrus (24 x 65), back-ins (24 x 50), mostly side by side hkups, 10 full hkups (30/50 amps), seasonal sites, cable, WiFi, laundry. Pets OK. 2015 rates: $24. Disc: AAA, military.
(903)887-4212 Lat: 32.3428973, Lon: -96.1091167
301 W Main Street, Gun Barrel City, TX 75156
Lakeridgervpark@aol.com
www.lakeridgervpark.com

HALLETTSVILLE — D7 *Lavaca*

HALLETTSVILLE CITY PARK (Public) From town, N 0.9 mi on North Main St, follow signs (R). 2015 rates: $10. (361)798-3246

K C RV PARK Ratings: 5.5/NA/7 (RV Park) From Jct of US 77 South & US 90 Alt, S 0.3 mi on US 90 Alt (L). **FAC:** Gravel rds. (89 spaces). Avail: 39 paved, patios, 18 pull-thrus (25 x 55), back-ins (20 x 45), some side by side hkups, 39 full hkups (30/50 amps), seasonal sites, cable, WiFi. **REC.** Pets OK. No tents. 2015 rates: $20.
AAA Approved
(361)798-2311 Lat: 29.43601, Lon: -96.95042
321 U.s. Hwy 77 South, Hallettsville, TX 77964
kchall2006@sbcglobal.net
www.kchall.com

Park policies vary. Ask about the cancellation policy when making a reservation.

OUTBACK RV CAMPGROUND **Ratings: 6.5/9.5★/7** (RV Park) 2015 rates: $22. (361)798-4645 1641 N Texana, Hallettsville, TX 77964

WINDING WAY RV PARK **Ratings: 5/NA/7** (RV Park) 2015 rates: $29.50. (361)648-4855 418 Country Road 1H, Hallettsville, TX 77964

HALLSVILLE — B9 *Harrison*

COWBOY CAMP RV PARK **Ratings: 5.5/9.5★/7.5** (RV Park) 2015 rates: $28. (903)660-2025 10212 Fm 968 West, Hallsville, TX 75650

HITCHIN' POST RV PARK
Ratings: 8/9.5★/8 (RV Park) From Jct of I-20 (exit 604) & FM-450: Go 500 feet N on FM-450 (L). **FAC:** Paved/gravel rds. (55 spaces). Avail: 10 gravel, 9 pull-thrus (22 x 80), back-ins (24 x 60), 10 full hkups (30/50 amps), seasonal sites, cable, WiFi, laundry, LP gas. **REC.** Pet restrict(B/Q). No tents. Big rig sites, 2015 rates: $27. Disc: military.
(903)668-3572 Lat: 32.47662, Lon: -94.58001
1674 Fm-450 S, Hallsville, TX 75650
sherri_skipper@yahoo.com
www.hitchingpostrvpark.com

HARLINGEN — M4 *Cameron*

HARLINGEN See also Brownsville, La Feria, Mercedes, San Benito.

CAREFREE VALLEY RV RESORT
Ratings: 7.5/6/6.5 (RV Park) From Bus 77 & Primiera, go E over RR tracks, go N, 1/4 mi (R). **FAC:** Paved rds. (231 spaces). Avail: 85 grass, patios, back-ins (23 x 40), 85 full hkups (30/50 amps), WiFi Hotspot, laundry. **REC:** heated pool, whirlpool, shuffleboard. Pet restrict(B/Q). Age restrict may apply, eco-friendly, 2015 rates: $35. No CC.
(956)425-2540 Lat: 26.23621, Lon: -097.72578
4506 N Bus 77, Harlingen, TX 78552
carefreevalley@gmail.com
www.carefreevalleyresort.com
See ad page 1122 (Spotlight South Texas Tropics).

EASTGATE MH & RV PARK
Ratings: 9/8★/7 (RV Area in MHP) From Jct of US-83 & US-77, N 2.3 mi on US-77 to Primera Rd (Loop 499), SE 5.2 mi to FM-106 (Harrison St), W 0.2 mi (R). **FAC:** Paved rds. (311 spaces). Avail: 80 paved, 30 all weather, patios, back-ins (25 x 40), 110 full hkups (30/50 amps), seasonal sites, cable, WiFi $, rentals, laundry. **REC:** heated pool, whirlpool, shuffleboard. Pet restrict(Q). Partial handicap access, no tents. Age restrict may apply, eco-friendly, 2015 rates: $36.
(800)499-3137 Lat: 26.19137, Lon: -97.66712
2801 E Harrison Ave, Harlingen, TX 78550
eastgatervpark@rgv.twcbc.com
www.eastgatervpark.net
See ad page 1123 (Spotlight South Texas Tropics).

FIG TREE RV RESORT **Ratings: 8.5/8.5★/8.5** (RV Park) 2015 rates: $33. (956)423-6699 15257 N. 83 Expressway, Harlingen, TX 78552

LAKEWOOD RV RESORT **Ratings: 9.5/8.5/8** (RV Park) 2015 rates: $36 to $37. (800)405-6188 4525 Graham Rd, Harlingen, TX 78552

PALM GARDENS MHP & RV COMMUNITY
Ratings: 8.5/8.5★/8 (RV Area in MHP) From Jct of US-77 & US-83 (Harlingen Downtown exit), W 0.6 mi on US-83 Bus (L). **FAC:** Paved rds. (241 spaces). 169 Avail: 33 paved, 136 gravel, patios, 26 pull-thrus (21 x 45), back-ins (25 x 50), 169 full hkups (30/50 amps), cable, WiFi $, laundry, controlled ac-

HARLINGEN (CONT)

PALM GARDENS MHP & RV (CONT)
cess. **REC:** heated pool, whirlpool, shuffleboard. Pet restrict(B/Q). No tents. Age restrict may apply, eco-friendly, 2015 rates: $36.
(956)423-7670 Lat: 26.18501, Lon: -97.73307
3401 W Bus 83, Harlingen, TX 78552
info@palmgardensresort.com
www.palmgardensresort.com
See ad opposite page.

PARADISE PARK RV RESORT **Ratings: 9/8/8** (RV Area in MHP) 2015 rates: $37. (800)405-6188 1201 N Expwy 77, Harlingen, TX 78552

PARK PLACE ESTATES & RV RESORT MHP **Ratings: 9/9.5★/9** (RV Resort) 2015 rates: $39. (956)428-4414 5401 W Bus 83, Harlingen, TX 78552

SUNSHINE RV RESORT **Ratings: 9.5/8.5/8.5** (RV Park) 2015 rates: $33 to $42. (800)405-6188 1900 Grace Ave, Harlingen, TX 78550

TROPIC WINDS RV RESORT **Ratings: 9.5/9★/8** (RV Park) 2015 rates: $36 to $38. (800)405-6188 1501 North Loop 499, Harlingen, TX 78550

HASKELL — B5 *Haskell*

HASKELL CITY PARK (Public) From Jct of US-277 & US-380, E 0.2 mi on US-380 to Ave B, S S 0.3 mi (E). First night free. 2015 rates: $16. (940)864-2333

HAWKINS — B8 *Wood*

LAKE HAWKINS RV PARK (Public) From Jct of Hwy 14 & US-80, W 3 mi on US-80 to CR-3440, N 1 mi (R). 2015 rates: $15 to $20. (903)769-4545

HIGHLANDS — D8 *Harris*

HOUSTON LEISURE RV RESORT **Ratings: 9/8.5★/8** (RV Park) 2015 rates: $44. (800)988-8285 1601 South Main Street, Highlands, TX 77562

SAN JACINTO RIVERFRONT RV PARK
Ratings: 10/10★/10 (RV Park) From Jct of I-10 & Exit 787 Highlands/Crosby-Lynchburg Rd (S. Main), N 1 mi on Crosby-Lynchburg/S. Main (L). **FAC:** Paved rds. (301 spaces). Avail: 100 paved, patios, 100 pull-thrus (30 x 70), 100 full hkups (30/50 amps), seasonal sites, cable, WiFi, rentals, dump, laundry, LP gas, controlled access. **REC:** pool, whirlpool, San Jacinto River: fishing, marina, playground. Pets OK. No tents. Big rig sites, eco-friendly, 2015 rates: $55.
(281)426-6919 Lat: 29.80906, Lon: -95.06108
540 S. Main, Highlands, TX 77562
riverfrontrvpark@yahoo.com
www.sjriverfrontrvresort.com
See ad pages 1158, 1108.

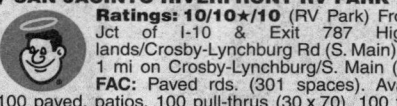

HOUSTON — D8 *Harris*

HOUSTON AREA MAP

Symbols on map indicate towns within a 50 mile radius of Houston where campgrounds are listed. Check listings for more information.

See also Alvin, Ames, Bacliff, Baytown, Brookshire, Cut and Shoot, Dickinson, Galveston, Highlands, Katy, Kemah, La Marque, League City, Magnolia, New Caney, Pasadena, Richmond, Spring, The Woodlands, Tomball, Waller & Willis.

ADVANCED RV RESORT
Ratings: 10/10★/10 (RV Park) From Jct of I-610 & Hwy 288, S 5.5 mi on US 288 to Beltway 8 exit, SE 0.5 mi on Beltway 8 Frontage Rd (R). **FAC:** Paved rds. (203 spaces). Avail: 155 paved, patios, 93 pull-thrus (30 x 65), back-ins (30 x 35), 155 full hkups (30/50 amps), seasonal sites, cable, WiFi, dump, laundry, LP gas, controlled access. **REC:** heated pool, whirlpool. Pet restrict(B/Q). Partial handicap access, no tents. Big rig sites, RV age restrict, eco-friendly, 2015 rates: $50 to $55. Disc: AAA, military.
(713)433-6950 Lat: 29.59623, Lon: -95.38083
2850 S Sam Houston Pkwy E, Houston, TX 77047
info@advancedrvpark.com
www.advancedrvpark.com
See ad pages 1161, 1108.

ALLSTAR RV RESORT
Ratings: 9.5/9.5★/9 (RV Park) S-bnd: From Jct of US-59 (southside of Houston) & Beltway 8 Frntg Rd exit, stay on Frntg Rd S. to U-turn under fwy, N 0.4 mi on Frntg Rd to SW Plaza Dr, E 0.1 mi (R); or N-bnd: From Jct of US-59 & Murphy Rd/Wilcrest Dr exit stay on Frontage Rd N 1.6 mi to SW Plaza Dr (R). **FAC:** Paved rds. (124 spaces). Avail: 109 paved, 15 pull-thrus (27 x 60), back-ins (27 x 40), some side by side hkups, 109 full hkups (30/50 amps), seasonal sites, cable, WiFi, rentals, laundry, LP gas. **REC:** heated pool. Pets OK. Partial handicap access, no tents. Eco-friendly, 2015 rates: $40 to $60. ATM.
AAA Approved
(713)981-6814 Lat: 29.66353, Lon: -95.55029
10650 SW Plaza Ct., Houston, TX 77074
allstar@qualityrvresorts.com
www.allstar-rv.com
See ad pages 1154-1155, 1108.

Know the name? Then you can use our special "Find-it-Fast" index to locate your campground on the map. The index arranges private and public campgrounds alphabetically, by state. Next to the name, you'll quickly find the name of the town the park is in, plus the Listing's page number.

TX

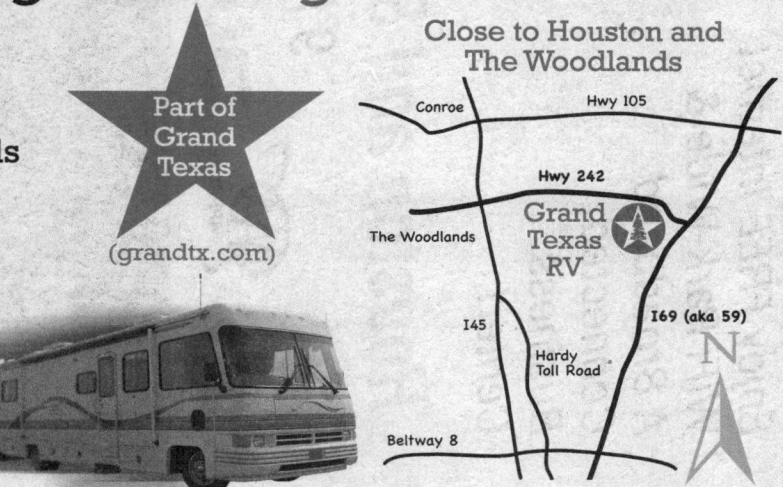

TX

JELLYSTONE PARK
Yogi Bear's
CAMP-RESORTS
1 & 2 BEDROOM CABINS
GRAND LODGE
FULL-HOOKUP RV SITES
TENT & GROUP SITES
Waller TX
THEMED WEEKENDS
PLANNED ACTIVITIES
RECREATION CENTER
ARTS & CRAFTS
WATER ZONE
SCREAMING WATERSLIDES
SPLASHPAD
LAZY RIVER
LONE STAR JELLYSTONE PARK
800-347-5106
Good Sam Park
www.LONESTARJELLYSTONE.com
34843 Betka Rd. Waller, TX. 77484
979-826-4111
YOGI BEAR™ and all related characters and elements are trademarks of and © of Hanna-Barbera. (s15)
See listing Waller, TX

TX

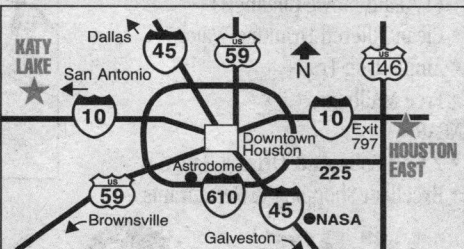

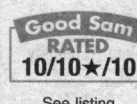

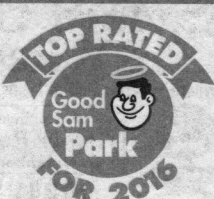

Rayford Crossing RV Resort

"Where Superior Service Meets Complete Tranquility"

Good Sam Park

See Our Sister Park Near Houston
Timber Ridge RV Village
www.timberridgervvillage.com

Good Sam RATED 10/10★/10

(281) 298-8008
29321 S. Plum Creek Dr. • Spring, TX 77386
www.RayfordCrossing.com

See listing The Woodlands, TX

San Jacinto Riverfront RV Resort

See listing Highlands, TX

Good Sam RATED 10/10★/10

Good Sam Park

540 S. Main • Highlands, Texas 77562
281-426-6919 • 1-866-426-6919
www.sjriverfrontrvresort.com

Directional arrows indicate the campground's position in relation to the nearest town.

Houston Central RV Park

A Friendly Park with Country Atmosphere & City Convenience

Close to Airport, Downtown, Medical, Shopping & Mall, Restaurants, Museums, Space Center

Wi-Fi 888-449-2267

Good Sam Park

houstoncentralrvpark.com
1620 Peach Leaf Street, Houston TX 77039
See listing Houston, TX

Riverbend RV Park

New RV Park

Country Quiet but Close to City Conveniences

- Large Wide & Long Pull-Thrus 30' x 84'
- 50 & 30 Amp at Each Site
- Laundry Room with 8 Washers & 8 Driers
- Beautiful Private Restrooms & Showers
- Free Hi-Speed WiFi - 6 Signals Throughout Park
- 48 Cable TV Channels - (17 Paid Movie Channels)
- Clean Filtered Drinking Water
- Ample Dog Trails
- Free Mailboxes

NEAR:

- 2 Golf Courses & Driving Range
- Excellent Shopping & Restaurants

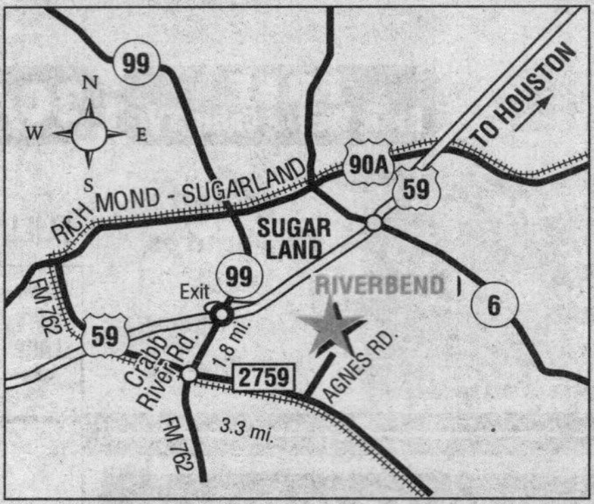

BIG RIGS WELCOME

Good Sam Park

See listing Richmond, TX

1055 Agnes Road
Richmond, TX 77469
Tel: (281) 343-5151
Web Site: www.riverbendrvpark.cc

Lone Star Lakes RV PARK

Fish Free in Our Private Lake
Only 15 miles north of Houston's Beltway 8
lonestarlakesrvpark.com
1-800-290-9301
20980 Hwy 59, New Caney, TX 77357

★ Full Time Security ★ Pool
★ Wide, Shaded Sites ★ Propane
★ Free Wi-Fi & Cable TV
★ Climate Controlled Laundry & Private Bathrooms ★ Dog Park
★ Warm Water Dog Wash

See listing New Caney, TX

CAMINO VILLA

Mobile Home & RV Park

JUST 15 MIN. FROM HOUSTON
Shaded Full Hookups
Near Shopping
Weekly, Monthly Rates
(281) 487-1759
3310 Space Center Blvd., Pasadena, TX 77505
See listing Pasadena, TX

RED • DOT RV PARK

CLEAN • CLOSE • CHEAP
2 PARKS

- Massive Shade Trees
- Oversized Patios
- Laundry

• CHECK OUT OUR SPECIAL RATES •

15703 N. Sellers Rd
Houston, TX 77061
281-448-3438

Only 10 Miles Outside Downtown Houston

See listing Houston, TX

www.RedDotRVPark.com

Van Manor RV Park

Small Town Rural Environment

Quick Hop to Shopping, Dining & World Class Health Care Services

9522 Telephone Rd.
Houston, TX 77075
713-991-1232

See listing Houston, TX

www.VanManorPark.com

Preston

Mobile Home Community

RV SPACES

- Full Hookups
- Special Rates
- Pet Friendly

3014 Preston Ave.
Pasadena, TX

See listing Pasadena, TX

713-991-1232

HOUSTON (CONT)

CAMINO VILLA MH & RV PARK

(RV Spaces) From Jct of I-610 & I-45, S 3.25 mi on I-45 to Exit 36 (College), E 6 mi on College (becomes Spencer Hwy) to Space Center Blvd, S 0.5 mi (R). **FAC:** Paved rds. (218 spaces). Avail: 9 grass, back-ins (30 x 50), accepts full hkup units only, 9 full hkups (30/50 amps). Pet restrict(B/Q). 2015 rates: $40. No CC.
(281)487-1759 Lat: 29.66031, Lon: -95.14481
3310 Space Center Blvd, Pasadena, TX 77505
See primary listing at Pasadena and ad page 1158.

EASTLAKE RV RESORT

Ratings: 10/9.5★/10 (RV Park) From Jct N Lake Houston Parkway & Lockwood Rd: Go N 2.1 mi (R). **FAC:** Paved rds. 240 paved, 40 pull-thrus (30 x 75), back-ins (30 x 41), 240 full hkups (30/50 amps), cable, WiFi, rentals, laundry, LP gas, controlled access. **REC:** heated pool, whirlpool, Eastlake: fishing, shuffleboard. Pets OK. Partial handicap access. Big rig sites, RV age restrict, eco-friendly, 2015 rates: $42.22 to $81. Disc: AAA, military. ATM.
AAA Approved
(832)243-6919 Lat: 29.89270, Lon: -095.21070
11802 Lockwood Road, Houston, TX 77044
eastlake@qualityrvresorts.com
www.eastlakervresort.com
See ad pages 1154-1155, 1108.

FALLBROOK RV RESORT

Ratings: 10/9.5★/10 (RV Resort) From I-45 S & Exit 59, go 1.1 mi S on West Rd (to end), then go W onto Veterans Memorial Dr, go 1/2 mi on Veterans Memorial Dr to Fallbrook Dr, then go W 1/2 mi on Fallbrook Dr (R). **FAC:** Paved rds. 186 paved, patios, 41 pull-thrus (30 x 60), back-ins (30 x 45), 186 full hkups (30/50 amps), cable, WiFi, rentals, laundry, controlled access. **REC:** heated pool, whirlpool, Fallbrook Lake: fishing. Pets OK. Partial handicap access. Big rig sites, 2015 rates: $42.22 to $63.33. ATM.
AAA Approved
(866)923-4988 Lat: 29.920584, Lon: -095.448840
3102 Fallbrook Dr, Houston, TX 77038
Fallbrook@qualityrvresorts.com
www.fallbrookrvresort.com
See ad pages 1154-1155, 1108.

HIGHWAY 6 RV RESORT

(RV Park) (Under Construction) **FAC:** Paved rds. 218 paved, 46 pull-thrus (30 x 65), back-ins (30 x 47), some side by side hkups, 218 full hkups (30/50 amps), cable, WiFi, laundry, controlled access. **REC:** heated pool, whirlpool, Highway 6 Lake. Pets OK. ATM.
Lat: 29.71852, Lon: -95.64050
14350 Schiller Rd., Houston, TX 77082
www.qualityrvresorts.com
See ad page 1154-1155.

HOUSTON CENTRAL RV PARK

Ratings: 9/8/8 (Campground) From N Jct of I-45 & Beltway 8 exit, E 3.5 mi on Beltway 8 to Aldine-Westfield, S 1 mi to Peachleaf, W 0.3 mi (L); or From N Jct of US-59 & Beltway 8 exit, W 3.5 mi on Beltway 8 to Aldine-Westfield, S 1 mi to Peach Leaf, W 0.3 mi (L). **FAC:** Paved rds. (64 spaces). Avail: 34 grass, patios, 34 pull-thrus (23 x 55), 34 full hkups (30/50 amps), seasonal sites, WiFi, tent sites, rentals, dump, laundry, groc, LP gas, controlled access. **REC:** pool, playground. Pet restrict(B). Eco-friendly, 2015 rates: $35 to $49.
(281)442-3700 Lat: 29.92373, Lon: -95.36086
1620 Peach Leaf St, Houston, TX 77039
houstonrvparkinfo@yahoo.com
www.houstoncentralrvpark.com
See ad opposite page.

Park owners want you to be satisfied with your stay. Get to know them.

HOUSTON (CONT)

KING PARKWAY MH COMMUNITY
Ratings: 8/NA/8.5 (RV Area in MHP) From US-90 & CE King Parkway: Go N on CE King Parkway 1.6 mi (R). **FAC:** Paved rds. (227 spaces). Avail: 40 grass, back-ins (40 x 80), 40 full hkups (30/50 amps), WiFi Hotspot, laundry. **REC:** pool, playground. Pet restrict(B/Q). Big rig sites, 2015 rates: $25.
(281)458-1806 Lat: 29.85453, Lon: -095.21389
8903 C.e. King Parkway, Houston, TX 77044
kingparkway@towermgmt.com
www.towerrvparks.com

LAKEVIEW RV RESORT
Ratings: 10/9.5★/9.5 (RV Park) From S Jct of I-610 & US-90A (South Main St): Go SW 1.9 mi on S Main St to Holmes Rd/Hiram Clark exit, E uturn under bridge to frontage rd, NE .01 (R). **FAC:** Paved rds. 245 paved, patios, 33 pull-thrus (31 x 75), back-ins (31 x 40), 245 full hkups (30/50 amps), cable, WiFi, rentals, dump, laundry, LP gas, controlled access. **REC:** heated pool, wading pool, whirlpool, pond, fishing. Pet restrict(B). Partial handicap access, no tents. Big rig sites, eco-friendly, 2015 rates: $41 to $54. Disc: AAA. ATM.
AAA Approved
(800)385-9122 Lat: 29.65260, Lon: -95.44563
11991 Main St, Houston, TX 77035
lakeviewrv@qualityrvresorts.com
www.lakeviewrvresort.com
See ad pages 1154-1155, 1108.

NORTHLAKE RV RESORT
Ratings: 10/9.5★/9.5 (RV Park) From Jct I-45 & FM 1960: Go 2 mi E on FM 1960, then go .05 mi S on Humble-Westfield Rd (R). **FAC:** Paved rds. 230 paved, patios, 32 pull-thrus (30 x 75), back-ins (30 x 40), 230 full hkups (30/50 amps), cable, WiFi, rentals, laundry, LP gas, controlled access. **REC:** heated pool, whirlpool, Northlake: fishing. Pets OK. Partial handicap access. Big rig sites, eco-friendly, 2015 rates: $43.33 to $65.55. ATM.
AAA Approved
(281)209-1770 Lat: 30.02251, Lon: -095.39792
1919 Humble-Westfield Road, Houston, TX 77073
northlake@qualityrvresorts.com
www.northlakervresort.com
See ad pages 1154-1155, 1108.

We rate what RVers consider important.

RED DOT NORTH **Ratings: 4.5/UI/6** (RV Park) 2015 rates: $26. (281)448-3438 15703 Seller Rd, Houston, TX 77060

RED DOT RV PARK
(RV Spaces) From jct I-45 (exit 60A) & Aldine Bender Rd: Go E 1.1 mi on Aldine Bender Rd to Sellers Rd, then S 0.3 mi (R). **FAC:** Paved rds. (80 spaces). Avail: 10 grass, 1 pull-thrus (25 x 70), back-ins (25 x 70), 10 full hkups (30/50 amps), seasonal sites, WiFi, laundry. Pet restrict(B). No tents. Big rig sites, 2015 rates: $26.
(281)448-3438 Lat: 29.91860, Lon: -95.38638
15703 Sellers Rd, Houston, TX 77060
www.reddotrvpark.com
See ad page 1159.

SAFARI MH COMMUNITY
Ratings: 7/6.5/7 (RV Area in MHP) From jct of I-45 & Calder (exit 22), W .01 mi to S Calder Dr, S 1.5 mi (R). **FAC:** Paved rds. (183 spaces). Avail: 50 gravel, patios, 11 pull-thrus (25 x 80), back-ins (25 x 45), 50 full hkups (30/50 amps), WiFi $, laundry. **REC:** pool. Pets OK. Eco-friendly, 2015 rates: $32. Disc: AAA, military.
(281)332-4131 Lat: 29.47160, Lon: -95.10545
2935 Calder Dr, League City, TX 77573
reservations@safarirvpark.com
www.safarirvpark.com
See primary listing at League City and ad page 1159.

SOUTH MAIN RV PARK Ratings: 7.5/8★/7.5 (RV Park) From south jct US 59 & Loop 610 S: Go 5-1/2 mi SE on Loop 610 S (South Main exit 2), then 1 block S on South Main. (R). **FAC:** Paved rds. 102 gravel, patios, 6 pull-thrus (24 x 75), back-ins (24 x 70), 102 full hkups (30/50 amps), cable, WiFi, rentals, laundry, controlled access. Pet restrict(B). Partial handicap access, no tents. 2015 rates: $46. Disc: military.
AAA Approved
(713)667-0120 Lat: 29.67557, Lon: -95.42979
10100 South Main, Houston, TX 77025
southmainrvpark@gmail.com
www.smrvpark.com

SOUTHLAKE RV RESORT
Ratings: 8.5/9.5★/10 (RV Park) From Jct Beltway 8 & SR 288: Go 1 mi N to Alameda Genoa, then .3 mi E on Alameda Genoa to Hycohn, then 1.3 mi S on Hycohn (L). **FAC:** Paved rds. 117 paved, patios, 12 pull-thrus (31 x 60), back-ins (31 x 45), 117 full hkups (30/50 amps), cable, WiFi, rentals, laundry, controlled access. **REC.** Pet restrict(B). Partial handicap access. Big rig sites, eco-friendly, 2015 rates: $53 to $67. ATM.
AAA Approved
(832)804-8088 Lat: 29.60817, Lon: -095.38416
13701 Hycohen Road, Houston, TX 77047
southlake@qualityrvresorts.com
www.southlakervresort.com
See ad pages 1154-1155, 1108.

TRADERS VILLAGE RV PARK
Ratings: 10/10★/9 (RV Park) From Jct of I-10 & Eldridge Rd (exit 753A), N 7.8 mi on Eldridge Rd (L); or From N Jct of I-45 & Beltway 8/Sam Houston Tollway (exit 60), W 12.6 mi on Beltway 8/Sam Houston Tollway to US-290, NW 2.2 mi to Eldridge Rd, S 0.6 mi (R).
ONLY @ TRADERS VILLAGE CAN YOU SHOP through thousands of shops, wheel and deal with the shop owners themselves and get the bargain of a lifetime. From furniture to flowers, you can find it all at Traders Houston.
FAC: Paved rds. (284 spaces). Avail: 179 paved, 140 pull-thrus (20 x 68), back-ins (32 x 40), 179 full hkups (30/50 amps), seasonal sites, WiFi, dump, laundry, LP gas, controlled access. **REC:** pool, shuffleboard, playground. Pet restrict(B/Q). Partial handicap access, no tents. Big rig sites, eco-friendly, 2015 rates: $32.95. Disc: AAA. ATM.
(281)890-5500 Lat: 29.89511, Lon: -95.60785
7979 N Eldridge, Houston, TX 77041
houstonrv@tradersvillage.com
www.tradersvillagervpark.com
See ad this page, 1108, 1102 (TX Map).

VAN MANOR MH & RV PARK
(RV Spaces) From Jct I-45 South & Alameda/Genoa Exit: Go W 3 mi to Telephone Rd, then N .03 mi (L) (Weekly Reservations only). **FAC:** Paved rds. 40 paved, back-ins (30 x 50), 40 full hkups (30/50 amps), WiFi Hotspot, laundry. **REC:**

County names help you follow the local weather report.

HOUSTON (CONT)

VAN MANOR MH & RV PARK (CONT)
pool. No pets. 2015 rates: $150 weekly. Disc: AAA, military.
(713)991-1232 Lat: 29.62727, Lon: -095.28584
9522 Telephone Rd, Houston, TX 77075
vcamacho@vanmanorpark.com
www.vanmanorpark.com
See ad page 1158.

WESTLAKE RV RESORT
Ratings: 10/9.5★/10 (RV Resort) From Jct of I-10 & Barker Cypress Rd exit: Go N 3 mi on Barker Cypress Rd to Clay Rd, W 0.2 mi (R). **FAC:** Paved rds. 197 paved, patios, 26 pull-thrus (30 x 66), back-ins (30 x 45), 197 full hkups (30/50 amps), cable, WiFi, rentals, dump, laundry, LP gas, controlled access. **REC:** heated pool, whirlpool, pond, fishing, shuffleboard. Pet restrict(B). Partial handicap access, no tents. Eco-friendly, 2015 rates: $45.55 to $73.33. Disc: AAA, military. ATM.
AAA Approved
(281)463-8566 Lat: 29.8312, Lon: -95.6899
18602 Clay Rd., Houston, TX 77084
westlake@qualityrvresorts.com
www.westlakervresort.com
See ad pages 1154-1155, 1108.

Things to See and Do

TRADERS VILLAGE 106 acres of bargain hunters paradise, thousands of dealers, thrill rides and festival foods. Plus special events & live entertainment. Partial handicap access. RV accessible. Restrooms, food. Hours: 10am to 5pm (Sat & Sun) ATM.
(281)890-5500 Lat: 29.89472, Lon: -95.60785
7979 N Eldridge Rd, Houston, TX 77041
houstonrv@tradersvillage.com
www.tradersvillage.com
See ad opposite page.

HUNTINGTON — C9 *Angelina*

HANKS CREEK PARK (Public Corps) From town, NE 0.5 mi on Hwy 147 to FR-2109, N 8 mi to FR-2801, E 2 mi (R). 2015 rates: $26 to $28. (409)384-5716

HUNTSVILLE — C8 *Walker*

HUNTSVILLE (State Pk) From Jct of I-45 & Park Rd 40 (exit 109), W 1.2 mi on Park Rd 40 (E) (Entrance fee). 2015 rates: $15 to $25. (936)295-5644

JACKSBORO — A6 *Jack*

FORT RICHARDSON STATE HISTORICAL PARK (State Pk) S-bnd: From Jacksboro town square, S 1 mi on US-281 (R); or N-bnd: From Jct of US-380 & US-281 (S of town), NW 1.6 mi on US-281 (L) (Entrance fee). 2015 rates: $20 to $25. (940)567-3506

HIDDEN LAKE RV RANCH AND SAFARI **Ratings: 8/NA/9** (RV Park) 2015 rates: $38. (940)567-5900 3100 Lowrance Rd, Jacksboro, TX 76458

JASPER — C9 *Jasper, Tyler*

DOUBLE HEART RV PARK **Ratings: 7.5/9.5★/9** (RV Park) 2015 rates: $25. (409)489-1515 14600 Tx Sh 63 W, Jasper, TX 75951

MARTIN DIES JR (State Pk) From Jct of US-96 & US-190 (in town), W 10.8 mi on US-190 (L) (Entrance fee). 2015 rates: $12 to $18. (409)384-5231

SANDY CREEK PARK (Public Corps) From town, W 15 mi on US-190 to FM-777, S 1.5 mi to CR-150, W 2.2 mi (E). For reservations call (877)444-6777. 2015 rates: $10 to $18. (409)429-3491

JEFFERSON — B9 *Marion*

ALLEY CREEK PARK (Public Corps) From town, NW 4 mi on Hwy 49 to Hwy 729, W 12 mi (L). 2015 rates: $22 to $42. Mar 1 to Sep 30. (903)755-2637

BUCKHORN CREEK PARK (Public Corps) From town, NW 4 mi on Hwy 49 to Hwy 729, W 3.5 mi to Hwy 726, S 2.4 mi (R). 2015 rates: $22 to $42. (903)665-8261

JOHNSON CREEK CAMPGROUND (Public Corps) From town, NW 4 mi on Hwy 49 to Hwy 729, W 8 mi, follow signs (L). 2015 rates: $26 to $30. (903)755-2435

JOHNSON CITY — C6 *Blanco*

PEDERNALES FALLS (State Pk) From Jct of US-281/290 & Ranch Rd 2766 (in town), E 9.2 mi on Ranch Rd 2766 (L) (Entrance fee). 2015 rates: $20. (830)868-7304

Take time now to plan a road trip with your pet for meaningful memories that last a lifetime. Read more in our Pampered Pet Parks feature at the front of the Guide.

ROADRUNNER RV PARK, LLC
Ratings: 8/9★/7.5 (RV Park) From Jct of US-290 & US-281 (in town): Go 3/4 mi S on US-290/281 (L). N Bnd: From S jct US 290 & US 281, Go 5 mi N on US 281 (R). **FAC:** Paved rds. (62 spaces). Avail: 42 paved, 42 pull-thrus (15 x 65), 42 full hkups (30/50 amps), seasonal sites, WiFi, rentals, laundry. **REC.** Pet restrict(B). No tents. Big rig sites, 2015 rates: $28 to $35.
(830)868-7449 Lat: 30.26895, Lon: -98.39752
501 US Hwy 281 South, Johnson City, TX 78636
rvpark@moment.net
www.roadrunnerrvparktexas.com
See ad pages 1125 (Spotlight Texas Hill Country), 1108.

JUNCTION — C5 *Kimble*

A SPOTLIGHT Introducing Junction's colorful attractions appearing at the front of the state section.

JUNCTION NORTH LLANO RIVER RV PARK
Ratings: 9/9★/9.5 (Campground) From Jct of I-10 & US-377 (exit 456), S 0.5 mi on US-377 (R). **FAC:** Paved/gravel rds. 52 gravel, patios, 51 pull-thrus (32 x 70), back-ins (32 x 35), 42 full hkups, 10 W, 10 E (30/50 amps), cable, WiFi, tent sites, rentals, dump, laundry, LP gas, fire rings, firewood, controlled access. **REC:** pool, North Llano River: fishing, playground. Pet restrict(B). Big rig sites, eco-friendly, 2015 rates: $36 to $39. Disc: AAA, military.
AAA Approved
(325)446-3138 Lat: 30.50130, Lon: -99.77870
2145 Main St, Junction, TX 76849
info@junctionriversrvpark.com
www.junctionnorthllanoriverrvpark.com
See ad pages 1118 (Spotlight Junction), 1108.

SOUTH LLANO RIVER (State Pk) From Jct of Bus Loop 481 & US-377 (in town), S 5.2 mi on US-377 to Park Rd 73, NE 2 mi (R) (Entrance fee). 2015 rates: $20. (325)446-3994

Heading to a privately owned park? Be sure to read how our inspection team rated it in the Guide "How to Use This Travel Guide" section.

SOUTH LLANO RIVER RV PARK & RESORT
(RV Park) (Too New to Rate) From of I-10 & US 377 (exit 456), S 1 mi on US 377, to Cedar Creek Rd, go W on Cedar Creek Rd. (R). **FAC:** Gravel rds. 50 gravel, patios, 50 pull-thrus (30 x 60), 50 full hkups (30/50 amps), tent sites, rentals, laundry, LP gas, fire rings, firewood. **REC:** South Llano River. Pet restrict(B). Partial handicap access. Big rig sites, 2015 rates: $40. Disc: AAA, military.
(325)446-3388 Lat: 30.48384, Lon: -99.75996
210 Cedar Creek Drive, Junction, TX 76849
Info@junctionriversrvpark.com
www.southllanoriverrvresort.com
See ad page 1118 (Spotlight Junction).

KARNACK — B9 *Harrison*

CADDO LAKE (State Pk) From Jct of SR-43 & FM-2198, E 0.4 mi on FM-2198 (L). CAUTION: Low Branches. 2015 rates: $10 to $20. (903)679-3351

KATY — D8 *Fort Bend*

KATY LAKE RV RESORT
Ratings: 10/10★/10 (RV Park) From I-10 & Fry Rd exit, Go N 2 1/2 mi N on Fry Rd to Morton Rd, Go W on Morton Rd 1/4 mi (R). **FAC:** Paved rds. 209 paved, patios, 64 pull-thrus (30 x 66), back-ins (30 x 45), 209 full hkups (30/50 amps), cable, WiFi, rentals, laundry, LP gas, controlled access. **REC:** heated pool, whirlpool, Katy Lake: fishing. Pet restrict(B/Q). Partial handicap access. Big rig sites, eco-friendly, 2015 rates: $49. Disc: AAA, military. No CC.
AAA Approved
(281)492-0044 Lat: 29.81000, Lon: -095.72043
20222 Morton Rd, Katy, TX 77449
info@katylakervresort.com
www.katylakervresort.com
See ad pages 1157, 1108.

Travel Services

CAMPING WORLD OF KATY/HOUSTON As the nation's largest retailer of RV supplies, accessories, services and new and used RVs, Camping World is committed to making your total RV experience better. RV Accessories: (866)337-4809. **SERVICES:** RV, RV appliance, MH mechanical, staffed RV wash, restrooms, RV Sales. RV

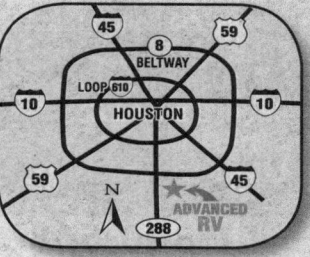

TX

KATY (CONT)

CAMPING WORLD OF (CONT)
supplies, emergency parking, RV accessible. waiting room. Hours: 8am to 6pm.
(888)730-2881 Lat: 29.776994, Lon: -95.854341
27905 A Katy Freeway, Katy, TX 77494
www.campingworld.com

Refer to the Table of Contents in front of the Guide to locate everything you need.

KEMAH — D9 *Galveston, Harris*

MARINA BAY RV RESORT **Ratings: 10/10★/9** (RV Park) 2015 rates: $58 to $89. (281)334-9944 925 Fm 2094, Kemah, TX 77565

Looking for a new or used RV? Camping World is America's largest retailer of RVs. Click CampingWorld.com or visit SuperCenters nationwide.

KERRVILLE — D6 *Kerr*

BUCKHORN LAKE RESORT
Ratings: 10/10★/10 (RV Park) Fron Jct of I-10 & Exit 501 (FM-1338/Goa Creek Rd) - on the NW corner of N ac cess rd & Goat Creek Rd, N 50 yds or Goat Creek Rd (L). **FAC:** Paved rds. 13 paved, patios, 41 pull-thrus (32 x 90), back-ins (32 x 65), 132 full hkups (30/50 amps), cable, WiFi rentals, laundry, groc, restaurant. **REC:** heated pool whirlpool, Goat Creek: fishing, playground. Pet re strict(Q). Partial handicap access, no tents. Big ri sites, eco-friendly, 2015 rates: $44 to $54. Disc: AAA military.
(830)895-0007 Lat: 30.11280, Lon: -99.20501
2885 Goat Creek Rd, Kerrville, TX 78028
info@buckhornlake.com
www.buckhornlake.com
See ad this page, 1108.

BY THE RIVER RV PARK & CAMPGROUND
Ratings: 8.5/8.5★/8 (Campground) From Jct of I-1 & Exit 505 (Harper Rd), S (right turn) 2.4 mi on Harpe Rd to Hwy 27, W (right turn) 3.7 mi to Riverview Rd S 0.5 mi (R). **FAC:** Paved rds. 59 grass, 11 pull-thru (24 x 60), back-ins (24 x 60), mostly side by side hkups, 59 full hkups (30/50 amps), WiFi, tent sites dump, laundry, firewood. **REC:** pool, Guadalupe Riv er: fishing. Pet restrict(B/Q). Eco-friendly, 2015 rates $30 to $40. Disc: AAA, military.
AAA Approved
(888)367-5566 Lat: 30.06917, Lon: -99.22465
175 Riverview Rd, Kerrville, TX 78028
info@bytheriver.com
www.bytheriver.com

GUADALUPE RIVER RV RESORT **Rat ings: 9.5/9★/9** (RV Park) 2015 rates: $39 to $49 (830)367-5676 2605 Junction Hwy, Kerrville, TX 78028

JOHNSON CREEK RV RESORT & PARK
Ratings: 10/10★/10 (RV Park) Fron Jct of Hwy 39 & Hwy 27, NW 4.9 mi o Hwy 27 (L); or From Jct of I-10 & Exit 48 (Hwy 27), E 9 mi on Hwy 27 (R). **FAC** Paved rds. 50 paved, patios, 23 pull thrus (30 x 80), back-ins (30 x 80), accepts full hku units only, 50 full hkups (30/50 amps), WiFi, rentals mobile sewer, laundry, LP gas. **REC:** pool, Johnso Creek: fishing, playground. Pet restrict(B/Q). Partia handicap access, no tents. Big rig sites, eco-friendly 2015 rates: $32 to $48. Disc: AAA, military.
AAA Approved
(830)367-3300 Lat: 30.11901, Lon: -99.29604
4279 Junction Hwy, Ingram, TX 78025
johnsoncreekrvresort@yahoo.com
www.johnsoncreekrvresortpark.com
See ad this page, 1108.

KERRVILLE KOA **Ratings: 8/8/8** (RV Park) 201 rates: $32.40. (830)895-1665 2400 Goat Creek Rd Kerrville, TX 78028

KERRVILLE (CONT)

KERRVILLE/SCHREINER (Public) From Jct of -10 & Hwy 16 (exit 508), S 0.4 mi on Hwy 16 to Loop 534, SE 4.2 mi to Hwy 173, S 0.2 mi (L). 2015 rates: $23 to $28. (830)257-7300

TAKE-IT-EASY RV RESORT
Ratings: 9.5/10★/8.5 (RV Park) From Jct of I-10 & FM-783 (exit 505), S 2.4 mi on FM-783/Harper Rd to Hwy 27, E 0.3 mi (R). **FAC:** Paved rds. (169 spaces). 81 Avail: 5 paved, 76 gravel, patios, 13 pull-thrus (24 x 60), back-ins (25 x 45), 81 full hkups (30/50 amps), seasonal sites, cable, WiFi, laundry. **REC:** heated pool, whirlpool, Guadalupe River: fishing, shuffleboard. Pet restrict(Q). Partial handicap access, no tents. Age restrict may apply, eco-friendly, 2015 rates: $38. No CC.
(800)828-6984 Lat: 30.05650, Lon: -99.15975
703 Junction Hwy, Kerrville, TX 78028
tie@ktc.com
www.takeiteasy.net
See ad opposite page, 1108.

TRIPLE T RV RESORT
Ratings: 9/10★/8.5 (RV Park) From Jct of I-10 & Exit 508 (Hwy 16/Sidney Baker St.), S 0.4 mi on Hwy 16 to Veterans Hwy, (Loop 534), SW 4.2 mi to Hwy 173 (Bandera Hwy), S 5.1 mi (R). **FAC:** Paved/gravel rds. 63 gravel, 34 pull-thrus (24 x 70), back-ins (24 x 60), 63 full hkups (30/50 amps), WiFi, rentals, dump, laundry, controlled access. **REC:** pool, whirlpool. Pet restrict(B/Q). No tents. Big rig sites, eco-friendly, 2015 rates: $35. Disc: AAA, military.
(830)634-3000 Lat: 29.94826, Lon: -99.10933
3900 Bandera Hwy, Kerrville, TX 78028
info@tripletrvresort.com
www.tripletrvresort.com
See ad opposite page.

Things to See and Do

KERRVILLE CONVENTION & VISITORS BUREAU Tourist information. Monday thru Friday 8:30am to 5pm. Saturday 9:00am to 3:00pm & Sunday 10:00am to 3:00pm. Hours: 8:30am to 5:00pm. No CC.
(830)792-3535 Lat: 30.06741, Lon: -99.11572
2108 Sidney Baker, Kerrville, TX 78028
kerrcvb@ktc.com
www.kerrvilletexascvb.com
See ad page 1106 (Welcome Section).

KILLEEN — C7 *Bell*

ELM GROVE MH COMMUNITY
Ratings: 7/NA/9 (RV Area in MHP) From jct US 190E and FM 3470/Stan Schlueter Loop: Go 1/4 mi N on FM 3470, then 1/2 mi W on MLK Blvd (FM 2410) (R). **FAC:** Paved rds. (203 spaces). Avail: 28 gravel, patios, 1 pull-thrus (30 x 80), back-ins (30 x 80), accepts self-contain units only, 28 full hkups (30/50 amps), seasonal sites, laundry. **REC:** pool, playground. Pet restrict(B/Q). Big rig sites, 2015 rates: $25.
(254)690-3838 Lat: 31.094304, Lon: -97.692694
1704 Mlk Jr Blvd, Killeen, TX 76543
elmgrove@towermgmt.com
www.elmgrovemhc.com

KINGSLAND — C6 *Burnet*

RIO VISTA RESORT Ratings: 8.5/8/7.5 (RV Park) From Jct FM 2342 & FM 1431: Go 3/4 mi W on FM 1431, then 3 blocks S on Reynolds St (R). **FAC:** Paved rds. (96 spaces). Avail: 76 grass, 2 pull-thrus (25 x 65), back-ins (25 x 60), 76 full hkups (30/50 amps), seasonal sites, cable, WiFi, rentals, laundry. **REC:** heated pool, whirlpool, Lake LBJ: swim, fishing, playground. Pet restrict(B). No tents. 2015 rates: $45 to $60. Disc: AAA, military.
AAA Approved
(325)388-6331 Lat: 30.65717, Lon: -98.43431
234 Rio Vista Dr, Kingsland, TX 78639
riovistaresort@RioVistaResort.com
www.riovistaresort.com

KINGSVILLE — K4 *Kleberg*

NATURE'S OWN RV RESORT
Ratings: 10/10★/9 (RV Park) From Jct of US-77 & FM-1356 (Gen Cavazos Rd), S 1.9 mi on US-77 (R). **FAC:** Paved rds. (105 spaces). Avail: 25 paved, 25 all weather, 50 pull-thrus (25 x 85), 50 full hkups (30/50 amps), seasonal sites, WiFi, laundry, controlled access. **REC:** pool. Pet restrict(B). Partial handicap access, no tents. Big rig sites, eco-friendly, 2015 rates: $40. No CC.
(361)221-2928 Lat: 27.46773, Lon: -97.85565
5151 S Hwy 77, Kingsville, TX 78363
naturesownrv@gmail.com
www.naturesownrvresort.com
See ad this page.

SEAWIND RV RESORT ON THE BAY
Ratings: 9/8.5★/9 (RV Park) From Jct of US-77 & E King Ave (Kingsville), go S 15 1/2 m on US-77, go E 9.8 mi on FM-628 (L). **FAC:** Paved rds. 184 paved, patios, 25 pull-thrus (35 x 70), back-ins (30 x 60), 159 full hkups, 25 W, 25 E (30/50 amps), WiFi, dump, laundry. **REC:** Baffin Bay: fishing, shuffleboard, playground. Pet restrict(B/Q). Partial handicap access. Big rig sites, eco-friendly, 2015 rates: $35.
(361)297-5738 Lat: 27.31681, Lon: -97.67923
1066 E Fm 628, Riviera, TX 78379
seawindrv@gmail.com
www.seawindrv.com
See primary listing at Riviera and ad page 1163.

KOPPERL — B7 *Bosque*

PLOWMAN CREEK (Public Corps) From town, S 1 mi on Hwy 56 (L). 2015 rates: $14 to $16. (254)694-3189

LA FERIA — M4 *Cameron*

KENWOOD RV RESORT
Ratings: 9.5/9★/7.5 (RV Park) From Jct of US-83 Expwy & La Feria/FM-506 exit, N 300 ft on FM-506 (L).

NESTLED IN THE RIO GRANDE VALLEY
This cozy RV resort offers amenities like an indoor pool and spa, fitness center and lots of activities for your enjoyment. Stay at a great location just minutes from shopping, golfing, historical sites and national parks.
FAC: Paved rds. (278 spaces). Avail: 178 grass, patios, back-ins (18 x 45), some side by side hkups, 178 full hkups (30/50 amps), seasonal sites, cable, WiFi $, rentals, laundry, controlled access. **REC:** heated pool, whirlpool, shuffleboard. Pet restrict(B). Partial handicap access, no tents. Age restrict may apply, eco-friendly, 2015 rates: $34. Disc: AAA, military.
AAA Approved
(888)904-3459 Lat: 26.16737, Lon: -97.82467
1201 North Main #1, La Feria, TX 78559
kenwood@suncommunities.com
www.kenwoodrv.com
See ad pages 1463 (Welcome Section), 1108 & RV Trips of a Lifetime, Snowbird Destinations in Magazine Section.

VIP-LA FERIA RV PARK
Ratings: 9.5/9.5★/8 (RV Park) From Jct of US-83 Expwy & La Feria/FM-506, exit to S frntg rd, E 0.4 mi (R). **FAC:** Paved rds. (360 spaces). 256 Avail: 4 paved, 252 grass, patios, 125 pull-thrus (30 x 60), back-ins (32 x 60), 256 full hkups (30/50 amps), seasonal sites, WiFi $, laundry, controlled access. **REC:** heated pool, whirlpool. Pet restrict(B/Q). Partial handicap access, no tents. Age restrict may apply, big rig sites, eco-friendly, 2015 rates: $32.
(956)797-1401 Lat: 26.16514, Lon: -97.81802
600 E Expressway 83, La Feria, TX 78559
info@viplaferia.com
www.viplaferia.com
See ad this page & Snowbird Destinations in Magazine Section.

LA GRANGE — D7 *Fayette*

COLORADO LANDING RV PARK
Ratings: 9.5/9.5★/10 (RV Park) From Jct of US-77 & Bus SR-71 (downtown La Grange), S 0.4 mi on US-77 to Cedar St, W 0.1 mi (E). **FAC:** Paved rds. 80 gravel, 18 pull-thrus (30 x 70), back-ins (40 x 90), 80 full hkups (30/50 amps), cable, WiFi, tent sites, laundry, LP gas. **REC:** pool, Colorado River: fishing. Pet restrict(B). Partial handicap access. Big rig sites, 2015 rates: $38. Disc: military.
(979)968-9465 Lat: 29.89613, Lon: -96.87387
64 East Bluffview, La Grange, TX 78945
coloradolanding@yahoo.com
www.coloradolanding.com
See ad pages 1164, 1108 & Snowbird Destinations in Magazine Section.

OAK THICKET PARK ON LAKE FAYETTE (Public) From Jct of Hwy 159 & FM-955 (in town), W 4.4 mi on Hwy 159 (L). 2015 rates: $15 to $20. (979)249-3504

LA MARQUE — D9 *Galveston*

OASIS RV PARK **Ratings: 8.5/8.5/7.5** (RV Park) 2015 rates: $40. (409)935-7101 1903 Gulf Fwy, La Marque, TX 77568

We shine "Spotlights" on interesting cities and areas.

TX

LAJITAS — D3 *Brewster*

MAVERICK RANCH RV PARK AT LAJITAS GOLF RESORT & SPA **Ratings: 9/10★/8** (RV Park) 2015 rates: $35 to $39. (432)424-5180 one Main Street, Lajitas, TX 79852

LAKEHILLS — D6 *Bandera*

LAKE MEDINA RV RESORT
Ratings: 9/9.5★/8.5 (RV Park) From jct PR 37 & Hwy 1283: Go 2 mi NW on Hwy 1283, then W at Lakewood Estates entrance and follow signs 2-1/2 miles. **FAC:** Paved rds. 95 gravel, 25 pull-thrus (30 x 72), back-ins (30 x 52), 93 full hkups, 2 W, 2 E (30/50 amps), cable, WiFi, rentals, dump, laundry, fire rings, firewood. **REC:** pool, whirlpool, Lake Medina: fishing, shuffleboard, playground. Pet restrict(B). Partial handicap access, no tents. Big rig sites, eco-friendly, 2015 rates: $29 to $35. Disc: AAA, military.
(888)722-2640 Lat: 29.62425, Lon: -98.96506
1218 Leibold's Point, Lakehills, TX 78063
resv@lmrvresort.com
www.lmrvresort.com
See ad page 1135.

MEDINA LAKE RV **Ratings: 9/8.5★/8** (Membership Pk) 2015 rates: $43.27. (800)405-6188 215 Spettle Rd., Lakehills, TX 78063

LAMESA — B4 *Dawson*

FORREST PARK (Public) At Jct of Hwy 137 & S 9th St (R) (Free camping limited to 4 days). 2015 rates: $0 to $20. (806)872-2124

LAMPASAS — C6 *Lampasas*

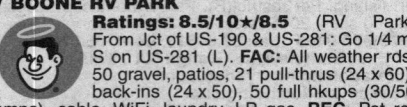

BOONE RV PARK
Ratings: 8.5/10★/8.5 (RV Park) From Jct of US-190 & US-281: Go 1/4 mi S on US-281 (L). **FAC:** All weather rds. 50 gravel, patios, 21 pull-thrus (24 x 60), back-ins (24 x 50), 50 full hkups (30/50 amps), cable, WiFi, laundry, LP gas. **REC.** Pet restrict(B/Q). Partial handicap access, no tents. Big rig sites, 2015 rates: $36.
(888)577-5171 Lat: 31.05115, Lon: -98.18093
1907 S Hwy 281, Lampasas, TX 76550
boonerv@sbcglobal.net
www.boonervpark.com
See ad this page, 1108.

LAREDO — K1 *Webb*

LAKE CASA BLANCA INTERNATIONAL (State Pk) At jct US 59 & Loop 20. Entrance fee required. 2015 rates: $18 to $21. (956)723-3826

LAVON — B7 *Collin*

LAVONIA PARK (Public Corps) From town, E 3 mi on Hwy 78 to CR-486 Lake Rd, W 0.5 mi, follow signs (E). 2015 rates: $30. Mar 31 to Oct 1. (972)442-3141

LEAGUE CITY — D8 *Galveston*

SAFARI MH COMMUNITY
Ratings: 7/6.5/7 (RV Area in MHP) From Jct of I-45 & Calder Dr (exit 22): Go W 0.1 mi to S Calder Dr, S 1.5 mi (R). **FAC:** Paved rds. (183 spaces). Avail: 50 gravel, patios, 11 pull-thrus (25 x 80), back-ins (25 x 45), 50 full hkups (30/50 amps), WiFi $, laundry. **REC:** pool. Pets OK. Partial handicap access, no tents. Eco-friendly, 2015 rates: $32. Disc: AAA, military.
(281)332-4131 Lat: 29.47160, Lon: -95.10545
2935 Calder Dr, League City, TX 77573
reservations@safarirvpark.com
www.safarirvpark.com
See ad page 1159.

SPACE CENTER RV PARK
Ratings: 10/9★/8 (RV Park) From Jct of I-45 & FM-518 (exit 23): Go S 0.2 mi on W Frontage Rd (R). Next to Cracker Barrel. **FAC:** Paved rds. 120 paved, 50 pull-thrus (20 x 60), back-ins (20 x 35), 120 full hkups (30/50 amps), cable, WiFi, laundry, groc. **REC:** pool, whirlpool, playground. Pet restrict(B/Q). Partial handicap access, no tents. RV age restrict, eco-friendly, 2015 rates: $39 to $41.
(888)846-3478 Lat: 29.50008, Lon: -95.11320
301 Gulf Fwy South, League City, TX 77573
scrvp@sbcglobal.net
www.spacecenterrvpark.com

LEANDER — C7 *Williamson*

LEANDER/NW AUSTIN KOA **Ratings: 9/9★/9** (RV Park) 2015 rates: $39 to $49. (512)259-7200 2689 Hero Way, Leander, TX 78641

LEGGETT — C9 *Polk*

EAGLES REST RV PARK **Ratings: 4.5/NA/7** (RV Park) 2015 rates: $25. (936)398-2631 522 E Fm 942, Livingston, TX 77351

LEWISVILLE — G3 *Denton*

LEWISVILLE LAKE PARK CAMPGROUND (Public) From Jct of I-35 E & Exit 454A (Highland Village): Go 1 mi E on Lake Park Rd (L). 2015 rates: $16 to $18. (972)219-3742

LIBERTY HILL — C7 *Williamson*

RIO BONITO RV & CABIN
Ratings: 10/10★/10 (RV Park) From Jct Hwy 29 & US 183: Go 3-3/4 mi N on US 183, then 1/4 mi E on FM 3405, then 1/2 mi S on CR 257, then 1/4 mi SE on CR 256 (R). **FAC:** All weather rds. (60 spaces). Avail: 10 all weather, 10 pull-thrus (30 x 60), 10 full hkups (30/50 amps), seasonal sites, cable, WiFi, rentals, laundry, LP gas, controlled access. **REC:** pool, North San Gabriel River: fishing, playground. Pet restrict(B/Q). No tents. Big rig sites, 2015 rates: $35. Disc: military.
(512)922-1383 Lat: 30.69919, Lon: -97.86611
1095 CR 256, Liberty Hill, TX 78642
ray@rbcabinresort.com
www.rbcabinresort.com
See ad page 1133.

Things change ... last year's rates serve as a guideline only.

LINDEN — A9 *Cass*

LINDEN CITY RV PARK (Public) From jct of FM125 and US59: Go 1/4 mi NE on US 59, then 1 Blk W on Center Hill Rd (L). 2015 rates: $20. (903)756-5591

LINN — L3 *Hidalgo*

LAZY PALMS RANCH RV PARK **Ratings: 8/5/7** (Membership Pk) 2015 rates: $21 to $23. (956)383-1020 35100 Lazy Palm Drive, Edinburg, TX 78541-9314

VALLEY GATEWAY RV PARK **Ratings: 5/6/5.5** (RV Park) 2015 rates: $22. (956)381-1883 34961 N Hwy 281, Edinburg, TX 78541

LITTLEFIELD — A4 *Lamb*

WAYLON JENNINGS RV PARK (Public) From Jct of US-84 & US-385, N 0.5 mi on US-385 (R). 2015 rates: $20. (806)385-5161

LIVINGSTON — C9 *Polk*

BUSTERTOWN RV PARK
Ratings: 6.5/NA/7.5 (RV Park) From Jct of US 59 & US 190, W 3.1 mi on US 190 (R). Note: Behind Buster McNutty's Restaurant. **FAC:** Gravel rds. 101 gravel, 98 pull-thrus (25 x 75), back-ins (25 x 65), 101 full hkups (30/50 amps), cable, WiFi, tent sites, laundry. **REC:** pond, fishing. Pets OK. Partial handicap access. 30 day max stay, 2015 rates: $40.
(936)967-0101 Lat: 30.73681, Lon: -94.99640
4700 Hwy 190 W, Livingston, TX 77351
bustertown@gmail.com

LAKE LIVINGSTON (State Pk) From Jct of US-59 & FM-1988 (exit 436A, exit S), W 3.7 mi on FM-1988 to FM-3126, N 0.4 mi (L) (Entrance fee). 2015 rates: $10 to $25. (936)365-2201

RAINBOW'S END RV PARK **Ratings: 8.5/8.5/8.5** (RV Park) 2015 rates: $27.50 to $28.50. (936)327-1279 140 Escapees Dr, Livingston, TX 77351

WOODSY HOLLOW CAMPGROUND & RV RESORT **Ratings: 8.5/8/8** (RV Park) 2015 rates: $30. (936)365-2267 248 Woodsy Hollow, Goodrich, TX 77335

LLANO — C6 *Llano*

LLANO RIVER GOLF & RV RESORT (Public) From Jct of Hwy 16/71 (Bessemer Ave) & TX 29, S 0.6 mi on Hwy 16/71 to Ranch Rd 152 (Main St), W 1.8 mi (R). 2015 rates: $27. (325)247-5100

ROBINSON CITY PARK (Public) From jct Hwy 16 & RR 152: Go 2 mi W on RR 152. 2015 rates: $20. (325)247-4158

LOCKHART — D7 *Caldwell*

LOCKHART (State Pk) From town, S 1 mi on US-183 to FM-20, SW 2 mi to Prk Rd 10, S 1 mi (L) (Entrance fee). 2015 rates: $18 to $21. (512)398-3479

LONE OAK — B8 *Hunt*

WIND POINT PARK (Public) From Jct of I-30 & Hwy 69, S 17 mi on Hwy 69 to FM-513, W 1 mi to FM-1571, W 2.7 mi, S 2.mi. 2015 rates: $25. (903)662-5134

Camping World offers new and used RV sales and so much more! Over 85 SuperCenters nationwide, a state-of-the-art call center and award-winning website. Find out more at CampingWorld.com

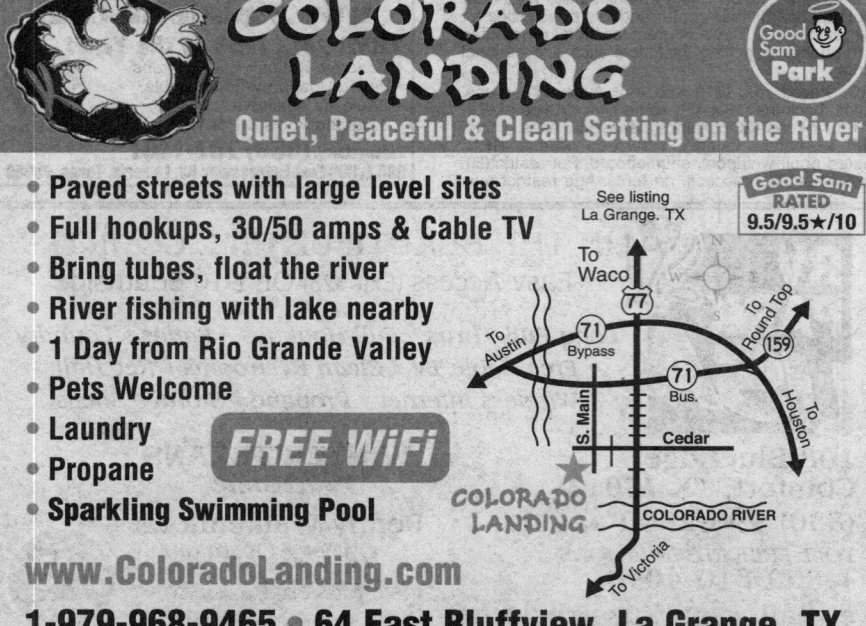

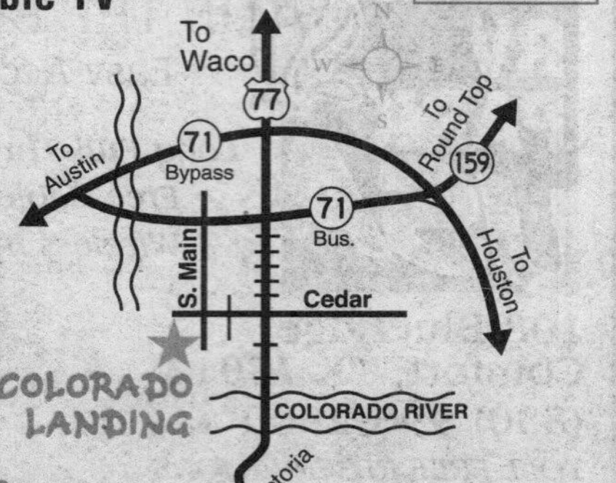

LONGVIEW — B9 *Gregg*

FERNBROOK PARK
Ratings: 10/10★/10 (RV Park) From Jct of I-20 (exit 591) & FM 2011: Go 2 mi SE on FM 2011. (L). **FAC:** Paved rds. (83 spaces). Avail: 43 paved, 32 pull-thrus (34 x 77), back-ins (34 x 65), 43 full hkups (30/50 amps), seasonal sites, cable, WiFi, dump, laundry, LP gas. **REC:** pool, playground. Pet restrict(B/Q). Partial handicap access, no tents. Big rig sites, 2015 rates: $35 to $40.
(903)643-8888 Lat: 32.41547, Lon: -94.76741
2073 Fm 2011, Longview, TX 75603
info@fernbrookpark.com
www.fernbrookpark.com
See ad this page, 1108.

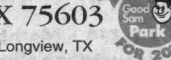

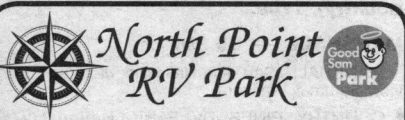

NORTH POINT RV PARK
Ratings: 7.5/10★/7 (RV Park) From jct Loop 281 & US 259: Go 5 mi N on US 259. (R). **FAC:** Gravel rds. 39 paved, 22 pull-thrus (24 x 55), back-ins (27 x 45), 39 full hkups (30/50 amps), cable, WiFi, laundry. **REC.** Pets OK. Partial handicap access. Big rig sites, 2015 rates: $35 to $50.
(903)663-6400 Lat: 32.6130236, Lon: -94.7544920
7552 U S Highway 259N, Longview, TX 75605
northpointrvpark@gmail.com
www.northpointrvpark.net
See ad this page.

WESTERN VILLA MH COMMUNITY Ratings: 5/NA/7.5 (RV Area in MHP) From jct I-20 & Hwy 42 (exit 587): Go 6 mi N on Hwy 42, then 3 1/4 mi E on US Hwy 80E, then 1 block N on West Loop 281 (R). **FAC:** Paved rds. (175 spaces). Avail: 18 gravel, back-ins (30 x 70), 18 full hkups (30/50 amps), seasonal sites. **REC:** playground. Pet restrict(B/Q). Big rig sites, 2015 rates: $35.
(903)753-7793 Lat: 32.48608, Lon: -94.76586
4522 W Loop 281 #56, Longview, TX 75604
Westernvilla@towermgmt.com
www.westernvillamhc.com

LUBBOCK — A4 *Lubbock*

LUBBOCK See also Slaton & Wolfforth.

BUFFALO SPRINGS LAKE (Public) From Jct of Loop 289 & E 50th St, E 4.5 mi on E 50th St, S .8 mi on CR 3100, High Meadow Rd. 2.8 mi around lake (R). 2015 rates: $15 to $35. (806)747-3353

CAMELOT VILLAGE RV PARK
Ratings: 8/9★/10 (RV Area in MHP) From Jct Loop 289W & W 34th St exit: Go 500 feet W on 34th St. (L). Elev 3240 ft. **FAC:** Paved rds. (193 spaces). Avail: 10 paved, patios, 10 pull-thrus (35 x 80), 10 full hkups (30/50 amps), seasonal sites, laundry. **REC:** pool. Pets OK. No tents. Big rig sites, 2015 rates: $27.50. Disc: military.
(806)792-6477 Lat: 33.56308, Lon: -101.94703
6001 34th St, Lubbock, TX 79407
camelot@evergreenmh.com
www.commanderspalacelubbock.com
See ad this page, 1108.

LOOP 289 RV PARK **Ratings: 8.5/10★/9** (RV Park) 2015 rates: $30. (806)792-4348 3436 W Loop 289, Lubbock, TX 79407

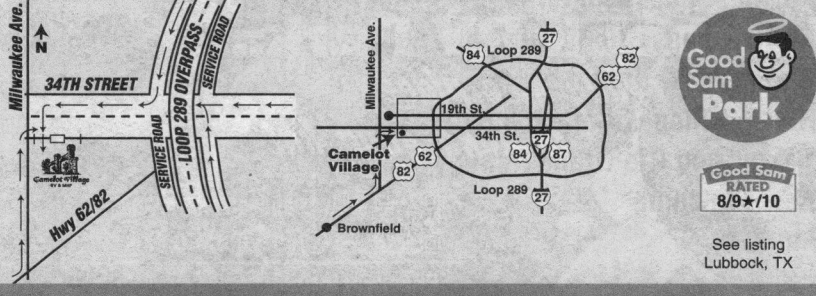

TX

LUBBOCK (CONT)

LUBBOCK KOA **Ratings: 8.5/9★/9** (Campground) 2015 rates: $29.95to $37.95. (806)762-8653 5502 CR-6300, Lubbock, TX 79416

LUBBOCK RV PARK, INC
Ratings: 9/9★/8 (RV Park) From Jct I-27 & Exit 9: Go 1/2 mi S on W Service Rd (R). Elev 3240 ft. **FAC:** Paved/gravel rds. (89 spaces). Avail: 39 paved, patios, 39 pull-thrus (25 x 70), 39 full hkups (30/50 amps), seasonal sites, WiFi, tent sites, laundry, LP gas. **REC:** heated pool, playground. Pet restrict(Q). Partial handicap access. Big rig sites, 2015 rates: $30. Disc: AAA, military.
AAA Approved
(806)747-2366 Lat: 33.64890, Lon: -101.83646
4811 N I-27, Lubbock, TX 79403
mail@lubbockrv.com
www.lubbockrvpark.com
See ad this page, 1108.

Travel Services

CAMPING WORLD OF LUBBOCK As the nation's largest retailer of RV supplies, accessories, services and new and used RVs, Camping World is committed to making your total RV experience better. RV Accessories: (855)830-0155. **SERVICES:** RV, tire, RV appliance, RV Sales. RV supplies, LP. Hours: 8am to 6pm. No CC. (888)688-5833 Lat: 33.528257, Lon: -101.855962 1701 S. Loop 289, Lubbock, TX 79423 www.campingworld.com

RV Park ratings you can rely on!

LUFKIN — C9 *Angelina*

LUFKIN KOA **Ratings: 9.5/8.5/7.5** (RV Park) 2015 rates: $42. (936)238-3721 250 Fm 2021, Lufkin, TX 75901

LULING — D7 *Caldwell, Guadalupe*

RIVERBEND RV PARK **Ratings: 7.5/7/7.5** (RV Park) 2015 rates: $30 to $35. (830)875-9548 1881 S. State Hwy 80, Luling, TX 78648

LUMBERTON — C9 *Hardin*

VILLAGE CREEK (State Pk) From US 96 (Dana St exit): Go 1/2 mi E on Dana St, then 1/2 block S on Village Creek Pkwy, then 1/2 mi E on Alma Dr. (Entrance fee). 2015 rates: $15. (409)755-7322

MAGNOLIA — C8 *Montgomery*

MAGNOLIA FOREST RV PARK **Ratings: 6.5/NA/9** (RV Park) 2015 rates: $45. (281)259-9700 30427 Nichols Sawmill, Magnolia, TX 77355

TIMBER RIDGE RV VILLAGE
Ratings: 7/10★/9 (RV Park) From Jct I-45 (Exit 76B) & Woodlands Pkwy: Go 10 mi W on Woodlands Pkwy then 2 mi S on Fm 2978 (R). **FAC:** Gravel rds. (43 spaces). Avail: 10 gravel, patios, back-ins (30 x 65), 10 full hkups (30/50 amps), seasonal sites, cable, WiFi, laundry. **REC:** pond, fishing. Pet restrict(B/Q). Big rig sites, 2015 rates: $33. Disc: military.
(281)356-1928 Lat: 30.16702, Lon: -95.59994
28323 Fm 2978, Magnolia, TX 77354
Timberridgervvillage@yahoo.com
www.timberridgervvillage.com
See ad page 1158.

MANSFIELD — j3 *Johnson*

DODGE CITY RV PARK **Ratings: 7.5/9★/8** (RV Park) 2015 rates: $27 to $33. (817)477-4433 412 CR 616, Alvarado, TX 76009

TEXAN RV RANCH
Ratings: 9/10★/9 (RV Park) From Jct of I-20 & US-287: Go 10 1/2 mi S on US-287, then 1/4 mi SW on Lone Star Rd (FM 157) (R). **FAC:** Gravel rds. (145 spaces). Avail: 51 gravel, 18 pull-thrus (27 x 70), back-ins (25 x 65), some side by side hkups, 51 full hkups (30/50 amps), seasonal sites, cable, WiFi, rentals, dump, laundry, groc, LP gas. **REC:** pool, playground. Pet restrict(B/Q). Partial handicap access, no tents. Big rig sites, 2015 rates: $40. Disc: AAA, military.
(817)473-1666 Lat: 32.53450, Lon: -97.10996
1961 Lone Star Rd, Mansfield, TX 76063
info@texanrvranch.com
www.texanrvranch.com
See ad pages 1115 (Spotlight Dallas/Fort Worth), 1108.

MARATHON — C3 *Brewster*

MARATHON MOTEL & RV PARK **Ratings: 5/7/7** (RV Park) 2015 rates: $25. (866)386-4241 703 West Hwy 90, Marathon, TX 79842

MARBLE FALLS — C6 *Burnet*

MARBLE FALLS See also Austin, Burnet & Johnson City.

SUNSET POINT ON LAKE LBJ
Ratings: 9.5/10★/10 (RV Park) From Jct of US 281 & FM 1431 (in Marble Falls): Go 3 1/4 mi W on FM 1431, then 2 1/4 mi S on Wirtz Dam Rd (R). **FAC:** Paved rds. 60 paved, patios, 26 pull-thrus (30 x 70), back-ins (32 x 70), 60 full hkups (30/50 amps), cable, WiFi, rentals, laundry, controlled access. **REC:** Lake LBJ: swim, fishing, marina. Pet restrict(B/Q). Partial handicap access, no tents. Big rig sites, eco-friendly, 2015 rates: $48 to $90. Disc: military.
(830)798-8199 Lat: 30.56545, Lon: -98.34361
2322 N Wirtz Dam Rd, Marble Falls, TX 78654
info@sunsetpointlbj.com
www.sunsetpointlbj.com
See ad pages 1124 (Spotlight Texas Hill Country), 1108.

MARSHALL — B9 *Harrison*

MARSHALL See also Hallsville, Jefferson, Longview, Tatum & Waskom.

COUNTRY PINES RV PARK **Ratings: 6/7/6.5** (RV Park) 2015 rates: $28 to $30. (903)935-4278 5935 Hwy 59N, Marshall, TX 75670

MASON — C6 *Mason*

FORT MASON CITY RV PARK (Public) From Jct of US 87 & SR 29, S 1.2 mi on US 87 (L). 2015 rates: $20. (325)347-6449

MATAGORDA — D8 *Matagorda*

MATAGORDA BAY NATURE PARK (Public) In Matagorda From Jct of Hwy 60 & FM 2031, S 6.4 mi on FM 2031 (R). 2015 rates: $25 to $35. (800)776-5272

MATHIS — E7 *Live Oak*

ADVENTURE TEXAS RV RESORT
Ratings: 8.5/8.5/8 (RV Park) From Jct of I-37 & exit 34, NW on E side frontage rd (R). **FAC:** Gravel rds. 72 gravel, 53 pull-thrus (35 x 70), back-ins (30 x 50), 72 full hkups (30/50 amps), cable, WiFi, laundry, LP gas. **REC:** pool. Pets OK. No tents. Big rig sites, 2015 rates: $35.
(361)547-5600 Lat: 28.09239, Lon: -97.80880
10754 North I-37, Exit 34, Mathis, TX 78368
trvresorts@trvresorts.com
www.trvresorts.com

MATHIS (CONT)

LAKE CORPUS CHRISTI (State Pk) From Jct of I-37 & SR-359 (exit 36), SW 5.8 mi on SR-359 to Park Rd 25, NW 1.4 mi (L) (Entrance fee). 2015 rates: $10 to $20. (361)547-2635

MUSTANG HOLLOW CAMPGROUND
Ratings: 8.5/8.5/8.5 (Campground) N-bnd: From Jct of I-37 & FM-888 (exit 40), W 0.25 mi on FM-888 to FM-3024, N 4 mi (L); or S-bnd: From Jct of I-37 & FM-3024 (exit 47), S 4 mi on FM-3024 (R). **FAC:** Gravel/dirt rds. 135 dirt, 123 pull-thrus (30 x 70), back-ins (30 x 50), 131 full hkups (30/50 amps), WiFi, tent sites, rentals, dump, laundry, groc, LP gas, fire rings, firewood. **REC:** pool, Lake Corpus Christi: fishing, shuffleboard, playground. Pet restrict(B) $. Partial handicap access. Big rig sites, eco-friendly, 2015 rates: $35 to $37.
(361)547-5201 Lat: 28.20743, Lon: -97.90310
101 C.r. 371, Mathis, TX 78368
mustanghollowcampground@gmail.com
www.mustanghollowcampground.com
See ad opposite page, 1108 & Snowbird Destinations in Magazine Section.

SUNRISE BEACH (Public) From jct I-37 & Hwy 359: Go 5-1/2 mi SW on Hwy 359, then 1-1/2 mi W on Park Rd 25, then 1 block S on FM 1068. (Entrance fee). 2015 rates: $16 to $20. (361)547-3004

WILDERNESS LAKES RV RESORT **Ratings: 6/9.5★/8** (RV Resort) 2015 rates: $30 to $32. (361)547-9995 22552 Park Rd 25, Mathis, TX 78368

MAUD — A9 *Bowie*

BIG CREEK LANDING (Public) From town, S 1 mi on FM-2624, E 5.5 mi to CR-1207, N 2 mi, follow signs (E). Pit toilets. 2015 rates: $13. (903)585-5453

KELLY CREEK LANDING (Public) From Jct of Hwy 67 & Hwy 8, S 0.5 mi on Hwy 8 to FM-2624, E 5.5 mi to unmarked paved rd, S 2 mi, follow signs (E). 2015 rates: $13. (903)585-5453

MCALLEN — M3 *Hidalgo*

CITRUS VALLEY RV PARK & MHP
Ratings: 8/7.5/7.5 (RV Park) From Jct of US 281 & Monte Cristo Rd, W 6.1 mi on Monte Cristo Rd to Ware Rd (FM 1925), S 2 mi to US 107, E 0.4 mi (R). **FAC:** Paved rds. (250 spaces). Avail: 50 grass, patios, back-ins (21 x 50), 50 full hkups (50 amps), seasonal sites, WiFi, laundry. **REC:** heated pool, whirlpool, shuffleboard. Pets OK. Partial handicap access, no tents. Age restrict may apply, 2015 rates: $36. No CC.
(956)383-8189 Lat: 26.31095, Lon: -98.23727
2901 State Hwy 107 West, Mcallen, TX 78504
citrusvalleyrvpark@yahoo.com
www.citrusvalleyrvpark.com
See ad this page.

MCALLEN MOBILE PARK
Ratings: 9/9★/8.5 (RV Area in MHP) From Jct of US-281 & Nolana Loop (Hwy 3461) exit, W 1.5 mi on Nolana Loop/Hwy 3461 to FM-2061/McColl Rd, N 0.5 mi (R). **FAC:** Paved rds. (465 spaces). 243 Avail: 111 paved, 132 grass, patios, 50 pull-thrus (25 x 45), back-ins (20 x 45), some side by side hkups, 243 full hkups (30/50 amps), seasonal sites, WiFi, rentals, laundry. **REC:** heated pool, whirlpool, shuffleboard. Pet restrict(Q). Partial handicap access, no tents. Eco-friendly, 2015 rates: $32 to $34. No CC.
(956)682-3304 Lat: 26.24497, Lon: -98.20538
4900 N Mccoll, Mcallen, TX 78504
mcallenmobile@aol.com
www.mcallenmobilepark.com
See ad opposite page.

SUNLIGHT TRAILER PARK **Ratings: 8/7.5/5.5** (RV Park) 2015 rates: $35. (956)682-7721 4821 W Business 83, Mc Allen, TX 78501

MEDINA — D6 *Bandera*

HILL COUNTRY RESORT AND EVENT CENTER **Ratings: 8.5/8.5★/8** (RV Park) 2015 rates: $37. (830)589-7475 17740 State Hwy 16 N, Medina, TX 78055

MEDINA HIGHPOINT RESORT
Ratings: 9.5/9.5★/9 (Campground) From Kerrville, S 16 mi on Hwy 173 to Hwy 2828, W 7 mi to Hwy 16, NW 11.3 mi (L).

IN THE HEART OF TEXAS HILL COUNTRY
The 95 acre resort sits at one of the highest points in the Texas Hill County providing guests with spectacular views. Now offering a new section known as The View features 11 new cabins with expansive views of the canyon.

FAC: Paved rds. 46 paved, patios, 20 pull-thrus (36 x 90), back-ins (43 x 60), 46 full hkups (30/50 amps), WiFi, tent sites, rentals, laundry, fire rings, restaurant. **REC:** pool, whirlpool, pond, fishing, playground. Pet restrict(B/Q). Partial handicap access. Big rig sites, 2015 rates: $44.99 to $49.99. Disc: military.
(800)225-0991 Lat: 29.90092, Lon: -99.25939
23195 Hwy 16 N, Medina, TX 78055
medinahighpoint@rvcoutdoors.com
http://rvcoutdoors.com/medina-highpoint-resort/
See ad pages 1175, 1108 & Family Camping, Snowbird Destinations in Magazine Section.

MERCEDES — M4 *Hidalgo*

LLANO GRANDE LAKE PARK RESORT & COUNTRY CLUB MHP **Ratings: 10/10★/10** (RV Area in MHP) 2015 rates: $33 to $55. (956)565-2638 2215 East West Blvd, Mercedes, TX 78570

PARADISE SOUTH RV RESORT **Ratings: 9/8.5/9** (RV Park) 2015 rates: $35. (800)405-6188 9099 N. Mile 2 West Road, Mercedes, TX 78570

MERIDIAN — B7 *Bosque*

MERIDIAN (State Pk) From Jct of SH-6 & Hwy 22, SW 2.4 mi on Hwy 22 (R) Note: Water & Elec. sites max. of 20 ft length.(Entrance fee). 2015 rates: $15 to $25. (254)435-2536

Like Us on Facebook.

MEXIA — B8 *Limestone*

FORT PARKER (State Pk) From Jct of SR-14 & US-84, S 6.5 mi on SR-14 to Park Rd 28 (R) (Entrance fee). 2015 rates: $12 to $20. (254)562-5751

MIDLAND — B4 *Midland*

MIDESSA OIL PATCH RV PARK
Ratings: 9.5/9.5★/8 (RV Park) From Jct Hwy 1788 & I-20 (Exit 126): Go 1 mi W on N Frontage Rd, then 1/4 mi N on CR-1290 (L). Elev 2890 ft.

YOUR EL PASO-DALLAS CONNECTION
We'll escort you to your site where service & amenities await. Enjoy our pool, pet park, & trees or tour area museums! We are the home of Presidents & Petroleum. Convenience and comfort plus a great gift store for you

FAC: Paved rds. (130 spaces). Avail: 50 gravel, patios, 50 pull-thrus (25 x 60), 50 full hkups (30/50 amps), seasonal sites, WiFi, tent sites, rentals, dump, laundry, groc, LP gas. **REC:** pool, shuffleboard, playground. Pet restrict(B/Q). Partial handicap access. Big rig sites, 2015 rates: $35. Disc: AAA.
(800)864-3204 Lat: 31.90730, Lon: -102.23057
4220 S County Rd 1290, Odessa, TX 79765
camping@midessaoilpatchrvpark.com
www.midessaoilpatchrvpark.com
See ad this page, 1108.

MIDLAND RV CAMPGROUND
Ratings: 7.5/8.5★/7 (RV Park) From Dallas (W on I-20): take exit 134. At ramp end (stop sign), continue W on the service road for 1 Mi. RT on Midland Dr. From El Paso (E on I-20): take exit 131. At ramp end, turn left at stop sign.Turn RT on the N Svc Rd. Go East 1 Mi. Turn Lt on Midland Dr. **FAC:** Gravel rds. (200 spaces). Avail: 21 gravel, 21 pull-thrus (25 x 50), 21 full hkups (30/50 amps), seasonal sites, cable, WiFi, showers $, dump, laundry, LP gas, controlled access. **REC:** playground. Pet restrict(B/Q). No tents. Big rig sites, 2015 rates: $35. Disc: military.
(432)697-0801 Lat: 31.96159, Lon: -102.12456
2134 South Midland dr, Midland, TX 79703
midlandrvpark@yahoo.com
www.midlandrvcampground.com
See ad this page.

Things to See and Do

MIDESSA OIL PATCH GIFT SHOP Welcome to Midessa Oil Patch RV Park in Odessa, Texas. Located in the Permian Basin of West Texas, the unmatched beauty of the region offers stunning sunsets and a warm and inviting climate. Hours: 9 to 6.
(432)563-2368 Lat: 31.90737, Lon: -102.23057
4220 S County Rd 1290, Odessa, TX 79765
camping@midessaoilpatchrvpark.com
www.midessaoilpatchrvpark.com
See ad this page.

MILAM — C9 *Sabine*

SABINE/RED HILLS LAKE REC. AREA (Natl Forest) From jct Hwy 21 & Hwy 87: Go 2-1/2 mi N on Hwy 87, then 1/4 mi E on FR 116. Pit toilets. 2015 rates: $6 to $10. May 1 to Sep 3. (409)625-1940

MINERAL WELLS — B6 *Palo Pinto, Parker*

LAKE MINERAL WELLS (State Pk) E-bnd: From Jct of US-281 & US-180, E 3.9 mi on US-180 (L); or W-bnd: From Jct of I-20 & Exit 406 (S Bowie Dr), N 2.1 mi on Bowie Dr to Hwy 180, W 14 mi (R) (Entrance fee). 2015 rates: $14 to $26. (940)328-1171

MINGUS — B6 *Palo Pinto*

CACTUS ROSE RV PARK
Ratings: 8.5/9★/8.5 (RV Park) From Jct of I-20 & Exit 370: Go 500 feet W on S Frontage Rd. (L). **FAC:** All weather rds. (17 spaces). Avail: 14 gravel, 11 pull-thrus (30 x 50), back-ins (30 x 50), 11 full hkups, 1 E (30/50 amps), seasonal sites, WiFi, dump, laundry. **REC:** pool. Pet restrict(B/Q). No tents. 7 day max stay. 2015 rates: $32 to $40. Disc: AAA, military.
(254)693-5976 Lat: 32.51307, Lon: -98.36965
115 W I-20, Mingus, TX 76463
cactusroserv@gmail.com
www.cactusroserv.com
See ad this page, 1108.

MISSION — M3 *Hidalgo*

AMERICANA RV RESORT MHP **Ratings: 9/8★/7.5** (RV Park) 2015 rates: $37. (956)581-1705 721 N Bentsen Palm Drive, Mission, TX 78572

BENTSEN GROVE RESORT MHP
Ratings: 9.5/9.5★/9 (RV Park) W-bnd: From Jct of US-83 (Expwy) & Hwy 364/La Homa Rd/Bentsen Palm Dr exit, W 1.5 mi on N Frntg Rd to Bentsen Palm Dr (second light), S 0.9 mi on Bentsen Palm Dr (L); E-bnd: From Jct of US Expwy 83 & Bentsen Palm Dr, S 0.9 mi on Bentsen Palm Dr (L).

SOAK UP SOME SUN THIS WINTER
Bentsen Grove Resort has the best of what South Texas has to offer. Warm sun, plus enough activities to keep you busy during the day so you'll sleep like baby all night. Great location, great facilities. Call today.

FAC: Paved rds. (831 spaces). Avail: 300 paved, patios, back-ins (30 x 60), accepts full hkup units only, 300 full hkups (30/50 amps), seasonal sites, cable, WiFi, rentals, laundry, controlled access. **REC:** heated pool, whirlpool, shuffleboard. Pets OK. Partial handicap access, no tents. Age restrict may apply, big rig sites, eco-friendly, 2015 rates: $36 to $39. No CC.
(956)585-7011 Lat: 26.21898, Lon: -98.37234
810 Bentsen Palm Drive, Mission, TX 78572
office@bentsengroveresort.com
www.bentsengroveresort.com
See ad opposite page, 1108 & Snowbird Destinations in Magazine Section.

BENTSEN PALM VILLAGE RV RESORT
Ratings: 10/10★/10 (RV Resort) From Jct of US-83 Expwy & Conway, go S 4 mi on Conway,to Military, go W 3 mi on Military to Bentsen Palm Dr, go S 1/4mi on Bentsen Palm Dr (L). **FAC:** Paved rds. 245 paved, patios, 90 pull-thrus (41 x 80), back-ins (30 x 65), 245 full hkups (30/50 amps), cable, WiFi, rentals, laundry, controlled access. **REC:** heated pool, whirlpool, Rio Grande River. Pet restrict(Q). Partial handicap access, no tents. Big rig sites, eco-friendly, 2015 rates: $45 to $62. Disc: AAA.
(877)247-3727 Lat: 26.18841, Lon: -98.37857
2500 S Bentsen Palm Drive, Mission, TX 78572
info@bentsenpalmvillage.com
www.bentsenpalmvillage.com
See ad this page, 1108 & Snowbird Destinations in Magazine Section.

CANYON LAKE RV RESORT OF MISSION **Ratings: 9/8.5/9** (RV Park) 2015 rates: $37. (877)550-7961 4770 N. Mayberry Rd., Mission, TX 78573

CHIMNEY PARK RV RESORT **Ratings: 8.5/8.5★/8** (RV Park) 2015 rates: $40 to $50. (956)585-5061 4224 S Conway, Mission, TX 78572

CIRCLE T RV PARK MHP
Ratings: 8/8.5★/6.5 (RV Park) From Jct of US-83 Expwy & Inspiration Rd exit, W 50 yds on N frntg rd to Jay Ave, N 50 yds (R). **FAC:** Paved rds. (270 spaces). 60 Avail: 18 gravel, 42 grass, patios, 18 pull-thrus (21 x 62), back-ins (24 x 40), some side by side hkups, 60 full hkups (30/50 amps), seasonal sites, WiFi $, rentals, laundry. **REC:** heated pool, whirlpool, shuffleboard. Pet restrict(B/Q). Partial handicap access, no tents. Age restrict may apply, big rig sites, eco-friendly, 2015 rates: $40.
(866)428-5500 Lat: 26.21876, Lon: -98.34855
1820 Clay Tolle, Mission, TX 78572
circletrvpark@rgv.rr.com
http://www.circletrvpark.net/
See ad page 1123 (Spotlight South Texas Tropics).

EL VALLE DEL SOL RESORT MHP **Ratings: 8.5/8/7** (RV Park) 2015 rates: $35. (956)585-5704 2500 E Bus 83, Mission, TX 78572

ELDORADO ACRES RV PARK **Ratings: 9.5/9★/7.5** (RV Park) 2015 rates: $35. (956)581-6718 610 N Fm 492, Mission, TX 78574

J FIVE RV & MOBILEHOME PARK **Ratings: 7.5/8★/7.5** (RV Park) 2015 rates: $30. (956)682-7495 3907 N Taylor Road, Mission, TX 78573

LEMON TREE RV INN **Ratings: 8/UI/7** (RV Park) 2015 rates: $35. (956)585-6861 1740 E Bus Hwy 83 C-1, Mission, TX 78572

MISSION BELL TRADEWINDS RV RESORT & MHP **Ratings: 8.5/9/7.5** (RV Park) 2015 rates: $35 to $45. (956)585-4833 1711 E Bus Highway 83, Mission, TX 78572

MISSION GARDEN RESORT & RV PARK **Ratings: 8.5/9★/8** (RV Park) 2015 rates: $39. (956)585-5671 930 W Expressway 83, Mission, TX 78572

MISSION WEST RV PARK **Ratings: 9/8★/7.5** (RV Park) 2015 rates: $40. (956)585-5551 511 E Loop 374, Palmview, TX 78572

OLEANDER ACRES MH & RV PARK **Ratings: 7/8.5★/6.5** (RV Park) 2015 rates: $30 to $40. (956)585-9093 2421 S Conway, Mission, TX 78572

SEVEN OAKS RESORT **Ratings: 9/8.5★/8.5** (RV Park) 2015 rates: $40 to $50. (956)581-0068 801 S Inspiration Rd #222, Mission, TX 78572

SHARYLAND VILLAS RV AND MHP **Ratings: 8/7.5★/7.5** (RV Park) 2015 rates: $28 (956)585-0966 417 N Shary Road, Mission, TX 78573

SLEEPY VALLEY RESORT **Ratings: 8/8/7.5** (RV Park) 2015 rates: $36. (956)581-1871 2301 N Abram Rd, Mission, TX 78572

SPLIT RAIL RV PARK **Ratings: 9/10★/9** (RV Park) 2015 rates: $38. (956)585-8135 513 N Los Ebanos, Mission, TX 78572

Things to See and Do

RETAMA VILLAGE Master planned South Texas gated 55+ community with uniquely designed RV Supersites and Coach Houses. A seperate area features Casita Coach Port Homes. Own in a community where people and nature grow together. Partial handicap access.
(956)381-1500 Lat: 26.19010, Lon: -98.37841
2209 Seagull Ln, Mission, TX 78572
Patti@mlrhodes.com
www.bentsenpalm.com
See ad this page.

WORLD BIRDING CENTER BENTSEN RIO GRANDE VALLEY HDQTRS. The World Birding Center is a network of nine unique and enchanting birding sites set along a 120 mile historic river road from Roma to South Padre Island Texas. Walk from Bentsen Palm Village RV Resort to the Center Headquarters. Hours: 7 AM to 10 PM during peak season. Adult fee: $5.00. No CC.
(956)585-1107 Lat: 26.18632, Lon: -98.37645
2800 S Bentsen Palm Dr, Mission, TX 78572
http://www.theworldbirdingcenter.com
See ad this page.

MONAHANS — C3 *Ward*

MONAHANS SANDHILLS (State Pk) From town E 6 mi on I-H 20 to Park Rd 41 (exit 86), N 0.25 mi (E) (Entrance fee). 2015 rates: $14. (432)943-209

MONTGOMERY — C8 *Montgomery*

LAKE CONROE/HOUSTON NORTH KOA **Ratings: 9.5/9.5★/8.5** (RV Park) 2015 rates: $42 to $57 (800)562-9750 19785 Hwy 105W, Montgomery, TX 77356

MOODY — C7 *McLennan*

MOTHER NEFF (State Pk) From jct Hwy 317 & FM 107: Go 6-1/2 mi W on FM 107, then 1-3/4 mi S on Hwy 236, then W on Park Rd 14. Entrance fee required. 2015 rates: $12 to $18. (254)853-2389

MOUNT PLEASANT — A8 *Titus*

LAKE BOB SANDLIN (State Pk) From Jct of US-271 & FM-127 (W of town), SW 10.5 mi on FM-127 to FM-21, S 1.1 mi (L); or N-bnd: From Jct of US-271 & SR-11, W 5.2 mi on SR-11 to FM-21, NW 4.8 mi (R) (Entrance fee). 2015 rates: $18. (903)572-5531

MOUNT PLEASANT KOA **Ratings: 9/9.5★/7** (RV Park) 2015 rates: $31.22 to $42.33. (903)572-500 2322 Greenhill Rd, Mount Pleasant, TX 75455

Take an RV Trip of a Lifetime! Check out trip ideas at the front of the Guide - you'll find something for the history buff, the food lover or even your wild side!

TX

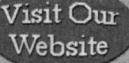

MOUNT VERNON — A8 *Franklin*

STILL MEADOW RV PARK
Ratings: 6.5/10★/9 (RV Park) From junction I-30 (West bound Exit 147, East bound exit 146) and FM 115: Go 1-1/2 mi S on FM 115, then 1/2 mi W on CR 3070 (R). **FAC:** Gravel rds. 30 Avail: 3 paved, 27 gravel, 17 pull-thrus (35 x 90), back-ins (35 x 60), 30 full hkups (30/50 amps), WiFi, laundry. **REC:** pond, fishing. Pets OK. No tents. Big rig sites, 2015 rates: $30 to $34.
(903)588-2230 Lat: 33.14008, Lon: -95.23266
571 County Road SE 3070, Mount Vernon, TX 75457
wafford@mt-vernon.com
www.stillmeadowrvpark.com
See ad this page, 1108.

WALLEYE PARK AT LAKE CYPRESS SPRINGS (Public) From Jct of I-30 & Exit 146/Hwy 37, S 0.9 mi to FM 21, E 1.5 mi to FM 2723, S 2.8 mi to FM 3122, E 1.5 mi to SE 4220, S 0.9 mi on SE 4220 (L) (Entrance fee). 2015 rates: $25. (903)537-4536

NACOGDOCHES — B9 *Nacogdoches*

CAMP TONKAWA SPRINGS RV PARK **Ratings: 7.5/8.5★/7.5** (Campground) 2015 rates: $27. (936)564-8888 4675 CR 153, Garrison, TX 75946

FAIRWAY RV PARK **Ratings: 7/NA/8.5** (RV Park) 2015 rates: $28. (936)462-9900 5393 US Hwy 59 South, Nacogdoches, TX 75964

FOREST COUNTRY RV PARK **Ratings: 7/NA/7** (Campground) 2015 rates: $30. (936)559-1645 5001 NW Stallings Dr, Nacogdoches, TX 75964

NAVASOTA — C8 *Brazos, Grimes*

CITY OF NAVASOTA RV PARK (Public) From west edge of town: Go 1 mi W on Hwy 105 (follow signs). 2015 rates: $10. (936)825-2241

NEW BRAUNFELS — D6 *Comal*

CANYON PARK (Public Corps) From Jct. of I-35 & SH-46, NW 2.7 mi on SH-46, NE 1.7 mi on Gruene Rd., NW 17 mi on Hwy 306, SE on Canyon Park Rd. Pit toilets. 2015 rates: $8 to $12. Apr 1 to Sep 30. (830)964-3341

CRANES MILL (Public Corps) From Jct of I-35 & Hwy 306, W 14 mi on Hwy 306 to FM-2673, S (following Guadalupe River crossing) to park entrance (E). 2015 rates: $26. (830)964-3341

HILL COUNTRY COTTAGE AND RV RESORT
Ratings: 9.5/9★/9 (RV Resort) From Jct of I-35 & Ruekle Rd (exit 184): Go E 0.1 mi on Ruekle Rd (L).

COTTAGE & RV HAVEN NEAR SAN ANTONIO
The perfect SNOWBIRD getaway for your Hill Country visit. Enjoy our many amenities and nearby attractions from your RV SITE or perfectly appointed CUSTOM COTTAGE furnished and ready for you. Reserve your vacation today.

FAC: Paved rds. (250 spaces). Avail: 100 gravel, patios, 60 pull-thrus (30 x 80), back-ins (30 x 46), 100 full hkups (30/50 amps), seasonal sites, cable, WiFi, rentals, laundry, groc, LP gas. **REC:** heated pool, whirlpool, shuffleboard, playground. Pet restrict(B/Q). Partial handicap access, no tents. Big rig sites, 2015 rates: $49 to $85. Disc: AAA, military. ATM.
(830)625-1919 Lat: 29.67225, Lon: -98.15284
131 Rueckle Rd, New Braunfels, TX 78130
Reservations@resortnb.com
www.hillcountryrvresortnb.com
See ad this page, 1108 & Snowbird Destinations in Magazine Section.

NORTH PARK (Public Corps) From Jct of I-35, NW 2.7 mi on SH-46, NE 1.7 mi on Gruene Rd., NW 16.7 mi on Hwy 306, S 1.2 mi on N Park Rd. Pit toilets. 2015 rates: $8 to $12. Apr 1 to Sep 30. (830)964-3341

POTTERS CREEK (Public Corps) From Jct of I-35 & FM-306, W 26 mi on FM-306 to Potters Creek Rd, S 2.3 mi (E). Pit toilets. 2015 rates: $26. (830)964-3341

RIVER RANCH RV RESORT **Ratings: 9/10★/8** (RV Park) 2015 rates: $45 to $62.50. (830)625-7788 420 North Business I-35, New Braunfels, TX 78130

SUMMIT VACATION & RV RESORT
Ratings: 9/9.5★/9.5 (RV Resort) From New Braunfels: Go 10mi NW on FM 306, then 1-1/2 mi S on FM2673, then 1-1/2mi E on River Road (R). **FAC:** Paved rds. (106 spaces). Avail: 94 gravel, 18 pull-thrus (45 x 80), back-ins (45 x 60), 94 full hkups (30/50 amps), seasonal sites, WiFi, rentals, dump, laundry, fire rings, firewood, restaurant, controlled access. **REC:** heated pool, wading pool, whirlpool, Guadalupe River: fishing, shuffleboard, playground. Pet restrict(B). No tents. Big rig sites, 2015 rates: $34 to $50. Disc: military.
(830)964-2531 Lat: 29.83273, Lon: -98.16363
13105 River Road, New Braunfels, TX 78132
reservations@summitresorttexas.com
www.summitresorttexas.com
See primary listing at Canyon Lake and ad page 1138.

Travel Services

CAMPING WORLD OF NEW BRAUNFELS As the nation's largest retailer of RV supplies, accessories, services and new and used RVs, Camping World is committed to making your total RV experience better. RV Accessories: (888)446-4290. **SERVICES:** RV, tire, RV appliance, MH mechanical, staffed RV wash, restrooms, RV Sales. RV supplies, LP, dump, emergency parking, RV accessible. waiting room. Hours: 8am - 6pm.
(888)614-3766 Lat: 29.762147, Lon: -98.017535
3891 South I-35 N, New Braunfels, TX 78130
www.campingworld.com

NEW CANEY — C8 *Montgomery*

FOREST RETREAT RV PARK
Ratings: 10/10★/10 (RV Park) From Jct of Hwy 59 & FM 1485 (New Caney exit): Go S 1 mi on Frontage Rd to McCleskey Rd, W 0.75 mi (R). **FAC:** Paved rds. (98 spaces). Avail: 68 paved, patios, 40 pull-thrus (30 x 70), back-ins (30 x 65), 68 full hkups (30/50 amps), seasonal sites, cable, WiFi,

NEW CANEY (CONT)

FOREST RETREAT RV PARK (CONT)
laundry, LP gas. **REC:** pool, shuffleboard. Pets OK. No tents. Big rig sites, 2015 rates: $45 to $55. Disc: military.
(281)354-9888 Lat: 30.14263, Lon: -95.23835
21711 McCleskey Rd, New Caney, TX 77357
Stay@forestretreatrvpark.com
www.forestretreatrvpark.com
See ad pages 1159, 1108.

GRAND TEXAS RV RESORT AND CAMPGROUND
(RV Resort) (Under Construction) From jct US Hwy 59 & SH 242: Go 3/4mi NW on SH 242 (L). **FAC.** 144 paved, no slide-outs, 98 pull-thrus (30 x 75), back-ins (30 x 50) (30/50 amps), cable, WiFi, laundry. Pet restrict(B). Disc: AAA, military.
(844)472-6389 Lat: 30.164901, Lon: -95.22126
22846 Hwy 242, New Caney, TX 77357
Info@grandtxrv.com
www.grandtxrv.com
See ad page 1153.

LONE STAR LAKES RV PARK
Ratings: 9/9★/8 (RV Park) From Jct of US-59 & FM 1485: Go S 0.9 mi on S-bnd Frntg Rd (R). **FAC:** Paved/gravel rds. (96 spaces). Avail: 13 paved, patios, 13 pull-thrus (20 x 70), 13 full hkups (30/50 amps), seasonal sites, cable, WiFi, rentals, laundry, LP gas, fire rings. **REC:** pool, Lake Redmond: fishing, playground. Pet restrict(B). No tents. 2015 rates: $32. Disc: military.
(800)290-9301 Lat: 30.14612, Lon: -95.22481
20980 US Hwy 59, New Caney, TX 77357
lonestarlakesrvpark@yahoo.com
www.lonestarlakesrvpark.com
See ad page 1158.

NEW WAVERLY — C8 *Walker*

TIMBER LODGE RV RESORT **Ratings: 6.5/NA/6.5** (RV Park) 2015 rates: $25. (936)767-4101 5260 Hwy 150W, New Waverly, TX 77358

NORTH RICHLAND HILLS — H2 *Tarrant*

LA CASITA MH COMMUNITY
Ratings: 7/NA/9.5 (RV Area in MHP) From Jct NE Loop 820 and Hwy 26: Go 1/4 mi NE on Hwy 26 (Grapevine Hwy), then 1 mi N on Davis Blvd (R). **FAC:** Paved rds. (190 spaces). Avail: 15 gravel, patios, back-ins (30 x 60), 15 full hkups (30/50 amps), seasonal sites, laundry. **REC:** pool. Pet restrict(B/Q). 2015 rates: $40.
(817)281-4353 Lat: 32.851587, Lon: -97.213419
7800 Mockingbird Lane, North Richland Hills, TX 76180
Lacasita@towermgmt.com
Lacasitamhc.com

ODESSA — B4 *Ector, Midland*

ODESSA See also Midland.

BARON MOBILE ESTATES & RV PARK (MHP)
Ratings: 5/8.5★/7 (RV Park) From Jct I-20 (exit 115) & FM-1882: Go 3-1/2 mi N on FM-1882 (County Rd W) (R). Elev 2890 ft. **FAC:** Paved/gravel rds. (104 spaces). Avail: 10 gravel, back-ins (25 x 80), 10 full hkups (30/50 amps), seasonal sites, cable, WiFi, laundry. Pet restrict(B). No tents. Big rig sites, 2015 rates: $35. No reservations.
(432)332-4976 Lat: 31.87023, Lon: -102.39850
1147 Gary Terrace, Odessa, TX 79764
baron@towermgmt.com
www.towerrvparks.com

Know the name? Then you can use our special "Find-it-Fast" index to locate your campground on the map. The index arranges private and public campgrounds alphabetically, by state. Next to the name, you'll quickly find the name of the town the park is in, plus the Listing's page number.

Travel Services

BILLY SIMS TRAILER TOWN Sales & Service 9-6 M-F, 9-5 Sat. Large parts supply in store, online parts catalog, special orders welcome, trailers, fifth wheels & fold down camping trailers. Elev 2890 ft. **SERVICES:** RV appliance, RV Sales. RV supplies, emergency parking, waiting room. Hours: 9am to 6pm.
(800)473-4678 Lat: 31.84820, Lon: -102.36273
520 E 2nd St, Odessa, TX 79761
billysims@anrv4u.net
www.anrv4u.net
See ad this page.

ONALASKA — C8 *Polk, Trinity*

LAKE LIVINGSTON/ONALASKA KOA **Ratings: 10/9/10** (RV Park) 2015 rates: $34 to $77. (936)646-3824 15152 US Hwy 190 West, Onalaska, TX 77360

NORTHSHORE RV RESORT **Ratings: 10/10★/9.5** (RV Park) 2015 rates: $35 to $55. (936)646-3124 168 Butler, Onalaska, TX 77360

ORE CITY — B9 *Upshur*

CEDAR SPRINGS PARK (COE-LAKE O'THE PINES) (Public Corps) From jct US-259 & Hwy-155: Go 1/2 mi E on Hwy-155. Pit toilets. (903)665-2336

OTTINE — D7 *Gonzales*

PALMETTO (State Pk) From Jct of I-10 & US-183, S 2.4 mi on US-183 to Park Rd 11, W 2 mi (R) (Entrance fee). 2015 rates: $18 to $20. (830)672-3266

PADRE ISLAND — K5 *Nueces*

PADRE ISLAND NATL SEASHORE/MALAQUITE (Natl Pk) From JFK Causeway, S 10 mi on PR-22 (E). Entrance fee required. 2015 rates: $8. (361)949-8068

PALACIOS — D8 *Matagorda*

SERENDIPITY BAY RESORT RV PARK & MARINA
Ratings: 9/9★/8 (RV Park) From Jct of Hwy 35 & Bus 35 (N of town), SW 1.7 mi on Bus 35 (L). **FAC:** Gravel rds. 150 Avail: 27 paved, 123 gravel, 27 pull-thrus (25 x 70), back-ins (22 x 48), 150 full hkups (30/50 amps), cable, WiFi, rentals, laundry. **REC:** pool, Matagorda Bay: fishing, marina, shuffleboard, playground. Pet restrict(B/Q). Partial handicap access, no tents. Eco-friendly, 2015 rates: $28 to $36.
(800)556-0534 Lat: 28.70081, Lon: -96.22452
1001 Main St, Palacios, TX 77465
serendipitybayresort@yahoo.com
www.serendipitybayresort.com
See ad page 1106 (Welcome Section).

PAMPA — F10 *Gray*

RECREATION PARK, CITY OF PAMPA (Public) From Jct of US-60 & US-70, E 2.3 mi on US-60 to Rodeo Dr, N 0.1 mi (L). 2015 rates: $15 to $20. (806)669-5750

PARIS — A8 *Lamar*

PAT MAYSE PARK/SANDERS COVE (Public Corps) From Jct of US-271 & FM-906, W 0.75 mi on FM-906 to CR-35920, SW 0.75 mi to park (E). Pit toilets. 2015 rates: $18 to $22. (903)732-3020

PAT MAYSE PARK/WEST (Public Corps) From Jct of Hwy 271 & FM-906, W 4 mi on FM-906 to FM-197, W 3 mi to CR-35810, S 1 mi to CR-35800, E to park (L). 2015 rates: $12 to $18. (903)732-3020

PASADENA — D8 *Houston*

CAMINO VILLA MH & RV PARK
(RV Spaces) From S Jct of I-610 & I-45, S 3.25 mi on I-45 to Exit 36 (College), E 6 mi on College (becomes Spencer Hwy) to Space Center Blvd, S 0.5 mi (R). **FAC:** Paved rds. (218 spaces). Avail: 9 grass, patios, back-ins (30 x 50), 9 full hkups (30/50 amps). Pet restrict(B/Q). No tents. 2015 rates: $40. No CC.
(281)487-1759 Lat: 29.66031, Lon: -95.14481
3310 Space Center Blvd., Pasadena, TX 77505
See ad page 1158.

PRESTON MOBILE HOME COMMUNITY
(RV Spaces) From Sam Houston Pkwy & Spencer Hwy, go W 1 mi on Spencer Hwy to Preston Ave, go N 1/8 mi on Preston Ave (L) (weekly reservations only). **FAC:** Paved rds. (80 spaces). Avail: 20 grass, back-ins (28 x 42), accepts full hkup units only, 20 full hkups (30/50 amps). Pet restrict(Q). 2015 rates: $160 weekly. Disc: AAA, military.
(713)991-1232 Lat: 29.66545, Lon: -95.17128
3014 Preston Ave, Pasadena, TX 77503
Vcamacho@prestonmhc.com
See ad page 1158.

PECOS — C3 *Reeves*

TRAPARK RV PARK **Ratings: 3.5/5/5** (Membership Pk) 2015 rates: $25 to $29. (432)447-2137 3100 Moore St, Pecos, TX 79772

PHARR — M3 *Hidalgo*

TEXAS TRAILS RV RESORT **Ratings: 9/8.5/9** (RV Resort) 2015 rates: $39. (956)787-6538 501 W Owassa Rd., Pharr, TX 78577

TIP O TEXAS MH & RV RESORT **Ratings: 9.5/9★/8.5** (RV Resort) 2015 rates: $39. (956)787-9959 101 E Sioux Rd, Pharr, TX 78577

TROPIC STAR RV RESORT **Ratings: 9/8.5★/9** (RV Resort) 2015 rates: $39. (956)787-5957 1401 S Cage Blvd., Pharr, TX 78577

PINELAND — C9 *San Augustine*

POWELL PARK MARINA (Public Corps) From town, NW 10 mi on FR-83 to FR-705, S 12 mi (L). 2015 rates: $28 to $30. (409)584-2624

RAYBURN PARK (Public Corps) From town, NW 10 mi on FR-83 to FR-705, S 11 mi to FR-3127, W 1.5 mi (L). 2015 rates: $14 to $28. Mar 1 to Dec 31. (409)384-5716

SAN AUGUSTINE PARK (Public Corps) From town, NW 6 mi on FR-83 to FR-1751, S 4 mi (E). 2015 rates: $16 to $26. (409)384-5716

PITTSBURG — B8 *Camp*

BAREFOOT BAY MARINA AND RESORT
Ratings: 8.5/9.5★/9 (RV Park) From jct US 271 & N Loop 179: Go 3/4 mi W on Loop 179, then 4 1/4 mi N on FM 1520 (L). **FAC:** Paved/gravel rds. 80 gravel, 26 pull-thrus (32 x 120), back-ins (32 x 100), 80 full hkups (30/50 amps), WiFi, tent sites, laundry, groc, LP gas, fire rings, firewood. **REC:** whirlpool, Lake Bob Sandlin: swim, marina, rec open to public. Pets OK. Big rig sites, 2015 rates: $25 to $35. Disc: military. ATM.
(903)856-3643 Lat: 33.05103, Lon: -95.02297
5244 Fm 1520, Pittsburg, TX 75686
info@barefootbaymarina.com
www.barefootbaymarina.com
See ad this page.

PLAINVIEW — A4 *Hale*

OLLIE LINER CENTER RV PARK (Public) S-bnd: From Jct of I-27 & Bus Lp 27 (Columbia St), S 6 mi on Columbia St to Ollie Liner Center, E 0.03 mi; E or W-bnd: From Jct of TX-70 & Bus Lp 27 (Columbia St), S 2.5 mi on Columbia St to Center, E 0.03 mi (E). 2015 rates: $10 to $15. (806)293-2183

POINTBLANK — C8 *San Jacinto*

HOLIDAY VILLAGES OF LIVINGSTON **Ratings: 5/5/7** (Membership Pk) 2015 rates: $40. (936)377-5500 700 Cooke Jones Road, Pointblank, TX 77364

TX

PORT ARANSAS — E7 *Nueces*

A SPOTLIGHT Introducing Port Aransas' colorful attractions appearing at the front of this state section.

ISLAND RV RESORT

Ratings: 9.5/9.5★/8.5 (RV Park) From Jct of Hwy 361 (Ave G) & Hwy 361 (Alistar Rd), NW 0.25 mi on Hwy 361/Ave G (L); or From ferry landing & Hwy 361 (Cut-Off Rd), S 0.6 on Hwy 361 (R).

PREMIER TEXAS GULF RESORT
Enjoy your exceptional island getaway at our RV park with lots of recreation & entertainment, world class sport fishing, beautiful beaches, golf, birding centers & vintage Airstream rentals!

FAC: Paved rds. (200 spaces). Avail: 197 paved, patios, 197 pull-thrus (24 x 60), mostly side by side hkups, 197 full hkups (30/50 amps), cable, WiFi, rentals, dump, laundry, LP gas. **REC:** pool, wading pool, whirlpool. Pet restrict(B/Q). Partial handicap access, no tents. Eco-friendly, 2015 rates: $50. Disc: AAA.
(361)749-5600 Lat: 27.83097, Lon: -97.07168
700 6th St, Port Aransas, TX 78373
info@islandrvresort.com
islandrvresort.com
See ad pages 1120 (Spotlight Port Aransas), 1108 & Snowbird Destinations in Magazine Section.

MUSTANG ISLAND (State Pk) From Corpus Christi: From Jct of Hwy 361 & Park Rd 22, N 4.9 mi on Hwy 361 (R); or From Port Aransas: From Jct of Ave G & Hwy 361, S 17.4 mi on Hwy 361 (L) (Entrance fee). 2015 rates: $20. (361)749-5246

PIONEER BEACH RESORT

Ratings: 10/10★/9 (RV Park) From Jct of ferry landing & Hwy 361 (Cutoff Rd), SE 1 mi on Hwy 361 to first light, SW 3.4 mi on Hwy 361 (L); or From Jct of Park Rd 22 (Hwy 358) & Hwy 361, N 13.7 mi on Hwy 361 (R). **FAC:** Paved rds. 361 paved, patios, 86 pull-thrus (25 x 65), back-ins (25 x 60), 361 full hkups (30/50 amps), cable, WiFi, rentals, dump, laundry, groc, LP gas. **REC:** pool, whirlpool, Gulf of Mexico: fishing, shuffleboard, playground. Pet restrict(B/Q). No tents. Big rig sites, eco-friendly, 2015 rates: $39 to $59. Disc: military.
(361)749-6248 Lat: 27.78723, Lon: -97.09763
120 Gulfwind Drive, Port Aransas, TX 78373
info@pioneerresorts.com
www.pioneerrvresorts.com
See ad page 1106 (Welcome Section).

PORT ARANSAS PARK (Public) E on Hwy 361 to Port Aransas. Leave ferry, stay on Cotter St to park (E). 2015 rates: $25. (361)749-6117

Things to See and Do

PORT ARANSAS CHAMBER/TOURIST BUREAU Visitor information Center for the Port Aransas area. Restrooms. Hours: 10am to 5pm. No CC.
(800)452-6278 Lat: 27.83746, Lon: -97.06692
403 W Cotter, Port Aransas, TX 78373
www.portaransas.org
See ad page 1105 (Welcome Section).

PORT ARTHUR — D9 *Nueces*

ACCESS RV PARK **Ratings: 8/9★/7.5** (RV Park) 2015 rates: $43 to $49. (409)729-8000 2565 95th St, Port Arthur, TX 77640

SEA RIM (State Pk) From town: Go 10 mi S on Hwy 87 to Sabine Pass Battleground, then 10 mi SW on Hwy 87.(Entrance fee) (Campground being rebuilt - Call for status). Pit toilets. 2015 rates: $10. (409)971-2559

PORT ISABEL — M5 *Cameron*

LONG ISLAND VILLAGE OWNERS ASSO. **Ratings: 9.5/6.5/9** (Condo Pk) 2015 rates: $46 to $52. (956)943-6449 33840 S. Garcia, Port Isabel, TX 78578

PORT ISABEL PARK CENTER INC MHP Ratings: 7.5/7.5/6.5 (RV Park) From Jct of Hwys 48 & 100, E 0.9 mi on Hwy 100 to Champion Ave, S 2 blks (R). **FAC:** Paved rds. (425 spaces). Avail: 235 grass, back-ins (25 x 45), some side by side hkups, 235 full hkups (30/50 amps), cable, WiFi, showers $, dump, laundry, controlled access. **REC:** Gulf of Mexico: shuffleboard. Pet restrict(Q). Partial handicap access, no tents. Big rig sites, 2015 rates: $32 to $35. Disc: AAA.
AAA Approved
(956)943-7340 Lat: 26.07055, Lon: -97.21340
702 Champion Ave., Port Isabel, TX 78578
info@piparkcenter.com
www.piparkcenter.com

PORT LAVACA — E7 *Calhoun*

LIGHTHOUSE BEACH RV PARK (Public) From Jct of Hwy 35 & Smith Rd (E side of town), SE 1 blk on Smith Rd (L). 2015 rates: $33 to $35. (361)552-5311

TEXAS LAKESIDE RV RESORT

Ratings: 10/10★/10 (RV Park) From Jct Hwy 87 & I-35: Go S .05 mi on Hwy 35, then go E 1 mi on County Road 101 (L). **FAC:** Paved rds. 97 paved, 20 pull-thrus (32 x 85), back-ins (30 x 75), 97 full hkups (30/50 amps), cable, WiFi, laundry, LP gas, controlled access. **REC:** pool, whirlpool. Pet restrict(B/Q). Partial handicap access. Big rig sites, RV age restrict, eco-friendly, 2015 rates: $45 to $60. Disc: military.
(361)551-2267 Lat: 28.59564, Lon: -096.64224
2499 W Austin St, Port Lavaca, TX 77979
reservations@texaslakesidervresort.com
www.texaslakesidervresort.com
See ad this page, 1108 & Snowbird Destinations in Magazine Section.

PORT MANSFIELD — L4 *Willacy*

THE PARK @ PORT MANSFIELD **Ratings: 7.5/8/6** (RV Park) 2015 rates: $30. (956)746-1530 1300 Mansfield Rd, Port Mansfield, TX 78598

PORTLAND — E7 *San Patricio*

SEA BREEZE RV PARK

Ratings: 9/9★/9 (RV Park) From Jct of US-181 & FM-893/Moore Ave exit, NW 1 mi on FM-893/Moore Ave to Marriott St, SW 0.5 mi to Doyle, S 0.2 mi (R). **FAC:** Gravel rds. (160 spaces). Avail: 100 gravel, patios, 42 pull-thrus (22 x 60), back-ins (22 x 40), some side by side hkups, 99 full hkups, 1 W, 1 E (30/50 amps), seasonal sites, WiFi, dump, laundry. **REC:** heated pool, wading pool, whirlpool, Corpus Christi Bay: fishing. Pet restrict(B/Q). Partial handicap access, no tents. Eco-friendly, 2015 rates: $34 to $39. Disc: AAA, military.
(361)643-0744 Lat: 27.88515, Lon: -97.34420
1026 Seabreeze Lane, Portland, TX 78374
seabreezrv@aol.com
www.seabreezerv.com
See ad pages 1141, 1108.

POTTSBORO — A7 *Grayson*

PRESTON BEND REC AREA (Public Corps) From town, N 9 mi on Hwy 120, follow signs (R). 2015 rates: $20. Apr 1 to Sep 30. (903)786-8408

PROCTOR — B6 *Comanche*

SOWELL CREEK PARK (Public Corps) From town, E 12 mi on US-377 to FM-1476, W 2.2 mi to recreation road 6, S 0.5 mi to park entrance (R) (Entrance fee). 2015 rates: $16 to $38. (254)879-2322

QUANAH — A5 *Hardeman*

COPPER BREAKS (State Pk) S-bnd: From Jct of US-287 & SR-6/Main St., S 12 mi on SR-6 (R); or N-bnd: From Jct of US-70 & SR-6, N 8 mi on SR-6 (L) (Entrance fee). 2015 rates: $10 to $20. (940)839-4331

QUITAQUE — A5 *Briscoe*

CAPROCK CANYONS (State Pk) From Jct of SR-86 & FM-1065, N 3.1 mi on FM-1065 (L) (Entrance fee). 2015 rates: $10 to $20. (806)455-1492

QUITMAN — B8 *Wood*

GOVERNOR JIM HOGG CITY PARK (Public) From jct Hwy 154 & Hwy 37 (at courthouse square): Go 6 blocks S on Hwy 37. 2015 rates: $20. (903)763-4411

RANGER — B6 *Eastland*

RL RV PARK **Ratings: 7.5/6/8** (RV Park) 2015 rates: $40. (254)647-1730 1424 W Loop 254, Ranger, TX 76470

REFUGIO — E7 *Refugio*

JETER RV PARK (Public) From jct US 77 & Hwy 774: Go 200 yds W on Hwy 774. 2015 rates: $20 (512)526-5361

RICHMOND — D8 *Fort Bend*

BRAZOS BEND (State Pk) From Jct of US-59 & FM-2759, S 1.9 mi on FM-2759 to FM-762, S 14.5 m (L) (Entrance fee). 2015 rates: $12 to $25. (979)553-5101

RIVERBEND RV PARK

Ratings: 7/8.5★/8 (RV Park) From Jct of US-59 & Grand Pkwy 99 (Crabb River Rd) SW 1.8 mi on Grand Pkwy 99 (Crabb River Rd) to FM 2759, E 3.1 mi to Agnes Rd, N 1 mi (L). **FAC:** Gravel rds 156 gravel, 150 pull-thrus (35 x 84), back-ins (45 x 50), 156 full hkups (30/50 amps), cable, WiFi showers $, laundry. **REC.** Pet restrict(B/Q). No tents Big rig sites, 2015 rates: $29.50.
(281)343-5151 Lat: 29.54245, Lon: -95.64398
1055 Agnes Rd, Richmond, TX 77469
elena2010texas@gmail.com
www.riverbendrvpark.cc
See ad page 1158.

SHILOH RV PARK **Ratings: 5.5/7/7** (RV Park) 2015 rates: $23. (281)344-2888 5539 Fm 762, Richmond, TX 77469

RIO GRANDE VALLEY — F7 *Starr*

RIO GRANDE VALLEY See also Alamo, Brownsville, Donna, Edinburg, Harlingen, La Feria, McAllen Mercedes, Mission, Weslaco.

RIO HONDO — M4 *Cameron*

TWIN PALMS RV RESORT **Ratings: 8.5/8/7.5** (RV Park) 2015 rates: $40 to $60. (956)748-0800 107 E Colorado, Rio Hondo, TX 78583

RIVERSIDE — C8 *Walker*

BETHY CREEK RV RESORT **Ratings: 7.5/7.5/8.5** (RV Park) 2015 rates: $35 to $50 (800)537-6251 136 Shorewood Dr, Riverside, TX 77320

RIVIERA — E7 *Kleberg*

SEAWIND RV RESORT ON THE BAY

Ratings: 9/8.5★/9 (Public) From Jct of US-77 & FM-628 (N of town), E 9.8 mi on FM-628 (L). **FAC:** Paved rds. 184 paved, patios, 25 pull-thrus (35 x 70), back-ins (30 x 60), 159 full hkups, 25 W, 25 E (30/50 amps), WiFi, dump, laundry. **REC:** Baffin Bay: fishing, shuffleboard, playground. Pet restrict(B/Q). Partial handicap access, no tents. Big rig sites, 2015 rates: $35.
(361)297-5738 Lat: 27.31681, Lon: -97.67923
1066 E Fm 628, Riviera, TX 78379
seawindrv@gmail.com
www.seawindrv.com
See ad pages 1163, 1108.

ROANOKE — G2 *Denton*

NORTHLAKE VILLAGE RV PARK

Ratings: 10/10★/10 (RV Park) From Jct I-35W (exit 70) & Hwy 114: Go 1 mi E on Hwy 114, then 1/4 mi N on Cleveland-Gibbs Rd (E).

QUIET COUNTRY LIVING NEAR DALLAS
Beautiful sites with paved patios and easy access close to all that DFW has to offer. Only 3 minutes to Texas Motor Speedway and 15 minutes to Fort Worth and Denton. Book your reservations now for a short or long term stay.

FAC: Paved rds. (176 spaces). Avail: 88 all weather patios, back-ins (30 x 60), 88 full hkups (30/50 amps), seasonal sites, WiFi, laundry, LP gas. **REC:** pool. Pet restrict(B/Q). Partial handicap access, no tents. Big rig sites, 2015 rates: $38 to $40. Disc: AAA, military
AAA Approved
(817)430-3303 Lat: 33.03099, Lon: -97.25084

ROANOKE (CONT)

NORTHLAKE VILLAGE RV PARK (CONT)
13001 Cleveland-Gibbs Rd #79, Roanoke, TX 76262
info@northlakevillagerv.com
www.northlakevillagerv.com
See ad pages 1114 (Spotlight Dallas/Fort Worth), 1108.

ROCKDALE — C7 *Milam*

ROCKDALE RV PARK **Ratings: 6/8.5/6.5** (RV Park) 2015 rates: $25. (512)446-9955 711 E Cameron Ave, Rockdale, TX 76567

ROCKPORT — E7 *Aransas*

A BAY BREEZE RV PARK
Ratings: 8/6/8 (RV Park) From Jct of Hwy 188 & US-35 Bypass: Go 1.5 mi SE on Hwy 188, then 0.8 mi N on Hwy 35 to Bishop Rd. Go W on Bishop Rd to Portia Ave, then 0.3 mi S on Portia Ave to Nell St (E). **FAC:** Paved/dirt rds. 34 paved, 10 pull-thrus (32 x 60), back-ins (35 x 60), 34 full hkups (30/50 amps), cable, WiFi, laundry. **REC:** pool, pond. Pet restrict(B). No tents. Big rig sites, 2015 rates: $35. Disc: AAA.
(361)727-2000 Lat: 27.96950, Lon: -97.10507
175 Nell Street, Rockport, TX 78382
mail@baybreezervpark.com
www.abaybreezervpark.com
See ad this page.

ANCIENT OAKS RV PARK
Ratings: 9.5/10★/9.5 (Campground) From Jct of Bus Hwy 35 & FM-1069, SW 0.7 mi on Bus Hwy 35 (L). **FAC:** Paved rds. (150 spaces). 110 Avail: 23 paved, 87 grass, 110 pull-thrus (24 x 60), some side by side hkups, 110 full hkups (30/50 amps), seasonal sites, cable, WiFi, tent sites, rentals, dump, laundry. **REC:** heated pool, whirlpool, pond, fishing, shuffleboard, playground. Pet restrict(B). Partial handicap access. Big rig sites, eco-friendly, 2015 rates: $32 to $40. Disc: AAA.
(361)729-5051 Lat: 28.01259, Lon: -97.06348
1222 Business Hwy 35 S, Rockport, TX 78382
ancientoaks@sbcglobal.net
www.ancientoaksrvpark.com
See ad this page, 1108 & Snowbird Destinations in Magazine Section.

BAY VIEW RV RESORT **Ratings: 8/7.5/8** (RV Park) 2015 rates: $35. (361)400-6000 5451 Hwy 35 N, Rockport, TX 78382

BUFFALO RV PARK & STORAGE **Ratings: 6.5/6.5/6.5** (RV Park) 2015 rates: $30 to $35. (361)727-0090 468 Griffith Dr, Rockport, TX 78382

CIRCLE W RV RANCH **Ratings: 8.5/8/7.5** (RV Park) 2015 rates: $40. (361)729-1542 1401 Smokehouse Rd, Rockport, TX 78382

COPANO BAY RV RESORT **Ratings: 9/9★/8.5** (RV Park) 2015 rates: $35. (361)790-9373 3101 Fm 1781, Rockport, TX 78382

FULTON OAKS PARK **Ratings: 7/8.5★/7** (RV Park) 2015 rates: $35. (361)729-4606 1301 Lone Star Rd, Fulton, TX 78358

GOOSE ISLAND SRA (State Pk) From Jct of SR-35 & Park Rd 13, E 1.4 mi on Park Rd 13 (R) (Entrance fee). 2015 rates: $18 to $22. (361)729-2858

SANDOLLAR RV RESORT **Ratings: 8/9★/7.5** (RV Park) 2015 rates: $38 to $48. (361)729-2381 919 N Fulton Beach Rd, Rockport, TX 78382

WILDERNESS OAKS RV RESORT **Ratings: 9/9★/7.5** (RV Park) 2015 rates: $35 to $55. (361)729-2307 4851 N Hwy 35, Rockport, TX 78382

WOODY ACRES MOBILE HOME & RV RESORT
Ratings: 8.5/9★/9 (RV Area in MHP) From Jct of Bus Hwy 35 & Bypass 35 (FM 3036), NW 0.3 mi on Bus Hwy 35 to Mesquite, W 0.2 mi (L). **FAC:** Paved rds. (360 spaces). 260 Avail: 16 paved, 244 grass, patios, 35 pull-thrus (25 x 50), back-ins (25 x 40), some side by side hkups, 260 full hkups (30/50 amps), cable, WiFi $, rentals, laundry. **REC:** heated pool, whirlpool, Sandpiper Lake: fishing, shuffleboard. Pet restrict(B/Q). Partial handicap access, no tents. Eco-friendly, 2015 rates: $34 to $38. Disc: AAA.
(800)526-9264 Lat: 28.06635, Lon: -97.04611
1202 West Mesquite St., Rockport, TX 78358
susan.woodyacres@gmail.com
www.woodyacres.us
See ad this page.

RUSK — B8 *Cherokee*

COUNTRY ESTATES RV PARK & MHP
Ratings: 7/7/7 (RV Park) From Jct of US 69 & US 84, W 2.3 mi on US 84 (L). **FAC:** Paved rds. 42 Avail: 23 gravel, 19 grass, 4 pull-thrus (20 x 60), back-ins (20 x 60), 42 full hkups (30/50 amps), WiFi, tent sites, laundry. **REC.** Pet restrict(B). Big rig sites, 2015 rates: $30. Disc: military. No CC. AAA Approved
(903)683-9684 Lat: 31.79735, Lon: -95.17611
1639 W. 6th St, Rusk, TX 75785
countryestatesrvpark@aol.com
www.countryestatesrvpark.com
See ad this page.

TEXAS STATE RAILROAD RV PARK & CAMPGROUND **Ratings: 8/7/7.5** (Campground) 2015 rates: $22 to $30. (877)726-7245 535 Park Road 76, U.s. Hwy 84W, Rusk, TX 75785

SALADO — C7 *Bell*

TRANQUIL GARDENS RV PARK
Ratings: 7.5/9.5★/9 (RV Park) From Jct of I-35 & Exit 286, W 2 mi on FM 2484 (R). **FAC:** Gravel rds. (25 spaces). Avail: 15 gravel, patios, 14 pull-thrus (30 x 80), back-ins (30 x 85), 15 full hkups (30/50 amps), seasonal sites, WiFi, laundry. **REC.** Pets OK. No tents. Big rig sites, 2015 rates: $36 to $40. Disc: AAA, military. No CC.
(254)947-5192 Lat: 30.97427, Lon: -97.56163
5644 Fm 2484, Salado, TX 76571
tranquilgarrv@yahoo.com
See ad pages 1136, 1108.

SAN ANGELO — C5 *Tom Green*

DRY CREEK PARK (COE-O.C. FISHER LAKE) (Public Corps) From jct US-67 & 87: Go 9 mi NW on US-87, then 1-1/4 mi S on FM-2288. (325)625-2322

GRANDVIEW PARK (COE-O.C. FISHER LAKE) (Public Corps) From jct US 87 & US 67: Go 3 mi SW on US 67, then 2 mi W on FM 853, then 8 mi N on FM 2288. Pit toilets. (325)625-2322

SAN ANGELO KOA
Ratings: 9/10★/7.5 (Campground) From Jct US 67 & US 87/277: Go 2 mi S on US 87, then 4-3/4 mi W on Knickerbocker Rd (R). **FAC:** Paved/gravel rds. (68 spaces). Avail: 46 gravel, 46 pull-thrus (20 x 45), mostly side by side hkups, 46 full hkups (30/50 amps), seasonal sites, cable, WiFi, rentals, dump, laundry, groc, LP gas, firewood. **REC:** pool, playground. Pet restrict(B). Partial handicap ac-

A campground rating is based on ALL facilities available at the park.

SAN ANGELO (CONT)

SAN ANGELO KOA (CONT)
cess, no tents. Big rig sites, 2015 rates: $27.95 to $34.95.
(800)562-7519 Lat: 31.38910, Lon: -100.49352
6699 Knickerbocker Rd, San Angelo, TX 76904
sanangelokoa@suddenlinkmail.com
www.koa.com
See ad this page.

SAN ANGELO/BALD EAGLE CREEK (State Pk) From town, NW 8 mi on US-87 to FM-2288, S 1 mi, follow signs (L) (Entrance fee). 2015 rates: $20. (325)949-4757

SAN ANGELO/ISABEL HARTE (State Pk) From jct US 67 & FM 2288: Go N on FM 2288. (Entrance fee). 2015 rates: $10. (325)949-4757

SAN ANGELO/LAKEVIEW (State Pk) From jct US 67 & US 87: Go 9 mi N on US 87, then 1-1/4 mi S on FM 2288. (Entrance fee). 2015 rates: $10. (325)949-4757

SAN ANGELO/NORTH CONCHO (State Pk) From Grape Creek, S 1.5 mi on FM-2288 (L). Entrance fee required. 2015 rates: $20. (325)949-4757

SAN ANGELO/RED ARROYO (State Pk) From jct US-67 & 87: Go 3 mi SW on US-67, then 2-1/2 mi W on FM-853 (Arden Rd), then 3 mi N on FM-2288. 2015 rates: $20. (325)949-8935

SAN ANGELO/RED ARROYO-SOUTH SHORE ENTRANCE (State Pk) From Jct of US-67 & US-87, SW 3 mi on US-67 to RR 853/Arden Rd, W 1.5 mi to FM-2288, NE 0.8 mi to Park Rd, follow signs (R) (Entrance fee). 2015 rates: $20. (325)949-4757

SAN ANGELO/SOUTH SHORE (State Pk) From jct US 87 & US 67: Go 3 mi SW on US 67, then 1-1/4 mi W on Hwy 853 (Arden Rd), then 3/4 mi N on FM 2288.(Entrance fee). 2015 rates: $20. (915)949-4757

SPRING CREEK MARINA & RV PARK, INC
Ratings: 7.5/8★/8.5 (RV Park) From Jct of US-67 & US 87/277: Go 2 mi S on US-87, then 6 mi SW on Knickerbocker Rd, then 1 1/2 mi W on Fisherman's Rd (end). **FAC:** Gravel rds. (72 spaces). Avail: 56 gravel, 45 pull-thrus (40 x 68), back-ins (35 x 50), 56 full hkups (30/50 amps), seasonal sites, cable, WiFi, tent sites, rentals, laundry, groc, LP gas, fire rings, firewood. **REC:** Lake Nasworthy: swim, fishing, marina, playground, rec open to public. Pet restrict(B). Partial handicap access. Big rig sites, 2015 rates: $37 to $59. Disc: AAA, military.
(325)944-3850 Lat: 31.37582, Lon: -100.51290
2680 Camper Rd, San Angelo, TX 76904
springcreek@springcreekmarina-rv.com
www.springcreekmarina-rv.com
See ad this page, 1108.

SAN ANTONIO — D6 *Bexar*

SAN ANTONIO See also Boerne, Bulverde, Canyon Lake, Castroville & Somerset.

ADMIRALTY RV RESORT

Ratings: 9.5/9.5★/9 (RV Park) From Jct of Loop 410 & Hwy 151, Sea World (Exit 9A), NW 2.7 mi on Hwy 151 to W. Military Dr, W 0.3 mi to Ellison S .02 mi (R). **FAC:** Paved rds. 200 paved, patios, 120 pull-thrus (22 x 60), back-ins (22 x 48), 200 full hkups (30/50 amps), WiFi $, rentals, laundry. **REC:** heated pool, playground. Pets OK. Partial handicap access, no tents. Eco-friendly, 2015 rates: $40 to $60. Disc: AAA, military.
(210)647-7878 Lat: 29.44700, Lon: -98.69116
1485 N Ellison Dr., San Antonio, TX 78251
stay@admiraltyrvresort.com
www.admiraltyrvresort.com
See ad this page, 1108 & Snowbird Destinations in Magazine Section.

ALSATIAN RV RESORT & GOLF CLUB

Ratings: 10/10★/10 (RV Resort) From jct Hwy 90 & CR 4516: Go 2.5 mi on CR 4516 (R). **FAC:** Paved rds. 69 paved, patios, 23 pull-thrus (41 x 110), back-ins (41 x 80), 69 full hkups (30/50 amps), cable, WiFi, rentals, laundry, groc, LP gas, restaurant, controlled access. **REC:** heated pool, whirlpool, pond, fishing, golf. Pet restrict(B). Partial handicap access. Big rig sites, RV age restrict, eco-friendly, 2015 rates: $35 to $85. Disc: AAA, military. ATM.
(830)931-9190 Lat: 29.36310, Lon: -098.94100
1581 CR 4516, Castroville, TX 78009
info@alsatianresort.com
www.alsatianresort.com
See primary listing at Castroville and ad page 1175.

BLAZING STAR LUXURY RV RESORT

Ratings: 10/10★/9.5 (RV Resort) (W Bnd from Houston) East Jct of I-10 & Loop 410, W 8.3 mi on I-10 to Hwy 90, W 11.7 mi on Hwy 90 to Loop 1604, N 4.5 mi (R) Located between Potranco Rd & Military Dr W (E Bnd from El Paso) W Jct of I-10 & Loop 1604, SW 14 mi on Loop 1604 to Potranco Rd. Turn around & go back 0.6 mi on Loop 1604 (R).

BEST IN SAN ANTONIO

Blazing Star Luxury RV Resort offers terrific location and luxury amenities for your RV vacation. Kick back in our beautiful 8,000 sq. ft. clubhouse, relax at the lagoon pool or enjoy a poolside game of ping pong!

FAC: Paved rds. 262 paved, patios, 185 pull-thrus (30 x 70), back-ins (30 x 55); 262 full hkups (30/50 amps), cable, WiFi, rentals, laundry, groc, LP gas. **REC:** heated pool, playground. Pets OK. Partial handicap access, no tents. Big rig sites, eco-friendly, 2015 rates: $46 to $79. Disc: AAA, military. AAA Approved
(888)838-7186 Lat: 29.44532, Lon: -98.71039
1120 W Loop 1604 N, San Antonio, TX 78251
blazingstar@suncommunities.com
www.blazingstarresort.com
See ad opposite page, 1463 (Welcome Section), 1108 & Snowbird Destinations in Magazine Section.

BRAUNIG LAKE RV RESORT

Ratings: 8.5/8/8 (RV Park) From S Jct of I-37 & I-410 (in San Antonio), S 3.4 mi on I-37 to exit 130 (Southton Rd/Donop Rd), N 0.3 mi on Donop Rd (R). **FAC:** All weather rds. (266 spaces). Avail: 166 paved, patios, 80 pull-thrus (22 x 65), back-ins (20 x 60), 166 full hkups (30/50 amps), seasonal sites, cable, WiFi, rentals, dump, laundry, LP gas. **REC:** pool, whirlpool, pond, fishing, shuffleboard. Pet restrict(B/Q). Partial handicap access, no tents. Big rig sites, RV age restrict, eco-friendly, 2015 rates: $43 to $59. Disc: AAA, military.
(877)633-3170 Lat: 29.28504, Lon: -98.39241
13550 Donop Rd, Elmendorf, TX 78112
info@brauniglakervresort.com
www.brauniglakervresort.com

Tell them you saw them in this Guide!

We appreciate your business!

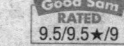

TX

SAN ANTONIO (CONT)

GREENLAKE RV RESORT
(RV Resort) (Too New to Rate) From I-410 & I-37S, go S 1.5 mi on I-37S to US-181 S (exit 132) onto US-181 S, continue S 1 mi on US-181 to S Presa St, go E, .3mi on S Presa St to Green Lake St., Go S 335' (R). **FAC:** Paved rds. 234 paved, patios, 39 pull-thrus (30 x 65), back-ins (30 x 40), 234 full hkups (30/50 amps), cable, WiFi, laundry, controlled access. **REC:** heated pool, whirlpool, Greenlake: fishing. Pets OK. Partial handicap access. Big rig sites, 2015 rates: $23.33 to $38.88. ATM.
AAA Approved
(866)682-4612 Lat: 29.30997, Lon: -098.38761
10842 Green Lake Dr., San Antonio, TX 78233
Greenlake@qualityrvresorts.com
www.greenlakervresort.com
See ad page 1154-1155.

GREENTREE VILLAGE RV PARK MHP
Ratings: 9/9★/9.5 (RV Area in MHP) From NE Jct of I-410 Loop & I-35, N 2.2 mi on I-35 to Wurzbach Pkwy/O'Connor Rd (exit 169), W 0.5 mi on O'Connor Rd, then NW 0.1 mi on O'Connor Rd (L). **FAC:** Paved rds. (190 spaces). Avail: 15 gravel, patios, 7 pull-thrus (30 x 95), back-ins (40 x 60), 15 full hkups (30/50 amps), seasonal sites, cable, WiFi, dump, laundry, groc. **REC:** pool, playground. Pet restrict(Q). Partial handicap access, no tents. Big rig sites, RV age restrict, eco-friendly, 2015 rates: $45.
(210)655-3331 Lat: 29.54926, Lon: -98.37626
12015 O'conner Rd, San Antonio, TX 78233
greentree@satx.rr.com
www.greentreevillage.com
See ad page 1175.

MISSION TRAIL RV **Ratings: 5.5/5.5/6** (RV Park) 2015 rates: $55. (210)928-8285 3500 Orkney Ave, San Antonio, TX 78223

RIVER WALK RV PARK
Ratings: 7.5/8★/6 (RV Park) From I-35 @ Exit 160 (AT & T Ctr Pkwy)-go 1/2 mi to Gembler.Turn left Go E 1 mi, (L); From I-10 @ exit 580 (WW White), go N 1/8 mi to Gembler. Go W-1/2 mi on Gembler (R). **FAC:** Paved rds. (150 spaces). 120 Avail: 60 gravel, 60 grass, patios, 30 pull-thrus (30 x 60), back-ins (30 x 60), 120 full hkups (30/50 amps), seasonal sites, cable, WiFi, tent sites, dump, laundry, firewood. **REC:** pool. Pet restrict(B/Q). Partial handicap access. Big rig sites, RV age restrict, 2015 rates: $34 to $39. Disc: AAA, military.
(210)337-6501 Lat: 29.43622, Lon: -98.41461
1011 Gembler Rd. @ At & T Pkwy., San Antonio, TX 78219
riverwalkrvpark@gmail.com
www.sariverwalkrvpark.com
See ad pages 1175, 1108.

SAN ANTONIO / ALAMO KOA **Ratings: 8.5/9.5★/9** (Campground) 2015 rates: $41 to $45. (210)224-9296 602 Gembler Rd, San Antonio, TX 78219

STONE CREEK RV PARK
Ratings: 9/9★/8.5 (Campground) From Jct of I-35 & Exit 177, S 0.4 mi on W Frntg Rd (R).

HOWDY FOLKS! WELCOME TO TEXAS FUN
With our western theme, we offer true Texas hospitality and a taste of the Old West. Only minutes to San Antonio & New Braunfels attractions, we are freeway close yet country quiet. Fun pet parks and a relaxing pool for you.

FAC: Paved rds. (225 spaces). Avail: 115 gravel, patios, 90 pull-thrus (33 x 60), back-ins (34 x 44), 115 full hkups (30/50 amps), seasonal sites, cable, WiFi, dump, laundry, LP gas. **REC:** pool, whirlpool. Pet restrict(B). No tents. Big rig sites, 2015 rates: $37.50 to $44. Disc: AAA, military.
AAA Approved
(830)609-7759 Lat: 29.61815, Lon: -98.26480
18905 Ih-35 N, Schertz, TX 78154
stonecreekrvpark@hotmail.com
www.stonecreekrvpark.com
See ad pages 1175, 1108 & Snowbird Destinations in Magazine Section.

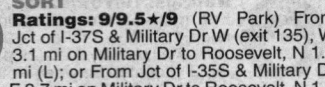

TRAVELERS WORLD CAREFREE RV RESORT
Ratings: 9/9.5★/9 (RV Park) From Jct of I-37S & Military Dr W (exit 135), W 3.1 mi on Military Dr to Roosevelt, N 1.3 mi (L); or From Jct of I-35S & Military Dr (exit 150B), E 2.7 mi on Military Dr to Roosevelt, N 1.3 mi (L). Do Not follow GPS.

TRAVELERS WORLD CAREFREE RV RESORT!
Highly rated for quality and the closest RV resort to the River Walk and Alamo! Explore the city and return to the resort for a relaxing swim, golf or a ride on the bike trails and enjoy our peaceful surroundings.

FAC: Paved rds. 165 gravel, patios, 29 pull-thrus (30 x 70), back-ins (21 x 45), 165 full hkups (30/50 amps), cable, WiFi, rentals, dump, laundry, LP gas. **REC:** heated pool, whirlpool, playground. Pet restrict(B/Q). No tents. Eco-friendly, 2015 rates: $42 to $47. Disc: AAA, military.
(210)532-8310 Lat: 29.37455, Lon: -98.48208
2617 Roosevelt Ave, San Antonio, TX 78214
travelersworld@carefreeresorts.com
www.carefreervresorts.com
See ad pages 1134, 1108 & Snowbird Destinations in Magazine Section.

SAN AUGUSTINE — C9 *San Augustine*

MISSION DOLORES CAMPGROUND (Public) From Jct of SR-21W & SR-147/S Broadway (in town), S 0.5 mi on SR-147/S Broadway (L); or From Jct of US-96 & SR-147, E 1.1 mi on SR-147 (R). 2015 rates: $24. (936)275-1108

SAN BENITO — M4 *Cameron*

FIRST COLONY MOBILE HOME & RV PARK **Ratings: 9/8.5/6.5** (RV Park) 2015 rates: $35. (956)399-8595 2800 Turner Rd, San Benito, TX 78586

FUN N SUN RV RESORT **Ratings: 8.5/7.5/8.5** (RV Area in MHP) 2015 rates: $39. (800)405-6188 1400 Zillock Rd, San Benito, TX 78586

PALMDALE RV RESORT **Ratings: 8.5/6/7** (RV Park) 2015 rates: $38. (800)456-7683 30910 State Hwy 100, San Benito, TX 78586

SAN JUAN — M3 *Hidalgo*

SAN JUAN GARDENS **Ratings: 8.5/8.5★/7.5** (RV Park) 2015 rates: $30. (956)781-1082 900 E US Business Hwy 83, San Juan, TX 78589

SAN LEON — D9 *Galveston*

TROPICAL GARDENS RV PARK & RESORT **Ratings: 7/8.5★/7** (RV Park) 2015 rates: $25 to $35. (281)339-1729 609 24th St., San Leon, TX 77539

SAN MARCOS — D7 *Hays*

CANYON TRAIL RV RESORT **Ratings: 8.5/9.5★/8.5** (RV Park) 2015 rates: $36.50 to $38.50. (512)805-9988 6050 I-H 35 S, San Marcos, TX 78666

PECAN PARK RIVERSIDE RV & CABINS
Ratings: 9/9.5★/9.5 (RV Park) From Jct I-35 (exit 205) & Hwy 80: Go 2 mi SE on Hwy 80 (1 mi past Blanco River Bridge), then 1 block S on Old Bastrop Hwy, then 1/2 mi E on Martindale Rd. (R).

STAY IN A BEAUTIFUL LUSH LOCATION
Relax in our scenic, peaceful location along the San Marcos River where you'll enjoy the shade of our huge pecan trees. Fish, float or just sit. Swim in our heated pool. Our mild winters make us a prime snowbird destination.

FAC: Paved/gravel rds. (145 spaces). Avail: 75 gravel, patios, 33 pull-thrus (35 x 75), back-ins (30 x 60), 75 full hkups (30/50 amps), seasonal sites, cable, WiFi, rentals, laundry, LP gas, firewood. **REC:** heated pool, whirlpool, San Marcos River: fishing, playground. Pet restrict(B). No tents. Big rig sites, 2015 rates: $40 to $58. Disc: military.
(512)396-0070 Lat: 29.86323, Lon: -97.88964
50 Squirrel Run, San Marcos, TX 78666
camping@pecanpark.com
www.pecanpark.com
See ad pages 1121 (Spotlight San Marcos), 1108, Family Camping & Snowbird Destinations in Magazine Section.

SANDERSON — D4 *Terrell*

CANYONS RV PARK **Ratings: 5/6/7** (RV Park) 2015 rates: $30. (432)345-2916 580 E Oak St, Sanderson, TX 79848

SANGER — A7 *Denton*

RAY ROBERTS LAKE/ISLE DU BOIS UNIT (State Pk) From Jct of I-35 & FM-455 (exit 467), E 11 mi on FM-455 (L); or From Jct of US-377 & FM-455, W 3.1 mi on FM-455 (R) (Entrance fee). 2015 rates: $25 to $26. (940)686-2148

WAGON MASTER RV PARK AND ALPACA FARM
Ratings: 8.5/9★/8.5 (RV Park) From jct I-35W (exit 478) and FM 455W (Chapman Dr): Go 1mi W on Chapman Dr (R). **FAC:** Gravel rds. (102 spaces). Avail: 10 gravel, 10 pull-thrus (50 x 75), 10 full hkups (30/50 amps), seasonal sites, WiFi, laundry. **REC:** pool. Pets OK. 2015 rates: $30. No CC.
(940)458-0077 Lat: 33.367793, Lon: -97.195873
3926 Fm 455W, Sanger, TX 76266
Wagonmasterrv@gmail.com
www.wagonmasterrv.com
See ad this page.

SANTO — B6 *Palo Pinto*

COFFEE CREEK RV RESORT & CABINS
Ratings: 10/10★/9 (RV Park) From Jct of I-20 & Exit 386 (US 281): Go 1/2 mi N on US 281 (R). **FAC:** All weather rds. (115 spaces). Avail: 95 paved patios, 95 pull-thrus (35 x 90), 95 full hkups (30/50 amps), seasonal sites, WiFi, rentals, laundry, LP gas. **REC:** pool, whirlpool, pond, Coffee Creek: fishing, playground. Pet restrict(B). Partial handicap access, no tents. Big rig sites, 2015 rates: $35.
(940)769-2277 Lat: 32.62168, Lon: -98.10923
13429 S Hwy 281, Santo, TX 76472
coffeecreekrvresort@yahoo.com
www.coffeecreek-rvresort.com

SCHULENBURG — D7 *Fayette*

SCHULENBURG RV PARK
Ratings: 7.5/9.5★/9 (RV Park) N-bnd: From Jct of US-90 & US-77, N 0.5 mi on US-77 (L); or S, E & W-bnd: From Jct of I-10 & US-77 (exit 674), S 0.2 mi on US-77 (R). **FAC:** Paved/gravel rds 49 gravel, 45 pull-thrus (32 x 60), back-ins (30 x 60) 49 full hkups (30/50 amps), WiFi, tent sites, laundry **REC:** pond, fishing. Pet restrict(B/Q). Partial hand-

What will it cost to catch a salmon in Alaska? State-by-state fishing license information is listed in the front section of the Guide.

Our rating system isn't just tough, it's thorough. We know the kinds of things that are important to you — like clean restrooms and showers, attractive, secure, well-tended grounds, and extras like swimming pools. We give the first rating for development of facilities, the second for cleanliness and physical characteristics of restrooms and showers, and the third for visual appearance.

We rate what RVers consider important.

SCHULENBURG (CONT)

SCHULENBURG RV PARK (CONT)
icap access. Big rig sites, eco-friendly, 2015 rates: $38.25.
(979)743-4388 Lat: 29.68995, Lon: -96.90304
65 North Kessler Ave, Schulenburg, TX 78956
camp@schulenburgrvpark.com
www.schulenburgrvpark.com
See ad opposite page.

SEALY — D8 *Austin*

STEPHEN F AUSTIN (State Pk) From Jct of I-10 & FM-1458 (exit 723), N 2 mi on FM-1458 to Park Rd 38, SW 0.8 mi (E) (Entrance fee). 2015 rates: $22. (979)885-3613

SEGUIN — D7 *Guadalupe*

RIVER SHADE RV PARK **Ratings: 6.5/6.5/7.5** (RV Park) 2015 rates: $37 to $42. (800)364-7275 3995 S 123 Bypass, Seguin, TX 78155

SEMINOLE — B4 *Andrews*

GAINES COUNTY PARK (Public) From town, N 8 mi on US-385 (L). 2015 rates: $4. (432)758-4002

SHERMAN — A7 *Grayson*

LAZY L RV PARK
Ratings: 9/9.5★/8.5 (RV Park) N-bnd Jct US-75/(Exit 57) & Park St: Go 1/4 mi N on Service Rd, then 500 ft E on Wilson (R) S-bnd Jct US-75 (Exit 57) & Park St: Go 3/4 mi S on W Service Rd, then 2 blocks E on Park St, then 1 block S on Columbia, then 100 ft E on Wilson (R). **FAC:** Paved/gravel rds. (97 spaces). Avail: 47 gravel, 43 pull-thrus (24 x 60), back-ins (24 x 60), 47 full hkups (30/50 amps), seasonal sites, cable, WiFi, dump, laundry. **REC:** pool, playground. Pet restrict(B). Partial handicap access, no tents. Big rig sites, 2015 rates: $30.50 to $32.50. Disc: military.
(903)870-7772 Lat: 33.61458, Lon: -96.60621
310 W Wilson, Sherman, TX 75090
Lazylrvpark@gmail.com
www.thelazylrvpark.com
See ad this page, 1108.

SILVERTON — A4 *Briscoe*

LAKE MACKENZIE PARK (MACKENZIE MUNICIPAL WATER AUTH) (Public) From jct Hwy-86 & Hwy-207: Go 7 mi N on Hwy-207. 2015 rates: $15. (806)633-4335

SINTON — E7 *San Patricio*

HITCHING POST RV PARK **Ratings: 5.5/5/7** (RV Park) 2015 rates: $30. (361)364-3615 900 W Sinton, Sinton, TX 78387

ROB & BESSIE WELDER PARK (Public) From Jct of US-77 & US-181, N 1.4 mi on US-181 (R). 2015 rates: $25. (361)437-6795

Need RV repair or service? Camping World has 700 certified and trained technicians, warranty-covered repairs, workmanship and a price match guarantee. Find out more at CampingWorld.com

SLATON — A4 *Lubbock*

TWIN PINE RV PARK
Ratings: 8/9.5★/10 (RV Park) At jct US Hwy 84 and Woodrow Road (East side of US 84). **FAC:** Paved/gravel rds. (66 spaces). 56 Avail: 19 paved, 37 gravel, 16 pull-thrus (32 x 70), back-ins (30 x 60), 56 full hkups (30/50 amps), seasonal sites, cable, WiFi, dump, laundry. **REC.** Pets OK. No tents. Big rig sites, 2015 rates: $30. Disc: military.
(866)708-3311 Lat: 33.44723, Lon: -101.66531
1202 N Hwy 84, Slaton, TX 79364
kcjv@twinpinervpark.com
www.twinpinervpark.com
See ad page 1165.

SMITHVILLE — D7 *Bastrop*

BUESCHER (State Pk) From Jct of SR-71 & FM-153, NE 0.5 mi on FM-153 (L). Caution: low tree clearance (Entrance fee). 2015 rates: $12 to $17. (512)237-2241

SOMERSET — D6 *Bexar*

A COUNTRY BREEZE RV PARK
Ratings: 6/7/8 (RV Park) From S jct Loop 1604 & I-35: Go 1 mi SW on I-35 (exit 139), then 2-1/4 mi S on Kinney Rd, then 1/2 mi E on Briggs Rd, then 1/4 mi S on Benton City Rd. **FAC:** Gravel rds. 46 paved, patios, 16 pull-thrus (45 x 70), back-ins (45 x 70), 46 full hkups (30/50 amps), cable, WiFi, laundry. **REC.** Pet restrict(B/Q). No tents. Big rig sites, 2015 rates: $35. Disc: AAA.
AAA Approved
(210)624-2665 Lat: 29.22954, Lon: -98.68193
19575 Benton City Rd, Somerset, TX 78069
management@acountrybreezervpark.com
www.acountrybreezervpark.com
See ad this page.

SOMERVILLE — C8 *Burleson, Washington*

BIG CREEK PARK (Public) From jct Hwy-36 & FM-60: Go 4 mi W on FM-60, then 3-1/2 mi S on Park Road 4. 2015 rates: $20 to $25. (866)596-1616

LAKE SOMERVILLE/BIRCH CREEK (State Pk) From Jct of FM 1361 & US 36 (in town), NW 3.4 mi on Hwy 36 to FM-60, SW 7 mi to Park Rd 57, S 4.1 mi (E) (Entrance fee). 2015 rates: $16. (979)535-7763

OVERLOOK PARK (Public Corps) From town, S 2 mi on Hwy 36 to FM-1948, E 0.2 mi to LBJ Dr, N 0.5 mi to park entrance (L). 2015 rates: $14 to $18. (979)596-1622

ROCKY CREEK (Public Corps) From town, S 2 mi on Hwy 36 to FM-1948, E 5 mi (R). 2015 rates: $24 to $28. (979)596-1622

YEGUA CREEK (Public Corps) From town, S 2 mi on Hwy 36 to FM-1948, E 3 mi (R). 2015 rates: $18 to $28. (979)596-1622

SONORA — C5 *Sutton*

CAVERNS OF SONORA RV PARK (RV Spaces) From I-10 & Exit 392 (FM-1989), S 5.3 mi on FM-1989 to Caverns of Sonora Rd, SE 1.5 mi (E). **FAC:** Dirt rds. 48 dirt, 12 pull-thrus (20 x 55), back-ins (20 x 40), some side by side hkups, 48 W, 48 E (30 amps), tent sites. **REC.** Pet restrict(B). 2015 rates: $20.
AAA Approved
(325)387-3105 Lat: 30.55539, Lon: -100.80950
1711 Pr 4468, Sonora, TX 76950
cavernsofsonora@cavernsofsonora.com
www.cavernsofsonora.com

SOUTH PADRE ISLAND — M5 *Cameron*

SOUTH PADRE ISLAND See also Brownsville & Port Isabel.

ISLA BLANCA (Public) From Hwy 100, E across Causeway, S 0.3 mi on Park Rd 100 (E). 2015 rates: $25 to $40. (956)761-5494

SOUTH PADRE KOA **Ratings: 9.5/9.5★/9** (RV Park) 2015 rates: $47.99 to $ 78.99. (800)562-9724 1 Padre Blvd, South Padre Island, TX 78597

SPRING — D8 *Harris*

TRINITY SPRINGS OAKS RV & MOBILE HOME COMMUNITY **Ratings: 7/NA/9** (RV Area in MHP) 2015 rates: $28. (281)350-2606 22014 Spring Oaks Dr, Spring, TX 77389

SPRING BRANCH — D6 *Comal*

GUADALUPE RIVER (State Pk) From Jct of US-281 & SR-46, W 7.3 mi on SR-46 to Park Rd 31, N 3 mi (E) (Entrance fee). 2015 rates: $16 to $20. (830)438-2656

SPRING BRANCH RV PARK
Ratings: 8/10★/8 (RV Park) From Jct SH 46 & US 281: Go 6-3/4 mi N on US 281. (R). **FAC:** All weather rds. (59 spaces). Avail: 39 all weather, patios, 31 pull-thrus (30 x 70), back-ins (30 x 65), 39 full hkups (30/50 amps), seasonal sites, WiFi, laundry, firewood. **REC:** playground. Pet restrict(B). Partial handicap access, no tents. Big rig sites, 2015 rates: $35 to $45.
(830)885-2491 Lat: 29.89470, Lon: -98.40889
10950 Hwy 281 N, Spring Branch, TX 78070
Sbrv@gvtc.com
www.springbranchrvpark.com
See ad page 1175.

STEPHENVILLE — B6 *Erath*

LOST CREEK RV PARK **Ratings: 7/NA/9** (RV Park) 2015 rates: $30. (254)965-6223 1962 US Hwy 281 South, Stephenville, TX 76401

STONEWALL — C6 *Gillespie*

PEACH COUNTRY RV PARK
Ratings: 7/9★/9 (RV Park) From Jct Hwy 16 & US-290: Go 14-1/2 mi E on US-290 (R). **FAC:** All weather rds. (52 spaces). Avail: 37 gravel, patios, 32 pull-thrus (30 x 100), back-ins (30 x 65), 37 full hkups (30/50 amps), seasonal sites, WiFi, rentals, laundry. **REC.** Pet restrict(Q). No tents. Big rig sites, 2015 rates: $30. Disc: military.
(830)644-2233 Lat: 30.23481, Lon: -98.65973
14789 Hwy 290 East, Stonewall, TX 78671
peachcountryrvpark@hotmail.com
www.peachcountryrv.com
See ad pages 1124 (Spotlight Texas Hill Country), 1108.

STRATFORD — E9 *Sherman*

STAR OF TEXAS RV PARK AND HORSE HOTEL
(RV Spaces) From jct US 54 & US 287: Go 1/4 mi S on US 287, then 1 Block E on TX 15 (R). **FAC:** Gravel rds. 60 gravel, 60 pull-thrus (30 x 75), 60 full hkups (30/50 amps), WiFi. Pets OK. Big rig sites, 2015 rates: $30. No CC.
(806)366-7827 Lat: 36.3277894, Lon: -102.0693890
5680 Texas Highway 15, Stratford, TX 79084
www.staroftexasrv.com
See ad this page.

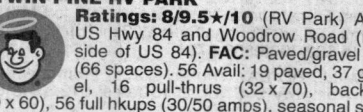

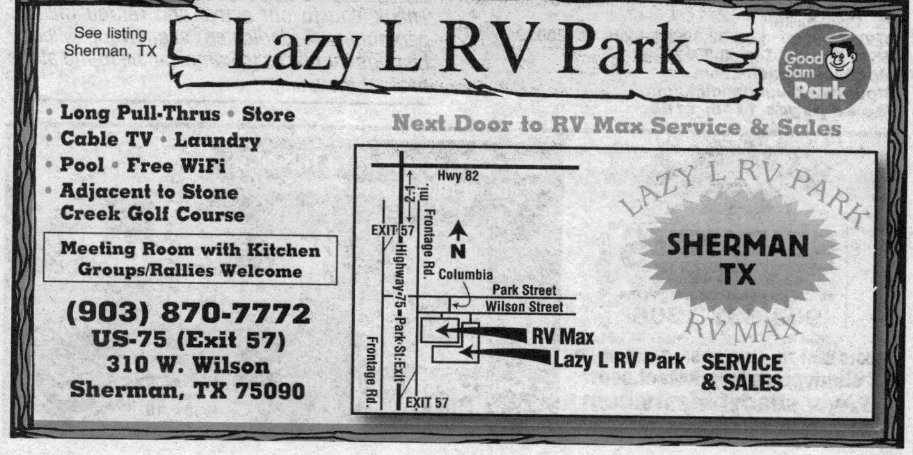

TX

SWEENY — D8 *Brazoria*

STONEBRIDGE RV PARK & RESORT **Ratings:** 9/8★/9 (RV Park) 2015 rates: $35. (979)245-1200 15804 Hwy 35 N, Sweeny, TX 77480

SWEETWATER — B5 *Nolan, Fisher*

BAR J HITCHIN POST RV
Ratings: 7.5/9.5★/7.5 (RV Park) From jct I20 and exit 242: Go 1 Blk N on CR142 (L). **FAC:** All weather rds. 50 Avail: 50 all weather, 33 pull-thrus (30 x 80), back-ins (30 x 60), 50 full hkups (30/50 amps), WiFi, laundry. **REC.** Pet restrict Partial handicap access. Big rig sites, 2015 rates: $40.
(325)236-3889 Lat: 32.4527934, Lon: -100.4428972
50 S Hopkins Rd, Sweetwater, TX 79556
www.barjhitchinpostrv.com/
See ad this page.

LAKE SWEETWATER BAIT SHOP (Public) From Jct of I-20 & Exit 249, S 5 mi on FM-1856 to FM-2035, E 0.5 mi (E). 2015 rates: $10 to $20. Mar 15 to Oct 1. (325)235-1223

TATUM — B9 *Rusk*

MARTIN CREEK LAKE (State Pk) From Jct of SR-149 & SR-43, SW 3.7 mi on SR-43 to CR-2183, S 0.7 mi to CR-2181D, SW 0.1 mi (E) (Entrance fee). 2015 rates: $13 to $17. (903)836-4336

TEMPLE — C7 *Bell*

CEDAR RIDGE PARK (Public Corps) From Jct of Hwy 317 & Hwy 36, NW 2 mi on Hwy 36 to Cedar Ridge Rd, S 1 mi (E). 2015 rates: $22 to $36. (254)986-1404

TERLINGUA — D3 *Brewster*

BIG BEND RESORT & ADVENTURES RV PARK
Ratings: 6.5/8/7 (RV Park) From Jct of Hwy 118 & FM-170W: Go 100 feet S on Hwy 118 (L). Elev 2680 ft. **FAC:** Dirt rds. 120 dirt, patios, 42 pull-thrus (25 x 55), back-ins (25 x 50), 120 full hkups (30/50 amps), WiFi, tent sites, rentals, laundry, groc, fire rings, restaurant. **REC:** golf. Pets OK. Big rig sites, 2015 rates: $29 to $32. ATM.
(432)371-2218 Lat: 29.32998, Lon: -103.53374
1 Main St, Terlingua, TX 79852
info@foreverlodging.com
www.bigbendresort.com
See ad pages 1112 (Spotlight Big Bend National Park), 1108 & Snowbird Destinations in Magazine Section.

TERRELL — B8 *Kaufman*

BLUEBONNET RIDGE RV PARK & COTTAGES
Ratings: 9.5/10★/10 (RV Park) From Jct of I-20 (exit 506) & FM-429: Go 1/2 mi N on FM-429 (L).

LESS THAN 30 MINUTES EAST OF DALLAS
Featuring true Texas Hospitality in a relaxing country setting, we are the perfect place to call home. Enjoy our 64 acres in a country setting with 90' long pull thru sites, a family pool and 5 acre fishing lake.

FAC: Paved rds. (90 spaces). Avail: 34 gravel, patios, 28 pull-thrus (33 x 90), back-ins (33 x 60), 34 full hkups (30/50 amps), seasonal sites, cable, WiFi, rentals, laundry, groc, LP gas. **REC:** pool, whirlpool, pond, fishing, playground. Pet restrict(B/Q). Partial handicap access, no tents. Big rig sites, 2015 rates: $42. Disc: military.
(972)524-9600 Lat: 32.69096, Lon: -96.20029
16543 Fm 429, Terrell, TX 75161
info@bluebonnetrv.com
http://www.bluebonnetrv.com
See ad pages 1145, 1108.

TEXARKANA — A9 *Bowie, Cass*

CLEAR SPRINGS CAMPGROUND (Public Corps) From town, S 10 mi on Hwy 59S to FM-2148, N 3 mi to Clear Springs Park, W 2 mi (E). 2015 rates: $12 to $32. (903)838-8781

MALLARD BAY (Public Corps) From town, SW 10 mi on Hwy 59S (L). 2015 rates: $12. (903)832-9161

PINEY POINT (COE-WRIGHT PATMAN LAKE) (Public Corps) From town: Go 12 mi SW on US 59 to first park road past Sulphur River bridge. Follow signs. 2015 rates: $22 to $24. Mar 1 to Nov 30. (903)838-8781

ROCKY POINT (Public Corps) From town, S 10 mi on US-59 (R). 2015 rates: $20 to $24. (903)838-8781

SHADY PINES RV PARK
Ratings: 9/10★/10 (RV Park) From Jct of US 59 & US 67 (W side of Texarkana): Go 6 mi W on US 67 (R). **FAC:** Paved rds. (48 spaces). Avail: 38 paved, patios, 18 pull-thrus (30 x 80), back-ins (30 x 60), 38 full hkups (30/50 amps), seasonal sites, WiFi, laundry, LP gas. **REC:** Shady Pines Lake: fishing. Pets OK. No tents. Big rig sites, 2015 rates: $30.
(903)832-1268 Lat: 33.39047, Lon: -94.19343
10010 W 7th St, Texarkana, TX 75501
sprvpark@aol.com
www.shadypinesrv.com
See ad this page, 1108.

TEXARKANA RV PARK **Ratings: 7/10★/8** (RV Park) 2015 rates: $35. (903)306-1364 5000 US Hwy 59 South, Texarkana, TX 75501

Travel Services

SHADY PINES RV CENTER, INC Your full line RV Dealer for Sales, Service & Supplies. **SERVICES:** RV, RV appliance, restrooms, RV Sales. RV supplies, LP, dump, emergency parking, RV accessible. waiting room. Hours: 8am to 5pm, Sat 8am to 3pm.
(903)838-5486 Lat: 33.39047, Lon: -94.19343
9956 W 7th, Texarkana, TX 75501
sptrlsls@aol.com
www.shadypinesrv.com
See ad this page.

THE COLONY — G4 *Denton*

HIDDEN COVE PARK (Public) From Jct of I-35E & Hwy 121 (exit 448), E 6 mi on Hwy 121 to FM-423, N 5.5 mi on FM 423 to Stonebrook, W 2.3 mi on Stonebrook to Hackberry Creek Pk Rd, W 0.9 mi (E) (Entrance fee). 2015 rates: $22 to $35. (972)294-1443

THE WOODLANDS — C8 *Montgomery*

RAYFORD CROSSING RV RESORT
Ratings: 10/10★/10 (RV Park) From Jct I-45 & Rayford Rd (Exit 73), Go 1.5 mi E on Rayford Rd then 1/2 mi S on Geneva Rd to dead end, then 1/4 mi E on N Plum Creek Dr (L) NOTE: No Pop up trailers.

LUXURY RESORT 20 MILES FROM HOUSTON
Enjoy an endless array of activities in the resort & in The Woodlands Town-Center and waterway nearby, always abuzz with concerts, outdoor cafes, shopping & home to some of the best golfing in the South. Good Sam Top Rated.

FAC: Paved rds. (115 spaces). Avail: 45 paved, patios, 45 pull-thrus (31 x 75), 45 full hkups (30/50 amps), seasonal sites, cable, WiFi, rentals, laundry, groc, LP gas, fire rings, firewood. **REC:** heated pool, wading pool, whirlpool, pond, fishing, shuffleboard, playground. Pet restrict(B/Q). Partial handicap access, no tents. Big rig sites, 2015 rates: $52 to $72. Disc: military.
(281)298-8008 Lat: 30.11341, Lon: -95.41498
29321 S. Plum Creek Dr, Spring, TX 77386
rayfordcrossing@sbcglobal.net
www.rayfordcrossing.com
See ad pages 1158, 1108 & Snowbird Destinations in Magazine Section.

Thank You to our active and retired military personnel. A dedicated section of Military Listings for places to camp can be found at the back of the Guide.

WOODLAND LAKES RV PARK
Ratings: 8/9★/9 (RV Park) From Jct I-45 (exit 79A) & SR-242: Go 1-1/2 mi E on SR-242, then 1 Block S on Firehouse Rd (E). **FAC:** Paved/gravel rds. (89 spaces). Avail: 29 gravel, patios, 22 pull-thrus (30 x 80), back-ins (30 x 45), 29 full hkups (30/50 amps), seasonal sites, cable, WiFi, laundry, LP gas. **REC:** Woodland Lakes: fishing. Pet restrict(B). No tents. Big rig sites, 2015 rates: $38 to $40.
(936)273-6666 Lat: 30.20638, Lon: -95.43198
17110 Fire House Rd, Conroe, TX 77385
woodlandlakesrvpark@yahoo.com
www.woodlandlakesrvpark.com
See ad pages 1159, 1108.

THREE RIVERS — E6 *Live Oak*

CHOKE CANYON/CALLIHAM UNIT (State Pk) From Jct of US-281 & Hwy 72, W 10.9 mi on Hwy 72 to Park Rd 8, N 1 mi (E). 2015 rates: $22. (361)786-3868

TOMBALL — D8 *Montgomery*

CORRAL RV PARK **Ratings: 7.5/9★/8.5** (RV Area in MHP) 2015 rates: $34 to $37. (281)351-2761 1402 S Cherry #37, Tomball, TX 77375

TOYAHVALE — C3 *Reeves*

BALMORHEA (State Pk) From I-10 & SR-17 (exit 209), SW 6.8 mi on SR-17 (L) (Entrance fee). 2015 rates: $11 to $17. (432)375-2370

TRINITY — C8 *Trinity*

MARINA VILLAGE RESORT **Ratings: 8/8/9.5** (Membership Pk) 2015 rates: $35. (936)594-0149 176 E Westwood Dr, Trinity, TX 75862

TYLER — B8 *Smith*

A SPOTLIGHT Introducing Tyler's colorful attractions appearing at the front of this state section.

TYLER See also Bullard, Gladewater, Hawkins & Mineola.

#1 RV PARK OF TYLER
Ratings: 8.5/9.5★/8.5 (RV Park) From Jct of W SW Loop 323 & State Hwy 31 W: Go 2 mi W on State Hwy 31 W. (L). **FAC:** Paved rds. (65 spaces). Avail: 35 paved, patios, 35 pull-thrus (19 x 62), 35 full hkups (30/50 amps), seasonal sites, cable, WiFi, dump, laundry, LP gas. **REC.** Pet restrict(B). No tents. 2015 rates: $34. Disc: AAA.
(903)593-9101 Lat: 32.33658, Lon: -95.37402
12421 State Hwy 31W, Tyler, TX 75709
office@numberonervpark.com
www.numberonervpark.com
See ad pages 1126 (Spotlight Tyler), 1108.

JELLYSTONE PARK AT WHISPERING PINES **Ratings: 9/6.5/8.5** (RV Park) 2015 rates: $35. (903)858-2405 5583 Fm 16E, Tyler, TX 75706

TYLER (CONT)

TYLER (State Pk) From Jct of I-20 & FM-14 (exit 562), N 2 mi on FM-14 (L) (Entrance fee). 2015 rates: $20 to $26. (903)597-5338

UNIVERSAL CITY — D6 *Bexar*

ABC RV PARK MHP

Ratings: 5/6.5/7 (RV Area in MHP) From Jct of I-35N & Hwy 218/Pat Booker Rd (exit 172), E 2 mi on Hwy 218 to Kitty Hawk Rd, N 0.1 mi (L); or From Jct of I-10 & Loop 1604, N 6.3 mi to Kitty Hawk Rd, E 0.9 mi (L). **FAC:** Paved rds. (55 spaces). Avail: 6 gravel, patios, 6 pull-thrus (35 x 65), accepts full hkup units only, 6 full hkups (30/50 amps), seasonal sites, laundry. Pet restrict Partial handicap access, no tents. Big rig sites, 2015 rates: $29.50. No CC.
(800)256-1770 Lat: 29.55371, Lon: -98.30223
271 Kitty Hawk, Universal City, TX 78148
See ad page 1174.

UVALDE — D5 *Uvalde*

PARKVIEW RIVERSIDE RV PARK

Ratings: 8.5/9.5★/9 (RV Park) From Jct of Hwy 83 & Hwy 1050 (north of Concan), E 1 mi on Hwy 1050 to CR-350, S 1.5 mi (R). **FAC:** Paved/gravel rds. 99 gravel, 17 pull-thrus (28 x 65), back-ins (35 x 55), 99 full hkups (30/50 amps), WiFi $, dump, laundry, groc, LP gas, fire rings, firewood. **REC:** Frio River: swim, fishing. Pets OK. Big rig sites, eco-friendly, 2015 rates: $42 to $60.
(877)374-6748 Lat: 29.58256, Lon: -99.72801
2561 County Road 350, Concan, TX 78838
parkviewrv@gmail.com
www.parkviewriversiderv.com
See primary listing at Concan and ad page 1140.

QUAIL SPRINGS RV PARK

Ratings: 7.5/9★/9 (RV Park) From Jct of US-83 & US-90 (in Uvalde), E 2.2 mi on US-90 (R). **FAC:** Paved rds. (83 spaces). Avail: 47 gravel, patios, 35 pull-thrus (30 x 60), back-ins (30 x 55), 47 full hkups (30/50 amps), seasonal sites, cable, WiFi, laundry. **REC:** Pet restrict(B). No tents. Big rig sites, 2015 rates: $26 to $28.
(830)278-8182 Lat: 29.22854, Lon: -99.75597
2727 E Main St, Uvalde, TX 78801
quail@hilconet.com
www.quailspringsrvpark.com
See ad this page.

VALLEY VIEW — A7 *Cook, Denton*

RAY ROBERTS LAKE/JOHNSON BRANCH (State Pk) From Jct of I-35 & Exit 483 (FM-3002), E 6.6 mi on FM-3002 (R) (Entrance fee). 2015 rates: $25 to $26. (940)637-2294

VAN HORN — C2 *Culberson*

DESERT WILLOW RV PARK

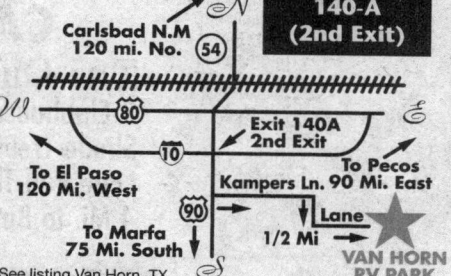

Ratings: 5.5/10★/7 (RV Park) Going East: From I-10 & US 90 (Exit 140A); Go 1/2 mi N on Van Horn St to Broadway, then go; 1/3 mi E on Broadway (R). Going West: From I-10 & Exit 140 B, go N 1/4 mi (L). Elev 3980 ft. **FAC:** Dirt rds. 26 dirt, 15 pull-thrus (30 x 55), back-ins (30 x 55), 26 full hkups

VAN HORN (CONT)

DESERT WILLOW RV PARK (CONT)
(30/50 amps), WiFi, tent sites, laundry. Pets OK. Big rig sites, 2015 rates: $25. Disc: AAA, military.
(432)283-2225 Lat: 31.039984, Lon: -104.826241
404 E Broadway, Van Horn, TX 79855
desertwillow@yahoo.com
www.desertwillowvanhorn.com
See ad page 1179.

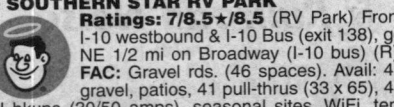

➔ MOUNTAIN VIEW RV PARK **Ratings: 5.5/7.5/7.5** (RV Park) 2015 rates: $30 to $35. (432)283-0005 810 S.E. Frontage Rd, Van Horn, TX 79855

SOUTHERN STAR RV PARK
Ratings: 7/8.5★/8.5 (RV Park) From I-10 westbound & I-10 Bus (exit 138), go NE 1/2 mi on Broadway (I-10 bus) (R). **FAC:** Gravel rds. (46 spaces). Avail: 41 gravel, patios, 41 pull-thrus (33 x 65), 41 full hkups (30/50 amps), seasonal sites, WiFi, tent sites, rentals, dump, laundry. **REC.** Pet restrict(B). Partial handicap access. Eco-friendly, 2015 rates: $30. Disc: AAA, military.
(432)283-2420 Lat: 31.03842, Lon: -104.84796
1605 W. Broadway, Van Horn, TX 79855
manager@southernstarrvpark.net
www.southernstarrvpark.net

VAN HORN RV PARK
Ratings: 8.5/8/9.5 (Campground) From Jct of I-10 (Exit 140-A) & US-90: Go 1/4 mi S on US-90, then E onto Kampers Lane (L). Elev 4078 ft. **FAC:** Gravel rds. (74 spaces). Avail: 72 gravel, 72 pull-thrus (30 x 75), 72 full hkups (30/50 amps), seasonal sites, cable, WiFi, tent sites, rentals, dump, laundry, groc, LP gas, restaurant. **REC:** pool, pond, fishing, playground. Pets OK. Partial handicap access. Big rig sites, eco-friendly, 2015 rates: $38. Disc: military.
(432)283-2728 Lat: 31.03056, Lon: -104.82601
#10 Kampers Lane, Van Horn, TX 79855
vanhornrvpark@windstream.net
www.vanhorntexasrvpark.com
See ad pages 1179, 1108.

Things to See and Do

VAN HORN RV PARK CAFE Dine in or delivery to your door nightly from 5:30pm to 8pm. Breakfast 7:30am-9:30am. Partial handicap access. Food. Hours: 7:30am-9:30am & 5:30pm-9:30pm.
(432)283-2728 Lat: 31.03109, Lon: -104.82599
10 Kampers Lane, Van Horn, TX 79855
vanhornrvpark@windstream.net
www.vanhorntexasrvpark.com
See ad page 1179.

Subscribe to MotorHome Magazine! Questions? Change of address? Call 800-678-1201.

VANDERPOOL — D6 *Bandera*

LOST MAPLES STATE NATURAL AREA (State Pk) From S Jct of Hwys 337 & 187, N 4.8 mi on Hwy 187 (L) (Entrance fee). 2015 rates: $20. (830)966-3413

VERNON — A6 *Wilbarger*

ROCKING "A" RV PARK
Ratings: 8/10★/8.5 (Campground) From Jct of US 70 & US 287 (W of town): Go 1/4 mi NW on N Service Rd, then 1 block E on Harrison St (past Wal Mart) (R). **FAC:** Paved/gravel rds. (75 spaces). Avail: 50 grass, 50 pull-thrus (30 x 60), 50 full hkups (30/50 amps), seasonal sites, cable, WiFi, tent sites, dump, laundry, LP gas. **REC:** pool, playground. Pet restrict(B). Big rig sites, 2015 rates: $30.
(940)552-2821 Lat: 34.16567, Lon: -99.31147
3725 Harrison, Vernon, TX 76384
info@rockingarvpark.com
www.rockingarvpark.com
See ad this page, 1108.

RV Park ratings you can rely on!

VICTORIA — D7 *Victoria*

DAD'S RV PARK **Ratings: 8.5/9★/7.5** (RV Park) 2015 rates: $35. (361)573-1231 203 Hopkins Street, Victoria, TX 77901

GATEWAY TO THE GULF RV PARK
Ratings: 9/9.5★/8 (RV Park) From N Jct of US-59 & Loop 463, NE 0.5 mi on US-59, then back S 0.1 mi on W Frntg Rd (R). **FAC:** Paved rds. 118 Avail: 95 paved, 23 gravel, 48 pull-thrus (32 x 80), back-ins (27 x 60), some side by side hkups, 118 full hkups (30/50 amps), cable, WiFi, laundry. **REC:** pool, pond. Pets OK. Partial handicap access, no tents. Big rig sites, RV age restrict, eco-friendly, 2015 rates: $30. Disc: military.
AAA Approved
(361)570-7080 Lat: 28.82334, Lon: -96.92044
9809 US Hwy 59 North, Victoria, TX 77905
info@gatewayrvpark.com
www.gatewayrvpark.com
See ad this page.

LAZY LONGHORN RV PARK
Ratings: 10/10★/9 (RV Park) From Jct of US-59 & Hwy 185, NW 1 mi on Hwy 185 (Laurent St) (R) or From Jct of Bus Hwy 59 & Laurent St (Hwy 185), SE 2 mi on Laurent St (L). **FAC:** Paved rds. 99 paved, patios, 32 pull-thrus (25 x 75), back-ins (25 x 45), 99 full hkups (30/50 amps), cable, WiFi, rentals, laundry, controlled access. **REC:** heated pool, whirlpool. Pet restrict(B/Q). Partial handicap access, no tents. RV age restrict, eco-friendly, 2015 rates: $30. Disc: AAA, military. No CC.
(361)485-1598 Lat: 28.78284, Lon: -96.98637
1402 S Laurent St., Victoria, TX 77901
www.lazylonghornrv.com
See ad this page, 1108.

RV PARK OF VICTORIA **Ratings: 8.5/8.5★/8** (RV Park) 2015 rates: $28. (361)580-2424 13202 N Navarro (US-77), Victoria, TX 77904

RV PARK OF VICTORIA (Public) From Jct of Vine St & Red River, N 0.3 mi on Vine St (L). 2015 rates: $28. (866)720-3496

VICTORIA COLETO CREEK LAKE KOA **Ratings: 9/10★/9.5** (RV Park) 2015 rates: $43 to $51. 500 Coleto Park Road, Victoria, TX 77905

VIDOR — C9 *Orange*

BOOMTOWN USA RV RESORT
Ratings: 6.5/9.5★/6.5 (RV Park) From jct I-10 & Asher Turn Around (exit 858) go E 1/2 mi on feeder road then go N under freeway (Enter). **FAC:** Paved/gravel rds. 117 Avail: 5 paved, 70 gravel, 42 grass, 10 pull-thrus (30 x 70), back-ins (30 x 70), 117 full hkups (30/50 amps), WiFi Hotspot, tent sites, rentals, dump, laundry. **REC:** Lake Tristan: swim, fishing. Pet restrict(B). Big rig sites, eco-friendly, 2015 rates: $33 to $55. Disc: AAA, military.
(409)769-6105 Lat: 30.112909, Lon: -094.045526
1495 W Freeway Blvd, Vidor, TX 77662
boomtownusa@sbcglobal.net
www.boomtownusarvresort.com
See ad page 1135.

SUGAR PINES MH COMMUNITY (RV Spaces) From I-10 & N Main St, go N 5.2 mi on N Main St to Circle Dr, go W on Circle Dr 1/4 mi (R) (monthly reservations only). **FAC:** Paved rds. 17 paved, back-ins (50 x 110), 17 full hkups (30/50 amps). Pet restrict(B/Q). 2015 rates: $195 monthly. No CC.
(409)681-0363 Lat: 30.20553, Lon: -094.02946
1205 W. Circle Drive, Vidor, TX 77662
sugarpines@towermgmt.com
www.towerrvparks.com

VON ORMY — D6 *Bexar*

ALAMO RIVER RV RESORT **Ratings: 8/8.5/9** (RV Park) 2015 rates: $39. (210)622-5022 12430 Trawalter, Von Ormy, TX 78073

WACO — C7 *McLennan*

WACO See also West.

AIRPORT PARK (Public Corps) From Jct of I-35 & Lake Shore Dr exit, W to Steinbeck Bend Rd, N to Airport Rd, E 2 mi (L). 2015 rates: $20 to $24. (254)756-5359

FLAT CREEK FARMS RV RESORT
Ratings: 5.5/8.5/9 (RV Park) From jct I-35 & Exit 328: Go 1 Block N on E service rd, then 1-3/4 mi NE on Greig Dr (R). **FAC:** Paved/gravel rds. 57 gravel, 17 pull-thrus (30 x 70), back-ins (30 x 70), 57 full hkups (30/50 amps), WiFi, laundry. **REC:** pond, fishing. Pets OK. Big rig sites, 2015 rates: $35. No reservations.
(254)662-9858 Lat: 31.46913, Lon: -97.14141
1633 Greig Dr, Waco, TX 76706
Flatcreekfarms@gmail.com
flatcreekfarmsrvresort.com
See ad this page.

HEART O'TEXAS FAIR COMPLEX (COUNTY FAIR ASSN.) (Public) From I-35 (exit 331 New Rd): Go NW on New Rd, then SW on Bosque Blvd. Follow signs. 2015 rates: $12 to $15. (254)776-1660

I 35 RV PARK & RESORT
Ratings: 9.5/9★/7.5 (RV Park) From Junction I-35 & Exit 346 (Northbound and Southbound): Go 3/4 mi S on W Service Rd (R). **FAC:** Paved rds. (215 spaces). 138 Avail: 128 gravel, 10 grass, 138 pull-thrus (24 x 75), 138 full hkups (30/50 amps), seasonal sites, WiFi, dump, laundry, LP gas, restaurant. **REC:** pool, pond, fishing. Pets OK. No tents. Big rig sites, 2015 rates: $33.50 to $35.50. Disc: military. ATM, no CC.
(254)829-0698 Lat: 31.70429, Lon: -97.10245
15131 N Ih-35, Elm Mott, TX 76640
info@i35rvpark.com
www.i35rvpark.com
See ad this page, 1108.

MIDWAY PARK (Public Corps) From Jct of I-35 & Hwy 6, W 5 mi on Hwy 6 to Midway Park exit, 0.5 mi on service rd. (E). 2015 rates: $20 to $36. (254)756-5359

QUAIL CROSSING RV PARK
Ratings: 6.5/8.5★/7 (RV Park) From jct I-35 exit 330B and US 6 go 9.5 mi NW on US 6, then 1/4 mi SW on Spur 412, then 1/4 mi SE on Speegle Rd, then 3/4 mi SW on Western, then 1/4 mi NW on Spanish Trail (E). **FAC:** Gravel rds. (55 spaces). Avail: 30 gravel, 30 pull-thrus (30 x 75), 30 full hkups (30/50 amps), seasonal sites, cable, WiFi, rentals, laundry. **REC:** pond, fishing. Pet restrict(B). Big rig sites, 2015 rates: $30 to $33. Disc: AAA, military.
(254)848-4818 Lat: 31.56187, Lon: -97.30421
824 Spanish Trail, Woodway, TX 76712
quailcrossingrvpark@hotmail.com
quailcrossingrvpark.com
See ad this page.

Tell your RV Campground that you found them in this Guide.

RIVERVIEW CAMPGROUND
Ratings: 8/8/7.5 (RV Park) From Jct of I-35 (Exit 330A) & Loop 340: Go 4 1/2 mi E on Loop 340, then 2 mi SE on FM-434 (S 3rd St), then 1 mi E on Riverview (R). **FAC:** All weather rds. (127 spaces). 60 Avail: 45 paved, 15 gravel, 50 pull-thrus (22 x 85), back-ins (25 x 40), 60 full hkups (30/50 amps), seasonal sites, cable, WiFi, laundry, LP bottles. **REC:** pool, Waco River: fishing, playground. Pets OK. No tents. 2015 rates: $28 to $30. Disc: military. No CC.
(254)662-0475 Lat: 31.50257, Lon: -97.05249
988 Riverview Rd, Waco, TX 76706
skippervoss@msn.com
www.riverviewcampgroundtx.com
See ad opposite page.

SPEEGLEVILLE I PARK (Public Corps) From Jct of I-35 & Hwy 6, W 7 mi on Hwy 6 to Speegleville Rd, N 2 mi to Overflow Rd (R). 2015 rates: $20. Mar 1 to Oct 31. (254)756-5359

WALLER — D8 *Waller*

LONESTAR YOGI
Ratings: 9/9★/9 (Campground) From Jct of US 290 & FM-1098 (E of Hempstead): Go S 4.1 mi on FM-1098 (E).

WHERE VACATIONS BECOME MEMORIES
Located in Waller, Texas, 35 miles northwest of Houston, Texas. Friendly, clean and active atmosphere will make your stay with us a memorable camping vacation experience. Perfect for family vacations.

FAC: Paved rds. 154 gravel, 72 pull-thrus (23 x 50), back-ins (25 x 55), 110 full hkups, 44 W, 44 E (30/50 amps), cable, WiFi Hotspot, tent sites, rentals, dump, laundry, groc, LP gas, firewood, controlled access. **REC:** pool, pond, fishing, playground, rec open to public. Pet restrict(B/Q). Partial handicap access. Big rig sites, 2015 rates: $34 to $58. Disc: AAA, military. ATM.
(979)826-4111 Lat: 30.02139, Lon: -95.98984
34843 Betka Rd, Waller, TX 77484
info@lonestarcamping.com
www.LoneStarJellystone.com
See ad pages 1156, 1108 & Family Camping in Magazine Section.

Did you know we sent 35 husband-wife RVing teams out this year to scour North America, rating and inspecting RV parks and campgrounds? You can rest easy when you read our listings, knowing we've already been there.

WASKOM — B9 *Harrison*

MISS ELLIE'S RV PARK
Ratings: 7/9★/7.5 (RV Park) From Jct I-20 & exit 633: Go 1/2 mi E on S Service Rd (R). **FAC:** Gravel rds. (68 spaces). Avail: 10 gravel, 10 pull-thrus (25 x 100), 10 full hkups (30/50 amps), seasonal sites, WiFi, dump, laundry, LP gas. **REC:** pond. Pet restrict(B). Partial handicap access, no tents. Big rig sites, 2015 rates: $27. Disc: military.
(903)687-3688 Lat: 32.47580, Lon: -94.07863
1517 S Interstate 20 W, Waskom, TX 75692
sherri_skipper@yahoo.com
www.missellliesrvpark.com

WEATHERFORD — B7 *Parker*

HOOVES N' WHEELS
Ratings: 8/9★/8 (RV Park) From Jct I-20 (Exit 408) & Hwy 51: Go 2 mi S on Hwy 51 (R). Service Rd (R). **FAC:** All weather rds. (70 spaces). Avail: 28 gravel, 22 pull-thrus (35 x 75), back-ins (35 x 70), 28 full hkups (30/50 amps), seasonal sites, WiFi, dump, laundry, LP gas. **REC:** Pet restrict(B). Partial handicap access, no tents. Big rig sites, 2015 rates: $31.
(817)599-4686 Lat: 32.69900, Lon: -97.77076
4128 Granbury Hwy, Weatherford, TX 76087
info@hoovesnwheels.com
www.hoovesnwheels.com
See ad this page.

Join the flock and head south during the winter. Use our handy Snowbird guide in the front of the Guide to find RV-friendly destinations throughout the Sunbelt. Snowbird Destinations features the top Snowbird roosts and lists great Campgrounds in compelling areas.

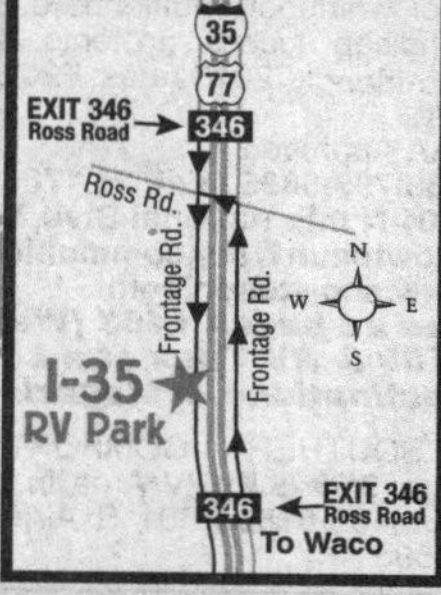

TX

WEATHERFORD (CONT)

OAK CREEK RV PARK
Ratings: 10/10★/10 (RV Park) From Jct FM 1189 & I-20 (Exit 397): Go 1/2 mi W on N Service Rd (R). **FAC:** Paved rds. (120 spaces). Avail: 72 paved, patios, 50 pull-thrus (30 x 70), back-ins (30 x 55), 72 full hkups (30/50 amps), seasonal sites, cable, WiFi, dump, laundry, LP gas. **REC:** pool, whirlpool, pond, fishing. Pets OK. No tents. Big rig sites, 2015 rates: $35.
(817)594-0200 Lat: 32.69953, Lon: -97.96760
7652 W I-20, Weatherford, TX 76088
oakcreekrvpark@yahoo.com
www.oakcreekrvpark.com
See ad page 1108.

WEATHERFORD/FORT WORTH WEST KOA
Ratings: 9/10★/8.5 (RV Park) W-Bnd: From Jct of I-20 (Exit 408): Go 1/2 mi W on N Service Rd, then 1 block S on Tin Top Rd. E-bnd: From the Jct of I-20 (exit 406): Go 2 mi E on S Service Rd, then 1 block S on Tin Top Rd. (L). **FAC:** Paved/gravel rds. (58 spaces). Avail: 25 gravel, 25 pull-thrus (20 x 60), mostly side by side hkups, 25 full hkups (30/50 amps), seasonal sites, cable, WiFi, tent sites, dump, laundry, groc, LP gas. **REC:** pool, playground. Pets OK. Big rig sites, eco-friendly, 2015 rates: $34.49.
(817)594-8801 Lat: 32.72536, Lon: -97.79628
2205 Tin Top Rd, Weatherford, TX 76087
info@weatherfordkoa.com
www.weatherfordkoa.com
See ad page 1148.

WECHES — C8 *Houston*

MISSION TEJAS (State Pk) From Jct of SR-21 & FM-227, NE 1.4 mi on SR-21 to Park Rd 44 (L) (Entrance fee). 2015 rates: $9 to $15. (936)687-2394

WEIMAR — D7 *Colorado*

WHISPERING OAKS RV PARK **Ratings: 8/8★/8** (RV Park) 2015 rates: $36.85. (979)732-9494 2965 Hwy 90, Weimar, TX 78962

WELLINGTON — F10 *Collingsworth*

COLLINGSWORTH COUNTY PIONEER'S PARK (Public) From town, N 7 mi on US-83 (L). 2015 rates: $15. (806)447-5408

WESLACO — M3 *Hidalgo*

COUNTRY SUNSHINE RV RESORT **Ratings: 9.5/7.5/8** (RV Area in MHP) 2015 rates: $37. (800)405-6188 1601 S Airport Dr, Weslaco, TX 78596

MAGIC VALLEY RV PARK MHP **Ratings: 9/7/7.5** (RV Park) 2015 rates: $36 to $40. (956)968-8242 2300 E Bus Hwy 83, Weslaco, TX 78596

SNOW TO SUN RV RESORT
Ratings: 9/9.5★/8.5 (RV Area in MHP) From Jct of Expwy 83 & FM-1015 (International Blvd), N 1.1 mi on International Blvd (L).

A RIO GRANDE VALLEY OASIS
Located just minutes from Hwy 83, this gated resort offers a friendly atmosphere with spacious sites and a full amenity package. Enjoy a heated pool and hot tub, shuffleboard, fitness center, billiards and planned activities!

FAC: Paved rds. (489 spaces). Avail: 152 grass, patios, back-ins (25 x 50), some side by side hkups, 152 full hkups (30/50 amps), seasonal sites, WiFi $, rentals, laundry, controlled access. **REC:** heated pool, whirlpool, shuffleboard. Pet restrict(B/Q). Partial handicap access, no tents. Age restrict may apply, eco-friendly, 2015 rates: $20 to $33. Disc: AAA, military.
AAA Approved
(888)799-5895 Lat: 26.17868, Lon: -97.96058
1701 N International Blvd, Weslaco, TX 78599
snowtosun@suncommunities.com
www.snowtosun.com
See ad pages 1463 (Welcome Section), 1108 & RV Trips of a Lifetime, Snowbird Destinations in Magazine Section.

SOUTHERN COMFORT RV RESORT **Ratings: 9/9★/8.5** (RV Area in MHP) 2015 rates: $37. (800)405-6188 1501 S Airport Drive, Weslaco, TX 78596

Nobody takes to the road like we do. In many listings we tell you the surface type and condition of interior campground roads.

WEST — B7 *McLennan*

WACO NORTH RV PARK
Ratings: 9/9★/7.5 (RV Park) N-bnd I-35 & Exit 354: Go 1 mi N on E Service Rd (R); or S-bnd & Exit 355: Go 3/4 mi S on E Frontage Rd (L). **FAC:** All weather rds. (75 spaces). Avail: 67 gravel, 64 pull-thrus (22 x 60), back-ins (22 x 45), some side by side hkups, 67 full hkups (30/50 amps), seasonal sites, WiFi, tent sites, rentals, dump, laundry, groc, firewood. **REC:** pool, pond, fishing, playground. Pets OK. Partial handicap access. Big rig sites, 2015 rates: $30 to $34. Disc: military.
(254)826-3869 Lat: 31.83310, Lon: -97.09075
24132 N Ih-35, West, TX 76691
info@waconorthrvpark.com
www.waconorthrvpark.com

WEST TAWAKONI — B8 *Hunt*

VETERAN'S MEMORIAL CITY PARK (Public) From Jct TX Hwy 34 & TX Hwy 276 (in Quinlan W of W Tawakoni), E 5 mi (L). 2015 rates: $17. (903)274-7180

WHITNEY — B7 *Bosque, Hill*

CEDRON CREEK (Public Corps) From town, N 3 mi on Hwy 933 to FM-1713, 2 mi to Cedron Rd, S 0.5 mi (follow signs). 2015 rates: $16 to $20. Apr 1 to Sep 30. (254)694-3189

LAKE WHITNEY (State Pk) From Jct of I-35 & SR-22 (exit 368A), W 15 mi on SR-22 to FM-933, N 0.6 mi to FM-1244, SW 2.2 mi (E) (Entrance fee). 2015 rates: $10 to $24. (254)694-3793

LAKE WHITNEY RV **Ratings: 7/6/7** (Membership Pk) 2015 rates: $40 to $48. (800)405-6188 417 Thousand Trails Dr, Whitney, TX 76692

LOFERS BEND EAST PARK (Public Corps) From town, SW 6 mi on Hwy 22 (R). 2015 rates: $10 to $16. Apr 1 to Sep 30. (254)694-3189

MCCOWN VALLEY PARK (Public Corps) From town, N 2.4 mi on SR-933 to FM-1713, SW 4.4 mi (L). 2015 rates: $16 to $20. Apr 1 to Sep 30. (254)694-3189

SUN COUNTRY RESORT **Ratings: 5/8.5★/7** (Membership Pk) 2015 rates: $28 to $32. (254)694-4023 255 Sun Country Dr, Whitney, TX 76692

WICHITA FALLS — A6 *Clay, Wichita*

LAKE ARROWHEAD (State Pk) From Jct of US-287/281 & US-281/79 (S of town), S 5.8 mi on US-281 to FM-1954, E 7.2 mi to Pk Rd 63 (E); or From Jct of US-287 & FM-2393, S 6.7 mi on FM-2393 to FM-1954, SE 3.2 mi (L) (Entrance fee). 2015 rates: $10 to $20. (940)528-2211

WICHITA FALLS RV PARK Ratings: 9/10★/9 (RV Park) N-bnd: From Jct of US 287 & Broad St exit: Go 3/4 mi N (stay right at split), then 1-1/4 mi W on 5th St/Seymour Hwy. (R) S-bnd: From Jct of US 287 & exit 1A: Go 1-1/4 mi SW on Bus 277 (5th/Seymour Hwy). (R). **FAC:** Paved rds. (145 spaces). Avail: 49 gravel, patios, 22 pull-thrus (27 x 70), back-ins (30 x 60), 49 full hkups (30/50 amps), seasonal sites, cable, WiFi, laundry. **REC:** pool, Wichita River: fishing. Pet restrict(B). No tents. Big rig sites, eco-friendly, 2015 rates: $30 to $38. Disc: AAA, military.
AAA Approved
(800)252-1532 Lat: 33.91081, Lon: -98.52480
2944 Seymour Hwy, Wichita Falls, TX 76301
wfrvpark@yahoo.com
www.wfrvpark.com

WICHITA RIVER BEND RV PARK (Public) From Jct of I-44 & US-277, N 1.5 mi on I-44, exit at Tourist Bureau, S 0.2 mi on frntg rd (E). 2015 rates: $17. (940)761-7491

YOGI BEAR'S JELLYSTONE PARK AT COYOTE RANCH **Ratings: 10/10★/8.5** (RV Park) 2015 rates: $60. (940)767-6700 14145 US Hwy 287 N, Wichita Falls, TX 76310

WILLIS — C8 *Montgomery*

LAKE CONROE RV **Ratings: 8.5/7.5/7.5** (Membership Pk) 2015 rates: $44. (800)405-6188 11720 Thousand Trails Rd, Willis, TX 77318

OMEGA FARMS RV PARK **Ratings: 6.5/8.5/7** (RV Park) 2015 rates: $34 to $39. (936)890-3800 11895 Old Montgoery Rd, Willis, TX 77318

VENICE ON THE LAKE **Ratings: 6/8/8** (RV Park) 2015 rates: $28 to $60. (936)856-1110 12765 Lake Conroe Bay Rd, Willis, TX 77318

Had a great stay? Let us know by emailing us travelguidecomments@goodsamfamily.com

WINNIE — D9 *Chambers*

WINNIE INN & RV PARK **Ratings: 6/NA/5.5** (RV Park) 2015 rates: $25. (409)296-2947 205 Spur 5, Winnie, TX 77665

WINTERS — B5 *Runnels*

ELM CREEK RESERVOIR (Public) From town, E 5 mi on Hwy 153 (L). 2015 rates: $9 to $12. (915)723-2081

WOLFFORTH — A4 *Lubbock*

MESA VERDE RV PARK
Ratings: 9/10★/9 (RV Park) From Jct W Loop 289 & US 62/82 (Lubbock): Go 5 mi SW on US 62/82 (Exit FM 179), then 1-1/4 mi N on E Service Rd (R). **FAC:** Paved rds. (78 spaces). Avail: 21 gravel, 21 pull-thrus (30 x 60), 21 full hkups (30/50 amps), seasonal sites, cable, WiFi, laundry. **REC:** pool. Pet restrict(Q). Partial handicap access, no tents. 2015 rates: $35. Disc: military.
(806)773-3135 Lat: 33.51413, Lon: -101.99806
503 E Hwy 62/82, Wolfforth, TX 79382
mesaverde@nts-online.net
www.rvlubbock.com
See ad page 1165.

WOODVILLE — C9 *Jasper, Tyler*

MAGNOLIA RIDGE PARK (Public Corps) From town, E 15 mi on US-190 to FM-92, N 1.5 mi to park entrance rd, E 1 mi (E). For reservations call (877)444-6777. 2015 rates: $10 to $18. (409)429-3491

WYLIE — G5 *Collin*

EAST FORK PARK (Public Corps) From town, E 2.5 mi on Hwy 78 to CR-434, N 0.05 mi to Sky View Dr, W 0.5 mi (R). 2015 rates: $30. (972)442-3141

YOAKUM — D7 *Lavaca*

HUB CITY RV PARK (Public) From Jct of Hwy 95/US-77A & FM-3475 (NE of Yoakum), SE 1.3 mi on FM-3475 (R). 2015 rates: $8 to $15. (361)293-5682

Tell your RV Campground that you found them in this Guide.

Tom Till

WELCOME TO
Utah

DATE OF STATEHOOD	WIDTH: 270 MILES (435 KM)	PROPORTION OF UNITED STATES
JAN. 4, 1896	LENGTH: 350 MILES (565 KM)	2.24% OF 3,794,100 SQ MI

This is the place. With more state parks than major cities, Utah practically owned the word "awesome" before it became downgraded to a better-than-average pizza. From the petrified forest of Escalante to the surreal canyons and mesas of Canyonlands or the ethereal reservoirs of Lake Powell, Utah's timeless landscapes will beguile, transfix and get your heart pumping, big time. With a mind-boggling area of outdoor pursuits, Utah is one of the nation's most diverse adventure playgrounds.

Dry, powdery snow yields some of the best skiing in the world and extreme-sport athletes push the boundaries with BASE jumping (illegal in many of the nation's national and state parks), skydiving, hang-gliding and extreme rope swings. Beyond Utah's primal landscapes, the Beehive State is a convivial land where squeaky clean, functional cities give way to neat Mormon outposts. State capital, Salt Lake City, is finally unbuttoning its collar. Along with a crop of hip new galleries and eclectic shops in the Sugar House district, a vibrant performing arts scene and an organic restaurant culture, the city is becoming ever more politically progressive.

Top 3 Tourism Attractions:
1) Bryce Canyon
2) Arches National Park
3) Latter-Day Saints Temple Square

Nickname: Beehive State

State Flower: Sego lily

State Bird: California Gull

People: Roseanne Barr, actress; Philo T. Farnsworth, inventor of TV; Merlin Olsen, football player and actor; Donny and Marie Osmond, singers and actors; Butch Cassidy, outlaw; James Woods, actor

Major Cities: Salt Lake City (capital), West Valley City, Provo, West Jordan, Orem

Topography: Southeast—High Colorado Plateau; west—desert-like Great Basin; northwest—Great Salt Lake, Bonneville Salt Flats; northeast—Middle Rockies

Climate: Generally semiarid to arid; favorable temperatures along the Wasatch Front, with relatively mild winters

Matt Morgan

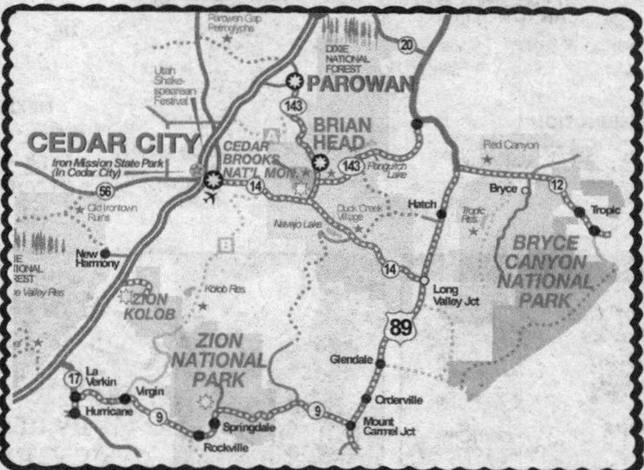

UT

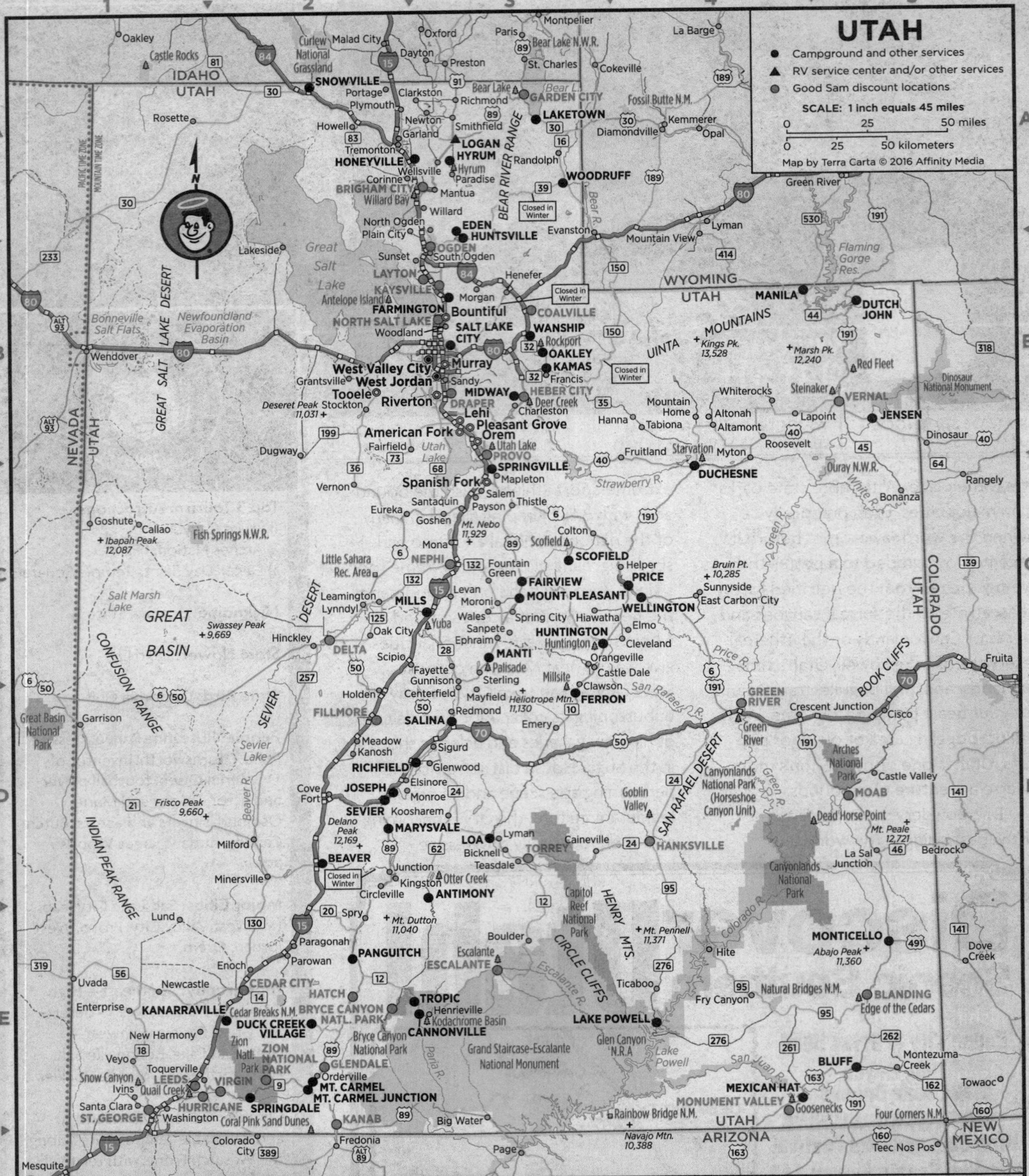
UTAH
Campground and other services
RV service center and/or other services
Good Sam discount locations
SCALE: 1 inch equals 45 miles
0 25 50 miles
0 25 50 kilometers
Map by Terra Carta © 2016 Affinity Media
SNOWVILLE
LOGAN
HYRUM
HONEYVILLE
LAKETOWN
WOODRUFF
EDEN
HUNTSVILLE
FARMINGTON
SALT LAKE CITY
WANSHIP
OAKLEY
KAMAS
MIDWAY
MANILA
DUTCH JOHN
JENSEN
DUCHESNE
SPRINGVILLE
SCOFIELD
PRICE
WELLINGTON
FAIRVIEW
MOUNT PLEASANT
MILLS
HUNTINGTON
MANTI
FERRON
SALINA
RICHFIELD
JOSEPH
SEVIER
MARYSVALE
LOA
BEAVER
ANTIMONY
PANGUITCH
MONTICELLO
TROPIC
CANNONVILLE
KANARRAVILLE
DUCK CREEK VILLAGE
LAKE POWELL
BLUFF
MEXICAN HAT
MT. CARMEL
MT. CARMEL JUNCTION
SPRINGDALE

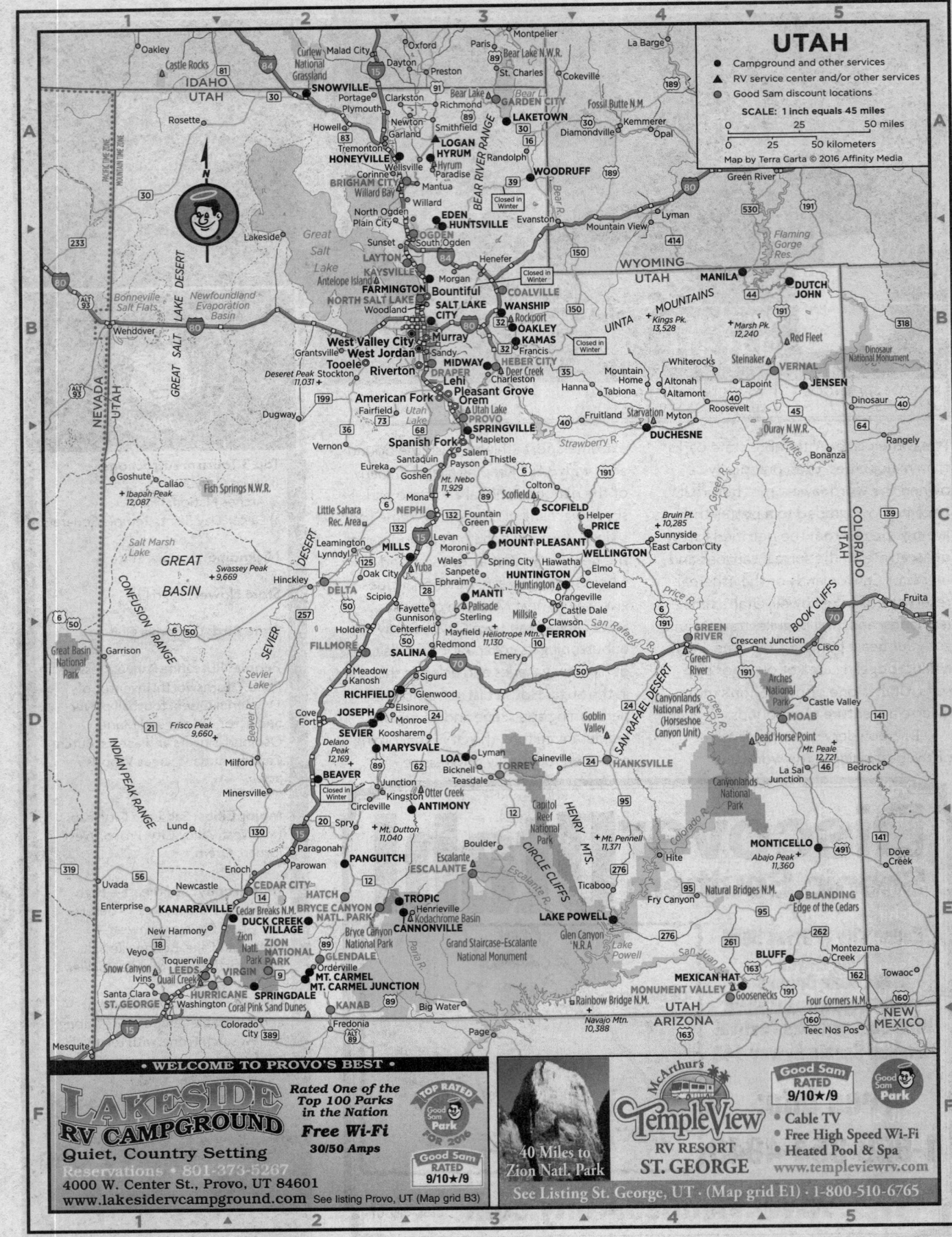

40 Miles to Zion Natl. Park

- STAY A WHILE -

Cedar City

Cedar City is a large town that sits on the edge of flat rangeland next to the heavily forested highland of the Markagunt Plateau. At an elevation of 5,800 feet, it is significantly cooler than St. George to the south.

Cedar City is a convenient base for exploring the Markagunt Plateau. In summer, the plateau offers good hiking, biking, horseback riding and fishing in beautiful natural settings. In winter, Brian Head Ski Resort (30 miles northeast) offers the best snow skiing in southern Utah as well as good cross-country skiing. Cedar City also works as a somewhat more distant base for visiting Zion National Park (60 miles south) and Bryce National Park (65 miles east). In late summer, Cedar City becomes a destination itself during its popular Utah Shakespearean Festival. Other fun festivals include the Neil Simon Fest and the Midsummer Renaissance Fair.

Cedar City is located on Highway 14 just off 1-15. It's 250 miles south of Salt Lake City and 170 miles north of Las Vegas. Cedar City has plenty of lodging and dining options as well as all other necessary visitor services.

Play

With 45 state parks, many of which are inaccessible to vehicles, Utah is a land for explorers. Sure, it's got Zion, it's got Canyonlands, it's got Bryce, plus Arches, but that's just a taster. And, if you want to see the landscape from a more intimate vantage point than a camper-van window, you can feel your thighs bellow and heart valves squeak with an organized bike tour. In Canyonlands, Utah's largest park, you can lose yourself in a Dalí-esque word of surreal rock formations, aptly named "Maze," "Needles" and "Island in the Sky." A haven for rock-climbers, Zion is Utah's first national park and its most visited. With rock formations that span more than 150 million years of geologic history, more than 100 miles of trails lead from the valley into narrow river canyons and scale the vertiginous terracotta hued walls of Navajo sandstone.

Amidst the primordial landscape of Monument Valley Navajo Tribal Park, isolated red mesas and buttes are infused with the spirits of the Navajo people. At Arches National Park, giant balanced rocks, spires, pinnacles and slick-rock domes carved and shaped by eons of weathering and erosion rise pierce a blue domed sky dotted with cotton ball clouds. In a state that brims with geologic oddities, Goblin Valley State Park, near Hansville, takes the cake when it comes to fantastical rock formations. Here thousands of hoodoos (totem-pole-shaped spires) rise from a biblical valley on the edge of the San Rafael Swell. One of the U.S.'s most popular ski towns, Park City hit every snow sport enthusiast's radar when it hosted the 2002 Winter

UT

Olympics. At an elevation of 6,900 feet, three distinct ski areas offer world-class skiing terrain, with deep powdery snow that furnishes excellent skiing terrain for beginners, hard-core backcountry zealots and everyone in between.

Experience

In January, you can ski on, arguably, the best snow in the world and then attend the Sundance Film Festival, one of the largest independent film festivals in the U.S. In April, the Tulip Festival at Thanksgiving Point showcases more than 250,000 tulips in 100 varieties. The Independence Day celebration at America's Freedom Festival Stadium of Fire is hailed as one of the most spectacular firework spectacles in the country. As October draws near, it's hard to trump Cornbelly's Corn Maze and Pumpkin Fest at Thanksgiving Point. You can navigate the intricate paths of a giant corn maze and cheer on the runts at the pig races and then, by night, tour Insanity Point, an extreme version of a Haunted House.

TRAVEL & TOURISM

Utah Office of Tourism
800-200-1160
www.utah.travel

Bear Lake CVB
208-945-2072, 800-448-2327

Beaver County Travel Council
435-438-5438
www.beavercounty.com

Cache Valley Visitors Bureau
435-755-1890, 800-882-4433
www.tourcachevalley.com

Cedar City & Brian Head Tourism Bureau
435-586-4484
www.cedarcitychamber.org

Duchesne Co. Travel Council
435-722-4598
www.duchesne.net

Emery County Travel Bureau
435-564-3600
www.emerycounty.com/travel

Moab Area Travel Council
800-635-6622 or 435-259-8825
www.discovermoab.com

Park City Chamber-Bureau
435-649-6100
www.parkcityinfo.com

St. George Area CVB
435-634-5747, 800-869-6635
www.utahstgeorge.com

Salt Lake Convention & Visitors Bureau
801-534-4900, 800-541-4955
www.visitsaltlake.com

Uintah County Travel and Tourism
800-477-5558
www.dinoland.com

Zion Canyon Visitors Bureau
888-518-7070
www.zionpark.com

OUTDOOR RECREATION

Ski Utah
801-534-1779
www.skiutah.com

Utah Division of Wildlife Resources
801-538-4700
www.wildlife.utah.gov

Utah Snowmobiling
800-200-1160
www.utah.com/snowmobile

SHOPPING

The Gateway
801-456-0000
www.shopthegateway.com

Featured Good Sam Parks

UTAH

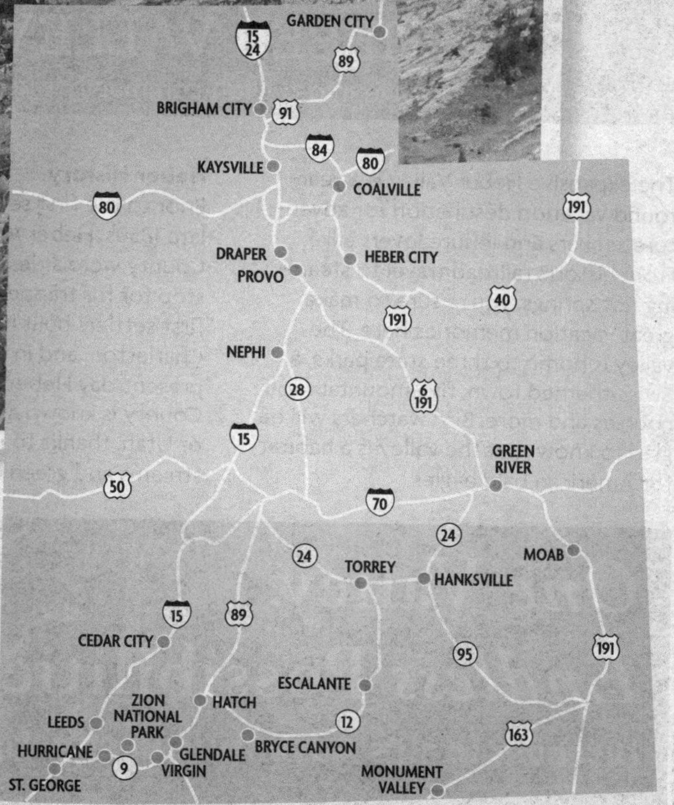

When you stay with Good Sam, you can expect the highest degree of cleanliness and friendliness, and better yet, you get 10% off campground fees.

If you're not already a Good Sam member you can purchase your membership at one of these locations:

BRIGHAM CITY
Golden Spike RV Park
(435)723-8858

BRYCE CANYON
Bryce Canyon Pines Store & Campground & RV Park
(800)892-7923

Red Canyon Village
(435)676-2690

CEDAR CITY
Cedar Breaks RV Park
(435)586-2550

COALVILLE
Holiday Hills RV Park
(435)336-4421

DRAPER
Mountain Shadows RV Park & MHP
(801)571-4024

ESCALANTE
Canyons Of Escalante RV Park
(888)241-8785

GARDEN CITY
Traveland RV Park Bear Lake
(435)946-8444

GLENDALE
Bauers Canyon Ranch RV Park
(888)648-2564

GREEN RIVER
Shady Acres RV Park
(800)537-8674

HANKSVILLE
Dukes Slickrock Campground & RV Park
(435)542-3235

HATCH
Riverside Resort & RV Park
(435)735-4223

HEBER CITY
Mountain Valley RV Resort
(435)657-6100

Rivers Edge At Deer Park
(888)754-4049

HURRICANE
WillowWind RV Park
(435)635-4154

KAYSVILLE
Cherry Hill Camping Resort
(801)451-5379

LEEDS
Leeds RV Park & Motel
(435)879-2450

MOAB
Spanish Trail RV Park
(800)787-2751

MONUMENT VALLEY
Goulding's Monument Valley & RV Park Campground
(435)727-3235

NEPHI
Big Mountain Campground RV Park
(435)623-4800

High Country RV Camp
(435)623-2624

PROVO
Lakeside RV Campground
(801)373-5267

ST GEORGE
McArthur's Temple View RV Resort
(800)510-6765

TORREY
Thousand Lakes RV Park & Campground
(800)355-8995

Wonderland Resort & RV Park
(435)425-3665

VIRGIN
Zion River Resort
(888)466-8594

ZION NATIONAL PARK
Zion RV & Campground
(435)648-3302

For more Good Sam Parks go to listing pages

Heber Valley Tourism and Economic Development

SPOTLIGHT UT

HEBER VALLEY/WASATCH

Dive into a Utah community ripe with adventure

The expansive Heber Valley is a year-round vacation destination for adventure seekers and leisure lovers alike. From historic railroad travel to steaming hot springs, you're sure to make great vacation memories here. The valley is home to three state parks, a Swiss-themed town, five mountain golf courses and more. Bird watchers will be glad to know that the valley is a habitat for American bald eagles.

Heber History

Prior to the first settlements here in the late 1850s, Heber Valley and Wasatch County were a destination and a rest stop for fur trappers and explorers. The first settlers built homes in Midway and Charleston, and in the area just north of present-day Heber City in 1859. Wasatch County is known as the Switzerland of Utah, thanks to its alpine climate, streams and green meadows—and, of course, the Swiss settlers who made Midway their home in the 1800s.

Daughters of the Utah Pioneers Museum in Wasatch County tells the story of early settlers through artifacts and portraits. The Commemorative Air Force Utah Wing Museum displays historic aircraft that have been restored to airworthy status to honor the nation's military aviation history. Displays also feature women in aviation and a history

Teeing off at Red Ledges Golf Course. Heber Valley Tourism and Economic Development

of commercial aircraft.

Uinta National Forest, at the southwestern edge of the valley, is a wilderness paradise with natural wonders. Cascade Springs send 7 million gallons of water each day down limestone terraces and into pools surrounded by lush vegetation. The fall leaves make for a picturesque hike to the springs when the weather turns cooler.

Soldier Hollow Golf Course above Heber Valley is uniquely designed to incorporate native vegetation.

Deer Creek State Park is a short drive from Uinta and offers year-round fishing for rainbow trout, brown trout, perch and bass in the early fall. Daniels Creek, east of Heber Valley in Daniels Canyon, is another popular spot for casting a line or enjoying the adjacent playground and nature trail with the family.

Under the Dome

Feel the warmth in the Homestead Crater mineral dome in Midway. This geothermal spring rests under a 55-foot-tall beehive-shaped limestone rock with a hole at the top that lets in sunlight and fresh air. The interior is a balmy 90 degrees Fahrenheit, and visitors are invited to take a dip in the warm mineral water or go scuba diving. The crater sits in a residential resort and is open to the public.

Get on board for a scenic trip on the Heber Valley Railroad. Historic steam locomotives take visitors on trips through farmland, across the Provo River and beside the foothills of the Wasatch Mountains down to the west bank of Deer Creek Reservoir, before descending into Provo Canyon.

Winter sports are a hallmark of the Utah adventure, and snow tubing at Soldier Hollow in Midway is one of the newest attractions. Slide down 1,200 feet of cool lanes day or night, then take a lift back to the top to enjoy the ride over and over. Deer Valley Resort provides top-notch facilities for downhill skiing, and Heber Ranger District offers several trails at various skill levels for cross-country skiing, snowshoeing and snowmobiling.

Tee off at the Lake and Mountain golf courses in Wasatch Mountain State Park. These picturesque courses were carved from the mountain and are frequented by the local wildlife as well as golfers of all skill levels. The Mountain course offers challenging terrain while the gentler Lake course is an all-skill favorite. Soldier Hollow Golf Course above Heber Valley is uniquely designed to incorporate native vegetation, inviting players to test their skills in the shadow of Mount Timpanogos.

Hike Heber

Stretch your legs and admire the natural beauty of Heber Valley on any of several hikes through Center Canyon, Clegg Canyon and Co-op Creek. The Center Canyon trail winds 4 miles through aspen forests and columbine-filled meadows and is frequently visited by wildlife. The Clegg Canyon trail wanders through oak, conifer and aspen stands. On the Co-op Creek trail, hikers often spot elk, moose and deer along the way.

Scenic drives are plentiful in the valley and perfect for taking in as much of the landscape as you can in a single day. Provo Canyon Scenic Byway stretches 32 miles along Highway 189 into Provo Canyon. Along the route, you'll see steep limestone cliffs and waterfalls rippling over the rock into the stream. Wolf Creek Highway climbs to more than 9,000 feet through spruce and fir forests, and in the fall the aspen groves turn gold.

Alpine Loop Scenic Byway, along Highway 92 from American Fork Canyon to Provo Canyon, stretches through the alpine canyons of the Wasatch Range and provides spectacular views of Mount Timpanogos and neighboring glacier-carved peaks. Travel during its open season, from May to October.

For More Information

Go Heber Valley
435-654-3666
www.gohebervalley.com

Utah Travel Council
800-200-1160
www.utah.com

UT

Getty Images/iStockphoto

ST GEORGE/WASHINGTON

Walk in the footsteps of southern Utah's intrepid pioneers

Washington County has served as the home of a diverse stream of visitors, from thriving Native American tribes to adventurous trappers to industrious missionaries. Today, this region of southwest Utah draws RV travelers to enjoy great golf, beautiful scenery and a splendid town.

The earliest settlers of the area were Pueblo and Paiute tribes. In later years, trappers and explorers made their mark, and settlers of the Mormon Church put down deep roots here. The settlers' cultivation of cotton and sugar cane in the 1860s earned the area the name of Utah's Dixie. Later, silver mining and cattle also helped grow the economy in Washington County and in its constituent communities.

Among the most significant historic sites in the area is the Jacob Hamblin House in nearby Santa Clara. The two-story homestead was built by the pioneer and Mormon missionary who founded the community in 1854. The home operates as a museum and invites guests to view replica period furniture and walk through the fruit orchards on the property.

The Road to Zion

Washington County is a popular destination today thanks in large part to the

A view of the Mormon Temple from Dixie Red Hills overlooking St. George.
Getty Images/iStockphoto

proximity of Zion National Park, which lies just 45 miles east of St. George. Declared a national park in 1919, Zion Canyon is the jewel in the park's crown, boasting breathtaking rock monoliths and canyon walls worn by the Virgin River, one of the nation's few remaining free-flowing waterways.

Other memorable sights in the park include the Great White Throne, a 2,400-foot mountain of white Navajo sandstone; Court of the Patriarchs, a set of sandstone cliffs; and the Kolob Arch in Kolob Canyon. At 310 feet, Kolob Arch is the world's second-largest natural arch.

Hiking is the best way to see the many features of Zion, and trails are abundant. Visitors looking for the perfect shot should take the short Canyon Overlook, which passes through ferns and trees on the way to the cliff that is the hallmark of the overlook. The view encompasses the expanse of the canyon, and East Temple rises above the Overlook.

Water features are hidden gems within the park, and the Emerald Pool Trail leads to waterfalls pouring over red canyon outcroppings. The Lower Pool Trail is the easiest hike while Middle Pool is steeper and longer; Upper Pool has the greatest degree of difficulty but provides stunning views of the waterfalls.

Weeping Rock Trail, less than half a mile round-trip, leads hikers to an overhanging cliff covered in moss and ferns where rivulets of water drizzle over the edge into pools below. Riverside Walk is bordered by cottonwood trees that provide shade, and hanging gardens cling to the walls along the way to Gateway of the Narrows. Stop here and cool off in the mouth of the Narrows before turning back to finish the 2-mile round trip.

Settle Down in St. George

Roughly 40 miles outside the park lies St. George, the county seat. St. George began as an Indian mission established by the Mormon Church and later was the site of farms that worked to grow semitropical crops as a way of becoming self-sustaining during the Civil War. As one of the fastest-growing communities in the nation, St. George offers a wide variety of recreational opportunities for all family members.

Challenging and immaculate golf courses carved out of the rugged landscape welcome golfers eager for long fairways and challenging hazards. The Red Rock Golf Trail welcomes players to explore Coral Canyon, Sunbrook, Green Spring, the Ledges and more.

For younger visitors, the St. George Children's Museum offers hands-on, interactive fun and a variety of ongoing and special programs. The Dinosaur Discovery Site at Johnson Farm shares the region's prehistoric treasures through exhibits and collections, including dinosaur tracks and a track-making area that gives children the chance to make their own footprints. Kids can learn how paleontologists go about uncovering and investigating dinosaur remains.

Explore Green Gate Village Historic Inn, a collection of pioneer-era and early Victorian homes in St. George. Some of these residences were built by the original homesteaders; others relocated here for preservation. A carriage house, granary and general store have also been restored and moved to the property, where they serve as an inn, restaurant and reception center.

St. George Outdoors

Municipal parks abound in St. George, welcoming visitors and residents to play and relax among pristine landscaping, fun playgrounds and serene ponds. The city also celebrates and displays the creative endeavors in the St. George Art Museum. Its exhibits include Western art, native crafts and permanent collections featuring works by Utah artists.

On the hottest of days, take the family to Sand Hollow Aquatic Center to cool off and have some fun. The center's leisure pool features a zero-depth entry, children's water toys, a water walk and slides. Nearby Sand Hollow State Park offers trails for riding ATVs through sand dunes, and a warm-water reservoir is ideal for boating and fishing. Angle for crappie, bluegill, bass and catfish.

Lees Ferry, below Lake Powell, is a tributary of the Colorado River that's ideal for boating and trout fishing. You can also cast a line in one of the small streams that carve their way around the mountains surrounding St. George. Gather up your gear and head to the upper and lower Tawa Ponds, Skyline Pond or Gunlock State Park.

For More Information

St. George Area Chamber of Commerce
435-628-1658
www.stgeorgechamber.com

Utah Office of Tourism
800-200-1160
www.travel.utah.gov

Utah

CONSULTANTS
Mike & Donna Oliverio

ANTIMONY — D3 *Garfield*

OTTER CREEK (State Pk) From town: Go 5 mi N on Hwy 22. 2015 rates: $16. (435)624-3268

BEAVER — D2 *Beaver*

BEAVER CAMPERLAND **Ratings: 8/7/6** (Campground) 2015 rates: $29.95 to $34.95. (877)438-2808 1603 S Camperworld Rd, Beaver, UT 84713

BEAVER CANYON CAMPGROUND **Ratings: 3.5/7.5/7** (Campground) 2015 rates: $24. Apr 15 to Nov 1. (435)438-5654 1419 E. 200 North, Beaver, UT 84713

BEAVER KOA **Ratings: 8/9★/8.5** (Campground) 2015 rates: $38 to $45. (435)438-2924 1428 Manderfield Rd, Beaver, UT 84713

MINERSVILLE (State Pk) From jct I-15 & Hwy-21: Go 11 mi W on Hwy-21. 2015 rates: $17. (801)438-5472

BLANDING — E5 *San Juan*

BLANDING RV PARK
Ratings: 5.5/8★/5 (Campground) From Jct of Center St & Main St (Hwy 191), S 0.9 mi on Hwy 191 (L). Elev 6200 ft. **FAC:** Gravel rds. (60 spaces). Avail: 48 gravel, 39 pull-thrus (22 x 40), back-ins (22 x 35), 48 full hkups (30/50 amps), seasonal sites, WiFi, tent sites, dump, laundry, groc, restaurant. Pets OK. Partial handicap access. 2015 rates: $30.
(435)678-2991 Lat: 37.61321, Lon: -109.47804
861 S Main St, Blanding, UT 84511
See ad this page.

BLUE MOUNTAIN RV PARK **Ratings: 6/9★/7** (RV Park) 2015 rates: $34 to $36. Mar 15 to Nov 1. (435)678-7840 1930 S Main, Blanding, UT 84511

BLUFF — E5 *San Juan*

CADILLAC RANCH RV PARK
Ratings: 6/8★/7.5 (RV Park) N-bnd: From Jct of SR-163 & US-191, N 4.4 mi on US-191 (R); or S-bnd: From Jct of US-191 & SR-163, S 1.6 mi on US-191 (L). Elev 4300 ft. **FAC:** Gravel rds. 15 gravel, 15 pull-thrus (29 x 65), 14 full hkups, 1 W, 1 E (30/50 amps), WiFi, tent sites, dump, firewood. **REC:** pond, fishing. Pets OK. Big rig sites, 2015 rates: $30. Disc: AAA.
(800)538-6195 Lat: 37.28281, Lon: -109.55129
630 E Main, Bluff, UT 84512
cadranch@frontiernet.net
cadillacranchrv.com
See ad this page.

Making campground reservations? Remember to ask about the cancellation policy when making your reservation.

COTTONWOOD RV PARK Ratings: 6/9★/8 (Campground) S-bnd: From Jct of Hwy 162 & Hwy 191, S 1 mi on Hwy 191 to 4th West St (past Cottonwood Wash), E 0.1 mi (L); or N-bnd: From Jct of Hwy 163 & Hwy 191, N 3.5 mi on Hwy 191 to 4th West St, E 0.1 mi (L). Elev 4300 ft. **FAC:** Gravel rds. 23 gravel, 15 pull-thrus (33 x 80), back-ins (30 x 50), 23 full hkups (30/50 amps), WiFi, tent sites, rentals, dump, firewood, restaurant. **REC:** playground. Pets OK. Partial handicap access. Big rig sites, 2015 rates: $29 to $30. Mar 5 to Nov 1.
(435)672-2287 Lat: 37.28045, Lon: -109.56421
32 W Main St, Bluff, UT 84512
cottonwoodrv_bluffutah@yahoo.com
www.cottonwoodrvpark.blogspot.com

BRIGHAM CITY — A3 *Box Elder*

BRIGHAM CITY PERRY SOUTH KOA Ratings: 7.5/8★/6.5 (Campground) S-bnd: From Jct of I-15 & US-91 (exit 362), E 2 mi on exit rd to Hwy 89, S 3 mi to 3600S St, W 0.1 mi (R); or N-bnd: From Jct of I-15 & exit 357, E 0.8 mi on exit rd to Hwy 89, N 1.5 mi to 3600S St, W 0.1 mi (L). Elev 4360 ft. **FAC:** Gravel rds. (72 spaces). 65 Avail: 63 gravel, 2 grass, 5 pull-thrus (26 x 100), back-ins (19 x 53), mostly side by side hkups, 58 full hkups, 7 W, 7 E (30/50 amps), seasonal sites, WiFi, tent sites, rentals, dump, laundry, groc, firewood. **REC:** pool, playground. Pet restrict(B). Big rig sites, 2015 rates: $33 to $47. Disc: AAA, military.
AAA Approved
(435)723-5503 Lat: 41.44485, Lon: -112.04073
1040 West 3600 South, Perry, UT 84302
brighamcitykoa@brigham.net
www.koa.com

GOLDEN SPIKE RV PARK
Ratings: 7.5/9.5★/8.5 (RV Park) From Jct of I-15 & US-91 (exit 362), E 1 mi on US-91 to 775 W (Medical Dr), N 300 ft to Georgia Dr, W 400 ft (L). Elev 4270 ft. **FAC:** Paved rds. (38 spaces). 23 Avail: 7 paved, 16 gravel, 23 pull-thrus (20 x 70), 23 full hkups (30/50 amps), seasonal sites, cable, WiFi, tent sites, laundry, LP gas. **REC.** Pets OK. Partial

BRIGHAM CITY (CONT)

GOLDEN SPIKE RV PARK (CONT)
handicap access. Big rig sites, eco-friendly. 2015 rates: $31.50. Disc: military.
(435)723-8858 Lat: 41.48734, Lon: -112.03031
905 W 1075 S, Brigham City, UT 84302
reservations@goldenspikerv.com
www.goldenspikerv.com
See ad opposite page, 1187.

BRYCE CANYON — E2 *Garfield*

BRYCE CANYON PINES STORE & CAMPGROUND & RV PARK
Ratings: 6.5/8★/7.5 (Campground) From Jct of US-89 & Hwy 12, E 9.7 mi on Hwy 12 (R); or From Bryce Cyn Nat'l Park, NW 3.8 mi on Hwy 12 (L). Elev 7600 ft. **FAC:** Gravel rds. 24 gravel, 17 pull-thrus (30 x 65), back-ins (26 x 50), some side by side hkups, 24 full hkups (30 amps), WiFi, tent sites, laundry, groc, fire rings, firewood. **REC.** Pets OK. 2015 rates: $35. Apr 1 to Nov 1.
(800)892-7923 Lat: 37.71169, Lon: -112.21724
Mp 10 Hwy 12, Bryce Canyon National Park, UT 84764
bcpines@color-country.net
http://www.brycecanyonmotel.com/bryce-campgrounds/
See ad opposite page, 1187.

BRYCE CANYON/NORTH CAMPGROUND (Natl Pk) From Jct of Hwys 12 & 63, S 4 mi on Hwy 63, follow signs (E). 2015 rates: $15. (435)834-5322

BRYCE CANYON/SUNSET CAMPGROUND (Natl Pk) From visitors center, S 6 mi Hwy 63 (R). 2015 rates: $15. May 10 to Oct 15. (435)834-5322

RED CANYON VILLAGE
Ratings: 5.5/8★/6.5 (RV Park) From Jct of Hwys 89 & 12, E 1 mi on Hwy 12 (L). Elev 6700 ft. **FAC:** Paved rds. 30 gravel, patios, 17 pull-thrus (30 x 70), back-ins (28 x 50), 30 full hkups (30/50 amps), cable, WiFi, tent sites, rentals, dump, fire rings, firewood. **REC.** Pets OK. Big rig sites, 2015 rates: $39. Apr 1 to Oct 31.
(435)676-2690 Lat: 37.74898, Lon: -112.36197
3279 E. Hwy 12, Panguitch, UT 84759
www.redcanyonvillage.com
See ad this page, 1187.

RUBY'S INN CAMPGROUND & RV PARK Ratings: 8.5/9.5★/8.5 (Campground) From Jct of Hwys 12 & 63, S 1.7 mi on Hwy 63 (R). Elev 7600 ft. **FAC:** Gravel rds. 170 gravel, 137 pull-thrus (29 x 70), back-ins (25 x 45), 156 full hkups, 14 W, 14 E (30/50 amps), cable, WiFi, tent sites, rentals, dump, laundry, groc, LP gas, fire rings, firewood, restaurant. **REC:** heated pool, whirlpool, Lake Minnie. Pets OK. Partial handicap access. Big rig sites, 2015 rates: $36.95 to $42.95. Apr 1 to Oct 30.
AAA Approved
(435)834-5301 Lat: 37.66831, Lon: -112.15819
300 S Main, Bryce Canyon City, UT 84764
rvpark@rubysinn.com
www.brycecanyoncampgrounds.com

BRYCE CANYON NATIONAL PARK — E2 *Garfield*

BRYCE CANYON NATIONAL PARK See also Cannonville, Glendale, Hatch & Panguitch.

CANNONVILLE — E3 *Garfield*

BRYCE CANYON KOA **Ratings: 8.5/9.5★/8** (Campground) 2015 rates: $28.95 to $53.95. Mar 15 to Oct 30. (435)679-8988 250 N Red Rocks Dr, Cannonville, UT 84718

KODACHROME BASIN (State Pk) From Jct of Hwy 12 & Main St (cnty rd), S 7.3 mi on Unnamed Cnty Rd, follow signs (E). 2015 rates: $16 to $32. (435)679-8562

CAPITOL REEF NATIONAL PARK — D3 *Wayne*

CAPITOL REEF NATIONAL PARK See also Hanksville & Torrey.

CEDAR CITY — E2 *Iron*

CEDAR BREAKS NATL MON/POINT SUPREME (Natl Pk) From Jct of Rtes 14 & 148, N 4 mi on Rte 148, follow signs (R). 2015 rates: $14. Jun 15 to Sep 15. (435)586-9451

CEDAR BREAKS RV PARK
Ratings: 6.5/8★/7 (RV Park) From Jct of I-15 & Main St (exit 62), S 1.7 mi on Main St (L). Elev 5800 ft. **FAC:** Paved/gravel rds. (53 spaces). Avail: 48 gravel, 42 pull-thrus (25 x 60), back-ins (25 x 65), some side by side hkups, 48 full hkups (30/50 amps), seasonal sites, cable, WiFi, tent sites, laundry. **REC.** Pets OK. Partial handicap access. Big rig sites, 2015 rates: $44 to $54. Disc: AAA, military. ATM.
(435)586-2550 Lat: 37.70767, Lon: -113.06207
1700 N Main St, Cedar City, UT 84721
cedarbreaksrv@gmail.com
www.cedarbreaksrv.com
See ad this page, 1187.

CEDAR CITY KOA KAMPGROUND **Ratings: 7.5/9.5★/8** (Campground) 2015 rates: $41 to $58. (435)586-9872 1121 N Main St, Cedar City, UT 84720

INDIAN PEAKS RV PARK **Ratings: 5/10★/7** (RV Park) 2015 rates: $25. (435)531-8913 4377 Old Hwy 91, Cedar City, UT 84720

THE INDIAN PEAKS RV PARK **Ratings: 5/10★/7** (RV Park) 2015 rates: $25. (435)531-8913 4377 Old Hwy 91, Cedar City, UT 84720

TOWN & COUNTRY RV PARK & HOTEL **Ratings: 8/NA/5** (Campground) 2015 rates: $35 to $40. (435)586-9900 50 W 200 North, Cedar City, UT 84720

Things to See and Do

CEDAR CITY & BRIAN HEAD TOURISM BUREAU & VISITOR CENTER Tourism & Convention Bureau for Iron County and Scenic Southern Utah. Elev 5800 ft. partial handicap access. RV accessible. Restrooms. Hours: 8:30am to 5pm. No CC.
(800)354-4849 Lat: 37.68893, Lon: -113.06259
581 North Main, Cedar City, UT 84721
maria@netutah.com
www.scenicsouthernutah.com
See ad page 1183 (Welcome Section).

COALVILLE — B3 *Summit*

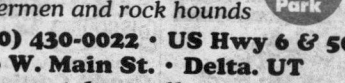

HOLIDAY HILLS RV PARK
Ratings: 7/8★/6.5 (RV Park) From Jct of I-80 & Exit 162 (Coalville), W 0.2 mi on Icy Springs Rd (L). Elev 5520 ft. **FAC:** Paved rds. (42 spaces). Avail: 38 paved, 38 pull-thrus (25 x 50), 38 full hkups (30/50 amps), seasonal sites, WiFi, tent sites, rentals, dump, laundry, groc, LP gas. **REC:** Weber River: fishing. Pets OK. 2015 rates: $27.50. Disc: AAA, military.
(435)336-4421 Lat: 40.91118, Lon: -111.40496
500 West 100 South, Coalville, UT 84017
bell@allwest.net
www.rvhills.com
See ad this page, 1187.

Say you saw it in our Guide!

DELTA — C2 *Millard*

ANTELOPE VALLEY RV PARK
Ratings: 6.5/9★/7 (RV Park) From Jct US-50 & US-6: Go 2 mi W on US-50 & US-6. Elev 4575 ft. **FAC:** Paved rds. (96 spaces). Avail: 82 gravel, patios, 8 pull-thrus (18 x 70), back-ins (30 x 44), 82 full hkups (30/50 amps), seasonal sites, WiFi, tent sites, dump, laundry. **REC.** Pets OK. Partial handicap access. 2015 rates: $32. Disc: AAA.
(800)430-0022 Lat: 39.35207, Lon: -112.59332
776 W Main (Hwy US 50 & US 6), Delta, UT 84624
anteloperv@yahoo.com
www.antelopevalleyrvpark.com
See ad this page.

DRAPER — B3 *Salt Lake*

MOUNTAIN SHADOWS RV PARK & MHP
Ratings: 9.5/10★/8.5 (Campground) From Jct of I-15 & 12300 South St (Draper exit 291), E 150 ft on 12300 South St to MinuteMan Dr (frntg rd), S 1.2 mi (L). Elev 4100 ft. **FAC:** Paved rds. (127 spaces). 65 Avail: 53 paved, 12 gravel, 49 pull-thrus (17 x 62), back-ins (20 x 50), mostly side by side hkups, 65 full hkups (30/50 amps), seasonal sites, WiFi, tent sites, dump, laundry, groc, LP gas. **REC:** heated pool, whirlpool, playground. Pets OK. Partial handicap access. Big rig sites, eco-friendly, 2015 rates: $20 to $39.25. Disc: military.
(801)571-4024 Lat: 40.51053, Lon: -111.88960
13275 S Minuteman Dr, Draper, UT 84020
apage@mountain-shadows.com
www.mountain-shadows.com
See ad pages 1194, 1187.

Travel Services

CAMPING WORLD STORE OF DRAPAR/SALT LAKE CITY As the nation's largest retailer of RV supplies, accessories, services and new and used RVs, Camping World is committed to making your total RV experience better. RV Accessories: (800)294-1240. Elev 4100 ft. **SERVICES:** RV, tire, RV appliance, restrooms, RV Sales. Rentals. RV supplies, LP, emergency parking, RV accessible. waiting room. Hours: 8am to 6pm.
(888)490-5818 Lat: 40.512612, Lon: -111.890673
13153 S Minuteman Dr., Draper, UT 84020
www.campingworld.com

DUCHESNE — C4 *Duchesne, Uintah*

CAMPERWORLD-LAKESIDE PARK (ANNEX) **Ratings: 6/7.5★/8** (Membership Pk) 2015 rates: $39 to $49. (435)738-2044 hc 63 Box 2, Duchesne, UT 84021

STARVATION (State Pk) From Jct of Hwys 191 & 40, W 0.5 mi on Hwy 40 to 2220 West St (Starvation Rd), NW 4 mi (E). 2015 rates: $10 to $25. (435)738-2326

DUCK CREEK VILLAGE — E2 *Kane*

PINEWOODS RESORT RV PARK Ratings: 6.5/8★/7.5 (RV Park) From Jct of SR 14 & Duck Creek Ridge Rd (MP 31.5), N on Duck Creek Ridge Rd .25 mi (L). Elev 8600 ft. **FAC:** Gravel rds. 11 gravel, back-ins (24 x 45), 11 full hkups (30/50 amps), WiFi, rentals, laundry, fire rings, firewood, restaurant. **REC:** playground. Pets OK. 2015 rates: $44. Apr 1 to Dec 1.
AAA Approved
(435)682-2512 Lat: 37.31004, Lon: -112.39020
1460 E Duck Creek Ridge Rd, Duck Creek Village, UT 84762
office@pinewoodsresort.com
www.pinewoodsresort.com

DUTCH JOHN — B5 *Daggett*

↑ DUTCH JOHN RESORT **Ratings: 6.5/9.5★/6.5** (RV Park) 2015 rates: $35 to $45. (435)885-3191 1050 South Boulevard, Dutch John, UT 84023

FLAMING GORGE/ANTELOPE FLAT CAMPGROUND (Natl Forest) From town: Go 5-1/2 mi NW on US 191, then 5 mi NW on FR 10145, then 1/2 mi W on FR 10343. 2015 rates: $16. May 16 to Sep 7. (435)784-3448

FLAMING GORGE/FIREFIGHTERS MEMORIAL CAMPGROUND (Natl Forest) From town: Go 6 mi SW on US 191, then 1/2 mi on FR 10195. 2015 rates: $18 to $20. May 9 to Sep 28. (435)784-3445

FLAMING GORGE/MUSTANG RIDGE CAMPGROUND (Natl Forest) From town: Go 1-1/2 mi NW on US 191, then 2 mi S on FR 10184, then 1/2 mi S on FR 10395. 2015 rates: $23. May 9 to Sep 7. (435)784-3445

EDEN — A3 *Weber*

NORTH FORK PARK (State Pk) At jct of Hwy 166 & Hwy 162: Go W 2.4 mi on Hwy 162,then 0.6 mi on N 3500 E (Hwy 162), continue W 2/10 mi on E 4100 N (Hwy 162), N 1-1/2 mi on N 3300 E (Hwy 162). Enter at S North Fork Rd. 2015 rates: $18. (801)625-3850

Our rating system isn't just tough, it's thorough. We know the kinds of things that are important to you — like clean restrooms and showers, attractive, secure, well-tended grounds, and extras like swimming pools. We give the first rating for development of facilities, the second for cleanliness and physical characteristics of restrooms and showers, and the third for visual appearance.

ESCALANTE — E3 *Garfield*

↓ **CANYONS OF ESCALANTE RV PARK**
Ratings: 7/9★/8 (RV Park) From Jct of Hwy 12 & Center St: Go S 0.5 mi on Hwy 12 (L). Elev 5800 ft. **FAC:** Gravel rds. 30 gravel, 30 pull-thrus (20 x 56), 30 full hkups (30/50 amps), WiFi, tent sites, rentals, laundry, firewood. **REC.** Pets OK. Partial handicap access. 2015 rates: $29 to $40. Mar 1 to Oct 31.
(888)241-8785 Lat: 37.77019, Lon: -111.60963
495 W Main St, Escalante, UT 84726
canyonsofescalantervpark@gmail.com
canyonsofescalantervpark.com
See ad this page, 1187.

↑ ESCALANTE PETRIFIED FOREST (State Pk) From Jct of Center St & Hwy 12, S 1.7 mi on Hwy 12 to park access rd (follow signs), NW 0.5 mi (E). 2015 rates: $19 to $25. (435)826-4466

← SHOOTING STAR RV RESORT **Ratings: 4/8.5★/7** (RV Park) 2015 rates: $35. Apr 1 to Oct 31. (435)826-4440 2020 W Hwy 12, Escalante, UT 84726

FAIRVIEW — C3 *Sanpete*

→ SKYLINE MOUNTAIN RESORT **Ratings: 6.5/9★/8.5** (Membership Pk) 2015 rates: $23. (435)427-9590 22130 N 11750E, Fairview, UT 84629

FARMINGTON — B3 *Davis*

↖ LAGOON RV PARK & CAMPGROUND **Ratings: 6.5/9★/6.5** (Campground) 2015 rates: $31 to $42. May 2 to Oct 25. (800)748-5246 375 N Lagoon Dr, Farmington, UT 84025

FERRON — D3 *Sanpete*

MILLSITE (State Pk) From jct Hwy 10 & Ferron Canyon Rd: Go 4 mi W on Ferron Canyon Rd. 2015 rates: $10 to $20. (435)384-2552

FILLMORE — D2 *Millard*

↓ FILLMORE KOA **Ratings: 9/9.5★/9.5** (Campground) 2015 rates: $42 to $44. Mar 1 to Nov 30. (435)743-4420 905 South Hwy 99, Fillmore, UT 84631

↑ **WAGONS WEST RV PARK AND CAMPGROUND**
Ratings: 7/8.5★/7.5 (Campground) From jct I-15 (exit 163) & Bus Loop I-15: Go 4 mi N on I-15 to (exit 167/Main St), then 1 mi S on Main St. Elev 5071 ft. **FAC:** Paved/gravel rds. (55 spaces). Avail: 45 gravel, 30 pull-thrus (24 x 120), back-ins (18 x 32), 45 full hkups (30/50 amps), seasonal sites, cable, WiFi, tent sites, dump, laundry. **REC.** Pets OK. 2015 rates: $35 to $40.
(435)743-6188 Lat: 38.98065, Lon: -112.32391
545 N Main St, Fillmore, UT 84631
wagonswestrvpark@hotmail.com
www.wagonswestrv.weebly.com
See ad this page.

FLAMING GORGE NATIONAL REC AREA — B5 *Daggett*

FLAMING GORGE NATIONAL RECREATION AREA See also Manila & Vernal.

GARDEN CITY — A3 *Rich*

↑ BEAR LAKE KOA **Ratings: 8/9★/7** (Campground) 2015 rates: $41 to $190. Apr 1 to Nov 1. (435)946-3454 485 N Bear Lake Blvd, Garden City, UT 84028

↖ **BEAVER MOUNTAIN SKI RESORT**
Ratings: 3.5/8.5★/6 (Campground) From jct Hwy 30 & US 89: Go 12 mi W on US 89, then 1-1/4 mi N on Hwy 243. Elev 7228 ft. **FAC:** Gravel/dirt rds. 39 Avail: 32 paved, 7 gravel, back-ins (22 x 50), mostly side by side hkups, 16 full hkups, 23 W, 23 E (20/30 amps), WiFi, tent sites, rentals, fire rings. **REC.** Pets OK. 2015 rates: $25 to $30. May 30 to Oct 15. No CC.
(435)563-5677 Lat: 41.96969, Lon: -111.54008
40000 E. Hwy 89, Garden City, UT 84028
info@skithebeav.com
www.skithebeav.com
See ad this page.

↖ **TRAVELAND RV PARK BEAR LAKE**
Ratings: 8/9★/7 (RV Park) From Jct of US 89 & SR-30, W 0.4 mi on US 89 to N300 West, N 0.2 mi on N300 West (L). Elev 6010 ft. **FAC:** Gravel rds. (64 spaces). Avail: 59 gravel, 59 pull-thrus (26 x 75), mostly side by side hkups, 59 full hkups (30/50 amps), seasonal sites, WiFi, tent sites, dump, laundry, fire rings, firewood. **REC:** playground. Pets OK. Partial handicap access. Big rig sites, eco-friendly, 2015 rates: $43. Disc: military. May 15 to Sep 15.
(435)946-8444 Lat: 41.94964, Lon: -111.40032
145 N 300 W, Garden City, UT 84028
information@travelandbearlake.com
www.travelandrvpark.net/bearlake.htm
See ad this page, 1187.

Like Us on Facebook.

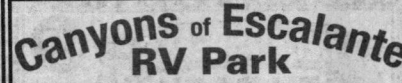

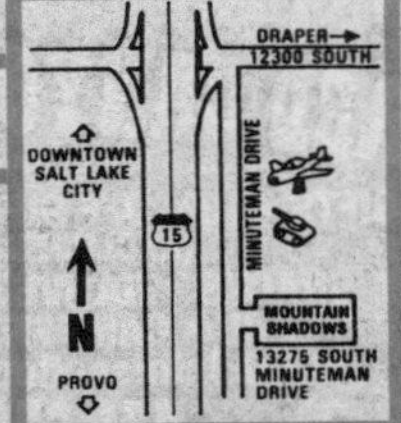

GLENDALE — E2 *Kane*

BAUERS CANYON RANCH RV PARK
Ratings: 7.5/9★/8 (RV Park) From Jct of Hwy 9 & US-89: Go N 10 mi on US-89 to Glendale (L). Elev 5900 ft. **FAC:** Gravel rds. 20 gravel, 15 pull-thrus (25 x 65), back-ins (26 x 48), 20 full hkups (30/50 amps), WiFi, tent sites, dump, laundry, firewood. **REC:** Virgin River: fishing. Pets OK. Partial handicap access. Big rig sites, 2015 rates: $33. Disc: military. Mar 1 to Nov 1.
(888)648-2564 Lat: 37.31819, Lon: -112.59894
90 W Mill St, Glendale, UT 84729
bauersrv@color-country.net
www.bauersrv.com
See ad opposite page, 1187.

BRYCE-ZION CAMPGROUND Ratings: 7/8.5★/7 (Campground) 2015 rates: $28 to $35. May 1 to Sep 30. (435)648-2490 175 E Koa Dr, Glendale, UT 84729

GREEN RIVER — D4 *Emery, Grand*

GOBLIN VALLEY (State Pk) From jct I-70 & Hwy 24: Go 25 mi S on Hwy 24, then 5 mi W at Temple Mtn. turnoff, then 7 mi S on gravel road. 2015 rates: $16. (435)275-4584

GREEN RIVER (State Pk) From Jct of I-70 & Exit 158 (bus loop), E 2 mi on bus loop to Green River Blvd, S 0.4 mi (L); or From Jct of I-70 & Exit 162 (bus loop), W 2 mi on bus loop to Green River Blvd, S 0.4 mi (L). 2015 rates: $16 to $20. Mar 1 to Nov 1. (435)564-3633

Tell them you saw them in this Guide!

GREEN RIVER KOA Ratings: 7.5/8.5★/7 (Campground) 2015 rates: $35 to $46. (800)562-5734 235 South 1780 East, Green River, UT 84525

SHADY ACRES RV PARK
Ratings: 8/10★/9 (Campground) From Jct of I-70 & Main St (exit 160/I-70 Bus Loop), E 1.5 mi on Main St (R); or From Jct of I-70 & Main St (exit 164/I-70 Bus Loop), W 2 mi on Main St (L). Elev 4080 ft.

NEAR UTAH'S SCENIC NATIONAL PARKS
Your perfect home base for exploring the natural wonders of Southeastern Utah. Enjoy spectacular mountain views from your campsite. Watch local wildlife as you stroll our lovely 16-acre park. Open year round.

FAC: Paved rds. 86 paved, 86 pull-thrus (26 x 60), some side by side hkups, 71 full hkups, 15 W, 15 E (30/50 amps), cable, WiFi, tent sites, rentals, dump, laundry, groc, LP bottles, fire rings, firewood, restaurant. **REC:** playground. Pets OK. Partial handicap access. Big rig sites, eco-friendly, 2015 rates: $32.99 to $38.99. Disc: AAA, military.
AAA Approved
(800)537-8674 Lat: 38.99521, Lon: -110.15388
690 E Main St, Green River, UT 84525
shadya@etv.net
www.shadyacresrv.com
See ad this page, 1187.

HANKSVILLE — D4 *Wayne*

DUKES SLICKROCK CAMPGROUND & RV PARK
Ratings: 5/8★/6.5 (Campground) From Jct of SR 24 & SR 95, W 0.1 mi on SR 24 (R). Elev 4443 ft. **FAC:** Gravel rds. 42 gravel, 36 pull-thrus (22 x 46), back-ins (28 x 46), 42 full hkups (30/50 amps), WiFi, tent sites, dump, laundry, fire rings, restaurant. **REC.** Pets OK. 2015 rates: $25 to $30. Mar 1 to Oct 31.
(435)542-3235 Lat: 38.37458, Lon: -110.70850
275 East 100 North, Hanksville, UT 84734
slickrock@hanksville.com
www.dukesslickrock.com
See ad this page, 1187.

We appreciate your business!

HATCH — E2 *Garfield*

MOUNTAIN RIDGE MOTEL & RV PARK
Ratings: 6/9.5★/7.5 (RV Park) From Hwy 89 & Hwy 12: Go 8-1/4 mi S on Hwy 89 (R). Elev 6889 ft. **FAC:** Gravel rds. 17 gravel, 11 pull-thrus (24 x 70), back-ins (24 x 54), 17 full hkups (30/50 amps), cable, WiFi, rentals. **REC.** Pets OK. Partial handicap access, no tents. Big rig sites, 2015 rates: $35 to $38. Disc: AAA, military. May 15 to Oct 31.
(435)735-4300 Lat: 37.64742, Lon: -112.43458
106 S Main St/Hwy 89, Hatch, UT 84735
info@mountainridgemotel.com
www.brycecanyonrv.com
See ad this page.

RIVERSIDE RESORT & RV PARK
Ratings: 7/8.5★/8 (RV Park) From Jct of US-89 & Hwy 12, S 7 mi on US-89 (L); or From Jct of Center & Main St/Hwy 89 (in Hatch), N 1 mi on Hwy 89 (R). Elev 6500 ft. **FAC:** Gravel rds. (67 spaces). 63 Avail: 46 gravel, 17 grass, 46 pull-thrus (24 x 60), back-ins (21 x 43), 47 full hkups, 16 W, 16 E (30 amps), seasonal sites, WiFi, tent sites, rentals, dump, laundry, groc, LP gas, firewood, restaurant. **REC:** Sevier River: fishing, playground. Pets OK. 2015 rates: $30 to $45. Disc: AAA, military.
(435)735-4223 Lat: 37.66055, Lon: -112.42879
594 N US 89, Hatch, UT 84735
info@riversideresort-utah.com
www.riversideresort-utah.com
See ad this page, 1187.

HEBER CITY — B3 *Wasatch*

DEER CREEK SRA (State Pk) From Jct of Hwys 40 & 189, S 9.6 mi on Hwy 189 (R). 2015 rates: $20 to $28. May 15 to Oct 15. (435)654-0171

JORDANELLE (State Pk) From Jct of US-40 & Mayflower Rd (exit 8), E 1 mi on Mayflower Rd (E). 2015 rates: $16 to $20. May 1 to Sep 15. (435)649-9540

Before you head north, know the rules and regulations for crossing the border into Canada. Read all about it in our Crossing into Canada section.

UT

Mountain Valley
RV RESORT
Welcome to One of the Finest RV Resorts in the Western United States and the Only 10/10★/10 Rated Park in Utah!
Good Sam Park
Good Sam RATED 10/10★/10
See listing Heber City, UT
Beautiful New RV Resort Located in the Heart of the Majestic Rocky Mountains
We Offer the Absolute Best in Full Service RV Lifestyle & Accommodations
Visit Heber Valley!
• Home to Blue Ribbon Fishing
• Over 90 Holes of Championship Golf
• Three Wonderful Water Sport Reservoirs
• Numerous Biking and Hiking Trails
• Many Scenic Byways and Excursions
• Shopping and Restaurants within Minutes of the Resort
• Minutes from Sundance and Park City
• Polaris RZR Rentals Available On Site
Coming 2016
• Grand Opening of Our Expansion
• New Adult Only Amenities
• Clubhouse, Pool, Spa
• Pickleball, Laundry and Much More
• Call for Details
FREE WIFI & CABLE
Located 20 Minutes South of I-80 (Park City) and 30 Minutes East of I-15 (Orem)
2120 South Hwy 40 • Heber City, UT 84032
www.mountainvalleyrv.com • (435) 657-6100 • 855-901-6100

HEBER CITY (CONT)

MOUNTAIN VALLEY RV RESORT

Ratings: 10/10★/10 (RV Resort) From Jct of SR 40 & SR 189 (in town), S 1.0 mi on SR 40 (R) (Park is under construction-targeted opening date Oct 2013). Elev 5778 ft. **FAC:** Paved rds. (94 spaces). Avail: 84 paved, patios, 83 pull-thrus (30 x 75), back-ins (25 x 45), 84 full hkups (30/50 amps), seasonal sites, cable, WiFi, tent sites, rentals, dump, laundry, LP gas, controlled access. **REC:** heated pool, whirlpool, playground. Pets OK. Partial handicap access. Big rig sites, eco-friendly, 2015 rates: $35 to $60. Disc: military.
(435)657-6100 Lat: 40.481377, Lon: -111.401861
2120 South Hwy 40, Heber City, UT 84032
info@mountainvalleyrv.com
www.mountainvalleyrv.com
See ad opposite page, 1189 (Spotlight Heber Valley/Wasatch), 1187.

RIVERS EDGE AT DEER PARK

Ratings: 8.5/9★/8.5 (RV Park) From Jct of I-80 (exit 146) & US 40/189, S 13 mi on Hwy 40/189 to SR-32, E 0.2 mi on SR-32 to Old Hwy 40, N 2.1 mi (R) or From Jct of US 40 W/189 (in Heber City) N 4.5 mi on US 40 W/189 to SR-32, E 0.2 mi on SR-32 to Old Hwy 40, N 2.1 mi (R). Elev 5835 ft. **FAC:** Paved/gravel rds. (30 spaces). Avail: 24 gravel, 22 pull-thrus (35 x 70), back-ins (30 x 60), mostly side by side hkups, 24 full hkups (50 amps), seasonal sites, WiFi, tent sites, rentals, laundry, groc, fire rings, firewood. **REC:** Middle Provo River: fishing, playground. Pets OK. Partial handicap access. Big rig sites, eco-friendly, 2015 rates: $37.95. Disc: AAA, military.
AAA Approved
(888)754-4049 Lat: 40.59339, Lon: -111.42749
7000 N Old Hwy 40, Heber City, UT 84032
riversedgeatdeerpark@gmail.com
riversedgeatdeerpark.com
See ad this page, 1187.

Things to See and Do

HEBER VALLEY TOURISM ECONOMIC DEVELOPMENT CHAMBER Situated only 45 mins from Salt Lake City, visit the Heber Valley Visitors Bureau for maps, brochures and lots of information about what to do when visiting the area. Elev 5588 ft. partial handicap access. RV accessible. Restrooms. Hours: 9am to 5pm. No CC.
(435)654-3666 Lat: 40.513846, Lon: -111.413352
475 North Main, Heber City, UT 84032
info@gohebervalley.com
www.gohebervalley.com
See ad page 1188 (Spotlight Heber Valley/Wasatch).

HONEYVILLE — A3 *Box Elder*

CRYSTAL HOT SPRINGS RV PARK **Ratings: 5.5/5.5/7.5** (RV Park) 2015 rates: $35. (435)279-8104 8215 North Hwy 38, Honeyville, UT 84314

HUNTINGTON — C3 *Emery*

HUNTINGTON (State Pk) From Jct of SR-10 & SR-31, N 1.8 mi on SR-10 to park access rd, W 0.3 mi (L). 2015 rates: $16. (435)687-2491

HUNTSVILLE — B3 *Weber*

CACHE/SOUTH FORK CAMPGROUND (Natl Forest) From town: Go 7 mi E on Hwy-39. Pit toilets. 2015 rates: $18 to $36. May 7 to Sep 19. (801)625-5112

WEBER MEMORIAL PARK (State Pk) From jct of Hwy 162 & Hwy 39 E: Go 8-1/2 mi E on Hwy 39 E, then 1-1/4 mi E on Camsey Rd. 2015 rates: $18. (801)625-3850

HURRICANE — E1 *Washington*

QUAIL CREEK (State Pk) From Jct of I-15 & Hwy 9 (exit 16), E 2.3 mi on Hwy 9 to Quail Creek Road (SR-317), N 2 mi (R). 2015 rates: $15. (435)879-2378

SOUTHERN UTAH RV PARK @ ZIONS GATE RV RESORT **Ratings: 8/8.5★/6** (RV Resort) 2015 rates: $30. (435)703-9585 150 North 3700 West, Hurricane, UT 84737

ST GEORGE KOA **Ratings: 8.5/8★/7** (RV Park) 2015 rates: $31 to $40. (800)405-6188 5800 N Hwy 91, Hurricane, UT 84737

WILLOWWIND RV PARK

Ratings: 9/10★/9.5 (RV Park) E-bnd: From Jct of I-15 & Hwy 9 (Exit 16), E 8 mi on Hwy 9 to 1150 West, S 0.1 mi (L); or W-bnd: From Jct of SR-9 & SR-17, 3.8 mi on SR-9 to S 1150 W, L 0.1 mi on S 1150 W (L). Elev 3200 ft.

PUT'ER IN PARK
Great home base for Zion, Bryce & Grand Canyon Parks! Big rigs, full hook-ups, tents, restrooms & showers. Laundry, free cable & Wi-fi. Easy access to ATV trails, groceries, banks, movies, restaurants, gasoline & Walgreens.

FAC: Paved rds. (164 spaces). Avail: 109 paved, 12 pull-thrus (25 x 66), back-ins (27 x 60), 109 full hkups (30/50 amps), seasonal sites, cable, WiFi, tent sites, laundry. **REC.** Pets OK. Partial handicap access. Big rig sites, 2015 rates: $35 to $45.
(435)635-4154 Lat: 37.17520, Lon: -113.30953
80 S 1150 W, Hurricane, UT 84737
office@willowwindrvpark.com
www.willowwindrvpark.net
See ad this page, 1187 & Snowbird Destinations in Magazine Section.

HYRUM — A3 *Cache*

HYRUM (State Pk) On north shore of Hyrum Lake. (435)245-6866

JENSEN — B5 *Uintah*

DINOSAUR NATL MON/GREEN RIVER CAMPGROUND (Natl Pk) From Jct of US-40 & Hwy 149, N 8.3 mi on Hwy 149 (L). Entrance fee required. 2015 rates: $12. Apr 15 to Oct 5. (970)374-3000

JOSEPH — D2 *Sevier*

FLYING U COUNTRY STORE, RV PARK & CAMPGROUND **Ratings: 5.5/7★/7** (Campground) 2015 rates: $30. (866)527-4758 45 South State St, Joseph, UT 84739

KAMAS — B3 *Summit*

WASATCH/LOST CREEK CAMPGROUND (Natl Forest) 27-1/2 mi E on Hwy-150. Note: Maximum length 40'. Pit toilets. 2015 rates: $18. Jun 20 to Sep 15. (435)783-4338

WASATCH/MIRROR LAKE CAMPGROUND (Natl Forest) 31-3/4 mi E on Hwy-150. Pit toilets. 2015 rates: $16 to $54. Jul 2 to Sep 27. (435)783-4338

WASATCH/MOOSEHORN LAKE CAMPGROUND (Natl Forest) 31 mi E on Hwy-150. Pit toilets. 2015 rates: $18. Jul 1 to Sep 2. (435)783-4338

WASATCH/TRIAL LAKE CAMPGROUND (Natl Forest) 26 mi E on Hwy-150. Pit toilets. 2015 rates: $18 to $36. Jun 20 to Sep 15. (435)783-4338

WASATCH/YELLOW PINE CAMPGROUND (Natl Forest) 6 mi E on Hwy-150. Pit toilets. 2015 rates: $10 to $30. May 19 to Sep 3. (435)783-4338

KANAB — E2 *Kane*

HITCH-N-POST RV PARK **Ratings: 5/6/6** (RV Park) 2015 rates: $27 to $29. (435)644-2142 196 E 300 South St, Kanab, UT 84741

Do you know how to read each part of a listing? Check the How to Use This Campground Guide in the front.

UT

Enjoy the scenery as you travel North America. We exclusively rate campgrounds for their visual appearance and environmental quality, and represent their score, 1 through 10, as the third rating in our Triple Rating System.

KANAB (CONT)

KANAB RV CORRAL
Ratings: 7.5/9.5★/8.5 (RV Park) From Jct of US-89 & US-89A, S 0.3 mi on US-89A (L). Elev 4900 ft. **FAC:** Paved/gravel rds. 41 gravel, 20 pull-thrus (22 x 70), back-ins (18 x 45), 41 full hkups (30/50 amps), WiFi, laundry. **REC:** pool. Pets OK. Partial handicap access, no tents. Big rig sites, eco-friendly, 2015 rates: $35. Disc: AAA. Mar 16 to Nov 1.
AAA Approved
(435)644-5330 Lat: 37.04000, Lon: -112.52520
483 S 100 East, Kanab, UT 84741
info@kanabrvcorral.com
www.kanabrvcorral.com
See ad page 1197.

KANARRAVILLE — E2 *Iron*

RED LEDGE RV PARK **Ratings: 5/7.5/6.5** (RV Resort) 2015 rates: $27. (435)586-9150 15 N Main St (Hwy 91), Kanarraville, UT 84742

Check out those views! From awe-inspiring redwood giants to the soaring towers of the Golden Gate Bridge, we've put the Spotlight on North America's most popular travel destinations. Turn to the Spotlight articles in our State and Province sections to learn more.

KAYSVILLE — B3 *Davis*

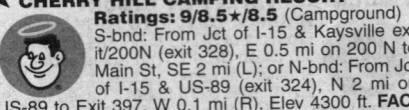

CHERRY HILL CAMPING RESORT
Ratings: 9/8.5★/8.5 (Campground) S-bnd: From Jct of I-15 & Kaysville exit/200N (exit 328), E 0.5 mi on 200 N to Main St, SE 2 mi (L); or N-bnd: From Jct of I-15 & US-89 (exit 324), N 2 mi on US-89 to Exit 397, W 0.1 mi (R). Elev 4300 ft. **FAC:** Paved/gravel rds. (124 spaces). 94 Avail: 34 paved, 60 grass, 80 pull-thrus (22 x 60), back-ins (22 x 42), some side by side hkups, 82 full hkups, 12 W, 12 E (30/50 amps), seasonal sites, WiFi, tent sites, dump, laundry, groc. **REC:** heated pool, wading pool, playground, rec open to public. Pets OK. Partial handicap access. 2015 rates: $38. Disc: AAA, military. Apr 1 to Nov 1. ATM.
AAA Approved
(801)451-5379 Lat: 41.01336, Lon: -111.91361
1325 S Main, Kaysville, UT 84037
info@cherry-hill.com
www.cherry-hill.com
See ad pages 1203, 1187.

Find it Fast! Use our alphabetized index of campgrounds and parks.

KAYSVILLE (CONT)

Travel Services

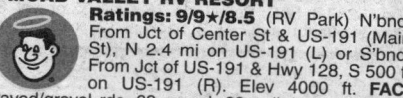

CAMPING WORLD OF KAYSVILLE As the nation's largest retailer of RV supplies, accessories, services and new and used RVs, Camping World is committed to making your total RV experience better. RV Accessories: (800)424-8844. Elev 4352 ft. **SERVICES:** RV, RV appliance, MH mechanical, staffed RV wash, restrooms, RV Sales. RV supplies, LP, dump, emergency parking, RV accessible. waiting room. Hours: 8am to 5pm. (888)497-4496 Lat: 41.045884, Lon: -111.9595 780 N 900 W, Kaysville, UT 84037 www.campingworld.com

LAKE POWELL — E4 *Kane*

BULLFROG RV PARK & CAMPGROUND **Ratings: 3/6.5/6.5** (Campground) 2015 rates: $46. (435)684-3032 bullfrog Resort & Marina Hwy276, Bullfrog, UT 84533

BULLFROG'S PAINTED HILLS RV PARK (Public) From the Bullfrog ferry dock (N): Go 1 mi N on Hwy 276. (435)684-3032

HALLS CROSSING RV RESORT & MARINA (Public) From the Hall's Crossing ferry dock: Go 2-1/4 mi S on Hwy 276. (435)684-7000

HALLS CROSSING TRAILER VILLAGE **Ratings: 5/6/6.5** (Campground) 2015 rates: $43. (435)684-7000 halls Crossing Hwy 276, Halls Crossing, UT 84533

LAKETOWN — A3 *Rich*

RENDEZVOUS BEACH (State Pk) From town, NW 2 mi on Hwy 30 (R). 2015 rates: $10 to $25. (435)946-3343

LAYTON — B3 *Morgan*

CIRCLE L MOBILE HOME COMMUNITY
Ratings: 6.5/8★/7 (RV Park) From Jct of I-15 & Hillfield Rd (exit 331), W 0.2 mi on Hillfield Rd to Main St, S 0.8 mi (R). Elev 4400 ft. **FAC:** Paved rds. (109 spaces). Avail: 64 gravel, back-ins (26 x 45), 64 full hkups (30/50 amps), seasonal sites, WiFi, dump, laundry. **REC:** playground. Pets OK. No tents. 2015 rates: $30.
(801)544-8945 Lat: 41.06253, Lon: -111.97025
231 North Main, Layton, UT 84041
circlel@towermgnt.com
www.circlelmhc.com

LEEDS — E1 *Washington*

LEEDS RV PARK & MOTEL
Ratings: 7.5/9★/9.5 (RV Park) N-Bnd: From Jct of I-15 & Hwy 228/Main St (exit 22), NE 0.7 mi on Main St to Center St, E 0.1 mi to Valley Rd, S 0.1 mi (L); or S-Bnd: From Jct of I-15 & Main St (exit 23), S 0.8 mi on Main St to Center St, E 0.1 mi to Valley Rd, S 0.1 mi (L). Elev 3550 ft. **FAC:** Gravel rds. (47 spaces). Avail: 23 gravel, patios, 8 pull-thrus (29 x 68), back-ins (30 x 44), some side by side hkups, 23 full hkups (30/50 amps), seasonal sites, cable, WiFi, tent sites, laundry. **REC.** Pets OK. Eco-friendly, 2015 rates: $37 to $40. Disc: AAA, military.
(435)879-2450 Lat: 37.23298, Lon: -113.36305
97 S Valley Rd, Leeds, UT 84746
leedsrvpark@infowest.com
www.leedsrvpark.com
See ad opposite page, 1187 & Snowbird Destinations in Magazine Section.

ZION WEST RV PARK
Ratings: 6/9.5★/9.5 (RV Park) N-bnd:From Jct of I-15 & Main St (exit 22), N 0.4 mi on Main St to Mulberry Ln, SE 0.1 mi to Valley N 100 ft (R); or S-bnd: From Jct of I-15 & Main St (exit 23), S 1 mi on Main St to Mulberry Ln, SE 0.1 mi to Valley, N 100 ft (R). Elev 3200 ft. **FAC:** Paved/gravel rds. (36 spaces). Avail: 24 gravel, 16 pull-thrus (18 x 60), back-ins (30 x 55), mostly side by side hkups, 24 full hkups (30/50 amps), seasonal sites, cable, WiFi, tent sites, laundry. Pets OK. 2015 rates: $37 to $40. Disc: military.
(435)879-2854 Lat: 37.23187, Lon: -113.36359
175 South Valley Rd, Leeds, UT 84746
zionwestrvpark@infowest.com
www.zionwestrv.com
See ad opposite page.

LOA — D3 *Wayne*

FISHLAKE/BOWERY CREEK (Natl Forest) 13 mi NW on Hwy-24, then 9 mi NE on Hwy-25. 2015 rates: $15.26. May 15 to Sep 14. (435)836-2811

We rate what RVers consider important.

FISHLAKE/MACKINAW CAMPGROUND (Natl Forest) 13 mi NW on Hwy-24, then 8 mi NE on Hwy-25. 2015 rates: $15.26. May 15 to Sep 14. (435)836-2811

LOGAN — A3 *Cache*

Things to See and Do

CACHE VALLEY VISITORS COUNCIL Information to visit Cache Valley. Maps, brochures and other info available. Elev 4400 ft. partial handicap access. RV accessible. Restrooms. Hours: 8:00am to 5:00pm. No CC.
(800)882-4433 Lat: 41.73525, Lon: -111.83477
199 N Main, Logan, UT 84321
cvinfo@visitloganutah.com
www.visitloganutah.com
See ad opposite page.

MANILA — B4 *Daggett*

FLAMING GORGE CAMPING RESORT KOA **Ratings: 7.5/9.5★/7** (Campground) 2015 rates: $34.50. Apr 15 to Nov 1. (435)784-3184 hwy 43 & 3rd West, Manila, UT 84046

MANTI — C3 *Sanpete*

PALISADE (State Pk) From Jct of US-89 & Palisade Dr, E 2 mi on Palisade Dr (E). 2015 rates: $20 to $28. (435)835-7275

TEMPLE HILL RESORT & RV CAMPGROUND **Ratings: 8/8.5★/9** (Campground) 2015 rates: $25 to $45. (435)835-2267 296 E Johnson Rd (800 N), Manti, UT 84642

MARYSVALE — D2 *Piute*

BIG ROCK CANDY MOUNTAIN RV **Ratings: 7/8★/7** (RV Park) 2015 rates: $29. May 15 to Oct 30. (800)519-2243 4550 S Hwy 89, Marysvale, UT 84750

LIZZIE & CHARLIE'S RV/ATV PARK **Ratings: 6/8★/6.5** (RV Park) 2015 rates: $31. Apr 1 to Oct 30. (435)326-4213 995 Main, Marysvale, UT 84750

SOUTH-FORTY RV PARK **Ratings: 6.5/9★/8.5** (RV Park) 2015 rates: $29 to $31. Apr 1 to Oct 30. (435)326-4404 1170 N Highway 89, Marysvale, UT 84750

MEXICAN HAT — E4 *San Juan*

VALLE'S RV PARK **Ratings: 2/6/4** (Campground) 2015 rates: $28. (435)683-2226 268 E Main St, Mexican Hat, UT 84531

MIDWAY — B3 *Wasatch*

WASATCH MOUNTAIN (State Pk) S-bnd: From Jct of US 40 & SR 113/SR 222, W 6.5 mi on SR 222 (L) N-bnd: From Jct of US 189 & SR 113, N 3.9 mi on SR 113 to SR-222, N 3.3 mi on SR 222 (L). 2015 rates: $13 to $25. Apr 15 to Oct 15. (435)654-1791

MILLS — C3 *Juab*

YUBA (State Pk) From town: Go 5 mi S on I-15 to exit 202, then 5 mi S on local paved road. (435)758-2611

MOAB — D5 *Grand*

ACT CAMPGROUND
Ratings: 7/9.5★/8.5 (RV Park) From Jct of Center St & Main St (in Moab) S 2.5 mi on Main St (Hwy 191) to S Mill Creek Rd, E .10 mi on S Mill Creek Rd (L). Elev 4375 ft. **FAC:** Gravel rds. 21 gravel, 6 pull-thrus (24 x 52), back-ins (24 x 40), 21 full hkups (30/50 amps), cable, WiFi, tent sites, rentals, laundry. Pets OK. Partial handicap access. Eco-friendly, 2015 rates: $39 to $49.
(435)355-0355 Lat: 38.55557, Lon: -109.52475
Us 191 at Mill Creek, Moab, UT 84532
info@actcampground.com
www.actcampground.com

ARCH VIEW RV PARK & CAMPGROUND
Ratings: 8.5/8.5★/8 (RV Park) N-bnd: From Jct of US-191 & SR-313, N 0.3 mi on Hwy 191 (R) S-bnd: From Jct I-70 & US-191 (Exit 182), S 20.1 mi on US-191 (L). Elev 5000 ft. **FAC:** Gravel rds. 97 gravel, 73 pull-thrus (26 x 60), back-ins (30 x 50), 97 full hkups (30/50 amps), WiFi, tent sites, rentals, laundry, groc, LP gas, firewood. **REC:** pool, playground. Pets OK. Partial handicap access. Big rig sites, eco-friendly, 2015 rates: $40 to $61. Disc: AAA. Mar 1 to Oct 31.
(800)813-6622 Lat: 38.67679, Lon: -109.68681
13701 North Highway 191, Moab, UT 84532
camp@archviewresort.com
www.archviewresort.com

ARCHES/DEVILS GARDEN (Natl Pk) From Jct of I-70 & US-191, S 28 mi on US-191 to park access rd, E 18 mi (R). Hilly rd. Pit toilets. 2015 rates: $20. Mar 1 to Oct 31. (435)719-2299

CANYONLANDS CAMPGROUND
Ratings: 8/9★/9 (RV Park) From Jct of Center St & Main St (US-191), S 0.6 mi on Main St (L). Elev 4000 ft. **FAC:** Gravel rds. 90 paved, patios, 90 pull-thrus (23 x 44), 66 full hkups, 24 W, 24 E (30/50 amps), cable, WiFi, tent sites, rentals, dump, laundry, groc, LP gas, firewood. **REC:** heated pool, playground. Pets OK. Partial handicap access. Eco-friendly, 2015 rates: $39 to $53. Disc: AAA. Mar 1 to Nov 7. ATM.
(800)522-6848 Lat: 38.56455, Lon: -109.54929
555 S Main St, Moab, UT 84532
canyonlandsmoab@gmail.com
www.canyonlandsrv.com

DEAD HORSE POINT (State Pk) From Jct of US-191 & SR-313, SW 21.5 mi on SR-313, follow signs (E). 2015 rates: $25. (435)259-2614

MOAB KOA Ratings: 8.5/8.5★/7.5 (Campground) From Jct of Center St & US-191 (Main St), S 4.9 mi on US-191 (L). Elev 4200 ft. **FAC:** Gravel/dirt rds. 132 gravel, 91 pull-thrus (25 x 55), back-ins (18 x 40), 96 full hkups, 36 W, 36 E (30/50 amps), cable, WiFi, tent sites, dump, laundry, groc, LP gas. **REC:** pool, playground. Pet restrict(B). Partial handicap access. 2015 rates: $34.90 to $69.90. Disc: AAA. Mar 1 to Oct 31.
AAA Approved
(435)259-6682 Lat: 38.52395, Lon: -109.49655
3225 S Hwy 191, Moab, UT 84532
info@moabkoa.com
www.moabkoa.com

MOAB RIM CAMPARK Ratings: 5.5/8.5★/7 (Campground) From Jct of Center St & Main St (in Moab) S 3 miles on Main St (Hwy 191) R. Elev 4483 ft. **FAC:** Gravel rds. (30 spaces). Avail: 28 gravel, patios, 25 pull-thrus (27 x 60), back-ins (22 x 36), 23 full hkups, 5 W, 5 E (30/50 amps), seasonal sites, cable, WiFi, tent sites, dump, laundry, dump, firewood. **REC:** playground. Pets OK. Partial handicap access. 2015 rates: $34 to $39. Disc: AAA, military.
AAA Approved
(435)259-5002 Lat: 38.544019, Lon: -109.518844
1900 S Hwy 191, Moab, UT 84532
moabrimcampark@gmail.com
www.moabrimrv.com

MOAB VALLEY RV RESORT
Ratings: 9/9★/8.5 (RV Park) N'bnd: From Jct of Center St & US-191 (Main St), N 2.4 mi on US-191 (L) or S'bnd: From Jct of US-191 & Hwy 128, S 500 ft on US-191 (R). Elev 4000 ft. **FAC:** Paved/gravel rds. 69 gravel, 69 pull-thrus (24 x 58), mostly side by side hkups, 62 full hkups, 7 W, 7 E (30/50 amps), cable, WiFi, tent sites, rentals, dump, laundry, groc, controlled access. **REC:** heated pool, whirlpool, playground. Pets OK. Partial handicap access. Eco-friendly, 2015 rates: $31 to $57. Disc: AAA. Mar 1 to Nov 9.
(435)259-4469 Lat: 38.60074, Lon: -109.57602
1773 N Hwy 191, Moab, UT 84532
moabvalley@highwaywestvacations.com
www.moabvalleyrv.com

O.K. RV PARK & CANYONLANDS STABLES **Ratings: 7/8.5★/7** (RV Park) 2015 rates: $39. (435)259-1400 3310 Spanish Valley Dr, Moab, UT 84532

SLICKROCK CAMPGROUND RV & TENT CAMPING RESORT **Ratings: 5.5/5.5/4** (Campground) 2015 rates: $38 to $44. Mar 1 to Oct 31. (800)448-8873 1301 N Hwy 191, Moab, UT 84532

Nobody takes to the road like we do. In many listings we tell you the surface type and condition of interior campground roads.

UT

MOAB (CONT)

SPANISH TRAIL RV PARK
Ratings: 7/10★/8.5 (RV Park) From Jct of Center & Main St (Hwy 191), S 4.4 mi on Hwy 191 (R). Elev 4200 ft. **FAC:** Gravel rds. 83 gravel, patios, 62 pull-thrus (27 x 60), back-ins (27 x 40), 83 full hkups (30/50 amps), cable, WiFi, laundry, groc. **REC.** Pet restrict(B/Q). Partial handicap access, no tents. Big rig sites, eco-friendly, 2015 rates: $44 to $60. Disc: military.
(800)787-2751 Lat: 38.52799, Lon: -109.50435
2980 S Hwy 191, Moab, UT 84532
spanishtrail@frontiernet.net
www.spanishtrailrvpark.com
See ad pages 1199, 1187.

Things to See and Do

MOAB TRAVEL COUNCIL Provides current weather & road information, interpretive displays, gift shop, guide books, maps, DVDs, posters, postcards and much more. Elev 4000 ft. partial handicap access. RV accessible. Restrooms. Hours: 9:00am to 5:00pm. No CC.
(435)259-8825 Lat: 38.61483, Lon: -109.73714
84 100 East, Moab, UT 84532
info2@discovermoab.com
www.discovermoab.com
See ad page 1198.

MONTICELLO — E5 *San Juan*

CANYONLANDS/SQUAW FLAT (Natl Pk) From town, N 15 mi on US-191, W 38 mi on Hwy 211, follow signs (E) Note: Maximum length 28'. Pit toilets. 2015 rates: $15. (435)719-2313

MOUNTAIN VIEW RV PARK **Ratings: 6/6.5/5** (RV Park) 2015 rates: $30. (435)587-2974 632 N Main, Monticello, UT 84535

MONUMENT VALLEY — E4 *San Juan*

GOULDING'S MONUMENT VALLEY & RV PARK CAMPGROUND
Ratings: 9/9★/9.5 (RV Park) From Kayenta, AZ, N 22 mi on US-163 to Monument Valley Rd, W 2 mi (R); or From Mexican Hat town center, SW 21 mi on US-163 to Monument Valley Rd, W 2 mi (R). Elev 5280 ft. **FAC:** Paved rds. 66 Avail: 33 gravel, 33 dirt, 34 pull-thrus (32 x 60), back-ins (27 x 30), 66 full hkups (30/50 amps), cable, WiFi, tent sites, rentals, dump, laundry, groc, fire rings, firewood. **REC:** heated pool. Pets OK. Partial handicap access. Big rig sites, eco-friendly, 2015 rates: $48. Disc: AAA, military.
(435)727-3235 Lat: 37.00648, Lon: -110.21509
2000 Main St, Monument Valley, UT 84536
campground@gouldings.com
www.gouldings.com
See ad this page, 1187.

MOUNT CARMEL — E2 *Kane*

EAST ZION RIVERSIDE RV PARK **Ratings: 5/9.5★/5.5** (Campground) 2015 rates: $18. (888)848-6358 4530 S State Street, Orderville, UT 84755

MOUNT CARMEL MOTEL & RV PARK **Ratings: 4/7★/6.5** (RV Park) 2015 rates: $25. Mar 15 to Oct 31. (435)648-2323 3000 S State, Mount Carmel, UT 84755

MOUNT CARMEL JUNCTION — E2 *Kane*

CORAL PINK SAND DUNES (State Pk) S-bnd: From Jct of Hwy 9 & US-89, S 4 mi on US-89 to Cnty Rd, S 12.1 mi (L); or N-bnd: From Jct of US-89A & US-89, N 8.2 mi on US-89 to Hancock Rd, SW 9.4 mi to Cnty Rd, S 3.2 mi (L). 2015 rates: $20. (801)322-3770

MOUNT PLEASANT — C3 *Sanpete*

CAMPERWORLD-PLEASANT CREEK **Ratings: 7/9★/8** (Membership Pk) 2015 rates: $39 to $49. (435)462-2010 2903 S 1700 E, Mount Pleasant, UT 84647

NEPHI — C3 *Juab*

BIG MOUNTAIN CAMPGROUND RV PARK
Ratings: 9/9.5★/8 (RV Park) From Jct of I-15 & Hwy 132 (Exit 225): Go E 5 mi on Hwy 132 (R). Elev 5700 ft. **FAC:** Paved rds. 52 gravel, 28 pull-thrus (28 x 60), back-ins (28 x 50), 27 full hkups, 25 W, 25 E (30 amps), WiFi, tent sites, rentals, dump, laundry, groc, firewood. **REC:** heated pool, Salt Creek: fishing, playground. Pets OK. Partial handicap access. 2015 rates: $39.75. May 15 to Sep 30.
(435)623-4800 Lat: 39.71223, Lon: -111.81026
5298 E Hwy 132, Nephi, UT 84648
reservations@bigmountainrv.com
www.bigmountainrv.com
See ad this page, 1187.

RV Park ratings you can rely on!

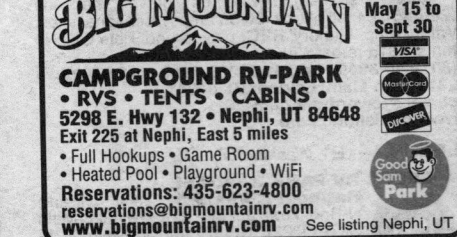

HIGH COUNTRY RV CAMP
Ratings: 6/8.5★/5.5 (RV Park) From Jct of I-15 & Main St (exit 222), N 1 mi on Main St (R). Elev 5100 ft. **FAC:** Gravel rds. (44 spaces). Avail: 37 gravel, 30 pull-thrus (16 x 45), back-ins (36 x 75), some side by side hkups, 37 full hkups (30/50 amps), seasonal sites, WiFi, tent sites, dump, laundry. Pets OK. Partial handicap access. Big rig sites, 2015 rates: $20 to $25.
(435)623-2624 Lat: 39.69539, Lon: -111.83520
899 S Main, Nephi, UT 84648
valjonesconstruction@gmail.com
www.nephirv.com
See ad this page, 1187.

OASIS (BLM) (Natl Pk) From jct Hwy 132 & Hwy 148: Go 9 mi N on Hwy 148, then 4 mi W on county road, then 5 mi SW on park road. (801)539-4001

WHITE SANDS (BLM) (State Pk) From jct Hwy-132 & Hwy-148: Go 9 mi NW on Hwy-148, then 4 mi W on paved county road, then 1 mi SW on paved road, then 1 mi N on dirt road. Pit toilets. (801)539-4001

NORTH SALT LAKE — B3 *Davis*

PONY EXPRESS RV RESORT
Ratings: 10/9.5★/8.5 (RV Park) S-bnd: From Jct of I-215 (exit 27) & SR 68 (Redwood Rd): Go S 0.2 mi on SR 68 (R); or N-bnd: From Jct of I-80 (exit 117) & I-215: Go N 5.2 mi on I-215 to SR 68 (exit 27), S 0.2 mi on SR 68 (Redwood Rd) (R). Elev 4300 ft. **FAC:** Paved rds. (175 spaces). Avail: 125 paved, 100 pull-thrus (28 x 60), back-ins (26 x 33), 125 full hkups (30/50 amps), seasonal sites, WiFi, rentals, laundry, groc, LP gas, controlled access.

NORTH SALT LAKE (CONT)

PONY EXPRESS RV RESORT (CONT)
REC: heated pool, Jordan River: playground. Pets OK. Partial handicap access, no tents. Big rig sites, eco-friendly, 2015 rates: $32 to $47. Disc: AAA, military.
(844)780-0170 Lat: 40.83037, Lon: -111.93858
2012 West Recreation Way, North Salt Lake, UT 84054
reserve@ponyexpressrvresort.com
www.ponyexpressrvresort.com

OAKLEY — B3 *Summit*

WASATCH/LEDGEFORK CAMPGROUND (State Pk) 12 mi NE on Hwy-213, then 4 mi S on FR-33. Pit toilets. 2015 rates: $19 to $38. May 24 to Oct 20. (435)783-4338

OGDEN — B3 *Weber*

CACHE/ANDERSON COVE CAMPGROUND (Natl Forest) From jct I-15 (exit 347-12th St) & Hwy 39: Go 12 mi E on Hwy 39. Pit toilets. 2015 rates: $18 to $36. May 9 to Oct 12. (801)524-3900

◄ CENTURY RV PARK & CAMPGROUND MHP
Ratings: 9.5/9.5★/8.5 (RV Park) From Jct of I-15 & 2100 South St (exit 343), W 0.1 mi on 2100 South St to Century Ln, S 0.1 mi (L). Do not use GPS. Elev 4300 ft. **FAC:** Paved rds. (150 spaces). Avail: 70 gravel, 70 pull-thrus (26 x 65), mostly side by side hkups, 70 full hkups (30/50 amps), seasonal sites, cable, WiFi, tent sites, dump, laundry. **REC:** heated pool, whirlpool, playground. Pets OK. Big rig sites, 2015 rates: $28 to $35. Disc: AAA, military.
(801)731-3800 Lat: 41.22753, Lon: -112.01303
1483 W 2100 S, West Haven, UT 84401
centuryrvpark@gmail.com
centuryparkrv.com
See ad opposite page.

FORT BUENAVENTURA (State Pk) From jct of 25th St & Lincoln Ave: Go N 1 blk on Lincoln Ave, then W 7/10 mi on 24th St, then S 1 blk on A Ave and E 6/10 mi on Capitol. 2015 rates: $18. (801)399-8099

◄ WILLARD BAY (State Pk) From Jct of I-15 & Exit 357 (SR-315), W 100 ft on SR-315 to park access rd, S 0.5 mi (E). 2015 rates: $16 to $25. (435)734-9494

PANGUITCH — E2 *Garfield*

✓ BEAR PAW FISHING RESORT & RV PARK **Ratings: 3/5.5/4** (RV Resort) 2015 rates: $28. May 10 to Oct 10. (888)553-8439 905 S Hwy 143, Panguitch, UT 84759

DIXIE/WHITE BRIDGE CAMPGROUND (Natl Forest) From town: Go 10 mi SW on Hwy 143. Pit toilets. 2015 rates: $15 to $30. May 22 to Nov 1. (435)865-3200

HITCH-N-POST RV CAMPGROUND **Ratings: 8/9★/8.5** (Campground) 2015 rates: $22 to $29. (435)676-2436 420 N Main, Panguitch, UT 84759

PANGUITCH BRYCE CANYON KOA
Ratings: 8.5/8.5★/7.5 (Campground) From Jct of US-89 & Main St (Hwy 143), S 0.6 mi on Main St (L). Elev 6700 ft. **FAC:** Gravel rds. 43 gravel, 43 pull-thrus (25 x 58), mostly side by side hkups, 26 full hkups, 17 W, 17 E (30/50 amps), WiFi, tent sites, rentals, dump, laundry, groc, LP gas, fire rings, firewood. **REC:** heated pool, playground. Pets OK. Big rig sites, eco-friendly, 2015 rates: $36 to $40. Disc: military. Apr 1 to Oct 7.
(435)676-2225 Lat: 37.81459, Lon: -112.43464
555 S Main St, Panguitch, UT 84759
zionkoa@color-country.net
www.koa.com/camp/panguitch
See ad this page.

PARADISE RV PARK & CAMPGROUND **Ratings: 5.5/7.5/5.5** (RV Park) 2015 rates: $13.95 to $14.95. May 1 to Oct 31. (435)676-8348 2153 Hwy 89, Panguitch, UT 84759

Things to See and Do

GARFIELD COUNTY OFFICE OF TOURISM
Maps, brochures and information for Bryce Canyon Country. Elev 6640 ft. partial handicap access. RV accessible. Restrooms. Hours: 9:00am to 5:00pm. No CC.
(800)444-6689 Lat: 37.82217, Lon: -112.43571
55 S Main, Panguitch, UT 84759
cravgar@color-country.net
www.brycecanyoncountry.com
See ad page 1186 (Welcome Section).

PRICE — C4 *Carbon*

◄ LEGACY INN & RV PARK Ratings: 4/8★/3 (RV Park) From Jct of Hwys 6 & 191 & Exit 240 (1st North St), E 0.3 mi on 100 North St to Carbonville Rd, N 800 ft (L). Elev 5500 ft. **FAC:** Poor paved/gravel rds. 30 gravel, 10 pull-thrus (16 x 60), back-ins (17 x 40), 30 full hkups (30/50 amps), WiFi, rentals, dump, laundry. Pets OK. Partial handicap access, no tents. Big rig sites, 2015 rates: $34. Disc: AAA. ATM.
AAA Approved
(435)637-2424 Lat: 39.60276, Lon: -110.82150
145 N Carbonville Rd, Price, UT 84501
legacyinnutah@gmail.com
legacyinnutah.com

PROVO — B3 *Utah*

PROVO See also Springville.

◄ LAKESIDE RV CAMPGROUND
Ratings: 9/10★/9 (Campground) S-bnd: From Jct of I-15 & Center St (exit 265), W 2.2 mi on Center St (R); or N-bnd: From Jct of I-15 & Center St (exit 265), W 2.2 mi on Center St (R). Elev 4491 ft. **FAC:** Paved/gravel rds. (125 spaces). Avail: 100 gravel, 100 pull-thrus (22 x 65), mostly side by side hkups, 100 full hkups (30/50 amps), seasonal sites, cable, WiFi, tent sites, dump, laundry, groc, LP gas, firewood. **REC:** heated pool, Provo River: fishing, playground. Pets OK. Eco-friendly, 2015 rates: $29.49 to $35.95. Disc: AAA, military.
AAA Approved
(801)373-5267 Lat: 40.23561, Lon: -111.72813
4000 West Center St, Provo, UT 84601
lakesiderv@aol.com
www.lakesidervcampground.com
See ad pages 1202, 1187, 1184 (UT Map).

◄ UTAH LAKE (State Pk) From Jct of I-15 & Center St (exit 265B), W 3 mi on Center St (E). 2015 rates: $20 to $40. (801)375-0731

How much will it all cost? Use this as a guide: Rates shown are the minimum and maximum for two adults in one RV at the time of inspection (excluding any additional fees for items not at the site). Remember, these rates serve as guidelines only. It's always best to call ahead for the most current rate information.

Snowbird Destinations

Join the flock and head south during the winter. Use our handy Snowbird section in the front of this Guide to find RV-friendly destinations throughout the sunbelt. Snowbird Destinations features the top Snowbird roosts and lists great campgrounds in compelling areas.

Time and rates don't stand still. Remember that last year's rates serve as a guideline only. Call ahead for the most current rate information.

UT

ICHFIELD — D2 *Sevier*

RICHFIELD'S KOA RV PARK & KAMPGROUND **atings: 8.5/9.5★/8.5** (Campground) 2015 rates: 35.89 to $39.89. Mar 1 to Oct 31. (435)896-6674 90 W 600 S, Richfield, UT 84701

ALINA — D3 *Sevier*

BUTCH CASSIDY CAMPGROUND **Rat-ngs: 8/8.5★/7** (Campground) 2015 rates: $27 to 35. (800)551-6842 1050 S State St, Salina, UT 4654

ALT LAKE CITY — B3 *Salt Lake*

SALT LAKE CITY AREA MAP

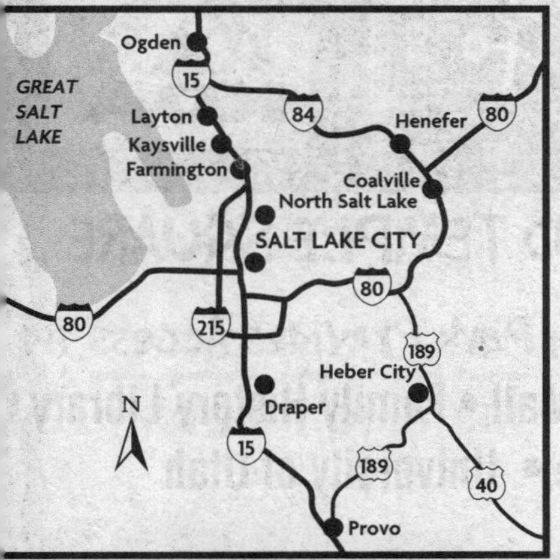

For more detail and a broader overview, please see our full-color state map at the front of the Utah state section.

Symbols on map indicate towns within a 50 mile radius of Salt Lake City where campgrounds are listed. Check listings for more information.

See also Coalville, Draper, Farmington, Heber City, Henefer, Kaysville, Layton, North Salt Lake, Ogden & Provo.

Things change ... last year's rates serve as a guideline only.

Know how to keep your four-legged travel companions happy and comfortable? Check out our Pampered Pet Parks feature at the front of the Guide.

EAST CANYON (State Pk) W-bnd: From Jct of I-84 & SR-65 (exit 115), SW 8.8 mi on SR-65 to SR-66, W 1.3 mi (L), E-bnd: From jct of I-84 & SR-66 (exit 103), SE 12 mi on SR-66, (R). 2015 rates: $24 to $28. (801)829-6866

SALT LAKE CITY KOA
Ratings: 10/9.5★/9 (RV Park) W-bnd: From Jct of I-15 & I-80 (exit 308), W 1.7 mi on I-80 to Redwood Rd exit (exit 118), N 0.3 mi on Redwood Rd to N Temple, E 0.3 mi to 1460 West, N on 1460 West 100 ft. (R) E-bnd: From Jct of I-80 & exit 115 (N Temple), E 3 mi on N Temple (follow signs) to 1460 West, N on 1460 West 100 ft (R). Elev 4300 ft.

The most friendly park in Salt Lake City area. Bus & tour service to & from campgrounds! 14 blocks from Temple Square & Family History Library. See our ad in the Directory for much more.

FAC: Paved rds. (180 spaces). Avail: 150 paved, patios, 150 pull-thrus (26 x 60), some side by side hkups, 150 full hkups (30/50 amps), seasonal sites, cable, WiFi, tent sites, rentals, dump, laundry, groc, LP gas, restaurant. **REC:** heated pool, whirlpool, Jordan River: fishing, playground. Pet restrict(B/Q). Partial handicap access. Big rig sites, eco-friendly, 2015 rates: $55.17 to $72.05. Disc: AAA, military.
AAA Approved
(801)328-0224 Lat: 40.77185, Lon: -111.93217
1400 W N Temple, Salt Lake City, UT 84116
saltlakekoa@gmail.com
www.slckoa.com
See ad page 1204.

Our travel services section will help you find services that you'll find handy in your travels.

Set a Destination for Family Fun!

Check out our camping destinations highlighting the best places for camping with the family in every state and province. Find a great destination, then select one of the family-friendly campgrounds listed by region throughout the article in the front of this Guide.

Want to Know How We Rate Campgrounds?

Understand our ratings! Turn to the "Understand the Campground Rating System" section at the front of this Guide to find out how we rate and inspect parks.

RATED
10/10★/10

The FIRST NUMBER represents
Development of Facilities

The SECOND NUMBER represents
Cleanliness and Physical Characteristics of Restrooms and Showers
(plus, a Star is awarded to parks who receive maximum points for cleanliness!)

The THIRD NUMBER represents
Visual Appearance/ Environmental Quality

UT

14 BLOCKS FROM DOWNTOWN CITY CENTER AND TEMPLE SQUARE

Guided Tours Leave Directly from our Campground

State Capitol
Great Salt Lake • City Tour
World's Largest Open Pit Mine

New Light Rail Directly from Park Provides Access To:

Temple Square • City Center Mall • Family History Library
Airport • Trolley Square • University of Utah

OPEN YEAR-ROUND

- 180 Full Hookups (30 & 50 Amp)
- Propane • Grassy Tent Sites
- Large Playground • Pavilion
- Heated Pool (Memorial Day to Labor Day)
- Laundry • Groceries
- RV Supplies • Gifts
- Free Cable TV • Sport Court
- Clean Restrooms
- Free Shuttle to Downtown

Kamping Kabins™

From I-15 N'bnd, S'bnd or I-80 W:

Take Exit 308 (I-80 W). Go 0.5 mi to Exit 118 (Redwood Rd). Turn R and head 0.5 mi to North Temple. Turn R and head 0.5 mi to 1460 West. Turn L at light and enter KOA.

From I-80 E:

Take Exit 115 (North Temple). Follow signs for North Temple and head East approx 3.5 mi to 1460 West. Turn L at light and enter KOA.

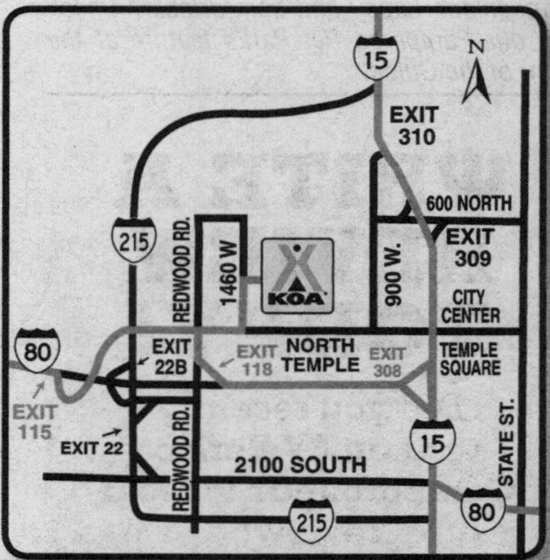

See listing Salt Lake City, UT

RESERVATIONS RECOMMENDED
(801) 328-0224 • 1-800-226-7752

WWW.SLCKOA.COM

REGISTRATION OFFICE AT
1400 W. North Temple • Salt Lake City, UT 84116

SCOFIELD — C3 *Carbon*

SCOFIELD (State Pk) From jct US-6 & Hwy-96: Go 13 mi S on Hwy-96. 2015 rates: $15 to $20. (435)448-9449

SEVIER — D2 *Sevier*

FREMONT INDIAN (State Pk) From town: Go 7 mi SW on I-70. 2015 rates: $13. (435)527-4631

SNOWVILLE — A2 *Box Elder*

← LOTTIE-DELL CAMPGROUND **Ratings: 4/6.5/6** (Campground) 2015 rates: $30. Mar 1 to Nov 1. (435)872-8273 490 West Main, Snowville, UT 84336

SPRINGDALE — E2 *Washington*

↑ **ZION CANYON CAMPGROUND & QUALITY INN AT ZION PARK**
Ratings: 8/8★/8.5 (RV Park) On Hwy 9, S 0.5 mi from South entrance to Zion Nat'l Park (L). Elev 3800 ft. **FAC:** Paved/gravel rds. 120 gravel, 56 pull-thrus (27 x 52), back-ins (25 x 36), some side by side hkups, 106 full hkups, 14 W, 14 E (30/50 amps), cable, WiFi, tent sites, rentals, dump, laundry, firewood. **REC:** heated pool, Virgin River: fishing, playground. No pets. Partial handicap access. 14 day max stay, 2015 rates: $45.
(435)772-3237 Lat: 37.19379, Lon: -112.99266
479 Zion Park Blvd, Springdale, UT 84767
zioncamp@infowest.com
www.zioncamp.com
See ad this page.

↓ ZION/SOUTH CAMPGROUND (Natl Pk) From Jct of I-15 & Hwy 17, S 7 mi on Hwy 17 to Hwy 9, E 20 mi, follow signs (R) Note: maximum height of 13'. 2015 rates: $16. (435)772-3256

↓ ZION/WATCHMAN (Natl Pk) From Jct of I-15 & Hwy 17, S 7 mi on Hwy 17 to Hwy 9, E 20 mi, follow signs (R). 2015 rates: $16 to $20. Feb 28 to Nov 30. (435)772-3256

SPRINGVILLE — C3 *Utah*

↖ **SPRINGVILLE/PROVO KOA Ratings: 10/9.5★/8** (RV Park) From Jct of I-15 & SR-75/1400 North (Exit 261), E 0.1 mi on SR-75/1400 North St to 1750 W, N 0.1 mi (R). Elev 4600 ft. **FAC:** Paved rds. (218 spaces). Avail: 188 paved, 136 pull-thrus (21 x 58), back-ins (20 x 50), 188 full hkups (30/50 amps), seasonal sites, WiFi, tent sites, rentals, dump, laundry. **REC:** heated pool, playground. Pet restrict(B/Q). Partial handicap access. Eco-friendly, 2015 rates: $43.89. Disc: AAA, military.
AAA Approved
(801)491-0700 Lat: 40.18948, Lon: -111.64148
1550 North 1750 West, Springville, UT 84663
Springville/Provokoa@outlook.com
www.koa.com

ST GEORGE — E1 *Washington*

A SPOTLIGHT Introducing St George's attractions appearing at the front of this state section.

ST GEORGE See also Leeds & Virgin.

↓ **MCARTHUR'S TEMPLE VIEW RV RESORT**
Ratings: 9/10★/9 (RV Park) From Jct of I-15 & Bluff St (exit 6), N 0.2 mi on Bluff St to Main St, NE 0.3 mi (R). Elev 2700 ft.

ZION, BRYCE AND MORE!
Located in the heart of St. George & convenient to everything! Stay with us while seeing Zion, Bryce & more. With a friendly staff, best wireless internet & most amenities of any RV Resort in Utah, you will love it here!

FAC: Paved rds. (270 spaces). Avail: 163 gravel, patios, 20 pull-thrus (30 x 60), back-ins (33 x 48), 163 full hkups (30/50 amps), seasonal sites, cable, WiFi, tent sites, dump, laundry. **REC:** heated pool, whirlpool, shuffleboard. Pets OK. Partial handicap access. Eco-friendly, 2015 rates: $41.95. Disc: AAA, military.
AAA Approved
(800)510-6765 Lat: 37.09155, Lon: -113.58302
975 S Main St, St George, UT 84770
mcarthur@templeviewrv.com
www.templeviewrv.com
See ad this page, 1191 (Spotlight St George/Washington), 1187, 1184 (UT Map).

↑ SNOW CANYON (State Pk) From Jct of I-15 & Exit 6 (Bluff St), N 3.5 mi on Bluff St to Snow Canyon Pkwy, NW 3.9 mi to Snow Canyon Dr, N 0.9 mi (E). 2015 rates: $16 to $20. (435)628-2255

→ ST GEORGE CAMPGROUND **Ratings: 7/8.5★/6** (Campground) 2015 rates: $33. (435)673-2970 2100 E Middleton Dr, St George, UT 84770

Travel Services

→ **CAMPING WORLD OF ST GEORGE** As the nation's largest retailer of RV supplies, accessories, services and new and used RVs, Camping World is committed to making your total RV experience better. RV Accessories: (888)218-8851. Elev 2700 ft. **SERVICES:** RV appliance, MH mechanical, staffed RV wash, restrooms, RV Sales. RV supplies, LP, dump, RV accessible. Hours: 8:00 am to 6:00 pm.
(888)569-6892 Lat: 37.081673, Lon: -113.584727
1500 South Hilton Drive, St George, UT 84770
www.campingworld.com

Things to See and Do

→ **ST GEORGE AREA CONVENTION & TOURISM** Location for information to visit to St George and Washington County. Elev 2900 ft. partial handicap access. RV accessible. Restrooms. Hours: 9am to 5pm. No CC.
(800)869-6635 Lat: 37.07842, Lon: -113.58283
1835 Convention Center Dr, St George, UT 84790
roxie@atozion.com
http://www.visitstgeorge.com/
See ad page 1190 (Spotlight St George/Washington).

TORREY — D3 *Wayne*

→ CAPITOL REEF/FRUITA CAMPGROUND (Natl Pk) From Jct of SR-12 & SR-24, E 10 mi on SR-24 to park access rd, follow signs (R). 2015 rates: $10. (435)425-3791

TORREY (CONT)

SANDCREEK RV PARK & CAMPGROUND **Ratings: 5.5/8★/6.5** (RV Park) 2015 rates: $25 to $30. Apr 1 to Oct 31. (435)425-3577 540 W Sr 24, Torrey, UT 84775

THOUSAND LAKES RV PARK & CAMPGROUND

Ratings: 8/9★/9 (RV Park) From Jct of Hwys 12 & 24, W 2.5 mi on Hwy 24 (R). Elev 6800 ft. **FAC:** Gravel rds. (52 spaces). Avail: 44 gravel, 36 pull-thrus (32 x 70), back-ins (33 x 44), 33 full hkups, 11 W, 11 E (30/50 amps), seasonal sites, WiFi, tent sites, rentals, dump, laundry, groc, LP gas, fire rings, firewood, restaurant. **REC:** heated pool, playground. Pets OK. Partial handicap access. Big rig sites, eco-friendly, 2015 rates: $31.50 to $32.50. Disc: AAA, military. Apr 1 to Oct 25.
AAA Approved
(800)355-8995 Lat: 38.30157, Lon: -111.44499
1110 West Sr 24, Torrey, UT 84775
reservations@thousandlakesrvpark.com
www.thousandlakesrvpark.com
See ad pages 1205, 1187.

WONDERLAND RESORT & RV PARK

Ratings: 7.5/10★/9 (RV Park) From Jct of Hwy 24 & Hwy 12, S 50 ft on Hwy 12 (R). Elev 7000 ft. **FAC:** Gravel rds. (36 spaces). Avail: 33 gravel, 12 pull-thrus (27 x 74), back-ins (30 x 60), 33 full hkups (30/50 amps), seasonal sites, cable, WiFi, tent sites, rentals, dump, laundry, firewood. **REC.** Pets OK. Partial handicap access. Big rig sites, eco-friendly, 2015 rates: $36. Disc: AAA, military. Apr 1 to Nov 1.
AAA Approved
(435)425-3665 Lat: 38.29856, Lon: -111.40246
44 South Hwy 12, Torrey, UT 84775
raydianepotter@yahoo.com
www.capitolreefrvpark.com
See ad this page, 1187.

TROPIC — E2 *Garfield*

BRYCE PIONEER VILLAGE RV PARK **Ratings: 5/8★/7** (RV Park) 2015 rates: $30. Apr 1 to Oct 31. (435)679-8546 80 South Main, Tropic, UT 84776

VERNAL — B5 *Uintah*

DINOSAURLAND KOA Ratings: 9/8.5★/8 (Campground) From Jct of US-40 (Main St) & US-191 (Vernal Ave), N 1 mi on US-191 (R). Elev 5200 ft. **FAC:** Paved/gravel rds. 62 grass, 58 pull-thrus (18 x 70), back-ins (30 x 50), 54 full hkups, 8 W, 8 E (30/50 amps), cable, WiFi, tent sites, rentals, dump, laundry, groc, LP gas, fire rings, firewood. **REC:** heated pool, playground. Pet restrict(B). Partial handicap access. Big rig sites, 2015 rates: $39 to $66. Disc: AAA, military. Apr 1 to Oct 31.
AAA Approved
(435)789-2148 Lat: 40.46955, Lon: -109.52854
930 N Vernal Ave, Vernal, UT 84078
dinokoa@ubtanet.com
www.koa.com/campgrounds/vernal

FOSSIL VALLEY RV PARK

Ratings: 6.5/8.5★/7 (RV Park) From Jct of Hwys 191N & 40, W 1 mi on Hwy 40 (L). Elev 5200 ft. **FAC:** Paved/gravel rds. (63 spaces). Avail: 40 gravel, 40 pull-thrus (25 x 60), 40 full hkups (30/50 amps), seasonal sites, cable, WiFi, showers $, dump, laundry. Pet restrict(B). Partial handicap access, no tents. Big rig sites, 2015 rates: $36 to $37. Disc: AAA, military.
AAA Approved
(435)789-6450 Lat: 40.45199, Lon: -109.54783
999 W Hwy 40, Vernal, UT 84078
fossilvalley@yahoo.com
www.fossilvalleyrvpark.com

RED FLEET (State Pk) From Jct of Main St & Vernal Ave, N 10 mi on SR-191 to Red Fleet Rd, E 2 mi (E). 2015 rates: $11 to $25. (435)789-4432

STEINAKER (State Pk) From Jct of Main & Verna Ave (SR-191), N 5.4 mi on SR-191 to Steinaker Par Rd, SW 1.7 mi (E). 2015 rates: $11 to $25. Apr 14 t Oct 15. (435)789-4432

Things to See and Do

UINTAH COUNTY TOURISM Dinosaur Nationa Monument, camping, hiking, biking, boatinc rafting, petroglyphs, museums and muc more. RV accessible. Restrooms. Hours: 9ar to 5pm. No CC.
(800)477-5558 Lat: 40.45587, Lon: -109.52750
152 East 100 North, Vernal, UT 84078
visitdinosaurland@gmail.com
www.dinoland.com
See ad page 1185 (Welcome Section).

VIRGIN — E2 *Washington*

ZION RIVER RESORT

Ratings: 10/9.5★/9.5 (RV Park) N-bnd: From Jct of I-15 & Hwy 9 (exit 16) E 18.9 mi on Hwy 9 to MP 19 (R); c S-bnd: From Jct of I-15 & Hwy 17 (ex 27), S 6 mi on Hwy 17 to Hwy 9, E 6.3 m to MP 19 (R). Elev 3582 ft. **FAC:** Paved rds. 7 paved, 38 all weather, 47 pull-thrus (30 x 65), back ins (25 x 35), 112 full hkups (30/50 amps), cable WiFi, tent sites, rentals, showers $, laundry, groc, L gas, fire rings, firewood. **REC:** heated pool, whirlpoo Virgin River: playground. Pet restrict(B/Q). Partia handicap access. Big rig sites, eco-friendly, 201 rates: $49 to $62. Disc: AAA, military.
(888)466-8594 Lat: 37.20310, Lon: -113.17744
551 E Hwy 9, Virgin, UT 84779
zionrv@zrr.com
www.zionriverresort.com
See ad this page, 1187.

WANSHIP — B3 *Summit*

ROCKPORT LAKE SRA (State Pk) From Jct c I-80 & Hwy 32 (exit 155), S 4.7 mi on Hwy 32 (L). 201 rates: $10 to $20. Apr 15 to Nov 1. (435)336-224

WELLINGTON — C4 *Carbon*

MOUNTAIN VIEW RV PARK **Ratings: 5/8★/** (Campground) 2015 rates: $21.95. (435)637-7980 5 South 700 E, Wellington, UT 84542

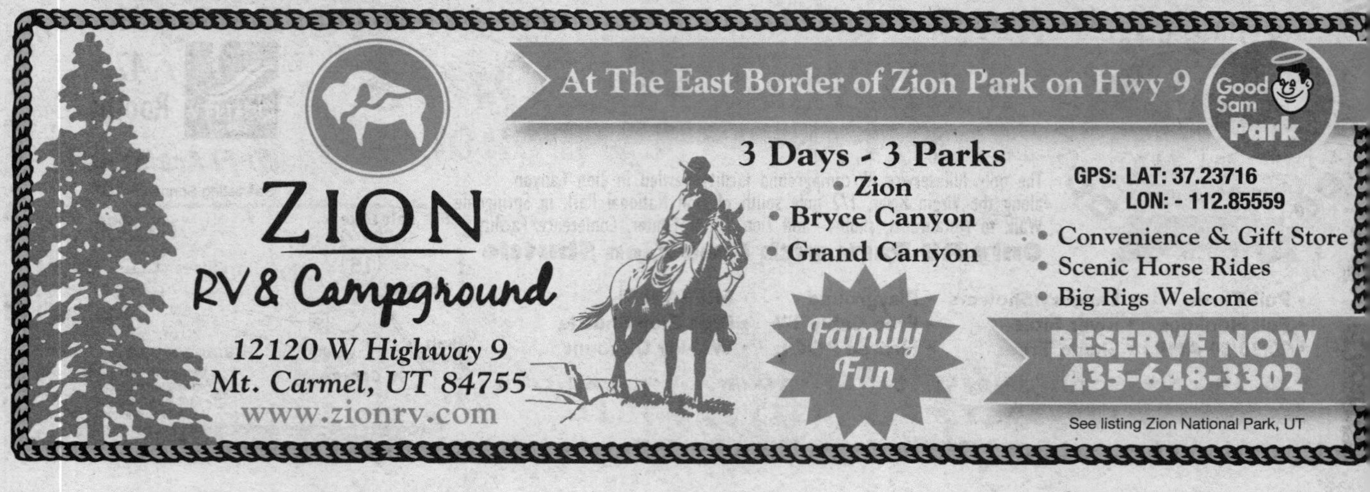

WOODRUFF — A3 *Rich*

CACHE/MONTE CRISTO CAMPGROUND (Natl Forest) 22 mi SW on Hwy-39. Pit toilets. 2015 rates: $18. Jun 25 to Sep 7. (801)625-5112

ZION NATIONAL PARK — E2 *Washington*

ZION NATIONAL PARK See also Cedar City, Glendale, Hurricane, Kanab, Leeds, Mount Carmel, Springdale, St George & Virgin.

← ZION PONDEROSA RANCH RESORT **Ratings: 8.5/8.5★/7.5** (RV Park) 2015 rates: $42 to $52. Apr 1 to Oct 31. (800)293-5444 5 Miles up North Fork Rd, Mount Carmel, UT 84755

← **ZION RV & CAMPGROUND**
Ratings: 5.5/8★/8 (Campground) N-bnd: S-bnd Jct of US 89 & UT 9, W 11.7 mi on UT 9 (L). Elev 5400 ft. **FAC:** Paved/gravel rds. 26 gravel, 22 pull-thrus (40 x 70), back-ins (29 x 40), 26 full hkups (30/50 amps), WiFi Hotspot, tent sites, dump, laundry, groc, firewood. **REC.** Pets OK. Partial handicap access. Big rig sites, 2015 rates: $35. Disc: AAA, military. Feb 15 to Nov 15.
(435)648-3302 Lat: 37.23716, Lon: -112.85559
12120 W Hwy 9, Mount Carmel, UT 84755
zionrvcampground@yahoo.com
www.zionrv.com
See ad opposite page, 1187.

We give campgrounds one rating for amenities, a second for restrooms and a third for visual appearance and environmental quality. That's the Triple Rating System.

UT

Getty Images/iStockphoto

WELCOME TO

Vermont

DATE OF STATEHOOD	WIDTH: 80 MILES (130 KM)	PROPORTION OF UNITED STATES
MARCH 4, 1791	LENGTH: 160 MILES (260 KM)	0.25% OF 3,794,100 SQ MI

With an intoxicating blend of pastoral farmland, majestic Green Mountains and chocolate-box villages with nary a golden arch in sight, Vermont is one of America's most alluring states. For outdoor enthusiasts, there's kayaking on the placid waters of Lake Champlain, hiking the Kingdom Trails Network and skiing on the vaunted slopes of classy Stowe, Killington and Sugarbush. Northern Vermont is home to Montpelier, an exemplary state capital where mom-and-pop shops nudge up against art-house movie theaters.

Burlington, the state's largest city, oozes charm with its tree-lined streets awash with boutiques and cafés that unfurl to the scenic pathways of Lake Champlain. Vermont's essence is embodied at Woodstock, a gorgeous village surrounded by woodlands. The town's lovely green, overlooked by Victorian painted ladies with wraparound porches, nestles at the heart of a pristine downtown.

Active travelers can tackle the state's portion of the 2,100-mile Appalachian trail, which enters southwest Vermont, crosses the rugged crest of the Green Mountains and then passes through wooded mountains.

With its small farming culture and craft-brewing density, Vermont is a paradise for lovers of all things fresh and local. In Bennington, the Blue Benn Diner, housed in a classic 1940s prefab diner complete with jukebox and lashings of stainless steel, serves hearty diner fare that includes lots of vegetarian options and heavenly buttery pies.

TRAVEL & TOURISM

Vermont Department of Tourism
802-828-3676, 800-VERMONT
www.vermontvacation.com

Bennington Area Chamber of Commerce
800-229-0252, 802-447-3311
www.bennington.com

Brandon Chamber of Commerce
802-247-6401
www.brandon.org

Brattleboro Area Chamber of Commerce
802-254-4565
www.brattleborochamber.com

Burke Area Chamber of Commerce
802-626-4124
www.burkevermont.com

Central Vermont Chamber of Commerce
802-229-5711
www.central-vt.com

Lake Champlain Islands Chamber of Commerce
802-372-8400, 800-262-5226
www.champlainislands.com

Vermont Chamber of Commerce
802-223-3443
www.vtchamber.com

Vermont Outdoor Guide Association
800-425-8747, 802-425-6211
www.voga.org

OUTDOOR RECREATION

Bike Vermont
802-457-3553
www.bikevt.com

Play Northeast Golf
800-639-1941, 802-496-7575
www.PlayNortheastGolf.com

Vermont Fish & Wildlife Dept.
802-241-3700
www.vtfishandwildlife.com

Top 3 Tourism Attractions:
1) Ben & Jerry's
2) Lake Champlain Maritime Museum
3) Killington Mountain Resort and Ski Area

Nickname: Green Mountain State

State Flower: Red Clover

State Bird: Hermit Thrush

People: John Deere, inventor; Rudy Vallee, singer and band leader; Henry Wells, founder of Wells Fargo; Brigham Young, president of the Church of Jesus Christ of Latter-day Saints

Major Cities: Burlington, South Burlington, Rutland, Essex Junction, Barre (Montpelier, capital)

Topography: Northwest—fertile farmland; northeast—mountains; central—Green Mountains; west—rivers, valleys; southwest—mountains, lakes; east—lakes, hills

Climate: Humid continental climate; frigid winters, sometimes humid summers

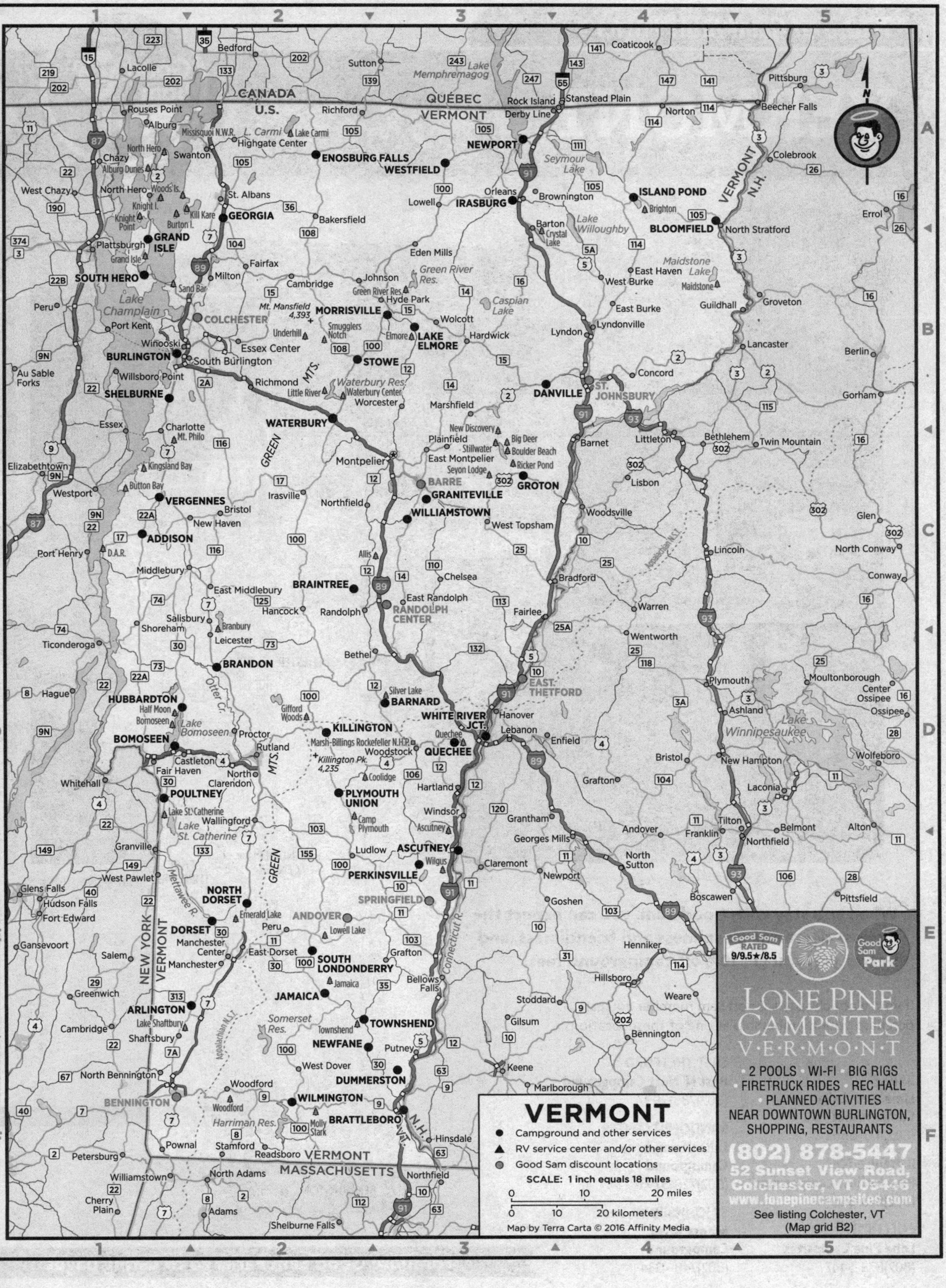

VERMONT
Campground and other services
RV service center and/or other services
Good Sam discount locations
SCALE: 1 inch equals 18 miles
0 10 20 miles
0 10 20 kilometers
Map by Terra Carta © 2016 Affinity Media
CANADA
U.S.
QUÉBEC
VERMONT
NEW YORK
VERMONT
N.H.
MASSACHUSETTS
GREEN MTS.
Lake Champlain
Lake Memphremagog
Seymour Lake
Lake Willoughby
Maidstone Lake
Caspian Lake
Green River Res.
Waterbury Res.
Lake Bomoseen
Lake St. Catherine
Somerset Res.
Harriman Res.
Lake Winnipesaukee
Connecticut R.
Otter Cr.
Mettawee R.
Appalachian N.S.T.
Mt. Mansfield 4,393
Killington Pk. 4,235
Lacolle
Bedford
Sutton
Coaticook
Pittsburg
Rouses Point
Alburg
Richford
Derby Line
Rock Island
Stanstead Plain
Norton
Beecher Falls
Chazy
Swanton
Highgate Center
ENOSBURG FALLS
WESTFIELD
NEWPORT
Colebrook
West Chazy
St. Albans
GEORGIA
Bakersfield
Lowell
IRASBURG
Orleans
Brownington
ISLAND POND
Brighton
BLOOMFIELD
North Stratford
Errol
Plattsburgh
GRAND ISLE
SOUTH HERO
Fairfax
Milton
Cambridge
Johnson
Hyde Park
Eden Mills
Barton
Crystal Lake
East Haven
West Burke
East Burke
Guildhall
Groveton
Peru
COLCHESTER
MORRISVILLE
Wolcott
LAKE ELMORE
Hardwick
Lyndon
Lyndonville
Lancaster
Port Kent
Winooski
BURLINGTON
Essex Center
South Burlington
STOWE
Berlin
Au Sable Forks
Willsboro Point
SHELBURNE
Richmond
Little River
Waterbury Center
Worcester
Marshfield
DANVILLE
Concord
ST. JOHNSBURY
Gorham
Essex
Charlotte
Mt. Philo
WATERBURY
Plainfield
New Discovery
Big Deer
Boulder Beach
Stillwater
Ricker Pond
Seyon Lodge
Barnet
Littleton
Bethlehem
Twin Mountain
Elizabethtown
Kingsland Bay
Montpelier
East Montpelier
BARRE
GRANITEVILLE
GROTON
Lisbon
Westport
Button Bay
VERGENNES
Bristol
Irasville
Northfield
WILLIAMSTOWN
West Topsham
Woodsville
Glen
New Haven
ADDISON
Port Henry
D.A.R.
Middlebury
Allis
Chelsea
Bradford
Lincoln
North Conway
Conway
East Middlebury
BRAINTREE
East Randolph
Hancock
Randolph
RANDOLPH CENTER
Fairlee
Warren
Salisbury
Branbury
Shoreham
Ticonderoga
Leicester
Wentworth
BRANDON
Bethel
EAST THETFORD
Moultonborough
Center Ossipee
Plymouth
Ashland
Ossipee
Hague
HUBBARDTON
Half Moon
Bomoseen
Silver Lake
BARNARD
Gifford Woods
WHITE RIVER JCT.
Hanover
BOMOSEEN
Proctor
Rutland
KILLINGTON
Quechee
Lebanon
Enfield
Marsh-Billings Rockefeller N.H.P.
Woodstock
QUECHEE
Castleton
Fair Haven
North Clarendon
Coolidge
Hartland
Bristol
New Hampton
Wolfeboro
Whitehall
POULTNEY
PLYMOUTH UNION
Grafton
Laconia
Lake St. Catherine
Wallingford
Camp Plymouth
Windsor
Grantham
Ascutney
Tilton
Belmont
Andover
Franklin
Alton
Northfield
Granville
Georges Mills
Ludlow
ASCUTNEY
Wilgus
West Pawlet
PERKINSVILLE
Claremont
Newport
North Sutton
Glens Falls
Hudson Falls
Fort Edward
NORTH DORSET
SPRINGFIELD
Goshen
Boscawen
Pittsfield
Emerald Lake
DORSET
ANDOVER
Peru
Lowell Lake
Gansevoort
Manchester Center
East Dorset
SOUTH LONDONDERRY
Grafton
Henniker
Salem
Manchester
Jamaica
Bellows Falls
Hillsboro
Greenwich
JAMAICA
Stoddard
Weare
ARLINGTON
Lake Shaftsbury
TOWNSHEND
Townshend
Gilsum
Cambridge
Shaftsbury
NEWFANE
Putney
Bennington
West Dover
Keene
North Bennington
DUMMERSTON
Woodford
Marlborough
BENNINGTON
WILMINGTON
BRATTLEBORO
Molly Stark
Hinsdale
Pownal
Stamford
Readsboro
Petersburg
Williamstown
North Adams
Northfield
Cherry Plain
Adams
Shelburne Falls

VT

Featured Good Sam Parks

VERMONT

Good Sam Park

When you stay with Good Sam, you can expect the highest degree of cleanliness and friendliness, and better yet, you get 10% off campground fees.

If you're not already a Good Sam member you can purchase your membership at one of these locations:

BARRE
Limehurst Lake Campground
(802)433-6662

BENNINGTON
Pine Hollow Campground
(802)823-5569

COLCHESTER
Lone Pine Campsites
(802)878-5447

EAST THETFORD
Rest N' Nest Campground
(802)785-2997

RANDOLPH CENTER
Lake Champagne Campground
(802)728-5293

ST JOHNSBURY
Moose River Campground
(802)748-4334

For more Good Sam Parks go to listing pages

Vermont

CONSULTANTS

Jeff & Peggy Harmann

ADDISON — C1 *Addison*

← DAR (State Pk) From Jct of Rte 22A & Rte 17 (in town), W 7 mi on Rte 17 (R). 2015 rates: $16 to $25. May 25 to Sep 7. (802)759-2354

ANDOVER — E2 *Windsor*

← **HORSESHOE ACRES**
Ratings: 8/8★/7.5 (Campground) From Jct of I-91 & SR-103 (exit 6), Go 11 mi N on SR-103 to SR-11 (in Chester), then 4 mi W to Andover-Weston Rd, then 3.5 mi N (R). **FAC:** Gravel rds. (175 spaces). Avail: 50 grass, 12 pull-thrus (40 x 58), back-ins (40 x 58), 12 full hkups, 38 W, 38 E (20/30 amps), seasonal sites, WiFi, tent sites, rentals, showers $, dump, mobile sewer, laundry, groc, LP gas, fire rings, firewood. **REC:** pool, wading pool, pond, Trout Brook: fishing, shuffleboard, playground. Pets OK. Eco-friendly, 2015 rates: $33.50 to $39. Disc: AAA, military. May 1 to Oct 18.
(802)875-2960 Lat: 43.28452, Lon: -72.71469
1978 Weston-Andover Rd, Andover, VT 05143
campers@vermontel.net
www.horseshoeacrescampground.com

ARLINGTON — E2 *Bennington*

↑ CAMPING ON THE BATTENKILL **Ratings: 4.5/6/7** (Campground) 2015 rates: $34 to $45. May 1 to Oct 15. (802)375-6663 48 Camping on the Battenkill, Arlington, VT 05250

ASCUTNEY — E3 *Windsor*

↓ ASCUTNEY (State Pk) From Jct of I-91 & exit 8 (US-5), N 2 mi on US-5 to VR-44A, NW 1 mi (L). 2015 rates: $16 to $27. May 25 to Oct 12. (802)674-2060

↓ GETAWAY MOUNTAIN CAMPGROUND **Ratings: 7.5/7/6** (Campground) 2015 rates: $27 to $30. May 1 to Oct 27. (802)674-2812 3628 Rte 5S, Ascutney, VT 05030

↓ RUNNING BEAR CAMPING AREA **Ratings: 6.5/5.5/6** (Campground) 2015 rates: $37 to $42. Apr 15 to Oct 15. (802)674-6417 6248 US Rte 5, Ascutney, VT 05030

Directional arrows indicate the campground's position in relation to the nearest town.

BARNARD — D3 *Windsor*

↑ SILVER LAKE (State Pk) From town, N 0.25 mi on Town Rd (R). 2015 rates: $16 to $27. May 22 to Sep 7. (802)234-9451

BARRE — C3 *Washington*

↓ **LIMEHURST LAKE CAMPGROUND**
Ratings: 8.5/9.5★/9.5 (Campground) From Jct of I-89 & Rte 63 (exit 6), Go 2 mi E on Rte 63 to Rte 14, then 6 mi S (R). **FAC:** Gravel rds. (57 spaces). Avail: 33 grass, 3 pull-thrus (20 x 70), back-ins (30 x 64), 24 full hkups, 9 W, 9 E (30/50 amps), seasonal sites, WiFi, tent sites, rentals, showers $, dump, mobile sewer, laundry, groc, LP gas, fire rings, firewood, controlled access. **REC:** Limehurst Lake: swim, fishing, shuffleboard, playground, rec open to public. Pet restrict(B). Big rig sites, eco-friendly, 2015 rates: $38 to $42. Disc: military. May 1 to Oct 15.
(802)433-6662 Lat: 44.10182, Lon: -72.54781
4104 Vt Rte 14, Williamstown, VT 05679
limehurstlakecampground@gmail.com
www.limehurstlake.com
See ad this page, 1210.

BENNINGTON — F1 *Bennington*

↙ **GREENWOOD LODGE & CAMPSITES**
Ratings: 7/9★/7.5 (Campground) From Jct of Rtes 7 & 9 (in Bennington), E 8 mi on Rte 9, to Prospect Ski Driveway/Parking Lot (R), to Greenwood Dr (L) or From Jct of I-91 & Rte 9 (exit 2), W 32 mi on Rte 9 (L). **FAC:** Gravel rds. 23 gravel, 8 pull-thrus (35 x 76), back-ins (30 x 74), 23 W, 23 E (30/50 amps), WiFi, tent sites, dump, mobile sewer, fire rings, firewood. **REC:** pond, swim. Pet restrict(B). Eco-friendly, 2015 rates: $33 to $37. May 20 to Oct 26. No CC.
(802)442-2547 Lat: 42.87838, Lon: -73.07641
311 Greenwood Drive, Woodford, VT 05201
campgreenwood@aol.com
www.campvermont.com/greenwood
See ad this page.

→ **PINE HOLLOW CAMPGROUND**
Ratings: 7.5/9.5★/9.5 (Campground) From VT/MA state line, Go 4.7 mi N on US 7 to Barber Pond Rd, then 1.5 mi SE to Old Military Rd, then 0.3 mi SW to Pine Hollow Rd, then 0.3 mi W. **FAC:** Gravel rds. 50 Avail: 6 gravel, 44 grass, 6 pull-thrus (24 x 70), back-ins (28 x 48), some side by side hkups, 27 full hkups, 23 W, 23 E (30/50 amps), WiFi, tent sites, dump, mobile sewer, fire rings, firewood. **REC:** pond, swim, fishing, playground. Pet restrict(B). Big rig sites, eco-friendly, 2015 rates: $35 to $42. May 15 to Oct 15. No CC.
(802)823-5569 Lat: 42.78608, Lon: -73.19944
342 Pine Hollow Rd, Pownal, VT 05261
www.pinehollowcamping.com
See ad this page, 1210.

→ WOODFORD (State Pk) From Jct of US-7 & SR-9, E 10 mi on SR-9 (R). 2015 rates: $16 to $27. May 24 to Oct 14. (802)447-7169

BLOOMFIELD — A4 *Essex*

↓ MAIDSTONE (State Pk) From Bloomfield, S 5 mi on SR-102 to Maidstone State Forest Hwy, SW 6 mi (E). 2015 rates: $16 to $27. May 24 to Sep 7. (802)676-3930

BOMOSEEN — D1 *Rutland*

↑ BOMOSEEN (State Pk) From Jct of US-A & Town Rd (exit 3), N 5 mi on Town Rd (R). 2015 rates: $16 to $27. May 25 to Sep 7. (802)265-4242

Like Us on Facebook.

↗ **LAKE BOMOSEEN KOA**
Ratings: 8.5/8★/7 (Campground) From Jct of US-4 & Rte 30 (exit 4), Go 4.8 mi N on Rte 30 (L). **FAC:** Paved rds. (127 spaces). 99 Avail: 8 paved, 20 gravel, 71 dirt, 11 pull-thrus (25 x 73), back-ins (27 x 56), 58 full hkups, 41 W, 41 E (30/50 amps), seasonal sites, WiFi, tent sites, rentals, showers $, dump, laundry, groc, LP gas, fire rings, firewood, controlled access. **REC:** pool, whirlpool, Lake Bomoseen: fishing, playground, rec open to public. Pet restrict(B/Q). Partial handicap access. Big rig sites, eco-friendly, 2015 rates: $29 to $69. May 1 to Oct 12.
(802)273-2061 Lat: 43.68472, Lon: -73.18913
18 Campground Dr, Bomoseen, VT 05732
camplbc@aol.com
www.lakebomoseen.com
See ad this page.

BRAINTREE — C2 *Orange*

↖ **ABEL MOUNTAIN CAMPGROUND Ratings: 8/9.5★/8** (Campground) From Jct of I-89 & Hwy 66 (Exit 4), Go 2.5 mi W on Hwy 66 to SR-12A, Then 2 mi N on SR-12A (L). **FAC:** Paved/gravel rds. (132 spaces). Avail: 77 grass, 11 pull-thrus (42 x 70), back-ins (37 x 65), 63 full hkups, 14 W, 14 E (30/50 amps), seasonal sites, cable, WiFi, tent sites, dump, laundry, LP gas, fire rings, firewood. **REC:** heated pool, White River - 3rd Branch: swim, fishing, playground. Pets OK. Partial handicap access. Big rig sites, eco-friendly, 2015 rates: $35 to $40. May 15 to Oct 15.
(802)728-5548 Lat: 43.93041, Lon: -72.70186
354 Mobile Acres Rd, Braintree, VT 05060
info@abelmountaincampground.com
www.abelmountain.com

BRANDON — D2 *Rutland, Addison*

↑ COUNTRY VILLAGE CAMPGROUND **Ratings: 7/6/7.5** (Campground) 2015 rates: $32. May 1 to Oct 14. (802)247-3333 40 US-Rte 7, Leicester, VT 05733

BRATTLEBORO — F3 *Windham*

↓ FORT DUMMER (State Pk) From Jct of I-91 & Exit 1 (CR-5), N 0.1 mi on CR-5 to Fairgrounds Rd, E 0.5 mi to S Main St (Old Guilford Rd), S 1 mi (E). 2015 rates: $16 to $25. May 25 to Sep 7. (802)254-2610

↘ **HINSDALE CAMPGROUND AT THICKET HILL VILLAGE**
Ratings: 7.5/9.5★/9 (Campground) From Jct of I-91 & Rte 5 (Exit 1 Brattleboro, VT), Go 1.1 mi NE on Rte 5 to Rte 119, then (in VT) 4.5 mi S (L). **FAC:** Gravel rds. (89 spaces). Avail: 33 gravel, 8 pull-thrus (35 x 60), back-ins (35 x 60), 17 full hkups, 16 W, 16 E (30/50 amps), seasonal sites, cable, WiFi, tent sites, dump, laundry, LP gas, fire rings, firewood. **REC:** pool, wading pool, playground. Pet restrict(B/Q). Partial handicap access. Big rig sites, 2015 rates: $39 to $43. Apr 17 to Oct 31.
(603)336-8906 Lat: 42.79731, Lon: -72.51586
29 Pine St, Hinsdale, NH 03451
hinsdale@campingnow.com
www.campingnow.com
See primary listing at Hinsdale, NH and ad page 769.

BURLINGTON — B1 *Chittenden*

BURLINGTON See also Colchester, Georgia, Shelburne & South Hero.

↑ NORTH BEACH CAMPGROUND (Public) From Jct of I-89 & US-2 (exit 14W), W 2 mi on US-2 (Main St) to Battery St, N 0.5 mi to Sherman St, W 0.1 mi to North Ave, N 1.5 mi to Institute Rd, W 0.3 mi (E). 2015 rates: $31 to $36. May 5 to Oct 12. (802)862-0942

COLCHESTER — B2 *Chittenden*

LONE PINE CAMPSITES
Ratings: 9/9.5★/8.5 (Campground) From Jct of I-89 & US 7 (Exit 16), Go 3.2 mi NW on US 7 to Jct of Rte 2A & Bay Rd, then 1 mi W on Bay Rd (R).

LONE PINE CAMPSITES WELCOMES YOU
Lone Pine Campsites wish to make your stay with us as enjoyable as possible. Our friendly staff is here to serve you any way we can. We want to put a smile in everything you do during your stay with us at Lone Pine Campsites.

FAC: Paved rds. (275 spaces). Avail: 145 grass, 7 pull-thrus (30 x 60), back-ins (39 x 66), some side by side hkups, 73 full hkups, 72 W, 72 E (30/50 amps), seasonal sites, cable, WiFi $, tent sites, rentals, showers $, dump, mobile sewer, laundry, groc, LP gas, fire rings, firewood. **REC:** heated pool, playground. Pet restrict(Q). Partial handicap access. Big rig sites, eco-friendly, 2015 rates: $36 to $61. May 1 to Oct 15.
(802)878-5447 Lat: 44.55551, Lon: -73.18538
52 Sunset View Rd, Colchester, VT 05446
Manager@lonepinecampsites.com
www.lonepinecampsites.com
See ad this page, 1210, 1209 (VT Map).

MALLETTS BAY CAMPGROUND **Ratings: 6.5/6.5/5** (Campground) 2015 rates: $48 to $50. May 1 to Oct 15. (802)863-6980 88 Malletts Bay Campground Rd, Colchester, VT 05446

DANVILLE — B3 *Caledonia*

SUGAR RIDGE RV VILLAGE & CAMPGROUND INC
Ratings: 9/10★/9.5 (Campground) From Jct of I-91 & Rte 2 (exit 21), Go 4.5 mi W on Rte 2 (L). **FAC:** Paved/gravel rds. (150 spaces). Avail: 100 gravel, 5 pull-thrus (32 x 100), back-ins (32 x 72), 82 full hkups, 18 W, 18 E (30/50 amps), seasonal sites, cable, WiFi $, tent sites, rentals, dump, laundry, groc, LP gas, fire rings, firewood, controlled access. **REC:** heated pool, pond, fishing, shuffleboard, playground, rec open to public. Pets OK. Partial handicap access. Big rig sites, eco-friendly, 2015 rates: $41.50 to $43.50. May 10 to Oct 12. ATM.
(802)684-2550 Lat: 44.42216, Lon: -72.11483
24 Old Stagecoach Rd, Danville, VT 05828
sugarridge@kingcon.com
www.sugarridgervpark.com
See ad this page.

DORSET — E2 *Bennington*

DORSET RV PARK
Ratings: 7.5/8.5★/8 (Campground) From Jct of US-7 & SR-30 (exit 4), NW 6 mi on Rte 30 (L); or From Jct of Historic Rte 7A & SR-30 (in Manchester Center), NW 4.3 mi on SR-30 (L). **FAC:** Gravel rds. 40 Avail: 36 gravel, 4 grass, 5 pull-thrus (32 x 93), back-ins (35 x 50), 30 full hkups, 4 W, 4 E (30/50 amps), cable, WiFi, tent sites, dump, mobile sewer, laundry, groc, LP gas, fire rings, firewood. **REC:** shuffleboard, playground. Pets OK. Partial handicap access. Big rig sites, eco-friendly, 2015 rates: $34 to $44. May 1 to Oct 31.
(802)867-5754 Lat: 43.23342, Lon: -73.08048
1567 Rte 30, Dorset, VT 05251
hasgas@aol.com
www.dorsetrvpark.com
See ad this page.

DUMMERSTON — F3 *Windham*

BRATTLEBORO NORTH KOA Ratings: 9/10★/10 (Campground) From Jct of I-91 & US-5 (exit 4), go S 2.8 mi on US-5 (L). **FAC:** Gravel rds. 40 gravel, 34 pull-thrus (44 x 65), back-ins (44 x 53), 21 full hkups, 19 W, 19 E (30/50 amps), cable, WiFi, tent sites, rentals, dump, mobile sewer, laundry, groc, LP gas, fire rings, firewood. **REC:** pool, playground. Pets OK. Big rig sites, eco-friendly, 2015 rates: $35 to $54. Disc: military. Apr 22 to Oct 12.
(800)562-5909 Lat: 42.92835, Lon: -72.53696
1238 US Rte 5, East Dummerston, VT 05346
koavt@svcable.net
www.brattleborokoa.com

HIDDEN ACRES CAMPING RESORT **Ratings: 8/7.5/7.5** (Campground) 2015 rates: $36 to $40. Apr 15 to Oct 15. (802)254-2098 792 US Rte 5, Dummerston, VT 05301

EAST THETFORD — D3 *Orange*

REST N' NEST CAMPGROUND
Ratings: 8/9★/8.5 (Campground) From Jct of I-91 & Rte 113 (exit 14), Go 0.1 E mi on Rte 113 to Latham Rd, then N 0.25 mi (R). **FAC:** Gravel rds. (80 spaces). 50 Avail: 37 gravel, 8 grass, 5 dirt, 7 pull-thrus (44 x 92), back-ins (35 x 50), 34 full hkups, 16 W, 16 E (30/50 amps), seasonal sites, WiFi, tent sites, rentals, dump, laundry, groc, LP gas, fire rings, firewood. **REC:** heated pool, pond, swim, playground. Pets OK. Big rig sites, eco-friendly, 2015 rates: $37 to $44. Apr 29 to Oct 9.
(802)785-2997 Lat: 43.81570, Lon: -72.21069
300 Latham Rd, East Thetford, VT 05043
info@restnnest.com
www.restnnest.com
See ad this page, 1210.

ENOSBURG FALLS — A2 *Franklin*

LAKE CARMI (State Pk) From town, W 3 mi on Rte 105 to Rte 236, N 3 mi (L). 2015 rates: $16 to $27. May 17 to Oct 12. (802)933-8383

GEORGIA — A2 *Franklin*

HOMESTEAD CAMPGROUND **Ratings: 7/6.5/5.5** (Campground) 2015 rates: $35 to $45. May 1 to Oct 6. (802)524-2356 864 Ethan Allen Hwy, Georgia, VT 05468

GRAND ISLE — B1 *Grand Isle*

GRAND ISLE (State Pk) From town: Go 1 mi S on US-2. May 9 to Oct 18. (802)372-4300

GRANITEVILLE — C3 *Washington*

LAZY LIONS CAMPGROUND **Ratings: 6.5/6/7.5** (Campground) 2015 rates: $35 to $38. May 1 to Oct 15. (802)479-2823 281 Middle Road, Graniteville, VT 05654

GROTON — C3 *Washington*

BIG DEER (State Pk) From Jct US-302 & SR-232, NW 5.3 mi on SR-232 to Boulder Beach Rd, NE 1.5 mi (L). 2015 rates: $16 to $27. May 25 to Sep 7. (802)584-3822

NEW DISCOVERY (State Pk) From Jct of US-2 & SR-232, S 5 mi on SR-232 (L). 2015 rates: $14 to $25. May 22 to Oct 12. (802)426-3042

RICKER POND (State Pk) From town: Go 2 mi W on US-302, then 2-1/2 mi N on Hwy-232. May 22 to Oct 12. (802)584-3821

STILLWATER (State Pk) From Jct US-302 & SR-232, N 5.5 mi on SR-232 to Boulder Beach Rd, NE 0.5 mi (R). 2015 rates: $16 to $27. May 17 to Sep 7. (802)584-3822

HUBBARDTON — D1 *Rutland*

HALF MOON (State Pk) From Jct of US-4 & SR-30, N 14 mi on SR-30 to Hubbardton Rd, S 1.5 mi to Black Pond Rd, E 2 mi (L). 2015 rates: $16 to $25. May 25 to Oct 12. (802)273-2848

IRASBURG — A3 *Orleans*

TREE CORNERS FAMILY CAMPGROUND LLC
Ratings: 9/9.5★/9 (Campground) From Jct of I-91 & Rte 58 (exit 26), Go 4 mi W on Rte 58 to Rte 14/58 (in town), then 1.4 mi N to Rte 58, then 0.1 mi W (L). **FAC:** Gravel rds. (131 spaces). Avail: 92 grass, 11 pull-thrus (30 x 50), back-ins (38 x 50), 57 full hkups, 35 W, 35 E (30/50 amps), seasonal sites, WiFi $, tent sites, rentals, showers $, dump, mobile sewer, laundry, groc, LP gas, fire rings, firewood, controlled access. **REC:** heated pool, whirlpool, shuffleboard, playground, rec open to public. Pet restrict(B). Partial handicap access. Big rig sites, eco-friendly, 2015 rates: $39 to $42. Disc: military. May 15 to Oct 15.
(802)754-6042 Lat: 44.81539, Lon: -72.29509
95 Rte 58 West, Irasburg, VT 05845
info@treecorners.com
www.treecorners.com
See ad this page.

ISLAND POND — A4 *Essex*

BRIGHTON (State Pk) From town, E 2 mi on SR-105 to Lakeshore Dr, S 0.75 mi (L). 2015 rates: $16 to $27. May 25 to Oct 12. (802)723-4360

LAKESIDE CAMPING AREA **Ratings: 7.5/6/5.5** (Campground) 2015 rates: $45 to $50. May 15 to Sep 8. (802)723-6649 1348 Rte 105 E Brighton Rd, Island Pond, VT 05846

JAMAICA — E2 *Windham*

JAMAICA (State Pk) In town, N 0.8 mi on Depot ST (L). 2015 rates: $16 to $27. May 9 to Oct 12. (802)874-4600

KILLINGTON — D2 *Rutland*

GIFFORD WOODS (State Pk) From town, E 10 mi on US-4 to VT-100, N 0.5 mi (L). 2015 rates: $16 to $27. May 17 to Oct 20. (802)775-5354

LAKE ELMORE — B3 *Lamoille*

ELMORE (State Pk) From Jct of SR-100 & SR-12, SE 5 mi on SR-12 (R). 2015 rates: $16 to $25. May 25 to Oct 12. (802)888-2982

MONTPELIER — C3 *Washington*

CHERRYSTONE FAMILY CAMPING RESORT
Ratings: 9/9.5★/9.5 (Campground) From I 89 in Montpelier: Go S on I 89 to I 91, S on I 91 to I 95, S on I 95 to Hwy 1 (in Delaware), S on Hwy 1 to Hwy 13, S on Hwy 13 to SR-680, W 1.5 mi (E). **FAC:** Paved/gravel rds. (539 spaces). 503 Avail: 5 gravel, 498 grass, 100 pull-thrus (30 x 70), back-ins (30 x 45), 358 full hkups, 145 W, 145 E (30/50 amps), seasonal sites, WiFi, tent sites, rentals, dump, mobile sewer, laundry, groc, LP gas, firewood, restaurant. **REC:** pool, Chesapeake Bay: swim, fishing, shuffleboard, playground. Pet restrict(B/Q). Partial handicap access. Big rig sites, eco-friendly, 2015 rates: $17 to $68. ATM.
(757)331-3063 Lat: 37.28557, Lon: -76.01077
1511 Townfield Dr, Cape Charles, VA 23310
info@cherrystoneva.com
www.cherrystoneva.com
See primary listing at Cheriton, VA and ad pages 1233, 587, 584 (MD Map), 1217 (VA Map) & ad Magazine Section page 103.

Tell them you saw them in this Guide!

MORRISVILLE — B3 *Lamoille*

MOUNTAIN VIEW CAMPGROUND Ratings: 8.5/7.5/7.5 (Campground) From Jct of I-89 & VT Rte 100 (Exit 10): Go N 19 mi on VT Rte 100 to VT Rte 15, then E 3 mi on VT Rte 15 (R). **FAC:** Gravel rds. 46 grass, back-ins (32 x 52), 30 full hkups, 16 W, 16 E (30 amps), WiFi, tent sites, rentals, showers $, dump, laundry, groc, LP gas, fire rings, firewood, controlled access. **REC:** heated pool, whirlpool, Lamoille River: fishing, shuffleboard, playground. Pets OK $. Partial handicap access. 2015 rates: $40 to $43. Disc: military. May 1 to Oct 12.
(802)888-2178 Lat: 44.56886, Lon: -72.53434
3154 Vermont Rte 15 E, Morrisville, VT 05661
info@mountainviewcamping.com
www.mountainviewcamping.com

NEW HAVEN — C2 *Addison*

RIVERS BEND CAMPGROUND
Ratings: 7/7.5★/7 (Campground) From Jct Hwy 125 & US-7 (in North Middlebury), Go 3 mi N on US-7 to Dog Team Rd, Then .7 mi L of Rivers Bend Rd (L). **FAC:** Gravel rds. (66 spaces). Avail: 50 grass, 3 pull-thrus (30 x 75), back-ins (46 x 60), 50 W, 50 E (20/30 amps), seasonal sites, WiFi, tent sites, showers $, dump, mobile sewer, LP gas, fire rings, firewood. **REC:** heated pool, New Haven River: swim, fishing, playground. Pet restrict(Q) $. 2015 rates: $35 to $42. May 15 to Oct 15.
(802)388-9092 Lat: 44.06321, Lon: -73.17763
722 Rivers Bend Rd, New Haven, VT 05472
rbc@gmavt.net
www.riversbendcamping.com
See ad this page.

NEWFANE — F2 *Windham*

KENOLIE VILLAGE **Ratings: 5.5/6.5/6.5** (Campground) 2015 rates: $23 to $25. Apr 1 to Nov 1. (802)365-7671 16 Kenolie Campground, Newfane, VT 05345

NEWPORT — A3 *Orleans*

PROUTY BEACH CAMPGROUND (Public) From jct I-91 (exit 27) & Hwy 191: Go 2 mi toward Newport, 1st traffic light continue straight, R at 2nd set of lights on to Union St. 2015 rates: $33 to $36. May 4 to Oct 8. (802)334-7951

NORTH DORSET — E2 *Bennington*

EMERALD LAKE (State Pk) From town, N 3 mi on US-7 (L). 2015 rates: $16 to $25. May 25 to Oct 12. (802)362-1655

PERKINSVILLE — E3 *Windsor*

CROWN POINT CAMPING AREA **Ratings: 6.5/7.5/8** (Campground) 2015 rates: $38. May 1 to Oct 15. (802)263-5555 131 Bishop Camp Rd, Perkinsville, VT 05151

PLYMOUTH UNION — D2 *Windsor*

COOLIDGE (State Pk) From town, E 17 mi on US-4 to SR-100, S 5 mi to SR-100A, NE 2 mi to Coolidge State Park Rd (R). Steep entrance. 2015 rates: $16 to $27. May 25 to Oct 12. (802)672-3612

POULTNEY — D1 *Rutland*

LAKE ST CATHERINE (State Pk) From Jct of US-4 & SR-30 (exit 4), S 10 mi on SR-30 (R). 2015 rates: $16 to $27. May 21 to Sep 7. (802)287-9158

QUECHEE — D3 *Windsor*

QUECHEE (State Pk) From Jct of I-89 & US 4 (exit 1), W 3 mi on US 4 (L). 2015 rates: $16 to $27. May 17 to Oct 20. (802)295-2990

RANDOLPH CENTER — C3 *Orange*

LAKE CHAMPAGNE CAMPGROUND
Ratings: 8.5/10★/9.5 (Campground) From Jct of I-89 & Hwy 66 (exit 4), Go 1 mi E on Hwy 66 to Furnace Rd, then 250 ft E (L). **FAC:** Gravel rds. (110 spaces). 70 Avail: 26 gravel, 44 grass, 31 pull-thrus (30 x 64), back-ins (36 x 64), 41 full hkups, 29 W, 29 E (30/50 amps), seasonal sites, cable, WiFi, tent sites, rentals, dump, laundry, LP gas, fire rings, firewood. **REC:** Lake Champagne: swim, shuffleboard, playground. Pets OK. Big rig sites, eco-friendly, 2015 rates: $30 to $40. Disc: AAA. May 21 to Oct 15.
AAA Approved
(802)728-5293 Lat: 43.94327, Lon: -72.60572
53 Lake Champagne Dr, Randolph Center, VT 05061
camp@lakechampagne.com
www.lakechampagne.com
See ad pages 1214, 1210.

RUTLAND — D2 *Rutland, Windsor*

SMOKE RISE CAMPGROUND (Campground) (Rebuilding) 2015 rates: $35. May 15 to Oct 15. (802)247-6984 2145 Grove St (Rte 7), Brandon, VT 05733

Find it fast! To locate a town on a map, follow these easy instructions: Look for the map grid code after the town heading in the listing section and match it to the letters and numbers on the map borders. Draw a line horizontally from the letter and vertically from the number. You'll find the town near the intersection of the two lines.

VT

SALISBURY — C2 Addison

LAKE DUNMORE KAMPERSVILLE
Ratings: 7.5/9★/7.5 (Campground) From Jct of US-7 & Hwy 53 (S of Middlebury), Go 1.5 mi E on Hwy 53 (L). **FAC:** Paved/gravel rds. (240 spaces). 148 Avail: 100 gravel, 48 dirt, 2 pull-thrus (25 x 57), back-ins (25 x 60), 81 full hkups, 60 W, 60 E (30/50 amps), seasonal sites, WiFi Hotspot, tent sites, dump, mobile sewer, laundry, groc, LP gas, fire rings, firewood, controlled access. **REC:** heated pool, wading pool, Lake Dunmore: swim, fishing, shuffleboard, playground. Pet restrict(Q). Partial handicap access. Big rig sites, eco-friendly, 2015 rates: $29 to $50. Apr 1 to Dec 1. ATM.
(802)352-4501 Lat: 43.92116, Lon: -73.08449
1457 Lake Dunmore Road, Salisbury, VT 05769
info@kampersville.com
www.kampersville.com
See ad this page.

SHELBURNE — B1 Chittenden

SHELBURNE CAMPING AREA
Ratings: 8/8.5★/7 (Campground) From Jct of I-89 (exit 13) & I-189, Go 1 mi W on I-189 to US-7, Then 4 mi S. (Campground is on East side of Hwy, 1 mi N of Shelburne Village). **FAC:** Gravel rds. (76 spaces). Avail: 56 gravel, 6 pull-thrus (28 x 58), back-ins (30 x 50), 30 full hkups, 26 W, 26 E (30/50 amps), seasonal sites, cable, WiFi, tent sites, rentals, dump, mobile sewer, laundry, groc, LP gas, fire rings, firewood, restaurant. **REC:** pool, playground. Pets OK. Partial handicap access. Big rig sites, eco-friendly, 2015 rates: $28 to $44.
AAA Approved
(802)985-2540 Lat: 44.39290, Lon: -73.21759
4385 Shelburne Rd, Shelburne, VT 05482
shelbcamp@aol.com
www.shelburnecamping.com
See ad this page.

Don't miss a thing! Check out the Table of Contents for everything the Guide has to offer.

SOUTH HERO — B1 Grand Isle

APPLE ISLAND RESORT
Ratings: 8.5/10★/9 (Campground) From Jct of I-89 & US-2 (exit 17), Go 6 mi W on US-2 (L).

APPLE ISLAND RESORT ON THE LAKE!
The best in RV camping directly on Lake Champlain. Features a 9-hole golf course, marina with boat rentals, general store, community center, fitness room, heated pool and hot tub. Cottage rentals and sleeping cabins.

FAC: Paved/gravel rds. (250 spaces). 113 Avail: 61 gravel, 52 grass, 16 pull-thrus (40 x 64), back-ins (35 x 61), 80 full hkups, 33 W, 33 E (30/50 amps), seasonal sites, WiFi, tent sites, rentals, dump, laundry, groc, LP gas, fire rings, firewood. **REC:** heated pool, whirlpool, Lake Champlain: fishing, marina, golf, playground. Pet restrict(B/Q). Partial handicap access. Big rig sites, eco-friendly, 2015 rates: $55 to $71. May 1 to Oct 20. ATM.
(802)372-3800 Lat: 44.63509, Lon: -73.26760
71 US Rte 2, South Hero, VT 05486
getinfo@appleislandresort.com
www.appleislandresort.com
See ad page 1212.

SOUTH LONDONDERRY — E2 Windham

WINHALL BROOK CAMPING AREA (COE-BALL MOUNTAIN LAKE) (Public Corps) From town: Go 2-1/2 mi S on Hwy 100, then E on Windhall Station Rd. 2015 rates: $18 to $22. May 17 to Oct 13. (802)874-4881

SPRINGFIELD — E3 Windsor

TREE FARM CAMPGROUND
Ratings: 6/8.5★/7.5 (Campground) From Jct of I-91 & Rte 11 (exit 7), Go 3.2 mi W on Rte 11 to Bridge St, then 0.5 mi N to Rte 143, Then 0.5 mi E. (R) Note: Follow directions, not GPS. **FAC:** Gravel rds. (101 spaces). 67 Avail: 38 grass, 29 dirt, 23 pull-thrus (25 x 73), back-ins (27 x 55), 48 full hkups, 19 W, 19 E (20/30 amps), seasonal sites, cable, WiFi, tent sites, dump, LP bottles, fire rings, firewood. **REC** playground. Pets OK. Eco-friendly, 2015 rates: $33 Disc: AAA. May 15 to Oct 31. No CC.
(802)885-2889 Lat: 43.28751, Lon: -72.46079
53 Skitchewaug Trail, Springfield, VT 05156
campvt@treefarmcampground.com
www.treefarmcampground.com

ST JOHNSBURY — B4 Caledonia

MOOSE RIVER CAMPGROUND
Ratings: 7.5/10★/9.5 (Campground) From Jct of I-91 (exit 19) & I-93 Go 3.5 mi E on I-93 (exit 1) to Rte 18 then 0.3 mi N to US-2, then 200 yds W (L). **FAC:** Gravel rds. (45 spaces). Avail 25 gravel, 6 pull-thrus (31 x 99), back-ins (30 x 52) some side by side hkups, 25 full hkups (30/50 amps) seasonal sites, cable, WiFi, tent sites, rentals, dump laundry, LP gas, fire rings, firewood. **REC:** Moose River: fishing. Pets OK. Big rig sites, eco-friendly 2015 rates: $37 to $42. May 1 to Oct 16.
(802)748-4334 Lat: 44.42921, Lon: -71.96533
2870 Portland St, St Johnsbury, VT 05819
info@mooserivercampground.com
www.mooserivercampground.com
See ad this page, 1210.

STOWE — B2 Lamoille, Washington

GOLD BROOK CAMPGROUND **Ratings: 6.5/7/7.5** (Campground) 2015 rates: $28 to $44. (802)253-7683 1900 Waterbury Rd, Stowe, VT 05672

SMUGGLERS NOTCH (State Pk) From Jct of SR-100 & SR-108 (in town), NW 6 mi on SR-108 (R) 2015 rates: $16 to $27. May 17 to Oct 14. (802)253 4014

TOWNSHEND — E2 Windham

BALD MOUNTAIN CAMPGROUND **Ratings: 5/5/6.5** (Campground) 2015 rates: $29 to $33 May 6 to Oct 16. (802)365-7510 1760 State Fores Rd, Townshend, VT 05353

TOWNSHEND (State Pk) From jct Hwy 30 & Town Rd: Go 3 mi N on Town Rd. Note: One vehicle pe site. May 22 to Sep 7. (802)365-7500

VERGENNES — C1 Addison

BUTTON BAY (State Pk) From town, S 0.5 mi on SR-22A to Panton Rd, W 1.2 mi to Basin Rd, NW 5. mi to Lake Rd, S 1 mi (L). 2015 rates: $16 to $27. May 25 to Oct 12. (802)475-2377

WATERBURY — B2 Washington

LITTLE RIVER (State Pk) From town, W 2 mi on US-2, follow signs (R). 2015 rates: $16 to $27. May 17 to Oct 12. (802)244-7103

WESTFIELD — A3 Orleans

BARREWOOD CAMPGROUND **Ratings: 5.5/6/7** (Campground) 2015 rates: $34 to $36. (802)744 6340 2998 Vt Rte 100, Westfield, VT 05874

WHITE RIVER JCT — D3 Windsor

QUECHEE PINE VALLEY KOA **Ratings: 8.5/8.5★/9** (Campground) 2015 rates: $35 to $70. May 1 to Oct 20. (802)296-6711 3700 Woodstock Rd, White River Jct, VT 05001

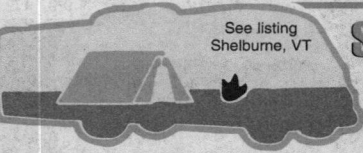

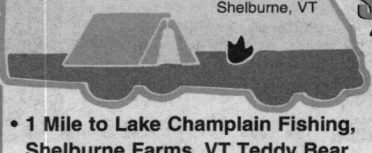

WILMINGTON — F2 *Windham*

➜ MOLLY STARK (State Pk) From Jct of I-91 & SR-9, exit 2 (in Brattleboro), W 15 mi on SR-9 (L); or From Wilmington, E 3 mi on SR-9 (R). 2015 rates: $16 to $25. May 22 to Oct 12. (802)464-5460

Reducing your speed to 55 mph from 65 mph may increase your fuel efficiency by as much as 15 percent; cut it to 55 from 70, and you could get a 23 percent improvement.

How can we make a great Travel Guide even better? We ask YOU! Please share your thoughts with us. Drop us a note and let us know if there's anything we haven't thought of.

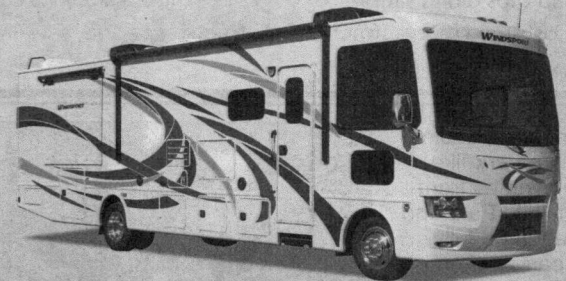

 See map page 1217

Sarah Hauser, Virginia Tourism Corporation.

WELCOME TO Virginia

DATE OF STATEHOOD	WIDTH: 200 MILES (322 KM)	PROPORTION OF UNITED STATES
JUNE 25, 1788	LENGTH: 430 MILES (692 KM)	1.13% OF 3,794,100 SQ MI

The birthplace of the nation and the primary staging ground for the unthinkable bloodshed of the Civil War, the Commonwealth of Virginia brims with museums, battlefields, presidential estates, colonial towns and plantations. State capital Richmond—the beating heart of the old Confederacy—is in the throes of a renaissance, as former tobacco warehouses have been recast as trendy lofts, hip restaurants and cutting-edge galleries. Thousands of acres of stunning natural beauty are preserved in two national parks, 25 state parks, two national forests and three national recreation areas, all of which afford more than 1,000 miles of hiking, biking and horseback riding through gorgeous mountain scenery.

If school field trips didn't satisfy your desire for costumed re-enactments of Patrick Henry's "Give Me Liberty, or Give Me Death!" speech, you can load up in the "historic triangle" of Williamsburg, Jamestown and Yorktown, home to the nation's best preserved colonial buildings. The former state capital, Colonial Williamsburg offers first-class art galleries, fine dining and outdoor pursuits to broaden the history lesson. The town of Charlottesville draws visitors to Thomas Jefferson's grand estate, Monticello, while the University of Virginia's neo-Classical Rotunda, the centerpiece of Jefferson's design, is a United Nations World Heritage Site. Etched with history, nearby Fredericksburg still retains the grace it exuded when illustrious former denizens George Washington, James Monroe and Confederate leader Robert E. Lee mused along its cobblestone streets.

Top 3 Tourism Attractions:
1) Arlington National Cemetery
2) Colonial Williamsburg
3) Presidential Estates

Nickname: The Old Dominion

State Flower: American Dogwood

State Bird: Cardinal

People: Arthur Ashe, tennis player; James Bridger, trapper, guide and storyteller; Ella Fitzgerald, singer; Walter Reed, army surgeon; George Washington, first president (seven other presidents were born in Virginia. For more info, see Welcome article).

Major Cities: Virginia Beach, Norfolk, Chesapeake, Richmond (capital), Newport News

Topography: West—valleys, mountains, including Blue Ridge Mountains; east—rolling piedmont plateau, tidewater, coastal plain

Climate: Despite its location in a humid, subtropical region, Virginia is generally temperate

Scott K. Brown Photography. Virginia Tourism Corporation

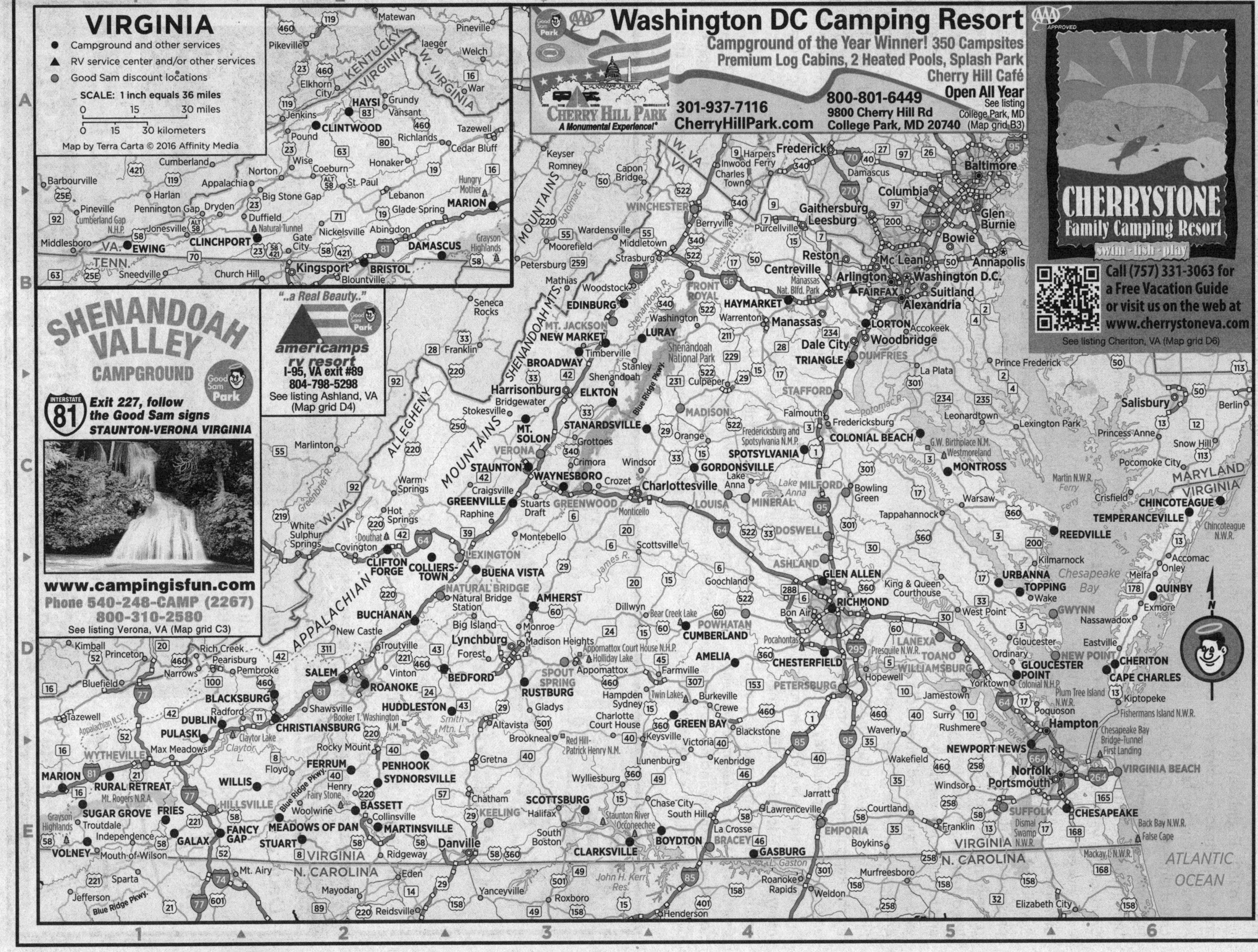
VIRGINIA
Campground and other services
RV service center and/or other services
Good Sam discount locations
SCALE: 1 inch equals 36 miles
0 15 30 miles
0 15 30 kilometers
Map by Terra Carta © 2016 Affinity Media
Washington DC Camping Resort
Campground of the Year Winner! 350 Campsites
Premium Log Cabins, 2 Heated Pools, Splash Park
Cherry Hill Café
Open All Year
See listing College Park, MD (Map grid B3)
CHERRY HILL PARK
A Monumental Experience!
301-937-7116
CherryHillPark.com
800-801-6449
9800 Cherry Hill Rd
College Park, MD 20740
CHERRYSTONE
Family Camping Resort
swim · fish · play
Call (757) 331-3063 for a Free Vacation Guide or visit us on the web at www.cherrystoneva.com
See listing Cheriton, VA (Map grid D6)
SHENANDOAH VALLEY
CAMPGROUND
Good Sam Park
INTERSTATE 81
Exit 227, follow the Good Sam signs
STAUNTON-VERONA VIRGINIA
www.campingisfun.com
Phone 540-248-CAMP (2267)
800-310-2580
See listing Verona, VA (Map grid C3)
"..a Real Beauty.."
americamps rv resort
I-95, VA exit #89
804-798-5298
See listing Ashland, VA (Map grid D4)
ATLANTIC OCEAN
Chesapeake Bay

History

In 1607, English settlers established the first permanent colony in North America when they built a fort they called Jamestowne. On October 19, 1781, following three weeks of continuous bombardment, British General Lord Charles Cornwallis surrendered to General George Washington in the Battle of Yorktown, to bring the American Revolution to an end. Yorktown's well-preserved battlefields and live military re-enactments provide an insight into life during those agonizing years. Sleepy and rural, known variously as "the garden of Virginia" and "the cradle of American democracy," the Northern Neck is a 61-mile peninsula bracketed by the Rappahannock and Potomac rivers and the Chesapeake Bay.

The Northern Neck was home to many of America's Founding Fathers and birthplace of three of the nation's first five presidents: George Washington, James Madison and James Monroe. George Washington's Virginia home, the Palladian-style Mount Vernon, has been artfully restored and affords an insight into the bygone days of rural gentility. Mount Vernon was first opened to the public in 1860. In addition to the mansion itself, more than 80 million visitors, to date, have viewed original and reconstructed buildings that include several barns, a blacksmith's shop, slave's quarters and the Pioneer Farm, George Washington's laboratory for testing and implementing innovative farming practices. Tobacco—the economic foundation of Virginia's economy—has been replaced by livestock as the state's most valuable source of agricultural income.

Play

Shenandoah National Park attracts nearly 2 million visitors a year to its 500 miles of hiking trails, complete with hollows, canyons, waterfalls and, if you are lucky, wildlife-viewing in the form of deer, bear, bobcat and wild turkey. Some 101 miles of the Appalachian Trail cross through Shenandoah and run parallel, in many places, to the Blue Ridge Parkway and the 105-mile Skylin Drive, one of America's most spectacu lar routes. In the Southwest Highlands Mount Rogers National Recreation occupies 117,000 wild and wonderful acres of forest. The park's namesake mountain is Virginia's highest peak. With hiking trails that flank swamp grass and placid tributaries, cavorting dolphins, migrating snow geese and tundra swans, there's more to Virginia Beach than just sun worshipping and cotton candy. At the Chincoteague National Wildlife Refuge, Assateague Island's famous wild ponies roam in solitude along 37 miles of virgin beach The island is also one of the best bird-watching sites in the country thanks tc its location on the Atlantic Flyway.

Experience

In February, Old Town Alexandria celebrates George Washington's birthday with the requisite pomp and circumstance. There are tours of the city's 140 Washington themed sites, an annual parade (the largest Washington celebration in the country) and the Birth Night Banquet and Ball at Gadsby's Tavern, which features character re-enactments, English country dancers and all manner of 18th-century shenanigans. In April, 250 Virginia landmarks, including historic homes and plantations, open their gardens to the public for the much loved statewide celebrations of Historic Garden Week. During April and May, classical musicians, actors, literary figures and performance artists appear at various venues throughout the state for the world-class Virginia Arts Festival. At Mount Vernon, each year on Christmas Day, Aladdin the Christmas Camel recreates Washington's 1787 hiring of a camel for 18 shillings to entertain his guests.

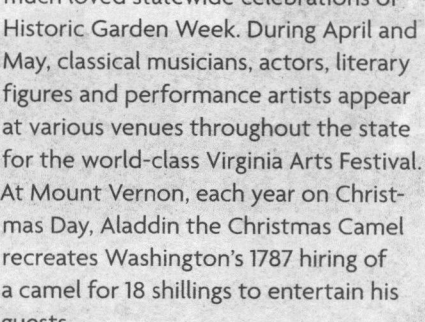

TRAVEL & TOURISM

Virginia Tourism Corporation
800-847-4882
www.virginia.org

Arlington County Visitors Center
800-296-7996, 703-416-0784
www.stayarlington.com

Fairfax County Visitors Center
800-732-4732
www.fxva.com

Fredericksburg Visitor Center
800-678-4748
www.visitfred.com

Newport News Tourism
888-493-7386, 757-926-1400
www.newport-news.org

Norfolk Convention & Visitors Bureau
757-664-6620, 800-368-3097
www.norfolkcvb.com

Roanoke Valley Visitor Information Center
800-635-5535
www.visitroanokeva.com

Shenandoah Valley Travel Association
800-847-4878
www.visitshenandoah.org

Virginia Beach Visitor Information Center
800-822-3224
www.vbfun.com

Greater Williamsburg Chamber & Tourism Alliance
757-229-6511, 800-368-6511
www.williamsburgcc.com

OUTDOOR RECREATION

Birding
804-367-8747

Civil War Reenactments
888-CIVIL WAR
www.civilwartraveler.com-virginia

Horseback Riding
877-TROT2VA
www.virginiahousecouncil.org

Featured Good Sam Parks

VIRGINIA

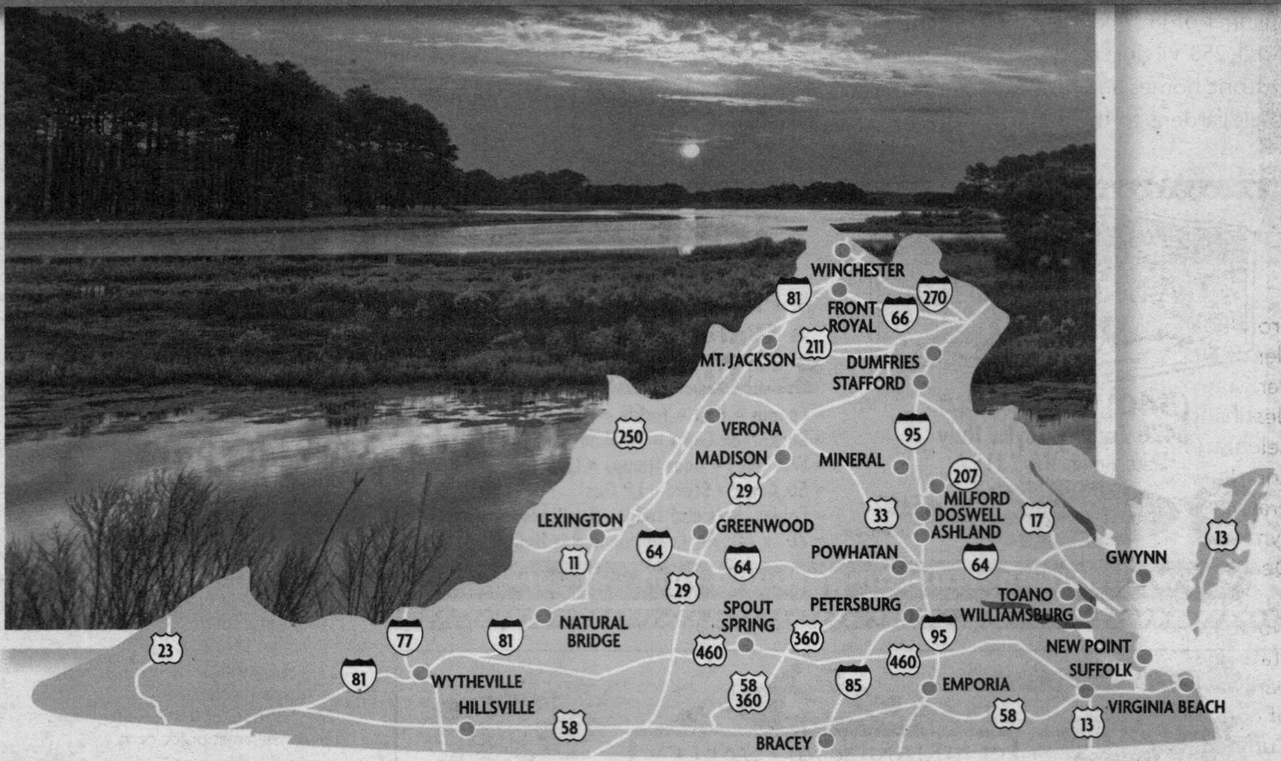

When you stay with Good Sam, you can expect the highest degree of cleanliness and friendliness, and better yet, you get 10% off campground fees.

If you're not already a Good Sam member you can purchase your membership at one of these locations:

ASHLAND
Americamps RV Resort
(804)798-5298

BRACEY
Lake Gaston Americamps
(434)636-2668

DOSWELL
Kings Dominion Camp Wilderness
(804)876-3006

DUMFRIES
Prince William Forest RV Campground
(888)737-5730

EMPORIA
Yogi Bear's Jellystone Park Camp-Resort Emporia
(434)634-3115

FRONT ROYAL
North Fork Resort
(540)636-2995

GREENWOOD
Misty Mountain Camp Resort
(888)647-8900

GWYNN
Gwynn's Island RV Resort & Campground
(888)699-4397

HILLSVILLE
Lake Ridge RV Resort
(866)513-1773

LEXINGTON
Lee Hi Campground
(540)463-3478

MADISON
Madison/Shenandoah Hills Campground
(540)948-4186

MILFORD
R & D Family Campground
(804)633-9515

MINERAL
Christopher Run Campground
(540)894-4744

MOUNT JACKSON
Shenandoah Valley Campground
(540)477-3080

NATURAL BRIDGE
Yogi Bear's Jellystone Park Camp Resort At Natural Bridge
(540)291-2727

NEW POINT
New Point RV Resort
(804)725-3084

PETERSBURG
Camptown Campground
(804)469-4569
Picture Lake Campground
(804)861-0174

POWHATAN
Cozy Acres Campground/ RV Park
(804)598-2470

SPOUT SPRING
Paradise Lake Family Campground
(434)993-3332

STAFFORD
Aquia Pines Camp Resort
(540)659-3447

SUFFOLK
Davis Lakes and Campground
(757)539-1191

TOANO
Williamsburg Christian Retreat Center
(757)566-2256

VERONA
Shenandoah Valley Campground
(540)248-CAMP(2267)

VIRGINIA BEACH
Holiday Trav-L-Park Of Virginia Beach
(866)850-9630
North Landing Beach RV Resort & Cottages
(757)426-6241

WILLIAMSBURG
American Heritage RV Park
(888)530-2267
Anvil Campground
(757)565-2300

WINCHESTER
Candy Hill Campground
(540)662-5198

WYTHEVILLE
Fort Chiswell RV Park
(276)637-6868

For more Good Sam Parks go to listing pages

Getty Images/iStockphoto

SPOTLIGHT

VA

BLUE RIDGE PARKWAY/SOUTHWEST VIRGINIA

Follow colorful Virginia trails to adventure

From Roanoke, Virginia, to the border of North Carolina, the Blue Ridge Parkway guides travelers to memorable destinations. The Blue Ridge Parkway celebrates its 80th anniversary in 2015 and remains an example of the cooperative, hardworking spirit that came to symbolize the New Deal of the 1930s.

At the Virginia-North Carolina state line sits the parkway's first point of construction, Cumberland Knob. Building began in 1935, but it wasn't completed until 1983. The parkway links Shenandoah National Park in Virginia with Great Smoky Mountains National Park in Tennessee.

At the southernmost point of the Plateau Region, on the Carolina side of the state line, sits Cumberland Knob Recreation Area. Take the paved Cumberland Knob Trail for a casual 20-minute hike around and stop for a quick bite at the scenic picnic area, nestled next to a meadow. Before the parkway, Cumberland Knob was home to a family graveyard.

> Hike to Rock Castle Gorge to see the remnants of the life lived by mountain families, whose apple orchards and stone chimneys remain.

Blue Ridge Music

The historic music of the region is preserved and celebrated at the Blue Ridge Music Center in Galax, Virginia, just across the line from Cumberland Knob. Traditional music concerts are held throughout the year and an onsite museum details the sound's origins. Interactive elements allow visitors to become part of the music-making process as well.

Further up the parkway, Fancy Gap beckons guests with a quaint Pickin' Porch that hosts live mountain music performances, along with locally grown produce and antique treasures. Local artisans craft log furniture and create one-of-a-kind art from wood and pottery. An alpaca farm welcomes visitors to meet its furry residents and browse gifts made from the wool.

Fancy Gap is also home to one of six rock churches built by Bob Childress, a Presbyterian minister who traveled the southern Appalachian region in the early part of the 20th century. Bluemont Presbyterian Rock Church, still an active church, was originally a wooden structure built in 1920 and was encased in stone in 1945.

One of Fancy Gap's more infamous landmarks is the Sidna Allen House, built for the eponymous local gangster convicted of a courthouse shooting in 1912. The home's current owners offer tours by appointment. Visits to Devil's Den are free—this 600-million-year-old cave inside Devil's Den Nature Preserve is where Allen reportedly hid after the shooting.

The mountain village of Meadows of Dan is a great spot to stop for a sweet treat. Nancy's Candy Company has created more than 100 flavors of fudge, at least 40 of which are available every day. The company also lets

One of many Blue Ridge Parkway vistas. Getty Images/iStockphoto

guests see the candy-making process in their factory. After satisfying that sweet tooth, visit Mabry's Mill and walk the mountain arts trail to see old-fashioned skills on display, such as grinding corn and making tools by hand.

Fine Wind on the Plateau

Taste the fruits of the Plateau Region at Chateau Morrissette Winery, which hosts music events and festivals throughout the year and provides several of its varieties for purchase along with meals at its onsite restaurant. Villa Appalaccia Winery offers limited tasting hours and live music on weekends.

Rocky Knob Recreation Area is known for its rustic, rural landscape. Hike to Rock Castle Gorge to see the remnants of the life lived by mountain families, whose apple orchards and stone chimneys remain.

At the northern tip of the Plateau Region lies the city of Roanoke, considered the cultural and recreational hub of the Blue Ridge Mountains. The Roanoke Valley hosts numerous festivals and events throughout the year, and the area also invites outdoor enthusiasts to enjoy fishing, hunting and hiking among the forests of the Blue Ridge.

View works of fine art at the Taubman Museum of Art and the Eleanor Wilson Museum, and take a self-guided bicycle tour through the city to view more than two dozen public art installations. Take in a live production at Mill Mountain Theatre or Moss Arts Center, and enjoy a night on the town with a craft-beer tour, which takes travelers to three breweries for a behind-the-scenes experience.

Blue Ridge on Foot

Take the quarter-mile, interactive Goode Railwalk and learn about Roanoke Valley's railroad history. The walk parallels active rail lines and reveals the industry's influence on the development of the region.

Smith Mountain Lake is a prime bass-fishing spot; whether on your own or with a knowledgeable guide, you're bound to snag some trophy-sized treasures. For trout, muskie or crappie, dip into the James River and Carvins Cove. Hunters in Roanoke Valley enjoy seasons for deer, elk and game birds.

The jewel of the Blue Ridge hiking trails is the Appalachian Trail, with its numerous paths for hikers of all levels. Experience grand views at the summit of McAfee Knob and Sharp Top Mountain, and hike to the top of Roanoke Star & Overlook for a view of the Roanoke Valley.

The Blue Ridge region is famed fo its fall color display, and popular spots for viewing include Cahas Knob Overlook, a scenic spot that rises 3,013 feet and provides views of the valley and Cahas Mountain. North of Roanoke is Natural Bridge Park, one of the nation' oldest landmarks. While visiting, walk Cedar Creek Trail, which runs under th Natural Bridge and is a great spot for viewing unique flora and fauna.

For More Information

Blue Ridge Parkway Association
828-670-1924
www.blueridgeparkway.org

Virginia Tourism Corporation
800-847-4882
www.virginia.org

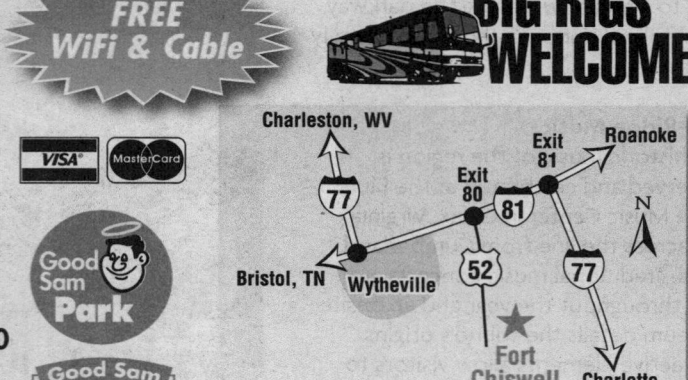

Getty Images/iStockphoto

HISTORIC TRIANGLE

Relive the formative years of America at three amazing destinations

A trip down scenic Colonial Parkway leads travelers to the Historic Triangle of Jamestown, Williamsburg and Yorktown. These picturesque towns are pivotal sites in the history of the nation as it rose from British colony to independent republic, and the story of their impact is brought to life through museums, reenactments and living history displays.

Colonial Williamsburg might easily be one of the most visited tourist spots on the mid-Atlantic Coast, but there's more to see and do than you might think. Colonial Williamsburg puts guests in the middle of Revolutionary action to experience the struggles of colonists in their fight for independence. Night tours introduce travelers to stories of witch trials, pirates and ghosts. When the sun comes up the next day, spend the morning hitting a few balls at the Golden Horseshoe Golf Club.

> In Jamestown Settlement, replicas of the ships that sailed from England allow visitors to board.

Swing over to Freedom Park and fly among the treetops at Go Ape Treetop Adventure. Zip lines, net bridges and rope ladders dot the challenge course that is sure to be a hit with older kids and adventurous grown-ups. Younger visitors are treated to their own Treetop Junior experience.

Find more thrills at Busch Gardens Williamsburg. This popular amusement park has something for everyone, from high-flying roller coasters to shows and kid-centric attractions. See high-stepping Celtic dancing, alpine hijinks and live-animal presentations, then get an up-close tour of the park's feathered and furry animal ambassadors.

Tour the sight of the first official Thanksgiving at Berkeley Plantation on the James River. President William Henry Harrison was born here, and the Civil War arrangement "Taps" was composed on-site when Berkeley served as a general's headquarters. The Georgian-style mansion was built in 1726 and a self-guided tour of the grounds reveals boxwood and flowering gardens and a monument to the first Thanksgiving. Guides dressed in period costumes lead visitors through the mansion to view 18th-century artifacts and antique furnishings.

March to Yorktown

Step onto the site of Yorktown Battlefield and see the earthworks that protected colonial militiamen from British fire during the pivotal battle of the Revolutionary War. Traipse through the battlefield and view the site of Washington's Headquarters, the Yorktown Victory Monument and Moore House, where terms of surrender were negotiated.

VA

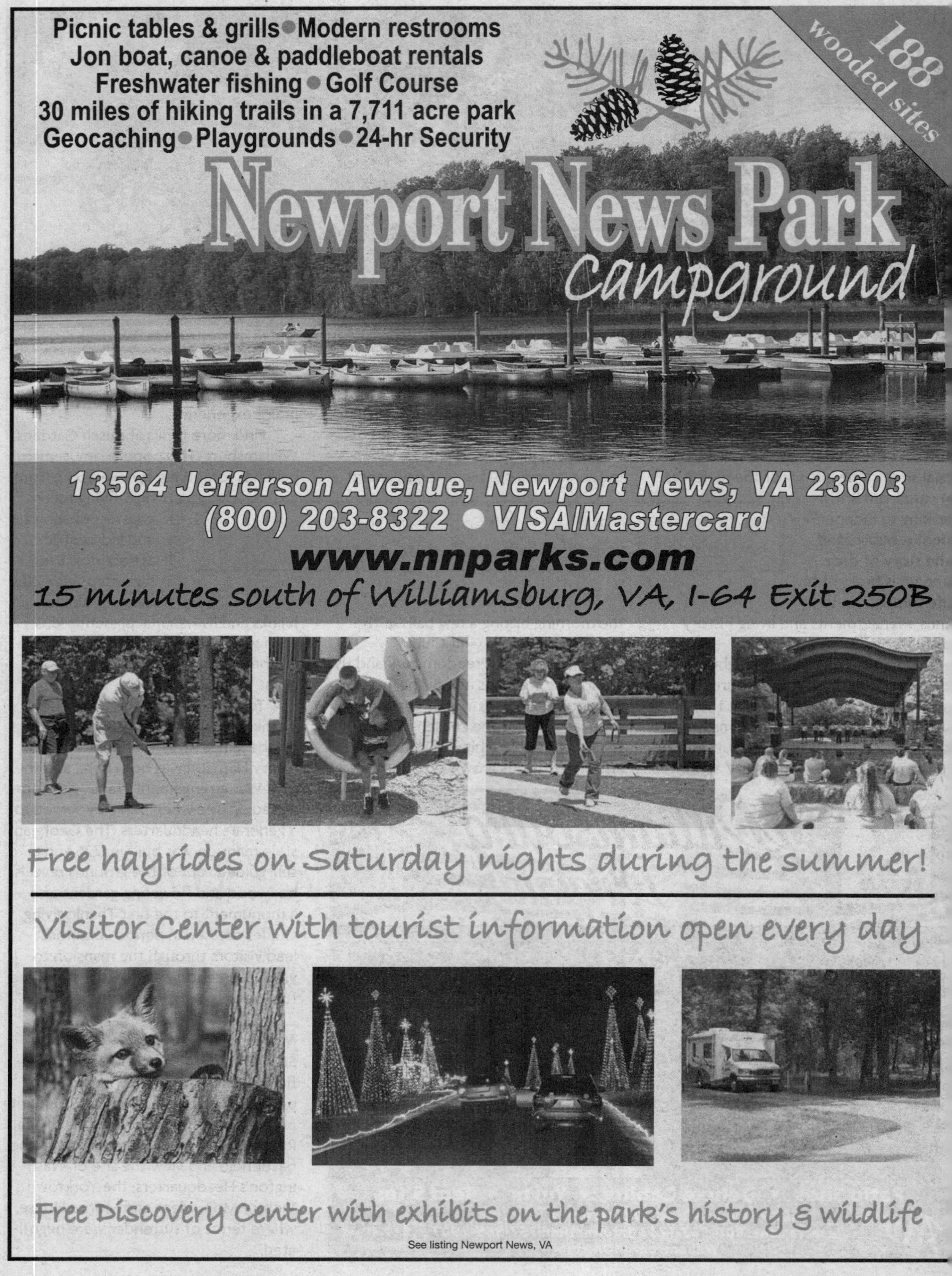
Picnic tables & grills • Modern restrooms
Jon boat, canoe & paddleboat rentals
Freshwater fishing • Golf Course
30 miles of hiking trails in a 7,711 acre park
Geocaching • Playgrounds • 24-hr Security
188 wooded sites
Newport News Park
Campground
13564 Jefferson Avenue, Newport News, VA 23603
(800) 203-8322 • VISA/Mastercard
www.nnparks.com
15 minutes south of Williamsburg, VA, I-64 Exit 250B
Free hayrides on Saturday nights during the summer!
Visitor Center with tourist information open every day
Free Discovery Center with exhibits on the park's history & wildlife
See listing Newport News, VA

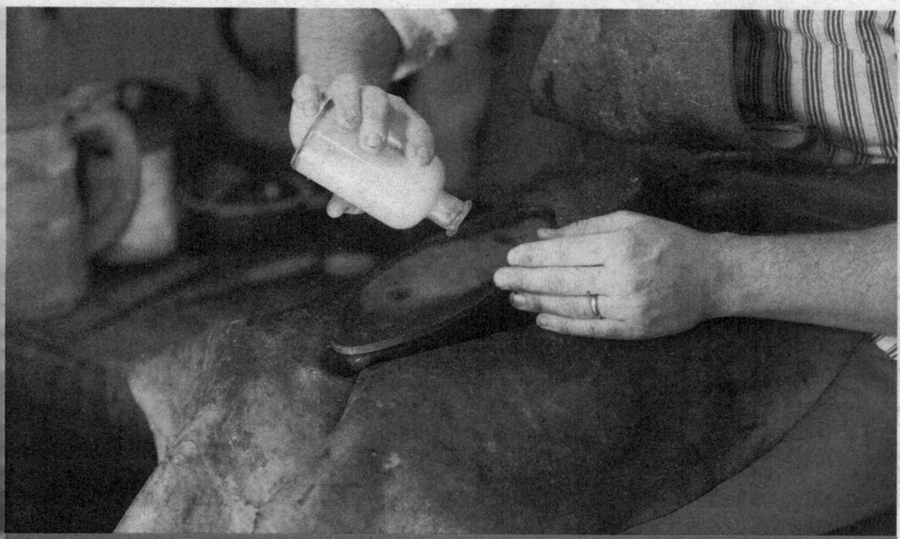
A colonial shoemaker in Williamsburg. Getty Images/iStockphoto

The Yorktown Victory Center tells the story of the Revolution through galleries and exhibits that detail the military and civilian life during wartime. The grounds feature a re-created military encampment and a simulated farm site that teaches visitors about agriculture and cloth-making in Colonial times.

Walk down Main Street and enjoy the variety of antique shops, galleries and dining options, or join a guided tour through Yorktown's historic streets. Riverwalk Landing on the York River offers views of the waterfront and access to the beach. Yorktown's Watermen's Museum reveals the lives and livelihoods of men and women who fished the rivers and tributaries of Chesapeake Bay.

Maritime victories were critical to the colonists' eventual success, and the ships they used have been re-created for guests to enjoy as living history lessons. Board the Schooner Serenity or Schooner Alliance. These tall ships sail down the river past the battlefield, occasionally joined in the water by schools of dolphins.

Enjoy the natural beauty of the Yorktown region at New Quarter Park, where diverse habitats make for great bird-watching. Tidal wetland, mature hardwoods and swampland, and meadows invite dozens of unique species to nest and find shelter here. Stay for a while and see if you can spot a yellow-crowned night heron, scarlet tanagers or wild turkeys. Bald eagles have been known to frequent the area year-round, perching on trees overlooking the river.

A Colonial First

Historic Jamestowne is legendary as the site of England's first permanent North American colony. Tales of John Smith and Pocahontas are highlights, but much more remains to be discovered on a trip to Virginia's 17th-century capital. Archeologists actively work to uncover and preserve artifacts from the 1607 site of James Fort. These artifacts are on display at the Archaearium, where stories about the settlement are shared alongside these treasures.

Rangers and archeologists lead walking tours of the island, where remains of the settlement's brick church still stand. Visitors are invited to view active dig sites and participate in behind-the-scenes tours of dig sites and artifact collections. Kids can get their hands dirty at the Ed Shed, an interactive space that lets visitors uncover genuine artifacts and search for clues on a Jamestown Adventure treasure hunt.

Jamestown Settlement, adjacent to Historic Jamestowne, is a living history presentation of life in the early colony. Replicas of the ships that sailed from England allow visitors to board, and a re-created Powhatan Indian village invites you to try your hand at grinding corn or making cordage as Pocahontas would have done. Historical interpreters help visitors take part in 17th-century games and try on period armor. Seasonal exhibits feature methods of cloth-making and the evolution and craft behind the log canoe.

Across the James River at Cobham Bay is Chippokes Plantation State Park. This unique state park, one of the oldest continually farmed plantations in America, has been a working farm since 1619 and is open to visitors for tours of the mansion and outbuildings. Guests can view antique equipment at the Chippokes Farm and Forestry Museum and take a dip in the park's pool.

For More Information

Virginia Tourism Corporation
800-847-4882
www.virginia.org

Bill Crabtree, Jr. Virginia Tour

SHENANDOAH VALLEY

Wine, natural wonders and Civil War history are among the treasures here

Along the western stretch of Virginia lies the Shenandoah Valley, composed of a handful of communities with a rich history and culture that embody the spirit of America. From Roanoke to Martinsburg, the Shenandoah Valley has more in store than you can uncover in a single road trip.

> Civil War troops who used the Grand Caverns for shelter during the conflict left behind hundreds of signatures.

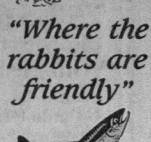

Open Air Fun

Folks in the Valley know how to have fun under open skies. Come to the Valley in late summer and enjoy live music at the Shenandoah Valley Music Festival in Orkney Springs. The intimate outdoor setting and great performances have brought in crowds for more than 50 years.

Kick off spring at the Shenandoah Apple Blossom Festival in the northern stretch of the valley, where arts and crafts share equal billing with musical guests and television personalities. The 10-day festival features a parade, a coronation for the festival queen and a talent show, along with many other family-friendly activities.

Get to know native and non-native animals that reside at Natural Bridge Zoo in Natural Bridge. In addition to viewer-friendly exhibits and a petting zoo for visitors, park guests can ride elephants and experience close encounters with other friendly species.

Kids are the special guests at Shenandoah Valley Discovery Museum in Winchester. In addition to interactive science-based activities, children and families can enjoy programs such as astronomy night and the family engineering challenge.

Valley Vineyards

Toast your Shenandoah Valley experience at any one of the vineyards along the Shenandoah Valley Wine Trail. At North Mountain Vineyard & Winery, you can sample handcrafted wines in the tasting room and pack a picnic to enjoy on the grounds of this family-friendly destination. Tour Barren Ridge Vineyards before enjoying one of the award-winning vintages on the patio while the sun sets.

Awaken your inner artist at the Shenandoah Valley Art Center in Waynesboro. Here you can take a class r just enjoy the work of local artisans s well as live music throughout the ear. Nature's creations are on display ear-round in Shenandoah National ark, which runs along the eastern edge f the valley and continues to attract isitors with opportunities for bird-vatching, canoeing and kayaking, hiking nd camping.

Shenandoah National Park's sight-eeing gems include two peaks that rise nore than 4,000 feet above sea level, igh-elevation streams that tumble over ocks to create rapids, cascades and vaterfalls, and stands of chestnut and ed oak.

;oing Deep

eauty also lives below the surface in ;rand Caverns, America's oldest contin-ously operated show cave. Rare shield ormations provide the centerpiece for nderground adventure and entertain-nent, but other attractions include undreds of signatures left by Civil War roops who used the caverns for shelter luring the conflict. The caverns are part f a multi-use park that has trails for iking and biking, a swimming pool and miniature golf course.

Take an elevator 60 feet down to he floor of Shenandoah Caverns and tep into a strange world where the valls seem to be melting. This phenom-enon is called "bacon" and is formed by vater running down walls and deposit-ng minerals over time. The bacon's stripes" are the result of various types f minerals found in the water. Peer up t the towering wall of flowstone in the ;rotto, the room where the Caverns vere first spotted through a natural pening at the surface.

'alley Waters

ihenandoah River Adventures in the own of Shenandoah promises a wild ide or a lazy day on the water—vhichever floats your boat. Canoeing, ayaking and tubing are popular ways to enjoy the beauty of the Shenandoah River. If you're angling to catch some fish, Shenandoah is prime bass territory. The smallmouth species is plentiful in the river—so much so, many anglers find they can snag at least two fish an hour. You'll also have luck with crappie, muskies and channel catfish.

Stop in the town of New Market for a history lesson, courtesy of the Virginia Museum of the Civil War and New Market Battlefield. The museum focuses on the battle at New Market, where young cadets from the Virginia Military Institute fought alongside Confederate troops to push back Union forces and secure the battlefield for the Confederacy.

A reenactment of the Civil War Battle of New Market at New Market Battlefield State Historical Park. Courtesy of Virginia Tourism Corporation

For More Information

Shenandoah Valley Inc.
800-847-4878
www.visitshenandoah.org

Virginia Tourism Corporation
800-847-4882
www.virginia.org

VA

THE VIRGINIA SHORELINE

Run with the horses on a superb Virginia Beach

Stretching south from the Maryland border and separating the Atlantic Ocean from the Chesapeake Bay, the Eastern Shore of Virginia exudes a wild, seafaring character that invites you to dig your toes in the sand and feel the ocean breeze on your face.

Getting there is easy: The Chesapeake Bay Bridge-Tunnel whisks you from Hampton Roads on the mainland out to the 70-mile-long peninsula, where coastal adventures await visitors.

A great place to start is the Chincoteague National Wildlife Refuge, a hot spot for horse lovers and curious onlookers, many of whom travel to the refuge in midsummer to see the wild, miniature ponies swim from Assateague Island to Chincoteague Island. The 90-year-old tradition, in which wild horses are rounded up before being herded into the water, has its roots in "pony penning." Today, foals are auctioned off each year to help control the size of the herd and raise funds for local volunteer firefighters.

> Take a canoe or kayak out on the water for a slow-paced tour that follows the Virginia Seaside Water Trail.

Chincoteague isn't just about ponies, though. With more than 14,000 acres of beach, dunes, marsh and maritime forest, the refuge is home to waterfowl of all kinds, as well as plants that are uniquely adapted to the environment. Visitors are permitted to fish and hunt, and wildlife photography and observation are also encouraged. Your guests can participate in ranger-guided programs at the visitor center to learn about archery, lighthouses, birds and animal tracks.

Follow the Light

The Assateague Lighthouse is open weekends for tours (with expanded hours during July and August), and it can be accessed by a walking-biking trail that leads from Chincoteague. The original lighthouse was built in 1833 and replaced by a larger one in 1867. The beacon's lights can be seen 19 miles out to sea, as it remains an active navigational aid. Though its first light was a candle lantern, today's lighthouse is outfitted with twin rotating electric lights that flash in tandem.

Enjoy a day in a Victorian-era town. Parksley sits on the north end of the peninsula and boasts a train station that harks back to the days when passenger trains made 14 stops per day here. Tour the Eastern Shore Railway Museum and its preserved lounge car, sleeper car and caboose, and browse railroad memorabilia. Quench your thirst at nearby Bloxom Vineyard and Winery, where several varieties of grapes are cultivated on a 35-acre Victorian farm.

Explore the outdoors at sea level in Wallops Island, home to the Marine Science Consortium. The field station's programs teach guests about marine life and the Wallops Island ecosystem through interactive programs for children and adults. Wallops is also home to NASA's primary facility for suborbital research programs. The Wallops Flight Facility visitor center hosts free public education programs as well as weekly activities, and it is an ideal viewing site

The historic Assateague Lighthouse overlooks the Atlantic.
Getty Images/iStockphoto

when rockets are launched.

During your visit, try some surf fishing off the shores of Wreck and Bone Island Natural Area Preserve near the town of Oyster. This piece of the barrier island chain is paralleled by shell mounds and consists mainly of beaches, sand dunes and salt marsh habitats. Nesting birds have the island to themselves during the last two weeks of April to ensure safe breeding.

Take a canoe or kayak out on the water for a slow-paced tour along the Virginia Seaside Water Trail. Essentially 100 miles of day-use paddling routes, the trail's 37 water courses stretch between the Virginia National Wildlife Refuge at Cape Charles and Chincoteague Island. North and South Raccoon Island are the recommended routes for beginner paddlers.

The whole family will appreciate a day at Kiptopeke State Park on the Chesapeake Bay. More than 5 miles of hiking and bicycle trails lead into upland hardwood forest, where deer and foxes make their homes. Bayside beaches invite visitors to cool off in calm waters; the southern beach is open to crabbing and surf fishing as well. Head out from the waterfront to a large fishing pier, or take a boat out to the concrete ships that form a breakwater, where many species make a home.

See what life in a coastal town is like on a trip to Cape Charles. Located on the Chesapeake Bay, Cape Charles delights guests with its resort feel and small-town charm. Cape Charles was built to serve the Pennsylvania Railroad; the town was mapped out in 1884 and trains began running that same year.

VA

Horses make the shore during the Chincoteague Pony Swim. Getty Images/iStockphoto

White Egret
Getty Images/iStockphoto

Diesel Power

Cape Charles Museum and Welcome Center resides in a former power plant with the diesel engine and generator still intact. Museum staff demonstrates the equipment upon request, along with a 4-foot-long locomotive model that runs in place. The museum also houses artifacts from the formation of the Chesapeake Bay crater, models of sailing ships and archival photographs from the town's development projects.

Though the trains have long gone, traffic continues to come to Cape Charles in waves of tourists seeking oceanside relaxation and fun. Cape Charles boasts the only public beach on Virginia's Eastern Shore that is free to use. The beach's southern end is adjacent to a public pier for saltwater fishing and watching boats sail through the Chesapeake Bay.

Central Park, located in the heart of the downtown historic district, is the site of year-round events and festivities. On quiet days, it's an ideal spot for strolling around the walking path or people-watching from the benches scattered around the park.

Enjoy a guided horseback ride through a 150-acre waterfront farm along wooded trails, or hit the links at Bay Creek Resort, marking the first time golf greats Arnold Palmer and Jack Nicklaus designed courses for the same club.

On the Chesapeake Bay shoreline, the Oyster Fram Seafood Eatery at Kings Creek serves up fresh seafood. Diners can enjoy stunning views of Chesapeake Bay during their visit, and when darkness falls, a candlit dinner with someone special should be on your menu.

In nearby Cheriton, Ballard Fish and Oyster Company has been producing shellfish since 1895 and opens its Cherrystone Aqua-Farms for tours. At Chatham Vineyards, 10 miles north on land founded in 1640, America's only authentic Kayak Winery Tour welcomes even inexperienced paddlers.

If you're visiting in October, head over to the narrow Delmarva Peninsula for the Eastern Shore Birding and Wildlife Festival. Each year, thousands of songbirds, hawks, butterflies and dragonflies follow this thin strip of land on a migration path. While there, visitors can explore historic towns and seaside villages.

Birders are encouraged to bring their binoculars and birding log books. During a recent festival, an incredible 162 species were observed. While visiting, take a boat trip to learn about the marshes, islands and bays that make up the Virginia Coastal Reserve, one of the last coastal wilderness areas on the Eastern Seaboard.

For More Information

Eastern Shore of Virginia Tourism
757-331-1660
www.esvatourism.org

Virginia Tourism Corporation
800-847-4882
www.virginia.org

Virginia

CONSULTANTS

Greg & Maureen Baron

AMELIA — D4 *Amelia*

AMELIA FAMILY CAMPGROUND Ratings: 5.5/8/7 (Campground) From Jct of US-360 & SR-153 (E of town), S 0.5 mi on SR-153 (Military Rd) (R). **FAC:** Gravel rds. (80 spaces). Avail: 50 gravel, 50 pull-thrus (14 x 65), mostly side by side hkups, 30 full hkups, 20 W, 20 E (30 amps), seasonal sites, tent sites, dump, laundry, LP gas, firewood. **REC:** pool, pond, Amelia Pond: fishing, playground, rec open to public. Pet restrict(B). 2015 rates: $30 to $35. No CC. AAA Approved
(804)561-3011 Lat: 37.35050, Lon: -77.88404
9720 Military Rd, Amelia, VA 23002
ameliacampground@tds.net
www.ameliafamilycampground.com

AMHERST — D3 *Amherst*

BLUE RIDGE PKWY/OTTER CREEK (Natl Pk) From Jct of US-501 & Blue Ridge Pkwy, N 3 mi on Blue Ridge Pkwy (R). 2015 rates: $20. May to Nov. (828)271-4779

APPOMATTOX — D3 *Appomattox*

APPOMATTOX See also Rustburg and Spout Spring.

HOLLIDAY LAKE (State Pk) From town: Go 9 mi E on Hwy-24, then 6 mi SE on Hwy-626 & 692. 2015 rates: $27. (434)248-6308

PARKVIEW RV PARK
Ratings: 5.5/NA/7.5 (RV Park) Take 2nd Appomattox exit on US 460-Bypass (from either direction) then at Jct of US 460 & Hwy 24, N 1 block on Hwy 24E, E 1 block on Clover Lane (R). **FAC:** Paved rds. 33 paved, 30 pull-thrus (30 x 70), back-ins (25 x 60), accepts full hkup units only, 33 full hkups (30/50 amps), WiFi. Pet restrict(B). No tents. Big rig sites, 2015 rates: $39. No CC.
(434)665-8418 Lat: 37.36987, Lon: -78.82317
174-A Clover Lane, Appomattox, VA 24522
See ad this page.

ASHLAND — D4 *Hanover*

AMERICAMPS RV RESORT
Ratings: 9/9.5★/9 (Campground) From Jct of I-95 & I-295, N 4 mi on I-95 to Jct of exit 89 (Lewistown Rd/Rte 802) & Rte 802, E 0.1 mi on Rte 802 to Air Park Rd, S 0.75 mi (L).

IDEAL HISTORIC RICHMOND LOCATION
Easy I-95 access: VA #89. Huge, FHU 50-amp level pull-thru sites. Propane. Updated bathhouses & fitness center. Free WiFi & Cable, free waffle breakfast. New rally room, kitchen and coffee bar. Hospitality Galore!

FAC: Paved/gravel rds. (200 spaces). 150 Avail: 9 paved, 141 gravel, 114 pull-thrus (30 x 68), back-ins (30 x 60), 150 full hkups (30/50 amps), seasonal sites, cable, WiFi, tent sites, dump, laundry, groc, LP gas, fire rings, firewood. **REC:** pool, playground. Pets OK. Partial handicap access. Big rig sites, 14 day max stay, eco-friendly, 2015 rates: $40 to $55. Disc: military.
(804)798-5298 Lat: 37.70995, Lon: -77.44720
11322 Air Park Rd, Ashland, VA 23005
info@americamps.com
www.americamps.com
See ad pages 1241, 1220, 1217 (VA Map) See ad inside back cover.

BASSETT — E2 *Patrick*

GOOSE POINT PARK (Public Corps) From town, W 8 mi on Hwy 57 to Rte 822, N 4 mi (E). 2015 rates: $20 to $25. (276)629-1847

BEDFORD — D3 *Bedford*

BLUE RIDGE PKWY/PEAKS OF OTTER (Natl Pk) From town, on Blue Ridge Pkwy at MP-86 (L). 2015 rates: $16 to $19. May 15 to Oct 15. (540)586-7321

BLACKSBURG — D2 *Montgomery*

NEW RIVER JUNCTION CAMPGROUND **Ratings: 6/4.5/7** (Campground) 2015 rates: $34. May 1 to Sep 30. (540)639-6633 2591 Big Falls Rd, Blacksburg, VA 24060

BOWLING GREEN — C5 *Caroline*

BOWLING GREEN See also Ashland, Colonial Beach, Doswell, Fredericksburg, Milford.

BOYDTON — E4 *Mecklenburg*

BUFFALO PARK (Public Corps) From town, W 6 mi on US-58 to SR-732, N 5 mi (E). 2015 rates: $18 to $48. May to Sep. (434)374-2063

NORTH BEND PARK (Public Corps) From Jct of US-58 & Rte 4, S 6 mi on Rte 4/Buggs Allen Rd to CR-678, W 1 mi (L). 2015 rates: $18 to $24. Apr 1 to Oct 31. (434)738-0059

RUDD'S CREEK (Public Corps) From town, W 3 mi on Hwy 58 (L). Pit toilets. 2015 rates: $18 to $48. Apr to Oct. (434)738-6827

BRACEY — E4 *Mecklenburg*

LAKE GASTON AMERICAMPS
Ratings: 8.5/9.5★/8.5 (Campground) From Jct of I-85 & Rte 903 (exit 4), E 5.4 mi on Rte 903 (R). **FAC:** Paved/gravel rds. (475 spaces). 125 Avail: 12 paved, 93 gravel, 20 dirt, 8 pull-thrus (25 x 55), back-ins (25 x 40), some side by side hkups, 10 full hkups, 115 W, 115 E (30 amps), seasonal sites, WiFi, tent sites, rentals, dump, mobile sewer, laundry, groc, LP gas, fire rings, firewood, controlled access. **REC:** pool, wading pool, Lake Gaston: swim, fishing, playground. Pets OK. Eco-friendly, 2015 rates: $42 to $45.
(434)636-2668 Lat: 36.56216, Lon: -78.07183
9 Lakeside Lane, Bracey, VA 23919
acamp@buggs.net
www.lakegastonamericamps.com
See ad pages 1218 (Welcome Section), 1220.

BRISTOL — B2 *Washington*

SUGAR HOLLOW RECREATION AREA (Public) From I-81 (exit 7): Go 1 mi N on US 11 (Robert E. Lee Hwy). 2015 rates: $12 to $15. (276)645-7376

BROADWAY — B3 *Rockingham*

HARRISONBURG/SHENANDOAH VALLEY KOA
Ratings: 8.5/9.5★/9 (Campground) From Jct of I-81 & US-11 (Mauzy-Exit 257), N 100 yds on US-11 to SR-608/Mauzy-Athlone Rd, E 3.2 mi on SR-608/Mauzy-Athlone Rd (E). Note: Entrance straight ahead past stop sign.

AWARD WINNING KOA-OPEN ALL YEAR
Friendly owners celebrating 8th season in the Shenandoah Valley; enjoy a heated pool, mini golf, stocked fishing pond, WiFi. Dog walk. Big rig friendly, escort site. In season, weekend food service. Our family welcomes you!

FAC: Gravel rds. 62 gravel, 36 pull-thrus (26 x 60), back-ins (26 x 45), 41 full hkups, 21 W, 21 E (30/50 amps), cable, WiFi, tent sites, rentals, dump, laundry, groc, LP gas, fire rings, firewood. **REC:** heated pool, pond, fishing, playground. Pets OK. Big rig sites, eco-friendly, 2015 rates: $38 to $65. ATM.
(540)896-8929 Lat: 38.53324, Lon: -78.70470
12480 Mountain Valley Road, Broadway, VA 22815
shenandoahvalleykoa@yahoo.com
www.koa.com/campgrounds/harrisonburg
See ad page 1227 (Spotlight Shenandoah Valley).

BUCHANAN — D2 *Botetourt*

MIDDLE CREEK CAMPGROUND **Ratings: 7/7/6.5** (Campground) 2015 rates: $32 to $36. (540)254-2550 1164 Middle Creek Road, Buchanan, VA 24066

BUENA VISTA — D3 *Rockbridge*

GLEN MAURY PARK (Public) From Jct of I-81 & US-60 (Buena Vista exit 188A), E 3.5 mi on US-60 to US-501S, S 2 mi to 10th St, W 0.25 mi, follow signs (R). 2015 rates: $27 to $32. (800)555-8845

CAPE CHARLES — D6 *Northampton*

KIPTOPEKE (State Pk) From Jct of US-13 & N end of The Chesapeake Bay Bridge Tunnel, N 3 mi on US-13 to Rte 704, W 0.5 mi (E). 2015 rates: $24 to $37. (757)331-2267

SUNSET BEACH INN & RV PARK
(RV Park) (Rebuilding) From Chesapeake Bay Bridge Tunnel & Hwy 13: Go 1/2 mi N on Hwy 13 from bridge toll booth (L). **FAC:** Paved/gravel rds. (94 spaces). 40 Avail: 20 grass, 20 dirt, 40 pull-thrus (28 x 44), 40 full hkups (30/50 amps), seasonal sites, cable, WiFi, rentals. **REC:** pool, Chesapeake Bay: swim, fishing, playground. Pets OK. 2015 rates: $39 to $49. Apr 1 to Dec 31.
(888)985-1761 Lat: 37.27990, Lon: -75.97210

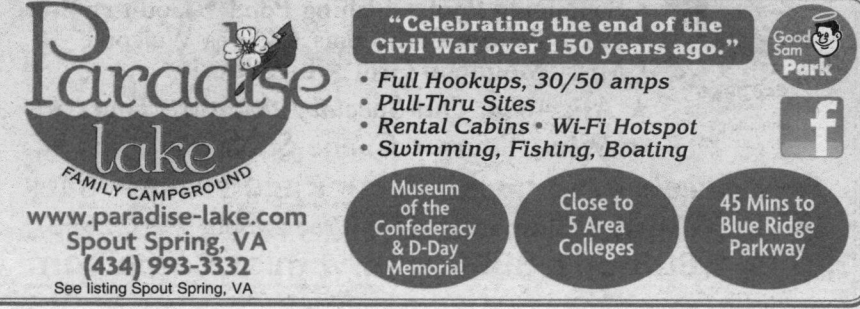

VA

CAPE CHARLES (CONT)

SUNSET BEACH INN & RV PARK (CONT)
32246 Lankford Highway, Cape Charles, VA 23310
frontdesk@sunsetbeachinn.com
www.sunsetbeachva.com
See ad page 1231.

CENTREVILLE — B4 *Fairfax*

BULL RUN REGIONAL PARK
(Public) From Jct of Rtes 28 & 29, S 3 mi on Rte 29 to Bull Run Post Office Rd, S 1.1 mi to Bull Run Dr, S 2 mi (R). Entrance fee required.

FUN FOR ALL & SPECTACULAR VIEWS
Bull Run's spacious fields accommodate groups by the hundreds, even thousands, for picnics, camping or special events. Bull Run's scenic woodland and trails offer miles of hiking and solitude. Come see us!

FAC: Paved rds. 89 gravel, 66 pull-thrus (30 x 55), back-ins (30 x 30), 32 full hkups, 57 E (30/50 amps), tent sites, rentals, dump, laundry, groc, LP gas, fire rings, firewood. **REC:** pool $, wading pool, Bull Run Stream: fishing, playground, rec open to public. Pets OK. Partial handicap access. 14 day max stay, 2015 rates: $30 to $45.50.
(703)631-0550 Lat: 38.801664, Lon: -77.491648
7700 Bull Run Dr, Centreville, VA 20121
bull_run@nvrpa.org
www.nvrpa.org
See ad pages 1238, 1232, 267, 1219 (Welcome Section).

CHARLOTTESVILLE — C3 *Albemarle*

CHARLOTTESVILLE KOA
Ratings: 9/9.5★/9 (Campground) From Jct of I-64 & SR20 (exit 121A), S 8 mi on SR20 to SR-708 (Red Hill Rd), W 1.5 mi (R). **FAC:** Paved/gravel rds. 45 gravel, 25 pull-thrus (25 x 65), back-ins (25 x 30), 40 full hkups, 5 W, 5 E (30/50 amps), cable, WiFi, tent sites, rentals, dump, laundry, groc, LP gas, fire rings, firewood. **REC:** pool, pond, fishing, playground. Pet restrict(Q). Eco-friendly, 2015 rates: $35 to $55. Mar 15 to Nov 13.
(434)296-9881 Lat: 37.93090, Lon: -78.56671
3825 Red Hill Rd, Charlottesville, VA 22903
charlottesville@koa.com
www.charlottesvillekoa.com
See ad this page.

"Full hookups" in a campground listing means there are water, electric and sewer hookups at the sites.

MISTY MOUNTAIN CAMP RESORT
Ratings: 9/9.5★/10 (Campground) From Jct of I-64 & US 250 (Exit 107/Crozet,13 miles W of Charlottesville), W 0.7 mi on US 250 (L). **FAC:** Paved/gravel rds. (122 spaces). Avail: 102 gravel, patios, 35 pull-thrus (30 x 70), back-ins (30 x 60), 78 full hkups, 24 W, 24 E (30/50 amps), seasonal sites, cable, WiFi, tent sites, rentals, dump, laundry, groc, LP gas, fire rings, firewood. **REC:** pool, pond, fishing, playground, rec open to public. Pet restrict(B/Q). Big rig sites, eco-friendly, 2015 rates: $38 to $55.
(888)647-8900 Lat: 38.03953, Lon: -78.73961
56 Misty Mountain Rd, Greenwood, VA 22943
contactus@mistymountaincampresort.com
www.mistycamp.com
See primary listing at Greenwood and ad this page.

CHERITON — D6 *Northampton*

CHERRYSTONE FAMILY CAMPING RESORT
Ratings: 9/9.5★/9.5 (Campground) From Jct of Chesapeake Bay Bridge Tunnel (N end) & US-13, N 11.1 mi on US-13 to SR-680, W 1.5 mi (E).

CHERRYSTONE FAMILY CAMPING RESORT
300 acres nestled along the beautiful lower Chesapeake Bay. Most of our sites are shaded by our tall growth pines and can accommodate almost any guest's rig or tent. Scenic water views with the best sunsets in Virginia.

FAC: Paved/gravel rds. (539 spaces). 503 Avail: 5 gravel, 498 grass, 100 pull-thrus (30 x 70), back-ins (30 x 45), 358 full hkups, 145 W, 145 E (30/50 amps), seasonal sites, WiFi, tent sites, rentals, dump, mobile sewer, laundry, groc, LP gas, firewood, restaurant. **REC:** pool, Chesapeake Bay: swim, fishing, shuffleboard, playground. Pet restrict(B/Q). Partial handicap access. Big rig sites, eco-friendly, 2015 rates: $17 to $68. ATM.
AAA Approved
(757)331-3063 Lat: 37.28557, Lon: -76.01077
1511 Townfield Dr, Cape Charles, VA 23310
info@cherrystoneva.com
www.cherrystoneva.com
See ad opposite page, 587, 584 (MD Map), 1217 (VA Map) & Family Camping, RV Trips of a Lifetime, ad page 103 in Magazine Section.

Things to See and Do

LITTLE NECK CAFE Family restaurant and ice cream shop. Serving breakfast, lunch and dinner. Restrooms, food. Hours: 11 am to 8 pm (weekend hrs in winter)
(757)331-4822 Lat: 37.28557, Lon: -76.01077
1511 Townfield Drive, Cheriton, VA 23316
bandbmarkets@gmail.com
See ad opposite page, 587, 584 (MD Map), 1217 (VA Map) & ad Magazine Section page 103.

See listing Cheriton, VA

CHESAPEAKE — E6 *Chesapeake City*

CHESAPEAKE CAMPGROUND Ratings: 7.5/6.5/6.5 (Campground) From Jct of I-64 & US-17 (Exit 296), S 4 mi on US-17 (L). **FAC:** Paved rds. (113 spaces). Avail: 10 paved, 10 pull-thrus (23 x 55), 10 W, 10 E (30 amps), seasonal sites, WiFi Hotspot, tent sites, rentals, dump, mobile sewer, laundry, groc, LP gas, fire rings, firewood, controlled access. **REC:** pool, pond, fishing, playground, rec open to public. Pet restrict(Q). 2015 rates: $30 to $37. AAA Approved
(757)485-0149 Lat: 36.7119, Lon: -76.3528
693 S George Washington Hwy, Chesapeake, VA 23323
chesapeakecampground@verizon.net
www.chesapeakecampgroundva.com

NORTHWEST RIVER PARK & CAMPGROUND (Public) From Jct Rt 168 & Hillcrest Pkwy E (Exit 86), S .25 mi to Battlefield Blvd, S on Battlefield Blvd to Indian Cree Rd, S .4 mi on Indian Creek Rd (R). 2015 rates: $21 to $26. Apr 1 to Nov 30. (757)421-7151

CHESTERFIELD — D4 *Chesterfield*

POCAHONTAS (State Pk) From Jct of I-95 & Hwy 10, W 7 mi on Hwy 10 to Beach Rd, S 4 mi (R). 2015 rates: $27. (804)796-4255

CHINCOTEAGUE — C6 *Accomack*

PINE GROVE CAMPGROUND & WATERFOWL PARK Ratings: 4.5/7/5.5 (Campground) From Jct of SR-175 & Main St across bridge (straight ahead Main St becomes Maddox Blvd) S 0.5 mi on Maddox Blvd. to Deep Hole Rd, E 0.8 mi (L). NOTE: RV size limit is 34 ft max. **FAC:** Gravel rds. (150 spaces). Avail: 100 grass, back-ins (20 x 35), mostly side by side hkups, 50 full hkups, 50 W, 50 E (30 amps), seasonal sites, cable, WiFi Hotspot, tent sites, groc, LP gas, firewood. **REC:** pool, pond. Pet restrict(B/Q). 2015 rates: $38 to $43. Disc: AAA. Apr 1 to Dec 1. AAA Approved
(757)336-5200 Lat: 37.93785, Lon: -75.35215
5283 Deep Hole Rd, Chincoteague, VA 23336
wjt_shore@verizon.net
www.pinegrovecampground.com

TALL PINES HARBOR WATERFRONT CAMPGROUND
Ratings: 9/10★/9.5 (Campground) From Jct of US-13 & VA-175 (west of Chincoteaque),S 3.7 mi on US-13 to Saxis Rd., W 6.7 mi(R). **FAC:** Gravel rds. (180 spaces). 120 Avail: 23 paved, 82 gravel, 15 grass, 67 pull-thrus (50 x 100), back-ins (24 x 50), 65 full hkups, 55 W, 55 E (30/50 amps), seasonal sites, cable, WiFi, tent sites, rentals, dump, mobile sewer, laundry, groc, LP gas, fire rings, firewood, controlled access. **REC:** pool, Pocomoke Sound: swim, fishing, playground. Pets OK. Partial handicap access. Big rig sites, eco-friendly, 2015 rates: $36 to $67. Mar 1 to Nov 1. ATM.
(757)824-0777 Lat: 37.93236, Lon: -75.65342
8107 Tall Pines Lane, Temperanceville, VA 23442
reservations@tallpinesharbor.com
www.tallpinesharbor.com
See primary listing at Temperanceville and ad page 1230 (Spotlight The Virginia Shoreline).

TOM'S COVE PARK
Ratings: 8/8.5★/8 (Campground) From Jct of SR-175 & Main St (in town), SW 1.5 mi on Main St to Beebe Rd, SE 0.25 mi (E). **FAC:** Paved/gravel rds. (920 spaces). Avail: 520 grass, 68 pull-thrus (35 x 50), back-ins (35 x 50), 240 full hkups, 280 W, 280 E (30/50 amps), seasonal sites, WiFi, tent sites, dump, laundry, groc, LP gas, firewood. **REC:** pool, Assateague Channel: fishing, playground. Pets OK. Partial handicap access. 2015 rates: $43 to $53. Mar 1 to Nov 30. ATM, no CC.
(757)336-6498 Lat: 37.91288, Lon: -75.38951
8128 Beebe Rd, Chincoteague, VA 23336
tomscovepark@verizon.net
www.tomscovepark.com
See ad this page.

CHINCOTEAGUE ISLAND — C6 *Accomack*

MADDOX FAMILY CAMPGROUND **Ratings: 6.5/8★/7** (Campground) 2015 rates: $44 to $56. Mar 1 to Nov 30. (757)336-3111 6742 Maddox Blvd, Chincoteague Island, VA 23336

CHRISTIANSBURG — D2 *Montgomery*

BLUE RIDGE PKWY/ROCKY KNOB CAMPGROUND (Natl Pk) From town, on Blue Ridge Parkway at MP-167 (R). 2015 rates: $16. May 24 to Nov 2. (540)745-9664

CLARKSVILLE — E3 *Mecklenburg*

IVY HILL CAMPGROUND DAY USE AREA (Public Corps) From town, S 10 mi on US-15 to NC-1501, E 7 mi to VA-825, N 3 mi (E). Pit toilets. 2015 rates: $10 to $12. Apr 1 to Oct 30. (434)738-6143

LONGWOOD CAMPGROUND (Public Corps) From town, S 4 mi on US-15 (R). 2015 rates: $18 to $36. Apr 1 to Oct 31. (434)374-2711

OCCONEECHEE (State Pk) From town: Go 1 mi E on US-58. Pit toilets. 2015 rates: $20 to $27. (804)374-2210

CLIFTON FORGE — C2 *Alleghany, Bath*

DOUTHAT (State Pk) From Jct of I-64 & SR-629 (exit 27), N 5 mi on SR-629 (R). 2015 rates: $26 to $27. May to Sep. (540)862-8100

THE BUCKHORNE COUNTRY STORE AND CAMPGROUND **Ratings: 6/6/7** (Campground) 2015 rates: $25 to $29. (877)301-3817 3508 Douthat Rd, Clifton Forge, VA 24422

CLINCHPORT — B2 *Scott*

NATURAL TUNNEL (State Pk) From Jct of US-23 & SR-871, E 1 mi on SR-871 (R). 2015 rates: $27. (276)940-2674

CLINTWOOD — A2 *Dickenson*

CRANE NEST CAMPSITE (COE-JOHN W FLANNAGAN RESERVOIR) (Public Corps) From town: Go 2 mi E on Hwy 83, then 3 mi W on FR. (276)835-9544

COLLIERSTOWN — D2 *Rockbridge*

LAKE A WILLIS ROBERTSON REC AREA (Public) From Jct of I-81 & US 60 (Exit 51), NW 2 mi on US 60 to US 11, SW 1 mi to SR-251, W 11 mi to SR-770, W 1.4 mi (R). Call park for reservations. Credit cards are not accepted. 2015 rates: $30. Apr 1 to Oct 30. (540)463-4164

COLONIAL BEACH — C5 *Westmoreland*

MONROE BAY CAMPGROUND
Ratings: 6/8★/7.5 (Campground) From Jct of Hwy 3 & Hwy 205: N 4 mi on Hwy 205 to Hwy 628 (Monroe Bay Circle), E 2 mi on Hwy 628 (Monroe Bay Circle) (E). **FAC:** Paved/gravel rds. (310 spaces). Avail: 60 gravel, 30 pull-thrus (25 x 50), back-ins (25 x 50), 12 full hkups, 48 W, 48 E (30/50 amps), seasonal sites, WiFi Hotspot, tent sites, dump, groc, LP gas, firewood. **REC:** Monroe Bay: swim, playground. Pets OK. 2015 rates: $35 to $45. Apr 1 to Nov 1. ATM.
(804)224-7418 Lat: 38.23932, Lon: -76.96856
1412 Monroe Bay Circle, Colonial Beach, VA 22443
cpc1932@verizon.net
www.monroebaycampground.com
See ad this page.

CUMBERLAND — D4 *Cumberland*

BEAR CREEK LAKE (State Pk) From town: Go 1/2 mi E on US-60, then 4-1/2 mi W on Hwy-622 & 629. 2015 rates: $20 to $30. Mar 1 to Dec 7. (804)492-4410

DAMASCUS — B2 *Washington*

LAUREL CREEK RV PARK Ratings: 3.5/NA/7.5 (Campground) From jct of US 58 & Orchard Hill Rd, SE 1 mi on Orchard Hill Rd (go over one lane bridge) (L). **FAC:** Gravel rds. 15 gravel back-ins (30 x 55), accepts full hkup units only, 15 full hkups (30/50 amps), WiFi. **REC:** Laurel Creek: swim, fishing. Pets OK. 2015 rates: $35. No CC.
(423)440-3042 Lat: 36.62941, Lon: -81.78005
812 Orchard Hill Rd, Damascus, VA 24236
laurelcreekrvpark@gmail.com
www.laurelcreekrvpark.com

DOSWELL — C4 *Hanover*

KINGS DOMINION CAMP WILDERNESS
Ratings: 9/9.5★/9.5 (Campground) From Jct of I-95 (exit 98/Doswell/Kings Dominion) & SR-30, E 0.6 mi on SR-30 (R).

CREATE MEMORIES AT KINGS DOMINION
Something for the whole family, in our newly updated campground, with pristine big rig sites, deluxe cabins and tent sites. Perfectly situated for family fun, with a complimentary shuttle to the Kings Dominion Amusement Park.

FAC: Paved rds. 180 Avail: 73 paved, 107 gravel, 34 pull-thrus (25 x 60), back-ins (30 x 55), some side by side hkups, 84 full hkups, 96 W, 96 E (30/50 amps), WiFi, tent sites, rentals, dump, laundry, groc, LP gas, fire rings, firewood. **REC:** pool. Pets OK. Partial handicap access. Big rig sites, eco-friendly, 2015 rates: $38 to $75. Disc: AAA, military. ATM.
(804)876-3006 Lat: 37.84917, Lon: -77.43954
10061 Kings Dominion Blvd, Doswell, VA 23047
camper@kingsdominion.com
www.kingsdominion.com
See ad pages 265 (Welcome Section), 1220.

Things to See and Do

KINGS DOMINION THEME PARK Family theme park of over 100 rides and attractions including Nickelodeon Central for children, plus Water Works Water Park. Voted Virginia's most exciting theme park. Apr 1 to Oct 31. partial handicap access. RV accessible. Restrooms, food. Hours: 10am to 10pm. Adult fee: $65. ATM.
(804)876-5400 Lat: 37.84729, Lon: -77.44538
16000 Theme Park Way, Doswell, VA 23047
info@kingsdominion.com
www.cedarfair.com/kingsdominion
See ad page 265 (Welcome Section).

DUBLIN — D1 *Pulaski*

CLAYTOR LAKE (State Pk) From Jct of I-81 & SR-660 (exit 101), S 2 mi on SR-660/State Park Rd (E). NOTE: Each pet incurs a $3 per day fee. 2015 rates: $20 to $27. Mar 1 to Dec 2. (540)643-2500

DUMFRIES — B5 *Prince William*

PRINCE WILLIAM FOREST RV CAMPGROUND
Ratings: 8.5/9★/9 (RV Park) From Jct of I-95 & SR-234 (exit 152B/Manassas), NW 2.5 mi on SR-234 (L). CAUTION: 42' max length. **FAC:** Paved rds. 72 paved, 54 pull-thrus (24 x 45), back-ins (24 x 35), 36 full hkups, 36 W, 36 E (30/50 amps), WiFi, tent sites, dump, laundry, LP gas, firewood. **REC:** pool, playground. Pets OK. Partial handicap

UMFRIES (CONT)

PRINCE WILLIAM FOREST RV (CONT)
:cess. 14 day max stay, eco-friendly, 2015 rates: 34 to $52.
AA Approved
88)737-5730 Lat: 38.60398, Lon: -77.35073
058 Dumfries Rd, Dumfries, VA 22025
rincewilliamrv@racpack.com
ww.princewilliamforestrvcampground.com
ee ad pages 267, 1220.

DINBURG — B3 *Shenandoah*

CREEKSIDE CAMPGROUND **Ratings: 6/8.5★/7.5** (Campground) 2015 rates: $30 to 50. (540)984-4299 108 Palmyra Rd, Edinburg, VA 2824

LKTON — C3 *Madison, Rockingham*

SHENANDOAH/BIG MEADOWS (Natl Pk) From wn, E 9 mi on Rte 211 to Skyline Dr, S 19 mi MP-51), follow signs (R). Entrance fee required. 015 rates: $20 to $32. Apr 26 to Nov 30. (540)999-500

SHENANDOAH/LEWIS MOUNTAIN (Natl Pk) rom town, E 7 mi on Rte 33 to Skyline Dr, N 7 mi, llow signs to MP-57 (R). Entrance fee required. 015 rates: $15. May to Dec. (540)999-3500

SHENANDOAH/LOFT MOUNTAIN (Natl Pk) rom town, E 5 mi on Rte 250 to Skyline Dr, N 25 mi, llow signs (R). Entrance fee required. 2015 rates: 15. May 13 to Oct 30. (540)999-3500

MPORIA — E4 *Greensville*

YOGI BEAR'S JELLYSTONE PARK CAMP-RESORT EMPORIA
Ratings: 9/9★/8.5 (Campground) From Jct of I-95 & US-301 (Exit 17), S 1.4 mi on US-301 (R). **FAC:** Gravel rds. (107 spaces). Avail: 75 gravel, 54 pull-thrus 25 x 60), back-ins (22 x 50), 54 full hkups, 21 W, 21 (30/50 amps), seasonal sites, cable, WiFi, tent tes, rentals, dump, laundry, groc, LP gas, fire rings, rewood. **REC:** pool, playground, rec open to public. ets OK. Big rig sites, 2015 rates: $37 to $45. Disc: AA, military.
434)634-3115 Lat: 36.74942, Lon: -77.48928
940 Sussex Dr, Emporia, VA 23847
anageremporiayogibear@gmail.com
ww.campingbear.com
See ad this page, 1220.

WING — B1 *Lee*

CUMBERLAND GAP NATL HIST ARK/WILDERNESS ROAD (Natl Pk) From Jct of S-25E & US-58, E 1.5 mi on US-58 (L). 2015 rates: 14 to $20. (606)248-2817

Had a great stay? Let us know by emailing us ravelguidecomments@goodsamfamily.com

FAIRFAX — B5 *Fairfax*

BURKE LAKE PARK (Public) From Jct of I-495 & exit 54, W 1.8 mi Braddock Rd. to Burke Lake Rd, S 4.5 mi, (L). 2015 rates: $28. Apr 18 to Oct 26. (703)323-6600

LAKE FAIRFAX PARK (Public Corps) From Jct of I-495 & Rte 7 (Exit 47A), W 6.5 mi on Rte 7 to Rte 606, S 0.1 mi to Lake Fairfax Dr, turn left (E). 2015 rates: $28 to $45. Mar 22 to Sep 7. (703)471-5415

FANCY GAP — E1 *Carroll*

FANCY GAP / BLUE RIDGE PARKWAY KOA **Ratings: 9/10★/10** (Campground) 2015 rates: $38 to $55. Mar 1 to Nov 15. (800)562-1876 47 Fox Trail Loop, Fancy Gap, VA 24328

UTT'S CAMPGROUND **Ratings: 7.5/8.5★/8** (Campground) 2015 rates: $28. May 1 to Nov 1. (276)728-7203 574 Campground Road, Fancy Gap, VA 24328

FERRUM — E2 *Franklin*

DEER RUN CAMPGROUND **Ratings: 5/8★/7** (Campground) 2015 rates: $25 to $28. May 23 to Nov 1. (276)930-1235 28 Fawn Road, Ferrum, VA 24088

HORSESHOE POINT PARK (Public Corps) From town, SE 7 mi on Rte 767 to Henry Rd, NW 3 mi to Horse Point Rd, W 4 mi (E). 2015 rates: $18 to $25. May 1 to Sep 29. (276)629-2703

SALTHOUSE BRANCH PARK (Public Corps) From town, W 2.5 mi on Henry Rd to Knob Church Rd/Salthouse Branch Rd, SW 2 mi (E). 2015 rates: $20 to $25. Mar 1 to Oct 31. (540)365-7005

FREDERICKSBURG — C4 *Spotsylvania*

FREDERICKSBURG See also Dumfries, Spotsylvania, Stafford.

FREDERICKSBURG/WASHINGTON DC SOUTH KOA **Ratings: 9/9.5★/9** (Campground) 2015 rates: $38 to $76.95. (800)562-1889 7400 Brookside Lane, Fredericksburg, VA 22408

FRIES — E1 *Grayson*

FRIES NEW RIVER TRAIL RV PARK **Ratings: 6/9★/9** (RV Park) 2015 rates: $38. (276)744-7566 26 Dalton Rd, Fries, VA 24330

FRONT ROYAL — B4 *Warren*

FRONT ROYAL RV CAMPGROUND
Ratings: 7.5/7.5/6.5 (Campground) From Jct of I-66 & US 340 (Exit 6), S 6.3 mi on US 340 to KOA Rd, E 0.6 mi to entrance (E). **FAC:** Paved/gravel rds. (150 spaces). Avail: 96 gravel, 34 pull-thrus (24 x 55), back-ins (20 x 45), some side by side hkups, 42 full hkups, 54 W, 54 E (30 amps), seasonal sites, WiFi, tent sites, rentals, dump, laundry, LP gas, fire rings, firewood. **REC:** pool, pond, fishing, playground, rec open to public. Pets OK. Partial handicap access. 2015 rates: $38 to $49. Disc: military. Apr 1 to Nov 1.
AAA Approved
(540)635-2741 Lat: 38.88839, Lon: -78.23032
585 Koa Drive, Front Royal, VA 22630
frrvcampground@aol.com
www.frontroyalcamp.com
See ad this page.

NORTH FORK RESORT
Ratings: 8/7.5/8 (Membership Pk) From Jct I-66 & Hwy 340 (Exit 6), S 1 mi on Hwy 340 to Hwy 55 (Strasburg Rd) W 2 mi on Hwy 55 to Homestead Rd, NE 0.3 mi (E). **FAC:** Paved/gravel rds. (500 spaces). Avail: 470 gravel, 50 pull-thrus (30 x 50), back-ins (30 x 50), 440 full hkups, 30 W, 30 E (30/50 amps), seasonal sites, WiFi Hotspot $, tent sites, rentals, dump, laundry, groc, LP gas, fire rings, firewood, controlled access. **REC:** pool, North Fork River: fishing, shuffleboard, playground. Pet restrict(B). 14 day max stay, 2015 rates: $42.
AAA Approved
(540)636-2995 Lat: 38.95503, Lon: -78.22952
301 North Fork Rd, Front Royal, VA 22630
res1@nfra.com
www.nfra.com
See ad this page, 1220.

SKYLINE RANCH RESORT **Ratings: 8.5/8★/8.5** (Membership Pk) 2015 rates: $60. (540)635-4169 751 Mountain Rd, Front Royal, VA 22630

GALAX — E1 *Grayson*

COOL BREEZE CAMPGROUND **Ratings: 7/9★/9** (Campground) 2015 rates: $34. Apr 1 to Nov 1. (866)342-0300 2330 Edmonds Road, Galax, VA 24333

OLD CRANKS CAMPGROUND & RV PARK
Ratings: 2.5/7/6.5 (Campground) From Jct of I-77 & US-58/US-221 (Exit 14), W 9.9 mi on US-58/US-221 to SR-89, S 0.4 mi to Grayson St, W 0.1 mi to Railroad Ave, S 0.5 mi (L). **FAC:** Gravel rds. 15 gravel, 15 pull-thrus (30 x 60), 15 full hkups (30/50 amps), tent sites. **REC:** rec open to public. No pets. Big rig sites, 2015 rates: $30. No CC.
(276)236-5114 Lat: 36.65587, Lon: -80.91887
407 Railroad Avenue, Galax, VA 24333
luv2fly53p@tcia.net
www.oldcranks.com

GASBURG — E4 *Brunswick*

LAKESIDE RESORT **Ratings: 8/6.5/6** (Membership Pk) 2015 rates: $40. Apr 1 to Oct 15. (434)577-2194 300 Lake Resort Dr, Gasburg, VA 23857

Follow the arrow. The arrow in each listing indicates where the facility is located in relation to the listed town.

We rate what RVers consider important.

See listing Hillsville, VA

GLEN ALLEN — D4 *Hanover*

KOSMO VILLAGE CAMPGROUND
Ratings: 4.5/NA/6.5 (Campground) From Jct of I-95 & Lewistown Rd (Exit 89-Rt 802), W 1 mi on Lewistown Rd to US 1 (Washington Hwy), S 0.2 mi (R). **FAC:** Gravel rds. 17 gravel, 11 pull-thrus (35 x 75), back-ins (35 x 50), accepts full hkup units only, 17 full hkups (30/50 amps), WiFi. **REC:** playground. Pets OK. No tents. Big rig sites, 2015 rates: $35.
(804)798-6689 Lat: 37.71038, Lon: -77.46684
11197 Washington Hwy (US1), Glen Allen, VA 23059
info@kosmovillage.com
www.kosmovillage.com
See ad page 1240.

GLOUCESTER POINT — D5 *Gloucester*

GLOUCESTER POINT See also Gwynn, New Point, Toano, Topping, Urbanna, Virginia Beach & Williamsburg.

YOGI BEAR'S JELLYSTONE PARK CAMP-RESORT AT GLOUCESTER POINT **Ratings: 9/9★/8.5** (Campground) 2015 rates: $39 to $75. (800)332-4316 3149 Campground Rd, Hayes, VA 23072

GORDONSVILLE — C4 *Orange*

SHENANDOAH CROSSING **Ratings: 8.5/9.5★/9.5** (Membership Pk) 2015 rates: $50. (540)832-9400 174 Horseshoe Cir, Gordonsville, VA 22942

GREEN BAY — D4 *Prince Edward*

TWIN LAKES (State Pk) From town, SW 4 mi on US-360 to SR-613, N 2 mi to SR-629, E 1 mi (E). 2015 rates: $27. (434)392-3435

GREENVILLE — C3 *Augusta*

STONEY CREEK RESORT CAMPGROUND **Ratings: 7.5/7/5.5** (Membership Pk) 2015 rates: $37 to $50. Apr 1 to Oct 31. (540)337-1510 277 Lake Dr, Greenville, VA 24440

GREENWOOD — C3 *Albemarle*

MISTY MOUNTAIN CAMP RESORT
Ratings: 9/9.5★/10 (Campground) From Jct of I-64 (exit 107/Crozet) & US-250 (13 mi W of Charlottesville), W 0.7 mi on US-250 (L). **FAC:** Paved/gravel rds. (122 spaces). Avail: 102 gravel, patios, 35 pull-thrus (30 x 70), back-ins (30 x 60), 78 full hkups, 24 W, 24 E (30/50 amps), seasonal sites, cable, WiFi, tent sites, rentals, dump, laundry, groc, LP gas, fire rings, firewood. **REC:** pool, pond, fishing, playground, rec open to public. Pet restrict(B/Q). Big rig sites, eco-friendly, 2015 rates: $38 to $55.
AAA Approved
(888)647-8900 Lat: 38.03953, Lon: -78.73961
56 Misty Mountain Rd, Greenwood, VA 22943
contactus@mistymountaincampresort.com
www.mistycamp.com
See ad pages 1232, 1220.

GWYNN — D6 *Mathews*

GWYNN'S ISLAND RV RESORT & CAMPGROUND
Ratings: 6/9.5★/8.5 (Campground) From Jct of US 17 & SR 198 (in Glenns), SE 21 mi on SR 198 to Rte 223 (Cricket Hill Rd), SW 0.5 mi to drawbridge (clearance 13 ft 9 in). Name changes over the bridge to Rte 633 (Old Ferry Rd), continue 2.1 mi on Rte 633, then SE 1 mi (at curve) on Rte 633 to Rte 740 (Buckchase Rd), SE 0.5 mi (L).

WELCOME TO HISTORIC GWYNN'S ISLAND
Located right on the Chesapeake Bay, Gwynn's Island is a great spot for boating, fishing or relaxing at the beach. Take in spectacular views from the fishing pier or explore the many waterways with the kayak and canoe launch.

FAC: Gravel rds. (126 spaces). Avail: 30 grass, 3 pull-thrus (30 x 50), back-ins (30 x 40), 30 W, 30 E (30 amps), seasonal sites, WiFi, tent sites, rentals, dump, mobile sewer, LP gas. **REC:** Chesapeake Bay: swim, playground. Pet restrict(B/Q). Eco-friendly, 2015 rates: $35 to $52. Apr 1 to Oct 31.
AAA Approved
(888)699-4397 Lat: 37.49088, Lon: -76.27467
551 Buckchase Rd., Gwynn, VA 23066
gwynnsisland@suncommunities.com
www.gwynnsislandrvresort.com
See ad pages 1463 (Welcome Section), 1220, 1229 (Spotlight The Virginia Shoreline) & Family Camping in Magazine Section.

RV Park ratings you can rely on!

HARRISONBURG — C3 *Rockingham*

HARRISONBURG/SHENANDOAH VALLEY KOA
Ratings: 8.5/9.5★/9 (Campground) From Jct of I-81 & US 33 (Exit247B, E of Harrisonburg), N 10.6 mi on I-81 to US 11(Exit 257,Jackson-Lee Memorial Hwy), N 100 yds to SR 608 (Mauzy-Athlone Rd., E 3.2 mi on SR 608/Mauzy-Athlone Rd. (E) Note: Entrance straight ahead past stop sign. **FAC:** Gravel rds. 62 gravel, 36 pull-thrus (26 x 60), back-ins (26 x 45), 41 full hkups, 21 W, 21 E (30/50 amps), cable, WiFi, tent sites, rentals, dump, laundry, groc, LP gas, fire rings, firewood. **REC:** heated pool, pond, fishing, playground. Pets OK. Big rig sites, eco-friendly, 2015 rates: $38 to $65. ATM.
(540)896-8929 Lat: 38.53324, Lon: -78.70470
12480 Mountain Valley Road, Broadway, VA 22815
shenandoahvalleykoa@yahoo.com
www.koa.com/campgrounds/Harrisonburg
See primary listing at Broadway and ad page 1227 (Spotlight Shenandoah Valley).

HAYMARKET — B4 *Prince William*

GREENVILLE FARM FAMILY CAMPGROUND
Ratings: 6.5/7/6.5 (Campground) From Jct of I-66 & US-15 (Exit 40), N 4 mi on US-15 to Rte 234 (Sudley Rd), SE 0.1 mi on Sudley Rd to Rte 601 (Shelter Lane), NE 1.3 mi on Shelter Lane (L). **FAC:** Paved/gravel rds. (125 spaces). Avail: 116 gravel, 46 pull-thrus (25 x 70), back-ins (20 x 50), some side by side hkups, 21 full hkups, 95 W, 95 E (30/50 amps), seasonal sites, tent sites, dump, laundry, LP gas, firewood. **REC:** pool, pond, fishing, playground. Pets OK. Partial handicap access. 2015 rates: $35 to $38.
(703)754-7944 Lat: 38.87638, Lon: -77.61081
14004 Shelter Lane, Haymarket, VA 20169
www.greenvillecampground.com
See ad page 266.

HAYSI — A2 *Dickenson*

BREAKS INTERSTATE PARK (State Pk) From Jct of SR-768 & SR-80, W 0.5 mi on SR-80 (R). 2015 rates: $15 to $24. Mar 1 to Dec 2. (276)865-4413

LOWER TWIN CAMPGROUND (COE-JOHN W FLANNAGAN RESERVOIR) (Public Corps) From town: Go 3 mi SW on Hwy-63, then 1/2 mi S on Hwy-614, then 2 mi NW on Hwy-739, then W on Hwy-611. 2015 rates: $5 to $6. May 11 to Oct 17. (270)835-9544

HILLSVILLE — E1 *Carroll*

LAKE RIDGE RV RESORT
Ratings: 9/9.5★/8.5 (Campground) From Jct of I-77 & US 58/221 (Exit 14), E 4.5 mi on US 221 to SR 100, N 4 mi on SR 100 to SR 783, SE 0.5 to SR 753 (Double Cabin Rd), E 0.5 mi (L) Note: Follow signs. Elev 2551 ft.

A MEMORABLE CAMPING EXPERIENCE
Enjoy the majestic Blue Ridge Mountains and Virginia area attractions, along with the two 400' waterslides, the two giant pools, and the lake activities, play mini-golf or simply relax with a good book.

FAC: Paved/gravel rds. (221 spaces). Avail: 138 gravel, 32 pull-thrus (40 x 70), back-ins (24 x 50), some side by side hkups, 101 full hkups, 37 W, 37 E (30/50 amps), seasonal sites, cable, WiFi, tent sites, rentals, dump, laundry, groc, LP gas, fire rings, firewood. **REC:** heated pool, wading pool, 4 Acre Lake: fishing, playground, rec open to public. Pet restrict(B/Q). Partial handicap access. Big rig sites, eco-friendly, 2015 rates: $34 to $57. ATM.
(866)513-1773 Lat: 36.83354, Lon: -80.71375
8736 Double Cabin Road, Hillsville, VA 24343
info@lakeridgerv.com
www.lakeridgerv.com
See ad opposite page, 1220 & Family Camping in Magazine Section.

HUDDLESTON — D3 *Bedford*

SMITH MOUNTAIN LAKE (State Pk) From jct Hwy 43 & Hwy 626: Go 14 mi SW on Hwy 626. 2015 rates: $20 to $27. (540)297-6066

KEELING — E3 *Pittsylvania*

PARADISE LAKE & CAMPGROUND
Ratings: 8.5/9★/8 (Campground) From Jct of US 29/Danville Expy & SR-726/Malmaison Rd (South of Blairs), E 0.7 mi on SR-726/Malmaison Rd to SR-716/Keeling Dr, NE 1.6 mi (L). **FAC:** Gravel rds. (64 spaces). Avail: 30 gravel, 11 pull-thrus (20 x 75), back-ins (20 x 30), 30 full hkups (30/50 amps), seasonal sites, WiFi, tent sites, rentals, dump, laundry, groc, fire rings, firewood. **REC:** pool, Paradise Lake: fishing, playground, rec open to public. Pet restrict(B). 2015 rates: $37.38 to $39.49. Disc: military.
(434)836-2620 Lat: 36.70186, Lon: -79.33355
593 Keeling Drive, Keeling, VA 24566
paradiselakeandcampground@verizon.net
www.campinparadise.com

LANEXA — D5 *New Kent*

ROCKAHOCK CAMPGROUNDS & RESORT RV PARK
Ratings: 8.5/8.5★/9.5 (Campground) From Jct. US 60 & Rte 649 (Rockahock Rd), SE 1 mi on 649, S 0.5 mi on Outpost Rd (E). **FAC:** Gravel rds. (500 spaces). 240 Avail: 6 paved, 204 gravel, 30 grass, patios, 98 pull-thrus (35 x 90), back-ins (35 x 98), 210 full hkups, 30 W, 30 E (30/50 amps), seasonal sites, cable, WiFi, tent sites, rentals, dump, laundry, groc, LP gas, fire rings, firewood, restaurant. **REC:** pool, Chickahominy River & Lake: swim, fishing, playground, rec open to public. Pet restrict(B). Partial handicap access. Big rig sites, eco-friendly, 2015 rates: $43 to $63. ATM.
(804)966-8362 Lat: 37.41452, Lon: -76.93736
1428 Outpost Rd, Lanexa, VA 23089
reservations@rockahock.com
www.rockahock.com

LEXINGTON — D3 *Rockbridge*

LEE HI CAMPGROUND
Ratings: 6.5/8.5★/6 (Campground) From Jct of I-81 and US 11 (Exit 195), S 0.75 mi on US 11 (L). **FAC:** Paved/gravel rds. (38 spaces). Avail: 33 gravel, 10 pull-thrus (24 x 60), back-ins (24 x 45), 18 full hkups, 15 W, 15 E (30/50 amps), seasonal sites, WiFi Hotspot $, tent sites, dump, laundry, groc, firewood, restaurant. **REC.** Pets OK. 2015 rates: $35. ATM.
(540)463-3478 Lat: 37.83161, Lon: -79.37811
2516 North Lee Hwy, Lexington, VA 24450
tcummings@leehi.com
www.leehi.com
See ad this page, 1220.

Travel Services

LEE HI TRAVEL PLAZA Open 24 hrs. Gas, diesel and food. **SERVICES:** Tire, MH mechanical, restaurant, restrooms. RV storage. RV supplies, dump, emergency parking, RV accessible. waiting room. Hours: 24 Hrs. ATM.
(540)463-3478 Lat: 37.83161, Lon: -79.37811
2516 North Lee Hwy, Lexington, VA 24450
tcummings@leehi.com
www.leehi.com
See ad this page.

Things to See and Do

BERKY'S RESTAURANT Open 24 hrs. RV accessible. Restrooms, food. Hours: 24 hrs. ATM.
(540)463-3478 Lat: 37.82771, Lon: -79.37402
2516 North Lee Hwy, Lexington, VA 24450
berkys@leehi.com
www.leehi.com
See ad this page.

LORTON — B5 *Fairfax*

POHICK BAY REGIONAL PARK
(Public) From Jct of I-95 & US1 (Ft. Belvoir exit 161), N 1.9 mi to Gunston Rd, SE 2 mi to park entrance (L). **FAC:** Paved rds. 150 gravel, back-ins (20 x 35), 10 full hkups, 14 W, 140 E (30/50 amps), tent sites, rentals, dump, laundry, LP gas, fire rings, firewood. **REC:** pool $, wading pool, Pohick Bay: fishing, golf, playground, rec open to public. Pets OK. Partial handicap access. 14 day max stay, 2015 rates: $30 to $45.50.
(703)339-6104 Lat: 38.671808, Lon: -77.174016
6501 Pohick Bay Dr, Lorton, VA 22079
pohick@nvrpa.org
www.nvrpa.org
See ad pages 1238, 1232, 267, 1219 (Welcome Section).

VA

LOUISA — C4 *Louisa*

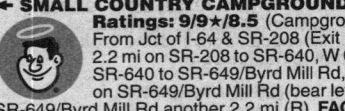

SMALL COUNTRY CAMPGROUND **Ratings: 9/9★/8.5** (Campground) From Jct of I-64 & SR-208 (Exit 143), NE 2.2 mi on SR-208 to SR-640, W 0.2 mi on SR-640 to SR-649/Byrd Mill Rd, N 2.2 mi on SR-649/Byrd Mill Rd (bear left), follow SR-649/Byrd Mill Rd another 2.2 mi (R). **FAC:** Gravel rds. (193 spaces). Avail: 169 gravel, 28 pull-thrus (25 x 60), back-ins (28 x 50), 102 full hkups, 67 W, 67 E (30/50 amps), seasonal sites, WiFi, tent sites, rentals, dump, mobile sewer, laundry, groc, LP bottles, fire rings, firewood. **REC:** pool, Lake Ruth Ann: swim, fishing, playground, rec open to public. Pet restrict(B). Partial handicap access. Big rig sites, eco-friendly, 2015 rates: $32 to $50. Disc: AAA, military.
AAA Approved
(540)967-2431 Lat: 38.02031, Lon: -78.09356
4400 Byrd Mill Rd, Louisa, VA 23093
camp@smallcountry.com
www.smallcountry.com
See ad page 1232.

LURAY — B3 *Page*

LURAY KOA **Ratings: 9.5/9.5★/10** (RV Park) From Jct of US 211 & US 340 (in Luray), N 2.3 mi on US 340 to SR-658/Kimball Rd, E 0.25 mi (L); or From Jct of I-66 & US 340 (Exit 6), S 23 mi on US 340 to SR-658/Kimball Rd, E 0.25 mi (L). **FAC:** Paved/gravel rds. 78 Avail: 78 all weather, 26 pull-thrus (40 x 70), back-ins (40 x 60), 78 full hkups (30/50 amps), WiFi, tent sites, rentals, laundry, fire rings, firewood. **REC:** pool, playground. Pets OK. Big rig sites, 2015 rates: $54 to $61. Mar 15 to Nov 15.
(800)562-2790 Lat: 38.70123, Lon: -78.43793
3402 Kimball Rd, Luray, VA 22835
camp@luraykoa.com
www.luraykoa.com

YOGI BEAR'S JELLYSTONE PARK CAMP-RESORT **Ratings: 8.5/8.5★/9** (Campground) From Jct of I-81 (exit 264) & US-211, E 18.1 mi on US-211 (R); or From Jct of Skyline Dr & US-211, W 5 mi on US-211 (L). **FAC:** Paved/gravel rds. 172 gravel, 87 pull-thrus (28 x 60), back-ins (28 x 50), 117 full hkups, 55 W, 55 E (30/50 amps), WiFi, tent sites, rentals, dump, laundry, groc, LP gas, fire rings, firewood. **REC:** pool, wading pool, pond, fishing, playground. Pet restrict(Q). Partial handicap access. Big rig sites, eco-friendly, 2015 rates: $40 to $106. Mar 30 to Nov 28. ATM.
(800)420-6679 Lat: 38.67333, Lon: -78.39173
2250 US Hwy 211 E, Luray, VA 22835
yogi@campluray.com
www.campluray.com

LYNCHBURG — D3 *Lynchburg City*

LYNCHBURG See also Appomattox, Monroe, Rustburg & Spout Spring.

MADISON — C4 *Madison*

MADISON/SHENANDOAH HILLS CAMPGROUND **Ratings: 9/9★/9** (Campground) From Jct of I-64 & US 29 (Exit 118), N 28 mi on US 29 (L). **FAC:** Paved/gravel rds. (64 spaces). 57 Avail: 45 gravel, 12 dirt, 16 pull-thrus (30 x 65), back-ins (30 x 37), 56 full hkups, 1 W, 1 E (30/50 amps), seasonal sites, cable, WiFi, tent sites, rentals, dump, laundry, groc, LP gas, fire rings, firewood, controlled access. **REC:** pool, pond, fishing, playground. Pet restrict(B). Big rig sites, eco-friendly, 2015 rates: $37 to $49. Disc: AAA.
AAA Approved
(540)948-4186 Lat: 38.35417, Lon: -78.28205
110 Campground Lane, Madison, VA 22727
ateam143@msn.com
www.shenandoahhills.com
See ad this page, 1220 & RV Trips of a Lifetime in Magazine Section.

MARION — E1 *Smyth*

HUNGRY MOTHER (State Pk) From Jct of I-81 & US-11 (exit 47), W 1 mi on US-11 to SR-16, N 4 mi (L). CAUTION: 35 ft max length on road through park (NOTE: $5 per day fee for each pet). 2015 rates: $20 to $30. (276)781-7400

MARTINSVILLE — E2 *Henry*

INDIAN HERITAGE RV PARK **Ratings: 6/9★/6.5** (RV Park) From Jct of US 220/Greensboro Rd & US 58 (A.L. Philpott Hwy), south of Martinsville. S 0.2 mi on US 220/ Greensboro Rd, to Tensbury Drive, E 0.1 mi (L). **FAC:** Gravel rds. (30 spaces). Avail: 22 gravel, patios, 11 pull-thrus (22 x 70), back-ins (24 x 60), 22 full hkups (30/50 amps), seasonal sites, WiFi, tent sites, rentals, dump, laundry, firewood. **REC:** Smith River: fishing. Pets OK. Eco-friendly, 2015 rates: $35.
(276)632-9500 Lat: 36.65770, Lon: -79.87880
184 Tensbury Dr, Martinsville, VA 24112
indianhrvp@outlook.com
www.indianheritagervpark.net

MEADOWS OF DAN — E2 *Patrick*

MEADOWS OF DAN CAMPGROUND **Ratings: 5.5/9★/7.5** (Campground) From Jct of US-58 Bus & Blue Ridge Parkway (MP 177.7), W 350 yds on US-58 (L). Elev 2900 ft. **FAC:** Paved/gravel rds. 26 gravel, 8 pull-thrus (32 x 60), back-ins (22 x 50), 26 full hkups (30/50 amps), WiFi Hotspot, tent sites, rentals, dump, laundry, fire rings, firewood. **REC:** pond, fishing, playground. Pets OK. Big rig sites, 2015 rates: $30 to $32.
AAA Approved
(866)952-2292 Lat: 36.73408, Lon: -80.41582
2182 Jeb Stuart Hwy, Meadows of Dan, VA 24120
modcampground@embarqmail.com
www.meadowsofdancampground.com
See ad this page.

MILFORD — C4 *Caroline*

HIDDEN ACRES FAMILY CAMPGROUND **Ratings: 6.5/7/6.5** (Campground) 2015 rates: $34 to $40. (804)633-7592 17391 Richmond Turnpike, Milford, VA 22514

R & D FAMILY CAMPGROUND **Ratings: 7.5/9★/8.5** (Campground) N-bnd: From Jct of I-95 & SR-30 (Exit 98), E 4 mi on SR-30 to US-301/SR-2 (Richmond Tpke), N 13 mi to SR-721/Sparta Rd, SE 4.5 mi (L); or S-bnd: From Jct of I-95 & SR 207 (Exit 104), NE 11 mi on SR-207 to US-301/SR-2 (Richmond Tpke), S 2.7 mi to SR-721/Sparta Rd, SE 4.5 mi (L). **FAC:** Gravel rds. (45 spaces). Avail: 35 gravel, 17 pull-thrus (25 x 55), back-ins (25 x 40), 35 full hkups (30/50 amps), seasonal sites, WiFi Hotspot, tent sites, rentals, dump, mobile sewer, laundry, groc, LP gas, fire rings, firewood. **REC:** pool, playground. Pet restrict(B). 2015 rates: $33. Disc: military.
(804)633-9515 Lat: 37.98732, Lon: -77.26550
22085 Sparta Rd (Rt 721), Milford, VA 22514
rdcampground@aol.com
www.rdfamilycampground.homestead.com
See ad pages 1235, 1220.

Everyone wants to be noticed. Tell your RV Park that you found them in the this Guide.

MINERAL — C4 *Louisa*

CHRISTOPHER RUN CAMPGROUND **Ratings: 6.5/8.5★/8.5** (Campground) From Jct of I-64 & Rte 522 (exit 159), N 27 mi on Rte 522 (R); or From Jct of I-95 & Rte 3 (exit 130B), W 12 mi on Rte 3 to Rte 20, SW 13 mi to Rte 522, S 13.3 mi, (on Lake Anna) (L). **FAC:** Gravel rds. (186 spaces). Avail: 106 gravel, 4 pull-thrus (22 x 55), back-ins (22 x 50), some side by side hkups, 36 full hkups, 70 W, 70 E (30/50 amps), seasonal sites, tent sites, rentals, dump, laundry, groc, LP gas, firewood, controlled access. **REC:** Lake Anna: swim, fishing,

Tell your RV Campground that you found them in this Guide.

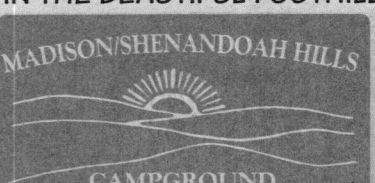

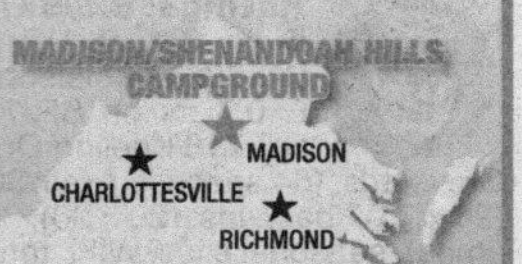

MINERAL (CONT)

CHRISTOPHER RUN (CONT)
playground, rec open to public. Pet restrict(B). 2015 rates: $35 to $40. Apr 1 to Oct 31.
AAA Approved
(540)894-4744 Lat: 38.09688, Lon: -77.89215
7149 Zachary Taylor Hwy, Mineral, VA 23117
reservations@christopherruncampground.com
www.christopherruncampground.com
See ad pages 1219 (Welcome Section), 1220.

MONTROSS — C5 *Westmoreland*

WESTMORELAND (State Pk) From Montross, N 5 mi on SR-3 to SR-347 and entrance (R). 2015 rates: $20 to $27. (804)493-8821

MOUNT JACKSON — B3 *Shenandoah*

SHENANDOAH VALLEY CAMPGROUND
Ratings: 9/9.5★/9 (Campground) N-Bnd: From Jct of I-81 & Exit 269 (Shenandoah Caverns) W on Caverns Rd., continue right onto Caverns Rd (SR 730 before high school.) W 0.8 mi to Industrial Park Rd, NE 0.2 mi (R) S-Bnd: from Jct: of I-81 & Exit 269 (Shenandoah Caverns) W on Caverns follow N-Bnd directions. **FAC:** Gravel rds. 43 gravel, 12 pull-thrus (40 x 80), back-ins (40 x 50), 43 full hkups (30/50 amps), cable, WiFi, tent sites, rentals, dump, laundry, groc, LP gas, fire rings, firewood. **REC:** pool, playground. Pets OK. Partial handicap access. Big rig sites, eco-friendly, 2015 rates: $35 to $47. Disc: military.
(540)477-3080 Lat: 38.71524, Lon: -78.66192
168 Industrial Park Road, Mount Jackson, VA 22842
dsaville@shenandoahfamilycampground.com
www.shenandoahfamilycampground.com
See ad pages 1219 (Welcome Section), 1220.

Things to See and Do

SHENANDOAH CAVERNS Underground Caverns, The Yellow Barn, Main Street of Yesteryear & American Celebration on Parade. RV accessible. Restrooms, food. Hours: 9am to 5pm. Adult fee: $23.
(540)477-3115 Lat: 38.71906, Lon: -78.66801
261 Caverns Rd, Shenandoah Caverns, VA 22842
shencave@shentel.net
www.shenandoahcaverns.com
See ad page 1219 (Welcome Section).

MOUNT SOLON — C3 *Augusta*

NATURAL CHIMNEYS REGIONAL PARK (Public) From Jct of SR-747 & SR-731, NW 0.5 mi on SR-731 (R). 2015 rates: $19 to $36. Apr 1 to Oct 31. (540)350-2510

NATURAL BRIDGE — D2 *Rockbridge*

NATURAL BRIDGE-LEXINGTON KOA Ratings: 9/9★/8 (Campground) S-bnd: From Jct of I-81 (Fancy Hill) & US-11 (exit 180B), cross US-11 to entrance rd (E); or N-bnd: From Jct of I-81 & US-11 (exit 180), NE .6 mi (under I-81) to entrance rd (L). **FAC:** Paved/gravel rds. 54 gravel, 54 pull-thrus (25 x 60), 31 full hkups, 23 W, 23 E (30/50 amps), WiFi, tent sites, rentals, dump, laundry, groc, LP gas, fire rings, firewood. **REC:** pool, playground, rec open to public. Pet restrict(B). Big rig sites, eco-friendly, 2015 rates: $34 to $64.
AAA Approved
(540)291-2770 Lat: 37.67624, Lon: -79.50627
214 Kildeer Lane, Natural Bridge, VA 24578
camp@naturalbridgekoa.info
www.naturalbridgekoa.com

YOGI BEAR'S JELLYSTONE PARK CAMP RESORT AT NATURAL BRIDGE
Ratings: 8.5/8.5/9 (Campground) S-bnd: From Jct I-81 & US-11 (exit 180A), S 4 mi on US-11 to Natural Bridge & Rte 130, E 3.5 mi to Rte 759, S 0.8 mi to Rte 782 (James River Rd.), E 0.8 mi (L); or N-bnd: From Jct of I-81 & US-11 (exit 175), N 2 mi on US-11 to Rte 130, follow above (L). **FAC:** Paved/gravel rds. 210 Avail: 178 gravel, 32 grass, 57 pull-thrus (30 x 60), back-ins (20 x 50), 152 full hkups, 58 W, 58 E (30/50 amps), cable, WiFi, tent sites, rentals, dump, laundry, groc, LP gas, fire rings, firewood. **REC:** pool, James River: swim, fishing, playground. Pet restrict(Q). Big rig sites, 2015 rates: $45 to $79. Mar 15 to Dec 1. ATM.
(540)291-2727 Lat: 37.61305, Lon: -79.48671
16 Recreation Lane, Natural Bridge, VA 24579
reservations@campnbr.com
www.campnbr.com
See ad pages 1227 (Spotlight Shenandoah Valley), 1220.

NEW MARKET — B3 *Shenandoah*

ENDLESS CAVERNS RV RESORT **Ratings: 8/9★/8.5** (Campground) 2015 rates: $30 to $40. Apr 1 to Nov 15. (540)896-2283 1800 Endless Caverns Rd, New Market, VA 22844

NEW POINT — D6 *Mathews*

NEW POINT RV RESORT
Ratings: 8.5/9★/8.5 (Campground) From Jct of US-17 & SR-14 (at Gloucester, VA), E 22.5 mi on SR-14 to Rte 602, E 0.8 mi (R).

GET AWAY TO THE CHESAPEAKE BAY
Our private beach and prime fishing location make New Point the perfect place to vacation on the Chesapeake Bay. Popular activities including crabbing and clamming, themed weekends and laser tag have guests wanting more!

FAC: Gravel rds. (321 spaces). 159 Avail: 20 gravel, 120 grass, 19 dirt, back-ins (25 x 50), 159 full hkups (30/50 amps), seasonal sites, WiFi, tent sites, rentals, dump, laundry, LP gas, fire rings, firewood. **REC:** pool, wading pool, Chesapeake Bay: fishing, marina, shuffleboard, playground. Pet restrict(B/Q). Eco-friendly, 2015 rates: $44 to $64. Apr 1 to Oct 31.
AAA Approved
(804)725-3084 Lat: 37.34339, Lon: -76.27740
846 Sand Bank Rd, New Point, VA 23125
newpoint@suncommunities.com
www.newpointcampground.com
See ad pages 1463 (Welcome Section), 1220, 1229 (Spotlight The Virginia Shoreline) & Family Camping in Magazine Section.

NEWPORT NEWS — E5 *City of Newport News, York*

NEWPORT NEWS PARK CAMPGROUND
(Public) From Jct of I-64 & SR-105 (exit 250B), E 0.1 mi on SR-105 to SR-143/Jefferson Ave, N 1 mi (R). **FAC:** Paved rds. 188 paved, back-ins (22 x 55), 155 W, 165 E (30/50 amps), tent sites, dump, laundry, groc, firewood. **REC:** Lee Hall Reservoir: fishing, golf, playground, rec open to public. Pets OK. Partial handicap access. 21 day max stay, 2015 rates: $34.
(800)203-8322 Lat: 37.18856, Lon: -76.55884
13564 Jefferson Avenue, Newport News, VA 23603
kbarber@nnva.gov
www.nnparks.com
See ad page 1224 (Spotlight Historic Triangle).

Things to See and Do

NEWPORT NEWS GOLF CLUB AT DEER RUN
Newport News Golf Club at Deer Run is a public facility with 36 holes of Championship golf. There is the renowned Deer Run Championship Course and the original Cardinal Championship Course. Partial handicap access. Restrooms, food. Hours: 7am to 7pm.
(757)886-7925 Lat: 37.17738, Lon: -76.52757
901 Clubhouse Way, Newport News, VA 23608
info@nngolfclub.com
www.nngolfclub.com
See ad page 1224 (Spotlight Historic Triangle).

NEWPORT NEWS VISITORS CENTER Travel & Tourism information about the local and state areas. Brochures on places to stay, things to do, restaurants, visitors guides & more. Partial handicap access. Restrooms. Hours: 9am to 5pm.
(888)493-7386 Lat: 37.17988, Lon: -76.55135
13560 Jefferson Ave, Newport News, VA 23603
tourism-mailing@nngov.com
www.newport-news.org
See ad page 1224 (Spotlight Historic Triangle).

PENHOOK — E2 *Pittsylvania*

SMITH MOUNTAIN CAMPGROUND **Ratings: 5/9.5★/9** (Campground) 2015 rates: $25. Apr 1 to Oct 31. (434)927-4198 1261 Smith Mountain Road, Penhook, VA 24137

PETERSBURG — D4 *Dinwiddie, Prince George*

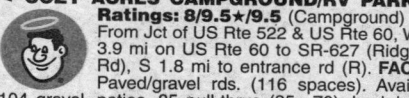

CAMPTOWN CAMPGROUND
Ratings: 5/9★/7.5 (Campground) S-bnd: From Jct of I-85 & US-1, (exit 63A), SW 5 mi on US-1 to Dabney Mill Rd (Rte 613-left side), SE (left turn) 1.3 mi to campground entrance rd (R); or N-bnd: From Jct of I-85 & Rte 703 (exit 53), W (lt turn) 1.1 mi to US-1, N 5.5 mi to Dabney Mill Rd, (Rte 613) SE 1.3 mi to entrance rd (R). **FAC:** Gravel rds. (19 spaces). Avail: 12 gravel, 5 pull-thrus (25 x 70), back-ins (25 x 55), 12 full hkups (30/50 amps), seasonal sites, cable, WiFi, tent sites, laundry, firewood. **REC.** Pets OK. Big rig sites, eco-friendly, 2015 rates: $35. No CC.
(804)469-4569 Lat: 37.13323, Lon: -77.50835
22819 Campton Dr, Petersburg, VA 23803
camptown123@comcast.net
See ad this page, 1220.

PICTURE LAKE CAMPGROUND
Ratings: 8.5/9★/8.5 (Campground) From Jct of I-85 & US 460 (Exit 61), E 0.4 mi on US 460 to US 1, S 1.8 mi (R). **FAC:** Paved/gravel rds. (200 spaces). Avail: 162 grass, 144 pull-thrus (35 x 60), back-ins (32 x 50), 57 full hkups, 105 W, 105 E (30/50 amps), seasonal sites, WiFi, tent sites, rentals, dump, mobile sewer, laundry, groc, LP gas, fire rings, firewood. **REC:** pool, Picture Lake: fishing, playground, rec open to public. Pets OK. 2015 rates: $28 to $35.
(804)861-0174 Lat: 37.16432, Lon: -77.51302
7818 Boydton Plank Rd, Petersburg, VA 23803
contactus@picturelakecampgrounds.com
www.picturelakecampgrounds.com
See ad pages 1240, 1220.

SOUTH FORTY RV RESORT AND CAMPGROUND
Ratings: 6.5/7.5/7.5 (Campground) From Jct of I-95 (Exit 41) & SR-35, S 0.6 mi on SR-35 (R). **FAC:** Gravel rds. (114 spaces). Avail: 92 gravel, 72 pull-thrus (32 x 60), back-ins (25 x 45), some side by side hkups, 44 full hkups, 48 W, 48 E (30/50 amps), seasonal sites, cable, WiFi Hotspot, tent sites, rentals, dump, mobile sewer, laundry, LP gas, fire rings, firewood. **REC:** pool, pond, fishing, playground. Pets OK. Big rig sites, 2015 rates: $42 to $47.
(877)732-8345 Lat: 37.07718, Lon: -77.35196
2809 Courtland Rd, Petersburg, VA 23805
southfortyrv@gmail.com
www.southfortycampground.com

POWHATAN — D4 *Powhatan*

COZY ACRES CAMPGROUND/RV PARK
Ratings: 8/9.5★/9.5 (Campground) From Jct of US Rte 522 & US Rte 60, W 3.9 mi on US Rte 60 to SR-627 (Ridge Rd), S 1.8 mi to entrance rd (R). **FAC:** Paved/gravel rds. (116 spaces). Avail: 104 gravel, patios, 85 pull-thrus (35 x 70), back-ins (30 x 70), 95 full hkups, 9 W, 9 E (30/50 amps), seasonal sites, WiFi Hotspot, tent sites, rentals, dump, laundry, groc, LP gas, firewood, controlled access. **REC:** pool, wading pool, pond, fishing, playground. Pets OK. Big rig sites, eco-friendly, 2015 rates: $43 to $75. Apr 1 to Nov 15.
(804)598-2470 Lat: 37.53970, Lon: -78.01788
2177 Ridge Road, Powhatan, VA 23139
cozyacrescamp@aol.com
www.cozyacres.com
See ad pages 1240, 1220.

PULASKI — D1 *Pulaski*

GATEWOOD PARK & RESERVOIR (Public) From Jct of Hwy 81 & Rte 99 (Exit 94), W 3.8 mi on Count Pulaski Dr./Main st. to Magazine St, NE 0.1 mi to Mt Olivet Rd (Rte 710), W 2.3 mi to Gatewood Ave, NW 6 mi (R). 2015 rates: $15 to $30. Apr 6 to Dec 1. (540)980-2561

QUINBY — D6 *Accomack*

VIRGINIA LANDING RV CAMPGROUND **Ratings: 8/7/8.5** (Membership Pk) 2015 rates: $36 to $44. Mar 28 to Oct 31. (757)442-5489 40226 Upshur Neck Road, Quinby, VA 23423

REEDVILLE — C6 *Northumberland*

CHESAPEAKE BAY CAMP-RESORT Ratings: 7/6.5/6.5 (Campground) From Jct of US-360 & SR-200 (in Burgess), E 5 mi on US-360 to Rte 652, NE 3 mi (follow Smith Island Cruise signs) to Rte 650, E 0.2 mi (R). **FAC:** Paved/gravel rds. 86 Avail: 43 gravel, 43 grass, 45 pull-thrus (20 x 60), back-ins (20 x 55), 45 full hkups, 41 W, 41 E (30/50 amps), cable, WiFi Hotspot, tent sites, rentals, dump, laundry, firewood. **REC:** pool, wading pool, Slough Creek:

VA

REEDVILLE (CONT)

CHESAPEAKE BAY CAMP-RESORT (CONT) playground. Pet restrict(B/Q). Big rig sites, 2015 rates: $50 to $55. Apr 7 to Nov 1.
(804)453-3430 Lat: 37.88252, Lon: -76.25872
382 Campground Rd, Reedville, VA 22539
info@chesapeakebaycampresort.com
www.chesapeakebaycampresort.com

RICHMOND — D4 *Richmond City*

RICHMOND See also Amelia, Ashland, Doswell, Glen Allen, Milford, Petersburg & Powhatan.

ROANOKE — D2 *Roanoke*

ROANOKE See also Buchanan, Natural Bridge, Salem & Willis.

BLUE RIDGE PKWY/ROANOKE MOUNTAIN (Natl Pk) From Jct of US-220 & Blue Ridge Pkwy, N 1 mi on Blue Ridge Pkwy to Mill Mt Rd., W 1.5 mi at MP-120.4 (E). 2015 rates: $16. May to Oct. (540)342-3051

We salute you! Our Military Listings indicate campgrounds for use exclusively by active and retired military personnel.

Travel Services

CAMPING WORLD OF ROANOKE As the nation's largest retailer of RV supplies, accessories, services and new and used RVs, Camping World is committed to making your total RV experience better. RV Accessories:(888)833-4454. **SERVICES:** RV, tire, RV appliance, MH mechanical, staffed RV wash, restrooms, RV Sales. RV supplies, LP, waiting room. Hours: 8am to 6pm.
(888)733-4021 Lat: 37.359094, Lon: -79.955393
8198 Gander Way, Roanoke, VA 24019
www.campingworld.com

Thank you for being one of our best customers!

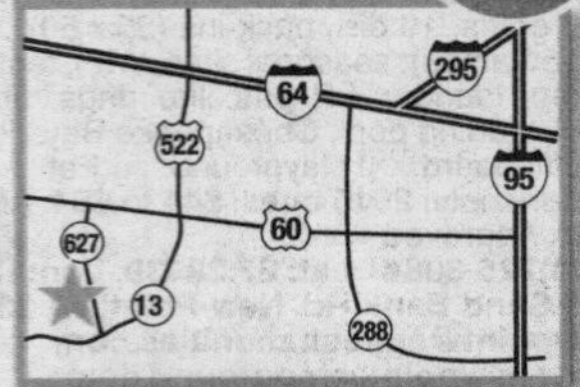

RURAL RETREAT — E1 *Wythe*

RURAL RETREAT FISHING LAKE & CAMPGROUND (Public) From Jct of I-81 & CR-79 (Exit 60), S 4 mi on Exit 60 to CR-677, W 2 mi (L). Call park for reservations. 2015 rates: $18 to $28. Apr 1 to Oct 1. (276)223-6022

RUSTBURG — D3 *Campbell*

LYNCHBURG RV **Ratings: 6.5/7.5/7.5** (Membership Pk) 2015 rates: $38 to $45. Apr 27 to Oct 20. (434)332-6672 405 Mollies Creek Road, Gladys, VA 24554

SALEM — D2 *Roanoke*

DIXIE CAVERNS CAMPGROUND
Ratings: 5.5/7.5/6.5 (Campground) From Jct of I-81, Exit 132 (Dixie Caverns) & Rte 647, SE 0.2 mi on Rte 647 to US-11/460 (Main St), SW (right turn) 0.1 mi (R). **FAC:** Paved/gravel rds. 62 gravel, 32 pull-thrus (24 x 55), back-ins (25 x 55), 62 full hkups (30/50 amps), cable, WiFi, tent sites, dump, LP gas, firewood. **REC:** rec open to public. Pets OK. 2015 rates: $34.
(540)380-2085 Lat: 37.25268, Lon: -80.17545
5757 W Main St, Salem, VA 24153
www.dixiecaverns.com
See ad this page.

Things to See and Do

DIXIE CAVERNS, POTTERY, GIFTS, ROCK SHOP & ANTIQUE MALL The only scenic underground caverns in SW Virginia, with rock shop, pottery, RV campground & antique mall. Open 7 days, discount to caverns for campers. RV accessible. Restrooms. Hours: 9am to 6pm. Adult fee: $14.
(540)380-2085 Lat: 37.25231, Lon: -80.17448
5757 W Main St, Salem, VA 24153
www.dixiecaverns.com
See ad this page.

SCOTTSBURG — E3 *Halifax*

STAUNTON RIVER (State Pk) From Town, Ne 7.3 mi. on US-360, SE 2.4 mi. on Scottsburg Rd., SE 7.8 mi. MacDonald Rd. 2015 rates: $20 to $27. (434)572-4623

SPOTSYLVANIA — C4 *Spotsylvania*

WILDERNESS PRESIDENTIAL RESORTS **Ratings: 7.5/7.5/7.5** (Membership Pk) 2015 rates: $20 to $30. (540)972-7433 9220 Plank Rd, Spotsylvania, VA 22553

SPOUT SPRING — D3 *Appomattox*

PARADISE LAKE FAMILY CAMPGROUND
Ratings: 7.5/8★/9 (Campground) W-bnd: From Appomattox, Jct of SR-24 & US 460, W 6 mi on US 460 to West Lake Rd, S 1 mi (E); or E-bnd: From Lynchburg, Jct of US-29 & US 460 (S Lynchburg), E 10.2 mi on US 460 to West Lake Rd, S 1 mi (E). **FAC:** Paved/gravel rds. (91 spaces). Avail: 71 gravel, 26 pull-thrus (30 x 60), back-ins (30 x 45), 39 full hkups, 32 W, 32 E (30/50 amps), seasonal sites, WiFi Hotspot, tent sites, rentals, dump, laundry, groc, LP bottles, fire rings, firewood. **REC:** pool, Paradise Lake: swim, fishing, playground, rec open to public. Pet restrict(B). 2015 rates: $33.50 to $36.50. Disc: military.
(434)993-3332 Lat: 37.33841, Lon: -78.93726
1105 West Lake Rd, Spout Spring, VA 24593
paradiselakecamp@juno.com
www.paradise-lake.com
See ad pages 1231, 1220.

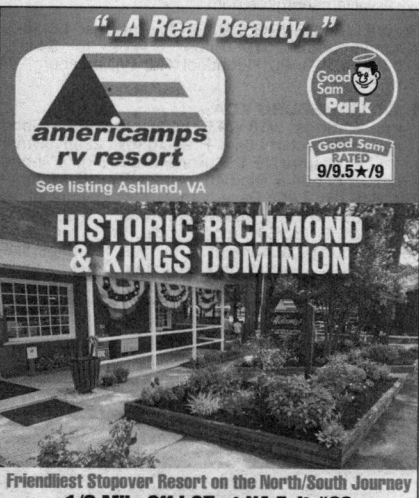

STAFFORD — C4 *Stafford*

AQUIA PINES CAMP RESORT
Ratings: 8/8.5★/8.5 (Campground) S-bnd: From Jct of I-95 (Aquia-Garrisonville/Exit 143A) & Rte 610, E 0.2 mi on Rte 610 to US 1, N 0.6 mi (L); or N-bnd: From Jct of I-95 (Aquia-Garrisonville/Exit 143A) & US 1, N 0.8 mi on US 1 (L). **FAC:** Paved/gravel rds. (100 spaces). Avail: 80 gravel, 80 pull-thrus (25 x 60), 80 full hkups (30/50 amps), seasonal sites, cable, WiFi, tent sites, rentals, dump, laundry, groc, LP gas, firewood. **REC:** pool, playground. Pets OK. Big rig sites, 2015 rates: $45 to $62.
(540)659-3447 Lat: 38.47028, Lon: -77.40011
3071 Jefferson Davis Hwy, Stafford, VA 22554
aquiapines@aol.com
www.aquiapines.com
See ad pages 266, 1220.

STANARDSVILLE — C3 *Greene*

HEAVENLY ACRES CAMPGROUND **Ratings: 7/7/7.5** (Campground) 2015 rates: $35 to $45. Mar 21 to Dec 1. (434)985-6601 2010 Madison Rd, Stanardsville, VA 22973

STAUNTON — C3 *Augusta*

STAUNTON / WALNUT HILLS KOA
Ratings: 9/9.5★/9 (Campground) N-bnd: From Jct of I-81 & US-11 (Exit 213), S (R) 0.2 mi on US-11 to US-340/Stuarts Draft Hwy, NE (L) 2.5 mi to SR-655/Walnut Hills Rd, N (L) 03. mi; or S-bnd: From Jct of I-81 & White Hill Rd (Exit 217), W (R) 0.4 mi on White Hill Rd to US-11, S (L) 1.5 mi to SR-655/Walnut Hills Rd, E (L) 1 mi (L). **FAC:** Paved/gravel rds. 126 gravel, 30 pull-thrus (30 x 60), back-ins (25 x 50), 63 full hkups, 63 W, 63 E (30/50 amps), cable, WiFi, tent sites, rentals, dump, laundry, groc, LP gas, fire rings, firewood. **REC:** pool, Kerplonken Lake: fishing, playground. Pets OK. Eco-friendly, 2015 rates: $34 to $65.
(800)699-2568 Lat: 38.04802, Lon: -79.09941
484 Walnut Hills Rd, Staunton, VA 24401
stauntonkoa@yahoo.com
www.walnuthillskoa.com
See ad page 1216 (Welcome Section).

STUART — E2 *Patrick*

FAIRY STONE (State Pk) From N jct US 58 & Hwy 8: go 4 mi N on Hwy 8, then 8 mi E on Hwy 57 (Fairystone Park Hwy), then 3/4 mi N on Hwy 346. 2015 rates: $27. (276)930-2424

STUARTS DRAFT — C3 *Waynesboro*

SHENANDOAH ACRES FAMILY CAMPGROUND **Ratings: 6/8.5★/8.5** (Campground) 2015 rates: $39 to $42. (540)337-2267 348 Lake Rd, Stuarts Draft, VA 24477

SUFFOLK — E5 *Isle of Wight, Suffolk*

DAVIS LAKES AND CAMPGROUND
Ratings: 8.5/9.5★/10 (Campground) From Jct of US 58 & US 13/Rte 32, S 2.2 mi on US13 to Horton Dr (South of Suffolk), NW 0.3 mi on Horton Dr to Byrd St, W 0.2 mi (E). **FAC:** Paved/gravel rds. (137 spaces). Avail: 50 gravel, patios, 7 pull-thrus (40 x 60), back-ins (40 x 60), 50 full hkups (30/50 amps), seasonal sites, cable, WiFi, rentals, dump, laundry, LP gas, fire rings, firewood. **REC:** Davis Lakes: swim, fishing, playground. Pet restrict(B). No tents. Big rig sites, 2015 rates: $38.70 to $46.
(757)539-1191 Lat: 36.70286, Lon: -76.60714
200 Byrd St, Suffolk, VA 23434
dlcamp83@verizon.net
www.davislakescampground.net
See ad pages 1235, 1220.

SUGAR GROVE — E1 *Smyth*

JEFFERSON/HURRICANE CAMPGROUND (Natl Forest) From town: Go 5 mi S on Hwy-16, then 1-1/2 mi NW on Hwy-650, then 1/2 mi N on FR-84. 2015 rates: $16 to $32. Apr 15 to Oct 31. (276)783-5196

SYDNORSVILLE — E2 *Franklin*

GOOSE DAM CAMPGROUND (Public) From Jct of US-220 & Hwy 40, S 8 mi on US-220 to Hwy 724 (Goose Dam Rd), W 1 mi (R). 2015 rates: $14 to $18. (540)483-2100

TEMPERANCEVILLE — C6 *Accomack*

TALL PINES HARBOR WATERFRONT CAMPGROUND
Ratings: 9/10★/9.5 (Campground) From Jct of SR-695 and US-13 in Temperanceville, W 6.5 mi on SR-695 to Entrance Rd (R). **FAC:** Gravel rds. (180 spaces). 120 Avail: 23 paved, 82 gravel, 15 grass, 67 pull-thrus (50 x 100), back-ins (24 x 50), 65 full hkups, 55 W, 55 E (30/50 amps), seasonal sites, cable, WiFi, tent sites, rentals, dump, mobile sewer, laundry, groc, LP gas, fire rings, firewood, controlled access. **REC:** pool, Pocomoke Sound: swim, fishing, playground. Pets OK. Partial handicap access. Big rig sites, eco-friendly, 2015 rates: $36 to $67. Mar 1 to Nov 1. ATM.
(757)824-0777 Lat: 37.93236, Lon: -75.65342
8107 Tall Pines Ln, Temperanceville, VA 23442
reservations@tallpinesharbor.com
www.tallpinesharbor.com
See ad page 1230 (Spotlight The Virginia Shoreline).

TOANO — D5 *James City*

TOANO See also Lanexa, Williamsburg.

WILLIAMSBURG CHRISTIAN RETREAT CENTER
Ratings: 7.5/8/8.5 (Campground) From Jct of I-64 & SR-30 (Exit 227), N 0.6 mi on SR-30 to SR-601/Barnes Rd, S (Left) 1 mi on SR-601/Barnes Rd (R). **FAC:** Gravel rds. 22 gravel, back-ins (20 x 50), 22 full hkups (30 amps), WiFi Hotspot, tent sites, rentals, dump, laundry, fire rings, firewood. **REC:** pool, wading pool, playground. Pets OK. Partial handicap access. Eco-friendly, 2015 rates: $30 to $35.
(757)566-2256 Lat: 37.42463, Lon: -76.85193
9275 Barnes Rd (Rt 601), Toano, VA 23168
wcrc@wcrc.info
www.wcrc.info
See ad pages 1242, 1220.

TOPPING — D5 *Middlesex*

GREY'S POINT CAMP
Ratings: 9.5/9.5★/10 (RV Park) From Jct of US 17 & SR-33 (in Saluda), E 8 mi on SR-33 to SR-3, NW approx 5 mi (L). **FAC:** Paved rds. (700 spaces). 150 Avail: 66 paved, 84 grass, 140 pull-thrus (30 x 62), back-ins (30 x 60), accepts full hkup units only, 150 full hkups (30/50 amps), cable, WiFi, dump, laundry, groc, LP gas, fire rings, firewood, controlled access. **REC:** pool, wading pool, Rappahannock River: swim, fishing, playground. Pets OK. No tents. Big rig sites, eco-friendly, 2015 rates: $40 to $83. Apr 1 to Nov 15.
(804)758-2485 Lat: 37.61020, Lon: -76.43783
3601 Greys Point Rd, Topping, VA 23169
greyspoint@rivahresorts.com
www.greyspointcamp.com
See ad page 1242.

VA

TRIANGLE — B5 *Prince William*

◄ PRINCE WILLIAM FOREST PARK/OAK RIDGE CAMPGROUND (Natl Pk) From Jct of I-95 & SR-619 (Exit 150), W 0.25 mi on SR-619 to park entrance rd, NW to Scenic Dr (R). Entrance fee required. Reservations only taken in high season. 2015 rates: $20. (703)221-7181

URBANNA — D5 *Middlesex*

BETHPAGE CAMP RESORT
Ratings: 9.5/9.5★/9.5 (RV Park) From Jct of US-17 & SR-33 (in Saluda), NW 1 mi on US-17 to Rte 616, E 2 mi to Rte 602, NW 0.1 mi to Rte 684, N 0.5 mi to entrance rd (R). **FAC:** Paved rds. (1000 spaces). 528 Avail: 30 paved, 498 grass, 264 pull-thrus (30 x 70), back-ins (30 x 70), 528 full hkups (30/50 amps), seasonal sites, cable, WiFi, rentals, dump, laundry, groc, LP gas, fire rings, firewood, controlled access. **REC:** pool, wading pool, Rappahannock River: swim, fishing, playground. Pets OK. No tents. Big rig sites, eco-friendly, 2015 rates: $45 to $100. Apr 1 to Nov 15.
(804)758-4349 Lat: 37.64929, Lon: -76.58634
679 Brown's Lane, Urbanna, VA 23175
bethpage@rivahresorts.com
www.bethpagecamp.com
See ad this page.

VERONA — C3 *Augusta*

◄ **SHENANDOAH VALLEY CAMPGROUND**
Ratings: 8.5/10★/9 (Campground) From Jct of I-81 & Rte 612 (exit 227), W 1 mi on Rte 612 to US-11, N 0.5 mi to Rte 781, W 1.2 mi (L). **FAC:** Paved/gravel rds. 132 gravel, 90 pull-thrus (25 x 50), back-ins (35 x 40), 39 full hkups, 93 W, 93 E (30 amps), WiFi, tent sites, rentals, dump, mobile sewer, laundry, groc, LP gas, fire rings, firewood. **REC:** pool, whirlpool, Middle River: swim, fishing, playground, rec open to public. Pet restrict(B). 2015 rates: $35 to $53. Apr 1 to Oct 31.
(540)248-CAMP(2267) Lat: 38.22324, Lon: -79.00636
476 Bald Rock Rd, Verona, VA 24482
camp@campingisfun.com
www.campingisfun.com
See ad pages 1226 (Spotlight Shenandoah Valley), 1220, 1217 (VA Map) & RV Trips of a Lifetime in Magazine Section.

VIRGINIA BEACH — E6 *Virginia Beach*

VIRGINIA BEACH See also Cheriton, Chesapeake, Gloucester Point & Suffolk.

▲ FIRST LANDING (State Pk) From Jct of I-64 & US-13N (North Hampton Blvd, exit 282), E 4.5 mi on 13N to Shore Dr (Rte 60), E 4.5 mi (R). 2015 rates: $24 to $30. Mar 1 to Dec 4. (757)412-2300

▼ **HOLIDAY TRAV-L-PARK OF VIRGINIA BEACH**
Ratings: 8.5/9/8 (Campground) From Jct of I-64 (exit 284) & I-264, E 10.5 mi on I-264 to Birdneck Rd (exit 22), S 3 mi to General Booth Blvd, SW 0.3 mi (R). **FAC:** Paved rds. 704 Avail: 62 paved, 284 gravel, 216 grass, 142 dirt, 600 pull-thrus (25 x 60), back-ins (25 x 60), 340 full hkups, 364 W, 364 E (30/50 amps), WiFi $, tent sites, rentals, dump, mobile sewer, laundry, groc, LP gas, firewood. **REC:** pool, wading pool, playground. Pet restrict(B/Q). Big rig sites, eco-friendly, 2015 rates: $32 to $87. Disc: AAA. ATM. AAA Approved
(866)850-9630 Lat: 36.80546, Lon: -75.99196
1075 General Booth Blvd, Virginia Beach, VA 23451
info@campingvb.com
www.campingvb.com
See ad pages 1228 (Spotlight The Virginia Shoreline), 1220.

▼ INDIAN COVE RESORT **Ratings: 9.5/9★/9** (Membership Pk) 2015 rates: $45.60. Mar 6 to Jan 4. (757)426-2601 1053 Sandbridge Rd, Virginia Beach, VA 23456

▼ NORTH BAY SHORE CAMPGROUND (Campground) (Rebuilding) 2015 rates: $45 to $50. May 1 to Oct 1. (757)426-7911 3257 Colechester Road, Virginia Beach, VA 23456

▼ **NORTH LANDING BEACH RV RESORT & COTTAGES**
Ratings: 8.5/8/8.5 (Campground) From Jct I-64 (Exit 286) & Indian River Rd, SE 12 mi to Princess Anne Rd, S 12.8 mi on Princess Anne Rd (R).

TOTAL RENOVATION! PRIVATE BEACH
Great South Virginia Beach Resort w/800 foot sandy beach. New amenities; 100 HUGE, FHU level RV sites, 90+ Studio/1-bed/2-bed cottages, Pool, spa, fitness center, 30 private bath suites, mini-golf, free WiFi & Cable TV.

FAC: Gravel rds. (65 spaces). 57 Avail: 47 gravel, 10 grass, 54 pull-thrus (45 x 60), back-ins (25 x 60), some side by side hkups, 57 full hkups (30/50 amps), seasonal sites, WiFi, tent sites, rentals, dump, laundry, groc, LP gas, fire rings, firewood, controlled access. **REC:** pool, North Landing River: fishing, playground, rec open to public. Pet restrict(B). Big rig sites, 2015 rates: $40 to $56. Disc: AAA, military. ATM.
(757)426-6241 Lat: 36.55768, Lon: -76.00685
161 Princess Anne Rd, Virginia Beach, VA 23457
info@northlandingbeach.com
www.northlandingbeach.com
See ad pages 1230 (Spotlight The Virginia Shoreline), 1220 See ad inside back cover & Family Camping in Magazine Section.

➘ OUTDOOR RESORTS-VIRGINIA BEACH **Ratings: 10/9.5★/10** (Condo Pk) 2015 rates: $82 to $92. (800)333-7515 3665 S Sandpiper Road, Virginia Beach, VA 23456

▼ VIRGINIA BEACH KOA **Ratings: 8/9★/7** (Campground) 2015 rates: $46 to $92. (800)562-4150 1240 General Booth Blvd., Virginia Beach, VA 23451

VOLNEY — E1 *Grayson*

▼ GRAYSON HIGHLANDS (State Pk) From Jct of I-81 & SR-16 exit, S 25 mi on SR-16 to US-58, W 8 mi (E). Pit toilets. 2015 rates: $20 to $27. (276)579-7092

WAYNESBORO — C3 *Augusta, Green*

▲ **WAYNESBORO NORTH 340 CAMPGROUND**
Ratings: 9/9★/9 (Campground) From Jct of I-64 & US-340 (exit 96), N 7 mi on US-340 (R); or From Jct of I-81 & SR-612 (exit 227), E 9.6 mi on SR-612 to US-340, S 2 mi (L). **FAC:** Paved rds. (165 spaces). 140 Avail: 20 paved, 60 gravel, 60 grass, 40 pull-thrus (28 x 70), back-ins (30 x 55), 140 full hkups (30/50 amps), seasonal sites, WiFi, tent sites, dump, laundry, groc, fire rings, firewood. **REC:** pool, playground. Pet restrict(B/Q). Big rig sites, 2015 rates: $36 to $40.
(540)943-9573 Lat: 38.12856, Lon: -78.84436
1125 Eastside Hwy (US-340), Waynesboro, VA 22980
waynesboron340@gmail.com
www.waynesboron340campground.com
See ad page 1227 (Spotlight Shenandoah Valley).

WILLIAMSBURG — D5 *James City, York*

WILLIAMSBURG See also Gloucester Point, Gwynn, Lanexa & Toano.

➚ **AMERICAN HERITAGE RV PARK**
Ratings: 9.5/10★/10 (RV Park) From Jct of I-64 & Rte 607 (exit 231A), SW 0.5 mi on Rte 607 to Maxton Ln on left, S 0.2 mi (L). **FAC:** Paved/gravel rds. 145 paved, patios, 70 pull-thrus (30 x 60), back-ins (30 x 60), 145 full hkups (30/50 amps), cable, WiFi, tent sites, rentals, dump, laundry, LP gas, fire rings, firewood. **REC:** pool, playground. Pets OK. Partial handicap access. Big rig sites, eco-friendly, 2015 rates: $50.25 to $74.99. Disc: AAA, military. ATM. AAA Approved
(888)530-2267 Lat: 37.37708, Lon: -76.76866
146 Maxton Lane, Williamsburg, VA 23188
americanheritagerv@gmail.com
www.americanheritagervpark.com
See ad pages 1225 (Spotlight Historic Triangle), 1220.

▲ **ANVIL CAMPGROUND**
Ratings: 10/10★/9 (Campground) From Jct of I-64 & Rte 143 (Camp Pearyexit 238), S 0.1 mi on Rte 143 to Rochambeau Dr, NW 1.4 mi to Rte 645 (Airport Rd), SW 1.8 mi to Rte 603 (Mooretown Rd), SE 0.3 mi (R); or From Jct of US-60 & Rte 645, NE 0.1 mi on Rte 645 to Rte 603, SE 0.3 mi (R). **FAC:** Paved rds. 49 Avail: 49 all weather, 9 pull-thrus (25 x 60), back-ins (25 x 50), 49 full hkups (30/50 amps), cable, WiFi, tent sites, rentals, dump, mobile sewer, laundry, groc, fire rings, firewood. **REC:** pool, playground. Pets OK. Eco-friendly, 2015 rates: $39.99 to $69.99. Disc: military.
(757)565-2300 Lat: 37.30687, Lon: -76.72889
5243 Mooretown Rd, Williamsburg, VA 23188
info@anvilcampground.com
www.anvilcampground.com
See ad this page, 1220.

▲ **COLONIAL CENTRAL KOA Ratings: 9/10★/10** (Campground) E-bnd: From Jct of I-64 (exit 234) & Rte 646 (Newman Rd), NE 1 mi on Rte 646 (R); or W-bnd: From Jct of I-64 (exit 234B) & Rte 646 (Newman Rd), NE 1 mi on Rte 646 (R). **FAC:** Paved/gravel rds. 175 gravel, 160 pull-thrus (30 x 55), back-ins (30 x 50), 107 full hkups, 68 W, 68 E (30/50 amps), cable, WiFi, tent sites, rentals, dump, laundry, groc, LP gas, fire rings, firewood. **REC:** heated pool, wading pool, Skimino Creek: playground. Pet restrict(B). 2015 rates: $27 to $73. Mar 1 to Dec 15.
(800)562-1733 Lat: 37.36066, Lon: -76.71413
4000 Newman Rd, Williamsburg, VA 23188
camp@williamsburgkoa.com
www.williamsburgkoa.com

➘ WILLIAMSBURG CAMPARK **Ratings: 4/5.5/5.5** (Campground) 2015 rates: $34.99 to $44.99. (757)565-2101 901 Lightfoot Rd, Williamsburg, VA 23188

▲ **WILLIAMSBURG KOA**
Ratings: 9/10★/9.5 (Campground) E-bnd: From Jct of I-64 & Rte 646 (exit 234/Newman Rd)lt turn, NE 1.5 mi on Rte 646 (R); or W-bnd: From Jct of I-64 & Rte 646 (exit 234B), NE 1.5 mi on Rte 646 (R). **FAC:** Paved/gravel rds. 110 gravel, 22 pull-thrus (20 x 55), back-ins (20 x 55), 73 full hkups, 37 W, 37 E (30/50 amps), cable, WiFi, tent sites, rentals, dump, laundry, groc, LP gas, fire rings, firewood. **REC:** heated pool, Skimino Creek: fishing,

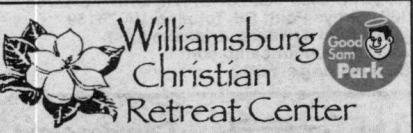

Our travel services section will help you find services that you'll find handy in your travels.

SAVE! Over $1,000 in coupons can be found at the front of the Guide!

WILLIAMSBURG (CONT)

WILLIAMSBURG KOA (CONT)
playground. Pet restrict(B). 2015 rates: $35 to $68. Mar 1 to Dec 15.
AAA Approved
(800)562-1733 Lat: 37.36505, Lon: -76.71505
5210 Newman Rd, Williamsburg, VA 23188
camp@williamsburgkoa.com
www.williamsburgkoa.com
See ad page 1223 (Spotlight Historic Triangle).

↑ WILLIAMSBURG OUTDOOR WORLD **Ratings: 7.5/7/6** (Membership Pk) 2015 rates: $45 to $55. Mar 15 to Nov 30. (757)566-3021 4301 Rochambeau Dr, Williamsburg, VA 23188

WILLIS — E2 *Floyd*

↘ DADDY RABBIT'S CAMPGROUND **Ratings: 4.5/6.5/7** (Campground) 2015 rates: $25 to $30. Apr 15 to Oct 31. (540)789-4150 2015 Union School Rd SW, Willis, VA 24380

WINCHESTER — B4 *Frederick*

← **CANDY HILL CAMPGROUND**
Ratings: 8/8.5★/8.5 (Campground) S-bnd: From Jct of I-81 & US 11/37 (Exit 317), SW 4.1 mi on Rte 37 to US 50, W 0.25 mi to Ward Ave, S 0.25 mi (E); or N-bnd: From Jct of N I-81 & Rte 37 (Exit 310), N 5.2 mi on Rte 37 to US 50, W 0.25 to Ward Ave, S 0.25 mi (E). **FAC:** Paved rds. 103 Avail: 47 paved, 45 gravel, 11 grass, 25 pull-thrus (25 x 50), back-ins (25 x 50), some side by side hkups, 74 full hkups, 29 W, 29 E (30/50 amps), cable, WiFi $, tent sites, rentals, dump, laundry, groc, LP gas, fire rings, firewood. **REC:** pool, playground, rec open to public. Pet restrict(Q). Eco-friendly, 2015 rates: $35 to $65. Disc: military.
(540)662-5198 Lat: 39.18746, Lon: -78.20373
165 Ward Ave, Winchester, VA 22602
reservations@candyhill.com
www.candyhill.com
See ad this page, 1220.

Travel Services

↓ **CAMPING WORLD OF WINCHESTER** As the nation's largest retailer of RV supplies, accessories, services and new and used RVs, Camping World is committed to making your total RV experience better. **SERVICES:** Tire, RV appliance, staffed RV wash, restrooms. RV supplies, LP, dump, emergency parking, RV accessible. waiting room. Hours: 8am to 6pm.
(888)615-6187 Lat: 39.126801, Lon: -78.192334
190 Commonwealth Ct, Winchester, VA 22602
www.campingworld.com

WYTHEVILLE — E1 *Wythe*

WYTHEVILLE See also Fancy Gap, Fries, Hillsville, Willis.

↖ **DEER TRAIL PARK & CAMPGROUND**
Ratings: 8.5/8.5★/9 (Campground) From Jct of I-81 & US-52/Stoney Fork Rd (Exit 70), N 9.1 mi on US-52/Stoney Fork Rd to Gullion Fork Rd, W 1 mi (L). **FAC:** Gravel rds. (70 spaces). 55 Avail: 34 gravel, 21 grass, 7 pull-thrus (20 x 60), back-ins (20 x 38), 30 full hkups, 25 W, 25 E (30/50 amps), seasonal sites, WiFi, tent sites, rentals, dump, laundry, groc, firewood. **REC:** heated pool, Stoney Fork Creek: fishing, playground, rec open to public. Pets OK. Eco-friendly, 2015 rates: $29 to $34. ATM.
(276)228-3636 Lat: 37.02628, Lon: -81.22357
599 Gullion Fork Rd., Wytheville, VA 24382
www.deertrailpark.com

→ **FORT CHISWELL RV PARK**
Ratings: 9/10★/9.5 (RV Park) From Jct of I-81/77 & US-52 (exit 80), S 0.5 mi on US-52 (L). **FAC:** Paved/gravel rds. 92 Avail: 8 paved, 84 gravel, patios, 81 pull-thrus (30 x 60), back-ins (30 x 60), 92 full hkups (30/50 amps), cable, WiFi, dump, laundry, groc, LP gas. **REC:** heated pool, pond, fishing, playground. Pets OK. Partial handicap access, no tents. Big rig sites, eco-friendly, 2015 rates: $35.
(276)637-6868 Lat: 36.94028, Lon: -80.94322
312 Ft. Chiswell Rd, Max Meadows, VA 24360
fcrv@psknet.com
www.fcrvpark.com
See ad pages 1222 (Spotlight Blue Ridge Parkway/Southwest Virginia), 1220.

↘ PIONEER VILLAGE CAMPGROUND **Ratings: 6.5/9.5★/8.5** (Campground) 2015 rates: $33. Apr 1 to Nov 30. (276)637-3777 3627 East Lee Hwy, Max Meadows, VA 24360

→ WYTHEVILLE KOA CAMPGROUND **Ratings: 9/8:5/9** (Campground) 2015 rates: $40 to $57. (800)562-3380 231 Koa Rd, Wytheville, VA 24382

VA

Getty Images

WELCOME TO
Washington

DATE OF STATEHOOD	WIDTH: 360 MILES (581 KM)	PROPORTION OF UNITED STATES
NOV. 11, 1889	LENGTH: 240 MILES (386 KM)	1.88% OF 3,794,100 SQ MI

With its poster child Space Needle, framed by the majestic Mount Rainier, Seattle is an enviable lifestyle-city that combines a glorious natural setting with a rich, spirited and diverse urban landscape. Even when it rains (which it does, a lot), there's a buzz to the city (and that's not just the caffeine) with its busy markets, dazzling skyscrapers, thrift stores, waterside sculpture park, warehouse district art walks and robust Indie music scene. The Fremont neighborhood, often invoked as "The People's Republic of Fremont," has transcended its counter-culture vibe to become the gentrified headquarters of choice for tech giants Adobe, Google and Getty Images.

Washington State's lauded outdoor attractions keep Seattleites faithful, despite the inclement weather. There's whale-watching on the Puget Sound, hiking or skiing in the Cascades and the Columbia River's scenic overlooks and world-class wines. Situated amid high desert, Spokane is hardly a tourist destination, but with a lovely park and a charming historic core dotted with fine hotels and restaurants, it's a worthy launch pad for exploring Lake Coeur

Top 3 Tourism Attractions:
1) Olympic National Park
2) Seattle
3) Mount Rainier National Park

Nickname: Evergreen State

State Flower: Coast Rhododendron

State Bird: Willow Goldfinch

People: Bob Barker, TV host; Bing Crosby, singer and actor; John Elway, Denver Broncos quarterback; Bill Gates, Microsoft co-founder

Major Cities: Seattle, Spokane, Tacoma, Vancouver, Bellevue, (Olympia, capital)

Topography: Northwest peninsula—Olympic Mountains; central—Puget Sound lowlands, Cascade Mountains; east—dry canyons, basins

Climate: East—continental climate with hot, dry summers; West—mild climate, high precipitation

Getty Images/iStockphoto

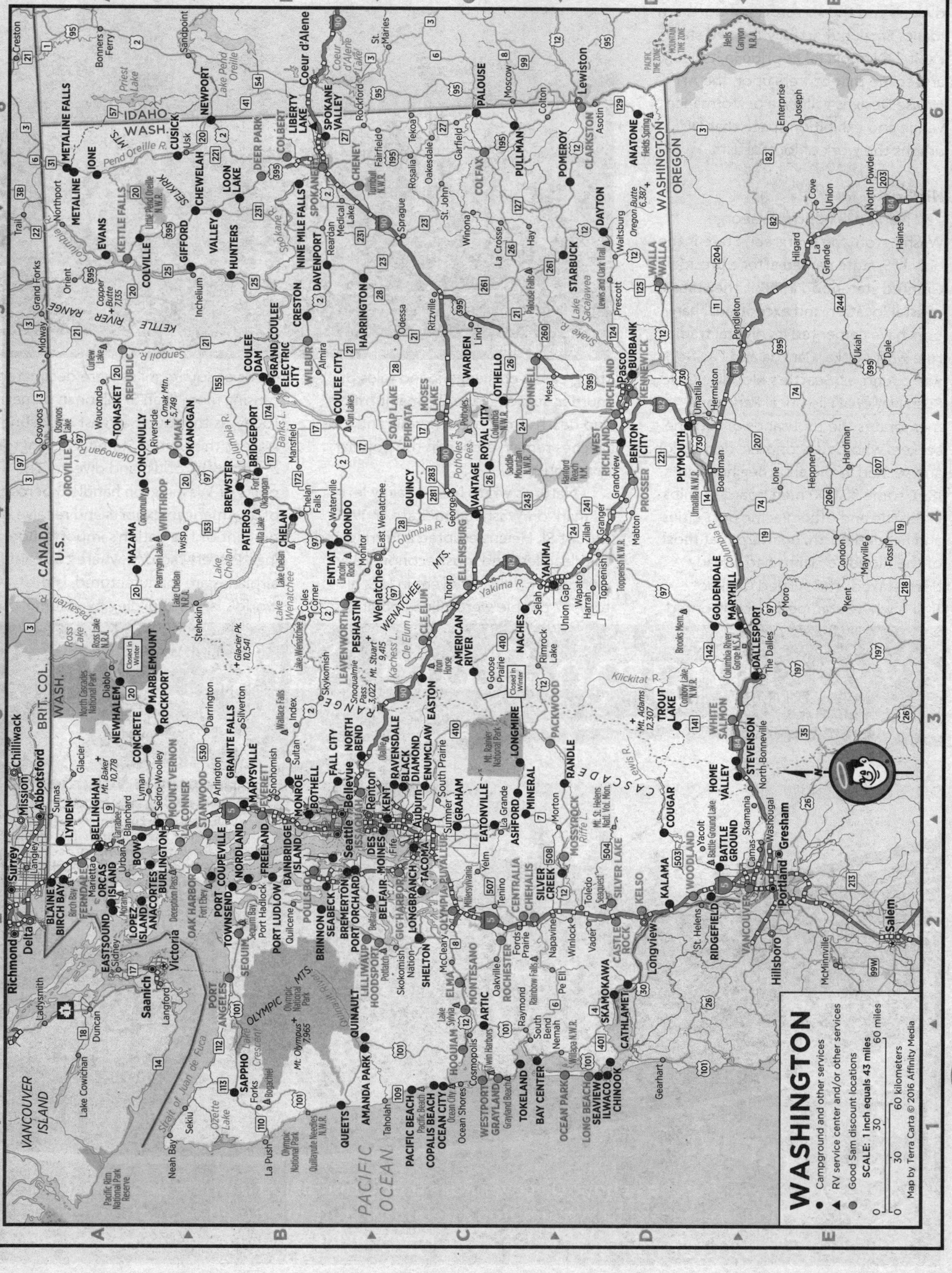
WASHINGTON
Campground and other services
RV service center and/or other services
Good Sam discount locations
SCALE: 1 inch equals 43 miles
0 30 60 miles
0 30 60 kilometers
Map by Terra Carta © 2016 Affinity Media
CANADA
U.S.
BRIT. COL.
WASH.
IDAHO
OREGON
PACIFIC OCEAN
VANCOUVER ISLAND

WA

d'Alene and the ski resorts of northern Idaho. Small but artfully formed state capital Olympia takes pride in its lively arts scene that centers upon the Art House Designs gallery, a performance venue and exhibition space that triumphs the work of local artists.

Seattle skyline Getty Images/iStockphoto

History

Named in honor of George Washington, the Evergreen State is the only U.S. state named after a president. Granted statehood in 1889, the state's coastal location and exceptional harbors have cemented its pivotal trading role with Alaska, Canada and Pacific Rim countries. Seattle's Klondike Gold Rush National Historical Park commemorates the thousands of fortune seekers who fled economic depression and settled in the area. Beginning in 1897, some 30,000 men boarded ships in Seattle and other Pacific port cities and headed north, unaware that most of the Klondike claims had already been staked. The storied Chilkoot Trail is where stampeders confronted the greatest challengers, and tales of murder, suicides, disease, malnutrition and deaths from hypothermia and avalanches remain etched in the popular consciousness.

Nature's wrath has certainly left its mark on Washington State. In 1980, Mount St. Helens erupted and triggered the deadliest and most economically destructive volcanic event in U.S. history; 57 people were killed and hundreds of square miles were decimated causing more than $1 billion in damage. Today, as the fourth largest exporting state in the United States, Washington's economy is robust and diverse. The ports of Washington handle 8 percent of all American exports and receive 6 percent of the nation's imports. Boeing's Everett factory, where twin-aisle airplanes are manufactured, is the world's largest building by volume.

- STAY A WHILE -

Ocean Park Area SW Washington's Beach & Bay

For a vacation close to nature, activities that the entire family will never forget, festivals or events nearly every weekend of the year, plus beautiful scenery, historic landmarks, walking trails and seafood that can't get any fresher, then treat yourself to SW Washington's Ocean Park Area.

Discover the five state parks, pristine bay, two lighthouses, diverse historic communities, beaches, art community, food, wildlife, deep sea lake and river fishing, two golf courses, horseback riding, go kart track, arcade, shopping and festivals, that made the region where the Columbia River meets the Pacific famous.

Why Ocean Park?
The quaint little town of Ocean Park lies at the heart of this beautiful Peninsula. In spite of being small, it contains all the facilities (gas stations, grocery stores, hardware store, restaurants, drinking establishments, gift shops, art galleries, accommodations and beach access) required for a pleasant visit to the seashore. In addition, the surrounding Peninsula, showcases all that is great and appealing about Washington. The Long Beach Peninsula measures 28 miles in length and is only 4 miles wide at its widest point. This 28-mile stretch of beach is recognized as one of the longest beaches in the world, and you can drive on it!

With this vast diversity of activities within such a small area, you can not go wrong choosing the Peninsula as your destination. Please come stay with us. Ocean Park will provide you with a pleasant, quiet and convenient home base close to any and all of our peninsula's attractions.

Washington is the nation's leading producer of apples, lentils, dry edible peas, pears, red raspberries and sweet cherries. A leading lumber producer, large stands of Douglas fir, hemlock, ponderosa and white pine, spruce, larch, and cedar thrive in Washington's forests.

Play

With eight national parks, 68 state parks and Puget Sound's 2,500 miles of shoreline, Seattle offers thrilling adventures on land and water. Soaring to 14,410 feet above sea level, Mount Rainier assumes the mantel of the most glaciated peak in the contiguous U.S., spawning six major rivers. Sub-alpine wildflower meadows encircle the lip of Rainier's active volcano, while ancient forests teeming with wildlife carpet the lower slopes. Only veteran hikers need attempt the 93-mile Wonderland Trail, a strenuous hike around Mount Rainier's rim. The San Juan Islands' emerald green forests, waterfalls, beaches and iridescent waters fulfill every traveler's idea of a pristine island escape, with myriad activities, including kayaking, cycling, Orca-whale-watching and bird-watching. One of the world's most beautiful and accessible mountain ranges, Washington Cascades (just two hour's drive north of Seattle) draws adrenaline seekers to its challenging hiking trails, mountain climbing, downhill and cross country skiing.

At Olympic National Park, it's hard to tear your eyes away from the stunning 1-million-acre tapestry of glaciers, sub-alpine meadows, deep river valleys, temperate rainforest and rugged Pacific coast crisscrossed by 611 miles of backcountry hiking trails. A UNESCO Biosphere Reserve and a World Heritage Site, with 95 percent of the park designated wilderness, Olympic's varied bioclimatic zones provide refuge to unique species, like the Olympic marmot and Piper's bellflower, that are found nowhere else on the planet.

Experience

Mid May, the 25-day Seattle International Film Festival previews 500 films from more than 80 countries as hundreds of directors, actors and industry professionals compete for coveted awards. Seattle celebrates Summer Solstice with the Fremont Fair, which triumphs the neighborhood's self-proclaimed status as the "Center of the Universe." The irreverent street fair fosters Fremont's "delibertas quirkas" (freedom to be peculiar) culture with live bands, art and craft exhibits and food and drink vendors. In late June,

WA

Spokane hosts the world's largest three-a-side street basketball tournament with 250,000 players and spectators competing at 450 courts throughout downtown. For 17 days in September, the town of Puyallup plays host to the Washington State Fair. One of the largest fairs in the world, the nation's top comedians and musicians take to the stage followed by a fireworks extravaganza each Friday evening. There are plenty of wholesome state-fair pursuits, including a petting zoo and parade.

Taste

At restaurants throughout Puget Sound, signature dishes include decadent clam chowder and cedar-plank salmon. Away from the coast, carnivorous tendencies prevail with unadorned steak and potatoes washed down with a local microbrew beer. Pike Place Market (in operation since 1907), overlooking Puget Sound, sells local produce including crisp apples, succulent peaches and gargantuan king crab legs the length of a man's arm; it's the perfect place to stock up before a road trip. In Seattle, the prevailing farm-to-table ethos reaches its zenith at Le Pichet (www.lepichetseattle.com), where bold diners seated at wooden banquettes graze on small, innovative French influenced plates.

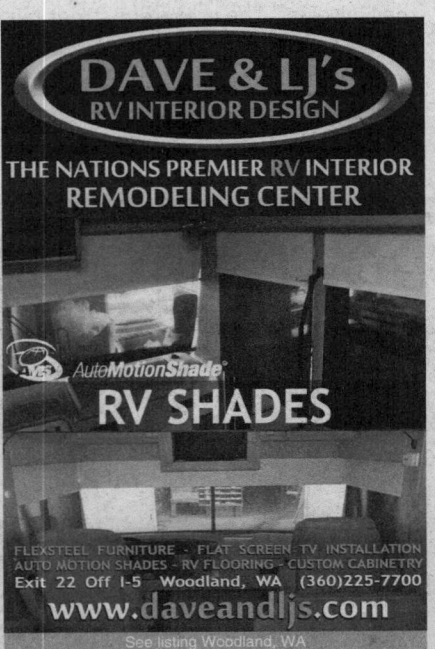

TRAVEL & TOURISM

Washington State Tourism
800-544-1800, 360-725-4000
www.experiencewa.com

Cascade Loop Assn.
509-662-3888
www.cascadeloop.com

Grant County Tourism
www.tourgrantcounty.com

Kitsap Peninsula CVB
800-337-0580
www.visitkitsap.com

Leavenworth Chamber of Commerce
509-548-5807
www.leavenworth.com

Long Beach Peninsula Visitors Burea
800-451-2542
www.funbeach.com

Olympia-Lacey-Tumwater VCB
360-704-7544
www.visitolympia.com

San Juan Islands Visitors Bureau
888-468-3701
www.visitsanjuans.com

Visit Seattle
www.visitseattle.org

Snohomish County Tourism Bureau
888-338-0976
www.snohomish.com

Spokane Regional CVB
888-SPOKANE
www.visitspokane.com

Yakima Valley VCB
800-221-0751
www.yakimavalleytourism.com

OUTDOOR RECREATION

Accessible Outdoor Recreation Guide
360-902-8844
www.parks.wa.gov/ada-rec

Washington Dept. of Fish & Wildlife
360-902-2200
wdfw.wa.gov

Washington Outfitters & Guides Assn.
509-997-1080
www.woga.org

FERRIES

Washington Ferries
360-902-2200
www.wsdot.wa.gov/ferries

SHOPPING

Centralia Outlets
360-736-3327
www.centraliafactoryoutlet.com

Factory Stores of North Bend
425-888-4505
www.premiumoutlets.com/northbend

Getty Images/iStockphoto

Featured Good Sam Parks

WASHINGTON

Good Sam Park

When you stay with Good Sam, you can expect the highest degree of cleanliness and friendliness, and better yet, you get 10% off campground fees.

If you're not already a Good Sam member you can purchase your membership at one of these locations:

CASTLE ROCK
Toutle River RV Resort
(360)274-8373

CENTRALIA
Midway RV Park
(800)600-3204

CHEHALIS
Riverside Golf Course & RV Park
(360)748-8182

CHENEY
Peaceful Pines RV Park & Campground
(800)985-2966

CLARKSTON
Chief Timothy Park
(509)758-9580
Granite Lake Premier RV Resort
(800)989-4578
Hells Canyon RV Resort & Marina
(509)758-6963
Hillview RV Park
(866)758-6299

CLE ELUM
Whispering Pines RV Park
(509)674-7278

COLFAX
Boyer Park and Marina
(509)397-3208

DEER PARK
Spokane RV Resort At Deer Park Golf Club
(877)276-1555

ELLENSBURG
E & J RV Park
(509)933-1500

ELMA
Elma RV Park
(866)211-3939

EPHRATA
Oasis RV Park & Golf Course
(877)754-5102
Sunny Springs Resort & Campground
(800)422-8447

EVERETT
Maple Grove RV Resort
(866)793-2200

GIG HARBOR
Gig Harbor RV Resort
(253)858-8138

GRAYLAND
Kenanna RV Park
(800)867-3515

HOODSPORT
Glen Ayr Resort
(360)877-9522
Skokomish Park At Lake Cushman
(360)877-5760
The Waterfront At Potlatch
(360)877-9422

HOQUIAM
Hoquiam River RV Park
(360)538-2870

ISSAQUAH
Issaquah Village RV Park
(425)392-9233

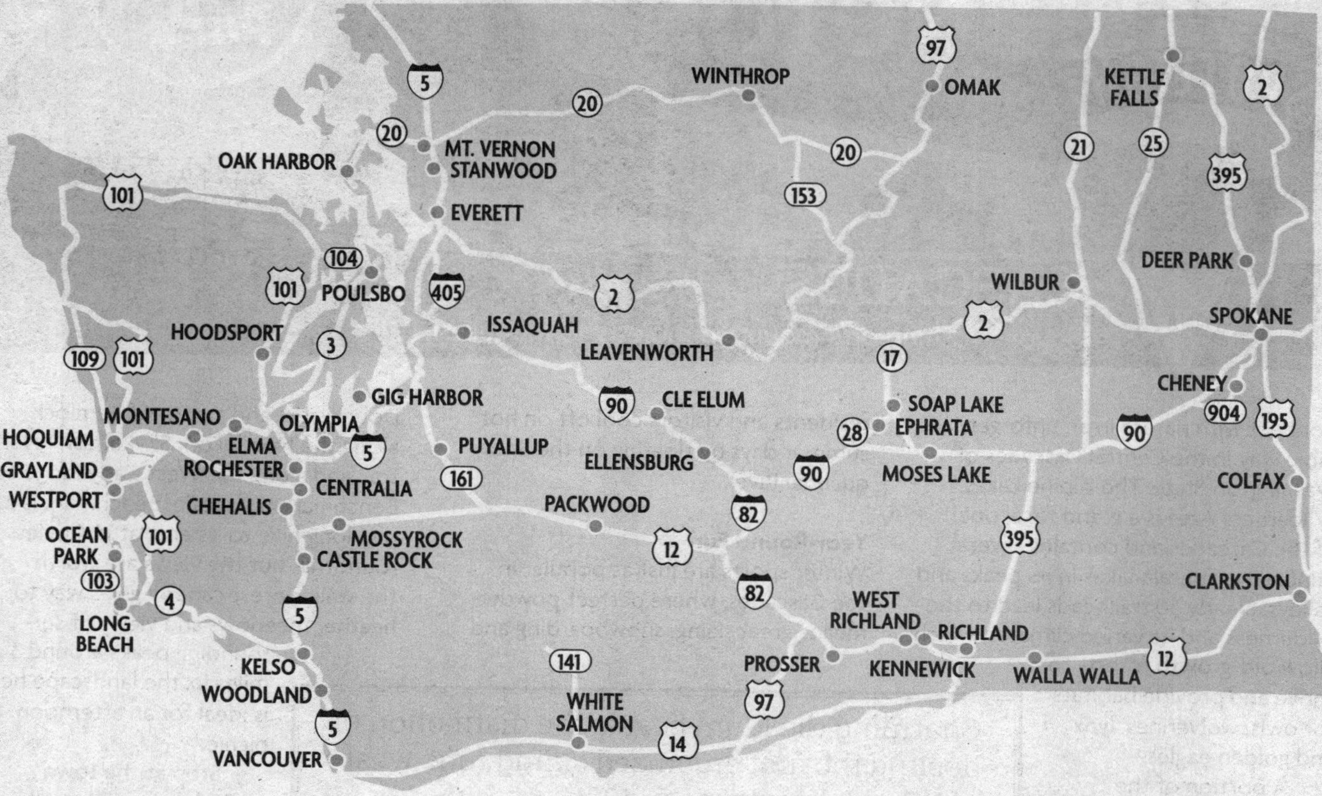

KELSO
Brookhollow RV Park
(800)867-0453

KENNEWICK
Columbia Sun RV Resort
(509)420-4880

KETTLE FALLS
Grandview Inn Motel & RV Park
(509)738-6733

LEAVENWORTH
Icicle River RV Resort
(509)548-5420

LONG BEACH
Driftwood RV Park
(888)567-1902

MONTESANO
Friends Landing
(360)249-5117
MonteSquare RV Park
(360)249-4424

MOSES LAKE
MarDon Resort at Potholes Reservoir
(800)416-2736

MOSSYROCK
Harmony Lakeside RV Park
(877)780-7275

MOUNT VERNON
Mount Vernon RV Park
(800)385-9895
Riverbend RV Park
(360)428-4044

OAK HARBOR
North Whidbey RV Park
(360)675-9597

OCEAN PARK
Westgate Cabins & RV Park
(360)665-4211

OLYMPIA
Riverbend Campground
(360)491-2534
Washington Land Yacht Harbor RV Park
(360)491-3750

OMAK
Carl Precht Memorial RV Park
(509)826-1170

PACKWOOD
Rainier Wings
(360)494-5145

POULSBO
Cedar Glen RV Park
(360)779-4305
Eagle Tree RV Park
(360)598-5988

PROSSER
Wine Country RV Park
(509)786-5192

PUYALLUP
Majestic Mobile Manor RV Park (MHP)
(800)348-3144

RICHLAND
Horn Rapids RV Resort
(866)557-9637
Wright's Desert Gold Motel & RV Park
(509)627-1000

ROCHESTER
Outback RV Park
(360)273-0585

SOAP LAKE
Smokiam RV Resort
(509)246-0413

SPOKANE
North Spokane RV Campground
(509)315-5561

STANWOOD
Cedar Grove Shores RV Park
(866)342-4981

VANCOUVER
Van Mall RV Park
(360)891-1091
Vancouver RV Park
(877)756-2972

WALLA WALLA
Blue Valley RV Park
(509)525-8282

WEST RICHLAND
RV Village Resort
(866)637-9900

WESTPORT
American Sunset RV Resort
(800)569-2267

WHITE SALMON
Bridge RV Park & Campground
(509)493-1111

WILBUR
Country Lane Campground & RV Park
(509)647-0100

WINTHROP
Riverbend RV Park
(509)997-3500
Silverline Resort
(509)996-2448

WOODLAND
Columbia Riverfront RV Park
(800)845-9842
Woodland Shores RV Park
(360)225-2222

WA

For more Good Sam Parks go to listing pages

CASCADES

Savor Washington's mountain majesty to the fullest

Connect with nature in an unforgettable way in the Central Cascades of Washington State. The Alpine Lakes Wilderness Area is a grand focal point of the Cascades and contains several hundred mountain lakes in its peaks and valleys. Nearly 50 trailheads lead to the wilderness and its varied climates, which allow old-growth forests to thrive and provide habitats for owls, wolverines, lynx and golden eagles.

A portion of the famed Pacific Crest Trail (PCT) runs through the Central Cascades, from Snoqualmie Pass to Stevens Pass. In the town of Snoqualmie, the Northwest Railway Museum operates a 5-mile interpretive railway and houses exhibits detailing the history of the railroad in the Northwest. The depot on-site was built in 1890 and remained in active service for 80 years.

Between Snoqualmie and Fall City, the Snoqualmie River plummets 270 feet to become Snoqualmie Falls. The falls were the site of the world's first underground power plant, which was built in 1898. Fall City is a picturesque, unincorporated community where residents and visitors cool off on hot summer days by floating on the Snoqualmie River.

Year-Round Fun

Winter sports are just as popular in the Cascades, where perfect powder means great skiing, snowboarding and snowmobiling at designated "Sno-Parks" located along Interstate 90. Hyak Sno-Park offers sledding and snowshoeing, and Crystal Springs offers tracks for dogsled runners and snowmobile operators.

> Charming Cle Elum boasts the distinction of hosting the first organized skiing runs west of Denver, beginning in 1921.

The town of Skykomish rests on the edge of Alpine Lakes Wilderness Area and welcomes kayakers and whitewater rafters to the Skykomish River. If a lazy day on the river appeals to you, check out a family float trip or just cast a line from the banks to catch steelhead or Chinook salmon.

Take a hike through old-growth Douglas firs and stands of hemlock along the North Fork Skykomish River trail and along the West Cady Ridge to Benchmark Mountain. Benchmark is a day-long hike to its end, at 14.4 miles roundtrip, but the views are worth the walk. Forest canopy gives way to heather meadows and views of surrounding peaks around 3 miles in; the landscape here is ideal for an afternoon picnic.

Stop at the town of Cashmere and stroll through the Cottage Avenue Historic District. The street is home to antique shops and 1900s-era Craftsman bungalows. More history resides at the Historic Museum and Pioneer Village, where children engage in an educational "treasure hunt" and grownups can learn about the museum's exhibits through an audio tour.

Unpack your golf clubs while you're in Cashmere and tee off at Mount Cashmere Golf Course. This petite nine-hole wonder is a feast for the eyes

Rapids on the Skykomish River. Getty Images/iStockphoto

Vineyards in the fall near Lake Chelan. Getty Images/iStockphoto

carved out among apple orchards at the foothills of the Cascade Mountains. Players of all skill levels will appreciate the driving range and putting green.

Alpine Attractions

Raise a glass and toast the ingenuity of Leavenworth and its Bavarian-flavored village feel. Inspired by the soaring mountains in the vicinity, the town remodeled itself to resemble an Alpine community, complete with authentic European architecture, beer gardens and a German restaurant. Tour the Leavenworth Nutcracker Museum or any of several galleries featuring the works of local artists.

Charming Cle Elum boasts the distinction of hosting the first organized skiing runs west of Denver, beginning in 1921. The town's Telephone Museum displays relics of another distinction: Cle Elum becoming Pacific Northwest Bell's last service area to convert from manual phone service to automatic dialing. Trek the nearby Coal Mines Trail and visit historic mining sites along the former railway bed. Points of interest abound along the 4.7-mile path, including former mine buildings, a company store and foundry.

The main attraction in the township of Chelan is Lake Chelan, where swimming, boating and fishing are among the area's popular activities. The lake is remarkably deep; at one-third of a mile down, the lake bottom is below sea level. Picnic sites and a 300-foot stretch of beach, along with boat access and playground equipment, line the shores of the lake. Lake trout, Kokanee and Chinook salmon are among the plentiful species that make for great trophy fishing.

Washington's fertile soil and alpine climate provide perfect conditions for growing wine grapes in the Cascades region. Chelan boasts several wineries that feature tasting rooms and special events, as well as winery tours.

Rustic solitude is on order in the tiny town of Index, where adventurous outdoor enthusiasts find easy access to day-hiking trails and rock-climbing locations. Keep both feet on the ground if you prefer, and visit Pickett Index Historical Museum. Mining and logging are the focal points, along with exhibits detailing the area's history with natural disasters.

Wallace Falls State Park, near the town of Monroe, is a 4,735-acre camping park on the shores of Wallace River, Wallace Lake, Jay Lake, Shaw Lake and the Skykomish River. The breathtaking scenery of Wallace Falls includes a 265-foot waterfall, old-growth forests and wildlife-viewing opportunities. Peregrine falcons and cougars have been spotted in the park. Travel north to Mount Pilchuck and take in the view from a historic fire lookout.

> Between Snoqualmie and Fall City, the Snoqualmie River plummets 270 feet to become Snoqualmie Falls.

For More Information

Washington State Tourism
800-544-1800
www.experiencewa.com

WA

Getty Images/iStockphoto

COULEE CORRIDOR

Take a beautiful byway that traverses a landscape carved by glaciers

The Coulee Corridor Scenic Byway is a compelling route that meanders 150 miles from Connell to Omak. Along this journey, travelers will discover numerous stops for recreation, relaxation and adventure.

The eastern Washington corridor follows the Columbia River's Ice-Age glacier path, where landscapes include semi-arid desert, pothole lakes, wetlands and canyons. The coulees, for which the corridor is named, are deep ravines carved into the bedrock by post-glacial flooding. The descendants of early inhabitants make up the Colville Confederated Tribes, and their legacy is memorialized at the Tribal Museum in Coulee Dam.

Coulee Corridor is a birder's dream come true. More than half of the 346 species recorded annually in Washington can be spotted along this route. From sandhill cranes to black-crowned night herons to bald eagles, birdwatching opportunities abound year-round.

The community of Connell was first established as a railroad stop in 1883. It preserves its history in the Connell Heritage Museum through a collection of archival photos and documents. Summertime travelers are welcome to cool off at the city's Pioneer Park Pool.

> The dam attracts thousands of guests to explore its visitor center and to stay later on summer evenings for a laser light show on the surface of the dam.

Othello is well-known for its springtime sandhill crane festival, which features education sessions and tours for crane viewing. But visitors are also welcome to tour the Old Hotel Art Gallery and to drop by one of the city's many other community celebrations, including the annual Adams County Fair and Rodeo.

Potholes State Park near Othello sits adjacent to Potholes Reservoir, which offers 6,000 feet of freshwater shoreline surrounded by desert and freshwater marsh terrain. Hike three miles of trails through the park, or take a boat out on the water from one of four ramps. Freshwater fishing in the reservoir is permitted with a state license.

Getting Creative in Moses Lake

There's plenty to explore in the town of Moses Lake. The Moses Lake Museum & Art Center is home to a collection of Native American artifacts, local history exhibits and fine art pieces, as well as a metal sculpture of a giant Columbian mammoth.

A local water park provides a cool respite on warm summer days, as do the Moses Lake Water Trails. The trails run through Moses Lake, which is 18 miles long and boasts more than 120 miles of shoreline. Kayaks, canoes and other non-motorized boats are ideal for exploring the parks along the trails.

Take a plunge into miraculous mud at Soap Lake, a mineral lake with a neighboring resort community touting the health benefits of getting down and dirty. Native American tribes took advantage of the mineralized waters and mud, and visitors flock to the shores of Soap Lake for the same reason. Once you're squeaky clean again, be sure to visit the Soap Lake Art Museum and Healing Water Gallery to see works by local artists, grab a bite to eat at a local European deli and browse a quirky antique store.

Dry Falls State Park is an arid oasis dotted with freshwater lakes. Once home to a massive waterfall, now all that remains is a 400-foot-high cliff that's 3.5 miles wide. The lakes still support wildlife, fishing and boating opportunities, and birdwatching. Golfers hit the links at a nine-hole golf course, and hikers traverse trails around geologic features and desert plants and animals.

In the town of Coulee City, an historic walking tour tells the story of the Grand Coulee Dam's construction and its impact on the people who lived there. Banks Lake is a warm-water fishery for black crappie, bluegill, channel catfish and largemouth bass, as well as rainbow trout and lake whitefish. Ice-fishing is popular in winter here, too.

A Steamboat and a Ski Loop

The north end of the lake is the site of Steamboat Rock State Park, with a sandy swimming area and several miles of horse trails, as well as a hiking trail to Northrup Lake. The Northrup Canyon hike features views of basalt cliffs and the remains of an old homestead.

Two miles above Grand Coulee Dam is the city of Grand Coulee. The dam attracts thousands of guests to explore its visitor center and to stay later on summer evenings for a laser light show. The city is home to a quirky collection of windmill folk art crafted by Emil Gehrke, a late resident

Grand Coulee Dam viewpoint at Steamboat Rock State Park. Mark Wagner

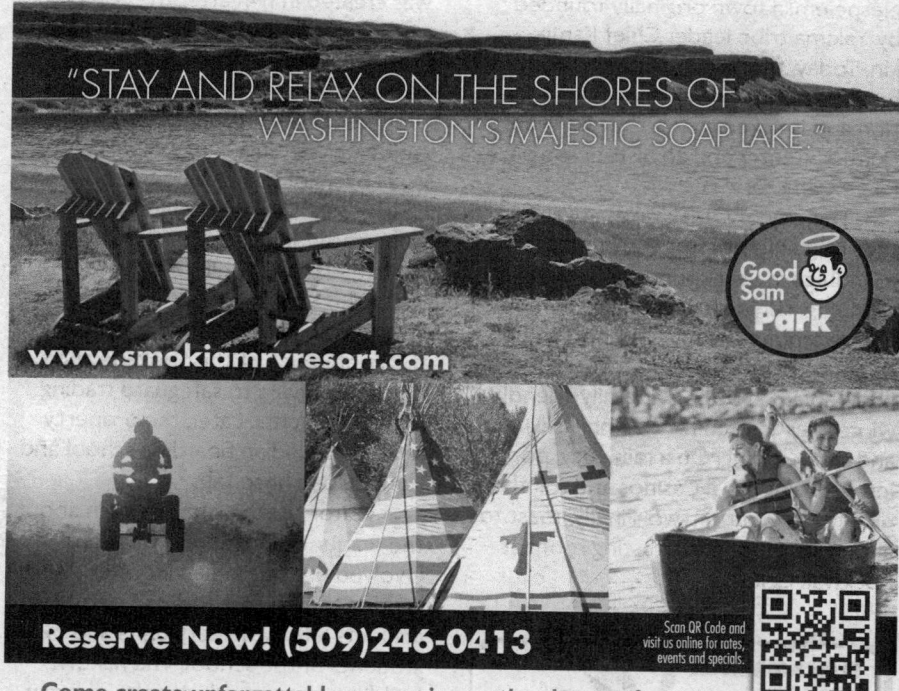

WA

Grand Coulee Dam and nearby town of Fiddle Creek. Gregg M. Erickson

Lake Roosevelt. Getty Images/iStockphoto

of nearby Electric City. More than 120 windmills populate the windmill garden, which is open to visitors.

Native American history and a legacy of mining form the backbone of Nespelem, a town originally founded by Yakima tribe leader Chief Kamiakin. Today, the small town rests in the borders of the Colville Indian Reservation and is home to the Colville Tribal Cultural Center and an historic Nez Perce Cemetery.

The city of Omak takes advantage of its high-desert surroundings to indulge in year-round recreation. Camping, fishing, skiing and snowmobiling are among the many opportunities to get out and enjoy the scenery. The Loup Loup Ski Bowl is a family-friendly winter destination for downhill skiing and snow tubing. On a rainy day, pop into Colville Tribal Casinos and roll the dice for an hour or two. Finally, toast to a fun-filled trip in the tasting room at Rockwall Cellars.

Life on Lake Roosevelt

No trip to the Coulee Corridor would be complete without visiting the Lake Roosevelt National Recreation Area. The centerpiece is the 130-mile lake that was created in 1941 after the completion of the Grand Coulee Dam. Named after President Franklin D. Roosevelt, the recreation area provides lots of opportunities for boating, swimming, fishing, canoeing, hunting.

Lovers of history should tour nearby Fort Spokane, built on land that was a gathering place for thousands of for native tribes fishing on the rapids of the Spokane River. In 1880, the U.S. Army established the fort above the confluence of the Spokane and Columbia Rivers to safeguard trading and settlements. Later, the property became an Indian boarding school and tuberculosis hospital.

Visitors to the site can learn about the unique uniforms and weapons involved on the "Indian Frontier." While touring the fort, visitors can peruse artifacts left by military units and by students of the school. The historic buildings are open during the summer season, and short walking trails around the grounds allow hikers to explore the surrounding wilderness.

Turn another chapter in history by visiting St. Paul's Mission, also located in the Roosevelt National Recreation Area. The mission's history stretches back to the mid-1800s when Catholic missionaries traveled the region to convert the Native Americans to Christianity. In 1840, Father DeSmet, a Belgian Jesuit, established a permanent mission near Kettle Falls for the more than 800 Indians who assembled in the area to fish.

Over the years, the building deteriorated, but it was restored in 1939 and still stands.

For More Information

Coulee Corridor Consortium
509-634-1608
www.couleecorridor.com

Washington State Tourism
800-544-1800
www.experiencewa.com

GATEWAY TO WASHINGTON

Find Evergreen State wonders just off the interstate

The stretch of Interstate 5 that runs from Vancouver to Olympia in Washington is a scenic journey through some of the state's most stunning natural beauty.

The obvious place to start is the city of Vancouver, located between the Pacific Ocean and the Cascade Mountains just across the border from Portland, Oregon. Its proximity to abundant freshwater makes this town a prime destination for sport fishing. The Columbia River is home to steelhead, coho and chinook salmon. Battling a 20-pound fish is a sport fisherman's dream tale to tell, and the fall salmon run beckons fishing enthusiasts by the hundreds.

Back on dry land, visit historic Fort Vancouver and step back in time to the days of fur traders and frontier life. The reconstructed fort is home to working trade houses dedicated to baking, carpentry and blacksmithing. Grab a bite at The Grant House, the oldest residence in the city and the namesake of former fort quartermaster and U.S. president, Ulysses S. Grant.

Vancouver's thriving arts scene encompasses live musical performances from the city's symphony orchestra and a popular Polynesian festival celebrating the heritage of the Hawaiian residents.

> Climb Seminary Hill, an urban natural space that overlooks the Chehalis and Skookumchuck River Valleys.

In the summer, the Pavilion at Esther Short Park welcomes audiences to outdoor concerts.

On the Wild Side

Sauvie Island is where bird hunters go to bag pheasant, dove, Canada goose and quail. This island, nestled in the middle of the Columbia River, receives more than 1 million visitors each year—many of whom flock to the island for its beaches, bike trails and boating opportunities. Bird-watchers enjoy sighting any of the more than 250 species that call the island home. Once the residence of Multnomah Indian tribes, the island is dedicated to wildlife preservation and farming as well as outdoor recreation.

Ridgefield National Wildlife Refuge rests on the banks of the Columbia River just north of Vancouver. It provides a wintering habitat for Canada goose subspecies and is home to neo-tropical songbirds and other native species. The refuge also preserves what's become the most intact archeological site on the lower portion of the river. The history and culture of the people who occupied this region for nearly 2,300 years are displayed at the Cathlapotle Plankhouse, which is open to visitors on weekends in spring and summer.

Castle Rock, known as the gateway to Mount St. Helens, earned its moniker from an impressive 190-foot-high monolith that once served as a landmark for fur traders and local tribes. Today, the town is a destination for outdoor recreation such as hiking, boating, hunting and fishing. The town's historic district is a prime spot for antiques shopping, gifts and locally sourced works of art. The Castle Rock Exhibit Hall and Visitors Center details the impact of the volcano's eruption on the region, and role of the logging industry in the development of the town.

See Mount St. Helens from the inside—sort of—at the Visitor Center at Silver Lake. This award-winning educational center features a step-in model of the volcano as well as interactive exhibits and theater programs. Mount St. Helens is part of the Gifford Pinchot National Forest, which covers more than 1.3 million acres and includes river valleys and waterfalls alongside the national volcanic monument. Known for its devastating 1980 eruption. Mount St.

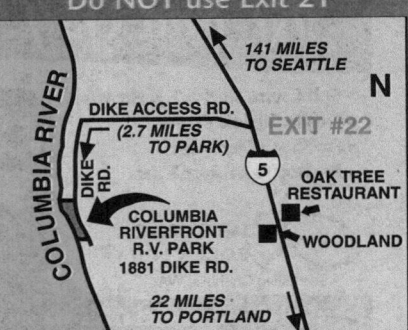

Mountain Sports

The town of Rainier celebrates the majesty of its namesake peak with heritage train rides and a railway museum, scenic driving tours and cross-country skiing trails. Mount Tahoma Trails hosts skiers in winter and hikers in summer, both of whom can traverse the paths that wind through the ridges and valleys of the Cascade range.

One of the most popular driving tours is the route circling Mount Rainier. At 78 miles long, the drive offers views of Mt. Rainier's snow-covered ridges and old-growth rainforests, as well as waterfalls and scenic vistas. Stops include Skate Creek for fall color displays. A stop at Longmire rewards visitors with a stunning shot of the mountain and views of the 40-foot Christine Falls.

Centralia's settler history is the backdrop for Fort Borst Park. Here, visitors can explore a replica of a one-room school house, a homestead and the Fort Borst Blockhouse, a hand-hewn log structure that was used to store grain. Get some fresh air at Seminary Hill, an urban natural space with more than 2 miles of trails that overlooks the town and the Chehalis and Skookumchuck River Valleys.

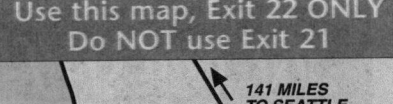

For More Information

Washington State Tourism
800-544-1800
www.experiencewa.com

Joe Mabel

GRAYS HARBOR/LONG BEACH/OCEAN PARK

Experience nirvana in three charming slices of Washington State

South of the Olympic Peninsula, Washington's Pacific Coast is rich in low-key cities and waterways that are ripe for fun and exploration. Small town charm meets maritime adventure in these gems of the West.

Start your adventure at Grays Harbor, where you'll find a slice of northwestern nirvana that's home to a lush northern rainforest. Here, ribbons of Pacific Ocean beachfront encircle a large, spade-shaped estuarine bay on the northwest coast of the state.

Home to seven inland bodies of water, portions of the Quinault Rainforest and more than 50 miles of pristine ocean shoreline, the Grays Harbor area

The Grays Harbor Historical Seaport Authority is home to the Lady Washington, a 90-ton tall-ship replica.

is a boon for anyone with a thirst for the great outdoors. You can paddle the coast by kayak in the morning, fetch some fresh fish for lunch in the middle of the day and then hike a rugged mountain trail in the afternoon. Or if big outdoor adventure isn't quite your pace, you can simply hop from waterfront town to waterfront town, exploring an endless supply of boutique shops and cozy mom-and-pop cafes. The choice is yours.

The three small cities of Aberdeen, Hoquiam and Cosmopolis constitute the economic hub of Grays Harbor. The trio is clustered around the eastern shores of Grays Harbor, where the Chehalis River, Hoquiam River and Wishkah River spill into the bay.

More Than Nirvana

In Aberdeen, visitors are greeted by a sign that says, "Come as you Are," the first of many references to famed alternative-rock band Nirvana's lead singer/guitarist, Kurt Cobain. The infamous grunge rocker grew up in Aberdeen, and it was here that the first glimmers of fame for Nirvana began to attract national attention.

Swing by the Aberdeen Museum of History—housed in an historic armory building dating to the early 1920s—for a thorough exploration of city and regional history. The collections are eclectic, to say the least, ranging from Cobain's couch to a fully restored blacksmith shop to an original Model T Ford.

The Grays Harbor Historical Seaport Authority is also housed in Aberdeen, and is home to the Lady Washington, a 90-ton tall-ship replica of the same sloop sailboat commissioned for explorer Robert Gray in 1787. The original Lady Washington was the first American vessel to navigate the west

The Lady Washington sets sail in Grays Harbor. Miso Beno

coast of North America. Today, the replica is as stunning as it is educational, and a guided walk on its deck is a rare opportunity to travel back in time.

From Aberdeen, head for the nearby town of Hoquiam, located a few miles to the west near the shores of a small harbor peninsula. Stroll the historic downtown core and spend an afternoon plundering the town's abundance of eclectic boutiques and antique shops. Between Wednesday and Saturday at any point in the year, the Grays Harbor Farmers Market and Craft Fair will likely be in full swing.

Love for Long Beach

About an hour's drive south on U.S. Route 101, the Long Beach peninsula is Washington's most commercial stretch of coast. Flanking 28 miles of beach, dunes and forests, a scattering of seaside towns cater to holiday makers of every generation, with resorts, motels, amusement parks, trinket shops, museums, galleries, lighthouses, restaurants and a lively festival calendar. When the sun finally shines, active Washingtonians take to the beaches for kite flying, horseback riding, fishing, razor clam digging and beachcombing.

The wild and rugged Long Beach coastline may not lend itself to gentle swimming, but swathes of open sands blasted by gusty winds create perfect conditions for kite flyers; and with a handful of kite stores in Long Beach, it's easy to partake in the ritual.

One of the few beaches on the west coast where you can ride horseback on the sand, Long Beach fulfills every equestrian's desire to gallop full throttle along the shore.

Head north along the peninsula for the low-key community of Ocean Park, which is worth a stroll for its handful of evocative structures and homes that speak to the town's origin as a station on the narrow gauge railroad: Ilwaco Railway and Navigation Company.

Housed in the Taylor Hotel building—one of the oldest buildings in the region, built in 1887—Adelaide's café/bookstore is a local institution, beloved for its excellent coffee, pastries and breakfast sandwiches. One of the oldest businesses in Washington State, Jack's Country Store, founded in 1885, oozes frontier charm with its parquet floors, rolling ladders, stained glass and beautiful oak display cases. An inventory of more than 200,000 items, include fresh fish and seafood (don't miss the smoked oysters from the in-house smokehouse) kitchen gadgets, retro children's toys and hardware supplies.

For More Information

Grays Harbor Tourism
800-621-9625
www.visitgraysharbor.com

Long Beach Peninsula
800-451-2542
www.funbeach.com

Washington State Tourism
800-544-1800
www.experiencewa.com

Getty Images/iStockphoto

GREATER SEATTLE

Explore every facet of the Pacific Northwest's crown jewel

Despite the Northwest's notorious precipitation, the "Emerald City" of Seattle forms the glittering epicenter of a region that passionately embraces outdoor adventure regardless of the season. Yes, it's the birthplace of Starbucks and REI, it's the cradle of grunge music and it's home to tech giants Microsoft and Amazon, as well as the beloved Pike Place Market, but the Greater Seattle area loves to defy cliché with its irreverence, authenticity and powers of reinvention.

> The oldest covered market in the country, Pike Place is a cornucopia of stands selling seafood and more.

From world-class arts to iconic music venues, not to mention its breathtaking setting, this magical tranche of the Pacific Northwest passionately embraces individualism and revels in its distinct cultural heritage.

The Beat Goes On

Orbiting a shimmering skyline defined by the iconic Space Needle, Seattle's eclectic constellation of diverse neighborhoods reveals the thrusting spirit and quest for inventiveness that defines the region. The best place to launch an urban tour is at Pioneer Square, where Seattle's gold-rush origins can be traced along the 21-block "Trail to Treasure." The oldest covered market in the country, Pike Place is a cornucopia of stands that purvey everything from fresh seafood to artfully arranged fruit and vegetables, curios and artisan products. Spend time in the Crafts Market, which sells handmade goods by local artisans. Here, you'll find a wide range of fashion accessories and apparel along with pottery goods and glass and metal sculpture.

Few neighborhoods can lay claim to a 1950s Cold War relic (the Fremont Rocket) as their community symbol. The "People's Republic of Fremont," with its off-beat stores, iconoclastic galleries and edgy cafés (and even a quirky troll and a statue of Lenin) still clings to its subculture status despite being the headquarters of choice for tech behemoths like Adobe and Getty Images. These days, it's all happening at South Lake Union, a former industrial wasteland that has been transformed into a dynamic urban village that boasts some of the city's most acclaimed art galleries, as well as innovative dining spots, funky stores and the shiny, happy Amazon campus.

River Deep, Mountain High

Draped with lush coniferous forests, the Seattle area combines excitement and unpredictability (and that's not just the weather) with stunning natural beauty. Rising to the west, the Olympic Mountains, a breathtaking vision of sawtooth peaks and colossal glaciers, are some of the most magnificent mountains in the world (in relation to their height). To the west, Mount Rainier, an active volcano, soars to 14,410 feet, the poster child for Washington's foreboding landscape. Within easy reach of Seattle's downtown, recreational opportunities abound.

The entire Seattle area is laced with terrific cycling paths; the Burke-Gilman Trail unfurls for 14 miles from Ballard to the northern fringes of Lake Washington. For urban kayaking, Lake Union affords great views of the Seattle skyline, and you can paddle alongside

WA

LAKE PLEASANT RV PARK
A Quiet Valley Setting... Close To All The Seattle Area Attractions
24025 Bothell Everett Hwy. S.E.
Bothell, WA 98021
Exit 26 Off I-405 Then Just 1 Mile South On Bothell Everett Highway
Big Rig Friendly
Paved Sites
Paved Interior Roads
Nature Trails
Park Your Rig While You Take a Cruise
Wi-Fi • Fishing
Easy access to Seattle & Tacoma
Reservations Recommended
(800) 742-0386
or (425) 487-1785
RATED
9/9.5★/9.5
See listing Bothell, WA
http://www.goodsamcamping.com.s3.amazonaws.com/gsparks/LakePleasant/LakePleasant.html

some restaurants and bars that line the waterfront. Park your kayak and grab a beer, or other cold refreshment.

Generally speaking, it's only athletes at the top of their game that challenge themselves to a vertiginous day hike to the top of Mount Si (less than an hour from Seattle). Rising sheer from the Snoqualmie River valley, the views from the top of Si are sublime.

Despite being on the fringes of a major metropolis, Discovery Park, on the Puget Sound waterfront, is a haven for wildlife with an inventory of around 300 bird species in addition to large mammals including coyotes, black bears and cougars. The Discovery Park Loop Trail, which was designated a National Recreation Trail in 1975, comprises a 3-mile path that links to 10 miles of gentle hiking trails.

Musical Nirvana

It's no wonder that the deeply introspective city that inspired Kurt Cobain and Jimi Hendrix beats to a different drum. Seattle's legacy may be grunge, but the city's venues run the gamut of every musical genre.

Across from Pike Place Market, the Showbox at the Market is a city institution, having played host to everyone from Nat King Cole to Blondie since it first opened its doors in 1939.

A veteran of the vaudeville scene, the Colombia City Theater was renovated in 2010. In the 1940s, the sumptuous theater played host to legends such Duke Ellington and Ella Fitzgerald before finding its new vocation in the 1990s as a hippy art commune.

The Art of Life

The newly redesigned Seattle Art Museum triumphs contemporary art with masterworks by Mark Tobey, Kenneth Callahan, Guy Anderson and Morris Graves. There's also a fine collection of furniture, sculptures and decorative arts from the Pacific Northwest, along with a worthy cache of Northwest Coast Native American art. Curators have expertly arranged art objects from a wide range of cultures.

An offshoot of the Seattle Art Museum, the waterfront Olympic Sculpture Park is the latest jewel in the crown of a city bestowed with unique cultural riches. A former industrial park framed by the glistening waters of the Puget Sound has been recast as a nine-acre showcase for world-class contemporary art works, including sculptures by Richard Serra, Alexander Calder and Mark di Suvero.

For an insight into Native American culture, Discovery Park's Daybreak Star Cultural Center hosts cultural events and workshops in addition to powwows and art exhibitions.

Invigorating the Frye Art Museum's collection of 19th-century portraits and landscape paintings, a series of modern and abstract artworks by Pacific Northwest artists, forms a great introduction—or the last stop of your visit—to learn about the region's fascinating cultural heritage.

For More Information

Visit Seattle
866-732-2695
www.visitseattle.org

Washington State Tourism
800-544-1800
www.experiencewa.com

WA

Getty Images/iStockphoto

HELLS CANYON

Don't let the name fool you—this is heaven for outdoors lovers

Hells Canyon. The name alone lights a fire in the imagination. Is it really and truly a landscape of precipitous peril and natural danger? Or is it simply an exaggeration, a relic from a bygone era of intrepid exploration?

Spend 10 minutes deep in the gullet of this mesmerizingly treacherous slice of the Snake River in southeastern Washington and you'll have your answer: This is rough country, through and through. It's considered so aggressively impassable, in fact, that in 1975 the U.S. Congress deemed 31.5 miles of the river from Hells Canyon Dam to Upper Pittsburg Landing as officially "wild." It's almost completely inaccessible by anything other than a river raft, so if your heart is set on exploring this scenic river ecosystem, buckle up and prepare for a wild ride.

The Lewis-Clark Valley in southeastern Washington is considered the Gateway to Hells Canyon, despite the fact that the canyon itself is largely found straddling the Oregon-Idaho border further south. The wilderness is so thick and impassable that tours and expeditions are organized in the sister cities of Lewiston and Clarkson, which sit at the confluence of the Snake and Clearwater rivers. From here, visitors can follow in the footsteps and paddlestrokes of some of history's most daring explorers, including Lewis and Clark, who tried and failed to battle the raging rapids and bone-shattering rocks of Hells Canyon in the 19th century.

> The Snake has to twist—sharply, frequently and aggressively—in order to wind its way downstream.

Today, many of the most dangerous rapids have been tamed by the damming of the river upstream from Hells Canyon, making a professionally guided tour of the river by jetboat, raft or kayak not only extremely enjoyable but also suitable for all ages.

As you set out on your journey down the Snake River and move closer to the stretch that comprises Hells Canyon, you'll gradually begin to discover what the flow of water can accomplish if given 13 million years to get the job done. The Snake River has slowly but surely carved out the deepest gorge on the continent, with walls topping out at 8,000-foot peaks at the canyon's highest point. Deeper, yes, than even the Grand Canyon.

If you're exploring the Snake River and Hells Canyon by jetboat from Lewis-Clark Valley, your trip will be divided into two sections. The first section is considered the "scenic" section of the river.

Dotted along the banks, beaches and cavernous rock shelves of the canyon is evidence of the Snake River's human history, from ancient Native American petroglyphs carved into the rock walls tens of thousands of years ago, to the ramshackle ruins of a bygone mining boom, which gripped the river from the 1860s to the 1920s.

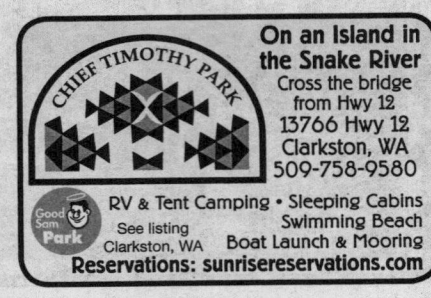

At its deepest point, Hells Canyon surpasses the Grand Canyon.
Art Bromage

There are plenty of places to stop, have a picnic, take a hike or go fishing before carrying on upstream.

Most guided expeditions make a stop at Cache Creek Ranch in the Hells Canyon National Recreation Area. An on-site permanently staffed visitor center provides informative exhibits and a chance to recharge before setting off into the second section of the river—the "wild" section.

As you close in on Pittsburg Landing you'll start to notice a change in the canyon walls and surrounding wilderness. The terrain begins to thicken and the walls begin to rise at a steeper grade, but this is only a taste of what's to come. Be sure to stop at Pittsburg Landing for a break. This is one of the busier stops along the river due to it being one of the last full-service stops on the trip upstream to Hells Canyon Dam. It features a boat launch, campground, access to the northern reaches of Hells Canyon National Recreation Area and a 6-mile marked trail to Kirkwood Historic Ranch.

Once you push off from the landing to complete the trip to Hells Canyon Dam you'll be seeing Hells Canyon at its finest. From this point on, it's just as easy to see how the Snake River got its name as it is to see how Hells Canyon acquired its own. The Snake has to twist—sharply, frequently and aggressively—in order to wind its way downstream through the choking gorge walls on either side.

The canyon's deepest sections—Hat Point, Heavens Gate and Kinney Point—are found here. Before the construction of the dam, this is also where you would have found some of the most dangerous whitewater rapids in the world, the very same that turned Lewis and Clark back the other way, to search for an alternate route.

From tip to tail, this mesmerizing slice of the Snake River is a dream come true for adventure-seekers.

For More Information

Hells Canyon Visitor Bureau
877-774-7248
www.visitlcvalley.com

Washington State Tourism
800-544-1800
www.experiencewa.com

Aerial photo of Hell's Canyon Dam. Samuel M Beebe, Ecotrust

WA

MOUNT RAINIER & MOUNT ST HELENS

Washington's two iconic peaks lure explorers with unforgettable trails

Visible from Seattle, Washington state's fabled Cascade Range comprises an 800-mile line of volcanoes that stretches from British Columbia to the tip of California. Formed from plate tectonics, some of the most powerful stratovolcanoes (tall, perfect cone volcanoes formed over centuries by layers of volcanic material) on earth can be found here: Mount Baker, Glacier Peak, Mount Rainier, Mount St. Helens and Mount Adams.

Mount Rainier:
The Power and the Glory

In 1899, Mount Rainier became the nation's fifth national park. Set off by its 26 glaciers, the hauntingly beautiful Rainier is inauspiciously deemed one of the world's most dangerous volcanoes due to its monumental size, the tremendous volume of ice and snow draped over its cone and its proximity to large population centers. Steam vents that gust from the mountain's peak suggest that while the volcano is currently dormant, the potential for an eruption should not be ignored. More reassuringly, scientists believe that Rainier's volcanic activity only occurs every 3,000 years.

Mount Rainier:
Trails of the Unexpected

Given its seductive beauty and mythical aura, Mount Rainier has become a rite of passage for serious climbers. The first documented summit of Mount Rainier was made in 1870 by Gen. Hazard Stevens. Certainly, climbing the 14,409-foot volcano is not for the faint of heart; an estimated 9,000 climbers attempt to summit each year, and more than half of those fail. For lesser mortals, the mountain's snow-capped peak and verdant lower foothills afford some 260 miles of hiking trails. If you have around two weeks to spare, the Wonderland Trail's 93-mile loop circles Mount Rainier, passing through

Mount Rainier with wildflowers in the foreground. Getty Images/iStockphoto

subalpine meadows, glacial streams, mountain passes and valley forests to an ultimate summit point of 6,500 feet at Panhandle Gap, which features some of the most awe-inspiring panoramas in the nation.

Despite the tourist onslaught during the summer, the best day hikes are Paradise and Sunrise alpine trails. At Paradise, the 5-mile Skyline Trail ascends through stunning meadows, while at Sunrise, the 5-mile Burroughs Mountain Trail and the 5 1/2-mile Mount Fremont Lookout Trail are scenic and afford wildlife-watching, most consistently in the form of mountain goats. If you are traveling with children, Rainier's most idyllic low-elevation hike is the 1.5-mile Grove of the Patriarchs Trail that weaves through a stunning grove of 1,000-year-old red cedars on an island in the Ohanapecosh River. For those who prefer a window seat, it takes around 5 hours to drive around the mountain (147 miles). Mount Rainier is open year-round, but many mountain roads are closed during their winter season, Nov. 1-May 1. Enshrouded with the Pacific's moisture-soaked air, Rainier's glaciated slopes remain snow-capped year-round.

Mount St Helens: The Sound and the Fury

Lording over mystical forests, the picture-perfect volcano of Mount St Helens, 178 miles south of Seattle, instilled the nation with horror on May 18, 1980, when it erupted with a violence unprecedented in the modern era. The cataclysmic eruption blasted off the side of the volcano and spliced the top 1,300 feet off the peak to set off the largest landslide on record. The blast, which spewed out ash at 650 miles per hour, was heard hundreds of miles away with ash scattered as far away as Denver. Some 57 people lost their lives.

Mount St. Helens: Close Encounters

Mount St Helens has been preserved as Mount St. Helens National Volcanic Monument. Several visitor centers provide state-of-the-art interpretive exhibits that examine the causes of the eruption and the ongoing reforestation project. Chiseled into the mountainside, the Johnston Ridge Observatory,

The Mount Freemont Lookout in Mount Rainier National Park. Getty Images/iStockphoto

A Stellar's jay on Mount Rainier. Getty Images/Hemera

located at the blast zone just five miles from the crater, provides the best vantage point to behold the sputtering volcano.

The Mount St. Helens National Volcanic Monument forms part of the Gifford Pinchot National Forest. Within the park's 1,368,300 acres, there are five high-altitude lakes within a 7-mile radius and 200 miles of hiking trails. These paths weave through meadows carpeted with wildflowers and berry fields, cross stunning river valleys and skirt St. Helens' growing volcanic crater, Washington's newest glacier. For wildlife watching, the areas of Lone Butte, Cayuse and Skookum Meadows are prime spots to view elk, deer, warblers and turtles.

Some of the best hiking trails in Gifford Pinchot include the Norway Pass to Mount Margaret (just over 10 miles round trip), which leads through wildflower fields to a ridge that offers jaw-dropping views of Rainier, Adams and Hood, as well as Mount St. Helens. A more challenging hike (narrow trails with steep drop-offs) to Harry's Ridge (8 miles round trip) leaves from the Johnston Ridge Observatory and affords incredible views of the crater's mouth along with Loowit Falls and an emerging glacier. On clear days, you can also see Spirit Lake, Mount Adams and Mount Hood. Along Eruption Trail, you can see the emerging lava dome and, heading east from the Johnston Ridge Observatory, the Boundary Ridge Trail provides surreal panoramas of the blast zone.

Going Ape

Follow the blazing trail of searing magma by exploring Ape Cave Lava Tube, one of the most popular attraction in Mount St. Helens National Monument. At more than two miles in length, Ape Cave is considered the longest lava tube in the continental United States. Ape Cave is located on the south side of the mountain and is accessible through Woodland.

For true spelunkers, nearby Lake Cave is harder to find but worth the trip. Parts of the underground chamber require crawling, so only serious explorers should consider entering this challenging space.

If you prefer treetop adventure to subterranean trails, drop in on Mount St. Helens Zipline Adventures. Located in Silver Lake, this attraction allows adventure-seekers to strap into harnesses and zip along lines strung between immense trees. When you're done speeding under the forest canopy, enjoy views of the mountain from Treehouse Island, with roomy observation decks that dish out spectacular views of the forest and beyond.

For More Information

Mount St. Helens
360-274-7750
www.mountsthelens.com

Washington State Tourism
800-544-1800
www.experiencewa.com

Getty Images/iStockphoto

NORTHWEST WASHINGTON

Don't overlook the superb swath of land between Seattle and the Canadian border

From Arlington to Blaine, Northwest Washington state is home to natural beauty and eclectic, inviting communities. Occupying the coastal region between Vancouver, British Columbia, to the north and Seattle to the south, this slice of the Pacific Northwest might surprise you with its many charming small towns and ample recreation opportunities.

Start your trip in Arlington, a picturesque town in Snohomish County with a thriving main street community atmosphere and activities to suit visitors from all over. Arlington sits at the forks of the Stillaguamish River, and its pioneer heritage is preserved at the Stillaguamish Valley Pioneer Museum. Here, guests can view artifacts from logging and dairy industries as well as from pioneer households and the railroad. Arlington celebrates its relationship with the Stillaguamish River every year with a summer festival and powwow hosted by the Stillaguamish Tribe.

If you're a hiker, the great outdoors beckon you to hike the Pacific Northwest National Scenic Trail.

West of Arlington lies Warm Beach on the shores of Puget Sound. This retreat-centered community hosts one of Snohomish County's largest horse herds and welcomes equestrian programs year-round. Warm Beach Camp offers riding lessons as well as weekend programs for parents and grandparents. The Lights of Christmas, a holiday festival of more than 1 million lights on display, features live entertainment and family activities.

Head north along state route 99 to Skagit Bay and the Skagit Wildlife Area. More than 16,700 acres provide habitat for estuarine species such as waterfowl, shorebirds, eagles and small mammals. Bald eagles use the wildlife area for winter nesting grounds, making Skagit a prime bird-watching spot.

Farther up Interstate 5/SR 99 is the town of Mount Vernon, which is named for George Washington's home on the Potomac River. Break out the golf clubs here and head to Eaglemont Golf Course, ranked among the state's Top 10 links. This dynamic course challenges golfers of all levels.

Mount Vernon's Skagit County Historical Museum showcases the agricultural heritage of the region on a barn tour of 55 registered historic barns. Self-guided tours reveal the family history of Skagit County pioneers. The rich soil of the region produces award-winning wines that can be enjoyed in the fall at the Skagit Wine and Beer Festival, and during visits to local wineries for afternoon tastings.

If winter brings you outside, head east to Mount Baker in the Snoqualmie National Forest for skiing, snowboarding and snowshoeing at any of the four resorts. Of course, the mountain and its surrounding forest are equally attractive in warmer months. Heather Meadows Visitor Center shares the region's cultural history and points visitors to scenic trails outfitted with interpretive signage.

If you're a hiker, the great outdoors beckon you to hike the Pacific Northwest National Scenic Trail. The 1,200-

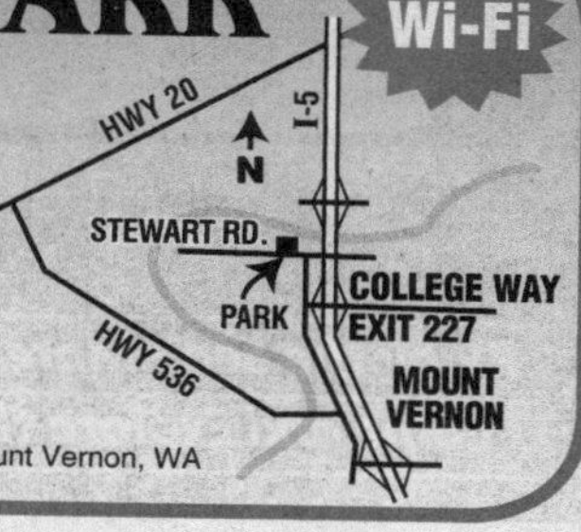

WA

Anacortes overlooks Puget Sound. Getty Images/iStockphoto

mile trail runs through the Mount Baker Wilderness area to the shores of Puget Sound.

Living Off the Sea

Back on the coast, live the fisherman's life in Anacortes, where the state's largest fishing fleet berths. Offshore, the San Juan Islands are a popular destination. This compelling archipelago is home to seabirds, seals and sea lions that live protected by the San Juan Wildlife Refuge. Orca whales are often spotted off the rocky islands.

Take a ferry to the islands in the morning, and come back to town to wander through local art galleries before grabbing a bite at a local hot spot. Water recreation is the gem of Anacortes, from kayak tours to whale watching around the islands.

As you plan your continuing trip north, make time for Bellingham, a thriving city with a rich maritime history. Nearby lakes invite fishing enthusiasts with licenses to try their luck at catching rainbow trout, bass, yellow perch and more. Lake Whatcom, the largest lake in the county at 5,003 acres, is stocked with kokanee, yellow perch, and largemouth and smallmouth bass. If salmon fishing is what you desire, head to the Nooksack River to cast for coho, chinook, chum and winter steelhead. Check out Whatcom Falls Park in the city, where the namesake cascades mesmerize visitors with their beauty.

Do something unusual here and take a ride on a camel. Camel Safaris introduce visitors to dromedary and Bactrian breeds for a fun ride on a desert creature. Also in town is Glen Echo Garden, a 7-acre botanical park that features nine different garden themes, including fern and moss, English-style, rose and tree stump gardens.

Wander the downtown cultural arts district and see the fruits of creative labor at Whatcom Museum and the Family Interactive Gallery. See how electricity spurred great minds at the Spark Museum of Electrical Invention, and enjoy a live performance at Mount Baker Theatre, home to the Whatcom Symphony Orchestra.

Going Dutch in Lynden

Directly north from Bellingham is Lynden, just 4 miles from the Canadian border. Lynden's fall music festival provides live entertainment, education and camaraderie for audiences and musicians. Lynden's Dutch heritage is celebrated in this small community.

Lynden is home to Berthusen Park, where old-growth cedars tower over bicyclists and hikers, and where the 100-year-old Berthusen Barn still stands. The park hosts an Antique Tractor and Machinery Show during the first weekend of August. Lynden also hosts the Northwest Washington Fair in August, with big-name musical acts, carnival rides, a rodeo and agriculture as the centerpiece.

End your Northwest journey under the Peach Arch monument in Blaine. This northernmost town's motto is "Where America Begins." Blaine hosts an annual birding festival in the spring that highlights brant geese and other shorebirds that pass through the region during migration season. In April, a two-day yacht race takes place on the border between Washington and Canada, bringing out the best of the Pacific Northwest fleets and their western Canadian counterparts for an exciting event.

For More Information

Washington State Tourism
800-544-1800
www.experiencewa.com

OLYMPIC PENINSULA

Take a trip around Washington's favorite mountain and coastal playground

Dense tracts of rugged northwestern wilderness drape across the thinly populated Olympic Peninsula in Washington state. Pockets of civilization ring the region's edges—you'll find towns on the rugged coastlines overlooking the Pacific Ocean, Strait of Juan de Fuca, Puget Sound and Hood Canal. Most of the peninsula's crusty and snow-capped inner core, on the other hand, is comprised of the Olympic Mountains, Olympic National Park and Olympic National Forest.

Make no mistake, if wilderness trails, fishing towns and whale-watching expeditions sound like your idea of a good time, then the Olympic Peninsula will positively knock your socks off.

Start with the Angels

Start your travels in the scenic seaside town of Port Angeles, which not only serves as the gateway to Olympic National Park, but also as a kind of regional hub for tourist exploration in general. From here, visitors can set off on quick and easy day trips deep into the heart of the peninsula or out across the Strait of Juan de Fuca to Vancouver Island and Victoria in Canada.

Take the time to explore the city of Port Angeles itself before jumping off into the wild. The downtown waterfront area is home to a 28-mile coastal sightseeing trail and more than 38 free public sculptures inspired by the geography and biodiversity of the northwest. The main attraction is undoubtedly City Pier, a vibrant public market area that offers the best views in the city of the Olympic Mountains to the south and Vancouver Island to the north. It's also home to a full slate of annual farmers markets, community festivals and fun fairs that unfold throughout the year.

Check out the Feiro Marine Life Center, which hosts public exhibits representative of the marine life of the Strait of Juan de Fuca. The center's

WA

exhibit on tidepools will make you see these little marine communities in a completely different way.

When you're ready to get a taste of what Olympic National Park has to offer, there's no better place to begin than in Port Angeles. One of the park's three main visitor centers is located directly in town, and from here, visitors can orient themselves to the types of activities and attractions available from the north-side park entrance.

The most accessible natural attraction of the park is Hurricane Ridge, which spans nearly a million square acres, so make this a top priority. From Port Angeles, the ridge is 17 miles away via a scenic paved byway. Alpine hiking trails overlooking glacier-carved gullies and traverses are the reward for hikers.

A short distance to the west sits another popular park destination, the Sol Duc Valley. This idyllic location is defined by its incredibly varied landscape. A combination of old-growth forests, snowy alpine peaks and glacial lakes line the river valley, which is also home to natural hot springs.

Rich farmlands in the Olympic Peninsula. Visit the Olympics

Other major points of interest in the park include the Hoh Rain Forest, Quinault Valley, Ozette, Rialto Beach, Kalaloch and Elwha Valley. Exploring Olympic National Park in full means jumping in and out by way of access points on the park's outer edges, so couple this with a tour of the Olympic Peninsula's charming small towns. To do this, simply jump on U.S. Highway 101, which rings the peninsula. Every major point of interest in and around the park is accessible via the 101.

Cool Small Town

In addition to its scenic splendor, the Olympic Peninsula also is home to one of the nation's "coolest" small towns. Port Townsend, located on the northeastern tip of the peninsula, made *Budget Travel's* Top 10 list in America's

Visit the Olympics

Coolest Small Towns in 2012. According to *Budget*, Port Townsend excels in serving up excellent seafood, cheeses and deserts. Its proximity to fantastic outdoor recreation also helped put it high up in the rankings. The town also made *Fodors* Top 10 list of America's Best Small Towns, praised for its dining options and lodging quality. Visitors can also find activities ranging from sailing to whale watching, biking to woodworking and from Christmas tree cutting to shell fishing.

Coastal Grandeur

The Olympic National Park protects 73 miles of untouched coastline. Following the trails here means unspoiled views of ocean, cliffs, headlands, islands and seastacks. It's considered one of the most primitive segments of shoreline in the 48 contiguous states, so hikers are advised to be mindful of their impact on the environment. For day hikes, always be aware of the changeable weather, and carry food, water, raingear and extra layers of clothing. Always stay on the trails to avoid injury or harming of vegetation, and pack all trash. Pets are not allowed on park trails or beaches, except in areas where leashed (up to six feet) pets are permitted.

Forest Fun

Along the way, you'll notice that Olympic National Forest seems to intertwine with Olympic National Park across the entire peninsula. The forest, in fact, largely encircles the park in three distinct sections: the Hood Canal Ranger District on the western side of the peninsula, the Pacific Ranger District North on the northwestern side and the Pacific Ranger District South on the southwestern side.

The forest is further subdivided into five distinct Recreation Areas: Forks, Dungeness, Hood-Canal-North, Hood-Canal-South, Wynochee and Quinault. Within each of these ranger-staffed areas, an abundance of trails and campgrounds are available to explore. Fishing, kayaking and canoeing are among the most popular activities because of the rich and seemingly never-ending supply of backcountry streams, creeks and rivers.

Major points of interest include Mount Walker Viewpoint and Kloshe

Marymere Falls and Trail
Getty Images/iStockphoto

Towering Mount Olympus in Olympic National Park. Getty Images/Purestock

Nanitch Lookout. The former is located on the western side of the peninsula, near the towns of Brinnon and Quilcene. A 2-mile hiking trail near the 2,804-foot summit unlocks spectacular panoramic views of Puget Sound and Seattle. Kloshe Nanitch Lookout, located in the northwestern corner of the peninsula, offers incredible views of Lake Crescent and the Strait of Juan de Fuca.

If you're a hiker, you'll want to make time for two of the best trails on the entire peninsula. Each is located within Olympic National Forest. The first, Interrorem Nature Trail, has a trailhead near the town of Hoodsport on Hood Canal. The second, Quinault Rain Forest Nature Trail, is located in the southwestern quadrant of the peninsula. These trails are renowned for their landscapes of ancient, old-growth trees, some with diameters of 9-feet or more.

Nature trails in Olympic National Forest are ideal for hikers seeking a less strenuous trip. These are generally less than one mile in length and have signs interpreting resources, features and history of the Olympic National Forest. Many of these trails have easy to moderate grades, making them highly accessible.

Birding Bonanza

The National Audubon Society has gone the extra mile to develop bird trails for avian watchers seeking to expand their knowledge of Pacific Northwest species. The Olympic Loop of the Great Washington State Birding Trails begins from the Nisqually River delta in south Puget Sound, then winds west, following rivers through moss-draped forests and touches the tip of the contiguous U.S. at Cape Flattery. The route follows the Strait of Juan de Fuca east over the Olympic Peninsula, then wends south along the inland waters of Hood Canal.

Along the Hood Canal, Hamma Hamma Beaver Pond and Mt. Walker Viewpoint have been designated as bird watching hot spots. On the Pacific Coast side, the Lake Quinault Rainforest Trail and Campell Tree Grove area give visitors prime viewpoints for observing a wide variety of birds associated with temperate old growth rainforests.

Visitors can download a free map of the Great Washington State Birding Trail from the U.S. Forest Service website.

Whether you're a weekend hiker or year-round outdoor adventure enthusiast, the Olympic Peninsula has something for everyone. Few places remain in the world with such a lush, untamed and undeveloped ecosystem, where hints of the past echo loudly into the present.

For More Information

Olympic Peninsula Tourism Commission
800-942-4042
www.olympicpeninsula.org

Washington State Tourism
800-544-1800
www.experiencewa.com

SPOKANE AND THE INLAND EMPIRE

Discover Washington's eastern half from this sparkling gem

The city of Spokane is the crown jewel of eastern Washington state. Tucked amongst the scenic foothills and low-lying mountains that drape across the border with neighboring Idaho, the city is a nature lover's paradise—bursting with outdoor adventures and day trip escapes into lush, wild countryside. You can fish, golf, hike, kayak and mountain climb all in a single weekend—taking advantage of 260 days of annual average sunshine each year—and a collection of 76 sparkling freshwater lakes all lie within short, easy reach of downtown.

> The stretch of river that pours through the heart of downtown is known as Spokane Falls.

Spokane began life as a fur-trading center, gaining its name from a Native American word that means "children of the sun," a nod to the area's idyllic climate. As with so many far-flung western frontier outposts, Spokane survived thanks to its transition into a role as a railway hub, connecting east to west.

The rest of Spokane's growth into a destination town for outdoor adventure enthusiasts was handled exclusively by Mother Nature. The community's picture-perfect placement means you can go for an early morning paddle by kayak before breakfast, brave whitewater rapids by lunch, tear up fresh mountain snow on skis in the afternoon and end the day with a spot of fishing at sunset. Find lots shopping in the city's diverse neighborhoods.

Fall for Spokane

But before you go stomping around the surrounding wilderness, start your exploring in downtown Spokane itself, where the Spokane River winds its way directly through the center of town. In the spring, the river level rises and the pace quickens to a delightful thundering roar. The stretch that pours through the heart of downtown is known as Spokane Falls. In peak season, the flow can carry as much as 31,000 cubic feet of water per second.

Riverfront Park and a portion of the Centennial Trail are the best ways to take in the beauty of Spokane Falls. Riverfront Park spans 100 acres and features a variety of scenic trails that include footbridges and lookouts over

WA

The Columbia Plateau State Park Trail near Spokane. Williamborg

Riverfront Park Clock Tower.
Getty Images/iStockphoto

the river. Centennial Trail stretches all the way east to Coeur d'Alene in Idaho, but the paved portion that runs through Riverside Park is a favorite for cyclists looking to take in Spokane Falls. Following the trail further west will take you to Riverside State Park, which bursts with more than 100 miles of hiking trails, biking trails and horse riding trails.

During the summer, Spokane offers several venues at which to see your favorite Hollywood films under the stars. Riverfront Park screens several popular movies to audiences, and each showings is accompanied by a vendor fair, live entertainment, trivia competitions, food trucks and giveaways.

Drive-in Movies also are shown at the Spokane Country Raceway and at Pavilion Park. Prepare some popcorn and partake in an all-American tradition.

If live entertainment is your preference, enjoy music performances at Riverfront Park's Fountain Cafe on Wednesday nights.

When you're ready to branch out for a day trip or two, you'll have plenty of options. About an hour's drive away to the north lies Mt. Spokane, one of the tallest mountain peaks in the state. It's home to Mount Spokane State Park, which spans more than 13,000 acres and is home to old-growth timber and granite rock outcroppings. In the winter months, the mountain opens up for downhill skiing, snowboarding, snowmobiling and snowshoeing. During the summer, adventure seekers can navigate the mountain's 90 miles of bike trails and 100 miles of hiking trails. If you reach the 5,883-foot summit on a clear day, you'll be able to see into Canada.

> The Turnbull National Wildlife Refuge is home to an abundance of wildlife and waterfowl.

Crossing the Border

To the east, in Idaho, Lake Coeur d'Alene sits less than 50 miles away. An on-site resort and an abundance of quaint lakeside cottages make this a great weekend spot for a mini-vacation within your vacation. More than 100 miles of freshwater shoreline provide access to the peaceful lake, which is popular for fishing, boating and canoeing. Cyclists can hop on the Trail of the Coeur d'Alenes, which winds to Wallace, a historic mining town.

Bird watchers and wildlife photographers will want to head 30 miles southwest of Spokane to Turnbull National Wildlife Refuge. In addition to an abundance of wildlife and waterfowl, the refuge's 18,217-acre expanse is full of rocky outcrops, thick pine bluffs, lush wetlands and sparkling lakes.

When it's time for a break from

A pedestrian bridge crosses the Spokane Falls. Getty Images/iStockphoto

ıiking trails and boat launches, there's ilverwood Theme Park, which is ocated just 50 miles east of downtown ›pokane in Idaho. The park is home o more than 60 rides and thrill rides, ncluding wooden roller coasters and ı log flume ride. It's also home to the Boulder Beach Water Park, which fea-ures a lazy river, tube slides and a wave ɔool.

History buffs and arts enthusi-ısts can stick closer to home for a ɔreak from the great outdoors. At he Northwest Museum of Arts and Culture, located in downtown Spokane ıear the banks of the Spokane River, guests can explore the history of the egion through a range of exhibits and ɔrograms. Items and artifacts on display nostly shed light on the history of ıortheastern Washington's indigenous ɔeople and the arrival of early pioneer-ıng explorers.

The city of Spokane and the sur-ounding area is a picture-perfect place o pull over the RV and set up camp for ı thoroughly rich taste of the American ıorthwest. Gorgeous freshwater lakes, oothill hiking trails, alpine vistas, tum-ɔling waterfalls and fantastic nationally protected parklands make Spokane a must-visit for nature lovers.

Spokane on Parade

Like the annual Rose Parade in Pasadena, Spokane has its own flower-themed parade. Held every May, the annual Spokane Lilac Festival culminates in the Spokane Lilac Festival Armed Forces Torchlight Parade, which focuses largely on its namesake flower. Started in 1938, the Lilac Festival and its accompanying parade grew to become one of Spokane's biggest annual events. Community organizations, marching bands, local leaders and skilled equestrians turn out to honor the military and celebrate their community.

Several local events are held to coincide with the big festival. Visitors can attend a car show, check out the float viewing or take part in the festival golf tournament.

Ironically, lilacs aren't indigenous to the region. As local historians will tell you, the first lilac came from Minnesota and flourished in the Spokane area.

Savor vine vintages at Arbor Crest Winery, Nodland Cellars and Latah Creek. Each winery serves rich selections of red and white Washington State wines. Arbor Crest sits atop a 450-foot cliff that overlooks the entire Valley region, offering stunning panoramic views that pair nicely with the quiet romantic setting. It's an experience that's a real treat for wine lovers.

For More Information

Visit Spokane
888-SPOKANE
www.visitspokane.com

Washington State Tourism
800-544-1800
www.experiencewa.com

WA

Visit Tri-Cities

TRI-CITIES

Three great reasons to visit this segment of Washington's Columbia River Basin

When taken as a whole, the Tri-Cities in southeastern Washington state constitutes a large metropolitan area of more than a quarter of a million people. Because of their convenient proximity to each other, it certainly makes sense to group the cities of Kennewick, Pasco and Richland together as a unit, but this betrays some of their greatest individual charms.

Remaining separate-but-connected has allowed each neighboring riverside city to develop its unique downtown core, avoiding the onset of increased urban density that so often chokes the charm straight out of other major cities The Tri-Cities is thus capable of offering all the amenities of a big city (gourmet restaurants, world-class entertainment alongside a small-town atmosphere and laid-back pace.

> If you're a golfer, landing in the Tri-Cities will seem like a dream come true. Ten courses are within close reach.

Carnivals on the Columbia

Start in Kennewick, which is found on

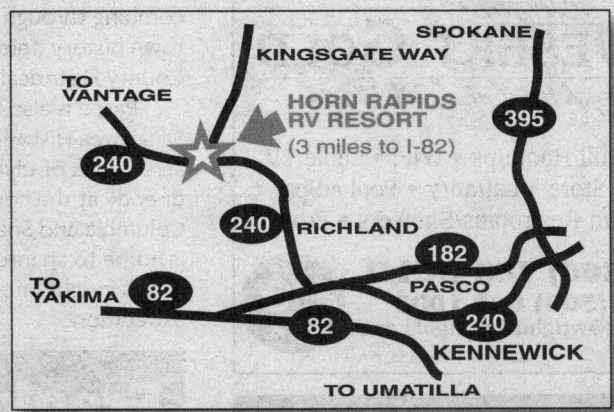

The lush Columbia Point Golf Club in Richland. Visit Tri-Cities

the south bank of the Columbia River, almost directly opposite Pasco. It's the largest of the three Tri-Cities in terms of population, but it feels decidedly small-town all the same. Stroll along the riverside in Columbia Park, a 5-mile-long greenbelt home to a waterpark, fishing pond, nature trails and picture-perfect views of the river. The downtown core features a healthy mix of upscale restaurants and trendy cafes.

For a bit of family fun, take a spin on the Gesa Carousel of Dreams in south Kennewick. This historic carnival attraction was built in 1910 and used for more than 60 years in St. Joseph, Michigan, before it was sold and moved to New Mexico. Decades later it was purchased and moved to Kennewick.

Pasco Pastimes

Pasco, on the northern shores of the Columbia River, is in many ways a mirror image of its south bank neighbor. Smaller in population and boasting even more of a small-town image than Kennewick or Richland, Pasco offers a similar assortment of charming riverside walks and parks, as well a healthy mix of wineries and tasting bars. The highlight of Pasco is the Pasco Farmers Market, which runs from May to October in the center of town. History buffs can choose to whittle away a few hours combing through the eclectic, small-town history items on display in Franklin County Historical Museum.

Pasco is also the gateway to Sacajawea Historical State Park, a 284-acre chunk of idyllic parkland located directly at the confluence of the Columbia and Snake rivers. The park is home to an interpretive center that offers insight into the Lewis and Clark expedition.

Make a Splash in Richmond

Richland is the farthest west of the three cities, found on the western shores of a sharp bend in the Columbia that points the river northward. Like Kennewick and Pasco, some of the most popular activities in Richland involve an enjoyment of the great outdoors. Kayaking, canoeing, hiking and biking are all possible here. And while all three cities feature a fantastic selection of wineries and tasting rooms, Richland serves as a kind of jumping-off point from the Tri-Cities on tours to the upper reaches of wine country in the Yakima Valley.

A short distance north of Richland, nature buffs can visit the Hanford Reach National Monument. This was once the home of nuclear reactors that developed the plutonium for "Fat Man," the atomic bomb dropped on Nagasaki, Japan, during World War II. Today it's a pristine, protected natural area full of scenic bluffs, wildflower fields, non-tidal marshes and reams of wildlife.

Finally, if you're a golfer, landing in the Tri-Cities will seem like a dream come true. Ten golf courses are located within easy reach of all three cities, including one with a championship putting course— Canyon Lakes.

Tri-City Country Club in Kennewick and Sun Willows in Pasco are popular courses for families, walk-ons and anyone with a bit of rust on their game. For those seeking a more moderately challenging course, head for Columbia Point Golf Course in Richland.

For More Information

Tri-Cities Visitor and Convention Bureau
800-254-5824
www.visittri-cities.com

Washington State Tourism
800-544-1800
www.experiencewa.com

WINE COUNTRY

Uncork a trip through Washington's superb wineries

lestled beneath the protective eastern lopes of the Cascade Mountains, Vashington State's award-winning Vine Country extends from the Yakima 'alley to the Tri-Cities and Walla Valla. And if you think the label "Wine Country" is little more than an exag-erated advertising slogan, think again: lew wineries pop up every month ere. "Wine Country" might, in fact, be utting it mildly.

The geography here is perfectly uned to growing fantastic grapes, so nuch so that it's a wonder the region lidn't carve out a space for itself on the nternational wine map even sooner. 'he aforementioned Cascades serve as barrier from the rainier weather pat-erns found on the coastal side of the tate, leaving the region east and south of Yakima warm and dry year-round. \n average of 300 days of sunshine ach year, coupled with volcanic-ash nriched soils (thanks to the fiery peaks of the Cascades' Volcanic Arc), makes or the perfect vineyard incubator.

/ineyard Roots

Geography can't take all of the credit hough, just a hefty chunk of it. The est goes to pioneer craft winemak-ers. Wine grapes were first introduced o the region in 1825 and the growth of wineries sputtered until the 1920s, vhen Prohibition sparked a wave of ousehold winemaking. By the time Prohibition was lifted, southeastern Vashington was primed with both erfect geography and a population of xperienced, self-trained grape growers.

By 1938, there were 42 wineries n the area. By 1960, commercial-scale vineyards were emerging. And by the 1970s, the wine industry in southeast-ern Washington State was in off to the races at a full-sprint, well on its way to evolving into the multi-billion dollar industry it is today, sporting more than 800 individual wineries.

Yakima Valley Vintages

The town of Yakima and the Yakima Valley at the northern reaches of Wine Country attract most of the attention. This is the head of Washington State's wine scene. The bulk of the Spirit and Hops Tasting Trail is found here, and visitors could spend a lifetime jumping from wine bar to wine bar and tasting room to tasting room.

If you're a history buff and need a break from acting as an amateur som-melier, head for Yakima Valley Museum in the center of town near Franklin Park. Small and eclectic, the museum is sur-prisingly impressive, with the highlight being a "Time Tunnel" exhibit, which portrays life in the valley more than 10,000 years ago.

If you're up for a day trip, then the eastern slopes and foothills of nearby Mount Rainier make for a nice break

Fort Simcoe kept peace between settlers and Native Americans in the 19th century.
Yakima Valley Tourism

Fly fishing on the Yakima River.
Yakima Valley Tourism

from city life. From downtown Yakima the entry point to Mount Rainier National Park is less than 70 miles to the east.

Moving south from Yakima, you can hop from winery to winery by way of Toppenish, Zillah, Prosser, the Tri-Cities (made up of the communities of Kennewick, Pasco and Richland) and finish up in Walla Walla—effectively the southern terminus for Wine Country.

Toppenish is known for its 70 public murals that are dotted throughout its small downtown area. Stroll the town center in between sips of red and enjoy the free open-air art show. The American Hop Museum is also found here, the only one of its kind in the world. History buffs will want to check out the Rail and Steam Museum and the 1911 Toppenish Train Depot.

Back to the Beginning

Prosser is regarded as the birthplace of Washington Wine Country. As such you'll find no shortage of wineries, tasting rooms and wine bars to sip and sample your way through. The rest of its main attractions pair well with the wineries: Jazz clubs, art galleries and antique shops abound.

Walla Walla makes for the perfect closing act to a valley-wide wine tour. The "town so nice they named it twice" is bursting with not just tasting rooms and wine bars, but also art galleries, night clubs and incredible restaurants.

When you arrive in town head straight for the Walla Walla Visitor Center on Main Street. Here, you can find the usual information on local events and important happenings, to be sure, but don't leave without grabbing a self-guided walking tour map. This is the perfect way to explore Walla Walla's historic downtown core at your own pace, leaving plenty of opportunity to peel off and pop into a tasting room or boutique shop whenever you feel like.

Fort Walla Walla Museum is one of the premier non-wine-related attractions, as is the Kirkman House Museum The former showcases artifacts and collections dating to early 19th century within the walls of Fort Walla Walla, an infantry outpost built in 1856. The fort alone is worthy of a visit. In similar vein the Kirkman House is one of the last remaining examples of perfectly preserved Victorian Italianate architecture in the country.

For More Information

Washington Wine Country
800-221-0751
www.winecountrywashington.com

Washington State Tourism
800-544-1800
www.experiencewa.com

Washington

CONSULTANTS

Bob & Becky Bazemore

AMANDA PARK — B1 *Grays Harbor*

OLYMPIC NATIONAL PARK (GRAVES CREEK CAMPGROUND) (Natl Pk) From town: Go 20 mi NE on gravel access road. Pit toilets. 2015 rates: $12. (360)365-3130

AMERICAN RIVER — C3 *Yakima*

WENATCHEE NF (BUMPING LAKE CAMPGROUND) (Natl Forest) From jct Hwy-410 & FR-174: Go 11 mi SW on FR-174, then 1/3 mi W on FR-174D. Pit toilets. 2015 rates: $20. May 20 to Sep 27. (509)672-2320

WENATCHEE NF (LODGEPOLE CAMPGROUND) (Natl Forest) From town: Go 11-1/2 mi W on Hwy-410. Pit toilets. 2015 rates: $18. May 20 to Sep 27. (509)653-2300

ANACORTES — A2 *Skagit*

ANACORTES See also Bellingham, Burlington, Mount Vernon, Oak Harbor, Port Townsend & Stanwood.

FIDALGO BAY RESORT

Ratings: 9/10★/9 (RV Park) From Jct of I-5 & Exit 230: Go 12 mi W on SR-20 to first Fidalgo Bay Rd Exit (500 ft past Whidrey Island turnoff), the 1-1/8 mi NW on Fidalgo Bay Rd (R). **FAC:** Paved/gravel rds. (142 spaces). Avail: 122 all weather, 43 pull-thrus (20 x 70), back-ins (22 x 60), 122 full hkups (30/50 amps), seasonal sites, cable, WiFi, rentals, laundry, groc, LP gas, fire rings, firewood. **REC:** Fidalgo Bay: swim, fishing, playground. Pets OK. Partial handicap access, no tents. Eco-friendly, 2015 rates: $34 to $62. Disc: military.
(800)727-5478 Lat: 48.481982, Lon: -122.593229
4701 Fidalgo Bay Rd, Anacortes, WA 98221
reserve@fidalgobay.com
www.fidalgobay.com
See ad page 1270 (Spotlight Northwest Washington).

LIGHTHOUSE RV PARK Ratings: 5.5/9★/6.5 (RV Park) From Anacortes, follow signs to Anacortes Ferry Terminal, then from jct of SR-20 Spur & Sunset Ave: Bear left at fork and go 1/2 mi W on Sunset Ave to Skyline Way, then 1/4 mi S on Skyline to Sands Way, then 1/8 mi W on Sands Way (L) (3/4 mile past Anacortes Ferry Terminal. **FAC:** Paved rds. (30 spaces). Avail: 15 all weather, 2 pull-thrus (20 x 40), back-ins (20 x 32), accepts self-contain units only, 15 full hkups (30/50 amps), seasonal sites, WiFi, laundry. **REC:** Puget Sound. Pet restrict(B). No tents. 2015 rates: $35. No CC.
(360)770-4334 Lat: 48.494943, Lon: -122.685330
5060 Sands Way, Anacortes, WA 98221
lighthousepark@yahoo.com
www.lighthouseministorageandrvpark.com

PIONEER TRAILS RV RESORT **Ratings: 7.5/8.5/8.5** (RV Park) 2015 rates: $36 to $49. (360)293-5355 7337 Miller Rd, Anacortes, WA 98221

SPENCER SPIT (State Pk) Board ferry at Anacortes, exit at Lopez Island, S 1 mi to Jct of Ferry Rd & Center Rd, S 1 mi on Center Rd to Cross Rd, E 0.75 mi to Port Stanley, S 0.25 mi to Bakerview Rd (E). For reservations call (888)226-7688. 2015 rates: $12 to $37. Mar 14 to Oct 30. (888)226-7688

SWINOMISH CASINO RV PARK **Ratings: 6/NA/6.5** (Campground) 2015 rates: $22 to $35. (888)288-8883 12885 Casino Dr, Anacortes, WA 98221

WASHINGTON PARK (Public) From Jct of I-5 & Hwy 20 (exit 230), W 16 mi on Hwy 20 to 12th St, W 3.5 mi to Sunset Ave, W 1 mi (E). 2015 rates: $17 to $25. (360)293-1927

ANATONE — D6 *Asotin*

FIELDS SPRING (State Pk) From Jct of Hwy 12 & 129 (in Clarkston), S 30 mi on Hwy 129 (L). 2015 rates: $12 to $42. (509)256-3332

ARLINGTON — B3 *Snohomish*

LAKE KI RV PARK **Ratings: 7/8/8** (Campground) 2015 rates: $30 to $40. (360)652-0619 2904 Lakewood Rd, Arlington, WA 98223

ARTIC — C1 *Grays Harbor*

ARTIC RV PARK **Ratings: 4.5/6.5/8** (Campground) 2015 rates: $20 to $25. May 1 to Oct 1. (360)533-4470 mm 75 Hwy 101, Artic, WA 98537

ASHFORD — C3 *Pierce*

MOUNTHAVEN RESORT **Ratings: 5/7.5/7.5** (Campground) 2015 rates: $44. (360)569-2594 38210 Sr 706 E, Ashford, WA 98304

BAINBRIDGE ISLAND — B2 *Kitsap*

FAY BAINBRIDGE (State Pk) Take ferry from Seattle to Bainbridge Island, N 5 mi on Hwy 305 to Day Rd NE, E 2 mi to Sunrise Dr NE, N 2 mi (R). 2015 rates: $12 to $34. (206)842-3931

BATTLE GROUND — D2 *Clark*

BATTLE GROUND LAKE (State Pk) From town, E 0.3 mi on Main St to Grace Ave, N 0.5 mi to N 229 St, E 2.5 mi (L). For reservations call (888)226-7688. 2015 rates: $12 to $42. (888)226-7688

BAY CENTER — C1 *Pacific*

BAY CENTER/WILLAPA BAY KOA **Ratings: 7.5/9.5★/9** (Campground) 2015 rates: $35.01 to $43.80. Apr 1 to Dec 1. (800)562-7810 457 Bay Center Rd, Bay Center, WA 98527

BELFAIR — C2 *Mason*

BELFAIR (State Pk) From Jct of SR-3 & SR-300, W 3 mi on SR-300 (L). 2015 rates: $12 to $42. (888)226-7688

POTHOLES (State Pk) From Jct of Sr-17 & Hwy 262 (O'Sullivan Dam Rd), W 11.8 mi on O'Sullivan Dam Rd (R). 2015 rates: $12 to $42. (888)226-7688

SUMMERTIDE RESORT & MARINA **Ratings: 5/7.5★/5** (Campground) 2015 rates: $30 to $40. (360)275-9313 15781 NE North Shore Rd, Tahuya, WA 98588

BELLEVUE — B3 *King*

BELLEVUE See also Bothell, Everett, Issaquah & Poulsbo.

BELLINGHAM — A2 *Whatcom*

BELLINGHAM See also Anacortes, Birch Bay, Burlington, Ferndale, Lynden, Mount Vernon & Stanwood.

BELLINGHAM RV PARK **Ratings: 8/9.5★/8.5** (RV Park) 2015 rates: $44.20. (888)372-1224 3939 Bennett Dr, Bellingham, WA 98225

LARRABEE

(State Pk) From Jct of I-5 & Old Fairhaven Pkwy (exit 250), W 1.4 mi on Old Fairhaven Pkwy to 12th St, S 0.1 mi to Chuckanut Dr, S 4.1 mi (R). **FAC:** Paved rds. 34 gravel, 12 pull-thrus (24 x 50), back-ins (24 x 35), 26 full hkups (20/30 amps), tent sites, showers $, dump, firewood. **REC:** Samish Bay: fishing, rec open to public. Pets OK. Partial handicap access. 10 day max stay, 2015 rates: $20 to $45.
(888)226-7688 Lat: 48.65334, Lon: -122.49034
245 Chukanut, Bellingham, WA 98226
infocent@parks.wa.gov
www.parks.wa.gov
See ad page 1246 (Welcome Section).

BENTON CITY — D4 *Benton*

BEACH RV PARK **Ratings: 6.5/8.5★/5.5** (RV Park) 2015 rates: $34.95. (509)588-5959 113 Abby Ave, Benton City, WA 99320

BIRCH BAY — A2 *Whatcom*

BEACHSIDE RV PARK Ratings: 5.5/8.5★/5 (RV Park) From Jct of I-5 & Birch Bay/Lynden Rd (exit 270): Go 3 mi W on Birch Bay Rd/Lynden Rd to Blaine Rd, then 1-1/8 mi S to Alderson Rd, then 3/4 mi W on Alderson Rd (R). **FAC:** Gravel/dirt rds. (78 spaces). Avail: 10 grass, 10 pull-thrus (14 x 40), 10 full hkups (30/50 amps), seasonal sites, WiFi Hotspot, tent sites, showers $, laundry. **REC.** Pet restrict(B). 2015 rates: $25 to $33. Disc: AAA, military.
AAA Approved
(360)371-5962 Lat: 48.918656, Lon: -122.744497
7630 Birch Bay Dr, Birch Bay, WA 98230
Beachsidervpark.com

BIRCH BAY RESORT -THOUSAND TRAILS **Ratings: 7.5/7/6** (Membership Pk) 2015 rates: $47 to $50. (877)362-6736 8418 Harborview Rd, Blaine, WA 98230

Say you saw it in our Guide!

LIGHTHOUSE BY THE BAY RV RESORT **Ratings: 6/7.5/7.5** (Campground) 2015 rates: $35 to $39. (360)371-5603 4700 Alderson Rd, Blaine, WA 98230

BLACK DIAMOND — C3 *King*

LAKE SAWYER RESORT-SUNRISE RESORTS **Ratings: 7.5/6.5/6** (Membership Pk) 2015 rates: $35 to $50. (360)886-2244 30250 224th Ave SE, Black Diamond, WA 98010

BLAINE — A2 *Whatcom*

BIRCH BAY (State Pk) S-bnd: From Jct of I-5 & Birch Bay/Lynden Rd (exit 270), W 3 mi on Birch Bay/Lynden Rd to Blaine Rd, S 2 mi to Bay Rd, W 1.1 mi to Jackson Rd, S 0.3 mi to Helwig Rd, W 0.5 mi (E); or N-bnd: From Jct of I-5 & Grandview Rd (exit 266), W 7 mi on Grandview Rd to Jackson Rd, N 0.8 mi (E). 2015 rates: $12 to $42. May 15 to Sep 15. (360)371-2800

BOTHELL — B3 *Snohomish*

BOTHELL See also Bellevue, Everett, Issaquah, Poulsbo & Seattle.

LAKE PLEASANT RV PARK

Ratings: 9/9.5★/9.5 (RV Park) S-bnd: From Jct of I-5 (Exit 182) & I-405: Go 3 mi S on I-405 to Bothell Hwy (Exit 26), then 1-1/8 mi S on Bothell Hwy to 242nd St (L). N-bnd: From Jct of I-5 & I-405: Go 26 mi N on I-405 to Bothell Hwy (Exit 26), then 1-1/8 mi S on Bothell Hwy to 242nd St (L).

STAY AWHILE & SEE IT ALL. CALL NOW!
We're the perfect park to stay & rest or explore the Seattle area. See the Space Needle-Pike Place Mkt-Boeing-Bellevue Shops-Snoqualmie Falls. Special RV Parking while cruising or flying out. Book early-we fill up in Summer.

FAC: Paved rds. (198 spaces). Avail: 119 paved, 46 pull-thrus (27 x 65), back-ins (29 x 65), accepts self-contain units only, 119 full hkups (30/50 amps), seasonal sites, WiFi $, dump, laundry, LP gas. **REC:** Lake Pleasant: fishing, playground. Pet restrict(B). Partial handicap access, no tents. Big rig sites, eco-friendly, 2015 rates: $44.
(425)487-1785 Lat: 47.777965, Lon: -122.217693
24025 Bothell Everett Hwy, Bothell, WA 98021
http://www.goodsamcamping.com.s3.amazonaws.com/gsparks/LakePleasant/LakePleasant.
See ad page 1262 (Spotlight Greater Seattle) & RV Trips of a Lifetime and ad Magazine Section page 113.

BOW — A2 *Skagit*

MOUNT VERNON RESORT **Ratings: 7.5/7/7** (Membership Pk) 2015 rates: $42 to $44. (360)724-4811 5409 N. Darrk Lane, Bow, WA 98232

BREMERTON — B2 *Kitsap*

ILLAHEE (State Pk) From town, NE 3 mi on Sylvan Way (E). 2015 rates: $12 to $42. (360)478-6460

BREWSTER — B4 *Okanogan*

COLUMBIA COVE RV PARK (Public) From Jct of US-97 & 7th St (in town), S 0.5 mi on 7th St (L). 2015 rates: $10 to $34. (509)689-3464

BRIDGEPORT — B4 *Douglas, Okanogan*

BRIDGEPORT

(State Pk) From Jct of SR-17 & park access rd, NE 3 mi on park access rd (E). **FAC:** Paved rds. 20 grass, patios, 9 pull-thrus (30 x 45), back-ins (30 x 45), 20 W, 20 E (30 amps), tent sites, dump, groc, firewood. **REC:** Columbia River: swim, fishing, golf, playground, rec open to public. Pets OK. Partial handicap access. 10 day max stay, 2015 rates: $20 to $45. Apr 1 to Oct 31. No reservations.
(888)226-7688 Lat: 48.01475, Lon: -119.60865
235A Half Sun Way, Bridgeport, WA 98813
infocent@parks.wa.gov
www.parks.wa.gov
See ad page 1246 (Welcome Section).

MARINA & RV PARK (Public) From Jct of SR-17 & SR-173, NW 1.4 mi on SR-173 to Columbia St, N 0.2 mi to 7th St, N 0.1 mi (E). 2015 rates: $20 to $25. (509)686-4747

BRINNON — B2 *Jefferson*

COVE RV PARK **Ratings: 6.5/7.5★/7** (RV Park) 2015 rates: $35. Apr 1 to Sep 30. (360)796-4723 303075 Hwy 101, Brinnon, WA 98320

DOSEWALLIPS (State Pk) From town, S 1 mi on Hood Canal (US-101), at MP-307 (R). 2015 rates: $12 to $42. (360)796-4415

BURBANK — D5 *Walla Walla*

HOOD PARK (COE - LAKE SACAJAWEA) (Public Corps) In town at jct Hwy-124 & US-12. 2015 rates: $11 to $24. May 16 to Sep 1. (509)547-7781

BURBANK (CONT)

LAKE SACAJEWEA/CHARBONNEAU PARK (Public Corps) From E Jct of US-12 & US-395, S 4 mi on US-12 to Hwy 124, E 8 mi to Sun Harbor Dr, N 1.5 mi to Charbonneau Rd, W 0.1 mi (R). 2015 rates: $11 to $28. May 16 to Sep 1. (509)547-2048

LAKE SACAJEWEA/FISHHOOK PARK (Public Corps) From E Jct of US-12 & US-395, S 4 mi on US-12 to Hwy 124, E 19 mi to Fishhook Park Rd, N 4 mi (L). 2015 rates: $8 to $28. May 16 to Sep 1. (509)547-2048

BURLINGTON — A2 *Skagit, Whatcom*

BAY VIEW (State Pk) From Jct of I-5 & Exit 230 (Hwy 20), W 7 mi on Hwy 20 to Bay View-Edison Rd, N 4 mi (R). For reservations call (888)226-7688. 2015 rates: $12 to $42. (888)226-7688

BURLINGTON/ANACORTES KOA **Ratings: 7.5/8.5★/7.5** (Campground) 2015 rates: $39 to $51. (800)562-9154 6397 N Green Rd, Burlington, WA 98233

FRIDAY CREEK CAMPGROUND **Ratings: 2/7★/6** (Campground) 2015 rates: $32 to $42. May 1 to Sep 30. (877)570-2267 4474 Friday Creek Rd, Burlington, WA 98233

Travel Services

CAMPING WORLD OF BURLINGTON As the nation's largest retailer of RV supplies, accessories, services and new and used RVs, Camping World is committed to making your total RV experience better. RV Accessories: (866)337-4810. **SERVICES:** RV, tire, RV appliance, MH mechanical, staffed RV wash, restrooms, RV Sales. RV supplies, LP, dump, emergency parking, RV accessible. waiting room. Hours: 8am to 6pm.
(888)865-4407 Lat: 48.485498, Lon: -122.333787
1240 Old Highway 99, Burlington, WA 98233
www.campingworld.com

CASTLE ROCK — D2 *Cowlitz*

LONGVIEW N/MOUNT ST HELEN'S KOA **Ratings: 8/8.5★/7.5** (Campground) 2015 rates: $34.17 to $58.50. (360)274-8522 167 Schaffran Rd, Castle Rock, WA 98611

TOUTLE RIVER RV RESORT
Ratings: 10/10★/8.5 (RV Park) From Jct of I-5 (Exit 52) & Barnes Rd: Go 1/8 mi on Barnes Rd to Happy Trails Rd (L). **FAC:** Paved rds. (246 spaces). Avail: 232 all weather, 116 pull-thrus (35 x 75), back-ins (30 x 70), 232 full hkups (30/50 amps), seasonal sites, WiFi, tent sites, rentals, dump, laundry, groc, LP gas, firewood, controlled access. **REC:** heated pool, whirlpool, Toutle River, Cowlitz River: fishing, playground. Pet restrict(B). Partial handicap access. Big rig sites, eco-friendly, 2015 rates: $42.
(360)274-8373 Lat: 46.32526, Lon: -122.91478
150 Happy Trails Rd, Castle Rock, WA 98611
greatrvresort@aol.com
www.greatrvresort.com
See ad pages 1250, 1268 (Spotlight Mount Rainier & Mount St Helens).

CATHLAMET — D2 *Wahkiakum*

ELOCHOMAN SLOUGH MARINA (Public) From Jct SR-4 & SR-409, NW 300 ft on SR-4 to 3rd Ave (Chester), W 0.2 mi (E). 2015 rates: $25. (360)795-3501

CENTRALIA — C2 *Lewis*

CENTRALIA See also Castle Rock, Chehalis, Kelso, Mossyrock, Oakville, Olympia, Rochester, Silver Lake & Toledo.

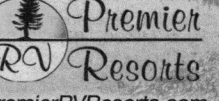

MIDWAY RV PARK
Ratings: 9/10★/9 (RV Park) From Jct of I-5 & Harrison Ave (exit 82), W 0.8 mi on Harrison Ave to Galvin Rd, S 0.3 mi (L). **FAC:** Paved rds. (62 spaces). Avail: 22 paved, 20 pull-thrus (27 x 66), back-ins (28 x 60), 22 full hkups (30/50 amps), seasonal sites, cable, WiFi, laundry, groc, LP gas. **REC.** Pets OK. Partial handicap access, no tents. Big rig sites, 2015 rates: $39. Disc: AAA, military.
(800)600-3204 Lat: 46.72211, Lon: -122.96448
3200 Galvin Rd, Centralia, WA 98531
Info@midwayrvparkwa.com
www.midwayrvparkwa.com
See ad pages 1266 (Spotlight Mount Rainier & Mount St Helens), 1250.

CHEHALIS — C2 *Lewis*

CHEHALIS RESORT **Ratings: 7/7/7.5** (Membership Pk) 2015 rates: $32 to $45. (800)405-6188 2228 Centralia Alpha Rd, Chehalis, WA 98532

LEWIS & CLARK (State Pk) From Jct of I-5 & Hwy 12 (exit 68), E 3 mi on Hwy 12 to Jackson Hwy, S 3 mi (R). 2015 rates: $12 to $42. Apr 1 to Oct 31. (360)864-2643

RAINBOW FALLS (State Pk) From Jct of I-5 & Exit 77 (Hwy 6), W 16 mi on Hwy 6 (R). 2015 rates: $12 to $42. (360)291-3767

RIVERSIDE GOLF COURSE & RV PARK
Ratings: 7.5/NA/7 (RV Park) From Jct of I-5 & Chamber Way (Exit 79): Go 1/8 mi W on Chamber Way to NW Louisiana Ave, then 1/2 mi S on NW Louisiana Ave to Airport Rd, then 1/2 mi W on Airport Rd. (L). **FAC:** Paved rds. 26 paved, patios, back-ins (24 x 60), accepts self-contain units only, 26 full hkups (30/50 amps), WiFi Hotspot, restaurant. **REC:** Chehalis River: fishing, golf, rec open to public. Pet restrict(B). No tents. Big rig sites, 2015 rates: $40. ATM.
(360)748-8182 Lat: 46.66449, Lon: -122.96722
1451 NW Airport Rd, Chehalis, WA 98532
riverside_golf_club@comcast.net
www.playriversidegolf.com
See ad pages 1257 (Spotlight Gateway to Washington), 1250.

STAN HEDWALL PARK (Public) From Jct of I-5 & Rice Rd (exit 76), W 0.5 mi on Rice Rd (R). 2015 rates: $15. Apr 1 to Nov 30. (360)748-0271

CHELAN — B4 *Chelan*

LAKE CHELAN (State Pk) From Jct of Woodin Ave & Alt US-97 (in town), S 3.9 mi on Alt US-97 to South Shore Rd/SR-971, W 6 mi (R). 2015 rates: $12 to $42. (509)687-3710

LAKESHORE RV PARK & MARINA (Public) From W Jct of US-Alt 97A & SR 150: Go 1/2 mi NW on SR 150/Manson Rd (L). No pets Memorial Day wknd and from last wknd of June thru Labor Day. 2015 rates: $28 to $55. (509)682-8023

TWENTY-FIVE MILE CREEK (State Pk) From jct US 97 & Hwy 150: Go 4 mi S on US 97, then 16 mi W on S Lakeshore Rd. 2015 rates: $12 to $42. (888)226-7688

CHENEY — B6 *Spokane*

KLINK'S WILLIAMS LAKE RESORT **Ratings: 7/8/7.5** (Campground) 2015 rates: $34.95 to $39.95. Apr 1 to Oct 1. (509)235-2391 18617 W Williams Lake Rd, Cheney, WA 99004

PEACEFUL PINES RV PARK & CAMPGROUND
Ratings: 7/8.5★/8 (Campground) From Jct of I-90 (Exit 257) & Hwy 904: Go 10 mi E on Hwy 904 (R); or From Jct of I-90 (Exit 270) & Hwy 904: Go 7 mi S on Hwy 904 (L). **FAC:** Gravel rds. (21 spaces). Avail: 18 gravel, 2 pull-thrus (20 x 60), back-ins (27 x 40), 9 full hkups, 9 W, 9 E (30/50 amps), seasonal sites, cable, WiFi, tent sites, rentals, dump, fire rings, firewood. **REC.** Pets OK. 2015 rates: $27 to $32. Disc: AAA, military.
AAA Approved
(800)985-2966 Lat: 47.475055, Lon: -117.597474
1231 W 1st St, Cheney, WA 99004
info@peacefulpinesrv.com
www.peacefulpinesrv.com
See ad pages 1277 (Spotlight Spokane and the Inland Empire), 1250.

CHEWELAH — B6 *Stevens*

CHEWELAH GOLF & COUNTRY CLUB **Ratings: 5/7/6** (Campground) 2015 rates: $26 to $28. Apr 1 to Oct 31. (509)935-6807 2537 Sand Canyon Rd, Chewelah, WA 99109

CHEWELAH PARK (CITY PARK) (Public) From town: Go 1/4 mi N on US-395. (509)935-8311

CHINOOK — D1 *Pacific*

COLUMBIA SHORES RV PARK **Ratings: 4.5/7/6** (Membership Pk) 2015 rates: $35 (360)777-8581 706 Hwy 101, Chinook, WA 98614

RIVERS END CAMPGROUND & RV PARK **Ratings: 6.5/8.5★/8.5** (Campground) 2015 rates: $30 May 1 to Oct 15. (360)777-8317 12 Bayview St, Chinook, WA 98614

CLARKSTON — D6 *Asotin*

CHIEF TIMOTHY PARK
Ratings: 8/8.5★/8.5 (RV Park) Wbnd- From Jct of US 12 & SR-128 (in Clarkston): Go 6-3/4 mi W on US 12 to entrance rd to park (R). Ebnd- Approaching Clarkston on US 12, entrance road btwn MM 425 & 426 (L). **FAC:** Paved rds. 50 paved patios, 46 pull-thrus (45 x 70), back-ins (30 x 35), 2[illegible] full hkups, 8 W, 8 E (30 amps), WiFi Hotspot, tent sites, rentals, showers $, dump, laundry, fire rings firewood. **REC:** Snake River: swim, fishing, playground. Pets OK. Partial handicap access. 28 day max stay, 2015 rates: $28 to $34. May 1 to Oct 31
(509)758-9580 Lat: 46.415503, Lon: -117.194222
13766 Hwy 12, Clarkston, WA 99403
Chief.timothy@clm-services.com
www.sunrisereservations.com
See ad pages 1264 (Spotlight Hells Canyon), 1250.

GRANITE LAKE PREMIER RV RESORT
Ratings: 9/10★/9.5 (RV Park) From Jct of Hwy 12 & 5th St (in town): Go 1/4 mi N on 5th St (L). **FAC:** Paved rds. 7[illegible] paved, patios, 18 pull-thrus (28 x 55) back-ins (26 x 50), 75 full hkups (30/50 amps), WiFi, laundry. **REC:** Granite Lake: fishing, rec open to public. Pets OK. Partial handicap access, no tents. 2015 rates: $42 to $53. Disc: AAA, military
(800)989-4578 Lat: 46.424214, Lon: -117.043018
306 Granite Lake Dr, Clarkston, WA 99403
premiergranite@msn.com
www.premierrvresorts.com
See ad this page, 1250.

HELLS CANYON RV RESORT & MARINA
Ratings: 10/10★/9.5 (RV Park) From Jct of SR-12 & SR 193 (15th St W-side of town): Go 1/8 mi N on SR-19[illegible] to Port Dr, then 100 yards west on Port Dr (L). **FAC:** Paved rds. (48 spaces) Avail: 38 paved, patios, 38 pull-thrus (32 x 64), 38 full hkups (30/50 amps), seasonal sites, WiFi, laundry groc. **REC:** heated pool, whirlpool, Snake River: fishing, marina. Pets OK. Partial handicap access, no tents. Big rig sites, 2015 rates: $33.39 to $44.43 Disc: AAA, military.
(509)758-6963 Lat: 46.420830, Lon: -117.069998
1560 Port Drive, Clarkston, WA 99403
hellscanyonrvpark@gmail.com
www.hellscanyon.net
See ad pages 1265 (Spotlight Hells Canyon), 1250.

HILLVIEW RV PARK
Ratings: 8/9.5★/7.5 (RV Park) On US-12 (Bridge St) between 12 St and 13 St. **FAC:** Paved rds. (104 spaces). Avail 25 all weather, 6 pull-thrus (30 x 65) back-ins (30 x 35), accepts self-contain units only, 25 full hkups (30/50 amps), seasonal sites cable, WiFi, laundry, LP gas. Pet restrict(B). Partial handicap access, no tents. Big rig sites, 2015 rates $30.
(866)758-6299 Lat: 46.420302, Lon: -117.054746
1224 Bridge St, Clarkston, WA 99403
hillviewrvpark@yahoo.com
See ad pages 1264 (Spotlight Hells Canyon), 1250.

Things to See and Do

SNAKE DANCER EXCURSIONS Jet Boat tours of Hells Canyon, plus fishing trips for steelhead, salmon, trout, sturgeon. Meals served on jet boat tours. Partial handicap access. RV accessible. Restrooms, food. Hours: 6am to 8pm Adult fee: $126 to $280.
(800)234-1941 Lat: 46.421091, Lon: -117.070581
1550 Port Dr, Suite B, Clarkston, WA 99403
Hellscanyontours@msn.com
www.snakedancerexcursions.com
See ad page 1265 (Spotlight Hells Canyon)

VISIT LEWIS CLARK VALLEY Visitor Information Center for Clarkston, WA, Lewiston, ID & Hells Canyon area. Information on the towns and the region. Partial handicap access. RV accessible. Restrooms. Hours: 9am to 5pm M-F. No CC.
(509)758-7489 Lat: 46.42522, Lon: -117.04850
847 Port Way, Clarkston, WA 99403
info@visitlcvalley.com
visitlcvalley.com
See ad page 1244 (Welcome Section).

CLE ELUM — C3 *Kittitas*

SUN COUNTRY GOLF AND RV **Ratings: 6.5/8/7.5** (RV Park) 2015 rates: $34 to $39. Apr 1 to Nov 1. (509)674-2226 841 St. Andrews Dr, Cle Elum, WA 98922

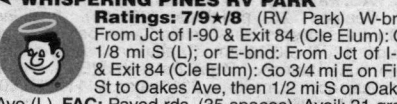

WHISPERING PINES RV PARK
Ratings: 7/9★/8 (RV Park) W-bnd: From Jct of I-90 & Exit 84 (Cle Elum): Go 1/8 mi S (L); or E-bnd: From Jct of I-90 & Exit 84 (Cle Elum): Go 3/4 mi E on First St to Oakes Ave, then 1/2 mi S on Oakes Ave (L). **FAC:** Paved rds. (35 spaces). Avail: 31 gravel, 14 pull-thrus (34 x 75), back-ins (30 x 65), 9 full hkups, 22 W, 22 E (30/50 amps), seasonal sites, cable, showers $, dump, laundry, LP gas. **REC:** Yakima River: fishing. Pet restrict(B). No tents. 2015 rates: $35. Disc: military.
(509)674-7278 Lat: 47.189420, Lon: -120.936748
100 Whispering Pines Dr, Cle Elum, WA 98922
whisperingpinespark@yahoo.com
www.whisperingpines.cjb.net
See ad pages 1253 (Spotlight Cascades), 1250.

COLBERT — B6 *Spokane*

WILD ROSE RV PARK
Ratings: 7/8.5★/8.5 (RV Park) From Jct of SR-395 & SR-2 (between MP 173-174): Go 9 mi N on SR-395 (R). **FAC:** Gravel rds. (57 spaces). Avail: 34 gravel, patios, 9 pull-thrus (32 x 55), back-ins (25 x 55), 34 full hkups (30/50 amps), seasonal sites, WiFi, showers $, laundry. **REC.** Pet restrict(B). Partial handicap access, no tents. 2015 rates: $30. No CC.
(509)276-8853 Lat: 47.869011, Lon: -117.421890
23106 N Hwy 395, Colbert, WA 99005
wildroserv@aol.com

COLFAX — C6 *Garfield*

BOYER PARK AND MARINA
Ratings: 8.5/9★/10 (RV Park) From Jct of US 195 & WA-194 (between Spokane and Clarkston) Go: 23 mi SW on WA-194 (R). **FAC:** Paved rds. (48 spaces). 36 Avail: 4 paved, 32 gravel, 1 pull-thrus (30 x 60), back-ins (60 x 65), 18 full hkups, 18 W, 18 E (30/50 amps), seasonal sites, WiFi, tent sites, rentals, showers $, dump, laundry, groc, fire rings, firewood, restaurant. **REC:** Snake River: swim, marina, playground. Pets OK. Big rig sites, 2015 rates: $37 to $40. Disc: military.
(509)397-3208 Lat: 46.68396, Lon: -117.44904
1753 Granite Rd, Colfax, WA 99111
boyerpark@colfax.com
www.boyerpark.com
See ad pages 1277 (Spotlight Spokane and the Inland Empire), 1250.

COLVILLE — A5 *Stevens*

COLVILLE FAIRGROUNDS RV PARK (Public) From Jct of Hwy 395 & Columbia Ave., W 0.1 mi on Columbia St (E). 2015 rates: $10 to $25. Apr 1 to Nov 30. (509)684-2585

CONCONULLY — A4 *Okanogan*

CONCONULLY
(State Pk) At Jct of Hwy 97 (Conconully Hwy) & W Broadway (L). **FAC:** Paved rds. 20 grass, back-ins (18 x 75), 20 W, 20 E (30 amps), tent sites, rentals, dump, laundry, firewood. **REC:** pool, Conconully Lake: fishing, rec open to public. Pets OK. Partial handicap access. 10 day max stay, 2015 rates: $20 to $45. May 1 to Oct 31.
(888)226-7688 Lat: 48.555528, Lon: -119.755111
1 South Lottie, Conconully, WA 98819
infocent@parks.wa.gov
www.parks.wa.gov
See ad page 1246 (Welcome Section).

CONCRETE — A3 *Skagit, Whatcom*

CONCRETE / GRANDY CREEK KOA **Ratings: 7.5/6.5/7** (RV Park) 2015 rates: $24 to $42. Mar 1 to Oct 31. (888)562-4236 7370 Russell Rd, Concrete, WA 98237

RASAR SP (State Pk) From town: Go 7 mi W on Hwy 20, then 3/4 mi S on Russell Rd, then 2 mi W on Cape Horn Rd. 2015 rates: $12 to $42. (360)826-3942

SWIFT CREEK CAMPGROUND (Natl Forest) From west town limits: Go 6 mi W on Hwy 20, then 20 mi N on Baker Lake Rd. Pit toilets. 2015 rates: $18 to $38. May 10 to Sep 23. (360)856-5700

Don't take any chances when it comes to cleanliness. We rate campground restrooms and showers for cleanliness and physical characteristics such as supplies and appearance.

CONNELL — C5 *Franklin*

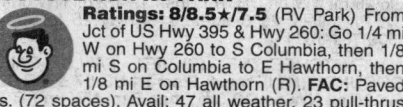

COYOTE RUN RV PARK
Ratings: 8/8.5★/7.5 (RV Park) From Jct of US Hwy 395 & Hwy 260: Go 1/4 mi W on Hwy 260 to S Columbia, then 1/8 mi S on Columbia to E Hawthorn, then 1/8 mi E on Hawthorn (R). **FAC:** Paved rds. (72 spaces). Avail: 47 all weather, 23 pull-thrus (30 x 85), back-ins (30 x 40), 47 full hkups (30/50 amps), seasonal sites, cable, WiFi, tent sites, rentals, dump, laundry, LP gas. **REC.** Pet restrict(B). Partial handicap access. Big rig sites, 2015 rates: $26 to $30. Disc: AAA.
(877)273-9484 Lat: 46.651024, Lon: -118.857967
351 E Hawthorn, Connell, WA 99326
info@coyoterunrvpark.com
www.coyoterunrvpark.com

COPALIS BEACH — C1 *Grays Harbor*

COPALIS BEACH RESORT-SUNRISE RESORTS **Ratings: 7.5/6/6.5** (Membership Pk) 2015 rates: $25 to $50. (360)289-4278 14 Heath Rd, Copalis Beach, WA 98535

COUGAR — D2 *Cowlitz*

GIFFORD PINCHOT NF (LOWER FALLS CAMPGROUND) (Natl Forest) From town: Go 25 mi E on FR 90. Pit toilets. 2015 rates: $15 to $35. May 1 to Nov 1. (360)247-3900

LONE FIR RESORT **Ratings: 8.5/9★/9** (RV Park) From Jct of I-5 & SR-503 (exit 21): Go 28-3/4 mi NE on SR-503/Lewis River Rd (L). **FAC:** Paved rds. (32 spaces). Avail: 29 grass, 2 pull-thrus (30 x 65), back-ins (33 x 60), 29 full hkups (30 amps), seasonal sites, WiFi, tent sites, rentals, showers $, laundry, fire rings, firewood, restaurant. **REC:** pool, playground. Pet restrict(B). Partial handicap access. 2015 rates: $35. Disc: AAA, military.
AAA Approved
(360)238-5210 Lat: 46.050815, Lon: -122.303840
16806 Lewis River Rd, Cougar, WA 98616
manager@lonefirresort.com
www.lonefirresort.com

COULEE CITY — B4 *Grant*

COULEE CITY COMMUNITY PARK (Public) From Jct of SR-17 & SR-2, E 2 mi on SR-2 (L). 2015 rates: $15 to $20. Apr 1 to Oct 31. (509)632-5331

SUN LAKES - DRY FALLS
(State Pk) From Jct of US-2 & SR-17, S 4 mi on SR-17 to Park Lake Rd, E 1.1 mi (L). **FAC:** Paved rds. 152 gravel, 3 pull-thrus (18 x 58), back-ins (16 x 40), 39 full hkups (30 amps), tent sites, dump, laundry, groc, LP bottles, fire rings, firewood. **REC:** Park Lake: swim, fishing, golf, playground, rec open to public. Pets OK. 10 day max stay, 2015 rates: $20 to $45.
(888)226-7688 Lat: 47.58964, Lon: -119.39058
34875 Park Lake Rd, Coulee City, WA 99115
infocent@parks.wa.gov
www.parks.wa.gov
See ad page 1246 (Welcome Section).

SUN LAKES PARK RESORT INC **Ratings: 8.5/7/7.5** (RV Park) 2015 rates: $27 to $45. Mar 30 to Oct 15. (509)632-5291 34228 Park Lake Road NE, Coulee City, WA 99115

COULEE DAM — B5 *Lincoln*

LAKE ROOSEVELT NRA/SPRING CANYON (Natl Pk) From Jct SR-155 & SR-174, E 3 mi on SR-174 (L). Pit toilets. 2015 rates: $5 to $13. (509)633-9441

COUPEVILLE — B2 *Island*

FORT CASEY
(State Pk) On Whidbey Island (from town): Go 3 mi S on Hwy 20 to Keystone ferry terminal exit. Park is by terminal (L). **FAC:** Paved rds. 14 gravel, 4 pull-thrus (18 x 40), back-ins (16 x 40), 14 W, 14 E (30 amps), tent sites, firewood. **REC:** Admiralty Inlet: fishing, rec open to public. Pets OK. Partial handicap access. 10 day max stay, 2015 rates: $20 to $45. No CC, no reservations.
(888)226-7688 Lat: 48.166139, Lon: -122.680722
1280 Engle Rd, Coupeville, WA 98239
infocent@parks.wa.gov
www.parks.wa.gov
See ad page 1246 (Welcome Section).

CRESTON — B5 *Lincoln*

LAKE ROOSEVELT NRA/HAWK CREEK (Natl Pk) From town, E 22 mi to SH-25, N 5 mi to Chase Rd., w 1.5 mi to Indian Creek Rd., NW 12.5 (E). Pit toilets. 2015 rates: $5 to $10. (509)633-9441

CUSICK — A6 *Pend Oreille*

BLUESLIDE RESORT **Ratings: 4.5/5.5/5** (Campground) 2015 rates: $25 to $50. Apr 15 to Oct 15. (509)445-1327 400041 Hwy 20, Cusick, WA 99119

DALLESPORT — E3 *Klickitat*

COLUMBIA HILLS (State Pk) From Jct of US-197 & Hwy 14, E 2 mi on Hwy 14 (R). 2015 rates: $12 to $42. (509)767-1159

DAVENPORT — B5 *Lincoln, Stevens*

LAKE ROOSEVELT NRA/FORT SPOKANE (Natl Pk) From E end of town, W 21 mi on SR-25 (R). Pit toilets. 2015 rates: $5 to $10. (509)633-3830

LAKE ROOSEVELT NRA/PORCUPINE BAY (Natl Pk) From town, N 19 mi on SR-25 to unnamed cnty rd, NW 4 mi (R). Pit toilets. 2015 rates: $5 to $10. (509)633-9441

TWO RIVERS CASINO RV & MARINA RESORT **Ratings: 8.5/8/9** (RV Park) 2015 rates: $28 to $39. (800)722-4031 6828 'd' Hwy 25 S, Davenport, WA 99122

DAYTON — D5 *Columbia*

LEWIS & CLARK TRAIL (State Pk) From town, W 5 mi on US-12 (R). 2015 rates: $12 to $42. Apr 1 to Oct 31. (509)337-6457

DEER PARK — B6 *Spokane*

SPOKANE RV RESORT AT DEER PARK GOLF CLUB
Ratings: 10/10★/10 (Condo Pk) From Jct of US-395 & Crawford St (between MP 180 & 181): Go 1-3/4 mi E on W Crawford St to N Country Club Dr, then 1 mi N on Country Club Dr (R). **FAC:** Paved rds. (127 spaces). Avail: 110 paved, patios, 11 pull-thrus (35 x 120), back-ins (30 x 85), accepts self-contain units only, 110 full hkups (30/50 amps), seasonal sites, cable, WiFi, laundry, restaurant, controlled access. **REC:** heated pool, whirlpool, golf, playground. Pets OK. Partial handicap access, no tents. Big rig sites, eco-friendly, 2015 rates: $41.
(877)276-1555 Lat: 47.972696, Lon: -117.447336
1205 Country Club Dr, Deer Park, WA 99006
info@spokanervresort.com
www.spokanervresort.com
See ad pages 1277 (Spotlight Spokane and the Inland Empire), 1250.

DES MOINES — C2 *King*

SALTWATER (State Pk) From Jct of I-5 & Des Moines Rd exit, W 4 mi on Des Moines Rd to SR-509, S 2 mi (R). 2015 rates: $12 to $42. Apr 23 to Oct 6. (253)661-4956

EASTON — C3 *Kittitas*

LAKE EASTON (State Pk) From I-90 (exit 70): Follow signs 1/2 mi. 2015 rates: $12 to $42. (509)656-2586

LAKE EASTON RESORT **Ratings: 7/6/5** (Membership Pk) 2015 rates: $25 to $45. (509)656-2255 581 Lake Easton Rd, Easton, WA 98925

EASTSOUND — A2 *San Juan*

MORAN (State Pk) From town: Go 5 mi E on Horseshoe Hwy. On Orcas Island. 2015 rates: $12 to $42. (885)226-7688

EATONVILLE — C2 *Pierce*

HENLEY'S SILVER LAKE RESORT (Public) From town, W 2.2 mi on Eatonville Hwy W, NW 4.5 mi on Hwy 7. 2015 rates: $32. (360)832-3580

RAINBOW RV RESORT
Ratings: 7.5/6/7 (RV Park) S-bnd: From Jct of SR-161 & SR-512 (Meridian), S 15 mi on SR-161 (MP 10-11) to Tanwax Dr, E 0.3 mi to Tanwax Court, S 0.2 mi (R); or N-bnd from center of Eatonville, N 8 mi on SR-161 (MP 10-11) to Tanwax Dr, E 0.3 mi to Tanwax Court, S 0.2 mi (R). **FAC:** Paved rds. (50 spaces). Avail: 16 gravel, back-ins (19 x 40), 16 full hkups (30 amps), seasonal sites, cable, WiFi, tent sites, rentals, showers $, laundry, groc, LP gas, firewood. **REC:** Tanwax Lake: fishing, rec open to public. Pet restrict(B). 2015 rates: $32 to $36.
(360)879-5115 Lat: 46.946005, Lon: -122.275548
34217 Tanwax Ct E, Eatonville, WA 98328
info@rainbowrvresort.com
www.rainbowrvresort.com
See ad page 1268 (Spotlight Mount Rainier & Mount St Helens).

ELECTRIC CITY — B5 *Grant*

COULEE PLAYLAND RESORT
Ratings: 6.5/8★/7 (Campground) From Jct of SR-174 & SR-155: Go 1 Mi S on SR-155 (R). **FAC:** Gravel/dirt rds. 59 Avail: 20 gravel, 39 grass, 18 pull-thrus (14 x 60), back-ins (24 x 50), 37 full hkups, 22 W, 22 E (30/50 amps), WiFi, tent sites, rentals, showers $, dump, laundry, groc, fire rings, firewood. **REC:** Banks Lake: swim, fishing, marina.

ELECTRIC CITY (CONT)

COULEE PLAYLAND RESORT (CONT)
Pets OK. Partial handicap access. 2015 rates: $38 to $46.
(509)633-2671 Lat: 47.934918, Lon: -119.027721
401 Coulee Blvd E, Electric City, WA 99123
www.couleeplayland.com
See ad page 1256 (Spotlight Coulee Corridor).

SUNBANKS RESORT **Ratings: 7/6/8.5** (RV Park) 2015 rates: $23 to $63. (888)822-7195 57662 Hwy 155 N, Electric City, WA 99123

ELLENSBURG — C4 *Kittitas*

E & J RV PARK
Ratings: 9.5/8/7 (RV Park) From Jct of I-90 & Canyon Rd (exit 109): Go 1/8 mi S on Canyon Rd to Berry Rd, then 1/16 mi E on Berry Rd (L) (Register in motel office). **FAC:** Paved rds. (79 spaces). Avail: 41 paved, no slide-outs, 21 pull-thrus (20 x 65), back-ins (20 x 65), mostly side by side hkups, 41 full hkups (30/50 amps), seasonal sites, WiFi, tent sites, rentals, laundry. **REC:** heated pool, whirlpool, rec open to public. Pets OK $. Partial handicap access. 2015 rates: $39.99 to $65. Disc: AAA, military. ATM. AAA Approved
(509)933-1500 Lat: 46.971040, Lon: -120.535115
901 Berry Rd, Ellensburg, WA 98926
eburgdaysinn@gmail.com
www.ellensburglodging.com
See ad pages 1281 (Spotlight Wine Country), 1250.

YAKIMA RIVER RV PARK
Ratings: 5/NA/6 (Campground) From I-90 (exit 109): Go 2 mi S on Canyon Rd to Ringer Loop Rd, then 1/2 mi W on Ringer Loop Rd. (R). **FAC:** Gravel rds. 36 Avail: 31 gravel, 5 grass, 32 pull-thrus (21 x 60), back-ins (25 x 40), mostly side by side hkups, 16 full hkups, 20 W, 20 E (30/50 amps), WiFi, tent sites, fire rings, firewood. **REC:** Yakima River: fishing. Pet restrict(B). 2015 rates: $27 to $42. Apr 1 to Sep 30.
(509)925-4734 Lat: 46.933558, Lon: -120.519351
791 Ringer Loop Rd, Ellensburg, WA 98926
yakimarvpark@yahoo.com
www.yakimarv.com

ELMA — C2 *Grays Harbor*

ELMA RV PARK
Ratings: 8/10★/9 (RV Park) From Jct of SR-8 & SR-12: Go 1/8 mi S on SR-12 to unnamed street (behind gas station), then 1/8 mi W (L). **FAC:** Paved/gravel rds. (81 spaces). Avail: 31 gravel, 4 pull-thrus (25 x 80), back-ins (25 x 42), 31 full hkups (30/50 amps), seasonal sites, cable, WiFi, tent sites, showers $, dump, laundry, LP gas. **REC.** Pets OK. Eco-friendly, 2015 rates: $35 to $39. Disc: AAA, military.
(866)211-3939 Lat: 47.002522, Lon: -123.387939
4730 State Route 12, Elma, WA 98541
elma1@surepost.net
www.elmarvpark.com
See ad pages 1273 (Spotlight Olympic Peninsula), 1250.

SCHAFER (State Pk) From town: Go 5 mi W on Hwy-410, then 10 mi N on E Satsop Rd. 2015 rates: $12 to $42. (888)226-7688

TRAVEL INN RESORT **Ratings: 9/7.5/8** (Membership Pk) 2015 rates: $40. (800)871-2888 801 East Main St, Elma, WA 98541

ENTIAT — B4 *Chelan*

ENTIAT CITY PARK (Public) From Jct of Hwy 2 & US-97 alternate, S 8.3 mi on US-97 Alternate (R). 2015 rates: $22 to $28. Apr 15 to Sep 15. (509)784-1500

WENATCHEE NF (COTTONWOOD CAMPGROUND) (Natl Forest) From jct US 97 & CR 371: Go 26 mi NW on CR 371, then 12-1/2 mi NW on FR 51. Pit toilets. 2015 rates: $10. May 25 to Sep 7. (509)784-1511

WENATCHEE NF (SILVER FALLS CAMPGROUND) (Natl Forest) From jct US 97 & CR 371: Go 26 mi NW on CR 371, then 5 mi NW on FR 51. Pit toilets. 2015 rates: $12. May 25 to Sep 7. (509)784-1511

ENUMCLAW — C3 *King, Pierce*

ENUMCLAW EXPO CENTER RV CAMPGROUND (Public) From Jct of Hwy 410 & 284th, N 0.2 mi on 284th (L). 2015 rates: $26. (360)615-5631

MT RAINIER/WHITE RIVER CAMPGROUND (Natl Pk) From town, E 38 mi on Hwy 410 to Sunrise Rd, W 5.5 mi (L). 2015 rates: $12. Jun 30 to Sep 30. (360)569-2211

EPHRATA — C4 *Grant*

EPHRATA See also Coulee City, Moses Lake & Soap Lake.

OASIS RV PARK & GOLF COURSE
Ratings: 8.5/7.5★/9 (RV Park) From Jct of SR-282 & SR-28 in Ephrata: Go 1-3/4 mi S on SR-28. (R). **FAC:** Paved rds. (67 spaces). Avail: 60 gravel, 6 pull-thrus (35 x 65), back-ins (30 x 55), 28 full hkups, 32 W, 32 E (30 amps), seasonal sites, cable, WiFi, tent sites, showers $, dump, laundry, groc, LP gas, fire rings, firewood. **REC:** heated pool, pond, fishing, golf, playground, rec open to public. Pets OK. Partial handicap access. 2015 rates: $25 to $33. Disc: AAA, military.
(877)754-5102 Lat: 47.285356, Lon: -119.578506
2541 Basin St SW, Ephrata, WA 98823
info@oasisrvandgolfcourse.com
www.oasisrvandgolfcourse.com
See ad pages 1256 (Spotlight Coulee Corridor), 1250.

SUNNY SPRINGS RESORT & CAMPGROUND
Ratings: 9/8.5★/7.5 (RV Park) From Jct of SR-28W & SR-283, W 0.3 mi on SR-28 between MP 41 & 42 (L). **FAC:** All weather rds. (73 spaces). Avail: 40 grass, 12 pull-thrus (19 x 70), back-ins (25 x 66), 40 full hkups (30/50 amps), seasonal sites, cable, WiFi, tent sites, rentals, dump, laundry, LP gas, firewood. **REC:** heated pool, playground. Pet restrict(B/Q). Big rig sites, 2015 rates: $25 to $33. Disc: AAA, military. AAA Approved
(800)422-8447 Lat: 47.246363, Lon: -119.611650
5707 Hwy 28W, Ephrata, WA 98823
stay@sunnysprings.com
www.sunnysprings.com
See ad this page, 1250.

EVANS — A5 *Stevens*

LAKE ROOSEVELT NRA/EVANS (Natl Pk) From town, S 2 mi on SR-25 (L). Pit toilets. 2015 rates: $5 to $10. (509)633-9441

EVERETT — B3 *Snohomish*

HARBOUR POINTE RV PARK Ratings: 7/6.5/5.5 (RV Park) From Jct I-5 (exit 186) & 128th St SW: Go 1-1/2 mi W on 128th St SW/Airport Rd to Hwy 99/Evergreen Way, then 4 3/4 mi N on Hwy 99/Evergreen Way. (R). **FAC:** Paved rds. (64 spaces). Avail: 4 gravel, 1 pull-thrus (25 x 60), back-ins (25 x 40), accepts self-contain units only, 4 full hkups (30/50 amps), seasonal sites, WiFi, dump, laundry, groc. Pet restrict(B/Q). No tents. Big rig sites, 2015 rates: $42 to $50. Disc: military.
(425)789-1169 Lat: 47.893665, Lon: -122.253784
11501 Hwy 99, Everett, WA 98204
parkinfo@harbourpointervpark.com
www.harbourpointervpark.com

LAKESIDE RV PARK Ratings: 8.5/9.5★/9 (RV Park) From Jct of I-5 & 128th St SW (Exit 186): Go .8 mi W on 128th St to Airport Rd, then .6 mi NW on Airport Rd to Hwy 99 (Evergreen Way), then .3 mi SW on Hwy 99 (L). **FAC:** Paved rds. (150 spaces). Avail: 50 paved, 30 pull-thrus (23 x 55), back-ins (22 x 39), 50 full hkups (30/50 amps), seasonal sites, cable, WiFi, tent sites, laundry, LP gas. **REC:** Lakeside Lake: fishing, playground. Pet restrict(B). Partial handicap access. 2015 rates: $38.80. Disc: AAA, military.
AAA Approved
(800)468-7275 Lat: 47.885856, Lon: -122.260500
12321 Hwy 99 S, Everett, WA 98204
lakesiderv@pcfre.com
www.lakesidervpark.net

MAPLE GROVE RV RESORT
Ratings: 8/10★/9.5 (RV Park) From Jct of I-5 & 128th St SW (Exit 186): Go .8 mi W on 128th St to Airport Rd, then .6 mi NW on Airport Rd to Hwy 99 (Evergreen Way), then .4 mi SW on Hwy 99 (L). **FAC:** Paved rds. (99 spaces). Avail: 57 paved, 12 all weather, 26 pull-thrus (23 x 55), back-ins (23 x 40), accepts self-contain units only, 57 full hkups, 12 W (30/50 amps), seasonal sites, cable, WiFi, dump, laundry, LP gas. Pet restrict(B/Q). Partial handicap access, no tents. 2015 rates: $44 to $55.50. Disc: AAA, military.
(866)793-2200 Lat: 47.885275, Lon: -122.262034
12417 Hwy 99, Everett, WA 98204
info@maplegroverv.com
www.maplegroverv.com
See ad pages 1263 (Spotlight Greater Seattle), 1250.

FALL CITY — B3 *King*

SNOQUALMIE RIVER RV PARK & CAMPGROUND **Ratings: 5/4.5/7.5** (Campground) 2015 rates: $34 to $43. Apr 1 to Oct 31. (425)222-5545 34807 SE 44th Place, Fall City, WA 98024

TALL CHIEF RV RESORT **Ratings: 7.5/8/6.5** (Membership Pk) 2015 rates: $48 to $50. (800)405-6188 29290 SE 8th St, Fall City, WA 98024

FERNDALE — A2 *Whatcom*

NOR'WEST RV PARK **Ratings: 7/8★/7.5** (RV Park) 2015 rates: $30. (360)384-5038 1627 Main St, Ferndale, WA 98248

THE CEDARS RV RESORT
Ratings: 9.5/9.5★/9 (RV Park) From Jct of I-5 & Portal Way (exit 263): Go 1 mi N on Portal Way (L). **FAC:** Paved rds. (163 spaces). 110 Avail: 73 gravel, 37 grass, 100 pull-thrus (25 x 68), back-ins (36 x 60), some side by side hkups, 100 full hkups, 10 W, 10 E (30/50 amps), seasonal sites, cable, WiFi $, tent sites, dump, laundry, groc, LP gas, fire rings, firewood. **REC:** heated pool, playground. Pets OK $. Partial handicap access. Big rig sites, eco-friendly, 2015 rates: $46 to $50. Disc: AAA, military.
(360)384-2622 Lat: 48.870074, Lon: -122.584599
6335 Portal Way, Ferndale, WA 98248
cedars@htr.ca
www.htr.ca

FIFE — C2 *Pierce*

Travel Services

CAMPING WORLD STORE OF FIFE/TACOMA
As the nation's largest retailer of RV supplies, accessories, services and new and used RVs, Camping World is committed to making your total RV experience better. **SERVICES:** Tire, RV appliance, staffed RV wash, restrooms. Rentals. RV supplies, emergency parking, RV accessible. waiting room. Hours: 8am to 6pm.
(800)526-4165 Lat: 47.242561, Lon: -122.366169
4650 16th St. East, Fife, WA 98424
www.campingworld.com

FORKS — B1 *Clallam*

BOGACHIEL (State Pk) From town: Go 6 mi S on US-101. 2015 rates: $12 to $42. (360)374-6356

FORKS 101 RV PARK **Ratings: 5/7.5★/7** (RV Park) 2015 rates: $35. Apr 1 to Oct 31. (360)374-5073 901 S Forks Ave, Forks, WA 98331

OLYMPIC/HOH (Natl Pk) From town, S 12 mi on US-101 to Upper Hoh River Rd, E 18 mi (R). Entrance fee required. 2015 rates: $12. (360)565-3130

OLYMPIC/MORA CAMPGROUND (Natl Pk) From town, N 1 mi on Hwy 101 to Mora-La Push Rd, W 9 mi to Mora, NW 2.5 mi (at 3 Rivers Resort), follow signs (L). 2015 rates: $12. (360)565-3130

RIVERVIEW RV PARK **Ratings: 8/NA/7.5** (RV Park) 2015 rates: $25 to $45. (360)374-3398 33 Mora Rd, Forks, WA 98363

FREELAND — B2 *Island*

SOUTH WHIDBEY (State Pk) Take ferry from Mukilteo to Whidbey Island, N 11 mi on Hwy 525 to Bushpoint, W 6 mi (L). For reservations call (888)226-7688. 2015 rates: $12 to $37. Feb 1 to Nov 30. (888)226-7688

GIFFORD — B5 *Stevens*

LAKE ROOSEVELT NRA/GIFFORD CAMPGROUND (Natl Pk) From S end of town, S 2 mi on SR-25 (R). Pit toilets. 2015 rates: $5 to $10. (509)633-9441

GIG HARBOR — C2 *Pierce*

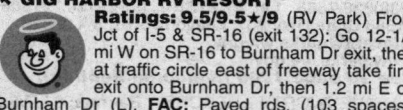

GIG HARBOR RV RESORT
Ratings: 9.5/9.5★/9 (RV Park) From Jct of I-5 & SR-16 (exit 132): Go 12-1/2 mi W on SR-16 to Burnham Dr exit, then at traffic circle east of freeway take first exit onto Burnham Dr, then 1.2 mi E on Burnham Dr (L). **FAC:** Paved rds. (103 spaces). Avail: 71 all weather, 35 pull-thrus (30 x 75), back-ins (27 x 50), 63 full hkups, 8 W, 8 E (30/50 amps), seasonal sites, cable, WiFi, tent sites, rentals, dump, laundry, LP gas. **REC:** pool, playground. Pets OK. Big rig sites, eco-friendly, 2015 rates: $30 to $45. Disc: AAA.
(253)858-8138 Lat: 47.344656, Lon: -122.599043
9515 Burnham Dr NW, Gig Harbor, WA 98332
info@gigharborrvresort.com
www.gigharborrvresort.com
See ad this page, 1250.

GOLDENDALE — D3 *Klickitat*

BROOKS MEMORIAL (State Pk) From Jct of SR-142 & US-97 in town, N 11.5 mi on US-97 (L). 2015 rates: $12 to $42. (509)773-4611

MARYHILL (State Pk) From Jct of SR-14 & US-97, (S of town), S 1.6 mi on US-97 (L); or From Jct of US-97 & I-84 (in Oregon), N 1 mi on US-97 (R). 2015 rates: $12 to $42. (888)226-7688

GRAHAM — C2 *Pierce*

CAMP LAKEVIEW Ratings: 6.5/8/8.5 (Campground) From Jct of SR-512 & SR-161 (Meridian): Go 13 mi S on SR-161 to 304th St E (Kapowsin Hwy), then 2 3/4 mi E on Kapowsin Hwy to 144th Ave E, then 3/4 mi S on 144th Ave (becomes Tanwax Lake) to Benbow Dr, then 1-3/4 mi W on Benbow Dr (R) Be Careful using GPS. **FAC:** Paved/gravel rds. (61 spaces). 21 Avail: 1 gravel, 20 grass, back-ins (20 x 42), 7 full hkups, 14 W, 14 E (30/50 amps), WiFi Hotspot, tent sites, rentals, dump, laundry, groc, fire rings, firewood. **REC:** Lake Tanwax: swim, fishing, playground, rec open to public. Pet restrict(B). 2015 rates: $25 to $27. Disc: AAA, military.
AAA Approved
(360)879-5426 Lat: 46.957249, Lon: -122.257640
32919 Benbow Dr E, Graham, WA 98338
info@camplakeview-wa.com
www.camplakeview-wa.com

GRAND COULEE — B5 *Grant*

GRAND COULEE RV PARK **Ratings: 6/5.5/5** (RV Park) 2015 rates: $31. (866)633-0750 22718 Hwy 174 East, Grand Coulee, WA 99133

STEAMBOAT ROCK
(State Pk) From town, S 10 mi on SR-155 to Steamboat Rock Rd, W 2 mi (E). **FAC:** Paved rds. 136 paved, patios, back-ins (30 x 50), 136 full hkups (20/30 amps), tent sites, dump, groc, firewood. **REC:** Banks Lake: swim, fishing, playground, rec open to public. Pets OK. Partial handicap access. 10 day max stay, 2015 rates: $20 to $45.
(888)226-7688 Lat: 47.85310, Lon: -119.13224
51052 Hwy 155, Electric City, WA 99123
infocent@parks.wa.gov
www.parks.wa.gov
See ad page 1246 (Welcome Section).

THE KING'S COURT RV PARK
Ratings: 6.5/6.5/5.5 (Campground) From Jct Hwy 155 & Hwy 174: Go 3/4 mi E on Hwy 174 (L). **FAC:** Gravel rds. (26 spaces). Avail: 10 gravel, 5 pull-thrus (21 x 45), back-ins (23 x 40), 10 full hkups (30/50 amps), seasonal sites, cable, WiFi, showers $, laundry, LP gas. Pets OK. No tents. 2015 rates: $35. Disc: AAA.
AAA Approved
(800)759-2608 Lat: 47.933954, Lon: -118.996782
212 East Grand Coulee Ave, Grand Coulee, WA 99133-0837
kingsco@bigdam.net
www.kingscourtrv.com
See ad page 1256 (Spotlight Coulee Corridor).

GRANITE FALLS — B3 *Snohomish*

GOLD BASIN CAMPGROUND (Natl Forest) From jct Hwy 92 & Mountain Loop Hwy: Go 13 mi E on Mountain Loop Hwy. 2015 rates: $22 to $35. May 15 to Sep 29. (360)436-1155

GRAYLAND — C1 *Grays Harbor, Pacific*

GRAYLAND BEACH (State Pk) From Jct of SR-105 & Cnty Line Rd (Cranberry Bch Rd), W 0.1 mi on Cranberry Bch Rd (L). 2015 rates: $12 to $42. (888)226-7688

Canada — know the rules, regulations and tips before crossing the border. This is listed at the beginning of the country.

KENANNA RV PARK
Ratings: 7/8.5★/7.5 (RV Park) From Grayland, WA: Go 3 mi S on SR-105 to Kenanna RV Park Rd (R). **FAC:** Gravel rds. (90 spaces). Avail: 85 grass, 85 pull-thrus (25 x 65), mostly side by side hkups, 85 full hkups (30 amps), seasonal sites, WiFi, tent sites, rentals, showers $, laundry, LP gas, fire rings, firewood. **REC:** playground. Pet restrict(Q). 2015 rates: $33. Disc: military.
(800)867-3515 Lat: 46.75393, Lon: -124.08686
2959 Sr 105, Grayland, WA 98547
kenannarv@yahoo.com
www.kenannarv.com
See ad pages 1259 (Spotlight Grays Harbor/Long Beach/Ocean Park), 1250.

HARRINGTON — B5 *Lincoln*

HARRINGTON HIDEAWAY RV PARK **Ratings: 4/7/6** (RV Park) 2015 rates: $25. (509)253-4788 208 W Adams St, Harrington, WA 99134

HOME VALLEY — D3 *Skamania*

TIMBERLAKE CAMPGROUND AND RV PARK **Ratings: 7/8.5★/8.5** (RV Park) 2015 rates: $36 to $39. Mar 1 to Oct 31. (509)427-2267 112 Bylin Rd, Home Valley, WA 98648

HOODSPORT — C2 *Mason*

DOW CREEK RESORT-SUNRISE RESORTS **Ratings: 6.5/8/7.5** (Membership Pk) 2015 rates: $30 to $40. (360)877-5022 2670 N Lake Cushman Rd, Hoodsport, WA 98548

GLEN AYR RESORT
Ratings: 8.5/9.5★/8.5 (RV Park) From Jct of US Hwy 101 & SR-119/N Lake Cushman Rd (in town): Go 1.2 mi N on US Hwy 101; Between MP 330 & 331 (L). **FAC:** All weather rds. 36 Avail: 36 all weather, patios, 9 pull-thrus (24 x 65), back-ins (27 x 40), accepts self-contain units only, 36 full hkups (30/50 amps), cable, WiFi, rentals, laundry, LP gas. **REC:** whirlpool, Hood Canal: fishing. Pet restrict(Q). No tents. Big rig sites, 2015 rates: $33 to $42. Disc: military.
(360)877-9522 Lat: 47.420311, Lon: -123.132038
25381 N Hwy 101, Hoodsport, WA 98548
glenayr@hctc.com
www.glenayr.com
See ad pages 1272 (Spotlight Olympic Peninsula), 1250.

OLYMPIC/STAIRCASE CAMPGROUND (Natl Pk) From Jct of US-101 & SR-119, NW 9 mi on SR-119 to FR-24, W 7 mi (E). Entrance fee required. Pit toilets. 2015 rates: $12. (360)565-3130

REST-A-WHILE RV PARK AND MARINA **Ratings: 5.5/7.5/5** (RV Park) 2015 rates: $40 to $45. (360)877-9474 27001 N US Hwy 101, Hoodsport, WA 98548

SKOKOMISH PARK AT LAKE CUSHMAN
Ratings: 6.5/7.5/8.5 (RV Park) From Jct of SR-119/N Lake Cushman Rd & US Hwy 101 (in town): Go W 7 mi on SR-119/N. Lake Cushman Rd (L). **FAC:** Paved rds. 36 paved, 12 pull-thrus (30 x 70), back-ins (30 x 45), 34 full hkups, 2 W, 2 E (30 amps), WiFi Hotspot, tent sites, showers $, dump, groc, fire rings, firewood. **REC:** Lake Cushman/Big Creek Inlet: swim, fishing. Pets OK. 2015 rates: $34 to $50. Disc: military.
(360)877-5760 Lat: 47.457100, Lon: -123.213878
7211 N Lake Cushman Rd, Hoodsport, WA 98548
info@skokomishpark.com
www.skokomishpark.com
See ad pages 1272 (Spotlight Olympic Peninsula), 1250.

THE WATERFRONT AT POTLATCH
Ratings: 9.5/9.5★/8.5 (RV Park) From Jct of US 101 & SR-119/N Lake Cushman Rd (in town): Go 2.7 mi S on US Hwy 101, between MP 334 & 335 (L). **FAC:** All weather rds. 14 paved, 2 all weather, patios, 3 pull-thrus (22 x 60), back-ins (24 x 48), 16 full hkups (30/50 amps), cable, WiFi, rentals, laundry, fire rings, firewood. **REC:** Hood Canal: swim, fishing. Pet restrict(B). No tents. 2015 rates: $40 to $60. Disc: military.
(360)877-9422 Lat: 47.370940, Lon: -123.158951
21660 North US Hwy 101, Shelton, WA 98584
canal@hctc.com
www.wfresort.com
See ad pages 1272 (Spotlight Olympic Peninsula), 1250.

County names are provided after the city names. If you're tracking the weather, this is the information you'll need to follow the reports.

Things to See and Do

LUCKY DOG CASINO All casino games plus entertainment. Partial handicap access. RV accessible. Restrooms, food. Hours: 8am to 1am.
(360)877-5656 Lat: 47.336823, Lon: -123.160692
19330 N US Hwy 101, Skokomish Nation, WA 98584
jschmitt@theluckydogcasino.net
www.myluckydogcasino.com
See ad page 1272 (Spotlight Olympic Peninsula).

HOQUIAM — C1 *Grays Harbor*

HOQUIAM RIVER RV PARK
Ratings: 7.5/9.5★/8.5 (RV Park) N-bnd: From Downtown Hoquiam: Go N 1.2 mi on Hwy 101 to Queen Ave, then E .1 mi on Queen Ave (L). **FAC:** Gravel rds. (75 spaces). Avail: 45 gravel, patios, 24 pull-thrus (23 x 70), back-ins (23 x 62), 45 full hkups (30/50 amps), seasonal sites, WiFi, tent sites, dump, laundry, LP gas, firewood. **REC:** Hoquiam River: fishing. Pet restrict(B/Q). 2015 rates: $38. Disc: military.
(360)538-2870 Lat: 46.97479, Lon: -123.88733
425 Queen Ave, Hoquiam, WA 98550
information@hoquiamriverrvpark.com
www.hoquiamriverrvpark.com
See ad pages 1273 (Spotlight Olympic Peninsula), 1250.

HUNTERS — B5 *Stevens*

LAKE ROOSEVELT NRA/HUNTERS (Natl Pk) From town, S 1 mi on CR-292 (E). 2015 rates: $5 to $10. (509)633-9441

ILWACO — D1 *Pacific*

CAPE DISAPPOINTMENT
(State Pk) From town, SW 3.2 mi on SR-100 (R). **FAC:** Paved rds. 215 paved, back-ins (25 x 42), 60 full hkups, 18 W, 18 E (20/30 amps), tent sites, rentals, dump, groc, firewood. **REC:** Pacific Ocean: fishing, rec open to public. Pets OK. Partial handicap access. 10 day max stay, 2015 rates: $20 to $45.
(888)226-7688 Lat: 46.28304, Lon: -124.05782
244 Robert Gray Dr, Ilwaco, WA 98624
infocent@parks.wa.gov
www.parks.wa.gov
See ad page 1246 (Welcome Section).

EAGLE'S NEST RESORT-SUNRISE RESORTS **Ratings: 8/7/7.5** (Membership Pk) 2015 rates: $30 to $45. (360)642-8351 700 W. North Head Rd, Ilwaco, WA 98624

ILWACO/LONG BEACH KOA CAMPGROUND **Ratings: 6/7.5/7.5** (Campground) 2015 rates: $35 to $75. May 1 to Oct 31. (360)642-3292 1509 Sr 101, Ilwaco, WA 98624

IONE — A6 *Pend Oreille*

COLVILLE NF (GILLETTE CAMPGROUND) (Natl Forest) From jct Hwy-31 & Hwy-20: Go 11 mi SW on Hwy-20, then 1/2 mi E on CR-647. 2015 rates: $14 to $16. May 25 to Sep 7. (509)684-7010

ISSAQUAH — B3 *King*

ISSAQUAH See also Bellevue, Bothell, Everett, Gig Harbor, Poulsbo & Seattle.

ISSAQUAH VILLAGE RV PARK
Ratings: 9/9.5★/7.5 (RV Park) From Jct of I-90 & Front St/E Lake Sammamish Rd (exit 17): Go 1/8 mi N on Front St to 229th Ave SE, then 50 ft NE to SE 66th St (keep right), then 1/16 mi E on 66th St to 1st Ave NE, then 1/4 mi S on 1st Ave (L).

CHARMING TOWN & EASY SEATTLE ACCESS
Issaquah Village RV is just 17 miles from Seattle but a world apart in Issaquah - with walking & bike paths, historic downtown, abundant dining, boutique & big-store shopping & outdoor destinations galore. And friendly staff!

FAC: Paved rds. (56 spaces). Avail: 29 paved, 1 all

WA

ISSAQUAH (CONT)

ISSAQUAH VILLAGE RV PARK (CONT)
weather, 2 pull-thrus (18 x 60), back-ins (21 x 60), accepts self-contain units only, 30 full hkups (30/50 amps), seasonal sites, cable, WiFi, dump, laundry, LP gas. **REC:** playground. Pet restrict(Q). Partial handicap access, no tents. Eco-friendly, 2015 rates: $48 to $55. Disc: military.
(425)392-9233 Lat: 47.536959, Lon: -122.030923
650 1st Ave NE, Issaquah, WA 98027
info@ivrvpark.com
ivrvpark.com
See ad pages 1261 (Spotlight Greater Seattle), 1250.

KALAMA — D2 *Cowlitz*

CAMP KALAMA RV PARK **Ratings: 6.5/4.5/5.5** (Campground) 2015 rates: $28 to $31. (360)673-2456 5055 N Meeker Dr, Kalama, WA 98625

LOUIS RASMUSSEN RV PARK (Public) S-bnd: From Jct of I-5 & Kalama exit, follow signs; or N-bnd: From Jct of I-5 & Todd Rd (exit 27), follow signs (L). 2015 rates: $15 to $20. (360)673-2626

KELSO — D2 *Cowlitz*

KELSO See also Castle Rock, Silver Lake & Woodland.

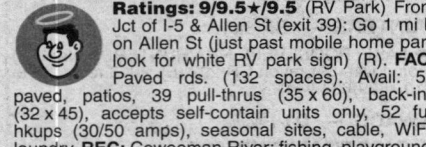

BROOKHOLLOW RV PARK
Ratings: 9/9.5★/9.5 (RV Park) From Jct of I-5 & Allen St (exit 39): Go 1 mi E on Allen St (just past mobile home park look for white RV park sign) (R). **FAC:** Paved rds. (132 spaces). Avail: 52 paved, patios, 39 pull-thrus (35 x 60), back-ins (32 x 45), accepts self-contain units only, 52 full hkups (30/50 amps), seasonal sites, cable, WiFi, laundry. **REC:** Coweeman River: fishing, playground. Pet restrict(B) $. Partial handicap access, no tents. Big rig sites, eco-friendly, 2015 rates: $35 to $38.
(800)867-0453 Lat: 46.14472, Lon: -122.87946
2506 Allen St, Kelso, WA 98626
brookhollowrv@ipgmhc.com
www.brookhollowrvpark.com
See ad pages 1266 (Spotlight Mount Rainier & Mount St Helens), 1250.

KENNEWICK — D5 *Benton*

COLUMBIA SUN RV RESORT
Ratings: 10/10★/10 (RV Resort) From Jct US 395 & I-82: Go 3-1/2 mi NW on I-82 to Badger Rd (Exit 109), then 1/2 mi SW on Badger Rd to Wiser Pkwy, then 3/4 mi W on Wiser Pkwy (L).

THE TRI-CITIES 10/10*/10 RV RESORT
Brand new resort, family operated, designed for big rigs. We offer non stop recreation for all ages. 145 full hk ups, 3000 sq ft event center, sport court, fitness ctr,pool & hot tub, rec rm, playground, private baths & more!

FAC: Paved rds. (145 spaces). Avail: 30 paved, 85 all weather, patios, 76 pull-thrus (38 x 80), back-ins (32 x 42), 115 full hkups (30/50 amps), seasonal sites, cable, WiFi, laundry, groc, LP gas. **REC:** heated pool, whirlpool, playground. Pet restrict(B/Q). Partial handicap access. Big rig sites, 2015 rates: $44.50 to $55. Disc: AAA, military.
(509)420-4880 Lat: 46.194902, Lon: -119.281763
103907 E Wiser Parkway, Kennewick, WA 99338
info@columbiasunrvresort.com
www.columbiasunrvresort.com
See ad pages 1278 (Spotlight Tri-Cities), 1250 & Family Camping in Magazine Section.

KENT — C3 *King*

SEATTLE/TACOMA KOA **Ratings: 9.5/8/7.5** (Campground) 2015 rates: $42.95 to $59.95. (800)562-1892 5801 S 212th St., Kent, WA 98032

WILLO VISTA ESTATES **Ratings: 4.5/7.5/5.5** (RV Area in MHP) 2015 rates: $55. (253)872-8264 22000 84th South, Kent, WA 98032

KETTLE FALLS — A5 *Ferry, Stevens*

GRANDVIEW INN MOTEL & RV PARK
Ratings: 7.5/8★/7.5 (RV Park) From Jct of WA-25 & SR-20/US-395: Go 1/8 mi N on US-395 (R). **FAC:** Gravel rds. (23 spaces). Avail: 17 gravel, back-ins (26 x 60), 17 full hkups (30 amps), seasonal sites, cable, WiFi, tent sites, rentals, dump, laundry, LP gas. **REC.** Pets OK. Partial handicap access. 2015 rates: $33. Disc: military.
(509)738-6733 Lat: 48.606423, Lon: -118.076981
978 Hwy 395N, Kettle Falls, WA 99141
gvmotel@gmail.com
www.grandviewinnmotelandrvpark.com
See ad pages 1276 (Spotlight Spokane and the Inland Empire), 1250.

LAKE ROOSEVELT NRA/HAAG COVE (Natl Pk) From Jct US-395 & Hwy 20, SW 4.22 mi on Hwy 20, S 2.3 mi on Inchelium Hwy/CH-3, E on Haag Rd. Pit toilets. 2015 rates: $5 to $10. (509)633-9441

LAKE ROOSEVELT NRA/KETTLE FALLS (Natl Pk) From Jct of US-395 & SR-25, W 4 mi on US-395 to unnamed cnty rd, S 2 mi (E). Pit toilets. 2015 rates: $5 to $10. (509)738-6266

NORTH LAKE RV PARK AND CAMPGROUND **Ratings: 6.5/8★/7.5** (Campground) 2015 rates: $15 to $28. Apr 1 to Dec 1. (509)738-2593 20 Roosevelt Rd, Kettle Falls, WA 99141

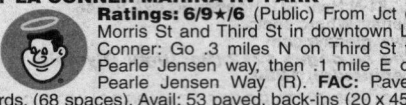

ROCK CUT RV PARK AND CAMPGROUND
Ratings: 8/7.5★/8 (Campground) From Jct of US-395/SR-20 and SR-25 (in Kettle Falls): Go 25-1/8 mi N on US-395 (R). **FAC:** All weather rds. 22 grass, 9 pull-thrus (24 x 65), back-ins (24 x 40), 3 full hkups, 6 W, 19 E (30 amps), WiFi, tent sites, rentals, dump, laundry, fire rings, firewood. **REC:** Kettle River: swim. Pets OK. 2015 rates: $20 to $35. No CC.
(509)684-7999 Lat: 48.98721, Lon: -118.22486
26430 Hwy 395 N, Kettle Falls, WA 99141
Info@rockcutrvpark.com
www.rockcutrvpark.com

LA CONNER — A2 *Skagit*

LA CONNER MARINA RV PARK
Ratings: 6/9★/6 (Public) From Jct of Morris St and Third St in downtown La Conner: Go .3 miles N on Third St to Pearle Jensen way, then .1 mile E on Pearle Jensen Way (R). **FAC:** Paved rds. (68 spaces). Avail: 53 paved, back-ins (20 x 45), 53 full hkups (30 amps), WiFi, dump, laundry. **REC:** Swinomish Channel: marina. Pets OK. 15 day max stay, 2015 rates: $32 to $40.
(360)466-3118 Lat: 48.401298, Lon: -122.492872
420 Pearle Jensen Way, La Conner, WA 98257
Visitor@portofskagit.com
Portofskagit.com

LA CONNER THOUSAND TRAILS **Ratings: 7/7.5/8** (Membership Pk) 2015 rates: $49.58. (800)405-6188 16362 Snee Oosh Rd, La Conner, WA 98257

LEAVENWORTH — B4 *Chelan*

ALPINE VIEW RV PARK & CAMPGROUND **Ratings: 3/8★/6** (Campground) 2015 rates: $30 to $38. (509)548-8439 9825 Duncan Rd, Leavenworth, WA 98826

ICICLE RIVER RV RESORT
Ratings: 9/9.5★/9.5 (RV Park) From Jct of US-2 & Icicle Rd exit (W end of town): Go 3 mi SW on Icicle Rd (L). **FAC:** Paved rds. (108 spaces). 96 Avail: 53 paved, 43 gravel, patios, back-ins (25 x 60), 92 full hkups, 4 W, 4 E (30/50 amps), seasonal sites, cable, WiFi, rentals, dump, laundry, groc, LP gas, firewood. **REC:** whirlpool, Icicle River: swim, fishing. Pet restrict(Q). Partial handicap access, no tents. Big rig sites, 2015 rates: $37 to $45. Disc: AAA. Apr 1 to Oct 16.
AAA Approved
(509)548-5420 Lat: 47.550220, Lon: -120.687258
7305 Icicle Rd, Leavenworth, WA 98826
icicleriverrv@yahoo.com
www.icicleriverrv.com
See ad this page, 1250.

LAKE WENATCHEE
(State Pk) From town, NW 17 mi on Hwy 97/US-2 to SR-207, N 4 mi (L). For reservations call (888)226-7688. **FAC:** Paved rds. 42 paved, 42 pull-thrus (20 x 40), 42 W, 42 E (30 amps), tent sites, dump, groc, LP gas, firewood. **REC:** Lake Wenatchee: swim, fishing, rec open to public. Pets OK. Partial handicap access. 10 day max stay, 2015 rates: $20 to $45.
(888)226-7688 Lat: 47.813167, Lon: -120.721306
21588 State Hwy 207, Leavenworth, WA 98826
infocent@parks.wa.gov
www.parks.wa.gov
See ad page 1246 (Welcome Section).

Looking for places the "locals" frequent? Make friends with park owners and staff to get the inside scoop!

LEAVENWORTH RESORT **Ratings: 6.5/7/6.5** (Membership Pk) 2015 rates: $42 to $56. (800)405-6188 20752 Chiwawa Loop Rd, Leavenworth, WA 98826

PINE VILLAGE KOA KAMPGROUND **Ratings: 8/8/8.5** (Campground) 2015 rates: $30 to $90. (800)562-5709 11401 River Bend Dr, Leavenworth, WA 98826

WENATCHEE NF (TUMWATER CAMPGROUND) (Natl Forest) From town: Go 10 mi NW on US-2. 2015 rates: $17. May 1 to Oct 15. (509)548-6977

LIBERTY LAKE — B6 *Spokane*

Travel Services

CAMPING WORLD OF LIBERTY LAKE/SPOKANE As the nation's largest retailer of RV supplies, accessories, services and new and used RVs, Camping World is committed to making your total RV experience better. RV Accessories: (855)418-8388. **SERVICES:** RV appliance, MH mechanical, staffed RV wash, restrooms, RV Sales. RV supplies, LP, dump, waiting room. Hours: 8am - 5pm.
(888)822-1996 Lat: 47.666508, Lon: -117.140086
19651 East Cataldo Ave., Liberty Lake, WA 99016
www.campingworld.com

LILLIWAUP — B2 *Mason*

MIKE'S BEACH RESORT
Ratings: 5.5/7.5★/6.5 (RV Park) On US Hwy 101 between Lilliwaup and Eldon: 3/10 mi north of MM 318 on US Hwy 101- park is on west side of highway, office is on east side. **FAC:** Gravel rds. (18 spaces). Avail: 14 grass, back-ins (24 x 55), 6 full hkups, 8 W, 8 E (30 amps), seasonal sites, tent sites, rentals, fire rings, firewood. **REC:** whirlpool, Hood Canal: playground. Pet restrict(Q). 2015 rates: $35. Disc: military. May 1 to Oct 31.
(360)877-5324 Lat: 47.568247, Lon: -123.015311
38470 North US Hwy 101, Lilliwaup, WA 98555
reservations@mikesbeachresort.com
www.mikesbeachresort.com

LONG BEACH — D1 *Pacific*

LONG BEACH See also Chinook, Grayland, Ilwaco, Ocean Park, Seaside; Astoria, OR; Warrenton, OR.

ANDERSEN'S ON THE OCEAN Ratings: 8/8.5★/9.5 (RV Park) From Jct of US-101 & SR-103: Go 5 mi N on SR-103 (L). **FAC:** Gravel rds. 60 Avail: 60 all weather, back-ins (22 x 65), accepts self-contain units only, 60 full hkups (30/50 amps), cable, WiFi, dump, laundry, LP gas, firewood. **REC:** Pacific Ocean: playground. Pets OK. No tents. Big rig sites, 2015 rates: $35 to $50. Disc: military.
(360)642-2231 Lat: 46.40210, Lon: -124.05312
1400 138th St, Long Beach, WA 98631
lorna@andersensrv.com
www.andersensrv.com

DRIFTWOOD RV PARK
Ratings: 6/7.5/6 (RV Park) From Jct of US-101 & SR-103: Go 2-1/8 mi N on SR-103 (R). **FAC:** Gravel rds. (57 spaces). Avail: 34 grass, 17 pull-thrus (20 x 60), back-ins (20 x 40), accepts self-contain units only, 34 full hkups (30 amps), seasonal sites, cable, WiFi, laundry. Pet restrict(B). Partial handicap access, no tents. Eco-friendly, 2015 rates: $31.50 to $43.50. Disc: military.
(888)567-1902 Lat: 46.361655, Lon: -124.053477
1512 Pacific Ave N, Long Beach, WA 98631
info@driftwood-rvpark.net
www.driftwood-rvpark.net
See ad pages 1260 (Spotlight Grays Harbor/Long Beach/Ocean Park), 1250.

PACIFIC HOLIDAY RV RESORT-SUNRISE RESORTS **Ratings: 8.5/9★/8** (Membership Pk) 2015 rates: $35 to $50. (360)642-2770 12109 Pacific Hwy, Long Beach, WA 98631

SAND CASTLE RV PARK **Ratings: 5/6.5/5** (RV Park) 2015 rates: $30 to $44. (360)642-2174 1100 Pacific Avenue North, Long Beach, WA 98631

LONGBRANCH — C2 *Pierce*

PENROSE POINT (State Pk) From Jct of SR-16 & SR-302, S 16 mi on SR-302 to Cornwall Rd, E 0.5 mi to Delano Rd, E 1 mi to 158th St, N 200 yds (E). For reservations call (888)226-7688. 2015 rates: $12 to $42. (888)226-7688

LONGMIRE — C3 *Pierce*

MT RAINIER/COUGAR ROCK CAMPGROUND (Natl Pk) From town, N 2.3 mi on Nisqually/SH-706 to Paradise Rd (L). For reservations call (800)365-CAMP. Over 35 feet and 27 feet not allowed. 2015 rates: $12 to $15. Jun 13 to Sep 27. (360)569-2211

LONGVIEW — D2 *Cowlitz*

LONGVIEW See also Castle Rock, Kelso, Silver Lake & Woodland.

LOON LAKE — B6 *Stevens*

DEER LAKE RESORT **Ratings: 8/8★/7.5** (Campground) 2015 rates: $38. (509)233-2081 3906 West Canyon Springs Way, Loon Lake, WA 99148

SHORE ACRES RESORT **Ratings: 5/5.5/6.5** (Campground) 2015 rates: $35 to $40. Apr 15 to Oct 15. (509)233-2474 41987 Shore Acres Rd, Loon Lake, WA 99148

LOPEZ ISLAND — A2 *San Juan*

LOPEZ ISLANDER RESORT
(Campground) (Rebuilding) From Lopez Island ferry terminal: Go 2 mi S on Ferry to Fisherman Bay Rd. then 2.7 mi SW on Fisherman Bay Rd. to resort (R). **FAC:** Paved/dirt rds. 14 grass, back-ins (16 x 40), some side by side hkups, 14 W, 14 E (20/30 amps), WiFi Hotspot, tent sites, rentals, pit toilets, dump, laundry, fire rings, restaurant. **REC:** heated pool, whirlpool, Fisherman Bay: marina. Pets OK. 2015 rates: $40. Disc: military. ATM.
(360)468-2233 Lat: 48.513821, Lon: -122.912832
2864 Fisherman Bay Rd., Lopez Island, WA 98261
desk@lopezfun.com
www.lopezfun.com
See ad page 1270 (Spotlight Northwest Washington).

LYNDEN — A2 *Whatcom*

HIDDEN VILLAGE RV PARK (MHP) **Ratings: 8.5/7.5/7** (RV Park) 2015 rates: $28 to $34. (800)843-8606 7062 Guide Meridian, Lynden, WA 98264

LYNDEN KOA **Ratings: 8/8.5★/9** (Campground) 2015 rates: $34 to $53. Mar 1 to Oct 1. (800)562-4779 8717 Line Rd, Lynden, WA 98264

LYNNWOOD — B2 *Snohomish*

TWIN CEDARS RV PARK Ratings: 7/8.5★/5 (RV Park) From Jct of I-5 & 164th St SW (exit 183): Go 2 mi W on 164th St/44th Ave W to 168th St, then 1/8 mi W on 168th St to Hwy 99, then 3/4 mi S on Hwy 99 (R). **FAC:** Paved rds. (69 spaces). Avail: 7 gravel, 7 pull-thrus (17 x 45), 7 full hkups (30/50 amps), seasonal sites, cable, WiFi Hotspot, dump, laundry, LP gas. **REC.** Pet restrict(B/Q). Partial handicap access, no tents. 2015 rates: $35.17. Disc: AAA, military.
AAA Approved
(800)878-9304 Lat: 47.837227, Lon: -122.302845
17826 Hwy 99, Lynnwood, WA 98037
twincedarsrv@pcfre.com

MARBLEMOUNT — A3 *Skagit, Whatcom*

NORTH CASCADES/GOODELL CREEK (Natl Pk) From town, E 13 mi on SR-20 (R). Pit toilets. 2015 rates: $10. (360)854-7200

MARYHILL — D3 *Klickitat*

PEACH BEACH CAMPGROUND **Ratings: 3/7.5★/7** (Campground) 2015 rates: $30 to $35. (509)773-4927 89 Maryhill Hwy, Goldendale, WA 98620

MARYSVILLE — B3 *Snohomish*

WENBERG COUNTY PARK (State Pk) From jct I-5 (exit 206) & Hwy 531: Go 6 mi W on Hwy 531. 2015 rates: $20.05 to $29.17. (425)388-6600

MAZAMA — A4 *Okanogan*

OKANOGAN NF (LONE FIR CAMPGROUND) (Natl Forest) From town: Go 11-1/2 mi W on Hwy 20. Pit toilets. 2015 rates: $12. May 24 to Oct 31. (509)996-4003

METALINE — A6 *Pend Oreille*

MT LINTON RV & TRAILER PARK **Ratings: 5.5/8★/7** (Campground) 2015 rates: $30. (509)446-4553 103 W. Metaline St, Metaline, WA 99152

METALINE FALLS — A6 *Pend Oreille*

COLVILLE NF (SULLIVAN LAKE CAMPGROUND-EAST) (Natl Forest) From town: Go 1-1/2 mi E on Hwy 31, then 5 mi E on CR 9345. Pit toilets. 2015 rates: $16 to $32. (509)446-7500

MINERAL — C3 *Lewis*

EASTCREEK CAMPGROUND **Ratings: 5/7/8** (Campground) 2015 rates: $35. Apr 20 to Sep 20. (360)492-3104 184 Naugle Rnd, Mineral, WA 98355

MONROE — B3 *Snohomish*

THUNDERBIRD RESORT **Ratings: 7.5/7.5/8** (Membership Pk) 2015 rates: $48.67 to $59.73. (800)405-6188 26702 Ben Howard Rd, Monroe, WA 98272

MONTESANO — C2 *Grays Harbor*

FRIENDS LANDING
Ratings: 5/7.5★/9.5 (Public) From the Jct of Hwy 12 and the Devonshire Rd Exit: Go 1.1 mi SW on Devonshire Rd to Katon Rd, then 1.7 mi S on Katon Rd to park (R). **FAC:** Paved rds. 18 paved, back-ins (32 x 65), 18 W, 18 E (30 amps), tent sites, showers $, dump, fire rings, firewood. **REC:** Chehalis River: fishing, rec open to public. Pets OK. 2015 rates: $25. Mar 15 to Nov 15.
(360)249-5117 Lat: 46.946690, Lon: -123.642373
300 Katon Rd, Montesano, WA 98563
friendslanding@portgrays.org
www.friendslanding.org
See ad pages 1271 (Spotlight Olympic Peninsula), 1250.

LAKE SYLVIA
(State Pk) From Jct of Hwy 12 & 3rd St, N 1 mi on 3rd St (E). **FAC:** Paved rds. 4 gravel, back-ins (12 x 30), 4 W, 4 E (30 amps), tent sites, dump, firewood. **REC:** Lake Sylvia: swim, fishing, rec open to public. Pets OK. Partial handicap access. 10 day max stay, 2015 rates: $20 to $45.
(888)226-7688 Lat: 47.000556, Lon: -123.590194
1812 N Lake Sylvia Rd, Montesano, WA 98563
infocent@parks.wa.gov
www.parks.wa.gov
See ad page 1246 (Welcome Section).

MONTESQUARE RV PARK
Ratings: 8/9.5★/7 (RV Park) From the Jct of WA 7 and Montesano Raymond exit: Go .1 mi straight to park. **FAC:** All weather rds. (55 spaces). Avail: 27 all weather, 27 pull-thrus (27 x 70), 27 full hkups (30/50 amps), seasonal sites, WiFi, rentals, laundry, groc, LP gas, firewood. **REC.** Pet restrict(B). Partial handicap access. 2015 rates: $35. ATM.
(360)249-4424 Lat: 46.977126, Lon: -123.601739
525 S 1st St, Montesano, WA 98563
montesquare@gmail.com
www.montesquarerv.com
See ad this page, 1250.

OLYMPIC NF (COHO CAMPGROUND) (Natl Forest) From town: Go 12 mi N on CR 58, then 20 mi N on FR 22, then 1-1/2 mi N on FR 2294. 2015 rates: $16 to $20. May 15 to Nov 15. (360)765-2200

MOSES LAKE — C4 *Grant*

MOSES LAKE See also Ephrata, Othello, Soap Lake & Warden.

MARDON RESORT AT POTHOLES RESERVOIR
Ratings: 8.5/8.5★/8 (RV Park) From Jct of I-90 & Dodson Rd (exit 164): Go 9 mi S on Dodson Rd to Frenchman Hills Rd, then 5 mi E on Frenchman Hills Rd to Hwy 262, then 6 mi E on Hwy 262 (L). **FAC:** Paved/gravel rds. (145 spaces). 84 Avail: 22 paved, 21 all weather, 41 gravel, patios, 30 pull-thrus (30 x 60), back-ins (25 x 38), 59 full hkups, 25 W, 25 E (30/50 amps), seasonal sites, WiFi, tent sites, rentals, showers $, dump, laundry, groc, LP gas, fire rings, firewood, restaurant, controlled access. **REC:** Potholes Reservoir: swim, fishing, marina, playground, rec open to public. Pet restrict(B) $. Partial handicap access. Big rig sites, 2015 rates: $19 to $45. ATM.
(800)416-2736 Lat: 46.966014, Lon: -119.321212
8198 Highway 262 SE, Othello, WA 99344
info@mardonresort.com
www.mardonresort.com
See ad pages 1254 (Spotlight Coulee Corridor), 1250.

We give campgrounds one rating for amenities, a second for restrooms and a third for visual appearance and environmental quality. That's the Triple Rating System.

SUNCREST RESORT
Ratings: 10/9.5★/9 (RV Park) From Jct of I-90 & Hansen Rd (exit 174): Go 1/4 mi N on Hansen Rd (R). **FAC:** Paved rds. 82 paved, 16 pull-thrus (24 x 65), back-ins (27 x 42), accepts self-contain units only, 82 full hkups (30/50 amps), WiFi, laundry, groc. **REC:** pool, whirlpool, playground. Pet restrict(B). Partial handicap access, no tents. Big rig sites, 2015 rates: $33 to $49. Disc: military.
(509)765-0355 Lat: 47.108147, Lon: -119.343536
303 Hansen Rd, Moses Lake, WA 98837
Suncrestrv@gmail.com
www.suncrestresort.com

SUNRISE RESORTS PIER 4 **Ratings: 9.5/7/6** (Membership Pk) 2015 rates: $35 to $45. (509)765-6319 3400 Sage Rd, Moses Lake, WA 98837

MOSSYROCK — D2 *Lewis*

HARMONY LAKESIDE RV PARK
Ratings: 8.5/10★/10 (RV Park) From Jct of I-5 & US-12 (exit 68): Go 13-3/4 mi E on US-12 to SR-122 (MP 86-87), then 5-1/2 mi NE on SR-122 (R). **FAC:** Gravel rds. (80 spaces). Avail: 55 gravel, 15 pull-thrus (30 x 65), back-ins (30 x 60), 55 full hkups (30/50 amps), seasonal sites, WiFi, rentals, showers $, laundry, fire rings, firewood. **REC:** Mayfield Lake: swim, fishing. Pet restrict(B) $. Partial handicap access, no tents. Big rig sites, eco-friendly, 2015 rates: $40.25 to $52.25. Disc: AAA, military.
AAA Approved
(877)780-7275 Lat: 46.557907, Lon: -122.503725
563 SR-122, Silver Creek, WA 98585
harmonyrvpark@aol.com
www.harmonylakesidervpark.com
See ad pages 1267 (Spotlight Mount Rainier & Mount St Helens), 1250.

IKE KINSWA
(State Pk) From Jct of US-12 & SR-122 (between MP-86 & MP-87), N 3.8 mi on SR-122 (R). **FAC:** Paved rds. 72 paved, 20 pull-thrus (16 x 60), back-ins (18 x 60), 41 full hkups, 31 W, 31 E (30/50 amps), tent sites, rentals, dump, firewood. **REC:** Lake Mayfield: swim, fishing, rec open to public. Pets OK. Partial handicap access. 10 day max stay, 2015 rates: $20 to $45.
(888)226-7688 Lat: 46.55413, Lon: -122.53011
873 State Hwy 122, Silver Creek, WA 98585
infocent@parks.wa.gov
www.parks.wa.gov
See ad page 1246 (Welcome Section).

LAKE MAYFIELD RV RESORT & MARINA **Ratings: 7/8.5★/7** (Campground) 2015 rates: $38 to $58. (360)985-2357 350 Hadaller Rd, Mossyrock, WA 98564

MAYFIELD LAKE PARK (Public) From Jct of I-5 & US-12, E 17 mi on US-12 to Beach Rd, N 0.25 mi (R). 2015 rates: $31 to $35. Apr 15 to Oct 15. (360)985-2364

MOUNT VERNON — A2 *Skagit*

BLAKES RV PARK & MARINA Ratings: 4.5/7/6.5 (RV Park) From Jct I-5 & exit 221: Go 5 mi W & N on Fir Island Rd to Rawlins Rd, then 1-1/4 mi W on Rawlins Rd (L). **FAC:** Gravel/dirt rds. (45 spaces). Avail: 32 gravel, back-ins (20 x 60), 18 full hkups, 8 W, 8 E (30 amps), seasonal sites, tent sites, rentals, dump, laundry, fire rings, firewood. **REC:** North Fork Skagit: fishing. Pet restrict(B) $. 2015 rates: $32 to $35. Disc: AAA.
AAA Approved
(360)445-6533 Lat: 48.355560, Lon: -122.449322
13739 Rawlins Rd, Mount Vernon, WA 98273
blakes@gotsky.com
www.blakesskagitresort.com

MOUNT VERNON (CONT)

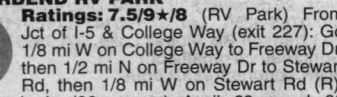

MOUNT VERNON RV PARK
Ratings: 8/8.5★/9.5 (RV Park) From Jct of I-5 & Kincaid St (exit 226): Go 1/8 mi W on Kincaid St to SR-536 (Third St), then 1 mi N on SR-536 (becomes Memorial Hwy) over bridge (R). **FAC:** Paved rds. (81 spaces). Avail: 16 all weather, 16 pull-thrus (24 x 82), 16 full hkups (30/50 amps), seasonal sites, cable, WiFi, laundry, LP gas. **REC.** Pet restrict(B). Partial handicap access, no tents. Big rig sites, eco-friendly, 2015 rates: $35. Disc: military.
(800)385-9895 Lat: 48.423405, Lon: -122.350874
1229 Memorial Hwy, Mount Vernon, WA 98273
mountvernonrvpark@hotmail.com
See ad pages 1289, 1250.

RIVERBEND RV PARK
Ratings: 7.5/9★/8 (RV Park) From Jct of I-5 & College Way (exit 227): Go 1/8 mi W on College Way to Freeway Dr, then 1/2 mi N on Freeway Dr to Stewart Rd, then 1/8 mi W on Stewart Rd (R). **FAC:** Gravel rds. (90 spaces). Avail: 60 gravel, 60 pull-thrus (22 x 63), 60 full hkups (30/50 amps), seasonal sites, cable, WiFi Hotspot, tent sites, showers $, dump, laundry. **REC:** Skagit River: fishing. Pet restrict(B/Q). Eco-friendly, 2015 rates: $34 to $38.
(360)428-4044 Lat: 48.443288, Lon: -122.345716
305 W Stewart Rd, Mount Vernon, WA 98273
See ad pages 1269 (Spotlight Northwest Washington), 1250.

NACHES — C4 *Yakima*

RIMROCK LAKE RESORT LLC **Ratings: 5/7.5★/7.5** (Campground) 2015 rates: $35 to $40. (509)672-2460 37590 US Hwy 12, Naches, WA 98937

NEWHALEM — A3 *Skagit*

NORTH CASCADES/COLONIAL CREEK (Natl Pk) From town, E 25 mi on SR-20. 2015 rates: $12. May 15 to Oct 14. (360)854-7200

NORTH CASCADES/HOZOMEEN (Natl Pk) From Jct of TCH-3 & Silver Skagit Rd, S 39 mi on Silver Skagit Rd (E). Pit toilets. Jun 21 to Oct 31. (360)856-5700

NORTH CASCADES/NEWHALEM CREEK (Natl Pk) From town, E 14 mi on SR-20, across the river on a single lane bridge (R). 2015 rates: $12 to $21. May 15 to Oct 31. (360)854-7200

NEWPORT — B6 *Pend Oreille*

LITTLE DIAMOND RESORT **Ratings: 7.5/8★/7.5** (Membership Pk) 2015 rates: $32 to $50. Apr 15 to Oct 4. (509)447-4813 1002 Mcgowen Rd, Newport, WA 99156

OLD AMERICAN KAMPGROUND **Ratings: 7/7/6** (Membership Pk) 2015 rates: $40. (509)447-3663 701 N Newport Ave, Newport, WA 99156

PEND OREILLE COUNTY PARK (Public) From town, S 17 mi on Hwy 2 (R). Pit toilets. 2015 rates: $10. May 25 to Sep 7. (509)447-4513

NINE MILE FALLS — B6 *Spokane*

WILLOW BAY RESORT **Ratings: 3.5/5.5/6** (Membership Pk) 2015 rates: $37. Mar 1 to Oct 31. (509)276-2350 6607 Highway 291, Nine Mile Falls, WA 99026

NORDLAND — B2 *Jefferson*

FORT FLAGLER (State Pk) From Jct of Oak Bay Rd & Irondale Rd/Chimacum Rd (in Port Hadlock), E 0.8 mi on Oak Bay Rd to Flagler Rd, N 8.5 mi (E). 2015 rates: $12 to $42. (360)385-1259

NORTH BEND — B3 *King*

DENNY CREEK CAMPGROUND (Public) From town: Go 17 mi SE on I-90 (exit 47), then 2-1/4 mi NE on FR 58 (Denny Creek Rd). 5 ton Wt. restriction on bridge (use exit 50 as alternate). 2015 rates: $20 to $24. May 17 to Sep 29. (425)888-1421

NOR' WEST RV PARK **Ratings: 5.5/7★/8** (RV Park) From Jct of I-90 & 468th Ave SE (exit 34): Go 1/8 mi N on 468th Ave SE to North Bend Way (Frontage Road), then 3/4 min W on North Bend Way. (R). **FAC:** Paved rds. (32 spaces). Avail: 6 gravel, backins (25 x 70), accepts self-contain units only, 6 full hkups (30/50 amps), seasonal sites, cable, WiFi Hotspot, laundry. **REC:** playground. Pet restrict(B/Q). No tents. RV age restrict, 2015 rates: $32.50. Disc: AAA, military. No CC.
AAA Approved
(425)888-9685 Lat: 47.47018, Lon: -121.72852
45810 SE North Bend Way, North Bend, WA 98045
Rv@norwestproperties.net
www.norwestproperties.net

OAK HARBOR — B2 *Island*

DECEPTION PASS (State Pk) From town, N 8 mi on SR-20 (L). For reservations call (888)226-7688. 2015 rates: $12 to $42. (360)675-2417

FORT EBEY (State Pk) From Mukilteo/Clinton Ferry: From Clinton (on Whidbey Island), N 32 mi on Hwy 525 (becomes Hwy 20) to Libbey Rd, W 1.5 mi to Hill Valley Dr, S 0.5 mi (E). For reservations call (888)226-7688. 2015 rates: $12 to $42. May 15 to Sep 15. (560)678-4636

NORTH WHIDBEY RV PARK
Ratings: 9/9.5★/9 (RV Park) From Jct of I-5 & SR-20 (exit 230): Go 18 mi W on SR-20, (at Jct of SR-20 & SR-20 Spur go S (left) toward Deception/Oak Harbor) to W Cornet Bay Rd (1 mi S of Deception Pass Bridge), then 1/8 mi E on Cornet Bay Rd (R). **FAC:** Paved rds. (98 spaces). Avail: 63 paved, 10 pull-thrus (30 x 60), back-ins (30 x 45), 63 full hkups (30/50 amps), seasonal sites, WiFi, tent sites, rentals, laundry, LP gas, fire rings, firewood. **REC:** playground. Pets OK $. Partial handicap access. Big rig sites, 2015 rates: $33. Disc: AAA, military.
(360)675-9597 Lat: 48.389054, Lon: -122.645970
565 W Cornet Bay Rd, Oak Harbor, WA 98277
managers@northwhidbeyrvpark.com
www.northwhidbeyrvpark.com
See ad this page, 1250.

OAK HARBOR CITY BEACH (Public) From Jct of SR-20, W Pioneer Way & 80th SW, S 300 ft on South Beeksma (L). 2015 rates: $12 to $20. (360)679-5551

OCEAN CITY — C1 *Grays Harbor*

OCEAN BREEZE RV RESORT & CAMPGROUND **Ratings: 6.5/8/8.5** (Membership Pk) 2015 rates: $35. (360)289-0628 2428 SR-109, Ocean City, WA 98569

OCEAN CITY (State Pk) From Jct of SR-109 & SR-115, S 1 mi on SR-115 (R) (Resv Advised from 5/15 to 9/15). 2015 rates: $12 to $42. (360)289-3553

SCREAMIN' EAGLE CAMPGROUND & RV PARK **Ratings: 5.5/8★/8.5** (Campground) 2015 rates: $30 to $35. (855)627-4673 17 2nd Ave, Ocean City, WA 98569

OCEAN PARK — D1 *Pacific*

OCEAN PARK See also Chinook, Grayland, Ilwaco, Long Beach & Seaview.

OCEAN PARK RESORT
Ratings: 6.5/8★/5 (Campground) From Jct of US-101 & WA-103/Pacific Way (in Seaview): Go 11 mi N on WA-103/Pacific Way to 259th Pl, then 1/8 mi E (R). **FAC:** Gravel/dirt rds. (100 spaces). Avail: 70 grass, 23 pull-thrus (28 x 60), back-ins (28 x 50), accepts self-contain units only, 70 full hkups (30 amps), seasonal sites, WiFi, tent sites, rentals, showers $, laundry, LP gas, firewood. **REC.** Pet restrict(B). 2015 rates: $28 to $34. Disc: military.
(800)835-4634 Lat: 46.489924, Lon: -124.047302
25904 R St, Ocean Park, WA 98640
info@opresort.com
www.opresort.com
See ad page 1260 (Spotlight Grays Harbor/Long Beach/Ocean Park).

Like Us on Facebook.

WESTGATE CABINS & RV PARK
Ratings: 6.5/7.5/6.5 (RV Park) From Jct of US-101 & SR-103: Go 8.5 mi N on SR-103 (L). **FAC:** Paved/gravel rds. (35 spaces). Avail: 31 gravel, 12 pull-thrus (22 x 40), back-ins (24 x 40), 31 full hkups (30 amps), seasonal sites, cable, WiFi, rentals, laundry, fire rings. **REC:** Pacific Ocean. Pets OK. No tents. Eco-friendly, 2015 rates: $38.
(360)665-4211 Lat: 46.45297, Lon: -124.05256
20803 Pacific Way, Ocean Park, WA 98640
westgaterv@centurytel.net
www.vacationwestgate.com
See ad pages 1260 (Spotlight Grays Harbor/Long Beach/Ocean Park), 1250.

Things to See and Do

OCEAN PARK AREA CHAMBER OF COMMERCE Ocean Park Chamber of Commerce assists tourists coming to the community by offering information on things to do and areas to see. Restrooms. Hours: 11am to 3pm. No CC.
(888)751-9354 Lat: 46.491672, Lon: -124.047743
1715 Bay Ave, Ocean Park, WA 98640
info@opwa.com
www.opwa.com
See ad page 1248 (Welcome Section).

OKANOGAN — A4 *Okanogan*

AMERICAN LEGION PARK (Public) From town, N 0.8 mi on 2nd Ave/SR-215 (R). 2015 rates: $12. Apr 15 to Oct 15. (509)422-3600

COUNTY FAIR GROUNDS (Public) From N end of town, N 1.75 mi on Rodeo Trail (L). 2015 rates: $18 to $20. Apr 15 to Oct 15. (509)422-1621

OLYMPIA — C2 *Thurston*

AMERICAN HERITAGE CAMPGROUND **Ratings: 8.5/8/8** (Campground) 2015 rates: $35 to $40. (360)943-8778 9610 Kimmie St. SW, Olympia, WA 98512

MILLERSYLVANIA (State Pk) From Jct of I-5 & Exit 95, E 2.5 mi on Maytown Rd to Tilley Rd, N 0.7 mi (L). 2015 rates: $12 to $42. (366)753-1519

OLYMPIA CAMPGROUND **Ratings: 6/7.5/6.5** (Campground) 2015 rates: $30 to $35. (360)352-2551 1441 83rd Ave SW, Olympia, WA 98512

RIVERBEND CAMPGROUND
Ratings: 7/8★/8 (Campground) From Jct I-5 & Brown Farm Rd (Exit 114): Go 1/8 mi S on Brown Farm Rd to Nisqually Cut Off Rd SE, then 1-1/8 mi S on Nisqually Cut Off Rd to Kuhlman Rd, then 1/2 mi SE on Kuhlman Rd to Old Pacific Hwy, then 1/8 mi SW on Pacific Hwy to Durgin Rd, then 3/4 mi SE on Durgin Rd to Clubhouse Lane (L). **FAC:** Paved/gravel rds. 42 gravel, 10 pull-thrus (30 x 60), back-ins (30 x 60), 14 full hkups, 28 W, 28 E (30/50 amps), WiFi, tent sites, showers $, dump, laundry, LP gas, fire rings, firewood, controlled access. **REC:** Nisqually River: fishing, playground. Pet restrict(B). Partial handicap access. 2015 rates: $32.44 to $41.71. Disc: military.
(360)491-2534 Lat: 47.048038, Lon: -122.694293
1040 Clubhouse Lane SE, Olympia, WA 98513
Riverbendcamp@hotmail.com
www.riverbendcampgroundwa.com
See ad this page, 1250.

WASHINGTON LAND YACHT HARBOR RV PARK
Ratings: 7/NA/7.5 (RV Park) From Jct I-5 and Marvin Rd (Exit 111): Go 1 mi S on Marvin Rd SE to Steilacoom Rd SE, then 1 mi E on Steilacoom Rd (R). **FAC:** Paved rds. 103 Avail: 103 all weather, back-ins (20 x 60), accepts self-contain units only, 103 full hkups (30 amps), WiFi, restrooms only, dump, controlled access. **REC.** Pets OK. 2015 rates: $27.
(360)491-3750 Lat: 47.050561, Lon: -122.746642
9101 Steilacoom Rd SE, Olympia, WA 98513
reservations@washingtonlandyachtharbor.com
www.washingtonlandyachtharbor.com
See ad pages 1274 (Spotlight Olympic Peninsula), 1250.

Things to See and Do

WASHINGTON STATE PARKS AND RECREATION Manages and markets Washington's State Parks, Recreation Areas, Discover Pass program and Park Volunteers. Partial handicap access. RV accessible. Restrooms. Hours: 9am to 5pm.
(360)902-8844 Lat: 46.98057, Lon: -122.91025
infocent@parks.wa.gov
www.parks.wa.gov
See ad page 1246 (Welcome Section).

Park owners and staff are rightly proud of their business. Let them know how much you enjoyed your stay.

)MAK — A4 *Okanogan*

CARL PRECHT MEMORIAL RV PARK
Ratings: 6/8/8.5 (Public) From Jct of US 97 & Hwy 155 (traffic light): Go .3 mi N on Dayton Street to Visitor's Center and Eastside Park complex and follow signs to RV park at back of complex. 'AC: Paved rds. 68 paved, 12 pull-thrus (22 x 75), ack-ins (24 x 35), some side by side hkups, 68 full ıkups (20/30 amps), WiFi, tent sites, showers $, lump, fire rings. **REC:** pool $, Okanogan River: swim, ishing, playground, rec open to public. Pets OK. 7 lay max stay, 2015 rates: $25. No CC, no reservaions.
509)826-1170 Lat: 48.41193, Lon: -119.51616
'25 Central Ave East, Omak, WA 98841
:onniet@omakcity.com
www.omakcity.com
See ad this page, 1250.

)RCAS ISLAND — A2 *San Juan*

WEST BEACH RESORT **Ratings: 5.5/7★/8** (RV Resort) 2015 rates: $33 to $49. (877)937-8224 190 Vaterfront Way, Eastsound, WA 98245

)RONDO — B4 *Douglas*

BEEBE BRIDGE PARK (Public) At Jct of US-97 MP-234 (R). 2015 rates: $15 to $30. Mar 28 to Nov . (509)661-4551

)ROVILLE — A4 *Okanogan*

BAINS RV PARK
Ratings: 6/8.5/7 (RV Park) From North city limits of Oroville: Go 2 mi N on Hwy 97 to Shirley Rd (between MP335-336), then 1/4 mi I on Shirley Rd to Swann Lane, then 1/8 mi W on Swann Lane. **FAC:** Gravel rds. 24 gravel, back-ins 30 x 60), 11 full hkups, 13 W, 13 E (30/50 amps), ViFi, tent sites, dump, laundry, fire rings. **REC.** Pet estrict(B). Partial handicap access. Big rig sites, '015 rates: $25 to $30.
509)476-4122 Lat: 48.988883, Lon: -119.460960
Swann Lane, Oroville, WA 98844
d1bains@gmail.com
www.bainsrvpark.com
See ad this page.

OSOYOOS LAKE STATE VETERANS MEMORI-L PARK (State Pk) From town, N 0.5 mi on US-97 R). For reservations call (888)226-7688. 2015 rates: 12 to $25. Mar to Oct. (509)476-2926

RIVER OAKS RV PARK
Ratings: 8/8.5★/9 (RV Park) From jct Hwy 97 & 12th Ave: Go 1/8 mi W on 12th Ave to Ironwood, then 1/8 mi N on Ironwood to Kernan St, then 1/16 mi W on Kernan St. (L). **FAC:** Paved rds. 48 Avail: 8 all weather, 2 pull-thrus (20 x 60), back-ins 21 x 56), 48 full hkups (30/50 amps), WiFi, tent sites, howers $, laundry, fire rings. **REC:** Similkameen River: fishing, playground. Pets OK. 2015 rates: $30 o $33.
509)476-2087 Lat: 48.937748, Lon: -119.442426
62 Kernan Rd, Oroville, WA 98844
iveroaksrv@hotmail.com
www.riveroaksrv.com

)THELLO — C5 *Grant*

O'SULLIVAN SPORTSMAN RESORT (CAMP RE-SORT) **Ratings: 9.5/8.5/8.5** (Membership Pk) 2015 ates: $40. (509)346-2447 6897 Hwy 262 SE, Othel-, WA 99344

THE LAST RESORT **Ratings: 3/NA/6** (Campround) 2015 rates: $25 to $30. (509)346-1657 6996 Hwy 262 SE, Othello, WA 99344

PACIFIC BEACH — C1 *Grays Harbor*

PACIFIC BEACH (State Pk) From Jct of Hwy 109 Main St, W 0.3 mi on Main St to 2nd St, S 0.3 mi E). For reservations call (888)226-7688. 2015 rates: 12 to $42. (888)226-7688

Tell them you saw them in this Guide!

PACKWOOD — C3 *Lewis*

MT RAINIER/OHANAPECOSH (Natl Pk) From town, N 7 mi on US-12 to SR-123, N 3 mi (L). For reservations call (800)365-CAMP. 2015 rates: $12 to $15. May 23 to Oct 12. (360)569-2211

RAINIER WINGS
Ratings: 5/8.5★/6 (RV Park) SE side of Hwy 12 in town. (L). **FAC:** Gravel rds. 63 grass, 11 pull-thrus (20 x 60), back-ins (20 x 35), some side by side hkups, 63 full hkups (30/50 amps), WiFi, tent sites, laundry, fire rings, firewood. Pet restrict(B). 2015 rates: $34.
(360)494-5145 Lat: 46.606166, Lon: -121.672533
12985 Hwy 12, Packwood, WA 98361
info@rainierwings.com
www.rainierwings.com
See ad pages 1268 (Spotlight Mount Rainier & Mount St Helens), 1250.

PALOUSE — C6 *Whitman*

PALOUSE RV PARK (Public) From Jct of SR-27 & Main St (in town), W 0.2 mi on Main St (R). 2015 rates: $25. (509)878-1811

PASCO — D5 *Franklin*

PASCO See also Kennewick, Pasco, Richland, Umatilla & West Richland.

FRANKLIN COUNTY RV PARK
(Public) From Jct of I-182 and Exit 9 (N Road 68): Go 1/4 mi N on Rd 68, then 1/8 mi E on Burden Blvd, then 1/4 mi S on Convention Pl, then 1/4 mi E on Home Run Rd to entrance (L) by large flagpole. **FAC:** Paved rds. (59 spaces). Avail: 24 paved, patios, back-ins (35 x 42), 11 full hkups, 13 W, 13 E (30/50 amps), cable, WiFi, showers $, laundry. Pet restrict(Q). Partial handicap access, no tents. 2015 rates: $37. Disc: AAA, military.
(509)542-5982 Lat: 46.26810, Lon: -119.17347
6333 Home Run Rd, Pasco, WA 99301
franklincountyrvpark@co.franklin.wa.us
www.franklincountyrvpark.com
See ad page 1280 (Spotlight Tri-Cities).

HORN RAPIDS RV RESORT
Ratings: 9.5/10★/10 (RV Resort) From Jct of I-182 & Hwy 240W (exit 4): Go 4 mi NE on Hwy 240W, then 2 mi NW on Hwy 240W to Kingsgate Wy, then 1/8 mi NE on Kingsgate Wy (R). **FAC:** Paved rds. (225 spaces). Avail: 100 all weather, patios, 20 pull-thrus (22 x 70), back-ins (30 x 50), 100 full hkups (30/50 amps), seasonal sites, cable, WiFi, dump, laundry, groc, LP gas. **REC:** heated pool, whirlpool, shuffleboard, playground. Pet restrict(B). Partial handicap access. 2015 rates: $39.95. Disc: AAA, military.
(866)557-9637 Lat: 46.32740, Lon: -119.31495
2640 Kingsgate Way, Richland, WA 99354
info@hornrapidsrvresort.com
www.hornrapidsrvresort.com
See primary listing at Richland and ad page 1279 (Spotlight Tri-Cities).

LAKE WALLULA/HOOD PARK (Public Corps) From Jct of US-12 & US-395, S 4 mi on US-12 to Hwy-124, E 0.2 mi (L). 2015 rates: $11 to $24. May 16 to Sep 1. (509)547-2048

PASCO SANDY HEIGHTS KOA **Ratings: 9.5/8/8** (RV Park) 2015 rates: $35. (800)562-2495 8801 St. Thomas Dr, Pasco, WA 99301

PATEROS — B4 *Okanogan*

ALTA LAKE (State Pk) From jct US 97 & Hwy 153: Go 1-1/4 mi W on Hwy 153, then 1-1/2 mi S on Alta Lake Rd/CR 1517. 2015 rates: $12 to $42. Apr 1 to Sep 30. (509)923-2473

PESHASTIN — B4 *Chelan*

BLU-SHASTIN RV PARK **Ratings: 7.5/8.5★/7** (Campground) 2015 rates: $36. (888)548-4184 3300 Hwy 97, Peshastin, WA 98847

We appreciate your business!

PLYMOUTH — D4 *Benton*

PLYMOUTH PARK (Public Corps) From Jct of I-82 & SR-14, W 1 mi on SR-14 to Old State Hwy (Plymouth Rd), S 1 mi to Christy Rd, W 300 ft (L). 2015 rates: $24 to $27. Apr 1 to Oct 30. (541)506-4807

POMEROY — D6 *Columbia, Whitman*

PATAHA CREEK RV PARK (Public) From Jct of US-12 & Port Way (west end of town): Go S 0.1 mi on Port Way (L). 2015 rates: $25. (509)843-3740

PORT ANGELES — B2 *Clallam*

CRESCENT BEACH & RV PARK **Ratings: 5/7/6.5** (RV Park) 2015 rates: $46 to $51. (866)690-3344 2860 Crescent Beach Rd, Port Angeles, WA 98363

ELWHA DAM RV PARK
Ratings: 9/9.5★/9.5 (Campground) From Jct of US 101 & Lincoln St (in town): Go 5-1/2 mi W on US 101 to SR-112, then 3/4 mi W on SR-112 to Lower Dam Rd, then 1/8 mi S on Dam Rd (L). **FAC:** Paved rds. (52 spaces). Avail: 32 all weather, 27 pull-thrus (25 x 60), back-ins (25 x 45), 32 full hkups (50 amps), seasonal sites, WiFi, tent sites, showers $, laundry, groc, firewood. **REC:** pond, playground. Pet restrict(B). Partial handicap access. Big rig sites, 2015 rates: $36.90 to $45. Disc: AAA, military.
(360)452-7054 Lat: 48.097749, Lon: -123.552677
47 Lower Dam Rd, Port Angeles, WA 98363
paradise@elwhadamrvpark.com
www.elwhadamrvpark.com
See ad this page.

LOG CABIN RESORT (Natl Pk) From Jct of US-101/SR-112 & Lincoln St (W end of town), 18 mi on US-101 to E Beach Rd (MP-232), N 3.2 mi (L). 2015 rates: $40. May 23 to Sep 30. (360)928-3325

OLYMPIC PENINSULA / PORT ANGELES KOA **Ratings: 8.5/9★/8** (Campground) 2015 rates: $29 to $85. Mar 1 to Oct 31. (360)457-5916 80 O'brien Rd, Port Angeles, WA 98362

OLYMPIC/SOL DUC (Natl Pk) From town, W 28 mi on US-101 to Soleduck River Rd, SE 12 mi (L). Entrance fee required. Pit toilets. 2015 rates: $14. (360)563-3130

SALT CREEK REC AREA (Public) From Jct of US-101 & SR-112, W 6 mi on SR-112 to Camp Hayden Rd, N 3 mi (R). 2015 rates: $19 to $27. (360)928-3441

SHADOW MOUNTAIN RV PARK & CAMPGROUND
Ratings: 8/9★/8.5 (RV Park) From Jct of US-101 & Lincoln St (W end of town): Go 16 mi W on US-101 to MP-233 (R). **FAC:** All weather rds. (40 spaces). 30 Avail: 2 paved, 28 gravel, back-ins (30 x 50), 30 full hkups (30/50 amps), seasonal sites, WiFi, tent sites, showers $, dump, laundry, groc, LP gas, fire rings, firewood, restaurant. **REC:** playground. Pet restrict(B). Partial handicap access. 2015 rates: $35. Disc: military. ATM.
(877)928-3043 Lat: 48.085806, Lon: -123.710089
232951 Hwy 101 W, Port Angeles, WA 98363
info@shadowmt.com
www.shadowmt.com
See ad page 1273 (Spotlight Olympic Peninsula).

PORT LUDLOW — B2 *Jefferson*

PORT LUDLOW RV PARK **Ratings: 4.5/8★/8** (Campground) 2015 rates: $25 to $35. (360)437-9377 40 Breaker Ln, Port Ludlow, WA 98365

PORT ORCHARD — B2 *Kitsap*

MANCHESTER (State Pk) From Jct of SR-16 & SR-160 E (Sedgwick Rd SE), E 2.5 mi on SR-160 E to Long Lake Rd SE, N 2.3 mi to Mile Hill Dr, E 1.5 mi to Colchester Dr, N 1.7 mi to Main St, W 100 ft to Beach Dr, N 2 mi to Hilldale, E 0.2 mi (E). 2015 rates: $12 to $42. (360)871-4065

WA

PORT TOWNSEND — B2 *Jefferson*

FORT WORDEN
(State Pk) From town: Go 1 mi N on Hwy 20 to Kearney St, then .4 mi W to Blaine St, E 0.2 mi to Walker/Cherry St, N 0.8 mi to Redwood St, NW 0.4 mi to W St, E 0.1 mi (L). Follow signs inside park. **FAC:** Paved rds. 80 Avail: 50 paved, 30 gravel, 16 pull-thrus (35 x 65), back-ins (35 x 65), 50 full hkups, 30 W, 30 E (30 amps), WiFi Hotspot, tent sites, rentals, dump, laundry, firewood, restaurant. **REC:** Admiralty Inlet: swim, fishing. Pets OK. Partial handicap access. 10 day max stay, 2015 rates: $20 to $45.
(360)344-4431 Lat: 48.13487, Lon: -122.76529
200 Battery Way, Port Townsend, WA 98368
fwcamping@parks.wa.gov
www.parks.wa.gov
See ad page 1246 (Welcome Section).

JEFFERSON COUNTY FAIRGROUNDS
(Public) From Jct of Hwy 20 & Kearney St (stoplight): Go 1/4-mi N on Kearney St to Blaine St (19th), then 1/8 mi W on Blaine St to San Juan, then 1-1/2 mi N on San Jaun to 49th St, then 1/8 mi W on 49th St to Jackman St, then 1/8 mi S on Jackman St (L). **FAC:** Gravel/dirt rds. 58 grass, 58 pull-thrus (20 x 40), mostly side by side hkups, 18 full hkups, 40 W, 40 E (20/30 amps), WiFi Hotspot, tent sites, dump. **REC:** rec open to public. Pets OK. Partial handicap access. 10 day max stay, 2015 rates: $10 to $25. No CC, no reservations.
(360)385-1013 Lat: 48.134415, Lon: -122.783013
4907 Landes St, Port Townsend, WA 98368
jeffcofairgrounds@olypen.com
www.jeffcofairgrounds.com
See ad page 1274 (Spotlight Olympic Peninsula).

OLD FORT TOWNSEND (State Pk) From town, S 4 mi on SR-20 to Old Fort Townsend Rd, W 0.5 mi (E). 2015 rates: $12 to $42. (360)385-3595

POINT HUDSON MARINA & RV PARK
(Public) From Jct of SR-20 & Ferry Landing (Water St): Go 1/2 mi N on Water St to Monroe St, then 1/8 mi W on Monroe St to Jefferson St, then 1/8 mi NE on Jefferson St (R). **FAC:** Gravel rds. (44 spaces). Avail: 34 gravel, 23 pull-thrus (16 x 45), back-ins (20 x 40), mostly side by side hkups, 34 full hkups (30/50 amps), cable, WiFi $, showers $, laundry, LP gas, restaurant. **REC:** Admiralty Inlet: marina. Pets OK. Partial handicap access, no tents. 2015 rates: $25 to $52.
(800)228-2803 Lat: 48.118289, Lon: -122.751886
103 Hudson St, Port Townsend, WA 98368
pointhudson@portofpt.com
www.portofpt.com
See ad page 1271 (Spotlight Olympic Peninsula).

POULSBO — B2 *Kitsap*

CEDAR GLEN RV PARK
Ratings: 9/9.5★/9 (RV Park) From Jct State Hwy 3 and State Hwy 305 (Poulsbo): Go 5 mi SE on State Hwy 305 to park office (L). **FAC:** Paved rds. (38 spaces). Avail: 20 all weather, back-ins (30 x 75), accepts self-contain units only, 20 full hkups (50 amps), seasonal sites, WiFi, laundry. **REC.** Pet restrict(B/Q). Partial handicap access. Big rig sites, 2015 rates: $40. Disc: AAA.
AAA Approved
(360)779-4305 Lat: 47.706030, Lon: -122.594494
16300 NE State Highway 305, Poulsbo, WA 98370
support@cedarglenmhp.com
www.cedarglenmhp.com
See ad pages 1274 (Spotlight Olympic Peninsula), 1250.

EAGLE TREE RV PARK
Ratings: 9/9★/8.5 (RV Park) From Jct State Hwy 3 & State Hwy 305 (Poulsbo): Go 5.5 mi SE on State Hwy 305 (L). **FAC:** Paved rds. (88 spaces). Avail: 48 all weather, 10 pull-thrus (17 x 63), back-ins (20 x 45), 48 full hkups (30/50 amps), seasonal sites, cable, WiFi, tent sites, showers $, laundry, LP gas, firewood. **REC.** Pet restrict(B). Partial handicap access. 2015 rates: $36.85.
AAA Approved
(360)598-5988 Lat: 47.706330, Lon: -122.590413
16280 Washington State Hwy 305, Poulsbo, WA 98370
basecamp@eagletreerv.com
www.eagletreerv.com
See ad pages 1273 (Spotlight Olympic Peninsula), 1250.

KITSAP MEMORIAL (State Pk) From town, N 5 mi on SR-3 to Park St, E 0.25 mi, follow signs (R). 2015 rates: $12 to $42. (888)226-7688

PROSSER — D4 *Benton*

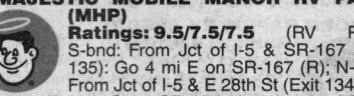

WINE COUNTRY RV PARK
Ratings: 10/10★/9 (RV Park) From Jct of I-82 & Wine Country Rd (exit 80): Go 1/8 mi SE on Wine Country Rd to Merlot Dr, then 1/4 mi E (R). **FAC:** Paved rds. (125 spaces). Avail: 60 paved, 42 all weather, 79 pull-thrus (29 x 60), back-ins (32 x 35), 102 full hkups (30/50 amps), seasonal sites, cable, WiFi, tent sites, showers $, laundry, groc, LP gas, firewood. **REC:** heated pool, whirlpool, playground. Pets OK. Partial handicap access. 2015 rates: $32 to $59. Disc: military.
(509)786-5192 Lat: 46.219755, Lon: -119.783890
330 Merlot Drive, Prosser, WA 99350
winecountry@winecountryrvpark.com
www.winecountryrvpark.com
See ad pages 1282 (Spotlight Wine Country), 1250.

PULLMAN — C6 *Whitman*

PULLMAN See also Clarkston, Colfax & Palouse.

PULLMAN RV PARK (Public) From Jct of US-195 & US-270, E 2.3 mi on US-270 to Spring St, N 0.5 mi (R). Pit toilets. 2015 rates: $10 to $25. Apr 1 to Nov 30. (509)338-3227

PUYALLUP — C2 *Pierce*

MAJESTIC MOBILE MANOR RV PARK (MHP)
Ratings: 9.5/7.5/7.5 (RV Park) S-bnd: From Jct of I-5 & SR-167 (Exit 135): Go 4 mi E on SR-167 (R); N-bnd: From Jct of I-5 & E 28th St (Exit 134), go .1 mi on E 28th St to SR-167, then go 4 mi E on SR-167 (R); From Jct of I-5 & SR-167 (Exit 135): Go 4 mi E on SR-167 (R). **FAC:** Paved rds. (88 spaces). Avail: 44 all weather, 1 pull-thrus (24 x 70), back-ins (22 x 55), 44 full hkups (30/50 amps), seasonal sites, cable, WiFi, dump, laundry, groc, LP gas. **REC:** heated pool, Clarks Creek: fishing. Pet restrict(B). No tents. 2015 rates: $34. No CC.
(800)348-3144 Lat: 47.209531, Lon: -122.336874
7022 River Rd E, Puyallup, WA 98371
majesticrvpark@juno.com
www.majesticrvpark.com
See ad pages 1267 (Spotlight Mount Rainier & Mount St Helens), 1250.

WASHINGTON STATE FAIR RV PARK **Ratings: 3.5/NA/5** (Campground) 2015 rates: $23 to $30. (253)845-1771 110 9th Ave SW, Puyallup, WA 98371

Things to See and Do

WASHINGTON STATE FAIR Headquarters for Washington State Fairs in spring and fall, plus year-round venue for events such as concerts, dog shows, craft, hobby and antiques shows. RV accessible. Restrooms. Hours: 8 am to 4:30 pm M-F. No CC.
(253)841-5045 Lat: 47.184282, Lon: -122.293928
110 9th Ave SW, Puyallup, WA 98371
www.thefair.com
See ad page 1247 (Welcome Section).

QUEETS — B1 *Jefferson*

OLYMPIC/KALALOCH (Natl Pk) From town, N 6 mi on Hwy 101 (L). 2015 rates: $14 to $18. (360)565-3130

QUINAULT — B1 *Grays Harbor*

OLYMPIC NF (FALLS CREEK CAMPGROUND) (Natl Forest) From jct US 101 & S Shore Rd: Go 2 mi NE on S Shore Rd. 2015 rates: $15 to $20. (360)288-2525

QUINCY — C4 *Grant*

CRESCENT BAR RESORT **Ratings: 6.5/8/8.5** (Membership Pk) 2015 rates: $65. Apr 15 to Oct 1. (800)288-7245 9252 Crescent Bar Rd NW, Quincy, WA 98848

Lend a hand. During the busy season park services are stretched to the max! Please do your best to keep your area "ship-shape".

RANDLE — D3 *Lewis*

CASCADE PEAKS RESORT **Ratings: 6.5/4/5.5** (Membership Pk) 2015 rates: $28.50 to $31.50. (360)494-7931 11519 US Highway 12, Randle, WA 98377

RAVENSDALE — C3 *King*

KANASKAT-PALMER
(State Pk) From Jct Hwy-410 & Farman Rd (east of town): Go 11 mi NE. **FAC:** Gravel rds. 19 gravel, 8 pull-thrus (20 x 65), back-ins (25 x 45), 19 E (30 amps), tent sites, rentals, dump, fire rings, firewood. **REC:** Green River: swim, fishing, rec open to public. Pets OK. Partial handicap access. 10 day max stay, 2015 rates: $20 to $45. No CC.
(888)226-7688 Lat: 47.311000, Lon: -121.899389
32101 Kanasket-Cumberland Rd, Ravensdale, WA 98051
infocent@parks.wa.gov
www.parks.wa.gov
See ad page 1246 (Welcome Section).

REPUBLIC — A5 *Ferry*

CURLEW LAKE (State Pk) From town, E 2.5 mi on SR-20 to SR-21, N 7 mi, follow signs (L). 2015 rates: $12 to $42. (509)775-3592

GOLD MOUNTAIN RV PARK **Ratings: 7.5/9.5★/7.5** (RV Park) 2015 rates: $32 to $35. (509)775-3700 4 Old Kettle Falls Rd, Republic, WA 99166

WINCHESTER RV PARK
Ratings: 8/10★/9 (RV Park) From Jct of US-20 & US-21N: Go 2-1/2 mi N on US-21N to W Curlew Lake Rd, then 1/8 mi W on Curlew Lake Rd (R). **FAC:** Paved/gravel rds. (33 spaces). Avail: 3 paved, 6 pull-thrus (20 x 105), back-ins (34 x 60), some side by side hkups, 31 full hkups (30/50 amps), seasonal sites, WiFi, tent sites, rentals, showers $, dump, laundry, LP gas, firewood. **REC:** wading pool, Curlew Creek: playground. Pet restrict(B/Q). Big rig sites, 2015 rates: $35.
(509)775-1039 Lat: 48.679083, Lon: -118.666480
8 West Curlew Lake Rd, Republic, WA 99166
relaxing@winchesterrvpark.com
www.winchesterrvpark.com

RICHLAND — D5 *Benton*

RICHLAND See also Benton City, Connell, Kennewick, Pasco, Prosser, Umatilla & West Richland.

HORN RAPIDS RV RESORT
Ratings: 9.5/10★/10 (RV Resort) From Jct of I-182 & Hwy 240W (exit 4): go 4 mi NE on Hwy 240W, then 2 mi NW on Hwy 240W to Kingsgate Wy, then 1/8 mi NE on Kingsgate Wy (R).

FIRST CLASS CUSTOMER CARE
Welcome to the largest top-rated RV resort in the Tri-Cities! Experience all the best the Columbia Valley has to offer: award-winning wineries, golf courses, art galleries, world-class fishing, boating & restaurants.

FAC: Paved rds. (225 spaces). Avail: 100 all weather patios, 20 pull-thrus (22 x 70), back-ins (30 x 50), 100 full hkups (30/50 amps), seasonal sites, cable, WiFi, dump, laundry, groc, LP gas. **REC:** heated pool, whirlpool, shuffleboard, playground. Pet restrict(B). Partial handicap access, no tents. 2015 rates: $39.95. Disc: AAA, military.
(866)557-9637 Lat: 46.32740, Lon: -119.31495
2640 Kingsgate Way, Richland, WA 99354
info@hornrapidsrvresort.com
www.hornrapidsrvresort.com
See ad pages 1279 (Spotlight Tri-Cities), 1250.

MOON RIVER RV RESORT **Ratings: 9.5/9.5★/8** (RV Park) 2015 rates: $40. (509)392-7127 1963 Saint St, Richland, WA 9935

WRIGHT'S DESERT GOLD MOTEL & RV PARK
Ratings: 9/9.5★/7.5 (RV Park) From Jct of US-395 & SR-240 (keep left at S end of US-395 Bridge): Go 5 mi W on SR-240 to Columbia Park Trail, then 1/2 mi W on Columbia Park Trail under overpass (L). **FAC:** Paved rds. (89 spaces). Avail: 49 paved, 1 pull-thrus (18 x 60), back-ins (17 x 35), some side by side hkups, 49 full hkups (30 amps), seasonal sites, cable, WiFi, laundry, groc, LP gas. **REC:** pool, whirlpool. Pets OK. No tents. 2015 rates: $30.
(509)627-1000 Lat: 46.23912, Lon: -119.25129
611 Columbia Park Trail, Richland, WA 99352
info@wrightsdesertgold.com
www.wrightsdesertgold.com
See ad pages 1280 (Spotlight Tri-Cities), 1250.

We rate what RVers consider important.

RIDGEFIELD — D2 *Cowlitz, Clark*

RIDGEFIELD See also Vancouver & Woodland; Fairview, Portland & Troutdale, OR.

TRI MOUNTAIN RV PARK **Ratings: 7.5/8.5★/7** (RV Park) 2015 rates: $35 to $37. (360)887-8983 109 South 65th Ave #C, Ridgefield, WA 98642

ROCHESTER — C2 *Thurston*

OUTBACK RV PARK
Ratings: 8/9★/8.5 (RV Park) From Jct of I-5 & Hwy 12 (exit 88): Go 2.5 mi W on Hwy 12 (L). **FAC:** Paved/gravel rds. (58 spaces). Avail: 33 gravel, 33 pull-thrus (22 x 55), 33 full hkups (30/50 amps), seasonal sites, WiFi, tent sites, laundry, LP gas. **REC:** playground. Pet restrict(Q). Partial handicap access. Eco-friendly, 2015 rates: $39.50. Disc: AAA.
AAA Approved
(360)273-0585 Lat: 46.809818, Lon: -123.056801
9100 Huntington St SW, Rochester, WA 98579
outbackrvpark@hotmail.com
www.outbackrvpark.com
See ad opposite page, 1250.

ROCKPORT — A3 *Skagit*

HOWARD MILLER STEELHEAD PARK/SKAGIT COUNTY (Public) From Jct of Hwy 20 & SR-530, S 0.25 mi on SR-530 (L). 2015 rates: $16 to $28. (360)853-8808

ROYAL CITY — C4 *Grant*

ROYAL CITY GOLF COURSE & RV PARK (Public) From the town of Royal City: Go 3-1/2 mi E on Hwy 26, then 1/2 mi NW on Dodson Rd. 2015 rates: $12. (509)346-2052

SAPPHO — B1 *Clallam*

OLYMPIC NF (KLAHOWYA CAMPGROUND) (Natl Forest) From town: Go 8 mi E on US-101. Pit toilets. 2015 rates: $17. (360)374-6522

SEABECK — B2 *Kitsap*

SCENIC BEACH (State Pk) From Jct of SR-3 & Newberry Hill Rd exit, S 2 mi on Newberry Hill Rd to Seabeck Hwy, W 2 mi to Scenic Beach Park Rd, W 1 mi (E). For reservations call (888)226-7688. 2015 rates: $12 to $42. (888)226-7688

SEATTLE — B2 *King*

SEATTLE See also Bellevue, Bothel, Bremerton, Everett, Fall City, Gig Harbor, Issaquah, Kent, Lynnwood, Port Orchard, Poulsbo, Renton & Stanwood.

ISSAQUAH VILLAGE RV PARK
Ratings: 9/9.5★/7.5 (RV Park) From Jct of I-90 & Front St/E Lake Sammamish Rd (Exit 17): Go 1/8 m N on Front St to 229th Ave SE, then 50 ft NE to SE 66th St (keep right), then 1/16 mi E on 66th St to 1st Ave NE, then 1/4 mi S on 1st Ave (L). **FAC:** Paved rds. (56 spaces). Avail: 29 paved, 1 all weather, 2 pull-thrus (18 x 60), back-ins (21 x 60), accepts self-contain units only, 30 full hkups (30/50 amps), seasonal sites, cable, WiFi, dump, laundry, LP gas. **REC:** playground. Pet restrict(Q). Partial handicap access, no tents. Eco-friendly, 2015 rates: $48 to $55. Disc: military.
(425)392-9233 Lat: 47.536959, Lon: -122.030923
650 1st Ave NE, Issaquah, WA 98027
info@ivrvpark.com
www.ivrvpark.com
See primary listing at Issaquah and ad page 1261 (Spotlight Greater Seattle).

LAKE PLEASANT RV PARK
Ratings: 9/9.5★/9.5 (RV Park) S-bnd: From Jct I-5 N & I-405 S (Exit 182): Go 3 mi S on I-405 to Bothell Hwy (Exit 26), then 1-1/8 mi S on Bothell Hwy to 242nd St (L). N-bnd: From Jct of I-5 & I-405: Go 26 mi N on I-405 to Bothell Hwy (Exit 26), then 1-1/8 mi S on Bothell Hwy to 242nd St (L). **FAC:** Paved rds. (198 spaces). Avail: 119 paved, 46 pull-thrus (27 x 65), back-ins (25 x 65), accepts self-contain units only, 119 full hkups (30/50 amps), seasonal sites, WiFi $, dump, laundry, LP gas. **REC:** Lake Pleasant: fishing, playground. Pet restrict(B). Partial handicap access. Big rig sites, eco-friendly, 2015 rates: $44.
(425)487-1785 Lat: 47.777965, Lon: -122.217693
24025 Bothell Everett Hwy SE, Bothell, WA 98021
http://www.goodsamcamping.com.s3.amazonaws.com/gsparks/LakePleasant/LakePleasant.
See primary listing at Bothell and ad page 1262 (Spotlight Greater Seattle).

So you're the one with "pooch" duty? Please make a clean sweep of it! Your fellow RVers will appreciate it!

MAPLE GROVE RV RESORT
Ratings: 8/10★/9.5 (RV Park) From Jct of I-5 & 128th St SW (Exit 186): Go .8 mi W on 128th St to Airport Rd, then .6 mi NW on Airport Rd to Hwy 99 (Evergreen Way), then .4 mi SW on Hwy 99 (L). **FAC:** Paved rds. (99 spaces). Avail: 57 paved, 12 all weather, patios, 26 pull-thrus (23 x 55), back-ins (23 x 40), accepts self-contain units only, 57 full hkups, 12 W (30/50 amps), seasonal sites, cable, WiFi, dump, laundry, LP gas. Pet restrict(B/Q). Partial handicap access. 2015 rates: $44 to $55.50. Disc: AAA, military.
(866)793-2200 Lat: 47.885275, Lon: -122.262034
12417 Hwy 99, Everett, WA 98204
info@maplegrovev.com
www.maplegrovev.com
See primary listing at Everett and ad page 1263 (Spotlight Greater Seattle).

TRAILER INNS OF BELLEVUE LLC
Ratings: 10/9★/6 (RV Park) W-bnd: From Jct of I-90 & 150th Ave (Exit 11A): Go 1/8 mi S on 150th Ave (over freeway) to SE 37th St, then 1/4 mi E on 37th St (R). E-bnd: From Jct of I-90 & 150th Ave (Exit 11A): At bottom of off-ramp go 1/4 mi E (straight) on 37th St (R). **FAC:** Paved rds. (102 spaces). Avail: 47 paved, 16 pull-thrus (21 x 62), back-ins (21 x 31), some side by side hkups, 47 full hkups (30/50 amps), seasonal sites, cable, WiFi, laundry, LP gas. **REC:** heated pool, whirlpool, playground. Pet restrict(Q). No tents. Eco-friendly, 2015 rates: $25 to $52. Disc: military.
(800)659-4684 Lat: 47.577412, Lon: -122.132675
15531 SE 37th St, Bellevue, WA 98006
tibellevue@aol.com
www.trailerinnsrv.com
See ad page 1276 (Spotlight Spokane and the Inland Empire).

SEAVIEW — D1 *Pacific*

LONG BEACH NACO **Ratings: 6.5/7.5/7** (Membership Pk) 2015 rates: $40 to $55. (800)405-6188 2215 Willows Rd, Seaview, WA 98644

SOU'WESTER HISTORIC LODGE & VINTAGE TRAVEL TRAILER RESORT **Ratings: 4.5/6/4** (Campground) 2015 rates: $30 to $45. (360)642-2542 3728 J Pl, Seaview, WA 98644

SEQUIM — B2 *Clallam*

DIAMOND POINT RESORT **Ratings: 6.5/7.5/7** (Membership Pk) 2015 rates: $40. (360)681-0590 294 Industrial Parkway, Sequim, WA 98382

DUNGENESS REC AREA (Public) From town, E 12 mi on Rte 101 to Kitchen Dick Rd, N 3 mi, into the park (L). 2015 rates: $19 to $22. (360)683-5847

GILGAL OASIS RV PARK
Ratings: 8/9.5★/9 (RV Park) From Jct of US 101 & River Rd exit: Go N to roundabout to Washington Ave, then 2-1/8 mi on Washington Ave to Lee Chatfield Ave, then 1/8 mi S on Lee Chatfield to Hammond St, then 1/8-mi W on Hammond to Brown, then 1/8 mi S (R). **FAC:** Paved rds. (28 spaces). Avail: 18 paved, 11 pull-thrus (25 x 60), back-ins (24 x 50), 18 full hkups (30/50 amps), seasonal sites, cable, WiFi, laundry. **REC.** Pet restrict(B). Partial handicap access, no tents. Big rig sites, eco-friendly, 2015 rates: $36.43 to $46.49. Disc: military.
(888)445-4251 Lat: 48.077279, Lon: -123.091393
400 S Brown Rd, Sequim, WA 98382
info@gilgaloasisrvpark.com
www.gilgaloasisrvpark.com

JOHN WAYNE'S WATERFRONT RESORT **Ratings: 7/9.5★/7.5** (RV Park) 2015 rates: $28 to $42. (360)681-3853 2634 W Sequim Bay Rd, Sequim, WA 98382

RAINBOW'S END RV PARK, LLC Ratings: 8/7.5/6.5 (RV Park) From Jct of US-101 & River Rd: Go 1-1/8 mi W on US-101 (R). **FAC:** Paved rds. (45 spaces). Avail: 22 gravel, 12 pull-thrus (19 x 45), back-ins (20 x 30), 19 full hkups, 3 W, 3 E (30/50 amps), seasonal sites, cable, WiFi, tent sites, dump, laundry, LP gas, firewood. **REC:** pond. Pet restrict(B). Eco-friendly, 2015 rates: $30 to $40. Disc: AAA, military.
AAA Approved
(360)683-3863 Lat: 48.078040, Lon: -123.160480
261831 Hwy 101, Sequim, WA 98382
office@rainbowsendrvpark.com
www.rainbowsendrvpark.com

SEQUIM BAY (State Pk) From town, E 4 mi on Hwy 101 at MP-269 (L). 2015 rates: $12 to $42. May 15 to Sep 15. (888)226-7688

You have high expectations, so we point out campgrounds, service centers and tourist attractions with elevations over 2,500 feet.

SHELTON — C2 *Mason*

LITTLE CREEK CASINO RESORT RV PARK **Ratings: 10/10★/9.5** (RV Resort) 2015 rates: $30 to $54. (800)667-7711 91 W State Route 108, Shelton, WA 98584

MINERVA BEACH (Public) From US 101 (Shelton exit): Go 12 mi N on US 101. (360)877-5145

POTLATCH (State Pk) From town, S 3.2 mi on US-101, btwn MP-335 & 336 (R). 2015 rates: $12 to $42. (888)226-7688

SILVER CREEK — C2 *Lewis*

SILVER CREEK See also Castle Rock, Centralia, Chehalis, Kelso, Mossy Rock & Silver Lake.

PARADISE RESORT **Ratings: 7/7.5/6.5** (Membership Pk) 2015 rates: $44 to $48. Apr 25 to Sep 22. (800)405-6188 173 Salem Plant Rd, Silver Creek, WA 98585

SILVER LAKE — D2 *Cowlitz*

SILVER LAKE See also Bothell, Castle Rock, Centralia, Chehalis, Everett, Kelso, Mossy Rock, Poulsbo, Silver Creek, Stanwood & Woodland.

MT ST HELENS RV RESORT **Ratings: 3.5/6.5/4.5** (Campground) 2015 rates: $18 to $30. (360)274-2701 4220 Spirit Lake Hwy, Silver Lake, WA 98645

SEAQUEST (State Pk) From jct I-5 (exit 49) & Hwy 504: Go 6 mi E on Hwy 504. 2015 rates: $12 to $42. (888)226-7688

SILVER COVE RV RESORT
Ratings: 9/8★/9 (RV Park) From Jct of I-5 (Exit 49) & Hwy 504: Go 9 mi E on Hwy 504 to Hall Rd, then 1/2 mi S on Hall Rd (R). **FAC:** Paved rds. (160 spaces). Avail: 120 all weather, 8 pull-thrus (32 x 62), back-ins (32 x 60), 120 full hkups (30/50 amps), seasonal sites, cable, WiFi, rentals, laundry, fire rings, firewood. **REC:** Silver Lake: fishing, playground. Pet restrict(B). Partial handicap access, no tents. Big rig sites, 2015 rates: $38 to $50. Disc: AAA.
AAA Approved
(877)380-7278 Lat: 46.313278, Lon: -122.763092
351 Hall Rd, Silver Lake, WA 98645
silvercove@highwaywestvacations.com
www.silvercovervresort.com

SILVER LAKE RESORT **Ratings: 5/7★/6.5** (Campground) 2015 rates: $30 to $45. (360)274-6141 3201 Spirit Lake Hwy, Silver Lake, WA 98645

SKAMOKAWA — D2 *Wahkiakum*

SKAMOKAWA VISTA PARK (Public) From town, W 0.25 mi on SR-4 to Vista Park Rd, W 100 yds (E). 2015 rates: $18 to $30. (360)795-8605

SOAP LAKE — C4 *Grant*

SMOKIAM CAMPGROUND (Public) From jct Hwy 28 & Hwy 17: Go 1 mi N on Hwy 17. 2015 rates: $10 to $20. (509)246-1211

SMOKIAM RV RESORT
Ratings: 9/8★/8 (RV Park) From Jct of WA Hwy 17 & WA Hwy 28 (in Soap Lake): Go 2 mi N on Hwy 17 (L).

A FAMILY-FRIENDLY WATER RESORT
With renovated big-rig sites, pool, 2 hot tubs, sauna, fitness & business center on the mineral waters of Soap Lake, it's truly nature's spa. Amenities: cafe, cabins, playground & dog park. Come relax, play & soak in the sun!

FAC: Paved rds. 19 all weather, 28 gravel, 28 pull-thrus (25 x 60), back-ins (35 x 55), 47 full hkups (30/50 amps), cable, WiFi, tent sites, rentals, dump, laundry, groc, LP gas, fire rings, firewood, controlled access. **REC:** heated pool, whirlpool, Soap Lake: playground. Pet restrict(B/Q). Big rig sites, 2015 rates: $39 to $48. Disc: AAA, military.
(509)246-0413 Lat: 47.423967, Lon: -119.498408
22818 Hwy 17 North, Soap Lake, WA 98851
Info@smokiamrvresort.com
www.smokiamrvresort.com
See ad pages 1255 (Spotlight Coulee Corridor), 1250.

SPOKANE — B6 *Spokane*

SPOKANE See also Cheney,Colbert, Davenport, Deer Park, Loon Lake, Spokane Valley & Wilbur.

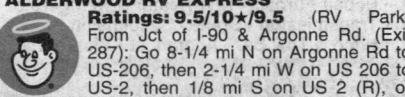

ALDERWOOD RV EXPRESS
Ratings: 9.5/10★/9.5 (RV Park) From Jct of I-90 & Argonne Rd. (Exit 287): Go 8-1/4 mi N on Argonne Rd to US-206, then 2-1/4 mi W on US 206 to US-2, then 1/8 mi S on US 2 (R), or S-Bnd: From Jct of US-2 & US-206: Go 1/8 mi S on US-2 (R). **FAC:** Paved rds. (102 spaces). Avail: 62 paved, patios, 40 pull-thrus (21 x 66), back-ins

WA

SPOKANE (CONT)

ALDERWOOD RV EXPRESS (CONT)
(24 x 34), 62 full hkups (30/50 amps), seasonal sites, cable, WiFi, dump, laundry, LP gas. **REC:** heated pool, playground. Pets OK. Partial handicap access, no tents. 2015 rates: $34 to $52. Disc: AAA.
(888)847-0500 Lat: 47.785360, Lon: -117.354620
14007 N Newport Hwy, Mead, WA 99021
alderwood@highwaywestvacations.com
www.alderwoodrv.com

→ KOA OF SPOKANE **Ratings: 8.5/8/7.5** (Campground) 2015 rates: $42 to $82. (509)924-4722 3025 N Barker Rd, Spokane Valley, WA 99027

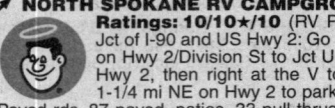

NORTH SPOKANE RV CAMPGROUND
Ratings: 10/10★/10 (RV Park) From Jct of I-90 and US Hwy 2: Go 5-3/4 mi N on Hwy 2/Division St to Jct US 395 and Hwy 2, then right at the V to continue 1-1/4 mi NE on Hwy 2 to park (R). **FAC:** Paved rds. 87 paved, patios, 33 pull-thrus (32 x 70), back-ins (30 x 60), 87 full hkups (30/50 amps), cable, WiFi, laundry, LP gas. **REC:** heated pool, playground. Pet restrict(B/Q). No tents. Big rig sites, 2015 rates: $40 to $54. Disc: military.
(509)315-5561 Lat: 47.757010, Lon: -117.394646
10904 Newport Hwy, Spokane, WA 99218
info@northspokanervcampground.com
www.northspokanervcampground.com
See ad pages 1275 (Spotlight Spokane and the Inland Empire), 1250.

RIVERSIDE
(State Pk) From town, NW 6 mi on SR-291, follow signs (L). **FAC:** Paved rds. 32 dirt, no slide-outs, back-ins (12 x 40), 16 W, 16 E (20 amps), tent sites, dump, groc, firewood. **REC:** Spokane River: fishing, rec open to public. Pets OK. Partial handicap access. 10 day max stay, 2015 rates: $20 to $45.
(509)465-5064 Lat: 47.717556, Lon: -117.497556
9711 W Charles Rd, Nine Mile Falls, WA 99026
riverside@parks.wa.gov
www.parks.wa.gov
See ad page 1246 (Welcome Section).

TRAILER INNS OF SPOKANE LLC
Ratings: 8.5/9★/7 (RV Park) E-bnd: From Jct of I-90 & Exit 285: Go 1/2 mi E on exit rd to Thierman Rd, then 1/8 mi S on Thierman Rd to 4th Ave, then 1/2 mi W on 4th Ave; or W-bnd: From Jct of I-90 & Exit 285 (Sprague Ave), go 1/2 mi E on Sprague to Thierman Rd, then 1/8 mi S on Thierman Rd to 4th Ave, then 1/2 mi W on 4th (R). **FAC:** Paved rds. (96 spaces). Avail: 26 paved, 9 pull-thrus (21 x 55), back-ins (22 x 35), 26 full hkups (30/50 amps), seasonal sites, cable, WiFi, tent sites, laundry, LP gas. **REC:** playground. Pet restrict(B). Partial handicap access. 2015 rates: $25 to $40. Disc: military.
(800)659-4864 Lat: 47.654544, Lon: -117.322920
6021 E 4th Ave, Spokane Valley, WA 99212
tispokane@aol.com
www.trailerinnsrv.com
See ad page 1276 (Spotlight Spokane and the Inland Empire).

Travel Services

→ **WASHINGTON AUTO CARRIAGE** Mechanical Repairs. Service, repair or replacement on: Air conditioners, refrigerators, water heaters, furnaces. Service generators. Workhorse chassis warranty center. Extended warranties honored. Roof Inspection. **SERVICES:** RV, RV appliance, MH mechanical, engine/chassis repair, restrooms. **TOW:** RV. RV supplies, emergency parking, RV accessible. waiting room. Hours: 8am to 5pm M-F.
(509)535-0363 Lat: 47.65869, Lon: -117.27631
5301 E Broadway Ave, Spokane, WA 99212
wac@waautocarriage.com
www.wacnw.com
See ad this page.

Subscribe to Trailer Life Magazine. For a subscription, call 800-825-6861.

SPOKANE VALLEY — B6 *Spokane*

→ PARK LANE MOTEL & RV PARK **Ratings: 6.5/NA/7** (RV Park) 2015 rates: $35 to $42. (509)535-1626 4412 E Sprague Ave, Spokane Valley, WA 99212

STANWOOD — B2 *Island, Snohomish*

CAMANO ISLAND (State Pk) From town, W 3 mi on Hwy 532 to E Camano Dr (left at fork), S 6 mi (rd becomes Elger Bay Rd) to Mountain View, W 2 mi to Lowell Point Rd, S 0.6 mi (E). 2015 rates: $12 to $42. (360)387-3031

← **CEDAR GROVE SHORES RV PARK**
Ratings: 9/9.5★/9 (RV Park) From Jct of I-5 & 172nd St (exit 206), W 2.2 mi on 172nd St to Lakewood Rd (SR-531), W 3.2 mi to West Lake Goodwin Rd, S 0.7 mi (L). **FAC:** Gravel rds. (62 spaces). Avail: 12 paved, 18 all weather, back-ins (22 x 40), accepts self-contain units only, 18 full hkups, 12 W, 12 E (30/50 amps), seasonal sites, WiFi, showers $, dump, laundry, LP bottles, controlled access. **REC:** Lake Goodwin: swim, fishing. Pet restrict(B/Q) $. Partial handicap access, no tents. Eco-friendly, 2015 rates: $40 to $45. No CC.
(866)342-4981 Lat: 48.13562, Lon: -122.30006
16529 W Lake Goodwin Rd, Stanwood, WA 98292
cgsrvpark@frontier.com
cgsrvpark.com
See ad pages 1269 (Spotlight Northwest Washington), 1250.

← LAKE GOODWIN RESORT **Ratings: 7.5/7.5/7** (Campground) From Jct of I-5 & 172nd St (exit 206), SW 2.2 mi on 172nd St to Lakewood Rd (SR-531) W 3.5 mi (L). **FAC:** Paved rds. (74 spaces). 49 Avail: 10 gravel, 39 grass, 8 pull-thrus (20 x 60), back-ins (17 x 60), some side by side hkups, 49 full hkups (30/50 amps), seasonal sites, cable, WiFi, tent sites, rentals, showers $, laundry, groc, LP gas, fire rings, firewood, controlled access. **REC:** Lake Goodwin: swim, fishing, playground. Pet restrict(Q). Partial handicap access. 2015 rates: $40 to $55.
AAA Approved
(800)242-8169 Lat: 48.14314, Lon: -122.29692
4726 Lakewood Rd, Stanwood, WA 98292
camp@lakegoodwinresort.com
www.lakegoodwinresort.com

STARBUCK — D5 *Franklin*

← KOA AT LYONS FERRY MARINA **Ratings: 6/7.5/7.5** (Campground) 2015 rates: $28.89 to $35.89. (800)562-5418 102 Lyons Ferry Rd, Starbuck, WA 99359

LYONS FERRY (Public Corps) From town, NW 8 mi on Hwy 261 (R). 2015 rates: $15 to $23.25. May 15 to Sep 7. (509)751-0240

TUCANNON RV PARK **Ratings: 5.5/8★/7.5** (RV Park) 2015 rates: $25. (888)399-2056 511 Hwy 261, Dayton, WA 99328

STEVENSON — D3 *Skamania*

→ THE RESORT AT SKAMANIA COVES **Ratings: 6/7.5/7.5** (RV Park) 2015 rates: $35. Apr 1 to Oct 31. (509)427-4900 45932 Hwy 14, Stevenson, WA 98648

→ WIND MOUNTAIN RV PARK & LODGE **Ratings: 5/5/6** (Campground) 2015 rates: $27.50. (509)607-3409 mile 50.5 State Hwy 14 (Columbia Gorge Scenic Byway), Stevenson, WA 98648

TACOMA — C2 *Pierce*

TACOMA See also Eatonville, Enumclaw, Gig Harbor, Graham, Kent, Olympia, Puyallup & South Prairie.

DASH POINT (State Pk) From I-5 (exit 143): Go 4-1/2 mi W on 320th St, then 1/2 mi N on 47th Ave, then 1-1/2 mi SW on Marine View Dr (Hwy 509). 2015 rates: $12 to $42. (253)661-4955

To get the most out of your Guide, refer to the Table of Contents in the front of the book.

← **MAJESTIC MOBILE MANOR RV PARK (MHP)**
Ratings: 9.5/7.5/7.5 (RV Park) From I-5 & WA-167N (Exit 135) toward Puyall up, slight left onto WA-167 for 3.8 mi (R) **FAC:** Paved rds. (88 spaces). Avail: 4 all weather, 1 pull-thrus (24 x 70), back-ins (22 x 55) 44 full hkups (30/50 amps), seasonal sites, cable WiFi, dump, laundry, groc, LP gas. **REC:** heated pool Clark's Creek: fishing. Pet restrict(B). 2015 rates $34. No CC.
(800)348-3144 Lat: 47.20939, Lon: -123.33744
7022 River Rd E, Puyallup, WA 98371
majesticrvpark@juno.com
www.majesticrvpark.com
See primary listing at Puyallup and ad page 1267 (Spotlight Mount Rainier & Mount St Helens).

TOKELAND — C1 *Pacific*

BAYSHORE BEACH RV RESORT **Ratings: 7.5/8★/8.5** (Campground) 2015 rates: $35 t $45. (360)267-2625 2941 Kindred Ave, Tokeland WA 98590

TONASKET — A4 *Okanogan*

SPECTACLE LAKE RESORT Ratings: 6.5/5.5/6 (Campground) From Tonasket at jc US 20 & US 97: Go 6-3/4 mi N on US 97, then 1/2 m W on Ellisforde Bridge Rd to dead end, then 1-1/4 m S on Hwy 7N to Loomis-Oroville Rd, then 5-3/4 mi NW on Loomis-Oroville Rd to Holmes Rd, then 3/4 mi S on Holmes Rd to McCammon Rd, then 1/8 mi W o McCammon Rd. (R). **FAC:** Poor gravel/dirt rds. 3 grass, back-ins (25 x 40), some side by side hkups 32 full hkups, 4 W, 4 E (30 amps), WiFi, tent sites rentals, laundry, groc, fire rings, firewood. **REC:** heat ed pool, Spectacle Lake: swim, fishing, playground Pets OK. 2015 rates: $32. Disc: AAA, military. Apr to Oct 31.
(509)223-3433 Lat: 48.809244, Lon: -119.532465
10 Mccammon Rd, Tonasket, WA 98855
spectaclelake@okcom.org
www.spectaclelakeresort.com

TONASKET CHAMBER OF COMMERCE R.V PARK (Public) N-bnd: From Jct Hwy 97 & Hwy 20 Go 1/2 mi N on Hwy 97 (L).S-bnd: From Oroville: G 15 mi S on Hwy 97 into Tonasket (R). 2015 rates: $20 (509)486-7155

TROUT LAKE — D3 *Klickitat*

ELK MEADOWS RV PARK **Ratings: 6/6/** (Campground) 2015 rates: $28 to $35. May 15 to No 15. (509)395-2400 78 Trout Lake Creek Rd, Trou Lake, WA 98650

GIFFORD PINCHOT NF (CULTUS CREEK CAMPGROUND) (Natl Forest) From town: Go 14 m W then N on FR 24. Pit toilets. 2015 rates: $10 to $20 Jul 15 to Oct 15. (509)395-3400

GIFFORD PINCHOT NF (PETERSON PRAIRIE CAMPGROUND) (Natl Forest) From town: Go 6 m W on FR 24. Pit toilets. 2015 rates: $16 to $30. Ju 12 to Sep 14. (360)569-0519

VALLEY — B5 *Stevens*

← WINONA BEACH RESORT **Ratings: 4.5/5.5/** (Campground) 2015 rates: $32. Apr 15 to Sep 30 (509)937-2231 33022 Winona Beach Rd, Valley, WA 99181

VANCOUVER — E2 *Clark*

VANCOUVER See also Corbett, Kelso, Wilsonville & Woodland.

VAN MALL RV PARK
Ratings: 8.5/10★/7.5 (RV Park N-bnd: From Jct of I-205 & SR-500 (exi 30A): Go 1/2 mi E on 30A to Gher Rd then 1/8 mi N on Gher Rd to 4th Plain Rd then 1/4 mi W to 102nd Ave, then 1/8 m S (L). S-bnd: From Jct of I-205 & Exit 30 (Mall exit) Go 1/2 mi SW on off-ramp rd to NE 4th Plain, then 1/ mi E to 102nd Ave, 1/8 mi S (L). **FAC:** Paved rds. (10 spaces). Avail: 16 paved, 16 pull-thrus (20 x 45), accepts self-contain units only, 16 full hkups (30/5 amps), seasonal sites, cable, WiFi, laundry. **REC.** Pe restrict(B/Q). Partial handicap access, no tents. 201 rates: $32 to $40.
(360)891-1091 Lat: 45.66062, Lon: -122.56637
10400 NE 53rd St, Vancouver, WA 98662
Manager@vanmallrv.com
www.vanmallrv.com
See ad pages 1257 (Spotlight Gateway to Washington), 1250.

Average site width and length are indicated in many campground listings to give you an idea of how much room and privacy you ca expect.

'ANCOUVER (CONT)

VANCOUVER RV PARK
Ratings: 8.5/10★/8.5 (RV Park) From Jct of I-5 & 78th St (exit 4): Go 1/4 mi E on 78th St to NE 13th Ave, then 1/8 mi S on 13th Ave (L). **FAC:** Paved rds. (176 spaces). Avail: 55 paved, patios, 28 ull-thrus (24 x 55), back-ins (20 x 54), accepts self-ontain units only, 55 full hkups (30/50 amps), sea-onal sites, WiFi, laundry. **REC.** Pet restrict(B). Par-al handicap access, no tents. 2015 rates: $34 to $47.)isc: AAA. No CC.
877)756-2972 Lat: 45.67723, Lon: -122.65878
'603 NE 13th Ave, Vancouver, WA 98665
'ancouverrv@juno.com
www.vancouverrvparks.com
See ad opposite page, 1250.

99 RV PARK Ratings: 7.5/9★/6.5 (RV Park) 'rom Jct of I-5 & I-205 (Exit 36/Hwy 99): Go 1/2 mi on Hwy 99 to Leichner Rd (R) or N-bnd: Jct of I 205 Exit 36): Go 1/8 mi W on 134th St to NE 20th Ave Hwy 99), then 1/4 mi S on Hwy 99 to Leichner Rd (R). 'AC: Paved rds. (88 spaces). Avail: 30 gravel, 15 ull-thrus (22 x 70), back-ins (30 x 40), 30 full hkups 30/50 amps), seasonal sites, WiFi, laundry. **REC.** 'et restrict(B/Q). Partial handicap access, no tents. ge restrict may apply, 2015 rates: $34. Disc: AAA. AA Approved
360)573-0351 Lat: 45.71384, Lon: -122.65161
913 NE Leichner Rd, Vancouver, WA 98686
vpark99@hotmail.com
9rvpark.net

'ANTAGE — C4 *Kittitas*

GINKGO/WANAPUM REC AREA
(State Pk) From Jct of I-90 & Huntzinger Rd (exit 136), S 3 mi on Huntzinger Rd to Wanapum Recreation Area (L). **FAC:** Paved/gravel ds. 50 gravel, 35 pull-thrus (35 x 60), back-ins 30 x 50), 50 full hkups (30 amps), tent sites, rest-ooms only, firewood. **REC:** Columbia River: swim, shing, rec open to public. Pets OK. Partial handicap ccess. 10 day max stay, 2015 rates: $15 to $45.
509)856-2700 Lat: 46.90053, Lon: -119.99285
511 Huntzinger Rd, Vantage, WA 98950
nfocent@parks.wa.gov
www.parks.wa.gov
ee ad page 1246 (Welcome Section).

VANTAGE RIVERSTONE RV & RETREAT **Rat-ngs: 5.5/6/6** (RV Park) 2015 rates: $30 to $35. 509)856-2800 551 Main St, Vantage, WA 98950

WALLA WALLA — D5 *Walla Walla*

BLUE VALLEY RV PARK
Ratings: 8.5/10★/9.5 (RV Park) From Jct of US 12 & 2nd Ave (in town): Go 1/8 mi N on 2nd Ave to 4th Ave N, then 1/8 mi N on 4th Ave to Rees St, then 1/8 mi E on Rees St to Burns, then 1/8 ni N on Burns to George St (R). **FAC:** Paved rds. (6 spaces). Avail: 24 paved, patios, back-ins (27 x 60), ccepts self-contain units only, 24 full hkups (30/50 mps), seasonal sites, cable, WiFi, laundry, con-rolled access. **REC:** playground. Pet restrict(B). Par-al handicap access, no tents. Big rig sites, 2015 ates: $39.
509)525-8282 Lat: 46.077189, Lon: -118.342891
0 W George, Walla Walla, WA 99362
tay@bluevalleyrv.com
www.bluevalleyrv.com
ee ad pages 1282 (Spotlight Wine Country), 1250.

RV RESORT FOUR SEASONS
Ratings: 8.5/9★/9.5 (RV Park) From Jct of US 12 & Prescott/Pendleton exit: Go 1-1/4 mi S on NE Myra Rd to Dalles Military Rd, then /2 mi E on Dalles Military Rd (L). **FAC:** Paved rds. 89 spaces). 69 Avail: 52 paved, 17 grass, 15 pull-hrus (24 x 68), back-ins (28 x 50), 69 full hkups 30/50 amps), seasonal sites, cable, WiFi, laundry. **REC:** Garrison Creek. Pet restrict(B). Partial hand-cap access, no tents. Big rig sites, 2015 rates: $37. AA Approved
509)529-6072 Lat: 46.048468, Lon: -118.357607
440 Dalles Military Rd, Walla Walla, WA 99362
vresort@gohighspeed.com
www.rvresortfourseasons.com
See ad this page.

WARDEN — C5 *Grant*

SAGE HILLS GOLF CLUB & RV RESORT **Rat-ngs: 7/7.5/6.5** (RV Park) 2015 rates: $20 to $31. 509)349-2603 10400 Sage Hill Rd SE, Warden, WA 8857

WENATCHEE — C4 *Chelan, Douglas*

DAROGA (State Pk) From Jct of US-2 & US-97 (at MP-219), NW 6.5 mi on US-97 (L). 2015 rates: $12 o $42. (509)664-6380

LINCOLN ROCK (State Pk) From town, N 8.4 mi on US-2/US-97 (L). 2015 rates: $12 to $42. Mar 9 to Oct 15. (888)226-7688

WENATCHEE CONFLUENCE (State Pk) From Jct of US-2 & US-97Alt exit, S 0.4 mi on US-97Alt to Euclid Ave, SE 0.4 to Olds Station Rd, W 0.25 mi (L); or From Jct of Wenatchee & Penny (Old Station exit), E 0.1 mi on Penny Rd to Chester Kim Rd, S 0.25 mi to Old Station Rd, E 0.25 mi (R). 2015 rates: $12 to $42. Apr 1 to Sep 20. (888)226-7688

WENATCHEE RIVER COUNTY PARK
(Public) From Jct of US-2 & US-97 (Wenatchee): Go 6 mi NW on US-2 (L). **FAC:** Paved rds. (49 spaces). Avail: 39 paved, 3 pull-thrus (28 x 70), back-ins (32 x 60), 33 full hkups, 4 W, 4 E (30/50 amps), WiFi, showers $, dump, laundry, LP gas, fire rings, firewood, controlled access. **REC:** Wenatchee River: swim, fishing, playground. Pets OK. Partial handicap access, no tents. Big rig sites, 2015 rates: $20 to $30. Apr 1 to Oct 31.
(509)667-7503 Lat: 47.484828, Lon: -120.409854
2924 State Hwy 2, Monitor, WA 98836
marylee.redline@co.chelan.wa.us
www.wenatcheeriverpark.org
See ad page 1253 (Spotlight Cascades).

WEST RICHLAND — D4 *Benton*

RV VILLAGE RESORT
Ratings: 9.5/8★/7 (RV Park) From Jct of I-82 & Hwy 224 & 225 (Exit 96), Go 6 mi NE on Hwy 244 (Van Giesen Rd) (L). **FAC:** Paved rds. (99 spaces). Avail: 21 paved, 21 pull-thrus (22 x 62), 21 full hkups (30/50 amps), seasonal sites, cable, WiFi, laundry, groc, LP gas. **REC:** heated pool, whirlpool. Pet restrict(B). Partial handicap access, no tents. 2015 rates: $30. Disc: AAA, military.
(866)637-9900 Lat: 46.29881, Lon: -119.38380
7300 W Van Giesen Ave, West Richland, WA 99353
rvvillageresort@gmail.com
www.rvvillageresort.com
See ad pages 1280 (Spotlight Tri-Cities), 1250.

WESTPORT — C1 *Grays Harbor*

AMERICAN SUNSET RV RESORT
Ratings: 9.5/10★/9 (RV Park) From Jct of SR-105 & Montesano St: Go 2.7 mi N on N Montesano (L). **FAC:** Paved rds. (120 spaces). Avail: 108 gravel, 60 pull-thrus (25 x 50), back-ins (25 x 50), 108 full hkups (30/50 amps), seasonal sites, WiFi, tent sites, rentals, laundry, groc, LP gas, fire rings, firewood. **REC:** heated pool, playground. Pet restrict(B/Q). Partial handicap access. Eco-friendly, 2015 rates: $38 to $39. Disc: AAA, military. AAA Approved
(800)569-2267 Lat: 46.899155, Lon: -124.106079
1209 North Montesano, Westport, WA 98595
info@americansunsetrv.com
www.americansunsetrv.com
See ad this page, 1259 (Spotlight Grays Harbor/Long Beach/Ocean Park), 1250.

PACIFIC MOTEL & RV Ratings: 6.5/6.5/7.5 (RV Park) From Jct of Hwy 105 & Montesano St: Go 1/2 mi S on Hwy 105 Spur to Forrest St, then 1/4 mi S on Forrest St (L). **FAC:** Poor paved/gravel rds. (80 spaces). Avail: 65 grass, 25 pull-thrus (15 x 55), back-ins (15 x 38), some side by side hkups, 65 full hkups (30/50 amps), seasonal sites, cable, WiFi, tent sites, rentals, showers $, laundry, LP gas, fire rings. **REC:** heated pool. Pet restrict(B). 2015 rates: $35. AAA Approved
(360)268-9325 Lat: 46.884291, Lon: -124.111106
330 S Forrest St, Westport, WA 98595
pacificmotelandrv@gmail.com
pacificmotelandrv.com

TWIN HARBORS (State Pk) From Jct of SR-105 & SR-105 Spur, E 0.2 mi on SR-105 (R). 2015 rates: $12 to $42. (360)268-9717

RV Park ratings you can rely on!

WHITE SALMON — D3 *Klickitat*

BRIDGE RV PARK & CAMPGROUND
Ratings: 8/10★/9 (RV Park) From Jct of I-84 & Exit 64 (Hood River Bridge, in OR): Go 1 mi N across toll bridge to SR-14, then 1/8 mi E on Sr-14 (R). Warning: Bridge is narrow. See park website for alternate big rig directions. **FAC:** Paved rds. (35 spaces). Avail: 29 paved, 16 pull-thrus (26 x 55), back-ins (24 x 48), 29 full hkups (30/50 amps), seasonal sites, cable, WiFi, tent sites, rentals, showers $, laundry, LP gas. **REC.** Pets OK $. Partial handicap access. Eco-friendly, 2015 rates: $45.48. Disc: AAA, military.
(509)493-1111 Lat: 45.72324, Lon: -121.48745
65271 Hwy 14, White Salmon, WA 98672
bridgerv@bridgerv.com
www.bridgerv.com
See ad pages 1257 (Spotlight Gateway to Washington), 1250.

WILBUR — B5 *Lincoln*

COUNTRY LANE CAMPGROUND & RV PARK
Ratings: 7.5/8.5★/7.5 (RV Park) From Jct of Hwy 2 & Hwy 174/21 (west of Wilbur): Go 1/8 mi E on Hwy 2 to Portland St, then N on Portland St (L). **FAC:** Gravel rds. 26 gravel, 10 pull-thrus (30 x 70), back-ins (30 x 40), 25 full hkups, 1 W, 1 E (30/50 amps), WiFi, tent sites, showers $, dump, laundry, fire rings, firewood, restaurant. **REC.** Pet restrict(Q). Partial handicap access. 2015 rates: $17 to $35.
(509)647-0100 Lat: 47.76091, Lon: -118.71281
14 Portland St NW, Wilbur, WA 99185
countrylanecampground@gmail.com
www.countrylanecampground.com
See ad pages 1254 (Spotlight Coulee Corridor), 1250.

LAKE ROOSEVELT NRA/KELLER FERRY (Natl Pk) From town, N 14 mi on SR-21 (L). Pit toilets. 2015 rates: $5 to $10. (509)633-9441

THE RIVER RUE RV PARK **Ratings: 6.5/7.5★/9** (Campground) 2015 rates: $32. (509)647-2647 44892 State Route 21 N, Wilbur, WA 99185

WINTHROP — A4 *Okanogan*

PEARRYGIN LAKE (State Pk) From Jct of Hwy 20 & Riverside Ave (Main St thru town), NW 1.6 mi on Riverside Ave/Bluff St to Bear Crk Rd, E 2 mi (R). 2015 rates: $12 to $42. (509)996-2370

PINE NEAR RV PARK & CAMPGROUND
Ratings: 7/9.5★/8 (Campground) From Jct of WA-20/Riverside St & Bridge St (Downtown): Go 1/16 mi N on Bridge St to Castle Ave, then 1/8 mi W on Castle Ave (L). **FAC:** Gravel rds. 38 grass, 23 pull-thrus (24 x 65), back-ins (30 x 55), 38 full hkups (30/50 amps), WiFi, tent sites, rentals, showers $, laundry, fire rings. **REC.** Pets OK. Big rig sites, 2015 rates: $35.50 to $38.50. Disc: AAA, military.
(509)341-4062 Lat: 48.476304, Lon: -120.179623
316 Castle Ave, Winthrop, WA 98862
info@pinenearpark.com
www.pinenearpark.com
See ad page 1253 (Spotlight Cascades).

RIVERBEND RV PARK
Ratings: 8.5/8.5★/8.5 (Campground) From town: Go 2 mi N on SR-20 (bet MP 199 & 200) (R); or From Winthrop: Go 6 mi S on SR-20 (L). **FAC:** Paved rds. (69 spaces). Avail: 64 gravel, 37 pull-thrus (26 x 80), back-ins (28 x 60), 56 full hkups, 8 W, 8 E (30/50 amps), seasonal sites, WiFi, tent sites, showers $, dump, laundry, groc, LP gas, fire rings, firewood. **REC:** Methow River: swim, fishing, playground. Pets OK $. Big rig sites, eco-friendly, 2015 rates: $39 to $41. Disc: AAA, military.
(509)997-3500 Lat: 48.391426, Lon: -120.135704
19961 Hwy 20, Twisp, WA 98856
reservations@riverbendrv.com
www.riverbendrv.com
See ad pages 1252 (Spotlight Cascades), 1250.

WINTHROP (CONT)

SILVERLINE RESORT
Ratings: 6.5/10★/9.5 (Campground) From Jct of SR-20 & Riverside Ave (North end of town): Go 1/16-mi NW on Riverside Ave to Bridge St, then 1/8 mi NW on Bridge St to Bluff St, then 1-1/4 mi E on Bluff St (name changes to E Chewuch Rd) to Bear Creek Rd, then 3/4 mi E on Bear Creek Rd (R) Follow Lake Pearrygin signs. **FAC:** Gravel/dirt rds. (48 spaces). Avail: 42 gravel, 5 pull-thrus (32 x 80), back-ins (25 x 40), some side by side hkups, 20 full hkups, 22 W, 22 E (30/50 amps), seasonal sites, WiFi, tent sites, rentals, showers $, dump, groc, fire rings, firewood. **REC:** Pearrygin Lake: swim, fishing. Pet restrict(Q) $. Big rig sites, 2015 rates: $33 to $38. Disc: military. Apr 25 to Oct 20.
(509)996-2448 Lat: 48.494748, Lon: -120.165655
677 Bear Creek Rd, Winthrop, WA 98862
info@silverlineresort.com
www.silverlineresort.com
See ad pages 1252 (Spotlight Cascades), 1250.

WINTHROP/NORTH CASCADES NAT'L PARK KOA **Ratings: 8.5/8.5★/7.5** (Campground) 2015 rates: $33.88 to $44.88. Apr 15 to Nov 1. (509)996-2258 1114 Hwy 20, Winthrop, WA 98862

WOODLAND — D2 *Cowlitz*

WOODLAND See also Castle Rock, Centralia, Chehalis, Kelso, Ridgefield, Rochester & Vancouver.

COLUMBIA RIVERFRONT RV PARK
Ratings: 10/10★/9 (RV Park) From Jct of I-5 & Exit 22: Go 1-1/2 mi W on Dike Access Rd to Dike Rd, then 1 mi S on Dike Rd (R).

ON THE BEACH OF THE COLUMBIA RIVER
Quiet Park. No Trains No Freeway No Airplanes. 800 ft of no-bank sandy beach. Watch large ships go by. Only 3 miles off I-5. Easy day trips: Mount St. Helens, Multnomah Falls (2nd largest in nation), 30 mi to Portland.

FAC: Paved rds. (76 spaces). Avail: 54 all weather, 9 pull-thrus (28 x 80), back-ins (28 x 40), 54 full hkups (30/50 amps), seasonal sites, cable, WiFi, laundry, groc, LP gas. **REC:** heated pool, Columbia River: fishing, shuffleboard, playground. Pet restrict(B). Partial handicap access, no tents. Big rig sites, eco-friendly, 2015 rates: $40 to $49. Disc: AAA. AAA Approved
(800)845-9842 Lat: 45.91295, Lon: -122.80332
1881 Dike Rd, Woodland, WA 98674
office@colriverfrontrv.com
www.columbiariverfrontrvpark.com
See ad pages 1258 (Spotlight Gateway to Washington), 1250.

PARADISE POINT (State Pk) From town, N 3 mi on I-5 to exit 16, follow sign on frntg rd (E). For reservations call (888)226-7688. 2015 rates: $12 to $42. Apr 1 to Sep 30. (888)226-7688

WOODLAND SHORES RV PARK
Ratings: 8.5/9★/8 (RV Park) From Jct of I-5 & SR-503 (exit 21), E 0.2 mi on SR-503 to Millard St, S 100 ft (L). **FAC:** Paved rds. (57 spaces). Avail: 47 paved, 26 pull-thrus (20 x 60), back-ins (20 x 48), accepts self-contain units only, 47 full hkups (30/50 amps), seasonal sites, WiFi, laundry. **REC:** North Fork Lewis River: fishing. Pet restrict(B). No tents. Eco-friendly, 2015 rates: $40. Disc: AAA, military.
(360)225-2222 Lat: 45.90637, Lon: -122.73927
1090 A St, Woodland, WA 98674
woodlandshores@aol.com
www.woodlandshoresrv.com
See ad this page, 1250.

Heading to a privately owned park? Be sure to read how our inspection team rated it in the Guide "How to Use This Travel Guide" section.

Travel Services

DAVE & LJ'S RV INTERIOR DESIGN Offers interior design & remodeling upgrades for any type RV. Furniture, flooring, TV installation, cabinetry. **SERVICES:** Restrooms. Emergency parking, RV accessible. waiting room. Hours: 9am to 5pm.
(360)225-7700 Lat: 45.91394, Lon: -122.74959
625 W Scott Avenue, Suite A, Woodland, WA 98674
www.daveandljs.com
See ad page 1248 (Welcome Section).

YAKIMA — C4 *Yakima*

SUNTIDES RV PARK & GOLF COURSE
Ratings: 8.5/8/9 (RV Park) From Jct of I-82 & SR-12 (exit 31): Go 4-1/8 mi W on SR-12 to Old Naches Hwy, then 1/16 mi N on Old Naches Hwy to Pence Rd, then 1/8 mi S on Pence Rd. (L). **FAC:** Paved rds. (60 spaces). Avail: 10 paved, 10 pull-thrus (35 x 64), mostly side by side hkups, 10 full hkups (30/50 amps), seasonal sites, WiFi, dump, laundry, restaurant. **REC:** golf, rec open to public. Pets OK. Partial handicap access, no tents. Big rig sites, 2015 rates: $38.
(800)376-8025 Lat: 46.636872, Lon: -120.590720
201 Pence Rd, Yakima, WA 98908
rvpark@suntidesgolf.com
www.suntidesgolf.com
See ad page 1281 (Spotlight Wine Country).

TRAILER INNS OF YAKIMA LLC
Ratings: 10/10★/8 (RV Park) From Jct of I-82 & N 1st St (exit 31): Go 1/8 mi S on N 1st St (R); or From Jct of SR-12 & N 1st St: Go 1/8 mi S on N 1st St (R). **FAC:** Paved rds. (135 spaces). Avail: 11 paved, 14 all weather, 25 pull-thrus (33 x 45), 25 full hkups (30/50 amps), seasonal sites, cable, WiFi, tent sites, laundry, LP gas. **REC:** heated pool, whirlpool, playground. Pet restrict(Q). 2015 rates: $35 to $50.
(800)659-4784 Lat: 46.622463, Lon: -120.512990
1610 N First St., Yakima, WA 98901
tiyakima@aol.com
www.trailerinnsrv.com
See ad page 1276 (Spotlight Spokane and the Inland Empire).

We appreciate your business!

YAKIMA SPORTSMAN
(State Pk) From Jct of I-82 & Hwy 24 (exit 34) E 0.7 mi on Hwy 24 to Keys Rd, N 1 mi (L) **FAC:** Paved rds. 37 Avail: 16 paved, 21 gravel, 16 pull-thrus (24 x 60), back-ins (30 x 40), 37 full hkups (30 amps), tent sites, dump, firewood. **REC** Yakima River: fishing, rec open to public. Pets OK Partial handicap access. 10 day max stay, 2015 rates: $20 to $45. Mar 1 to Nov 30.
(888)226-7688 Lat: 46.57184, Lon: -120.43323
904 University Pkwy, Yakima, WA 98901
infocent@parks.wa.gov
www.parks.wa.gov
See ad page 1246 (Welcome Section).

Things to See and Do

SUNTIDES GOLF COURSE Beautiful golf course surrounded by fruit orchards with adjacent RV park. Partial handicap access. RV accessible. Restrooms, food. Hours: 7am to 9pm. Adult fee: $30 to $45.
(509)966-9065 Lat: 46.636872, Lon: -120.590720
231 Pence Rd, Yakima, WA 98908
suntidesgolf@charter.net
suntidesgolf.com
See ad page 1281 (Spotlight Wine Country).

Look in the Guide to Seasonal Sites to find places you can stay for a month, a season or longer.

CLEAN RESTROOMS GET A STAR

Campgrounds that receive the maximum 5 points for restroom cleanliness (toilets, showers, floors, walls and sinks/counters/mirrors) are honored with a star beside their total restroom rating.

RATED 10/10★/10

Getty Images/iStockphoto

WELCOME TO West Virginia

DATE OF STATEHOOD	WIDTH: 130 MILES (210 KM)	PROPORTION OF UNITED STATES
JUNE 20, 1863	LENGTH: 240 MILES (386 KM)	0.64% OF 3,794,100 SQ MI

A lush paradise with green mountains, gushing whitewater rivers and dramatic snowcapped peaks, few states deliver such unexpected scenic wonders and outdoor pursuits as the Mountain State. Sprinkled across this beautiful tranche of Appalachia, historic sites provide soul-stirring insight into the seminal events in American history.

With two national parks, two national forests, 34 state parks and eight state forests, West Virginia offers a wealth of recreational opportunities. The 1,400 square miles of the Monongahela National Forest draws more than 3 million visitors a year with its rushing rivers, yawning caves and the highest peak in the state (Spruce Knob).

In the southeast, the New River Gorge National River Recreation Area boasts the finest whitewater rapids in the eastern U.S., as well as horseback riding, fishing and boating. For prime leaf-peeping and history, Cass Scenic Railroad State Park offers vintage steam train rides on the Cass Scenic Railroad.

For more than 80 years, the annual State Fair of West Virginia—staged in mid-August at the State Fairgrounds in Lewisburg—has been a standard bearer for state fairs, with livestock exhibits, harness racing and a beauty pageant.

Every October, Fayetteville hosts "Bridge Day" in honor of the city's masterstroke New River Gorge Bridge, one of the longest steel arch bridges in the world. During the festival, the bridge is closed to traffic as thrill-seekers parachute and bungee jump from the span and into the deep valley below.

Top 3 Tourism Attractions:
1) Monongahela National Forest
2) The Town of Harpers Ferry
3) New River Gorge Bridge

Nickname: Mountain State

State Flower: Rhododendron

State Bird: Cardinal

People: Pearl Buck, author; Don Knotts, actor; Mary Lou Retton, Olympic gymnast; Walter Reuther, labor leader

Major Cities: Charleston (capital), Huntington, Parkersburg, Morgantown, Wheeling

Topography: Most of West Virginia lies within the Appalachian forest's ecoregion; higher elevations are along eastern border

Climate: Humid continental climate with hot summers and cool to cold winters

TRAVEL & TOURISM

West Virginia Division of Tourism
800-225-5982
www.wvtourism.com

Berkeley Springs CVB
800-447-8797
www.berkeleysprings.com

Greater Bridgeport CVB
800-368-4324
www.greater-bridgeport.com

Greater Clarksburg CVB
304-622-2157
www.cityofclarksburgwv.com

Charleston CVB
304-344-5075
www.charlestonwv.com

Ohio County CVB
304-233-7709
www.visitwheelinwv.com

Summersville CVB
304-872-3722
www.summersvillecvb.com

West Virginia Div. of Natural Resources
304-558-2758
www.wvhunt.com/wizard/hflw000.asp

West Virginia Mountain Highlands
877-WVA-MTNS
www.mountainhighlands.com

OUTDOOR RECREATION

West Virginia Scenic Trails Association
800-225-5982
www.wvscenictrails.org

West Virginia Skiing
www.westvirginiaski.com

West Virginia Pro River Outfitters
877-4-A-WVPRO
www.americasbestwhitewater.com

SHOPPING

Appalachian
304-296-0163
www.appalachiansupplyinc.com

MountainMade Artisan Gallery
www.mountainmade.com

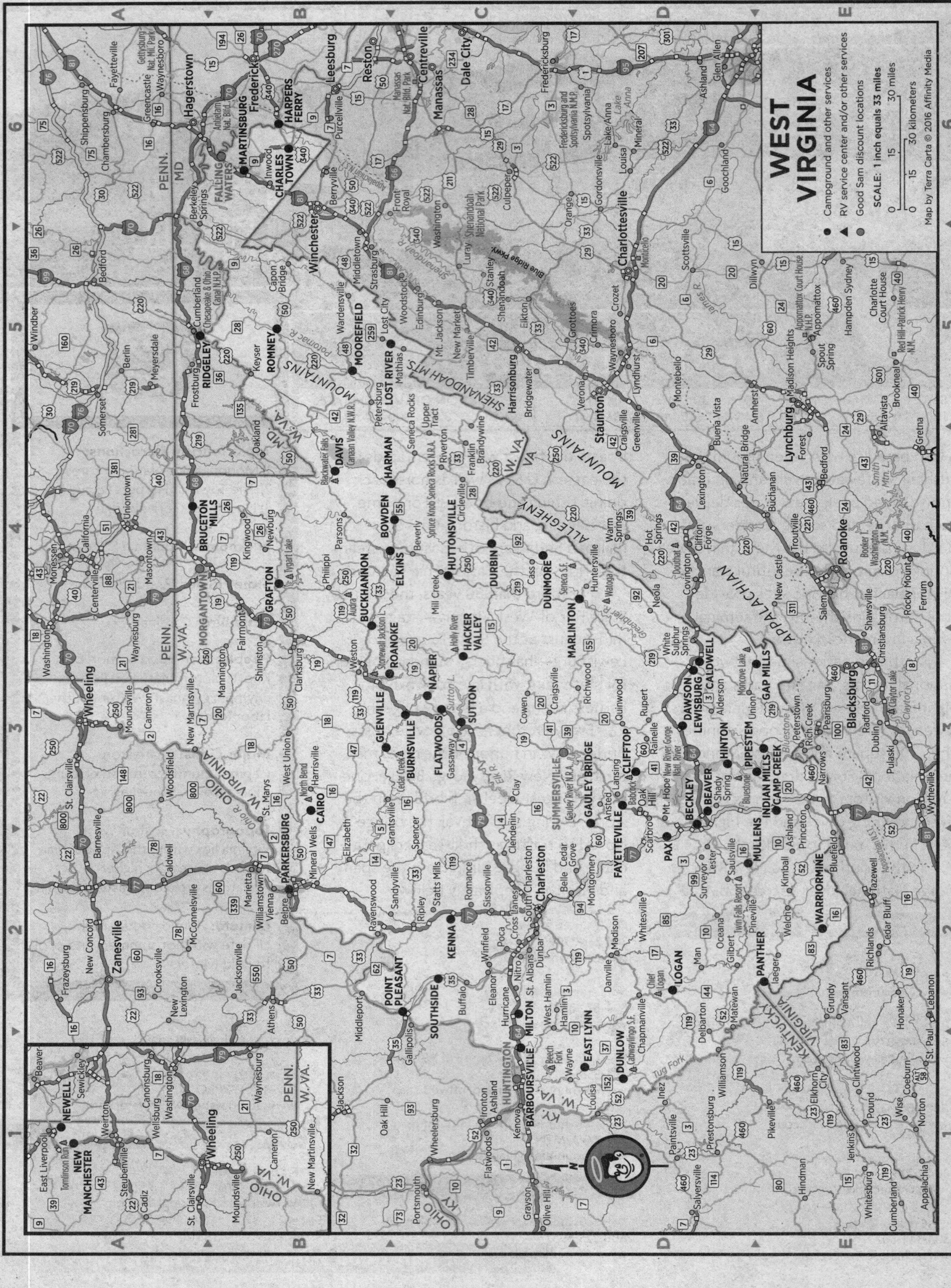
WEST VIRGINIA
Campground and other services
RV service center and/or other services
Good Sam discount locations
SCALE: 1 inch equals 33 miles
0 15 30 miles
0 15 30 kilometers
Map by Terra Carta © 2016 Affinity Media

Featured Good Sam Parks

WEST VIRGINIA

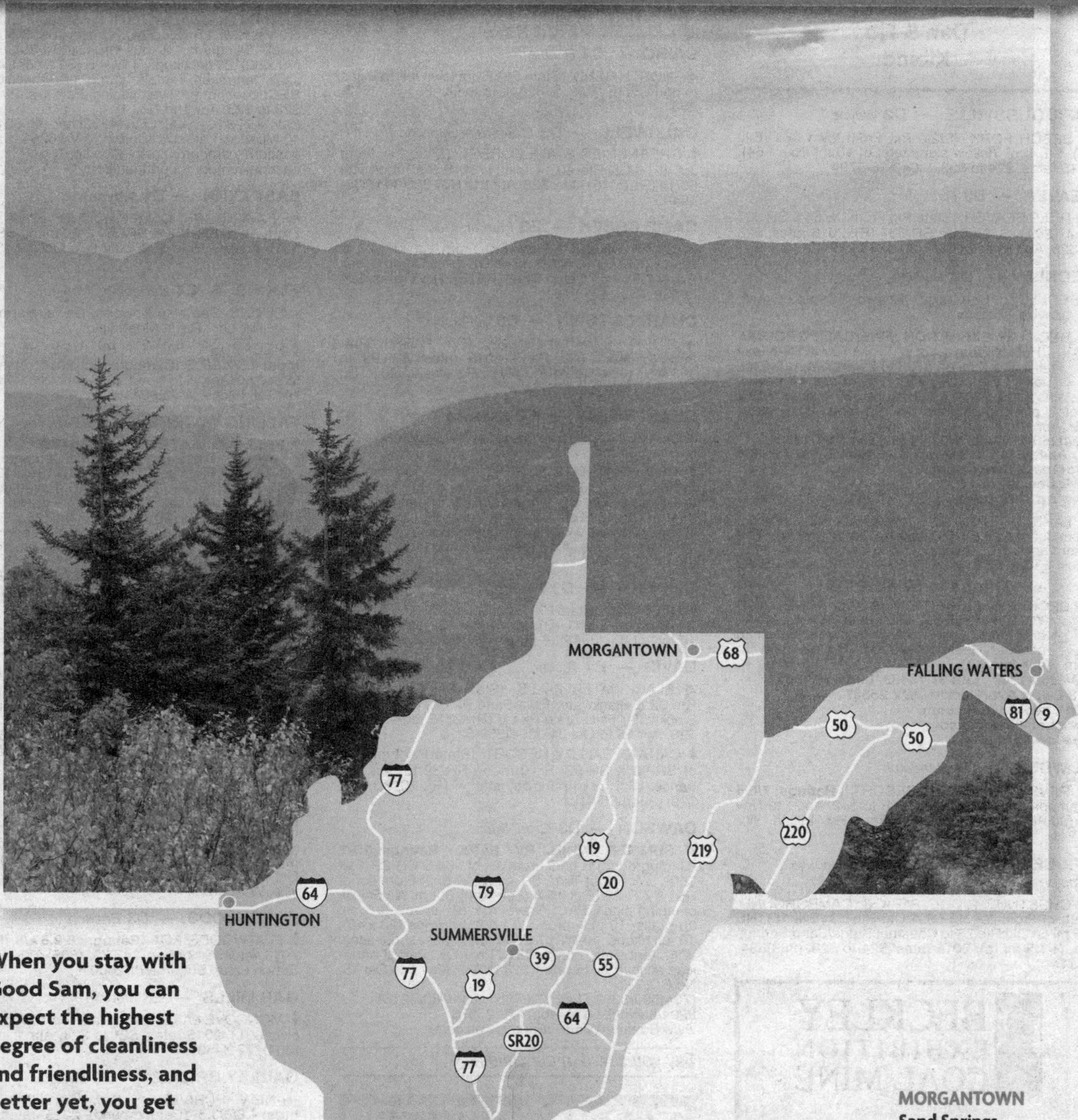

When you stay with Good Sam, you can expect the highest degree of cleanliness and friendliness, and better yet, you get 10% off campground fees.

If you're not already a Good Sam member you can purchase your membership at one of these locations:

FALLING WATERS
Falling Waters Campsite
(800)527-4902

HUNTINGTON
Robert Newlon RV Park & Camping
(304)733-1240

MORGANTOWN
Sand Springs Camping Area
(304)594-2415

SUMMERSVILLE
Summersville Lake Retreat
(888)872-5580

For more Good Sam Parks go to listing pages

West Virginia

CONSULTANTS

Dan & Flo Kleine

BARBOURSVILLE — D2 *Wayne*

BEECH FORK (State Pk) From town I-64 (Exit 11), SE 4 mi, (follow signs total of 10 mi from I-64). 2015 rates: $24 to $33. (304)528-5794

BEAVER — D3 *Raleigh*

LITTLE BEAVER (State Pk) From US 64 & SR 307 (exit 129A), S. 2 mi on SR 307 (E). 2015 rates: $25 to $28. Apr 15 to Oct 31. (304)763-2494

BECKLEY — D3 *Raleigh*

BECKLEY See also Beaver, Camp Creek, Fayetteville, Mullens.

BECKLEY EXHIBITION MINE CAMPGROUND (Public) From Jct of WV Tpke/I-77 & SR-3 (exit 44), E 1.7 mi on SR-3 to Ewart Ave, N 0.5 mi, follow signs (R). **FAC:** Paved rds. 17 paved, back-ins (20 x 50), 17 full hkups (30 amps). **REC:** pool $, playground. Pets OK. No tents. 2015 rates: $22. Apr 1 to Nov 1.
(304)256-1747 Lat: 37.78439, Lon: -81.19631
PO Box 2514 - 513 Ewart Ave, Beckley, WV 25801
info@beckleymine.com
www.beckley.org
See ad this page.

LAKE STEPHENS CAMPGROUND (Public) From Jct of I-77 & SR-3 (exit 44), W 8.1 mi on SR-3 to entrance (R), then 2.5 mi to campground. 2015 rates: $30 to $33. May 1 to Sep 30. (304)934-5322

Things to See and Do

BECKLEY EXHIBITION COAL MINE AND YOUTH MUSEUM Museum of WV coal mine and tours. Apr 1 to Nov 1. partial handicap access. Restrooms, food. Hours: 10am to 6pm. Adult fee: $20.
(304)256-1747 Lat: 37.78439, Lon: -81.19631
513 Ewart Ave, Beckley, WV 25801
info@beckleymine.com
www.beckleymine.com
See ad this page.

BOWDEN — C4 *Randolph*

REVELLES RIVER RESORT **Ratings: 7/6/5** (Campground) 2015 rates: $36 to $42. Apr 1 to Nov 1. (304)636-0023 5 1/2 Faulkner Rd, Elkins, WV 26241

BRUCETON MILLS — B5 *Monongalia, Preston*

CHESTNUT RIDGE PARK & CAMPGROUND (Public) From Jct of I-68 & Old Rte 73 (Exit 15), NE 0.6 mi on Old Rte 73 to Chestnut Ridge/Sand Springs Rd, N 1.5 mi (L). 2015 rates: $24 to $28. (888)594-3111

COOPERS ROCK STATE FOREST (State Pk) From town, W 9 mi on I-68 to exit 15/park access rd, S 1.25 mi (L). 2015 rates: $26. Apr 1 to Nov 30. (304)594-1561

BUCKHANNON — C5 *Webster*

AUDRA (State Pk) From Jct of SR-20 & US-119, NE 6 mi on US-119 to Audra Park Rd, E 8 mi (R). 2015 rates: $21 to $25. Apr 15 to Oct 15. (304)457-1162

BURNSVILLE — C3 *Braxton*

BURNSVILLE LAKE/RIFFLE RUN CAMPGROUND (Public Corps) From Jct of US-79 & exit 79, E 3.5 mi on 5th St./CH-5. 2015 rates: $12 to $26. May 18 to Sep 5. (304)853-2371

CAIRO — C4 *Ritchie*

NORTH BEND (State Pk) From town follow signs to park. 2015 rates: $26. Apr 15 to Oct 31. (304)643-2931

CALDWELL — D3 *Greenbrier, Monroe*

GREENBRIER STATE FOREST (State Pk) From Jct of I-64 & Rte 60/14 (exit 175), S 3.5 mi on Rte 60/14 (R). 2015 rates: $23. Apr 9 to Nov 30. (304)536-1944

CAMP CREEK — E3 *Mercer*

CAMP CREEK (State Pk) From Jct of I-77 & US-19 (Exit 20), SW 0.3 mi on US-19 to Camp Creek Rd, N 1.7 mi on Camp Creek Rd (E). 2015 rates: $24 to $30. (304)425-9481

CHARLES TOWN — B6 *Jefferson*

TURF STAY & PLAY RV PARK **Ratings: 5.5/NA/7** (RV Park) 2015 rates: $39.99 to $59.99. (304)725-2081 741 E Washington St, Charles Town, WV 25414

CHARLESTON — C2 *Kanawha*

CHARLESTON See also Gauley Bridge, Kenna, Milton, Summersville.

KANAWHA STATE FOREST (State Pk) From Jct of I-64 & US 119 (Exit 58A, Oakwood Rd), S 0.8 mi to Oakwood Rd. SE 1 mi to (CR23, Bridge Rd), NE 3 mi to Connell Rd, 2 mi to entrance E. Note: Road is very narrow & winding, with switchbacks. Rigs over 28' not advisable. 2015 rates: $28. Apr 15 to Nov 30. (304)558-3500

CLIFFTOP — D3 *Fayette*

BABCOCK (State Pk) From Jct of US-60 & SR-41, S 3.8 mi on SR-41 (R). 2015 rates: $21 to $24. Apr 15 to Oct 31. (304)438-3004

DAVIS — B4 *Tucker*

BLACKWATER FALLS (State Pk) From Jct of Rte 32 & Blackwater Falls State Pk Rd, SW 2 mi on Blackwater Falls State Pk Rd (R). 2015 rates: $20 to $23. Apr 15 to Oct 31. (304)259-5216

CANAAN VALLEY RESORT (State Pk) From Jct of SR-93 & SR-32, S 10 mi on SR-32 to park entrance, W 1 mi to park pay station (R). 2015 rates: $29. (304)866-4121

DAWSON — D3 *Greenbrier*

SUMMER WIND RV PARK Ratings: 5/7/7 (Campground) E-bnd: From Jct of I-64 & CR-29 (Exit 150), SW (Right Turn) 0.1 mi (L) W-bnd: From Jct of I-64 & CR-29 (Exit 150) (Left Turn) 0.2 mi (L) Follow camping signs. **FAC:** Gravel rds. (21 spaces). Avail: 20 grass, 10 pull-thrus (20 x 60), back-ins (20 x 40), 10 full hkups, 10 W, 10 E (30 amps), seasonal sites, WiFi, tent sites, dump. **REC.** Pets OK. Partial handicap access. 2015 rates: $26 to $29. May 1 to Oct 15. No CC.
(704)560-6392 Lat: 37.85051, Lon: -80.72181
2204 Lawn Rd, Dawson, WV 25976
www.SummerWindRvPark.vpweb.com

Say you saw it in our Guide!

DUNLOW — D1 *Wayne*

CABWAYLINGO STATE FOREST (State Pk) From Huntington, S 42 mi on US Rte 152 and follow signs. 2015 rates: $23. Apr 1 to Oct 3. (304)385-425

DUNMORE — C4 *Pocahontas*

SENECA STATE FOREST (State Pk) From Jct of Hwys 92 & 28, S 5 mi on Hwy 28, NW 1.3 mi Cabi Rd. Pit toilets. 2015 rates: $12. Apr 15 to Dec 1 (304)799-6213

DURBIN — C4 *Pocahontas*

EAST FORK CAMPGROUND & LODGING Ratings: 4/5.5/6 (Campground) From Jct of SR-250 River Rd (in town), W 100 ft to Meadow Ln, N 200 on Meadow Ln (E). **FAC:** Gravel rds. (35 spaces Avail: 24 grass, 2 pull-thrus (30 x 60), back-in (30 x 60), 20 full hkups, 4 W, 4 E (30 amps), seasona sites, tent sites, rentals, dump, fire rings, firewood **REC:** Greenbrier River: fishing. Pets OK. 2015 rates $23 to $25. Apr 1 to Nov 1.
(304)456-3101 Lat: 38.54428, Lon: -79.82408
43 Meadow Lane Dr., Durbin, WV 26264
eastfork_campground@yahoo.com
eastforkcampgrounddurbin.com

EAST LYNN — D1 *Wayne*

EAST FORK CAMPGROUND (Public Corps From Jct of SR-152 & SR-37, E 20 mi on SR-37 (R 2015 rates: $16 to $22. May 9 to Oct 19. (304)849-5000

ELKINS — C4 *Randolph, Webster*

ELKINS See also Bowden, Davis, Harman, Huttonsville, Lost River, Moorefield.

PEGASUS FARM RV RETREAT **Ratings: 4.5/7.5/7.5** (Campground) 2015 rates: $37.50 to $42.50. Apr 15 to Nov 1. (304)642-2351 480 Arnold Hill Rd, Elkins, WV 26241

FALLING WATERS — B6 *Berkeley*

FALLING WATERS CAMPSITE Ratings: 6/8.5★/7 (Campground) From Jct of I-81 & US-11 (exit 23), S 0. mi on US-11 (R). **FAC:** Paved/gravel rds (48 spaces). Avail: 43 gravel, 15 pull thrus (20 x 50), back-ins (25 x 50), 22 fu hkups, 21 W, 21 E (30/50 amps), seasonal sites cable, WiFi, tent sites, laundry, LP gas, fire rings. Pet OK. 2015 rates: $38 to $40.
(800)527-4902 Lat: 39.56817, Lon: -77.88333
7685 Williamsport Pike, Falling Waters, WV 2541
lynnleatherman@yahoo.com
www.fallingwaterscampsite.com
See ad this page, 1299.

Travel Services

FALLING WATERS RV SUPPLIES Trailer Hitches, RV Supplies & Propane. RV supplies LP, emergency parking, RV accessible. waiting room. Hours: 9am to 7pm.
(800)527-4902 Lat: 39.58933, Lon: -77.88333
7685 Williamsport Pike, Falling Waters, WV 2541
lynnleatherman@yahoo.com
www.fallingwaterscampsite.com
See ad this page.

FAYETTEVILLE — D3 *Fayette*

RIFRAFTERS CAMPGROUND **Ratings: 4/5.5/6** (Campground) 2015 rates: $40. Apr 1 to Oct 31. (304)574-1065 286 Rifrafters Lane, Fayetteville, WV 25840

FLATWOODS — C3 *Braxton*

FLATWOODS KOA **Ratings: 9/9.5★/8** (RV Park 2015 rates: $43.46 to $47.70. (866)700-7284 2000 Sutton Lane, Sutton, WV 26601

GAP MILLS — E3 *Monroe*

MONCOVE LAKE (State Pk) From town, N 6 mi on Hwy 8 (L). 2015 rates: $21 to $24. Apr 1 to Oct 31 (304)772-3450

GAULEY BRIDGE — D3 *Fayette*

NEW RIVER CAMPGROUND **Ratings: 4.5/6/3.5** (Campground) 2015 rates: $31 to $34. (304)632-9821 rt 60 East, Gauley Bridge, WV 25085

GLENVILLE — B3 *Braxton*

CEDAR CREEK (State Pk) From Jct of US-33/119 & SR-17, SE 4 mi on SR-17 (R). 2015 rates: $28. Apr 15 to Oct 15. (304)462-7158

GRAFTON — B4 *Taylor*

TYGART LAKE (State Pk) From Jct of US-119 & Tygart Lake access rd, S 4 mi on McVicker Rd, follow signs (E). 2015 rates: $20 to $23. Apr 15 to Oct 31 (304)265-6144

HACKER VALLEY — C3 *Webster*

HOLLY RIVER (State Pk) From Jct of SR-15 & SR-20, N 12 mi on SR-20 (R). 2015 rates: $23. Apr 2 to Nov 30. (304)493-6353

HARMAN — B4 *Randolph*

HARMAN MOUNTAIN FARM CAMPGROUND **Ratings: 4/7.5★/7.5** (Campground) 2015 rates: $20. May 1 to Oct 31. (304)227-3647 hc 70, Box 67-A, Harman, WV 26270

HARPERS FERRY — B6 *Jefferson*

HARPERS FERRY/CIVIL WAR BATTLEFIELDS KOA **Ratings: 9/7.5/8** (Campground) 2015 rates: $40 to $65. (800)562-9497 343 Campground Rd, Harpers Ferry, WV 25425

HINTON — D3 *Summers*

BLUESTONE (State Pk) From Jct of I-64 & WV-20, S 16 mi on WV-20 (R). 2015 rates: $21 to $27. Apr 1 to Oct 31. (304)466-2805

HUNTINGTON — C1 *Cabell*

HUNTINGTON See also Barboursville, Charleston, Milton and Ashland, KY.

HUNTINGTON KOA
Ratings: 9/10★/8 (Campground) W-bnd: Jct of I-64 & Mason Rd (exit 28), S 0.3 mi on Mason Rd to US-60, W 2.5 mi, N at Fox Fire Rd (NOTE: sharp right, hairpin turn). 0.25 mi on access rd (E) E-bnd: Jct of I-64 & Mall Rd (exit 20B), S 0.2 mi on Mall Rd to US-60, E (L) 5 mi on US-60 to Fox Fire Rd on left, 0.25 mi on access rd (E). **FAC:** Paved rds. (110 spaces). 81 Avail: 41 gravel, 40 grass, 70 pull-thrus (30 x 65), back-ins (30 x 55), some side by side hkups, 81 full hkups (30/50 amps), seasonal sites, cable, WiFi, tent sites, rentals, dump, laundry, groc, LP gas, firewood. **REC:** KOA Lake: swim, fishing, playground. Pet restrict(B). Partial handicap access. Big rig sites, eco-friendly, 2015 rates: $37 to $65.
(800)562-0898 Lat: 38.43251, Lon: -82.16936
290 Fox Fire Rd, Milton, WV 25541
foxfirekoa@gmail.com
www.foxfirekoa.com
See ad this page.

ROBERT NEWLON RV PARK & CAMPING
Ratings: 8/9.5★/7 (Campground) From Jct of I-64 & SR-193N/Merritts Creek Connector (Exit 18), N 3.3 mi on Merritts Creek Connector to SR-2 (Ohio River R), S 0.2 mi on SR-2 to Kyle Ln, W 0.3 mi on Kyle Ln (R). **FAC:** Gravel rds. 42 gravel, 42 pull-thrus (28 x 57), 22 full hkups, 20 W, 20 E (30/50 amps), WiFi, tent sites, rentals, dump, laundry, LP gas, firewood, restaurant. **REC:** Ohio River: swim, fishing. Pets OK. 2015 rates: $33 to $38. ATM.
(304)733-1240 Lat: 38.46092, Lon: -82.31013
6090 Kyle Lane, Huntington, WV 25702
robertnewlonairpark@gmail.com
www.skydivewv.com
See ad this page, 1299.

Park policies vary. Ask about the cancellation policy when making a reservation.

HUTTONSVILLE — C4 *Randolph*

KUMBRABOW STATE FOREST (Public) From town, S 7 mi on US 219 to Kumbrabow Forest Rd and follow signs. RV longer than 20' may experience difficulty. Pit toilets. 2015 rates: $14. Apr 15 to Oct 31. (304)335-2219

INDIAN MILLS — E3 *Summers*

BLUESTONE STATE WILDLIFE MGMT. AREA (State Pk) From town: Go 2 mi S on Hwy 12, then 3 mi SW on Indian Mills Rd. Pit toilets. (304)466-3398

KENNA — B5 *Jackson*

RIPPLING WATERS CHURCH OF GOD CAMPGROUND Ratings: 7.5/7/8 (Campground) From Jct of I-77 & SR-21 (exit 116 Sissonville), N 1.3 mi on SR-21 to Middle Fork Rd, E 3 mi (L) Note: Middle Fork Rd is bumpy & windy. **FAC:** Gravel rds. (120 spaces). 50 Avail: 8 paved, 37 gravel, 5 grass, 13 pull-thrus (38 x 80), back-ins (28 x 50), 31 full hkups, 19 W, 19 E (30/50 amps), seasonal sites, WiFi Hotspot, rentals, dump, laundry, LP bottles, fire rings, firewood. **REC:** pool, White Swan Lake: fishing, playground. Pets OK. Partial handicap access, no tents. Big rig sites, 2015 rates: $20 to $30. Disc: AAA.
AAA Approved
(304)988-2607 Lat: 38.57515, Lon: -81.60614
2271 Middle Fork Rd (Cr-42), Kenna, WV 25248
rwcogcamp@hotmail.com
www.ripplingwaterscampground.com

LEWISBURG — D3 *Greenbrier*

GREENBRIER RIVER CAMPGROUND Ratings: 7.5/7/7 (Campground) From Jct of I-64 & Rte 12 (exit 161), S 11.3 mi on Rte 12 to Rte 63, E 4 mi (R). **FAC:** Gravel rds. (33 spaces). Avail: 10 gravel, back-ins (28 x 45), 10 W, 10 E (30/50 amps), seasonal sites, WiFi, tent sites, rentals, dump, mobile sewer, laundry, LP bottles, firewood. **REC:** Greenbrier River: swim, fishing. Pets OK. 2015 rates: $28 to $42. Apr 1 to Oct 31.
(304)445-2203 Lat: 37.74141, Lon: -80.57200
4316 Highland Tr (Hwy 63), Alderson, WV 24910
info@greenbrierriver.com
www.greenbrierriver.com

STATE FAIR OF WEST VIRGINIA CAMPGROUND
(RV Spaces) From Jct of Rt 219 & I-64 (Exit 169), S 3 mi on Rte 219 (L). **FAC:** Gravel rds. 562 grass, 5 pull-thrus (35 x 90), back-ins (18 x 50), 403 full hkups, 159 W, 159 E (30/50 amps), WiFi Hotspot, dump. Pets OK. No tents. 2015 rates: $20 to $25. Disc: AAA.
(304)645-1090 Lat: 37.78067, Lon: -80.44501
891 Maplewood Ave, Lewisburg, WV 24902
statefairofwv@statefairofwv.com
www.statefairofwv.com
See ad this page.

County names help you follow the local weather report.

Things to See and Do

GREENBRIER COUNTY CVB Maps & information for local attractions & campgrounds. Partial handicap access. Restrooms. Hours: 9am to 5pm. No CC.
(800)833-2068 Lat: 37.80200, Lon: -80.44600
200 W Washington St, Lewisburg, WV 24901
www.greenbrierwv.com
See ad this page.

STATE FAIRGROUNDS OF WEST VIRGINIA
Site of State Fair & Flea Markets. Partial handicap access. RV accessible. Restrooms, food. Hours: 7am to 10pm. Adult fee: $8 to $10.
(304)645-1090 Lat: 37.78067, Lon: -80.44511
891 Maplewood Ave, Lewisburg, WV 24902
statefairofwv@statefairofwv.com
www.statefairofwv.com
See ad this page.

LOGAN — D2 *Logan*

CHIEF LOGAN (State Pk) From Jct of US 119 (Corridor G) & Rte 10 (in Chapmanville), S 8 mi on Rte 10 (R). 2015 rates: $27. Mar 1 to Nov 30. (304)792-7125

LOST RIVER — B5 *Hardy*

LOST RIVER CAMPGROUND **Ratings: 4/8★/7** (Campground) 2015 rates: $25. (304)897-8500 337 Kimsey Run Rd, Lost River, WV 26810

MARLINTON — D4 *Pocahontas*

MONONGAHELA NF (TEA CREEK CAMPGROUND) (Natl Pk) From jct US 219 & Hwy 150: Go 7 mi W on Hwy 150, then 2 mi W on FR 86. Pit toilets. (304)799-4334

WATOGA (State Pk) From Jct of SR-39 & SR-21, S 9 mi on SR-21, follow signs (R). 2015 rates: $21 to $24. Apr 1 to Dec 1. (304)799-4087

MARTINSBURG

NAHKEETA CAMPSITE (RV Spaces) From Jct of I-81& SR 9 (exit 12), E 3 mi to Charles Town Rd (follow signs) (E). **FAC:** Gravel rds. (45 spaces). Avail: 35 grass, 10 pull-thrus (30 x 100), back-ins (30 x 60), accepts full hkup units only, 35 full hkups (30/50 amps), seasonal sites, WiFi Hotspot. **REC:** Opequon Creek. Pets OK. Big rig sites, 2015 rates: $35. No CC.
(304)263-5382 Lat: 39.42473, Lon: -77.93646
1435 Charles Town Rd, Martinsburg, WV 25405
nahkeetacamp@gmail.com

MILTON — C2 *Cabell*

JIM'S CAMPING Ratings: 5/4/4 (Campground) From Jct I-64 & US-60 (exit 28), W 1.5 on US-60 (L). **FAC:** Paved/gravel rds. (82 spaces). 40 Avail: 20 gravel, 20 grass, 10 pull-thrus (22 x 100), back-ins (22 x 50), mostly side by side hkups, 15 full hkups, 25 W, 25 E (30/50 amps), seasonal sites, WiFi, tent sites, dump, laundry, LP gas, fire rings, firewood.

MILTON (CONT)

JIM'S CAMPING (CONT)
REC: Mudd River: fishing. Pets OK. 2015 rates: $20 to $25. No CC.
(304)743-4560 Lat: 38.43257, Lon: -82.15031
1794 US Route 60 West, Milton, WV 25541
wvcamping@aol.com

MOOREFIELD — B5 *Hardy*

RIVERSIDE CABINS & RV PARK **Ratings: 7/5.5/6.5** (Campground) 2015 rates: $30 to $35. (304)538-6467 3822 River Rd, Fisher, WV 26818

MORGANTOWN — A4 *Monongalia*

MORGANTOWN See also Bruceton Mills & Grafton.

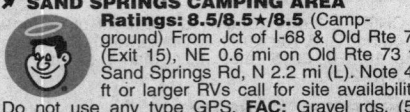

SAND SPRINGS CAMPING AREA
Ratings: 8.5/8.5★/8.5 (Campground) From Jct of I-68 & Old Rte 73 (Exit 15), NE 0.6 mi on Old Rte 73 to Sand Springs Rd, N 2.2 mi (L). Note 40 ft or larger RVs call for site availability. Do not use any type GPS. **FAC:** Gravel rds. (54 spaces). Avail: 41 gravel, 10 pull-thrus (30 x 60), back-ins (30 x 40), 34 full hkups, 7 W, 7 E (30/50 amps), seasonal sites, WiFi Hotspot, tent sites, showers $, dump, laundry, fire rings, firewood. **REC:** pool, playground. Pets OK. Eco-friendly, 2015 rates: $35 to $46.
(304)594-2415 Lat: 39.68523, Lon: -79.77473
Sand Springs Rd, Morgantown, WV 26507
sandspringsrv@gmail.com
www.sandspringscampground.com
See ad this page, 1299.

MULLENS — D2 *Wyoming*

TWIN FALLS RESORT (State Pk) From Jct of I-77 & SR-16, S 4 mi on SR-16 to SR-54, S 14 mi to SR-97, W 5.4 mi to Cabin Creek Rd, S 1 mi (E). Steep & winding rd 4.3 mi. 2015 rates: $23. (304)294-4000

NAPIER — C3 *Braxton*

BURNSVILLE LAKE/BULLTOWN CAMPGROUND (Public Corps) From Jct of US-79 & US-19 (exit 67), N 10 mi on US-19. 2015 rates: $20 to $26. May 19 to Sep 1. (304)853-2371

NEW MANCHESTER — A4 *Hancock*

TOMLINSON RUN (State Pk) From Jct of Rtes 2 & 8, NE 3 mi on Rte 8 (R); or From Jct of Rtes 30 & 8, S 5.5 mi on Rte 8 (R). 2015 rates: $20 to $24. Apr 1 to Oct 31. (304)564-3651

NEWELL — A1 *Hancock*

KENNEDY MARINA PARK (Public) From Jct of US-30 & SR-2, S 2 mi on SR-2 (R). 2015 rates: $27 to $37. May 15 to Sep 15. (304)387-3063

Explore America's Top RV Destinations! Turn to the Spotlight articles in our State and Province sections to learn more.

PANTHER — E2 *McDowell*

PANTHER (Public) From town, W 3.5 mi on Forest Rd to park entrance. Pit toilets. 2015 rates: $13. (304)938-2252

PARKERSBURG — B2 *Wood*

MOUNTWOOD PARK CAMPGROUND (WOOD COUNTY PARK) (Public) From jct I-77 & US 50: Go 14 mi E on US 50, then N on Borland Springs Rd. Follow signs. 2015 rates: $20 to $35. Apr 1 to Oct 31. (304)679-3694

PAX — D2 *Fayette*

PLUM ORCHARD LAKE WILDLIFE MANAGEMENT AREA (Public) From the Pax (Exit 54) off the I-77, take CR-23 to the lake. (R). Pit toilets. 2015 rates: $12. (304)469-9905

PIPESTEM — E3 *Mercer, Summers*

PIPESTEM RESORT (State Pk) From Jct of I-77 & CR-7 (Athens exit 14), N 3.5 mi on CR-7 to SR-20, NE 13 mi (L). 2015 rates: $23 to $32. (304)466-1800

POINT PLEASANT — C2 *Mason*

KRODEL PARK (CITY PARK) (Public) From Jct of SR-2 & SR-62, E 1 mi on SR-2 (L). 2015 rates: $14 to $20. Apr 1 to Oct 31. (304)675-1068

RIDGELEY — B5 *Mineral*

EAGLE'S NEST CAMPGROUND **Ratings: 6/NA/5** (Campground) 2015 rates: $38. May 1 to Oct 31. (304)298-4380 1714 Patterson Creek Rd (Off Route 28), Ridgeley, WV 26753

ROANOKE — B3 *Lewis*

STONEWALL RESORT (State Pk) From Jct of I-79 & US-19 (exit 91), E 2.7 mi on US-19 (L). 2015 rates: $44 to $48. (304)269-7400

ROMNEY — B5 *Hampshire*

WAPOCOMA CAMPGROUND Ratings: 5.5/7.5/7 (Campground) From Jct of US 50 & S Branch River Rd (West of Romney), S 4.1 mi on Branch River Rd (R). **FAC:** Gravel rds. (300 spaces). Avail: 155 grass, 30 pull-thrus (25 x 60), back-ins (25 x 40), 44 full hkups, 111 W, 111 E (30/50 amps), seasonal sites, WiFi, tent sites, dump, groc, LP gas, fire rings, firewood. **REC:** So. Branch Potomac: swim, fishing, playground, rec open to public. Pet restrict(B/Q). Partial handicap access. Big rig sites, 2015 rates: $24 to $28. Apr 15 to Oct 31. No CC, no reservations.
(304)822-5528 Lat: 39.28791, Lon: -78.80745
hc-66, Box 11, Romney, WV 26757
www.wapocomacampground.com

SOUTHSIDE — C2 *Mason*

CHIEF CORNSTALK STATE PUBLIC HUNTING & FISHING AREA (State Pk) From town: Go 6 mi W on CR 29. Pit toilets. (304)675-0871

SUMMERSVILLE — C3 *Nicholas*

SUMMERSVILLE See also Fayetteville & Gauley Bridge.

BATTLE RUN CAMPGROUND (Public Corps) From Jct of US-19 & SR-129, W 3.3 mi on SR-129 (R). 2015 rates: $16 to $24. May 1 to Oct 6. (304)872-3459

Tell them you saw them in this Guide!

MOUNTAIN LAKE CAMPGROUND LLC **Ratings: 7.5/7.5/7.5** (Campground) 2015 rates: $24 to $48. Mar 1 to Nov 30. (877)686-6222 1898 Summersville Airport Rd, Summersville, WV 26651

SUMMERSVILLE LAKE RETREAT
Ratings: 6/9.5★/9.5 (Campground) From Jct of US 19 & SR-129, W 0.2 mi on 129 W (R) Note: Please follow directions as some GPS devices will route you 0.25 mi past entrance. **FAC:** Gravel rds. 32 gravel, 10 pull-thrus (50 x 100), back-ins (30 x 50), 11 full hkups, 21 W, 21 E (30/50 amps), WiFi, tent sites, rentals, fire rings, firewood, controlled access. **REC:** Summersville Lake: playground, rec open to public. Pets OK. 2015 rates: $34 to $46. Disc: AAA.
AAA Approved
(888)872-5580 Lat: 38.19948, Lon: -80.86556
278 Summersville Lake Rd, Mount Nebo, WV 26679
reservations@summersvillelakeretreat.com
www.summersvillelakeretreat.com
See ad this page, 1299.

WV NAZARENE CAMP MUSIC PARK Ratings: 3/7/6.5 (Campground) From Jct of I-79 & US Rt 19 (Exit 57), W .1 mi to Rt 41 (Webster Rd) (traffic light at McDonald's), N 1.4 mi on Rt 41 (L). **FAC:** Gravel rds. 250 Avail: 100 gravel, 150 grass, 150 pull-thrus (25 x 60), back-ins (25 x 40), some side by side hkups, 26 full hkups, 102 W, 102 E (20/30 amps), WiFi Hotspot, tent sites, dump, mobile sewer, firewood. **REC:** Glade Creek. Pets OK. 2015 rates: $25. Apr 1 to Oct 31. No CC.
(304)872-6698 Lat: 38.31766, Lon: -80.80925
7441 Webster Rd (Hwy 41 N), Summersville, WV 26651
jcpourbaix@frontier.com

Things to See and Do

SUMMERSVILLE LAKE LIGHTHOUSE 100 ft high Lighthouse with daily tours April thru October (November thru March by appointment). RV accessible. Restrooms. Hours: 9am to 6pm. Adult fee: $7.
(888)872-5580 Lat: 38.19948, Lon: -80.86556
278 Summersville Lake Rd, Mount Nebo, WV 26679
reservations@summersvillelakeretreat.com
www.summersvillelakeretreat.com
See ad this page.

SUTTON — C3 *Braxton*

BAKERS RUN CAMPGROUND (Public Corps) From town, S 5 mi on US-19 to CR-17, E 10 mi (L). 2015 rates: $12 to $14. Apr 23 to Nov 31. (304)765-5631

GERALD R FREEMAN CAMPGROUND (Public Corps) From town, N 3 mi on US-19 to CR-15, E 12 mi (R). 2015 rates: $16 to $30. Apr 18 to Dec 1. (304)765-7756

WARRIORMINE — E2 *McDowell*

BERWIND LAKE WILDLIFE MANAGEMENT AREA (Public) From Princeton, take I-77 to Exit 9, WV Rt. 460W. Stay on 460W to Tazwell, VA. At Exit 2, take WV Rt. 16N to War, WV. Go to end of city limits and left across bridge. Follow road to park entrance. (R). Pit toilets. 2015 rates: $11 to $16. May 25 to Sep 7. (304)875-2577

Tell your RV Campground that you found them in this Guide.

Nick Collura, Travel Wisconsin

WELCOME TO

Wisconsin

DATE OF STATEHOOD	WIDTH: 260 MILES (420 KM)	PROPORTION OF UNITED STATES
MAY 29, 1848	LENGTH: 310 MILES (500 KM)	1.73% OF 3,794,100 SQ MI

With its green and gentle landscape, dotted with red barns and cherry orchards, it's easy to see why Old World immigrants were so enamored with the state of Wisconsin. Thanks in no small part to German and Scandinavian farming techniques, Wisconsin today produces 25 percent of the nation's cheese supply. Unassuming Wisconsinites revel in their state's cheesy preeminence, referring to themselves with pride as "cheese heads."

Carpeted with swathes of forestland and home to more than 90 glacial lakes, Wisconsin offers enough hiking, biking, camping, fishing and even downhill skiing to keep outdoor enthusiasts invigorated regardless of the season. Petite state capital Madison is a dynamic university city with verdant city parks and arty cafés.

When you think of Milwaukee, the image of a blue-collar, beer-and-brats kind of town generally holds sway. But, over the last decade, Milwaukee has gained serious kudos as an unassuming Great Lakes city that has created its own brand of freethinking, urban cool. The gentrified riverfront features upscale shopping, music and art.

Learn

Until the mid-18th century, France controlled the area that is now Wisconsin, which explains the prevalence of French sounding cities: La Crosse, Fond du Lac, Eau Claire and Benoit. Wisconsin became known as the Badger State, not because of its population of badgers, but due to its first white population: lead miners who lived in burrows in the hills. By 1829, more than 4,000 miners worked in southwestern Wisconsin, producing 13 million pounds of lead a year. Miners from Cornwall, England, settled in the historic town of Mineral Point during the 1830s. Mineral Point's picturesque historic district, dotted with restored miners' cottages, studios, galleries and antique shops, provides insight into the Midwest's architectural history and its role as a cultural melting pot. In the town of Eagle, some 60 historic structures were dismantled and reconstructed to create a working pioneer community dedicated to the history of rural life during the 19th century.

Play

With two national parks and 64 state parks, Wisconsinites revel in the wooded bluffs, misty forests, windswept beaches, glistening lakes and lush valleys of their enchanted state. In northern Wisconsin, Copper Falls State Park combines stunning scenery and recreational opportunities. In addition to three spectacular waterfalls, 17 miles of hiking trails and deep gorges, the North Country National Scenic Trail passes through the park.

Top 3 Tourism Attractions:
1) Wisconsin Dells
2) Door County
3) Harley-Davidson Museum

Nickname: Badger State

State Flower: Wood Violet

State Bird: Robin

People: Eric Heiden, Olympic speed skater; Liberace, entertainer and pianist; Georgia O'Keeffe, artist; Laura Ingalls Wilder, author; Frank Lloyd Wright, architect

Major Cities: Milwaukee, Madison (capital), Green bay, Kenosha, Racine

Topography: Five areas: Lake Superior Lowland; Eastern Ridges and Lowlands; Northern Highland; Central Plain; Western Upland

Climate: Continental climate; warm summers and cold, snowy winters; some variations by Lake Michigan and Lake Superior

Travel Wisconsin

WI

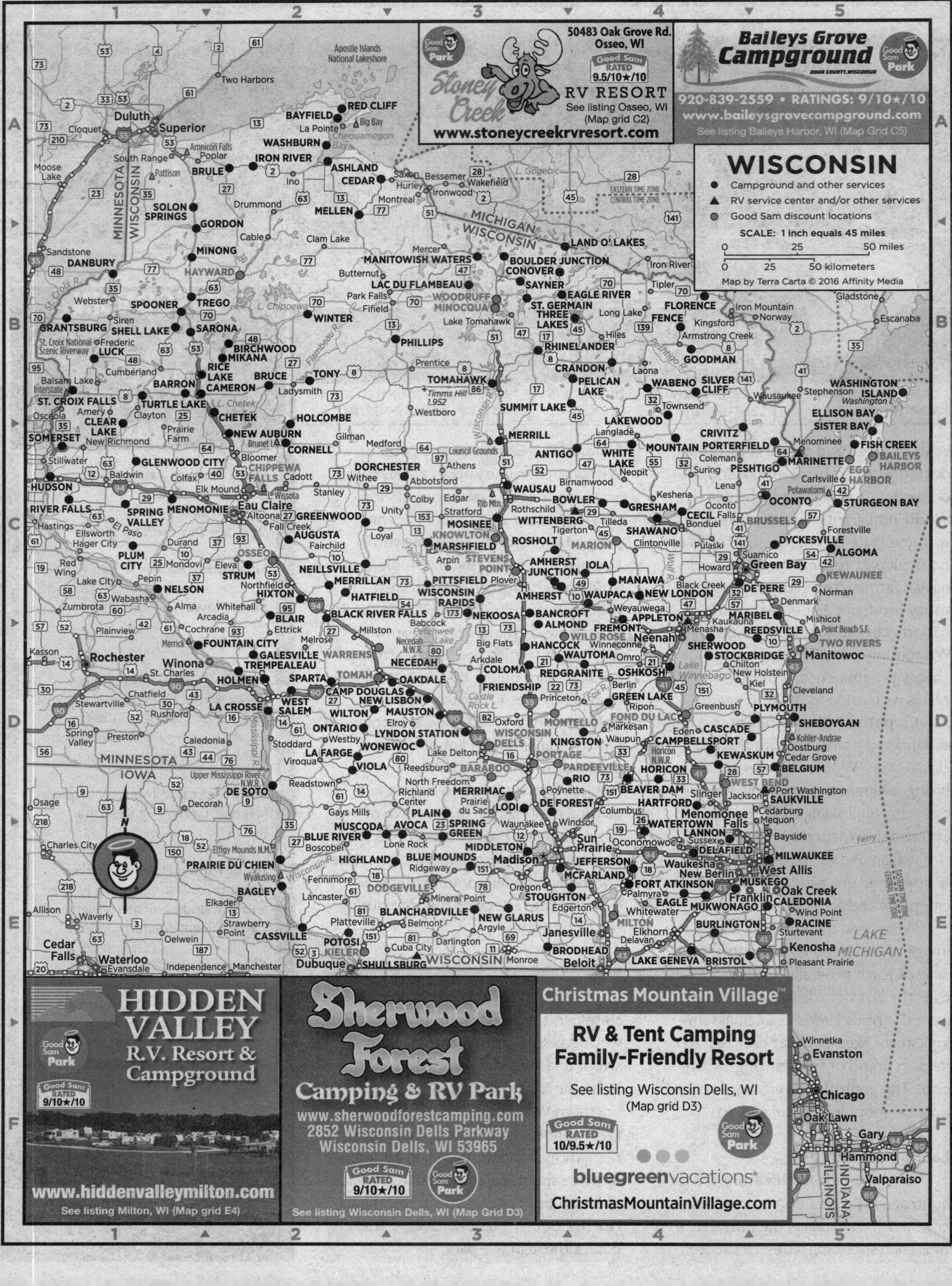

WISCONSIN
Campground and other services
RV service center and/or other services
Good Sam discount locations
SCALE: 1 inch equals 45 miles
0 25 50 miles
0 25 50 kilometers
Map by Terra Carta © 2016 Affinity Media
Good Sam Park
50483 Oak Grove Rd. Osseo, WI
Good Sam RATED 9.5/10★/10
Stoney Creek RV RESORT
See listing Osseo, WI (Map grid C2)
www.stoneycreekrvresort.com
Baileys Grove Campground
DOOR COUNTY, WISCONSIN
Good Sam Park
920-839-2559 • RATINGS: 9/10★/10
www.baileysgrovecampground.com
See listing Baileys Harbor, WI (Map Grid C5)
HIDDEN VALLEY R.V. Resort & Campground
Good Sam Park
Good Sam RATED 9/10★/10
www.hiddenvalleymilton.com
See listing Milton, WI (Map grid E4)
Sherwood Forest Camping & RV Park
www.sherwoodforestcamping.com
2852 Wisconsin Dells Parkway
Wisconsin Dells, WI 53965
Good Sam RATED 9/10★/10
Good Sam Park
See listing Wisconsin Dells, WI (Map Grid D3)
Christmas Mountain Village™
RV & Tent Camping
Family-Friendly Resort
See listing Wisconsin Dells, WI
(Map grid D3)
Good Sam RATED 10/9.5★/10
Good Sam Park
bluegreenvacations®
ChristmasMountainVillage.com

The self-declared "Waterpark Capital of the World," Wisconsin Dells is more than just wave pools, squirt guns and resort-style accommodation. In addition to 15 miles of salted sandstone cliffs that can be appreciated from the deck of the world's largest fleet of "Ducks" (restored WWII amphibious vehicles), visitors can kayak or canoe on the Wisconsin River, fish on Lake Delton or paddle board at Mirror Lake State Park. With 300 miles of rocky coastline, five state parks, 11 picturesque lighthouses, cherry orchards galore and tidy 19th-century villages, idyllic Door County is easy on the eye.

Experience

In June, in Little Chute, the Great Wisconsin Cheese Festival triumphs the state's cheese-making kudos with three action-packed days of cheese tastings, cheese-carving demonstrations, a cheese-curd eating contest and a cheesecake competition. For the lactose intolerant, there's live music, carnival rides, children's activities, an animal petting zoo and a cheese-themed parade. At the end of June/early July, Milwaukee's 11-day Summerfest is purportedly the "World's Largest Music Festival," hosting more than 700 bands on 11 stages along the shores of Lake Michigan. Late April through early November, Capitol Square provides the setting for Dane County Farmer's Market (www.dcfm.org), every Wednesday and Saturday, with its kaleidoscopic array of local produce, cheese (of course), flowers and arts and crafts. At Baraboo's Circus World Museum, the former winter haven for the Ringling Brothers, the history of the circus is presented through compelling artifacts.

Taste

While, at heart, Milwaukee remains a meat and potatoes sort of town, a crop of innovative bistros, trendy cafés and upscale restaurants have ignited the city's gastronomic culture. Sanford Restaurant (www.sanfordrestaurant.com), the veteran restaurant located in an intimate town home just outside downtown, steals the show with its superb haute cuisine served with flawless, understated style. In Madison, the Great Dane Pub & Brewing Co. (www.greatdanepub.com) serves upscale bar food staples—burgers, sandwiches, wings, tacos—washed down with a dozen craft beers. The Old Fashioned (www.theoldfashioned.com) is a characterful tavern, which adheres to the mantra, "Where Wisconsin is King." Not surprisingly, comfort food reigns here.

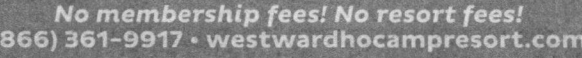

TRAVEL & TOURISM

Wisconsin Dept. of Tourism
800-432-8747, 608-266-2161
www.travelwisconsin.com

Door County Visitor Bureau
800-52-RELAX, 920-743-4456
www.doorcounty.com

Greater Green Bay CVB
888-867-3342, 920-494-9507
www.greenbay.com

Green County Tourism
888-222-9111
www.greencounty.org

Lake Geneva Convention and Visitors Bureau
262-248-4416
www.lakegenevawi.com

Sheboygan County Chamber of Commerce
920-457-9491
www.sheboygan.org

Wisconsin Dells CVB
800-223-3557
www.wisdells.com

OUTDOOR RECREATION

Bicycling Wisconsin
800-236-3649
www.northwoodsbiking.com

Hiking Wisconsin
800-236-3649
www.vilas.org

Snowmobiling Association of Wisconsin
920-734-5530
www.awsc.org

Wisconsin ATV Association
920-565-7531
www.watva.org

Wisconsin Dept. of Natural Resources
608-266-2621, 877-945-4236
www.dnr.state.wi.us

Wisconsin State Horse Council
920-623-0393
www.wisconsinstatehorsecouncil.org

SHOPPING

Burnstad's European Village
608-372-4040
www.burnstads.com

Cedar Creek Settlement
866-377-4788

Columbus Antiques Mall & Museum
920-623-1992
www.columbusantiquemall.com

Dane Co. Farmers' Market on the Square
www.dcfm.org

Fox River Mall
920-739-4100
www.foxrivermall.com

WI

Featured Good Sam Parks

WISCONSIN

Good Sam Park

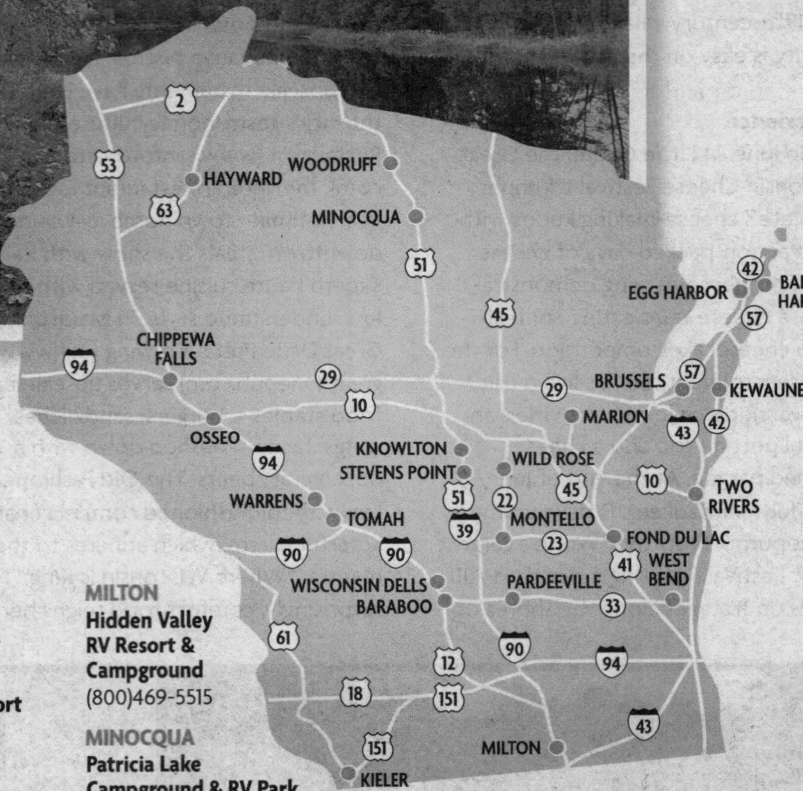

When you stay with Good Sam, you can expect the highest degree of cleanliness and friendliness, and better yet, you get 10% off campground fees.

If you're not already a Good Sam member you can purchase your membership at one of these locations:

BAILEYS HARBOR
Baileys Grove Campground
(920)839-2559

BARABOO
Fox Hill RV Park & Campground
(608)356-5890

Ho-Chunk Houisa Chi' Nuk RV Park
(800)746-2486

BRUSSELS
Quietwoods South Camping Resort
(920)825-7065

CHIPPEWA FALLS
O'Neil Creek Campground
(715)723-6581

EGG HARBOR
Rustic Timbers Door County Camping
(920)868-3151

FOND DU LAC
Westward Ho RV Resort & Campground
(888)712-9617

HAYWARD
Treeland Farm RV Resort
(715)462-4987

KEWAUNEE
Kewaunee Village RV Park & Campground
(920)388-4851

KIELER
Rustic Barn Campground & RV Park
(608)568-7797

KNOWLTON
Lake Dubay Shores Campground
(715)457-2484

MARION
Farmer Gene's Campground
(715)754-5900

MILTON
Hidden Valley RV Resort & Campground
(800)469-5515

MINOCQUA
Patricia Lake Campground & RV Park
(715)356-3198

MONTELLO
Buffalo Lake Camping Resort
(608)297-2915

OSSEO
Stoney Creek RV Resort
(715)597-2102

PARDEEVILLE
Indian Trails Campground
(608)429-3244

STEVENS POINT
Rivers Edge Campground
(715)344-8058

TOMAH
Holiday Lodge Golf Resort & RV Park
(608)372-9314

TWO RIVERS
Village Inn On the Lake Hotel & RV Park
(920)794-8818

WARRENS
Jellystone Park Warrens
(888)386-9644

WEST BEND
Lake Lenwood Beach & Campground
(262)334-1335

WILD ROSE
Evergreen Campsites & Resort
(866)450-2267

WISCONSIN DELLS
Christmas Mountain Village Campground
(608)253-1000

Sherwood Forest Camping & RV Park
(877)474-3796

WOODRUFF
Hiawatha Trailer Resort
(888)429-2842

For more Good Sam Parks go to listing pages

DOOR COUNTY

Take a trip to the Cape Cod of the Midwest

Door County, a popular destination for vacationers and tourists from around the United States, is named after the strait between the Door Peninsula and Washington Island. It is said that because of the natural hazards of the strait, where the waters of Green Bay meet Lake Michigan, early French explorers gave it the name *Porte des Morts*, which translates to Death's Door.

Slightly scary stuff, but don't worry, despite the name, the Door County you will encounter on your trip will be absolutely teeming with life. And the good news is that you don't have to hazard the sea—simply drive in your RV to the peninsula that many consider to be the "Cape Cod of the Midwest."

> Door County features more than 2,500 acres of cherry orchards, and visitors flock each year to pick the harvest.

Beautiful Beacons

Lighthouse lovers will enjoy visiting the county's most majestic beacons. Looming over Sturgeon Bay is the Sturgeon Bay Canal Lighthouse. Located at a Coast Guard station, it was originally constructed in 1899 and then reinforced with additional steel in 1903. Another must-see is Pottawatomie Lighthouse, which ranks as the oldest lighthouse in Wisconsin, having started duty in 1836. While the original was demolished in the late 1850s, a new light was constructed and lit in 1858. Today, it is open for summertime tours under the name of the Pottawatomie Lighthouse Museum.

There are a number of intriguing shipwreck sites in the area. One of the most popular for visitors is the site of the schooner *Fleetwing*, a lumber cargo vessel that ran aground in Door County in September of 1888. Today, the broken hull of the *Fleetwing* lies on the lake bottom close to shore, little more than 10 feet below the surface, making it easily accessible for divers, snorkelers and kayak enthusiasts.

Those who would like to learn more about the nautical history around Door County without getting wet can visit the Door County Maritime Museum. The museum features a detailed rundown of the region's shipbuilding history, as well as a larger ship model collection, a collection of classic boats and a restored steamship pilothouse.

Another water-based attraction that makes Door County unique is its array of surrounding islands. Accessible only by boat, the islands give the visitor a sense of seclusion that is enhanced by a total absence of motor vehicles. The most famous of these getaways is Washington Island, which is situated just beyond the tip of the Door County Peninsula. Take hikes in local trails, duck into a museum to learn about history and folklore of Door County here. Also of note is Cana Island, which features

Kayaking at Cave Point County Park. Jon Jarosh

Eagle Bluff Lighthouse.
Door County Visitor Bureau

the Cana Island Lighthouse, one of the most recognizable landmarks in Door County. The attraction's keeper's house, oil house and tower are open for tours May through October.

Cherries on Top

Door County is a haven for lovers of the great outdoors. Peninsula State Park features an 18-hole championship golf course, camping sites, hiking trails and bicycle paths. Snow on the ground doesn't mean an end to the frivolity. Instead, prepare to bust out the skis for groomed ski trails, snowmobiling and sledding. Bring the kids to family-friendly White Cedar Nature Center, which hosts a number of hikes, nature-based arts and crafts, and outdoor skills workshops to keep the kids' minds off the TV remote control and into the beauty of the surrounding forest.

Whitefish State Dunes, on the other hand, offers more than 860 acres of ground on the Lake Michigan shoreline, including a mile of sand beach and the tallest sand dunes in the Badger State. Visitors can enjoy swimming, hiking and fishing in the summer and snowshoeing in winter.

At the end of a busy day, there often is nothing better than a nice adult beverage, and Door County has offerings for you. If beer is your thing, make sure to check out Door County Brewing Company. The Baileys Harbor brewer, established in 2012, has made a tremendous reputation for itself as a brewer of distinctive beers. The taproom serves up a number of selections for the sophisticated beer sampler, including farmhouse ale, a pale ale, a smoked imperial stout and a witbier.

However, if it's the smashed grapes you are about, there are many that are worth your attention, including Simon Creek Vineyard & Winery, Orchard Country Winery & Market and Red Oak Winery. Take your pick of these Midwest vintages.

Don't leave Door County without taking in the fruit of choice in the region: the cherry. Because of the region's distinctive geography, climate and soil, cherry trees grow in abundance. As a result, Door County features over 2,500 acres of blossoming cherry orchards, and visitors flock each year to pick the harvest. If you are visiting during the summer, make sure you make this Door County tradition part of your itinerary at a destination such as Choice Orchards or the aforementioned Orchard Country Winery & Market.

For More Information

Door County Visitor Bureau
800-52-RELAX
www.doorcounty.com

Wisconsin Department of Tourism
800-432-8747
www.travelwisconsin.com

WISCONSIN DELLS

Slide into fun in the Midwest's watery playground

There's no shortage of things to do and places to experience in Wisconsin Dells. This Midwestern hamlet is a true destination with activities and entertainment for every family member. Wisconsin Dells is known as the Waterpark Capital of the World, thanks to an abundance of parks with slides, pools and lazy rivers.

Water recreation is a little wilder on the Upper and Lower Dells of the Wisconsin River. Jet-boat tours take guests zipping over the water, while kayaking and canoeing serve up stunning views of Wisconsin scenery at a more leisurely pace. The rock formations of the Upper Dells are a must-see attraction. Some of the cliffs here rise as high as 100 feet above the river.

Bring your rod and reel—and your fishing license—to the banks of the river and fish for Northern pike, walleye, bass, muskie and sturgeon. Boat launches are found at several points along the river at both Upper and Lower Dells. Lake Delton is a source of panfish year-round, and game fish from May to March. The wilds of Wisconsin Dells are home to deer and turkey, and hunting seasons for both are open to licensed non-residents and residents.

Enjoy a fine wine or well-crafted brew in Wisconsin Dells, where wineries and breweries in the region offer tasting opportunities with a side of casual dining and interaction with the local crowd. Spend an evening enjoying live entertainment at Crystal Grand Music Theater or the Rick Wilcox Magic Theater. Crystal Grand hosts concerts from acts of all musical styles as well as live stage performances. Shows at Rick Wilcox Magic Theater promise entertaining and mind-bending illusions for audiences, with a touch of comedic timing thrown in.

Fun for the Kids

Younger audiences will get a thrill at Mr. Marvel's Wondertorium, a live show where classic circus tricks and

WI

oddities on display will delight and intrigue everyone. Continue the thrill at MagiQuest, where kids play a four-story, live-action adventure game with magic wands, mystical creatures and a dragon.

Hands-on learning and fun are the main attraction at Tommy Bartlett Exploratory Interactive Science Center. Guests get in on the action with more than 175 interactive activities, including a Russian Space Station MIR module. The strongest will find themselves able to lift a car off the ground—with the help of a giant lever, of course.

Head to Timberland Playhouse at the Wilderness Resort and let the high-energy set explore the four-story playhouse, with 30,000 square feet of interactive fun for kids ages 1 to 12. Crawl spaces, slides and obstacle courses are highlights.

The scenic RiverWalk near downtown is a prime opportunity to enjoy views of the river and sandstone bluffs. Amble down the quarter-mile path and take a peek at the outdoor game tables, or stop to catch the sunset.

Just a short jaunt from the RiverWalk is H.H. Bennett Studio, the oldest operating business in the city that was opened by one of the 19th century's most lauded landscape photographers. Bennett's original workspace is preserved and open for tours, and visitors can see homemade cameras, darkroom equipment and glass-plate collections. The photography museum showcases many of Bennett's celebrated images.

Walk in Bennett's footsteps and visit Witches Gulch. This stretch of canyon was discovered by the photographer in 1871 during an excursion. The gulch is a moss-covered sandstone slot with a wooden boardwalk built for visitors to trek through—in some spots, the walls are close enough to touch.

Rocky Arbor High

The forested seclusion of Rocky Arbor State Park welcomes visitors to hike its one-mile nature trail or snowshoe through the woods in wintertime. Rocky outcrops of sandstone are hallmarks of this 244-acre park.

Riding in the snow at Red Ridge Ranch. Wisconsin Dells Visitor and Convention Bureau

Get up close and personal with alligators and other reptiles at Alligator Alley Adventures. This family-friendly destination teaches visitors about these scaly creatures and several other species of reptiles on display. The Alligator Alley staff even lets guests feed the toothy residents.

If you're lucky enough to be in Wisconsin Dells when the snow falls, Christmas Mountain Village is a popular place for skiers, snowboarders and snow tubers. If it's too warm for snow, head to Christmas Mountain with your clubs for a day on the fairways. Oaks Course is a championship layout that's nearly 7,000 yards from the back tees. The Pines Course welcomes golfers of all skill levels, and its unique layout is surrounded by towering pine trees.

Train lovers and rail enthusiasts should chug over to Riverside and Great Northern Railway for a living-museum experience that offers rides on 15-gauge live steam trains through three miles of canyons, woods and rock cuts alongside the Wisconsin River.

For More Information

Wisconsin Dells Visitor & Convention Bureau
800-223-3557
www.wisdells.com

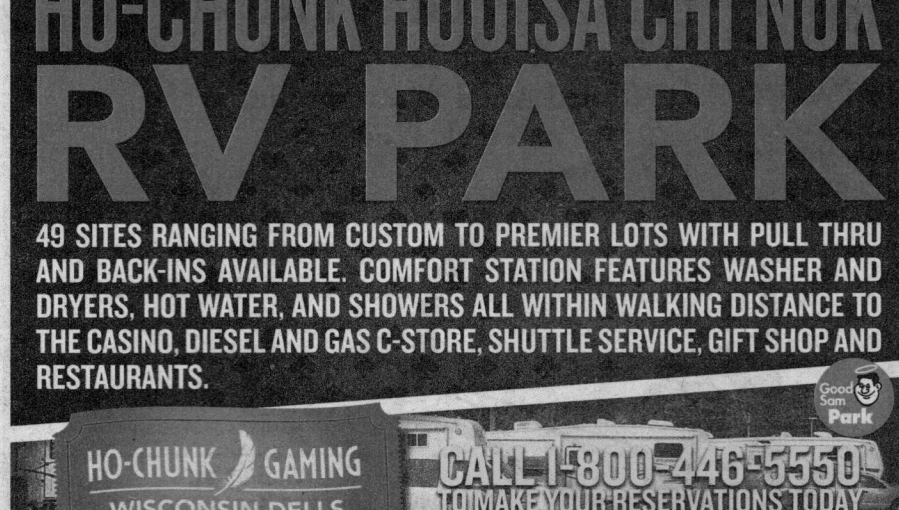

Wisconsin Department of Tourism
800-432-8747
www.travelwisconsin.com

Wisconsin

CONSULTANTS

Tim & Sheryl Heath

ALGOMA — C5 *Kewaunee*

AHNAPEE RIVER TRAILS CAMPGROUND **Ratings: 8/9/8** (Campground) 2015 rates: $32 to $36. May 1 to Oct 15. (920)487-5777 E 6053 W Wilson Rd, Algoma, WI 54201

BIG LAKE CAMPGROUND **Ratings: 6.5/7/7.5** (Campground) 2015 rates: $33 to $38. May 1 to Oct 15. (920)487-2726 2427 Lake St, Algoma, WI 54201

TIMBER TRAIL CAMPGROUND **Ratings: 7/8.5/9** (Campground) 2015 rates: $35 to $39. Apr 15 to Oct 15. (920)487-3707 N 8326 County Rd M, Algoma, WI 54201

ALMOND — D3 *Portage*

FOUNTAIN LAKE RV PARK **Ratings: 6.5/9★/8** (Campground) 2015 rates: $28. May 1 to Oct 1. (715)366-2954 8599 16th Rd, Almond, WI 54909

AMHERST — C3 *Portage*

WILD WEST CAMPGROUND & CORRAL **Ratings: 6/8.5/7.5** (Campground) 2015 rates: $30. Apr 15 to Oct 15. (715)824-5112 9495 Hwy 54, Amherst, WI 54406

AMHERST JUNCTION — C3 *Portage*

LAKE EMILY COUNTY PARK (Public) From town, W 1 mi on Old US-18 (L). 2015 rates: $16 to $18. May 1 to Oct 31. (715)824-3175

ANTIGO — C4 *Langlade*

ANTIGO LAKE RV CAMPGROUND (Public) From Jct of Hwy 45 & 2nd Ave, E 0.3 mi on 2nd Ave. to Hudson St, S 0.1 mi (L). Note: 45' RV length limit. 2015 rates: $20. May 1 to Oct 1. (715)623-3633

APPLETON — C4 *Winnebago*

Travel Services

TRUCK COUNTRY Full RV service. **SERVICES:** MH mechanical, engine/chassis repair, emergency rd svc, restrooms. **TOW:** RV. RV accessible. waiting room. Hours: M-F 6am to 1am, Sa & Sun 6am to 6pm.
(800)236-5271 Lat: 44.30418, Lon: -88.25791
2401 Progress Way, Kaukauna, WI 54130
www.truckcountry.com
See ad pages 488, 1311.

ARKDALE — D3 *Adams*

PINELAND CAMPING PARK **Ratings: 8/9/9** (Campground) 2015 rates: $37 to $55. Apr 15 to Dec 1. (608)564-7818 916 Hwy 13, Arkdale, WI 54613

ASHLAND — A2 *Ashland*

KREHER RV PARK (Public) From Jct of SR-13 & US 2, E 0.2 mi on US 2 to N Prentice Ave, N 0.2 mi, follow signs (R). Reservations for MONTH LONG ONLY. 2015 rates: $25 to $30. May 1 to Oct 1. (715)682-7059

PRENTICE PARK (Public) At West city limits on US-2. 2015 rates: $25 to $30. May 1 to Oct 30. (715)682-7061

AUGUSTA — C2 *Eau Claire*

COON FORK LAKE PARK (EAU CLAIRE COUNTY PARK) (Public) From town: Go 1 mi E on US 12, then 4 mi N on CR CF. 2015 rates: $15 to $25. (715)839-4738

AVOCA — E3 *Iowa*

AVOCA LAKESIDE CAMPGROUND (Public) From Jct of SR-133 & 6th St (in town), N 0.2 mi on 6th St to Clyde St, E 0.3 mi to 8th St, N 0.2 mi (R). Call or email for reservations. 2015 rates: $24. Apr 15 to Nov 30. (608)532-6188

Like Us on Facebook.

BAGLEY — E2 *Grant*

RIVER OF LAKES CAMPGROUND **Ratings: 4.5/6.5/5.5** (Campground) 2015 rates: $23 to $25. Apr 1 to Nov 1. (608)996-2275 132 Packer Dr, Bagley, WI 53801

WYALUSING/WISCONSIN RIDGE (State Pk) From town, N 10 mi on CR-X, through village of Wyalusing (L). Entrance fee required. Pit toilets. 2015 rates: $12 to $22. (888)947-2757

YOGI BEAR'S JELLYSTONE PARK CAMP-RESORT **Ratings: 8.5/9★/9** (Campground) 2015 rates: $24 to $51. May 1 to Oct 11. (608)996-2201 11354 Cnty Rd X, Bagley, WI 53801

BAILEYS HARBOR — C5 *Door*

BAILEYS GROVE CAMPGROUND
Ratings: 9/10★/10 (Campground) From Jct of Hwy 57 & CR-F: Go W 3/4 mi on CR-F (R). **FAC:** Gravel rds. (95 spaces). 66 Avail: 38 gravel, 28 grass, 51 pull-thrus (30 x 55), back-ins (30 x 60), 40 full hkups, 26 W, 26 E (30/50 amps), seasonal sites, WiFi, tent sites, dump, mobile sewer, laundry, groc, fire rings, firewood. **REC:** heated pool, playground. Pet restrict(B). Big rig sites, eco-friendly, 2015 rates: $36 to $41. Disc: military. May 1 to Oct 18.
(920)839-2559 Lat: 45.07145, Lon: -87.13546
2552 Cty Rd F, Baileys Harbor, WI 54202
campnowwi@yahoo.com
www.baileysgrovecampground.com
See ad pages 1307 (Spotlight Door County), 1306, 1304 (WI Map) & RV Trips of a Lifetime in Magazine Section.

BAILEYS WOODS CAMPGROUND **Ratings: 6.5/9★/8.5** (Campground) 2015 rates: $30 to $32. May 15 to Oct 15. (262)470-7091 2701 County Road Ee, Baileys Harbor, WI 54202

BEANTOWN CAMPGROUND **Ratings: 9/9★/8.5** (Campground) 2015 rates: $38. May 1 to Oct 31. (920)839-1439 8398 Cty Rd F, Baileys Harbor, WI 54202

BANCROFT — C3 *Portage*

VISTA ROYALLE CAMPGROUND **Ratings: 8/9.5★/9.5** (Campground) 2015 rates: $28.49 to $46.42. Apr 20 to Oct 20. (715)335-6860 8025 Isherwood Rd, Bancroft, WI 54921

BARABOO — D3 *Sauk*

DEVIL'S LAKE (State Pk) From Jct of I-90/94 & Hwy 33, W 13 mi on Hwy 33 to Hwy 123, S 4 mi (E). Entrance fee required. Pit toilets. 2015 rates: $12 to $17. (608)356-8301

Got a different point of view? We want to know. Rate the campgrounds you visit using the rating guidelines located in front of this Guide, then compare your ratings to ours.

FOX HILL RV PARK & CAMPGROUND
Ratings: 8.5/9.5★/10 (Campground) From Jct of I-90/94 & SR-12 (Exit 92): Take SR-12 E 2-1/2 mi to N Reedsburg Rd (Exit 214), then take 3rd exit on the roundabout to N Reedsburg Rd, then go E 1-1/2 mi (R). **FAC:** Paved/gravel rds. (108 spaces). 83 Avail: 75 gravel, 8 grass, 26 pull-thrus (35 x 80), back-ins (35 x 65), 34 full hkups, 49 W, 49 E (30/50 amps), seasonal sites, WiFi, tent sites, rentals, dump, mobile sewer, laundry, groc, LP bottles, fire rings, firewood. **REC:** heated pool, golf, playground. Pets OK. Partial handicap access. Big rig sites, 30 day max stay, eco-friendly, 2015 rates: $39 to $52. Disc: AAA, military. Apr 24 to Oct 12. ATM. AAA Approved
(608)356-5890 Lat: 43.52772, Lon: -89.75431
E 11371 N Reedsburg Rd, Baraboo, WI 53913
foxhill@foxhillrvpark.com
www.foxhillrvpark.com
See ad pages 1310 (Spotlight Wisconsin Dells), 1306.

HO-CHUNK HOUISA CHI' NUK RV PARK
Ratings: 8.5/10★/9.5 (RV Park) From I-90/94 (Exit 92): Go S 2-1/2 mi on US Hwy 12 to Jct Hwy 12 & N Reedsbug Rd (Exit 214), then E 3/4 mi on N Reedsburg Rd (R). **FAC:** Paved rds. 49 Avail: 6 paved, 43 gravel, 33 pull-thrus (41 x 73), back-ins (41 x 73), 38 full hkups, 11 E (30/50 amps), WiFi Hotspot, rentals, dump, laundry, groc, LP bottles, fire rings, firewood, restaurant. **REC:** heated pool, whirlpool, playground, rec open to public. Pets OK. Partial handicap access, no tents. Big rig sites, 2015 rates: $26 to $54. ATM.
(800)746-2486 Lat: 43.5280151, Lon: -89.7768107
S3214 County Rd Bd, Baraboo, WI 53913
hchotel@ho-chunk.com
www.ho-chunkgaming.com/wisconsindells/
See ad pages 1310 (Spotlight Wisconsin Dells), 1306.

RED OAK CAMPGROUND **Ratings: 5.5/7.5/7.5** (Campground) 2015 rates: $20 to $30. May 1 to Oct 1. (608)356-7304 s2350 Timothy Lane, Baraboo, WI 53913

WHEELER'S CAMPGROUND **Ratings: 5.5/8.5★/8.5** (Campground) 2015 rates: $41 to $47. Apr 15 to Oct 15. (608)356-4877 e11329 Hwy 159, Baraboo, WI 53913

Things to See and Do

HO-CHUNK GAMING WISCONSIN DELLS Full service casino with table games, slots, bingo, and a steakhouse, buffet, cafe', bar & grille. Partial handicap access. RV accessible. Restrooms, food. Hours: 24 hours. ATM.
(800)746-2486 Lat: 43.523897, Lon: -89.777871
S3214 County Rd Bd, Baraboo, WI 53913
www.ho-chunkgaming.com/wisconsindells/
See ad page 1310 (Spotlight Wisconsin Dells).

BARRON — B1 *Barron*

→ BARRON MOTEL & RV CAMPGROUND **Ratings: 5/6.5/7.5** (Campground) 2015 rates: $32 to $41. May 1 to Oct 1. (715)637-3154 1521 E Division Ave, Hwy 8, Barron, WI 54812

BAYFIELD — A2 *Bayfield*

↗ APOSTLE ISLANDS AREA CAMPGROUND **Ratings: 4.5/6.5/7** (Campground) 2015 rates: $36 to $45. May 20 to Oct 9. (715)779-5524 85150 Trailer Court Rd, Bayfield, WI 54814

APOSTLE ISLANDS NATIONAL LAKESHORE (PRESQUE ISLE-STOCKTON) (Natl Pk) Access by excursion boat (Jul & Aug) or private boat. 16 mi NE of Bayfield on Stockton Island. Pit toilets. (715)779-3397

→ BIG BAY (State Pk) Take ferry from Bayfield to Madeline Island, follow signs. 2015 rates: $12 to $17. (715)747-6425

↑ LEGENDARY WATERS CAMPGROUND & MARINA **Ratings: 7/9.5★/8.5** (Campground) 2015 rates: $35. May 1 to Oct 15. (800)226-8478 37600 Onigamiing Dr., Bayfield, WI 54814

BEAVER DAM — D4 *Dodge*

DERGE (Public) From Beaver Dam, NW 4 mi on Hwy G to Hwy CP, NE 1 mi (L). 2015 rates: $20. (920)887-0365

BELGIUM — D5 *Ozaukee*

→ HARRINGTON BEACH (State Pk) From jct I-43 (exit 107) & CR D: Go 2-1/4 mi E on CR D, then 3/4 mi S on Sauk Trail Rd. 2015 rates: $12 to $14. May 7 to Oct 25. (262)285-3015

BIRCHWOOD — B2 *Sawyer, Barron*

↑ DOOLITTLE VILLAGE PARK (Public) From Jct of US-53 & CR-V, E 10 mi on CR-V to Hwy 48, NE 7 mi (Birchwood Village) to Main St, left 1 mi to Hinman Dr, right 0.5 mi (R). 2015 rates: $20. May 1 to Sep 30. (715)354-3300

BLACK RIVER FALLS — C2 *Jackson*

↘ BLACK RIVER/CASTLE MOUND (State Pk) From town, SE 1 mi on US-12 (R). Entrance fee required. 2015 rates: $9 to $17. (715)284-4103

↗ BLACK RIVER/PIGEON CREEK CAMPGROUND (State Pk) From Jct of I-94 (Exit 128) & CR-O, E 0.25 mi on CR-O to N Settlement Rd, NE 2 mi (R). Entrance fee required. Boating with no power available. Pit toilets. 2015 rates: $12 to $14. (715)284-4103

→ LOST FALLS CAMPGROUND **Ratings: 5.5/8.5★/7.5** (Campground) 2015 rates: $35 to $40. May 15 to Oct 1. (800)329-3911 n2974 E Sunnyvale Rd, Black River Falls, WI 54615

→ PARKLAND VILLAGE CAMPGROUND **Ratings: 7/9.5★/7.5** (Campground) 2015 rates: $40 to $45. Apr 15 to Nov 15. (715)284-9700 n6150 Julianna Rd 409, Black River Falls, WI 54615

Things to See and Do

→ **HO-CHUNK GAMING BLACK RIVER FALLS** Full service casino with slots, table games, bingo, and a buffet and cafe'. Partial handicap access. RV accessible. Restrooms, food. Hours: 24 hours. ATM.
(800)657-4621 Lat: 44.305141, Lon: -90.829544
w9010 Hwy 54 E, Black River Falls, WI 54615
www.ho-chunkgaming.com/blackriverfalls/
See ad page 1310 (Spotlight Wisconsin Dells).

BLAIR — C2 *Trempealeau*

↑ RIVERSIDE MEMORIAL PARK (Public) From town, Hwy 95 to Park Rd, S 0.25 mi (L). 2015 rates: $15 to $20. Apr 15 to Sep 1. (608)989-2517

Replace clogged air filters. A clogged air filter can cut a vehicle's fuel efficiency by 10 percent.

BLANCHARDVILLE — E3 *Green*

↗ YELLOWSTONE LAKE (State Pk) From town, SW 9 mi on CR-F, follow signs (L). Entrance fee required. Pit toilets. 2015 rates: $12 to $14. (608)523-4427

BLUE MOUNDS — E3 *Dane*

↑ BLUE MOUND (State Pk) From Jct of US-18/151 & Blue Mound Rd, NW 1 mi on Blue Mound Rd, follow signs (R) Entrance fee required. 2015 rates: $12 to $14. (608)437-5711

↗ BRIGHAM (Public) From Jct of US-18 & CR-F, NE 2 mi on CR-F (R). Pit toilets. 2015 rates: $15 to $20. (608)242-4576

BLUE RIVER — E2 *Grant*

← EAGLE CAVE RESORT **Ratings: 5.5/8.5★/7** (Campground) 2015 rates: $20. May 22 to Sep 7. (608)537-2988 16320 Cavern Lane, Blue River, WI 53518

BOULDER JUNCTION — B3 *Vilas*

↗ **CAMP HOLIDAY Ratings: 8.5/9.5★/9** (Campground) From Woodruff, N 12 mi on Hwy 51 to CR-H, then E 3 mi to Rudolph Lake Rd, then E 0.1 mi (R). **FAC:** Paved/gravel rds. (227 spaces). 102 Avail: 56 gravel, 46 grass, 36 pull-thrus (45 x 70), back-ins (40 x 55), some side by side hkups, 57 full hkups, 45 W, 45 E (30/50 amps), seasonal sites, cable, WiFi, tent sites, dump, mobile sewer, laundry, groc, LP bottles, fire rings, firewood. **REC:** Lake Rudolph: swim, fishing, playground. Pets OK. Partial handicap access. Big rig sites, eco-friendly, 2015 rates: $35 to $45. May 1 to Nov 1.
(715)385-2264 Lat: 46.09470, Lon: -89.71725
11475 Rudolph Lake Lane, PO Box 67, Boulder Junction, WI 54512
campholiday@centurytel.net
www.camp-holiday.com

↗ NO HIGHLAND AMERICAN LEGION SF/BIG LAKE (State Pk) From the Jct of US-51 & Hwy W, N 2.5 mi on Hwy W to Hwy K, E 4.5 mi to Hwy P, N 1.5 mi (R). Entrance fee required. Pit toilets. 2015 rates: $12 to $14. (715)385-3352

↗ NO HIGHLAND AMERICAN LEGION SF/MUSKY LAKE (State Pk) From Woodruff, N 6 mi on US-51 to Hwy M, NE 3 mi to Hwy N, E 3 mi, follow SF sign (L). Entrance fee required. 2015 rates: $9 to $14. (715)385-2704

↑ NO HIGHLAND AMERICAN LEGION SF/SOUTH TROUT LAKE CAMPGROUND (State Pk) From Jct of US-51 & Hwy M, N 4 mi on Hwy M to Lake Shore Dr, W 0.25 mi (L). Entrance fee required. Pit toilets. 2015 rates: $12 to $14. May 19 to Sep 2. (715)385-2727

↗ NO HIGHLAND AMERICAN LEGION SF/UPPER GRESHAM LAKE (State Pk) From S end of town, S 4 mi on CR-M to N Creek Rd, W 5 mi (R). Entrance fee required. Pit toilets. 2015 rates: $12. May 1 to Oct 14. (715)385-2727

BOWLER — C4 *Shawano*

→ MOHICAN RV PARK **Ratings: 6/NA/8.5** (RV Park) 2015 rates: $25 to $35. (800)775-CASH(2274) W 12180 Cty Rd A, Bowler, WI 54416

BRISTOL — E4 *Kenosha*

↖ HAPPY ACRES KAMPGROUND **Ratings: 7.5/8/9** (Campground) 2015 rates: $36.95 to $47.95. May 1 to Oct 1. (262)857-7373 22230 45th St, Bristol, WI 53104

BRODHEAD — E3 *Green*

← CRAZY HORSE CAMPGROUND **Ratings: 7/10★/9** (Campground) 2015 rates: $41 to $51. May 1 to Oct 31. (608)897-2207 n3201 Crazy Horse Ln, Brodhead, WI 53520

BRUCE — B2 *Rusk*

↖ AUDIE LAKE PARK (Public) From town, N 1 mi on SR-40 to CR-0, NW 7 mi to Fire Lane Rd, NW 3.5 mi to Perch Lake Rd, W 1 mi (L). Pit toilets. 2015 rates: $18 to $23. May 1 to Dec 1. (715)532-2113

BRULE — A2 *Douglas*

BRULE RIVER/BOIS BRULE (State Pk) From jct Hwy 27 & US 2: Go 1 mi W on US 2, then 1/2 mi W & 1 mi S on Ranger Rd. Pit toilets. 2015 rates: $7 to $9. (715)372-5678

The RVers' Guide to NASCAR helps RV travelers get the most out of North America's most thrilling sporting event. Turn to the front of the Guide and we'll give you the inside track on how to get high-speed thrills at major NASCAR venues.

BRUSSELS — C5 *Door*

↗ **QUIETWOODS SOUTH CAMPING RESORT**
Ratings: 8.5/10★/10 (Campground) From Jct of Hwy 57 & CR-C: Go N 2-1/2 mi on CR-C to CR-K, then E 1-1/2 mi to Lovers Ln, then N 1/3 mi (L). **FAC:** Gravel rds. (217 spaces). 122 Avail: 76 gravel, 46 grass, 51 pull-thrus (40 x 100), back-ins (40 x 50), 6 full hkups, 116 W, 116 E (30/50 amps), seasonal sites, WiFi, tent sites, rentals, dump, mobile sewer, laundry, groc, fire rings, firewood, restaurant. **REC:** heated pool, wading pool, pond, fishing, playground, rec open to public. Pets OK. Partial handicap access. Big rig sites, eco-friendly, 2015 rates: $40 to $55. Apr 17 to Oct 25. ATM.
(920)825-7065 Lat: 44.77582, Lon: -87.59158
9245 Lovers Lane, Brussels, WI 54204
qws@centurytel.net
www.quietwoodscamping.com
See ad pages 1308 (Spotlight Door County), 1306 & RV Trips of a Lifetime in Magazine Section.

BURLINGTON — E4 *Walworth*

↗ RICHARD BONG SRA/SUNRISE - SUNSET (State Pk) From Jct of Hwys 75 & 142, W 1 mi on Hwy 142 (L). Entrance fee required. 2015 rates: $12 to $14. (262)878-5600

CALEDONIA — E5 *Racine*

↑ **YOGI BEAR'S JELLYSTONE PARK CAMP-RESORT**
Ratings: 8.5/10★/10 (Campground) From Jct of I-94 & Seven Mile Rd (exit 326), E 2 mi on Seven Mile Rd to Hwy 38, N 0.4 mi (R) Rate does not include amenity fee. **FAC:** Paved/gravel rds. (223 spaces). 196 Avail: 96 gravel, 100 grass, 27 pull-thrus (35 x 65), back-ins (35 x 45), 95 full hkups, 101 W, 101 E (30/50 amps), seasonal sites, WiFi, tent sites, rentals, dump, laundry, groc, LP bottles, fire rings, firewood, controlled access. **REC:** heated pool $, wading pool, pond, fishing, playground, rec open to public. Pets OK. Partial handicap access. Big rig sites, eco-friendly, 2015 rates: $23 to $66. May 1 to Oct 15. ATM.
(262)835-2565 Lat: 42.83548, Lon: -87.91214
8425 State Rd 38, Caledonia, WI 53108
reservations@jellystone-caledonia.com
www.jellystone-caledonia.com
See ad this page.

CAMERON — B1 *Barron*

↓ **BUCK 'N BEAM'S CAMPGROUND 'N BAR Ratings: 6/9.5★/9** (Campground) From Jct Hwy 53 & Hwy 8: Go E 1/2 mi on Hwy 8, then go S 1/4 mi on 20th St (L). **FAC:** Gravel rds. (20 spaces). Avail: 12 gravel, back-ins (35 x 70), 12 W, 12 E (30/50 amps), seasonal sites, WiFi Hotspot, tent sites, showers $, dump, mobile sewer, groc, fire rings, firewood, restaurant. **REC:** playground. Pets OK. Partial handicap access. Eco-friendly, 2015 rates: $30. May 1 to Nov 1. ATM.
(715)458-2990 Lat: 45.391921, Lon: -91.745748
1277 20th St, Cameron, WI 54822
bucknbeams@chibardun.net
www.bucknbeams.com

VETERANS MEMORIAL PARK (Public) Go 1-1/2 mi S on CR-'SS', then 1 mi E on 12-1/2 Ave. Pit toilets. 2015 rates: $10 to $15. May 1 to Oct 1. (715)458-4125

CAMP DOUGLAS — D3 *Juneau*

↗ MILL BLUFF (State Pk) From jct I-90 (exit 55) & US 12/16: Go 3 mi E on US 12/16. Pit toilets. 2015 rates: $12 to $14. (608)337-4775

CAMPBELLSPORT — D4 *Fond du Lac*

↗ BENSON'S CENTURY CAMPING RESORT **Ratings: 6/6.5/8** (Campground) 2015 rates: $30. May 15 to Oct 15. (920)533-8597 n3845 Hwy 67, Campbellsport, WI 53010

↗ KETTLE MORAINE/LONG LAKE CAMPGROUND (State Pk) From Jct of US-45 & Hwy 67, E 6 mi on Hwy 67 to Dundee, N 2.5 mi to Kettle Moraine Dr, follow signs (L). Entrance fee required. 2015 rates: $12 to $14. (920)533-8612

CASCADE — D4 *Sheboygan*

↗ HOEFT'S RESORT & CAMPGROUND **Ratings: 6.5/8★/7.5** (Campground) 2015 rates: $32. May 1 to Oct 15. (262)626-2221 w9070 Crooked Lake Dr, Cascade, WI 53011

CASSVILLE — E2 *Grant*

→ BIG H CAMPGROUND **Ratings: 3/5.5/7** (Campground) 2015 rates: $21. May 1 to Oct 31. (608)725-5921 4929 Cty Rd N, Cassville, WI 53806

CASSVILLE (CONT)

NELSON DEWEY (State Pk) From Jct of Hwy 133 & Cnty Trunk VV, W 1 mi on Cnty Trunk VV (R). Entrance fee required. Pit toilets. 2015 rates: $12 to $14. Apr 1 to Nov 30. (608)725-5374

WHITETAIL BLUFF CAMP & RESORT **Ratings: 7.5/9/7.5** (RV Park) 2015 rates: $20 to $38. (608)725-5577 8973 Irish Ridge Rd, Cassville, WI 53806

CECIL — C4 *Shawano*

CECIL LAKEVIEW PARK (Public) In town on Hwy 22. May 15 to Sep 1. (715)745-4428

CEDAR — A2 *Iron*

FRONTIER RV PARK & CAMPGROUND **Ratings: 5.5/8/7.5** (RV Park) 2015 rates: $27 to $34. May 15 to Oct 15. (715)893-2461 11296 W US Hwy 2, Saxon, WI 54559

CHETEK — B2 *Barron*

CHETEK RIVER CAMPGROUND **Ratings: 8/9★/8** (Campground) 2015 rates: $33 to $35. May 1 to Sep 30. (715)924-2440 590 24th St, Chetek, WI 54728

NORTHERN EXPOSURE RESORT & CAMPGROUND **Ratings: 6/7.5/6** (Campground) 2015 rates: $25 to $30. May 1 to Oct 1. (800)731-2887 1075 Bronstad Beach Rd, Chetek, WI 54822

SIX LAKES RESORT & RV PARK **Ratings: 7/8.5★/7.5** (Campground) 2015 rates: $32 to $39. Apr 25 to Oct 1. (715)924-3680 2535 8-7/8 Ave, Chetek, WI 54728

SOUTHWORTH MEMORIAL PARK (Public) From town: Go 1-1/2 mi S on CR SS, then 1 mi E on 6th Ave, then 3/4 mi N on 26-1/2 St. Pit toilets. 2015 rates: $15 to $23. May 1 to Oct 1. (715)537-6295

CHIPPEWA FALLS — C2 *Chippewa*

COUNTRY VILLA MOTEL & COUNTRY CAMPING **Ratings: 6.5/8.5★/8** (Campground) 2015 rates: $28 to $34. May 1 to Nov 1. (715)288-6376 10765 County Hwy Q, Chippewa Falls, WI 54729

LAKE WISSOTA (State Pk) From Jct of US-124 & Hwy 29, N 3 mi on US-124 to Cnty Rd S, NE 3 mi to Cnty Rd O, E 2 mi (R). Entrance fee required. Pit toilets. 2015 rates: $12 to $14. (715)382-4574

O'NEIL CREEK CAMPGROUND
Ratings: 8/10★/9.5 (Campground) N-bnd: From Jct of US-53 & CR-S (exit 99), E 2 mi on CR-S to Hwy 124, N 2 mi to CR-B, E 0.9 mi (L); or S-bnd: From Jct of US-53 & CR-B (exit 102), E 0.1 mi on CR-B, N 3.8 on CR-B (L). **FAC:** Paved rds. (355 spaces). 90 Avail: 10 paved, 80 grass, 10 pull-thrus (30 x 80), back-ins (30 x 60), 10 full hkups, 80 W, 80 E (30/50 amps), seasonal sites, WiFi Hotspot, tent sites, rentals, dump, mobile sewer, laundry, groc, LP bottles, fire rings, firewood. **REC:** O'Neil Creek: swim, fishing, playground, rec open to public. Pet restrict(B). Partial handicap access. Big rig sites, eco-friendly, 2015 rates: $34 to $49. Apr 15 to Oct 15. ATM.
(715)723-6581 Lat: 44.99709, Lon: -91.36694
14912 105th Ave, Chippewa Falls, WI 54729
office@oneilcreek.com
www.oneilcreek.com
See ad pages 653, 1306.

PINE HARBOR CAMPGROUND **Ratings: 6/7/9** (Campground) 2015 rates: $29. May 1 to Oct 15. (715)723-9865 7181 185th St, Chippewa Falls, WI 54729

CLEAR LAKE — C1 *Polk*

CLEAR LAKE PARK (Public) From Jct of SR-63 & 7th St., N 0.5 mi on park access rd (E). 2015 rates: $25. May 1 to Oct 31. (715)263-2157

COLOMA — D3 *Waushara*

COLOMA CAMPERLAND **Ratings: 8.5/9.5★/8** (Campground) 2015 rates: $25 to $31. (715)228-3600 n1130 5th Rd, Coloma, WI 54930

CONOVER — B3 *Vilas*

BUCKATABON LODGE & LIGHTHOUSE INN **Ratings: 5.5/7/6** (Campground) 2015 rates: $28. May 1 to Nov 1. (715)479-4660 5630 Rush Rd, Conover, WI 54519

NO HIGHLAND AMERICAN LEGION SF/STAR LAKE (State Pk) From Woodruff, N 5 mi on US-51 to Hwy M, N 9 mi to Hwy K, E 12 mi to Hwy N, S 1 mi (R). Entrance fee required. Pit toilets. 2015 rates: $12 to $14. May 19 to Sep 2. (715)385-3352

CORNELL — C2 *Chippewa*

BRUNET ISLAND (State Pk) From Jct of Hwy 64 & Park Rd, N 1 mi on Park Rd (E). Entrance fee required. 2015 rates: $12 to $14. (715)239-6888

CRANDON — B4 *Forest*

VETERANS MEMORIAL PARK (Public) From town, S 3 mi on East Shore Dr (R). 2015 rates: $19. May 1 to Sep 15. (715)478-2040

CRIVITZ — C4 *Marinette*

PESHTIGO RIVER CAMPGROUND **Ratings: 7.5/9★/8** (Campground) 2015 rates: $32 to $34. May 1 to Oct 15. (715)854-2986 W 7948 Airport Rd, Crivitz, WI 54114

DANBURY — B1 *Burnett*

EAGLES LANDING CAMPGROUND **Ratings: 8/7/7.5** (Campground) 2015 rates: $20. May 1 to Oct 15. (715)656-4402 30158 Highway 35, Danbury, WI 54830

DE FOREST — D3 *Dane*

MADISON KOA
Ratings: 9/10★/9.5 (Campground) From Jct of I-90/94 & CR-V (exit 126), E 0.25 mi on CR-V (R). **FAC:** Gravel rds. 81 gravel, 81 pull-thrus (32 x 80), 81 full hkups (30/50 amps), WiFi, tent sites, rentals, dump, laundry, groc, LP gas, fire rings, firewood. **REC:** heated pool, playground. Pets OK. Big rig sites, eco-friendly, 2015 rates: $35 to $ 50. Disc: military. Apr 1 to Oct 31.
(800)562-5784 Lat: 43.24986, Lon: -89.37015
4859 County Rd V, De Forest, WI 53532
madison@koa.com
www.koa.com
See ad page 1316.

TOKEN CREEK PARK (Public) From Jct of I-90 & SR-51, N 0.5 mi on SR-51 (R). 2015 rates: $18 to $27. Apr 27 to Oct 12. (608)242-4576

Travel Services

CAMPING WORLD OF DEFOREST/MADISON
As the nation's largest retailer of RV supplies, accessories, services and new and used RVs, Camping World is committed to making your total RV experience better. RV Accessories: (888)833-4430. **SERVICES:** Tire, RV appliance, MH mechanical, staffed RV wash, restrooms, RV Sales. RV supplies, LP, dump, emergency parking, RV accessible. waiting room. Hours: 8am to 5pm.
(888)722-5114 Lat: 43.184853, Lon: -89.325209
6195 Metro Drive, De Forest, WI 53532
www.campingworld.com

DE PERE — C4 *Brown*

APPLE CREEK CAMPGROUND **Ratings: 8.5/8/8** (Campground) 2015 rates: $35 to $37. Apr 15 to Oct 15. (920)532-4386 3831 Cty Rd U, De Pere, WI 54115

DE SOTO — D2 *Vernon*

BLACKHAWK PARK (COE-MISSISSIPPI RIVER POOL #9) (Public Corps) From jct Hwy 82 & Hwy 35: Go 3 mi N on Hwy 35. 2015 rates: $18 to $24. May 31 to Oct 30. (608)648-3314

DELAFIELD — E4 *Dane, Waukesha*

NAGA-WAUKEE PARK (Public) From jct I-94 & Hwy-83: Go 1/2 mi N on Hwy-83, then 1/2 mi W on Mariner Dr. Pit toilets. Apr 1 to Nov 2. (262)548-7801

DODGEVILLE — E3 *Iowa*

GOVERNOR DODGE (State Pk) From town, N 3 mi on State Hwy 23 (R). Entrance fee required. Pit toilets. 2015 rates: $12 to $17. (608)935-2315

TOM'S CAMPGROUND **Ratings: 5.5/8.5★/8** (Campground) 2015 rates: $26 to $35. Apr 1 to Oct 31. (608)935-5446 2626 Spring Rd, Dodgeville, WI 53533

DOOR COUNTY — C5 *Door*

A SPOTLIGHT Introducing the Door County attractions appearing at the front of state section.

DORCHESTER — C3 *Clark*

DORCHESTER REC PARK CORP (Public) From Jct of SR-29 & SR-13, N 4 mi on SR-13 to CR-A, W 0.5 mi (L). 2015 rates: $10. May 1 to Nov 11. (715)654-5098

DYCKESVILLE — C5 *Kewaunee*

BAY SHORE (Public) From Jct of I-43 & Hwy 57, NE 12 mi on Hwy 57 (L). 2015 rates: $15 to $25. May 15 to Oct 15. (920)448-4466

EAGLE — E4 *Waukesha*

KETTLE MORAINE/OTTAWA LAKE REC AREA (State Pk) From Jct of Hwys 59 & 67, N 6 mi on Hwy 67 to Hwy ZZ, W 0.1 mi (R). Entrance fee required. Pit toilets. 2015 rates: $12 to $14. (262)594-6220

EAGLE RIVER — B3 *Vilas*

CHAIN O' LAKES CAMPGROUND Ratings: 7.5/8/7 (Membership Pk) From Jct of US-45/32 & Hwy 70: Go E 3-3/4 mi on Hwy 70 to E Cranberry Lake Rd, then S 1 mi to East Bass Lk Rd, then E 1/2 mi to Campground Rd (R). **FAC:** Dirt rds. (197 spaces). Avail: 75 gravel, 50 pull-thrus (40 x 60), back-ins (35 x 60), 75 W, 75 E (20/30 amps), seasonal sites, WiFi Hotspot, tent sites, rentals, dump, mobile sewer, laundry, groc, LP gas, fire rings, firewood. **REC:** heated pool, Cranberry Lake: fishing, shuffleboard, playground. Pets OK. Partial handicap access. Eco-friendly, 2015 rates: $33. Disc: military. May 1 to Oct 7.
(715)479-6708 Lat: 45.91198, Lon: -89.15217
3165 Campground Rd, Eagle River, WI 54521
camp@colcamp.com
www.colcamp.com

HI-PINES EAGLE RIVER CAMPGROUND **Ratings: 7/10★/9** (RV Park) 2015 rates: $31 to $43. May 1 to Oct 15. (715)479-9124 1919 Hwy 45 N, Eagle River, WI 54521

ROHR'S WILDERNESS TOURS **Ratings: 5/7.5/7** (Campground) 2015 rates: $20 to $28. (715)547-3639 5230 Razorback Rd, Conover, WI 54519

EGG HARBOR — C5 *Door*

EGG HARBOR CAMPGROUND & RV RESORT **Ratings: 8.5/9.5★/10** (Campground) 2015 rates: $40 to $46. May 15 to Oct 23. (920)868-3278 8164 State Hwy 42, Egg Harbor, WI 54209

FRONTIER WILDERNESS CAMPGROUND **Ratings: 8/10★/9.5** (Campground) 2015 rates: $38. May 1 to Oct 31. (920)868-3349 4375 Hillside Rd, Egg Harbor, WI 54209

MONUMENT POINT CAMPING **Ratings: 4/9★/7** (Campground) 2015 rates: $30. May 1 to Oct 20. (920)743-9411 5718 Monument Point Rd, Sturgeon Bay, WI 54235

RUSTIC TIMBERS DOOR COUNTY CAMPING
Ratings: 8/9.5★/10 (Campground) From Jct of Cnty Rds G, E & Hwy 42, S 3 mi on Hwy 42 to Sunnypoint Rd, E 0.25 mi to Court Rd, E 0.5 mi (L). **FAC:** Gravel rds. (226 spaces). Avail: 127 gravel, 18 pull-thrus (30 x 90), back-ins (30 x 50), 28 full hkups, 99 W, 99 E (30/50 amps), seasonal sites, WiFi Hotspot, tent sites, rentals, dump, mobile sewer, laundry, groc, LP gas, fire rings, firewood, controlled access. **REC:** heated pool, playground. Pets OK. Partial handicap access. Big rig sites, eco-friendly, 2015 rates: $45 to $50. May 1 to Oct 19. ATM.
(920)868-3151 Lat: 45.00252, Lon: -87.29505
4906 Court Rd, Egg Harbor, WI 54209
rustictimbersdcc@gmail.com
www.rustictimbersdoorcountycamping.com
See ad pages 1307 (Spotlight Door County), 1306 & RV Trips of a Lifetime in Magazine Section.

ELLISON BAY — B5 *Door*

HY-LAND COURT RV PARK **Ratings: 7/8.5★/9.5** (Campground) 2015 rates: $35 to $39. May 1 to Nov 1. (920)854-4850 11503 Hwy 42, Ellison Bay, WI 54210

WAGON TRAIL CAMPGROUND **Ratings: 7/10★/10** (Campground) 2015 rates: $38 to $55.50. May 8 to Oct 19. (920)854-4818 1190 County Road Zz, Ellison Bay, WI 54210

FENCE — B4 *Florence*

WEST BASS LAKE (Public) From Pembine, W 24 mi on Rte 8 to Hwy 101, N 7 mi to Cnty Trunk Hwy C, E 5 mi to Fire Lane Rd, N 1 mi (L). Pit toilets. 2015 rates: $8. (888)889-0049

FISH CREEK — C5 *Door*

FISH CREEK CAMPGROUND
Ratings: 7/8.5/9 (Campground) From Jct of Hwy 42 & CR-F (Fish Creek): Go E 1/3 mi on CR-F (R). **FAC:** Gravel rds. (70 spaces). 43 Avail: 22 gravel, 21 grass, 23 pull-thrus (35 x 58), back-ins (40 x 54), 43 W, 43 E (30 amps), seasonal sites, WiFi, tent sites, dump, mobile sewer, laundry, fire rings, firewood. **REC:** playground. Pets OK. Eco-friendly, 2015 rates: $30 to $32. May 6 to Oct 19.
(920)495-CAMP Lat: 45.12155, Lon: -87.21583
3709 Cty Rd F, Fish Creek, WI 54212
info@fishcreekcampground.com
www.fishcreekcampground.com
See ad page 1308 (Spotlight Door County).

PENINSULA (State Pk) From town, W 100' on Hwy 42. Entrance fee required. Pit toilets. 2015 rates: $12 to $17. (920)868-3258

WI

FLORENCE — B4 *Florence*

KEYES LAKE CAMPGROUND **Ratings: 5/7.5/6.5** (RV Park) 2015 rates: $21.50. (715)528-4907 n4918 Hwy 101, Florence, WI 54121

FOND DU LAC — D4 *Byron*

BREEZY HILL CAMPGROUND **Ratings: 8.5/10★/9.5** (Campground) 2015 rates: $40 to $59. Apr 15 to Oct 15. (920)477-2300 n4177 Cearns Lane, Fond du Lac, WI 54937

WESTWARD HO RV RESORT & CAMPGROUND

Ratings: 9/10★/10 (Campground) From Jct US-41 & Hwy 23: Go 16 mi E on Hwy 23, then 3 mi S on CR-G, then 1/2 mi E on CR-T & follow signs.

THE PERFECT FAMILY VACATION

Explore 103 acres of scenic grounds with spacious tent and RV sites and cozy vacation rentals. Resort amenities include a petting zoo, heated pools, miniature golf, volleyball, basketball, RC car track, crafts and much more!

FAC: Paved rds. (311 spaces). Avail: 94 gravel, 3 pull-thrus (45 x 100), back-ins (45 x 60), 11 full hkups, 83 W, 83 E (30/50 amps), seasonal sites, WiFi $, tent sites, rentals, dump, laundry, groc, LP bottles, fire rings, firewood. **REC:** heated pool, wading pool, shuffleboard, playground. Pets OK. Partial handicap access. Big rig sites, eco-friendly, 2015 rates: $32 to $60. Disc: AAA, military. Apr 15 to Oct 15. ATM. AAA Approved

(888)712-9617 Lat: 43.73522, Lon: -88.16576
N5456 Division Rd, Glenbeulah, WI 53023
westwardho@suncommunities.com
www.westwardhocampresort.com
See ad pages 1463 (Welcome Section), 1305 (Welcome Section), 1306 & Family Camping in Magazine Section.

FORT ATKINSON — E4 *Jefferson*

JELLYSTONE PARK OF FORT ATKINSON **Ratings: 8.5/8.5★/8.5** (Membership Pk) 2015 rates: $45 to $52. May 1 to Oct 15. (877)BEAR-FUN n551 Wishing a Well Ln, Fort Atkinson, WI 53538

FOUNTAIN CITY — D1 *Buffalo*

MERRICK (State Pk) From town, N 2 mi on Hwy 35 (L). Entrance fee required. Pit toilets. 2015 rates: $12 to $14. (608)687-4936

FREMONT — D4 *Waupaca*

BLUE TOP RESORT & CAMPGROUND **Ratings: 5/8.5★/10** (Campground) 2015 rates: $22 to $32. Apr 15 to Oct 31. (920)446-3343 1460 Wolf River Dr, Fremont, WI 54940

YOGI BEAR'S JELLYSTONE PARK CAMP-RESORT **Ratings: 8/8.5★/8.5** (Campground) 2015 rates: $35 to $88. Apr 15 to Oct 15. (800)258-3315 e6506 Hwy 110, Fremont, WI 54940

Visit CampingWorld.com where you can get deals on over 10,000 RV and camping related products!

FRIENDSHIP — D3 *Adams*

CASTLE ROCK PARK (Public) From jct CR J & Hwy 13 (in town): Go 3-1/2 mi S on Hwy 13, then 6 mi W on CR F, then 1/2 mi S on CR Z. 2015 rates: $15 to $22. (608)339-7713

PETENWELL LAKE COUNTY PARK (Public) From Jct of Hwys 13 & 21, W 8 mi on Hwy 21 to CR-Z, N 6 mi to Bighorn Dr, W 1 mi (E). 2015 rates: $15 to $22. (608)564-7513

ROCHE A' CRI (State Pk) From Jct of SR-21 & SR-13, S 1.5 mi on SR-13 (R). Entrance fee required. Pit toilets. 2015 rates: $12 to $14. (608)565-2789

GALESVILLE — D2 *Trempealeau*

CHAMPION'S RIVERSIDE RESORT **Ratings: 7/7.5/5.5** (Campground) 2015 rates: $38 to $45. Apr 15 to Oct 31. (608)582-2995 w16751 Pow Wow Ln, Galesville, WI 54630

GLENWOOD CITY — C1 *St Croix*

GLEN HILLS COUNTY PARK (Public) From town, S 1.8 mi on Hwy 128 to Rustic Rd 3, S 2 mi (L). Pit toilets. 2015 rates: $20. May 1 to Oct 31. (715)265-4613

GOODMAN — B4 *Marinette*

LAKE HILBERT CAMPGROUND **Ratings: 4.5/7/7.5** (Campground) 2015 rates: $21 to $28. May 2 to Oct 24. (715)336-3013 N 20470 Town Park Rd, Goodman, WI 54120

GORDON — B1 *Douglas*

GORDON DAM PARK (Public) From Jct of US-53 & Cnty Hwy Y, W 7 mi on Cnty Hwy Y (R). Pit toilets. 2015 rates: $15 to $18. (715)378-2219

HAPPY OURS RV PARK **Ratings: 5/9.5★/5** (RV Park) 2015 rates: $25. (715)376-2302 14627 S East Mail Rd, Gordon, WI 54838

GRANTSBURG — B1 *Burnett*

JAMES N MCNALLY CAMPGROUND (Public) From Jct of Hwy 70/48 & S Pine St, N 0.4 mi on S Pine St to Olson St, W 0.3 mi (R). 2015 rates: $26. Apr 15 to Oct 15. (715)463-5832

GREEN LAKE — D4 *Green Lake*

GREEN LAKE CAMPGROUND **Ratings: 8/9/9.5** (Campground) 2015 rates: $48 to $57. Apr 18 to Oct 18. (920)294-3543 W 2360 Hwy 23, Green Lake, WI 54941

HATTIE SHERWOOD CAMPGROUND (Public) From Jct SR-23 & CR-A, SW 1.2 mi on SR-23B, E .6 mi Lawson Dr. Reservations strongly recommended. 2015 rates: $27.50. May 1 to Oct 15. (920)294-6380

GREENWOOD — C2 *Clark*

NORTH MEAD LAKE COUNTY PARK (Public) From town, N 15 mi on Hwy 73 to CR-G, W 2.5 mi to CR-0, N 2 mi to CR-MM, W 5 mi (L). Pit toilets. 2015 rates: $16 to $21. May 1 to Nov 1. (888)252-7594

ROCK DAM PARK CAMPGROUND (Public) From town, N 6 mi on CR-H to Rock Dam Rd (turns into Camp Globe Rd), continue N 3 mi (passed the TV tower) to the two curves in the rd, E 6 mi on the 2nd curve in the road (L). 2015 rates: $16 to $28. May 1 to Nov 1. (715)267-6845

GRESHAM — C4 *Shawano*

ANNIE'S CAMPGROUND **Ratings: 6.5/7/8.5** (Campground) 2015 rates: $37 to $46. (715)787-3632 w12505 Roosevelt Rd, Gresham, WI 54128

CAPTAIN'S COVE RESORT AND COUNTRY CLUB **Ratings: 8/8.5/8** (Membership Pk) 2015 rates: $45. May 1 to Oct 31. (715)787-3535 N 9099 Big Lake Rd, Gresham, WI 54128

Refer to the Table of Contents in front of the Guide to locate everything you need.

HANCOCK — D3 *Waushara*

HANCOCK/STEVENS POINT SOUTH KOA

Ratings: 9/10★/9.5 (Campground) From Jct I-39 & Exit 131: Go W on Beachnut Dr 1/8 mi, then R on Elizabeth Lane (E). **FAC:** Gravel rds. 74 gravel, 74 pull-thrus (35 x 80), 74 full hkups (30/50 amps), WiFi, tent sites, rentals, dump, laundry, groc, LP gas, fire rings, firewood, controlled access. **REC:** heated pool, pond, swim, playground. Pets OK. Partial handicap access. Big rig sites, eco-friendly, 2015 rates: $49.80 to $126.89. Disc: military. May 1 to Oct 31.

(715)249-3322 Lat: 44.13728, Lon: -89.53561
N4398 Elizabeth Lane, Hancock, WI 54943
intotocamp@hotmail.com
www.koa.com/campgrounds/hancock
See ad this page.

VILLAGE HANCOCK CAMPGROUND (Public) From Jct of US-51 & CR-V, E 1.3 mi on CR-V to CR-GG, SE 0.75 mi (R). Pit toilets. 2015 rates: $7.50 to $10. (715)249-5521

HARTFORD — D4 *Washington*

KETTLE MORAINE/PIKE LAKE (State Pk) From Jct of SR-83 & SR-60, E 2.8 mi on SR-60 (R). Entrance fee required. 2015 rates: $12 to $14. Apr 18 to Nov 1. (262)670-3400

HATFIELD — C2 *Jackson*

BLACK RIVER/EAST FORK (State Pk) From Jct of I-94 & Hwy 54, E 8 mi on Hwy 54 to S Cementary Rd (unposted, follow signs), N 4 mi to Old Hwy 54, E 0.5 mi to campground rd, N 2 mi (E). Entrance fee required. Pit toilets. 2015 rates: $12 to $14. Apr 15 to Nov 30. (715)284-4103

RUSSELL MEMORIAL COUNTY PARK (Public) From town, SW 13 mi on Hwy 95 to CR-J, S 3 mi (L). 2015 rates: $16 to $28. May 1 to Nov 1. (715)333-7948

HAYWARD — B2 *Sawyer*

CAMP NAMEKAGON **Ratings: 6/9.5★/8** (Campground) 2015 rates: $37. Apr 15 to Oct 15. (715)766-2277 w2108 Larson Rd, Springbrook, WI 54875

HAYWARD KOA

Ratings: 8.5/10★/10 (Campground) From Jct of US-77 & US-63: Go N 3 mi on US-63 (R). **FAC:** Gravel rds. (166 spaces). Avail: 162 gravel, 103 pull-thrus (35 x 50), back-ins (30 x 40), 48 full hkups, 107 W, 114 E (30/50 amps), seasonal sites, WiFi, tent sites, rentals, dump, mobile sewer, laundry, groc, LP gas, fire rings, firewood. **REC:** heated pool, playground, rec open to public. Pets OK. Partial handicap access. Big rig sites, eco-friendly, 2015 rates: $45 to $69. May 1 to Oct 6. ATM.

(715)634-2331 Lat: 46.04954, Lon: -91.44092
11544 N US Hwy 63, Hayward, WI 54843
haywardkoa@yahoo.com
www.haywardkoa.com
See ad this page.

LAKE CHIPPEWA CAMPGROUND **Ratings: 7.5/10★/9** (Campground) 2015 rates: $35 to $51. May 1 to Nov 1. (715)462-3672 8380 N CR-Cc, Hayward, WI 54843

RIVER ROAD RV CAMPGROUND **Ratings: 4/NA/7** (RV Park) 2015 rates: $35. Apr 1 to Oct 15. (715)634-2054 W 449 East River Rd, Hayward, WI 54843

SISKO'S PINE POINT RESORT **Ratings: 5.5/5.5/7** (Campground) 2015 rates: $26 to $30. May 1 to Oct 15. (715)462-3700 8677 N CR-Cc, Hayward, WI 54843

Tell them you saw them in this Guide!

HAYWARD (CONT)

SUNRISE BAY CAMPGROUNDS & RV PARK **Ratings: 4.5/5/6** (Campground) 2015 rates: $28. May 1 to Oct 1. (715)634-2213 16269 W Jolly Fisherman Rd, Hayward, WI 54843

TREELAND FARM RV RESORT
Ratings: 9/10★/10 (RV Park) From Jct of Hwy 27 & CR-B: Go E on CR-B 14 1/2 mi (L). **FAC:** Gravel rds. (75 spaces). Avail: 60 gravel, patios, 50 pull-thrus (30 x 90), back-ins (30 x 50), 60 full hkups (30/50 amps), seasonal sites, WiFi, tent sites, dump, laundry, groc, fire rings, firewood, restaurant, controlled access. **REC:** heated pool, Lake Chippewa Flowage: swim, fishing, marina, playground. Pet restrict(Q). Partial handicap access. Big rig sites, eco-friendly, 2015 rates: $42 to $67. Disc: military. May 1 to Oct 15. ATM.
(715)462-4987 Lat: 45.98259, Lon: -91.19332
10138 W CR-B, Hayward, WI 54843
treelandrvresort@gmail.com
www.treelandresorts.com
See ad opposite page, 1306.

HIGHLAND — E3 *Iowa*

BLACKHAWK LAKE REC AREA (Public) From Jct of Hwy 80 & CR-BH, E 3 mi on CR-BH (E). Entrance fee required. 2015 rates: $12 to $18. Apr 15 to Nov 1. (608)623-2707

HIXTON — C2 *Jackson*

KOA HIXTON/ALMA CENTER **Ratings: 9/10★/9** (Campground) 2015 rates: $26 to $50. May 1 to Nov 1. (800)562-2680 N 9657 State Hwy 95, Alma Center, WI 54611

HOLCOMBE — C2 *Chippewa*

PINE POINT COUNTY PARK (Public) From town, W 2.5 mi on CR-M (R). Pit toilets. 2015 rates: $16 to $27. May 2 to Oct 31. (715)726-7882

HOLMEN — D2 *La Crosse*

WHISPERING PINES CAMPGROUND **Ratings: 8/10★/9.5** (Campground) 2015 rates: $38 to $46. Apr 15 to Oct 15. (608)526-4956 N 8905 Hwy 53, Holmen, WI 54636

HORICON — D4 *Dodge*

LEDGE PARK (Public) From Jct of SR-33 & SR-28, NE 0.2 mi on SR-28 to Raaschs Hill Rd, E 2.5 mi (E). 2015 rates: $15 to $20. (920)387-5450

PLAYFUL GOOSE CAMPGROUND **Ratings: 6/5.5/6** (Campground) 2015 rates: $36 to $43. May 1 to Oct 12. (920)485-4744 2001 S. Main St., Horicon, WI 53032

HUDSON — C1 *St Croix*

WILLOW RIVER (State Pk) From town, E 3 mi on I-94 to Hwy 12, N 2 mi to CR-A, N 2 mi (L). Entrance fee required. Pit toilets. 2015 rates: $14 to $17. (715)386-5931

IOLA — C4 *Waupaca*

IOLA PINES CAMPGROUND **Ratings: 7/8/8** (Campground) 2015 rates: $30. May 1 to Nov 30. (715)445-3489 100 Fairway Dr, Iola, WI 54945

IRON RIVER — A2 *Bayfield*

DELTA LAKE PARK (Public) From jct US 2 & CR H: Go 5 mi S on CR H, then 5 mi S on Scenic Drive Rd: Pit toilets. (715)372-8767

MOON LAKE PARK (Public) From town, S 0.5 mi on County Trunk H (R). 2015 rates: $15 to $20. May 1 to Oct 15. (218)591-0905

TOP O THE MORN RESORT & CAMPGROUND **Ratings: 8/8.5★/8.5** (Campground) 2015 rates: $33 to $36. May 1 to Oct 15. (715)372-4546 6080 Iron Lake Rd, Iron River, WI 54847

TWIN BEAR PARK (Public) From jct US 2 & CR H: Go 7 mi S on CR H. Pit toilets. 2015 rates: $22 to $27. (715)372-8610

JEFFERSON — E4 *Jefferson*

BARK RIVER CAMPGROUND **Ratings: 5.5/5/8** (Campground) 2015 rates: $36. Apr 3 to Oct 26. (262)593-2421 w2340 Hanson Rd, Jefferson, WI 53549

JEFFERSON COUNTY FAIR PARK CAMPGROUND (Public) From Jct of US-26 & US-18: Go E 1/3 mi on US-18 to N Jackson Ave (L), then 3 blocks to park (L). **FAC:** Paved/gravel rds. 199 Avail: 20 paved, 40 gravel, 139 grass, 50 pull-thrus (30 x 70), back-ins (30 x 60), 10 full hkups, 189 W, 189 E (30/50 amps), WiFi $, tent sites, dump, restaurant. **REC:** rec open to public. Pets OK. Partial handicap access. Big rig sites, 2015 rates: $30 to $40. ATM.
(920)674-7148 Lat: 43.01294, Lon: -88.81893
503 N Jackson Ave, Jefferson, WI 53549
info@jeffersoncountywi.gov
www.JcFairPark.com

KEWASKUM — D4 *Fond du Lac*

KETTLE MORAINE/MAUTHE LAKE CAMPGROUND (Public) From Jct of Hwy 28 & Hwy S, N 6 mi on Hwy S to Hwy GGG, N 1 mi (E). Entrance fee required. Pit toilets. 2015 rates: $12 to $14. (262)626-4305

KEWAUNEE — C5 *Kewaunee*

CEDAR VALLEY CAMPGROUND **Ratings: 7.5/8.5/9.5** (Campground) 2015 rates: $42 to $45. Apr 25 to Oct 10. (920)388-4983 n5098 Cedar Valley Rd, Kewaunee, WI 54216

KEWAUNEE MARINA & CAMPGROUNDS (Public) From jct Hwy 29 & Hwy 42: Go 1/4 mi N on Hwy 42. (920)388-3300

KEWAUNEE VILLAGE RV PARK & CAMPGROUND
Ratings: 8.5/9.5★/9.5 (Campground) From Jct of Hwy 42 & Hwy 29: Go N 1 mi on Hwy 42 to Terraqua Dr, then W 1/4 mi (R). **FAC:** Gravel rds. (74 spaces). 50 Avail: 25 gravel, 25 grass, 41 pull-thrus (35 x 60), back-ins (35 x 60), 26 full hkups, 24 W, 24 E (30/50 amps), seasonal sites, WiFi Hotspot, tent sites, rentals, dump, laundry, groc, LP gas, fire rings, firewood. **REC:** heated pool, playground, rec open to public. Pets OK. Big rig sites, eco-friendly, 2015 rates: $35 to $42. May 1 to Oct 1.
(920)388-4851 Lat: 44.47591, Lon: -87.50444
333 Terraqua Dr, Kewaunee, WI 54216
camp@kewauneevillage.com
www.kewauneevillage.com
See ad this page, 1306.

KIELER — E2 *Grant*

RUSTIC BARN CAMPGROUND & RV PARK
Ratings: 7/9.5★/9 (RV Park) From Hwy 151/61/35, Exit CR-HHH (Exit 5), W 0.2 mi to Prism Lane, N 0.3 mi on Prism Lane to Dry Hollow Rd, N 0.1 mi (R). **FAC:** Gravel rds. (58 spaces). Avail: 42 gravel, patios, 20 pull-thrus (25 x 75), back-ins (40 x 50), some side by side hkups, 2 full hkups, 40 W, 40 E (30/50 amps), seasonal sites, WiFi, tent sites, dump, mobile sewer, laundry, groc, LP bottles, fire rings, firewood. **REC:** playground. Pets OK. Partial handicap access. Big rig sites, eco-friendly, 2015 rates: $32 to $38. Apr 15 to Oct 31.
(608)568-7797 Lat: 42.58166, Lon: -90.61077
3854 Dry Hollow Rd, PO Box 68, Kieler, WI 53812
rusticbarncampground@gmail.com
www.rusticbarnrvpark.com
See ad this page, 1306.

KINGSTON — D4 *Green Lake*

GRAND VALLEY CAMPGROUND **Ratings: 8/9.5★/9.5** (Campground) 2015 rates: $32 to $37. Apr 1 to Dec 1. (920)394-3643 W 5855 CR-B, Dalton, WI 53926

KNOWLTON — C3 *Marathon*

LAKE DUBAY SHORES CAMPGROUND
Ratings: 8/9★/8.5 (Campground) From Jct of I-39/US-51 & SR-34 (exit 175): Go SW 2 mi on SR-34 to DuBay Dr (turn left), then 500 ft (R). **FAC:** Gravel rds. (225 spaces). Avail: 120 grass, 10 pull-thrus (45 x 60), back-ins (45 x 50), 23 full hkups, 97 W, 97 E (30/50 amps), seasonal sites, WiFi, tent sites, rentals, dump, mobile sewer, laundry, groc, LP gas, fire rings, firewood. **REC:** Lake DuBay: swim, fishing, marina, playground, rec open to public. Pets OK $. Partial handicap access. Big rig sites, eco-friendly, 2015 rates: $32 to $50.
(715)457-2484 Lat: 44.42614, Lon: -89.41779
1713 Dubay Dr, Mosinee, WI 54455
camp@dubayshores.com
www.dubayshores.com
See ad this page, 1306.

LA CROSSE — D2 *La Crosse*

GOOSE ISLAND CAMPGROUND
(Public) From Jct of I-90 & WI-16 (Exit 5): Go 9 3/4 mi S on WI-16 to US-14E/US-61/WI-35, then go 1 1/2 mi on SR-35 S to CR GI (R). **FAC:** Paved rds. 239 Avail: 97 paved, 28 gravel, 114 grass, back-ins (50 x 55), 140 W, 239 E (30/50 amps), WiFi Hotspot, tent sites, showers $, dump, mobile sewer, laundry, groc, LP gas, fire rings, firewood. **REC:** Mississippi River: swim, fishing, playground, rec open to public. Pets OK. Partial handicap access. 2015 rates: $20.25 to $26.75. Apr 15 to Oct 30.
(608)788-7018 Lat: 43.72898, Lon: -91.20113
w6488 County Rd Gi, Stoddard, WI 54658
gisland@lacrossecounty.org
www.lacrossecountycamping.com
See ad this page.

PETTIBONE RESORT **Ratings: 8/8.5/9** (RV Park) 2015 rates: $39. Apr 15 to Nov 1. (608)782-5858 333 Park Plaza Dr, La Crosse, WI 54601

Things to See and Do

LA CROSSE COUNTY FACILITIES DEPARTMENT Provides parks, campgrounds (including Goose Island Campground & Veterans Memorial Campground) and other outdoor facilities that will afford an opportunity for the public to enjoy a quality experience in the out-of-doors. Partial handicap access. Restrooms. Hours: M-F 8am to 4:30pm. ATM.
(608)785-9770 Lat: 43.815205, Lon: -91.249011
www.lacrossecounty.org
See ad this page.

LA FARGE — D2 *Vernon*

LA FARGE VILLAGE PARK (Public) From Jct of US-14 & SR-131, NE 16 mi on SR-131 to Adams St, E 0.2 mi, follow signs (L). 2015 rates: $10 to $20. Apr 1 to Dec 1. (608)625-4422

We shine "Spotlights" on interesting cities and areas.

WI

LAC DU FLAMBEAU — B3 *Vilas*

LAC DU FLAMBEAU TRIBAL CAMPGROUND & MARINA **Ratings: 6/6/7.5** (Campground) 2015 rates: $35 to $38. May 1 to Sep 30. (715)588-4211 2549 State Hwy 47N, Lac Du Flambeau, WI 54538

LAKE GENEVA — E4 *Walworth*

BIG FOOT BEACH (State Pk) From Jct of Hwys 50 & 120, S 1.5 mi on Hwy 120 (L). Pit toilets. 2015 rates: $12 to $14. Apr 15 to Oct 27. (262)248-2528

COACHMAN'S TERRACE
Ratings: 8/7/7 (RV Park) From intersection of Hwy 120 & Hwy 50: Go W 1 1/2 mi on Hwy 50. Enter (R).

CLOSE TO BEAUTIFUL LAKE GENEVA
Come enjoy the Lake Geneva cool waters, beaches, boating, golfing, shopping and much more! The Historic downtown is filled with more than 100 shops and restaurants for your enjoyment.

FAC: Paved rds. (63 spaces). Avail: 12 gravel, 9 pull-thrus (30 x 45), back-ins (30 x 45), 12 full hkups (30/50 amps), seasonal sites, WiFi, dump, laundry, fire rings, firewood. **REC:** pool. Pet restrict(B). No tents. Big rig sites, 2015 rates: $40 to $45. Disc: military. May 1 to Nov 1.
(262)248-3636 Lat: 42.59124, Lon: -88.47623
W 3540 State Rd 50, Lake Geneva, WI 53147
info@coachmansterrace.com
www.coachmansterrace.com
See ad this page.

LAKEWOOD — B4 *Oconto*

HEAVEN'S UP NORTH FAMILY CAMPGROUND Ratings: 8/9.5★/9 (Campground) From Jct of Hwy 32 & CR-F: Go E 1-3/4 mi on CR-F, then N 3 mi on Lake John Rd (R). **FAC:** Gravel rds. (113 spaces). Avail: 21 gravel, 6 pull-thrus (40 x 80), back-ins (42 x 60), 19 W, 21 E (20/30 amps), seasonal sites, WiFi Hotspot, tent sites, rentals, showers $, dump, mobile sewer, laundry, fire rings, firewood. **REC:** heated pool, playground. Pets OK. Partial handicap access. Eco-friendly, 2015 rates: $28 to $31. May 1 to Oct 15.
(715)276-6556 Lat: 45.20316, Lon: -88.29911
18344 Lake John Rd, Lakewood, WI 54138
heavnsupno@centurytel.net
www.heavensupnorth.com

MAPLE HEIGHTS CAMPGROUND **Ratings: 8/8.5★/8** (Campground) 2015 rates: $32 to $33. May 1 to Oct 31. (715)276-6441 16091 E Chain Lake Rd, Lakewood, WI 54138

LAND O'LAKES — B3 *Vilas*

BORDERLINE RV PARK **Ratings: 5/7/6.5** (Campground) 2015 rates: $25. May 1 to Oct 31. (715)547-6169 6078 Hwy 45, Land O' Lakes, WI 54540

LANNON — E4 *Waukesha*

MENOMONEE PARK (Public) From jct Hwy 74 & CR V: Go 1-1/2 mi N on CR V. Pit toilets. 2015 rates: $12 to $16. Apr 1 to Nov 2. (262)548-7801

Check out the travel services section of this Guide to find services that you'll find handy in your travels.

LODI — D3 *Columbia*

CRYSTAL LAKE CAMPGROUND & RV PARK
Ratings: 8.5/8.5★/8.5 (Campground) From Jct of I-90/94 & Hwy 60 (exit 119), W 10 mi on Hwy 60 to Gannon Rd, S 0.75 mi (L). **FAC:** Paved/gravel rds. (430 spaces). 50 Avail: 25 gravel, 25 grass, 12 pull-thrus (25 x 80), back-ins (30 x 40), 50 W, 50 E (30/50 amps), seasonal sites, WiFi Hotspot, tent sites, rentals, dump, mobile sewer, laundry, groc, LP bottles, fire rings, firewood, restaurant. **REC:** heated pool, wading pool, Crystal Lake: swim, fishing, playground. Pets OK. Eco-friendly, 2015 rates: $30 to $53. Disc: military. Apr 15 to Oct 15. ATM.
(608)592-5607 Lat: 43.29411, Lon: -89.63341
N550 Gannon Rd, Lodi, WI 53555
info@crystallakewicamping.com
www.CrystalLakewiCamping.com
See ad this page.

SMOKEY HOLLOW CAMPGROUND **Ratings: 7.5/10★/10** (Campground) 2015 rates: $45 to $65. (608)635-4806 w9935 Mcgowan Rd, PO Box 18, Lodi, WI 53555

LUCK — B1 *Polk*

PINE GROVE RESORT **Ratings: 4.5/6.5/7.5** (Campground) 2015 rates: $38 to $43. May 1 to Oct 31. (715)857-5335 1095 238th Ave, Luck, WI 54853

LYNDON STATION — D3 *Juneau*

HO-CHUNK RV RESORT & CAMPGROUND **Ratings: 7/9/8.5** (Campground) 2015 rates: $55. Apr 15 to Oct 15. (608)666-2040 N 2884 28th Ave, Lyndon Station, WI 53944

MADISON — E3 *Dane*

LAKE FARM PARK (Public) From Jct of US12/18 & Exit 264 (South Town Dr), S 0.75 mi on South Town Dr to Moorland Rd, E .8 mi (rd becomes Lake Farm Rd) (L). 2015 rates: $18 to $27. Apr 27 to Nov 2. (608)242-4576

Travel Services

TRUCK COUNTRY Freightliner dealer. **SERVICES:** MH mechanical, engine/chassis repair, emergency rd svc, restrooms. **TOW:** RV. RV accessible. waiting room. Hours: M-F 6am-midnight, Sa 6am-4pm, Su closed.
(800)837-7367 Lat: 43.17129, Lon: -89.32082
4195 Anderson Rd, De Forest, WI 53532
www.truckcountry.com
See ad pages 488, 1311.

Things to See and Do

HO-CHUNK GAMING MADISON Full service casino with slots, poker room, and a restaurant for casual dining. Partial handicap access. RV accessible. Restrooms, food. Hours: 24 hours. ATM.
(608)223-9576 Lat: 43.039505, Lon: -89.272099
4002 Evan Acres Rd, Madison, WI 53718
www.ho-chunkgaming.com/madison/
See ad page 1310 (Spotlight Wisconsin Dells).

MANAWA — C4 *Waupaca*

BEAR LAKE CAMPGROUND **Ratings: 6.5/7.5/7.5** (Campground) 2015 rates: $27 to $35. May 1 to Oct 15. (920)596-3308 n4715 Hwy 110 & 22, Manawa, WI 54949

MANITOWISH WATERS — B3 *Vilas*

NO HIGHLAND AMERICAN LEGION SF/SANDY BEACH (State Pk) From town, SE 3.8 mi on US-51, S 4.5 mi on SR-47 to Powell Rd, N 0.25 mi to Sandy Beach (E). Entrance fee required. Pit toilets. 2015 rates: $12 to $14. May 19 to Sep 2. (715)385-2727

MARIBEL — C5 *Manitowoc*

DEVILS RIVER CAMPGROUND **Ratings: 4.5/7/8.5** (Campground) 2015 rates: $30 to $34. May 1 to Oct 1. (920)863-2812 16612 County Hwy R, Maribel, WI 54227

We appreciate your business!

MARINETTE — C5 *Marinette*

Travel Services

TRUCK COUNTRY Full RV service. **SERVICES:** MH mechanical, engine/chassis repair, emergency rd svc, restrooms. **TOW:** RV. RV accessible. waiting room. Hours: M-F 7am-5pm, Sa 7am-3:30pm.
(888)315-5995 Lat: 45.08592, Lon: -87.64670
2890 Cleveland Ave, Marinette, WI 54143
www.truckcountry.com
See ad pages 488, 1311.

MARION — C4 *Waupaca*

FARMER GENE'S CAMPGROUND
Ratings: 8/8.5/8.5 (Campground) From Jct of US-45 & SR-110: Go S 2-1/2 mi on SR-110 to CR-G, then W 3-1/4 mi to Kinney Lake Rd, then N 1/4 mi (E). **FAC:** Paved/gravel rds. (530 spaces). Avail: 180 grass, back-ins (40 x 50), 180 W, 180 E (30/50 amps), seasonal sites, WiFi Hotspot, tent sites, rentals, showers $, dump, mobile sewer, laundry, groc, LP bottles, fire rings, firewood, restaurant, controlled access. **REC:** heated pool, wading pool, whirlpool, Lake Kinney: swim, fishing, shuffleboard, playground. Pets OK. Partial handicap access. Eco-friendly, 2015 rates: $43 to $46. Disc: military. ATM.
(715)754-5900 Lat: 44.65333, Lon: -88.96648
N11301 Kinney Lake Rd, Marion, WI 54950
info@farmergenescampground.com
www.farmergenescampground.com
See ad this page, 1306.

MARSHFIELD — C3 *Wood*

NORTH WOOD COUNTY PARK (Public) From town, W 14 mi on Hwy 13 to CR-A, N 5 mi (L). 2015 rates: $16 to $28. May 1 to Oct 31. (715)421-8422

MAUSTON — D3 *Juneau*

CASTLE ROCK COUNTY PARK (Public) From Jct of I-90 & Rte 82 (exit 69), W 0.6 mi on Rte 82 to Rte 58, N 6.8 mi on Rte 58 to CR-G, S 5.1 mi (L). 2015 rates: $19. (608)847-7089

MCFARLAND — E3 *Dane*

BABCOCK PARK (Public) From Jct of SR-12 & SR-51, S 3 mi on SR-51 (R). 2015 rates: $27. Apr 27 to Oct 12. (608)242-4576

MELLEN — A2 *Ashland*

COPPER FALLS (State Pk) From town, NE 2 mi on SR-169 (L). Entrance fee required. 2015 rates: $12 to $17. (715)274-5123

MENOMONIE — C1 *Dunn*

TWIN SPRINGS CAMPGROUND **Ratings: 4/8.5★/5.5** (Campground) 2015 rates: $27 to $44. May 1 to Oct 31. (715)235-9321 N 6572 530th St, Menomonie, WI 54751

MERRILL — C3 *Lincoln*

COUNCIL GROUNDS (State Pk) From Jct US-51 & SR-64, W 2 mi on SR-64 to SR-107N, NW 2 mi (L). Entrance fee required. 2015 rates: $12 to $17. (715)536-8773

MERRILLAN — C2 *Jackson*

JACKSON COUNTY/EAST ARBUTUS (Public) From Jct of US-12 & SH-54, E 5.8 mi to CH-K, N 6.4 mi to Clay School Rd, E 1.5 mi to Klima Rd., N .5 mi. 2015 rates: $12 to $18. (715)333-5832

JACKSON COUNTY/WEST ARBUTUS (Public) From Jct of US-12 & SH-54, E 5.8 mi to CH-K, N 7.8 mi to Hatfield, follow signs (R). 2015 rates: $15 to $23. May 15 to Sep 1. (715)333-5832

MERRIMAC — D3 *Sauk*

MERRY MAC'S CAMPGROUND **Ratings: 8.5/10★/9.5** (Campground) 2015 rates: $35 to $52. Apr 15 to Oct 15. (608)493-2367 e12995 Halweg Rd, Merrimac, WI 53561

MIDDLETON — E3 *Dane*

MENDOTA PARK (Public) From Jct of I-90 & US-12, W 17 mi on US-12 to CR-M Century Ave, E 2.5 mi (R). 2015 rates: $27. Apr 27 to Oct 12. (608)242-4576

MIKANA — B2 *Barron*

WALDO CARLSON PARK (Public) From Jct of I-53 & Hwy 48, NE 12.5 mi on Hwy 48 to park access rd, E 0.5 mi (E). 2015 rates: $15 to $23. May 1 to Oct 1. (800)272-9829

MILTON — E4 *Rock*

BLACKHAWK CAMPING RESORT **Ratings: 7.5/8/9** (Campground) 2015 rates: $32 to $52. Apr 15 to Oct 15. (608)868-2586 3407 E Blackhawk Dr, Milton, WI 53563

HIDDEN VALLEY RV RESORT & CAMPGROUND

Ratings: 9/10★/10 (RV Park) From Jct of I-90 & Hwy 59E (exit 163): Go E 1/2 mi on State Rd 59E (R).

PREMIER BIG RIG SITES

We have a clean modern facility with immaculately manicured grounds & wifi with activities every weekend. Concerts in May, Christmas in July & six weekends of Halloween fun with our own Haunted Barn!

FAC: Gravel rds. (232 spaces). 132 Avail: 7 paved, 125 gravel, 32 pull-thrus (34 x 90), back-ins (32 x 55), 80 full hkups, 52 W, 52 E (30/50 amps), seasonal sites, WiFi $, rentals, dump, laundry, groc, LP gas, fire rings, firewood, controlled access. **REC:** heated pool, whirlpool, Rock River: fishing, playground. Pets OK. Partial handicap access, no tents. Big rig sites, eco-friendly, 2015 rates: $38 to $76. Apr 25 to Oct 20. ATM.

(800)469-5515 Lat: 42.82674, Lon: -89.01620
872 E State Rd 59, Milton, WI 53563
hiddenvalleymilton@gmail.com
www.hiddenvalleymilton.com
See ad pages 1318, 1306, 1304 (WI Map).

Find it Fast! Use our alphabetized index of campgrounds and parks.

LAKELAND CAMPING RESORT **Ratings: 8/7/9** (Campground) 2015 rates: $42 to $58. Apr 15 to Oct 15. (608)868-4700 2803 E State are 59, Milton, WI 53563

PETTIT'S LAKEVIEW CAMPGROUND

Ratings: 6/6.5/7.5 (Campground) From Jct of I-39 & Exit 163 WI-59 (Milton/Edgerton): Go E 1-1/4 mi on WI-59 (L). **FAC:** Paved/gravel rds. (81 spaces). 28 Avail: 26 gravel, 2 grass, 2 pull-thrus (30 x 60), back-ins (30 x 60), 28 full hkups (30/50 amps), seasonal sites, WiFi Hotspot, rentals, dump, LP bottles, fire rings, firewood, restaurant. **REC:** Lake Koshkonong: swim, fishing, playground, rec open to public. Pets OK. Partial handicap access, no tents. 2015 rates: $42. ATM.

(608)868-7800 Lat: 42.82760, Lon: -89.00108
1901 E State Rd 59, Milton, WI 53563
lakeviewcampgroundllc@yahoo.com
www.lakeviewcampgroundandbar.com
See ad this page.

Things change ... last year's rates serve as a guideline only.

According to some studies, almost 50 percent of RVers camp with pets! Find out more about the joys of traveling with your four-legged companions in our Pampered Pet Parks feature at the front of the Guide.

WI

MILWAUKEE — E5 *Milwaukee*

MILWAUKEE See also Caledonia & Mukwonago.

WISCONSIN STATE FAIR RV PARK (Public) From Jct of I-94 & 84th St exit, (exit 306) S 50 ft on 84th St (L). 2015 rates: $33 to $75. (414)266-7035

Travel Services

TRUCK COUNTRY Full RV service. **SERVICES:** MH mechanical, engine/chassis repair, emergency rd svc, restrooms. **TOW:** RV. RV accessible. waiting room. Hours: M-F 6am to 12am, Sat 6am to 4pm.
(800)236-6061 Lat: 42.87354, Lon: -87.94454
2222 W Ryan Rd, Oak Creek, WI 53154
www.truckcountry.com
See ad pages 488, 1311.

TRUCK COUNTRY Truck Country is the largest Freightliner/Western Star dealer group in the United States, with 21 locations in Iowa, Indiana, Ohio and Wisconsin. **SERVICES:** RV Sales. RV supplies, waiting room. Hours: 7 am - 4 pm.
(844)753-7728 Lat: 48.185157, Lon: -88.041358
9202 N 107th St., Milwaukee, WI 53224
www.truckcountry.com
See ad pages 488, 1311.

MINOCQUA — B3 *Vilas, Oneida*

PATRICIA LAKE CAMPGROUND & RV PARK
Ratings: 8.5/9★/9 (Campground) From Jct of Hwys 51 & 70: Go W 2-1/2 mi on Hwy 70 to Camp Pinemere Rd, then S 1/2 mi (L). **FAC:** Paved/gravel rds. (100 spaces). 31 Avail: 14 gravel, 17 grass, 5 pull-thrus (50 x 80), back-ins (50 x 60), 30 full hkups, 1 W, 1 E (30/50 amps), seasonal sites, cable, WiFi, tent sites, rentals, showers $, dump, laundry, groc, LP gas, fire rings, firewood. **REC:** Patricia Lake: swim, fishing, playground. Pet restrict(Q). Big rig sites, 30 day max stay, eco-friendly, 2015 rates: $30 to $42. Disc: AAA, military. May 1 to Oct 15.
(715)356-3198 Lat: 45.87697, Lon: -89.75629
8508 Camp Pinemere Rd, Minocqua, WI 54548
info@patricialakecampground.com
www.patricialakecampground.com
See ad this page, 1306.

Travel Services

TRUCK COUNTRY Full RV service. **SERVICES:** MH mechanical, engine/chassis repair, emergency rd svc, restrooms. **TOW:** RV. RV accessible. waiting room. Hours: M-F 7:30am to 5pm.
(715)358-5200 Lat: 45.84667, Lon: -89.83056
7854 US Hwy 51 South, Minocqua, WI 54548
www.truckcountry.com
See ad pages 488, 1311.

MINONG — B1 *Washburn*

TOTOGATIC PARK (Public) From town, NW 7 mi on CR-I (R). Pit toilets. 2015 rates: $10 to $15. May 1 to Oct 31. (715)635-4490

MONTELLO — D3 *Marquette*

BUFFALO LAKE CAMPING RESORT
Ratings: 8.5/9.5★/10 (Campground) From Jct of SR-23 & W Jct of SR 22 (in town), W 0.1 mi on SR-23 to CR-C (left turn), W 0.7 mi on CR-C (R). **FAC:** Gravel rds. (112 spaces). Avail: 47 grass, 8 pull-thrus (40 x 80), back-ins (40 x 60), 8 full hkups, 39 W, 39 E (30/50 amps), seasonal sites, cable, WiFi, tent sites, rentals, dump, mobile sewer, laundry, groc, LP gas, fire rings, firewood, restaurant. **REC:** heated pool, Buffalo Lake: fishing, playground. Pets OK. Partial handicap access. Big rig sites, eco-friendly, 2015 rates: $34 to $45. Apr 15 to Oct 15.
(608)297-2915 Lat: 43.79221, Lon: -89.34488
555 Lake Ave, Montello, WI 53949
info@buffalolakecamping.com
www.buffalolakecamping.com
See ad this page, 1306.

CROOKED RIVER CAMPGROUND **Ratings: 7/9/9** (Campground) 2015 rates: $40 to $55. Apr 15 to Oct 15. (608)297-7307 W 4054 11th Rd, Montello, WI 53949

KILBY LAKE CAMPGROUND **Ratings: 6.5/6.5/8.5** (Campground) 2015 rates: $32 to $50. Apr 15 to Oct 15. (877)497-2344 N 4492 Fern Ave, Montello, WI 53949

LAKE ARROWHEAD CAMPGROUND **Ratings: 8.5/9★/8.5** (Campground) 2015 rates: $39 to $66. Apr 15 to Oct 15. (920)295-3000 w781 Fox Ct, Montello, WI 53949

WILDERNESS CAMPGROUND Ratings: 8/10★/8.5 (Campground) From Jct of SR-22 & SR-23, S 7.7 mi on SR-22 to Wilderness Rd, W 0.7 mi (L). **FAC:** Gravel rds. (365 spaces). 145 Avail: 15 gravel, 130 grass, 35 pull-thrus (50 x 100), back-ins (47 x 90), 8 full hkups, 137 W, 137 E (20/50 amps), seasonal sites, WiFi Hotspot, tent sites, rentals, showers $, dump, mobile sewer, laundry, groc, LP gas, fire rings, firewood. **REC:** heated pool, Bonnie Lake: swim, fishing, playground. Pets OK. Partial handicap access. Big rig sites, eco-friendly, 2015 rates: $42 to $49. Apr 17 to Oct 11.
AAA Approved
(608)297-2002 Lat: 43.69301, Lon: -89.33166
N 1499 State Hwy 22, Montello, WI 53949
info@wildernesscampground.com
www.wildernesscampground.com

MOSINEE — C3 *Marathon*

BIG EAU PLEINE COUNTY PARK (Public) From town, W 6 mi on SR-153 to Eau Pleine Parks Rd, S 3 mi (E). Pit toilets. 2015 rates: $11 to $17. May 2 to Oct 31. (715)261-1566

MOUNTAIN — C4 *Oconto*

CHUTE POND/FISCHER MEMORIAL PARK (Public) From town: Go 5 mi S on Hwy-32/64. 2015 rates: $25. Apr 1 to Nov 30. (715)276-6261

MUKWONAGO — E4 *Waukesha*

COUNTRY VIEW CAMPGROUND
Ratings: 7/10★/8 (Campground) From Jct of I-43 & Hwy 83 (exit 43), S 0.3 mi on Hwy 83 to E. Wolf Run Rd, E .2 mi to Maple Rd, S 1.3 mi to Craig Rd, S. 1.1 mi. (L). **FAC:** Gravel rds. 150 Avail: 132 gravel, 18 grass, 68 pull-thrus (30 x 60), back-ins (40 x 50), some side by side hkups, 37 full hkups, 113 W, 113 E (20/30 amps), tent sites, dump, mobile sewer, laundry, groc, LP gas, fire rings, firewood. **REC:** heated pool, playground, rec open to public. Pets OK. Partial handicap access. Eco-friendly, 2015 rates: $24 to $34. May 1 to Oct 15. ATM.
(262)662-3654 Lat: 42.84219, Lon: -88.27515
S 110 W 26400 Craig Ave, Mukwonago, WI 53149
www.countryviewcamp.com
See ad this page.

MUKWONAGO PARK (Public) From jct US-83 & US-99: Go 3 mi W on US-99. Pit toilets. 2015 rates: $12 to $16. Apr 1 to Nov 2. (262)548-7801

MUSCODA — E2 *Grant*

RIVERSIDE CAMPGROUND (Public) From Hwy-80 north of town, follow signs. May 1 to Oct 30. (608)739-3786

VICTORIA RIVERSIDE PARK (Public) From Jct of Hwys 80 & 133, N 1 mi on Hwy 80 to River St, E 0.2 mi (R). 2015 rates: $10 to $25. May 15 to Oct 1. (608)604-7094

MUSKEGO — E4 *Waukesha*

MUSKEGO PARK (Public) From jct I-43 & CR Y(Racine Ave): Go 2-1/2 mi S on CR Y, then 3/4 mi W on CR L (Janesville Rd). Pit toilets. 2015 rates: $12 to $22. Apr 1 to Nov 2. (262)548-7801

NECEDAH — D3 *Juneau*

BUCKHORN (State Pk) From jct Hwy 21 & Hwy 80/CR Q: Go 3-1/4 mi S on Hwy 80/CR Q, then 4-1/2 mi E on CR G. Pit toilets. 2015 rates: $12 to $14. (608)565-2789

MOONLITE TRAILS CAMPGROUND **Ratings: 4/8/7.5** (Campground) 2015 rates: $22. Apr 15 to Nov 30. (608)565-6936 W 4641 9th St East, Necedah, WI 54646

ST JOSEPH RESORT **Ratings: 6/8/8.5** (Campground) 2015 rates: $23.70. May 1 to Oct 15. (608)565-7258 W 5630 Hwy 21, Necedah, WI 54646

WILDERNESS COUNTY PARK (Public) From Jct of Hwy 21 & Cnty G (E edge of town), N 9 mi on Cnty G to 8th St E 4 mi (R). 2015 rates: $19. May 1 to Oct 1. (608)565-7285

NEILLSVILLE — C2 *Clark*

SHERWOOD PARK (Public) From town, SE 17 mi on Hwy 73 to CR-Z, S 2 mi to Badger Ave (E). Pit toilets. 2015 rates: $15 to $20. May 1 to Nov 1. (715)743-5140

SNYDER COUNTY PARK (Public) From town, W 6 mi on Hwy 10 to CR-B, N 0.5 follow signs (R). Pit toilets. 2015 rates: $12 to $16. May 1 to Dec 1. (715)743-5140

NEKOOSA — C3 *Wood*

DEER TRAIL PARK CAMPGROUND **Ratings: 6.5/7/7** (Campground) 2015 rates: $27 to $36. Apr 15 to Nov 30. (715)886-3871 13846 County Road Z, Nekoosa, WI 54457

HOMEGROUNDS RV PARK (RV Park) (Too New to Rate) 2015 rates: $30 to $45. Apr 15 to Nov 1. (715)310-0380 1312 Akron Drive, Nekoosa, WI 54457

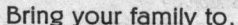

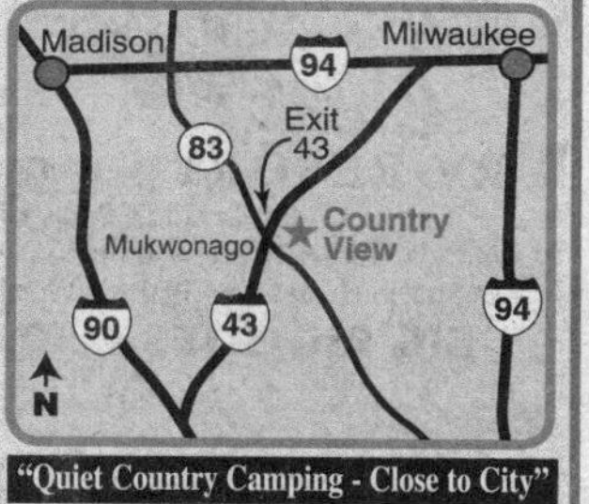

NEKOOSA (CONT)

Things to See and Do

HO-CHUNK GAMING NEKOOSA Full service casino with slots, table games, poker room, and a grille, snack bar and lounge. Partial handicap access. RV accessible. Restrooms, food. Hours: 24 hours. ATM.
(800)782-4560 Lat: 44.280868, Lon: -89.962502
949 County Rd G, Nekoosa, WI 54457
www.ho-chunkgaming.com/nekoosa/
See ad page 1310 (Spotlight Wisconsin Dells).

NELSON *Buffalo*

NELSON'S LANDING RV PARK (RV Park) (Not Visited) From Jct of Hwy 35 & 25: Go N 1-1/4 mi on Hwy 35, then E 1/4 mi on Cleveland St (R). **FAC:** Gravel rds. (55 spaces). Avail: 35 gravel, 10 pull-thrus (50 x 70), back-ins (50 x 70), 35 full hkups (50 amps), seasonal sites, WiFi, laundry, groc, fire rings. Pets OK. Partial handicap access. Eco-friendly, 2015 rates: $38. May 1 to Oct 31.
(507)951-2842 Lat: 44.42138, Lon: -92.00685
Cleveland St, Nelson, WI 54756
nelsonslandingrvpark@gmail.com
www.nelsonslandingrvpark.com

NEW AUBURN — C2 *Chippewa*

GREEN ACRES FAMILY CAMPGROUND **Ratings: 5.5/9★/9.5** (Campground) 2015 rates: $37 to $40. (715)967-2067 30714 152nd St, New Auburn, WI 54757

MORRIS-ERICKSON (Public) From town: Go 8 mi NE on CR M & Hwy 40. Pit toilets. 2015 rates: $16 to $20. May 2 to Oct 31. (715)726-7880

NEW GLARUS — E3 *Green*

NEW GLARUS WOODS (State Pk) From jct Hwy 69 & CR NN: Go 1/8 mi W on CR NN. Pit toilets. 2015 rates: $12 to $14. (608)527-2335

NEW LISBON — D3 *Juneau*

RIVERSIDE PARK (Public) From Jct of I-90/94 & Hwy 80 (exit 61), W 0.6 mi on Hwy 80 to Hog Island Rd, N 0.05 mi (R). 2015 rates: $15 to $25. May 15 to Oct 15. (608)562-3534

NEW LONDON — C4 *Waupaca*

HUCKLBERRY ACRES CAMPGROUND **Ratings: 6/7.5/7.5** (Campground) 2015 rates: $26 to $34. May 1 to Oct 15. (920)982-4628 9005 Hucklberry Rd, New London, WI 54961

WOLF RIVER TRIPS & CAMPGROUND **Ratings: 6.5/8.5/8** (Campground) 2015 rates: $25 to $36. Apr 15 to Oct 15. (920)982-2458 e8041 County Hwy X, New London, WI 54961

OAKDALE — D3 *Monroe*

GRANGER'S CAMPGROUND **Ratings: 5/7.5/3.5** (Campground) 2015 rates: $30. Apr 1 to Nov 1. (608)372-4511 566 N Oakwood St, Tomah, WI 54660

OAKDALE KOA **Ratings: 9/10★/8.5** (Campground) 2015 rates: $34 to $45. Apr 1 to Nov 1. (800)562-1737 200 Jay St, Oakdale, WI 54649

OCONTO — C5 *Oconto*

HOLTWOOD CAMPGROUND (Public) From Jct of US-41 & SR-22, S 0.5 mi on US-41 to McDonald St, W 0.1 mi to Holtwood Way, N 0.05 mi (R). 2015 rates: $15 to $23. May 15 to Oct 1. (920)834-7732

NORTH BAY SHORE (State Pk) From town: Go 9 mi NE on CR-Y. 2015 rates: $25. (920)834-6825

ONTARIO — D2 *Vernon*

WILDCAT MOUNTAIN (State Pk) From Jct of Hwys 131 & 33, E 1.5 mi on Hwy 33 to park office rd (L). Entrance fee required. Pit toilets. 2015 rates: $12 to $14. (888)947-2757

OSHKOSH — D4 *Winnebago*

HICKORY OAKS FLY IN & CAMPGROUND **Ratings: 5.5/8/7.5** (Campground) 2015 rates: $28 to $33. May 1 to Nov 1. (920)235-8076 3485 Vinland Rd, Oshkosh, WI 54901

KALBUS' COUNTRY HARBOR
Ratings: 7/10★/9 (Campground) From jct US 41 (exit 113) & Hwy 26/CR N: Go 3 mi E on CR N (becomes Fisk Rd), then 1-1/2 mi S on US 45, then 1/2 mi E on Nekimi Ave, then 1/4 mi N on Lake Rd. **FAC:** Gravel rds. (72 spaces). 47 Avail: 41 gravel, 6 grass, 15 pull-thrus (35 x 70), back-ins (40 x 60), 8 full hkups, 39 W, 39 E (30/50 amps), seasonal sites, WiFi, tent sites, showers $, dump, mobile sewer, laundry, LP bottles, fire rings, firewood. **REC:** Lake Winnebago: swim, fishing, marina, rec open to public. Pets OK. Partial handicap access. Big rig sites, eco-friendly, 2015 rates: $35 to $50. May 1 to Oct 31.
(920)426-0062 Lat: 43.94087, Lon: -88.47924
5309 Lake Rd, Oshkosh, WI 54902
kchinc@charter.net
www.kalbuscountryharbor.com
See ad this page.

OSSEO — C2 *Trempealeau*

STONEY CREEK RV RESORT
Ratings: 9.5/10★/10 (Campground) From Jct of Hwy 10 & I-94 (exit 88), E 0.1 mi on Hwy 10 to Oak Grove Rd, S 0.4 mi (R). **FAC:** Paved rds. (176 spaces). Avail: 114 gravel, patios, 17 pull-thrus (45 x 90), back-ins (45 x 65), 83 full hkups, 31 W, 31 E (30/50 amps), seasonal sites, cable, WiFi, tent sites, rentals, showers $, dump, laundry, groc, fire rings, firewood, restaurant. **REC:** heated pool, wading pool, playground, rec open to public. Pet restrict(B). Partial handicap access. Big rig sites, eco-friendly, 2015 rates: $31 to $55. Apr 1 to Nov 1. ATM.
(715)597-2102 Lat: 44.57436, Lon: -91.19509
50483 Oak Grove Rd, Osseo, WI 54758
info@stoneycreekrvresort.com
www.stoneycreekrvresort.com
See ad this page, 1306, 1304 (WI Map).

PARDEEVILLE — D3 *Columbia*

DUCK CREEK CAMPGROUND
Ratings: 8/9★/10 (Campground) From Jct of Hwys 16 & 22, N 0.4 mi on Hwy 22 to CR-G, W 1 mi (R). **FAC:** Gravel rds. (128 spaces). 50 Avail: 15 gravel, 35 grass, 2 pull-thrus (35 x 80), back-ins (40 x 50), 16 full hkups, 34 W, 34 E (30 amps), seasonal sites, WiFi, tent sites, rentals, showers $, dump, mobile sewer, laundry, groc, fire rings, firewood, restaurant. **REC:** pond, swim, fishing, playground. Pet restrict(Q). Partial handicap access. Eco-friendly, 2015 rates: $35 to $50. Apr 25 to Oct 12. ATM.
(608)429-2425 Lat: 43.49971, Lon: -89.32843
W6560 County Rd G, Pardeeville, WI 53954
duckcrcg@frontier.com
www.duckcreekcampground.com
See ad this page.

GLACIER VALLEY CAMPGROUND **Ratings: 6.5/8/8** (Campground) 2015 rates: $30 to $40. Apr 15 to Oct 15. (920)348-5488 n8129 Larson Rd, Cambria, WI 53923

We rate what RVers consider important.

INDIAN TRAILS CAMPGROUND
Ratings: 8/9.5★/10 (Campground) From Jct of Hwys 44 & 22, N 1 mi on Hwy 22 to Haynes Rd, W 1 mi (L). **FAC:** Gravel rds. (324 spaces). 184 Avail: 32 gravel, 152 grass, 12 pull-thrus (30 x 70), back-ins (35 x 60), 28 full hkups, 156 W, 156 E (30/50 amps), seasonal sites, WiFi Hotspot, tent sites, rentals, dump, laundry, groc, LP bottles, fire rings, firewood, restaurant. **REC:** heated pool, pond, swim, playground. Pets OK. Partial handicap access. Big rig sites, eco-friendly, 2015 rates: $35 to $57. Disc: military. Apr 15 to Oct 15. ATM.
(608)429-3244 Lat: 43.55395, Lon: -89.32422
W6445 Haynes Rd, Pardeeville, WI 53954
itcinfo@indiantrailscampground.com
www.indiantrailscampground.com
See ad this page, 1306.

PELICAN LAKE — B4 *Oneida*

PELICAN LAKE CAMPGROUND Ratings: 8/9.5★/9 (Campground) From jct US 45 & CR B: Go 2 mi N on US 45, then 1mi W on CR Q (R). **FAC:** Gravel rds. (100 spaces). Avail: 30 gravel, back-ins (35 x 60), 8 full hkups, 22 W, 22 E (30/50 amps), seasonal sites, WiFi, tent sites, showers $, dump, laundry, fire rings, firewood. **REC:** Pelican Lake: swim, fishing, shuffleboard, playground. Pets OK. Partial handicap access. Eco-friendly, 2015 rates: $30. May 1 to Oct 15. No CC.
(715)487-4600 Lat: 45.51927, Lon: -89.18437
2060 Cty Road Q, Pelican Lake, WI 54463
pelicanlakecpgd@peoplepc.com
www.pelicanlakec.com

PESHTIGO — C5 *Marinette*

BADGER PARK (Public) From Jct of Hwy 41 & Emery Ave (in town), N .25 mi on Emery Ave (E). Call for reservations. 2015 rates: $20. May to Sep 26 (715)582-4321

PHILLIPS — B3 *Price*

SOLBERG PARK (Public) From town, N 2.5 mi on Old Hwy 13 to West Solberg Lake Rd, N 2.5 mi (R) 2015 rates: $20 to $25. (715)339-6371

PITTSVILLE — C3 *Wood*

DEXTER PARK (Public) From Jct of Hwys 80 & 54, W 1 mi on Hwy 54 (R). 2015 rates: $16 to $28 May 1 to Oct 31. (715)421-8422

PLAIN — D3 *Sauk*

WHITE MOUND CAMPGROUND (Public) From jct Hwy 23 & CR GG: Go 2 mi W on CR GG, then 1/2 mi N on Lake Rd. 2015 rates: $5 to $10. (608)546 5011

PLUM CITY — C1 *Pierce*

NUGGET LAKE COUNTY PARK (Public) From center of town: Go 3-1/2 mi W on US 10, then 3 mi N on CR CC, then 2 mi E on CR HH. 2015 rates: $20 (715)639-5611

PLYMOUTH — D5 *Sheboygan*

PLYMOUTH ROCK CAMPING RESORT **Ratings: 8.5/8.5/8.5** (Campground) 2015 rates: $35 to $63. Apr 15 to Oct 15. (800)405-6188 n7271 Lando St, Plymouth, WI 53073

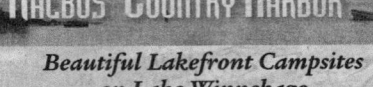

PORTAGE — D3 *Columbia*

➜ PRIDE OF AMERICA CAMPING RESORT **Ratings: 8.5/10★/10** (RV Park) 2015 rates: $47 to $67.50. Apr 15 to Oct 15. (800)236-6395 w7520 West Bush Rd, Pardeeville, WI 53954

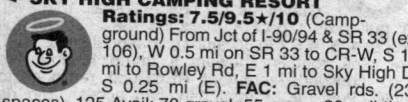

➜ **SKY HIGH CAMPING RESORT**
Ratings: 7.5/9.5★/10 (Campground) From Jct of I-90/94 & SR 33 (exit 106), W 0.5 mi on SR 33 to CR-W, S 1.5 mi to Rowley Rd, E 1 mi to Sky High Dr, S 0.25 mi (E). **FAC:** Gravel rds. (230 spaces). 125 Avail: 70 gravel, 55 grass, 20 pull-thrus (40 x 100), back-ins (40 x 60), 38 full hkups, 87 W, 87 E (30/50 amps), seasonal sites, WiFi Hotspot, tent sites, rentals, dump, mobile sewer, laundry, groc, LP gas, fire rings, firewood. **REC:** heated pool, wading pool, shuffleboard, playground. Pets OK. Partial handicap access. Big rig sites, eco-friendly, 2015 rates: $28 to $52. ATM.
(608)742-2572 Lat: 43.48255, Lon: -89.51285
n5740 Sky High Dr, Portage, WI 53901
info@skyhighcampingresort.com
www.skyhighcampingresort.com

PORTERFIELD — C5 *Marinette*

➘ DIAMOND LAKE FAMILY CAMPGROUND **Ratings: 5.5/8.5/7.5** (Campground) 2015 rates: $30 to $34. May 1 to Oct 31. (715)789-2113 w5449 Loomis Rd, Porterfield, WI 54159

POTOSI — E2 *Grant*

↓ GRANT RIVER (Public Corps) From town, S 3 mi on SR-133 (L). 2015 rates: $16 to $18. Apr 10 to Oct 25. (563)582-0881

PRAIRIE DU CHIEN — E2 *Crawford*

➘ SPORTS UNLIMITED CAMPGROUND & BARN YARD 9 GOLF COURSE **Ratings: 7.5/9.5★/8.5** (Campground) 2015 rates: $30 to $42. Apr 15 to Oct 15. (608)326-2141 32750 Cty Rd K, Prairie du Chien, WI 53821

RACINE — E5 *Racine*

➜ CLIFFSIDE PARK (Public) From Jct of I-94 & Seven Mile Rd (Exit 326), E 4.5 mi from Seven Mile Rd to SR-32/Douglas Ave, (R) 1 mi on SR-32/Douglas to Six Mile Rd (L) go 2 mi to Michna Rd (L). Park is on the right. 2015 rates: $23. Apr 15 to Oct 15. (800)272-2463

↙ SANDERS PARK (Public) From Jct of I-94 & Cnty 'KR' (exit 337), E 5.5 mi on Cnty 'KR' to Wood Rd, N 0.5 mi (R). 2015 rates: $23. Apr 15 to Oct 15. (262)886-8440

RED CLIFF — A2 *Bayfield*

↑ BUFFALO BAY (Public) From N end of town, N 3 mi on SR-13 (R). Call park for reservations. 2015 rates: $30 to $35. May 15 to Oct 15. (715)779-3712

REDGRANITE — D4 *Waushara*

➘ FLANAGAN'S PEARL LAKE CAMPSITE **Ratings: 7/7/7** (Campground) 2015 rates: $36 to $39. Apr 15 to Oct 15. (920)566-2758 w4585 Pearl Lake Rd, Redgranite, WI 54970

REEDSVILLE — D5 *Manitowoc*

➜ **RAINBOW'S END CAMPGROUND**
Ratings: 7/7.5/8.5 (Campground) From Jct of Hwy 10 & CR-W: Go E 1-1/3 mi on Hwy 10 (R); or From Jct of I-43 & Hwy 10: Go W 10-3/4 mi on Hwy 10 (L). **FAC:** Gravel rds. (89 spaces). Avail: 44 grass, 17 pull-thrus (30 x 75), back-ins (30 x 50), some side by side hkups, 44 W, 44 E (20/30 amps), seasonal sites, WiFi, tent sites, rentals, showers $, dump, laundry, groc, LP gas, fire rings, firewood. **REC:** pond, swim, playground. Pet restrict(B). Partial handicap access. Eco-friendly, 2015 rates: $27. May 1 to Oct 15. ATM, no CC.
(920)754-4142 Lat: 44.15186, Lon: -87.93966
18227 US Hwy 10, Reedsville, WI 54230
rainbowscamp@tm.net
www.rainbowsendcampgrounds.homestead.com
See ad this page.

RHINELANDER — B3 *Oneida*

➜ WEST BAY CAMPING RESORT **Ratings: 7.5/9★/8.5** (Membership Pk) 2015 rates: $34. May 1 to Oct 1. (715)362-3481 4330 South Shore Dr, Rhinelander, WI 54501

RICE LAKE — B1 *Barron*

➜ NORTHWOOD SHORES CAMPGROUND **Ratings: 8/8.5/9** (Campground) 2015 rates: $39. May 1 to Oct 13. (715)234-1150 1876 29-3/4 Avenue, Rice Lake, WI 54868

A campground rating is based on ALL facilities available at the park.

RIO — D3 *Columbia*

➜ SILVER SPRINGS CAMPSITES **Ratings: 9/10★/10** (Campground) 2015 rates: $37 to $55. Apr 15 to Sep 30. (920)992-3537 n5048 Ludwig Rd, Rio, WI 53960

↑ WILLOW MILL CAMPSITE **Ratings: 8/7/9** (RV Park) 2015 rates: $36 to $38. May 1 to Oct 1. (800)582-0393 N 5830 County Hwy Ss, Rio, WI 53960

RIVER FALLS — C1 *St Croix*

↑ HOFFMAN PARK (Public) From Jct of I-94 & Hwy 35 (Exit 3), S 8 mi on Hwy 35 to Division St, E 0.2 mi to Division St (Cty M), W 0.3 mi on Hanson, N 0.2 mi (L). 2015 rates: $15. Apr 15 to Oct 15. (715)426-3420

ROSHOLT — C3 *Portage*

↗ COLLINS PARK (Public) From town, NE 12 mi on SR-66 to CR-I, S 1.5 mi (L). Pit toilets. 2015 rates: $16 to $22. May 15 to Sep 30. (715)346-1433

SARONA — B1 *Washburn*

➜ WHITETAIL RIDGE CAMPGROUND & RV PARK **Ratings: 5/9/8.5** (Campground) 2015 rates: $35. Apr 1 to Oct 1. (715)469-3309 N 753 Shallow Lake Rd, Sarona, WI 54870

SAUKVILLE — D5 *Ozaukee*

Travel Services

➜ **CAMPING WORLD OF SAUKVILLE** As the nation's largest retailer of RV supplies, accessories, services and new and used RVs, Camping World is committed to making your total RV experience better. RV Accessories:(877)479-4582. **SERVICES:** Staffed RV wash, RV Sales. RV supplies, LP, dump, emergency parking. Hours: 8am - 6pm.
(888)827-0779 Lat: 43.385820, Lon: -87.924560
800 E. Green Bay Avenue, Saukville, WI 53080
www.campingworld.com

SAYNER — B3 *Vilas*

↗ NO HIGHLAND AMERICAN LEGION SF/FIREFLY LAKE (State Pk) From Boulder Junction, N 5 mi on US-51 to Hwy M, NE 3 mi to Hwy M, E 1.5 mi, follow sign (R). Entrance fee required. Pit toilets. 2015 rates: $15 to $17. (715)385-2727

← NO HIGHLAND AMERICAN LEGION SF/PLUM LAKE (State Pk) From town, W 1 mi on Hwy N (R). Entrance fee required. Pit toilets. 2015 rates: $12 to $14. May 19 to Sep 2. (715)385-2727

↖ NO HIGHLAND AMERICAN LEGION SF/RAZORBACK LAKE (State Pk) From town, W 2.5 mi on Hwy N to Razorback Rd, N 5 mi (R). Entrance fee required. Pit toilets. 2015 rates: $12 to $14. (715)385-2727

↘ NO HIGHLAND AMERICAN LEGION SF/STARRETT LAKE (State Pk) From town, S 7.5 mi on Hwy M to N Muskellunge Rd, W 5 mi (L). Entrance fee required. Pit toilets. 2015 rates: $12 to $14. May 1 to Oct 14. (715)385-2727

SHAWANO — C4 *Shawano*

← PINE GROVE CAMPGROUND **Ratings: 8/10★/10** (Campground) 2015 rates: $30 to $51. Apr 15 to Nov 30. (715)787-4555 n5999 Campground Rd, Shawano, WI 54166

↑ SHAWANO LAKE PARK (Public) From town, NE 5 mi on CR-H, follow signs (R). 2015 rates: $25 to $30. May 15 to Oct 15. (715)524-4986

SHEBOYGAN — D5 *Sheboygan*

↓ KOHLER-ANDRAE (State Pk) From Jct of I-43 & exit 120 (V St), E 1 mi on V St to CR-KK, S 1 mi to Old Park Rd, E 0.25 mi (E). Entrance fee required. 2015 rates: $12 to $17. (920)451-4080

Travel Services

↙ **TRUCK COUNTRY** Truck Country is the largest Freightliner/Western Star dealer group in the United States, with 21 locations in Iowa, Indiana, Ohio and Wisconsin. **SERVICES:** Engine/chassis repair, emergency rd svc, RV Sales. Waiting room. Hours: 7 am - 5 pm.
(844)920-9600 Lat: 43.704258, Lon: -87.758851
4530 S. Taylor Dr., Sheboygan, WI 53081
www.truckcountry.com
See ad pages 488, 1311.

SHELL LAKE — B1 *Washburn*

➜ RED BARN CAMPGROUND **Ratings: 5.5/7/9** (Campground) 2015 rates: $34 to $37. May 1 to Oct 10. (715)468-2575 w6820 Cty Hwy B, Shell Lake, WI 54871

➜ SHELL LAKE PARK (Public) From Jct of Hwy 63 & CR-B, S 0.4 mi on Hwy 63 (L). 2015 rates: $27 to $35. May 1 to Oct 15. (715)468-7846

SHERWOOD — D4 *Calument*

➘ HIGH CLIFF (State Pk) From Appleton, E 5 mi on Hwy 10 to Hwy 114, E 3 mi to State Park Rd, S 3 mi to Entrance (E). 2015 rates: $10 to $17. (920)989-1106

SHULLSBURG — E3 *Lafayette*

Travel Services

➘ **TRUCK COUNTRY** Full RV service. **SERVICES:** RV, MH mechanical, engine/chassis repair, emergency rd svc, restrooms. **TOW:** RV. RV accessible. waiting room. Hours: M-F 7am-midnight, Sa 7am-noon.
(800)362-1313 Lat: 42.57708, Lon: -90.23489
119 Hwy 11, Shullsburg, WI 53586
www.truckcountry.com
See ad pages 488, 1311.

SILVER CLIFF — B4 *Marinette*

➘ KOSIR'S RAPID RAFTS & CAMPGROUND **Ratings: 4/7/7** (Campground) 2015 rates: $15. Apr 1 to Sep 15. (715)757-3431 W 14073 Highway C, Silver Cliff, WI 54104

➘ **MCCASLIN MOUNTAIN CAMPGROUND Ratings: 5/7/8** (Campground) From Jct Hwy 32 & County Rd F (in Lakewood): Go 10 mi E on CR-F (L). **FAC:** Gravel rds. (109 spaces). Avail: 35 gravel, back-ins (30 x 50), 35 W, 35 E (20/30 amps), seasonal sites, tent sites, rentals, showers $, dump, groc, LP bottles, fire rings, firewood. **REC:** playground. Pets OK. Partial handicap access. Eco-friendly, 2015 rates: $25 to $35. May 15 to Dec 1.
(715)757-3734 Lat: 45.37763, Lon: -88.38856
W 15720 County F, Silver Cliff, WI 54104
info@mccaslinmountain.com
www.mccaslinmountain.com

SISTER BAY — C5 *Door*

↓ AQUALAND CAMPGROUND **Ratings: 6.5/8.5/9.5** (Campground) 2015 rates: $35. May 15 to Oct 15. (920)854-4573 2445 Cty Rd Q, Sister Bay, WI 54234

SOLON SPRINGS — A1 *Douglas*

LUCIUS WOODS (Public) From jct CR A & US 53: Go 1/4 mi S, then 1/10 mi E on Marion Ave. 2015 rates: $15 to $18. May 17 to Sep 8. (715)378-4528

SOMERSET — C1 *St Croix*

➜ APPLE RIVER FAMILY CAMPGROUND **Ratings: 7/6/8** (Campground) 2015 rates: $40 to $60. (715)247-3600 345 Church Hill Rd, Somerset, WI 54025

➜ RIVER'S EDGE CAMPING RESORT **Ratings: 7/7/7.5** (Campground) 2015 rates: $30 to $40. May 15 to Sep 30. (715)247-3305 1820 Raleigh Rd, New Richmond, WI 54017

SPARTA — D2 *La Crosse*

↓ LEON VALLEY CAMPGROUND **Ratings: 6.5/8.5/7.5** (Campground) 2015 rates: $38. Apr 1 to Oct 31. (608)269-6400 9050 Jancing Ave, Sparta, WI 54656

SPOONER — B1 *Washburn*

↓ THE COUNTRY HOUSE MOTEL & RV PARK **Ratings: 5.5/9★/8** (RV Park) 2015 rates: $36. May 1 to Oct 10. (715)635-8721 717 South River St. (Hwy 63), Spooner, WI 54801

SPRING GREEN — E3 *Sauk*

← FIRESIDE CAMPGROUND **Ratings: 7.5/8★/8** (Campground) 2015 rates: $30 to $40. Apr 6 to Nov 30. (608)583-5111 33533 Jay Ln, Lone Rock, WI 53556

SPRING GREEN (CONT)

TOWER HILL (State Pk) 3 mi SE via US-14 and Hwy-23. Pit toilets. May 15 to Oct 15. (608)588-2116

WISCONSIN RIVERSIDE RESORT Ratings: 9.5/9.5★/10 (RV Park) From Jct of Hwy 23 & Hwy 14, S 0.8 mi on Hwy 23 to Madison St, W 0.7 mi on Madison St to Shifflet Rd, S 0.75 mi (E). **FAC:** Paved rds. (145 spaces). 61 Avail: 26 gravel, 35 grass, patios, 9 pull-thrus (30 x 65), back-ins (35 x 60), 61 full hkups (30/50 amps), seasonal sites, WiFi, tent sites, rentals, showers $, laundry, groc, LP bottles, fire rings, firewood, restaurant. **REC:** heated pool, Wisconsin River: swim, fishing, shuffleboard, playground. Pets OK. Partial handicap access. Big rig sites, eco-friendly, 2015 rates: $38 to $60. Apr 1 to Nov 1. ATM.
(608)588-2826 Lat: 43.16220, Lon: -90.07524
S13220 Shifflet Rd, Spring Green, WI 53588
info@wiriverside.com
www.wiriverside.com

SPRING VALLEY — C1 *St Croix*

HIGHLAND RIDGE CAMPGROUND (Public Corps) From Jct of I-94 & exit 24, S 2 mile on CR-B (exit 24) to CR-N, E 2 mi to CR-NN, S 2 mi (R). 2015 rates: $16 to $20. Apr 1 to Nov 30. (715)778-5562

ST CROIX FALLS — B1 *Polk*

INTERSTATE (State Pk) From Jct of US-8 & SR-35, S 0.5 mi on SR-35 (R). 2015 rates: $12 to $14. (715)483-3747

ST GERMAIN — B3 *Vilas*

LYNN ANN'S CAMPGROUND **Ratings: 8/8/7.5** (Campground) 2015 rates: $33 to $39. May 1 to Oct 12. (715)542-3456 1597 S Shore, St Germain, WI 54558

STEVENS POINT — C3 *Portage*

DUBAY PARK (Public) From Jct of US-51 & Hwy 10, W 7 mi on Hwy 10 to CR-E, N 8 mi (R). Pit toilets. 2015 rates: $16 to $22. May 1 to Oct 31. (715)346-1433

JORDAN PARK (Public) From town, NE 4 mi on Hwy 66 to CR-Y, N 0.25 mi (L). 2015 rates: $16. May 1 to Oct 31. (715)346-1433

RIVERS EDGE CAMPGROUND
Ratings: 8.5/9.5★/9 (Campground) From Jct US-51 & I-39: Take Casimir (Exit 163), then N 4-1/2 mi on N Second Dr, then W 1/2 mi on Maple Dr, then N 1/2 mi on Campsite Dr (L). **FAC:** Paved rds. (192 spaces). 92 Avail: 62 gravel, 30 grass, 33 pull-thrus (30 x 80), back-ins (30 x 50), 92 W, 92 E (30/50 amps), seasonal sites, WiFi Hotspot, tent sites, rentals, showers $, dump, mobile sewer, laundry, groc, LP bottles, fire rings, firewood, restaurant. **REC:** heated pool, Wisconsin River: swim, fishing, playground. Pet restrict(Q) $. Partial handicap access. Eco-friendly, 2015 rates: $42. May 1 to Oct 15. ATM.
(715)344-8058 Lat: 44.63118, Lon: -89.63737
3266 Campsite Dr, Stevens Point, WI 54482
camp@riversedgewisconsin.com
www.riversedgewisconsin.com
See ad this page, 1306.

Things to See and Do

BULLHEADS BAR & GRILL Prime destination for lunch, dinner or drinks - offering a full bar & seasonal outdoor dining along the Wisconsin River. Also available for meetings, receptions & special events. Partial handicap access. RV accessible. Restrooms, food. Hours: W-Th noon to 9pm, F-Su 11am to 10 pm. ATM.
(715)344-5990 Lat: 44.63118, Lon: -89.63737
3368 Campsite Dr, Stevens Point, WI 54482
www.bullheadsbargrill.com
See ad this page.

Look in the Guide to Seasonal Sites to find places you can stay for a month, a season or longer.

STOCKBRIDGE — D4 *Calumet*

CALUMET COUNTY PARK (Public) From town, N 2 mi on Hwy 55 to Cnty Trunk Rd, W 2 mi (E). Note: 40' RV length limit. 2015 rates: $18 to $24. Apr 1 to Nov 1. (920)439-1008

LAKEVIEW CAMPGROUND **Ratings: 6/9/9** (Campground) 2015 rates: $39.50. Apr 15 to Oct 15. (920)439-1495 n4475 Ledge Rd, Chilton, WI 53014

STOUGHTON — E4 *Dane*

BADGERLAND CAMPGROUND **Ratings: 5.5/9/8** (Campground) 2015 rates: $38 to $42. Apr 3 to Nov 1. (608)873-5800 2671 Circle Dr, Stoughton, WI 53589

LAKE KEGONSA (State Pk) From Jct of I-90 & CR-N (exit 147), S 1 mi on CR-N to Koshkonong Rd, W 1.5 mi to Door Creek Rd, S 1 mi. Entrance fee required. 2015 rates: $12 to $28. (608)873-9695

VIKING VILLAGE CAMPGROUND & RESORT **Ratings: 6/9/9.5** (Campground) 2015 rates: $45.75 to $48.75. May 1 to Oct 1. (608)873-6601 1648 County Rd N, Stoughton, WI 53589

STRUM — C2 *Trempealeau*

CRYSTAL LAKE PARK (Public) From Jct of I-94 & Hwy 10, W 9 mi on Hwy 10 to Woodland Dr, S 100 ft (L). 2015 rates: $20 to $22. May 15 to Oct 1. (715)695-3601

STURGEON BAY — C5 *Door*

HARBOUR VILLAGE RESORT **Ratings: 7.5/7.5/9** (Membership Pk) 2015 rates: $32 to $60. May 15 to Oct 15. (920)743-0274 5840 Hwy 42, Sturgeon Bay, WI 54235

POTAWATOMI (State Pk) From Hwy 42/57 (in Green Bay), N 40 mi to County Trunk PD, S 1 mi (R).Entrance fee required. Pit toilets. 2015 rates: $15 to $17. (920)746-2890

TRANQUIL TIMBERS CAMPING RETREAT **Ratings: 8/8★/9** (Campground) 2015 rates: $38 to $53. Apr 15 to Oct 15. (800)405-6188 3668 Grondin Rd, Sturgeon Bay, WI 54235

YOGI BEAR'S JELLYSTONE PARK **Ratings: 8.5/9/9** (Campground) 2015 rates: $37.50 to $57.50. May 16 to Sep 10. (920)743-9001 3677 May Rd, Sturgeon Bay, WI 54235

SUMMIT LAKE — B4 *Langlade*

LANGLADE COUNTY VETERANS MEMORIAL PARK (Public) From Jct of Hwy 45 & Cnty Trunk J, E 3 mi on Cnty Trunk J (E). 2015 rates: $20. May 1 to Dec 1. (715)623-6214

SUPERIOR — A1 *Douglas*

AMNICON FALLS (State Pk) From town, E 10 mi on Hwy 2 to CR-U, N 0.5 mi (L). Entrance fee required. 2015 rates: $12 to $14. (715)398-3000

NORTHLAND CAMPING & RV PARK
Ratings: 8/6.5/8.5 (Campground) From Jct of US-2/53 & Hwy 13: Go E 0.1 mi on Hwy 13S (2.5 mi SE of town) (L). **FAC:** Gravel rds. (72 spaces). 60 Avail: 17 paved, 43 gravel, 39 pull-thrus (35 x 70), back-ins (35 x 60), 60 full hkups (30/50 amps), seasonal sites, WiFi, tent sites, dump, laundry, fire rings, firewood. **REC:** heated pool, whirlpool, playground. Pets OK. Partial handicap access. Big rig sites, 2015 rates: $32 to $36. May 15 to Oct 15. No CC.
(715)398-3327 Lat: 46.64782, Lon: -91.97462
6377 E State Rd 13, South Range, WI 54874
www.northlandcamprv.com
See ad page 651.

PATTISON (State Pk) From town, S 13 mi on Hwy 35 (L). Entrance fee required. Pit toilets. 2015 rates: $12 to $17. (715)399-3111

THREE LAKES — B4 *Oneida*

HARBOR CAMPGROUND **Ratings: 5/7.5/6.5** (Campground) 2015 rates: $30 to $45. May 1 to Oct 1. (715)546-3520 6812 Connors Rd, Three Lakes, WI 54562

TOMAH — D2 *Monroe*

HOLIDAY LODGE GOLF RESORT & RV PARK
Ratings: 7.5/8/8 (Campground) From Jct I-94 & Hwy 21: Go 6 mi E on Hwy 21, then 3/4 mi S on Excelsior Ave. **FAC:** Gravel rds. (27 spaces). Avail: 18 gravel, 11 pull-thrus (36 x 60), back-ins (36 x 60), 14 full hkups, 4 W, 4 E (30/50 amps), seasonal sites, WiFi, tent sites, rentals, showers $, dump, laundry, fire rings, firewood, restaurant. **REC:** golf, rec open to public. Pets OK. Partial handicap access. Big rig sites, eco-friendly, 2015 rates: $37 to $43. May 1 to Sep 1. ATM.
(608)372-9314 Lat: 44.01988, Lon: -90.37908
10558 Freedom Rd, Tomah, WI 54660
holidaylodge@centurytel.net
www.holidaylodgegolf.com
See ad this page, 1306.

Things to See and Do

HO-CHUNK GAMING TOMAH Casino with your favorite slots and conveniently connected to Whitetail Crossing Convenience Store. Partial handicap access. RV accessible. Restrooms. Hours: Su-Thurs 8am to MN, Fri & Sat 8am to 2am. ATM.
(866)880-9822 Lat: 44.030148, Lon: -90.437292
27867 Hwy 21 East, Tomah, WI 54660
www.ho-chunkgaming.com/tomah/
See ad page 1310 (Spotlight Wisconsin Dells).

HOLIDAY LODGE GOLF RESORT Regulation 18 hole golf course with RV park, motel & vacation home rentals. Full Pro Shop. Full service bar, fresh sandwiches & burgers served. Rental golf clubs & special rates for guests. May 1 to Sep 1. partial handicap access. RV accessible. Restrooms, food. Hours: 7am to 7pm. Adult fee: $38 to $45. ATM.
(608)372-9314 Lat: 44.01988, Lon: -90.37908
10555 Fredom Rd, Tomah, WI 54660
holidaylodge@centurytel.net
ww.holidaylodgegolf.com
See ad this page.

TOMAHAWK — B3 *Lincoln, Oneida*

BIRKENSEE CAMPGROUND **Ratings: 6/8/7.5** (Campground) 2015 rates: $35 to $40. May 1 to Oct 1. (715)453-5103 n9350 Hwy H, Tomahawk, WI 54487

NORTHFOREST CAMPGROUND **Ratings: 7/7/7** (Campground) 2015 rates: $25 to $35. May 1 to Oct 1. (715)453-2522 w2504 Northforest Rd, Tomahawk, WI 54487

OTTER LAKE RECREATION AREA (Public) From town: Go 3 mi S on US-51, then 7 mi E on CR-S, Stevenson Rd, Grundy Rd, Bear Trail Rd & Otter Lake Rd. Pit toilets. 2015 rates: $10. May 2 to Oct 31. (715)536-0327

TERRACE VIEW CAMPSITES **Ratings: 6/6.5/7.5** (Campground) 2015 rates: $26 to $28. Apr 1 to Dec 1. (715)453-8352 w5220 Terrace View Rd, Tomahawk, WI 54487-9428

TOMAHAWK CAMPGROUND & RV PARK **Ratings: 3.5/7.5/6.5** (RV Park) 2015 rates: $20 to $25 May 1 to Oct 1. (715)525-9600 n11046 County Rd A Tomahawk, WI 54487

TONY — B2 *Rusk*

JOSIE CREEK PARK (Public) From town, E 1 mi on Hwy 8 to CR-X, N 2 mi (L). Pit toilets. 2015 rates $18 to $23. May 1 to Dec 1. (715)532-2113

TREGO — B1 *Washburn*

LOG CABIN RESORT & CAMPGROUND **Ratings: 6/7/8.5** (Campground) 2015 rates: $37 to $42 May 1 to Oct 15. (715)635-2959 N 7470 Log Cabin Dr, Trego, WI 54888

TREMPEALEAU — D2 *Trempealeau*

PERROT (State Pk) From town, W 3.5 mi on park rd (E). Pit toilets. 2015 rates: $12 to $14. (608)534-6409

TURTLE LAKE — B1 *Barron, Polk*

ST CROIX RV PARK **Ratings: 7.5/7.5/7** (Campground) 2015 rates: $25. May 1 to Oct 31. (715)986-4777 777 Hwy 8 & 63, Turtle Lake, WI 54889

TURTLE LAKE RV PARK Ratings: 6/8/7.5 (Campground) E-bnd: From Jct of US-63S & US-8, E 500 ft on US-8 (R) W-bnd: From Jct of US 63N & US 8, West 1 mi (L). **FAC:** Gravel rds. (70 spaces). Avail 50 gravel, 25 pull-thrus (32 x 90), back-ins (32 x 70), 50 full hkups (30/50 amps), seasonal sites, WiFi, tent sites, fire rings, firewood. **REC:** heated pool. Pets OK

RV Park ratings you can rely on!

TURTLE LAKE (CONT)

TURTLE LAKE RV PARK (CONT)
Partial handicap access. Big rig sites, eco-friendly, 2015 rates: $29. Apr 15 to Oct 15.
(715)986-4140 Lat: 45.39478, Lon: -92.16238
750 US Hwy 8 & 63S, Turtle Lake, WI 54889
tlrvpark@gmail.com
www.turtlelakervpark.com

TWO RIVERS — D5 *Manitowoc*

POINT BEACH (State Pk) From town, N 4 mi on Cnty Hwy O to park access rd, E 0.3 mi (L). Entrance fee required. Pit toilets. 2015 rates: $12 to $22. (920)794-7480

SCHEFFEL'S HIDEAWAY CAMPGROUND **Ratings: 7/9.5★/10** (Campground) 2015 rates: $35 to $42. Apr 1 to Dec 1. (920)657-1270 6511 County Rd O, Two Rivers, WI 54241

SEA GULL MARINA & CAMPGROUND **Ratings: 4.5/8/7** (Campground) 2015 rates: $20 to $31. May 15 to Oct 15. (920)794-7533 1400 Lake St, Two Rivers, WI 54241

VILLAGE INN ON THE LAKE HOTEL & RV PARK
Ratings: 8.5/10★/8.5 (RV Park) From Jct of Hwy 42 & Hwy 310: S 2 mi on Hwy 42 (R). **FAC:** Paved/gravel rds. 24 gravel, 12 pull-thrus (24 x 60), back-ins (25 x 35), 24 full hkups (30/50 amps), WiFi, rentals, laundry, fire rings, firewood. **REC:** heated pool, whirlpool, Lake Michigan: playground. Pets OK. Partial handicap access, no tents. Big rig sites, eco-friendly, 2015 rates: $35 to $50. Disc: AAA, military. ATM.
AAA Approved
(920)794-8818 Lat: 44.13291, Lon: -87.60047
3310 Memorial Dr, Two Rivers, WI 54241
info@villageinnwi.com
www.villageinnwi.com
See ad this page, 1306 & RV Trips of a Lifetime in Magazine Section.

Visit Camping World on your RV travels to stock up on accessories and supplies while on the road. Find the nearest SuperCenter at CampingWorld.com

VIOLA — D2 *Vernon*

BANKER PARK (Public) At jct Hwy-131 & Hwy-56. (608)627-1831

WABENO — B4 *Forest, Langlade*

S-J & W HAM LAKE CAMPGROUND **Ratings: 5/5.5/6** (Campground) 2015 rates: $28 to $37. May 1 to Oct 15. (715)674-2201 3490 State Hwy 32, Wabeno, WI 54566

WARRENS — D2 *Monroe*

JELLYSTONE PARK WARRENS
Ratings: 8.5/10★/10 (RV Park) From Jct of I-94 & CR-EW (Warren exit 135), E 0.4 mi on CR-EW (L).

ENJOY A VACATION THAT HAS IT ALL!
For 30+ yrs Jellystone Warrens is the choice for families & friends to enjoy the great outdoors: daily activities, mini golf, paddleboats, campfires & more. A unique 1st class campground w/water park & resort facilities.

FAC: Paved/gravel rds. (653 spaces). 393 Avail: 27 paved, 300 gravel, 66 grass, patios, 157 pull-thrus (35 x 60), back-ins (40 x 50), 393 full hkups (30/50 amps), seasonal sites, cable, WiFi Hotspot, tent sites, rentals, dump, laundry, groc, LP gas, fire rings, firewood, restaurant, controlled access. **REC:** heated pool, wading pool, whirlpool, pond, swim, fishing, shuffleboard, playground, rec open to public. Pets OK. Partial handicap access. Big rig sites, eco-friendly, 2015 rates: $49 to $69. Disc: AAA, military. Apr 15 to Oct 15. ATM.
(888)386-9644 Lat: 44.12523, Lon: -90.52354
1500 Jellystone Park Dr, Warrens, WI 54666
info@jellystonewarrens.com
www.JellystoneWarrens.com
See ad pages 1324, 1306 & Family Camping in Magazine Section.

Take an RV Trip of a Lifetime! Check out trip ideas at the front of the Guide - you'll find something for the history buff, the food lover or even your wild side!

Enjoy the scenery as you travel North America. We exclusively rate campgrounds for their visual appearance and environmental quality, and represent their score, 1 through 10, as the third rating in our Triple Rating System.

Explore America's Top RV Destinations!

From fishing along the Cape to boating on the Great Lakes, we've put the Spotlight on North America's most popular travel destinations. Turn to the Spotlight articles in our State and Province sections to learn more.

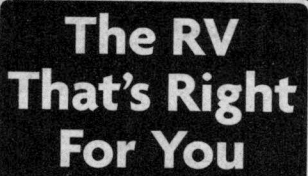

The RV That's Right For You

Which recreational vehicle is right for you? Our handy overview in the front of this Guide helps prospective buyers decide which RV type fits their lifestyle, travel needs and budget, from folding camping trailers to motorhomes.

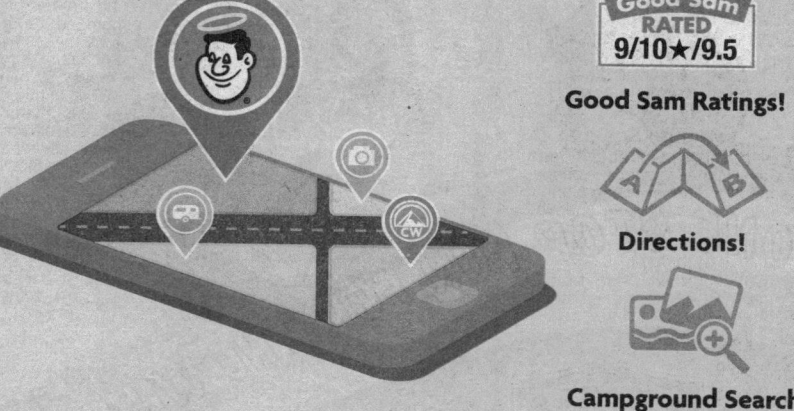

See listing Warrens, WI

WASHBURN — A2 *Bayfield*

MEMORIAL PARK (Public) From town: Go N on Memorial Park Lane. 2015 rates: $20 to $25. May 15 to Oct 15. (715)373-6160

WEST END THOMPSON PARK (Public) From Jct of Hwy 13 & 8th St, S 0.3 mi on 8th St (E). 2015 rates: $25. Apr 15 to Oct 15. (715)373-6160

WASHINGTON ISLAND — B5 *Door*

WASHINGTON ISLAND CAMPGROUND
Ratings: 7.5/8/9 (Campground) At Northport, take the ferry to the Island. From Ferry Landing: Go 1-3/4 mi NE on Lobdells Point Rd, then 1/3 mi N on Main Rd, then 2 mi E on Lake View Rd, then 1/2 mi S on East Side Rd. **FAC:** Gravel rds. (45 spaces). Avail: 38 gravel, 1 pull-thrus (35 x 60), back-ins (25 x 50), 38 W, 38 E (30/50 amps), seasonal sites, WiFi Hotspot, tent sites, rentals, dump, mobile sewer, laundry, groc, fire rings, firewood. **REC:** pond, swim, playground. Pets OK. Partial handicap access. Eco-friendly, 2015 rates: $35. May 1 to Oct 14. ATM.
(920)847-2622 Lat: 45.35667, Lon: -86.88895
745 East Side Rd, Washington Island, WI 54246
info@washingtonislandcampground.com
www.washingtonislandcampground.com
See ad page 1308 (Spotlight Door County).

Things to See and Do

REEL DREAMS SALMON CHARTERS Coast Guard licensed salmon charter service. Rods, reels, lures & bait provided. Cleaning & bagging of catch. Fishing license and salmon & trout stamp needed. Bring rain gear, food & drinks. Call for reservations and details. May 1 to Oct 14. RV accessible. Restrooms. Adult fee: $500. ATM.
(920)535-0073 Lat: 45.35667, Lon: -86.88895
745 East Side Rd, Washington Island, WI 54246
reeldreamswi@yahoo.com
See ad page 1308 (Spotlight Door County).

WATERTOWN — E4 *Dodge, Jefferson*

RIVER BEND RV RESORT
Ratings: 8.5/10★/9.5 (RV Resort) From Jct of 26 & 19, W 6 mi on 19 to Q St, S 1 mi to Hubbleton Rd, W 1 mi to Riverbend Rd, S 1 mi to Rubidell, W 0.7 mi (R). **FAC:** Paved rds. (630 spaces). Avail: 82 gravel, 5 pull-thrus (46 x 100), back-ins (50 x 50), 82 W, 82 E (30/50 amps), seasonal sites, WiFi Hotspot, tent sites, rentals, dump, mobile sewer, laundry, groc, LP gas, fire rings, firewood, restaurant, controlled access. **REC:** heated pool, whirlpool, Crawfish River: swim, fishing, shuffleboard, playground, rec open to public. Pets OK. Partial handicap access. Eco-friendly, 2015 rates: $50 to $95. ATM.
(920)261-7505 Lat: 43.16384, Lon: -88.87328
W 6940 Rubidell Rd, Watertown, WI 53094
info@rbresort.com
www.rbresort.com
See ad this page.

WAUPACA — C4 *Waupaca*

HARTMAN CREEK (State Pk) From town, W 6 mi on Hwy 54 to Hartman Creek Rd, S 1.6 mi (L). 2015 rates: $12 to $17. (715)258-2372

WAUPACA S'MORE FUN CAMPGROUND **Ratings: 7/9.5★/9** (Campground) 2015 rates: $31 to $39. Apr 19 to Oct 13. (715)258-8010 e2411 Holmes Rd, Waupaca, WI 54981

WAUSAU — C3 *Marathon*

MARATHON PARK (Public) From Jct of I-39/51 & Hwy 52E (exit 192), E 0.6 mi on Hwy 52E/Stewart Ave (R). Note: No fire allowed. 2015 rates: $14 to $20. May 2 to Oct 31. (715)261-1566

Travel Services

TRUCK COUNTRY Full RV service. **SERVICES:** MH mechanical, engine/chassis repair, emergency rd svc, restrooms. **TOW:** RV. RV accessible. waiting room. Hours: M-F 6am-12:30am, Sa 6am-4:30pm.
(715)359-9989 Lat: 44.85542, Lon: -89.63512
2435 Trailwood Ln, Rothschild, WI 54474
www.truckcountry.com
See ad pages 488, 1311.

WAUTOMA — D3 *Marquette*

LAKE OF THE WOODS CAMPGROUND **Ratings: 7/8.5/8** (Campground) 2015 rates: $44 to $59. (920)787-3601 n9070 14th Ave, Wautoma, WI 54982

WEST BEND — D4 *Washington*

LAKE LENWOOD BEACH & CAMPGROUND
Ratings: 7/9.5★/9 (Campground) From Jct of Hwy 45 & CR-D (Exit 73): Go E 1-1/2 mi on CR-D (Exit 73) (becomes Main St) to Hwy 144, then N 1 mi to Wallace Lake Rd, then E 200 ft to Lenwood Dr (R). **FAC:** Paved/gravel rds. (130 spaces). Avail: 60 grass, 7 pull-thrus (40 x 60), back-ins (40 x 60), 45 full hkups, 15 W, 15 E (30/50 amps), seasonal sites, WiFi, tent sites, showers $, dump, fire rings, firewood. **REC:** Lake Lenwood: swim, fishing, playground, rec open to public. Pet restrict(B/Q). Big rig sites, eco-friendly, 2015 rates: $40.50 to $43.50. Apr 15 to Oct 19.
(262)334-1335 Lat: 43.44726, Lon: -88.16544
7053 Lenwood Dr, West Bend, WI 53090
www.lakelenwood.com
See ad pages 1319, 1306.

TIMBER TRAIL CAMPGROUND **Ratings: 5/5/7.5** (Campground) 2015 rates: $25 to $35. May 15 to Oct 15. (262)338-8561 7590 Good Luck Lane, West Bend, WI 53090

WEST SALEM — D2 *La Crosse*

NESHONOC LAKESIDE CAMP-RESORT **Ratings: 9.5/9.5★/10** (Campground) 2015 rates: $40 to $85. Apr 15 to Oct 15. (608)786-1792 N 5334 Neshonoc Rd, West Salem, WI 54669

VETERANS MEMORIAL CAMPGROUND
(Public) From Jct of I-90 & SR 16 (exit 5): Go 3 3/4 mi N on SR 16 to CR-VP (R). **FAC:** Gravel rds. 120 grass, 16 pull-thrus (33 x 70), back-ins (50 x 55), 56 W, 57 E (30/50 amps), tent sites, showers $, dump, laundry, groc, fire rings, firewood. **REC:** La Crosse River: fishing, shuffleboard, playground, rec open to public. Pets OK. Partial handicap access. 2015 rates: $20.25 to $26.75. Apr 15 to Oct 15. No CC, no reservations.
(608)786-4011 Lat: 43.89095, Lon: -91.11643
n4668 County Rd Vp, West Salem, WI 54669
facilities@lacrossecounty.org
www.lacrossecountycamping.com
See ad this page.

Nobody said it was easy being a 10. And our rating system makes it even tougher.

WHITE LAKE — C4 *Langlade*

RIVER FOREST RAFTING CAMPGROUND **Ratings: 4/5.5/6** (Campground) 2015 rates: $10 to $30. May 1 to Oct 1. (715)882-3351 W 510 County Road Ww, White Lake, WI 54491

9 MILE ALL SPORT RESORT **Ratings: 6/8/8** (Campground) 2015 rates: $20 to $25. (715)484-8908 n5751 Hwy 55, White lake, WI 54491

WILD ROSE — D3 *Waushara*

EVERGREEN CAMPSITES & RESORT
Ratings: 9/10★/10 (Campground) From Jct of SR-22 & CRs-G & H: Go E 3 mi on CR-H to Archer Ln, then E 1-3/4 mi (R). **FAC:** Paved rds. (426 spaces). 144 Avail: 6 paved, 138 grass, 30 pull-thrus (45 x 90), back-ins (40 x 60), 28 full hkups, 116 W, 116 E (30/50 amps), seasonal sites, WiFi, tent sites, rentals, showers $, dump, mobile sewer, laundry, groc, LP bottles, fire rings, firewood, restaurant, controlled access. **REC:** heated pool, wading pool, Kusel Lake: swim, fishing, playground, rec open to public. Pets OK. Partial handicap access. Big rig sites, eco-friendly, 2015 rates: $41 to $63. Apr 15 to Oct 15. ATM.
AAA Approved
(866)450-2267 Lat: 44.10424, Lon: -89.09375
W5449 Archer Lane, Wild Rose, WI 54984
evergreencampsites@gmail.com
www.evergreencampsites.com
See ad this page, 1306.

LUWISOMO CAMPGROUND **Ratings: 5.5/9★/8** (Campground) 2015 rates: $25 to $35. May 1 to Oct 15. (608)343-5265 w5202 Aspen Rd, Wild Rose, WI 54984

WILTON — D2 *Monroe*

TUNNEL TRAIL CAMPGROUND Ratings: 7.5/8.5/9.5 (Campground) From Jct of Hwys 131 & 71, E 1.2 mi on Hwy 71 (R). **FAC:** Paved/gravel rds. 84 Avail: 8 paved, 38 gravel, 38 grass, 11 pull-thrus (40 x 45), back-ins (35 x 45), 84 W, 84 E (30/50 amps), WiFi Hotspot, tent sites, rentals, dump, laundry, groc, fire rings, firewood. **REC:** heated pool, wading pool, playground. Pets OK. Partial handicap access. 30 day max stay, eco-friendly, 2015 rates: $40. May 1 to Oct 15.
(608)435-6829 Lat: 43.82550, Lon: -90.45251
26983 State Hwy 71, Wilton, WI 54670
reservations@tunneltrail.com
www.tunneltrail.com

WINTER — B2 *Sawyer*

FLAMBEAU RIVER/CONNORS LAKE (State Pk) From Jct of US-8 & SR M, N 17 mi on SR M to Connors Lake (L). Entrance fee required. Note: 45' RV length limit. Pit toilets. 2015 rates: $12 to $14. May 24 to Sep 2. (715)332-5271

FLAMBEAU RIVER/LAKE OF THE PINES (State Pk) From Jct of SR-13 & SR-W, NW 18 mi on SR-W to Lake of the Pines Rd, N 1.5 mi; or From Jct of Hwys 70 & W, SE 17 mi on Hwy W to Lake of the Pines Rd, N 1.5 mi (E). Entrance fee required. Pit toilets. 2015 rates: $14. Apr 15 to Dec 15. (715)332-5271

WISCONSIN DELLS — D3 *Adams, Columbia, Juneau, Sauk*

WISCONSIN DELLS AREA MAP

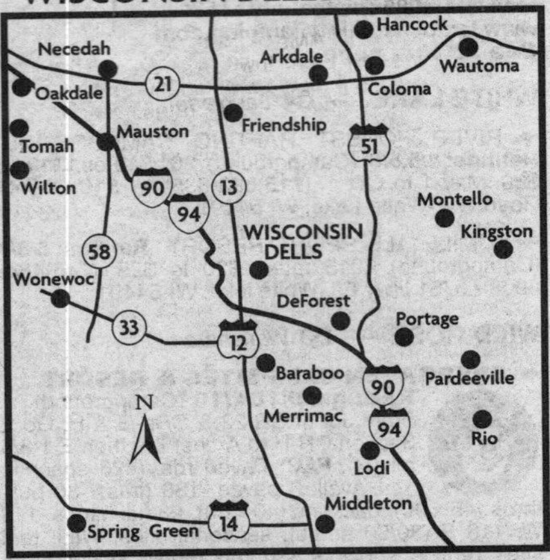

Symbols on map indicate towns within a 50 mile radius of Wisconsin Dells where campgrounds are listed. Check listings for more information.

See also Arkdale, Baraboo, Coloma, DeForest, Friendship, Hancock, Kingston, Lodi, Mauston, Merrimac, Middleton, Montello, Necedah, Oakdale, Pardeeville, Portage, Rio, Spring Green, Tomah, Wautoma, Wilton & Wonewoc.

A SPOTLIGHT Introducing the Wisconsin Dells attractions appearing at the front of state section.

ARROWHEAD RESORT CAMPGROUND **Ratings: 8/9.5★/9** (Campground) 2015 rates: $21 to $60. Apr 15 to Oct 15. (608)254-7344 w1530 Arrowhead Rd, Wisconsin Dells, WI 53965

BARABOO HILLS CAMPGROUND **Ratings: 8.5/10★/10** (Campground) 2015 rates: $37 to $68. Apr 15 to Oct 15. (608)356-8505 e10545 Terrytown Rd, Baraboo, WI 53913

BASS LAKE CAMPGROUND **Ratings: 7/7.5/9** (Campground) 2015 rates: $40to $43. May 1 to Oct 1. (608)666-2311 N 1497 Southern Rd, Lyndon Station, WI 53944

BONANZA CAMPGROUND **Ratings: 7.5/8/8.5** (Campground) 2015 rates: $55 to $60. Apr 1 to Oct 20. (608)254-8124 1770 Wisconsin Dells Pkwy, Wisconsin Dells, WI 53965

CHRISTMAS MOUNTAIN VILLAGE CAMPGROUND
Ratings: 10/9.5★/10 (RV Park) From Jct I-90/94 (Exit 87) & Hwy 13: Go 1/2 mi E on Hwy 13, then 4 mi NW on CR-H, then 1/2 mi S on Lyndon Rd. **FAC:** Paved rds. 91 paved, 5 pull-thrus (40 x 60), back-ins (40 x 60), 91 full hkups (30/50 amps), cable, WiFi, tent sites, rentals, laundry, groc, LP bottles, fire rings, firewood, restaurant, controlled access. **REC:** heated pool, wading pool, whirlpool, pond, fishing, golf, shuffleboard, playground. Pet restrict(Q). Partial handicap access. Big rig sites, 14 day max stay, eco-friendly. 2015 rates: $55. ATM.
(608)253-1000 Lat: 43.60943, Lon: -89.86195
s944 Christmas Mtn Rd, Wisconsin Dells, WI 53965
www.christmasmountainvillage.com
See ad pages 1309 (Spotlight Wisconsin Dells), 1306, 1304 (WI Map).

COUNTRY ROADS MOTORHOME & RV PARK **Ratings: 7.5/10★/10** (RV Park) 2015 rates: $34 to $39. Apr 15 to Oct 7. (608)253-2132 s1633 Hwy 23, Lake Delton, WI 53940

DELL BOO FAMILY CAMPGROUND
Ratings: 9/10★/9.5 (Campground) From Jct of I-90/94 & US-12 (exit 92), L to Baraboo, then take exit 214 L to stop light, then L on Business 12 Cty Trunk BD 1mi, then L on Shady Lane Rd, then go 3/4 mi (R). **FAC:** Paved/gravel rds. (141 spaces). Avail: 91 grass, 8 pull-thrus (50 x 70), back-ins (35 x 50), 54 full hkups, 37 W, 37 E (30/50 amps), seasonal sites, WiFi, tent sites, rentals, dump, mobile sewer, laundry, groc, LP bottles, fire rings, firewood. **REC:** heated pool, shuffleboard, playground. Pets OK. Partial handicap access. Big rig sites, eco-friendly. 2015 rates: $44 to $52. May 1 to Oct 1. AAA Approved
(608)356-5898 Lat: 43.54874, Lon: -89.79522
E10562 Shady Lane Rd, Baraboo, WI 53913
dairystate@centurytel.net
www.dellboo.com
See ad this page.

DELLS TIMBERLAND CAMPING RESORT **Ratings: 8.5/9.5★/8.5** (Campground) 2015 rates: $30 to $50. Apr 15 to Oct 15. (800)774-0535 N 1005 US 12, Wisconsin Dells, WI 53965

EDGE-O-DELLS CAMPING & RV RESORT Ratings: 7/9.5★/9 (RV Park) From Jct of I-94 (Exit 85) & Hwy 16 W .5 mi on Hwy 16(L). Note: 21 & older. **FAC:** Gravel rds. 54 Avail: 10 paved, 44 gravel, 35 pull-thrus (25 x 70), back-ins (25 x 45), 54 W, 54 E (30/50 amps), WiFi Hotspot, tent sites, rentals, dump, mobile sewer, laundry, groc, fire rings, firewood, restaurant. **REC:** heated pool, whirlpool. Pets OK. Partial handicap access. Age restrict may apply. 2015 rates: $25 to $70. Disc: military. May 1 to Sep 30. ATM.
(608)253-4275 Lat: 43.65894, Lon: -89.82934
n555 US Hwys 12 and 16, Wisconsin Dells, WI 53965
camping@edgeodells.com
www.edgeodells.com

HOLIDAY SHORES CAMPGROUND & RESORT **Ratings: 8.5/10★/9** (Campground) 2015 rates: $34 to $52. May 1 to Oct 15. (608)254-2717 3901 River Rd, Wisconsin Dells, WI 53965

K & L CAMPGROUND **Ratings: 6.5/7.5/7.5** (Campground) 2015 rates: $30. May 1 to Sep 15. (608)586-4720 3503 Cnty Rd G, Wisconsin Dells, WI 53965

MIRROR LAKE (State Pk) From Jct of I-90/94 & Hwy 12 (exit 92), S 0.5 mi on Hwy 12 to Fern Dell Rd, W 1.5 mi (R). Entrance fee required. 2015 rates: $12 to $17. (608)254-2333

MT. OLYMPUS CAMP RESORT **Ratings: 9/9.5★/8** (RV Park) 2015 rates: $25 to $189. Apr 1 to Nov 1. (800)800-4997 400 County Rd A & Hwy 12, Wisconsin Dells, WI 53965

RIVER BAY CAMPING RESORT & MARINA **Ratings: 8.5/10★/9.5** (Campground) 2015 rates: $47 to $50. Apr 15 to Oct 15. (608)254-7193 w1147 River Bay Rd, Lyndon Station, WI 53944

ROCKY ARBOR (State Pk) From jct I-90/94 (exit 92) & US 12: Go 200 yds W on US 12, then 2 mi W on Fern Dell Rd. 2015 rates: $12 to $14. May 25 to Sep 7. (608)254-8001

Want to see what our inspectors see? The exact reproductions of the rating guidelines our inspectors used for this edition of the Guide are printed in the front of the book. Try using them on your next trip to perform your own inspection. Since our rating system is based on objective criteria, we're confident that your ratings will be similar to ours.

SHERWOOD FOREST CAMPING & RV PARK
Ratings: 9/10★/10 (Campground) From Jct of I-90/94 & SR-13 (exit 87), E 0.25 mi on SR-13 to US-12/SR-16, NW 0.4 mi (R).

LOCATED IN THE HEART OF THE DELLS
Quiet family camping within walking distance to downtown Dells. Easy on/off Interstate access. Huge heated pool and splashpad, themed weekends, planned activities and events. Cabin rentals and Big Rig friendly!

FAC: Paved rds. (184 spaces). 148 Avail: 41 gravel, 107 grass, 25 pull-thrus (30 x 60), back-ins (30 x 50), 54 full hkups, 76 W, 94 E (30/50 amps), seasonal sites, WiFi, tent sites, rentals, dump, laundry, groc, LP bottles, fire rings, firewood. **REC:** heated pool, playground. Pets OK. Partial handicap access. Big rig sites, eco-friendly. 2015 rates: $32 to $57. Disc: AAA, military. May 1 to Oct 1. ATM.
(877)474-3796 Lat: 43.63178, Lon: -89.78841
2852 Wisconsin Dells Parkway, Wisconsin Dells, WI 53965
info@sherwoodforestcamping.com
www.sherwoodforestcamping.com
See ad pages 1309 (Spotlight Wisconsin Dells), 1306, 1304 (WI Map) & RV Trips of a Lifetime in Magazine Section.

STAND ROCK CAMPGROUND **Ratings: 7.5/10★/9.5** (Campground) 2015 rates: $47 to $49. Apr 15 to Oct 15. (608)253-2169 n570 County Rd N, Wisconsin Dells, WI 53965

WANNA BEE CAMPGROUND & RV RESORT **Ratings: 8/9/9** (RV Park) 2015 rates: $36 to $48. Apr 15 to Oct 15. (608)253-3122 E 10096 Trout Rd, Wisconsin Dells, WI 53965

WISCONSIN DELLS KOA **Ratings: 9.5/10★/9.5** (Campground) 2015 rates: $39 to $73. Apr 17 to Oct 25. (800)254-4177 s235 A Stand Rock Rd, Wisconsin Dells, WI 53965

YOGI BEAR'S JELLYSTONE PARK CAMP-RESORT Ratings: 9/10★/9.5 (Campground) From Jct of I-90/94 & US-12 (exit 92), NW 0.5 mi on US-12 to Gasser Rd, W 1 mi to Ishnala Rd, S 100 ft (R). **FAC:** Paved rds. (203 spaces). 196 Avail: 12 paved, 184 gravel, patios, 8 pull-thrus (40 x 60), back-ins (40 x 45), 61 full hkups, 135 W, 135 E (20/50 amps), seasonal sites, WiFi, tent sites, rentals, dump, mobile sewer, laundry, groc, LP bottles, fire rings, firewood, restaurant, controlled access. **REC:** heated pool, wading pool, whirlpool, Mirror Lake: fishing, shuffleboard, playground. Pets OK. Partial handicap access. Big rig sites, eco-friendly. 2015 rates: $39 to $133. Disc: AAA, military. May 8 to Sep 20. ATM. AAA Approved
(800)462-9644 Lat: 43.57854, Lon: -89.79753
S1915 Ishnala Rd, Wisconsin Dells, WI 53965
reservations@dellsjellystone.com
www.dellsjellystone.com

YUKON TRAILS CAMPING **Ratings: 7/8/8.5** (Campground) 2015 rates: $38 to $46. Apr 15 to Oct 15. (608)666-3261 n2330 Cty Rd Hh, Lyndon Station, WI 53944

WISCONSIN RAPIDS — C3 *Wood*

SOUTH WOOD COUNTY PARK (Public) From Jct of Hwy 13 & CR-Z, E 3.5 mi on CR-Z to 64th St, N 1 mi (R). Pit toilets. 2015 rates: $16 to $21. May 1 to Oct 31. (715)421-8422

WITTENBERG — C4 *Shawano*

Things to See and Do

HO-CHUNK GAMING WITTENBERG Full service casino with penny slots, video poker keno, and more, along with a snack bar. Partial handicap access. RV accessible. Rest rooms, food. Hours: 24 hours. ATM.
(866)910-0150 Lat: 44.827117, Lon: -89.143416
n7198 US Hwy 45, Wittenberg, WI 54499
http://www.ho-chunkgaming.com/wittenberg/
See ad page 1310 (Spotlight Wisconsin Dells).

WONEWOC — D3 *Sauk*

CHAPPARAL CAMPGROUND & RESORT Ratings: 8.5/9.5★/10 (Campground) From Jct of SR-58 & SR-33, W 3.8 mi on SR-33 (R). **FAC:** Paved/gravel rds. (116 spaces). Avail: 78 grass, 30 pull-thrus (35 x 60), back-ins (35 x 60), 45 full hkups, 33 W, 33 E (30/50 amps), seasonal sites, WiFi, tent sites, rentals, showers $, dump, laundry, groc, fire rings, firewood, restaurant. **REC:** heated pool, pond, swim fishing, playground. Pets OK. Partial handicap access. Big rig sites, eco-friendly. 2015 rates: $40 to $43. Disc: military. Apr 15 to Oct 31.
(608)464-3200 Lat: 43.63278, Lon: -90.17447
s316 Dreamland Dr, Wonewoc, WI 53968
chapparal@mwt.net
www.chapparal.com

WOODRUFF — B3 *Oneida*

ARBOR VITAE CAMPGROUND Ratings: 6.5/8/7.5 (Campground) From Jct of US-51 & SR-70: Go E 1-1/2 mi on SR-70 to Big Arbor Vitae Dr (exit on curve), then N 1/2 mi on Big Arbor Vitae Dr (R). **FAC:** Gravel rds. (110 spaces). 46 Avail: 23 gravel, 23 grass, 11 pull-thrus (25 x 100), back-ins (25 x 50), 22 full hkups, 6 W, 18 E (30/50 amps), seasonal sites, WiFi, tent sites, rentals, dump, groc, fire rings, firewood. **REC:** Lake Big Arbor Vitae: swim, fishing, playground, rec open to public. Pets OK. Partial handicap access. Big rig sites, eco-friendly, 2015 rates: $25 to $30. May 1 to Oct 15.
(715)356-5146 Lat: 45.91654, Lon: -89.65609
10545 Big Arbor Vitae Dr, Arbor Vitae, WI 54568
avc@arborvitaecampground.com
www.arborvitaecampground.com

HIAWATHA TRAILER RESORT
Ratings: 9/10★/9.5 (RV Park) From Jct of Hwys 51 & 47: Go E 1/3 mi on Hwy 47 to Old Hwy 51 (Balsam St), then N 1/2 mi (L). **FAC:** Paved rds. (170 spaces). Avail: 20 grass, patios, 10 pull-thrus (25 x 65), back-ins (21 x 50), 20 full hkups (30/50 amps), seasonal sites, WiFi, laundry, fire rings, firewood. **REC:** Lake Arrowhead: swim, fishing, playground. Pets OK. Partial handicap access, no tents. Big rig sites, eco-friendly, 2015 rates: $34 to $39. Disc: military. May 1 to Oct 15.
(888)429-2842 Lat: 45.90269, Lon: -89.68811
1077 Old Hwy 51S, Woodruff, WI 54568
info@hiawathatrailerresort.com
www.hiawathatrailerresort.com
See ad opposite page, 1306.

Don't camp without it ... Our 2016 listings are your key to travel satisfaction.

INDIAN SHORES RV & COTTAGE RESORT Ratings: 9/9.5★/9 (RV Park) From Jct of Hwys 51 & 47: Go SE 4-1/2 mi on Hwy 47 (R). **FAC:** Paved rds. (263 spaces). 130 Avail: 15 paved, 115 gravel, 12 pull-thrus (60 x 80), back-ins (35 x 55), 130 full hkups (30/50 amps), seasonal sites, cable, WiFi Hotspot, tent sites, rentals, dump, laundry, groc, LP gas, fire rings, firewood, restaurant, controlled access. **REC:** heated pool, Lake Tomahawk: swim, fishing, marina, shuffleboard, playground. Pets OK. Partial handicap access. Big rig sites, eco-friendly, 2015 rates: $49 to $77. May 1 to Oct 31. ATM.
(715)356-5552 Lat: 45.83909, Lon: -89.64557
7750 Indian Shores Rd, Woodruff, WI 54568
info@indian-shores.com
www.indian-shores.com

NO HIGHLAND AMERICAN LEGION SF/BUFFALO LAKE (State Pk) From town, S 2 mi on Hwy 47 to Hwy J, E 7.5 mi to Buffalo Lake Rd, N 1 mi (L). Entrance fee required. Pit toilets. 2015 rates: $12 to $14. (715)385-3352

County names help you follow the local weather report.

NO HIGHLAND AMERICAN LEGION SF/CARROL LAKE (State Pk) From Jct of US-51 & Hwy 47, S 2 mi on Hwy 47 to Hwy J, E 3 mi (L). Entrance fee required. Pit toilets. 2015 rates: $12 to $14. (715)385-2727

NO HIGHLAND AMERICAN LEGION SF/CLEAR LAKE (State Pk) From town, S 4 mi on Hwy 47 to Woodruff Rd, NE 1 mi to Clear Lake Rd, E 0.5 mi (R). Entrance fee required. 2015 rates: $15 to $17. (715)385-2727

NO HIGHLAND AMERICAN LEGION SF/CRYSTAL-MUSKIE LAKES (State Pk) From Woodruff, N 6 mi on US-51 to Hwy M, NE 3 mi to Hwy N, E 2 mi (L). Entrance fee required. 2015 rates: $15 to $17. (715)385-2727

NO HIGHLAND AMERICAN LEGION SF/INDIAN MOUNDS AREA (State Pk) From Woodruff, SE 5 mi on Hwy 47 (R). Entrance fee required. Pit toilets. 2015 rates: $12 to $14. (715)385-2727

NO HIGHLAND AMERICAN LEGION SF/NORTH TROUT LAKE (State Pk) From Jct of US-51 & CT-M, N 5.5 mi on CT-M (L). Entrance fee required. Pit toilets. 2015 rates: $12 to $14. (715)385-2727

Got something to tell us? We welcome your comments and suggestions regarding the ratings for a particular campground, or our rating system in general. Please email them to: travelguidecomments@goodsamfamily.com

 See map page 1329

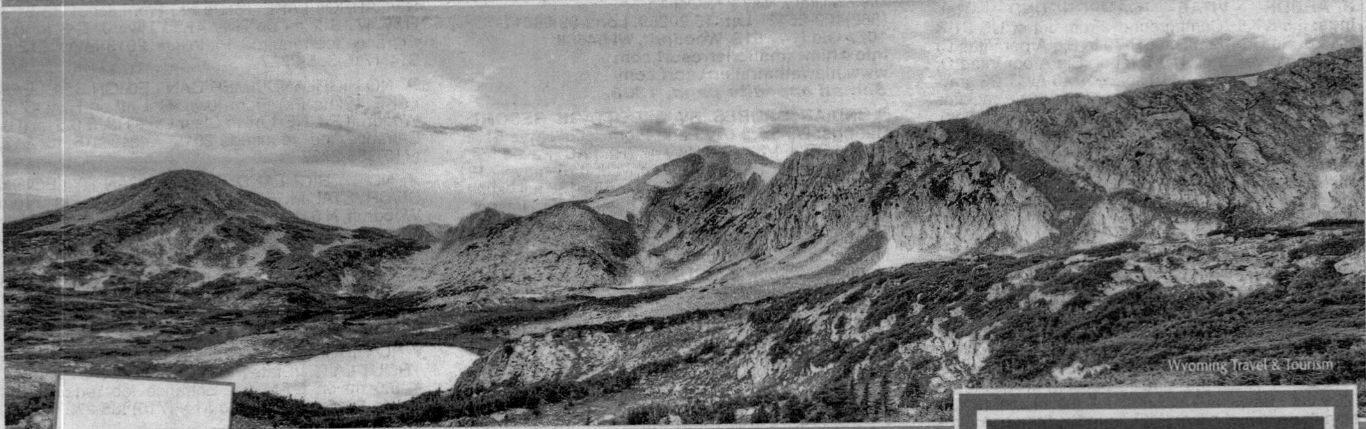
Wyoming Travel & Tourism

WELCOME TO

Wyoming

DATE OF STATEHOOD JULY 10, 1890	WIDTH: 360 MILES (581 KM) LENGTH: 280 MILES (451 KM)	PROPORTION OF UNITED STATES 2.58% OF 3,794,100 SQ MI

Top 3 Tourism Attractions:
1) Yellowstone National Park
2) Devils Tower
3) Hot Springs State Park

Nickname: Equality State

State Flower: Indian Paintbrush

State Bird: Western Meadowlark

People: Curt Gowdy, sportscaster; Leonard S. Hobbs, turbo jet engine developer

Major Cities: Cheyenne (capital), Casper, Laramie, Gillette, Rock Springs

Topography: Eastern Great Plains rise to the foothills of the Rocky Mountains; Continental Divide crosses the state

Climate: Generally semi-arid with local desert conditions

Curtis Bullock

With its big blue skies, primal winds and flat plains encircled by mile-high mountains, Wyoming is a wilderness of soul-satisfying majesty. Ever since the early 19th century, when French fur trappers entered Jackson Hole from what is now Yellowstone National Park, visitors have been awe-struck by the state's fire-and-brimstone landscapes. It's a place where herds of roaming deer and buffalo commandeer the roadside, wolves howl as you perfect your smore's technique over the campfire and the air crackles with every sulfurous belch of steam that erupts from Old Faithful. The Western town of Jackson, ever chic, ever sophisticated and perpetually adrenaline-infused (the average age of its denizens is just 32), provides the launch pad for superb skiing, climbing and hiking.

In Jackson's backyard, Grand Teton soars to some 13,770-feet, making it one of North America's most abiding natural wonders. Grand Teton and Yellowstone National Parks form a network six times the size of Yellowstone: the Greater Yellowstone Ecosystem. Here you'll find blue-ribbon trout streams, hiking trails and Wild West towns with their gaze set firmly on the great outdoors. The laid-back prairie town of Cheyenne, the largest city in Wyoming and also its capital, provides an authentic slice of western culture and a clutch of worthy attractions, including the eye-catching Renaissance-revival Capitol Building and the 1904 Historic Governor's Mansion.

Learn

When, in 1807, John Colter discovered a region of glacier-carved valleys, volcanic plateaus and bubbling geysers, he found it so foreboding that he named the area "Colter's Hell." In 1872, the area became known as Yellowstone, the world's first National Park. In the mid 19th century, Fort Laramie bore witness to the epic narrative of America's western expansion and Indian resistance. Proclaimed a national monument in 1938 by President Franklin D. Roosevelt, Fort Laramie National Historic Site comprises 22 structures that reveal the life of one of the country's most important military posts. Originally established as a private fur-trading fort in 1834, Fort Laramie provided gold prospectors, weary frontiersmen and homesteaders with vital reprieve.

Another fascinating historic site, Fort Phil Kearny in northern Wyoming

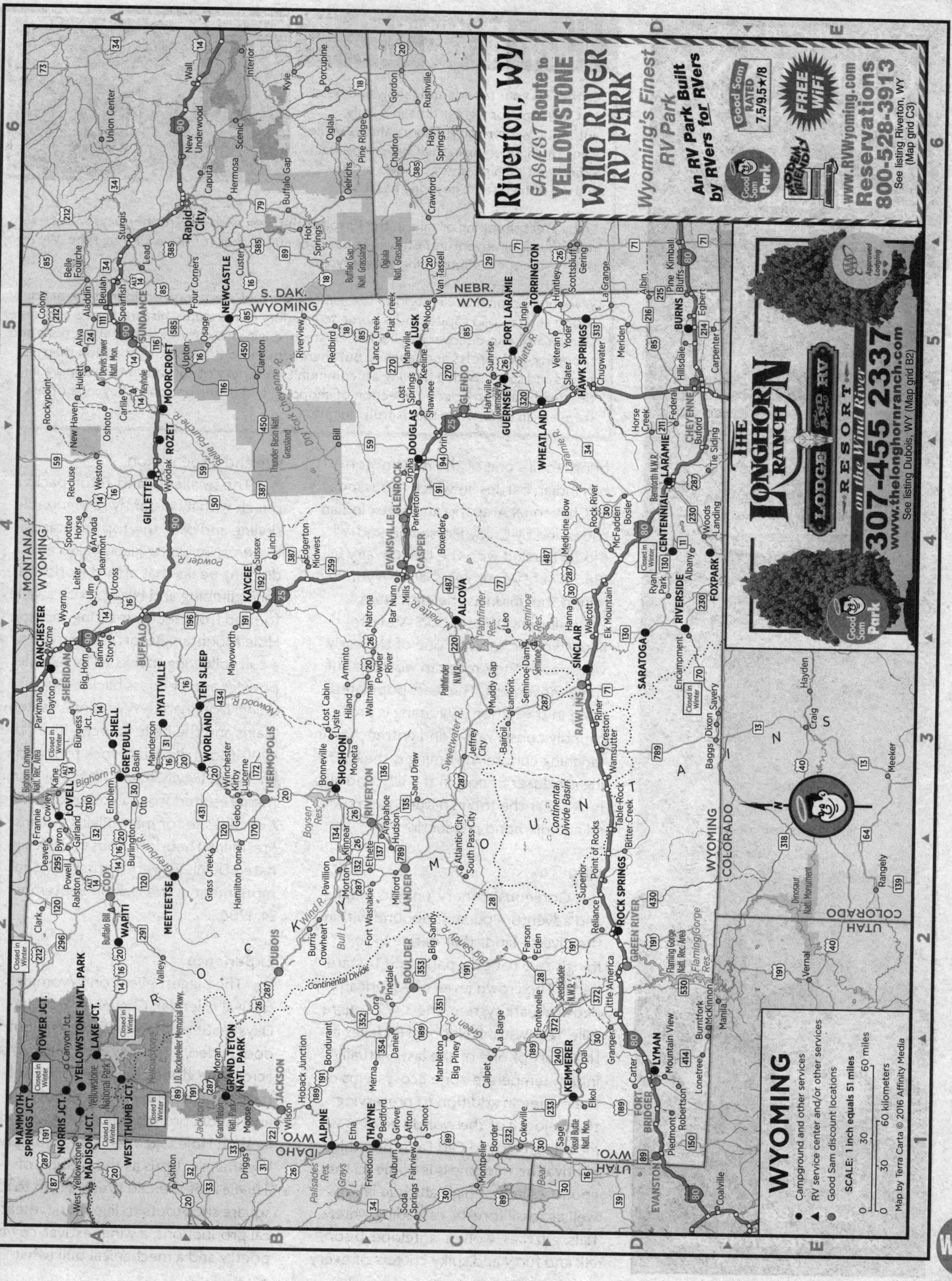
WYOMING
Campground and other services
RV service center and/or other services
Good Sam discount locations
SCALE: 1 inch equals 51 miles
0 30 60 miles
0 30 60 kilometers
Map by Terra Carta © 2016 Affinity Media
THE LONGHORN RANCH
LODGE AND RV
RESORT
on the Wind River
307-455 2337
www.thelonghornranch.com
See listing Dubois, WY (Map grid B2)
Riverton, WY
EASIEST Route to YELLOWSTONE
WIND RIVER RV PARK
Wyoming's Finest RV Park
An RV Park Built by RVers for RVers
Good Sam RATED 7.5/9.5★/8
FREE WiFi
www.RVWyoming.com
Reservations
800-528-3913
See listing Riverton, WY (Map grid C3)

- STAY A WHILE -

Visit Cheyenne

Gather up your friends and family and head to Cheyenne for a great time in a truly authentic western city! There's always something fun happening in the Cheyenne area. Whether it's a high-energy rodeo or the culture of high tea, Cheyenne has it all.

Enjoy great shopping or take in the flavor of the west with our Frontier Days. Want even more outdoor adventure? Cheyenne has over 600 caches for the exploring type. We're pretty sure there's something for everyone.

Wyoming's capital city embodies the spirit of the Old West. It is considered the nation's rodeo and railroad capital and is home to a variety of museums, historic hotels and mansions. You'll also discover a collection of steam engines Western-themed attractions and shopping, and resorts and ranches. But there is more to this iconic destination than just boots and spurs. With a thriving art community, a variety of soft adventure opportunities nearby and an eclectic selection of shopping and dining options, Cheyenne offers travelers an experience that is truly unique.

brings to life one of the most notorious Indian battles, in which thousands of Cheyenne, Arapaho and Sioux Indian tribes, led by Crazy Horse and Red Cloud, battled with the U.S. Cavalry in 1866. Twenty-four years later, Wyoming joined the union as the 44th state. Wyoming was the first U.S. state to allow women to vote, one of the early victories of the American women's suffrage movement. The least populated state in the nation, Wyoming is profoundly conservative and entrenched in ranching culture. Wyoming is the leading producer of coal in the U.S. and also ranks near the top in natural gas, crude oil and diamond production.

Play

Gorgeous scenery, unique wildlife and adventure pursuits abound within the diverse lands that define Wyoming's two national parks and 12 state parks. The crown jewel of American's national park system, the 3,472-square-mile Yellowstone National Park lies at the heart of one of the last, virtually intact, temperate-zone ecosystems on the planet. In addition to preserving the majority of the world's geysers—including beloved Old Faithful—this captivating wilderness is home to the country's largest high-altitude lake as well as fossil forests, cascading waterfalls, grizzlies, wolves, antelope, bison, elk and furry and spiky critters of every size and dispensation.

The smaller Grand Teton packs a punch with its instantly recognizable skyline and over-the-top spectacular features, including glacial lakes and dizzying peaks that afford world-class rock-climbing and hiking. With a valley formed from tectonic tilting, Jackson Hole Mountain Resort has garnered a cult following thanks to its reliable powder and peerless backcountry skiing. Dominating Wyoming's eastern plains and the Belle Fourche River, the 1,200-foot-tall natural rock formation known as Devils Tower National Monument resulted from a volcanic intrusion. A sacred site for many Plains Indians, President Theodore Roosevelt designated Devils Tower the first national monument in the U.S. on September 24, 1906.

Experience

The biggest event on Wyoming's festival calendar, Cheyenne Frontier Days features the world's largest outdoor rodeo. Every July, spectators from across the globe converge for barrel racing, team penning, steer wrestling and saddle bronco riding. Late May, the Jackson Hole Old West Days triumphs Wyoming's status as the bastion of "The Last of the Old West." From town square shootouts to live music, theatrical productions, a wine festival, cowboy poetry and a mechanical bull (what would an Old West festival be without one), it's an all-embracing Wild West extravaganza. At the end of August, the Fort Bridger Rendezvous is one of the largest mountain men gatherings in the nation. The Rendezvous re-enacts the annual gathering of mountain men traders and Indians that took place in the Rocky Mountains between 1825 and 1840 with archery contests, a mountain run, a hilarious toss the frying pan competition, cook-offs and seminars by leading historians.

Taste

Jackson Hole has come a long way. Chic sushi bars serve fish flown in daily, mixologists conjure fabulous cocktails in sleek lounge bars and elegant restaurants prepare gourmet cuisine for Jackson's gilded denizens. At the high end, the award-winning Snake River Grill (www.snakerivergrill.com), with its log cabin ambience and innovative interpretations of western classics (local beef tenderloin with pesto and tomato-bacon jam), is the best in town. Smack bang in Grand Teton National Park, the Jenny Lake Lodge Dining Room (www.gtlc.com/lodging/jenny-lake-lodge-dining.aspx) offers salads, sandwiches and entrée specials including snake river trout for lunch and gourmet five-course dinners, which spike homespun ranch classics with more exotic flavors such as ceviche and rabbit gnocchi.

TRAVEL & TOURISM

Wyoming Travel & Tourism
800-225-5996, 307-777-7777
www.wyomingtourism.org

Albany County Tourism Board
307-745-4195, 800-445-5303
www.visitlaramie.org

Basin Chamber
307-568-3055
www.basincc.com

Campbell County Chamber
www.gillettechamber.com

Carbon County Visitor Council
800-228-3547
www.wyomingcarboncounty.com

Casper Area Chamber
307-234-5311, 866-234-5311
www.casperwyoming.org

Visit Cheyenne
800-426-5009
www.cheyenne.org

Cody Country Chamber
307-587-2777, 800-393-2639
www.codychamber.org

Cokeville Chamber
307-279-3200
www.cokevillewy.com

Converse County Tourism Promotion Board
www.conversecountytourism.com

Douglas Chamber
307-358-2950, 877-937-4996
www.jackalope.org

Dubois Chamber
www.duboiswyoming.org

East Yellowstone Valley Chamber
307-587-9595
www.eastyellowstonechamber.com

Evanston Chamber
307-783-0370, 800-328-9708
www.etownchamber.com

Gillette CVB
307-686-0040
www.visitgillette-wrightwyo.org

Glenrock Chamber
307-436-5652
www.glenrockwyomingchamber.com

Green River Chamber
307-875-5711, 800-354-6743
www.grchamber.com

Greater Bridger Valley Chamber
307-787-6738
www.bridgervalleychamber.com

Visit Cheyenne
307-638-3388, 800-426-5009
www.cheyennechamber.org

Greybull Area Chamber
307-765-2100, 877-765-2100
www.greybull.com

Jackson Hole Chamber
307-733-3316
www.jacksonholechamber.com

Kaycee Area Chamber
307-738-2444
www.kayceewyoming.org

Kemmerer Chamber
307-877-9761, 888-300-3413
www.kemmererchamber.com

Visit Riverton
www.rivertonchamber.org/visit

OUTDOOR RECREATION

Snowmobiling Wyoming
877-996-7275
snowmo@state.wy.us

Wyoming Game and Fish Department
wgfd.wyo.gov

Featured Good Sam Parks

WYOMING

Good Sam Park

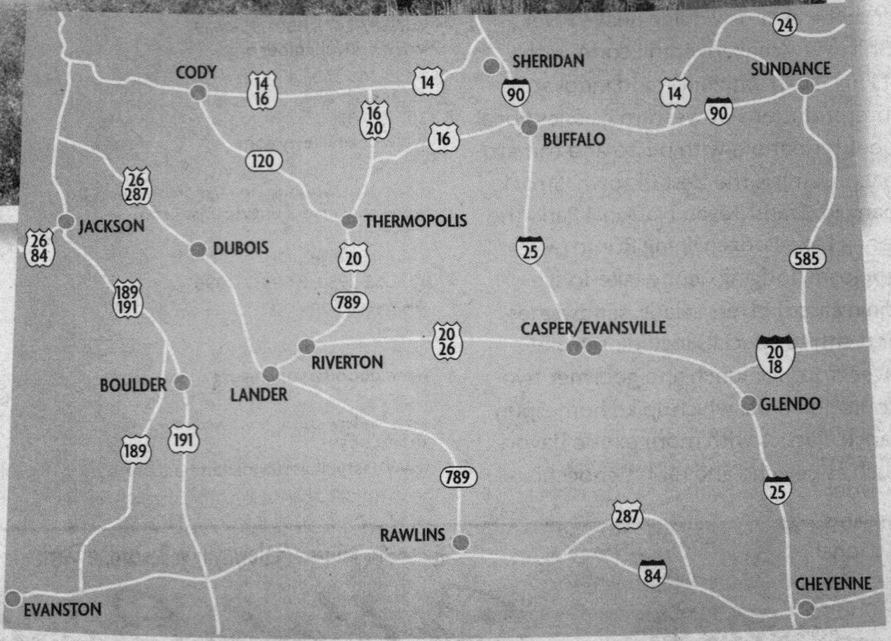

When you stay with Good Sam, you can expect the highest degree of cleanliness and friendliness, and better yet, you get 10% off campground fees.

If you're not already a Good Sam member you can purchase your membership at one of these locations:

BOULDER
Highline Trail RV Park
(307)537-3080

BUFFALO
Deer Park
(307)684-5722
Indian Campground & RV Park
(866)808-9601

CASPER
Casper East RV Park & Campground
(888)294-8551

CHEYENNE
AB Camping RV Park
(307)634-7035
Terry Bison Ranch RV Park
(307)634-4171

CODY
Absaroka Bay RV Park
(800)557-7440
Ponderosa Campground
(307)587-9203
Yellowstone Valley Inn & RV
(307)587-3961

DUBOIS
The Longhorn Ranch Lodge & RV Resort
(307)455-2337

EVANSTON
Phillips RV Park
(800)349-3805

EVANSVILLE
Rivers Edge RV & Cabins Resort
(307)234-0042

GLENDO
Glendo Lakeside RV Park
(307)735-4161

JACKSON
The Virginian RV Resort
(800)321-6982

LANDER
Sleeping Bear RV Park & Campground
(307)332-5159
Twin Pines RV Park & Campground
(800)986-4008

RAWLINS
RV World Campground
(307)328-1091
Western Hills Campground
(307)324-2592

RIVERTON
Wind River RV Park
(307)857-3000

SHERIDAN
Peter D's RV Park
(888)673-0597

SUNDANCE
Mountain View RV Park & Campground
(800)792-8439

THERMOPOLIS
Eagle RV Park
(307)864-5262

For more Good Sam Parks go to listing pages

Getty Images/iStockphoto

SPOTLIGHT

WY

BUFFALO

The West never stopped being wild in this rugged corner of Wyoming

Go a little wild in the historic Old West town of Buffalo. Resting in the foothills of the Big Horn Mountains, Buffalo is a popular destination for hunters, wilderness enthusiasts and aficionados of the cowboy way. From here, visitors can make day trips to a variety of destinations certain to quench the thirsts of adventure seekers of all ages.

The Sporting Life

If you like to ski, boat, fish or hike, Buffalo serves as your gateway to a sportsman's paradise. Take a watercraft out on Lake DeSmet just north of the town and take advantage of clear, cool days on the water. Jet skis and water skis are permitted on this popular lake, as is fishing.

Anglers can cast their lines at Healy Reservoir and in the Middle Fork of the Powder River, as well as in the mountain streams and lakes throughout Bighorn National Forest and Cloud Peak Wilderness. With a little patience, you're bound to hook one of several trout species, or maybe even some bass, perch and bluegill.

Big-game hunting in Johnson County, where Buffalo resides, is open to nonresidents who are accompanied by a resident companion or licensed guide. You can also set your sights on elk, black bear, pronghorn antelope and white-tailed deer in the national wilderness areas of the county. If you prefer to capture big game with your camera, the open spaces along major roadways and leading into wilderness areas are great spots to camp out and wait for the perfect photo.

The Big Horn Mountains beckon hikers and horseback riders to traverse the range's trails, which follow lakes and streams. The U.S. Forest Service provides detailed trail maps and tips for making the most of a hike. Area guest ranches and outfitters offer visitors the opportunity to ride at their leisure, whether for a half-day or an overnight camping trip.

Hunting for Photos

From the comfort of your vehicle, you can still experience the beauty of the region. Cloud Peak Skyway—U.S. 16—crosses the southern Big Horns and showcases views of snowcapped peaks on its 45-mile route. Equally thrilling are views of Hospital Hill, Meadowlark Lake and Tensleep Canyon.

Medicine Wheel Passage, also known as US 14A, rises from the Bighorn Basin near the town of Lovell and crosses through steep canyons and alpine meadows, but the main attraction is the largest intact Medicine Wheel in North America. Because of the fragile nature of the stones that make up the wheel, visitors are encouraged to observe at a distance.

Wyoming's frontier history is preserved at Fort Phil Kearny. The fort's historic site features a museum and visitor center that share the story of conflict between Native Americans and U.S. soldiers. Butch Cassidy's famous Hole in the Wall hideout is nearby.

For More Information

Discover Historic Buffalo
800-227-5122
www.buffalowyoming.org

Wyoming Travel & Tourism
800-225-5996
www.wyomingtourism.org

A bridge crosses a creek in the Bighorn Mountains. Getty Images/iStockphoto

See listing Buffalo, WY

Wyoming

CONSULTANTS

Mike & Donna Oliverio

ALCOVA — C4 *Natrona*

ALCOVA LAKE CAMPGROUND (Public) From Casper, W 26 mi on Hwy 220 to CR-407, S 0.9 mi (L). Pit toilets. 2015 rates: $10. (307)235-9311

PATHFINDER NATIONAL WILDLIFE REFUGE (State Pk) From town, W 32 mi on Hwy 220 (follow signs) to CR-409, S 6.4 mi (R). Pit toilets. 2015 rates: $10. (307)235-9325

ALPINE — B1 *Lincoln*

GREYS RIVER COVE RV PARK Ratings: 5/8★/5.5 (RV Park) From Jct US 26 & US 89 (Alpine Jct): Go S 1/2 mile. Elev 5650 ft. **FAC:** Gravel rds. (28 spaces). Avail: 15 gravel, 10 pull-thrus (18 x 75), back-ins (18 x 40), 15 full hkups (30/50 amps), seasonal sites, WiFi, tent sites, laundry, fire rings, firewood. **REC:** Snake River: fishing. Pet restrict(B). Big rig sites, 2015 rates: $40. Disc: AAA, military.
AAA Approved
(307)880-2267 Lat: 43.16454, Lon: -111.01707
25 Hwy 89, Alpine, WY 83128
greysrivercove@silverstar.com
www.greysrivercove.com

TARGHEE/ALPINE CAMPGROUND (Natl Forest) From town: Go 1/4 mi NW on US-89, then 2-2/3 mi NW on US-26. Pit toilets. 2015 rates: $10 to $20. May 27 to Sep 12. (208)523-1412

BOULDER — C2 *Sublette*

HIGHLINE TRAIL RV PARK
Ratings: 6.5/9.5★/8.5 (RV Park) From Jct I-80 & US 191: Go 84-1/4 mi N on US 191 (3/4 mi S of town). Elev 6998 ft. **FAC:** Gravel rds. (53 spaces). Avail: 43 gravel, 16 pull-thrus (45 x 110), back-ins (30 x 70), 43 full hkups (30/50 amps), seasonal sites, WiFi, tent sites, dump, laundry, fire rings. Pets OK. Partial handicap access. Big rig sites, 2015 rates: $33.
(307)537-3080 Lat: 42.73858, Lon: -109.71461
8718 Hwy 191, Boulder, WY 82923
jbkochever@wyoming.com
www.highlinetrailrvpark.com
See ad this page, 1332.

WIND RIVER VIEW CAMPGROUND **Ratings: 5.5/7★/6** (Membership Pk) 2015 rates: $30. (307)537-5453 8889 US Hwy 191, Boulder, WY 82923

BUFFALO — A4 *Johnson*

A SPOTLIGHT Introducing Buffalo's colorful attractions appearing at the front of this state section.

BUFFALO KOA
Ratings: 9/9.5★/9.5 (Campground) From Jct of I-90 & US-16 (exit 58), W 1 mi on US-16 (L); or From Jct of I-25 & US-16 (exit 299), E 0.3 mi on US-16 (R). Elev 4768 ft. **FAC:** Gravel rds. 58 gravel, 37 pull-thrus (30 x 60), back-ins (30 x 50), 45 full hkups, 13 W, 13 E (30/50 amps), cable, WiFi, tent sites, rentals, dump, laundry, groc, LP gas, fire rings, firewood. **REC:** heated pool, French Creek: fishing, playground. Pets OK. Partial handicap access. Big rig sites, eco-friendly, 2015 rates: $38 to $48. Disc: military. Apr 15 to Nov 1.
(307)684-5423 Lat: 44.35351, Lon: -106.68134
87 U S Hwy 16E, Buffalo, WY 82834
info@buffalowykoa.com
www.koa.com/campgrounds/buffalo-wyoming
See ad this page.

DEER PARK
Ratings: 9/9.5★/9 (Campground) From Jct of I-90 & US-16 (exit 58), W 0.7 mi on US-16 (R); or From Jct of I-25 & US-16 (exit 299), E 0.7 mi on US-16 (L). Elev 4550 ft. **FAC:** Gravel rds. 70 Avail: 67 gravel, 3 grass, 36 pull-thrus (25 x 65), back-ins (30 x 35), 41 full hkups, 29 W, 29 E (30/50 amps), cable, WiFi, tent sites, rentals, dump, laundry, groc, fire rings, firewood. **REC:** heated pool, Buffalo Stream. Pets OK. Big rig sites, eco-friendly, 2015 rates: $32 to $42. Disc: AAA, military. May 1 to Sep 30.
AAA Approved
(307)684-5722 Lat: 44.35643, Lon: -106.66970
146 U S Hwy 16E @ Deer Park Rd, Buffalo, WY 82834
info@deerparkrv.com
www.deerparkrv.com
See ad pages 1337, 1332.

INDIAN CAMPGROUND & RV PARK
Ratings: 8.5/9.5★/9 (Campground) N or S-bnd: From Jct of I-25 & US-16 (exit 299), W 0.1 mi on US-16 (R); or W-bnd: From Jct of I-90 & I-25 (exit 56B), S 1 mi on I-25 to Exit 299, W 0.1 mi (R). Elev 4640 ft. **FAC:** Gravel rds. 90 Avail: 76 gravel, 14 grass, 49 pull-thrus (24 x 75), back-ins (33 x 45), 79 full hkups, 11 W, 11 E (30/50 amps), cable, WiFi, tent sites, rentals, dump, laundry, groc, LP gas, fire rings, firewood. **REC:** heated pool, French Creek: fishing, playground. Pets OK. Big rig sites, eco-friendly, 2015 rates: $36 to $41. Disc: AAA. Apr 15 to Oct 15.
AAA Approved
(866)808-9601 Lat: 44.35534, Lon: -106.68842
660 E Hart St, Buffalo, WY 82834
info@indiancampground.com
www.indiancampground.com
See ad pages 1336, 1332.

Things to See and Do

BOZEMAN TRAIL STEAK HOUSE Serving the best beef, elk, and bison for lunch and dinner. Elev 4640 ft. RV accessible. Restrooms, food. Hours: 11:00 am to 9:00 pm.
(307)684-5555 Lat: 44.35375, Lon: -106.68824
675 E Hart St, Buffalo, WY 82834
bozemantrailsteakhouse@hotmail.com
www.thebozemantrailsteakhouse.com
See ad page 1336.

BUFFALO CHAMBER OF COMMERCE (JOHNSON COUNTY TOURISM ASSOC.) Area information for Johnson County including maps, calendar of events and things to do. Elev 4550 ft. RV accessible. Restrooms. Hours: 8am to 5pm. No CC.
(307)684-5544 Lat: 44.34777, Lon: -106.69899
55 N Main St, Buffalo, WY 82834
www.buffalowyo.com
See ad page 1334 (Spotlight Buffalo).

CREEKSIDE CLUBHOUSE & GREENS Miniature golf course, ice cream and fudge. Elev 4640 ft. May 30 to Sep 5. Hours: 12:00 pm to 9:00 pm.
(307)684-7347 Lat: 44.35417, Lon: -106.68879
665 E Hart St, Buffalo, WY 82834
creeksideclubhouse@gmail.com
www.creeksideclubhouse.com
See ad page 1336.

The RVers' Guide to NASCAR - We'll give you the inside track on how to get high-speed thrills at major NASCAR venues. Turn to the front of the Guide to get the most out of North America's most thrilling sporting event.

Set a Destination for Family Fun!

Check out our camping destinations highlighting the best places for camping with the family in every state and province. Find a great destination, then select one of the family-friendly campgrounds listed by region throughout the article in the front of this Guide.

 See map page 1329

INDIAN
Campground & RV Park
★ True Western Hospitality ★

HALF WAY BETWEEN YELLOWSTONE & MT. RUSHMORE

YOUR HOSTS HAROLD AND KATRINA WELCOME YOU!

Large Shade Trees

FAMILY OWNED & OPERATED

Free Wi-Fi • Cable TV • Coffee • and A Smile

- Full Hookups • 50-30 Amp
- Sparkling Clean Hot Showers
- Gravel Sites w/Grass & Picnic Table
- 24 hr Large Laundry/Lounge
- Propane • City Water
- Snacks • RV Supplies
- Exceptional Gift Shop
- Walking Trails • Horseshoes
- Heated 22 x 50 Pool
- Camping Cabins
- Grassy Tent Sites by a Stream

- Walk to Several Local Restaurants
- Buffalo Golf Course
- Jim Gatchell Museum
- Big Horn Mountains
- Historic Fort McKinney
- Fort Phil Kearney
- Fetterman Battlefield
- Crazy Woman Canyon Drive

Dish Friendly Sites

LARGEST & LONGEST PULL-THRUS IN BUFFALO

EZ ON EZ OFF

BIG RIGS WELCOME

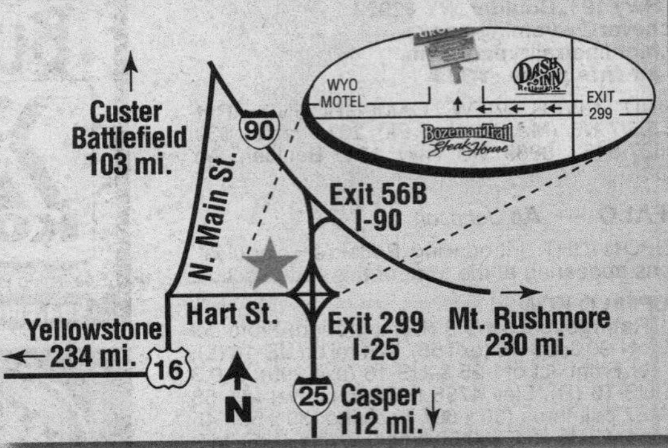

YEAR-ROUND RESERVATIONS

TOLL FREE 1-866-808-9601 • (307) 684-9601

www.indiancampground.com

N 44° 21.257 W 106° 41.320

VISA MasterCard DISCOVER

Good Sam RATED 8.5/9.5★/9

See listing Buffalo, WY

Good Sam Park

Walk Across the Street from Indian Campground to

CREEKSIDE Clubhouse and greens

- MINIATURE GOLF
- HAND-DIPPED ICE CREAM
- SHAKES & MALTS
- HOMEMADE FUDGE
- AIR CONDITIONED SEATING
- PATIO SEATING

- CONFERENCE CENTER FOR GROUPS & FAMILY GATHERINGS
- FEATURING BUFFALO BURGERS & BUFFALO STEAKS

Bozeman Trail Steak House

www.creeksideclubhouse.com

www.thebozemantrailsteakhouse.com

Family Owned Since 1980

DEER PARK

Exceptional CAMPING

Free Wi-Fi
Camping Cabins
Available

Buffalo, Wyoming

Buffalo — A National Historic District, a small, friendly town at the foot of the Big Horn Mountains

Halfway between
Mt. Rushmore and Yellowstone
DEER PARK is the Perfect Campground:

Stay in a park-like setting with grass, trees and flowers
Large 35′ x 80′ 50-Amp Full Hookup Pull-thrus

Big Rigs, Small Rigs and Tents Welcome
Shady or Sunny Sites

Sparkling Clean Restrooms and Showers

Cable TV 24 Channels - 24 hour Laundry - Heated Pool

Private one mile walking path • Nearby Restaurants
Shopping, Fishing, Golf and Wildlife

10% Discount for all Camping Discount Card Holders

Spend your summer with us!
Separate 55+ monthly area - Attractive rates
Open May 1 thru September 30

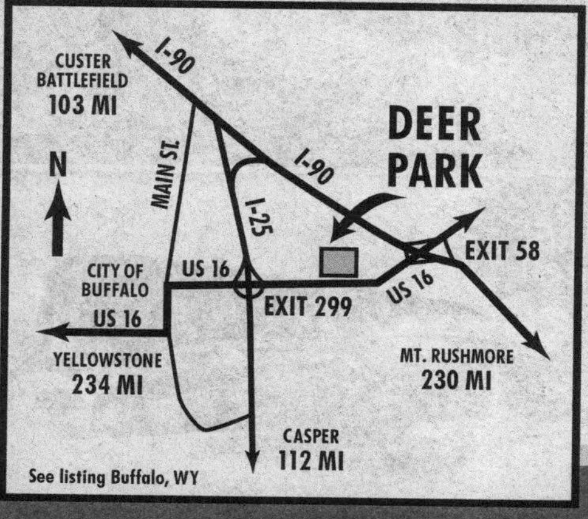

307-684-5722

AAA

Good Sam RATED 9/9.5★/9

Good Sam Park

GPS 44.3542N 106.6697W

146 Highway 16E @ Deer Park Road, Buffalo, WY 82834

WWW.DEERPARKRV.COM

WY

BURNS — D5 *Laramie*

↓ WYO CAMPGROUND **Ratings: 7.5/6/3** (Campground) 2015 rates: $35.50 to $55. May 1 to Oct 1. (307)547-2244 4066 I-80 Service Rd, Burns, WY 82053

CASPER — C4 *Natrona*

CASPER See also Evansville.

Our Guide to Seasonal Sites will help you find places you can stay for extended periods of time.

➔ **CASPER EAST RV PARK & CAMPGROUND**

Ratings: 9/9★/7.5 (Campground) From Jct of I-25 & Curtis St (exit 185), N 0.2 mi on Curtis St to US-20/26 (Yellowstone Hwy), W 0.8 mi (R). Elev 5300 ft.

FAC: Paved/gravel rds. (60 spaces). 55 Avail: 45 gravel, 10 grass, 32 pull-thrus (30 x 55), back-ins

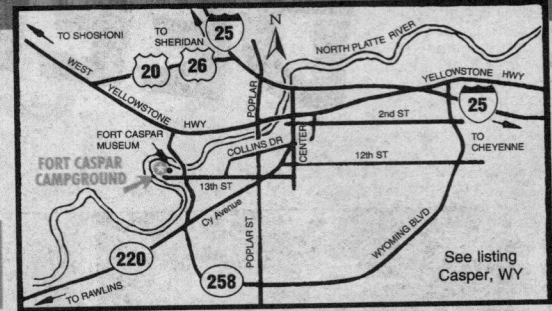

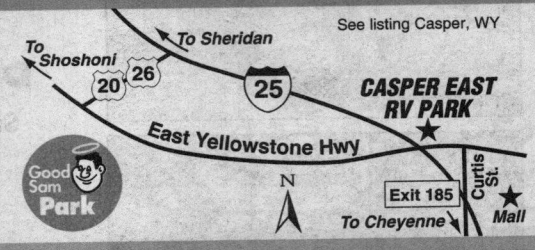

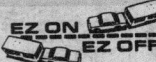

CASPER (CONT)

CASPER EAST RV PARK & (CONT)
(30 x 40), some side by side hkups, 50 full hkups, 5 W, 5 E (30/50 amps), seasonal sites, WiFi, tent sites, rentals, dump, laundry, groc, LP gas. **REC:** heated pool, playground. Pets OK. Partial handicap access. 2015 rates: $29 to $35.75. Disc: AAA, military. AAA Approved
(888)294-8551 Lat: 42.85634, Lon: -106.28867
2800 E Yellowstone Hwy, Casper, WY 82609
manager@caspereastrvpark.com
www.caspereastrvpark.com
See ad opposite page, 1332.

FORT CASPAR CAMPGROUND
Ratings: 6.5/9★/7.5 (Campground) From Jct of I-25 & Poplar St (exit 188B), S 1.2 mi on Poplar St to Collins Dr, W 1.8 mi to Wyoming Blvd, cross over Wyoming Blvd to Fort Caspar entrance, continue W 0.5 mi (R). Elev 5140 ft. **FAC:** Gravel rds. (89 spaces). Avail: 30 gravel, 20 pull-thrus (24 x 60), back-ins (20 x 45), 30 full hkups (30/50 amps), seasonal sites, WiFi Hotspot, tent sites, laundry. **REC:** North Platte River: fishing, playground. Pets OK. Big rig sites, 2015 rates: $44. Disc: AAA, military.
(307)234-3260 Lat: 42.83838, Lon: -106.37503
4205 Fort Caspar Rd, Casper, WY 82604
www.fortcasparcamp.com
See ad opposite page.

GRAY REEF RESERVOIR (Public) From town, W 30 mi on Hwy 220 to CR-412, S 0.5 mi (R). Pit toilets. 2015 rates: $10. (307)235-9311

RIVERS EDGE RV & CABINS RESORT
Ratings: 8/9.5★/9.5 (RV Park) From Jct of I-25 & Exit 182 (Hat Six Rd), N 1 mi on Hat Six Rd, becomes Cole Creek Rd (L). Elev 5130 ft. **FAC:** Gravel rds. (73 spaces). Avail: 53 gravel, 38 pull-thrus (35 x 65), back-ins (32 x 63), 53 full hkups (30/50 amps), seasonal sites, cable, WiFi, tent sites, rentals, dump, laundry, fire rings, firewood. **REC:** North Platte: fishing, playground. Pets OK. Partial handicap access. Big rig sites, 2015 rates: $35.50 to $40.50. Disc: military.
(307)234-0042 Lat: 42.85778, Lon: -106.21467
6820 Sante Fe Circle, Evansville, WY 82636
rvreservations@riversedgervresort.net
www.riversedgervresort.net
See primary listing at Evansville and ad page 1338.

Read many of our brand new RV Trips of a Lifetime for 2016 in the front of the Guide. Find the rest Online!

CENTENNIAL — D4 *Albany*

MEDICINE BOW NATIONAL FOREST (LIBBY CREEK/WILLOW CAMPGROUND) (Natl Pk) From town: Go 2 mi NW on Hwy-130, then 1/4 mi W on FR-351. Pit toilets. 2015 rates: $10. May 24 to Sep 30. (307)745-2300

CHEYENNE — D5 *Laramie*

AB CAMPING RV PARK
Ratings: 7/9★/8.5 (Campground) From Jct of I-80 & I-25, S 0.5 mi on I-25 to College Dr (exit 7), E 1.5 mi (R); or From Jct of I-80 & exit 364, SW 4.5 mi on College Dr (L). Elev 6100 ft. **FAC:** Gravel rds. 115 gravel, patios, 82 pull-thrus (20 x 60), back-ins (18 x 27), some side by side hkups, 89 full hkups, 26 E (30/50 amps), cable, WiFi, tent sites, dump, laundry, LP gas, restaurant. **REC:** playground. Pets OK. Big rig sites, eco-friendly, 2015 rates: $30.30 to $55. Disc: AAA, military. Apr 1 to Oct 15.
(307)634-7035 Lat: 41.10205, Lon: -104.82174
1503 W College Dr, Cheyenne, WY 82007
abcamping@gmail.com
www.campcheyenne.com
See ad this page, 1332.

CHEYENNE KOA **Ratings: 8.5/9.5★/8.5** (Campground) 2015 rates: $48.99 to $107.79. (800)562-1507 8800 Hutchins Dr, Cheyenne, WY 82007

CURT GOWDY (State Pk) From jct I-80 & I-25: Go 1-3/4 mi N on I-25 (exit 5) then 1/2 mi E on Missille Dr., then 18 mi W on Hwy-210 (Happy Jack Rd.). Pit toilets. 2015 rates: $10 to $17. (307)632-7946

GREENWAY TRAILER PARK & CAMPGROUND **Ratings: 4.5/9★/3.5** (Campground) 2015 rates: $30. (307)634-6696 3829 Greenway Street, Cheyenne, WY 82001

Say you saw it in our Guide!

JOLLEY ROGERS RV CAMPGROUND **Ratings: 4/8★/5.5** (Campground) 2015 rates: $25. May 1 to Sep 30. (307)634-8457 6102 E Hwy 30, Cheyenne, WY 82001

RESTWAY TRAVEL PARK Ratings: 6.5/8★/4.5 (Campground) From Jct of I-80 & Exit 364 (E Lincoln Way SR-212), N 1.3 mi on Bus 80 to Hwy 30 (E Lincoln Way) to Whitney Rd, E 2 mi on Whitney Rd (L). Elev 6100 ft. **FAC:** Gravel rds. (59 spaces). Avail: 30 gravel, 20 pull-thrus (22 x 50), back-ins (30 x 35), 29 full hkups, 1 W, 1 E (30/50 amps), seasonal sites, WiFi, tent sites, dump, laundry. **REC:** pool, playground. Pet restrict(B/Q). 2015 rates: $33.50. Disc: AAA, military.
(800)443-2751 Lat: 41.156944, Lon: -104.733333
4212 Whitney Rd, Cheyenne, WY 82001
www.restwaytravelpark.weebly.com

TERRY BISON RANCH RV PARK
Ratings: 7/8★/5 (RV Park) From Jct of I-80 & I-25, S 6 mi on I-25 to Exit 2 (Terry Ranch Rd) S 2.7 mi (L). Elev 6200 ft. **FAC:** Gravel rds. (92 spaces). Avail: 72 gravel, 72 pull-thrus (24 x 70), 72 full hkups (30/50 amps), seasonal sites, WiFi, tent sites, rentals, dump, laundry, groc, LP gas, fire rings, firewood, restaurant. **REC:** pond, fishing, playground, rec open to public. Pets OK. Partial handicap access. Big rig sites, eco-friendly, 2015 rates: $41.95 to $57.95. Disc: AAA. ATM.
AAA Approved
(307)634-4171 Lat: 41.00047, Lon: -104.90528
51 I-25 Service Rd E, Cheyenne, WY 82007
info@terrybisonranch.com
www.terrybisonranch.com
See ad this page, 1332.

Things to See and Do

VISIT CHEYENNE Brochures, maps, and someone to answer all your questions about Cheyenne. Elev 5900 ft. partial handicap access. RV accessible. Restrooms. Hours: 9am to 4pm. No CC.
(800)426-5009 Lat: 41.13193, Lon: -104.81374
121 W 15th St, Ste 202, Cheyenne, WY 82001
darren@cheyenne.org
www.cheyenne.org
See ad page 1330 (Welcome Section).

CODY — A2 *Park*

CODY See also Meeteetse & Wapiti.

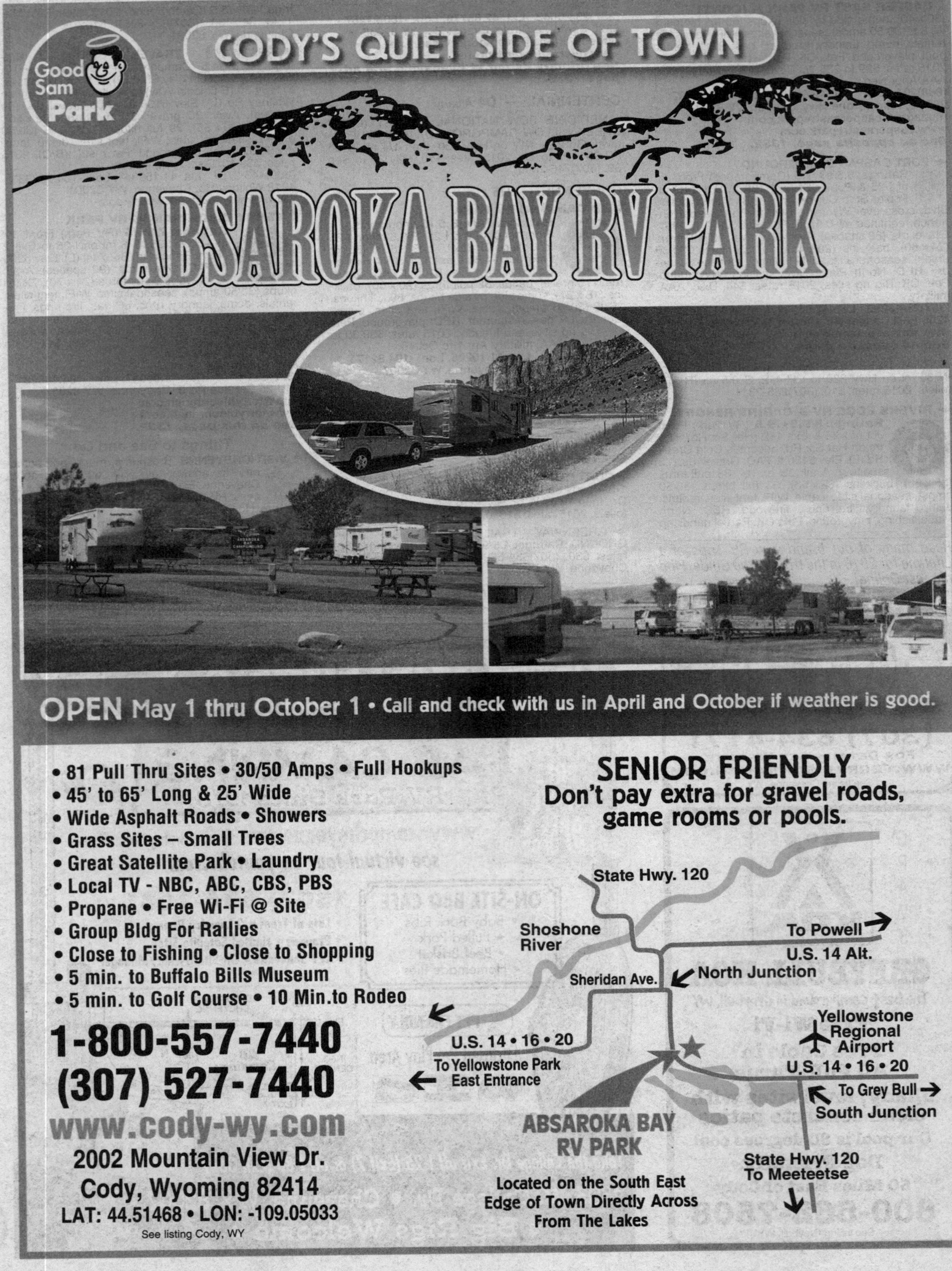
Good Sam Park
CODY'S QUIET SIDE OF TOWN
ABSAROKA BAY RV PARK
OPEN May 1 thru October 1 • Call and check with us in April and October if weather is good.
• 81 Pull Thru Sites • 30/50 Amps • Full Hookups
• 45' to 65' Long & 25' Wide
• Wide Asphalt Roads • Showers
• Grass Sites – Small Trees
• Great Satellite Park • Laundry
• Local TV - NBC, ABC, CBS, PBS
• Propane • Free Wi-Fi @ Site
• Group Bldg For Rallies
• Close to Fishing • Close to Shopping
• 5 min. to Buffalo Bills Museum
• 5 min. to Golf Course • 10 Min.to Rodeo
1-800-557-7440
(307) 527-7440
www.cody-wy.com
2002 Mountain View Dr.
Cody, Wyoming 82414
LAT: 44.51468 • LON: -109.05033
See listing Cody, WY
SENIOR FRIENDLY
Don't pay extra for gravel roads, game rooms or pools.
State Hwy. 120
Shoshone River
To Powell
U.S. 14 Alt.
North Junction
Sheridan Ave.
U.S. 14 • 16 • 20
To Yellowstone Park East Entrance
Yellowstone Regional Airport
U.S. 14 • 16 • 20
To Grey Bull
South Junction
ABSAROKA BAY RV PARK
State Hwy. 120 To Meeteetse
Located on the South East Edge of Town Directly Across From The Lakes

PONDEROSA CAMPGROUND

Good Sam Park

YOU CAN'T BEAT OUR LOCATION

Come Join Us for our Western Weekend Entertainment

The Richardson Family Extends To You a Warm Welcome and Western Hospitality

BIG RIGS WELCOME

UP TO 70' PULL-THRU SITES • 50 AMP

EZ Enter & Exit

Heated Camping Cabins with Porch Swing

- 137 Full Hookups
- Large Grass, Shade or Sun Sites with Mtn. Views
- Picnic Tables • Video Game Room
- 2 Restrooms & Showers • New Large Laundry
- E-Mail Access / Wi-Fi • ATM Machine / Fax
- New Enclosed Pet Corral
- Groups & Clubs Welcome
- Ponderosa Trading Post-Largest Selection of Authentic Indian Jewelry, Rugs, Pottery, Etc.
- Walk to Cody's Shops & Restaurants
- 3 Blks to Buffalo Bill Historical Center

- **We Book Tours to Yellowstone**
- **River Float Trips & Horseback Rides**
- **Rodeo Tickets • Trolley Stop to Rodeo**

FREE 75 CHANNEL CABLE TV

OPEN APR 15 TO OCT 15

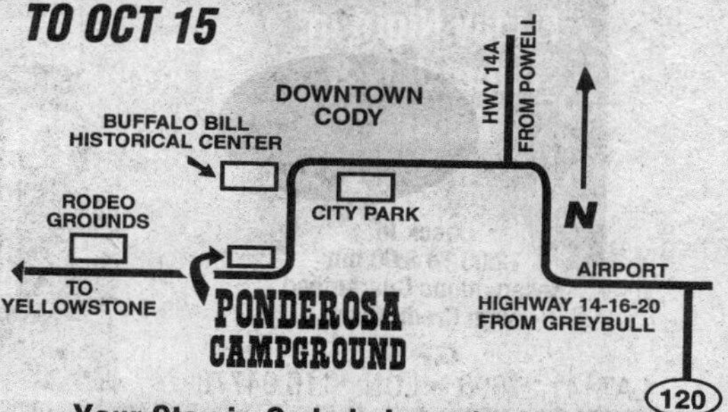

www.codyponderosa.com

info@codyponderosa.com

INFORMATION - RESERVATIONS

1815 8th St. • P.O. Box 1477, Cody, WY 82414

(307) 587-9203

YEAR-ROUND RESERVATIONS

Your Stay in Cody is Important to Us. We Offer & Provide Complete Tourist Information

See listing Cody, WY

CODY (CONT)

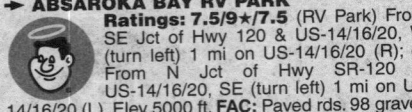

ABSAROKA BAY RV PARK
Ratings: 7.5/9★/7.5 (RV Park) From SE Jct of Hwy 120 & US-14/16/20, W (turn left) 1 mi on US-14/16/20 (R); or From N Jct of Hwy SR-120 & US-14/16/20, SE (turn left) 1 mi on US 14/16/20 (L). Elev 5000 ft. **FAC:** Paved rds. 98 gravel, 81 pull-thrus (25 x 60), back-ins (25 x 32), 98 full hkups (30/50 amps), WiFi, tent sites, laundry, LP gas. **REC.** Pets OK. Partial handicap access. Big rig sites, 2015 rates: $36.67. Disc: AAA, military. May 1 to Oct 1.
(800)557-7440 Lat: 44.51468, Lon: -109.05033
2002 Mountain View Dr, Cody, WY 82414
abc@cody-wy.com
www.cody-wy.com
See ad pages 1340, 1332, 1328 (Welcome Section).

BUFFALO BILL/NORTH FORK (State Pk) From town, W 13.5 mi on US-14/16/20 (L). Entrance fee & camping permit required. 2015 rates: $10 to $17. (307)587-9227

Like Us on Facebook.

BUFFALO BILL/NORTH SHORE BAY (State Pk) From town, W 9 mi on US-14/16/20 (L) Entrance fee & camping permit required. 2015 rates: $10 to $17. (307)587-9227

CODY KOA **Ratings: 8/9.5★/7** (Campground) 2015 rates: $44.95 to $74.47. May 1 to Oct 1. (800)562-8507 5561 Greybull Hwy, Cody, WY 82414

PARKWAY RV CAMPGROUND **Ratings: 4.5/5.5/7** (Campground) 2015 rates: $30. (307)527-5927 132 Yellowstone Ave, Cody, WY 82414

Find 'em fast. Our advertisers often include extra information or provide a detailed map in their ads to help you find their facilities quickly and easily.

PONDEROSA CAMPGROUND
Ratings: 7/9★/7.5 (Campground) From Jct of Hwy 120 & US-14/16/20 (in town), W 1.3 mi on US-14/16/20-Yellowstone Park Hwy (R). Elev 5000 ft. **FAC:** Paved/gravel rds. 137 Avail: 87 paved, 50 gravel, 32 pull-thrus (18 x 65), back-ins (21 x 35), some side by side hkups, 137 full hkups (30/50 amps), cable, WiFi, tent sites, rentals, dump, laundry, groc. **REC:** Shoshone River: fishing, playground. Pets OK. Big rig sites, eco-friendly, 2015 rates: $35 to $49. Disc: AAA, military. Apr 15 to Oct 15. No CC.
AAA Approved
(307)587-9203 Lat: 44.51769, Lon: -109.07279
1815 8th St, Cody, WY 82414
info@codyponderosa.com
www.codyponderosa.com
See ad pages 1341, 1332.

SHOSHONE NATIONAL FOREST (FOX CREEK CAMPGROUND) (Natl Forest) From town: Go 7-1/2 mi SE on US-212 (in Wyoming). Pit toilets. 2015 rates: $20. May 18 to Sep 20. (307)527-6241

SHOSHONE NATIONAL FOREST (WAPITI CAMPGROUND) (Natl Forest) From town: Go 8 mi W on US-16. Pit toilets. 2015 rates: $15 to $20. May 11 to Sep 16. (307)527-6921

Keeping pets quiet and on a leash is common courtesy. "Pet Restrictions" which you'll find in some listings refers to limits on size, breed or quantity of pets allowed.

CODY (CONT)

➔ **YELLOWSTONE VALLEY INN & RV**
Ratings: 7.5/8.5★/8 (RV Park) From Jct of Hwy 14/16/20 & 8th St (W edge of Cody), W 18 mi on Hwy 14/16/20 Yellowstone Hwy (L). Elev 5250 ft. **FAC:** Gravel rds. 60 gravel, 50 pull-thrus (30 x 62), back-ins (33 x 50), 23 full hkups, 37 W, 37 E (30/50 amps), WiFi, rentals, dump, mobile sewer, laundry, LP gas, fire rings, firewood, restaurant. **REC:** heated pool, whirlpool, Shoshone River: fishing, playground. Pets OK. Partial handicap access, no tents. Big rig sites, eco-friendly, 2015 rates: $48 to $58. Disc: military. May 1 to Oct 31.
(307)587-3961 Lat: 44.28511, Lon: -109.24636
3324 Yellowstone Hwy, Cody, WY 82414
yvicody@vcn.com
www.yellowstonevalleyinn.com
See ad opposite page, 1332.

Things to See and Do

➔ **BUFFALO BILL'S CODY YELLOWSTONE COUNTRY** All area information for Cody & Yellowstone Nat'l Park. Maps, calendars of events and things to do. Elev 5000 ft. partial handicap access. RV accessible. Restrooms. Hours: 8am to 5pm. No CC.
(307)587-2297 Lat: 44.52569, Lon: -109.07019
836 Sheridan Ave, Cody, WY 82414
pctc@codychamber.org
www.codycountry.org
See ad page 1331 (Welcome Section).

DEVILS TOWER — A5 *Crook*

➔ DEVILS TOWER KOA **Ratings: 8/6.5/9** (Campground) 2015 rates: $28 to $80. May 15 to Sep 30. (800)562-5785 60 Hwy 110, Devils Tower, WY 82714

↑ DEVILS TOWER NATL MON/BELLE FOURCHE CAMPGROUND (Natl Pk) From Jct of US 14 & WY Hwy 24, N 7 mi on WY Hwy 24, follow signs (E) Entrance fee required. 2015 rates: $12. Apr 23 to Oct 30. (307)467-5283

DOUGLAS — C4 *Converse*

↑ **DOUGLAS KOA**
Ratings: 9/9★/9 (Campground) From Jct of I-25 & exit 140 (Hwy 91/94), S 0.25 mi on Hwy 91/94 exit (right) to Jct of Hwys 91 & 94, NW (right) 1.5 mi on Hwy 91 (L). Right under I-25. Elev 4900 ft. **FAC:** Paved/gravel rds. (113 spaces). Avail: 52 gravel, 37 pull-thrus (24 x 50), back-ins (24 x 35), 52 full hkups (30/50 amps), seasonal sites, cable, WiFi, tent sites, rentals, dump, laundry, groc, LP gas, firewood. **REC:** heated pool, playground. Pets OK. 2015 rates: $33 to $35. Disc: military.
(800)562-2469 Lat: 42.76413, Lon: -105.43693
168 Cold Spring Rd, Douglas, WY 82633
douglaskoa@yahoo.com
www.douglaskoa.com
See ad opposite page.

DUBOIS — B2 *Fremont*

↓ DUBOIS WIND RIVER KOA **Ratings: 9/9★/8** (Campground) 2015 rates: $45 to $60. May 11 to Sep 30. (800)562-0806 225 Welty St, Dubois, WY 82513

➔ **THE LONGHORN RANCH LODGE & RV RESORT**
Ratings: 7.5/9.5★/9 (Campground) From town, E 3 mi on Hwy 26 (L). Elev 6900 ft. **FAC:** Gravel rds. (42 spaces). Avail: 37 gravel, 24 pull-thrus (40 x 85), back-ins (40 x 60), 37 full hkups (30/50 amps), seasonal sites, WiFi, tent sites, rentals, laundry, groc, LP gas, fire rings, firewood. **REC:** Wind River: fishing, playground. Pets OK. Big rig sites, eco-friendly, 2015 rates: $38 to $54. Disc: AAA, military. May 1 to Nov 1.
AAA Approved
(307)455-2337 Lat: 43.51754, Lon: -109.59067
5810 US Hwy 26, Dubois, WY 82513
info@thelonghornranch.com
www.thelonghornranch.com
See ad opposite page, 1332, 1329 (WY Map).

EVANSTON — D1 *Uinta*

➔ **PHILLIPS RV PARK**
Ratings: 7/9.5★/7.5 (Campground) From Jct of I-80 & I-80 Bus Loop (E Evanston exit 6), W 0.6 mi on I-80 Bus Loop/Bear River Dr (L) (Note: Do Not Use GPS). Elev 6748 ft. **FAC:** Gravel rds. (61 spaces). 56 Avail: 48 gravel, 8 grass, 52 pull-thrus (24 x 75), back-ins (25 x 45), 56 full hkups (30/50 amps), seasonal sites, cable, WiFi, tent sites, laundry. **REC:** playground. Pets OK. Big rig sites, eco-friendly, 2015 rates: $33.50 to $45. Disc: AAA. Apr 1 to Oct 15.
AAA Approved
(800)349-3805 Lat: 41.27096, Lon: -110.94778
225 Bear River Dr, Evanston, WY 82930
phillipsrvpark@nglconnection.net
www.phillipsrvpark.com
See ad opposite page, 1332.

EVANSVILLE — C4 *Natrona*

➔ **RIVERS EDGE RV & CABINS RESORT**
Ratings: 8/9.5★/9.5 (RV Park) From Jct of I-25 & Exit 182 (Hat Six Rd), N 1 mi on Hat Six Rd - becomes Cole Creek Rd (L). Elev 5130 ft. **FAC:** Gravel rds. (73 spaces). Avail: 53 gravel, 38 pull-thrus (35 x 65), back-ins (32 x 63), 53 full hkups (30/50 amps), seasonal sites, cable, WiFi, tent sites, rentals, dump, laundry, fire rings, firewood. **REC:** North Platte: fishing, playground. Pets OK. Partial handicap access. Big rig sites, 2015 rates: $35.50 to $40.50. Disc: military.
(307)234-0042 Lat: 42.85778, Lon: -106.21467
6820 Santa Fe Circle, Evansville, WY 82636
rvreservations@riversedgervresort.net
www.riversedgervresort.net
See ad pages 1338, 1332.

FORT BRIDGER — D1 *Uinta*

↓ **FORT BRIDGER RV CAMP**
Ratings: 6/8.5★/6.5 (Campground) From Jct of I-80 & Exit 34 (Fort Bridger/Bus Loop), S 2.2 mi on I-80 Bus Loop (turn S on street between fort entrance & trading post). Elev 6700 ft. **FAC:** Gravel rds. (38 spaces). Avail: 28 grass, 14 pull-thrus (50 x 100), back-ins (50 x 100), 28 full hkups (30/50 amps), seasonal sites, WiFi, laundry. Pets OK. No tents. Big rig sites, 2015 rates: $35. Disc: AAA, military. May 1 to Oct 15. No CC.
(307)782-3150 Lat: 41.31618, Lon: -110.38860
64 Groshon Rd, Fort Bridger, WY 82933
fbrv@bvea.net
users.bvea.net/fbrv
See ad this page.

FORT LARAMIE — C5 *Goshen*

➔ **CHUCK WAGON RV Ratings: 5/8★/5** (RV Park) From Jct of Hwy 26 & SR-160, SW on SR-160 300 ft (R). Elev 4125 ft. **FAC:** Gravel rds. 14 Avail: 13 paved, 1 gravel, 10 pull-thrus (24 x 60), back-ins (18 x 40), some side by side hkups, 14 full hkups (30/50 amps), WiFi, tent sites, laundry, LP gas, restaurant. Pets OK. Big rig sites, 2015 rates: $30. (307)837-2828 Lat: 42.21130, Lon: -104.52523 306 Pioneer Ct, Fort Laramie, WY 82212 acd4021@vistabeam.com www.chuckwagonrv.com

Don't miss a thing! Check out the Table of Contents for everything the Guide has to offer.

FOXPARK — D4 *Albany*

MEDICINE BOW NATIONAL FOREST (LAKE OWEN CAMPGROUND) (Natl Forest) From town: Go 7 mi NE on FR-517, then 3 mi S on FR-540. Pit toilets. 2015 rates: $10. Jun 1 to Oct 15. (307)745-2300

GILLETTE — A4 *Campbell*

➚ **GREEN TREE'S CRAZY WOMAN CAMPGROUND**
Ratings: 7/8.5★/7 (Campground) From Jct I-90 & Business I-90 (exit 124): Go N .2 mi to W 2nd St; Turn E and go .6 mi (R). Elev 4550 ft. **FAC:** Gravel rds. (90 spaces). Avail: 50 gravel, 15 pull-thrus (26 x 46), back-ins (24 x 42), some side by side hkups, 27 full hkups, 23 W, 23 E (30/50 amps), seasonal sites, WiFi, tent sites, dump, mobile sewer, laundry, firewood. **REC:** playground. Pets OK. Partial handicap access. 2015 rates: $32.55 to $36.27. No CC.
AAA Approved
(307)682-3665 Lat: 44.29281, Lon: -105.51655
1001 W 2nd St., Gillette, WY 82716
crazywomancampground@gmail.com
http://crazywomancampground.com
See ad this page.

GLENDO — C5 *Platte*

➔ GLENDO (State Pk) From Jct of I-25 & Glendo Park Rd, E 2 mi on Glendo Park Rd, follow signs (L) Entrance fee required. 2015 rates: $10 to $17. (307)735-4433

➔ **GLENDO LAKESIDE RV PARK**
Ratings: 8/10★/9 (Campground) From jct of I-25 & exit 111, E 500 yards on A St to SR 319/Yellowstone Hwy, N 1 mi on SR 319 to Lakeshore Dr, E 0.5 mi (R). Elev 4900 ft. **FAC:** Paved rds. 44 gravel, 44 pull-thrus (38 x 75), 44 full hkups (30/50 amps), WiFi, showers $, laundry, LP gas, fire rings. **REC.** Pets OK. Partial handicap access, no tents. Big rig sites, 2015 rates: $35. Disc: military. Mar 15 to Nov 15.
(307)735-4161 Lat: 42.51158, Lon: -105.01404
631 Lakeshore Dr, Glendo, WY 82213
nancy@glendolakesiderv.com
www.glendolakesiderv.com
See ad this page, 1332.

GLENROCK — C4 *Converse*

↓ DEER CREEK VILLAGE RV PARK **Ratings: 5.5/8.5★/4.5** (RV Park) 2015 rates: $25 to $33.75. (307)436-8121 302 Millat Lane, Glenrock, WY 82637

↑ **PLATTE RIVER RV & CAMPGROUND**
Ratings: 6.5/7.5★/6.5 (Campground) From Jct of I-25 & Exit 165 (Hwy 95), N 2.0 on Hwy 95 to Birch St, W .60 on Birch St to Hwy 95, N .40 mi on Hy 95 (L). Elev 5200 ft. **FAC:** Gravel rds. (55 spaces). Avail: 20 gravel, 20 pull-thrus (35 x 60), some side by side hkups, 20 full hkups (30/50 amps), seasonal sites, WiFi, tent sites, dump, LP gas, fire-

Tell them you saw them in this Guide!

GLENROCK (CONT)

PLATTE RIVER RV & (CONT)
wood. **REC:** playground. Pets OK. 2015 rates: $30 to $35. Disc: military.
(307)262-9768 Lat: 42.86858, Lon: -105.88054
131 Shawnie Ln, Glenrock, WY 82637
platteriverrv@gmail.com
www.platteriverrv.com

GRAND TETON NATIONAL PARK — B1
Teton

COLTER BAY CAMPGROUND **Ratings: 4/7.5/6.5** (RV Park) 2015 rates: $24 to $50. May 21 to Sep 20. (307)543-2811 hwy 89, Moran, WY 83013

COLTER BAY VILLAGE RV PARK **Ratings: 6.5/8★/7.5** (RV Park) 2015 rates: $57 to $67. May 27 to Sep 30. (800)628-9988 hwy 89, Moran, WY 83013

GRAND TETON NP (COLTER BAY CAMPGROUND) (Natl Pk) From Moran, NW 10 mi on Hwy 89/191/287 toward Yellowstone, follow signs (L) Entrance fee required. 2015 rates: $11 to $22. May 22 to Sep 21. (307)543-2811

GRAND TETON NP (GROS VENTRE CAMPGROUND) (Natl Pk) From Jackson, N 6.5 mi on Hwy 89/191 to Gros Ventre Jct, E 4.5 mi (R) Entrance fee required. 2015 rates: $10 to $20.50. May 3 to Oct 4. (800)628-9988

GRAND TETON NP (LIZARD CREEK CAMPGROUND) (Natl Pk) From town: Go 17 mi N on US-89/287 (Teton Park Rd). RVs up to 30 ft are permitted. 2015 rates: $21. Jun 7 to Sep 2. (800)672-6012

GRAND TETON NP (SIGNAL MOUNTAIN CAMPGROUND) (Natl Pk) From Moran, NW 5 mi on US-89/287 to Teton Park Rd, S 3 mi, follow signs (R) Camping permit required. Vehicle size limited to 30 feet. 2015 rates: $21 to $45. May 10 to Oct 13. (800)672-6012

HEADWATERS LODGE & CABINS AT FLAGG RANCH
Ratings: 5.5/8.5★/7.5 (Campground) From Jct of US-26/287 & US-26/89/191 (Moran Jct), NW 26.5 mi on US-191, 0.6 mi N of Flagg Ranch Village (L); or From S gate of Yellowstone Park, S 2 mi on US-191 (R). Entrance fee required to access this campground. Elev 7000 ft. **FAC:** Gravel/dirt rds. 97 gravel, 97 pull-thrus (30 x 60), 97 full hkups (30/50 amps), tent sites, rentals, laundry, LP gas, firewood. **REC:** rec open to public. Pets OK. Partial handicap access. 2015 rates: $69. Jun 1 to Sep 30.
(307)543-2861 Lat: 44.10505, Lon: -110.66826
Us Hwy 89 2 Mi S Of Yellowstone, Yellowstone National Park, WY 83813
info@flaggranch.com
www.flaggranch.com
See ad page 1349.

JENNY LAKE CAMPGROUND (Natl Pk) 8 miles north of Moose on Grand Teton Road. 2015 rates: $11.50 to $23. May 9 to Sep 28. (800)628-9988

SIGNAL MOUNTAIN CAMPGROUND **Ratings: 4.5/NA/7** (Campground) 2015 rates: $22 to $45. May 10 to Oct 13. (307)739-3300 1 Inner Park Rd, Grand Teton National Park, WY 83013

Things to See and Do

TRIANGLE X RANCH Guided scenic floats in Grand Teton National Park on the Snake River. Western style cookout. Guided fly fishing, half and full days, lessons, equipment, flies. N-bnd: From Jct of West Broadway & Hwy 89/191 (in Jackson), N 13 mi on Hwy 89/191 to Moose Jct, W 1/2 mi (over Snake River to 4-way stop, N into prkg lot. S-bnd: From Jct of Hwy 26/89/191 (at Moran Jct), S 18 mi on Hwy 26/89/191 to Moose Jct, W 1/2 mi (over Snake River to 4-way stop, N into prkg lot). Elev 6200 ft.

SCENIC FLOATS-GRAND TETON NTL PARK
Guest ranch specializing in scenic sunrise and evening wildlife floats, dinner cookout trips and more! Relax, stay dry and bring your camera. Great opportunity for wildlife viewing. Knowledgeable and informative guides.

May 1 to Sep 30. Restrooms. Hours: 7am to 9pm.
(307)733-5500 Lat: 43.65524, Lon: -110.71628
rivertrips@trianglex.com
www.nationalparkfloattrips.com
See ad this page.

GREEN RIVER — D2 *Sweetwater*

THE TRAVEL CAMP
Ratings: 7/8.5★/5.5 (RV Park) From Jct I-80 & Exit 85, S 0.1 on Covered Wagon Rd to Hwy 374, E 1.4 mi (R) or From Jct I-80 & Exit 91, SW 2 mi on Flaming Gorge Way to Hwy 374, W 2.4 mi (L). Elev 6100 ft. **FAC:** Paved rds. (54 spaces). Avail: 34 paved, 19 pull-thrus (18 x 40), back-ins (20 x 40), 19 full hkups (30/50 amps), seasonal sites, cable, WiFi, tent sites, dump, laundry, groc, firewood. Pets OK. Partial handicap access. 2015 rates: $35. Disc: AAA, military. No CC.
(307)875-2630 Lat: 41.55507, Lon: -109.51738
4626 4th St, Green River, WY 82935
www.thetravelcamp.com

GREYBULL — A3 *Big Horn*

CAMPBELLS GREEN OASIS CAMPGROUND **Ratings: 5/10★/5** (RV Park) 2015 rates: $32. (307)765-2856 540 12th Ave N, Greybull, WY 82426

GREYBULL KOA
Ratings: 10/10★/9 (Campground) From Jct of US-14 (Greybull Ave) & US-16/14 (6th St), N 0.4 mi on 6th St to 4th Ave, E 0.4 mi (E). Elev 3800 ft. **FAC:** All weather rds. 40 paved, patios, 19 pull-thrus (23 x 60), back-ins (21 x 34), 37 full hkups, 3 W, 3 E (30/50 amps), cable, WiFi, tent sites, rentals, dump, laundry, LP gas, firewood. **REC:** heated pool, playground. Pet restrict(B). Partial handicap access. Eco-friendly. 2015 rates: $41 to $55. Disc: AAA. Apr 15 to Oct 15.
(800)562-7508 Lat: 44.49304, Lon: -108.04899
399 N 2nd St, Greybull, WY 82426
info@greybullkoa.com
www.koa.com/campgrounds/greybull
See ad page 1339.

GUERNSEY — C5 *Platte*

GUERNSEY (State Pk) From town, W 0.5 mi on Hwy 26, N 2 mi on Hwy 319 (E) Entrance fee required. 2015 rates: $10 to $17. (307)836-2334

LARSON PARK CAMPGROUND (Public) From town, S 1 mi on Wyoming Ave (L). Call park for reservations. 2015 rates: $14 to $20. Apr 15 to Oct 15. (307)836-2255

HAWK SPRINGS — D5 *Goshen*

HAWK SPRINGS STATE RECREATION AREA (State Pk) From town: Go 3 mi S on US 85, then 3 mi E on dirt county road. Pit toilets. 2015 rates: $10 to $17. (307)836-2334

HYATTVILLE — A3 *Big Horn*

MEDICINE LODGE STATE ARCHAEOLOGICAL SITE (State Pk) From Hwy 31 in town: Go 6 mi NW on dirt local road. Pit toilets. 2015 rates: $6 to $11. (307)469-2234

JACKSON — B1 *Teton*

JACKSON See also Grand Teton National Park.

SNAKE RIVER PARK KOA **Ratings: 7/9.5★/7** (Campground) 2015 rates: $49 to $110. Apr 15 to Oct 15. (800)562-1878 9705 S U S Hwy 89, Jackson, WY 83001

THE VIRGINIAN RV RESORT
Ratings: 7.5/9★/6 (RV Park) N-bnd: From Jct of Hwy 22 & US-26/89, NE 0.5 mi on US-26/89 (W Broadway) to Virginian Ln, S 500 yds (L); or S-bnd: From Jct of US-26/89 & W Broadway (center of town), SW 0.9 mi on W Broadway to Virginia LN, S 500 yds (L). Elev 6200 ft. **FAC:** Gravel rds. 103 grass, 68 pull-thrus (20 x 40), back-ins (22 x 28), 103 full hkups (30/50 amps), cable, WiFi, laundry, restaurant. **REC:** heated pool, whirlpool. Pets OK. No tents

ACKSON (CONT)

THE VIRGINIAN RV RESORT (CONT)
Eco-friendly, 2015 rates: $75 to $80. Disc: AAA, mili-
ary. May 1 to Oct 15.
AAA Approved
800)321-6982 Lat: 43.47188, Lon: -110.77892
50 W Broadway, Jackson, WY 83001
nfo@virginianlodge.com
www.virginianlodge.com
See ad opposite page, 1332.

ACKSON HOLE — B1 *Teton*

JACKSON HOLE See also Grand Teton National
Park & Jackson.

KAYCEE — B4 *Johnson*

KAYCEE RV PARK **Ratings: 4/NA/4.5** (RV
Park) 2015 rates: $30. (307)738-2233 42 Mayoworth
Rd, Kaycee, WY 82639

POWDER RIVER CAMPGROUND **Rat-
ings: 3/5/5** (Campground) 2015 rates: $30.
307)738-2233 101 Old Barnum Rd, Kaycee, WY
82639

KEMMERER — D1 *Lincoln*

FONTENELLE RESERVOIR CAMPGROUND
BUREAU OF LAND MGMT.) (State Pk) From town:
Go 30 mi NE on US 189. 2015 rates: $7. May 20 to
Oct 15. (307)828-4500

RIVERSIDE RV PARK
Ratings: 3.5/NA/7 (RV Park) From Jct of Hwys 30 & 189 (in town), N 0.5 mi on Hwy 189 to sign (Aspen Ave), S 0.3 mi to sign (Spinel St), E 0.1 mi (R). Elev 6927 ft. **FAC:** Paved/gravel rds. 34 Avail: 13 paved, 21 gravel, 16 pull-thrus (25 x 57), back-ins (25 x 30), 34 full hkups (30/50 amps), WiFi, dump. **REC:** Hams Fork River: fishing. Pets OK. No tents. 2015 rates: $35. May 15 to Oct 15. No CC.
AAA Approved
307)877-3416 Lat: 41.79735, Lon: -110.53495
216 Spinel St, Kemmerer, WY 83101
See ad this page.

LAKE JUNCTION — A1 *Park*

YELLOWSTONE/CANYON CAMPGROUND (Natl Pk) From Canyon Junction, E 0.25 mi on County Rd, follow signs (L). 2015 rates: $26. May 30 to Sep 4. (307)344-7311

YELLOWSTONE/FISHING BRIDGE RV PARK (Natl Pk) From Lake Jct, E 1 mi on US-14/16/20, 0.5 mi E of Fishing Bridge (L). Entrance fee required to access this campground (hard sided vehicles only). 2015 rates: $50. May 11 to Sep 30. (307)344-7311

LANDER — C2 *Fremont*

HOLIDAY LODGE MOTEL AND CAMP-GROUND
Ratings: 6/8★/6 (Campground) From Jct of Hwy 287 & SR-789 (in town), E .10 mi on SR-789 (L). Elev 5300 ft. **FAC:** Paved rds. 7 gravel, back-ins (25 x 60), 7 full hkups (30/50 amps), WiFi, tent sites, laundry, firewood. **REC.** Pets OK. Partial handicap access. 2015 rates: $38. Disc: AAA, military. No CC.
(307)332-2511 Lat: 42.49952, Lon: -108.43418
210 Mcfarlane Dr, Lander, WY 82520
holidaylodgebusiness@yahoo.com
www.landerholidaylodge.com
See ad this page.

Treat your pet to a fabulous camping experience by staying at one of the Pampered Pet Parks featured in the front of the Guide.

MAVERICK RV PARK/MHP
Ratings: 3.5/6.5/4.5 (RV Park) From Jct of Hwy 287 (Main St) & SR-789, W 0.3 mi on Hwy 287 to 2nd St, N 0.7 mi (R). Elev 5300 ft. **FAC:** Paved/gravel rds. (50 spaces). Avail: 35 grass, 15 pull-thrus (30 x 65), back-ins (30 x 60), 35 full hkups (30/50 amps), seasonal sites, WiFi, tent sites, laundry. Pets OK. Big rig sites, 2015 rates: $28. No CC.
(307)332-3142 Lat: 42.84278, Lon: -108.72496
1104 N Second St, Lander, WY 82520
maverickrvpark@yahoo.com
www.maverickrv.com
See ad this page.

Had a great stay? Let us know by emailing us travelguidecomments@goodsamfamily.com

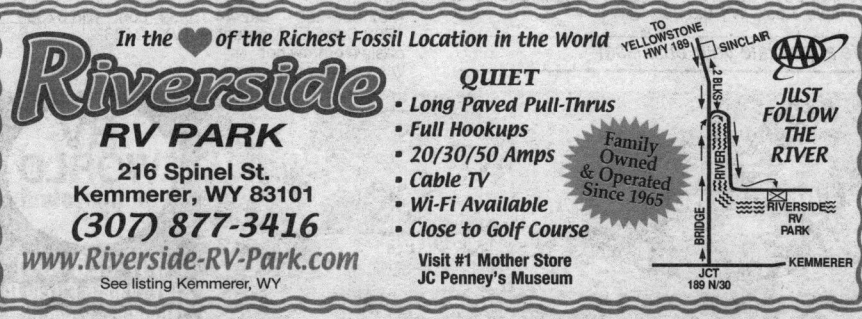

SHOSHONE NATIONAL FOREST (LOUIS LAKE CAMPGROUND) (Natl Forest) From jct US 287 & Hwy 131: Go 26 mi S on Hwy 131 & FR 300 (Loop Rd). No trailers over 24 ft. Pit toilets. 2015 rates: $10. (307)332-5460

SHOSHONE NATIONAL FOREST (WORTHEN MEADOWS CAMPGROUND) (Natl Forest) From jct US 287 & Hwy 131: Go 13 mi S on Hwy 131 & FR 300 (Loop Rd). Pit toilets. 2015 rates: $15. Jun 1 to Sep 7. (307)332-5460

SINKS CANYON (State Pk) From town: Go 6 mi W on Hwy 131. Pit toilets. 2015 rates: $10 to $17. (307)332-6333

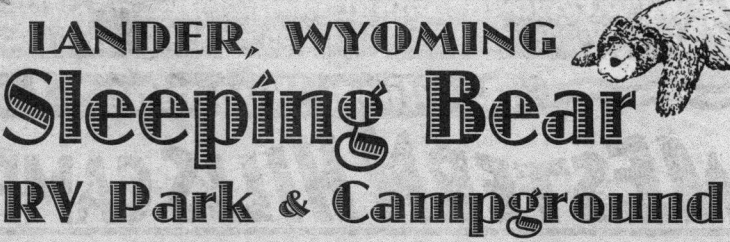

SLEEPING BEAR RV PARK & CAMP-GROUND
Ratings: 7.5/9★/8.5 (RV Park) From W Jct of Hwy 287 & SR-789 (in town), S 0.5 mi on Hwy 287/SR-789 (R). E edge of town on Hwy 287. Elev 5381 ft. **FAC:** Gravel rds. (45 spaces). Avail: 37 gravel, 32 pull-thrus (30 x 65), back-ins (25 x 35), 34 full hkups, 3 W, 3 E (30/50 amps), seasonal sites, WiFi, tent sites, rentals, dump, laundry, LP gas, fire rings, firewood. **REC:** playground, rec open to public. Pets OK. Partial

LANDER (CONT)

SLEEPING BEAR RV PARK & (CONT)
handicap access. Eco-friendly, 2015 rates: $24.50 to $44.03. Disc: AAA, military.
AAA Approved
(307)332-5159 Lat: 42.82516, Lon: -108.71869
715 E Main, Lander, WY 82520
slpbear@yahoo.com
www.sleepingbearrvpark.com
See ad pages 1345, 1332.

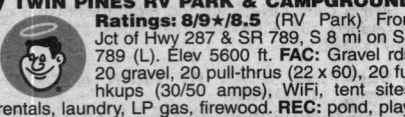

TWIN PINES RV PARK & CAMPGROUND Ratings: 8/9★/8.5 (RV Park) From Jct of Hwy 287 & SR 789, S 8 mi on SR 789 (L). Elev 5600 ft. **FAC:** Gravel rds. 20 gravel, 20 pull-thrus (22 x 60), 20 full hkups (30/50 amps), WiFi, tent sites, rentals, laundry, LP gas, firewood. **REC:** pond, playground. Pets OK. Big rig sites, eco-friendly, 2015 rates: $39. Disc: AAA, military.
AAA Approved
(800)986-4008 Lat: 42.73738, Lon: -108.64835
7345 Hwy 789, Lander, WY 82520
info@twinpinesrvpark.com
www.twinpinesrvpark.com
See ad pages 1345, 1332.

LARAMIE — D4 *Albany*

LARAMIE KOA **Ratings: 6.5/9.5★/6** (Campground) 2015 rates: $47 to $50. (800)562-4153 1271 W Baker St, Laramie, WY 82072

LOVELL — A3 *Big Horn*

BIGHORN CANYON NRA/HORSESHOE BEND (Natl Pk) From Lovell, E 3 mi on 14A to SR-37, N 9.7 mi to park access rd, E 2 mi (E). 2015 rates: $15. (307)548-2251

LOVELL CAMPER PARK (Public) From Jct of US-310 & Quebec Ave, N 0.2 mi on Quebec Ave (L). (307)548-6551

LUSK — C5 *Niobrara*

BJ'S CAMPGROUND **Ratings: 6/9★/8** (Campground) 2015 rates: $35 to $38. (307)334-2314 902 S Maple, Lusk, WY 82225

We appreciate your business!

LYMAN — D1 *Uinta*

LYMAN KOA
Ratings: 8/8.5★/7 (Campground) From Jct of I-80 & Hwy 413 (exit 41), S 1 mi on Hwy 413 (R). Elev 6700 ft. **FAC:** Gravel rds. 36 Avail: 18 gravel, 18 grass, 36 pull-thrus (21 x 90), 18 full hkups, 18 W, 18 E (30/50 amps), WiFi, tent sites, rentals, dump, laundry, groc, fire rings, firewood. **REC:** heated pool, playground. Pet restrict(B). 2015 rates: $30 to $36. May 15 to Oct 1.
(800)562-2762 Lat: 41.35012, Lon: -110.29915
1531 N Hwy 413, Lyman, WY 82937
lyman@koa.com
www.koa.com/campgrounds/lyman
See ad this page.

MADISON JUNCTION — A1 *Teton*

YELLOWSTONE/MADISON JUNCTION CAMPGROUND (Natl Pk) From Jct of Hwys 20 & 191 (W entrance), E 14 mi on Hwy 20, follow signs (L). 2015 rates: $21.50. May 2 to Oct 19. (307)344-7311

MAMMOTH SPRINGS JUNCTION — A1 *Park*

YELLOWSTONE/INDIAN CREEK (Natl Pk) From Mammoth Jct, S 7.5 mi, follow signs (R). Entrance fee required. Pit toilets. 2015 rates: $15. Jun 8 to Sep 17. (307)344-7381

YELLOWSTONE/MAMMOTH (Natl Pk) From Jct of Hwys 89 & 212 (N entrance), S 5 mi on Hwy 89, follow signs (R). Entrance fee required. 2015 rates: $20. (307)344-7381

MEETEETSE — A2 *Park*

OASIS MOTEL & RV PARK Ratings: 6.5/7★/5.5 (Campground) From Jct of Hwy 120 & Mary Ave (N edge of town), S 600 ft (L). Elev 4900 ft. **FAC:** Gravel rds. 11 gravel, 4 pull-thrus (20 x 60), back-ins (20 x 60), 11 full hkups (30/50 amps), cable, WiFi, tent sites, rentals, laundry. **REC:** Grey Bull River: fishing. Pets OK. 2015 rates: $23.25. Disc: AAA, military.
(307)868-2551 Lat: 44.15939, Lon: -108.87369
1702 State St, Meeteetse, WY 82433
oasis@ommw.net
www.ommw.net

MOORCROFT — A5 *Crook*

KEYHOLE (State Pk) From town, E 11.3 mi or I-90 to Pine Ridge Rd., N 6 mi on Pine Ridge Rd. follow signs (L). Entrance fee required. Pit toilets 2015 rates: $10 to $17. (307)756-3596

NEWCASTLE — B5 *Weston*

AUTO-INN MOTEL & RV PARK
Ratings: 5/8.5★/6.5 (RV Park) From Jct o US-85 & US-16: W 0.5 mi on US-16 to US-16 Bypass, NW 1.9 mi to Main St, W 0.3 mi (R or From Jct of Hwy 450 & US-16, E 1.9 mi on US-1 (L). Elev 4300 ft. **FAC:** Poor gravel rds. (38 spaces) Avail: 28 gravel, 24 pull-thrus (20 x 45), back-ins (30 x 55), mostly side by side hkups, 28 full hkups (30/50 amps), seasonal sites, WiFi, tent sites, rentals laundry. **REC.** Pets OK. Big rig sites, 2015 rates $35.50 to $40.50. Disc: AAA.
AAA Approved
(307)746-2734 Lat: 43.85134, Lon: -104.23389
2503 W Main, Newcastle, WY 82701
autoinnmotel@yahoo.com
See ad this page.

NORRIS JUNCTION — A1 *Park*

YELLOWSTONE/NORRIS (Natl Pk) From Mammoth Jct, S 20 mi. 2015 rates: $20. May 15 to Sep 27 (307)344-7381

RANCHESTER — A3 *Sheridan*

LAZY R CAMPGROUND & RV PARK Ratings: 4/7★/6 (RV Park) From Jct of I-90 & Hwy 14 (exit 9), W 1 mi on Hwy 14 (L). Elev 3725 ft. **FAC** Gravel rds. (44 spaces). 33 Avail: 9 paved, 24 gravel 22 pull-thrus (25 x 68), back-ins (25 x 55), 33 fu

RANCHESTER (CONT)

LAZY R CAMPGROUND & RV PARK (CONT)
hkups (30/50 amps), seasonal sites, cable, WiFi, tent sites, rentals. Pets OK. Big rig sites, 2015 rates: $30. (888)655-9284 Lat: 44.90787, Lon: -107.16709
652 U S Hwy 14, Ranchester, WY 82839
lazyr@vcn.com
www.lazyrcampground.com

RAWLINS — D3 *Carbon*

RAWLINS KOA Ratings: 8/9.5★/7 (Campground) From Jct of I-80 & Exit 214, exit to N Frontage Rd W 0.1 mi on Frontage Rd (R). Elev 6977 ft. **FAC:** Gravel rds. (51 spaces). Avail: 44 gravel, 44 pull-thrus (25 x 63), 38 full hkups, 6 W, 6 E (30/50 amps), seasonal sites, cable, WiFi, tent sites, rentals, dump, laundry, LP gas, firewood. **REC:** playground. Pet restrict(B). Partial handicap access. 2015 rates: $28 to $44. Disc: AAA, military.
(800)562-7559 Lat: 41.77991, Lon: -107.22974
205 E Hwy 71, Rawlins, WY 82301
rawlinskoa@gmail.com
koa.com

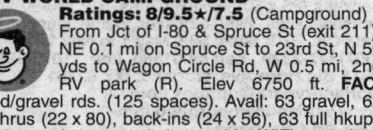

RV WORLD CAMPGROUND
Ratings: 8/9.5★/7.5 (Campground) From Jct of I-80 & Spruce St (exit 211), NE 0.1 mi on Spruce St to 23rd St, N 50 yds to Wagon Circle Rd, W 0.5 mi, 2nd RV park (R). Elev 6750 ft. **FAC:** Paved/gravel rds. (125 spaces). Avail: 63 gravel, 62 pull-thrus (22 x 80), back-ins (24 x 56), 63 full hkups (30/50 amps), seasonal sites, cable, WiFi, tent sites, dump, laundry, groc, LP gas. **REC:** playground. Pets OK. Partial handicap access. 2015 rates: $26 to $32. Disc: AAA, military.
AAA Approved
(307)328-1091 Lat: 41.78338, Lon: -107.27221
3101 Wagon Circle Rd, Rawlins, WY 82301
info@rvworldcamp.com
www.rvworldcampground.com
See ad opposite page, 1332.

WESTERN HILLS CAMPGROUND
Ratings: 8/9★/8 (Campground) From Jct of I-80 & Spruce St (Exit 211), NE 0.3 mi on Spruce St to 23rd St, N 50 yds on 23rd St to Wagon Circle Rd, W 0.2 mi (R). Elev 6750 ft. **FAC:** Gravel rds. (83 spaces). Avail: 45 gravel, 45 pull-thrus (24 x 65), 35 full hkups, 10 E (30/50 amps), seasonal sites, cable, WiFi, tent sites, rentals, dump, laundry. **REC:** playground. Pets OK. Big rig sites, 2015 rates: $27.75 to $35.50. Disc: AAA, military.
AAA Approved
(307)324-2592 Lat: 41.78523, Lon: -107.26664
2500 Wagon Circle Road, Rawlins, WY 82301
stay@westernhillscampground.com
www.westernhillscampground.com
See ad opposite page, 1332.

RIVERSIDE — D4 *Carbon*

LAZY ACRES CAMPGROUND & MOTEL **Ratings: 7/8★/7.5** (Campground) 2015 rates: $33 to $35. May 15 to Oct 31. (307)327-5968 110 Fields Ave, Riverside, WY 82325

RIVERTON — B3 *Fremont*

OWL CREEK KAMPGROUND LLC **Ratings: 6/8.5★/5** (Campground) 2015 rates: $35 to $45. May 1 to Nov 1. (307)856-2869 11124 U S Hwy 789, Riverton, WY 82501

WIND RIVER RV PARK
Ratings: 7.5/9.5★/8 (RV Park) E-bnd: From Jct of US-26 & SR-789 (in town), N 0.2 mi on US-26 (Federal Ave) to Park Ave, E 0.6 mi (L); or W bnd: From Jct of US-26 & Park Ave (in town at Pizza Hut), E 0.6 mi on Park Ave (L). Elev 4960 ft. **FAC:** Gravel rds. 60 gravel, 38 pull-thrus (27 x 70), back-ins (27 x 52), mostly side by side hkups, 60 full hkups (30/50 amps), WiFi, showers $, dump, laundry, firewood. **REC.** Pet restrict(B). Partial handicap access, no tents. Big rig sites, eco-friendly, 2015 rates: $30.86 to $39.86. Disc: AAA, military.
(307)857-3000 Lat: 43.02769, Lon: -108.37064
1618 E Park Ave, Riverton, WY 82501
jpepper@bresnan.net
See ad this page, 1332, 1329 (WY Map).

Things to See and Do

WIND RIVER CASINO 24 hour casino featuring over 750 slot machines and table games. Elev 4950 ft. partial handicap access. RV accessible. Restrooms, food. ATM, no CC.
(866)657-1604 Lat: 43.12430, Lon: -108.31628
10269 Hwy 789, Riverton, WY 82501
wrcinfo@windrivercasino.com
www.windrivercasino.com
See ad this page.

ROCK SPRINGS — D2 *Sweetwater*

ROCK SPRINGS - GREEN RIVER KOA **Ratings: 7.5/9.5★/6.5** (Campground) 2015 rates: $40 to $56. (800)562-8699 86 Foothill Blvd, Rock Springs, WY 82901

ROZET — A4 *Campbell*

ALL SEASONS RV PARK **Ratings: 4/8★/7.5** (RV Park) 2015 rates: $35. (307)686-2552 1000 Mcintosh Lane, Rozet, WY 82727

SARATOGA — D3 *Carbon*

DEER HAVEN RV PARK/MHP **Ratings: 4.5/NA/6** (RV Park) 2015 rates: $40. May 15 to Oct 31. (307)326-8746 706 N 1st St, Saratoga, WY 82331

SARATOGA LAKE CAMPGROUND (Public) From town, N 1 mi on Hwy 230/130 to Saratoga Lake Rd, E 1 mi (S). 2015 rates: $10 to $15. (307)326-8335

SHELL — A3 *Big Horn*

SHELL CAMPGROUND **Ratings: 4.5/8★/8** (Campground) 2015 rates: $35. May 1 to Oct 31. (307)765-9924 102 1st St, Shell, WY 82441

SHERIDAN — A3 *Sheridan*

PETER D'S RV PARK
Ratings: 6.5/9.5★/8.5 (RV Park) From Jct of I-90 & Exit 23/5th St, W 0.3 mi on 5th St to Joe St, N 0.2 mi (R) Note: be sure to use Exit 23. Elev 3700 ft. **FAC:** Gravel rds. 54 gravel, 54 pull-thrus (22 x 60), 54 full hkups (30/50 amps), cable, WiFi, laundry. Pets OK. No tents. 2015 rates: $35 to $38. Disc: AAA. Apr 1 to Oct 1.
(888)673-0597 Lat: 44.80948, Lon: -106.94183
1105 Joe St, Sheridan, WY 82801
pschutte@vcn.com
www.wyomingrvpark.com
See ad this page, 1332.

SHERIDAN BIG HORN MTN KOA **Ratings: 7.5/8/7.5** (Campground) From Jct of I-90 & Main St (exit 20), S 0.1 mi on Main St to Hwy 338 (Decker Rd), N 0.5 mi (R). Elev 3700 ft. **FAC:** Paved/gravel rds. (65 spaces). Avail: 53 gravel, 53 pull-thrus (23 x 70), 17 full hkups, 36 W, 36 E (30/50 amps), seasonal sites, WiFi, tent sites, rentals, dump, laundry, groc, firewood. **REC:** heated pool, whirlpool, Sheridan Stream: fishing, playground. Pets OK. 2015 rates: $33 to $46. Disc: AAA, military. Apr 1 to Oct 31.
AAA Approved
(800)562-7621 Lat: 44.83664, Lon: -106.96368
63 Decker Rd, Sheridan, WY 82801
sheridankoa@hotmail.com
www.koa.com

SHOSHONI — B3 *Fremont*

BOYSEN (State Pk) From Jct of US-26 & US-20, N 13 mi on US-20, follow signs (E). Entrance fee required. 2015 rates: $10 to $17. (307)876-2796

SINCLAIR — D3 *Carbon*

SEMINOE (State Pk) From town, N 34 mi on CR-351, follow signs (R) Entrance fee required. 2015 rates: $10 to $17. (307)320-2234

SUNDANCE — A5 *Crook*

BLACK HILLS NATIONAL FOREST (COOK LAKE CAMPGROUND) (Natl Forest) From town: Go 2 mi W on Hwy 14, then 14 mi N on FR 838, then 5 mi E on FR 843, then 1 mi NW on FR 842. Pit toilets. 2015 rates: $14 to $18. May 16 to Sep 6. (307)283-1361

SUNDANCE (CONT)

➔ MOUNTAIN VIEW RV PARK & CAMPGROUND
Ratings: 9/9.5★/8.5 (Campground) From Jct of I-90 & Hwy 14 (exit 189, E of town), N 0.1 mi on exit rd to Hwy 14, W 0.4 mi to Government Valley Rd, N 0.2 mi (L). Elev 4750 ft. **FAC:** Gravel rds. 56 Avail: 41 gravel, 15 grass, 34 pull-thrus (26 x 53), back-ins (30 x 35), 34 full hkups, 22 W, 22 E (30/50 amps), cable, WiFi, tent sites, rentals, dump, laundry, groc, LP gas. **REC:** heated pool, playground. Pets OK. Big rig sites, eco-friendly, 2015 rates: $30 to $42. Disc: AAA, military. Apr 1 to Nov 1.
AAA Approved
(800)792-8439 Lat: 44.41743, Lon: -104.35292
117 Government Valley Rd, Sundance, WY 82729
info@mtnviewcampground.com
www.mtnviewcampground.com
See ad this page, 1342, 1332.

TEN SLEEP — B3 *Washakie*

BIGHORN NATIONAL FOREST (BOULDER PARK CAMPGROUND) (Natl Pk) From town: Go 20 mi NE on US 16, then 1/2 mi W on FR 27, then 1-1/2 mi S on FR 212. Pit toilets. 2015 rates: $12. May 22 to Sep 23. (307)684-7806

← TEN BROEK RV PARK & CABINS Ratings: 6/8.5★/8 (Campground) From Jct of US-16 & SR-434, W 50 ft on US-16 (L). Elev 4300 ft. **FAC:** Gravel rds. 52 gravel, 11 pull-thrus (36 x 40), back-ins (36 x 40), 52 full hkups (30/50 amps), WiFi, tent sites, rentals, dump, laundry, LP gas. **REC.** Pets OK. 2015 rates: $31 to $34. Disc: military. Apr 1 to Nov 1.
(307)366-2250 Lat: 44.03291, Lon: -107.45142
98 2nd St, Ten Sleep, WY 82442
tenbroekrv@tctwest.net
http://tenbroekrvpark.com

THAYNE — C1 *Lincoln*

↓ FLAT CREEK RV PARK & CABINS Ratings: 6.5/7.5★/7 (RV Park) S edge of town on Hwy 89 (L). Elev 5950 ft. **FAC:** Gravel rds. (26 spaces). 20 Avail: 17 gravel, 3 grass, back-ins (38 x 60), 20 full hkups (30/50 amps), seasonal sites, WiFi, tent sites, rentals, laundry, firewood. **REC.** Pets OK. 2015 rates: $33.
(307)883-2231 Lat: 42.91045, Lon: -110.99740
74 Flat Creek Road, Thayne, WY 83127
http://www.flatcreekrv.com

↑ STAR VALLEY RANCH RESORT **Ratings: 9.5/9.5★/8.5** (Membership Pk) 2015 rates: $30. May 1 to Oct 15. (307)883-2670 3522 Muddy String Rd, Thayne, WY 83127

↑ WOLF DEN RV PARK **Ratings: 6/9★/8.5** (RV Park) 2015 rates: $38 to $40. Apr 1 to Oct 31. (307)883-2226 55 County Road 115/Us Hwy 89, Thayne, WY 83127

THERMOPOLIS — B3 *Hot Springs*

↓ EAGLE RV PARK
Ratings: 8/10★/8 (RV Park) From Jct of SR-120 (Broadway) & US-20 (6th St), S 2 mi on US-20 (R). Elev 4300 ft. **FAC:** Gravel rds. (33 spaces). Avail: 23 gravel, 23 pull-thrus (22 x 50), 23 full hkups (30/50 amps), seasonal sites, cable, WiFi, tent sites, rentals, laundry, LP gas, fire rings. **REC:** playground. Pets OK. Eco-friendly, 2015 rates: $37 to $42. Disc: AAA, military.
(307)864-5262 Lat: 43.37454, Lon: -108.13254
204 Hwy 20 S, Thermopolis, WY 82443
eaglervpark@bresnan.net
www.eaglervpark.com
See ad this page, 1332.

TORRINGTON — C5 *Goshen*

← PIONEER PARK (Public) From Jct of US-85 & 15th St, W 0.2 mi on 15th St, follow signs (L). 2015 rates: $10. (307)532-5666

TOWER JUNCTION — A1 *Park*

↗ YELLOWSTONE/PEBBLE CREEK (Natl Pk) From Via Cooke City Mt entrance, SW 7 mi on Via Cooke City MT entrance rd (R). Entrance fee required. Pit toilets. 2015 rates: $15. Jun 15 to Sep 29. (307)344-7381

↗ YELLOWSTONE/SLOUGH CREEK CAMPGROUND (Natl Pk) From Tower Jct, NE 6 mi on Tower Rd to gravel rd, N 2.5 mi, follow signs (L). Entrance fee required. Pit toilets. 2015 rates: $15. Jun 15 to Oct 7. (307)344-7381

↑ YELLOWSTONE/TOWER FALL CAMPGROUND (Natl Pk) From Tower Jct, S 2.5 mi on Tower Canyon Rd, follow signs (R). Entrance fee required. Pit toilets. 2015 rates: $15. May 23 to Sep 29. (307)344-7381

WAPITI — A2 *Wapiti*

SHOSHONE NATIONAL FOREST (NEWTON CREEK CAMPGROUND) (Natl Forest) From town: Go 16 mi W on US-16. Pit toilets. 2015 rates: $15. May 2 to Sep 24. (307)527-6921

WEST THUMB JUNCTION — A1 *Park*

↓ YELLOWSTONE/GRANT VILLAGE CAMPGROUND (Natl Pk) From West Thumb Jct, S 2 mi, follow signs (L). 2015 rates: $26. Jun 21 to Sep 21. (307)344-7311

↓ YELLOWSTONE/LEWIS LAKE (Natl Pk) From town, S 10 mi on Thumb Jct Rd, follow signs (R). Entrance fee required. Pit toilets. 2015 rates: $15. Jun 15 to Nov 1. (307)344-7381

WHEATLAND — C5 *Platte*

↑ A-OK RV PARK Ratings: 3/8.5★/5.5 (RV Park) From Jct of I-25 & Exit 94, W 0.2 mi on exit rd to Fish Creek Rd, N 500 ft (14 miles north of the town of Wheatland) (R). Elev 4889 ft. **FAC:** Gravel rds. 26 gravel, 26 pull-thrus (25 x 100), 20 full hkups, 4 W, 6 E (30/50 amps), tent sites, laundry. **REC.** Pets OK. Partial handicap access. 2015 rates: $25. Apr 1 to Oct 15.
(307)322-8109 Lat: 42.26380, Lon: -105.04131
26 Fish Creek Rd, Wheatland, WY 82201
aokrvpark@gmail.com

↗ LEWIS PARK (Public) From Jct of I-25 & Mariposa Pkwy (exit 78), E 0.1 mi on Mariposa Pkwy to 16th St, N 0.5 mi to Gilchrist, E 0.6 mi to 8th St, S 0.2 mi, follow signs (R). (307)322-2962

We rate what RVers consider important.

← MOUNTAIN VIEW RV PARK
Ratings: 6/10★/6 (RV Park) From Jct of I-25 & Mariposa (exit 78), W 0.2 mi on Mariposa (L). Elev 4900 ft. **FAC:** Paved/gravel rds. (24 spaces). Avail: 12 grass, patios, 10 pull-thrus (30 x 75), back-ins (50 x 75), 12 full hkups (30/50 amps), seasonal sites, cable, WiFi, showers $, laundry. Pets OK. Partial handicap access, no tents. 2015 rates: $35. No CC.
(307)322-4858 Lat: 42.04557, Lon: -104.96999
77 N 20th St, Wheatland, WY 82201
info@wheatlandrvpark.com
www.wheatlandrvpark.com
See ad this page.

WORLAND — B3 *Hot Springs, Washakie*

BIGHORN NATIONAL FOREST (SITTING BULL CAMPGROUND) (Natl Forest) From town: Go 23 mi NE on Hwy 16, then 1 mi N on FR 432. Pit toilets. 2015 rates: $16. May 30 to Sep 16. (406)587-9054

➔ WORLAND RV PARK AND CAMPGROUND
(RV Park) (Not Visited) From Jct of US Hwy 16 and US Hwy 16/20 (center of town), E 1.0 mi on Hwy 16 (L). Elev 4065 ft. **FAC:** Gravel rds. (39 spaces). Avail: 30 gravel, 23 pull-thrus (26 x 60), back-ins (25 x 50), 27 full hkups, 3 E (30/50 amps), seasonal sites, WiFi, tent sites, dump, laundry. **REC.** Pets OK. 2015 rates: $33. May 1 to Nov 1.
(307)347-2329 Lat: 44.01686, Lon: -107.93881
2313 Big Horn Ave, Worland, WY 82401
worlandrvpark@outlook.com
www.worlandcampground.info
See ad this page.

Are you using a friend's Guide? Want one of your own? Call 877-209-6655.

YELLOWSTONE NATIONAL PARK — A1
Teton

YELLOWSTONE AREA MAP

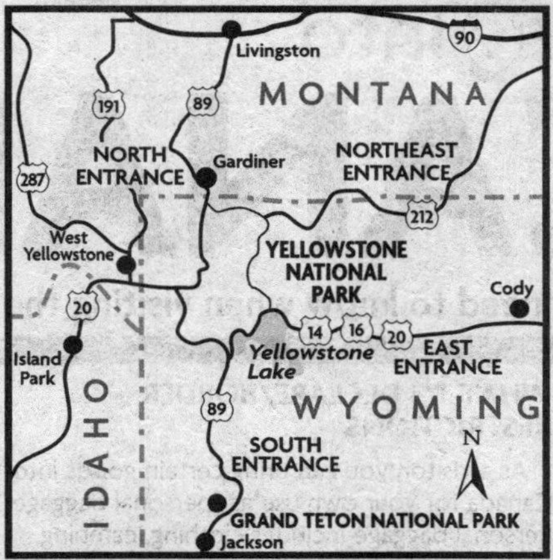

Symbols on map indicate towns within a 55 mile radius of Yellowstone National Park where campgrounds are listed. Check listings for more information.

In WY, see also Cody, Grand Teton National Park & Jackson.

In ID, see also Island Park.

In MT, see also Gardiner, Livingston & West Yellowstone.

REDROCK RV AND CAMPING PARK
Ratings: 8.5/10★/10 (RV Park) From Jct US 89 & US 191/US 287: Go 14 mi W on US 191/US 287 to US 20, then 17-1/2 miles W on US 20 to Red Rock Rd (MP 398), then 5 mi W on Red Rock Rd (R). Elev 6600 ft. **FAC:** Paved/gravel rds. 54 gravel, 46 pull-thrus (32 x 60), back-ins (45 x 42), 54 full hkups (30/50 amps), WiFi, tent sites, dump, laundry, groc, fire rings, firewood, controlled access. **REC:** Henry's Lake: swim, fishing, playground, rec open to public. Pet restrict(B). Partial handicap access. Big rig sites, eco-friendly, 2015 rates: $50 to $54. May 1 to Sep 25.
(800)473-3762 Lat: 44.60347, Lon: -111.41653
3707 Red Rock Rd, Island Park, ID 83429
office@redrockrvpark.com
www.redrockrvpark.com
See primary listing at Island Park, ID and ad page 722.

→ YELLOWSTONE/BRIDGE BAY (Natl Pk) In town, SW 3 mi on Lake Village Rd, follow signs (R). 2015 rates: $21. May 27 to Sep 11. (307)344-7381

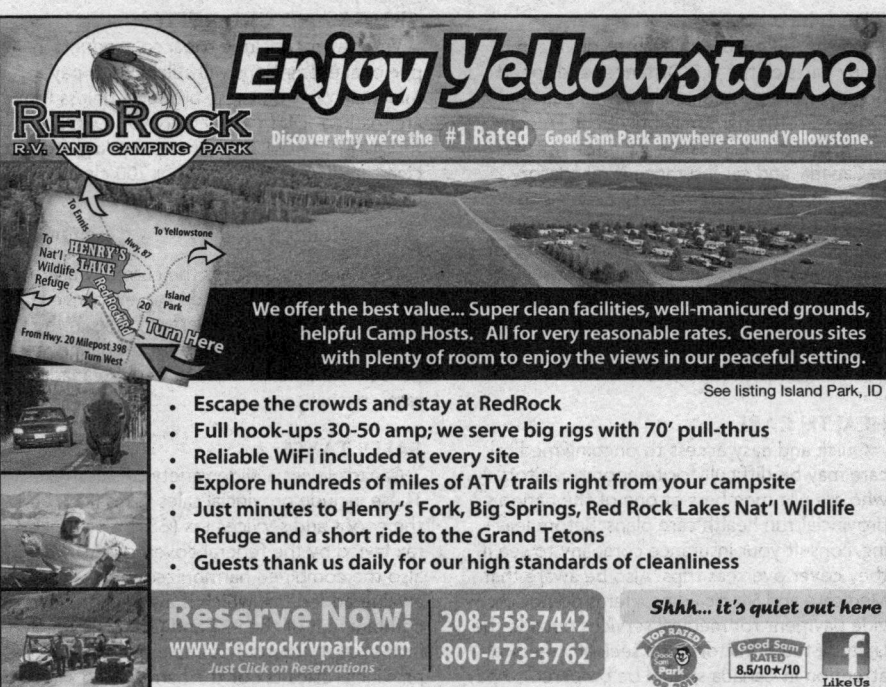

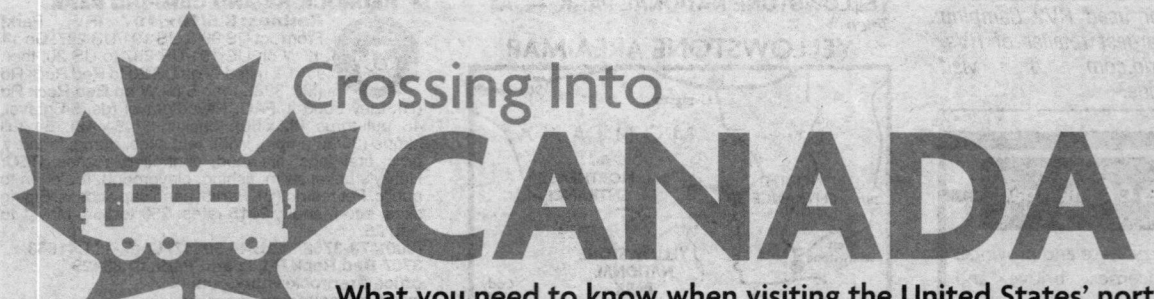

Crossing Into CANADA

What you need to know when visiting the United States' northern neighbor

It's not hard to see why Canada is such a popular destination among RV travelers. Fabulous scenery, compelling history and a welcoming environment lure U.S. tourists across the international border again and again. But don't visit the United States' neighbor to the north without making sure you're aware of Canada's laws regarding identification, customs, driving and importation.

REQUIRED IDENTIFICATION

Upon entering Canada, U.S. citizens are required in most cases to show a passport to the Canada Border Services Agency (CBSA) as proof of identity and as a document that denotes citizenship. If you are a U.S. permanent resident, carry proof of your status, such as a U.S. Permanent Resident Card, in addition to a passport.

Citizens and permanent U.S. residents who are members of the NEXUS or FAST programs may present their membership cards to the CBSA. This identification only applies to travelers arriving by land or by the sea.

All travelers are encouraged to visit the CBSA website, cbsa-asfc.gc.ca, for more information. Also helpful is the U.S. Customs and Border Protection's website, cbp.gov.

DRIVING

Driving in Canada is similar to driving in many parts of the U.S. Distances and speeds, however, are posted in kilometers per hour. In Quebec, some signs may only be in French.

U.S. driver's licenses are valid for visitors in Canada, and car insurance is mandatory. Many visitors choose to carry a Canadian Non-Resident Insurance Card. Valid anywhere in Canada, the card is proof of financial responsibility and is available through U.S. insurance companies. Motor vehicle and RV registration cards should be carried with you. If the vehicle is registered to someone else, you should have a letter that authorizes use.

HEALTH CARE

Quick and easy access to ongoing medical care may be difficult for temporary visitors who are not members of one of the nation's provincial-run health care plans. Before leaving, consult your insurance company to see if they cover overseas trips. Also be aware that Medicare and Medicaid programs do not provide payment for medical services outside the United States. Visitors who seek any medical attention in Canada should be prepared to pay cash in full at the time the service is rendered.

WHAT TO DECLARE/BORDER RESTRICTIONS

As a visitor, you can bring certain goods into Canada for your own use as "personal baggage." Personal baggage includes clothing, camping and sports equipment, cameras and personal computers. This also includes your mode of transportation, including vehicles.

You must declare all goods at the port of entry with the CBSA. Border service officers sometimes conduct examinations of goods being imported or exported to verify declarations. If you declare goods when you arrive and take them back with you when you leave, you will not have to pay any duty or taxes. These goods can't be used by a resident of Canada, used on behalf of a business based in Canada, given as a gift to a Canadian resident or disposed of or left behind in Canada.

ALCOHOL

Visitors are allowed to import only one of the following categories to avoid taxes: a maximum of 1.14 liters of liquor (40 fl. oz. or about 1 bottle), 1.5 liters of wine (53 fl. oz. or two 750 ml bottles), or 8.5 liters of beer or ale (287 fl. oz. or about 24 cans). Alcohol quantities above this amount incur duties.

CIGARS AND CIGARETTES

Visitors who include tobacco products in personal exemptions will still have to pay a minimum duty on these products unless they are marked "DUTY PAID CANADA DROIT ACQUITTÉ." Adults can transport duty-free 50 cigars (not of Cuban origin) or 200 cigarettes (1 carton) back to the United States.

MONEY

The Canadian Dollar is the currency used in all of Canada's provinces. You can exchange U.S. dollars and Canadian dollars at banks in the U.S. or Canada. To find the current exchange rate, consult the Bank of Canada, bankofcanada.ca/rates/exchange.

SALES TAXES

Canada levies a wide variety of sales taxes. These include provincial sales taxes (PST) and the goods and services tax (GST), a value-added tax levied by the federal government. There's also the combined harmonized sales tax, also a value-added tax, which is a single, blended combination of the PST and GST. Every province except Alberta has implemented either a provincial sales tax or the harmonized sales tax. The federal GST rate is 5 percent.

PERSONAL EXEMPTIONS FOR DUTY AND TAXES

When re-entering the U.S., be sure to list you purchases, have your sales receipts handy and pack your purchases separately for convenienc or inspection.

If you've been traveling in Canada for longer than 48 hours, you may bring back, duty-free, US$800 (based on fair retail value in Canada) worth of articles for personal or household use if less than 48 hours, the maximum is US$200. You will also qualify for this exemption if you have used your personal exemption on a previous trip outside the U.S. within the previous 30 days.

SAFETY AND SECURITY

As in the U.S., emergency assistance can be reached by calling 911. If you or someone you know becomes the victim of a crime in Canada you should contact the local police and the nearest U.S. embassy or consulate.

TRAVEL WITH MINORS

If you plan to travel to Canada with a minor who is not your own child or for whom you do not have full legal custody, CBSA may require you to present a notarized affidavit of consent from the minor's parents.

FIREARMS

Firearms are more strictly controlled in Canada than in the U.S. Violations of firearms restrictions may result in prosecution and imprisonment.

PETS

Dogs and cats may enter Canada if they are accompanied by rabies certification. The Canadian Food Inspection Agency establishes import requirements for all animals and animal products entering Canada. See inspection.gc.ca for more information.

For More Information:

Canada Border Services Agency (CBSA), 204-983-3500; 800-461-9999 within Canada, cbsa-asfc.gc.ca

U.S. Customs and Border Protection (CBP), cbp.gov, 877-CBP-5511; 202-325-8000 if you are outside the U.S., cpb.gov

Assistance for U.S. Citizens

U.S. Embassy Ottawa, 490 Sussex Drive, K1N 1G8 Ottawa, Ontario, Canada, 613-688-5335. Emergency After-Hours: 613-238-5335, canada.usembassy.gov, ottawacons@state.gov

Paul Zizka Photography

WELCOME TO
Alberta

JOINED CONFEDERATION SEPT 1,1905	WIDTH: 410 MILES (660 KM) LENGTH: 760 MILES (1,223 KM)	PROPORTION OF CANADA 6.63% OF 9,984,670 SQ KM

lberta is blessed with stunning rasslands, endless fields of wheat and ye-popping mountain scenery. The anadian Rockies run along its south-vestern border, providing the setting or national parks that draw visitors rom around the world. Stampede to algary, immerse yourself in the ulti-nate shopping excursion at the West dmonton Mall or escape to the seem-ngly endless plains to scope out bison nd whooping cranes.

earn

Alberta reveals about as much of ne planet's prehistoric times as any ther region on the planet. The Cana-ian Badlands of the Red River Valley ontain some of the richest dinosaur ields in the world. Bus tours of Dino-aur Provincial Park explore the eroded ground where the "terrible lizards" roamed. In Drumheller, the "Dinosaur Capital of the World," the Royal Tyrrell Museum assembles the Alberta fossil record into fascinating clarity. Highway 10 South will lead you to the Hoodoo site where millions of years of erosion have left 20-foot-tall pillars under large capstones.

Much of that Paskapoo sandstone in southern Alberta was used to construct Calgary, the "Sandstone City." It was a rough-and-tumble cowtown until February 13, 1947, when the province's greatest oil reserves were tapped. You can still see those heritage stone buildings along Stephen Avenue, a pedestrian mall in downtown Calgary, but much of the rest of the city is a modern steel-and-glass oil town.

The Bar U Ranch in Longview, now

Top 3 Tourism Attractions:
1) Banff National Park
2) Calgary Stampede
3) West Edmonton Mall

Nickname: Princess Province

State Flower: Wild Rose

State Bird: Great Horned Owl

People: Kurt Browning, figure skater; Crowfoot, Blackfoot chief; John Firth, author; Michael J. Fox, actor; K. D. Lang, singer and songwriter; Darryl Sutter, hockey player and coach

Major Cities: Calgary, Edmonton (capital), Strathcona County, Red Deer, Lethbridge

Topography: North—forest; southwest—Rocky Mountains; south—prairie; central—most fertile soil; southeast—badlands

Climate: Dry continental climate with warm, dry summers and extremely cold winters; snowfall is irregular

Travel Alberta

ALBERTA
Campground and other services
RV service center and/or other services
Good Sam discount locations
SCALE: 1 inch equals 45 miles
0 35 70 miles
0 35 70 kilometers
Map by Terra Carta © 2016 Affinity Media
FORT MCMURRAY
Anzac
La Loche
Peerless Lake
Loon Lake
Little Buffalo
Queen Elizabeth
Hines Creek
PEACE RIVER
Grimshaw
Berwyn
Fairview
Moonshine L.
SPIRIT RIVER
DUNVEGAN
RYCROFT
Dawson Creek
WABASCA-DESMARAIS
Atikameg
FALHER
MCLENNAN
Winagami Lake
GROUARD
HIGH PRAIRIE
Lesser Slave Lake
SLAVE LAKE
KINUSO
CALLING LAKE
Saskatoon Island
Sexsmith
Clairmont
HYTHE
BEAVERLODGE
WEMBLEY
GRANDE PRAIRIE
Young's Pt.
Sturgeon Heights
Williamson
VALLEYVIEW
Lac la Biche
Sir Winston Churchill
LAC LA BICHE
ATHABASCA
Cross Lake
BOYLE
CASLAN
FAWCETT
Long Lake
FORK LAKE
IRON RIVER
COLD LAKE
Cold Lake
GLENDON
Moose Lake
BONNYVILLE
Swan Hills
FOX CREEK
Carson-Pegasus
WHITECOURT
Thunder Lake
BARRHEAD
WESTLOCK
Clyde
Thorhild
Goodfish Lake
Garner Lake
SPEDDEN
SMOKY LAKE
ST. PAUL
Saddle Lake
ELK POINT
Whitney Lakes
GRANDE CACHE
Willmore Wilderness Park
LAC LA NONNE
Legal
Redwater
Mayerthorpe
MORINVILLE
GIBBONS
Lamont
Andrew
TWO HILLS
Onion Lake
ALBERTA BEACH
ONOWAY
Cardiff
Fort Saskatchewan
Pembina River
SPRUCE GROVE
ST. ALBERT
Elk Island N.P.
MARWAYNE
EDSON
William A. Switzer
ENTWISTLE
WABAMUN
SHERWOOD PARK
VEGREVILLE
HINTON
STONY PLAIN
EDMONTON
SPRING LAKE
DEVON
Beaumont
TOFIELD
Vermilion
Kitscoty
Mannville
VERMILION
Lloydminster
ROBB
DRAYTON VALLEY
CALMAR
Miquelon Lake
Ryley
Thorsby
LEDUC
NEW SAREPTA
Breton
Warburg
CAMROSE
Viking
LODGEPOLE
Millet
Valemount
Mt. Robson
JASPER
BUCK LAKE
Pigeon L.
WESTEROSE
WETASKIWIN
Irma
Manitou L.
Samson
Daysland
Killam
WAINWRIGHT
Jasper National Park
Rimbey
Ponoka
SEDGEWICK
Hardisty
CHAUVIN
Dillberry Lake
BASHAW
FORESTBURG
Crimson Lake
Gull Lake
GULL LAKE
Aspen Beach
Big Knife
NORDEGG
Bentley
Lacombe
MIRROR
Buffalo L.
Provost
Macklin
ROCKY MOUNTAIN HOUSE
Sylvan L.
Blackfalds
Alix
STETTLER
Cline River
SYLVAN LAKE
RED DEER
ERSKINE
Castor
PENHOLD
Coronation
Gooseberry Lake
Consort
CAROLINE
DELBURNE
BIG VALLEY
Kinbasket L.
Continental Divide
Innisfail
Red Lodge
BOWDEN
TROCHU
Sullivan L.
OLDS
SUNDRE
DIDSBURY
THREE HILLS
HANNA
Banff National Park
CARSTAIRS
Cremona
CARBON
Nacmine
DRUMHELLER
Youngstown
Crossfield
Little Fish Lake
OYEN
LAKE LOUISE
Golden
Yoho National Park
Glacier National Park
Adams L.
Airdrie
Beiseker
Irricana
Mt. Revelstoke National Park
KANANASKIS VILLAGE
COCHRANE
Balzac
BANFF
CANMORE
STRATHMORE
Blind Bay
Revelstoke
Exshaw
CALGARY
Chestermere
Malakwa
Chase
Sicamous
Mt. Assiniboine
BRAGG CREEK
CARSELAND
Bassano
Dinosaur
Duchess
Buffalo
Salmon Arm
Kootenay National Park
MILLARVILLE
OKOTOKS
Siksika
Enderby
Edgewater
TURNER VALLEY
BLACK DIAMOND
MOSSLEIGH
BROOKS
Kinbrook Island
Tillebrook
Armstrong
Radium Hot Springs
Invermere
HIGH RIVER
Windermere
LONGVIEW
South Saskatchewan R.
Vernon
Coldstream
NANTON
Vulcan
Nakusp
Fairmont Hot Springs
L. Newell
CHAMPION
Chain Lakes
Little Bow
REDCLIFF
Winfield
Canal Flats
Willow Creek
Stavely
Dunmore
Kelowna
CLARESHOLM
Vauxhall
MEDICINE HAT
Kaslo
Elkford
GRANUM
Bow Island
Grassy Lake
Sparwood
CROWSNEST PASS
FORT MACLEOD
Coalhurst
Taber
TABER
Elkwater
Kimberley
Marysville
Coaldale
Cypress Hills Interprov. Park
Balfour
BLAIRMORE
LETHBRIDGE
STIRLING
Cranbrook
Fernie
BELLEVUE
LUNDBRECK
Foremost
PINCHER CREEK
Beauvais L.
Stand Off
Raymond
Pakowki L.
Jaffray
Hill Spring
MAGRATH
Wynndel
CARDSTON
Woolford
MILK RIVER
Creston
WATERTON LAKES
Waterton Lakes N.P.
Police Outpost
Porthill
Eastport
Eureka
Roosville
Glacier N.P.
WATERTON PARK
Sweetgrass
Sunburst
CANADA
U.S.
ALBERTA
MONTANA
BRITISH COLUMBIA
SASKATCHEWAN
CENTRAL TIME ZONE
MOUNTAIN TIME ZONE
PACIFIC TIME ZONE
Peace R.
Smoky R.
Athabasca R.
Pembina R.
McLeod R.
Columbia R.
Red Deer R.
Battle R.
Milk R.
N

national historic site, was one of :anada's largest ranching operations ı those cowtown days. Cattle are still aised on the Bar U, but 35 historic tructures are open for public touring. wo hours to the south, Fort Macleod vas constructed in 1874 as the home f the North West Mounted Police, vho sought to bring order to Alberta. Nowadays the fort tells the stories of he internationally famous Mounties nd the settlement of Alberta.

'lay

In the 1880s, he Canadian acific Railway vas building its vay across the ontinent when officials got their first ɔok at the Rocky Mountains. It did not ake long for Canada to have its first ıational park and only the world's third. oday, Banff National Park boasts more niles of trail—topping 1,000—than nost other mountain parks, providing ɔts of space for the park's estimated our million annual visitors.

While Banff serves a cosmopolitan lientele with its world-famous Banff prings Hotel, nearby Jasper National 'ark delivers more of a wilderness xperience. One of Canada's most xpansive protected spaces, Jasper s the second largest Dark Sky Preerve on earth. The mountain lakes in he two parks—Maligne, Louise and Moraine—are all national symbols.

Banff and Jasper are connected by one of North America's most magnificent drives, the 140 miles of the Icefields Parkway. It earns the name honestly by winding past more than 100 glaciers. At the Athabasca Glacier, hiking or riding glacier-equipped motorcoaches on the green-blue ice is just a short distance from the parking lot. Or you can walk out onto The Glacier Skywalk on a glass-floored platform suspended 1,000 feet above the Columbia Icefields.

Waterton Lakes National Park on the United States border, adjoining Glacier National Park in Montana, is the smallest of the Canadian Rockies national parks. It's also the only Canadian park that preserves fescue grasslands, which blanket the foothills. Upper Waterton Lake is the deepest lake in the Canadian Rockies and the star of the park. Here, the Prince of Wales railway hotel was built as a resort in 1927. Mount Blakiston is the park's roof at 9,550 feet. The 2.5-mile Lineham Creek Trail runs along its southern slopes, and experienced scramblers can ascend the rubble rock to the top.

One of Canada's most expansive protected spaces, Jasper is the second largest Dark Sky Preserve on earth.

At the other extreme, Wood Buffalo National Park is Canada's largest park, and its vast expanses hold the world's largest free-roaming herd of bison. This is also the birthplace of North America's largest bird—the Whooping Crane.

Experience

For 10 days in July, Alberta is transformed into "the Greatest Outdoor Show on Earth" during the Calgary Stampede. Highlights include one of the world's largest rodeos, the Rangeland Derby chuck wagon races and exhibitions from five First Nation tribes. There are nightly grandstand shows, and the ever-present aroma of pancake breakfasts and barbecues from Alberta's high-quality beef.

Musicians from around the globe converge on Alberta for three big events: the four-day Edmonton Folk Festival, the Canmore Folk Festival—the province's longest running musical extravaganza—and the Big Valley Jamboree, one of the largest country music festivals on the continent.

Taste

In Edmonton, a snack that has its roots in northern China tantalizes the taste buds of locals and visitors alike. Green onion cakes are a delectable street food made from fried dough, green onions and soy sauce. The snack didn't make its appearance in the Alberta heartland until the 1980s, but has since become a a staple in local festivals, including the Taste of Edmonton.

TRAVEL & TOURISM

Travel Alberta
800-ALBERTA
www.TravelAlberta.com

Alberta North
800-756-4351, 780-427-4321
www.travelalbertanorth.com

Alberta Central
800-252-3782
www.travelalbertacentral.com

Alberta South
800-252-3782
www.travelalbertasouth.com

Chinook Country Tourist Association
403-320-1222, 800-661-1222
info@chinookcountry.com

Tourism Calgary
800-661-1678, 403-218-7892
www.tourismcalgary.com

Canadian Rockies Tourism Destination Region
800-252-3782
www.travelalberta.us

Edmonton Tourism World Trade Centre Edmonton
800-463-4667, 780-496-8400
www.edmonton.com

Tourism Medicine Hat
800-481-2822
www.tourismmedicinehat.com

Visit Red Deer
403-346-0180
www.visitreddeer.com

OUTDOOR RECREATION

Alberta Speleological Society
www.caving.ab.ca

Alberta Golf Association
888-414-4849
www.albertagolf.org

Sustainable Resource Development
www.srd.gov.ab.ca/fw/fishing/index.html

SHOPPING

Altan Duty Free Shop
403-344-3000

West Edmonton Mall
780-444-5321
www.wem.ca

Featured Good Sam Parks

ALBERTA

Good Sam Park

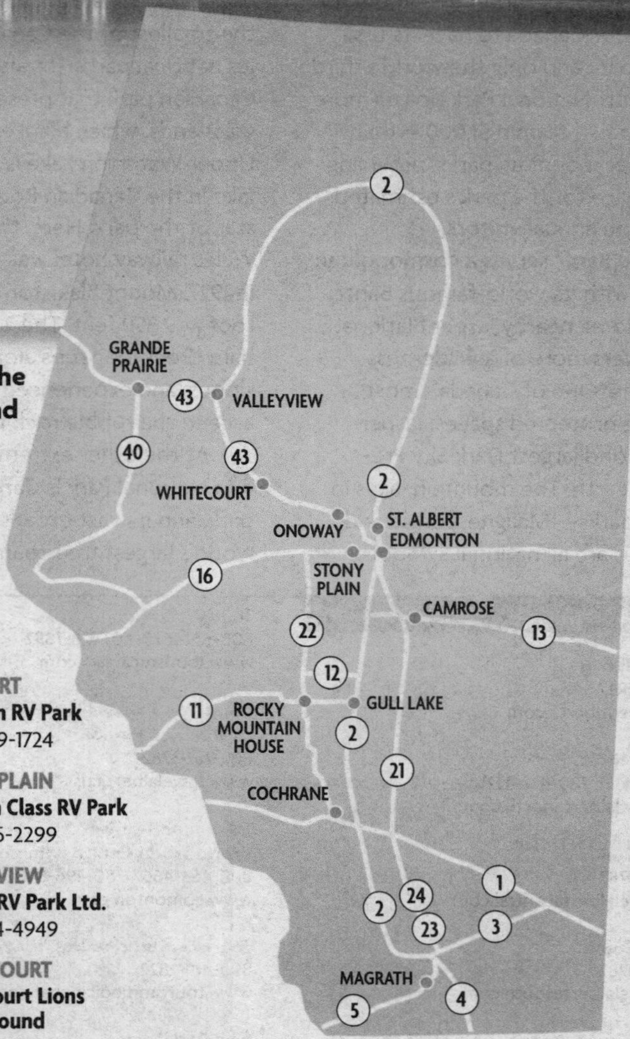

When you stay with Good Sam, you can expect the highest degree of cleanliness and friendliness, and better yet, you get 10% off campground fees.

If you're not already a Good Sam member you can purchase your membership at one of these locations:

CAMROSE
Camrose Exhibition Trail RV Park
(780)678-2888

COCHRANE
Bow RiversEdge Campground
(877)932-4675

EDMONTON
Diamond Grove RV Campground
(780)962-8003
Glowing Embers RV Park & Travel Centre
(877)785-7275

GRANDE PRAIRIE
Camp Tamarack RV Park
(877)532-9998

GULL LAKE
Summerland Leisure RV Park
(403)748-4855

MAGRATH
Covered Wagon RV Park
(403)758-3572

ONOWAY
Memory Lane Campground
(780)995-5555

ROCKY MOUNTAIN HOUSE
Riverview Campground
(403)845-4422

ST ALBERT
Kinsmen RV Park
(888)459-1724

STONY PLAIN
Camp 'n Class RV Park
(855)455-2299

VALLEYVIEW
Sherk's RV Park Ltd.
(780)524-4949

WHITECOURT
Whitecourt Lions Campground
(780)778-6782

For more Good Sam Parks go to listing pages

Travel Alberta

SPOTLIGHT
AB

EDMONTON

Discover Canadian culture in all its variations

Edmonton is a delightful destination with year-round attractions for culture buffs, outdoorsy folks and everyone in between. Whether you prefer hiking through the woods or strolling past shops, you'll be pleased with what Edmonton has to offer.

Edmonton Traditions

Revisit the past at Rutherford House Provincial Historic Site. The Edwardian-era home has been restored and furnished to look the way it would have in the days of Alberta's first premier, Alexander Rutherford. Costumed storytellers guide visitors through the house and share stories of Rutherford's time in the home with his family.

The Ukrainian community of Alberta is a treasured part of its history, and the Ukrainian Culture Heritage Village recreates life for early settlers who carved out their lives there at the turn of the 20th century and into the 1930s. This open-air museum encompasses 35 restored historic buildings such as Eastern Byzantine churches, farmsteads, a two-room school and a working grain elevator. Costumed role-players portray the pioneers and interact with guests.

Turn back the clock even further at Royal Alberta Museum. Here, you're greeted by petroglyphs, dinosaurs and representatives of Canada's first peoples. Crawl through a replica bear den to see how they live in the wild, and inspect sparkling minerals and gems that were given up by the earth.

When the water's up, see Edmonton and the river valley glide by from the deck of a riverboat as you sail down the North Saskatchewan River. Whether it's a leisure cruise or dinnertime jaunt, a riverboat excursion is a unique way to admire the cityscape.

> Take an evening paddle in a canoe on Astotin Lake to see red-necked grebes, common loons, ducks and double-crested cormorants on the water.

Museums and Munching

Edmonton's arts scene is varied and rich, from symphonies and ballets to dinner theater and live soap operas. And the venues where you'll see great shows are just as memorable as the performances. Francis Winspear Centre for Music is an acoustic wonder of a facility set in the heart of Sir Winston Churchill Square in downtown. Step into the Commons for a cold brew, or dine at one of the gourmet restaurants that line the streets of the neighborhood.

Edmonton Valley Zoo is a family destination where more than 350 animals reside in natural habitats and provide visitors with up-close views of everyday life for seals, arctic foxes and more. Zoo staff brings many species out to guests to learn more about them through programs and demonstrations.

Young explorers learn about the life of a roughneck and the birth of western Canada's oil industry at Leduc #1 Energy Discovery Centre. This hands-on facility teaches visitors about the origins of oil and the mighty equipment used to extract it from the earth.

Taste the local fare and savor the company of Edmonton's residents at Old Strathcona Farmers' Market. The year-round venue showcases artisan goodies, local produce and handmade treasures in an airy warehouse.

Take time out from a busy schedule or a rainy day and pop into Hexagon Board Game Café, where friends and family gather for rousing games of Monopoly, Jenga, Sorry! and more. Staff also host game education nights to teach players how to master the toughest ones.

Speed

Pick a winner and see the dirt fly on the

track at Northlands Park, a horse track that's been entertaining race fans since 1882. Northlands is the home of the annual Canadian Derby and a unique, tiered restaurant that can seat upwards of 600 guests at once.

If the younger family members are with you, give them a chance to say they've played at the world's largest indoor amusement park. Galaxyland in West Edmonton Mall is a space-themed attraction with activities and rides for patrons young and young at heart.

See the wonder of the night sky open up at Edmonton's Observatory in Coronation Park, just southeast of the TELUS World of Science. Large telescopes bring the moon, sun, stars and planets into plain view, and local volunteers share their expertise with visitors.

Outside the City

The region's natural beauty is the star of Elk Island National Park, outside the city. Elk Island is home to a thriving bison population thanks to conservation efforts, and its aspen woodlands and prairie meadows also support elk and coyotes. A Bison Backstage Tour welcomes guests to the park's bison handling facility, where they learn about the conservation efforts through demonstrations and hands-on activities.

Enjoy the rest of the park by hiking one of its many trails through spruce bogs and past shallow lakes and ponds. Or, take an evening paddle in a canoe on Astotin Lake. You're bound to see red-necked grebes, common loons, ducks and double-crested cormorants while you're on the water.

Fishing is a way of life here, as much as it is a sporting pursuit, and Edmonton's waterways are brimming with trophies just waiting to be claimed. Angle for walleye, sturgeon, sauger or northern pike in the lakes and the North Saskatchewan River. The city also stocks ponds at Hermitage Park with rainbow trout by the thousands.

For More Information

Edmonton Tourism
800-463-4667
www.exploreedmonton.com

Travel Alberta
800-252-3782
www.travelalberta.com

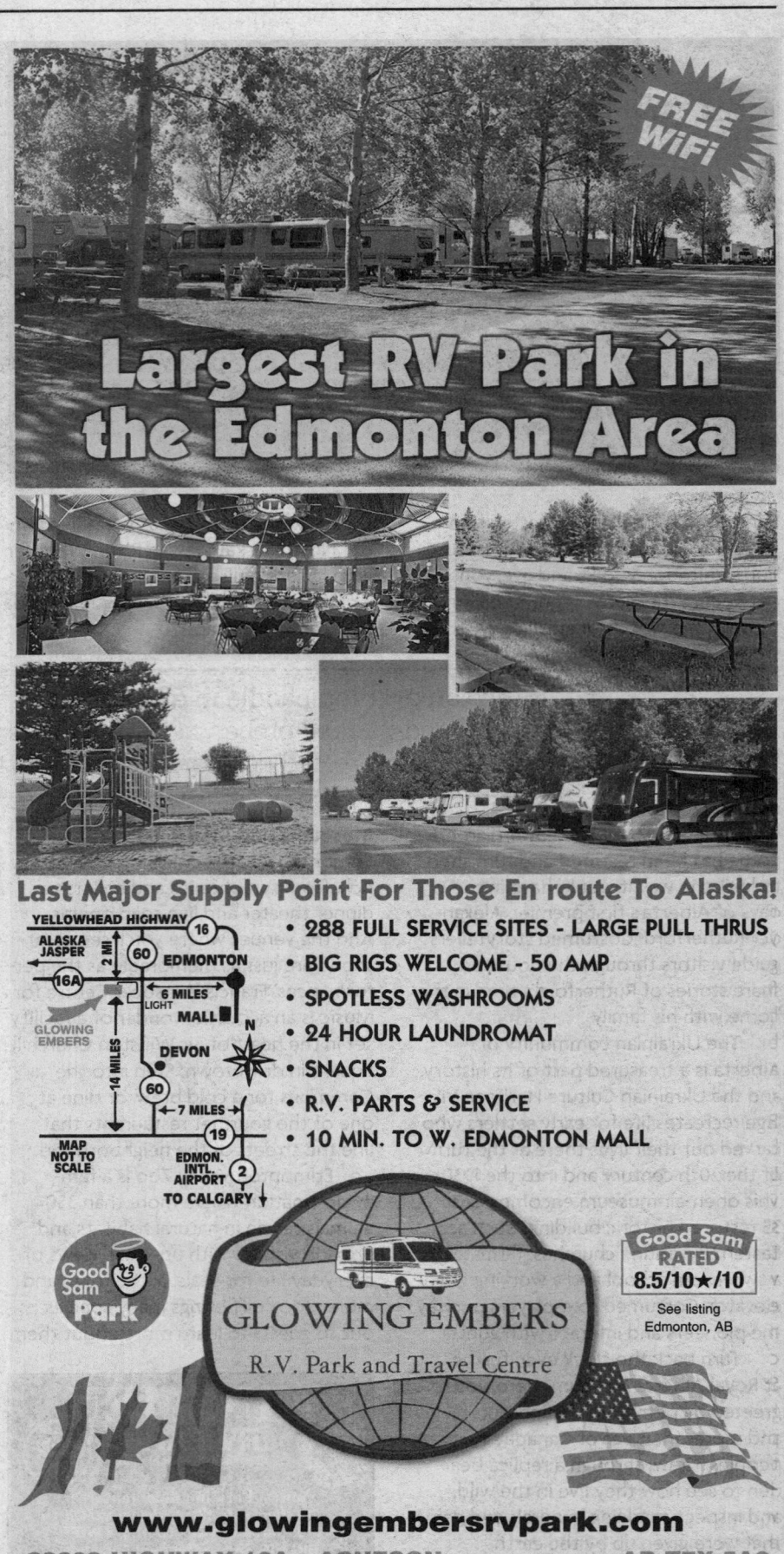

GRANDE PRAIRIE

Trumpeter swans and prehistoric fossils make this a fun destination

From dinosaur bones to wildness hikes and picture-perfect golf, the Grande Prairie region is a land where prehistoric monsters, frontier spirit and contemporary élan coalesce. Situated some 280 miles northwest of Edmonton, Alberta's "Peace Country" boasts 10 provincial parks and recreation areas within just an hour's drive of Grande Prairie, the regional hub that goes by the moniker of "Swan City" due to its proximity to the trumpeter swan's migration route.

Into the Great Wide Open

You don't have to explore too far in the Grande Prairie region to feel like you have crossed the last frontier. From gushing rivers where black bears hunt for salmon to bright-white canola fields brimming with butterflies, Alberta combines a raw beauty with recreational activities for every traveler.

Located 16 miles west of Grande Prairie, Saskatoon Island Provincial Park between Saskatoon Lake and Little Lake is Alberta's second oldest provincial park. A federal migratory bird sanctuary, Saskatoon provides a haven to the threatened trumpeter swan as well as tundra swans, northern harriers and a variety of mammals including moose, muskrats, beavers, deer and coyotes. In addition to foraging for Saskatoon's (purple berries), visitors can take advantage of a boat launch, several playgrounds and cross-country skiing in the winter.

With its majestic trees, plunging waterfalls, kaleidoscopic meadows, emerald lakes and translucent creeks, the Kakwa Wildland Park is a land of ethereal beauty. Located in the alpine and subalpine regions of the Rocky Mountain Natural Region, Sulphur Ridge and Coal Ridge form the park's northern boundary. One of the park's highlights is Kakwa Falls, Alberta's tallest waterfall, which drops nearly 100 feet.

Jurassic World

Just 25 minutes by car southwest of Grande Prairie, Pipestone Creek is one of the richest dinosaur bone beds in the world. In 1974, science teacher Al Lakusta went for a ramble at Pipestone Creek and uncovered the remains of a type of as yet undiscovered horned dinosaur, the Pachyrhinosaurus lakustai (named after its founder). The new Phillip J. Currie Dinosaur Museum, named after Canada's leading paleontologist Dr. Philip Currie, was unveiled in 2015. Dr. Currie excavated fossils at what is considered the world's largest site for Pachyrhinosaurus fossils.

Parks and Recreation

The community of Grande Prairie makes for a pleasant and convenient base for exploring the region. A series of walking/bike paths run around the entire circumference nearby Crystal Lake, and Golfing is big here. The Dunes Golf & Winter Club, south of Grande Prairie, offers the region's most civilized golfing experience. The course's green fairways, fringed with jackpine and spruce, provide stunning views.

For More Information

City of Grande Prairie Regional Tourism Association
866-202-2202
www.gptourism.ca

Travel Alberta
800-ALBERTA
www.travelalberta.com

Trumpeter Swans on Saskatoon Lake. Getty Images/iStockphoto

CONSULTANTS

Ron & Marg Hobkirk

ALBERTA BEACH — C3 *Lac Ste Anne*

ALBERTA BEACH CAMPGROUND (TOWN PARK) (Public) From jct Hwy 43 & Secondary Hwy 633: Go 8 km/5 mi W on Secondary Hwy 633, then 1.6 km/1 mi N on 47th St, then 1 block W. Follow signs. 2015 rates: $30 to $37. May 1 to Sep 30. (780)924-2333

ALBERTA BEACH GOLF RESORT **Ratings: 6/7.5/7.5** (Campground) 2015 rates: $40. May 1 to Sep 30. (780)924-2421 4438 44th Street, Alberta Beach, AB T0E 0A0

ATHABASCA — B4 *Athabasca*

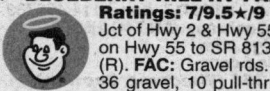

BLUEBERRY HILL RV PARK
Ratings: 7/9.5★/9 (RV Park) From Jct of Hwy 2 & Hwy 55, E 0.9 km (0.5 mi) on Hwy 55 to SR 813, N 2.4 km (1.5 mi) (R). **FAC:** Gravel rds. (49 spaces). Avail: 36 gravel, 10 pull-thrus (30 x 90), back-ins (30 x 60), 29 full hkups (15/30 amps), seasonal sites, WiFi Hotspot, showers $, dump, laundry, fire rings, firewood, restaurant. **REC:** golf, playground, rec open to public. Pet restrict(B). Partial handicap access, no tents. Eco-friendly, 2015 rates: $38. May 1 to Oct 1.
(780)675-3733 Lat: 54.737543, Lon: -113.284883
hwy 813, Athabasca, AB T9S 2A6
judy@blueberryhillrvpark.ca
www.blueberryhillrvpark.ca
See ad this page.

BANFF — D3 *Banff National Park*

BANFF See also Canmore, Kananaskis Village & Lake Louise.

BANFF/CASTLE MOUNTAIN (Natl Pk) From Jct of TCH 1 & Hwy 1A, E 1 km on Hwy 1A (Bow Valley Pkwy) (R). 2015 rates: $21.50. May 29 to Sep 15. (403)762-1550

Things change ... last year's rates serve as a guideline only.

Start planning your RV travels at
GoodSamClub.com!
Use GoodSamClub.com's online navigation tools to chart a course for your next RV adventures. Good Sam's Plan A Trip will help you find Good Sam Parks, Camping World SuperCenters and other resources on the road so that you get the most out of your travels.

BANFF/JOHNSTON CANYON (Natl Pk) From Jct of Hwy 1A & TCH-1, W 10 mi on Hwy 1A (Bow Valley Pkwy), follow signs (L). 2015 rates: $27.40. May 29 to Sep 15. (403)762-1550

BANFF/TUNNEL MOUNTAIN TRAILER COURT (Natl Pk) From Hwy 1 & Lake Minnewanka exit (Banff Ave), S .06 mi on Banff Ave to Tunnel Mtn Rd, E 2 mi to entrance (R). 2015 rates: $38.20. May 15 to Oct 5. (403)762-1550

BANFF/TUNNEL MOUNTAIN VILLAGE 2 (Natl Pk) From Hwy 1 & Lake Minnewanka exit (Banff Ave), S 0.6 mi on Banff Ave to Tunnel Mtn Rd, E 2 mi to entrance (R). 2015 rates: $27.40 to $32.30. (403)762-1550

BANFF/TWO JACK LAKESIDE (Natl Pk) From Banff, NE 7.5 on Minnewanka Rd (L). 2015 rates: $27.40. May 15 to Oct 5. (403)762-1550

BANFF/TWO JACK MAIN CAMPGROUND (Natl Pk) From Banff, NE 8 mi on Lake Minnewanka Rd (L). 2015 rates: $21.50. Jun 26 to Sep 2. (403)762-1550

BANFF/WATERFOWL LAKES (Natl Pk) From Jct of TCH-1 & Hwy 93, N 35 mi on Hwy 93 (L). 2015 rates: $21.50. Jun 27 to Sep 1. (403)522-3833

BARRHEAD — B3 *Barrhead*

THUNDER LAKE (Prov Pk) From town, W 13 mi on Hwy 18 (E). 2015 rates: $23 to $29. Apr 15 to Oct 13. (780)674-4051

BASHAW — C4 *Camrose*

BASHAW MUNICIPAL CAMPGROUND (Public) From Jct of Hwys 21 & 53, E 0.3 mi on Hwy 53 (R). Pit toilets. 2015 rates: $5. (780)372-3911

BEAVERLODGE — B1 *Grande Prairie County No. 1*

HANS O. HOMMY MEMORIAL PARK (GRANDE PRAIRIE COUNTY #1) (Public) From town: Go 4 mi NW on Hwy 43. Pit toilets. 2015 rates: $15 to $20. May 15 to Oct 15. (780)354-8039

BELLEVUE — E3 *Crowsnest Pass*

BEAVER MINES LAKE PROVINCIAL RECREATION AREA (Prov Pk) From town: Go 4-3/4 km/3 mi E, then 22-1/2 km/14 mi S on local roads. Pit toilets. 2015 rates: $20. May 1 to Nov 30. (403)563-5395

BIG VALLEY — D4 *Stettler County No. 6*

MCKENZIE CROSSING REC AREA (Public Corps) From town, W 9.3 mi on Hwy 590 (L). Pit toilets. 2015 rates: $15. (403)876-2269

BLACK DIAMOND — E3 *Foothills*

FOOTHILLS LIONS CENTENNIAL CAMPGROUND (Public) From Jct of Hwy 2 & Hwy 7, W 16 mi on Hwy 7 to Hwy 22 (Centre Ave), N 0.4 mi to 5th St, W 0.2 mi (R). 2015 rates: $21 to $31.50. (403)933-5785

BLAIRMORE — E3 *Crowsnest*

LOST LEMON RV PARK & CAMPGROUND **Ratings: 7.5/9★/6.5** (Campground) 2015 rates: $40 to $42. (403)562-2932 11001 19th Avenue, Blairmore, AB T0K 0E0

BONNYVILLE — B5 *Bonnyville*

FRANCHERE BAY REC AREA (Prov Pk) From Jct of Hwy 28 & park access rd, N 8 mi on park access rd, follow signs (R). 2015 rates: $23 to $35. May 14 to Oct 14. (780)594-7856

MOOSE LAKE (Prov Pk) From Jct of PR-28 & PR-41, N 3 mi on PR-41 to CR-660, W 7 mi (L). Pit toilets. 2015 rates: $23 to $29. May 14 to Oct 14. (780)594-7856

MURIEL LAKE MD PARK (Public) From town, S 2 mi on SR-890 to unmarked CR, E 4 mi to unmarked CR, S 3 mi (E). 2015 rates: $17 to $20. May 15 to Sep 15. (780)826-4140

PELICAN POINT MD PARK (Public) From Jct of Hwys 41 & 660, W 13 mi on Hwy 660 to Franchere Bay Prov Park, S 1.5 mi, follow signs (L); or From Edmonton: From Jct of Hwys 882 & 28, N 6 mi to Hwy 660, E 6 mi to Franchere Bay Prov Park, S 1.5 mi, Follow signs (L). Pit toilets. 2015 rates: $20. May 15 to Sep 15. (780)635-3825

BOWDEN — D3 *Red Deer*

RED LODGE (Prov Pk) From town, W 8.3 mi on Hwy 587 (R). 2015 rates: $23 to $29. May 14 to Oct 13. (403)224-2547

BOYLE — B4 *Athabasca*

LONG LAKE (Prov Pk) From Jct SR-63 & CR-661, E 5 mi on CR-661 to CR-831, N 10 mi (R). 2015 rates: $23 to $29. May 2 to Oct 31. (780)576-3959

BRAGG CREEK — D3 *Rocky View*

BEAVER FLATS CAMPGROUND (Public) From jct Hwy 22 & Hwy 66: Go 29-1/2 km/18-1/2 mi SW on Hwy 66. Pit toilets. 2015 rates: $23. May 16 to Sep 6. (403)949-3132

GOOSEBERRY LAKE CAMPGROUND (Prov Pk) From jct Hwy 22 & Hwy 66: Go 9-1/2 km/6 mi SW on Hwy 66. 2015 rates: $22 to $28. May 15 to Oct 14. (403)577-3873

LITTLE ELBOW CAMPGROUND PROV. REC. AREA (Prov Pk) From jct Hwy 22 & Hwy 66: Go 49-1/2 km/31 mi SW on Hwy 66. 2015 rates: $23 to $29. May 15 to Sep 22. (403)897-3933

MCLEAN CREEK PROVINCIAL RECREATION AREA (Prov Pk) From jct Hwy 22 & Hwy 66: Go 14-1/2 km/9 mi SW on Hwy 66. 2015 rates: $23 to $29. (403)949-3132

PADDY'S FLAT CAMPGROUND (Prov Pk) From Hwy 22 & Hwy 66: Go 20 km/12-1/2 mi SW on Hwy 66. Pit toilets. 2015 rates: $23. May 15 to Sep 22. (403)949-3132

BROOKS — E4 *Newell*

DINOSAUR (Prov Pk) From town, N 5 mi on Hwy 873 to Hwy 544, E 20 mi on Hwy 544, N at Patricia Turnoff, Follow signs (R). 2015 rates: $23 to $29. (403)378-4342

KINBROOK ISLAND PROVINCIAL PARK (Prov Pk) From town, S 9 mi on Hwy 873 to access rd, W 1 mi (E). 2015 rates: $23 to $29. (403)362-2962

TILLEBROOK (Prov Pk) From town: Go 7 km/4-1/4 mi E on Trans Canada Hwy 1. Note: 44' RV length limit. 2015 rates: $23 to $29. Apr 17 to Oct 13. (403)362-4525

BUCK LAKE — C3 *Westaskiwin*

BUCK LAKE PROVINCIAL RECREATION AREA (Prov Pk) From jct Hwy 13 & Buck Lake Rd: Go 10.5 km/6-1/2 mi N on Buck Lake Rd, then 2 km/1.2 mi E on gravel road. Pit toilets. 2015 rates: $18. May 1 to Oct 14. (780)586-2864

CALHOUN BAY PROVINCIAL REC. AREA (Prov Pk) From jct Hwy 13 & Buck Mountain Rd: Go 5 km/3 mi N on Buck Mountain Rd (gravel) and follow signs. Pit toilets. 2015 rates: $18. May 1 to Oct 14. (780)586-2864

CALGARY — D3 *Calgary, Foothills, Rocky View*

CALGARY See also Carseland, Cochrane, Okotoks & Strathmore.

CALAWAY RV PARK & CAMPGROUND Ratings: 7/9★/8 (RV Park) From Jct of Hwy 1 & Springbank Rd (Exit 169), S 0.3 mi on Springbank Rd (R). Elev 3924 ft. **FAC:** Gravel rds. 104 gravel, 20 pull-thrus (20 x 60), back-ins (35 x 55), 56 full hkups, 41 E (15/30 amps), WiFi $, tent sites, showers $, dump, laundry, groc, LP bottles, controlled access. **REC.** Pets OK. Partial handicap access. 2015 rates: $26 to $39. May 16 to Sep 1. ATM.
AAA Approved
(403)249-7372 Lat: 51.083570, Lon: -114.352867
245033 Range Road 33, Calgary, AB T3Z 2E9
campground@calawaypark.com
www.calawaypark.com

CALGARY WEST CAMPGROUND Ratings: 8.5/8.5★/6 (Campground) E-bnd: From Jct Hwy 1 & Valley Ridge Blvd, E 0.8 mi on Valley Ridge Blvd/Crestmont to 101 St, S 0.1 mi (R) Follow blue signs W-bnd: From Jct Hwy 1 & Valley Ridge Blvd/Crestmont Blvd exit, N 0.1 mi to Roundabout, then S .9 mi on Valley Ridge Blvd to 101 St, S 0.1 mi (R) Follow blue signs. Elev 3806 ft. **FAC:** Gravel rds. 250 Avail: 230 gravel, 20 grass, 60 pull-thrus (28 x 60), back-ins (28 x 40), some side by side hkups, 120 full hkups, 130 W, 130 E (20/30 amps), WiFi, tent sites, dump, laundry, groc, LP gas. **REC:**

Everyone wants to be noticed. Tell your RV Park that you found them in the this Guide.

CALGARY (CONT)

CALGARY WEST CAMPGROUND (CONT)
heated pool, playground. Pets OK. 14 day max stay, 2015 rates: $48 to $56. Apr 15 to Oct 15. ATM.
AAA Approved
(888)562-0842 Lat: 51.083372, Lon: -114.234893
221 101 St SW, Calgary, AB T3B 5T2
www.calgarycampground.com

MOUNTAIN VIEW CAMPING Ratings: 8/8.5/6.5 (Campground) From Jct of Hwy 2 & Trans Canada Hwy 1 (Hwy 1), E 7 mi (3.4 km) on Hwy 1 (L). Elev 3451 ft. **FAC:** Paved rds. (142 spaces). Avail: 130 all weather, patios, 2 pull-thrus (22 x 70), back-ins (22 x 55), mostly side by side hkups, 114 full hkups, 16 W, 16 E (30/50 amps), seasonal sites, WiFi $, showers $, dump, laundry, groc, LP gas, fire rings, firewood. **REC:** playground. Pet restrict Partial handicap access, no tents. 2015 rates: $42 to $50. Mar 15 to Nov 15.
AAA Approved
(403)293-6640 Lat: 51.069062, Lon: -113.864380
244024 Range Rd 284, Calgary, AB T2M 4L5
information@calgarycamping.com
www.calgarycamping.com

WHISPERING SPRUCE RV PARK & STORAGE Ratings: 5.5/7.5/5.5 (RV Park) 2015 rates: $24 to $38. May 1 to Oct 31. (403)226-0097 262195 Balzac Blvd, Balzac, AB T4B 2T3

CALLING LAKE — B4 *Opportunity No. 17*

CALLING LAKE PROVINCIAL PARK (Prov Pk) From town: Go 1-1/2 km/1 mi S on Hwy 813. Pit toilets. 2015 rates: $29. May 7 to Oct 13. (780)327-9812

TANASIUK ROCK ISLAND LAKE CAMPGROUND (Public) From Hwy 813 in town: Go 40 km/25 mi N on improved road to Rock Island Lake. Pit toilets. 2015 rates: $15. May 1 to Oct 31. (855)953-3358

CALMAR — C3 *Leduc*

WIZARD LAKE JUBILEE PARK (Public) From jct Hwy 616 & Hwy 795: Go 3-1/2 km/2 mi N on Hwy 795, then 1-1/2 km/.9 mi W on Twp Rd 481, then 3/4 km/.5 mi S on Range Rd 271. 2015 rates: $27.30 to $36.75. (780)985-2499

CAMROSE — C4 *Camrose*

CAMROSE EXHIBITION TRAIL RV PARK
Ratings: 8.5/10★/9 (RV Park) From Jct of Hwy 21 & Hwy 13, E 7.3 mi on Hwy 13 to Exhibition Drive, S 0.1 mi to Exhibition Trail (R). **FAC:** Paved rds. (107 spaces). Avail: 62 all weather, 50 pull-thrus (30 x 60), back-ins (30 x 60), 62 full hkups (30/50 amps), seasonal sites, cable, WiFi, tent sites, showers $, dump, laundry, fire rings, firewood. **REC:** pond, playground. Pets OK. Partial handicap access. Big rig sites, eco-friendly, 2015 rates: $45 to $50.
(780)678-2888 Lat: 53.008996, Lon: -112.791317
4250 Exhibition Trail, Camrose, AB T4V 4Z8
reservations@camroservpark.com
www.camroservpark.com
See ad this page, 1354.

MIQUELON LAKE (Prov Pk) From town, E 14.25 mi on Hwy 623(L). 2015 rates: $23 to $29. (780)672-7274

Things to See and Do

CAMROSE REGIONAL EXHIBITION (CRE)
CRE offers a multitude of agricultural, entertainment, education & leisure programs throughout the year. The annual Big Valley Jamboree features some of the biggest names in country music. Partial handicap access. RV accessible. Restrooms, food. Hours: 8am to 4:30pm. Adult fee: $10 to $100. ATM.
(780)672-3640 Lat: 53.00794, Lon: -112.78629
4250 Exhibition Dr, Camrose, AB T4V 4Z8
cre@cre.ab.ca
www.cre.ab.ca
See ad this page.

CANMORE — D3 *Canmore*

BOW RIVER CAMPGROUND (Prov Pk) From Calgary, W 89 km on Hwy 1 (R). Pit toilets. 2015 rates: $23. May 1 to Sep 28. (403)673-2163

BOW VALLEY CAMPGROUND (Prov Pk) From Jct of Hwy 1 & Seebe-Exshaw exit, N 0.75 mi on Seebe-Exshaw Hwy/Hwy 1X (L). 2015 rates: $23 to $35. May 1 to Oct 13. (403)673-2163

LAC DES ARCS (Prov Pk) From town, W 80 km on Hwy 1 (R). Pit toilets. 2015 rates: $23. May 1 to Sep 1. (403)673-2163

SPRING CREEK RV CAMPGROUND
Ratings: 7/9.5★/7.5 (RV Park) From Jct of Hwy 1 & Main St (Exit 89), S 0.2 mi to Bow Valley Trail, E 0.3 mi on Bow Valley Trail to Spring Creek Gate roundabout, S 0.1 mi (L). Elev 4306 ft. **FAC:** Paved/gravel rds. (123 spaces). Avail: 101 gravel, 31 pull-thrus (24 x 75), back-ins (22 x 50), 91 full hkups, 10 W (30/50 amps), seasonal sites, WiFi, showers $, dump, laundry, fire rings, firewood. **REC:** playground. Pets OK $. Partial handicap access, no tents. Eco-friendly, 2015 rates: $28 to $49.
AAA Approved
(403)678-5111 Lat: 51.08369, Lon: -115.34741
1 Spring Creek Gate, Canmore, AB T1W 0A7
info@springcreekrv.ca
www.springcreekrv.ca
See ad this page.

THREE SISTERS CAMPGROUND (Prov Pk) From town, W 86 km on Hwy 1 (R). Pit toilets. 2015 rates: $23. Apr 12 to Nov 24. (403)673-2163

CARBON — D4 *Carbon*

CARBON MUNICIPAL CAMPGROUND (Public) From Jct of Hwys 21 & 575, E 5 mi on Hwy 575 to SR-836 (Carbon exit), S 1.5 mi (R). 2015 rates: $30 to $35. May 15 to Sep 15. (403)572-3244

CARDSTON — F4 *Cardston*

LEE CREEK CAMPGROUND (Public) From jct Hwy 5 & Hwy 2: Go 1.1 km/3/4 mi S on Hwy 2 (Main St), 0.4km/1/4 mi W on 7 Ave W. 2015 rates: $24 to $30. Apr to Oct. (877)471-2267

POLICE OUTPOST (Prov Pk) From town, S 6.5 mi on Hwy 2, W 10 mi on dirt rd, S 2 mi on dirt rd (E). Pit toilets. 2015 rates: $21. Apr 1 to Nov 1. (403)653-4060

CAROLINE — D3 *Clearwater*

TAY RIVER PROVINCIAL RECREATION AREA (Prov Pk) From town: Go 16 km/10 mi SW on Hwy 591. Pit toilets. 2015 rates: $23. May 1 to Oct 14. (403)845-8349

CARSELAND — E4 *Wheatland*

WYNDHAM-CARSELAND PARK (Prov Pk) From Jct Hwys 1 & 24, S 18 mi (30 km) on Hwy 24 (R). Closed due to Flooding, expecting to reopen Spring 2015. Pit toilets. 2015 rates: $23. Apr 19 to Oct 14. (403)934-3523

CARSTAIRS — D3 *Mountain View*

CARSTAIRS MUNICIPAL CAMPGROUND (Public) From jct Hwy 2 & Hwy 581: Go 4-3/4 km/3 mi W on Hwy 581, then 3 blocks N on Hwy 2A. 2015 rates: $27. May 1 to Oct 31. (403)990-2059

CASLAN — B4 *Athabasca*

NORTH BUCK LAKE CAMPGROUND (Prov Pk) From Hwy 663 in town: Go 4 km/2-1/2 mi N on access road. Pit toilets. 2015 rates: $23 to $29. May 9 to Oct 14. (780)689-4602

CHAMPION — E4 *Vulcan*

LITTLE BOW PROVINCIAL PARK (Prov Pk) From Jct PR-23 & CR-529, E 12 mi on CR-529 to park access rd, S 1 mi (R). 2015 rates: $23 to $29. Apr 17 to Oct 13. (403)897-3933

CHAUVIN — C5 *Wainwright*

DILLBERRY LAKE (Prov Pk) From town, S 10 mi on Hwy 17 (L). 2015 rates: $29 to $35. May 14 to Oct 15. (780)853-8221

CLARESHOLM — E4 *Willow Creek No. 26*

CLARESHOLM CENTENNIAL PARK (Public) From Jct of Hwy 2 and Secondary Hwy 520, W 0.3 mi on Hwy 520 to 4th St W, N 0.5 mi. 2015 rates: $12 to $25. (403)625-2751

COCHRANE — D3 *Rockyview*

BOTTREL STORE AND CAMPGROUND (Public) From Jct of TCH & Hwy 22 exit (Cochrane), N 23.5 mi on Cochrane to Bottrel St, W 1.8 mi (L). 2015 rates: $10 to $15. May 1 to Oct 31. (403)932-5423

BOW RIVERSEDGE CAMPGROUND
Ratings: 8.5/10★/9.5 (Public) From Jct of Hwy 22 & Griffin Rd, E 1.9 mi / 3km on Griffin Rd to Arena sign, W 0.2 mi /0.3km (R). Elev 3671 ft. **FAC:** Paved rds. (144 spaces). Avail: 114 all weather, 75 pull-thrus (30 x 75), back-ins (30 x 70), 114 full hkups (30/50 amps), WiFi $, tent sites, showers $, dump, laundry, fire rings, firewood, controlled access. **REC:** Bow River: fishing, playground. Pet restrict(Q) $. Partial handicap access. Big rig sites, 2015 rates: $40 to $45. Apr 1 to Nov 1.
(877)932-4675 Lat: 51.175417, Lon: -114.455753
900 Griffen Rd E, Cochrane, AB T4C 2B8
info@bowriversedge.com
www.bowriversedge.com
See ad pages 1351 (Welcome Section), 1354.

BURNT TIMBER CAMPGROUND (Prov Pk) From jct Hwy 1A & Hwy 40: Go 68 km/42-1/4 mi W on Hwy 40 (Forestry Trunk Rd). Pit toilets. 2015 rates: $28. May 1 to Sep 9. (403)637-2198

FALLEN TIMBER PROVINCIAL RECREATION AREA-SOUTH (Prov Pk) From jct Hwy 1A & Hwy 40: Go 54 km/33-1/2 mi NW on Hwy 40 (Forestry Trunk Rd). Pit toilets. 2015 rates: $28. May 1 to Oct 15. (403)637-2198

GHOST RESERVOIR P.R.A. (Prov Pk) From town: Go 21-1/2 km/13-1/2 mi W on Hwy 1A. Pit toilets. 2015 rates: $20. May 1 to Oct 31. (403)851-0766

NORTH GHOST PROVINCIAL RECREATION AREA (Prov Pk) From jct Hwy 1A & Hwy 40: Go 40 km/24.8 mi NW on Hwy 40 (Forestry Trunk Rd). Pit toilets. 2015 rates: $28. May 1 to Oct 14. (403)637-2198

SPRING HILL RV PARK Ratings: 7/10★/9 (RV Park) From Jct of Hwy 22 & Hwy 567, E 0.1 mi on Hwy 567 (L). Elev 4321 ft. **FAC:** Gravel rds. (115 spaces). Avail: 90 gravel, 46 pull-thrus (30 x 75), back-ins (30 x 60), 90 full hkups (30/50 amps), seasonal sites, WiFi, tent sites, showers $, dump, laundry, groc, LP gas, fire rings, firewood, controlled access. **REC:** pond, Meaghan's Pond: fishing, playground. Pets OK. Partial handicap access. Big rig sites, eco-friendly, 2015 rates: $40 to $50. Disc: AAA. ATM.
AAA Approved
(403)932-2010 Lat: 51.272086, Lon: -114.466527
41216 Big Hill Springs Road, Cochrane, AB T4C 1A1
info@springhillrvpark.com
www.springhillrvpark.com

WAIPAROUS CREEK PROV. REC. AREA (Prov Pk) From jct Hwy 1A & Hwy 40: Go 37 km/23 mi NW on Hwy 40 (Forestry Trunk Rd). Pit toilets. 2015 rates: $28. May 1 to Oct 14. (403)637-2198

COLD LAKE — B5 *Bonnyville*

COLD LAKE MD CAMPGROUND (Public) From Jct of Hwy 28 & Hwy 55, NE 1.5 mi on Hwy 28 to Cold Lake town, follow signs (R). 2015 rates: $22 to $24. (780)639-4121

COLD LAKE PROVINCIAL PARK (Prov Pk) From town, E 2 mi on Hwy 28, follow signs (E). 2015 rates: $29 to $35. May 14 to Oct 14. (780)594-7856

CROWSNEST PASS — E3 *Crowsnest Pass*

CASTLE FALLS PROVINCIAL RECREATION AREA (Prov Pk) From town: Go 28-3/4 km/18 mi SW on local roads. Pit toilets. 2015 rates: $17. May 1 to Nov 30. (403)563-5395

CASTLE RIVER BRIDGE PROVINCIAL RECREATION AREA (Prov Pk) From town: Go 22-3/4 km/14-1/4 mi SW on local roads. Pit toilets. 2015 rates: $17. May 1 to Nov 30. (403)563-5395

CROWSNEST PASS (CONT)

DUTCH CREEK PROVINCIAL RECREATION AREA (Prov Pk) From town: Go 30-1/2 km/19 mi NE on Hwy 940. Pit toilets. 2015 rates: $17. May 1 to Oct 14. (403)563-5395

LYNX CREEK PROVINCIAL RECREATION AREA (Prov Pk) From town: Go 19-1/2 km/12-1/4 mi SW on local roads. Pit toilets. 2015 rates: $14. May 1 to Oct 14. (403)563-5395

RACEHORSE PROVINCIAL RECREATION AREA (Prov Pk) From town: Go 24 km/15 mi N on Hwy 940. Pit toilets. 2015 rates: $17. May 1 to Nov 30. (403)563-5395

DELBURNE — D4 *Red Deer*

FAWN MEADOWS LODGE & RV PARK **Ratings: 6/9.5★/7** (Campground) 2015 rates: $34. (403)749-2099 2201 18th Avenue, Delburne, AB T0M 0V0

DEVON — C3 *Edmonton*

DEVON LIONS CLUB CAMPGROUND (Public) N/bnd or S/bnd -From Jct of Hwy 60 & Athabaska Dr., E 190 yds/174m on Athabaska Dr. to Superior St., N 140 yds/128m to Saskatchewan Ave, E 1.2 mi/1.9km (E). 2015 rates: $32.55 to $46.20. May 1 to Oct 15. (780)987-4777

DIDSBURY — D3 *Mountain View*

ROSEBUD VALLEY PARK & CAMPGROUND (Public) From Jct of Hwy 2 & SR-582 (exit 326), W 4 mi/6.4km on SR-582 (R). 2015 rates: $23 to $26. Apr 1 to Oct 15. (403)335-8578

DRAYTON VALLEY — C3 *Brazeau*

WILLEY WEST PARK (Public) From Jct of Hwys 39 & 22, W 2.5 mi to park entrance rd (R). 2015 rates: $25 to $40. May 1 to Oct 31. (780)542-5821

DRUMHELLER — D4 *Starland*

BLERIOT FERRY REC AREA (Prov Pk) From Bleriot Ferry crossing to Hwy 837, W 300 yds (E). Pit toilets. 2015 rates: $18. May 15 to Sep 15. (403)823-1749

DINOSAUR RV PARK & DINO NEST **Ratings: 6.5/9/6.5** (RV Park) 2015 rates: $48 to $53. May 1 to Oct 31. (403)823-3291 500 N. Dinosaur Trail, Drumheller, AB T0J 0Y0

DINOSAUR TRAIL RV RESORT **Ratings: 9/8.5★/8** (RV Park) 2015 rates: $58 to $65. May 1 to Sep 30. (403)823-9333 294004 N Dinosaur Trail, Drumheller, AB T0J 0Y0

LITTLE FISH LAKE (Prov Pk) From Jct of Hwys 10 & 573, E 13.6 mi on Hwy 573 (R). Pit toilets. 2015 rates: $16. May 15 to Sep 15. (403)823-1749

RIVER GROVE CAMPGROUND & CABINS **Ratings: 7/9/7.5** (Campground) 2015 rates: $40 to $46. May 1 to Sep 22. (403)823-6655 25 Poplar St., Drumheller, AB T0J 0Y0

THE HOODOO RV RESORT & CAMPGROUND **Ratings: 5.5/7/7** (Campground) 2015 rates: $35 to $40. May 1 to Oct 15. (866)923-2790 5075 Hwy 10E, Drumheller, AB T0J 0Y0

THE POPE LEASE PINES BED & BREAKFAST AND RV RESORT **Ratings: 3.5/7/8.5** (RV Park) 2015 rates: $37. May 1 to Oct 1. (403)823-8281 232922 W of Fourth, Drumheller, AB T0J 0Y0

DUNVEGAN — A1 *Fairviewe No. 136*

DUNVEGAN (Prov Pk) From town, S 15 mi on Hwy 2 (L). 2015 rates: $30. May 1 to Oct 15. (780)538-5350

EDMONTON — C4 *Edmonton, Parkland, Sturgeon*

A SPOTLIGHT Introducing Edmonton's colorful attractions appearing in this province section.

EDMONTON See also Acheson, Devon, Gibbons, Morinville, Sherwood Park, Spruce Grove, St Albert & Stony Plain.

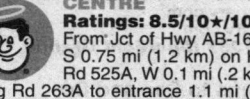

DIAMOND GROVE RV CAMPGROUND
Ratings: 9/10★/9 (RV Resort) From Jct of Hwy 16A & Hwy 60, W 8km/5 mi on Hwy16A to Century Rd, S 1.3km/0.8 mi to Century Close, W 316 yds/ 310 m (L). **FAC:** All weather rds. 242 Avail: 242 all weather, patios, 180 pull-thrus (35 x 90), back-ins (35 x 66), 242 full hkups (30/50 amps), WiFi, showers $, dump, laundry, groc, fire rings, firewood, controlled access. **REC:** whirlpool. Pets OK. Partial handicap access, no tents. Big rig sites, eco-friendly, 2015 rates: $45 to $55.
(780)962-8003 Lat: 53.529813, Lon: -113.890254
41 Century Close, Spruce Grove, AB T7X 3B3
diamondgrovervpark@gmail.com
www.diamondgrove.ca
See ad this page, 1354.

ELK ISLAND NATIONAL PARK (SANDY BEACH) (Natl Pk) From town: Go 35 km/21-3/4 mi E on Hwy 16, then 14 km/8-1/2 mi N on Elk Island Pkwy, then W into Astotin Lake Area, then 200 meters N at first right. 2015 rates: $25.50. May 1 to Oct 1. (780)992-2950

GLOWING EMBERS RV PARK & TRAVEL CENTRE
Ratings: 8.5/10★/10 (RV Park) From Jct of Hwy AB-16A & Hwy AB-60, S 0.75 mi (1.2 km) on Hwy-60 to Twshp Rd 525A, W 0.1 mi (.2 km) (R); N-bnd on Frntg Rd 263A to entrance 1.1 mi (1.8 km) (L). Elev 2900 ft.

*** GREAT PARK ON ROUTE TO ALASKA ***
With over 200 full-service sites, we offer something for everyone; from families to large groups needing banquet facilities. We are conveniently located near many golf courses, shopping and the world-famous West Edmonton Mall

FAC: All weather rds. (288 spaces). Avail: 223 all weather, 25 pull-thrus (25 x 70), back-ins (25 x 45), 223 full hkups (30/50 amps), seasonal sites, WiFi, tent sites, showers $, dump, laundry, LP gas. **REC:** playground. Pets OK. Partial handicap access. Big rig sites, eco-friendly, 2015 rates: $45 to $50. Disc: AAA.
(877)785-7275 Lat: 53.53913, Lon: -113.77012
26309 Hwy 16A, Acheson, AB T7X 5A6
www.glowingembersrvpark.com
See ad pages 1356 (Spotlight Edmonton), 1354, 1352 (AB Map).

RAINBOW VALLEY CAMPGROUND (Public) From Jct of Whitemud Fwy & 119th St, S 1 blk on 119th St to Whitemud Park (45th Ave), W 2 blks (E). 2015 rates: $30 to $36. Apr 15 to Oct 10. (780)434-5531

SHAKERS ACRES RV PARK **Ratings: 6/7/7** (Campground) 2015 rates: $31 to $50. (877)447-3565 21530 103Rd Ave, Edmonton, AB T5S 2C4

EDSON — C2 *Yellowhead*

EDSON LIONS PARK CAMPGROUND (Public) From Jct of Yellowhead Hwy 16 & 40th St, N 0.05 mi (R). 2015 rates: $21 to $26.25. May 1 to Oct 1. (780)723-3169

FICKLE LAKE PROVINCIAL RECREATION AREA (Prov Pk) From town: Go 38-1/2 km/24 mi SW on Hwy 47. Pit toilets. 2015 rates: $22. May 1 to Oct 14. (780)723-0738

WILLMORE RECREATION PARK (Public) From Jct of Hwy 16 & 63rd St, S 3 mi on 63rd St (L). Pit toilets. 2015 rates: $17. May 15 to Oct 15. (780)723-7141

WOLF LAKE WEST RECREATION AREA (Prov Pk) From town: Go 30-3/4 km/19-1/4 mi E on Hwy 16, then 54-1/2 km/34 mi S on local road. Pit toilets. 2015 rates: $22. May 1 to Oct 13. (780)797-4154

ELK POINT — B5 *St Paul*

WHITNEY LAKE CAMPGROUND (Prov Pk) From town, E 15 mi on Hwy 646 (L). 2015 rates: $23 to $29. May 14 to Oct 13. (780)645-6295

ENTWISTLE — C3 *Parkland*

PEMBINA RIVER (Prov Pk) From Jct of Hwy 16 & Hwy 16A at Entwistle, NW 1 mi on Hwy 16A (R). 2015 rates: $29. May 15 to Sep 30. (780)727-3643

ERSKINE — D4 *Stettler*

ROCHON SANDS PROVINCIAL PARK (Prov Pk) From town: Go 13-1/4 km/8-1/4 mi N on Hwy 835, then 1-1/2 km/1 mi W. Pit toilets. 2015 rates: $25. May 15 to Oct 15. (403)742-4338

FALHER — A2 *Smoky River No. 130*

FALHER MUNICIPAL CAMPGROUND (Public) In town on Hwy 49. 2015 rates: $15.75 to $21. (780)837-2247

FAWCETT — B3 *Westlock*

CROSS LAKE PROVINCIAL PARK (Prov Pk) From town, N 0.5 mi on Hwy 44 to Hwy 663, NE 13 mi (L). 2015 rates: $29. May 9 to Oct 31. (780)675-8213

FORESTBURG — C4 *Flagstaff*

BIG KNIFE (Prov Pk) From Jct of Hwys 53 & 855, S 8.5 mi on Hwy 855 (R). Pit toilets. 2015 rates: $20. May 15 to Oct 15. (403)742-7516

FORK LAKE — B4 *Lac la Biche*

FORK LAKE PROVINCIAL RECREATION AREA (Prov Pk) From jct Hwy 55 & Hwy 867: Go 2-1/2 km/1-1/2 mi S on Hwy 867. Pit toilets. 2015 rates: $18.90 to $25.20. (780)623-1747

FORT MACLEOD — E4 *Fort Macleod*

DAISY MAY CAMPGROUND
Ratings: 8.5/9★/8.5 (Campground) From Jct of Hwy-3 & Lyndon Rd, W 0.8 km/0.5 mi on Lyndon Rd (R) Note: Do not use GPS. Elev 3136 ft. **FAC:** Gravel rds. 110 Avail: 24 gravel, 86 grass, 5 pull-thrus (30 x 70), back-ins (30 x 60), 24 full hkups, 64 W, 64 E (30/50 amps), WiFi, tent sites, rentals, showers $, dump, laundry, groc, LP bottles, fire rings, firewood. **REC:** heated pool, whirlpool, Old Man River: fishing, playground. Pet restrict(Q). Big rig sites, eco-friendly, 2015 rates: $35 to $50. Apr 1 to Oct 31.
(888)553-2455 Lat: 49.723480, Lon: -113.420873
249 Lyndon Road, Fort Macleod, AB T0L 0Z0
questions@daisymaycampground.com
www.daisymaycampground.com
See ad this page.

FORT MCMURRAY — A4 *Wood Buffalo*

CENTENNIAL RV PARK (Public) N-bnd: From Jct of Hwy 63 & McKenzie Blvd exit, E 1 blk on McKenzie Blvd to Gregoire Dr, N 4 blks to Hwy 63, S 2 blks (L). 2015 rates: $27 to $30. (780)714-9790

GREGOIRE LAKE (Prov Pk) From town, S 11.78 mi on Hwy 63 to Hwy 881, E 6 mi (L). 2015 rates: $28 to $34. May 1 to Oct 15. (780)743-7437

HANGINGSTONE RIVER P.R.A. (Prov Pk) From town, S 22 mi Hwy 63 (R). Pit toilets. 2015 rates: $23. May 15 to Sep 15. (780)743-7437

FOX CREEK — B2 *Greenview No. 16*

FOX CREEK RV CAMPGROUND (Public) From jct Hwy 43 & Kaybob Dr: Go 1 block E on Kaybob Dr, then 2 blocks N on Campground Rd. 2015 rates: $20 to $35. (780)622-3896

IOSEGUN LAKE CAMPGROUND (TOWN PARK) (Public) From town: Go 11-1/4 km/7 mi N on Hwy 43. Pit toilets. 2015 rates: $20. May 17 to Sep 30. (780)622-2418

SMOKE LAKE CAMPGROUND (TOWN PARK) (Public) From town: Go 8-3/4 km/5-1/2 mi SW on Hwy 43. Pit toilets. 2015 rates: $20. May 24 to Oct 1. (780)538-5350

GIBBONS — C4 *Sturgeon*

LONGRIDERS RV PARK **Ratings: 4.5/8.5★/6** (RV Park) 2015 rates: $42 to $46. (780)923-3300 23136 Secondary Hwy 643, Gibbons, AB T0A 1N0

GLENDON — B5 *Bonnyville No. 87*

LAKELAND PROV. REC AREA (SEIBERT LAKE CG) (Prov Pk) From town: Go 9-1/2 km/6 mi W on Hwy 660, then 40 km/25 mi N on Hwy 881, then 9-1/2 km/6 mi E on Hwy 55, then 30-1/2 km/19 mi N on local road/forestry trail. 2-wheel drive recommended in dry weather only. Pit toilets. 2015 rates: $23. May 17 to Oct 31. (403)623-5434

Take time now to plan a road trip with your pet. Read more in our Pampered Pet Parks feature at the front of the Guide.

GRANDE CACHE — B1 *Greenview*

GRANDE CACHE MUNICIPAL CAMPGROUND (Public) From Jct of Hwy 40 & Shand Ave, E 0.4 mi on Shand Ave to 97th St, N 0.2 mi to 104th Ave, E 0.3 mi to Memorial Dr, N 0.6 mi to Campground Dr (E). 2015 rates: $26 to $32. May 15 to Oct 15. (780)827-2404

GRANDE PRAIRIE — B1 *Grand Prairie, Greenview, West End*

CAMP TAMARACK RV PARK
Ratings: 8/10★/9.5 (RV Park) From Jct Hwy 43 & Hwy 40, S 5.5 mi (9 km) on Hwy 40 (L).

COME VISIT THE PINE & ASPEN FOREST!
Big sites, clean facilities; Camp Tamarack is your home away from home. Minutes from shopping, parks, walking trails, ATV area, Rec Centre & new Dinosaur Museum. Stay with us & enjoy all that we & Grande Prairie have to offer

FAC: All weather rds. (89 spaces). Avail: 59 gravel, 29 pull-thrus (34 x 75), back-ins (34 x 60), 29 full hkups, 30 W, 30 E (30/50 amps), seasonal sites, WiFi, tent sites, dump, laundry, groc, LP gas, fire rings, firewood. **REC:** playground. Pets OK. Partial handicap access. Big rig sites, eco-friendly, 2015 rates: $42 to $49. Disc: AAA. Apr 15 to Oct 15.
(877)532-9998 Lat: 55.09466, Lon: -118.81274
704063 Range Rd, Grande Prairie, AB T8W 5B3
reservations@camptamarackrv.com
www.camptamarackrv.com
See ad pages 1358 (Spotlight Grande Prairie), 1354.

COUNTRY ROADS RV PARK
Ratings: 7.5/9.5★/9 (Campground) From Jct of 43 & 116 St, N 6.6 km (4 mi) on 116 St to Hwy 43X, W 1.2km/0.7 mi to park entrance (L); or W-bnd: From Jct of Hwy 43 & Hwy 2, W 4.4 km (2.5 mi) on Hwy 43X (L). **FAC:** Gravel rds. (115 spaces). Avail: 80 gravel, 60 pull-thrus (36 x 60), back-ins (24 x 50), 80 full hkups (30/50 amps), seasonal sites, WiFi, tent sites, rentals, showers $, dump, laundry, groc, LP gas, fire rings, firewood, controlled access. **REC:** pond, fishing, playground. Pet restrict(B/Q). Partial handicap access. Big rig sites, eco-friendly, 2015 rates: $45. ATM.
(866)532-6323 Lat: 55.227726, Lon: -118.864339
63061A Twp. Rd.722, Grande Prairie, AB T8X 4K7
rvpark@countryroadsrvpark.com
www.countryroadsrvpark.com
See ad page 1358 (Spotlight Grande Prairie).

GRANDE PRAIRIE ROTARY RV PARK **Ratings: 6/9★/7.5** (RV Park) 2015 rates: $39 to $43. May 1 to Sep 30. (780)532-1137 10747 108 St, Grande Prairie, AB T8V 7T8

NITEHAWK WILDERNESS RV PARK
Ratings: 5.5/8★/7.5 (Campground) From Jct of Hwy 43 & Hwy 40, S 11.6km/7.2 mi on Hwy 40 to Hwy 666 (Nitehawk Exit), W 3.9km/2.4 mi to Nitehawk Ski Hill (R). **FAC:** Gravel rds. (73 spaces). Avail: 15 gravel, 3 pull-thrus (32 x 70), back-ins (32 x 70), 15 W, 15 E (30/50 amps), seasonal sites, WiFi Hotspot, tent sites, dump, mobile sewer, laundry, fire rings, firewood. **REC:** Wapiti River: playground. Pet restrict(Q). Eco-friendly, 2015 rates: $35 to $39.
(888)754-6778 Lat: 55.05551, Lon: -118.86213
6356 Twp Rd 702A (Hwy 666W), Grovedale, AB T8V 4B5
info@gonitehawk.com
www.gonitehawk.com
See ad page 1358 (Spotlight Grande Prairie).

Travel Services

MCGOVERNS RV & MARINE CENTRE Provides service and parts for RV and Marine in the greater Grande Prairie area. **SERVICES:** RV, RV appliance, restrooms, RV Sales. RV storage. RV supplies, emergency parking, RV accessible. waiting room. Hours: 8am to 6pm.
(780)539-1814 Lat: 55.21229, Lon: -118.79348
14525 100 St, Grande Prairie, AB T8V 7C1
sales@mcgovernsrv.com
www.mcgovernsrv.com
See ad page 1358 (Spotlight Grande Prairie).

Things to See and Do

GRANDE PRAIRIE REGIONAL TOURISM ASSOC. Visitor info centre - Grande Prairie & N. Alberta offers FREE snacks & beverages Wed. & free city tours Tues, Wed,Thur 7pm. Grande Prairie Regional Tourism offers information on Northern travel & the Deh Cho Travel Connection. Partial handicap access. RV accessible. Restrooms. Hours: 8:30am to 7pm. ATM.
(866)202-2202 Lat: 55.18172, Lon: -118.81757
#114-11330 106th st, Grande Prairie, AB T8V 7X9
info@gptourism.ca
www.gptourism.ca
See ad page 1358 (Spotlight Grande Prairie).

PHILIP J. CURRIE DINOSAUR MUSEUM New Dinosaur Museum located west of Grande Prairie AB. Partial handicap access. Restrooms. Hours: 10 to 6. Adult fee: $14.
(587)771-0662 Lat: 55.168255, Lon: -119.129970
9301-112 Ave, Wembley, AB T0H 3S0
info@dinomuseum.ca
dinomuseum.ca
See ad page 1358 (Spotlight Grande Prairie).

THE HERITAGE DISCOVERY CENTRE A family friendly, hands on museum depicting the history of the Peace River country, from the Ice Age until the present day. Its featured attraction is a life size animatronic dinosaur named Piper. Partial handicap access. RV accessible. Restrooms. Hours: 8:30am to 4:30pm.
(780)532-5790 Lat: 55.18172, Lon: -118.81757
11330 106th St- Lower Level, Grande Prairie, AB T8V 7X9
kpfau@cityofgp.com
www.cityofgp.com
See ad page 1358 (Spotlight Grande Prairie).

GRANUM — E4 *Willow Creek*

GRANVIEW RV PARK (Public) From Jct of Hwy 2 & Hwy 519, E 0.4 mi on Hwy 519, follow signs (R). 2015 rates: $16.80 to $28.35. (403)687-3830

GROUARD — A2 *Big Lakes*

HILLIARD'S BAY PROVINCIAL PARK (Prov Pk) From town: Go 8 km/5 mi E on access road. 2015 rates: $24 to $30. May 14 to Oct 15. (780)849-7100

GULL LAKE — C3 *Lacombe*

ASPEN BEACH (Prov Pk) From Jct of Hwys 2 & 12, W 7 mi on Hwy 12 to Aspen Beach Prov Park sign (R). 2015 rates: $23 to $47. May 1 to Oct 13. (903)748-4066

ASPEN BEACH PROVINCIAL PARK (BREWER'S CAMPGROUND) (Prov Pk) From jct Hwy 2 & Hwy 12: Go 9 km/5.6 mi W on Hwy 12. 2015 rates: $23 to $41. May 1 to Oct 14. (403)748-4066

SUMMERLAND LEISURE RV PARK
Ratings: 7.5/9.5★/10 (RV Park) From Jct of Hwy 2 & Hwy 12, W 10 km (6.2 mi) on Hwy 12 to Rge Rd 282, S 100 meters (0.6 mi) (L). Elev 3095 ft. **FAC:** Gravel rds. 31 Avail: 31 all weather, back-ins (30 x 60), 31 full hkups (30 amps), WiFi, showers $, laundry, fire rings, firewood. **REC:** playground, rec open to public. Pets OK. Partial handicap access, no tents. Eco-friendly, 2015 rates: $44. May 1 to Oct 1.
(403)748-4855 Lat: 52.46038, Lon: -113.93890
40325 Rge Rd 282, Lacombe, AB T4L 2N1
summerlandleisurepark@shaw.ca
www.summerlandleisurepark.com
See ad this page, 1354.

Things to See and Do

SUMMERLAND MINI GOLF & DRIVING RANGE 18 hole mini golf and driving range 375 yards & twenty stalls open 7 days week 10am to 9pm mid May to mid Sep. Licensed concession. Elev 3095 ft. May 1 to Sep 30. partial handicap access. Hours: 10am to 9pm. Adult fee: $8.25. No CC.
(403)748-4855 Lat: 52.46038, Lon: -113.9389
40325 Rge Rd 282, Lacombe, AB T4L 2N1
summerlandleisurepark@shaw.ca
summerlandleisurepark.com
See ad this page.

HANNA — D4 *Special Area No. 2*

FOX LAKE PARK (TOWN PARK) (Public) From jct Hwy 9 & Palliser Trail at west city limits: Go 1 mi N on Palliser Trail, then 2 mi W on Fox Lake Trail. 2015 rates: $20 to $30. (403)854-4433

HANNA MUSEUM TRAILER PARK (TOWN PARK) (Public) From jct Hwy 9 & Pioneer Trail at east city limits: Go 2 mi on Pioneer Trail. 2015 rates: $31.50. (403)854-4433

HIGH PRAIRIE — A2 *Big Lakes*

ELKS RV PARK Ratings: 4/UI/8 (RV Park) From Hwy 749 N in town, N 3/4 mi (1.5 km) on Hwy 749 (L). **FAC:** Gravel rds. 54 Avail: 25 gravel, 29 grass, 54 pull-thrus (40 x 108), accepts full hkup units only, 54 full hkups (30/50 amps), WiFi, tent sites, dump, fire rings, firewood. **REC:** West Prairie River: fishing. Pets OK. Big rig sites, 2015 rates: $28. Apr 15 to Oct 1.
(780)507-0399 Lat: 55.450237, Lon: -116.491295
74508 Hwy 749 (48th St), High Prairie, AB T0G 1E0
hpelks@telus.net
www.elkshp.com

HIGH PRAIRIE CAMPGROUND (Public) From jct Hwy 749 & Hwy 2: Go 2.4 km/1-1/2 mi E on Hwy 2, then 90 m/100 yds N on access road. 2015 rates: $$20 to $25. May 1 to Sep 30. (780)523-3724

SHAW'S POINT RESORT **Ratings: 8/9.5★/7.5** (Campground) 2015 rates: $40 to $48. May 1 to Oct 1. (780)751-3900 751-15A Range Rd 141, High Prairie, AB T0G 1E0

HIGH RIVER — E3 *Foothills No. 31*

GEORGE LANE MEMORIAL PARK (Public) From Jct of Hwys 23 (12th Ave) & Hwy 2, W 2 mi on Hwy 23 (12th Ave) to 1st St SW, N 1 mi to 5th Ave, W (E). Reservations recommended. 2015 rates: $20 to $29.50. May 1 to Sep 30. (403)652-2529

HINTON — C2 *Yellowhead*

HINTON/JASPER KOA
Ratings: 8.5/9.5★/9.5 (RV Park) From Jct of Hwy 40N & Hwy 16, W 0.7mi/1.1km (L); or From Jasper Natl Park East Gate, E 11.2 mi (18 km) on Hwy 16 (R). Elev 3409 ft. **FAC:** All weather rds. 88 Avail: 88 all weather, 77 pull-thrus (35 x 75), back-ins (35 x 45), 77 full hkups, 11 W, 11 E (30/50 amps), cable, WiFi, tent sites, rentals, dump, laundry, groc, firewood, controlled access. **REC:** Maskuta

HINTON (CONT)

HINTON/JASPER KOA (CONT)
Creek: fishing, playground. Pet restrict(B/Q). Partial handicap access. Big rig sites, eco-friendly, 2015 rates: $40 to $55. Disc: AAA. May 15 to Oct 1. AAA Approved
(888)562-4714 Lat: 53.339308, Lon: -117.661591
50409B Hwy 16, Hinton, AB T7V 1X3
brownkoa4@shaw.ca
www.koa.com
See ad opposite page.

PIERRE GREY'S LAKE PROVINCIAL RECREATION AREA (Prov Pk) From town: Go 120 km/74-1/2 mi NW on Hwy 40. Pit toilets. 2015 rates: $23 to $29. May 14 to Oct 15. (780)827-7393

ROCK LAKE PROVINCIAL RECREATION AREA (Prov Pk) From town: Go 86 km/53-1/2 mi NW on Hwy 40. Pit toilets. 2015 rates: $16. May 15 to Oct 14. (780)865-2154

WATSON CREEK RECREATION AREA (Prov Pk) From town: Go 48 km/30 mi S on Hwy 40. Pit toilets. 2015 rates: $11. May 1 to Sep 30. (780)865-2154

WHITEHORSE CREEK RECREATION AREA (Prov Pk) From town: Go 71-1/4 km/44-1/2 mi S on Hwy 40 and local roads. Pit toilets. 2015 rates: $11. May 1 to Sep 30. (780)865-2154

WILLIAM A SWITZER (Prov Pk) From town, W 2 mi on Hwy 16 to Hwy 40, NW 12.75 mi (R). 2015 rates: $21 to $35. (780)865-5600

HYTHE — A1 *Grande Prairie County No. 1*

HYTHE MUNICIPAL CAMPGROUND (Public) From Jct of Hwy 2 & 100th St, NW 0.2 mi on Hwy-2 (R). 2015 rates: $20. May to Oct. (780)356-3888

IRON RIVER — B5 *Bonnyville No. 87*

WOLF LAKE RECREATION AREA (Prov Pk) From jct Hwy 41 & Hwy 55: Go 18-1/2 km/11-1/2 mi W on Hwy 55, then 30-3/4 km/19-1/4 mi N on access road. Pit toilets. 2015 rates: $20. May 15 to Sep 14. (780)826-3171

JASPER — C1 *Edson*

JASPER NATIONAL PARK (JONAS CREEK) (Natl Pk) From town: Go 76-3/4 km/ 48 mi on Icefields Pkwy S (Hwy 93). Pit toilets. 2015 rates: $16.80. May 17 to Sep 2. (780)852-6176

JASPER/HONEYMOON LAKE (Natl Pk) From town, S 32.3 mi on Hwy 93 (L). Pit toilets. 2015 rates: $16.80. Jun 21 to Sep 2. (780)852-6176

JASPER/MT KERKESLIN (Natl Pk) From Jct of Hwys 93 & 16, S 22.5 mi on Hwy 93 (R). Pit toilets. 2015 rates: $16.80. Jun 20 to Sep 1. (780)852-6176

JASPER/POCAHONTAS (Natl Pk) From Jct of Hwys 93 & 16, NE 22 mi on Hwy 16 to Miette Rd, S .25 mi (R). 2015 rates: $21.50. May 16 to Sep 7. (780)852-6176

JASPER/SNARING RIVER (Natl Pk) From town, N 6.8 mi on Hwy 16 to Snaring Rd, W 3 mi (L). Pit toilets. 2015 rates: $16.80. May 16 to Sep 14. (780)852-6176

JASPER/WABASSO (Natl Pk) From town, S 10 mi on Hwy 93A (L). 2015 rates: $21.50. Jun 20 to Sep 1. (780)852-6176

JASPER/WAPITI (Natl Pk) From Jct of Hwy 93 & Hwy 16, S 3 mi on Hwy 93 (L). 2015 rates: $27.40 to $32.30. (780)852-6176

JASPER/WHISTLERS (Natl Pk) From Jct of Hwys 93 & 16, S 1.5 mi on Hwy 93 (R). 2015 rates: $27.40 to $38.20. May 2 to Oct 13. (780)852-6176

JASPER/WILCOX CREEK (Natl Pk) From Jct of Hwy 16 & Hwy 93, S 65 mi on Hwy 93 (L). Pit toilets. 2015 rates: $15.70. Jun 6 to Sep 28. (780)852-6176

KANANASKIS VILLAGE — D3 *Kanaskis*

BOULTON CREEK CAMPGROUND (Public) From jct Hwy 1 & Hwy 40: Go 53 km/33 mi S on Hwy 40, then 10 km/6.2 mi SW on Kananaskis Lake Trail. 2015 rates: $23 to $35. May 8 to Oct 13. (403)591-7226

DAWSON EQUESTRIAN (Prov Pk) From jct Hwy 1 & Hwy 40: Go 8 km/5 mi S on Hwy 40, then 11.7 km/7 mi E on Hwy 68, then 5 km/3 mi S on Powderface Trail. Pit toilets. 2015 rates: $23. (403)673-2163

EAU CLAIRE CAMPGROUND (Prov Pk) From jct Hwy 1 & Hwy 40: Go 38 km/23.6 mi S on Hwy 40. Pit toilets. 2015 rates: $23. May 15 to Sep 2. (403)591-7226

ELKWOOD CAMPGROUND (Prov Pk) From jct Hwy 1 & Hwy 40: Go 53 km/33 mi S on Hwy 40, then 5 km/3-3/4 mi SW on Kananaskis Lake Trail. 2015 rates: $23 to $35. May 14 to Oct 13. (403)591-7226

INTERLAKES CAMPGROUND (Prov Pk) From jct Hwy 1 & Hwy 40: Go 53 km/33 mi S on Hwy 40, then 15 km/9.3 mi SW on Kananaskis Lake Trail. Pit toilets. 2015 rates: $23. May 14 to Oct 13. (403)591-7226

LOWER LAKE CAMPGROUND (Prov Pk) From jct Hwy 1 & Hwy 40: Go 53 km/33 mi S on Hwy 40, then 10.5 km/6-1/2 mi SW on Kananaskis Lake Trail. Pit toilets. 2015 rates: $23. May 15 to Sep 15. (403)591-7226

MOUNT KIDD RV PARK (Public) From Jct of Hwy 1 & Hwy 40, S 16 mi on Hwy 40 (R). 2015 rates: $32.50 to $48. (403)591-7700

SIBBALD LAKE CAMPGROUND (Prov Pk) From jct Hwy 1 & Hwy 40: Go 8 km/5 mi S on Hwy 40, then 12 km/7-1/2 mi E on Hwy 68. Pit toilets. 2015 rates: $23. May 1 to Oct 13. (403)673-3985

SPRAY LAKES WEST CAMPGROUND (Prov Pk) From jct Hwy 1 & Hwy 40: Go 53 km/33 mi S on Hwy 40, then 2 km/1.3 mi SW on Kananaskis Lake Trail, then 50 km/31 mi N on Smith Dorrien/Spray Trail (gravel road). (Across 3 Sister Dam.). Pit toilets. 2015 rates: $23. May 14 to Sep 14. (403)591-7226

KINUSO — B3 *Big Lakes*

SPRUCE POINT PARK (Public) From town, N 7 mi on Hwy 2, follow signs (R). 2015 rates: $29 to $32. May 15 to Sep 15. (780)775-2117

LAC LA BICHE — B4 *Bonnyville*

FISH'N FRIENDS BEAVER LAKE CAMPGROUND (Public) From jct Hwy 55 & Hwy 36: Go 2 km/1.2 mi S on Hwy 36, then 5 km/3 mi E on Hwy 663. 2015 rates: $23 to $29. (780)623-9222

LAKELAND PROVINCIAL RECREATION AREA (IRONWOOD LAKE CAMPGROUND) (Prov Pk) From town: Go 20 km/12.4 mi S on Hwy 36, then 30 km/18.6 mi E. Pit toilets. 2015 rates: $23. May 17 to Oct 31. (780)623-5235

LAKELAND PROVINCIAL RECREATION AREA (PINEHURST LAKE CAMPGROUND) (Prov Pk) From town: Go 20 km/12.4 mi S on Hwy 36, then 30 km/18.6 mi E. Pit toilets. 2015 rates: $23. May 17 to Oct 31. (780)623-5235

LAKELAND PROVINCIAL RECREATION AREA (TOUCHWOOD LAKE CAMPGROUND) (Prov Pk) From town: Go 12-3/4 km/8 mi E on Secondary Hwy 881, then 29-1/2 km/18-1/2 mi E. Pit toilets. 2015 rates: $23. May 17 to Oct 31. (780)623-5235

SIR WINSTON CHURCHILL (Prov Pk) From town, N 6 mi on Hwy 881 (L). 2015 rates: $29. May 7 to Oct 13. (780)623-4144

LAC LA NONNE — B3 *Lac Ste Anne*

ELKS BEACH (Public) From Jct of Hwy 33 & Secondary Hwy 651, E 2 mi on Secondary Hwy 651 to Elks Beach Rd, S 1.5 mi (R). 2015 rates: $12 to $18. May 1 to Oct 10. (780)967-5029

LAKE LOUISE — D2 *Improvement District No. 9 Banff*

BANFF/LAKE LOUISE-TRAILER PARK (Natl Pk) From Jct TCH 1 & Whitehorn Rd exit, W 0.7 mi on Whitehorn Rd (becomes Lake Louise Dr) to Fairview Rd, S .80 mi (E). 2015 rates: $32.30. (403)762-1550

BANFF/MOSQUITO CREEK (Natl Pk) At Milepost 14.5 on Banff Rte 93 (Icefields Pkwy) (L). Pit toilets. 2015 rates: $17.60. May 16 to Oct 14. (403)762-1550

BANFF/PROTECTION MOUNTAIN (Natl Pk) At Jct of Hwy 1A & TCH 1 W 25 mi on Hwy 1A (Bow Valley Pkwy) (R). 2015 rates: $21.50. Jun 27 to Sep 1. (403)762-1550

BANFF/RAMPART CREEK (Natl Pk) From Jct of TCH 1 & Hwy 93, N 55 mi on Hwy 93 (Icefields Pkwy) to park access rd (E). Pit toilets. 2015 rates: $17.60. Jun 6 to Oct 14. (403)762-1550

LEDUC — C4 *Leduc*

LEDUC LIONS CLUB RV PARK & CAMPGROUND (Public) From Jct of Hwy 2 & 50th St (Exit 519), S 2.4 mi on 50th St to Rollyview Rd, E 1.2 mi to Lions Park Rd, N 0.3 mi (L). 2015 rates: $33 to $44. Apr 15 to Oct 15. (780)986-1882

LETHBRIDGE — E4 *Lethbridge*

LETHBRIDGE See also Magrath & Stirling.

BRIDGEVIEW RV RESORT **Ratings: 9.5/10★/8.5** (RV Park) 2015 rates: $48 to $70. (403)381-2357 1501 2nd Avenue, Lethbridge, AB T1J 4S5

PARK LAKE (Prov Pk) From town, W 3 mi on Crows Nest #3 to Picture Butte exit, N 3 mi, follow signs (L). Pit toilets. 2015 rates: $21 to $27. May 12 to Oct 31. (403)382-4097

LODGEPOLE — C3 *Brazeau*

BRAZEAU RESERVOIR PROVINCIAL RECREATION AREA (Prov Pk) From town: Go 24-3/4 km/15-1/2 mi SW on Hwy 620. Pit toilets. 2015 rates: $23 to $29. May 1 to Oct 13. (780)894-0006

LONGVIEW — E3 *Foothills No. 31*

CATARACT CREEK PROVINCIAL REC. AREA (Prov Pk) From jct Hwy 22 & Hwy 541: Go 44 km/26-1/2 mi W on Hwy 541, then 15 km/9 mi S on Hwy 940 Secondary (gravel road). Pit toilets. 2015 rates: $23. May 15 to Sep 2. (403)591-7226

ETHERINGTON CREEK (Prov Pk) From jct Hwy 22 & Hwy 541: Go 44 km/26-1/2 mi W on Hwy 541, then 7.6 km/4-1/2 mi S on Hwy 940 Secondary (gravel road). Pit toilets. 2015 rates: $23. May 15 to Oct 14. (403)591-7226

GREENFORD PROVINCIAL REC AREA (Prov Pk) From jct Hwy 22 & Hwy 541: Go 24 km/15 mi W on Hwy 541. Pit toilets. 2015 rates: $23. May 15 to Sep 2. (403)591-7226

LUNDBRECK — E3 *Pincher Creek No. 9*

LUNDBRECK FALLS PROVINCIAL REC. AREA (Prov Pk) From town: Go 1-1/2 km/1 mi W on Hwy 3, then follow signs. Pit toilets. 2015 rates: $20 to $24. May 1 to Oct 14. (403)563-5395

MAGRATH — F4 *Cardston*

COVERED WAGON RV PARK
Ratings: 8/9★/9 (RV Park) From Jct of Hwy 5 & SR-62, S 1.1 mi (2 km) on SR-62 to 2nd Ave S, W 0.2 mi to 2nd St W, S 0.4 mi (0.6km) to 5th Ave S, W 330 ft (L). Elev 3215 ft. **FAC:** Gravel rds. (59 spaces). 34 Avail: 7 gravel, 27 grass, patios, 9 pull-thrus (25 x 68), back-ins (25 x 50), 23 full hkups, 8 W, 11 E (30/50 amps), seasonal sites, WiFi, tent sites, rentals, showers $, dump, laundry, fire rings, firewood. **REC:** Pothole Creek: fishing, playground. Pets OK. Big rig sites, eco-friendly, 2015 rates: $25 to $37. Apr 1 to Oct 31.
(403)758-3572 Lat: 49.40674, Lon: -112.87333
234 W 5th Avenue South, Magrath, AB T0K 1J0
info@coveredwagon.ca
www.coveredwagon.ca
See ad this page, 1354.

MARWAYNE — C5 *Vermillion River*

MARWAYNE CHAMBER OF COMMERCE CAMPGROUND JUBILEE REGIONAL PARK (Public) From Jct of Hwys 16 & 897, N 10 mi on Hwy 897 (L). 2015 rates: $20 to $25. (780)847-2273

MCLENNAN — A2 *Smoky River*

WINAGAMI LAKE (Prov Pk) From Jct of PR-2 & PR-679, E 7 mi on PR-679 (L). Pit toilets. 2015 rates: $24 to $30. May 1 to Oct 13. (780)523-0041

MEDICINE HAT — E5 *Cypress, Medicine Hat*

CYPRESS HILLS PROVINCIAL PARK (Prov Pk) From Jct of TCH 1 & DR-41, S 21 mi on DR-41 (R). 2015 rates: $18 to $41. (403)893-3833

GAS CITY CAMPGROUND (Public) From Jct of Hwy 1 W & 7th St SW, W 1 mi on 7th St SW (R). 2015 rates: $28.45 to $49.25. May 12 to Sep 30. (403)529-8158

ROSS CREEK RV PARK LTD **Ratings: 4.5/NA/5.5** (RV Park) Pit toilets. 2015 rates: $38 to $45. Apr 1 to Oct 15. (403)526-5809 2990 54th St SE, Medicine Hat, AB T1B 0N2

MILK RIVER — F4 *Warner County No. 5*

UNDER EIGHT FLAGS CAMPGROUND (Public) From jct Hwy 501 & Hwy 4: Go .4 km/1/4 mi S on Hwy 4. 2015 rates: $15 to $25.

WRITING-ON-STONE PROVINCIAL PARK (Prov Pk) From town: Go 32 km/20 mi E on Hwy 501, then 10 km/6 mi S on local access road. 2015 rates: $21 to $27. (403)647-2364

MILLARVILLE — E3 *Foothills No. 31*

MESA BUTTE PROVINCIAL REC. AREA (Prov Pk) From jct Hwy 22 & Hwy 549 (secondary): Go 15 km/9.3 mi W on Hwy 549 (Equestrian Camping). Pit toilets. 2015 rates: $29. May 15 to Sep 15. (403)949-3132

NORTH FORK PROV. REC. AREA (Prov Pk) From jct Hwy 22 & Hwy 549 (secondary): Go 13 km/8 mi W on Hwy 549. Pit toilets. 2015 rates: $23. May 15 to Sep 15. (403)949-3132

MIRROR — C4 *Lacombe*

THE NARROWS PROVINCIAL REC. AREA (Prov Pk) From town: Go 3 km/1-3/4 mi S on Hwy 21, then 3 km/1-3/4 mi E and 1 km/1/2 mi N on access roads. Pit toilets. 2015 rates: $21. May 15 to Oct 14. (403)742-4338

MORINVILLE — C4 *Sturgeon*

MORINVILLE RV PARK **Ratings: 6/6.5★/6.5** (Campground) 2015 rates: $43 to $44. Apr 15 to Oct 15. (780)939-6040 55529 Range Rd 254, Morinville, AB T8R 1R9

MOSSLEIGH — E4 *Vulcan*

ASPEN CROSSING **Ratings: 6/9.5/10** (RV Park) 2015 rates: $26 to $46. Apr 1 to Oct 31. (866)440-3500 203079 Range Rd 251, Mossleigh, AB T0L 1P0

NANTON — E3 *Willow Creek No. 26*

CHAIN LAKES PROVINCIAL PARK (Prov Pk) From Jct of Hwy 2 & Hwy 533, W 25 mi on Hwy 533 (R). Pit toilets. 2015 rates: $19 to $26. (403)382-4097

INDIAN GRAVES PROVINCIAL RECREATION AREA (Prov Pk) From town: Go 38-1/2 km/24 mi W on Hwy 533, then 11-1/4 km/7 mi N on Hwy 22, then 12-3/4 km/8 mi W on Hwy 532. Pit toilets. 2015 rates: $23. May 17 to Set 28. (403)995-5554

NEW SAREPTA — C4 *Leduc*

JOSEPH LAKE CENTENNIAL (LEDUC COUNTY PARK) (Public) From jct Hwy 21 & Twp Rd 500: Go 7 km/4-1/4 mi E on Twp Rd 500. 2015 rates: $23 to $27. May 18 to Sep 7. (780)941-2124

NORDEGG — C2 *Clearwater*

FISH LAKE (Prov Pk) From town, W 3 mi on Hwy 11 (L). Pit toilets. 2015 rates: $29 to $35. May 1 to Oct 13. (403)721-3975

GOLDEYE LAKE PRA (Prov Pk) From town, W 7 mi on Hwy 11 (R). 2015 rates: $29. May 1 to Oct 14. (403)721-3975

RAM FALLS PROVINCIAL RECREATION AREA (Prov Pk) From town: Go 64 km/40 mi S on Hwy 940. Pit toilets. 2015 rates: $23. May 1 to Oct 13. (403)845-8349

THOMPSON CREEK (Prov Pk) From town, W 54 mi on Hwy 11 (L). Pit toilets. 2015 rates: $24. May 1 to Oct 14. (855)721-3975

TWO O'CLOCK CREEK (Public Corps) From town, W 41.5 mi on Hwy 11 (R). Pit toilets. 2015 rates: $24. May 1 to Nov 26. (855)721-3975

UPPER SHUNDA CREEK CAMPGROUND (Public) From town, W 1.5 mi on Hwy 11 (R) Note: 30' RV length limit. Pit toilets. 2015 rates: $17 to $20. May 1 to Sep 30. (403)845-8250

OKOTOKS — E3 *Calgary*

OKOTOKS LIONS SHEEP RIVER CAMPGROUND **Ratings: 5.5/9.5★/8** (RV Park) 2015 rates: $38. May 1 to Sep 30. (403)938-4282 99 Woodhaven Dr, Okotoks, AB T1S 2L2

OLDS — D3 *Mountain View*

O.R. HEDGES (LIONS) CAMPGROUND (Public) From jct Hwy 2A & Hwy 27 (46 St): Go 3 blocks W on Hwy 27 (46 St), then 5 blocks S on 50th Ave, then 1 block W on 54th St. 2015 rates: $15 to $28. (403)556-2299

WESTWARD HO PARK & CAMPGROUND (Public) From town, W 18 mi on Hwy 27 (L). 2015 rates: $20. (403)556-2568

ONOWAY — C3 *Lac Ste Anne*

MEMORY LANE CAMPGROUND
Ratings: 5.5/9.5★/8 (Campground) From Hwy 642 & Range Road 13, N 3 mi 5 km on Range Road 13 (R). **FAC:** Gravel rds. 45 gravel, 1 pull-thrus (40 x 130), back-ins (35 x 65), 45 full hkups (30/50 amps), tent sites, showers $, groc, LP gas, fire rings, firewood, controlled access. **REC:** pond, fishing, playground. Pet restrict Eco-friendly, 2015 rates: $35. May 1 to Sep 30.
(780)995-5555 Lat: 53.850303, Lon: -114.072518
56401 Range Road 13, Onoway, AB T0E 1V0
memorylanecampground@hotmail.ca
www.memorylanecampground.ca
See ad this page, 1354.

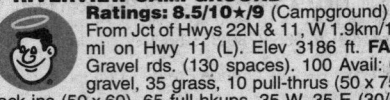

OYEN — D5 *Special Area No. 3*

OYEN CENTENNIAL PARK (TOWN PARK) (Public) From jct Hwy 9 & Hwy 41: Go 3 km/1-3/4 mi S on Hwy 41, then 3 blocks on West Frontage Rd. 2015 rates: $25. (403)664-9711

PEACE POINT — B4 *Peace Point Indian Reserve 222*

WOOD BUFFALO/PINE LAKE CAMPGROUND (Natl Pk) From Fort Smith, Northwest Terr: Go 2 km/1-1/4 mi E on Hwy 5, then 57 km/35-1/4 mi S on Pine Lake Rd into Alberta, then W into Pine Lake. Approx. 55 km/34 mi N of Peace Point, AB. Pit toilets. 2015 rates: $15.70. May 17 to Sep 7. (867)872-7900

PEACE RIVER — A2 *Saddle Hills*

PEACE RIVER LIONS PINES CAMPSITE
Ratings: 7/7.5★/5 (Campground) From jct Hwy 2 & Hwy 684 (Shaftsbury Trail South exit): Go SE 550 m/600 yds SE on Hwy 684. (L). **FAC:** Paved rds. (104 spaces). Avail: 48 gravel, 10 pull-thrus (25 x 40), back-ins (25 x 40), 36 full hkups, 12 W, 12 E (15/30 amps), seasonal sites, WiFi, tent sites, showers $, dump, laundry, LP bottles, fire rings, firewood. **REC:** playground. Pets OK. 2015 rates: $25 to $30. Apr 1 to Nov 1.
(780)624-2120 Lat: 56.234286, Lon: -117.313070
8700-100 Ave, Peace River, AB T8S 1R8
See ad this page.

STRONG CREEK PARK (MUNICIPAL PARK) (Public) From town: Go 12-3/4 km/8 mi S on Shaftsbury Trail (Secondary 684). Pit toilets. (780)338-3845

PENHOLD — D3 *Red Deer*

A-SOO-WUH-UM CAMPGROUND (RED DEER COUNTY PARK) (Public) From jct Hwy 2 & Hwy 42 W: Go 3.5 km/2.2 mi W on Hwy 42, then 6.5 km/4 mi W on Secondary Hwy 592. May 1 to Oct 15. (403)886-2001

PINCHER CREEK — E3 *Pincher Creek No. 9*

BEAUVAIS LAKE PROVINCIAL PARK (Prov Pk) From town, W 8 mi on Hwy 507 to Hwy 775, S 5 mi (L). Pit toilets. 2015 rates: $18 to $26. (403)627-2021

RED DEER — D3 *Red Deer*

LION'S CAMPGROUND-WASKASOO PARK (Public) From Jct of Hwy 2 & 67th St (Exit 401), E 2.1 mi on 67th St to Riverside Dr, S 0.5 mi (L). 2015 rates: $27 to $37. May 1 to Sep 30. (403)342-8183

WESTERNER CAMPGROUND **Ratings: 6.5/9.5★/8.5** (RV Park) 2015 rates: $43 to $ 46. (403)352-8801 4847D 19 St, Red Deer, AB T4R 2N7

REDCLIFF — E5 *Cypress*

REDCLIFF CAMPGROUND (CITY PARK) (Public) From jct Trans Canada Hwy 1 & Broadway Ave: Go 6 blocks W on Broadway to 3rd St SW. 2015 rates: $21 to $26.25. (403)548-9253

RV Park ratings you can rely on!

ROBB — C2 *Yellowhead*

FAIRFAX LAKE PROVINCIAL RECREATION AREA (Prov Pk) From jct Hwy 47 & Hwy 40: Go 45-1/2 km/28-1/2 mi SE on Hwy 40. Pit toilets. 2015 rates: $11. May 1 to Sep 30. (780)865-2154

ROCKY MOUNTAIN HOUSE — D3 *Clearwater*

ASPEN CAMPGROUND (TOWN PARK) (Public) From jct Hwy 11 & Hwy 11A: Go 3/4 km/1/2 mi N on Hwy 11. May 15 to Sep 15. (403)845-2866

CHAMBERS CREEK PROVINCIAL RECREATION AREA (Public Corps) From town, W 15 mi on Hwy 11 (L). Pit toilets. 2015 rates: $29. May 1 to Oct 14. (403)721-3975

CRIMSON LAKE PROVINCIAL PARK (Prov Pk) From town, W 5 mi on Hwy 11 to Hwy 756, N 4 mi (L). 2015 rates: $23 to $29. (403)845-2330

MEDICINE LAKE PROVINCIAL RECREATION AREA (Prov Pk) From town: Go 47 km/31 mi N on Hwy 22, then 8 km SE on access road. Pit toilets. 2015 rates: $28. May 1 to Oct 13. (780)388-2223

NEW OLD TOWN COTTAGES & RV PARK **Ratings: 3.5/6.5/7.5** (Campground) 2015 rates: $36.75. Apr 1 to Oct 15. (403)844-4442 4203 62 St, Rocky Mountain House, AB T4T 1B3

RIVERVIEW CAMPGROUND
Ratings: 8.5/10★/9 (Campground) From Jct of Hwys 22N & 11, W 1.9km/1.2 mi on Hwy 11 (L). Elev 3186 ft. **FAC:** Gravel rds. (130 spaces). 100 Avail: 65 gravel, 35 grass, 10 pull-thrus (50 x 75), back-ins (50 x 60), 65 full hkups, 35 W, 35 E (30/50 amps), seasonal sites, WiFi, tent sites, rentals, showers $, dump, mobile sewer, laundry, fire rings, firewood, controlled access. **REC:** North Saskatchewan River: swim, fishing, playground. Pet restrict(B/Q). Partial handicap access. Eco-friendly, 2015 rates: $36 to $38. Disc: AAA.
AAA Approved
(403)845-4422 Lat: 52.407674, Lon: -114.953577
400009 Range Rd 7-3A, Rocky Mountain House, AB T4T 2A4
riverviewcampground@telus.net
www.riverview-campground.com
See ad this page, 1354.

STRACHAN PROVINCIAL REC AREA (Prov Pk) From town, SW 15 mi on Hwy 752 (R). Pit toilets. 2015 rates: $23. May 1 to Oct 13. (403)845-8349

TWIN LAKES (Prov Pk) From town: Go 12 km/7-1/2 mi W on Hwy 11, then 2 km/1.2 mi N on Hwy 756. Pit toilets. 2015 rates: $23. May 1 to Oct 14. (403)845-2330

WILDERNESS VILLAGE RESORT **Ratings: 8/10★/9** (RV Park) 2015 rates: $70. May 1 to Oct 15. (403)845-2145 se-14-40-08-W5, Rocky Mountain House, AB T4T 1A9

RYCROFT — A1 *Spirit River*

NARDAM RV PARK (Public) From Jct of Hwy 2 & Hwy 49: Go W 1 mi (1.6 km) on Hwy 49, then 1000 ft (300 meters) on Range Road 54 (L). 2015 rates: $25. May 15 to Oct 15. (780)864-8286

SEDGEWICK — C4 *Flagstaff*

SEDGEWICK LAKE CAMPGROUND (Public) From town, N 0.5 mi on Hwy 13 (R). 2015 rates: $20 to $30. May 1 to Sep 30. (780)384-2256

SHERWOOD PARK — C4 *Strathcona*

HALF MOON LAKE RESORT **Ratings: 7.5/5.5/7.5** (Campground) 2015 rates: $44 to $49. May 15 to Oct 15. (780)922-3045 21524 Twp Rd 520, Sherwood Park, AB T8E 1E5

SLAVE LAKE — B3 *Lesser Slave River No. 124*

LESSER SLAVE LAKE/MARTEN RIVER CAMPGROUND (Prov Pk) From Jct of Hwys 2 & 88, N 20.5 mi on Hwy 88 to park access rd, SW 3 mi (E). 2015 rates: $23 to $29. May 14 to Oct 15. (780)849-7100

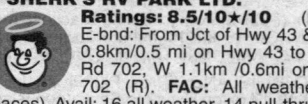

SMOKY LAKE — B4 *Smoky Lake*

HANMORE LAKE CAMPGROUND (Public) From jct Hwy 28 & Hwy 855 (Secondary): Go 17.6 km/11 mi N on Hwy 855, then 3.2 km/2 mi W on access road. Pit toilets. 2015 rates: $15. (780)383-2263

SPEDDEN — B4 *Smoky Lake*

GARNER LAKE PROVINCIAL PARK (Prov Pk) From Hwy 28 in town: Go 4-3/4 km/3 mi N on paved road. 2015 rates: $23 to $29. May 14 to Oct 14. (780)594-7856

SPIRIT RIVER — A1 *Spirit River No. 133*

MOONSHINE LAKE (Prov Pk) From town, W 19 mi on Hwy 49 to Hwy 725, N 3 mi (L). 2015 rates: $24 to $30. May 1 to Oct 13. (780)538-5350

SPRING LAKE — C3 *Parkland*

SPRING LAKE RV RESORT **Ratings: 7/7.5/8.5** (Campground) 2015 rates: $42 to $56. May 1 to Sep 30. (780)963-3993 499 Lakeside Dr., Spring Lake, AB T7Z 2V5

ST ALBERT — C4 *Sturgeon*

KINSMEN RV PARK
Ratings: 8/10★/10 (RV Park) From Jct of Hwy 16 (Yellowhead Hwy) & Hwy 216 (Anthony Henday Dr): NE 1.5km/.9 mi on Hwy 216 (Anthony Henday Dr) to Ray Gibbon Dr (Exit 27), N 2.3km/1.4 mi to LeClair Way, E 0.3km/0.2 mi to Riel Dr, N 1.3km/.8 mi (E). **FAC:** Paved rds. 93 Avail: 93 all weather, 33 pull-thrus (30 x 72), back-ins (30 x 64), 93 full hkups (50 amps), WiFi. **REC:** playground. Pet restrict(B). Partial handicap access, no tents. Big rig sites, RV age restrict, eco-friendly, 2015 rates: $48. May 1 to Oct 1.
(888)459-1724 Lat: 53.620525, Lon: -113.651094
47 Riel Dr., St Albert, AB T8N 3Z2
host@sakin.ca
www.stalbertrvpark.ca
See ad pages 1355 (Spotlight Edmonton), 1354.

ST PAUL — B5 *St Paul County No. 19*

ST PAUL OVERNIGHT CAMPGROUND (TOWN PARK) (Public) In town, from west end at jct Hwy 28 & 55th St: Go 1 block S. 2015 rates: $15 to $20. May 15 to Sep 23. (780)645-5313

WESTCOVE MUNICIPAL RECREATION AREA (Public) From jct Hwy 28 & 50th St: Go 8 km/5 mi N, then follow signs. 2015 rates: $20 to $25. May 11 to Aug 28. (780)645-6688

STETTLER — D4 *West End*

BUFFALO LAKE PROVINCIAL RECREATION AREA (Prov Pk) From town: Go 20-3/4 km/13 mi N on Hwy 56, then 6-3/4 km/4-1/4 mi W on access road. Pit toilets. 2015 rates: $20. May 15 to Sep 15. (403)742-9575

OL' MACDONALD'S RESORT **Ratings: 7/6/7.5** (RV Park) 2015 rates: $25 to $50. May 15 to Sep 15. (403)742-6603 sw 15-40-21 West of 4, Erskine, AB T0C 1G0

STETTLER LIONS CAMPGROUND (Public) From Jct of Hwys 56 & 12, W 0.5 mi on Hwy 12 to 62nd St, S 0.3 mi (L). 2015 rates: $20 to $28. (403)742-4411

STETTLER ROTARY PARK (Public) From Jct of SR-12 & SR-56, S 0.3 mi on SR-56 to 45th Ave, E 0.05 mi (R). 2015 rates: $10 to $12. (403)740-6425

TOWN OF STETTLER CAMPGROUND (Public) From jct Hwy 12 (50th Ave) W & 62nd St: Go 2 blocks S.

STIRLING — E4 *Warner County No. 5*

CENTENNIAL REUNION SQUARE (VILLAGE PARK) (Public) From jct Hwy 4 & Stirling turnoff: Go 3/4 km/1/2 mi S, then 3/4 km/1/2 mi W on 4th Ave. 2015 rates: $25. (403)756-3379

STONY PLAIN — C3 *Parkland*

CAMP 'N CLASS RV PARK
Ratings: 8/10★/10 (Campground) E-Bnd: From Jct of Hwy 16 & Hwy 16A (Exit 344), SE 10.3 km/6.4 mi on Hwy 16A Bear right onto Service Rd. 0.8 km/0.5 mi to 50th St, S 210m/230 yds (L). W-Bnd: From Jct Hwy 16A & Stony Plain Overpass(Rd 779), S 0.6km/0.4mi on Rd 779 to 44th Ave, W395m/433 yds to 50th St, N 376m/412 yds (R). **FAC:** Paved rds. 77 Avail: 77 all weather, patios, 33 pull-thrus (30 x 70), back-ins (30 x 60), 77 full hkups (30/50 amps), cable, WiFi, showers $, laundry, controlled access. **REC.** Pet restrict(B/Q) $. Partial handicap access, no tents. Big rig sites, RV age restrict, eco-friendly, 2015 rates: $52.
(855)455-2299 Lat: 53.539294, Lon: -114.007909
4107 50 Street, Stony Plain, AB T7Z 1L5
info@campinclass.com
www.campinclass.com
See ad pages 1355 (Spotlight Edmonton), 1354.

Say you saw it in our Guide!

STONY PLAIN LION'S CAMPGROUND **Ratings: 5.5/8.5★/7** (Campground) 2015 rates: $35. Apr 15 to Oct 15. (780)963-4505 #9 Granite Drive, Stony Plain, AB T7Z 1V8

STRATHMORE — D4 *Calgary, Wheatland*

EAGLE LAKE RV RESORT **Ratings: 6/6/7** (Campground) 2015 rates: $38 to $45. May 8 to Sep 13. (403)934-4283 234036 Range Rd 243, Strathmore, AB T1P 1J6

SUNDRE — D3 *Mountain View*

COYOTE CREEK GOLF & RV RESORT **Ratings: 8.5/10★/10** (RV Park) 2015 rates: $43. (403)638-1215 32351 Range Rd 55, Sundre, AB T0M 1X0

GREENWOOD CAMPGROUND (TOWN PARK) (Public) From jct Hwy 22 (Main Ave) & Center St: Go 2 blocks S on Center St. 2015 rates: $20 to $30. May 18 to Sep 7. (403)638-2130

WAGONS WEST RV PARK & STORAGE
Ratings: 6/9.5/9.5 (Campground) From Jct of Hwy 22 & Hwy 584, W 0.5mi/0.8km on Hwy 584 to 5446/Hwy 584 (R). Elev 3694 ft. **FAC:** Gravel rds. (62 spaces). Avail: 43 gravel, 1 pull-thrus (25 x 110), back-ins (30 x 60), 43 full hkups (30 amps), seasonal sites, WiFi Hotspot, tent sites, showers $, dump, laundry, LP bottles, fire rings, firewood, controlled access. **REC:** playground. Pets OK. Partial handicap access. Eco-friendly, 2015 rates: $33.
(403)638-4402 Lat: 51.796309, Lon: -114.676409
103 5446 Hwy 584, Site 103, Sundre, AB T0M 1X0
info@wagonswestrvpark.com
www.wagonswestrvpark.com

SYLVAN LAKE — D3 *Red Deer*

JARVIS BAY (Prov Pk) From town, N 3 mi on Hwy 20 (L). 2015 rates: $23 to $29. May 14 to Oct 13. (403)887-5522

TABER — E4 *Taber*

M.D. OF TABER MUNICIPAL PARK (Public) From jct Hwy 3 & Hwy 864: Go 2-3/4 km/1-3/4 mi N on Hwy 864. 2015 rates: $25 to $30. Apr 15 to Oct 30. (403)223-0091

THREE HILLS — D4 *Kneehill*

KEIVER'S LAKE REC PARK (Public) From Jct of Hwy 21 & Hwy 583, W 11 mi on Hwy 583 to Keiver's Rd, S 1 mi (R). 2015 rates: $20. May 17 to Sep 30. (866)443-5541

TOFIELD — C4 *Beaver*

LINDBROOK STAR GAZER CAMPGROUND & RV PARK **Ratings: 6.5/8.5/8** (RV Park) 2015 rates: $39 to $44. May 15 to Oct 1. (780)662-4439 51123 Range Rd 200, Tofield, AB T0B 4J0

TROCHU — D4 *Kneehill*

TOLMAN BRIDGE REC. AREA (Prov Pk) From town: Go 20 km/13-1/2 mi E on Hwy 585. Pit toilets. (403)442-4211

TURNER VALLEY — E3 *Foothills No. 31*

BLUEROCK CAMPGROUND (Public) From jct Hwy 22 & Hwy 546: Go 36.6 km/22 mi W on Hwy 546. Pit toilets. 2015 rates: $23 to $29. May 15 to Sep 21. (403)949-4261

HELL'S HALF ACRE CAMPGROUND (Public) From Jct of Hwy 2 & Hwy 22, S 24 mi on Hwy 22 (L). 2015 rates: $20 to $24. May to Oct. (403)993-8538

SANDY MCNABB (Prov Pk) From jct Hwy 22 & Hwy 546: Go 20 km/12.5 mi W on Hwy 546. 2015 rates: $29. May 1 to Oct 13. (403)949-3132

TWO HILLS — C4 *Two Hills County No. 21*

SANDY LAKE RECREATION PARK (TWO HILLS COUNTY PARK) (Public) From jct Hwy 861 & Hwy 45: Go 4.8 km/3 mi E on Hwy 45, then 12.8 km/8 mi N on Hwy 831. 2015 rates: $12 to $16. May to Sep. (780)768-2330

Don't miss the best part! Look in the front of most state sections for articles that focus on areas of special interest to RVers. These "Spotlights" tell you about interesting tourist destinations you might otherwise miss.

VALLEYVIEW — B2 *Greenview*

SHERK'S RV PARK LTD.
Ratings: 8.5/10★/10 (RV Park) E-bnd: From Jct of Hwy 43 & Hwy 49, S 0.8km/0.5 mi on Hwy 43 to Twp Range Rd 702, W 1.1km /0.6mi on Range Rd 702 (R). **FAC:** All weather rds. (56 spaces). Avail: 16 all weather, 14 pull-thrus (35 x 80), back-ins (35 x 65), 16 full hkups (15/30 amps), seasonal sites, WiFi, tent sites, showers $, laundry, fire rings, firewood. **REC:** playground. Pets OK. Partial handicap access. Eco-friendly, 2015 rates: $42. Disc: AAA. May 1 to Sep 30.
(780)524-4949 Lat: 55.05491, Lon: -117.29852
22362 Township Road 702, Valleyview, AB T0H 3N0
www.sherksrvpark.com
See ad this page, 1354.

WILLIAMSON (Prov Pk) From town, W 10.5 mi on Hwy 43 to access rd, N 1 mi (L). Pit toilets. 2015 rates: $24 to $30. May 1 to Oct 13. (780)538-5350

YOUNG'S POINT (Prov Pk) From town, W 16 mi on Hwy 43 to park access rd, N 6.25 mi (E). 2015 rates: $24 to $30. May 1 to Oct 15. (780)538-5350

VEGREVILLE — C4 *Minburn*

VEGREVILLE MUNICIPAL CAMPGROUND (Public) From Jct of PR-16 & 43rd St, N 0.1 mi on 43rd St (R). 2015 rates: $23 to $25. May 1 to Sep 1. (780)632-6800

VERMILION — C5 *Wainwright*

VERMILION (Prov Pk) From Jct of Hwys 16 & 41 (in town), N 1 mi on Hwy 41 to 50th Ave, W 1.5 mi on entrance rd, N 0.25 mi (R). 2015 rates: $23 to $41. (780)853-4372

WABAMUN — C3 *Parkland*

WABAMUN LAKE (Prov Pk) From Jct of Hwys 16 & 30, S 0.5 mi on Hwy 30 (R) Note: 49' RV length limit. 2015 rates: $23 to $29. May 1 to Oct 31. (780)892-2702

WABASCA-DESMARAIS — A3 *Opportunity No. 17*

WABASCA LIONS CLUB CAMPGROUND (Public) From town: At 4 way stop, go 15 km/9 mi N following Mistassiniy Rd N. Pit toilets. 2015 rates: $20. May 15 to Sep 15. (780)891-2093

WAINWRIGHT — C5 *Wainwright*

DR MIDDLEMASS CAMPGROUND (Public) From Jct of Hwy 14 & 15th St, S 0.4 mi on 15th St (L). 2015 rates: $32. May 1 to Oct 15. (780)842-3541

RIVERDALE MINI PARK (MUNICIPAL PARK) (Public) From jct Hwy 14 & Hwy 41: Go 17 km/10-1/2 mi N on Hwy 41. 2015 rates: $12 to $24. May 1 to Sep 30. (780)842-2996

WATERTON LAKES — F3 *Improvement District No. 4 Waterton*

WATERTON LAKES/CRANDELL MOUNTAIN (Natl Pk) From Jct PR-6 & PR-5, SW 2.5 mi on PR-5 to Red Rock Canyon Rd, NE 5 mi (L). 2015 rates: $21.50. May 15 to Sep 1. (403)859-5133

WATERTON PARK — F3 *Cardston*

WATERTON LAKES/BELLY RIVER (Natl Pk) From Jct of PR-6 & PR-5, W 1 mi on PR-5/6, S 10 mi on PR-6 (R). 2015 rates: $15.70 to $38.20. May 10 to Sep 10. (403)859-5133

WATERTON LAKES/TOWNSITE (Natl Pk) From Jct of PR-6 & PR-5, SW 5 mi on PR-5 (R). 2015 rates: $22.50 to $38.20. May 10 to Oct 15. (403)859-5133

WATERTON SPRINGS CAMPGROUND **Ratings: 6.5/8/6.5** (Campground) 2015 rates: $32 to $35. May 1 to Sep 30. (403)859-2247 hwy 6 & Waterton Park Boundary, Waterton Park, AB T0K 2M0

Tell your RV Campground that you found them in this Guide.

WEMBLEY — B1 *Grande Prairie County No. 1*

PIPESTONE CREEK PARK (GRANDE PRAIRIE COUNTY #1) (Public) From jct Hwy 2 & access road into Wembley: Go 16 km/10 mi S following signs. 2015 rates: $20. May 15 to Oct 15. (780)766-2391

SASKATOON ISLAND (Prov Pk) From Jct of Hwys 34 & 2, W 17 mi on Hwy 2 to Saskatoon Island Rd, N 2.5 mi (E). 2015 rates: $24 to $30. May 1 to Oct 15. (780)538-5350

WESTEROSE — C3 *Leduc, Wetaskiwin*

PIGEON LAKE (Prov Pk) From town, W 3 mi on Hwy 13 to Hwy 771, N 4 mi to Park Access Rd, E 0.5 mi (L). 2015 rates: $23 to $29. May 14 to Oct 13. (780)586-2864

PIGEON LAKE/ZEINER CAMPGROUND (Prov Pk) From town, W 3 mi on Hwy 13 to Hwy 771, NW 11 mi (R). Reservations strongly recommended. 2015 rates: $23 to $29. May 14 to Oct 13. (780)586-2644

WESTLOCK — B3 *Westlock*

MOUNTIE PARK CAMPGROUND (Public) From Jct of Hwys 44 & 18, W 1 mi on Hwy 18 (L). 2015 rates: $25 to $27. May 18 to Oct 3. (780)349-4444

WETASKIWIN — C4 *Wetaskiwin*

PRAIRIE BREEZE INN, RV & CAMPING **Ratings: 5/6/7** (Campground) 2015 rates: $28 to $35. May 1 to Oct 31. (780)352-7220 west 1/2 Of NE 9-46-24-W4, Wetaskiwin, AB T9A 1W8

WETASKIWIN LIONS RV CAMPGROUND (Public) From Jct of Hwy 2A & Hwy 13, E 1.7 mi on Hwy 13 (R). 2015 rates: $20 to $33. May 1 to Sep 30. (780)352-7258

WHITECOURT — B3 *Lac Ste Anne*

CARSON/PEGASUS (Prov Pk) From town, W 3 mi on Hwy 43 to Hwy 32, N 7 mi to park access rd, E 3 mi, follow signs (E). 2015 rates: $23 to $29. May 15 to Sep 30. (780)778-2664

EAGLE RIVER TOURISM RV PARK
Ratings: 5/9.5★/8 (Campground) From Jct of Hwy 43 and Hwy 32N: Go N .2 Mi (.3 Km) on Hwy 32 to Township Road 602A, W .1 mi (E). Elev 2635 ft. **FAC:** Gravel/dirt rds. (107 spaces). Avail: 60 gravel, 24 pull-thrus (30 x 75), back-ins (30 x 70), 60 full hkups (30/50 amps), seasonal sites, WiFi, tent sites, dump, laundry, groc, LP bottles, fire rings, firewood, restaurant, controlled access. **REC:** playground. Pet restrict(Q). Partial handicap access. Eco-friendly, 2015 rates: $45 to $50. ATM.
(587)773-2497 Lat: 54.195765, Lon: -115.788436
hwy 43 at Hwy 32N, Whitecourt, AB T7S 2A1
www.eagleriverrv.com

SAGITAWAH RV PARK **Ratings: 5/7.5/7** (RV Park) 2015 rates: $35 to $40. May 15 to Oct 15. (780)778-3734 river Boat Park Rd, Whitecourt, AB T7S 1N9

WHITECOURT LIONS CAMPGROUND
Ratings: 7.5/10★/8.5 (Campground) From Jct of Hwy 43 & Hwy 32: Go E 2.9 mi (5 km) on Hwy 43 to 33rd St, S 0.1 mi (L). **FAC:** Gravel rds. (72 spaces). Avail: 46 gravel, 14 pull-thrus (25 x 70), back-ins (25 x 60), 8 full hkups, 38 W, 38 E (30/50 amps), seasonal sites, WiFi, tent sites, showers $, dump, mobile sewer, laundry, fire rings, firewood, controlled access. **REC:** playground. Pets OK. Partial handicap access. Eco-friendly, 2015 rates: $35 to $39. Apr 15 to Oct 15.
(780)778-6782 Lat: 54.113425, Lon: -115.647659
3001 33 Street, Whitecourt, AB T7S 1P3
wtclionscamp@live.ca
See ad this page, 1354.

Canada — know the rules, regulations and tips before crossing the border. This is listed at the beginning of the country.

BC

Kenneth J Dyck

WELCOME TO British Columbia

JOINED CONFEDERATION JULY 20, 1871	WIDTH: 640 MILES (1,030 KM) LENGTH: 730 MILES (1,180 KM)	PROPORTION OF CANADA 9.46% OF 9,984,670 SQ KM

From high tea and scones in a Victorian dining room to exhilarating outdoor Shakespeare performances, totem poles and epic verticals doused in powder, British Columbia is a feast for the mind, body and soul. The island city of Victoria—the provincial capital—with its quaint harbor, stately government buildings and historic monuments—oozes European charm.

And then there's Vancouver, one of the world's most desirable lifestyle cities. Few places combine the cosmopolitan verve of a modern city with sandy beaches, forests and an outstanding ski resort just two hours away. From the historic streets of Gastown to the salty seafront of Kitsilano and the funky enclave of SoMa, Vancouver is hip, yet unpretentious, a city that balances work and play, the cerebral and the corporeal, with flair. The Sea-to-Sky Highway, a two-lane route carved into the walls of the steep fiord which flanks scenic Howe Sound, rates as one of the world's most spectacular road trips. The scenic highway funnels north from Vancouver to the quaint but effortlessly worldly Whistler Village, which marries an unpretentious vibe with sophisticated shopping and dining.

Learn

For more than 10,000 years, First Nations people lived and flourished on the region's prolific animal, marine and plant life. Coastal tribes like the Haida and Nisga'a were renowned for their intricate Aboriginal art forms, trading skills, tribal nature (they are often compared to the Vikings) and practice of slavery.

Top 3 Tourism Attractions:
1) Stanley Park
2) Butchart Gardens
3) Victoria

Nickname: The Pacific Province

State Flower: Pacific Dogwood

State Bird: Steller's Jay

People: Pamela Anderson, actress; Jason Priestley, actor; Raymond Burr, actor; Margaret Trudeau, former first lady

Major Cities: Vancouver, Surrey, Burnaby, Richmond, Abbotsford, (Victoria, capital)

Topography: Majority of terrain is forested and mountainous; only about 5% is arable

Climate: Most temperate climate in Canada. Temps are warmer in the south and rainfall is heavier on the coast

<No data from link>

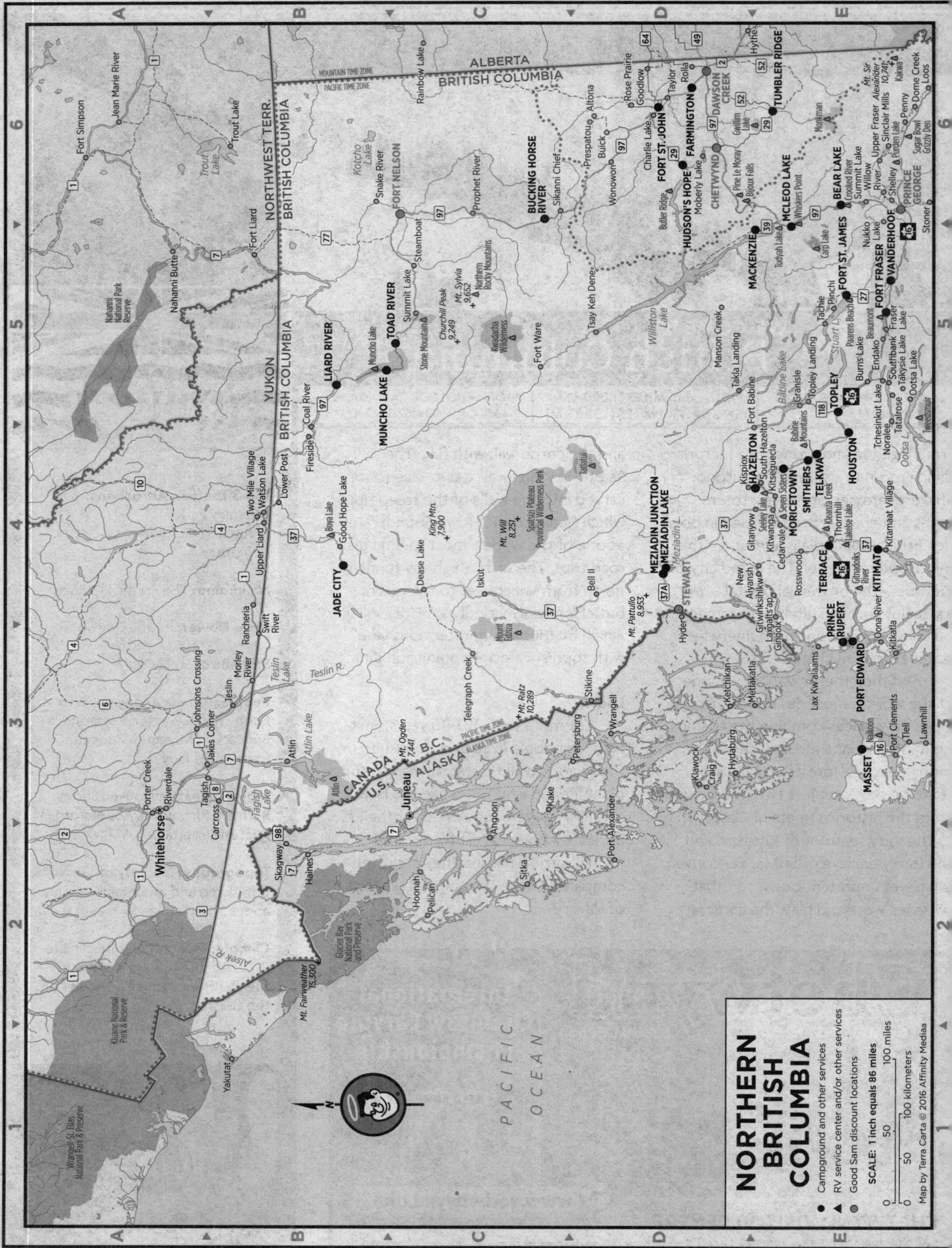
NORTHERN BRITISH COLUMBIA
Campground and other services
RV service center and/or other services
Good Sam discount locations
SCALE: 1 inch equals 86 miles
0 50 100 miles
0 50 100 kilometers
Map by Terra Carta © 2016 Affinity Media
PACIFIC OCEAN
YUKON
BRITISH COLUMBIA
NORTHWEST TERR.
ALBERTA
ALASKA
CANADA
U.S.
B.C.
MOUNTAIN TIME ZONE
PACIFIC TIME ZONE
ALASKA TIME ZONE
Whitehorse
Juneau
Skagway
Haines
Yakutat
Sitka
Petersburg
Wrangell
Ketchikan
Atlin
Teslin
Watson Lake
Fort Nelson
LIARD RIVER
MUNCHO LAKE
TOAD RIVER
JADE CITY
Dease Lake
Iskut
Stewart
Hyder
MEZIADIN JUNCTION
MEZIADIN LAKE
BUCKING HORSE RIVER
FORT ST. JOHN
HUDSON'S HOPE
FARMINGTON
DAWSON CREEK
CHETWYND
TUMBLER RIDGE
MACKENZIE
MCLEOD LAKE
BEAR LAKE
PRINCE GEORGE
FORT ST. JAMES
FORT FRASER
VANDERHOOF
TOPLEY
HOUSTON
TELKWA
SMITHERS
MORICETOWN
HAZELTON
TERRACE
KITIMAT
PRINCE RUPERT
PORT EDWARD
MASSET
Mt. Fairweather 15,300
Mt. Ratz 10,289
Mt. Pattullo 8,953
Mt. Ogden 7,441
Kluane National Park & Reserve
Wrangell-St. Elias National Park & Preserve
Glacier Bay National Park and Preserve
Nahanni National Park Reserve
Spatsizi Plateau Provincial Wilderness Park
Williston Lake
Teslin Lake
Atlin Lake

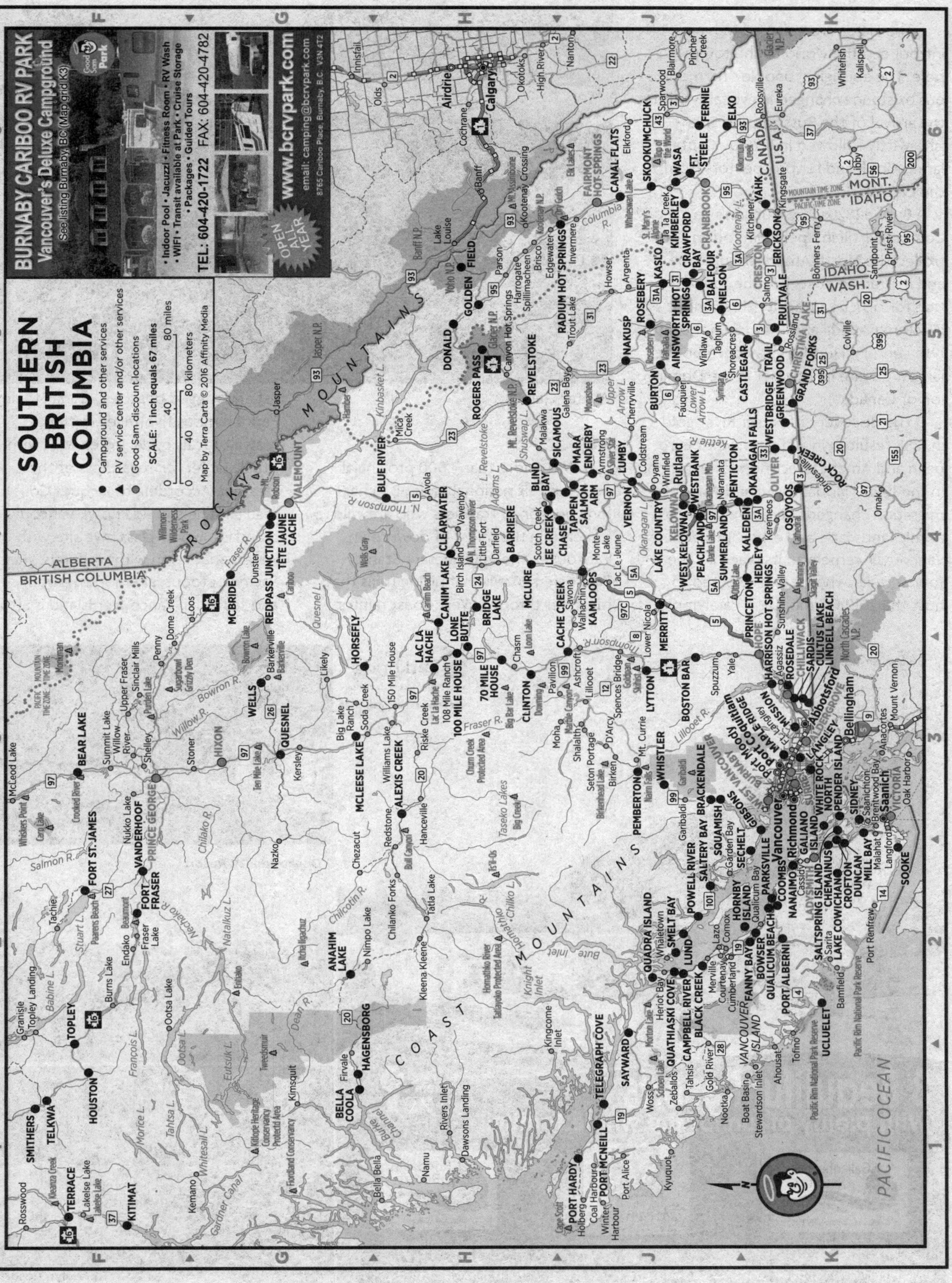
SOUTHERN BRITISH COLUMBIA
Campground and other services
RV service center and/or other services
Good Sam discount locations
SCALE: 1 inch equals 67 miles
40 80 miles
40 80 kilometers
Map by Terra Carta © 2016 Affinity Media
PACIFIC OCEAN
COAST MOUNTAINS
ROCKY MOUNTAINS
ALBERTA
BRITISH COLUMBIA

Vancouver waterfront. HelloBC

The Haida are believed to have introduced the world to the totem pole. The aboriginal people's harmonious existence changed irrevocably with the arrival of the Russians and Spanish, swiftly followed in 1778 by Captain James Cook and fur prospectors from the Old World.

By the 1820s, the Hudson's Bay Company (still in operation today) controlled the North American fur trade, and its trading posts laid the foundation for official authority throughout Western Canada and the U.S. In the late 19th century, Hudson's Bay became the largest private landowner in the Dominion of Canada.

The discovery of Fraser River gold in 1858 resulted in a huge wave of European and American economic migration. In the 1990s, global travel and Asian migration changed the province's economic landscape and ethnic makeup. Vancouver cemented its place on the tourist radar when it was selected to host the 2010 Olympic and Paralympic Winter Games.

Play

With more than 1,000 provincial parks and six national parks, B.C. has long beckoned travelers who are wild of heart. In the midst of downtown Vancouver, the 400-hectare Stanley Park offers 16 miles of hiking trails that meander through West Coast rainforest and rugged beaches. Along Stanley Park's famous five-mile stretch of seawall, locals cycle, jog or walk with ritualistic fervor, regardless of the weather. According to Jacques Cousteau (and he should know), Vancouver Island is a world-class dive site with waters that teem with wolf eels, giant Pacific octopus, anemones, harbor sea and sea lions. Vancouver Island is also the site of HMCS Saskatchewan, British Columbia's most successful artificial reef. The extraordinary Gwaii Haanas National Park, a UNESCO World Heritage Site, occupies around 15 percent of the Queen Charlotte Islands, also known as the "Canadian Galapagos" due to the number of endemic species that have evolved here. In the village of Ninstints, remains of houses along with carved mortuary and totem poles celebrate the cultural richness of the Haida people, who occupied Haida Gwaii for over 17,000 years.

Glacier National Park is a hiker's Shangri La. Carved from the rugged Selkirk and Purcell Mountains by glaciers, over 700 miles of trails crisscross rugged mountains, forests and alpine meadows dotted with Native American sites. A highlight of Glacier, the Nakimu Caves rank as one of Canada's largest cave systems.

With more than 8,100 acres of awe-inspiring ski trails, reliably doused with powdery snow, Whistler delivers more vertical runs and ski lifts than any of its North American peers. During Spring and Summer, Whistler seduces nature enthusiasts with its pristine forests—home to marmots, eagles, bears and wolves—that afford excellent recreational opportunities in the form of rafting, hiking and golfing.

British Columbia's capital city is also one of its most beautiful. Victoria, located on Vancouver Island, is accessible from both British Columbia and Washington by ferry. After reaching the city, rent a carriage and take a tour of this charming and sophisticated town.

Experience

In August, the Victoria Symphony Splash hosts one of the largest annual classical music events in North America. The Victoria Symphony Orchestra performs their concert series from a floating stage in Victoria's Inner Harbor. Recitals reach a crescendo with a performance of the 1812 Overture accompanied by the festival's fireworks.

TRAVEL & TOURISM

Destination British Columbia
800-HELLOBC
www.hellobc.com

BC Ferry Services, Inc.
www.bcferries.com

Cariboo Chilcotin Coast Tourism Association
800-663-5885, 250-392-2838
www.landwithoutlimits.com

Kootenay Rockies Tourism Association
250-427-4838, 800-661-6603
www.kootenayrockies.com

Northern BC
800-663-8843, 250-561-0432
www.northernbctourism.com

Thompson Okanagan Tourism Association
250-860-5999, 800-567-2275
www.thompsonokanagon.com

Vancouver, Coast & Mountains Tourism Region
604-739-9011, 800-667-3306
www.604pulse.com

Tourism Vancouver Island
250-754-3500
www.vancouverisland.travel

Tourism Victoria
800-663-3883
www.tourismvictoria.com

OUTDOOR ADVENTURES

BC Fishing Resorts and Outfitters Association
250-374-6836, 866-374-6836
www.bcfroa.ca

Fisheries and Oceans Canada
604-666-0384
www.pac.dfo-mpo.gc.ca

Ministry of the Environment, Fish and Wildlife Branch
250-387-9771
www.env.gov.bc.ca

Ministry of Water, Land and Air Protection
www.gov.bc.ca

Association of Canadian Mountain Guides
403-678-2885
www.acmg.ca

Outdoor Recreation Council of British Columbia
604-873-5546
www.orcbc.ca

SHOPPING

Sasquatch Trading
250-386-9033
www.cowichantrading.com

The Salt Spring Market
www.saltspringmarket.com

The Sinclair Centre
800-622-6232

- STAY A WHILE -

Chetwynd: A Four Season Outdoor Adventure Destination

Located in the eastern foothills of the Northern Rocky Mountains, Chetwynd offers a unique balance of prairies, mountains, wilderness areas and a full-service community.

The area is well known for its breathtaking scenery and countryside. The surrounding area contains mountains for hiking and skiing. Visitors also will discover lakes and rivers for swimming, canoeing and fishing, and a countryside and park system that provides some of the best camping, snowmobiling, hunting and wildlife spotting in Canada.

The Annual Chetwynd International Chainsaw Carving Championship has visually shaped Chetwynd into a one-of-a-kind locale. Artists from all over the world participate in this unique competition. The District of Chetwynd keeps each intricate carved piece from the championship and places the art throughout the town.

- Spectators can watch the artists carve their creations over the three days from start to finish
- Today, competitors come from as far as Wales and Japan to vie for the title.
- Don't miss the quick carve competition held on Sunday and your chance to bid on a piece at the auction!
- Take a self-guided walking tour
- 120 carvings and more added each year—a must-see!

Chetwynd Visitor Centre
250-788-1943
tourist@gochetwynd.com
www.gochetwynd.com

 See map pages 1368 and 1369

Featured Good Sam Parks

BRITISH COLUMBIA

Good Sam Park

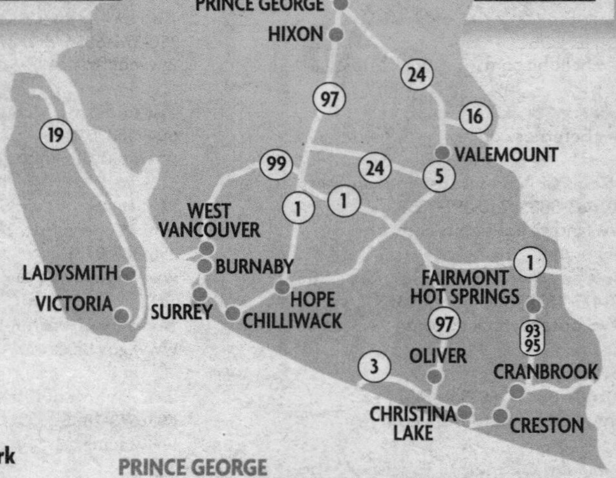

When you stay with Good Sam, you can expect the highest degree of cleanliness and friendliness, and better yet, you get 10% off campground fees.

If you're not already a Good Sam member you can purchase your membership at one of these locations:

BURNABY
Burnaby Cariboo RV Park and Campground
(604)420-1722

CHETWYND
Westwind RV Park
(250)788-2190

CHILLIWACK
Cottonwood Meadows RV Country Club
(604)824-7275

CHRISTINA LAKE
Cascade Cove RV Park & Campground
(250)447-6662

CRANBROOK
Mount Baker RV Park
(877)501-2288

CRESTON
Pair-A-Dice RV Park & Campground
(866)223-3423

DAWSON CREEK
Northern Lights RV Park (2010)
(250)782-9433

FAIRMONT HOT SPRINGS
Fairmont Hot Springs Resort Ltd
(800)663-4979

FORT NELSON
Triple "G" Hideaway RV Park & Restaurant
(250)774-2340

HIXON
Canyon Creek Campground & RV Park
(250)998-4384

HOPE
Wild Rose RV Park
(604)869-9842

LADYSMITH
Rondalyn Resort Family RV & Tenting - Parkbridge
(250)245-3227

OLIVER
Desert Gem RV Resort
(888)925-9966
Gallagher Lake Resort - Parkbridge
(250)498-3358

PRINCE GEORGE
Bee Lazee RV Park & Campground
(866)963-7263
Sintich RV Park
(877)791-1152

SURREY
Hazelmere RV Park & Campground
(604)538-1167
Tynehead RV Camp
(877)599-1161

VALEMOUNT
Irvin's Park & Campground
(250)566-4781

VICTORIA
Oceanside RV Resort - Parkbridge
(250)544-0508

WEST VANCOUVER
Capilano River RV Park
(604)987-4722

For more Good Sam Parks go to listing pages

BC

Western Canada's largest city might technically qualify as a major metropolitan area, but it certainly doesn't feel like one. The downtown core is packed into a small geographic footprint, one that's sequestered on a scenic peninsula, making the heart of the city not only highly walkable but also a visual treat to roam and explore on foot.

You'll quickly find that multiple bodies of water help define the layout and diversity of greater Vancouver eclectic neighborhoods. Burrard Inlet separates the downtown peninsula from the North Shore, where you'll find snow-capped mountains less than a 30-minute drive away. Coal Harbour is tucked between downtown and world-famous Stanley Park. False Creek separates the south side of downtown from a handful of trendy urban neighborhoods, including Granville Island, Kitsilano and West Point Grey. And English Bay offers some of the best beachfront in the city, opening out into the Straight of Georgia.

With the water theme set firmly in place, start your exploring with two of the city's most cherished attractions—the seawall and Stanley Park. The latter buffers the tip of the downtown peninsula while the former lines the waterfront of not just Stanley Park but also much of the city itself. This is, in fact, the longest uninterrupted waterfront path in the world, spanning just over 17 miles. Roughly one-third of the seawall is located in Stanley Park, and this is easily the most popular stretch for tourists.

Superb Stanley

Stanley Park itself—often cited as one of the best city parks in the world—annually attracts more than 8 million visitors. At nearly 1,000 acres, the park offers visitors and locals alike an opportunity to escape the big city in the blink of an eye. Miles and miles of walking trails snake through the park's core, while the Stanley Park Seawall follows the rocky peninsula shoreline, featuring incredible views of the North Shore, Lions Gate Bridge, Burrard Inlet, Spanish Banks and Kitsilano.

The park is also home to the Vancouver Aquarium, a must-visit for anyone traveling with children. The aquarium rescues, rehabilitates and houses more than 50,000 marine animals at a time, including sharks, eels, dolphins, beluga whales, sea otters and penguins. There's also an on-site rainforest tucked deep inside the aquarium, where guests can walk through an open environment full of exotic birds and one very lazy resident sloth.

> There's a rainforest tucked deep inside the aquarium, where guests can see a lush setting with exotic birds.

Science World, located a few blocks from the downtown core, is another must-visit for those with kids. Housed in an unmistakable giant silver sphere, the facility is packed with interactive displays and exhibits that teach kids (and their parents) about a variety of ever-changing science themes and topics. The on-site OMNIMAX Theatre is five stories high and features a rotating lineup of the latest educational IMAX films.

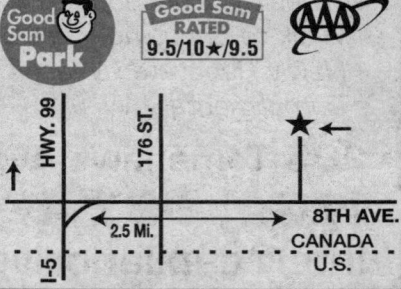

From here, head across Burrard Inlet to the North Shore, where the Capilano Suspension Bridge blends sightseeing, outdoor adventure and education. The main attraction is the 450-foot long suspension bridge, slung 230 feet above the Capilano River.

But the complex offers visitors more than a topsy-turvy walk across a bouncy sky-high rope bridge. Head for the Cliffwalk section of the park to navigate a series of bridges, stairs and lookouts that are anchored into the sides of granite cliffs. There's also Treetops Adventure, which gives visitor's a "squirrel's eye view" of the rainforest from an observation deck atop a 1,300-year-old Douglas fir tree.

Of course, no trip to Vancouver would be complete without an exploration of some of its most renowned neighborhoods. Topping them all is Granville Island, a tiny spit of land found in the middle of False Creek (and directly under the Granville Street Bridge). This spot features boutiques, food market stalls, theaters and industrial design studios. If you're on the downtown peninsula, the fastest (and most delightful) way to get to Granville Island is to hop on a water taxi, which skips across False Creek in minutes.

Humpback Whale off of Vancouver Island Getty Images/iStockphoto

Have a Gas

Gastown, located just east of the downtown core, near the shores of Burrard Inlet, is another must-visit. This is the oldest section of the city, boasting a cobblestone street and Victorian-era architecture alongside upscale shops and high-end art galleries. Gift shops abound here, as do sidewalk cafes and fashionable pubs.

For More Information

Vancouver Tourism
604-682-2222
www.tourismvancouver.com

Destination British Columbia
800-HELLOBC
www.hellobc.com

British Columbia

CONSULTANTS

Mike & Mary Lou Dillon

100 MILE HOUSE — H3 *Bulkley-Nechako*

CARIBOO BONANZA RESORT (Campground) (Phone Update) 2015 rates: $31 to $33. (250)395-3766 6384 Watson Rd, Lone Butte, BC V0K 1X3

WELLS GRAY PROVINCIAL PARK (MAHOOD LAKE CAMPGROUND) (Prov Pk) From town: Go 1-1/2 km/1 mi S on Hwy 97, then 88 km/55 mi E on Horsefly Rd (gravel). Pit toilets. 2015 rates: $16. (250)674-2194

70 MILE HOUSE — H3 *Cariboo*

GREEN LAKE (Prov Pk) From Jct of Hwy 97 & Green Lake Rd, NE 8 mi on Green Lake Rd (E). Pit toilets. 2015 rates: $16. May 15 to Sep 30. (250)397-2523

GREEN LAKE PROVINCIAL PARK (SUNSET VIEW) (Prov Pk) From town: Go 19-1/4 km/12 mi E on Green Lake South Rd. Pit toilets. 2015 rates: $16. May 15 to Sep 8. (250)397-2523

AINSWORTH HOT SPRINGS — J5 *Thompson-Nicola*

WOODBURY RESORT & MARINA Ratings: 7.5/7/6.5 (RV Resort) From Jct of Hwy 3A & Hwy 31 (Balfour Ferry), N 18kms/11.3 mi on Hwy 31 (R). **FAC:** Gravel rds. (88 spaces). 33 Avail: 13 paved, 20 gravel, 1 pull-thrus (25 x 75), back-ins (25 x 40), mostly side by side hkups, 33 W, 33 E (15/30 amps), WiFi, tent sites, rentals, showers $, dump, laundry, LP gas, firewood, restaurant. **REC:** heated pool, Kootenay Lake: fishing, marina, playground. Pets OK. Partial handicap access. RV age restrict, 2015 rates: $25 to $35. Disc: AAA.
AAA Approved
(877)353-7717 Lat: 49.77537, Lon: -116.90676
4112 Hwy 31, Ainsworth Hot Springs, BC V0G 1A0
woodburyresort@netidea.com
www.woodburyresort.com

ALDERGROVE — K3 *Langley, Lower Mainland*

EAGLE WIND RV PARK
Ratings: 10/9.5★/9 (RV Park) From Hwy 1 (TCH) & 264th St (Exit 73) S 0.2km/0.1 mi to 52nd Ave, E 1km/0.6 mi (R). **FAC:** Paved rds. (60 spaces). Avail: 45 all weather, back-ins (25 x 50), 45 full hkups (30/50 amps), seasonal sites, WiFi, rentals, showers $, laundry, firewood, controlled access. **REC:** heated pool, whirlpool. Pets OK. Partial handicap access, no tents. Big rig sites, RV age restrict, eco-friendly, 2015 rates: $38 to $52.
(604)856-6674 Lat: 49.09510, Lon: -122.47877
26920 52nd Ave, Aldergrove, BC V4W 1N6
sales@eaglewindrv.ca
www.eaglewindrv.ca

Thank you for being one of our best customers!

ALEXIS CREEK — H3 *Cariboo*

BULL CANYON (Prov Pk) From town, W 5 mi on Hwy 20 (L) NOTE: Fishing restrictions. Pit toilets. 2015 rates: $16. Jun 15 to Sep 15. (250)397-2523

ANAHIM LAKE — G2 *Kitimat-Stikine*

ANAHIM LAKE RESORT & RV PARK (RV Park) (Phone Update) 2015 rates: $24 to $32. (250)742-3242 2799 Reed Rd, Anahim Lake, BC V0L 1C0

BALFOUR — J5 *Thompson-Nicola*

BIRCH GROVE CAMPGROUND **Ratings: 5/8★/7.5** (Campground) 2015 rates: $40. Apr 15 to Oct 31. (877)247-8774 7048 Lee Rd, Nelson, BC V1L 6R9

BARKERVILLE — G3 *Cariboo*

BARKERVILLE (Public) From Jct of Hwy 26 & Hwy 97, E 50 mi on Hwy 26 (R). 2015 rates: $13.95. Jun to Oct. (250)994-3297

BARKERVILLE CAMPGROUNDS (LOWHEE/FOREST ROSE) **Ratings: 2.5/4.5/7.5** (Campground) 2015 rates: $23 to $28. May 15 to Sep 29. (866)994-3297 13500 Hwy 26, Barkerville, BC V0K 1B0

BOWRON LAKE PROVINCIAL PARK (Prov Pk) From town: Go 17-1/2 km/11 mi E on secondary road. Pit toilets. 2015 rates: $16 to $30. May 15 to Sep 30. (250)992-3101

BARRIERE — H4 *Thompson*

DEE JAY RV PARK/MHP **Ratings: 5.5/5.5/5.5** (Campground) 2015 rates: $28 to $30. (866)872-5685 4626 Summer Rd, Barriere, BC V0E 1E0

BEAR LAKE — F3 *Peace River*

CROOKED RIVER PROVINCIAL PARK (Prov Pk) From town: Go 1-1/2 km/1 mi N on Hwy 97. 2015 rates: $16. May 16 to Sep 8. (250)964-3489

BELLA COOLA — G1 *Central Coast*

GNOMES HOME RV PARK AND CAMPGROUND (RV Park) (Phone Update) From Ferry Dock & Hwy 20, W 14.5 mi on Hwy 20 (R). **FAC:** Paved/gravel rds. 35 gravel, 1 pull-thrus (25 x 70), back-ins (35 x 40), 15 full hkups, 5 E (15/30 amps), WiFi Hotspot, tent sites, showers $, dump, laundry, fire rings, firewood. **REC:** Fish Creek: fishing. Pets OK. RV age restrict, 2015 rates: $18 to $20. Apr 15 to Oct 15.
(250)982-2504 Lat: 52.39098, Lon: -126.55354
1875 Hwy 20, Hagensborg, BC V0T 1C0
gnome@belco.bc.ca
www.gnomeshome.ca

TWEEDSMUIR SOUTH (Prov Pk) From Williams Lake, W 240 mi on Hwy 20 (L). 2015 rates: $16. Jun 15 to Sep 30. (250)397-2523

BLACK CREEK — G3 *East Island*

PACIFIC PLAYGROUNDS RV PARK COTTAGES MARINA **Ratings: 8.5/9.5★/9** (RV Park) 2015 rates: $25 to $50. (877)239-5600 9082 Clarkson Ave, Black Creek, BC V9J 1B3

BLIND BAY — H4 *Okanagan, Thompson*

BLIND BAY RESORT **Ratings: 9/9/8** (Campground) 2015 rates: $43 to $58. (250)675-2595 2698 Blind Bay Rd, Blind Bay, BC V0E 1H1

BLUE RIVER — H4 *Columbia*

BLUE RIVER CAMPGROUND
Ratings: 6/7/7.5 (Campground) From Jct Hwy 5 & Harwood Rd, W 30m/100 ft on Harwood Rd to Blue River W Frontage Rd, N 0.2kms/0.1 mi (L). **FAC:** Gravel rds. 30 gravel, 20 pull-thrus (25 x 70), back-ins (20 x 40), mostly side by side hkups, 14 full hkups, 12 W, 12 E (15/30 amps), WiFi, tent sites, rentals, dump, laundry, groc, fire rings, firewood. **REC:** playground. Pets OK. RV age restrict, 2015 rates: $32 to $38. May 1 to Oct 31.
(866)675-8203 Lat: 52.11502, Lon: -119.30418
991 W Frontage Rd, Blue River, BC V0E 1J0
bluerivercampground@gmail.com
www.bluerivercampground.ca
See ad this page.

BOSTON BAR — J3 *Thompson Region*

ANDERSON CREEK CAMPGROUND **Ratings: 3.5/8/8** (Campground) 2015 rates: $28 to $33. Apr 1 to Oct 31. (604)867-9089 48500 Tuckkwiowhum, Boston Bar, BC V0K 1C0

CANYON ALPINE RV PARK & CAMPGROUND **Ratings: 5.5/10★/8.5** (RV Park) 2015 rates: $30 to $37. Apr 1 to Nov 1. (604)867-9734 50490 Hwy 1, Boston Bar, BC V0K 1C0

BOWSER — K2 *East Island*

DEEP BAY RV PARK **Ratings: 5/7★/5** (Campground) 2015 rates: $29 to $39. May 1 to Sep 30. (250)757-8424 5315 Deep Bay Dr, Bowser, BC V0R 1G0

BRACKENDALE — J3 *Squamish*

WONDERLAND VALLEY RESORT **Ratings: 4.5/9/7.5** (Campground) 2015 rates: $50. Apr 15 to Oct 15. (604)390-4200 1796 Depot Rd, Squamish, BC V8B 0C2

BRIDGE LAKE — H4 *Cariboo*

BRIDGE LAKE PROVINCIAL PARK (Prov Pk) From town: Go N on Hwy 24. Pit toilets. 2015 rates: $16. Jun 15 to Sep 18. (250)397-2523

MOONDANCE BAY RESORT (Campground) (Phone Update) 2015 rates: $35 to $38. May 15 to Oct 15. (604)986-1500 7237 Johnstone Rd, Lone Butte, BC V0K 1X2

BUCKING HORSE RIVER — C6 *Peace River*

BUCKINGHORSE RIVER WAYSIDE (Prov Pk) From town, NE 128 mi (205 km) on Hwy 97 (AK Hwy) to MP-175 (L). Pit toilets. 2015 rates: $16. May 15 to Sep 30. (250)772-4999

BURNABY — K3 *Mount Waddington*

BURNABY CARIBOO RV PARK AND CAMPGROUND
Ratings: 9.5/10★/9.5 (RV Park) From Jct of Hwy 1 & Gaglardi Way (exit 37) W 9.6km/6 mi (W of Port Mann Bridge), N 91m/300 ft to traffic light, E 91m/300 ft on Cariboo Rd, N 0.3km/0.2 mi on Cariboo Rd (under overpass) to Cariboo Pl (E).

CENTRAL TO VANCOUVER AND AREA
BCRV offers RVers and Campers an opportunity to enjoy Vancouver while nestled in a park like setting in a deluxe RV park with all amenities. Easy access to the city by rapid transit or tours.

FAC: Paved rds. 212 paved, patios, back-ins (30 x 45), 212 full hkups (30 amps), cable, WiFi, tent sites, dump, laundry, groc. **REC:** heated pool, whirlpool, Brunette River: fishing, playground. Pets OK. Partial handicap access. RV age restrict, eco-friendly, 2015 rates: $62 to $69.75. ATM.
AAA Approved
(604)420-1722 Lat: 49.24864, Lon: -122.91216
8765 Cariboo Place, Burnaby, BC V3N 4T2
camping@bcrvpark.com
www.bcrv.com
See ad pages 1368 (BC Map), 1375 (Spotlight Vancouver Area), 1372 & RV Trips of a Lifetime in Magazine Section.

BURTON — J5 *West Kootenay*

BURTON HISTORICAL PARK (Campground) (Phone Update) 2015 rates: $30 to $32. May 1 to Sep 30. (250)265-4982 145 Lakeview Park Rd, Burton, BC V0G 1E0

CACHE CREEK — J3 *Cariboo, Thompson*

BROOKSIDE CAMPSITE Ratings: 7.5/9/8 (Campground) From Jct of Hwys 1 & 97 (in town), E 1.1km/0.7 mi on Hwy 1 (L). **FAC:** Gravel rds. (56 spaces). Avail: 48 gravel, 48 pull-thrus (25 x 60), 33 full hkups, 15 W, 15 E (30 amps), seasonal sites, WiFi, tent sites, dump, laundry, fire rings, firewood. **REC:** heated pool, Cache Creek: playground. Pets OK. RV age restrict, 2015 rates: $35 to $40. Disc: AAA.
(250)457-6633 Lat: 50.80963, Lon: -121.30732
1621 E Trans Canada Hwy, Cache Creek, BC V0K 1H0
Info@brooksidecampsite.com
www.brooksidecampsite.com

JUNIPER BEACH (Prov Pk) From town, E 12 mi on Hwy 1 (R). Pit toilets. 2015 rates: $21 to $25. Apr 18 to Dec 31. (250)457-6794

CACHE CREEK (CONT)

MARBLE CANYON PARK (Prov Pk) From Jct of Hwy 97 & Hwy 99, W 18 mi on Hwy 99 (L). Pit toilets. 2015 rates: $16. (250)378-5334

CAMPBELL RIVER — J2 *East Island*

ELK FALLS (Prov Pk) From Jct of Hwy 19 & Hwy 28, W 2 mi on Hwy 28. 2015 rates: $11 to $18. (250)474-1336

FRIENDSHIP INN MOTEL & TRAILER PARK (RV Park) (Rebuilding) 2015 rates: $28. (250)287-9591 3900 North Island Hwy, Campbell River, BC V9W 2J2

LOVELAND BAY (Prov Pk) From town, W 20 km on Hwy 28 (L). Pit toilets. 2015 rates: $18. May 17 to Sep 30. (250)474-1336

MORTON LAKE (Prov Pk) From town, NW 17 mi on Hwy 19 (R). Pit toilets. 2015 rates: $11 to $16. (250)474-1336

RIPPLE ROCK RV PARK AT BROWN'S BAY RESORT **Ratings: 8.5/10★/9** (RV Park) 2015 rates: $40 to $45. Apr 1 to Oct 31. (877)361-7847 P.O.box 285, Campbell River, BC V9W 5B1

SALMON POINT RESORT RV PARK & MARINA **Ratings: 9/9.5★/9.5** (RV Park) 2015 rates: $38 to $52. (866)246-6605 2176 Salmon Point Rd, Campbell River, BC V9H 1E5

STRATHCONA/BUTTLE LAKE (Prov Pk) From Jct of Hwy 19 & Hwy 28, SW 33 mi on Hwy 28 (L). For reservations call 1-800-689-9025. Pit toilets. 2015 rates: $18. Apr 1 to Oct 31. (250)474-1336

STRATHCONA/RALPH RIVER (Prov Pk) From Jct of Hwy 19 & Hwy 28, SW 47 mi on Hwy 28 to Western Mines Rd, S 17 mi (E). Pit toilets. 2015 rates: $18. May 15 to Sep 30. (250)248-9460

THUNDERBIRD RV PARK

Ratings: 8.5/9.5★/7.5 (RV Park) From Jct of Hwy 19A & Spit Rd, W 0.8kms/0.5 mi on Spit Rd (L). **FAC:** All weather rds. (75 spaces). Avail: 29 all weather, 9 pull-thrus (24 x 60), back-ins (24 x 40), mostly side by side hkups, 29 full hkups (30/50 amps), seasonal sites, cable, WiFi, tent sites, showers $, dump, laundry, fire rings, firewood, restaurant. **REC:** Discovery Passage: swim, fishing, playground. Pet restrict(B). Partial handicap access. Big rig sites, RV age restrict, 2015 rates: $36 to $39.
(250)286-3344 Lat: 50.04266, Lon: -125.25002
2660 Spit Rd, Campbell River, BC V9W 6E3
tbirdrvpark@telus.net
www.thunderbirdrvpark.com
See ad this page.

CANAL FLATS — J6 *Columbia-Shuswap*

KOOTENAY RIVER RV RESORT **Ratings: 5.5/8.5/7** (RV Resort) 2015 rates: $32 to $42. (250)349-8212 9110 Hwy 93/95, Canal Flats, BC V0B 1B0

WHITESWAN LAKE PARK (Prov Pk) From town, S 3 mi on Hwy 93/95 to gravel logging rd, E 13 mi (L). Pit toilets. 2015 rates: $18. (250)422-3003

CANIM LAKE — H4 *Fraser-Fort George*

PONDEROSA RESORT (Campground) (Phone Update) 2015 rates: $38 to $45. May 15 to Oct 15. (250)397-2243 7405 Canim Lake Rd, Canim Lake, BC V0K 1J0

CASTLEGAR — K5 *Kootenay West*

CASTLEGAR CABINS RV PARK & CAMPGROUND Ratings: 5.5/8★/7 (Campground) From Jct of Hwy 3 & Hwy 22, W 4 kms/2.5 mi on Hwy 3 (L). Elev 2500 ft. **FAC:** Gravel rds. (36 spaces). 29 Avail: 11 gravel, 18 grass, back-ins (22 x 42), 29 full hkups (15/30 amps), seasonal sites, WiFi, tent sites, rentals, showers $, dump, laundry, firewood. **REC:** Judkin Creek. Pets OK $. RV age restrict, 2015 rates: $34. AAA Approved
(866)687-7275 Lat: 49.27139, Lon: -117.67866
1725 Hwy 3, Castlegar, BC V1N 4W1
www.castlegarrvpark.com

CASTLEGAR GOLF CLUB & RV PARK **Ratings: 5/9.5★/8** (RV Park) 2015 rates: $$21 to $30. Apr 15 to Oct 15. (800)666-0324 1602 Aaron Rd, Castlegar, BC V1N 4L6

SYRINGA PARK (Prov Pk) From N-end of town, N 2 mi on Hwy 3A to Robson Turnoff, W 12 mi (R). Pit toilets. 2015 rates: $21. May 2 to Sep 30. (250)837-5734

CHASE — J4 *Okanagan, Thompson*

SHUSWAP LAKE PARK (Prov Pk) From Jct of Hwy 1 & Squilax-Anglemont Rd, NE 13 mi on Squilax-Anglemont Rd (R). 2015 rates: $16. May 1 to Sep 30. (250)836-2958

SILVER BEACH PROVINCIAL PARK (Prov Pk) From town: Go 11-1/4 km/7 mi NE on Hwy 1 to Squilax, then 64 km/40 mi NE on Squilax-Anglemont-Seymour Arm Rd. Pit toilets. 2015 rates: $16. Apr 1 to Oct 31. (250)836-2958

CHEMAINUS — K2 *North Cowichan*

CHEMAINUS GARDEN HOLIDAY RESORT **Ratings: 4.5/8/8** (RV Park) 2015 rates: $30 to $50. (250)246-3569 3042 River Rd, Chemainus, BC V0R 1K3

COUNTRY MAPLES RV RESORT **Ratings: 9/9.5★/9** (Campground) 2015 rates: $32 to $64. (250)246-2078 9010 Trans Canada Hwy, Chemainus, BC V0R 1K4

CHETWYND — D6 *Peace River*

GWILLIM LAKE PROVINCIAL PARK (Prov Pk) From town: Go 4 km/2-1/2 mi E on Hwy 97, then 56 km/35 mi S on Hwy 29. Pit toilets. 2015 rates: $16. May 21 to Sep 15. (250)242-1146

MOBERLY LAKE PARK (Prov Pk) From Jct of Hwys 97 & 29, NW 15 mi (24 km) on Hwy 29 to park access rd, W 1.5 mi (2.4 km) (R). Pit toilets. 2015 rates: $16. May 15 to Sep 1. (250)964-2243

WESTWIND RV PARK

Ratings: 6/9.5★/7 (RV Park) From Jct of Hwy 97 & 29, N 1.2 mi on Hwy 97N (R). **FAC:** Gravel rds. 50 gravel, 50 pull-thrus (20 x 65), 50 full hkups (30 amps), WiFi, tent sites, dump, laundry, fire rings, firewood. **REC:** playground. Pets OK. Partial handicap access. RV age restrict, 2015 rates: $35. Disc: AAA. May 1 to Oct 31.
AAA Approved
(250)788-2190 Lat: 55.68752, Lon: -121.60345
4441 53rd Ave, Chetwynd, BC V0C 1J0
wwrvpark@hotmail.com
See ad this page, 1372.

Things to See and Do

DISTRICT OF CHETWYND District offices that promote Chetwynd and the area. Sculptured carvings with a chainsaw adorn the city. Hours: 9am to 5pm. No CC.
(250)788-1943 Lat: 55.69526, Lon: -121.63893
5400 N Access Rd, Chetwynd, BC V0C 1J0
emcavany@gochetwynd.com
www.gochetwynd.com
See ad page 1367 (Welcome Section).

CHILLIWACK — K3 *Fraser Valley*

COTTONWOOD MEADOWS RV COUNTRY CLUB

Ratings: 8/10★/9 (RV Park) From Jct of Hwy 1 & Lickman Rd (exit 116), S 0.2km/0.1 mi on Lickman Rd to Luckakuck Way, E 0.6km/0.4 mi (R). **FAC:** Paved rds. (118 spaces). Avail: 73 gravel, 17 pull-thrus (30 x 64), back-ins (28 x 65), 73 full hkups (30/50 amps), seasonal sites, cable, WiFi, dump, laundry, controlled access. **REC:** Athelix Creek. Pet restrict(B). Partial handicap access, no tents. Big rig sites, RV age restrict, eco-friendly, 2015 rates: $36 to $43.
(604)824-7275 Lat: 49.14358, Lon: -121.99952
44280 Luckakuck Way, Chilliwack, BC V2R 4A7
camping@cottonwoodrvpark.com
www.cottonwoodrvpark.com
See ad this page, 1372.

CULTUS LAKE PROVINCIAL PARK (CLEAR CREEK CAMPGROUND) (Prov Pk) From Hwy 1 (Sardis exit): Go 11-1/4 km/7 mi S. 2015 rates: $30. Apr 1 to Oct 14. (604)986-9371

CULTUS LAKE PROVINCIAL PARK (DELTA GROVE CAMPGROUND) (Prov Pk) From Hwy 1 (Sardis exit): Go 11-1/4 km/7 mi S. 2015 rates: $30. Mar 28 to Oct 13. (604)986-9371

CULTUS LAKE PROVINCIAL PARK (ENTRANCE BAY CAMPGROUND) (Prov Pk) From Hwy 1 (Sardis exit): Go 10-1/2 km/6-1/2 mi S. 2015 rates: $30. Mar 28 to Oct 13. (604)986-9371

CULTUS LAKE PROVINCIAL PARK (MAPLE BAY CAMPGROUND) (Prov Pk) From Hwy 1 (Sardis exit): Go 12 km/7-1/2 mi S. 2015 rates: $30. Apr 1 to Oct 13. (604)986-9371

CHRISTINA LAKE — K5 *Kootenay West*

CASCADE COVE RV PARK & CAMPGROUND

Ratings: 7/8.5/8.5 (Campground) From Jct of Hwy 3 & Hwy 395 (11 mi E of Grand Forks), E 0.5 mi on Hwy 3 to River Rd, S 0.5 mi (E). **FAC:** All weather rds. (100 spaces). 50 Avail: 18 gravel, 32 grass, 18 pull-thrus (30 x 60), back-ins (30 x 45), 50 full hkups (15/30 amps), seasonal sites, WiFi, tent sites, rentals, showers $, laundry, fire rings, firewood. **REC:** Kettle River: swim, fishing, playground. Pet restrict(B) $. Partial handicap access. RV age restrict, eco-friendly, 2015 rates: $40 to $45. Apr 1 to Oct 31.
(250)447-6662 Lat: 49.02482, Lon: -118.21531
1209 River Rd, Christina Lake, BC V0H 1E0
cascadecovervpark@hotmail.com
www.christinalake.com/cascadecove/
See ad this page, 1372.

CHRISTINA PINES CAMPGROUND **Ratings: 7.5/8/7.5** (Condo Pk) 2015 rates: $30 to $42. Apr 15 to Oct 15. (250)447-9587 1528 Neimi Rd, Christina Lake, BC V0H 1E0

GLADSTONE/TEXAS CREEK PARK (Prov Pk) From town, E 15 mi on Hwy 3 to Christina Lake, N 4 mi to Eastlake Dr (E). 2015 rates: $25. May 1 to Sep 15. (250)548-0076

CLEARWATER — H4 *Thompson*

CLEARWATER VALLEY RESORT KOA **Ratings: 8.5/9★/8.5** (Campground) 2015 rates: $31.90 to $41.90. May 1 to Oct 1. (250)674-3909 373 Clearwater Valley Rd, Clearwater, BC V0E 1N1

DUTCH LAKE RESORT & RV PARK **Ratings: 6/8★/8** (RV Park) 2015 rates: $34 to $42. Apr 1 to Oct 15. (888)884-4424 361 Ridge Dr, Clearwater, BC V0E 1N2

NORTH THOMPSON RIVER PROVINCIAL PARK (Prov Pk) From town: Go 4-3/4 km/3 mi S on Hwy 5. Pit toilets. 2015 rates: $21. (250)674-2194

WELLS GRAY GOLF RESORT & RV PARK (Campground) (Phone Update) 2015 rates: $25 to $40. Apr 15 to Sep 30. (250)674-0009 6624 Clearwater Valley Rd, Clearwater, BC V0E 1N0

WELLS GRAY/CLEARWATER LAKE (Prov Pk) From Jct of Hwy 5 & Clearwater Valley Rd, N 40 km on Clearwater Valley Rd (E). Pit toilets. 2015 rates: $16. May 12 to Sep 30. (250)674-2194

CLINTON — H3 *Cariboo*

BIG BAR LAKE PARK (Prov Pk) From N end of town, N 5 mi on Hwy 97 to Big Bar Lake Rd, NW 21 mi (R). Pit toilets. 2015 rates: $16. May 15 to Sep 30. (250)397-2523

COOMBS — K2 *East Island*

COOMBS COUNTRY CAMPGROUND & RV PARK **Ratings: 6.5/7/8** (Campground) 2015 rates: $40 to $45. May 13 to Sep 30. (800)925-3888 2619 Alberni Hwy, Coombs, BC V0R 1M0

COURTENAY — J2 *East Island*

BATES BEACH OCEANFRONT & RV PARK **Ratings: 7/8.5★/7** (RV Park) 2015 rates: $30 to $40. (250)334-4154 5726 Coral Rd, Courtenay, BC V9N 5M9

MAPLE POOL CAMPSITE Ratings: 6.5/5.5/4 (Campground) From Courtenay Town Centre: Go .6 km/1/4 mi NW on Cliffe Ave, then 1.1 km/ 1/2 mi NE on 5th St/Old Island Hwy, then .5 km/ 1/4 mi NW on Headquaters Rd. **FAC:** Gravel rds. (100 spaces). Avail: 47 grass, 2 pull-thrus (24 x 50), back-ins (25 x 40), some side by side hkups, 12 full hkups, 35 W, 35 E (30 amps), seasonal sites, cable, WiFi Hotspot, tent sites, dump, laundry, fire rings, controlled access. **REC:** Tsolum River: swim. Pet restrict(Q). RV age restrict, 2015 rates: $27 to $30. Disc: AAA.
AAA Approved
(250)338-9386 Lat: 49.70360, Lon: -124.99529
4685 Headquarters Rd, Courtenay, BC V9N 9H3
maplepool@shaw.ca
www.maplepoolcampsite.com

MIRACLE BEACH PARK (Prov Pk) From town, N 14 mi on Hwy 19 to Miracle Beach Dr, E 1 mi (L). 2015 rates: $11 to $28. (250)474-1336

PUNTLEDGE RV CAMPGROUND & NIM NIM INTERPRETIVE CENTRE (RV Park) (Phone Update) 2015 rates: $23 to $33. May 1 to Sep 30. (250)334-3773 4624 Condensory Rd, Courtenay, BC V9J 1R6

SEAL BAY RV PARK & CAMPGROUND **Ratings: 7/9★/9** (RV Park) 2015 rates: $29 to $37. (250)339-1837 1901 Larch Rd, Courtenay, BC V9J 1X7

CRANBROOK — J6 *Kootenay East*

JIMSMITH LAKE PARK (Prov Pk) From town, S 1 mi on Hwy 3/95, 2 mi on Jimsmith Lake Rd (L). Pit toilets. 2015 rates: $21. May 15 to Oct 11. (250)422-3003

MOUNT BAKER RV PARK
Ratings: 7/9.5★/7.5 (RV Park) S-bnd: From Jct of Hwy 3 & Victoria Ave, S 1.4 km (0.9 mi) on Victoria Ave to 2nd St N, W 0.3 km (0.2 mi) on 2nd St N to 17th St, S 0.4 km (0.25 mi) on 17th St to 1st St S, W 0.2 km (0.1 mi) on 1st St S to entrance. Elev 3022 ft. **FAC:** All weather rds. (47 spaces). Avail: 38 gravel, 7 pull-thrus (25 x 60), back-ins (27 x 40), some side by side hkups, 38 full hkups (30/50 amps), seasonal sites, cable, WiFi, tent sites, dump, laundry. **REC:** playground. Pet restrict(B) $. Partial handicap access. Big rig sites, RV age restrict, eco-friendly, 2015 rates: $26 to $38. Apr 1 to Oct 31.
(877)501-2288 Lat: 49.51004, Lon: -115.76060
1501 1st Street South, Cranbrook, BC V1C 1B7
parkhost@mountbakerrvpark.com
www.mountbakerrvpark.com
See ad this page, 1372.

MOYIE LAKE PARK (Prov Pk) From town, S 12 mi on Hwy 3/95 (R). 2015 rates: $28. May 12 to Sep 30. (250)422-3003

CRAWFORD BAY — J5 *Kootenay West*

KOKANEE CHALETS, CABINS, MOTEL & RV CAMPGROUND (Campground) (Phone Update) 2015 rates: $32 to $39.90. Apr 15 to Oct 15. (800)448-9292 15981 Hwy 3A, Crawford Bay, BC V0B 1E0

Like Us on Facebook.

CRESTON — K5 *Kootenay West*

KOZY RV PARK/MHP **Ratings: 4.5/5.5/6.5** (Campground) 2015 rates: $21 to $25.50. (250)428-4143 3003 Hwy 3, Creston, BC V0B 1G1

LOCKHART CREEK (Prov Pk) From town, N 18 mi on Hwy-3A (R). Pit toilets. 2015 rates: $21. May 9 to Sep 30. (250)422-3003

PAIR-A-DICE RV PARK & CAMPGROUND
Ratings: 7/9.5★/8 (RV Park) From Jct of Hwy 3A & Hwy 3 (West side of Town), E 0.8kms/0.5 mi on Hwy 3 (L) or N-bnd From Jct of Hwy 21 & Erickson St, N 4kms/2.5 mi on Hwy 21 to Jct of Hwy 21 & Hwy 3, E 2.2kms/1.4 mi on Hwy 3 (L). **FAC:** Gravel rds. (26 spaces). Avail: 22 gravel, 10 pull-thrus (30 x 65), back-ins (30 x 45), 22 full hkups (30 amps), seasonal sites, cable, WiFi, tent sites, dump, laundry, firewood. **REC:** playground. Pets OK. Partial handicap access. RV age restrict, eco-friendly, 2015 rates: $28 to $37.
(866)223-3423 Lat: 49.11124, Lon: -116.52311
1322 Hwy 3, Creston, BC V0B 1G6
pairadice@shaw.ca
www.pairadicepark.com
See ad this page, 1372.

CROFTON — K2 *South Island*

OSBORNE BAY RESORT **Ratings: 6.5/8/8** (RV Resort) 2015 rates: $32 to $39. (800)567-7275 1450 Charlotte St, Box 39, Crofton, BC V0R 1R0

CULTUS LAKE — K3 *Lower Mainland*

CULTUS LAKE (Prov Pk) From Jct of TCH-1 & Sardis exit (Vedder Rd), S 5 mi on Vedder Rd to Cultus Lake Rd, S 3.5 mi, follow signs. 2015 rates: $11 to $30. Mar 28 to Oct 14. (604)986-9371

SUNNYSIDE CAMPGROUND (Public) From Jct of Prov Hwy 1 & Vedder Rd, S 5 mi on Vedder Rd (across Vedder River bridge) to Jct of Cultus Lake Rd & Vedder Mountain Rd, S 2 mi on Cultus Lake Rd (R). 2015 rates: $43 to $45. Apr 15 to Sep 30. (604)858-5253

VEDDER RIVER CAMPGROUND (Public) From town, W 3 mi on Vedder Rd to Vedder Mt Rd, W 2.5 mi to Giesbrecht Rd, N 0.5 mi (R). 2015 rates: $26 to $37. (604)823-6012

DAWSON CREEK — D6 *Peace River*

MILE 0 RV PARK (Public) From AK Hwy MP-0, N 1.5 mi (2.4 km) on AK Hwy to PR-97, W 1/4 mi (.04 km) on PR-97 (R). 2015 rates: $25 to $45. May 1 to Oct 1. (250)782-2590

NORTHERN LIGHTS RV PARK (2010)
Ratings: 7/9.5★/7.5 (RV Park) W-bnd: From Jct Hwy 2 & Dangerous Goods Rte, W 4.1 mi on Dangerous Good Rte to Hwy 97 S, W 0.6 mi (L); or N-bnd: From Jct of Hwy 97 N, S 2 mi on Hwy 97 S (L). **FAC:** All weather rds. 90 Avail: 90 all weather, 70 pull-thrus (24 x 60), back-ins (18 x 32), 90 full hkups (30/50 amps), WiFi, tent sites, showers $, laundry, fire rings, firewood. **REC.** Pets OK. Big rig sites, eco-friendly, 2015 rates: $40 to $45.
AAA Approved
(250)782-9433 Lat: 55.76532, Lon: -120.29120
9636 Friesen Sub, Dawson Creek, BC V1G 4T9
nlrv2010@gmail.com
www.nlrv.com
See ad this page, 1372.

ONE ISLAND LAKE PROVINCIAL PARK (Prov Pk) From town: Go 36-3/4 km/23 mi SE on Hwy 2, then 29-1/2 km/18-1/2 mi S on secondary road. Pit toilets. 2015 rates: $16. May 21 to Sep 15. (780)876-1393

SWAN LAKE PARK (Prov Pk) From town, SE 35 km on Hwy 2 (R). Pit toilets. 2015 rates: $16. May 11 to Sep 3. (250)786-5960

TUBBY'S RV PARK & CAR WASH **Ratings: 4.5/9.5★/7** (RV Park) 2015 rates: $35 to $40. (250)782-2584 1913 96th Ave # 4, Dawson Creek, BC V1G 1M2

DONALD — H5 *Division No. 14*

CAMPER'S HAVEN RV TENTING & MOTEL Ratings: 6/8.5/7 (Campground) From Jct Hwy 95 & Hwy 1, W 15.7 mi on Hwy 1 to Dejordie Rd, N 0.3 mi (L). Elev 2621 ft. **FAC:** Dirt rds. (49 spaces). Avail: 39 grass, 36 pull-thrus (25 x 65), back-ins (25 x 35), 39 full hkups (15/30 amps), seasonal sites, WiFi, tent sites, rentals, showers $, dump, laundry, groc, fire rings, firewood. **REC:** playground. Pets OK. RV age restrict, eco-friendly, 2015 rates: $28.95 to $37.95. Disc: AAA.
AAA Approved
(800)563-6122 Lat: 51.48946, Lon: -117.16221
2779 Dejordie Rd, Donald, BC V0A 1H1
nor.von@hotmail.com
www.campershavenrvpark.com

DUNCAN — K2 *Cowichan Valley*

RIVERSIDE RV & CAMPING **Ratings: 4.5/8.5★/7** (RV Park) 2015 rates: $26 to $30. (250)746-4352 #1-3065 Allenby Road, Duncan, BC V9L 6W5

ELKO — J6 *Columbia-Shuswap*

KIKOMUN CREEK PARK (Prov Pk) From town, W 3 mi on Hwy 3/93, W 5 mi on paved rd, follow signs (L). 2015 rates: $30 to $35. May 5 to Sep 30. (250)422-3003

ENDERBY — J4 *North Okanagan*

RIVERSIDE RV PARK (Public) From Jct Hwy 97 & Regent Ave, E 0.1 mi on Regent Ave to Belvedere Rd, N 0.4 mi to Howard St, Howard St to Kate St, N 0.5 mi on Kate St to Kildonan Ave, E 0.2 mi (R). 2015 rates: $23 to $36. (250)838-0155

SHUSWAP FALLS RV RESORT **Ratings: 8/8/8.5** (Condo Pk) 2015 rates: $35 to $50. Apr 15 to Oct 15. (250)838-6100 2202 Mabel Lake Rd, Enderby, BC V0E 1V5

ERICKSON — K5 *Kootenay West*

MOUNTAIN PARK RESORT Ratings: 6/9.5/7.5 (Campground) From Jct of Hwy 3 & Erickson Rd, E2.5km/1.5 mi on Hwy 3 (R). **FAC:** All weather rds. 46 dirt, 5 pull-thrus (25 x 60), back-ins (25 x 40), mostly side by side hkups, 46 W, 46 E (15/30 amps), WiFi, tent sites, rentals, dump, laundry, groc, firewood. **REC:** Goat River: swim, fishing, playground. Pets OK. RV age restrict, 2015 rates: $33 to $52. Disc: AAA. ATM.
AAA Approved
(877)428-2954 Lat: 49.10281, Lon: -116.45426
4020 Hwy 3, Erickson, BC V0B 1K0
mt_park@hotmail.com
www.mountainprk.com

FAIRMONT HOT SPRINGS — J6 *Columbia Valley*

FAIRMONT HOT SPRINGS RESORT LTD
Ratings: 10/9.5★/10 (RV Park) From Jct of Hwy 93/95 & Fairmont Resort Rd, E 0.8kms/ 0.5 mi on Fairmont Resort Rd (E). Elev 3232 ft. **FAC:** Paved rds. 85 paved, 150 all weather, patios, 67 pull-thrus (30 x 60), back-ins (30 x 50), 220 full hkups (30/50 amps), cable, WiFi, dump, laundry, groc, LP bottles, restaurant. **REC:** heated pool $, whirlpool, Fairmont Creek: golf, playground, rec open to public. Pet restrict(Q) $. Partial handicap access, no tents. Big rig sites, RV age restrict, eco-friendly, 2015 rates: $40 to $65. ATM.
AAA Approved
(800)663-4979 Lat: 50.32932, Lon: -115.84250
5225 Fairmont Resort Rd, Fairmont Hot Springs, BC V0B 1L1
rvpark@fhsr.com
www.fhsr.com
See ad page 1372.

SPRUCE GROVE RV PARK AND CAMPGROUND Ratings: 7/8/8.5 (Campground) From Jct of Hwy 93/95 & Fairmont Hot Springs Rd, S 1.6kms/1 mi on Hwy 93/95 (L). Elev 2672 ft. **FAC:** Gravel rds. (117 spaces). Avail: 72 gravel, 11 pull-thrus (21 x 55), back-ins (30 x 50), 11 full hkups, 50 W, 50 E (15/30

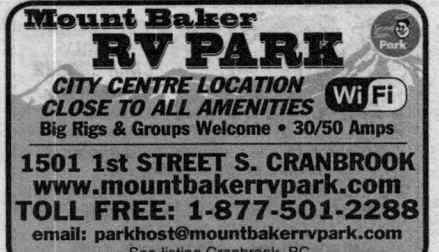

BC

FAIRMONT HOT SPRINGS (CONT)

SPRUCE GROVE RV PARK AND (CONT) amps), seasonal sites, WiFi, tent sites, dump, laundry, groc, fire rings, firewood, controlled access. **REC:** heated pool, Columbia River: fishing. Pets OK. Partial handicap access. RV age restrict, eco-friendly, 2015 rates: $39.50 to $48.50. Apr 15 to Oct 15.
AAA Approved
(888)629-4004 Lat: 50.32157, Lon: -115.86617
5225 Fairmont Resort Rd, Fairmont Hot Springs, BC V0B 1L1
camp@sprucegroveresort.com
www.sprucegroveresort.com

FANNY BAY — K2 *Central Coast*

LIGHTHOUSE RV PARK **Ratings: 6/9★/7** (RV Park) 2015 rates: $40 to $42. Apr 1 to Oct 31. (250)335-1667 8256 E Island Hwy S, Fanny Bay, BC V0R 1W0

FARMINGTON — D6 *Peace River*

KISKATINAW PROVINCIAL PARK (Prov Pk) On the Alaska Hwy at milepost 21. Pit toilets. 2015 rates: $16. May 21 to Sep 15. (250)843-0074

FERNIE — J6 *Columbia-Shuswap*

MOUNT FERNIE PARK (Prov Pk) From town, W 2 mi on Hwy 3 (R). 2015 rates: $25. Jun 1 to Sep 30. (250)422-3003

FIELD — H5 *Division No. 14*

YOHO NATIONAL PARK (CHANCELLOR PEAK CAMPGROUND) (Natl Pk) From town: Go 25-1/2 km/16 mi W on Hwy 1. Pit toilets. (250)343-6012

YOHO NATIONAL PARK (HOODOO CREEK CAMPGROUND) (Natl Pk) From town: Go 22-1/2 km/14 mi W Trans Canada Hwy. Pit toilets. 2015 rates: $17.60. Jun 27 to Sep 1. (250)343-6783

YOHO NATIONAL PARK (TAKAKKAW FALLS) (Natl Pk) From town: Go 3-1/4 km/2 mi E on Trans Canada Hwy, then 14-1/2 km/9 mi N on Takakkaw Falls Rd, then walk into campground 1/2 km/1/4 mi. Pit toilets. 2015 rates: $17.60. Jun 28 to Oct 14. (250)343-6100

YOHO/KICKING HORSE (Natl Pk) From Jct of TCH 1 & Yoho Valley Rd, N 1 mi on Yoho Valley Rd (L). 2015 rates: $27.40. May 23 to Oct 3. (250)343-6100

FORT FRASER — F2 *Bulkley-Nechako*

BEAUMONT PROVINCIAL PARK (Prov Pk) From town: Go 6-1/2 km/4 mi W on Hwy 16, then 1/2 km/1/4 mi off Hwy on gravel road. 2015 rates: $16. May 14 to Sep 10. (250)964-3489

FORT NELSON — C6 *Peace River*

TETSA RIVER LODGE
Ratings: 5.5/7/6.5 (Campground) N-bnd on Alaska Hwy at Mile 375 (L)-(72mls N of Fort Nelson). Elev 2577 ft. **FAC:** Gravel rds. 30 Avail: 15 gravel, 15 grass, 7 pull-thrus (25 x 60), back-ins (20 x 40), 30 W, 30 E (15 amps), WiFi Hotspot, tent sites, rentals, dump, laundry, LP gas, fire rings, firewood. **REC:** Tetsa River: fishing. Pets OK. 2015 rates: $30. Apr 15 to Oct 30.
(250)774-1005 Lat: 58.65340, Lon: -124.23445
Mile 375 Alaska Hwy, Fort Nelson, BC V0C 1R0
tetsariverlodge@gmail.com
www.tetsariver.com

TETSA RIVER REGIONAL PARK (Public) From town: Go 95-1/4 km/59-1/2 mi NW on Hwy 97 (Alaska Hwy), then 3/4 km/ 1/2 mi S on secondary road. Pit toilets. 2015 rates: $17. May to Sep. (250)774-2541

TRIPLE "G" HIDEAWAY RV PARK & RESTAURANT
Ratings: 5.5/8★/8 (Campground) N-bnd: W edge of Fort Nelson on AK Hwy (L). **FAC:** Gravel rds. 130 gravel, 31 pull-thrus (20 x 60), back-ins (20 x 40), 130 full hkups (15/30 amps), WiFi, tent sites, showers $, laundry, fire rings, firewood, restaurant. **REC.** Pets OK. RV age restrict, 2015 rates: $40. May 1 to Oct 31.
AAA Approved
(250)774-2340 Lat: 58.80463, Lon: -122.72092
5651 Alaska Hwy, Fort Nelson, BC V0C 1R0
tripleghideaway@outlook.com
www.tripleghideaway.com
See ad this page, 1372.

FORT ST JAMES — F2 *Stikine*

PAARENS BEACH PROVINCIAL PARK (Prov Pk) From town: Go 4-3/4 km/3 mi W on secondary road. Pit toilets. 2015 rates: $16. May 1 to Oct 30. (250)964-3489

SOWCHEA BAY PROVINCIAL RECREATION AREA (Prov Pk) From Hwy 27: Go 4 km/2-1/2 mi W of Paaren Beach, Stuart Lake on secondary road. Pit toilets. 2015 rates: $16. May 15 to Sep 1. (250)964-3489

FORT ST JOHN — D6 *Peace River*

BEATTON (Prov Pk) From town, NW 3 mi (8 km) on Hwy 97 (AK Hwy), N 5 mi on Rd 271, W 1 mi on access rd to entrance of park. Pit toilets. 2015 rates: $16. May 15 to Sep 1. (250)964-2243

CHARLIE LAKE PARK (Prov Pk) From Jct of Prov Hwy 2 & Prov Hwy 97, NW 54 mi (74 km) on Prov Hwy 97 to park access rd (R). Pit toilets. 2015 rates: $16. May 15 to Sep 7. (250)787-1894

ROSS H MACLEAN ROTARY RV PARK (Public) N-bnd: On AK Hwy at MP-52, 3.5 mi N of town (R). 2015 rates: $29 to $38. May 1 to Sep 30. (250)785-1700

FORT STEELE — J6 *Kootenay East*

FORT STEELE RESORT & RV PARK **Ratings: 7.5/7.5/7** (RV Park) 2015 rates: $40 to $45. (250)489-4268 10 Wardner-Fort Steele Rd, Fort Steele, BC V0B 1N0

NORBURY LAKE PARK (Prov Pk) From town, SE 10 mi on CR-3/Dull River Rd (Secondary Rd), follow signs (R). Pit toilets. 2015 rates: $16. (250)422-3003

FRUITVALE — K5 *Thompson-Nicola*

CHAMPION LAKES PARK (Prov Pk) From NE end of town, NE 4 mi on Hwy 3B to Champion Lakes Rd, NW 6 mi (L). 2015 rates: $21. (250)825-4293

GALIANO ISLAND — K3 *Mount Waddington*

MONTAGUE HARBOUR PROVINCIAL PARK (Prov Pk) Accessible by car ferry only from Swartz Bay & Tsawwassen. On west coast of Galiano Island. Pit toilets. 2015 rates: $21. (250)539-2115

GIBSONS — K3 *South Coast*

LANGDALE HEIGHTS RV PAR 3 GOLF RESORT **Ratings: 6/9★/8** (RV Resort) 2015 rates: $39. (604)886-2182 rr 6 2170 Port Mellon Hwy, Unit 100, Gibsons, BC V0N 1V6

ROBERTS CREEK PARK (Prov Pk) From town, SE 3 mi on Hwy 101 (R). Pit toilets. 2015 rates: $18. Jun 15 to Sep 15. (604)885-3714

GOLDEN — H5 *Columbia Valley*

GOLDEN ECO ADVENTURE RANCH **Ratings: 6/9.5★/7.5** (Campground) 2015 rates: $38.10 to $43.81. May 4 to Sep 30. (250)344-6825 872 Mcbeath Rd, Golden, BC V0A 1H2

GOLDEN MUNICIPAL CAMPGROUND
(Public) From Jct of TCH 1 & Hwy 95, S 0.5 mi on Hwy 95 to 9th St, E 0.3 Kms/ 0.2 mi (L). Elev 2500 ft. **FAC:** Gravel rds. 35 gravel, 4 pull-thrus (30 x 60), back-ins (30 x 50), mostly side by side hkups, 35 W, 35 E (15/30 amps), WiFi, tent sites, showers $, dump, laundry, groc, fire rings, firewood. **REC:** pool $, Kicking Horse River: fishing, playground. Pets OK. Partial handicap access. RV age restrict, 14 day max stay, 2015 rates: $31 to $35.
(866)538-6625 Lat: 51.29700, Lon: -116.95221
1411 9th St South, Golden, BC VOA 1HO
info@goldenmunicipalcampground.com
www.goldenmunicipalcampground.com
See ad this page.

WHISPERING SPRUCE CAMPGROUND AND RV PARK
Ratings: 6.5/7.5/7 (Campground) From Jct Hwy of 95 & Hwy 1, E 0.9 mi on Hwy 1/Golden View Rd (R). Elev 2960 ft. **FAC:** Gravel rds. (114 spaces). 108 Avail: 60 gravel, 48 grass, 69 pull-thrus (32 x 58), back-ins (32 x 36), 35 full hkups, 51 W, 22 E (15/30 amps), seasonal sites, WiFi, tent sites, dump, laundry, fire rings, firewood. **REC:** playground. Pets OK. RV age restrict, 2015 rates: $35 to $40. Apr 15 to Oct 15.
AAA Approved
(250)344-6680 Lat: 51.30157, Lon: -116.94833
1430 Golden View Rd, Golden, BC V0A 1H1
wsc@whisperingsprucecampground.com
www.whisperingsprucecampground.com
See ad this page.

Explore America's Top RV Destinations! Turn to the Spotlight articles in our State and Province sections to learn more.

GRAND FORKS — K5 *Kootenay West*

GRAND FORKS CITY PARK (Public) From Jct of Hwy 3 & Fifth St, S 0.1 mi on Fifth St (R). 2015 rates: $23 to $33. May 15 to Sep 15. (250)442-5853

RIVIERA RV PARK & CAMPGROUND **Ratings: 6.5/7.5/6.5** (Campground) 2015 rates: $30.95. (877)700-2158 6331 Hwy 3 East, Grand Forks, BC V0H 1H9

GREENWOOD — K5 *Okanagan*

BOUNDARY CREEK PARK (Prov Pk) From town, SW 3 mi on Hwy 3 (R). 2015 rates: $16. May 15 to Sep 16. (250)766-1835

HAGENSBORG — G1 *Skeena-Queen Charlotte*

RIP RAP CAMPSITE (RV Park) (Phone Update) 2015 rates: $23 to $28. (250)982-2752 1854 Hwy 20, Hagensborg, BC V0T 1H0

HARRISON HOT SPRINGS — K3 *Lower Mainland*

SASQUATCH PARK (Prov Pk) From town, N 4 mi on Rockwell Dr (E). Pit toilets. 2015 rates: $21. Mar 28 to Oct 13. (604)986-9371

HAZELTON — E4 *Bulkley Valley*

KSAN CAMPGROUND **Ratings: 6.5/8.5/8.5** (Campground) 2015 rates: $37.50. May 1 to Oct 31. (250)842-5940 1450 River Road, Hazelton, BC V0J 1Y0

SEELEY LAKE PARK (Prov Pk) From town, W 4 mi on Hwy 16 (L). Pit toilets. 2015 rates: $16. May 15 to Sep 30. (250)638-8490

HEDLEY — K4 *Okanagan*

STEMWINDER PARK (Prov Pk) From town, W 2 mi on Hwy 3 (R). Pit toilets. 2015 rates: $16. (250)840-8807

HIXON — G3 *Central Interior*

CANYON CREEK CAMPGROUND & RV PARK
Ratings: 8.5/9★/10 (Campground) From Jct of Hwy 97 & Thorley Rd, N 0.6 mi (1 km) on Hwy 97 (L). **FAC:** Paved rds. (35 spaces). Avail: 31 all weather, 12 pull-thrus (25 x 75), back-ins (30 x 40), 13 full hkups, 12 W, 12 E (15/30 amps), seasonal sites, WiFi $, tent sites, rentals, dump, mobile sewer, laundry, fire rings, firewood, controlled access. **REC:** Hixon Creek: swim, fishing, playground. Pets OK. RV age restrict, eco-friendly, 2015 rates: $24 to $33. May 1 to Sep 30.
(250)998-4384 Lat: 53.42401, Lon: -122.59153
39035 Hwy 97S, Hixon, BC V0K 1S0
rvpark@canyoncreekcampground.com
www.canyoncreekcampground.com
See ad pages 1382, 1372.

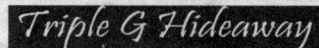

HOPE — K3 *Fraser Valley*

COQUIHALLA CAMPGROUND **Ratings: 6.5/8/8** (Campground) 2015 rates: $36 to $53. Mar 1 to Nov 1. (888)869-7118 800 Kawkawa Lake Rd, Hope, BC V0X 1L0

EMORY BAR RV PARK **Ratings: 5/7.5/7** (RV Park) 2015 rates: $28 to $35. Apr 1 to Oct 31. (604)863-2423 28775 Hwy 1, Hope, BC V0X 1L3

EMORY CREEK PARK (Prov Pk) From Jct Hwy 3 & TCH 1, N 11 mi on TCH 1, follow signs. 2015 rates: $21. May to Oct. (604)869-1167

HOPE VALLEY RV & CAMPGROUND
Ratings: 8/8/7.5 (Campground) E-bnd: From Jct of Hwy 1 & Flood Hope Rd (exit 165), E 0.6km/0.4 mi on Flood Hope Rd (R); or W-bnd: From Jct of Hwy 1 & Flood Hope Rd (exit 168), W 2km/1.3 mi on Flood Hope Rd (L). **FAC:** Paved/gravel rds. (122 spaces). 73 Avail: 68 gravel, 5 grass, no slide-outs, 65 pull-thrus (25 x 60), back-ins (25 x 40), some side by side hkups, 32 full hkups, 41 W, 41 E (30/50 amps), seasonal sites, cable, WiFi, tent sites, rentals, dump, laundry, LP gas, fire rings, firewood. **REC:** heated pool, playground. Pets OK. Big rig sites, RV age restrict, eco-friendly, 2015 rates: $38 to $42. Disc: AAA, military.
(604)869-9857 Lat: 49.36652, Lon: -121.50678
62280 Flood-Hope Rd, Hope, BC V0X 1L2
hopevalleyrv@hotmail.com
www.hopevalleyrv.ca

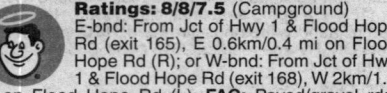

MANNING PARK (Prov Pk) From Jct of TCH-1 & Hwy 3, W 40 mi on Hwy 3 (E). Pit toilets. 2015 rates: $11 to $28. May to Oct. (250)840-8822

MANNING PROVINCIAL PARK (LIGHTNING LAKE CAMPGROUND) (Prov Pk) From town: Go 64 km/40 mi E on Hwy 3. Pit toilets. 2015 rates: $28. Jun 6 to Oct 13. (250)840-8822

OTHELLO TUNNELS CAMPGROUND & RV PARK **Ratings: 4.5/7.5/6.5** (Campground) 2015 rates: $32 to $35. (877)869-0543 67851 Othello Rd, Hope, BC V0X 1L1

SKAGIT VALLEY (Prov Pk) From Jct of Hwy 3 & TCH 1, W 2 mi on TCH 1 to Skagit Valley Rd, S 27 mi, follow signs (E). Pit toilets. 2015 rates: $16. May 1 to Oct 13. (604)986-9371

SUNSHINE VALLEY RV RESORT & CAMPING CABINS **Ratings: 9.5/10★/9** (RV Park) 2015 rates: $40 to $65. (604)869-0066 14850 Alpine Blvd, Hope, BC V0X 1L5

WILD ROSE RV PARK
Ratings: 8/9★/9 (RV Park) E-bnd: From Jct of Hwy 1 & Flood-Hope Rd (exit 165), E 0.5km/0.3 mi on Flood Hope Rd (R); or W-bnd: From Jct of Hwy 1 & Flood-Hope Rd (exit 168), W 2.2km/1.4 mi on Flood-Hope Rd (L). **FAC:** Paved rds. (58 spaces). 45 Avail: 10 gravel, 35 grass, 15 pull-thrus (27 x 60), back-ins (33 x 45), 32 full hkups, 10 W, 10 E (30/50 amps), seasonal sites, cable, WiFi, tent sites, dump, laundry, fire rings, firewood. **REC:** playground. Pets OK. Big rig sites, RV age restrict, eco-friendly, 2015 rates: $42 to $50.40. Disc: AAA. AAA Approved
(604)869-9842 Lat: 49.36572, Lon: -121.51315
62030 Flood-Hope Rd, Hope, BC V0X 1L2
wildrose@uniserve.com
www.wildrosecamp.com
See ad this page, 1372.

HORNBY ISLAND — K2 *Central Coast*

BRADSDADSLAND RESORT (Campground) (Phone Update) 2015 rates: $34.50 to $54. (250)335-0757 2105 Shingle Spit Rd, Hornby Island, BC V0R 1Z0

TRIBUNE BAY CAMPSITE (Campground) (Phone Update) Pit toilets. 2015 rates: $35 to $40. Jun 15 to Sep 15. (250)335-2359 5200 Shields Rd, Hornby Island, BC V0R 1Z0

Tell them you saw them in this Guide!

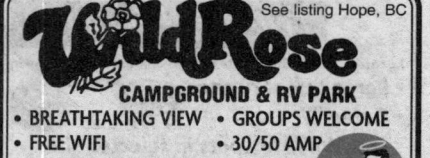

HORSEFLY — G3 *Bulkley-Nechako*

HORSEFLY LAKE (Prov Pk) From Jct of Hwy 97 & Horsefly-Quesnel Lake Rd, E 42 mi on Horsefly-Quesnel Lake Rd (R). Pit toilets. 2015 rates: $21. May 15 to Sep 15. (250)397-2523

HOUSTON — F1 *Bulkley Valley*

SHADY REST RV PARK/MHP **Ratings: 6/10★/8** (Campground) 2015 rates: $21 to $30. May 15 to Sep 15. (250)845-2314 3960 Drive In Road, Houston, BC V0J 1Z2

HUDSON'S HOPE — D6 *Peace River*

DINOSAUR LAKE CAMPGROUND (DISTRICT PARK) (Public) From south town limits: Go 6.4 km/4 mi S on Hwy 29, then 1.6 km/1 mi W on Peace Canyon Dam Rd. Pit toilets. 2015 rates: $20 to $29. May 22 to Sep 7. (250)783-9154

ISKUT — C4 *Cassiar Mountains*

MOUNTAIN SHADOW RESORT **Ratings: 5.5/8.5★/7.5** (RV Park) 2015 rates: $20 to $38. May 1 to Sep 30. (250)234-3333 hwy 37, Km 254, Iskut, BC V0J 1K0

TATOGGA LAKE RV RESORT **Ratings: 5.5/7/7.5** (Campground) 2015 rates: $15 to $25. May 15 to Nov 1. (250)234-3526 km 390 - Hwy 37, Iskut, BC V0J 1K0

JADE CITY — B4 *Stikine*

BOYA LAKE PARK (Prov Pk) From Jct of Hwy 37 & Boya Lake Rd, E 1.5 mi on Boya Lake Rd (E). Pit toilets. 2015 rates: $18. May 15 to Sep 15. (250)638-8490

KALEDEN — K4 *South Okanagan*

BANBURY GREEN RV & CAMPING RESORT **Ratings: 5.5/7/8** (RV Resort) 2015 rates: $40 to $55. May 15 to Sep 30. (250)497-5221 930 Pineview Drive, Kaleden, BC V0H 1K0

KAMLOOPS — J4 *Thompson*

KAMLOOPS RV PARK (Public) From Jct of Hwy 5N & Hwy 1, E 10 mi on Hwy 1/Exit 390 (LaFarge Rd) (R). 2015 rates: $35 to $40. (250)573-3789

LAC LE JEUNE PARK (Prov Pk) From town, SW 23 mi on Hwy 5 to Lac Le Jeune Rd exit, E 3 mi (R). 2015 rates: $21. May 15 to Sep 30. (250)377-8888

PAUL LAKE PARK (Prov Pk) From Jct of Prov Hwy 5 & Paul Lake Rd, E 14 mi on Paul Lake Rd (R). 2015 rates: $16. May 15 to Sep 15. (250)578-7376

KASLO — J5 *Kootenay West*

KOOTENAY LAKE/LOST LEDGE (Prov Pk) From town, N 15 mi on Hwy-31 (R). Pit toilets. 2015 rates: $21. (250)825-4212

MIRROR LAKE CAMPGROUND **Ratings: 5/8/8** (Campground) 2015 rates: $24 to $27. Apr 15 to Oct 15. (250)353-7102 5777 Arcola Rd, Kaslo, BC V0G 1M0

SCHROEDER CREEK RESORT **Ratings: 6.5/7.5★/7** (Campground) 2015 rates: $35. Apr 1 to Oct 31. (250)353-7383 128 Bickel Rd, Kaslo, BC V0G 1M0

KELOWNA — J4 *Central Okanagan*

BEAR CREEK PROVINCIAL PARK (Prov Pk) From town: Go 8-3/4 km/5-1/2 mi S on Hwy 97, then 8 km/5 mi NW on Westside Rd. 2015 rates: $30. Apr 1 to Oct 14. (250)548-0076

HIAWATHA RV PARK **Ratings: 7.5/8★/7** (RV Park) 2015 rates: $44 to $60. Mar 1 to Sep 30. (250)861-4837 3795 Lakeshore Rd, Kelowna, BC V1W 3K3

HOLIDAY PARK RESORT
Ratings: 9.5/9.5★/9.5 (Condo Pk) From Jct Hwy 97 & Commonwealth Rd, 0.6km/0.4 mi on Commonwealth Rd (L). **FAC:** Paved rds. (570 spaces). Avail: 100 paved, patios, back-ins (30 x 75), 100 full hkups (30/50 amps), WiFi $, laundry, groc, LP bottles, restaurant, controlled access. **REC:** heated pool, whirlpool, Duck Lake: fishing, golf, shuffleboard, playground. Pets OK. Partial handicap access, no tents. Big rig sites, RV age restrict, eco-friendly, 2015 rates: $45 to $70. Disc: AAA.
(250)766-4255 Lat: 50.00765, Lon: -119.39306
i-415 Commonwealth Rd, Kelowna, BC V4V 1P4
holiday@sweetlife.com
www.sweetlife.com

KIMBERLEY — J6 *Kimberley, Kootenay East*

KIMBERLEY RIVERSIDE CAMPGROUND (Public) From Jct of Hwy 95A North & St Mary Lake Rd, W 2.7kms/ 1.7 mi on St Mary Lake Rd (L). Elev 3205 ft. **FAC:** Paved/gravel rds. (130 spaces). Avail: 106 gravel, 45 pull-thrus (35 x 85), back-ins (25 x 55), 81 full hkups, 25 W, 25 E (30/50 amps), WiFi Hotspot, tent sites, dump, laundry, fire rings, firewood. **REC:** heated pool, St Mary 's River: fishing, playground. Pets OK. Partial handicap access. Big rig sites, RV age restrict, 2015 rates: $30 to $41. Apr 15 to Oct 15. AAA Approved
(877)999-2929 Lat: 49.63494, Lon: -115.99763
site 500, St Mary Lake Rd, Kimberley, BC V1A 3B9
info@kimberleycampground.com
www.kimberleycampground.com

KITIMAT — F1 *Kitimat-Stikine*

RADLEY PARK (MUNICIPAL PARK) (Public) In town on Commercial St next to Kitimat River. Follow signs. Pit toilets. 2015 rates: $18 to $24. (250)632-8955

LAC LA HACHE — H3 *Cariboo*

BIG COUNTRY CAMPGROUND & RV PARK **Ratings: 8/9★/7.5** (Campground) 2015 rates: $29 to $34. May 15 to Sep 30. (250)396-4181 4239 Caraboo Hwy 97S, Lac La Hache, BC V0K 1T0

KOKANEE BAY MOTEL & CAMPGROUND **Ratings: 5.5/7/7** (Campground) 2015 rates: $29 to $33. May 1 to Oct 15. (250)396-7345 3728 Hwy 97 Cariboo Hwy, Lac La Hache, BC V0K 1T1

LAC LA HACHE PARK (Prov Pk) From town, N 15 mi on Hwy 97 (R). 2015 rates: $16. May 15 to Sep 30. (250)397-2523

LADYSMITH — K2 *Lower Island, Nanaimo District*

RONDALYN RESORT FAMILY RV & TENTING - PARKBRIDGE
Ratings: 8.5/9.5★/9.5 (RV Resort) From Jct of Hwy 1 & Timberlands Rd, W 2.2km/1.4 mi on Timberlands Rd (R). **FAC:** Gravel rds. (98 spaces). Avail: 65 gravel, 16 pull-thrus (34 x 65), back-ins (30 x 65), 35 full hkups, 30 W, 30 E (15/30 amps), WiFi, tent sites, rentals, dump, laundry, fire rings, firewood, controlled access. **REC:** heated pool, whirlpool, Haslam Creek: golf, playground. Pet restrict(B). Partial handicap access. RV age restrict, 2015 rates: $33 to $52.
(250)245-3227 Lat: 49.03990, Lon: -123.90266
1350 Timberlands Road, Ladysmith, BC V9G 1L5
rondalyn@parkbridge.com
www.parkbridge.com/rondalyn
See ad pages 1370 (Welcome Section), 1372.

LAKE COUNTRY — J4 *Cariboo*

WOOD LAKE RV PARK AND MARINA Ratings: 7.5/9.5★/7.5 (RV Park) From Jct of Hwy 97 & Woodsdale Rd, E 0.5km/0.3 mi on Woodsdale Rd. (L). **FAC:** Paved/gravel rds. 188 gravel, 20 pull-thrus (20 x 50), back-ins (20 x 50), 188 full hkups (30/50 amps), WiFi, tent sites, dump, laundry, fire rings, firewood. **REC:** Wood Lake: swim, fishing, marina, playground. Pets OK $. RV age restrict, 2015 rates: $20 to $80.
(250)766-1881 Lat: 50.04963, Lon: -119.40877
2930 Woodsdale Rd, Lake Country, BC V4V 1Y1
info@woodlakerv.com
www.woodlakerv.com

LAKE COWICHAN — K2 *Mount Waddington*

GORDON BAY PROVINCIAL PARK (Prov Pk) From town: Go 12-3/4 km/8 mi W on Hwy 18. 2015 rates: $11 to $30. (250)474-1336

LANGLEY — K3 *Lower Mainland*

FORT CAMPING IN BRAE ISLAND REGIONAL PARK **Ratings: 8/9★/9** (Campground) 2015 rates: $34 to $48. (604)888-3678 9451 Glover Rd, Langley, BC V1M 2R9

LEE CREEK — H4 *Thompson Okanagan*

COTTONWOOD COVE RESORT **Ratings: 6.5/9★/9** (Campground) 2015 rates: $50 to $65. May 1 to Oct 31. (866)931-3572 2604 Squilax-Anglemont Hwy, Lee Creek, BC V0E 1M4

LIARD RIVER — B5 *Northern Rockies*

LIARD RIVER HOT SPRINGS (Prov Pk) From town, NE 36 mi on Hwy 97 (R). Pit toilets. 2015 rates: $16 to $24. (250)776-7000

LINDELL BEACH — K3 *Strathcona*

THOUSAND TRAILS - CULTUS LAKE **Ratings: 8/9★/9** (Membership Pk) 2015 rates: $51 to $58. (800)405-6188 1855 Columbia Valley Rd., Lindell Beach, BC V2R 0E1

LONE BUTTE — H3 *Cariboo*

LOON BAY RESORT **Ratings: 7.5/8.5★/8** (Campground) 2015 rates: $33 to $36. May 15 to Oct 15. (250)593-4431 7250 Texas Rd, Lone Butte, BC V0K 1X1

LONE BUTTE (CONT)

SHERIDAN LAKE RESORT **Ratings: 6/9★/8** (Campground) 2015 rates: $30 to $33. Apr 30 to Oct 15. (250)593-4611 7510 Magnussen Rd, Lone Butte, BC V0K 1X1

LUMBY — J4 *Cariboo*

MABEL LAKE PARK (Prov Pk) From Jct of Hwys 97 & 6, E 32 mi on Hwy 6 to Mabel Lake Rd, NE 47 mi (E). Pit toilets. 2015 rates: $21. (250)547-6862

LUND — J2 *Sunshine Coast*

LUND See also Black Creek, Campbell River, Comox, Courtenay, Powell River & Quadra Island.

SUNLUND BY-THE-SEA RV CAMPGROUND & CABINS **Ratings: 6.5/8.5★/8** (RV Park) 2015 rates: $32. May 1 to Sep 30. (604)483-9220 1496 Murray Rd, Lund, BC V0N 2G0

LYTTON — J3 *Cariboo*

SKIHIST PARK (Prov Pk) From town, E 8 km (5 mi) on Hwy 1 (R). 2015 rates: $21. May 1 to Sep 30. (250)455-2708

MACKENZIE — E5 *Peace River*

MACKENZIE MUNICIPAL RV PARK (Public) From Jct of Hwys 97 & 39, N 18 mi on Hwy 39, at entrance to town (R). Sites without hookups are free for first 3 days, then $10 for each additional day. 2015 rates: $20 to $29. May to Oct. (250)997-3221

MAPLE RIDGE — K3 *Greater Vancouver*

GOLDEN EARS PARK (Prov Pk) From E end of town, E 3.5 mi on Hwy 7 to 232nd St, N 2.5 mi to Fern Crescent Rd, E 2.5 mi (E). 2015 rates: $30. Jun 20 to Sep 1. (604)795-6169

MARA — J4 *Okanagan, Thompson*

WHISPERING PINES TENT & RV PARK **Ratings: 7/8/8** (Campground) 2015 rates: $35 To $47.50. May 21 to Oct 12. (250)838-6775 11 Hamilton Rd, Mara, BC V0E 2K0

MASSET — E3 *Skeena-Queen Charlotte*

NAIKOON PARK-MISTY MEADOWS (Prov Pk) Take ferry from Prince Rupert to Skidgate, N 20.5 mi (45 km) on Hwy 16 (R). Pit toilets. 2015 rates: $16. (250)626-3337

NAIKOON/AGATE BEACH CAMPGROUND (Prov Pk) From town, E 25 km on Hwy 16 to Toll Hill Rd (L). Pit toilets. 2015 rates: $16. (250)626-3337

MCBRIDE — G4 *Cariboo*

BEAVERVIEW RV PARK & CAMPGROUND **Ratings: 5.5/8★/8** (Campground) 2015 rates: $30 to $34. May 1 to Sep 30. (250)569-2513 2435 Hwy 16E, Mcbride, BC V0J 2E0

N.V. MOUNTAIN VIEW CHALETS & RV RESORT **Ratings: 6.5/9★/6.5** (RV Park) 2015 rates: $23 to $37. May 15 to Nov 15. (250)569-0185 5306 Hwy 10 East, Mcbride, BC V0J 2E0

MCLEESE LAKE — G3 *Cariboo*

MCLEESE LAKE RESORT **Ratings: 6.5/8.5★/7** (Campground) 2015 rates: $26 to $35. May 1 to Oct 15. (250)297-6525 6721 Cariboo Hwy 97 N, Mcleese Lake, BC V0L 1P0

MCLEOD LAKE — E6 *Fraswer-Fortt George*

CARP LAKE PROVINCIAL PARK (Prov Pk) From town: Go 32 km/20 mi W on gravel, secondary road. Check locally before proceeding. Pit toilets. 2015 rates: $16. May 16 to Sep 1. (250)964-3489

TUDYAH LAKE PROVINCIAL PARK (Prov Pk) From town: Go 8-3/4 km/5-1/2 mi N on Hwy 97. Pit toilets. 2015 rates: $11. May 15 to Sep 30. (250)964-3489

WHISKERS POINT PROVINCIAL PARK (Prov Pk) From town: Go 9-1/2 km/6 mi S on Hwy 97. 2015 rates: $18. May 17 to Sep 8. (250)964-3489

MCLURE — H4 *Thompson*

PINEGROVE CAMPGROUND AND RV PARK
Ratings: 7.5/7.5/7.5 (Campground) N-bnd: From Jct of Hwy 5 & Hwy 1 in Kamloops, N 41kms/25.6 mi on Hwy 5 (L). **FAC:** Gravel rds. 25 gravel, 19 pull-thrus (20 x 65), back-ins (23 x 50), 6 full hkups, 19 W, 19 E (30/50 amps), cable, WiFi $, tent sites, dump, laundry, groc, fire rings, firewood, controlled access. **REC:** playground. Pets OK. RV age restrict, eco-friendly, 2015 rates: $24 to $38. Disc: AAA. AAA Approved
(877)672-5529 Lat: 51.01118, Lon: -120.22257
421 Walterdale Rd, General Delivery, Mclure, BC V0E 2H0
pinegrove2011@gmail.com
www.pinegrovecampground.net

MERRITT — J4 *Thompson Region*

CLAYBANKS RV PARK (Public) From Jct of Hwy 5 & Voght St (exit 290), S 2.4 mi on Voght St, follow Sani-Station signs (L). 2015 rates: $25 to $30. (250)378-6441

KENTUCKY-ALLEYNE PROVINCIAL PARK (Prov Pk) From town: Go 31-1/2 km/19-3/4 mi S on Hwy 5, then 6 km/3-3/4 mi E on secondary road. Pit toilets. 2015 rates: $16. May 15 to Sep 30. (250)378-5334

MONCK PARK (Prov Pk) From city center, NE 11 mi on Prov Hwy 5A to Monck Park access rd, E 5 mi (R). 2015 rates: $21. Apr 25 to Sep 30. (250)315-0253

MOON SHADOWS RV PARK **Ratings: 5.5/9★/7** (RV Park) 2015 rates: $28 to $40. (888)344-2267 1145 Neilson St, Merritt, BC V1K 1B8

MEZIADIN JUNCTION — D4 *Kitimat-Stikine*

KINASKAN LAKE (Prov Pk) From town, S 85 mi on Hwy 37 (R). Pit toilets. 2015 rates: $16. May 15 to Sep 30. (250)638-8490

MEZIADIN LAKE (Prov Pk) From Jct of Hwy 16 & Hwy 37, N 150 mi, follow signs (L). Pit toilets. 2015 rates: $18. May 15 to Sep 15. (250)638-8490

MEZIADIN LAKE — D4 *Kitimat-Stikine*

BELL 2 LODGE **Ratings: 4/9/6.5** (RV Park) 2015 rates: $35. (250)275-4770 km 249 Hwy 37, Meziadin Lake, BC V0J 3S0

MILL BAY — K3 *South Island*

BAMBERTON PROVINCIAL PARK (Prov Pk) From town: Go 8 km/5 mi S on Hwy 1. Pit toilets. 2015 rates: $11 to $16. (250)474-1336

MISSION — K3 *Greater Vancouver*

KILBY (Prov Pk) From Jct of SR-7 & School Rd, S 0.4 mi on School Rd, follow signs. Pit toilets. 2015 rates: $10 to $25. (604)796-9576

ROLLEY LAKE PARK (Prov Pk) From Jct of Hwy 7 (Maple Ridge) & Dewdney Trunk Rd, NW 8 mi on Dewdney Trunk Rd to Rolley Lake Rd, N 2 mi (L). 2015 rates: $30. Apr 1 to Oct 14. (604)466-8325

MONTE LAKE — J4 *Thompson*

HERITAGE CAMPSITE & RV PARK (RV Park) (Phone Update) 2015 rates: $25 to $33. Apr 15 to Oct 15. (250)375-2434 3961 Hwy 97, Monte Lake, BC V0E 2N0

MORICETOWN — E4 *Bulkley-Nechako*

MORICETOWN RV PARK (Campground) (Phone Update) 2015 rates: $22 to $32. May 15 to Sep 15. (250)847-1461 163 Telkwa High Rd, Smithers, BC V0J 2N1

MUNCHO LAKE — B5 *Liard, Peace River*

MUNCHO LAKE LODGE & RV PARK **Ratings: 3.5/6.5/7.5** (Campground) 2015 rates: $37. May 15 to Sep 15. (250)776-3005 mile 463 Alaska Hwy, Muncho Lake, BC V0C 1Z0

MUNCHO LAKE PARK (Prov Pk) From town, S 3 km on Hwy 97 (R). Pit toilets. 2015 rates: $16. May 1 to Sep 15. (250)776-7000

NORTHERN ROCKIES LODGE & RV PARK **Ratings: 5.5/9★/8** (Campground) 2015 rates: $42 to $58. (800)663-5269 mile 462 Alaska Hwy, Muncho Lake, BC V0C 1Z0

NAKUSP — J5 *Kootenay West*

COACHMAN CAMPSITE (Campground) (Phone Update) 2015 rates: $22.50 to $31.50. Apr 15 to Oct 31. (250)265-4212 1701 Hwy 23N, Nakusp, BC V0G 1R0

HALCYON HOT SPRINGS RESORT (Campground) (Phone Update) 2015 rates: $70. (888)689-4699 5655 Hwy 23, Nakusp, BC V0G 1R0

NAKUSP HOT SPRINGS CAMPGROUND (Public) From Jct of Hwy 6 & Hwy 23, (6th Ave NW & W Broadway), N 1.6 mi on Hwy 6 to Hot Springs Rd, E 7.5 mi (E). 2015 rates: $26.75 to $30. May 1 to Oct 15. (866)999-4528

NAKUSP VILLAGE CAMPGROUND (Public) In town from jct Hwy 23 & 4th St NW: Go 200 meters/220 yards W on 4th St NW, then 30 meters/100 feet S on 8th Ave NW. 2015 rates: $19 to $27. May 15 to Oct 15. (250)265-4019

THREE ISLANDS RESORT RV & CAMPING (Campground) (Phone Update) 2015 rates: $26 to $30. May 1 to Sep 30. (250)265-3023 2384 Hwy 6, Nakusp, BC V0G 1R0

We appreciate your business!

NANAIMO — K2 *East Island*

BRANNEN LAKE RV PARK & CAMPSITE **Ratings: 6.5/8.5/9** (Campground) 2015 rates: $33 to $35. (866)756-0404 4220 Biggs Rd, Nanaimo, BC V9T 5P9

JINGLEPOT RV PARK & CAMPGROUNDS **Ratings: 6/8/6.5** (Campground) 2015 rates: $30 to $34. (250)758-1614 4012 Jinglepot Rd, Nanaimo, BC V9T 5P9

LIVING FOREST OCEANSIDE CAMPGROUND & RV PARK **Ratings: 9/8.5/9.5** (RV Park) 2015 rates: $25 to $51. (250)755-1755 6 Maki Rd, Nanaimo, BC V9R 6N7

MOUNTAINAIRE CAMPGROUND & RV PARK **Ratings: 6.5/8/7.5** (Campground) 2015 rates: $38. (250)245-1169 1092 Spruston Rd, Nanaimo, BC V9X 1R2

NELSON — J5 *Kootenay West*

KOKANEE CREEK (Prov Pk) From town, NE 12 mi on Hwy 3A (R). 2015 rates: $30 to $35. May 1 to Sep 30. (250)825-4293

NELSON CITY CAMPGROUND (Public) From Jct of Hwys 6 & 3A, NE 0.7 mi on Hwy 3A to Edgewood, N 0.2 mi, follow signs (E). 2015 rates: $20 to $30. May 1 to Sep 30. (250)352-7618

NORTH PENDER ISLAND — K3 *Mount Waddington*

GULF ISLANDS PRIOR CENTENNIAL PARK (Natl Pk) Take ferry from Swartz Bay to Pender Island, S 3 mi, follow signs (L). Pit toilets. 2015 rates: $13.70. May 15 to Sep 30. (250)654-4000

OKANAGAN FALLS — K4 *South Okanagan*

OKANAGAN FALLS PARK (Prov Pk) From town, N 1 mi on Hwy 97 to Green Lake Rd (L). 2015 rates: $21. Mar 28 to Oct 14. (250)548-0076

SUN & SAND TENT & TRAILER PARK **Ratings: 6/9★/7** (Campground) 2015 rates: $30 to $55. Apr 15 to Oct 15. (250)497-8289 5356 8th Ave, Okanagan Falls, BC V0H 1R0

OLIVER — K4 *South Okanagan*

APPLE BEACH RV PARK **Ratings: 6/8★/8** (RV Park) 2015 rates: $25 to $44. (855)358-3287 915 Bulrush Road, Oliver, BC V0H 1T2

BEL-AIR CEDAR RESORT **Ratings: 7.5/8.5/8** (RV Park) 2015 rates: $30 to $44. (800)801-0999 5650 Hwy 97 S, Oliver, BC V0H 1T9

DESERT GEM RV RESORT
Ratings: 8/10★/9.5 (RV Park) From Jct of Fairway Ave & Hwy 97 (in town), S 1km/0.6 mi on Main St. (Hwy 97) (L). **FAC:** Paved rds. 65 paved, patios, 17 pull-thrus (25 x 62), back-ins (25 x 50), 65 full hkups (15/50 amps), cable, WiFi, rentals, laundry, controlled access. **REC:** Pet restrict(B/Q). Partial handicap access, no tents. Big rig sites, RV age restrict, eco-friendly, 2015 rates: $37 to $51.
(888)925-9966 Lat: 49.17269, Lon: -119.55439
5753 Main St (Hwy 97), Oliver, BC V0H 1T0
info@desertgemrv.com
www.desertgemrv.com
See ad this page, 1372.

GALLAGHER LAKE RESORT - PARKBRIDGE
Ratings: 7.5/9/8.5 (Campground) From town, N 8kms/5 mi on Hwy 97 (R). **FAC:** Paved rds. (110 spaces). Avail: 95 gravel, 20 pull-thrus (28 x 62), back-ins (26 x 40), 58 full hkups, 27 W, 27 E (15/30 amps), seasonal sites, WiFi, tent sites, rentals, showers $, dump, laundry, groc. **REC:** Gallagher Lake: swim, fishing, playground. Pets OK. RV age restrict, 2015 rates: $38 to $54. May 1 to Oct 1.
(250)498-3358 Lat: 49.24372, Lon: -119.52436
8439 Hwy 97, Oliver, BC V0H 1T2
gallagherlake@parkbridge.com
www.gallagherlakeresort.com
See ad pages 1370 (Welcome Section), 1372.

OLIVER (CONT)

OLIVER CENTENNIAL RV PARK **Ratings: 6/6.5/5.5** (RV Park) 2015 rates: $25 to $39. Apr 1 to Oct 6. (877)965-4837 256 Fairview Rd, Oliver, BC V0H 1T0

THE LAKESIDE RESORT **Ratings: 7/6.5/7.5** (Campground) 2015 rates: $27 to $45. (800)220-7330 6707 Lakeside Dr, Oliver, BC V0H 1T4

OSOYOOS — K4 *South Okanagan*

BROOKVALE HOLIDAY RESORT **Ratings: 6/8.5★/8** (Campground) 2015 rates: $36 to $46. May 20 to Sep 1. (250)495-7514 1219 Lakeshore Dr, Osoyoos, BC V0H 1V6

HAYNES POINT PARK (Prov Pk) From town, S 1 mi on Hwy 97 to 32nd Ave (R). 2015 rates: $30. Apr 1 to Oct 14. (250)548-0076

NK'MIP CAMPGROUND & RV PARK **Ratings: 8.5/9★/9** (RV Park) 2015 rates: $40 to $52. (250)495-7279 8000 45th St, Osoyoos, BC V0H 1V6

WALTON'S LAKEFRONT RESORT **Ratings: 9/9.5★/9.5** (Condo Pk) 2015 rates: $35 to $80. (800)964-1148 3207 Lakeshore Drive, Osoyoos, BC V0H 1V6

PARKSVILLE — K2 *East Island*

ENGLISHMAN RIVER FALLS (Prov Pk) From town, W 3.5 mi on Hwy 4 to Errington Rd, S 5 mi (E). For reservations call 1-800-689-9025. Pit toilets. 2015 rates: $21. May 1 to Sep 30. (250)474-1336

FILLONGLEY PARK (Prov Pk) From ferry (Buckley Bay to Denman Island), E 9 mi on PR-19 (R). Pit toilets. 2015 rates: $11 to $21. (250)474-1336

LITTLE QUALICUM FALLS (Prov Pk) From Jct of Hwy 19 & Hwy 4, W 12 mi on Hwy 4 (R). 2015 rates: $21. May 1 to Sep 30. (250)474-1336

PARADISE SEA SIDE RESORT **Ratings: 8/10★/9** (RV Park) 2015 rates: $27 to $47. Mar 1 to Oct 31. (250)248-6612 375 W Island Hwy, Parksville, BC V9P 1A1

PARRYS RV PARK & CAMPGROUND Ratings: 8.5/8.5★/9 (RV Park) From Jct 19 & 19A (exit 46), N 3.7km/2.3 mi on Hwy 19A to Martindale Rd, W 0.5 km/0.3 mi (L). **FAC:** Gravel rds. (125 spaces). Avail: 106 grass, 74 pull-thrus (25 x 55), back-ins (25 x 55), 79 full hkups, 21 W, 21 E (20/30 amps), seasonal sites, cable, WiFi, tent sites, showers $, dump, laundry, groc, firewood. **REC:** heated pool, Englishman River: swim, playground. Pets OK. Partial handicap access. RV age restrict, 2015 rates: $40 to $49. Disc: AAA. May 1 to Sep 30.
AAA Approved
(250)248-6242 Lat: 49.31269, Lon: -124.28568
380 Martingdale Rd, Parksville, BC V9P 1R7
info@parrysrvpark.com
www.parrysrvpark.com

RATHTREVOR BEACH PARK (Prov Pk) From town, S 2 mi on Hwy 19A (R). 2015 rates: $11 to $30. (250)474-1336

SURFSIDE RV RESORT **Ratings: 9/9.5★/9.5** (Membership Pk) 2015 rates: $35 to $65. (866)642-2001 200 N Corfield St, Parksville, BC V9P 2H5

PEACHLAND — J4 *Central Okanagan*

TODD'S RV & CAMPING **Ratings: 4.5/7/6.5** (Campground) 2015 rates: $35 to $67. Apr 1 to Oct 15. (866)255-6864 3976 Beach Ave, Peachland, BC V0H 1X1

Get the Facts! Essential tips and travel info for can be found in the Welcome Section at the beginning of each State/Province.

PEMBERTON — J3 *Cariboo*

BIRKENHEAD LAKE PARK (Prov Pk) From Pemberton-D'Arcy Hwy, NW 11 mi on gravel rd (L). Pit toilets. 2015 rates: $18. May 15 to Sep 15. (604)986-9371

NAIRN FALLS PARK (Prov Pk) From town, S 2 mi on Hwy 99 (L). Pit toilets. 2015 rates: $20. May 15 to Sep 30. (604)986-9371

PENTICTON — J4 *South Okanagan*

CAMP-ALONG RESORT **Ratings: 6.5/8.5★/7.5** (Campground) 2015 rates: $20 to $45. Apr 1 to Oct 15. (800)968-5267 100 Ash Ave, Kaleden, BC V0H 1K0

OKANAGAN LAKE (Prov Pk) From town, N 20 mi on Hwy 97 (R). 2015 rates: $30. Mar 28 to Oct 14. (250)548-0076

SOUTH BEACH GARDENS RV PARK **Ratings: 7/7.5/5.5** (Campground) 2015 rates: $29 to $46. May 15 to Sep 15. (250)492-0628 3815 Skaha Lake Rd, Penticton, BC V2A 6G8

WRIGHT'S BEACH CAMP **Ratings: 7.5/8/6.5** (Campground) 2015 rates: $32 to $64. Mar 15 to Oct 15. (250)492-7120 4200 Skaha Lake Rd, Penticton, BC V2A 6J7

PORT ALBERNI — K2 *East Island*

CHINA CREEK CAMPGROUND & MARINA (REG PARK) (Public) From jct Hwy 4 & 10th Ave: Go S on 10th Ave following signs to Bamfield Rd, then 16 km/10 mi on Bamfield Rd. 2015 rates: $20 to $37.36. (250)723-9812

SPROAT LAKE PARK (Prov Pk) From town, NW 8 mi on SR-4 (R). 2015 rates: $21 to $25. (250)474-1336

STAMP RIVER PARK (Prov Pk) From Jct of Hwy 4 & Beaver Creek Rd, N 9 mi on Beaver Creek Rd (L). Pit toilets. 2015 rates: $11 to $16. (250)474-1336

TIMBERLODGE & RV CAMPGROUND Ratings: 6.5/8★/7.5 (RV Park) From Jct of Hwy 19 & Hwy 4, W 33km/20.7mi on Hwy 4 to Timberlane Rd, S 80m/85yds (L). **FAC:** Gravel rds. (39 spaces). Avail: 24 gravel, back-ins (25 x 45), 21 full hkups, 3 W, 3 E (30/50 amps), seasonal sites, cable, WiFi, tent sites, rentals, laundry, restaurant. **REC:** heated pool. Pets OK. Partial handicap access. RV age restrict, 2015 rates: $35 to $42. Disc: AAA.
AAA Approved
(250)723-9415 Lat: 49.26450, Lon: -124.75396
2404 Timberlane Rd, Port Alberni, BC V9Y 8P2
timberlodge@shaw.ca
www.timberlodgerv.ca

PORT EDWARD — E3 *Skeena-Queen Charlotte*

KINNIKINNICK CAMPGROUND & RV PARK **Ratings: 4/6/7** (Campground) 2015 rates: $24 to $32. (866)628-9449 333 Skeena Dr, Port Edward, BC V0V 1G0

PORT HARDY — J1 *North Island*

PORT HARDY RV RESORT (RV Park) (Phone Update) 2015 rates: $39. Jun 1 to Sep 14. (855)949-8118 8080 Goodspeed Rd, Port Hardy, BC V0N 2P0

QUATSE RIVER CAMPGROUND (N. VANCOUVER ISLAND SALMONID ENHANCEMENT ASSOC.) (Public) From south city limits: Go 1-1/2 km/1 mi S on Hwy 19, then 3/4 km/1/2 mi W on Coal Harbour Rd. 2015 rates: $18 to $29. (866)949-2395

PORT MCNEILL — J1 *North Island*

ALDER BAY RESORT **Ratings: 7/8.5★/8** (Campground) 2015 rates: $32 to $34. (888)956-4117 #1 Alder Bay Dr, Port Mcneill, BC V0N 2R0

CLUXEWE RESORT **Ratings: 5/8.5/8** (RV Park) 2015 rates: $20 to $26. (250)949-0378 1 Cluxewe Campground Rd, Port Mcneill, BC V0N 2R0

POWELL RIVER — J2 *South Coast*

POWELL RIVER See also Comox, Courtenay, Garden Bay, Lund & Saltery Bay.

HAYWIRE BAY REGIONAL PARK (POWELL RIVER REG DISTRICT) (Public) From town: Go N on Manson Ave, then right on Cranberry St, then left on Haslam St, turn left on gravel road, then 7-1/4 km/4-1/2 mi on gravel road to park. Pit toilets. 2015 rates: $21. May 3 to Sep 29. (604)483-1097

SHELTER POINT REGIONAL PARK (POWELL RIVER REG DISTRICT) (Public) From Powell River: Take Texada Island ferry to Blubber Bay terminal. Follow Hwy, turn S toward Gillies Bay at only intersection. On SW coast of Texada Isl. 33-1/2 km/21 mi from ferry terminal. 2015 rates: $16 to $21. (604)485-2260

WILLINGDON BEACH CAMPSITE (Public) From Ferry, N 1 mi on Marine Ave (L). 2015 rates: $24 to $32. (604)485-2242

WILLINGDON BEACH MUNICIPAL CAMPSITE (Public) From Jct of Hwy 101 & Alberni St, N 0.5 km on Hwy 101 (L). 2015 rates: $24 to $32. (604)485-2242

PRINCE GEORGE — F3 *Central Interior*

BEE LAZEE RV PARK & CAMPGROUND Ratings: 8.5/9.5★/9 (Campground) From Jct of Hwys 16 & 97, S 9.4 mi on Hwy 97, 8 mi S of Simon Fraser Bridge (L). **FAC:** All weather rds. 35 Avail: 35 all weather, 26 pull-thrus (32 x 60), back-ins (34 x 40), 30 full hkups, 5 W, 5 E (15/30 amps), WiFi, tent sites, dump, laundry, fire rings, firewood, controlled access. **REC:** heated pool. Pets OK. Partial handicap access. RV age restrict, eco-friendly, 2015 rates: $30 to $32. May 1 to Sep 30.
(866)963-7263 Lat: 53.78196, Lon: -122.65516
15910 Hwy 97 S, Prince George, BC V2N 5Y3
drone@pgonline.com
beelazee.ca
See ad this page, 1372.

BLUE CEDARS CAMPGROUND **Ratings: 6/8/7** (Campground) 2015 rates: $37. (888)964-7271 4433 Kimball Road, Prince George, BC V2N 5N7

HARTWAY RV PARK **Ratings: 6.5/9★/8** (RV Park) 2015 rates: $35 to $38. (866)962-8848 7729 Kelly Rd S, Prince George, BC V2K 2H5

MAMAYEH RV PARK (Campground) (Too New to Rate) From Jct of Hwy 16 & Hwy 97, S 18kms/11mi on Hwy 97 to White Rd, E 0.3km/0.2mi (L). **FAC:** Gravel rds. 24 gravel, 11 pull-thrus (84 x 120), back-ins (45 x 50), some side by side hkups, 24 full hkups (20/50 amps), WiFi, tent sites. Pets OK. Big rig sites, RV age restrict, 2015 rates: $28 to $36. Jun 1 to Oct 15. No CC.
AAA Approved
(250)963-8828 Lat: 53.76291, Lon: -122.64930
5235 White Rd, Prince George, BC V2N 5Y5
Service@mamayeh.com
www.mamayeh.com

NORTHLAND RV PARK **Ratings: 6/7.5★/6** (RV Park) 2015 rates: $35. May 15 to Oct 15. (250)962-5010 10180 Hart Hwy, Prince George, BC V2K 5X6

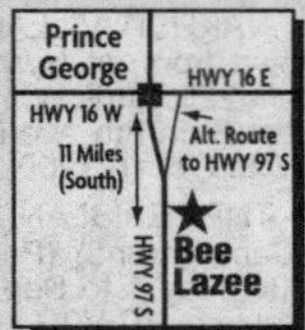

PRINCE GEORGE (CONT)

PURDEN LAKE PROVINCIAL PARK (Prov Pk) From town: Go 64 km/40 mi E on Hwy 16. 2015 rates: $16. May 1 to Sep 22. (250)964-3489

ROCKIN'S RIVER RESORT **Ratings: 3/5/4.5** (Campground) 2015 rates: $28. May 1 to Oct 1. (250)971-2223 3865 Salmon Valley Road, Prince George, BC V2K 5X3

SINTICH RV PARK
Ratings: 7/8.5★/7.5 (RV Park) S-bnd: From Jct of Hwys 16 & 97, S 3-3/4 mi (6 km) on Hwy 97 (R); or N-bnd: From Jct of Hwy 97 & Sintich Rd, N 1/2 mi (.08 km) on Hwy 97 to left turn lane, W to entrance. **FAC:** All weather rds. (131 spaces). Avail: 43 gravel, 15 pull-thrus (25 x 70), back-ins (30 x 40), 41 full hkups, 2 W, 2 E (30 amps), cable, WiFi, tent sites, dump, laundry. **REC.** Pets OK. Age restrict may apply, RV age restrict, eco-friendly, 2015 rates: $28 to $38. Disc: AAA.
(877)791-1152 Lat: 53.85352, Lon: -122.71475
7817 Hwy 97S, Prince George, BC V2N 6P6
info@sintichpark.bc.ca
www.sintichpark.bc.ca
See ad opposite page, 1372.

SOUTHPARK RV CAMPGROUND (RV Park) (Not Visited) From Jct of Hwys 16 & 97, S 5.1 mi on Hwy 97 (L); or W-bnd: From Jct of Hwy 16 & Old Cariboo Rd (1st traffic light), S 5.8 mi on Old Cariboo Rd to Holmes Rd, W .3 mi to Hwy 97, N .3 mi (R). **FAC:** All weather rds. (63 spaces). Avail: 60 gravel, 15 pull-thrus (35 x 100), back-ins (35 x 50), 44 full hkups, 14 W, 14 E (30 amps), seasonal sites, WiFi, tent sites, dump, laundry, LP gas. **REC:** playground. Pet restrict(Q). Eco-friendly, 2015 rates: $33 to $39.50. Disc: AAA.
AAA Approved
(250)963-7577 Lat: 53.84302, Lon: -122.69279
9180 Hwy 97 S., Prince George, BC V2N 6E2
mail@southparkrv.com

PRINCE RUPERT — E3 *North Coast*

PARK AVENUE CAMPGROUND (CITY PARK) (Public) From Ferry Terminal: Go 1.6 km/1 mi E on Yellowhead Hwy 16 (Park Avenue). (877)624-5861

PRUDHOMME LAKE PARK (Prov Pk) From town, E 15 mi on Yellowhead Hwy 16 (L). Pit toilets. 2015 rates: $16. May 9 to Sep 15. (250)638-8490

PRINCETON — K4 *Similkameen*

ALLISON LAKE PARK (Prov Pk) From town, N 17.4 mi on Hwy 5A (R). Pit toilets. 2015 rates: $16. Jun 15 to Sep 15. (604)795-6169

MANNING PROVINCIAL PARK (HAMPTON CAMPGROUND) (Prov Pk) From town: Go 62-1/2 km/39 mi SW on Hwy 3. Pit toilets. 2015 rates: $21. Jun 27 to Sep 1. (250)840-8822

MANNING PROVINCIAL PARK (MULE DEER CAMPGROUND) (Prov Pk) From town: Go 56 km/35 mi SW on Hwy 3. Pit toilets. 2015 rates: $21. May 16 to Sep 15. (250)840-8822

OTTER LAKE PARK (Prov Pk) From Princeton, NW 47 km on Hwy 5A (at Tulameen), follow signs (R). 2015 rates: $21. May 15 to Sep 28. (250)840-8807

PRINCETON GOLF CLUB AND RV SITES **Ratings: 6.5/9★/7** (Campground) 2015 rates: $25 to $30. Apr 1 to Oct 15. (250)295-6123 365 Darcy Mountain Rd, Princeton, BC V0X 1W0

PRINCETON MUNICIPAL RV PARK (Public) From Jct of Hwy 3 & Bridge St (Hwy 5A), E 1.6 mi on Hwy 3 (L). 2015 rates: $25 to $28. May 1 to Sep 30.

QUADRA ISLAND — J2 *Central Coast*

WE WAI KAI CAMPSITE **Ratings: 5/9★/7** (Campground) 2015 rates: $38 to $42. May 15 to Sep 15. (250)285-3111 1 Rebecca Spit Rd, Quathiaski Cove, BC V0P 1N0

QUALICUM BEACH — K2 *East Island*

CEDAR GROVE RV PARK & CAMPGROUND **Ratings: 7/8★/7** (Campground) 2015 rates: $31 to $39. (250)752-2442 246 Riverbend Rd, Qualicum Beach, BC V9K 2N2

QUALICUM BAY RESORT **Ratings: 7.5/9★/8.5** (RV Park) 2015 rates: $34 to $36. (250)757-2003 5970 West Island Hwy, Qualicum Beach, BC V9K 2N1

RIVERSIDE RESORT **Ratings: 7/8★/8** (RV Park) 2015 rates: $32 to $45. (250)752-9544 3506 W Island Hwy, Qualicum Beach, BC V9K 2H4

QUATHIASKI COVE — J2 *East Island*

TSA-KWA-LUTEN LODGE & RV PARK **Ratings: 6.5/9★/8** (RV Park) 2015 rates: $30 to $45. (250)285-2042 1 Lighthouse Road, Quathiaski Cove, BC V0P 1N0

QUESNEL — G3 *Cariboo*

AIRPORT INN MOTEL & RV PARK Ratings: 7/8.5★/7.5 (RV Park) From Jct of Hwys 97 & Front St(in town)N 4kms/2.4 mi on Hwy 97(L). **FAC:** Paved/gravel rds. (50 spaces). Avail: 40 grass, 40 pull-thrus (27 x 70), 20 full hkups, 10 W, 20 E (15/30 amps), seasonal sites, cable, WiFi, tent sites, rentals, showers $, dump, laundry, firewood. **REC:** playground. Pets OK. RV age restrict, 2015 rates: $30 to $35. Disc: AAA.
AAA Approved
(250)992-5942 Lat: 53.00857, Lon: -122.50570
3101 Hwy 97N, Quesnel, BC V2J 5Y8
airportinn@shaw.ca
www.airportinnrv.com

LAZY DAZE MOTEL & CAMPSITE **Ratings: 5/9★/8** (Campground) 2015 rates: $30. May 1 to Sep 30. (250)992-6700 714 Ritchie Rd, Quesnel, BC V2J 6X2

TEN MILE LAKE (Prov Pk) From town, N 10 mi on Hwy 97 (L). 2015 rates: $16 to $21. May 15 to Sep 30. (250)397-2523

RADIUM HOT SPRINGS — J6 *Columbia Valley*

CANYON RV RESORT **Ratings: 6.5/9.5★/10** (RV Park) 2015 rates: $45.50 to $65. Apr 15 to Oct 30. (250)347-9564 5012 Sinclair Creek Rd, Radium Hot Springs, BC V0A 1M0

DRY GULCH PARK (Prov Pk) From town, S 5 mi on Hwy 93/95 (L). 2015 rates: $21. May 1 to Oct 11. (250)422-3003

KOOTENAY NATIONAL PARK (MARBLE CANYON CAMPGROUND) (Natl Pk) From town: Go 85-1/2 km/53-1/2 mi N on Hwy 93. 2015 rates: $21.50. Jun 27 to Sep 1. (250)347-9505

KOOTENAY/MCLEOD MEADOWS (Natl Pk) From town, N 16 mi on Hwy 93 (R). 2015 rates: $21.50. Jun 27 to Sep 1. (250)347-9505

KOOTENAY/RED STREAK (Natl Pk) From Jct of Hwy 93/95 & Red Streak Rd, E 1.4 mi on Red Streak Rd., E 1.2 mi on Red Streak Rd (E) Note: Entrance fee & reservations required for full service sites. 2015 rates: $27.40 to $38.20. May 2 to Oct 13. (250)347-9505

RADIUM VALLEY VACATION RESORT **Ratings: 9.5/10★/9** (Condo Pk) 2015 rates: $58.75 to $73.75. Apr 1 to Nov 30. (250)347-9715 7274 Radium Valley Rd, Radium Hot Springs, BC V0A 1M0

REDPASS JUNCTION — G4 *Fraser-Fort George*

MOUNT ROBSON PARK (Prov Pk) From Jct of Hwys 5 & 16, E 10 mi on Hwy 16 (E). 2015 rates: $18 to $25. May 15 to Sep 30. (250)964-2243

REVELSTOKE — H5 *Columbia*

BLANKET CREEK (Prov Pk) From town S 14 mi on Hwy 23 (L). 2015 rates: $21. May 1 to Sep 30. (250)837-5734

CANADA WEST RV PARK **Ratings: 6.5/8/7.5** (Campground) 2015 rates: $30 to $55. (250)837-4420 3069 Hwy 1, Revelstoke, BC V0E 2S0

CANYON HOT SPRINGS RESORT LTD
Ratings: 7.5/9.5★/9 (Campground) From the town of Revelstoke: Go E 21.7 mi (35 km) on Hwy Number 1 (R) Maximum length of motor home 40ft. **FAC:** Paved rds. 62 gravel, 25 pull-thrus (25 x 55), back-ins (25 x 55), 62 W, 62 E (15/30 amps), WiFi Hotspot, tent sites, rentals, showers $, dump, laundry, fire rings, firewood. **REC:** heated pool $, whirlpool. Pet restrict(Q). Partial handicap access. RV age restrict, eco-friendly, 2015 rates: $42 to $51. May 15 to Sep 20. ATM.
AAA Approved
(250)837-2420 Lat: 51.13953, Lon: -117.85512
7050 Trans Canada Hwy Number 1, Revelstoke, BC V0E 2S0
info@canyonhotsprings.com
www.canyonhotsprings.com
See ad this page.

LAMPLIGHTER CAMPGROUND **Ratings: 7/9.5★/8.5** (Campground) 2015 rates: $35 to $40. May 1 to Sep 30. (250)837-3385 1760 Nixon Rd, Revelstoke, BC V0E 2S0

REVELSTOKE CAMPGROUND Ratings: 8/8.5★/8 (Campground) From Jct of Hwy 1 & Victoria Ave (in town), E 3 mi on Hwy 1 (R). **FAC:** Paved/gravel rds. 157 Avail: 80 gravel, 77 grass, 100 pull-thrus (30 x 50), back-ins (30 x 30), 70 full hkups, 23 W, 23 E (30/50 amps), cable, WiFi, tent sites, rentals, dump, laundry, groc, fire rings, firewood. **REC:** heated pool, Illecillewaet River: playground. Pets OK. Partial handicap access. RV age restrict, 2015 rates: $28 to $47. Disc: AAA. May 1 to Oct 1. (250)837-2085 Lat: 50.99173, Lon: -118.15345 2411 Koa Rd, Revelstoke, BC V0E 2S0
revkoa@yahoo.com
www.revelstokecampground.com

We rate what RVers consider important.

WILLIAMSON LAKE CAMPGROUND (Public) From Jct of Hwy #1 & Victoria Rd, S 1.8 mi on Victoria Rd to Fourth St (changes to Airport Way), E 2.2 mi to Williamson Lake Rd, E 300 ft to park entrance (E). 2015 rates: $29 to $35. Apr 15 to Oct 20. (250)837-5512

ROCK CREEK — K4 *South Okanagan, Boundary Region*

KETTLE RIVER REC AREA (Prov Pk) From town, N 2 mi on Hwy 33 (R). 2015 rates: $28. May 1 to Sep 28. (250)548-0076

ROGERS PASS — H5 *Fraser-Fort George*

GLACIER NATIONAL PARK (ILLECILLEWAET) (Natl Pk) From town: Go 3-1/4 km/2 mi W on Hwy 1. 2015 rates: $21.50. Jun to Oct. (250)837-7500

GLACIER NATIONAL PARK (LOOP BROOK CAMPGROUND) (Natl Pk) From town: Go 5-1/2 km/3-1/2 mi W on Hwy 1. 2015 rates: $21.50. (250)837-7500

ROSEBERY — J5 *Thompson-Nicola*

MARTHA CREEK (Prov Pk) From town, N 11 mi on Hwy 23 (L). Pit toilets. 2015 rates: $21. May 2 to Sep 29. (250)837-5734

ROSEDALE — K3 *Fraser Valley*

CAMPERLAND BRIDAL FALLS **Ratings: 9/9★/9** (Membership Pk) 2015 rates: $40 to $65. (604)794-7361 53730 Bridal Falls Rd, Rosedale, BC V0X 1X1

SALMON ARM — J4 *Okanagan, Thompson*

PIERRE'S POINT CAMPGROUND **Ratings: 6.5/6.5/6.5** (Campground) 2015 rates: $40 to $65. May 1 to Oct 1. (877)832-9523 2569 Campground Rd, Salmon Arm, BC V1E 3A1

SALMON ARM CAMPING RESORT **Ratings: 8/8.5/8.5** (Campground) 2015 rates: $37 to $49. Apr 15 to Oct 15. (866)979-1659 381 Hwy 97B, Salmon Arm, BC V1E 1X5

SALTERY BAY — J2 *Central Coast*

SALTERY BAY PARK (Prov Pk) From Jct of Saltery Bay ferry landing & Hwy 101, W 0.75 mi on Hwy 101 (L). Pit toilets. 2015 rates: $18. (604)885-3714

SALTSPRING ISLAND — K3 *Mount Waddington*

RUCKLE PROVINCIAL PARK (Prov Pk) On Saltspring Island. Accessible by car ferry from Swartz Bay, Crofton or Tsawwassen. 8-3/4 km/5-1/2 mi E of Fulford on country road. Pit toilets. 2015 rates: $11 to $18. (250)539-2115

SARDIS — K3 *Lower Mainland*

CHILLIWACK LAKE PARK (Prov Pk) From town, S 6 mi on Vedder Rd to Chilliwack Lake Rd, E 25.5 mi, follow signs. Pit toilets. 2015 rates: $20. May 1 to Oct 13. (604)795-6169

SAYWARD — J2 *North Island*

SAYWARD VALLEY RESORT/FISHERBOY PARK **Ratings: 6.5/9★/8.5** (Campground) 2015 rates: $33. (866)357-0598 1546 Sayward Rd, Sayward, BC V0P 1R0

RV Park ratings you can rely on!

SECHELT — K2 *South Coast*

BAYSIDE CAMPGROUND & RV PARK **Ratings: 5/8/8** (Campground) 2015 rates: $30 to $35. (877)885-7444 6040 Sechelt Inlet Rd, Sechelt, BC V0N 3A3

CREEKSIDE CAMPGROUND **Ratings: 5.5/8★/6** (Campground) 2015 rates: $35. (800)565-9222 4314 Sunshine Coast Hwy, Sechelt, BC V0N 3A1

PORPOISE BAY PARK (Prov Pk) From town, N 3 mi on Porpoise Bay Rd(L). 2015 rates: $26. (604)885-3714

SICAMOUS — H4 *Okanagan, Thompson*

CEDARS CAMPGROUND & RV PARK **Ratings: 7/7/7** (Campground) 2015 rates: $40 to $48. Jun 25 to Sep 10. (877)836-3988 3499 Luoma Rd, Malakwa, BC V0E 2J0

SICAMOUS KOA **Ratings: 6/9★/8** (Campground) 2015 rates: $36 to $48. May 1 to Sep 30. (800)562-0797 3250 Oxbow Frontage Rd, Malakwa, BC V0E 2V0

YARD CREEK PROVINCIAL PARK (Public) From town: Go 12-3/4 km/8 mi E on Hwy 1. Pit toilets. 2015 rates: $20. May 21 to Sep 30. (250)836-4663

SIDNEY — K3 *South Island*

MCDONALD CREEK (Prov Pk) From town, S 6 mi on Hwy 6 (R). Pit toilets. 2015 rates: $21. May 2 to Sep 29. (250)265-3590

MCDONALD PARK (Natl Pk) From Jct of Hwy 14 & Hwy 17 N 9 mi on Hwy 17 to Exit 31 (McDonald Park Rd/Wain Rd) E 1 mi (R). Pit toilets. 2015 rates: $21. Mar 3 to Sep 30. (250)265-3590

SKOOKUMCHUCK — J6 *Kootenay East*

PREMIER LAKE PARK (Prov Pk) From town, N 0.6 mi on Hwy 93/95 to Sheep Creek Rd, E 6.6 mi on Sheep Creek Rd to Premier Ridge Rd, S 2.4 mi (E). Pit toilets. 2015 rates: $21. (250)422-3003

SMELT BAY — J2 *Central Coast*

SMELT BAY PARK (Prov Pk) Take ferry from Campbell River to Quadra Island, cross island, take ferry from Quadra Island to Cortes Island, follow signs. Pit toilets. 2015 rates: $18. May 15 to Sep 30. (250)474-1336

SMITHERS — F1 *Bulkley Valley*

GLACIER VIEW RV PARK Ratings: 6/9.5★/7 (Campground) From town: Go 9.6 km/6 mi W on Hwy 16 Nouch Frontage Rd, then 300 meters/330 yrds SE on Nouch Frontage Rd.(R). **FAC:** Gravel rds. 18 gravel, no slide-outs, 5 pull-thrus (25 x 50), back-ins (25 x 40), some side by side hkups, 18 full hkups (30 amps), WiFi, tent sites, rentals, dump, laundry, fire rings, firewood, controlled access. **REC.** Pets OK. Partial handicap access. RV age restrict, 2015 rates: $24 to $32. May 15 to Sep 30.
AAA Approved
(250)847-3961 Lat: 54.85149, Lon: -127.22227
9028 Nouch Frontage Rd, Smithers, BC V0J 2N2
camping@glacierviewrvpark.com
www.glacierviewrvpark.com

RIVERSIDE PARK CAMPGROUND (Public) From Jct of Hwy 16 & Main St, N 0.75 mi on Main St (L). 2015 rates: $23 to $27. May to Oct. (250)847-1600

SOOKE — K2 *South Island*

FRENCH BEACH PROVINCIAL PARK (Prov Pk) From town: Go 26-3/4 km/16-3/4 mi W on Hwy 14. Pit toilets. 2015 rates: $11 to $23. (250)474-1336

SUNNY SHORES RESORT AND MARINA **Ratings: 6/7/6.5** (Campground) 2015 rates: $30. (250)642-5731 5621 Sooke Rd, Sooke, BC V9Z 0C6

SQUAMISH — J3 *Howe Sound*

ALICE LAKE PARK (Prov Pk) From town, N 3 mi on Hwy 99 (R). 2015 rates: $21 to $30. Mar 14 to Oct 31. (604)898-3678

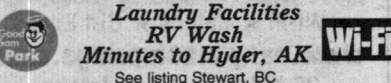

EAGLE VISTA RV RESORT & CAMPGROUND **Ratings: 6/10★/8.5** (RV Park) 2015 rates: $38 to $48. (877)898-3343 1940 Centennial Way, Squamish, BC V8B 0A8

PORTEAU COVE (Prov Pk) From Horseshoe Bay, N 15 mi on Hwy 99 (L). 2015 rates: $24 to $38. (604)986-9371

STEWART — D4 *North Coast Inland, Skeena District*

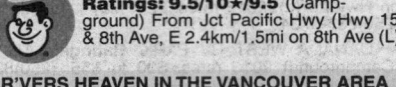

BEAR RIVER RV PARK
Ratings: 7/9★/8 (RV Park) From Jct of Hwy 37 & Hwy 37A, W 59kms/36.8 mi on Hwy 37A (L). **FAC:** Gravel rds. 72 gravel, 20 pull-thrus (30 x 80), back-ins (30 x 80), 72 full hkups (30 amps), WiFi, tent sites, rentals, showers $, laundry, firewood. **REC:** Airport Creek: rec open to public. Pets OK. RV age restrict, eco-friendly, 2015 rates: $40.53. May 1 to Sep 30.
(250)636-9205 Lat: 55.95138, Lon: -129.97879
2200 Davis St, Stewart, BC V0T 1W0
info@bearriverrvpark.com
www.bearriverrvpark.com
See ad this page.

RAINEY CREEK CAMPGROUND & RV PARK (Public) From Jct Hwy 37A Conway St & 5th Ave, N 0.2 mi on Hwy 37A to 8th Ave, W 0.4 mi (E). 2015 rates: $12 to $21. May 15 to Sep 15. (250)636-2537

SUMMERLAND — J4 *South Okanagan*

PEACH ORCHARD CAMPGROUND (Public) From Jct of Hwy 97 & Rosedale Ave, W 0.05 mi on Rosedale Ave, E 0.7 mi on Peach Orchard Rd (R). 2015 rates: $28 to $34. May 15 to Sep 15. (250)494-9649

SURREY — K3 *Lower Mainland*

DOGWOOD CAMPGROUNDS Ratings: 7/7.5/6.5 (Campground) W-bnd: Jct Hwy 1 & 160th St (Exit 50), N 1.4km/0.9 mi on 160th St to 112th Ave, W 1.6km/1 mi (R); or E-Bnd: Jct Hwy 1 & 104th Ave (Exit 50), E 0.2km/0.1 mi on 104th Ave to 160th Ave, N 1.8km/1.1 mi to 112th Ave, W 1.6km/1 m (R). **FAC:** Paved/gravel rds. (180 spaces). 60 Avail: 35 paved, 25 grass, 6 pull-thrus (16 x 50), back-ins (16 x 45), 60 full hkups (30 amps), seasonal sites, cable, WiFi Hotspot, tent sites, dump, laundry, groc. **REC:** heated pool, playground. Pet restrict(B). Partial handicap access. RV age restrict, eco-friendly, 2015 rates: $41 to $45. Disc: AAA.
AAA Approved
(604)583-5585 Lat: 49.20638, Lon: -122.80085
15151 112th Ave, Surrey, BC V3R 6G8
manager@dogwoodcampgrounds.com
www.dogwoodcampgrounds.com

HAZELMERE RV PARK & CAMPGROUND
Ratings: 9.5/10★/9.5 (Campground) From Jct Pacific Hwy (Hwy 15) & 8th Ave, E 2.4km/1.5mi on 8th Ave (L).

R'VERS HEAVEN IN THE VANCOUVER AREA
Country close to the city you'll love the quiet, beautiful setting surrounded by a mature forest, rolling meadows, streams and pond. Pool, hot tub & children's playground.

FAC: Paved rds. (198 spaces). Avail: 53 all weather, 2 pull-thrus (24 x 60), back-ins (24 x 40), 28 full hkups, 25 W, 25 E (30 amps), seasonal sites, cable, WiFi, tent sites, rentals, showers $, dump, laundry, groc, LP bottles, fire rings, firewood. **REC:** heated pool, whirlpool, Little Campbell River: playground. Pets OK. Partial handicap access. RV age restrict, eco-friendly, 2015 rates: $38 to $45. Disc: AAA.
AAA Approved
(604)538-1167 Lat: 49.01691, Lon: -122.70072
18843-8th Ave, Surrey, BC V3S 9R9
camping@hazelmere.ca
www.hazelmere.ca
See ad pages 1374 (Spotlight Vancouver Area), 1372 & RV Trips of a Lifetime in Magazine Section.

PEACE ARCH RV PARK **Ratings: 8.5/9/7.5** (RV Park) 2015 rates: $39.50 to $49.50. (604)594-7009 14601 40th Ave, Surrey, BC V3Z 1E7

TYNEHEAD RV CAMP
Ratings: 8.5/8.5/8 (Campground) From Jct of Hwy 1 & 160 St (exit 50), S 0.1 mi on 160 St to 103rd Ave, E 0.3 mi (103rd Ave becomes 102nd Ave), follow signs (L). **FAC:** Paved rds. (123 spaces). Avail: 53 gravel, 17 pull-thrus (22 x 55), back-ins (22 x 55), some side by side hkups, 53 full hkups (30 amps), seasonal sites, cable, WiFi, tent sites, showers $, dump, laundry, groc, LP bottles. **REC:** heated pool, playground. Pets OK $. Partial handicap access. RV age restrict, eco-friendly, 2015 rates: $45 to $47. Disc: AAA.
AAA Approved
(877)599-1161 Lat: 49.18805, Lon: -122.77071
16275 102nd Ave, Surrey, BC V4N 2K7
tynehead@telus.net
www.tynehead.com
See ad opposite page, 1372.

TAPPEN — J4 *Cariboo*

HERALD PARK (Prov Pk) From Trans Canada Hwy at Tappen, N 9 mi (R). 2015 rates: $30. May 1 to Sep 30. (250)835-0103

TELEGRAPH COVE — J1 *North Island*

TELEGRAPH COVE MARINA & RV PARK **Ratings: 7.5/9/7.5** (RV Park) 2015 rates: $33.34 to $42.86. (877)835-2683 1642B Telegraph Cove Road, Telegraph Cove, BC V0N 3J0

TELEGRAPH COVE RESORT-FOREST CAMPGROUND **Ratings: 5.5/7.5/7** (Campground) 2015 rates: $33 to $35. May 1 to Sep 30. (800)200-4665 #5 Telegraph Cove Rd, Telegraph Cove, BC V0N 3J0

TELKWA — F1 *Bulkley Valley*

FORT TELKWA RV PARK LTD **Ratings: 6/9★/7.5** (RV Park) 2015 rates: $31 to $33. May 1 to Oct 31. (250)846-5012 11939 Hwy 16 East, Telkwa, BC V0J 2X0

TYHEE LAKE PARK (Prov Pk) From Jct of PR-16 & Coal Mine Rd, W 0.2 mi on PR-16 to Telkwa High Rd, N 0.2 mi to Cemetery Rd, E 0.1 mi (L). 2015 rates: $25. May 9 to Sep 15. (250)638-8490

TERRACE — F1 *North Coast Inland*

FERRY ISLAND MUNICIPAL CAMPGROUND (Public) At east edge of town on Hwy 16 E. Pit toilets. 2015 rates: $20 to $25. May 6 to Sep 30. (250)615-9657

KLEANZA CREEK PARK (Prov Pk) From town, E 19 km on Hwy 16 (R). Pit toilets. 2015 rates: $16. May 9 to Sep 14. (250)638-8490

LAKELSE LAKE PARK (Prov Pk) From Jct of Prov Hwy 37 & Yellowhead 16, S 20 km on Prov Hwy 37 (R). 2015 rates: $25. May 9 to Sep 15. (250)638-8490

WILD DUCK MOTEL & RV PARK **Ratings: 6.5/9/7.5** (RV Park) 2015 rates: $20 to $23. (250)638-1511 5504 Hwy 16 W, Terrace, BC V8G 0C6

TETE JAUNE CACHE — G4 *Fraser-Fort George*

MOUNT ROBSON PROVINCIAL PARK (ROBSON MEADOWS) (Prov Pk) From town: Go 19-1/4 km/12 mi E on Hwy 16. 2015 rates: $25. May 15 to Sep 30. (250)964-2243

TOAD RIVER — C5 *Liard, Peace River*

STONE MOUNTAIN PROVINCIAL PARK (Prov Pk) On the Alaska Hwy at milepost 387. Pit toilets. 2015 rates: $16. May 1 to Sep 15. (250)776-7000

TOAD RIVER LODGE & RV PARK **Ratings: 7/8.5/8.5** (RV Park) 2015 rates: $32.50. (855)878-8623 mile 422 Alaska Hwy, Toad River, BC V0C 2X0

TOFINO — K2 *West Island*

BELLA PACIFICA **Ratings: 5.5/7/7.5** (Campground) 2015 rates: $30 to $54. Mar 1 to Nov 1. (250)725-3400 400 Mackenzie Beach Road, Tofino, BC V0R 2Z0

CRYSTAL COVE BEACH RESORT **Ratings: 8.5/8.5/9** (RV Park) 2015 rates: $50 to $62. (877)725-4213 1165 Cedarwood Place, Tofino, BC V0R 2Z0

TOPLEY — F2 *Kitimat-Stikine*

RED BLUFF PROVINCIAL PARK (Prov Pk) From town: Go 56 km/34-3/4 mi N on secondary road to Granisle. Pit toilets. 2015 rates: $18. May 15 to Sep 7. (250)697-6264

TRAIL — K5 *Thompson-Nicola*

TRAIL MUNICIPAL RV PARK (Public) In town on Hwy 3B. 2015 rates: $25. May 1 to Sep 30. (250)368-3144

TUMBLER RIDGE — E6 *Peace River*

DISTRICT OF TUMBLER RIDGE LIONS FLAT BED CREEK CAMPGROUND (Public) From south town limits at jct Monkman Way & Hwy 29: Go 2 km/1-1/4 mi SW on Hwy 29. 2015 rates: $15. May to Oct. (250)242-3123

Say you saw it in our Guide!

TUMBLER RIDGE (CONT)

MONKMAN PROVINCIAL PARK (Prov Pk) From town: Go 10 km/6-1/4 mi E on paved local road, then 44-3/4 km/28 mi S on gravel secondary road. Pit toilets. 2015 rates: $16. May 21 to Nov 15. (250)787-3407

MONKMAN WAY RV PARK (DISTRICT PARK) (Prov Pk) From north town limits at jct Heritage Hwy & Mackenzie Way: Go .8 km/1/2 mi S on Mackenzie Way, then 91 meters/100 yards W on Monkman Way. May 15 to Nov 15. (250)257-0700

UCLUELET — K2 *West Island*

PACIFIC RIM NATIONAL PARK (GREEN POINT CAMPGROUND) (Natl Pk) From town: Go 12-3/4 km/8 mi N on Hwy 4 (Pacific Rim Hwy). 2015 rates: $17.60 to $23.50. May 1 to Oct 15. (250)726-7721

SURF JUNCTION CAMPGROUND **Ratings: 4/6.5/7** (Campground) 2015 rates: $20 to $40. Mar 15 to Sep 30. (250)726-7214 2650 Pacific Rim Hwy, Ucluelet, BC V0R 3A0

UCLUELET CAMPGROUND **Ratings: 4/8.5★/7** (Campground) 2015 rates: $25 to $48. (250)726-4355 260 Seaplane Base Rd, Ucluelet, BC V0R 3A0

VALEMOUNT — G4 *Columbia*

CANOE RIVER CAMPGROUND **Ratings: 6/7.5/7.5** (Campground) 2015 rates: $25 to $30. Apr 1 to Oct 31. (250)566-9112 6190 Hwy 5 South, Valemount, BC V0E 2Z0

IRVIN'S PARK & CAMPGROUND
Ratings: 7.5/10★/9 (RV Park) From Jct Hwy 5 & 5th Ave, N 0.6kms/0.4 mi on Hwy 5 to Loseth Rd, E 0.2kms/0.1 mi (R). Elev 2600 ft. **FAC:** All weather rds. 68 gravel, 68 pull-thrus (32 x 62), 68 full hkups (30/50 amps), WiFi, tent sites, dump, laundry, groc, LP gas, firewood. **REC.** Pets OK. Partial handicap access. Big rig sites, RV age restrict, eco-friendly, 2015 rates: $34 to $40. Disc: AAA. Apr 1 to Oct 30.
AAA Approved
(250)566-4781 Lat: 52.84285, Lon: -119.28320
360 Loseth Rd, Valemount, BC V0E 2Z0
irvins@valemount.com
www.irvinsrvpark.com
See ad this page, 1372.

VALEMOUNT PINES GOLF CLUB & RV PARK **Ratings: 5/9★/8** (Campground) 2015 rates: $22 to $27. Apr 20 to Oct 15. (250)566-4550 1110 Hwy N #5, Valemount, BC V0E 2Z0

YELLOWHEAD RV PARK & CAMPGROUND Ratings: 5/8.5★/7 (Campground) W-Bnd:from Jct of Hwy 5 & 5th Ave (in Valemount) NW 100m on Hwy 5 (L). Elev 2600 ft. **FAC:** Gravel rds. 44 gravel, 14 pull-thrus (24 x 50), back-ins (24 x 30), 44 W, 44 E (30 amps), WiFi, tent sites, dump, laundry, fire rings, firewood. **REC:** playground. Pets OK. RV age restrict, 2015 rates: $30 to $35. May 1 to Sep 30.
AAA Approved
(250)566-0078 Lat: 52.83693, Lon: -119.28295
325 North Hwy #5, Valemount, BC V0E 2Z0
camping@yellowheadcampground.com
www.yellowheadcampground.com

Wasn't that a beautiful campground you visited ten years ago? But can you remember where it was? Use our "Find-it-Fast" index, located in the back of the Guide. It's an alphabetical list, by state, of every private and public park and campground in the Guide.

VANCOUVER — K3 *Lower Mainland*

VANCOUVER AREA MAP

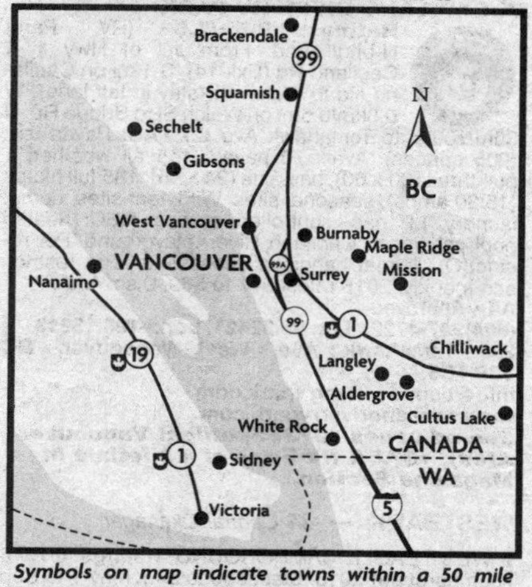

Symbols on map indicate towns within a 50 mile radius of Vancouver where campgrounds are listed. Check listings for more information.

See also Aldergrove, Brackendale, Burnaby, Chilliwack, Cultus Lake, Gibsons, Langley, Maple Ridge, Mission, Nanaimo, Sechelt, Sidney, Squamish, Surrey, Victoria, West Vancouver & White Rock.

A SPOTLIGHT Introducing Vancouver's colorful attractions appearing in this province section.

HAZELMERE RV PARK & CAMPGROUND
Ratings: 9.5/10★/9.5 (RV Park) From Jct of TCH 1 and Hwy 7A (Hastings Ave) SE 28km/17.3 mi to Hwy 15 (176th Ave), S 18.4 km/11.5mi to 8th St, E 2.4km/1.5mi on 8th Ave (L). **FAC:** Paved rds. (198 spaces). Avail: 53 all weather, 2 pull-thrus (24 x 69), back-ins (24 x 40), 28 full hkups, 25 W, 25 E (30 amps), seasonal sites, cable, WiFi, tent sites, rentals, showers $, dump, laundry, groc, LP bottles, fire rings, firewood. **REC:** heated pool, whirlpool, Little Campbell River: playground. Pets OK. Partial handicap access. RV age restrict, eco-friendly, 2015 rates: $38 to $45. Disc: AAA.
(604)538-1167 Lat: 49.01691, Lon: -122.70072
18843-8th Ave, Surrey, BC V3S 9R9
camping@hazelmere.ca
www.hazelmere.ca
See primary listing at Surrey and ad page 1374 (Spotlight Vancouver Area).

VANDERHOOF — F2 *Bulkley, Nechako*

DAVE'S RV PARK
Ratings: 8.5/10★/9.5 (RV Park) From town, E 1.6kms/1 mi on Hwy 16 to Derksen Rd, N 1.3kms/0.7 mi(R). **FAC:** All weather rds. 43 Avail: 43 all weather, patios, 31 pull-thrus (27 x 65), back-ins (27 x 45), 35 full hkups, 8 W, 8 E (30/50 amps), cable, WiFi $, tent sites, dump, laundry. **REC.** Pets OK. Big rig sites, RV age restrict, eco-friendly, 2015 rates: $32 to $36. Apr 15 to Oct 15.
(250)567-3161 Lat: 53.99696, Lon: -123.97765
1048 Derksen Rd, Vanderhoof, BC V0J 3A0
camping@davesrvpark.com
www.davesrvpark.com
See ad page 1382.

RIVERSIDE CAMPSITE (Public) From Jct of Hwy 16 & Burrard Ave, N 0.6 mi on Burrard Ave to park entrance (L). 2015 rates: $23 to $30. May 16 to Oct 13. (250)847-1600

TACHICK LAKE RESORT (Campground) (Phone Update) 2015 rates: $25 to$30. May 15 to Oct 15. (877)567-4929 11512 Tachick Lake Rd, Vanderhoof, BC V0J 3A0

VERNON — J4 *North Okanagan*

ELLISON PARK (Prov Pk) From town, SW 10 mi on Okanagan Landing Rd (R). 2015 rates: $30. Apr 1 to Oct 31. (250)545-9943

SILVER STAR RV PARK **Ratings: 7.5/10★/7.5** (RV Park) 2015 rates: $40 to $44. (250)542-2808 6310 Stickle Rd, Vernon, BC V1B 3V1

SWAN LAKE RV PARK & CAMPGROUND **Ratings: 5.5/7/7.5** (Campground) 2015 rates: $38 to $43. (250)545-2300 7235 Old Kamloops Rd, Vernon, BC V1H 1W6

SWAN LAKE RV RESORT **Ratings: 9.5/9.5★/9** (Membership Pk) 2015 rates: $45 to $55. (250)558-1116 8000 Highland Rd, Box 1010, Vernon, BC V1B 3W5

VICTORIA — K3 *Metchosin, South Island, View Royal, West Shore*

VICTORIA See also Sooke, Sidney, Mill Bay, North Pender Island & Saltspring Island.

CEDAR SPRINGS RANCH (Campground) (Phone Update) From Jct of Hwy 1 & Hwy 17, N 16 mi on Hwy 1 (L) Use U-turn Rte. Caution: Sharp turn off highway & steep narrow access road. **FAC:** Paved/gravel rds. 39 grass, back-ins (25 x 45), some side by side hkups, 8 full hkups, 19 W, 6 E (15/30 amps), WiFi Hotspot, tent sites, rentals, dump, laundry, groc. **REC:** heated pool, playground. Pets OK. Partial handicap access. RV age restrict, 2015 rates: $42 to $53. Disc: AAA. Jun 1 to Sep 30.
AAA Approved
(250)478-3332 Lat: 48.54321, Lon: -123.56574
230 Trans Canada Hwy 1, Malahat, BC V0R 2L0
cedarspringsranch@shaw.ca

FORT VICTORIA RV PARK **Ratings: 6.5/9.5★/7** (RV Park) 2015 rates: $43. (250)479-8112 340 Island Hwy 1A, Victoria, BC V9B 1H1

GOLDSTREAM PARK (Prov Pk) From Jct of Hwy 1 & Sooke Lake Rd, N 0.4 mi on Sooke Lake Rd to Golden Gate Rd, W 0.1 mi (R). 2015 rates: $11 to $30. (250)478-9414

OCEANSIDE RV RESORT - PARKBRIDGE
Ratings: 8.5/9.5/10 (RV Park) From Jct of Hwy 17 & Mt Newton X Rd, E 0.5km/0.3 mi on Mt Newton X Rd to Stautw Rd, E 1.1km/0.7 mi (R). **FAC:** Paved rds. (182 spaces). Avail: 68 all weather, 15 pull-thrus (30 x 60), back-ins (30 x 50), 68 full hkups (30/50 amps), seasonal sites, cable, WiFi Hotspot, tent sites, showers $, dump, laundry, firewood. **REC:** Pacific Ocean: swim, playground. Pet restrict(B/Q). Partial handicap access. Big rig sites, RV age restrict, 2015 rates: $35 to $56.
(250)544-0508 Lat: 48.58849, Lon: -123.37716
3000 Stautw Rd, Saanichton, BC V8M 2K5
oceanside@parkridge.com
www.parkbridge.com
See ad pages 1370 (Welcome Section), 1372.

PEDDER BAY RV RESORT & MARINA Ratings: 8/9.5★/10 (RV Park) From Jct of Hwy 1 & Hwy 14 (Exit 14), S 5.8 km (4 mi) on Hwy 14 (Millstream Rd/Veterans Memorial Pkwy) to Latoria, W 2 km (1.2 mi) to Happy Valley Rd, SW 4.9 km (3 mi) to Rocky Point Rd, S 5.1 km (3.2 mi) to Pedder Bay Dr, S 150 meters (0.1 mi) (L). **FAC:** Paved rds. (79 spaces). Avail: 69 all weather, 16 pull-thrus (30 x 45), back-ins (30 x 45), 69 full hkups (30/50 amps), seasonal sites, WiFi, tent sites, showers $, laundry, fire rings, firewood. **REC:** Juan de Fuca Strait: fishing, marina. Pets OK. RV age restrict, 2015 rates: $27 to $66. Disc: AAA.
AAA Approved
(250)478-1771 Lat: 48.34911, Lon: -123.57388
925 Pedder Bay Dr, Victoria, BC V9C 4H1
reservations@pedderbay.com
www.pedderbay.com

VICTORIA (CONT)

THETIS LAKE CAMPGROUND **Ratings: 4.5/6/4** (Campground) 2015 rates: $25 to $30. (250)478-3845 1938 W Park Lane, Victoria, BC V9B 5Z6

WEIR'S BEACH RV RESORT **Ratings: 8.5/9★/9.5** (RV Park) 2015 rates: $37 to $58. (866)478-6888 5191 William Head Rd, Victoria, BC V9C 4H5

WASA — J6 *Columbia-Shuswap*

WASA LAKE PARK (Prov Pk) From Jct of Hwy 93/95 & Hwy 3/93, N 25 mi on Hwy 93/95 (R). 2015 rates: $25. May 5 to Sep 30. (250)422-3003

WELLS — G3 *Bulkley-Nechako*

CARIBOO JOY RV PARK **Ratings: 4/7.5★/8** (RV Park) 2015 rates: $30 to $45. May 31 to Sep 25. (888)996-4653 12566 Hwy 26, Barkerville, BC V0K 1B0

NUGGET HILLS RV PARK **Ratings: 4/8★/6.5** (Campground) 2015 rates: $23.75 to $29.75. May 20 to Oct 15. (250)994-2333 3885 Ski Hill Rd, Barkerville, BC V0K 1B0

WEST KELOWNA — J4 *Cariboo*

WEST BAY BEACH RESORT **Ratings: 6.5/8.5★/8** (Campground) 2015 rates: $30.40 to $66.50. Apr 1 to Oct 15. (250)768-3004 3745 West Bay Rd, Westbank, BC V4T 2B9

Get the Facts!

Essential tips and travel info can be found in the Welcome Section at the beginning of each State/Province.

WEST VANCOUVER — K3 *Mount Waddington*

CAPILANO RIVER RV PARK

Ratings: 9/9.5★/7.5 (RV Park) N-bnd/S-bnd: From Jct of Hwy 1 & Capilano Rd (Exit 14), S 1 mi on Capilano Rd to Welch St (stay in left lane), W 0.8km/0.5mi on Welch St to Bridge Rd, N 30m/100 ft to Tomahawk Ave (L). **FAC:** Paved rds. (205 spaces). Avail: 70 paved, 115 all weather, 1 pull-thrus (30 x 60), back-ins (24 x 45), 185 full hkups (15/30 amps), seasonal sites, WiFi, tent sites, dump, laundry, LP gas, controlled access. **REC:** heated pool, whirlpool, Capilano River: playground. Pet restrict(Q). Partial handicap access. RV age restrict, eco-friendly, 2015 rates: $47 to $69. Disc: AAA. AAA Approved

(604)987-4722 Lat: 49.32421, Lon: -123.13213
295 Tomahawk Ave, West Vancouver, BC V7P 1C5
info@capilanoriverrvpark.com
www.capilanoriverrvpark.com

See ad pages 1373 (Spotlight Vancouver Area), 1372 & RV Trips of a Lifetime in Magazine Section.

WESTBANK — J4 *Central Okanagan*

WEST EAGLE CAMPGROUND **Ratings: 5/7.5/6** (Campground) 2015 rates: $30 to $45. May 1 to Sep 30. (250)768-7426 2325 Old Okanagan Hwy, Westbank, BC V4T 1V3

WESTBRIDGE — K4 *Thompson-Nicola*

JOHNSTONE CREEK PARK (Prov Pk) From town, E 7 mi on Hwy 3 (R). Pit toilets. 2015 rates: $16. May 15 to Sep 16. (250)548-0076

How much does a fishing license cost in Idaho? Can you turn right on a red light in Rhode Island? Check the Table of Contents for the page location for annual updates of important towing laws, rules of the road, bridge and tunnel information and fishing license fees.

WHALETOWN — J2 *Coastal*

GORGE HARBOUR MARINA RESORT (RV Resort) (Phone Update) 2015 rates: $32.50 to $42.50. (250)935-6433 1374 Hunt Rd, Whaletown, BC V0P 1Z0

WHISTLER — J3 *Home Sound*

RIVERSIDE RESORT **Ratings: 9/10★/10** (RV Park) 2015 rates: $35 to $58. (604)905-5533 8018 Mons Rd, Whistler, BC V0N 1B8

WHISTLER RV PARK & CAMPGROUND **Ratings: 6/9★/9** (RV Park) 2015 rates: $43 to $55. (604)905-2523 55 Hwy 99, Whistler, BC V0N 1B1

WHITE ROCK — K3 *Lower Mainland*

SEACREST MOTEL & RV PARK **Ratings: 5.5/8.5/7** (RV Park) 2015 rates: $35 to $44. (604)531-4720 864 160th St (Stayte Rd), White Rock, BC V4A 4W4

WILLIAMS LAKE — H3 *Cariboo*

WILLIAMS LAKE STAMPEDE CAMPGROUND **Ratings: 5/8.5★/7** (Campground) 2015 rates: $28 to $38. (250)398-6718 800 South Mckenzie Ave, Williams Lake, BC V2G 2V2

YAHK — K6 *Columbia-Shuswap*

YAHK PARK (Prov Pk) From Jct of SR-95 & SR-3, N 3 mi on SR-95/3 (R). Pit toilets. 2015 rates: $16. May 17 to Oct 1. (250)422-3003

You can be the king of the road, but you still have to be safe. Be sure to use the valuable information provided in the Road and Highway Safety Information pages, and check out the Road and Highway Information Telephone Numbers. You can locate both by referring to the Table of Contents at the front of the Guide.

MB

Travel Manitoba

WELCOME TO Manitoba

JOINED CONFEDERATION	WIDTH: 260-279 MILES (418-449 KM)	PROPORTION OF CANADA
JULY 15, 1870	LENGTH: 761 MILES (1,225 KM)	6.49% OF 9,984,670 SQ KM

A vast and unpopulated wilderness of rolling pastures, translucent lakes and horizons that stretch seemingly to eternity, the human touch feels light on the Canadian province of Manitoba.

Standing at a geographical and cultural crossroads where prairies, wildflower meadows and farmlands give way subarctic boreal forests, Manitoba doesn't feel the need to court tourist affection. The province's exceptional national parks offer abundant wildlife—moose, bears, bison, lynx and beaver—and first-rate fishing, canoeing and exhilarating hikes along endless trails.

In the north, the town of Churchill is synonymous with its polar bear population and 2,000 beluga whales that convene at the mouth of the Churchill River waiting for the ice to form and the commencement of hunting season.

Gateway to the prairies, the metropolis of Winnipeg boasts an array of fine restaurants and a cutting-edge performing-arts scene. The gentrified riverside development, the Forks, draws young urbanites to its eclectic stores and outdoor patio cafés in the summertime. About 60 miles north of Winnipeg, Gimli is a fascinating tranche of Icelandic cultural heritage.

An 1,800-mile wilderness, renowned for its superb hiking (250 miles of trails) and abundant wildlife, Riding Mountain National Park's rich and diverse landscape spans boreal forest, majestic hills and stunning alpine lakes. On the south shore of Clear Lake, the town of Wasagaming provides an ideal base to let summer days unfold.

Top 3 Tourism Attractions:
1) Churchill
2) Canadian Museum for Human Rights
3) Assiniboine Park Zoo

Nickname: Keystone Province

State Flower: Prairie Crocus

State Bird: Great Gray Owl

People: Deanna Durbin, actress and singer; Monty Hall, TV game show host; Anna Paquin, actress; David Steinberg, comedian and actor; Jonathan Toews, hockey player

Major Cities: Winnipeg (capital), Brandon, Thompson, Portage la Prairie, Steinbach

Topography: Over 110,000 lakes; south—flat, fertile; north and east lie on Canadian Shield

Climate: Mostly sunny, clear-sky days; very little winter precipitation; northern regions are sub-arctic

TRAVEL & TOURISM

Travel Manitoba
800-665-0040, 204-927-7800
www.travelmanitoba.com

Brandon
204-729-2141
www.brandontourism.com

Everything Churchill
800-665-0040
www.everythingchurchill.com

The Forks National Historic Site
888-773-8888, 204-983-2221
www.pc.gc.ca

International Peace Garden
888-432-6733
www.peacegarden.com

Tourism Winnipeg
800-665-0204, 204-943-1970
www.destinationwinnipeg.ca

OUTDOOR RECREATION

Golf Manitoba
204-925-5730
www.golfmanitoba.mb.ca

Manitoba Conservation
204-945-6640, 204-945-4683, 204-945-6784

Manitoba Cycling Association
204-925-5686
www.cycling.mb.ca

Manitoba Cross-Country Ski Association
204-925-5639
www.ccski.mb.ca

Manitoba Lodges & Outfitters Association
204-772-1912, 800-305-0013
www.mloa.com

SHOPPING

Bayat Gallery
204-475-5873, 888-884-6848

Emerson Duty-free Shop
204-373-2600, 800-268-6088
www.vec.ca-english-2-duty-free-canada.cfm

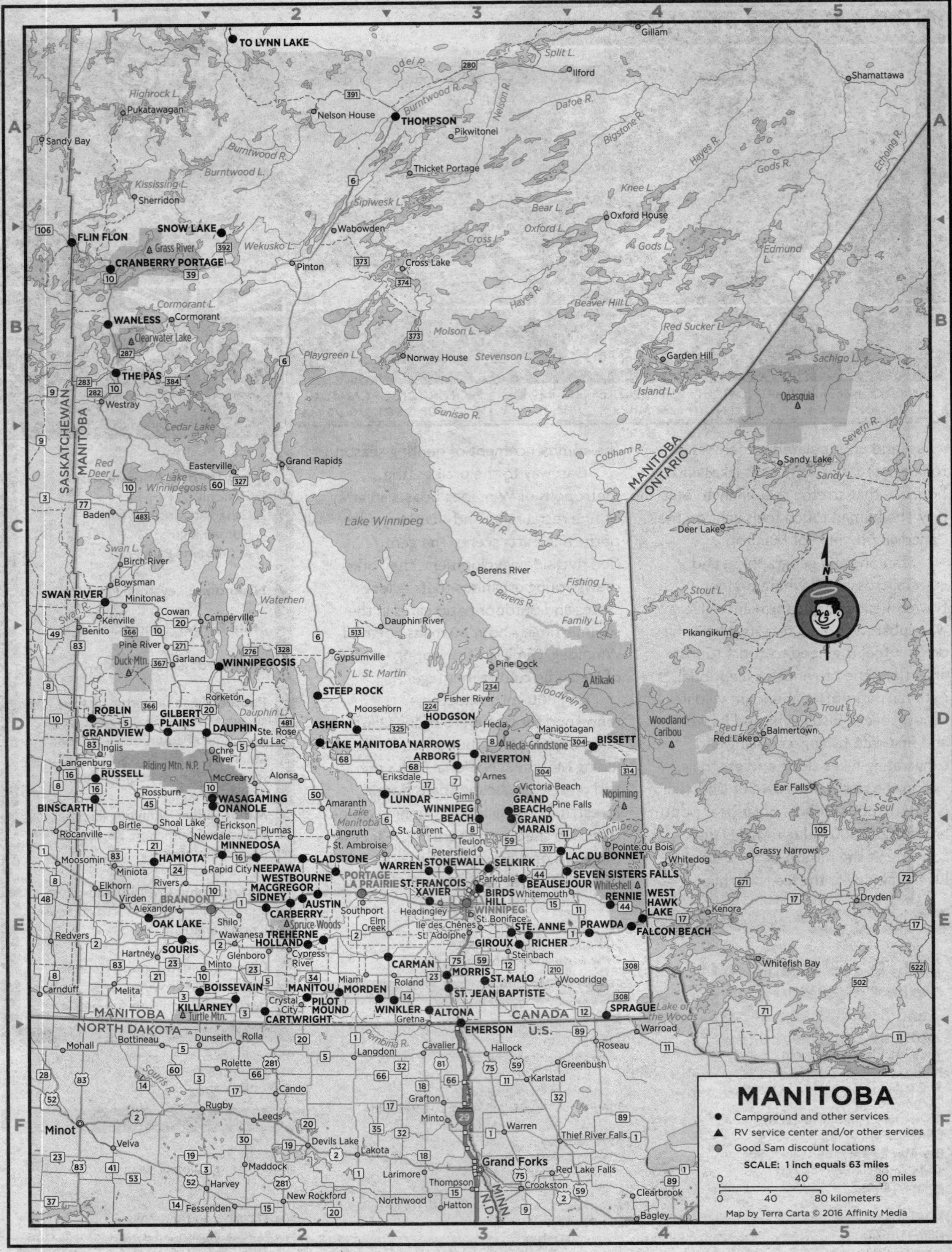
MANITOBA
Campground and other services
RV service center and/or other services
Good Sam discount locations
SCALE: 1 inch equals 63 miles
0 40 80 miles
0 40 80 kilometers
Map by Terra Carta © 2016 Affinity Media
TO LYNN LAKE
Gillam
Split L.
Ilford
Shamattawa
Odei R.
Burntwood R.
Nelson R.
Dafoe R.
Highrock L.
Pukatawagan
Nelson House
THOMPSON
Pikwitonei
Sandy Bay
Burntwood L.
Thicket Portage
Bigstone R.
Hayes R.
Gods R.
Echoing R.
Kississing L.
Sherridon
Sipiwesk L.
Knee L.
Bear L.
Oxford House
Oxford L.
FLIN FLON
SNOW LAKE
Grass River
Wabowden
Wekusko L.
Cross L.
Gods L.
Edmund L.
CRANBERRY PORTAGE
Pinton
Cross Lake
Cormorant L.
Hayes R.
Beaver Hill L.
WANLESS
Cormorant
Clearwater Lake
Molson L.
Red Sucker L.
Garden Hill
Sachigo L.
Playgreen L.
Norway House
Stevenson L.
THE PAS
Westray
Island L.
Opasquia
Gunisao R.
Cedar Lake
SASKATCHEWAN
MANITOBA
ONTARIO
Cobham R.
Severn R.
Grand Rapids
Sandy Lake
Sandy L.
Red Deer L.
Easterville
Lake Winnipegosis
Lake Winnipeg
Poplar R.
Baden
Deer Lake
Swan L.
Birch River
Berens River
Bowsman
Fishing L.
SWAN RIVER
Minitonas
Waterhen L.
Berens R.
Stout L.
Swan R.
Kenville
Cowan
Camperville
Benito
Dauphin River
Family L.
Pikangikum
Pine River
Garland
Gypsumville
Duck Mtn.
WINNIPEGOSIS
L. St. Martin
Pine Dock
Atikaki
STEEP ROCK
Fisher River
Bloodvein R.
Rorketon
Dauphin L.
Moosehorn
Woodland Caribou
Trout
ROBLIN
GILBERT PLAINS
HODGSON
GRANDVIEW
DAUPHIN
ASHERN
Hecla
Manigotagan
Balmertown
Ste. Rose du Lac
Red L.
Red Lake
Inglis
Ochre River
LAKE MANITOBA NARROWS
Hecla-Grindstone
BISSETT
Langenburg
Riding Mtn. N.P.
ARBORG
RIVERTON
RUSSELL
McCreary
Alonsa
Eriksdale
Arnes
Victoria Beach
Ear Falls
Rossburn
Nopiming
BINSCARTH
WASAGAMING
ONANOLE
Amaranth
LUNDAR
WINNIPEG BEACH
GRAND BEACH
Pine Falls
L. Seul
GRAND MARAIS
Birtle
Shoal Lake
Lake Manitoba
Gimli
Rocanville
Erickson
Plumas
Langruth
St. Laurent
Newdale
St. Ambroise
Teulon
Winnipeg
Pointe du Bois
Moosomin
HAMIOTA
MINNEDOSA
GLADSTONE
Petersfield
LAC DU BONNET
Whitedog
Grassy Narrows
Miniota
Rapid City
NEEPAWA
WARREN
STONEWALL
SELKIRK
Parkdale
SEVEN SISTERS FALLS
Elkhorn
Rivers
WESTBOURNE
PORTAGE LA PRAIRIE
ST. FRANCOIS XAVIER
BEAUSEJOUR
Whiteshell
Virden
BRANDON
MACGREGOR
BIRDS HILL
Whitemouth
WEST HAWK LAKE
Dryden
Alexander
SIDNEY
AUSTIN
Southport
Headingley
WINNIPEG
RENNIE
Kenora
OAK LAKE
CARBERRY
Spruce Woods
Elm Creek
St. Boniface
Shilo
Ile des Chênes
STE. ANNE
PRAWDA
FALCON BEACH
Redvers
Wawanesa
TREHERNE
St. Adolphe
HOLLAND
SOURIS
GIROUX
RICHER
Hartney
Glenboro
Cypress River
Steinbach
Minto
CARMAN
Whitefish Bay
MORRIS
ST. MALO
Woodridge
Carnduff
Melita
BOISSEVAIN
Roland
Miami
MANITOU
MORDEN
ST. JEAN BAPTISTE
KILLARNEY
Turtle Mtn.
Crystal City
PILOT MOUND
WINKLER
ALTONA
SPRAGUE
Lake of the Woods
CARTWRIGHT
Gretna
EMERSON
CANADA
U.S.
NORTH DAKOTA
Warroad
Mohall
Bottineau
Dunseith
Rolla
Pembina R.
Langdon
Cavalier
Hallock
Roseau
Souris R.
Rolette
Greenbush
Karlstad
Cando
Grafton
Rugby
Leeds
Minto
Minot
Warren
Thief River Falls
Velva
Devils Lake
Lakota
Maddock
Grand Forks
Red Lake Falls
Larimore
Harvey
Thompson
Crookston
Fessenden
New Rockford
Northwood
Hatton
N.D.
MINN.
Clearbrook
Bagley

MB

Featured Good Sam Parks

MANITOBA

Good Sam Park

When you stay with Good Sam, you can expect the highest degree of cleanliness and friendliness, and better yet, you get 10% off campground fees.

If you're not already a Good Sam member you can purchase your membership at one of these locations:

BRANDON
Bry-Mar RV Park and Campground
(204)573-7067

PORTAGE LA PRAIRIE
Miller's Camping Resort
(204)857-4255

WINNIPEG
Arrowhead RV Park
(888)878-4203

For more Good Sam Parks go to listing pages

Manitoba

CONSULTANTS

Ron & Marg Hobkirk

ALTONA — E3 *Central*

ALTONA CENTENNIAL PARK (Public) From town, W 1 mi on 10th Ave (L). 2015 rates: $22. May 22 to Oct 1. (204)324-9005

ARBORG — D3 *Interlake*

HNAUSA CAMPGROUND (Prov Pk) From Winnipeg: Go 100 km/62 mi N on Hwy 8, then 1 km/1/2 mi E on PTH 68, then 1 km/1/2 mi S on PR 222. 2015 rates: $18.90 to $23.10. May 1 to Sep 1. (888)482-2267

ASHERN — D2 *Interlake*

PORCUPINE PROVINCIAL FOREST (NORTH STEEPROCK LAKE PROVINCIAL PARK) (Prov Pk) From jct Hwy 10 & Hwy 365: Go NW on Hwy 365. 2015 rates: $13.96. (204)734-3429

AUSTIN — E2 *North Central*

MANITOBA AGRICULTURAL MUSEUM THREE CREEKS CAMPGROUND **Ratings: 2/8★/6.5** (Campground) 2015 rates: $20. May 15 to Sep 30. (204)637-2354 site 62105 Hwy 34, Austin, MB R0H 0C0

BEAUSEJOUR — E3 *Eastern*

GREAT WOODS PARK Ratings: 7/8/9 (Campground) From Jct of Hwy 44 & 12N & Mile 73N, E 1.2 mi on Mile 73N (R). **FAC:** All weather rds. (250 spaces). Avail: 150 all weather, back-ins (35 x 50), 150 W, 150 E (30 amps), seasonal sites, tent sites, dump, mobile sewer, groc, LP bottles, fire rings, firewood, controlled access. **REC:** Brokenhead River: swim, fishing, golf, playground, rec open to public. Pets OK. Partial handicap access. Eco-friendly, 2015 rates: $25 to $30. May 15 to Oct 1.
AAA Approved
(204)268-2814 Lat: 50.079919, Lon: -96.472069
#73 Great Woods Park Rd, Beausejour, MB R0E 0C0
park@greatwoodspark.com
www.greatwoodspark.com

BINSCARTH — D1 *Parkland*

BINSCARTH PARK & POOL (Public) From Jct of Hwy 41 & 16 (Yellowhead), N 0.4 mi on Hwy 16 (R). 2015 rates: $15 to $30. May 16 to Oct 13. (204)532-2102

BIRDS HILL — E3 *Interlake*

BIRDS HILL PROVINCIAL PARK (Prov Pk) From Town, NE 12 mi on Hwy 59 (R). 2015 rates: $17.85 to $25.20. May 1 to Oct 15. (888)482-2267

BISSETT — D4 *Northern*

NOPIMING PROVINCIAL PARK (BERESFORD LAKE CAMPGROUND) (Prov Pk) From town: Go 70 km/43-1/2 mi SE on Hwy 304. Follow signs. 2015 rates: $10.50 to $19.95. (888)482-2267

BOISSEVAIN — E1 *Western*

BOISSEVAIN LIONS CAMPGROUND (Public) From Jct of Hwy 10 & P Rd 348 exit, W 0.05 mi on Hwy 10 (L). 2015 rates: $15 to $18. (204)534-6250

INTERNATIONAL PEACE GARDEN (Public) From Jct of Hwy 10 & secondary Rd 443, S 16 mi on Hwy 10 (R). $10 entrance fee. 2015 rates: $16 to $22. (888)432-6733

TURTLE MOUNTAIN PROVINCIAL PARK (ADAM LAKE CAMPGROUND) (Prov Pk) From Jct of Hwy 10 & Secondary Hwy 443, S 15 mi on Hwy 10 (R). 2015 rates: $16.80 to $26.25. May 1 to Sep 1. (888)482-2267

TURTLE MOUNTAIN PROVINCIAL PARK (MAX LAKE CAMPGROUND) (Prov Pk) From jct Hwy 10 & Hwy 3: Go 8 km/5 mi W on Hwy 3, then 11-1/4 km/7 mi S. 2015 rates: $16.80. May 15 to Sep 15. (204)534-2578

WILLIAM LAKE PROVINCIAL PARK (Prov Pk) From Jct of Hwy 10 & Secondary Rd 443, S 8 mi on Hwy 10 to Sec Hwy 341, E 4 mi to Lake William Rd, S 5 mi (E). 2015 rates: $21. May 1 to Sep 15. (888)482-2267

BRANDON — E2 *Brandon*

BRY-MAR RV PARK AND CAMPGROUND
Ratings: 8/10★/8.5 (Campground) From town go 9.5 Kim's (6 miles) east on Hwy 1 (L). **FAC:** All weather rds. (82 spaces). Avail: 78 gravel, 23 pull-thrus (35 x 75), back-ins (35 x 75), 57 full hkups, 2 W, 2 E (30 amps), seasonal sites, WiFi, tent sites, rentals, dump, laundry, fire rings, firewood. **REC:** Willow Creek: fishing, playground. Pets OK. Partial handicap access. Eco-friendly, 2015 rates: $21 to $40. May 1 to Oct 31.
(204)573-7067 Lat: 49.88821, Lon: -99.801474
Site 520 Road 102 (Hwy 1), Douglas, MB R7A 5Y5
Brymar4u@hotmail.com
www.brymarrvpark.ca
See ad this page, 1389.

MEADOWLARK CAMPGROUND Ratings: 6.5/8/8 (Campground) (E-bnd Hwy 1 or N-bnd Hwy 10) From W Jct of Hwys 1 & 10, E 0.3 mi on N Service Rd; or (W-bnd Hwy 1 or S-bnd Hwy 10) From E Jct of Hwys 1 & 10, W 0.5 mi on Hwy 1 to N Service Rd, W 200 ft to park entrance (R). **FAC:** Gravel rds. (75 spaces). Avail: 70 gravel, 35 pull-thrus (30 x 94), back-ins (30 x 55), some side by side hkups, 60 full hkups, 10 W, 10 E (30/50 amps), seasonal sites, WiFi, tent sites, dump, laundry, controlled access. **REC:** playground. Pets OK. Big rig sites, eco-friendly, 2015 rates: $34 to $38. Apr 15 to Oct 15.
AAA Approved
(800)363-6434 Lat: 49.888315, Lon: -99.956037
100 Meadowlark Trailer Park, Brandon, MB R7C 0C1
info@meadowlarkcampground.ca
www.meadowlarkrvpark.com

RIVERS PROVINCIAL PARK (Prov Pk) From Jct of Hwy 25 & Hwy 250, N .5 mi on Hwy 250 to Memorial Dr. E 1.6 mi (E). 2015 rates: $11.55 to $28.35. May 11 to Sep 1. (888)482-2267

TURTLE CROSSING **Ratings: 3.5/8.5★/7.5** (Campground) 2015 rates: $24 to $29. Apr 1 to Sep 30. (204)571-0750 4100 Grand Valley Rd, Brandon, MB R7A 5Y3

CARBERRY — E2 *Southwest*

SPRUCE WOODS/KICHE MANITOU (Prov Pk) From Jct of Hwys 2 & 5, N 6 mi on Hwy 5 (R). 2015 rates: $15.75 to $18.90. May 1 to Sep 15. (204)827-2458

CARMAN — E2 *Pembina Valley*

KING'S PARK (CITY PARK) (Public) From jct Hwys 13, Hwy 3 & Secondary Hwy 245: Go 3/4 km/1/2 mi W on Hwy 245. 2015 rates: $15 to $25. May 20 to Sep 1. (204)745-2684

CARTWRIGHT — E2 *Western*

CARTWRIGHT CAMPGROUND (Public) From Jct of Hwys 5 & 3, W 0.25 mi on Hwy 3 (L). Donation. 2015 rates: $5. May to Sep. (204)529-2363

CRANBERRY PORTAGE — B1 *Northern*

CRANBERRY PORTAGE CAMPGROUND (Public) From Jct of Prov Hwy 10 & Portage Rd, W 0.5 mi on Portage Rd (L). 2015 rates: $10 to $20. May 15 to Sep 15. (204)472-3219

GRASS RIVER CAMPGROUND/REED LAKE (Prov Pk) From Jct of Hwy 10 & Hwy 39, E 38 mi on Hwy 39 (L). Pit toilets. 2015 rates: $16.80. May 1 to Sep 15. (888)482-2267

DAUPHIN — D1 *Parkland, Western*

RAINBOW BEACH CAMPGROUND (Prov Pk) From Town, E 11 mi on Hwy 20 (L). 2015 rates: $11.55 to $26.25. May to Sep. (888)482-2267

VERMILLION TRAILER PARK & CAMPGROUND (Public) From Jct of Hwy 5 (2nd St) & 2nd Ave (in town), W 0.1 mi on 2nd Ave (R). 2015 rates: $15 to $35. May 15 to Sep 15. (204)622-3125

EMERSON — E3 *South Central*

EMERSON PARK (Public) From jct Hwy 75 & I-29: Go E to Banks St. Pit toilets. 2015 rates: $10. May 15 to Oct 15. (204)373-2002

FALCON BEACH — E4 *Eastern*

WHITESHELL PROVINCIAL PARK (FALCON BEACH CAMPGROUND) (Prov Pk) From Town, S 0.6 mi on Hwy 1 (R). 2015 rates: $19.95 to $27.30. May 1 to Oct 1. (888)482-2267

WHITESHELL PROVINCIAL PARK FALCON (LAKESHORE CAMPGROUND) (Prov Pk) From Town, S 0.6 mi on Hwy 1 (R). 2015 rates: $17.85 to $23.10. May to Sep. (888)482-2267

FALCON LAKE — E4 *Eastern*

WHITESHELL PROVINCIAL PARK (FALCON CREEK CAMPGROUND) (Prov Pk) From Hwy 1: Go 2 km/1-1/4 mi S. On South Shore Rd. Pit toilets. 2015 rates: $19.95 to $27.30. May 1 to Oct 1. (204)349-2201

FLIN FLON — B1 *Northern*

BAKER'S NARROWS PROVINCIAL RECREATION AREA (Prov Pk) From the Jct of Hwy 10 & Bakers Narrows (L). 2015 rates: $18.90 to $23.10 May 16 to Sep 1. (888)482-2267

FLIN FLON TOURIST BUREAU & CAMPGROUND (Public) On Hwy 10A at E edge of town (R). 2015 rates: $9 to $11. May 1 to Sep 15. (204)687-7674

GILBERT PLAINS — D1 *Parklands*

GILBERT PLAINS CENTENNIAL PARK (CITY PARK) (Public) From jct Hwy 5 & Main St: Go 2 blocks N, then 2 blocks W on Gordon Ave W. 2015 rates: $25. (204)548-2063

GIROUX — E3 *Southeast*

RIDGEWOOD SOUTH GOLF COURSE & CAMPGROUND **Ratings: 5.5/6.5/7.5** (Campground) 2015 rates: $26.97. May 1 to Oct 10 (204)326-5722 hwy 311, Giroux, MB R5G 1R7

GLADSTONE — E2 *Central*

WILLIAMS PARK (Public) From Jct of SR-16 & CR-460, N 1 mi on CR-460 (L). 2015 rates: $19 to $26. May 15 to Sep 30. (204)212-3047

GRAND BEACH — D3 *Eastern*

GRAND BEACH PROVINCIAL PARK (Prov Pk) From Jct of Hwy 12 & Hwy 59, W 6 mi on Hwy 12 (E) 2015 rates: $17.85 to $22.05. May 1 to Sep 15 (888)482-2267

GRAND MARAIS — D3 *Interlake*

GRAND MARAIS COMMUNITY CENTRAL & RV PARK (Public) Located on Hwy 12 in the Town of Grand Marais. (R) .5 km (.3 mi.) from West Gate of Grand Beach. 2015 rates: $25. May 15 to Oct 15 (204)754-3596

GRANDVIEW — D1 *Western, Parkland*

DUCK MOUNTAIN PROVINCIAL PARK (SINGUSH LAKE CAMPGROUND) (Prov Pk) From town Go 25 km/15-1/2 mi W on Hwy 367. Pit toilets. 2015 rates: $16.80. May 1 to Sep 1. (204)546-2701

WILSON CENTENNIAL PARK (Public) From Jct of Hwy 5 & Main St, NE 0.1 mi on Main St to Railway North Rd, W 0.3 mi (R). May 15 to Sep 1. (204)546-5250

HAMIOTA — E1 *Western*

HAMIOTA MUNICIPAL CAMPGROUND (Public) From Jct of Hwy 21 & Main St, E 0.5 mi on Main St (R). 2015 rates: $17 to $27.50. May 1 to Oct 1 (204)764-3050

HODGSON — D3 *Interlake*

LAKE ST GEORGE CAMPGROUND (PROVINCIAL WAYSIDE PARK) (Prov Pk) From town: Go 2 km/15 mi N on Hwy 224 to Dallas, then 40 km/25 mi N on gravel access road. Pit toilets. 2015 rates $16.80. May 1 to Sep 1. (888)482-2267

HOLLAND — E2 *North Central*

HOLLAND AGRICULTURAL SOCIETY CAMPGROUND **Ratings: 2/6/7** (Campground) 2015 rates $20. May 15 to Oct 15. (204)526-2005 hwy 34, Holland, MB R0G 0X0

KILLARNEY — E2 *Southwest*

← KERRY PARK CAMPGROUND **Ratings: 6/7/7.5** (Campground) 2015 rates: $25 to $30. May 1 to Sep 30. (204)523-6000 402 South Railway St, Killarney, MB R0K 1G0

← KILLARNEY AGRICULTURAL SOCIETY CAMPGROUNDS (Public) From jct Hwy 18 & Hwy 3W: Go .5 km/1/3 mi W on Hwy 3. 2015 rates: $14 to $20. (204)523-4699

LAC DU BONNET — E3 *Southeast*

← **CHAMPAGNE'S RV PARK Ratings: 8/9.5★/9** (RV Park) From jct Hwy 11 & Hwy 313: Go .4 km/1/4 mi W on gravel road. **FAC:** All weather rds. (55 spaces). Avail: 44 all weather, 10 pull-thrus (30 x 60), back-ins (30 x 45), 44 full hkups (15/30 amps), seasonal sites, WiFi, tent sites, showers $, dump, laundry, fire rings. **REC:** playground, rec open to public. Pets OK. Partial handicap access. Eco-friendly, 2015 rates: $25 to $30. May 1 to Oct 1. No CC. (204)345-2414 Lat: 50.280956, Lon: -96.037264 102 Tinant Road, Lac Du Bonnet, MB R0E 1A0 champagnesrv@hotmail.com

↑ NOPIMING PROVINCIAL PARK (BIRD LAKE CAMPGROUND) (Prov Pk) From town: Go 72.5 km/45 mi N on Hwys 314 & 315. Follow signs. 2015 rates: $10.50 to $19.95. (888)482-2267

→ NOPIMING PROVINCIAL PARK (BLACK LAKE CAMPGROUND) (Prov Pk) Travel 3 km N on Pth 11 to PR 313; drive E 20 km, then N on PR 315. Pit toilets. 2015 rates: $10.50 to $19.95. (888)482-2267

↓ NOPIMING PROVINCIAL PARK (TULABI FALLS CAMPGROUND) (Prov Pk) From town: Go 60 km/37-1/4 mi S. Follow signs. 2015 rates: $10.50 to $19.95. (888)482-2267

LAKE MANITOBA NARROWS — D2 *Interlake*

← LAKE MANITOBA NARROWS LODGE (NARROWS TOURIST LODGE) (Campground) (Phone Update) 2015 rates: $20 to $30. May 15 to Oct 15. (204)768-2749 hwy 68, Oakview, MB R0C 2K0

LUNDAR — D2 *Interlake*

← LUNDAR BEACH CAMPGROUND (Prov Pk) From Jct of Hwy 6 & Secondary Hwy 419, W 12 mi on Secondary Rd 419 (L) - 3 day park entrance fee req'd ($5.95). 2015 rates: $18.90 to $23.10. May 1 to Sep 15. (888)482-2267

LYNN LAKE — A2 *Northern*

↑ ZED LAKE PROVINCIAL PARK (Prov Pk) From town, N 13 mi on PR-394 to park access rd, SW .25 mi (E). Pit toilets. 2015 rates: $11 to $23. May 1 to Sep 15. (204)356-2413

MACGREGOR — E2 *North Central*

MACGREGOR LIONS RV PARK (Public) Downtown, follow signs. 2015 rates: $8 to $20. May 1 to Oct 15. (204)685-2582

MANITOU — E2 *South Central*

← STEPHENFIELD PROVINCIAL PARK (Prov Pk) From Jct of Hwys 13, 3 & Secondary Hwy 245, W 10 mi on Hwy 245 (R). 2015 rates: $11.55 to $28.35. May 11 to Oct 13. (204)828-3366

MINNEDOSA — E2 *Central*

→ MINNEDOSA CAMPGROUND (Public Corps) From N Jct of Hwys 10 & 16A, E 2.5 mi on Hwy 16A to clock tower (Downtown), follow signs to PR-262, E 0.5 mi (L). 2015 rates: $22 to $33. May to Sep. (204)867-3450

MOOSEHORN — D2 *Interlake*

← WATCHORN BAY CAMPGROUND (Prov Pk) From Jct of Hwy 6 & Secondary Rd 237, W 7 mi on Secondary Rd 237 (E). 2015 rates: $18.90 to $23.10. May 1 to Sep 15. (888)482-2267

MORDEN — E2 *Pembina Valley*

↗ COLERT BEACH AND MORDEN CAMPGROUND (Public) From Jct of Hwy 3 & Hwy 432, W 1.2 mi on Hwy 3 to Colert Rd, S 0.5 mi (E). 2015 rates: $20 to $25. May 15 to Sep 3. (204)822-4991

← LAKE MINNEWASTA RECREATION AREA (Public) From town: Go 1-1/2 km/1 mi W on Hwy 3, then 1-1/4 km/3/4 mi S to Colert Beach. 2015 rates: $20 to $25. (204)822-5431

MORRIS — E3 *South Central*

BIG M CENTENNIAL PARK (MORRIS & DISTRICT CENTENNIAL MUSEUM) (Public) At jct Hwy 75 & Hwy 23 E, adjacent to fairgrounds. 2015 rates: $15. Jun 1 to Sep 30. (204)746-2169

MUSEUM CAMPGROUND (Public) At jct Hwy 75 & Hwy 23 E, adjacent to Fairgrounds. 2015 rates: $10 to $20. May 15 to Sep 30. (204)746-2169

→ SCRATCHING RIVER CAMPGROUND (CITY PARK) (Public) From jct Hwy 75 & Hwy 23 E: Go 3/4 km/1/2 mi E on Hwy 23 E. Pit toilets. 2015 rates: $8 to $10. (204)746-2531

NEEPAWA — E2 *Central*

→ LIONS RIVERBEND CAMPGROUND (Public) From Jct of Hwy 16 & Hwy 5, E 1 mi on Hwy 16 (L). 2015 rates: $15 to $28. May 1 to Sep 30. (204)476-7676

OAK LAKE — E1 *Southwest*

← ASPEN GROVE CAMPGROUND **Ratings: 6.5/7.5/8** (Campground) 2015 rates: $34.50 to $39.50. May 8 to Oct 3. (204)855-2260 nw 25-9-25W, Oak Lake, MB R0M 1P0

↓ FOUR SEASONS ISLAND RESORT (OAK ISLAND RESORT) **Ratings: 7.5/7/8** (Campground) 2015 rates: $30 to $42. May 1 to Oct 1. (204)855-2307 hwy 254, Oak Lake, MB R0M 1P0

ONANOLE — D2 *Southwest*

→ ONANOLE RV PARK AND CAMPGROUND (Campground) (Phone Update) 2015 rates: $44 .77. May 15 to Sep 15. (204)848-2398 5 Elk Dr, Onanole, MB R0J 1N0

PILOT MOUND — E2 *South Central*

← MOUNT PARK CAMPGROUND (VILLAGE PARK) (Public) From jct Hwy 3 & Hwy 253: Go .8 km/1/2 mi W on Hwy 253. (204)825-2587

PORTAGE LA PRAIRIE — E2 *Central*

→ **MILLER'S CAMPING RESORT Ratings: 8.5/9.5★/9** (Campground) From town, E 6 mi on Hwy 1, follow signs (L). **FAC:** All weather rds. (192 spaces). Avail: 68 gravel, 20 pull-thrus (40 x 80), back-ins (40 x 50), some side by side hkups, 30 full hkups, 25 W, 25 E (30/50 amps), seasonal sites, WiFi, tent sites, showers $, dump, laundry, groc, LP bottles, fire rings, firewood, controlled access. **REC:** heated pool, playground. Pet restrict(Q). Partial handicap access. Big rig sites, eco-friendly, 2015 rates: $25 to $40. May 1 to Oct 1. **(204)857-4255 Lat: 49.97557, Lon: -98.136613 hwy 1, Portage La Prairie, MB R1N 3C3 info@millerscampground.com www.millerscampground.com**
See ad this page, 1389.

PRAWDA — E4 *Southeast*

→ **PINE TREE CAMPGROUND & TRAILER PARK** (Campground) (Seasonal Stay Only) From Jct of TCH 1 & PR 74E, N 100 yds on PR 74E to River Rd, W 200 yds (R). **FAC:** Gravel rds. (44 spaces). Avail: 8 gravel, 4 pull-thrus (27 x 50), back-ins (20 x 55), 8 W, 8 E (15/30 amps), seasonal sites, WiFi, tent sites, dump, laundry, fire rings, firewood, restaurant. **REC:** Birch River: fishing, playground. Pets OK. 2015 rates: $25 to $40. May 17 to Oct 10.
AAA Approved
(204)426-5413 Lat: 49.38992, Lon: -95.46505 group 8, Box 11, Prawda, MB R0E 0X0 info@pinetreecampground.com www.pinetreecampground.com

RENNIE — E4 *Eastern*

↗ WHITESHELL PROVINCIAL PARK (BIG WHITESHELL LAKE CAMPGROUND) (Prov Pk) From Jct of Hwy 307 & Hwy 309, E 6.3 mi on Hwy 309 NE 1.1 mi on un-named rd (L). 2015 rates: $13.85 to $18.90. May 1 to Oct 1. (888)482-2267

↑ WHITESHELL PROVINCIAL PARK (BRERETON LAKE CAMPGROUND) (Prov Pk) From Jct of Hwy 44 & Hwy 307, N 5.5 mi on Hwy 307 (L). 2015 rates: $13.85 to $17.85. May 11 to Oct 1. (888)482-2267

↑ WHITESHELL PROVINCIAL PARK (WHITE LAKE CAMPGROUND) (Prov Pk) From town: Go 26 km/16 mi N on Hwy 307. 2015 rates: $13.85. May 1 to Oct 1. (888)482-2267

RICHER — E3 *Eastern*

→ CRIPPLE CREEK CAMPGROUND **Ratings: 5/6/7.5** (Campground) 2015 rates: $25 to $36. Apr 26 to Sep 30. (204)771-0242 44154 Trudeau Road, Richer, MB R0J 0N0

↑ ROCK GARDEN CAMPGROUND **Ratings: 7.5/7/8** (Campground) 2015 rates: $25 to $38. Apr 1 to Oct 15. (866)422-5441 44025 Mun. Rd 46 N, Richer, MB R0E 1S0

↑ **WILD OAKS CAMPGROUND Ratings: 7/6.5/8.5** (Campground) From Jct of TCH 1 & PR 302, N 0.8 mi on PR 302 (L). **FAC:** Gravel rds. (135 spaces). 45 Avail: 27 gravel, 18 grass, 18 pull-thrus (30 x 70), back-ins (50 x 42), 45 W, 45 E (15/30 amps), seasonal sites, WiFi Hotspot, tent sites, dump, laundry, fire rings, firewood, controlled access. **REC:** heated pool, whirlpool, pond, swim, playground, rec open to public. Pets OK. 2015 rates: $32. May 1 to Oct 15. No CC.
AAA Approved
(204)422-6175 Lat: 49.675194, Lon: -96.457956 45136 Pr 302, Richer, MB R0E 1S0 wildoaks@simplyconnected.ca www.wildoaks.ca

RIVERTON — D3 *Interlake*

↑ BEAVER CREEK PROVINCIAL PARK (Prov Pk) Take Hwy 8 N of Riverton then N on to Hwy 234 & follow for approx 35 km. Pit toilets. 2015 rates: $16.80. May 15 to Sep 1. (888)4U2-CAMP

↗ HECLA PROVINCIAL PARK (GULL HARBOUR CAMPGROUND) (Prov Pk) From Town, NE 5 mi on Hwy 8 (E) - 3 day park entrance fee req'd ($5.95). 2015 rates: $17.85 to $23.10. May 1 to Sep 15. (888)482-2267

ROBLIN — D1 *Parklands*

↑ ASESSIPPI PROVINCIAL PARK (Prov Pk) From Jct of Hwy 16 & Hwy 83, N 12 mi on Hwy 83 to Secondary Rd 482, W 5 mi (R). 2015 rates: $10.50 to $19.95. May 22 to Sep 30. (888)482-2267

↑ DUCK MOUNTAIN PROVINCIAL PARK (CHILDS LAKE CAMPGROUND) (Prov Pk) From Jct of Hwy 5 & Secondary Hwy 366, NW 30 mi on Secondary Rd 366 to Secondary Rd 367, W 12 mi (R). 2015 rates: $18.90 to $24.15. May 1 to Sep 1. (888)482-2267

↓ PYOTT'S WEST CAMPGOUND (Campground) (Phone Update) 2015 rates: $28 to $30. May 10 to Sep 30. (204)564-2308 hwy 482, Roblin, MB R0L 1P0

RUSSELL — D1 *Western, Parkland*

← PEACE PARK (Public) At Jct of Hwys 16 & 83, in town (R). May to Sep. (204)773-2456

SELKIRK — E3 *Interlake*

← SELKIRK MUNICIPAL PARK (Public) From Jct of Hwy 9 & Queen Ave, SE 0.1 mi on Queen Ave (E). 2015 rates: $11.75 to $15.25. May 21 to Oct 15. (204)785-4958

SEVEN SISTERS FALLS — E3 *Eastern*

→ WHITESHELL PROVINCIAL PARK (BETULA LAKE CAMPGROUND) (Prov Pk) From town: Go 42 km/26 mi E on Hwy 307. 2015 rates: $15.75. May 1 to Oct 1. (888)482-2267

→ WHITESHELL PROVINCIAL PARK (NUTIMIK LAKE CAMPGROUND) (Prov Pk) From town: Go 33 km/21 mi E on Hwy 307. 2015 rates: $13.85 to $18.90. May 1 to Oct 1. (888)482-2267

→ WHITESHELL PROVINCIAL PARK (OPAPISKAW CAMPGROUND) (Prov Pk) From Town, E 26 mi on Hwy 307 (L). 2015 rates: $13.85 to $17.85. May 9 to Oct 13. (888)482-2267

→ WHITESHELL PROVINCIAL PARK (OTTER FALLS) (Prov Pk) From Jct of Hwy 408 & Hwy 307, E 11.3 mi on Hwy 307 (L). 2015 rates: $13.65 to $17.85. May 1 to Oct 1. (888)482-2267

SIDNEY — E2 *Central*

→ SHADY OAKS RV RESORT & CAMPGROUND **Ratings: 7.5/6/7.5** (Campground) 2015 rates: $26 to $32. May 14 to Sep 30. (866)466-2777 box 149, Sidney, MB R0H 1L0

SNOW LAKE — B2 *Northern*

↓ WEKUSKO FALLS PROVINCIAL PARK (Prov Pk) From town: Go 10 km/6-1/4 mi S on Hwy 392. 2015 rates: $17.85 to $22.05. May 1 to Sep 1. (888)482-2267

SOURIS — E1 *Glenwood*

↓ VICTORIA PARK (Public) From Jct Hwy 2 & 3rd St, S 0.9 mi on 3rd St (E). 2015 rates: $18. May to Oct. (204)483-5212

SPRAGUE — E4 *Southeast*

BIRCH POINT PROVINCIAL PARK (BIRCH POINT CAMPGROUND) (Prov Pk) From town: Go 40 km/24-3/4 mi NE on Hwy 308. (Entrance fee). Pit toilets. 2015 rates: $11.55. May 1 to Sep 1. (888)482-2267

MOOSE LAKE PROVINCIAL PARK (Prov Pk) From town: Go 32 km/20 mi NE on Hwy 308 (16 km/10 mi paved, 16 km/10 mi gravel). 2015 rates: $11.55 to $15.75. May 1 to Sep 1. (888)482-2267

ST FRANCOIS XAVIER — E3 *Central*

WINNIPEG WEST KOA
Ratings: 8/9/8 (Campground) From Jct of TCH 1 & Perimeter Hwy 100/101, W 8.1 mi on TCH 1 (L). **FAC:** All weather rds. (75 spaces). Avail: 71 all weather, 40 pull-thrus (40 x 80), back-ins (30 x 50), 40 full hkups, 23 W, 23 E (30/50 amps), seasonal sites, WiFi, tent sites, dump, laundry, groc, LP bottles, fire rings, firewood. **REC:** heated pool, Assiniboine River: fishing, playground. Pets OK. Partial handicap access. Big rig sites, eco-friendly, 2015 rates: $29 to $43. Apr 15 to Oct 15. ATM.
(800)562-0378 Lat: 49.53242, Lon: -97.30561
588 Hwy #1 West, St Francois Xavier, MB R4L 1A1
welcomestop@gmail.com
koa.com/campground/winnipeg-west
See ad this page.

ST JEAN BAPTISTE — E3 *Southeastern*

ST JEAN REGIONAL REC PARK (Public) From N end of town, E 0.25 mi on Park rd (L). 2015 rates: $10 to $12. Jun 1 to Oct 1. (204)758-3881

ST MALO — E3 *Eastern*

DEBONAIR CAMPGROUND **Ratings: 6/7.5/8.5** (Campground) 2015 rates: $22 to $28. May 1 to Oct 10. (204)347-5336 22079 Pr 403, St Malo, MB R0A 1T0

ST MALO PROVINCIAL PARK (Prov Pk) From Jct of Hwy 59 & Beach Rd, E 0.5 mi (E). 2015 rates: $17.85 to $22.05. May 9 to Sep 7. (204)347-5283

STE ANNE — E3 *Eastern*

LILAC RESORT LTD **Ratings: 7.5/8.5★/8** (Campground) 2015 rates: $24 to $52. Apr 15 to Oct 15. (866)388-6095 911 Marker: Hwy 1 East, 37162, Ste Anne, MB R5H 1C1

STEEP ROCK — D2 *Interlake*

NORTH STEEPROCK LAKE PROVINCIAL PARK (Prov Pk) From jct Hwy 239 & gravel road on south end of town: Go 3.9 km/6-1/4 mi N on gravel road. 2015 rates: $10.50 to $19.95. (888)482-2267

STONEWALL — E3 *Interlake*

QUARRY PARK CAMPGROUND (Public) From Jct of Hwys 67 & 236, N 0.4 mi on Hwy 236 (L). 2015 rates: $25 to $35. May 1 to Sep 30. (204)467-7980

SWAN RIVER — C1 *Parklands*

BELL LAKE PROVINCIAL PARK (Prov Pk) North of Birch River, turn W from PTH and continue on PR 365 for about 18 km (11 mi). Pit toilets. 2015 rates: $16.80. May 1 to Sep 1. (888)4U2-CAMP

DUCK MOUNTAIN PROVINCIAL PARK (WELLMAN LAKE CAMPGROUND) (Prov Pk) From Jct of Hwy 10 & Secondary Hwy 366, S 15.5 mi on Secondary Rd 366 (E). 2015 rates: $16.80 to $24.15. May 1 to Oct 1. (888)482-2267

GREEN ACRES CAMPGROUND (Campground) (Phone Update) 2015 rates: $17 to $22.50. Apr 15 to Oct 15. (204)734-3334 312 Centennial Drive, Swan River, MB R0L 1Z0

WHITEFISH LAKE PROVINCIAL PARK (Prov Pk) From jct Hwy 10 & Hwy 279: Go 25-1/2 km/16 mi NW on Hwy 279. 2015 rates: $13.86. (888)482-2267

THE PAS — B1 *Northern*

CLEARWATER LAKE PROVINCIAL PARK (CAMPERS COVE CAMPGROUND) (Prov Pk) From town, NW 15 mi on Hwy 287 (L). 2015 rates: $10.50 to $19.95. May 1 to Sep 15. (888)482-2267

KINSMEN KAMPGROUND (TOWN PARK) (Public) In town, from jct Hwy 10 & Edwards Ave: Go 1 block NW on Edwards Ave, then follow signs. May 1 to Oct 1. (204)623-2233

THOMPSON — A3 *Northern*

MCCREEDY CAMPGROUND (Public) From Burntwood Bridge to Hwy 6, NE 0.5 mi, follow signs (R). Pit toilets. 2015 rates: $10 to $16. May 21 to Oct 1. (204)778-8810

PAINT LAKE PROVINCIAL PARK (Prov Pk) From Town, S 17.3 mi on Hwy 6 to SR 375, SE 3.6 mi (R). 2015 rates: $10.50 to $19.95. May to Sep. (204)677-6444

TREHERNE — E2 *Central*

COTTONWOOD CAMP SITE (Public) From Jct of Hwy 2 & Railway St, SE 0.1 mi on Railway St to Vanzile St, S 0.25 mi (R). 2015 rates: $16 to $29. May 15 to Sep 15. (204)723-5040

WANLESS — B1 *Northern*

ROCKY LAKE (Public) From The Pas, N 30 mi on Hwy 10 to Wanless, W 1.5 mi to unnamed Rd, S 0.25 mi, follow signs (L). 2015 rates: $18 to $23. May 22 to Oct 1. (204)682-7423

WARREN — E2 *Central*

RUBBER DUCKY RESORT & CAMPGROUND **Ratings: 7.5/8.5/8** (RV Park) 2015 rates: $34.95 to $40.95. Apr 15 to Oct 15. (204)322-5286 road 76.5N, Warren, MB R0C 3E0

WASAGAMING — D2 *Riding Mountain*

RIDING MTN/LAKE AUDY (Natl Pk) From Jct of Hwy 10 & Lake Audy Rd, W 16 mi on Lake Audy Rd (R). Pit toilets. 2015 rates: $27.40. May to Oct. (204)848-7275

RIDING MTN/MOON LAKE (Natl Pk) From Jct of Yellowhead Hwy 16 & Hwy 10, N 48 mi on Hwy 10 (R). Pit toilets. 2015 rates: $15.70. May to Oct. (204)848-7275

RIDING MTN/WASAGAMING CAMPGROUND (Natl Pk) From Jct of Hwy 10 & Yellowhead Hwy 16, N 26 mi on Hwy 10 (L). 2015 rates: $27.40 to $38.20. May 15 to Oct 15. (204)848-7275

SPORTSMAN'S PARK **Ratings: 7.5/7/7.5** (RV Park) 2015 rates: $39 to $42. May 1 to Sep 30. (204)848-2520 545 Pth 10, Onanole, MB R0J 1N0

WEST HAWK LAKE — E4 *Eastern*

WHITESHELL PROVINCIAL PARK (CADDY LAKE CAMPGROUND) (Prov Pk) From town, W 5 mi on Hwy 44 (R). 2015 rates: $13.65. May to Oct. (888)482-2267

WHITESHELL PROVINCIAL PARK (WEST HAWK LAKE) (Prov Pk) From Jct of Hwy 17 & Hwy 44, E 500 yds (L). Pit toilets. 2015 rates: $15.75 to $23.10. May 1 to Oct 1. (888)482-2267

WESTBOURNE — E2 *Central*

OFTY'S RIVERSIDE CAMPGROUND (Campground) (Phone Update) 2015 rates: $28 to $35. May 15 to Sep 30. (204)274-2705 pr 242N, Westbourne, MB R0H 1P0

SPORTSMAN'S CORNER CAMPGROUND (Campground) (Phone Update) Pit toilets. 2015 rates: $22. May 1 to Sep 30. (204)274-2015 48071, Rd 81 North, Westbourne, MB R0H 0C0

WINKLER — E3 *Central*

WINKLER TOURIST PARK (Public) From Jct of Hwy 14 & Park St (exit 2nd), S 0.1 mi on Park St (R). 2015 rates: $20. May to Sep. (204)325-8212

WINNIPEG — E3 *Eastern*

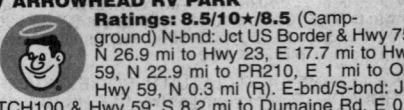

ARROWHEAD RV PARK
Ratings: 8.5/10★/8.5 (Campground) N-bnd: Jct US Border & Hwy 75: N 26.9 mi to Hwy 23, E 17.7 mi to Hwy 59, N 22.9 mi to PR210, E 1 mi to Old Hwy 59, N 0.3 mi (R). E-bnd/S-bnd: Jct TCH100 & Hwy 59: S 8.2 mi to Dumaine Rd, E 0.2 mi to Old Hwy 59, S 1 mi (L). W-bnd: Jct TCH1 & PR206: S 7.6 mi to PR210, W 8 mi to Old Hwy 59, N 0.3 mi (R). **FAC:** All weather rds. 54 Avail: 54 all weather, 41 pull-thrus (24 x 65), back-ins (20 x 55) mostly side by side hkups, 54 full hkups (30/50 amps), WiFi $, laundry, fire rings, firewood, controlled access. **REC:** playground. Pets OK. No tents. Big rig sites, eco-friendly, 2015 rates: $34 to $44. Apr 15 to Oct 31.
(888)878-4203 Lat: 49.69691, Lon: -96.98386
1375 A Major Trail, Ile des Chenes, MB R0A 0T0
info@arrowheadrvpark.ca
www.arrowheadrvpark.ca
See ad this page, 1389.

TOWN & COUNTRY CAMPGROUND **Ratings: 7.5/7/8** (Campground) 2015 rates: $34 to $39. Apr 15 to Oct 15. (204)615-1995 56001 Murdock Road, Winnipeg, MB R2C 2Z3

WINNIPEG BEACH — D3 *Interlake*

CAMP MORTON PROVINCIAL PARK (Prov Pk) From town: Go 6 km/4 mi N on Park Rd 222. 2015 rates: $16.80. May 1 to Sep 1. (888)482-2267

HNAUSA BEACH PROVINCIAL PARK (Prov Pk) Follow PR 222, 22 km N of Gimli. 2015 rates: $10.50 to $19.95. (888)4U2-CAMP

NORRIS LAKE PROVINCIAL PARK (Prov Pk) Approx 1 hour from Winnipeg, take PTH 7 N 45 km to Teulon. Then NW 20 km on PTH 17. 2015 rates: $11.55. May 1 to Sep 15. (888)4U2-CAMP

WINNIPEG BEACH PROVINCIAL PARK (Prov Pk) Leaving Winnipeg, go N on PTH 8 for 45 km/28 mi, turn right at PR 229 drive 5 km/3.1 mi to Winnipeg Beach. 2015 rates: $25.20. May 1 to Oct 1. (888)4U2-CAMP

WINNIPEGOSIS — D2 *Western*

MANIPOGO PROVINCIAL RECREATION PARK (Prov Pk) From Jct of Secondary Hwy 276 & Secondary Hwy 364, N 12 mi on Secondary Hwy 276 (R). 3 day park entrance fee req'd ($5.95). 2015 rates: $14.90. May 11 to Sep 8. (888)482-2267

WINNIPEGOSIS PARK BEACH CAMPGROUND (Public Corps) From Jct of Hwys 20A & 20, N 35 mi on Hwy 20, follow signs (R). 2015 rates: $15. May 1 to Oct 1. (204)656-4791

Don't take any chances when it comes to cleanliness. We rate campground restrooms and showers for cleanliness and physical characteristics such as supplies and appearance.

Snowbird Destinations

Join the flock and head south during the winter. Use our handy Snowbird section in the front of this Guide to find RV-friendly destinations throughout the sunbelt. Snowbird Destinations features the top Snowbird roosts and lists great campgrounds in compelling areas.

WELCOME TO
New Brunswick

JOINED CONFEDERATION JULY 1, 1867	WIDTH: 114 MILES (183 KM) LENGTH: 188 MILES (302 KM)	PROPORTION OF CANADA 0.73% OF 9,984,670 SQ KM

Sprawling beaches, stunning mountains and legendary waterways have made New Brunswick a popular destination among outdoors enthusiasts. During summer, warm water greets beachgoers and fantastic golf courses challenge RVers who travel with a bag of clubs.

New Brunswick's Bay of Fundy has the highest tidal range in the world, with waters fluctuating 40 feet twice every day. Out on the water, sightseeing cruises encounter sea mammals and several species of whale. On shore, tide pool explorers get up close to towering formations like the Hopewell Rocks, which disappear at high tide.

The pristine spruce forests of Fundy National Park engulf hikers along the cliffs above the bay. The coastline at Kouchibouguac National Park on the Northumberland Strait boasts the warmest Atlantic Ocean waters north of Virginia.

The Acadian culture in New Brunswick comes to life for a summer fortnight during the Festival Acadien de Caraquet, which began as a simple village party in Caraquet, the unofficial "capital of Acadia," in 1963. Today, more than 400 artists appear in cabaret shows and main stage parties.

In Edmundston on the banks of St. Johns River, Canada's largest French festival outside of Quebec takes place during the Foire Brayonne. The culinary star of the festivities is the ploye, a pancake-type mix of water and buckwheat flour. The highlight of the five-day event comes during the Party du Parking, when the town parking lot erupts into a non-stop dance party.

The centerpiece of the Shediac Lobster Festival in the town that fancies itself "The Lobster Capital of the World" is a 1,000-foot Long Table Lobster Dinner set up on Main Street.

Top 3 Tourism Attractions:
1) Fredericton
2) Bay of Fundy
3) Sightseeing Tour

Nickname: Picture Province

State Flower: Purple Violet

State Bird: Black-Capped Chickadee

People: Gordon "Gordie" Drillon, hockey player; Donald Sutherland, actor; Franklin D. Roosevelt Jr., son of the 32nd president of the U.S.; Ron Turcotte, thoroughbred race horse jockey; Robb Wells, actor and screenwriter

Major Cities: Saint John, Moncton, Fredericton (capital), Dieppe, Miramichi

Topography: Mostly forested; Appalachian Mountains dominate interior; east-central—Gulf of St. Lawrence lowlands; south—Bay of Fundy

Climate: Continental climate; warm summers, cold winters; south-moderate maritime climate, cooler summers, milder winters

TRAVEL & TOURISM

New Brunswick Dept. of Tourism and Parks
800-561-0123
www.tourismnewbrunswick.ca

Albert County Tourism Association
506-882-2349
www.albertcountytourism.com

City of Dieppe
506-877-7900
www.dieppe.ca

City of Fredericton
506-460-2041, 888-888-4768
www.tourismfredericton.ca

Grand Manan Tourism Association
506-662-3442
www.grandmanannb.com

City of Miramichi-Community Dev. Tourism
506-623-2200
www.miramichi.org

City of Moncton
800-363-4558
www.gomoncton.com

Trinity Power Centre
www.knowmoncton.com

Greater Woodstock Tourism Partnership
www.town.woodstock.nb.ca

OUTDOOR RECREATION

Canoe Kayak New Brunswick
www.canoekayak-nb.org

Golf New Brunswick
877-TEE-IN-NB
www.golfnb.ca

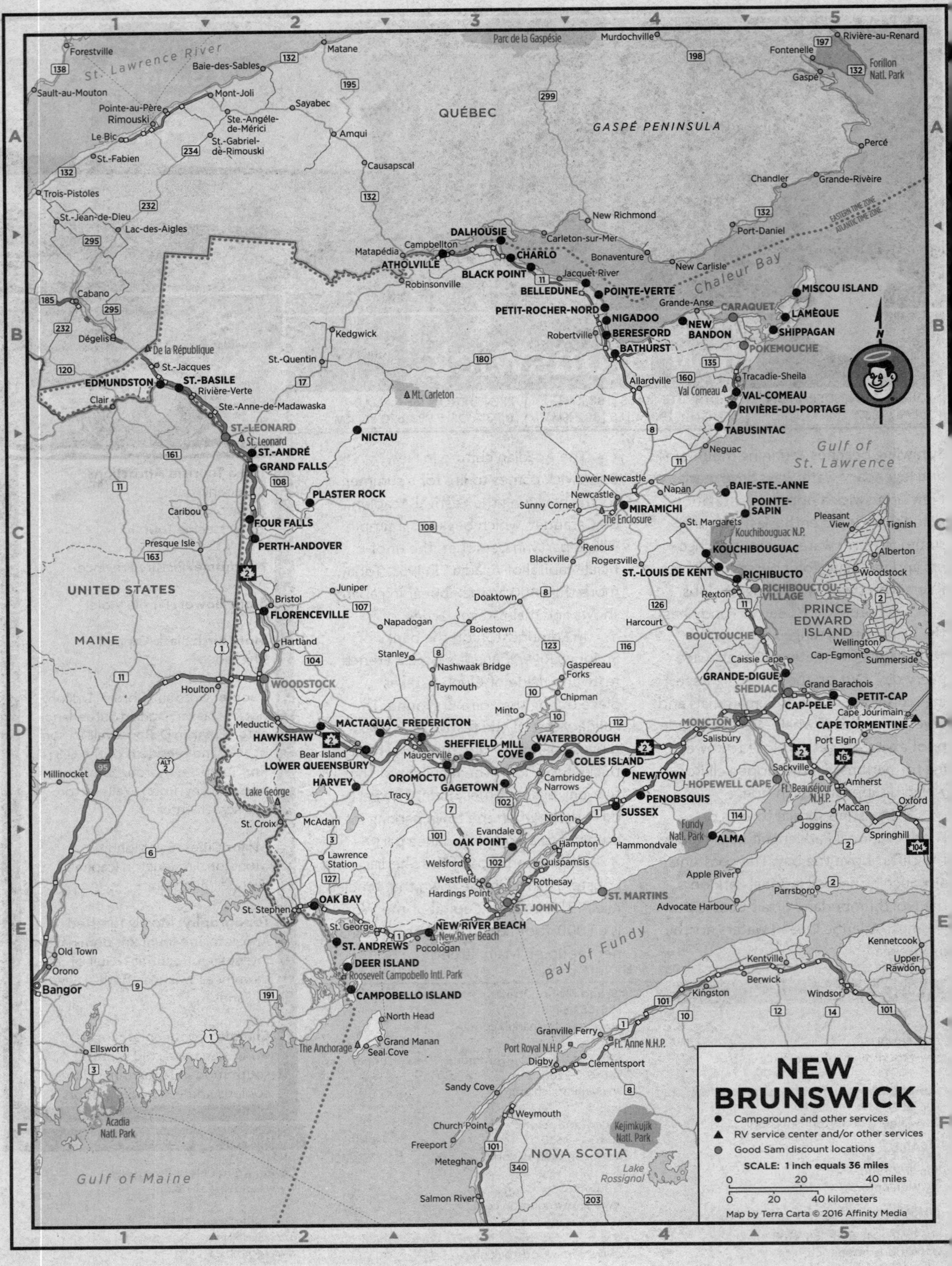
NEW BRUNSWICK
Campground and other services
RV service center and/or other services
Good Sam discount locations
SCALE: 1 inch equals 36 miles
0 20 40 miles
0 20 40 kilometers
Map by Terra Carta © 2016 Affinity Media
QUÉBEC
GASPÉ PENINSULA
UNITED STATES
MAINE
PRINCE EDWARD ISLAND
NOVA SCOTIA
St. Lawrence River
Chaleur Bay
Gulf of St. Lawrence
Bay of Fundy
Gulf of Maine
EASTERN TIME ZONE
ATLANTIC TIME ZONE
Parc de la Gaspésie
Forillon Natl. Park
Mt. Carleton
Kouchibouguac N.P.
Fundy Natl. Park
Acadia Natl. Park
Kejimkujik Natl. Park
Port Royal N.H.P.
Ft. Anne N.H.P.
Ft. Beauséjour N.H.P.
Roosevelt Campobello Intl. Park
Forestville
Baie-des-Sables
Matane
Murdochville
Fontenelle
Rivière-au-Renard
Gaspé
Sault-au-Mouton
Mont-Joli
Pointe-au-Père
Rimouski
Sayabec
Ste.-Angéle-de-Méríci
Le Bic
St.-Gabriel-de-Rimouski
Amqui
St.-Fabien
Causapscal
Percé
Chandler
Grande-Rivèire
Trois-Pistoles
St.-Jean-de-Dieu
Lac-des-Aigles
New Richmond
Port-Daniel
DALHOUSIE
Carleton-sur-Mer
Matapédia
Campbellton
ATHOLVILLE
Robinsonville
CHARLO
Bonaventure
New Carlisle
BLACK POINT
Jacquet River
BELLEDUNE
POINTE-VERTE
MISCOU ISLAND
Grande-Anse
CARAQUET
LAMÈQUE
PETIT-ROCHER-NORD
NIGADOO
NEW BANDON
SHIPPAGAN
Cabano
Dégelis
Kedgwick
Robertville
BERESFORD
BATHURST
POKEMOUCHE
De la République
St.-Jacques
St.-Quentin
EDMUNDSTON
ST.-BASILE
Rivière-Verte
Allardville
Tracadie-Sheila
Val Comeau
VAL-COMEAU
RIVIÈRE-DU-PORTAGE
Clair
Ste.-Anne-de-Madawaska
TABUSINTAC
ST.-LEONARD
St. Leonard
NICTAU
Neguac
ST.-ANDRÉ
GRAND FALLS
Lower Newcastle
Napan
BAIE-STE.-ANNE
PLASTER ROCK
Newcastle
Sunny Corner
MIRAMICHI
POINTE-SAPIN
Caribou
The Enclosure
St. Margarets
Pleasant View
Tignish
FOUR FALLS
PERTH-ANDOVER
Presque Isle
Renous
KOUCHIBOUGUAC
Alberton
Blackville
Rogersville
ST.-LOUIS DE KENT
RICHIBUCTO
Woodstock
Juniper
Doaktown
Rexton
RICHIBOUCTOU-VILLAGE
Bristol
FLORENCEVILLE
Napadogan
Boiestown
Harcourt
Hartland
BOUCTOUCHE
Wellington
Stanley
Nashwaak Bridge
Caissie Cape
Cap-Egmont
Summerside
Taymouth
Gaspereau Forks
GRANDE-DIGUE
Grand Barachois
WOODSTOCK
Houlton
Chipman
SHEDIAC
PETIT-CAP
CAP-PELE
Minto
Cape Jourimain
Meductic
MACTAQUAC
FREDERICTON
MONCTON
CAPE TORMENTINE
HAWKSHAW
Salisbury
Port Elgin
Bear Island
SHEFFIELD
MILL COVE
WATERBOROUGH
Maugerville
COLES ISLAND
Millinocket
LOWER QUEENSBURY
Sackville
NEWTOWN
Cambridge-Narrows
HOPEWELL CAPE
Amherst
HARVEY
OROMOCTO
GAGETOWN
Oxford
Lake George
Tracy
PENOBSQUIS
SUSSEX
Maccan
Norton
St. Croix
McAdam
Joggins
Evandale
Springhill
Hampton
ALMA
OAK POINT
Hammondvale
Lawrence Station
Welsford
Quispamsis
Apple River
Westfield
Rothesay
Parrsboro
Hardings Point
ST. MARTINS
OAK BAY
ST. JOHN
Advocate Harbour
St. Stephen
St. George
NEW RIVER BEACH
New River Beach
ST. ANDREWS
Pocologan
Kennetcook
Old Town
DEER ISLAND
Kentville
Upper Rawdon
Orono
Berwick
Bangor
CAMPOBELLO ISLAND
Kingston
Windsor
North Head
Granville Ferry
Ellsworth
Grand Manan
The Anchorage
Seal Cove
Digby
Clementsport
Sandy Cove
Weymouth
Church Point
Freeport
Meteghan
Lake Rossignol
Salmon River

Featured Good Sam Parks

NEW BRUNSWICK

Good Sam Park

NB

When you stay with Good Sam, you can expect the highest degree of cleanliness and friendliness, and better yet, you get 10% off campground fees.

If you're not already a Good Sam member you can purchase your membership at one of these locations:

CARAQUET
Camping Colibri
(506)727-2222

HOPEWELL CAPE
Ponderosa Pines Park
(800)822-8800

MONCTON
Camper's City RV Resort
(877)512-7868

SAINT-JOHN
Hardings Point Campground Inc.
(506)763-2517

SAINT-MARTINS
Century Farm Family Campground
(866)394-4400

SHEDIAC
Ocean Surf RV Park
(506)532-5480

For more Good Sam Parks go to listing pages

New Brunswick

CONSULTANTS

Bob & Raissa Maroney

ALMA — E4 *Albert*

FUNDY/CHIGNECTO NORTH CAMPGROUND (Natl Pk) From town, NW 4 km (2.48 mi) on Rte 114 (R). 2015 rates: $25 to $40. May 16 to Oct 13. (506)887-6000

FUNDY/HEADQUARTERS CAMPGROUND (Natl Pk) From town, NW 0.5 km on Rte 114 (R). 2015 rates: $25 to $40. May 16 to Oct 13. (506)887-6000

FUNDY/POINT WOLFE CAMPGROUND (Natl Pk) From Alma & Rte 114, SW 10 km (6.2 mi) on 114/Pointe Wolfe Rd (R). 2015 rates: $25 to $27. Jun 20 to Sep 1. (506)887-6000

FUNDY/WOLFE LAKE CAMPGROUND (Natl Pk) From town, NW 20 km (12.40 mi) on Rte 114(L). Pit toilets. 2015 rates: $25. May 21 to Oct 10. (506)887-6000

ATHOLVILLE — B3 *Restigouche*

SUGARLOAF PROVINCIAL PARK (Prov Pk) From Jct of Hwy 11 & Exit 415 (Chemin Val D'Amour Rd), W 0.4 mi (L). 2015 rates: $25 to $39. May 31 to Sep 30. (506)789-2366

BAIE-SAINTE-ANNE — C4 *Northumberland*

SANDY POINT PARK **Ratings: 8/8.5★/8** (Campground) 2015 rates: $22 to $29. May 19 to Oct 9. (506)228-1122 160 Chemin Pointe au Sable, Baie-Sainte-Anne, NB E9A 1J7

BATHURST — B4 *Gloucester*

BATHURST WILDLIFE CAMPING Ratings: 6.5/8★/8.5 (Campground) From Hwy 11 (exit 311): Go 1.4 km/1 mi W on Sunset Dr. **FAC:** Gravel rds. (43 spaces). Avail: 33 grass, 26 pull-thrus (30 x 40), back-ins (30 x 40), some side by side hkups, 8 full hkups, 8 W, 8 E (30/50 amps), seasonal sites, WiFi, tent sites, laundry, groc, fire rings, firewood, controlled access. **REC:** playground. Pets OK. Big rig sites, eco-friendly, 2015 rates: $30 to $45. May 15 to Oct 15.
(506)546-8987 Lat: 47.64966, Lon: -65.72131
2476 Sunset Dr, Bathurst, NB E2A 7K8
sunsetberrypatch@hotmail.com

BELLEDUNE — B4 *Restigouche*

JACQUET RIVER PARK (Public) From Hwy 11 (exit 351): Go 2.6 km/1-1/2 mi E on Jacquet River Rd, then 90 meters/100 yards S on Hwy 134. 2015 rates: $20. May 30 to Sep 7. (506)237-3239

BERESFORD — B4 *Gloucester*

PARC MALYBEL **Ratings: 8.5/9.5★/9** (Campground) 2015 rates: $32 to $44. May 15 to Sep 14. (506)545-6888 1121 Bryar Rd, Beresford, NB E8K 1B2

BLACK POINT — B3 *Restigouche*

CAMPING BY THE BAY **Ratings: 5/7.5★/7.5** (Campground) 2015 rates: $16 to $25. Jun 1 to Sep 8. (506)237-5291 55 Black Point Rd, Black Point, NB E8G 1P8

BOUCTOUCHE — D5 *Kent*

BOUCTOUCHE BAIE CHALETS ET CAMPING
Ratings: 8.5/9.5★/9 (Campground) From Jct of Hwy 11 & Exit 32-A (Rte 515 & 475), E 0.6 mi on exit Rd (Rte 515) to Rte 475, N 6.75 mi (L). **FAC:** Gravel rds. (200 spaces). Avail: 110 grass, 13 pull-thrus (33 x 72), back-ins (36 x 72), 101 full hkups, 9 W, 9 E (30 amps), seasonal sites, WiFi, tent sites, rentals, dump, laundry, groc, LP bottles, fire rings, firewood, controlled access. **REC:** heated pool, Northumberland Strait: swim, fishing, playground. Pets OK. Partial handicap access. Eco-friendly, 2015 rates: $32 to $35. May 16 to Sep 14.
(506)743-8883 Lat: 46.543143, Lon: -64.7056628
2239 Rte 475, Saint-Edouard-de-Kent, NB E4S 4W4
reservation@bouctouchecamping.com
www.bouctouchecamping.com

CAMPOBELLO ISLAND — E2 *Charlotte*

HERRING COVE (Prov Pk) From Jct of US-1 & SR-189 (in ME), NE 6.2 mi on SR-189, cross bridge at Lubec to Hwy 774, follow signs (R). 2015 rates: $25 to $39. May 23 to Sep 21. (506)752-7010

CAP-PELE — D5 *Westmorland*

CAMPING PLAGE GAGNON BEACH Ratings: 9/9.5★/9 (Campground) From Shediac: From Jct of Hwy 15 & Exit 46 (Rte 133), E 0.8 mi on exit 46 to Rte 133E, E 2.25 mi (L). **FAC:** Gravel rds. (250 spaces). 100 Avail: 21 gravel, 79 grass, 78 pull-thrus (25 x 65), back-ins (30 x 45), 78 full hkups, 22 W, 22 E (30/50 amps), seasonal sites, WiFi, tent sites, rentals, showers $, dump, laundry, groc, LP bottles, fire rings, firewood, controlled access. **REC:** heated pool, wading pool, Northumberland Strait: swim, fishing, playground. Pets OK. Partial handicap access. Big rig sites, eco-friendly, 2015 rates: $40 to $45. May 15 to Sep 30. No CC.
(800)658-2828 Lat: 46.22467, Lon: -64.33145
30 Chemin Plage Gagnon, Grand-Barachois, NB E4P 7Z6
www.campinggagnon.com

SANDY BEACH TRAILER PARK 1988 LTD **Ratings: 7.5/8.5★/8.5** (Campground) 2015 rates: $34 to $45. May 18 to Sep 20. (506)577-2218 380 Rte 950, Cap-Pele, NB E4N 1J1

CAPE TORMENTINE — D5 *Westmorland*

CAPE TORMENTINE BEACH CG **Ratings: 6/9★/9** (Campground) 2015 rates: $33. May 15 to Sep 30. (506)538-7229 rte 955, Cape Tormentine, NB E4M 2A3

MURRAY BEACH (Prov Pk) From Cape Tormentine (Hwy 16), E 10 km (6.2 mi) on Hwy 955 (R). 2015 rates: $25 to $39. May 30 to Sep 7. (506)538-2628

CARAQUET — B4 *Gloucester*

CAMPING CARAQUET Ratings: 7/8.5★/7.5 (Campground) At W end of town on Rte 11 (R). **FAC:** Paved/gravel rds. (120 spaces). Avail: 70 grass, 30 pull-thrus (30 x 75), back-ins (30 x 75), mostly side by side hkups, 30 full hkups, 10 W, 10 E (15/30 amps), seasonal sites, WiFi $, tent sites, rentals, dump, laundry, fire rings, firewood, controlled access. **REC:** Bay of Caraquet: swim, playground. Pets OK. Partial handicap access. 2015 rates: $28 to $34. May 15 to Oct 15.
AAA Approved
(506)726-2696 Lat: 47.772764, Lon: -65.01862
619 Boulevard St. Pierre Ouest, Caraquet, NB E1W 1A2
campcara@nbnet.nb.ca
www.campingcaraquet.com

CAMPING COLIBRI
Ratings: 9.5/10★/9.5 (Campground) At W-end of town on Rte 11 (L). **FAC:** Paved rds. (306 spaces). 146 Avail: 106 gravel, 40 grass, 24 pull-thrus (25 x 90), back-ins (30 x 62), some side by side hkups, 106 full hkups, 40 W, 40 E (30/50 amps), seasonal sites, WiFi, tent sites, rentals, showers $, dump, laundry, groc, LP bottles, fire rings, firewood, restaurant, controlled access. **REC:** heated pool, wading pool, playground, rec open to public. Pets OK. Big rig sites, eco-friendly, 2015 rates: $32 to $45. May 16 to Sep 20.
(506)727-2222 Lat: 47.762797, Lon: -65.048159
913 Boul des Acadiens Rte 11, Caraquet, NB E1W 1H5
info@lecolibri.ca
www.lecolibri.ca
See ad this page, 1395.

CAMPING MARINA **Ratings: 5/9★/8.5** (Campground) 2015 rates: $26. May 15 to Sep 15. (506)726-8900 c.p. 5585, Caraquet, NB E1W 1B7

MAISON TOURISTIQUE DUGAS CAMPING **Ratings: 8/8.5★/8** (Campground) 2015 rates: $28 to $30. May 1 to Oct 30. (506)727-3195 683 Blvd. St Pierre Quest, Caraquet, NB E1W 1A1

CHARLO — B3 *Restigouche*

BLUE HERON CAMPING HERON BLEU (Public) From Jct of Hwy 11 & Exit 385 (Rte 134), E 0.6 mi on Ch. Craig Rd (exit rd) to Rte 134, N 1.25 mi to Rte 280 (Cove Rd), W 600 ft, Follow Signs (L). 2015 rates: $20 to $35. May 30 to Sep 14. (506)684-7860

COLES ISLAND — D4 *Queens*

RIVERRUN CAMPGROUND **Ratings: 6/8★/8** (Campground) 2015 rates: $25 to $30. May 15 to Sep 3. (506)362-9198 8976 Rte 112, Coles Island, NB E4C 2V2

TNT CAMPGROUND Ratings: 8.5/9★/9 (Campground) From Jct of TCH-2 & Exit 365 (Rtes 10 & 112), E 1.5 mi on Rte 10 to Rte 112, E 2 mi to TNT Campground Rd, S 0.5 mi (L). **FAC:** Paved rds. (230 spaces). Avail: 70 gravel, 12 pull-thrus (18 x 46), back-ins (32 x 32), mostly side by side hkups, 30 full hkups, 40 W, 40 E (15/30 amps), seasonal sites, WiFi $, tent sites, dump, laundry, groc, LP bottles, fire rings, firewood, controlled access. **REC:** Canaan River: swim, fishing, golf, playground. Pets OK. 2015 rates: $34. May 9 to Sep 30.
(506)362-5372 Lat: 45.56237, Lon: -65.44995
131 Boyd Loop Rd, Coles Island, NB E4C 2W9
smillie@nbnet.nb.ca

DALHOUSIE — B3 *Restigouche*

INCH ARRAN PARK (Public) S'bnd: From jct of Hwy 11 & Exit 397 (Rte 134), E 0.5 mi on Blair Malcom Rd to Rte 134, S 5 mi to Victoria St, S 1.4 mi, (R), follow signs. N'bnd: From Jct of Hwy 11 & Exit 391A, E 1 mi on Rte 275 to Rte 134, N 1 mi on 134 to Goderich St, E 1 mi to Inch Arran, N 20 ft to entrance (R). 2015 rates: $21 to $31.50. May to Aug. (506)684-7363

DEER ISLAND — E2 *Charlotte*

DEER ISLAND POINT CAMPGROUND (Public) Located at Campobello-Eastport ferry dock. 2015 rates: $25 to $30. (506)747-2423

EDMUNDSTON — B1 *Madawaska*

CAMPING PANORAMIC '86 Ratings: 8/9.5★/8.5 (Campground) From Jct of TCH 2 & Exit 8 (Rte 144), E 0.5 mi on Rte 144 (Principale St) to St-Joseph Rd, N 0.25 mi to Ch Riviere Madawaska, E 1 mi to Albert St, W 300 ft, follow signs (E). **FAC:** Paved/gravel rds. (185 spaces). Avail: 40 grass, 12 pull-thrus (33 x 90), back-ins (37 x 60), 35 full hkups (30 amps), seasonal sites, WiFi, tent sites, dump, laundry, groc, fire rings, firewood, restaurant. **REC:** heated pool, wading pool, Madawaska River: fishing, playground. Pets OK. 2015 rates: $36. May 1 to Oct 31.
(506)739-6544 Lat: 47.41848, Lon: -68.37457
86 Albert St, Saint-Jacques, NB E7B 1Z5
campingpanoramic@NB.AIBN.com
www.sn2000.nb.ca/comp/camping-panoramic/

DE LA REPUBLIQUE (Prov Pk) From Edmundston, W 5 mi on TCH 2, exit 8 (R). 2015 rates: $28 May 30 to Sep 1. (506)735-2525

RIVERSIDE (IROQUOIS) RV PARK **Ratings: 3.5/6.5/6.5** (RV Park) 2015 rates: $33 to $39 May 30 to Sep 5. (506)739-9060 1318 Rue Principale, Site 6, Edmundston, NB E7C 1L9

FLORENCEVILLE — C2 *Carleton*

RIVER COUNTRY CAMPGROUND & CABINS **Ratings: 7/8★/8.5** (Campground) 2015 rates: $30 to $40. May 15 to Sep 15. (506)278-3700 32 Tapley Road, Florenceville, NB E7L 2E1

FOUR FALLS — C2 *Victoria*

SPRING WATER CAMPGROUND **Ratings: 7.5/8★/8** (Campground) 2015 rates: $35 to $40. May 15 to Sep 30. (506)273-3682 2539 Route 130, Four Falls, NB E3Z 2H3

FREDERICTON — D3 *Sunbury*

HARTT ISLAND RV RESORT **Ratings: 9/10★/** (Campground) 2015 rates: $55 to $65. May 1 to Oct 31. (506)462-9400 2475 Woodstock Rd Rte 102 Fredericton, NB E3C 1P6

WOOLASTOOK PARK **Ratings: 8/10★/8.** (Campground) 2015 rates: $32 to $40. May 15 to Oct 15. (506)472-5584 5171 Rte 102, Upper Kingsclear NB E3E 1P9

GAGETOWN — D3 *Queens*

COY LAKE CAMPING RV PARK LTD **Ratings: 7.5/8★/8.5** (Campground) 2015 rates: $27 to $38. May 15 to Oct 15. (506)488-2567 1805 Rte 102 Upper Gagetown, NB E5N 1N3

NB

GRAND FALLS — C2 *Victoria*

→ MULHERIN'S CAMPGROUND **Ratings: 7/7.5/9** (Campground) 2015 rates: $31 to $34. May 22 to Sep 8. (506)473-3050 170 Mccluskey Rd., Grand Falls, NB E3Z 1L3

↓ RAPID BROOK CAMPING **Ratings: 3.5/6/6** (Campground) 2015 rates: $20 to $29. May 15 to Oct 15. (506)473-1036 59 Michaud Rd, Grand Falls, NB E3Z 2K3

GRAND MANAN ISLAND — F2 *Charlotte*

↑ THE ANCHORAGE (Prov Pk) From ferry terminal, S 5 mi on Rte 776, follow signs (L). 2015 rates: $25 to $39. May 30 to Sep 28. (506)662-7022

GRANDE-ANSE — B4 *Gloucester*

→ CAMPING & MOTEL DOIRON **Ratings: 4/7.5★/7.5** (Campground) 2015 rates: $22 to $27. May 1 to Sep 30. (506)732-5316 575 Acadie St., Grande Anse, NB E8N 1E9

↓ MOTEL & CAMPING BAIE DES CHALEURS LTD **Ratings: 6/5/8.5** (Campground) 2015 rates: $28 to $30. May 15 to Oct 1. (506)732-2948 480 Rue Acadie, Grande Anse, NB E8N 1E4

GRANDE-DIGUE — D5 *Kent*

↑ BEACH VIEW CAMPING **Ratings: 5.5/8★/7.5** (Campground) 2015 rates: $29 to $35. May 20 to Sep 30. (506)576-1118 2449 Rte 530, Grande Digue, NB E4R 5M7

HARVEY — D2 *York*

↖ LAKE GEORGE FAMILY CAMPGROUND (CITY PARK) (Public) From jct Hwy 3 & Hwy 636: Go 12.8 km/8 mi N on Hwy 636. 2015 rates: $25 to $30. (506)366-2933

HAWKSHAW — D2 *York*

↘ **SUNSET VIEW CAMPGROUND Ratings: 8.5/10★/9.5** (Campground) From Jct of TCH 2 & Hawkshaw Rd (Exit 231) NE 0.4 mi on exit rd, follow signs (R). **FAC:** All weather rds. (70 spaces). Avail: 61 grass, 12 pull-thrus (40 x 85), back-ins (30 x 42), some side by side hkups, 27 full hkups, 19 W, 19 E (30 amps), seasonal sites, WiFi, tent sites, rentals, showers $, dump, laundry, groc, LP bottles, fire rings, firewood. **REC:** pool, St John River: swim, fishing, playground. Pet restrict Eco-friendly, 2015 rates: $30 to $34. Jun 1 to Sep 15.
AAA Approved
(506)575-2592 Lat: 45.97004, Lon: -67.23538
45 Hawkshaw Rd, Hawkshaw, NB E6G 1N8
walfield@hotmail.com
www.walfield.ca

HOPEWELL CAPE — D5 *Albert*

↗ **PONDEROSA PINES PARK**
Ratings: 8.5/9★/9.5 (Campground) From Jct of Rte 114 & Hopewell Rock Entrance (in town), W 1 mi on Rte 114 (L). **FAC:** Gravel rds. 57 all weather, 48 grass, 18 pull-thrus (30 x 75), back-ins (30 x 50), some side by side hkups, 55 full hkups, 26 W, 26 E (30/50 amps), WiFi, tent sites, rentals, dump, laundry, groc, LP bottles, fire rings, firewood, controlled access. **REC:** heated pool, Bay of Fundy: fishing, playground. Pets OK. Big rig sites, 14 day max stay, eco-friendly, 2015 rates: $34 to $51. May 12 to Oct 24.
(800)822-8800 Lat: 45.81907, Lon: -64.59628
4325 Rte 114, Hopewell Cape, NB E4H 4W7
ponderosa@nb.aibn.com
www.ponderosapines.ca
See ad this page, 1395.

KOUCHIBOUGUAC — C4 *Kent*

↑ SOUTH KOUCHIBOUGUAC CAMPGROUND (Natl Pk) From Jct of TCH-11 & Rd 117, E 2 mi on Rd 117 (R). 2015 rates: $21.50 to $32.30. Jun 28 to Sep 1. (506)876-2443

We appreciate your business!

LAMEQUE — B5 *Gloucester*

← CAMPING ILE LAMEQUE **Ratings: 7/8★/8** (Campground) 2015 rates: $24 to $29. May 31 to Sep 7. (506)344-3292 237 Gauvin Rd, Petite Lameque, NB E8T 2N1

↖ CHALETS ET CAMPING DES ILES JEANNOT **Ratings: 8.5/9.5★/8.5** (Campground) 2015 rates: $30. May 15 to Sep 15. (506)344-2590 110 Allee Jeaunnot Lane, Petite Lameque, NB E8T 4R8

LOWER QUEENSBURY — D2 *York*

↘ HERITAGE COUNTRY CAMPING **Ratings: 5.5/8★/7** (Campground) 2015 rates: $32 to $38. May 15 to Oct 15. (506)363-3338 2400 Rte 105, Lower Queensbury, NB E6L 1G3

MACTAQUAC — D2 *York*

↘ EVERETT'S CAMPGROUND **Ratings: 3.5/7.5★/7** (Campground) 2015 rates: $30 to $35. May 15 to Sep 30. (506)363-3248 2137 Rte 105, Lower Queensbury, NB E6L 1E6

↑ MACTAQUAC PARK (Prov Pk) From Jct of TCH 2 & Hwy 105 (exit 274), W 6 mi on Hwy 105 (L). 2015 rates: $25 to $28. May 17 to Oct 13. (506)363-4747

MILL COVE — D3 *Queens*

→ LAKESIDE CAMPGROUND & RECREATION PARK (Prov Pk) From Jemseg, E 9 mi on TCH 2 (L). 2015 rates: $28 to $42. May 17 to Oct 13. (506)488-2321

MIRAMICHI — C4 *Northumberland*

← ENCLOSURE CAMPGROUND **Ratings: 6.5/6/7** (Campground) 2015 rates: $32. May 15 to Oct 15. (506)622-8638 rte 420, Miramichi, NB E1V 3V4

↗ FAMILY LAND CAMPGROUND **Ratings: 5.5/7/6.5** (Campground) 2015 rates: $28. May 20 to Sep 30. (506)773-6666 187 E Point Road, Miramichi, NB E1N 4P3

→ **OAK POINT FAMILY CAMPGROUND Ratings: 6/6.5/6.5** (Campground) From jct Hwy 8 & Hwy 11 (at Centennial Bridge): Go 18-3/4 km/11-1/2 mi N on Hwy 11, then 2 km/1-1/4 mi E on Ch.Oak Point Rd. **FAC:** Gravel rds. (130 spaces). Avail: 88 grass, 20 pull-thrus (45 x 85), back-ins (30 x 60), some side by side hkups, 88 full hkups (15/30 amps), seasonal sites, tent sites, showers $, dump, laundry, groc, fire rings, firewood. **REC:** pool, whirlpool. Pets OK. 2015 rates: $29 to $32. May 15 to Oct 15. No CC.
(506)778-9400 Lat: 47.11621, Lon: -65.26806
187 Shore Rd, Oak Point, NB E1V 1H0
kburch_8@hotmail.com

→ **SUNRISE CAMPGROUND Ratings: 8.5/8.5★/8** (Campground) In Miramichi, From Jct of Hwy 11 & Rte 8, N 7 mi on Hwy 11 (R). **FAC:** Gravel rds. (125 spaces). Avail: 45 grass, 38 pull-thrus (30 x 60), back-ins (30 x 50), some side by side hkups, 45 full hkups (30 amps), seasonal sites, WiFi, tent sites, dump, laundry, groc, LP bottles, fire rings, firewood, controlled access. **REC:** pool, Miramichi River: playground. Pets OK. Eco-friendly, 2015 rates: $29 to $32. May 20 to Oct 11.
(506)778-2282 Lat: 47.08895, Lon: -65.36994
504 Rte 11, Lower Newcastle, NB E1V 7G1
sunrisecampground@gmail.com

MISCOU ISLAND — B5 *Gloucester*

↓ CAMPING LA VAGUE **Ratings: 6.5/7★/7.5** (Campground) 2015 rates: $25 to $32. Jun 23 to Sep 15. (506)344-8531 3 Herring Pte Rd., Miscou Island, NB E8T 2G2

Wasn't that a beautiful campground you visited ten years ago? But can you remember where it was? Use our "Find-it-Fast" index, located in the back of the Guide. It's an alphabetical list, by state, of every private and public park and campground in the Guide.

MONCTON — D4 *Westmorland*

↗ **CAMPER'S CITY RV RESORT**
Ratings: 9/10★/9.5 (Campground) From Jct of TCH-2 & Exit 454 (Mapleton Rd), N 500 ft on Mapleton Rd to Queensway Dr, E 0.25 mi (L). **FAC:** Paved/gravel rds. (185 spaces). 151 Avail: 109 gravel, 42 grass, 73 pull-thrus (35 x 65), back-ins (25 x 55), 109 full hkups, 22 W, 22 E (30/50 amps), seasonal sites, WiFi $, tent sites, rentals, showers $, dump, laundry, groc, LP bottles, fire rings, firewood, controlled access. **REC:** heated pool, pond, playground. Pets OK. Big rig sites, eco-friendly, 2015 rates: $31 to $42. May 1 to Oct 12.
(877)512-7868 Lat: 46.133401, Lon: -64.827864
138 Queensway Dr, Moncton, NB E1G 2L2
camperscity@killamproperties.com
www.killamleisureliving.com/camperscity/
See ad this page, 1395.

← STONEHURST GOLF COURSE & TRAILER PARK **Ratings: 8/8★/8.5** (Campground) 2015 rates: $32 to $47. May 15 to Oct 15. (506)852-4162 47915 Homestead Rd., Berry Mills, NB E1G 2R5

NEW BANDON — B4 *Gloucester*

↗ BACK HOME FAMILY CAMPGROUND (Campground) (Phone Update) 2015 rates: $30 to $35. May 1 to Oct 31. (506)365-8920 7195 Route 8, New Bandon, NB E9C 2B9

NEW RIVER BEACH — E3 *Charlotte*

← NEW RIVER BEACH (Prov Pk) From St John, W 31 mi on Hwy 1 (L). 2015 rates: $25 to $39. May 16 to Sep 21. (506)755-4078

NEWTOWN — D3 *Kings*

↗ ALL DONE RV CAMPING **Ratings: 6.5/NA/9** (Campground) Pit toilets. 2015 rates: $40. May 1 to Nov 1. (506)869-0547 1468 Route 890, Newtown, NB E4G 1N2

NICTAU — C2 *Victoria*

→ MOUNT CARLETON (Prov Pk) From Hwy 385 (in town), N 20 mi on private rd (R). 2015 rates: $25. May 30 to Sep 14. (506)235-0793

NIGADOO — B4 *Gloucester*

↑ MOTEL CAMPING HACHE **Ratings: 8.5/9.5★/9.5** (Campground) 2015 rates: $28 to $36. May 10 to Sep 30. (506)783-3739 264 Rue Principale, Nigadoo, NB E8K 3T3

OAK BAY — E2 *Charlotte*

→ **OAK BAY CAMPGROUND Ratings: 7/8★/7.5** (Campground) W-bnd: From Jct of Rte 1 & exit 13, (L) 3 mi on Rte 170 (L). E-bnd: From Town, E 5 mi on Rte 170 (R). **FAC:** Gravel rds. (121 spaces). Avail: 66 gravel, 13 pull-thrus (35 x 60), back-ins (30 x 40), some side by side hkups, 18 full hkups, 20 W, 20 E (15/30 amps), seasonal sites, WiFi, tent sites, dump, laundry, fire rings, firewood. **REC:** Passamaquoddy/Bay of Fundy: swim, playground. Pets OK. Partial handicap access. Eco-friendly, 2015 rates: $36 to $42. May 8 to Oct 14.
(506)466-4999 Lat: 45.22746, Lon: -67.19127
742 Rte 170, Oak Bay, NB E3L 4A4
info@oakbaycampground.ca
http://www.oakbay-campground.com/

OAK POINT — E3 *Kings*

↑ KIWANIS OAK POINT CAMPGROUND & PARK (Public) From Jct of Hwys 7 & 102 (Westfield), N 18.6 mi on Hwy 102 (R). 2015 rates: $32 to $45. May 17 to Sep 15. (506)468-2266

OROMOCTO — D3 *Sunbury*

↘ SUNBURY-OROMOCTO PARK **Ratings: 6/7.5★/7.5** (Campground) 2015 rates: $32 to $35. May 15 to Sep 14. (506)357-3708 413 Smith Rd., Oromocto, NB E2V 3S9

PENOBSQUIS — D4 *Kings*

➔ LONE PINE PARK & CABINS **Ratings: 7/8/8** (Campground) 2015 rates: $26 to $40. May 15 to Sep 18. (506)432-4007 45 Lone Pine Rd, Penobsquis, NB E4E 5T3

➔ PINE CONE CAMPING **Ratings: 8.5/6/9.5** (Campground) 2015 rates: $35.50 to $37.50. May 15 to Sep 15. (506)433-4389 rte 114 Hwy, Sussex, NB E4E 5L9

➔ **THREE BEARS FAMILY CAMPING & RV PARK Ratings: 8/9★/9** (Campground) From Jct of Hwy 1 & exit 211 (Rte 114), W 0.25 mi (L). **FAC:** Gravel rds. (190 spaces). 90 Avail: 20 gravel, 70 grass, 15 pull-thrus (25 x 65), back-ins (35 x 45), some side by side hkups, 59 full hkups, 21 W, 21 E (15/30 amps), seasonal sites, WiFi, tent sites, rentals, dump, laundry, groc, LP gas, fire rings, firewood, controlled access. **REC:** heated pool, wading pool, South Branch: swim, fishing, playground. Pets OK. Eco-friendly, 2015 rates: $34 to $38. May 10 to Sep 23.
(506)433-2870 Lat: 45.785416, Lon: -65.349165
12049 Rte 114, Penobsquis, NB E4G 2Y2
tim@atlanticsigns.com
www.threebearscamping.com

PERTH-ANDOVER — C2 *Victoria*

➔ ROBERT E BAIRD MEMORIAL PARK **Ratings: 6/7.5★/7.5** (Campground) 2015 rates: $32 to $36. May 15 to Oct 20. (506)273-3080 12255 Rte 105, Perth-Andover, NB E7H 3X2

PETIT-CAP — D5 *Westmorland*

← SILVER SANDS CAMPGROUND **Ratings: 5/5/5** (Campground) 2015 rates: $44 to $66. May 20 to Sep 30. (506)577-6771 64 Chemin Du Camp, Petit Cap, NB E4N 2W2

PETIT-ROCHER-NORD — B4 *Gloucester*

↑ CAMPING MURRAYWOOD PARK LTD **Ratings: 9/9★/9** (Campground) 2015 rates: $26 to $42. May 15 to Sep 26. (506)783-2137 281 Route 134, Petit-Rocher-Nord, NB E8J 2E5

PLASTER ROCK — C2 *Victoria*

↓ PLASTER ROCK TOURIST PARK (Public) From town, S 1 mi on Rte 108 (L). 2015 rates: $20 to $25. Jun 17 to Aug 31. (506)356-6077

POINTE-SAPIN — C4 *Kent*

↑ CAMPING L'ETOILE DE MER (Public) From Richucto, N 23 mi on Rte 117, exit at Kouchibouguac (R). 2015 rates: $15 to $17. May to Oct. (506)876-2282

POINTE-VERTE — B4 *Gloucester*

↑ CEDAR COVE CAMPGROUND **Ratings: 6/8★/7.5** (RV Park) 2015 rates: $30 to $35. May 15 to Sep 15. (506)783-2648 115 Rue Principale St, Pointe-Verte, NB E8J 2Z3

POKEMOUCHE — B4 *Gloucester*

↓ **POKEMOUCHE**
Ratings: 9.5/10★/10 (Campground) From Jct of Hwy 11 & 113, S 1.5 mi (L). **FAC:** Paved rds. (238 spaces). 78 Avail: 74 gravel, 4 grass, 5 pull-thrus (40 x 60), back-ins (40 x 60), 49 full hkups, 25 W, 25 E (30/50 amps), seasonal sites, WiFi $, tent sites, rentals, dump, laundry, groc, LP bottles, fire rings, firewood, restaurant, controlled access. **REC:** heated pool, Pokemouche River: fishing, marina, playground, rec open to public. Pet restrict(Q). Partial handicap access. Big rig sites, eco-friendly, 2015 rates: $35 to $46. May 15 to Sep 14.
AAA Approved
(506)727-6090 Lat: 47.6598, Lon: -64.8698
11220, Rte 11, Pokemouche, NB E8P 1J8
info@campingpokemouche.com
www.campingpokemouche.com

We rate what RVers consider important.

RICHIBOUCTOU-VILLAGE — C4 *Kent*

↓ **CAMPING CAP LUMIERE BEACH**
Ratings: 7/9★/8 (RV Park) On New Brunswick Hwy 11, (exit 42 or 53), follow Rte 505 to Chemin Cap Lumiere Rd, then Cap Lumiere Rd to the lighthouse, campground is at the lighthouse. **FAC:** All weather rds. (54 spaces). Avail: 44 grass, 6 pull-thrus (35 x 70), back-ins (35 x 50), 30 full hkups, 7 W, 7 E (30/50 amps), seasonal sites, WiFi, tent sites, dump, laundry, groc, LP bottles, fire rings, firewood. **REC:** Northumberland Strait: swim, fishing, playground. Pets OK. Eco-friendly, 2015 rates: $25 to $39. May 15 to Sep 15. No CC.
(506)523-0994 Lat: 46.669911, Lon: -64.712373
239 Ch Cap Lumiere, Richibouctou-Village, NB E4W 1C9
campingcaplumiere@live.ca

RICHIBUCTO — C4 *Kent*

↓ PARC MUNICIPAL JARDINE MUNICIPAL PARK **Ratings: 8.5/9★/9.5** (Campground) 2015 rates: $30 to $34. May 15 to Sep 1. (506)523-7874 9235 Rue Main St., Richibucto, NB E4W 4B4

RIVIERE-DU-PORTAGE — B4 *Northumberland*

← PLAGE TRACADIE BEACH CAMPING **Ratings: 7.5/7.5★/7.5** (Campground) 2015 rates: $33 to $42. May 15 to Sep 14. (506)395-4010 5903 Rte 11, Riviere-du-Portage, NB E9H 1W7

SAINT-ANDRE — C2 *Madawaska*

↑ CAMPING PARADIS DE LA P'TITE MONTAGNE **Ratings: 8/8.5★/9** (RV Park) 2015 rates: $32 to $42. May 15 to Sep 15. (506)473-6683 472 Chemin de la P'tite Montagne, Saint-Andre, NB E3Y 1H4

SAINT-ANDREWS — E2 *Charlotte*

➔ ISLAND VIEW CAMPING **Ratings: 7.5/8/7.5** (Campground) 2015 rates: $32 to $38. May 15 to Oct 15. (506)529-3787 3406, Rte127, St Andrews, NB E5B 2V1

↓ KIWANIS OCEAN FRONT CAMPING **Ratings: 7.5/9★/8.5** (Campground) 2015 rates: $37 to $52. May 1 to Oct 15. (506)529-3439 550 Water St, St Andrews, NB E5B 2R6

SAINT-BASILE — B1 *Madawaska*

➔ CAMPING ST BASILE **Ratings: 6.5/7.5/8** (Campground) 2015 rates: $33 to $35. May 15 to Sep 7. (506)263-1183 14411 Rte 144, Edmundston, NB E7B 2L2

SAINT-JOHN — E3 *Saint John*

↖ **HARDINGS POINT CAMPGROUND INC.**
Ratings: 8.5/9★/8.5 (Campground) From Jct of Hwy 7 & Exit 80 (Rte 177), E 0.75 mi on exit rd (Rte 102) to Rte 177, S 1.5 mi to Ferry Landing, take (free) Ferry (R). **FAC:** Gravel rds. (175 spaces). 75 Avail: 40 gravel, 35 grass, 15 pull-thrus (28 x 70), back-ins (25 x 65), 65 full hkups, 10 W, 10 E (30/50 amps), seasonal sites, WiFi Hotspot, tent sites, showers $, dump, laundry, groc, fire rings, firewood, controlled access. **REC:** heated pool, Saint John River: swim, fishing, playground. Pets OK. Big rig sites, eco-friendly, 2015 rates: $35 to $40. May 18 to Sep 30.
(506)763-2517 Lat: 45.352074, Lon: -66.217707
71 Hardings Point Landing Rd., Carters Point, NB E5S 1N8
www.hardingspointcampground.com
See ad this page, 1395.

↑ ROCKWOOD PARK **Ratings: 7/6/8** (Campground) 2015 rates: $29 to $39. May 25 to Sep 30. (506)652-4050 142 Lake Drive South, Saint John, NB E2K 5S2

Check our family camping destinations article in the front of the Guide highlighting the best places to camp in every state and province.

SAINT-LEONARD — C2 *Madawaska*

↗ **CAMPING ST LEONARD**
Ratings: 7/9★/9.5 (Campground) From Jct Hwy 2 & Exit 58, N 2 mi on Rte 17 (L). **FAC:** Paved/gravel rds. (110 spaces). Avail: 30 gravel, 10 pull-thrus (40 x 65), back-ins (40 x 45), 20 full hkups, 5 W, 5 E (30/50 amps), seasonal sites, tent sites, dump, laundry, fire rings, firewood, restaurant, controlled access. **REC:** heated pool, pond, fishing, playground. Pets OK. Partial handicap access. 2015 rates: $35 to $40. May 29 to Sep 29.
(506)423-6536 Lat: 47.173983, Lon: -67.879899
470 Rte #17, Saint-Leonard, NB E7E 2L7
campingstleonardnb@hotmail.ca

SAINT-LOUIS-DE-KENT — C4 *Kent*

↓ EVERGREEN ACRES CAMPGROUNDS LIMITED **Ratings: 6.5/6/7.5** (Campground) 2015 rates: $30 to $35. May 15 to Sep 30. (506)876-4897 10374 Route 134, Portage St-Louis, NB E4X 2L2

↑ MUNICIPAL PARK DAIGLE **Ratings: 8.5/8.5★/8.5** (Campground) 2015 rates: $27 to $35. May 15 to Sep 15. (506)876-4540 10787 Rte 134, St Louis De Kent, NB E4X 1W4

SAINT-MARTINS — E4 *St John*

↓ **CENTURY FARM FAMILY CAMPGROUND**
Ratings: 8.5/10★/10 (Campground) In town, From Jct of Rte 111 & Main St (access rd), E 0.7 mi on Main St (R). **FAC:** Paved rds. (180 spaces). 80 Avail: 60 gravel, 20 grass, 25 pull-thrus (30 x 80), back-ins (30 x 40), 50 full hkups, 15 W, 15 E (30 amps), seasonal sites, WiFi, tent sites, rentals, dump, laundry, LP bottles, fire rings, firewood, controlled access. **REC:** Bay of Fundy: swim, golf, playground. Pets OK. Partial handicap access. Eco-friendly, 2015 rates: $28 to $32. May 1 to Sep 30.
(866)394-4400 Lat: 45.351170, Lon: -65.542942
67 Ocean Wave Dr., St Martins, NB E5R 2E8
cenfarcg@nbnet.nb.ca
www.centuryfarmcampground.com
See ad this page, 1395.

➔ SEA SIDE TENT & TRAILER PARK **Ratings: 6/5/6.5** (RV Park) 2015 rates: $27 to $33. May 15 to Sep 30. (506)833-4413 234 Main St., St Martins, NB E5R 1B8

SHEDIAC — D5 *Westmorland*

↘ BEAUSEJOUR CAMPING **Ratings: 8/8★/8.5** (Campground) 2015 rates: $35 to $55. May 1 to Oct 1. (506)532-5885 747 Lino Rd, Shediac, NB E4P 1Z5

← CAMPING OCEANIC **Ratings: 6.5/10★/9** (Campground) 2015 rates: $37 to $42.50. May 15 to Sep 15. (506)533-7006 221 Chemin Ohio, Shediac, NB E4P 2J8

↓ CAMPING PARASOL **Ratings: 6/6.5/7.5** (Campground) 2015 rates: $30 to $37. May 15 to Oct 15. (506)532-8229 205 Rue Main, Shediac, NB E4P 2A5

➔ **OCEAN SURF RV PARK**
Ratings: 9/10★/9.5 (Campground) From Jct of Hwy 15 & Exit 37 (Parlee Beach Rd-Rte 140), NE 1 mi on Rte 140 to Rte 133, E 0.3 mi to Ch Belliveau Beach Rd, N 0.5 mi (R). **FAC:** Paved/gravel rds. (450 spaces). Avail: 100 gravel, 5 pull-thrus (30 x 75), back-ins (35 x 65), 100 full hkups (30/50 amps), seasonal sites, WiFi, showers $, dump, laundry, groc, fire rings, firewood, controlled access. **REC:** pool, Northhumberland Strait: swim, playground. Pets OK. Partial handicap access, no tents. 2015 rates: $35 to $45. May 1 to Oct 10.
(506)532-5480 Lat: 46.233685, Lon: -64.503411
73 Chemin Plage Belliveau Beach Rd, Pointe-Du-Chene, NB E4P 3W2
oceansurf@nb.aibn.com
www.oceansurf.ca
See ad this page, 1395.

← OCEAN VIEW PARK **Ratings: 8/8★/8.5** (Campground) From Jct of Hwy 15 & exit 43 (Rte 933), N 0.8 mi on Rte 933 to Rte 133, E 1.5 mi (L) **FAC:** Paved/gravel rds. (122 spaces). Avail: 38

SHEDIAC (CONT)

OCEAN VIEW PARK (CONT)
grass, back-ins (30 x 50), 7 full hkups, 25 W, 25 E (20/30 amps), seasonal sites, WiFi, tent sites, showers $, dump, laundry, groc, LP bottles, fire rings, firewood, restaurant, controlled access. **REC:** Northumberland Strait: swim, playground. Pets OK. 2015 rates: $36 to $40. May 19 to Sep 25.
(506)532-3520 Lat: 46.219905, Lon: -64.393376
1586 Rte 133, Grand-Barachois, NB E4P 8H2
www.oceanviewcamping.ca

PARC HORIZON PARK **Ratings: 6/8/8.5** (Campground) 2015 rates: $31 to $63. May 15 to Oct 1. (506)532-5755 37 Belliveau Beach Rd., Shediac, NB E4P 3W2

PARLEE BEACH **Ratings: 7.5/9.5★/9** (Campground) 2015 rates: $28 to $37. May 20 to Sep 6. (506)532-1500 25 Gould Beach Rd, Pointe-du-Chene, NB E4P 4S8

SOUTH-COVE CAMPING & GOLF **Ratings: 7.5/9.5★/9** (Campground) 2015 rates: $35 to $45. May 15 to Oct 1. (506)532-6713 55 South Cove Rd., Shediac, NB E4P 2T4

WISHING STAR CAMPGROUND **Ratings: 7/8.5★/8.5** (RV Park) 2015 rates: $40 to $47. May 20 to Oct 15. (506)532-6786 218 Main St, Shediac, NB E4P 2E1

SHEFFIELD — D3 *Sunbury*

CASEY'S CAMPGROUND **Ratings: 4/5.5/7** (Campground) 2015 rates: $22 to $32. May 1 to Oct 13. (506)357-8592 2511 Rte 105, Sheffield, NB E3A 9K3

SHIPPAGAN — B5 *Gloucester*

CAMPING JANINE DU HAVRE **Ratings: 7.5/8★/8.5** (Campground) 2015 rates: $28 to $30. May 1 to Oct 31. (506)336-8884 48 Chemin Chiasson, Shippagan, NB E8S 3A6

CAMPING SHIPPAGAN (Public) From Jct of Rtes 11 & 113, N 10 mi on Rte 113 to blvd J.D. Gauthier, W 2.5 mi (R). 2015 rates: $25 to $30. Jun 1 to Sep 30. (506)336-3960

SUSSEX — D4 *Kings*

TOWN & COUNTRY CAMPARK Ratings: 9/9.5★/9.5 (Campground) From Jct of Hwy 1 & Exit 195, (R) Follow Signs. **FAC:** Paved/gravel rds. (322 spaces). Avail: 49 grass, 5 pull-thrus (30 x 70), back-ins (30 x 50), 22 full hkups, 16 W, 16 E (20/30 amps), seasonal sites, WiFi, tent sites, rentals, dump, laundry, LP bottles, fire rings, firewood, controlled access. **REC:** heated pool, wading pool, Kennebecasis River: fishing, playground. Pets OK. Partial handicap access. Eco-friendly, 2015 rates: $37 to $39. May 25 to Sep 15.
(506)432-9114 Lat: 45.735674, Lon: -65.486378
133 Aiton Rd, Sussex, NB E4G 2V5
sussexdrivein@nb.aibn.com
http://sussexdrivein.com

TABUSINTAC — B4 *Northumberland*

RIVER HAVEN CAMPGROUND **Ratings: 7.5/9★/8** (Campground) 2015 rates: $27 to $30. May 15 to Sep 30. (506)779-8067 119 J Mackenzie Rd., Tabusintac, NB E9H 2B8

TRACADIE-SHEILA — B4 *Gloucester*

AQUAPARC DE LA RIVIERE TRACADIE **Ratings: 7.5/8.5★/7.5** (Campground) 2015 rates: $25 to $35. May 15 to Sep 30. (506)393-7759 3205 Rue Alcide, Tracadie-Sheila, NB E1X 1A5

CHALETS ET CAMPING DE LA POINTE **Ratings: 9/9★/9** (Campground) 2015 rates: $30 to $35. May 15 to Sep 9. (506)393-0987 c.p. 20003 - Centre Ville, Tracadie Sheila, NB E1X 1G6

VAL-COMEAU — B4 *Gloucester*

VAL COMEAU (Prov Pk) N-bnd: In town on Rte 11, end of peninsula (R). 2015 rates: $25 to $36. Jun 1 to Sep 8. (506)393-4137

WATERBOROUGH — D3 *Queens*

MOHAWK CAMPING **Ratings: 7.5/5.5/8** (Campground) 2015 rates: $28 to $32. May 15 to Oct 15. (506)362-5250 6249 Rte 105, Waterborough, NB E4C 2Y5

Park policies vary. Ask about the cancellation policy when making a reservation.

WOODSTOCK — D2 *Carleton*

CONNELL PARK CAMPGROUND (Public) From Jct of TCH 2 & exit 188 (Connell Rd), S 0.75 mi on Connell Rd (R). 2015 rates: $25 to $32. May 17 to Sep 18. (506)325-4979

COSY CABINS CAMPGROUND **Ratings: 5.5/4.5/7.5** (RV Park) 2015 rates: $30 to $45. Apr 15 to Oct 15. (506)328-3344 2335 Rte165, Lower Woodstock, NB E7M 4A4

YOGI BEAR'S JELLYSTONE PARK
Ratings: 9.5/10★/9.5 (Campground) From Jct of TCH-2 & Exit 191 (Beardsley Rd/Woodstock Direction), N 0.25 mi on Beardsley Rd to Hemlock St, W 0.25 mi, follow signs (E). **FAC:** Paved rds. 140 Avail: 140 all weather, 120 pull-thrus (35 x 60), back-ins (27 x 60), 140 W, 140 E (30/50 amps), cable, WiFi, tent sites, rentals, dump, mobile sewer, laundry, groc, LP bottles, fire rings, firewood, controlled access. **REC:** heated pool, wading pool, playground, rec open to public. Pets OK. Partial handicap access. Eco-friendly, 2015 rates: $62 to $65. Jun 1 to Sep 7.
(506)328-6287 Lat: 46.126365, Lon: -67.605145
174, Hemlock St., Lower Woodstock, NB E7M 4E5
yoginb@nb.aibn.com
www.jellystoneparknb.com
See ad this page.

Say you saw it in our Guide!

Newfoundland and Labrador Tourism

WELCOME TO

Newfoundland & Labrador

JOINED CONFEDERATION MARCH 31, 1949	WIDTH: 374 MILES (602 KM) LENGTH: 868 MILES (1,396 KM)	PROPORTION OF CANADA 4.06% OF 9,984,670 SQ KM

Newfoundland and Labrador combine past and present in compelling ways. Here, you'll find a restored Viking settlement that dates back to A.D 1000. You'll also discover vibrant waterfront communities that honor centuries-old traditions with exciting festivals. Founded in Canada's Atlantic region, this province incorporates the island of Newfoundland and the mainland region of Labrador with a combined area of more than 405,000 square miles and a population of just over 500,000.

In this province, you might meet locals who consider themselves "Newfoundlanders" and not Canadians. Newfoundland was an independent country until 1949, when it joined Canada as a province, and old habits die hard.

Gros Morne is Newfoundland's second highest mountain and the centerpiece of the spectacular Gros Morne National Park. More than 20 miles of footpaths include a tramp to the 2,644-foot peak. Some of the best hiking in the park traverses the Tablelands, where the barren rocks more resemble the earth's core than the lush forests and bogs found elsewhere in the park.

Where fingers of the North Atlantic Ocean reach into central Newfoundland to find the boreal forests of the inner island is Canada's easternmost national park, Terra Nova.

Many festivals are bunched together in the provincial capital during St. John's Time in June. These include the Busker's Festival, the Newfoundland and Labrador Folk Festival and the Royal St. John's Regatta. Any day is special on George Street in St. John. With more public houses per square foot than any North American street, this street is closed to vehicle traffic except for re-stocking hours in the mornings.

Ancient paths lead out of town to Ferryland Head and its familiar bright red lighthouse, built in 1870.

Top 3 Tourism Attractions:
1) St. John's
2) Cape St. Mary's Ecological Reserve
3) Gros Morne National Park

Nickname: The Rock

State Flower: Pitcher Plant

State Bird: Atlantic Puffin

People: D'Arcy Broderick, musician and singer; Vincent P. Bryan, composer and lyricist; Mark Critch, comedian; Natasha Henstridge, model and actress; Sara Canning, actress

Major Cities: St. John's (capital), Conception Bay South, Mount Pearl, Corner Brook, Grand Falls-Windsor

Topography: Composed largely of hills, mountain ranges, hundreds of bays, coves, islands and small inlets

Climate: Radically changing short summers of approximately six weeks; high winds, sudden rain, snow storms

TRAVEL & TOURISM

Newfoundland and Labrador Tourism
800-563-6353
www.newfoundlandlabrador.com

Coast of Bays Tourism Association
709-538-3552
www.coastofbays.nl.ca

Destination St. John's
877-739-8899
www.destinationstjohns.com

Dorset Trail Tourism Association
709-532-4242

Murray Premises
709-739-8899, 877-739-8899
www.destinationstjohns.com

Western Newfoundland DMO
709-458-3604
www.westernnl.com

OUTDOOR RECREATION

Grey River Lodge Fly Fishing
www.flyfishinggreyriver.com

Iceberg Spotting
www.icebergfinder.com

SHOPPING

Chapel Arm Woodcrafts
709-592-2240
www.chapelarmwoodcrafts.com

King's Point Pottery
709-268-2216
www.kingspointpottery.com

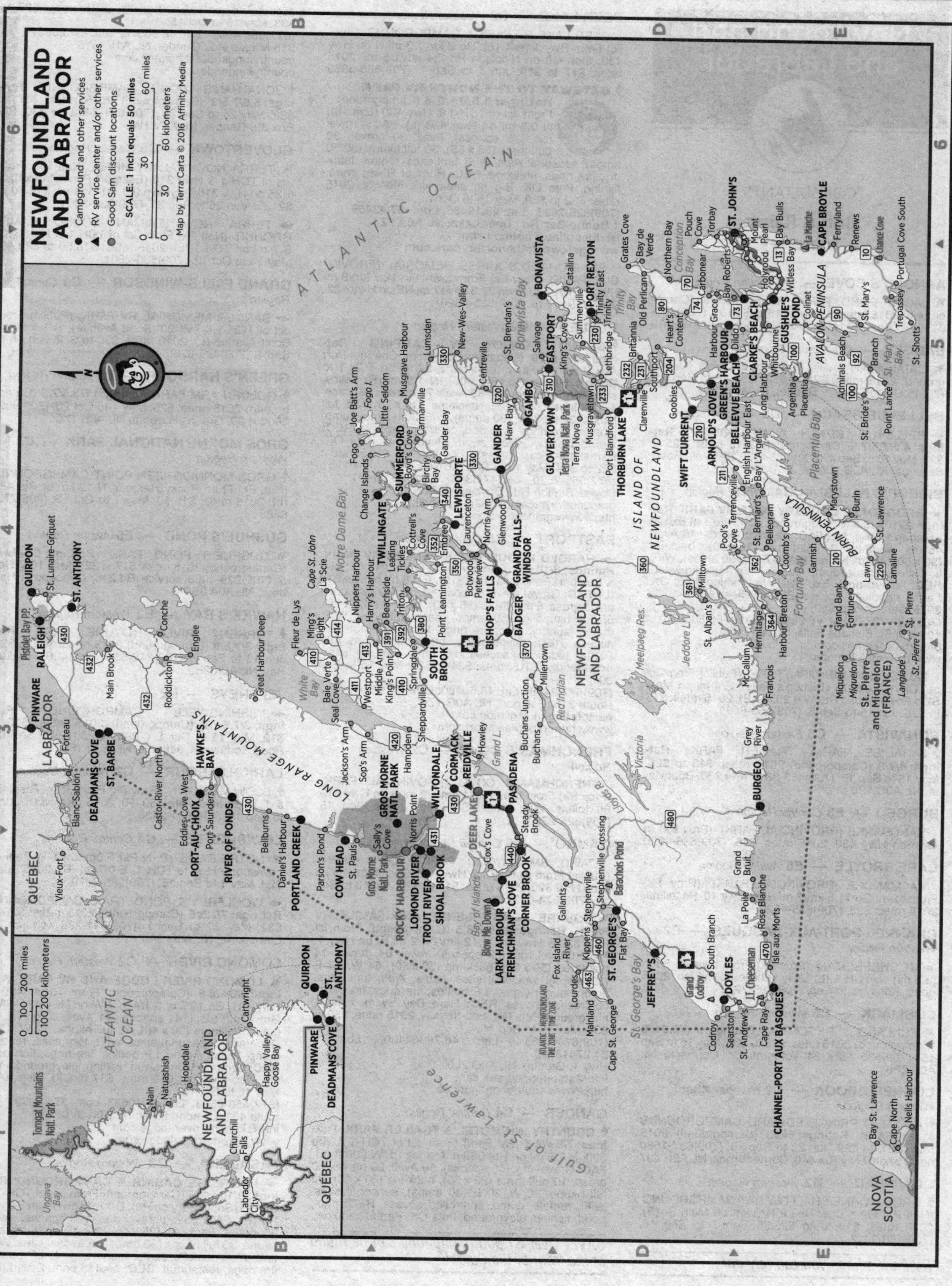
NEWFOUNDLAND AND LABRADOR
Campground and other services
RV service center and/or other services
Good Sam discount locations
SCALE: 1 inch equals 50 miles
Map by Terra Carta © 2016 Affinity Media
ATLANTIC OCEAN
LONG RANGE MOUNTAINS
ISLAND OF NEWFOUNDLAND
AVALON PENINSULA
BURIN PENINSULA
Gulf of St. Lawrence
NOVA SCOTIA
QUÉBEC
LABRADOR
St. Pierre and Miquelon (FRANCE)

Newfoundland and Labrador

CONSULTANTS

Bob & Raissa Maroney

ARNOLD'S COVE — D5 *Avalon Region*

JACKS POND PARK **Ratings: 5/8/8** (Campground) 2015 rates: $30. May 15 to Sep 30. (709)463-0150 PO Box 394 Hwy 1, Arnolds Cove, NL A0B 1A0

BADGER — C4 *Central Region*

CATAMARAN PARK **Ratings: 8/8.5★/8** (Campground) 2015 rates: $24 to $32. May 16 to Sep 15. (709)539-5115 hwy 1, Badger, NL A0H 1A0

BELLEVUE BEACH — D5 *Avalon Region*

BELLEVUE BEACH CAMPGROUND **Ratings: 4.5/7.5/7.5** (Campground) 2015 rates: $25 to $32. May 15 to Sep 4. (709)442-4536 239 Main Road, Bellevue, NL A0B 1B0

BISHOP'S FALLS — C4 *Central Region*

BROOKDALE COUNTRY INN & RV PARK Ratings: 9/10★/8.5 (Campground) TCH, Rte 1 at Exit 21 - Bishop's Falls, NL. **FAC:** All weather rds. 46 Avail: 46 all weather, 8 pull-thrus (30 x 70), back-ins (30 x 60), 40 full hkups, 6 W, 6 E (30/50 amps), WiFi, tent sites, rentals, dump, laundry, fire rings, firewood. **REC:** heated pool, Exploits River: fishing. Pets OK. Partial handicap access. Big rig sites, eco-friendly, 2015 rates: $25 to $40.
(709)258-7377 Lat: 48.988652, Lon: -55.535975
10 Main St, Bishops Falls, NL A0H 1C0
brookdale@email.com
www.brookdaleinn.com

FALLSVIEW MUNICIPAL PARK (Public) From Jct of TCH-1 & exit 21 (Bishop's Falls), S 4 mi on Main St to Powerhouse Rd, W 0.25 mi (E). 2015 rates: $15 to $25. Jun 15 to Sep 3. (709)258-6581

BONAVISTA — C5 *Eastern Region*

PARADISE FARM TRAILER PARK **Ratings: 4/7/8** (Campground) 2015 rates: $18 to $25. May 15 to Sep 15. (709)468-8811 hwy 230, Bonavista, NL A0C 1B0

BURGEO — E3 *Central Region*

SANDBANKS (PROVINCIAL PARK) (Prov Pk) In town on Hwy 480. 2015 rates: $15. (709)635-4520

CAPE BROYLE — E5 *Avalon Region*

LA MANCHE (PROVINCIAL PARK) (Prov Pk) From town: Go 11.5 km/7 mi N on Hwy 10. Pit toilets. 2015 rates: $23. (709)635-4520

CHANNEL-PORT-AUX-BASQUES — E2 *Western Region*

JT CHEESEMAN (Prov Pk) From town, E 6 km (3.6 mi) on TCH 1 (L) Daily vehicle permit fee. 2015 rates: $23. May to Sep. (709)695-7222

CORMACK — C3 *Western Region*

FUNLAND RESORT **Ratings: 7.5/8.5★/8** (Campground) 2015 rates: $25 to $30. May 15 to Sep 15. (709)635-7227 34 Veterans Dr, Cormack, NL A8A 2P8

CORNER BROOK — C2 *Humber West, Western Region*

KINSMEN PRINCE EDWARD CAMPGROUNDS & RV PARK **Ratings: 6/6/8** (Campground) 2015 rates: $26 to $29. Jun 23 to Sep 15. (709)637-1580 north Shore Hwy Rte 440, Corner Brook, NL A2H 6J7

COW HEAD — B2 *Western Region*

GROS MORNE/SHALLOW BAY CAMPGROUND (Natl Pk) From Cow Head, N 2 km on Main St (E). 2015 rates: $18.60 to $25.50. Jun 7 to Sep 16. (709)458-2417

RV Park ratings you can rely on!

DEER LAKE — C2 *Western Region*

DEER LAKE RV PARK & CAMPGROUND (Public) From Hwy 1 (exit 16): Go 2 km/1.3 mi N on Hwy 430, then left on Nicolson Rd 2.4 km/1.5 mi. 2015 rates: $17 to $19. Jun 1 to Sep 1. (709)635-5885

GATEWAY TO THE NORTH RV PARK Ratings: 6.5/9★/8.5 (Campground) From Jct of TCH-1 & Hwy 430 (Exit 16), N 0.3 mi on Hwy 430 (L). **FAC:** Gravel rds. (75 spaces). Avail: 30 gravel, 30 pull-thrus (35 x 65), 30 full hkups (30/50 amps), seasonal sites, WiFi, tent sites, rentals, laundry, fire rings, firewood. **REC:** Humber River: swim, fishing. Pets OK. Big rig sites, eco-friendly, 2015 rates: $32 to $39. May 15 to Oct 1.
(709)635-2693 Lat: 49.19436, Lon: -57.43459
1 Bonne Bay Rd., Deer Lake, NL A8A 2Z4
geribeaulieu@hotmail.com
www.gatewaytothenorthrvpark.com

SIR RICHARD SQUIRES MEMORIAL (PROVINCIAL PARK) (Prov Pk) From town: Go 12.7 km/8 mi NW on Hwy 430, then 27.3 km/17 mi NE on Hwy 422. 2015 rates: $15. (709)635-4520

DOYLES — D2 *Western Region*

GRAND CODROY RV CAMPING Ratings: 8/10★/10 (Campground) From Channel-Port Aux Basques Ferry Terminal, E 22 mi on TCH-1 to Doyle's Station Rd (Rte 406), N 1.5 mi (R) Follow signs. **FAC:** Gravel rds. 82 Avail: 70 gravel, 12 grass, 4 pull-thrus (30 x 55), back-ins (40 x 75), 38 full hkups, 32 W, 32 E (30 amps), WiFi, tent sites, dump, laundry, fire rings, firewood, controlled access. **REC:** Grand Codroy River: swim, playground. Pets OK. Partial handicap access. Eco-friendly, 2015 rates: $22 to $34. May 15 to Sep 30. No CC.
(877)955-2520 Lat: 47.83457, Lon: -59.20471
Doyles Station Rd., Doyles, NL A0N 1J0
grandcodroyrvcamping@nf.sympatico.ca
http://www.grandcodroy.com

EASTPORT — C5 *Central Region*

HAROLD W. DUFFETT SHRINERS RV PARK Ratings: 8/10★/9 (Campground) From Jct of TCH-1 & Eastport Peninsula (Rte 310), E 8.5 mi on Rte 310 (L). **FAC:** Gravel rds. (153 spaces). 56 Avail: 45 gravel, 11 grass, 8 pull-thrus (25 x 60), back-ins (25 x 60), 56 full hkups (30/50 amps), seasonal sites, WiFi, dump, laundry, groc, fire rings, firewood, controlled access. **REC:** shuffleboard, playground. Pets OK. Partial handicap access, no tents. Big rig sites, eco-friendly, 2015 rates: $34 to $37. May 15 to Sep 30.
(709)677-2438 Lat: 48.66460, Lon: -53.80441
Route 310, Eastport, NL A0G 1Z0
eastportrvpark@nf.aibn.com
www.shrinersparkeastport.com

FRENCHMAN'S COVE — C2 *Western Region*

FRENCHMAN'S COVE (PROVINCIAL PARK) (Prov Pk) From town: Go 1 km/1/2 mi S on Hwy 210. Pit toilets. 2015 rates: $15. May 15 to Sep 15. (709)826-2753

GAMBO — C5 *Central Region*

DAVID SMALLWOOD PARK (TOWN PARK) (Public) From jct Hwy 1 & Hwy 320: Go 7.1 km/4.3 mi N on Hwy 320. 2015 rates: $16 to $20. Jun 10 to Sep 10. (709)674-0122

SQUARE POND FRIENDS AND FAMILY RV PARK Ratings: 8/10★/8.5 (Campground) From jct Hwy 320 & Hwy 1: Go 12 km/7-1/2 mi W on Hwy 1. **FAC:** Gravel rds. (89 spaces). Avail: 64 gravel, 14 pull-thrus (50 x 60), back-ins (50 x 50), 64 W, 64 E (30 amps), seasonal sites, cable, WiFi, tent sites, dump, laundry, groc, LP bottles, fire rings, firewood, controlled access. **REC:** Hare Bay: swim, fishing, playground. Pets OK. Eco-friendly, 2015 rates: $30 to $36. May 16 to Sep 15.
(709)674-7566 Lat: 48.79862400, Lon: -54.27413800
Hwy 1, Gambo, NL A0G 2L0
info@squarepondpark.ca
http://www.squarepondpark.ca

GANDER — C4 *Central Region*

COUNTRY INN MOTEL & TRAILER PARK Ratings: 7/8★/8.5 (RV Park) From Jct of TCH-1 & Rte 330, N 2.5 mi on Rte 330 to Magee St, W 200 ft (L). **FAC:** Gravel rds. (66 spaces). 50 Avail: 20 gravel, 30 grass, 10 pull-thrus (22 x 55), back-ins (20 x 40), 30 full hkups, 20 W, 20 E (30 amps), seasonal sites, WiFi, rentals, dump, controlled access. **REC:** pool, pond, fishing, playground. Pets OK. Partial handicap access, no tents. Eco-friendly, 2015 rates: $25 to $35. May 15 to Oct 15.
(877)956-4005 Lat: 48.98516, Lon: -54.60657
315 Magee Rd., Gander, NL A1V 1W6
countryinngander@hotmail.com
countryinngander.ca

SAVE! Over $1,000 in coupons can be found at the front of the Guide!

JONATHAN'S POND CAMPGROUND **Ratings: 5.5/7.5/8** (Campground) 2015 rates: $17 to $32. May 24 to Sep 30. (709)651-2492 rte 330, PO Box 89, Gander, NL A1V 1W5

GLOVERTOWN — C5 *Central Region*

TERRA NOVA/MALADY HEAD (Natl Pk) From Jct of TCH 1 & Hwy 310 (Eastport Peninula exit), N 1.25 on Hwy 310/Traytown (R). 2015 rates: $15.70 to $21.50. Jun 25 to Aug 31. (709)533-2801

TERRA NOVA/NEWMAN SOUND CAMPGROUND (Natl Pk) From Jct of TCH 1 & Hwy 310, S 7 mi on TCH 1 (L). 2015 rates: $18.60 to $29.40. May 14 to Oct 12. (709)533-2801

GRAND FALLS-WINDSOR — C4 *Central Region*

SANGER MEMORIAL RV PARK (Public) From Jct of TCH-1 & exit 20 (Scott Avenue), S 1.5 mi on Scott Avenue (L). 2015 rates: $30 to $32. Jun 16 to Sep 1. (709)489-8780

GREEN'S HARBOUR — D5 *Avalon Region*

GOLDEN ARM PARK **Ratings: 7/5.5/7.5** (Campground) 2015 rates: $25. May 1 to Oct 20. (709)582-3600 rt 80, Greens Harbour, NL A0B 1X0

GROS MORNE NATIONAL PARK — C3 *Western Region*

GROS MORNE/GREEN POINT CAMPGROUND (Natl Pk) From Rocky Harbour, N 12 km or Rte 430 (L). 2015 rates: $15.70. May 1 to Oct 13. (888)773-8888

GUSHUE'S POND — E5 *Avalon Region*

GUSHUE'S POND PARK **Ratings: 5.5/8★/7** (Campground) 2015 rates: $17 to $25. May 16 to Sep 5. (709)229-4003 service Rd.210, Conception Harbour, NL A0A 3S0

HAWKE'S BAY — B3 *Western Region*

TORRENT RIVER NATURE PARK **Ratings: 3/7.5/8** (Campground) 2015 rates: $25 to $29. Jun 18 to Sep 7. (709)248-5344 hwy 430, Hawke's Bay, NL A0K 3B0

JEFFREYS — D2

WISHINGWELL CAMPGROUND **Ratings: 3/7.5★/7** (Campground) 2015 rates: $10 to $12. May 15 to Oct 1. (709)645-2501 520 Seaside Road Southwest, Jeffreys, NL A0N 1P0

LARK HARBOUR — C2 *Western Region*

BLOW ME DOWN (Prov Pk) From Jct of Rtes 450 & 1, W 36 mi on Rte 450 (R). 2015 rates: $15. Jun 1 to Sep 15. (709)681-2430

LEWISPORTE — C4 *Central Region*

NOTRE DAME (Prov Pk) From town, W 7 mi on Lewisporte Hwy to TCH 1, E 0.7 mi (R). 2015 rates: $23. May 1 to Sep 15. (709)535-2379

WOOLFREY'S POND TRAIL CAMPGROUND **Ratings: 7/7.5/8** (Campground) 2015 rates: $20 to $32. May 31 to Sep 1. (709)541-2267 church St, Lewisporte, NL A0G 3A0

LOMOND RIVER — C2 *Western Region*

LOMOND RIVER LODGE AND RV PARK Ratings: 6/8★/8.5 (Campground) From Hwys 430 & Hwy 431: Go 10 km/ 6-1/4 mi NW on Hwy 431. **FAC:** Gravel/dirt rds. (141 spaces). 41 Avail: 20 gravel, 21 grass, back-ins (30 x 40), 29 full hkups, 12 W, 12 E (15 amps), seasonal sites, WiFi, tent sites, rentals, dump, laundry, groc, LP bottles, fire rings, firewood. **REC:** Lomond River: swim, fishing, playground. Pets OK. Eco-friendly, 2015 rates: $17 to $30. Disc: AAA. May 15 to Oct 15.
(877)456-6663 Lat: 49.40623, Lon: -57.72879
route 431, Lomond River, NL A0K 3V0
info@lomond-river-lodge.com
www.lomond-river-lodge.com

PASADENA — C3 *Western Region*

PINERIDGE CABINS & CAMPGROUND Ratings: 9/10★/8.5 (Campground) From Jct of TCH-1 & Exit 13 (South Service Rd), E 0.5 mi on South Service Rd (R). **FAC:** Paved/gravel rds. (128 spaces). Avail: 30 grass, back-ins (25 x 45), mostly side by side hkups, 30 full hkups (30 amps), seasonal sites, WiFi, tent sites, rentals, dump, laundry, groc, LP bottles, fire rings, restaurant. **REC:** heated pool, Deer Lake:

PASADENA (CONT)

PINERIDGE CABINS & (CONT)
swim, fishing, playground. Pets OK. Eco-friendly. 2015 rates: $30. May 15 to Sep 25. (709)686-2541 Lat: 49.03854, Lon: -57.57624 south Service Rd, Pasadena, NL A0L 1K0 dermon.piercy@nf.sympatico.ca

PINWARE — A3 *Labrador Region*

PINWARE RIVER (PROVINCIAL PARK) (Prov Pk) From Trans-Labrador Hwy/NL-510 N at West St Modeste: Go 2.2 km SE to Pinware, then go 700 m (E). Pit toilets. 2015 rates: $15. Jun 1 to Sep 15. (709)635-4520

PORT REXTON — D5 *Eastern Region*

LOCKSTON PATH (PROVINCIAL PARK) (Prov Pk) From town: Go 6.8 km/4 mi N on Hwy 236. 2015 rates: $15 to $23. (709)464-3553

PORT-AU-CHOIX — B3 *Western Region*

OCEANSIDE RV PARK **Ratings: 4.5/8.5★/7.5** (Campground) 2015 rates: $25. May 24 to Sep 30. (709)861-2133 route 430, Port Au Choix, NL A0K 4H0

PORTLAND CREEK — B3 *Western Region*

MOUNTAIN WATERS RESORT **Ratings: 6.5/9★/8.5** (RV Park) 2015 rates: $17 to $28. Jun 1 to Oct 10. (709)898-2490 rt 430, Portland Creek, NL A0K 4G0

QUIRPON — A4 *Western Region*

VIKING RV PARK
Ratings: 5/7/7.5 (Campground) From Jct of Rtes 430 & 436 (St Lunaire-Griquet), W 15 mi on Rte 436 to Quirpon Rd, N 500 ft (L). **FAC:** Gravel rds. 30 Avail: 15 gravel, 15 grass, 2 pull-thrus (30 x 65), back-ins (30 x 35), 30 W, 30 E (15/30 amps), WiFi, tent sites, dump, laundry, groc, fire rings, firewood. **REC:** pond. Pets OK. Eco-friendly. 2015 rates: $28. Jun 1 to Sep 30.
(709)623-2425 Lat: 51.56791, Lon: -55.48035
Main St, Quirpon, NL A0K 2X0
vikingrvpark@hotmail.com
See ad this page.

RALEIGH — A4 *Western Region*

PISTOLET BAY (Prov Pk) From Jct of Rtes 430 & 437, S 16 mi on Rte 437 (R). 2015 rates: $15 to $23. May 1 to Sep 15. (709)635-4520

REIDVILLE — C3

Things to See and Do

NEWFOUNDLAND INSECTARIUM & BUTTERFLY PAVILION Live and mounted exhibits feature butterflies, beetles and other insects from around the world and those from NFL & Labrador. May 15 to Oct 15. partial handicap access. Hours: 9am to 6pm. Adult fee: $12.00.
(866)635-5454 Lat: 49.185198, Lon: -57.418216
2 Bonne Bay Rd, Reidville, NL A8A 2V1
www.nfinsectarium.com

Tell them you saw them in this Guide!

RIVER OF PONDS — B3 *Western Region*

RIVER OF PONDS PARK **Ratings: 5.5/6.5/7** (Campground) 2015 rates: $15 to $21. Jun 1 to Sep 16. (709)225-3130 hwy 430, River of Ponds, NL A0K 4M0

ROCKY HARBOUR — C2 *Western Region*

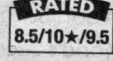

GROS MORNE RV CAMPGROUND & MOTEL UNITS
Ratings: 8/10★/9.5 (Campground) From Jct of Rte 430 & West Link Rd, W 0.5 mi on West Link Rd (E). **FAC:** Gravel rds. 72 gravel, 8 pull-thrus (30 x 60), back-ins (30 x 60), 53 full hkups, 19 W, 19 E (30/50 amps), WiFi, tent sites, rentals, dump, laundry, groc, LP bottles, fire rings, firewood, controlled access. **REC:** playground. Pets OK. Partial handicap access. Eco-friendly. 2015 rates: $25 to $34. May 15 to Oct 11.
(877)488-3133 Lat: 49.58092, Lon: -57.91343
10 West Link Rd, Rocky Harbour, NL A0K 4N0
info@grosmornervcampground.com
www.grosmornervcampground.com
See ad this page.

GROS MORNE/BERRY HILL CAMPGROUND (Natl Pk) From Rocky Harbour, N 4 km on Rte 430 (R). 2015 rates: $18.60 to $25.50. Jun 13 to Sep 8. (709)458-2417

GROS MORNE/NORRIS POINT KOA
Ratings: 8.5/10★/9.5 (Campground) From Jct of Rte 430 & Information Center Rd, (Norris Point), W 1.2 mi on Inf Center Rd to Park Entrance (L). **FAC:** Gravel rds. (103 spaces). 85 Avail: 60 gravel, 25 grass, 12 pull-thrus (25 x 85), back-ins (25 x 65), 60 full hkups, 20 W, 20 E (30/50 amps), seasonal sites, WiFi, tent sites, rentals, dump, laundry, groc, LP bottles, fire rings, firewood, controlled access. **REC:** pond, swim, fishing, playground. Pets OK. Partial handicap access. Big rig sites, eco-friendly. 2015 rates: $25 to $43. May 14 to Oct 14.
(709)458-2229 Lat: 49.55642, Lon: -57.87421
PO Box 382, Rocky Harbour, NL A0K 4N0
koa.grosmorne@warp.nfld.net
www.koa.com/campgrounds/gros-morne
See ad this page.

SHOAL BROOK — C2 *Western Region*

THE WATER'S EDGE RV PARK (Natl Pk) From Hwy 430 & 431: Go 33.4 km/20 3/4 mi W on 431. 2015 rates: $15 to $20. Jun 1 to Oct 15. (709)453-2020

SOUTH BROOK — C3 *Central Region*

KONA BEACH CAMPGROUND RV PARK **Ratings: 7.5/8.5★/8** (Campground) 2015 rates: $19 to $25. May 19 to Sep 24. (709)657-2400 hwy 1, South Brook, NL A0J 1S0

ST ANTHONY — A4 *Western Region*

TRIPLE FALLS RV PARK **Ratings: 7.5/8/8.5** (RV Park) 2015 rates: $20 to $30. May 21 to Sep 24. (709)454-2599 rt 430, St Anthony, NL A0K 4S0

ST BARBE — A3 *Western Region*

ST BARBE RV PARK **Ratings: 5.5/10★/8** (RV Area in MHP) 2015 rates: $35. Jun 1 to Sep 20. (709)877-2515 main Road 430, Black Duck Cove, NL A0K 1M0

ST GEORGE'S — D2 *Western Region*

BARACHOIS POND (PROVINCIAL PARK) (Prov Pk) From town: Go 4.8 km/3 mi SE on paved road, then 14.8 km/9 mi N on Hwy 1. 2015 rates: $15 to $23. May 15 to Sep 15. (877)214-2267

ST JOHN'S — D6 *Avalon Region*

BLUE FIN RV TRAILER PARK **Ratings: 7/8★/8** (RV Park) 2015 rates: $30 to $35. May 15 to Sep 30. (709)229-5500 22 Tch 1, Holyrood, NL A0A 2R0

BUTTER POT (PROVINCIAL PARK) (Prov Pk) From town: Go 32 km/20 mi SW on Hwy 1. 2015 rates: $15. May 15 to Sep 15. (709)635-1853

PIPPY PARK CAMPGROUND (Public) From Jct of TCH & Prince Philip Pkwy, E 1.5 mi on Prince Philip Pkwy to Allandale Rd, N 0.25 mi to Nagle Pl, N 0.1 mi (R). 2015 rates: $29 to $45. May 15 to Oct 17. (709)737-3669

SUMMERFORD — C4 *Central Region*

DILDO RUN (PROVINCIAL PARK) (Prov Pk) From town: Go 15.4 km/9-1/2 mi NW on Hwy 340 (on New World Island). 2015 rates: $15. May 25 to Sep 1. (877)214-2267

SWIFT CURRENT — D5 *Eastern Region*

KILMORY RESORT **Ratings: 4/8★/7.5** (Campground) 2015 rates: $25. May 20 to Oct 15. (888)884-2410 rte 210, Swift Current, NL A0E 2W0

THORBURN LAKE — D5 *Eastern Region*

LAKESIDE RV RESORT **Ratings: 5/7.5/7** (Campground) 2015 rates: $28 to $35. May 15 to Oct 15. (709)427-7668 hwy 1, Clarenville, NL A5A 2C2

TROUT RIVER — C2 *Western Region*

GROS MORNE/TROUT RIVER POND CAMPGROUND (Natl Pk) From Trout River, S 2 km on Hwy 431, follow sign (E). 2015 rates: $18.60 to $25.50. Jun 7 to Sep 17. (709)458-2417

TWILLINGATE — B4 *Central Region*

PEYTON'S WOODS RV PARK AND CAMPGROUND **Ratings: 4/5/6.5** (Campground) 2015 rates: $20 to $29. May 15 to Oct 30. (709)884-2000 PO Box 314 Hwy 340, Twillingate, NL A0G 4M0

WILTONDALE — C3 *Western Region*

GROS MORNE/LOMOND CAMPGROUND (Natl Pk) From Jct of Rtes 430 & 431, W 17km on Rte 431, NE 4 km on Lomond Rd (R). 2015 rates: $18.60 to $25.50. May 17 to Oct 14. (709)458-2417

 See map page 1405

Getty Images/iStockphoto

WELCOME TO
Northwest Territories

JOINED CONFEDERATION JULY 15, 1870	WIDTH: 783 MILES (1,260 KM) LENGTH: 1,440 MILES (2,317 KM)	PROPORTION OF CANADA 13.48% OF 9,984,670 SQ KM

Travelers venture into Canada's Northwest Territories to see wilderness in its most elemental form. Endless arctic sky, aurora borealis and some of North America's most spectacular natural wonders reveal themselves to RVers. In an area twice as large as Texas, the entire population could fit comfortably into Houston's Astrodome.

The best way to learn about the vast lands of the Northwest Territory is to drive the ribbons of roadway that penetrate the wilderness. The star road is the Dempster Highway, an all-weather passage that traverses more than 400 miles and offers the rare chance to drive across the Arctic Circle. The Northwest Territory boasts two critical ferry crossings and two settlements between Dawson City, Yukon, and Inuvik near the Arctic Ocean. Along the way, the Nitainlaii Territorial Park Visitor Centre relates the long history of trade and settlement at Fort McPherson in the Mackenzie Delta, one of the most remote settlements in Canada.

The Waterfalls Route on Highway 1 leads to pristine hydro-spectaculars at Twin Falls Park, Lady Evelyn Falls Park and Sambaa Deh Falls Park. The Nahanni National Park Reserve provides air access to the magnificent Virginia Falls that thunder down 315 feet of sheer rock around a spire of basaltic rock. On your driving tours, be certain to stop at a Northwest Territories Visitor Center for a well-earned "North of 60" certificate for explorers who have ventured beyond the 60-degree latitude, the boundary of the Arctic Circle.

The Northwest Territories are far from frozen from May to September. Temperatures routinely top 80 degrees, and weeks will pass without rain. For birders, about one-fifth of all of North America's ducks, swans and geese nest here. The area's biggest city, Yellowknife, boasts a vibrant cultural scene.

Canada set aside 17,300 square miles in the Northwest Territory and Alberta to protect the world's largest herd of free-roaming bison. The result, Wood Buffalo National Park, is the world's second-largest national park.

June and July bring long days for fishing. Two lakes where the fish are sure to bite are Great Bear Lake and Great Slave Lake, the territory's two largest lakes. Great Slave Lake is the deepest lake in the continent.

Top 3 Tourism Attractions:
1) Nahanni National Park Reserve
2) Wood Buffalo National Park
3) Baffin Island

Nickname: Canada's Last Frontier

State Flower: Mountain Avens

State Bird: Gyrfalcon

People: Ethel Blondin-Andrew, First Nation woman elected to parliament; Jason Elliott, hockey player; Charlie Panigoniak, singer-songwriter; Donald Morton Stewart, politician

Major Cities: Yellowknife (NWT capital), Hay City, Inuvik

Topography: Two regions: taiga-boreal forest that circles the subarctic zone; tundra-rocky arctic with stunted vegetation

Climate: Harsh climate seven months of year; climate warms the farther south one travels

Getty Images/iStockphoto

TRAVEL & TOURISM

NWT Arctic Tourism
800-661-0788
www.spectacularnwt.com

Hay River
www.hayriver.com/visitors

Visit Yellowknife
867-873-4262
www.visityellowknife.com

SHOPPING

Acho Dene Native Crafts
www.adnc.ca

Gallery of the Midnight Sun
www.gallerymidnightsun.com

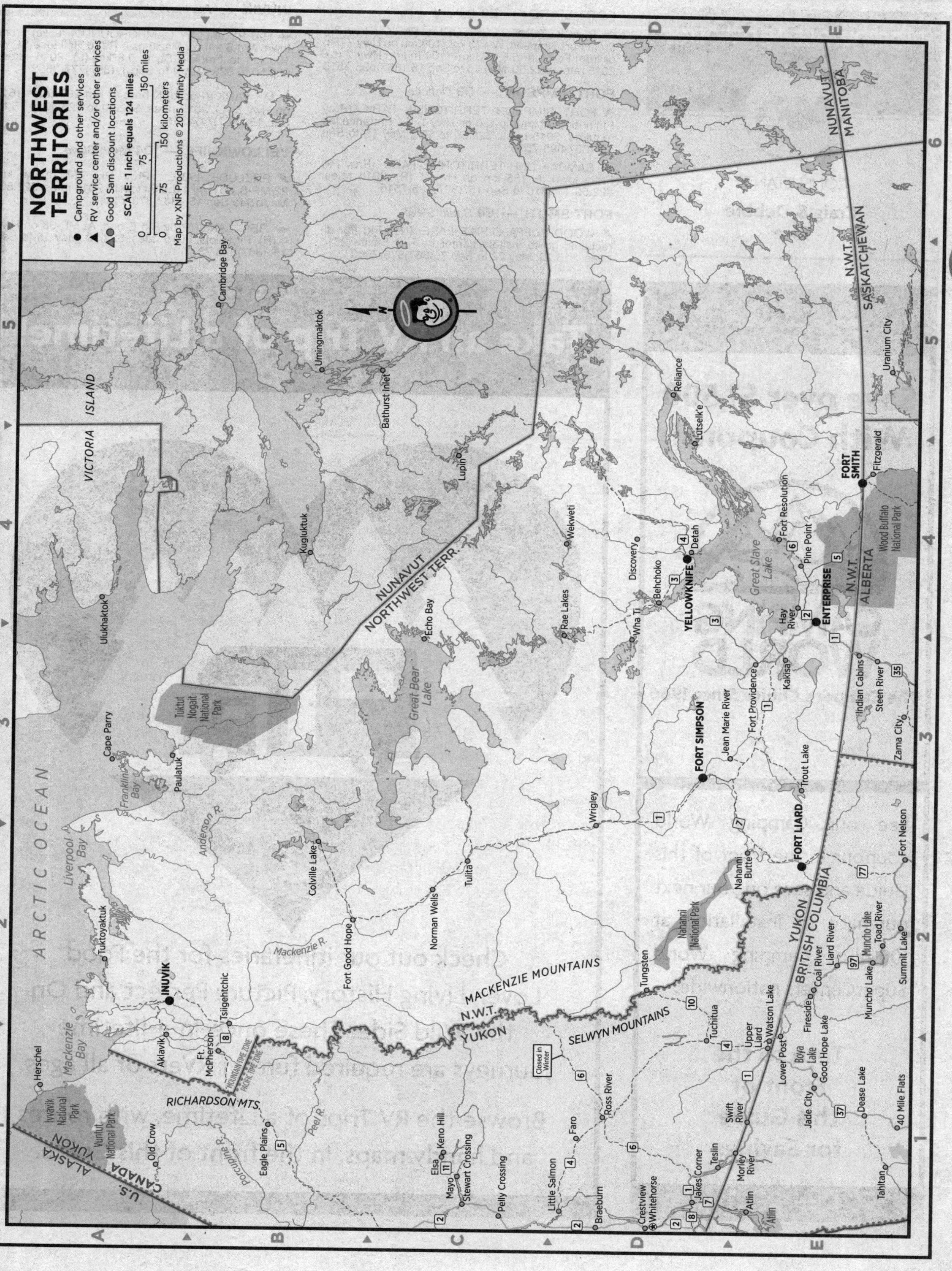
NORTHWEST TERRITORIES
Campground and other services
RV service center and/or other services
Good Sam discount locations
SCALE: 1 inch equals 124 miles
0 75 150 miles
0 75 150 kilometers
Map by XNR Productions © 2015 Affinity Media
ARCTIC OCEAN
VICTORIA ISLAND
NUNAVUT
NORTHWEST TERR.
N.W.T.
YUKON
BRITISH COLUMBIA
ALBERTA
SASKATCHEWAN
MANITOBA
ALASKA
U.S.
CANADA
MACKENZIE MOUNTAINS
SELWYN MOUNTAINS
RICHARDSON MTS.
MOUNTAIN TIME ZONE
PACIFIC TIME ZONE
Great Bear Lake
Great Slave Lake
Mackenzie Bay
Liverpool Bay
Franklin Bay
Mackenzie R.
Anderson R.
Peel R.
Porcupine R.
Ivvavik National Park
Vuntut National Park
Tuktut Nogait National Park
Nahanni National Park
Wood Buffalo National Park
Closed in Winter
INUVIK
YELLOWKNIFE
FORT SIMPSON
FORT LIARD
ENTERPRISE
FORT SMITH
Herschel
Aklavik
Ft. McPherson
Tsiigehtchic
Tuktoyaktuk
Paulatuk
Cape Parry
Ulukhaktok
Kugluktuk
Cambridge Bay
Umingmaktok
Bathurst Inlet
Lupin
Fort Good Hope
Colville Lake
Norman Wells
Tulita
Echo Bay
Wrigley
Rae Lakes
Wekweti
Wha Ti
Behchoko
Discovery
Detah
Reliance
Lutselk'e
Fort Resolution
Pine Point
Hay River
Fitzgerald
Uranium City
Fort Providence
Kakisa
Jean Marie River
Trout Lake
Nahanni Butte
Tungsten
Indian Cabins
Steen River
Zama City
Fort Nelson
Toad River
Muncho Lake
Summit Lake
Liard River
Coal River
Fireside
Watson Lake
Upper Liard
Lower Post
Boya Lake
Good Hope Lake
Jade City
Dease Lake
40 Mile Flats
Tahltan
Tuchitua
Ross River
Faro
Swift River
Teslin
Morley River
Jakes Corner
Atlin
Whitehorse
Crestview
Braeburn
Little Salmon
Pelly Crossing
Stewart Crossing
Mayo
Elsa
Keno Hill
Eagle Plains
Old Crow

Northwest Territories

CONSULTANTS

Craig & Debbie Rice

FORT LIARD — E2 *Dehcho*

➔ BLACKSTONE TERRITORIAL PARK (Prov Pk) From Fort Simpson, W 173 km (104 mi) on Hwy 7 (R); or from Fort Liard, E 173 km (104 mi) on Hwy 7 (L). 2015 rates: $22.50. May 15 to Sep 15. (867)695-7515

FORT SIMPSON — D3 *Dehcho*

➘ FORT SIMPSON TERRITORIAL PARK (Prov Pk) N-bnd: At km/mp 480 on Hwy 1, (L). Entrance fee required. 2015 rates: $22.50 to $28. May 15 to Sep 15. (867)695-7515

➔ SAMBAA DEH TERRITORIAL PARK (Prov Pk) From town, E 155 km on Hwy 1 (R). 2015 rates: $22.50. May 15 to Sep 15. (867)695-7515

FORT SMITH — E4 *South Slave*

➚ WOOD BUFFALO/PINE LAKE (Natl Pk) For directions, go to visitors center in Fort Smith. 2015 rates: $15.70. May 22 to Sep 7. (867)875-7960

INUVIK — A2 *Inuvik*

➔ HAPPY VALLEY CAMPGROUND (Public) From town, N 1.5 km on Mackenzie Rd to Reliance St, W 100 km to Franklin St, N 0.8 km (L). 2015 rates: $22.50 to $28. May 4 to Sep 1. (867)777-3652

⬇ JAK PARK (Public) N-bnd: At Km 267 (mile 161) on Hwy 8 (L). 2015 rates: $22.50 to $28. May 15 to Sep 15. (867)777-3613

YELLOWKNIFE — D4 *North Slave*

➚ PRELUDE LAKE (Prov Pk) N-bnd: At km 22/MP-8, on Hwy 4 (L). Pit toilets. 2015 rates: $22.50. May 15 to Sep 15. (867)873-7184

➔ REID LAKE (Prov Pk) E-bnd: At MP-38 on Hwy 4 (R). Pit toilets. 2015 rates: $22.50. May 15 to Sep 15. (867)873-7317

Getty Images/iStockphoto

NS

WELCOME TO
Nova Scotia

JOINED CONFEDERATION	WIDTH: 314 MILES (505 KM)	PROPORTION OF CANADA
JULY 1, 1867	LENGTH: 85 MILES (137 KM)	0.55% OF 9,984,670 SQ KM

With a shoreline that stretches more than 4,000 miles, Nova Scotia is a haven for sightseers and lovers of water recreation. Prepare a driving itinerary along the rugged peninsula that includes stops at the compelling city of Halifax and the charming town of Peggy's Cove. The Cabot Trail is considered to be one of the world's most breathtaking drives, but take time to stop and explore the province's many beautiful villages and natural wonders.

Baddeck is a popular starting point on the world-famous Cabot Trail. This scenic driving route loops Cape Breton Island for 185 miles, crossing the scenic Margaree Valley and hugging the sea cliffs and beaches of the Cape Breton Highlands, Canada's first Atlantic Provinces national park. Along the route are stops for 26 hiking trails in the park, including the breathtaking hike along a ridgetop on the Skyline Trail.

Cape Chignecto is Nova Scotia's largest provincial park and is located at the end of a dramatic, arrow-shaped peninsula that thrusts into the Bay of Fundy.

With so much coastline, Nova Scotia packs more than its share of sea adventures. Digby Neck provides the best whale and dolphin watching, along with lots of charter tour boats. Sea kayakers can challenge those 40-foot tides on the Bay of Fundy, and beachgoers will find lots sand on the shores of Melmerby Beach Provincial Park on the waters of the Northumberland Strait.

Top 3 Tourism Attractions:
1) Cape Breton Island
2) Halifax
3) Bay of Fundy

Nickname: Bluenose Country

State Flower: Mayflower

State Bird: Osprey

People: David Brine, hockey player; Holly Cole, singer; Samuel Edison, father of Thomas Edison; Anne Murray, singer; Joshua Slocum, first man to sail solo around world; Sydney Crosby, hockey player

Major Cities: Halifax (capital), Cape Breton (Sydney), Truro, Amherst, New Glasgow

Topography: Atlantic Ocean nearly surrounds peninsula; contains hundreds of small, freshwater lakes and numerous rivers, bays, estuaries.

Climate: Mid-temperate; closer to continental than maritime climate; warm, balmy summers; cold, wet winters

TRAVEL & TOURISM

Nova Scotia Tourism Agency (NSTA)
800-565-0000
www.novascotia.com

Amherst
902-667-8429
Vic-amh@gov.ns.ca

Central Nova Tourism Association Glooscap-Sunrise Trail
902-893-8782
www.cnta.ns.ca

Destination Cape Breton
902-563-4636
www.cbisland.com

Destination Eastern and Northumberland Shores Association
902-752-6383, 877-81-OCEAN
www.northumberlandshore.com
www.easternshorenovascotia.com

Destination Halifax
877-422-9334, 902-422-9334
www.destinationhalifax.com

Digby
902-245-2201
vic-digby@gov.ns.ca

Halifax Stanfield International Airport
902-873-1223
vic-airport@gov.ns.ca

Halifax Waterfront
902-424-4248
vic-water@gov.ns.ca

Peggy's Cove
902-823-2253
vic-peggy@gov.ns.ca

Port Hastings
902-625-4201
vic-phast@gov.ns.ca

Seaside Tourism Association
866-736-8217
www.seacoasttrail.com

St. Margaret's Bay
902-857-3249
www.peggyscovearea.com

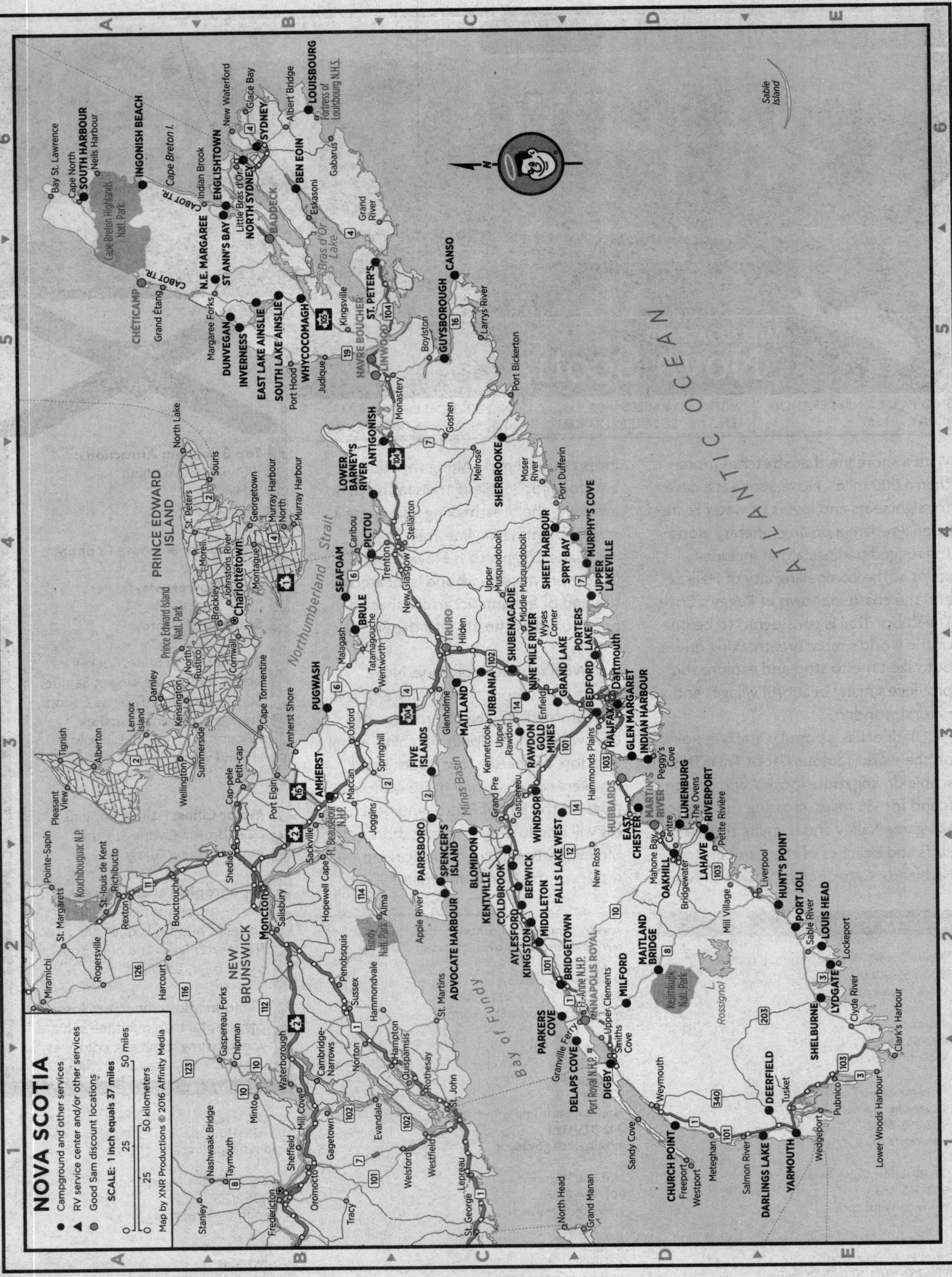
NOVA SCOTIA
Campground and other services
RV service center and/or other services
Good Sam discount locations
SCALE: 1 inch equals 37 miles
0 25 50 miles
0 25 50 kilometers
Map by XNR Productions © 2016 Affinity Media
A B C D E
1 2 3 4 5 6
NEW BRUNSWICK
PRINCE EDWARD ISLAND
ATLANTIC OCEAN
Bay of Fundy
Northumberland Strait
Minas Basin
Bras d'Or Lake
Cape Breton I.
Cape Breton Highlands Natl. Park
Prince Edward Island Natl. Park
Kejimkujik Natl. Park
Fundy Natl. Park
Kouchibouguac N.P.
Ft. Beauséjour N.H.P.
Ft. Anne N.H.P.
Port Royal N.H.P.
Fortress of Louisbourg N.H.S.
Sable Island
CABOT TR.
CHETICAMP
SOUTH HARBOUR
INGONISH BEACH
N.E. MARGAREE
ST. ANN'S BAY
ENGLISHTOWN
NORTH SYDNEY
SYDNEY
LOUISBOURG
BEN EOIN
BADDECK
DUNVEGAN
INVERNESS
EAST LAKE AINSLIE
SOUTH LAKE AINSLIE
WHYCOCOMAGH
HAVRE BOUCHER
LINWOOD
ST. PETER'S
CANSO
GUYSBOROUGH
ANTIGONISH
LOWER BARNEY'S RIVER
PICTOU
SEAFOAM
BRULE
PUGWASH
AMHERST
TRURO
MAITLAND
URBANIA
SHUBENACADIE
NINE MILE RIVER
GRAND LAKE
PORTERS LAKE
SHERBROOKE
SHEET HARBOUR
SPRY BAY
MURPHY'S COVE
UPPER LAKEVILLE
BEDFORD
Dartmouth
HALIFAX
GLEN MARGARET
INDIAN HARBOUR
RAWDON GOLD MINES
FIVE ISLANDS
PARRSBORO
SPENCER'S ISLAND
ADVOCATE HARBOUR
BLOMIDON
WINDSOR
FALLS LAKE WEST
KENTVILLE
COLDBROOK
BERWICK
AYLESFORD
KINGSTON
MIDDLETON
BRIDGETOWN
ANNAPOLIS ROYAL
PARKERS COVE
DELAPS COVE
DIGBY
MILFORD
MAITLAND BRIDGE
HUBBARDS
EAST CHESTER
MARTIN'S RIVER
LUNENBURG
RIVERPORT
OAKHILL
LAHAVE
HUNT'S POINT
PORT JOLI
LOUIS HEAD
LYDGATE
SHELBURNE
DEERFIELD
DARLINGS LAKE
YARMOUTH
CHURCH POINT
Moncton
Charlottetown
Fredericton
St. John

Featured Good Sam Parks

NOVA SCOTIA

Good Sam Park

NS

When you stay with Good Sam, you can expect the highest degree of cleanliness and friendliness, and better yet, you get 10% off campground fees.

If you're not already a Good Sam member you can purchase your membership at one of these locations:

BADDECK

Baddeck Cabot Trail Campground
(902)295-2288

Bras d'Or Lakes Campground
(902)295-2329

MARTIN'S RIVER

Rayport Campground
(902)627-2678

For more Good Sam Parks go to listing pages

Nova Scotia

CONSULTANTS

Bob & Raissa Maroney

ADVOCATE HARBOUR — C2 *Cumberland*

CAPE CHIGNECTO PP (Prov Pk) From town: Go 2.5 km/1-1/2 mi W on Hwy 209, then 1 km/1/2 mi S on West Advocate Rd. Pit toilets. 2015 rates: $23. May 17 to Oct 14. (902)392-2085

AMHERST — B3 *Cumberland*

AMHERST SHORE (Prov Pk) From town, E 4 mi on Tyndal Rd/Rte 366 (R). 2015 rates: $25.90. Jun 13 to Oct 13. (902)661-6002

LOCH LOMOND TENT & TRAILER PARK **Ratings: 8.5/9★/10** (Campground) 2015 rates: $33 to $35. May 15 to Sep 30. (902)667-3890 rr 6, Amherst, NS B4H 3Y4

ANNAPOLIS ROYAL — D2 *Annapolis*

DUNROMIN CAMPSITE
Ratings: 8.5/10★/9.5 (Campground) From Jct of Hwy 101 & Exit 22 (Rtes 8 & 1), N 3.8 mi on Rte 8 to Rte 1, E 1.4 mi (R). **FAC:** Gravel rds. (162 spaces). 132 Avail: 57 gravel, 75 grass, 30 pull-thrus (30 x 55), back-ins (30 x 50), 75 full hkups, 57 W, 57 E (30/50 amps), seasonal sites, WiFi Hotspot, tent sites, rentals, showers $, dump, laundry, groc, LP gas, fire rings, firewood, restaurant, controlled access. **REC:** pool, whirlpool, Annapolis River: swim, fishing, playground. Pets OK. Partial handicap access. Big rig sites, eco-friendly, 2015 rates: $32 to $45. May 15 to Oct 15.
(902)532-2808 Lat: 44.75753, Lon: -65.50716
4618 Hwy 1, Granville Ferry, NS B0S 1K0
office@dunromincampsite.com
www.dunromincampsite.com

ANTIGONISH — B4 *Antigonish*

AE WHIDDEN TRAILER COURT LTD (Campground) (Phone Update) 2015 rates: $40 to $47. May 1 to Oct 15. (902)863-3736 4 Park Lane, Antigonish, NS B2G 2M5

SALSMAN (Prov Pk) From Goshen, S 16.3 mi on Rte 316 (R). 2015 rates: $25.90. Jun 13 to Sep 8. (902)328-2999

AYLESFORD — C2 *Kings*

KLAHANIE KAMPING **Ratings: 8.5/8.5★/8** (Campground) 2015 rates: $33 to $36. May 15 to Oct 15. (902)847-9316 1144 Victoria Rd, Coldbrook, NS B0P 1C0

BADDECK — B5 *Victoria*

ADVENTURES EAST CAMPGROUND & COTTAGES **Ratings: 7.5/10★/9.5** (Membership Pk) 2015 rates: $29 to $36. Jun 5 to Oct 17. (800)507-2228 9585 Hwy 105, Baddeck, NS B0E 1B0

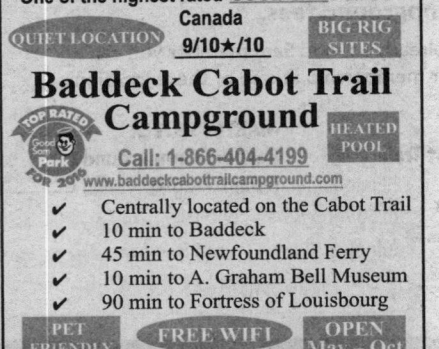

BADDECK CABOT TRAIL CAMPGROUND
Ratings: 9/10★/10 (Campground) W-bnd: From town, W 5 mi on TCH-105 (R); or E-bnd: From Jct of TCH-105 & Exit 7 (Cabot Trail Entrance), E 0.5 mi on TCH-105 (L). **FAC:** Paved/gravel rds. (175 spaces). 150 Avail: 110 gravel, 40 grass, 62 pull-thrus (25 x 80), back-ins (25 x 40), 42 full hkups, 47 W, 47 E (30/50 amps), seasonal sites, WiFi, tent sites, rentals, dump, laundry, groc, LP bottles, fire rings, firewood. **REC:** heated pool, Baddeck River: fishing, playground. Pets OK. Big rig sites, eco-friendly, 2015 rates: $36 to $48. May 14 to Oct 13.
AAA Approved
(902)295-2288 Lat: 46.090520, Lon: -60.852559
9584 Hwy 105, Baddeck, NS B0E 1B0
camp@baddeckcabottrailcampground.com
www.baddeckcabottrailcampground.com
See ad this page, 1409.

BRAS D'OR LAKES CAMPGROUND
Ratings: 9/10★/10 (Campground) From town, W 3 mi on TCH-105 (L) Between Exit 7 & 8, MM 80. **FAC:** Gravel rds. 88 Avail: 73 gravel, 15 grass, 8 pull-thrus (35 x 85), back-ins (32 x 65), 73 full hkups (30/50 amps), WiFi, tent sites, rentals, dump, laundry, groc, LP bottles, fire rings, firewood. **REC:** pool, Bras d'Or Lake: swim, fishing, playground. Pets OK. Big rig sites, eco-friendly, 2015 rates: $45 to $53. Disc: AAA, military. Jun 9 to Sep 30.
AAA Approved
(902)295-2329 Lat: 46.079114, Lon: -60.819352
box 595, 8885 Hwy 105, Baddeck, NS B0E 1B0
brasdorlakescamp@aol.com
www.brasdorlakescampground.com
See ad this page, 1409.

BEDFORD — D3 *Halifax*

DOLLAR LAKE (Prov Pk) From town, N 20 km on Hwy 102 to Hwy 212, E 18 km on Hwy 212, follow the signs (R). 2015 rates: $25.90. Jun 13 to Oct 13. (902)384-2770

BEN EOIN — B6 *Cape Breton*

BEN EOIN BEACH RV RESORT & CAMPGROUND **Ratings: 8.5/9★/8.5** (Campground) 2015 rates: $44 to $53. Jun 15 to Sep 15. (902)828-3100 6140 East Bay Hwy, Big Pond, NS B0A 1H0

BERWICK — C2 *Kings*

FOX MOUNTAIN CAMPING PARK **Ratings: 3.5/7/7** (Campground) 2015 rates: $32 to $36. May 15 to Oct 30. (902)847-3747 6128 Aylesford Road, Aylesford, NS B0P 1C0

THE PLANTATION CAMPGROUND **Ratings: 7.5/8.5★/8** (Campground) 2015 rates: $39 to $47. May 15 to Oct 15. (888)363-8882 rr 2-210 West Steadman Rd, Berwick, NS B0P 1E0

BLOMIDON — C3 *Kings*

BLOMIDON (Prov Pk) From town, NE 10 mi on Hwy 358 (R). 2015 rates: $25.90. May 16 to Sep 1. (902)582-7319

BRIDGETOWN — C2 *Annapolis*

VALLEY VIEW (Prov Pk) From Bridgetown, N 3 mi on Church St, at top of mtn (R). Pit toilets. 2015 rates: $19.40. Jun 13 to Sep 8. (902)665-2559

BRULE — B4 *Colchester*

SUNSET WATCH CAMPGROUND **Ratings: 7/8.5★/7.5** (Campground) 2015 rates: $33 to $36. May 15 to Oct 8. (902)657-0009 rr 1 242 Peninsula Pt Rd., Tatamagouche, NS B0K 1V0

CANSO — C5 *Guysborough*

SEABREEZE CAMPGROUND & COTTAGES **Ratings: 7/9★/8.5** (Campground) 2015 rates: $32 to $35. May 15 to Oct 15. (902)366-2352 230 Fox Island Main Rd., Canso, NS B0H 1H0

Say you saw it in our Guide!

CHETICAMP — A5 *Inverness*

CAPE BRETON HIGHLANDS NATIONAL PARK (CORNEY BROOK CAMPGROUND) (Natl Pk) From town: Go 8-3/4 km/5-1/2 mi N on the Cabot Trail. (No potable water). 2015 rates: $23.50. May 17 to Oct 15. (902)224-2306

CAPE BRETON HIGHLANDS/CHETICAMP CAMPGROUND (Natl Pk) From town, N 4 mi on Cabot Trail to park entrance, N 0.5 mi (L) Entrance fee required (reservations accepted for wheelchair-accessible sites only). 2015 rates: $25.50 to $35.30. May 17 to Oct 15. (902)224-2306

PLAGE SAINT PIERRE BEACH AND CAMPGROUND
Ratings: 8/9★/9.5 (Campground) From town, S 2.5 mi on Cabot Trail Rd to Cheticamp Island, W 2 mi (L). **FAC:** Gravel rds. (106 spaces). 61 Avail: 40 gravel, 21 grass, 16 pull-thrus (25 x 70), back-ins (25 x 45), some side by side hkups, 33 full hkups, 28 W, 28 E (30 amps), seasonal sites, WiFi $, tent sites, rentals, dump, laundry, groc, LP bottles, fire rings, firewood, controlled access. **REC:** Atlantic Ocean: swim, playground, rec open to public. Pets OK. Eco-friendly, 2015 rates: $33.50 to $35. May 14 to Oct 14.
(800)565-0000 Lat: 46.607783, Lon: -61.047811
635 Cheticamp Island Rd., Cheticamp, NS B0E 1H0
plagestpierre@ns.sympatico.ca
www.plagestpierrebeachandcampground.com
See ad this page.

CHURCH POINT — D1 *Yarmouth, Digby*

BELLE BAIE PARK **Ratings: 7.5/7.5★/8.5** (Campground) 2015 rates: $23 to $43. May 7 to Sep 30. (902)769-3160 rr 1, 2135 Hwy 1, Church Point, NS B0W 1M0

CHURCH POINT CAMPGROUND **Ratings: 4.5/5/7** (Campground) 2015 rates: $35. May 15 to Sep 30. (902)769-0070 164 Bonnenfant Rd., Church Point, NS B0W 1M0

COLDBROOK — C2 *Kings*

SHERWOOD FOREST CAMPING PARK **Ratings: 8/8.5★/8.5** (Campground) 2015 rates: $39 to $41. May 15 to Sep 30. (902)679-6632 6890 Hwy 1 Coldbrook, NS B4R 1B6

DARLINGS LAKE — E1 *Yarmouth*

LAKE BREEZE CAMPGROUND & COTTAGES **Ratings: 5.5/7/7.5** (Campground) 2015 rates: $31 to $34. May 15 to Oct 15. (902)649-2332 2560 Hwy 1 Yarmouth, NS B5A 4A5

DEERFIELD — E1 *Yarmouth*

ELLENWOOD LAKE (Prov Pk) From Yarmouth NE 12 mi on Rte 340 (L). 2015 rates: $25.90. May 1 to Sep 1. (902)761-2400

DELAPS COVE — D1 *Annapolis*

FUNDY TRAIL CAMPGROUND & COTTAGES **Ratings: 8/8.5★/8.5** (Campground) 2015 rates: $3 to $34. May 15 to Sep 30. (902)532-7711 rr 3, 6 Deplaps, Granville Ferry, NS B0S 1K0

DIGBY — D1 *Digby*

DIGBY CAMPGROUND & FUN PARK **Ratings: 6.5/7.5★/8** (Campground) 2015 rates: $30 to $38. May 15 to Sep 30. (902)245-1985 230 Victoria St, Digby, NS B0V 1A0

FUNDY SPRAY CAMPGROUND Ratings: 8/8★/8 (Campground) From Jct of Hwy 101 & Exit 25 (Rte 1), E 0.5 mi on Rte 1 (R). **FAC:** Gravel rds. (99 spaces). 19 Avail: 14 gravel, 5 grass, 1 pull-thrus (25 x 100), back-ins (28 x 37), some side by side hkups, 19 full hkups (30/50 amps), seasonal sites, tent sites, dump, laundry, groc, LP gas, fire rings, firewood, controlled access. **REC:** heated poo

Enjoy shopping over 10,000 RV products at great prices, at CampingWorld.com.

DIGBY (CONT)

FUNDY SPRAY CAMPGROUND (CONT)
playground. Pets OK. Eco-friendly, 2015 rates: $36 to $45. May 9 to Sep 29.
AAA Approved
(902)245-4884 Lat: 44.60362, Lon: -65.73365
Route1 100, Smiths Cove, NS B0S 1S0
fundyspray@tartannet.ns.ca

WHALE COVE CAMPGROUND Ratings: 6.5/9★/7 (Campground) Jct Hwy 101 towards Digby, take Middle Cross Rd to access Hwy 217, follow 217 to Whale Cove Rd turn right, campground is on top of hill. **FAC:** Dirt rds. 36 grass, back-ins (30 x 60), 18 W, 18 E (20/30 amps), WiFi Hotspot, tent sites, rentals, dump, laundry, groc, LP bottles, fire rings, firewood. **REC:** playground. Pets OK. Partial handicap access. Eco-friendly, 2015 rates: $35. May 1 to Oct 15.
Lat: 44.2611, Lon: -66.1028
50 Whale Cove, Digby, NS B0V 1E0
www.whalecovecampground.com

DUNVEGAN — B5 *Inverness*

MACLEOD'S BEACH CAMPSITE **Ratings: 8/8.5★/8** (Campground) 2015 rates: $34 to $38. Jun 7 to Oct 6. (902)258-2433 rr 1 1485 Broad Cove Marsh Rd, Inverness, NS B0E 1N0

EAST CHESTER — D3 *Lunenburg*

GRAVES ISLAND PARK (Prov Pk) From Chester, E 2 mi on Rte 3 to access rd, S 0.5 mi (R). 2015 rates: $25.90. May 16 to Oct 13. (902)275-4425

EAST LAKE AINSLIE — B5 *Inverness*

MACKINNON'S CAMPGROUNDS **Ratings: 8.5/10★/8.5** (Campground) 2015 rates: $28 to $39. May 1 to Oct 15. (902)756-2790 rr 1 2457 Hwy 395, Whycocomagh, NS B0E 3M0

ENGLISHTOWN — B6 *Victoria*

ENGLISHTOWN RIDGE CAMPGROUND Ratings: 8/10★/8 (Campground) From Jct of TCH-105 & Exit 12 (Rte 312), NE 3 mi on Rte 312 (R). **FAC:** Gravel rds. (73 spaces). Avail: 45 grass, 6 pull-thrus (30 x 50), back-ins (30 x 60), some side by side hkups, 30 full hkups, 8 W, 8 E (15/30 amps), seasonal sites, WiFi, tent sites, rentals, showers $, laundry, groc, LP bottles, fire rings, firewood, controlled access. **REC:** pool, playground. Pets OK. Partial handicap access. Eco-friendly, 2015 rates: $31 to $34. May 18 to Oct 15.
(902)929-2598 Lat: 46.27686, Lon: -60.54339
938 Englishtown Rd, Englishtown, NS B0C 1H0
englishtownridge@ns.sympatico.ca
www.englishtown_ridge.com

FALLS LAKE WEST — C3 *Hants*

FALLS LAKE RECREATIONAL FACILITY (Public) From Hwy 101 (exit 5): Go 24.1 km/15 mi on Hwy 14 W, then R on New Ross Rd, 3.2 km/2 mi (watch for signs), then R 3.2 km/2 mi on Pioneer (dirt) Rd. From Hwy 103 (exit 8): Go N 30 km/17 mi on Hwy 14, then L on New Ross Rd 3.2 km, then R on Pioneer Rd. 2015 rates: $20 to $35. May 17 to Dec 1. (877)325-5253

FIVE ISLANDS — C3 *Colchester*

DIAMOND SHORES CAMPGROUND **Ratings: 4.5/5.5/5.5** (Campground) 2015 rates: $25 to $35. May 21 to Sep 30. (902)254-2903 538 Hwy #2, Five Islands, NS B0M 1N0

FIVE ISLAND OCEAN RESORT **Ratings: 9/9★/9** (RV Resort) 2015 rates: $30 to $50. May 15 to Oct 15. (902)254-2824 482 Hwy 2, Lower Five Islands, NS B0M 1N0

FIVE ISLANDS PARK (Prov Pk) From Jct of TCH 104 & Hwy 2, W 30 mi on Hwy 2 to Five Islands Rd, SE 2 mi (L). 2015 rates: $25.90. Jun 13 to Oct 13. (902)254-2980

Don't camp without it ... Our 2016 listings are your key to travel satisfaction.

GLEN MARGARET — D3 *Halifax*

WAYSIDE R.V. PARK **Ratings: 6.5/5/6.5** (Campground) 2015 rates: $20 to $35. Apr 1 to Nov 30. (902)823-2547 10295 Peggy's Cove Rd, Glen Margaret, NS B3Z 3H1

GRAND LAKE — C3 *Halifax*

LAURIE (Prov Pk) From town, N on Hwy 102 to exit 5 (Waverley Rd), N 13 km on Waverley Rd to park entrance (L). Closed for renovations. Will re-open in 2011. Pit toilets. 2015 rates: $25.90. Jun 13 to Sep 8. (902)861-1623

GRAND PRE — C3 *Hants*

LAND OF EVANGELINE FAMILY CAMPING RESORT LTD **Ratings: 8/9.5★/9** (Campground) 2015 rates: $33 to $46. May 1 to Oct 1. (902)542-5309 84 Evangeline Beach Rd, Grand Pre, NS B4P 1W4

GUYSBOROUGH — C5 *Guysborough*

BOYLSTON (Prov Pk) From Guysborough, E 2 mi Hwy 16 (L). Pit toilets. 2015 rates: $19.40. Jun 13 to Sep 8. (902)533-3326

HALIFAX — D3 *Halifax*

HALIFAX WEST KOA
Ratings: 8.5/10★/10 (Campground) From Jct of Hwy 101 & Exit 3 (Rte 1), SE 1.25 mi on Rte 1 (R). **FAC:** Gravel rds. 91 Avail: 62 gravel, 29 grass, 15 pull-thrus (30 x 75), back-ins (33 x 63), 31 full hkups, 57 W, 56 E (30/50 amps), WiFi, tent sites, rentals, dump, laundry, groc, LP bottles, fire rings, firewood, controlled access. **REC:** pool, Sackville River: swim, fishing, playground. Pet restrict(B). Partial handicap access. Big rig sites, eco-friendly, 2015 rates: $36 to $47. Disc: AAA. May 1 to Oct 28.
(888)562-4705 Lat: 44.831822, Lon: -63.784158
3070 Sackville Dr., Upper Sackville, NS B4E 3C9
halifaxwestkoa@gmail.com
www.halifaxwestkoa.com
See ad this page.

SHUBIE CAMPGROUND **Ratings: 7.5/8.5★/8.5** (Campground) 2015 rates: $43.50 to $52. May 18 to Oct 13. (800)440-8450 30 John Brenton Dr., Dartmouth, NS B2X 2V5

WOODHAVEN RV PARK OF HALIFAX **Ratings: 8/7/9** (RV Park) 2015 rates: $38 to $48. May 1 to Oct 15. (902)835-2271 1757 Hammonds Plains Rd, Halifax, NS B4B 1P5

HAVRE BOUCHER — B5 *Antigonish*

HYCLASS OCEAN CAMPGROUND
Ratings: 7/8.5★/10 (Campground) Jct Hwy 104 Exit 37 (Monastery) follow signs (L) From Cape Breton Jct Hwy 104 Exit 38 follow signs. **FAC:** Gravel rds. (75 spaces). 60 Avail: 35 gravel, 25 grass, 9 pull-thrus (22 x 65), back-ins (30 x 45), 10 full hkups, 25 W, 25 E (15/30 amps), seasonal sites, WiFi, tent sites, rentals, showers $, dump, laundry, groc, LP bottles, fire rings, firewood, controlled access. **REC:** Atlantic Ocean: swim, fishing, playground. Pets OK. Eco-friendly, 2015 rates: $37to $44. May 15 to Sep 30.
(866)892-3117 Lat: 45.645599, Lon: -61.579412
PO Box 107 11373 Hwy 4, Havre Boucher, NS B0H 1P0
info@hyclass-campground.com
www.hyclass-campground.com
See ad this page.

HUBBARDS — D3 *Halifax, Lunenburg*

HUBBARDS BEACH CAMPGROUND & COTTAGES
Ratings: 8/8.5★/8.5 (Campground) From Jct of Rte 103 & exit 6 (Rte 3), S 0.25 mi on Access Rd to Rte 3, E 1.5 mi to Shankel Rd/Hubbards sign, S 100 ft to Shore Club Rd, W 0.5 mi (L). **FAC:** Paved/gravel rds. (129 spaces). 35 Avail: 26 gravel, 9 grass, 2 pull-thrus (22 x 50), back-ins (22 x 63), 33 full hkups (15/30 amps), seasonal sites, WiFi, tent sites, rentals, showers $, dump, laundry, fire rings, firewood, restaurant, controlled access. **REC:** St. Margarets Bay: swim, playground. Pets OK. Eco-friendly, 2015 rates: $38 to $45. May 15 to Oct 1.
(902)857-9460 Lat: 44.633764, Lon: -64.056515
226 Shore Club Rd, Hubbards, NS B0J 1T0
inquiries@hubbardsbeach.com
www.hubbardsbeach.com
See ad this page.

HUNT'S POINT — E2 *Queens*

FISHERMAN'S COVE RV & CAMPGROUND Ratings: 7.5/8.5★/7.5 (Campground) From Jct of Hwy 103 & exit 20 (Rte 3), E 3.4 mi on Rte 3 (L). **FAC:** Gravel rds. (19 spaces). Avail: 14 gravel, 7 pull-thrus (45 x 40), back-ins (30 x 40), 14 full hkups (30 amps), seasonal sites, WiFi, tent sites, dump, mobile sewer, laundry, LP bottles, fire rings, firewood. **REC:** Atlantic Ocean: swim, playground. Pets OK. Partial handicap access. Eco-friendly, 2015 rates: $38 to $40. May 15 to Oct 31.
(902)683-2772 Lat: 43.95478, Lon: -64.76667
6718 #3 Hwy, Hunts Point, NS B0T 1G0
dvhuskins@eastlink.ca
www.fishermanscoverv.netfirms.com

INDIAN HARBOUR — D3 *Halifax*

KING NEPTUNE CAMPGROUND **Ratings: 4/8/7.5** (Campground) 2015 rates: $25 to $31. Jun 1 to Sep 30. (902)823-2582 8536 Peggy's Cove Rd, Indian Harbour, NS B3Z 3P4

INGONISH BEACH — A6 *Victoria*

CAPE BRETON HIGHLANDS/BROAD COVE (Natl Pk) From E park entrance, N 7 mi on Cabot Trail (R) Entrance fee required (reservations accepted for wheelchair-accessible sites only). 2015 rates: $25.50 to $35.30. May 17 to Oct 15. (902)224-2306

CAPE BRETON HIGHLANDS/INGONISH (Natl Pk) From town, N 4 mi on Cabot Trail to E park entrance, N 0.5 mi (L) Entrance fee. 2015 rates: $25.50. May 17 to Oct 15. (902)224-3406

INVERNESS — B5 *Victoria*

INVERNESS BEACH VILLAGE **Ratings: 6.5/7.5★/7.5** (Campground) 2015 rates: $33 to $37. Jun 7 to Oct 20. (902)258-2653 PO Box 617 50 Beach Village Rd., Inverness, NS B0E 1N0

KENTVILLE — C2 *Kings*

HIGHBURY GARDENS FAMILY CAMPING **Ratings: 8/9.5★/9.5** (Campground) 2015 rates: $41 to $47. May 15 to Oct 15. (902)678-8011 121 New Canaan Rd, Kentville, NS B4N 4K1

SOUTH MOUNTAIN PARK FAMILY CAMPING & RV RESORT **Ratings: 8.5/9★/8.5** (Campground) 2015 rates: $45 to $47. May 15 to Oct 15. (866)860-6092 3022 Hwy 12, Kentville, NS B4N 3X9

KINGSTON — C2 *Kings*

YOGI BEAR'S JELLYSTONE PARK CAMP RESORT **Ratings: 9/10★/8** (Campground) 2015 rates: $45 to $55. May 9 to Sep 30. (888)225-7773 rr 1-43 Boo Boo Blvd, Kingston, NS B0P 1R0

LAHAVE — D3 *Lunenburg*

RISSER'S BEACH (Prov Pk) From Jct of Hwy 103 & exit 15, exit to town, E 1 mi on Rte 331 (R). 2015 rates: $25.90 to $34.55. May 16 to Oct 13. (902)688-2034

LINWOOD — B5 *Antigonish*

LINWOOD HARBOUR CAMPGROUND
Ratings: 8/9.5★/9.5 (Campground) From Jct of TCH-104 & exit 37 (Rte 4), E 3.25 mi on Rte 4 (L) or; From Cape Breton, exit 38 (Rte 4) W 4.5 mi on Rte 4. **FAC:** Gravel rds. (41 spaces). 38 Avail: 33 gravel, 5 grass, 13 pull-thrus (35 x 80), back-ins (35 x 50), 33 full hkups (30/50 amps), seasonal sites, WiFi, tent sites, showers $, dump, laundry, groc, LP bottles, fire rings, firewood. **REC:** St Georges Bay: fishing, playground. Pets OK. Partial

Like Us on Facebook.

NS

LINWOOD (CONT)

LINWOOD HARBOUR (CONT)
handicap access. Big rig sites, eco-friendly, 2015 rates: $29 to $39. May 22 to Sep 30.
(866)661-9145 Lat: 45.63643, Lon: -61.58495
11089 Hwy 4, Linwood, NS B0H 1P0
infolinwoodcampground@bellaliant.net
www.linwoodcampground.com
See ad this page.

LOUIS HEAD — E2 *Shelburne*

← LOUIS HEAD BEACH CAMPGROUND **Ratings: 4/7.5/7.5** (Campground) 2015 rates: $16 to $22. May 30 to Sep 30. (902)656-3129 1668 Louis Head Rd, Sable River, NS B0T 1L0

LOUISBOURG — B6 *Cape Breton*

← LAKEVIEW TREASURES CAMPGROUND & RV PARK **Ratings: 7.5/7.5/7.5** (Campground) 2015 rates: $31 to $37. May 15 to Oct 15. (902)733-2058 5785 Louisbourg Hwy, Catalone, NS B1C 2G4

↑ LOUISBOURG MOTORHOME RV PARK & CAMPGROUND **Ratings: 5/9★/8** (Campground) 2015 rates: $29 to $40. Jun 15 to Oct 15. (866)733-3631 24 Harbourfront Crescent, Louisbourg, NS B1C 1C4

← RIVERDALE RV PARK **Ratings: 5/9★/7.5** (RV Park) 2015 rates: $20 to $28. May 15 to Oct 15. (902)733-2531 9 Riverdale St., Louisbourg, NS B1C 2H9

LOWER BARNEY'S RIVER — B4 *Pictou*

← CRANBERRY CAMPGROUND **Ratings: 7.5/8.5★/8** (Campground) 2015 rates: $32 to $36. May 14 to Oct 9. (902)926-2571 135 Weir Rd, Merigomish, NS B0K 1G0

LUNENBURG — D3 *Lunenburg*

↗ **LUNENBURG BOARD OF TRADE CAMPGROUND Ratings: 4.5/8★/6.5** (Campground) From Jct of Hwy 103 & Exit 11 (Rte 324), S 6 mi on Rte 324, follow visitors information signs 1.5 mi (R). **FAC:** All weather rds. 55 Avail: 55 all weather, 2 pull-thrus (30 x 70), back-ins (30 x 50), mostly side by side hkups, 22 full hkups, 23 W, 23 E (30 amps), WiFi, tent sites, dump. Pets OK. Eco-friendly, 2015 rates: $40 to $42. May 1 to Oct 31.
AAA Approved
(902)634-8100 Lat: 44.377362, Lon: -64.303660
PO Box1300, 11 Blockhouse Hill Rd., Lunenburg, NS B0J 2C0
lbt@ns.aliantzinc.ca
www.explorelunenburg.ca

LYDGATE — E2 *Shelburne*

← LOCKEPORT COTTAGES & CAMPGROUND **Ratings: 7.5/7/7.5** (Campground) 2015 rates: $35 to $50. May 15 to Sep 30. (866)656-2876 3318 Hwy 3 PO Box 515, Lydgate, NS B0T 1L0

MAHONE BAY — D3 *Lunenburg*

MAHONE BAY See also Martins River.

MAITLAND — C3 *Hants*

↓ MAITLAND FAMILY CAMPGROUND **Ratings: 6/5.5/7.5** (Campground) 2015 rates: $25 to $35. May 13 to Oct 8. (902)261-2267 520 Cedar Rd, Maitland, NS B0N 1T0

MAITLAND BRIDGE — D2 *Annapolis*

↑ KEJIMKUJIK/JEREMYS BAY (Natl Pk) From Annapolis Royal, S 28.5 mi on Rte 8, near Maitland Bridge (R); or From Liverpool, N 45 mi on Rte 8, near Maitland Bridge (L). 2015 rates: $22 to $29.40. May 16 to Oct 13. (902)682-2772

We make finding the perfect campground easier. Just use the "Find-it-Fast" index in the back of the Guide. It's a complete, state-by-state, alphabetical listing of our private and public park listings.

MARTIN'S RIVER — D3 *Lunenburg*

↑ **RAYPORT CAMPGROUND**
Ratings: 8.5/10★/9.5 (Campground) From Jct of Hwy 103 & Exit 10 (Rte 3), S. 0.5 mi on access rd to Rte 3, E 2 mi, Follow signs (L) Note: Maximum length 75 ft. **FAC:** Gravel rds. (86 spaces). Avail: 26 gravel, 4 pull-thrus (40 x 75), back-ins (40 x 45), 21 W, 21 E (30/50 amps), seasonal sites, cable, WiFi, tent sites, dump, mobile sewer, laundry, groc, LP bottles, fire rings, firewood, controlled access. **REC:** pool, Martin's River: swim, fishing, playground. Pets OK. Eco-friendly, 2015 rates: $34 to $38. May 10 to Oct 15.
AAA Approved
(902)627-2678 Lat: 44.48876, Lon: -64.34227
165 Shingle Mill Rd, Martin's River, NS B0J 2E0
rayport@hotmail.com
www.rayport.ca
See ad this page, 1409.

MIDDLETON — C2 *Annapolis*

→ ORCHARD QUEEN MOTEL & CAMPGROUND **Ratings: 8.5/8.5★/8** (Campground) 2015 rates: $30 to $40. May 1 to Oct 15. (902)825-4801 PO Box 249-425 Main St, Middleton, NS B0S 1P0

→ VIDITO FAMILY CAMPGROUND & COTTAGES **Ratings: 7/5.5/7.5** (Campground) 2015 rates: $25 to $30. May 1 to Oct 30. (902)825-4380 rr 1, 13736 Hwy 1, Middleton, NS B0P 1W0

MILFORD — D2 *Annapolis*

↙ RAVEN HAVEN BEACHSIDE FAMILY PARK (CITY TOWN) (Public) From jct Hwy 101 (exit 22) & Rt 8: Go 20 km/12 mi S on Rt 8, then 5 km/3 mi W on Virginia Rd. to West Springhill. 2015 rates: $20 to $24. (902)532-7320

MURPHY'S COVE — D4 *Halifax*

→ MURPHY'S CAMPING ON THE OCEAN **Ratings: 7.5/7.5★/7.5** (Campground) 2015 rates: $27 to $39. May 15 to Oct 15. (902)772-2700 308 Murphy's Rd., Tangier, NS B0J 3H0

N.E. MARGAREE — B5 *Inverness*

↓ **THE LAKES CAMPGROUND Ratings: 7/8.5★/8** (Campground) From jct Hwy 19 & Cabot Trail: Go 16 km/10 mi S on Cabot Trail. **FAC:** Gravel rds. (64 spaces). Avail: 35 grass, back-ins (32 x 60), 10 full hkups, 18 W, 18 E (15/30 amps), seasonal sites, WiFi Hotspot, tent sites, rentals, showers $, dump, laundry, groc, LP bottles, fire rings, firewood, restaurant. **REC:** Lake O'Law: swim, fishing, playground. Pets OK. Eco-friendly, 2015 rates: $26 to $29. Disc: military. May 15 to Oct 20.
(902)248-2360 Lat: 46.281279, Lon: -60.964573
4932 Cabot Trail, North East Margaree, NS B0E 2H0
a.taylor@ns.sympatico.ca
www.thelakesresort.com

NINE MILE RIVER — C3 *Hants*

↙ **RENFREW CAMPGROUND Ratings: 7.5/7.5/7** (Campground) From jct Hwy 214 & Hwy 14: Go 3.5 km/2-1/3 mi W on Hwy 14, then 2 km/1-1/3 mi SW on Renfrew Road. **FAC:** Gravel rds. (210 spaces). Avail: 148 gravel, 9 pull-thrus (40 x 50), back-ins (40 x 45), some side by side hkups, 96 full hkups, 52 W, 52 E (30 amps), seasonal sites, WiFi, tent sites, showers $, dump, laundry, groc, LP bottles, fire rings, firewood. **REC:** pool, playground. Pets OK. Partial handicap access. Eco-friendly, 2015 rates: $28.50 to $40,25. May 16 to Oct 14.
(902)883-1681 Lat: 45.02575, Lon: -63.59100
824 Renfrew Road, Nine Mile River, NS B2S 2W5

← RIVERLAND CAMPGROUND **Ratings: 7.5/8★/7** (Campground) 2015 rates: $46. May 1 to Sep 30. (902)883-7115 419 Cp Thompson Rd, Nine Mile River, NS B2S 2X8

NORTH SYDNEY — B6 *Cape Breton*

↑ **ARM OF GOLD CAMPGROUND Ratings: 8/10★/9** (Campground) From Jct of TCH-105 & Exit 18 (Georges River Rd), SW 0.1 mi on Georges River Rd (R). **FAC:** Gravel rds. 140 grass, 120 pull-thrus (28 x 75), back-ins (30 x 60), some side by side hkups, 120 full hkups (30/50 amps), WiFi, tent sites, rentals, showers $, dump, laundry, fire rings, firewood. **REC:** whirlpool, Bras d'Or Lake: playground. Pets OK. Partial handicap access. Big rig sites, eco-friendly, 2015 rates: $32 to $48. Jun 1 to Oct 1.
(866)736-6516 Lat: 46.250056, Lon: -60.289648
24 Church Rd., Little Bras D'or, NS B1Y 2Y2
camp@armofgoldcamp.com
www.armofgoldcamp.com

← **NORTH SYDNEY CABOT TRAIL KOA Ratings: 7.5/9.5★/8** (Campground) E-bnd: From Bras D'Or Bridge, W 0.5 mi on TCH-105 to New Harris Rd, SE 1200 ft (R). **FAC:** Gravel/dirt rds. (145 spaces). Avail: 135 gravel, 38 pull-thrus (25 x 60), back-ins (25 x 40), some side by side hkups, 106 full hkups, 29 W, 29 E (30/50 amps), seasonal sites, WiFi, tent sites, rentals, dump, laundry, groc, LP gas, fire rings, firewood. **REC:** Bras d'Or Lake: swim, playground. Pets OK. Partial handicap access. Eco-friendly, 2015 rates: $35 to $70. Disc: AAA. May 15 to Oct 15.
(902)674-2145 Lat: 46.23994, Lon: -60.49986
rr 1, 3779 New Harris Rd., New Harris, NS B1X 1T1
koansct@koansct.com
www.koansct.com

OAKHILL — D2 *Luneburg*

↗ OAKHILL PINES CAMPGROUND **Ratings: 8/8★/8.5** (Campground) 2015 rates: $30 to $35. May 15 to Oct 1. (902)543-2885 rr 7, 388 Oakhill Rd, Bridgewater, NS B4V 3J5

PARKERS COVE — C2 *Annapolis*

→ **COVE OCEANFRONT CAMPGROUND Ratings: 8.5/9.5★/9.5** (Campground) E-bnd: From Jct of Hwy 101 & Exit 22 (Rtes 8 & 1), N 3.75 mi on Rte 8 to Rte 1, E 2 mi to Parker Mountain Rd, N 4 mi to Shore Rd, W 400 ft (R). **FAC:** Gravel rds. 62 grass, 6 pull-thrus (30 x 60), back-ins (30 x 40), some side by side hkups, 62 full hkups (30 amps), WiFi, tent sites, showers $, laundry, LP bottles, fire rings, firewood, controlled access. **REC:** heated pool, Bay of Fundy: swim, fishing, playground. Pet restrict(Q). Eco-friendly, 2015 rates: $40 to $100. May 8 to Oct 20.
AAA Approved
(902)532-5166 Lat: 44.81199, Lon: -65.53310
4405 Shore Rd. West, Parkers Cove, NS B0S 1K0
stay@oceanfront-camping.com
www.oceanfront-camping.com

PARRSBORO — C3 *Cumberland*

↖ GLOOSCAP CAMPGROUND (Public) From Jct of TCH-104 & Hwy 2 (in Glenholme), W 35 mi on Hwy 2 to Parrsboro Tourist Bureau, continue on Hwy 2 to War Memorial, left 3.5 mi (R). 2015 rates: $25 to $30. May 16 to Sep 30. (902)254-2529

PEGGY'S COVE — D3 *Halifax*

PEGGY'S COVE See also Glen Margaret.

PICTOU — B4 *Pictou*

↙ BIRCHWOOD CAMPGROUND & CABINS **Ratings: 7/8.5/8.5** (Campground) 2015 rates: $32 to $35. May 1 to Oct 15. (902)485-8565 2521 Hwy 376, Pictou, NS B0K 1H0

→ CARIBOU & MUNROES ISLAND (PROV PARK) (Prov Pk) From Jct TCH-106 & Pictou Rotary, P.E.I. Ferry Rd NE 4 mi to Three Brooks Rd 1.5 mi (L). 2015 rates: $25.90. Jun 13 to Oct 13. (902)485-6134

↑ **HARBOUR LIGHT TRAILER COURT & CAMPGROUND**
Ratings: 7.5/7/7.5 (Campground) From Pictou Rotary (Pictou exit): Go 1.5 km/1 mi E through town, then E fork at Y in center of Pictou, then follow signs 4.5 km/2-3/4 mi beyond Golf Course. **FAC:** Gravel rds. (200 spaces). Avail: 80 grass, 14 pull-thrus (30 x 50), back-ins (25 x 30), some side by side hkups, 60 full hkups, 20 W, 20 E (30/50 amps) seasonal sites, WiFi, dump, laundry, groc, LP gas, fire rings, firewood. **REC:** pool, Northumberland Strait: swim, fishing, playground. Pets OK. No tents.

PICTOU (CONT)

HARBOUR LIGHT TRAILER COURT (CONT)
Eco-friendly, 2015 rates: $33 to $38. May 25 to Oct 15.
(902)485-5733 Lat: 45.694888, Lon: -62.667401
Brae Shore Rr 1 2881-Three Brooks Rd, Pictou, NS B0K 1H0
harbour.light@ns.sympatico.ca
See ad opposite page.

PORT JOLI — E2 *Queens*

⬅ THOMAS RADDALL PROVINCIAL PARK (Prov Pk) From Jct of Hwy 103 & East Port L'Hebert Rd to Thomas Raddall Rd (park entrance), E 2 mi (E). 2015 rates: $25.90. May 16 to Oct 13. (902)683-2664

PORTERS LAKE — D3 *Halifax*

⬅ PORTER'S LAKE (Prov Pk) From Jct of Hwy 107 & exit 19, 3 km on Porters Lake Rd (L). 2015 rates: $25.90. May 16 to Oct 13. (902)827-2250

PUGWASH — B3 *Colchester*

➡ GULF SHORE CAMPING PARK (Campground) (Phone Update) 2015 rates: $22 to $33. Jun 15 to Sep 15. (902)243-2489 rr 4 2167 Gulf Shore Rd, Pugwash, NS B0K 1L0

RAWDON GOLD MINES — C3 *Hants*

➡ RGM CAMPING PARK **Ratings: 6.5/8★/8** (RV Park) 2015 rates: $30 to $46. May 15 to Oct 15. (902)632-2050 2980 Rt 14, Rr 1, Upper Rawdon, NS B0N 2N0

RIVERPORT — D3 *Lunenburg*

⬇ **THE OVENS NATURAL PARK Ratings: 6.5/5.5/6** (Campground) From Jct of Hwy 103 & Exit 11 (Rte 324), S 6 mi on Rte 324 to Rte 332, W 6.5 mi to Feltzen South Rd, S 1.5 mi to park rd, W 1 mi (E). **FAC:** Paved/gravel rds. (200 spaces). Avail: 194 grass, back-ins (22 x 60), 32 full hkups, 30 W, 30 E (30 amps), seasonal sites, tent sites, rentals, dump, firewood, restaurant, controlled access. **REC:** pool, Atlantic Ocean: swim, playground. Pets OK. Partial handicap access. 2015 rates: $43 to $60. May 18 to Sep 30.
AAA Approved
(902)766-4621 Lat: 44.39938, Lon: -64.51268
326 Feltsen South Rd, Riverport, NS B0J 2W0
ovenspark@ns.sympatico.ca
www.ovenspark.com

SEAFOAM — B4 *Pictou*

➡ SEAFOAM CAMPGROUND **Ratings: 7.5/8.5★/7.5** (Campground) 2015 rates: $38 to $39. May 15 to Sep 30. (902)351-3122 58 Harris Ave., Truro, NS B2N 3N2

SHEET HARBOUR — C4 *Buysborough*

↗ EAST RIVER LODGE CAMPGROUND & TRAILER PARK **Ratings: 6/5.5/7.5** (Campground) 2015 rates: $25 to $35. May 1 to Oct 30. (902)885-2057 200 Pool Rd, Sheet Harbour, NS B0J 3B0

SHELBURNE — E2 *Shelburne*

↗ THE ISLANDS (Prov Pk) From Shelbourne, W 3 mi on Rte 3 (L). 2015 rates: $25.90. Jun 13 to Oct 13. (902)875-4304

SHERBROOKE — C4 *Guysborough*

⬅ NIMROD'S CAMPGROUND **Ratings: 5.5/6.5/7** (Campground) 2015 rates: $25 to $32. May 15 to Oct 15. (902)522-2441 159 Rte 211, Sherbrooke, NS B0J 3C0

⬇ RIVERSIDE CAMPGROUNDS **Ratings: 6/8/7.5** (Campground) 2015 rates: $22 to $30. May 15 to Oct 31. (902)522-2913 3987 Sonora Rd, Sherbrooke, NS B0J 3C0

SHUBENACADIE — C3 *Colchester, Hants*

↘ WHISPERING WINDS FAMILY CAMPING **Ratings: 7.5/5.5/7** (Campground) 2015 rates: $33 to $36. May 2 to Oct 15. (902)758-2177 rr 4, Shubenacadie, NS B0N 2H0

⬇ WILD NATURE CAMPING GROUND **Ratings: 3/7.5★/8.5** (Campground) 2015 rates: $22 to $30. May 30 to Sep 30. (902)758-1631 20961 Hwy 2, Shubenacadie, NS B0N 2H0

SOUTH HARBOUR — A6 *Victoria*

⬇ HIDEAWAY CAMPGROUND AND OYSTER MARKET (Campground) (Phone Update) 2015 rates: $30 to $34. May 15 to Oct 15. (902)383-2116 401 Shore Rd., Dingwall, NS B0C 1G0

SOUTH LAKE AINSLIE — B5 *Inverness*

⬆ AINSLIE VILLAGE CAMPGROUND **Ratings: 6/7.5/7.5** (Campground) 2015 rates: $22 to $27. May 15 to Sep 30. (902)756-2255 1321 Lake Ainslie, Whycocomagh, NS B0E 3M0

SPENCER'S ISLAND — C2 *Colchester*

⬇ **THE OLD SHIPYARD BEACH CAMPGROUND Ratings: 6/8★/7.5** (Campground) From Jct of Rtes 2 & 209, W 23 mi on Rte 209 to Spencer Beach Rd, SW 1 mi (L). **FAC:** Gravel rds. (30 spaces). Avail: 24 gravel, back-ins (34 x 40), 13 full hkups, 11 W, 11 E (30 amps), seasonal sites, WiFi, tent sites, rentals, showers $, laundry, fire rings, firewood, restaurant. **REC:** Bay of Fundy: swim, fishing. Pets OK. Eco-friendly, 2015 rates: $30 to $32. Jun 1 to Oct 1.
(902)392-2487 Lat: 45.35483, Lon: -64.71037
774 Beach Rd, Spencer's Island, NS B0M 1S0
noreenbob2000@yahoo.com
http://www.oldshipyardbeachcampground.com

SPRY BAY — D4 *Halifax*

➡ SPRYBAY CAMPGROUND & CABINS **Ratings: 7/8.5★/8** (Campground) 2015 rates: $30 to $45. May 15 to Oct 30. (902)772-2554 19867 Hwy 7, Tangier, NS B0J 3H0

ST ANN'S BAY — B6 *Victoria*

⬆ JOYFULL JOURNEYS CAMPARK (Campground) (Phone Update) 2015 rates: $33 to $36. May 15 to Oct 15. (866)791-9960 1762 Hwy 312, Englishtown, NS B0C 1H0

ST PETERS — B5 *Richmond*

BATTERY PROVINCIAL PARK (Prov Pk) From town: Go 3/4 km/1/2 mi E on Hwy 4. 2015 rates: $25.90. Jun 13 to Sep 8. (902)535-3094

SYDNEY — B6 *Cape Breton*

⬅ MIRA RIVER PROVINCIAL PARK (Prov Pk) From Jct of Hwy 125 & Exit 8 (Rte 22), S 10 mi on Rte 22 to Brickyard Rd, E 1.2 mi (L). 2015 rates: $25.90. Jun 6 to Sep 8. (902)563-3373

TRURO — C3 *Colchester*

➡ ELM RIVER RV PARK LTD **Ratings: 9/10★/10** (Campground) 2015 rates: $39 to $42. May 15 to Oct 15. (888)356-4356 rr 1, 85 Elm River Parkway, Debert, NS B0M 1G0

⬅ HIDDEN HILLTOP CAMPGROUND **Ratings: 8/6/8** (Campground) 2015 rates: $31 to $38. May 9 to Oct 15. (866)662-3391 PO Box 1131, 2600 Hwy 4, Truro, NS B2N 5H1

⬇ **SCOTIA PINE CAMPGROUND**
Ratings: 9/10★/9.5 (Campground) From Jct of Hwy 102 & Exit 12 (Rte 289), E 0.6 mi on Rte 289 to Rte 2, N 2.4 mi (R). **FAC:** Paved/gravel rds. (170 spaces). Avail: 86 grass, 42 pull-thrus (25 x 65), back-ins (25 x 45), mostly side by side hkups, 40 full hkups, 8 W, 8 E (30/50 amps), seasonal sites, WiFi, tent sites, showers $, dump, laundry, LP bottles, fire rings, firewood, controlled access. **REC:** pool, playground. Pets OK. Partial handicap access. Big rig sites, eco-friendly, 2015 rates: $32 to $43. May 13 to Oct 14.
(877)893-3666 Lat: 45.286415, Lon: -63.289395
1911 Hwy 2, Brookfield, NS B0N 1C0
info@scotiapine.ca
www.scotiapine.ca
See ad this page.

UPPER LAKEVILLE — D4 *Halifax*

⬅ E AND F WEBBER'S LAKESIDE PARK **Ratings: 7.5/8★/8** (Campground) From Dartmouth, E 35 mi on Rte 7 to Upper Lakeville Rd, N 2.5 mi (E). **FAC:** Gravel rds. (52 spaces). Avail: 18 gravel, 6 pull-thrus (40 x 45), back-ins (30 x 45), 15 full hkups, 3 W, 3 E (15/30 amps), seasonal sites, WiFi, tent sites, rentals, dump, laundry, groc, LP bottles, fire rings, firewood, controlled access. **REC:** Lake Charlotte: swim, fishing, marina, playground. Pets OK. Partial handicap access. 2015 rates: $30 to $45. May 2 to Oct 9.
AAA Approved
(800)589-2282 Lat: 44.79907, Lon: -62.96390
738 Upper Lakeville Rd, Lake Charlotte, NS B0J 1W0
info@webberslakesideresort.com
www.webberslakesideresort.com

URBANIA — C3 *Hants*

⬆ WIDE OPEN WILDERNESS FAMILY CAMPGROUND **Ratings: 7.5/8★/9** (Campground) 2015 rates: $32.50 to $39.50. May 15 to Oct 15. (902)261-2228 11129 Hwy 215, Shubenacadie, NS B0N 2H0

WHYCOCOMAGH — B5 *Inverness*

⬆ GLENVIEW CAMPGROUND **Ratings: 8/8★/8** (Campground) 2015 rates: $25 to $35. May 15 to Oct 15. (902)756-3198 PO Box 12 40 Hwy 252, Whycocomagh, NS B0E 3M0

⬆ WHYCOCOMAGH (Prov Pk) From Whycocomagh, E 0.25 mi on Hwy 105 (L). 2015 rates: $25.90 to $34.55. Jun 13 to Oct 20. (902)756-2448

WINDSOR — C3 *Hants*

➡ SMILEY'S PARK (Prov Pk) From town, E 9 mi on Rte 14 to MacKay Rd, E 0.2 mi (E). 2015 rates: $25.90. Jun 13 to Sep 22. (902)757-3131

YARMOUTH — E1 *Yarmouth*

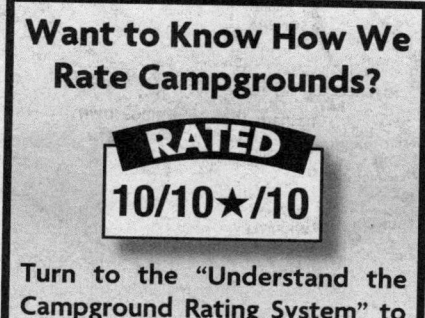

➡ **CAMPER'S HAVEN CAMPGROUND** (Campground) (Phone Update) From Jct of Hwys 103 & 101 & Old Rte 3 (in Yarmouth), W 0.5 mi on Hwy 101 to Rte 3, E 3.6 mi (L). **FAC:** Gravel rds. (215 spaces). 144 Avail: 72 gravel, 72 grass, 17 pull-thrus (40 x 80), back-ins (25 x 45), some side by side hkups, 32 full hkups, 75 W, 75 E (30/50 amps), seasonal sites, WiFi, tent sites, rentals, dump, laundry, groc, LP bottles, fire rings, firewood. **REC:** heated pool, whirlpool, Trefry's Lake: swim, fishing, golf, playground. Pets OK. Partial handicap access. Big rig sites, eco-friendly, 2015 rates: $25 to $45. May 16 to Sep 28.
AAA Approved
(902)742-4848 Lat: 43.829041, Lon: -66.038634
9700 Hwy 3, Arcadia, NS B5A 5J8
camping@campershavencampground.com
www.campershavencampground.com

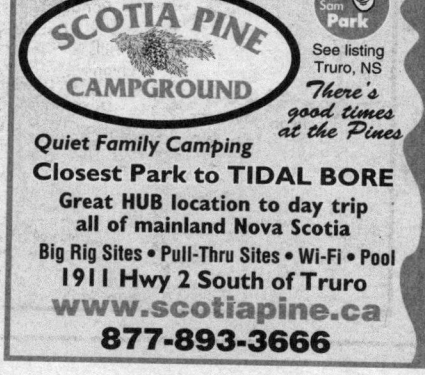

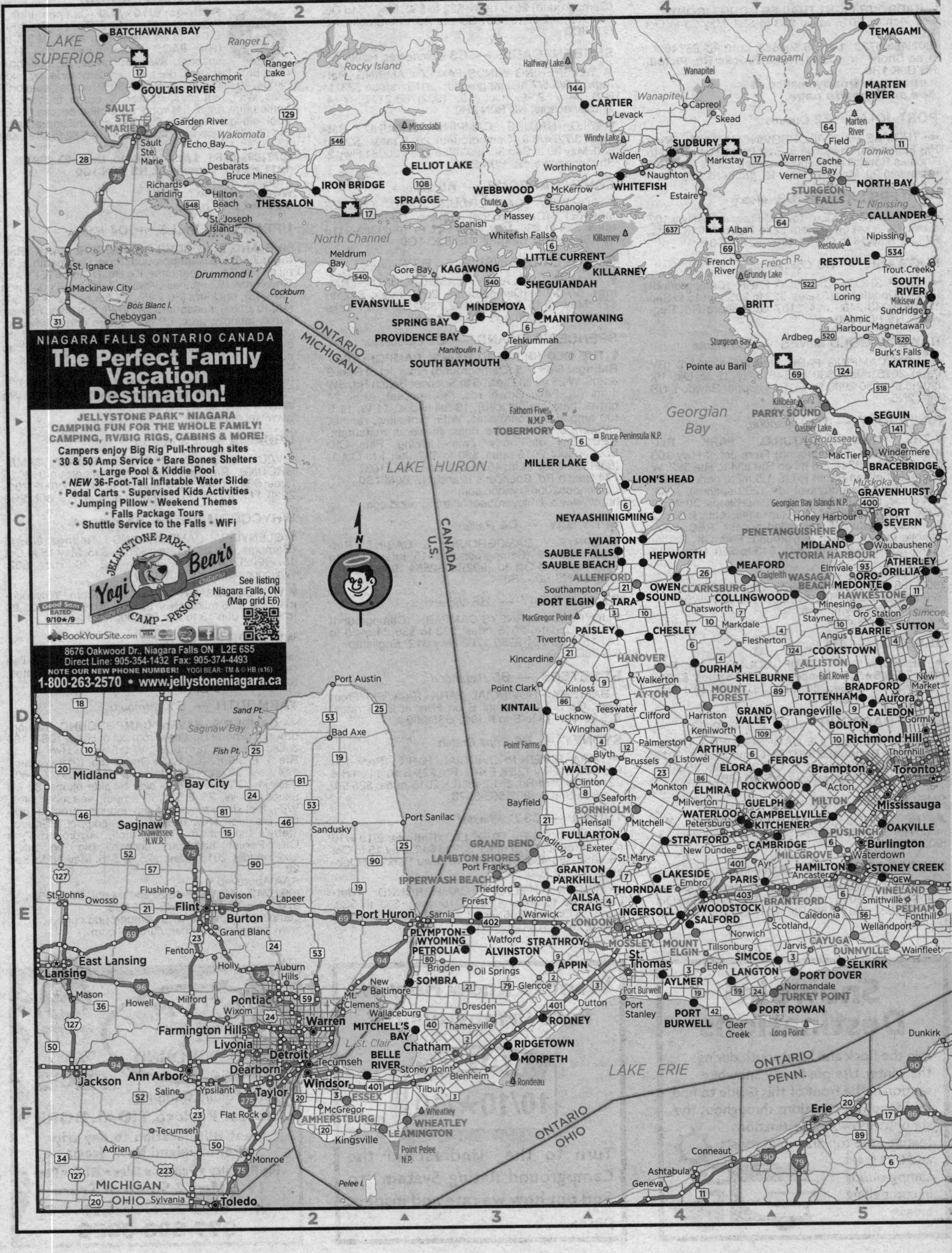

LAKE SUPERIOR
BATCHAWANA BAY
GOULAIS RIVER
Searchmont
Ranger L.
Ranger Lake
Rocky Island L.
SAULT STE. MARIE
Sault Ste. Marie
Garden River
Echo Bay
Wakomata L.
Desbarats
Bruce Mines
Richards Landing
Hilton Beach
St. Joseph Island
THESSALON
IRON BRIDGE
ELLIOT LAKE
SPRAGGE
Mississiabi
Halfway Lake
CARTIER
Levack
Wanapitei
Wanapitei L.
Capreol
Skead
L. Temagami
TEMAGAMI
MARTEN RIVER
Windy Lake
SUDBURY
Walden
Worthington
Naughton
WHITEFISH
Markstay
Warren
Verner
Cache Bay
Field
Tomiko L.
STURGEON FALLS
NORTH BAY
L. Nipissing
CALLANDER
WEBBWOOD
McKerrow
Chutes
Massey
Espanola
Estaire
Spanish
North Channel
Whitefish Falls
Killarney
Alban
Nipissing
Restoule
RESTOULE
Meldrum Bay
Gore Bay
KAGAWONG
LITTLE CURRENT
KILLARNEY
French River
French R.
Grundy Lake
Trout Creek
SOUTH RIVER
Mikisew
Sundridge
Port Loring
Ahmic Harbour
Magnetawan
St. Ignace
Drummond I.
Cockburn I.
Mackinaw City
Bois Blanc I.
Cheboygan
EVANSVILLE
SHEGUIANDAH
MINDEMOYA
SPRING BAY
PROVIDENCE BAY
MANITOWANING
Tehkummah
Manitoulin I.
SOUTH BAYMOUTH
BRITT
Ardbeg
Burk's Falls
KATRINE
Sturgeon Bay
Pointe au Baril
ONTARIO
MICHIGAN
Fathom Five N.M.P.
TOBERMORY
Bruce Peninsula N.P.
Georgian Bay
Killbear
PARRY SOUND
SEGUIN
Oastler Lake
L. Rosseau
MacTier
Windermere
BRACEBRIDGE
L. Muskoka
GRAVENHURST
Georgian Bay Islands N.P.
Honey Harbour
PORT SEVERN
LAKE HURON
MILLER LAKE
LION'S HEAD
NEYAASHIINIGMIING
WIARTON
PENETANGUISHENE
MIDLAND
Waubaushene
VICTORIA HARBOUR
Elmvale
ATHERLEY
ORO-MEDONTE
ORILLIA
HAWKESTONE
SAUBLE FALLS
SAUBLE BEACH
HEPWORTH
MEAFORD
Craigleith
WASAGA BEACH
ALLENFORD
OWEN SOUND
CLARKSBURG
COLLINGWOOD
Southampton
PORT ELGIN
TARA
Chatsworth
Minesing
Oro Station
L. Simcoe
MacGregor Point
Markdale
Stayner
BARRIE
SUTTON
PAISLEY
CHESLEY
Flesherton
Angus
Tiverton
Kincardine
HANOVER
DURHAM
COOKSTOWN
ALLISTON
Walkerton
Earl Rowe
New Market
Point Clark
Kinloss
AYTON
MOUNT FOREST
SHELBURNE
BRADFORD
KINTAIL
TOTTENHAM
Aurora
Teeswater
Clifford
Harriston
GRAND VALLEY
Orangeville
CALEDON
Lucknow
Wingham
Kenilworth
BOLTON
Gormley
Richmond Hill
Point Farms
Palmerston
Thornhill
Blyth
Brussels
Listowel
ARTHUR
FERGUS
WALTON
ELORA
Brampton
Toronto
Clinton
Monkton
ELMIRA
ROCKWOOD
Acton
Bayfield
Seaforth
Milverton
GUELPH
MILTON
Mississauga
BORNHOLM
WATERLOO
CAMPBELLVILLE
Hensall
Mitchell
Petersburg
KITCHENER
OAKVILLE
Crediton
FULLARTON
PUSLINCH
GRAND BEND
STRATFORD
CAMBRIDGE
Burlington
Exeter
New Dundee
MILLGROVE
Waterdown
LAMBTON SHORES
St. Marys
Ayr
HAMILTON
STONEY CREEK
Port Franks
GRANTON
Ancaster
IPPERWASH BEACH
PARKHILL
LAKESIDE
Embro
PARIS
QEW
VINELAND
Thedford
THORNDALE
Arkona
AILSA CRAIG
BRANTFORD
Smithville
PELHAM
Forest
INGERSOLL
WOODSTOCK
Fonthill
Warwick
LONDON
SALFORD
Caledonia
Wellandport
Sarnia
Port Huron
PLYMPTON-WYOMING
Watford
STRATHROY
MOSSLEY
MOUNT ELGIN
Norwich
Scotland
Tillsonburg
CAYUGA
PETROLIA
ALVINSTON
St. Thomas
Jarvis
DUNNVILLE
Wainfleet
Brigden
Oil Springs
APPIN
SIMCOE
Eden
LANGTON
SELKIRK
New Baltimore
SOMBRA
Glencoe
Port Burwell
AYLMER
PORT DOVER
Normandale
TURKEY POINT
Mt. Clemens
Wallaceburg
Dresden
Dutton
Port Stanley
PORT BURWELL
PORT ROWAN
Clear Creek
Long Point
Thamesville
RODNEY
MITCHELL'S BAY
L. St. Clair
Chatham
RIDGETOWN
MORPETH
BELLE RIVER
Stoney Point
Blenheim
Rondeau
LAKE ERIE
ONTARIO
PENN.
Dunkirk
Tecumseh
Windsor
ESSEX
Tilbury
McGregor
Wheatley
WHEATLEY
AMHERSTBURG
LEAMINGTON
Kingsville
Point Pelee N.P.
Pelee I.
OHIO
Erie
Conneaut
Ashtabula
Geneva
Port Austin
Sand Pt.
Saginaw Bay
Bad Axe
Fish Pt.
Midland
Bay City
Saginaw
Shiawassee N.W.R.
Port Sanilac
Sandusky
Flushing
St. Johns
Owosso
Davison
Lapeer
Flint
Burton
Grand Blanc
East Lansing
Lansing
Fenton
Holly
Auburn Hills
Mason
Howell
Milford
Pontiac
Wixom
Warren
Farmington Hills
Livonia
Detroit
Dearborn
Jackson
Ann Arbor
Saline
Ypsilanti
Taylor
Flat Rock
Tecumseh
Adrian
Monroe
MICHIGAN
Sylvania
Toledo
CANADA
U.S.

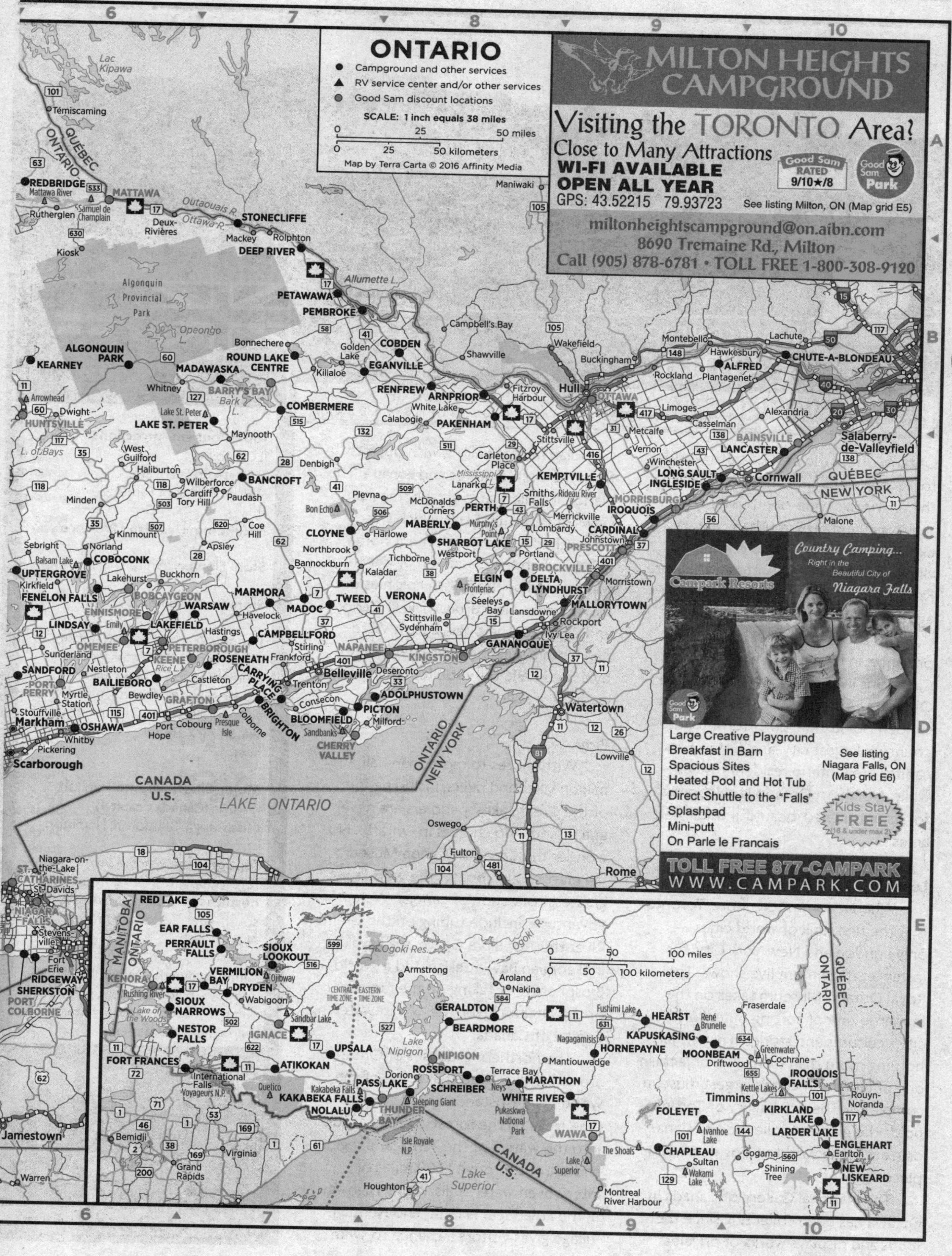
6
7
8
9
10
ONTARIO
Campground and other services
RV service center and/or other services
Good Sam discount locations
SCALE: 1 inch equals 38 miles
0 25 50 miles
0 25 50 kilometers
Map by Terra Carta © 2016 Affinity Media
A
B
C
D
E
F
Lac Kipawa
Témiscaming
QUÉBEC
ONTARIO
REDBRIDGE
Mattawa River
MATTAWA
Samuel de Champlain
Rutherglen
Kiosk
Outaouais R.
Ottawa R.
Deux-Rivières
STONECLIFFE
Mackey
Rolphton
DEEP RIVER
Algonquin Provincial Park
Allumette L.
PETAWAWA
PEMBROKE
Opeongo L.
ALGONQUIN PARK
KEARNEY
Arrowhead
Dwight
HUNTSVILLE
L. of Bays
Whitney
MADAWASKA
BARRY'S BAY
Bark L.
Lake St. Peter
LAKE ST. PETER
Maynooth
Bonnechere
ROUND LAKE CENTRE
Golden Lake
COBDEN
EGANVILLE
Killaloe
COMBERMERE
RENFREW
ARNPRIOR
White Lake
Calabogie
PAKENHAM
Campbell's Bay
Shawville
Fitzroy Harbour
Maniwaki
Wakefield
Buckingham
Hull
OTTAWA
Stittsville
Carleton Place
Mississippi
Lanark
KEMPTVILLE
Smiths Falls
Rideau River
PERTH
Merrickville
Lombardy
Murphy's Point
MABERLY
SHARBOT LAKE
Westport
Portland
ELGIN
DELTA
LYNDHURST
Frontenac
Seeleys Bay
Lansdowne
MALLORYTOWN
Rockport
Ivy Lea
GANANOQUE
BROCKVILLE
Morristown
PRESCOTT
Johnstown
CARDINAL
IROQUOIS
MORRISBURG
INGLESIDE
LONG SAULT
Cornwall
LANCASTER
BAINSVILLE
Winchester
Vernon
Metcalfe
Casselman
Limoges
Rockland
Plantagenet
ALFRED
Hawkesbury
Montebello
Lachute
CHUTE-A-BLONDEAU
Alexandria
Salaberry-de-Valleyfield
QUÉBEC
NEW YORK
Malone
West Guilford
Haliburton
Wilberforce
BANCROFT
Cardiff
Tory Hill
Paudash
Minden
Denbigh
Plevna
McDonalds Corners
Bon Echo
CLOYNE
Harlowe
Northbrook
Coe Hill
Apsley
Kinmount
Norland
Sebright
Balsam Lake
COBOCONK
UPTERGROVE
Kirkfield
FENELON FALLS
Lakehurst
Buckhorn
BOBCAYGEON
ENNISMORE
WARSAW
Havelock
MARMORA
MADOC
TWEED
Bannockburn
Kaladar
Tichborne
VERONA
Stittsville
Sydenham
LINDSAY
Emily
LAKEFIELD
Hastings
CAMPBELLFORD
Stirling
NAPANEE
KINGSTON
OMEMEE
Sunderland
PETERBOROUGH
KEENE
Rice L.
ROSENEATH
Frankford
SANDFORD
Nestleton
BAILIEBORO
Castleton
CARRYING PLACE
Trenton
Belleville
Deseronto
PORT PERRY
Myrtle Station
Bewdley
GRAFTON
BRIGHTON
Consecon
ADOLPHUSTOWN
Stouffville
Markham
OSHAWA
Whitby
Port Hope
Cobourg
Presque Isle
Colborne
BLOOMFIELD
Sandbanks
PICTON
Milford
CHERRY VALLEY
Pickering
Scarborough
CANADA
U.S.
LAKE ONTARIO
ONTARIO
NEW YORK
Watertown
Lowville
Oswego
Fulton
Rome
Niagara-on-the-Lake
ST. CATHARINES
St. Davids
NIAGARA FALLS
Stevensville
Fort Erie
RIDGEWAY
SHERKSTON
PORT COLBORNE
Jamestown
Warren
MANITOBA
ONTARIO
RED LAKE
EAR FALLS
PERRAULT FALLS
SIOUX LOOKOUT
VERMILION BAY
Ojibway
KENORA
Rushing River
DRYDEN
Wabigoon
SIOUX NARROWS
Lake of the Woods
NESTOR FALLS
Sandbar Lake
IGNACE
FORT FRANCES
International Falls
Voyageurs N.P.
Quetico
ATIKOKAN
UPSALA
CENTRAL TIME ZONE
EASTERN TIME ZONE
Ogoki Res.
Ogoki R.
Armstrong
Aroland
Nakina
GERALDTON
BEARDMORE
Lake Nipigon
NIPIGON
Dorion
ROSSPORT
SCHREIBER
Terrace Bay
Neys
MARATHON
PASS LAKE
Kakabeka Falls
KAKABEKA FALLS
NOLALU
THUNDER BAY
Sleeping Giant
Isle Royale N.P.
Houghton
Lake Superior
CANADA
U.S.
WHITE RIVER
Pukaskwa National Park
WAWA
Lake Superior
Montreal River Harbour
0 50 100 miles
0 50 100 kilometers
Fushimi Lake
HEARST
René Brunelle
KAPUSKASING
Nagagamisis
HORNEPAYNE
Mantiouwadge
MOONBEAM
Fraserdale
Greenwater
Cochrane
Driftwood
IROQUOIS FALLS
Kettle Lakes
Timmins
FOLEYET
Ivanhoe Lake
The Shoals
CHAPLEAU
Sultan
Wakami Lake
Gogama
Shining Tree
KIRKLAND LAKE
LARDER LAKE
ENGLEHART
Earlton
NEW LISKEARD
Rouyn-Noranda
ONTARIO
QUÉBEC
Bemidji
Grand Rapids
Virginia
ON

 See map pages 1414 and 1415

WELCOME TO Ontario

JOINED CONFEDERATION JULY 1, 1867	WIDTH: 692 MILES (1,114 KM) LENGTH: 998 MILES (1,606 KM)	PROPORTION OF CANADA 10.78% OF 9,984,670 SQ KM

Ontario offers the best of both worlds for RV travelers. Go camping and hiking the province's wide-open spaces or hit the stores and sites at urban centers like Toronto. Ontario also is home to vineyards between Toronto and Niagara Falls. In autumn, the province's fall foliage attracts legions of leaf peepers.

This is Canada's most populous province. In fact, one in every four Canadians lives in an area around Lake Ontario's western shores known as the Golden Horseshoe. Both Toronto, the country's largest city, and Ottawa, its capital, are Ontario residents. Meanwhile, Northern Ontario is celebrated for its untouched, beautiful wilderness areas.

Learn

When it comes to culture, Toronto is at the first rank of world cities—only London and New York City, for instance, stage more live shows. The Royal Ontario Museum takes on the immense task of sorting out all of the city's cultures and stories. That entails housing more than six million objects in one of North America's largest museum complexes. The Art Gallery of Toronto holds the greatest collection of Canadian art in the world among its 80,000 pieces.

The National Gallery of Canada in Ottawa has been collecting since the 1880s and displays works of priceless Canadian heritage along with objects from the United States and Europe. The National Gallery affords spectacular views of Parliament Hill, which was established as the government home in 1867 when the Dominion of Canada was formed by the British colonies of Nova Scotia, New Brunswick, Ontario and Quebec. The original High Victorian Gothic buildings were destroyed by a fire in 1916 but rebuilt in the same distinctive style.

Play

With shores to more than half a million lakes and rivers, including four of the Great Lakes, paddlers are never at a loss for trip choices in Ontario. No wonder the Canadian Canoe Museum in Peterborough boasts the world's greatest collection of canoes. Water adventures include tubing on the Grand River through Elora Gorge, sea kayaking in Georgian Bay—designated a World Biosphere—or taking on the rapids of the Ottawa River, the "Whitewater Capital of Canada."

The northern expanses of Ontario are so lightly visited that some of the world's largest stands of old growth pine trees fill the forests. Push a canoe into the waters of the Temagami region and set out through 1,500 miles of interwoven water trails. Along Highway 11, the Polar Bear Habitat and Heritage Village gives visitors a chance to swim

Top 3 Tourism Attractions:
1) CN Tower
2) Stratford Festival
3) Hockey Hall of Fame

Nickname: Heartland Province

State Flower: White Trillion

State Bird: Common Loon

People: Wayne Gretzky, hockey player and coach; Peter Jennings, journalist and TV news anchor; Howie Mandel, comedian and actor; Brian Orser, Olympic figure skater; Alex Trebek, TV game show host

Major Cities: Toronto (capital), Ottawa (Canada's capital), Mississauga, Brampton, Hamilton

Topography: Northwest/central—forests, uplands, lakes, rivers; north/northeast—swampy lowlands; south—fertile, lowland forests, Niagara Falls

Climate: North—subarctic climate; central—colder winters, pleasant summers; south—cold winters and warm, humid summers

with polar bears—on the other side of a thick plexiglass window.

On Lake Ontario, the sand blows into 180-foot dunes. On Lake Huron, you'll find places like Wasaga Beach, the world's longest stretch of freshwater beach at more than eight miles. Out on the water, visitors can choose from more than 30,000 freshwater islands to explore. At the tip of the rugged Bruce Peninsula, which bisects Lake Huron, visitors will discover Five Fathom National Marine Park and Bruce Peninsula National Park. These sit atop the geographical phenomenon known as the Niagara Escarpment. The world-famous Bruce Trail begins its serpentine 550-mile journey here, eventually leading truly adventurous explorers to Niagara Falls.

- STAY A WHILE -

Take a Fun Ferry Ride Across Georgian Bay

The MS Chi-Cheemaun is a passenger and vehicle ferry that crosses Georgian Bay between Tobermory and South Baymouth on Manitoulin Island, connecting two portions of Hwy. 6. The ferry service runs seasonally from mid-May to mid-October. Traveling on the Chi-Cheemaun not only takes to you an island full of good spirits and native lore, but it also does so in a way that keeps you in good spirits, too. You can have a nice meal, sit on a deck chair surrounded with breathtaking views, ask local historians about the region or simply relax with a drink while the kids play. Compared to long highway driving, this is heaven. So when you arrive on the island of even more spirits and legends, the best part is you'll have arrived in good spirits as well.

ON

Experience

Ontario sponsors more than 3,000 annual festivals, so you should be able to find a party any weekend. Celebrations don't get any bigger than the Canadian National Exhibition, which takes up much of the month of August to fit everything in. "The Ex" began as a simple agriculture and technology fair in 1879. Today's event is now the country's largest fair, with more than one million visitors coming to the shores of Lake Ontario for shows, exhibits, concerts and an old-fashioned carnival midway.

Celebrated across three weekends in February, Ottawa's Winterlude offers skating on the world's largest ice rink: the Rideau Canal Skateway. Illuminated ice sculptures in Confederation Park and workshops in the art of igloo building also make up a big part of the event. In the summer, when the ice thaws, the family-friendly Rideau Canal Festival leads the way in environmentally conscious big events by aiming for a zero carbon footprint.

Taste

Ontario is about as far away from its British origins as it is possible to stray. It also boasts quite a mix of ethnicities and cultures. Almost half of the population was born outside of Canada, and that cultural diversity is reflected in the provincial cuisine. Hakka, a dish of masala fried rice and thread chicken that was bred in India, is a Toronto menu tradition that is scarcely found outside of India. Food carts in the city's six Chinatowns, Little Italy, Koreatown and the Greek enclave of The Danforth all dispense their own ethnic culinary delights.

Toronto's signature sandwich is peameal bacon, a trimmed boneless pork loin rolled into cornmeal and grilled to a crisp exterior. The St. Lawrence Market, one of the world's most esteemed fresh-food markets, serves as a reliable destination for lovers of peameal bacon. If it is after dinner time in Ottawa, the dessert of choice is the BeaverTail, which is whole wheat dough fried and hand-stretched into a flat oval and smeared with butter. From there, any sweet topping is on offer, from brown sugar and cinnamon to chocolate and fresh fruit. Create the dessert sensation of your dreams.

In the countryside, you can enjoy award-winning cheddar cheeses from the province's many small dairies or nosh on wild blueberries that grow in abundance across northern Ontario. And working sugar bushes make Lanark County the "Maple Syrup Capital of Ontario."

Cavorting in an Ontario park. Ontario Travel

TRAVEL & TOURISM

Ontario Travel
800-ONTARIO
www.ontariotravel.net

Bruce County Tourism
www.explorethebruce.com

Cambridge Tourism
519-622-2336, 800-749-7560
www.cambridgetourism.com

Niagara Falls Tourism
905-356-6061
www.niagarafallstourism.com

Norfolk County – South Coast Tourism
519-426-9497, 800-699-9038
www.norfolktourism.ca

North of Superior Tourism
800-265-3951
www.northofsuperior.org

Northumberland Tourism
866-401-3278, 905-372-3329
www.northumberlandtourism.com

Ontario East Economic Development Commission
613-528-1472
www.onteast.com

Ontario's Near North
800-387-0516, 705-474-6634
www.ontariosnearnorth.on.ca

Rainbow Country Travel Association
800-465-6655, 705-522-0104
www.rainbowcountry.com

See Toronto Now
800-499-2514
www.seetorontonow.com

Tourism London
519-661-5000, 800-265-2602
www.londontourism.ca

Town of Milton Visitor & Community Information Service
905-878-7252, 800-418-5494
www.town.milton.on.ca

Wiarton
800-268-3838, 519-534-5344
www.naturalretreat.com

OUTDOOR RECREATION

Bicycle Ontario
www.bicycleontario.com

Ontario Golf
www.ontgolf.com

Canoe and Kayaking Adventures
www.paddlingontario.com

SHOPPING

Locke Street
www.lockestreetshops.com

Toronto Eaton Centre
www.torontoeatoncentre.com

Vaughan Mills
www.vaughanmills.com

Village of St. Jacobs
www.stjacobs.com/village-of-st-jacobs

Featured Good Sam Parks

ONTARIO

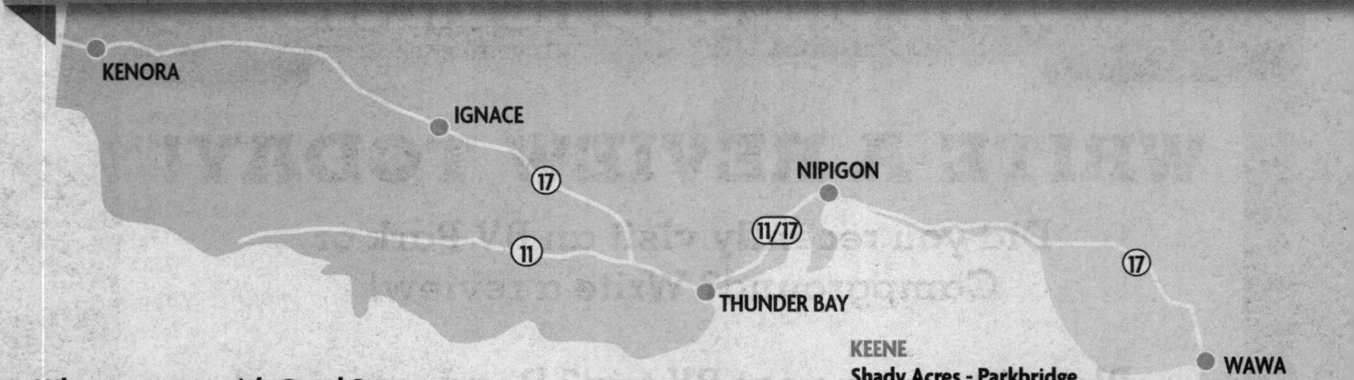

When you stay with Good Sam, you can expect the highest degree of cleanliness and friendliness, and better yet, you get 10% off campground fees.

If you're not already a Good Sam member you can purchase your membership at one of these locations:

ALLENFORD
Arran Lake Carefree RV Resort
(519)934-1224

ALLISTON
Nicolston Dam Campground
(705)435-7946

AMHERSTBURG
Willowood Carefree RV Resort
(519)736-3201

AYTON
Silent Valley Park Resort - Parkbridge
(519)665-7787

BAINSVILLE
Maplewood Acres RV Park
(613)347-2130

BARRY'S BAY
Chippawa Resort and Easy Living Camping & RV Resort
(800)267-8507

BOBCAYGEON
Lonesome Pine Cottage and RV Resort - Parkbridge
(705)738-2684

BORNHOLM
Woodland Lake Carefree RV Resort
(519)347-2315

BRANTFORD
Willow Lake Carefree RV Resort
(519)446-2513

BROCKVILLE
Happy Green Acres Tent & Trailer Park
(613)342-9646

CAYUGA
Grand Oaks Carefree RV Resort
(905)772-3713

CHERRY VALLEY
Lake Avenue Carefree RV Resort
(613)476-4990

Quinte's Isle Campark
(613)476-6310

CLARKSBURG
Craigleith Carefree RV Resort
(519)599-3840

DUNNVILLE
Grand River RV Resort - Parkbridge
(905)774-4257

ENNISMORE
Grandview Cottage and RV Resort - Parkbridge
(705)292-7717

Skyline Cottage and RV Resort - Parkbridge
(705)292-9811

ESSEX
Wildwood Golf & RV Resort
(866)994-9699

GRAFTON
Cobourg East Campground
(905)349-2594

GRAND BEND
Rus-Ton Family Campground
(519)243-2424

HANOVER
Saugeen Springs RV Park Inc
(519)369-5136

HAWKESTONE
Heidi's Campground
(705)487-3311

HUNTSVILLE
Deer Lake Carefree RV Resort
(705)789-3326

IGNACE
Davy Lake Campground
(877)374-3113

IPPERWASH BEACH
Silver Birches Carefree RV Resort
(519)243-2480

KEENE
Shady Acres - Parkbridge
(705)295-6815

KENORA
The Willows RV Park & Campground
(807)548-1821

KINGSTON
Rideau Acres Camping Resort
(800)958-5830

LAMBTON SHORES
Oakridge Resort - Parkbridge
(519)243-2500

Our Ponderosa RV & Golf Resort - Parkbridge
(888)786-CAMP

LEAMINGTON
Leisure Lake Resort - Parkbridge
(888)274-8817

LONDON
Campers Corner RV Campground
(844)287-9313

MATTAWA
Sid Turcotte Park
(705)744-5375

MILTON
Milton Heights Campground Ltd.
(800)308-9120

MORRISBURG
Upper Canada Campground
(613)543-2201

MOSSLEY
Golden Pond R V Resort
(888)990-9920

MOUNT ELGIN
Spring Lake R.V. Resort - Parkbridge
(877)877-9265

MOUNT FOREST
Spring Valley Resort - Parkbridge
(519)323-2581

NAPANEE
Pickerel Park Carefree RV Resort
(613)373-2812

NIAGARA FALLS
Campark Resorts
(877)CAMPARK

Knights Hide-Away Park
(905)894-1911

Riverside Park Motel & Campground
(905)382-2204

Scott's Tent & Trailer Park
(905)356-6988

Yogi Bear's Jellystone Park Camp-Resort
(800)263-2570

NIPIGON
Stillwater Tent & RV Park
(877)887-3701

OTTAWA
Camp Hither Hills
(613)822-0509

Wesley Clover Parks Campground
(613)828-6632

PARRY SOUND
Trailside Carefree RV Resort
(705)378-2844

PELHAM
Bissell's Hideaway Resort
(888)236-0619

PENETANGUISHENE
Lafontaine Carefree RV Resort
(705)533-2961

PETERBOROUGH
Bailey's Bay Resort - Parkbridge
(705)748-9656

PORT COLBORNE
Sherkston Shores Carefree RV Resort
(877)482-3224

PORT PERRY
Goreski's Landing - Parkbridge
(800)331-9935

ST CATHARINES
Jordan Valley Campground
(866)526-2267

Shangri-La Park Niagara Campground
(905)562-5851

STURGEON FALLS
Glenrock Cottages & Trailer Park
(866)592-1157

THUNDER BAY
Happy Land RV Park
(866)473-9003

TOBERMORY
Lands End Park
(519)596-2523

TURKEY POINT
Hidden Valley Carefree RV Resort
(519)426-5666

VICTORIA HARBOUR
Victoria Harbour Beach and Marine Resort - Parkbridge
(705)534-7551

VINELAND
N.E.T. Camping Resort
(866)490-4745

ON

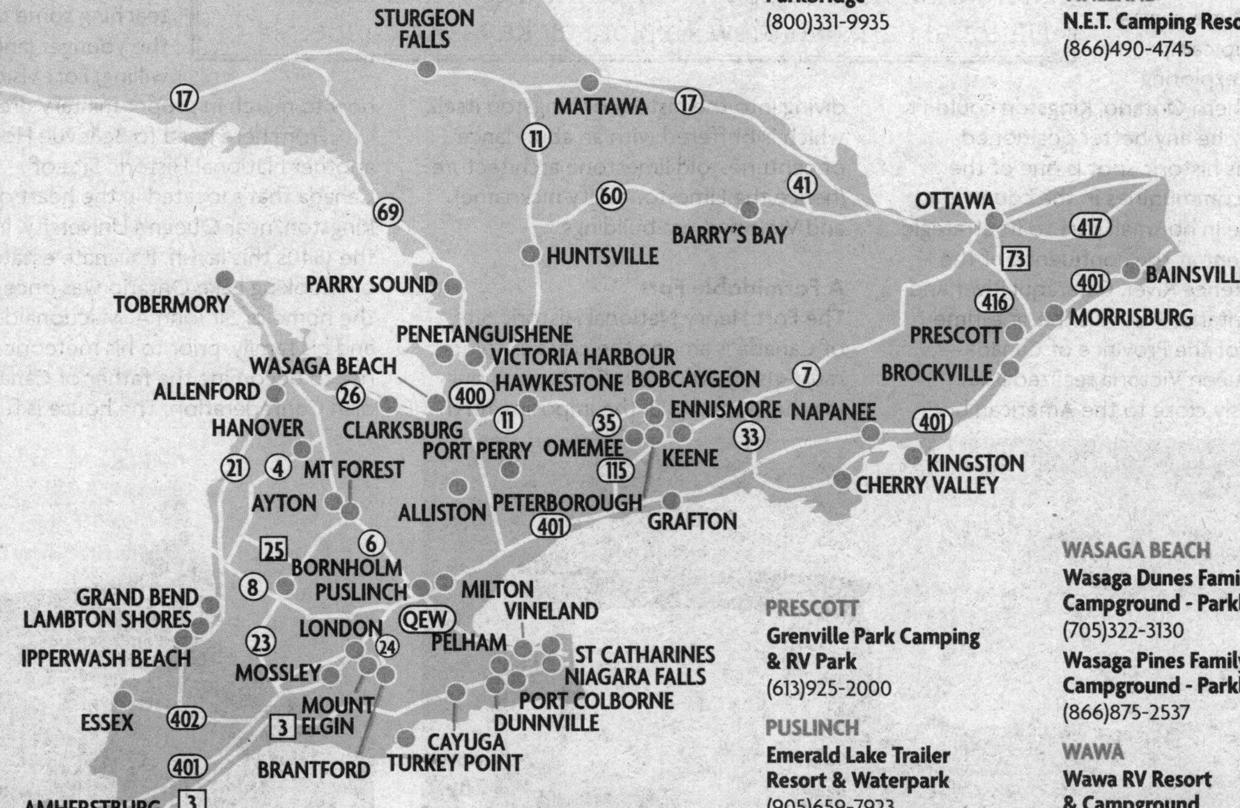

OMEMEE
Beaver Narrows - Parkbridge
(705)799-6221

PRESCOTT
Grenville Park Camping & RV Park
(613)925-2000

PUSLINCH
Emerald Lake Trailer Resort & Waterpark
(905)659-7923

SAULT STE MARIE
Glenview Cottages & Campground
(705)759-3436

WASAGA BEACH
Wasaga Dunes Family Campground - Parkbridge
(705)322-3130

Wasaga Pines Family Campground - Parkbridge
(866)875-2537

WAWA
Wawa RV Resort & Campground
(877)256-4368

WHEATLEY
Campers Cove
(519)825-4732

For more Good Sam Parks go to listing pages

Getty Images/iStockphoto

KINGSTON

History lives in Ontario's Limestone City

Kingston, also known as Canada's Limestone City, sits in an enviable position. Less than three hours away from Toronto, Ottawa and Montreal, the city also sits on the shores of both the St. Lawrence River and Lake Ontario, as well as on the doorstep of the Thousand Islands. If you're looking for somewhere central to set up camp and go exploring in Southern Ontario, Kingston couldn't possibly be any better positioned.

This historic spot is one of the oldest communities in the country, a fact due in no small part to its strategic placement at the confluence of the St. Lawrence River, Cataraqui River and Lake Ontario. This was the one-time capital of the Province of Canada—until Queen Victoria realized it lay perilously close to the American border—and the early stomping grounds of Canada's first prime minister, Sir John A. Macdonald.

As such, history lives large here, and those who like to disappear into museums and roam historic sites will find no shortage of attractions. Start by diving into the history of Kingston itself, which is buffered with an abundance of centuries-old limestone architecture (hence the Limestone City nickname) and Victorian-era buildings.

> More than 20 islands lie within the Thousand Islands National Park overview. Explore by kayak or canoe.

A Formidable Fort

The Fort Henry National Historic Site of Canada is among the city's absolute must-visit attractions. Established during the War of 1812, the imposing fortification sits on an elevated overlook at the confluence of the Cataraqui and St Lawrence rivers. Today, both self-guided and professionally guided tours through the old British military outpost are available. The experience is designed to give visitors an impression of 19th-century military life up to and including teaching some of the younger (and willing) Fort visitors how to march in proper military dress.

From here head to Bellevue House, another National Historic Site of Canada that's located in the heart of Kingston, near Queen's University. In the 1840s this lavish, Italianate estate overlooking Lake Ontario was once the home of Sir John A. Macdonald and his family, prior to his meteoric rise to becoming the father of Canadian Confederation. The house is fully

One of Kingston's Martello Towers. Getty Images/iStockphoto

Kingston's city hall showcases 19th-century architecture. Getty Images/Ingram Publishing

restored, back to its 1840s splendor, and staff is adorned in full period costume. Guided tours of the house, gardens and grounds are available daily.

Rounding out the big historic attractions in Kingston is Kingston City Hall. Built between 1841 and 1843, this was supposed to be Canada's very first capitol building before the capital was moved to Montreal. Today it stands as one of the finest examples of 19th century architecture in the country. Free guided tours are available during the week from May to October, and on weekends in July and August.

History buffs will also want to check out the city's collection of more than 20 museums, including the Royal Military College of Canada Museum, Canada's Penitentiary Museum and the Marine Museum of the Great Lakes. While touring the city, keep an eye out for the Martello Towers, built on the city's waterfront to ward off invasion.

Those travelling with kids can visit the Pump House Steam Museum (where animated steam-powered pumps and model trains will enthrall younger visitors) or the Frontenac County Schools Museum (where life as a grade-school student at the turn of the century is demonstrated with hands-on activities).

A Thousand Islands

When you're ready for a break from museums and historic sites, you can savor a taste of the great outdoors at Thousand Islands National Park, just a half hour away to the northeast. This is where the Canadian Shield meets the Adirondack Mountains, a transitional axis known as the Frontenac Arch. The islands serve as steppingstones for wildlife, helping to form one contiguous ecosystem.

The park features campgrounds and cottages for extended visits, as well as picnic areas, boat launches, playgrounds and informative visitors centers. More than 20 islands lie within the Thousand Islands National Park overview itself, making this an idyllic area to explore by kayak or canoe.

Hikers can hit any number of trails, with an abundance of trailheads conveniently located at Mallorytown Landing, Landon Bay and around the Jones Creek area. The larger islands have their own networks of well-marked trails as well.

Fishing and birdwatching are also popular in Thousand Islands National Park. You'll need a valid fishing license to dip your lure in the water, but the effort is worth it—large stocks of rock bass, largemouth bass, smallmouth bass, yellow perch, pike, walleye and pumpkinseed are ready to bite year-round. Bird-watchers, meanwhile, can look for more the diverse species of avians that inhabit the park.

It's no coincidence that the city of Kingston has been attracting visitors for so long. Its placement at the confluence of two historic rivers, on the shores of scenic Lake Ontario, near the American border and equal distance from three of the country's largest cities all add up to picture-perfect centrality.

For More Information

Kingston Tourist Information Office
888-855-4555
tourism.kingstoncanada.com

Ontario Travel
800-668-2746
www.ontariotravel.net

ON

NIAGARA FALLS

Feel the power of an iconic spectacle

Photos simply don't do Niagara Falls justice. Six million cubic feet of water gush over Horseshoe Falls on the Canadian side of the river every minute of every day. The roar is deafening, the view visceral. The power of the falls is so vicious that behind the mesmerizing veil of plummeting, tumbling, raging water the 12,000-year-old Niagara Escarpment rock shelf is being chewed and chipped away at a rate of 12 inches per year.

This is nature unleashed. And it's a sight to behold.

> An observation deck at the very foot of the falls outside offers the closest and most riveting views available.

If this is your first visit to the Niagara Falls region, you'll want to orient yourself to the area. As the Niagara River flows north from Lake Erie to Lake Ontario, it forms part of the international border between Ontario and New York State. Halfway between the two Great Lakes the river is split and divided into three massive waterfalls—Horseshoe Falls on the Canadian side and American Falls and Bridal Veil Falls on the New York side. The best views of all three are found on the Canadian ide of the river, and the Canadian falls :arry nine times more water than their American counterparts.

As such, most visitors to the Niagara area aim for the city of Niagara Falls, Ontario, which offers an abundance of waterfall-themed attractions o truly enhance and expand the experience far beyond a simple act of sightseeing.

> Six million cubic feet of water gush over Horseshoe Falls on the Canadian side of the river every minute of every day.

Exploring the Falls

Queen Victoria Park serves as the doorstep to the falls themselves, running along the shores of the river and providing direct access to Horseshoe Falls. Five different Welcome Centers are located throughout the park and it's worth your time to stop at one of them if you plan on visiting any of the other attractions in the area, such as Journey Behind the Falls, White Water Walk or Niagara's Fury. Passes can be purchased in advance, and in some cases, guests can reserve timed-ticket access to popular attractions.

If you're short on time, then Journey Behind the Falls is the absolute must-do activity. The self-guided walk winds below and behind the roaring waters of Horseshoe Falls via a series of open-ended tunnels. Safety rails are in place to prevent visitors from getting too close to the edge of the tunnels, past which water falls from a height of 13 stories at more than 40 miles per hour. An observation deck at the very foot of the falls outside offers the closest and most riveting views available though the deck is more than a bit misty, so mind your expensive camera.

Having seen the power of Niagara Falls up close, head for Niagara's Fury next. This high-tech immersive experience tells the story of how the Niagara River Gorge and its famous waterfalls were created over the course of 12,000

The view of American Falls. Getty Images/iStockphoto

A resident of the Butterfly Conservator
Getty Images/iStockphoto

years. The floor will tilt, water will spray and snow will fall as you're taken on a wild ride that showcases the incredible power of the natural world.

If you prefer indoor pursuits, checkout the Niagara IMAX Theatre, which brings the thundering falls to life with state-of-the-art projection and sound. Learn about the area's rich history of human habitation, and get acquainted with some of the brave souls who floated over the falls at the Niagara Daredevil Exhibit. You can even touch the sturdy craft that carried these larger-than-life characters through the white water and into history. Of particular note is Annie Edson Taylor, a charm-school teacher from Bay City who, in 1901, became the first person to go over Horseshoe Falls in a barrel and live to tell the tale. The feat earned her the nickname, "Queen of Niagara Falls."

The quintessential Niagara Falls experience, however, isn't found inside a 4D theater or from the relative comfort of an observation deck.

Anne Edson Taylor in the barrel she used to go over Niagara Falls.
Getty Images

Adventure seekers prepare to take the Journey Behind the Falls tour. Getty Images/iStockphoto

For that, you have to head out on a Hornblower Niagara Cruise. These world-famous catamaran boat tours take guests straight into the pluming mists of all three falls, bringing poncho-covered guests up-close to Bridal Veil Falls, American Falls and straight into the thundering crosshairs of deafening Horseshoe Falls.

Butterflies and Birds

When you're ready for a change of pace head a few miles upstream to White Water Walk. Here the power of the Niagara River is on display with a stretch of some of the roughest whitewater rapids in the world. This section of the Niagara River Gorge acts like an acceleration chute, channeling the water toward the falls at upwards of 30 miles per hour. Visitors can explore the rapids by way of a scenic quarter-mile boardwalk, reached by a trip down to the riverbank in an elevator.

Niagara Falls (the city) isn't all about fast-flowing water and struggling to keep your hair dry, though. Two of the most popular attractions on the Canadian side of the river are the Butterfly Conservatory and Bird Kingdom.

At the Butterfly Conservatory, visitors enter a world of more than 2,000 tropical butterflies living and floating about in a lush rainforest setting. Ponds, waterfalls and walkways weave through the conservatory, and tours are self-guided.

At Bird Kingdom, located just a short walk from Horseshoe Falls, visitors enjoy an experience that's one part show, one part tour and one part zoo visit. The experience is designed to bring guests back in time to the age of fearless explorers, navigating a world of exotic plants, animals, birds and reptiles. The experience culminates with an entry into the world's largest aviary, home to a 40-foot waterfall, living jungle and free-flying exotic birds.

For More Information

Tourism Partnership of Niagara
800-563-2557
www.visitniagaracanada.com

Ontario Travel
800-668-2746
www.ontariotravel.net

ON

Dwayne Brown Studio

PRINCE EDWARD COUNTY

Vacation in a recreation-rich corner of Ontario

At less than 270 square miles, Prince Edward County in southeastern Ontario might seem like an easy spot to overlook while exploring the north shore of Lake Ontario. But this small headland community packs a hefty punch when it comes to summer vacationing, annually attracting more than 100,000 visitors on the prowl for charming lakeside towns, quiet campgrounds and world-renowned parks.

The appeal isn't a new trend either. As you kick about Prince Edward County's abundance of parks and trails you might be lucky enough to find a fluted spear point, left behind by the region's first inhabitants who swept into the area with the retreat of ice-age glaciers 12,000 years ago. Since that time, the Prince Edward County headland has been populated by hunter-gatherers, prehistoric farmers, and the Iroquois and the Mississauga Indians. British, French and Dutch fur traders appeared on the scene in the 17th century, sparking periodic trade wars and often drawing in military intervention.

When the area fell under British rule, it was decided that no European settlement was allowed, in a measure to ensure peace. But the appeal of Prince Edward County, it would seem, was too great. Following the American Revolution, Loyalists moved north and began settling on the headland near modern-day Prinyer Cove. The next 200 years brought with them the gradual development of a thriving agricultural industry, which today is paired with a thriving tourism industry.

> Birdhouse City consists of more than 100 decorated birdhouses. Many are designed after world-famous buildings.

Edward's Abundance

As you move about the headland from campsite to campsite and town to tow (often on picturesque, unpaved countr roads), both farm stands and farmlan vistas line the way. Charm is the defining characteristic o this rural community. The manmade attractions here are humble, to say the least.

Birdhouse City, near Fawcettville, is one such attraction. Tucked into the northern edges of Macaulay Mountain Conservation Area, Birdhouse City consists of more than 100 ornately decorated and designed birdhouses. Many are miniatures modeled after

Running the dunes in Sandbanks Provincial Park. Dwayne Brown Studio

Apples ready for cider in Picton.
Prince Edward County

world-famous buildings. They sit atop tall poles jammed into the ground along the roadside and annually attract thousands upon thousands of curious shutterbugs.

Not far from Birdhouse City is the Glenora Ferry, another of the headland's humble manmade attractions. Every half-hour the ferry makes the short hop across the water to Adolphustown, linking the route between Prince Edward County and Kingston further east. The ride is short but incredibly scenic.

Prince Edward County's truly world-class attractions, though, are all found in the natural environment. Three provincial parks and 14 conservation areas are found on the headland. Whatever your preferred recreational activity is Prince Edward County has the natural terrain to accommodate. Kayaking, canoeing, fishing, hiking and even cross-country skiing are all popular pastimes here.

Start with a trip to Sandbanks Provincial Park, which can be found near West Lake on the southwestern shores of the headland. Sandbanks is home to the largest formation of baymouth sandbar dunes, a type that completely closes off an inland bay from a larger body of water.

Sandbanks is a popular summer destination due to its three nationally renowned beaches, often cited as the best in the country. A robust network of walking and hiking trails are also available to explore. The park's visitor center houses exhibits about the unique geological history of the area, and during the summer months it organizes daily guided hikes, talks and educational programs for kids.

A Mysterious Lake

On the northwestern side of the headland, near Glenora, Lake on the Mountain Provincial Park is another popular destination. On all scientific grounds, the Lake on the Mountain is a geological abomination. It sits near the headland coast and the Bay of Quinte, but at a height of 200 feet. There's no consensus on how the lake formed or, since it has no known water source, how it manages a constant flow of clean water. It certainly makes for one of the more dramatic natural settings one could ever hope to find.

Most theories on the formation of Lake on the Mountain revolve around the county's limestone bedrock. And while the jury is still out on that, we do know for sure that the headland's limestone-enriched soil is the reason behind Prince Edward County's booming, award-winning wine industry.

More than 40 wineries now call the headland home. A self-guided tasting trail is sponsored by the local community and takes visitors on a whirlwind tour of barn-house tasting rooms and wine cellars.

Take the time to stop and explore this often overlooked but richly rewarding headland community.

For More Information

Prince Edward County
800-640-4717
www.prince-edward-county.com

Ontario Travel
800-668-2746
www.ontariotravel.net

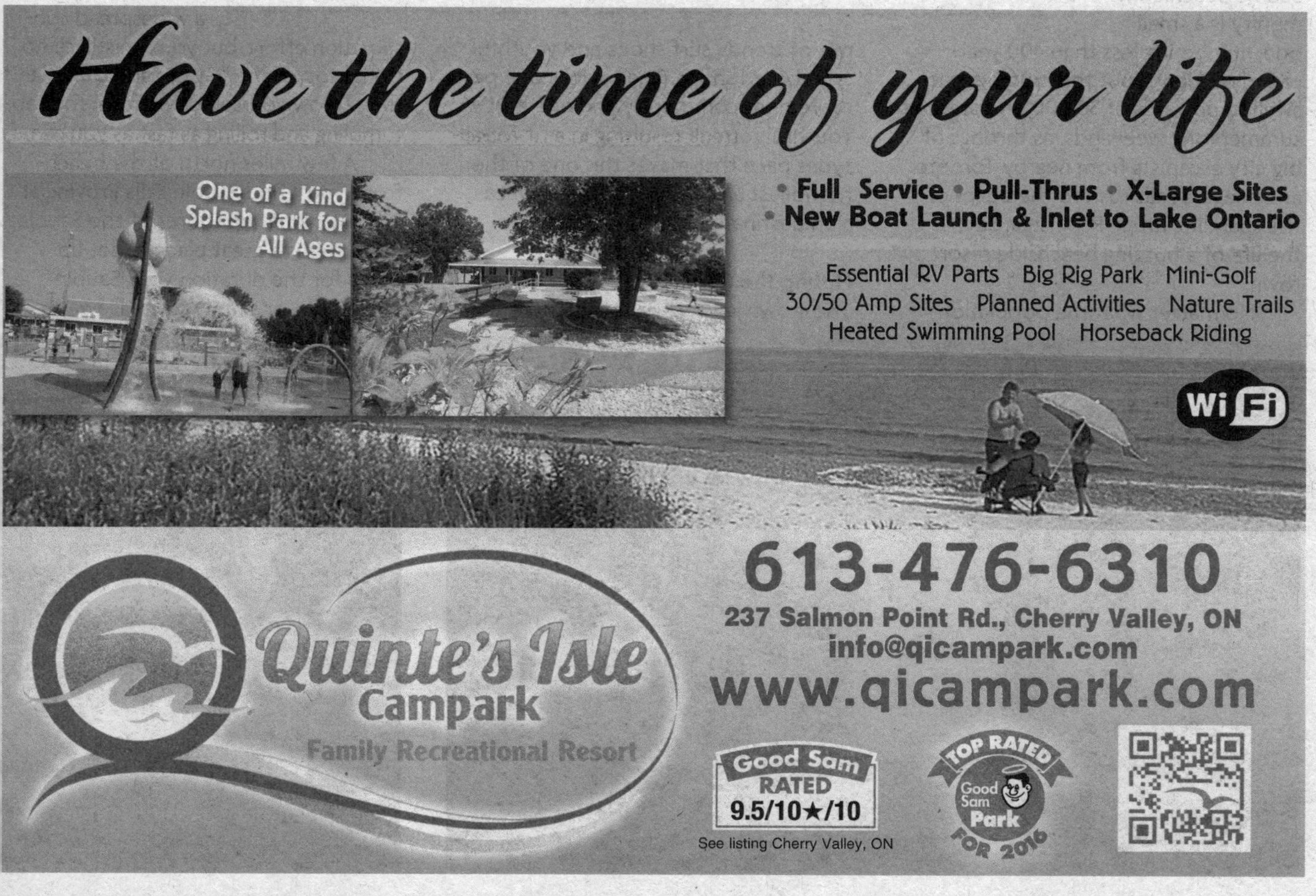

Pyzote

SAUBLE BEACH

Sand, sun and stunning coastlines make this a standout slice of Ontario

The official motto of Sauble Beach, Ontario, is "Live Life Slow." Once you're here, it's easy to take that advice to heart. Great parks, a small-town atmosphere and picturesque beachfront placement combine to make this an attractive spot to relax, unwind and escape.

Perched on the eastern shores of Lake Huron, the Sauble Beach community is a small one, numbering less than 400 year-round residents. But that number can swell to upwards of 30,000 on gorgeous summer long weekends, as throngs of big city escapists from nearby Toronto and Niagara Falls rush to the edges of the sparkling Bruce Peninsula. Such is the life of a buzzing beachside resort town.

No matter what the population is at any given time, however, Sauble Beach manages to retain (and proudly display) all of its small-town bonafides with classic, casual charm. Mom-and-pop shops line Main Street, which looks as if it's been pulled from the pages of a 1950s catalogue. There's also a healthy mix of trendy surf shops and youthful skateboard shops. The town is one part retirement community and one part youthful retreat, resulting in a fit-for-all-types pace that makes this one of the friendliest and most welcoming vacation destinations around.

> Rising above Georgia Bay, Bruce Peninsula National Park is filled with old growth forests, curious black bears, rare reptiles and incredible hiking trails.

Hitting the Beach

The crown jewel of Sauble Beach is the waterfront itself. At just over 7 miles in length, this is said to be the second longest freshwater beach in the world, sitting behind only Wasaga Beach—which just so happens to sit about 70 miles away to the east. It's also buffered with a spread of ancient sand dunes that are part of eastern Lake Huron's dune system. They're under attack from intense erosion, and part of a widespread conservation effort, but you can still climb to the top of the "Giant Sand Dune" and then throw yourself down from the top, tumbling and rolling as fast as you can.

A few miles north of the beachfront you'll find Sauble Falls Provincial Park. Flanking the shores of the Sauble River, this is a great place to set up camp for the duration your Sauble Beach stay, or simply to steal away a

Bridal Veil Falls Getty Images/iStockphoto

Flower pot stone formations stand on the rugged coast.
Getty Images/iStockphoto

day or two of hiking, camping, fishing or kayaking. The Falls themselves are small and easy to splash around in, even for kids. Canoe and kayak rentals are available to explore the length of the river, and an Adventure Playground is available for those with children.

Don't miss taking a hike on the Sauble Trail, which offers incredible views of the Sauble River. The trail route begins on the eastern end of the park and winds through a red pine plantation to the sand dunes further west. If you're an angler visiting in spring or fall be sure to pack your rod and reel. Rainbow trout and Chinook salmon burst from the waters of the Sauble River in abundant supply. Portions of the river are closed to fishing across all seasons, so be sure to seek out a designated area.

Park at the Peninsula

Further north still—about an hour's drive from Sauble Beach—sits Bruce Peninsula National Park, which clings to cliffs that rise from the waters of Georgian Bay. The park is filled with old growth forests, curious black bears, rare reptiles and incredible hiking trails. Stop in at the park visitor center in the town Tobermory for up-to-date information on the status of certain trails and activities.

Hop on the Bruce Trail (the longest and oldest footpath in Canada) for a chance to explore the Niagara Escarpment, a UNESCO World Biosphere Reserve. Or hop on the Georgian Bay-Marr Lake Trail for the quickest and easiest access to the park's dramatic lakeside cliffs. For easy-on-the-knees and back hiking, head for the Singing Sands Day Use area—it's home to a variety of trailheads that provide lower difficulty casual day hikes.

For more adventurous types, Bruce Peninsula is also one of the best caving and spelunking areas in the country. Ancient holes and crevices that were carved out of the Niagara Escarpment more than 7,000 years ago during the last ice age are ripe for exploration. Greig's Caves, the Grotto, Bruce's Caves and a loop trail on Flowerpot Island are among the most popular.

Ancient holes and crevices that were carved out of the Niagara Escarpment more than 7,000 years ago during the last ice age are ripe for exploration.

The community of Sauble Beach and the surrounding area is a rewarding and highly relaxing spot to set up camp and enjoy the great outdoors. You'll have plenty of company if you're visiting in the summer, but the pace and vibe of this charming small town handles the influx with ease.

ON

For More Information

Sauble Beach Tourism Office
519-422-1262
www.saublebeach.com

Ontario Travel
800-668-2746
www.ontariotravel.net

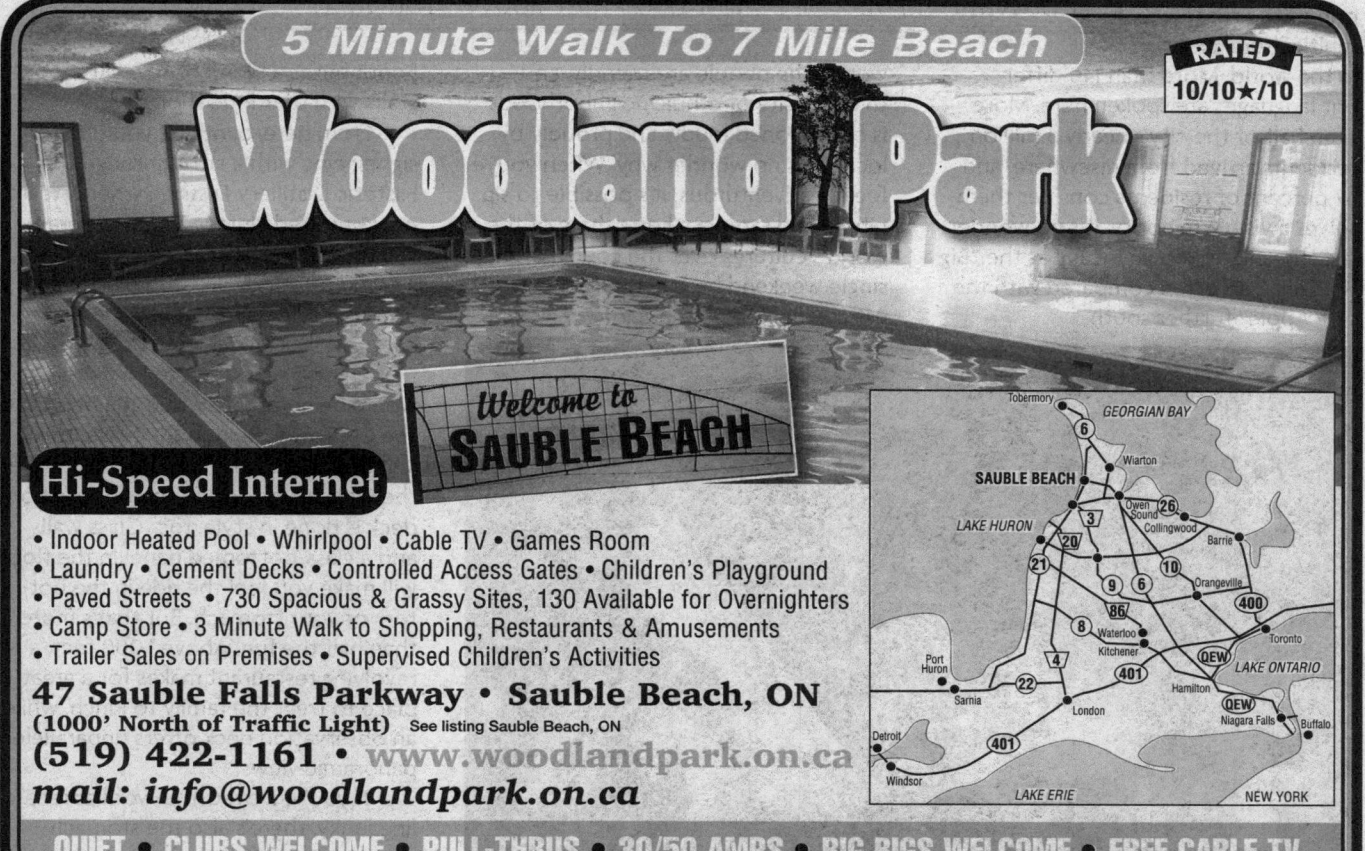

Getty Images/iStockphoto

TORONTO

Feel the buzz of a world-class metropolis

For all of its world-class attractions and thriving cultural scene, Toronto's greatest feature might just be something that's impossible to define adequately or properly quantify: its people.

Blessed with a kaleidoscope of diverse neighborhoods, an easy-to-navigate layout and an astoundingly friendly atmosphere, this is also one of the most multicultural cities in the world. More than 140 different languages are spoken here. More than half of the city's nearly 3 million residents arrived from elsewhere, and 47 percent of residents consider themselves a visible minority. It's no wonder why the city is known locally as the "Big Smoke" is so often compared with the "Big Apple" further south.

But the comparisons between New York and Canada's largest metropolis mostly end after the first glance. Dig any deeper or spend any amount of time here at all and you'll discover a city that's remarkably free from violent crime and racial intolerance, regularly ranking in the top 10 safest cities in the world. The people are friendly, and the diversity of ethnic neighborhoods is championed loudly and proudly by locals. It's no wonder why. When you're feeling adventurous, it's possible to sip, nibble and sample a lion's share of the world's cultures over the course of a single weekend here in the fourth largest city in North America.

> For the dyed-the-wool adrenaline junky, a visit to the CN Tower isn't complete without the stomach-churning EdgeWalk. Stroll more than 1,600 feet above ground.

The Royal Ontario Museum with the Michael Lee-Chin Crystal addition.
www.torontowide.com

Brews, Big Buildings and More

One of the best places to start is St. Lawrence Market. If Toronto is a comin together of the world's ethnicities and cultures, St. Lawrence Market is where Toronto itself comes together. Established in 1803, the modern day market i split into two: Market North and Market South. Market North teems with fresh produce and baked goods from local farmers and bakeries. Market South mixes a blend of specialty food stalls with boutique shops.

From here, continue your city sightseeing with a stroll through the Historic Distillery District, where steam punk-inspired vintage Victorian-era warehouses have been converted into a world of trendy art studios, design houses, coffee shops and gourmet eateries.

Of course, no trip to Toronto would be complete without a ride to u the CN Tower. Built in the 1970s, this is still the tallest freestanding structure o the planet. The ride to the observation deck is done in style, too. Glass walls and a glass-bottomed panel in the floo will make you feel the ride in the bottom of your stomach. But that's more than half the fun. Above 1,000 feet, a revolving restaurant makes for a great place to treat the family to lunch, while an observation deck offers unparallelec panoramic views.

If you're a dyed-the-wool adrenaline junky, there's also the stomach-churning EdgeWalk option, which is exactly what it sounds like. You don a jumpsuit and safety harness, clip into a rail on the outside of the tower and go for a nice leisurely stroll around the top rim of the observation deck, more than 1,600 feet above the surface of the earth.

Trips to the Past

When your feet are back firmly on the ground, downtown Toronto is perfectly tailored to please all interest and all age groups.

History buffs will want to spend some time spelunking about in the depths of the massive Royal Ontario Museum. More than 6 million items, artifacts and specimens are found here, and truly curious visitors can expect to spend at least an entire day combing the collections. The museum is spread across four floors and divided into two sections: The Natural History Galleries (showcasing the biological history and diversity of the world's plant and animal species) and the World Culture Galleries (full of artifacts spanning the history of civilization, from Ancient Egypt to the turn of the twentieth century).

For sports enthusiasts, a trip to the Hockey Hall of Fame should be high on the must-visit list. In Canada, the significance of this timeless institution borders on being spiritual. The hall offers a high-tech overview of the history of the game of hockey through a mix of visual displays and interactive exhibits. Highlights include a virtual reality experience with Wayne Gretzky, the evolution of the goalie mask exhibit and, of course, the Stanley Cup itself.

Animal lovers can make their way to the north side of Roundhouse Park, where Ripley's brand new Aquarium of Canada displays more than 15,000 marine animals. After your done there, the Toronto Zoo is located about a half-hour away on the north side of the city. Home to more than 5,000 exotic animals and occupying 700 acres, it's one of the largest zoos in the world.

The Distillery District as seen from the Main Gate with Gooderham and Worts sign.
The Distillery Historic District

ON

For More Information

Toronto Convention and Visitors Association
800-499-2514
www.seetorontonow.com

Ontario Travel
800-668-2746
www.ontariotravel.net

Welcome to

ONTARIO

KOA

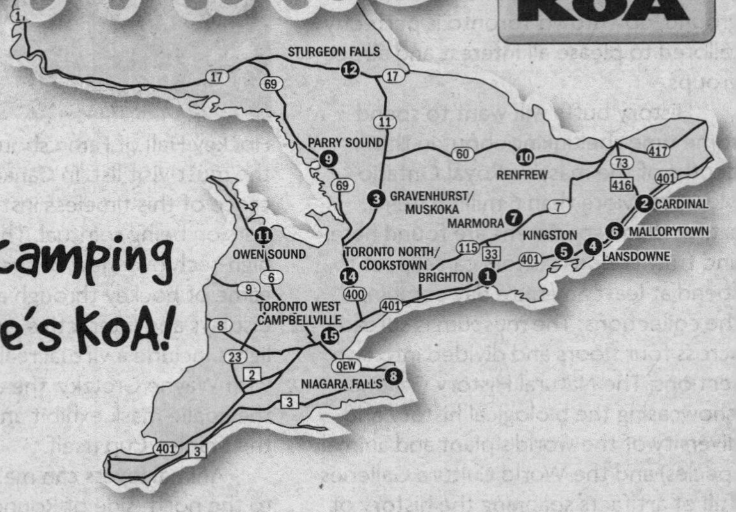

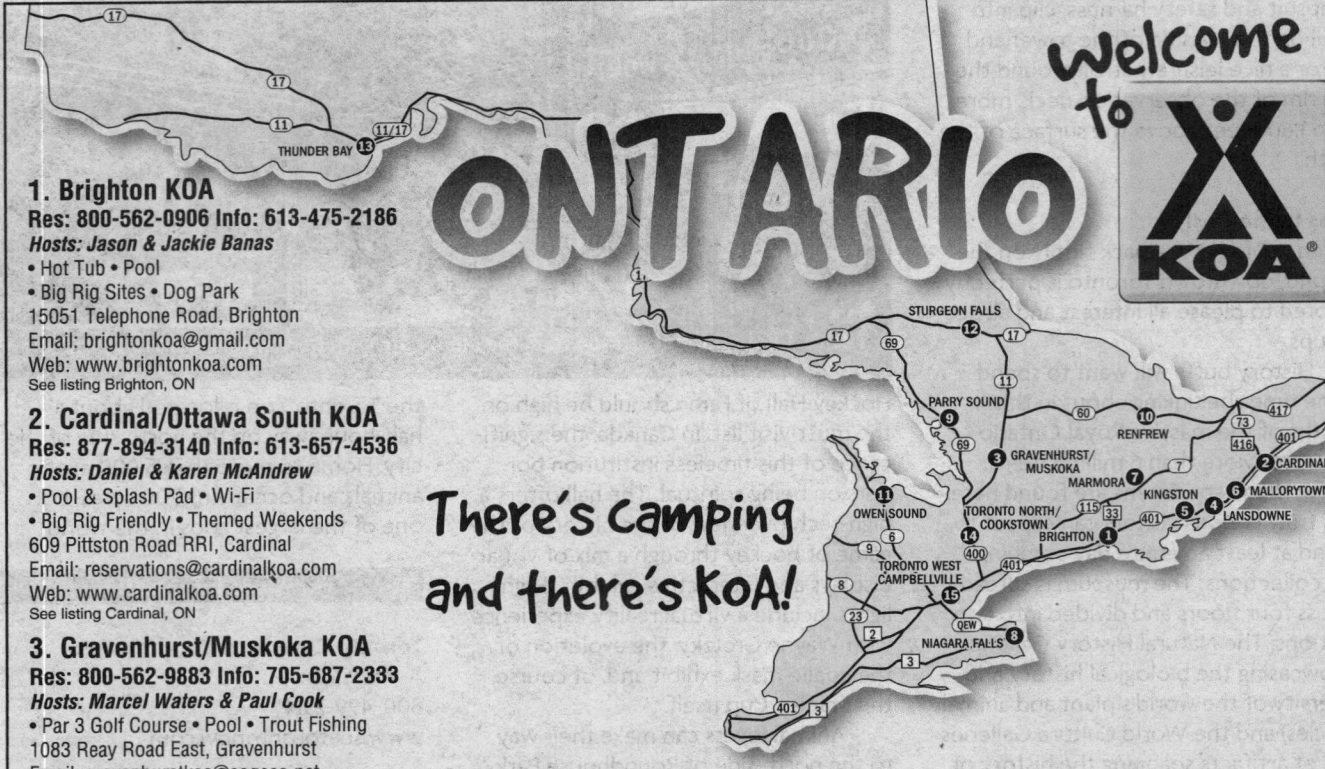

There's camping and there's KOA!

1. Brighton KOA

Res: 800-562-0906 Info: 613-475-2186

Hosts: Jason & Jackie Banas

- Hot Tub • Pool
- Big Rig Sites • Dog Park

15051 Telephone Road, Brighton
Email: brightonkoa@gmail.com
Web: www.brightonkoa.com
See listing Brighton, ON

2. Cardinal/Ottawa South KOA

Res: 877-894-3140 Info: 613-657-4536

Hosts: Daniel & Karen McAndrew

- Pool & Splash Pad • Wi-Fi
- Big Rig Friendly • Themed Weekends

609 Pittston Road RRI, Cardinal
Email: reservations@cardinalkoa.com
Web: www.cardinalkoa.com
See listing Cardinal, ON

3. Gravenhurst/Muskoka KOA

Res: 800-562-9883 Info: 705-687-2333

Hosts: Marcel Waters & Paul Cook

- Par 3 Golf Course • Pool • Trout Fishing

1083 Reay Road East, Gravenhurst
Email: gravenhurstkoa@cogeco.net
Web: www.koa.com/campgrounds/gravenhurst/
See listing Gravenhurst, ON

4. 1000 Islands Ivy Lea KOA

Res: 800-562-2471 Info: 613-659-2817

Hosts: Dave & Susan Barton

- Wi-Fi • Big Rig Friendly
- Pull-Thru Sites, 50 AMP

514-1000 Islands Parkway, Lansdowne
Email: campinfo@1000islandskoa.com
Web: www.1000islandskoa.com
See listing Gananoque, ON

5. 1000 Islands/Kingston KOA

Res: 800-562-9178 Info: 613-546-6140

Hosts: Patrick, Amanda & Hans Wagner

- Big Rig Friendly • Pull-Thru Sites
- Heated Pool • Close to Fort Henry

2039 Cordukes Road, Kingston
Email: koakingston@hotmail.com
Web: www.kingstonkoa.com
See listing Kingston, ON

6. 1000 Islands/Mallorytown KOA

Res: 800-562-9725 Info: 613-923-5339

Hosts: Richard & Susan Marcoux

- Big Rig Friendly • Long Pull-Thru Sites
- Htd Pool w/Slide, Hydrotherapy Jets & Kiddie Pool
- Jumping Pilllow • A/C Cabins w/BBQs

1477 County Road 2, Mallorytown
Email: koa@1000islandscamping.com
Web: www.1000islandscamping.com
See listing Mallorytown, ON

7. Marmora KOA

Res: 800-562-9156 Info: 613-472-2233

Hosts: Dan & Alexandra Petr

- Indoor & Outdoor Pool • Fishing
- ATV & Cyclist Trails
- Trailer & Cabin Rentals

178 KOA Campground Road, Marmora
Email: marmorakoa@bellnet.ca
Web: www.marmorakoa.com
See listing Marmora, ON

8. Niagara Falls KOA

Res: 800-562-6478 Info: 905-356-2267

Host: Lisa Thompson

- Minutes to the Falls • Heated Indoor Pool
- Outdoor Pools • Deluxe Cabins

8625 Lundys Lane, Niagara Falls
Email: niagara@koa.net
Web: www.niagarakoa.net
See listing Niagara Falls, ON

9. Parry Sound KOA

Res: 800-562-2681 Info: 705-378-2721

Hosts: Don & Michelle Berry

- Big Rig Friendly Pull-Thru Sites
- ATV Trails from Park
- Heated Pool • Free WiFi
- Deluxe Cabins • Basic Cabins

276 Rankin Lake Rd, Seguin
Email: parrysoundkoa@gmail.com
Web: www.parrysoundkoa.com
See listing Seguin, ON

10. Renfrew/Ottawa West KOA

Res: 800-562-3980 Info: 613-432-6280

Hosts: Greg & Angela Burgess

- Splash Pad • Driving Range
- Wi-Fi • Fishing • Jump Pad

2826 Johnston Road, Renfrew
Email: info@renfrewkoa.com
Web: www.koa.com/campgrounds/renfrew/
See listing Renfrew, ON

11. Rocksprings KOA Owen Sound

Res: 800-562-8675 Info: 519-371-1331

Hosts: Christian & Elisabeth Thomann

- Pull-Thru Sites
- Spacious Open & Shaded Sites
- Kamping Kabins • Swimming Pool

RR 6 – 398235 28 Ave East, Owen Sound
Email: owensoundkoa@hotmail.com
Web: www.koa.com/campgrounds/owen-sound/
See listing Owen Sound, ON

12. Sturgeon Falls KOA

Res: 800-562-7798 Info: 705-753-5759

Hosts: Greg & Gina Demers

- Big Rig Sites • Swimming in the River
- Fishing • Marina Slips • Cabin Rentals

818 Lalande Road, Sturgeon Falls
Email: sturgeonfallskoa@gmail.com
Web: www.koa.com/campgrounds/sturgeon-falls/
See listing Sturgeon Falls, ON

13. Thunder Bay KOA

Res: 800-562-4162 Info: 807-683-6221

Hosts: The Kuper Family

- Big Rig Friendly • 2 Heated Pools
- Wi-Fi • Catch & Release Trout Pond

162 Spruce River Road, Shuniah
Email: tbaykoa@tbaytel.net
Web: www.thunderbaykoa.com
See listing Thunder Bay, ON

14. Toronto North/Cookstown KOA

Res: 800-562-2691 Info: 705-458-2267

Hosts: Matt & Allison Stovold

- On Hwy 400 • Heated Pool • Cabin Rentals
- Big Rig Friendly • Pull-Thru Sites

139 Reive Blvd, Cookstown
Email: info@torontonorthkoa.com
Web: www.torontonorthkoa.com
See listing Cookstown, ON

15. Toronto West KOA

Res: 800-562-1523 Info: 905-854-2495

Hosts: Shawn & Bridget Saulnier

- New Deluxe Cabins w/AC, Heating, Fridge, BBQ, Patio • Heated Pool • Free WiFi
- Close to Toronto and 7 Conversation Parks

9301 Second Line, Campbellville
Email: info@torontowestkoa.on.ca
Web: www.koa.com/campgrounds/toronto-west
See listing Campbellville, ON

Ontario

CONSULTANTS

Fred & Susan Denischuk

ADOLPHUSTOWN — D8 *Lennox, Addington*

UNITED EMPIRE LOYALIST HERITAGE CENTRE & PARK (Public) E-bnd: At W-end of town, on Hwy 33 (Loyalist Parkway) (R) Fee to museum included in camping fee). 2015 rates: $33 to $42. May 15 to Oct 8. (613)373-2196

AILSA CRAIG — E3 *Middlesex*

SHADY PINES CAMPGROUND **Ratings: 7/8.5★/8.5** (Campground) 2015 rates: $42. May 1 to Oct 8. (519)232-4210 rr 1, 11316 Petty Street, Ailsa Craig, ON N0M 1A0

ALFRED — B9 *Prescott-Russell*

CEDAR SHADE CAMPGROUND **Ratings: 8/9★/9** (Campground) 2015 rates: $49 to $53. May 15 to Sep 30. (613)679-4447 530 Peladeau Rd, Alfred, ON K0B 1A0

EVERGREEN CAMPING RESORT **Ratings: 8/8.5★/9** (Campground) 2015 rates: $50 to $55. May 1 to Oct 1. (888)679-4059 5279 CR 17, Alfred, ON K0B 1A0

ALGONQUIN PARK — B6 *Nipissing*

ALGONQUIN/CANISBAY LAKE (Prov Pk) From W Park Gate, E 24 km (15 mi) on Hwy 60 to Canisbay Campground Rd, N 1.6 km (1 mi) (L). Use of generators is allowed. 2015 rates: $43.22 to $49.44. May 18 to Nov 14. (705)633-5572

ALGONQUIN/COON LAKE (Prov Pk) From W Park Gate, E 38.6 km (24 mi) on Hwy 60 to Rock Lake Rd, S 5 km (3.1 mi) (R). Generators allowed. Pit toilets. 2015 rates: $38.44. Jun 14 to Sep 3. (705)633-5572

ALGONQUIN/KEARNEY LAKE (Prov Pk) From W Park Gate, E 39.4 km (24.5 mi) on Hwy 60 (R). 2015 rates: $43.22. May 18 to Sep 7. (705)633-5572

ALGONQUIN/KIOSK (Prov Pk) From Jct of Hwys 17 & 630, S 19.3 km (12 mi) on Hwy 630 (E). 2015 rates: $38.14. Apr 26 to Nov 14. (705)633-5572

ALGONQUIN/LAKE OF TWO RIVERS (Prov Pk) From W Park Gate, E 33.8 km (21 mi) on Hwy 60 (L). 2015 rates: $43.22. May 18 to Nov 14. (705)633-5572

ALGONQUIN/MEW LAKE (Prov Pk) From W Park Gate, E 33 km (20.5 mi) on Hwy 60 (L). 2015 rates: $43.22. (705)633-5572

ALGONQUIN/POG LAKE (Prov Pk) From W Park Gate, E 37 km (23 mi) on Hwy 60 (L). 2015 rates: $43.22. May 18 to Sep 3. (705)633-5572

ALGONQUIN/ROCK LAKE (Prov Pk) From W Park Gate, E 38.6 km (24 mi) on Hwy 60 to Rock Lake Rd, S 6.4 km (4 mi) (E). 2015 rates: $43.22. Apr 26 to Nov 14. (705)633-5572

ALGONQUIN/TEA LAKE (Prov Pk) From W Park Gate, E 12 km (7.5 mi) on Hwy 60 (L). Generators allowed. 2015 rates: $39.55. May 18 to Sep 3. (705)633-5572

ALLENFORD — C4 *Bruce*

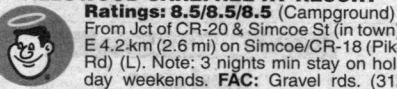

ARRAN LAKE CAREFREE RV RESORT
Ratings: 7/7/7 (Campground) From Hwy 21 go E to Bruce Road 3, turn S for 21 km (13.5 mi) turn E onto Sideroad 6 2.7 km (1.68 mi) to Concession Road 12, 1/2 km (1/4 mi). **FAC:** Gravel rds. (175 spaces). Avail: 50 grass, 6 pull-thrus (50 x 75), back-ins (45 x 60), mostly side by side hkups, 50 full hkups (30 amps), seasonal sites, WiFi, tent sites, rentals, showers $, dump, mobile sewer, laundry, groc, fire rings, firewood, controlled access. **REC:** Arran Lake: swim, fishing, playground. Pet restrict(B). Eco-friendly, 2015 rates: $40 to $56. May 9 to Oct 20.
(519)934-1224 Lat: 44.497463, Lon: -81.263963
53 Concession 12 West, Allenford, ON N0H 1A0
arranlake@carefreeRVresorts.com
www.carefreeRVresorts.ca/arranlake
See ad pages 1445, 1420.

Use our handy Snowbird Destinations guide in the front of the Guide to find RV-friendly destinations throughout the Sunbelt.

ALLISTON — D5 *Simcoe*

EARL ROWE (Prov Pk) From town, W 1 mi on Hwy 89 to Concession 7, N 0.5 mi (L). 2015 rates: $12.75 to $43.75. May 9 to Oct 14. (705)435-2498

NICOLSTON DAM CAMPGROUND
Ratings: 8.5/8★/8 (Campground) From jct Hwy 400 & 89: Go 11 km/7 mi W on Hwy 89. **FAC:** Gravel rds. (78 spaces). Avail: 53 grass, 15 pull-thrus (30 x 75), back-ins (30 x 45), mostly side by side hkups, 53 W, 53 E (15/30 amps), seasonal sites, WiFi, tent sites, rentals, dump, mobile sewer, laundry, groc, fire rings, firewood, controlled access. **REC:** heated pool, Nottawasage River: fishing, playground. Pet restrict(B/Q). Eco-friendly, 2015 rates: $35.40 to $62. Disc: AAA, military. May 1 to Oct 15.
(705)435-7946 Lat: 44.167450, Lon: -79.807160
5140 5th Line Essa, Alliston, ON L9R 1V2
nicolston-dam@sympatico.ca
www.nicolstondam.vpweb.ca
See ad this page, 1420.

ALVINSTON — E3 *Middlesex*

A W CAMPBELL CONSERVATION AREA (Public) From Jct of Hwy 402 & Hwy 79 (Nauvoo Rd), S 11.2 mi to Shiloh Line, E 1.7 mi (R). 2015 rates: $33. Apr 23 to Oct 11. (519)847-5357

AMHERSTBURG — F2 *Essex*

HOLIDAY BEACH CONSERVATION AREA (Public) From town, S 6 mi on Hwy 18 to Malden Center, S (right) 2 mi on CR-50 (R). 2015 rates: $25 to $35. Apr 19 to Oct 15. (519)736-3772

WILLOWOOD CAREFREE RV RESORT
Ratings: 8.5/8.5/8.5 (Campground) From Jct of CR-20 & Simcoe St (in town), E 4.2 km (2.6 mi) on Simcoe/CR-18 (Pike Rd) (L). Note: 3 nights min stay on holiday weekends. **FAC:** Gravel rds. (312 spaces). 251 Avail: 4 gravel, 247 grass, 4 pull-thrus (35 x 62), back-ins (45 x 50), 17 full hkups, 221 W, 221 E (15/50 amps), seasonal sites, WiFi $, tent sites, rentals, dump, mobile sewer, laundry, groc, LP bottles, fire rings, firewood. **REC:** pool, wading pool, shuffleboard, playground. Pet restrict(B). Partial handicap access. Eco-friendly, 2015 rates: $48 to $55. Disc: AAA. Apr 15 to Oct 15. ATM.
(519)736-3201 Lat: 42.09881, Lon: -83.05509
4610 Essex County Rd 18, Rr 1 (Pike Rd), Amherstburg, ON N9V 2Y7
willowood@carefreervresorts.com
www.carefreervresorts.com/willowood
See ad pages 1445, 1420.

APPIN — E3 *Middlesex*

SILVER DOVE ESTATES (Campground) (Phone Update) 2015 rates: $36 to $39. May 1 to Oct 8. (519)289-2100 4838 Switzer Dr, Appin, ON N0L 1A0

ARNPRIOR — B8 *Renfrew*

FITZROY (Prov Pk) From town, E 13 mi on Hwy 17, (L). 2015 rates: $32.90 to $43.75. May 9 to Oct 14. (613)623-5159

ARTHUR — D4 *Wellington*

CONESTOGA FAMILY CAMPGROUNDS INC **Ratings: 8/9★/9** (Campground) 2015 rates: $40. May 15 to Oct 18. (877)88-CAMP8 8772 Concession #9, Wellington North, ON N0G 2K0

ATHERLEY — C5 *Simcoe*

MARA (Prov Pk) From Orillia, E 3 mi on Hwy 12 S to Courtland St, S 1 mi (E). 2015 rates: $12.75 to $43.75. May 9 to Sep 1. (705)326-4451

ATIKOKAN — F7 *Rainy River*

BUNNELL PARK CAMPGROUND (Public) From Jct of SR-622 & Saturn Ave, E 0.1 mi on Saturn Ave (R). 2015 rates: $13 to $16. May 1 to Sep 30. (807)597-1234

QUETICO/DAWSON TRAIL CAMPGROUND (Prov Pk) From town, E 30 mi on Hwy 11 to access rd, S 1 mi (E). 2015 rates: $12.75 to $43.75. (807)597-2735

AYLMER — E4 *Elgin*

SPRINGWATER CONSERVATION AREA (CATFISH CREEK CONS AUTH.) (Prov Pk) From town: Go 5 km/3 mi W on Hwy 3, then 3 km/1-3/4 mi S on Springwater Rd at Orwell. 2015 rates: $35 to $43. (519)773-9037

AYTON — D4 *Grey*

RIVER PLACE PARK CAMPGROUND LTD. **Ratings: 6/7/7** (Campground) 2015 rates: $38. May 15 to Oct 15. (519)338-3010 232352 Concession 2 West Grey, Ayton, ON N0G 1C0

SHAMADON RV RESORT **Ratings: 7.5/8.5★/8** (RV Resort) 2015 rates: $45 to $120. May 13 to Oct 15. (519)323-4592 231764 Concession 2, Rr3, Ayton, ON N0G 1C0

SILENT VALLEY PARK RESORT - PARKBRIDGE
Ratings: 8/8/8 (Campground) From Jct of Hwys 89 & 6, N 9.6 km (6 mi) on Hwy 6 to Grey Rd 9, W 2.9 km (1.5 mi) to Concession 2 WGR, N 2 km (1.25 mi) (R). Min. stay 3 ngts on holiday weekends. **FAC:** All weather rds. (335 spaces). 57 Avail: 8 gravel, 49 grass, patios, 5 pull-thrus (40 x 75), back-ins (25 x 60), mostly side by side hkups, 28 full hkups, 18 W, 14 E (15/30 amps), seasonal sites, WiFi Hotspot, tent sites, dump, laundry, groc, fire rings, firewood, controlled access. **REC:** heated pool, wading pool, Murray's Lake: swim, fishing, playground. Pets OK. RV age restrict, eco-friendly, 2015 rates: $48 to $56. May 15 to Oct 15.
(519)665-7787 Lat: 44.06360, Lon: -80.83296
142571 Road 35, Rr 3, Ayton, ON N0G 1C0
silentvalleyinfo@parkbrige.ca
http://www.parkbridge.com/en-ca/rv-cottages/Silent-Valley
See ad pages 1417 (Welcome Section), 1420.

ON

BAILIEBORO — D6 *Peterborough*

BENSFORT BRIDGE RESORT, LTD
Ratings: 7/8★/7.5 (Campground) From Jct of Hwy 28 & Lakeview Rd go E 6 km (4.5 mi) to stop sign, at stop sign turn left and continue on CR-2 (R). Min. 2 days stay on holiday weekends. **FAC:** All weather rds. (50 spaces). Avail: 18 grass, 3 pull-thrus (40 x 50), back-ins (40 x 50), some side by side hkups, 13 full hkups, 5 W, 5 E (30 amps), seasonal sites, tent sites, rentals, dump, laundry, fire rings, firewood, controlled access. **REC:** Otonabee River: swim, fishing, marina, playground, rec open to public. Pet restrict(B). Partial handicap access. Eco-friendly, 2015 rates: $35 to $40. May 5 to Oct 15. AAA Approved
(705)939-6515 Lat: 44.20518, Lon: -78.27701
1821 CR 2, Bailieboro, ON K0L 1B0
jenni.greyer@nexicom.net
www.bensfortbridgeresort.com
See ad page 1436.

Clean Green! Vinegar and baking soda can be used to clean almost anything. Mix in a little warm water with either of these and you've got yourself an all-purpose cleaner.

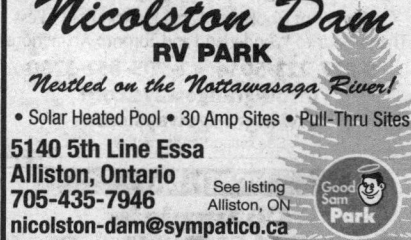

Camping Around Ontario

BAILIEBORO
Bensfort Bridge Resort, LTD
• Cottage Rentals • RV Sites-Full Hookups
• Fishing • Boating & Marina
1821 County Rd. 2 • 705-939-6515
jenni.greyer@nexicom.net
www.bensfortbridgeresort.com
See listing Bailieboro, ON

CARRYING PLACE
North Shore RV Park
Open May 1st to Thanksgiving
• Spacious Full Hookups • Big Rig Friendly
• 30/50 Amp • WiFi • Excellent Fishing
1675 County Road 64 • 613-475-2036
nshore@northshorepark.com
www.northshorepark.com
See listing Carrying Place, ON

CHESLEY
Cedar Rail Family Campground
• Big Rig Pull-Thru Sites • 30 & 50 Amp • Heated Pool
• Wedding Venues • 2 Rec Halls • Fishing
015259 Grey Bruce Line R R 3 • 519-363-3387
cedarrailcamp@bellnet.ca
www.cedarrailcamp.com
See listing Chesley, ON

EDEN
Red Oak Travel Park
• Swimming Pool • Internet • Group Camping Area
• Serviced & Unserviced Sites
Located on Hwy #3
54428 Talbot Line • 519-866-3504
camp@redoaktravelpark.com
www.redoaktravelpark.com
See listing Eden, ON

HAMILTON
Flamboro Valley Camping Resort
• Big Rig Friendly • Heated Pool/Hot Tub
• Water Park-Wading Pool • Trailer & Cabin Rentals
1158 Hwy 97 • 1-905-659-5053
info@flamborovalley.com
www.flamborovalley.com
See listing Hamilton, ON

KINCARDINE
Aintree Trailer Park LTD
• Shady Cedar Bordered RV Sites • Sunny Sand Beaches of Lake Huron • 1 Mile West of Hiway 21
10-20% Off-Season Discounts!
1-877-396-8533
aintreepark@hotmail.com
www.aintreepark.com
See listing Kincardine, ON

MANITOULIN ISLAND
Manitoulin Resort
• Family Campground & Cottages • Beach Area
• Boat Docking & Rentals • Great Fishing
• Recreation Facilities • Big Rig Friendly
705-859-3550
info@manitoulinresort.com
www.manitoulinresort.com
See listing Manitowaning, ON

KAGAWONG/MANITOULIN ISLAND
Norm's Tent & Trailer Park
• 15/30 Amp Power • Cabin Rentals
• Fishing • Swimming
1125B Lakeshore Rd.
705-282-2827
normsttpk@yahoo.ca
See listing Kagawong, ON

MIDLAND
Smith's Trailer Park & Camp
• Heated Pool • On Little Lake • Pull-Thru Sites
• Fishing & Boating • Ramp • Clean Washrooms
736 King Street • info@smithscamp.ca
705-526-4339 • 1-855-728-4760
www.smithscamp.ca
See listing Midland, ON

NIAGARA FALLS
Riverside Park Motel & Campground
Quiet Family Camping by the Majestic Niagara River
• Heated Pool • Bike Trail
• Super Clean Washrooms
905-382-2204
www.riversidepark.net
See listing Niagara Falls, ON

SANDFORD
Grangeways RV Park & Family Campground
• 30 Amp 3 pt Hookups • Large Circular Pool • Less Than 1 Hour to Wonderland and Toronto Attractions
1-877-223-5034 • 1-905-852-3260
info@grangeways.com
www.grangeways.com
See listing Sandford, ON

THESSALON
Brownlee Lake Park Resort
• Pull-Thru Sites • Rental Cabins
• Fishing • Licensed European Restaurant
(Fri & Sat Only) Reservations Required
136 Brownlee Rd. N. • 1-705-842-2118
www.brownleelake.com
See listing Thessalon, ON

TOBERMORY
Happy Hearts Park
• Fully Serviced Sites • 3 km to Ferry
• Pool • Cabin Rentals • Free WiFi
• Mini-Golf • Shuffleboard
1-519-596-2455
wilson@amtelecom.net
www.happyheartspark.com
See listing Tobermory, ON

NORTH BAY
Champlain Tent, RV & Trailer Park
• Pull-Thru & Back-In Sites
• WiFi • Fishing & Swimming • Pet Friendly
1-705-474-4669 • 1202 Premier Rd.
info@champlaintrailerpark.com
www.champlaintrailerpark.com
See listing North Bay, ON

VERMILION BAY
Crystal Lake Campground & RV Park
• Paved Big Rig Pull-Thru Sites • Sandy Beach • WiFi
• Fishing • Swimming • Easy On/Easy Off Hwy 17
807-220-5467
info@crystallakecampground.ca
www.crystallakecampground.ca
See listing Vermillion Bay ON

WOODSTOCK
Willow Lake Park
• Pull-Thru 50 Amp Sites
• Extended Stay Sites
• Heated Pool
519-537-7301
willowlake@xplornet.com
www.willowlakepark.on.ca
See listing Woodstock, ON

WASAGA BEACH
Cedar Grove Park
• Located on Sandy Beach • 30 Amp
• Chip Truck • Mini Golf
100 Cedar Grove Pkwy.
705-429-2134
See listing Wasaga Beach, ON

PORT DOVER
Shore Acres Park
On the Shores of Lake Erie
• Fully Serviced Overnight & Seasonal Sites
• Pet/Tent Free Resort
Close to Port Dover Downtown
Season Opens April 15 – October 15, 2016
574 Radical Road • 519-583-2222
camping@kwic.com
www.shoreacres.ca
See listing Port Dover, ON

BAINSVILLE
Maplewood Acres RV Park
• Big Rig Friendly • Lg Pull-Thru Sites
• Free WiFi • Pool with Splash Pad
Eay On/Easy Off Hwy 401 Near Quebec Border
21848 Concession 3 • 613-347-2130
info@maplewoodacres.com
www.maplewoodacres.com
See listing Bainsville, ON

BAINSVILLE — C10 *Stormont, Dundas, Glengarry*

MAPLEWOOD ACRES RV PARK
Ratings: 8.5/9.5★/9 (Campground) From Hwy 401 east exit 825 - 4th Line Road (last exit in Ontario). 4th Line Rd N for 3 km (1.8 mi). R on Concession 3 road. R. **FAC:** Gravel rds. (92 spaces). Avail: 42 gravel, 13 pull-thrus (40 x 85), back-ins (40 x 50), 29 full hkups, 13 W, 13 E (30/50 amps), seasonal sites, WiFi, tent sites, dump, laundry, groc, LP bottles, fire rings, firewood. **REC:** heated pool, playground. Pets OK. Partial handicap access. Big rig sites, eco-friendly, 2015 rates: $43.25 to $46.51. May 8 to Sep 27.
(613)347-2130 Lat: 45.225637, Lon: -74.405180
21848 Concession Road 3, Bainsville, ON K0C 1E0
info@maplewoodacres.com
maplewoodacres.com
See ad opposite page, 1420.

BANCROFT — C7 *Hastings*

BANCROFT CAMPGROUND **Ratings: 7/7/7** (Campground) 2015 rates: $26 to $32. (877)404-4160 98 Bird Lake Road, Bancroft, ON K0L 1C0

SILENT LAKE (Prov Pk) From town, S 6 mi on Hwy 28 (L). 2015 rates: $12.75 to $43.75. May 9 to Oct 14. (613)339-2807

THE HOMESTEAD TRAILER PARK **Ratings: 7.5/8.5★/8.5** (RV Area in MHP) 2015 rates: $40 to $45. May 15 to Oct 15. (613)339-2500 1123 Homestead Rd, Bancroft, ON K0L 1C0

BARRIE — D5 *Springwater*

BARRIE KOA **Ratings: 8.5/9.5★/8.5** (Campground) 2015 rates: $43 to $99. May 1 to Oct 15. (800)562-7397 3138 Pentanguishene Road, Rr 1, Barrie, ON L4M 4Y8

BARRY'S BAY — B7 *Renfrew*

CHIPPAWA RESORT AND EASY LIVING CAMPING & RV RESORT
Ratings: 7/9.5★/8 (Campground) From Jct of Hwy 60 & CR-62, S 10.3 km (6.4 mi) on CR-62 to Chippawa Rd, W 2.3 km (1.4 mi), follow signs (L). Note: Min. 3 night stay on holiday weekends. **FAC:** Gravel rds. (46 spaces). Avail: 36 grass, 14 pull-thrus (35 x 75), back-ins (35 x 40), 28 full hkups, 8 W, 8 E (30 amps), seasonal sites, WiFi Hotspot, tent sites, rentals, dump, laundry, fire rings, firewood, restaurant. **REC:** Kamaniskeg Lake: swim, fishing, playground. Pet restrict(B). Eco-friendly, 2015 rates: $55 to $80. May 15 to Oct 15.
(800)267-8507 Lat: 45.39213, Lon: -77.65537
Rr1, 835 Chippawa Road, Barry's Bay, ON K0J 1B0
chippawa@igs.net
www.chippawaresort.com
See ad this page, 1420.

BATCHAWANA BAY — A1 *Algoma*

PANCAKE BAY (Prov Pk) From Sault Ste Marie, N 47 mi on Hwy 17 (L). 2015 rates: $36.75 to $43.75. May 2 to Oct 14. (705)882-2209

BEARDMORE — F8 *Thunder Bay*

HIGH HILL HARBOUR MARINA & CAMPGROUND (Public) From Jct of Hwy 11 & Hwy 580, W 11 mi on Hwy 580(L). Proceed to Poplar Lodge Park for registration. 2015 rates: $29.75. May 14 to Sep 6. (807)875-2639

POPLAR LODGE PARK (Public) From Jct of Hwys 11 & 580, W 7 mi on Hwy 580 (E). 2015 rates: $28.85 to $33.90. May 14 to Sep 6. (807)875-2639

BELLE RIVER — F2 *Essex*

ROCHESTER PLACE RV, GOLF & MARINE RESORT **Ratings: 7.5/9.5★/7.5** (RV Park) 2015 rates: $40 to $47. May 1 to Oct 31. (800)563-5940 981 Country Road 2, Belle River, ON N0R 1A0

BLOOMFIELD — D7 *Prince Edward*

HIDEAWAY TRAILER PARK **Ratings: 6/5/7** (Campground) 2015 rates: $49 to $54. May 8 to Oct 8. (888)928-8488 1024 CR 12, Picton, ON K0K 2T0

SANDBANKS (Prov Pk) From town, SW 3 mi on CR-10 to CR-11, W (right) 4 mi (E). 2015 rates: $28.75 to $43.75. Apr 24 to Oct 12. (613)393-3319

BOBCAYGEON — C6 *Peterborough*

BOBCAYGEON BEACH PARK (Public) From Jct of Hwy 36 & King St, W 0.5 mi on King St to Sherwood St, N 0.2 mi to Park St, W 0.2 mi (R). 2015 rates: $25. May to Oct. (705)738-2435

LONESOME PINE COTTAGE AND RV RESORT - PARKBRIDGE
Ratings: 7/7★/7.5 (Campground) From Jct of Hwy 7 & Hwy 17 turn R on Pigeon Lake Rd/County Rd 17 for 13.2 km (8.2 mi) (R). **FAC:** Gravel rds. (299 spaces). Avail: 12 gravel, back-ins (25 x 50), 12 full hkups (30 amps), seasonal sites, rentals, laundry, groc, LP bottles, fire rings, firewood, controlled access. **REC:** heated pool, Pigeon Lake: swim, playground. Pets OK. Eco-friendly, 2015 rates: $42. May 2 to Oct 14. No CC.
(705)738-2684 Lat: 44.441588, Lon: -78.509221
2346 Pigeon Lake Road, Bobcaygeon, ON K0M 1A0
lonesomepineinfo@parkbridge.com
http://www.parkbridge.com/en-ca/rv-cottages/Lonesome-Pine
See ad pages 1417 (Welcome Section), 1420.

BOLTON — D5 *Peel*

ALBION HILLS CAMPGROUND (Public) From Bolton, N 8.8 km (5.5 mi) on Hwy 50 (L). Minimum stay of 3 ngts on holiday w/ends. 2015 rates: $27 to $32.50. May 1 to Oct 31. (855)811-0111

BORNHOLM — E4 *Perth*

WOODLAND LAKE CAREFREE RV RESORT
Ratings: 7.5/8.5/7.5 (Campground) From Jct of Hwys 8 & 23, NE 9.7 km (6 mi) on Hwy 23 to Logan Rd 46, NW 4.2 km (3 mi). (R) Note: 3 night min stay on holiday weekends. **FAC:** Gravel rds. (235 spaces). Avail: 70 grass, 22 pull-thrus (30 x 80), back-ins (35 x 45), mostly side by side hkups, 70 full hkups (30/50 amps), seasonal sites, WiFi Hotspot, tent sites, showers $, dump, laundry, LP bottles, fire rings, firewood, controlled access. **REC:** heated pool, Woodland Lake: swim, fishing, playground. Pets OK. RV age restrict, eco-friendly, 2015 rates: $46 to $52. May 1 to Oct 15.
(519)347-2315 Lat: 43.572139, Lon: -81.186403
6710 Line 46, Rr 1, Bornholm, ON N0K 1A0
www.woodland@carefreervresorts.com
http://www.carefreervresorts.com/rv-parks/ontario/woodland-lake/
See ad pages 1445, 1420.

BRACEBRIDGE — C5 *Muskoka*

MUSKOKA RIDGE TRAILER PARK **Ratings: 6.5/7.5/7.5** (Campground) 2015 rates: $60. May 1 to Oct 15. (705)646-1259 1005 Stephens Bay Road, Bracebridge, ON P1L 1X2

BRADFORD — D5 *Simcoe*

YOGI BEAR'S JELLYSTONE PARK & CAMP-RESORT **Ratings: 7.5/9/8.5** (Campground) 2015 rates: $39.95 to $99.95. May 1 to Sep 30. (905)775-1377 3666 Simcoe Road County Road 88, Bradford, ON L3Z 2A4

BRANTFORD — E5 *Brant*

BRANT CONSERVATION AREA (Public) From Jct of Hwy 403 & Hwy 24 South, S 1.7 mi on Hwy 24 South to Robinson Rd, E 2.8 mi (L). 2015 rates: $35 to $50.50. May 1 to Oct 15. (519)752-2040

WILLOW LAKE CAREFREE RV RESORT
Ratings: Between 6.5/7.5/7 (Campground) From Town go East on Hwy 4 (Oakland Rd) 1.1 km (.7 mi) turn L onto Willow Road. **FAC:** Gravel rds. (380 spaces). Avail: 60 grass, 5 pull-thrus (40 x 60), back-ins (40 x 50), some side by side hkups, 60 full hkups (15 amps), seasonal sites, WiFi Hotspot, tent sites, showers $, dump, laundry, groc, fire rings, firewood, controlled access. **REC:** Willow Lake: swim, fishing, playground. Pet restrict(B). Eco-friendly, 2015 rates: $32 to $36. May 1 to Oct 15. ATM.
(519)446-2513 Lat: 43.145, Lon: -80.2144
14 Willow Lake Road, Scotland, ON N0E 1R0
willowlake@carefreeRVresorts.com
www.carefreervresorts.ca/willowlake
See ad pages 1445, 1420.

BRIGHTON — D7 *Northumberland*

BRIGHTON KOA
Ratings: 8.5/10★/8.5 (Campground) From Jct of Hwy 401 & CR-30 (Exit 509), N 0.16 km (0.1 mi) on CR 30 to Telephone Rd (runs adjacent to Hwy 401), W 1.2 km (0.75 mi) (L). **FAC:** Gravel rds. (97 spaces). 75 Avail: 49 gravel, 26 grass, patios, 40 pull-thrus (35 x 65), back-ins (45 x 50), 44 full hkups, 31 W, 31 E (15/50 amps), seasonal sites, WiFi, tent sites, rentals, dump, laundry, groc, fire rings, firewood. **REC:** heated pool, whirlpool, playground. Pets OK. Partial handicap access. Big rig sites, eco-friendly, 2015 rates: $55.58 to $83.68. May 1 to Oct 15.
(800)562-0906 Lat: 44.06946, Lon: -77.78355
15051 Telephone Road, Brighton, ON K0K 1H0
brightonkoa@gmail.com
www.brightonkoa.com
See ad page 1434.

PRESQU'ILE (Prov Pk) From Jct of Hwy 401 (exit 509) & Hwy 30, S 3.2 mi on Hwy 30 to Hwy 2, W 0.2 mi on Hwy 2 (Main St) to Presqu'ile Parkway, S 2.4 mi (E). 2015 rates: $34.92 to $43.75. Apr 24 to Oct 11. (613)475-4324

BRITT — B4 *Parry Sound*

GRUNDY LAKE (Prov Pk) From town, N 12 mi on Hwy 69 (R). 2015 rates: $12.75 to $43.75. May 9 to Oct 14. (705)383-2286

KILLBEAR (Prov Pk) From town, N 8 mi on Hwy 69 to Hwy 559, W 12.6 mi (E). 2015 rates: $10 to $43.75. May 9 to Oct 14. (705)342-5492

STURGEON BAY (Prov Pk) From Jct of TCH-69 & Hwy 529, NW 2 mi on Hwy 529 (L). 2015 rates: $12.75 to $43.75. May 9 to Oct 14. (705)366-2521

BROCKVILLE — C9 *Grenville, Leeds*

HAPPY GREEN ACRES TENT & TRAILER PARK
Ratings: 7.5/8★/8.5 (Campground) From Jct of Hwys 401 & CR-2 (Exit 687), W 2.3 km (1.4 mi) on CR-2 (L). **FAC:** Paved/gravel rds. (89 spaces). Avail: 49 grass, 45 pull-thrus (30 x 60), back-ins (30 x 40), mostly side by side hkups, 49 full hkups (15/30 amps), seasonal sites, WiFi $, tent sites, showers $, dump, laundry, fire rings, firewood. **REC:** pool, playground. Pets OK. Eco-friendly, 2015 rates: $36 to $48. May 1 to Oct 15. No CC.
(613)342-9646 Lat: 44.52446, Lon: -75.79410
2 Happy Green Acres Road, Rr3, Brockville, ON K6V 5T3
See ad this page, 1420.

PLEASURE PARK RV RESORT INC **Ratings: 8/8.5/8** (Campground) 2015 rates: $42 to $49. May 3 to Sep 15. (613)923-5490 80 Graham Lake Road, Mallorytown, ON K0E 1R0

ST LAWRENCE PARK (Public) In town, on Hwy 2 (R). 2015 rates: $33 to $39. May 15 to Sep 15. (613)345-1341

CALEDON — D5 *York*

LEISURE TIME PARK & TRAILER SALES INC **Ratings: 8/8/8.5** (Campground) 2015 rates: $48 to $52. May 1 to Oct 31. (888)280-0018 18478 Duffy's Lane, Caledon, ON L7E 0E8

CALLANDER — B5 *Nipissing*

BAYVIEW CAMP & COTTAGES **Ratings: 6/7/7.5** (Campground) 2015 rates: $30 to $40. May 15 to Oct 15. (877)752-2095 35 Camp Road, Rr 1, Callander, ON P0H 1H0

CAMBRIDGE — E5 *Hamilton-Wentworth, Wellington*

CHURCHILL PARK (Public) From Jct of Hwy 97 & Hwy 24, S 0.07 mi on Hwy 24 (L) Note: Maximum 3 day stay. 2015 rates: $15. Apr 30 to Oct 11. (519)740-4681

Tell them you saw them in this Guide!

ON

CAMBRIDGE (CONT)

VALENS CONSERVATION AREA (Public) From town, E 6 mi on Hwy 97 (L) Refundable entrance fee required to access this campground when office closed. (Min 2 day stay on holiday weekends). 2015 rates: $33 to $36. (905)525-2183

CAMPBELLFORD — D7 *Northumberland*

FERRIS (Prov Pk) From Jct of Hwys 401 & 30, N 18.6 mi on Hwy 30 to Campbellford, follow signs (R). 2015 rates: $12.75 to $43.75. May 9 to Oct 14. (705)653-3575

CAMPBELLVILLE — E5 *Halton*

TORONTO WEST KOA
Ratings: 8.5/10★/7 (Campground) From Jct of Hwy 401 & Guelph Line (Exit 312), N 2.6 km (1.6 mi) on Guelph Line to 10th Side Rd, SW 0.9 mi to Nassagaweya/2nd Line, S 1.9 km (1.2 mi) (L). Min 3 night stay on holiday weekends. **FAC:** Gravel rds. 86 gravel, 10 pull-thrus (30 x 60), back-ins (20 x 55), some side by side hkups, 50 full hkups, 36 W, 36 E (30/50 amps), WiFi, tent sites, rentals, dump, laundry, groc, fire rings, firewood, controlled access. **REC:** heated pool, playground. Pets OK. Partial handicap access. Eco-friendly, 2015 rates: $49 to $89. May 1 to Oct 31. ATM.
(800)562-1523 Lat: 43.48376, Lon: -80.00312
9301 2nd Line, Campbellville, ON L0P 1B0
info@torontowestkoa.on.ca
www.koa.com/campgrounds/toronto-west
See ad page 1434.

CARDINAL — C9 *Grenville, Leeds*

CARDINAL/OTTAWA SOUTH KOA
Ratings: 8.5/10★/8 (Campground) From Jct of Hwy 401 & CR-22 (Shanly Rd, exit 730), N 6.4 km (4 mi) on CR-22 to Pittston Rd, E 0.4 km (0.25 mi) (R). Min. stay 2 ngts on weekends, 3 ngts stay holiday weekends. **FAC:** Gravel rds. (140 spaces). Avail: 118 gravel, patios, 42 pull-thrus (30 x 70), back-ins (30 x 50), mostly side by side hkups, 118 W, 118 E (30/50 amps), seasonal sites, WiFi, tent sites, rentals, dump, mobile sewer, laundry, groc, LP gas, fire rings, firewood, controlled access. **REC:** heated pool, playground. Pet restrict(B). RV age restrict, eco-friendly, 2015 rates: $48 to $77. May 2 to Oct 18.
(877)894-3140 Lat: 44.86150, Lon: -75.44334
609 Pittston Road, Cardinal, ON K0E 1E0
reservations@cardinalkoa.com
www.cardinalkoa.com
See ad page 1434.

CARRYING PLACE — D7 *Hastings, Northumberland*

CAMP BARCOVAN TENT & RV RESORT **Ratings: 7.5/7/7** (Campground) 2015 rates: $40 to $50. May 11 to Oct 17. (888)859-2369 133 Carter Road, Carrying Place, ON K0K 1L0

CEDARDALE FAMILY CAMPGROUND & COTTAGE RESORT **Ratings: 7/7/8** (Campground) 2015 rates: $38 to $58. May 9 to Oct 19. (800)363-5638 rr 2, 107A Cedardale Road, Carrying Place, ON K0K 1L0

NORTH SHORE RV PARK
Ratings: 9.5/10★/9.5 (RV Park) E-bnd: From Jct of Hwy 401 & Hwy 30 (Exit 509), S 4.8 km (3 mi) on Hwy 30 to CR-64, E 10 km (6.3 mi) to Shoreline Rd, S 0.8 km (0.5 mi) (E). W-bnd; From Jct of Hwy 40 (Wooler Rd, exit 522) go S till no. 40 ends at Hwy 33, turn right until you cross the Murray Canal, turn on CR 64, 4 km (2.8 mi). **FAC:** All weather rds. (125 spaces). 20 Avail: 6 gravel, 14 grass, 9 pull-thrus (30 x 90), back-ins (30 x 75), 20 full hkups (30/50 amps), seasonal sites, WiFi $, tent sites, rentals, showers $, dump, laundry, LP bottles, fire rings, firewood. **REC:** heated pool, Lake Ontario (Wellers Bay): swim, fishing, marina, playground. Pet restrict(B). Partial handicap access. Eco-friendly, 2015 rates: $46 to $49.50. May 1 to Oct 19.
(613)475-2036 Lat: 44.03340, Lon: -77.62437
1675 County Rd 64, Carrying Place, ON K0K 1L0
nshore@northshorepark.com
www.northshorepark.com
See ad page 1436.

CARTIER — A4 *Sudbury*

HALFWAY LAKE (Prov Pk) From town, N 10 mi on Hwy 144 (L). 2015 rates: $12.75 to $43.75. May 16 to Sep 28. (705)965-2702

Your neighbor just told you about a great little campground in Kentucky — what was the name of it again? The "Find-it-Fast" index in the back of the Guide can help. It's an alphabetical listing, by state, of every private and public park in the Guide.

CAYUGA — E5 *Haldimand-Norfolk*

GRAND OAKS CAREFREE RV RESORT
Ratings: 8/7.5/6.5 (Campground) From Hwy 3 and CR 54 turn N 1 km (.6 mi). **FAC:** Gravel rds. (253 spaces). Avail: 30 grass, 5 pull-thrus (40 x 65), back-ins (30 x 45), some side by side hkups, 17 W, 17 E (30 amps), seasonal sites, WiFi Hotspot, tent sites, dump, laundry, fire rings, firewood, controlled access. **REC:** heated pool, Grand River: fishing, shuffleboard, playground. Pets OK. Eco-friendly, 2015 rates: $34 to $50. May 1 to Oct 15.
(905)772-3713 Lat: 42.961119, Lon: -79.871073
107 Haldimand Hwy 54, Cayuga, ON N0A 1E0
grandoaks@carefreeRVresorts.com
www.carefreeRVresorts.ca/grandoaks
See ad pages 1445, 1420.

CHAPLEAU — F9 *Algoma*

MISSINAIBI (Prov Pk) From Jct of Hwy 101 & Missinaibi Lake Rd, N 55 mi on Missinaibi Lake Rd (E). Pit toilets. 2015 rates: $23.75 to $30.95. May 2 to Sep 21. (705)234-2222

WAKAMI LAKE (Prov Pk) From town, S 20 mi on Hwy 129 to Hwy 667, follow signs, E 16 mi (R). Pit toilets. 2015 rates: $12.75 to $40. May to Sep. (705)233-2853

CHERRY VALLEY — D7 *Prince Edward*

LAKE AVENUE CAREFREE RV RESORT
Ratings: 8/7.5/7.5 (Campground) From Jct of CR-10 & CR-18 (Cherry Valley), W 4.8 km (3 mi) on CR-18 (R). Minimum 3 night stay on holiday weekends. **FAC:** Gravel rds. (112 spaces). Avail: 11 gravel, 4 pull-thrus (35 x 55), back-ins (20 x 40), 11 full hkups (30 amps), seasonal sites, WiFi Hotspot, tent sites, rentals, dump, mobile sewer, laundry, groc, LP bottles, fire rings, firewood, controlled access. **REC:** heated pool, East Lake: swim, fishing, playground, rec open to public. Pet restrict(Q). Partial handicap access. Eco-friendly, 2015 rates: $53 to $57. May 1 to Oct 15.
(613)476-4990 Lat: 43.89542, Lon: -77.20054
rr 1, 37 Lake Avenue Lane, Cherry Valley, ON K0K 1P0
lakeavenuepark@carefreeRVresorts.com
www.carefreeRVresorts.ca/lakeavenue
See ad pages 1445, 1420.

QUINTE'S ISLE CAMPARK
Ratings: 9.5/10★/10 (Campground) From Jct of Hwys 401 & 62 (Exit 543A), S 46.6 km (29 mi) on Hwy 62 to Hwy 33, E 9.6 km (6 mi) to CR-10 (Lake St, in Picton), S 8 km (5 mi) to CR-18, SW 8 km (5 mi) to Salmon Pt Rd, S 2 km (1.25 mi) (L). Note: 3 night minimum stay on holiday weekends. **FAC:** All weather rds. (620 spaces). Avail: 320 gravel, 94 pull-thrus (40 x 90), back-ins (40 x 60), 160 full hkups (30/50 amps), seasonal sites, WiFi $, tent sites, rentals, showers $, dump, laundry, groc, LP bottles, fire rings, firewood, controlled access. **REC:** heated pool, Lake Ontario: swim, fishing, shuffleboard, playground, rec open to public. Pets OK. Partial handicap access. Big rig sites, eco-friendly, 2015 rates: $59 to $77.50. Apr 15 to Nov 1. ATM.
(613)476-6310 Lat: 43.87610, Lon: -77.21199
237 Salmon Point Road, Cherry Valley, ON K0K 1P0
info@qicampark.com
www.qicampark.com
See ad pages 1429 (Spotlight Prince Edward County), 1420.

Travel Services

QUINTE'S ISLE CAMPARK & TRAILER SALE
Trailer sales division. **SERVICES:** RV appliance, mobile RV svc, restaurant, restrooms, RV Sales. RV storage. RV supplies, LP, dump, RV accessible. Hours: 9am to 5pm. ATM.
(613)476-6310 Lat: 43.87610, Lon: -77.21199
237 Salmon Pt Rd, Cherry Valley, ON K0K 1P0
info@qicampark.com
www.qicampark.com
See ad page 1429 (Spotlight Prince Edward County).

Things to See and Do

QUINTE'S ISLE DIAMOND "J" RANCH Scenic trail rides & guided tours. Winetasting. May 15 to Oct 15. Hours: 9am to 7pm. Adult fee: $20. ATM.
(613)476-6310 Lat: 43.87248, Lon: -77.20690
rr 1 237 Salmon Pt. Rd, Cherry Valley, ON K0K 1P0
info@qicampark.com
See ad page 1429 (Spotlight Prince Edward County).

Are you using a friend's Guide? Want one of your own? Call 877-209-6655.

CHESLEY — D4 *Grey*

CEDAR RAIL FAMILY CAMPGROUND
Ratings: 8.5/8★/8.5 (Campground) From Jc of CR10 & Grey Bruce Line, N 0.6 km (0.4 mi on Grey Bruce Line (R). **FAC:** Gravel rds. (20 spaces). Avail: 39 grass, 13 pull-thrus (33 x 60) back-ins (33 x 50), some side by side hkups, 31 fu hkups, 8 W, 8 E (30/50 amps), seasonal sites, WiF $, tent sites, rentals, dump, laundry, groc, fire rings firewood, controlled access. **REC:** heated pool, North Branch Saugeen River: fishing, shuffleboard, playground, rec open to public. Pets OK. RV age restric 2015 rates: $36 to $42. May 1 to Oct 15.
(519)363-3387 Lat: 44.31119, Lon: -81.07427
015259 Grey Bruce Line, Rr 3, Chesley, O N0G 1L0
cedarrailcamp@bellnet.ca
www.cedarrailcamp.com
See ad page 1436.

CHUTE-A-BLONDEAU — B10 *Ontario*

VOYAGEUR (Prov Pk) From Jct of Hwy 417 CR-14 (exit 5), N 0.6 mi on CR-14 (R). 2015 rates $25.25 to $37.35. May to Oct. (613)674-2825

CLARKSBURG — C4 *Grey*

CRAIGLEITH CAREFREE RV RESORT
Ratings: 6.5/7.5/8 (RV Park) Fron Hwy 26 and CR40 turn S for 2.7 km (mi), turn R onto CR 2 for 700 meters, o L. **FAC:** Gravel rds. (103 spaces). Avai 33 gravel, 3 pull-thrus (35 x 55), back-in (35 x 50), mostly side by side hkups, 8 full hkups (3 amps), seasonal sites, WiFi Hotspot, tent sites, ren als, dump, fire rings, firewood, controlled acces **REC:** heated pool, Indian Brook: fishing, playgroun Pets OK. Eco-friendly, 2015 rates: $42 to $56. Ma 15 to Oct 15.
(519)599-3840 Lat: 44.541262, Lon: -80.433663
496875 Grey Rd 2, Rr2, Clarksburg, ON N0H 1J
craigleith@carefreeRVresorts.com
www.carefreeRVresorts.ca/craigleith
See ad pages 1445, 1420.

CLOYNE — C7 *Frontenac*

BON ECHO (Prov Pk) From Jct of Hwys 7 & 4 (Kaladar), N 20 mi on Hwy 41 (R). 2015 rates: $13.8 to $43.75. Apr 23 to Oct 11. (613)336-2228

SHERWOOD PARK CAMPGROUND **Ratings: 5.5/7.5/7.5** (Campground) 2015 rates: $30.4 to $40.42. May 1 to Oct 8. (888)419-3026 1141 Nort Frontenac Rd, Cloyne, ON K0H 1K0

COBDEN — B8 *Renfrew*

CEDAR HAVEN TENT & TRAILER PARK **Ratings: 5.5/5.5/6.5** (Campground) 2015 rates: $4 May 10 to Oct 1. (613)646-7989 423 Cedar Have Road, Rr 1, Cobden, ON K0J 1K0

LOGOS LAND RESORT **Ratings: 8/9.5★/8.** (Campground) 2015 rates: $46 to $49. May 15 to O 12. (877)816-6605 15906 Hwy 17, Cobden, O K0J 1K0

COBOCONK — C6 *Kawartha Lakes*

BALSAM LAKE (Prov Pk) From town, E 7.5 mi o Hwy 48 (R). 2015 rates: $28.75 to $43.75. May 12 Nov 20. (705)454-3324

COBOURG — D7 *Northumberland*

VICTORIA PARK/COBOURG CAMPGROUN (Public) From Jct of Hwy 401 & Division St (Exit 474 S 3.2 km (2 mi) on Division St (L). 2015 rates: $36 $42. May 15 to Oct 8. (905)373-7321

COLLINGWOOD — C5 *Grey*

CRAIGLEITH PROVINCIAL PARK (Prov P From Jct of Hwys 24 & 26, NW 7 mi on Hwy 26 (R 2015 rates: $36.75 to $43.75. Apr 11 to Oct 2 (705)445-4467

COMBERMERE — B7 *Renfrew*

PINE CLIFF RESORT **Ratings: 7.5/7.5/7.5** (R Resort) 2015 rates: $65. May 1 to Oct 8. (888)75 3014 21 Allingham Lane, Box 99, Combermere, C K0J 1L0

COOKSTOWN — D5 *Simcoe*

TORONTO NORTH/COOKSTOWN KOA
Ratings: 8.5/9.5★/9 (Campground) S-Bn From Jct of Hwys 400 & 89 (Exit 75), E 64 (70 yds) on Hwy 89 to Reive Blvd, N 0.6 k (0.4 mi) (R); or N-bnd: From Jct of Hwys 400 & 8 (Exit 75), continue directly across Hwy 89 to Reiv Blvd, N 0.6 km (0.4 mi) (R). Min 3 night stay on holida weekends. **FAC:** Gravel rds. 106 Avail: 106 all weat er, patios, 66 pull-thrus (30 x 70), back-ins (26 x 5 53 full hkups, 53 W, 53 E (30/50 amps), WiFi, te sites, rentals, dump, laundry, groc, fire rings, fir wood, controlled access. **REC:** heated pool, wadir

COOKSTOWN (CONT)

TORONTO NORTH/COOKSTOWN (CONT)
pool, playground. Pets OK. Partial handicap access. Big rig sites, eco-friendly, 2015 rates: $51 to $85. May 1 to Oct 13.
(800)562-2691 Lat: 44.12360, Lon: -79.39416
139 Reive Blvd, Cookstown, ON L0L 1L0
info@torontonorthkoa.com
www.torontonorthkoa.com
See ad page 1434.

DEEP RIVER — B7 *Renfrew*

← DRIFTWOOD (Prov Pk) From Mattawa, E 30 mi on Hwy 17 to Driftwood Rd (R). 2015 rates: $12.75 to $43.75. May 16 to Sep 21. (613)586-2553

← RYAN'S CAMPSITE **Ratings: 5/5.5/6.5** (Campground) 2015 rates: $35 to $40. May 1 to Oct 8. (613)584-3453 34572 Hwy 17, Deep River, ON K0J 1P0

DELTA — C8 *Grenville, Leeds*

↑ LOWER BEVERLEY LAKE PARK (Public) From Lyndhurst, N 10 mi on Hwy 33 to Hwy 42, W 2 mi (L). 2015 rates: $27.50 to $50. May 7 to Oct 11. (613)928-2881

DEUX RIVIERES — A6 *Renfrew*

→ ANTLER'S KINGFISHER LODGE & TRAILER PARK **Ratings: 5.5/7/7.5** (Campground) 2015 rates: $39.83. May 9 to Oct 10. (705)747-0851 46980 Hwy 17, Rr1, Deux Rivieres, ON K0J 1R0

DRYDEN — E7 *Kenora*

→ AARON PARK (Prov Pk) From town, E 9 mi on Hwy 17 (L). 2015 rates: $34.47 to $39.55. May 16 to Sep 20. (807)938-6534

← BIRCHLAND TRAILER PARK **Ratings: 4.5/7/8** (Campground) 2015 rates: $34. May 1 to Oct 31. (807)937-4938 17122 Hwy 17, Dryden, ON P8N 2Z2

← NATURES INN RV PARK & MARINA (Campground) (Rebuilding) 2015 rates: $33 to $34.95. May 15 to Oct 15. (807)223-6800 80 Claybanks Road, Dryden, ON P8N 3H4

→ THE NORTHWESTERN TENT & RV PARK **Ratings: 7/8★/6.5** (RV Park) 2015 rates: $39 to $42. Apr 15 to Oct 31. (807)223-4945 559 Government St, Dryden, ON P8N 2Y8

DUNNVILLE — E5 *Haldimand*

↓ BYNG ISLAND CONSERVATION AREA (Public) From Jct of Hwy 3 & Reg Rd 3, W 0.2 mi on Reg Rd 3 to Reg Rd 20, N 0.1 mi (R). 2015 rates: $27 to $46. May 1 to Oct 15. (905)774-5755

← CHIPPAWA CREEK CONSERVATION AREA (Public) From Jct of Niagara Hwy 27 & Niagara Hwy 4, S 0.2 mi on Niagara Hwy 4 to CR-45, W 1.7 mi (R). 2015 rates: $32 to $42. May 17 to Oct 11. (905)386-6387

↖ **GRAND RIVER RV RESORT - PARKBRIDGE**
Ratings: 7/7/7.5 (RV Park) From Jct of Hwy 3 & Reg Rd 17, W 7.2 km (4.5 mi) on Reg Rd 17 (L). Note: 3 day min. stay on holiday weekends. **FAC:** Paved/gravel rds. (332 spaces). Avail: 10 grass, patios, back-ins (30 x 65), mostly side by side hkups, 10 W, 10 E (30 amps), seasonal sites, dump, mobile sewer, LP bottles, fire rings, firewood, controlled access. **REC:** heated pool, Grand River: fishing, shuffleboard, playground. Pet restrict(B). No tents. 2015 rates: $50. May 15 to Oct 31.
(905)774-4257 Lat: 42.92108, Lon: -79.73179
Rr #1, 1001 Haldimand Rd 17, Cayuga, ON N0A 1E0
grandriverinfo@parkbrige.ca
www.niagaratrailers.com
See ad pages 1417 (Welcome Section), 1420.

← KNIGHT'S BEACH RESORT **Ratings: 7.5/9.5★/8.5** (Campground) 2015 rates: $42 to $55. May 1 to Oct 19. (888)581-8775 2190 Lakeshore Road, Dunnville, ON N1A 2W8

← ROCK POINT (Prov Pk) From Jct of Hwy 3 & RR 3 (Dunnville), E 5.5 mi on RR 3 to Niece Rd, W 0.5 mi (L). 2015 rates: $36.75 to $43.75. May 7 to Oct 12. (905)774-6642

DURHAM — D4 *Grey*

↑ AMAZING ROCKY PARK CAMPGROUND **Ratings: 6.5/7★/7.5** (Campground) 2015 rates: $36 to $40. Apr 15 to Oct 15. (519)369-6450 423059 Rocky Saugenn Road, Rr 1, Durham, ON N0G 1R0

↑ DURHAM CONSERVATION AREA (Public) From Jct of Hwy 6 & Old Durham Rd, E 1 mi on Old Durham Rd (R). 2015 rates: $30 to $39. (519)369-2074

We appreciate your business!

EAR FALLS — E7 *Kenora*

↑ PAKWASH (Prov Pk) From town, N 13 mi on Hwy 105 (L). 2015 rates: $32.25 to $43.75. May 16 to Sep 1. (807)222-3346

EDEN — E4 *Elgin*

← **RED OAK TRAVEL PARK**
Ratings: 8/9★/8.5 (Campground) From Jct of Hwy 3 & Culloden Rd, W 0.4 km (0.25 mi) on Hwy 3 (R). **FAC:** Gravel rds. (105 spaces). Avail: 17 grass, 6 pull-thrus (25 x 60), back-ins (20 x 30), 17 W, 17 E (15/30 amps), seasonal sites, WiFi, tent sites, rentals, dump, mobile sewer, laundry, groc, LP bottles, fire rings, firewood, controlled access. **REC:** pool, playground. Pets OK. RV age restrict, eco-friendly, 2015 rates: $33 to $45. May 1 to Oct 15.
(519)866-3504 Lat: 42.792333, Lon: -80.833796
54428 Talbot Line (Hwy 3), Eden, ON N0J 1H0
camp@redoaktravelpark.com
www.redoaktravelpark.com
See ad page 1436.

EGANVILLE — B7 *Renfrew*

↑ LAKE DORE RV RESORT **Ratings: 6/6.5/8.5** (Campground) 2015 rates: $43 to $46. May 8 to Sep 30. (613)628-2615 130 Camelot Lane, Eganville, ON K0J 1T0

ELGIN — C8 *Leeds and Grenville*

↙ SAND LAKE CAMPGROUND & COTTAGES **Ratings: 6/6.5/7** (Campground) 2015 rates: $42 to $52. May 1 to Oct 1. (866)359-6361 5 Powell Bay Road, Rr #3, Elgin, ON K0G 1E0

ELLIOT LAKE — A3 *Algoma*

↑ MISSISSAGI (Prov Pk) From town, N 16 mi on Hwy 108/639 (R). 2015 rates: $12.75 to $43.75. May 16 to Sep 7. (705)865-2021

↑ WESTVIEW PARK TRAILER PARK (Public) From town, N 1 mi on Hwy 108 (R). 2015 rates: $30. May 1 to Oct 1. (705)848-7737

ELMIRA — D4 *Wellington*

↖ CONESTOGO LAKE CONSERVATION AREA (Public) From Jct of Hwy 86 & CR-11, NE 1.7 mi on CR-11, SE 0.7 mi on CR-145/CR-11, NE 0.5 mi on CR-11 (L). 2015 rates: $26 to $44. May 1 to Oct 15. (519)638-2873

ELORA — D4 *Wellington*

← ELORA GORGE CONSERVATION AREA (Public) From Jct of CR-7 & CR-21, SW 0.7 mi on CR-21 (R). 2015 rates: $28 to $46. May 1 to Oct 15. (519)846-9742

ENGLEHART — F10 *Timiskaming*

KAP-KIG-IWAN PROVINCIAL PARK (Prov Pk) From town: Go 3/4 km/1/2 mi W on Hwy 11, then 2-1/2 km/1-1/2 mi S on 5th St. Pit toilets. 2015 rates: $28.75 to $43.75. May 16 to Sep 28. (705)544-2050

ENNISMORE — D6 *Peterborough*

↙ ANCHOR BAY CAMP **Ratings: 7.5/7.5★/7.5** (Campground) 2015 rates: $38 to $42. May 1 to Oct 8. (705)657-8439 197 Anchor Bay Road, Peterborough, ON K9J 6X2

↑ **GRANDVIEW COTTAGE AND RV RESORT - PARKBRIDGE**
Ratings: 8.5/8.5★/8 (Campground) From Town turn R on Tara Rd/County Rd-16 for 4.5 km (2.7 mi) turn R on Kerry Line for 1.6 km (1 mi) on L. **FAC:** Paved rds. (272 spaces). Avail: 10 gravel, back-ins (20 x 35), 10 full hkups (30 amps), seasonal sites, WiFi $, dump, laundry, LP bottles, fire rings, firewood, controlled access. **REC:** heated pool, Buckhorn Lake: swim, playground. Pet restrict(B/Q). Eco-friendly, 2015 rates: $60. May 1 to Oct 15.
(705)292-7717 Lat: 44.449225, Lon: -78.436506
626 Kerry Lane, Ennismore, ON K0L 1T0
grandviewinfo@parkbridge.com
parkbridge.com/grandview
See ad pages 1417 (Welcome Section), 1420.

→ **SKYLINE COTTAGE AND RV RESORT - PARKBRIDGE**
Ratings: 7.5/9★/8.5 (Campground) From Hwy 7 TC go E onto Lindsay Rd/ON 7B/County Rd for 6.6 km (4.1 mi), turn L onto Chemong Rd/County Rd 18, 4.5 km (2.7) turn L onto County Rd 14/Bridge Rd for 1.4 km (.8 mi), turn R on Robinson Rd. 2 km (1.2 mi), turn R onto Skyline Rd 2.3km (1.4 mi) on L. **FAC:** Paved rds. (325 spaces). Avail: 43 gravel, 25 pull-thrus (50 x 50), back-ins (40 x 40), 43 full hkups (30 amps), seasonal sites, rentals, laundry, groc, LP bottles, fire rings, firewood, restaurant, controlled access. **REC:** heated pool, Chemong Lake: swim, fishing, shuffleboard, playground. Pets OK. Partial handicap access. Eco-friendly, 2015 rates: $36 to $52. May 1 to Oct 15.
(705)292-9811 Lat: 44.408257, Lon: -78.387314
920 Skyline Road, Ennismore, ON L0L 1T0
skylineinfo@parkbridge.com
www.parkbridge.com/skyline
See ad pages 1417 (Welcome Section), 1420.

↙ WOODLAND CAMP SITE **Ratings: 6/8★/7** (Campground) 2015 rates: $40 to $45. May 1 to Oct 18. (705)657-8946 209 Allen's Road, Lakehurst, ON K0L 1J0

ESSEX — F2 *Essex*

→ **WILDWOOD GOLF & RV RESORT**
Ratings: 9.5/9.5★/9.5 (Campground) From Jct of Hwy 401 & CR-19 (Manning Rd) Exit 21, S 4.7 km (2.9 mi) on CR-19 to Hwy 3, SE 4.8 km (3 mi) to N. Malden Rd, SW 9.2 km (5.7 mi) to 11th Conc Rd, W 0.6 km (0.4 mi) (R). **FAC:** Paved rds. (374 spaces). Avail: 82 all weather, patios, 82 pull-thrus (22 x 75), some side by side hkups, 82 full hkups (30/50 amps), seasonal sites, cable, WiFi Hotspot, laundry, fire rings, firewood, restaurant, controlled access. **REC:** heated pool, golf, playground, rec open to public. Pet restrict(B). Partial handicap access, no tents. Big rig sites, eco-friendly, 2015 rates: $48. Disc: AAA. May 1 to Oct 31. No CC.
(866)994-9699 Lat: 42.13936, Lon: -82.94960
11112, 11th Concession Road, Essex, ON N0R 1J0
joelucier@aol.com
www.wildwoodgolfandrvresort.com
See ad pages 1453, 1420.

EVANSVILLE — B3 *Manitoulin*

↓ LAKE WOLSEY OBEJEWUNG PARK **Ratings: 6/5/6.5** (Campground) 2015 rates: $26 to $30. May 24 to Oct 8. (705)282-2174 225 Lake Wolsey Rd, Evansville, ON P0P 1E0

FENELON FALLS — C6 *Kawartha Lakes*

↑ LOG CHATEAU PARK **Ratings: 7.5/8.5★/7.5** (Campground) 2015 rates: $17 to $34. May 1 to Oct 12. (705)887-3960 1691 C.r #121, Rr 2, Fenelon Falls, ON K0M 1N0

↑ SUNNY ACRES **Ratings: 3.5/7/6.5** (Campground) 2015 rates: $37. May 10 to Oct 8. (705)887-3416 24 Sunny Acres Road, Fenelon Falls, ON K0M 1N0

FERGUS — D5 *Wellington*

↗ **HIGHLAND PINES CAMPGROUND & RV SALES** **Ratings: 8/10★/9.5** (Campground) From Jct of Hwy 6 (Garafraxa St) & CR-19, NE 9 km (5.6 mi) on CR-19 (R). 3 day minimum stay on holiday weekends. **FAC:** Paved/gravel rds. (650 spaces). 107 Avail: 4 gravel, 103 grass, 4 pull-thrus (35 x 84), back-ins (45 x 60), 89 full hkups, 18 W, 18 E (15/50 amps), seasonal sites, WiFi Hotspot, tent sites, rentals, dump, laundry, fire rings, firewood, controlled access. **REC:** heated pool, wading pool, Lake Belwood: swim, fishing, marina, golf, shuffleboard, playground. Pets OK. Partial handicap access. Big rig sites, eco-friendly, 2015 rates: $52 to $68. May 8 to Oct 12.
AAA Approved
(877)211-7044 Lat: 43.778531, Lon: -80.340443
8523 Wellington Rd. 19, Belwood, ON N0B 1J0
camping@highlandpines.com
www.highlandpines.com

FOLEYET — F9 *Sudbury*

← IVANHOE LAKE (Prov Pk) From town, W 5 mi on Hwy 101 (L). 2015 rates: $12.75 to $43.75. May 16 to Sep 1. (705)899-2644

FORT FRANCES — F7 *Rainy River*

→ PITHERS POINT MUNICIPAL PARK (Public) From town, E 0.5 mi on Hwy 11 (R). 2015 rates: $16.95 to $33.90. May 18 to Sep 1. (807)274-9893

FULLARTON — E4 *Perth*

↓ **WINDMILL FAMILY CAMPGROUND Ratings: 8/7/7** (Campground) From jct Hwy 23 & County Rd 163: Go S 9.2 km/5-3/4 mi. **FAC:** Gravel rds. (205 spaces). Avail: 24 grass, back-ins (40 x 60), mostly side by side hkups, 17 full hkups, 7 W, 7 E (15/30 amps), seasonal sites, WiFi $, tent sites, rentals, showers $, dump, laundry, groc, fire rings, firewood, controlled access. **REC:** heated pool, shuffleboard, playground, rec open to public. Pets OK. Eco-friendly, 2015 rates: $34 to $38. May 1 to Oct 25.
AAA Approved
(519)229-8982 Lat: 43.354750, Lon: -81.209975
2778 Perth Rd 163, Fullarton, ON N0K 1H0
windmillpark@ebtech.net
www.windmillfamilycampground.com

We rate what RVers consider important.

GANANOQUE — D9 *Grenville, Leeds*

IVY LEA PARK (Prov Pk) From Jct Hwy 401 & (Hill Islands) (Exit 661), S 0.8 km (0.5 mi) on CR-137 to 1000 Islands Pkwy, W 90 m (300 ft) (L). Note: Two night min. stay on holiday weekends. 2015 rates: $40.50. May 17 to Oct 14. (800)437-2233

THE LANDON BAY CENTRE **Ratings: 6/6.5/7** (Campground) 2015 rates: $34 to $38. May 15 to Oct 15. (613)382-2719 302 1000 Island Parkway, Lansdown, ON K7G 2V2

1000 ISLANDS IVY LEA KOA
Ratings: 9/9.5★/9 (Campground) From Jct of Hwy 401 & Reynolds Rd (Exit 659), S 2.4 km (1.5 mi) on Reynolds Rd to 1000 Island Pkwy, W 3.2 km (2 mi) (R). Note: Min. 3 night stay on holiday weekends & 2 nights on event weekends. **FAC:** Gravel rds. (121 spaces). 110 Avail: 62 gravel, 48 grass, 38 pull-thrus (38 x 60), back-ins (30 x 50), 74 full hkups, 36 W, 36 E (15/50 amps), seasonal sites, WiFi, tent sites, rentals, dump, mobile sewer, laundry, groc, LP bottles, fire rings, firewood, controlled access. **REC:** heated pool, whirlpool, playground. Pets OK. Big rig sites, eco-friendly, 2015 rates: $57.95 to $94.95. May 13 to Oct 17. ATM.
(613)659-2817 Lat: 44.36160, Lon: -76.02295
514-1000 Islands Parkway, Lansdowne, ON K0E 1L0
campinfo@1000islandskoa.com
www.1000islandskoa.com
See ad page 1434.

GERALDTON — F8 *Thunder Bay*

MACLEOD (Prov Pk) From town, E 6 mi on Hwy 11 (R). 2015 rates: $12.75 to $43.75. May 16 to Sep 28. (807)854-0370

WILD GOOSE LAKE CAMPGROUND Ratings: 7/7.5/7.5 (Campground) From Jct of Hwy 11 & CR-584, W 19.3 km (12 mi) on Hwy 11 to Kuengs Rd, N 1.2 km (0.75 mi) (L). **FAC:** Gravel rds. (47 spaces). Avail: 27 gravel, 16 pull-thrus (35 x 90), back-ins (30 x 50), 27 full hkups (20/30 amps), seasonal sites, WiFi $, tent sites, showers $, dump, laundry, fire rings, firewood. **REC:** Wild Goose Lake: swim, fishing, marina, playground. Pets OK. Eco-friendly, 2015 rates: $32 to $38. May 15 to Sep 30.
AAA Approved
(866)465-4404 Lat: 49.71114, Lon: -87.18449
8 Kuengs Road, Geraldton, ON P0T 1M0
wildgooselake@yahoo.ca
www.wildgooselakecampground.com

GODERICH — D3 *Huron*

AUBURN RIVERSIDE RETREAT **Ratings: 8/7.5/8.5** (Campground) 2015 rates: $30 to $38. May 1 to Oct 15. (519)526-7238 38382 Blythe Road, Auburn, ON N0M 1E0

FALLS RESERVE CONSERVATION AREA (Public) From Jct of Hwy 21 & CR-31, SE 6 mi on CR-31 (R). 2015 rates: $32 to $47. Apr 15 to Oct 30. (519)524-6429

LAKE HURON RESORT **Ratings: 8/8/7.5** (Campground) 2015 rates: $55 to $60. May 1 to Oct 29. (519)524-5343 82803 Bluewater Hwy (21), Goderich, ON N7A 3X9

POINT FARMS (Prov Pk) From town, N 3 mi on Hwy 21 (L). 2015 rates: $12.75 to $43.75. May 9 to Oct 14. (519)524-7124

SHELTER VALLEY CAMPGROUND Ratings: 9/9★/8.5 (Campground) From Jct of Hwys 21 & 8, E 8.4 km (5.2 mi) on Hwy 8 (L). 3 ngts min. stay on long weekends. **FAC:** Paved/gravel rds. (178 spaces). 34 Avail: 2 paved, 9 gravel, 23 grass, 7 pull-thrus (25 x 60), back-ins (25 x 40), mostly side by side hkups, 34 W, 34 E (30 amps), seasonal sites, WiFi $, tent sites, rentals, dump, mobile sewer, laundry, groc, LP bottles, fire rings, firewood, controlled access. **REC:** heated pool, Maitland River: swim, fishing, shuffleboard, playground, rec open to public. Pets OK. Partial handicap access. RV age restrict, eco-friendly, 2015 rates: $35 to $45. May 15 to Oct 15.
(519)524-4141 Lat: 43.68821, Lon: -81.62991
36534 Huron Road, Rr 2, Clinton, ON N0M 1L0
Info@sheltervalleycampground.ca
www.sheltervalleycampground.ca

GOULAIS RIVER — A1 *Algoma*

BLUEBERRY HILL MOTEL & CAMPGROUND LTD **Ratings: 7.5/7.5★/7.5** (Campground) 2015 rates: $34 to $36. (800)811-4411 2528 Hwy 17 N, Goulais River, ON P0S 1E0

GRAFTON — D7 *Northumberland*

COBOURG EAST CAMPGROUND
Ratings: 8/8/8.5 (Campground) From Jct of Hwy 401 & Exit 487, S 1.6 km (1 mi) on Lyle St to Hwy 2, E 1.3 km (0.8 mi) to Benlock Rd, S 0.8 km (0.5 mi) (R). **FAC:** Gravel rds. (160 spaces). Avail: 75 gravel, 24 pull-thrus (25 x 50), back-ins (20 x 40), some side by side hkups, 8 full hkups, 45 W, 45 E (20/30 amps), seasonal sites, WiFi Hotspot, tent sites, dump, mobile sewer, laundry, groc, fire rings, firewood. **REC:** pool, Shelter Valley Creek: fishing, playground, rec open to public. Pet restrict(Q). Eco-friendly, 2015 rates: $36. Disc: AAA. May 1 to Oct 15.
(905)349-2594 Lat: 43.99191, Lon: -77.99983
253 Benlock Road, Grafton, ON K0K 2G0
ceccamp@outlook.com
www.ceccamp.ca
See ad this page, 1420.

GRAND BEND — E3 *Huron, Lambton*

BIRCH BARK TENT & TRAILER PARK **Ratings: 7/8.5/8** (Campground) 2015 rates: $45 to $50. May 1 to Oct 15. (519)238-8256 rr1, 36501 Dashwood Road, Dashwood, ON N0M 1N0

PINERY PROVINCIAL PARK (Prov Pk) From town, S 4 mi on Hwy 21 (R). Min 3 ngt stay on holiday weekends. 2015 rates: $34.92 to $38. (519)243-2220

RUS-TON FAMILY CAMPGROUND
Ratings: 8/9.5★/9 (Campground) From Jct of Hwy 81 & Lakeshore Rd, S 6.4 km (4 mi) on Lakeshore Rd (L). Min 3 night stay on holiday weekends. **FAC:** Paved/gravel rds. (244 spaces). Avail: 24 grass, back-ins (40 x 48), 14 full hkups, 10 W, 10 E (15/30 amps), seasonal sites, WiFi Hotspot $, tent sites, rentals, dump, laundry, groc, LP bottles, fire rings, controlled access. **REC:** heated pool, wading pool, playground. Pet restrict(B). RV age restrict, eco-friendly, 2015 rates: $50. May 1 to Oct 15.
(519)243-2424 Lat: 43.25881, Lon: -81.80650
box 604, 9787 Lakeshore Road, Grand Bend, ON N0M 1T0
info@rustoncampground.com
www.rustoncampground.com
See ad this page, 1420.

GRAND VALLEY — D5 *Dufferin*

SUMMER PLACE **Ratings: 6.5/7.5/8** (Campground) 2015 rates: $32 to $37. May 9 to Oct 8. (519)928-5408 #174366 County Rd 25 North, Grand Valley, ON L9W 0L9

GRANTON — E4 *Perth*

PROSPECT HILL CAMPGROUND **Ratings: 7.5/7/7** (Campground) 2015 rates: $42. May 15 to Oct 13. (519)225-2405 rr 2, 1142 Perth Road 139, Granton, ON N0M 1V0

GRAVENHURST — C5 *Muskoka*

CAMP HILLBILLY ESTATES **Ratings: 7/8★/7.** (Campground) 2015 rates: $48 to $53. May 1 to Oc 13. (705)689-2366 1633 Hwy 11S, Kilworthy, O P0E 1G0

GRAVENHURST/MUSKOKA KOA
Ratings: 8/8.5/8.5 (Campground) From N J of Hwys 11 & District Rd 6 (Exit 175), E 0.1 km (0.1 mi) on District Rd 6 to Gravenhurs Pkwy, N 2.4 km (1.5 mi) to Reay Rd, E 0.4 km (0.2 mi) (L). Note: Min 3 night stay on holiday weekends **FAC:** Paved/gravel rds. (160 spaces). 77 Avail: 3 gravel, 47 grass, 20 pull-thrus (32 x 60), back-in (20 x 40), 10 full hkups, 67 W, 67 E (15/30 amps) seasonal sites, WiFi, tent sites, rentals, dump, mobil sewer, laundry, groc, LP bottles, fire rings, firewoo **REC:** heated pool, wading pool, Duck Lake: fishing golf, playground, rec open to public. Pets OK Eco-friendly, 2015 rates: $48. May 8 to Oct 18.
(800)562-9883 Lat: 44.958085, Lon: -79.318666
1083 Reay Road, Gravenhurst, ON P1P 1R3
gravenhurstkoa@cogeco.net
www.koa.com/campgrounds/gravenhurst
See ad page 1434.

GUELPH — E5 *Wellington*

GUELPH LAKE CONSERVATION AREA (Public From Jct of Hwy 7 West & Hwy 6 North, N 1.3 mi o Hwy 6 North to Conservation Rd, E 2.4 mi (E). 201 rates: $35 to $42. May 1 to Oct 15. (866)ONT-CAM

HAMILTON — E5 *Hamilton-Wentworth*

FLAMBORO VALLEY CAMPING RESORT
Ratings: 8.5/8.5/7.5 (Campground) From J of Hwy 6 & Reg Rd 97, W 3.5 km (2.2 mi) o Reg Rd 97 (L). Note: Min. 3 nights stay o holiday weekends. **FAC:** All weather rds. (26 spaces). 89 Avail: 58 gravel, 31 grass, 68 pull-thru (30 x 85), back-ins (25 x 65), mostly side by sid hkups, 28 full hkups, 60 W, 60 E (30/50 amps), sea sonal sites, WiFi $, tent sites, rentals, showers dump, laundry, groc, fire rings, firewood, controlle access. **REC:** heated pool, wading pool, whirlpoo pond, fishing, playground, rec open to public. P restrict(B). Partial handicap access. Big rig site eco-friendly, 2015 rates: $44 to $50. May 1 to Oct 1
(905)659-5053 Lat: 43.38982, Lon: -80.07255
#1158 Regional Road 97, Puslinch, ON N0B 2J0
info@flamborovalley.com
www.flamborovalley.com
See ad page 1436.

OLYMPIA VILLAGE TRAILER PARK **Ra ings: 6.5/6.5/7** (Campground) 2015 rates: $42 $48. Apr 15 to Oct 31. (905)627-1923 1161 4th Co Road W., R.r.2, Waterdown, ON L0R 2H2

HANOVER — D4 *Grey*

SAUGEEN CEDARS FAMILY CAMPGROUN **Ratings: 5.5/5.5/6.5** (Campground) 2015 rates: $3 Apr 25 to Oct 17. (519)364-2069 # 401563, Gre Road 4, Rr1, Hanover, ON N4N 3B8

SAUGEEN SPRINGS RV PARK INC
Ratings: 8/9★/9.5 (Campground) From Jct of West Grey County Rd 4 Mulock Rd, N 4.5 km (2.8 mi) on Muloc Rd (L). Min 3 nights stay on holida weekends. **FAC:** All weather rds. (2 spaces). 100 Avail: 35 gravel, 65 grass, 3 pull-thr (36 x 78), back-ins (47 x 90), mostly side by si hkups, 17 full hkups, 41 W, 41 E (30 amps), seasona sites, WiFi $, tent sites, rentals, showers $, dum mobile sewer, laundry, groc, LP bottles, fire ring firewood, controlled access. **REC:** Saugeen Rive swim, fishing, shuffleboard, playground, rec open public. Pets OK. Partial handicap access. RV ag restrict, eco-friendly, 2015 rates: $38 to $66. Apr 1 Nov 15.
(519)369-5136 Lat: 44.21187, Lon: -80.91791
173844 Mulock Road, Rr3, Hanover, ON N4N 3B
info@saugeenspringspark.com
www.saugeenspringspark.com
See ad this page, 1420.

HAWKESTONE — C5 *Simcoe*

HEIDI'S CAMPGROUND
Ratings: 8.5/9/9 (Campground) From Jct of Hwy 400 & Hwy 11N, N 14.5 km (9 mi) on Hwy 11N to Oro/Medonte Line 11, (over the overpass) NW 0.16 km (0.1 mi) (R). Min stay 3 ngts on holiday w/ends. **FAC:** All weather rds. (160 spaces). Avail: 40 gravel, patios, 21 pull-thrus (30 x 55), back-ins (20 x 40), 40 full hkups (30 amps), seasonal sites, WiFi $, tent sites, rentals, dump, laundry, groc, fire rings, firewood, controlled access. **REC:** heated pool, whirlpool, Heidis Creek: playground. Pet restrict(B). Partial handicap access. RV age restrict, eco-friendly, 2015 rates: $41.95 to $47.95. Disc: AAA. May 1 to Oct 15.
(705)487-3311 Lat: 44.506279, Lon: -79.480461
3982 Hwy 11S, Oro-Medonte, ON L0L 1T0
heidis@heidisrv.com
www.heidisrv.com/camp/
See ad opposite page, 1420.

Travel Services

HEIDI'S RV SUPERSTORE Offers RV sales dealership, RV repair and RV parts & accessories. **SERVICES:** RV, RV appliance, MH mechanical, mobile RV svc, restrooms, RV Sales. Rentals, RV storage. **TOW:** RV. RV supplies, dump, emergency parking, RV accessible. waiting room. Hours: 8am to 7pm.
(705)487-2214 Lat: 44.503971, Lon: -79.483482
3982 Hwy 11 S., Oro-Medonte, ON L0L 1T0
heidis@heidisrv.com
www.heidisrv.com
See ad opposite page.

HEARST — F9 *Cochrane*

FUSHIMI LAKE (Prov Pk) From town, W 15 mi on Hwy 11 to Fushimi Forest Access Rd, N 10 mi (R). 2015 rates: $12.75 to $43.75. May 16 to Sep 1. (705)372-5909

VEILLEUX CAMPING & MARINA **Ratings: 6/7/7** (Campground) 2015 rates: $35.64. May 15 to Sep 15. (705)362-5379 20 Desgroseillers Road, Hearst, ON P0L 1N0

HEPWORTH — C4 *Grey*

WHISPERING PINES FAMILY CAMPGROUND **Ratings: 7.5/6.5/7.5** (RV Park) 2015 rates: $38 to $42. May 1 to Oct 8. (519)935-2571 719601 Hwy 6, Hepworth, ON N0H 1P0

HORNEPAYNE — F9 *Hearst*

NAGAGAMISIS (Prov Pk) From Jct of Hwy 11 & Hwy 631, S 26 mi on Hwy 631 (L). 2015 rates: $12.75 to $43.75. May 16 to Sep 28. (807)868-2254

HUNTSVILLE — C6 *Muskoka*

ARROWHEAD (Prov Pk) From Jct of Hwy 11 (exit 226) & Muskoka Rd 3, E 0.1 mi on Muskoka Rd 3 to Arrowhead Park Rd, N 0.75 mi (E). 2015 rates: $30.50 to 43.75. (705)789-5105

DEER LAKE CAREFREE RV RESORT
Ratings: 7.5/8.5★/7.5 (Campground) From jct Hwy 60 & Hwy 11: Go 1.6 km/1 mi S on Hwy 11 (exit 221), then 1.6 km/1 mi N on Muskoka Rd 2, then .8 km/1/2 mi S on Hutchinson Beach Rd. **FAC:** Gravel rds. (250 spaces). Avail: 28 grass, 5 pull-thrus (25 x 70), back-ins (45 x 50), some side by side hkups, 28 W, 28 E (30 amps), seasonal sites, WiFi Hotspot, tent sites, rentals, dump, mobile sewer, laundry, groc, fire rings, firewood, controlled access. **REC:** heated pool, Deer Lake: fishing, playground. Pet restrict(B). Eco-friendly, 2015 rates: $48 to $54. May 15 to Oct 15.
(705)789-3326 Lat: 45.33946, Lon: -79.25555
85 Hutchinson Beach Rd, Huntsville, ON P1H 1N4
deerlake@carefreervresorts.com
http://www.carefreervresorts.com/rv-parks/ontario/deer-lake/
See ad pages 1445, 1420.

LAGOON TENT & TRAILER PARK **Ratings: 6/7/7** (Campground) 2015 rates: $47. May 15 to Oct 15. (705)789-5011 100 Lagoon Trailer Park Rd, Huntsville, ON P1H 2J4

SILVER SANDS TENT & TRAILER PARK **Ratings: 6/7/7** (Campground) 2015 rates: $39 to $41. May 15 to Oct 15. (705)789-5383 58 Silver Sands Rd., Huntsville, ON P1H 2J4

IGNACE — F7 *Kenora*

COBBLESTONE LODGE **Ratings: 4.5/6.5/6.5** (Campground) 2015 rates: $27. May 20 to Sep 30. (807)934-2345 375 Raleigh Lake Road, Ignace, ON P0T 1T0

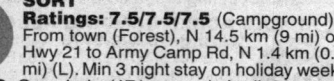

DAVY LAKE CAMPGROUND
Ratings: 8/10★/8.5 (Campground) From Jct of Hwy 17 & Hwy 599, W 0.5 km (0.3 mi) on Hwy 17 to Davy Lake Rd, SW 0.8 km (0.5 mi) (L). **FAC:** Gravel rds. (54 spaces). 50 Avail: 29 gravel, 21 grass, 18 pull-thrus (46 x 100), back-ins (30 x 45), some side by side hkups, 19 full hkups, 23 W, 23 E (15/50 amps), seasonal sites, cable, WiFi, tent sites, rentals, dump, laundry, groc, fire rings, firewood, controlled access. **REC:** Davy Lake: swim, fishing, playground. Pets OK. Eco-friendly, 2015 rates: $35 to $45. May 15 to Oct 1.
(877)374-3113 Lat: 49.41009, Lon: -91.65237
400 Davy Lake Road, Ignace, ON P0T 1T0
smorin@davylakecampground.com
www.davylakecampground.com
See ad this page, 1420.

SANDBAR LAKE (Prov Pk) From town, E 0.5 mi on Hwy 17 to Hwy 599, N 7 mi (L). 2015 rates: $12.75 to $43.75. May 16 to Sep 21. (807)934-2995

INGERSOLL — E4 *Oxford*

CENTENNIAL PARK (Public) From Jct of Hwy 401 & 19 (exit 218), N 0.7 mi on Hwy 19 (L) (Registration at Victoria Park Community Center). 2015 rates: $16.50. May 20 to Sep 1. (519)425-1181

INGLESIDE — C9 *Stormont, Dundas & Glengarry*

FARRAN PARK (TOWNSHIP PARK) (Public) From west town limits: Go 4-1/4 km/2-3/4 mi W on Hwy 2. (613)537-8600

UPPER CANADA MIGRATORY BIRD SANCTUARY/CAMPSITE (Prov Pk) From town, W 2 mi on forest service rd. (E). 2015 rates: $33 to $43. May 15 to Oct 25. (800)437-2233

IPPERWASH BEACH — E3 *Lambton*

SILVER BIRCHES CAREFREE RV RESORT
Ratings: 7.5/7.5/7.5 (Campground) From town (Forest), N 14.5 km (9 mi) on Hwy 21 to Army Camp Rd, N 1.4 km (0.9 mi) (L). Min 3 night stay on holiday weekends. **FAC:** Gravel rds. (171 spaces). Avail: 30 grass, back-ins (45 x 60), mostly side by side hkups, 2 full hkups, 8 W, 8 E (15/30 amps), seasonal sites, WiFi Hotspot, tent sites, rentals, dump, laundry, fire rings, firewood, controlled access. **REC:** heated pool, playground. Pet restrict(B/Q). Eco-friendly, 2015 rates: $46 to $54. May 1 to Oct 30.
(519)243-2480 Lat: 43.20122, Lon: -81.94950
9537 Army Camp Rd, Lambton Shores, ON N0N 1J3
silverbirches@carefreervresorts.com
www.carefreervresorts.ca/silverbirches
See ad pages 1445, 1420.

IRON BRIDGE — A2 *Algoma*

VIKING TENT & TRAILER PARK **Ratings: 5/6.5/6** (Campground) 2015 rates: $32 to $35. May 1 to Oct 15. (705)843-2834 21715 Hwy 17, Iron Bridge, ON P0R 1H0

IROQUOIS — C9 *South Dundas*

IROQUOIS MUNICIPAL PARK (Prov Pk) From jct Hwy 401 & Hwy 2 (Carman Rd): Go 3/4 km/1/2 mi S on Hwy 2. (613)652-2506

IROQUOIS FALLS — F10 *Cochrane*

CAMERON'S BEACH TRAILER PARK (Campground) (Phone Update) 2015 rates: $32 to $36. May 15 to Sep 15. (705)232-4905 1011 Cameron Ave, Iroquois Falls, ON P0K 1G0

KETTLE LAKES (Prov Pk) From town, E 24 mi on Hwy 101 to Hwy 67, N 2 mi (R). 2015 rates: $12.75 to $43.75. May 16 to Oct 14. (705)363-3511

KAGAWONG — B3 *Manitoulin*

NORM'S TENT & TRAILER PARK
Ratings: 6/6.5/7 (Campground) From Jct of Hwy 540 & Lake Shore Rd, S 1.4 km (0.9 mi) on Lake Shore Rd (R). **FAC:** Gravel rds. (55 spaces). Avail: 25 grass, 8 pull-thrus (25 x 40), back-ins (25 x 40), mostly side by side hkups, 25 W, 25 E (15/30 amps), seasonal sites, tent sites, rentals, dump, mobile sewer, laundry, groc, fire rings, firewood. **REC:** Lake Kagawong: swim, fishing, playground, rec open to public. Pets OK. Partial handicap access. Eco-friendly, 2015 rates: $33. May 8 to Oct 8.
(705)282-2827 Lat: 45.888437, Lon: -82.260597
rr 1, 1125B Lakeshore Road, Kagawong, ON P0P 1J0
normsttpk@yahoo.ca
www.manitoulintourism.com
See ad page 1436.

KAKABEKA FALLS — F8 *Thunder Bay*

KAKABEKA FALLS (Prov Pk) From Thunder Bay, W 20 mi on Hwy 11/17 (L). 2015 rates: $36.75 to $43.75. May 16 to Oct 14. (807)473-9231

KAPUSKASING — F9 *Cochrane*

RENE BRUNELLE (Prov Pk) From Jct of Hwys 11 & 581, N 6 mi on Hwy 581 (R). 2015 rates: $12.75 to $43.75. May 16 to Sep 1. (705)367-2692

KATRINE — B5 *Parry Sound*

ALMAGUIN CAMPGROUND **Ratings: 7.5/9★/8** (Campground) 2015 rates: $40 to $50. May 15 to Oct 15. (705)382-3802 419 Owl Lake Road, Katrine, ON P0A 1L0

KEARNEY — B6 *Parry Sound*

GRANITE RIDGE CAMPGROUND **Ratings: 6/7.5/7.5** (Campground) 2015 rates: $40 to $50. May 14 to Sep 7. (705)636-1474 rr 1, 2900 518 East, Kearney, ON P0A 1M0

KEENE — D7 *Peterborough*

HOPE MILL (OTONABEE REGION CONS AUTH) (Prov Pk) From town: Go 3-1/4 km/2 mi N on CR 34. Pit toilets. (705)750-0545

SHADY ACRES - PARKBRIDGE
Ratings: 8/7.5/8.5 (Campground) From Hwy 7E turn R on Heritage Line/County Rd-34, 9 km (5.5 mi) Heritage Line/County Rd becomes Serpent Mounds Rd, 3 km (1.8 mi) (R). **FAC:** All weather rds. (281 spaces). Avail: 27 gravel, back-ins (25 x 50), 2 full hkups, 25 W, 25 E (15/30 amps), seasonal sites, rentals, dump, laundry, groc, fire rings, firewood, controlled access. **REC:** heated pool, Rice Lake: swim, fishing, shuffleboard, playground. Pets OK. Eco-friendly, 2015 rates: $35. May 1 to Oct 15.
(705)295-6815 Lat: 44.214378, Lon: -78.158241
740 Serpent Mounds Rd, Keene, ON L0L 2G0
shadyacresinfo@parkbridge.com
www.parkbridge.com
See ad pages 1417 (Welcome Section), 1420.

KEMPTVILLE — C9 *Stormont, Dundas & Glengarry*

RIDEAU RIVER (Prov Pk) From town, NW 2.5 mi on CR-44 (becomes CR-5), NE 1 mi (R). 2015 rates: $12.75 to $43.75. May 9 to Sep 21. (613)258-2740

SANDY MOUNTAIN CAMP & GOLF **Ratings: 7/6.5/7** (Campground) 2015 rates: $31 to $36. May 15 to Oct 15. (613)989-2058 10152 CR 43, Rr2, Mountain, ON K0E 1S0

KENORA — E6 *Kenora*

ANICINABE PARK **Ratings: 8/9.5★/9** (Campground) From Jct of Trans-Canada Hwy 17 & Mikana Way, S 0.8 km (0.5 mi) to park entrance (R). Minimum 2 ngts stay on holiday weekends. **FAC:** Gravel rds. 87 Avail: 87 all weather, back-ins (30 x 60), 28 full hkups, 42 W, 42 E (15/30 amps), WiFi, tent sites, dump, laundry, groc, fire rings, firewood, restaurant,

ON

KENORA (CONT)

ANICINABE PARK (CONT) controlled access. **REC:** Lake of the Woods: swim, fishing, golf, playground, rec open to public. Pets OK. Partial handicap access. 28 day max stay, eco-friendly, 2015 rates: $34 to $39. May 1 to Oct 15. ATM.
(807)467-2700 Lat: 49.75345, Lon: -94.47953
955 Golf Course Road, Kenora, ON P9N 4J1
anicinabepark@live.com
www.anicinabepark.ca

→ RUSHING RIVER (Prov Pk) From Jct of Hwys 17 & 71, S 3 mi on Hwy 71 (L). 2015 rates: $12.75 to $43.75. May 16 to Sep 21. (807)548-4351

→ **THE WILLOWS RV PARK & CAMPGROUND**
Ratings: 7.5/9★/8.5 (Campground) From Jct of Hwy 17 & Longbow Lake Rd, SE 350 m on Longbow Lake Rd to Heritage Rd, N 200 m (R). **FAC:** Gravel rds. (75 spaces). Avail: 35 gravel, 6 pull-thrus (30 x 90), back-ins (30 x 60), 15 full hkups, 20 W, 20 E (15/50 amps), seasonal sites, WiFi, tent sites, rentals, dump, laundry, groc, fire rings, firewood, controlled access. **REC:** pond, fishing, playground. Pets OK. Big rig sites, RV age restrict, eco-friendly, 2015 rates: $34 to $45. May 10 to Oct 15.
(807)548-1821 Lat: 49.73048, Lon: -94.29684
41 Longbow Lake Road, Longbow Lake, ON P0X 1H0
willowscampground@hotmail.com
www.willowscampground.ca
See ad pages 1441, 1420.

KILLARNEY — B4 *Algoma*

↗ KILLARNEY/GEORGE LAKE (Prov Pk) From Jct of Hwys 69 & 637, W 45 mi on Hwy 637 (R). 2015 rates: $10.75 to $43.75. (705)287-2900

KINCARDINE — D3 *Bruce*

↙ **AINTREE TRAILER PARK LTD**
Ratings: 7.5/8.5★/8.5 (Campground) From Jct of Hwy 21 & Hwy 9, SW 3.2 km (2 mi) on Hwy 21 to Conc #12, NW 1.9 km (1.2 mi) (L). **FAC:** Gravel rds. (171 spaces). 18 Avail: 6 gravel, 12 grass, patios, 6 pull-thrus (22 x 65), back-ins (30 x 65), mostly side by side hkups, 6 full hkups, 12 W, 12 E (30 amps), seasonal sites, WiFi Hotspot, tent sites, showers $, dump, laundry, LP bottles, fire rings, firewood. **REC:** Lake Huron: swim, fishing, shuffleboard, playground. Pets OK. Eco-friendly, 2015 rates: $33.05 to $36.73. Apr 15 to Oct 13.
(877)396-8533 Lat: 44.148936, Lon: -81.667515
2435 Huron Concession 12 Road, Kincardine, ON N2Z 2X3
aintreepark@hotmail.com
www.aintreepark.com
See ad page 1436.

BLUEWATER TRAILER PARK (CITY PARK) (Public) From jct Hwy 9 & Hwy 21: Go 1/2 km/1/4 mi S on Hwy 21, then 1/2 km/1/4 mi W on Durham St. 2015 rates: $35. (519)396-8698

↓ **FISHERMAN'S COVE TENT & TRAILER PARK**
Ratings: 10/10★/10 (Campground) From Jct of Hwys 21 & 9, E 18 km (11.25 mi) on Hwy 9 to Bruce CR-1, S 2 km (1.3 mi) to Southline, SE 0.8 km (0.5 mi) (E). Note: Min 3 ngt stay on holiday weekends. **FAC:** Paved rds. (530 spaces). Avail: 155 all weather, patios, 13 pull-thrus (40 x 100), back-ins (35 x 50), 145 full hkups, 10 W, 10 E (30/50 amps), seasonal sites, WiFi $, tent sites, rentals, showers $, dump, laundry, groc, LP bottles, fire rings, firewood, controlled access. **REC:** heated pool, whirlpool, Otter Lake: swim, fishing, marina, shuffleboard, playground. Pet restrict(B). Partial handicap access. Big rig sites, RV age restrict, eco-friendly, 2015 rates: $51 to $61. May 15 to Oct 1. ATM.
(519)395-2757 Lat: 44.074340, Lon: -81.4147565
13 Southline Ave, Huron-Kinloss, ON N2Z 2X5
info@fishermanscove.com
www.fishermanscove.com
See ad this page.

↓ GREEN ACRES CAMPGROUND & RV PARK **Ratings: 8.5/9★/8** (Campground) 2015 rates: $39 to $42. May 1 to Oct 15. (519)395-2808 2310 Concession 12, Rr 1, Kincardine, ON N2Z 2X3

KINGSTON — D8 *Frontenac*

A SPOTLIGHT Introducing Kingston's colorful attractions appearing at the front of this state section.

↗ **RIDEAU ACRES CAMPING RESORT**
Ratings: 8.5/9.5★/8 (Campground) From Jct of Hwys 401 & 15 (Exit 623), N 1.6 km (1 mi) on Hwy 15 to entrance on Cunningham Rd (L). **FAC:** Gravel rds. (530 spaces). 294 Avail: 244 gravel, 50 grass, 89 pull-thrus (30 x 60), back-ins (30 x 60), 169 full hkups, 80 W, 80 E (30/50 amps), seasonal sites, WiFi, tent sites, dump, mobile sewer, laundry, groc, LP gas, fire rings, firewood, controlled access. **REC:** heated pool, Colonel By Lake: swim, fishing, playground, rec open to public. Pets OK. Partial handicap access. Big rig sites, eco-friendly, 2015 rates: $43.5[...] Disc: AAA.
AAA Approved
(800)958-5830 Lat: 44.30502, Lon: -76.42098
1014 Cunningham Road, Kingston, ON K7L 4V3
info@rideauacres.com
www.rideauacres.com
See ad pages 1423 (Spotlight Kingston), 1420.

↖ **1000 ISLANDS/KINGSTON HOLIDAY KOA**
Ratings: 8.5/10★/9 (Campground) From J[...] of Hwy 401 & Hwy 38 (Exit 611), N 0.8 km (0.[...] mi) on Hwy 38 to Cordukes Rd, NE 0.8 km (0.[...] mi) (L). Minimum 3 ngt stay on holiday weekends. **FAC:** Paved/gravel rds. (83 spaces). Avail: 60 grave[...] patios, 44 pull-thrus (37 x 65), back-ins (40 x 55), 6[...] W, 60 E (30/50 amps), seasonal sites, WiFi, te[...] sites, rentals, dump, mobile sewer, laundry, groc, fi[...] rings, firewood. **REC:** heated pool, playground, re[...] open to public. Pet restrict(B). Partial handicap ac[...]cess. Eco-friendly, 2015 rates: $53 to $92.50. May [...] to Oct 15.
(800)562-9178 Lat: 44.30162, Lon: -76.57525
2039 Cordukes Road Rr 8, Kingston, ON K7L 4V[...]
koakingston@hotmail.com
www.kingstonkoa.com
See ad page 1434.

KINTAIL — D3 *Huron*

← MACKENZIE'S TRAILER PARK **Ratings: 5/7/[...]** (Campground) 2015 rates: $30 to $40. May 10 to O[...] 8. (519)529-7536 85324 Mackenzie Camp Rd South[...] Goderich, ON N7A 3X9

KIRKLAND LAKE — F10 *Timiskaming*

→ ESKER LAKES (Prov Pk) From Jct of TCH-11 [...] Hwy 112, N 12 mi on Hwy 112 to Hwy 66, E 9 mi [...] Hwy 672, N 10 mi to park access rd, E 1 mi (E). 201[...] rates: $12.75 to $43.75. May 16 to Sep 1. (705)56[...] 7677

KITCHENER — E4 *Waterloo*

↗ **BINGEMANS CAMPING RESORT Ra[...]ings: 8/7/8** (Campground) E-Bnd: From Jct of Hwy 86 & 7, E 3.2 km (2 mi) on Hwy 7 (Victoria St) [...] Bingemans Centre Dr, N 0.3 km (0.2 mi) (R) W-Bn[...] From Jct of Wellington St. N & Shirley Ave, SE 2.3 k[...] (1.4 mi) on Shirley Ave. 3rd Bingemans entrance o[...] left. (3 day minimum stay on holiday weekends[...] **FAC:** Paved/gravel rds. (450 spaces). 300 Avail: [...] gravel, 287 grass, 13 pull-thrus (30 x 75), back-in[...] (40 x 40), mostly side by side hkups, 100 full hkup[...] 200 W, 200 E (15/50 amps), seasonal sites, Wi[...] Hotspot, tent sites, rentals, dump, mobile sewe[...] laundry, groc, fire rings, firewood, restaurant, co[...]trolled access. **REC:** heated pool, wading pool, whi[...]pool, Grand River: fishing, golf, playground, rec ope[...] to public. Pet restrict(B). Partial handicap acces[...] Eco-friendly, 2015 rates: $50 to $85. Disc: AAA. Ma[...] 8 to Oct 30. ATM.
AAA Approved
(800)565-4631 Lat: 43.47383, Lon: -80.44343
425 Bingemans Centre Drive, Kitchener, O[...] N2B 3X7
camping@bingemans.com
www.bingemans.com

LAKE ST PETER — C7 *Hastings*

↑ LAKE SAINT PETER (Prov Pk) From Jct of Hwy[...] 62 & 127, NW 15 mi on Hwy 127 to North Rd, N 1[...] mi (R). 2015 rates: $12.75 to $43.75. May 9 to Oct 1[...] (613)338-5312

LAKEFIELD — D6 *Peterborough*

← GALVIN BAY PARK RESORT **Ratings: 8/10★[...]** (Membership Pk) 2015 rates: $38 to $43. May 15 [...] Oct 15. (705)657-8055 2707 Buckhorn Rd, Lakefiel[...] ON K0L 2H0

→ LAKEFIELD CAMPGROUND (Public) Jct 33 [...] CR 20 E CR 29 1/2 km W on CR 29 1/4 km N o[...] Clement St. Follow signs. 2015 rates: $32 to $3[...] May 1 to Oct 15. (705)652-8610

↑ LAKEFIELD PARK (Public) From Jct of Hwys 11[...] 135 & 28, N 0.5 mi to Parkway, E 0.5 mi to Land[...] down, N 0.2 mi to George St, E 1 mi to Water St, [...] to Lakefield, follow signs (E). 2015 rates: $27 to $3[...] May 2 to Sep 30. (705)652-8610

LAKESIDE — E4 *Oxford*

↓ LAKESIDE RESORT **Ratings: 6.5/6/7** (Cam[...]ground) 2015 rates: $40 to $45. May 1 to Oct [...] (519)349-2820 256440 Sunova Crescent, Lakesid[...] ON N0M 2G0

Say you saw it in our Guide!

AMBTON SHORES — E3 *Lambton*

CAROLINIAN FOREST FAMILY CAMP-ROUND **Ratings: 7.5/7.5/8** (Campground) 2015 ...tes: $50. May 1 to Oct 12. (519)243-2258 rr 2, 9589 ...perwash Road, Lambton Shores, ON N0N 1J3

OAKRIDGE RESORT - PARKBRIDGE
Ratings: 7.5/7.5/8 (Campground) From Jct of Hwy 79 & 21 (Lakeshore Rd), NW 0.8 km (0.5 mi) on Hwy 21 (Lakeshore Rd) to Northville Cr, W 0.3 km (0.2 mi) (R). Min 3 day stay on holiday week-...nds. **FAC:** Paved/gravel rds. (292 spaces). Avail: 86 ...rass, 4 pull-thrus (25 x 45), back-ins (23 x 38), ...ostly side by side hkups, 61 W, 61 E (15/30 amps), ...easonal sites, WiFi Hotspot, tent sites, rentals, ...ump, laundry, groc, LP bottles, fire rings, firewood, ...ontrolled access. **REC:** heated pool, wading pool, ...huffleboard, playground, rec open to public. Pet re-...rict(B). Partial handicap access. RV age restrict, ...co-friendly, 2015 rates: $42 to $52. May 1 to Oct 15.
...19)243-2500 Lat: 43.22066, Lon: -81.87120
...910 Northville Cres, Rr1, Thedford, ON N0M 2N0
...vere@parkbridge.ca
...ttp://www.parkbridge.com/en-ca/rv-cottages/ ...akridge
...ee ad pages 1417 (Welcome Section), ...420.

OUR PONDEROSA RV & GOLF RESORT - PARKBRIDGE
Ratings: 8.5/8.5/8 (Campground) From Jct of Hwy 21/CR 7 (Lakeshore Rd) & W Ipperwash Rd, N 1.3 km (0.8 mi) on W Ipperwash Rd (R). Min 2 nights stay ...n weekends & min 3 nights stay on holiday week-...nds. **FAC:** All weather rds. (410 spaces). 73 Avail: ...6 gravel, 47 grass, 9 pull-thrus (45 x 72), back-ins ...40 x 60), mostly side by side hkups, 53 full hkups, 20 ...V, 20 E (15/50 amps), seasonal sites, WiFi Hotspot, ...ent sites, rentals, dump, mobile sewer, laundry, groc, ...P bottles, fire rings, firewood, controlled access. **...EC:** heated pool, whirlpool, golf, shuffleboard, play-...round. Pets OK. Partial handicap access. RV age ...estrict, eco-friendly, 2015 rates: $52 to $135. May 1 ...Oct 12.
...88)786-CAMP Lat: 43.18939, Lon: -81.98885
...338 West Ipperwash Road, Rr #2, Lambton ...hores, ON N0N 1J2
...amping@ourponderosa.com
...ttp://www.parkbridge.com/en-ca/rv-cottages/ ...ur-ponderosa
...ee ad pages 1417 (Welcome Section), ...420.

...ANCASTER — C10 *Stormont, Dundas & ...lengarry*

GLENGARRY PARK (Prov Pk) W-bnd: From Jct ...f Hwy 401 & Hwy 2 (Exit 814), S 0.5 km (0.3 mi) on ...wy 2 to S Service Rd, E 3.4 km (2.1 mi) (R) Note: ...hree night min. stay on holiday weekends. 2015 ...ates: $34.50 to $38.25. May 16 to Oct 13. (800)437-...233

LANCASTER PARK OUTDOOR RESORT **Rat-...ngs: 7/7/7.5** (Campground) 2015 rates: $44 to ...49.56. May 1 to Oct 15. (613)347-3452 20716 South ...ervice Road, Lancaster, ON K0C 1N0

...ANGTON — E4 *Norwich*

DEER CREEK CONSERVATION AREA (Public) ...rom town, S 3 mi on Hwy 59 to Regional Rd 45, W ....25 mi (R). Pit toilets. 2015 rates: $34 to $46. May ...to Sep 7. (877)990-9934

...ARDER LAKE — F10 *Timiskaming*

RAVEN BEACH PARK (Public) At Jct of Hwy 66 ...E 2nd Ave (R). 2015 rates: $20 to $30. May 15 to ...Oct 15. (705)643-2171

...EAMINGTON — F2 *Essex*

LEISURE LAKE RESORT - PARKBRIDGE
Ratings: 8/8.5★/8 (Campground) From Jct of Hwy 401 & French Line Rd 31 (formerly St. Joachim Rd) (Exit 40), S 16.1 km (10 mi) on CR-31 (L). Note: Min 3 night stay on holiday weekends. **FAC:** ...ravel rds. (406 spaces). Avail: 61 grass, 4 pull-thrus ...21 x 60), back-ins (35 x 50), 11 full hkups, 50 W, 27 ...E (30/50 amps), seasonal sites, WiFi Hotspot, tent ...ites, rentals, dump, laundry, groc, LP bottles, fire ...ings, firewood, controlled access. **REC:** heated pool, ...vading pool, Leisure Lake: swim, fishing, playground, ...ec open to public. Pet restrict(B/Q). Partial handicap ...ccess. Eco-friendly, 2015 rates: $50 to $77. May 1 ...o Oct 31.
...888)274-8817 Lat: 42.08717, Lon: -82.64158
...510 Essex Rd #31, Ruthven, ON N0P 2G0
...eisurelakeinfo@parkbridge.ca
...www.parkbridge.ca
...ee ad pages 1417 (Welcome Section), ...1420.

LINDSAY — D6 *Kawartha Lakes*

DOUBLE "M" RV RESORT & CAMPGROUND **Ratings: 6.5/7/8.5** (Campground) 2015 rates: $40 to $50. May 15 to Oct 15. (705)324-9317 101 Ridgewood Rd, Lindsay, ON K9V 4R2

RIVERWOOD PARK **Ratings: 8/9.5★/7.5** (Campground) 2015 rates: $39.83. May 18 to Oct 8. (705)324-1655 78 Riverwood Park Drive, Lindsay, ON K9V 0K2

LION'S HEAD — C4 *Bruce*

LION'S HEAD BEACH PARK (Prov Pk) From jct Hwy 6 & CR 9 at Ferndale: Go 4km/2 1/2 mi E on CR9A, then .4 km/ 1/4 mi N on Main St. Then 1 block E on Webster St. (519)793-3522

LITTLE CURRENT — B3 *Manitoulin*

SILVER BIRCHES **Ratings: 6.5/6/6** (Campground) 2015 rates: $55. Apr 15 to Dec 1. (705)368-2669 110 Bay Street, Little Current, ON P0H 1K0

LONDON — E4 *Middlesex*

CAMPERS CORNER RV CAMPGROUND
Ratings: 8.5/9★/8 (Campground) From Jct of Hwys 401 & 74 (Exit 195), E 0.4 km (0.25 mi) on Cromarty Dr (L). **FAC:** Gravel rds. (118 spaces). 116 Avail: 94 gravel, 22 grass, 55 pull-thrus (25 x 65), back-ins (20 x 50), mostly side by side hkups, 21 full hkups, 95 W, 95 E (15/50 amps), seasonal sites, WiFi, tent sites, rentals, dump, laundry, groc, fire rings, firewood. **REC:** heated pool, whirlpool, playground. Pets OK. Big rig sites, eco-friendly, 2015 rates: $49. Disc: AAA. May 1 to Oct 15.
(844)287-9313 Lat: 42.949287, Lon: -81.097621
136 Cromarty Drive Rr 18, London, ON N6M 1H6
camperscorner.london@gmail.com
http://camperscorner.ca
See ad this page, 1420.

FANSHAWE CONSERVATION AREA (Public) From Jct of Hwys 401 & Airport Rd, N 4 mi on Airport Rd to Oxford St, W 2 mi to Clark Rd, N 2 mi (R). 2015 rates: $35 to $45. Apr 22 to Oct 16. (519)951-6181

LONG SAULT — C9 *Stormont, Dundas & Glengarry*

MCLAREN CAMPSITE (Public) From Jct of Hwy 401 & Moulinette Rd (Exit 778), S 2.6 km (1.6 mi) on Moulinette Rd to Long Sault Pkwy, W 10.5 km (6.5 mi) (L). Note: Three night min stay on holiday weekends. 2015 rates: $31.07 to $43.73. May 17 to Oct 14. (800)437-2233

MILLE ROCHE AREA CAMPSITE & BEACH (Public) From Hwy 401 & Moulinette Rd (Exit 778), S 2.6 km (1.6 mi) on Moulinette Rd to Long Sault Pkwy, S 3.2 km (2 mi) on Long Sault Pkwy (R). Min. three night stay on holiday weekend. 2015 rates: $31.07 to $43.73. May 17 to Sep 1. (613)543-8202

WOODLANDS AREA CAMPSITE & BEACH (Prov Pk) From Hwy 401 & Moulinette Rd (Exit 778), S 2.6 km (1.6 mi) on Moulinette Rd to Long Sault Parkway, S 9 km (5.6 mi) (R). Note: Three night min. stay on holiday weekends. 2015 rates: $34.50 to $38.25. May 17 to Sep 1. (800)437-2233

LYNDHURST — C8 *Leeds and Grenville*

CHARLESTON LAKE (Prov Pk) From Jct of Hwy 401 CR-3 (exit 659), N 12 mi on CR-3 (R). 2015 rates: $12.75 to $43.75. May 9 to Oct 14. (613)659-2065

WILSON'S TENT & TRAILER PARK **Ratings: 5/5/6** (Campground) 2015 rates: $29. May 1 to Sep 30. (613)928-2557 465 Lyndhurst Rd, Lyndhurst, ON K0E 1N0

MABERLY — C8 *Lanark*

SILVER LAKE (Prov Pk) From town, W 2 mi on Hwy 7 (R). 2015 rates: $12.75 to $43.75. May 15 to Sep 14. (613)268-2000

MADAWASKA — B7 *Nipissing*

RIVERLAND LODGE & CAMP **Ratings: 6/6.5/7.5** (Campground) 2015 rates: $39.82. (613)637-5338 98 Hwy 60, Madawaska, ON K0J 2C0

MADOC — C7 *Hastings*

CRYSTAL BEACH RESORT **Ratings: 7.5/7.5/6** (Campground) 2015 rates: $35 to $45. (613)473-4296 51 Crystal Beach Lane, Madoc, ON K0K 2K0

MALLORYTOWN — C9 *Leeds and Grenville*

1000 ISLANDS/MALLORYTOWN KOA
Ratings: 8.5/10★/8.5 (Campground) From Jct of Hwy 401 & CR-5 (Exit 675), N 0.8 km (0.5 mi) on CR-5 to CR-2, W 0.8 km (0.5 mi) (L). Min stay 3 ngts on holiday w/ends. **FAC:** All weather rds. (160 spaces). 145 Avail: 45 gravel, 100 grass, patios, 69 pull-thrus (30 x 75), back-ins (30 x 50), mostly side by side hkups, 35 full hkups, 110 W, 110 E (15/50 amps), seasonal sites, WiFi, tent sites, rentals, dump, mobile sewer, laundry, groc, LP gas, fire rings, firewood, controlled access. **REC:** heated pool, wading pool, pond, playground. Pets OK. Partial handicap access. Big rig sites, RV age restrict, eco-friendly, 2015 rates: $40 to $88. Apr 10 to Oct 31.
(800)562-9725 Lat: 44.47364, Lon: -75.88285
1477 Country Rd 2, Box 29, Mallorytown, ON K0E 1R0
koa@1000islandscamping.com
www.1000islandscamping.com
See ad page 1434.

MANITOWANING — B3 *Manitoulin*

MANITOULIN RESORT
Ratings: 7.5/9★/9 (Campground) From Jct of Hwy 6 & Bidwell Rd: Go NW .6 km (.4 mi) on Bidwell Rd to Holiday Haven Rd, then W .8 km (.5 mi) (R). **FAC:** Paved/gravel rds. (130 spaces). 30 Avail: 15 gravel, 15 grass, 4 pull-thrus (40 x 60), back-ins (30 x 50), 23 W, 23 E (30 amps), seasonal sites, WiFi Hotspot, tent sites, rentals, dump, mobile sewer, laundry, groc, fire rings, firewood, controlled access. **REC:** Lake Manitou: swim, fishing, playground. Pets OK. RV age restrict, eco-friendly, 2015 rates: $38 to $40. May 9 to Sep 28.
(705)859-3550 Lat: 45.75688, Lon: -81.87251
152 Holiday Haven Road, Manitowaning, ON P0P 1N0
info@manitoulinresort.com
www.manitoulinresort.com
See ad page 1436.

MARATHON — F8 *Thunder Bay*

NEYS (Prov Pk) From town, W 16 mi on Hwy 17 (L). 2015 rates: $12.75 to $43.75. May 16 to Sep 21. (807)229-1624

NEYS LUNCH & CAMPGROUND **Ratings: 5/8★/7.5** (Campground) 2015 rates: $35. Apr 1 to Dec 1. (807)229-1869 hwy 17 Neys, Marathon, ON P0T 2E0

MARMORA — C7 *Hastings*

MARMORA KOA
Ratings: 8.5/9.5★/8 (Campground) From Jct of Hwy 62 & Hwy 7 (in Madoc), W 8 km (4.8 mi) on Hwy 7 to KOA Campground Rd. S 1 km (0.5 mi) (R). Min 3 ngt stay on holiday weekends. **FAC:** Gravel rds. (175 spaces). 81 Avail: 32 gravel, 49 grass, 23 pull-thrus (35 x 55), back-ins (22 x 48), mostly side by side hkups, 3 full hkups, 65 W, 65 E (20/30 amps), seasonal sites, WiFi $, tent sites, rentals, dump, mobile sewer, laundry, groc, fire rings, firewood. **REC:** heated pool, whirlpool, Lily Creek: fishing, playground, rec open to public. Pet restrict(B). Eco-friendly, 2015 rates: $41 to $49.50. May 1 to Oct 15.
(800)562-9156 Lat: 44.48872, Lon: -77.62572
178 Koa Campground Road, Rr2, Marmora, ON K0K 2M0
marmorakoa@bellnet.ca
www.marmorakoa.com
See ad page 1434.

MARTEN RIVER — A5 *Nipissing*

MARTEN RIVER (Prov Pk) From Jct of Trans-Canada 11 & Trans-Canada 17, N 36 mi on Trans-Canada 11 (L). 2015 rates: $12.75 to $43.75. May 16 to Sep 28. (705)892-2200

MATTAWA — A6 *Nipissing*

SAMUEL DE CHAMPLAIN (Prov Pk) From town, W 8 mi on Hwy 17 (L). 2015 rates: $12.75 to $43.75. May 16 to Oct 14. (705)744-2276

SID TURCOTTE PARK
Ratings: 8/8.5★/9 (Campground) From Jct of Hwy 17 & Turcotte Park Rd, N 0.3 km (0.2 mi) on Turcotte Park Rd to Mattawan St, E 46 m (50 yds) (L). **FAC:** All weather rds. (85 spaces). Avail: 27 grass, 22 pull-thrus (30 x 50), back-ins (30 x 50), 15 full hkups, 12 W, 12 E (15/30 amps), seasonal sites, WiFi Hotspot, tent sites, rentals, dump, laundry, fire rings, firewood, controlled access. **REC:** Mattawa

MATTAWA (CONT)

SID TURCOTTE PARK (CONT)
River: swim, fishing, playground. Pet restrict(B). RV age restrict, eco-friendly, 2015 rates: $36 to $39. May 12 to Oct 11.
(705)744-5375 Lat: 46.31180, Lon: -78.71560
750 Mattawan St, Mattawa, ON P0H 1V0
stp@sidturcottepark.com
www.sidturcottepark.com
See ad this page, 1420.

MEAFORD — C4 *Grey*

MEAFORD MEMORIAL PARK (Public) From Jct of Hwy 26 & CR-7, N 0.1 mi on CR-7 to Aitken St, E 0.25 mi to Grant Ave, SE 0.3 mi (E). 2015 rates: $35 to $49. May 1 to Oct 18. (800)399-6323

MIDLAND — C5 *Simcoe*

BAYFORT TENT AND TRAILER PARK **Ratings: 5.5/7/7.5** (Campground) 2015 rates: $41.50. May 1 to Oct 15. (705)526-8704 3321 Ogden's Beach Road, Midland, ON L4R 4K6

SMITH'S TRAILER PARK & CAMP
Ratings: 7.5/7.5/7.5 (RV Area in MHP) From Jct of Hwy 93 & Hwy 12, E 3.2 km (2 mi) on Hwy 12 to King St, N 0.8 km (0.5 mi) (L). **FAC:** Paved/gravel rds. (179 spaces). Avail: 19 grass, 7 pull-thrus (30 x 70), back-ins (35 x 45), some side by side hkups, 5 full hkups, 14 W, 14 E (15/50 amps), seasonal sites, WiFi, tent sites, showers $, dump, groc, fire rings, firewood. **REC:** heated pool, wading pool, Little Lake: swim, fishing, shuffleboard, playground. Pet restrict(B). RV age restrict, eco-friendly, 2015 rates: $47.50 to $52.75. May 16 to Oct 13.
(705)526-4339 Lat: 44.73645, Lon: -79.87666
736 King St, Midland, ON L4R 0B9
info@smithscamp.ca
www.smithscamp.ca
See ad page 1436.

MILLER LAKE — C4 *Bruce*

SUMMER HOUSE PARK
Ratings: 8.5/10★/10 (Campground) From Jct of Hwy 6 & Miller Lake Rd, E 3.2 km (2 mi) on Miller Lake Rd (L). Min 3-5 nights stay on holiday weekends. **FAC:** Paved/gravel rds. (236 spaces). Avail: 76 gravel, 14 pull-thrus (25 x 65), back-ins (20 x 45), 30 full hkups, 29 W, 29 E (30/50 amps), seasonal sites, WiFi $, tent sites, rentals, dump, mobile sewer, laundry, groc, LP bottles, fire rings, firewood, restaurant, controlled access. **REC:** Miller Lake: swim, fishing, marina, shuffleboard, playground, rec open to public. Pet restrict(B). Partial handicap access. RV age restrict, eco-friendly, 2015 rates: $35 to $55. May 1 to Oct 17. ATM.
(519)795-7712 Lat: 45.098626, Lon: -81.402174
197 Miller Lake Shore Road, Miller Lake, ON N0H 1Z0
info@summerhousepark.ca
www.summerhousepark.ca
See ad this page.

Got something to tell us? We welcome your comments and suggestions regarding the ratings for a particular campground, or our rating system in general. Please email them to: travelguidecomments@goodsamfamily.com

MILLGROVE — E5 *Hamilton*

GULLIVER'S LAKE CAREFREE RV RESORT
Ratings: 6.5/7.5/8 (RV Park) From Hwy 6N turn onto Safari Rd E for 2.4 km (1.8 mi) on L. **FAC:** Paved/gravel rds. (198 spaces). Avail: 10 gravel, back-ins (40 x 55), some side by side hkups, accepts self-contain units only, 10 full hkups (30 amps), seasonal sites, WiFi Hotspot, fire rings, firewood, controlled access. **REC:** Gulliver's Lake: swim, playground, rec open to public. Pets OK. Eco-friendly, 2015 rates: $36. May 11 to Oct 15.
(905)659-7300 Lat: 43.361946, Lon: -80.021476
792 Safari Road, Millgrove, ON L0R 1V0
gulliverslake@carefreervresorts.com
www.carefreervresorts.com
See ad opposite page.

MILTON — E5 *Halton*

MILTON HEIGHTS CAMPGROUND LTD.
Ratings: 9/10★/8 (Campground) From Jct of Hwys 401 & 25 (Exit 320), N 1.6 km (1 mi) on Hwy 25 to RR #9 (#5 Sideroad), W 2.1 km (1.3 mi) to Tremaine Rd, S 0.3 km (0.2 mi) (R). Note: Min. 2 day stay on holiday weekends. **FAC:** Paved rds. (164 spaces). 131 Avail: 42 paved, 14 gravel, 75 grass, 31 pull-thrus (30 x 60), back-ins (30 x 50), 81 full hkups, 48 W, 48 E (15/50 amps), seasonal sites, WiFi, tent sites, rentals, dump, laundry, groc, fire rings, firewood, controlled access. **REC:** heated pool, playground. Pet restrict(B). Partial handicap access. Eco-friendly, 2015 rates: $40 to $45.
(800)308-9120 Lat: 43.52215, Lon: -79.93723
8690 Tremaine Road, Rr3, Milton, ON L9T 2X7
miltonheightscampground@on.aibn.com
www.miltonhgtscampgrd.com
See ad pages 1433 (Spotlight Toronto), 1420, 1414 (ON Map).

MINDEMOYA — B3 *Manitoulin*

MINDEMOYA COURT COTTAGES & CAMPGROUND **Ratings: 7/6/7.5** (Campground) 2015 rates: $34. May 15 to Oct 10. (705)377-5778 604 Ketchankookem Trail, Mindemoya, ON P0P 1S0

MITCHELL'S BAY — F3 *Chatham-Kent*

MITCHELLS BAY MARINE PARK LTD **Ratings: 7/8★/7.5** (RV Park) 2015 rates: $40 to $50. May 1 to Oct 31. (519)354-8423 3 Allen St, Mitchell's Bay, ON N0P 1L0

MONTREAL RIVER HARBOUR — F9 *Algoma*

TWILIGHT RESORT (Campground) (Phone Update) 2015 rates: $30 to $34. May 1 to Oct 31. (705)882-2183 hwy 17 N, Montreal River Harbour, ON P0S 1H0

MOONBEAM — F9 *Cochrane*

REMI LAKE TRAILER PARK (RV Area in MHP) (Phone Update) 2015 rates: $35 to $42. May 15 to Sep 15. (705)367-2213 80 Remi Lake Road, Moonbeam, ON P0L 1V0

TWIN LAKES CAMPING Ratings: 8/9.5★/9 (Campground) From Jct of Hwys 11 & 581, N 3.2 km (2 mi) on Hwy 581 (L). **FAC:** All weather rds. (200 spaces). Avail: 35 gravel, 5 pull-thrus (35 x 100), back-ins (30 x 65), 25 full hkups, 10 W, 10 E (30 amps), seasonal sites, WiFi $, tent sites, rentals, showers $, dump, mobile sewer, laundry, fire rings, firewood, controlled access. **REC:** Twin Lakes: swim, fishing, shuffleboard, playground, rec open to public. Pets OK. Eco-friendly, 2015 rates: $35 to $39. May 15 to Sep 15.
(705)367-9000 Lat: 49.37802, Lon: -82.16644
35 Hwy 581, Moonbeam, ON P0L 1V0
twinlakescamping1@gmail.com
www.twinlakescamping.ca

To get the most out of your Guide, refer to the Table of Contents in the front of the book.

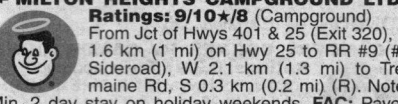

MORPETH — F3 *Chatham-Kent*

RONDEAU (Prov Pk) From Jct of Hwy 401 & 15 (exit 101), SE 9.8 mi on CR 15 (E). Follow sig 2015 rates: $34.91 to $43.75. Apr 4 to Oct (519)674-1750

MORRISBURG — C9 *Dundas, Glengarry, Stormont*

RIVERSIDE/CEDAR PARK CAMPSITE (P Pk) From Jct of Hwy 401 & Upper Canada Rd (l 758), SE 1.6 km (1 mi) on Upper Canada Rd to 2, SW 1.9 km (1.2 mi) (L). Min. three night stay holiday weekends. 2015 rates: $34.50 to $38.25. M 18 to Oct 8. (800)437-2233

UPPER CANADA CAMPGROUND
Ratings: 8/9★/8.5 (Campground) From Jct of Hwy 401 & Upper Canada N (exit 758), W 0.25 mi on Upper Can Rd N (R). Min. 2 night stay on weeker **FAC:** All weather rds. (247 spaces). Avail: 25 gravel, 22 grass, 5 pull-thrus (30 x 6 back-ins (30 x 50), some side by side hkups, 47 47 E (15/30 amps), seasonal sites, WiFi Hotspot, sites, rentals, showers $, dump, mobile sewer, la dry, groc, LP bottles, fire rings, firewood, contro access. **REC:** pool, pond, swim, fishing, playgrou rec open to public. Pets OK. RV age restr eco-friendly, 2015 rates: $35 to $38. May 1 to Sep ATM.
(613)543-2201 Lat: 44.95336, Lon: -75.11371
13390 Upper Canada Road, Morrisburg, K0C 1X0
info@uppercanadacampground.com
www.uppercanadacampground.com
See ad this page, 1420.

MOSSLEY — E4 *Middlesex*

GOLDEN POND R V RESORT
Ratings: 8.5/10★/9 (Campground) From Jct of Hwy 401 & Putnam Rd (E 208), S 0.8 km (0.5 mi) on Putnam R Cromarty Dr, E 0.3 km (0.2 mi) (L). FA Paved/gravel rds. (270 spaces). Av 60 gravel, 15 pull-thrus (30 x 70), back-ins (30 x 4 mostly side by side hkups, 60 full hkups (30 amps), seasonal sites, WiFi $, tent sites, renta showers $, dump, laundry, groc, fire rings, firewo restaurant, controlled access. **REC:** heated p pond, fishing, playground, rec open to public. restrict(Q). Partial handicap access. Big rig sites, age restrict, eco-friendly, 2015 rates: $44 to $48.
(888)990-9920 Lat: 42.97034, Lon: -80.94368
4340 Cromarty Drive, Mossley, ON N0L 1V0
info@goldenpondrv.com
www.goldenpondrv.com
See ad this page, 1420.

MOUNT ELGIN — E4 *Oxford*

SPRING LAKE R.V. RESORT - PAR BRIDGE
Ratings: 8.5/7.5/7.5 (Campgroun From jct Hwy 401 (exit 216) & Culloo Rd: Go 10.4 km/6-1/2 mi S on Culloo Rd, then .4 km/1/4 mi W on CR (Prouse Rd). **FAC:** All weather rds. (296 space Avail: 11 grass, patios, 2 pull-thrus (35 x 120), ba ins (35 x 60), mostly side by side hkups, 11 full hku (30/50 amps), seasonal sites, WiFi $, rentals, sho ers $, laundry, groc, LP bottles, fire rings, control access. **REC:** pond, swim, fishing, shuffleboard, pl ground. Pet restrict(Q). Partial handicap access, tents. Eco-friendly, 2015 rates: $43 to $58. May 1 Oct 30.
(877)877-9265 Lat: 42.917824, Lon: -80.86329
263459 Prouse Rd, Mount Elgin, ON N0J 1N0
gmcelhinney@parkbridge.com
www.parkbridge.com/springlake
See ad pages 1417 (Welcome Section), 1420.

EXCLUSIVE! Every listing includes a spec "arrow" symbol. This valuable tool shows y where the facility is located (N, S, E, W, N NW, SE, SW) in relation to the town.

MOUNT FOREST — D4 *Wellington*

SPRING VALLEY RESORT - PARKBRIDGE
Ratings: 8/7.5/7.5 (Campground) From Jct of Hwys 89 & 6, S 8.4 km (5.2 mi) on Hwy 6 to Sideroad 5, NE 1.1 km (0.7 mi) (R). Note: 3 night min stay during holiday weekends. **FAC:** Gravel rds. (256 spaces). 13 Avail: 8 gravel, 5 grass, 4 pull-thrus (40 x 63), back-ins (40 x 65), 8 W, 8 E (30 amps), seasonal sites, WiFi Hotspot, tent sites, rentals, showers $, dump, mobile sewer, laundry, LP bottles, firewood, controlled access. **REC:** heated pool, wading pool, Greenwood Lake: swim, fishing, playground. Pet restrict(B/Q). Partial handicap access. 2015 rates: $39 to $52. May 15 to Oct 17.
(519)323-2581 Lat: 43.93738, Lon: -80.64464
7489 Side Road 5E, Rr #6, Mount Forest, ON N0G 2L0
springvalley@rogers.com
http://www.parkbridge.com/en-ca/rv-cottages/Spring-Valley
See ad pages 1417 (Welcome Section), 1420.

NAPANEE — D8 *Lennox, Addington*

PICKEREL PARK CAREFREE RV RESORT
Ratings: 6.5/7/7 (Campground) From Jct of Hwy 401 & CR-8 (Exit 579), S 20 km (12.5 mi) on CR-8 (South Shore Hay Bay Rd) to South Shore Rd, NW 3.4 km (2.1 mi) (R). Min 3 day stay on holiday weekends. **FAC:** Gravel rds. (255 spaces). Avail: 50 grass, 1 pull-thrus (30 x 50), back-ins (30 x 40), some side by side hkups, 20 W, 20 E (15/30 amps), seasonal sites, tent sites, rentals, showers $, dump, mobile sewer, laundry, fire rings, firewood. **REC:** heated pool, Hay Bay (Lake Ontario): swim, fishing, playground. Pet restrict(Q). Partial handicap access. Eco-friendly, 2015 rates: $42 to $48. May 1 to Oct 15.
(613)373-2812 Lat: 44.14795, Lon: -76.95483
665 South Shore Road, Napanee, ON K7R 3K7
pickerelpark@carefreervresorts.com
www.carefreeRVresorts.ca/pickerelpark
See ad this page, 1420.

NESTOR FALLS — F6 *Rainy River, Kenora*

CALIPER LAKE (Prov Pk) From town, S 3 mi on Hwy 71 (R). 2015 rates: $12.75 to $43.75. May 16 to Sep 14. (807)484-2181

PARKVIEW RV RESORT **Ratings: 5.5/7/7** (Campground) 2015 rates: $34.50. May 1 to Sep 30. (807)484-2337 641 Hwy 71, Nestor Falls, ON P0X 1K0

NEW LISKEARD — F10 *Timiskaming*

SUTTON BAY PARK (Campground) (Phone Update) 2015 rates: $31 to $36. May 15 to Oct 15. (705)647-8510 841514 Waugh's Hill Road, New Liskeard, ON P0J 1P0

NEYAASHIINIGMIING — C4 *Bruce*

CAPE CROKER PARK **Ratings: 6.5/7/7** (RV Park) 2015 rates: $35 to $45. May 1 to Oct 15. (519)534-0571 112 Park Road, Wiarton, ON N0H 2T0

Got something to tell us? We welcome your comments and suggestions regarding the ratings for a particular campground, or our rating system in general. Please email them to: travelguidecomments@goodsamfamily.com

NIAGARA FALLS — E6 *Niagara*

NIAGARA FALLS AREA MAP

Symbols on map indicate towns within a 80 km/50 mile radius of Niagara Falls where campgrounds are listed. Check listings for more information.

In ON, see also Cayuga, Dunnville, Hamilton, Pelham, Port Colborne, Ridgeway, Sherkston, St Catharines & Vineland.

In NY, see also Akron, Barker, Darien Center, Gasport, Holland, Lockport, Medina, Ransomville & Youngstown.

A SPOTLIGHT Introducing Niagara Falls's colorful attractions appearing in this province section.

EXCLUSIVE! Military Listings in the back of the Guide indicate campgrounds for use exclusively by active and retired military personnel.

ON

NIAGARA FALLS (CONT)

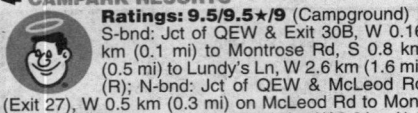

CAMPARK RESORTS
Ratings: 9.5/9.5★/9 (Campground) S-bnd: Jct of QEW & Exit 30B, W 0.16 km (0.1 mi) to Montrose Rd, S 0.8 km (0.5 mi) to Lundy's Ln, W 2.6 km (1.6 mi) (R); N-bnd: Jct of QEW & McLeod Rd (Exit 27), W 0.5 km (0.3 mi) on McLeod Rd to Montrose Rd, N 2 km (1.3 mi) to Lundy's Ln, W 2.6 km (1.6 mi) (R). Min. 2 ngts stay holiday weekends.

NIAGARA FALLS ONTARIO CAMPING
Along Lundy's Lane, just minutes from everything Niagara Falls has to offer, Campark Resorts is a preferred camping destination for families from all over the world. We give you the best in comfort and affordable family fun.

FAC: All weather rds. (350 spaces). 270 Avail: 139 gravel, 131 grass, 43 pull-thrus (30 x 75), back-ins (30 x 49), some side by side hkups, 140 full hkups, 130 W, 130 E (30/50 amps), seasonal sites, cable, WiFi, tent sites, rentals, dump, laundry, groc, LP bottles, fire rings, firewood, restaurant, controlled access. **REC:** heated pool, whirlpool, golf, playground, rec open to public. Pets OK. Partial handicap access. Big rig sites, eco-friendly, 2015 rates: $47 to $62. Disc: AAA.
AAA Approved
(877)CAMPARK Lat: 43.08631, Lon: -79.15514
9387 Lundy's Lane, Niagara Falls, ON L2E 6S4
info@campark.com
www.campark.com
See ad pages 838, 1426 (Spotlight Niagara Falls), 1420, 1414 (ON Map) & ad Magazine Section page 144.

KING WALDORF'S TENT & TRAILER PARK **Ratings: 7.5/8/8** (Campground) 2015 rates: $35 to $67. May 15 to Sep 14. (877)700-0477 9015 Stanley Ave, Niagara Falls, ON L2E 6X8

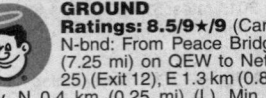

KNIGHTS HIDE-AWAY PARK
Ratings: 8/7.5/7 (Campground) From Jct of Peace Bridge & Hwy 3, W 9.7 km (6 mi) on Hwy 3 to Gorham Rd (RR 116), N 91 m (100 yds) (R); or From Jct of QEW & RR 116 (Exit 16), S 9.7 km (6 mi) on RR 116 (L). Minimum 2 day stay on holiday weekends. **FAC:** Gravel rds. (137 spaces). 49 Avail: 19 gravel, 30 grass, 19 pull-thrus (25 x 75), back-ins (22 x 40), mostly side by side hkups, 19 full hkups, 30 W, 30 E (15/50 amps), seasonal sites, WiFi Hotspot, tent sites, rentals, dump, mobile sewer, laundry, groc, fire rings, firewood, controlled access. **REC:** heated pool, playground. Pets OK. Partial handicap access. Big rig sites, eco-friendly, 2015 rates: $34 to $38. May 1 to Oct 30.
AAA Approved
(905)894-1911 Lat: 42.90575, Lon: -79.05720
1154 Gorham Road, Ridgeway, ON L0S 1N0
campinginfo@knightsfamilycamping.com
www.knightsfamilycamping.com
See ad this page, 1420.

NIAGARA FALLS KOA
Ratings: 9/10★/9 (Campground) S-bnd: From jct of QEW & Exit 30B, W 0.16 km (0.1 mi) to Montrose Rd, S 0.8 km (0.5 mi) to Lundy's Lane, W 1.6 km (1 mi) (R); or N-bnd: From Jct of QEW & McLeod Rd (Exit 27), W 0.48 km (0.3 mi) on McLeod Rd to Montrose Rd, N 2.1 km (1.3 mi) to Lundy's Lane, W 1.6 km (1 mi) (R). **FAC:** Paved rds. 268 Avail: 52 paved, 94 gravel, 122 grass, 45 pull-thrus (30 x 70), back-ins (21 x 40), 125 full hkups, 120 W, 143 E (15/50 amps), WiFi, tent sites, rentals, dump, laundry, groc, fire rings, firewood, restaurant, controlled access. **REC:** heated pool, wading pool, whirlpool, shuffleboard, playground. Pet restrict(B). Partial handicap access. Big rig sites, eco-friendly, 2015 rates: $53 to $100. Apr 13 to Oct 28. ATM.
(800)KOA-MIST Lat: 43.08892, Lon: -79.14240
8625 Lundy's Lane, Niagara Falls, ON L2H 1H5
niagara@koa.net
www.niagarakoa.net
See ad page 1434.

RIVERSIDE PARK MOTEL & CAMPGROUND
Ratings: 8.5/9★/9 (Campground) N-bnd: From Peace Bridge, N 11.7 km (7.25 mi) on QEW to Netherby Rd (RR 25) (Exit 12), E 1.3 km (0.8 mi) to Niagara Pkwy, N 0.4 km (0.25 mi) (L). Min 3 ngt stay on holiday w/ends. **FAC:** Gravel rds. (90 spaces). 76 Avail: 49 gravel, 27 grass, 11 pull-thrus (25 x 55), back-ins (30 x 42), mostly side by side hkups, 47 full hkups, 29 W, 29 E (15/50 amps), seasonal sites, WiFi $, tent sites, rentals, dump, laundry, groc, fire rings, firewood, controlled access. **REC:** heated pool, Niagara River: fishing, playground. Pet restrict(B). Eco-friendly, 2015 rates: $38 to $55. May 1 to Oct 13.
(905)382-2204 Lat: 42.98485, Lon: -79.02689
13541 Niagara Parkway, Niagara Falls, ON L2E 6S6
camp@riversidepark.net
www.riversidepark.net
See ad pages 1436, 1420.

SCOTT'S TENT & TRAILER PARK
Ratings: 8.5/9★/8.5 (Campground) S-Bnd: From Jct of QEW & Exit 30B, W 0.16 km (0.1 mi) to Montrose Rd, S 0.8 km (0.5 mi) to Lundy's Ln, W 1.9 km (1.2 mi) (R); N-bnd: From Jct of QEW & McLeod Rd (Exit 27), W 0.5 km (0.3 mi) on McLeod Rd to Montrose Rd, N 2.1 km (1.3 mi) to Lundy's Ln, W 1.9 km (1.2 mi) (R). **FAC:** Paved/gravel rds. (265 spaces). Avail: 235 gravel, 15 pull-thrus (35 x 65), back-ins (35 x 65), mostly side by side hkups, 113 full hkups, 52 W, 52 E (15/50 amps), seasonal sites, WiFi, tent sites, dump, laundry, groc, LP bottles, fire rings, firewood, controlled access. **REC:** heated pool, wading pool, playground. Pet restrict(B). Eco-friendly, 2015 rates: $42 to $52. May 1 to Oct 31.
(905)356-6988 Lat: 43.08843, Lon: -79.14705
8845 Lundy's Lane, Niagara Falls, ON L2H 1H5
scottscamping@outlook.com
www.scottstrailerpark.com
See ad pages 1427 (Spotlight Niagara Falls), 1420.

YOGI BEAR'S JELLYSTONE PARK CAMP-RESORT
Ratings: 9/10★/9 (Campground) From Jct of QEW & McLeod Rd (Exit 27), E 182 m (200 yds) on McLeod Rd to Oakwood Dr, S 2.4 km (1.5 mi) (L). NOTE: Min. 3 day stay on summer holiday weekends.

CLOSEST CAMPGROUND TO NIAGARA FALLS
Yogi Bear's Jellystone Park in Niagara Falls, Ontario, Canada offers fun & affordable camping for the whole family. Large wooded sites, big rig pull-thru sites, furnished cabins & rental trailers, just minutes from the Falls!

FAC: Paved/gravel rds. (221 spaces). Avail: 216 gravel, patios, 57 pull-thrus (30 x 80), back-ins (30 x 60), 211 full hkups, 5 W, 5 E (15/50 amps), seasonal sites, WiFi $, tent sites, rentals, dump, laundry, groc, fire rings, firewood, controlled access. **REC:** heated pool, wading pool, playground. Pet restrict(B). Partial handicap access. Big rig sites, eco-friendly, 2015 rates: $44 to $72. May 1 to Oct 15.
(800)263-2570 Lat: 43.050850, Lon: -79.121206
8676 Oakwood Dr, Niagara Falls, ON L2E 6S5
yogibear@jellystoneniagara.ca
www.jellystoneniagara.ca
See ad pages 839, 1424 (Spotlight Niagara Falls), 1420, 1414 (ON Map).

NIPIGON — F8 *Thunder Bay*

STILLWATER TENT & R.V. PARK
Ratings: 7/7.5★/7.5 (Campground) W-Bnd: From town, W 2.6 km (1.6 mi) on TCH-11/17 (R); or E-Bnd: 106 km (66 mi) E of Thunder Bay (L). **FAC:** Gravel rds. (50 spaces). 45 Avail: 14 gravel, 31 grass, 28 pull-thrus (15 x 50), back-ins (20 x 40), 15 full hkups, 29 W, 29 E (15/30 amps), seasonal sites, WiFi, tent sites, dump, mobile sewer, laundry, groc, fire rings, firewood. **REC:** Stillwater Creek: swim, fishing, playground. Pets OK. 2015 rates: $35 to $40. Disc: AAA. May 15 to Oct 1.
AAA Approved
(877)887-3701 Lat: 49.01191, Lon: -88.31826
358 Hwy 11/17, Nipigon, ON P0T 2J0
reservations@stillwaterpark.ca
www.stillwaterpark.ca
See ad this page, 1420.

Tell them you saw them in this Guide!

NOLALU — F7 *Thunder Bay*

ST URHO'S CAMPGROUND **Ratings: 5.5/7★/5** (Campground) 2015 rates: $23 to $25. May 1 to Oct 31. (807)475-8814 2165 Hwy 588, Nolalu, ON P0T 2K0

NORTH BAY — A5 *Nipissing*

CHAMPLAIN TENT RV & TRAILER PARK
Ratings: 6.5/8.5★/8.5 (Campground) From Jct of Hwy 11 & Lakeshore Dr (Exit 338), W 3.2 km (2 mi) on Lakeshore Dr (11B) to Premier Rd, S 1.6 km (1 mi) (L). **FAC:** Gravel rds. (56 spaces). 41 Avail: 8 gravel, 33 grass, 6 pull-thrus (25 x 42), back-ins (30 x 50), 16 full hkups, 16 W, 16 E (15/50 amps), seasonal sites, WiFi, tent sites, dump, laundry, fire rings, firewood. **REC:** Lake Nipissing: swim, fishing, playground. Pet restrict(B/Q) Eco-friendly, 2015 rates: $36 to $50. May 15 to Oc 15.
(705)474-4669 Lat: 46.245003, Lon: -79.422455
1202 Premier Road, North Bay, ON P1A 2J4
info@champlaintrailerpark.com
www.champlaintrailerpark.com
See ad page 1436.

DREANY HAVEN CAMPGROUND
Ratings: 6/8.5★/9 (Campground) From S Jc of Hwy 11 & Hwy 17: Go E 4 mi (6.4 km) o Hwy 17 (R). **FAC:** Gravel rds. (60 spaces) Avail: 10 grass, 6 pull-thrus (30 x 40), back-ins (30 x 40), 10 W, 10 E (15/30 amps), seasonal sites tent sites, dump, fire rings, firewood, controlled ac cess. **REC:** pool, Dreany Lake: fishing, playground Pet restrict(B). Eco-friendly, 2015 rates: $35. May 1 to Sep 30.
(705)752-2800 Lat: 46.290049, Lon: -79.346583
Hwy 17E 1859, Corbeil, ON P0H 1K0
camping@dreanyhaven.ca
www.dreanyhaven.ca
See ad this page.

FAIRVIEW PARK CAMPING & MARINA **Ratings: 6/7/7** (RV Area in MHP) 2015 rates: $30 to $34 May 15 to Oct 15. (705)474-0903 395 Riverbend Ro North Bay, ON P1B 8Z4

FRANKLIN MOTEL TENT & TRAILER PARK **Ratings: 5/6.5/7** (Campground) 2015 rates: $40 t $45. May 15 to Oct 15. (705)472-1360 444 Lakeshor Drive, North Bay, ON P1A 2E1

OAKVILLE — E5 *Halton*

BRONTE CREEK PROVINCIAL PARK (Prov Pk From Jct of Hwy 403 (QEW) & Bronte Rd (Exit 111) NW 1.7 mi on Bronte Rd to Upper Middle Rd, SW 0. mi (E). 2015 rates: $13.88 to $43.75. Apr 4 to Oct 26 (905)827-6911

OMEMEE — D6 *Victoria*

BEAVER NARROWS - PARKBRIDGE
Ratings: 7.5/7★/8.5 (Campground) From East go to Hwy 28N 30 km (18. mi) to Hwy 7 turn L 10 km (6.2 mi) t Omemee. Turn R at lights 1 km N (.6 m turn R on Beaver Rd 1 km (.6 mi) (L **FAC:** All weather rds. (367 spaces). Avail: 10 grave 2 pull-thrus (30 x 50), back-ins (30 x 50), 4 full hkups 6 W, 6 E (30 amps), seasonal sites, rentals, dum mobile sewer, laundry, groc, LP bottles, restauran controlled access. **REC:** heated pool, Pigeon Rive swim, fishing, playground. Pets OK. Partial handica access. Eco-friendly, 2015 rates: $40. May 8 to Oc 13.
(705)799-6221 Lat: 44.313435, Lon: -78.556480
433 Beaver Road, Omemee, ON K0L 2W0
beavernarrowsinfo@parkbridge.com
http://www.parkbridge.com/properties/en-ca/Pages/home.aspx?pbCommunityId=MKB
See ad pages 1417 (Welcome Section), 1420.

OMEMEE (CONT)

EMILY (Prov Pk) From town, E 3 mi on Hwy 7 to CR-10, N 3 mi (L). 2015 rates: $12.75 to $43.75. May 9 to Oct 14. (705)799-5170

ORILLIA — C5 *Simcoe*

BASS LAKE (Prov Pk) From Jct of Hwys 11 & 12, W 2 mi on Hwy 12 to Bass Lake Side Rd, S 1 mi (R). 2015 rates: $13.88 to $42.75. May 1 to Sep 7. (705)326-7054

HAMMOCK HARBOUR RV PARK **Ratings: 7/7.5/6.5** (Campground) 2015 rates: $34. Apr 21 to Oct 13. (705)326-7885 4569 Concession12, Ramara Rr 6, Ramara, ON L3V 6H6

ORO-MEDONTE — C5 *Simcoe*

ORO FAMILY CAMPGROUND **Ratings: 6/7/6** (Campground) 2015 rates: $30 to $36. May 15 to Oct 13. (866)312-2267 3096 Hwy 11, Oro-Medonte, ON L0L 2E0

OSHAWA — D6 *Durham*

DARLINGTON (Prov Pk) From Jct of Hwy 401 & Courtice Rd (Exit 425), S 0.2 mi on Courtice Rd to Darlington Park Rd, W 1 mi (E). 2015 rates: $28.75 to $43.75. May 2 to Oct 14. (905)436-2036

OTTAWA — B9 *Ottawa*

OTTAWA AREA MAP

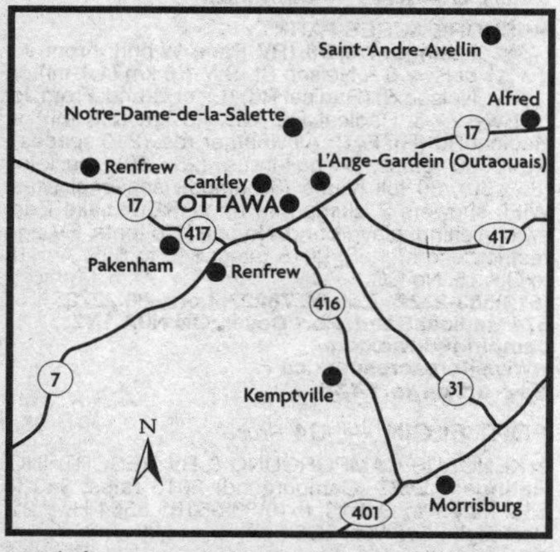

Symbols on map indicate towns within a 80 km/ 50 mile radius of Ottawa where campgrounds are listed. Check listings for more information.

In ON, see also Alfred, Kemptville, Morrisburg, Pakenham & Renfrew.

In QC, see also Cantley, L'Ange-Gardein (Outaouais), Notre-Dame-de-la-Salette & Saint-Andre-Avellin.

BREEZY HILL CAMPING & RV PARK **Ratings: 5.5/7.5★/7.5** (Campground) 2015 rates: $40 to $45. May 1 to Oct 15. (613)839-5202 rr 1, 3798 Grainger Park Rd, Kinburn, ON K0A 2H0

CAMP HITHER HILLS
Ratings: 8.5/10★/8.5 (Campground) E-bnd: From Jct of Hwy 417 & 416S (Exit 131), S 17.7 km (11 mi) on Hwy 416S to Bankfield Rd (Exit 57), E 4.5 km (2.8 mi) to Manotick Main St, SE 0.3 km (0.2 mi) to Bridge St, NE 11 km (6.8 mi) to Bank St, NW 1.3 km (0.8 mi) (R). Min 3 ngts stay on July 1 weekend. **FAC:** Paved/gravel rds. 80 Avail: 25 gravel, 55 grass, 13 pull-thrus (30 x 100), back-ins (30 x 70), 70 full hkups, 10 W, 10 E (15/50 amps), WiFi, tent sites, showers $, dump, laundry, fire rings, firewood. **REC:** heated pool, playground. Pets OK. Partial handicap access. Big rig sites, eco-friendly, 2015 rates: $32 to $43. May 1 to Oct 15.
(613)822-0509 Lat: 45.29080, Lon: -75.57530
5227 Bank Street, Ottawa, ON K1X 1H2
terry@camphitherhills.com
www.camphitherhills.com
See ad this page, 1420.

OTTAWA'S POPLAR GROVE CAMPGROUND/RV PARK **Ratings: 8.5/8/7** (Campground) 2015 rates: $39 to $44. May 1 to Oct 31. (613)821-2973 6154 Bank St, Ottawa, ON K4P 1B4

RECREATIONLAND **Ratings: 7/5.5/7.5** (Campground) 2015 rates: $26 to $33.50. Apr 15 to Oct 15. (613)833-2974 1566 Canaan Rd, PO Box 89, Cumberland, ON K4C 1E5

SLEEPY CEDARS FAMILY CAMPING **Ratings: 7.5/7.5/8.5** (Campground) 2015 rates: $25 to $40. May 15 to Oct 8. (613)821-0756 1893 Manotick Station Rd, Greely, ON K4P 1H2

WESLEY CLOVER PARKS CAMPGROUND
Ratings: 7.5/8★/9 (Campground) From Jct of Hwy 417 & March Rd (Exit 138), N 0.4 km (0.25 mi) on March Rd to Corkstown Rd, NE 2.2 km (1.3 mi) (L). **FAC:** Paved rds. 176 gravel, back-ins (25 x 70), 105 W, 130 E (15/30 amps), WiFi Hotspot, tent sites, rentals, dump, laundry, groc, fire rings, firewood, controlled access. **REC:** playground, rec open to public. Pets OK. Partial handicap access. 28 day max stay, eco-friendly, 2015 rates: $36 to $39.75. Disc: AAA. May 1 to Oct 13.
(613)828-6632 Lat: 45.32993, Lon: -75.86730
411 Corkstown Road, Kanata, ON K2K 0J5
don.murphy@ottawa.ca
www.wesleycloverparks.com
See ad this page, 1420.

OWEN SOUND — C4 *Grey*

HARRISON PARK (Public) From Jct of Hwy 6 & 2nd Ave, S 0.5 mi on 2nd Ave (E). 2015 rates: $32. May 1 to Oct 24. (519)371-9734

KELSO BEACH (CITY PARK) (Public) From town: Go 3/4 km/1/2 mi W on Hwy 21, then 2-1/2 km/1-1/2 mi N on 4th Ave West. 2015 rates: $30. (519)371-9734

ROCKSPRINGS/OWEN SOUND KOA
Ratings: 8/9.5★/9 (Campground) From Jct of Hwys 26 & 28th Ave E (E side of town), S 1.2 km (0.75 mi) (L). **FAC:** Gravel rds. (113 spaces). 73 Avail: 47 gravel, 26 grass, 16 pull-thrus (32 x 70), back-ins (30 x 60), 53 full hkups, 20 W, 20 E (30/50 amps), seasonal sites, WiFi $, tent sites, rentals, dump, laundry, groc, fire rings, firewood. **REC:** heated pool, pond, playground, rec open to public. Pets OK. Eco-friendly, 2015 rates: $42 to $47. May 1 to Oct 13.
(800)562-8675 Lat: 44.56466, Lon: -80.89111
398235 28 Ave East, Owen Sound, ON N4K 5N8
owensoundkoa@hotmail.com
http://koa.com/camp/owen-sound
See ad page 1434.

SUNNY VALLEY PARK **Ratings: 8/7★/8.5** (Campground) 2015 rates: $32 to $40. May 5 to Oct 15. (519)794-3297 rr#4 062703 Sunny Valley Rd, Georgian Bluffs, ON N4K 5N6

Things to See and Do

OWEN SOUND TRANSPORTATION COMPANY
Ontario Ferries. May 2 to Oct 19. Restrooms. Hours: 9am to 6 pm.
(800)265-3163 Lat: 44.560945, Lon: -80.990930
717875 Hwy 6 North, Owen Sound, ON N4K 5N7
susanschrempf@ostmarine.com
www.ontarioferries.com
See ad page 1418 (Welcome Section).

Park policies vary. Ask about the cancellation policy when making a reservation.

PAISLEY — D4 *Bruce*

SAUGEEN BLUFF CONSERVATION AREA (Public) From town, N 2.5 mi on Bruce County Rd-3, follow signs (L). 2015 rates: $30.40. May 1 to Sep 15. (519)353-7206

PAKENHAM — B8 *Lanark*

RIVERBEND PARK **Ratings: 5/6.5/7** (Campground) 2015 rates: $35. May 15 to Oct 16. (613)624-5426 2918 County Road 29, Pakenham, ON K0A 2X0

PARIS — E5 *Brant*

PINEHURST LAKE CONSERVATION (Public) From N side of town, N 3.5 mi on Hwy 24A (R). 2015 rates: $27 to $46. May 1 to Oct 15. (519)442-4721

PARKHILL — E3 *Middlesex*

GREAT CANADIAN HIDEAWAY **Ratings: 7.5/8/8** (Campground) 2015 rates: $44. May 1 to Oct 13. (800)539-5226 32910 Centre Road, Parkhill, ON N0M 2K0

PARRY SOUND — B5 *Parry Sound*

HORSESHOE LAKE CAMP & COTTAGES **Ratings: 7/7.5/7.5** (Campground) 2015 rates: $37.50 to $50. May 15 to Oct 15. (705)732-4928 55 North Sandy Plains Road, Seguin, ON P2A 2W8

OASTLER LAKE (Prov Pk) From Jct of Hwys 124 & 69, S 8 mi on Hwy 69 (L). 2015 rates: $12.75 to $43.75. May 9 to Oct 14. (705)378-2401

TRAILSIDE CAREFREE RV RESORT
Ratings: 7/8/8 (Campground) From Jct of Hwy 400 & Oastler Park Dr (Exit 217), W 1.6 km (1 mi) on Oastler Park Dr to James Bay Jct South, SW 1.6 km (1 mi) to Blue Lake Rd, S 1.6 km (1 mi) (R). Min 3 day stay on holiday weekends. **FAC:** Gravel rds. (235 spaces). Avail: 10 gravel, 5 pull-thrus (35 x 80), back-ins (30 x 40), 5 full hkups, 5 W, 5 E (30/50 amps), seasonal sites, WiFi Hotspot, tent sites, dump, mobile sewer, laundry, fire rings, firewood, controlled access. **REC:** Lingerlong Lake and McDonald Lake and Levi Lake: swim, fishing, playground. Pet restrict(Q). Eco-friendly, 2015 rates: $52.89 to $56. May 8 to Oct 23.
(705)378-2844 Lat: 45.294758, Lon: -79.978967
105 Blue Lake Rd, Seguin, ON P2A 0B2
trailside@carefreeRVresorts.com
www.carefreeRVresorts.ca/trailside
See ad pages 1445, 1420.

PASS LAKE — F8 *Thunder Bay*

MIRROR LAKE RESORT & CAMPGROUND **Ratings: 6/6.5/7.5** (Campground) 2015 rates: $28. May 1 to Oct 1. (807)977-2840 3495 Hwy 11/17, Shuniah, ON P0T 2M0

SLEEPING GIANT (Prov Pk) From Thunder Bay, E 24 mi on Hwy 11/17 to Hwy 587, S 21 mi (R). 2015 rates: $12.75 to $43.75. May 16 to Oct 14. (807)977-2526

PELHAM — E5 *Niagara*

BISSELL'S HIDEAWAY RESORT
Ratings: 10/10★/10 (Campground) From Jct of QEW & RR 24 (Exit 57), S 13.8 km (8.6 mi) on RR 24 (Victoria Ave) to Metler Rd, E 6.9 km (4.3 mi) on Metler Rd (L). Note: Min 3 night stay on holiday weekends.

LOOK NO FURTHER!
Bissell's Hideaway offers something for everyone. Large, quiet campsites, mini log cabins, enormous one acre swimming pool, giant water slide, kiddie's splash pool, daily activities & a host of sports & leisure facilities.

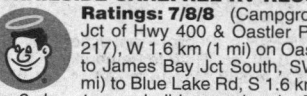

FAC: Paved rds. (400 spaces). Avail: 240 paved, patios, 9 pull-thrus (35 x 100), back-ins (30 x 50), 190 full hkups, 50 W, 50 E (30/50 amps), seasonal sites, WiFi, tent sites, rentals, showers $, dump, mobile

PELHAM (CONT)

BISSELL'S HIDEAWAY RESORT (CONT)
sewer, laundry, groc, LP bottles, fire rings, firewood, restaurant, controlled access. **REC:** pool, wading pool, pond, fishing, shuffleboard, playground, rec open to public. Pet restrict(B). Partial handicap access. Big rig sites, eco-friendly, 2015 rates: $40 to $90. May 8 to Oct 12. ATM.
(888)236-0619 Lat: 43.06227, Lon: -79.30328
205 Metler Rd, Rr1, Ridgeville, ON L0S 1M0
bissellshideaway@aol.com
www.bissellshideaway.com
See ad pages 1425 (Spotlight Niagara Falls), 1420.

PEMBROKE — B7 *Renfrew*

PINE RIDGE PARK & RESORT
Ratings: 7/7.5/7.5 (Campground) From Jct of Hwy 17 & B-Line Rd (In Petawawa), NW 6.9 km (4.3 mi) on B-Line Rd to CR-51, W 1 km (0.6 mi) to River Dr, NE 2 km (1.3 mi) (L). For GPS put in Petawawa. Reservations req'd for evening arrival on weekdays. **FAC:** All weather rds. (55 spaces). 18 Avail: 10 grass, 8 dirt, 2 pull-thrus (40 x 135), back-ins (30 x 45), 9 full hkups, 9 W, 9 E (30 amps), seasonal sites, WiFi, tent sites, rentals, dump, mobile sewer, laundry, groc, fire rings, firewood, restaurant. **REC:** Ottawa River: swim, fishing, playground. Pets OK. RV age restrict, eco-friendly, 2015 rates: $39. May 1 to Sep 30.
(888)746-3743 Lat: 45.86703, Lon: -77.20338
419 River Drive, Rr 6, Pembroke, ON K8A 6W7
pineridgepark@hotmail.com
www.pineridgepark.com
See ad this page.

RIVERSIDE PARK (Public) From Jct of Hwy 17 & CR 40, NW 7.8 mi on CR 40 to Pembroke St W (R). 2015 rates: $26 to $32. May 15 to Oct 11. (613)735-6821

PENETANGUISHENE — C5 *Simcoe*

AWENDA (Prov Pk) From town, W 7 mi on Hwy 93 (R). 2015 rates: $28.75 to $43.75. (705)549-2231

LAFONTAINE CAREFREE RV RESORT
Ratings: 7.5/8.5/9 (Campground) From Jct of Hwy 93 & CR-25 (Balm Beach Rd), W 6.4 km (4 mi) on CR-25 to CR-6, N 9.7 km (6 mi) to CR-26 (Lafontaine Rd), E 1.6 km (1 mi) (L). Note: Min 3 night stay on holiday weekends. **FAC:** All weather rds. (250 spaces). 79 Avail: 25 gravel, 54 grass, 11 pull-thrus (40 x 80), back-ins (20 x 40), 11 full hkups, 24 W, 24 E (15/50 amps), seasonal sites, tent sites, rentals, showers $, dump, laundry, firewood, controlled access. **REC:** heated pool, playground. Pet restrict(B/Q). Eco-friendly, 2015 rates: $47.46 to $51.98. May 1 to Oct 15.
(705)533-2961 Lat: 44.78029, Lon: -80.01138
240 Lafontaine Road E, Tiny, ON L9M 0S2
lafontainepark@carefreeresorts.com
www.carefreeRVresorts.ca/lafontaine
See ad pages 1445, 1420.

PERRAULT FALLS — E7 *Kenora*

GAWLEY'S PARKVIEW CAMP LTD **Ratings: 5.5/7.5/7.5** (RV Park) 2015 rates: $30. May 15 to Sep 21. (807)529-3147 1 Gawleys Parkview Road, Perrault Falls, ON P0V 2K0

PERTH — C8 *Lanark*

LAST DUEL PARK CAMPGROUND (Public) From town, E 0.1 mi on Hwy 43 (R). 2015 rates: $22.60 to $39.55. May 15 to Oct 15. (613)812-0020

MURPHYS POINT (Prov Pk) From town, SE 4 mi on CR-1 to Elmgrove Rd/CR-21, S 6.6 mi (L). 2015 rates: $36.75 to $43.75. May 9 to Oct 14. (613)267-5060

PETAWAWA — B7 *Renfrew*

BLACK BEAR CAMPGROUND (Public Corps) From Jct of Hwy 17 & Paquette Rd, NE 2.4 km (1.5 mi) on Paquette Rd to Menin Rd, N 1.6 km (1 mi) to Passchendale Rd, NE 366 m (400 yds) to Lieven Rd, E 0.6 km (0.4 mi) (L). 2015 rates: $25 to $35. May 1 to Oct 11. (613)687-7268

PETERBOROUGH — D6 *Peterborough*

BAILEY'S BAY RESORT - PARKBRIDGE
Ratings: 8/9★/7.5 (Campground) From jct Hwy 7 & Hwy 7B: Go 305 m/1000 feet E on Hwy 7B. **FAC:** All weather rds. (364 spaces). Avail: 10 gravel, back-ins (50 x 75), mostly side by side hkups, 10 full hkups (30 amps), seasonal sites, cable, WiFi Hotspot, rentals, dump, laundry, LP bottles, fire rings, firewood, controlled access. **REC:** heated pool, wading pool, whirlpool, Chemong Lake: swim, fishing, playground. Pet restrict(Q). No tents. Eco-friendly, 2015 rates: $36 to $47. May 1 to Oct 14.
(705)748-9656 Lat: 44.32458, Lon: -78.43477
78 Lindsay Road, Selwyn, ON K9J 0C5
baileybayinfo@parkbridge.ca
www.baileysbayresort.com
See ad pages 1417 (Welcome Section), 1420.

PETERSBURG — E4 *Waterloo*

COUNTRY GARDENS RV PARK **Ratings: 6.5/9.5★/7** (Campground) 2015 rates: $45. May 1 to Oct 31. (866)224-0503 1335 Witmer Road, Petersburg, ON N0B 2H0

PETROLIA — E3 *Lambton*

LORNE C. HENDERSON AREA (ST CLAIR REGION CONS AUTH.) (Prov Pk) From town: Go 2 km/1-1/4 mi W on CR 4. (519)882-2280

PICTON — D7 *Prince Edward*

MARTIN'S RIVER COUNTRY
Ratings: 7/7.5★/8 (Campground) From town at jct CR 10 & CR 18: Go 9.6 km/6 mi S on CR 18. **FAC:** All weather rds. (150 spaces). Avail: 65 all weather, 1 pull-thrus (60 x 60), back-ins (40 x 60), 19 full hkups, 43 W, 43 E (30 amps), seasonal sites, WiFi Hotspot, tent sites, showers $, dump, LP bottles, fire rings, firewood, controlled access. **REC:** Outlet River: swim, fishing, playground, rec open to public. Pets OK. Partial handicap access. Eco-friendly, 2015 rates: $50. May 1 to Oct 15.
(613)393-5645 Lat: 43.901582, Lon: -77.227441
#1854 County Road 18, Picton, ON K0K 2T0
information@martinsrivercountry.ca
www.martinsrivercountry.ca
See ad this page.

SMUGGLERS COVE RV RESORT LTD **Ratings: 8/9★/8** (Campground) 2015 rates: $43 to $55. May 1 to Oct 15. (613)476-4125 3187 CR 13, Rr 3, Picton, ON K0K 2T0

PLYMPTON-WYOMING — E3 *Lambton*

LAKEWOOD CHRISTIAN CAMPGROUND **Ratings: 8.5/7/8.5** (Campground) 2015 rates: $35 to $45. May 1 to Oct 15. (519)899-4415 4297 Lakeshore Rd, Plympton-Wyoming, ON N0N 1J6

PARADISE VALLEY CAMPGROUND **Ratings: 8/7/7.5** (Campground) 2015 rates: $43 to $68. May 1 to Oct 25. (877)389-1147 4895 Lakeshore Road, Unit A 100, Plympton-Wyoming, ON N0N 1J6

PORT BURWELL — F4 *Norfolk*

PORT BURWELL (Prov Pk) From Jct of Hwys 3 & 19S, S 0.25 mi on Hwy 19S to CR-42, E 300 ft (E). 2015 rates: $30.20 to $43.75. May 9 to Oct 14. (519)874-4691

SAND HILL PARK **Ratings: 6.5/7/8** (Campground) 2015 rates: $50 to $66. May 1 to Oct 8. (519)586-3891 930 Lakeshore Road, Port Burwell, ON N0J 1T0

PORT COLBORNE — E6 *Niagara*

LONG BEACH CONSERVATION AREA (Public) From Jct of Hwy 3 & Reg Rd, W 4 mi on Reg Rd (L). Min 3 night stay on holiday weekends. 2015 rates: $32 to $42. May 14 to Oct 20. (905)899-3462

We appreciate your business!

SHERKSTON SHORES CAREFREE RV RESORT
Ratings: 8.5/9.5★/9.5 (RV Park) From Jct of Hwy 140 (Elizabeth St) & Hwy 3, E 8.2 km (5.1 mi) on Hwy 3 to Empire Rd, S 2.4 km (1.5 mi) (R). Minimum stay 3 nights.

SHERKSTON SHORES CAREFREE RV RESORT
A premier RV & vacation home resort situated on 2.5 mi of Lake Erie, ON waterfront. Spend the day on the beach or in the pool or take off and explore 560 acres of magnificent landscapes. Come for a day, enjoy for a lifetime.

FAC: Paved/gravel rds. (1719 spaces). 239 Avail: 95 paved, 85 gravel, 59 grass, patios, 136 pull-thrus (25 x 100), back-ins (33 x 65), 169 full hkups, 70 W, 70 E (30/50 amps), seasonal sites, WiFi, tent sites, rentals, dump, laundry, groc, LP bottles, fire rings, firewood, restaurant, controlled access. **REC:** heated pool, wading pool, whirlpool, Lake Erie: swim, fishing, playground. Pet restrict(B). Partial handicap access. Big rig sites, eco-friendly, 2015 rates: $60 to $100. May 1 to Oct 31. ATM.
(877)482-3224 Lat: 42.87224, Lon: -79.13698
490 Empire Road, Sherkston, ON L0S 1R0
reservations@sherkston.com
www.sherkston.com
See ad pages 1445, 1420 & Family Camping in Magazine Section.

PORT DOVER — E5 *Norfolk*

SHORE ACRES PARK
Ratings: 7/8.5/8 (RV Park) W-bnd: From Jct of Hwy 6 & Nelson St, SW 1.8 km (1.1 mi) on Nelson St (Radical Rd) (L); or E-bnd: From Jct of Hwy 24 & Radical Rd, NE 4.5 km (2.8 mi) on Radical Rd (R). **FAC:** All weather rds. (210 spaces). Avail: 30 grass, 7 pull-thrus (25 x 60), back-ins (35 x 50), 30 full hkups (30 amps), seasonal sites, WiFi, showers $, dump, fire rings. **REC:** Lake Erie: swim, fishing, playground. No pets. No tents. RV age restrict, eco-friendly, 2015 rates: $45 to $55. Apr 15 to Oct 15. No CC.
(519)583-2222 Lat: 42.78227, Lon: -80.22705
574 Radical Road, Port Dover, ON N0A 1N2
camping@kwic.com
www.shoreacrespark.ca
See ad page 1436.

PORT ELGIN — C4 *Bruce*

KENORUS CAMPGROUND & RV RESORT, INC **Ratings: 7.5/8/7** (Campground) 2015 rates: $40 to $55. May 1 to Oct 15. (519)832-5183 5564 Hwy 21, Port Elgin, ON N0H 2C6

MACGREGOR POINT (Prov Pk) From town, S 3 mi on Hwy 21, follow signs (R). 2015 rates: $12.75 to $43.75. (519)389-9056

PORT ELGIN MUNICIPAL TOURIST CAMP (Public) In town, at Jct of Johnson Ave & Bruce St (E). 2015 rates: $20. May 1 to Oct 31. (519)832-2512

PORT PERRY — D6 *Durham*

GORESKI'S LANDING - PARKBRIDGE
Ratings: 7.5/8.5/9 (Campground) From Jct of Hwys 12 & 7A, E 6.4 km (4 mi) on Hwy 7A to Island Rd 7, N 5.8 km (3.6 mi) to Stephenson Pt Rd, W 0.5 km (0.3 mi) to Platten Blvd, N 1 km (0.6 mi) (R). Note: Min 3 day stay on long weekends. **FAC:** Paved rds. (530 spaces). 20 Avail: 12 gravel, 8 grass, back-ins (25 x 45), 20 W, 20 E (30 amps), seasonal sites, WiFi $, tent sites, showers $, dump, LP bottles, fire rings, firewood, restaurant, controlled access. **REC:** heated pool, wading pool, whirlpool, Lake Scugog: swim, fishing, marina, playground. Pet restrict(B). Partial handicap access. Eco-friendly, 2015 rates: $39 to $60. May 7 to Oct 18. ATM.
(800)331-9935 Lat: 44.16135, Lon: -78.91229
225 Platten Boulevard, Port Perry, ON L9L 1B4
goreskis@wcshighspeed.com
www.parkbridge.ca
See ad pages 1417 (Welcome Section), 1420.

PORT ROWAN — F4 *Haldimand-Norfolk*

BACKUS HERITAGE CONSERVATION AREA (Public) From town, N 2 mi on Regional Rd 42, to CR-2 (E). 2015 rates: $35 to $41. May 1 to Oct 15. (519)586-2201

LONG POINT (Prov Pk) From town, S 2 mi on Hwy 59 (E). 2015 rates: $12.75 to $43.75. May 9 to Oct 14. (519)586-2133

PORT SEVERN — C5 *Muskoka Lakes*

SIX MILE LAKE (Prov Pk) From Jct of Hwys 400 & 34 (exit 162), W 1 mi on Hwy 34 (R). 2015 rates: $12.75 to $43.75. May 9 to Oct 14. (705)756-2746

We rate what RVers consider important.

PRESCOTT — C9 *Leeds and Grenville*

GRENVILLE PARK CAMPING & RV PARK
Ratings: 8/9★/8.5 (Campground) From Jct of Hwys 401 & 16/416, E-bnd: On Hwy 401 (Exit 721B); or W-bnd: On Hwy 401 (Exit 721); or S-bnd: On Hwy 416 (Exit 1), S 3 km (1.9 mi) on Hwy 16/416 to Hwy 2, E 1 km (0.6 mi) (R). Minimum 3 night stay on holiday weekends. **FAC:** Gravel rds. (168 spaces). 48 Avail: 10 gravel, 38 grass, patios, 6 pull-thrus (35 x 60), back-ins (35 x 60), 48 W, 48 E (15/30 amps), seasonal sites, WiFi $, tent sites, rentals, showers $, dump, mobile sewer, laundry, groc, LP bottles, fire rings, firewood, controlled access. **REC:** St Lawrence River: swim, fishing, playground, rec open to public. Pets OK. Partial handicap access. Eco-friendly, 2015 rates: $35 to $40. Apr 1 to Nov 1.
(613)925-2000 Lat: 44.75095, Lon: -75.45294
2323 County Road, Johnstown, ON K0E 1T1
grenvillepark@xplornet.ca
www.grenvillepark.com
See ad this page, 1420.

PROVIDENCE BAY — B3 *Manitoulin*

PROVIDENCE BAY TENT-TRAILER PARK **Ratings: 4.5/7.5/7.5** (Campground) 2015 rates: $38 to $43.50. May 1 to Oct 1. (877)269-2018 5466 Hwy 551, Providence Bay, ON P0P 1T0

PUSLINCH — E5 *Wellington*

EMERALD LAKE TRAILER RESORT & WATERPARK
Ratings: 9.5/9.5★/9 (RV Park) From Jct of Hwy 401 & Hwy 6S, (Exit 299), S 4.8 km (3 mi) on Hwy 6S to Flamborough Conc 11 West (then becomes Gore Rd), W 4.8 km (3 mi) (R). **FAC:** All weather rds. (228 spaces). Avail: 48 all weather, 10 pull-thrus (35 x 60), back-ins (40 x 60), some side by side hkups, 28 full hkups, 20 W, 20 E (30/50 amps), seasonal sites, WiFi Hotspot, tent sites, rentals, showers $, dump, laundry, LP bottles, fire rings, firewood, controlled access. **REC:** pool, wading pool, whirlpool, Emerald Lake: swim, playground, rec open to public. Pet restrict(B). Partial handicap access. Big rig sites, eco-friendly, 2015 rates: $75 to $85. May 1 to Oct 15.
(905)659-7923 Lat: 43.41004, Lon: -80.12919
7248 Gore Road, Rr2, Puslinch, ON N0B 2J0
emeraldlake@bellnet.ca
www.emeraldlake.ca
See ad this page, 1420.

RED LAKE — E7 *Kenora*

SOUTH BAY ON GULL ROCK (Campground) (Phone Update) 2015 rates: $35. May 15 to Oct 15. (866)300-5330 1 Gull Rock Road, Red Lake, ON P0V 2M0

REDBRIDGE — A6 *Nipissing*

CAMP CONEWANGO CAMPGROUND **Ratings: 6/7/7** (Campground) 2015 rates: $35 to $38. May 15 to Oct 15. (866)802-6644 1875 Songis Road, Redbridge, ON P0H 2A0

RENFREW — B8 *Renfrew*

RENFREW/OTTAWA WEST KOA
Ratings: 8/9★/9.5 (Campground) From Jct of Hwy 17 & CR-4 (Storyland Rd), N 0.4 km (0.25 mi) on CR-4 (Storyland Rd) to Johnston Rd, E 0.8 km (0.5 mi) (L). **FAC:** Gravel rds. (101 spaces). Avail: 61 grass, 17 pull-thrus (25 x 60), back-ins (25 x 45), 43 full hkups, 8 W, 8 E (30/50 amps), seasonal sites, WiFi, tent sites, rentals, dump, laundry, groc, fire rings, firewood. **REC:** Yuill's Lake: swim, fishing, playground. Pets OK. Big rig sites, eco-friendly, 2015 rates: $37 to $58. May 1 to Oct 15.
(800)562-3980 Lat: 45.53111, Lon: -76.68191
2826 Johnston Road, Renfrew, ON K7V 3Z8
info@renfrewkoa.com
http://koa.com/campgrounds/renfrew/
See ad page 1434.

RV Park ratings you can rely on!

SERENITY HILLS **Ratings: 5.5/6.5/6.5** (Campground) 2015 rates: $35 to $45. May 1 to Oct 8. (613)432-5767 435 Castleford Road, Renfrew, ON K7V 3Z8

RESTOULE — B5 *Nipissing*

RESTOULE (Prov Pk) From town, N 6 mi on Hwy 534 (E). 2015 rates: $25.25 to $37.35. Apr 14 to Nov 26. (705)729-2010

RIDGETOWN — F3 *Chatham-Kent*

CLEARVILLE PARK & CAMPGROUND (Public) From Jct of Hwy 401 & CR 103 (Furnnal Rd) SE 5.8 mi on CR 103 to CR 3, SW 5.9 mi to Clearville Rd. SE 1.2 mi (E). 2015 rates: $25.69 to $27.84. May 1 to Oct 15. (519)674-5583

RIDGEWAY — E6 *Niagara*

WINDMILL POINT PARK **Ratings: 8/8.5/8** (Campground) 2015 rates: $48 to $55. May 1 to Oct 15. (888)977-8888 2409 Dominion Rd, Ridgeway, ON L0S 1N0

ROCKWOOD — D5 *Wellington*

ROCKWOOD CONSERVATION AREA (Public) From Jct of Hwys 6 & 7, NE 7 mi on Hwy 7 (R). 2015 rates: $31 to $54. Apr 24 to Oct 12. (866)668-2267

RODNEY — F3 *Elgin*

PORT GLASGOW TRAILER PARK (Public) From Jct of Hwy 401 & Furnival Rd (exit 129), SE 6.8 mi on Furnival Rd (L). 2015 rates: $23 to $25. May 1 to Oct 30. (519)785-0069

ROSENEATH — D7 *Northumberland*

GOLDEN BEACH RESORT AND TRAILER PARK **Ratings: 8/9★/9** (Campground) 2015 rates: $48 to $58. May 1 to Oct 15. (905)342-5366 7100 CR 18, Roseneath, ON K0K 2X0

ROSSPORT — F8 *Thunder Bay*

RAINBOW FALLS/WHITESAND LAKE (Prov Pk) From town, E 5 mi on Hwy 17 (L). 2015 rates: $12.75 to $43.75. May 16 to Sep 21. (807)824-2298

ROUND LAKE CENTRE — B7 *Renfrew*

BONNECHERE (Prov Pk) From town, NE 0.5 mi on Rte-58 (L). 2015 rates: $13.88 to $43.75. May 16 to Oct 14. (613)757-2103

SALFORD — E4 *Oxford*

CASEY'S PARK **Ratings: 5.5/6.5/7** (Campground) 2015 rates: $35. May 1 to Oct 26. (519)485-3992 333585 Plank Line (Hwy 19), R R 1, Salford, ON N0J 1W0

SANDFORD — D6 *Durham Region*

GRANGEWAYS RV PARK & FAMILY CAMPGROUND
Ratings: 7.5/9★/8.5 (Campground) From Jct of Hwy 404 & Davis Dr (Exit 51), E 9.2 km (5.7 mi) on Davis Dr to Hwy 48, N 2.1 km (1.3 mi) to Herald Rd, E 6.8 km (4.2 mi) to 3rd Conc, N 1.3 km (0.8 mi) (L). Min 3 day on holiday weekends. **FAC:** Paved/gravel rds. (300 spaces). Avail: 40 all weather, back-ins (40 x 60), 40 full hkups (15/30 amps), seasonal sites, tent sites, showers $, laundry, groc, LP bottles, fire rings, firewood, controlled access. **REC:** pool, wading pool, Pefferlaw River: swim, fishing, playground. Pets OK. RV age restrict, eco-friendly, 2015 rates: $38.40 to $56. May 1 to Oct 13.
(877)223-5034 Lat: 44.141178, Lon: -79.239655
9700 3rd Concession, Sandford, ON L0C 1E0
info@grangeways.com
www.grangeways.com
See ad page 1436.

SAUBLE BEACH — C4 *Bruce*

A SPOTLIGHT Introducing Sauble Beach's colorful attractions appearing at the front of this state section.

Say you saw it in our Guide!

CARSONS' CAMP LIMITED **Ratings: 9.5/9★/9.5** (Campground) 2015 rates: $40 to $52. May 1 to Oct 8. (519)422-1143 110 Southampton Parkway, Sauble Beach, ON N0H 2G0

FIDDLEHEAD RESORT CAMP **Ratings: 6/8★/8** (Campground) 2015 rates: $45. May 1 to Oct 8. (519)534-0405 50 Oliphant Way, South Bruce Peninsula, ON N0H 2T0

SAUBLE BEACH RESORT CAMP **Ratings: 7/8.5/8** (Campground) 2015 rates: $45. May 1 to Sep 15. (519)422-1101 877 Main St, Sauble Beach, ON N0H 2G0

SAUBLE FALLS (Prov Pk) From town, N 3 mi on Rd 21 (E). 2015 rates: $12.75 to $43.75. Apr 25 to Oct 26. (519)422-1952

WOODLAND PARK
Ratings: 10/10★/10 (Campground) From Jct of CR-8 & CR-13 (Sauble Falls Pkwy), N 0.4 km (0.25 mi) on CR-13/Sauble Falls Pkwy (R) Note: Min. 3 nights stay on holiday weekends. **FAC:** Paved rds. (737 spaces). Avail: 137 paved, patios, 13 pull-thrus (40 x 65), back-ins (40 x 65), 127 full hkups, 10 W, 10 E (30/50 amps), seasonal sites, cable, WiFi $, tent sites, rentals, showers $, dump, laundry, groc, LP bottles, fire rings, firewood, controlled access. **REC:** heated pool, whirlpool, playground. Pet restrict(B). Partial handicap access. Big rig sites, RV age restrict, eco-friendly, 2015 rates: $32 to $56. May 1 to Oct 8.
(519)422-1161 Lat: 44.63431, Lon: -81.26333
47 Sauble Falls Parkway, Sauble Beach, ON N0H 2G0
info@woodlandpark.on.ca
www.woodlandpark.on.ca
See ad page 1431 (Spotlight Sauble Beach).

SAUBLE FALLS — C4 *Bruce*

SAUBLE FALLS TENT & TRAILER PARK **Ratings: 6/8/8** (Campground) 2015 rates: $42 to $48. May 1 to Sep 7. (519)422-1322 849 Sauble Falls Parkway, South Bruce Peninsula, ON N0H 2T0

SAULT STE MARIE — A1 *Algoma*

GLENVIEW COTTAGES & CAMPGROUND
Ratings: 8/8.5/7.5 (Campground) From Jct of International Bridge & Queen St W, W 259 m (850 ft) on Queen St W to Carmens Way, N 2.3 km (1.4 mi) to Second Line, E 2.1 km (1.3 mi) to Great Northern Rd/Hwy 17 N, N 8.1 km (5 mi) (L). **FAC:** Paved/gravel rds. 44 gravel, 23 pull-thrus (35 x 50), back-ins (20 x 40), mostly side by side hkups, 19 full hkups, 25 W, 25 E (15/30 amps), WiFi, tent sites, rentals, dump, laundry, fire rings, firewood. **REC:** heated pool, pond, playground. Pets OK. Eco-friendly, 2015 rates: $40 to $44. May 15 to Oct 8.
(705)759-3436 Lat: 46.60153, Lon: -84.29473
2611 Great Northern Road, Sault Ste Marie, ON P6A 5K7
info@glenviewcottages.com
www.glenviewcottages.com
See ad this page, 1420.

POINTE DES CHENES CAMPGROUND **Ratings: 6.5/6.5/7** (Campground) 2015 rates: $27 to $42. May 14 to Sep 30. (705)779-2696 57 Des Chene Dr, Sault Ste Marie, ON P6A 5K6

SAULT STE MARIE KOA **Ratings: 8.5/10★/8.5** (Campground) 2015 rates: $42 to $61. May 1 to Oct 12. (800)562-0847 501 Fifth Line East, Sault Ste Marie, ON P6A 6J8

SCHREIBER — F8 *Thunder Bay*

RAINBOW FALLS/ROSSPORT (Prov Pk) From town, W 17 mi on Hwy 17, follow signs. 2015 rates: $12.75 to $43.75. May 16 to Oct 14. (807)824-2298

Nobody said it was easy being a 10. And our rating system makes it even tougher. Check out 10/10/10 RV parks and campgrounds in the front of the guide.*

SEGUIN — C5 *Parry Sound*

PARRY SOUND KOA
Ratings: 8/9★/8.5 (Campground) From Jct of Hwy 400 & Seguin Trail Rd/Horseshoe Lake Rd (Exit 214), S 1.4 km (0.9 mi) on Horseshoe Lake Rd to Black Rd, W 1 km (0.6 mi) to Rankin Lake Rd, W 1 km (0.6 mi) (R). Note: Min 3 day stay on holiday weekends. **FAC:** All weather rds. (72 spaces). Avail: 64 gravel, 14 pull-thrus (30 x 90), back-ins (30 x 55), 64 W, 64 E (15/50 amps), seasonal sites, WiFi, tent sites, rentals, dump, mobile sewer, laundry, groc, fire rings, firewood. **REC:** heated pool, pond, playground. Pet restrict(B). Eco-friendly, 2015 rates: $47.29 to $54.26. May 1 to Oct 15.
(800)562-2681 Lat: 45.29929, Lon: -79.90502
276 Rankin Lake Road, Seguin, ON P2A 0B2
parrysoundkoa@gmail.com
www.parrysoundkoa.com
See ad page 1434.

SELKIRK — E5 *Haldimand-Norfolk*

HALDIMAND CONSERVATION AREA (Public) From Jct of Hwy 3 & Regional Rd 18 S 7 mi on Regional Rd 18 to Lakeshore Rd, E. 0.6 mi (R). 2015 rates: $25 to $35. May 1 to Oct 15. (905)776-2700

SELKIRK (Prov Pk) From Jct of Hwy 3 & Reg Rd 53, S 5 mi on Reg Rd 53 to Reg Rd 3, W 1 mi to Wheelers Rd, S 0.5 mi (R). 2015 rates: $12.75 to $43.75. May 9 to Sep 1. (905)776-2600

SHARBOT LAKE — C8 *Frontenac*

SHARBOT LAKE (Prov Pk) From town, W 3.2 mi on Hwy 7 (L). 2015 rates: $12.75 to $43.75. May 9 to Sep 28. (613)335-2814

SHEGUIANDAH — B3 *Manitoulin*

BATMAN'S COTTAGES & CAMPGROUND Ratings: 7/8★/8 (Campground) From town, S 1.6 km (1 mi) on Hwy 6 (L). **FAC:** Gravel rds. (142 spaces). Avail: 61 grass, 6 pull-thrus (35 x 90), back-ins (20 x 50), mostly side by side hkups, 15 full hkups, 46 W, 46 E (30/50 amps), seasonal sites, WiFi Hotspot, tent sites, rentals, dump, mobile sewer, laundry, groc, LP bottles, fire rings, firewood. **REC:** Sheguiandah Bay: swim, fishing, marina, playground, rec open to public. Pets OK. Eco-friendly, 2015 rates: $38 to $45. May 1 to Oct 15.
AAA Approved
(877)368-2180 Lat: 45.87882, Lon: -81.89897
11408 Hwy 6, Sheguiandah, ON P0P 1W0
info@batmanscamping.com
www.batmanscamping.com

GREEN ACRES TENT & TRAILER PARK Ratings: 5.5/6.5/7 (Campground) From Jct of Hwys 17 & 6, S 56 km (35 mi) on Hwy 6 (S edge of town) (L). **FAC:** Gravel rds. (68 spaces). Avail: 30 grass, 4 pull-thrus (25 x 50), back-ins (20 x 40), mostly side by side hkups, 30 W, 30 E (15/30 amps), seasonal sites, WiFi Hotspot, tent sites, dump, mobile sewer, laundry, groc, fire rings, firewood, restaurant. **REC:** Sheguiandah Bay: swim, fishing, playground. Pets OK. 2015 rates: $38. May 10 to Oct 10.
AAA Approved
(705)368-2420 Lat: 45.88953, Lon: -81.92081
10944 Hwy 6, Sheguiandah, ON P0P 1W0
greenacres@campingmanitoulin.ca
www.campingmanitoulin.ca

SHELBURNE — D5 *Dufferin*

PRIMROSE PARK **Ratings: 7/8.5/8** (Campground) 2015 rates: $30 to $41. May 1 to Oct 12. (519)925-2848 635687 Hwy 10, Mono, ON L9V 0Z8

SHERKSTON — E6 *Niagara*

PLEASANT BEACH CAMPGROUND **Ratings: 4/7.5/6** (Campground) 2015 rates: $27 to $37. May 1 to Oct 15. (905)894-4249 342 Pleasant Beach Road, Sherkston, ON L0S 1R0

SIMCOE — E5 *Haldimand-Norfolk*

NORFOLK CONSERVATION AREA (Public) From Simcoe, S 7 mi on Hwy 24, follow signs to township rds, S 1 mi to Lakeshore Rd (R). 2015 rates: $26 to $36. May 1 to Oct 15. (519)428-1460

TURKEY POINT (Prov Pk) From Jct of Hwy 24 & Reg Rd 10, S 2.5 mi on Reg Rd 10 to park access rd, E 200 yds (R). 2015 rates: $34.92 to 43.75. May 9 to Oct 14. (519)426-3239

SIOUX LOOKOUT — E7 *Kenora*

ABRAM LAKE PARK (Campground) (Phone Update) 2015 rates: $37 to $44. May 15 to Oct 15. (807)737-1247 1041 Hwy 72, Sioux Lookout, ON P8T 1A5

OJIBWAY (Prov Pk) From town, S 13 mi on Hwy 72 (R). 2015 rates: $12.75 to $43.75. May 16 to Sep 21. (807)223-7535

SIOUX NARROWS — F6 *Kenora*

LAUGHING WATER TRAILER PARK **Ratings: 7.5/10★/8.5** (Campground) 2015 rates: $35 to $37. May 15 to Sep 30. (807)226-5462 30 Heithecker Lane, Sioux Narrows, ON P0X 1N0

PARADISE POINT RV PARK & MARINA **Ratings: 5/7/6.5** (Campground) 2015 rates: $33. May 1 to Sep 30. (807)226-5269 16 Paradise Point Road, Sioux Narrows, ON P0X 1N0

SIOUX NARROWS (Prov Pk) From town, N 5 mi on Hwy 71 (R). 2015 rates: $12.75 to $43.75. May 16 to Sep 14. (807)226-5223

TOMAHAWK RESORT RV PARK **Ratings: 8/7.5/8** (Campground) 2015 rates: $49 to $53. May 1 to Oct 15. (800)465-1091 111 Tomahawk Road, Sioux Narrows, ON P0X 1N0

SOMBRA — E3 *Lambton*

BRANTON-CUNDICK PARK (Public) From N-end of town, N 1 mi on CR-33 to W Wilksport Line, E 0.1 mi (R). 2015 rates: $38. May 15 to Oct 15. (519)892-3968

CATHCART PARK (Public) From town, N 2 mi on St Clair Pkwy (L). 2015 rates: $33.25 to $38. May to Oct. (519)892-3342

SOUTH BAYMOUTH — B3 *Manitoulin*

SOUTH BAY RESORT **Ratings: 6/7.5★/7** (Campground) 2015 rates: $32 to $40. May 18 to Sep 15. (705)859-3106 21214 Hwy 6, South Baymouth, ON P0P 1Z0

SOUTH RIVER — B5 *Parry Sound*

MIKISEW PARK (Prov Pk) From Jct of Hwy 11 & Eagle Lake Rd, W 12 mi on Eagle Lake Rd (L). 2015 rates: $12.75 to $43.75. Jun 20 to Sep 28. (705)386-7762

SPRAGGE — A3 *Algoma*

SERPENT RIVER CAMPGROUND Ratings: 8.5/9.5★/8 (Campground) From Jct of Hwys 17 & 108, W 2.3 km (1.4 mi) on Hwy 17 (L). **FAC:** Gravel rds. (105 spaces). 49 Avail: 25 gravel, 24 grass, 25 pull-thrus (35 x 60), back-ins (35 x 50), 49 W, 49 E (30 amps), seasonal sites, WiFi, tent sites, rentals, dump, mobile sewer, laundry, groc, fire rings, firewood. **REC:** pool, Serpent River: swim, fishing, playground, rec open to public. Pets OK. RV age restrict, eco-friendly, 2015 rates: $36.28. Disc: AAA. May 1 to Oct 13.
AAA Approved
(877)849-2210 Lat: 46.21069, Lon: -82.60069
4696 Hwy 17W, Spragge, ON P0R 1K0
src@vanalong.com
www.serpentrivercampground.com

SPRING BAY — B3 *Manitoulin*

SANTA MARIA TRAILER RESORT & COTTAGES LTD **Ratings: 7/9★/8** (Campground) 2015 rates: $40. May 1 to Sep 30. (705)377-5870 249 Square Bay Road, Spring Bay, ON P0P 2B0

STANLEY PARK **Ratings: 7/9★/8** (RV Park) 2015 rates: $30 to $35. May 1 to Oct 1. (705)377-4661 1702 Monument Road, Rr 1, Spring Bay, ON P0P 2B0

Like Us on Facebook.

ST CATHARINES — E6 *Niagara*

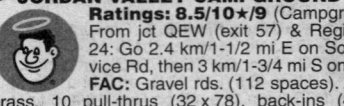

JORDAN VALLEY CAMPGROUND
Ratings: 8.5/10★/9 (Campground) From jct QEW (exit 57) & Regional Rd 24: Go 2.4 km/1-1/2 mi E on South Service Rd, then 3 km/1-3/4 mi S on 21st St. **FAC:** Gravel rds. (112 spaces). Avail: 76 grass, 10 pull-thrus (32 x 78), back-ins (40 x 50), mostly side by side hkups, 9 full hkups, 10 W, 10 E (15/30 amps), seasonal sites, WiFi $, tent sites, dump, laundry, fire rings, firewood, controlled access. **REC:** pool, Twenty Mile Creek: fishing, playground. Pet restrict(B). Eco-friendly, 2015 rates: $36.20 to $46.43. May 1 to Oct 15.
(866)526-2267 Lat: 43.150877, Lon: -79.375373
3902 21st St, Jordan Station, ON L0R 1S0
jvc@campingniagara.com
www.campingniagara.com
See ad this page, 1420.

SHANGRI-LA PARK NIAGARA CAMPGROUND
Ratings: 8/8★/8 (Campground) From jct QEW (exit 55) & Jordan Rd: Go 4.8 km/3 mi S on Jordan Rd, then 500 feet E on Regional Rd 81, then 1.6 km/1 mi S on 17th St. **FAC:** All weather rds. (205 spaces). 75 Avail: 9 gravel, 66 grass, 17 pull-thrus (30 x 60), back-ins (30 x 50), mostly side by side hkups, 75 W, 75 E (30/50 amps), seasonal sites, WiFi, tent sites, rentals, dump, mobile sewer, laundry, groc, LP bottles, fire rings, firewood, controlled access. **REC:** pool, shuffleboard, playground, rec open to public. Pets OK. Partial handicap access. Eco-friendly, 2015 rates: $28 to $39. Disc: AAA. May 15 to Oct 15.
AAA Approved
(905)562-5851 Lat: 43.130273, Lon: -79.358244
3425 17th Street, St Catharines, ON L2R 6P7
info@shangrilaniagara.com
www.shangrilaniagara.com
See ad this page, 1420.

STONECLIFFE — B7 *Renfrew*

MORNING MIST RESORT **Ratings: 7.5/9.5★/8** (Campground) 2015 rates: $33 to $39. May 1 to Oct 31. (888)356-1113 1256 Pine Valley Road, Stonecliffe, ON K0J 2K0

STONEY CREEK — E5 *Hamilton*

FIFTY POINT CONSERVATION AREA & MARINA (Public) From Jct of QEW & Fifty Rd (Exit 78), N 0.2 km (0.1 mi) on Fifty Rd to N Service Rd, SE 0.3 km (0.2 mi) to Lockport Way, NE 61 m (200 ft) to Baseline Rd, SE 0.3 km (0.2 mi) (L). Note: 2 nights min. stay on holiday weekends. 2015 rates: $47 to $52. Apr 3 to Nov 29. (905)525-2187

STRATFORD — E4 *Perth*

WILDWOOD CONSERVATION AREA (Public) From Stratford, SW 7 mi on Hwy 7 (L). 2015 rates: $10 to $45. Apr 25 to Oct 19. (866)668-2267

STRATHROY — E3 *Middlesex*

TROUT HAVEN PARK **Ratings: 7.5/9.5★/8.5** (Campground) 2015 rates: $32.74. May 1 to Oct 31. (519)245-4070 24749 Park St, Strathroy, ON N7G 3H5

STURGEON FALLS — A5 *Nipissing*

DUTRISAC COTTAGES & CAMPING **Ratings: 6.5/6.5/7** (Campground) 2015 rates: $26 to $38. May 15 to Oct 8. (705)753-2419 270 Pierre Rd, Sturgeon Falls, ON P2B 2W8

GLENROCK COTTAGES & TRAILER PARK
Ratings: 7.5/9.5★/7.5 (Campground) From Jct of Hwy 17 & Nipissing St, S 3.2 km (2 mi) on Nipissing St to Marleau Rd, W 0.8 km (0.5 mi) to Glenrock Rd, S 0.8 km (0.5 mi) (E). **FAC:** Paved/gravel rds. (93 spaces). Avail: 22 grass, 6 pull-thrus (30 x 50), back-ins (30 x 45), 22 full hkups (30 amps), seasonal sites, cable, WiFi, tent sites, rentals, dump, laundry, groc, fire rings, firewood, controlled access. **REC:** Lake Nipissing: swim, fishing, marina, play-

STURGEON FALLS (CONT)

GLENROCK COTTAGES & (CONT)
ground, rec open to public. Pets OK. RV age restrict, eco-friendly, 2015 rates: $38. May 15 to Oct 15.
(866)592-1157 Lat: 46.329445, Lon: -79.938315
100 Glenrock Road, Sturgeon Falls, ON P2B 2M5
glenrock@persona.ca
www.glenrock.ca
See ad opposite page, 1420.

STURGEON FALLS KOA
Ratings: 8/10★/8.5 (Campground) From town Hwy 17 (S) to Leblanc Rd 2 km (1.8 m), to Lalande Rd 1 km (.6 m) (L). **FAC:** Gravel rds. (52 spaces). Avail: 24 gravel, 8 pull-thrus (35 x 60), back-ins (30 x 60), 24 full hkups (30/50 amps), seasonal sites, WiFi, tent sites, rentals, laundry, groc, fire rings, firewood. **REC:** Sturgeon River: swim, fishing, marina, playground, rec open to public. Pet restrict(B). Partial handicap access. Big rig sites, eco-friendly, 2015 rates: $44.50 to $60. May 8 to Oct 15.
(800)562-7798 Lat: 46.349503, Lon: -79.968323
818 Lalande Road, Sturgeon Falls, ON P2B 2V4
sturgeonfallskoa@gmail.com
koa.com/campgrounds/sturgeon-falls/
See ad page 1434.

SUDBURY — A4 *Sudbury (City)*

CAROL'S CAMPSITE Ratings: 7.5/8★/7 (Campground) From Jct of Hwy 17 SW bypass & Hwy 69, S 3.2 km (2 mi) on Hwy 69 (L). **FAC:** Gravel rds. (152 spaces). Avail: 82 gravel, 4 pull-thrus (40 x 50), back-ins (30 x 35), mostly side by side hkups, 82 full hkups (30 amps), seasonal sites, WiFi, tent sites, dump, laundry, groc, LP bottles, fire rings, firewood, controlled access. **REC:** Richard Lake: swim, fishing, playground. Pets OK. Partial handicap access. Eco-friendly, 2015 rates: $35. May 1 to Oct 15.
AAA Approved
(705)522-5570 Lat: 46.43246, Lon: -80.91693
2388 Richard Lake Drive, Sudbury, ON P3G 0A3
info@carolscampsite.com
www.carolscampsite.com

MINE MILL 598/CAW CAMPGROUND **Ratings: 7/7/6.5** (Campground) 2015 rates: $35. May 1 to Oct 14. (705)522-5076 2550 Richard Lake Drive, Sudbury, ON P3E 0A3

WINDY LAKE (Prov Pk) From town, N 35 mi on Hwy 144 N (L). 2015 rates: $16.25 to $49.44. May 16 to Sep 1. (705)966-2315

SUTTON — D5 *York*

SIBBALD POINT (Prov Pk) From town, E 3 mi on Hwy 48 (L). 2015 rates: $12.75 to $43.75. May 9 to Oct 14. (905)722-8061

TARA — C4 *Bruce*

KILSYTH COUNTRY CAMPGROUND **Ratings: 7.5/7/6.5** (Campground) 2015 rates: $30 to $35. May 1 to Oct 8. (519)371-3856 rr 4 101739 Grey Rd 5, Tara, ON N0H 2N0

TEMAGAMI — A5 *Nipissing*

FINLAYSON POINT (Prov Pk) From town, S 0.6 mi on Hwy 11 to access rd, W 0.25 mi (E). 2015 rates: $16.25 to $49.44. May 15 to Sep 27. (705)569-3205

HAPPY HOLIDAY CAMPGROUND AND COTTAGES (Campground) (Phone Update) From town, N 9.6 km (6 mi) on Hwy 11 to Happy Holidays Rd, E 0.8 km (0.5 mi) (E). **FAC:** Gravel rds. (69 spaces). Avail: 44 grass, 8 pull-thrus (30 x 50), back-ins (20 x 40), mostly side by side hkups, 12 full hkups, 32 W, 32 E (15/30 amps), seasonal sites, WiFi Hotspot, tent sites, rentals, dump, mobile sewer, laundry, fire rings, firewood, controlled access. **REC:** Duncan Lake: swim, fishing, playground. Pet restrict(B). 2015 rates: $38 to $44. May 15 to Oct 1.
AAA Approved
(705)569-3540 Lat: 47.14574, Lon: -79.75366
7727 Hwy 11 North, Temagami, ON P0H 2H0
happyholiday@ontera.net
www.camping-in-temagami.com

THESSALON — A2 *Algoma*

BROWNLEE LAKE PARK RESORT & CAMPGROUND
Ratings: 6.5/9★/9 (Campground) From Jct of Hwys 129 & 17, E 9.6 km (6 mi) on Hwy 17 to Brownlee Rd, N 1.6 km (1 mi) (E). **FAC:** All weather rds. (37 spaces). Avail: 12 gravel, 8 pull-thrus (30 x 60), back-ins (20 x 30), 12 full hkups (15/30 amps), seasonal sites, WiFi Hotspot, tent sites, rentals, laundry, fire rings, firewood, restaurant. **REC:** Brownlee Lake: swim, fishing. Pets OK. Partial handicap access. Eco-friendly, 2015 rates: $31 to $39. May 20 to Oct 15.
(705)842-2118 Lat: 46.29668, Lon: -83.43229
136 Ingram Road, Thessalon, ON P0R 1L0
brownleelake@yahoo.com
www.brownleelake.com
See ad page 1436.

THESSALON LAKESIDE PARK (Public) In town on Hwy 17B (L). 2015 rates: $21.63. May 1 to Oct 1. (705)842-2523

THORNDALE — E4 *Middlesex*

RIVER VIEW CAMPGROUND **Ratings: 6.5/6.5/6.5** (Campground) 2015 rates: $45. May 1 to Oct 18. (866)447-7197 22164 Valleyview Rd, Rr1, Thorndale, ON N0M 2P0

THUNDER BAY — F8 *Thunder Bay*

CHIPPEWA PARK
(Public) From Jct of Hwys 11/17, 11B/17B & 61, S 5.1 km (3.2 mi) on Hwy 61 to Chippewa Rd/City Rd, E 9.7 km (6 mi) on Chippewa Rd (becomes City Rd) (L). **FAC:** Paved/gravel rds. 26 gravel, 16 pull-thrus (38 x 58), back-ins (20 x 40), mostly side by side hkups, 26 W, 26 E (30/50 amps), WiFi Hotspot, tent sites, rentals, dump, laundry, groc, fire rings, firewood, controlled access. **REC:** Lake Superior: swim, fishing. Pets OK. Partial handicap access. 21 day max stay, 2015 rates: $30 to $35. May 24 to Sep 4. ATM.
(807)623-3912 Lat: 48.347832, Lon: -89.225552
2465 City Road, Thunder Bay, ON P7J 1J3
chippewaparkcampgrounds@live.com
www.chippewapark.ca
See ad this page.

HAPPY LAND RV PARK
Ratings: 9/8.5★/8.5 (Campground) From Jct of Hwys 61 and 11/17 (in town), go W 24.8 km (15.4 mi) on Hwy 11/17 (R). **FAC:** Gravel rds. 60 gravel, 54 pull-thrus (33 x 70), back-ins (30 x 60), 38 full hkups, 22 W, 22 E (30/50 amps), WiFi, tent sites, rentals, dump, laundry, groc, fire rings, firewood, controlled access. **REC:** heated pool, whirlpool, playground, rec open to public. Pets OK. Partial handicap access. Big rig sites, eco-friendly, 2015 rates: $43 to $48. May 1 to Oct 10.
AAA Approved
(866)473-9003 Lat: 48.392932, Lon: -89.598792
I-4650 Hwy 11-17, Kakabeka Falls, ON P7K 0J1
taltmann@tbaytel.net
www.happylandpark.com
See ad this page, 1420.

County names help you follow the local weather report.

THUNDER BAY KOA
Ratings: 8.5/10★/9 (Campground) From Jct of Hwy 11/17 & Hwy 527 (Spruce River Rd) at E city limits, S 0.4 km (0.25 mi) on Spruce River Rd (L). **FAC:** Gravel rds. 205 gravel, 122 pull-thrus (30 x 60), back-ins (20 x 40), 126 full hkups, 79 W, 79 E (15/50 amps), cable, WiFi, tent sites, rentals, dump, laundry, groc, LP gas, fire rings, firewood, controlled access. **REC:** heated pool, pond, fishing, shuffleboard, playground. Pets OK. Eco-friendly, 2015 rates: $42 to $49. Apr 15 to Oct 15.
(800)562-4162 Lat: 48.49905, Lon: -89.12916
162 Spruce River Road, Shuniah, ON P7A 0P4
tbaykoa@tbaytel.net
www.thunderbaykoa.com
See ad page 1434.

TROWBRIDGE FALLS PARK
(Public) From Jct of Hwy 17/11 & Hodder-Copenhagen exit (NE edge of town), NW 274 m (300 yds) on Copenhagen Rd (L). **FAC:** Paved rds. 122 gravel, 25 pull-thrus (18 x 50), back-ins (18 x 35), 36 W, 64 E (15 amps), tent sites, dump, laundry, fire rings, firewood. **REC:** Current River: swim, fishing, playground. Pets OK. Partial handicap access. 21 day max stay, 2015 rates: $30 to $35. May 20 to Sep 5.
(807)683-6661 Lat: 48.49072, Lon: -89.18620
125 Copenhagen Road, Thunder Bay, ON P7B 6B3
www.thunderbay.ca
See ad this page.

TOBERMORY — C3 *Bruce*

BRUCE PENINSULA/CYPRUS LAKE CAMPGROUND (Natl Pk) From town, S 6 mi on Hwy 6 (L). Pit toilets. 2015 rates: $15.70 to $23.50. (519)596-2233

HAPPY HEARTS TENT & TRAILER PARK
Ratings: 8/7.5/7.5 (Campground) From Jct of Hwy 6 & Cape Hurd Rd, W 0.8 km (0.5 mi) on Cape Hurd Rd (L). Min stay 3 nights on holiday weekends. **FAC:** Gravel rds. (150 spaces). 130 Avail: 65 gravel, 65 grass, 1 pull-thrus (30 x 40), back-ins (30 x 40), mostly side by side hkups, 32 full hkups, 98 W, 98 E (15/50 amps), seasonal sites, WiFi, tent sites, rentals, dump, laundry, groc, fire rings, firewood, controlled access. **REC:** pool, playground. Pets OK. 2015 rates: $38 to $48. May 1 to Oct 15.
(519)596-2455 Lat: 45.23478, Lon: -81.65698
93 Cape Hurd Road, Tobermory, ON N0H 2R0
wilson@amtelecom.net
www.happyheartspark.com
See ad page 1436.

LANDS END PARK
Ratings: 8/9★/10 (Campground) From Jct of Hwy 6 & Hay Bay Rd, W 2.6 km (1.6 mi) on Hay Bay Rd (L). Min 3 or 7 nghts. stay on holiday weekends. **FAC:** All weather rds. (122 spaces). Avail: 96 all weather, 17 pull-thrus (30 x 60), back-ins (30 x 60), 65 W, 65 E (15/50 amps), seasonal sites, WiFi, tent sites, rentals, showers $, dump, mobile sewer, groc, fire rings, firewood. **REC:** Georgian Bay: swim, fishing, playground, rec open to public. Pets OK. Eco-friendly, 2015 rates: $38 to $53. May 1 to Oct 13.
AAA Approved
(519)596-2523 Lat: 45.239390, Lon: -81.682947
59 Corey Crescent, Tobermory, ON N0H 2R0
mail@landsendpark.com
www.landsendpark.com
See ad this page, 1420.

Heading South? We have lots of Snowbird Destination ideas to explore at the front of the Guide.

ON

TOBERMORY (CONT)

TOBERMORY VILLAGE CAMPGROUND & CABINS
Ratings: 8.5/10★/9.5 (Campground) From S city limits, S 1.6 km (1 mi) on Hwy 6 (R). Min. 3 night stay on holiday weekends. **FAC:** Gravel rds. (100 spaces). 85 Avail: 26 gravel, 59 grass, 16 pull-thrus (30 x 120), back-ins (30 x 60), 43 full hkups, 42 W, 42 E (15/50 amps), seasonal sites, WiFi, tent sites, rentals, showers $, dump, laundry, groc, fire rings, firewood, controlled access. **REC:** heated pool, pond, playground, rec open to public. Pet restrict(B). Partial handicap access. RV age restrict, eco-friendly, 2015 rates: $44 to $53. May 1 to Oct 12.
(519)596-2689 Lat: 45.23646, Lon: -81.64052
7159, Hwy 6, Tobermory, ON N0H 2R0
contact@tobermoryvillagecamp.com
www.tobermoryvillagecamp.com
See ad page 1451.

Things to See and Do

MS CHI-CHEEMAUN FERRY Ferry from Tobermory to Manitoulin Island. May 2 to Oct 19. RV accessible. Restrooms, food. Hours: 8:00 am to 6 pm. Adult fee: $16.50 to $90.95.
(800)265-3163 Lat: 45.256975, Lon: -81.664229
8 Eliza Street, Tobermory, ON N0H 2R0
info@ontarioferries.com
www.ontarioferries.com
See ad page 1418 (Welcome Section).

TORONTO — D5 *Toronto, York*

TORONTO AREA MAP

Symbols on map indicate towns within a 80 km/50 mile radius of Toronto where campgrounds are listed. Check listings for more information.

See also Alliston, Bolton, Bradford, Caledon, Campbellville, Cookstown, Hamilton, Millgrove, Milton, Oshawa, Port Perry, Puslinch, Sandford & Waterdown.

A SPOTLIGHT Introducing Toronto's colorful attractions appearing at the front of this state section.

GLEN ROUGE CAMPGROUND (Public) From Jct of Hwy 401 & (E-bnd) exit 390 (W-bnd) exit 392, E 0.6 mi on Kingston Rd (L). 2015 rates: $32.50. May 13 to Nov 1. (855)811-0111

INDIAN LINE CAMPGROUND (Public) From Jct of Hwy 401 & Hwy 427, N 5.6 km (3.5 mi) on Hwy 427 to Finch Ave, W 0.8 km (0.5 mi) (R). 2015 rates: $28.50 to $44. May 1 to Oct 31. (855)811-0111

TOTTENHAM — D5 *Simcoe*

TOTTENHAM CONSERVATION AREA (TOWN OF NEW TECUMSETH) (Prov Pk) From jct Hwy 9 & CR 10: Go 6.4 km/4 mi N on CR 10, then 1/2 km/1/4 mi W on Mill St. 2015 rates: $20 to $35. (905)729-1260

TURKEY POINT — E5 *Norfolk*

HIDDEN VALLEY CAREFREE RV RESORT
Ratings: 8/8/8 (Campground) From Jct of Hwy 24 & CR-10, S 4.2 km (2.6 mi) on CR-10 to Front Rd, E 2.1 km (1.3 mi) to Mole Side Rd (R). Min 3 nights stay on holiday weekends. **FAC:** Gravel rds. (243 spaces). Avail: 35 grass, back-ins (40 x 55), 26 W, 26 E (30 amps), seasonal sites, WiFi Hotspot, tent sites, rentals, dump, laundry, fire rings, firewood, controlled access. **REC:** heated pool, playground, rec open to public. Pet restrict(B/Q). Partial handicap access. RV age restrict, eco-friendly, 2015 rates: $45 to $54. May 1 to Oct 15.
(519)426-5666 Lat: 42.71043, Lon: -80.32352
61 Mole Side Road, Vittoria, ON N0E 1W0
hiddenvalley@carefreeRVresorts.com
www.carefreeRVresorts.ca/hiddenvalley
See ad pages 1445, 1420.

TWEED — C7 *Hastings*

TIPPER'S FAMILY CAMPGROUND **Ratings: 5/7/7.5** (Campground) 2015 rates: $39. May 15 to Oct 13. (613)478-6844 115 Varty Rd, Tweed, ON K0K 3J0

UPSALA — F7 *Thunder Bay*

OPEN BAY LODGE **Ratings: 5.5/7/7** (Campground) 2015 rates: $35. (807)986-2356 321 Lac Des Mille Lacs Rd, Upsala, ON P0T 2Y0

PINE POINT RESORT **Ratings: 6/7/7.5** (Campground) 2015 rates: $30 to $33. (807)986-1300 lac Des Milles Lac Road South, Upsala, ON P0T 2Y0

UPSALA CAMPGROUND **Ratings: 4.5/6.5/6.5** (Campground) 2015 rates: $30. May 15 to Sep 15. (807)986-2312 4850 Hwy 17, Upsala, ON P0T 2Y0

UPTERGROVE — C6 *Simcoe*

MCRAE POINT (Prov Pk) From Jct of Hwys 11 & 12, E 7 mi on Hwy 12 to Muley Point Rd, SE 2.5 mi (E). 2015 rates: $12.75 to $43.75. May 9 to Oct 14. (705)325-7290

VERMILION BAY — E7 *Kenora*

BLUE BIRD TRAILER & CAMPSITE **Ratings: 5/6.5/7** (Campground) 2015 rates: $33 to $45. May 15 to Sep 30. (807)227-2042 144 Myers Road, Vermilion Bay, ON P0V 2V0

BLUE LAKE (Prov Pk) From town, N 5 mi on Hwy 647 (L). 2015 rates: $13.88 to $43.75. (807)227-2601

CRYSTAL LAKE CAMPGROUND RV PARK
Ratings: 8/8.5★/9.5 (Campground) From town, W 4.8 km (3 mi) on Hwy 17 to Hanslips Rd, S 0.8 km (0.5 mi) (L). **FAC:** Paved/gravel rds. 28 Avail: 5 paved, 23 gravel, 5 pull-thrus (30 x 100), back-ins (30 x 50), 15 full hkups, 13 W, 13 E (30/50 amps), WiFi, tent sites, rentals, dump, laundry, fire rings, firewood. **REC:** Crystal Lake: swim, fishing, playground. Pets OK. Big rig sites, eco-friendly, 2015 rates: $36.50. May 15 to Sep 15.
(807)220-5467 Lat: 49.829984, Lon: -93.456771
167 Hanslips Road, Vermilion Bay, ON P0V 2V0
info@crystallakecampground.ca
www.crystallakecampground.ca
See ad page 1436.

VERONA — C8 *Frontenac*

DESERT LAKE FAMILY RESORT **Ratings: 7.5/8.5★/7.5** (Campground) 2015 rates: $45 to $50. Apr 15 to Oct 15. (866)421-2956 rr 1, 1009 Chester Ln, Hartington, ON K0H 1W0

VICTORIA HARBOUR — C5 *Simcoe*

VICTORIA HARBOUR BEACH AND MARINE RESORT - PARKBRIDGE
Ratings: 6.5/8★/7.5 (Campground) From Hwy12 turn R on William St .4 km (.2 mi) turn L on Winfield Dr. **FAC:** Gravel rds. (178 spaces). Avail: 11 gravel, back-ins (30 x 50), 11 full hkups (30 amps), seasonal sites, laundry, fire rings, firewood. **REC:** heated pool, Georgian Bay: swim, fishing, playground. Pets OK. 2015 rates: $51. May 10 to Oct 10. No CC.
(705)534-7551 Lat: 44.745032, Lon: -79.780874
10 Winfield Dr, Victoria Harbour, ON L0K 2A0
victoriaharbourinfo@parkbridge.com
http://www.parkbridge.com/en-ca/rv-cottages/Victoria-Harbour
See ad pages 1417 (Welcome Section), 1420.

VINELAND — E5 *Niagara*

N.E.T. CAMPING RESORT
Ratings: 10/10★/9 (Campground) W-bnd: From Jct of QEW & N Service Rd, NW 0.16 km (0.1 mi) on N Service Rd to Victoria Ave (RR24), S 11.6 km (7.2 mi) (L); or E-bnd: From Jct of QEW & S Service Rd (Exit 57), W 0.16 km (0.1 mi) on S Service Rd to Victoria Ave (RR 24) S 11.3 km (7 mi) (L). Min. 3 day stay on holiday weekends. **FAC:** All weather rds. (356 spaces). Avail: 112 all weather, 25 pull-thrus (35 x 80), back-ins (40 x 50), 112 full hkups (30/50 amps), seasonal sites, WiFi, tent sites, rentals, showers $, dump, laundry, groc, fire rings, firewood, controlled access. **REC:** pool, wading pool, Sixteen Mile Creek: fishing, playground, rec open to public. Pet restrict(B/Q). Partial handicap access. Big rig sites, eco-friendly, 2015 rates: $36 to $55. May 1 to Oct 12.
(866)490-4745 Lat: 43.08270, Lon: -79.38842
2325 Regional Road 24, Vineland, ON L0R 2C0
netcamping@bell.net
www.netcampingresort.com
See ad pages 1427 (Spotlight Niagara Falls), 1420.

Refer to the Table of Contents in front of the Guide to locate everything you need.

WABIGOON — E7 *Kenora*

WABIGOON LAKE RV PARK **Ratings: 7/9.5★/7** (RV Park) 2015 rates: $29.50 to $31.50. May 15 to Oct 12. (807)938-6432 10188 Hwy 17, Wabigoon, ON P0V 2W0

WALTON — D4 *Huron*

FAMILY PARADISE CAMPGROUND **Ratings: 7.5/9★/8** (Campground) 2015 rates: $38 to $57. May 1 to Oct 18. (877)591-1961 43835 Hullett-Mckillop Road, Rr 4, Walton, ON N0K 1Z0

WARSAW — D6 *Peterborough*

WARSAW CAVES (OTONABEE REGION CONS AUTH) (Prov Pk) From town: Go 4 km/2-1/2 mi N on CR 4. May 10 to Oct 14. (705)652-3161

WARWICK — E3 *Lambton*

WARWICK CONSERVATION AREA (Public) From Jct of Hwy 402 & CR 9 (exit 44), N 0.9 mi to CR 22, W 3.5 mi (L). 2015 rates: $30.40. May 1 to Oct 11. (519)849-6770

WASAGA BEACH — C5 *Simcoe*

CEDAR GROVE PARK
Ratings: 6.5/7/6.5 (RV Park) Located on Hwy 26 at the W city limits. **FAC:** Gravel rds. (150 spaces). Avail: 75 grass, back-ins (25 x 40), mostly side by side hkups, 75 full hkups (30 amps), seasonal sites, tent sites, showers $, dump, laundry, fire rings, firewood. **REC:** Georgian Bay: swim. Pet restrict Eco-friendly, 2015 rates: $60 to $65. May 1 to Oct 1. ATM, no CC.
(705)429-2134 Lat: 44.469372, Lon: -80.107716
100 Cedar Grove Parkway, Wasaga Beach, ON L9Z 1T5
See ad page 1436.

GATEWAY CAMPING **Ratings: 6/7/7** (Campground) 2015 rates: $47 to $59. May 15 to Oct 15. (705)429-5862 186 Main St, Wasaga Beach, ON L9Z 2L2

WASAGA DUNES FAMILY CAMPGROUND - PARKBRIDGE
Ratings: 7.5/8★/7.5 (Campground) From Jct Hwy 92 & CR 29: Go 7.1 km (4-1/4 mi) N on CR 29. (L). **FAC:** Gravel rds. (202 spaces). 41 Avail: 8 gravel, 33 grass, back-ins (30 x 40), 8 full hkups (30/50 amps), seasonal sites, WiFi Hotspot, tent sites, rentals, dump, laundry, LP bottles, fire rings, controlled access. **REC:** heated pool, playground. Pets OK. Partial handicap access. Eco-friendly, 2015 rates: $33 to $46. May 15 to Oct 15.
(705)322-3130 Lat: 44.607359, Lon: -79.979185
4300 Crossland Rd, County Road 29, Tiny, ON L0L 2T0
wasagadunesinfo@parkbridge.com
www.parkbridge.com
See ad pages 1417 (Welcome Section), 1420.

WASAGA PINES FAMILY CAMPGROUND - PARKBRIDGE
Ratings: 7.5/8.5/8.5 (Campground) From E city limits, E 5.8 km (3.6 mi) on County Rd 92 (L). **FAC:** All weather rds. (238 spaces). Avail: 36 gravel, back-ins (45 x 55), 11 full hkups, 25 W, 25 E (30 amps), seasonal sites, WiFi Hotspot, tent sites, rentals, dump, laundry, LP bottles, fire rings, firewood, controlled access. **REC:** heated pool, playground. Pets OK. Partial handicap access. Eco-friendly, 2015 rates: $53. May 10 to Oct 20.
(866)875-2537 Lat: 44.56591, Lon: -79.90810
1780 County Rd 92, Elmvale, ON L0L 1P0
wasagapinesinfo@parkbridge.ca
www.parkbridge.ca
See ad pages 1417 (Welcome Section), 1420.

WATERLOO — E4 *Waterloo*

GREEN ACRE PARK **Ratings: 8.5/8.5★/9** (RV Park) 2015 rates: $48 to $54. Mar 1 to Dec 31. (877)885-7275 580 Beaver Creek Road, Waterloo, ON N2J 3Z4

LAUREL CREEK CONSERVATION AREA (Public) From Jct of Hwy 86 North & Northfield Dr (CR-22), W 1 mi on CR-22 to Westmount Rd N, N 0.2 mi (L). 2015 rates: $26 to $44. May 1 to Oct 15. (866)668-2267

Tell them you saw them in this Guide!

WAWA — F9 *Algoma*

LAKE SUPERIOR/AGAWA BAY (Prov Pk) On Hwy 17, 5 mi N of S Park boundary (L). 2015 rates: $32.90 to $43.75. May 2 to Oct 14. (705)856-2284

LAKE SUPERIOR/CRESCENT LAKE (Prov Pk) On Hwy 17, 1 mi N of S Park boundary (R). Pit toilets. 2015 rates: $28.75. Jun 20 to Sep 14. (705)856-2284

LAKE SUPERIOR/RABBIT BLANKET LAKE CAMPGROUND (Prov Pk) From town, 17 mi S on Hwy 17 (L). 2015 rates: $32.90 to $43.75. May 16 to Oct 26. (705)856-2284

WAWA RV RESORT & CAMPGROUND
Ratings: 8.5/8.5★/9 (Campground) N-bnd: From Jct of Hwys 101 & 17 N, W 1.6 km (1 mi) on Hwy 17 N to Magpie River Rd, S 275 m (900 ft) (L). **FAC:** Paved/gravel rds. 68 gravel, 19 pull-thrus (25 x 60), back-ins (30 x 40), 10 full hkups, 58 W, 58 E (15/50 amps), WiFi, tent sites, rentals, dump, mobile sewer, laundry, fire rings, firewood, controlled access. **REC:** heated pool, whirlpool, Magpie River: fishing, playground. Pets OK. Partial handicap access. Eco-friendly, 2015 rates: $35 to $45. May 1 to Oct 31.
(877)256-4368 Lat: 47.98430, Lon: -84.80159
634A Hwy 17 N, Wawa, ON P0S 1K0
contact@wawarv.com
www.wawarv.com
See ad this page, 1420.

WEBBWOOD — A3 *Sudbury*

CHUTES (Prov Pk) From town, N 0.5 mi on Hwy 553 (R). 2015 rates: $12.75 to $43.75. May 16 to Oct 14. (705)865-2021

WHEATLEY — F3 *Chatham-Kent*

CAMPERS COVE
Ratings: 8.5/10★/10 (Campground) From Jct of Erie S & Hwy 3 (business center), E 2.9 km (1.8 mi) on Hwy 3 to Campers Cove Rd, S 0.8 km (0.5 mi) (L) Note: Min. 3 days stay on holiday weekends. **FAC:** All weather rds. (324 spaces). Avail: 85 gravel, 8 pull-thrus (36 x 75), back-ins (45 x 50), 72 full hkups, 13 W, 13 E (30/50 amps), seasonal sites, WiFi $, tent sites, rentals, dump, laundry, groc, fire rings, firewood, controlled access. **REC:** Lake Erie: swim, fishing, shuffleboard, playground. Pet restrict(B/Q). Partial handicap access. Big rig sites, eco-friendly, 2015 rates: $50 to $56. May 1 to Sep 27. AAA Approved
(519)825-4732 Lat: 42.10319, Lon: -82.42649
21097 Campers Cove Road, Wheatley, ON N0P 2P0
info@camperscove.ca
www.camperscove.ca
See ad this page, 1420.

HOLIDAY HARBOUR RESORT **Ratings: 7/8.5★/8** (Campground) 2015 rates: $44 to $68. May 1 to Oct 31. (519)825-7396 20951 Pier Road, Wheatley, ON N0P 2P0

LAKESIDE VILLAGE MOTEL & CAMPGROUND **Ratings: 8/9★/9** (Campground) 2015 rates: $38.75 to $40.75. May 1 to Oct 13. (888)505-4550 2416 Talbot Trail Rr1, Wheatley, ON N0P 2P0

WHEATLEY (Prov Pk) From Jct of Hwy 3 & CR 1, E 0.6 mi on Hwy 3 to Klondike Rd S (E). 2015 rates: $16.25 to $49.44. Apr 11 to Oct 14. (888)668-7275

WHITE RIVER — F9 *Thunder Bay*

OBATANGA (Prov Pk) From town, E 22 mi on Hwy 17 (L). 2015 rates: $32.90 to $37.35. (807)822-2447

WHITE LAKE (Prov Pk) From town, w 20 mi on Hwy 17 (L). 2015 rates: $16.25 to $49.44. May 9 to Sep 28. (807)822-2447

WHITEFISH — A4 *Sudbury (District)*

FAIRBANK (Prov Pk) From town, N 2 mi on CR-4 (R). 2015 rates: $12.75 to $43.75. May 16 to Sep 1. (705)866-0530

WIARTON — C4 *Bruce*

BLUEWATER PARK CAMPGROUND (Public) From Jct of SR-6 & William St, E 0.1 mi on William St (L). 2015 rates: $40. May 15 to Oct 15. (519)534-2592

WINDSOR — F2 *Essex*

WINDSOR CAMPGROUND INC **Ratings: 8/8★/9** (Campground) 2015 rates: $40 to $47. Apr 15 to Oct 15. (866)258-5554 4855 9th Concession, Windsor, ON N0R 1K0

WOODSTOCK — E4 *Oxford*

PITTOCK CONSERVATION AREA (Public) From Jct of Hwy 401 (exit 230) & Sweaburg Rd, N 2 mi on Sweaburg Rd (Mill St) to Hwy 2, E 100 yds to Hwy 59, N 3.9 mi on Hwy 59 to Pittock Park Rd, NE 0.9 mi (R). 2015 rates: $35 to $45. Apr 23 to Oct 18. (519)539-5088

WILLOW LAKE PARK
Ratings: 8.5/8.5★/9 (Campground) From Jct of Hwy 401 & Sweaburg Rd (Exit 230), N 3.2 km (2 mi) on Sweaburg Rd (Mill St) to Hwy 2, E 91 m (100 yds) to Hwy 59 (Van Sittart Ave), N 4.8 km (3 mi) (L). **FAC:** All weather rds. (84 spaces). 47 Avail: 25 gravel, 22 grass, 10 pull-thrus (25 x 70), back-ins (25 x 45), 47 full hkups (30/50 amps), seasonal sites, WiFi Hotspot, tent sites, rentals, showers $, laundry, groc, fire rings, firewood, controlled access. **REC:** heated pool, pond, shuffleboard, playground, rec open to public. Pet restrict(B). Partial handicap access. Big rig sites, eco-friendly, 2015 rates: $40 to $46. Disc: AAA. May 1 to Oct 15.
(519)537-7301 Lat: 43.172356, Lon: -80.782249
595487 County Road 59, Woodstock, ON N4S 7W1
willowlake@xplorenet.com
www.willowlakepark.on.ca
See ad page 1436.

WYOMING — E3 *Lambton*

COUNTRY VIEW MOTEL & CAMPING RESORT
Ratings: 9/10★/9 (Campground) From Jct of Hwy 402 & Hwy 21 (Exit 25), S 1.2 km (0.75 mi) on Hwy 21 to CR-22 (London Line), E 91 m (300 ft) (R). **FAC:** All weather rds. (200 spaces). Avail: 30 grass, 19 pull-thrus (25 x 85), back-ins (30 x 30), 15 full hkups, 15 W, 15 E (30/50 amps), seasonal sites, WiFi $, tent sites, rentals, dump, laundry, LP bottles, fire rings, firewood. **REC:** pool, Lake Albert: fishing, playground, rec open to public. Pet restrict(B). Big rig sites, eco-friendly, 2015 rates: $36 to $45. Apr 15 to Oct 23.
(519)845-3394 Lat: 42.97945, Lon: -82.11344
rr1 4569 London Line Hwy 22, Wyoming, ON N0N 1T0
cvmandr@mnsi.net
www.sarnia.com/countryview
See ad this page.

Like Us on Facebook.

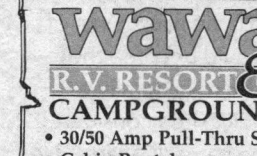

ON

 See map page 1455

Getty Images/iStockphoto

WELCOME TO

Prince Edward Island

JOINED CONFEDERATION	WIDTH: 40 MILES (64 KM)	PROPORTION OF CANADA
JULY 1, 1873	LENGTH: 139 MILES (224 KM)	0.06% OF 9,984,670 SQ KM

Prince Edward Island is home to the famous *Anne of Green Gables* novels as well as exquisite seafood, lush farmlands and beautiful sandy beaches. The island province boasts diverse cultures and once played a pivotal role Canada's formation.

Despite its big historic influence, Prince Edward Island is Canada's smallest province in size. It isn't even the country's largest island—there are 22 in Canada that are larger. Since 1997, islanders have been connected to the rest of the country by the eight-mile Confederation Bridge, which spans the Northumberland Strait.

Learn

Prince Edward, the fourth son of King George III, would become the first member of the royal family to live in North America; he's considered the first to use the name "Canada." He had a strong influence on the province, along with the rest of the country, during the late 18th century. He also participated in the capture of the island from defending French forces. Fort Amherst, which played a pivotal role in that conflict, is now a National Historic Site and interprets both British and French rule of the island.

Prince Edward Island is considered the cradle of Canada. In fact, the Charlottetown Conference to discuss political independence from Great Britain was held here in 1864. Canada became a reality in 1867, but Prince Edward Island officials chose to remain a colony and did not shift allegiances for six more years. The Province House, built in 1847, which hosted the Fathers of Confederation, has been restored and brings those fateful meetings to life with audio-visual exhibits and guided tours.

The Cavendish region of Prince Edward Island may be the best known place in the province, thanks to author Lucy Maud Montgomery. Her first novel, *Anne of Green Gables*, was published in 1908, and the coming-of-age tale has sold 50 million copies world-

Top 3 Tourism Attractions:
1) Confederation Trail
2) Lucy Maud Montgomery Birthplace
3) Prince Edward Island National Park

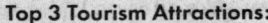

Nickname: The Garden Province

State Flower: Lady's Slipper

State Bird: Blue Jay

People: Milton Acorn, poet; Claire Rankin, singer and dancer; Lucy Maud Montgomery, author; Heather Moyse, Olympic bobsledder

Major Cities: Charlottetown (capital), Summerside

Topography: Landscape is pastoral, rolling hills, woods, reddish white sand beaches, ocean coves, red soil

Climate: Mild climate; summers are warm with low humidity, winters are cold with blizzards and frequent severe storms

- STAY A WHILE -

Prince Edward Island

Prince Edward Island is noted for its beaches, Charlottetown fine dining and live theater—*Anne of Green Gables* in particular. The province also boasts festivals from June to October. You can take a trolley and explore 25 miles of Sand dunes on Cavendish and museums, golf courses and lobster dinners.

Yvonne Duivenvoorden

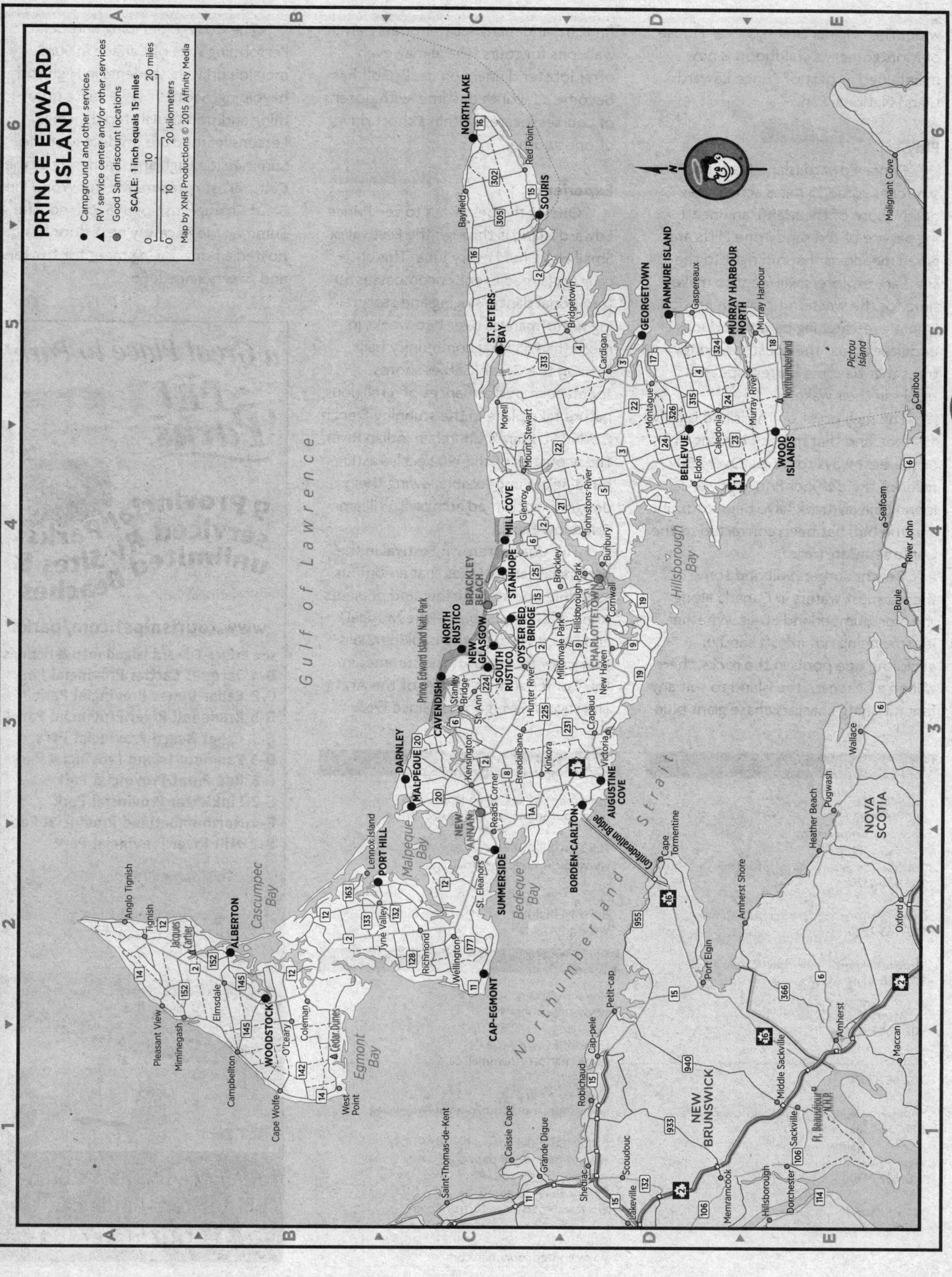
PRINCE EDWARD ISLAND
Campground and other services
RV service center and/or other services
Good Sam discount locations
SCALE: 1 inch equals 15 miles
0 10 20 miles
0 10 20 kilometers
Map by XNR Productions © 2015 Affinity Media
Gulf of Lawrence
Northumberland Strait
NORTH LAKE
SOURIS
Red Point
Bayfield
ST. PETERS BAY
GEORGETOWN
PANMURE ISLAND
MURRAY HARBOUR NORTH
Murray Harbour
Murray River
Gaspereaux
Cardigan
Bridgetown
Montague
Morell
Mount Stewart
BELLEVUE
WOOD ISLANDS
Caledonia
Eldon
Pictou Island
Caribou
MILL COVE
Glenroy
Johnstons River
STANHOPE
BRACKLEY BEACH
Brackley
Bunbury
Hillsborough Bay
CHARLOTTETOWN
Cornwall
Hillsborough Park
OYSTER BED BRIDGE
NORTH RUSTICO
SOUTH RUSTICO
NEW GLASGOW
Prince Edward Island Natl. Park
CAVENDISH
Stanley Bridge
St. Ann
Hunter River
Miltonvale Park
New Haven
Crapaud
Victoria
DARNLEY
MALPEQUE
Kensington
Breadalbane
Kinkora
NEW ANNAN
Reads Corner
AUGUSTINE COVE
BORDEN-CARLTON
Confederation Bridge
SUMMERSIDE
St. Eleanors
Bedeque Bay
Malpeque Bay
Lennox Island
PORT HILL
Tyne Valley
Richmond
Wellington
CAP-EGMONT
Egmont Bay
West Point
Cedar Dunes
Coleman
O'Leary
WOODSTOCK
Elmsdale
ALBERTON
Cascumpec Bay
Jacques Cartier
Tignish
Anglo Tignish
Pleasant View
Miminegash
Campbellton
Cape Wolfe
Cape Tormentine
NEW BRUNSWICK
NOVA SCOTIA
Port Elgin
Petit-cap
Cap-pele
Robichaud
Caissie Cape
Grande Digue
Saint-Thomas-de-Kent
Shediac
Lakeville
Scoudouc
Memramcook
Hillsborough
Dorchester
Sackville
Ft. Beausejour N.H.P.
Middle Sackville
Amherst
Maccan
Amherst Shore
Oxford
Heather Beach
Pugwash
Wallace
Brule
River John
Seafoam
Malignant Cove
PE

wide. The original Green Gables House of Montgomery's childhood is now maintained as part of Prince Edward Island National Park.

Play

Prince Edward Island National Park stretches some 25 miles across the north shore of the island, an unending parade of red sandstone cliffs and green meadows that run right to the sea. Park explorers will want to make time for the western tip of Greenwich, where eye-catching parabolic dunes undulate across the coast, covering trees that become barren, spectral trunks in their wake.

The high point on the island is only 459 feet, and that makes bicycling one of the best ways to travel. Over 300 miles of the defunct Prince Edward Island Railway track have been torn out, and the bed has been converted to the Confederation Trail.

Beachcombers will find some of the warmest waters in Canada along the Northumberland Strait. Whether it's stretching out in soft sand or exploring tide pools in the rocks, there will be a beach on the island to suit any fancy. Fishing charters chase giant bluefin tuna, and many lobster boats permit walk-ons for tours. These may even offer lobster dinners on deck. Golf has become a favorite pastime, with dozens of courses located within a short drive of one another.

Experience

One of the best ways to see Prince Edward Island is through the Festival of Small Halls, held every June. This critically acclaimed event encompasses 50 traditional dance, singing and storytelling performances over two weeks in more than 45 rural community halls.

On the Green Gables shores, spectacular performances of a religious nature take place in the stunning French Gothic St. Mary's Church in Indian River. The acoustics of the 1902 ecclesiastic building are impeccable, owing their design to acclaimed architect William Critchlow Harris.

The Charlottetown Festival in the provincial capital takes that ambitious schedule one step further and presents "Anne of Green Gables—the Musical" and "Alice Through the Looking Glass" every day throughout the summer in the Confederation Centre of the Arts. The shows have gone on since 1965.

The College of Piping and Celtic Performing Arts of Canada in Summerside drills its students in Highland bagpiping, Scottish-style snare drumming and traditional step dancing. Lessons learned are on display at the Summerside Highland Gathering as the Celtic artists prepare for the World Pipe Band Championships in Scotland. The Summerside Raceway next door has hosted a horse racing meet for trotters and pacers since 1886.

TRAVEL & TOURISM

Tourism PEI
800-463-4734
www.tourismpei.com

Borden-Carleton Visitor Information Centre
902-437-8570

Cavendish Visitor Information Centre
902-963-7830

Charlottetown Visitor Information Centre
902-368-4444

St. Peters Visitor Information Centre
902-961-3540

Souris Visitor Information Centre
902-687-7030

Summerside Visitor Information Centre
877-734-2382

West Prince
902-831-7930

Wood Islands
902-962-7411

OUTDOOR RECREATION

Authentic PEI Experiences
www.tourismpei.com/pei-experiences

The Confederation Trail
www.tourismpei.com/trail

Golf
887-894-3980
www.golfpei.ca

SHOPPING

Anne of Green Gables Store
www.annestore.ca

Charlottetown Mall
www.charlottetownmall.ca

Gateway Village
www.tourismpei.com/pei-gateway-villag

Prince Edward Island Preserve Co.
www.preservecompany.com

Spinnakers' Landing
www.summersidewaterfront.com

The Shops of Confederation Court Mall
www.confedcourtmall.com

Featured Good Sam Parks

PRINCE EDWARD ISLAND

Good Sam Park

When you stay with Good Sam, you can expect the highest degree of cleanliness and friendliness, and better yet, you get 10% off campground fees.

If you're not already a Good Sam member you can purchase your membership at one of these locations:

BRACKLEY BEACH
Vacationland RV Park
(902)672-2317

CHARLOTTETOWN
Pine Hills RV Park
(877)226-2267

For more Good Sam Parks go to listing pages

PE

Prince Edward Island

CONSULTANTS

Bob & Raissa Maroney

ALBERTON — D4 *Prince*

JACQUES CARTIER
(Prov Pk) From Jct of Hwys 2 & 150, W 12 mi on Hwy 150 to Hwy 12, N 20 mi to Jacques Cartier Entrance, NE 0.25 mi (R). **FAC:** Paved/gravel rds. 34 grass, 4 pull-thrus (14 x 35), back-ins (14 x 35), 34 W, 34 E (15/30 amps), tent sites, dump, laundry, fire rings, firewood, controlled access. **REC:** North Umberland Straight: swim, playground. Pets OK. Partial handicap access. 2015 rates: $28 to $35. Jun 12 to Sep 20.
(902)853-8632 Lat: 46.84848, Lon: -64.0152
16448 Rt 12 Kildare, Alberton, PE C0B 1B0
jacquescartiercampground@gov.pe.ca
www.gov.pe.ca
See ad page 1456 (Welcome Section).

AUGUSTINE COVE — D3 *Prince*

CUMBERLAND COVE CAMPGROUND **Ratings: 5.5/4.5/6** (Campground) 2015 rates: $24 to $27. Jun 25 to Sep 8. (902)855-2961 rr #1, Albany, PE C0B 1A0

BELLEVUE — D4 *Queens*

BEN'S LAKE TROUT FISHING & CAMPGROUND **Ratings: 4.5/5/7.5** (Campground) 2015 rates: $30 to $33. May 15 to Sep 30. (902)838-2706 2741 Road 24, Belfast, PE C0A 1A0

BORDEN-CARLETON — D3 *Prince*

JELLYSTONE PARK PEI
Ratings: 9/10★/9.5 (Campground) From town, NE 1.25 mi on Hwy 1 (L). **FAC:** Paved rds. (98 spaces). Avail: 89 grass, 7 pull-thrus (21 x 65), back-ins (21 x 90), 66 full hkups, 13 W, 13 E (30/50 amps), seasonal sites, WiFi, tent sites, rentals, dump, laundry, groc, LP bottles, fire rings, firewood. **REC:** heated pool, shuffleboard, playground. Pets OK. Partial handicap access. Eco-friendly, 2015 rates: $32 to $44. May 16 to Oct 3.
(844)734-9644 Lat: 46.254044, Lon: -63.673517
23714 Tch-1, Borden-Carleton, PE C0B 1X0
www.jellystonepei.com
See ad this page.

BRACKLEY BEACH — C4 *Queens*

VACATIONLAND RV PARK
Ratings: 8/9.5★/9.5 (Campground) In Charlottetown: From Jct of TCH-1 (Arterial Hwy) & Rte 15, N 9 mi on Rte 15 to Britain Shore Rd, E 1 mi (R). **FAC:** Paved/gravel rds. (328 spaces). Avail: 124 grass, 60 pull-thrus (35 x 70), back-ins (30 x 45), some side by side hkups, 67 full hkups, 57 W, 57 E (30/50 amps), seasonal sites, WiFi Hotspot, tent sites, showers $, dump, laundry, groc, LP gas, fire rings, firewood, controlled access. **REC:** heated pool, Black River: playground. Pets OK. Big rig sites, eco-friendly, 2015 rates: $35 to $49. Disc: AAA. May 15 to Sep 7.
(902)672-2317 Lat: 46.403591, Lon: -63.173551
29 Britain Shore Rd, Brackley Beach, PE C1E 1Z3
moreinfo@vacationlandrv.pe.ca
www.vacationlandpei.com
See ad this page, 1457.

CAP-EGMONT — C2 *Prince*

CEDAR DUNES
(Prov Pk) From Jct of Hwys 2 & 14, SW 12 mi on Hwy 14 (L). **FAC:** Gravel rds. 40 grass, 10 pull-thrus (26 x 45), back-ins (20 x 40), 40 W, 40 E (15 amps), tent sites, dump, laundry, fire rings, firewood, controlled access. **REC:** North Umberland Straits: swim, fishing, playground. Pets OK. Partial handicap access. 2015 rates: $28 to $33. Jun 12 to Sep 20.
(902)859-8785 Lat: 46.623711, Lon: -64.38635
256 Cedar Hanes Park Rd, Rte 14, O'leary, PE C0B 1V0
cedardunescampground@gov.pe.ca
www.gov.pe.ca
See ad page 1456 (Welcome Section).

CAVENDISH — C3 *Queens*

CAVENDISH KOA **Ratings: 9/10★/9.5** (Campground) 2015 rates: $34 to $68. May 31 to Oct 1. (800)562-1879 198 Forest Hill Lane, Hunter River, PE C0A 1N0

CAVENDISH SUNSET CAMPGROUND Ratings: 8.5/9.5★/9 (Campground) From Jct of Rtes 6 & 13, W 1.6 mi on Rte 6 (L). **FAC:** Paved/gravel rds. (475 spaces). 365 Avail: 245 grass, 120 dirt, 59 pull-thrus (39 x 63), back-ins (33 x 45), some side by side hkups, 145 full hkups, 115 W, 115 E (30/50 amps), seasonal sites, cable, WiFi, tent sites, dump, laundry, groc, LP bottles, fire rings, firewood, restaurant, controlled access. **REC:** heated pool, playground. Pets OK. Partial handicap access. Big rig sites, 2015 rates: $39.50 to $44.50. Disc: AAA. Jun 12 to Sep 7. ATM. AAA Approved
(902)963-2440 Lat: 46.482465, Lon: -63.408257
9115 Rte 6, Cavendish, PE C0A 1M0
camp@cavendishsunsetcampground.com
www.cavendishsunsetcampground.com

MARCO POLO LAND INC
Ratings: 9/10★/10 (Campground) From Jct of Rtes 6 & 13, S 0.5 mi on Rte 13 (L). **FAC:** Paved/gravel rds. (543 spaces). Avail: 343 grass, 59 pull-thrus (35 x 85), back-ins (40 x 90), 257 full hkups, 76 W, 76 E (30/50 amps), seasonal sites, WiFi, tent sites, rentals, dump, laundry, groc, LP bottles, fire rings, firewood, restaurant. **REC:** heated pool, wading pool, pond, fishing, playground. Pets OK. Partial handicap access. Big rig sites, eco-friendly, 2015 rates: $38 to $45. May 25 to Sep 03. ATM.
AAA Approved
(902)963-2352 Lat: 46.482455, Lon: -63.370724
7406 Route 13, Hunter River, PE C0A 1N0
hennie@marcopololand.com
www.marcopololand.com
See ad this page.

PRINCE EDWARD ISLAND/CAVENDISH CAMPGROUND (Natl Pk) From town, W 2 mi off Rte 6 on Gulf Shore Pky (E). Natl Park personal use permit required. 2015 rates: $28 to $35.30. Jun 11 to Sep 14. (902)672-6350

RED ROCK RETREAT CAMPGROUND Ratings: 8.5/8.5★/9 (Campground) From jct of Rte 6 & Rte 13, S 4 km on Rte 13, then R on Toronto Rd. 2.5 km (R). **FAC:** Gravel rds. 18 grass, 18 pull-thrus (30 x 100), 18 full hkups (30 amps), WiFi, tent sites, rentals, dump, laundry, groc, LP bottles, fire rings, firewood. **REC:** heated pool, playground. Pets OK. 2015 rates: $38. May 20 to Sep 30.
(902)963-3757 Lat: 46.46265, Lon: -63.38387
230 Toronto Rd Extension, Green Gables, PE C0A 1N0
rrcottages@gmail.com
www.redrockcottages.com

CHARLOTTETOWN — D4 *Queens*

CORNWALL KOA **Ratings: 9/10★/10** (Campground) 2015 rates: $37 to $68. May 15 to Oct 12. (902)566-2421 208 Ferry Rd., Cornwall, PE C0A 1H0

PINE HILLS RV PARK
Ratings: 9/10★/9.5 (Campground) In Charlottetown: From Jct of TCH 1 (Arterial Hwy) & Rte 15, N 6 mi on Rte 15 (L); or W-bnd: From Wood Island, W 32 mi on TCH-1 to Hillsborough Bridge, cross bridge, take first right (Riverside Dr), NE 4 mi to Rte 15, N 6 mi (L). **FAC:** Paved/gravel rds. (200 spaces). Avail: 104 grass, 4 pull-thrus (35 x 65), back-ins (35 x 65), some side by side hkups, 40 full hkups, 64 W, 64 E (30/50 amps), seasonal sites, WiFi, tent sites, rentals, dump, laundry, groc, LP bottles, fire rings, firewood, controlled access. **REC:** heated pool, playground. Pets OK. Big rig sites, eco-friendly, 2015 rates: $41 to $50. May 15 to Sep 15.
(877)226-2267 Lat: 46.35703, Lon: -63.17546
1531 Brackley Pt Rd (Harrington), Charlottetown, PE C1E 1R1
pinehillsrv@aol.com
www.pinehillsrvpark.com
See ad this page, 1457.

New to RVing? Be sure to check out the all the great articles on getting the most out of your RV, at the front of the Guide.

CHARLOTTETOWN (CONT)

Things to See and Do

PEI PROVINCIAL PARKS 10 province parks, heritage sites, day parks & golf courses. Hours: 9 am to 5 pm. No CC.
(902)368-6556 Lat: 46.234117, Lon: -63.133258
105 Rochford St, 3rd floor, Charlottetown, PE C1A 7N8
klmaclaren@gov.pe.ca
www.peiplay.com/parks
See ad page 1456 (Welcome Section).

DARNLEY — C3 *Prince*

TWIN SHORES CAMPING AREA
Ratings: 9/10★/10 (Campground) In Kensington; From Jct of Hwy 2 & Rte 20, N 10 mi on Rte 20 to Lower Darnley Rd, W 2.5 mi (E) Note: Park does not honor CAA discount. **FAC:** Paved/gravel rds. (670 spaces). Avail: 78 all weather, 355 grass, 71 pull-thrus (35 x 70), back-ins (37 x 55), 240 full hkups, 124 W, 124 E (30/50 amps), seasonal sites, WiFi, tent sites, rentals, showers $, dump, laundry, groc, LP bottles, fire rings, firewood, restaurant, controlled access. **REC:** Gulf of St Lawrence: swim, shuffleboard, playground. Pets OK. Partial handicap access. Big rig sites, eco-friendly, 2015 rates: $39 to $55. Jun 1 to Oct 1. ATM.
(877)734-2267 Lat: 46.562994, Lon: -63.664926
702 Lower Darnley Rd., Kensington, PE C0B 1M0
info@twinshores.com
www.twinshores.com
See ad opposite page.

GEORGETOWN — D5 *Kings*

BRUDENELL RIVER
(Prov Pk) From Jct of Hwys 3 & 4, E 5 mi on Hwy 3 to Brundenel Provincial Rd S 0.1 mi (L). **FAC:** Gravel rds. (95 spaces). Avail: 43 grass, 18 pull-thrus (20 x 55), back-ins (20 x 35), 25 full hkups, 18 W, 18 E (15/30 amps), tent sites, dump, laundry, fire rings, firewood, controlled access. **REC:** Brudenell River: swim, marina, golf, playground. Pets OK. Partial handicap access. 2015 rates: $28 to $35. May 15 to Oct 3.
(902)652-8966 Lat: 46.20026, Lon: -62.58027
283 Brundell Island Blvd, Rye 3, Montague, PE C0A 1R0
brudenellcampground@gov.pe.ca
www.gov.pe.ca
See ad page 1456 (Welcome Section).

MALPEQUE — C3 *Prince*

CABOT BEACH PROVINCIAL PARK
(Prov Pk) Jct of Hwys 2 & 20 6 mi on Rte 20 follow signs (L). **FAC:** Gravel/dirt rds. (163 spaces). Avail: 58 grass, back-ins (25 x 40), 28 full hkups, 30 W, 30 E (15/30 amps), tent sites, dump, laundry, fire rings, firewood, controlled access. **REC:** Malpeque Bay: swim, playground. Pets OK. 2015 rates: $28 to $35. Jun 9 to Sep 6.
(902)836-8945 Lat: 46.2895316, Lon: -63.1707989
449 Malpeque Rt 20, Malpeque, PE C1E 1V4
www.peiplay.com/parks
See ad page 1456 (Welcome Section).

MILL COVE — C4 *Queens*

WINTER BAY TENT & TRAILER PARK **Ratings: 6.5/5.5/6.5** (Campground) 2015 rates: $30 to $35. May 15 to Sep 25. (902)672-2834 rr 1 95 Donaldston, Mount Stewart, PE C0A 1P0

MURRAY HARBOUR NORTH — D5 *Kings*

SEAL COVE CAMPGROUND **Ratings: 7.5/8★/8.5** (Campground) 2015 rates: $30 to $42. May 16 to Sep 21. (902)962-2745 rr 4, Murray Harbour N, Montague, PE C0A 1R0

MURRAY RIVER — E5 *Kings*

RIVER R.V. CAMPGROUND **Ratings: 5.5/6.5/7** (RV Park) 2015 rates: $28. May 3 to Oct 15. (902)962-3738 25 Park Ave, Murray River, PE C0A 1W0

NEW ANNAN — C3 *Prince*

CRYSTAL BEACH CAMPGROUND
Ratings: 8/8.5/7 (Campground) From Jct of Hwy 1A & Hwy 2, E 1.6 mi on Hwy 2 to Rte 120 (Waterview Rd), N 0.4 mi to Rte 180 (Barbara Weit Rd), E 0.3 mi to Crystal Dr (L). **FAC:** Paved rds. (200 spaces). 150 Avail: 75 gravel, 75 grass, 28 pull-thrus (30 x 55), back-ins (20 x 40), some side by side hkups, 85 full hkups, 65 W, 65 E (15/30 amps), seasonal sites, WiFi $, tent sites, rentals, dump, laundry, groc, LP bottles, fire rings, firewood. **REC:** heated pool, Malpeque Bay: playground. Pets OK. Eco-friendly, 2015 rates: $32 to $35. May 16 to Sep 29.
(902)436-4984 Lat: 46.436343, Lon: -63.711869
1 Crystal Dr., New Annan, PE C1N 4J8
stay@crystalbeachcampground.net
www.crystalbeachcampground.net

NEW GLASGOW — C3 *Queens*

NEW GLASGOW HIGHLANDS **Ratings: 8.5/9.5★/9.5** (Campground) 2015 rates: $35 to $44. May 1 to Oct 31. (902)964-3232 rr3 2497 Hwy 224, Hunter River, PE C0A 1N0

NORTH LAKE — C6 *Kings*

CAMPBELL'S COVE CAMPGROUND (Campground) (Phone Update) 2015 rates: $29 to $32. May 20 to Sep 20. (902)357-2233 538 Rr #4, Elmira, PE C0A 2B0

NORTH RUSTICO — C3 *Queens*

WHITE SANDS COTTAGES & CAMPGROUND **Ratings: 6.5/8.5★/7** (Campground) 2015 rates: $35 to $45. May 5 to Sep 30. (902)963-2532 226 Cape Rd, North Rustico, PE C0A 1X0

OYSTER BED BRIDGE - C4 *Queens*

BAYSIDE RV CAMPGROUND **Ratings: 8/6/9.5** (Campground) 2015 rates: $30 to $34. May 30 to Sep 14. (902)621-0144 112 Camp Rd, Oyster Bed Bridge, PE C1E 0L4

PANMURE ISLAND — D5 *Kings*

PANMURE ISLAND PROVINCIAL PARK
(Prov Pk) From Jct of Hwys 1&4 N 12 mi on Rte 4 to Rte 17 11 mi follow signs to Rte 347 (R). **FAC:** Gravel/dirt rds. 22 grass, back-ins (25 x 40), some side by side hkups, 22 W, 22 E (15 amps), tent sites, dump, laundry, fire rings, firewood, controlled access. **REC:** Northumberland Strait: swim, fishing. Pets OK. 2015 rates: $28 to $35. Jun 27 to Sep 15.
(902)838-0668 Lat: 46.138786, Lon: -62.50122
350 Rte 347, Montague, PE C0A 1R0
panmurecampground@gov.pe.ca
www.peiplay.com/parks
See ad page 1456 (Welcome Section).

PORT HILL — B2 *Prince*

GREEN PARK CAMPGROUND **Ratings: 5/7.5★/8** (Campground) 2015 rates: $28 to $30. Jun 1 to Sep 15. (902)831-2021 364 Greenpark Rd., Tyne Valley, PE C0B 1V0

SOURIS — C6 *Kings*

RED POINT
(Prov Pk) On Rte 16, E 6 mi to Souris (R). **FAC:** Paved/gravel rds. 78 dirt, back-ins (20 x 40), 58 full hkups, 20 W, 20 E (15/30 amps), tent sites, dump, laundry, fire rings, firewood, controlled access. **REC:** North Umberland Straight: swim, playground. Pets OK. 2015 rates: $28 to $35. May 31 to Sep 20.
(902)357-3075 Lat: 46.37113, Lon: -62.13555
249 Red Point Park Rd Rte 16, Souris, PE C0A 2B0
redpointcampground@gov.pe.ca
www.gov.pe.ca
See ad page 1456 (Welcome Section).

SOUTH RUSTICO — C3 *Queens*

CYMBRIA TENT & TRAILER PARK **Ratings: 8/9★/7.5** (Campground) 2015 rates: $33 to $39. May 28 to Sep 8. (902)963-2458 rr 3 0729 Grandpere Point Rd, Hunter River, PE C0A 1N0

ST PETERS BAY — C5 *Kings*

ST PETERS PARK (Public) From Jct of Rtes 2 & 313, W 0.8 mi on Rte 2 (R). 2015 rates: $22 to $28. Jun 15 to Sep 17. (902)961-2786

STANHOPE — C4 *Queens*

PRINCE EDWARD ISLAND/STANHOPE CAMPGROUND (Natl Pk) From Jct of Hwy 2 & Hwy 15, N 15 mi on Hwy 15 to Gulf Shore Hwy, E 4.5 mi (R). Natl park personal use permit required. 2015 rates: $28 to $35.30. Jun 11 to Sep 14. (902)672-6350

SUMMERSIDE — C2 *Prince*

LINKLETTER PROVINCIAL PARK
(Prov Pk) From Jct Hwys 1 & 11 W 5 mi follow signs to 437 Linkletter Rd (R). **FAC:** Gravel/dirt rds. (93 spaces). Avail: 42 grass, back-ins (25 x 40), 25 full hkups, 17 W, 17 E (30/50 amps), tent sites, dump, laundry, fire rings, firewood, controlled access. **REC:** Bedeque Bay: swim, playground. Pets OK. 2015 rates: $28 to $35. May 31 to Sep 22.
(902)888-8366 Lat: 46.3989421, Lon: -63.8567089
437 Linkletter Rd, Summerside, PE C0B 1V0
linklettercampground@gov.pe.ca
www.peiplay.com/parks
See ad page 1456 (Welcome Section).

WOOD ISLANDS — E4 *Kings*

NORTHUMBERLAND
(Prov Pk) From ferry terminal, E 2 mi on Hwy 4 (R). **FAC:** Paved/gravel rds. 48 grass, 6 pull-thrus (30 x 65), back-ins (20 x 40), 10 full hkups, 38 W, 38 E (15 amps), tent sites, rentals, dump, laundry, groc, fire rings, firewood, controlled access. **REC:** Northumberland Strait: swim, playground. Pets OK. Partial handicap access. 2015 rates: $28 to $35. May 29 to Sep 20.
(902)962-7418 Lat: 45.96224, Lon: -62.71750
12547 Shore Rd, Rte 4, Wood Islands, PE C0A 1R0
northumberlandcampground@gov.pe.ca
www.gov.pe.ca
See ad page 1456 (Welcome Section).

WOODSTOCK — B2 *West Prince*

MILL RIVER PROVINCIAL PARK
(Prov Pk) From Jct of Hwys 2 & 136, N 200 ft on Hwy 136 (L). **FAC:** Gravel/dirt rds. 54 grass, 36 pull-thrus (30 x 60), back-ins (30 x 60), some side by side hkups, 18 W, 18 E (15/30 amps), tent sites, dump, laundry, fire rings, firewood, controlled access. **REC:** pool $, Mill River: swim, marina, golf, playground. Pets OK. Partial handicap access. 2015 rates: $28 to $35. May 15 to Sep 27.
(902)859-8786 Lat: 46.73913, Lon: -64.17068
3 Mill Pines Resort Rd, Rte 136, Woodstock, PE C0B 1V0
millrivercampground@gov.pe.ca
www.gov.pe.ca
See ad page 1456 (Welcome Section).

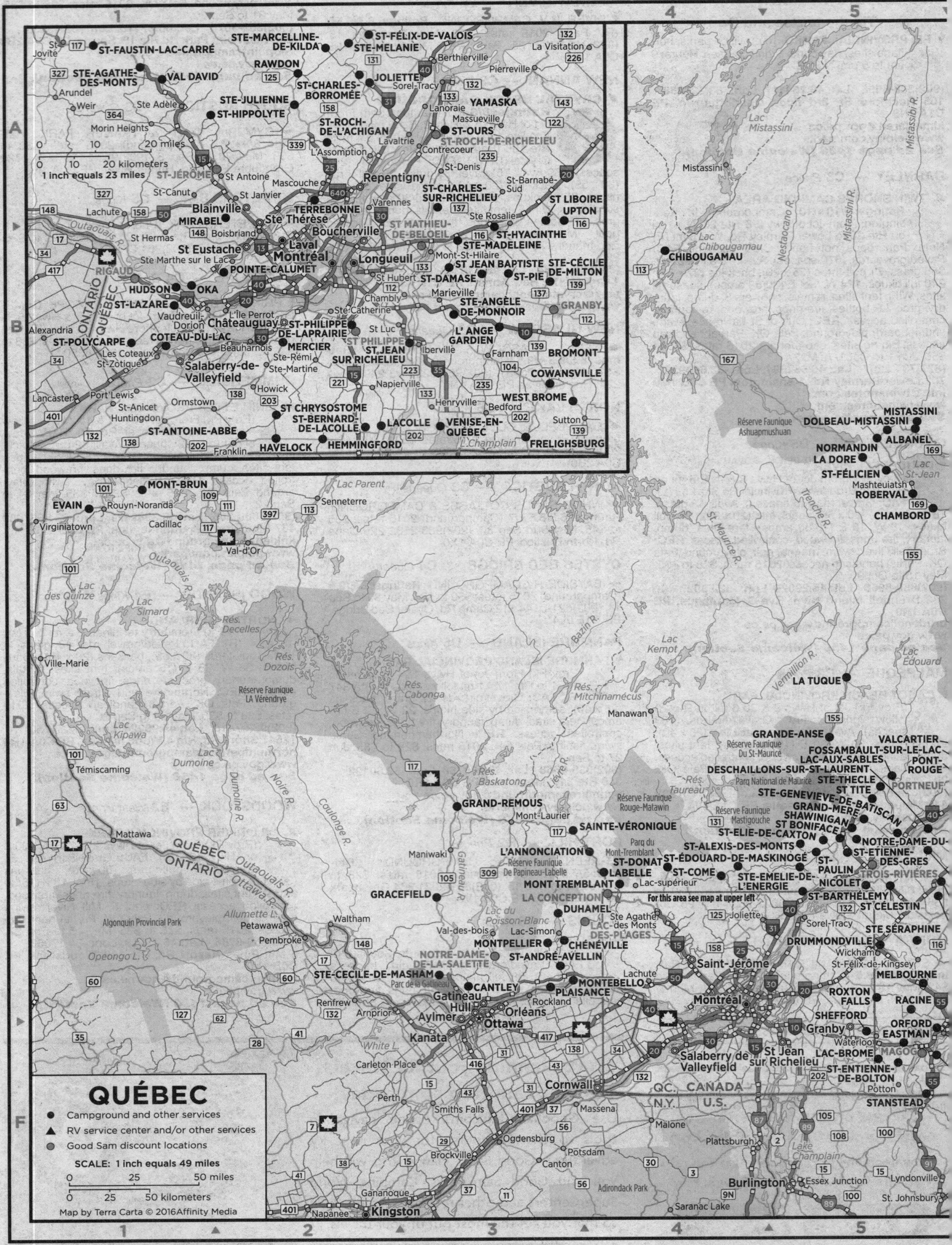
QUÉBEC
Campground and other services
RV service center and/or other services
Good Sam discount locations
SCALE: 1 inch equals 49 miles
0 25 50 miles
0 25 50 kilometers
Map by Terra Carta © 2016Affinity Media
1 inch equals 23 miles
0 10 20 miles
0 10 20 kilometers
For this area see map at upper left
ST-FAUSTIN-LAC-CARRÉ
STE-MARCELLINE-DE-KILDA
ST-FÉLIX-DE-VALOIS
STE-MELANIE
STE-AGATHE-DES-MONTS
VAL DAVID
RAWDON
JOLIETTE
ST-CHARLES-BORROMÉE
STE-JULIENNE
ST-HIPPOLYTE
YAMASKA
ST-ROCH-DE-L'ACHIGAN
ST-OURS
ST-ROCH-DE-RICHELIEU
ST-JÉRÔME
Repentigny
ST-CHARLES-SUR-RICHELIEU
TERREBONNE
Blainville
MIRABEL
Ste Thérèse
ST LIBOIRE
UPTON
ST MATHIEU-DE-BELOEIL
ST-HYACINTHE
STE-MADELEINE
Boucherville
St Eustache
Laval
Montréal
Longueuil
RIGAUD
POINTE-CALUMET
ST JEAN BAPTISTE
ST-DAMASE
STE-CÉCILE-DE-MILTON
ST-PIE
HUDSON
OKA
ST-LAZARE
STE-ANGÈLE-DE-MONNOIR
GRANBY
Châteauguay
ST-PHILIPPE-DE-LAPRAIRIE
ST PHILIPPE
L' ANGE GARDIEN
ST-POLYCARPE
COTEAU-DU-LAC
MERCIER
ST JEAN SUR RICHELIEU
BROMONT
Salaberry-de-Valleyfield
COWANSVILLE
WEST BROME
ST CHRYSOSTOME
ST-BERNARD-DE-LACOLLE
LACOLLE
VENISE-EN-QUÉBEC
ST-ANTOINE-ABBE
HAVELOCK
HEMMINGFORD
FRELIGHSBURG
ONTARIO
QUÉBEC
CHIBOUGAMAU
Lac Mistassini
Mistassini
Lac Chibougamau
Réserve Faunique Ashuapmushuan
MISTASSINI
DOLBEAU-MISTASSINI
ALBANEL
NORMANDIN
LA DORE
ST-FÉLICIEN
Lac St-Jean
Mashteuiatsh
ROBERVAL
CHAMBORD
MONT-BRUN
EVAIN
Rouyn-Noranda
Virginiatown
Cadillac
Val-d'Or
Senneterre
Lac Parent
Réserve Faunique LA Vérendrye
Rés. Dozois
Rés. Cabonga
Rés. Decelles
Ville-Marie
Lac Kempt
LA TUQUE
Rés. Mitchinamécus
Manawan
Lac Kipawa
Témiscaming
Lac Dumoine
GRANDE-ANSE
Réserve Faunique Du St-Maurice
VALCARTIER
FOSSAMBAULT-SUR-LE-LAC
LAC-AUX-SABLES
PONT-ROUGE
DESCHAILLONS-SUR-ST-LAURENT
Parq National de Mauricie
STE-THECLE
ST TITE
PORTNEUF
STE-GENEVIEVE-DE-BATISCAN
GRAND-MERE
SHAWINIGAN
ST BONIFACE
GRAND-REMOUS
Mont-Laurier
Réserve Faunique Rouge-Matawin
Réserve Faunique Mastigouche
SAINTE-VÉRONIQUE
ST-ELIE-DE-CAXTON
NOTRE-DAME-DU-
ST-ÉTIENNE-DES-GRES
ST-ALEXIS-DES-MONTS
ST-ÉDOUARD-DE-MASKINOGÉ
ST-PAULIN
TROIS-RIVIÈRES
L'ANNONCIATION
Réserve Faunique De Papineau-Labelle
ST-DONAT
ST-COME
STE-EMELIE-DE-L'ENERGIE
NICOLET
LABELLE
MONT TREMBLANT
Lac-supérieur
LA CONCEPTION
ST-BARTHÉLEMY
ST CÉLESTIN
Mattawa
Algonquin Provincial Park
GRACEFIELD
DUHAMEL
Ste Agathe
LAC-DES-PLAGES
Joliette
Sorel-Tracy
STE SÉRAPHINE
DRUMMONDVILLE
MONTPELLIER
CHÉNÉVILLE
NOTRE-DAME-DE-LA-SALETTE
ST-ANDRÉ-AVELLIN
Saint-Jérôme
STE-CECILE-DE-MASHAM
CANTLEY
MONTEBELLO
PLAISANCE
MELBOURNE
Montréal
ROXTON FALLS
RACINE
SHEFFORD
ORFORD
EASTMAN
Granby
Gatineau
Hull
Orléans
Aylmer
Ottawa
Kanata
LAC-BROME
MAGOG
Salaberry de Valleyfield
St Jean sur Richelieu
ST-ENTIENNE-DE-BOLTON
Cornwall
QC. CANADA
N.Y. U.S.
STANSTEAD
Burlington
Kingston
Adirondack Park

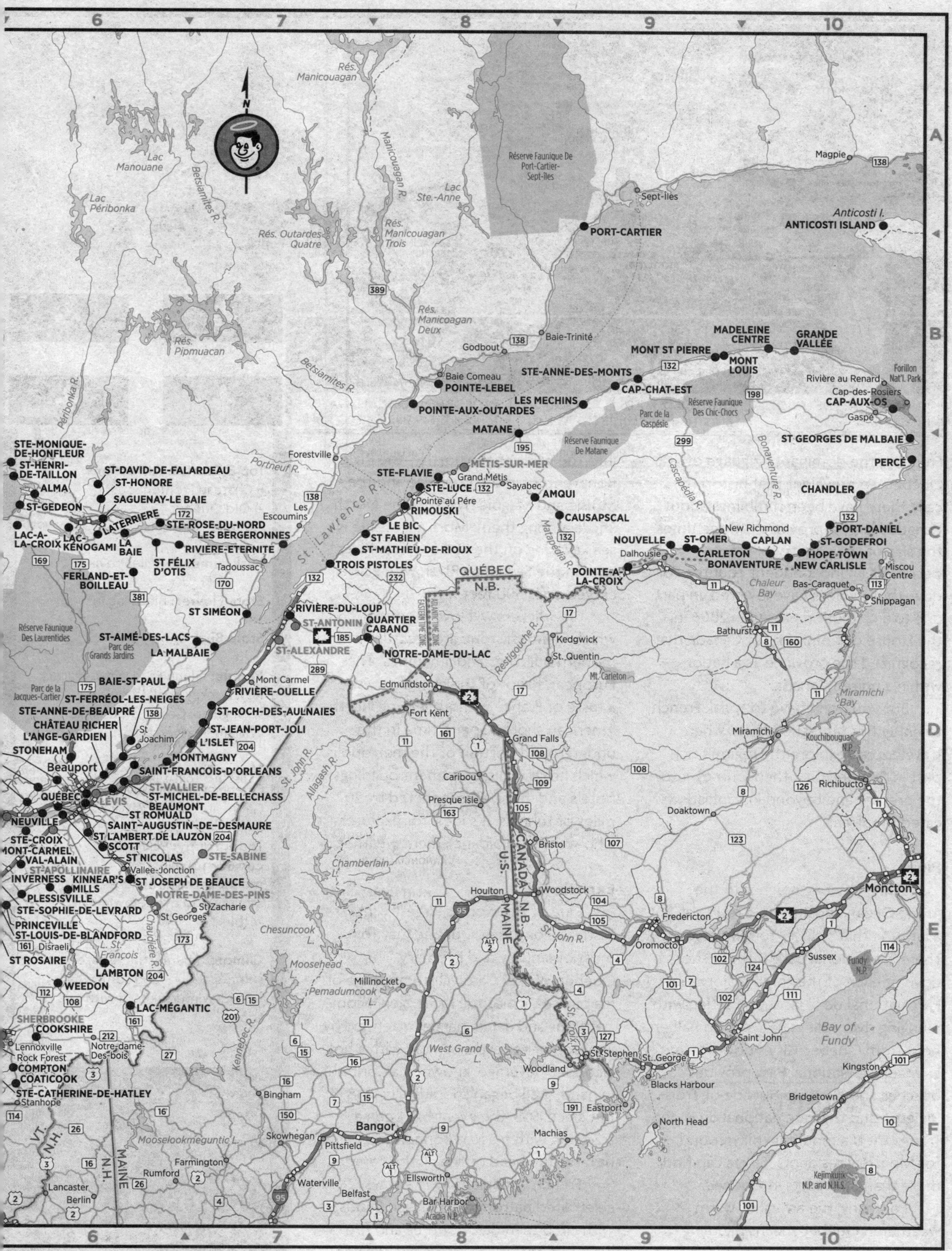
6
7
8
9
10
A
B
C
D
E
F
Rés. Manicouagan
Lac Manouane
Lac Péribonka
Betsiamites R.
Manicouagan R.
Lac Ste.-Anne
Rés. Outardes Quatre
Rés. Manicouagan Trois
Réserve Faunique De Port-Cartier-Sept-Îles
Sept-Îles
PORT-CARTIER
Magpie
138
Anticosti I.
ANTICOSTI ISLAND
389
Rés. Manicoagan Deux
Rés. Pipmuacan
Godbout
Baie-Trinité
MADELEINE CENTRE
GRANDE VALLÉE
MONT ST PIERRE
MONT LOUIS
132
STE-ANNE-DES-MONTS
CAP-CHAT-EST
Baie Comeau
POINTE-LEBEL
Betsiamites R.
Péribonka R.
LES MECHINS
POINTE-AUX-OUTARDES
Parc de la Gaspésie
Réserve Faunique Des Chic-Chocs
198
Rivière au Renard
Forillon Nat'l. Park
Cap-des-Rosiers
CAP-AUX-OS
Gaspé
MATANE
Réserve Faunique De Matane
299
ST GEORGES DE MALBAIE
195
PERCÉ
STE-MONIQUE-DE-HONFLEUR
ST-HENRI-DE-TAILLON
ALMA
ST-GEDEON
ST-DAVID-DE-FALARDEAU
ST-HONORE
SAGUENAY-LE BAIE
Portneuf R.
Forestville
MÉTIS-SUR-MER
Grand Métis
STE-FLAVIE
STE-LUCE
Pointe au Pére
Sayabec
AMQUI
Cascapédia R.
Bonaventure R.
CHANDLER
LAC-A-LA-CROIX
LAC-KENOGAMI
LATERRIERE
LA BAIE
172
ST-ROSE-DU-NORD
LES BERGERONNES
RIVIERE-ETERNITE
ST FÉLIX D'OTIS
Les Escoumins
St. Lawrence R.
RIMOUSKI
LE BIC
ST FABIEN
ST-MATHIEU-DE-RIOUX
CAUSAPSCAL
Matapédia R.
New Richmond
PORT-DANIEL
NOUVELLE
ST-OMER
CARLETON
CAPLAN
ST-GODEFROI
BONAVENTURE
HOPE TOWN
NEW CARLISLE
Dalhousie
POINTE-A-LA-CROIX
169
175
FERLAND-ET-BOILLEAU
Tadoussac
170
381
TROIS PISTOLES
232
QUÉBEC
N.B.
Chaleur Bay
Bas-Caraquet
Miscou Centre
113
Shippagan
Réserve Faunique Des Laurentides
ST SIMÉON
RIVIÈRE-DU-LOUP
ST-ANTONIN
QUARTIER CABANO
185
ST-ALEXANDRE
NOTRE-DAME-DU-LAC
ATLANTIC TIME ZONE
EASTERN TIME ZONE
Restigouche R.
17
Kedgwick
St. Quentin
Bathurst
160
ST-AIMÉ-DES-LACS
Parc des Grands Jardins
LA MALBAIE
289
Mont Carmel
Edmundston
Mt. Carleton
Parc de la Jacques-Cartier
BAIE-ST-PAUL
RIVIÈRE-OUELLE
ST-FERRÉOL-LES-NEIGES
STE-ANNE-DE-BEAUPRÉ
ST-ROCH-DES-AULNAIES
Fort Kent
Miramichi Bay
CHÂTEAU RICHER
L'ANGE-GARDIEN
St Joachim
ST-JEAN-PORT-JOLI
L'ISLET
204
Grand Falls
Miramichi
Kouchibouguac N.P.
STONEHAM
Beauport
MONTMAGNY
SAINT-FRANCOIS-D'ORLEANS
St. John R.
Allagash R.
Caribou
108
109
126
Richibucto
QUÉBEC
LÉVIS
ST-VALLIER
ST-MICHEL-DE-BELLECHASS
BEAUMONT
ST ROMUALD
Presque Isle
163
105
Doaktown
NEUVILLE
SAINT-AUGUSTIN-DE-DESMAURE
ST LAMBERT DE LAUZON
STE-CROIX
MONT-CARMEL
VAL-ALAIN
SCOTT
ST NICOLAS
STE-SABINE
Vallee-Jonction
Chamberlain
CANADA
U.S.
Bristol
107
123
ST-APOLLINAIRE
INVERNESS
KINNEAR'S MILLS
ST JOSEPH DE BEAUCE
PLESSISVILLE
NOTRE-DAME-DES-PINS
STE-SOPHIE-DE-LEVRARD
St Zacharie
St Georges
Houlton
Woodstock
Moncton
95
104
Fredericton
PRINCEVILLE
ST-LOUIS-DE-BLANDFORD
Chaudière R.
Chesuncook L.
MAINE
N.B.
105
Oromocto
St. John R.
161
Disraeli
L. St. François
173
ST ROSAIRE
LAMBTON
Moosehead L.
Sussex
Fundy N.P.
114
WEEDON
Millinocket
Pemadumcook L.
St. Croix R.
SHERBROOKE
COOKSHIRE
LAC-MÉGANTIC
201
Kennebec R.
Bay of Fundy
Saint John
Lennoxville
Rock Forest
Notre-dame-Des-bois
West Grand L.
St. Stephen
St. George
COMPTON
COATICOOK
STE-CATHERINE-DE-HATLEY
Stanhope
Woodland
Blacks Harbour
Kingston
Bingham
Bridgetown
Eastport
North Head
Bangor
Skowhegan
Pittsfield
Machias
VT.
N.H.
N.H.
MAINE
Mooselookmeguntic L.
Farmington
Rumford
Lancaster
Berlin
Waterville
Ellsworth
Belfast
Bar Harbor
Acadia N.P.
Kejimkujik N.P. and N.H.S.

Tourisme Quebec

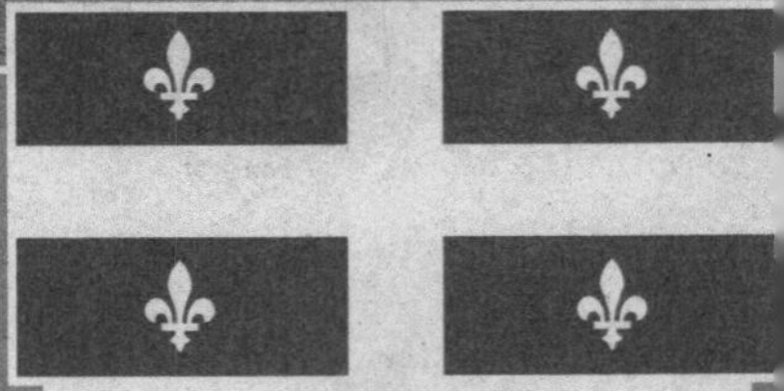

JOINED CONFEDERATION JULY 1, 1867	WIDTH: 842 MILES (1,355 KM) LENGTH: 1,102 MILES (1,773 KM)	PROPORTION OF CANADA 15.44% OF 9,984,670 SQ KM

French is the dominant language of Québec, so prevalent that historically there have been rumblings about Canada's largest province—three times the size of the country of France—becoming an independent country. For now, those voices have lowered, in part due to a resolution passed in 2006 in the House of Commons of Canada that recognized the province as a nation within a united Canada.

But you don't have to speak French to enjoy this fantastic region, where travelers can explore the region's rich past in Québec City, then journey into the present and beyond in sophisticated Montréal.

Play

While Québec reaches to the Arctic Ocean, most people reside at a latitude that's closer to Minnesota. There is a national park within a short drive of each of the three major cities: Parc national de la Jacques-Cartier, with plunging river valleys, is less than half an hour from Québec City's downtown; La Mauricie National Park provides beaches and 150 lakes outside of Trois-Rivières; and the Parc national du Mont-Tremblant is a mountain playground for Montréal residents. Skiers can find more than 80 resorts in Québec.

For many, the arrival of warm weather in Québec means paddling. Adventure touring companies lead trips into the wilds of the north—the Rivière Bonaventure in the Gaspésie and the Moisie and Magpie rivers on the North Shore among them. More accessible is sea kayaking on the St. Lawrence River and on the Saguenay River, with glacier-carved cliffs 500 feet high.

City slickers will love Montréal, which blends historic architecture with modern buildings and amenities. The European flavor of the city gives visitors a taste of France without leaving North American shores. Spend time in the underground portion of the metropolis, which hosts malls, apartment buildings, hotels and more, all connected by 20 miles of tunnels. It's ideal for explorers who want to avoid inclement weather.

Experience

One of the world's largest winter festivals consumes Québec City for most of January and February. The Québec Winter Carnival is a mélange of ice palaces, ice canoe races, sleigh competitions and dance parties attended by a million or so revelers, most with a hot alcoholic beverage, known as a Caribou, in hand. It all began sporadically in 1894, but since 1955, the event has been a tradition with mascot Bonhomme Carnaval at the head of the all the parades.

French Canadians have always celebrated patron saint St. Jean Baptiste with circus parades, bonfires and fireworks so heartily that the day became

Top 3 Tourism Attractions:
1) Château Frontenac
2) Old Québec
3) Gaspe Peninsula

Nickname: La Belle Province

State Flower: Blue Flag Iris

State Bird: Snowy Owl

People: Glenn Ford, actor; Patrick Roy, hockey goalie; Louis Cyr, strongman; Céline Dion, singer; William Shatner, actor

Major Cities: Montréal, Québec (capital), Laval, Gatineau, Longueuil

Topography: 95% within Canadian Shield; flat, mountainous, with lakes, bogs, streams and rivers; lowland is fertile

Climate: Four distinct seasons; summers—hot and somewhat humid; winters—cold with lots of snow

Getty Images/iStockphoto

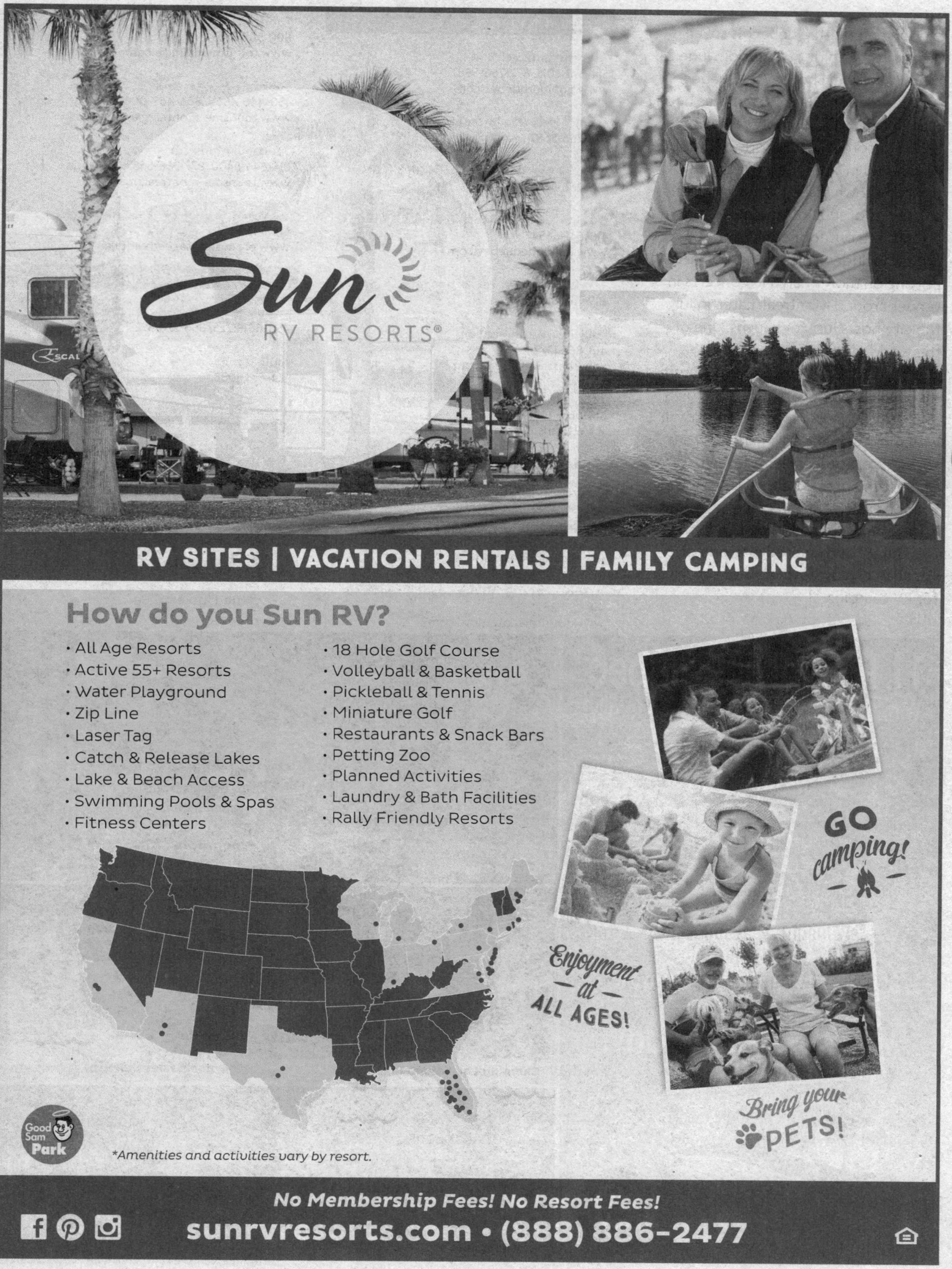

synonymous with Québecois sovereignty. In the spirit of inclusion, June 24 is now a national holiday in Québec.

International Jazz Festival has been recognized in the *Guinness Book of World* Records for its enormous scope. For 10 days in late June and early July, the downtown streets close to vehicles so crowds of 100,000 and more can attend free outdoor concerts. All told, the bill includes more than 3,000 artists putting on more than 650 concerts in venues around Montréal. Later, in July the city hosts Just for Laughs, one of the world's largest comedy fests.

The Mondial des Cultures in Drummondville's Woodyatt Park has grown into the country's biggest folk festival, with musicians and folk dancers from some 90 countries filling eleven days of performances. The Gatineau Hot Air Balloon Festival began in 1988 as a late summer mass ascension for balloonists, but it has morphed into one of Canada's biggest festivals and a magnet for RV camping.

TRAVEL & TOURISM

Tourism Québec
514-873-2015, 877-266-5687
www.bonjourquebec.com

Montréal Centre Infotouriste
877-266-5687

Québec City Centre Infotouriste
877-266-5687

Québec City and Area Québec City Tourism
418-641-6654
www.regiondequebec.com

Tourisme, Abitibi-Témiscamingue
819-762-8181

Tourisme Bas-Saint Laurent
418-867-1272
www.bassaintlaurent.com

Tourisme Charlevoix
418-665-4454
www.tourisme-charlevoix.com

Tourisme Lanaudière
450-834-2535
www.lanaudiere.ca

Tourisme Laurentides
450-224-7007
www.laurentides.com

Association Touristique de Manicouagan
418-294-2876
www.tourismecote-nord.com

Tourisme Mauricie
800-567-7603
www.tourismemauricie.com

Tourisme Montérégie
450-466-4666, 866-469-0069
www.tourisme-monteregie.qc.ca

Tourisme Montréal
514-844-5400, 877-266-5687
www.tourisme-montreal.org

Tourisme Saguenay - Lac-Saint-Jean
418-543-9778
www.promotionsaguenay.qc.ca

OUTDOOR RECREATION

Aventure Écotourisme Québec
450-661-2225, 866-278-5923

Golf Quebec
514-633-1088

Ressources Naturelles et Faune Québec
418-627-8600

Québec Ski Areas Association
514-493-1810

SHOPPING

Fédération des clubs de motoneigistes du Québec
514-252-3076

Featured Good Sam Parks

QUEBEC

Good Sam Park

When you stay with Good Sam, you can expect the highest degree of cleanliness and friendliness, and better yet, you get 10% off campground fees.

If you're not already a Good Sam member you can purchase your membership at one of these locations:

GRANBY
Camping L'EstriVal-Parkbridge
(450)378-9410

LA CONCEPTION
Camping Parc la Conception - Parkbridge
(819)686-5596

MAGOG
Domaine Parc-Estrie - Parkbridge
(819)868-6944

NOTRE-DAME-DE-LA-SALETTE
Royal Papineau - Parkbridge
(819)766-2826

NOTRE-DAME-DES-PINS
Camping la Roche d'Or - Parkbridge
(418)774-9191

PORTNEUF
Camping Panoramique - Parkbridge
(418)286-3655

SAINT-ANTONIN
Camping Lido 2002
(418)862-6933

SAINT-APOLLINAIRE
Domaine de la Chute - Parkbridge
(418)831-1311

SAINTE-SABINE
Camping Caravelle - Parkbridge
(450)293-7637

SAINT-JEROME
Camping Lac Lafontaine - Parkbridge
(450)431-7373

SAINT-MATHIEU-DE-BELOEIL
Camping Alouette - Parkbridge
(450)464-1661

SAINT-ROCH-DE-RICHELIEU
Camping Domaine des Erables - Parkbridge
(450)785-2805

For more Good Sam Parks go to listing pages

Quebec

CONSULTANTS

Bob & Raissa Maroney

ALBANEL — C5 *Saguenay-Lac-Saint-Jean*

◄ CAMPING MUNICIPAL ALBANEL (Public) In center town on Rte 169 (L). 2015 rates: $30 to $34. May 15 to Sep 4. (418)279-3374

ALMA — C6 *Saguenay-Lac-Saint-Jean*

↖ CAMPING COLONIE NOTRE DAME (Campground) (Phone Update) 2015 rates: $23 to $32. May 24 to Sep 1. (418)662-9113 700, chemin de la Baie-Moise, Alma, QC G8B 5V5

↑ COMPLEXE TOURISTIQUE DE LA DAM-EN-TERRE (Campground) (Phone Update) 2015 rates: $35 to $39. May 16 to Sep 7. (418)668-3016 1385 Chemin De La Marina (C.p. 836), Alma, QC G8B 5W1

↑ RESERVE FAUNIQUE DES LAURENTIDES-CAMPING BELLE-RIVIERE (Prov Pk) From jct Hwy 175 & Hwy 169: Go NW on Hwy 169 N to Laurentides Wildlife Reserve. 2015 rates: $30.75 to $42.75. May 16 to Aug 30. (418)864-2161

AMQUI — C8 *Gaspesie*

◄ CAMPING AMQUI (Public) In Town: From S Jct of Rtes 195 & 132, W 3 mi on Rte 132 (R). 2015 rates: $27 to $37. Jun 13 to Sep 1. (418)629-3433

ANTICOSTI ISLAND — A10 *Cote-Nord*

PARC NATIONAL D'ANTICOSTI/BAIE-DE-LA-TOUR (Prov Pk) Take ferry from Rimouski or Sept-Iles, also by plane from Montreal, Quebec, Mont-Joli or Sept-Iles. Jun 28 to Aug 19. (418)535-0231

BAIE-SAINT-PAUL — D6 *Quebec*

↗ CAMPING DU GOUFFRE **Ratings: 8/10★/9** (Campground) 2015 rates: $37 to $41. May 9 to Sep 29. (418)435-2143 439 St Laurent (C.p. 3164), Baie-Saint-Paul, QC G3Z 3B6

► CAMPING LE GENEVRIER **Ratings: 8/8.5★/8.5** (Campground) 2015 rates: $30 to $49. May 1 to Oct 16. (418)435-6520 1175 Mgr de Laval (Rte 138), Baie-Saint-Paul, QC G3Z 2X4

PARC NATIONAL DES GRANDS-JARDINS (Natl Forest) From Hwy 138 & 381 N. (418)439-1227

BAIE-TRINITE — B9 *Manicouagan*

◄ CAMPING DOMAINE ENSOLEILLE 2000 (Campground) (Phone Update) 2015 rates: $30 to $35. May 16 to Sep 14. (418)939-2002 15 Rte 138 Est, Baie-Trinite, QC G0H 1A0

BEAUMONT — D6 *Chaudiere-Appalaches*

► CAMPING GUILMETTE **Ratings: 8/9★/9** (Campground) 2015 rates: $30 to $40. May 15 to Sep 30. (418)837-6900 152 Rue du Fleuve, Beaumont, QC G0R 1C0

BERGERONNES — C7 *Manicouagan*

► CAMPING BON DESIR (Public) From overpass Rue de la Mer in Grandes Bergeronnes, E 2.5 mi on Rte 138 (R). 2015 rates: $23.35 to $31.59. Jun 1 to Oct 10. (418)232-6297

BIC — C8 *Bas-Saint-Laurent*

PARC NATIONAL DU BIC/CAMPING RIOUX (Prov Pk) On Hwy 132 E. 2015 rates: $28.50 to $37.75. (800)665-6527

BONAVENTURE — C10 *Gaspesie*

◄ CAMPING PLAGE BEAUBASSIN (Public) From Center of Town, E 0.25 mi on Hwy 132 to Chemin Plage-De-Beaubassin, S 500 ft to Marina Drive, E 1000 ft (R). 2015 rates: $14.79 to $41.75. May 5 to Sep 28. (418)534-3246

BROMONT — B3 *Cantons de l'Est*

◄ CAMPING PARC BROMONT **Ratings: 7.5/9★/8** (Campground) 2015 rates: $30 to $44. Apr 27 to Oct 15. (450)534-2712 24 Rue Lafontaine, Bromont, QC J2L 2S9

◄ CAMPING VACANCES BROMONT **Ratings: 8/9★/8** (Campground) 2015 rates: $34 to $58. Apr 25 to Oct 25. (877)534-4434 22 rue Bleury St, Bromont, QC J2L 1B3

↓ **GRANBY/BROMONT KOA**

Ratings: 10/10★/9.5 (Campground) From Jct of Hwy 10 & Exit 74 (Rte Pierre Laporte), S 3.5 mi on Rte Pierre Laporte to Shefford Rd, E 100 ft (R). **FAC:** Paved/gravel rds. (255 spaces). Avail: 120 all weather, 16 pull-thrus (35 x 65), back-ins (30 x 55), 120 full hkups (30/50 amps), seasonal sites, cable, WiFi, tent sites, rentals, dump, laundry, groc, LP gas, fire rings, firewood, controlled access. **REC:** heated pool, Lake Bromont: swim, playground. Pets OK. Big rig sites, eco-friendly, 2015 rates: $50 to $55. Disc: AAA. Apr 15 to Oct 15.
(450)534-2404 Lat: 45.29309, Lon: -72.70189
1699 Shefford, Bromont, QC J2L 3N8
koa4u2@gmail.com
http://koa.com/campgrounds/granby/
See ad this page.

CABANO — D7 *Bas-Saint-Laurent*

↑ CAMPING TEMILAC INC **Ratings: 7.5/10★/8.5** (Campground) 2015 rates: $32 to $37. May 15 to Sep 15. (418)854-7660 33 Rue de La Plage, Cabano, QC G0L 1E0

CANTLEY — E3 *Outaouais*

↖ CAMPING CANTLEY **Ratings: 8.5/8.5★/8.5** (Campground) 2015 rates: $38 to $44. May 15 to Sep 15. (819)827-1056 100 Ch Ste Elisabeth, Cantley, QC J8V 3G4

CAP-CHAT-EST — B9 *Gaspesie*

► CAMPING AU BORD DE LA MER **Ratings: 7.5/8★/7** (Campground) 2015 rates: $23 to $36. Jun 1 to Sep 30. (418)809-3675 173 Notre Dame Est, Cap-Chat-Est, QC G0J 1G0

CAPLAN — C10 *Gaspesie*

↗ CAMPING RUISSELET **Ratings: 8/8.5★/7.5** (Campground) 2015 rates: $25 to $30. Jun 1 to Sep 5. (418)388-2138 322 Blvd Perron Est (Cp.1955), Caplan, QC G0C 1H0

CARLETON — C9 *Gaspesie*

↓ CAMPING CARLETON (Public) From Jct of Rte 132 & Avenue Du Phare in E part of town, S on Avenue Du Phare access road (L). 2015 rates: $25 to $47. May 30 to Sep 21. (418)364-3992

CAUSAPSCAL — C9 *Gaspesie*

↑ CAMPING DE CAUSAPSCAL (Public) From town, W 1.5 mi on Rte 132 (R). 2015 rates: $18 to $22. Jun 9 to Sep 5. (418)756-5621

CHAMBORD — C5 *Saguenay-Lac-Saint-Jean*

◄ CAMPING PLAGE BLANCHET (Public) From Town: N 1 mi on Rte 169 to Ch Du Domaine Norois, NE 0.25 mi (E). 2015 rates: $21 to $33. Jun 22 to Aug 18. (418)346-5436

◄ CAMPING VAL-JALBERT (Public) From Jct of Rtes 155 & 169 (in town), N 4 mi on Rte 169 (L). 2015 rates: $27.50 to $43. May 16 to Sep 21. (888)675-3132

CHANDLER — C10 *Gaspesie*

◄ PARC DU BOURG DE PABOS **Ratings: 7.5/8.5★/7.5** (Campground) 2015 rates: $25 to $38. May 11 to Sep 30. (418)689-6043 75 De la Plage Rd., Chandler, QC G0C 2J0

CHANDLER (PABOS) — C10 *Gaspesie*

↗ CENTRE DE PLAIN AIR LA SEIGNEURIE **Ratings: 6.5/8.5★/7** (Campground) 2015 rates: $28 to $36. Jun 1 to Sep 30. (418)689-3031 99 Rte de L'eglise, Pabos, QC G0C 2H0

CHATEAU-RICHER — D6 *Quebec*

◄ CAMPING TURMEL ENR **Ratings: 8.5/9/8.5** (Campground) 2015 rates: $46. May 15 to Sep 15. (418)824-4311 7000 Boul Ste-Anne, Chateau-Richer, QC G0A 1N0

CHENEVILLE — E3 *Outaouais*

↓ CAMPING LA PINEDE **Ratings: 5/8★/8.5** (Campground) 2015 rates: $35 to $45. May 4 to Sep 27. (819)428-3264 1735 De La Pinede St, Lac-Simon, QC J0V 1E0

CHIBOUGAMAU — B4 *Nord du Quebec*

RESERVE FAUNIQUE ASSINICA ET DES LACS-ALBANEL-MISTASSINI-ET WACONICHI/CAMPING BAIE PENICOU (Prov Pk) Road 167 N. 2015 rates: $29.25 to $40.75. May 31 to Sep 2. (418)748-7748

COATICOOK — F6 *Cantons de l'Est*

↓ CAMPING DU LAC LYSTER (PISKIART-LA SEQUINIERE) (Campground) (Phone Update) 2015 rates: $34 to $38. May 15 to Oct 10. (819)849-3929 385 Chemin Sequin, Coaticook, QC J1A 2S4

COMPTON — F6 *Cantons de l'Est*

◄ CAMPING DE COMPTON **Ratings: 9/10★/10** (Membership Pk) 2015 rates: $36.50 to $46.50. Apr 13 to Oct 8. (800)563-5277 24 Chemin de la Station, Compton, QC J0B 1L0

COOKSHIRE — F6 *Cantons de l'Est*

↓ CAMPING CO-OP PREVERT **Ratings: 8.5/8.5★/8** (Campground) 2015 rates: $34 to $38. May 1 to Sep 30. (819)875-3186 530 Chemin Chute, Cookshire, QC J0B 1M0

COTEAU-DU-LAC — B1 *Monteregie*

◄ KOA MONTREAL WEST **Ratings: 9/10★/9.5** (Campground) 2015 rates: $42 to $53. Apr 20 to Oct 20. (800)562-9395 171 Rte 338, Coteau-Du-Lac, QC J0P 1B0

COWANSVILLE — B3 *Cantons de l'Est*

↑ CAMPING DOMAINE TOURNESOL **Ratings: 7.5/8.5★/7.5** (Campground) 2015 rates: $38 to $43. Apr 26 to Oct 26. (450)263-9515 327 Chemin Brosseau, Cowansville, QC J2K 3S7

DESCHAILLONS-SUR-SAINT-LAURENT — E5 *Centre du Quebec*

◄ **CAMPING CAP A LA ROCHE Ratings: 8/9★/9.5** (Campground) From Jct of Hwy 20 & exit 253 (Rte 265), N 18 mi on Rte 265 to Rte 132, W 1 mi (R). **FAC:** Gravel rds. (199 spaces). Avail: 108 gravel, 34 pull-thrus (30 x 60), back-ins (25 x 60), 96 full hkups, 5 W, 5 E (30 amps), seasonal sites, WiFi tent sites, showers $, dump, laundry, groc, LP bottles fire rings, firewood, controlled access. **REC:** whirlpool, St Lawrence River: swim, fishing, playground Pet restrict(B). Partial handicap access. 2015 rates $31 to $48.50. May 10 to Oct 19.
(819)292-1212 Lat: 46.549962, Lon: -72.131662
1820 Marie-Victorin, Deschaillons-Sur-Saint-Laurent, QC G0S 1G0
info@capalaroche.com
www.capalaroche.com

DOLBEAU-MISTASSINI — C5 *Saguenay-Lac-Saint-Jean*

↙ CAMPING DES CHUTES (Public) From Jct of Rtes 373 & 169, (in town) S 2 mi on Rte 169 (R). 2015 rates: $20.50 to $30.50. May 16 to Sep 7. (418)276-5675

DRUMMONDVILLE — E5 *Centre du Quebec, Monterigie*

↘ CAMPING DES VOLTIGEURS (Prov Pk) From Jct of Hwy 20 & Exit 181, S 0.6 mi on Exit 181 to Montplaisir St, S 0.4 mi (R). 2015 rates: $34 to $38 May 15 to Sep 7. (819)477-1360

↖ CAMPING LA DETENTE **Ratings: 8/7.5/7.5** (Campground) 2015 rates: $24 to $35. May 15 to Sep 15. (819)478-0651 1580, Fontainebleau, Drummondville, QC J2B 7T5

↗ CAMPING LE DOMAINE DU REPOS **Ratings: 6.5/7.5/6.5** (Campground) 2015 rates: $33 May 1 to Oct 1. (819)478-1758 1400 rue du Repos Drummondville, QC J2B 7T5

DUHAMEL — E3 *Outaouais*

CENTRE TOURISTIQUE DU LAC-SIMON (Prov Pk) 2 km/1-1/4 mi from Duhamel on Hwy 321 N. 2015 rates: $31.75 to $43.50. May 10 to Oct 14. (819)428-7931

EASTMAN — F5 *Cantons de l'Est*

CAMPING DO RE MI **Ratings: 7.5/9★/7.5** (Campground) 2015 rates: $45 to $48. May 15 to Oct 15. (450)297-2983 351 rue Principale, Eastman, QC J0E 1P0

CAMPING LA MINE DE CUIVRE **Ratings: 8/8.5★/8** (Campground) 2015 rates: $40 to $45. May 15 to Oct 15. (450)297-3226 33 Chemin de la Mine de Cuivre, Eastman, QC J0E 1P0

CAMPING LEROUX **Ratings: 5.5/8.5★/8** (Campground) 2015 rates: $46 to $48. May 9 to Oct 15. (450)297-3219 1050 Chemin des Diligences, Eastman, QC J0E 1P0

EVAIN — C1 *Abitibi-Tmiscamingue*

CAMPING AUX PETITS TREMBLES (LAC FLAVRIAN) (Campground) (Phone Update) 2015 rates: $25. Jun 1 to Sep 15. (819)768-3759 3000 rang du Lac Flavrian, Rouyn-Noranda, QC J0Z 1Y1

FERLAND-ET-BOILLEAU — C6 *Saguenay-Lac-Saint-Jean*

DOMAINE DU LAC HA! HA! (MUNICIPAL PARK) (Public) From church at Boilleau: Go 12 km/7-1/2 mi S on Hwy 381. May 19 to Sep 7. (418)676-2373

FORESTVILLE — C7 *Manicouagan*

CAMPING LAC AUX PINS (Campground) (Phone Update) 2015 rates: $20 to $30. Jun 1 to Oct 1. (418)587-6529 1025 Rte. 385, Forestville, QC G0T 1E0

FOSSAMBAULT-SUR-LE-LAC — D6 *Quebec*

PLAGE LAC SAINT-JOSEPH **Ratings: 7/8.5★/9** (Campground) 2015 rates: $53 to $73. Jun 19 to Sep 1. (877)522-3224 7001 Rte de Fossambault, Fossambault-sur-le-Lac, QC G0A 3M0

FRELIGHSBURG — C3 *Cantons de l'Est*

CAMPING DES CHUTES HUNTER **Ratings: 7.5/9★/8** (Campground) 2015 rates: $43 to $46. May 13 to Oct 15. (450)298-5005 18 Chemin des Chutes, Frelighsburg, QC J0J 1C0

CAMPING ECOLOGIQUE DE FRELIGHSBURG **Ratings: 6/7.5/7.5** (Campground) 2015 rates: $30 to $40. May 15 to Sep 15. (450)298-5259 174 Route 237 Sud, Frelighsburg, QC J0J 1C0

GASPE — B10 *Gaspesie*

CAMPING BAIE DE GASPE **Ratings: 6.5/8.5★/7** (Campground) 2015 rates: $24 to $35. Jun 1 to Sep 1. (418)892-5503 2107 Blvd. Grande Greve, Gaspe, QC G4X 6L7

CAMPING DES APPALACHES **Ratings: 8/8.5★/8.5** (Campground) 2015 rates: $28 to $38. Jun 1 to Sep 30. (418)269-7775 367 Montee Riviere Morris, Gaspe, QC G4X 5P7

CAMPING GASPE **Ratings: 7.5/8.5★/7** (Campground) 2015 rates: $28 to $32. Jun 1 to Oct 1. (418)368-4800 1029 Rte. Haldimand, Gaspe, QC G4X 2H7

CAMPING GRIFFON **Ratings: 7.5/8.5★/8.5** (Campground) 2015 rates: $30 to $40. May 1 to Oct 31. (418)892-5938 421 Blvd Griffon, Gaspe, QC G4X 6A1

CAMPING 4 VENTS **Ratings: 3/5/6** (Campground) 2015 rates: $20 to $35. May 1 to Oct 31. (418)892-5256 1986 Blvd Grande Greve, Gaspe, QC G0E 1J0

FORILLON/CAMPING DES ROSIERS (Natl Pk) From town, E 1.5 mi on Rte 132 to access rd (L). 2015 rates: $25.50 to $29.40. Jun 21 to Sep 2. (877)737-3783

FORILLON/PETIT GASPE (Natl Pk) From village of Cap-Aux-Os, W 3 mi on Rte 132 to access rd (R). 2015 rates: $25.50 to $29.40. May 17 to Oct 13. (877)737-3783

FORT RAMSAY CAMPING & MOTELS **Ratings: 6/7/7** (Campground) 2015 rates: $24 to $34. May 15 to Sep 30. (418)368-5094 254 Boul Gaspe, Gaspe, QC G4X 1B1

GRACEFIELD — E3 *Outaouais*

CAMPING PIONNIER **Ratings: 6.5/8.5★/8** (Campground) 2015 rates: $30 to $35. May 1 to Sep 30. (819)463-4163 180 Route 105, Gracefield, QC J0X 1W0

GRANBY — B3 *Cantons de l'Est*

CAMPING BON-JOUR **Ratings: 8/8★/7** (Campground) 2015 rates: $46 to $59. Apr 15 to Oct 15. (450)378-0213 1633 Principale Rte 112, Granby, QC J2G 0M7

CAMPING L'ESTRIVAL-PARKBRIDGE

Ratings: 9/10★/9 (Campground) From Jct of Hwy 10 & Exit 68 (Rte 139), N 5 mi on Rte 139 to Rte 112, W 2.8 mi (L). **FAC:** Paved/gravel rds. (721 spaces). 182 Avail: 20 gravel, 162 grass, 20 pull-thrus (25 x 60), back-ins (30 x 50), 137 full hkups, 45 W, 45 E (30/50 amps), seasonal sites, WiFi $, tent sites, showers $, dump, laundry, groc, LP gas, fire rings, firewood, restaurant, controlled access. **REC:** pool, pond, swim, shuffleboard, playground. Pets OK. Big rig sites, eco-friendly, 2015 rates: $43 to $47. May 1 to Oct 1. ATM.
(450)378-9410 Lat: 45.426518, Lon: -72.819414
1680 Principale Rte 112, Granby, QC J2J 0M6
lestrival@parkbridge.com
www.parkbridge.com/lestrival
See ad pages 1464 (Welcome Section), 1465.

GRAND-MERE — E5 *Mauricie*

LA MAURICIE NATIONAL PARK (RIVIERE-A-LA-PECHE) (Prov Pk) From Hwy 55 (exit 226): Go 16 km/10 mi N. 4-8/10 km/3 mi NW of St-Jean des Piles entrance. 2015 rates: $29.40 to $29.50. May 16 to Oct 13. (819)533-7272

GRAND-REMOUS — D3 *Outaouais*

RESERVE FAUNIQUE LA VERENDRYE OUTAOUAIS-CAMPING LAC RAPIDE (Prov Pk) Hwy 15/Hwy 117N. 2015 rates: $35.77 to $55. May 16 to Sep 8. (819)435-2246

RESERVE FAUNIQUE LA VERENDRYE-OUTAOUAIS-CAMPING DE LA VIEILLE (Prov Pk) Hwy 15N/117N. 2015 rates: $18.76. May 14 Sep 13. (819)438-2017

RESERVE FAUNIQUE LA VERENDRYE-OUTAOUAIS-CAMPING LAC SAVARY (Prov Pk) Hwy 15 N, then at Sainte-Agathe-des-Monts follow 117 N. 2015 rates: $21.10. May 13 to Sep 14. (819)438-2017

GRANDE-VALLEE — B10 *Gaspesie*

CAMPING AU SOLEIL COUCHANT **Ratings: 7.5/7.5/6** (Campground) 2015 rates: $26 to $33. Jun 1 to Sep 30. (418)393-2489 73 St Francois Xavier Est, Grande-Vallee, QC G0E 1K0

HAVELOCK — C2 *Monteregie*

CAMPING GEMEAUX **Ratings: 7.5/9★/8.5** (Campground) 2015 rates: $26 to $34. Apr 15 to Oct 15. (877)826-0193 330 Rang St Charles, Havelock, QC J0S 2C0

DOMAINE FRONTIERE ENCHANTEE **Ratings: 7/8.5★/8.5** (Campground) 2015 rates: $32 to $39. May 1 to Sep 30. (450)826-4490 474 Covey Hill Rd, Havelock, QC J0S 2C0

HEMMINGFORD — C2 *Monteregie*

CANNE DE BOIS DE HEMMINGFORD INC. **Ratings: 8/8★/8** (Campground) 2015 rates: $35 to $45. May 2 to Sep 14. (450)247-2031 306 Rte 219 S, Hemmingford, QC J0L 1H0

HOPE TOWN — C10 *Bonaventure*

CAMPING DES ETOILES **Ratings: 7.5/8★/7.5** (Campground) 2015 rates: $34 to $39. May 17 to Sep 11. (418)752-6553 269 Rte 132, Hope Town, QC G0C 3C1

HUDSON — B1 *Monteregie*

CAMPING D'AOUST Ratings: 8/8/8 (Campground) From Jct of Hwy 40 W & Exit 28 (Rte 342), N 0.6 mi on Rte Harwood W 1.5 mi (L). **FAC:** Paved/gravel rds. (214 spaces). 111 Avail: 30 gravel, 81 grass, 6 pull-thrus (30 x 55), back-ins (25 x 50), mostly side by side hkups, 43 full hkups, 68 W, 45 E (20/30 amps), seasonal sites, WiFi $, tent sites, rentals, dump, laundry, groc, LP gas, fire rings, firewood, restaurant, controlled access. **REC:** pool, playground, rec open to public. Pets OK. Partial handicap access. Eco-friendly, 2015 rates: $39 to $40. Disc: AAA. May 1 to Oct 31.
AAA Approved
(450)458-7301 Lat: 45.440704, Lon: -74.137382
3844 Harwood Route, Hudson, QC J7V 0G1
camping.daoust@qc.aira.com
www.campingdaoust.com

INVERNESS — E6 *Centre du Quebec*

CAMPING INVERNESS **Ratings: 6/8★/7** (Campground) 2015 rates: $30 to $35. May 9 to Sep 8. (418)453-2400 1771 Chemin Gosford Nord, Inverness, QC G0S 1K0

KINNEAR'S MILLS — E6 *Chaudiere-Appalaches*

CAMPING SOLEIL **Ratings: 7.5/8.5★/7.5** (Campground) 2015 rates: $44 to $46. May 9 to Sep 7. (418)424-3372 111 des Eglises Rd, Kinnear's Mills, QC G0N 1K0

L'ANGE GARDIEN (OUTAOUAIS) — B3 *Monteregie*

CAMPING ANGE GARDIEN **Ratings: 8.5/9★/8** (Campground) 2015 rates: $33 to $40. Apr 15 to Oct 31. (819)281-5055 671 Lamarche Rd, L'ange-Gardien, QC J8L 0S1

LE DOMAINE DE L'ANGE GARDIEN **Ratings: 7/8.5★/8** (Campground) 2015 rates: $41 to $49. May 1 to Oct 30. (819)281-0299 1031 Pierre Laporte Rd, L'ange-Gardien, QC J8L 2W7

L'ANGE-GARDIEN — D6 *Quebec*

CAMPING PLAGE FORTIER (K.F.A.) **Ratings: 7/8.5★/7** (Campground) 2015 rates: $35 to $46. May 1 to Sep 15. (888)226-7387 1400 Chemin Lefrancois, L'ange Gardien, QC G0A 2K0

L'ANNONCIATION — E4 *Laurentides*

RESERVE FAUNIQUE/ROUGE MATAWIN-CAMPING LAC DES SUCREREIES (Prov Pk) North on Hwy 117. Pit toilets. 2015 rates: $19.50 to $31.50. May 9 to Nov 2. (819)275-1811

L'ISLET — D7 *Chaudiere-Appalaches*

CAMPING MUNICIPAL ROCHER PANET (Public) From Jct of Hwy 20 & Exit 400 (Rte 285), N 2.3 mi on Rte 285 to Rte 132, E 0.8 mi (L). 2015 rates: $30. May 15 to Oct 15. (418)247-3193

LA CONCEPTION — E4 *Laurentides*

CAMPING LA MONTAGNE D'ARGENT **Ratings: 7/8.5★/8** (Campground) 2015 rates: $37.50 to $50. May 15 to Sep 7. (819)686-5207 PO Box 44, Rte 117 Labelle, Labelle, QC J0T 1H0

CAMPING PARC LA CONCEPTION - PARKBRIDGE

Ratings: 8.5/9.5★/9.5 (Campground) N-Bnd: From Jct of Rtes 117 & 323, N 3.6 mi on Rte 117 to Montagne D'Argent Rd, W 4.2 mi to Rue Des Erables, S 0.3 mi to Rue Des Ormes, SE 1.5 (L). **FAC:** Gravel rds. (227 spaces). Avail: 119 grass, patios, 6 pull-thrus (30 x 55), back-ins (35 x 50), 100 full hkups, 19 W, 19 E (20/30 amps), seasonal sites, WiFi $, tent sites, rentals, showers $, dump, laundry, groc, LP gas, fire rings, firewood, controlled access. **REC:** pool, Riviere Rouge: swim, fishing, shuffleboard, playground. Pet restrict(B) $. Eco-friendly, 2015 rates: $40 to $48. Disc: AAA. May 15 to Oct 12.
(819)686-5596 Lat: 46.12909, Lon: -74.69171
1158 Chemin Des Ormes, La Conception, QC J0T 1M0
parclaconception@parkbridge.com
www.parkbridge.com/laconception
See ad pages 1464 (Welcome Section), 1465.

LA DORE — C5 *Saguenay-Lac-Saint-Jean*

RESERVE FAUNIQUE ASHUAPMUSHUAN CAMPING LAC CHIBOUBICHE (Prov Pk) From Road 175 N & Hwy 169: Go 33 km on Hwy 167. May 24 to Oct 28. (418)256-3806

LA MALBAIE — D7 *Charlevoix*

CAMPING AU BORD DE LA RIVIERE **Ratings: 8/8.5★/8.5** (Campground) 2015 rates: $41 to $47. May 15 to Oct 13. (418)665-9999 1510 Boul de Comporte, La Malbaie, QC G5A 1M8

CAMPING CHUTES FRASER **Ratings: 7/8.5★/7.5** (Campground) 2015 rates: $35 to $44. May 11 to Oct 21. (418)665-2151 500 Chemin De La Vallee, La Malbaie, QC G5A 1C2

VILLAS ET CAMPING DES ERABLES **Ratings: 4/8★/7** (Campground) 2015 rates: $25 to $30. Jun 1 to Sep 9. (418)665-4212 635 Cote Bellevue, La Malbaie, QC G5A 3B2

LA TUQUE — D5 *Mauricie*

LA TUQUE MUNICIPAL CAMPGROUND (Public) In town at Hwy 155 N. 2015 rates: $28 to $39. (819)523-4561

LABELLE — E4 *Laurentides*

CAMPING CHUTES AUX IROQUOIS **Ratings: 8.5/10★/8.5** (Campground) 2015 rates: $38 to $51. May 1 to Sep 28. (819)686-2337 36 du Camping, Labelle, QC J0T 1H0

Things change ... last year's rates serve as a guideline only.

QC

LAC-A-LA-CROIX — C6 *Saguenay-Lac-Saint-Jean*

CAMPING VILLA DES SABLES (Campground) (Phone Update) 2015 rates: $28 to $45. May 28 to Sep 12. (418)345-2655 60 Chemin 10, Rte 170 Est, Metabetchouan-Lac-a-la-Croix, QC G8G 1P1

LAC-AUX-SABLES — D5 *Mauricie*

CAMPING LAC-AUX-SABLES **Ratings: 7.5/8.5★/8** (Campground) 2015 rates: $34 to $42. May 18 to Sep 18. (418)365-8282 200 rue Sainte-Marie, Lac-Aux-Sables, QC G0X 1M0

LAC-BROME — F5 *Monteregie*

CAMPING FAIRMOUNT **Ratings: 6.5/8/7** (Campground) 2015 rates: $33 to $36. May 9 to Sep 21. (450)266-0928 127 Chemin Fairmount, Lac-Brome, QC J0E 1K0

DOMAINE DES ERABLES **Ratings: 6.5/8.5★/7.5** (Campground) 2015 rates: $37 to $45. May 15 to Sep 15. (450)242-8888 688 Bondville (Foster), Lac Brome, QC J0E 1R0

LAC-DES-PLAGES — E4 *Outaouais*

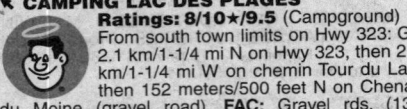

CAMPING LAC DES PLAGES
Ratings: 8/10★/9.5 (Campground) From south town limits on Hwy 323: Go 2.1 km/1-1/4 mi N on Hwy 323, then 2.2 km/1-1/4 mi W on chemin Tour du Lac, then 152 meters/500 feet N on Chenail du Moine (gravel road). **FAC:** Gravel rds. (134 spaces). Avail: 74 gravel, back-ins (25 x 45), 51 full hkups, 23 W, 23 E (30 amps), seasonal sites, WiFi Hotspot, tent sites, rentals, dump, laundry, groc, LP gas, fire rings, firewood, controlled access. **REC:** pool, Lake Papoeau: swim, fishing, shuffleboard, playground. Pet restrict(B/Q). Eco-friendly, 2015 rates: $35 to $52. May 15 to Oct 12.
(819)426-2576 Lat: 46.00882, Lon: -74.89996
10 Chenail du Moine, Lac-Des-Plages, QC J0T 1K0
www.lacdesplages.com

LAC-KENOGAMI — C6 *Saguenay-Lac-Saint-Jean*

CENTRE TOURISTIQUE DU LAC KENOGAMI (Prov Pk) From jct Hwy 175 & Hwy 169: Go N on Hwy 169. 2015 rates: $28.75 to $47.25. Jun 13 to Sep 1. (418)344-1142

LAC-MEGANTIC — E6 *Cantons de l'Est*

CAMPING BAIE DES SABLES (Public) From town, W 2 mi on Hwy 161 to Hwy 263, S 0.5 mi to Marsboro (L). 2015 rates: $30 to $41. May 9 to Oct 14. (819)583-3965

LACOLLE — C2 *Monteregie*

CAMPING GREGOIRE **Ratings: 7/8/8** (Campground) 2015 rates: $37 to $44. May 15 to Sep 15. (450)246-3385 347 Rte 221, Lacolle, QC J0J 1J0

LAMBTON — E6 *Cantons de l'Est*

PARC NATIONAL DE FRONTENAC, BAIE SAUVAGE (Prov Pk) From Hwy 112 or 108. 2015 rates: $26 to $35. May 16 to Oct 12. (418)486-2300

LATERRIERE — C6 *Saguenay-Lac-Saint-Jean*

DOMAINE DE VACANCES LA ROCAILLE (Campground) (Phone Update) 2015 rates: $22 to $45. May 30 to Sep 14. (418)678-2657 7894 Portage des Roches Nord, Laterriere, QC G7N 2A1

LES ESCOUMINS — C7 *Manicouagan*

CAMPING LE TIPI (Campground) (Phone Update) 2015 rates: $27 to $48. May 23 to Sep 7. (888)868-6666 46 De La Reserve, Les Escoumins, QC G0T 1K0

LES MECHINS — B9 *Bas-Saint-Laurent*

CAMPING AUX PIGNONS VERTS **Ratings: 4.5/8★/7** (Campground) 2015 rates: $26 to $34. May 1 to Sep 30. (418)729-3423 218 Rte Bellevue est, Les Mechins, QC G0T 1T0

LEVIS — D6 *Chaudiere-Appalaches*

CAMPING DU FORT DE LA MARTINIERE **Ratings: 6/8.5★/6** (Campground) 2015 rates: $30 to $45. Apr 15 to Oct 15. (418)835-9060 9825 Boul de la Rivesud (132), Levis, QC G6V 9R4

CAMPING LA JOLIE ROCHELLE **Ratings: 9.5/10★/9.5** (RV Park) 2015 rates: $52. May 15 to Sep 15. (418)243-1320 135 Petite Troisieme, Saint-Raphael, QC G0R 4C0

CAMPING TRANSIT
Ratings: 9/10★/9.5 (Campground) E-bnd: From Jct of Hwy 20 & Exit 330 (Rte Lallemand/Chemin St-Roch), E 2.5 mi on Chemin St-Roch, follow signs (L); or W-bnd: From Jct of Hwy 20 & Exit 337 (Rte 279), S 0.5 mi on Rte 279 to Chemin St-Roch Rd, W 2 mi (R). **FAC:** Paved/gravel rds. (217 spaces). Avail: 157 gravel, 105 pull-thrus (40 x 70), back-ins (30 x 50), 101 full hkups, 56 W, 56 E (30/50 amps), seasonal sites, WiFi $, tent sites, showers $, dump, laundry, groc, LP bottles, fire rings, firewood, restaurant, controlled access. **REC:** pool, wading pool, whirlpool, pond, shuffleboard, playground. Pets OK. Partial handicap access. Big rig sites, 2015 rates: $45 to $55. Apr 15 to Oct 30.
(418)838-0948 Lat: 46.812179, Lon: -71.051488
600 Chemin St. Roch, Levis, QC G6Y 0W3
info@campingtransit.com
www.campingtransit.com
See ad this page.

MADELEINE-CENTRE — B10 *La Cote-de Gaspe*

CAMPING BEL-AIR **Ratings: 6/8.5★/7** (Campground) 2015 rates: $20 to $32. May 15 to Sep 30. (418)281-3449 99 Rte Principale, Madeleine-Centre, QC G0E 1P0

MAGOG — F5 *Cantons de l'Est*

CAMPING MAGOG-ORFORD **Ratings: 7/8.5★/8** (Campground) 2015 rates: $39 to $41. May 1 to Oct 31. (819)843-2500 611 Alfred Desrochers, Orford, QC J1X 6J4

DOMAINE PARC-ESTRIE - PARKBRIDGE
Ratings: 8.5/10★/10 (Campground) From Jct of Hwy 10 & Exit 123 (Rte 112), W 0.25 mi on Rte 112 and follow signs (L). **FAC:** Paved/gravel rds. (388 spaces). Avail: 150 gravel, patios, 12 pull-thrus (35 x 70), back-ins (40 x 60), 80 full hkups, 70 W, 70 E (15/30 amps), seasonal sites, WiFi $, tent sites, rentals, showers $, dump, laundry, groc, LP bottles, fire rings, firewood, controlled access. **REC:** heated pool, wading pool, pond, fishing, shuffleboard, playground. Pet restrict Partial handicap access. Eco-friendly, 2015 rates: $40 to $46. Apr 24 to Oct 24.
(819)868-6944 Lat: 45.29380, Lon: -72.10290
19 Rue du Domaine, Magog, QC J1X 5Z3
parcestrie@parkbridge.com
www.parkbridge.com/parcestrie
See ad pages 1464 (Welcome Section), 1465.

MASHTEUIATSH — C5 *Saguenay-Lac-Saint-Jean*

CAMPING PLAGE ROBERTSON (Campground) (Phone Update) 2015 rates: $28 to $38. May 30 to Oct 8. (418)275-1375 2202 Rue Ouiatchouan, Mashteuiatsh, QC G0W 2H0

MATANE — C8 *Gaspesie*

CAMPING PARC SIROIS LA BALEINE **Ratings: 6.5/8.5★/7** (Campground) 2015 rates: $19 to $28. Jun 1 to Oct 1. (866)876-2242 2345 Ave Du Phare Ouest, Matane, QC G4W 3M6

RESERVE FAUNIQUE DE MATANE ET DE DUNIERE/CAMPING ETANG A LA TRUITE (Prov Pk) Hwy I-20 E & 195 S. 2015 rates: $28 to $46.50. Jun 8 to Sep 3. (418)562-3700

RESERVE FAUNIQUE DE MATANE/CAMPING JOHN (Prov Pk) From jct Hwy 132 & Hwy 195: Go S on Hwy 195. 2015 rates: $27.50 to $42.75. Jun 8 to Sep 3. (418)224-3345

MELBOURNE — E5 *Cantons de l'Est*

CAMPING MELBOURNE 2000 **Ratings: 7.5/8.5★/8** (Campground) 2015 rates: $36 to $38. May 5 to Oct 1. (819)826-6222 1185 Belmont St, Melbourne, QC J0B 2B0

MERCIER — B2 *Nord du Quebec*

DOMAINE DU BEL AGE **Ratings: 6/7★/6** (Campground) 2015 rates: $39 to $48. May 1 to Oct 31. (450)691-0306 475 St Jean Baptiste, Mercier, QC J6R 2A9

A campground rating is based on ALL facilities available at the park.

METIS-SUR-MER — C8 *Bas-Saint-Laurent*

CAMPING ANNIE
Ratings: 9/10★/9.5 (Campground) From Jct of Rtes 132 & 234, E 6 mi on Rte 132 (R). **FAC:** All weather rds. (165 spaces). 125 Avail: 25 gravel, 100 grass, 6 pull-thrus (30 x 60), back-ins (30 x 50), 72 full hkups, 53 W, 53 E (15/30 amps), seasonal sites, cable, WiFi, tent sites, rentals, showers $, dump, laundry, groc, LP bottles, fire rings, firewood, controlled access. **REC:** heated pool, St Lawrence River: playground. Pets OK. Partial handicap access. 2015 rates: $38 to $42.75. Jun 1 to Oct 1.
(418)936-3825 Lat: 48.67079, Lon: -68.03552
394 Rte 132, Metis-Sur-Mer, QC G0J 1S0
info@campingunion.com
www.campingunion.com

MIRABEL — A2 *Laurentides*

CAMPING MIRABEL **Ratings: 8/9★/7.5** (Campground) 2015 rates: $57 to $60. May 1 to Oct 31. (450)475-7725 8500 Chemin Bourgeois, Mirabel, QC J7N 2K1

MISTASSINI — C5 *Saguenay-Lac-Saint-Jean*

CAMPING ST-LOUIS (Campground) (Phone Update) 2015 rates: $35 to $41. May 16 to Sep 15. (418)276-4670 543 Rang St Louis, Dolbeau-Mistassini, QC G8L 5H6

MONT-BRUN — C1 *Abitibi-Tmiscamingue*

PARC NATIONAL AIGUEBELLE/CAMPING ABIJEVIS (Prov Pk) From Hwy 117-111 or 101 Follow signs. 2015 rates: $27.25 to $36.50. May 17 to Oct 14. (819)637-2480

MONT-LOUIS — B9 *Gaspesie*

CAMPING PARC ET MER MONT LOUIS (Public) 2015 rates: $28.88 to $31.31. May 18 to Oct 11. (418)797-5270

MONT-SAINT-PIERRE — B9 *Gaspesie*

CAMPING MUNICIPAL MONT SAINT PIERRE (Public) In town, From Jct of Rte 132 & Pierre-Godefroi Coulombe St., S 1.4 mi on PG Coulombe St (L) 2015 rates: $21 to $30. Jun 10 to Sep 16. (418)797-2250

MONT-TREMBLANT — E4 *Lanaudiere*

CAMPING DE LA DIABLE **Ratings: 8/8.5★/8** (Campground) 2015 rates: $36 to $45. May 15 to Oc 12. (819)425-5501 140 Regimbald St, Mont-Trem blant, QC J8E 3C5

PARC DU MONT-TREMBLANT/SECTEUR DE LA DIABLE (Prov Pk) From Jct of Hwy 117 & loca rd (St Faustin exit), N 14 mi on paved local rd, follow signs (R). 2015 rates: $38. May 12 to Oct 9. (819)688 2281

PARC NATIONAL DU MONT-TREMBLANT/LAC CACHE (Prov Pk) From Hwy 117-125-329 or 343 Jun 21 to Sep 2. (877)688-2289

MONTEBELLO — E3 *Outaouais*

AUBERGE MONTEBELLO CAMPING & MARINA (Prov Pk) From jct Hwy 148 & rue Laurier in town: G 152 m/500 feet S on rue Laurier. May 15 to Oct 15 (877)423-0001

MONTMAGNY — D6 *Chaudiere-Appalaches*

CAMPING DES ERABLES **Ratings: 8/10★/8.** (Campground) 2015 rates: $31 to $34. May 15 to Se 10. (418)248-8953 860 Boul Tacheouest PO Bo 512, Montmagny, QC G5V 3R8

CAMPING POINTE AUX OIES **Rat ings: 9/10★/9.5** (Campground) 2015 rates: $31 t $40. May 9 to Oct 20. (418)248-9710 45 Bassin Nor Ave, Montmagny, QC G5V 4E5

MONTPELLIER — E3 *Outaouais*

RESERVE FAUNIQUE DE PAPINEAU LABELLE/LAC ECHO (Prov Pk) From jct Hwy 148 Hwy 315: Go N on Hwy 315 to Montpellier (Accue Mulet). (819)454-2011

Our rating system isn't just tough, it thorough. We know the kinds of things tha are important to you — like clean restroom and showers, attractive, secure, well-tende grounds, and extras like swimming pools. W give the first rating for development facilities, the second for cleanliness an physical characteristics of restrooms an showers, and the third for visual appearanc

We rate what RVers consider important.

MONTREAL — B2 *Montreal*

MONTREAL AREA MAP

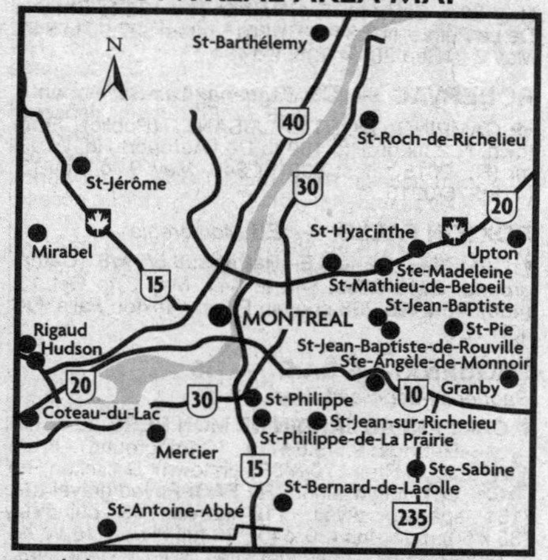

Symbols on map indicate towns within a 80 km/50 mile radius of Montreal where campgrounds are listed. Check listings for more information.

See also Coteau-du-Lac, Granby, Hudson, Mercier, Mirabel, Rigaud, St-Antoine-Abbe, St-Barthelemy, St-Bernard-de-Lacolle, St-Hyacinthe, St-Jean-Baptiste, St-Jean-Baptiste-de-Rouville, St-Jean-sur-Richelieu, St-Jerome, St-Mathieu-de-Beloeil, St-Philippe, St-Philippe-de-La Prairie, St-Pie, St-Roch-de-Richelieu, Ste-Angele-de-Monnoir, Ste-Madeleine, Ste-Sabine & Upton.

NEUVILLE — D6 *Quebec*

CAMPING L'EGARE **Ratings: 5.5/6.5/6.5** (Campground) 2015 rates: $28 to 35. May 10 to Oct 15. (418)876-3359 1069 Rte 138 Ouest, Neuville, QC G0A 2R0

NEW CARLISLE — C10 *Gaspesie*

CAMPING LE MOULIN ROUGE **Ratings: 6/8★/7** (Campground) 2015 rates: $28 to $35. May 30 to Sep 30. (418)752-2724 PO Box 36/11 Green St, New Carlisle, QC G0C 1Z0

NICOLET — E5 *Bois, Centre du Quebec, Francs, Mauricie*

CAMPING PORT ST FRANCOIS **Ratings: 8.5/8.5★/8** (Campground) 2015 rates: $38 to $40. May 1 to Oct 15. (819)293-5091 25 Des Bains, Nicolet, QC J3T 1P9

NORMANDIN — C5 *Saguenay-Lac-Saint-Jean*

CAMPING CHUTE A L'OURS (Public) From Jct of Rte 169 & Du Rocher Ave, W 2 mi on Du Rocher Ave to Rang 4, S 4 mi to LS-Ovide Bouchard Rd, W 1.75 mi (E). Follow signs. 2015 rates: $24 to $35. Jun 14 to Sep 9. (418)274-3411

NOTRE-DAME-DE-LA-SALETTE — E3 *Outaouais*

ROYAL PAPINEAU - PARKBRIDGE
Ratings: 9/9.5★/9 (Campground) From Rte 309 (in town), N 8 mi on Thomas Rd S (E). **FAC:** Paved/gravel rds. (292 spaces). Avail: 51 gravel, patios, 18 pull-thrus (35 x 60), back-ins (40 x 60), 47 full hkups, 4 W, 4 E (30/50 amps), seasonal sites, WiFi, tent sites, rentals, showers $, dump, laundry, groc, LP bottles, fire rings, firewood, restaurant, controlled access. **REC:** pool, Lac De L'Argile: swim, fishing, playground. Pet restrict(Q). Partial handicap access. Big rig sites, eco-friendly, 2015 rates: $50 to $54. May 1 to Oct 15.
(819)766-2826 Lat: 45.84028, Lon: -75.53877
237 Chemin Du Golf, Notre Dame De La Salette, QC J0X 2L0
royalpapineau@parkbridge.com
www.parkbridge.com/royalpapineau
See ad pages 1464 (Welcome Section), 1465.

NOTRE-DAME-DES-PINS — E6 *Chaudiere-Appalaches*

CAMPING LA ROCHE D'OR - PARKBRIDGE
Ratings: 9/9.5★/9 (Campground) From St-Georges De Beauce, N 5 mi on Rte 173 (R). **FAC:** All weather rds. (320 spaces). Avail: 188 all weather, 2 pull-thrus (26 x 45), back-ins (26 x 45), 124 full hkups, 61 W, 61 E (30 amps), seasonal sites, WiFi Hotspot, tent sites, dump, laundry, groc, LP gas, fire rings, firewood, restaurant, controlled access. **REC:** pool, Gilbert Stream: playground, rec open to public. Pets OK. Partial handicap access. 2015 rates: $45. May 10 to Sep 15.
(418)774-9191 Lat: 46.18510, Lon: -70.70757
3005 Rte 173, Notre-Dame-Des-Pins, QC G0M 1K0
larochedor@parkbridge.com
www.parkbridge.com/larochedor
See ad pages 1464 (Welcome Section), 1465.

NOTRE-DAME-DU-LAC — D8 *Bas-Saint-Laurent*

CAMPING MUNICIPAL NOTRE DAME DU LAC (Public) From Jct of Rte 185 & exit 29 (N.D. Du Lac), E 0.5 mi on Rue de l'Eglise to Rue Commerciale, S 0.6 mi (L). 2015 rates: $20 to $40. May 15 to Oct 1. (418)899-6820

NOTRE-DAME-DU-MONT-CARMEL — E5 *Mauricie*

CAMPING LAC MORIN **Ratings: 5.5/8.5★/7.5** (Campground) 2015 rates: $40 to $43. May 15 to Oct 31. (819)376-1479 1430 Rang Saint-Flavien, Notre-Dame-du-Mont-Carmel, QC G0X 3J0

CAMPING PARADISO **Ratings: 7.5/8.5★/8.5** (Campground) 2015 rates: $44 to $47. May 15 to Sep 15. (819)375-1569 1281 Rang St-Flavien, Notre Dame du Mont Carmel, QC G0X 3J0

NOUVELLE — C9 *Gaspesie*

CAMPING L'ERABLIERE **Ratings: 3.5/5/5.5** (Campground) 2015 rates: $24. May 10 to Oct 10. (418)794-2913 28 Rte Miguasha Est, Nouvelle, QC G0C 2E0

OKA — B1 *Laurentides*

PARC NATIONAL D'OKA (Prov Pk) From Jct of Hwys 13 & 640, W 9.4 mi on Hwy 640 (E) (park entrance). 2015 rates: $28.50 to $42. (450)479-8365

ORFORD — F5 *Cantons de l'Est*

PARC NATIONAL DU MONT-ORFORD/CAMPING LAC STUKELY (Prov Pk) From I-10 or Hwy 220, follow signs. 2015 rates: $29 to $44.75. May 9 to Oct 12. (819)843-9855

PERCE — C10 *Gaspesie*

BAIE DE PERCE (Prov Pk) In center of town, W 1 mi on Rte 132 (L). 2015 rates: $29 to $38. May 31 to Sep 2. (418)782-5102

CAMPING AU PANORAMA DE PERCE **Ratings: 7.5/8/6.5** (Campground) 2015 rates: $32 to $45. May 1 to Oct 1. (418)782-2208 (Cp 250) 382 Rte 132 Ouest, Perce, QC G0C 2L0

CAMPING COTE SURPRISE **Ratings: 6/8.5★/7** (Campground) 2015 rates: $35 to $48. May 1 to Oct 30. (418)782-5443 335 Rte 132 (C.p. 296), Perce, QC G0C 2L0

CAMPING DU PHARE A PERCE **Ratings: 7/9.5★/8.5** (Campground) 2015 rates: $28 to $70. May 1 to Oct 15. (877)332-5588 385 Rte 132 Ouest, Perce, QC G0C 2L0

CAMPING DU VILLAGE **Ratings: 6/8.5★/6.5** (Campground) 2015 rates: $35 to $40. May 1 to Sep 30. (418)782-2020 230 Rte 132 Ouest, Perce, QC G0C 2L0

CAMPING HAVRE DE LA NUIT **Ratings: 7/8.5★/7.5** (RV Park) 2015 rates: $30 to $40. May 15 to Sep 30. (418)782-2924 16 Biard St (C.p. 424), Perce, QC G0C 2L0

CHALETS & CAMPING NATURE OCEAN **Ratings: 6.5/8.5★/7.5** (Campground) 2015 rates: $28 to $42. May 20 to Sep 20. (418)782-2400 400 Rte 132 Ouest, Perce, QC G0C 2L0

PLAISANCE — E3 *Outaouais*

PARC NATIONAL DE PLAISANCE (Natl Forest) On Hwy 148, follow signs 8 km/5mi. (819)427-5334

PLESSISVILLE — E6 *Centre du Quebec*

CAMPING MON PLAISIR **Ratings: 7.5/8★/7.5** (Campground) 2015 rates: $30 to $47. May 11 to Sep 10. (819)362-7591 149 Sainte-Sophie Rd, Plessisville, QC G6L 2Y2

POINTE-A-LA-CROIX — C9 *Gaspesie*

CAMPING LA MAISON VERTE DU PARC GASPESIEN **Ratings: 6.5/8.5★/7** (Campground) 2015 rates: $25 to $30. Apr 13 to Nov 14. (418)788-2342 79 Rue Des Meandres, Pointe-A-La-Croix, QC G0C 1L0

POINTE-AUX-OUTARDES — B8 *Cote-Nord*

CAMPING PARC DE LA RIVE (Campground) (Phone Update) 2015 rates: $24 to $30. Jun 1 to Sep 7. (418)567-4021 197 Chemin de la Baie, Les Buissons, QC G0H 1H0

POINTE-CALUMET — B2 *Laurentides*

CAMPING L'ESCALE (Campground) (Phone Update) 2015 rates: $38 to $50. Apr 15 to Oct 15. (450)472-6789 880 - Rue Andre Soucy St., Pointe-Calumet, QC J0N 1G2

POINTE-LEBEL — B8 *Cote-Nord*

CAMPING DE LA MER (Campground) (Phone Update) 2015 rates: $32 to $35. May 15 to Oct 10. (418)589-6576 72 Rue Chounard, Baie-Comeau, QC G0H 1N0

PONT-ROUGE — D6 *Quebec*

UN AIR D'ETE 2005 **Ratings: 8.5/10★/8.5** (Campground) 2015 rates: $33 to $42. May 1 to Oct 1. (877)873-4791 459 Rte Grand Capsa (Rt 358), Pont-Rouge, QC G3H 1L3

PORT-CARTIER — A9 *Cote-Nord*

CAMPING LE PARADIS (Public) From Jct of Rte 138 & Boul Portage des Mousses (E end of town), S 0.2 mi, follow signs (R). 2015 rates: $30. Jun 7 to Sep 21. (418)766-7137

RESERVE FAUNIQUE DE PORT-CARTIER-SEPT-ILES/CAMPING LAC WALKER (Prov Pk) From Hwy 138 E follow sign for Reserve. 2015 rates: $27.50 to $39.25. May 31 to Sep 1. (418)766-4743

PORT-DANIEL — C10 *Gaspesie*

RESERVE FAUNIQUE DE/CAMPING PORT-DANIEL (Prov Pk) In town, at church: Go 1 km/3/4 mi E on Hwy 132. 2015 rates: $30.75 to $49.25. May 31 to Sep 28. (418)396-2789

PORTNEUF — D6 *Quebec*

QC

CAMPING PANORAMIQUE - PARKBRIDGE
Ratings: 8.5/10★/9.5 (Campground) From Jct of Hwy 40 & Exit 261 (Rte 138), S E 0.5 mi on exit Rd to Rte 138, W 0.5 mi to Francois Gignac Rd, N 0.25 mi (L). **FAC:** Paved/gravel rds. (608 spaces). Avail: 58 gravel, 10 pull-thrus (50 x 70), back-ins (50 x 50), 52 full hkups (30/50 amps), seasonal sites, WiFi $, tent sites, showers $, dump, laundry, groc, LP bottles, fire rings, firewood, restaurant, controlled access. **REC:** pool, golf, playground. Pets OK. Partial handicap access. Big rig sites, eco-friendly, 2015 rates: $50. May 1 to Oct 15.
(418)286-3655 Lat: 46.686816, Lon: -71.902359
464 Francois-Gignac Rd, Portneuf, QC G0A 2Y0
panoramique@parkbridge.com
www.parkbridge.com/panoramique
See ad pages 1464 (Welcome Section), 1465.

RIVIERE FAUNIQUE DE PORTNEUF/CAMPING LAC BELLEVUE (Prov Pk) From Hwy 40 (exit 281): Go N on Hwy 365 to Saint-Raymond, then NW on Hwy 367 to Wildlife Reserve. Pit toilets. 2015 rates: $19.50 to $30.75. Jun 13 to Sep 1. (418)323-2021

Remember, ratings are based on ALL available facilities.

PRINCEVILLE — E6 *Centre du Quebec*

CAMPING PLAGE DES SABLES **Ratings: 6.5/8.5★/6.5** (Campground) 2015 rates: $37 to $41. May 8 to Sep 7. (819)364-5769 1444 Route 116 Ouest, Princeville, QC G6L 4K7

QUARTIER CABANO — D7
Bas-Saint-Laurent

CAMPING CABANO Ratings: 8.5/10★/8.5 (RV Park) From Hwy 20 E to Hwy 185 S toward NB. Exit 40 turn R twice. Park on L. From NB Hwy 185 N Exit 40, turn L then R (L). **FAC:** Gravel rds. (150 spaces). Avail: 110 gravel, 2 pull-thrus (25 x 65), back-ins (27 x 53), some side by side hkups, 100 full hkups, 10 W, 10 E (15/30 amps), seasonal sites, WiFi, tent sites, dump, laundry, groc, LP bottles, fire rings, firewood, restaurant, controlled access. **REC:** heated pool, Ruisseau Bernard: fishing, playground. Pets OK. 2015 rates: $32 to $35. Disc: AAA. Apr 1 to Nov 1.
(418)854-9133 Lat: 47.68040, Lon: -68.90472
1155 Ch du Golf Quartier Cabano, Quartier Cabano, QC G0L 1E0
campingcabano@gmail.com
www.campingcabano.com

QUEBEC CITY — D6 *Quebec*

QUEBEC CITY AREA MAP

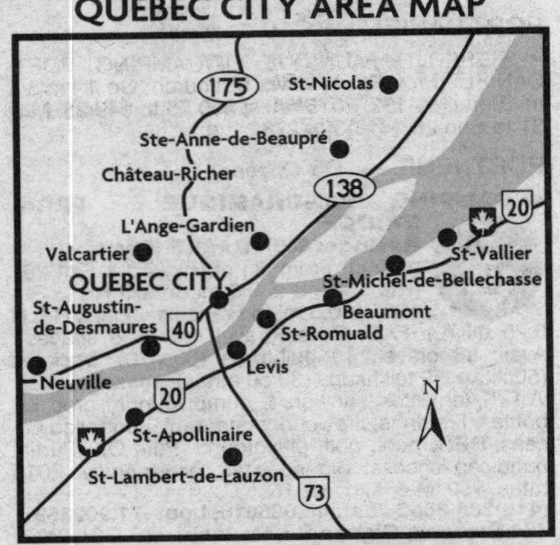

Symbols on map indicate towns within a 80 km/50 mile radius of Quebec City where campgrounds are listed. Check listings for more information.

See also Beaumont, Chateau-Richer, L'Ange-Gardien, Levis, Neuville, St-Apollinaire, St-Augustin-de-Desmaures, St-Lambert-de-Lauzon, St-Michel-de-Bellechasse, St-Nicolas, St-Romuald, St-Vallier, Ste-Anne-de-Beaupre & Valcartier.

CAMPING DE LA JOIE **Ratings: 8/8/7** (Campground) 2015 rates: $30 to $42. May 15 to Sep 15. (877)849-2264 640 Georges Muir, Quebec City, QC G2N 2H3

CAMPING MUNICIPAL DE BEAUPORT (Public) From Jct of Hwy 40 & Exit 321 (Boul Raymond)), E 0.1 mi on Yves Prevost St to Boul Raymond (Labelle St), N 2 mi to Boul Louis XIV, E 0.5 mi, follow signs (L). 2015 rates: $36 to $44. Jun 6 to Sep 1. (418)641-6112

CAMPING QUEBEC EN VILLE **Ratings: 8.5/6/7.5** (Campground) 2015 rates: $35 to $48. May 1 to Oct 31. (418)871-1574 2050 Rte De L'aeroport, Quebec, QC G2E 3L9

PARC NATIONAL RUSTIQUE DE LA JACQUES-CARTIER SECTEUR DE LA PALLIC (Prov Pk) On Hwy 175 N. (418)848-3169

RESERVE FAUNIQUE DES LAURENTIDES-CAMPING LA LOUTRE (Prov Pk) On 175 N. 2015 rates: $30.75 to $42.75. May 23 to Aug 30. (418)846-2201

RACINE — E5 *Cantons de l'Est*

CAMPING PLAGE MCKENZIE **Ratings: 7.5/8.5★/8** (Campground) 2015 rates: $39 to $45. May 8 to Sep 15. (819)846-2011 842 Rte 222, Racine, QC J0E 1Y0

RAWDON — A2 *Lanaudiere*

CAMPING PARC ENSOLEILLE 2002 INC. **Ratings: 7.5/7/7** (Campground) 2015 rates: $35 to $45. May 9 to Oct 1. (450)834-3332 3163 1E Ave, Rawdon, QC J0K 1S0

RIGAUD — B1 *Monteregie*

CAMPING CHOISY
Ratings: 9/10★/9 (Campground) From Jct of Hwy 40 & Exit 17 (Rte 201), S 1.8 mi on Hwy 201 (L). **FAC:** All weather rds. (430 spaces). Avail: 92 grass, 13 pull-thrus (30 x 45), back-ins (30 x 45), some side by side hkups, 49 full hkups, 35 W, 35 E (30/50 amps), seasonal sites, WiFi Hotspot, tent sites, rentals, dump, laundry, groc, LP gas, fire rings, firewood, restaurant, controlled access. **REC:** heated pool, wading pool, whirlpool, River Raquette: shuffleboard, playground. Pets OK. Partial handicap access. Eco-friendly. 2015 rates: $46 to $53. May 1 to Sep 15.
(450)458-4900 Lat: 45.433975, Lon: -74.234730
209 Rte 201, Rigaud, QC J0P 1P0
info@campingchoisy.com
www.campingchoisy.com

CAMPING TRANS-CANADIEN **Ratings: 7.5/8.5★/7.5** (Campground) 2015 rates: $39 to $44. May 1 to Oct 30. (514)867-4515 960 Chemin de la Baie, Rigaud, QC J0P 1P0

RIMOUSKI — C8 *Bas-Saint-Laurent*

CAMPING & MOTEL DE L'ANSE **Ratings: 7.5/8.5★/8.5** (Campground) 2015 rates: $38 to $51. May 1 to Oct 14. (418)721-0322 1105 Boul St-Germain, Rimouski, QC G5L 8Y9

RESERVE FAUNIQUE DE RIMOUSKI/CAMPING LAC RIMOUSKI (Prov Pk) From jct Hwy 20 & Hwy 232: Go E on Hwy 232. 2015 rates: $27.50 to $45.75. May 23 to Sep 1. (418)735-5672

RIVIERE-DU-LOUP — C7 *Bas-Saint-Laurent*

CAMPING DU QUAI Ratings: 8.5/9.5★/8.5 (Campground) From Jct of Hwy 20 & exit 507 (Boul. Cartier), N 1000 ft on Boul. Cartier to Rue De L'Ancrage, W 0.5 mi (R). **FAC:** Gravel rds. (150 spaces). Avail: 115 gravel, 37 pull-thrus (30 x 65), back-ins (30 x 50), 80 full hkups, 16 W, 16 S (30/50 amps), seasonal sites, WiFi, tent sites, rentals, dump, laundry, groc, LP bottles, fire rings, firewood. **REC:** heated pool, whirlpool, playground. Pets OK. Partial handicap access. Big rig sites, 2015 rates: $30 to $38. May 6 to Sep 30.
AAA Approved
(418)860-3111 Lat: 47.85521, Lon: -69.55537
70 Rue de L'ancrage (70), Riviere-du-Loup, QC G5R 6B1
info@campingduquai.com
www.campingduquai.com

CAMPING MUNICIPAL DE LA POINTE (Public) From Jct of Hwy 20 & exit 507 (Boul. Cartier), NE 0.5 mi on Boul. Cartier (L). 2015 rates: $23 to $38.50. May 9 to Sep 22. (418)862-4281

RIVIERE-ETERNITE — C6
Saguenay-Lac-Saint-Jean

PARC NATIONAL DU SAGUENAY, BAIE-ETERNITE (Prov Pk) From Hwy 138 & Hwy 170: Go NE on Hwy 170 to Riviere Eternite. 2015 rates: $29 to $38.25. May 16 to Oct 13. (877)272-1556

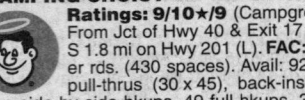

RV Park ratings you can rely on!

RIVIERE-OUELLE — D7 *Bas-Saint-Laurent*

CAMPING RIVIERE-OUELLE (Public) From Jct of Hwy 20 & Exit 444, E 1.4 mi on Rte 132 to Chemin De La Pointe, N 2.3 mi (R). 2015 rates: $27.90 to $40. May 2 to Sep 28. (418)856-1484

ROBERVAL — C5 *Saguenay-Lac-Saint-Jean*

CAMPING MONT PLAISANT (Public) From town, N 2 mi on Rte 169 to De l'Aeroport Rd, W 0.6 mi (R). 2015 rates: $30 to $40. May 9 to Oct 13. (418)275-0910

ROXTON FALLS — E5 *Monteregie*

CAMPING DE L'ILE **Ratings: 8.5/9★/8** (Campground) 2015 rates: $40 to $41. May 3 to Oct 13. (450)548-2495 238 chemin Pepin, Roxton Falls, QC J0H 1E0

SAGUENAY-LA BAIE — C6
Saguenay-Lac-Saint-Jean

CAMPING AU JARDIN DE MON PERE
Ratings: 9.5/9.5★/10 (Campground) From Jct of Rtes 170 & 381 (in town), S 1 mi on Rte 381, follow signs (R). **FAC:** Paved/gravel rds. (151 spaces). Avail: 112 gravel, 13 pull-thrus (35 x 50), back-ins (30 x 40), 96 full hkups, 16 W, 16 E (30/50 amps), seasonal sites, WiFi $, tent sites, rentals, showers $, dump, laundry, groc, fire rings, firewood, restaurant, controlled access. **REC:** heated pool, River A Mars: fishing, shuffleboard, playground. Pets OK. Partial handicap access. Eco-friendly. 2015 rates: $36 to $40. May 13 to Sep 14.
(418)544-6486 Lat: 48.32261, Lon: -70.91320
3736 Chemin St Louis, La Baie, QC G7B 4M8
http://camping.riviereamars.com
See ad this page.

SAINT-AIME-DES-LACS — D7 *Quebec*

PARC NATIONAL HAUTES-GORGES-DE-LA-RIVIERE-MALBAIE (Prov Pk) Hwy 138 & 172. 2015 rates: $28.50. May 15 to Oct 30. (418)439-1227

SAINT-ALEXANDRE — D7
Bas-Saint-Laurent

CAMPING LE RAYON DE SOLEIL
Ratings: 8/9★/9 (Campground) From Jct of Hwy 20 & Exit 488 (Rte 289), S 0.25 mi on Rte 289 to service rd, W 0.5 mi (E). **FAC:** Gravel rds. (117 spaces). Avail: 63 grass, 60 pull-thrus (30 x 60), back-ins (30 x 50), 12 full hkups, 24 W, 28 E (15/30 amps), seasonal sites, WiFi, tent sites, rentals, dump, laundry, groc, LP bottles, fire rings, firewood. **REC:** heated pool, playground. Pets OK. 2015 rates: $32 to $39. May 16 to Oct 1.
(418)495-2677 Lat: 47.698420, Lon: -69.661098
571 Rang St Edouard Ouest, St Alexandre de Kamouraska, QC G0L 2G0
camping.lerayondesoleil@gmail.com
www.campinglerayondesoleil.com

SAINT-ALEXIS-DES-MONTS — E5 *Mauricie*

RESERVE FAUNIQUE MASTIGOUCHE/LAC SAINT-BERNARD (Prov Pk) From jct Hwy 40 & Hwy 348: Go N on Hwy 348 to Saint-Alexis-des-Monts. 2015 rates: $19.50 to $38. May 9 to Oct 20. (819)265-6055

SAINT-ANDRE-AVELLIN — E3 *Outaouais*

CAMPING AU PETIT LAC SIMON **Ratings: 6.5/7/7.5** (Campground) 2015 rates: $40 to $45. Apr 30 to Oct 30. (819)983-6584 1203 Rte 321 Nord, Saint-Andre-Avellin, QC J0V 1W0

CAMPING ST ANDRE AVELLIN **Ratings: 8/8★/8.5** (Campground) 2015 rates: $40 to $43. May 9 to Oct 13. (819)983-3777 20 Duquette St, Saint-Andre-Avellin, QC J0V 1W0

SAINT-ANTOINE-ABBE — C2 *Monteregie*

CAMPING LAC DES PINS **Ratings: 9/9.5★/8.5** (Campground) 2015 rates: $30 to $40. May 15 to Oct 1. (450)827-2353 3625 Rte 201, Franklin, QC J0S 1N0

SAINT-ANTONIN — C7 *Bas-Saint-Laurent*

CAMPING CHEZ JEAN **Ratings: 9/9★/1**[illegible] (Campground) 2015 rates: $27 to $34. May 16 to Sep 30. (418)862-3081 434 Principale, Saint-Antonin, QC G0L 2J0

CAMPING LIDO 2002
Ratings: 8.5/9.5★/9.5 (Campground) From Jct of Rte 185 & Chemin Riviere Verte (1.75 mi S of town), E 50 ft on Chemin Riviere Verte, follow signs (L). **FAC:** Paved/gravel rds. (15[illegible] spaces). Avail: 38 grass, 24 pull-thrus (35 x 70), back-ins (30 x 60), 34 full hkups, 4 W, 4 E (30/50 amps), seasonal sites, WiFi, tent sites, showers $, dump, laundry, groc, LP gas, fire rings, firewood, co[illegible]

SAINT-ANTONIN (CONT)

CAMPING LIDO 2002 (CONT)
trolled access. **REC:** heated pool, playground. Pets OK. Eco-friendly, 2015 rates: $33 to $38. Disc: AAA. May 1 to Oct 1.
(418)862-6933 Lat: 47.768030, Lon: -69.439044
928 Chemin Riviere Verte, Saint-Antonin, QC G0L 2J0
info@camping-lido.net
www.camping-lido.net
See ad opposite page, 1465.

SAINT-APOLLINAIRE — D6
Chaudiere-Appalaches

DOMAINE DE LA CHUTE - PARKBRIDGE
Ratings: 9/10★/10 (Campground) E-bnd: From Jct of Hwy 20 & Exit 296 (Rte Du Cap), S 0.7 mi on Rte Du Cap to Chemin de la Chute, E 1.5 mi, follow signs (E). **FAC:** All weather rds. (847 spaces). Avail: 218 grass, 17 pull-thrus (40 x 60), back-ins (40 x 40), 146 full hkups, 72 W, 72 E (30/50 amps), seasonal sites, WiFi $, tent sites, rentals, showers $, dump, laundry, groc, LP gas, fire rings, firewood, restaurant, controlled access. **REC:** heated pool, Aulneuse River: swim, fishing, shuffleboard, playground. Pets OK $. Partial handicap access. Big rig sites, eco-friendly, 2015 rates: $39 to $53. May 15 to Sep 30.
(418)831-1311 Lat: 46.635875, Lon: -71.419792
74 Chemin de La Chute, Saint-Apollinaire, QC G0S 2E0
domainedelachute@parkbridge.com
www.parkbridge.com/lachute
See ad pages 1464 (Welcome Section), 1465.

SAINT-AUGUSTIN-DE-DESMAURES — D6
Quebec

CAMPING CANADIEN AMERICAIN **Ratings: 4.5/8★/7** (Campground) 2015 rates: $32 to $34. May 1 to Oct 24. (418)878-4254 209 Rte 138, Saint-Augustin-De-Desmaures, QC G3A 1W7

CAMPING JUNEAU CHALETS **Ratings: 7.5/8/7** (Campground) 2015 rates: $40 to $52. May 1 to Oct 31. (866)871-9090 153 Chemin du Lac, Saint-Augustin-De-Desmaures, QC G3A 1W7

SAINT-BARTHELEMY — E5 *Lanaudiere*

CAMPING DU VIEUX MOULIN INC
Ratings: 8/8.5★/8 (Campground) From Jct of Hwy 40 & exit 155, N 5 mi on exit rd (Mtee St-Laurent-Mtee Des Laurentides) to St-Joachim Rd, E 1 mi (E) Follow Signs. **FAC:** Gravel rds. (410 spaces). Avail: 94 grass, back-ins (40 x 50), mostly side by side hkups, 64 full hkups, 30 W, 30 E (15/30 amps), seasonal sites, WiFi Hotspot, tent sites, showers $, dump, laundry, fire rings, firewood, restaurant, controlled access. **REC:** pool, pond, playground. Pet restrict(B). Eco-friendly, 2015 rates: $32 to $45. May 15 to Sep 30.
(450)885-3591 Lat: 46.224091, Lon: -73.137980
2780 Rue Buteau, St Barthelemy, QC J0K 1X0
ginetbut@yahoo.com
www.campingduvieuxmoulin.com
See ad page 1469.

SAINT-BERNARD-DE-LACOLLE — C2
Monteregie

CAMPING COOLBREEZE **Ratings: 7/8★/8** (Campground) 2015 rates: $30 to $38. Apr 21 to Oct 21. (450)246-3785 144 Montee Glass, Saint-Bernard-De-Lacolle, QC J0J 1V0

CAMPING DU LAC CRISTAL **Ratings: 6/8★/8** (Campground) 2015 rates: $50. May 3 to Sep 2. (450)246-3773 251 Route 162, Chemin Grande Ligne, Saint-Rosaire, QC G0Z 1K0

SAINT-BONIFACE — E5 *Mauricie*

CAMPING ST BONIFACE **Ratings: 7.5/7.5/8** (Campground) 2015 rates: $34 to $38. May 16 to Oct 14. (819)535-7047 1850 Boul Trudel Est, Saint-Boniface-de-Shawinigan, QC G0X 2L0

SAINT-CELESTIN — E5 *Centre du Quebec*

CAMPING VAL-LERO **Ratings: 8/8.5★/7.5** (Campground) 2015 rates: $27 to $35. May 9 to Sep 21. (819)229-3545 1000 Rang Val-Lero, Saint-Celestin, QC J0C 1G0

SAINT-CHARLES-BORROMEE — A2
Lanaudiere

CAMPING DE LA RIVE **Ratings: 8.5/8.5★/8.5** (Campground) 2015 rates: $30 to $43. May 1 to Oct 30. (450)755-6555 45 Sansregret, Saint-Charles-Borromee, QC J6E 7Y8

Find it Fast! Use our alphabetized index of campgrounds and parks.

SAINT-CHARLES-SUR-RICHELIEU — A3
Monteregie

DOMAINE MADALIE **Ratings: 6.5/8.5★/8** (Campground) 2015 rates: $32 to $41. May 1 to Oct 10. (450)584-2444 512-3e Rang N, Saint-Charles-Sur-Richelieu, QC J0H 2G0

SAINT-CHRYSOSTOME — B2 *Monteregie*

CAMPING RUSSELTOWN **Ratings: 8/9★/7.5** (Campground) 2015 rates: $27 to $40. May 15 to Oct 31. (450)826-4841 258 Rang Notre Dame, Saint-Chrysostome, QC J0S 1R0

SAINT-COME — E4 *Lanaudiere*

CAMPING SUMMUM DE ST COME (Campground) (Phone Update) 2015 rates: $30 to $40. May 9 to Sep 28. (800)559-1968 2340 Rg Versaille (Hwy 347 N), Saint-Come, QC J0K 2B0

PARC NATIONAL DU MONT-TREMBLANT/CAMPING SECTEUR DE L'ASSOMPTION (Prov Pk) From Hwy 117-125-329 or 343. 2015 rates: $29. May 9 to Oct 13. (877)688-2281

SAINT-DAMASE — B3 *Monteregie*

BASE PLEIN AIR SAINT-DAMASE **Ratings: 6.5/8.5★/7.5** (Campground) 2015 rates: $29 to $36. May 15 to Sep 23. (418)776-2828 302 Rte 297 Sud, Saint-Damase-De-Matapedia, QC G0J 2J0

SAINT-DAVID-DE-FALARDEAU — C6
Saguenay-Lac-Saint-Jean

MUNICIPAL L'OASIS (Campground) (Phone Update) 2015 rates: $32 to $35. May 30 to Sep 1. (418)673-3066 694 Lac Emmuraille, Falardeau, QC G0V 1C0

SAINT-DONAT — E4 *Lanaudiere*

PARC NATIONAL DU MONT-TREMBLANT/CAMPING SECTEUR DE LA PIMBINA (Prov Pk) From Hwy 117-125-329 or 343. 2015 rates: $22.50 to $38.25. May 9 to Oct 13. (877)688-2281

SAINT-EDOUARD-DE-MASKINONGE — E5
Mauricie

CAMPING ZOO DE ST EDOUARD **Ratings: 8.5/8.5★/8** (Campground) 2015 rates: $48 to $50. May 9 to Sep 28. (819)268-2422 3371 Rang Des Chutes, Saint-Edouard-De-Maskinonge, QC J0K 2H0

SAINT-ELIE-DE-CAXTON — E5 *Mauricie*

FLORIBELL **Ratings: 7/9★/9.5** (Campground) 2015 rates: $41 to $50. May 5 to Sep 23. (819)221-5731 391 Lac Bell, Saint-Elie-de-Caxton, QC G0X 2N0

SAINT-ETIENNE-DE-BOLTON — F5
Cantons de l'Est

DOMAINE DES CANTONS **Ratings: 8.5/10★/8** (RV Park) 2015 rates: $48. May 1 to Oct 31. (450)297-2444 315 Rte 112, Saint-Etienne-De-Bolton, QC J0E 2E0

DOMAINE DU LAC LIBBY **Ratings: 7/9★/8** (Campground) 2015 rates: $37 to $40. May 15 to Sep 15. (450)297-2221 426 Rang 1, Saint-Etienne-De-Bolton, QC J0E 2E0

SAINT-ETIENNE-DES-GRES — E5 *Mauricie*

CAMPING DU LAC BLAIS **Ratings: 6.5/8.5★/7.5** (Campground) 2015 rates: $25 to $34. May 9 to Sep 14. (819)535-2783 2191 7E Rang, Saint-Etienne-des-Gres, QC G0X 2P0

SAINT-FABIEN — C7 *Bas-Saint-Laurent*

BIC/ST FABIEN (Public) In town N Hwy 132 (S). 2015 rates: $20.38 to $32. May 1 to Oct 1. (418)869-3333

SAINT-FAUSTIN-LAC-CARRE — A1
Laurentides

DOMAINE DESJARDINS **Ratings: 6.5/8.5★/8** (Campground) 2015 rates: $39 to $43. May 15 to Sep 2. (819)688-2179 1045 Rue De La Pisciculture, Saint-Faustin-Lac-Carre, QC J0T 1J3

SAINT-FELICIEN — C5
Saguenay-Lac-Saint-Jean

CAMPING MUNICIPAL ST-FELICIEN INC (Public) From Jct of Rtes 167 & 169, N 4 mi on Rte 167 (R). 2015 rates: $25 to $45. May 16 to Oct 7. (418)679-1719

It's the law! Rules of the Road and Towing Laws are updated each year. Be sure to consult this chart to find the laws for every state on your traveling route.

SAINT-FELIX-D'OTIS — C6 *Charlevoix, Saguenay-Lac-Saint-Jean*

CAMPING MUNICIPAL DE ST-FELIX-D'OTIS (Public) From town, W 6 mi on Rte 170 to Sentier St-Hilaire, NE 1 mi (E). 2015 rates: $25 to $43. May 19 to Sep 20. (418)697-1617

SAINT-FELIX-DE-VALOIS — A2 *Lanaudiere*

CAMPING AUX BOULEAUX ARGENTES **Ratings: 7/8.5★/8.5** (Campground) 2015 rates: $48 to $50. May 15 to Sep 15. (450)889-5809 2294 Rg St-Leon, Saint-Felix-De-Valois, QC J0K 2M0

CAMPING GLOBE TROTTER **Ratings: 7/8.5★/7.5** (Campground) 2015 rates: $37 to $39. May 15 to Sep 15. (450)889-5832 1200 Chemin de Ligne Brandon, Saint-Felix-De-Valois, QC J0K 2M0

CAMPING LE PETIT BONHEUR **Ratings: 5.5/8.5★/7.5** (Campground) 2015 rates: $30 to $40. May 10 to Sep 30. (450)889-4638 201 Des Sources, Saint-Felix-De-Valois, QC J0K 2M0

SAINT-FERREOL-LES-NEIGES — D6
Quebec

CAMPING MONT STE-ANNE **Ratings: 6.5/7.5/8.5** (Campground) 2015 rates: $49 to $53. May 15 to Oct 14. (418)826-2323 st Ferreol Les Neiges C.p. 300, Beaupre, QC G0A 1E0

SAINT-FRANCOIS-D'ORLEANS — D6
L'Ile-d' Orl'eans

CAMPING ILE D'ORLEANS **Ratings: 8/9.5★/9** (Campground) 2015 rates: $42 to $52. May 16 to Oct 9. (418)829-2953 357 Chemin Royal, Saint-Francois-D'orleans, QC G0A 3S0

QC

SAINT-GEDEON — C6
Saguenay-Lac-Saint-Jean

CAMPING 2 RIVIERES (Campground) (Phone Update) 2015 rates: $28 to $35. May 15 to Sep 15. (418)582-3278 rr 204, Saint-Gedeon, QC G0M 1T0

SAINT-GEORGES-DE-MALBAIE — C10
Gaspesie

AUBERGE FORT - PREVEL (Prov Pk) Hwy 132 E. Jun 20 to Sep 21. (418)368-2281

CAMPING CAP-ROUGE **Ratings: 5.5/7.5/7** (Campground) 2015 rates: $32 to $35. May 15 to Sep 30. (418)645-3804 cp 73-St Georges de Malabaie, Perce, QC G0C 2X0

CAMPING TETE D'INDIEN **Ratings: 8.5/8★/8** (Campground) 2015 rates: $38. May 1 to Oct 10. (877)530-8383 1669 Rte 132 E, Saint-Georges-de-Malbaie, QC G0C 2X0

SAINT-GODEFROI — C10 *Gaspesie*

CAMPING MUNICIPAL ST-GODEFROI (Public) In center town on Rte 132 (R). 2015 rates: $28 to $35. Jun 20 to Sep 10. (418)752-6316

SAINT-HENRI-DE-TAILLON — C6
Saguenay-Lac-Saint-Jean

CAMPING BELLEY (Campground) (Phone Update) 2015 rates: $38 to $49. May 23 to Oct 13. (418)347-3612 109 Chemin Belley, Taillon, QC G0W 2X0

PARC NATIONAL DE LA POINTE-TAILLON (Prov Pk) From Hwy 169. (418)347-5371

SAINT-HIPPOLYTE — A2 *Laurentides*

CAMPING AU PIN D'ERABLE **Ratings: 7/8★/8** (Campground) 2015 rates: $29 to $43. May 10 to Sep 10. (514)436-8319 161 Chemin Du Lac Bertrand, Saint-Hippolyte, QC J5J 2M1

SAINT-HONORE — C6
Saguenay-Lac-Saint-Jean

CAMPING LAC JOLY (Campground) (Phone Update) 2015 rates: $25 to $45. May 28 to Sep 12. (418)673-4777 100 Lac Joly, Saint-Honore-de-Chicoutimi, QC G0V 1L0

SAINT-HYACINTHE — B3 *Monteregie*

CAMPING BELLE ROSE **Ratings: 8/8★/7.5** (Campground) 2015 rates: $30 to $35. Apr 20 to Oct 30. (450)799-5169 7280-4E Rang, Saint-Hyacinthe, QC J2R 1S1

CAMPING DE L'ETE **Ratings: 9/8.5★/7.5** (Campground) 2015 rates: $34 to $42. May 1 to Oct 1. (450)799-1110 5960-5e Rang, Saint-Hyacinthe, QC J2R 2A4

Traveling with a Fido? Many campground listings indicate pet-friendly amenities and pet restrictions.

SAINT-JEAN-BAPTISTE — B3 *Monteregie*

CAMPING AU PIED DU MONT **Ratings: 6.5/7/7.5** (Campground) 2015 rates: $39 to $40. Apr 20 to Oct 20. (450)467-6318 3225 Rang du Cordon, Saint-Jean-Baptiste, QC J0L 2B0

CAMPING AUCLAIR **Ratings: 8/8.5★/9** (Campground) 2015 rates: $38 to $40. May 11 to Sep 30. (450)467-1898 4450 Rg. des Etangs, Saint-Jean-Baptiste, QC J0L 2B0

CAMPING LAC DU REPOS **Ratings: 8.5/10★/9.5** (Campground) 2015 rates: $35 to $49. May 1 to Oct 15. (450)467-3671 5715 Rang de La Riviere Nord, Saint-Jean-Baptiste, QC J0L 2B0

LE DOMAINE DE ROUVILLE INC. **Ratings: 8.5/9★/9.5** (Campground) 2015 rates: $35 to $55. May 10 to Oct 31. (450)467-6867 1925 Chemin Rouville, Saint-Jean-Baptiste, QC J0L 2B0

SAINT-JEAN-PORT-JOLI — D7
Chaudiere-Appalaches

CAMPING AU BONNET ROUGE **Ratings: 6.5/8.5★/6.5** (Campground) 2015 rates: $35 to $40. May 1 to Oct 15. (418)598-1919 76 Ave de Gaspe Est, Saint-Jean-Port-Joli, QC G0R 3G0

CAMPING DE LA DEMI-LIEUE Ratings: 8.5/9.5★/8.5 (Campground) From Jct of Hwy 20 & exit 414 (Rte 204), E 2 mi on Rte 204 to Rte 132, E 3 mi (L). **FAC:** Paved rds. (339 spaces). Avail: 171 grass, 38 pull-thrus (38 x 60), back-ins (30 x 60), some side by side hkups, 100 full hkups, 71 W, 71 E (15/30 amps), seasonal sites, tent sites, rentals, showers $, dump, laundry, groc, LP bottles, fire rings, firewood, controlled access. **REC:** heated pool, wading pool, St Lawrence River: shuffleboard, playground. Pets OK. Partial handicap access. 2015 rates: $38 to $43. May 9 to Sep 28.
AAA Approved
(418)598-6108 Lat: 47.245181, Lon: -70.232720
589 ave de Gaspe Est, Saint-Jean-Port-Joli, QC G0R 3G0
demi-lieue@campingunion.com
www.campingunion.com

SAINT-JEAN-SUR-RICHELIEU — B3
Monteregie

CAMPING JOIE DE VIVRE **Ratings: 6/6.5/7** (Campground) 2015 rates: $44 to $50. Apr 15 to Oct 15. (450)348-9383 977 Blvd Saint Luc, Saint-Jean-Sur-Richelieu, QC J2W 2G6

CAMPING LES CEDRES **Ratings: 8.5/9★/9** (Campground) 2015 rates: $35 to $54. May 1 to Oct 1. (450)346-9276 658 Route 219, Saint-Jean-sur-Richelieu, QC J2Y 1C4

SAINT-JEROME — A2 *Laurentides*

CAMPING LAC LAFONTAINE - PARKBRIDGE
Ratings: 8/9.5★/8 (Campground) N-bnd: From Jct of Hwy 15 & exit 41 (Boulevard Du Grand-Heron), SW 0.75 mi (at end of exit follow Boulevard Du Grand-Heron signs) (R); S-bnd: From Jct of Hwy 15 & exit 41 (JF Kennedy Boul), SW 0.25 mi on JFK to Roland Godard Boul, S 0.25 mi to Boulevard Du Grand-Heron, W 0.1 mi (R). **FAC:** Paved/gravel rds. (362 spaces). Avail: 143 gravel, 14 pull-thrus (30 x 60), back-ins (35 x 50), 36 full hkups, 107 W, 107 E (30/50 amps), seasonal sites, WiFi $, tent sites, showers $, dump, laundry, groc, LP gas, fire rings, firewood, restaurant, controlled access. **REC:** Lake Lafontaine: swim, shuffleboard, playground. Pet restrict(B). Partial handicap access. Eco-friendly, 2015 rates: $35 to $54.
(450)431-7373 Lat: 45.755648, Lon: -74.023540
1100 Boulevard Du Grand-Heron, St Jerome, QC J5L 1G2
laclafontaine@parkbridge.com
www.parkbridge.com/laclafontaine
See ad pages 1464 (Welcome Section), 1465.

SAINT-JOSEPH-DE-BEAUCE — E6
Chaudiere-Appalaches

CAMPING MUNICIPAL ST JOSEPH (Public) From Jct of Rtes 173 & 276, W 3 mi on Rte 276 (L). 2015 rates: $23 to $32. May 10 to Sep 10. (418)397-5953

SAINT-LAMBERT-DE-LAUZON — E6
Chaudiere-Appalaches

CAMPING LE RUISSEAU BLEU **Ratings: 7/7.5/7.5** (Campground) 2015 rates: $32 to $36. May 15 to Sep 15. (418)889-9100 1635 des Erables St, Saint-Lambert-De-Lauzon, QC G0S 2W0

SAINT-LAZARE — B1 *Monteregie*

CAMPING LAC DES CEDRES **Ratings: 7/8.5★/8** (Campground) 2015 rates: $40 to $45. Apr 26 to Oct 26. (450)455-2131 1717 Des Cedres, Saint-Lazare, QC J7T 2S6

SAINT-LIBOIRE — A3 *Monteregie*

CAMPING PLAGE LA LIBERTE **Ratings: 7/9★/9** (Campground) 2015 rates: $40 to $42. May 1 to Sep 15. (450)793-2716 129 Rang Charlotte, Saint-Liboire, QC J0H 1R0

SAINT-LOUIS-DE-BLANDFORD — E5
Centre du Quebec

DOMAINE DU LAC LOUISE INC **Ratings: 8/8.5★/7.5** (Campground) 2015 rates: $36 to $46. May 1 to Oct 15. (819)364-7002 950 Rte 263 N, Saint-Louis-De-Blandford, QC G0Z 1B0

SAINT-MATHIEU-DE-BELOEIL — B3
Monteregie

CAMPING ALOUETTE - PARKBRIDGE
Ratings: 10/10★/10 (Campground) From Jct of TCH 20 & Exit 105, E 1 mi on N service rd (De L'Industrie St) (L). **FAC:** Paved rds. (402 spaces). Avail: 34 paved, 183 all weather, 143 pull-thrus (33 x 90), back-ins (30 x 40), 170 full hkups, 33 W, 33 E (30/50 amps), seasonal sites, WiFi $, tent sites, rentals, showers $, dump, laundry, groc, LP gas, fire rings, firewood, restaurant, controlled access. **REC:** heated pool, playground. Pets OK $. Partial handicap access. Big rig sites, eco-friendly, 2015 rates: $45 to $54. Disc: AAA. Apr 15 to Oct 15.
AAA Approved
(450)464-1661 Lat: 45.590141, Lon: -73.268652
3449, de L'industrie, St Mathieu de Beloeil, QC J3G 4S5
alouette@parkbridge.com
www.parkbridge.com/alouette
See ad pages 1464 (Welcome Section), 1465.

SAINT-MATHIEU-DE-RIOUX — C7
Bas-Saint-Laurent

KOA BAS-ST-LAURENT CAMPGROUND
Ratings: 10/10★/10 (Campground) From Rt 132 in St Simonde Rimouski, go NE toward Rue d'Anjou 0.9 mi on Rt 132. R (SE) on Route de Saint Simon Saint Mathieu 2.7 mi. R at stop sign go SW 0.4 mi. On 3e Rang 0. L (SE) on Chemin Du Lac Sud 1.6 mi. Follow KOA sign. **FAC:** All weather rds. (145 spaces). Avail: 35 all weather, 31 pull-thrus (35 x 70), back-ins (35 x 60), 35 full hkups (30/50 amps), seasonal sites, cable, WiFi, tent sites, rentals, dump, laundry, groc, LP bottles, fire rings, firewood, restaurant, controlled access. **REC:** pool, wading pool, Lac Saint Mathieu: swim, fishing, marina, playground, rec open to public. Pets OK. Partial handicap access. Big rig sites, eco-friendly, 2015 rates: $42 to $54. Disc: AAA. May 14 to Oct 12. ATM.
AAA Approved
(800)562-2482 Lat: 48.159038, Lon: -69.010917
109 Chemin du Lac Sud, Saint-Mathieu-de-Rioux, QC G0L 3T0
info@koabasstlaurent.com
www.koabasstlaurent.com
See ad this page.

SAINT-MICHEL-DE-BELLECHASSE — D6
Chaudiere-Appalaches

CAMPING PARC ST MICHEL **Ratings: 6.5/6/8.5** (Campground) 2015 rates: $28 to $40. May 15 to Sep 15. (418)884-2621 7 Chemin des Campings, Saint-Michel-De-Bellechasse, QC G0R 3S0

SAINT-NICOLAS — D6
Chaudiere-Appalaches

CAMPING AU SOUS-BOIS DU CAMPEUR **Ratings: 7.5/9.5★/8.5** (Campground) 2015 rates: $36 to $50. May 1 to Sep 30. (888)731-1788 1932 Chemin Filteau, Saint-Nicolas, QC G7A 2N4

CAMPING BERNIERES **Ratings: 8/6.5/8** (Campground) 2015 rates: $37 to $45. May 15 to Oct 1. (418)831-8665 1012 Oliver, Saint-Nicolas, QC G7A 2M9

KOA QUEBEC CITY Ratings: 9/10★/9.5 (Campground) E-bnd: From Jct of Hwy 20 & Exit 311 (Rte 116), SE 0.1 mi on Arena St to Rte 116, E 0.4 mi to Chemin Olivier (N Service Rd), W 1 mi (R); or W-bnd: From Jct of Hwy 20 & exit 311, N 200 ft on exit rd to Chemin Olivier, W 1 mi (R). **FAC:** Paved/gravel rds. (201 spaces). 198 Avail: 168 gravel, 30 grass, patios, 151 pull-thrus (35 x 60), back-ins (30 x 40), 137 full hkups, 57 W, 39 E (30/50 amps), seasonal sites, WiFi, tent sites, rentals, dump, laundry, groc, LP bottles, fire rings, firewood, controlled access. **REC:** heated pool, whirlpool, playground. Pets OK. Partial handicap access. Big rig sites, eco-friendly, 2015 rates: $40 to $80. Disc: AAA. May 1 to Oct 12.
AAA Approved
(418)831-1813 Lat: 46.699138, Lon: -71.301418
684 Chemin Oliver, Saint-Nicolas, QC G7A 2N6
camp@koaquebec.com
www.koa.com

SAINT-OMER — C9 *Gaspesie*

CAMPING AUX FLOTS BLEUS **Ratings: 5.5/8★/7.5** (Campground) 2015 rates: $32 to $40. May 1 to Sep 30. (418)364-3659 279 Rte 132 Ouest, Saint-Omer, QC G0C 2Z0

SAINT-OURS — A3 *Monteregie*

CAMPING BELLERIVE (MARINA) **Ratings: 7.5/9.5★/8.5** (Campground) 2015 rates: $33 to $51. May 8 to Sep 15. (450)785-2272 1992 Chemin des Patriotes, Saint-Ours, QC J0G 1P0

SAINT-PAULIN — E5 *Mauricie*

CAMPING BELLE MONTAGNE (1999) **Ratings: 7/8★/8** (Campground) 2015 rates: $39 to $45 May 15 to Oct 15. (819)268-2881 2470 Belle Montagne, Saint-Paulin, QC J0K 3G0

SAINT-PHILIPPE — B2 *Monteregie*

CAMPING BON-AIR **Ratings: 6.5/7/6.5** (Campground) 2015 rates: $24 to $44. Apr 25 to Oct 25. (450)659-8868 110 Rang St Andre, Saint-Philippe QC J0L 2K0

CAMPING LA CLE DES CHAMPS RV RESORT
Ratings: 10/10★/10 (Campground) From Jct of Hwy 30 & Exit 104 (Rte 104) E 1.7 mi on Rte 104 to Rang St-Raphael S 2 mi to Montee St-Claude, W 0.5 mi (R). **FAC:** All weather rds. (200 spaces). Avail: 33 all weather, patios, 6 pull-thrus (30 x 75), back-ins (30 x 45), 33 full hkups (30/50 amps), seasonal sites WiFi, dump, laundry, groc, LP gas, fire rings, firewood, controlled access. **REC:** heated pool, shuffleboard, playground. Pet restrict(B). Partial handicap access, no tents. Big rig sites, eco-friendly, 2015 rates: $47 to $55. Apr 10 to Oct 15.
(450)659-3389 Lat: 45.361975, Lon: -73.446600
415 Montee St Claude, Saint-Philippe, QC J0L 2K0
info@campinglacledeschamps.com
www.campinglacledeschamps.com
See ad this page.

SAINT-PHILIPPE (CONT)

← KOA MONTREAL SOUTH **Ratings: 8.5/10★/9.5** (Campground) 2015 rates: $34 to $68. May 15 to Sep 30. (450)659-8626 130 Boul Monette, Saint-Philippe, QC J0L 2K0

SAINT-PHILIPPE-DE-LAPRAIRIE — B2
Monteregie

↓ CAMPING AMERIQUE **Ratings: 6.5/7/6** (Campground) 2015 rates: $32 to $34. Apr 1 to Oct 31. (450)659-8282 40 Chemin St Andre, Saint-Philippe, QC J0L 2K0

SAINT-PIE — B3 *Monteregie*

↑ CAMPING AQUA-PARC ST-PIE **Ratings: 7.5/9.5★/7** (Campground) 2015 rates: $40 to $48. May 15 to Sep 15. (450)772-2614 289 Chemin St-Dominique, Saint-Pie, QC J0H 1W0

↗ CAMPING AU VIEUX FOYER ENR. **Ratings: 8/8.5★/7.5** (Campground) 2015 rates: $42.50 to $46. May 15 to Sep 15. (450)772-5177 105 Chemin St Dominique, Saint-Pie, QC J0H 1W0

SAINT-POLYCARPE — B1 *Monteregie*

↓ CAMPING ST POLYCARPE **Ratings: 7/8/8** (Campground) 2015 rates: $30 to $40. May 15 to Sep 14. (450)265-3815 1400 Ch St-Philippe, Saint-Polycarpe, QC J0P 1X0

SAINT-ROCH-DE-L'ACHIGAN — A2
Lanaudiere

← CAMPING HORIZON **Ratings: 8/8★/7.5** (Campground) 2015 rates: $32 to $49. May 7 to Sep 15. (450)588-5607 170 St Philippe Rd, Saint-Roch-De-L'achigan, QC J0K 3H0

SAINT-ROCH-DE-RICHELIEU — A3
Monteregie

→ **CAMPING DOMAINE DES ERABLES - PARKBRIDGE**
Ratings: 8.5/9.5★/9.5 (Campground) From Jct of Hwy 30 & Exit 126 (Rte 223S), S 2 mi on Rte 223 to St-Pierre St, E 1 mi (L). **FAC:** Gravel rds. (442 spaces). 110 Avail: 34 gravel, 76 grass, 51 pull-thrus (35 x 65), back-ins (35 x 45), 76 full hkups, 34 W, 34 E (30 amps), seasonal sites, WiFi, tent sites, showers $, dump, laundry, groc, LP gas, fire rings, firewood, restaurant, controlled access. **REC:** heated pool, wading pool, whirlpool, pond, swim, fishing, playground. Pet restrict(B). 2015 rates: $43 to $50. May 1 to Oct 12.
(450)785-2805 Lat: 45.90150, Lon: -73.15579
500 rue St-Pierre, Saint-Roch-De-Richelieu, QC J0L 2M0
domainedeserables@parkbridge.com
www.parkbridge.com/erables
See ad pages 1464 (Welcome Section), 1465.

SAINT-ROCH-DES-AULNAIES — D7
Chaudiere-Appalaches

← CAMPING DES AULNAIES **Ratings: 8.5/9.5★/9.5** (Campground) 2015 rates: $38 to $46. May 11 to Sep 20. (418)354-2225 1399 Rte de La Seigneurie, Saint-Roch-Des-Aulnaies, QC G0R 4E0

SAINT-ROMUALD — D6
Chaudiere-Appalaches

← CAMPING LA RELACHE **Ratings: 3.5/6.5/5.5** (Campground) 2015 rates: $25 to $40. May 15 to Oct 15. (418)839-4743 1355 boul Rive-Sud, Saint-Romuald, QC G6W 5M6

↘ MOTEL ET CAMPING ETCHEMIN **Ratings: 7/7/8** (Campground) 2015 rates: $35 to $55. May 1 to Oct 15. (418)839-6853 2774 Boul de la Rive Sud, Saint-Romuald, QC G6W 7Y1

SAINT-ROSAIRE — E5 *Centre du Quebec*

→ CAMPING DOMAINE DU LAC CRISTAL **Ratings: 8/8.5★/7.5** (Campground) 2015 rates: $50 to $53. May 1 to Oct 15. (819)752-4275 251 Rte 162, Chemin Grande-Ligne, Saint-Rosaire, QC G0Z 1K0

SAINT-SIMEON — C7 *Quebec*

← CAMPING FAMILLE MORIN **Ratings: 6/8★/8** (Campground) 2015 rates: $30 to $35. May 30 to Sep 15. (418)514-8547 1640 Rte 138, Saint-Simeon, QC G0T 1X0

→ CAMPING LEVESQUE **Ratings: 6/8★/8** (Campground) 2015 rates: $20 to $30. May 10 to Oct 1. (418)638-5220 40 Rte Port-Aux-Quilles (138), Saint-Simeon, QC G0T 1X0

↘ CAMPING MUNICIPAL DE ST-SIMEON (Public) From Jct of Rtes 170 & 138, W 0.25 mi on Rte 138 to Ferry Rd (Festival St), S 0.5 mi (L). 2015 rates: $19.50 to $30. May 16 to Oct 12. (418)638-5253

SAINT-TITE — D5 *Mauricie*

↑ CAMPING LA GERVAISIE **Ratings: 7/8.5★/8.5** (Campground) 2015 rates: $42. May 15 to Sep 15. (418)365-7171 1 Lac Trottier, Saint-Tite, QC G0X 3H0

SAINT-VALLIER — D6 *Chaudiere-Appalaches*

↓ **CAMPING LE DOMAINE CHAMPETRE**
Ratings: 9.5/10★/10 (Campground) From Jct of Hwy 20 & exit 356 (Montee De La Station), E .4 km on Chemin D'Azur (exit Rd) to Montee De La Station, S 2.7 km (L). **FAC:** All weather rds. (176 spaces). 126 Avail: 15 gravel, 111 grass, patios, 5 pull-thrus (30 x 90), back-ins (40 x 70), 106 full hkups, 20 W, 20 E (30/50 amps), seasonal sites, WiFi $, tent sites, showers $, dump, laundry, groc, LP bottles, fire rings, firewood, controlled access. **REC:** heated pool, shuffleboard, playground. Pet restrict Partial handicap access. Big rig sites, 2015 rates: $33 to $55. May 15 to Sep 30.
(418)884-2270 Lat: 46.851305, Lon: -70.774162
888 Montee de La Station, Saint-Vallier, QC G0R 4J0
cdc@campingdomainechampetre.com
www.campingdomainechampetre.com

SAINTE-AGATHE-DES-MONTS — A1
Laurentides

↑ CAMPING DU DOMAINE LAUSANNE **Ratings: 7/8.5★/8** (Campground) 2015 rates: $32 to $48. May 9 to Sep 7. (819)326-3550 150 Rte 117, Sainte-Agathe-Des-Monts, QC J8C 2Z8

↑ CAMPING SAINTE-AGATHE-DES-MONTS **Ratings: 7/8.5★/8** (Campground) 2015 rates: $40 to $51. May 15 to Oct 15. (800)561-7360 2 Chemin Du Lac Des Sables, Sainte-Agathe-Des-Monts, QC J8C 2Z7

SAINTE-ANGELE-DE-MONNOIR — B3
Monteregie

↗ CAMPING DOMAINE DU REVE **Ratings: 8/10★/10** (Campground) 2015 rates: $35 to $425. May 1 to Oct 15. (450)469-2524 85 Rang dela Cote-Double, Sainte-Angele-De-Monnoir, QC J0L 1P0

SAINTE-ANNE-DE-BEAUPRE — D6
Quebec

← CAMPING LAC AUX FLAMBEAUX **Ratings: 6.5/8.5★/7** (Campground) 2015 rates: $27 to $35. Apr 25 to Oct 15. (418)827-3977 9491 Boul Ste-Anne, Sainte-Anne-De-Beaupre, QC G0A 3C0

SAINTE-ANNE-DES-MONTS — B9
Gaspesie

← CAMPING DU RIVAGE **Ratings: 6.5/5.5/7** (Campground) 2015 rates: $25 to $34. May 15 to Oct 15. (418)763-3529 500 1Ere Ave Ouest, Sainte-Anne-Des-Monts, QC G4V 1H4

PARC NATIONAL DE LA GASPESIE (Prov Pk) From Hwy 132 & Hwy 299: Go S on Hwy 299 to Gite Mont-Albert. (418)763-7494

PARC NATIONAL DE LA GASPESIE, LAC CASCAPEDIA (Prov Pk) From Hwy 132 in Sainte-Anne-des-Monts: Go S on Hwy 299 to Gite Mont-Albert. Jun 1 to Sep 30. (866)727-2427

PARC NATIONAL DE LA GASPESIE, MONT-ALBERT (Prov Pk) From Hwy 132 E in Sainte-Anne-des-Monts: Go S on Hwy 299 to Gite du Mont-Albert. 2015 rates: $28.50 to $32.25. Jun 13 to Oct 12. (866)727-2427

SAINTE-CATHERINE-DE-HATLEY — F5
Cantons de l'Est

↓ CAMPING HATLEY **Ratings: 7/8.5★/7** (Campground) 2015 rates: $37. May 15 to Oct 15. (819)843-5337 250 Chemin Magog, Sainte-Catherine-de-Hatley, QC J0B 1W0

SAINTE-CECILE-DE-MASHAM — E3
Outaouais

GATINEAU PARK (LA PECHE LAKE) (Prov Pk) From jct Hwy 105 & Hwy 366: Go 12-3/4 km/8 mi W on Hwy 366, then S on Eardley Rd. Sites accessible by boat or canoe only. Pit toilets. (819)456-3016

GATINEAU PARK (PHILIPPE LAKE) (Prov Pk) From jct Hwy 105 & Hwy 366: Go 8 km/5 mi W on Hwy 366. 2015 rates: $39. (819)456-3016

SAINTE-CECILE-DE-MILTON — B3
Monteregie

↑ CAMPING OASIS **Ratings: 7.5/8/7** (Campground) 2015 rates: $38 to $42. May 1 to Oct 15. (450)378-2181 974-1er Rang Ouest, Sainte-Cecile-De-Milton, QC J0E 2C0

SAINTE-CROIX — E6 *Chaudiere-Appalaches*

↖ CENTRE DE VILLEGIATURE BELLE-VUE **Ratings: 8.5/10★/8.5** (Campground) 2015 rates: $40 to $50. May 15 to Oct 15. (418)926-3482 6940 Pointe Platon, Sainte-Croix, QC G0S 2H0

SAINTE-EMELIE-DE-L'ENERGIE — E4
Lanaudiere

↑ CAMPING SAINTE-EMILIE **Ratings: 7.5/8.5★/7.5** (Campground) 2015 rates: $37 to $40. May 15 to Sep 15. (450)886-5879 1551 Rte Saint-Joseph, Sainte-Emelie-de-L'energie, QC J0K 2K0

SAINTE-FLAVIE — C8 *Bas-Saint-Laurent*

← CAMPING CAPITAINE HOMARD **Ratings: 5.5/7.5★/6** (Campground) 2015 rates: $26 to $36. May 15 to Sep 7. (418)775-8046 180 Rte de La Mer (Rte 132), Sainte-Flavie, QC G0J 2L0

SAINTE-GENEVIEVE-DE-BATISCAN — E5
Mauricie

↑ CAMPING PARC DE LA PENINSULE **Ratings: 8/8★/8.5** (Campground) 2015 rates: $43 to $45. May 9 to Sep 21. (418)362-2043 250 Grande Pointe Rd, Sainte-Genevieve-De-Batiscan, QC G0X 2R0

SAINTE-JULIENNE — A2 *Lanaudiere*

↑ CAMPING KELLY **Ratings: 7.5/8★/7.5** (Campground) 2015 rates: $38 to $40. May 15 to Sep 30. (450)831-2422 2795 rue du Camping, Sainte-Julienne, QC J0K 2T0

SAINTE-LUCE — C8 *La Mitis*

← CAMPING CHALETS LA LUCIOLE **Ratings: 5.5/8.5★/7.5** (Campground) 2015 rates: $32 to $45. Jun 17 to Sep 7. (418)739-3258 118 Rte 132 Ouest Cp 897, Sainte-Luce, QC G0K 1P0

SAINTE-MADELEINE — B3 *Monteregie*

↑ CAMPING SAINTE MADELEINE **Ratings: 8/10★/9** (Campground) 2015 rates: $41 to $44. Apr 30 to Oct 15. (450)795-3888 10 St Simon St, Sainte-Madeleine, QC J0H 1S0

SAINTE-MARCELLINE-DE-KILDARE — A2
Lanaudiere

↓ CAMPING SOL AIR **Ratings: 7.5/8.5★/8.5** (Campground) 2015 rates: $45. May 16 to Sep 14. (450)883-3400 760 9e Rang, Sainte-Marcelline-De-Kildare, QC J0K 2Y0

SAINTE-MELANIE — A2 *Lanaudiere*

↘ CAMPING BERNARD **Ratings: 7.5/8.5★/7.5** (Campground) 2015 rates: $30 to $40. May 7 to Sep 2. (450)756-2560 100 Boul Bernard, Sainte-Melanie, QC J0K 3A0

↑ CAMPING CAMPUS **Ratings: 6.5/8.5★/7.5** (Campground) 2015 rates: $35 to $50. May 14 to Sep 14. (450)883-2337 6571 Rte de Sainte-Beatrix, Sainte-Melanie, QC J0K 3A0

SAINTE-MONIQUE-DE-HONFLEUR — C6
Saguenay-Lac-Saint-Jean

↙ CENTRE TOURISTIQUE SAINTE-MONIQUE (Prov Pk) From S City Limit on Hwy 169: Go .05 km/1/4 mi S on Hwy 169, then 1 km/3/4 mi W on Rang 6 Ouest. (418)347-3124

SAINTE-ROSE-DU-NORD — C6
Saguenay-Lac-Saint-Jean

↓ CAMPING LA DESCENTE DES FEMMES (Campground) (Phone Update) 2015 rates: $30. Jun 1 to Oct 12. (418)675-2581 154 De La Montagne, Sainte-Rose-Du-Nord, QC G0V 1T0

SAINTE-SABINE — E7
Chaudiere-Appalaches

↗ **CAMPING CARAVELLE - PARKBRIDGE**
Ratings: 8.5/9★/7.5 (Campground) From Jct of Hwy 10 & exit 48 (Rte 233), S 6 mi on Rte 233 to Rte 104, E 2 mi to Rte 235, S 3 mi to Rang De La Gare, W 0.6 mi (L). **FAC:** Gravel rds. (445 spaces). 61 Avail: 40 gravel, 21 grass, back-ins (50 x 50), some side by side hkups, 61 full hkups (30/50 amps), seasonal sites, WiFi, tent sites, showers $, dump, laundry, groc, LP bottles, fire rings, firewood, restaurant, controlled access. **REC:** pool, wading pool, shuffleboard, playground. Pets OK. 2015 rates: $28 to $40. Apr 20 to Oct 20.
(450)293-7637 Lat: 45.23055, Lon: -72.99826
180 Rang de la Gare, Sainte-Sabine, QC J0J 2B0
caravelle@parkbridge.com
www.parkbridge.com/caravelle
See ad pages 1464 (Welcome Section), 1465.

QC

SAINTE-SERAPHINE — E5 *Centre du Quebec*

CAMPING LAC DES CYPRES **Ratings: 6.5/7.5/7** (Campground) 2015 rates: $39 to $45. May 1 to Oct 1. (819)336-3443 175 des Cypres, Sainte-Seraphine, QC J0A 1E0

SAINTE-SOPHIE-DE-LEVRARD — E5 *Centre du Quebec*

CAMPING PLAGE PARIS **Ratings: 7.5/8★/7** (Campground) 2015 rates: $38 to $46. May 16 to Sep 14. (819)288-5948 315 Rang St-Antoine, Sainte-Sophie-de-Levrard, QC G0X 3C0

SAINTE-THECLE — D5 *Mauricie*

DOMAINE LAC ET FORET **Ratings: 8/8.5★/8.5** (Campground) 2015 rates: $48. May 17 to Sep 22. (418)289-3871 131, 12e Av. du Lac-Croche Sud, Sainte-Thecle, QC G0X 3G0

SAINTE-VERONIQUE — E3 *Laurentides*

MUNICIPAL DE STE VERONIQUE (Public) From town, N 1 mi on Hwy 117 (R). 2015 rates: $30.46 to $38.28. May 10 to Oct 13. (819)275-2155

SCOTT — E6 *Chaudiere-Appalaches*

CAMPING PARC DE LA CHAUDIERE **Ratings: 8/10★/8** (Campground) 2015 rates: $39 to $48. May 9 to Sep 29. (866)882-5759 100 du Camping St, Scott, QC G0S 3G0

SHAWINIGAN — E5 *Mauricie*

CAMPING OTAMAC **Ratings: 8.5/9★/8.5** (Campground) 2015 rates: $59. May 15 to Sep 15. (819)538-9697 5431 Av Tour Du Lac, Lac-a-la-Tortue, QC G0X 1L0

CAMPING ROUILLARD **Ratings: 8.5/8.5★/7.5** (Campground) 2015 rates: $30 to $42. May 15 to Oct 1. (819)538-2159 5095 Ave Tour-du-Lac, Lac-a-la-Tortue, QC G0X 1L0

LA MAURICIE NATIONAL PARK (MISTAGANCE) (Prov Pk) From jct Hwy 55 (exit 217) & Hwy 351 S: Go 24 km/15 mi N on Hwy 351. 2015 rates: $25.50 to $29.40. Dec 1 to Mar 1. (819)538-3232

LA MAURICIE NATIONAL PARK (WAPIZAGONKE) (Prov Pk) From jct Hwy 55 (exit 217) & Hwy 351: Go 48 km/30 mi N on Hwy 351. North of Lake Wapizagonka. 2015 rates: $25.50 to $29.40. May 16 to Oct 13. (819)538-3232

PARC DE L'ILE MELVILLE (Public) From Jct of Hwy 55 & Exit 211 (Rte 153), N 2.7 mi on Rte 153 to Rte 157, S 0.6 mi (L). 2015 rates: $ 25.35 to $39.25. May 15 to Oct 1. (819)536-0222

RESERVE FAUNIQUE DU SAINT-MAURICE/LAC NORMAND (Prov Pk) From jct I-40 & Hwy 55: Go N on Hwy 55, then N on Hwy 155. 2015 rates: $26.50. May 9 to Sep 1. (819)646-5687

SHEFFORD — F5 *Cantons de l'Est*

CAMPING DE L'ESTRIE **Ratings: 8/8.5★/7.5** (Campground) 2015 rates: $33 to $38. Apr 15 to Oct 1. (450)539-3728 630 Chemin de Frost Village, Shefford, QC J2M 1C1

SHERBROOKE — F5 *Cantons de l'Est*

CAMPING BEAU-LIEU **Ratings: 8.5/8.5★/8** (Campground) 2015 rates: $32 to $38. May 1 to Sep 30. (819)864-4531 5153 Chemin Ste Catherine, Sherbrooke, QC J1N 3B8

CAMPING ILE-MARIE **Ratings: 7/8★/7.5** (Campground) 2015 rates: $39 to $43. May 1 to Sep 15. (819)820-0330 225 Rue St Francis, Sherbrooke, QC J1M 0B3

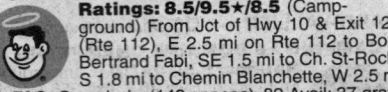

CAMPING LAC MAGOG
Ratings: 8.5/9.5★/8.5 (Campground) From Jct of Hwy 10 & Exit 128 (Rte 112), E 2.5 mi on Rte 112 to Boul Bertrand Fabi, SE 1.5 mi to Ch. St-Roch, S 1.8 mi to Chemin Blanchette, W 2.5 mi (L). **FAC:** Gravel rds. (149 spaces). 82 Avail: 37 gravel, 45 grass, 7 pull-thrus (40 x 75), back-ins (35 x 50), some side by side hkups, 59 full hkups, 23 W, 23 E (15/30 amps), seasonal sites, WiFi $, tent sites, showers $, dump, laundry, groc, LP bottles, fire rings, firewood, controlled access. **REC:** pool, Lake Magog: swim, fishing, playground. Pet restrict(B). 2015 rates: $38 to $47. May 9 to Sep 29.
(819)864-4401 Lat: 45.32459, Lon: -72.02088
7255 Chemin Blanchette, Sherbrooke, QC J1N 0G7
lacmagog@campingunion.com
https://www.campingunion.com/fr/sherbrooke-lac-magog

STANSTEAD — F5 *Estrie*

CAMPING LAC FRONTIERE (BORDER LAKE) **Ratings: 8/8★/7.5** (Campground) 2015 rates: $32 to $35. May 10 to Oct 4. (819)876-5505 150, Route 143 North, Stanstead, QC J0B 3E1

STONEHAM — D6 *Quebec*

CAMPING STONEHAM **Ratings: 9/8.5★/9** (Campground) 2015 rates: $33 to $57. May 9 to Sep 7. (418)848-2233 71 Chemin Saint-Edmond, Stoneham-et-Tewkesbury, QC G3C 1G3

TADOUSSAC — C7 *Manicouagan*

CAMPING TADOUSSAC INC (Campground) (Phone Update) 2015 rates: $31 to $48. May 24 to Sep 22. (888)868-6666 428 Du Bateau Passeur (Rte 138), Tadoussac, QC G0T 2A0

TERREBONNE — A2 *Lanaudiere*

CAMPING AU PLATEAU 5 ETOILES (Campground) (Phone Update) 2015 rates: $38 to $45. Apr 15 to Oct 15. (450)471-6266 1770 Cote Terrebonne, Terrebonne, QC J6Y 1E2

TROIS-PISTOLES — C7 *Bas-Saint-Laurent*

CAMPING MUNICIPAL TROIS PISTOLES (Public) From Jct of Rtes 132 7 293 W 1 mi on Rte 132 to Rue Chanoine-Cote, N 0.6 mi (E). 2015 rates: $30 to $37. May 31 to Sep 2. (418)851-1377

CAMPING PLAGE TROIS-PISTOLES **Ratings: 7/8.5★/8.5** (Campground) 2015 rates: $33 to $38. Jun 1 to Sep 15. (418)851-2403 130 Chemin Rioux, Trois-Pistoles, QC G0L 4K0

TROIS-RIVIERES — E5 *Centre du Quebec*

CAMPING LA ROCHELLE **Ratings: 8/8.5★/7.5** (Campground) 2015 rates: $38 to $42. May 1 to Sep 15. (819)372-9636 471 Rue des Marguerites, Trois-Rivieres, QC G8W 2B6

CAMPING LAC ST MICHEL
Ratings: 8.5/9★/9 (Campground) From Jct of Hwy 55 & Exit 191 (St Michel Blvd), E 1.5 mi on St-Michel Blvd to Des Forges Blvd, N 2.2 mi (R) Follow Signs. **FAC:** Paved/gravel rds. (141 spaces). Avail: 76 grass, 12 pull-thrus (30 x 50), back-ins (40 x 55), 51 full hkups, 25 W, 25 E (20/30 amps), seasonal sites, WiFi $, tent sites, rentals, dump, laundry, groc, LP bottles, fire rings, firewood, controlled access. **REC:** pool, Lac St-Michel: swim, fishing, shuffleboard, playground. Pets OK. Eco-friendly, 2015 rates: $38 to $46. May 9 to Sep 28.
(819)374-8474 Lat: 46.40755, Lon: -72.68376
11650 Du Clairon, Trois-Rivieres, QC G9A 5E1
lacstmichel@campingunion.com
https://www.campingunion.com/fr/trois-rivieres-saint-michel

DOMAINE AU GRAND 'R' INC **Ratings: 7/7.5/8** (Campground) 2015 rates: $65. May 10 to Sep 14. (819)378-3723 761 Rue des Prairies, Trois-Rivieres, QC G8W 2E5

UPTON — A3 *Monteregie*

CAMPING WIGWAM **Ratings: 7/8/8** (Campground) 2015 rates: $41. May 1 to Oct 13. (450)549-4513 425 Rue Principale St, Upton, QC J0H 2E0

VAL-ALAIN — E6 *Chaudiere-Appalaches*

CAMPING LAC GEORGES **Ratings: 8/10★/8** (Campground) 2015 rates: $49 to $62. May 10 to Sep 28. (418)744-3510 150, Seigneuriale St, Val-Alain, QC G0S 3H0

VAL-DAVID — A1 *Laurentides*

CAMPING LAURENTIEN **Ratings: 5.5/7.5/8** (Campground) 2015 rates: $37 to $40. May 16 to Oct 14. (819)322-2281 1949 Guertin St, Val David, QC J0T 2N0

VALCARTIER — D6 *Quebec*

CAMPING VALCARTIER (Campground) (Phone Update) 2015 rates: $45 to $60. Jun 13 to Aug 31. (418)844-2200 1860 Boul Valcartier, Valcartier, QC G0A 4S0

VENISE-EN-QUEBEC — C3 *Monteregie*

CAMPING PLAGE CHAMPLAIN **Ratings: 7.5/9.5★/8.5** (Campground) 2015 rates: $29 to $36. May 15 to Sep 15. (450)244-5317 29 Avenue Venise W, Venise En Quebec, QC J0J 2K0

CAMPING PLAGE VENISE **Ratings: 6.5/5.5/6.5** (Campground) 2015 rates: $30 to $40. May 15 to Oct 1. (514)979-5325 94 Ave Venise Est, Venise-En-Quebec, QC J0J 2K0

DOMAINE FLORENT **Ratings: 7/8.5★/7.5** (Campground) 2015 rates: $23 to $40. May 15 to Sep 15. (450)244-5607 272 23Eme Ave E, Venise en Quebec, QC J0J 2K0

KIRKLAND CAMPING PLAGE KIRKLAND **Ratings: 7.5/9★/9** (Campground) 2015 rates: $28 to $50. May 1 to Sep 30. (450)244-5337 39 Ave Venise E, Venise En Quebec, QC J0J 2K0

WEEDON — E6 *Cantons de l'Est*

CAMPING BEAU-SOLEIL **Ratings: 7.5/8.5★/7.5** (Campground) 2015 rates: $33 to $39. May 15 to Sep 15. (819)877-5000 1225 Route 112, Weedon, QC J0B 3J0

WEST BROME — B3 *Cantons de l'Est*

CAMPING VALLEE BLEUE **Ratings: 7.5/8.5★/8** (Campground) 2015 rates: $28 to $37. May 15 to Oct 15. (450)263-4804 50 Haman, West Brome, QC J0E 2P0

YAMASKA — A3 *Centre du Quebec*

PARC NATIONAL DE LA YAMASKA (Prov Pk) From I-10 (exit 68) & Hwy 139: Go on Hwy 139. 2015 rates: $28.50 to $37.75. (450)776-7182

Tourism Saskatchewan

WELCOME TO Saskatchewan

JOINED CONFEDERATION SEPT 1, 1905	WIDTH: 344 MILES (553 KM) LENGTH: 753 MILES (1212 KM)	PROPORTION OF CANADA 6.53% OF 9,984,670 SQ KM

Saskatchewan offers endless water sports, rich wildlife, uncrowded parks, ample outdoors adventures and delightful farm tours. You'll even find lots of golf opportunities in its vast, wide-open spaces. Don't worry about traffic jams or long lines—the province has room to spare. But Saskatchewan isn't only for lovers of the country. City slickers will find lots of urban excitement in places like Regina and Saskatoon, where metropolitan life buzzes throughout the year.

Saskatchewan is land-locked, but freshwater resources are abundant. More than 100,000 lakes dot the province, and it would require several lifetimes to travel all the canoe routes in the region—there are more than 50 in Prince Albert National Park alone.

The park has also carved out three auto routes, including one to the old homestead of Grey Owl, an English-born wilderness explorer who adopted a First Nations identity and emerged as one of Canada's most influential early conservationists.

Those efforts have paid off in Saskatchewan, where more than three million acres have been set aside as national and provincial parks. Saskatchewan also enjoys more sunny days than any other Canadian province.

Public lands here are varied. The flat-topped Cypress Hills region claims the highest elevations in the province, topping out close to 5,000 feet. Grasslands National Park, on the other hand, contains some of the last mixed-prairie ecosystems in North America.

Top 3 Tourism Attractions:
1) Royal Canadian Mounted Police
2) Western Development Museum
3) Athabasca Sand Dunes Provincial Park

Nickname: Bread Basket of Canada

State Flower: Western Red Lily

State Bird: Sharp-Tailed Grouse

People: Gordie Howe, hockey player; Leonard Lee, founder of Lee Valley Tools; Art Linkletter, radio and TV host; Leslie Nielsen, actor; Jon Vickers, tenor

Major Cities: Saskatoon, Regina (capital), Prince Albert, Moose Jaw

Topography: Landlocked, prairie province; north—Canadian Shield, boreal forests, sand dunes; south—plains, sand dunes

Climate: Four distinct seasons: summers—warm, dry; winters—very cold with temps remaining below freezing; occasional blizzards

TRAVEL & TOURISM

Tourism Saskatchewan
306-787-2300, 877-237-2273
www.sasktourism.com

Battlefords Tourism
800-243-0394, 306-445-2000
www.tourism.battlefords.com

East Central Tourism Region
306-783-8707, 877-250-6454
www.eastcentral.sask.info

Estevan Tourism, City Hall
306-634-6044
www.estevan.ca

Lloydminster Tourism & Convention Authority
800-825-6184, 306-871-8345
www.lloydminster.ca

City of Melfort
306-752-5911
www.cityofmelfort.ca

Tourism Moose Jaw Inc.
306-693-8097, 866-693-8097
www.moosejaw.ca-tourism-index.shtml

Northern Saskatchewan Tourism, Inc.
306-427-2202
www.northern.sask.info

Prince Albert & District Tourism
306-953-4385, 877-868-7470

West Central Tourism Region
800-665-4600, 306-446-3600
www.westcentral.sask.info

Saskatchewan SE Tourism Association
306-842-4648, 866-676-7111
www.southeast.sask.info

Saskatchewan SW Tourism Association
306-693-1883, 800-670-1093
www.southwest.sask.info

OUTDOOR RECREATION

Canoeing
www.canoesaskatchewan.rkc.ca

Saskatchewan Golf Association
www.saskgolf.ca

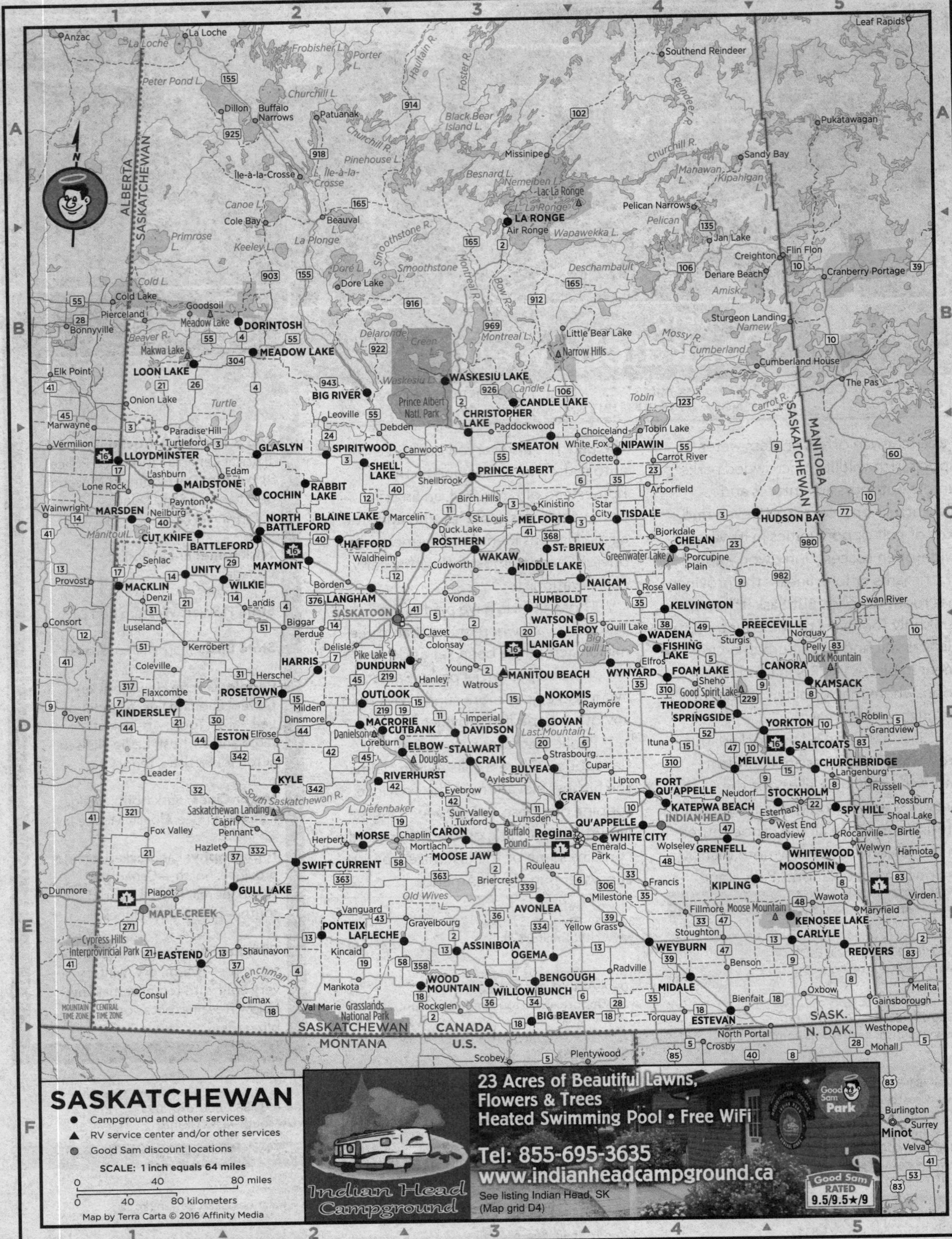
SASKATCHEWAN
Campground and other services
RV service center and/or other services
Good Sam discount locations
SCALE: 1 inch equals 64 miles
0 40 80 miles
0 40 80 kilometers
Map by Terra Carta © 2016 Affinity Media
23 Acres of Beautiful Lawns, Flowers & Trees
Heated Swimming Pool • Free WiFi
Tel: 855-695-3635
www.indianheadcampground.ca
See listing Indian Head, SK (Map grid D4)
Indian Head Campground
Good Sam Park
Good Sam RATED 9.5/9.5★/9

Featured Good Sam Parks

SASKATCHEWAN

Good Sam Park

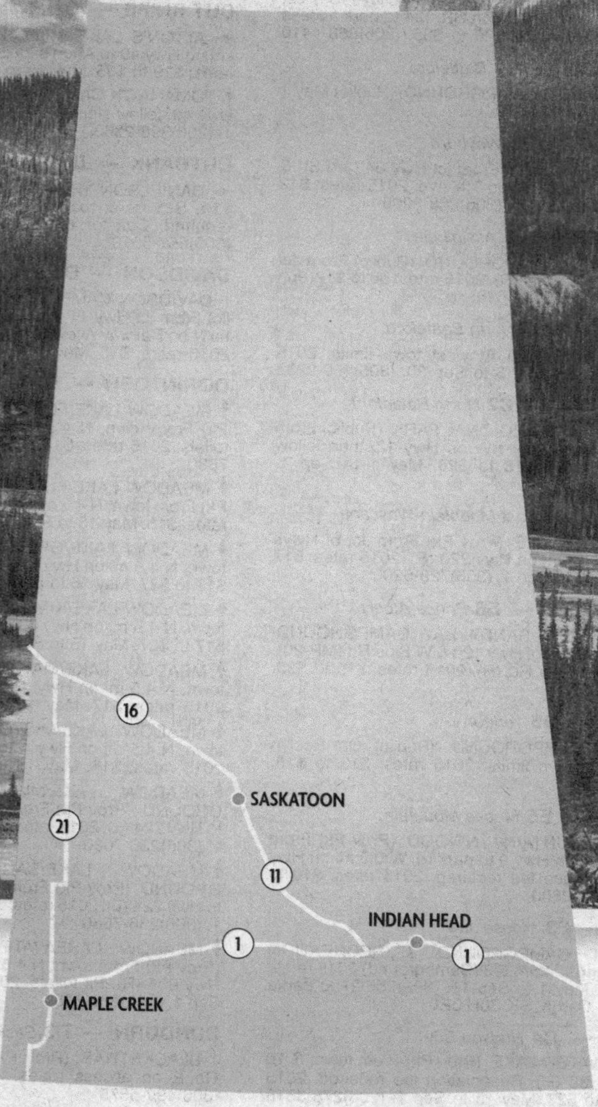

When you stay with Good Sam, you can expect the highest degree of cleanliness and friendliness, and better yet, you get 10% off campground fees.

If you're not already a Good Sam member you can purchase your membership at one of these locations:

INDIAN HEAD
Indian Head Campground
(855)695-3635

MAPLE CREEK
Eagle Valley Park Campground Ltd.
(306)662-2788

SASKATOON
Campland RV Resort
(306)477-7444

For more Good Sam Parks go to listing pages

Saskatchewan

CONSULTANTS

Ron & Marg Hobkirk

ASSINIBOIA — E3 *Assiniboia*

ASSINIBOIA REGIONAL PARK & GOLF COURSE (Public) From jct Hwy 13 & Hwy 2: Go .9 km/1/2 mi S on Hwy 2. 2015 rates: $15 to $25. May 21 to Sep 30. (306)642-5442

AVONLEA — E3 *Moose Jaw*

DUNNET REGIONAL PARK (Public) From Jct SR-339 & SR-334, S 2 mi on SR-334 to park access rd, E 2 mi. 2015 rates: $20 to $35. (306)868-4410

BATTLEFORD — C2 *Battleford*

EILING KRAMER CAMPGROUND (Public) May 1 to Sep 30. (306)937-6212

BENGOUGH — E3 *Weyburn*

BENGOUGH (Public) From jct Hwy 34 (3rd St) & 7th Ave: Go 1 block W on 7th Ave. 2015 rates: $12 to $30. May 1 to Oct 15. (306)268-2909

BIG BEAVER — F3 *Assiniboia*

BIG BEAVER CAMPGROUND (Public) From Jct of Hwys 18, N 0.75 mi (R). 2015 rates: $8 to $12. Jun 1 to Sep 30. (306)267-4520

BIG RIVER — B2 *North Battleford*

BIG RIVER (Public) At west town limits. 2015 rates: $22 to $35. May 5 to Sep 30. (306)469-2232

BLAINE LAKE — C2 *North Battleford*

MARTIN'S LAKE REGIONAL PARK (Public) From town: Go 24 km/15 mi NW on Hwy 12, then follow signs. 2015 rates: $15 to $20. May 1 to Sep 1. (306)466-4438

BULYEA — D3 *Last Mountain-Wascana*

ROWANS RAVINE (Prov Pk) From Jct of Hwys 20 & 220, W 13 mi on Hwy 220 (E). 2015 rates: $17 to $27. May 15 to Sep 1. (306)725-5200

CANDLE LAKE — B3 *Prince Albert*

CANDLE LAKE/SANDY BAY CAMPGROUND (Prov Pk) From Jct of Hwy 120 & W Side Rd (MP-20), W 6 mi on W Side Rd (R). 2015 rates: $15 to $35. (306)929-8400

CANORA — D5 *Yorkton*

CANORA CAMPGROUND (Public) On Roslyn Ave at north town limits. 2015 rates: $13 to $18. (306)563-4355

CARLYLE — E5 *Moose Mountain*

MOOSE MOUNTAIN/LYNWOOD (Prov Pk) From town, N 16 mi on Hwy 9 to park rd, W 0.5 mi on Hwy 209 (E). Entrance fee required. 2015 rates: $10 to $20. (306)577-2600

CARON — E3 *Moose Jaw*

BESANT CAMPGROUND & RECREATION AREA **Ratings: 4.5/4.5/8** (Campground) 2015 rates: $30 to $35. May 1 to Sep 15. (306)756-2700 parka Access Rd, Caron, SK S0H 0R0

CHELAN — C4 *Hudson Bay*

GREENWATER LAKE (Prov Pk) From town, S 10 mi on Hwy 38 (R). Reservation fee required. 2015 rates: $17 to $27. May 15 to Sep 1. (306)278-3515

CHRISTOPHER LAKE — C3 *Prince Albert*

ANGLIN LAKE PROV RECREATION SITE (ANDERSON POINT CG) (Prov Pk) From jct Hwy 2N & Hwy 953: Go 8 km/5 mi W on Hwy 953. Pit toilets. 2015 rates: $12 to $17. (306)982-6250

EMMA LAKE PROV RECREATION SITE (MURRAY POINT/NORTH CG) (Prov Pk) From jct Hwy 2 & Hwy 263: Go 10 km/6-1/4 mi W on Hwy 263, then 5 km/3 mi N on Hwy 953. 2015 rates: $17 to $26. (306)982-2002

Nobody said it was easy being a 10. And our rating system makes it even tougher.

CHURCHBRIDGE — D5 *Yorkton*

CHURCHBRIDGE CAMPGROUND (Public) From Jct of Hwys 8, 16 & 80, S 0.25 mi on Hwy 80 (L). 2015 rates: $17 to $20. May 15 to Sep 1. (306)896-2240

COCHIN — C2 *Lloydminster*

THE BATTLEFORDS PROVINCIAL PARK (Prov Pk) From jct Hwy 26 & Hwy 4: Go 17.3 km/ 10-3/4 mi N on Hwy 4. 2015 rates: $17 to $27. (306)386-2212

CRAIK — D3 *Moose Jaw*

CRAIK & DISTRICT REGIONAL PARK (Public) NW on Hwy 11, at Craik Town exit, turn right on gravel park access rd, N 1.5 mi (follow white sail signs) to entrance (E). 2015 rates: $14 to $22. May 15 to Sep 15. (306)734-5102

CRAVEN — D3 *Regina*

CRAVEN WORLD CAMPGROUND **Ratings: 5.5/8/8** (Campground) 2015 rates: $28. May 1 to Sep 30. (306)731-3336 hwy 20, Craven, SK S0G 0N0

CUT KNIFE — C1 *Battleford*

ATTON'S LAKE (Public) From Cut Knife, E 14 km on Hwy 40 to Atton's Lake Rd, N 14 km (E). 2015 rates: $19 to $35. May 15 to Sep 30. (306)398-2814

TOMAHAWK CAMPGROUND (Public) In town on Hwy 40, follow signs. 2015 rates: $12. May 15 to Oct 1. (306)398-2363

CUTBANK — D2 *Saskatoon*

DANIELSON (Prov Pk) From Jct of Hwys 44 & 219, S 3 mi on park access rd (R). Entrance fee required: Call for rates. 2015 rates: $17 to $27. (306)857-5510

DAVIDSON — D3 *Saskatoon*

DAVIDSON CAMPGROUND (CITY PARK) (Public) From jct Hwy 11 & S Davidson exit: Go 2 km/1.3 mi N on Railway Ave, then 4 blocks E on Hamilton St. 2015 rates: $15. May 15 to Sep 15. (306)567-2908

DORINTOSH — B2 *Meadow Lake*

MEADOW LAKE/FLOTTEN LAKE NORTH (Prov Pk) From town, N 4.5 mi on Hwy 4 to 904 (L). Pit toilets. 2015 rates: $15. May 15 to Sep 1. (306)236-7680

MEADOW LAKE/FLOTTEN LAKE SOUTH (Prov Pk) From town, N 4.5 mi on Hwy 4 (L). Pit toilets. 2015 rates: $15. May 15 to Sep 1. (306)236-7680

MEADOW LAKE/GREIG LAKE (Prov Pk) From town, N 4.5 mi on Hwy 4 to Hwy 224 (L). 2015 rates: $17 to $27. May 15 to Sep 1. (306)236-7680

MEADOW LAKE/KIMBALL LAKE (Prov Pk) From town, N 4.5 mi on Hwy 4 to Hwy 224 (L). 2015 rates: $17 to $27. May 15 to Sep 1. (306)236-7680

MEADOW LAKE/MATHESON (Prov Pk) From town, N 4.5 mi on Hwy 4 to Hwy 224 (L). Pit toilets. 2015 rates: $17. May 15 to Sep 1. (306)236-7680

MEADOW LAKE/MISTOHAY (Prov Pk) From town, N 4.5 mi on Hwy 4 to Hwy 224 (L). Pit toilets. 2015 rates: $15. May 15 to Sep 1. (306)236-7680

MEADOW LAKE/MURRAY DOELL CAMPGROUND (Prov Pk) From town, N 4.5 mi on Hwy 4 to Hwy 224 (L). 2015 rates: $15 to $27. May 15 to Sep 1. (306)236-7680

MEADOW LAKE/SANDY BEACH CAMPGROUND (Prov Pk) From town, N 4.5 mi on Hwy 4 to Hwy 224 (L). 2015 rates: $17 to $27. May 15 to Sep 1. (306)236-7680

MEADOW LAKE/WATERHEN LAKE SOUTH (Prov Pk) From town, N 4.5 mi on Hwy 4, N 10 mi on Hwy 904 (R). Pit toilets. 2015 rates: $23. May 15 to Sep 1. (306)236-7680

DUNDURN — D3 *Saskatoon*

BLACKSTRAP (Prov Pk) From Hwy 11 in town: Go E on access roads. 2015 rates: $15 to $35. (306)492-5675

EASTEND — E1 *Maple Creek*

EASTEND TOWN PARK (Public) From jct Hwy 13 (Red Coat Dr) & Tamarack Ave N: Go 2 blocks N on Tamarack Ave N. (306)295-3322

ELBOW — D3 *Moose Jaw*

DOUGLAS (Prov Pk) From S end of town, S 7 mi on SR-19 (R). Entrance fee required. 2015 rates: $17 to $27. (306)854-6266

ESTEVAN — E4 *Weyburn*

WOODLAWN REGIONAL PARK (Public) From town, S 2 mi on Hwy 47 (L). 2015 rates: $10. May 17 to Sep 30. (306)634-2324

ESTON — D1 *Swift Current*

ESTON RIVERSIDE REGIONAL PARK (Public) From south town limits on Hwy 30: Go 21 km/13 mi S on Hwy 30. 2015 rates: $13 to $25. May 1 to Sep 30. (306)962-3845

FISHING LAKE — D4 *Quill Lakes*

FISHING LAKE REGIONAL PARK (Public) From Jct SR-16 & CR-310, N 10 mi on CR-310 (R). Entrance fee required. 2015 rates: $20. May 1 to Oct 31. (306)272-3968

FOAM LAKE — D4 *Wynyard*

FOAM LAKE CAMPGROUND (CITY PARK) (Public) In town at jct Hwy 16 & Hwy 310. 2015 rates: $18 to $35. (306)272-3714

FORT QU'APPELLE — D4 *Regina*

ECHO VALLEY (Prov Pk) From town, W 5.25 mi on Hwy 210 (E). 2015 rates: $17 to $35. May 15 to Sep 1. (306)332-3215

FORT QU'APPELLE CAMPGROUND (Public) From Jct of Hwy 10 & Boundary Rd, N 1 mi on Boundary Rd to Fort Trail, W 200 yds(E). 2015 rates: $20 to $25. May 12 to Sep 7. (306)332-4614

GLASLYN — C2 *Lloydminster*

LITTLE LOON REGIONAL PARK (Public) From jct Hwy 4 & Hwy 3: Go 4-3/4 km/3 mi E on Hwy 3, then 1-1/2 km/1 mi S on gravel road. 2015 rates: $19 to $26. May 1 to Sep 30. (306)342-2176

GOVAN — D3 *Saskatoon*

LAST MOUNTAIN REGIONAL PARK (Public) From north town limits: Go 5 km/3 mi N on Hwy 20, then 14 km/8-3/4 mi W on grid road. 2015 rates: $18 to $25. May 9 to Sep 14. (306)484-4483

GRENFELL — E4 *Moose Mountain*

CROOKED LAKE (Prov Pk) From jct Trans Canada Hwy 1 & Hwy 47: Go 31 km/19-1/4 mi N on Hwy 47, then E on Hwy 247. 2015 rates: $17 to $27. May 15 to Sep 1. (306)728-7480

GRENFELL RECREATIONAL PARK (Public) From Jct of Trans-Canada Hwy & Desmond St, N 0.75 mi on Desmond St to Front St, W 0.5 mi (L). 2015 rates: $17 to $25. May 15 to Sep 30. (306)697-3055

GULL LAKE — E2 *Swift Current*

ANTELOPE LAKE (Public) From jct Hwy 1 & Hwy 37: Go 19 km/12 mi N on Hwy 37, then 3-1/4 km/2 mi E (follow signs). 2015 rates: $20. May 15 to Sep 15. (306)672-3933

GULL LAKE CAMPGROUND (Public) From Jct of Hwy 37 & 6th St (in town), E 0.3 mi on 6th St (L). 2015 rates: $20 to $25. May 15 to Sep 30. (306)672-3447

HAFFORD — C2 *Dundurn-Rosthern*

REDBERRY LAKE REGIONAL PARK (Public) From Hafford, E 5 mi on Hwy 40 to park access rd, S 3 mi, follow signs (E). 2015 rates: $20 to $40. May 1 to Sep 30. (306)549-2149

HARRIS — D2 *Battleford*

CRYSTAL BEACH REGIONAL PARK (Public) From south town limits on Hwy 7: Go 3 km/1-3/4 m S on Hwy 7. May 17 to Sep 15. (306)656-2134

HUDSON BAY — C5 *Hudson Bay*

HUDSON BAY REGIONAL PARK (Public) From town, S 1.5 mi, adjacent to Hwy 9 (R). 2015 rates: $1[illegible] to $26. May 15 to Sep 15. (306)865-2263

HUMBOLDT — C3 *Prince Albert*

HUMBOLDT HISTORICAL PARK AND CAMPGROUND (Public) From jct Hwys 20 & 5: Go 4 blk E on Hwy 5. 2015 rates: $20 to $25. May 1 to Oct 31 (306)682-4990

WALDSEA LAKE REGIONAL PARK (Public From jct Hwy 5 & Hwy 20: Go 4.8 km/3 mi N on Hw 20, then go 3 1/4 km/2 mi W on Gravel Rd. May 1[illegible] to Sep 17. (306)682-3528

Did you know we sent 35 husband-wife RVin teams out this year to scour North America rating and inspecting RV parks an campgrounds? You can rest easy when yo read our listings, knowing we've already bee there.

INDIAN HEAD — E4 *Wascana*

➔ INDIAN HEAD CAMPGROUND
Ratings: 9.5/9.5★/9 (Campground) From Jct of Hwy 1 & East Entrance to Indian Head, N (across railway tracks) 0.3km/0.2 mi (L). **FAC:** All weather rds. (160 spaces). Avail: 70 all weather, patios, 50 pull-thrus (30 x 80), back-ins (20 x 30), 50 full hkups, 20 W, 3 E (30/50 amps), seasonal sites, WiFi, tent sites, rentals, dump, laundry, groc, LP bottles, fire rings, firewood. **REC:** heated pool, playground. Pet restrict(B/Q) $. Big rig sites, eco-friendly, 2015 rates: $39 to $43. May 1 to Sep 30.
(855)695-3635 Lat: 50.53062, Lon: -103.65668
1100 Mckay St., Indian Head, SK S0G 2K0
indianheadcampground@sasktel.net
www.indianheadcampground.ca
See ad this page, 1476 (SK Map), 1477.

KAMSACK — D5 *Yorkton*

➔ DUCK MOUNTAIN (Prov Pk) From town, E 13 mi on Hwy 57 to park entry, E 3 mi (E). 2015 rates: $17 to $35. (306)542-5500

KATEPWA BEACH — D4 *Regina*

↓ SOUTH KATEPWA RV PARK **Ratings: 6/8.5★/9** (RV Park) 2015 rates: $32. May 15 to Sep 15. (306)695-3330 hwy 56 (Rm156-Indian Head), Katepwa Beach, SK S0G 2K0

KELVINGTON — C4 *Melfort*

KELVINGTON LIONS PARK (Public) At south end of town on Hwy 38. Follow signs. (306)327-4481

KENOSEE LAKE — E5 *Estevan*

↑ MOOSE MOUNTAIN/FISH CREEK CAMPGROUND (Prov Pk) From town, N 17 mi on Hwy 9 (L). 2015 rates: $10 to $24. May to Oct. (306)577-2600

KINDERSLEY — D1 *Kindersley*

KINDERSLEY REGIONAL PARK (Public) From jct Hwy 7 & Ditson Dr: Go 1.5 km/1-1/4 mi S on Ditson Dr. 2015 rates: $24 to $26. May 1 to Sep 30. (306)463-2788

KIPLING — E4 *Melville*

↓ KIPLING CAMPGROUND (Public) From Jct Hwy 65 & Hwy 48: Go W 1/2 mi (.09 km) on Hwy 48, then S 1/2 mi (.08 km) on 6th Ave./Louisa Ave, then W 55 yards (50 meters) on Clare St. (E). 2015 rates: $25 to $30. May 1 to Oct 15. (306)736-8440

KYLE — D2 *Swift Current*

SASKATCHEWAN LANDING PROVINCIAL PARK (Prov Pk) From town: Go 11 km/7 mi S on Hwy 4, then 4-3/4 km/3 mi E on park road. 2015 rates: $17 to $27. (306)375-5527

LA RONGE — B3 *La Ronge*

↑ LAC LA RONGE PROVINCIAL PARK (Prov Pk) From town, N 15 mi on Hwy 2 (L). 2015 rates: $15 to $27. (306)425-4234

LAC LA RONGE PROVINCIAL PARK (NUT POINT CAMPGROUND) (Prov Pk) From jct Brown St & La Ronge Ave: Go 3.6 km/2-1/4 mi E on La Ronge Ave. 2015 rates: $17 to $27. (306)425-4234

LAC LA RONGE PROVINCIAL PARK (WADIN BAY CAMPGROUND) (Prov Pk) From jct Brown St & Hwy 102 N: Go 27 km/16-3/4 mi N on Hwy 102 N, then .9 km/1/2 mi N on service road. 2015 rates: $17 to $27. (306)425-4234

LAFLECHE — E3 *Assiniboia*

THOMSON LAKE REGIONAL PARK (Public) From jct Hwy 13 & Hwy 58: Go 8 km/5 mi N on Hwy 58. 2015 rates: $19 to $37. May 1 to Sep 30. (306)472-3752

LANGHAM — C2 *Saskatoon*

⬅ RIVER VALLEY R.V. PARK **Ratings: 4.5/9★/9** (RV Park) 2015 rates: $31 to $33. Apr 15 to Oct 31. (306)283-4672 201 Service Rd West, Langham, SK S0K 2L0

LANIGAN — D3 *Saskatoon*

LANIGAN LIONS CAMPGROUND (Public) From jct Hwy 16 & Hoover St: Go 4 blocks N on Hoover St, then 3 blocks E on Downing Dr. 2015 rates: $12 to $20. May 1 to Oct 15.

LEROY — D3 *Wynyard*

LEROY LEISURELAND REGIONAL PARK (Public) From Hwy 6: Go 12 mi W. 2015 rates: $30. May 15 to Sep 30. (306)286-3437

LLOYDMINSTER — C1 *Battleford*

➔ WEAVER PARK CAMPGROUND (Public) From Jct of Hwy 17 & Hwy 16, E 1 mi on Hwy 16 to 45th Ave, S 0.1 mi (R). 2015 rates: $40. May 1 to Sep 30. (306)825-3726

LOON LAKE — B1 *Meadow Lake*

⬅ MAKWA LAKE/MEWASIN (Prov Pk) From town, SW 3 mi on Grid 699 (L). Entrance fee required. Pit toilets. 2015 rates: $17. (306)837-2410

⬅ MAKWA/JUMBO BEACH CAMPGROUND (Prov Pk) From town, SW 3 mi on Grid 699 (L). Entrance fee required. Pit toilets. 2015 rates: $17. May 16 to Sep 2. (306)837-2410

MACKLIN — C1 *Kindersley*

MACKLIN LAKE REGIONAL PARK (Prov Pk) From jct Hwy 14 & Hwy 31: Go 3-1/4 km/2 mi S on Hwy 31 (through town), then 450 meters/500 yards SW. 2015 rates: $20 to $30. May 1 to Oct 31. (306)753-3252

MACRORIE — D2 *Kindersley*

COLDWELL PARK REC SITE (Natl Pk) From town, SE 8 mi on Hwy 44, follow signs (E). Pit toilets. 2015 rates: $17. Jun 27 to Sep 1. (306)857-2155

MAIDSTONE — C1 *Battleford*

MAIDSTONE CAMPGROUND (CITY PARK) (Public) From jct Hwy 21 & Hwy 16: Go 6-1/2 km/4 mi W on Hwy 16. Pit toilets. 2015 rates: $7 to $10. (306)893-2373

↑ SILVER LAKE REGIONAL PARK (Public) From Jct of Hwys 16 & 21, N 9 mi on Hwy 21 to Silver Lake Cnty Rd, E 1 mi to Regional Park access rd, N 0.5 mi (N). 2015 rates: $17 to $25. Apr 15 to Oct 15. (306)893-2831

MANITOU BEACH — D3 *Quill Lakes*

↓ MANITOU & DISTRICT REGIONAL PARK (Public) From Watrous, N 3.5 mi on Hwy 365, follow signs (R). Entrance fee required. 2015 rates: $19 to $29. May 1 to Oct 12. (306)946-2588

MAPLE CREEK — E1 *Cypress Hills*

↓ CYPRESS HILLS (Prov Pk) From town, S 18 mi on Hwy 21 (R). 2015 rates: $17 to $35. (306)662-5411

↑ EAGLE VALLEY PARK CAMPGROUND LTD.
Ratings: 8/9.5★/9.5 (Campground) From Jct of Trans Cda Hwy 1 & Hwy 21, W 3 mi (4 km) on Trans Cda Hwy 1 (L) - 88kms/54.7 mi E of Medicine Hat. Elev 2515 ft. **FAC:** All weather rds. (116 spaces). 50 Avail: 39 paved, 11 grass, 37 pull-thrus (24 x 65), back-ins (20 x 35), 11 full hkups, 22 W, 22 E (30 amps), seasonal sites, WiFi Hotspot, tent sites, rentals, dump, laundry, fire rings, firewood, restaurant. **REC:** heated pool $, Maple Creek: fishing, playground. No pets. Eco-friendly, 2015 rates: $36 to $38. Disc: AAA. May 1 to Sep 30.
(306)662-2788 Lat: 49.97544, Lon: -109.52677
sw Q-8 of 12 of 26 W 3rd., Maple Creek, SK S0N 1N0
eaglevalley@sasktel.net
www.eaglevalleypark.ca
See ad this page, 1477.

MARSDEN — C1 *Kindersley*

SUFFERN LAKE REGIONAL PARK (Public) From town: Go 6 km/3-3/4 mi SE on Hwy 40. 2015 rates: $15 to $20. May 1 to Sep 30. (306)826-5410

MAYMONT — C2 *North Battleford*

GLENBURN REGIONAL PARK (Public) From town: Go 8 km/5 mi S on Hwy 376. 2015 rates: $15 to $30. May 15 to Sep 15. (306)389-4700

MEADOW LAKE — B2 *Lloydminster*

MEADOW LAKE LIONS REGIONAL PARK & MUSEUM (Public) In town on Hwy 4. 2015 rates: $25. May 25 to Sep 7. (306)236-4447

MELFORT — C3 *Melfort*

MELFORT SOUTH CAMPGROUND (Public) From jct Hwys 3/6/41: Go 270 meters/300 yds W on Hwy 41. 2015 rates: $20 to $25. (306)752-5560

MELVILLE — D4 *Yorkton*

➚ MELVILLE REGIONAL PARK (Public) From Jct of Hwys 47 & 10 (Queen St), S 0.2 mi on Queen St to Halfax St, E 0.2 mi to Prince Edward St, S 0.1 mi (L). 2015 rates: $20 to $25. May 1 to Sep 30. (306)728-4111

MIDALE — E4 *Weyburn*

➚ MAINPRIZE REG PARK (Public) From Jct Hwy 39 & Hwy 606, S 0.3 mi on Hwy 606 to Stop Sign, W 5 mi on Hwy 606 to Stop Sign, S 1 mi on Hwy 606 to Unamed Access Rd, W 3.8 mi (E). 2015 rates: $20 to $38. May 15 to Sep 15. (306)458-2865

MIDDLE LAKE — C3 *Quill Lakes*

⬅ LUCIEN LAKE REGIONAL PARK (Public) From Jct of Hwy 20 & Lucien Lake Rd, W 1 mi on Lucien Lake Rd (E). 2015 rates: $14 to $25. May 15 to Sep 15. (306)367-4300

MOOSE JAW — E3 *Moose Jaw*

↑ BUFFALO POUND/ELMVIEW (Prov Pk) From town, N 11 mi on Hwy 2 to Hwy 202, E 6.8 mi (L) Entrance fee required. 2015 rates: $15 to $35. (306)694-3229

↑ BUFFALO POUND/MAPLE VALE (Prov Pk) From town, N 11 mi on Hwy 2 to Hwy 202, E 6.8 mi (E) Entrance fee required. 2015 rates: $15 to $35. (306)694-3229

↑ BUFFALO POUND/SHADY LANE (Prov Pk) From town, N 11 mi on Hwy 2 to Hwy 202, E 6.8 mi (E) Entrance fee required. 2015 rates: $15 to $35. (306)694-3229

➚ **PRAIRIE OASIS TOURIST COMPLEX Ratings: 6/10★/8.5** (RV Park) From Jct of Hwy 1 & Thatcher Dr East, W 0.16 km/0.1 mi on Thatcher Dr East (L). **FAC:** Paved rds. (94 spaces). 54 Avail: 28 paved, 26 gravel, 28 pull-thrus (25 x 70), back-ins (20 x 30), 28 full hkups, 26 W, 26 E (15/50 amps), seasonal sites, WiFi, tent sites, rentals, dump, laundry, groc, LP gas, restaurant. **REC:** wading pool, pond, fishing, playground. Pets OK. Partial handicap access. Big rig sites, 2015 rates: $36 to $39. Apr 1 to Oct 31.
AAA Approved
(800)854-8855 Lat: 50.410851, Lon: -105.509576
955 Thatcher Dr E, Moose Jaw, SK S6H 4N9
prairieoasis@sasktel.net
www.prairie-oasis.com

SK

MOOSOMIN — E5 *Moose Mountain*

↑ FIELDSTONE CAMPGROUND & RV RESORT **Ratings: 6/6.5/8** (Campground) 2015 rates: $25 to $38. May 1 to Oct 31. (800)511-2677 route 8, Moosomin, SK S0G 3N0

MOOSOMIN AND DISTRICT REGIONAL PARK (Prov Pk) From jct Hwy 1 & Hwy 8: Go 4-3/4 km/3 mi S on Hwy 8, then 3 mi W on Secondary Hwy 709, then 3-1/4 km/2 mi S. 2015 rates: $21 to $37.75. May 15 to Sep 30. (306)435-3531

MORSE — E2 *Moose Jaw*

➚ TOWN OF MORSE CAMPGROUND (Public) From Hwy 1: Go N on Railway Ave. Pit toilets. 2015 rates: $25. (306)629-3300

NAICAM — C4 *Quill Lakes*

LAKE CHARRON REGIONAL PARK (Public) From town, S 1 mi on Hwy 6 to access rd, E 8 mi follow signs (R). 2015 rates: $10. May 15 to Sep 15. (306)874-8292

NIPAWIN — C4 *Prince Albert*

↑ NIPAWIN & DISTRICT REGIONAL PARK (Public) From town, S 1.5 mi on Hwy 55 (L). Entrance fee required. 2015 rates: $28 to $35. May 15 to Oct 7. (306)862-3237

NOKOMIS — D3 *Saskatoon*

NOKOMIS CAMPGROUND (CITY PARK) (Public) From jct of Hwy 15 & Hwy 20: Go 1-1/2 km/1 mi N on Hwy 20 (through town to 7th Ave). Pit toilets. (306)528-2010

NORTH BATTLEFORD — C2 *North Battleford*

➔ DAVID LAIRD CAMPGROUND (Public) From Jct of Hwy 40 & Hwy 16E, E 1 mi on Hwy 16 to Unmarked Rd, N 0.75 mi (L). 2015 rates: $17 to $30. May 1 to Sep 30. (306)445-3552

OGEMA — E3 *Weyburn*

OGEMA REGIONAL PARK (Prov Pk) In town on Hwy 13. 2015 rates: $15 to $25. May 19 to Sep 2. (306)459-2709

OUTLOOK — D2 *Saskatoon*

OUTLOOK & DISTRICT REGIONAL PARK (Prov Pk) From town: Go 45 km/28 mi S on Hwy 45. (306)867-8846

PONTEIX — E2 *Assiniboia*

NOTUKEU REGIONAL PARK (Prov Pk) From jct Hwy 13 & town access road (Centre St): Go 2.3 km/1-1/2 mi N on Centre St, then 1 block W on Railway Ave. 2015 rates: $20 to $25. May 25 to Sep 30. (306)625-3959

PREECEVILLE — D4 *Yorkton*

PREECEVILLE CAMPGROUND (Prov Pk) Second street and eighth avenue NW in Preeceville. (306)547-2276

SASKATCHEWAN WILDLIFE FEDERATION CAMPGROUND (Public Corps) From jct of Hwy 49 & 2nd St NE: Go E to 7th Ave. NW. (306)547-2810

PRINCE ALBERT — C3 *North Central, Saskatchewan*

MARY NISBET CAMPGROUND (Public) From N jct Hwy 55 & Hwy 2: Go 1.5 km/1 mi N on Hwy 2, then 120 m/130 yds SE on local Rd. 2015 rates: $15 to $20. May 15 to Sep 15. (306)953-4880

➔ PRINCE ALBERT EXHIBITION RV CAMPGROUND (Public) From Jct of Hwy 2 & 15th St W, E 0.9 mi on 15th St W (becomes 15th St E) to 6th Ave E, N 0.3 mi to Exhibition Dr, E 0.1 mi (E). 2015 rates: $17 to $25. May 1 to Sep 30. (306)764-1611

QU'APPELLE — E4 *Regina*

➔ CREEKSIDE GARDENS **Ratings: 3/8★/6.5** (Campground) 2015 rates: $25. May 1 to Sep 30. (306)699-7466 95-9th Ave, Qu'appelle, SK S0G 4A0

RABBIT LAKE — C2 *Battleford*

MEETING LAKE REGIONAL PARK (Public) From Jct Hwy 378 & Rabbit Lake Rd., N 6 mi on Hwy 378 to Meeting Lake Rd, N 1.6 mi (R) $5 Park Gate Fee. 2015 rates: $23 to $30. May 16 to Sep 1. (306)824-4812

REDVERS — E5 *Estevan*

REDVERS (TOURISM) LOG CABIN CAMPGROUND (Prov Pk) From jct Hwy 8 & Hwy 13: Go .9 km/1/2 mi W on Hwy 13, then 100 metres/110 yds S on Methuen St. May 17 to Sep 1. (306)452-3276

REGINA — E3 *Wascana*

➔ BUFFALO LOOKOUT RV PARK & CAMPING **Ratings: 6/5/7** (RV Park) 2015 rates: $35 to $42. Apr 1 to Nov 1. (306)525-1448 south East 201718 W 2, Regina, SK S4N 7L2

➔ KINGS ACRES CAMPGROUND **Ratings: 6/7.5/6.5** (RV Park) 2015 rates: $36 to $45. (306)522-1619 hwy 1 E & East Gate Dr, Regina, SK S4L 7C6

RIVERHURST — D2 *Moose Jaw*

➔ PALLISER REGIONAL PARK (Public) From Jct of Hwys 19 & 42, W 18 mi on Hwy 42 to park access rd, S 1.5 mi, follow signs (R). Entrance fee required. 2015 rates: $30 to $45. May 25 to Sep 7. (306)353-4604

ROSETOWN — D2 *Kindersley*

➔ PRAIRIE VIEW PARK **Ratings: 2/7/7.5** (RV Park) 2015 rates: $30. May 1 to Oct 30. (306)882-4257 marshall Ave., Rosetown, SK S0L 2V0

ROSTHERN — C3 *Dundurn-Rosthern*

VALLEY REGIONAL PARK (Public) From town, N 2 km on Hwy 11 (R) Entrance fee required. 2015 rates: $24 to $30. Apr 15 to Oct 1. (306)232-5000

SALTCOATS — D5 *Yorkton*

➔ SALTCOATS REGIONAL PARK (Prov Pk) From town, E 0.6 mi on Hwy 16 (Yellowhead Hwy) to access rd, N 0.2 mi (E). 2015 rates: $15 to $20. May 20 to Sep 3. (306)744-2254

SASKATOON — C3 *Dundurn-Rosthern*

CAMPLAND RV RESORT

Ratings: 8.5/10★/9 (RV Park) From the city of Saskatoon, NW 9 km (5.5 mi) on Hwy 16 to Lutheran Rd, E 0.7 km (0.4 mi) on Lutheran Rd (R). **FAC:** Gravel rds. 132 gravel, 132 pull-thrus (30 x 70), 132 full hkups (30/50 amps), WiFi, tent sites, showers $, laundry, groc, LP bottles, fire rings, firewood. **REC:** heated pool $, playground. Pet restrict(Q). Partial handicap access. Big rig sites, eco-friendly. 2015 rates: $40 to $44. Apr 4 to Nov 1.
(306)477-7444 Lat: 52.259534, Lon: -106.781449
hwy 16 & Lutheran Rd, Saskatoon, SK S7K 3N2
camplandrvresort@sasktel.net
www.camplandrvresort.com
See ad this page, 1477.

➔ **GORDON HOWE CAMPGROUND**

(Public) From Jct of Idylwyld Dr & 22nd St, W 1.6km/1 mi on 22nd St to Ave P South, S 2.4km/1.5 mi (E). **FAC:** Paved rds. 135 gravel, 8 pull-thrus (35 x 60), back-ins (35 x 55), 135 W, 135 E (30/50 amps), WiFi, tent sites, dump, mobile sewer, laundry, groc, fire rings, firewood, controlled access. **REC:** playground. Pets OK. Partial handicap access. 2015 rates: $34 to $40. Apr 16 to Oct 13. ATM.
(306)975-3328 Lat: 52.10739, Lon: -106.69353
1640 Ave. P South, Saskatoon, SK S7M 2X8
gordonhowe.campground@saskatoon.ca
www.saskatoon.ca/go/camp
See ad this page.

PIKE LAKE (Prov Pk) From town, S 14.5 mi on Hwy 60 (E). 2015 rates: $27. May 15 to Sep 1. (306)933-6966

SASKATOON 16 WEST RV PARK **Ratings: 4.5/8★/5.5** (RV Park) 2015 rates: $40 to $44. Apr 15 to Oct 15. (800)478-7833 site 401, Box 91 Rr4, Saskatoon, SK S7K 3J7

Things to See and Do

➔ **HOLIDAY PARK GOLF COURSE** Features an 18-hole championship course plus an executive 9-hole course. the 6538-yard championship course nestled in the south Saskatchewan River Valley. Combines great golf with natural scenic beauty. Apr 15 to Oct 15. RV accessible. Rest rooms, food. Hours: 5am to 10pm. Adult fee: $24.25 to 48.50.
(306)975-3325 Lat: 52.10909, Lon: -106.706103
1630 Avenue U South-11th Street W, Saskatoon, SK S7M 1H4
leisure.services@saskatoon.ca
www.saskatoon.ca/go/golf
See ad this page.

➔ **RIVERSDALE OUTDOOR POOL** Riversdale Pool features 180 ft waterslide, zero depth water for toddlers, diving boards, playground, volleyball court, basketball, lawn area with electric BBQ & concession. Jun 12 to Sep 4. partial handicap access. Food. Hours: 11am to 8pm. Adult fee: $7.35. No CC.
(306)975-3353 Lat: 52.108965, Lon: -106.700932
822 Avenue Hs, Saskatoon, SK S7K 0J5
www.saskatoon.ca
See ad this page.

SASKATOON FORESTRY FARM PARK & ZOO Find yourself eye to eye with native prairie animals and exotic reptiles, birds of prey and monkeys and other at Saskatchewan's only Caza accredited Zoo. Apr 1 to Oct 31. partial handicap access. Food. Hours: 9am to 9pm. Adult fee: $11 youth $6.60 family $22.
(306)975-3382 Lat: 52.15669, Lon: -106.58212
1903 Forestry Farm Park Drive, Saskatoon, SK S7K 0J5
www.saskatoon.ca
See ad this page.

SHELL LAKE — C2 *Dundurn-Rosthern*

MEMORIAL LAKE REGIONAL PARK (Public) From Jct of Hwys 3 & 12, N 0.25 mi on Hwy 12/park access rd (R). Entrance fee required. 2015 rates: $22 to $27.50. May 1 to Sep 30. (306)427-2281

SMEATON — C3 *Melfort*

NARROW HILLS PROVINCIAL PARK (Prov Pk) From jct Hwy 55 & Hwy 106: Go 69 km/43 mi N on Hwy 106. 2015 rates: $15 to $27. (306)426-2622

Park owners want you to be satisfied with your stay. Get to know them.

Say you saw it in our Guide!

SPIRITWOOD — C2 *Meadow Lake*

↑ CHITEK LAKE (Prov Pk) From town, NW 35 mi on Hwy 24 (E). 2015 rates: $15 to $35. May 15 to Oct 21. (306)984-2343

SPRINGSIDE — D4 *Yorkton*

↑ GOOD SPIRIT LAKE (Prov Pk) From town, NE 16 mi on Hwy 47 to park access road, E 4 mi (E). 2015 rates: $17 to $26. May to Sep. (306)792-4750

SPY HILL — D5 *Yorkton*

↑ CARLTON TRAIL (Public) From town, N 4 mi on Hwy 8 (L). 2015 rates: $28. May 1 to Sep 30. (306)534-4724

ST BRIEUX — C3 *Prince Albert*

ST BRIEUX REGIONAL PARK & GOLF COURSE (Public) At jct of Hwy 368 & Barbier Dr: Go 1 km/6/10 mi W of St. Brieux. 2015 rates: $23 to $32. May 16 to Sep 16. (306)275-4433

STALWART — D3 *Saskatoon*

RESORT VILLAGE OF ETTERS BEACH CAMPGROUND (VILLAGE PARK) (Prov Pk) From jct Hwy 2 & Hwy 11: Go N to Stalwart, then 7.2 km/4-1/2 mi E on Grid Rd. 2015 rates: $20 to $30. May 15 to Sep 27. (306)963-2532

STOCKHOLM — D5 *Melville*

BIRD'S POINT (Public) From jct Hwy 1 & Hwy 9: Go 16 km/10 mi N on Hwy 9, then 11.2 km/7 mi W on Hwy 247 (follow signs). May 1 to Sep 1. (306)793-4552

SWIFT CURRENT — E2 *Moose Jaw, Swift Current*

LAC PELLETIER REGIONAL PARK (Prov Pk) From east jct Hwy 1 & Hwy 4: Go 48 km/29 mi S on Hwy 4, then 14 km/10 mi W on grid road. 2015 rates: $25 to $40. May 1 to Sep 30. (306)627-3595

↗ **PONDAROSA MH & RV PARK**
Ratings: 6/7.5★/7.5 (Campground) From jct Hwy 4 & Hwy 1: Go .8 km / .5 mi E on Hwy 1, to exit road, 33 yds S on exit road, to frontage road then 220 yds W (L). **FAC:** Gravel rds. (97 spaces). Avail: 77 gravel, 22 pull-thrus (22 x 80), back-ins (25 x 60), some side by side hkups, 70 full hkups, 7 W, 7 E (30/50 amps), seasonal sites, WiFi, tent sites, dump, laundry, fire rings, firewood. **REC:** Swift Current Creek: fishing, playground. Pets OK. 2015 rates: $34 to $36.
AAA Approved
(306)773-5000 Lat: 50.307863, Lon: -107.766369
hwy 1 -Trans Canada Hwy-East side, Swift Current, SK S9H 3X6
camppondarosa@shaw.ca
www.pondarosacampground.ca
See ad this page.

↖ TRAIL CAMPGROUND **Ratings: 5.5/7/6.5** (Campground) 2015 rates: $25 to $38. May 1 to Oct 15. (306)773-8088 53-701 11th Ave NW, Swift Current, SK S9H 4M5

The RVers' Guide to NASCAR helps RV travelers get the most out of North America's most thrilling sporting event. Turn to the front of the Guide and we'll give you the inside track on how to get high-speed thrills at major NASCAR venues.

THEODORE — D4 *Yorkton*

SAND WHITE REGIONAL PARK (Public) From jct Hwy 16 & Grid Rd 651: Go 6.4 km/4 mi N on Grid Rd 651, then 2.4 km/1-1/2 mi E. Follow signs. May 1 to Sep 15. (306)647-2191

TISDALE — C4 *Melfort*

KIPABISKAU REGIONAL PARK (Public) From town: Go 29 km/18 mi S on Hwy 35, then 11-1/4 km/7 mi W on gravel road. 2015 rates: $22.50 to $27.50. May 16 to Sep 7. (306)873-4335

UNITY — C1 *Kindersley*

UNITY AND DISTRICT REGIONAL PARK (Public) From west town limits on Hwy 14: Go 2 km/1-1/4 mi W on Hwy 14. Apr 15 to Oct 1. (306)228-2621

WADENA — D4 *Wynyard*

WADENA CAMPGROUND (Public) From jct Pamela Wallin Dr & Jim Headington Way: Go 1/2 block E on Pamela Wallin Drive. Follow signs. May 1 to Oct 31. (888)338-2145

WAKAW — C3 *Prince Albert*

WAKAW LAKE REGIONAL PARK (Public) From town: Go 3-1/4 km/2 mi N on Hwy 2, then 9-1/2 km/6 mi E on Secondary Rd. 2015 rates: $27 to $35. May 1 to Sep 30. (306)233-5744

WASKESIU LAKE — B3 *North Battleford*

PRINCE ALBERT NP (BEAVER GLEN) (Prov Pk) From jct Hwy 2 & Hwy 264: Go 12 km/7-1/2 mi NW on Hwy 264, then 1/2 km/1/3 mi W on Ajawaan St. (306)663-4522

PRINCE ALBERT NP (NAMEKUS LAKE) (Prov Pk) From jct Hwy 264 & Hwy 263: Go 15-1/4 km/9-1/2 mi S on Hwy 263. Pit toilets. (306)663-4522

PRINCE ALBERT NP (NARROWS) (Prov Pk) From Waskesiu Lake townsite: Go 25 km/15-1/2 mi NW on park road. Pit toilets. (306)663-4522

PRINCE ALBERT NP (SANDY LAKE) (Prov Pk) From jct Hwy 240 & Hwy 263: Go 5 km/3 mi N on Hwy 263. Pit toilets. (306)663-4522

PRINCE ALBERT NP (WASKESIU TRAILER PARK) (Prov Pk) From jct Hwy 2 & Hwy 264: Go 12 km/7-1/2 mi NW on Hwy 264, then 1/2 km/1/3 mi W on Ajawaan St. (306)663-4522

WATSON — C4 *Wynyard*

MCNAB REGIONAL PARK (Public) From jct Hwy 5 & Hwy 6: Go .5 km/1/4 mi N on Hwy 6. 2015 rates: $10 to $35. Apr 15 to Oct 15. (306)287-4240

WEYBURN — E4 *Weyburn*

↓ CITY OF WEYBURN RIVER PARK CAMPGROUND (Public) From jct Hwy 35 & Hwy 39: Go 300 m/300 yds E on Hwy 39, then 100 m/110 yds S on 3rd St S, then 200 m/220 yds E on 2nd Ave SE. 2015 rates: $16 to $26. May 25 to Sep 15. (306)848-3290

Check out those views! From awe-inspiring redwood giants to the soaring towers of the Golden Gate Bridge, we've put the Spotlight on North America's most popular travel destinations. Turn to the Spotlight articles in our State and Province sections to learn more.

NICKLE LAKE REGIONAL PARK (Prov Pk) From jct 16th St & Hwy 39: Go 6.6 km/4 mi S on Hwy 39, then 1.7 km/1 mi S on grid road, then .8 km/1/2 mi W on access road. 2015 rates: $23.75 to $35. May 15 to Sep 15. (306)842-7522

Travel Services

↓ **MINARD'S LEISURE WORLD** Sales and service in the greater Weyburn area. Mobile RV Service and RV Towing. **SERVICES:** RV appliance, mobile RV svc, RV Sales. **TOW:** RV. RV supplies. Hours: 8am to 5pm.
(877)842-3288 Lat: 49.65006, Lon: -103.85830
921 Government Rd S, Weyburn, SK S4H 2B6
mlw@minards.ca
www.minardsleisureworld.com

WHITE CITY — E4 *Regina*

→ COMFORT PLUS CAMPGROUND **Ratings: 7.5/8★/7** (Campground) 2015 rates: $30 to $38. May 1 to Sep 30. (306)781-2810 north Service Road, Hwy 48 & Hwy 1 E., White City, SK S0G 5B0

WHITEWOOD — E5 *Melville*

↑ LARSON PARK (Public) From Jct of Hwy 1 & Hwy 9: S 5 1/4 mi/.06 km on Hwy 9 to Lalonde St.,NW 1/2 mi/.08 km (R). 2015 rates: $24 to $32. May 1 to Sep 30. (306)735-2210

WILKIE — C2 *Kindersley*

WILKIE REGIONAL PARK (Public) From jct Hwy 14 & Hwy 29: Go 3/4 km/1/2 mi N on Hwy 29. 2015 rates: $15 to $20. May 1 to Sep 30. (306)843-2692

WILLOW BUNCH — E3 *Assiniboia*

JEAN LOUIS LEGARE REGIONAL PARK (Public) From Hwy 36 at south town limits: Go .5 km/1/4 mi W on grid road, then 1.8 km/1 mi SW on grid road. 2015 rates: $23 to $27. May 19 to Sep 7. (306)473-2621

WOOD MOUNTAIN — E3 *Assiniboia*

WOOD MOUNTAIN REGIONAL PARK (Public) From town: Go 13 km/8 mi S on Hwy 18. 2015 rates: $15 to $40. May 19 to Sep 7. (306)266-4249

WYNYARD — D4 *Wynyard*

WYNYARD & DISTRICT REGIONAL PARK (Public) From jct Hwy 16 & Grid Rd 640: Go 2.4 km/1.5 mi S on Grid Rd 640. 2015 rates: $15 to $20. May 19 to Sep 30. (306)554-3661

YORKTON — D5 *Yorkton*

↖ CITY OF YORKTON CAMPGROUND (Public) From NW section of town, N on Gladstone Ave, W at York Rd/16A, past lake (L). 2015 rates: $20 to $27. Apr 15 to Sep 30. (306)786-1757

↓ YORK LAKE REGIONAL PARK (Public) From Jct of Hwys 16 & 9, W 0.5 mi on Queen St to Gladstone Ave, S 2.5 mi (E). 2015 rates: $20 to $25. May 17 to Oct 10. (306)782-7080

We rate what RVers consider important.

SK

CLEAN RESTROOMS GET A STAR

Campgrounds that receive the maximum 5 points for restroom cleanliness (toilets, showers, floors, walls and sinks/counters/mirrors) are honored with a star beside their total restroom rating.

RATED 10/10★/10

WELCOME TO
Yukon

JOINED CONFEDERATION JUNE 13, 1898	WIDTH: 575 MILES (925 KM) LENGTH: 719 MILES (1,157 KM)	PROPORTION OF CANADA 4.83% OF 9,984,670 SQ KM

A state of mind rather than a place, the Yukon is a land that feels untouched by time. Home to the Inuit, Dene, Inuvialuit and northern First Nations peoples, Canada's northern wilderness is a vast, sparsely populated (34,000 people) landscape with a raw, untamed beauty. Home to the five highest mountains in Canada, the world's largest subarctic ice fields, vast herds of wildlife—including ten thousand black bears—foreboding tundra and stunted forest, the Yukon is a land rich in superlatives. A quintessential frontier town, Dawson City was at the center of the Klondike Gold Rush.

With its buckled clapboard buildings, dirt streets and inhospitable climate (-60° C in the winter), Dawson's charms aren't of the warm and cozy variety. After decades of decline, Parks Canada has made admirable efforts to restore Dawson City, and with a buoyant arts community and counterculture vibe, it's a thought-provoking place to rest for a couple of days. Two of the continent's great highways—the Alaska and the Klondike—cross through Yukon's amiable capital, Whitehorse. Only a handful of pioneer buildings remain in Whitehorse, but the town's atmospheric bars, cafés and restaurants ripple with creative energy, thanks to the city's well-funded arts community.

History

The Inuit and Dene form the majority of the Yukon's population. Around 1576, Martin Frobisher, an English seaman and licensed pirate (or "privateer") made contact with the Inuit during his quest to find a passage to the Orient. Frobisher's written account of his bizarre encounters with the Inuit—the earliest on record—makes for fascinating reading. Hospitality has always been the Inuit's overarching characteristic. It was the Inuit's sage knowledge of land and sea that came to the rescue of European whalers caught in the furies of violent storms and shipwrecks. In 1870, the Yukon became part of the Northwest Territories (NWT). The

Top 3 Tourism Attractions:
1) Kluane National Park and Reserve
2) Yukon Wildlife Preserve
3) Klondike National Historic Site

Nickname: Land of the Midnight Sun

State Flower: Fireweed

State Bird: Raven

People: Jerry Alfred, musician; Skookum Jim Mason, gold prospector; Greg Wiltjer, basketball player

Major Cities: Whitehorse (capital)

Topography: Most of province in watershed of Yukon River; snow-capped mountains, glacier-fed alpine lakes, rivers, coniferous forests, frozen tundra

Climate: Subarctic climate; summers are warm with continuous sunlight; bitterly cold winters with little daylight; short growing season

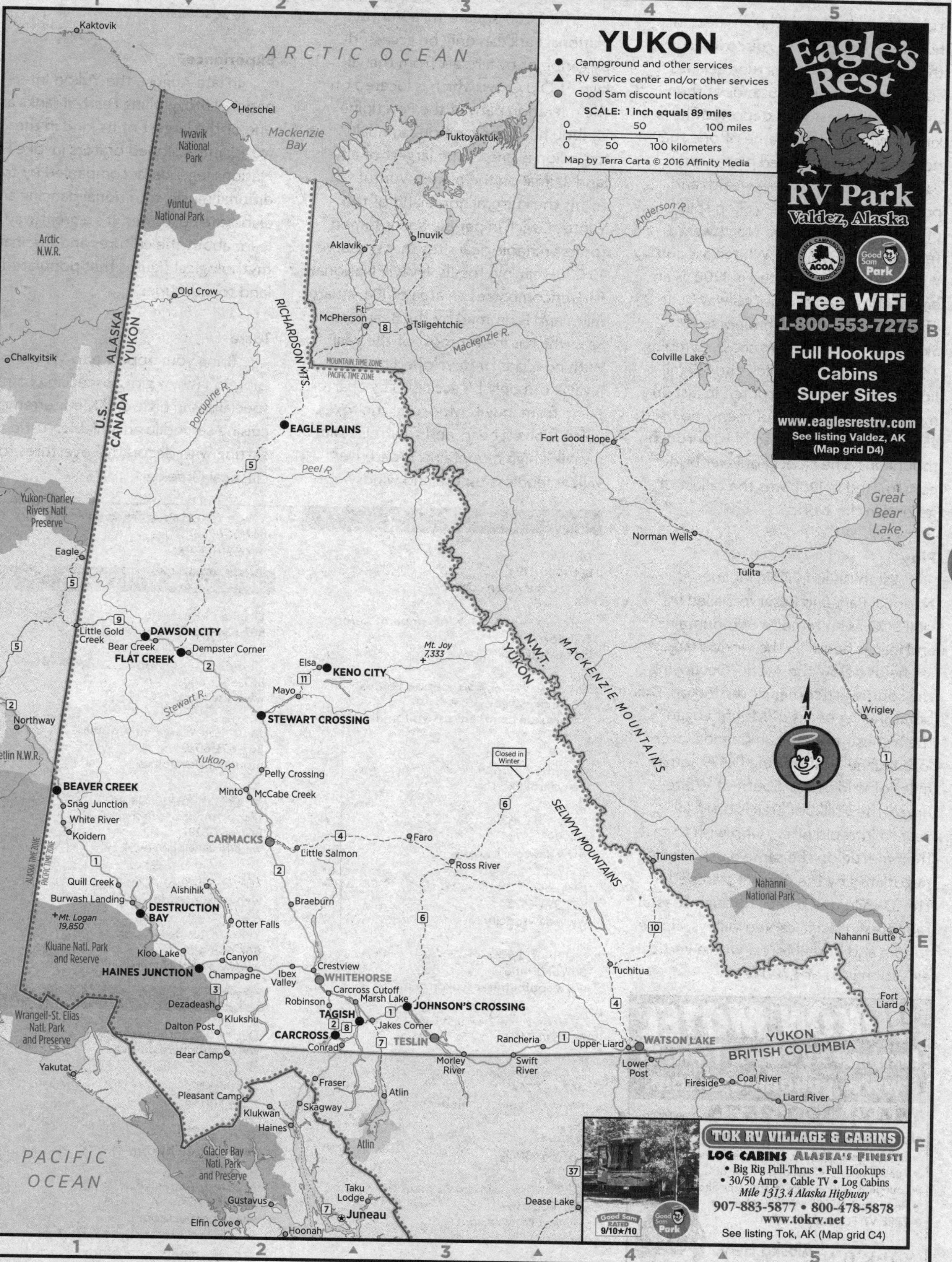
YUKON
Campground and other services
RV service center and/or other services
Good Sam discount locations
SCALE: 1 inch equals 89 miles
0 50 100 miles
0 50 100 kilometers
Map by Terra Carta © 2016 Affinity Media
ARCTIC OCEAN
PACIFIC OCEAN
Mackenzie Bay
Kaktovik
Herschel
Ivvavik National Park
Vuntut National Park
Arctic N.W.R.
Tuktoyaktuk
Inuvik
Aklavik
Ft. McPherson
Tsiigehtchic
Mackenzie R.
Anderson R.
Old Crow
Chalkyitsik
RICHARDSON MTS.
MOUNTAIN TIME ZONE
PACIFIC TIME ZONE
Porcupine R.
U.S.
CANADA
ALASKA
YUKON
EAGLE PLAINS
Peel R.
Colville Lake
Fort Good Hope
Great Bear Lake
Norman Wells
Tulita
Yukon-Charley Rivers Natl. Preserve
Eagle
Little Gold Creek
DAWSON CITY
Bear Creek
FLAT CREEK
Dempster Corner
Elsa
KENO CITY
Mt. Joy 7,333
Mayo
Stewart R.
STEWART CROSSING
N.W.T.
YUKON
MACKENZIE MOUNTAINS
Wrigley
Northway
Tetlin N.W.R.
Yukon R.
Pelly Crossing
Minto
McCabe Creek
Closed in Winter
BEAVER CREEK
Snag Junction
White River
Koidern
SELWYN MOUNTAINS
CARMACKS
Little Salmon
Faro
Ross River
Tungsten
Nahanni National Park
ALASKA TIME ZONE
PACIFIC TIME ZONE
Quill Creek
Aishihik
Burwash Landing
DESTRUCTION BAY
Mt. Logan 19,850
Otter Falls
Braeburn
Kluane Natl. Park and Reserve
Kloo Lake
Canyon
HAINES JUNCTION
Champagne
Ibex Valley
Crestview
WHITEHORSE
Carcross Cutoff
Marsh Lake
Robinson
JOHNSON'S CROSSING
Tuchitua
Nahanni Butte
Fort Liard
Wrangell-St. Elias Natl. Park and Preserve
Dezadeash
Klukshu
Dalton Post
TAGISH
Jakes Corner
CARCROSS
Conrad
TESLIN
Rancheria
Upper Liard
WATSON LAKE
YUKON
BRITISH COLUMBIA
Yakutat
Bear Camp
Morley River
Swift River
Lower Post
Fireside
Coal River
Liard River
Fraser
Atlin
Pleasant Camp
Skagway
Klukwan
Haines
Glacier Bay Natl. Park and Preserve
Taku Lodge
Gustavus
Juneau
Elfin Cove
Hoonah
Dease Lake
YT

Yukon Gold Rush was the greatest in history. When gold was discovered in the Klondike in 1896, fortune seekers converged in their thousands at the site of the largest gold deposit of its kind. Dawson City became of one the richest and most storied places on earth. Reveling in its new wealth and population growth, the Yukon split off from the rest of the Northwest Territories in 1898. The White Pass and Yukon railway, completed in 1900, is an engineering marvel. The "railway built of gold" connected Whitehorse to Skagway on the Alaskan coast. Climbing 3,000 feet in just 20 miles, the $10 million project was constructed in just 26 months by thousands of men who used 450 tons of explosives to blast through mountains. The steel cantilever bridge, constructed in 1901, was the tallest of its kind in the world.

Play

Established in 1972, Kluane National Park and Reserve, hailed by UNESCO as an "empire of mountains and ice," is home to the world's largest ice fields below the Arctic. Occupying the southwest corner of the Yukon, the breathtaking peaks of Mount Logan, the highest mountain in Canada, overlord Kluane's unforgiving 13,679 square miles of wilderness. South of Whitehorse, the Chilkoot Trail is open all year to intrepid hikers who wish to test their mettle on the same harsh terrain negotiated by the original stampeders. The 33-mile trail passes through coastal rainforest, glacier-carved valleys, alpine tundra and boreal forest with a vertical elevation gain of 3,700 feet.

The 3,000-square-mile Vuntut National Park can only be accessed by canoe or by aircraft from the village of Old Crow, which is located on the migration path of the Porcupine caribou herd; the caribou's annual migration is one of the largest of any land animal on the planet. Vuntut forms the cultural homeland of the Vuntut Gwich'in people and is famed for its archeological sites that preserve 40,000-year-old fossils. Ivvavik National Park encompasses an area of 104 square miles and is rimmed by the Beaufort Sea, which is ice for most of the year. With no roads or developed trails, Ivvavik can only be accessed by charter plane from Inuvik. Moose, arctic foxes, voles, wolves, bears and squirrels roam Ivvavik's high mountains, broad river valleys, endless tundra and windswept Arctic seacoast.

Experience

In late August, the Yukon International Storytelling Festival ranks as one of the largest of its kind in the world. Impassioned orators invoke First Nations legends, accompanied by traditional music, traditional dancing and elaborate costumes. It's a great way to learn about the cultures and fascinating mythological figures that populated the land for centuries.

Taste

Bring your appetite to Whitehorse. Giorgio's (www.giorgioscuccina.com) specializes in high-end Mediterranean cuisine served in an amiable, rustic setting with decorative overtures to classical Greek art.

TRAVEL & TOURISM

Dept. of Tourism Yukon
800-661-0494
www.travelyukon.com

Beaver Creek Visitor Information Centre
867-862-7321
vic.beavercreek@gov.yk.ca

Carcross Visitor Information Centre
Vic.carcross@gov.yk.ca
travelyukon.com/carcross-visitor-information-centre-0

Campbell Region Interpretive Centre
www.faroyukon.ca

Dawson City
867-993-5575
www.dawsoncity.ca

Klondike Visitors Association
867-993-5575
www.dawsoncity.ca

Southern Lakes Visitor Association
867-660-4106
www.southernlakesyukon.com

Watson Lake Visitor Information Centre
867-536-7469

Whitehorse Chamber of Commerce
867-667-7545
www.whitehorsechamber.com

Whitehorse Yukon
867-667-3084

Wilderness Tourism Assn. of the Yukon
867-668-3369
www.yukonwild.com

Yukon First Nations Tourism Association
867-667-7627
www.yfnta.org

OUTDOOR RECREATION

Fishing Licenses
867-634-7250

Klondike Snowmobile Association
867-667-7680
www.ksa.yk.ca

Mountain View Golf Course
867-633-6020
mountainviewgolf.ca

Wildlife Viewing Program, Department of Environment
867-667-8291
wildlife.viewing@gov.yk.ca

Yukon Outdoors Club
www.yukonoutdoorsclub.ca

Yukon Outfitters' Assn.
867-668-4118
www.yukonoutfitters.net

SHOPPING

Caribou Crossing Trading Post
www.cariboucrossing.ca

Klondike Nugget & Ivory Shop Ltd.
www.knis.ca

The Northern Beaver Post
www.nuggetcity.com

Sportees Activewear
867-668-2691
www.sportees.com

Whitehorse General Store
867-393-8203

Featured Good Sam Parks

YUKON/ALASKA

Good Sam Park

YT

When you stay with Good Sam, you can expect the highest degree of cleanliness and friendliness, and better yet, you get 10% off campground fees.

If you're not already a Good Sam member you can purchase your membership at one of these locations:

ALASKA

ANCHORAGE

Anchorage Ship Creek RV Park
(907)277-0877

Creekwood Inn Motel & RV Park
(907)258-6006

CANTWELL

Cantwell RV Park
(800)940-2210

DENALI NATIONAL PARK

Denali Rainbow Village RV Park & Motel
(907)683-7777

Denali RV Park & Motel
(800)478-1501

FAIRBANKS

River's Edge RV Park & Campground
(907)474-0286

Riverview RV Park
(888)488-6392

GLENNALLEN

Northern Nights Campground & RV Park
(907)822-3199

HAINES

Haines Hitch-Up RV Park Inc
(907)766-2882

Oceanside RV Park
(907)766-2437

HOMER

Baycrest RV Park
(907)435-7995

Oceanview RV Park
(907)235-3951

KENAI

Beluga Lookout Lodge & RV Park
(907)283-5999

Diamond M Ranch Resort
(907)283-9424

NINILCHIK

Alaskan Angler RV Resort & Cabins
(800)347-4114

All Seasons Campground
(907)567-3396

PALMER

Mountain View RV Park
(907)745-5747

SKAGWAY

Garden City RV Park
(866)983-2378

TOK

Tok RV Village & Cabins
(907)883-5877

TRAPPER CREEK

Trapper Creek Inn & RV Park
(907)733-2302

VALDEZ

Eagle's Rest RV Park & Cabins
(800)553-7275

WASILLA

Big Bear RV Park
(907)745-7445

YUKON

CARMACKS

Carmacks Hotel & RV Park
(867)863-5221

TESLIN

Yukon Motel & Lakeshore RV Park
(867)390-2089

WHITEHORSE

Caribou RV Park
(867)668-2961

Hi Country RV Park
(877)458-3806

For more Good Sam Parks go to listing pages

Yukon

CONSULTANTS

Craig & Debbie Rice

BEAVER CREEK — C1 *Kluane Region*

DISCOVERY YUKON LODGINGS & RV PARK **Ratings: 6/9.5★/9.5** (RV Park) 2015 rates: $20 to $45. May 1 to Sep 30. (867)862-7408 km 1818 Alaska Hwy, Beaver Creek, YT Y0B 1A0

LAKE CREEK (YUKON GOV'T) (Prov Pk) From Beaver Creek: Go 81 km/50 mi E on Alaska Hwy to km 1854/milepost 1152. Pit toilets. 2015 rates: $12. (867)667-5652

CARCROSS — E2 *Whitehorse Region*

CARCROSS GROCERY & RV PARK **Ratings: 5.5/8/5.5** (RV Park) 2015 rates: $24.95 to $29.95. May 20 to Oct 1. (867)821-3998 mile 104 S Klondike, Carcross, YT Y0B 1B0

CARMACKS — D2 *Klondike Region*

CARMACKS HOTEL & RV PARK
Ratings: 6.5/8/7.5 (RV Park) On N Klondike Hwy at MP 102.3. **FAC:** Gravel rds. 15 gravel, 5 pull-thrus (22 x 60), back-ins (20 x 32), 15 full hkups (30/50 amps), WiFi, rentals, dump, laundry, groc, restaurant. **REC:** Yukon River: fishing. Pets OK. No tents. 2015 rates: $27 to $37. May 15 to Sep 15.
(867)863-5221 Lat: 62.05386, Lon: -136.16900
35607 Klondike Hwy N, Carmacks, YT Y0B 1C0
info@hotelcarmacks.com
www.hotelcarmacks.com
See ad this page, 1485.

THE COAL MINE CAMPGROUND & CANTEEN **Ratings: 5/5.5/7** (Campground) 2015 rates: $21 to $24. May 15 to Sep 10. (867)863-6363 km 359 Klondike Hwy N, Carmacks, YT Y0B 1C0

DAWSON CITY — C2 *Klondike Region*

BONANZA GOLD MOTEL & RV PARK
Ratings: 6.5/9.5★/8.5 (RV Park) From town, S 1 mi on Klondike Hwy at KM-712 (R). NOTE: Limited facilities early & late season. **FAC:** All weather rds. 102 gravel, 11 pull-thrus (20 x 55), back-ins (20 x 60), some side by side hkups, 50 full hkups, 39 W, 39 E (30/50 amps), cable, WiFi, tent sites, rentals, showers $, dump, laundry, firewood. **REC.** Pets OK. Partial handicap access. 2015 rates: $15 to $46. May 1 to Sep 30.
(888)993-6789 Lat: 64.02474, Lon: -139.24171
km 712 Klondike Hwy N, Dawson City, YT Y0B 1G0
bonanzagold.dawson@gmail.com
www.bonanzagold.ca
See ad this page.

DAWSON CITY RV PARK & CAMPGROUND **Ratings: 6/6.5/7.5** (Campground) 2015 rates: $17.25 to $39.75. May 15 to Sep 15. (867)993-5142 km 712 Klondike Hwy N, Dawson City, YT Y0B 1G0

GOLD RUSH RV PARK **Ratings: 6/9★/7** (Campground) 2015 rates: $37 to $44. May 7 to Sep 15. (867)993-5247 1207 York St., Dawson City, YT Y0B 1G0

KLONDIKE RIVER (YUKON GOV'T) (Prov Pk) From town: Go S on Klondike Hwy 2 to km marker 698 (milepost 433). Pit toilets. 2015 rates: $12. (867)667-5200

YUKON RIVER (YUKON GOV'T) (Prov Pk) In town on the Top of the World Hwy at km marker .3 (milepost 0). Pit toilets. (867)667-5652

DESTRUCTION BAY — D2 *Kluane Region*

CONGDON CREEK (YUKON GOV'T) (Prov Pk) From town: Go 19 km/12 mi S on Alaska Hwy 1 to km marker 1724.3 (milepost 1071.5). Pit toilets. 2015 rates: $12. (867)667-5200

COTTONWOOD RV PARK
Ratings: 5/10★/9 (Campground) N-Bnd: On AK Hwy 1 at MP-1067/ KM 1658, 16 mi S of Destruction Bay (R). Elev 2592 ft. **FAC:** Gravel rds. 60 gravel, 20 pull-thrus (35 x 50), back-ins (35 x 40), 20 W, 33 E (15 amps), WiFi Hotspot, tent sites, rentals, dump, groc, fire rings, firewood. **REC:** Kluane Lake: fishing. Pets OK. 2015 rates: $30 to $35. Jun 1 to Sep 1. No CC.
(867)841-4066 Lat: 61.08818, Lon: -138.53355
km 1658 Alaska Hwy, Destruction Bay, YT Y0B 1H0
maryanne_glenn@cottonwoodpark.ca
www.cottonwoodpark.ca
See ad this page.

DESTRUCTION BAY RV LODGE **Ratings: 7.5/9★/8** (RV Park) 2015 rates: $29.95 to $36.95. May 15 to Sep 15. (867)841-4332 PO Box 48, Burwash Landing, YT Y0B 1V0

EAGLE PLAINS — C2 *North Yukon Region*

ROCK RIVER (YUKON GOV'T) (Prov Pk) From Eagle Plains: Go 78 km/49 mi N on Dempster Hwy 5. Pit toilets. 2015 rates: $12. (867)667-5652

FLAT CREEK — D2 *Klondike Region*

TOMBSTONE MOUNTAIN CAMPGROUND (YUKON GOV'T) (Prov Pk) From town: Go 72 km/45 mi N on Dempster Hwy 5 to km marker 73 (milepost 45.4). Pit toilets. 2015 rates: $12. (867)667-5652

HAINES JUNCTION — D2 *Kluane Region*

DEZADEASH LAKE (YUKON GOV'T) (Prov Pk) From jct Alaska Hwy 1 & Haines Rd 3: Go 50 km/3 mi S on Haines Rd 3. Pit toilets. 2015 rates: $12. (867)667-5200

KLUANE NATIONAL PARK (KATHLEEN LAKE CAMPGROUND) (Prov Pk) From town: Go 27 km/17 mi S on the Haines Hwy 3 to km marker 229.4 (milepost 142). Pit toilets. 2015 rates: $15.70. May 16 to Sep 1. (867)634-7250

KLUANE RV KAMPGROUND **Ratings: 6/5.5/5.5** (Campground) 2015 rates: $28 to $30. (867)634-2709 km 1635.9, Haines Junction, YT Y0B 1L0

MILLION DOLLAR FALLS (YUKON GOV'T) (Prov Pk) From town: Go S on the Haines Rd to km marker 167 (milepost 103.7). Pit toilets. 2015 rates: $12. (867)667-5652

OTTER FALLS CUTOFF RV PARK **Ratings: 5/7.5/7** (RV Park) 2015 rates: $19.95 to $29.95. (867)634-2812 km 1546 Alaska Hwy, Otter Falls, YT Y0B 1L0

PINE LAKE (YUKON GOV'T) (Prov Pk) In town on Alaska Hwy 1 at km marker 1628 (milepost 1013). Pit toilets. 2015 rates: $12. (867)667-5652

JOHNSON'S CROSSING — D2 *Johnson's Crossing*

QUIET LAKE (YUKON GOV'T) (Prov Pk) From jct Alaska Hwy 1 & Hwy 6 (Canol Rd): Go 77 km/48 mi N on Hwy 6 (Canol Rd). Pit toilets. 2015 rates: $12. (867)667-5652

KENO CITY — D2 *Silver Trail Region*

KENO CITY CAMPGROUND (Prov Pk) From jct Hwy 2 (Klondike Hwy) & Hwy 11: Go 106.8 km/66-1/2 mi NE on Hwy 11, then 120 metres/130 yrds SE on Yukon Ave. Pit toilets. (867)995-3103

STEWART CROSSING — D2 *Silver Trail Region*

MOOSE CREEK (YUKON GOV'T) (Prov Pk) From jct Hwy 11 (The Silver Trail) & Klondike Hwy 2: Go 24 km/15 mi NW on Klondike Hwy 2 to km marker 562 (milepost 349.2). Pit toilets. 2015 rates: $12. (862)667-5652

TAGISH — E3 *Southern Lakes Region*

TAGISH (YUKON GOV'T) (Prov Pk) In town on Hwy 8 at km marker 21 (milepost 13). Pit toilets. 2015 rates: $12. (867)667-5652

TESLIN — E2 *Yukon*

TESLIN LAKE (YUKON GOV'T) (Prov Pk) From town: Go 15.5 km/9-1/2 mi W on Alaska Hwy to km 1309/milepost 813. Pit toilets. 2015 rates: $12. (867)667-5652

YUKON MOTEL & LAKESHORE RV PARK
Ratings: 6.5/10★/9.5 (RV Park) On Alaska Hwy at MP-804 or KM-1244. **FAC:** Gravel rds. 58 gravel, 39 pull-thrus (20 x 60), back-ins (20 x 40), some side by side hkups, 58 W, 58 E (15/30 amps), WiFi Hotspot, tent sites, rentals, dump, laundry, LP gas, restaurant. **REC:** Teslin Lake: fishing. Pets OK. 2015 rates: $15 to $30. May 15 to Sep 30. ATM.
(867)390-2089 Lat: 60.10078, Lon: -132.42596
mile 804 Alaska Hwy (Km 1244), Teslin, YT Y0A 1B0
yukonmotel@northwestel.net
www.yukonmotel.com
See ad pages 1484 (Welcome Section), 1485.

WATSON LAKE — E3

BABY NUGGET RV PARK
Ratings: 7/10★/8 (RV Park) From Jct of Alaska Hwy & Hwy 37, W 0.5 mi on Alaska Hwy at mi 622/KM 1003 (L). **FAC:** Gravel rds. 83 gravel, 73 pull-thrus (40 x 100), back-ins (25 x 40), 83 W, 83 E (30/50 amps), WiFi Hotspot, tent sites, rentals, showers $, dump, laundry, groc, restaurant, controlled access. **REC:** Butterfly Lake: fishing. Pets OK. Partial handicap access. 2015 rates: $39.99 to $55. May 1 to Sep 30.
(867)536-2307 Lat: 60.02801, Lon: -129.08102
milepost 627/Km 1003 Alaska Hwy, Watson Lake, YT Y0A 1C0
nuggetcityyukon@gmail.com
www.nuggetcity.com

DOWNTOWN RV PARK
Ratings: 6.5/10★/7.5 (RV Park) From Jct of AK Hwy & 8th St, N 200 ft on 8th St (L). **FAC:** Gravel rds. 78 gravel, 35 pull-thrus (16 x 75), back-ins (16 x 60), 78 full hkups (30/50 amps), WiFi, dump, laundry. **REC.** Pets OK. No tents. 2015 rates: $35 to $52. Disc: AAA. Apr 15 to Oct 15.
AAA Approved
(867)536-2646 Lat: 60.03825, Lon: -128.42398
105 8th St N, Watson Lake, YT Y0A 1C0
atannock@hotmail.com

FRANCES LAKE (YUKON GOV'T) (Prov Pk) From jct Alaska Hwy 1 & Robert Campbell Hwy 4: Go N on Robert Campbell Hwy 4 to km 177/milepost 110. Pit toilets. 2015 rates: $12. (867)667-5200

RANCHERIA MOTEL **Ratings: 3/NA/6** (Campground) Pit toilets. 2015 rates: $10 to $20. May 15 to Oct 15. (867)851-6456 mile 710 Alaska Hwy, Watson Lake, YT Y0A 1C0

WATSON LAKE (YUKON GOV'T) (Prov Pk) Just outside of town on Alaska Hwy 1 at km marker 1025 (milepost 636.5), then 1.6 km/1 mi on access road. Pit toilets. 2015 rates: $12. (867)667-5652

Exclusive! According to our research, restroom cleanliness is of the utmost concern to RVers. Of course, you knew that already. The cleanest campgrounds have a star in their restroom rating!

WHITEHORSE — D2 *Whitehorse Region*

➛ **CARIBOU RV PARK**

Ratings: 7/10★/8.5 (Campground) From Whitehorse, E 13 mi on AK Hwy, at MP-904 (L) Season dates: Weather permitting. **FAC:** Gravel rds. 47 Avail: 27 gravel, 20 dirt, 19 pull-thrus (20 x 60), back-ins (20 x 30), 27 W, 27 E (15/30 amps), WiFi, tent sites, dump, laundry, firewood, restaurant. **REC.** Pets OK. Partial handicap access. 2015 rates: $42. Disc: AAA. May 1 to Sep 30.
(867)668-2961 Lat: 60.597415, Lon: -134.851809
mile 904/ Km 1403 Alaska Hwy, Whitehorse, YT Y1A 7A1
info@caribou-rv-park.com
www.caribou-rv-park.com
See ad this page, 1485.

FOX LAKE CAMPGROUND (YUKON GOV'T) (Prov Pk) From town: Go N on Klondike Hwy 2 to km marker 248 (milepost 141.7). Pit toilets. 2015 rates: $12. (867)667-5200

⬇ **HI COUNTRY RV PARK**

Ratings: 7/10★/10 (RV Park) At Jct of Robert Service Way & Alaska Hwy (L). **FAC:** Gravel rds. 125 gravel, 27 pull-thrus (24 x 50), back-ins (20 x 35), 55 full hkups, 52 W, 52 E (20/30 amps), cable, WiFi, tent sites, dump, laundry, groc, fire rings, firewood. **REC:** playground. Pets OK. Partial handicap access. 14 day max stay, 2015 rates: $22 to $42. Disc: AAA. May 15 to Sep 15. ATM.
(877)458-3806 Lat: 60.683962, Lon: -135.060620
91374 Alaska Hwy, Whitehorse, YT Y1A 6E4
reservations@hicountryrv.com
www.hicountryrvyukon.com
See ad pages 1482 (Welcome Section), 1485.

KUSAWA LAKE (YUKON GOV'T) (Prov Pk) From town: Go 67 km/42 mi W on Alaska Hwy 1 to km marker 1543.1 (milepost 959), then 22-1/2 km/14 mi S on Kusawa Lake Rd. Pit toilets. 2015 rates: $12. (867)667-5652

MARSH LAKE CAMPGROUND & RECREATION SITE (YUKON GOV'T) (Prov Pk) From town: Go 45 km/28 mi E on Alaska Hwy 1 to km marker 1429.6 (milepost 888.4). Pit toilets. 2015 rates: $12.

⬇ MOUNTAIN RIDGE MOTEL & SMALL RIG RV PARK **Ratings: 6/8.5/5.5** (Campground) 2015 rates: $35. Apr 15 to Sep 1. (867)667-4202 91297 Alaska Hwy, Whitehorse, YT Y1A 7A3

⬇ PIONEER RV PARK **Ratings: 6.5/9★/6.5** (RV Park) 2015 rates: $25 to $34. May 15 to Sep 30. (867)668-5944 91091 Alaska Hwy, Whitehorse, YT Y1A 5V9

ROBERT SERVICE CAMPGROUND (CITY OF WHITEHORSE) (Public) In town on Alaska Hwy 1 at km marker 1467.8 (milepost 917.4). 2015 rates: $20. May 15 to Sep 30. (403)668-3721

➛ TAKHINI HOT SPRINGS CAMPGROUND **Ratings: 5/NA/6** (Campground) Pit toilets. 2015 rates: $37. (867)456-8000 mile 6 Hot Springs Rd, Whitehorse, YT Y1A 7A2

WOLF CREEK CAMPGROUND & RECREATION SITE (YUKON GOV'T) (Prov Pk) From town: Go E on Alaska Hwy 1 to km marker 1458.6 (milepost 906). Pit toilets. 2015 rates: $12.

Find it fast! To locate a town on a map, follow these easy instructions: Look for the map grid code after the town heading in the listing section and match it to the letters and numbers on the map borders. Draw a line horizontally from the letter and vertically from the number. You'll find the town near the intersection of the two lines.

YT

Looking for Mexico?
Mexico's listings have moved online.
Check them out at:
www.GoodSamCamping.com

SEASONAL SITES GUIDE

Turn off the ignition and stay for a week, a month or an entire season. The Seasonal Sites Guide to RV Parks and Campgrounds for 2016 provides comprehensive listings and informative display ads of RV parks that cater to seasonal and extended stay RV travelers.

Each listing includes hookups, pet restrictions, wi-fi availability and more. Some of the parks listed also have display ads, which elaborate on a park's features and may include information pertaining to local attractions, special prices, park model sales and more. Look for the "See ad" line at the bottom of the listing to find the corresponding display ad.

The listings and advertisements in the guide are organized alphabetically, first by state or province, then by town. Use this section to find the location of your next extended stay vacation.

ALABAMA

MONTGOMERY — D4 *Montgomery*

THE WOODS RV PARK & CAMPGROUND (RV Park) From Jct of I-65 & US 80/82 (exit 168) E 0.1 mi (one block) on US 80/82 to Sassafras Cir. (R); or From US 231 N & US 80/82, W 5 mi on US 80/82 to Sassafras Cir (L). **FAC:** Gravel rds. (105 spaces). Avail: 93 gravel, 93 pull-thrus (30 x 80), 93 full hkups (30/50 amps), cable, WiFi, dump, laundry, LP gas, fire rings, firewood. **REC:** pond, fishing, playground. Pets OK. Partial handicap access, big rig sites, RV age restrict, eco-friendly.
(334)356-1887 Lat: 32.32544, Lon: -86.33126
4350 Sassafras Circle, Montgomery, AL 36105
shanajirik@yahoo.com
www.woodsrvpark.com

ARIZONA

APACHE JUNCTION — D3 *Maricopa, Pinal*

VIP RV RESORT (RV Park) From Jct of US Hwy 60 & Ironwood Dr (Exit 195), N 1.8 mi on Ironwood Dr (R). **FAC:** Paved rds. (128 spaces). Avail: 41 all weather, back-ins (30 x 45), 41 full hkups (30/50 amps), WiFi, laundry. **REC:** shuffleboard. Pet restrict(B/Q). Partial handicap access, age restrict may apply, eco-friendly.
AAA Approved
(480)983-0847 Lat: 33.41203, Lon: -111.56219
401 S Ironwood Drive, Apache Junction, AZ 85120
Waymary60@msn.com
www.viprvresort.com

TUCSON — E4 *Pima*

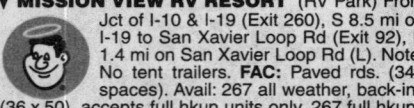

MISSION VIEW RV RESORT (RV Park) From Jct of I-10 & I-19 (Exit 260), S 8.5 mi on I-19 to San Xavier Loop Rd (Exit 92), E 1.4 mi on San Xavier Loop Rd (L). Note: No tent trailers. **FAC:** Paved rds. (342 spaces). Avail: 267 all weather, back-ins (36 x 50), accepts full hkup units only, 267 full hkups (30/50 amps), WiFi, rentals, laundry. **REC:** heated pool, whirlpool, shuffleboard. Pet restrict(B/Q). Age restrict may apply, eco-friendly.
(800)444-8439 Lat: 32.11721, Lon: -110.97208
31 West Los Reales, Tucson, AZ 85756
missionviewrv@aol.com
www.missionviewrv.com
See ad this page.

CALIFORNIA

BEAUMONT — N6 *Riverside*

COUNTRY HILLS RV PARK (RV Park) From Jct of Hwy I-10 & Beaumont Ave (exit94), S 3.6mi on Beaumont Ave to 1st St,E 0.5 mi to Michigan Ave, S 0.6 mi on Michigan Ave which becomes Manzanita Park Rd, S 0.6mi (E). **FAC:** Gravel rds. (85 spaces). Avail: 45 all weather, 12 pull-thrus (25 x 60), back-ins (23 x 38), some side by side hkups, 35 full hkups (20/50 amps), WiFi, rentals, showers $, dump, laundry, controlled access. **REC:** pool, whirlpool, playground. Pets OK $. RV age restrict, eco-friendly.
(951)845-5919 Lat: 33.90882, Lon: -116.96811
14711 Manzanita Park Rd, Beaumont, CA 92223
Countryhills@newportpacific.com
www.countryhillsrv.com

Check out those views! From awe-inspiring redwood giants to the soaring towers of the Golden Gate Bridge, we've put the Spotlight on North America's most popular travel destinations. Turn to the Spotlight articles in our State and Province sections to learn more.

DESERT HOT SPRINGS — J5 *Riverside*

CALIENTE SPRINGS RESORT (RV Resort) E-bnd: From Jct of I-10 & Palm Dr (Exit 123), N 3.1 mi on Palm Dr to Dillon Rd, E 3.7 mi (L). **FAC:** Paved rds. (679 spaces). 200 Avail: 10 gravel, 190 dirt, 4 pull-thrus (28 x 52), back-ins (33 x 55), 200 full hkups (30/50 amps), cable, WiFi $, rentals, laundry, controlled access. **REC:** heated pool, whirlpool, golf, shuffleboard. Pet restrict(B/Q). Partial handicap access, big rig sites, RV age restrict, eco-friendly.
(760)329-8400 Lat: 33.92611, Lon: -116.43606
70-200 Dillon Rd, Desert Hot Springs, CA 92241
info@calientesprings.com
www.calientesprings.com

SAM'S FAMILY SPA (RV Park) From Jct of I-10 & Palm Dr (exit 123), N 3 mi on Palm Dr to Dillon Rd, E 4.2 mi (R). **FAC:** Paved rds. (350 spaces). Avail: 175 all weather, back-ins (32 x 45), 175 full hkups (30/50 amps), WiFi $, rentals, laundry, groc. **REC:** heated pool, whirlpool, playground, rec open to public. Pets OK. Partial handicap access, big rig sites, RV age restrict.
(760)329-6457 Lat: 33.92488, Lon: -116.42535
70875 Dillon Rd, Desert Hot Springs, CA 92241
samsfamilyspa@aol.com
www.samsfamilyspa.com

SKY VALLEY RESORT (RV Resort) E-bnd: From Jct of I-10 & Palm Dr (Exit 123), N 3.1 mi on Palm Dr to Dillon Rd, E 8.5 mi (R); W-bnd: From Jct of I-10 & Dillon Rd, NW 18.6 mi on Dillon Rd (L). **FAC:** Paved rds. (891 spaces). 100 Avail: 4 gravel, 96 dirt, 6 pull-thrus (32 x 50), back-ins (30 x 50), 100 full hkups (30/50 amps), cable, WiFi $, rentals, dump, laundry, groc, restaurant, controlled access. **REC:** heated pool, whirlpool, pond, shuffleboard. Pet restrict(B/Q). Partial handicap access, RV age restrict, eco-friendly.
(760)329-2909 Lat: 33.90341, Lon: -116.35998
74-711 Dillon Rd, Desert Hot Springs, CA 92241
info@skyvalleyresort.com
www.rvwell.com

ENCINITAS — J4 *San Diego*

TRAILER RANCHO RV PARK (RV Park) From Jct of I-5 & La Costa Ave (Exit 44), W 0.5 mi on La Costa Ave to N Vulcan Ave, S 0.5 mi (L). **FAC:** Paved rds. (83 spaces). Avail: 50 all weather, back-ins (28 x 36), 50 full hkups (30/50 amps), WiFi, laundry. **REC.** Pet restrict(B/Q). Partial handicap access, RV age restrict.
(760)753-2741 Lat: 33.07549, Lon: -117.30527
1549 N Vulcan Ave, Encinitas, CA 92024
trailerrancho@jandhmgt.com
www.goodsamcamping.com.s3.amazonaws.com/gsparks/840000652/index.html

INDIO — J5 *Riverside*

INDIAN WATERS RV RESORT & COTTAGES (RV Resort) From Jct of I-10 & Golf Center Pky (Exit 144): Go SW 0.9 mi on Golf Center Pkwy to Hwy 111, then W 0.3 mi to Jackson St, then S 0.7 mi (L). **FAC:** Paved rds. 265 paved, 15 pull-thrus (26 x 60), back-ins (35 x 48), 265 full hkups (50 amps), WiFi, rentals, dump, laundry, controlled access. **REC:** heated pool, whirlpool, pond, shuffleboard. Pets OK. Partial handicap access, RV age restrict, eco-friendly.
(760)342-8100 Lat: 33.70674, Lon: -116.21637
47202 Jackson St, Indio, CA 92201
info@iwrvr.com
www.indianwatersrvresort.com

Looking for a new or used RV? Camping World is America's largest retailer of RVs. Click CampingWorld.com or visit SuperCenters nationwide.

NEWPORT BEACH — O3 *Orange*

NEWPORT DUNES WATERFRONT RESORT & MARINA (RV Park) From Jct of Pacific Coast Hwy (Hwy 1) & Jamboree Rd exit, N 0.2 mi on Jamboree Rd to Back Bay Dr, W 0.1 mi (L); or From Jct of I-405 & Jamboree Rd exit (in Irvine), S 5 mi on Jamboree Rd to Back Bay Dr, W 0.1 mi (L). **FAC:** Paved rds. (377 spaces). 287 Avail: 5 paved, 282 dirt, 8 pull-thrus (24 x 80), back-ins (24 x 40), 287 full hkups (30/50 amps), WiFi, rentals, laundry, groc, LP bottles, fire rings, firewood, restaurant, controlled access. **REC:** heated pool, whirlpool, Newport Bay: swim, playground, rec open to public. Pet restrict(B/Q) $. Partial handicap access, RV age restrict, eco-friendly, ATM.
(800)765-7661 Lat: 33.61480, Lon: -117.89670
1131 Back Bay Drive, Newport Beach, CA 92660
info@newportdunes.com
www.newportdunes.com

OCEANSIDE — J4 *San Diego*

OCEANSIDE RV PARK (RV Park) From Jct of I-5 & Oceanside Blvd (exit 52), W 0.5 mi on Oceanside Blvd to S. Coast Hwy, S 0.1 mi across railway track-4th Entrance (L). **FAC:** Paved rds. 139 paved, 33 pull-thrus (20 x 45), back-ins (22 x 40), 139 full hkups (30 amps), cable, WiFi, dump, laundry, LP gas, controlled access. **REC:** heated pool, whirlpool. Pet restrict(B/Q) $. RV age restrict, eco-friendly.
(760)722-4404 Lat: 33.18222, Lon: -117.36663
1510 S Coast Hwy, Oceanside, CA 92054
oceansidervpark@yahoo.com
www.oceansidervpark.com

POMONA — M4 *Los Angeles*

LOS ANGELES KOA (RV Park) W-bnd: From I-10 & Garey Ave onto Orangegrove, SW under Fwy 300 ft to McKinley, NW 0.6 mi to White Ave, N 0.8 mi (R); or E-bnd: From Jct of I-10 & White Ave, N 1.4 mi on White Ave (R). E-bnd or W-bnd: From Jct of I-210 & Fruit St (Exit 48), S 2 mi on Fruit St (becomes White Ave) (L). **FAC:** Paved rds. (182 spaces). Avail: 122 paved, 122 pull-thrus (18 x 55), 122 full hkups (30/50 amps), WiFi, rentals, dump, laundry, groc, restaurant. **REC:** pool, whirlpool, golf. Pet restrict(B/Q). Partial handicap access, RV age restrict, ATM.
(888)562-4230 Lat: 34.08981, Lon: -117.76391
2200 N White Ave, Pomona, CA 91768
koa@fairplex.com
www.fairplex.com
See ad this page.

SAN DIEGO — K4 *San Diego*

CAMPLAND ON THE BAY (RV Park) N-bnd: Jct of I-5 & Grand/Garnet exit 23A (becomes Mission Bay Dr), N 0.2 mi to Grand Ave, W 0.8 mi to Olney, S 0.2 mi to Pacific Beach Dr(R) S-bnd: Jct of I-5 & Balboa/Garnet St (Mission Bay Dr), S 0.5 mi to Mission Bay Dr to Grand Ave, follow N-bnd directions (E). **FAC:** Paved rds. 568 paved, 26 pull-thrus (20 x 45), back-ins (18 x 37), some side by side hkups, 405 full hkups, 145 W, 145 E (30 amps), cable, WiFi, dump, laundry, groc, LP gas, firewood, controlled access. **REC:** heated pool, whirlpool, Mission Bay: swim, fishing, marina, playground. Pet restrict(B/Q) $. Partial handicap access, eco-friendly, ATM.
(800)422-9386 Lat: 32.79630, Lon: -117.22390
2211 Pacific Beach Drive, San Diego, CA 92109
reservations@campland.com
www.campland.com

We rate what RVers consider important.

SAN DIMAS — M4 *Los Angeles*

EAST SHORE RV PARK (Campground) From Jct of I-10 & Fairplex Dr (exit 44), N 0.5 mi on Fairplex Dr to Via Verde, W 0.6 mi to Camper View Rd, N 0.3 mi (E). **FAC:** Paved rds. (518 spaces). Avail: 138 paved, 15 pull-thrus (33 x 45), back-ins (27 x 50), 138 full hkups (30/50 amps), cable, WiFi Hotspot, dump, laundry, groc, LP gas, fire rings, firewood, controlled access. **REC:** pool, Puddingstone Lake: fishing, playground. Pet restrict $. Partial handicap access, RV age restrict, eco-friendly, ATM.
AAA Approved
(800)809-3778 Lat: 34.08404, Lon: -117.79150
1440 Camper View Rd, San Dimas, CA 91773
eastshore@linkline.com
www.eastshorervpark.com

VAN NUYS — L1 *Los Angeles*

BALBOA RV PARK (RV Park) From Jct of US-101 & Balboa Blvd (Exit 21), N 2.8 mi on Balboa Blvd (R); or From Jct of I-405 & Roscoe Blvd (Exit 68), W 1.7 mi on Roscoe Blvd to Balboa Blvd, S 0.7 mi (L). **FAC:** Paved rds. (192 spaces). Avail: 130 all weather, 6 pull-thrus (26 x 60), back-ins (18 x 32), some side by side hkups, 130 full hkups (30/50 amps), cable, WiFi, laundry. **REC.** Pet restrict(B). Partial handicap access, RV age restrict, eco-friendly.
(818)785-0949 Lat: 34.21121, Lon: -118.49930
7740 Balboa Blvd, Van Nuys, CA 91406
info@balboarvpark.com
www.balboarvpark.com

VISTA — J4 *San Diego*

OLIVE AVE RV RESORT (RV Park) From Jct of N Melrose Dr & Olive Ave, W 450 ft on Olive Ave (R). **FAC:** Paved rds. (60 spaces). Avail: 40 paved, 31 pull-thrus (25 x 62), back-ins (36 x 40), 40 full hkups (50 amps), cable, WiFi, laundry. **REC:** heated pool, whirlpool. Pet restrict(B) $. Partial handicap access, RV age restrict, eco-friendly.
(877)633-3557 Lat: 33.20471, Lon: -117.25660
713 Olive Ave, Vista, CA 92083
reservations@oliveavervresort.com
www.oliveavervresort.com

FLORIDA

BRADENTON — L2 *Manatee*

SARASOTA BAY RV PARK (RV Park) From Jct of I-75 (exit 217) & SR-70: Go W 13 mi on SR-70, then W 2 mi on SR-684/Cortez Rd (L). **FAC:** Paved rds. (240 spaces). Avail: 100 paved, back-ins (25 x 55), 100 full hkups (30/50 amps), WiFi, dump, laundry. **REC:** heated pool, whirlpool, Sarasota Bay: fishing, shuffleboard. No pets. Age restrict may apply.
(941)794-1200 Lat: 27.46314, Lon: -82.66993
10777 Cortez Rd W, Bradenton, FL 34210
info@sarabayrvpark.com
www.sarabayrvpark.com

FORT MYERS — E3 *Lee*

UPRIVER RV RESORT (RV Park) From Jct of I-75 & SR-78 (exit 143/Bayshore Rd), E 1.6 mi on SR-78 (R). **FAC:** Paved rds. (351 spaces). 226 Avail: 196 paved, 30 grass, 65 pull-thrus (35 x 100), back-ins (32 x 60), 226 full hkups (30/50 amps), cable, WiFi, rentals, dump, laundry, LP gas. **REC:** heated pool, whirlpool, Caloosahatchee River: fishing, golf, shuffleboard. Pet restrict(B/Q). Partial handicap access, age restrict may apply, big rig sites, RV age restrict, eco-friendly.
AAA Approved
(239)543-3330 Lat: 26.71156, Lon: -81.78521
17021 Upriver Dr, North Fort Myers, FL 33917
info@upriver.com
www.upriver.com

WOODSMOKE CAMPING RESORT (RV Park) From Jct of I-75 & Corkscrew Rd (exit 123), W 2 mi on Corkscrew Rd to US-41, N 2 mi (R). **FAC:** Paved rds. (300 spaces). 160 Avail: 35 paved, 80 gravel, 45 grass, 18 pull-thrus (35 x 75), back-ins (35 x 55), 160 full hkups (30/50 amps), cable, WiFi, rentals, dump, laundry. **REC:** heated pool, whirlpool, Cypress Head Lake: fishing, shuffleboard, playground. Pet restrict(B/Q). Partial handicap access, big rig sites, eco-friendly.
AAA Approved
(800)231-5053 Lat: 26.45666, Lon: -81.82332
19551 S Tamiami Trail (US 41S), Fort Myers, FL 33908
woodsmokeresort@gmail.com
www.woodsmokecampingresort.com
See ad this page.

FORT PIERCE — L6 *St Lucie*

ROAD RUNNER TRAVEL RESORT (RV Park) From Jct of FL Tpke & SR-713 (exit 152), N 5 mi on SR-713 to CR-608, E 1.2 mi (L); or From Jct of I-95 & Indrio Rd (exit 138), E 3.2 mi on Indrio Rd to SR-713, S 2.5 mi to CR-608 (St Lucie Blvd), E 1.2 mi (L). **FAC:** Paved rds. (452 spaces). Avail: 275 grass, 14 pull-thrus (30 x 55), back-ins (30 x 55), 275 full hkups (30/50 amps), WiFi, rentals, laundry, groc, LP gas, restaurant, controlled access. **REC:** heated pool, pond, fishing, golf, shuffleboard. Pet restrict(B/Q). Partial handicap access, big rig sites, eco-friendly, ATM.
AAA Approved
(800)833-7108 Lat: 27.48544, Lon: -80.38001
5500 St Lucie Blvd, Fort Pierce, FL 34946
info@roadrunnerresort.com
www.roadrunnertravelresort.com

KEY WEST — F4 *Monroe*

BLUEWATER KEY RV RESORT (Condo Pk) S-bnd: On US-1 at MP-14.5 (L). **FAC:** Paved rds. (81 spaces). Avail: 66 paved, back-ins (35 x 75), accepts full hkup units only, 66 full hkups (30/50 amps), cable, WiFi, laundry, controlled access. **REC:** heated pool, Bluewater Bay: fishing. Pet restrict(Q). Partial handicap access, big rig sites.
AAA Approved
(305)745-2494 Lat: 24.62358, Lon: -81.60033
2950 US Hwy 1, Key West, FL 33040
bluekeyrv@aol.com
www.bluewaterkey.com

MALABAR — K5 *Brevard*

CAMELOT RV PARK, INC (RV Park) From Jct of I-95 (exit 173) & SR-514 (Malabar Rd): Go E 4.2 mi on Malabar Rd, then S 0.3 mi on US-1 (R). **FAC:** Paved rds. (177 spaces). 150 Avail: 50 paved, 100 gravel, 25 pull-thrus (20 x 60), back-ins (35 x 50), some side by side hkups, 150 full hkups (30/50 amps), cable, WiFi, laundry, LP gas, controlled access. **REC:** heated pool, Indian River Lagoon: fishing, shuffleboard. Pet restrict(B). Partial handicap access, big rig sites.
(321)724-5396 Lat: 28.00009, Lon: -80.56114
1600 S US-1, Malabar, FL 32950
camelot@camelotrvpark.com
www.camelotrvpark.com

Take an RV Trip of a Lifetime! Check out trip ideas at the front of the Guide - you'll find something for the history buff, the food lover or even your wild side!

OKEECHOBEE — D4 *Glades, Okeechobee*

BRIGHTON RV RESORT (RV Park) From jct US 441 & Hwy 70:Go 16 mi W on Hwy 70, then 13 mi S on SR 721 (R). **FAC:** Paved rds. (56 spaces). Avail: 50 paved, back-ins (40 x 75), 50 full hkups (30/50 amps), WiFi, rentals, dump, laundry, groc, LP bottles. **REC:** heated pool, rec open to public. Pet restrict(B/Q). Partial handicap access, ATM.
(863)357-6644 Lat: 27.04331, Lon: -81.06901
14685 Reservation Rd, Okeechobee, FL 34974
reservation@semtribe.com
www.brightonrvresort.com

PALM HARBOR — K1 *Pinellas*

SHERWOOD FOREST RV PARK (RV Park) From Jct of Alt US-19 & SR-584 (Tampa Rd): Go S 100 ft on Alt US-19 (R). **FAC:** Paved rds. (106 spaces). Avail: 49 grass, back-ins (30 x 45), 49 full hkups (30/50 amps), WiFi, laundry. **REC:** heated pool, pond, fishing. Pet restrict(B/Q). Partial handicap access, big rig sites.
AAA Approved
(727)784-4582 Lat: 28.06702, Lon: -82.77018
175 Alt 19S, Palm Harbor, FL 34683
sherwoodrv@aol.com
www.sherwoodrvresort.com

POLK CITY — K3 *Polk*

LE LYNN RV RESORT (RV Park) From Jct of I-4 & SR-559 (exit 44), N 0.3 mi on SR-559 (L). **FAC:** Paved rds. (370 spaces). Avail: 220 paved, 10 pull-thrus (25 x 66), back-ins (34 x 60), 220 full hkups (30/50 amps), WiFi $, dump, laundry, LP gas. **REC:** pool, Little Lake Agnes: fishing, shuffleboard. Pet restrict(B/Q). Partial handicap access, big rig sites.
(800)736-0409 Lat: 28.16321, Lon: -81.80183
1513 SR-559, Polk City, FL 33868

PORT CHARLOTTE — D3 *De Soto*

RIVERSIDE RV RESORT & CAMPGROUND (RV Park) From Jct of I-75 & CR-769 (Exit 170), NE 4.5 mi on CR-769/Kings Hwy (R). **FAC:** Paved rds. (499 spaces). Avail: 449 all weather, 5 pull-thrus (35 x 70), back-ins (45 x 80), 449 full hkups (30/50 amps), cable, WiFi, dump, laundry, groc, LP gas, fire rings, firewood, controlled access. **REC:** heated pool, whirlpool, Peace River: fishing, shuffleboard, playground. Pets OK. Partial handicap access, big rig sites, eco-friendly.
AAA Approved
(800)795-9733 Lat: 27.07961, Lon: -82.01331
9770 SW Cr-769 Kings Hwy, Arcadia, FL 34269
riverside@desoto.net
www.riversidervresort.com
See ad this page.

RUSKIN — L2 *Hillsborough*

SUN LAKE RV RESORT (RV Park) From Jct of I-75 (Exit 240) & SR-674: Go W 1.0 mi on SR-674, then S 0.5 mi on 27th St SE, then E 0.3 mi on 14th Ave SE (L). **FAC:** Paved rds. (49 spaces). Avail: 30 grass, 18 pull-thrus (25 x 50), back-ins (40 x 60), some side by side hkups, 30 full hkups (30/50 amps), WiFi $, dump, laundry. **REC:** pool, Sun Lake: fishing. Pet restrict(Q). Age restrict may apply, big rig sites.
(813)645-7860 Lat: 27.70636, Lon: -82.39371
3006 14th Ave SE, Ruskin, FL 33570
sunlakerv@aol.com

Thank You to our active and retired military personnel. A dedicated section of Military Listings for places to camp can be found at the back of the Guide.

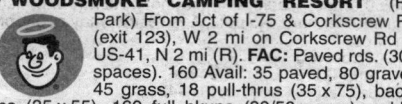

SANFORD — H4 *Seminole, Volusia*

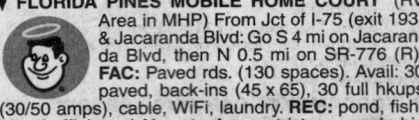

WEKIVA FALLS RESORT (Campground) From Jct of I-4 (exit 101C) & SR-46: Go W 5.5 mi on SR-46, then S 1.4 mi on Wekiva River Rd (L). **FAC:** Paved/gravel rds. (817 spaces). Avail: 569 grass, back-ins (40 x 60), 569 full hkups (30/50 amps), cable, WiFi $, laundry, groc, LP gas, controlled access. **REC:** heated pool, Wekiva River: swim, fishing, shuffleboard, playground, rec open to public. Pet restrict(B). Partial handicap access, big rig sites.
(352)383-8055 Lat: 28.79477, Lon: -81.42585
30700 Wekiva River Rd, Sorrento, FL 32776
info@wekivafallsresort.com
www.wekivafalls.com

SEBRING — L4 *Highlands*

OUTBACK RV RESORT AT TANGLEWOOD (RV Park) From Jct of US-27 & CR-634A: Go N 0.7 mi on US-27 (L). **FAC:** Paved rds. (151 spaces). 147 Avail: 31 paved, 116 grass, back-ins (50 x 85), 147 full hkups (30/50 amps), cable, WiFi, rentals, dump, laundry, controlled access. **REC:** heated pool, pond, fishing, shuffleboard. Pet restrict(B/Q). Partial handicap access, age restrict may apply, big rig sites.
(888)364-3729 Lat: 27.51860, Lon: -81.50798
3000 Tanglewood Pkwy, Sebring, FL 33872
Tammy.Martin@hometownamerica.com
www.OutbackRvResort.com

ST AUGUSTINE — B4 *St Johns*

ST JOHNS RV PARK (Campground) From Jct of I-95 & SR-207 (exit 311), E 0.1 mi on SR-207 (L). **FAC:** Paved/gravel rds. (60 spaces). Avail: 37 gravel, 15 pull-thrus (30 x 70), back-ins (25 x 60), some side by side hkups, 15 full hkups, 7 W, 7 E (30/50 amps), cable, WiFi Hotspot, dump, laundry. **REC:** pond. Pet restrict(B). Partial handicap access, big rig sites.
AAA Approved
(904)824-9840 Lat: 29.83230, Lon: -81.37794
2493 SR-207, St Augustine, FL 32086
www.stjohnsfleamarket.com

TAMPA — K2 *Hillsborough*

BAY BAYOU RV RESORT (RV Park) From Jct of I-275 (exit 47) & SR-580/Hillsborough Ave: Go W 10.8 mi, then N 0.5 mi on Country Way Blvd, then W 0.75 mi on Memorial Hwy (L). **FAC:** Paved rds. (274 spaces). 173 Avail: 99 gravel, 74 grass, back-ins (40 x 60), accepts full hkup units only, 173 full hkups (30/50 amps), cable, WiFi, dump, laundry, LP gas, controlled access. **REC:** heated pool, whirlpool, Double Branch Creek: fishing, shuffleboard. Pet restrict(B/Q). Partial handicap access, big rig sites, RV age restrict.
(813)855-1000 Lat: 28.02971, Lon: -82.63068
8492 Manatee Bay Dr, Tampa, FL 33635
info@baybayou.com
www.baybayou.com

TITUSVILLE — H5 *Brevard*

THE GREAT OUTDOORS RV, NATURE & GOLF RESORT (Condo Pk) From Jct of I-95 (exit 215) & SR-50: Go W 0.5 mi on SR-50 (Cheney Hwy) to entrance rd (L). **FAC:** Paved rds. (600 spaces). Avail: 100 paved, back-ins (40 x 80), 100 full hkups (30/50 amps), WiFi $, dump, laundry, LP gas, restaurant, controlled access. **REC:** heated pool, whirlpool, pond, fishing, golf, shuffleboard. Pet restrict(Q). Partial handicap access, big rig sites.
(321)269-5004 Lat: 28.55026, Lon: -80.86089
125 Plantation Dr, Titusville, FL 32780
info@tgoresort.com
www.tgoresort.com

VENICE — D3 *Sarasota*

FLORIDA PINES MOBILE HOME COURT (RV Area in MHP) From Jct of I-75 (exit 193) & Jacaranda Blvd: Go S 4 mi on Jacaranda Blvd, then N 0.5 mi on SR-776 (R). **FAC:** Paved rds. (130 spaces). Avail: 30 paved, back-ins (45 x 65), 30 full hkups (30/50 amps), cable, WiFi, laundry. **REC:** pond, fishing, shuffleboard. No pets. Age restrict may apply, big rig sites.
AAA Approved
(941)493-0019 Lat: 27.04838, Lon: -82.40494
150 Satulah Cir, Venice, FL 34293
http://www.goodsamcamping.com.s3.amazonaws.com/gsparks/731000284/index.html

ZEPHYRHILLS — J2 *Pasco*

RALPH'S TRAVEL PARK (RV Park) From S Jct of US-301 & SR-54: Go W 2.5 mi on SR-54 (L). **FAC:** Paved rds. (385 spaces). Avail: 75 grass, 15 pull-thrus (16 x 45), back-ins (16 x 40), some side by side hkups, 75 full hkups (30/50 amps), WiFi Hotspot, dump, laundry. **REC:** pool, pond, shuffleboard. Pet restrict(B).
(813)782-8223 Lat: 28.21859, Lon: -82.24739
34408 State Rd. 54 West, Zephyrhills, FL 33543
ralphs33543@aol.com
ralphstravelpark.net

GEORGIA

BRUNSWICK — E5 *Glynn*

GOLDEN ISLES RV PARK (Campground) From Jct of I-95 (Exit 29) & US Hwy 82/17: Go 1/2 mi W on US Hwy 82/17, then 1/4 mi N on GA 303 (L). **FAC:** Paved/gravel rds. (165 spaces). Avail: 125 dirt, 96 pull-thrus (28 x 60), back-ins (28 x 45), 115 full hkups, 10 W, 10 E (30/50 amps), cable, WiFi, dump, laundry, LP gas, firewood, restaurant. **REC:** pool, playground. Pets OK. Partial handicap access, big rig sites.
(912)261-1025 Lat: 31.14542, Lon: -81.57653
7445 Blythe Island Hwy, Brunswick, GA 31523
goldenislesrv@bellsouth.net
www.goldenislesrvpark.com

CLEVELAND — A2 *Habersham, Hall, Lumpkin, White*

LEISURE ACRES CAMPGROUND (Campground) S-bnd: From Cleveland, From Jct of US 129 & Hwy 115: Go 3-3/4 mi S on US-129, then 1/2 mi W on Westmoreland Rd (L); N-bnd: From Clermont, From Jct of US 129 & Hwy 254: Go 2-3/4 N on US 129 then 1/2 mi W on Westmoreland Rd (L). **FAC:** Gravel rds. (94 spaces). Avail: 54 gravel, 29 pull-thrus (25 x 60), back-ins (25 x 45), 54 full hkups (30/50 amps), WiFi, dump, laundry, LP gas, fire rings, firewood. **REC:** pool, wading pool, pond, fishing, playground. Pet restrict(B). Partial handicap access, big rig sites.
(706)865-6466 Lat: 34.53684, Lon: -83.76715
3840 Westmoreland Rd, Cleveland, GA 30528
info@leisureacrescampground.com
www.leisureacrescampground.com
See ad this page.

JACKSON — B2 *Butts*

FOREST GLEN MOBILE HOME & RV PARK (RV Park) From Jct of I-75 (exit 205) & Hwy 16: Go 1/4 mi W on Hwy 16, then 500 ft S on Windy Lane Circle, then 1/2 mi E on Forest Glen Rd, then 500 ft S on Entrance Rd (E). **FAC:** Paved rds. (148 spaces). Avail: 44 paved, 42 pull-thrus (22 x 50), back-ins (22 x 50), 44 full hkups (30/50 amps), WiFi Hotspot, laundry. **REC:** pool. Pet restrict(B).
(770)228-3399 Lat: 33.25707, Lon: -84.09341
218 Glade Rd, Jackson, GA 30233

RV Park ratings you can rely on!

SAVANNAH — D5 *Chatham*

SAVANNAH OAKS RV RESORT (Campground) From Jct of I-95 (exit 94) & SR 204: Go 2-1/2 mi W on SR 204 (L). **FAC:** Paved/gravel rds. (139 spaces). 99 Avail: 21 paved, 78 gravel, 76 pull-thrus (24 x 60), back-ins (24 x 60), 86 full hkups, 13 W, 13 E (30/50 amps), cable, WiFi, rentals, dump, laundry, groc, LP gas, controlled access. **REC:** pool, Ogeechee River: fishing, playground. Pets OK. Partial handicap access, big rig sites.
(800)851-0717 Lat: 32.025745, Lon: -81.31976
805 Fort Argyle Rd Hwy 204, Savannah, GA 31419
campinginsavannah@yahoo.com
www.savannahoaks.net
See ad this page.

TYBEE ISLAND — D5 *Chatham*

RIVER'S END CAMPGROUND & RV PARK (Public) From Jct I-95 (Exit 94) & Hwy 204: Go 10 mi E on Hwy 204, then 8 mi N on Harry Truman Parkway, then 15-1/2 mi E on US 80E, then 1/4 mi N on Polk St, then 500 ft E on Fort Ave (L). **FAC:** Paved/gravel rds. (87 spaces). Avail: 82 gravel, 30 pull-thrus (20 x 45), back-ins (20 x 40), 75 full hkups, 7 W, 7 E (30/50 amps), cable, WiFi, rentals, dump, laundry, LP gas, fire rings, firewood. **REC:** pool. Pet restrict(Q). Partial handicap access, eco-friendly, ATM.
(800)786-1016 Lat: 32.02274, Lon: -80.85020
5 Fort Ave, Tybee Island, GA 31328
riversend@cityoftybee.org
www.riversendcampground.com
See ad this page.

MAINE

MOOSE RIVER — C2 *Somerset*

MOOSE RIVER CAMPGROUND & CABINS (Campground) From Jct of Rtes 201 & 15/6, N 3.5 mi on Rte 201 to Heald Stream Rd, E 1.4 mi (R). **FAC:** Gravel rds. (26 spaces). Avail: 16 gravel, 6 pull-thrus (24 x 84), back-ins (33 x 57), 4 full hkups, 12 W, 12 E (30/50 amps), cable, WiFi, rentals, dump, mobile sewer, fire rings, firewood. **REC:** Heald Stream: fishing, playground. Pets OK. Partial handicap access, big rig sites, eco-friendly, May 15 to Oct 15.
AAA Approved
(207)668-4400 Lat: 45.65070, Lon: -70.24356
107 Heald Stream Rd, Moose River, ME 04945
littlebigwood@hotmail.com
www.mooserivercampground.org

SCARBOROUGH — E2 *Cumberland*

WASSAMKI SPRINGS CAMPGROUND (Campground) From Jct I-95 (Exit 46) & Hwy 22: Go 3 mi W on Hwy 22, then 1/4 mi N on Saco St (L). **FAC:** Paved/gravel rds. (256 spaces). 156 Avail: 45 grass, 111 dirt, 22 pull-thrus (30 x 60), back-ins (30 x 45), 126 full hkups, 30 W, 30 E (30/50 amps), cable, WiFi, dump, mobile sewer, laundry, groc, LP gas, fire rings, firewood, controlled access. **REC:** Wassamki Springs Lake: swim, fishing, playground, rec open to public. Pet restrict(B). Partial handicap access, big rig sites, eco-friendly, May 1 to Oct 15.
AAA Approved
(207)839-4276 Lat: 43.64687, Lon: -70.39875
56 Saco St., Scarborough, ME 04074
wassamkisprings@aol.com
www.wassamkisprings.com

Find it fast! To locate a town on a map, follow these easy instructions: Look for the map grid code after the town heading in the listing section and match it to the letters and numbers on the map borders. Draw a line horizontally from the letter and vertically from the number. You'll find the town near the intersection of the two lines.

MISSISSIPPI

TUPELO — A4 *Lee*

NATCHEZ TRACE RV PARK (Campground) From Jct of Natchez Trace Pkwy & US-78, SW 12.5 mi on Natchez Trace Pkwy to CR-506 (between MP-251 & MP-252 Pontocola Rd), E 400 ft (R); or From Jct of US 245 & Pontocola Rd (CR-506), W 7 mi on CR-506 (L). **FAC:** Gravel rds. 27 gravel, 21 pull-thrus (25 x 65), back-ins (30 x 40), 21 full hkups, 6 W, 6 E (30/50 amps), dump, laundry, LP gas, firewood. **REC:** pool, pond, fishing. Pets OK. Big rig sites, eco-friendly.
(662)767-8609 Lat: 34.14589, Lon: -88.81812
189 CR-506, Shannon, MS 38868
wez@dixieconnect.com
www.natcheztracervpark.com

MISSOURI

BRANSON — E2 *Stone, Taney*

CARSON'S COUNTRY COURT (RV Area in MHP) From Hwy 65 S & Exit 248 (Shepherd of the Hills Expressway); Go W 1.6 mi on Rt 248 and stay right (R). **FAC:** Paved/gravel rds. (53 spaces). Avail: 10 gravel, 5 pull-thrus (16 x 48), back-ins (18 x 34), 10 full hkups (30/50 amps), WiFi, laundry. **REC.** Pets OK. Eco-friendly.
AAA Approved
(417)334-3084 Lat: 36.668452, Lon: -93.249186
2166 State Hwy 248, Branson, MO 65616
office@carsonsrvpsrk.com
www.carsonsrvpark.com

NEVADA

LAS VEGAS — E4 *Clark, Las Vegas*

ARIZONA CHARLIE'S BOULDER RV PARK (RV Park) From Jct of I-515 (US 93/95 Expwy) & Boulder Hwy (exit 70): Go 2 mi S on Boulder Hwy (L). **FAC:** Paved rds. (221 spaces). Avail: 201 paved, 92 pull-thrus (20 x 70), back-ins (20 x 40), 201 full hkups (30/50 amps), cable, WiFi, laundry, restaurant. **REC:** heated pool, whirlpool. Pet restrict(B/Q). Partial handicap access.
(800)970-7280 Lat: 36.12466, Lon: -115.07733
4445 Boulder Hwy, Las Vegas, NV 89121
www.arizonacharlies.com
See ad this page.

HITCHIN' POST RV PARK (RV Park) S-bnd: From Jct of I-15 & Exit 50 (Lamb): Go 2 mi S on Lamb, then 500 ft S on Las Vegas Blvd (L) or N-bnd: From Jct of I-15 & Craig Rd (exit 48): Go 1-1/4 mi E on Craig Rd, then 1 mi SE on Lamb Blvd, then 500 ft on Las Vegas Blvd (L) Note: Call for updated directions. **FAC:** Paved rds. (196 spaces). Avail: 98 gravel, 98 pull-thrus (30 x 70), 98 full hkups (30/50 amps), cable, WiFi, rentals, laundry, restaurant, controlled access. **REC:** heated pool. Pet restrict(Q). Partial handicap access, big rig sites, eco-friendly, ATM.
AAA Approved
(888)433-8402 Lat: 36.24390, Lon: -115.05432
3640 Las Vegas Blvd North, Las Vegas, NV 89115
office@hprvp.com
www.hprvp.com
See ad this page.

PAHRUMP — E4 *Nye*

LAKESIDE CASINO & RV RESORT (RV Resort) From Jct of Hwy 160 & Homestead Rd (S end of town): Go S 3-3/4 mi on Homestead Rd, then W 100 ft on Thousandaire Rd (R). Elev 2700 ft. **FAC:** Paved rds. (159 spaces). Avail: 129 paved, 15 pull-thrus (30 x 70), back-ins (30 x 58), 129 full hkups (30/50 amps), WiFi, laundry, groc, LP gas, firewood, restaurant. **REC:** pool, whirlpool, Lakeside Lake: fishing, playground. Pet restrict(Q). Partial handicap access, big rig sites, eco-friendly, ATM.
(888)558-5253 Lat: 36.12054, Lon: -115.96387
5870 S Homestead Road, Pahrump, NV 89048
infogcg@goldencasinogroup.com
www.lakesidecasinopahrump.com
See ad this page.

NEVADA TREASURE RV RESORT (RV Resort) From Jct of SR-372 & SR-160: Go N 7-1/2 mi on SR-160, then go 500 ft on Leslie St (L). Elev 2699 ft. **FAC:** Paved rds. (202 spaces). Avail: 167 paved, back-ins (36 x 50), 167 full hkups (30/50 amps), WiFi, laundry, LP gas, restaurant, controlled access. **REC:** heated pool, whirlpool, rec open to public. Pets OK. Partial handicap access, big rig sites, eco-friendly.
AAA Approved
(800)429-6665 Lat: 36.30349, Lon: -116.01604
301 West Leslie St., Pahrump, NV 89060
frontdesk@nvtreasure.com
www.nvtreasure.com
See ad this page.

RENO — C1 *Washoe*

SILVER SAGE RV PARK (RV Park) From Jct of US-395, I-80(Exit 64) Moana Lane: Go W on Moana Lane 1/2 mi to S Virginia St, then N 1/4 mi on S Virginia St (R). Elev 4458 ft. **FAC:** Paved rds. (43 spaces). Avail: 30 paved, back-ins (23 x 50), 30 full hkups (30/50 amps), cable, WiFi, laundry, controlled access. **REC.** Pets OK. Partial handicap access, eco-friendly.
AAA Approved
(888)823-2002 Lat: 39.47937, Lon: -119.78943
2760 S. Virginia St., Reno, NV 89502
info@silversagervpark.com
www.silversagervpark.com
See ad this page.

SEARCHLIGHT — F5 *Clark*

COTTONWOOD COVE RESORT (RV Park) From Jct of US-95 & SR 164 (Cottonwood Cove Rd) in Searchlight: Go E 14 mi on Cottonwood Cove Rd (E). **FAC:** Dirt rds. 72 dirt, 29 pull-thrus (18 x 80), back-ins (20 x 32), some side by side hkups, 72 full hkups (30/50 amps), rentals, dump, laundry, groc, LP gas, firewood, restaurant. **REC:** Lake Mohave: swim, fishing, marina, shuffleboard, rec open to public. Pet restrict(Q). Partial handicap access, eco-friendly, ATM.
(702)297-1464 Lat: 35.49122, Lon: -114.68630
10000 Cottonwood Cove Rd, Searchlight, NV 89046
ccarter@foreverresorts.com
www.cottonwoodcoveresort.com
See ad this page.

SPARKS — C1 *Washoe*

VICTORIAN RV PARK (RV Park) From Jct of Hwy 395 & I-80 (Exit 19): Go 1/4 mi N on McCarren Blvd, then 1/4 mi W on Nichols Blvd (L). Elev 4600 ft. **FAC:** Paved rds. (85 spaces). Avail: 45 paved, 21 pull-thrus (24 x 60), back-ins (25 x 30), 45 full hkups (30/50 amps), cable, WiFi, dump, laundry, groc. **REC:** heated pool, whirlpool. Pets OK. Partial handicap access, eco-friendly.
(800)955-6405 Lat: 39.5354284, Lon: -119.7407624
205 Nichols Blvd, Sparks, NV 89431
info@victorianrvpark.com
www.victorianrvpark.com
See ad this page.

NEW HAMPSHIRE

FREEDOM — D4 *Carroll*

THE BLUFFS RV RESORT (RV Park) From Jct of Rte 16 & Rte 41 (in West Ossipee), Go 0.5 mi E on Rte 41 to Ossipee Lake Rd, then 4.8 mi SE to Shawtown Rd, then 1 mi NE (R). One week minimum stay, age 50 and older. **FAC:** Paved/gravel rds. (297 spaces). Avail: 12 gravel, back-ins (30 x 65), accepts full hkup units only, 12 full hkups (30/50 amps), cable, WiFi, rentals, laundry, groc, LP gas, fire rings, firewood, controlled access. **REC:** heated pool, pond, fishing. Pet restrict(Q). Partial handicap access, age restrict may apply, big rig sites, eco-friendly, Apr 18 to Nov 2.
(603)539-2069 Lat: 43.83240, Lon: -71.11064
196 Shawton Rd, Freedom, NH 03836
seasonal@danforthbay.com
www.nhrvresort.com
See ad page 1494.

Explore America's Top RV Destinations! Turn to the Spotlight articles in our State and Province sections to learn more.

NEW JERSEY

NEW GRETNA — E3 *Burlington, Ocean, Wrightstown*

CHIPS FOLLY FAMILY CAMPGROUND (Campground) N-bnd: From Jct of Garden State Pkwy & US 9 (Exit 50), N 1 mi on US 9 to CR-542, NW 3 mi to CR-653, E 0.1 mi to access rd, N 1 mi (E); or S-bnd: From Jct of Garden State Parkway & CR 654 (Exit 52), N 1.3 mi on CR 654 to CR 653, W 2.8 mi (R). **FAC:** Gravel rds. (300 spaces). Avail: 30 dirt, 7 pull-thrus (30 x 45), back-ins (18 x 32), some side by side hkups, 24 full hkups, 6 W, 6 E (30/50 amps), WiFi Hotspot, rentals, dump, mobile sewer, laundry, groc, LP gas, fire rings, firewood, controlled access. **REC:** pool, Wading River: fishing, playground. Pet restrict(B).
(609)296-4434 Lat: 39.63378, Lon: -74.49723
100 Chips Folly Rd, New Gretna, NJ 08224
www.chipsfolly.com
See ad this page.

NEW YORK

LAKE GEORGE — C10 *Warren*

LAKE GEORGE RV PARK (RV Park) From Jct of I-87 & US-9 (exit 20), N 0.5 mi on US-9 to SR-149, E 0.5 mi (R) Note: 3 night minimum on holiday weekends. **FAC:** Paved rds. (368 spaces). Avail: 356 all weather, 280 pull-thrus (30 x 60), back-ins (30 x 56), 356 full hkups (50 amps), cable, WiFi, rentals, dump, laundry, groc, LP gas, fire rings, firewood, controlled access. **REC:** heated pool, wading pool, pond, fishing, shuffleboard, playground. Pets OK. Partial handicap access, big rig sites, eco-friendly, May 6 to Oct 10. ATM.
AAA Approved
(518)792-3775 Lat: 43.36922, Lon: -73.69109
74 SR-149, Lake George, NY 12845
info@lakegeorgervpark.com
www.lakegeorgervpark.com

OREGON

EUGENE — C2 *Lane*

EUGENE KAMPING WORLD (Campground) From Jct of I-5 & Van Duyn Rd (exit 199): Go W 0.3 mi on Van Duyn Rd/E Pearl St to S Stuart Way, then S 0.2 mi (E) Note: first turn after stop light. **FAC:** Paved rds. (110 spaces). 60 Avail: 37 paved, 23 gravel, 55 pull-thrus (22 x 65), back-ins (22 x 40), 47 full hkups, 13 W, 13 E (30/50 amps), WiFi, dump, laundry, LP gas. **REC:** playground. Pet restrict(B). Eco-friendly.
AAA Approved
(800)343-3008 Lat: 44.13420, Lon: -123.05683
90932 S Stuart Way, Coburg, OR 97408
eugenekampingworld2@yahoo.com
www.eugenekampingworld.com

FAIRVIEW — A2 *Multnomah*

PORTLAND FAIRVIEW RV PARK (RV Park) From Jct of I-84 & 207th Ave N (exit 14): Go N 0.1 mi on 207th Ave to NE Sandy Blvd, then E 0.3 mi (L). **FAC:** Paved rds. (407 spaces). Avail: 257 paved, 105 pull-thrus (25 x 60), back-ins (25 x 35), accepts full hkup units only, 257 full hkups (30/50 amps), cable, WiFi, laundry. **REC:** heated pool, whirlpool, pond. Pet restrict(B). Big rig sites, eco-friendly.
(877)777-1047 Lat: 45.54333, Lon: -122.44438
21401 NE Sandy Blvd, Fairview, OR 97024
customerservice@portlandfairviewrv.com
www.portlandfairviewrv.com

PORTLAND — A2 *Multnomah*

JANTZEN BEACH RV PARK (RV Park) From Jct of I-5 & Jantzen Beach (exit 308/N of Portland), take exit rd to N Hayden Island Dr, W 0.3 mi (R). **FAC:** Paved rds. (169 spaces). Avail: 69 paved, 9 pull-thrus (27 x 68), back-ins (30 x 50), 69 full hkups (30/50 amps), cable, WiFi, laundry. **REC:** heated pool, wading pool, Columbia River: playground. Pet restrict(B). Big rig sites, eco-friendly.
AAA Approved
(800)443-7248 Lat: 45.61613, Lon: -122.68609
1503 N Hayden Island Dr., Portland, OR 97217
mail@jbrv.com
www.jantzenbeachrv.com

SISTERS — C3 *Deschutes, Jefferson, Linn*

BEND/SISTERS GARDEN RV RESORT (RV Resort) From Jct of US-20 & Hwy 126 (E edge of Sisters), SE 4 mi on US-20 (R). Elev 3200 ft. **FAC:** Paved rds. (105 spaces). Avail: 99 paved, 66 pull-thrus (30 x 70), back-ins (30 x 45), 99 full hkups (30/50 amps), WiFi, rentals, laundry, groc, LP gas, fire rings, firewood. **REC:** heated pool, whirlpool, pond, fishing, playground. Pet restrict(Q) $. Partial handicap access, big rig sites, eco-friendly.
(541)516-3036 Lat: 44.25039, Lon: -121.48825
67667 Hwy 20, Bend, OR 97701
bendsistersgardenrv@gmail.com
www.bendsistersgardenrv.com
See ad this page.

TEXAS

CONCAN — D5 *Uvalde*

PARKVIEW RIVERSIDE RV PARK (RV Park) From Jct of Hwy 83 & Hwy 1050 (North of Concan), E 1.1mi on Hwy 1050 to CR-350, S 1.5 mi (R). **FAC:** Paved/gravel rds. 99 gravel, 17 pull-thrus (28 x 65), back-ins (35 x 55), 99 full hkups (30/50 amps), WiFi $, dump, laundry, groc, LP gas, fire rings, firewood. **REC:** Frio River: swim, fishing. Pets OK. Partial handicap access, big rig sites, eco-friendly.
(877)374-6748 Lat: 29.58256, Lon: -99.72801
2561 County Road 350, Concan, TX 78838
parkviewrv@gmail.com
parkviewriversiderv.com
See ad this page.

MISSION — M3 *Hidalgo*

BENTSEN GROVE RESORT MHP (RV Park) W-bnd: From Jct of US-83 (Expwy) & Hwy 364/La Homa Rd/Bentsen Palm Dr exit, W 1.5 mi on N Frntg Rd to Bentsen Palm Dr (second light), S 0.9 mi on Bentsen Palm Dr (L); E-bnd: From Jct of US Expwy 83 & Bentsen Palm Dr, S 0.9 mi on Bentsen Palm Dr (L). **FAC:** Paved rds. (831 spaces). Avail: 300 paved, back-ins (30 x 60), accepts full hkup units only, 300 full hkups (30/50 amps), cable, WiFi, rentals, laundry, controlled access. **REC:** heated pool, whirlpool, shuffleboard. Pets OK. Partial handicap access, age restrict may apply, big rig sites, eco-friendly.
(956)585-7011 Lat: 26.21898, Lon: -98.37234
810 Bentsen Palm Drive, Mission, TX 78572
office@bentsengroveresort.com
www.bentsengroveresort.com
See ad this page.

PASADENA — D8 *Houston*

CAMINO VILLA MH & RV PARK (RV Spaces) From S Jct of I-610 & I-45, S 3.25 mi on I-45 to Exit 36 (College), E 6 mi on College (becomes Spencer Hwy) to Space Center Blvd, S 0.5 mi (R). **FAC:** Paved rds. (218 spaces). Avail: 9 grass, back-ins (30 x 50), 9 full hkups (30/50 amps). Pet restrict(B/Q).
(281)487-1759 Lat: 29.66031, Lon: -95.14481
3310 Space Center Blvd., Pasadena, TX 77505

PORTLAND — E7 *San Patricio*

SEA BREEZE RV PARK (RV Park) From Jct of US-181 & FM-893/Moore Ave exit, NW 1 mi on FM-893/Moore Ave to Marriott St, SW 0.5 mi to Doyle, S 0.2 mi (R). **FAC:** Gravel rds. (160 spaces). Avail: 100 gravel, 42 pull-thrus (22 x 60), back-ins (22 x 40), some side by side hkups, 99 full hkups, 1 W, 1 E (30/50 amps), WiFi, dump, laundry. **REC:** heated pool, wading pool, whirlpool, Corpus Christi

SAVE! Over $1,000 in coupons can be found at the front of the Guide!

Visit Camping World on your RV travels to stock up on accessories and supplies while on the road. Find the nearest SuperCenter at CampingWorld.com

PORTLAND (CONT)

SEA BREEZE RV PARK (CONT)
Bay: fishing. Pet restrict(B/Q). Partial handicap access, eco-friendly.
(361)643-0744 Lat: 27.88515, Lon: -97.34420
1026 Seabreeze Lane, Portland, TX 78374
seabreezrv@aol.com
www.seabreezerv.com
See ad opposite page.

WASHINGTON

KELSO — D2 *Cowlitz*

BROOKHOLLOW RV PARK (RV Park) From Jct of I-5 & Allen St (exit 39): Go 1 mi E on Allen St (just past mobile home park look for white RV park sign) (R). **FAC:** Paved rds. (132 spaces). Avail: 52 paved, 39 pull-thrus (35 x 60), back-ins (32 x 45), accepts self-contain units only, 52 full hkups (30/50 amps), cable, WiFi, laundry. **REC:** Coweeman River: fishing, playground. Pet restrict(B) $. Partial handicap access, big rig sites, eco-friendly.
(800)867-0453 Lat: 46.14472, Lon: -122.87946
2506 Allen St, Kelso, WA 98626
brookhollowrv@ipgmhc.com
www.brookhollowrvpark.com
See ad this page.

KENNEWICK — D5 *Benton*

COLUMBIA SUN RV RESORT (RV Resort) From Jct US 395 & I-82: Go 3-1/2 mi NW on I-82 to Badger Rd (Exit 109), then 1/2 mi SW on Badger Rd to Wiser Pkwy, then 3/4 mi W on Wiser Pkwy (L). **FAC:** Paved rds. (145 spaces). Avail: 30 paved, 85 all weather, 76 pull-thrus (38 x 80), back-ins (32 x 42), 115 full hkups (30/50 amps), cable, WiFi, laundry, groc, LP gas. **REC:** heated pool, whirlpool, playground. Pet restrict(B/Q). Partial handicap access, big rig sites.
(509)420-4880 Lat: 46.194902, Lon: -119.281763
103907 E Wiser Parkway, Kennewick, WA 99338
info@columbiasunrvresort.com
www.columbiasunrvresort.com
See ad this page.

Got a big rig? Look for listings indicating "big rig sites." These campgrounds are made for you, with 12'-wide roads and 14' overhead clearance. They guarantee that 25% or more of their sites measure 24' wide by 60' long or larger, and have full hookups with 50-amp electricity.

RICHLAND — D5 *Benton*

HORN RAPIDS RV RESORT (RV Resort) From Jct of I-182 & Hwy 240W (exit 4): go 4 mi NE on Hwy 240W, then 2 mi NW on Hwy 240W to Kingsgate Wy, then 1/8 mi NE on Kingsgate Wy (R). **FAC:** Paved rds. (225 spaces). Avail: 100 all weather, 20 pull-thrus (22 x 70), back-ins (30 x 50), 100 full hkups (30/50 amps), cable, WiFi, dump, laundry, groc, LP gas. **REC:** heated pool, whirlpool, shuffleboard, playground. Pet restrict(B). Partial handicap access.
(866)557-9637 Lat: 46.32740, Lon: -119.31495
2640 Kingsgate Way, Richland, WA 99354
info@hornrapidsrvresort.com
www.hornrapidsrvresort.com
See ad this page.

BRITISH COLUMBIA

KIMBERLEY — J6 *Kimberley, Kootenay East*

KIMBERLEY RIVERSIDE CAMPGROUND (Public) From Jct of Hwy 95A North & St Mary Lake Rd, W 2.7kms/ 1.7 mi on St Mary Lake Rd (L). Elev 3205 ft. **FAC:** Paved/gravel rds. (130 spaces). Avail: 106 gravel, 45 pull-thrus (35 x 85), back-ins (25 x 55), 81 full hkups, 25 W, 25 E (30/50 amps), WiFi Hotspot, dump, laundry, fire rings, firewood. **REC:** heated pool, St Mary 's River: fishing, playground. Pets OK. Partial handicap access, big rig sites, RV age restrict, eco-friendly, Apr 15 to Oct 15.
AAA Approved
(877)999-2929 Lat: 49.63494, Lon: -115.99763
Site 500, St Mary Lake Rd, Kimberley, BC V1A 3B9
info@kimberleycampground.com
www.kimberleycampground.com

MANITOBA

BRANDON — E2 *Brandon*

MEADOWLARK CAMPGROUND (Campground) (E-bnd Hwy 1 or N-bnd Hwy 10) From W Jct of Hwys 1 & 10, E 0.3 mi on N Service Rd; or (W-bnd Hwy 1 or S-bnd Hwy 10) From E Jct of Hwys 1 & 10, W 0.5 mi on Hwy 1 to N Service Rd, W 200 ft to park entrance (R). **FAC:** Gravel rds. (75 spaces). Avail: 70 gravel, 35 pull-thrus (30 x 94), back-ins (30 x 55), some side by side hkups, 60 full hkups, 10 W, 10 E (30/50 amps), WiFi, dump, laundry, controlled access. **REC:** playground. Pets OK. Big rig sites, eco-friendly, Apr 15 to Oct 15.
AAA Approved
(800)363-6434 Lat: 49.888315, Lon: -99.956037
100 Meadowlark Trailer Park, Brandon, MB R7C 0C1
info@meadowlarkcampground.ca
www.meadowlarkrvpark.com

QUEBEC

HUDSON — B1 *Monteregie*

CAMPING D'AOUST (Campground) From Jct of Hwy 40 W & Exit 28 (Rte 342), N 0.6 mi on Rte Harwood W 1.5 mi (L). **FAC:** Paved/gravel rds. (214 spaces). 111 Avail: 30 gravel, 81 grass, 6 pull-thrus (30 x 55), back-ins (25 x 50), mostly side by side hkups, 43 full hkups, 68 W, 45 E (20/30 amps), WiFi $, rentals, dump, laundry, groc, LP gas, fire rings, firewood, restaurant, controlled access. **REC:** pool, playground, rec open to public. Pets OK. Partial handicap access, eco-friendly, May 1 to Oct 31.
AAA Approved
(450)458-7301 Lat: 45.440704, Lon: -74.137382
3844 Harwood Route, Hudson, QC J7V 0G1
camping.daoust@qc.aira.com
www.campingdaoust.com

SAINT-NICOLAS — D6
Chaudiere-Appalaches

KOA QUEBEC CITY (Campground) E-bnd: From Jct of Hwy 20 & Exit 311 (Rte 116), SE 0.1 mi on Arena St to Rte 116, E 0.4 mi to Chemin Olivier (N Service Rd), W 1 mi (R); or W-bnd: From Jct of Hwy 20 & exit 311, N 200 ft on exit rd to Chemin Olivier, W 1 mi (R). **FAC:** Paved/gravel rds. (201 spaces). 198 Avail: 168 gravel, 30 grass, 151 pull-thrus (35 x 60), back-ins (30 x 40), 137 full hkups, 57 W, 39 E (30/50 amps), WiFi, rentals, dump, laundry, groc, LP bottles, fire rings, firewood, controlled access. **REC:** heated pool, whirlpool, playground. Pets OK. Partial handicap access, big rig sites, eco-friendly, May 1 to Oct 12.
AAA Approved
(418)831-1813 Lat: 46.699138, Lon: -71.301418
684 Chemin Oliver, Saint-Nicolas, QC G7A 2N6
camp@koaquebec.com
www.koa.com

Nobody takes to the road like we do. In many listings we tell you the surface type and condition of interior campground roads.

Set a Destination for Family Fun!

Check out our camping destinations highlighting the best places for camping with the family in every state and province. Find a great destination, then select one of the family-friendly campgrounds listed by region throughout the article in the front of this Guide.

Travel Services & Pilot Flying J Locations

Within this special Yellow Pages section, you'll find information on businesses that offer a variety of RV services to ensure your vacation stays on course. You'll find information on vital RV services you may need should your windshield crack or your transmission make a strange new sound.

Organized by state and province, the Good Sam RV Travel & Savings Guide's Yellow Pages section puts vital information at your fingertips. Whether you're passing through or planning an extended stay, the businesses listed in the RV-friendly Yellow Pages can help you find what you need.

How to Read:

Town Name
Where the facility is located, or the nearest town.
Location on Map
The letter and number next to a town correspond to the coordinates on the state map noted at the top of the page.
Name of Facility
Name of facility or service center.
PISMO BEACH — G2 San Luis Obispo
Travel Services
PISMO COAST RV SERVICE Your full service RV repair facility. SERVICES: RV, tire, RV appliance. RV storage. RV supplies, LP, RV parking. Hours: 9am to 5pm. V, MC, D, Debit.
(805)773-3868 Lat: 35.13438, Lon: -120.63577
180 S. Dolliver St, Pismo Beach, CA 93449
rv@pismocoastvillage.com
www.pismocoastvillage.com
See ad this page.
County Name(s)
County names make it easier to follow weather forecasts.
Phone Number
Address

Pilot® FLYING J®

You'll also find a list of Pilot Flying J locations located throughout the United States and Canada where Good Sam Members get discounts on gas, diesel, propane and dump station fees. From checking your tire pressure to getting a hearty meal, Pilot Flying J provides all of the services needed by an RV traveler on the go. And with more than 700 locations across North America, you're never far from a Pilot Flying J location.

Use your Good Sam Club membership card to save 3 cents on every gallon of gas and diesel at Pilot Flying J Travel Centers. Plus, members can save even more when applying for the Pilot Flying J RV Plus Charge Card. Save at least 4 cents per gallon on gas and at least 5 cents on diesel. For Good Sam Club members with recreational vehicles requiring diesel exhaust fluid, Pilot Flying J has America's largest network of DEF dispensers.

ALASKA

FAIRBANKS — B4 *Burrough, Fairbanks, North Star*

Travel Services

GABE'S TRUCK & AUTO REPAIR, L.L.C. Napa Truck Care Center. Auto, truck and RV service. General automotive repair for RVs, trucks and cars. Towing services (not for Class A motorhomes). **SERVICES:** MH mechanical, engine/chassis repair, emergency rd svc, restrooms. **TOW:** RV, auto. Emergency parking, RV accessible. waiting room. Hours: 7:30 am to 6 pm.
(907)456-6156 Lat: 64.48598, Lon: -147.45975
2015 Frank Ave, Fairbanks, AK 99707
marty.frey@gabesauto.com
www.gabesauto.com
See ad this page.

ARIZONA

PARKER — C1 *La Paz*

Travel Services

SPANKY'S RV & MARINE SUPPLY The largest RV & Marine supplier on the Colorado River. **SERVICES:** Restrooms. RV supplies, RV accessible. Hours: 8am to 5pm.
(928)669-1600 Lat: 34.14934, Lon: -114.29025
1012 Joshua Ave, Parker, AZ 85344
traveltrees@juno.com
www.spankysrvonline.com
See ad this page.

TUCSON — E4 *Pima*

Travel Services

ALL-RV SERVICE CENTER RV service & parts. Specialists in hard-to-find specialty parts and have available tent-trailer parts, Winnebago parts, Holiday Rambler, Monaco, and more. Elev 3800 ft. **SERVICES:** RV, MH mechanical, engine/chassis repair, mobile RV svc, emergency rd svc. RV storage. **TOW:** RV. RV supplies, dump. Hours: 8 am to 5 pm.
(520)622-1578 Lat: 32.25011, Lon: -110.98026
537 W Grant Rd, Tucson, AZ 85705
allrvtucson@aol.com
www.allrvtucson.com
See ad this page.

ARKANSAS

WEST MEMPHIS — C5 *Crittenden*

Travel Services

RIKARD & SONS, INC As well as selling parts this is a mobile service center. **SERVICES:** RV appliance, mobile RV svc, restrooms. RV supplies, emergency parking, RV accessible. Hours: 8am to 5pm Mon-Fri.
(870)735-2141 Lat: 35.14722, Lon: -90.14941
203 N Walker Ave, West Memphis, AR 72301
parts@rikardandsons.com
www.rikardandsons.com
See ad this page.

We rate what RVers consider important.

CALIFORNIA

ESCONDIDO — J4 *San Diego*

Travel Services

SONRISE RV SERVICE & PARTS Service, parts, body & paint, 50 ft. paint booth, appliances, and plumbing. **SERVICES:** RV, RV appliance. RV supplies, emergency parking, waiting room. Hours: 8am to 5pm.
(760)745-2444 Lat: 33.12735, Lon: -117.11945
1931 Don Lee Place, Escondido, CA 92029
jrashforth@sonriserv.com
www.sonriserv.com
See ad this page.

PISMO BEACH — G2 *San Luis Obispo*

Travel Services

PISMO COAST RV SERVICE Full service RV repair facility. **SERVICES:** RV, RV appliance, mobile RV svc, staffed RV wash. RV storage. RV supplies, LP. Hours: 9am to 5pm.
(805)773-3868 Lat: 35.134770, Lon: -120.637282
180 S Dolliver St, Pismo Beach, CA 93449
rv@pismocoastvillage.com
www.pismocoastvillage.com
See ad this page.

Dispose of old paint, chemicals, and oil properly. Don't put batteries, antifreeze, paint, motor oil, or chemicals in the trash. Use proper toxics disposal sites.

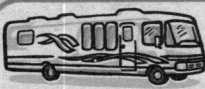

PLACENTIA — N3

Travel Services

FAIRWAY FORD RV CENTER Full service RV shop. Complete body repair shop. Extended warranties accepted. **SERVICES:** RV, tire, RV appliance, MH mechanical. **TOW:** RV, auto. RV supplies, emergency parking, waiting room. Hours: 7:30am to 6pm.
(714)524-1200 Lat: 33.88788, Lon: -117.83850
1350 E Yorba Linda Blvd, Placentia, CA 92870
rvservice@go2fairway.com
www.go2fairway.com
See ad this page.

REDDING — B2 *Shasta*

Travel Services

ALL WHEEL AUTO, TRUCK & RV REPAIR Services: motor homes, trailers, autos pickups vans, semi trucks buses, home of the trailer, wheel alignment, tires, shocks, complete auto, truck & RV service and repairs. **SERVICES:** Tire, MH mechanical, engine/chassis repair, restrooms. **TOW:** Auto. Emergency parking, RV accessible. waiting room. Hours: 8am to 5pm M-F.
(530)241-1010 Lat: 40.63958, Lon: -122.36792
18730 Old Oasis Rd, Redding, CA 96003
allwheelalignment@msn.com
www.allwheelinc.com
See ad this page.

CONNECTICUT

SOUTH WINDSOR — B4 *Hartford*

Travel Services

CUSSON AUTOMOTIVE INC. Service and repair all makes and models of motorhome chassis components including engine, transmission, suspension, air conditioning, tires, brakes and more. Cummins Service and Warranty Center.

AUTHORIZED CUMMINS, SPARTA, ONAN DLR
We are a family owned business that has been providing honest & professional quality care & maintenance to South Windsor, CT and surrounding areas since 1993. We specialize in all makes & models. A/C repair. 24 hr towing.
SERVICES: RV, tire, MH mechanical, engine/chassis repair, emergency rd svc, restrooms. **TOW:** RV, auto. RV supplies, LP, emergency parking, RV accessible. waiting room. Hours: 7:30am to 5:30pm M-F.
(860)289-2389 Lat: 41.82240, Lon: -72.60780
29 Mascolo Road, South Windsor, CT 06074
don@cussonautomotive.com
www.cussonautomotive.com
See ad this page.

FLORIDA

JUPITER — D5 *Palm Beach*

Travel Services

LAND YACHTS, INC Motorhome repair and warranty center. **SERVICES:** RV, tire, RV appliance, MH mechanical, engine/chassis repair, staffed RV wash, restrooms. RV storage. RV supplies, RV accessible. waiting room. Hours: 8am to 5pm.
(561)745-0242 Lat: 26.93012, Lon: -80.12064
1414 Commerce Ln, Jupiter, FL 33458
landyachtsinc@bellsouth.net
www.landyachtsinc.com

MARY ESTHER — F1

Travel Services

OPEN ROAD INC Large Selection of RV parts and supplies, as well as used RVs. RV supplies, RV accessible. waiting room. Hours: 9am to 5pm.
(850)244-4020 Lat: 30.40944, Lon: -86.66289
135 E Miracle Strip Parkway, Mary Esther, FL 32569
ken@openroad.gcoxmail.com
www.openroadrvinc.com
See ad this page.

WEST PALM BEACH — D5 *Palm Beach*

Travel Services

PALM BEACH RV Full service RV dealership. Sells new and used fifth-wheels, toy haulers, and travel trailers. Parts, repair, and service. **SERVICES:** RV, RV appliance, restrooms, RV Sales. RV supplies, LP, waiting room. Hours: 8am to 5pm.
(561)689-5788 Lat: 26.76335, Lon: -80.10851
5757 N Military Trail, West Palm Beach, FL 33407
mary.waits@palmbeachrv.com
www.palmbeachrv.com
See ad this page.

We've listened to thousands of RVers like you, so we know exactly how to rate campgrounds. Got feedback? Call us!877-209-6655

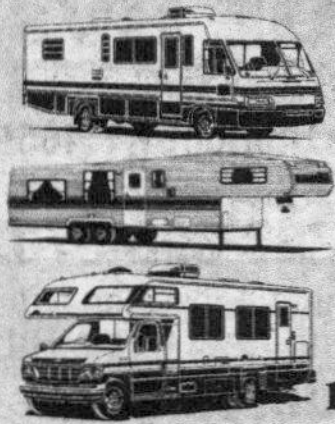

INDIANA

BURNS HARBOR — A2 *Porter*

Travel Services

CAMP-LAND RV RV Dealership with RV sales, part supplies and repair. **SERVICES:** RV, RV appliance, MH mechanical, engine/chassis repair, restrooms, RV Sales. RV supplies, LP, emergency parking, RV accessible. waiting room. Hours: 9am to 5:30pm.
(219)787-1040 Lat: 41.60519, Lon: -87.11882
1171 Lions Dr, Burns Harbor, IN 46304
sales@camplandrv.com
www.camplandrv.com
See ad this page.

GREENFIELD — C4 *Hancock*

Travel Services

S & H RV SERVICE & PARTS CENTER Onsite RV repairs and upgrades at campgrounds. 10% Good Sam/AAA discounts on parts and service. **SERVICES:** Tire, RV appliance, MH mechanical, mobile RV svc, emergency rd svc, staffed RV wash, restrooms. Rentals. **TOW:** RV, auto. RV supplies, LP, dump, emergency parking, RV accessible. Hours: 9am to 9 pm.
(317)326-3208 Lat: 39.79832, Lon: -85.85059
2573 W 100 N, Greenfield, IN 46140
reservations@sandhcampground.com
www.shservicecenter.com
See ad this page.

NEW CARLISLE — A3 *St Joseph*

Travel Services

S & H RV SERVICE & PARTS CENTER Onsite RV repairs and upgrades at campgrounds. 10% Good Sam/AAA discounts on parts and service. **SERVICES:** Tire, RV appliance, MH mechanical, mobile RV svc, emergency rd svc, staffed RV wash, restrooms. Rentals. **TOW:** RV, auto. RV supplies, LP, dump, emergency parking, RV accessible. Hours: 9am to 9pm.
(574)654-3307 Lat: 41.67206, Lon: -86.49600
32351 State Rd 2, New Carlisle, IN 46552
reservations@sandhcampground.com
www.shservicecenter.com
See ad this page.

KENTUCKY

LEXINGTON — C4 *Fayette, Madison*

Travel Services

NORTHSIDE RV'S, INC. Sales of new and used recreational vehicles. Repairs of RVs, sales of accessories and parts. Sales, Service and Rentals. **SERVICES:** RV, RV appliance, RV Sales. Rentals. RV storage. RV supplies, LP, emergency parking, RV accessible. waiting room. Hours: 8:30am to 5:00pm.
(859)299-8386 Lat: 38.06855, Lon: -84.47117
1630 N. Broadway, Lexington, KY 40505
gecklar@northsidervs.com
www.northsidervs.com
See ad this page.

Looking for a new or used RV? Camping World is America's largest retailer of RVs. Click CampingWorld.com or visit SuperCenters nationwide.

LOUISVILLE — C3 *Fayette, Meade*

Travel Services

LOUISVILLE RV CENTER Sales, Service and Parts. Repair all aspects of RVs. Rent Class "C" RVs. **SERVICES:** RV, tire, RV appliance, MH mechanical, RV Sales. Rentals, RV storage. **TOW:** RV, auto. RV supplies, LP, emergency parking, RV accessible. waiting room. Hours: 8am to 5pm.
(502)966-0911 Lat: 38.13251, Lon: -85.72842
2103 Outer Loop, Louisville, KY 40219
tim@louisvillerv.com
www.louisvillerv.com
See ad this page.

LOUISIANA

BATON ROUGE — D4 *East Baton Rouge*

Travel Services

BLANCHARD TRAILER SALES RV sales of towables and fifth wheels, parts and supplies and service. **SERVICES:** RV, RV appliance, restrooms, RV Sales. RV supplies, dump, emergency parking, RV accessible. waiting room. Hours: 8:30am to 5:30pm.
(225)355-4449 Lat: 30.49212, Lon: -91.12421
6632 Airline Hwy, Baton Rouge, LA 70805
btsrv@hotmail.com
www.blanchardbr.com

MARYLAND

ANNAPOLIS — B4

Travel Services

ANNAPOLIS RV SERVICE RV Service and Repair, including mechanical, appliance and engine repair. **SERVICES:** RV, RV appliance, MH mechanical, engine/chassis repair, restrooms. Rentals. RV supplies, LP, dump, emergency parking, RV accessible. waiting room. Hours: 8am to 5pm.
(410)280-0800 Lat: 38.57654, Lon: -76.12138
117 Rental Lane, Grasonville, MD 21638
Parts@annapolisrv.com
www.annapolisrv.com
See ad this page.

Take time now to plan a road trip with your pet. Read more in our Pampered Pet Parks feature at the front of the Guide.

MICHIGAN

CHESANING — H5 *Saginaw*

Travel Services

PARSHALLBURG CAMPERS, INC Parshallburg Campers is a family owned business since 1968 offering a wide selection of RVs, Accessories and Parts. **SERVICES:** RV, tire, RV appliance, restrooms, RV Sales. RV supplies, LP, emergency parking, RV accessible. waiting room. Hours: 9am to 6pm.
(989)845-3189 Lat: 43.18943, Lon: -84.16870
15775 S Oakley (M-52), Chesaning, MI 48616
parshallburgcampers@yahoo.com
www.parshallburgcampers.com
See ad this page.

CLIO — H5

Travel Services

LEISURE DAYS A family-owned and operated RV business that has been selling trailers since 1971.. **SERVICES:** RV, RV appliance, MH mechanical, RV Sales. RV storage. RV supplies, LP, dump, emergency parking, RV accessible. waiting room. Hours: 9 am to 5:30 pm.
(810)686-2090 Lat: 43.17813, Lon: -83.68203
1354 E Vienna Rd (M-57), Clio, MI 48420
leisuredaysrv@aol.com
www.leisuredays-rv.com
See ad this page.

MISSOURI

BEVIER — B3 *Macon*

Travel Services

SHOEMAKER'S RV SALES & SERVICE RV sales & service, RV rentals, RV appliance repair; arrangement can be made for towing, tire replacement & repair, and propane through Rick's Towing/Service immediately next door. **SERVICES:** RV, RV appliance, MH mechanical, mobile RV svc, restrooms, RV Sales. Rentals. RV supplies, dump, emergency parking, RV accessible. waiting room. Hours: M-F 8am to 5pm Sat 10am to 5pm.
(660)773-5313 Lat: 39.7563, Lon: -92.56458
955 Macon St, Bevier, MO 63532
shoemakers@cvalley.net
www.shoemakersrv.com
See ad this page.

SPRINGFIELD — D2 *Greene*

Travel Services

THOMAS & SONS RV SUPPLY Offering service, repairs, parts and accessories for RVs. **SERVICES:** RV, RV appliance, MH mechanical, restrooms. RV storage. RV supplies, emergency parking, RV accessible. waiting room. Hours: 8am to 5pm M-F, 8am to 12pm Sat.
(417)865-6125 Lat: 37.19559, Lon: -93.28629
1930 N Glenstone Ave, Springfield, MO 65803
parts@thomassonsrv.com
www.thomassonsrv.com
See ad this page.

SAVE! Over $1,000 in coupons can be found at the front of the Guide!

MONTANA

BILLINGS — C4 *Yellowstone*

Travel Services

HANSER'S RV TOWING & SERVICE Hanser's RV mechanics are trained & certified to work on the complex engine, transmission, A/C & brake systems on RV's and coaches and travel trailer suspension. 50 years in business and specialized equipment for damage free repairs. Elev 3100 ft. **SERVICES:** tire, MH mechanical, engine/chassis repair, mobile RV svc, emergency rd svc, restrooms. RV storage. **TOW:** RV, auto. Emergency parking, RV accessible. waiting room. Hours: 7:30am to 5:30pm.
(406)869-2390 Lat: 45.76130, Lon: -108.53603
430 S Billings Blvd, Billings, MT 59101
dispatch@hansers.com
www.hansers.com
See ad this page.

NEBRASKA

LINCOLN — C5 *Lancaster*

Travel Services

STEPHENSON TRUCK REPAIR, INC One stop repair shop, mechanical & full body repair and paint, engine & transmission service. **SERVICES:** RV, MH mechanical, engine/chassis repair, restrooms. **TOW:** RV, auto. Emergency parking, RV accessible. Hours: 8 AM to 5:30 PM.
(402)466-8532 Lat: 40.85751, Lon: -96.67963
4201 Industrial Ave, Lincoln, NE 68504
www.stephensonrepair.com

We give you what you want. First, we surveyed thousands of RVers just like you. Then, we developed our exclusive Triple Rating System for campgrounds based on the results. That's why our rating system is so good at explaining the quality of facilities and cleanliness of campgrounds.

NORTH PLATTE — C3 *Lincoln*

Travel Services

LARRY'S RV SALES & SERVICE In business for over 30 years, Larry's RV has established itself as your complete and trusted RV dealer. The expert service department along with the large parts and accessories store, guarantees your satisfaction. Elev 2800 ft. **SERVICES:** RV, RV appliance, RV Sales. RV storage. RV supplies, LP, emergency parking, waiting room. Hours: 8 AM to 5:30 PM, M-F; 8 AM to 4 PM Sat.
(308)532-5474 Lat: 41.13342, Lon: -100.74139
1802 East 4th St, North Platte, NE 69101
larrysrv@charter.net
www.larrysrvsales.com
See ad this page.

NEW YORK

WADING RIVER — A4 *Suffolk*

Travel Services

W E S TRAILER SALES, INC Trailer sales & service. **SERVICES:** RV, RV appliance, restrooms, RV Sales. RV storage. RV supplies, LP, dump, emergency parking, RV accessible. waiting room. Hours: 8am to 5pm.
(631)727-5852 Lat: 40.91477, Lon: -72.83493
6166 Route 25, Wading River, NY 11792
www.westrailersales.com

How much does a fishing license cost in Idaho? Can you turn right on a red light in Rhode Island? Check the Table of Contents for the page location for annual updates of important towing laws, rules of the road, bridge and tunnel information and fishing license fees.

NORTH CAROLINA

GOLDSBORO — B4 *Wayne*

Travel Services

DALY RV Family owned & operated since 1997 - One Stop shop for all your RV needs. **SERVICES:** RV, RV appliance, restrooms, RV Sales. RV supplies, LP. Hours: 8:30am to 5:00pm (closed Mon)
(800)972-8995 Lat: 35.43785, Lon: -78.08336
3369 Hwy 70 W, Goldsboro, NC 27530
info@dalyrv.com
www.dalyrv.com
See ad this page.

OREGON

BEND — C3 *Deschutes*

Travel Services

JERRY'S RV SERVICE CENTER RV service, supplies, parts and accessories and a complete service department. Elev 3600 ft. **SERVICES:** RV appliance, restrooms. RV supplies, emergency parking, RV accessible. waiting room. Hours: 8am to 5:30pm.
(541)382-2372 Lat: 44.03749, Lon: -121.30476
1165 SE 3rd. St (US Bus 97), Bend, OR 97702
jim@jerrys-rv.com
www.jerrysrvservice.com

How much will it all cost? Use this as a guide: Rates shown are the minimum and maximum for two adults in one RV at the time of inspection (excluding any additional fees for items not at the site). Remember, these rates serve as guidelines only. It's always best to call ahead for the most current rate information.

PENNSYLVANIA

BROOKVILLE — C3 *Jefferson*

Travel Services

DALE SMITH CAMPER SALES Sales of new Jayco & pre-owned travel trailers, fifth wheels, park trailers, toy haulers, motorcycle trailers, cargo trailers, hitches, RV parts & service. **SERVICES:** RV, tire, RV appliance, mobile RV svc, emergency rd svc, restrooms, RV Sales. RV supplies, LP, RV accessible. Hours: Mon-Fri 8am to 5pm Sat 9am to 3pm.
(814)849-2911 Lat: 41.191302, Lon: -79.10535
1648 Route 36 North, Brookville, PA 15825
dscamper@windstream.net
www.dalesmithcampersales.com
See ad this page.

LANCASTER — E8 *Lancaster*

Travel Services

MELLOTT BROTHERS TRAILER SALES Sales of new and used motorhomes, fifth wheels and towables. Service and repair. Extensive inventory of parts and supplies. (Extended Spring, Summer & Fall Hrs.). **SERVICES:** RV, RV appliance, MH mechanical, engine/chassis repair, restrooms, RV Sales. RV supplies, LP, dump, emergency parking, RV accessible. waiting room. Hours: 8am to 5pm, Mon-Fri.
(717)464-2311 Lat: 39.985806, Lon: -76.283627
2718 Willow Street Pike, Rte 272 North, Willow Street, PA 17584
sales@mellottbrothers.com
www.mellottbrothers.com
See ad this page.

Set a destination for family fun! Check our family camping destinations article highlighting the best places to camp in every state and province. Find a great destination, then select one of the family-friendly campgrounds listed by region.

TENNESSEE

MEMPHIS — C1 *Shelby*

Travel Services

DAVIS MOTORHOME / D & N CAMPER SALES Sale of new and pre-owned RVs/trailers. Sales of RV supplies, parts and accessories. Repair of RVs. **SERVICES:** RV, RV appliance, MH mechanical, restrooms, RV Sales. RV supplies, dump, RV accessible. waiting room. Hours: 8 am to 5 pm.
(800)772-3414 Lat: 35.06138, Lon: -90.02590
1145 East Brooks Rd, Memphis, TN 38116
jody@dandncampersales.com
dandncampersales.com
See ad this page.

PARKERS CROSSROADS — B2
Henderson

Travel Services

PARKERS CROSSROADS RV Repair RVs, all sizes & types, including Electrical Systems, Roofs, Awnings & Steps, Generators, Water Heaters, Refrigerators, Air Conditioners & just about anything else wrong with your RV. Located halfway between Memphis & Nashville. **SERVICES:** RV, RV appliance, MH mechanical, mobile RV svc, restrooms. RV supplies, LP, dump, emergency parking, RV accessible. waiting room. Hours: 8am - 7pm.
(731)968-9939 Lat: 35.809162, Lon: -88.389067
22580 Hwy 22 North, Yuma, TN 38390
Pcrvrepair@gmail.com
www.pcrvrepair.com
See ad this page.

TEXAS

EL PASO — B1 *El Paso*

Travel Services

MISSION RV PARTS & SERVICE CENTER Services RV, RV appliance, RV supplies, LP, Dump, emergency parking, waiting room. Elev 3500 ft. **SERVICES:** RV, RV appliance. RV storage. RV supplies, LP, dump, emergency parking, waiting room. Hours: 9am to 5pm. ATM.
(915)859-3344 Lat: 31.70105, Lon: -106.28031
1420 Rv Drive, El Paso, TX 79928
www.missionrvparklp.com
See ad this page.

Visit CampingWorld.com where you can get deals on over 10,000 RV and camping related products!

WASHINGTON

MARYSVILLE — B3 *Snohomish*

Travel Services

RV & MARINE SUPPLY BY CASCADE LLC Sells RV supplies, RV parts and accessories. **SERVICES:** Restrooms. RV supplies. Hours: 9am to 5pm.
(360)659-7833 Lat: 48.060844, Lon: -122.176564
1108 State Ave, Marysville, WA 98270
louise@rvmarinesupply.com
www.rvmarinesupply.com
See ad this page.

SEQUIM — B2 *Clallam*

Travel Services

ERIC'S RV PERFORMANCE CENTER RV parts, service & supplies. **SERVICES:** RV appliance, MH mechanical, engine/chassis repair, mobile RV svc, staffed RV wash, restrooms. RV storage. RV supplies, emergency parking, RV accessible. waiting room. Hours: 8am to 5pm.
(800)488-3697 Lat: 48.07802, Lon: -123.11339
275 S 7th Ave, Sequim, WA 98382
eric@ericsrv.com
www.ericsrv.com
See ad this page.

WISCONSIN

KIELER — E2 *Grant*

Travel Services

KIELER SERVICE CENTER RV Engine & chasis service, full service RV wash, 24 hour towing. **SERVICES:** Tire, MH mechanical, engine/chassis repair, mobile RV svc, emergency rd svc, staffed RV wash, restrooms. **TOW:** RV, auto. Emergency parking, RV accessible. waiting room. Hours: 7am to 10pm M-Th, 7am to 6pm F, Sat hrs. ATM.
(608)568-7265 Lat: 42.587451, Lon: -90.604903
3722 Contractors Lane, Kieler, WI 53812
brian@kielerservicecenter.com
www.kielerservicecenter.com
See ad this page.

From fishing along the Cape to boating on the Great Lakes, we've put the Spotlight on North America's most popular travel destinations. Turn to the Spotlight articles in our State and Province sections to learn more.

The RV That's Right For You

Which recreational vehicle is right for you? Our handy overview in the front of this Guide helps prospective buyers decide which RV type fits their lifestyle, travel needs and budget, from folding camping trailers to motorhomes.

NEW BRUNSWICK

MONCTON — D4 *Westmorland*

Travel Services

ED'S TRAVEL TRAILER PARTS & SERVICE RV Repairs, Trailer Sales, RV Supplies. **SERVICES:** RV, tire, RV appliance. RV storage. RV supplies, emergency parking. Hours: 8am to 5pm Mon - Fri, 8am to 12pm Sat.
(506)856-5001 Lat: 46.12500, Lon: -64.70366
1500 Shediac Rd., Moncton, NB E1A 7A7
info@edstraveltrailer.com
www.edstraveltrailer.com
See ad this page.

SASKATCHEWAN

SASKATOON — C3 *Dundurn-Rosthern*

Travel Services

MR. RV RV Sales and Service in the greater Saskatoon area. Mobile RV service available. **SERVICES:** RV, RV appliance, mobile RV svc, restrooms, RV Sales. RV supplies, waiting room. Hours: 8am to 5pm.
(306)653-0078 Lat: 52.18766, Lon: -106.66985
3510 Idylwyld Drive N, Saskatoon, SK S7L 6G3
mrrv@sasktel.net
www.mrrv.net

YUKON

WATSON LAKE — E3

Travel Services

A NICE MOTEL A Nice Motel in Watson Lake has gas, diesel, an auto & RV wash, propane, movie rentals, convenience store & motel. **SERVICES:** Self RV wash, restrooms. LP, RV accessible. Hours: 6am to 11pm.
(867)536-2555 Lat: 60.03729, Lon: -128.42278
705 Frank Trail, Watson Lake, YT Y0A 1C0
duranais@hotmail.com
www.anicemotel.com
See ad this page.

WHITEHORSE — D2 *Whitehorse Region*

Travel Services

PHILMAR RV CENTRE Philmar RV Centre carries a large supply of RV parts & accessories. They service refrigerators, furnaces, water systems, springs & brakes. They also provide RV storage. **SERVICES:** RV, RV appliance, MH mechanical. RV supplies, emergency parking. Hours: 8am to 5pm.
(867)668-6129 Lat: 60.40294, Lon: -135.03041
91280 Alaska Hwy, Whitehorse, YT Y1A 6E4
PhilmarRV@Yukon.net
www.PhilmarRV.com
See ad this page.

According to the Wall Street Journal, 100 billion plastic shopping bags are consumed in the United States annually. Consider toting your own reusable shopping bags instead of using plastic.

ALABAMA

Flying J
I-65 & SR 94 Exit 264
224 Daniel Payne Drive
Birmingham, AL 35207
Denny's, Hot Food & Pizza

Pilot Travel Center
I-20/59/65/AL 78 Exit 123
901 Bankhead Highway West
Birmingham, AL 35204
Wendy's

Flying J
Ross Clark Hwy/Hwy 231
2190 Ross Clark Circle
Dothan, AL 36301
Denny's, Hot Food & Pizza

Flying J
I-65 Exit 158
900 Tyson Road
Hope Hull, AL 36043
Denny's, Hot Food & Pizza

Pilot Travel Center
I-20 Exit 165
121 Honda Drive
Lincoln, AL 35096
Subway

Flying J
I-20/I-59 Exit 104
6098 MacAshan Dr
McCalla, AL 35111
Subway

Pilot Travel Center
I-65 Exit 334
3240 Point Mallard Parkway
Priceville, AL 35603
Subway, Wendy's

Pilot Travel Center
I-65 Exit 19
6109 US 43 South
Satsuma, AL 36572
Arby's

Pilot Travel Center
I-10 Exit 13
6955 Theodore Dawes Road
Theodore, AL 36582
Wendy's

Pilot Travel Center
I-20/59 Exit 76
4416 Skyland Boulevard East
Tuscaloosa, AL 35405
Subway

ARIZONA

Pilot Travel Center
I-10 Exit 133
900 North 99th Avenue
Avondale, AZ 85323
Subway, Wendy's

Pilot Travel Center
I-40 Exit 185
12500 West I-40
Bellemont, AZ 86015
McDonald's, Subway

Flying J
I-10 Exit 1
Box 801 I-10 Exit 1 S Frontage
Ehrenberg, AZ 85334
Wendy's

Flying J
I-10 Exit 208A
16189 S Sunshine Blvd
Eloy, AZ 85231
Denny's

Pilot Travel Center
I-10 Exit 208
619 South Sunshine Boulevard
Eloy, AZ 85231
Dairy Queen, Subway

Flying J
I-40 Exit 53
3300 E Andy DeVine Ave
Kingman, AZ 86401
Deli

Pilot Travel Center
I-40 & AZ 95 Exit 9
14750 South Highway 95
Lake Havasu City, AZ 86404
Wendy's

Flying J
I-10 Exit 137
6700 West Latham
Phoenix, AZ 85043
Denny's, Hot Food & Pizza

Pilot Travel Center
I-10 & US 95 Exit 17
1201 West Main Street
Quartzsite, AZ 85359
Dairy Queen, Subway

Pilot Travel Center
I-19 & SR 289 Exit 12
769 East Frontage Road
Rio Rico, AZ 85648
Wendy's

Pilot Travel Center
I-10, Exit 268
5570 E. Travel Plaza Way
Tucson, AZ 85756
Subway, Taco Bell

Flying J
I-40 Exit 255
400 Transcon Lane
Winslow, AZ 86047
Denny's

Flying J Dealer
I-8 Exit 12
108000 North Frontage Road
Yuma, AZ 85367
Day Breaker's Café

ARKANSAS

Pilot Travel Center
I-30 Exit 121
7801 Alcoa Road
Benton, AR 72015
Subway

Pilot Travel Center
I-30, Exit 78 & Hwy 7
170 Valley Street
Caddo Valley, AR 71923
Cinnabon, Hot Food & Pizza

Pilot Travel Center
I-40 Exit 161 Galloway Rd
3300 Highway 391 North
North Little Rock, AR 72117
Chester's Chicken, Subway

Pilot Travel Center
I-40 Exit 84
215 SR 331 North
Russellville, AR 72802
Subway, Wendy's

Flying J
I-40 Exit 84
42 Bradley Cove Road
Russellville, AR 72801
Denny's

Pilot Travel Center
US 412 & 71 Bypass
5660 West Sunset Avenue
Springdale, AR 72762
Burger King

Flying J
I-30 Exit 7
Rt 12 Box 254B I30 & Hwy 108
Texarkana, AR 71854
Denny's

Pilot Travel Center
I-40 Exit 280
1100 Martin Luther King Boulevard
West Memphis, AR 72301
Subway, Wendy's

Flying J
I-40 Exit 280/I-55 Exit 4
3400 Service Loop Road
West Memphis, AR 72301
Denny's

CALIFORNIA

Flying J
Hwy 99 Exit Merced Ave.
17047 Zachary Ave
Bakersfield, CA 93308
Denny's, Subway

Pilot Travel Center
I-15/40/US 58 Lenwood Rd
2591 Commerce Parkway
Barstow, CA 92311
Subway

Flying J
I-15 & Lenwood Exit
2611 Fisher Blvd.
Barstow, CA 92311
Denny's, Hot Food & Pizza

Pilot Travel Center
US 395/US 58
5725 Highway 58
Boron, CA 93516
Subway

Pilot Travel Center
I-5 & Lake Hughes Exit
31642 Castaic Road
Castaic, CA 91384
Wendy's

Pilot Travel Center
I-5 Road 8 Exit
30035 County Road 8
Dunnigan, CA 95937
Wendy's

Flying J
I-5 Frazier Park Exit 205
42810 Frazier Mountain Park Rd
Frazier Park, CA 93243
Denny's

Pilot Travel Center
I-15 & US 395
8701 Highway 395
Hesperia, CA 92345
Wendy's

Flying J
I-5/Hwy 12 Exit Fairfield
15100 North Thornton Rd
Lodi, CA 95242
Denny's, Hot Food & Pizza, Subway

Pilot Travel Center
I-5 & SR 46
14808 Warren Street
Lost Hills, CA 93249
Wendy's

Pilot Travel Center
I-99 at Ave 18.5
22717 Avenue 18 1/2
Madera, CA 93637
Dairy Queen, Denny's, Subway

Pilot Travel Center
I-10 Garnet / Indian Ave
6605 N. Indian Canyon Drive
PO Box 581236
North Palm Springs, CA 92258
Dairy Queen, Wendy's

Flying J
Hwy 99 Exit Jack Tone Rd
1501 North Jack Tone Road
Ripon, CA 95366
Denny's

Pilot Dealer
I-80 Exit 85
2828 El Centro Road
Sacramento, CA 95833
Silver Skillet Restaurant

Pilot Travel Center
US 101 & Sanborn
951 Work Street
Salinas, CA 93901
Subway

Pilot Travel Center
I-805 Exit 1B CA 905
1497 Piper Ranch Road
San Diego, CA 92154
Dairy Queen, Wendy's

Flying J
I-10 Ramon Exit
72235 Varner Rd
Thousand Palms, CA 92276
Deli

Pilot Travel Center
I-5 Exit 745
395 E. Vista Drive
Weed, CA 96094
Subway

COLORADO

Flying J
I-70 Exit 285 (South)
16751 East 32nd Ave
Aurora, CO 80011
Denny's, Hot Food & Pizza

Pilot Travel Center
I-70 Exit 276A
4640 Steele Street
Denver, CO 80216
Wendy's

Pilot Travel Center
I-70 Exit 26
2195 Hwy 6 and 50
Grand Junction, CO 81505
McDonald's

Flying J
I-70 & Exit 359
2495 Williams Ave
Limon, CO 80828
Hot Food & Pizza, IHOP

CONNECTICUT

Pilot Travel Center
I-95 Exit 40
433 Old Gate Lane
Milford, CT 06460
Wendy's

Pilot Dealer
I-95 Exit 93
273 Clarks Falls Road
North Stonington, CT 06359
Johnny Pastrami, Nathan's Famous

FLORIDA

Pilot Travel Center
I-10 Exit 343
1050 US 301 South
Baldwin, FL 32234
Subway

Pilot Travel Center
I-95 Exit 201
4455 King Street
Cocoa, FL 32926
Subway

Flying J
I-75 Exit 285 & SR52
29933 State Road 52
Dade City, FL 33576
Denny's

Pilot Travel Center
I-75 Exit 224
1526 51st Avenue East
Ellenton, FL 34222
Deli

Pilot Travel Center
I-75 Exit 139 Luckett Rd
6050 Plaza Drive
Fort Myers, FL 33905
Subway

Flying J
I-95 Hwy 68 Exit 131
100 North Kings Hwy
Fort Pierce, FL 34945
Denny's, Hot Food & Pizza, Subway

Pilot Travel Center
I-95 Exit 129
7300 West Okeechobee Road
Fort Pierce, FL 34945
McDonald's

Pilot Travel Center
US Hwy 27 North
35647 US Hwy 27 North
Haines City, FL 33845
Denny's

Pilot Travel Center
I-95 Exit 329
1625 County Road 210 West
Jacksonville, FL 32259
McDonald's

Pilot Travel Center
I-75 Exit 460
8067 State Road 6 West
Jasper, FL 32052
Cinnabon, Subway

Pilot Travel Center
I-10/FL 71 Exit 141
2209 Highway 71
Marianna, FL 32448
Arby's

Pilot Dealer
Hwy 27 N
12200 NW South River Drive
Medley, FL 33178
Sunshine Café

Pilot Dealer
US 41 & SR 997
17696 SW 8th Street
Miami, FL 33194
Subway

Pilot Dealer
SR 826 Exit SR 817
16650 NW 27th Avenue
Miami Gardens, FL 33054

Pilot Travel Center
I-10 Exit 192
33333 Blue Star Highway
Midway, FL 32343
Subway

Pilot Travel Center
I-75 & FL 484 Exit 341
2020 SW 135th Street
Ocala, FL 34473
Dairy Queen, Wendy's

Pilot Travel Center
I-75 Exit 358
4032 West Highway 326
Ocala, FL 34482
Arby's

Pilot Travel Center
I-75 Exit 358
4255 NW Highway 326
Ocala, FL 34482
Wendy's

Pilot Travel Center
FL Turnpike Exit 193
3051 State Road 60
Okeechobee, FL 34972
Subway

Pilot Travel Center
I-75 Exit 161
26505 Jones Loop Road
Punta Gorda, FL 33950
Arby's

Flying J
I-10 Exit 192
32670 Blue Star Hwy
Quincy, FL 32343
Denny's, Hot Food & Pizza

Flying J
I-95 Hwy 206 Exit 305
950 State Road 206 West
St. Augustine, FL 32086
Denny's, Hot Food & Pizza, Subway

Flying J
I-4 & SR 579 Exit 10
11555 East Sligh Ave.
Tampa, FL 33584
Hot Food & Pizza

Pilot Travel Center
I-75 Exit 329
493 East State Route 44
Wildwood, FL 34785
Deli

GEORGIA

Pilot Travel Center
Hwy 300 & Clark Ave
310 Cordele Road
Albany, GA 31705
Subway

Pilot Travel Center
I-285 Exit 51
2605 Bouldercrest
Atlanta, GA 30316
Wendy's

Pilot Travel Center
I-20 Exit 200
2975 Gun Club Road
Augusta, GA 30907
Wendy's

Pilot Travel Center
I-20 Exit 194
4091 Jimmie Dyess Parkway
Augusta, GA 30909
Subway

Pilot Travel Center
I-85 Exit 129
5888 Highway 53
Braselton, GA 30517
McDonald's

Flying J
I-95 Exit 29
2990 US Hwy 17 South
Brunswick, GA 31523
Denny's, Hot Food & Pizza

Pilot Travel Center
I-75 Exit 146
2965 Highway 247C
Byron, GA 31008
Arby's

Flying J
I-85 Exit 160
10226 Old Federal Road
Carnesville, GA 30521
Hot Food & Pizza

Pilot Travel Center
I-75 Exit 296
968 Cassville-White Road
Cartersville, GA 30120
McDonald's, Subway

Pilot Travel Center
I-75 Exit 101
2201 East 16 Avenue
Cordele, GA 31015
Arby's

Pilot Travel Center
I-75 Exit 326
142 Carbondale Road
Dalton, GA 30721
McDonald's, Subway

Pilot Travel Center
I-75 Exit 328
243 Connector 3 SW
Dalton, GA 30720
Arby's

Pilot Travel Center
I-16 Exit 51
2185 US 441
Dublin, GA 31021
Deli

Flying J
I-75 Exit 201
I-75 & Exit 201 Bucksnort Road
Jackson, GA 30233
Denny's

Pilot Travel Center
I-85 Exit 13
1960 Whitesvillle Road
LaGrange, GA 30240
Subway

Flying J
I-75 Exit 2
7001 Lake Park Bellville Road
Lake Park, GA 31636
Denny's, Hot Food & Pizza, Subway

Pilot Travel Center
I-20 Exit 114
1881 Eatonton Road
Madison, GA 30650
Denny's

Pilot Travel Center
I-85 Exit 41
1645 South Highway 29
Newnan, GA 30263
Subway, Wendy's

Pilot Travel Center
I-95 Exit 109
7001 Highway 21
Port Wentworth, GA 31407
McDonald's, Subway

Flying J
I-75 Exit 320
288 Resaca Beach Blvd
Resaca, GA 30735
Denny's

Pilot Travel Center
I-59 Exit 4
319 Deer Head Cover Road
Rising Fawn, GA 30738
Subway

Pilot Travel Center
I-16 Exit 160
1504 Dean Forrest Road
Savannah, GA 31408
Subway

Pilot Travel Center
I-95, Exit 1
491 W St. Mary's St
St. Mary's, GA 31558
Subway

Pilot Travel Center
I-20 & GA 100 Exit 5
882 Georgia Highway 100
Tallapoosa, GA 30176
KFC, Taco Bell

Flying J
I-20 & Hwy 113 Exit 19
15 Villa Rosa Road
Temple, GA 30179
Hot Food & Pizza

Pilot Travel Center
I-20 Exit 19
625 Carrollton Street
Temple, GA 30179
Subway, Wendy's

Pilot Travel Center
I-75 Exit 60
4431 Old Union Road
Tifton, GA 31794
Steak n Shake, Subway

Flying J
I-20 & Exit 138
3600 Highway 77 South
Union Point, GA 30669
Denny's, Hot Food & Pizza

Pilot Travel Center
I-75 Exit 11
3495 Madison Highway
Valdosta, GA 31601
Subway

Pilot Travel Center
I-75 Exit 109
39 Victory Lane
Vienna, GA 31092
McDonald's

Pilot Travel Center
I-24/59 Exit 169
650 Highway 299
Wildwood, GA 30757
Subway

IDAHO

Flying J
I-84 Exit 29
3512 Franklin Road
Caldwell, ID 83605
Denny's

Flying J
I-84 Exit 54 (Federal Way)
3353 Federal Way
East Boise, ID 83705
Hot Food & Pizza

Flying J
I-15 Exit 113
6485 West Overland Drive
Idaho Falls, ID 83402
Subway

Flying J
I-84 Exit 173
5350 Hwy 93 I-84 & Exit 173
Jerome, ID 83338
Hot Food & Pizza

Flying J
I-15 Exit 47
587 E. US HWY 30
McCammon, ID 83250
Hot Food & Pizza

Pilot Travel Center
I-84 & US 20 Exit 95
1050 Highway 20
Mountain Home, ID 83647
Arby's

Flying J
I-90 Exit 2
3636 W. 5th Street
Post Falls, ID 83854
Subway

ILLINOIS

Flying J
I-255 & Exit 17a
140 Racehorse Dr.
Alorton, IL 62207
Denny's, Hot Food & Pizza

Pilot Travel Center
I-55/74/IL 9 Exit 160
1522 West Market Street
Bloomington, IL 61701
Wendy's

Pilot Deal
Road Ranger
I-57 Exit 240
4910 Market Street
Champaign, IL 61821
McDonald's

Pilot Travel Center
I-55 Exit 248
23841 West Eames Street
Channahon, IL 60410
Dunkin' Donuts, Subway

Pilot Deal
Road Ranger
I-55 Exit 288
3401 South California Avenue
Chicago, IL 60632

Pilot Travel Center
I-72 Exit 144
4030 East Boyd Road
Decatur, IL 62521
McDonald's, Subway

Pilot Deal
Road Ranger
I-88 Exit 54
1801 South Galena Avenue
Dixon, IL 61021
Subway

Pilot Travel Center
I-55/70 Exit 4
699 State Route 203
East St. Louis, IL 62201
Subway, Taco Bell

Flying J
I-70 & I-57 Exit 160
1701 W Evergreen/I-70 & I-55
Effingham, IL 62401
Denny's, Hot Food & Pizza

Pilot Travel Center
I-57/70 Exit 162
2500 North 3rd Street
Effingham, IL 62401
McDonald's

Pilot Travel Center
I-57 Exit 283
815 Hwy 24 West
Gilman, IL 60938
Denny's

Pilot Deal
Road Ranger
I-64 Exit 130
1776 South Court Street
Grayville, IL 62844

Pilot Deal
Road Ranger
I-90 Exit 36
19 N 681 US Highway 20
Hampshire, IL 60140
McDonald's, Subway

Flying J
I-80 Exit 77
343 Civic Road
LaSalle, IL 61301
Denny's, Hot Food & Pizza

Pilot Deal
Thorntons
I-55 Exit 126
2903 Woodlawn Road
Lincoln, IL 62656

Pilot Deal
Road Ranger
I-90 Riverside Blvd
7500 E Riverside Boulevard
Loves Park, IL 61111
Subway

Pilot Travel Center
I-57 Exit 54
2611 Vernell Road
Marion, IL 62959
Subway

Pilot Deal
Road Ranger
Illinois Hwy
2003 Illinois Hwy 1
Marshall, IL 62441
Hot Food & Pizza

Pilot Deal
Road Ranger
I-55 Exit 145
501 South Main Street
McLean, IL 61754

Pilot Deal
Road Ranger
I-39 Exit 72
2705 12th Street
Mendota, IL 61342
McDonald's, Subway

Pilot Deal
Road Ranger
I-39 Exit 27
1311 Carolyn Drive
Minonk, IL 61760

Pilot Travel Center
I-80 Exit 122
301 Ridge Road
Minooka, IL 60447
Arby's

Pilot Travel Center
I-57 Exit 335
6002 Monee-Manhattan Road
Monee, IL 60449
McDonald's

Pilot Travel Center
I-80 Exit 112
3801 N Division Street
Morris, IL 60450
Cinnabon, Subway

Pilot Travel Center
I-57 Exit 95
4610 Broadway
Mount Vernon, IL 62864
Denny's

Flying J Dealer
I-64/57 and Hwy 15
101 South 45th Street
Mt. Vernon, IL 62864
Huddle House

Pilot Deal Road Ranger
I-72 Exit 82
700 King Road
New Berlin, IL 62670

Pilot Travel Center
I-74, Exit 206
503 N. Oakwood Street
Oakwood, IL 61858
Cinnabon, Hot Food & Pizza

Pilot Deal Road Ranger
I-64 Exit 41
905 Hen House Road
Okawville, IL 62271
Burger King

Pilot Deal Road Ranger
I-80 Exit 93
3041 North IL Route 71
Ottawa, IL 61350

Flying J
I-270 & Exit 6B
1310 East Chain of Rocks Road
Pontoon Beach, IL 62040
Denny's, Hot Food & Pizza

Pilot Deal Road Ranger
I-80 Exit 56
2835 N Main Street
Princeton, IL 61356
Dan's Big Slice Pizza

Pilot Deal Road Ranger
I-39 Exit 99 at IL 38
890 E Highway 38
Rochelle, IL 61068
Dan's Big Slice Pizza, Subway

Pilot Deal Road Ranger
I-90 Exit US 20 to IL 2
4980 S Main Street
Rockford, IL 61102
Subway

Flying J
I-90 & HWY 75
16049 Willowbrook Road
South Beloit, IL 61080
Denny's, Hot Food & Pizza

Pilot Deal Road Ranger
I-90 Exit 1
6070 Gardner Street
South Beloit, IL 61080
Beef-A-Roo, Dan's Big Slice Pizza

Pilot Deal Road Ranger
I-55 Exit 100-A
3752 Camp Butler Road
Springfield, IL 62707
Star 66 Café, Subway

Pilot Deal Road Ranger
I-55 Exit 90
500 Toronto Road
Springfield, IL 62711

Pilot Travel Center
I-55/70/IL 162 Exit 18
820 Edwardsville Road
Troy, IL 62294
Arby's

Pilot Deal Road Ranger
I-57 Exit 212
1112 East Southline Drive
Tuscola, IL 61953
Deli

Pilot Deal Road Ranger
US 20 Mile Marker #8
902 N Elida Street
Winnebago, IL 61088
McDonald's

Pilot Travel Center
I-74 Exit 32
900 Plaza Avenue
Woodhull, IL 61490
Hot Food & Pizza

INDIANA

Pilot Travel Center
I-70 Exit 23
4376 North SR 59
Brazil, IN 47834
McDonald's, Subway

Pilot Deal Road Ranger
I-70 Exit 23
990 W SR 42
Brazil, IN 47834
Subway

Pilot Travel Center
I-94 Exit 22
243 Melton Road
Burns Harbor, IN 46304
McDonald's, Subway

Pilot Travel Center
I-74 & SR 63 Exit 4
16502 North State Road 63
Covington, IN 47932
Arby's

Pilot Travel Center
I-74 Exit 39
4403 East State Route 32
Crawfordsville, IN 47933
Subway

Pilot Travel Center
I-69 Exit 34
15151 Commerce Road
Daleville, IN 47334
Subway

Pilot Travel Center
I-69 Exit 34
15876 West Commerce Road
Daleville, IN 47334
Denny's

Pilot Dealer
I-69 Exit 109 A
3037 Goshen Road
Fort Wayne, IN 46808
McDonald's, Subway, The Point Restaurant

Pilot Travel Center
I-80/69 Exit 157
6900 Old US 27
Fremont, IN 46737
Wendy's

Pilot Travel Center
I-80/94 Exit 6
2501 Burr Street
Gary, IN 46406
Subway

Mr. Fuel
I-80 & I-94 Exit 6
2945 Burr Street
Gary, IN 46406
Deli

Pilot Travel Center
I-70 Exit 96
2640 North 600 West
Greenfield, IN 46140
Pizza Hut

Pilot Deal Road Ranger
I-65 Exit 99
1615 E Main Street
Greenwood, IN 46143
Subway

Pilot Travel Center
I-64 Exit 25
1042 East Warrenton Road
Route 2 Box 109E
Haubstadt, IN 47639
Subway, Taco Bell

Flying J
I-64 & SR 41 Exit 25B
844 East 1250 South
Haubstadt, IN 47639
Denny's, Hot Food & Pizza

Pilot Travel Center
I-65 Exit 240
18011 Colorado Street
Hebron, IN 46341
McDonald's

Flying J
Rt 2 & I-65 Exit 240
3231 East 181st Avenue
Hebron, IN 46341
Denny's, Hot Food & Pizza

Pilot Travel Center
I-80/94 Exit 2
8150 Indianapolis Boulevard
Highland, IN 46322
Hot Stuff Pizza

Flying J
I-465 Exit 4
1720 W Thompson Rd
Indianapolis, IN 46217
Denny's

Pilot Travel Center
I-465 & IN 37 Exit 4
4607 South Harding Street
Indianapolis, IN 46217
Subway

Mr. Fuel
I-465 & IN 37 Exit 4
4610 South Harding
Indianapolis, IN 46217
Hot Food & Pizza

Mr. Fuel
I-80 & I-94, Exit 15B
1235 Ripley Street
Lake Station, IN 46405

Flying J
I-94 & Exit 15b
1401 Ripley Street Lake Station, IN 46405
Denny's

Pilot Deal Road Ranger
I-80 Exit 15A
2151 Ripley Street
Lake Station, IN 46405
Subway

Pilot Travel Center
I-64 Exit 92
6921 South SR 66
Leavenworth, IN 47137
Subway

Flying J
I-65 Exit 139
520 South State Road #39 I-65
Lebanon, IN 46052
Hot Food & Pizza

Pilot Travel Center
I-65 Exit 16
14013 Memphis Blue Lick Road
Memphis, IN 47143
Arby's

Flying J
I-469 Exit 19
3105 Doyle Rd & Hwy 30
New Haven, IN 46774
Huddle House, Subway

Pilot Travel Center
I-69 Exit 14
7455 South State Road 13
Pendleton, IN 46064
Subway

Pilot Travel Center
US Hwy 30 & 31
10619 9A Road
Plymouth, IN 46563
Subway

Pilot Travel Center
I-65 Exit 201
4154 West US Highway 24
Remington, IN 47977
Subway

Pilot Travel Center
I-74 Exit 109
1851 West 400 North
Shelbyville, IN 46176
McDonald's

Pilot Travel Center
I-80 Exit 72
6424 West Brick Road
South Bend, IN 46628
Subway

Mr. Fuel
I-74 Exit 4
140 Holwager Road
Spiceland, IN 47385
Hot Food & Pizza

Flying J
I-70 Exit 123
5300 South State Rte. 3
Spiceland, IN 47385
Denny's, Hot Food & Pizza, Subway

Pilot Travel Center
I-70 & IN 46 Exit 11
5555 E. Margaret Avenue
Terre Haute, IN 47803
Subway

Pilot Travel Center
US 30 & SR 49
4105 US 30 East
Valparaiso, IN 46383
Subway

Pilot Travel Center
I-65 Exit 95
2962 East 500 North
Whiteland, IN 46184
McDonald's

Flying J
I-65 Whiteland Rd Exit 95
4982 North 350 East
Whiteland, IN 46184
Denny's, Hot Food & Pizza

IOWA

Flying J
I-80 Exit 142
3231 Adventureland Drive I-80 & US 65
Altoona, IA 50009
Grandma Max's, Max's Highway Diner

Pilot Travel Center
I-80 Exit 265
2086 Atalissa Road
Atalissa, IA 52720
Chester's Chicken

Pilot Dealer
I-80 Exit 40
7005 North Chestnut Street
Avoca, IA 51521
American Pie Café, Maid Rite, Taco John's

Pilot Travel Center
I-80 Exit 201
4126 Highway 21
Brooklyn, IA 52211
Subway

Pilot Travel Center
I-35 Exit 194
2411 US Highway 18 East
Clear Lake, IA 50428
Denny's, Subway

Pilot Travel Center
I-80/29 Exit 1B
2647 South 24th Street
Council Bluffs, IA 51501
Arby's

Flying J
I-80 Exit 292
8200 N.W. Blvd.
Davenport, IA 52806
Denny's

Pilot Travel Center
I-35/80 Ext 126
11957 Douglas Avenue
Des Moines, IA 50322
Grandma Max's

Pilot Deal Road Ranger
Highway 20 Exit 68
100 Plaza Drive
Elk Run Heights, IA 50707
Junie's Restaurant, Subway

Flying J
I-380 & Evansdale Dr.
445 Evansdale Drive
Evansdale, IA 50707
Hot Food & Pizza

Pilot Travel Center
Washington Street Exit
1300 N Grande Avenue
Mt. Pleasant, IA 52641
Arby's, Cinnabon

Pilot Travel Center
I-35 Exit 34
2010 West Clay Street
Osceola, IA 50213
Subway

Pilot Travel Center
I-29 Exit 10
2495 210th Ave
Percival, IA 51648
Subway

Pilot Travel Center
I-29 Exit 43
2815 Singing Hills Blvd
Sioux City, IA 51111
Subway, Moe's

Pilot Travel Center
I-80 Exit 284 & CR Y40
2975 North Plainview Road
Walcott, IA 52773
Subway

Pilot Travel Center
I-80 Exit 284
3500 North Plainview Road
Walcott, IA 52773
Arby's

Flying J
I-35 Exit 144
3040 220th St
Williams, IA 50271
Subway

KANSAS

Pilot Travel Center
I-70 Exit 54
1100 East Willow Street
Colby, KS 67701
Wendy's

Flying J
Hwy 400 & Hwy 283
2524 E Wyatt Earp Blvd
Dodge City, KS 67801
Hot Food & Pizza

Flying J
I-35 & US 50 Exit 127
4215 West Hwy 50
Emporia, KS 66801
Hot Food & Pizza, Huddle House

Pilot Dealer
I-635 Exit 3
4610 Kansas Avenue
Kansas City, KS 66106

Pilot Travel Center
I-70 Exit 252
1944 N. 9th Street
Salina, KS 67401
Grandma Max's

Flying J
I-70 Exit 253
2250 North Ohio Street
Salina, KS 67401
Hot Food & Pizza

KENTUCKY

Flying J
I-64 SR 180 Exit 185
15236 State Route 180
Catlettsburg, KY 41129
Denny's

Pilot Travel Center
I-75 & US 25E Exit 29
249 West Cumberland Gap Parkway
Corbin, KY 40701
McDonald's, Subway

Pilot Travel Center
I-65 Exit 6
2929 Scottsville Road
Franklin, KY 42134
Subway

Pilot Travel Center
I-65 Exit 6
2940 Scottsville Road
Highway 100 & I-65 Exit 6
Franklin, KY 42134
Wendy's

Flying J
I-65 US Hwy 31W Exit 2
4380 Nashville Road
Franklin, KY 42134
Denny's, Hot Food & Pizza

Pilot Travel Center
I-75 Exit 129
110 Triport Road
Georgetown, KY 40324
Wendy's

Pilot Travel Center
I-75 Exit 129
259 Cherry Blossom Way
Georgetown, KY 40324
McDonald's

Pilot Travel Center
I-65 Exit 86
58 Glendale-Hodgenville Road
Glendale, KY 42740
McDonald's

Pilot Dealer
I-64 Exit 172
960 N Carol Malone Blvd
Grayson, KY 41143

Pilot Dealer
I-24 Exit 40 & US Hwy 62
2299 US Hwy 62W
Kuttawa, KY 42055
Grillin Zone, Quizno's Subs

Pilot Travel Center
I-65 Exit 105
150 Park Plaza Boulevard
Lebanon Junction, KY 40150
McDonald's, Subway

Pilot Travel Center
Hwy 813
95 Free Henry Ford Road
Madisonville, KY 42440
Subway

Pilot Travel Center
Hwy 25 Route 2
3000 US Highway 25E
Middlesboro, KY 40965
Deli

Pilot Travel Center
I-64 Exit 113
3060 Owingsville Road
Mount Sterling, KY 40353
McDonald's, Subway

Pilot Travel Center
I-24 Exit 86
12900 Fort Campbell Boulevard
Oak Grove, KY 42262
Subway, Wendy's

Flying J
I-24 Exit 86
18750 Herndon Oak Grove Rd.
Oak Grove, KY 42262
Denny's, Hot Food & Pizza

Pilot Travel Center
I-24 Exit 89
8190 Pembroke-Oak Grove Road
Oak Grove, KY 42262
McDonald's

Pilot Travel Center
I-24 & KY 305 Exit 3
5353 Cairo Road
Paducah, KY 42001
Subway

Pilot Travel Center
I-71 Exit 28
205 Pendleton Road
Pendleton, KY 40055
Subway

Pilot Travel Center
I-65 Exit 121 Brooks Rd
2050 East Blue Lick Road
Shepherdsville, KY 40165
Subway, Taco Bell

Pilot Travel Center
I-64 Exit 28 Veechdale Rd
819 Buck Creek Road
Simpsonville, KY 40067
Wendy's

Pilot Travel Center
I-65 Exit 81
450 East Western Avenue
Sonora, KY 42776
Subway

Pilot Travel Center
I-71 Exit 28
489 Pendleton Road
Sulphur, KY 40070
McDonald's

Flying J
I-64 & HWY 395 Exit 43
1670 Waddy Road
Waddy, KY 40076
Denny's

Pilot Travel Center
I-75/71/KY 338 Exit 175
11229 Frontage Road
Walton, KY 41094
Subway

Pilot Travel Center
I-75/71/KY 338 Exit 175
118 Richwood Road
Walton, KY 41094
Subway

Flying J
I-75 Exit 171
13019 Walton Verona Rd
Walton, KY 41094
Denny's

Pilot Travel Center
I-75 Exit 11
481 West Highway 92
Williamsburg, KY 40769
Wendy's

LOUISIANA

Pilot Travel Center
I-10 Exit 109
2112 Rees Street
Breaux Bridge, LA 70517
Arby's

Pilot Travel Center
I-12 Exit 10
2601 South Range Avenue
Denham Springs, LA 70726
Subway

Flying J
I-20 Exit 3
9510 Greenwood Road
Greenwood, LA 71033
Denny's

Pilot Travel Center
I-12/55/US 51 Exit 40
2111 SW Railroad Avenue
Hammond, LA 70403
Arby's

Pilot Travel Center
I-20 & Hwy 157 Exit 33
490 North Elm Street
Haughton, LA 71037
Arby's

Pilot Travel Center
I-10/55 Exit 209
4301 South Main Street
LaPlace, LA 70068
Subway

Pilot Travel Center
I-20 & LA 137 Exit 138
103 Grimshaw Street
Rayville, LA 71269
Wendy's

Pilot Travel Center
I-20 Exit 112
300 Well Road
West Monroe, LA 71292
Subway, Wendy's

MARYLAND

Flying J Dealer
I-95 Exit 109A
221 Belle Hill Road
Elkton, MD 21921
Golden Corral

Pilot Travel Center
I-68 Exit 22
3000 Chestnut Ridge Road
Grantsville, MD 21536
Arby's

Pilot Travel Center
I-70 & US 63
11633 Greencastle Pike
Hagerstown, MD 21740
Subway

Pilot Travel Center
I-81 Exit 5B
16921 Halfway Boulevard
Hagerstown, MD 21740
McDonald's, Subway

Flying J
I-95 Exit 100
1 Center Drive I-95 Exit 100
Northeast, MD 21901
Denny's, Hot Food & Pizza

Pilot Travel Center
I-95 & MD 222 Exit 93
31 Heather Lane
Perryville, MD 21903
Subway

MASSACHUSETTS

Pilot Travel Center
I-84 Exit 1
400 Route 15 (Haynes Street)
Sturbridge, MA 01566
Deli

MICHIGAN

Pilot Travel Center
I-94 Exit 104
15901 Eleven Mile Road
Battle Creek, MI 49014
McDonald's

Pilot Travel Center
I-94 Exit 30
1860 East Napier Ave.
Benton Harbor, MI 49022
Wendy's

Pilot Travel Center
I-94 Exit 167
195 Baker Road
Dexter, MI 48130
Arby's

Pilot Travel Center
I-94 Exit 167
750 Baker Road
Dexter, MI 48130
Subway

Flying J
I-96 & Exit 90/I-69 & Exit 81
7800 West Grand River Ave.
Grand Ledge, MI 48837
Denny's, Hot Food & Pizza

Pilot Travel Center
I-96 Exit 67
7205 South State Road
Ionia, MI 48846
Subway

Pilot Travel Center
I-75 Exit 15
1100 North Dixie Highway
Monroe, MI 48162
Subway

Pilot Travel Center
I-75 Exit 18
1200 Nadeau Road
Monroe, MI 48161
Arby's

Pilot Travel Center
US 23 Exit 5
6158 US 223
Ottawa Lake, MI 49267
McDonald's

Flying J
I-75 & Washington St. Exit 151
3475 E Washington
Saginaw, MI 48601
Wendy's

Pilot Travel Center
I-69 Exit 196
2424 Wadhams Rd
Smiths Creek, MI 48074
Subway

Flying J Dealer
I-75 Exit 32A
21055 West Road
Woodhaven, MI 48183
IHOP, Subway

MINNESOTA

Pilot Travel Center
I-94 Exit 100
2812 Evergreen Lane
Alexandria, MN 56308
Subway

Pilot Travel Center
Hwy 52 & 117 St
11650 Courthouse Blvd
Inver Grove Heights, MN 55077
Subway

Flying J
I-35 Exit 69
8051 Bagley Avenue
Northfield, MN 55057
Big Steer Restaurant, Subway

Pilot Travel Center
I-94 Exit 171 (CR 75)
4231 Clearwater Road
St. Cloud, MN 56301
Hot Stuff Pizza

MISSISSIPPI

Flying J
I-10 Exit 31
9351 Canal Road
Gulfport, MS 39503
Denny's

Pilot Travel Center
I-55/20 Exit 45
2520 South Gallatin Street
Jackson, MS 39204
McDonald's

Pilot Travel Center
I-59 Exit 151
1555 Tommy Webb Drive
Meridian, MS 39307
Subway

Pilot Travel Center
I-10 Exit 69
6705 Hwy 63
Moss Point, MS 39563
Moe's, Hot Food & Pizza

Pilot Travel Center
US 78 Exit 64
500 State Highway 15 South
New Albany, MS 38652
Arby's

Flying J
HWY 78 and Bethel Road
4740 Bethel Road
Olive Branch, MS 38654
Hot Food & Pizza, Subway

Flying J
I-20/I-55 Exit 47
685 Highway 80 East
Pearl, MS 39208
Denny's

Pilot Deal
The Pantry
I-55 Exit 265
510 E Main Street
Senatobia, MS 38668
Baskin Robbins, Huddle House

Pilot Travel Center
I-55 & Hwy 82
403 SW Frontage Road
Winona, MS 38967
Taco Bell

MISSOURI

Pilot Travel Center
I-70 Exit 101
1701 Ashley Road
Boonville, MO 65233
Wendy's

Flying J
I-57 Exit 12
2460 East Highway 60
Charleston, MO 63834
Huddle House

Pilot Travel Center
US 54 & Hwy 13 South
Hwy 13 South and US 54
Collins, MO 64738
Subway

Pilot Deal
Road Ranger
I-44 Exit 275
205 North Highway Drive
Fenton, MO 63026
Subway

Mr. Fuel
I-70 Exit 203
11 Highway W
Foristell, MO 63348
Hot Food & Pizza

Pilot Travel Center
I-55 Exit 19
1701 Highway 84 East
Hayti, MO 63851
Arby's

Pilot Travel Center
I-70 Exit 49
6676 Highway 13
Higginsville, MO 64037
McDonald's, Subway

Flying J
I-44 U.S. 71 Exit 11A
11570 Hwy FF
Joplin, MO 64804
Denny's, Hot Food & Pizza

Pilot Travel Center
I-44 & MO 43S Exit 4
4500 Highway 43 South
Joplin, MO 64804
Wendy's

Flying J
I-435 Front Street
1300 N. Corrington Avenue
Kansas City, MO 64120
Hot Food & Pizza

Pilot Travel Center
I-35 Exit 26
600 West SR 92
Kearney, MO 64060
Taco Bell

Pilot Travel Center
I-55 Exit 40
917 East Elm Street
Marston, MO 63866
Subway

Flying J
I-55 Exit 58
703 State Hwy 80
Matthews, MO 63867
Denny's

Pilot Travel Center
US 71
2424 East Austin Road
Nevada, MO 64772
Hot Food & Pizza

Pilot Travel Center
I-44 Exit 257
1475 Thornton Street
Pacific, MO 63069
Subway

Flying J
US Hwy 71 Exit J
700 J Hwy
Peculiar, MO 64078
Denny's, Hot Food & Pizza

Mr. Fuel
I-55 Exit 180
8915 Weier Road
Pevely, MO 63070
Hot Food & Pizza

Pilot Deal
Road Ranger
I-44 Exit 163
22345 Highway 28
St. Robert, MO 65584
Chester's Chicken, Subway

Flying J
I-44/Hwy. 185 Exit 226
1500 AF Highway
Sullivan, MO 63080
Denny's, Hot Food & Pizza

Mr. Fuel
I-44 Exit 251
3324 Highway 100
Villa Ridge, MO 63089
Hot Food & Pizza

Flying J
I-70 Exit 188
#1 Camp Branch Rd
Warrenton, MO 63383
Denny's

Flying J
Hwy 136 & Hwy 61
102 Fore Drive
Wayland, MO 63472
Denny's

MONTANA

Pilot Deal
Town Pump
I-90 Exit 298
561 Business Hub Road
Belgrade, MT 59714
Hot Food & Pizza

Flying J Deal
Broadway
I-90 Exit 298
6505 Jack Rabit Lane
Belgrade, MT 59701
Broadway Diner

Pilot Deal
Town Pump
I-90 Exit 455
2775 Old Hardin Road
Billings, MT 59101
McDonald's

Pilot Deal
Town Pump
I-15 Exit 122 & I-90 MM 220
122000 W Browns Gulch Road
Butte, MT 59701

Pilot Deal
Town Pump
US 2 & Hwy 40
6102 Highway 2 West
Columbia Falls, MT 59912
Deli

Pilot Deal
Town Pump
I-90 Exit 408
602 8th Avenue North
Columbus, MT 59019
McDonald's

Pilot Deal
Town Pump
I-15 Exit 277 31st Street
3100 Tri-Hill Frontage Road
Great Falls, MT 59404
Subway

Pilot Deal
Town Pump
I-15 & 31st Street Exit 277
3715 31st Street SW
Great Falls, MT 59404
Denny's

Flying J Deal
Broadway
I-90 Exit 495
315 E 13th Street
Hardin, MT 59034
Subway

Pilot Deal
Town Pump
US 12 & US 93
11882 Highway 93 S
Lolo, MT 59847
McDonald's

Pilot Deal
Town Pump
I-94 Exit 138
1210 South Haynes
Miles City, MT 59301
McDonald's

Pilot Deal
Town Pump
I-90 Exit 109
7985 Highway 200
Milltown, MT 59851
Arby's, Hot Stuff Pizza

Pilot Deal
Town Pump
I-90 Exit 96
8475 Highway 93 N Suite B
Missoula, MT 59808
McDonald's

Pilot Deal
Town Pump
I-90 Exit 122
1000 Grizzly Trail
Rocker, MT 59701
Arby's, McDonald's

Pilot Deal
Town Pump
I-15 Exit 363
1350 Roosevelt
Shelby, MT 59474
Country Skillet, Subway

Flying J Deal
Town Pump
Hwy 200
3150 S Central Avenue
Sidney, MT 59270

Pilot Deal
Town Pump
I-90 Exit 47
27 Diamond Road
Superior, MT 59872
Deli

Pilot Deal
Town Pump
I-90 & US 287
10800 Highway 287
Three Forks, MT 59751
Subway

NEBRASKA

Flying J
I-80 Exit 107
I-80 & Big Springs Road
Big Springs, NE 69122
Grandma Max's, Little Caesars, Sam Bass Steakhouse, Subway

Pilot Travel Center
I-80 & US 183 Exit 257
5085 Buffalo Creek Rd
Elm Creek, NE 68836
Little Caesars, Subway, Taco Express

Pilot Deal
Bosselman
I-80 & US 281 Exit 312
3335 West Wood River Road
Grand Island, NE 68801
Grandma Max's, Little Caesars, Subway, Taco Express

Flying J
I-80 Exit 432
15010 South State Hwy 31
Gretna, NE 68028
Denny's

Flying J
I-80 Exit 179
3400 So. Newberry Rd.
North Platte, NE 69101
Denny's, Hot Food & Pizza

Pilot Travel Center
I-80 Exit 300
I-80 and Highway 11 Exit 300
Wood River, NE 68883
Grandma Max's, Subway

NEVADA

Flying J Deal
Broadway
I-80 Exit 231
650 W Front Street
Battle Mountain, NV 89820
Blimpie's, Broadway Diner

Pilot Travel Center
I-80 & NV 278 Exit 280
791 Tenth Street
Carlin, NV 89822
Subway

Pilot Travel Center
I-80 & US 95 Exit 46
465 Pilot Road
Fernley, NV 89408
Dairy Queen, Wendy's

Flying J
I-80 Exit 48
480 Truck Inn Way
Fernley, NV 89408
Denny's, Cinnabon

Pilot Travel Center
I-15 Exit 48
3812 East Craig Road
North Las Vegas, NV 89031
KFC, Pizza Hut

Flying J Dealer
I-15 Exit 1
115 West Primm Blvd
Primm, NV 89019

Flying J
I-80 & HWY 93 Exit 352 (South)
156 Hwy 93 South
Wells, NV 89835
Hot Food & Pizza

Pilot Travel Center
I-80 Peppermill Casino
1200 West Wendover Boulevard
West Wendover, NV 89883
Arby's

Flying J
I-80 Exit 176
1880 W. Winnemucca Blvd
Winnemucca, NV 89445
Hot Food & Pizza

Pilot Travel Center
I-80 & W. Interchange
5625 I-80 West Winnemucca Exchange
Winnemucca, NV 89445
Subway

NEW HAMPSHIRE

Pilot Dealer
I-93 EXIT 11/12C
728 SR 3A
Bow, NH 03304
Deli

NEW JERSEY

Pilot Travel Center
I-78 & NJ 173 Exit 7
979 Route 173
Bloomsbury, NJ 08804
Subway

Flying J
I-295 Exit 2C
326 Slapes Corner/I295 Ex 2C
Carney's Point, NJ 08069
Denny's, Hot Food & Pizza

Pilot Travel Center
I-295 Exit 2B NJT
600 Pennsville-Auburn Road
Carneys Point, NJ 08069
Subway

Pilot Travel Center
I-78 Exit 12
66 Route 173 West
Hampton, NJ 08827
Subway

Pilot Travel Center
230 Route 17 South
230 Route 17 South
Mahwah, NJ 07430
Deli

Pilot Dealer
I-84 Exit 1
15 Route 23
Montague, NJ 07827
Subway

Pilot Dealer
Route 46 East
1470 Route 46 East
Roxbury, NJ 07852

NEW MEXICO

Flying J
I-40 Exit 153
9911 Avalon Road NW
Albuquerque, NM 87105
Denny's, Hot Food & Pizza

Pilot Thomas Cardlock
E Main Street
210 E Main Street
Artesia, NM 88210

Pilot Fuel Center
US 285 & US 180
3202 S Canal Street
Carlsbad, NM 88221
Hot Food & Pizza

Pilot Travel Center
Carlsbad Hwy
3710 W Carlsbad Hwy
Hobbs, NM 88240
Cinnabon, Subway

Pilot Travel Center
I-40 Exit 39
1 Giant Crossing
Jamestown, NM 87347
Denny's, Subway

Pilot Travel Center
I-10 & NM 292 Exit 139
2681 West Amador
Las Cruces, NM 88005
Subway

Pilot Travel Center
I-10 Exit 24
1050 East Motel Drive
Lordsburg, NM 88045
Arby's

Flying J
I-10 Exit 24
11 Old Hwy 70
Lordsburg, NM 88045
Denny's, Hot Food & Pizza

Pilot Travel Center
I-40 and Hwy 41
305 Abrahams Rd. W
Moriarty, NM 87035
Subway

Flying J
I-40 & Exit 333
2021 S. Mountain Rd
Tucumcari, NM 88401
Denny's, Hot Food & Pizza

NEW YORK

Pilot Travel Center
I-86 Exit 37
7767 State Route 53
Bath, NY 14810
Subway

Pilot Travel Center
I-90 Exit 12
995 US Route 9
Castleton - On - Hudson, NY 12033
Subway

Pilot Travel Center
I-81/90 Exit 25
107 Seventh North Street
Liverpool, NY 13088
McDonald's

Pilot Travel Center
I-84 Exit 6
239 Route 17K
Newburgh, NY 12550
Arby's

Flying J
I-90 Exit 48A
8484 Allegheny Road
Pembroke, NY 14036
Denny's, Hot Food & Pizza

Pilot Travel Center
I-88. Exit 25
1128 Duanesburg Road
Rotterdam, NY 12306
Dunkin' Donuts, Subway

NORTH CAROLINA

Pilot Travel Center
I-85/77 Exit 39
3807 Statesville Avenue
Charlotte, NC 28206
Subway

Pilot Dealer
I-95 Exit 75
65 Sadler Road
Dunn, NC 28334
Dairy Queen, Milestone Dinner, Quizno's Subs

Pilot Deal The Pantry
I-95 Exit 71
873 Longbranch Road
Dunn, NC 28334
Hardee's

Flying J
I-85 & I-40 Exit 150
1043 Jimmie Kerr Rd
Graham, NC 27258
Denny's, Hot Food & Pizza

Pilot Travel Center
I-85 Exit 63
2825 Lane Street
Kannapolis, NC 28083
Subway

Flying J
I-95 & Exit 106
1800 Princeton-Kenly Road
Kenly, NC 27542
Denny's

Pilot Travel Center
I-40/85 Exit 152
1342 Trollingwood Road
Mebane, NC 27302
McDonald's

Flying J Dealer
I-77 Exit 100
125 Plaza Lane
Mount Airy, NC 27030

Pilot Travel Center
I-95 Exit 180
2032 Highway 48
Pleasant Hill, NC 27866
Subway

Pilot Travel Center
I-40 & NC 209 Exit 24
3712 Crabtree Road
Waynesville, NC 28786
Subway

NORTH DAKOTA

Flying J
I-94 & Hwy 16
I-94 & Hwy 16
Beach, ND 58621
Subway

Flying J
I-29 Exit 62
3150 39th St SW Suite A
Fargo, ND 58104
Hot Food & Pizza

Flying J
I-29 Exit 12
4401 32nd Avenue South
Grand Forks, ND 58201
Milestone Dinner, Subway

Flying J Dealer
I-94 Exit 147
3825 Business Loop I-94
Mandan, ND 58554
Hot Food & Pizza

Flying J
Hwy 2 & 52 Exit 83
3800 Highway 2 and 52 W
Minot, ND 58701
Cinnabon, Subway

Pilot Travel Center
Hwy 2 and Hwy 85
13553 Hwy 2 NE side of Hwy 2 @ Hwy 85 and Hwy 2
Williston, ND 58801
Subway

OHIO

Pilot Travel Center
I-90 Exit 223
2246 State Route 45
Austinburg, OH 44010
Subway

Flying J
I-90 & State Rd 45 Exit 223
2349 Center Road
Austinburg, OH 44010
Denny's, Hot Food & Pizza

Pilot Travel Center
I-80 Exit 223
1150 North Canfield-Niles Road
Austintown, OH 44515
McDonald's

Pilot Travel Center
I-90 Exit 151
39115 Colorado Road
Avon, OH 44011
Subway

Pilot Travel Center
I-75 Exit 135
427 East Main Street
Beaver Dam, OH 45808
McDonald's, Subway

Flying J
I-75 Exit 135
420 East Main Street
Beaverdam, OH 45808
Denny's

Pilot Travel Center
I-70 Exit 208
66377 Belmont-Morristown Road
Belmont, OH 43718
Cinnabon, Subway

Flying J
I-71 Exit 131
7735 East State Rt 37
Berkshire, OH 43074
Denny's

Pilot Travel Center
I-71 & OH 83 Exit 204
10048 Avon Lake Road
Burbank, OH 44214
Wendy's

Pilot Travel Center
I-77 Exit 25
44133 Fairground Road
Caldwell, OH 43724
Arby's

Pilot Travel Center
I-70 Exit 178
61700 Southgate Road
Cambridge, OH 43725
Subway

Pilot Travel Center
I-77, Exit 101
2320 Faircrest St.
Canton, OH 44706
Subway

Pilot Travel Center
Hwy 35
1111 East Main Street
Chillicothe, OH 45601
Cinnabon, Moe's

Pilot Travel Center
US 23 Pittsburg Rd
25600 US 23
Circleville, OH 43113
Pizza Hut

Pilot Travel Center
I-70 Exit 94 Wilson Rd
3600 Interchange Road
Columbus, OH 43204
Wendy's

Pilot Travel Center
I-70 & OH 127 Exit 10
6141 US 127 North
Eaton, OH 45320
Subway

Pilot Travel Center
I-75 & OH 613 Exit 164
11471 State Route 613W
Findlay, OH 45840
Subway, Taco Bell

Pilot Travel Center
I-75 Exit 36
6830 Franklin-Lebanon Road
Franklin, OH 45005
Pizza Hut, Subway

Pilot Travel Center
I-80 Exit 226
2786 Salt Springs Road
Girard, OH 44420
Subway

Mr. Fuel
I-80 Exit 226
2840 Salt Spring Road
Girard, OH 44420
Hot Food & Pizza

Pilot Travel Center
I-70 & OH 37 Exit 126
10258 Lancaster Road SW
Hebron, OH 43025
Chester's Chicken, Subway

Flying J
I-80 & Hwy 62 Exit 234B (Eastbound)
2226 North Main
Hubbard, OH 44425
Denny's, Hot Food & Pizza

Flying J
I-71 Exit 69
9935 SR 41
Jeffersonville, OH 43128
Denny's, Hot Food & Pizza

Flying J
I-280 Exit 1B
26415 Warns Road
Lake Township, OH 43551
Denny's

Pilot Travel Center
I-70 Exit 79
1365 SR 42 NE
London, OH 43140
Arby's

Pilot Travel Center
I-71 Exit 140
488 State Route 61
Marengo, OH 43334
Arby's

Flying J
I-70 St Rd 158 Exit 122
10480 Baltimore
Millersport, OH 43046
Denny's, Hot Food & Pizza

Pilot Travel Center
Route 24
905 American Road Route 24
Napoleon, OH 43545
Subway

Pilot Travel Center
I-76 Exit 232
10920 Market Street
North Lima, OH 44452
McDonald's

Pilot Travel Center
I-80/90 Exit 71
3430 Libbey Road
Perrysburg, OH 43551
McDonald's

Pilot Travel Center
I-77 Exit 146 / I-80 Exit 173
5219 Brecksville Road
Richfield, OH 44286
Wendy's

Pilot Travel Center
I-71 Exit 209
8924 Lake Road
Seville, OH 44273
Subway

Pilot Travel Center
I-71 Exit 131
7680 East State Route 36
Sunbury, OH 43074
Subway

Pilot Travel Center
I-75 Exit 210
5820 Hagman Road
Toledo, OH 43612
Subway

Pilot Travel Center
State Hwy 23 & 30
1600 East Wyandot Avenue
Upper Sandusky, OH 43351
Subway

Flying J
I-75, Exit 64
175 Northwoods Blvd.
Vandalia, OH 45377
Subway

Pilot Travel Center
I-71 Exit 50
5772 US 68 North
Wilmington, OH 45177
Subway

OKLAHOMA

Flying J
I-35 & Exit 33
2450 Cooper Drive
Ardmore, OK 73401
Hot Food & Pizza
Huddle House

Flying J
US Hwy 69 & US Hwy 266
1255 Gentry
Checotah, OK 74426
Denny's, Hot Food & Pizza

Pilot Dealer
I-40 Exit 166
7501 Choctaw Rd
Choctaw, OK 73020

Flying J
I-35 & N.E. 122nd Street
4801 NE 122nd St.
Edmond, OK 73013
Hot Food & Pizza,
Huddle House

Pilot Dealer
US Hwy 412 & 42nd Street
106 South 42nd Street
Enid, OK 73701
Hot Food & Pizza

Pilot Travel Center
US 69 & US 51
3000 North 32nd Street
Muskogee, OK 74401
Subway

Pilot Travel Center
I-40 Exit 140
400 South Morgan Road
Oklahoma City, OK 73128
McDonald's

Flying J
I-40 Exit 140
701 South Morgan Road
Oklahoma City, OK 73128
Hot Food & Pizza,
Huddle House

Pilot Travel Center
I-40 Exit 325
302 West Ray Fine Boulevard
Roland, OK 74954
Wendy's

Flying J
I-40 & US 283 Exit 20
2400 So 4th Route
Sayre, OK 73662
Denny's, Hot Food & Pizza

Pilot Travel Center
I-35 Exit 214
16600 West South Avenue
Tonkawa, OK 74653
Cinnabon, Taco Bell

Flying J
I-44 & Exit 236
121 North 129 E/I-44 Exit 236
Tulsa, OK 74116
Denny's, Hot Food & Pizza

OREGON

Flying J
I-5, Exit 278
12334 Ehlen Road
Aurora, OR 97002
Cinnabon, Subway

Pilot Travel Center
I-5 Exit 263
4220 Brooklake Road
Brooks, OR 97305
Subway, Taco Bell

Pilot Travel Center
I-5 Exit 33
1600 East Pine Street
Central Point, OR 97502
Subway, Taco Bell

Pilot Travel Center
109450 Hwy 97
341 Damon Street 109450
Highway 97
Chemult, OR 97731
Subway

Pilot Travel Center
Hwy 97
3817 N. Hwy 97
Klamath Falls, OR 97601
Subway

Pilot Travel Center
I-84 Exit 265
I-84 & Exit 265 PO Box 3298
LaGrande, OR 97850
Deli

Pilot Travel Center
I-5 Exit 148
800 John Long Road
Oakland, OR 97462
Denny's, Subway

Pilot Travel Center
I-84 Exit 376A
653 East Idaho Avenue
Ontario, OR 97914
Arby's

Pilot Travel Center
I-84/82 Exit 188
2115 Highway 395
Stanfield, OR 97875
McDonald's, Subway

Pilot Travel Center
I-84 & US 97
91485 Biggs Rufus Highway
Wasco, OR 97065
McDonald's

PENNSYLVANIA

Pilot Travel Center
I-70 Exit 32B
205 Wilson Road
Bentleyville, PA 15314
Dairy Queen, Subway

Pilot Deal
All American
I-70 Exit 147; I-76 Exit 161
167 Post House Road
Breezewood, PA 15533
Perkins, Pizza Shop,
Taco Maker

Flying J
I-80 Exit 78
246 Allegheny Blvd
Brookville, PA 15825
Denny's, Hot Food & Pizza

Flying J
I-81 Exit 52/I-76 & Exit 226
1501 Harrisburg Pike
Carlisle, PA 17013
Denny's

Pilot Travel Center
I-80/81/PA 93 Exit 256
SR 93 Box 1114
Drums, PA 18222
Subway

Pilot Travel Center
I-80 & Hwy 219 Exit 97
1742 Rich Highway
DuBois, PA 15801
Arby's

Pilot Travel Center
US 22 & 322
30 Benvenue Road
Duncannon, PA 17020
Iron Kettle, Subway

Pilot Travel Center
I-90 & PA 97 Exit 27
8035 Perry Highway
Erie, PA 16509
Subway

Pilot Travel Center
I-78 Exit 10 (PA 645)
2210 Camp Swatara Road
Frystown, PA 17067
Subway

Pilot Travel Center
I-81 & PA 39 Exit 77
7961 Linglestown Road
Harrisburg, PA 17112
Pizza Hut

Flying J
I-80 and Exit 173
5609 Nittany Valley Drive
Mill Hall, PA 17751
Denny's, Hot Food & Pizza

Pilot Travel Center
I-80 Exit 173
5868 Nittany Valley Drive
Mill Hall, PA 17751
Subway

Flying J Dealer
I-80 Exit 215
1460 North Ridge Rd
Milton, PA 17847
Penn 80 Grill, Subway

Flying J
I-81 Exit 219
1623 Oliver Road
New Milford, PA 18834
Denny's, Hot Food & Pizza

Pilot Dealer
I-81 Exit 100 / PA 443
473 Suedberg Road
Pine Grove, PA 17963

Pilot Dealer
I-81 Exit 100
482 Suedberg Road
Pine Grove, PA 17963
Auntie Anne's, Dairy Queen,
Gooseberry Farms, Subway

Pilot Travel Center
I-81N Exit 175
417 Route 315
Pittston, PA 18640
Wendy's

Pilot Travel Center
I-79 Exit 99
2010 New Castle Road
Portersville, PA 16051
McDonald's, Subway

Flying J
I-70 Exit 49
122 Fitzhenry Road
Smithton, PA 15479
Denny's

SOUTH CAROLINA

Flying J
I-85 Exit 102
1011 North Mountain St
Blacksburg, SC 29702
Denny's

Pilot Travel Center
I-26 Exit 159
2064 Homestead Road
Bowman, SC 29018
McDonald's

Pilot Deal
The Pantry
I-26 Exit 5
8998 SC Highway 11
Campobello, SC 29322
Subway

Pilot Travel Center
I-26/77 Exit 115
3008 Highway 321
Cayce, SC 29033
Dairy Queen, Wendy's

Pilot Travel Center
I-26 Exit 52
12818 Highway 56 North
Clinton, SC 29325
Subway

Flying J
I-20 Exit 70
5901 Fairfield Road
Columbia, SC 29203
Denny's

Pilot Travel Center
I-85 & SC 290 Exit 63
1405 East Main Street
Duncan, SC 29334
Wendy's

Pilot Travel Center
I-95 & US 52 Exit 164
2015 West Lucas Street
Florence, SC 29501
Subway, Taco Bell

Pilot Travel Center
I-95 Exit 170
3006 North Williston Road
Florence, SC 29506
Wendy's

Pilot Travel Center
I-85 Exit 90
909 Hyatt Street
Gaffney, SC 29341
Arby's

Flying J
I-95 Exit 181A
111 Mill Branch Road
Latta, SC 29565
Hot Food & Pizza

Pilot Travel Center
I-20 & US 601 Exit 92
522 Highway 601 South
Lugoff, SC 29078
Dairy Queen, Subway

Pilot Travel Center
I-85 Exit 35
110 Frontage Road
Piedmont, SC 29673
McDonald's

Flying J
I-77 & Hwy 901 Exit 73
2435 Mount Holly Road
Rock Hill, SC 29730
Denny's, Hot Food & Pizza

Flying J
I-95 Exit 77
113 Motel Drive
St. George, SC 29477
Denny's, Cinnabon

Pilot Travel Center
I-26 Exit 199
1521 North Main Street
Summerville, SC 29483
McDonald's

SOUTH DAKOTA

Flying J Franchise
Hwy 79
25 Heartland Express Hwy 79
Hermosa, SD 57744
Hot Food & Pizza

Pilot Travel Center
I-90 Exit 192
601 E. Fifth St.
Murdo, SD 57559
Subway

Pilot Travel Center
I-90 Exit 55
2783 Deadwood Avenue
Rapid City, SD 57702
Subway

Flying J Franchise
I-90 Exit 61
4200 N I-90 Service Road
Rapid City, SD 57701
Country Market

Flying J
I-29 Exit 83
5201 Granite Lane
Sioux Falls, SD 57107
Denny's, Hot Food & Pizza

TENNESSEE

Pilot Travel Center
I-40 Exit 287
1111 South Jefferson
Cookeville, TN 38501
Deli

Pilot Travel Center
I-65 Exit 22
9211 Lewisburg Highway
Cornersville, TN 37047
Hot Stuff Pizza

Pilot Travel Center
I-40 Exit 320
2449 Genesis Road
Crossville, TN 38571
Wendy's

Pilot Travel Center
I-40 Exit 417
505 Patriot Drive
Dandridge, TN 37725
Subway

Pilot Travel Center
I-40 Exit 172
2320 Highway 46 South
Dickson, TN 37055
Wendy's

Flying J
I-40 & Hwy 96 Exit 182
1420 Hwy 96 North
Fairview, TN 37062
Denny's, Hot Food & Pizza

Pilot Travel Center
I-81 Exit 36
11190 Baileyton Road
Greeneville, TN 37745
Subway

Pilot Travel Center
I-75 Exit 117
1915 East Raccoon Valley Road
Heiskel, TN 37754
Deli

Pilot Travel Center
I-40 Exit 143
15559 Highway 13 South
Hurricane Mills, TN 37078
Arby's

Pilot Travel Center
I-40 Exit 85
30 Sand Pebble Road
Jackson, TN 38305
Denny's

Pilot Travel Center
I-40/75 Exit 374
314 Lovell Road
Knoxville, TN 37922
Wendy's

Pilot Travel Center
I-40 Exit 398
7210 Straw Plains Pike
Knoxville, TN 37914
Subway

Flying J
I-40 & I-75 Exit 369
800 Watt Road
Knoxville, TN 37932
Denny's

Pilot Travel Center
I-24 Exit 64
535 Waldron Road
Lavergne, TN 37086
Subway

Pilot Travel Center
I-40 Exit 238
921 Murfreesboro
Lebanon, TN 37090
Dairy Queen, Subway

Pilot Travel Center
I-75 Exit 20
281 Pleasant Grove Rd SW
McDonald, TN 37353
Subway, Pizza Hut, Cinnabon

Pilot Travel Center
I-240 & Hwy 78S
4949 Lamar Avenue
Memphis, TN 38118
Subway

Pilot Travel Center
US 78 Pleasant Hill
5021 Highway 78
Memphis, TN 38118
Arby's

Pilot Travel Center
I-24 Exit 81
2441 South Church Street
Murfreesboro, TN 37127
Arby's

Pilot Travel Center
Hwy 155 Exit 26
6418 Centennial Boulevard
Nashville, TN 37209
Subway

Pilot Travel Center
I-75 Exit 141
304 Howard Baker Highway
Pioneer, TN 37847
Subway

Pilot Travel Center
I-40 Exit 42
7720 Highway 222
Stanton, TN 38069
Chester's Chicken, Subway

Pilot Travel Center
I-81 Exit 4
3624 Roy Messer Highway
White Pine, TN 37890
McDonald's

TEXAS

Pilot Travel Center
I-40 Exit 75
715 South Lakeside Drive
Amarillo, TX 79118
McDonald's, Subway

Flying J
I-40 Exit 76
9601 I-40 E Exit 76
Amarillo, TX 79118
Denny's

Flying J
Hwy 75 Exit 48
714 South Central Expressway
Anna, TX 75409
Huddle House

Pilot Travel Center
I-10 Exit 0
2015 Antonio Street
Anthony, TX 79821
Subway, Wendy's

Flying J
I-10 Exit 0
3001 Mountain Pass Blvd
Anthony, TX 79821
Denny's

Flying J
I-10 & Exit 789 Thompson Road
1876 East Freeway
Baytown, TX 77521
Denny's, Hot Food & Pizza

Pilot Travel Center
Highway 59
525 1st Street
Beasley, TX 77417
Arby's, Cinnabon

Pilot Travel Center
Hwy 67
1312 E Hwy 67
Big Lake, TX 76932
Cinnabon, Taco Bell

Pilot Travel Center
I-20 Exit 178
706 East I-20
Big Spring, TX 79720
McDonald's, Hot Food & Pizza

Flying J
I-10 Exit 732
204 South Waller Ave
Brookshire, TX 77423
Denny's, Hot Food & Pizza

Pilot Travel Center
I-45 & Hwy 79, Exit 178
2605 West Commerce Street
Buffalo, TX 75831
Taco Bell, Cinnabon

Pilot Travel Center
I-30 Exit 88
2226 FM-1903 I-30 & FM 1903 Exit 87
Caddo Mills, TX 75135
McDonald's

Pilot Deal The Pantry
I-20 Exit 533
9800 Interstate 20
Canton, TX 75103
A&W, Hot Skillet, Long John Silvers

Pilot Travel Center
Highway 83
1045 S Highway 83
Carrizo Springs, TX 78834
Moe's, Cinnabon

Pilot Travel Center
Hwy 287 & Hwy 83
2301 Avenue F NW
Childress, TX 79201
Arby's, Cinnabon

Flying J Dealer
I-20 & SH 206 Exit 330
16851 IH 20
Cisco, TX 76437
Denny's

Flying J
I-35, Exit 69
921 N. IH35 LaSalle County
Cotulla, TX 78014
Subway

Flying J
I-20 Exit 472
7425 Bonnie View Road
Dallas, TX 75241
Denny's

Pilot Travel Center
I-20 Exit 470
8787 South Lancaster Road
Dallas, TX 75241
Wendy's

Pilot Dealer
86A US Hwy 57
3002 US 57
Eagle Pass, TX 78852

Flying J
Hwy 281 & FM 1925
1305 East Monte Cristo Road
Edinburg, TX 78539
Denny's

Flying J
I-10 and Exit 37
1301 Horizon Blvd
El Paso, TX 79928
Denny's, Hot Food & Pizza

Flying J
I-10 Exit 259
2571 N. Front St.
Fort Stockton, TX 79735
Cinnabon, Subway

Pilot Travel Center
I-35 Exit 65
2400 Alliance Gateway
Fort Worth, TX 76177
McDonald's, Subway

Flying J
I-37, Exit 56
4066 Hwy 59
George West, TX 78022
McDonald's

Flying J
I-45 Exit 64 & Richey Rd
15919 North Freeway
Houston, TX 77090
Denny's, Hot Food & Pizza

Pilot Travel Center
I-610 & US 90E Exit 24A
4440 North McCarty Street
Houston, TX 77013
McDonald's

Pilot Travel Center
I-45 Exit 118
639 State Highway 75 North
Huntsville, TX 77320
Wendy's

Flying J Dealer
I-35 Exit 275
11710 North Interstate 35
Jarrell, TX 76537
Burger King, Denny's, Q Eats

Pilot Travel Center
I-40 Exit 456
2342 North Main Street
Junction, TX 76489
Cinnabon, Subway

Flying J
I-35 & Exit 13
1011 Beltway Parkway
Laredo, TX 78041
Denny's, Hot Food & Pizza

Pilot Travel Center
I-35 Exit 13
1101 Uniroyal Drive
Laredo, TX 78045
McDonald's, Subway

Flying J
I-27 & 4th Street Exit
602 4th Street
Lubbock, TX 79401
Subway

Pilot Travel Center
Hwy 69/Loop 287
1920 East Denman Avenue
Lufkin, TX 75901
Moe's, Cinnabon

Pilot Thomas Cardlock
Garden City Hwy
3015 Garden City Hwy
Midland, TX 79701

Flying J
I-20, Exit 138
3302 Garden City Highway
Midland, TX 79706
Moe's, Cinnabon

Pilot Travel Center
I-20&FM 1788 Exit 126
4015 South FM 1788
Midland, TX 79706
McDonald's

Pilot Travel Center
I-35 Exit 184
4142 Loop 337
New Braunfels, TX 78132
McDonald's, Subway

Flying J
US 59 & Exit 242
23412 Hwy 242
New Caney, TX 77357
Denny's, Hot Food & Pizza

Pilot Thomas Cardlock
42st Street
3479 W 42nd Street
Odessa, TX 79764

Flying J
I-20 Exit 121
5900 E Interstate 20
Odessa, TX 79766
McDonald's, Hot Food & Pizza

Pilot Thomas Cardlock
Grandview Ave
715 S Grandview Avenue
Odessa, TX 79761

Pilot Travel Center
I-10 Exit 873
2205 North Highway 62
Orange, TX 77630
Subway

Flying J
I-10 Exit 873
7112 I-10 West
Orange, TX 77630
Denny's

Flying J
I-20 Exit 42
100 E Pinehurst 120 US Hwy 285
Pecos, TX 79772
Denny's

Pilot Travel Center
I-35 Exit 328
8055 South I-35
Robinson, TX 76706
Subway, Wendy's

Flying J
I-10 Exit 583
1815 N Foster Road
San Antonio, TX 78244
Denny's

Pilot Travel Center
I-37, Exit 125
4105 Loop 1604
San Antonio, TX 78264
Subway

Pilot Travel Center
I-10 Exit 582 Ackerman Rd
5619 I-10 East
San Antonio, TX 78219
Subway

Pilot Dealer
Hwy 180
1100 E Hwy 180
Snyder, TX 79549

Pilot Travel Center
I-30 Exit 122
1200 South Hillcrest
Sulphur Springs, TX 75482
Arby's

Pilot Travel Center
Hwy 16
3080 N Hwy 16
Tilden, TX 78072
Cinnabon, Subway

Pilot Dealer
I-27 Exit 74
2901 W Highway 86
Tulia, TX 79088
Krispy Krunchy Chicken, Noble Roman's Pizza, Subway

Flying J
I-20 & FM 707 Exit 277
101 N FM 707
Tye, TX 79563
Denny's, Hot Food & Pizza

Pilot Travel Center
I-20 & FM 14
12881 FM 14 A
Tyler, TX 75706
McDonald's

Pilot Travel Center
I-10 Exit 140
501 Van Horn Drive
Van Horn, TX 79855
Wendy's

Pilot Travel Center
I-35 Exit 140
14555 IH35 South
Von Ormy, TX 78073
Cinnabon, Subway

Flying J
I-35 & New Road
2409 So New Road
Waco, TX 76711
Denny's, Hot Food & Pizza

Pilot Travel Center
I-20 Exit 406
1201 I-20 West
Weatherford, TX 76087
Wendy's

Flying J
US 287 & Jacksboro Highway
2311 Jacksboro Highway
Wichita Falls, TX 76301
Denny's, Wendy's

UTAH

Flying J Dealer
I-15 Exit 112
653 West 1400 North
Beaver, UT 84713
Roberto's Taco Shop, Wendy's

Pilot Dealer
I-70 Exit 164
1085 East Main Street
Green River, UT 84525
Hot Food & Pizza

Flying J
I-80 Exit 99
1605 East Saddleback Blvd.
Lake Point, UT 84074
Denny's, Hot Food & Pizza

Flying J
I-15 Exit 222
1597 South Main
Nephi, UT 84648
Denny's, Hot Food & Pizza

Flying J
I-215 & Redwood Rd Exit 27
885 West North Point Circle
North Salt Lake, UT 84054
Hot Food & Pizza

Flying J
I-15 Exit 343
1172 West 21st Street
Ogden, UT 84401
Denny's, Hot Food & Pizza

Pilot Travel Center
I-15 & UT 39 Exit 344
1670 West 12th Street
Ogden, UT 84404
Subway, Taco Bell

Pilot Dealer
I-15 Exit 362
1674 West 1100 South
Perry, UT 84302
Dairy Queen

Flying J
I-70 Exit 40
35 East Flying J Drive
Richfield, UT 84701
Hot Food & Pizza

Flying J
I-15 & I-80 SR201 Exit 17
2025 S 900 W
Salt Lake City, UT 84116
Denny's, Hot Food & Pizza

Flying J Dealer
I-15 Exit 188
810 North 800 West
Scipio, UT 84656
Dairy Queen

Flying J
I-84 Exit 7
90 South Stone Road
Snowville, UT 84336
Hot Food & Pizza

Flying J
I-15 Exit 261
1460 North 1750 West
Springville, UT 84663
Denny's

Pilot Travel Center
I-15 Exit 4
2841 South 60 East
St. George, UT 84790
Hot Food & Pizza

Flying J
I-15 Exit 357
600 West 750 North
Willard, UT 84340
Hot Food & Pizza, Subway

VIRGINIA

Flying J
I-95 Exit 104
24279 Rogers Clark Blvd.
Carmel Church, VA 22546
Denny's, Hot Food & Pizza

Pilot Travel Center
I-95 Exit 58
2126 Ruffin Mill Road
Colonial Heights, VA 23834
Wendy's

Pilot Travel Center
Hwy 58 & Hwy 29
110 River Point Drive
Danville, VA 24541
Arby's

Pilot Dealer
I-295 & Rt 460 Exit 3A
4610 County Drive
Disputanta, VA 23842
Wendy's

Pilot Dealer
I-95 Exit 11 (Hwy 58)
918 West Atlantic
Emporia, VA 23847
Five Guys, Fosho Italian Sport Grill, Milestone Dinner, Quizno's Subs

Flying J
I-81 & I-77 Exit 80
139 Factory Outlet Drive
Fort Chiswell, VA 24360
Denny's, Wendy's

Pilot Travel Center
I-81 Exit 251
3634 North Valley Pike
Harrisonburg, VA 22802
Subway

Pilot Travel Center
I-64 Exit 211
6721 Emmaus Church Road
Providence Forge, VA 23140
Subway

Pilot Dealer
I-81/I-64 Exit 205
713 Oakland Circle
Raphine, VA 24472
Wendy's

Mr. Fuel
I-95 Exit 104
23818 Rogers Clark Blvd
Ruther Glen, VA 22546
Hot Food & Pizza

Flying J
I-95 Exit 104
23866 Rogers Clark Blvd.
Ruther Glen, VA 22546
Golden Corral, Wendys

Pilot Dealer
I-95 Exit 4
781 Moores Ferry Road
Skippers, VA 23879
Subway

Pilot Dealer
Philpott Hwy 58
2190 Philpott Highway 58
South Boston, VA 24592

Pilot Dealer
I-85 Exit 12 (Hwy 58)
1011 E. Atlantic Street
South Hill, VA 23970
Bill Ellis BBQ, Hunts Brothers Pizza

Pilot Travel Center
I-81 Exit 213A
3541 Lee Jackson Highway
Staunton, VA 24401
Arby's

Pilot Dealer
I-81 Exit 291
1014 Mt. Olive Road
Tom's Brook, VA 22660
Dairy Queen, Subway

Pilot Travel Center
I-81 Exit 150A or B
2966 Lee Highway South
Troutville, VA 24175
Subway

Flying J
I-81 Exit 323
1530 Rest Church Rd
Winchester, VA 22624
Denny's, Hot Food & Pizza, Subway

Pilot Dealer
I-81/I-77 Exit 77
1318 East Lee Highway
Wytheville, VA 24382
Arby's, Dairy Queen

Flying J
I-77 & I-81 Exit 77
3249 Chapman Road
Wytheville, VA 24382
Denny's

WASHINGTON

Flying J Deal Broadway
I-90 Canyon Rd Exit 109
2300 Canyon Road
Ellensburg, WA 98926
Broadway Diner

Pilot Travel Center
I-5 Exit 262
1678 Main St #3
Ferndale, WA 98248
Subway

Flying J Deal Broadway
US Hwy 395
2216 E Hillsboro Road
Pasco, WA 99301
Deli

Flying J Deal Broadway
I-90 Exit 276
3709 S Geiger Blvd
Spokane, WA 99224
Subway

Flying J Deal Broadway
I-90 Exit 286
E 6606 Broadway
Spokane, WA 99212
Broadway Diner

Pilot Travel Center
I-5 Exit 99 NE
2430 93rd Avenue SW
Tumwater, WA 98512
McDonald's, Subway

WEST VIRGINIA

Pilot Travel Center
I-79 Exit 146
2309 Smithton Road I-79 Exit 146
Morgantown, WV 26508
Cinnabon, Hot Food & Pizza

Pilot Travel Center
I-64 & SR 25 Exit 45
4304 First Avenue
Nitro, WV 25143
Arby's

Pilot Travel Center
I-79 Exit 67
270 Scott Fork - Bonnie Rd
Sutton, WV 26601
Moe's

WISCONSIN

Pilot Travel Center
I-43/90/WI 81 Exit 185A
3001 Milwaukee Road
Beloit, WI 53511
Taco Bell

Flying J
I-94 & Exit 116
780 State Hwy 54
Black River Falls, WI 54615
Denny's

Pilot Deal Road Ranger
I-90 Exit 147
2762 County Highway N
Cottage Grove, WI 53589
Subway

Pilot Deal Road Ranger
I-43 Exit 38
1946 A Energy Drive
East Troy, WI 53120
Subway, Hot Food & Pizza

Pilot Travel Center
I-94 & CR K Exit 329
13712 Northwestern Avenue
Franksville, WI 53126
Arby's

Pilot Travel Center
I-90/94 Exit 69
1101 State Road 82 East
Mauston, WI 53948
Wendy's

Pilot Travel Center
I-94 Exit 322
2031 West Ryan Road
Oak Creek, WI 53154
Subway

Pilot Deal Road Ranger
I-90/I-94 Exit 48
102 E Woody Drive
Oakdale, WI 54649
Subway

Pilot Travel Center
US 65 & I-94
1191 70th Ave
Roberts, WI 54023
Subway

WYOMING

Flying J
I-25 Exit 185
41 SE Wyoming Blvd.
Casper, WY 82609
Subway

Flying J
I-25 Exit 7
2250 Etchepare Drive
Cheyenne, WY 82007
Denny's

Pilot Travel Center
I-80 Exit 367
8020 Campstool Road
Cheyenne, WY 82007
Subway

Flying J
US HWY 30/SR 232
10501 US Hwy 30
Cokeville, WY 83114
Hot Food & Pizza

Flying J
I-80 Exit 3
1920 Harrison Drive
Evanston, WY 82930
Subway

Pilot Travel Center
I-80 Exit 6
289 Bear River Drive
Evanston, WY 82930
Subway

Flying J
I-90 & Hwy 59
1810 South Douglas Hwy.
Gillette, WY 82718
Hot Food & Pizza

Pilot Travel Center
I-80 Exit 310
1564 McCue Street
Laramie, WY 82072
Wendy's

Flying J
I-80 Exit 209
I-80 Johnson Road
Rawlins, WY 82301
Denny's

Flying J
I-80 Exit 104
650 Stage Coach Dr.
Rock Springs, WY 82901
Denny's

CANADIAN LOCATIONS

ALBERTA

Flying J Cardlock
Lake Cres
85 East Lake Cres
Airdrie, AB T4B 2B5

Flying J Fuel Stop
Cassils Road
1260 Cassils Road East
Brooks, AB T1R 0G4

Flying J
11511 40th Street SE
11511 - 40 St. S.E
Calgary, AB T2H 1L4
Hot Food & Pizza

Flying J Cardlock
23 Street
2525 23 Street NE
Calgary, AB T2E 7M1

Flying J Fuel Stop
72 Ave
4216 72 Avenue SE
Calgary, AB T2C 2C1
Hot Food & Pizza

Flying J Dealer
Barlow Trail
4949 Barlow Trail SE
Calgary, AB T2B 3B5
J's Wok and Grill

Flying J Cardlock
Jubilee Ave
5505 Jubilee Ave
Drayton Valley, AB T7A 1S3

Flying J Cardlock
121 A Ave
15609-121 A Avenue NW
Edmonton, AB T5V 1B1

Flying J Dealer
118 Ave
16806 118 Avenue
Edmonton, AB T5V 1M8

Flying J Cardlock
2 Ave
2520-2 Avenue
Edson Motco, AB T7E 1T9

Flying J Fuel Stop
Sakitawaw Trail
345 Sakitawaw Trail
Fort McMurray, AB T9H 4E4

Flying J Cardlock
108 St
9212-108 Street
Grande Prairie, AB T8V 4C9

Flying J Dealer
Hwy 63
1st Ave & 1st Street
Grassland, AB T0A 1V0
Family Restaurant

Flying J Dealer
Hwy 9 & Hwy 36
Hwy 9 & Hwy 36 South
Hanna, AB T0J 1P0

Flying J Cardlock
Kelly Rd
294 Kelly Road
Hinton, AB T7V 1H2

Flying J Cardlock
43 St
1005 43 Street
Lethbridge, AB T1K 7B8

Flying J Cardlock
63 St
5109 63 Street
Lloydminster, AB T9V 2E7

Flying J Fuel Stop
Hwy 2
2810 21st Avenue
Nanton, AB T0L 1R0

Flying J Fuel Stop
20th Ave
302 20 Avenue
Nisku, AB T9E 7Z9
Hot Food & Pizza

Flying J Fuel Stop
67th Ave & 67 Street
6607 67th Street
Red Deer, AB T4P 1A4
Hot Food & Pizza

Flying J Cardlock
Lockwood St
115 Lockwood Street
Redcliff, AB T1A 7T9

Flying J Fuel Stop
Hwy 49 & Hwy 2
Hwy 49 & 2
Rycroft, AB T0H 3A0
Hot Food & Pizza

Flying J
Yellowhead Hwy 16/ Broadmoor Blvd.
50 Pembina Rd.
Sherwood Park, AB T8H 2G9
Denny's, Hot Food & Pizza

Flying J Cardlock
Hwy 43
Hwy 43 & West Mountain Road
Whitecourt, AB T7N 1S9
Hot Food & Pizza

BRITISH COLUMBIA

Flying J Cardlock
Coutts Way
929 Coutts Way & Sumas Way
Abbotsford, BC V2S 4N2

Flying J Fuel Stop
Cliveden Ave
1291 Cliveden Avenue
Annacis Island Delta, BC V5M 6G4
Hot Food & Pizza

Flying J Dealer
Lickman Rd
7970 Lickman Road
Chilliwack, BC V2R 1A9
Hot Food & Pizza

Flying J Cardlock
Theatre Rd
2209 Theatre Road
Cranbrook, BC V1C 4H4

Flying J Cardlock
Northwest Blvd
1411 Northwest Blvd
Creston, BC V0B 1G6

Flying J Cardlock
Alaska Ave
1725 Alaska Ave
Dawson Creek, BC V1G 1P5

Flying J Cardlock
Alaska Hwy
9407 109th Street
Fort St. John, BC V1J 6K6

Flying J
Hwy 1 Exit 168
63100 Flood Hope Road
Hope, BC V0X 1L2
Subway, Hot Food & Pizza

Flying J Dealer
Kokanee Way
175 Kokanee Way
Kamloops, BC V2C 6Z2
Billy Miner's Roadhouse

Flying J Cardlock
Braid St
24 Braid Street
New Westminster, BC V3L 3P3

Flying J Fuel Stop
Continental Way
4869 Continental Way
Prince George, BC V2N 5S5

Flying J Cardlock
Marine Way
8655 Boundary Road
Vancouver, BC V5S 4H3

MANITOBA

Flying J
Hwy #1 & Camp Manitou Rd.
4100 Portage Ave
Headingley, MB R4H 1C5
Denny's, Hot Food & Pizza

Flying J Fuel Stop
Hwy 1 East
Highway 1 East
Portage La Prairie, MB R1N 3B2

Flying J Cardlock
Hwy 59
131 Warman Road & Hwy 59
Winnipeg, MB R2J 3R3

Flying J Fuel Stop
Brookside Blvd
1747 Brookside Blvd
Winnipeg, MB R2C 2E8

ONTARIO

Flying J
Hwy 401 & Hwy 97 Exit 268
2492 Cedar Creek Road
Ayr, ON N0B 1E0
Papa Joe's Hot Kettle

Flying J Dealer
Hwy 401 Exit 825
6115 4th Line Road
Bainsville, ON K0C 1E0

Flying J Cardlock
Sinclair Blvd
11 Sinclair Blvd
Brantford, ON N3S 7X6

Flying J Dealer
Hwy 401 Exit 730
2085 Shanly Road
Cardinal, ON K0E 1E0

Flying J Fuel Stop
Hwy 27
1765 Albion Road
Etobicoke, ON M9W 5S7

Flying J
QEW Exit 5
1637 Pettit Road
Ft. Erie, ON L2A 5M4
Denny's, Hot Food & Pizza

Flying J Fuel Stop
Government Road
410 Government Road East
Kapuskasing, ON P5N 2X7
Hot Food & Pizza

Flying J
Hwy 401
20382 Old Highway #2
Lancaster, ON K0C 1N0
Denny's

Flying J
HWY 401 & Highbury Ave. Exit 189
3700 Highbury Ave. South
London, ON N6N 1P3
Denny's, Hot Food & Pizza

Flying J Fuel Stop
Britannia Rd
1400 Britannia Road
Mississauga, ON L4W 1C8
Hot Food & Pizza

Flying J
401 & Cnty Rd 41 Exit 579
628 County Road #41 RR6
Napanee, ON K7R 3L1
Denny's, Hot Food & Pizza

Flying J Dealer
Hwy 401
2000 Clements Road
Pickering, ON L1W 4A1
Hot Food & Pizza

Flying J Cardlock
Great Northern Rd
987 Great Northern Road
Sault Ste Marie, ON P6A 5K7

Flying J Dealer
Hwy 11/17 @ Hwy 587
3200 Hwy 11/17
Shuniah, ON P0T 2M0

Flying J Cardlock
Duhamel Rd
17 Duhamel Road
Sudbury, ON P3E 4N1

Pilot Travel Center
Hwy 401 Exit 56
19325 Essex County Road 42
Tilbury, ON N0P2L0
Subway

Flying J Dealer
Hwy 402 Exit 25
5906 Oil Heritage Road
Wyoming, ON N0N 1T0

QUÉBEC

Flying J Dealer
Ave Gilles Villeneuve
1181 Ave Gilles Villeneuve
Berthierville, QC J0K 1A0

Flying J Dealer
Hwy 15 Exit 21
1 Rang Saint Andre
Napierville, QC J0J 1L0
Hot Food & Pizza

Flying J Dealer
152 Highway 20
569 Rue Principlae
Sainte Helene de Bagot, QC J0H 1M0
Hot Food & Pizza

SASKATCHEWAN

Flying J Dealer
Hwy 11 & Hwy 44 Junction
Hwy 11 & Hwy 44 Junction
Davidson, SK S0G 1A0

Flying J Fuel Stop
Hwy 1
370 North Service Road
Moose Jaw, SK S6H 4N9
Hot Food & Pizza

Flying J Fuel Stop
Ross Ave East
1511 Ross Ave East
Regina, SK S4R 1J2

Flying J
3850 Idylwylde Drive North
3850 Idylwyld Dr. N.
Saskatoon, SK S7P 0A1
Denny's

Flying J Cardlock
Hwy 16A Bypass on York
191 York Road West
Yorkton, SK S3N 2W8

MILITARY LISTINGS

The following listings are for military camping facilities where active and retired members of the military (and civilian Department of Defense employees) may camp. Please note that this does not include veterans, but only those people who are career-military personnel. These facilities require proper identification from the appropriate branch of the armed forces for admittance. If you are unsure of your eligibility to camp at a listed facility, please call ahead.

In addition, all listed facilities and any or all information about them are subject to change. Again, it is advisable to telephone ahead for verification. Telephone numbers are included in each listing.

ALABAMA

Alexander City

LAKE MARTIN MAXWELL/GUNTER REC AREA (Maxwell AFB) Off base. From Jct of I-85 & Exit 32/AL-49 (E of Montgomery), N on AL-49 to CR-34 (Stillwater Rd), W 2.5 mi, follow signs. Good paved interior rds. No pets. SITES: 64 gravel, 66 full hookups, 10W, 10E (30/50 amps), 12 tent. FAC: Restrooms & showers, dump, laundry. REC: Lake Martin Reservoir: fishing, swimming, boating: marina, rentals. Playground. Last year's rates $12 to $18, reservations accepted. Min. 2 nights stay. V, MC (334) 953-3509

Fort Rucker

RUCKER OUTDOOR REC AREA (Fort Rucker) On base. Jan to Dec. From Jct of US-231 & Andrew Ave, (L) on Andrew to Ozark gate, right on first street through gate, right on Whittaker, right on Christian Rd, right at sign. Fair dirt interior rds. No pets. SITES: 18 grass with patios, 18W, 18E (30 amps). FAC: Restrooms & showers, dump. REC: Golf, archery, pistol range. Last year's rates $12 to $15, call for availability. (334) 255-4305

Huntsville

REDSTONE ARSENAL CAMPGROUND (Redstone Arsenal) On base. Water in winter. From Jct of I-65 & I-565, E 15 mi on I-565 to Jordan Ln (Patton Rd) S 2 mi to Gate 10; Gate is open 5am to 12am. Good paved interior rds. SITES: 48 paved, 48 full hookups (20/30/50 amps). FAC: Restrooms & showers, REC: Tennessee River: boating, ramp. Playground, rec field, pavilions. Rigs over 30' will have problems. Last year's rates $20, call for availability. (256) 876-6854/4868

Montgomery

MAXWELL/GUNTER FAMCAMP (Maxwell AFB) On base. From Jct of I-85S & I-65, I-85S to Day St or I-65N to Herron exit, to Bell St. Good paved interior rds. SITES: 56 paved, 56 full hookups (30/50 amps) w/patios, 4W, 4E. FAC: Restrooms & showers, dump, phone, laundry, grill, WiFi. REC: Rec hall, rec field, rec equip rental, golf. Last year's rates $18, $10 overflow, call for availability. (334) 953-5161

ALASKA

Anchorage

BLACK SPRUCE ARMY TRAVEL CAMP (Fort Richardson) On base. May 1 to Oct 1. From AK1/Glenn Hwy & main gate entrance (NE Anchorage), N to main gate, follow "D" St, E 100 yds on Otter Loop Rd (L). Good gravel interior rds. SITES: 40 gravel, mostly shaded, 39 full hookups, 4W, 4E (30 amps), 7 tent. FAC: Restrooms & showers, dump, laundry, phone. REC: Upper Otter Lake: fishing, boating: rental, rec equip rental, golf. Last year's rates $15 to $18, no reservations. (907) 384-1476/7740

ELMENDORF FAMCAMP (Elmendorf AFB) On base. May to Sep. From Jct of Glenn Hwy & Muldoon exit, N 200 ft (E). Good gravel interior rds. SITES: 60 gravel, 60W, 60E. (30/50 amps), 8 tents. Mostly shaded. 14 day max stay. FAC: Dump, restrooms & showers, laundry, phone. REC: Hiking, playground, tour boats. Last year's rates $18, no reservations. Note: Camping may be restricted to active duty participants when full. (907) 552-2023

Fairbanks

BIRCH LAKE REC AREA (Eielson AFB) Off base. May 28 to Sep 6. From base, S 38 mi on AK-2/Richardson Hwy at milepost 305. Good dirt interior rds. SITES: 40 gravel, 34E (30 amps), 22 cabins, 14 tent. FAC: Restrooms & showers. REC: Birch Lake: trout fishing, boating: ramp, dock rental. Playground, pavilion. Last year's rates $18, reservations accepted, 8-day cancellation policy. (907) 488-6161

EIELSON FAMCAMP (Eielson AFB) On base. May 15 to Sep 7. From Fairbanks, NW 26 mi on Richardson Hwy. Good dirt interior rds. SITES: 41 paved, 41W, 41E (30 amps). 14 day max stay. FAC: Dump. Last year's rates $16, call for availability. (907) 377-1232

Seward

SEWARD MILITARY REC RESORT (Fort Richardson) Off base. May 15 to Sep 15. On AK-9/Seward Hwy, (R) S end of town. Fair paved interior rds. SITES: 40 gravel, 40W, 40E (30 amps) 15 tent, 1 cabin. Some shaded. 14 day max stay. FAC: Restrooms & showers, dump, laundry, phone, WiFi. REC: Tackle, tour boat, rec hall, billiards, playground. Last year's rates $23 to $27, call for availability. V, MC. (907) 224-2659/2654

ARIZONA

Flagstaff

FORT TUTHILL REC AREA (Luke AFB) Off base May 1 to Oct 15. Elev: 7000 ft. From Jct of I-17 & Flagstaff Airport Rd/ Exit 337, W on Flagstaff Airport Rd thru intersection of US-89A & Fort Tuthill Rd, straight to rec area. Good gravel interior rds. SITES: 34 gravel, 27W, 27E (20/30 amps), 13 tent. FAC: Restrooms & showers, dump, laundry, ltd groceries, WiFi. REC: Playground, rec field. Last year's rates $12 to $14, reservations recommended. (928) 774-8893

Fort Huachuca

APACHE FLATS CAMPGROUND (Fort Huachuca). On base. Elev: 5000 feet. From Jct of I-10 & AZ-90, S 25 mi on AZ-90 to main gate & follow signs. Good, paved interior rds. SITES: 50 paved, 50 full hookups (30/50 amps), CATV, BBQ's & picnic tables. FAC: Restrooms & showers, laundry, propane site. REC: Support activities, rec facilities, commissary. Last year's rates $14. Reservations highly recommended. (520) 533-1335

Gila Bend

GILA BEND FAMCAMP (Gila Bend AF Auxiliary Field) Off base. From Jct of I-10 & AZ-85/ Exit 112, S 45 mi on AZ-85 to Gila Bend AFAF/Ajo sign, W 4.5 mi (L). Good dirt interior rds. SITES: 40 gravel pull-thrus with patios, 37 full hookups (15/30/50 amps). FAC: Free laundry. REC: Fitness area, tennis, basketball, jogging. Last year's rates $7, no reservations. (928) 683-5290/6238.

Tucson

AGAVE GULCH FAMCAMP (Davis-Monthan AFB) On base. W-bnd: From Jct of I-10 & Kolb Rd exit 270, N 6 mi on Kolb Rd to Golf Links Rd, W 2 mi to Craycroft Ave, left to base, through main gate to Quijota Blvd, E .75 mi (R); E-bnd: From Jct of I-10 & Alvernon Way exit 265, S 4 mi on Alvernon Way (becomes Golf Links Rd.) to Craycroft Ave, E to gate. Good paved interior rds. SITES: 162 paved, 144 full hookups (20/30/50 amps). 14 day max stay. FAC: Restrooms & showers, dump, laundry, WiFi. REC: Rec hall, rec field, golf, archery, skeet, tennis. Rec equip rental. Last year's rates $16. No reservations. (520) 747-9144

Yuma

DESERT BREEZE TRAVEL CAMP (Yuma Proving Ground). On base. From Jct I-8 & So. Fortuna Ave, N 2 mi to US-95 (R) 10.5 mi to Imperial Dam Rd. main gate (L) 5.2 mi. Good paved interior rds, 2 pet limit. SITES: 115 gravel, 113 full hookups, 2W, 2E (20/30/50) amps), CATV. FAC: Restrooms, showers, laundry, dump, rec hall, WiFi. REC: Swimming, horseshoes, playground, tennis. Last year's rates $10 to $25. V, MC. No reservations. (928) 328-3989

MARTINEZ LAKE RECREATION AREA (MCAS Yuma). Off base. From town, NE 32 mi to Martinez Lake Rd turnoff, 7 mi to Red Cloud Mine Rd, rt 2.5 mi, follow signs. Good paved interior rds. SITES: 20 dirt, 20W, 20E (20/30/50 amps). FAC: Restrooms & showers. REC: Boat and fishing rentals, fishing, swimming, horseshoes, playground, picnic area. Last year's rates $12. Reservations accepted. (928) 269-2262

ARKANSAS

Fort Chaffee

CHAFFEE TRAILER PARK (Fort Chaffee) On base. From Jct of I-40 & I-540, S 2 mi on I-540 to AR-22/Rogers Ave, E thru Barling to base. Fair gravel interior rds. SITES: 39 grass/gravel, full hookups (20/30/50 amps), 12 cabins. FAC: Restrooms & showers, laundry. REC: Last year's rates $8.50, reservations for cabins only, V, D, MC, AmX. (479) 484-2252/2917

Jacksonville

LITTLE ROCK FAMCAMP (Little Rock AFB) On base. At Jct of US-67/167 & AFB exit (in town). Good paved interior rds. SITES: 8 paved, 10 grass, 6 gravel 10 full hookups (30/50 amps) 14W, 14E 6 tent. FAC: Restrooms & showers, laundry, dump. REC: Playground, rec field, golf, tennis. Last year's rates $12, no reservations. (501) 987-3365

CALIFORNIA

El Centro

EL CENTRO NAF CAMPGROUND (El Centro Naval Air Facility) On base. From Jct of I-8 & Forester Rd to Evan Hewen, left, to Bennet Rd, N 0.75 mi (R) Register at bldg. 318. Good paved interior rds. SITES: 91 paved, 82 full hookups, (30/50 amps). FAC: Restrooms & showers, laundry, dump, compost space. REC: Pool, rec field, racquet sports, volleyball, mini-golf course, batting cage, bowling alley, rec equip. RV lounge, fitness ctr, All Hands Club, auto hobby, library. Last year's rates $18, Reservations accepted 30 days in advance. (760) 339-2486

Fairfield

TRAVIS FAMCAMP (Travis AFB) On base. From Jct of 1-80 & Fairfield Airbase Pkwy, E 8 mi on Airbase Pkwy to Main Gate (R). Good paved interior rds. SITES: 72 gravel, 72 full hookups (30/50 amps), 4 tent, CATV. FAC: Restrooms & showers, laundry, dump. REC: Fitness center, shopping, hospital, gas station. Last year's rates $17, reservations accepted 30 days in advance. (707) 424-3583

Lemoore

NAS LEMOORE CAMPGROUNDS (NAS Lemoore) On base. From Jct 99 & 198, E on 198 19 mi to main gate, right at traffic light, .5 mi to Ranger Ave, left .25 mi. Good paved interior rds. SITES: 18 paved, 18 full hookups (30/50 amps), CATV. FAC: Restrooms & showers, dump, laundry, RV storage. REC: Pool, horseshoes, basketball, volleyball, playground, gym. Last year's rates $25, reservations accepted. V, MC (559) 998-0837/0838

Lompoc

VANDENBERG FAMCAMP (Vandenberg AFB) On base. From Jct of US-101 & CA-1, W on CA-1. Good paved interior rds. SITES: 49 paved, 49 full hookups (20/50 amps), 20 tent. FAC: Restrooms & showers, dump, laundry, ltd RV supplies, limited WiFi. REC: Adult lounge, rec hall, playground, rec field. Last year's rates $20 to $22, no reservations. (805) 606-8579

Marysville

BEALE FAMCAMP (Beale AFB) Off base. From Marysville, S 1 mi on US-70 to N Beale Rd exit, E 6 mi. Good paved interior rds. SITES: 44 paved, 41 full hookups (30/50 amps). FAC: Dump, laundry, WiFi. REC: Rec hall, golf, skeet, playground. Last year's rates $14 to $19, reservations accepted. (530) 634-3382

Monterey

MONTEREY PINES (NSA Monterey Bay) On base. From Jct of Hwy 18 and Casaverde Rd, W 5 mi to Fairgrounds Rd, N .2 mi (L). Good paved interior roads. SITES: 30 paved, 30 full hookups (30/50 amps) 8W, 8E. 14 day max stay. FAC: Restrooms & showers, laundry, WiFi. REC: Boat ramp, pool. Last years rates $26 to $30, reservations recommended. V, MC. (831)656-7563

Oceanside

LAKE O'NEILL REC PARK (MCB Camp Pendleton) On base. From Jct of I-5N & Camp Pendleton exit, to Vandergrift Blvd, NE 12 mi. Good paved interior rds. SITES: 61 paved, 18 full hookups, 43W, 43E (30 amps), 77 tent. FAC: Restrooms & showers, dump. REC: Lake O'Neill: fishing, bait, boat rental, horseshoes, rec field, playground, miniature golf. Last year's rates $20 to $25.V, MC, D. Reservations accepted. (760) 725-5611

Oxnard

FAIRWAY RV RESORT (Port Hueneme) On base. From Jct of Hwy 1 & Wooley Rd., W 1 mi on Wooley Rd. to S. Ventura Rd, S 1.5 mi to Cutting Rd. (E) Good paved interior roads. SITES: 34 paved, 34 full hookups (30/50 amps), CATV, 30 day max stay. FAC: Restrooms and showers, dump. REC: Boat ramp, pool, playground, swimming. Last year's rates $30 to $34. Reservations recommended. (805) 982-6123

POINT MUGU REC AREA (NAS Point Mugu) On base. From Jct of Hwy 101 & Las Posas Rd, S 5 mi on Las Posas Rd. Good paved interior rds. SITES: 71 paved, 71 full hookups (30/50 amps), 10 tent. FAC: Laundry, WiFi. REC: Ocean: fishing. Last year's rates $23 to $27, reservations accepted. (805) 989-8407

Rosamond

EDWARDS FAMCAMP (Edwards AFB) On base. From Jct of Hwy 14 & Edwards AFB exit/Rosamond Blvd, E 18 mi on Rosamond Blvd, follow signs. From Barstow, NW 40 mi on CA-58, follow signs. Good paved interior rds. SITES: 25 paved, 25 full hookups (30/50 amps), 4 tent. FAC: Restrooms & showers. REC: Rec field, rec equip rental, golf. Last year's rates $15 to $25. No reservations. (661) 275-2267

Ridgecrest

SIERRA VISTA RV PARK (NAWS China Lake) Check in at outdoor recreation office, Bldg 21; then return to N Richmond Rd and go left; then turn right onto Nimitz Ave & then immediate left on to Halsey St (L). FAC: 60 paved, 60 full hkups (30/50 amps), WiFi Hotspot, restrooms & showers, dump, laundry, commissary. REC: Swimming, fitness center, golf, hiking. Pets OK, big rig sites, 30 day max stay. Reservations accepted. (877) 628-9233.

San Clemente

SAN ONOFRE REC BEACH (MCB Camp Pendleton) On base. From Jct of I-5 & Basilone Rd exit, E 1.6 mi on Basilone Rd. Good paved interior rds. SITES: 46 paved, 51 dirt, 46 sand, 46 full hookups, 97W, 97E (15/30/50 amps), 46 tent. FAC: Restrooms & showers, dump. REC: Ocean, playground, rec field. Last year's rates $30 to $40. Reservations accepted. (760) 763-7873

DEL MAR BEACH RV PARK (MCB Camp Pendleton) On base. From S I-5 exit Camp Pendleton, from N I-5 exit Oceanside to main gate. From main gate to Wire Mountain Rd., left to 12th St., left to end. SITES: 81 Full Hookup sites, 42 paved, 39 dirt. Seasonal: Summer (April–Oct. 31) Winter (Nov.1–March 31) Last year's rates $40 to $55 Reservations Call: (760) 725-2134/2313 or Fax: (760) 725-2396 or online www.mccscp.com.

San Diego

ADMIRAL BAKER FIELD CAMPGROUND (NAS San Diego) On base. From Jct I-8 at Friars Road, follow Friars Rd (E) to Santo Rd left, then right on Admiral Baker Road, park entrance on right. Good paved interior roads. SITES: 48 paved, 48 full hookups (20/30/50 amps), CATV. FAC: Restrooms, showers, laundry, dump, WiFi. REC: Pool, tennis, horseshoes, basketball, rec field, playground. Last year's rates $30 to $35. V, MC ,D, AmX. Reservations accepted. (619) 487-0090

FIDDLERS COVE RV PARK (NAS North Island) On base. From Jct of Hwy 75 & Orange Ave. to base entrance (E). Good paved interior roads. SITES: 50 paved, 2 tent, 47W, 47E (30 amps). FAC: Restrooms & showers, dump, WiFi $. REC: Fishing, swimming, playground. Last year's rates $22 to $28. Reservations accepted. (619) 522-8680

San Luis Obispo

CAMP SAN LUIS OBISPO RV PARK (San Luis Obispo) On base. From Jct of US 101 & CA-1 NW 5 mi on CA-1 Good gravel interior rds. No pets. SITES: 12 grass, 12W, 4S, 12E, (20/30 amps), some shaded. 30 day max stay. FAC: Restrooms & showers, dump, laundry, groceries. REC: Playground. Last year's rates $20 to $23. V, MC, AmX. Reservations accepted. (805) 594-6500

Stockton

SHARPE TRAVEL CAMP (Lanthrop USMRA) On base. From Jct of I-5 & Roth Rd, E on Roth Rd to depot (R) Good paved interior rds. SITES: 20 gravel, 20 full hookups (30/50 amps), some shaded. FAC: Restrooms & showers, laundry. REC: Pool, playground, gym, rec field, picnic area, racquetball, tennis, rec equip. rental. Last year's rates $12, Golden Age/Access accepted. No reservations. (209) 639-1016

Twentynine Palms

TWILIGHT DUNES (MCAGCC 29 Palms) On base. From Jct I-10 & SR-62, N 20 mi, L at Adobe Rd. 3 mi to main gate, right 1.25 mi to traffic signal, right to Sunshine Peak Rd., left to entrance. Good paved interior roads. SITES: 75 paved, 75 full hookups (15/30/50 amps), CATV. FAC: Laundry, dump, no restrooms, store. REC: Pool, tennis, basketball, more nearby. Last year's rates $20. V, MC, D, AmX. Reservations accepted. (760) 830-6573

COLORADO

Colorado Springs

FARISH REC AREA (USAF Academy) Off base. Elev 9150. Limited winter facilities. From Jct of I-25 & US-24, W on US-24 to Woodland Park, N 6 mi on Rampart Range Rd, follow signs. Call ahead due to weather. CAUTION: RVs over 26 ft call for special directions. SITES: 15 gravel, 15E (20/30 amps), 15 tent, 15 cabins. FAC: Restrooms & showers, groceries, pit toilets. REC: Lakes: fishing & ice fishing. Rec equip, playground, cross-country skiing. Limited winter camping, cabins only. Last year's rates $15 to $25. Reservations - highly recommended. (719) 687-9098

PEREGRINE PINES FAMILY CAMPING (USAF Academy) On base. From Jct. of I-25 & North Gate Blvd (exit 156), W 1 mi. on North Gate Blvd, to Stadium Blvd, NW 1.3 mi on Stadium Blvd. to base entrance (L) Good paved interior roads. SITES: 105 full hookups (30/50 amps), 8 tent. FAC: Restrooms & showers, dump, laundry, community room, WiFi. REC: Swimming, playground, horseshoes, pool, pet restrictions, no open fires. Last year's rates $16 to $18. Reservations highly recommended. (719) 333-4356/4980

FLORIDA

Destin

DESTIN ARMY INFANTRY CENTER REC AREA (Fort Benning) Off base. From Jct of Hwy 98 & Benning Dr, N 1 mi on Benning Dr to Calhoon Ave (E). Good paved interior rds. SITES: 46 sites, 46 full hookups (30/50 amps), CATV. FAC: Restrooms & showers, laundry, phone, WiFi $. REC: Bay fishing, swimming, boat marina, launch & rentals, pool, playground, pavilion, picnic area, rec & water sports equip. rental. Last year's rates $19. Reservations accepted up to 4 mos. in advance. (800) 642-0466 or (850) 837-6423

Hurlburt Field

HURLBURT FAMCAMP (Hurlburt AFB) Off base. US-98 E of main gate to Hurlburt AFT, 100 yds on left. SITES: 50 paved, 50 full hookups (30/50 amps), 10 tent. FAC: Restrooms & showers, dump, laundry, ltd groceries. REC: Golf, picnic area, tennis, rec fields, water sports, boating rentals. Last year's rates $20. V, MC. No reservations. (850) 884-6939

Key West

SIGSBEE RV PARK (Key West NAS) On base. From Jct of US-1 & N Roosevelt Blvd, 1 mi on N Roosevelt Blvd to Kennedy St, turn right. Good paved interior rds. SITES: 70 paved, 90 full hookups (30/50 amps), 300 tent, handicap access. 14 day max stay. FAC: Restrooms & showers, laundry, phone, grills, ice. REC: Gulf: boating, fishing, swimming, paddle boats, playground, marina, rentals. Adult lounge, rec field. Last year's rates $21 to $23, reservations accepted up to 30 days in advance from active duty only. (305) 293-4432/4433

Melbourne

MANATEE COVE CAMPGROUND (Patrick AFB) On base. From Jct of I-95 & Wickham Rd (exit 73), E 3 mi on Wickham Rd to FL-404 (Pineda Causeway) to S Patrick Dr. Fair gravel interior rds. SITES: 80 gravel, 80W, 80E (20/30/50 amps) 47S, 5 tent. FAC: Restrooms & showers, dump, laundry, email. REC: Banana River: fishing. Golf, skeet, playground, boat rentals, swimming, biking. Last year's rates $9 to $15. Reservations accepted up to 30 days in advance from Active Duty only. (321) 494-4787

Niceville

EGLIN FAMCAMP (Eglin AFB) On base. From Jct of I-10 & FL-85, S 18 mi on FL-85 to John Simms Pkwy, follow signs. Good paved interior rds. SITES: 22 gravel, 20W, 20E (30/50 amps), 20 tent, CATV. FAC: Restrooms & showers, dump, laundry. REC: Gulf: boating, ramp, marina, rentals. Rec field, playground, golf, rec equip rental. Last year's rates $20, no reservations. Call for availability. (850) 883-1243

MID BAY SHORES MAXWELL/ GUNTER REC AREA (Maxwell AFB) Off base. Lower rates in winter. From Jct of Rte 85 & I-10, S 20 mi on Rte 85 to Hwy 20, E 8 mi to SR-293, S 1 mi to White Point Rec Area/Lake Pippin sign (R). Good paved/gravel interior rds. SITES: 26 gravel, 26 full hookups, 6W, 6E (30/50 amps). Mostly shaded. No pets. FAC: Restrooms & showers, dump, laundry. REC: Lake, swimming, boat launch, canoe rental, fishing, picnic area, playground. Call for rates, reservations accepted. (334) 953-3509.

Orange Park

JACKSONVILLE RV PARK (NAS Jacksonville) on base. From Jct of I-95 & I-295, S 10 mi on I-295 to 17N, N 3 mi to Yorktown gate (E). Good paved/gravel interior rds. SITES: 28 full hookups, 9 partial (water, elec), 7 primitive 11W, 11E (30/50 amps) 8 tent. Mostly shaded. 14 day max stay. FAC: Free laundry, restrooms & showers, grills, dump, WiFi $. REC: St. John's River: fishing, boat marina, picnic area. Call for rates, reservations recommended. (904) 542-3227

Panama City

SHADY PINES PANAMA CITY CSS OUTDOOR REC/MARINA (Panama City Coastal Systems Station) On base. In Panama City Beach, on US-98 at W end of Hathaway Bridge (L). SITES: 45 paved, 45 full hookups (30/50 amps). FAC: Restrooms & showers, ice, snacks, WiFi. REC: Gulf, St. Andrews Bay, beach, swimming, fishing, windsurfing, boating: ramp, marina rental. Pool, playground, rec field. Camp & rec equip rental, snacks. Last year's rates $10 to $18. Reservations required. (850) 234-4402

RAPTOR RANCH (Tyndall AFB) On base. From Jct of US-231 & US-98, E 11 mi on US-98. Good gravel interior rds. SITES: 100 paved, 62 full hookups, 16 overflow 54W/E (30/50 amps), FAC: CATV, restrooms & showers, grills, dump, laundry, WIFI. REC: Gulf, boating: marina, swimming, rental. Shuffleboard, playground, rec field, golf, stables, archery, skeet, tennis. Last year's rates $15 to $19, no reservations for campsites. (850) 283-2798

Pensacola

BLUE ANGEL NAVY REC PARK (Corry Station) Off base. From Jct of I-10 & Exit 2, S 1.5 mi on Hwy 297 to SR-173 (Blue Angel Pkwy), S 8 mi to US-98, W 3 mi (L) SITES: 83 dirt, 34 concrete 83W, 83E (30/50 amps), 5 tent. FAC: Restrooms & showers, dump, laundry, metered gas. REC: Perdido Bay, fishing, swimming, boating, boat rental, playground, paintball, tackle, fishing (license available). Camp & rec equip rental. Last year's rates $12 to $19. No reservations for campsites. (850) 453-9435/4530

OAK GROVE TRAILER PARK (Pensacola NAS) On base. From Jct of I-10 & R297S (Pine Forest), take R297S to Blue Angel Pkwy (R173S), enter through back gate. Fair gravel interior rds. 81 SITES: 56 gravel, 56 full hookups (30/50 amps), 8 tent. FAC: Restrooms & showers, dump, WiFi $. REC: Gulf, boating: ramp, marina, fishing, swimming, rentals. Last year's rates $19 to $29, reservations required. (850) 452-2535

Tampa

RACCOON CREEK REC AREA (Mac Dill AFB) On base. From Jct of I-275 & Dale Mabry (Exit 23B), S 5 mi on Dale Mabry. Fair paved interior rds. SITES: 346 full hookups 36W, 36E (30/50 amps), CATV. FAC: Restrooms & showers, dump, laundry, ice, snacks, propane. REC: Tampa Bay, fishing, boating: ramp, marina, rental. Pool, playground, rec field, golf. Last year's rates $9 to $18, reservations recommended up to 1 year in advance. V, MC. (813) 840-6919 or (800) 821-4982 (toll-free)

GEORGIA

Appling

POINTES WEST ARMY RESORT (Fort Gordon) Off base. From Jct of I-20 & GA-47, N 15 mi on GA-47 to Rte 104, 1.5 mi. Good paved interior rds. SITES: 90 gravel, 75 full hookups (30/50 amps) 65 tents. FAC: Restrooms & showers, ltd groceries, snacks. REC: Thurmond Lake, playground. Last year's rates $10 to $18. Now accepting reservations. (706) 541-1057

Cartersville

LAKE ALLATOONA ARMY REC AREA (Fort McPherson) Off base. From Jct of I-75N & Exit 283E, E 2.7 mi on exit rd. Good paved interior rds. No pets. SITES: 12 paved, 12 full hookups (30 amps), 15 tent, 28 cabins, CATV. FAC: Restrooms & showers, dump, laundry, phone, ltd groceries. REC: Lake Allatoona: boating, ramp, marina, fishing, swimming, mini-golf, hiking trails. Rec hall, playground, pavilions. Last year's rates $14 to $20, reservations required only for cabins. (770) 974-3413/9420

Fort Benning

UCHEE CREEK ARMY CAMPGROUND & MARINA (Fort Benning) S on I-85 through Columbus to end on Fort Benning, W 1 mi on First Division Rd. to Dixie Rd., S 2.8 mi to Uchee Creek Rd., N 1.5 mi (L). Good paved interior rds. SITES: 85 paved, patios, most shaded, 8 pull-thrus (30x60), back-ins (30x60), big rig sites, 85 full hookups (30/50 amps), CATV, phone each site, 61 rental units. FAC: Rally site for 200 rigs with trail vehicle, activity site with seating for 500. Restrooms & shower, dump, security, public phone, laundry, ltd groceries, ltd RV supplies, LP gas, WIFI $. REC: Chattahoochee River: freshwater fishing, tackle, boating: ramp, dock, marina, rentals. Golf, basketball, volleyball, pool, horseshoes, rec hall, playground, rec field. Last year's rates $12 to $19. V, MC, AmX. Reservations accepted. (706) 545-4053/7238

Hinesville

HOLBROOK POND REC AREA & CAMPGROUND (Fort Stewart) On base. From Jct of I-95 & Exit 15, W 17 mi on Hwy 144 to Brown Holbrook Recreation Area, follow sign (L). Good dirt interior rds. SITES: 20 sites, 20W, 20E (30/50 amps), 20 tent. Mostly shaded. FAC: Restrooms & showers, dump, laundry, phone. REC: Boating, boat rental, fishing, golf, volleyball, skeet/trap range, pavilions, picnic area, playgrounds. Last year's rates $15, reservations accepted. (912) 435-8205/8209

Valdosta

GRASSY POND REC AREA (Moody AFB) Off base. From Jct of I-75 & GA-376 (exit 5), W on GA-376 to Loch Laurel Rd, turn left and follow signs to gate, N 1.8 mi. Good paved interior rds. SITES: 39 gravel, 39 full hookups (30/50 amps). FAC: Restrooms & showers, dump, laundry, phone, snacks. REC: Grassy Pond: bass fishing, tackle, boating. Playgrounds. Last year's rates $13 to $16. No reservations (229) 559-5840

Warner-Robins

ROBINS FAMCAMP (Robins AFB) On base. From Jct of I-129 & GA-247 (at Warner Robins), E 7 mi on GA-247. Good paved interior rds. SITES: 18 gravel, 18 full hook ups (20/30 amps), 3 tent. FAC: Restrooms & showers. REC: Luna Lake, playground. Last year's rates $12, 7 spaces can be reserved. (478) 926-4500

IDAHO

Mountain Home

MOUNTAIN HOME FAMCAMP (Mtn Home AFB) On base. From Jct of I-84 & ID-67, SW 12 mi on ID-67. Good paved interior rds. SITES: 22 paved, some shaded, 22 full hookups, (20/30 amps) 6 tent. FAC: Restrooms & showers, dump laundry. REC: Playground, skeet, golf. Rec equip rent horseshoes,pool, tennis, gym. Last year's rates $12 to $14 no reservations. (208) 828-6333

ILLINOIS

Bellville

SCOTT FAMCAMP (Scott AFB) On base. From Jct of I-64 & SR-158, S 1 mi on SR-158 to base (L). Good paved interior rds. SITES: 12 paved, 10 dirt, many tent, 22W, 22E (30 amps). Mostly shaded. FAC: Restrooms & showers, dump, ltd groceries, laundry. REC: Picnic area, rec field, tennis, Scott Lake fishing, racquet sports, skeet/trap range, rec. equip. rental. Last year's rates $15, reservations recommended. (618) 256-2067

INDIANA

Taylorsville

CAMP ATTERBURY (Indiana Nat'l Guard) On base. Apr to Oct. From Jct I-65 & 31, Exit 76B N to Hwy 31 (Hospital Road/252) approx. 3 mi to main camp entrance, E one block. Good gravel interior rds. SITES: 33 gravel, 33 full hookups (30/50 amps), 2 cabins, tables, grills. FAC: Restrooms & showers, laundry, dump, ice, wood, internet, cabins. REC: Pool, basketball, volleyball, gym, rentals. Last year's rates $15 to $17, reservations accepted. MC, V, D, AmX (812) 526-1298

KENTUCKY

Louisville

CAMP CARLSON ARMY TRAVEL CAMP (Fort Knox) Off base. From Jct of I-65 & I-264, W 9.5 mi on I-264 to US-31W, S 20 mi to US-60, W 2.5 mi (R). Fair gravel interior rds. SITES: 35 gravel, 53 full hookups, 18W, 18E (30/50 amps), 10 cabins. FAC: Restrooms & showers, dump, laundry, ice. REC: Playground, rec field. Last year's rates $15 to $18, no reservations. (502) 624-4836

LOUISIANA

Leesville

TOLEDO BEND REC SITE (Fort Polk) Off base. From Leesville, N on US-171 to LA-111, W 15 mi (bear right onto LA-392) to LA-191, N 5 mi to Army Travel Camp sign, W on Army Rec Rd. Good paved interior rds. SITES: 15 gravel, no slide-outs, 13W, 13E (30/50 amps), 12 park mobile homes, 2 cabins. FAC: Restrooms & showers, dump, ltd groceries. REC: Toledo Bend Lake: swimming, beach, boating: ramp, marina, rental. Playground, rec field. Last year's rates $15, reservations accepted. (888) 718-9088 or (318) 531-1974

Shreveport

BARKSDALE FAMCAMP (Barksdale AFB) On base. From Jct I-20 and US-71, S on US-71 to base entrance. Good paved interior rds. SITES: 42 paved, 36 full hookups (20/30/50 amps), unlimited tent, 6 mobile homes. FAC: Restrooms & showers, dump, groceries, laundry, WiFi. REC: Boat rentals, launch, golf, playground, picnic area, equip rentals, fishing, hunting. Last year's rate $16. Pet restrictions, No reservations for campsites. (318) 456-2679

MARYLAND

Andrews AFB

ANDREWS FAMCAMP (Andrews AFB) On base. From Jct of I-95 & Exit 11A S 0.25 mi on exit rd. SE .5 mi on PA Ave, right on Suitland Pkwy 400 yds (R). Good gravel interior rds. SITES: 47 gravel, 30 full hookups, 14E (30 amps), 30 day max stay. FAC: Restrooms & showers, dump, laundry. REC: Rec hall, horseshoes, modem, rec field, golf. Last year's rates $13 to $16. MC, V. Reservations accepted. (301) 981-3279

Annapolis

ANNAPOLIS FAMCAMP (United States Naval Academy/ Annapolis Naval Station) On base. From Hwys 450 & 648N, N 0.5 mi on 648N to Kinkaid Rd (E) Good gravel interior rds. SITES: 14 paved, 14W, 14E (30 amps). Mostly shaded. FAC: Restrooms & showers, dump, ltd. groceries. REC: Swimming pools, boat marina, boat rental, picnic area, playground, rec field, rec hall, tennis, racquetball, golf, fishing. Last year's rates $18, reservations accepted. (410) 293-9200

Patuxent River

GOOSE CREEK/WEST BASIN REC AREA (NAS Patuxent River) On base. Feb to Nov. From Jct of I-95 (east portion of Capital Beltway, I-495) & Exit 7A, SE on exit rd to Branch Ave S (MD-5), S 25 mi (MD-5 turns onto MD-235), SE 24 mi to NAS (L). SITES: 14 gravel, 14W, 14E (30 amps), 30 tent. FAC: Restrooms & showers, dump, laundry, phone, gas. REC: Pool, playground, picnic area, rec center, pavilion, golf, hunting, waterskiing, swimming, fishing, boating: marina, launch, rentals. Last year's rates $12. V, MC. Reservations required. (301) 342-3648

Prince Frederick

SOLOMONS ISLAND NAVY REC CENTER (NRC Solomons) From Beltway (295) & Exit 11A, S to 4S, S 65 mi to base (E). Good paved/gravel interior rds. SITES: 361 paved/gravel. 146 full hookups, 6W, 6E, (20/30 amps), 29 tent, 62 rentals. Mostly shaded. 7 day max stay April 1 to October 15. FAC: Restrooms & showers, dump, WiFi. REC: Patuxent River, fishing, golf, tennis, swimming, pool, boat marina, launch, rental, rec. field, golf, tennis, racquetball, mini-golf, picnic area, playground, sports equip. rental, pavilions. Call for rates. Reservations required. (410) 286-5529/7301

MASSACHUSETTS

Bedford

HANSCOM FAMCAMP (Hanscom AFB) Off base. May to Oct. From Jct of MA-90 & Exit 128/95N, N 9 mi on Exit 128/95N to Exit 31B, W 0.25 mi to Rte 4/225, turn right 1 mi on Hartwell Ave to McGuire Rd (E). Good paved interior rds. SITES: 21 gravel, 46 paved, 46 full hookups, 21W, 21E, (30/50 amps), 10 tent. FAC: Restrooms & showers, dump, laundry, phone, WiFi. REC: Bowling, swimming, golf, bicycling, rec equip rental. No water Nov. to May. Last year's rates $16 to $18, no reservations. (781) 377-4670

Humarock

FOURTH CLIFF REC AREA (Hanscom AFB) Off base. Only self-contained units in winter. From Jct of I-93 & Rte-3, S 11 mi on Rte-3 to Rte-139 (Exit 12), E 1.5 mi to Marshfield, S 1.5 mi to Furnace St, E 2 mi to Ferry St, S 3.5 mi to Sea St, E 100 yds (over bridge) to Central Ave (bear left). Good paved interior rds. SITES: 11 paved, 11 full hookups (30/50 amps), many tent. FAC: Restrooms & showers, dump, phone, laundry, ice, snacks. REC: Ocean, rec hall, playground. Last year's rates $15 to $25, reservations accepted. (781) 837-6785 or (800) 468-9547

MICHIGAN

Grayling

CAMP GRAYLING TRAILER PARK (Camp Grayling) On base. May to Sep. From Jct of I-75 & MI-72, W 3 mi to Hwy 93, S 3 mi to Main Gate. Good paved interior rds. SITES: 70 grass, 50 full hookups, (20/30/50 amps), 10 tent. FAC: Restrooms & showers free WiFi for 14 days. REC: Lake, fishing, boating. Last year's rates $15, reservations accepted. (989) 348-9033

MISSISSIPPI

Biloxi

KEESLER FAMCAMP (Keesler AFB) Off base. From town, W 3 mi on Pass Rd to Jim Money Rd, N 0.75 mi to Thrower Park Military Housing (E). Good paved interior rds. SITES: 60 paved, 42 full hookups (20/30/50 amps). CATV. FAC: Restrooms & showers, laundry, snacks, ltd groceries. REC: Playground. Last year's rates $20, no reservations. (228) 377-9050

Hattiesburg

LAKE WALKER FAMILY CAMPGROUND (Camp Shelby) On base. From town, S 11 mi on Hwy 49 to Gulf Coast Hwy, S 4 mi to Camp Shelby North Gate Exit (L). SITES: 32 paved, 4 grass, 32 full hookups (30/50 amps). FAC: Restrooms, grills, laundry. REC: Dogwood Lake: fishing. Rec equip rental. Last year's rates $10, no reservations. (601) 558-2397

MISSOURI

Jefferson City

LAKE OF THE OZARKS REC AREA (Fort Leonard Wood) Off base. From Jct of I-70 and Hwy 63, S 21 mi on Hwy 63 to US-54, SW 40 mi to SR-A, E 6 mi to McCubbins Dr, N 5 mi to travel camp. SITES: 38 gravel, 17W, 17E (30/50 amp), 21 tent, 21 cabins, 21 mobile homes, CATV. FAC: Restrooms & showers, dump, laundry. REC: Picnic area, playground, pavilion, swimming, fishing, watersports, boating: rentals. Last year's rates $15. V, MC, AmX. Reservations recommended. (573) 346-5640

MONTANA

Great Falls

GATEWAY FAMCAMP (Malmstrom AFB) On base. May to Oct. From Jct of I-15 & 10th Ave & S exit, E 6 mi on 10th Ave to bypass, follow signs. Fair gravel interior rds. SITES: 55 gravel, 25 full hookups (30/50 amps). FAC: Restrooms & showers, laundry, dump, phone, WiFi. REC: Tennis, swimming, rec field, rec equip avail. Last year's rates $15 to $19, call for availability, no reservations. (406) 731-5140

NEBRASKA

Bellevue

OFFUTT FAMCAMP (Offut AFB) Off base. From Jct of I-80E and Exit 439, follow exit rd/ Rte 755 to Hwy 370E into Bellevue, to

Hancock St (R). Good paved interior rds. SITES: 40 gravel, 40 full hookups (30/50 amps). FAC: Restrooms & showers, free WiFi. REC: Playground, rec field, golf, archery, skeet, tennis. Last year's rates $17, reservations recommended. (402) 294-6311

NEVADA

Fallon

FALLON RV PARK & REC AREA (NAS Fallon) On base. Limited facilities in winter. From town, S 8 mi on US-95 to Union Ln, N to pasture rd, follow signs. Good dirt interior rds. SITES: 32 dirt, 32 full hookups (30/50 amps). FAC: Restrooms & showers, dump, laundry, groceries, WiFi. REC: Fishing, boating, jet skis, pavilion. Last year's rate $15, reservations accepted. (775) 426-2598

Las Vegas

DESERT EAGLE RV PARK (Nellis AFB) Off base. From Jct of I-15 & Craig Rd exit, E 2 mi on Craig Rd to Las Vegas Blvd N, 1.5 mi to N gate, left on Range Road. Good paved interior rds. SITES: 148 paved, 116 full hookups, 32W, 32E, (30/50 amps). FAC: Restrooms & showers, dump, laundry, WIFI. REC: Pool, rec field, rec equip rental, golf. Last year's rates $17 to $21, reservations recommended. (702) 643-3060

NEW MEXICO

Alamogordo

HOLLOMAN FAMCAMP (Holloman AFB) On base. From Jct of US-70 & Mesquite Rd (10 mi SW of town), left 500 ft on Mesquite Rd. Good paved interior rds. SITES: 24 paved, 24 full hookups (30/50 amps) 30 day max stay. FAC: Restrooms & showers, laundry, WiFi. REC: Pool, playground, golf. Last year's rates $20, no reservations. (575) 572-5369

Albuquerque

KIRTLAND FAMCAMP (Kirtland AFB) On base. From Jct of I-40 & Wyoming Blvd (Exit 164, E of Albuquerque), S 3 blks on Wyoming Blvd. Good paved interior rds. SITES: 72 paved, 72 full hookups, (30/50 amps), 24 tent, 14 day max stay. FAC: Restrooms & showers, dump, laundry. REC: Heated pool, playground, rec field, golf, gym, rec center, bowling. Last year's rates $18, no reservations. (505) 846-0337

NEW YORK

West Point

ROUND POND REC AREA (US Military Academy, West Point) Off base. Apr 1 to Oct 30. From Jct of I-87 & US-6 (Exit 16), E on US-6 to NY-293, E 8 mi. Good paved interior rds. SITES: 39 gravel, 28W, 28E (30/50 amps), 20 tent. FAC: 10 cabins, restrooms & showers, dump, laundry, LP gas. REC: Round Pond: fishing. Playground. Last year's rates $15 to $25, reservations accepted. (845) 938-2503/8811

NORTH CAROLINA

Fayetteville

SMITH LAKE ARMY TRAVEL CAMP (Fort Bragg) On base. From Jct of I-95 & Bus Loop 95/US-301/NC-24/87/210, N 8.2 mi on NC-87/210 to SE border of Fort Bragg, continue to Smith Lake sign, right. Gravel interior rds. SITES: 30 gravel, 22 full hookups, 8W, 8E (30/50 amps). 14-day max stay. FAC: Restrooms and showers, dump, laundry, phone, ice. REC: Smith Lake, beach, riding stable, golf. Last year's rates $15 to $20, no alcohol, reservations accepted. (910)396-5979

Havelock

CHERRY POINT MWR FAMCAMP (Cherry Pt MCAS) On base. From Jct of US-70 & NC-101, E 0.1 mi on NC-101 to entrance. SITES: 15 grass, 15 full hookups (30/50 amps). FAC: Dump. REC: Neuse Waterway: fishing, boating: marina, rental. Rec field, tennis, golf, rec equip rental. Last year's rates $15, reservations accepted. (252) 466-2197

Jacksonville

ONSLOW BEACH REC AREA (MCB Camp Lejeune) On base. Apr to Oct. From Jct. US-17 & Hwy 24, E to main gate, S 5 mi on Holcomb Blvd, left on Sneads Ferry Rd, merge w/Hwy 172, left on Beach Rd., over bridge. Gravel interior rds. SITES: 36 gravel/ grass, 36 full hookups (20/30/50 amps), 5 tent. 14 day max stay. FAC: Restrooms & showers, dump, laundry, free WiFi. REC: Basketball, volleyball, horseshoes, playground, rec field, mini-golf. Last year's rates $15. Reservations accepted. MC, V, D, AmX. (910) 440-7502

Wilmington

FORT FISHER AIR FORCE RECREATION AREA (Seymour Johnson AFB) Off base. From Wilmington, S 20 mi on Hwy 421 to Fort Fisher Rec Area sign, W to base. Go to bldg. 118 (E) Good paved interior rds. SITES: 24 full hookups (20/30/50 amps), 50 tent, 40 cottages some shaded. FAC: Restrooms & showers, dump, groceries, laundry. REC: Swimming pool, Jacuzzi, sauna, rec field, enc. rec hall, restaurant, beach, rec equip rental, boat ramp, tennis, gym, racquetball, gift shop, fishing. Call for rates, reservations accepted. (910) 458-6549

NORTH DAKOTA

Grand Forks

GRAND FORKS FAMCAMP (Grand Forks AFB) On base. May 1 to Oct 1. From Grand Forks, W 15 mi on US-2 to Grand Forks Air Force Base exit, N 1 mi to gate (E). Fair paved interior rds. SITES: 21 gravel, 21 full hookups (30/50 amps), 40 tents, CATV. Some shaded. FAC: Restrooms & showers, dump, laundry. REC: Boat rental, playground, bowling alley, golf course, camping & fishing equip. rental, picnic area & theatre. Last year's rates $12, no reservations. (701) 747-3688

Minot

MINOT FAMCAMP (Minot AFB) On base May 15 to Sep 15. From Jct. US-2 & Hwy 83, take Hwy 83 approx 15 mi to Missile Ave, left into base, 2 mi to park entrance on left. Good paved interior rds. SITES: 6 paved, 6W, 6E (30 amps). FAC: Restrooms & showers, dump, commissary. REC: Basketball, volleyball, bowling, playground, gym, equip rental. Last year's rates $7 to $10, MC, V. No reservations. (701) 723-3648

OHIO

Dayton

WRIGHT-PATTERSON FAMCAMP (Wright-Patterson AFB) On base. From Jct of I-75 & Hwy 4, NE 5 mi on Hwy 4 to SR-444, proceed to Gate 12A. SITES: 54 gravel, 40 full hookups, (20/30/50 amps), unlimited tents, CATV. FAC: Dump, gas, phone laundry, showers. REC: Picnic area, playground, rec equip, fishing, boating: rentals. No water in winter. Last year's rates $22 to $23. V, MC. Reservations accepted. (937) 257-2579

OKLAHOMA

Medicine Park

LAKE ELMER THOMAS REC AREA (Fort Sill) On base. From Jct. US-62 & I-44, go NW to Medicine Park exit, take Hwy 49 W 6 miles. Good paved interior rds. SITES: 58 gravel/ grass, 45 pull-thrus, 58 full hookups, (50 amps), 10 tent. FAC: Restrooms & showers, laundry, restaurant, dump, convenience store. REC: Beach swimming, volleyball, horseshoes, mini-golf, waterslide, boat rental. Last year's rates $17. MC, V. Call for availability. (580) 442-5854

Savanna

MURPHY'S MEADOW (McAlester Army Ammunition Plant) On base. From McAlester, S 7 mi on US-69. Fair paved interior rds. SITES: 17 paved, 51 full hookups (30/50 amps). FAC: Restrooms & showers, dump, laundry, groceries. REC: Brown Lake: boating, ramp, rental. Playground, tennis, rec equip rental, pavilion. Last year's rates $12, no reservations, call for availablity. (918) 420-7484

Oklahoma City

TINKER FAMCAMP (Tinker AFB) On base. From Jct of I-40 & Air Depot Blvd, 1 mi on Air Depot Blvd. Good paved interior rds. SITES: 29 paved, 29 full hookups (30/50 amps). FAC: Restrooms & showers, dump, laundry. REC: Pond: fishing. Playground, golf. Last year's rates $13 to $15, no reservations. (405) 734-2847

OREGON

Klamath Falls

KINGSLEY FIELD CAMPGROUND (Oregon ANG) On base. From Jct. US-97 & Hwy 140, 3.3 mi E on Joe Wright Rd. to main gate entrance at Airport Dr., S 100 yds. Good paved interior rds. SITES: 5 grass, 5W, 5E (30 amps) FAC: restrooms & showers, laundry, dump, BX. REC: Gym, volleyball. Last year's rates $12. No reservations. No credit cards. (541) 885-6365.

RHODE ISLAND

Newport

CARR POINT REC AREA (NS Newport) Off base. May to Oct. From Jct Hwy 24 & 114, S 1.7 mi on 114 to Stringham Rd, 2.3 mi past Melville Pond Marina sign. Good paved/gravel interior rds. SITES: 6 gravel, 6W, 6E (30/50 amps). 14 day max stay. FAC: Port-O-Johns, On-base restrooms and showers, laundry. REC: On-base pool. Last year's rates $20 to $24, reservations recommended. V, MC. (401) 841-3116

SOUTH CAROLINA

Camden

WATEREE REC AREA (Shaw AFB) Off base. From Jct of I-20 & Camden exit, W 13 mi on Camden (turns into Hwy 521) to Hwy 97, W 9.5 mi to Wateree Rec sign, S 1.8 mi to base (L). Fair paved interior rds. SITES: 22 paved, W/E (30/50 amps), unlimited tent. Mostly shaded. 30 day max stay. FAC: Restrooms & showers, dump. REC: Lake Wateree: fishing, swimming, tackle, boat marina, ramp, dock, playground, picnic area, water sports equip. rental, pavilions. Last year's rates $16 to $19, reservations accepted. (877) 928-8373

Charleston

SHADY OAKS FAMILY CAMPGROUND (Charleston AFB) On base. From Jct of I-26 & W Aviation Ave, E 1 mi on W Aviation Ave to Arthur Rd, thru gate. Good paved interior rds. SITES: 17 paved, 6 grass, 17W, 17E (30 amps), 6 tent. FAC: Restrooms & showers, dump. REC: Playground, rec field, tennis. Last year's rates $10, call for availability. (803) 566-5271/5270

SHORT STAY (Charleston Naval Station) Off base. From town, N 30 mi on US-52 (follow signs). Good gravel interior rds. SITES: 83 gravel, 83W, 83E (30 amps), 17 tent. FAC: Restrooms & showers, dump, laundry, ltd groceries, ice, snacks. REC: Lake Moultrie: fishing, tackle, boating: marina, rental. Game room, playground, rec equip rental. Last year's rates $9 to $19, reservations accepted. (800) 447-2178

Columbia

WESTON LAKE REC AREA & TRAVEL CAMP (Fort Jackson) On base. From town, E 12 mi on SC-262 (Leesburg Rd), 4 mi past gate 5. Good paved interior rds. SITES: 16 paved, 6 full hookups, 4W, 10E (30/50 amps), 11 tent, 20 cabins. FAC: Restrooms & showers, dump, groceries REC: Weston Lake: fishing, swimming, boating, marina & rental. Rec field. No pets. Last year's rates $9 to $11, reservations for cabins only. (803) 751-5253

Shaw

FALCON'S NEST FAMCAMP (Shaw AFB) On base. From Sumter, W 9mi on Hwy 378 (E). SITES: 20 paved, 20 full hookups (30/50 amps), 5 tent. FAC: Restroom and showers, dump, grills, convenience store. REC: Playground, fishing, boat & equip rentals. Last year's rates $20, reservations accepted 60 days in advance. MC, V. (803) 895-0449/0450

SOUTH DAKOTA

Rapid City

ELLSWORTH FAMCAMP (Ellsworth AFB) On base. May 15 to Oct 15. From Jct of I-90 & Exit 66, right 2.5 mi Good paved interior rds. SITES: 30 paved, 30 full hookups, 12E (15/30/50 amps), 30 tent, 14 day max stay. FAC: Restrooms & showers, dump, phone, laundry, ltd groceries. REC: Playground. Last year's rates $20, reservations accepted PCS & TDY only. (605) 385-2997

TENNESSEE

Millington

NAVY LAKE REC AREA (NSA Mid-South) Off base. From Jct SR-51 N at Navy Road, R 3.5 mi to Bethel Rd., L 1.9 mi to Kerr-Rosemark Rd. L to entrance. Good paved interior rds. SITES: 24 paved/gravel, 7 full hookups, (30/50 amps), all pull-thrus. 30 day max stay. FAC: Restrooms & showers, laundry, dump, free WiFi. REC: Boating, fishing, horseshoes, volleyball, equip. rental. Last year's rates $17.50 to $22.50, no reservations. V, MC. (901) 872-3660

Tullahoma

ARNOLD FAMCAMP (Arnold AFB) On base. Apr 1 to Oct 1. From Jct of I-29 & Exit 117, E 3.5 mi on Wallendorf Hwy (pass Gate #2) to Pump Station Rd. (L). Good gravel interior rds. SITES: 32 paved, 32W, 32E (30/50 amps), 6 tent. Mostly shaded. 14 days max stay. Max RV length 25 ft. FAC: Restrooms & showers, dump, laundry, grills, food service, WiFi. REC: Lake (Woods Reservoir), fishing, boat marina, boat rental, swimming, beach, playground, racquet sports, golf, picnic area, rec equip. rental. Last year's rates $15 to $20, reservations accepted. (931) 454-4062/6084

TEXAS

Corpus Christi

NASKING RECREATION FAMCAMP (Kingsville NAS) On base. From Jct of I-37 & Hwy 77, S 30 mi on Hwy 77 to Carlos Truan Blvd, E 1.5 mi to security gate. SITES: 15 paved, full hookups, 10W, (20/30/50 amps), 10 tent. 14 day max stay. FAC: Restrooms & showers, dump, phone, WiFi. REC: pools, rec field, picnic areas, tennis, bowling, hunting, horseshoes, boating: rentals. Last year's rates $12. V, MC. No reservations accepted (361) 516-6191

SHIELDS PARK NAS REC AREA (Corpus Christi NAS) On base. From Jct of I-37 & TX-358, E 14 mi on TX-358. Good paved interior rd. SITES: 52 paved, 80 full hookups, 23W, 23E (30/50 amps), 5 tent. FAC: Restrooms, dump, ltd groceries, showers 0.5 mi. from camp, WiFi $. REC: Gulf, fishing, swimming, boating: ramp, marina, rental. Rec field, golf, skeet, trap. Rec equip rental. Last year's rates $15 to $17, reservations accepted up to 6 months in advance. (361) 961-1293/1294/1295

Del Rio

LAUGHLIN FAMCAMP (Laughlin AFB) On base. From town, E 7 mi on US-90 to AFB. Good paved interior rds. SITES: 20 paved, 20 full hookups (30/50 amps), all pull-thrus, CATV. FAC: Restrooms only. REC: Pool, playground, rec equip rental, fitness center, golf, bowling, tennis. Last year's rates $15, reservations accepted. (830) 298-5830

El Paso

FORT BLISS RV PARK (Fort Bliss) Off base. From Jct of I-10 & Hwy 54, E 4 mi on Hwy 54 to Exit 5, W to RV park (E). Good paved interior rds. SITES: 73 paved, 73 full hookups (30/50 amps), all pull-thrus. FAC: Restrooms & showers, laundry, dump, grills, RV storage WiFi. REC: Picnic area, golf, rec. field, bowling, miniature golf, pavilion. Last year's rates $16 to $17, no reservations. (915) 568-0106

Hooks

ELLIOT LAKE REC AREA (Red River Army Depot) On base. From Jct of I-30 & US-82, E on US-82 to Red River Army Depot exit (cross US-82 to exit). Good paved interior rds. SITES: 16 paved, 16 gravel, 16 full hookups, 21W, 21E (30/50 amps), 20 tent, 16 cabins. FAC: Restrooms & showers, dump, laundry, free WiFi. REC: Elliott Lake: swimming, boating, ramp, fishing, marina, rental. Playground, horseshoes. Last year's rates $9 to $12, no reservations. (903) 334-2254

Killeen

BELTON LAKE OUTDOOR REC AREA (Fort Hood) On base. From Jct of I-35 & US-190(Killeen/Ft Hood exit), W on US-190 to Loop 121, exit to Sparta Rd, N 6 mi. Good gravel interior rds. SITES: 81 paved, 10 full hookups, 52W, 52E (30 amps), 60 tent. FAC: Restrooms & showers, dump, laundry, ice, snacks. REC: Belton Lake: boating, ramp, fishing, marina, rental. Public beach, waterslides, playground, rec field, rec equip rental. Last year's rates $12 to $15, no reservations. (254) 287-4907

WEST FORT HOOD TRAVEL CAMP (Fort Hood) On base. From Jct of I-35 & US-190 (Killeen/Ft Hood exit), W on US-l90 to W Ft Hood turnoff, S 0.25 mi. Good paved interior rds. SITES: 80 paved, narrow 40 ft max length, 80 full hookups (20/30/50 amps) CATV. 30 day max stay in pull thru sites. FAC: Restrooms & showers, dump, laundry, ltd groceries, restaurant. REC: Playground. Last year's rates $10.50 to $18, no reservations. (254) 288-9926

New Braunfels

CANYON LAKE ARMY REC AREA (Fort Sam Houston) Off base. From Jct of I-35 & FM-306, W 16 mi on FM-306. Good paved interior rds. Large breed pets restricted. SITES: 32 paved, (30/50 amps), 35 cottages, 10 cabanas w/ electric, 50 tent. FAC: Restrooms & showers, dump, free WiFi. REC: Canyon Lake: fishing, tackle, boating: ramp, marina, rental. Rec hall, playground. Last year's rates $15, no reservations . (888) 882-9878

San Angelo

GOODFELLOW AIR FORCE BASE FAMCAMP (Goodfellow AFB) Open Thu-Mon. Off base. From US-87 & Loop 306, S on Loop 306 to Knickerbocker Rd. (around Loop 306) to lake (E). Good paved interior rds. SITES: 20 gravel sites, 20 full hookups (20/30 amps), unlimited tents. 30 day max stay. Mostly shaded. FAC: Restrooms & showers, food service, WiFi in some sites. REC: Lake Nasworthy, boat rental, boat marina, fishing, picnic area, racquet courts, rec field, rec equip, pavilion, volleyball, horseshoes. Last year's rates $10 to $15, reservations between March 1 - July 30 only. (325) 944-1012

San Antonio

FORT SAM HOUSTON RV PARK (Fort Sam Houston) On base. From Jct. I-35 S at Exit 161, right at Binz-Englemann to base entrance, right on S-33. Good paved interior rds. SITES: 68 gravel, 68 full hookups (30/50 amps), all pull-thrus, 30 day max stay. FAC: Restrooms & showers, tables, grills, laundry, convenience store. REC: Pool, basketball, volleyball, archery, playground, gym, rec equip rental. Last year's rates $17, reservations accepted up to 1 year in advance. (210) 221-5502

LACKLAND FAMCAMP (Lackland AFB) On base. From town W on US-90 to Exit 17, S on Military Drive to Luke East gate. Good paved interior roads. SITES: 41 paved, 29 full hookups, 12W, 12E (20/30/50 amp), CATV. FAC: Laundry, modem hookup. REC: Golf, stables. Last year's rate $16 to $22. No reservations. Pet restrictions. (210) 671-5179

Whitesboro

SHEPPARD REC ANNEX (Sheppard AFB) Off base. From Jct of US-82 & US-377, N 12 mi on US-377 to FM-901, N 1.5 mi to Rock Creek Rd. Good paved interior rds. SITES: 41 gravel, 25 full hookups, 16W, 16E (30/50 amps), many tent, 47 cabins. FAC: Restrooms & showers, dump, ltd groceries. REC: Lake Texoma: boating, fishing, ramp, rental. Rec hall, playground, rec equip rental, restaurant, golf. Last year's rates $15 to $20. Reservations accepted. (903) 523-4613

UTAH

Layton

HILL FAMCAMP (Hill AFB) On base. From Jct of I-15 (N of SLC) & Cut Off 334, exit to Hill Field Rd, N approx 2 mi, left to South Gate, E 2 mi on UT-193 to S gate entrance. Good paved interior rds. SITES: 28 gravel, 28 full hookups (20/30/50 amps), 6 tent, 14 day max stay April - September. FAC: Restrooms & showers, dump, laundry. REC: Lake, swimming, boating: rental. Rec equip rental, clubhouse, playground, golf. Last year's rates $10 to $14. Reservations accepted 14 days in advance. (801) 775-3250

VIRGINIA

Bowling Green

CHAMPS CAMP RV PARK (Fort AP Hill) On base. S-bnd: From Jct of I-95 & US-17 (Bowling Green/Ft AP Hill exit), E 6 mi on US-17 to VA-2, S 14 mi to US-301, NE 2 mi; N-bnd: From Jct of I-95 & VA-207, N 12 mi on VA-207 to Bowling Green, N 2 mi. Good paved interior rds. SITES: 49 paved, 49 full hookups (20/30/50 amps), 20 cottages/lodge/cabins. FAC: None. REC: Lakes, fishing, hunting, boating: Pool, rec hall, lodge. Rec equip rental. Last year's rates $21, reservations accepted. (804) 633-8244

Chesapeake

STEWART CAMPGROUND (NSA Norfolk Northwest Annex) On base. May 1 to Oct 31. From Jct of I-64 & VA-168, S 16 mi on VA-168 to Ballahock Rd, W 3mi to Relay Rd, S through gate to Olympic Ave, E to campground. Fair gravel interior roads. SITES: 18 gravel, 8E (110V/50A), 3 tent. FAC: Restrooms & showers, dump, gas, ltd groceries. REC: Playground, picnic area, bowling, pool, tennis, fishing, boating: rentals. Last year's rates $10. V, MC. Reservations accepted. (757) 421-8264

Hampton

THE COLONIES TRAVEL PARK (Fort Monroe) On base. From Jct of I-64 & Exit 268 (in town), E 2 mi on exit rd, follow signs. Good paved interior rds. SITES: 13 paved (35 ft max length), 13 full hookups, 6W, 6E (20/30 amps). FAC: Restrooms & showers, dump, laundry. REC: Pool ($), playground, archery, tennis. Rec equip rental. Last year's rates $17 to $20, reservations accepted up to 6 months in advance. (757) 788-2384/5304

Norfolk

LITTLE CREEK MWR RV PARK (Little Creek Naval Amphibious Base) On base. From Jct of I-64 & North Hampton Blvd/US-13 (S of town), N on Hampton Blvd to Amphibious Base exit, exit to Independence Blvd/VA-225, N to Gate 5; or from Jct of US-13 (Chesapeake Bay Bridge Tunnel) & US-60, W on US-60 to Gate 5. SITES: 51 paved, 45 full hookups (30/50 amps), CATV($), 6 tent. FAC: Restrooms & showers, dump, phone, laundry, WiFi. REC: Ocean, swimming, boating: marina, rental. Playground, golf. Last year's rates $18. Reservations accepted up to 6 months in advance. (757) 462-7282

Quantico

LUNGA PARK (MC Combat Development Command) On base. From Jct of I-95 & MCB-4 (MC CDC Quantico, Exit 148), W 7 mi on MCB-4. Fair paved interior rds. SITES: 18 gravel, 18 full hookups, 7W, 7E (50 amps), 27 tent. FAC: Pit toilets, dump. REC: Lunga Reservoir: boating: ramp, tackle, ltd. groceries. Playground, golf. Last year's rates $16 to $26. Reservations accepted. (703) 784-5270

Virginia Beach

CAPE HENRY RV PARK (Fort Story) On base. From Jct of US-13 & US-60 (Shore Dr), E 5 mi on US-60 to Atlantic Ave, 2 mi. Good gravel interior rds. SITES: 24 gravel, 24W, 24E (50 amps), FAC: Restrooms & showers, dump. REC: Rec field, tennis, canoes, kayaks, rec equip rental. Last year's rates $16, reservations required. (757) 422-7601

Williamsburg

CHEATHAM ANNEX REC CABINS & RV PARK (Naval Weapons Station Yorktown) On base. From Jct of I-64 & VA-199 (Exit 242B), E 2.5 mi on VA-199. Fair gravel interior rds. SITES: 19 paved, 19 full hookups (50 amps), 6 tent, 31 cabins, 9 camper rentals, CATV. FAC: Restrooms & showers, dump, laundry, store, gym. REC: Cheatham Lake: boating, rentals, fishing. Playground, golf, rec field, tennis. Last year's rates $15 to $18, reservations accepted 6 months in advance. (757) 887-7224/7418

WASHINGTON

Cheney

CLEAR LAKE REC AREA (Fairchild AFB) Off base. Apr to Sep. From Jct of I-90 & Salnave Rd (Exit 264), N on Salnave Rd to Clear Lake Rd, E 1 mi, follow signs. Good paved interior rds. SITES: 24 full hookups 3E (30/50 amps), 14 tent. FAC: Restrooms & showers, dump, snacks. REC: Clear Lake: fishing, tackle, swimming, boating: ramp, rental. Playground, camp & rec equip rental. Last year's rates $12 to $17. V, MC. Reservations accepted. (509) 299-5129

Oak Harbor

CLIFFSIDE RV PARK (Whidbey Island NAS) On base. From town, NW 4 mi on WA-20 to Ault Field Rd, 3 mi to Langley Blvd, right to main gate (5th St), left to Saratoga, right to N St, then left. Fair paved interior rds. SITES: 20 gravel, 20W, 20E, 6 tent, 14 day max stay May to September. FAC: Showers only, dump. REC: Ocean, fishing, boating: ramp, marina, rental. Last year's rates $18 to $19, reservations accepted up to 6 months in advance. (360) 257-2702/2432

Pacific Beach

PACIFIC BEACH RESORT (NS Everett) Off base. From Olympia, Jct of I-5 & US-8/Exit 104 (Aberdeen/Port Angeles exit), W on US-8 (becomes US-8/12) thru Aberdeen to Hoquiam (becomes US-101), NW 4 mi on US-101 to Beaches sign, left on Ocean Beach Rd, NW 20 mi to Pacific Beach, camp located adjacent to Pacific Beach Resort main bldg. Good paved interior rds. SITES: 43 paved, 45 hookups, 43W, 43E, 19 tent. FAC: Restrooms & showers, laundry, phone, free WiFi in hotel lobby. REC: Ocean, fishing, adult lounge, game room, planned activities, bowling, hot tubs. Last year's rates $15 to $19, reservations recommended. (888) 463-6697

Spokane

FAIRCHILD FAMCAMP (Fairchild AFB) On base. From Jct of I-90 & US Hwy 2, exit through Airway Heights, base entrance on left. Good gravel interior roads. SITES: 32 gravel, 32 full hookups (30/50 amps). FAC: Restrooms & showers, dump, laundry, phone, ltd groceries, ice, free WiFi, horse shoes, bowling. REC: Pool, playground, picnic areas, tennis, golf, skeet, horseshoes, bowling, archery, swimming, fishing, boating: rentals. Last year's rates $17. V, MC. No reservations. (509) 247-5920/3247

Tacoma

CAMP MURRAY BEACH (Camp Murray) On base. From Jct of I-5 & Exit 122, W across railroad tracks to beach (R). Good gravel interior rds. SITES: 24 gravel, 24 full hookups (30 amps). 14 day max stay on water front row. Mostly shaded. FAC: Restrooms & showers, laundry. REC: Picnic area, boat marina, beach. Last year's rates $14. V, MC. Reservations accepted & recommended. (800) 588-6420

HOLIDAY PARK FAMCAMP (McChord AFB) On base. From Jct of I-5 & Exit 125E, 0.25 mi on exit rd, follow signs. Good paved interior rds. SITES: 37 paved, 19 full hookups, 18W, 18E (30 amps), 12 tent. FAC: Restrooms & showers, dump. REC: Playground, rec field, horseshoes. Last year's rates $10 to $11, no reservations. (253) 982-5488

LEWIS TRAVEL CAMP (Fort Lewis) On base. From Jct of I-5 & Exit 120 to North Fort past guard shack, right at stop light. Check-in at the North West Adventure Center on left. Good paved interior rds. SITES: 29 hard stand, 48 full hookups, (30/50 amps) 14 day max stay May 1 - September 30, 7 cabins, 5 tent, CATV. FAC: Restrooms & showers, dump, phone, laundry. REC: American Lake: fishing, boating: marina, rental. Adult lounge, game room, playground, golf. Last year's rates $5 to $20. Reservations accepted up to 90 days in advance. (253) 967-5415

WISCONSIN

Sparta

PINE VIEW REC AREA (Fort McCoy) On base. From Jct of I-90 & WI-21, NE 8 mi on WI-21 to Gate 5. Good paved interior rds. SITES: 127 paved, 85 full hookups, 17E (15/30/50 amps), 9 yurts/cabins/duplex. FAC: Restrooms & showers, dump, laundry, CATV. REC: Squaw Lake: bass fishing, boating: rental. Archery, playground, golf, mini-golf, volleyball, horseshoes, pavilions, rec equip rental. Last year's rates $20 to $45, reservations accepted. (608) 388-3517

WYOMING

Cheyenne

WARREN FAMCAMP (Francis E Warren AFB) On base. From Jct of I-80 & I-25, N 2 mi on I-25. Ltd. facilities in Winter. Good gravel interior rds. SITES: 40 gravel, 40 full hook-ups, (20/30/50 amps) 50 tent, 166 overflow. 30 day max stay. FAC: Restrooms & showers, dump, laundry. REC: Rec equip rental, pool. Last year's rates $10 to $20, reservations accepted 30 days in advance. (307) 773-2988/3874.

FIND-IT-FAST INDEX

WHEN To Use This Section

Use the alphabetical index to reference campground listings when you know the name of a campground, but can't remember the city in which it is located.

After determining the listing city and page number, turn to the appropriate state/provincial section and find the campground listing. Use the map coordinates under the city heading to find the city in which the campground is located on the state or provincial map.

HOW to Use the Alphabetical Index (step-by-step instructions)

The information in each alphabetical listing is as follows: Good Sam discount location (designated by a black dot), campground name, listing city, and page number for listing.

1. Locate the state or province in which the campground is found in the following pages.
2. A black dot (•) in front of a location indicates that it is part of the Good Sam RV Park & Resort Network, and offers a 10% discount to Good Sam Club members on an overnight stay for two people in one RV. Members must present a valid Good Sam Club membership card at the time of registration.
3. Locate the name of the campground; campgrounds are listed alphabetically within each state and province.
4. The listing city is that city under which the campground listing may be found in the main campground section of this Guide.
5. The page number will lead you directly to the listing.

Example:

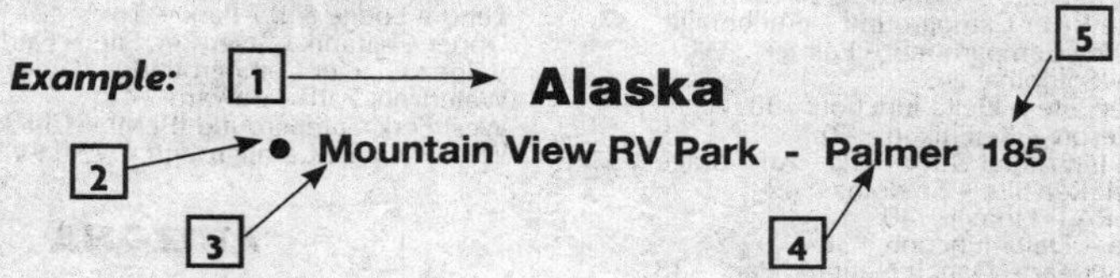

INDEX

USA

ALABAMA

ALASKA

ARIZONA

ARKANSAS

CALIFORNIA

INDEX

COLORADO

CONNECTICUT

DELAWARE

FLORIDA

GEORGIA

INDEX

IDAHO

ILLINOIS

INDIANA

IOWA

INDEX

KANSAS

KENTUCKY

LOUISIANA

MAINE

MARYLAND

MASSACHUSETTS

MICHIGAN

MINNESOTA

MISSISSIPPI

MISSOURI

MONTANA

NEBRASKA

NEVADA

NEW HAMPSHIRE

NEW JERSEY

NEW MEXICO

NEW YORK

NORTH CAROLINA

INDEX

NORTH DAKOTA

OHIO

OKLAHOMA

OREGON

PENNSYLVANIA

RHODE ISLAND

SOUTH CAROLINA

SOUTH DAKOTA

TENNESSEE

TEXAS

UTAH

VERMONT

VIRGINIA

WASHINGTON

WEST VIRGINIA

WISCONSIN

WYOMING

CANADA

ALBERTA

INDEX

BRITISH COLUMBIA

MANITOBA

NEW BRUNSWICK

NEWFOUNDLAND AND LABRADOR

NORTHWEST TERRITORIES

NOVA SCOTIA

ONTARIO

INDEX

PRINCE EDWARD ISLAND

QUEBEC

SASKATCHEWAN

YUKON